Features

Features

You may visit us on the Web at
http://www.census.gov/statab/www/ccdb.html

County and City
Data Book: 2000

A Statistical Abstract Supplement

13th Edition

Updated as of March 2002

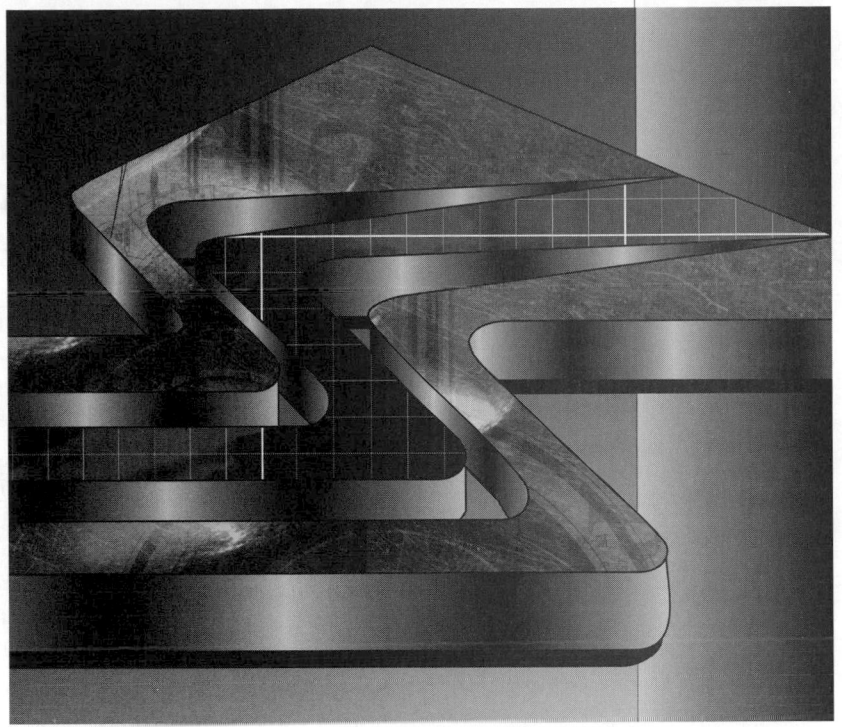

Issued November 2001

U.S. Department of Commerce
Donald L.Evans,
Secretary

**Economics and Statistics
Administration**
Kathleen B. Cooper,
Under Secretary for Economic Affairs

U.S. CENSUS BUREAU
William G. Barron, Jr.,
Acting Director

SUGGESTED CITATION

U.S. Census Bureau,
County and City Data Book: 2000
(13th edition)
Washington, DC, 2001

Library of Congress
Card No. 52-4576

**Economics
and Statistics
Administration**

Kathleen B. Cooper,
Under Secretary
for Economic Affairs

U.S. CENSUS BUREAU

William G. Barron, Jr.,
Acting Director

William G. Barron, Jr.,
Deputy Director

Nancy A. Potok,
Principal Associate Director
and Chief Financial Officer

Ted A. Johnson, Associate Director
for Finance and Administration

Walter C. Odom, Chief, Administrative
and Customer Services Division

Acknowledgments

Wanda K. Cevis was responsible for the technical supervision and coordination
of this volume under the general direction of **Glenn W. King,** Chief, Statistical
Compendia Branch. Subject development and analytical review were provided by
Lars B. Johanson, Rosemary E. Clark, and **Edward C. Jagers. Kathleen A. Siemer**
was responsible for computer operations and data processing. Support activities and
data review were provided by **Edward C. Jagers** and **Mary Grace Lynch.** Data entry
and other support activities were provided by **Kristen M. Iversen** and **Daphanie M.
Smallwood.**

Penny Heiston, Elizabeth J. Williams, Shirley Clark, and **Barbara Blount** of the
Administrative and Customer Services Division, **Walter C. Odom,** Chief, performed
publications and printing management, graphics design and composition, and editorial
review for print and electronic media. General direction and production management
were provided by **Michael G. Garland,** Assistant Chief, and **Gary J. Lauffer,** Chief,
Publication Services Branch.

Nick Padfield, Scott Wilcox, Deanna Fowler, and **Michael DeGennaro** of the Carto-
graphic Operations Branch under the direction of **Connie Beard** of Geography Division,
Robert Marx, Chief, designed and produced the maps in this volume. Maps were edited
by **Rashida Abul-Qasim** and **Barbara Saville** of the Geographic Areas Branch, Geography Division, under the direction of **Dorothy Stroz.**

The cooperation of many contributors to this volume is gratefully acknowledged. The
source notes below each table and in appendix A credits the various government and
private agencies which have furnished information for the *County and City Data Book.*
In a few instances, contributors have requested that their data be designated as subject
to copyright restrictions, as indicated in the source notes. Permission to use copyright
material should be obtained directly from the copyright owner.

Reprinted without alteration on acid-free paper
National Technical Information Service (NTIS) Springfield, VA
Updated as of March 2002
Telephone: 703-605-6000 or 1-800-553-6847
ISBN 0-934213-88-7
PB number: PB2002-101674

Preface

The *County and City Data Book* (CCDB), published intermittently since 1944, is a local area supplement to the *Statistical Abstract of the United States*. This 2000 edition is the thirteenth in the series. The first edition featured city data only; the second, in 1947, county data only. Beginning with the third edition in 1949, the book was redesigned to include both county and city data and renamed the *County and City Data Book*. Subsequent editions were published in 1952, 1956, 1962, 1967, 1972, 1977, 1983, 1988, and 1994.

The CCDB is a convenient summary of statistics on the social and economic structure of the counties and cities of the United States. It is designed to serve as a statistical reference and guide to other data publications and sources. The latter function is served by the source citations appearing below each table and in Appendix A, Source Notes and Explanations.

This volume includes a selection of data from many statistical publications and electronic sources, both government and private. Publications and Internet sites listed as sources usually contain additional detail and more comprehensive discussions of definitions and concepts than can be presented here. Data not available in publications issued by the contributing agency but obtained from unpublished records are identified in the source notes as "unpublished data." More information on the subjects covered in the tables so noted may generally be obtained from the source.

Although emphasis in this *Data Book* is primarily given to county and city data, Table A includes U.S. and state totals and Table D includes population data for all places of 2,500 or more population.

Changes in this edition—The presentation of the various tables has been changed such that one data table for all counties or cities is shown before the next data table; earlier editions presented all the data tables for a specific group of counties or cities before repeating the data tables for the next group of counties or cities. This change has enabled us to include county and city references in Appendix D, Subject Guide for ease in locating these data.

We have changed the presentation of state data to an alphabetic one. Selected rankings may be found on the Census Bureau's Internet site at <http://www.census.gov/statab/www/ccdb.html>.

Source notes now appear at the bottom of each table page, as well as in the source notes and explanations appendix. Some citations provide Internet addresses either as the sole citation or as a supplement to the printed or electronic source. In addition, we now include a Contact List which provides a guide to Federal agencies with major statistical programs and includes their mailing address, phone number, and Internet address.

Statistics in this edition—Data are generally shown for the most recent year or period available by spring 2001. Initial results from the 2000 Census of Population and Housing are included, as well as 1997 Economic Census data.

States—Data are presented for the United States, the 50 states, and the District of Columbia. 191 data items are presented for these areas in 13 tables, A-1 through A-13. The states and the District of Columbia are presented in alphabetic order under the U.S. total.

Counties—Data are presented for the 3,142 counties and county equivalents defined as of January 1, 1992, as well as the United States, the 50 states, and the District of Columbia. 191 data items are presented for these areas in 13 tables, B-1 through B-13. The counties and county equivalents are presented in Federal Information Processing Standards (FIPS) code order, which lists counties alphabetically under their respective states; independent cities in Maryland, Missouri, Nevada, and Virginia are listed alphabetically at the end of the respective county listing.

Cities—Data are presented for the 1,070 incorporated places with 25,000 or more population in the 1990 census, as well as the 50 states, the District of Columbia, 8 census designated places (CDPs) with 25,000 or more population in 1990 in Hawaii which has no incorporated places, and the 5 boroughs of New York city. This list is based on population counts from the 1990 census. 103 data items are presented for these areas in 7 tables, C-1 through C-7. The cities and CDPs are presented in FIPS code order, which lists these areas alphabetically under their respective states; the 5 New York city boroughs are listed under the city.

Places—Census 2000 population data are presented for the 8,888 incorporated places and census designated places (CDPs) with 2,500 or more population as of April 1, 2000 in Table D-1. Table D-2 presents the same 11 Census 2000 data items for the 2,759 functioning minor civil divisions (MCDs) with 2,500 or more population as of April 1, 2000 in the following 12 states: Connecticut, Maine, Massachusetts, Michigan, Minnesota, New Hampshire, New Jersey, New York, Pennsylvania, Rhode Island, Vermont, and Wisconsin. Both tables also present state totals for all states shown. The places in Table D-1 and the MCDs in Table D-2 are presented in FIPS code order, as described above.

Statistical reliability and responsibility—The contents of this volume were taken from many sources. All data from either censuses and surveys or from administrative records are subject to error arising from a number of factors: Sampling variability (for statistics based on samples), reporting errors in the data for individual units, incomplete coverage, nonresponse, imputations, and processing error. The Census Bureau cannot accept the responsibility for the accuracy or limitations of the data presented here, other than those for which it collects. The responsibility for selection of the material and for proper presentation, however, rests with the Bureau.

Maps—For a map of the United States with the 50 states and the District of Columbia, as well as census regions and divisions, see the inside of the front cover. Maps of all 50 states and the District of Columbia showing county and metropolitan area boundaries and names, as well as the locations of cities of 25,000 or more population, can be found in Appendix C.

Appendixes—Appendix A presents a discussion of source notes and explanations for the data items in Tables A through D. Appendix B presents a discussion of the geographic concepts and codes relevant to this volume, as well as the current definitions for metropolitan areas. Appendix C is a set of state maps with county and metropolitan area boundaries and names, as well as locations of cities of 25,000 or more population. Appendix D is a guide to subjects by geographic area.

For additional information on data presented—Please consult the source publications available in local libraries, write to the agency indicated in the source notes, or visit the Internet site listed. Contact the Census Bureau only if it is cited as the source.

Statistics for the nation—Extensive data at the national level can be found in the Statistical Abstract of the United States: 2001, an annual national data book, released each fall. Several editions of this publication are available on the Internet at <http://www.census.gov/statab/www/>.

USA Statistics in Brief, a pocket-size pamphlet highlighting many statistical series in the *Abstract,* is available separately; single copies of this pamphlet can be obtained free from U.S. Census Bureau, Customer Services Center, Washington, DC 20233 (telephone 301-763-4636).

Statistics for states and metropolitan areas—Data for states and metropolitan areas may be found in the *State and Metropolitan Area Data Book: 1997-98;* available in print, on CD-ROM, or on the Internet at <http://www.census.gov/statab/www/smadb.html>.

Additional statistics for counties—While this book contains approximately 200 data items for all counties and county equivalents in the United States, an extensive county database featuring over 5,000 data items for these areas can be found on USA Counties: 1998, a CD-ROM product or on the Internet at <http://www.census.gov/statab/www/county.html>.

Suggestions and comments—Users of the *County and City Data Book* and related publications (see inside back cover) are urged to make their data needs known for consideration in planning future editions. Suggestions and comments for improving coverage and presentation of data should be sent to the Director, U.S. Census Bureau, Washington, DC 20233.

CONTENTS

Places/MCDs of 2,500 or More Population

Guide to Tabular Presentation

EXAMPLE OF TABLE STRUCTURE

Table B-8. Counties — Personal Income and Earnings

[Includes United States, states, and 3,142 counties/county equivalents defined as of January 1, 1992. For changes to these areas since January 1, 1992, see appendix B. Geographic Information]

County	Personal income, 1998												
			Per capita			Earnings (mil. dol.)							
								Percent by selected industry—					
							Goods-related		Service-related				
	Total (mil. dol.)	Percent change, 1990-1998	Amount (dollars)	Percent of national averages	Transfer payments (mil. dol.)	Total [2] (mil. dol.)	Total [3]	Manufac- turing	Total [4]	Retail trade	FIRE [5]	Services	Govern- ment
UNITED STATES ..	7,351,547.0	50.5	27,203	100.0	983,530.0	5,302,066.0	23.4	16.8	75.8	8.8	9.0	28.4	16.0
ALABAMA.........	95,955.6	49.7	22,054	81.1	15,961.2	66,930.1	27.7	20.5	70.8	9.4	5.6	23.1	20.0
Autauga...........	890.0	72.0	21,093	77.5	118.8	336.1	D	30.3	D	15.2	4.3	15.3	17.3
Baldwin...........	3,203.0	104.5	24,109	88.6	440.1	1,364.8	22.4	12.8	76.7	15.7	9.9	23.3	17.8
Barbour...........	521.5	52.7	19,360	71.2	111.2	330.7	41.9	37.5	53.1	7.9	3.2	13.5	17.7
Bibb	345.8	64.6	18,214	67.0	72.5	132.5	D	19.8	D	8.8	D	14.1	24.5
Blount	917.2	70.5	19,813	72.8	144.0	313.4	29.7	18.8	57.1	9.7	4.6	15.2	16.5

[1] Based on resident population estimated as of July 1, 1998. [2] Includes farm earnings; see table B-10 for these data. [3] Includes mining and construction, not shown separately. [4] Includes agricultural services, forestry, and fisheries; transportation and public utilities; and wholesale trade, not shown separately. [5] Finance, insurance, and real estate.

Source: Personal Income and Earnings—U.S. Bureau of Economic Analysis. "Regional Economic Information System (REIS) 1989-1998" on CD-ROM (related Internet site <http://www.bea.doc.gov/bea/regional/data.htm>).

Headnotes immediately below table titles provide information on the geographic areas presented in the table.

Unit indicators show the specified quantities in which data items are presented. They are used for two primary reasons. Sometimes data are not available in absolute form. Other times we round the numbers in order to save space to show more data, as in the case above.

If no unit indicator is shown, data presented are in absolute form (see table B-1 for an example). When needed, unit indicators are found in the column or spanner headings for the data items as shown above.

Footnotes below the bottom rule of table pages give information relating to specific data items or figures within the table.

Source notes below footnotes provide a guide to the the original source and related Internet site, when applicable.

Example of Unit Indicator Interpretation From Table

Geography or area	Year	Item	Unit indicator	Number shown	Multiply by
UNITED STATES......................	1998	Personal income	(mil. dol.)	7,351,547.0	$1,000,000

To Determine the Figure it Is Necessary to Multiply the Number Shown by the Unit Indicator:

Personal income, 1998 = 7,351,547.0 * 1,000,000 or 7,351,547,000,000 (over 7 trillion dollars)

In many tables, details will not add to the totals shown because of rounding.

EXPLANATION OF SYMBOLS AND TERMS

The following symbols are used in the tables throughout this book.

-	Represents zero or rounds to less than half the unit of measurement shown.
B	Base figure too small to meet statistical standards for reliability of a derived figure.
D	Figure withheld to avoid disclosure pertaining to a specific organization or individual.
NA	Data not enumerated, tabulated, or otherwise available separately.
S	Figure does not meet publication standards for reasons other than that covered by symbol B, above.
X	Figure not applicable because column heading and stub line make entry impossible, absurd, or meaningless.
Z	Entry would amount to less than half the unit of measurement shown.

The following terms are also used throughout this publication:

Averages. An average is a single number or value that is often used to represent the "typical value" of a group of numbers. It is regarded as a measure of "location" or "central tendency" of a group of numbers.

The *arithmetic* mean is the type of average used most frequently. It is derived by summing the individual item values of a particular group and dividing the total by the number of items. The arithmetic mean is often referred to simply as the "mean" or "average."

The *median* of a group of numbers is the middle number or value when each item in the group is arranged according to size (lowest to highest or visa versa); it generally has the same number of items above it as well as below it. If there is an even number of items in the group, the median is taken to be the average of the two middle numbers.

Rates. Rate is a quantity or amount of an item measured in relation to a specified number of units of another item. For example, unemployment rate is the number of unemployed persons per 100 persons in the civilian labor force. Examples of other rates found in this publication include birth rate, which is the number of births per 1,000 population; infant death rate, the number of infant deaths per 1,000 live births; and crime rate, which is the number of serious offenses per 100,000 population.

A *per capita* figure represents a specific type of rate computed for every person in a specified group (or population). It is derived by taking the total for a data item (such as income, taxes, or retail sales) and dividing it by the number of persons in the specified population.

Contact List

To help *County and City Data Book* users find more data and information about statistical publications, we are issuing this list of contacts for Federal agencies with major statistical programs. The intent is to give a single, first-contact point-of-entry for users of statistics. These agencies will provide general information on their statistical programs and publications, as well as specific information on how to order their publications. We are also including the Internet (World Wide Web) addresses for many of these agencies. These URL's were current in September 2001.

Executive Office of the President

Office of Management and Budget
Administrator
Office of Information and Regulatory Affairs
Office of Management and Budget
725 17th Street, N.W.
Washington, DC 20503
Information: 202-395-3080
Internet address: http://www.whitehouse.gov/omb

Department of Agriculture

Economic Research Service
Information Center
U.S. Department of Agriculture
1800 M St. N.W., Rm. North 3050
Washington, DC 20036 5831
Information and Publications:
 202-694-5050
Internet address: http://www.ers.usda.gov/

National Agricultural Statistics Service
National Agricultural Statistics Service
U.S. Department of Agriculture
1400 Independence Ave., S.W.,
 Room 5829
Washington, DC 20250
Information hotline: 1-800-727-9540
Internet address: http://www.usda.gov/nass/

Department of Commerce

U.S. Census Bureau
Customer Services Branch
U.S. Census Bureau
U.S. Department of Commerce
Washington, DC 20233
Information and Publications:
 301-763-4636
Internet address: http://www.census.gov/

Bureau of Economic Analysis
Bureau of Economic Analysis
U.S. Department of Commerce
Washington, DC 20230
Information and Publications:
 202-606-9900
Internet address: http://www.bea.doc.gov/

Department of Commerce—Con.

International Trade Administration
Trade Statistics Division
Office of Trade and Economic Analysis
International Trade Administration
Room 2814 B
U.S. Department of Commerce
Washington, DC 20230
Information and Publications:
 202-482-2185
Internet address: http://www.ita.doc.gov/tradestats/

*National Oceanic and Atmospheric
 Administration*
National Oceanic and Atmospheric Administration
 Central Library
U.S. Department of Commerce
1315 East-West Highway
2nd Floor
Silver Spring MD 20910
Library: 301-713-2600
Internet address: http://www.lib.noaa.gov/

Department of Defense

Department of Defense
Office of the Assistant Secretary of Defense
 (Public Affairs)
Room 3A750
Attention: Directorate for Public
 Communications
1400 Defense Pentagon
Washington, DC 20301-1400
Information: 703-697-5737
Internet address:
 http://web1.whs.osd.mil/diorhome.htm

Department of Education

National Library of Education
U.S. Department of Education
400 Maryland Avenue, S.W.
Washington, DC 20202-5621
Education Information and Statistics 1-800-424-1616
Education Publications 1-877-433-7827
Internet address: http://www.ed.gov/

Department of Energy

Energy Information Administration
National Energy Information Center
U.S. Department of Energy
1000 Independence Ave., SW
1E238-EI-30
Washington, DC 20585
Information and Publications:
   202-586-8800
Internet address: http://www.eia.doe.gov/

Department of Health and Human Services

*Health Resources and Services
Administration*
HRSA Office of Communications
5600 Fishers Lane, Room 14-45
Rockville, MD 20857
Information Center: 301-443-3376
Internet address: http://www.hrsa.gov/

Substance Abuse Mental Health Services Administration
U.S. Department of Health and Human Services
5600 Fishers Lane
Room 12-105
Rockville, MD 20857
Information: 301-443-4795
Publications: 1-800-729-6686
Internet address: http://www.samhsa.gov/

Centers for Disease Control and Prevention
Office of Public Affairs
1600 Clifton Road, N.E.
Atlanta, GA 30333
Public Inquiries: 1-800-311-3435
Internet address: http://www.cdc.gov/

*Centers for Medicare and Medicaid
Services (CMS)*
Office of Public Affairs
U.S. Department of Health and Human Services
Room 303D, Humphrey Building
200 Independence Ave., S.W.
Washington, DC 20201
Media Relations: 202-690-6145
Internet address: http://www.cms.gov/

National Center for Health Statistics
U.S. Department of Health and Human Services
   Centers for Disease Control and Prevention
National Center for Health Statistics
Data Dissemination Branch
6525 Belcrest Rd., Rm. 1064
Hyattsville, MD 20782 301-458-INFO
Internet address: http://www.cdc.gov/nchswww

U.S. Department of Housing and Urban Development

*Office of the Assistant Secretary for
Community Planning and Development*
451 7th St., S.W.
Washington, DC 20410-0555
Information and Publications:
   1-800-998-9999
Internet address: http://www.hud.gov/

Department of the Interior

Geological Survey
Earth Science Information Center
Geological Survey
U.S. Department of the Interior
507 National Center
Reston, VA 20192
Information and Publications:
   1-888-275-8747
Internet address for minerals:
   http://minerals.usgs.gov/
Internet address for other materials:
   http://ask.usgs.gov/

Department of Justice

Bureau of Justice Statistics
Statistics Division
810 7th St., N.W. 2nd Floor
Washington, DC 20531
Information and Publications:
   202-307-0765
Internet address: http://www.ojp.usdoj.gov/bjs/

National Criminal Justice Reference Service
Box 6000
Rockville, MD 20849-6000
Information and Publications:
   301-519-5500
Publications: 1-800-732-3277
Internet address: http://www.ncjrs.org/

Federal Bureau of Investigation
U.S. Department of Justice
J. Edgar Hoover FBI Building
935 Pennsylvania Ave., N.W.
Washington, DC 20535-0001
202-324-3000
Information and Publications:
   202-324-3691
Research and Communications Unit:
   202-324-5611
Internet address: http://www.fbi.gov/

Department of Justice—Con.

Immigration and Naturalization Service
Statistics Branch
Immigration and Naturalization Service
U.S. Department of Justice
425 I St., NW, Rm. 4034
Washington, DC 20536
Information and Publications:
202-305-1613
*Internet address: http://www.ins.gov/graphics/
index.htm*

Department of Labor

Bureau of Labor Statistics
Office of Publications and Special Studies Services
Division of Information
Bureau of Labor Statistics
2 Mass. Ave., N.E., Room 2850
Washington, DC 20212
Information and Publications:
202-691-5200
Internet address: http://www.bls.gov/

Employment and Training Administration
Office of Public Affairs
Employment and Training Administration
U.S. Department of Labor
200 Constitution Ave., N.W., Room S4231
Washington, DC 20210
Information and Publications:
202-693-3900
Internet address: http://www.doleta.gov/

Department of Transportation

Federal Aviation Administration
U.S. Department of Transportation
800 Independence Ave., S.W.
Washington, DC 20591
Information and Publications:
202-267-3484
Internet address: http://www.faa.gov/

Bureau of Transportation Statistics
400 7th St., S.W. Room 3430
Washington, DC 20590
Products: 202-366-3282
Statistical Information:800-853-1351
Internet address: http://www.bts.gov/

Federal Highway Administration
Office of Public Affairs
Federal Highway Administration
U.S. Department of Transportation
400 7th St., S.W.
Washington, DC 20590
Information: 202-366-0660
Internet address: http://www.fhwa.dot.gov/

Department of Transportation—Con.

*National Highway Traffic Safety
Administration*
Office of Public & Consumer Affairs
National Highway Traffic Safety
Administration
U.S. Department of Transportation
400 7th St., S.W.
Washington, DC 20590
Information: 202-366-4000
Publications: 202-366-8892
Internet address: http://www.nhtsa.dot.gov/

Department of the Treasury

Internal Revenue Service
Statistics of Income Division
Internal Revenue Service
P.O. Box 2608
Washington, DC 20013-2608
Information and Publications:
202-874-0410
Internet address:
http://www.irs.ustreas.gov/cover.html

Department of Veterans Affairs

Office of Public Affairs
Department of Veterans Affairs
810 Vermont Ave., N.W.
Washington, DC 20420
Information: 202-273-5400
Internet address: http://www.va.gov/

Independent Agencies

Administrative Office of the U.S. Courts
Statistics Division
1 Columbus Circle, N.E.
Washington, DC 20544
Information: 202-502-1455
Internet address: http://www.uscourts.gov/

Environmental Protection Agency
Information Resource Center, Rm. M2904
Environmental Protection Agency
1200 Pennsylvania Ave., N.W.
Mail Code 3201
Washington, DC 20460
Information: 202-260-9152
Internet address: http://www.epa.gov/

Federal Reserve Board
Division of Research and Statistics
Federal Reserve Board
Washington, DC 20551
Information: 202-452-3301
Publications: 202-452-3245
Internet address: http://www.federalreserve.gov/

Independent Agencies—Con.

National Science Foundation
Office of Legislation and Public Affairs
National Science Foundation
4201 Wilson Boulevard
Arlington, Virginia 22230
Information: 703-292-5111
Publications: 703-292-8129
Internet address: http://www.nsf.gov/

Securities and Exchange Commission
Office of Public Affairs
Securities and Exchange Commission
450 5th St., N.W.
Room 2500
Mail Stop 0213
Washington, DC 20549
Information: 202-942-0020
Publications: 202-942-4040
Internet address: http://www.sec.gov/

Independent Agencies—Con.

Social Security Administation
6400 Security Blvd
Baltimore, MD 21235
Information and Publications:
1-800-772-1213
Internet Address: http://www.ssa.gov/

States

Table A

Page

You may visit us on the Web at
http://www.census.gov/statab/www/ccdb.html

States

Table A

Figure 1.
Percent Population Change by State: 1990 to 2000

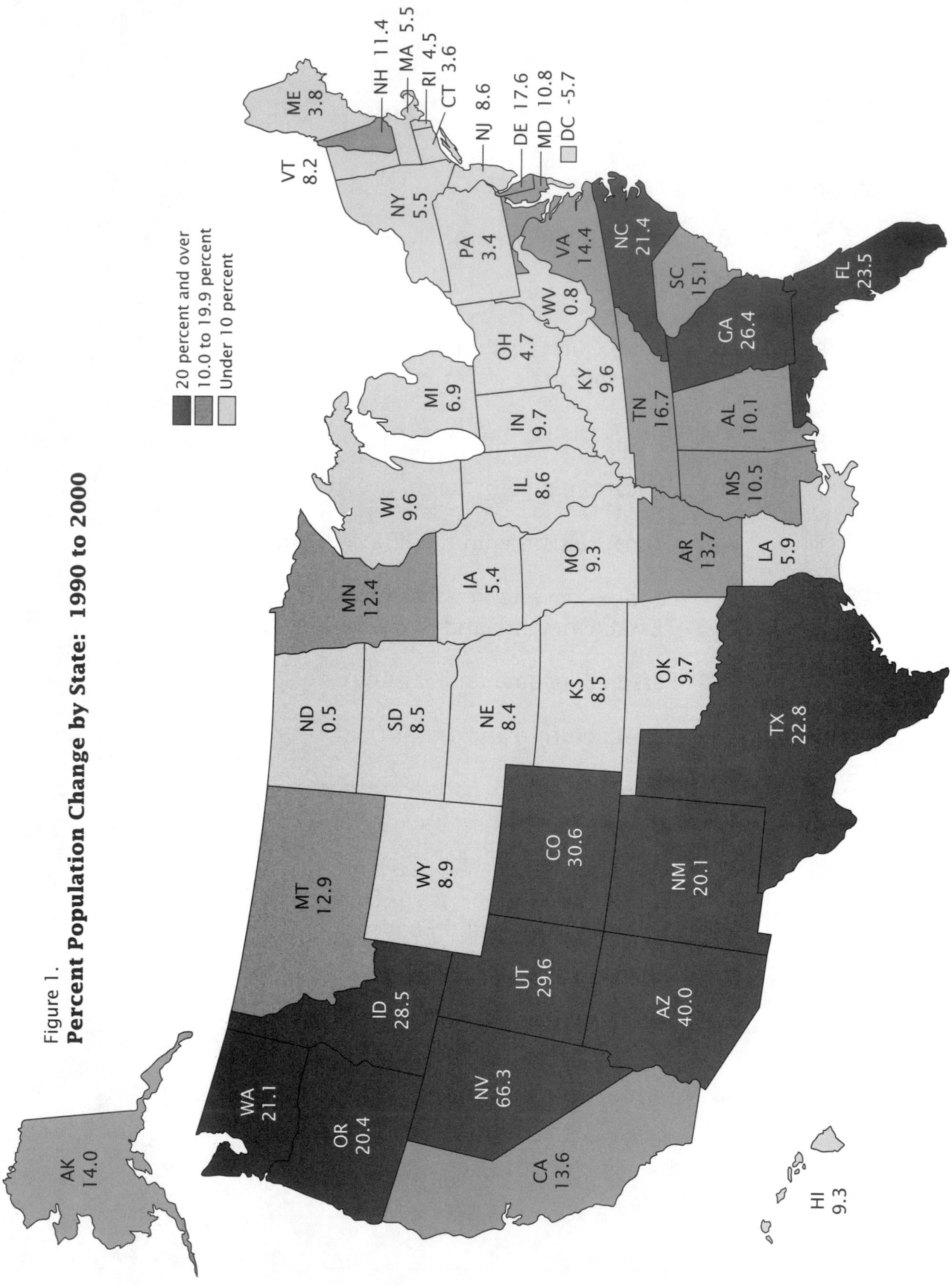

Legend:
- 20 percent and over
- 10.0 to 19.9 percent
- Under 10 percent

ME 3.8
NH 11.4
MA 5.5
RI 4.5
CT 3.6
VT 8.2
NY 5.5
NJ 8.6
DE 17.6
MD 10.8
DC -5.7
PA 3.4
VA 14.4
WV 0.8
NC 21.4
SC 15.1
FL 23.5
GA 26.4
OH 4.7
KY 9.6
TN 16.7
AL 10.1
MI 6.9
IN 9.7
IL 8.6
MS 10.5
LA 5.9
WI 9.6
AR 13.7
MN 12.4
IA 5.4
MO 9.3
OK 9.7
TX 22.8
ND 0.5
SD 8.5
NE 8.4
KS 8.5
CO 30.6
NM 20.1
MT 12.9
WY 8.9
UT 29.6
AZ 40.0
ID 28.5
NV 66.3
WA 21.1
OR 20.4
CA 13.6
AK 14.0
HI 9.3

Source: Chart prepared by U.S. Census Bureau, for data see Table A-1.

State code[1]	State	Land area,[2] 2000 (sq. miles)	Population (April 1) 2000 Number	Rank	Per square mile	1990[3] Number	Rank	1980	Net change 1990–2000	1980–1990	Percent change 1990–2000	1980–1990	Hispanic or Latino,[4] 2000 Number	Percent
00	UNITED STATES	3 537 441	281 421 906	X	79.6	248 790 925	X	226 542 199	32 630 981	22 248 726	13.1	9.8	35 305 818	12.5
01	Alabama	50 744	4 447 100	23	87.6	4 040 389	22	3 894 025	406 711	146 364	10.1	3.8	75 830	1.7
02	Alaska	571 951	626 932	48	1.1	550 043	49	401 851	76 889	148 192	14.0	36.9	25 852	4.1
04	Arizona	113 635	5 130 632	20	45.2	3 665 339	24	2 716 546	1 465 293	948 793	40.0	34.9	1 295 617	25.3
05	Arkansas	52 068	2 673 400	33	51.3	2 350 624	33	2 286 357	322 776	64 267	13.7	2.8	86 866	3.2
06	California	155 959	33 871 648	1	217.2	29 811 427	1	23 667 764	4 060 221	6 143 663	13.6	26.0	10 966 556	32.4
08	Colorado	103 718	4 301 261	24	41.5	3 294 473	26	2 889 735	1 006 788	404 738	30.6	14.0	735 601	17.1
09	Connecticut	4 845	3 405 565	29	702.9	3 287 116	27	3 107 564	118 449	179 552	3.6	5.8	320 323	9.4
10	Delaware	1 954	783 600	45	401.0	666 168	46	594 338	117 432	71 830	17.6	12.1	37 277	4.8
11	District of Columbia	61	572 059	X	9 378.0	606 900	X	638 432	–34 841	–31 532	–5.7	–4.9	44 953	7.9
12	Florida	53 927	15 982 378	4	296.4	12 938 071	4	9 746 961	3 044 307	3 191 110	23.5	32.7	2 682 715	16.8
13	Georgia	57 906	8 186 453	10	141.4	6 478 149	11	5 462 982	1 708 304	1 015 167	26.4	18.6	435 227	5.3
15	Hawaii	6 423	1 211 537	42	188.6	1 108 229	41	964 691	103 308	143 538	9.3	14.9	87 699	7.2
16	Idaho	82 747	1 293 953	39	15.6	1 006 734	42	944 127	287 219	62 607	28.5	6.6	101 690	7.9
17	Illinois	55 584	12 419 293	5	223.4	11 430 602	6	11 427 409	988 691	3 193	8.6	Z	1 530 262	12.3
18	Indiana	35 867	6 080 485	14	169.5	5 544 156	14	5 490 210	536 329	53 946	9.7	1.0	214 536	3.5
19	Iowa	55 869	2 926 324	30	52.4	2 776 831	30	2 913 808	149 493	–136 977	5.4	–4.7	82 473	2.8
20	Kansas	81 815	2 688 418	32	32.9	2 477 588	32	2 364 236	210 830	113 352	8.5	4.8	188 252	7.0
21	Kentucky	39 728	4 041 769	25	101.7	3 686 892	23	3 660 324	354 877	26 568	9.6	.7	59 939	1.5
22	Louisiana	43 562	4 468 976	22	102.6	4 221 826	21	4 206 116	247 150	15 710	5.9	.4	107 738	2.4
23	Maine	30 862	1 274 923	40	41.3	1 227 928	38	1 125 043	46 995	102 885	3.8	9.1	9 360	.7
24	Maryland	9 774	5 296 486	19	541.9	4 780 753	19	4 216 933	515 733	563 820	10.8	13.4	227 916	4.3
25	Massachusetts	7 840	6 349 097	13	809.8	6 016 425	13	5 737 093	332 672	279 332	5.5	4.9	428 729	6.8
26	Michigan	56 804	9 938 444	8	175.0	9 295 287	8	9 262 044	643 157	33 243	6.9	.4	323 877	3.3
27	Minnesota	79 610	4 919 479	21	61.8	4 375 665	20	4 075 970	543 814	299 695	12.4	7.4	143 382	2.9
28	Mississippi	46 907	2 844 658	31	60.6	2 575 475	31	2 520 770	269 183	54 705	10.5	2.2	39 569	1.4
29	Missouri	68 886	5 595 211	17	81.2	5 116 901	15	4 916 766	478 310	200 135	9.3	4.1	118 592	2.1
30	Montana	145 552	902 195	44	6.2	799 065	44	786 690	103 130	12 375	12.9	1.6	18 081	2.0
31	Nebraska	76 872	1 711 263	38	22.3	1 578 417	36	1 569 825	132 846	8 592	8.4	.5	94 425	5.5
32	Nevada	109 826	1 998 257	35	18.2	1 201 675	39	800 508	796 582	401 167	66.3	50.1	393 970	19.7
33	New Hampshire	8 968	1 235 786	41	137.8	1 109 252	40	920 610	126 534	188 642	11.4	20.5	20 489	1.7
34	New Jersey	7 417	8 414 350	9	1 134.5	7 747 750	9	7 365 011	666 600	382 739	8.6	5.2	1 117 191	13.3
35	New Mexico	121 356	1 819 046	36	15.0	1 515 069	37	1 303 302	303 977	211 767	20.1	16.2	765 386	42.1
36	New York	47 214	18 976 457	3	401.9	17 990 778	2	17 558 165	985 679	432 613	5.5	2.5	2 867 583	15.1
37	North Carolina	48 711	8 049 313	11	165.2	6 632 448	10	5 880 095	1 416 865	752 353	21.4	12.8	378 963	4.7
38	North Dakota	68 976	642 200	47	9.3	638 800	47	652 717	3 400	–13 917	.5	–2.1	7 786	1.2
39	Ohio	40 948	11 353 140	7	277.3	10 847 115	7	10 797 603	506 025	49 512	4.7	.5	217 123	1.9
40	Oklahoma	68 667	3 450 654	27	50.3	3 145 576	28	3 025 487	305 078	120 089	9.7	4.0	179 304	5.2
41	Oregon	95 997	3 421 399	28	35.6	2 842 337	29	2 633 156	579 062	209 181	20.4	7.9	275 314	8.0
42	Pennsylvania	44 817	12 281 054	6	274.0	11 882 842	5	11 864 720	398 212	18 122	3.4	.2	394 088	3.2
44	Rhode Island	1 045	1 048 319	43	1 003.2	1 003 464	43	947 154	44 855	56 310	4.5	5.9	90 820	8.7
45	South Carolina	30 110	4 012 012	26	133.2	3 486 310	25	3 120 729	525 702	365 581	15.1	11.7	95 076	2.4
46	South Dakota	75 885	754 844	46	9.9	696 004	45	690 768	58 840	5 236	8.5	.8	10 903	1.4
47	Tennessee	41 217	5 689 283	16	138.0	4 877 203	17	4 591 023	812 080	286 180	16.7	6.2	123 838	2.2
48	Texas	261 797	20 851 820	2	79.6	16 986 335	3	14 225 513	3 865 485	2 760 822	22.8	19.4	6 669 666	32.0
49	Utah	82 144	2 233 169	34	27.2	1 722 850	35	1 461 037	510 319	261 813	29.6	17.9	201 559	9.0
50	Vermont	9 250	608 827	49	65.8	562 758	48	511 456	46 069	51 302	8.2	10.0	5 504	.9
51	Virginia	39 594	7 078 515	12	178.8	6 189 197	12	5 346 797	889 318	842 400	14.4	15.8	329 540	4.7
53	Washington	66 544	5 894 121	15	88.6	4 866 669	18	4 132 353	1 027 452	734 316	21.1	17.8	441 509	7.5
54	West Virginia	24 078	1 808 344	37	75.1	1 793 477	34	1 950 186	14 867	–156 709	.8	–8.0	12 279	.7
55	Wisconsin	54 310	5 363 675	18	98.8	4 891 954	16	4 705 642	471 721	186 312	9.6	4.0	192 921	3.6
56	Wyoming	97 100	493 782	50	5.1	453 589	50	469 557	40 193	–15 968	8.9	–3.4	31 669	6.4

[1] Federal Information Processing Standards (FIPS) codes for states and DC.   [2] Dry land and land temporarily or partially covered by water.   [3] Includes count resolution corrections through 1997 and adjustments based on Census 2000 dress rehearsal results.   [4] Persons of Hispanic or Latino origin may be of any race.

Sources: Land Area—U.S. Census Bureau, unpublished data file from Geography Division based on TIGER data base.   2000 Population—U.S. Census Bureau, Census of Population and Housing, Census 2000 Redistricting Data (Public Law 94-171) Summary Files (related Internet site <http://www.census.gov/dmd/www/2kresult.html>).   1990 Population—U.S. Census Bureau, (CO-99-8) County Population Estimates and Demographic Components of Population Change: Annual Time Series, July 1, 1990 to July 1, 1999 (includes revised April 1, 1990 Population Estimates Base)"; published 9 March 2000; <http://www.census.gov/population/estimates/county/co-99-8/99C8_00.txt>.   1980 Population—U.S. Census Bureau, "1980–1990 Intercensal Population Estimates by County" on diskette (related Internet site <http://www.census.gov/population/www/estimates/countypop.html>).

State	Population by age, 2000 (April 1) Percent—								Median age (years)	Males per 100 females, 2000 (April 1)	Population by race, 2000 (April 1) One race						Two or more races[2]
	Under 5 years	5 to 17 years	18 to 24 years	25 to 44 years	45 to 64 years	65 to 74 years	75 to 84 years	85 years and over			White	Black or African American	American Indian and Alaska Native	Asian	Native Hawaiian and Other Pacific Islander	Some other race[1]	
UNITED STATES	6.8	18.9	9.6	30.2	22.0	6.5	4.4	1.5	35.3	96.3	211 460 626	34 658 190	2 475 956	10 242 998	398 835	15 359 073	6 826 228
Alabama	6.7	18.6	9.9	29.0	22.8	7.1	4.4	1.5	35.8	93.3	3 162 808	1 155 930	22 430	31 346	1 409	28 998	44 179
Alaska	7.6	22.8	9.1	32.5	22.3	3.6	1.7	.4	32.4	107.0	434 534	21 787	98 043	25 116	3 309	9 997	34 146
Arizona	7.5	19.2	10.0	29.5	20.9	7.1	4.6	1.3	34.2	99.7	3 873 611	158 873	255 879	92 236	6 733	596 774	146 526
Arkansas	6.8	18.7	9.8	28.1	22.7	7.4	4.8	1.7	36.0	95.3	2 138 598	418 950	17 808	20 220	1 668	40 412	35 744
California	7.3	20.0	9.9	31.6	20.5	5.6	3.8	1.3	33.3	99.3	20 170 059	2 263 882	333 346	3 697 513	116 961	5 682 241	1 607 646
Colorado	6.9	18.7	10.0	32.6	22.2	5.3	3.3	1.1	34.3	101.4	3 560 005	165 063	44 241	95 213	4 621	309 931	122 187
Connecticut	6.6	18.2	8.0	30.3	23.2	6.8	5.1	1.9	37.4	93.9	2 780 355	309 843	9 639	82 313	1 366	147 201	74 848
Delaware	6.6	18.3	9.6	30.2	22.4	7.2	4.4	1.3	36.0	94.4	584 773	150 666	2 731	16 259	283	15 855	13 033
District of Columbia	5.7	14.4	12.7	33.1	21.9	6.3	4.4	1.6	34.6	89.0	176 101	343 312	1 713	15 189	348	21 950	13 446
Florida	5.9	16.9	8.3	28.6	22.7	9.1	6.4	2.1	38.7	95.3	12 465 029	2 335 505	53 541	266 256	8 625	477 107	376 315
Georgia	7.3	19.2	10.2	32.4	21.3	5.3	3.2	1.1	33.4	96.8	5 327 281	2 349 542	21 737	173 170	4 246	196 289	114 188
Hawaii	6.5	18.0	9.5	29.9	22.9	7.0	4.8	1.4	36.2	101.0	294 102	22 003	3 535	503 868	113 539	15 147	259 343
Idaho	7.5	21.0	10.7	28.0	21.5	5.9	4.0	1.4	33.2	100.5	1 177 304	5 456	17 645	11 889	1 308	54 742	25 609
Illinois	7.1	19.1	9.8	30.6	21.5	6.2	4.3	1.5	34.7	95.9	9 125 471	1 876 875	31 006	423 603	4 610	722 712	235 016
Indiana	7.0	18.9	10.1	29.5	22.1	6.5	4.4	1.5	35.2	96.3	5 320 022	510 034	15 815	59 126	2 005	97 811	75 672
Iowa	6.4	18.6	10.2	27.6	22.2	7.2	5.4	2.2	36.6	96.3	2 748 640	61 853	8 989	36 635	1 009	37 420	31 778
Kansas	7.0	19.5	10.3	28.6	21.4	6.5	4.8	1.9	35.2	97.7	2 313 944	154 198	24 936	46 806	1 313	90 725	56 496
Kentucky	6.6	18.0	9.9	30.0	23.0	6.8	4.3	1.4	35.9	95.6	3 640 889	295 994	8 616	29 744	1 460	22 623	42 443
Louisiana	7.1	20.2	10.6	28.9	21.6	6.3	3.9	1.3	34.0	93.8	2 856 161	1 451 944	25 477	54 758	1 240	31 131	48 265
Maine	5.5	18.1	8.1	29.1	24.8	7.5	5.0	1.8	38.6	94.8	1 236 014	6 760	7 098	9 111	382	2 911	12 647
Maryland	6.7	18.9	8.5	31.4	23.1	6.1	4.0	1.3	36.0	93.4	3 391 308	1 477 411	15 423	210 929	2 303	95 525	103 587
Massachusetts	6.3	17.4	9.1	31.3	22.4	6.7	5.0	1.8	36.5	93.0	5 367 286	343 454	15 015	238 124	2 489	236 724	146 005
Michigan	6.8	19.4	9.4	29.8	22.4	6.5	4.4	1.4	35.5	96.2	7 966 053	1 412 742	58 479	176 510	2 692	129 552	192 416
Minnesota	6.7	19.5	9.6	30.4	21.8	6.0	4.3	1.7	35.4	98.1	4 400 282	171 731	54 967	141 968	1 979	65 810	82 742
Mississippi	7.2	20.1	10.9	28.4	21.4	6.5	4.0	1.5	33.8	93.4	1 746 099	1 033 809	11 652	18 626	667	13 784	20 021
Missouri	6.6	18.9	9.6	29.1	22.3	7.0	4.7	1.8	36.1	94.6	4 748 083	629 391	25 076	61 595	3 178	45 827	82 061
Montana	6.1	19.4	9.5	27.2	24.4	6.9	4.8	1.7	37.5	99.3	817 229	2 692	56 068	4 691	470	5 315	15 730
Nebraska	6.8	19.5	10.2	28.5	21.5	6.8	4.8	2.0	35.3	97.2	1 533 261	68 541	14 896	21 931	836	47 845	23 953
Nevada	7.3	18.3	9.0	31.5	23.0	6.6	3.5	.9	35.0	103.9	1 501 886	135 477	26 420	90 266	8 426	159 354	76 428
New Hampshire	6.1	18.9	8.4	30.9	23.8	6.3	4.2	1.5	37.1	96.8	1 186 851	9 035	2 964	15 931	371	7 420	13 214
New Jersey	6.7	18.1	8.0	31.2	22.7	6.8	4.8	1.6	36.7	94.3	6 104 705	1 141 821	19 492	480 276	3 329	450 972	213 755
New Mexico	7.2	20.8	9.8	28.4	22.2	6.5	3.9	1.3	34.6	96.7	1 214 253	34 343	173 483	19 255	1 503	309 882	66 327
New York	6.5	18.2	9.3	30.7	22.3	6.7	4.5	1.6	35.9	93.1	12 893 689	3 014 385	82 461	1 044 976	8 818	1 341 946	590 182
North Carolina	6.7	17.7	10.0	31.1	22.5	6.6	4.1	1.3	35.3	96.0	5 804 656	1 737 545	99 551	113 689	3 983	186 629	103 260
North Dakota	6.1	18.9	11.4	27.2	21.6	7.1	5.3	2.3	36.2	99.6	593 181	3 916	31 329	3 606	230	2 540	7 398
Ohio	6.6	18.8	9.3	29.3	22.7	7.0	4.8	1.6	36.2	94.4	9 645 453	1 301 307	24 486	132 633	2 749	88 627	157 885
Oklahoma	6.8	19.0	10.3	28.3	22.3	7.0	4.5	1.7	35.5	96.6	2 628 434	260 968	273 230	46 767	2 372	82 898	155 985
Oregon	6.5	18.2	9.6	29.1	23.7	6.4	4.7	1.7	36.3	98.4	2 961 623	55 662	45 211	101 350	7 976	144 832	104 745
Pennsylvania	5.9	17.9	8.9	28.6	23.1	7.9	5.8	1.9	38.0	93.4	10 484 203	1 224 612	18 348	219 813	3 417	188 437	142 224
Rhode Island	6.1	17.5	10.2	29.6	22.0	7.0	5.5	2.0	36.7	92.5	891 191	46 908	5 121	23 665	567	52 616	28 251
South Carolina	6.6	18.6	10.2	29.6	23.0	6.7	4.1	1.3	35.4	94.5	2 695 560	1 185 216	13 718	36 014	1 628	39 926	39 950
South Dakota	6.8	20.1	10.3	27.3	21.2	7.0	5.2	2.1	35.6	98.5	669 404	4 685	62 283	4 378	261	3 677	10 156
Tennessee	6.6	18.0	9.6	30.2	23.2	6.7	4.2	1.4	35.9	94.9	4 563 310	932 809	15 152	56 662	2 205	56 036	63 109
Texas	7.8	20.4	10.5	31.1	20.2	5.5	3.3	1.1	32.3	98.6	14 799 505	2 404 566	118 362	562 319	14 434	2 438 001	514 633
Utah	9.4	22.8	14.2	28.1	17.0	4.5	3.0	1.0	27.1	100.4	1 992 975	17 657	29 684	37 108	15 145	93 405	47 195
Vermont	5.6	18.6	9.3	29.0	24.8	6.7	4.4	1.6	37.7	96.1	589 208	3 063	2 420	5 217	141	1 443	7 335
Virginia	6.5	18.0	9.6	31.6	23.0	6.1	3.9	1.2	35.7	96.3	5 120 110	1 390 293	21 172	261 025	3 946	138 900	143 069
Washington	6.7	19.0	9.5	30.8	22.8	5.7	4.1	1.4	35.3	99.1	4 821 823	190 267	93 301	322 335	23 953	228 923	213 519
West Virginia	5.6	16.6	9.5	27.7	25.2	8.2	5.3	1.8	38.9	94.6	1 718 777	57 232	3 606	9 434	400	3 107	15 788
Wisconsin	6.4	19.1	9.7	29.5	22.2	6.6	4.7	1.8	36.0	97.6	4 769 857	304 460	47 228	88 763	1 630	84 842	66 895
Wyoming	6.3	19.8	10.1	28.1	24.0	6.3	4.0	1.4	36.2	101.2	454 670	3 722	11 133	2 771	302	12 301	8 883

[1] Includes all other responses not included in the other five race categories shown. Also includes write-in entries such as multiracial, mixed, interracial, or a Hispanic/Latino group. [2] Refers to combinations of two or more of the six race categories shown under one race.

Source: Population by Age, Sex, and Race—U.S. Census Bureau; 2000 Census of Population and Housing, "Census 2000 Profiles of General Demographic Characteristics" data files, published May 2001 (related Internet site <http://www.census.gov/mp/www/pub/2000cen/mscen01.html>).

Table A–3. States — Group Quarters Population and Households

State	Group quarters population, 2000[1] Number	Institutionalized population[2]	Households, 2000 (April 1) Number	Percent change, 1990–2000	Persons per household	One-person	With 1 or more persons under 18 years	With 1 or more persons 65 years and over	Family households (families) Number	Percent with own children under 18 years	Married-couple Number	Percent with own children under 18 years[3]	Female householder[4] Number	Percent with own children under 18 years[3]	Nonfamily households Number	Percent change, 1990–2000
UNITED STATES	7 778 633	4 059 039	105 480 101	14.7	2.59	25.8	36.0	23.4	71 787 347	48.2	54 493 232	45.6	12 900 103	58.6	33 692 754	22.8
Alabama	114 720	65 363	1 737 080	15.3	2.49	26.1	36.1	24.1	1 215 968	46.2	906 916	43.1	246 466	57.2	521 112	29.3
Alaska	19 349	4 824	221 600	17.3	2.74	23.5	42.9	11.9	152 337	58.1	116 318	54.4	23 937	72.0	69 263	23.5
Arizona	109 850	63 768	1 901 327	38.9	2.64	24.8	35.4	24.5	1 287 367	47.2	986 303	43.5	210 781	61.4	613 960	43.2
Arkansas	73 908	45 152	1 042 696	17.0	2.49	25.6	35.6	25.3	732 261	45.7	566 401	41.9	126 561	60.7	310 435	29.6
California	819 754	413 656	11 502 870	10.8	2.87	23.5	39.7	22.3	7 920 049	52.0	5 877 084	50.9	1 448 510	57.6	3 582 821	10.5
Colorado	102 955	52 741	1 658 238	29.3	2.53	26.3	35.3	17.7	1 084 461	50.1	858 671	47.2	158 979	64.2	573 777	34.0
Connecticut	107 939	55 256	1 301 670	5.8	2.53	26.4	34.7	25.1	881 170	47.6	676 467	45.4	157 411	57.9	420 500	14.9
Delaware	24 583	11 510	298 736	20.7	2.54	25.0	35.4	23.9	204 590	46.5	153 136	42.8	38 986	58.9	94 146	31.4
District of Columbia	35 562	7 964	248 338	-.5	2.16	43.8	24.6	21.5	114 166	43.0	47 032	36.6	56 631	52.2	134 172	5.2
Florida	388 945	248 350	6 337 929	23.4	2.46	26.6	31.3	30.7	4 210 760	42.3	3 192 266	38.1	759 000	57.7	2 127 169	31.1
Georgia	233 822	126 023	3 006 369	27.0	2.65	23.6	39.1	18.8	2 111 647	49.8	1 548 800	47.3	435 410	59.3	894 722	36.9
Hawaii	35 782	7 690	403 240	13.2	2.92	21.9	37.9	27.4	287 068	45.0	216 077	44.8	49 923	47.3	116 172	25.2
Idaho	31 496	17 717	469 645	30.2	2.69	22.4	38.7	21.5	335 588	50.8	276 511	47.8	40 849	66.3	134 057	37.5
Illinois	321 781	174 727	4 591 779	9.3	2.63	26.8	36.2	23.2	3 105 513	48.8	2 353 892	47.3	563 718	56.0	1 486 266	16.4
Indiana	178 154	90 885	2 336 306	13.1	2.53	25.9	35.7	22.5	1 602 501	47.9	1 251 458	44.4	259 372	61.8	733 805	25.4
Iowa	104 169	50 256	1 149 276	8.0	2.46	27.2	33.3	25.4	769 684	46.9	633 254	43.4	98 270	65.5	379 592	17.3
Kansas	81 950	45 396	1 037 891	9.9	2.51	27.0	35.5	23.3	701 547	49.2	567 924	45.9	96 661	64.9	336 344	17.6
Kentucky	114 804	62 057	1 590 647	15.3	2.47	26.0	35.5	22.8	1 104 398	46.8	857 944	43.7	187 957	58.8	486 249	33.7
Louisiana	135 965	90 002	1 656 053	10.5	2.62	25.3	39.2	22.5	1 156 438	49.5	809 498	46.2	275 075	58.7	499 615	22.0
Maine	34 912	13 091	518 200	11.4	2.39	27.0	32.4	24.7	340 685	46.2	272 152	41.4	49 022	66.0	177 515	29.9
Maryland	134 056	69 318	1 980 859	13.3	2.61	25.0	37.3	21.7	1 359 318	48.7	994 549	46.4	279 876	56.9	621 541	23.5
Massachusetts	221 216	88 453	2 443 580	8.7	2.51	28.0	32.9	24.7	1 576 696	47.5	1 197 917	45.8	289 944	56.4	866 884	18.4
Michigan	249 889	126 132	3 785 661	10.7	2.56	26.2	35.6	22.8	2 575 699	48.0	1 947 710	44.8	473 802	59.9	1 209 962	23.4
Minnesota	135 883	63 058	1 895 127	15.0	2.52	26.9	34.8	21.3	1 255 141	49.9	1 018 245	46.9	168 782	66.0	639 986	23.7
Mississippi	95 414	50 826	1 046 434	14.8	2.63	24.6	39.6	23.7	747 159	48.6	520 844	45.0	180 705	58.8	299 275	26.3
Missouri	162 058	90 430	2 194 594	11.9	2.48	27.3	34.7	24.0	1 476 516	47.4	1 140 866	43.6	253 760	61.7	718 078	21.1
Montana	24 762	12 068	358 667	17.1	2.45	27.4	33.3	23.4	237 407	47.1	192 067	42.9	32 016	66.2	121 260	28.3
Nebraska	50 818	26 011	666 184	10.6	2.49	27.6	34.5	23.7	443 411	49.1	360 996	46.0	60 343	65.8	222 770	19.2
Nevada	33 675	22 173	751 165	61.1	2.62	24.9	35.3	21.3	498 333	47.9	373 201	44.5	83 482	60.7	252 832	59.1
New Hampshire	35 539	13 784	474 606	15.4	2.53	24.4	35.5	21.5	323 651	48.9	262 438	45.9	42 952	63.5	150 955	27.3
New Jersey	194 821	110 169	3 064 645	9.7	2.68	24.5	36.6	25.9	2 154 539	47.6	1 638 322	47.4	387 012	50.9	910 106	17.7
New Mexico	36 307	19 178	677 971	24.9	2.63	25.4	38.6	22.4	466 515	50.4	341 818	46.1	89 622	62.6	211 456	39.8
New York	580 461	262 262	7 056 860	6.3	2.61	28.1	35.0	25.0	4 639 387	48.1	3 289 514	46.4	1 038 176	55.2	2 417 473	12.4
North Carolina	253 881	106 659	3 132 013	24.4	2.49	25.4	35.3	21.8	2 158 869	46.1	1 645 346	43.0	389 997	58.3	973 144	38.0
North Dakota	23 631	9 688	257 152	6.8	2.41	29.3	32.7	24.7	166 150	48.4	137 433	45.1	20 148	67.7	91 002	22.0
Ohio	299 121	172 368	4 445 773	8.8	2.49	27.3	34.5	23.8	2 993 023	47.1	2 285 798	43.6	536 878	60.2	1 452 750	21.8
Oklahoma	112 375	66 746	1 342 293	11.3	2.49	26.7	35.7	23.8	921 750	47.2	717 611	43.4	152 575	61.9	420 543	19.9
Oregon	77 491	37 901	1 333 723	20.9	2.51	26.1	33.4	22.9	877 671	46.8	692 532	42.8	130 782	63.6	456 052	29.4
Pennsylvania	433 301	213 790	4 777 003	6.3	2.48	27.7	32.6	27.8	3 208 388	44.6	2 467 673	42.3	554 693	53.7	1 568 615	17.1
Rhode Island	38 816	13 801	408 424	8.1	2.47	28.6	32.9	26.3	265 398	47.0	196 757	43.6	52 609	60.3	143 026	20.1
South Carolina	135 037	60 533	1 533 854	21.9	2.53	25.0	36.5	22.6	1 072 822	46.2	783 142	42.6	226 958	57.7	461 032	39.8
South Dakota	28 418	14 387	290 245	12.0	2.50	27.6	34.8	25.0	194 330	49.0	157 391	45.2	26 205	67.3	95 915	21.8
Tennessee	147 946	83 397	2 232 905	20.5	2.48	25.8	35.2	22.5	1 547 835	45.7	1 173 960	42.5	287 899	57.6	685 070	35.5
Texas	561 109	374 704	7 393 354	21.8	2.74	23.7	40.9	19.9	5 247 794	51.9	3 989 741	50.2	937 589	60.2	2 145 560	24.2
Utah	40 480	19 467	701 281	30.5	3.13	17.8	45.8	18.6	535 294	56.0	442 931	55.5	65 941	61.2	165 987	31.3
Vermont	20 760	5 663	240 634	14.2	2.44	26.2	33.6	22.5	157 763	48.4	126 413	44.2	22 272	66.4	82 871	26.0
Virginia	231 398	111 484	2 699 173	17.8	2.54	25.1	35.9	20.9	1 847 796	47.7	1 426 044	45.3	320 290	58.3	851 377	28.5
Washington	136 382	57 218	2 271 398	21.3	2.53	26.2	35.2	20.4	1 499 127	49.5	1 181 995	45.8	224 618	65.4	772 271	27.1
West Virginia	43 147	24 009	736 481	7.0	2.40	27.1	31.8	27.3	504 055	42.3	397 499	39.5	79 120	53.5	232 426	23.4
Wisconsin	155 958	79 073	2 084 544	14.4	2.50	26.8	33.9	23.0	1 386 815	48.0	1 108 597	44.5	200 300	64.4	697 729	27.6
Wyoming	14 083	7 861	193 608	14.7	2.48	26.3	35.0	20.8	130 497	48.5	106 179	44.3	16 837	68.9	63 111	28.8

[1] As of April 1.   [2] Includes people under formally authorized, supervised care or custody in institutions at the time of enumeration (such as correctional institutions, nursing homes, and juvenile institutions).   [3] Under 18 years.   [4] No husband present.

Sources: Group Quarters Population—U.S. Census Bureau; 2000 Census of Population and Housing, "Census 2000 Profiles of General Demographic Characteristics" data files, published May 2001 (related Internet site <http://www.census.gov/mp/www/pub/2000cen/mscen01.html>).   Households, 2000—U.S. Census Bureau; 2000 Census of Population and Housing, "Census 2000 Profiles of General Demographic Characteristics" data files, published May 2001 (related Internet site <http://www.census.gov/mp/www/pub/2000cen/mscen01.html>).   Households, 1990—U.S. Census Bureau, 1990 Census of Population and Housing, Summary Tape File (STF) 1C on CD-ROM (related Internet site <http://homer.ssd.census.gov/cdrom/lookup>).

Table A–4. States — **Vital Statistics and Health**

| State | Births, 1997 | | Deaths, 1997 | | | | Physicians,[4] 1999 | | Community hospitals,[6] 1998 | | | Nursing and personal care facilities,[7] 1997 | | Medicare program enrollment,[9] 1999 | |
| | | | Total | | Infant[2] | | | | | Beds | | | | | |
	Number	Rate[1]	Number	Rate[1]	Number	Rate[3]	Number	Rate[5]	Number	Number	Rate[5]	Estab-lishments	Em-ployees[8]	Total[10]	Aged
UNITED STATES	3 880 894	14.5	2 314 245	8.6	28 045	7.2	693 345	254	5 015	839 988	311	33 140	2 013 278	[11]138 299 382	[11]133 237 188
Alabama	60 914	14.1	43 258	10.0	581	9.5	8 733	200	110	16 998	391	349	27 346	676 569	553 223
Alaska	9 947	16.3	2 575	4.2	75	7.5	1 054	170	17	1 240	202	21	694	40 062	33 338
Arizona	75 699	16.6	37 066	8.1	536	7.1	9 714	203	64	10 857	233	355	22 514	658 193	576 916
Arkansas	36 478	14.5	27 844	11.0	316	8.7	4 906	192	82	9 876	389	332	21 305	435 880	357 554
California	524 840	16.3	224 592	7.0	3 104	5.9	82 176	248	405	74 482	228	2 949	138 273	3 837 080	3 385 486
Colorado	56 533	14.5	25 626	6.6	397	7.0	9 914	244	69	9 179	231	333	23 669	458 380	394 517
Connecticut	43 109	13.2	29 415	9.0	310	7.2	11 859	361	33	6 949	212	470	45 140	511 611	455 570
Delaware	10 253	13.9	6 510	8.9	80	7.8	1 791	238	6	1 977	266	56	5 130	109 575	95 615
District of Columbia	7 927	15.0	6 129	11.6	105	13.2	3 935	758	12	3 552	681	115	4 839	75 619	66 219
Florida	192 383	13.1	154 497	10.5	1 366	7.1	36 760	243	204	49 231	330	1 222	98 391	2 770 576	2 472 896
Georgia	118 221	15.8	59 351	7.9	1 022	8.6	16 470	211	156	25 236	330	530	36 512	897 503	736 497
Hawaii	17 393	14.6	7 892	6.6	114	6.6	3 184	269	20	2 791	234	37	3 303	161 787	148 077
Idaho	18 582	15.3	8 976	7.4	127	6.8	1 944	155	42	3 414	277	143	7 570	161 362	141 679
Illinois	180 803	15.1	102 914	8.6	1 523	8.4	31 928	263	203	39 218	325	1 336	97 115	1 628 744	1 436 573
Indiana	83 436	14.2	53 130	9.0	682	8.2	11 753	198	111	19 401	328	1 010	56 307	844 835	731 685
Iowa	36 659	12.8	27 694	9.7	229	6.2	5 009	175	116	12 219	427	779	41 340	475 854	427 230
Kansas	37 289	14.3	23 750	9.1	276	7.4	5 424	204	129	10 923	414	505	29 755	389 103	346 757
Kentucky	53 203	13.6	37 998	9.7	387	7.3	8 382	212	106	15 240	387	375	31 174	615 436	487 877
Louisiana	66 025	15.2	40 006	9.2	630	9.5	10 975	251	126	17 820	408	610	35 225	597 485	494 949
Maine	13 669	11.0	11 993	9.6	70	5.1	2 913	232	38	3 768	302	271	14 851	213 210	178 598
Maryland	70 215	13.8	41 794	8.2	616	8.8	19 592	379	51	12 670	247	593	39 982	634 527	562 188
Massachusetts	80 364	13.1	54 685	8.9	421	5.2	26 062	422	82	16 493	268	1 311	78 804	954 180	825 864
Michigan	133 714	13.7	83 301	8.5	1 092	8.2	22 246	226	151	27 168	277	1 706	64 579	1 389 107	1 193 930
Minnesota	64 499	13.8	36 913	7.9	382	5.9	12 125	254	136	16 486	349	1 350	62 598	648 272	578 935
Mississippi	41 533	15.2	27 503	10.1	442	10.6	4 533	164	96	13 005	473	206	15 218	413 900	327 980
Missouri	74 037	13.7	54 322	10.0	564	7.6	12 695	232	122	20 685	380	952	54 694	854 472	734 440
Montana	10 849	12.3	7 769	8.8	75	6.9	1 683	191	53	4 413	502	149	7 235	135 415	117 593
Nebraska	23 319	14.1	15 282	9.2	173	7.4	3 679	221	86	8 133	490	269	19 097	252 231	226 916
Nevada	26 911	16.1	13 380	8.0	175	6.5	3 209	177	20	3 528	202	66	4 237	228 631	199 819
New Hampshire	14 313	12.2	9 458	8.1	62	4.3	2 813	234	28	2 841	240	139	8 869	166 751	144 530
New Jersey	113 279	14.1	72 137	9.0	719	6.3	24 525	301	83	26 353	326	629	52 372	1 194 539	1 064 754
New Mexico	26 871	15.6	12 653	7.3	164	6.1	3 717	214	36	3 489	201	147	9 633	229 124	196 179
New York	257 238	14.2	158 653	8.7	1 727	6.7	71 840	395	222	68 511	377	2 005	145 728	2 694 015	2 333 581
North Carolina	107 015	14.4	66 022	8.9	985	9.2	18 166	237	116	23 297	309	977	57 239	1 111 273	925 041
North Dakota	8 353	13.0	5 893	9.2	52	6.2	1 420	224	43	3 978	624	152	10 185	103 066	93 029
Ohio	152 033	13.6	105 345	9.4	1 189	7.8	26 731	237	172	35 187	313	1 756	119 587	1 692 072	1 473 557
Oklahoma	48 269	14.6	33 944	10.2	361	7.5	5 614	167	109	11 022	330	517	29 694	503 506	436 048
Oregon	43 809	13.5	28 771	8.9	256	5.8	7 519	227	60	6 809	207	561	22 470	483 898	428 641
Pennsylvania	144 224	12.0	127 925	10.6	1 098	7.6	35 148	293	212	44 739	373	2 027	119 728	2 088 116	1 864 828
Rhode Island	12 455	12.6	9 820	9.9	87	7.0	3 362	339	12	2 581	261	209	13 892	170 331	147 537
South Carolina	52 214	13.8	33 690	8.9	501	9.6	8 294	213	65	11 518	300	397	19 085	555 082	454 448
South Dakota	10 173	13.9	6 865	9.4	78	7.7	1 379	188	49	4 401	602	138	9 604	118 979	106 219
Tennessee	74 478	13.8	52 665	9.8	637	8.6	13 626	248	122	20 682	381	554	37 081	815 231	672 228
Texas	333 974	17.3	142 776	7.4	2 150	6.4	41 084	205	400	56 573	287	1 992	111 222	2 223 175	1 942 812
Utah	43 059	20.8	11 578	5.6	249	5.8	4 312	202	41	4 010	191	203	10 238	201 217	178 271
Vermont	6 607	11.2	5 053	8.6	40	6.1	1 860	313	14	1 671	283	95	4 925	87 644	74 923
Virginia	91 862	13.6	53 852	8.0	714	7.8	16 717	243	93	17 890	264	440	39 276	875 799	747 960
Washington	78 190	14.0	41 463	7.4	440	5.6	13 616	237	86	10 739	189	545	36 772	725 018	635 190
West Virginia	20 730	11.4	20 881	11.5	198	9.6	3 962	219	58	8 117	448	286	14 416	335 529	270 449
Wisconsin	66 557	12.8	44 891	8.6	431	6.5	12 167	232	123	16 693	320	944	51 644	777 273	689 270
Wyoming	6 387	13.3	3 745	7.8	37	5.8	825	172	25	1 935	403	27	2 721	64 448	56 549

[1] Per 1,000 resident population estimated as of July 1, 1997.   [2] Deaths of infants under 1 year old.   [3] Infant deaths per 1,000 live births.   [4] Active, nonfederal physicians as of December 31. Data subject to copyright; see below for source citation.   [5] Per 100,000 resident population estimated as of July 1 of the year shown.   [6] Nonfederal, short-stay (average length of stay less than 30 days) hospitals except hospital units of institutions.   Data subject to copyright; see below for source citation.   [7] SIC 805 includes skilled nursing care facilities; intermediate care facilities; and nursing and personal care, not elsewhere classified.   [8] Full- and part-time employees on the payroll in the pay period including March 12.   [9] Unduplicated count of persons enrolled in either hospital and/or supplemental medical insurance as of July 1.   [10] Includes disabled, not shown separately.   [11] Includes data not distributed by state.

Sources: Births—U.S. National Center for Health Statistics, "Vital Statistics of the United States, Vol. I, Natality," annual, and unpublished data.   Deaths—U.S. National Center for Health Statistics, "Vital Statistics of the United States, Vol. II, Mortality," annual, and unpublished data.   Physicians—American Medical Association, Chicago, IL, "Physician Characteristics and Distribution in the U.S., annual (copyright).   Community Hospitals—Health Forum, LLC, an American Hospital Association Company, Chicago, IL, "Hospital Statistics" 2000 edition and unpublished data (copyright).   Nursing and Personal Care Facilities—U.S. Census Bureau, County Business Patterns 1997 on CD-ROM (related Internet site <http://www.census.gov/epcd/cbp/view/cbpview.html>).   Medicare—U.S. Health Care Financing Administration, "Medicare County Enrollment as of July 1, 1999 - Aged and Disabled 3/2000 update," <http://www.hcfa.gov/stats/enroll/default.htm>.

State	Public school enrollment			Educational attainment, 1990			Median household income[2]			Persons below poverty level,[2] 1997				
	Fall				Percent—					Number			Percent	
										Persons of all ages				
	1998–1999	1994–1995[1]	1990	Persons 25 years and over	High school graduate or higher	Bachelor's degree or higher	1997 (dollars)	1989 (dollars)	Percent change, 1989–1997	Total	Net change, 1989–1997	Persons under 18 years	Persons of all ages	Persons under 18 years
UNITED STATES	46 368 903	43 993 459	41 058 718	158 868 436	75.2	20.3	37 005	30 056	23.1	35 573 858	3 830 994	14 113 067	13.3	19.9
Alabama	737 639	727 989	716 155	2 545 969	66.9	15.7	30 790	23 597	30.5	700 944	−22 670	260 970	16.2	23.8
Alaska	135 374	126 348	108 967	323 429	86.6	23.0	43 657	41 408	5.4	68 409	20 503	31 968	11.2	16.2
Arizona	847 416	735 752	635 900	2 301 177	78.7	20.3	34 751	27 540	26.2	720 713	156 351	305 109	15.5	23.2
Arkansas	452 267	448 109	425 717	1 496 150	66.3	13.3	27 875	21 147	31.8	442 856	5 767	169 089	17.5	25.0
California	5 844 111	5 342 071	5 002 596	18 695 499	76.2	23.4	39 595	35 798	10.6	5 195 477	1 567 892	2 223 674	16.0	24.6
Colorado	699 135	640 521	567 007	2 107 072	84.4	27.0	40 853	30 140	35.5	403 410	28 196	155 960	10.2	14.6
Connecticut	544 698	506 824	473 898	2 198 963	79.2	27.2	46 648	41 721	11.8	291 242	73 895	121 256	8.9	14.7
Delaware	113 735	107 228	96 156	428 499	77.5	21.4	41 315	34 875	18.5	73 868	17 645	28 193	10.0	15.4
District of Columbia	71 889	80 450	72 810	409 131	73.1	33.3	34 980	30 727	13.8	96 253	−25	33 503	19.3	33.7
Florida	2 337 757	2 108 968	1 812 155	8 887 168	74.4	18.3	32 877	27 483	10.6	2 120 825	525 639	775 012	14.4	21.0
Georgia	1 401 291	1 270 948	1 134 100	4 023 420	70.9	19.3	36 372	29 021	25.3	1 113 562	190 477	470 440	14.7	22.8
Hawaii	188 069	183 869	167 841	709 820	80.1	22.9	43 627	38 829	12.4	130 644	42 236	48 849	11.1	16.2
Idaho	244 722	240 601	214 664	601 292	79.7	17.7	33 612	25 257	33.1	159 237	28 649	61 496	13.0	17.3
Illinois	2 011 530	1 929 153	1 824 313	7 293 930	76.2	21.0	41 179	32 252	27.7	1 353 506	26 775	564 675	11.3	17.5
Indiana	989 015	969 419	947 784	3 489 470	75.6	15.6	37 909	28 797	31.6	583 055	9 423	228 246	9.9	14.8
Iowa	499 819	500 414	479 505	1 776 798	80.1	16.9	35 427	26 229	35.1	280 797	−26 623	100 262	9.9	13.7
Kansas	469 758	460 905	430 595	1 565 936	81.3	21.1	36 488	27 291	33.7	283 038	8 415	109 324	10.9	15.4
Kentucky	653 128	639 708	632 679	2 333 833	64.6	13.6	31 730	22 534	40.8	624 219	−57 608	229 043	16.0	23.1
Louisiana	768 734	799 237	765 022	2 536 994	68.3	16.1	30 466	21 949	38.8	793 472	−173 530	316 991	18.4	26.0
Maine	210 080	212 225	212 465	795 613	78.8	18.8	33 140	27 854	19.0	132 809	4 343	44 122	10.7	14.9
Maryland	841 671	790 938	703 379	3 122 665	78.4	26.5	45 289	39 386	15.0	484 987	99 691	194 703	9.5	14.9
Massachusetts	937 647	893 727	830 138	3 962 223	80.0	27.2	43 015	36 952	16.4	649 293	129 954	250 244	10.7	17.0
Michigan	1 698 501	1 604 141	1 636 182	5 842 642	76.8	17.4	38 883	31 020	25.3	1 127 886	−62 812	468 947	11.5	18.0
Minnesota	856 410	821 404	747 713	2 770 562	82.4	21.8	41 591	30 909	34.6	417 797	−17 534	167 853	8.9	13.1
Mississippi	503 742	505 962	509 252	1 538 997	64.3	14.7	28 527	20 136	41.7	494 044	−136 985	188 272	18.1	24.5
Missouri	913 689	864 301	808 221	3 291 579	73.9	17.8	34 502	26 362	30.9	658 159	−4 916	252 485	12.2	17.7
Montana	159 988	164 341	153 344	507 851	81.0	19.8	29 672	22 988	29.1	135 691	10 838	49 055	15.5	21.3
Nebraska	291 140	287 100	272 985	996 049	81.8	18.9	35 337	26 016	35.8	158 962	−11 654	57 013	9.6	12.6
Nevada	311 236	250 910	190 335	789 638	78.8	15.3	39 280	31 011	26.7	186 345	66 685	74 006	10.7	15.4
New Hampshire	204 713	189 286	171 104	713 894	82.2	24.4	42 023	36 329	15.7	87 975	18 871	30 356	7.5	10.0
New Jersey	1 259 166	1 173 960	1 097 317	5 166 233	76.7	24.9	47 903	40 927	17.0	749 198	176 046	302 459	9.3	14.8
New Mexico	328 715	327 253	301 380	922 590	75.1	20.4	30 836	24 087	28.0	333 013	27 979	139 054	19.3	27.5
New York	2 877 142	2 766 208	2 650 601	11 818 569	74.8	23.1	36 369	32 965	10.3	2 814 460	537 164	1 121 585	15.6	24.7
North Carolina	1 254 821	1 156 786	1 091 659	4 253 494	70.0	17.4	35 320	26 647	32.5	940 547	110 689	361 170	12.6	18.6
North Dakota	114 927	120 900	120 680	396 550	76.7	18.1	31 764	23 213	36.8	78 461	−9 815	27 807	12.5	16.8
Ohio	1 849 182	1 829 761	1 779 522	6 924 764	75.7	17.0	36 029	28 706	25.5	1 223 791	−101 977	465 752	11.0	16.0
Oklahoma	628 522	609 743	571 787	1 995 424	74.6	17.8	30 002	23 577	27.3	536 804	26 950	210 470	16.3	23.7
Oregon	542 809	519 945	471 013	1 855 369	81.5	20.6	37 284	27 250	36.8	379 506	34 639	134 932	11.6	16.3
Pennsylvania	1 816 414	1 764 946	1 666 743	7 872 932	74.7	17.9	37 267	29 069	28.2	1 297 614	13 985	482 596	10.9	16.6
Rhode Island	154 785	147 493	138 054	658 956	72.0	21.3	36 699	32 181	14.0	108 836	16 166	41 893	11.2	17.3
South Carolina	655 650	640 756	633 545	2 167 590	68.3	16.6	33 325	26 256	26.9	569 045	51 252	224 380	14.9	23.0
South Dakota	132 495	143 482	132 431	430 500	77.1	17.2	31 354	22 503	39.3	100 537	−5 768	38 270	14.0	19.0
Tennessee	892 936	870 594	806 796	3 139 066	67.1	16.0	32 047	24 807	29.2	734 108	−10 833	258 288	13.6	18.9
Texas	3 945 367	3 670 193	3 303 198	10 310 605	72.1	20.3	34 478	27 016	27.6	3 259 559	259 044	1 350 837	16.7	23.6
Utah	479 854	473 308	438 499	897 321	85.1	22.3	38 884	29 470	31.9	210 783	18 368	89 867	10.0	12.5
Vermont	105 120	104 593	95 243	357 245	80.8	24.3	35 210	29 792	18.2	56 967	3 598	18 244	9.7	12.7
Virginia	1 120 819	1 060 809	985 675	3 974 814	75.2	24.5	40 209	33 328	20.6	782 827	171 216	286 182	11.6	17.0
Washington	999 616	938 314	814 938	3 126 390	83.8	22.9	41 715	31 183	33.8	579 789	61 856	227 904	10.2	15.2
West Virginia	297 129	310 511	320 282	1 171 766	66.0	12.3	27 432	20 795	31.9	302 521	−42 572	102 253	16.8	24.7
Wisconsin	879 542	860 686	800 466	3 094 226	78.6	17.7	39 800	29 442	35.2	478 698	−29 847	196 327	9.2	14.3
Wyoming	94 988	100 369	95 907	277 769	83.0	18.8	33 197	27 096	22.5	57 421	4 968	20 080	12.0	15.3

[1] Revised. [2] 1997 data are model-based estimates; 1989 data are census estimates. For more information on these estimates, see appendix A. Source Notes and Explanations or <http://www.census.gov/hhes/www/saipe.html>.

Sources: Public School Enrollment, 1998-1999 and 1994-1995—U.S. National Center for Education Statistics, <http://nces.ed.gov/ccd/pubagency.html> (accessed: 16 March 2001). Public School Enrollment and Educational Attainment, 1990—U.S. Census Bureau, 1990 Census of Population and Housing, Summary Tape File (STF) 3C on CD-ROM (related Internet site <http://homer.ssd.census.gov/cdrom/lookup>). Income and Poverty, 1997—U.S. Census Bureau, "State and County Income and Poverty Estimates - 1997," published 22 November 2000, <http://www.census.gov/housing/saipe/estmod97/est97ALL.dat>. Income and Poverty, 1989—U.S. Census Bureau, 1990 Census of Population and Housing, Summary Tape File (STF) 3C on CD-ROM (related Internet site <http://homer.ssd.census.gov/cdrom/lookup>).

Table A–6. States — Crime, Housing, and Building Permits

State	Serious crimes known to police (as reported to the FBI) [1] Number 1999 Total	Violent[2]	Property[3]	Number 1990	Rate[4] 1999	Rate[4] 1990	Housing, 2000 Total units	Percent change, 1990–2000	Occupied units Number	Percent owner-occupied	New private housing units authorized by building permits, 2000 Number	Percent in structures with— One unit	Five units or more	Valuation ($1,000)
UNITED STATES	10 674 012	1 328 303	9 345 709	13 900 249	4 347	5 826	115 904 641	13.3	105 480 101	66.2	1 592 267	75.2	20.7	185 743 965
Alabama	184 492	20 432	164 060	189 406	4 433	5 181	1 963 711	17.6	1 737 080	72.5	17 406	78.5	19.1	1 718 032
Alaska	24 280	3 497	20 783	27 115	4 281	5 104	260 978	12.2	221 600	62.5	2 147	74.8	10.9	332 576
Arizona	278 661	25 931	252 730	286 187	5 870	7 933	2 189 189	31.9	1 901 327	68.0	61 485	79.4	18.3	7 157 587
Arkansas	102 269	10 731	91 538	113 661	4 016	4 839	1 173 043	17.2	1 042 696	69.4	9 203	75.3	15.0	858 621
California	1 260 684	207 900	1 052 784	1 955 842	3 805	6 572	12 214 549	9.2	11 502 870	56.9	145 575	72.1	24.9	23 343 968
Colorado	157 843	13 268	144 575	198 540	3 939	6 027	1 808 037	22.4	1 658 238	67.3	54 596	70.7	26.2	6 822 090
Connecticut	111 084	11 366	99 718	176 751	3 385	6 266	1 385 975	4.9	1 301 670	66.8	9 376	87.0	10.4	1 425 048
Delaware	35 927	5 005	30 922	35 431	4 765	5 319	343 072	18.3	298 736	72.3	4 611	84.9	15.1	414 089
District of Columbia	41 868	8 448	33 420	65 435	8 067	10 782	274 845	-1.3	248 338	40.8	806	23.2	74.9	53 993
Florida	931 961	128 332	803 629	1 095 149	6 204	8 477	7 302 947	19.7	6 337 929	70.1	155 269	68.6	28.0	17 462 405
Georgia	384 791	39 799	344 992	417 321	5 053	6 551	3 281 737	24.4	3 006 369	67.5	91 820	75.0	23.3	8 722 256
Hawaii	57 324	2 785	54 539	67 676	4 837	6 107	460 542	18.1	403 240	56.5	4 905	86.7	10.4	823 362
Idaho	39 684	3 112	36 572	40 552	3 190	4 075	527 824	27.7	469 645	72.4	10 915	88.7	5.5	1 358 936
Illinois	267 004	53 068	213 936	671 512	7 750	5 886	4 885 615	8.4	4 591 779	67.3	51 944	72.8	21.2	6 527 982
Indiana	177 355	17 954	159 401	195 840	4 069	4 823	2 532 319	12.7	2 336 306	71.4	37 903	80.2	15.3	4 414 450
Iowa	87 021	7 513	79 508	112 339	3 262	4 078	1 232 511	7.8	1 149 276	72.3	12 500	67.8	25.3	1 333 198
Kansas	34 327	3 035	31 292	128 415	7 588	5 195	1 131 200	8.3	1 037 891	69.2	12 542	74.1	19.9	1 397 050
Kentucky	56 767	7 938	48 829	121 043	4 846	3 286	1 750 927	16.2	1 590 647	70.8	18 460	80.3	14.8	1 767 186
Louisiana	241 847	30 579	211 268	241 822	5 737	6 827	1 847 181	7.6	1 656 053	67.9	14 720	89.1	7.3	1 552 997
Maine	35 460	1 243	34 217	45 394	2 845	3 697	651 901	11.0	518 200	71.6	6 177	93.1	4.1	722 989
Maryland	186 989	23 561	163 428	278 747	4 136	5 830	2 145 283	13.4	1 980 859	67.7	30 358	82.8	16.1	3 232 130
Massachusetts	195 639	33 256	162 383	238 901	3 236	5 044	2 621 989	6.0	2 443 580	61.7	18 000	78.9	15.4	2 741 246
Michigan	406 393	54 885	351 508	545 020	4 281	5 961	4 234 279	10.0	3 785 661	73.8	52 489	81.8	15.0	6 255 876
Minnesota	169 982	13 061	156 921	159 526	3 559	3 646	2 065 946	11.8	1 895 127	74.6	32 814	77.9	17.2	4 203 938
Mississippi	90 385	8 063	82 322	71 574	5 106	4 590	1 161 953	15.0	1 046 434	72.3	11 270	67.6	29.5	917 766
Missouri	234 794	25 496	209 298	249 123	4 909	5 369	2 442 017	11.0	2 194 594	70.3	24 321	73.7	17.8	2 569 413
Montana	18 674	974	17 700	31 834	3 699	4 289	412 633	14.3	358 667	69.1	2 572	60.8	19.0	235 126
Nebraska	67 049	7 030	60 019	65 847	4 049	4 189	722 668	9.4	666 184	67.4	9 105	71.5	23.9	830 398
Nevada	84 185	10 311	73 874	67 611	4 654	6 081	827 457	59.5	751 165	60.9	32 285	79.7	19.4	3 312 244
New Hampshire	13 194	694	12 500	39 045	2 705	3 651	547 024	8.6	474 606	69.7	6 680	91.3	5.8	936 637
New Jersey	277 000	33 539	243 461	421 079	3 402	5 447	3 310 275	7.6	3 064 645	65.6	34 585	73.0	20.7	3 375 991
New Mexico	92 600	12 733	79 867	78 703	6 055	6 853	780 579	23.5	677 971	70.0	8 869	92.3	6.8	1 072 810
New York	537 078	101 781	435 297	1 137 857	3 401	6 346	7 679 307	6.3	7 056 860	53.0	44 105	54.1	30.1	4 991 541
North Carolina	384 312	40 401	343 911	353 425	5 105	5 397	3 523 944	25.0	3 132 013	69.4	78 376	75.4	22.3	8 643 196
North Dakota	14 608	467	14 141	14 583	2 443	3 024	289 677	4.8	257 152	66.6	2 128	59.1	31.2	190 198
Ohio	354 710	30 181	324 529	468 698	4 151	5 028	4 783 051	9.4	4 445 773	69.1	49 745	76.4	17.8	6 153 635
Oklahoma	157 263	17 064	140 199	176 026	4 685	5 599	1 514 400	7.7	1 342 293	68.4	11 148	80.5	17.1	1 204 001
Oregon	165 062	12 418	152 644	159 755	4 991	5 635	1 452 709	21.7	1 333 723	64.3	19 877	78.6	16.0	2 533 336
Pennsylvania	345 405	47 614	297 791	356 245	3 030	3 126	5 249 750	6.3	4 777 003	71.3	41 076	84.0	12.1	4 616 212
Rhode Island	35 498	2 839	32 659	53 712	3 582	5 381	439 837	6.1	408 424	60.0	2 596	86.9	7.3	296 394
South Carolina	208 987	33 360	175 627	209 842	5 383	6 023	1 753 670	23.1	1 533 854	72.2	32 812	75.8	21.6	3 532 670
South Dakota	16 182	1 041	15 141	18 486	2 933	3 052	323 208	10.5	290 245	68.2	4 196	74.9	20.9	369 138
Tennessee	248 849	37 037	211 812	218 433	4 680	5 445	2 439 443	20.4	2 232 905	69.9	32 203	75.9	21.0	3 377 637
Texas	1 002 171	111 635	890 536	1 328 954	5 010	7 830	8 157 575	16.4	7 393 354	63.8	141 231	76.9	20.1	15 418 421
Utah	104 315	5 840	98 475	95 937	4 950	5 612	768 594	28.4	701 281	71.5	17 638	83.4	10.4	2 137 948
Vermont	16 078	653	15 425	22 794	2 795	4 173	294 382	8.5	240 634	70.6	2 506	88.3	7.6	319 491
Virginia	215 373	20 350	195 023	275 475	3 138	4 452	2 904 192	16.3	2 699 173	68.1	48 402	82.1	16.4	5 051 607
Washington	295 660	21 344	274 316	298 711	5 214	6 186	2 451 075	20.6	2 271 398	64.6	39 021	65.3	28.5	4 426 088
West Virginia	37 289	4 831	32 458	44 890	2 451	2 503	844 623	8.1	736 481	75.2	3 763	87.6	9.5	359 560
Wisconsin	171 155	12 796	158 359	214 899	3 284	4 396	2 321 144	12.9	2 084 544	68.4	34 154	70.3	19.0	3 916 846
Wyoming	16 484	1 112	15 372	19 086	3 449	4 210	223 854	10.1	193 608	70.0	1 582	90.3	6.8	313 656

[1] Data on serious crimes have not been adjusted for underreporting; this may affect comparability over time or among geographic areas.   [2] Includes murder and nonnegligent manslaughter, forcible rape, robbery, and aggravated assault.   [3] Includes burglary, larceny-theft, and motor vehicle theft.   [4] Per 100,000 resident population provided by the U.S. Federal Bureau of Investigation.

Sources: Serious Crimes Known to Police—U.S. Federal Bureau of Investigation, Uniform Crime Reporting Program, unpublished data, annual (related Internet site <http://www.fbi.gov/ucr/ucr.htm>).   Housing, 2000—U.S. Census Bureau, 2000 Census of Population and Housing, "Census 2000 Profiles of General Demographic Characteristics" data files, published May 2001 (related Internet site <http://www.census.gov/mp/www/pub/2000cen/mscen01.html>).   Housing, 1990—U.S. Census Bureau, 1990 Census of Population and Housing, Summary Tape File (STF) 1C on CD-ROM (related Internet site <http://homer.ssd.census.gov/cdrom/lookup>).   Building Permits—U.S. Census Bureau, "New Residential Construction–Building Permits," e-mail from Manufacturing and Construction Division/Residential Construction Branch, subject: building permits by place 2000, 22 May 2001 (related Internet site <http://www.census.gov/const/www/permitsindex.html>).

Table A–7. States — Labor Force and Private Business Establishments and Employment

State	Civilian labor force, 2000		Unemployment		Private nonfarm businesses								Annual payroll per employee, 1998	
					Establishments				Employment[2]					
	Total	Percent change, 1999–2000	Total	Rate[1]	1998	Percent change, 1990–1998	1995	1990	1998	Percent change, 1990–1998	1995	1990	Amount (dollars)	Percent of national average
UNITED STATES	140 863 000	1.1	5 655 000	4.0	6 941 822	12.4	6 613 218	6 175 563	108 117 731	15.7	100 334 745	93 476 087	30 609	100.0
Alabama	2 154 273	.6	99 092	4.6	100 316	15.9	96 053	86 537	1 604 110	19.4	1 553 309	1 342 993	25 142	82.1
Alaska	321 964	1.0	21 296	6.6	18 212	23.3	17 264	14 773	196 135	24.3	181 975	157 798	35 098	114.7
Arizona	2 346 997	-.5	91 223	3.9	110 245	27.5	99 583	86 489	1 763 508	42.6	1 507 132	1 236 401	27 815	90.9
Arkansas	1 238 151	.7	54 930	4.4	62 353	16.7	60 231	53 409	944 935	25.8	891 175	750 877	23 033	75.2
California	17 090 815	3.0	845 192	4.9	773 925	3.8	740 583	745 686	12 026 989	6.3	10 959 318	11 318 516	33 797	110.4
Colorado	2 275 545	.5	62 501	2.7	130 354	34.6	118 192	96 828	1 757 628	40.8	1 558 141	1 248 022	30 604	100.0
Connecticut	1 746 489	2.2	39 345	2.3	92 362	-.5	91 189	92 816	1 493 964	.8	1 415 400	1 482 023	38 974	127.3
Delaware	409 058	5.0	16 247	4.0	22 871	21.9	20 991	18 761	354 643	14.0	324 498	311 017	33 361	109.0
District of Columbia	278 875	-.7	16 112	5.8	19 571	-.1	19 451	19 587	402 070	-5.8	413 757	426 959	43 172	141.0
Florida	7 490 307	1.8	268 808	3.6	420 638	16.4	390 232	361 330	5 756 353	24.9	5 208 285	4 607 247	26 047	85.1
Georgia	4 173 274	2.3	154 398	3.7	194 213	23.2	179 006	157 667	3 198 950	28.0	2 920 361	2 498 877	29 599	96.7
Hawaii	595 432	.4	25 517	4.3	29 603	1.0	29 942	29 313	416 571	-3.7	423 822	432 663	27 107	88.6
Idaho	657 712	1.0	31 914	4.9	35 961	35.6	32 972	26 513	423 615	41.1	379 161	300 163	25 012	81.7
Illinois	6 419 316	.6	279 433	4.4	304 533	11.7	293 694	272 738	5 221 782	12.4	4 950 462	4 647 094	33 648	109.9
Indiana	3 084 135	.3	100 203	3.2	146 197	13.9	141 253	128 311	2 540 866	18.2	2 403 189	2 150 168	28 115	91.9
Iowa	1 563 063	-.6	40 922	2.6	80 838	10.5	78 464	73 130	1 213 285	20.4	1 138 402	1 007 900	25 064	81.9
Kansas	1 411 024	-1.6	52 323	3.7	74 019	12.4	70 894	65 858	1 081 941	21.0	982 066	893 830	26 570	86.8
Kentucky	1 981 868	.8	81 752	4.1	89 593	13.4	85 123	79 006	1 443 015	21.7	1 347 087	1 186 001	25 564	83.5
Louisiana	2 029 566	-1.1	112 475	5.5	100 667	14.0	96 063	88 290	1 577 220	24.1	1 452 355	1 271 219	25 870	84.5
Maine	688 754	2.8	24 153	3.5	38 334	10.0	36 298	34 840	456 715	7.7	432 290	424 027	25 309	82.7
Maryland	2 804 827	1.1	108 284	3.9	126 577	10.2	122 350	114 874	1 938 727	7.1	1 820 731	1 810 796	30 854	100.8
Massachusetts	3 236 597	-1.4	85 610	2.6	167 929	6.1	160 350	158 329	2 924 913	5.5	2 735 963	2 772 444	36 196	118.3
Michigan	5 201 404	1.1	185 356	3.6	235 403	11.9	226 973	210 303	3 919 567	14.9	3 704 315	3 411 784	32 822	107.2
Minnesota	2 738 685	1.3	89 540	3.3	134 981	20.3	125 927	112 187	2 271 671	24.0	2 072 503	1 832 156	30 856	100.8
Mississippi	1 326 349	4.6	75 285	5.7	59 771	13.0	57 095	52 888	937 023	29.6	871 814	723 174	22 483	73.5
Missouri	2 929 827	3.1	101 447	3.5	143 912	10.5	139 980	130 287	2 310 122	14.7	2 169 026	2 013 560	27 994	91.5
Montana	479 132	1.1	23 524	4.9	30 957	23.7	29 109	25 028	277 144	24.9	260 973	221 851	21 508	70.3
Nebraska	924 298	1.4	27 537	3.0	48 655	11.2	47 128	43 749	720 252	22.7	674 779	587 044	25 239	82.5
Nevada	986 052	4.7	39 978	4.1	44 613	49.0	37 219	29 932	800 861	49.2	672 260	536 607	27 280	89.1
New Hampshire	685 511	2.6	19 191	2.8	36 842	10.8	34 647	33 249	518 526	17.9	464 122	439 636	28 666	93.7
New Jersey	4 187 899	-.4	157 410	3.8	230 860	7.8	220 991	214 076	3 368 365	4.6	3 184 458	3 220 178	37 344	122.0
New Mexico	832 835	2.9	40 400	4.9	42 608	19.4	40 031	35 700	540 186	29.2	506 634	417 986	24 313	79.4
New York	8 941 082	.7	407 769	4.6	481 962	3.3	467 262	466 762	6 993 814	-1.2	6 782 174	7 075 441	39 268	128.3
North Carolina	3 958 354	2.3	144 079	3.6	198 690	20.4	181 972	165 076	3 223 178	20.3	2 992 175	2 678 669	26 924	88.0
North Dakota	338 822	.6	10 106	3.0	20 288	6.9	20 269	18 979	249 476	26.8	230 090	196 675	22 182	72.5
Ohio	5 782 649	.5	236 536	4.1	270 343	8.7	263 739	248 694	4 806 046	13.2	4 550 590	4 245 977	29 185	95.3
Oklahoma	1 648 017	-.4	50 048	3.0	84 881	13.7	81 395	74 663	1 167 709	24.1	1 055 227	940 800	24 550	80.2
Oregon	1 802 889	2.4	87 486	4.9	99 183	22.3	93 468	81 077	1 310 750	28.9	1 185 415	1 017 239	28 780	94.0
Pennsylvania	5 971 913	-.1	249 922	4.2	292 659	4.7	283 998	279 595	4 906 190	6.7	4 702 892	4 598 441	29 670	96.9
Rhode Island	504 800	.1	20 586	4.1	28 245	1.9	27 766	27 726	402 485	2.3	379 595	393 456	27 618	90.2
South Carolina	1 985 249	1.1	76 504	3.9	94 985	19.1	87 990	79 743	1 526 106	20.5	1 395 070	1 266 320	25 266	82.5
South Dakota	401 151	.4	9 145	2.3	23 521	14.8	22 708	20 492	289 422	34.5	268 483	215 104	22 125	72.3
Tennessee	2 798 336	-.6	110 174	3.9	131 110	15.7	124 014	113 292	2 299 348	23.0	2 153 264	1 869 268	27 156	88.7
Texas	10 324 527	1.0	437 488	4.2	462 875	17.3	438 262	394 482	7 570 820	29.1	6 786 893	5 864 637	30 272	98.9
Utah	1 104 208	1.7	35 837	3.2	52 025	42.2	45 882	36 586	866 146	51.7	744 430	570 830	25 631	83.7
Vermont	331 574	-1.3	9 657	2.9	21 261	7.2	20 542	19 839	239 034	11.1	224 327	215 222	24 716	80.7
Virginia	3 609 703	2.3	79 801	2.2	172 182	15.0	162 378	149 695	2 700 589	16.3	2 481 306	2 321 517	30 090	98.3
Washington	3 045 244	-1.0	157 714	5.2	161 473	22.4	151 925	131 919	2 134 598	21.1	1 948 923	1 762 046	34 324	112.1
West Virginia	824 578	1.0	45 626	5.5	41 703	10.7	40 599	37 687	547 234	13.4	530 596	482 517	24 265	79.3
Wisconsin	2 934 931	1.6	103 769	3.5	138 635	13.5	133 238	122 142	2 319 343	19.0	2 186 060	1 948 856	27 987	91.4
Wyoming	266 945	1.9	10 377	3.9	17 888	22.3	17 133	14 630	163 791	24.0	157 472	132 061	24 300	79.4

[1] Civilian unemployed as a percent of total civilian labor force.   [2] For pay period including March 12 of the year shown.

Sources: Civilian Labor Force—U.S. Bureau of Labor Statistics; Local Area Unemployment Statistics; 2000 data published 2 May 2001, 1999 data published 30 May 2001; <ftp://ftp.bls.gov/pub/time.series/la/> (related Internet site <http://www.bls.gov/lauhome.htm>).   Private Business Establishments and Employment—U.S. Census Bureau; County Business Patterns on CD-ROM; annual (related Internet site <http://www.census.gov/epcd/cbp/view/cbpview.html>).

Table A–8. States — Personal Income and Earnings

State	Personal income, 1998													Manufacturing earnings		
		Per capita[1]				Earnings										
									Percent, by selected industry—							
							Goods-related		Service-related							
	Total (mil. dol.)	Percent change, 1990–1998	Amount (dollars)	Percent of national average	Transfer payments (mil. dol.)	Total[2] (mil. dol.)	Total[3]	Manufacturing	Total[4]	Retail trade	FIRE[5]	Services	Government	1998 ($1,000)	1997 ($1,000)	1996 ($1,000)
UNITED STATES	7 351 547.0	50.5	27 203	100.0	983 530.0	5 302 066.0	23.4	16.8	75.8	8.8	9.0	28.4	16.0	891 190 000	847 972 000	800 423 000
Alabama	95 955.6	49.7	22 054	81.1	15 961.2	66 930.1	27.7	20.5	70.8	9.4	5.6	23.1	20.0	13 753 680	13 376 333	12 886 639
Alaska	17 124.0	36.3	27 835	102.3	2 440.9	13 111.9	D	4.3	81.2	8.9	4.0	20.8	33.1	565 686	583 074	601 083
Arizona	112 973.9	78.4	24 206	89.0	15 261.1	79 155.1	21.8	13.5	77.2	10.4	9.5	28.6	15.9	10 709 917	9 634 054	8 774 355
Arkansas	53 725.4	57.3	21 167	77.8	9 607.4	37 066.7	28.0	21.9	67.9	10.9	4.9	21.5	16.5	8 114 421	7 739 513	7 469 080
California	920 452.2	40.4	28 163	103.5	109 387.7	677 217.3	20.8	15.2	78.0	8.8	8.9	31.6	15.6	102 939 260	95 856 549	87 524 160
Colorado	119 043.7	82.9	29 994	110.3	11 098.4	90 240.5	20.3	11.0	78.9	9.0	9.0	28.6	16.0	9 915 018	9 169 829	8 532 923
Connecticut	122 190.7	39.0	37 338	137.3	14 121.6	86 121.4	25.1	20.1	74.7	7.5	13.7	29.5	11.9	17 311 162	16 436 269	15 337 069
Delaware	21 863.1	51.0	29 383	108.0	2 551.7	16 947.2	28.7	22.7	70.6	8.4	14.9	24.5	14.0	3 843 055	3 660 919	3 553 879
District of Columbia	18 987.9	18.1	36 415	133.9	2 584.3	40 652.7	D	2.3	96.6	2.2	5.7	39.4	43.6	941 922	901 726	867 065
Florida	400 208.5	54.8	26 845	98.7	62 522.9	248 372.2	14.4	8.2	84.6	11.0	9.9	33.0	17.0	20 489 647	19 431 632	18 637 071
Georgia	197 318.7	71.0	25 839	95.0	22 733.9	151 756.3	21.5	15.6	77.3	8.8	7.8	26.0	16.2	23 644 729	22 168 568	21 008 774
Hawaii	31 856.2	27.9	26 759	98.4	3 794.2	23 309.3	8.8	3.1	90.5	10.8	8.5	28.7	30.5	716 754	709 654	754 378
Idaho	27 177.4	69.3	22 079	81.2	3 552.1	18 941.1	D	17.1	D	10.1	5.2	22.3	18.2	3 241 927	3 093 699	2 937 750
Illinois	360 317.1	51.7	29 853	109.7	41 565.5	263 398.3	24.2	18.6	75.4	7.7	10.3	29.3	13.2	48 995 852	47 625 156	44 523 708
Indiana	148 650.9	51.8	25 163	92.5	19 383.1	106 049.3	37.1	30.1	62.4	9.1	6.2	21.8	13.1	31 920 916	30 060 690	28 630 204
Iowa	70 797.1	46.5	24 745	91.0	9 742.0	49 141.5	27.5	21.1	69.0	9.2	7.7	22.3	15.8	10 356 843	9 803 023	9 189 590
Kansas	67 383.4	49.4	25 537	93.9	8 466.9	47 411.8	25.3	18.3	74.7	9.6	6.1	23.4	17.2	8 676 091	8 164 979	7 515 145
Kentucky	87 273.9	52.6	22 183	81.5	15 063.9	61 248.0	29.2	21.1	69.1	9.9	5.0	22.4	18.0	12 937 809	12 394 354	11 589 170
Louisiana	96 877.7	50.8	22 206	81.6	16 964.7	67 725.1	26.4	13.6	73.0	9.0	5.4	26.3	18.7	9 191 117	8 839 756	8 390 466
Maine	29 315.8	36.2	23 499	86.4	4 964.7	19 645.5	24.2	17.7	75.3	11.6	6.6	27.0	18.3	3 481 402	3 411 038	3 256 430
Maryland	156 759.3	41.9	30 557	112.3	16 347.9	101 409.6	15.2	8.5	84.5	9.0	8.1	31.9	23.7	8 617 296	8 180 182	7 785 154
Massachusetts	205 813.6	47.2	33 496	123.1	26 554.9	154 005.8	20.9	16.0	79.0	8.3	10.6	35.6	12.3	24 677 689	23 543 236	22 254 146
Michigan	264 016.0	49.1	26 885	98.8	35 055.9	192 095.9	36.9	31.2	62.9	8.1	5.7	24.2	13.2	59 879 767	57 000 561	54 581 721
Minnesota	138 306.9	57.5	29 263	107.6	15 427.7	101 523.0	D	20.5	D	8.9	8.9	26.5	13.3	20 817 967	19 779 198	18 675 862
Mississippi	54 410.1	60.4	19 776	72.7	10 307.0	36 726.4	27.9	20.7	69.8	9.7	4.5	22.8	21.1	7 609 819	7 169 938	6 960 763
Missouri	136 753.8	50.3	25 150	92.5	20 233.1	99 230.4	24.9	18.2	74.7	9.4	7.9	27.0	15.0	18 044 814	17 752 493	16 737 354
Montana	18 671.5	50.4	21 229	78.0	3 063.2	12 009.4	17.9	7.9	80.1	11.8	5.9	26.6	21.8	949 555	853 721	817 339
Nebraska	43 053.2	50.6	25 924	95.3	5 494.6	31 163.1	19.9	13.7	75.4	8.6	7.3	25.2	17.0	4 260 189	4 091 261	3 852 984
Nevada	50 918.5	102.1	29 200	107.3	5 279.8	37 227.0	18.2	4.7	81.6	9.4	8.5	38.4	14.6	1 735 424	1 592 163	1 489 979
New Hampshire	34 958.3	51.8	29 480	108.4	3 806.7	23 207.7	29.0	22.3	70.8	11.6	7.3	28.0	11.5	5 180 331	4 894 033	4 509 226
New Jersey	278 348.6	44.9	34 383	126.4	31 392.7	190 545.7	19.7	15.2	80.2	7.5	9.5	31.3	14.1	28 890 291	27 789 456	26 587 411
New Mexico	36 688.2	61.3	21 164	77.8	5 593.0	25 319.8	17.0	7.3	80.6	10.6	5.2	27.2	27.2	1 851 778	1 820 127	1 680 938
New York	583 061.2	38.9	32 108	118.0	93 972.1	432 571.5	15.3	11.6	84.6	6.4	20.7	31.0	14.5	50 071 702	47 925 703	46 366 814
North Carolina	190 008.5	64.4	25 181	92.6	26 130.9	138 538.5	29.3	22.5	69.1	9.2	7.0	22.6	17.7	31 119 905	30 152 031	28 669 590
North Dakota	14 600.4	44.3	22 892	84.2	2 292.5	10 196.3	16.6	8.0	77.9	9.5	5.6	25.0	20.8	818 283	754 696	686 991
Ohio	292 999.2	43.5	26 073	95.8	42 197.2	208 359.9	31.4	25.5	68.1	9.2	6.8	24.8	14.6	53 090 841	51 501 318	49 364 389
Oklahoma	73 349.9	43.7	21 964	80.7	11 445.4	51 096.2	25.9	16.0	72.8	9.4	5.3	24.0	20.5	8 151 721	7 724 507	7 314 517
Oregon	85 043.5	63.0	25 912	95.3	11 139.7	60 103.3	26.1	18.6	72.7	10.4	7.1	25.2	15.7	11 151 563	10 617 275	9 686 341
Pennsylvania	329 687.1	39.8	27 469	101.0	53 391.1	226 718.2	26.9	20.6	72.8	8.7	8.0	29.9	13.3	46 774 842	45 013 390	43 118 436
Rhode Island	27 914.2	37.6	28 262	103.9	4 691.5	17 890.2	22.6	17.6	77.2	8.8	8.0	31.2	17.9	3 154 097	3 088 475	2 986 736
South Carolina	85 897.9	53.0	22 372	82.2	13 265.7	60 400.1	30.1	22.9	69.4	10.6	6.2	22.1	19.5	13 813 387	13 425 772	12 907 490
South Dakota	17 331.0	53.2	23 715	87.2	2 430.2	11 909.9	20.9	14.2	71.2	10.0	7.0	23.8	17.0	1 694 918	1 542 794	1 419 254
Tennessee	132 756.5	61.4	24 437	89.8	20 540.0	98 605.3	27.0	20.4	72.8	10.4	6.8	27.7	13.5	20 152 760	19 683 235	18 911 753
Texas	500 086.8	68.1	25 369	93.3	59 395.9	388 313.5	25.3	14.1	74.0	8.9	7.4	26.5	14.8	54 748 360	49 906 807	46 321 126
Utah	46 717.0	80.1	22 240	81.8	4 857.4	35 540.3	23.0	13.9	76.5	10.3	7.9	26.7	18.2	4 955 043	4 798 736	4 487 879
Vermont	14 529.4	42.5	24 602	90.4	2 046.8	9 988.8	27.4	20.2	71.1	10.0	5.6	28.5	16.0	2 018 648	1 906 589	1 829 927
Virginia	190 528.1	49.3	28 063	103.2	18 822.9	138 258.4	18.2	11.9	81.6	8.1	7.2	29.6	24.3	16 445 718	15 868 028	15 224 623
Washington	163 347.9	66.4	28 719	105.6	19 389.8	118 132.7	22.5	15.9	76.3	8.9	6.5	29.0	17.8	18 811 380	17 770 966	15 998 788
West Virginia	36 569.4	39.9	20 185	74.2	8 561.0	22 682.7	27.3	15.0	72.7	9.5	4.1	25.0	21.3	3 393 792	3 296 656	3 313 567
Wisconsin	137 256.4	54.2	26 284	96.6	17 160.5	96 051.0	33.6	27.2	65.6	8.7	6.9	23.2	14.4	26 116 131	25 050 743	23 492 974
Wyoming	11 670.9	43.0	24 312	89.4	1 474.7	7 804.1	28.6	5.7	70.6	9.7	4.9	18.6	24.3	444 781	417 095	409 989

[1] Based on resident population estimated as of July 1, 1998. [2] Includes farm earnings; see table A-10 for these data. [3] Includes mining and construction, not shown separately. [4] Includes agricultural services, forestry, and fisheries; transportation and public utilities; and wholesale trade, not shown separately. [5] Finance, insurance, and real estate.

Source: Personal Income and Earnings—U.S. Bureau of Economic Analysis, "Regional Economic Information System (REIS) 1969-1998" on CD-ROM (related Internet site <http://www.bea.doc.gov/bea/regional/data.htm>).

State	Manufacturing, 1997								Water use per day,[3] 1995					
	Establishments		All employees		Production workers		Value added by manufacture (mil. dol.)	Value of shipments (mil. dol.)	Withdrawals					
	Total	Percent with 20 or more employees	Number[1]	Annual payroll (mil. dol.)	Number[2]	Wages (mil. dol.)			Total (mil. gal.)	Percent ground water	By selected major use— (mil. gal.)			Consumptive use (mil. gal.)
											Irrigation	Public supply	Industrial	
UNITED STATES	363 753	33.1	16 888 016	572 101.1	12 124 001	339 723.0	1 826 590.0	3 842 061.4	398 514	19.4	133 626	39 779	22 367	101 052
Alabama	5 444	38.4	352 618	10 187.8	275 637	6 928.4	29 221.5	67 970.1	7 097	6.3	139	813	733	532
Alaska	488	20.9	10 770	331.2	8 805	238.2	1 159.3	3 305.0	329	40.3	1	81	57	35
Arizona	4 917	27.9	193 616	6 753.6	121 994	3 000.1	26 898.9	43 030.3	6 830	41.7	5 672	807	39	3 843
Arkansas	3 316	37.6	230 153	5 778.4	187 493	4 192.7	19 346.8	45 186.0	8 767	62.2	5 936	381	187	4 761
California	49 418	30.9	1 809 667	65 762.8	1 181 865	31 140.0	195 872.8	379 612.4	45 937	31.9	28 894	5 622	575	25 558
Colorado	5 480	23.1	173 069	6 176.8	115 308	3 177.7	20 673.0	40 012.8	13 840	16.4	12 735	705	123	5 235
Connecticut	5 844	33.0	252 330	10 452.1	153 045	4 895.3	27 295.2	46 938.2	4 453	3.7	28	393	10	171
Delaware	675	34.4	41 084	1 474.3	28 959	899.8	5 389.5	13 397.3	1 495	7.4	48	89	64	74
District of Columbia	200	17.5	2 858	101.1	1 926	60.9	170.8	320.2	10	4.9	–	–	1	15
Florida	15 992	22.7	433 149	13 185.1	291 452	6 826.0	40 213.4	77 477.5	18 183	23.9	3 469	2 065	353	2 782
Georgia	9 083	36.3	533 830	15 534.1	410 713	10 173.4	55 550.1	124 526.8	5 818	20.5	722	1 153	664	1 173
Hawaii	921	17.3	15 109	405.0	9 899	231.6	1 262.4	3 192.5	1 934	27.5	652	214	20	551
Idaho	1 647	25.4	66 184	2 099.8	50 362	1 277.2	6 393.1	16 952.9	15 141	18.7	13 048	189	47	4 342
Illinois	17 953	36.6	887 350	31 837.9	629 423	18 713.8	95 287.3	200 020.0	19 922	4.8	180	1 823	452	882
Indiana	9 303	42.4	625 692	22 121.4	478 248	14 956.5	67 210.9	142 270.7	9 139	7.8	116	669	2 275	505
Iowa	3 749	37.7	235 880	7 573.3	175 933	4 936.1	28 673.3	62 413.7	3 035	17.4	39	373	258	290
Kansas	3 309	34.8	193 742	6 532.5	141 169	4 052.5	17 650.6	46 296.4	5 235	67.1	3 383	370	53	3 620
Kentucky	4 218	40.6	288 405	9 198.1	223 868	6 251.6	38 337.6	86 636.1	4 420	5.1	12	496	347	318
Louisiana	3 545	33.0	165 777	6 054.5	123 566	3 967.7	29 066.9	80 424.0	9 848	13.7	769	638	2 582	1 925
Maine	1 812	28.3	82 288	2 591.1	62 647	1 746.0	6 530.6	14 097.6	326	24.6	27	100	11	50
Maryland	3 996	30.4	163 992	5 840.5	109 564	3 249.2	18 721.6	36 505.9	7 729	3.2	62	834	326	229
Massachusetts	9 554	34.7	417 135	16 379.0	257 050	7 734.8	44 337.8	77 876.6	5 511	6.4	82	725	85	186
Michigan	16 045	35.9	833 429	34 418.9	630 390	23 486.0	93 809.5	214 900.7	12 064	7.1	227	1 300	1 854	668
Minnesota	8 091	33.7	382 530	13 126.1	260 158	7 250.1	36 629.9	76 244.9	3 392	21.0	157	485	140	417
Mississippi	3 008	42.6	227 800	5 599.4	182 630	3 905.8	17 088.5	39 658.3	3 200	80.8	1 742	344	290	1 572
Missouri	7 497	33.3	371 448	11 647.1	270 297	7 197.3	43 186.1	93 115.5	7 029	12.7	567	699	39	692
Montana	1 160	15.4	19 611	560.1	14 988	394.0	1 732.2	4 866.3	8 860	2.5	8 546	143	60	1 957
Nebraska	1 960	31.2	106 690	3 040.5	84 085	2 132.7	10 822.7	27 859.2	10 548	58.8	7 550	286	30	7 021
Nevada	1 615	25.3	37 849	1 178.0	26 247	677.2	3 298.1	6 361.8	2 301	39.0	1 644	468	15	1 364
New Hampshire	2 328	32.5	98 934	3 361.4	68 942	1 935.5	11 320.1	19 813.1	1 323	6.2	6	98	43	35
New Jersey	11 812	32.4	409 788	15 430.2	275 840	8 152.1	50 101.7	97 060.8	6 113	9.5	125	1 037	396	257
New Mexico	1 593	18.4	39 664	1 135.8	29 334	721.4	13 440.2	17 906.1	3 505	48.6	2 993	311	8	1 980
New York	23 908	28.0	785 891	26 515.8	538 186	14 695.8	76 999.8	146 720.2	16 782	6.0	30	3 000	259	603
North Carolina	11 306	40.9	773 548	21 297.9	601 190	14 061.0	78 638.0	161 900.5	9 286	5.8	239	769	369	730
North Dakota	704	26.7	21 956	604.8	16 364	386.9	1 802.4	5 115.9	1 122	10.9	117	73	11	181
Ohio	17 974	38.4	984 201	35 950.5	730 170	23 561.0	112 491.4	241 902.9	10 523	8.6	27	1 420	557	791
Oklahoma	4 087	29.1	164 060	4 963.2	122 705	3 229.5	17 233.7	37 453.2	2 040	59.7	864	567	21	716
Oregon	5 768	29.0	213 111	7 095.3	158 506	4 545.8	25 077.2	47 666.0	7 906	13.2	6 168	504	378	3 206
Pennsylvania	17 128	37.1	826 521	27 641.3	597 544	17 045.1	86 212.1	172 193.2	9 685	8.9	16	1 546	1 682	565
Rhode Island	2 535	27.8	75 599	2 288.6	52 889	1 279.8	5 484.2	10 482.0	411	6.7	2	114	1	24
South Carolina	4 450	42.1	346 142	10 369.4	267 548	6 856.0	33 657.8	70 797.0	6 203	5.2	52	543	700	321
South Dakota	888	32.9	46 539	1 162.6	33 230	707.4	3 880.9	12 305.5	460	40.7	269	88	5	249
Tennessee	7 407	39.2	483 823	14 351.9	375 121	9 468.8	44 355.2	98 503.1	10 076	4.3	24	777	863	233
Texas	21 808	31.1	959 665	32 760.8	663 929	18 163.1	129 390.0	297 657.0	29 608	29.7	9 451	3 294	2 296	11 124
Utah	2 860	30.1	119 140	3 726.1	84 129	2 218.7	11 343.5	24 014.4	4 459	17.7	3 533	497	86	2 333
Vermont	1 226	27.7	42 533	1 459.6	29 318	758.0	4 044.6	7 803.0	565	8.8	4	47	9	24
Virginia	5 986	34.1	370 595	11 557.8	279 682	7 412.2	43 563.0	83 814.0	8 262	4.3	30	786	583	226
Washington	7 801	27.7	328 511	13 004.1	213 330	7 046.4	30 434.8	78 852.5	8 860	19.9	6 469	1 179	649	3 081
West Virginia	1 505	34.4	72 813	2 460.7	55 643	1 658.9	9 311.0	18 293.3	4 619	3.2	Z	176	1 316	353
Wisconsin	9 936	39.3	562 479	18 766.4	416 254	11 952.6	54 947.1	117 383.0	7 252	10.5	169	600	441	443
Wyoming	503	17.9	8 448	256.4	6 426	174.8	1 031.1	2 955.1	7 059	4.8	6 595	90	3	2 809

[1] Average number of production workers plus the number of other (nonproduction) employees for the pay period including March 12. [2] Average number of production workers for the pay periods including the 12th of March, May, August, and November. [3] In millions of gallons per day.

Sources: Manufacturing—U.S. Census Bureau, 1997 Economic Census – Manufacturing, generated by Statistical Compendia Branch, using American Factfinder at <http://www.census.gov/>, (June 2000) [related Internet site <http://www.census.gov/epcd/www/97EC31.HTM>]. Water Use—U.S. Geological Survey, "Water Use in the United States," individual state/county and US by state files from <http://water.usgs.gov/watuse/spread95.html>, (accessed: September 1999).

Table A–10. States — Farm Population, Farm Earnings, and Agriculture

State	Farm population, 1990 Number	Farm population, 1990 Percent of total[1]	Farm earnings 1998 Total ($1,000)	Farm earnings 1998 Percent of total[2]	Farm earnings 1997 ($1,000)	Farms Number	Farms Percent Less than 50 acres	Farms Percent 500 acres or more	Land in farms Total acreage (1,000)	Land in farms Net change, 1992–1997[3] (1,000)	Land in farms Average size of farm	Land in farms Total cropland (1,000)	Value of farm products sold Total ($1,000)	Value of farm products sold Average per farm (dollars)	Value Percent from Crops[4]	Value Percent from Livestock and poultry[5]
UNITED STATES	3 871 583	1.6	43 016 000	.8	45 698 000	1 911 859	29.5	18.4	931 795	–13 736	487	431 145	196 864 649	102 970	49.8	50.2
Alabama................	59 349	1.5	1 045 235	1.6	932 599	41 384	33.8	9.2	8 704	254	210	4 198	3 098 989	74 884	20.4	79.6
Alaska.................	1 160	.2	18 649	.1	21 672	548	35.4	16.4	881	–42	1 608	95	24 650	44 982	64.8	35.2
Arizona................	6 967	.2	800 723	1.0	648 200	6 135	44.8	27.1	26 867	–8 171	4 379	1 277	1 903 408	310 254	64.2	35.8
Arkansas	63 589	2.7	1 515 409	4.1	1 700 883	45 142	24.1	16.4	14 365	237	318	10 062	5 479 692	121 388	39.9	60.1
California	150 535	.5	8 002 197	1.2	8 407 862	74 126	60.6	11.7	27 699	–1 280	374	10 804	23 032 259	310 718	74.0	26.0
Colorado	45 118	1.4	719 814	.8	599 652	28 268	28.4	34.2	32 634	–1 349	1 154	10 509	4 534 213	160 401	29.3	70.7
Connecticut	5 250	.2	188 342	.2	161 504	3 687	54.7	2.8	359	1	97	181	421 648	114 361	62.6	37.4
Delaware	6 486	1.0	118 522	.7	86 564	2 460	47.6	11.9	580	–10	236	487	690 794	280 811	25.3	74.7
District of Columbia	–	–	–	–	–	X	X	X	X	X	X	X	X	X	X	X
Florida	47 436	.4	2 492 670	1.0	2 169 340	34 799	57.9	8.7	10 454	–312	300	3 640	6 004 554	172 550	80.2	19.8
Georgia	80 083	1.2	1 774 258	1.2	1 802 887	40 334	31.4	12.6	10 671	646	265	5 371	4 992 918	123 789	38.5	61.5
Hawaii.................	6 277	.6	164 304	.7	159 179	5 473	89.0	2.6	1 439	–150	263	292	496 935	90 798	80.8	19.2
Idaho.................	44 869	4.5	867 410	4.6	648 342	22 314	39.0	22.6	11 830	–1 639	530	6 309	3 345 864	149 945	53.0	47.0
Illinois	207 016	1.8	1 115 205	.4	1 729 734	73 051	23.1	25.1	27 205	–46	372	23 921	8 556 486	117 130	76.8	23.2
Indiana	188 133	3.4	507 141	.5	922 905	57 916	31.4	15.1	15 111	–508	261	12 849	5 229 977	90 303	62.1	37.9
Iowa	256 562	9.2	1 693 638	3.4	3 030 950	90 792	18.3	22.8	31 167	–180	343	26 822	11 947 894	131 596	51.8	48.2
Kansas	108 083	4.4	1 201 726	2.5	1 325 029	61 593	14.9	37.9	46 089	–583	748	30 021	9 207 130	149 483	35.0	65.0
Kentucky	174 204	4.7	1 065 729	1.7	1 065 618	82 273	33.9	5.9	13 334	–332	162	8 549	3 064 460	37 247	51.5	48.5
Louisiana	40 103	1.0	380 617	.6	573 615	23 823	34.1	17.3	7 877	39	331	5 331	2 031 277	85 265	69.5	30.5
Maine	11 008	.9	100 487	.5	79 231	5 810	29.6	9.3	1 212	–47	209	540	438 673	75 503	48.4	51.6
Maryland	32 596	.7	300 133	.3	226 722	12 084	43.3	8.2	2 155	–69	178	1 613	1 312 086	108 580	35.0	65.0
Massachusetts	9 342	.2	165 502	.1	195 405	5 574	56.0	2.7	518	–8	93	224	454 404	81 522	78.6	21.4
Michigan	120 496	1.3	468 037	.2	513 620	46 027	31.9	10.7	9 873	–215	215	7 892	3 567 825	77 516	61.7	38.3
Minnesota	207 956	4.8	965 470	1.0	734 669	73 367	18.0	20.8	25 995	328	354	21 492	8 290 264	112 997	50.7	49.3
Mississippi	56 225	2.2	839 778	2.3	828 297	31 318	22.3	14.5	10 125	–64	323	5 947	3 127 383	99 859	41.3	58.7
Missouri	180 097	3.5	424 624	.4	995 172	98 860	20.1	15.5	28 826	279	292	19 229	5 367 813	54 297	43.0	57.0
Montana	45 718	5.7	244 124	2.0	172 663	24 279	18.4	53.0	58 608	–1 035	2 414	17 629	1 870 732	77 051	48.3	51.7
Nebraska	117 658	7.5	1 481 636	4.8	1 610 749	51 454	14.2	42.2	45 525	1 132	885	22 093	9 831 519	191 074	38.6	61.4
Nevada	4 831	.4	61 446	.2	47 573	2 829	39.6	26.1	6 409	–2 854	2 266	847	356 565	126 039	42.5	57.5
New Hampshire	5 576	.5	35 293	.2	36 105	2 937	41.2	5.2	415	29	141	133	149 467	50 891	49.3	50.7
New Jersey	17 283	.2	249 918	.1	228 337	9 101	66.5	3.8	833	–15	91	595	697 380	76 627	85.0	15.0
New Mexico	15 090	1.0	600 214	2.4	522 883	14 094	37.0	35.5	45 787	–1 062	3 249	2 179	1 617 708	114 780	28.6	71.4
New York	82 256	.5	551 355	.1	346 757	31 757	24.3	10.7	7 254	–204	228	4 722	2 834 512	89 256	35.3	64.7
North Carolina	116 801	1.8	2 174 674	1.6	2 984 233	49 406	39.6	8.2	9 122	186	185	5 608	7 676 523	155 376	33.8	66.2
North Dakota	60 288	9.4	563 763	5.5	–41 978	30 504	6.4	63.9	39 359	–79	1 290	27 025	2 869 322	94 064	76.5	23.5
Ohio	198 914	1.8	1 009 065	.5	1 453 217	68 591	30.7	10.0	14 103	–145	206	11 341	4 684 277	68 293	60.4	39.6
Oklahoma	82 929	2.6	658 277	1.3	711 656	74 214	20.5	21.6	33 219	1 076	448	14 844	4 146 351	55 870	21.9	78.1
Oregon	68 729	2.4	747 932	1.2	790 214	34 030	56.3	12.9	17 449	–160	513	5 286	2 969 194	87 252	71.2	28.8
Pennsylvania...........	117 119	1.0	696 848	.3	582 340	45 457	29.2	5.4	7 168	–22	158	5 032	3 997 565	87 942	32.1	67.9
Rhode Island	1 124	.1	27 214	.2	23 131	735	59.6	2.0	55	6	75	26	48 200	65 578	81.8	18.2
South Carolina	48 565	1.4	306 125	.5	445 975	20 189	34.4	10.6	4 593	121	228	2 463	1 588 173	78 665	49.8	50.2
South Dakota	76 170	10.9	941 499	7.9	804 134	31 284	11.5	52.2	44 355	–473	1 418	19 355	3 569 951	114 114	46.3	53.7
Tennessee.............	111 680	2.3	110 619	.1	268 145	76 818	39.5	5.0	11 122	–47	145	7 069	2 178 389	28 358	52.5	47.5
Texas	192 392	1.1	2 511 051	.6	2 579 353	194 301	27.6	21.4	131 308	422	676	37 662	13 766 527	70 852	31.2	68.8
Utah	11 685	.7	192 929	.5	171 817	14 181	46.3	16.4	12 025	2 400	848	2 070	877 295	61 864	28.2	71.8
Vermont	11 810	2.1	147 264	1.5	112 250	5 828	25.0	10.0	1 262	–16	217	617	476 343	81 734	12.5	87.5
Virginia	80 560	1.3	373 498	.3	379 798	41 095	32.0	9.0	8 228	–69	200	4 322	2 343 518	57 027	33.3	66.7
Washington	60 243	1.2	1 503 168	1.3	1 291 353	29 011	51.4	16.2	15 180	–546	523	7 914	4 767 727	164 342	68.2	31.8
West Virginia	23 753	1.3	–4 845	Z	–6 461	17 772	21.1	7.5	3 456	188	194	1 337	447 428	25 176	14.5	85.5
Wisconsin	195 550	4.0	839 302	.9	456 193	65 602	19.5	9.2	14 900	–563	227	10 353	5 579 861	85 056	29.4	70.6
Wyoming	15 919	3.5	58 011	.7	167 912	9 232	16.9	50.5	34 089	1 213	3 692	2 968	898 527	97 327	19.3	80.7

[1] For 1990 corrected population, see table A-1. Percent is based on 1990 uncorrected population because only total population is corrected. [2] For total earnings, see table A-8. [3] Most data are comparable between 1992 and 1997; however, it should be noted that farms with all acreage in Conservation or Wetlands Reserve Programs (excluded in 1992) are included in 1997, as are short rotation woody crops which includes Christmas trees and maple sap gathering (in Forestry in 1992). [4] Includes nursery and greenhouse crops. [5] Includes related products.

Sources: Farm Population—U.S. Census Bureau, 1990 Census of Population and Housing, Summary Tape File (STF) 3C on CD-ROM (related Internet site <http://homer.ssd.census.gov/cdrom/lookup>). Farm Earnings—U.S. Bureau of Economic Analysis, "Regional Economic Information System (REIS) 1969-1998" on CD-ROM (related Internet site <http://www.bea.doc.gov/bea/regional/reis/ca45/>). Agriculture—U.S. Department of Agriculture, National Agricultural Statistics Service, 1997 Census of Agriculture, Volume 1, Geographic Area Series, 1A, 1B, 1C CD-ROM Set (related Internet site <http://www.nass.usda.gov/census/>).

Table A–11. States — Wholesale Trade and Retail Trade

State	Wholesale trade[1] (NAICS 42), 1997 Estab-lishments	Sales Total (mil. dol.)	Sales Merchant wholesalers (mil. dol.)	Paid em-ployees[2]	Annual payroll (mil. dol.)	Operating expenses (mil. dol.)	Retail trade[1] (NAICS 44-45), 1997 Estab-lishments	Sales Total (mil. dol.)	Per capita[3] Amount (dollars)	Per capita[3] Percent of national average	Percent from general mer-chandise stores	Annual payroll Paid em-ployees[2]	Annual payroll Total (mil. dol.)	Per paid em-ployee (dollars)
UNITED STATES	453 470	4 059 657.8	2 333 131.2	5 796 557	214 915.4	443 572.9	1 118 447	2 460 886.0	9 190	100.0	13.4	13 991 103	237 195.5	16 953
Alabama	6 315	40 986.3	26 045.8	79 229	2 394.7	4 844.9	20 163	36 623.3	8 477	92.2	15.5	231 665	3 381.7	14 598
Alaska	784	2 989.8	2 148.8	6 860	256.8	507.9	2 866	6 251.4	10 268	111.7	20.0	32 502	670.5	20 628
Arizona	6 689	45 899.1	26 412.6	80 155	2 748.9	5 311.0	16 283	43 960.9	9 657	105.1	13.0	232 050	4 223.9	18 202
Arkansas	3 619	27 515.4	14 409.6	41 385	1 136.6	2 271.9	12 600	21 643.7	8 575	93.3	18.4	132 335	1 904.4	14 391
California	57 841	548 864.5	342 227.7	757 294	29 875.0	64 165.6	106 357	263 118.3	8 167	88.9	13.1	1 354 797	26 362.7	19 459
Colorado	7 383	60 310.4	27 610.4	88 364	3 282.0	6 213.5	18 299	40 536.0	10 417	113.4	12.8	225 647	4 163.3	18 451
Connecticut	5 283	76 167.9	54 110.8	77 716	3 595.3	7 560.0	14 574	34 938.9	10 690	116.3	9.5	186 935	3 634.3	19 442
Delaware	906	12 585.5	2 943.2	13 509	619.5	1 262.7	3 736	8 237.0	11 206	121.9	13.5	47 116	798.7	16 952
District of Columbia	348	3 918.6	1 091.0	5 008	223.0	411.3	2 075	2 788.8	5 274	57.4	6.3	19 608	351.5	17 925
Florida	31 214	187 079.9	121 260.1	296 139	9 678.2	20 378.7	66 643	151 191.2	10 297	112.0	13.0	841 814	14 169.5	16 832
Georgia	13 978	163 782.6	69 922.1	191 087	7 519.7	15 252.1	33 073	72 212.5	9 646	105.0	12.9	420 676	6 943.6	16 506
Hawaii	1 872	7 147.5	5 088.7	18 532	576.0	1 213.5	5 088	11 317.8	9 516	103.5	20.1	64 218	1 161.8	18 092
Idaho	1 980	10 127.8	6 081.3	22 828	628.0	1 303.0	5 848	11 649.6	9 623	104.7	13.1	63 732	1 079.7	16 941
Illinois	21 951	275 968.4	142 923.4	325 752	13 324.5	27 788.1	44 568	108 002.2	8 992	97.8	13.0	610 790	10 596.0	17 348
Indiana	8 896	66 350.1	38 354.0	112 705	3 737.8	7 412.2	24 954	57 241.7	9 748	106.1	15.4	337 867	5 273.8	15 609
Iowa	5 399	35 453.7	25 728.6	63 596	1 820.1	3 746.2	14 695	26 723.8	9 362	101.9	13.0	175 694	2 633.4	14 989
Kansas	5 085	42 209.9	23 579.8	59 954	1 946.8	3 921.6	12 271	22 571.9	8 627	93.9	15.3	140 412	2 191.1	15 604
Kentucky	5 051	37 242.9	23 683.8	69 309	2 071.2	4 190.9	17 369	33 332.7	8 530	92.8	16.1	212 189	3 128.1	14 742
Louisiana	6 390	46 972.3	34 931.9	76 350	2 375.2	4 827.7	17 863	35 807.9	8 229	89.5	16.2	224 412	3 307.9	14 740
Maine	1 726	7 305.6	6 051.1	19 932	616.2	1 231.5	7 074	12 737.1	10 229	111.3	10.9	72 897	1 164.2	15 970
Maryland	6 283	54 906.7	31 714.9	92 458	3 656.3	7 019.8	19 798	46 428.2	9 116	99.2	12.5	274 260	4 914.0	17 917
Massachusetts	9 993	112 792.4	61 530.3	146 827	6 484.8	12 686.7	26 209	58 578.0	9 579	104.2	10.1	335 736	5 894.8	17 558
Michigan	13 936	159 432.3	70 982.0	189 057	7 629.6	15 704.7	39 564	93 706.1	9 576	104.2	16.1	529 441	8 922.3	16 852
Minnesota	9 348	99 444.5	56 577.7	131 787	5 024.0	10 030.4	20 888	48 098.0	10 260	111.6	12.9	282 413	4 528.5	16 035
Mississippi	3 173	18 445.2	13 925.7	36 520	1 012.1	2 143.3	12 791	20 774.5	7 605	82.8	17.3	138 372	1 935.3	13 986
Missouri	9 522	91 411.9	47 744.0	125 929	4 639.8	9 354.1	24 181	51 269.9	9 482	103.2	15.2	297 556	4 945.0	16 619
Montana	1 574	7 596.8	6 045.5	14 356	371.6	765.3	5 042	7 779.1	8 853	96.3	14.7	48 337	746.5	15 443
Nebraska	3 157	38 015.4	17 741.8	41 002	1 170.2	2 461.1	8 295	16 529.3	9 981	108.6	13.3	102 684	1 554.6	15 140
Nevada	2 253	12 806.9	8 185.7	27 251	918.5	1 865.4	6 222	18 220.8	10 874	118.3	13.5	89 452	1 798.2	20 103
New Hampshire	2 033	11 371.1	7 618.2	22 631	875.0	1 731.7	6 645	15 812.0	13 477	146.6	13.1	84 170	1 422.0	16 894
New Jersey	17 812	227 309.0	129 415.1	266 944	11 886.1	26 750.7	34 837	79 914.9	9 922	108.0	10.2	420 724	7 926.0	18 839
New Mexico	2 182	7 397.6	5 400.6	21 344	601.1	1 201.7	7 421	14 984.5	8 697	94.6	14.2	86 300	1 455.5	16 865
New York	37 499	319 697.6	217 216.8	414 249	17 185.8	37 754.1	75 241	139 303.9	7 678	83.5	11.4	805 200	14 329.8	17 796
North Carolina	12 284	98 080.1	48 386.9	157 774	5 574.1	11 039.1	35 563	72 356.8	9 740	106.0	11.9	416 287	6 697.4	16 088
North Dakota	1 604	8 618.4	7 464.2	16 992	454.4	934.3	3 569	6 702.1	10 457	113.8	13.9	40 685	616.1	15 144
Ohio	17 322	160 415.6	76 172.9	254 226	9 192.2	18 406.0	44 521	102 938.8	9 181	99.9	14.6	630 098	9 924.5	15 751
Oklahoma	5 191	32 132.3	20 292.5	59 641	1 756.1	3 612.6	14 352	27 065.6	8 166	88.9	16.7	161 613	2 406.9	14 893
Oregon	5 943	53 679.1	38 230.9	74 790	2 578.7	5 192.5	14 467	33 396.8	10 297	112.0	16.8	178 349	3 308.8	18 552
Pennsylvania	17 138	159 354.2	80 673.7	237 567	8 588.2	17 081.0	50 208	109 948.5	9 150	99.6	11.5	650 144	10 561.9	16 245
Rhode Island	1 590	7 602.7	5 058.1	18 762	635.2	1 276.1	4 169	7 505.8	7 605	82.8	10.2	45 747	752.2	16 442
South Carolina	5 035	34 179.8	19 994.2	58 910	1 866.8	3 763.1	18 481	33 634.3	8 874	96.6	13.0	209 256	3 107.2	14 849
South Dakota	1 402	7 874.2	6 181.7	15 509	389.8	794.3	4 311	11 707.1	16 018	174.3	8.2	45 867	689.6	15 034
Tennessee	8 234	82 626.4	47 023.5	120 228	3 975.4	8 044.6	24 808	50 813.2	9 448	102.8	15.3	304 452	4 810.3	15 800
Texas	33 346	323 111.7	170 652.6	425 750	15 504.9	31 787.8	74 105	182 516.1	9 430	102.6	14.2	950 848	16 197.1	17 034
Utah	3 277	21 271.9	13 618.2	44 312	1 420.4	2 763.4	7 656	19 964.6	9 666	105.2	12.8	114 474	1 856.9	16 221
Vermont	941	4 731.4	4 109.5	10 987	330.6	740.3	4 093	5 898.6	10 020	109.0	7.5	36 306	603.3	16 618
Virginia	7 868	61 046.7	34 446.6	106 365	3 784.4	7 276.7	29 032	62 569.9	9 293	101.1	13.8	379 039	6 202.6	16 364
Washington	10 039	75 397.8	47 863.7	118 810	4 376.0	8 684.1	22 841	52 472.9	9 363	101.9	14.2	283 653	5 385.9	18 988
West Virginia	1 956	10 290.4	6 503.4	23 805	681.1	1 396.6	8 082	14 057.9	7 743	84.3	16.2	90 087	1 309.3	14 534
Wisconsin	8 025	57 192.9	35 760.6	110 309	3 764.9	7 173.4	21 717	50 520.5	9 715	105.7	13.4	305 255	4 826.2	15 810
Wyoming	800	2 547.1	1 995.0	5 761	161.9	323.7	2 939	4 530.5	9 438	102.7	14.7	26 934	426.7	15 841

[1] Includes only establishments with payroll. [2] For pay period including March 12. [3] Based on resident population estimated as of July 1, 1997.

Sources: Wholesale Trade—U.S. Census Bureau, 1997 Economic Census, ECON97 Report Series CD-ROM, CD-EC97-1, Disc 1E, issued February 2001 (related Internet site <http://www.census.gov/epcd/www/97EC42.HTM>). Retail Trade—U.S. Census Bureau, 1997 Economic Census, ECON97 Report Series CD-ROM, CD-EC97-1, Disc 1E, issued February 2001 (related Internet site <http://www.census.gov/epcd/www/97EC44.HTM>).

Table A–12. States — Accommodation and Foodservices, Banking, and Federal Funds

State	Accommodation and foodservices[1] (NAICS 72), 1997 — Sales					Banking,[4] 1999		Federal funds and grants, 1999		Per capita[5] (dollars)				
	Estab-lishments	Total ($1,000)	Percent from food-services[2]	Paid employ-ees[3]	Annual payroll ($1,000)	Offices	Deposits (mil. dol.)	Total expenditures or obligations (mil. dol.)	Percent change, 1990–1999	Total	Direct payments for individuals	Procure-ment contract awards	Salaries and wages	Grant awards
UNITED STATES	545 068	350 399 194	71.9	9 451 226	97 007 396	83 684	3 749 761.0	1 516 775.0	51.6	5 562	2 946	760	646	1 058
Alabama	6 955	3 881 782	84.0	134 719	1 059 642	1 419	52 700.3	26 775.6	54.3	6 127	3 449	846	640	1 060
Alaska	1 763	1 065 459	68.5	20 587	301 523	137	4 542.6	5 278.7	60.9	8 521	1 912	1 365	2 053	3 114
Arizona	9 094	6 634 744	66.5	184 382	1 823 706	947	40 171.6	26 959.3	77.9	5 642	2 869	1 001	557	950
Arkansas	4 663	2 179 696	81.9	73 397	589 917	1 198	31 798.8	13 630.8	62.8	5 343	3 421	183	437	1 025
California	62 629	42 312 641	73.8	1 054 106	11 455 306	6 103	427 750.1	166 049.7	41.2	5 010	2 532	778	535	1 097
Colorado	10 073	6 710 540	68.7	195 262	1 939 282	1 202	45 923.9	21 755.4	47.0	5 364	2 409	1 095	863	850
Connecticut	6 903	3 746 560	83.5	96 556	1 062 812	1 202	58 734.2	19 240.5	30.2	5 862	3 098	1 108	411	1 172
Delaware	1 605	1 008 954	85.3	26 969	280 815	254	52 948.8	3 765.7	71.3	4 997	3 002	294	539	1 095
District of Columbia	1 700	2 263 498	52.2	42 650	701 354	206	10 903.4	27 033.7	52.8	52 088	5 100	12 338	23 074	10 198
Florida	28 999	24 165 336	63.5	608 834	6 239 469	4 509	200 783.4	87 214.9	69.1	5 772	3 872	572	518	741
Georgia	13 829	9 689 927	76.7	274 322	2 695 138	2 252	89 625.3	39 215.0	84.3	5 035	2 597	661	808	867
Hawaii	3 081	5 007 899	39.6	88 083	1 507 538	306	17 844.3	8 568.2	52.1	7 228	2 981	963	2 055	1 126
Idaho	2 980	1 233 215	72.5	42 087	345 955	435	10 141.7	6 164.7	61.2	4 925	2 521	695	554	940
Illinois	23 984	14 826 805	79.4	397 300	4 018 697	3 881	220 296.8	55 836.0	50.3	4 604	2 769	287	495	873
Indiana	11 705	6 646 318	84.1	215 710	1 865 305	2 239	70 354.5	26 828.1	57.5	4 514	2 773	374	332	792
Iowa	6 830	2 762 766	80.3	99 148	769 461	1 499	41 705.2	15 601.5	54.2	5 437	2 889	313	338	904
Kansas	5 677	2 685 732	83.9	91 173	757 095	1 374	38 835.0	14 447.0	50.4	5 443	2 868	476	660	822
Kentucky	6 546	4 056 107	83.3	129 442	1 140 617	1 591	48 237.3	22 198.1	61.9	5 604	3 126	574	660	1 110
Louisiana	7 151	5 259 921	69.4	147 016	1 408 910	1 462	44 762.9	24 384.3	59.1	5 577	3 121	610	495	1 196
Maine	3 716	1 510 182	70.5	39 657	429 143	509	13 472.1	7 281.5	46.9	5 811	3 143	641	634	1 328
Maryland	9 049	5 972 467	81.2	161 273	1 644 729	1 671	60 524.0	41 990.2	53.9	8 119	3 057	2 046	1 614	1 111
Massachusetts	14 827	9 282 541	78.4	227 898	2 579 922	1 987	131 158.7	37 803.0	24.9	6 122	3 209	932	473	1 431
Michigan	18 958	10 158 693	84.8	320 014	2 835 825	2 983	111 363.8	43 871.6	49.1	4 448	2 880	209	297	990
Minnesota	9 982	5 934 155	74.4	179 487	1 688 779	1 557	66 928.2	21 665.8	44.9	4 537	2 425	378	372	942
Mississippi	4 050	3 064 753	55.7	84 834	814 454	1 101	27 913.6	16 487.9	61.6	5 955	3 237	700	613	1 223
Missouri	11 150	6 780 812	74.7	203 849	1 933 340	2 066	74 262.9	33 231.0	36.1	6 077	3 123	1 043	606	1 002
Montana	3 280	1 199 251	71.8	38 551	325 510	336	9 013.6	6 225.0	81.9	7 052	3 034	589	755	1 585
Nebraska	4 070	1 726 647	83.5	61 048	488 208	930	27 225.8	8 793.3	44.5	5 278	2 755	282	596	991
Nevada	3 633	15 323 751	12.8	241 682	4 665 524	403	16 689.3	7 941.9	89.9	4 390	2 719	443	499	690
New Hampshire	3 033	1 544 942	76.4	43 996	450 258	408	19 430.6	5 301.4	47.0	4 414	2 646	401	377	932
New Jersey	16 975	13 416 088	53.6	252 031	3 610 740	2 967	141 283.2	40 397.6	41.9	4 961	3 052	517	442	892
New Mexico	3 827	2 146 558	73.1	67 203	599 757	501	14 092.2	13 580.2	56.2	7 805	2 893	2 259	946	1 581
New York	38 051	21 680 529	74.5	473 481	6 104 432	4 548	418 861.5	101 808.6	45.6	5 595	3 134	372	413	1 587
North Carolina	14 579	8 624 993	80.2	262 848	2 393 158	2 458	101 651.7	37 227.6	81.0	4 866	2 834	268	689	994
North Dakota	1 827	684 930	77.7	26 330	188 982	401	9 793.1	4 535.2	54.0	7 157	2 844	402	975	1 593
Ohio	22 631	12 410 978	86.6	401 206	3 444 193	3 863	156 316.7	53 262.2	38.9	4 732	2 947	400	386	911
Oklahoma	6 534	3 151 332	86.7	105 934	856 753	1 118	36 602.8	19 188.7	60.4	5 714	3 215	497	822	962
Oregon	8 371	4 388 304	77.3	124 506	1 237 426	953	28 345.5	15 592.3	58.2	4 702	2 866	231	454	1 061
Pennsylvania	24 465	12 227 177	80.9	365 158	3 364 117	4 509	175 347.4	69 448.0	52.3	5 790	3 640	495	452	1 096
Rhode Island	2 617	1 220 865	85.0	34 162	340 552	217	12 771.8	6 036.1	39.2	6 092	3 439	425	729	1 424
South Carolina	7 775	4 835 839	75.0	150 621	1 313 837	1 214	35 959.9	20 833.2	50.6	5 361	3 008	654	628	998
South Dakota	2 259	888 148	69.6	30 136	234 413	417	12 271.1	4 909.0	71.6	6 696	2 942	714	762	1 440
Tennessee	9 604	6 790 159	74.7	197 881	1 880 279	1 981	68 584.7	30 866.8	73.3	5 629	3 140	824	496	1 076
Texas	34 160	22 698 848	80.1	638 333	6 175 414	4 620	207 774.7	97 987.6	68.3	4 889	2 507	724	589	916
Utah	3 785	2 313 309	71.8	74 481	650 041	561	19 248.8	9 238.7	41.7	4 338	2 053	595	690	936
Vermont	1 932	910 188	57.4	27 088	277 161	261	7 523.4	3 114.3	75.1	5 245	2 722	465	508	1 488
Virginia	12 343	8 281 218	74.4	233 639	2 320 695	2 442	79 684.8	57 842.2	58.4	8 416	3 052	2 771	1 753	691
Washington	13 124	7 001 716	79.8	195 157	1 965 223	1 633	57 817.3	31 993.1	59.2	5 558	2 792	802	846	994
West Virginia	3 290	1 633 164	77.0	51 529	462 334	616	20 888.8	11 028.1	64.0	6 103	3 821	346	504	1 378
Wisconsin	13 253	5 649 870	79.1	190 520	1 550 660	2 071	72 446.0	22 603.8	49.2	4 305	2 667	273	288	922
Wyoming	1 751	808 887	56.9	24 950	218 995	166	6 453.5	2 916.2	57.6	6 081	2 740	415	854	1 946

[1] Includes only establishments with payroll. [2] Foodservices and drinking places (NAICS 722) includes full-service restaurants, limited-service eating places, special food services, and drinking places (alcoholic beverages). [3] For pay period including March 12. [4] As of June 30. Covers all FDIC-insured commercial banks and savings institutions. [5] Based on resident population estimated as of July 1, 1999.

Sources: Accommodation and Foodservices—U.S. Census Bureau, 1997 Economic Census, ECON97 Report Series CD-ROM, CD-EC97-1, Disc 1E, issued February 2001 (related Internet site <http://www.census.gov/epcd/www/97EC72.HTM>). Banking—U.S. Federal Deposit Insurance Corporation and Office of Thrift Supervision, "1999 Bank and Thrift Branch Office Data Book: Summary of Deposits," national and 6 regional data books (related Internet site <http://www2.fdic.gov/sod/>). Federal Funds and Grants—U.S. Census Bureau, County Aggregate files for each state, <http://www.census.gov/govs/www/cffr99.html>, (accessed: August 2000).

Table A–13. States — Government Programs, Employment, and Finances

State	Social Security Program beneficiaries, December 1999 — Total — Number	Percent change, 1990–1999	Rate[1]	Retired workers	Supplemental Security Income Program recipients, December 1999	Government employment, 1998 — Federal — Civilian	Military	State and local	Local government employment, full-time equivalent, March 1997	Local government finances, 1996–1997 — General revenue — Total (mil. dol.)	Taxes — Total (mil. dol.)	Per capita[2]	Percent property	Direct general expenditure (mil. dol.)
UNITED STATES	43 521 432	11.9	160	27 251 862	6 555 989	2 808 000	2 098 000	17 042 000	10 227 429	747 030.3	284 397.7	1 062	73.3	723 603.9
Alabama	810 196	14.3	185	444 171	160 292	53 249	42 064	288 880	175 369	8 918.4	2 474.0	573	36.5	8 853.0
Alaska	51 320	52.5	83	29 287	8 165	17 041	22 707	53 138	23 132	2 464.6	792.5	1 302	80.1	2 453.1
Arizona	772 631	30.8	162	502 824	79 490	44 070	32 672	266 516	165 331	11 241.3	3 825.0	840	71.3	11 031.2
Arkansas	517 826	10.2	203	294 498	87 732	20 728	19 178	158 504	90 806	4 424.0	1 343.7	532	60.1	4 277.2
California	4 105 728	12.0	124	2 621 878	1 065 323	268 568	230 324	1 881 006	1 194 169	109 714.6	28 850.0	895	67.9	105 593.7
Colorado	522 116	23.8	129	321 477	54 685	53 973	42 580	270 700	153 146	11 434.3	4 809.8	1 236	61.7	11 101.4
Connecticut	567 637	7.8	173	394 490	47 669	22 175	16 986	185 623	104 338	8 526.0	4 965.5	1 519	98.7	8 309.0
Delaware	128 935	23.5	171	83 720	11 849	5 407	8 946	49 245	18 865	1 434.3	412.5	561	82.9	1 419.7
District of Columbia	73 176	-5.4	141	46 809	20 009	183 932	23 335	41 950	46 246	5 279.0	2 637.4	4 988	26.5	4 335.8
Florida	3 139 437	18.4	208	2 121 056	366 966	119 348	111 309	823 269	543 525	41 196.5	14 647.4	998	78.8	40 665.5
Georgia	1 073 388	21.5	138	620 139	196 959	93 207	94 817	491 328	324 480	19 321.4	7 273.0	972	67.5	10 353.7
Hawaii	178 000	19.8	150	125 755	20 417	30 127	55 253	80 967	14 319	1 449.2	760.7	640	79.8	1 440.5
Idaho	190 674	21.2	152	120 373	17 813	12 728	9 768	86 918	46 035	2 631.0	758.5	627	93.8	2 689.4
Illinois	1 816 192	3.6	150	1 170 184	251 058	95 718	58 239	715 325	459 893	33 167.7	15 718.2	1 309	80.9	31 001.6
Indiana	986 207	8.0	166	619 639	88 314	38 659	21 888	357 365	220 747	14 293.6	5 623.5	958	90.5	13 512.6
Iowa	537 366	2.5	187	348 253	40 484	20 040	13 979	212 503	112 667	7 291.4	2 509.1	879	92.4	7 069.7
Kansas	435 613	6.9	164	281 732	36 298	26 060	29 108	215 634	118 302	6 597.1	2 529.8	967	80.9	6 540.0
Kentucky	729 134	12.8	184	375 154	172 253	36 894	47 221	245 003	134 740	6 772.7	2 076.7	531	53.6	6 871.3
Louisiana	702 105	7.7	161	352 364	168 025	35 309	41 812	324 870	169 976	9 650.3	3 760.4	864	37.5	9 197.5
Maine	246 214	14.6	196	150 290	29 365	13 021	10 838	79 403	46 260	2 743.3	1 535.2	1 233	96.4	2 585.2
Maryland	704 867	15.7	136	456 463	86 748	153 567	51 984	303 307	171 635	12 632.0	6 206.5	1 219	58.1	12 361.1
Massachusetts	1 046 655	7.9	169	684 047	166 825	54 691	24 278	360 422	213 917	15 350.4	6 814.3	1 114	97.0	13 649.6
Michigan	1 620 377	8.7	164	996 670	209 957	56 255	21 763	577 804	332 671	26 844.5	6 760.6	691	89.1	27 426.6
Minnesota	728 088	8.8	152	476 167	63 632	33 229	20 084	328 799	188 845	15 010.8	4 507.6	962	94.7	15 262.1
Mississippi	505 731	12.2	183	265 231	131 379	26 375	35 509	197 560	122 256	5 740.6	1 345.3	492	91.8	5 781.0
Missouri	993 174	8.7	182	611 577	111 040	58 899	37 557	351 621	201 609	11 391.4	4 779.4	884	58.4	11 314.6
Montana	155 072	12.6	176	95 734	13 723	12 647	8 474	61 856	32 676	1 821.7	622.2	708	94.8	1 799.4
Nebraska	282 661	5.5	170	183 101	21 054	15 840	15 873	129 070	75 377	4 250.2	1 944.2	1 174	81.7	4 088.8
Nevada	271 205	61.2	150	183 219	24 395	14 155	11 329	96 433	56 607	5 169.5	1 522.8	909	61.5	5 356.3
New Hampshire	195 065	20.7	162	129 909	11 445	8 083	4 374	68 780	38 830	2 539.4	1 836.7	1 566	98.8	2 454.8
New Jersey	1 322 550	7.6	162	902 780	145 376	65 637	30 205	491 838	298 363	24 746.9	12 988.6	1 613	98.4	24 199.8
New Mexico	270 658	23.6	156	158 310	45 911	29 867	18 427	138 207	69 941	3 850.4	881.0	511	55.1	3 966.0
New York	2 966 658	4.8	163	1 919 252	608 986	138 893	57 885	1 242 103	860 168	86 743.9	40 603.8	2 238	59.4	80 961.2
North Carolina	1 322 399	23.1	173	813 306	191 841	61 370	120 100	533 782	203 505	18 000.2	5 002.0	662	75.2	17 582.4
North Dakota	114 171	1.4	180	69 430	8 264	8 985	13 097	49 267	21 221	1 363.0	515.1	804	89.8	1 319.7
Ohio	1 893 896	5.0	168	1 146 261	242 752	83 126	36 706	683 434	421 092	29 022.3	12 647.7	1 128	65.9	27 841.2
Oklahoma	586 802	10.3	175	357 236	72 665	44 493	41 819	227 140	129 462	6 625.4	2 065.3	623	53.0	6 516.8
Oregon	553 547	12.4	167	366 633	50 623	29 971	12 704	213 424	117 999	9 528.2	3 120.2	962	81.2	9 377.6
Pennsylvania	2 332 589	4.3	194	1 522 467	277 998	111 517	45 066	601 726	365 556	30 375.9	12 502.3	1 040	70.4	29 086.6
Rhode Island	190 681	5.4	192	129 804	26 837	10 591	9 676	54 934	29 102	2 130.8	1 234.5	1 251	98.6	1 996.7
South Carolina	672 353	24.2	173	398 766	108 198	29 258	56 340	278 278	143 952	7 907.3	2 421.1	639	86.0	7 776.0
South Dakota	135 165	5.4	184	84 435	12 756	10 767	8 260	50 252	26 567	1 419.0	695.1	951	76.7	1 400.2
Tennessee	970 895	17.7	177	558 215	166 435	50 308	23 782	329 985	194 274	11 286.5	4 009.8	746	58.2	11 575.0
Texas	2 575 745	17.4	129	1 516 987	408 084	184 577	165 408	1 308 218	850 380	46 587.8	20 537.1	1 061	79.6	45 113.0
Utah	234 587	22.5	110	148 879	19 999	30 620	16 037	145 215	63 884	4 554.1	1 532.4	742	71.6	4 386.0
Vermont	102 729	17.3	173	64 531	12 520	5 478	4 501	39 543	17 841	1 157.9	720.7	1 224	98.8	1 112.0
Virginia	1 008 033	20.8	147	614 617	131 989	163 596	164 865	450 499	253 219	15 415.7	7 200.6	1 069	72.6	16 054.0
Washington	825 281	15.5	143	535 485	98 067	66 840	73 524	388 621	185 152	16 138.7	5 167.5	922	63.5	15 729.7
West Virginia	390 558	5.5	216	198 667	70 972	21 583	9 662	118 538	59 926	3 379.8	925.9	510	82.5	3 270.5
Wisconsin	890 588	6.2	170	591 942	86 544	29 494	19 338	344 990	201 633	15 575.4	5 438.6	1 046	94.6	15 921.8
Wyoming	74 688	20.6	156	47 617	5 783	7 034	6 349	48 207	27 423	1 619.6	485.1	1 011	78.0	1 622.6

[1] Per 1,000 resident population estimated as of July 1, 1999. [2] Based on resident population estimated as of July 1, 1997.

Sources: Social Security Program—U.S. Social Security Administration, OASDI Beneficiaries by State and County - December 1999, <http://www.ssa.gov/statistics/oasdi_sc/1999/oasdi_sc99.pdf> (accessed: 7 March 2001) for 1999 -- annual publication of same title for 1990. Supplemental Security Income Program—U.S. Social Security Administration, SSI Recipients by State and County, <http://www.ssa.gov/statistics/ssi_st_cty/1999/ssi_st_cty.pdf> (accessed: November 2000). Government employment, 1998—U.S. Bureau of Economic Analysis, "Regional Economic Information System (REIS) 1969-1998" on CD-ROM (related Internet site <http://www.bea.doc.gov/bea/regional/data.htm>). Local government employment, 1997—U.S. Census Bureau, 1997 Census of Governments, Compendium of Public Employment, <http://www.census.gov/govs/apes/97coar2.dat> (accessed: 14 January 2000). Local government finances—U.S. Census Bureau, 1997 Census of Governments, Compendium of Government Finances, <http://www.census.gov/prod/gc97/gc974-5.pdf> (accessed: 16 February 2001).

Figure 2.
Counties With 1 Million or More Population in the United States: 2000

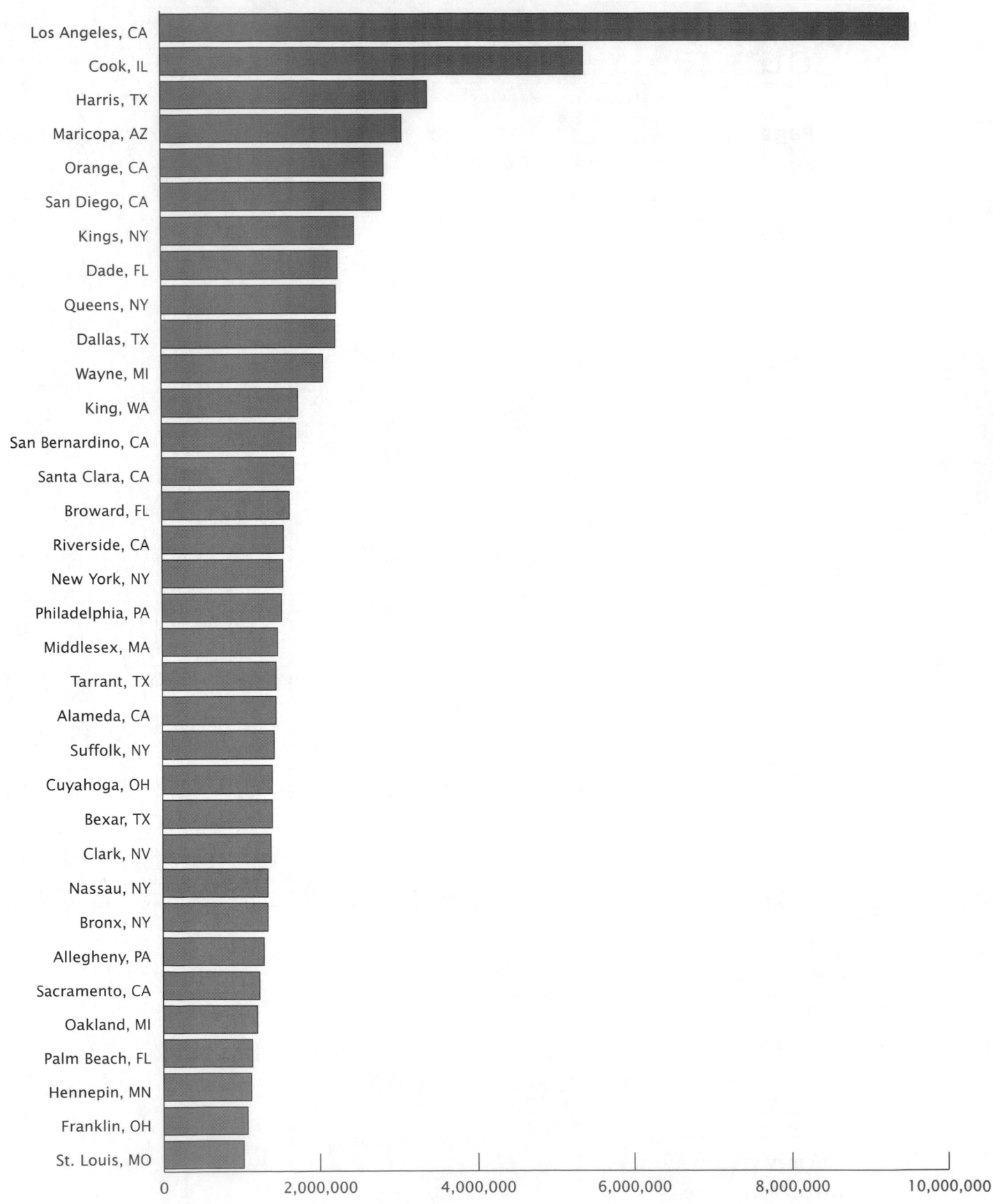

U.S. Census Bureau, County and City Data Book: 2000

Counties

Table B

Page

You may visit us on the Web at
http://www.census.gov/statab/www/ccdb.html

Counties

B

Table B

Table B–1. Counties — Area and Population

[Includes U.S., states, and 3,142 counties/county equivalents defined as of January 1, 1992. For changes to these areas since January 1, 1992, see appendix B. Geographic Information]

Metropolitan area code[1]	State and county code[2]	County	Land area,[3] 2000 (sq. miles)	Population (April 1) 2000 Number	2000 Rank[4]	Per square mile	1990[5] Number	1990 Rank[4]	1980	Net change 1990–2000	Net change 1980–1990	Percent change 1990–2000	Percent change 1980–1990	Hispanic or Latino,[6] 2000 Number	Hispanic or Latino,[6] 2000 Percent
	00 000	UNITED STATES	3 537 441	281 421 906	X	79.6	248 790 925	X	226 542 199	32 630 981	22 248 726	13.1	9.8	35 305 818	12.5
	01 000	ALABAMA	50 744	4 447 100	X	87.6	4 040 389	X	3 894 025	406 711	146 364	10.1	3.8	75 830	1.7
5240	01 001	Autauga	596	43 671	1 022	73.3	34 222	1 160	32 259	9 449	1 963	27.6	6.1	610	1.4
5160	01 003	Baldwin	1 596	140 415	390	88.0	98 280	467	78 556	42 135	19 724	42.9	25.1	2 466	1.8
...	01 005	Barbour	885	29 038	1 424	32.8	25 417	1 450	24 756	3 621	661	14.2	2.7	478	1.6
...	01 007	Bibb	623	20 826	1 743	33.4	16 598	1 878	15 723	4 228	875	25.5	5.6	210	1.0
1000	01 009	Blount	646	51 024	909	79.0	39 248	1 019	36 459	11 776	2 789	30.0	7.6	2 718	5.3
...	01 011	Bullock	625	11 714	2 318	18.7	11 042	2 289	10 596	672	446	6.1	4.2	322	2.7
...	01 013	Butler	777	21 399	1 718	27.5	21 892	1 584	21 680	–493	212	–2.3	1.0	143	.7
0450	01 015	Calhoun	608	112 249	478	184.6	116 032	396	119 761	–3 783	–3 729	–3.3	–3.1	1 753	1.6
...	01 017	Chambers	597	36 583	1 200	61.3	36 876	1 079	39 191	–293	–2 315	–.8	–5.9	280	.8
...	01 019	Cherokee	553	23 988	1 593	43.4	19 543	1 696	18 760	4 445	783	22.7	4.2	204	.9
...	01 021	Chilton	694	39 593	1 124	57.1	32 458	1 202	30 612	7 135	1 846	22.0	6.0	1 152	2.9
...	01 023	Choctaw	914	15 922	2 025	17.4	16 018	1 922	16 839	–96	–821	–.6	–4.9	107	.7
...	01 025	Clarke	1 238	27 867	1 454	22.5	27 240	1 382	27 702	627	–462	2.3	–1.7	180	.6
...	01 027	Clay	605	14 254	2 145	23.6	13 252	2 116	13 703	1 002	–451	7.6	–3.3	253	1.8
...	01 029	Cleburne	560	14 123	2 151	25.2	12 730	2 164	12 595	1 393	135	10.9	1.1	198	1.4
...	01 031	Coffee	679	43 615	1 026	64.2	40 240	994	38 533	3 375	1 707	8.4	4.4	1 183	2.7
2650	01 033	Colbert	595	54 984	859	92.4	51 666	818	54 519	3 318	–2 853	6.4	–5.2	618	1.1
...	01 035	Conecuh	851	14 089	2 155	16.6	14 054	2 052	15 884	35	–1 830	.2	–11.5	102	.7
...	01 037	Coosa	652	12 202	2 282	18.7	11 063	2 287	11 377	1 139	–314	10.3	–2.8	158	1.3
...	01 039	Covington	1 034	37 631	1 171	36.4	36 478	1 091	36 850	1 153	–372	3.2	–1.0	292	.8
...	01 041	Crenshaw	610	13 665	2 187	22.4	13 635	2 089	14 110	30	–475	.2	–3.4	87	.6
...	01 043	Cullman	738	77 483	654	105.0	67 613	657	61 642	9 870	5 971	14.6	9.7	1 688	2.2
2180	01 045	Dale	561	49 129	928	87.6	49 633	845	47 821	–504	1 812	–1.0	3.8	1 642	3.3
...	01 047	Dallas	981	46 365	975	47.3	48 130	867	53 981	–1 765	–5 851	–3.7	–10.8	290	.6
...	01 049	DeKalb	778	64 452	754	82.8	54 651	788	53 658	9 801	993	17.9	1.9	3 578	5.6
5240	01 051	Elmore..................	621	65 874	741	106.1	49 210	854	43 390	16 664	5 820	33.9	13.4	805	1.2
...	01 053	Escambia	947	38 440	1 151	40.6	35 518	1 111	38 440	2 922	–2 922	8.2	–7.6	379	1.0
2880	01 055	Etowah	535	103 459	514	193.4	99 840	460	103 057	3 619	–3 217	3.6	–3.1	1 763	1.7
...	01 057	Fayette	628	18 495	1 869	29.5	17 962	1 790	18 809	533	–847	3.0	–4.5	152	.8
...	01 059	Franklin	636	31 223	1 370	49.1	27 814	1 357	28 350	3 409	–536	12.3	–1.9	2 316	7.4
...	01 061	Geneva	576	25 764	1 525	44.7	23 647	1 507	24 253	2 117	–606	9.0	–2.5	453	1.8
...	01 063	Greene	646	9 974	2 449	15.4	10 153	2 373	11 021	–179	–868	–1.8	–7.9	58	.6
...	01 065	Hale	644	17 185	1 941	26.7	15 498	1 953	15 604	1 687	–106	10.9	–.7	157	.9
...	01 067	Henry	562	16 310	2 003	29.0	15 374	1 966	15 302	936	72	6.1	.5	249	1.5
2180	01 069	Houston	580	88 787	587	153.1	81 331	559	74 632	7 456	6 699	9.2	9.0	1 122	1.3
...	01 071	Jackson.................	1 079	53 926	869	50.0	47 796	879	51 407	6 130	–3 611	12.8	–7.0	610	1.1
1000	01 073	Jefferson	1 113	662 047	77	594.8	651 520	71	671 371	10 527	–19 851	1.6	–3.0	10 284	1.6
...	01 075	Lamar	605	15 904	2 027	26.3	15 715	1 941	16 453	189	–738	1.2	–4.5	207	1.3
2650	01 077	Lauderdale	669	87 966	593	131.5	79 661	572	80 546	8 305	–885	10.4	–1.1	894	1.0
2030	01 079	Lawrence	693	34 803	1 258	50.2	31 513	1 230	30 170	3 290	1 343	10.4	4.5	367	1.1
0580	01 081	Lee	609	115 092	469	189.0	87 146	524	76 283	27 946	10 863	32.1	14.2	1 645	1.4
3440	01 083	Limestone	568	65 676	742	115.6	54 135	794	46 005	11 541	8 130	21.3	17.7	1 740	2.6
...	01 085	Lowndes	718	13 473	2 195	18.8	12 658	2 171	13 253	815	–595	6.4	–4.5	85	.6
...	01 087	Macon	611	24 105	1 590	39.5	24 928	1 465	26 829	–823	–1 901	–3.3	–7.1	173	.7
3440	01 089	Madison	805	276 700	205	343.7	238 912	209	196 966	37 788	41 946	15.8	21.3	5 226	1.9
...	01 091	Marengo	977	22 539	1 668	23.1	23 084	1 534	25 047	–545	–1 963	–2.4	–7.8	219	1.0
...	01 093	Marion	741	31 214	1 371	42.1	29 830	1 302	30 041	1 384	–211	4.6	–.7	360	1.2
...	01 095	Marshall	567	82 231	630	145.0	70 832	625	65 622	11 399	5 210	16.1	7.9	4 656	5.7
5160	01 097	Mobile	1 233	399 843	148	324.3	378 643	134	364 980	21 200	13 663	5.6	3.7	4 887	1.2
...	01 099	Monroe	1 026	24 324	1 582	23.7	23 968	1 493	22 651	356	1 317	1.5	5.8	190	.8
5240	01 101	Montgomery	790	223 510	253	282.9	209 085	239	197 038	14 425	12 047	6.9	6.1	2 665	1.2
2030	01 103	Morgan	582	111 064	487	190.8	100 043	458	90 231	11 021	9 812	11.0	10.9	3 645	3.3
...	01 105	Perry	719	11 861	2 301	16.5	12 759	2 161	15 012	–898	–2 253	–7.0	–15.0	102	.9
...	01 107	Pickens	881	20 949	1 739	23.8	20 699	1 645	21 481	250	–782	1.2	–3.6	147	.7
...	01 109	Pike	671	29 605	1 412	44.1	27 595	1 369	28 050	2 010	–455	7.3	–1.6	365	1.2
...	01 111	Randolph	581	22 380	1 674	38.5	19 881	1 684	20 075	2 499	–194	12.6	–1.0	272	1.2
1800	01 113	Russell	641	49 756	919	77.6	46 860	893	47 356	2 896	–496	6.2	–1.0	744	1.5
1000	01 115	St. Clair	634	64 742	751	102.1	49 811	843	41 205	14 931	8 606	30.0	20.9	686	1.1
1000	01 117	Shelby	795	143 293	380	180.2	99 363	462	66 298	43 930	33 065	44.2	49.9	2 910	2.0
...	01 119	Sumter	905	14 798	2 103	16.4	16 174	1 913	16 908	–1 376	–734	–8.5	–4.3	165	1.1
...	01 121	Talladega	740	80 321	639	108.5	74 109	608	73 826	6 212	283	8.4	.4	812	1.0
...	01 123	Tallapoosa	718	41 475	1 068	57.8	38 826	1 028	38 766	2 649	60	6.8	.2	242	.6
8600	01 125	Tuscaloosa	1 324	164 875	326	124.5	150 500	310	137 541	14 375	12 959	9.6	9.4	2 130	1.3
...	01 127	Walker	794	70 713	702	89.1	67 670	656	68 660	3 043	–990	4.5	–1.4	607	.9
...	01 129	Washington	1 081	18 097	1 893	16.7	16 694	1 869	16 821	1 403	–127	8.4	–.8	160	.9
...	01 131	Wilcox	889	13 183	2 213	14.8	13 568	2 096	14 755	–385	–1 187	–2.8	–8.0	97	.7
...	01 133	Winston	614	24 843	1 563	40.5	22 053	1 573	21 953	2 790	100	12.7	.5	372	1.5

[1] Federal Information Processing Standards (FIPS) codes for metropolitan areas defined as of June 30, 1999. [2] FIPS codes for states and counties/county equivalents. [3] Dry land and land temporarily or partially covered by water. [4] Based on 3,140 counties/county equivalents; excludes Yellowstone National Park in MT and South Boston independent city in VA which are no longer counties. When counties share the same rank, the next lower rank is omitted. [5] Includes count resolution corrections through 1997 and adjustments based on Census 2000 dress rehearsal results and boundary changes reported as legally effective as of January 1, 1998. [6] Persons of Hispanic or Latino origin may be of any race.

Sources: Land Area—U.S. Census Bureau, unpublished data file from Geography Division based on TIGER data base. 2000 Population—U.S. Census Bureau, Census of Population and Housing, Census 2000 Redistricting Data (Public Law 94-171) Summary Files (related Internet site <http://www.census.gov/dmd/www/2kresult.html>). 1990 Population—U.S. Census Bureau, "(CO-99-8) County Population Estimates and Demographic Components of Population Change: Annual Time Series, July 1, 1990 to July 1, 1999 (includes revised April 1, 1990 Population Estimates Base)"; published 9 March 2000; <http://www. census.gov/population/estimates/county/co-99-8/99C8_00.txt>. 1980 Population—U.S. Census Bureau, "1980–1990 Intercensal Population Estimates by County" on diskette (related Internet site <http://www.census.gov/population/www/estimates/countypop.html>).

[Includes U.S., states, and 3,142 counties/county equivalents defined as of January 1, 1992. For changes to these areas since January 1, 1992, see appendix B. Geographic Information]

Metro-politan area code[1]	State and county code[2]	County	Land area,[3] 2000 (sq. miles)	Population (April 1)										
				2000			1990[5]		1980	Net change		Percent change		Hispanic or Latino,[6] 2000	
				Number	Rank[4]	Per square mile	Number	Rank[4]		1990–2000	1980–1990	1990–2000	1980–1990	Number	Percent
	02 000	ALASKA	571 951	626 932	X	1.1	550 043	X	401 851	76 889	148 192	14.0	36.9	25 852	4.1
...	02 013	Aleutians East	6 988	2 697	3 014	.4	2 464	3 023	[7]1 643	233	[7]821	9.5	[7]50.0	339	12.6
...	02 016	Aleutians West	4 397	5 465	2 819	1.2	9 478	2 436	[7]6 125	−4 013	[7]3 353	−42.3	[7]54.7	573	10.5
0380	02 020	Anchorage	1 697	260 283	212	153.4	226 338	218	174 431	33 945	51 907	15.0	29.8	14 799	5.7
...	02 050	Bethel	40 633	16 006	2 021	.4	13 660	2 085	10 999	2 346	2 661	17.2	24.2	140	.9
...	02 060	Bristol Bay	505	1 258	3 102	2.5	1 410	3 100	1 094	−152	316	−10.8	28.9	7	.6
...	02 068	Denali	12 750	1 893	3 074	.1	1 682	3 086	(8)	211	NA	12.5	NA	47	2.5
...	02 070	Dillingham	18 675	4 922	2 854	.3	4 010	2 918	[7]3 232	912	[7]778	22.7	[7]24.1	111	2.3
...	02 090	Fairbanks North Star	7 366	82 840	627	11.2	77 720	583	53 983	5 120	23 737	6.6	44.0	3 440	4.2
...	02 100	Haines	2 344	2 392	3 031	1.0	2 117	3 061	1 680	275	437	13.0	26.0	33	1.4
...	02 110	Juneau	2 717	30 711	1 380	11.3	26 752	1 399	19 528	3 959	7 224	14.8	37.0	1 040	3.4
...	02 122	Kenai Peninsula	16 013	49 691	922	3.1	40 802	982	25 282	8 889	15 520	21.8	61.4	1 087	2.2
...	02 130	Ketchikan Gateway	1 233	14 070	2 158	11.4	13 828	2 072	11 316	242	2 512	1.8	22.2	372	2.6
...	02 150	Kodiak Island	6 560	13 913	2 167	2.1	13 309	2 113	9 939	604	3 370	4.5	33.9	848	6.1
...	02 164	Lake and Peninsula	23 782	1 823	3 078	.1	1 666	3 088	[7]1 384	157	[7]282	9.4	[7]20.4	21	1.2
...	02 170	Matanuska-Susitna	24 682	59 322	810	2.4	39 683	1 008	17 816	19 639	21 867	49.5	122.7	1 485	2.5
...	02 180	Nome.................	23 001	9 196	2 514	.4	8 288	2 538	6 537	908	1 751	11.0	26.8	92	1.0
...	02 185	North Slope	88 817	7 385	2 649	.1	5 986	2 760	4 199	1 399	1 787	23.4	42.6	175	2.4
...	02 188	Northwest Arctic	35 898	7 208	2 666	.2	6 106	2 743	4 831	1 102	1 275	18.0	26.4	57	.8
...	02 201	Prince of Wales-Outer Ketchikan	7 411	6 146	2 768	.8	6 278	2 726	3 822	−132	2 456	−2.1	64.3	107	1.7
...	02 220	Sitka	2 874	8 835	2 541	3.1	8 588	2 504	7 803	247	785	2.9	10.1	290	3.3
...	02 231	Skagway-Yakutat-Angoon ..	15 546	4 244	2 899	.3	4 404	2 881	3 478	−160	926	−3.6	26.6	103	2.4
...	02 240	Southeast Fairbanks......	24 815	6 174	2 765	.2	5 925	2 766	5 676	249	249	4.2	4.4	167	2.7
...	02 261	Valdez-Cordova	34 319	10 195	2 429	.3	9 920	2 392	8 348	275	1 572	2.8	18.8	286	2.8
...	02 270	Wade Hampton	17 194	7 028	2 681	.4	5 789	2 779	4 665	1 239	1 124	21.4	24.1	23	.3
...	02 280	Wrangell-Petersburg......	5 835	6 684	2 719	1.1	7 042	2 654	6 167	−358	875	−5.1	14.2	132	2.0
...	02 290	Yukon-Koyukuk	145 900	6 551	2 734	Z	6 798	2 676	[8]7 873	−247	NA	−3.6	NA	78	1.2
	04 000	ARIZONA	113 635	5 130 632	X	45.2	3 665 339	X	2 716 546	1 465 293	948 793	40.0	34.9	1 295 617	25.3
...	04 001	Apache	11 205	69 423	714	6.2	61 591	709	52 108	7 832	9 483	12.7	18.2	3 119	4.5
...	04 003	Cochise...............	6 169	117 755	459	19.1	97 624	471	85 686	20 131	11 938	20.6	13.9	36 134	30.7
2620	04 005	Coconino	18 617	116 320	463	6.2	96 591	477	75 008	19 729	21 583	20.4	28.8	12 727	10.9
...	04 007	Gila	4 768	51 335	901	10.8	40 216	995	37 080	11 119	3 136	27.6	8.5	8 546	16.6
...	04 009	Graham	4 629	33 489	1 300	7.2	26 554	1 405	22 862	6 935	3 692	26.1	16.1	9 054	27.0
...	04 011	Greenlee	1 847	8 547	2 564	4.6	8 008	2 565	11 406	539	−3 398	6.7	−29.8	3 681	43.1
...	04 012	La Paz	4 500	19 715	1 810	4.4	13 844	2 068	[7]12 557	5 871	[7]1 287	42.4	[7]10.2	4 420	22.4
6200	04 013	Maricopa	9 203	3 072 149	4	333.8	2 122 101	7	1 509 175	950 048	612 926	44.8	40.6	763 341	24.8
4120	04 015	Mohave	13 312	155 032	344	11.6	93 497	495	55 865	61 535	37 632	65.8	67.4	17 182	11.1
...	04 017	Navajo	9 953	97 470	532	9.8	77 674	586	67 629	19 796	10 045	25.5	14.9	8 011	8.2
8520	04 019	Pima	9 186	843 746	53	91.9	666 957	68	531 443	176 789	135 514	26.5	25.5	247 578	29.3
6200	04 021	Pinal	5 370	179 727	307	33.5	116 397	395	90 918	63 330	25 479	54.4	28.0	53 671	29.9
...	04 023	Santa Cruz	1 238	38 381	1 154	31.0	29 676	1 309	20 459	8 705	9 217	29.3	45.1	31 005	80.8
9360	04 025	Yavapai	8 123	167 517	322	20.6	107 714	429	68 145	59 803	39 569	55.5	58.1	16 376	9.8
9360	04 027	Yuma	5 514	160 026	333	29.0	106 895	432	[7]76 205	53 131	[7]30 690	49.7	[7]40.3	80 772	50.5
	05 000	ARKANSAS	52 068	2 673 400	X	51.3	2 350 624	X	2 286 357	322 776	64 267	13.7	2.8	86 866	3.2
...	05 001	Arkansas..............	988	20 749	1 750	21.0	21 653	1 595	24 175	−904	−2 522	−4.2	−10.4	157	.8
...	05 003	Ashley	921	24 209	1 568	26.3	24 319	1 485	26 538	−110	−2 219	−.5	−8.4	776	3.2
...	05 005	Baxter	554	38 386	1 153	69.3	31 186	1 239	27 409	7 200	3 777	23.1	13.8	385	1.0
2580	05 007	Benton	846	153 406	346	181.3	97 530	472	78 115	55 876	19 415	57.3	24.9	13 469	8.8
...	05 009	Boone	591	33 948	1 281	57.4	28 297	1 345	26 067	5 651	2 230	20.0	8.6	360	1.1
...	05 011	Bradley	651	12 600	2 255	19.4	11 793	2 229	13 803	807	−2 010	6.8	−14.6	1 040	8.3
...	05 013	Calhoun	628	5 744	2 806	9.1	5 826	2 777	6 079	−82	−253	−1.4	−4.2	86	1.5
...	05 015	Carroll	630	25 357	1 550	40.2	18 623	1 758	16 203	6 734	2 420	36.2	14.9	2 471	9.7
...	05 017	Chicot	644	14 117	2 153	21.9	15 713	1 942	17 793	−1 596	−2 080	−10.2	−11.7	407	2.9
...	05 019	Clark	865	23 546	1 614	27.2	21 437	1 606	23 326	2 109	−1 889	9.8	−8.1	566	2.4
...	05 021	Clay	639	17 609	1 922	27.6	18 107	1 785	20 616	−498	−2 509	−2.8	−12.2	140	.8
...	05 023	Cleburne	553	24 046	1 592	43.5	19 411	1 710	16 909	4 635	2 502	23.9	14.8	282	1.2
...	05 025	Cleveland	598	8 571	2 561	14.3	7 781	2 597	7 868	790	−87	10.2	−1.1	139	1.6
...	05 027	Columbia	766	25 603	1 531	33.4	25 691	1 432	26 644	−88	−953	−.3	−3.6	269	1.1
...	05 029	Conway...............	556	20 336	1 770	36.6	19 151	1 724	19 505	1 185	−354	6.2	−1.8	359	1.8
3700	05 031	Craighead.............	711	82 148	631	115.5	68 956	642	63 239	13 192	5 717	19.1	9.0	1 739	2.1
2720	05 033	Crawford	595	53 247	879	89.5	42 493	946	36 892	10 754	5 601	25.3	15.2	1 743	3.3
4920	05 035	Crittenden	610	50 866	912	83.4	49 939	842	49 499	927	440	1.9	.9	720	1.4
...	05 037	Cross	616	19 526	1 816	31.7	19 225	1 718	20 434	301	−1 209	1.6	−5.9	181	.9
...	05 039	Dallas	667	9 210	2 511	13.8	9 614	2 423	10 515	−404	−901	−4.2	−8.6	177	1.9
...	05 041	Desha	765	15 341	2 068	20.1	16 798	1 860	19 760	−1 457	−2 962	−8.7	−15.0	485	3.2

[1] Federal Information Processing Standards (FIPS) codes for metropolitan areas defined as of June 30, 1999. [2] FIPS codes for states and counties/county equivalents. [3] Dry land and land temporarily or partially covered by water. [4] Based on 3,140 counties/county equivalents; excludes Yellowstone National Park in MT and South Boston independent city in VA which are no longer counties. When counties share the same rank, the next lower rank is omitted. [5] Includes count resolution corrections through 1997 and adjustments based on Census 2000 dress rehearsal results and boundary changes reported as legally effective as of January 1, 1998. [6] Persons of Hispanic or Latino origin may be of any race. [7] 1980 population based on 1990 county boundaries. [8] Denali Borough included with Yukon-Koyukuk Census Area; data not available separately.

Sources: Land Area—U.S. Census Bureau, unpublished data file from Geography Division based on TIGER data base. 2000 Population—U.S. Census Bureau, Census of Population and Housing, Census 2000 Redistricting Data (Public Law 94-171) Summary Files (related Internet site <http://www.census.gov/dmd/www/2kresult.html>). 1990 Population—U.S. Census Bureau, "(CO-99-8) County Population Estimates and Demographic Components of Population Change: Annual Time Series, July 1, 1990 to July 1, 1999 (includes revised April 1, 1990 Population Estimates Base)"; published 9 March 2000; <http://www. census.gov/population/estimates/county/co-99-8/99C8_00.txt>. 1980 Population—U.S. Census Bureau, "1980–1990 Intercensal Population Estimates by County" on diskette (related Internet site <http://www.census.gov/population/www/estimates/countypop.html>).

[Includes U.S., states, and 3,142 counties/county equivalents defined as of January 1, 1992. For changes to these areas since January 1, 1992, see appendix B. Geographic Information]

Metropolitan area code[1]	State and county code[2]	County	Land area,[3] 2000 (sq. miles)	Population (April 1)										Hispanic or Latino,[6] 2000	
				2000			1990[5]			Net change		Percent change			
				Number	Rank[4]	Per square mile	Number	Rank[4]	1980	1990–2000	1980–1990	1990–2000	1980–1990	Number	Percent
		ARKANSAS—Con.													
...	05 043	Drew	828	18 723	1 860	22.6	17 369	1 829	17 910	1 354	−541	7.8	−3.0	329	1.8
4400	05 045	Faulkner	647	86 014	605	132.9	60 006	724	46 192	26 008	13 814	43.3	29.9	1 509	1.8
...	05 047	Franklin	610	17 771	1 913	29.1	14 897	1 995	14 705	2 874	192	19.3	1.3	310	1.7
...	05 049	Fulton	618	11 642	2 323	18.8	10 037	2 381	9 975	1 605	62	16.0	.6	62	.5
...	05 051	Garland	677	88 068	591	130.1	73 397	613	70 531	14 671	2 866	20.0	4.1	2 254	2.6
...	05 053	Grant	632	16 464	1 992	26.1	13 948	2 061	13 008	2 516	940	18.0	7.2	189	1.1
...	05 055	Greene	578	37 331	1 182	64.6	31 804	1 218	30 744	5 527	1 060	17.4	3.4	434	1.2
...	05 057	Hempstead	729	23 587	1 608	32.4	21 621	1 597	23 635	1 966	−2 014	9.1	−8.5	1 946	8.3
...	05 059	Hot Spring	615	30 353	1 389	49.4	26 115	1 418	26 819	4 238	−704	16.2	−2.6	384	1.3
...	05 061	Howard	587	14 300	2 140	24.4	13 569	2 094	13 459	731	110	5.4	.8	727	5.1
...	05 063	Independence	764	34 233	1 274	44.8	31 192	1 238	30 147	3 041	1 045	9.7	3.5	523	1.5
...	05 065	Izard	581	13 249	2 208	22.8	11 364	2 264	10 768	1 885	596	16.6	5.5	133	1.0
...	05 067	Jackson	634	18 418	1 873	29.1	18 944	1 739	21 646	−526	−2 702	−2.8	−12.5	234	1.3
6240	05 069	Jefferson	885	84 278	617	95.2	85 487	537	90 718	−1 209	−5 231	−1.4	−5.8	810	1.0
...	05 071	Johnson	662	22 781	1 655	34.4	18 221	1 777	17 423	4 560	798	25.0	4.6	1 527	6.7
...	05 073	Lafayette	527	8 559	2 563	16.2	9 643	2 420	10 213	−1 084	−570	−11.2	−5.6	88	1.0
...	05 075	Lawrence	587	17 774	1 911	30.3	17 455	1 824	18 447	319	−992	1.8	−5.4	121	.7
...	05 077	Lee	602	12 580	2 258	20.9	13 053	2 136	15 539	−473	−2 486	−3.6	−16.0	276	2.2
...	05 079	Lincoln	561	14 492	2 122	25.8	13 690	2 082	13 369	802	321	5.9	2.4	263	1.8
...	05 081	Little River	532	13 628	2 188	25.6	13 966	2 059	13 952	−338	14	−2.4	.1	235	1.7
...	05 083	Logan	710	22 486	1 672	31.7	20 557	1 651	20 144	1 929	413	9.4	2.1	273	1.2
4400	05 085	Lonoke	766	52 828	882	69.0	39 268	1 018	34 518	13 560	4 750	34.5	13.8	922	1.7
...	05 087	Madison	837	14 243	2 146	17.0	11 618	2 247	11 373	2 625	245	22.6	2.2	436	3.1
...	05 089	Marion	598	16 140	2 013	27.0	12 001	2 219	11 334	4 139	667	34.5	5.9	122	.8
8360	05 091	Miller	624	40 443	1 106	64.8	38 467	1 041	37 766	1 976	701	5.1	1.9	641	1.6
...	05 093	Mississippi	898	51 979	893	57.9	57 525	756	59 517	−5 546	−1 992	−9.6	−3.3	1 169	2.2
...	05 095	Monroe	607	10 254	2 421	16.9	11 333	2 272	14 052	−1 079	−2 719	−9.5	−19.3	132	1.3
...	05 097	Montgomery	781	9 245	2 508	11.8	7 841	2 589	7 771	1 404	70	17.9	.9	234	2.5
...	05 099	Nevada	620	9 955	2 451	16.1	10 101	2 377	11 097	−146	−996	−1.4	−9.0	151	1.5
...	05 101	Newton	823	8 608	2 557	10.5	7 666	2 605	7 756	942	−90	12.3	−1.2	93	1.1
...	05 103	Ouachita	732	28 790	1 428	39.3	30 574	1 262	30 541	−1 784	33	−5.8	.1	210	.7
...	05 105	Perry	551	10 209	2 427	18.5	7 969	2 574	7 266	2 240	703	28.1	9.7	120	1.2
...	05 107	Phillips	693	26 445	1 505	38.2	28 830	1 336	34 772	−2 385	−5 942	−8.3	−17.1	382	1.4
...	05 109	Pike	603	11 303	2 349	18.7	10 086	2 379	10 373	1 217	−287	12.1	−2.8	403	3.6
...	05 111	Poinsett	758	25 614	1 530	33.8	24 664	1 475	27 032	950	−2 368	3.9	−8.8	366	1.4
...	05 113	Polk	859	20 229	1 778	23.5	17 347	1 830	17 007	2 882	340	16.6	2.0	708	3.5
...	05 115	Pope	812	54 469	865	67.1	45 883	906	38 964	8 586	6 919	18.7	17.8	1 123	2.1
...	05 117	Prairie	646	9 539	2 486	14.8	9 518	2 432	10 140	21	−622	.2	−6.1	77	.8
4400	05 119	Pulaski	771	361 474	163	468.8	349 569	147	340 597	11 905	8 972	3.4	2.6	8 816	2.4
...	05 121	Randolph	652	18 195	1 887	27.9	16 558	1 883	16 834	1 637	−276	9.9	−1.6	149	.8
...	05 123	St. Francis	634	29 329	1 420	46.3	28 497	1 343	30 858	832	−2 361	2.9	−7.7	1 431	4.9
4400	05 125	Saline	723	83 529	622	115.5	64 183	684	53 156	19 346	11 027	30.1	20.7	1 090	1.3
...	05 127	Scott	894	10 996	2 366	12.3	10 205	2 371	9 685	791	520	7.8	5.4	628	5.7
...	05 129	Searcy	667	8 261	2 585	12.4	7 841	2 589	8 847	420	−1 006	5.4	−11.4	86	1.0
2720	05 131	Sebastian	536	115 071	470	214.7	99 590	461	95 172	15 481	4 418	15.5	4.6	7 710	6.7
...	05 133	Sevier	564	15 757	2 035	27.9	13 637	2 088	14 060	2 120	−423	15.5	−3.0	3 107	19.7
...	05 135	Sharp	604	17 119	1 948	28.3	14 109	2 046	14 607	3 010	−498	21.3	−3.4	167	1.0
...	05 137	Stone	607	11 499	2 335	18.9	9 775	2 407	9 022	1 724	753	17.6	8.3	124	1.1
...	05 139	Union	1 039	45 629	988	43.9	46 719	895	48 573	−1 090	−1 854	−2.3	−3.8	520	1.1
...	05 141	Van Buren	712	16 192	2 008	22.7	14 008	2 054	13 357	2 184	651	15.6	4.9	215	1.3
2580	05 143	Washington	950	157 715	338	166.0	113 409	405	100 494	44 306	12 915	39.1	12.9	12 932	8.2
...	05 145	White	1 034	67 165	731	65.0	54 676	787	50 835	12 489	3 841	22.8	7.6	1 264	1.9
...	05 147	Woodruff	587	8 741	2 551	14.9	9 520	2 431	11 222	−779	−1 702	−8.2	−15.2	69	.8
...	05 149	Yell	928	21 139	1 727	22.8	17 759	1 800	17 026	3 380	733	19.0	4.3	2 691	12.7
	06 000	CALIFORNIA	155 959	33 871 648	X	217.2	29 811 427	X	23 667 764	4 060 221	6 143 663	13.6	26.0	10 966 556	32.4
7362	06 001	Alameda	738	1 443 741	21	1 956.3	1 304 347	21	1 105 379	139 394	198 968	10.7	18.0	273 910	19.0
...	06 003	Alpine	739	1 208	3 103	1.6	1 113	3 109	1 097	95	16	8.5	1.5	94	7.8
...	06 005	Amador	593	35 100	1 247	59.2	30 039	1 294	19 314	5 061	10 725	16.8	55.5	3 126	8.9
1620	06 007	Butte	1 639	203 171	270	124.0	182 120	266	143 851	21 051	38 269	11.6	26.6	21 339	10.5
...	06 009	Calaveras	1 020	40 554	1 100	39.8	31 998	1 211	20 710	8 556	11 288	26.7	54.5	2 765	6.8
...	06 011	Colusa	1 151	18 804	1 855	16.3	16 275	1 906	12 791	2 529	3 484	15.5	27.2	8 752	46.5
7362	06 013	Contra Costa	720	948 816	38	1 317.8	803 731	47	656 331	145 085	147 400	18.1	22.5	167 776	17.7
...	06 015	Del Norte	1 008	27 507	1 466	27.3	23 460	1 517	18 217	4 047	5 243	17.3	28.8	3 829	13.9
6922	06 017	El Dorado	1 711	156 299	342	91.3	125 995	368	85 812	30 304	40 183	24.1	46.8	14 566	9.3

[1] Federal Information Processing Standards (FIPS) codes for metropolitan areas defined as of June 30, 1999.   [2] FIPS codes for states and counties/county equivalents.   [3] Dry land and land temporarily or partially covered by water.   [4] Based on 3,140 counties/county equivalents; excludes Yellowstone National Park in MT and South Boston independent city in VA which are no longer counties. When counties share the same rank, the next lower rank is omitted.   [5] Includes count resolution corrections through 1997 and adjustments based on Census 2000 dress rehearsal results and boundary changes reported as legally effective as of January 1, 1998.   [6] Persons of Hispanic or Latino origin may be of any race.

Sources: Land Area—U.S. Census Bureau, unpublished data file from Geography Division based on TIGER data base.   2000 Population—U.S. Census Bureau, Census of Population and Housing, Census 2000 Redistricting Data (Public Law 94-171) Summary Files (related Internet site <http://www.census.gov/dmd/www/2kresult.html>).   1990 Population—U.S. Census Bureau, "(CO-99-8) County Population Estimates and Demographic Components of Population Change: Annual Time Series, July 1, 1990 to July 1, 1999 (includes revised April 1, 1990 Population Estimates Base)"; published 9 March 2000; <http://www. census.gov/population/estimates/county/co-99-8/99C8_00.txt>.   1980 Population—U.S. Census Bureau, "1980–1990 Intercensal Population Estimates by County" on diskette (related Internet site <http://www.census.gov/population/www/estimates/countypop.html>).

[Includes U.S., states, and 3,142 counties/county equivalents defined as of January 1, 1992. For changes to these areas since January 1, 1992, see appendix B. Geographic Information]

Metro-politan area code[1]	State and county code[2]	County	Land area,[3] 2000 (sq. miles)	Population (April 1)										
				2000		Per square mile	1990[5]		1980	Net change		Percent change		Hispanic or Latino,[6] 2000	
				Number	Rank[4]		Number	Rank[4]		1990–2000	1980–1990	1990–2000	1980–1990	Number	Percent
		CALIFORNIA—Con.													
2840	06 019	Fresno	5 963	799 407	58	134.1	667 479	67	514 621	131 928	152 858	19.8	29.7	351 636	44.0
...	06 021	Glenn	1 315	26 453	1 503	20.1	24 798	1 471	21 350	1 655	3 448	6.7	16.1	7 840	29.6
...	06 023	Humboldt	3 572	126 518	429	35.4	119 118	389	108 525	7 400	10 593	6.2	9.8	8 210	6.5
...	06 025	Imperial	4 175	142 361	384	34.1	109 303	421	92 110	33 058	17 193	30.2	18.7	102 817	72.2
...	06 027	Inyo	10 203	17 945	1 902	1.8	18 281	1 775	17 895	–336	386	–1.8	2.2	2 257	12.6
0680	06 029	Kern	8 141	661 645	78	81.3	544 981	88	403 089	116 664	141 892	21.4	35.2	254 036	38.4
...	06 031	Kings	1 391	129 461	414	93.1	101 469	450	73 738	27 992	27 731	27.6	37.6	56 461	43.6
...	06 033	Lake	1 258	58 309	820	46.4	50 631	832	36 366	7 678	14 265	15.2	39.2	6 639	11.4
...	06 035	Lassen	4 557	33 828	1 286	7.4	27 598	1 368	21 661	6 230	5 937	22.6	27.4	4 681	13.8
4472	06 037	Los Angeles	4 061	9 519 338	1	2 344.1	8 863 052	1	7 477 238	656 286	1 385 814	7.4	18.5	4 242 213	44.6
2840	06 039	Madera	2 136	123 109	440	57.6	88 090	518	63 116	35 019	24 974	39.8	39.6	54 515	44.3
7362	06 041	Marin	520	247 289	235	475.6	230 096	212	222 592	17 193	7 504	7.5	3.4	27 351	11.1
...	06 043	Mariposa	1 451	17 130	1 947	11.8	14 302	2 031	11 108	2 828	3 194	19.8	28.8	1 329	7.8
...	06 045	Mendocino	3 509	86 265	603	24.6	80 345	568	66 738	5 920	13 607	7.4	20.4	14 213	16.5
4940	06 047	Merced	1 929	210 554	264	109.2	178 403	272	134 558	32 151	43 845	18.0	32.6	95 466	45.3
...	06 049	Modoc	3 944	9 449	2 491	2.4	9 678	2 414	8 610	–229	1 068	–2.4	12.4	1 088	11.5
...	06 051	Mono	3 044	12 853	2 243	4.2	9 956	2 390	8 577	2 897	1 379	29.1	16.1	2 274	17.7
7120	06 053	Monterey	3 322	401 762	147	120.9	355 660	144	290 444	46 102	65 216	13.0	22.5	187 969	46.8
7362	06 055	Napa	754	124 279	433	164.8	110 765	417	99 199	13 514	11 566	12.2	11.7	29 416	23.7
....	06 057	Nevada	958	92 033	555	96.1	78 510	576	51 645	13 523	26 865	17.2	52.0	5 201	5.7
4472	06 059	Orange	789	2 846 289	5	3 607.5	2 410 668	5	1 932 921	435 621	477 747	18.1	24.7	875 579	30.8
6922	06 061	Placer	1 404	248 399	233	176.9	172 796	260	117 247	75 603	55 549	43.8	47.4	24 019	9.7
...	06 063	Plumas	2 554	20 824	1 745	8.2	19 739	1 689	17 340	1 085	2 399	5.5	13.8	1 177	5.7
4472	06 065	Riverside	7 207	1 545 387	16	214.4	1 170 413	26	663 199	374 974	507 214	32.0	76.5	559 575	36.2
6922	06 067	Sacramento	966	1 223 499	29	1 266.6	1 066 789	29	783 381	156 710	283 408	14.7	36.2	195 890	16.0
...	06 069	San Benito	1 389	53 234	880	38.3	36 697	1 082	25 005	16 537	11 692	45.1	46.8	25 516	47.9
4472	06 071	San Bernardino	20 053	1 709 434	13	85.2	1 418 380	16	895 016	291 054	523 364	20.5	58.5	669 387	39.2
7320	06 073	San Diego	4 200	2 813 833	6	670.0	2 498 016	4	1 861 846	315 817	636 170	12.6	34.2	750 965	26.7
7362	06 075	San Francisco	47	776 733	62	16 526.2	723 959	55	678 974	52 774	44 985	7.3	6.6	109 504	14.1
8120	06 077	San Joaquin	1 399	563 598	97	402.9	480 628	101	347 342	82 970	133 286	17.3	38.4	172 073	30.5
7460	06 079	San Luis Obispo	3 304	246 681	236	74.7	217 162	229	155 435	29 519	61 727	13.6	39.7	40 196	16.3
7362	06 081	San Mateo	449	707 161	70	1 575.0	649 623	72	587 329	57 538	62 294	8.9	10.6	154 708	21.9
7480	06 083	Santa Barbara	2 737	399 347	149	145.9	369 608	139	298 694	29 739	70 914	8.0	23.7	136 668	34.2
7362	06 085	Santa Clara	1 291	1 682 585	14	1 303.3	1 497 577	14	1 295 071	185 008	202 506	12.4	15.6	403 401	24.0
7362	06 087	Santa Cruz	445	255 602	220	574.4	229 734	214	188 141	25 868	41 593	11.3	22.1	68 486	26.8
6690	06 089	Shasta	3 785	163 256	320	40.1	147 036	320	115 613	16 220	31 423	11.0	27.2	8 998	5.5
...	06 091	Sierra	953	3 555	2 950	3.7	3 318	2 970	3 073	237	245	7.1	8.0	213	6.0
...	06 093	Siskiyou	6 287	44 301	1 010	7.0	43 531	931	39 732	770	3 799	1.8	9.6	3 354	7.6
7362	06 095	Solano	829	394 542	150	475.9	339 469	150	235 203	55 073	104 266	16.2	44.3	69 598	17.6
7362	06 097	Sonoma	1 576	458 614	125	291.0	388 222	130	299 681	70 392	88 541	18.1	29.5	79 511	17.3
5170	06 099	Stanislaus	1 494	446 997	132	299.2	370 522	137	265 900	76 475	104 622	20.6	39.3	141 871	31.7
9340	06 101	Sutter	603	78 930	649	130.9	64 409	677	52 246	14 521	12 163	22.5	23.3	17 529	22.2
...	06 103	Tehama	2 951	56 039	842	19.0	49 625	846	38 888	6 414	10 737	12.9	27.6	8 871	15.8
...	06 105	Trinity	3 179	13 022	2 230	4.1	13 063	2 134	11 858	–41	1 205	–.3	10.2	517	4.0
8780	06 107	Tulare	4 824	368 021	160	76.3	311 932	160	245 738	56 089	66 194	18.0	26.9	186 846	50.8
...	06 109	Tuolumne	2 235	54 501	863	24.4	48 456	863	33 928	6 045	14 528	12.5	42.8	4 445	8.2
4472	06 111	Ventura	1 845	753 197	64	408.2	669 016	66	529 174	84 181	139 842	12.6	26.4	251 734	33.4
6922	06 113	Yolo	1 013	168 660	321	166.5	141 212	337	113 374	27 448	27 838	19.4	24.6	43 707	25.9
9340	06 115	Yuba	631	60 219	803	95.4	58 234	744	49 733	1 985	8 501	3.4	17.1	10 449	17.4
	08 000	COLORADO	103 718	4 301 261	X	41.5	3 294 473	X	2 889 735	1 006 788	404 738	30.6	14.0	735 601	17.1
2082	08 001	Adams	1 192	363 857	162	305.2	265 038	186	245 944	98 819	19 094	37.3	7.8	102 585	28.2
...	08 003	Alamosa	723	14 966	2 093	20.7	13 617	2 091	11 799	1 349	1 818	9.9	15.4	6 197	41.4
2082	08 005	Arapahoe	803	487 967	116	607.7	391 572	129	293 300	96 395	98 272	24.6	33.5	57 612	11.8
...	08 007	Archuleta	1 350	9 898	2 456	7.3	5 345	2 815	3 664	4 553	1 681	85.2	45.9	1 659	16.8
...	08 009	Baca	2 556	4 517	2 878	1.8	4 556	2 867	5 419	–39	–863	–.9	–15.9	317	7.0
...	08 011	Bent	1 514	5 998	2 781	4.0	5 048	2 836	5 945	950	–897	18.8	–15.1	1 814	30.2
2082	08 013	Boulder	742	291 288	194	392.6	225 339	221	189 625	65 949	35 714	29.3	18.8	30 456	10.5
...	08 015	Chaffee	1 013	16 242	2 005	16.0	12 684	2 167	13 227	3 558	–543	28.1	–4.1	1 393	8.6
...	08 017	Cheyenne	1 781	2 231	3 049	1.3	2 397	3 031	2 153	–166	244	–6.9	11.3	181	8.1
...	08 019	Clear Creek	395	9 322	2 503	23.6	7 619	2 608	7 308	1 703	311	22.4	4.3	361	3.9
...	08 021	Conejos	1 287	8 400	2 573	6.5	7 453	2 618	7 794	947	–341	12.7	–4.4	4 949	58.9
...	08 023	Costilla	1 227	3 663	2 943	3.0	3 190	2 984	3 071	473	119	14.8	3.9	2 476	67.6
...	08 025	Crowley	789	5 518	2 816	7.0	3 946	2 922	2 988	1 572	958	39.8	32.1	1 244	22.5
...	08 027	Custer	739	3 503	2 954	4.7	1 926	3 071	1 528	1 577	398	81.9	26.0	88	2.5

[1] Federal Information Processing Standards (FIPS) codes for metropolitan areas defined as of June 30, 1999. [2] FIPS codes for states and counties/county equivalents. [3] Dry land and land temporarily or partially covered by water. [4] Based on 3,140 counties/county equivalents; excludes Yellowstone National Park in MT and South Boston independent city in VA which are no longer counties. When counties share the same rank, the next lower rank is omitted. [5] Includes count resolution corrections through 1997 and adjustments based on Census 2000 dress rehearsal results and boundary changes reported as legally effective as of January 1, 1998. [6] Persons of Hispanic or Latino origin may be of any race.

Sources: Land Area—U.S. Census Bureau, unpublished data file from Geography Division based on TIGER data base. 2000 Population—U.S. Census Bureau, Census of Population and Housing, Census 2000 Redistricting Data (Public Law 94-171) Summary Files (related Internet site <http://www.census.gov/dmd/www/2kresult.html>). 1990 Population—U.S. Census Bureau, "(CO-99-8) County Population Estimates and Demographic Components of Population Change: Annual Time Series, July 1, 1990 to July 1, 1999 (includes revised April 1, 1990 Population Estimates Base)"; published 9 March 2000; <http://www. census.gov/population/estimates/county/co-99-8/99C8_00.txt>. 1980 Population—U.S. Census Bureau, "1980–1990 Intercensal Population Estimates by County" on diskette (related Internet site <http://www.census.gov/population/www/estimates/countypop.html>).

[Includes U.S., states, and 3,142 counties/county equivalents defined as of January 1, 1992. For changes to these areas since January 1, 1992, see appendix B. Geographic Information]

Metro-politan area code[1]	State and county code[2]	County	Land area,[3] 2000 (sq. miles)	2000 Number	2000 Rank[4]	2000 Per square mile	1990[5] Number	1990[5] Rank[4]	1980	Net change 1990–2000	Net change 1980–1990	Percent change 1990–2000	Percent change 1980–1990	Hispanic or Latino,[6] 2000 Number	Hispanic or Latino,[6] 2000 Percent
		COLORADO—Con.													
...	08 029	Delta	1 142	27 834	1 455	24.4	20 980	1 631	21 225	6 854	−245	32.7	−1.2	3 171	11.4
2082	08 031	Denver	153	554 636	101	3 625.1	467 549	106	492 686	87 087	−25 137	18.6	−5.1	175 704	31.7
...	08 033	Dolores	1 067	1 844	3 077	1.7	1 504	3 096	1 658	340	−154	22.6	−9.3	71	3.9
2082	08 035	Douglas	840	175 766	311	209.2	60 391	717	25 153	115 375	35 238	191.0	140.1	8 886	5.1
...	08 037	Eagle	1 688	41 659	1 064	24.7	21 928	1 581	13 320	19 731	8 608	90.0	64.6	9 682	23.2
...	08 039	Elbert	1 851	19 872	1 798	10.7	9 646	2 419	6 850	10 226	2 796	106.0	40.8	766	3.9
1720	08 041	El Paso	2 126	516 929	107	243.1	397 014	125	309 424	119 915	87 590	30.2	28.3	58 401	11.3
...	08 043	Fremont	1 533	46 145	979	30.1	32 273	1 207	28 676	13 872	3 597	43.0	12.5	4 776	10.3
...	08 045	Garfield	2 947	43 791	1 021	14.9	29 974	1 299	22 514	13 817	7 460	46.1	33.1	7 300	16.7
...	08 047	Gilpin	150	4 757	2 862	31.7	3 070	2 995	2 441	1 687	629	55.0	25.8	202	4.2
...	08 049	Grand	1 847	12 442	2 269	6.7	7 966	2 575	7 475	4 476	491	56.2	6.6	543	4.4
...	08 051	Gunnison	3 239	13 956	2 164	4.3	10 273	2 362	10 689	3 683	−416	35.9	−3.9	700	5.0
...	08 053	Hinsdale	1 118	790	3 124	.7	467	3 135	408	323	59	69.2	14.5	12	1.5
...	08 055	Huerfano	1 591	7 862	2 617	4.9	6 009	2 756	6 440	1 853	−431	30.8	−6.7	2 763	35.1
...	08 057	Jackson	1 613	1 577	3 090	1.0	1 605	3 090	1 863	−28	−258	−1.7	−13.8	103	6.5
2082	08 059	Jefferson	772	527 056	105	682.7	438 430	113	371 753	88 626	66 677	20.2	17.9	52 449	10.0
...	08 061	Kiowa	1 771	1 622	3 088	.9	1 688	3 085	1 936	−66	−248	−3.9	−12.8	51	3.1
...	08 063	Kit Carson	2 161	8 011	2 605	3.7	7 140	2 639	7 599	871	−459	12.2	−6.0	1 095	13.7
...	08 065	Lake	377	7 812	2 623	20.7	6 007	2 757	8 830	1 805	−2 823	30.0	−32.0	2 823	36.1
...	08 067	La Plata	1 692	43 941	1 018	26.0	32 284	1 206	27 195	11 657	5 089	36.1	18.7	4 571	10.4
2670	08 069	Larimer	2 601	251 494	227	96.7	186 136	260	149 184	65 358	36 952	35.1	24.8	20 811	8.3
...	08 071	Las Animas	4 773	15 207	2 075	3.2	13 765	2 076	14 897	1 442	−1 132	10.5	−7.6	6 304	41.5
...	08 073	Lincoln	2 586	6 087	2 772	2.4	4 529	2 871	4 663	1 558	−134	34.4	−2.9	519	8.5
...	08 075	Logan	1 839	20 504	1 761	11.1	17 567	1 817	19 800	2 937	−2 233	16.7	−11.3	2 439	11.9
2995	08 077	Mesa	3 328	116 255	464	34.9	93 145	498	81 530	23 110	11 615	24.8	14.2	11 651	10.0
...	08 079	Mineral	876	831	3 121	.9	558	3 132	804	273	−246	48.9	−30.6	17	2.0
...	08 081	Moffat	4 742	13 184	2 211	2.8	11 357	2 266	13 133	1 827	−1 776	16.1	−13.5	1 247	9.5
...	08 083	Montezuma	2 037	23 830	1 598	11.7	18 672	1 752	16 510	5 158	2 162	27.6	13.1	2 263	9.5
...	08 085	Montrose	2 241	33 432	1 301	14.9	24 423	1 480	24 352	9 009	71	36.9	.3	4 967	14.9
...	08 087	Morgan	1 285	27 171	1 476	21.1	21 939	1 580	22 513	5 232	−574	23.8	−2.5	8 473	31.2
...	08 089	Otero	1 263	20 311	1 772	16.1	20 185	1 665	22 567	126	−2 382	.6	−10.6	7 642	37.6
...	08 091	Ouray	540	3 742	2 938	6.9	2 295	3 039	1 925	1 447	370	63.1	19.2	152	4.1
...	08 093	Park	2 201	14 523	2 121	6.6	7 174	2 636	5 333	7 349	1 841	102.4	34.5	628	4.3
...	08 095	Phillips	688	4 480	2 883	6.5	4 189	2 899	4 542	291	−353	6.9	−7.8	527	11.8
...	08 097	Pitkin	970	14 872	2 101	15.3	12 661	2 170	10 338	2 211	2 323	17.5	22.5	973	6.5
...	08 099	Prowers	1 640	14 483	2 123	8.8	13 347	2 110	13 070	1 136	277	8.5	2.1	4 766	32.9
6560	08 101	Pueblo	2 389	141 472	388	59.2	123 051	374	125 972	18 421	−2 921	15.0	−2.3	53 710	38.0
...	08 103	Rio Blanco	3 221	5 986	2 783	1.9	6 051	2 751	6 255	−65	−204	−1.1	−3.3	296	4.9
...	08 105	Rio Grande	912	12 413	2 270	13.6	10 770	2 310	10 511	1 643	259	15.3	2.5	5 172	41.7
...	08 107	Routt	2 362	19 690	1 812	8.3	14 088	2 049	13 404	5 602	684	39.8	5.1	634	3.2
...	08 109	Saguache	3 168	5 917	2 792	1.9	4 619	2 865	3 935	1 298	684	28.1	17.4	2 678	45.3
...	08 111	San Juan	387	558	3 133	1.4	745	3 127	833	−187	−88	−25.1	−10.6	41	7.3
...	08 113	San Miguel	1 287	6 594	2 728	5.1	3 653	2 944	3 192	2 941	461	80.5	14.4	439	6.7
...	08 115	Sedgwick	548	2 747	3 011	5.0	2 690	3 014	3 266	57	−576	2.1	−17.6	314	11.4
...	08 117	Summit	608	23 548	1 613	38.7	12 881	2 148	8 848	10 667	4 033	82.8	45.6	2 306	9.8
...	08 119	Teller	557	20 555	1 757	36.9	12 468	2 183	8 034	8 087	4 434	64.9	55.2	718	3.5
...	08 121	Washington	2 521	4 926	2 853	2.0	4 812	2 855	5 304	114	−492	2.4	−9.3	310	6.3
2082	08 123	Weld	3 992	180 936	305	45.3	131 821	350	123 438	49 115	8 383	37.3	6.8	48 935	27.0
...	08 125	Yuma	2 366	9 841	2 462	4.2	8 954	2 475	9 682	887	−728	9.9	−7.5	1 268	12.9
	09 000	CONNECTICUT	4 845	3 405 565	X	702.9	3 287 116	X	3 107 564	118 449	179 552	3.6	5.8	320 323	9.4
5483	09 001	Fairfield	626	882 567	47	1 409.9	827 645	42	807 143	54 922	20 502	6.6	2.5	104 835	11.9
3283	09 003	Hartford	735	857 183	51	1 166.2	851 783	38	807 766	5 400	44 017	.6	5.4	98 968	11.5
...	09 005	Litchfield	920	182 193	301	198.0	174 092	278	156 769	8 101	17 323	4.7	11.1	3 894	2.1
3283	09 007	Middlesex	369	155 071	343	420.2	143 196	332	129 017	11 875	14 179	8.3	11.0	4 649	3.0
5483	09 009	New Haven	606	824 008	54	1 359.7	804 219	46	761 325	19 789	42 894	2.5	5.6	83 131	10.1
5523	09 011	New London	666	259 088	215	389.0	254 957	195	238 409	4 131	16 548	1.6	6.9	13 236	5.1
3283	09 013	Tolland	410	136 364	395	332.6	128 699	360	114 823	7 665	13 876	6.0	12.1	3 873	2.8
...	09 015	Windham	513	109 091	495	212.7	102 525	449	92 312	6 566	10 213	6.4	11.1	7 737	7.1
	10 000	DELAWARE	1 954	783 600	X	401.0	666 168	X	594 338	117 432	71 830	17.6	12.1	37 277	4.8
2190	10 001	Kent	590	126 697	426	214.7	110 993	414	98 219	15 704	12 774	14.1	13.0	4 069	3.2
6162	10 003	New Castle	426	500 265	112	1 174.3	441 946	112	398 115	58 319	43 831	13.2	11.0	26 293	5.3
...	10 005	Sussex	938	156 638	341	167.0	113 229	407	98 004	43 409	15 225	38.3	15.5	6 915	4.4
	11 000	DISTRICT OF COLUMBIA	61	572 059	X	9 378.0	606 900	X	638 432	−34 841	−31 532	−5.7	−4.9	44 953	7.9
8872	11 001	District of Columbia	61	572 059	94	9 378.0	606 900	76	638 432	−34 841	−31 532	−5.7	−4.9	44 953	7.9

[1] Federal Information Processing Standards (FIPS) codes for metropolitan areas defined as of June 30, 1999. [2] FIPS codes for states and counties/county equivalents. [3] Dry land and land temporarily or partially covered by water. [4] Based on 3,140 counties/county equivalents; excludes Yellowstone National Park in MT and South Boston independent city in VA which are no longer counties. When counties share the same rank, the next lower rank is omitted. [5] Includes count resolution corrections through 1997 and adjustments based on Census 2000 dress rehearsal results and boundary changes reported as legally effective as of January 1, 1998. [6] Persons of Hispanic or Latino origin may be of any race.

Sources: Land Area—U.S. Census Bureau, unpublished data file from Geography Division based on TIGER data base. 2000 Population—U.S. Census Bureau, Census of Population and Housing, Census 2000 Redistricting Data (Public Law 94-171) Summary Files (related Internet site <http://www.census.gov/dmd/www/2kresult.html>). 1990 Population—U.S. Census Bureau, "(CO-99-8) County Population Estimates and Demographic Components of Population Change: Annual Time Series, July 1, 1990 to July 1, 1999 (includes revised April 1, 1990 Population Estimates Base)"; published 9 March 2000; <http://www. census.gov/population/estimates/county/co-99-8/99C8_00.txt>. 1980 Population—U.S. Census Bureau, "1980-1990 Intercensal Population Estimates by County" on diskette (related Internet site <http://www.census.gov/population/www/estimates/countypop.html>).

Table B–1. Counties — **Area and Population**–Con.

[Includes U.S., states, and 3,142 counties/county equivalents defined as of January 1, 1992. For changes to these areas since January 1, 1992, see appendix B. Geographic Information]

Metro-politan area code[1]	State and county code[2]	County	Land area,[3] 2000 (sq. miles)	Population (April 1): 2000 Number	2000 Rank[4]	2000 Per square mile	1990[5] Number	1990[5] Rank[4]	1980	Net change 1990–2000	Net change 1980–1990	Percent change 1990–2000	Percent change 1980–1990	Hispanic or Latino,[6] 2000 Number	Hispanic or Latino,[6] 2000 Percent
	12 000	FLORIDA	53 927	15 982 378	X	296.4	12 938 071	X	9 746 961	3 044 307	3 191 110	23.5	32.7	2 682 715	16.8
2900	12 001	Alachua	874	217 955	259	249.4	181 596	268	151 369	36 359	30 227	20.0	20.0	12 493	5.7
...	12 003	Baker	585	22 259	1 682	38.0	18 486	1 763	15 289	3 773	3 197	20.4	20.9	419	1.9
6015	12 005	Bay	764	148 217	366	194.0	126 994	365	97 740	21 223	29 254	16.7	29.9	3 591	2.4
...	12 007	Bradford	293	26 088	1 513	89.0	22 515	1 554	20 023	3 573	2 492	15.9	12.4	622	2.4
4900	12 009	Brevard	1 018	476 230	120	467.8	398 978	124	272 959	77 252	126 019	19.4	46.2	21 970	4.6
4992	12 011	Broward	1 205	1 623 018	15	1 346.9	1 255 531	23	1 018 257	367 487	237 274	29.3	23.3	271 652	16.7
...	12 013	Calhoun	567	13 017	2 231	23.0	11 011	2 291	9 294	2 006	1 717	18.2	18.5	492	3.8
6580	12 015	Charlotte	694	141 627	387	204.1	110 975	415	58 460	30 652	52 515	27.6	89.8	4 667	3.3
...	12 017	Citrus	584	118 085	458	202.2	93 513	494	54 703	24 572	38 810	26.3	70.9	3 141	2.7
3600	12 019	Clay	601	140 814	389	234.3	105 986	437	67 052	34 828	38 934	32.9	58.1	6 059	4.3
5345	12 021	Collier	2 025	251 377	228	124.1	152 099	305	85 971	99 278	66 128	65.3	76.9	49 296	19.6
...	12 023	Columbia	797	56 513	838	70.9	42 613	943	35 399	13 900	7 214	32.6	20.4	1 546	2.7
4002	12 025	Dade	1 946	2 253 362	8	1 157.9	1 937 194	10	1 625 509	316 168	311 685	16.3	19.2	1 291 737	57.3
...	12 027	DeSoto	637	32 209	1 341	50.6	23 865	1 497	19 039	8 344	4 826	35.0	25.3	8 019	24.9
...	12 029	Dixie	704	13 827	2 171	19.6	10 585	2 329	7 751	3 242	2 834	30.6	36.6	249	1.8
3600	12 031	Duval	774	778 879	61	1 006.3	672 971	63	571 003	105 908	101 968	15.7	17.9	31 946	4.1
6080	12 033	Escambia	662	294 410	192	444.7	262 445	191	233 794	31 965	28 651	12.2	12.3	7 935	2.7
2020	12 035	Flagler	485	49 832	918	102.7	28 701	1 338	10 913	21 131	17 788	73.6	163.0	2 537	5.1
...	12 037	Franklin	544	11 057	2 362	20.3	8 967	2 473	7 661	2 090	1 306	23.3	17.0	268	2.4
8240	12 039	Gadsden	516	45 087	996	87.4	41 116	978	41 674	3 971	–558	9.7	–1.3	2 782	6.2
...	12 041	Gilchrist	349	14 437	2 127	41.4	9 667	2 417	5 767	4 770	3 900	49.3	67.6	404	2.8
...	12 043	Glades	774	10 576	2 391	13.7	7 591	2 610	5 992	2 985	1 599	39.3	26.7	1 594	15.1
...	12 045	Gulf	555	13 332	2 201	24.0	11 504	2 256	10 658	1 828	846	15.9	7.9	270	2.0
...	12 047	Hamilton	515	13 327	2 203	25.9	10 930	2 303	8 761	2 397	2 169	21.9	24.8	847	6.4
...	12 049	Hardee	637	26 938	1 486	42.3	19 499	1 702	20 357	7 439	–858	38.2	–4.2	9 611	35.7
...	12 051	Hendry	1 153	36 210	1 208	31.4	25 773	1 429	18 599	10 437	7 174	40.5	38.6	14 336	39.6
8280	12 053	Hernando	478	130 802	409	273.6	101 115	454	44 469	29 687	56 646	29.4	127.4	6 587	5.0
...	12 055	Highlands	1 028	87 366	600	85.0	68 432	645	47 526	18 934	20 906	27.7	44.0	10 542	12.1
8280	12 057	Hillsborough	1 051	998 948	35	950.5	834 054	41	646 939	164 894	187 115	19.8	28.9	179 692	18.0
...	12 059	Holmes	482	18 564	1 867	38.5	15 778	1 936	14 723	2 786	1 055	17.7	7.2	358	1.9
...	12 061	Indian River	503	112 947	476	224.5	90 208	507	59 896	22 739	30 312	25.2	50.6	7 381	6.5
...	12 063	Jackson	916	46 755	966	51.0	41 375	972	39 154	5 380	2 221	13.0	5.7	1 361	2.9
...	12 065	Jefferson	598	12 902	2 241	21.6	11 296	2 275	10 703	1 606	593	14.2	5.5	290	2.2
...	12 067	Lafayette	543	7 022	2 683	12.9	5 578	2 792	4 035	1 444	1 543	25.9	38.2	642	9.1
5960	12 069	Lake	953	210 528	265	220.9	152 104	304	104 870	58 424	47 234	38.4	45.0	11 808	5.6
2700	12 071	Lee	804	440 888	136	548.4	335 113	154	205 266	105 775	129 847	31.6	63.3	42 042	9.5
8240	12 073	Leon	667	239 452	240	359.0	192 493	249	148 655	46 959	43 838	24.4	29.5	8 407	3.5
...	12 075	Levy	1 118	34 450	1 266	30.8	25 912	1 426	19 870	8 538	6 042	32.9	30.4	1 339	3.9
...	12 077	Liberty	836	7 021	2 684	8.4	5 569	2 793	4 260	1 452	1 309	26.1	30.7	316	4.5
...	12 079	Madison	692	18 733	1 859	27.1	16 569	1 882	14 894	2 164	1 675	13.1	11.2	600	3.2
7510	12 081	Manatee	741	264 002	209	356.3	211 707	237	148 445	52 295	63 262	24.7	42.6	24 540	9.3
5790	12 083	Marion	1 579	258 916	217	164.0	194 835	247	122 488	64 081	72 347	32.9	59.1	15 616	6.0
2710	12 085	Martin	556	126 731	425	227.9	100 900	455	64 014	25 831	36 886	25.6	57.6	9 506	7.5
...	12 087	Monroe	997	79 589	644	79.8	78 024	580	63 188	1 565	14 836	2.0	23.5	12 553	15.8
3600	12 089	Nassau	652	57 663	828	88.4	43 941	927	32 894	13 722	11 047	31.2	33.6	873	1.5
2750	12 091	Okaloosa	936	170 498	317	182.2	143 777	330	109 920	26 721	33 857	18.6	30.8	7 302	4.3
...	12 093	Okeechobee	774	35 910	1 222	46.4	29 627	1 311	20 264	6 283	9 363	21.2	46.2	6 684	18.6
5960	12 095	Orange	907	896 344	45	988.3	677 491	62	470 865	218 853	206 626	32.3	43.9	168 361	18.8
5960	12 097	Osceola	1 322	172 493	315	130.5	107 728	428	49 287	64 765	58 441	60.1	118.6	50 727	29.4
8960	12 099	Palm Beach	1 974	1 131 184	31	573.0	863 503	37	576 758	267 681	286 745	31.0	49.7	140 675	12.4
8280	12 101	Pasco	745	344 765	170	462.8	281 131	176	193 661	63 634	87 470	22.6	45.2	19 603	5.7
8280	12 103	Pinellas	280	921 482	41	3 291.0	851 659	39	728 531	69 823	123 128	8.2	16.9	42 760	4.6
3980	12 105	Polk	1 874	483 924	119	258.2	405 382	122	321 652	78 542	83 730	19.4	26.0	45 933	9.5
...	12 107	Putnam	722	70 423	705	97.5	65 070	673	50 549	5 353	14 521	8.2	28.7	4 168	5.9
3600	12 109	St. Johns	609	123 135	439	202.2	83 829	547	51 303	39 306	32 526	46.9	63.4	3 244	2.6
2710	12 111	St. Lucie	572	192 695	285	336.9	150 171	312	87 182	42 524	62 989	28.3	72.3	15 733	8.2
6080	12 113	Santa Rosa	1 017	117 743	460	115.8	81 961	554	55 988	35 782	25 973	43.7	46.4	2 968	2.5
7510	12 115	Sarasota	572	325 957	177	569.9	277 776	178	202 251	48 181	75 525	17.3	37.3	14 142	4.3
5960	12 117	Seminole	308	365 196	161	1 185.7	287 521	170	179 752	77 675	107 769	27.0	60.0	40 731	11.2
...	12 119	Sumter	546	53 345	876	97.7	31 577	1 228	24 272	21 768	7 305	68.9	30.1	3 356	6.3
...	12 121	Suwannee	688	34 844	1 256	50.6	26 780	1 397	22 287	8 064	4 493	30.1	20.2	1 703	4.9
...	12 123	Taylor	1 042	19 256	1 830	18.5	17 111	1 845	16 532	2 145	579	12.5	3.5	295	1.5
...	12 125	Union	240	13 442	2 197	56.0	10 252	2 363	10 166	3 190	86	31.1	.8	477	3.5
2020	12 127	Volusia	1 103	443 343	135	401.9	370 737	136	258 762	72 606	111 975	19.6	43.3	29 111	6.6
...	12 129	Wakulla	607	22 863	1 650	37.7	14 202	2 037	10 887	8 661	3 315	61.0	30.4	443	1.9
...	12 131	Walton	1 058	40 601	1 098	38.4	27 759	1 360	21 300	12 842	6 459	46.3	30.3	880	2.2
...	12 133	Washington	580	20 973	1 738	36.2	16 919	1 855	14 509	4 054	2 410	24.0	16.6	483	2.3

[1] Federal Information Processing Standards (FIPS) codes for metropolitan areas defined as of June 30, 1999. [2] FIPS codes for states and counties/county equivalents. [3] Dry land and land temporarily or partially covered by water. [4] Based on 3,140 counties/county equivalents; excludes Yellowstone National Park in MT and South Boston independent city in VA which are no longer counties. When counties share the same rank, the next lower rank is omitted. [5] Includes count resolution corrections through 1997 and adjustments based on Census 2000 dress rehearsal results and boundary changes reported as legally effective as of January 1, 1998. [6] Persons of Hispanic or Latino origin may be of any race.

Sources: Land Area—U.S. Census Bureau, unpublished data file from Geography Division based on TIGER data base. 2000 Population—U.S. Census Bureau, Census of Population and Housing, Census 2000 Redistricting Data (Public Law 94-171) Summary Files (related Internet site <http://www.census.gov/dmd/www/2kresult.html>). 1990 Population—U.S. Census Bureau, "(CO-99-8) County Population Estimates and Demographic Components of Population Change: Annual Time Series, July 1, 1990 to July 1, 1999 (includes revised April 1, 1990 Population Estimates Base)"; published 9 March 2000; <http://www. census.gov/population/estimates/county/co-99-8/99C8_00.txt>. 1980 Population—U.S. Census Bureau, "1980–1990 Intercensal Population Estimates by County" on diskette (related Internet site <http://www.census.gov/population/www/estimates/countypop.html>).

[Includes U.S., states, and 3,142 counties/county equivalents defined as of January 1, 1992. For changes to these areas since January 1, 1992, see appendix B. Geographic Information]

Metro-politan area code[1]	State and county code[2]	County	Land area,[3] 2000 (sq. miles)	Population (April 1) 2000 Number	2000 Rank[4]	2000 Per square mile	1990[5] Number	1990 Rank[4]	1980	Net change 1990–2000	Net change 1980–1990	Percent change 1990–2000	Percent change 1980–1990	Hispanic or Latino,[6] 2000 Number	Hispanic Percent
	13 000	GEORGIA	57 906	8 186 453	X	141.4	6 478 149	X	5 462 982	1 708 304	1 015 167	26.4	18.6	435 227	5.3
...	13 001	Appling	509	17 419	1 928	34.2	15 744	1 937	15 565	1 675	179	10.6	1.2	792	4.5
...	13 003	Atkinson	338	7 609	2 635	22.5	6 213	2 731	6 141	1 396	72	22.5	1.2	1 290	17.0
...	13 005	Bacon	285	10 103	2 437	35.4	9 566	2 426	9 379	537	187	5.6	2.0	342	3.4
...	13 007	Baker	343	4 074	2 914	11.9	3 615	2 949	3 808	459	–193	12.7	–5.1	111	2.7
...	13 009	Baldwin	258	44 700	1 005	173.3	39 530	1 012	34 686	5 170	4 844	13.1	14.0	607	1.4
...	13 011	Banks	234	14 422	2 128	61.6	10 308	2 358	8 702	4 114	1 606	39.9	18.5	493	3.4
0520	13 013	Barrow	162	46 144	980	284.8	29 721	1 306	21 354	16 423	8 367	55.3	39.2	1 460	3.2
0520	13 015	Bartow	459	76 019	659	165.6	55 915	774	40 760	20 104	15 155	36.0	37.2	2 524	3.3
...	13 017	Ben Hill	252	17 484	1 924	69.4	16 245	1 911	16 000	1 239	245	7.6	1.5	800	4.6
...	13 019	Berrien	452	16 235	2 006	35.9	14 153	2 041	13 525	2 082	628	14.7	4.6	384	2.4
4680	13 021	Bibb	250	153 887	345	615.5	150 137	313	150 256	3 750	–119	2.5	–.1	2 023	1.3
...	13 023	Bleckley	217	11 666	2 321	53.8	10 430	2 346	10 767	1 236	–337	11.9	–3.1	107	.9
...	13 025	Brantley	444	14 629	2 111	32.9	11 077	2 285	8 701	3 552	2 376	32.1	27.3	152	1.0
...	13 027	Brooks	494	16 450	1 993	33.3	15 398	1 964	15 255	1 052	143	6.8	.9	505	3.1
7520	13 029	Bryan	442	23 417	1 621	53.0	15 438	1 959	10 175	7 979	5 263	51.7	51.7	465	2.0
...	13 031	Bulloch	682	55 983	843	82.1	43 125	936	35 785	12 858	7 340	29.8	20.5	1 052	1.9
...	13 033	Burke	830	22 243	1 684	26.8	20 579	1 650	19 349	1 664	1 230	8.1	6.4	316	1.4
...	13 035	Butts	187	19 522	1 818	104.4	15 326	1 970	13 665	4 196	1 661	27.4	12.2	277	1.4
...	13 037	Calhoun	280	6 320	2 755	22.6	5 013	2 841	5 717	1 307	–704	26.1	–12.3	189	3.0
...	13 039	Camden	630	43 664	1 024	69.3	30 167	1 291	13 371	13 497	16 796	44.7	125.6	1 585	3.6
...	13 043	Candler	247	9 577	2 482	38.8	7 744	2 599	7 518	1 833	226	23.7	3.0	882	9.2
0520	13 045	Carroll	499	87 268	601	174.9	71 422	620	56 346	15 846	15 076	22.2	26.8	2 243	2.6
1560	13 047	Catoosa	162	53 282	878	328.9	42 464	947	36 991	10 818	5 473	25.5	14.8	621	1.2
...	13 049	Charlton	781	10 282	2 419	13.2	8 496	2 513	7 343	1 786	1 153	21.0	15.7	81	.8
7520	13 051	Chatham	438	232 048	248	529.8	216 774	230	202 226	15 274	14 548	7.0	7.2	5 403	2.3
1800	13 053	Chattahoochee	249	14 882	2 100	59.8	16 934	1 853	21 732	–2 052	–4 798	–12.1	–22.1	1 551	10.4
...	13 055	Chattooga	313	25 470	1 541	81.4	22 236	1 569	21 856	3 234	380	14.5	1.7	537	2.1
0520	13 057	Cherokee	424	141 903	385	334.7	90 204	508	51 699	51 699	38 505	57.3	74.5	7 695	5.4
0500	13 059	Clarke	121	101 489	520	838.8	87 594	520	74 498	13 895	13 096	15.9	17.6	6 436	6.3
...	13 061	Clay	195	3 357	2 967	17.2	3 364	2 966	3 553	–7	–189	–.2	–5.3	32	1.0
0520	13 063	Clayton	143	236 517	245	1 654.0	181 436	269	150 357	55 081	31 079	30.4	20.7	17 728	7.5
...	13 065	Clinch	809	6 878	2 699	8.5	6 160	2 736	6 660	718	–500	11.7	–7.5	54	.8
0520	13 067	Cobb	340	607 751	89	1 787.5	447 745	111	297 718	160 006	150 027	35.7	50.4	46 964	7.7
...	13 069	Coffee	599	37 413	1 179	62.5	29 592	1 314	26 894	7 821	2 698	26.4	10.0	2 550	6.8
...	13 071	Colquitt	552	42 053	1 057	76.2	36 645	1 084	35 376	5 408	1 269	14.8	3.6	4 554	10.8
0600	13 073	Columbia	290	89 288	579	307.9	66 031	664	40 118	23 257	25 913	35.2	64.6	2 313	2.6
...	13 075	Cook	229	15 771	2 033	68.9	13 456	2 104	13 490	2 315	–34	17.2	–.3	485	3.1
0520	13 077	Coweta	443	89 215	580	201.4	53 853	798	39 268	35 362	14 585	65.7	37.1	2 797	3.1
...	13 079	Crawford	325	12 495	2 265	38.4	8 991	2 471	7 684	3 504	1 307	39.0	17.0	301	2.4
...	13 081	Crisp	274	21 996	1 693	80.3	20 011	1 677	19 489	1 985	522	9.9	2.7	382	1.7
1560	13 083	Dade	174	15 154	2 081	87.1	13 183	2 125	12 318	1 971	865	15.0	7.0	137	.9
...	13 085	Dawson	211	15 999	2 023	75.8	9 429	2 440	4 774	6 570	4 655	69.7	97.5	254	1.6
...	13 087	Decatur	597	28 240	1 442	47.3	25 517	1 447	25 495	2 723	22	10.7	.1	905	3.2
0520	13 089	De Kalb	268	665 865	76	2 484.6	546 174	87	483 024	119 691	63 150	21.9	13.1	52 542	7.9
...	13 091	Dodge	500	19 171	1 836	38.3	17 607	1 813	16 955	1 564	652	8.9	3.8	248	1.3
...	13 093	Dooly	393	11 525	2 332	29.3	9 901	2 398	10 826	1 624	–925	16.4	–8.5	537	4.7
0120	13 095	Dougherty	330	96 065	539	291.1	96 321	479	100 710	–256	–4 389	–.3	–4.4	1 292	1.3
0520	13 097	Douglas	199	92 174	553	463.2	71 120	622	54 573	21 054	16 547	29.6	30.3	2 640	2.9
...	13 099	Early	511	12 354	2 277	24.2	11 854	2 227	13 158	500	–1 304	4.2	–9.9	152	1.2
...	13 101	Echols	404	3 754	2 936	9.3	2 334	3 036	2 297	1 420	37	60.8	1.6	739	19.7
7520	13 103	Effingham	479	37 535	1 176	78.4	25 687	1 435	18 327	11 848	7 360	46.1	40.2	531	1.4
...	13 105	Elbert	369	20 511	1 759	55.6	18 949	1 738	18 758	1 562	191	8.2	1.0	489	2.4
...	13 107	Emanuel	686	21 837	1 699	31.8	20 546	1 652	20 795	1 291	–249	6.3	–1.2	745	3.4
...	13 109	Evans	185	10 495	2 398	56.7	8 724	2 491	8 428	1 771	296	20.3	3.5	625	6.0
...	13 111	Fannin	386	19 798	1 801	51.3	15 992	1 923	14 748	3 806	1 244	23.8	8.4	130	.7
0520	13 113	Fayette	197	91 263	564	463.3	62 415	696	29 043	28 848	33 372	46.2	114.9	2 582	2.8
...	13 115	Floyd	513	90 565	569	176.5	81 251	561	79 800	9 314	1 451	11.5	1.8	4 983	5.5
0520	13 117	Forsyth	226	98 407	529	435.4	44 083	925	27 958	54 324	16 125	123.2	57.7	5 477	5.6
...	13 119	Franklin	263	20 285	1 775	77.1	16 650	1 873	15 185	3 635	1 465	21.8	9.6	187	.9
0520	13 121	Fulton	529	816 006	55	1 542.5	648 776	73	589 904	167 230	58 872	25.8	10.0	48 056	5.9
...	13 123	Gilmer	427	23 456	1 618	54.9	13 368	2 108	11 110	10 088	2 258	75.5	20.3	1 815	7.7
...	13 125	Glascock	144	2 556	3 022	17.8	2 357	3 035	2 382	199	–25	8.4	–1.0	12	.5
...	13 127	Glynn	422	67 568	725	160.1	62 496	695	54 981	5 072	7 515	8.1	13.7	2 019	3.0
...	13 129	Gordon	356	44 104	1 015	123.9	35 067	1 130	30 070	9 037	4 997	25.8	16.6	3 268	7.4
...	13 131	Grady	458	23 659	1 604	51.7	20 279	1 662	19 845	3 380	434	16.7	2.2	1 222	5.2
...	13 133	Greene	388	14 406	2 131	37.1	11 793	2 229	11 391	2 613	402	22.2	3.5	420	2.9

[1] Federal Information Processing Standards (FIPS) codes for metropolitan areas defined as of June 30, 1999.   [2] FIPS codes for states and counties/county equivalents.   [3] Dry land and land temporarily or partially covered by water.   [4] Based on 3,140 counties/county equivalents; excludes Yellowstone National Park in MT and South Boston independent city in VA which are no longer counties. When counties share the same rank, the next lower rank is omitted.   [5] Includes count resolution corrections through 1997 and adjustments based on Census 2000 dress rehearsal results and boundary changes reported as legally effective as of January 1, 1998.   [6] Persons of Hispanic or Latino origin may be of any race.

Sources: Land Area—U.S. Census Bureau, unpublished data file from Geography Division based on TIGER data base.   2000 Population—U.S. Census Bureau, Census of Population and Housing, Census 2000 Redistricting Data (Public Law 94-171) Summary Files (related Internet site <http://www.census.gov/dmd/www/2kresult.html>).   1990 Population—U.S. Census Bureau, "(CO-99-8) County Population Estimates and Demographic Components of Population Change: Annual Time Series, July 1, 1990 to July 1, 1999 (includes revised April 1, 1990 Population Estimates Base)"; published 9 March 2000; <http://www. census.gov/population/estimates/county/co-99-8/99C8_00.txt>.   1980 Population—U.S. Census Bureau, "1980–1990 Intercensal Population Estimates by County" on diskette (related Internet site <http://www.census.gov/population/www/estimates/countypop.html>).

Table B–1. Counties — **Area and Population**–Con.

[Includes U.S., states, and 3,142 counties/county equivalents defined as of January 1, 1992. For changes to these areas since January 1, 1992, see appendix B. Geographic Information]

Metro-politan area code[1]	State and county code[2]	County	Land area,[3] 2000 (sq. miles)	Population (April 1)										
				2000			1990[5]		1980	Net change		Percent change		Hispanic or Latino,[6] 2000	
				Number	Rank[4]	Per square mile	Number	Rank[4]		1990–2000	1980–1990	1990–2000	1980–1990	Number	Percent
		GEORGIA—Con.													
0520	13 135	Gwinnett	433	588 448	92	1 359.0	352 910	146	166 808	235 538	186 102	66.7	111.6	64 137	10.9
...	13 137	Habersham	278	35 902	1 223	129.1	27 622	1 367	25 020	8 280	2 602	30.0	10.4	2 750	7.7
...	13 139	Hall	394	139 277	392	353.5	95 434	484	75 649	43 843	19 785	45.9	26.2	27 242	19.6
...	13 141	Hancock	473	10 076	2 438	21.3	8 908	2 479	9 466	1 168	–558	13.1	–5.9	54	.5
...	13 143	Haralson	282	25 690	1 528	91.1	21 966	1 578	18 422	3 724	3 544	17.0	19.2	143	.6
1800	13 145	Harris	464	23 695	1 602	51.1	17 788	1 798	15 464	5 907	2 324	33.2	15.0	260	1.1
...	13 147	Hart	232	22 997	1 642	99.1	19 712	1 691	18 585	3 285	1 127	16.7	6.1	196	.9
...	13 149	Heard	296	11 012	2 364	37.2	8 628	2 500	6 520	2 384	2 108	27.6	32.3	116	1.1
0520	13 151	Henry	323	119 341	455	369.5	58 741	741	36 309	60 600	22 432	103.2	61.8	2 692	2.3
4680	13 153	Houston	377	110 765	489	293.8	89 208	514	77 605	21 557	11 603	24.2	15.0	3 363	3.0
...	13 155	Irwin	357	9 931	2 455	27.8	8 649	2 498	8 988	1 282	–339	14.8	–3.8	202	2.0
...	13 157	Jackson	342	41 589	1 066	121.6	30 005	1 295	25 343	11 584	4 662	38.6	18.4	1 249	3.0
...	13 159	Jasper	370	11 426	2 339	30.9	8 453	2 517	7 553	2 973	900	35.2	11.9	236	2.1
...	13 161	Jeff Davis	333	12 684	2 248	38.1	12 032	2 216	11 473	652	559	5.4	4.9	651	5.1
...	13 163	Jefferson	528	17 266	1 935	32.7	17 408	1 827	18 403	–142	–995	–.8	–5.4	259	1.5
...	13 165	Jenkins	350	8 575	2 560	24.5	8 247	2 544	8 841	328	–594	4.0	–6.7	287	3.3
...	13 167	Johnson	304	8 560	2 562	28.2	8 329	2 532	8 660	231	–331	2.8	–3.8	78	.9
4680	13 169	Jones	394	23 639	1 605	60.0	20 739	1 643	16 579	2 900	4 160	14.0	25.1	169	.7
...	13 171	Lamar	185	15 912	2 026	86.0	13 038	2 138	12 215	2 874	823	22.0	6.7	172	1.1
...	13 173	Lanier	187	7 241	2 661	38.7	5 531	2 798	5 654	1 710	–123	30.9	–2.2	126	1.7
...	13 175	Laurens	812	44 874	1 001	55.3	39 988	1 000	36 990	4 886	2 998	12.2	8.1	529	1.2
0120	13 177	Lee...................	356	24 757	1 565	69.5	16 250	1 909	11 684	8 507	4 566	52.4	39.1	300	1.2
...	13 179	Liberty	519	61 610	789	118.7	52 745	804	37 583	8 865	15 162	16.8	40.3	5 022	8.2
...	13 181	Lincoln	211	8 348	2 576	39.6	7 442	2 620	6 716	906	726	12.2	10.8	81	1.0
...	13 183	Long	401	10 304	2 415	25.7	6 202	2 732	4 524	4 102	1 678	66.1	37.1	870	8.4
...	13 185	Lowndes	504	92 115	554	182.8	75 981	591	67 972	16 134	8 009	21.2	11.8	2 447	2.7
...	13 187	Lumpkin	284	21 016	1 735	74.0	14 573	2 015	10 762	6 443	3 811	44.2	35.4	728	3.5
0600	13 189	McDuffie	260	21 231	1 723	81.7	20 119	1 669	18 546	1 112	1 573	5.5	8.5	284	1.3
...	13 191	McIntosh	433	10 847	2 377	25.1	8 634	2 499	8 046	2 213	588	25.6	7.3	99	.9
...	13 193	Macon	403	14 074	2 157	34.9	13 114	2 130	14 003	960	–889	7.3	–6.3	364	2.6
0500	13 195	Madison	284	25 730	1 526	90.6	21 050	1 626	17 747	4 680	3 303	22.2	18.6	507	2.0
...	13 197	Marion	367	7 144	2 674	19.5	5 590	2 791	5 297	1 554	293	27.8	5.5	413	5.8
...	13 199	Meriwether	503	22 534	1 669	44.8	22 411	1 559	21 229	123	1 182	.5	5.6	191	.8
...	13 201	Miller	283	6 383	2 750	22.6	6 280	2 725	7 038	103	–758	1.6	–10.8	44	.7
...	13 205	Mitchell	512	23 932	1 595	46.7	20 275	1 663	21 114	3 657	–839	18.0	–4.0	491	2.1
...	13 207	Monroe	396	21 757	1 706	54.9	17 113	1 844	14 610	4 644	2 503	27.1	17.1	281	1.3
...	13 209	Montgomery	245	8 270	2 584	33.8	7 379	2 623	7 011	891	368	12.1	5.2	271	3.3
...	13 211	Morgan	350	15 457	2 053	44.2	12 883	2 147	11 572	2 574	1 311	20.0	11.3	248	1.6
...	13 213	Murray	344	36 506	1 202	106.1	26 147	1 415	19 685	10 359	6 462	39.6	32.8	2 006	5.5
1800	13 215	Muscogee	216	186 291	295	862.5	179 280	271	170 108	7 011	9 172	3.9	5.4	8 372	4.5
0520	13 217	Newton	276	62 001	784	224.6	41 808	960	34 666	20 193	7 142	48.3	20.6	1 157	1.9
0500	13 219	Oconee	186	26 225	1 508	141.0	17 618	1 812	12 427	8 607	5 191	48.9	41.8	833	3.2
...	13 221	Oglethorpe	441	12 635	2 253	28.7	9 763	2 408	8 929	2 872	834	29.4	9.3	174	1.4
0520	13 223	Paulding	313	81 678	636	261.0	41 611	967	26 110	40 067	15 501	96.3	59.4	1 398	1.7
4680	13 225	Peach	151	23 668	1 603	156.7	21 189	1 621	19 151	2 479	2 038	11.7	10.6	998	4.2
0520	13 227	Pickens	232	22 983	1 644	99.1	14 432	2 023	11 652	8 551	2 780	59.3	23.9	467	2.0
...	13 229	Pierce	343	15 636	2 047	45.6	13 328	2 111	11 897	2 308	1 431	17.3	12.0	357	2.3
...	13 231	Pike	218	13 688	2 185	62.8	10 224	2 368	8 937	3 464	1 287	33.9	14.4	167	1.2
...	13 233	Polk	311	38 127	1 161	122.6	33 815	1 170	32 382	4 312	1 433	12.8	4.4	2 921	7.7
...	13 235	Pulaski	247	9 588	2 481	38.8	8 108	2 554	8 950	1 480	–842	18.3	–9.4	270	2.8
...	13 237	Putnam	345	18 812	1 853	54.5	14 137	2 043	10 295	4 675	3 842	33.1	37.3	407	2.2
...	13 239	Quitman	152	2 598	3 020	17.1	2 210	3 054	2 357	388	–147	17.6	–6.2	13	.5
...	13 241	Rabun	371	15 050	2 088	40.6	11 648	2 241	10 466	3 402	1 182	29.2	11.3	683	4.5
...	13 243	Randolph	429	7 791	2 626	18.2	8 023	2 562	9 599	–232	–1 576	–2.9	–16.4	92	1.2
0600	13 245	Richmond	324	199 775	277	616.6	189 719	253	181 629	10 056	8 090	5.3	4.5	5 545	2.8
0520	13 247	Rockdale	131	70 111	709	535.2	54 091	795	36 570	16 020	17 521	29.6	47.9	4 182	6.0
...	13 249	Schley	168	3 766	2 933	22.4	3 590	2 951	3 433	176	157	4.9	4.6	89	2.4
...	13 251	Screven	648	15 374	2 062	23.7	13 842	2 069	14 043	1 532	–201	11.1	–1.4	147	1.0
...	13 253	Seminole	238	9 369	2 501	39.4	9 010	2 468	9 057	359	–47	4.0	–.5	347	3.7
0520	13 255	Spalding	198	58 417	819	295.0	54 457	792	47 899	3 960	6 558	7.3	13.7	947	1.6
...	13 257	Stephens	179	25 435	1 545	142.1	23 436	1 519	21 761	1 999	1 675	8.5	7.7	250	1.0
...	13 259	Stewart	459	5 252	2 835	11.4	5 654	2 788	5 896	–402	–242	–7.1	–4.1	79	1.5
...	13 261	Sumter	485	33 200	1 308	68.5	30 232	1 285	29 360	2 968	872	9.8	3.0	891	2.7
...	13 263	Talbot	393	6 498	2 739	16.5	6 524	2 706	6 536	–26	–12	–.4	–.2	82	1.3
...	13 265	Taliaferro	195	2 077	3 061	10.7	1 915	3 073	2 032	162	–117	8.5	–5.8	19	.9
...	13 267	Tattnall	484	22 305	1 679	46.1	17 722	1 802	18 134	4 583	–412	25.9	–2.3	1 883	8.4

[1] Federal Information Processing Standards (FIPS) codes for metropolitan areas defined as of June 30, 1999. [2] FIPS codes for states and counties/county equivalents. [3] Dry land and land temporarily or partially covered by water. [4] Based on 3,140 counties/county equivalents; excludes Yellowstone National Park in MT and South Boston independent city in VA which are no longer counties. When counties share the same rank, the next lower rank is omitted. [5] Includes count resolution corrections through 1997 and adjustments based on Census 2000 dress rehearsal results and boundary changes reported as legally effective as of January 1, 1998. [6] Persons of Hispanic or Latino origin may be of any race.

Sources: Land Area—U.S. Census Bureau, unpublished data file from Geography Division based on TIGER data base. 2000 Population—U.S. Census Bureau, Census of Population and Housing, Census 2000 Redistricting Data (Public Law 94-171) Summary Files (related Internet site <http://www.census.gov/dmd/www/2kresult.html>). 1990 Population—U.S. Census Bureau, "(CO-99-8) County Population Estimates and Demographic Components of Population Change: Annual Time Series, July 1, 1990 to July 1, 1999 (includes revised April 1, 1990 Population Estimates Base)"; published 9 March 2000; <http://www. census.gov/population/estimates/county/co-99-8/99C8_00.txt>. 1980 Population—U.S. Census Bureau, "1980–1990 Intercensal Population Estimates by County" on diskette (related Internet site <http://www.census.gov/population/www/estimates/countypop.html>).

[Includes U.S., states, and 3,142 counties/county equivalents defined as of January 1, 1992. For changes to these areas since January 1, 1992, see appendix B. Geographic Information]

Metropolitan area code[1]	State and county code[2]	County	Land area,[3] 2000 (sq. miles)	Population (April 1)										
				2000			1990[5]		1980	Net change		Percent change		Hispanic or Latino,[6] 2000	
				Number	Rank[4]	Per square mile	Number	Rank[4]		1990–2000	1980–1990	1990–2000	1980–1990	Number	Percent
		GEORGIA—Con.													
...	13 269	Taylor	377	8 815	2 544	23.4	7 642	2 606	7 902	1 173	–260	15.3	–3.3	163	1.8
...	13 271	Telfair	441	11 794	2 306	26.7	11 000	2 293	11 445	794	–445	7.2	–3.9	215	1.8
...	13 273	Terrell	335	10 970	2 369	32.7	10 653	2 322	12 017	317	–1 364	3.0	–11.4	136	1.2
...	13 275	Thomas	548	42 737	1 043	78.0	38 943	1 024	38 098	3 794	845	9.7	2.2	734	1.7
...	13 277	Tift	265	38 407	1 152	144.9	34 998	1 133	32 862	3 409	2 136	9.7	6.5	2 944	7.7
...	13 279	Toombs	367	26 067	1 514	71.0	24 072	1 490	22 592	1 995	1 480	8.3	6.6	2 310	8.9
...	13 281	Towns	167	9 319	2 504	55.8	6 754	2 680	5 638	2 565	1 116	38.0	19.8	67	.7
...	13 283	Treutlen	201	6 854	2 704	34.1	5 994	2 758	6 087	860	–93	14.3	–1.5	79	1.2
...	13 285	Troup	414	58 779	816	142.0	55 532	779	50 003	3 247	5 529	5.8	11.1	1 004	1.7
...	13 287	Turner	286	9 504	2 489	33.2	8 703	2 492	9 510	801	–807	9.2	–8.5	244	2.6
4680	13 289	Twiggs	360	10 590	2 390	29.4	9 806	2 403	9 354	784	452	8.0	4.8	112	1.1
...	13 291	Union	323	17 289	1 933	53.5	11 993	2 220	9 390	5 296	2 603	44.2	27.7	153	.9
...	13 293	Upson	325	27 597	1 464	84.9	26 300	1 411	25 998	1 297	302	4.9	1.2	327	1.2
1560	13 295	Walker	447	61 053	797	136.6	58 310	743	56 470	2 743	1 840	4.7	3.3	565	.9
0520	13 297	Walton	329	60 687	799	184.5	38 586	1 038	31 211	22 101	7 375	57.3	23.6	1 163	1.9
...	13 299	Ware	902	35 483	1 233	39.3	35 471	1 112	37 180	12	–1 709	Z	–4.6	688	1.9
...	13 301	Warren	286	6 336	2 753	22.2	6 078	2 748	6 583	258	–505	4.2	–7.7	51	.8
...	13 303	Washington	680	21 176	1 726	31.1	19 112	1 726	18 842	2 064	270	10.8	1.4	134	.6
...	13 305	Wayne	645	26 565	1 496	41.2	22 356	1 561	20 750	4 209	1 606	18.8	7.7	1 013	3.8
...	13 307	Webster	210	2 390	3 032	11.4	2 263	3 046	2 341	127	–78	5.6	–3.3	66	2.8
...	13 309	Wheeler	298	6 179	2 764	20.7	4 903	2 844	5 155	1 276	–252	26.0	–4.9	219	3.5
...	13 311	White	242	19 944	1 795	82.4	13 006	2 141	10 120	6 938	2 886	53.3	28.5	311	1.6
...	13 313	Whitfield	290	83 525	623	288.0	72 462	617	65 775	11 063	6 687	15.3	10.2	18 419	22.1
...	13 315	Wilcox	380	8 577	2 559	22.6	7 008	2 658	7 682	1 569	–674	22.4	–8.8	139	1.6
...	13 317	Wilkes	471	10 687	2 386	22.7	10 597	2 328	10 951	90	–354	.8	–3.2	212	2.0
...	13 319	Wilkinson	447	10 220	2 425	22.9	10 228	2 367	10 368	–8	–140	–.1	–1.4	101	1.0
...	13 321	Worth	570	21 967	1 695	38.5	19 744	1 687	18 064	2 223	1 680	11.3	9.3	240	1.1
	15 000	HAWAII	6 423	1 211 537	X	188.6	1 108 229	X	964 691	103 308	143 538	9.3	14.9	87 699	7.2
...	15 001	Hawaii	4 028	148 677	363	36.9	120 317	383	92 053	28 360	28 264	23.6	30.7	14 111	9.5
3320	15 003	Honolulu	600	876 156	48	1 460.3	836 231	40	762 565	39 925	73 666	4.8	9.7	58 729	6.7
...	15 005	Kalawao	13	147	3 139	11.3	130	3 139	144	17	–14	13.1	–9.7	6	4.1
...	15 007	Kauai	622	58 463	818	94.0	51 177	823	39 082	7 286	12 095	14.2	30.9	4 803	8.2
...	15 009	Maui	1 159	128 094	422	110.5	100 374	457	70 847	27 720	29 527	27.6	41.7	10 050	7.8
	16 000	IDAHO	82 747	1 293 953	X	15.6	1 006 734	X	944 127	287 219	62 607	28.5	6.6	101 690	7.9
1080	16 001	Ada	1 055	300 904	188	285.2	205 775	242	173 125	95 129	32 650	46.2	18.9	13 467	4.5
...	16 003	Adams	1 365	3 476	2 956	2.5	3 254	2 979	3 347	222	–93	6.8	–2.8	54	1.6
6340	16 005	Bannock	1 113	75 565	663	67.9	66 026	665	65 421	9 539	605	14.4	.9	3 540	4.7
...	16 007	Bear Lake	971	6 411	2 749	6.6	6 084	2 747	6 931	327	–847	5.4	–12.2	154	2.4
...	16 009	Benewah	776	9 171	2 516	11.8	7 937	2 579	8 292	1 234	–355	15.5	–4.3	142	1.5
...	16 011	Bingham	2 095	41 735	1 061	19.9	37 583	1 056	36 489	4 152	1 094	11.0	3.0	5 550	13.3
...	16 013	Blaine	2 645	18 991	1 846	7.2	13 552	2 097	9 841	5 439	3 711	40.1	37.7	2 030	10.7
...	16 015	Boise	1 902	6 670	2 720	3.5	3 509	2 956	2 999	3 161	510	90.1	17.0	228	3.4
...	16 017	Bonner	1 738	36 835	1 193	21.2	26 622	1 402	24 163	10 213	2 459	38.4	10.2	604	1.6
...	16 019	Bonneville	1 868	82 522	618	44.2	72 207	618	65 980	10 315	6 227	14.3	9.4	5 703	6.9
...	16 021	Boundary	1 269	9 871	2 459	7.8	8 332	2 531	7 289	1 539	1 043	18.5	14.3	335	3.4
...	16 023	Butte	2 233	2 899	2 999	1.3	2 918	3 004	3 342	–19	–424	–.7	–12.7	120	4.1
...	16 025	Camas	1 075	991	3 111	.9	727	3 128	818	264	–91	36.3	–11.1	55	5.5
1080	16 027	Canyon	590	131 441	406	222.8	90 076	510	83 756	41 365	6 320	45.9	7.5	24 455	18.6
...	16 029	Caribou	1 766	7 304	2 655	4.1	6 963	2 663	8 695	341	–1 732	4.9	–19.9	289	4.0
...	16 031	Cassia	2 566	21 416	1 717	8.3	19 532	1 698	19 427	1 884	105	9.6	.5	4 013	18.7
...	16 033	Clark	1 765	1 022	3 110	.6	762	3 126	798	260	–36	34.1	–4.5	350	34.2
...	16 035	Clearwater	2 461	8 930	2 532	3.6	8 505	2 510	10 390	425	–1 885	5.0	–18.1	165	1.8
...	16 037	Custer	4 925	4 342	2 893	.9	4 133	2 903	3 385	209	748	5.1	22.1	183	4.2
...	16 039	Elmore	3 078	29 130	1 423	9.5	21 205	1 620	21 565	7 925	–360	37.4	–1.7	3 492	12.0
...	16 041	Franklin	665	11 329	2 348	17.0	9 232	2 452	8 895	2 097	337	22.7	3.8	591	5.2
...	16 043	Fremont	1 867	11 819	2 303	6.3	10 937	2 300	10 813	882	124	8.1	1.1	1 255	10.6
...	16 045	Gem	563	15 181	2 077	27.0	11 844	2 228	11 972	3 337	–128	28.2	–1.1	1 050	6.9
...	16 047	Gooding	731	14 155	2 149	19.4	11 633	2 244	11 874	2 522	–241	21.7	–2.0	2 414	17.1
...	16 049	Idaho	8 485	15 511	2 052	1.8	13 768	2 074	14 769	1 743	–1 001	12.7	–6.8	243	1.6
...	16 051	Jefferson	1 095	19 155	1 839	17.5	16 543	1 887	15 304	2 612	1 239	15.8	8.1	1 907	10.0
...	16 053	Jerome	600	18 342	1 878	30.6	15 138	1 978	14 840	3 204	298	21.2	2.0	3 150	17.2

[1] Federal Information Processing Standards (FIPS) codes for metropolitan areas defined as of June 30, 1999.   [2] FIPS codes for states and counties/county equivalents.   [3] Dry land and land temporarily or partially covered by water.   [4] Based on 3,140 counties/county equivalents; excludes Yellowstone National Park in MT and South Boston independent city in VA which are no longer counties. When counties share the same rank, the next lower rank is omitted.   [5] Includes count resolution corrections through 1997 and adjustments based on Census 2000 dress rehearsal results and boundary changes reported as legally effective as of January 1, 1998.   [6] Persons of Hispanic or Latino origin may be of any race.

Sources: Land Area—U.S. Census Bureau, unpublished data file from Geography Division based on TIGER data base.   2000 Population—U.S. Census Bureau, Census of Population and Housing, Census 2000 Redistricting Data (Public Law 94-171) Summary Files (related Internet site <http://www.census.gov/dmd/www/2kresult.html>).   1990 Population—U.S. Census Bureau, "(CO-99-8) County Population Estimates and Demographic Components of Population Change: Annual Time Series, July 1, 1990 to July 1, 1999 (includes revised April 1, 1990 Population Estimates Base)"; published 9 March 2000; <http://www. census.gov/population/estimates/county/co-99-8/99C8_00.txt>.   1980 Population—U.S. Census Bureau, "1980–1990 Intercensal Population Estimates by County" on diskette (related Internet site <http://www.census.gov/population/www/estimates/countypop.html>).

Table B–1. Counties — **Area and Population**–Con.

[Includes U.S., states, and 3,142 counties/county equivalents defined as of January 1, 1992. For changes to these areas since January 1, 1992, see appendix B. Geographic Information]

Metro-politan area code[1]	State and county code[2]	County	Land area,[3] 2000 (sq. miles)	Population (April 1) 2000 Number	Rank[4]	Per square mile	1990[5] Number	Rank[4]	1980	Net change 1990–2000	1980–1990	Percent change 1990–2000	1980–1990	Hispanic or Latino,[6] 2000 Number	Percent
		IDAHO—Con.													
...	16 055	Kootenai	1 245	108 685	496	87.3	69 795	635	59 770	38 890	10 025	55.7	16.8	2 528	2.3
...	16 057	Latah	1 077	34 935	1 251	32.4	30 617	1 260	28 749	4 318	1 868	14.1	6.5	740	2.1
...	16 059	Lemhi	4 564	7 806	2 625	1.7	6 899	2 671	7 460	907	−561	13.1	−7.5	170	2.2
...	16 061	Lewis	479	3 747	2 937	7.8	3 516	2 955	4 118	231	−602	6.6	−14.6	71	1.9
...	16 063	Lincoln	1 206	4 044	2 918	3.4	3 308	2 975	3 436	736	−128	22.2	−3.7	542	13.4
...	16 065	Madison	472	27 467	1 469	58.2	23 674	1 505	19 480	3 793	4 194	16.0	21.5	1 078	3.9
...	16 067	Minidoka	760	20 174	1 782	26.5	19 361	1 712	19 718	813	−357	4.2	−1.8	5 137	25.5
...	16 069	Nez Perce	849	37 410	1 180	44.1	33 754	1 172	33 220	3 656	534	10.8	1.6	721	1.9
...	16 071	Oneida	1 200	4 125	2 907	3.4	3 492	2 957	3 258	633	234	18.1	7.2	95	2.3
...	16 073	Owyhee	7 678	10 644	2 388	1.4	8 392	2 521	8 272	2 252	120	26.8	1.5	2 459	23.1
...	16 075	Payette	408	20 578	1 756	50.4	16 434	1 897	15 825	4 144	609	25.2	3.8	2 453	11.9
...	16 077	Power	1 406	7 538	2 640	5.4	7 086	2 648	6 844	452	242	6.4	3.5	1 638	21.7
...	16 079	Shoshone	2 634	13 771	2 175	5.2	13 931	2 063	19 226	−160	−5 295	−1.1	−27.5	266	1.9
...	16 081	Teton	450	5 999	2 780	13.3	3 439	2 960	2 897	2 560	542	74.4	18.7	705	11.8
...	16 083	Twin Falls	1 925	64 284	759	33.4	53 580	801	52 927	10 704	653	20.0	1.2	6 026	9.4
...	16 085	Valley	3 678	7 651	2 633	2.1	6 109	2 741	5 604	1 542	505	25.2	9.0	150	2.0
...	16 087	Washington	1 456	9 977	2 448	6.9	8 550	2 509	8 803	1 427	−253	16.7	−2.9	1 372	13.8
	17 000	**ILLINOIS**	55 584	12 419 293	X	223.4	11 430 602	X	11 427 409	988 691	3 193	8.6	Z	1 530 262	12.3
...	17 001	Adams	857	68 277	721	79.7	66 090	662	71 622	2 187	−5 532	3.3	−7.7	567	.8
...	17 003	Alexander	236	9 590	2 480	40.6	10 626	2 324	12 264	−1 036	−1 638	−9.7	−13.4	138	1.4
...	17 005	Bond	380	17 633	1 921	46.4	14 991	1 988	16 224	2 642	−1 233	17.6	−7.6	253	1.4
6880	17 007	Boone	281	41 786	1 059	148.7	30 806	1 249	28 630	10 980	2 176	35.6	7.6	5 219	12.5
...	17 009	Brown	306	6 950	2 691	22.7	5 836	2 776	5 411	1 114	425	19.1	7.9	273	3.9
...	17 011	Bureau	869	35 503	1 232	40.9	35 688	1 107	39 114	−185	−3 426	−.5	−8.8	1 732	4.9
...	17 013	Calhoun	254	5 084	2 846	20.0	5 322	2 816	5 867	−238	−545	−4.5	−9.3	32	.6
...	17 015	Carroll	444	16 674	1 976	37.6	16 805	1 859	18 779	−131	−1 974	−.8	−10.5	340	2.0
...	17 017	Cass	376	13 695	2 184	36.4	13 437	2 105	15 084	258	−1 647	1.9	−10.9	1 162	8.5
1400	17 019	Champaign	997	179 669	308	180.2	173 025	279	168 392	6 644	4 633	3.8	2.8	5 203	2.9
...	17 021	Christian	709	35 372	1 238	49.9	34 418	1 153	36 446	954	−2 028	2.8	−5.6	345	1.0
...	17 023	Clark	502	17 008	1 952	33.9	15 921	1 929	16 913	1 087	−992	6.8	−5.9	54	.3
...	17 025	Clay	469	14 560	2 116	31.0	14 460	2 019	15 283	100	−823	.7	−5.4	88	.6
7040	17 027	Clinton	474	35 535	1 230	75.0	33 944	1 165	32 617	1 591	1 327	4.7	4.1	570	1.6
...	17 029	Coles	508	53 196	881	104.7	51 644	819	52 260	1 552	−616	3.0	−1.2	737	1.4
1602	17 031	Cook	946	5 376 741	2	5 683.7	5 105 044	2	5 253 628	271 697	−148 584	5.3	−2.8	1 071 740	19.9
...	17 033	Crawford	444	20 452	1 763	46.1	19 464	1 704	20 818	988	−1 354	5.1	−6.5	351	1.7
...	17 035	Cumberland	346	11 253	2 353	32.5	10 670	2 320	11 062	583	−392	5.5	−3.5	68	.6
1602	17 037	DeKalb	634	88 969	585	140.3	77 932	582	74 628	11 037	3 304	14.2	4.4	5 830	6.6
...	17 039	De Witt	398	16 798	1 970	42.2	16 516	1 891	18 108	282	−1 592	1.7	−8.8	213	1.3
...	17 041	Douglas	417	19 922	1 797	47.8	19 464	1 704	19 774	458	−310	2.4	−1.6	690	3.5
1602	17 043	DuPage	334	904 161	42	2 707.1	781 689	49	658 858	122 472	122 831	15.7	18.6	81 366	9.0
...	17 045	Edgar	624	19 704	1 811	31.6	19 595	1 693	21 725	109	−2 130	.6	−9.8	154	.8
...	17 047	Edwards	222	6 971	2 688	31.4	7 440	2 621	7 961	−469	−521	−6.3	−6.5	32	.5
...	17 049	Effingham	479	34 264	1 272	71.5	31 704	1 222	30 944	2 560	760	8.1	2.5	252	.7
...	17 051	Fayette	716	21 802	1 702	30.4	20 893	1 634	22 167	909	−1 274	4.4	−5.7	174	.8
...	17 053	Ford	486	14 241	2 147	29.3	14 275	2 032	15 265	−34	−990	−.2	−6.5	176	1.2
...	17 055	Franklin	412	39 018	1 138	94.7	40 319	992	43 201	−1 301	−2 882	−3.2	−6.7	249	.6
...	17 057	Fulton	866	38 250	1 159	44.2	38 080	1 050	43 687	170	−5 607	.4	−12.8	478	1.2
...	17 059	Gallatin	324	6 445	2 743	19.9	6 909	2 670	7 590	−464	−681	−6.7	−9.0	56	.9
1602	17 061	Greene	543	14 761	2 105	27.2	15 317	1 971	16 661	−556	−1 344	−3.6	−8.1	77	.5
...	17 063	Grundy	420	37 535	1 176	89.4	32 337	1 205	30 582	5 198	1 755	16.1	5.7	1 552	4.1
...	17 065	Hamilton	435	8 621	2 556	19.8	8 499	2 511	9 172	122	−673	1.4	−7.3	55	.6
...	17 067	Hancock	795	20 121	1 785	25.3	21 373	1 615	23 877	−1 252	−2 504	−5.9	−10.5	105	.5
...	17 069	Hardin	178	4 800	2 859	27.0	5 189	2 826	5 383	−389	−194	−7.5	−3.6	51	1.1
...	17 071	Henderson	379	8 213	2 590	21.7	8 096	2 555	9 114	117	−1 018	1.4	−11.2	72	.9
1960	17 073	Henry	823	51 020	910	62.0	51 159	824	57 968	−139	−6 809	−.3	−11.7	1 467	2.9
...	17 075	Iroquois	1 116	31 334	1 365	28.1	30 787	1 252	32 976	547	−2 189	1.8	−6.6	1 217	3.9
...	17 077	Jackson	588	59 612	806	101.4	61 067	713	61 649	−1 455	−582	−2.4	−.9	1 443	2.4
...	17 079	Jasper	494	10 117	2 435	20.5	10 609	2 327	11 318	−492	−709	−4.6	−6.3	48	.5
...	17 081	Jefferson	571	40 045	1 113	70.1	37 020	1 072	36 558	3 025	462	8.2	1.3	531	1.3
7040	17 083	Jersey	369	21 668	1 709	58.7	20 539	1 653	20 538	1 129	1	5.5	Z	162	.7
...	17 085	Jo Daviess	601	22 289	1 681	37.1	21 821	1 589	23 520	468	−1 699	2.1	−7.2	342	1.5
...	17 087	Johnson	345	12 878	2 242	37.3	11 347	2 268	9 624	1 531	1 723	13.5	17.9	368	2.9
1602	17 089	Kane	520	404 119	146	777.2	317 471	159	278 405	86 648	39 066	27.3	14.0	95 924	23.7

[1] Federal Information Processing Standards (FIPS) codes for metropolitan areas defined as of June 30, 1999. [2] FIPS codes for states and counties/county equivalents. [3] Dry land and land temporarily or partially covered by water. [4] Based on 3,140 counties/county equivalents; excludes Yellowstone National Park in MT and South Boston independent city in VA which are no longer counties. When counties share the same rank, the next lower rank is omitted. [5] Includes count resolution corrections through 1997 and adjustments based on Census 2000 dress rehearsal results and boundary changes reported as legally effective as of January 1, 1998. [6] Persons of Hispanic or Latino origin may be of any race.

Sources: Land Area—U.S. Census Bureau, unpublished data file from Geography Division based on TIGER data base. 2000 Population—U.S. Census Bureau, Census of Population and Housing, Census 2000 Redistricting Data (Public Law 94-171) Summary Files (related Internet site <http://www.census.gov/dmd/www/2kresult.html>). 1990 Population—U.S. Census Bureau, "(CO-99-8) County Population Estimates and Demographic Components of Population Change: Annual Time Series, July 1, 1990 to July 1, 1999 (includes revised April 1, 1990 Population Estimates Base)"; published 9 March 2000; <http://www.census.gov/population/estimates/county/co-99-8/99C8_00.txt>. 1980 Population—U.S. Census Bureau, "1980–1990 Intercensal Population Estimates by County" on diskette (related Internet site <http://www.census.gov/population/www/estimates/countypop.html>).

[Includes U.S., states, and 3,142 counties/county equivalents defined as of January 1, 1992. For changes to these areas since January 1, 1992, see appendix B. Geographic Information]

Metro-politan area code[1]	State and county code[2]	County	Land area,[3] 2000 (sq. miles)	Population (April 1) 2000 Number	2000 Rank[4]	2000 Per square mile	1990[5] Number	1990[5] Rank[4]	1980	Net change 1990–2000	Net change 1980–1990	Percent change 1990–2000	Percent change 1980–1990	Hispanic or Latino,[6] 2000 Number	Hispanic or Latino,[6] 2000 Percent
		ILLINOIS—Con.													
1602	17 091	Kankakee	677	103 833	511	153.4	96 255	480	102 926	7 578	−6 671	7.9	−6.5	4 959	4.8
1602	17 093	Kendall	321	54 544	862	169.9	39 413	1 014	37 202	15 131	2 211	38.4	5.9	4 086	7.5
...	17 095	Knox	716	55 836	845	78.0	56 393	770	61 607	−557	−5 214	−1.0	−8.5	1 896	3.4
1602	17 097	Lake	448	644 356	84	1 438.3	516 418	90	440 388	127 938	76 030	24.8	17.3	92 716	14.4
...	17 099	La Salle	1 135	111 509	484	98.2	106 913	431	112 033	4 596	−5 120	4.3	−4.6	5 791	5.2
...	17 101	Lawrence	372	15 452	2 054	41.5	15 972	1 925	17 807	−520	−1 835	−3.3	−10.3	137	.9
...	17 103	Lee	725	36 062	1 214	49.7	34 392	1 154	36 328	1 670	−1 936	4.9	−5.3	1 147	3.2
...	17 105	Livingston	1 044	39 678	1 120	38.0	39 301	1 017	41 381	377	−2 080	1.0	−5.0	1 056	2.7
...	17 107	Logan	618	31 183	1 372	50.5	30 798	1 250	31 802	385	−1 004	1.3	−3.2	503	1.6
...	17 109	McDonough	589	32 913	1 322	55.9	35 244	1 124	37 467	−2 331	−2 223	−6.6	−5.9	488	1.5
1602	17 111	McHenry	604	260 077	213	430.6	183 241	262	147 897	76 836	35 344	41.9	23.9	19 602	7.5
1040	17 113	McLean	1 184	150 433	357	127.1	129 180	358	119 149	21 253	10 031	16.5	8.4	3 833	2.5
2040	17 115	Macon	581	114 706	472	197.4	117 206	394	131 375	−2 500	−14 169	−2.1	−10.8	1 120	1.0
...	17 117	Macoupin	864	49 019	931	56.7	47 679	880	49 384	1 340	−1 705	2.8	−3.5	305	.6
7040	17 119	Madison	725	258 941	216	357.2	249 238	200	247 661	9 703	1 577	3.9	.6	3 925	1.5
...	17 121	Marion	572	41 691	1 063	72.9	41 561	969	43 523	130	−1 962	.3	−4.5	378	.9
...	17 123	Marshall	386	13 180	2 214	34.1	12 846	2 151	14 479	334	−1 633	2.6	−11.3	138	1.0
...	17 125	Mason	539	16 038	2 019	29.8	16 269	1 907	19 492	−231	−3 223	−1.4	−16.5	80	.5
...	17 127	Massac	239	15 161	2 079	63.4	14 752	2 003	14 990	409	−238	2.8	−1.6	123	.8
7880	17 129	Menard	314	12 486	2 266	39.8	11 164	2 280	11 700	1 322	−536	11.8	−4.6	94	.8
...	17 131	Mercer	561	16 957	1 955	30.2	17 290	1 834	19 286	−333	−1 996	−1.9	−10.3	216	1.3
7040	17 133	Monroe	388	27 619	1 461	71.2	22 422	1 557	20 117	5 197	2 305	23.2	11.5	203	.7
...	17 135	Montgomery	704	30 652	1 383	43.5	30 728	1 256	31 686	−76	−958	−.2	−3.0	326	1.1
...	17 137	Morgan	569	36 616	1 198	64.4	36 397	1 093	37 502	219	−1 105	.6	−2.9	496	1.4
...	17 139	Moultrie	336	14 287	2 141	42.5	13 930	2 064	14 546	357	−616	2.6	−4.2	68	.5
6880	17 141	Ogle	759	51 032	908	67.2	45 957	904	46 338	5 075	−381	11.0	−.8	3 066	6.0
6120	17 143	Peoria	620	183 433	298	295.9	182 827	263	200 466	606	−17 639	.3	−8.8	3 827	2.1
...	17 145	Perry	441	23 094	1 639	52.4	21 412	1 610	21 714	1 682	−302	7.9	−1.4	406	1.8
...	17 147	Piatt	440	16 365	1 999	37.2	15 548	1 950	16 581	817	−1 033	5.3	−6.2	101	.6
...	17 149	Pike	830	17 384	1 929	20.9	17 577	1 816	18 896	−193	−1 319	−1.1	−7.0	87	.5
...	17 151	Pope	371	4 413	2 886	11.9	4 373	2 886	4 404	40	−31	.9	−.7	40	.9
...	17 153	Pulaski	201	7 348	2 652	36.6	7 523	2 614	8 840	−175	−1 317	−2.3	−14.9	107	1.5
...	17 155	Putnam	160	6 086	2 773	38.0	5 730	2 784	6 085	356	−355	6.2	−5.8	171	2.8
...	17 157	Randolph	578	33 893	1 284	58.6	34 583	1 149	35 652	−690	−1 069	−2.0	−3.0	521	1.5
...	17 159	Richland	360	16 149	2 012	44.9	16 545	1 886	17 587	−396	−1 042	−2.4	−5.9	124	.8
1960	17 161	Rock Island	427	149 374	361	349.8	148 723	318	166 759	651	−18 036	.4	−10.8	12 791	8.6
7040	17 163	St. Clair	664	256 082	219	385.7	262 852	190	267 531	−6 770	−4 679	−2.6	−1.7	5 604	2.2
...	17 165	Saline	383	26 733	1 493	69.8	26 551	1 406	28 448	182	−1 897	.7	−6.7	258	1.0
7880	17 167	Sangamon	868	188 951	292	217.7	178 386	273	176 070	10 565	2 316	5.9	1.3	2 000	1.1
...	17 169	Schuyler	437	7 189	2 667	16.5	7 498	2 616	8 365	−309	−867	−4.1	−10.4	39	.5
...	17 171	Scott	251	5 537	2 814	22.1	5 644	2 789	6 142	−107	−498	−1.9	−8.1	10	.2
...	17 173	Shelby	759	22 893	1 649	30.2	22 261	1 565	23 923	632	−1 662	2.8	−6.9	110	.5
...	17 175	Stark	288	6 332	2 754	22.0	6 534	2 704	7 389	−202	−855	−3.1	−11.6	54	.9
...	17 177	Stephenson	564	48 979	934	86.8	48 052	870	49 536	927	−1 484	1.9	−3.0	747	1.5
6120	17 179	Tazewell	649	128 485	420	198.0	123 692	372	132 078	4 793	−8 386	3.9	−6.3	1 331	1.0
...	17 181	Union	416	18 293	1 881	44.0	17 619	1 811	17 765	674	−146	3.8	−.8	481	2.6
...	17 183	Vermilion	899	83 919	620	93.3	88 257	516	95 222	−4 338	−6 965	−4.9	−7.3	2 504	3.0
...	17 185	Wabash	223	12 937	2 237	58.0	13 111	2 131	13 713	−174	−602	−1.3	−4.4	95	.7
...	17 187	Warren	543	18 735	1 858	34.5	19 181	1 721	21 943	−446	−2 762	−2.3	−12.6	507	2.7
...	17 189	Washington	563	15 148	2 082	26.9	14 965	1 990	15 472	183	−507	1.2	−3.3	108	.7
...	17 191	Wayne	714	17 151	1 946	24.0	17 241	1 839	18 059	−90	−818	−.5	−4.5	103	.6
...	17 193	White	495	15 371	2 063	31.1	16 522	1 890	17 864	−1 151	−1 342	−7.0	−7.5	103	.7
...	17 195	Whiteside	685	60 653	800	88.5	60 186	721	65 970	467	−5 784	.8	−8.8	5 347	8.8
1602	17 197	Will	837	502 266	111	600.1	357 313	143	324 460	144 953	32 853	40.6	10.1	43 768	8.7
1602	17 199	Williamson	423	61 296	794	144.9	57 733	753	56 538	3 563	1 195	6.2	2.1	763	1.2
6880	17 201	Winnebago	514	278 418	203	541.7	252 913	198	250 884	25 505	2 029	10.1	.8	19 206	6.9
6120	17 203	Woodford	528	35 469	1 234	67.2	32 653	1 198	33 320	2 816	−667	8.6	−2.0	241	.7
	18 000	INDIANA	35 867	6 080 485	X	169.5	5 544 156	X	5 490 210	536 329	53 946	9.7	1.0	214 536	3.5
2760	18 001	Adams	339	33 625	1 295	99.2	31 095	1 243	29 619	2 530	1 476	8.1	5.0	1 118	3.3
2760	18 003	Allen	657	331 849	176	505.1	300 836	164	294 335	31 013	6 501	10.3	2.2	13 877	4.2
...	18 005	Bartholomew	407	71 435	692	175.5	63 657	687	65 088	7 778	−1 431	12.2	−2.2	1 598	2.2
...	18 007	Benton	406	9 421	2 493	23.2	9 441	2 439	10 218	−20	−777	−.2	−7.6	245	2.6
...	18 009	Blackford	165	14 048	2 160	85.1	14 067	2 051	15 570	−19	−1 503	−.1	−9.7	83	.6
3480	18 011	Boone	423	46 107	982	109.0	38 147	1 049	36 446	7 960	1 701	20.9	4.7	534	1.2
...	18 013	Brown	312	14 957	2 094	47.9	14 080	2 050	12 377	877	1 703	6.2	13.8	131	.9
...	18 015	Carroll	372	20 165	1 783	54.2	18 809	1 747	19 722	1 356	−913	7.2	−4.6	591	2.9
...	18 017	Cass	413	40 930	1 082	99.1	38 413	1 042	40 936	2 517	−2 523	6.6	−6.2	2 905	7.1

[1] Federal Information Processing Standards (FIPS) codes for metropolitan areas defined as of June 30, 1999. [2] FIPS codes for states and counties/county equivalents. [3] Dry land and land temporarily or partially covered by water. [4] Based on 3,140 counties/county equivalents; excludes Yellowstone National Park in MT and South Boston independent city in VA which are no longer counties. When counties share the same rank, the next lower rank is omitted. [5] Includes count resolution corrections through 1997 and adjustments based on Census 2000 dress rehearsal results and boundary changes reported as legally effective as of January 1, 1998. [6] Persons of Hispanic or Latino origin may be of any race.

Sources: Land Area—U.S. Census Bureau, unpublished data file from Geography Division based on TIGER data base. 2000 Population—U.S. Census Bureau, Census of Population and Housing, Census 2000 Redistricting Data (Public Law 94-171) Summary Files (related Internet site <http://www.census.gov/dmd/www/2kresult.html>). 1990 Population—U.S. Census Bureau, "(CO-99-8) County Population Estimates and Demographic Components of Population Change: Annual Time Series, July 1, 1990 to July 1, 1999 (includes revised April 1, 1990 Population Estimates Base)"; published 9 March 2000; <http://www. census.gov/population/estimates/county/co-99-8/99C8_00.txt>. 1980 Population—U.S. Census Bureau, "1980–1990 Intercensal Population Estimates by County" on diskette (related Internet site <http://www.census.gov/population/www/estimates/countypop.html>).

[Includes U.S., states, and 3,142 counties/county equivalents defined as of January 1, 1992. For changes to these areas since January 1, 1992, see appendix B. Geographic Information]

Metro-politan area code[1]	State and county code[2]	County	Land area,[3] 2000 (sq. miles)	Population (April 1) 2000 Number	2000 Rank[4]	2000 Per square mile	1990[5] Number	1990[5] Rank[4]	1980	Net change 1990–2000	Net change 1980–1990	Percent change 1990–2000	Percent change 1980–1990	Hispanic or Latino,[6] 2000 Number	Hispanic or Latino,[6] 2000 Percent
		INDIANA—Con.													
4520	18 019	Clark	375	96 472	536	257.3	87 774	519	88 838	8 698	−1 064	9.9	−1.2	1 799	1.9
8320	18 021	Clay	358	26 556	1 499	74.2	24 705	1 473	24 862	1 851	−157	7.5	−.6	155	.6
3920	18 023	Clinton	405	33 866	1 285	83.6	30 974	1 246	31 545	2 892	−571	9.3	−1.8	2 478	7.3
...	18 025	Crawford	306	10 743	2 380	35.1	9 914	2 393	9 820	829	94	8.4	1.0	100	.9
...	18 027	Daviess	431	29 820	1 402	69.2	27 533	1 373	27 836	2 287	−303	8.3	−1.1	620	2.1
1642	18 029	Dearborn	305	46 109	981	151.2	38 835	1 027	34 291	7 274	4 544	18.7	13.3	266	.6
...	18 031	Decatur	373	24 555	1 573	65.8	23 645	1 508	23 841	910	−196	3.8	−.8	132	.5
2760	18 033	De Kalb	363	40 285	1 108	111.0	35 324	1 120	33 606	4 961	1 718	14.0	5.1	676	1.7
5280	18 035	Delaware	393	118 769	456	302.2	119 659	386	128 587	−890	−8 928	−.7	−6.9	1 304	1.1
...	18 037	Dubois	430	39 674	1 121	92.3	36 616	1 086	34 238	3 058	2 378	8.4	6.9	1 103	2.8
2330	18 039	Elkhart	464	182 791	299	393.9	156 198	300	137 330	26 593	18 868	17.0	13.7	16 300	8.9
...	18 041	Fayette	215	25 588	1 535	119.0	26 015	1 420	28 272	−427	−2 257	−1.6	−8.0	132	.5
4520	18 043	Floyd	148	70 823	701	478.5	64 404	678	61 205	6 419	3 199	10.0	5.2	772	1.1
...	18 045	Fountain	396	17 954	1 901	45.3	17 808	1 797	19 033	146	−1 225	.8	−6.4	190	1.1
...	18 047	Franklin	386	22 151	1 685	57.4	19 580	1 694	19 612	2 571	−32	13.1	−.2	104	.5
...	18 049	Fulton	369	20 511	1 759	55.6	18 840	1 744	19 335	1 671	−495	8.9	−2.6	473	2.3
...	18 051	Gibson	489	32 500	1 332	66.5	31 913	1 215	33 156	587	−1 243	1.8	−3.7	229	.7
...	18 053	Grant	414	73 403	681	177.3	74 169	607	80 934	−766	−6 765	−1.0	−8.4	1 787	2.4
...	18 055	Greene	542	33 157	1 311	61.2	30 410	1 274	30 416	2 747	−6	9.0	Z	268	.8
3480	18 057	Hamilton	398	182 740	300	459.1	108 936	423	82 027	73 804	26 909	67.7	32.8	2 911	1.6
3480	18 059	Hancock	306	55 391	851	181.0	45 527	909	43 939	9 864	1 588	21.7	3.6	526	.9
4520	18 061	Harrison	485	34 325	1 270	70.8	29 890	1 301	27 276	4 435	2 614	14.8	9.6	331	1.0
3480	18 063	Hendricks	408	104 093	508	255.1	75 717	594	69 804	28 376	5 913	37.5	8.5	1 162	1.1
...	18 065	Henry	393	48 508	939	123.4	48 139	866	53 336	369	−5 197	.8	−9.7	387	.8
3850	18 067	Howard	293	84 964	614	290.0	80 827	564	86 896	4 137	−6 069	5.1	−7.0	1 709	2.0
2760	18 069	Huntington	383	38 075	1 162	99.4	35 427	1 116	35 596	2 648	−169	7.5	−.5	363	1.0
...	18 071	Jackson	509	41 335	1 070	81.2	37 730	1 054	36 523	3 605	1 207	9.6	3.3	1 112	2.7
...	18 073	Jasper	560	30 043	1 395	53.6	24 823	1 468	26 138	5 220	−1 315	21.0	−5.0	733	2.4
...	18 075	Jay	384	21 806	1 700	56.8	21 512	1 603	23 239	294	−1 727	1.4	−7.4	390	1.8
...	18 077	Jefferson	361	31 705	1 352	87.8	29 797	1 304	30 419	1 908	−622	6.4	−2.0	332	1.0
...	18 079	Jennings	377	27 554	1 465	73.1	23 661	1 506	22 854	3 893	807	16.5	3.5	193	.7
3480	18 081	Johnson	320	115 209	468	360.0	88 109	517	77 240	27 100	10 869	30.8	14.1	1 591	1.4
...	18 083	Knox	516	39 256	1 132	76.1	39 884	1 007	41 838	−628	−1 954	−1.6	−4.7	322	.8
...	18 085	Kosciusko	538	74 057	673	137.7	65 294	671	59 555	8 763	5 739	13.4	9.6	3 722	5.0
...	18 087	Lagrange	380	34 909	1 252	91.9	29 477	1 317	25 550	5 432	3 927	18.4	15.4	1 097	3.1
1602	18 089	Lake	497	484 564	118	975.0	475 594	103	522 917	8 970	−47 323	1.9	−9.0	59 128	12.2
...	18 091	La Porte	598	110 106	493	184.1	107 066	430	108 632	3 040	−1 666	2.8	−1.4	3 402	3.1
...	18 093	Lawrence	449	45 922	986	102.3	42 836	940	42 472	3 086	364	7.2	.9	416	.9
3480	18 095	Madison	452	133 358	402	295.0	130 669	355	139 336	2 689	−8 667	2.1	−6.2	1 993	1.5
3480	18 097	Marion	396	860 454	50	2 172.9	797 159	48	765 233	63 295	31 926	7.9	4.2	33 290	3.9
...	18 099	Marshall	444	45 128	994	101.6	42 182	955	39 155	2 946	3 027	7.0	7.7	2 664	5.9
...	18 101	Martin	336	10 369	2 407	30.9	10 369	2 351	11 001	−	−632	−	−5.7	42	.4
...	18 103	Miami	376	36 082	1 211	96.0	36 897	1 077	39 820	−815	−2 923	−2.2	−7.3	478	1.3
1020	18 105	Monroe	394	120 563	450	306.0	108 978	422	98 783	11 585	10 195	10.6	10.3	2 235	1.9
...	18 107	Montgomery	505	37 629	1 172	74.5	34 436	1 152	35 501	3 193	−1 065	9.3	−3.0	611	1.6
3480	18 109	Morgan	406	66 689	733	164.3	55 920	773	51 999	10 769	3 921	19.3	7.5	490	.7
...	18 111	Newton	402	14 566	2 115	36.2	13 551	2 098	14 844	1 015	−1 293	7.5	−8.7	422	2.9
...	18 113	Noble	411	46 275	997	112.6	37 877	1 052	35 443	8 398	2 434	22.2	6.9	3 299	7.1
1642	18 115	Ohio	87	5 623	2 812	64.6	5 315	2 818	5 114	308	201	5.8	3.9	25	.4
...	18 117	Orange	400	19 306	1 828	48.3	18 409	1 769	18 677	897	−268	4.9	−1.4	108	.6
...	18 119	Owen	385	21 786	1 705	56.6	17 281	1 835	15 841	4 505	1 440	26.1	9.1	164	.8
...	18 121	Parke	445	17 241	1 938	30.7	15 410	1 963	16 372	1 831	−962	11.9	−5.9	104	.6
...	18 123	Perry	381	18 899	1 849	49.6	19 107	1 727	19 346	−208	−239	−1.1	−1.2	133	.7
...	18 125	Pike	336	12 837	2 244	38.2	12 509	2 181	13 465	328	−956	2.6	−7.1	74	.6
1602	18 127	Porter	418	146 798	370	351.2	128 932	359	119 816	17 866	9 116	13.9	7.6	7 079	4.8
2440	18 129	Posey	409	27 061	1 480	66.2	25 968	1 422	26 414	1 093	−446	4.2	−1.7	118	.4
...	18 131	Pulaski	434	13 755	2 176	31.7	12 780	2 157	13 258	975	−478	7.6	−3.6	191	1.4
...	18 133	Putnam	480	36 019	1 216	75.0	30 315	1 279	29 163	5 704	1 152	18.8	4.0	412	1.1
...	18 135	Randolph	453	27 401	1 470	60.5	27 148	1 385	29 997	253	−2 849	.9	−9.5	333	1.2
...	18 137	Ripley	446	26 523	1 501	59.5	24 616	1 476	24 398	1 907	218	7.7	.9	247	.9
...	18 139	Rush	408	18 261	1 882	44.8	18 129	1 781	19 604	132	−1 475	.7	−7.5	92	.5
7800	18 141	St. Joseph	457	265 559	208	581.1	247 052	203	241 617	18 507	5 435	7.5	2.2	12 557	4.7
4520	18 143	Scott	190	22 960	1 645	120.8	20 991	1 630	20 422	1 969	569	9.4	2.8	222	1.0
3480	18 145	Shelby	413	43 445	1 029	105.2	40 307	993	39 887	3 138	420	7.8	1.1	497	1.1
...	18 147	Spencer	399	20 391	1 767	51.1	19 490	1 703	19 361	901	129	4.6	.7	303	1.5
...	18 149	Starke	309	23 556	1 611	76.2	22 747	1 546	21 997	809	750	3.6	3.4	514	2.2
...	18 151	Steuben	309	33 214	1 306	107.5	27 446	1 378	24 694	5 768	2 752	21.0	11.1	683	2.1
...	18 153	Sullivan	447	21 751	1 707	48.7	18 993	1 735	21 107	2 758	−2 114	14.5	−10.0	179	.8
...	18 155	Switzerland	221	9 065	2 523	41.0	7 738	2 600	7 153	1 327	585	17.1	8.2	78	.9
3920	18 157	Tippecanoe	500	148 955	362	297.9	130 598	356	121 702	18 357	8 896	14.1	7.3	7 834	5.3

[1] Federal Information Processing Standards (FIPS) codes for metropolitan areas defined as of June 30, 1999. [2] FIPS codes for states and counties/county equivalents. [3] Dry land and land temporarily or partially covered by water. [4] Based on 3,140 counties/county equivalents; excludes Yellowstone National Park in MT and South Boston independent city in VA which are no longer counties. When counties share the same rank, the next lower rank is omitted. [5] Includes count resolution corrections through 1997 and adjustments based on Census 2000 dress rehearsal results and boundary changes reported as legally effective as of January 1, 1998. [6] Persons of Hispanic or Latino origin may be of any race.

Sources: Land Area—U.S. Census Bureau, unpublished data file from Geography Division based on TIGER data base. 2000 Population—U.S. Census Bureau, Census of Population and Housing, Census 2000 Redistricting Data (Public Law 94-171) Summary Files (related Internet site <http://www.census.gov/dmd/www/2kresult.html>). 1990 Population—U.S. Census Bureau, "(CO-99-8) County Population Estimates and Demographic Components of Population Change: Annual Time Series, July 1, 1990 to July 1, 1999 (includes revised April 1, 1990 Population Estimates Base)"; published 9 March 2000; <http://www. census.gov/population/estimates/county/co-99-8/99C8_00.txt>. 1980 Population—U.S. Census Bureau, "1980–1990 Intercensal Population Estimates by County" on diskette (related Internet site <http://www.census.gov/population/www/estimates/countypop.html>).

[Includes U.S., states, and 3,142 counties/county equivalents defined as of January 1, 1992. For changes to these areas since January 1, 1992, see appendix B. Geographic Information]

Metro-politan area code[1]	State and county code[2]	County	Land area,[3] 2000 (sq. miles)	Population (April 1) 2000 Number	2000 Rank[4]	2000 Per square mile	1990[5] Number	1990[5] Rank[4]	1980	Net change 1990–2000	Net change 1980–1990	Percent change 1990–2000	Percent change 1980–1990	Hispanic or Latino,[6] 2000 Number	Hispanic or Latino,[6] 2000 Percent
		INDIANA—Con.													
3850	18 159	Tipton	260	16 577	1 985	63.8	16 119	1 916	16 819	458	−700	2.8	−4.2	201	1.2
...	18 161	Union	162	7 349	2 651	45.4	6 976	2 662	6 860	373	116	5.3	1.7	22	.3
2440	18 163	Vanderburgh	235	171 922	316	731.6	165 058	289	167 515	6 864	−2 457	4.2	−1.5	1 679	1.0
8320	18 165	Vermillion	257	16 788	1 971	65.3	16 773	1 863	18 229	15	−1 456	.1	−8.0	107	.6
8320	18 167	Vigo	403	105 848	501	262.7	106 107	436	112 385	−259	−6 278	−.2	−5.6	1 275	1.2
...	18 169	Wabash	413	34 960	1 250	84.6	35 069	1 129	36 640	−109	−1 571	−.3	−4.3	414	1.2
...	18 171	Warren	365	8 419	2 571	23.1	8 176	2 548	8 976	243	−800	3.0	−8.9	37	.4
2440	18 173	Warrick	384	52 383	892	136.4	44 920	913	41 474	7 463	3 446	16.6	8.3	340	.6
...	18 175	Washington	514	27 223	1 474	53.0	23 717	1 502	21 932	3 506	1 785	14.8	8.1	200	.7
...	18 177	Wayne	404	71 097	699	176.0	71 951	619	76 058	−854	−4 107	−1.2	−5.4	971	1.4
2760	18 179	Wells	370	27 600	1 462	74.6	25 948	1 423	25 401	1 652	547	6.4	2.2	397	1.4
...	18 181	White	505	25 267	1 556	50.0	23 265	1 527	23 867	2 002	−602	8.6	−2.5	1 349	5.3
2760	18 183	Whitley	336	30 707	1 381	91.4	27 651	1 365	26 215	3 056	1 436	11.1	5.5	276	.9
	19 000	IOWA	55 869	2 926 324	X	52.4	2 776 831	X	2 913 808	149 493	−136 977	5.4	−4.7	82 473	2.8
...	19 001	Adair	569	8 243	2 587	14.5	8 409	2 519	9 509	−166	−1 100	−2.0	−11.6	58	.7
...	19 003	Adams	424	4 482	2 882	10.6	4 866	2 846	5 731	−384	−865	−7.9	−15.1	26	.6
...	19 005	Allamakee	640	14 675	2 110	22.9	13 855	2 067	15 108	820	−1 253	5.9	−8.3	520	3.5
...	19 007	Appanoose	496	13 721	2 181	27.7	13 743	2 077	15 511	−22	−1 768	−.2	−11.4	135	1.0
...	19 009	Audubon	443	6 830	2 707	15.4	7 334	2 627	8 559	−504	−1 225	−6.9	−14.3	33	.5
...	19 011	Benton	716	25 308	1 552	35.3	22 429	1 556	23 649	2 879	−1 220	12.8	−5.2	156	.6
8920	19 013	Black Hawk	567	128 012	423	225.8	123 798	371	137 961	4 214	−14 163	3.4	−10.3	2 359	1.8
...	19 015	Boone	571	26 224	1 509	45.9	25 186	1 455	26 184	1 038	−998	4.1	−3.8	218	.8
...	19 017	Bremer	438	23 325	1 628	53.3	22 813	1 541	24 820	512	−2 007	2.2	−8.1	130	.6
...	19 019	Buchanan	571	21 093	1 732	36.9	20 844	1 638	22 900	249	−2 056	1.2	−9.0	131	.6
...	19 021	Buena Vista	575	20 411	1 765	35.5	19 965	1 679	20 774	446	−809	2.2	−3.9	2 560	12.5
...	19 023	Butler	580	15 305	2 071	26.4	15 731	1 939	17 668	−426	−1 937	−2.7	−11.0	89	.6
...	19 025	Calhoun	570	11 115	2 357	19.5	11 508	2 255	13 542	−393	−2 034	−3.4	−15.0	100	.9
...	19 027	Carroll	569	21 421	1 716	37.6	21 423	1 608	22 951	−2	−1 528	Z	−6.7	115	.5
...	19 029	Cass	564	14 684	2 108	26.0	15 128	1 979	16 932	−444	−1 804	−2.9	−10.7	101	.7
...	19 031	Cedar	580	18 187	1 889	31.4	17 444	1 825	18 635	743	−1 191	4.3	−6.4	171	.9
...	19 033	Cerro Gordo	568	46 447	974	81.8	46 733	894	48 458	−286	−1 725	−.6	−3.6	1 291	2.8
...	19 035	Cherokee	577	13 035	2 229	22.6	14 098	2 048	16 238	−1 063	−2 140	−7.5	−13.2	124	1.0
...	19 037	Chickasaw	505	13 095	2 221	25.9	13 295	2 115	15 437	−200	−2 142	−1.5	−13.9	82	.6
...	19 039	Clarke	431	9 133	2 519	21.2	8 287	2 539	8 612	846	−325	10.2	−3.8	369	4.0
...	19 041	Clay	569	17 372	1 930	30.5	17 585	1 815	19 576	−213	−1 991	−1.2	−10.2	196	1.1
...	19 043	Clayton	779	18 678	1 862	24.0	19 054	1 730	21 098	−376	−2 044	−2.0	−9.7	142	.8
...	19 045	Clinton	695	50 149	914	72.2	51 040	827	57 122	−891	−6 082	−1.7	−10.6	627	1.3
...	19 047	Crawford	714	16 942	1 956	23.7	16 775	1 862	18 935	167	−2 160	1.0	−11.4	1 482	8.7
2120	19 049	Dallas	586	40 750	1 090	69.5	29 755	1 305	29 513	10 995	242	37.0	.8	2 199	5.4
...	19 051	Davis	503	8 541	2 565	17.0	8 312	2 533	9 104	229	−792	2.8	−8.7	61	.7
...	19 053	Decatur	532	8 689	2 552	16.3	8 338	2 530	9 794	351	−1 456	4.2	−14.9	148	1.7
...	19 055	Delaware	578	18 404	1 874	31.8	18 035	1 789	18 933	369	−898	2.0	−4.7	121	.7
...	19 057	Des Moines	416	42 351	1 048	101.8	42 614	942	46 203	−263	−3 589	−.6	−7.8	740	1.7
...	19 059	Dickinson	381	16 424	1 996	43.1	14 909	1 992	15 629	1 515	−720	10.2	−4.6	109	.7
2200	19 061	Dubuque	608	89 143	583	146.6	86 403	528	93 745	2 740	−7 342	3.2	−7.8	1 065	1.2
...	19 063	Emmet	396	11 027	2 363	27.8	11 569	2 251	13 336	−542	−1 767	−4.7	−13.2	475	4.3
...	19 065	Fayette	731	22 008	1 691	30.1	21 843	1 587	25 488	165	−3 645	.8	−14.3	330	1.5
...	19 067	Floyd	501	16 900	1 959	33.7	17 058	1 847	19 597	−158	−2 539	−.9	−13.0	222	1.3
...	19 069	Franklin	582	10 704	2 383	18.4	11 364	2 264	13 036	−660	−1 672	−5.8	−12.8	642	6.0
...	19 071	Fremont	511	8 010	2 606	15.7	8 226	2 546	9 401	−216	−1 175	−2.6	−12.5	174	2.2
...	19 073	Greene	568	10 366	2 408	18.3	10 045	2 380	12 119	321	−2 074	3.2	−17.1	172	1.7
...	19 075	Grundy	503	12 369	2 275	24.6	12 029	2 217	14 366	340	−2 337	2.8	−16.3	72	.6
...	19 077	Guthrie	591	11 353	2 346	19.2	10 935	2 301	11 983	418	−1 048	3.8	−8.7	120	1.1
...	19 079	Hamilton	577	16 438	1 994	28.5	16 071	1 919	17 862	367	−1 791	2.3	−10.0	234	1.4
...	19 081	Hancock	571	12 100	2 290	21.2	12 638	2 174	13 833	−538	−1 195	−4.3	−8.6	301	2.5
...	19 083	Hardin	569	18 812	1 853	33.1	19 094	1 728	21 776	−282	−2 682	−1.5	−12.3	455	2.4
...	19 085	Harrison	697	15 666	2 042	22.5	14 730	2 004	16 348	936	−1 618	6.4	−9.9	113	.7
...	19 087	Henry	434	20 336	1 770	46.9	19 226	1 717	18 890	1 110	336	5.8	1.8	256	1.3
...	19 089	Howard	473	9 932	2 453	21.0	9 809	2 401	11 114	123	−1 305	1.3	−11.7	55	.6
...	19 091	Humboldt	434	10 381	2 404	23.9	10 756	2 311	12 246	−375	−1 490	−3.5	−12.2	100	1.0
...	19 093	Ida	432	7 837	2 620	18.1	8 365	2 527	8 908	−528	−543	−6.3	−6.1	37	.5
...	19 095	Iowa	586	15 671	2 041	26.7	14 630	2 010	15 429	1 041	−799	7.1	−5.2	152	1.0
...	19 097	Jackson	636	20 296	1 773	31.9	19 950	1 681	22 503	346	−2 553	1.7	−11.3	121	.6
...	19 099	Jasper	730	37 213	1 186	51.0	34 795	1 140	36 425	2 418	−1 630	6.9	−4.5	375	1.0
...	19 101	Jefferson	435	16 181	2 010	37.2	16 310	1 902	16 316	−129	−6	−.8	Z	297	1.8
3500	19 103	Johnson	614	111 006	488	180.8	96 119	482	81 717	14 887	14 402	15.5	17.6	2 781	2.5
...	19 105	Jones	575	20 221	1 779	35.2	19 444	1 706	20 401	777	−957	4.0	−4.7	213	1.1
...	19 107	Keokuk	579	11 400	2 341	19.7	11 624	2 246	12 921	−224	−1 297	−1.9	−10.0	61	.5

[1] Federal Information Processing Standards (FIPS) codes for metropolitan areas defined as of June 30, 1999.   [2] FIPS codes for states and counties/county equivalents.   [3] Dry land and land temporarily or partially covered by water.   [4] Based on 3,140 counties/county equivalents; excludes Yellowstone National Park in MT and South Boston independent city in VA which are no longer counties. When counties share the same rank, the next lower rank is omitted.   [5] Includes count resolution corrections through 1997 and adjustments based on Census 2000 dress rehearsal results and boundary changes reported as legally effective as of January 1, 1998.   [6] Persons of Hispanic or Latino origin may be of any race.

Sources: Land Area—U.S. Census Bureau, unpublished data file from Geography Division based on TIGER data base.   2000 Population—U.S. Census Bureau, Census of Population and Housing, Census 2000 Redistricting Data (Public Law 94-171) Summary Files (related Internet site <http://www.census.gov/dmd/www/2kresult.html>).   1990 Population—U.S. Census Bureau, "(CO-99-8) County Population Estimates and Demographic Components of Population Change: Annual Time Series, July 1, 1990 to July 1, 1999 (includes revised April 1, 1990 Population Estimates Base)"; published 9 March 2000; <http://www.census.gov/population/estimates/county/co-99-8/99C8_00.txt>.   1980 Population—U.S. Census Bureau, "1980–1990 Intercensal Population Estimates by County" on diskette (related Internet site <http://www.census.gov/population/www/estimates/countypop.html>).

[Includes U.S., states, and 3,142 counties/county equivalents defined as of January 1, 1992. For changes to these areas since January 1, 1992, see appendix B. Geographic Information]

Metro-politan area code[1]	State and county code[2]	County	Land area,[3] 2000 (sq. miles)	Population (April 1) 2000 Number	2000 Rank[4]	2000 Per square mile	1990[5] Number	1990[5] Rank[4]	1980	Net change 1990–2000	Net change 1980–1990	Percent change 1990–2000	Percent change 1980–1990	Hispanic or Latino,[6] 2000 Number	Hispanic or Latino,[6] 2000 Percent
		IOWA—Con.													
...	19 109	Kossuth	973	17 163	1 944	17.6	18 591	1 759	21 891	−1 428	−3 300	−7.7	−15.1	139	.8
...	19 111	Lee	517	38 052	1 163	73.6	38 687	1 036	43 106	−635	−4 419	−1.6	−10.3	902	2.4
1360	19 113	Linn	717	191 701	286	267.4	168 767	284	169 775	22 934	−1 008	13.6	−.6	2 722	1.4
...	19 115	Louisa	402	12 183	2 284	30.3	11 592	2 249	12 055	591	−463	5.1	−3.8	1 537	12.6
...	19 117	Lucas	431	9 422	2 492	21.9	9 070	2 463	10 313	352	−1 243	3.9	−12.1	82	.9
...	19 119	Lyon	588	11 763	2 312	20.0	11 952	2 223	12 896	−189	−944	−1.6	−7.3	42	.4
...	19 121	Madison	561	14 019	2 162	25.0	12 483	2 182	12 597	1 536	−114	12.3	−.9	105	.7
...	19 123	Mahaska	571	22 335	1 677	39.1	21 532	1 602	22 867	803	−1 335	3.7	−5.8	190	.9
...	19 125	Marion	554	32 052	1 344	57.9	30 001	1 296	29 669	2 051	332	6.8	1.1	257	.8
...	19 127	Marshall	572	39 311	1 129	68.7	38 276	1 046	41 652	1 035	−3 376	2.7	−8.1	3 523	9.0
...	19 129	Mills	437	14 547	2 118	33.3	13 202	2 122	13 406	1 345	−204	10.2	−1.5	179	1.2
...	19 131	Mitchell	469	10 874	2 375	23.2	10 928	2 304	12 329	−54	−1 401	−.5	−11.4	63	.6
...	19 133	Monona	693	10 020	2 443	14.5	10 034	2 383	11 692	−14	−1 658	−.1	−14.2	70	.7
...	19 135	Monroe	433	8 016	2 603	18.5	8 114	2 553	9 209	−98	−1 095	−1.2	−11.9	40	.5
...	19 137	Montgomery	424	11 771	2 310	27.8	12 076	2 212	13 413	−305	−1 337	−2.5	−10.0	153	1.3
...	19 139	Muscatine	439	41 722	1 062	95.0	39 907	1 006	40 436	1 815	−529	4.5	−1.3	4 973	11.9
...	19 141	O'Brien	573	15 102	2 084	26.4	15 444	1 958	16 972	−342	−1 528	−2.2	−9.0	267	1.8
...	19 143	Osceola	399	7 003	2 686	17.6	7 267	2 630	8 371	−264	−1 104	−3.6	−13.2	125	1.8
...	19 145	Page	535	16 976	1 954	31.7	16 870	1 858	19 063	106	−2 193	.6	−11.5	265	1.6
...	19 147	Palo Alto	564	10 147	2 434	18.0	10 669	2 321	12 721	−522	−2 052	−4.9	−16.1	77	.8
...	19 149	Plymouth	864	24 849	1 562	28.8	23 388	1 520	24 743	1 461	−1 355	6.2	−5.5	328	1.3
...	19 151	Pocahontas	578	8 662	2 554	15.0	9 525	2 430	11 369	−863	−1 844	−9.1	−16.2	77	.9
2120	19 153	Polk	569	374 601	156	658.3	327 140	156	303 170	47 461	23 970	14.5	7.9	16 490	4.4
5920	19 155	Pottawattamie	954	87 704	596	91.9	82 628	550	86 561	5 076	−3 933	6.1	−4.5	2 892	3.3
...	19 157	Poweshiek	585	18 815	1 852	32.2	19 033	1 733	19 306	−218	−273	−1.1	−1.4	226	1.2
...	19 159	Ringgold	538	5 469	2 818	10.2	5 420	2 806	6 112	49	−692	.9	−11.3	13	.2
...	19 161	Sac	576	11 529	2 331	20.0	12 324	2 192	14 118	−795	−1 794	−6.5	−12.7	111	1.0
1960	19 163	Scott	458	158 668	334	346.4	150 973	309	160 022	7 695	−9 049	5.1	−5.7	6 445	4.1
...	19 165	Shelby	591	13 173	2 215	22.3	13 230	2 118	15 043	−57	−1 813	−.4	−12.1	88	.7
...	19 167	Sioux	768	31 589	1 357	41.1	29 903	1 300	30 813	1 686	−910	5.6	−3.0	808	2.6
...	19 169	Story	573	79 981	642	139.6	74 252	606	72 326	5 729	1 926	7.7	2.7	1 238	1.5
...	19 171	Tama	721	18 103	1 892	25.1	17 419	1 826	19 533	684	−2 114	3.9	−10.8	679	3.8
...	19 173	Taylor	534	6 958	2 690	13.0	7 114	2 643	8 353	−156	−1 239	−2.2	−14.8	265	3.8
...	19 175	Union	424	12 309	2 279	29.0	12 750	2 163	13 858	−441	−1 108	−3.5	−8.0	125	1.0
...	19 177	Van Buren	485	7 809	2 643	16.1	7 676	2 603	8 626	133	−950	1.7	−11.0	60	.8
...	19 179	Wapello	432	36 051	1 215	83.5	35 696	1 106	40 241	355	−4 545	1.0	−11.3	799	2.2
2120	19 181	Warren	572	40 671	1 094	71.1	36 033	1 098	34 878	4 638	1 155	12.9	3.3	441	1.1
...	19 183	Washington	569	20 670	1 753	36.3	19 612	1 692	20 141	1 058	−529	5.4	−2.6	564	2.7
...	19 185	Wayne	526	6 730	2 716	12.8	7 067	2 650	8 199	−337	−1 132	−4.8	−13.8	48	.7
...	19 187	Webster	715	40 235	1 109	56.3	40 342	991	45 953	−107	−5 611	−.3	−12.2	944	2.3
...	19 189	Winnebago	400	11 723	2 316	29.3	12 122	2 206	13 010	−399	−888	−3.3	−6.8	237	2.0
...	19 191	Winneshiek	690	21 310	1 721	30.9	20 847	1 636	21 876	463	−1 029	2.2	−4.7	170	.8
7720	19 193	Woodbury	873	103 877	510	119.0	98 276	468	100 884	5 601	−2 608	5.7	−2.6	9 468	9.1
...	19 195	Worth	400	7 909	2 614	19.8	7 991	2 567	9 075	−82	−1 084	−1.0	−11.9	124	1.6
...	19 197	Wright	581	14 334	2 137	24.7	14 269	2 033	16 319	65	−2 050	.5	−12.6	706	4.9
	20 000	KANSAS	81 815	2 688 418	X	32.9	2 477 588	X	2 364 236	210 830	113 352	8.5	4.8	188 252	7.0
...	20 001	Allen	503	14 385	2 134	28.6	14 638	2 008	15 654	−253	−1 016	−1.7	−6.5	278	1.9
...	20 003	Anderson	583	8 110	2 597	13.9	7 803	2 594	8 749	307	−946	3.9	−10.8	88	1.1
...	20 005	Atchison	432	16 774	1 972	38.8	16 932	1 854	18 397	−158	−1 465	−.9	−8.0	327	1.9
...	20 007	Barber	1 134	5 307	2 829	4.7	5 874	2 773	6 548	−567	−674	−9.7	−10.3	107	2.0
...	20 009	Barton	894	28 205	1 445	31.5	29 382	1 318	31 343	−1 177	−1 961	−4.0	−6.3	2 344	8.3
...	20 011	Bourbon	637	15 379	2 061	24.1	14 966	1 989	15 969	413	−1 003	2.8	−6.3	199	1.3
...	20 013	Brown	571	10 724	2 381	18.8	11 128	2 281	11 955	−404	−827	−3.6	−6.9	249	2.3
9040	20 015	Butler	1 428	59 482	808	41.7	50 580	833	44 782	8 902	5 798	17.6	12.9	1 336	2.2
...	20 017	Chase	776	3 030	2 992	3.9	3 021	2 998	3 309	9	−288	.3	−8.7	53	1.7
...	20 019	Chautauqua	642	4 359	2 891	6.8	4 407	2 880	5 016	−48	−609	−1.1	−12.1	59	1.4
...	20 021	Cherokee	587	22 605	1 665	38.5	21 374	1 614	22 304	1 231	−930	5.8	−4.2	291	1.3
...	20 023	Cheyenne	1 020	3 165	2 981	3.1	3 243	2 980	3 678	−78	−435	−2.4	−11.8	82	2.6
...	20 025	Clark	975	2 390	3 032	2.5	2 418	3 029	2 599	−28	−181	−1.2	−7.0	96	4.0
...	20 027	Clay	644	8 822	2 543	13.7	9 158	2 455	9 802	−336	−644	−3.7	−6.6	73	.8
...	20 029	Cloud	716	10 268	2 420	14.3	11 023	2 290	12 494	−755	−1 471	−6.8	−11.8	62	.6
...	20 031	Coffey	630	8 865	2 537	14.1	8 404	2 520	9 370	461	−966	5.5	−10.3	137	1.5
...	20 033	Comanche	788	1 967	3 066	2.5	2 313	3 038	2 554	−346	−241	−15.0	−9.4	35	1.8
...	20 035	Cowley	1 126	36 291	1 205	32.2	36 915	1 076	36 824	−624	91	−1.7	.2	1 304	3.6
...	20 037	Crawford	593	38 242	1 160	64.5	35 582	1 109	37 916	2 660	−2 334	7.5	−6.2	910	2.4
...	20 039	Decatur	894	3 472	2 957	3.9	4 021	2 916	4 509	−549	−488	−13.7	−10.8	34	1.0
...	20 041	Dickinson	848	19 344	1 826	22.8	18 958	1 737	20 175	386	−1 217	2.0	−6.0	445	2.3

[1] Federal Information Processing Standards (FIPS) codes for metropolitan areas defined as of June 30, 1999.   [2] FIPS codes for states and counties/county equivalents.   [3] Dry land and land temporarily or partially covered by water.   [4] Based on 3,140 counties/county equivalents; excludes Yellowstone National Park in MT and South Boston independent city in VA which are no longer counties. When counties share the same rank, the next lower rank is omitted.   [5] Includes count resolution corrections through 1997 and adjustments based on Census 2000 dress rehearsal results and boundary changes reported as legally effective as of January 1, 1998.   [6] Persons of Hispanic or Latino origin may be of any race.

Sources: Land Area—U.S. Census Bureau, unpublished data file from Geography Division based on TIGER data base.   2000 Population—U.S. Census Bureau, Census of Population and Housing, Census 2000 Redistricting Data (Public Law 94-171) Summary Files (related Internet site <http://www.census.gov/dmd/www/2kresult.html>).   1990 Population—U.S. Census Bureau, "(CO-99-8) County Population Estimates and Demographic Components of Population Change: Annual Time Series, July 1, 1990 to July 1, 1999 (includes revised April 1, 1990 Population Estimates Base)"; published 9 March 2000; <http://www. census.gov/population/estimates/county/co-99-8/99C8_00.txt>.   1980 Population—U.S. Census Bureau, "1980–1990 Intercensal Population Estimates by County" on diskette (related Internet site <http://www.census.gov/population/www/estimates/countypop.html>).

Table B–1. Counties — **Area and Population**–Con.

[Includes U.S., states, and 3,142 counties/county equivalents defined as of January 1, 1992. For changes to these areas since January 1, 1992, see appendix B. Geographic Information]

Metro-politan area code[1]	State and county code[2]	County	Land area,[3] 2000 (sq. miles)	Population (April 1) 2000 Number	2000 Rank[4]	2000 Per square mile	1990[5] Number	1990[5] Rank[4]	1980	Net change 1990–2000	Net change 1980–1990	Percent change 1990–2000	Percent change 1980–1990	Hispanic or Latino,[6] 2000 Number	Hispanic or Latino,[6] 2000 Percent
		KANSAS—Con.													
...	20 043	Doniphan	392	8 249	2 586	21.0	8 134	2 551	9 268	115	−1 134	1.4	−12.2	96	1.2
4150	20 045	Douglas	457	99 962	525	218.7	81 798	556	67 640	18 164	14 158	22.2	20.9	3 268	3.3
...	20 047	Edwards	622	3 449	2 960	5.5	3 787	2 932	4 271	−338	−484	−8.9	−11.3	335	9.7
...	20 049	Elk	647	3 261	2 976	5.0	3 327	2 968	3 918	−66	−591	−2.0	−15.1	71	2.2
...	20 051	Ellis	900	27 507	1 466	30.6	26 004	1 421	26 098	1 503	−94	5.8	−.4	652	2.4
...	20 053	Ellsworth	716	6 525	2 737	9.1	6 586	2 700	6 640	−61	−54	−.9	−.8	234	3.6
...	20 055	Finney	1 302	40 523	1 103	31.1	33 070	1 188	23 825	7 453	9 245	22.5	38.8	17 548	43.3
...	20 057	Ford	1 099	32 458	1 334	29.5	27 463	1 377	24 315	4 995	3 148	18.2	12.9	12 231	37.7
...	20 059	Franklin	574	24 784	1 564	43.2	21 994	1 576	22 062	2 790	−68	12.7	−.3	650	2.6
...	20 061	Geary	385	27 947	1 453	72.6	30 453	1 271	29 852	−2 506	601	−8.2	2.0	2 362	8.5
...	20 063	Gove	1 071	3 068	2 987	2.9	3 231	2 981	3 726	−163	−495	−5.0	−13.3	38	1.2
...	20 065	Graham	898	2 946	2 995	3.3	3 543	2 954	3 995	−597	−452	−16.9	−11.3	23	.8
...	20 067	Grant	575	7 909	2 614	13.8	7 159	2 637	6 977	750	182	10.5	2.6	2 742	34.7
...	20 069	Gray	869	5 904	2 793	6.8	5 396	2 809	5 138	508	258	9.4	5.0	579	9.8
...	20 071	Greeley	778	1 534	3 093	2.0	1 774	3 079	1 845	−240	−71	−13.5	−3.8	177	11.5
...	20 073	Greenwood	1 140	7 673	2 632	6.7	7 847	2 587	8 764	−174	−917	−2.2	−10.5	132	1.7
...	20 075	Hamilton	996	2 670	3 017	2.7	2 388	3 032	2 514	282	−126	11.8	−5.0	550	20.6
...	20 077	Harper	801	6 536	2 736	8.2	7 124	2 641	7 778	−588	−654	−8.3	−8.4	70	1.1
9040	20 079	Harvey	539	32 869	1 323	61.0	31 028	1 245	30 531	1 841	497	5.9	1.6	2 620	8.0
...	20 081	Haskell	577	4 307	2 895	7.5	3 886	2 926	3 814	421	72	10.8	1.9	1 015	23.6
...	20 083	Hodgeman	860	2 085	3 059	2.4	2 177	3 055	2 269	−92	−92	−4.2	−4.1	56	2.7
...	20 085	Jackson	656	12 657	2 251	19.3	11 525	2 254	11 644	1 132	−119	9.8	−1.0	189	1.5
...	20 087	Jefferson	536	18 426	1 871	34.4	15 905	1 931	15 207	2 521	698	15.9	4.6	236	1.3
...	20 089	Jewell	909	3 791	2 929	4.2	4 251	2 894	5 241	−460	−990	−10.8	−18.9	27	.7
3760	20 091	Johnson	477	451 086	131	945.7	355 021	145	270 269	96 065	84 752	27.1	31.4	17 957	4.0
...	20 093	Kearny	871	4 531	2 876	5.2	4 027	2 914	3 435	504	592	12.5	17.2	1 203	26.6
...	20 095	Kingman	863	8 673	2 553	10.0	8 292	2 536	8 960	381	−668	4.6	−7.5	125	1.4
...	20 097	Kiowa	722	3 278	2 975	4.5	3 660	2 942	4 046	−382	−386	−10.4	−9.5	67	2.0
...	20 099	Labette	649	22 835	1 651	35.2	23 693	1 504	25 682	−858	−1 989	−3.6	−7.7	700	3.1
...	20 101	Lane	717	2 155	3 055	3.0	2 375	3 034	2 472	−220	−97	−9.3	−3.9	31	1.4
3760	20 103	Leavenworth	463	68 691	718	148.4	64 371	679	54 809	4 320	9 562	6.7	17.4	2 620	3.8
...	20 105	Lincoln	719	3 578	2 946	5.0	3 653	2 944	4 145	−75	−492	−2.1	−11.9	37	1.0
...	20 107	Linn	599	9 570	2 483	16.0	8 254	2 543	8 234	1 316	20	15.9	.2	87	.9
...	20 109	Logan	1 073	3 046	2 991	2.8	3 081	2 994	3 478	−35	−397	−1.1	−11.4	50	1.6
...	20 111	Lyon	851	35 935	1 220	42.2	34 732	1 144	35 108	1 203	−376	3.5	−1.1	6 010	16.7
...	20 113	McPherson	900	29 554	1 413	32.8	27 268	1 381	26 855	2 286	413	8.4	1.5	573	1.9
...	20 115	Marion	943	13 361	2 200	14.2	12 888	2 146	13 522	473	−634	3.7	−4.7	257	1.9
...	20 117	Marshall	903	10 965	2 370	12.1	11 705	2 232	12 787	−740	−1 082	−6.3	−8.5	83	.8
...	20 119	Meade	978	4 631	2 871	4.7	4 247	2 895	4 788	384	−541	9.0	−11.3	505	10.9
3760	20 121	Miami	577	28 351	1 436	49.1	23 466	1 516	21 618	4 885	1 848	20.8	8.5	451	1.6
...	20 123	Mitchell	700	6 932	2 692	9.9	7 203	2 632	8 117	−271	−914	−3.8	−11.3	61	.9
...	20 125	Montgomery	645	36 252	1 207	56.2	38 816	1 030	42 281	−2 564	−3 465	−6.6	−8.2	1 118	3.1
...	20 127	Morris	697	6 104	2 770	8.8	6 198	2 733	6 419	−94	−221	−1.5	−3.4	136	2.2
...	20 129	Morton	730	3 496	2 955	4.8	3 480	2 958	3 454	16	26	.5	.8	493	14.1
...	20 131	Nemaha	718	10 717	2 382	14.9	10 446	2 343	11 211	271	−765	2.6	−6.8	76	.7
...	20 133	Neosho	572	16 997	1 953	29.7	17 035	1 848	18 967	−38	−1 932	−.2	−10.2	494	2.9
...	20 135	Ness	1 075	3 454	2 959	3.2	4 033	2 913	4 498	−579	−465	−14.4	−10.3	52	1.5
...	20 137	Norton	878	5 953	2 788	6.8	5 947	2 765	6 689	6	−742	.1	−11.1	141	2.4
...	20 139	Osage	704	16 712	1 975	23.7	15 248	1 974	15 319	1 464	−71	9.6	−.5	255	1.5
...	20 141	Osborne	892	4 452	2 885	5.0	4 867	2 845	5 959	−415	−1 092	−8.5	−18.3	17	.4
...	20 143	Ottawa	721	6 163	2 766	8.5	5 634	2 790	5 971	529	−337	9.4	−5.6	80	1.3
...	20 145	Pawnee	754	7 233	2 662	9.6	7 555	2 611	8 065	−322	−510	−4.3	−6.3	301	4.2
...	20 147	Phillips	886	6 001	2 779	6.8	6 590	2 699	7 406	−589	−816	−8.9	−11.0	40	.7
...	20 149	Pottawatomie	844	18 209	1 886	21.6	16 128	1 915	14 782	2 081	1 346	12.9	9.1	411	2.3
...	20 151	Pratt	735	9 647	2 474	13.1	9 702	2 412	10 275	−55	−573	−.6	−5.6	298	3.1
...	20 153	Rawlins	1 070	2 966	2 994	2.8	3 404	2 964	4 105	−438	−701	−12.9	−17.1	24	.8
...	20 155	Reno	1 254	64 790	749	51.7	62 389	697	64 983	2 401	−2 594	3.8	−4.0	3 661	5.7
...	20 157	Republic	716	5 835	2 799	8.1	6 482	2 711	7 569	−647	−1 087	−10.0	−14.4	55	.9
...	20 159	Rice	727	10 761	2 379	14.8	10 610	2 326	11 900	151	−1 290	1.4	−10.8	604	5.6
...	20 161	Riley	610	62 843	774	103.0	67 139	658	63 505	−4 296	3 634	−6.4	5.7	2 872	4.6
...	20 163	Rooks	888	5 685	2 809	6.4	6 039	2 752	7 006	−354	−967	−5.9	−13.8	60	1.1
...	20 165	Rush	718	3 551	2 951	4.9	3 842	2 929	4 516	−291	−674	−7.6	−14.9	37	1.0
...	20 167	Russell	885	7 370	2 650	8.3	7 835	2 591	8 868	−465	−1 033	−5.9	−11.6	67	.9
...	20 169	Saline	720	53 597	871	74.4	49 301	851	48 905	4 296	396	8.7	.8	3 228	6.0
...	20 171	Scott	718	5 120	2 842	7.1	5 289	2 820	5 782	−169	−493	−3.2	−8.5	323	6.3
9040	20 173	Sedgwick	999	452 869	130	453.3	403 662	123	367 088	49 207	36 574	12.2	10.0	36 397	8.0
...	20 175	Seward	640	22 510	1 670	35.2	18 743	1 748	17 071	3 767	1 672	20.1	9.8	9 486	42.1
8440	20 177	Shawnee	550	169 871	319	308.9	160 976	297	154 916	8 895	6 060	5.5	3.9	12 330	7.3
...	20 179	Sheridan	896	2 813	3 005	3.1	3 043	2 997	3 544	−230	−501	−7.6	−14.1	41	1.5

[1] Federal Information Processing Standards (FIPS) codes for metropolitan areas defined as of June 30, 1999. [2] FIPS codes for states and counties/county equivalents. [3] Dry land and land temporarily or partially covered by water. [4] Based on 3,140 counties/county equivalents; excludes Yellowstone National Park in MT and South Boston independent city in VA which are no longer counties. When counties share the same rank, the next lower rank is omitted. [5] Includes count resolution corrections through 1997 and adjustments based on Census 2000 dress rehearsal results and boundary changes reported as legally effective as of January 1, 1998. [6] Persons of Hispanic or Latino origin may be of any race.

Sources: Land Area—U.S. Census Bureau, unpublished data file from Geography Division based on TIGER data base. 2000 Population—U.S. Census Bureau, Census of Population and Housing, Census 2000 Redistricting Data (Public Law 94-171) Summary Files (related Internet site <http://www.census.gov/dmd/www/2kresult.html>). 1990 Population—U.S. Census Bureau, "(CO-99-8) County Population Estimates and Demographic Components of Population Change: Annual Time Series, July 1, 1990 to July 1, 1999 (includes revised April 1, 1990 Population Estimates Base)"; published 9 March 2000; <http://www. census.gov/population/estimates/county/co-99-8/99C8_00.txt>. 1980 Population—U.S. Census Bureau, "1980–1990 Intercensal Population Estimates by County" on diskette (related Internet site <http://www.census.gov/population/www/estimates/countypop.html>).

[Includes U.S., states, and 3,142 counties/county equivalents defined as of January 1, 1992. For changes to these areas since January 1, 1992, see appendix B. Geographic Information]

Metro-politan area code[1]	State and county code[2]	County	Land area,[3] 2000 (sq. miles)	Population (April 1)											
				2000			1990[5]		1980	Net change		Percent change		Hispanic or Latino,[6] 2000	
				Number	Rank[4]	Per square mile	Number	Rank[4]		1990–2000	1980–1990	1990–2000	1980–1990	Number	Percent
		KANSAS—Con.													
...	20 181	Sherman	1 056	6 760	2 714	6.4	6 926	2 667	7 759	−166	−833	−2.4	−10.7	571	8.4
...	20 183	Smith	895	4 536	2 875	5.1	5 078	2 834	5 947	−542	−869	−10.7	−14.6	33	.7
...	20 185	Stafford	792	4 789	2 861	6.0	5 365	2 812	5 694	−576	−329	−10.7	−5.8	259	5.4
...	20 187	Stanton	680	2 406	3 029	3.5	2 333	3 037	2 339	73	−6	3.1	−.3	570	23.7
...	20 189	Stevens	728	5 463	2 820	7.5	5 048	2 836	4 736	415	312	8.2	6.6	1 187	21.7
...	20 191	Sumner	1 182	25 946	1 519	22.0	25 841	1 428	24 928	105	913	.4	3.7	929	3.6
...	20 193	Thomas	1 075	8 180	2 595	7.6	8 258	2 542	8 451	−78	−193	−.9	−2.3	151	1.8
...	20 195	Trego	888	3 319	2 971	3.7	3 694	2 941	4 165	−375	−471	−10.2	−11.3	26	.8
...	20 197	Wabaunsee	797	6 885	2 696	8.6	6 603	2 698	6 867	282	−264	4.3	−3.8	128	1.9
...	20 199	Wallace	914	1 749	3 083	1.9	1 821	3 076	2 045	−72	−224	−4.0	−11.0	84	4.8
...	20 201	Washington	898	6 483	2 740	7.2	7 073	2 649	8 543	−590	−1 470	−8.3	−17.2	42	.6
...	20 203	Wichita	719	2 531	3 024	3.5	2 758	3 012	3 041	−227	−283	−8.2	−9.3	466	18.4
...	20 205	Wilson	574	10 332	2 411	10.0	10 289	2 300	12 128	43	−1 839	.4	−15.2	173	1.7
...	20 207	Woodson	501	3 788	2 930	7.6	4 116	2 906	4 600	−328	−484	−8.0	−10.5	52	1.4
3760	20 209	Wyandotte	151	157 882	337	1 045.6	162 026	293	172 335	−4 144	−10 309	−2.6	−6.0	25 257	16.0
	21 000	**KENTUCKY**	39 728	4 041 769	X	101.7	3 686 892	X	3 660 324	354 877	26 568	9.6	.7	59 939	1.5
...	21 001	Adair	407	17 244	1 936	42.4	15 360	1 967	15 233	1 884	127	12.3	.8	132	.8
...	21 003	Allen	346	17 800	1 910	51.4	14 628	2 011	14 128	3 172	500	21.7	3.5	147	.8
...	21 005	Anderson	203	19 111	1 842	94.1	14 571	2 016	12 567	4 540	2 004	31.2	15.9	153	.8
...	21 007	Ballard	251	8 286	2 581	33.0	7 902	2 581	8 798	384	−896	4.9	−10.2	52	.6
...	21 009	Barren	491	38 033	1 164	77.5	34 001	1 163	34 009	4 032	−8	11.9	Z	355	.9
...	21 011	Bath	279	11 085	2 359	39.7	9 692	2 413	10 025	1 393	−333	14.4	−3.3	89	.8
...	21 013	Bell	361	30 060	1 394	83.3	31 506	1 231	34 330	−1 446	−2 824	−4.6	−8.2	194	.6
1642	21 015	Boone	246	85 991	607	349.6	57 589	755	45 842	28 402	11 747	49.3	25.6	1 702	2.0
4280	21 017	Bourbon	291	19 360	1 825	66.5	19 236	1 716	19 405	124	−169	.6	−.9	503	2.6
3400	21 019	Boyd	160	49 752	920	311.0	51 096	825	55 513	−1 344	−4 417	−2.6	−8.0	558	1.1
...	21 021	Boyle	182	27 697	1 458	152.2	25 590	1 439	25 066	2 107	524	8.2	2.1	398	1.4
...	21 023	Bracken	203	8 279	2 583	40.8	7 766	2 598	7 738	513	28	6.6	.4	39	.5
...	21 025	Breathitt	495	16 100	2 016	32.5	15 703	1 943	17 004	397	−1 301	2.5	−7.7	106	.7
...	21 027	Breckinridge	572	18 648	1 863	32.6	16 312	1 901	16 861	2 336	−549	14.3	−3.3	134	.7
4520	21 029	Bullitt	299	61 236	796	204.8	47 567	881	43 346	13 669	4 221	28.7	9.7	383	.6
...	21 031	Butler	428	13 010	2 232	30.4	11 245	2 278	11 064	1 765	181	15.7	1.6	135	1.0
...	21 033	Caldwell	347	13 060	2 226	37.6	13 232	2 117	13 473	−172	−241	−1.3	−1.8	80	.6
...	21 035	Calloway	386	34 177	1 276	88.5	30 735	1 254	30 031	3 442	704	11.2	2.3	473	1.4
1642	21 037	Campbell	152	88 616	588	580.0	83 866	540	83 317	4 750	549	5.7	.7	765	.9
...	21 039	Carlisle	192	5 351	2 825	27.9	5 238	2 824	5 487	113	−249	2.2	−4.5	44	.8
...	21 041	Carroll	130	10 155	2 431	78.1	9 292	2 445	9 270	863	22	9.3	.2	330	3.2
3400	21 043	Carter	411	26 889	1 488	65.4	24 340	1 484	25 060	2 549	−720	10.5	−2.9	158	.6
...	21 045	Casey	446	15 447	2 055	34.6	14 211	2 035	14 818	1 236	−607	8.7	−4.1	198	1.3
1660	21 047	Christian	721	72 265	688	100.2	68 941	643	66 878	3 324	2 063	4.8	3.1	3 494	4.8
4280	21 049	Clark	254	33 144	1 313	130.5	29 496	1 316	28 322	3 648	1 174	12.4	4.1	393	1.2
...	21 051	Clay	471	24 556	1 572	52.1	21 746	1 591	22 752	2 810	−1 006	12.9	−4.4	333	1.4
...	21 053	Clinton	197	9 634	2 475	48.9	9 135	2 457	9 321	499	−186	5.5	−2.0	118	1.2
...	21 055	Crittenden	362	9 384	2 498	25.9	9 196	2 454	9 207	188	−11	2.0	−.1	48	.5
...	21 057	Cumberland	306	7 147	2 673	23.4	6 784	2 678	7 289	363	−505	5.4	−6.9	43	.6
5990	21 059	Daviess	462	91 545	560	198.1	87 189	522	85 949	4 356	1 240	5.0	1.4	845	.9
...	21 061	Edmonson	303	11 644	2 322	38.4	10 357	2 353	9 962	1 287	395	12.4	4.0	65	.6
...	21 063	Elliott	234	6 748	2 715	28.8	6 455	2 713	6 908	293	−453	4.5	−6.6	40	.6
...	21 065	Estill	254	15 307	2 070	60.3	14 614	2 012	14 495	693	119	4.7	.8	81	.5
4280	21 067	Fayette	285	260 512	211	914.1	225 366	220	204 165	35 146	21 201	15.6	10.4	8 561	3.3
...	21 069	Fleming	351	13 792	2 173	39.3	12 292	2 197	12 323	1 500	−31	12.2	−.3	103	.7
...	21 071	Floyd	394	42 441	1 047	107.7	43 586	930	48 764	−1 145	−5 178	−2.6	−10.6	260	.6
...	21 073	Franklin	210	47 687	957	227.1	44 143	923	41 830	3 544	2 313	8.0	5.5	531	1.1
...	21 075	Fulton	209	7 752	2 629	37.1	8 271	2 540	8 971	−519	−700	−6.3	−7.8	56	.7
1642	21 077	Gallatin	99	7 870	2 616	79.5	5 393	2 810	4 842	2 477	551	45.9	11.4	82	1.0
...	21 079	Garrard	231	14 792	2 104	64.0	11 579	2 250	10 853	3 213	726	27.7	6.7	195	1.3
1642	21 081	Grant	260	22 384	1 673	86.1	15 737	1 938	13 308	6 647	2 429	42.2	18.3	232	1.0
...	21 083	Graves	556	37 028	1 189	66.6	33 550	1 176	34 049	3 478	−499	10.4	−1.5	888	2.4
...	21 085	Grayson	504	24 053	1 591	47.7	21 050	1 626	20 854	3 003	196	14.3	.9	186	.8
...	21 087	Green	289	11 518	2 333	39.9	10 371	2 350	11 043	1 147	−672	11.1	−6.1	109	.9
3400	21 089	Greenup	346	36 891	1 192	106.6	36 796	1 081	39 132	95	−2 336	.3	−6.0	204	.6
...	21 091	Hancock	189	8 392	2 574	44.4	7 864	2 585	7 742	528	122	6.7	1.6	64	.8
...	21 093	Hardin	628	94 174	545	150.0	89 240	513	88 011	4 934	329	5.5	.4	3 159	3.4
...	21 095	Harlan	467	33 202	1 307	71.1	36 574	1 088	41 889	−3 372	−5 315	−9.2	−12.7	216	.7
...	21 097	Harrison	310	17 983	1 898	58.0	16 248	1 910	15 166	1 735	1 082	10.7	7.1	207	1.2
...	21 099	Hart	416	17 445	1 926	41.9	14 890	1 996	15 402	2 555	−512	17.2	−3.3	150	.9

[1] Federal Information Processing Standards (FIPS) codes for metropolitan areas defined as of June 30, 1999.   [2] FIPS codes for states and counties/county equivalents.   [3] Dry land and land temporarily or partially covered by water.   [4] Based on 3,140 counties/county equivalents; excludes Yellowstone National Park in MT and South Boston independent city in VA which are no longer counties. When counties share the same rank, the next lower rank is omitted.   [5] Includes count resolution corrections through 1997 and adjustments based on Census 2000 dress rehearsal results and boundary changes reported as legally effective as of January 1, 1998.   [6] Persons of Hispanic or Latino origin may be of any race.

Sources: Land Area—U.S. Census Bureau, unpublished data file from Geography Division based on TIGER data base.   2000 Population—U.S. Census Bureau, Census of Population and Housing, Census 2000 Redistricting Data (Public Law 94-171) Summary Files (related Internet site <http://www.census.gov/dmd/www/2kresult.html>).   1990 Population—U.S. Census Bureau, "(CO-99-8) County Population Estimates and Demographic Components of Population Change: Annual Time Series, July 1, 1990 to July 1, 1999 (includes revised April 1, 1990 Population Estimates Base)"; published 9 March 2000; <http://www. census.gov/population/estimates/county/co-99-8/99C8_00.txt>.   1980 Population—U.S. Census Bureau, "1980–1990 Intercensal Population Estimates by County" on diskette (related Internet site <http://www.census.gov/population/www/estimates/countypop.html>).

Table B–1. Counties — **Area and Population**–Con.

[Includes U.S., states, and 3,142 counties/county equivalents defined as of January 1, 1992. For changes to these areas since January 1, 1992, see appendix B. Geographic Information]

Metropolitan area code[1]	State and county code[2]	County	Land area,[3] 2000 (sq. miles)	Population (April 1) 2000 Number	Rank[4]	Per square mile	1990[5] Number	Rank[4]	1980	Net change 1990–2000	1980–1990	Percent change 1990–2000	1980–1990	Hispanic or Latino,[6] 2000 Number	Percent
		KENTUCKY—Con.													
2440	21 101	Henderson	440	44 829	1 003	101.9	43 044	937	40 849	1 785	2 195	4.1	5.4	433	1.0
...	21 103	Henry	289	15 060	2 087	52.1	12 823	2 153	12 740	2 237	83	17.4	.7	339	2.3
...	21 105	Hickman	244	5 262	2 834	21.6	5 566	2 794	6 065	-304	-499	-5.5	-8.2	54	1.0
...	21 107	Hopkins	551	46 519	972	84.4	46 126	900	46 174	393	-48	.9	-.1	423	.9
...	21 109	Jackson	346	13 495	2 194	39.0	11 955	2 222	11 996	1 540	-41	12.9	-.3	72	.5
4520	21 111	Jefferson	385	693 604	73	1 801.6	665 123	69	684 638	28 481	-19 515	4.3	-2.9	12 370	1.8
4280	21 113	Jessamine	173	39 041	1 137	225.7	30 508	1 268	26 065	8 533	4 443	28.0	17.0	512	1.3
...	21 115	Johnson	262	23 445	1 620	89.5	23 248	1 528	24 432	197	-1 184	.8	-4.8	143	.6
1642	21 117	Kenton	162	151 464	354	935.0	142 005	335	137 058	9 459	4 947	6.7	3.6	1 669	1.1
...	21 119	Knott	352	17 649	1 919	50.1	17 906	1 793	17 940	-257	-34	-1.4	-.2	112	.6
...	21 121	Knox	388	31 795	1 350	81.9	29 676	1 309	30 239	2 119	-563	7.1	-1.9	180	.6
...	21 123	Larue	263	13 373	2 199	50.8	11 679	2 239	11 922	1 694	-243	14.5	-2.0	140	1.0
...	21 125	Laurel	436	52 715	884	120.9	43 438	932	38 982	9 277	4 456	21.4	11.4	291	.6
...	21 127	Lawrence	419	15 569	2 049	37.2	13 998	2 057	14 121	1 571	-123	11.2	-.9	64	.4
...	21 129	Lee	210	7 916	2 613	37.7	7 422	2 622	7 754	494	-332	6.7	-4.3	29	.4
...	21 131	Leslie	404	12 401	2 272	30.7	13 642	2 087	14 882	-1 241	-1 240	-9.1	-8.3	77	.6
...	21 133	Letcher	339	25 277	1 554	74.6	27 000	1 389	30 687	-1 723	-3 687	-6.4	-12.0	110	.4
...	21 135	Lewis	484	14 092	2 154	29.1	13 029	2 139	14 545	1 063	-1 516	8.2	-10.4	62	.4
...	21 137	Lincoln	336	23 361	1 625	69.5	20 096	1 671	19 053	3 265	1 043	16.2	5.5	208	.9
...	21 139	Livingston	316	9 804	2 464	31.0	9 062	2 465	9 219	742	-157	8.2	-1.7	74	.8
...	21 141	Logan	556	26 573	1 495	47.8	24 416	1 481	24 138	2 157	278	8.8	1.2	288	1.1
...	21 143	Lyon	216	8 080	2 599	37.4	6 624	2 693	6 490	1 456	134	22.0	2.1	59	.7
...	21 145	McCracken	251	65 514	746	261.0	62 879	693	61 310	2 635	1 569	4.2	2.6	694	1.1
...	21 147	McCreary	428	17 080	1 949	39.9	15 603	1 946	15 634	1 477	-31	9.5	-.2	106	.6
...	21 149	McLean	254	9 938	2 452	39.1	9 628	2 422	10 090	310	-462	3.2	-4.6	83	.8
4280	21 151	Madison	441	70 872	700	160.7	57 508	757	53 352	13 364	4 156	23.2	7.8	685	1.0
...	21 153	Magoffin	309	13 332	2 201	43.1	13 077	2 133	13 515	255	-438	1.9	-3.2	56	.4
...	21 155	Marion	346	18 212	1 885	52.6	16 499	1 892	17 910	1 713	-1 411	10.4	-7.9	144	.8
...	21 157	Marshall	305	30 125	1 393	98.8	27 205	1 383	25 637	2 920	1 568	10.7	6.1	229	.8
...	21 159	Martin	231	12 578	2 259	54.5	12 526	2 180	13 925	52	-1 399	.4	-10.0	78	.6
...	21 161	Mason	241	16 800	1 969	69.7	16 666	1 871	17 760	134	-1 094	.8	-6.2	160	1.0
...	21 163	Meade	309	26 349	1 506	85.3	24 170	1 488	22 854	2 179	1 316	9.0	5.8	567	2.2
...	21 165	Menifee	204	6 556	2 732	32.1	5 092	2 832	5 117	1 464	-25	28.8	-.5	73	1.1
...	21 167	Mercer	251	20 817	1 746	82.9	19 148	1 725	19 011	1 669	137	8.7	.7	265	1.3
...	21 169	Metcalfe	291	10 037	2 441	34.5	8 963	2 474	9 484	1 074	-521	12.0	-5.5	53	.5
...	21 171	Monroe	331	11 756	2 313	35.5	11 401	2 261	12 353	355	-952	3.1	-7.7	170	1.4
...	21 173	Montgomery	199	22 554	1 667	113.3	19 561	1 695	20 046	2 993	-485	15.3	-2.4	259	1.1
...	21 175	Morgan	381	13 948	2 165	36.6	11 648	2 241	12 103	2 300	-455	19.7	-3.8	85	.6
...	21 177	Muhlenberg	475	31 839	1 349	67.0	31 318	1 235	32 238	521	-920	1.7	-2.9	232	.7
...	21 179	Nelson	423	37 477	1 178	88.6	29 710	1 308	27 584	7 767	2 126	26.1	7.7	395	1.1
...	21 181	Nicholas	197	6 813	2 710	34.6	6 725	2 685	7 157	88	-432	1.3	-6.0	37	.5
...	21 183	Ohio	594	22 916	1 647	38.6	21 105	1 625	21 765	1 811	-660	8.6	-3.0	231	1.0
4520	21 185	Oldham	189	46 178	978	244.3	33 263	1 185	27 795	12 915	5 468	38.8	19.7	602	1.3
...	21 187	Owen	352	10 547	2 394	30.0	9 035	2 466	8 924	1 512	111	16.7	1.2	105	1.0
...	21 189	Owsley	198	4 858	2 857	24.5	5 036	2 840	5 709	-178	-673	-3.5	-11.8	35	.7
1642	21 191	Pendleton	281	14 390	2 133	51.2	12 062	2 213	10 989	2 328	1 073	19.3	9.8	97	.7
...	21 193	Perry	342	29 390	1 417	85.9	30 283	1 280	33 763	-893	-3 480	-2.9	-10.3	154	.5
...	21 195	Pike	788	68 736	716	87.2	72 584	616	81 123	-3 848	-8 539	-5.3	-10.5	450	.7
...	21 197	Powell	180	13 237	2 210	73.5	11 686	2 236	11 101	1 551	585	13.3	5.3	88	.7
...	21 199	Pulaski	662	56 217	841	84.9	49 489	849	45 803	6 728	3 686	13.6	8.0	454	.8
...	21 201	Robertson	100	2 266	3 044	22.7	2 124	3 060	2 270	142	-146	6.7	-6.4	21	.9
...	21 203	Rockcastle	318	16 582	1 984	52.1	14 803	2 000	13 973	1 779	830	12.0	5.9	102	.6
...	21 205	Rowan	281	22 094	1 688	78.6	20 353	1 658	19 049	1 741	1 304	8.6	6.8	235	1.1
4280	21 207	Russell	254	16 315	2 002	64.2	14 716	2 005	13 708	1 599	1 008	10.9	7.4	140	.9
...	21 209	Scott	285	33 061	1 317	116.0	23 867	1 496	21 813	9 194	2 054	38.5	9.4	531	1.6
...	21 211	Shelby	384	33 337	1 304	86.8	24 824	1 467	23 328	8 513	1 496	34.3	6.4	1 505	4.5
...	21 213	Simpson	236	16 405	1 997	69.5	15 145	1 976	14 673	1 260	472	8.3	3.2	150	.9
...	21 215	Spencer	186	11 766	2 311	63.3	6 801	2 675	5 929	4 965	872	73.0	14.7	132	1.1
...	21 217	Taylor	270	22 927	1 646	84.9	21 146	1 622	21 178	1 781	-32	8.4	-.2	189	.8
...	21 219	Todd	376	11 971	2 296	31.8	10 940	2 298	11 874	1 031	-934	9.4	-7.9	199	1.7
...	21 221	Trigg	443	12 597	2 256	28.4	10 361	2 352	9 384	2 236	977	21.6	10.4	113	.9
...	21 223	Trimble	149	8 125	2 596	54.5	6 090	2 745	6 253	2 035	-163	33.4	-2.6	111	1.4
...	21 225	Union	345	15 637	2 046	45.3	16 557	1 884	17 821	-920	-1 264	-5.6	-7.1	244	1.6
...	21 227	Warren	545	92 522	551	169.8	77 720	583	71 828	14 802	5 892	19.0	8.2	2 466	2.7
...	21 229	Washington	301	10 916	2 373	36.3	10 441	2 344	10 764	475	-323	4.5	-3.0	175	1.6
...	21 231	Wayne	459	19 923	1 796	43.4	17 468	1 823	17 022	2 455	446	14.1	2.6	291	1.5
...	21 233	Webster	335	14 120	2 152	42.1	13 955	2 060	14 832	165	-877	1.2	-5.9	268	1.9
...	21 235	Whitley	440	35 865	1 224	81.5	33 326	1 182	33 396	2 539	-70	7.6	-.2	249	.7
...	21 237	Wolfe	223	7 065	2 679	31.7	6 503	2 710	6 698	562	-195	8.6	-2.9	36	.5
4280	21 239	Woodford	191	23 208	1 632	121.5	19 955	1 680	17 778	3 253	2 177	16.3	12.2	695	3.0

[1] Federal Information Processing Standards (FIPS) codes for metropolitan areas defined as of June 30, 1999.   [2] FIPS codes for states and counties/county equivalents.   [3] Dry land and land temporarily or partially covered by water.   [4] Based on 3,140 counties/county equivalents; excludes Yellowstone National Park in MT and South Boston independent city in VA which are no longer counties. When counties share the same rank, the next lower rank is omitted.   [5] Includes count resolution corrections through 1997 and adjustments based on Census 2000 dress rehearsal results and boundary changes reported as legally effective as of January 1, 1998.   [6] Persons of Hispanic or Latino origin may be of any race.

Sources: Land Area—U.S. Census Bureau, unpublished data file from Geography Division based on TIGER data base.   2000 Population—U.S. Census Bureau, Census of Population and Housing, Census 2000 Redistricting Data (Public Law 94-171) Summary Files (related Internet site <http://www.census.gov/dmd/www/2kresult.html>).   1990 Population—U.S. Census Bureau, "(CO-99-8) County Population Estimates and Demographic Components of Population Change: Annual Time Series, July 1, 1990 to July 1, 1999 (includes revised April 1, 1990 Population Estimates Base)"; published 9 March 2000; <http://www. census.gov/population/estimates/county/co-99-8/99C8_00.txt>.   1980 Population—U.S. Census Bureau, "1980–1990 Intercensal Population Estimates by County" on diskette (related Internet site <http://www.census.gov/population/www/estimates/countypop.html>).

Table B–1. Counties — **Area and Population**–Con.

[Includes U.S., states, and 3,142 counties/county equivalents defined as of January 1, 1992. For changes to these areas since January 1, 1992, see appendix B. Geographic Information]

Metropolitan area code[1]	State and county code[2]	County	Land area,[3] 2000 (sq. miles)	Population (April 1) 2000 Number	2000 Rank[4]	2000 Per square mile	1990[5] Number	1990[5] Rank[4]	1980	Net change 1990–2000	Net change 1980–1990	Percent change 1990–2000	Percent change 1980–1990	Hispanic or Latino,[6] 2000 Number	Hispanic or Latino,[6] 2000 Percent
	22 000	LOUISIANA	43 562	4 468 976	X	102.6	4 221 826	X	4 206 116	247 150	15 710	5.9	.4	107 738	2.4
3880	22 001	Acadia..................	655	58 861	813	89.9	55 882	775	56 427	2 979	–545	5.3	–1.0	538	.9
	22 003	Allen	765	25 440	1 544	33.3	21 226	1 619	21 408	4 214	–182	19.9	–.9	1 146	4.5
0760	22 005	Ascension	292	76 627	656	262.4	58 214	745	50 068	18 413	8 146	31.6	16.3	1 883	2.5
...	22 007	Assumption	339	23 388	1 624	69.0	22 753	1 545	22 084	635	669	2.8	3.0	284	1.2
...	22 009	Avoyelles	832	41 481	1 067	49.9	39 159	1 020	41 393	2 322	–2 234	5.9	–5.4	404	1.0
...	22 011	Beauregard	1 160	32 986	1 320	28.4	30 083	1 293	29 692	2 903	391	9.6	1.3	468	1.4
...	22 013	Bienville	811	15 752	2 036	19.4	16 232	1 912	16 387	–480	–155	–3.0	–.9	149	.9
7680	22 015	Bossier	839	98 310	530	117.2	86 088	531	80 721	12 222	5 367	14.2	6.6	3 063	3.1
7680	22 017	Caddo	882	252 161	224	285.9	248 253	201	252 437	3 908	–4 184	1.6	–1.7	3 750	1.5
3960	22 019	Calcasieu	1 071	183 577	297	171.4	168 134	285	167 223	15 443	911	9.2	.5	2 463	1.3
...	22 021	Caldwell	529	10 560	2 393	20.0	9 806	2 403	10 761	754	–955	7.7	–8.9	157	1.5
...	22 023	Cameron	1 313	9 991	2 446	7.6	9 260	2 448	9 336	731	–76	7.9	–.8	215	2.2
...	22 025	Catahoula	704	10 920	2 372	15.5	11 065	2 286	12 287	–145	–1 222	–1.3	–9.9	101	.9
...	22 027	Claiborne	755	16 851	1 964	22.3	17 405	1 828	17 095	–554	310	–3.2	1.8	128	.8
...	22 029	Concordia	696	20 247	1 777	29.1	20 828	1 639	22 981	–581	–2 153	–2.8	–9.4	300	1.5
...	22 031	De Soto	877	25 494	1 540	29.1	25 668	1 436	25 727	–174	–59	–.7	–.2	396	1.6
0760	22 033	East Baton Rouge........	455	412 852	145	907.4	380 105	132	366 191	32 747	13 914	8.6	3.8	7 363	1.8
...	22 035	East Carroll	421	9 421	2 493	22.4	9 709	2 411	11 772	–288	–2 063	–3.0	–17.5	112	1.2
...	22 037	East Feliciana	453	21 360	1 720	47.2	19 211	1 720	19 015	2 149	196	11.2	1.0	157	.7
...	22 039	Evangeline	664	35 434	1 237	53.4	33 274	1 184	33 343	2 160	–69	6.5	–.2	368	1.0
...	22 041	Franklin	624	21 263	1 722	34.1	22 387	1 560	24 141	–1 124	–1 754	–5.0	–7.3	160	.8
...	22 043	Grant	645	18 698	1 861	29.0	17 526	1 818	16 703	1 172	823	6.7	4.9	213	1.1
...	22 045	Iberia	575	73 266	684	127.4	68 297	647	63 752	4 969	4 545	7.3	7.1	1 101	1.5
...	22 047	Iberville	619	33 320	1 305	53.8	31 049	1 244	32 159	2 271	–1 110	7.3	–3.5	343	1.0
...	22 049	Jackson.................	570	15 397	2 059	27.0	15 859	1 932	17 321	–462	–1 462	–2.9	–8.4	94	.6
5560	22 051	Jefferson...............	307	455 466	128	1 483.6	448 306	110	454 592	7 160	–6 286	1.6	–1.4	32 418	7.1
...	22 053	Jefferson Davis	652	31 435	1 362	48.2	30 722	1 257	32 168	713	–1 446	2.3	–4.5	312	1.0
3880	22 055	Lafayette...............	270	190 503	288	705.6	164 762	290	150 017	25 741	14 745	15.6	9.8	3 320	1.7
3350	22 057	Lafourche	1 085	89 974	574	82.9	85 860	535	82 483	4 114	3 377	4.8	4.1	1 284	1.4
...	22 059	La Salle................	624	14 282	2 142	22.9	13 662	2 084	17 004	620	–3 342	4.5	–19.7	117	.8
...	22 061	Lincoln.................	471	42 509	1 046	90.3	41 745	963	39 763	764	1 982	1.8	5.0	492	1.2
0760	22 063	Livingston..............	648	91 814	558	141.7	70 523	629	58 806	21 291	11 717	30.2	19.9	1 017	1.1
...	22 065	Madison	624	13 728	2 179	22.0	12 463	2 184	15 682	1 265	–3 219	10.2	–20.5	288	2.1
...	22 067	Morehouse	794	31 021	1 377	39.1	31 938	1 214	34 803	–917	–2 865	–2.9	–8.2	230	.7
...	22 009	Natchitoches	1 255	39 080	1 135	31.1	37 254	1 065	39 863	1 826	–2 609	4.9	–6.5	566	1.4
5560	22 071	Orleans.................	181	484 674	117	2 677.8	496 938	98	557 927	–12 264	–60 989	–2.5	–10.9	14 826	3.1
5200	22 073	Ouachita................	611	147 250	368	241.0	142 191	334	139 241	5 059	2 950	3.6	2.1	1 747	1.2
5560	22 075	Plaquemines	845	26 757	1 492	31.7	25 575	1 440	26 049	1 182	–474	4.6	–1.8	433	1.6
...	22 077	Pointe Coupee...........	557	22 763	1 658	40.9	22 540	1 553	24 045	223	–1 505	1.0	–6.3	245	1.1
0220	22 079	Rapides.................	1 323	126 337	430	95.5	131 556	352	135 282	–5 219	–3 726	–4.0	–2.8	1 739	1.4
...	22 081	Red River	389	9 622	2 477	24.7	9 526	2 429	10 433	96	–907	1.0	–8.7	97	1.0
...	22 083	Richland	558	20 981	1 737	37.6	20 629	1 648	22 187	352	–1 558	1.7	–7.0	227	1.1
...	22 085	Sabine	865	23 459	1 617	27.1	22 646	1 551	25 280	813	–2 634	3.6	–10.4	642	2.7
5560	22 087	St. Bernard.............	465	67 229	728	144.6	66 631	660	64 097	598	2 534	.9	4.0	3 425	5.1
5560	22 089	St. Charles	284	48 072	951	169.3	42 437	948	37 259	5 635	5 178	13.3	13.9	1 346	2.8
...	22 091	St. Helena	408	10 525	2 395	25.8	9 874	2 399	9 827	651	47	6.6	.5	104	1.0
5560	22 093	St. James	246	21 216	1 724	86.2	20 879	1 635	21 495	337	–616	1.6	–2.9	130	.6
5560	22 095	St. John the Baptist ...	219	43 044	1 036	196.5	39 996	998	31 924	3 048	8 072	7.6	25.3	1 230	2.9
3880	22 097	St. Landry..............	929	87 700	597	94.4	80 312	570	84 128	7 388	–3 816	9.2	–4.5	794	.9
3880	22 099	St. Martin..............	740	48 583	938	65.7	44 097	924	40 214	4 486	3 883	10.2	9.7	405	.8
...	22 101	St. Mary................	613	53 500	875	87.3	58 086	747	64 253	–4 586	–6 167	–7.9	–9.6	1 152	2.2
5560	22 103	St. Tammany.............	854	191 268	287	224.0	144 500	328	110 869	46 768	33 631	32.4	30.3	4 737	2.5
...	22 105	Tangipahoa..............	790	100 588	521	127.3	85 709	536	80 698	14 879	5 011	17.4	6.2	1 536	1.5
...	22 107	Tensas	602	6 618	2 725	11.0	7 103	2 645	8 525	–485	–1 422	–6.8	–16.7	83	1.3
3350	22 109	Terrebonne..............	1 255	104 503	506	83.3	96 982	474	94 393	7 521	2 589	7.8	2.7	1 631	1.6
...	22 111	Union	878	22 803	1 654	26.0	20 796	1 640	21 167	2 007	–371	9.7	–1.8	461	2.0
...	22 113	Vermilion	1 174	53 807	870	45.8	50 055	841	48 458	3 752	1 597	7.5	3.3	742	1.4
...	22 115	Vernon	1 328	52 531	888	39.6	61 961	704	53 475	–9 430	8 486	–15.2	15.9	3 111	5.9
...	22 117	Washington	670	43 926	1 019	65.6	43 185	935	44 207	741	–1 022	1.7	–2.3	334	.8
7680	22 119	Webster	595	41 831	1 058	70.3	41 989	956	43 631	–158	–1 642	–.4	–3.8	378	.9
0760	22 121	West Baton Rouge	191	21 601	1 714	113.1	19 419	1 709	19 086	2 182	333	11.2	1.7	313	1.4
...	22 123	West Carroll	359	12 314	2 278	34.3	12 093	2 209	12 922	221	–829	1.8	–6.4	166	1.3
...	22 125	West Feliciana	406	15 111	2 083	37.2	12 915	2 145	12 186	2 196	729	17.0	6.0	157	1.0
...	22 127	Winn	950	16 894	1 961	17.8	16 498	1 893	17 253	396	–755	2.4	–4.4	147	.9

[1] Federal Information Processing Standards (FIPS) codes for metropolitan areas defined as of June 30, 1999.   [2] FIPS codes for states and counties/county equivalents.   [3] Dry land and land temporarily or partially covered by water.   [4] Based on 3,140 counties/county equivalents; excludes Yellowstone National Park in MT and South Boston independent city in VA which are no longer counties. When counties share the same rank, the next lower rank is omitted.   [5] Includes count resolution corrections through 1997 and adjustments based on Census 2000 dress rehearsal results and boundary changes reported as legally effective as of January 1, 1998.   [6] Persons of Hispanic or Latino origin may be of any race.

Sources: Land Area—U.S. Census Bureau, unpublished data file from Geography Division based on TIGER data base.   2000 Population—U.S. Census Bureau, Census of Population and Housing, Census 2000 Redistricting Data (Public Law 94-171) Summary Files (related Internet site <http://www.census.gov/dmd/www/2kresult.html>).   1990 Population—U.S. Census Bureau, "(CO-99-8) County Population Estimates and Demographic Components of Population Change: Annual Time Series, July 1, 1990 to July 1, 1999 (includes revised April 1, 1990 Population Estimates Base)"; published 9 March 2000; <http://www.census.gov/population/estimates/county/co-99-8/99C8_00.txt>.   1980 Population—U.S. Census Bureau, "1980–1990 Intercensal Population Estimates by County" on diskette (related Internet site <http://www.census.gov/population/www/estimates/countypop.html>).

[Includes U.S., states, and 3,142 counties/county equivalents defined as of January 1, 1992. For changes to these areas since January 1, 1992, see appendix B. Geographic Information]

Metropolitan area code[1]	State and county code[2]	County	Land area,[3] 2000 (sq. miles)	Population (April 1) 2000 Number	Rank[4]	Per square mile	1990[5] Number	Rank[4]	1980	Net change 1990–2000	1980–1990	Percent change 1990–2000	1980–1990	Hispanic or Latino,[6] 2000 Number	Percent
	23 000	MAINE...............	30 862	1 274 923	X	41.3	1 227 928	X	1 125 043	46 995	102 885	3.8	9.1	9 360	.7
4243	23 001	Androscoggin............	470	103 793	512	220.8	105 259	438	99 509	−1 466	5 750	−1.4	5.8	988	1.0
...	23 003	Aroostook..............	6 672	73 938	676	11.1	86 936	525	91 344	−12 998	−4 408	−15.0	−4.8	441	.6
6403	23 005	Cumberland............	836	265 612	207	317.7	243 135	206	215 789	22 477	27 346	9.2	12.7	2 526	1.0
...	23 007	Franklin..............	1 698	29 467	1 415	17.4	29 008	1 329	27 447	459	1 561	1.6	5.7	159	.5
...	23 009	Hancock...............	1 588	51 791	895	32.6	46 948	891	41 781	4 843	5 167	10.3	12.4	336	.6
...	23 011	Kennebec..............	868	117 114	462	134.9	115 904	397	109 889	1 210	6 015	1.0	5.5	852	.7
...	23 013	Knox	366	39 618	1 123	108.2	36 310	1 095	32 941	3 308	3 369	9.1	10.2	225	.6
...	23 015	Lincoln...............	456	33 616	1 296	73.7	30 357	1 276	25 691	3 259	4 666	10.7	18.2	155	.5
...	23 017	Oxford................	2 078	54 755	860	26.3	52 602	806	49 043	2 153	3 559	4.1	7.3	292	.5
0733	23 019	Penobscot.............	3 396	144 919	377	42.7	146 601	321	137 015	−1 682	9 586	−1.1	7.0	882	.6
...	23 021	Piscataquis............	3 966	17 235	1 939	4.3	18 653	1 755	17 634	−1 418	1 019	−7.6	5.8	89	.5
...	23 023	Sagadahoc.............	254	35 214	1 241	138.6	33 535	1 177	28 795	1 679	4 740	5.0	16.5	391	1.1
...	23 025	Somerset	3 927	50 888	911	13.0	49 767	844	45 049	1 121	4 718	2.3	10.5	234	.5
...	23 027	Waldo	730	36 280	1 206	49.7	33 018	1 190	28 414	3 262	4 604	9.9	16.2	215	.6
...	23 029	Washington	2 568	33 941	1 282	13.2	35 308	1 121	34 963	−1 367	345	−3.9	1.0	274	.8
...	23 031	York..................	991	186 742	294	188.4	164 587	291	139 739	22 155	24 848	13.5	17.8	1 301	.7
	24 000	MARYLAND............	9 774	5 296 486	X	541.9	4 780 753	X	4 216 933	515 733	563 820	10.8	13.4	227 916	4.3
1900	24 001	Allegany	425	74 930	666	176.3	74 946	600	80 548	−16	−5 602	Z	−7.0	571	.8
8872	24 003	Anne Arundel..........	416	489 656	114	1 177.1	427 239	117	370 775	62 417	56 464	14.6	15.2	12 902	2.6
8872	24 005	Baltimore.............	599	754 292	63	1 259.3	692 134	60	655 615	62 158	36 519	9.0	5.6	13 774	1.8
8872	24 009	Calvert...............	215	74 563	671	346.8	51 372	822	34 638	23 191	16 734	45.1	48.3	1 135	1.5
...	24 011	Caroline	320	29 772	1 404	93.0	27 035	1 388	23 143	2 737	3 892	10.1	16.8	789	2.7
8872	24 013	Carroll...............	449	150 897	356	336.1	123 372	373	96 356	27 525	27 016	22.3	28.0	1 489	1.0
6162	24 015	Cecil	348	85 951	608	247.0	71 347	621	60 430	14 604	10 917	20.5	18.1	1 306	1.5
8872	24 017	Charles	461	120 546	451	261.5	101 154	453	72 751	19 392	28 403	19.2	39.0	2 722	2.3
...	24 019	Dorchester	558	30 674	1 382	55.0	30 236	1 283	30 623	438	−387	1.4	−1.3	385	1.3
8872	24 021	Frederick.............	663	195 277	283	294.5	150 208	311	114 792	45 069	35 416	30.0	30.9	4 664	2.4
...	24 023	Garrett...............	648	29 846	1 401	46.1	28 138	1 347	26 490	1 708	1 648	6.1	6.2	131	.4
8872	24 025	Harford...............	440	218 590	258	496.8	182 132	265	145 930	36 458	36 202	20.0	24.8	4 169	1.9
8872	24 027	Howard	252	247 842	234	983.5	187 328	258	118 572	60 514	68 756	32.3	58.0	7 490	3.0
...	24 029	Kent	279	19 197	1 833	68.8	17 842	1 796	16 695	1 355	1 147	7.6	6.9	546	2.8
8872	24 031	Montgomery...........	496	873 341	49	1 760.8	762 875	51	579 053	110 466	183 822	14.5	31.7	100 604	11.5
8872	24 033	Prince George's........	485	801 515	57	1 652.6	722 705	56	665 071	78 810	57 634	10.9	8.7	57 057	7.1
8872	24 035	Queen Anne's	372	40 563	1 099	109.0	33 953	1 164	25 508	6 610	8 445	19.5	33.1	444	1.1
...	24 037	St. Mary's	361	86 211	604	238.8	75 974	592	59 895	10 237	16 079	13.5	26.8	1 720	2.0
...	24 039	Somerset	327	24 747	1 566	75.7	23 440	1 518	19 188	1 307	4 252	5.6	22.2	334	1.3
...	24 041	Talbot	269	33 812	1 287	125.7	30 549	1 264	25 604	3 263	4 945	10.7	19.3	615	1.8
8872	24 043	Washington	458	131 923	404	288.0	121 393	379	113 086	10 530	8 307	8.7	7.3	1 570	1.2
...	24 045	Wicomico	377	84 644	615	224.5	74 339	605	64 540	10 305	9 799	13.9	15.2	1 842	2.2
...	24 047	Worcester	473	46 543	970	98.4	35 028	1 132	30 889	11 515	4 139	32.9	13.4	596	1.3
		Independent City													
8872	24 510	Baltimore city	81	651 154	82	8 038.9	736 014	53	786 741	−84 860	−50 727	−11.5	−6.4	11 061	1.7
	25 000	MASSACHUSETTS	7 840	6 349 097	X	809.8	6 016 425	X	5 737 093	332 672	279 332	5.5	4.9	428 729	6.8
0743	25 001	Barnstable	396	222 230	256	561.2	186 605	259	147 925	35 625	38 680	19.1	26.1	3 000	1.3
6323	25 003	Berkshire	931	134 953	399	145.0	139 352	342	145 110	−4 399	−5 758	−3.2	−4.0	2 286	1.7
1123	25 005	Bristol	556	534 678	104	961.7	506 325	94	474 641	28 353	31 684	5.6	6.7	19 242	3.6
...	25 007	Dukes	104	14 987	2 091	144.1	11 639	2 243	8 942	3 348	2 697	28.8	30.2	155	1.0
1123	25 009	Essex	501	723 419	69	1 444.0	670 080	65	633 688	53 339	36 392	8.0	5.7	79 871	11.0
...	25 011	Franklin..............	702	71 535	691	101.9	70 086	632	64 317	1 449	5 769	2.1	9.0	1 425	2.0
8003	25 013	Hampden	618	456 228	127	738.2	456 310	109	443 018	−82	13 292	Z	3.0	69 197	15.2
8003	25 015	Hampshire	529	152 251	352	287.8	146 568	322	138 813	5 683	7 755	3.9	5.6	5 212	3.4
1123	25 017	Middlesex	823	1 465 396	19	1 780.6	1 398 468	18	1 367 034	66 928	31 434	4.8	2.3	66 707	4.6
...	25 019	Nantucket	48	9 520	2 488	198.3	6 012	2 755	5 087	3 508	925	58.3	18.2	212	2.2
1123	25 021	Norfolk...............	400	650 308	83	1 625.8	616 087	75	606 587	34 221	9 500	5.6	1.6	11 990	1.8
1123	25 023	Plymouth..............	661	472 822	121	715.3	435 276	114	405 437	37 546	29 839	8.6	7.4	11 537	2.4
1123	25 025	Suffolk...............	59	689 807	74	11 691.6	663 906	70	650 142	25 901	13 764	3.9	2.1	107 031	15.5
1123	25 027	Worcester	1 513	750 963	65	496.3	709 711	59	646 352	41 252	63 359	5.8	9.8	50 864	6.8

[1] Federal Information Processing Standards (FIPS) codes for metropolitan areas defined as of June 30, 1999. [2] FIPS codes for states and counties/county equivalents. [3] Dry land and land temporarily or partially covered by water. [4] Based on 3,140 counties/county equivalents; excludes Yellowstone National Park in MT and South Boston independent city in VA which are no longer counties. When counties share the same rank, the next lower rank is omitted. [5] Includes count resolution corrections through 1997 and adjustments based on Census 2000 dress rehearsal results and boundary changes reported as legally effective as of January 1, 1998. [6] Persons of Hispanic or Latino origin may be of any race.

Sources: Land Area—U.S. Census Bureau, unpublished data file from Geography Division based on TIGER data base. 2000 Population—U.S. Census Bureau, Census of Population and Housing, Census 2000 Redistricting Data (Public Law 94-171) Summary Files (related Internet site <http://www.census.gov/dmd/www/2kresult.html>). 1990 Population—U.S. Census Bureau, "(CO-99-8) County Population Estimates and Demographic Components of Population Change: Annual Time Series, July 1, 1990 to July 1, 1999 (includes revised April 1, 1990 Population Estimates Base)"; published 9 March 2000; <http://www. census.gov/population/estimates/county/co-99-8/99C8_00.txt>. 1980 Population—U.S. Census Bureau, "1980–1990 Intercensal Population Estimates by County" on diskette (related Internet site <http://www.census.gov/population/www/estimates/countypop.html>).

[Includes U.S., states, and 3,142 counties/county equivalents defined as of January 1, 1992. For changes to these areas since January 1, 1992, see appendix B. Geographic Information]

Metro-politan area code[1]	State and county code[2]	County	Land area,[3] 2000 (sq. miles)	Population (April 1)										Hispanic or Latino,[6] 2000	
				2000			1990[5]			Net change		Percent change			
				Number	Rank[4]	Per square mile	Number	Rank[4]	1980	1990–2000	1980–1990	1990–2000	1980–1990	Number	Percent
	26 000	MICHIGAN	56 804	9 938 444	X	175.0	9 295 287	X	9 262 044	643 157	33 243	6.9	.4	323 877	3.3
...	26 001	Alcona	674	11 719	2 317	17.4	10 145	2 374	9 740	1 574	405	15.5	4.2	81	.7
...	26 003	Alger	918	9 862	2 460	10.7	8 972	2 472	9 225	890	−253	9.9	−2.7	99	1.0
3000	26 005	Allegan	827	105 665	503	127.8	90 509	505	81 555	15 156	8 954	16.7	11.0	6 040	5.7
...	26 007	Alpena	574	31 314	1 366	54.6	30 605	1 261	32 315	709	−1 710	2.3	−5.3	181	.6
...	26 009	Antrim	477	23 110	1 637	48.4	18 185	1 779	16 194	4 925	1 991	27.1	12.3	284	1.2
...	26 011	Arenac	367	17 269	1 934	47.1	14 906	1 994	14 706	2 363	200	15.9	1.4	238	1.4
...	26 013	Baraga	904	8 746	2 550	9.7	7 954	2 577	8 484	792	−530	10.0	−6.2	81	.9
...	26 015	Barry	556	56 755	834	102.1	50 057	840	45 781	6 698	4 276	13.4	9.3	831	1.5
6960	26 017	Bay	444	110 157	492	248.1	111 723	411	119 881	−1 566	−8 158	−1.4	−6.8	4 308	3.9
...	26 019	Benzie	321	15 998	2 024	49.8	12 200	2 201	11 205	3 798	995	31.1	8.9	233	1.5
0870	26 021	Berrien	571	162 453	330	284.5	161 378	294	171 276	1 075	−9 898	.7	−5.8	4 888	3.0
...	26 023	Branch	507	45 787	987	90.3	41 502	970	40 188	4 285	1 314	10.3	3.3	1 365	3.0
3720	26 025	Calhoun	709	137 985	394	194.6	135 982	345	141 579	2 003	−5 597	1.5	−4.0	4 351	3.2
...	26 027	Cass	492	51 104	905	103.9	49 477	850	49 499	1 627	−22	3.3	Z	1 233	2.4
...	26 029	Charlevoix	417	26 090	1 512	62.6	21 468	1 605	19 907	4 622	1 561	21.5	7.8	272	1.0
...	26 031	Cheboygan	716	26 448	1 504	36.9	21 398	1 611	20 649	5 050	749	23.6	3.6	202	.8
...	26 033	Chippewa	1 561	38 543	1 149	24.7	34 604	1 148	29 029	3 939	5 575	11.4	19.2	599	1.6
...	26 035	Clare	567	31 252	1 368	55.1	24 952	1 464	23 822	6 300	1 130	25.2	4.7	340	1.1
4040	26 037	Clinton	571	64 753	750	113.4	57 893	749	55 893	6 860	2 000	11.8	3.6	1 688	2.6
...	26 039	Crawford	558	14 273	2 143	25.6	12 260	2 199	9 465	2 013	2 795	16.4	29.5	142	1.0
...	26 041	Delta	1 170	38 520	1 150	32.9	37 780	1 053	38 947	740	−1 167	2.0	−3.0	187	.5
4040	26 043	Dickinson	766	27 472	1 468	35.9	26 831	1 395	25 341	641	1 490	2.4	5.9	187	.7
...	26 045	Eaton	576	103 655	513	180.0	92 879	499	88 337	10 776	4 542	11.6	5.1	3 323	3.2
2162	26 047	Emmet	468	31 437	1 361	67.2	25 040	1 461	22 992	6 397	2 048	25.5	8.9	285	.9
...	26 049	Genesee	640	436 141	137	681.5	430 459	116	450 449	5 682	−19 990	1.3	−4.4	10 152	2.3
...	26 051	Gladwin	507	26 023	1 516	51.3	21 896	1 583	19 957	4 127	1 939	18.8	9.7	249	1.0
...	26 053	Gogebic	1 102	17 370	1 931	15.8	18 052	1 788	19 686	−682	−1 634	−3.8	−8.3	153	.9
...	26 055	Grand Traverse	465	77 654	653	167.0	64 273	682	54 899	13 381	9 374	20.8	17.1	1 155	1.5
...	26 057	Gratiot	570	42 285	1 050	74.2	38 982	1 022	40 448	3 303	−1 466	8.5	−3.6	1 875	4.4
...	26 059	Hillsdale	599	46 527	971	77.7	43 431	933	42 071	3 096	1 360	7.1	3.2	558	1.2
...	26 061	Houghton	1 012	36 016	1 217	35.6	35 446	1 113	37 872	570	−2 426	1.6	−6.4	251	.7
...	26 063	Huron	837	36 079	1 212	43.1	34 951	1 135	36 459	1 128	−1 508	3.2	−4.1	591	1.6
4040	26 065	Ingham	559	279 320	202	499.7	281 912	175	275 520	−2 592	6 392	−.9	2.3	16 190	5.8
...	26 067	Ionia	573	61 518	791	107.4	57 024	764	51 815	4 494	5 209	7.9	10.1	1 711	2.8
...	26 069	Iosco	549	27 339	1 471	49.8	30 209	1 288	28 349	−2 870	1 860	−9.5	6.6	269	1.0
...	26 071	Iron	1 166	13 138	2 218	11.3	13 175	2 126	13 635	−37	−460	−.3	−3.4	84	.6
...	26 073	Isabella	574	63 351	765	110.4	54 624	789	54 110	8 727	514	16.0	.9	1 419	2.2
3520	26 075	Jackson	707	158 422	335	224.1	149 756	316	151 495	8 666	−1 739	5.8	−1.1	3 493	2.2
3720	26 077	Kalamazoo	562	238 603	242	424.6	223 411	223	212 378	15 192	11 033	6.8	5.2	6 311	2.6
...	26 079	Kalkaska	561	16 571	1 986	29.5	13 497	2 102	10 952	3 074	2 545	22.8	23.2	142	.9
3000	26 081	Kent	856	574 335	93	671.0	500 631	97	444 506	73 704	56 125	14.7	12.6	40 183	7.0
...	26 083	Keweenaw	541	2 301	3 038	4.3	1 701	3 083	1 963	600	−262	35.3	−13.3	18	.8
...	26 085	Lake	567	11 333	2 347	20.0	8 583	2 506	7 711	2 750	872	32.0	11.3	191	1.7
2162	26 087	Lapeer	654	87 904	595	134.4	74 768	602	70 038	13 136	4 730	17.6	6.8	2 731	3.1
...	26 089	Leelanau	348	21 119	1 731	60.7	16 527	1 888	14 007	4 592	2 520	27.8	18.0	694	3.3
2162	26 091	Lenawee	751	98 890	526	131.7	91 476	503	89 948	7 414	1 528	8.1	1.7	6 884	7.0
2162	26 093	Livingston	568	156 951	339	276.3	115 645	398	100 289	41 306	15 356	35.7	15.3	1 953	1.2
...	26 095	Luce	903	7 024	2 682	7.8	5 763	2 783	6 659	1 261	−896	21.9	−13.5	123	1.8
...	26 097	Mackinac	1 022	11 943	2 298	11.7	10 674	2 319	10 178	1 269	496	11.9	4.9	107	.9
2162	26 099	Macomb	480	788 149	60	1 642.0	717 400	57	694 600	70 749	22 800	9.9	3.3	12 435	1.6
...	26 101	Manistee	544	24 527	1 576	45.1	21 265	1 617	23 019	3 262	−1 754	15.3	−7.6	639	2.6
...	26 103	Marquette	1 821	64 634	752	35.5	70 887	624	74 101	−6 253	−3 214	−8.8	−4.3	444	.7
...	26 105	Mason	495	28 274	1 438	57.1	25 537	1 444	26 365	2 737	−828	10.7	−3.1	852	3.0
...	26 107	Mecosta	556	40 553	1 101	72.9	37 308	1 064	36 961	3 245	347	8.7	.9	520	1.3
...	26 109	Menominee	1 044	25 326	1 551	24.3	24 920	1 466	26 201	406	−1 281	1.6	−4.9	190	.8
6960	26 111	Midland	521	82 874	626	159.1	75 651	595	73 578	7 223	2 073	9.5	2.8	1 287	1.6
...	26 113	Missaukee	567	14 478	2 124	25.5	12 147	2 203	10 009	2 331	2 138	19.2	21.4	169	1.2
2162	26 115	Monroe	551	145 945	375	264.9	133 600	348	134 659	12 345	−1 059	9.2	−.8	3 110	2.1
...	26 117	Montcalm	708	61 266	795	86.5	53 059	802	47 555	8 207	5 504	15.5	11.6	1 394	2.3
...	26 119	Montmorency	548	10 315	2 413	18.8	8 936	2 476	7 492	1 379	1 444	15.4	19.3	67	.6
3000	26 121	Muskegon	509	170 200	318	334.4	158 983	298	157 589	11 217	1 394	7.1	.9	6 001	3.5
...	26 123	Newaygo	842	47 874	955	56.9	38 206	1 048	34 917	9 668	3 289	25.3	9.4	1 845	3.9
2162	26 125	Oakland	873	1 194 156	30	1 367.9	1 083 592	28	1 011 793	110 564	71 799	10.2	7.1	28 999	2.4

[1] Federal Information Processing Standards (FIPS) codes for metropolitan areas defined as of June 30, 1999.   [2] FIPS codes for states and counties/county equivalents.   [3] Dry land and land temporarily or partially covered by water.   [4] Based on 3,140 counties/county equivalents; excludes Yellowstone National Park in MT and South Boston independent city in VA which are no longer counties. When counties share the same rank, the next lower rank is omitted.   [5] Includes count resolution corrections through 1997 and adjustments based on Census 2000 dress rehearsal results and boundary changes reported as legally effective as of January 1, 1998.   [6] Persons of Hispanic or Latino origin may be of any race.

Sources: Land Area—U.S. Census Bureau, unpublished data file from Geography Division based on TIGER data base.   2000 Population—U.S. Census Bureau, Census of Population and Housing, Census 2000 Redistricting Data (Public Law 94-171) Summary Files (related Internet site <http://www.census.gov/dmd/www/2kresult.html>).   1990 Population—U.S. Census Bureau, "(CO-99-8) County Population Estimates and Demographic Components of Population Change: Annual Time Series, July 1, 1990 to July 1, 1999 (includes revised April 1, 1990 Population Estimates Base)"; published 9 March 2000; <http://www. census.gov/population/estimates/county/co-99-8/99C8_00.txt>.   1980 Population—U.S. Census Bureau, "1980–1990 Intercensal Population Estimates by County" on diskette (related Internet site <http://www.census.gov/population/www/estimates/countypop.html>).

[Includes U.S., states, and 3,142 counties/county equivalents defined as of January 1, 1992. For changes to these areas since January 1, 1992, see appendix B. Geographic Information]

Metropolitan area code[1]	State and county code[2]	County	Land area,[3] 2000 (sq. miles)	Population (April 1) 2000 Number	2000 Rank[4]	2000 Per square mile	1990[5] Number	1990[5] Rank[4]	1980	Net change 1990–2000	Net change 1980–1990	Percent change 1990–2000	Percent change 1980–1990	Hispanic or Latino,[6] 2000 Number	Hispanic or Latino,[6] 2000 Percent
		MICHIGAN—Con.													
...	26 127	Oceana	540	26 873	1 489	49.8	22 455	1 555	22 002	4 418	453	19.7	2.1	3 119	11.6
...	26 129	Ogemaw	564	21 645	1 711	38.4	18 681	1 751	16 436	2 964	2 245	15.9	13.7	252	1.2
...	26 131	Ontonagon	1 312	7 818	2 622	6.0	8 854	2 484	9 861	–1 036	–1 007	–11.7	–10.2	58	.7
...	26 133	Osceola	566	23 197	1 633	41.0	20 146	1 668	18 928	3 051	1 218	15.1	6.4	230	1.0
...	26 135	Oscoda	565	9 418	2 495	16.7	7 842	2 588	6 858	1 576	984	20.1	14.3	89	.9
...	26 137	Otsego	515	23 301	1 629	45.2	17 957	1 791	14 993	5 344	2 964	29.8	19.8	175	.8
3000	26 139	Ottawa	566	238 314	243	421.0	187 768	257	157 174	50 546	30 594	26.9	19.5	16 692	7.0
...	26 141	Presque Isle	660	14 411	2 130	21.8	13 743	2 077	14 267	668	–524	4.9	–3.7	79	.5
...	26 143	Roscommon	521	25 469	1 542	48.9	19 776	1 686	16 374	5 693	3 402	28.8	20.8	204	.8
6960	26 145	Saginaw	809	210 039	266	259.6	211 946	236	228 059	–1 907	–16 113	–.9	–7.1	14 075	6.7
2162	26 147	St. Clair	724	164 235	328	226.8	145 607	325	138 802	18 628	6 805	12.8	4.9	3 593	2.2
...	26 149	St. Joseph	504	62 422	777	123.9	58 913	738	56 083	3 509	2 830	6.0	5.0	2 488	4.0
...	26 151	Sanilac	964	44 547	1 007	46.2	39 928	1 004	40 789	4 619	–861	11.6	–2.1	1 239	2.8
...	26 153	Schoolcraft	1 178	8 903	2 533	7.6	8 302	2 535	8 575	601	–273	7.2	–3.2	83	.9
...	26 155	Shiawassee	539	71 687	689	133.0	69 770	636	71 140	1 917	–1 370	2.7	–1.9	1 295	1.8
...	26 157	Tuscola	812	58 266	821	71.8	55 498	781	56 961	2 768	–1 463	5.0	–2.6	1 342	2.3
3720	26 159	Van Buren	611	76 263	658	124.8	70 060	633	66 814	6 203	3 246	8.9	4.9	5 634	7.4
2162	26 161	Washtenaw	710	322 895	179	454.8	282 937	173	264 740	39 958	18 197	14.1	6.9	8 839	2.7
2162	26 163	Wayne	614	2 061 162	11	3 356.9	2 111 687	8	2 337 843	–50 525	–226 156	–2.4	–9.7	77 207	3.7
...	26 165	Wexford	565	30 484	1 386	54.0	26 360	1 410	25 102	4 124	1 258	15.6	5.0	307	1.0
	27 000	MINNESOTA	79 610	4 919 479	X	61.8	4 375 665	X	4 075 970	543 814	299 695	12.4	7.4	143 382	2.9
...	27 001	Aitkin	1 819	15 301	2 072	8.4	12 425	2 188	13 404	2 876	–979	23.1	–7.3	92	.6
5120	27 003	Anoka	424	298 084	189	703.0	243 641	205	195 998	54 443	47 643	22.3	24.3	4 961	1.7
...	27 005	Becker	1 310	30 000	1 396	22.9	27 881	1 354	29 336	2 119	–1 455	7.6	–5.0	230	.8
...	27 007	Beltrami	2 505	39 650	1 122	15.8	34 384	1 155	30 982	5 266	3 402	15.3	11.0	394	1.0
6980	27 009	Benton	408	34 226	1 275	83.9	30 185	1 289	25 187	4 041	4 998	13.4	19.8	307	.9
...	27 011	Big Stone	497	5 820	2 802	11.7	6 285	2 723	7 716	–465	–1 431	–7.4	–18.5	20	.3
...	27 013	Blue Earth	752	55 941	844	74.4	54 044	797	52 314	1 897	1 730	3.5	3.3	988	1.8
...	27 015	Brown	611	26 911	1 487	44.0	26 984	1 392	28 645	–73	–1 661	–.3	–5.8	545	2.0
...	27 017	Carlton	860	31 671	1 353	36.8	29 259	1 321	29 936	2 412	–677	8.2	–2.3	266	.8
5120	27 019	Carver	357	70 205	707	196.7	47 915	874	37 046	22 290	10 869	46.5	29.3	1 791	2.6
...	27 021	Cass	2 018	27 150	1 477	13.5	21 791	1 590	21 050	5 359	741	24.6	3.5	220	.8
...	27 023	Chippewa	583	13 088	2 223	22.4	13 228	2 119	14 941	–140	–1 713	–1.1	–11.5	251	1.9
5120	27 025	Chisago	418	41 101	1 078	98.3	30 521	1 267	25 717	10 580	4 804	34.7	18.7	473	1.2
2520	27 027	Clay	1 045	51 229	903	49.0	50 422	837	49 327	807	1 095	1.6	2.2	1 872	3.7
...	27 029	Clearwater	995	8 423	2 570	8.5	8 309	2 534	8 761	114	–452	1.4	–5.2	65	.8
...	27 031	Cook	1 451	5 168	2 839	3.6	3 868	2 927	4 092	1 300	–224	33.6	–5.5	39	.8
...	27 033	Cottonwood	640	12 167	2 286	19.0	12 694	2 166	14 854	–527	–2 160	–4.2	–14.5	267	2.2
...	27 035	Crow Wing	997	55 099	857	55.3	44 249	921	41 722	10 850	2 527	24.5	6.1	381	.7
5120	27 037	Dakota	570	355 904	165	624.4	275 210	180	194 279	80 694	80 931	29.3	41.7	10 459	2.9
...	27 039	Dodge	440	17 731	1 915	40.3	15 731	1 939	14 773	2 000	958	12.7	6.5	530	3.0
...	27 041	Douglas	634	32 821	1 324	51.8	28 674	1 339	27 839	4 147	835	14.5	3.0	193	.6
...	27 043	Faribault	714	16 181	2 010	22.7	16 937	1 852	19 714	–756	–2 777	–4.5	–14.1	566	3.5
...	27 045	Fillmore	861	21 122	1 730	24.5	20 777	1 642	21 930	345	–1 153	1.7	–5.3	113	.5
...	27 047	Freeborn	708	32 584	1 329	46.0	33 060	1 189	36 329	–476	–3 269	–1.4	–9.0	2 049	6.3
...	27 049	Goodhue	758	44 127	1 014	58.2	40 690	984	38 749	3 437	1 941	8.4	5.0	473	1.1
...	27 051	Grant	546	6 289	2 758	11.5	6 246	2 729	7 171	43	–925	.7	–12.9	33	.5
5120	27 053	Hennepin	557	1 116 200	32	2 003.9	1 032 431	30	941 411	83 769	91 020	8.1	9.7	45 439	4.1
3870	27 055	Houston	558	19 718	1 809	35.3	18 497	1 761	18 382	1 221	115	6.6	.6	121	.6
...	27 057	Hubbard	922	18 376	1 875	19.9	14 939	1 991	14 098	3 437	841	23.0	6.0	124	.7
5120	27 059	Isanti	439	31 287	1 367	71.3	25 921	1 425	23 600	5 366	2 321	20.7	9.8	259	.8
...	27 061	Itasca	2 665	43 992	1 016	16.5	40 844	981	43 069	3 148	–2 225	7.7	–5.2	263	.6
...	27 063	Jackson	702	11 268	2 352	16.1	11 677	2 240	13 690	–409	–2 013	–3.5	–14.7	210	1.9
...	27 065	Kanabec	525	14 996	2 090	28.6	12 802	2 156	12 161	2 194	641	17.1	5.3	140	.9
...	27 067	Kandiyohi	796	41 203	1 073	51.8	38 761	1 033	36 763	2 442	1 998	6.3	5.4	3 295	8.0
...	27 069	Kittson	1 097	5 285	2 830	4.8	5 767	2 782	6 672	–482	–905	–8.4	–13.6	67	1.3
...	27 071	Koochiching	3 102	14 355	2 136	4.6	16 299	1 904	17 571	–1 944	–1 272	–11.9	–7.2	81	.6
...	27 073	Lac qui Parle	765	8 067	2 601	10.5	8 924	2 477	10 592	–857	–1 668	–9.6	–15.7	21	.3
...	27 075	Lake	2 099	11 058	2 361	5.3	10 415	2 348	13 043	643	–2 628	6.2	–20.1	63	.6
...	27 077	Lake of the Woods	1 297	4 522	2 897	3.5	4 076	2 910	3 764	446	312	10.9	8.3	29	.6
...	27 079	Le Sueur	449	25 426	1 546	56.6	23 239	1 529	23 434	2 187	–195	9.4	–.8	997	3.9
...	27 081	Lincoln	537	6 429	2 747	12.0	6 890	2 672	8 207	–461	–1 317	–6.7	–16.0	55	.9
...	27 083	Lyon	714	25 425	1 547	35.6	24 789	1 472	25 207	636	–418	2.6	–1.7	1 009	4.0
...	27 085	McLeod	492	34 898	1 253	70.9	32 030	1 210	29 657	2 868	2 373	9.0	8.0	1 268	3.6
...	27 087	Mahnomen	556	5 190	2 837	9.3	5 044	2 839	5 535	146	–491	2.9	–8.9	46	.9
...	27 089	Marshall	1 772	10 155	2 431	5.7	10 993	2 296	13 027	–838	–2 034	–7.6	–15.6	298	2.9
...	27 091	Martin	709	21 802	1 702	30.8	22 914	1 537	24 687	–1 112	–1 773	–4.9	–7.2	421	1.9
...	27 093	Meeker	609	22 644	1 663	37.2	20 846	1 637	20 594	1 798	252	8.6	1.2	487	2.2

[1] Federal Information Processing Standards (FIPS) codes for metropolitan areas defined as of June 30, 1999. [2] FIPS codes for states and counties/county equivalents. [3] Dry land and land temporarily or partially covered by water. [4] Based on 3,140 counties/county equivalents; excludes Yellowstone National Park in MT and South Boston independent city in VA which are no longer counties. When counties share the same rank, the next lower rank is omitted. [5] Includes count resolution corrections through 1997 and adjustments based on Census 2000 dress rehearsal results and boundary changes reported as legally effective as of January 1, 1998. [6] Persons of Hispanic or Latino origin may be of any race.

Sources: Land Area—U.S. Census Bureau, unpublished data file from Geography Division based on TIGER data base. 2000 Population—U.S. Census Bureau, Census of Population and Housing, Census 2000 Redistricting Data (Public Law 94-171) Summary Files (related Internet site <http://www.census.gov/dmd/www/2kresult.html>). 1990 Population—U.S. Census Bureau, "(CO-99-8) County Population Estimates and Demographic Components of Population Change: Annual Time Series, July 1, 1990 to July 1, 1999 (includes revised April 1, 1990 Population Estimates Base)"; published 9 March 2000; <http://www. census.gov/population/estimates/county/co-99-8/99C8_00.txt>. 1980 Population—U.S. Census Bureau, "1980–1990 Intercensal Population Estimates by County" on diskette (related Internet site <http://www.census.gov/population/www/estimates/countypop.html>).

[Includes U.S., states, and 3,142 counties/county equivalents defined as of January 1, 1992. For changes to these areas since January 1, 1992, see appendix B. Geographic Information]

Metro-politan area code[1]	State and county code[2]	County	Land area,[3] 2000 (sq. miles)	Population (April 1)										Hispanic or Latino,[6] 2000	
				2000			1990[5]			Net change		Percent change			
				Number	Rank[4]	Per square mile	Number	Rank[4]	1980	1990–2000	1980–1990	1990–2000	1980–1990	Number	Percent
		MINNESOTA—Con.													
...	27 095	Mille Lacs	574	22 330	1 678	38.9	18 670	1 753	18 430	3 660	240	19.6	1.3	214	1.0
...	27 097	Morrison	1 125	31 712	1 351	28.2	29 604	1 313	29 311	2 108	293	7.1	1.0	203	.6
...	27 099	Mower	712	38 603	1 148	54.2	37 385	1 061	40 390	1 218	−3 005	3.3	−7.4	1 646	4.3
...	27 101	Murray	704	9 165	2 517	13.0	9 660	2 418	11 507	−495	−1 847	−5.1	−16.1	135	1.5
...	27 103	Nicollet	452	29 771	1 405	65.9	28 076	1 348	26 929	1 695	1 147	6.0	4.3	535	1.8
...	27 105	Nobles	715	20 832	1 742	29.1	20 098	1 670	21 840	734	−1 742	3.7	−8.0	2 325	11.2
...	27 107	Norman	876	7 442	2 645	8.5	7 975	2 572	9 379	−533	−1 404	−6.7	−15.0	227	3.1
6820	27 109	Olmsted	653	124 277	434	190.3	106 470	435	92 006	17 807	14 464	16.7	15.7	2 959	2.4
...	27 111	Otter Tail	1 980	57 159	833	28.9	50 714	831	51 937	6 445	−1 223	12.7	−2.4	957	1.7
...	27 113	Pennington	617	13 584	2 191	22.0	13 306	2 114	15 258	278	−1 952	2.1	−12.8	169	1.2
...	27 115	Pine	1 411	26 530	1 500	18.8	21 264	1 618	19 871	5 266	1 393	24.8	7.0	465	1.8
...	27 117	Pipestone	466	9 895	2 457	21.2	10 491	2 336	11 690	−596	−1 199	−5.7	−10.3	69	.7
2985	27 119	Polk	1 970	31 369	1 363	15.9	32 589	1 200	34 844	−1 220	−2 255	−3.7	−6.5	1 502	4.8
...	27 121	Pope	670	11 236	2 354	16.8	10 745	2 314	11 657	491	−912	4.6	−7.8	57	.5
5120	27 123	Ramsey	156	511 035	108	3 275.9	485 760	100	459 784	25 275	25 976	5.2	5.6	26 979	5.3
...	27 125	Red Lake	432	4 299	2 896	10.0	4 525	2 872	5 471	−226	−946	−5.0	−17.3	13	.3
...	27 127	Redwood	880	16 815	1 966	19.1	17 254	1 838	19 341	−439	−2 087	−2.5	−10.8	192	1.1
...	27 129	Renville	983	17 154	1 945	17.5	17 673	1 807	20 401	−519	−2 728	−2.9	−13.4	876	5.1
...	27 131	Rice	498	56 665	836	113.8	49 183	855	46 087	7 482	3 096	15.2	6.7	3 117	5.5
...	27 133	Rock	483	9 721	2 468	20.1	9 806	2 403	10 703	−85	−897	−.9	−8.4	124	1.3
...	27 135	Roseau	1 663	16 338	2 001	9.8	15 026	1 985	12 574	1 312	2 452	8.7	19.5	71	.4
2240	27 137	St. Louis	6 225	200 528	275	32.2	198 232	245	222 229	2 296	−23 997	1.2	−10.8	1 597	.8
5120	27 139	Scott	357	89 498	577	250.7	57 846	752	43 784	31 652	14 062	54.7	32.1	2 381	2.7
5120	27 141	Sherburne	436	64 417	756	147.7	41 945	957	29 908	22 472	12 037	53.6	40.2	709	1.1
...	27 143	Sibley	589	15 356	2 064	26.1	14 366	2 025	15 448	990	−1 082	6.9	−7.0	834	5.4
6980	27 145	Stearns	1 345	133 166	403	99.0	119 324	388	108 161	13 842	11 163	11.6	10.3	1 827	1.4
...	27 147	Steele	430	33 680	1 291	78.3	30 729	1 255	30 328	2 951	401	9.6	1.3	1 266	3.8
...	27 149	Stevens	562	10 053	2 439	17.9	10 634	2 323	11 322	−581	−688	−5.5	−6.1	90	.9
...	27 151	Swift	744	11 956	2 297	16.1	10 724	2 317	12 920	1 232	−2 196	11.5	−17.0	320	2.7
...	27 153	Todd	942	24 426	1 578	25.9	23 363	1 523	24 991	1 063	−1 628	4.5	−6.5	463	1.9
...	27 155	Traverse	574	4 134	2 906	7.2	4 463	2 877	5 542	−329	−1 079	−7.4	−19.5	50	1.2
...	27 157	Wabasha	525	21 610	1 712	41.2	19 744	1 687	19 335	1 866	409	9.5	2.1	364	1.7
...	27 159	Wadena	535	13 713	2 182	25.6	13 154	2 127	14 192	559	−1 038	4.2	−7.3	128	.9
...	27 161	Waseca	423	19 526	1 816	46.2	18 079	1 787	18 448	1 447	−369	8.0	−2.0	566	2.9
5120	27 163	Washington	392	201 130	272	513.1	145 860	324	113 571	55 270	32 289	37.9	28.4	3 892	1.9
...	27 165	Watonwan	435	11 876	2 300	27.3	11 682	2 238	12 361	194	−679	1.7	−5.5	1 804	15.2
...	27 167	Wilkin	751	7 138	2 675	9.5	7 516	2 615	8 454	−378	−938	−5.0	−11.1	110	1.5
...	27 169	Winona	626	49 985	915	79.8	47 828	878	46 256	2 157	1 572	4.5	3.4	686	1.4
5120	27 171	Wright	661	89 986	573	136.1	68 710	644	58 681	21 276	10 029	31.0	17.1	994	1.1
...	27 173	Yellow Medicine	758	11 080	2 360	14.6	11 684	2 237	13 653	−604	−1 969	−5.2	−14.4	195	1.8
	28 000	MISSISSIPPI	46 907	2 844 658	X	60.6	2 575 475	X	2 520 770	269 183	54 705	10.5	2.2	39 569	1.4
...	28 001	Adams	460	34 340	1 269	74.7	35 356	1 119	38 071	−1 016	−2 715	−2.9	−7.1	273	.8
...	28 003	Alcorn	400	34 558	1 263	86.4	31 722	1 220	33 036	2 836	−1 314	8.9	−4.0	443	1.3
...	28 005	Amite	730	13 599	2 190	18.6	13 328	2 111	13 369	271	−41	2.0	−.3	113	.8
...	28 007	Attala	735	19 661	1 814	26.7	18 481	1 764	19 865	1 180	−1 384	6.4	−7.0	280	1.4
...	28 009	Benton	407	8 026	2 602	19.7	8 046	2 560	8 153	−20	−107	−.2	−1.3	84	1.0
...	28 011	Bolivar	876	40 633	1 096	46.4	41 875	958	45 965	−1 242	−4 090	−3.0	−8.9	477	1.2
...	28 013	Calhoun	587	15 069	2 086	25.7	14 908	1 993	15 664	161	−756	1.1	−4.8	318	2.1
...	28 015	Carroll	628	10 769	2 378	17.1	9 237	2 451	9 776	1 532	−539	16.6	−5.5	79	.7
...	28 017	Chickasaw	502	19 440	1 821	38.7	18 085	1 786	17 851	1 355	234	7.5	1.3	445	2.3
...	28 019	Choctaw	419	9 758	2 465	23.3	9 071	2 462	8 996	687	75	7.6	.8	79	.8
...	28 021	Claiborne	487	11 831	2 302	24.3	11 370	2 262	12 279	461	−909	4.1	−7.4	94	.8
...	28 023	Clarke	691	17 955	1 899	26.0	17 313	1 832	16 945	642	368	3.7	2.2	120	.7
...	28 025	Clay	409	21 979	1 694	53.7	21 120	1 624	21 082	859	38	4.1	.2	190	.9
...	28 027	Coahoma	554	30 622	1 384	55.3	31 665	1 225	36 918	−1 043	−5 253	−3.3	−14.2	276	.9
...	28 029	Copiah	777	28 757	1 429	37.0	27 592	1 370	26 503	1 165	1 089	4.2	4.1	332	1.2
...	28 031	Covington	414	19 407	1 823	46.9	16 527	1 888	15 927	2 880	600	17.4	3.8	155	.8
4920	28 033	DeSoto	478	107 199	498	224.3	67 910	652	53 930	39 289	13 980	57.9	25.9	2 516	2.3
3285	28 035	Forrest	467	72 604	686	155.5	68 314	646	66 018	4 290	2 296	6.3	3.5	912	1.3
...	28 037	Franklin	565	8 448	2 568	15.0	8 377	2 525	8 208	71	169	.8	2.1	45	.5
...	28 039	George	478	19 144	1 840	40.1	16 673	1 870	15 297	2 471	1 376	14.8	9.0	307	1.6
...	28 041	Greene	713	13 299	2 204	18.7	10 220	2 370	9 827	3 079	393	30.1	4.0	106	.8
...	28 043	Grenada	422	23 263	1 630	55.1	21 555	1 600	21 115	1 708	440	7.9	2.1	145	.6
0920	28 045	Hancock	477	42 967	1 037	90.1	31 760	1 219	24 496	11 207	7 264	35.3	29.7	775	1.8
0920	28 047	Harrison	581	189 601	290	326.3	165 365	288	157 665	24 236	7 700	14.7	4.9	4 910	2.6
3560	28 049	Hinds	869	250 800	229	288.6	254 441	197	250 998	−3 641	3 443	−1.4	1.4	1 978	.8
...	28 051	Holmes	756	21 609	1 713	28.6	21 604	1 598	22 970	5	−1 366	Z	−5.9	194	.9
...	28 053	Humphreys	418	11 206	2 356	26.8	12 134	2 204	13 931	−928	−1 797	−7.6	−12.9	168	1.5
...	28 055	Issaquena	413	2 274	3 043	5.5	1 909	3 074	2 513	365	−604	19.1	−24.0	10	.4

[1] Federal Information Processing Standards (FIPS) codes for metropolitan areas defined as of June 30, 1999. [2] FIPS codes for states and counties/county equivalents. [3] Dry land and land temporarily or partially covered by water. [4] Based on 3,140 counties/county equivalents; excludes Yellowstone National Park in MT and South Boston independent city in VA which are no longer counties. When counties share the same rank, the next lower rank is omitted. [5] Includes count resolution corrections through 1997 and adjustments based on Census 2000 dress rehearsal results and boundary changes reported as legally effective as of January 1, 1998. [6] Persons of Hispanic or Latino origin may be of any race.

Sources: Land Area—U.S. Census Bureau, unpublished data file from Geography Division based on TIGER data base.   2000 Population—U.S. Census Bureau, Census of Population and Housing, Census 2000 Redistricting Data (Public Law 94-171) Summary Files (related Internet site <http://www.census.gov/dmd/www/2kresult.html>).   1990 Population—U.S. Census Bureau, "(CO-99-8) County Population Estimates and Demographic Components of Population Change: Annual Time Series, July 1, 1990 to July 1, 1999 (includes revised April 1, 1990 Population Estimates Base)"; published 9 March 2000; <http://www.census.gov/population/estimates/county/co-99-8/99C8_00.txt>.   1980 Population—U.S. Census Bureau, "1980–1990 Intercensal Population Estimates by County" on diskette (related Internet site <http://www.census.gov/population/www/estimates/countypop.html>).

Table B–1. Counties — Area and Population–Con.

[Includes U.S., states, and 3,142 counties/county equivalents defined as of January 1, 1992. For changes to these areas since January 1, 1992, see appendix B. Geographic Information]

Metropolitan area code[1]	State and county code[2]	County	Land area,[3] 2000 (sq. miles)	Population (April 1)										
				2000			1990[5]		1980	Net change		Percent change		Hispanic or Latino,[6] 2000	
				Number	Rank[4]	Per square mile	Number	Rank[4]		1990–2000	1980–1990	1990–2000	1980–1990	Number	Percent
		MISSISSIPPI—Con.													
...	28 057	Itawamba	532	22 770	1 657	42.8	20 017	1 676	20 518	2 753	–501	13.8	–2.4	226	1.0
0920	28 059	Jackson	727	131 420	407	180.8	115 243	400	118 015	16 177	–2 772	14.0	–2.3	2 807	2.1
...	28 061	Jasper	676	18 149	1 890	26.8	17 114	1 843	17 265	1 035	–151	6.0	–.9	117	.6
...	28 063	Jefferson	519	9 740	2 467	18.8	8 653	2 495	9 181	1 087	–528	12.6	–5.8	64	.7
...	28 065	Jefferson Davis	408	13 962	2 163	34.2	14 051	2 053	13 846	–89	205	–.6	1.5	107	.8
...	28 067	Jones	694	64 958	748	93.6	62 031	702	61 912	2 927	119	4.7	.2	1 271	2.0
...	28 069	Kemper	766	10 453	2 401	13.6	10 356	2 354	10 148	97	208	.9	2.0	76	.7
...	28 071	Lafayette	631	38 744	1 146	61.4	31 826	1 217	31 030	6 918	796	21.7	2.6	427	1.1
3285	28 073	Lamar	497	39 070	1 136	78.6	30 424	1 272	23 821	8 646	6 603	28.4	27.7	426	1.1
...	28 075	Lauderdale	704	78 161	650	111.0	75 555	596	77 285	2 606	–1 730	3.4	–2.2	888	1.1
...	28 077	Lawrence	431	13 258	2 207	30.8	12 458	2 185	12 518	800	–60	6.4	–.5	89	.7
...	28 079	Leake	583	20 940	1 740	35.9	18 436	1 766	18 790	2 504	–354	13.6	–1.9	440	2.1
...	28 081	Lee	450	75 755	661	168.3	65 579	668	57 061	10 176	8 518	15.5	14.9	882	1.2
...	28 083	Leflore	592	37 947	1 167	64.1	37 341	1 063	41 525	606	–4 184	1.6	–10.1	720	1.9
...	28 085	Lincoln	586	33 166	1 310	56.6	30 278	1 281	30 174	2 888	104	9.5	.3	229	.7
...	28 087	Lowndes	502	61 586	790	122.7	59 308	732	57 304	2 278	2 004	3.8	3.5	684	1.1
3560	28 089	Madison	717	74 674	670	104.1	53 794	799	41 613	20 880	12 181	38.8	29.3	742	1.0
...	28 091	Marion	542	25 595	1 532	47.2	25 544	1 443	25 708	51	–164	.2	–.6	158	.6
...	28 093	Marshall	706	34 993	1 249	49.6	30 361	1 275	29 296	4 632	1 065	15.3	3.6	425	1.2
...	28 095	Monroe	764	38 014	1 165	49.8	36 582	1 087	36 404	1 432	178	3.9	.5	261	.7
...	28 097	Montgomery	407	12 189	2 283	29.9	12 387	2 190	13 366	–198	–979	–1.6	–7.3	103	.8
...	28 099	Neshoba	570	28 684	1 430	50.3	24 800	1 470	23 789	3 884	1 011	15.7	4.2	332	1.2
...	28 101	Newton	578	21 838	1 698	37.8	20 291	1 661	19 967	1 547	324	7.6	1.6	198	.9
...	28 103	Noxubee	695	12 548	2 260	18.1	12 604	2 177	13 212	–56	–608	–.4	–4.6	141	1.1
...	28 105	Oktibbeha	458	42 902	1 040	93.7	38 375	1 043	36 018	4 527	2 357	11.8	6.5	461	1.1
...	28 107	Panola	684	34 274	1 271	50.1	29 996	1 297	28 164	4 278	1 832	14.3	6.5	384	1.1
...	28 109	Pearl River	811	48 621	936	60.0	38 714	1 035	33 795	9 907	4 919	25.6	14.6	686	1.4
...	28 111	Perry	647	12 138	2 288	18.8	10 865	2 307	9 864	1 273	1 001	11.7	10.1	122	1.0
...	28 113	Pike	409	38 940	1 143	95.2	36 882	1 078	36 173	2 058	709	5.6	2.0	284	.7
...	28 115	Pontotoc	497	26 726	1 494	53.8	22 237	1 568	20 918	4 489	1 319	20.2	6.3	481	1.8
...	28 117	Prentiss	415	25 556	1 537	61.6	23 278	1 526	24 025	2 278	–747	9.8	–3.1	176	.7
...	28 119	Quitman	405	10 117	2 435	25.0	10 490	2 337	12 636	–373	–2 146	–3.6	–17.0	55	.5
3560	28 121	Rankin	775	115 327	467	148.8	87 161	523	69 427	28 166	17 734	32.3	25.5	1 520	1.3
...	28 123	Scott	609	28 423	1 434	46.7	24 137	1 489	24 556	4 286	–419	17.8	–1.7	1 660	5.8
...	28 125	Sharkey	428	6 580	2 730	15.4	7 066	2 651	7 964	–486	–898	–6.9	–11.3	86	1.3
...	28 127	Simpson	589	27 639	1 460	46.9	23 953	1 495	23 441	3 686	512	15.4	2.2	318	1.2
...	28 129	Smith	636	16 182	2 009	25.4	14 798	2 001	15 077	1 384	–279	9.4	–1.9	96	.6
...	28 131	Stone	445	13 622	2 189	30.6	10 750	2 312	9 716	2 872	1 034	26.7	10.6	170	1.2
...	28 133	Sunflower	694	34 369	1 268	49.5	35 129	1 127	34 844	–760	285	–2.2	.8	448	1.3
...	28 135	Tallahatchie	644	14 903	2 098	23.1	15 210	1 975	17 157	–307	–1 947	–2.0	–11.3	137	.9
...	28 137	Tate	404	25 370	1 548	62.8	21 432	1 607	20 119	3 938	1 313	18.4	6.5	223	.9
...	28 139	Tippah	458	20 826	1 743	45.5	19 523	1 699	18 739	1 303	784	6.7	4.2	434	2.1
...	28 141	Tishomingo	424	19 163	1 837	45.2	17 683	1 806	18 434	1 480	–751	8.4	–4.1	343	1.8
...	28 143	Tunica	455	9 227	2 510	20.3	8 164	2 549	9 652	1 063	–1 488	13.0	–15.4	233	2.5
...	28 145	Union	415	25 362	1 549	61.1	22 085	1 572	21 741	3 277	344	14.8	1.6	413	1.6
...	28 147	Walthall	404	15 156	2 080	37.5	14 352	2 027	13 761	804	591	5.6	4.3	201	1.3
...	28 149	Warren	587	49 644	923	84.6	47 880	876	51 627	1 764	–3 747	3.7	–7.3	514	1.0
...	28 151	Washington	724	62 977	771	87.0	67 935	651	72 344	–4 958	–4 409	–7.3	–6.1	531	.8
...	28 153	Wayne	810	21 216	1 724	26.2	19 517	1 700	19 135	1 699	382	8.7	2.0	134	.6
...	28 155	Webster	422	10 294	2 416	24.4	10 222	2 369	10 300	72	–78	.7	–.8	174	1.7
...	28 157	Wilkinson	677	10 312	2 414	15.2	9 678	2 414	10 021	634	–343	6.6	–3.4	45	.4
...	28 159	Winston	607	20 160	1 784	33.2	19 433	1 708	19 474	727	–41	3.7	–.2	243	1.2
...	28 161	Yalobusha	467	13 051	2 227	27.9	12 033	2 215	13 183	1 018	–1 150	8.5	–8.7	127	1.0
...	28 163	Yazoo	919	28 149	1 446	30.6	25 506	1 448	27 349	2 643	–1 843	10.4	–6.7	1 233	4.4
	29 000	MISSOURI	68 886	5 595 211	X	81.2	5 116 901	X	4 916 766	478 310	200 135	9.3	4.1	118 592	2.1
...	29 001	Adair	567	24 977	1 560	44.1	24 577	1 478	24 870	400	–293	1.6	–1.2	315	1.3
7000	29 003	Andrew	435	16 492	1 989	37.9	14 632	2 009	13 980	1 860	652	12.7	4.7	138	.8
...	29 005	Atchison	545	6 430	2 745	11.8	7 457	2 617	8 605	–1 027	–1 148	–13.8	–13.3	43	.7
...	29 007	Audrain	693	25 853	1 523	37.3	23 599	1 509	26 458	2 254	–2 859	9.6	–10.8	189	.7
...	29 009	Barry	779	34 010	1 280	43.7	27 547	1 371	24 408	6 463	3 139	23.5	12.9	1 713	5.0
...	29 011	Barton	594	12 541	2 274	21.1	11 312	2 274	11 292	1 229	20	10.9	.2	119	.9
...	29 013	Bates	848	16 653	1 981	19.6	15 025	1 986	15 873	1 628	–848	10.8	–5.3	179	1.1
...	29 015	Benton	706	17 180	1 942	24.3	13 859	2 066	12 183	3 321	1 676	24.0	13.8	153	.9
...	29 017	Bollinger	621	12 029	2 293	19.4	10 619	2 325	10 301	1 410	318	13.3	3.1	68	.6
1740	29 019	Boone	685	135 454	398	197.7	112 379	409	100 376	23 075	12 003	20.5	12.0	2 413	1.8
7000	29 021	Buchanan	410	85 998	606	209.8	83 083	548	87 888	2 915	–4 805	3.5	–5.5	2 086	2.4
...	29 023	Butler	698	40 867	1 087	58.5	38 765	1 032	37 693	2 102	1 072	5.4	2.8	412	1.0
...	29 025	Caldwell	429	8 969	2 529	20.9	8 380	2 524	8 660	589	–280	7.0	–3.2	67	.7
...	29 027	Callaway	839	40 766	1 089	48.6	32 809	1 195	32 252	7 957	557	24.3	1.7	377	.9

[1] Federal Information Processing Standards (FIPS) codes for metropolitan areas defined as of June 30, 1999.   [2] FIPS codes for states and counties/county equivalents.   [3] Dry land and land temporarily or partially covered by water.   [4] Based on 3,140 counties/county equivalents; excludes Yellowstone National Park in MT and South Boston independent city in VA which are no longer counties. When counties share the same rank, the next lower rank is omitted.   [5] Includes count resolution corrections through 1997 and adjustments based on Census 2000 dress rehearsal results and boundary changes reported as legally effective as of January 1, 1998.   [6] Persons of Hispanic or Latino origin may be of any race.

Sources: Land Area—U.S. Census Bureau, unpublished data file from Geography Division based on TIGER data base.   2000 Population—U.S. Census Bureau, Census of Population and Housing, Census 2000 Redistricting Data (Public Law 94-171) Summary Files (related Internet site <http://www.census.gov/dmd/www/2kresult.html>).   1990 Population—U.S. Census Bureau, "(CO-99-8) County Population Estimates and Demographic Components of Population Change: Annual Time Series, July 1, 1990 to July 1, 1999 (includes revised April 1, 1990 Population Estimates Base)"; published 9 March 2000; <http://www. census.gov/population/estimates/county/co-99-8/99C8_00.txt>.   1980 Population—U.S. Census Bureau, "1980–1990 Intercensal Population Estimates by County" on diskette (related Internet site <http://www.census.gov/population/www/estimates/countypop.html>).

[Includes U.S., states, and 3,142 counties/county equivalents defined as of January 1, 1992. For changes to these areas since January 1, 1992, see appendix B. Geographic Information]

| Metro-politan area code[1] | State and county code[2] | County | Land area,[3] 2000 (sq. miles) | Population (April 1) ||||||||||||
| | | | | 2000 ||| 1990[5] || | Net change || Percent change || Hispanic or Latino,[6] 2000 ||
				Number	Rank[4]	Per square mile	Number	Rank[4]	1980	1990–2000	1980–1990	1990–2000	1980–1990	Number	Percent
		MISSOURI—Con.													
...	29 029	Camden	655	37 051	1 188	56.6	27 495	1 375	20 017	9 556	7 478	34.8	37.4	346	.9
...	29 031	Cape Girardeau	579	68 693	717	118.6	61 633	708	58 837	7 060	2 796	11.5	4.8	624	.9
...	29 033	Carroll	695	10 285	2 418	14.8	10 748	2 313	12 131	-463	-1 383	-4.3	-11.4	73	.7
...	29 035	Carter	508	5 941	2 789	11.7	5 515	2 801	5 428	426	87	7.7	1.6	72	1.2
3760	29 037	Cass	699	82 092	632	117.4	63 808	686	51 029	18 284	12 779	28.7	25.0	1 816	2.2
...	29 039	Cedar	476	13 733	2 178	28.9	12 093	2 209	11 894	1 640	199	13.6	1.7	153	1.1
...	29 041	Chariton	756	8 438	2 569	11.2	9 202	2 453	10 489	-764	-1 287	-8.3	-12.3	47	.6
7920	29 043	Christian	563	54 285	867	96.4	32 644	1 199	22 402	21 641	10 242	66.3	45.7	714	1.3
...	29 045	Clark	507	7 416	2 647	14.6	7 547	2 612	8 493	-131	-946	-1.7	-11.1	52	.7
3760	29 047	Clay	396	184 006	296	464.7	153 411	302	136 488	30 595	16 923	19.9	12.4	6 594	3.6
3760	29 049	Clinton	419	18 979	1 847	45.3	16 595	1 879	15 916	2 384	679	14.4	4.3	205	1.1
...	29 051	Cole	391	71 397	693	182.6	63 579	688	56 663	7 818	6 916	12.3	12.2	915	1.3
...	29 053	Cooper	565	16 670	1 978	29.5	14 835	1 998	14 643	1 835	192	12.4	1.3	143	.9
7040	29 055	Crawford	743	22 804	1 653	30.7	19 173	1 722	18 300	3 631	873	18.9	4.8	176	.8
...	29 057	Dade	490	7 923	2 612	16.2	7 449	2 619	7 383	474	66	6.4	.9	67	.8
...	29 059	Dallas	542	15 661	2 043	28.9	12 646	2 172	12 096	3 015	550	23.8	4.5	147	.9
...	29 061	Daviess	567	8 016	2 603	14.1	7 865	2 584	8 905	151	-1 040	1.9	-11.7	55	.7
...	29 063	DeKalb	424	11 597	2 325	27.4	9 967	2 389	8 222	1 630	1 745	16.4	21.2	125	1.1
...	29 065	Dent	754	14 927	2 097	19.8	13 702	2 080	14 517	1 225	-815	8.9	-5.6	112	.8
...	29 067	Douglas	815	13 084	2 224	16.1	11 876	2 225	11 594	1 208	282	10.2	2.4	110	.8
...	29 069	Dunklin	546	33 155	1 312	60.7	33 112	1 187	36 324	43	-3 212	.1	-8.8	824	2.5
7040	29 071	Franklin	923	93 807	546	101.6	80 603	565	71 233	13 204	9 370	16.4	13.2	678	.7
...	29 073	Gasconade	521	15 342	2 066	29.4	14 006	2 056	13 181	1 336	825	9.5	6.3	64	.4
...	29 075	Gentry	492	6 861	2 702	13.9	6 854	2 673	7 887	7	-1 033	.1	-13.1	44	.6
7920	29 077	Greene	675	240 391	239	356.1	207 949	240	185 302	32 442	22 647	15.6	12.2	4 434	1.8
...	29 079	Grundy	436	10 432	2 403	23.9	10 536	2 332	11 959	-104	-1 423	-1.0	-11.9	165	1.6
...	29 081	Harrison	725	8 850	2 539	12.2	8 469	2 515	9 890	381	-1 421	4.5	-14.4	89	1.0
...	29 083	Henry	702	21 997	1 692	31.3	20 044	1 675	19 672	1 953	372	9.7	1.9	201	.9
...	29 085	Hickory	399	8 940	2 531	22.4	7 335	2 626	6 367	1 605	968	21.9	15.2	68	.8
...	29 087	Holt	462	5 351	2 825	11.6	6 034	2 753	6 882	-683	-848	-11.3	-12.3	21	.4
...	29 089	Howard	466	10 212	2 426	21.9	9 631	2 421	10 008	581	-377	6.0	-3.8	88	.9
...	29 091	Howell	928	37 238	1 184	40.1	31 447	1 232	28 807	5 791	2 640	18.4	9.2	450	1.2
...	29 093	Iron	551	10 697	2 384	19.4	10 726	2 316	11 084	-29	-358	-.3	-3.2	64	.6
3760	29 095	Jackson	605	654 880	81	1 082.4	633 234	74	629 266	21 646	3 968	3.4	.6	35 160	5.4
3710	29 097	Jasper	640	104 686	504	163.6	90 465	506	86 958	14 221	3 507	15.7	4.0	3 615	3.5
7040	29 099	Jefferson	657	198 099	279	301.5	171 380	282	146 183	26 719	25 197	15.6	17.2	2 002	1.0
...	29 101	Johnson	830	48 258	943	58.1	42 514	944	39 059	5 744	3 455	13.5	8.8	1 407	2.9
...	29 103	Knox	506	4 361	2 890	8.6	4 482	2 876	5 508	-121	-1 026	-2.7	-18.6	26	.6
...	29 105	Laclede	766	32 513	1 330	42.4	27 158	1 384	24 323	5 355	2 835	19.7	11.7	401	1.2
3760	29 107	Lafayette	629	32 960	1 321	52.4	31 107	1 241	29 931	1 853	1 176	6.0	3.9	386	1.2
...	29 109	Lawrence	613	35 204	1 242	57.4	30 236	1 283	28 973	4 968	1 263	16.4	4.4	1 195	3.4
...	29 111	Lewis	505	10 494	2 399	20.8	10 233	2 365	10 901	261	-668	2.6	-6.1	77	.7
7040	29 113	Lincoln	630	38 944	1 141	61.8	28 892	1 333	22 193	10 052	6 699	34.8	30.2	444	1.1
...	29 115	Linn	620	13 754	2 177	22.2	13 885	2 065	15 495	-131	-1 610	-.9	-10.4	104	.8
...	29 117	Livingston	535	14 558	2 117	27.2	14 592	2 013	15 739	-34	-1 147	-.2	-7.3	94	.6
...	29 119	McDonald	540	21 681	1 708	40.2	16 938	1 851	14 917	4 743	2 021	28.0	13.5	2 030	9.4
...	29 121	Macon	804	15 762	2 034	19.6	15 345	1 968	16 313	417	-968	2.7	-5.9	121	.8
...	29 123	Madison	497	11 800	2 305	23.7	11 127	2 283	10 725	673	402	6.0	3.7	66	.6
...	29 125	Maries	528	8 903	2 533	16.9	7 976	2 570	7 551	927	425	11.6	5.6	103	1.2
...	29 127	Marion	438	28 289	1 437	64.6	27 682	1 363	28 638	607	-956	2.2	-3.3	252	.9
...	29 129	Mercer	454	3 757	2 935	8.3	3 723	2 937	4 685	34	-962	.9	-20.5	11	.3
...	29 131	Miller	592	23 564	1 610	39.8	20 700	1 644	18 539	2 864	2 161	13.8	11.7	231	1.0
...	29 133	Mississippi	413	13 427	2 198	32.5	14 442	2 021	15 726	-1 015	-1 284	-7.0	-8.2	129	1.0
...	29 135	Moniteau	417	14 827	2 102	35.6	12 298	2 196	12 068	2 529	230	20.6	1.9	435	2.9
...	29 137	Monroe	646	9 311	2 505	14.4	9 104	2 460	9 716	207	-612	2.3	-6.3	52	.6
...	29 139	Montgomery	537	12 136	2 289	22.6	11 355	2 267	11 537	781	-182	6.9	-1.6	94	.8
...	29 141	Morgan	597	19 309	1 827	32.3	15 574	1 949	13 807	3 735	1 767	24.0	12.8	161	.8
...	29 143	New Madrid	678	19 760	1 805	29.1	20 928	1 633	22 945	-1 168	-2 017	-5.6	-8.8	183	.9
3710	29 145	Newton	626	52 636	886	84.1	44 445	920	40 555	8 191	3 890	18.4	9.6	1 147	2.2
...	29 147	Nodaway	877	21 912	1 696	25.0	21 709	1 592	21 996	203	-287	.9	-1.3	155	.7
...	29 149	Oregon	791	10 344	2 409	13.1	9 470	2 437	10 238	874	-768	9.2	-7.5	113	1.1
...	29 151	Osage	606	13 062	2 225	21.6	12 018	2 218	12 014	1 044	4	8.7	Z	77	.6
...	29 153	Ozark	742	9 542	2 485	12.9	8 598	2 503	7 961	944	637	11.0	8.0	90	.9
...	29 155	Pemiscot	493	20 047	1 791	40.7	21 921	1 582	24 987	-1 874	-3 066	-8.5	-12.3	315	1.6
...	29 157	Perry	475	18 132	1 891	38.2	16 648	1 874	16 784	1 484	-136	8.9	-.8	93	.5
...	29 159	Pettis	685	39 403	1 127	57.5	35 437	1 115	36 378	3 966	-941	11.2	-2.6	1 527	3.9
...	29 161	Phelps	673	39 825	1 117	59.2	35 248	1 123	33 633	4 577	1 615	13.0	4.8	485	1.2
...	29 163	Pike	673	18 351	1 876	27.3	15 969	1 926	17 568	2 382	-1 599	14.9	-9.1	295	1.6
3760	29 165	Platte	420	73 781	680	175.7	57 867	750	46 341	15 914	11 526	27.5	24.9	2 211	3.0
...	29 167	Polk	637	26 992	1 483	42.4	21 826	1 588	18 822	5 166	3 004	23.7	16.0	350	1.3

[1] Federal Information Processing Standards (FIPS) codes for metropolitan areas defined as of June 30, 1999. [2] FIPS codes for states and counties/county equivalents. [3] Dry land and land temporarily or partially covered by water. [4] Based on 3,140 counties/county equivalents; excludes Yellowstone National Park in MT and South Boston independent city in VA which are no longer counties. When counties share the same rank, the next lower rank is omitted. [5] Includes count resolution corrections through 1997 and adjustments based on Census 2000 dress rehearsal results and boundary changes reported as legally effective as of January 1, 1998. [6] Persons of Hispanic or Latino origin may be of any race.

Sources: Land Area—U.S. Census Bureau, unpublished data file from Geography Division based on TIGER data base. 2000 Population—U.S. Census Bureau, Census of Population and Housing, Census 2000 Redistricting Data (Public Law 94-171) Summary Files (related Internet site <http://www.census.gov/dmd/www/2kresult.html>). 1990 Population—U.S. Census Bureau, "(CO-99-8) County Population Estimates and Demographic Components of Population Change: Annual Time Series, July 1, 1990 to July 1, 1999 (includes revised April 1, 1990 Population Estimates Base)"; published 9 March 2000; <http://www. census.gov/population/estimates/county/co-99-8/99C8_00.txt>. 1980 Population—U.S. Census Bureau, "1980–1990 Intercensal Population Estimates by County" on diskette (related Internet site <http://www.census.gov/population/www/estimates/countypop.html>).

Table B–1. Counties — **Area and Population**–Con.

[Includes U.S., states, and 3,142 counties/county equivalents defined as of January 1, 1992. For changes to these areas since January 1, 1992, see appendix B. Geographic Information]

Metro-politan area code[1]	State and county code[2]	County	Land area,[3] 2000 (sq. miles)	Population 2000 Number	Population 2000 Rank[4]	Population 2000 Per square mile	Population 1990[5] Number	Population 1990[5] Rank[4]	1980	Net change 1990–2000	Net change 1980–1990	Percent change 1990–2000	Percent change 1980–1990	Hispanic or Latino,[6] 2000 Number	Hispanic or Latino,[6] 2000 Percent
		MISSOURI—Con.													
...	29 169	Pulaski	547	41 165	1 076	75.3	41 307	975	42 011	−142	−704	−.3	−1.7	2 404	5.8
...	29 171	Putnam	518	5 223	2 836	10.1	5 079	2 833	6 092	144	−1 013	2.8	−16.6	32	.6
...	29 173	Ralls	471	9 626	2 476	20.4	8 476	2 514	8 984	1 150	−508	13.6	−5.7	42	.4
...	29 175	Randolph	482	24 663	1 568	51.2	24 370	1 482	25 460	293	−1 090	1.2	−4.3	282	1.1
3760	29 177	Ray	569	23 354	1 626	41.0	21 968	1 577	21 378	1 386	590	6.3	2.8	253	1.1
...	29 179	Reynolds	811	6 689	2 718	8.2	6 661	2 688	7 230	28	−569	.4	−7.9	55	.8
...	29 181	Ripley	629	13 509	2 193	21.5	12 303	2 194	12 458	1 206	−155	9.8	−1.2	132	1.0
7040	29 183	St. Charles	560	283 883	198	506.9	212 751	234	144 107	71 132	68 644	33.4	47.6	4 176	1.5
...	29 185	St. Clair	677	9 652	2 473	14.3	8 457	2 516	8 622	1 195	−165	14.1	−1.9	95	1.0
...	29 186	Ste. Genevieve	502	17 842	1 908	35.5	16 037	1 921	15 180	1 805	857	11.3	5.6	132	.7
...	29 187	St. Francois	449	55 641	848	123.9	48 904	858	42 600	6 737	6 304	13.8	14.8	447	.8
7040	29 189	St. Louis	508	1 016 315	34	2 000.6	993 508	31	974 180	22 807	19 328	2.3	2.0	14 577	1.4
...	29 195	Saline	756	23 756	1 600	31.4	23 523	1 512	24 913	233	−1 390	1.0	−5.6	1 050	4.4
...	29 197	Schuyler	308	4 170	2 902	13.5	4 236	2 897	4 979	−66	−743	−1.6	−14.9	27	.6
...	29 199	Scotland	438	4 983	2 850	11.4	4 822	2 854	5 415	161	−593	3.3	−11.0	42	.8
...	29 201	Scott	421	40 422	1 107	96.0	39 376	1 015	39 647	1 046	−271	2.7	−.7	448	1.1
...	29 203	Shannon	1 004	8 324	2 579	8.3	7 613	2 609	7 885	711	−272	9.3	−3.4	77	.9
...	29 205	Shelby	501	6 799	2 712	13.6	6 942	2 665	7 826	−143	−884	−2.1	−11.3	43	.6
...	29 207	Stoddard	827	29 705	1 408	35.9	28 895	1 332	29 009	810	−114	2.8	−.4	231	.8
...	29 209	Stone	463	28 658	1 431	61.9	19 078	1 729	15 587	9 580	3 491	50.2	22.4	298	1.0
...	29 211	Sullivan	651	7 219	2 664	11.1	6 326	2 719	7 434	893	−1 108	14.1	−14.9	634	8.8
...	29 213	Taney	632	39 703	1 118	62.8	25 561	1 441	20 467	14 142	5 094	55.3	24.9	962	2.4
...	29 215	Texas	1 179	23 003	1 641	19.5	21 476	1 604	21 070	1 527	406	7.1	1.9	221	1.0
...	29 217	Vernon	834	20 454	1 762	24.5	19 041	1 732	19 806	1 413	−765	7.4	−3.9	172	.8
7040	29 219	Warren	431	24 525	1 577	56.9	19 534	1 697	14 900	4 991	4 634	25.6	31.1	314	1.3
...	29 221	Washington	760	23 344	1 627	30.7	20 380	1 657	17 983	2 964	2 397	14.5	13.3	170	.7
...	29 223	Wayne	761	13 259	2 206	17.4	11 543	2 253	11 277	1 716	266	14.9	2.4	65	.5
7920	29 225	Webster	593	31 045	1 376	52.4	23 753	1 501	20 414	7 292	3 339	30.7	16.4	400	1.3
...	29 227	Worth	267	2 382	3 034	8.9	2 440	3 026	3 008	−58	−568	−2.4	−18.9	7	.3
...	29 229	Wright	682	17 955	1 899	26.3	16 758	1 864	16 188	1 197	570	7.1	3.5	139	.8
		Independent City													
7040	29 510	St. Louis city	62	348 189	168	5 616.0	396 685	126	452 801	−48 496	−56 116	−12.2	−12.4	7 022	2.0
	30 000	**MONTANA**	145 552	902 195	X	6.2	799 065	X	786 690	103 130	12 375	12.9	1.6	18 081	2.0
...	30 001	Beaverhead	5 542	9 202	2 513	1.7	8 424	2 518	8 186	778	238	9.2	2.9	246	2.7
...	30 003	Big Horn	4 995	12 671	2 249	2.5	11 337	2 270	11 096	1 334	241	11.8	2.2	465	3.7
...	30 005	Blaine	4 226	7 009	2 685	1.7	6 728	2 684	6 999	281	−271	4.2	−3.9	70	1.0
...	30 007	Broadwater	1 191	4 385	2 887	3.7	3 318	2 970	3 267	1 067	51	32.2	1.6	58	1.3
...	30 009	Carbon	2 048	9 552	2 484	4.7	8 080	2 556	8 099	1 472	−19	18.2	−.2	169	1.8
...	30 011	Carter	3 340	1 360	3 099	.4	1 503	3 097	1 799	−143	−296	−9.5	−16.5	8	.6
3040	30 013	Cascade	2 698	80 357	638	29.8	77 691	585	80 696	2 666	−3 005	3.4	−3.7	1 949	2.4
...	30 015	Chouteau	3 973	5 970	2 787	1.5	5 452	2 804	6 092	518	−640	9.5	−10.5	40	.7
...	30 017	Custer	3 783	11 696	2 319	3.1	11 697	2 234	13 109	−1	−1 412	Z	−10.8	177	1.5
...	30 019	Daniels	1 426	2 017	3 064	1.4	2 266	3 044	2 835	−249	−569	−11.0	−20.1	32	1.6
...	30 021	Dawson	2 373	9 059	2 525	3.8	9 505	2 433	11 805	−446	−2 300	−4.7	−19.5	81	.9
...	30 023	Deer Lodge	737	9 417	2 496	12.8	10 356	2 354	12 518	−939	−2 162	−9.1	−17.3	155	1.6
...	30 025	Fallon	1 620	2 837	3 003	1.8	3 103	2 992	3 763	−266	−660	−8.6	−17.5	11	.4
...	30 027	Fergus	4 339	11 893	2 299	2.7	12 083	2 211	13 076	−190	−993	−1.6	−7.6	96	.8
...	30 029	Flathead	5 098	74 471	672	14.6	59 218	735	51 966	15 253	7 252	25.8	14.0	1 061	1.4
...	30 031	Gallatin	2 606	67 831	723	26.0	50 484	834	42 865	17 347	X	34.4	X	1 047	1.5
...	30 033	Garfield	4 668	1 279	3 101	.3	1 589	3 091	1 656	−310	−67	−19.5	−4.0	5	.4
...	30 035	Glacier	2 995	13 247	2 209	4.4	12 121	2 207	10 628	1 126	1 493	9.3	14.0	159	1.2
...	30 037	Golden Valley	1 175	1 042	3 109	.9	912	3 116	1 026	130	−114	14.3	−11.1	13	1.2
...	30 039	Granite	1 727	2 830	3 004	1.6	2 548	3 020	2 700	282	−152	11.1	−5.6	36	1.3
...	30 041	Hill	2 896	16 673	1 977	5.8	17 654	1 808	17 985	−981	−331	−5.6	−1.8	208	1.2
...	30 043	Jefferson	1 657	10 049	2 440	6.1	7 939	2 578	7 029	2 110	910	26.6	12.9	149	1.5
...	30 045	Judith Basin	1 870	2 329	3 036	1.2	2 282	3 041	2 646	47	−364	2.1	−13.8	13	.6
...	30 047	Lake	1 494	26 507	1 502	17.7	21 041	1 628	19 056	5 466	1 985	26.0	10.4	668	2.5
...	30 049	Lewis and Clark	3 461	55 716	847	16.1	47 495	884	43 039	8 221	4 456	17.3	10.4	843	1.5
...	30 051	Liberty	1 430	2 158	3 054	1.5	2 295	3 039	2 329	−137	−34	−6.0	−1.5	4	.2
...	30 053	Lincoln	3 613	18 837	1 851	5.2	17 481	1 821	17 752	1 356	−271	7.8	−1.5	271	1.4
...	30 055	McCone	2 643	1 977	3 065	.7	2 276	3 043	2 702	−299	−426	−13.1	−15.8	19	1.0
...	30 057	Madison	3 587	6 851	2 705	1.9	5 989	2 759	5 448	862	541	14.4	9.9	130	1.9
...	30 059	Meagher	2 392	1 932	3 069	.8	1 819	3 077	2 154	113	−335	6.2	−15.6	29	1.5
...	30 061	Mineral	1 220	3 884	2 925	3.2	3 315	2 974	3 675	569	−360	17.2	−9.8	61	1.6
5140	30 063	Missoula	2 598	95 802	540	36.9	78 687	575	76 016	17 115	2 671	21.8	3.5	1 543	1.6
...	30 065	Musselshell	1 867	4 497	2 880	2.4	4 106	2 908	4 428	391	−322	9.5	−7.3	72	1.6
...	30 067	Park	2 802	15 694	2 038	5.6	14 515	2 018	12 869	1 179	X	8.1	X	288	1.8
...	30 069	Petroleum	1 654	493	3 135	.3	519	3 134	655	−26	−136	−5.0	−20.8	6	1.2

[1] Federal Information Processing Standards (FIPS) codes for metropolitan areas defined as of June 30, 1999. [2] FIPS codes for states and counties/county equivalents. [3] Dry land and land temporarily or partially covered by water. [4] Based on 3,140 counties/county equivalents; excludes Yellowstone National Park in MT and South Boston independent city in VA which are no longer counties. When counties share the same rank, the next lower rank is omitted. [5] Includes count resolution corrections through 1997 and adjustments based on Census 2000 dress rehearsal results and boundary changes reported as legally effective as of January 1, 1998. [6] Persons of Hispanic or Latino origin may be of any race.

Sources: Land Area—U.S. Census Bureau, unpublished data file from Geography Division based on TIGER data base. 2000 Population—U.S. Census Bureau, Census of Population and Housing, Census 2000 Redistricting Data (Public Law 94-171) Summary Files (related Internet site <http://www.census.gov/dmd/www/2kresult.html>). 1990 Population—U.S. Census Bureau, "(CO-99-8) County Population Estimates and Demographic Components of Population Change: Annual Time Series, July 1, 1990 to July 1, 1999 (includes revised April 1, 1990 Population Estimates Base)"; published 9 March 2000; <http://www. census.gov/population/estimates/county/co-99-8/99C8_00.txt>. 1980 Population—U.S. Census Bureau, "1980–1990 Intercensal Population Estimates by County" on diskette (related Internet site <http://www.census.gov/population/www/estimates/countypop.html>).

Table B–1. Counties — **Area and Population**–Con.

[Includes U.S., states, and 3,142 counties/county equivalents defined as of January 1, 1992. For changes to these areas since January 1, 1992, see appendix B. Geographic Information]

Metro-politan area code[1]	State and county code[2]	County	Land area,[3] 2000 (sq. miles)	Population (April 1) 2000 Number	Rank[4]	Per square mile	1990[5] Number	Rank[4]	1980	Net change 1990–2000	Net change 1980–1990	Percent change 1990–2000	Percent change 1980–1990	Hispanic or Latino,[6] 2000 Number	Percent
		MONTANA—Con.													
...	30 071	Phillips	5 140	4 601	2 872	.9	5 163	2 829	5 367	−562	−204	−10.9	−3.8	53	1.2
...	30 073	Pondera	1 625	6 424	2 748	4.0	6 433	2 714	6 731	−9	−298	−.1	−4.4	54	.8
...	30 075	Powder River	3 297	1 858	3 075	.6	2 090	3 063	2 520	−232	−430	−11.1	−17.1	11	.6
...	30 077	Powell	2 326	7 180	2 668	3.1	6 620	2 695	6 958	560	−338	8.5	−4.9	140	1.9
...	30 079	Prairie	1 737	1 199	3 104	.7	1 383	3 103	1 836	−184	−453	−13.3	−24.7	8	.7
...	30 081	Ravalli	2 394	36 070	1 213	15.1	25 010	1 462	22 493	11 060	2 517	44.2	11.2	678	1.9
...	30 083	Richland	2 084	9 667	2 472	4.6	10 716	2 318	12 243	−1 049	−1 527	−9.8	−12.5	209	2.2
...	30 085	Roosevelt	2 356	10 620	2 389	4.5	10 999	2 294	10 467	−379	532	−3.4	5.1	131	1.2
...	30 087	Rosebud	5 012	9 383	2 499	1.9	10 505	2 335	9 899	−1 122	606	−10.7	6.1	219	2.3
...	30 089	Sanders	2 762	10 227	2 423	3.7	8 669	2 494	8 675	1 558	−6	18.0	−.1	159	1.6
...	30 091	Sheridan	1 677	4 105	2 908	2.4	4 732	2 860	5 414	−627	−682	−13.3	−12.6	44	1.1
...	30 093	Silver Bow	718	34 606	1 262	48.2	33 941	1 166	38 092	665	−4 151	2.0	−10.9	950	2.7
...	30 095	Stillwater	1 795	8 195	2 594	4.6	6 536	2 703	5 598	1 659	938	25.4	16.8	165	2.0
...	30 097	Sweet Grass	1 855	3 609	2 944	1.9	3 154	2 988	3 216	455	−62	14.4	−1.9	54	1.5
...	30 099	Teton	2 273	6 445	2 743	2.8	6 271	2 727	6 491	174	−220	2.8	−3.4	73	1.1
...	30 101	Toole	1 911	5 267	2 833	2.8	5 046	2 838	5 559	221	−513	4.4	−9.2	61	1.2
...	30 103	Treasure	979	861	3 118	.9	874	3 119	981	−13	−107	−1.5	−10.9	13	1.5
...	30 105	Valley	4 921	7 675	2 631	1.6	8 239	2 545	10 250	−564	−2 011	−6.8	−19.6	60	.8
...	30 107	Wheatland	1 423	2 259	3 045	1.6	2 246	3 051	2 359	13	−113	.6	−4.8	25	1.1
...	30 109	Wibaux	889	1 068	3 107	1.2	1 191	3 108	1 476	−123	−285	−10.3	−19.3	4	.4
0880	30 111	Yellowstone	2 635	129 352	415	49.1	113 419	404	108 035	15 933	5 384	14.0	5.0	4 788	3.7
...	30 113	Yellowstone National Park	X	X	X	X	X	X	66	X	X	X	X	X	X
	31 000	**NEBRASKA**	76 872	1 711 263	X	22.3	1 578 417	X	1 569 825	132 846	8 592	8.4	.5	94 425	5.5
...	31 001	Adams	563	31 151	1 373	55.3	29 625	1 312	30 656	1 526	−1 031	5.2	−3.4	1 428	4.6
...	31 003	Antelope	857	7 452	2 644	8.7	7 965	2 576	8 675	−513	−710	−6.4	−8.2	52	.7
...	31 005	Arthur	715	444	3 136	.6	462	3 136	513	−18	−51	−3.9	−9.9	6	1.4
...	31 007	Banner	746	819	3 122	1.1	852	3 120	918	−33	−66	−3.9	−7.2	46	5.6
...	31 009	Blaine	711	583	3 132	.8	675	3 131	867	−92	−192	−13.6	−22.1	1	.2
...	31 011	Boone	687	6 259	2 760	9.1	6 667	2 687	7 391	−408	−724	−6.1	−9.8	56	.9
...	31 013	Box Butte	1 075	12 158	2 287	11.3	13 130	2 128	13 696	−972	−566	−7.4	−4.1	930	7.6
...	31 015	Boyd	540	2 438	3 027	4.5	2 835	3 009	3 331	−397	−496	−14.0	−14.9	2	.1
...	31 017	Brown	1 221	3 525	2 953	2.9	3 657	2 943	4 377	−132	−720	−3.6	−16.4	29	.8
...	31 019	Buffalo	968	42 259	1 052	43.7	37 447	1 060	34 797	4 812	2 650	12.9	7.6	1 970	4.7
...	31 021	Burt	493	7 791	2 626	15.8	7 868	2 583	8 813	−77	−945	−1.0	−10.7	98	1.3
...	31 023	Butler	584	8 767	2 548	15.0	8 601	2 502	9 330	166	−729	1.9	−7.8	145	1.7
5920	31 025	Cass	559	24 334	1 581	43.5	21 318	1 616	20 297	3 016	1 021	14.1	5.0	355	1.5
...	31 027	Cedar	740	9 615	2 478	13.0	10 131	2 375	11 375	−516	−1 244	−5.1	−10.9	41	.4
...	31 029	Chase	895	4 068	2 915	4.5	4 381	2 884	4 758	−313	−377	−7.1	−7.9	139	3.4
...	31 031	Cherry	5 961	6 148	2 767	1.0	6 307	2 720	6 758	−159	−451	−2.5	−6.7	57	.9
...	31 033	Cheyenne	1 196	9 830	2 463	8.2	9 494	2 434	10 057	336	−563	3.5	−5.6	438	4.5
...	31 035	Clay	573	7 039	2 680	12.3	7 123	2 642	8 106	−84	−983	−1.2	−12.1	245	3.5
...	31 037	Colfax	413	10 441	2 402	25.3	9 139	2 456	9 890	1 302	−751	14.2	−7.6	2 732	26.2
...	31 039	Cuming	572	10 203	2 428	17.8	10 117	2 376	11 664	86	−1 547	.9	−13.3	559	5.5
...	31 041	Custer	2 576	11 793	2 307	4.6	12 270	2 198	13 877	−477	−1 607	−3.9	−11.6	108	.9
7720	31 043	Dakota	264	20 253	1 776	76.7	16 742	1 866	16 573	3 511	169	21.0	1.0	4 581	22.6
...	31 045	Dawes	1 396	9 060	2 524	6.5	9 021	2 467	9 609	39	−588	.4	−6.1	220	2.4
...	31 047	Dawson	1 013	24 365	1 580	24.1	19 940	1 683	22 304	4 425	−2 364	22.2	−10.6	6 178	25.4
...	31 049	Deuel	440	2 098	3 058	4.8	2 237	3 052	2 462	−139	−225	−6.2	−9.1	57	2.7
...	31 051	Dixon	476	6 339	2 752	13.3	6 143	2 740	7 137	196	−994	3.2	−13.9	348	5.5
...	31 053	Dodge	534	36 160	1 209	67.7	34 500	1 150	35 847	1 660	−1 347	4.8	−3.8	1 421	3.9
5920	31 055	Douglas	331	463 585	124	1 400.6	416 444	121	397 038	47 141	19 406	11.3	4.9	30 928	6.7
...	31 057	Dundy	920	2 292	3 040	2.5	2 582	3 017	2 861	−290	−279	−11.2	−9.8	74	3.2
...	31 059	Fillmore	576	6 634	2 722	11.5	7 103	2 645	7 920	−469	−817	−6.6	−10.3	110	1.7
...	31 061	Franklin	576	3 574	2 947	6.2	3 938	2 923	4 377	−364	−439	−9.2	−10.0	23	.6
...	31 063	Frontier	975	3 099	2 985	3.2	3 101	2 993	3 647	−2	−546	−.1	−15.0	30	1.0
...	31 065	Furnas	718	5 324	2 828	7.4	5 553	2 796	6 486	−229	−933	−4.1	−14.4	61	1.1
...	31 067	Gage	855	22 993	1 643	26.9	22 794	1 544	24 456	199	−1 662	.9	−6.8	196	.9
...	31 069	Garden	1 704	2 292	3 040	1.3	2 460	3 024	2 802	−168	−342	−6.8	−12.2	33	1.4
...	31 071	Garfield	570	1 902	3 073	3.3	2 141	3 058	2 363	−239	−222	−11.2	−9.4	19	1.0
...	31 073	Gosper	458	2 143	3 057	4.7	1 928	3 070	2 140	215	−212	11.2	−9.9	27	1.3
...	31 075	Grant	776	747	3 128	1.0	769	3 125	877	−22	−108	−2.9	−12.3	10	1.3
...	31 077	Greeley	570	2 714	3 013	4.8	3 006	2 999	3 462	−292	−456	−9.7	−13.2	23	.8
...	31 079	Hall	546	53 534	874	98.0	48 925	857	47 690	4 609	1 235	9.4	2.6	7 497	14.0
...	31 081	Hamilton	544	9 403	2 497	17.3	8 862	2 483	9 301	541	−439	6.1	−4.7	107	1.1
...	31 083	Harlan	553	3 786	2 931	6.8	3 810	2 930	4 292	−24	−482	−.6	−11.2	29	.8
...	31 085	Hayes	713	1 068	3 107	1.5	1 222	3 107	1 356	−154	−134	−12.6	−9.9	27	2.5
...	31 087	Hitchcock	710	3 111	2 984	4.4	3 750	2 935	4 079	−639	−329	−17.0	−8.1	44	1.4
...	31 089	Holt	2 413	11 551	2 329	4.8	12 599	2 178	13 552	−1 048	−953	−8.3	−7.0	82	.7

[1] Federal Information Processing Standards (FIPS) codes for metropolitan areas defined as of June 30, 1999. [2] FIPS codes for states and counties/county equivalents. [3] Dry land and land temporarily or partially covered by water. [4] Based on 3,140 counties/county equivalents; excludes Yellowstone National Park in MT and South Boston independent city in VA which are no longer counties. When counties share the same rank, the next lower rank is omitted. [5] Includes count resolution corrections through 1997 and adjustments based on Census 2000 dress rehearsal results and boundary changes reported as legally effective as of January 1, 1998. [6] Persons of Hispanic or Latino origin may be of any race.

Sources: Land Area—U.S. Census Bureau, unpublished data file from Geography Division based on TIGER data base. 2000 Population—U.S. Census Bureau, Census of Population and Housing, Census 2000 Redistricting Data (Public Law 94-171) Summary Files (related Internet site <http://www.census.gov/dmd/www/2kresult.html>). 1990 Population—U.S. Census Bureau, "(CO-99-8) County Population Estimates and Demographic Components of Population Change: Annual Time Series, July 1, 1990 to July 1, 1999 (includes revised April 1, 1990 Population Estimates Base)"; published 9 March 2000; <http://www. census.gov/population/estimates/county/co-99-8/99C8_00.txt>. 1980 Population—U.S. Census Bureau, "1980–1990 Intercensal Population Estimates by County" on diskette (related Internet site <http://www.census.gov/population/www/estimates/countypop.html>).

[Includes U.S., states, and 3,142 counties/county equivalents defined as of January 1, 1992. For changes to these areas since January 1, 1992, see appendix B. Geographic Information]

Metro-politan area code[1]	State and county code[2]	County	Land area,[3] 2000 (sq. miles)	Population (April 1)											
				2000			1990[5]			Net change		Percent change		Hispanic or Latino,[6] 2000	
				Number	Rank[4]	Per square mile	Number	Rank[4]	1980	1990–2000	1980–1990	1990–2000	1980–1990	Number	Percent
		NEBRASKA—Con.													
...	31 091	Hooker	721	783	3 125	1.1	793	3 124	990	−10	−197	−1.3	−19.9	8	1.0
...	31 093	Howard	569	6 567	2 731	11.5	6 057	2 750	6 773	510	−716	8.4	−10.6	66	1.0
...	31 095	Jefferson	573	8 333	2 578	14.5	8 759	2 489	9 817	−426	−1 058	−4.9	−10.8	109	1.3
...	31 097	Johnson	376	4 488	2 881	11.9	4 673	2 863	5 285	−185	−612	−4.0	−11.6	129	2.9
...	31 099	Kearney	516	6 882	2 698	13.3	6 629	2 692	7 053	253	−424	3.8	−6.0	161	2.3
...	31 101	Keith	1 061	8 875	2 535	8.4	8 584	2 505	9 364	291	−780	3.4	−8.3	375	4.2
...	31 103	Keya Paha	773	983	3 112	1.3	1 029	3 111	1 301	−46	−272	−4.5	−20.9	38	3.9
...	31 105	Kimball	952	4 089	2 911	4.3	4 108	2 907	4 882	−19	−774	−.5	−15.9	136	3.3
...	31 107	Knox	1 108	9 374	2 500	8.5	9 564	2 427	11 457	−190	−1 893	−2.0	−16.5	85	.9
4360	31 109	Lancaster	839	250 291	230	298.3	213 641	233	192 884	36 650	20 757	17.2	10.8	8 437	3.4
...	31 111	Lincoln	2 564	34 632	1 261	13.5	32 508	1 201	36 455	2 124	−3 947	6.5	−10.8	1 880	5.4
...	31 113	Logan	571	774	3 126	1.4	878	3 118	983	−104	−105	−11.8	−10.7	7	.9
...	31 115	Loup	570	712	3 131	1.2	683	3 130	859	29	−176	4.2	−20.5	12	1.7
...	31 117	McPherson	859	533	3 134	.6	546	3 133	593	−13	−47	−2.4	−7.9	8	1.5
...	31 119	Madison	573	35 226	1 240	61.5	32 655	1 197	31 382	2 571	1 273	7.9	4.1	3 042	8.6
...	31 121	Merrick	485	8 204	2 592	16.9	8 062	2 557	8 945	142	−883	1.8	−9.9	168	2.0
...	31 123	Morrill	1 424	5 440	2 821	3.8	5 423	2 805	6 085	17	−662	.3	−10.9	549	10.1
...	31 125	Nance	441	4 038	2 920	9.2	4 275	2 891	4 740	−237	−465	−5.5	−9.8	46	1.1
...	31 127	Nemaha	409	7 576	2 638	18.5	7 980	2 569	8 367	−404	−387	−5.1	−4.6	76	1.0
...	31 129	Nuckolls	575	5 057	2 848	8.8	5 786	2 780	6 726	−729	−940	−12.6	−14.0	51	1.0
...	31 131	Otoe	616	15 396	2 060	25.0	14 252	2 034	15 183	1 144	−931	8.0	−6.1	377	2.4
...	31 133	Pawnee	432	3 087	2 986	7.1	3 317	2 972	3 937	−230	−620	−6.9	−15.7	21	.7
...	31 135	Perkins	883	3 200	2 979	3.6	3 367	2 965	3 637	−167	−270	−5.0	−7.4	74	2.3
...	31 137	Phelps	540	9 747	2 466	18.1	9 715	2 409	9 769	32	−54	.3	−.6	220	2.3
...	31 139	Pierce	574	7 857	2 618	13.7	7 827	2 592	8 481	30	−654	.4	−7.7	56	.7
...	31 141	Platte	678	31 662	1 354	46.7	29 820	1 303	28 852	1 842	968	6.2	3.4	2 072	6.5
...	31 143	Polk	439	5 639	2 811	12.8	5 655	2 787	6 320	−16	−665	−.3	−10.5	61	1.1
...	31 145	Red Willow	717	11 448	2 338	16.0	11 705	2 232	12 615	−257	−910	−2.2	−7.2	281	2.5
...	31 147	Richardson	553	9 531	2 487	17.2	9 937	2 391	11 315	−406	−1 378	−4.1	−12.2	100	1.0
...	31 149	Rock	1 008	1 756	3 082	1.7	2 019	3 065	2 383	−263	−364	−13.0	−15.3	9	.5
...	31 151	Saline	575	13 843	2 170	24.1	12 715	2 165	13 131	1 128	−416	8.9	−3.2	911	6.6
5920	31 153	Sarpy	241	122 595	443	508.7	102 583	448	86 015	20 012	16 568	19.5	19.3	5 358	4.4
...	31 155	Saunders	754	19 830	1 799	26.3	18 285	1 774	18 716	1 545	−431	8.4	−2.3	205	1.0
...	31 157	Scotts Bluff	739	36 951	1 191	50.0	36 025	1 100	38 344	926	−2 319	2.6	−6.0	6 352	17.2
...	31 159	Seward	575	16 496	1 988	28.7	15 450	1 957	15 789	1 046	−339	6.8	−2.1	179	1.1
...	31 161	Sheridan	2 441	6 198	2 762	2.5	6 750	2 681	7 544	−552	−794	−8.2	−10.5	91	1.5
...	31 163	Sherman	566	3 318	2 972	5.9	3 718	2 939	4 226	−400	−508	−10.8	−12.0	34	1.0
...	31 165	Sioux	2 067	1 475	3 094	.7	1 549	3 093	1 845	−74	−296	−4.8	−16.0	34	2.3
...	31 167	Stanton	430	6 455	2 742	15.0	6 244	2 730	6 549	211	−305	3.4	−4.7	149	2.3
...	31 169	Thayer	575	6 055	2 775	10.5	6 635	2 691	7 582	−580	−947	−8.7	−12.5	61	1.0
...	31 171	Thomas	713	729	3 129	1.0	851	3 121	973	−122	−122	−14.3	−12.5	6	.8
...	31 173	Thurston	394	7 171	2 670	18.2	6 936	2 666	7 186	235	−250	3.4	−3.5	174	2.4
...	31 175	Valley	568	4 647	2 870	8.2	5 169	2 827	5 63.	−522	−464	−10.1	−8.2	75	1.6
5920	31 177	Washington	390	18 780	1 856	48.2	16 607	1 877	15 508	2 173	1 099	13.1	7.1	202	1.1
...	31 179	Wayne	443	9 851	2 461	22.2	9 364	2 441	9 858	487	−494	5.2	−5.0	146	1.5
...	31 181	Webster	575	4 061	2 917	7.1	4 279	2 890	4 858	−218	−579	−5.1	−11.9	22	.5
...	31 183	Wheeler	575	886	3 117	1.5	948	3 115	1 060	−62	−112	−6.5	−10.6	5	.6
...	31 185	York	576	14 598	2 112	25.3	14 428	2 024	14 798	170	−370	1.2	−2.5	205	1.4
	32 000	NEVADA	109 826	1 998 257	X	18.2	1 201 675	X	800 508	796 582	401 167	66.3	50.1	393 970	19.7
...	32 001	Churchill	4 929	23 982	1 594	4.9	17 938	1 792	13 917	6 044	4 021	33.7	28.9	2 076	8.7
4120	32 003	Clark	7 910	1 375 765	25	173.9	741 368	52	463 087	634 397	278 281	85.6	60.1	302 143	22.0
...	32 005	Douglas	710	41 259	1 072	58.1	27 637	1 366	19 421	13 622	8 216	49.3	42.3	3 057	7.4
...	32 007	Elko	17 179	45 291	993	2.6	33 463	1 178	17 269	11 828	16 194	35.3	93.8	8 935	19.7
...	32 009	Esmeralda	3 589	971	3 113	.3	1 344	3 104	777	−373	567	−27.8	73.0	99	10.2
...	32 011	Eureka	4 176	1 651	3 087	.4	1 547	3 094	1 198	104	349	6.7	29.1	158	9.6
...	32 013	Humboldt	9 648	16 106	2 015	1.7	12 844	2 152	9 449	3 262	3 395	25.4	35.9	3 040	18.9
...	32 015	Lander	5 494	5 794	2 804	1.1	6 266	2 728	4 076	−472	2 190	−7.5	53.7	1 073	18.5
...	32 017	Lincoln	10 634	4 165	2 903	.4	3 775	2 933	3 732	390	43	10.3	1.2	221	5.3
...	32 019	Lyon	1 994	34 501	1 264	17.3	20 001	1 678	13 594	14 500	6 407	72.5	47.1	3 784	11.0
...	32 021	Mineral	3 756	5 071	2 847	1.4	6 475	2 712	6 217	−1 404	258	−21.7	4.1	428	8.4
4120	32 023	Nye	18 147	32 485	1 333	1.8	17 781	1 799	9 048	14 704	8 733	82.7	96.5	2 713	8.4
...	32 027	Pershing	6 037	6 693	2 717	1.1	4 336	2 889	3 408	2 357	928	54.4	27.2	1 294	19.3
...	32 029	Storey	263	3 399	2 963	12.9	2 526	3 021	1 503	873	1 023	34.6	68.1	174	5.1
6720	32 031	Washoe	6 342	339 486	172	53.5	254 667	196	193 623	84 819	61 044	33.3	31.5	56 301	16.6
...	32 033	White Pine	8 876	9 181	2 515	1.0	9 264	2 447	8 167	−83	1 097	−.9	13.4	1 008	11.0
		Independent City													
...	32 510	Carson City city	143	52 457	891	366.8	40 443	988	32 022	12 014	8 421	29.7	26.3	7 466	14.2

[1] Federal Information Processing Standards (FIPS) codes for metropolitan areas defined as of June 30, 1999. [2] FIPS codes for states and counties/county equivalents. [3] Dry land and land temporarily or partially covered by water. [4] Based on 3,140 counties/county equivalents; excludes Yellowstone National Park in MT and South Boston independent city in VA which are no longer counties. When counties share the same rank, the next lower rank is omitted. [5] Includes count resolution corrections through 1997 and adjustments based on Census 2000 dress rehearsal results and boundary changes reported as legally effective as of January 1, 1998. [6] Persons of Hispanic or Latino origin may be of any race.

Sources: Land Area—U.S. Census Bureau, unpublished data file from Geography Division based on TIGER data base. 2000 Population—U.S. Census Bureau, Census of Population and Housing, Census 2000 Redistricting Data (Public Law 94-171) Summary Files (related Internet site <http://www.census.gov/dmd/www/2kresult.html>). 1990 Population—U.S. Census Bureau, "(CO-99-8) County Population Estimates and Demographic Components of Population Change: Annual Time Series, July 1, 1990 to July 1, 1999 (includes revised April 1, 1990 Population Estimates Base)"; published 9 March 2000; <http://www.census.gov/population/estimates/county/co-99-8/99C8_00.txt>. 1980 Population—U.S. Census Bureau, "1980–1990 Intercensal Population Estimates by County" on diskette (related Internet site <http://www.census.gov/population/www/estimates/countypop.html>).

Table B–1. Counties — **Area and Population**–Con.

[Includes U.S., states, and 3,142 counties/county equivalents defined as of January 1, 1992. For changes to these areas since January 1, 1992, see appendix B. Geographic Information]

Metro-politan area code[1]	State and county code[2]	County	Land area,[3] 2000 (sq. miles)	Population (April 1): 2000			1990[5]			Net change		Percent change		Hispanic or Latino,[6] 2000	
				Number	Rank[4]	Per square mile	Number	Rank[4]	1980	1990–2000	1980–1990	1990–2000	1980–1990	Number	Percent
	33 000	NEW HAMPSHIRE	8 968	1 235 786	X	137.8	1 109 252	X	920 610	126 534	188 642	11.4	20.5	20 489	1.7
...	33 001	Belknap	401	56 325	839	140.5	49 216	853	42 884	7 109	6 332	14.4	14.8	418	.7
...	33 003	Carroll	934	43 666	1 023	46.8	35 410	1 118	27 931	8 256	7 479	23.3	26.8	209	.5
...	33 005	Cheshire	707	73 825	678	104.4	70 121	631	62 116	3 704	8 005	5.3	12.9	529	.7
...	33 007	Coos	1 800	33 111	1 315	18.4	34 828	1 139	35 147	–1 717	–319	–4.9	–.9	201	.6
...	33 009	Grafton	1 713	81 743	635	47.7	74 929	601	65 806	6 814	9 123	9.1	13.9	914	1.1
1123	33 011	Hillsborough	876	380 841	153	434.8	335 838	152	276 608	45 003	59 230	13.4	21.4	12 166	3.2
...	33 013	Merrimack	934	136 225	396	145.9	120 240	385	98 302	15 985	21 938	13.3	22.3	1 362	1.0
1123	33 015	Rockingham	695	277 359	204	399.1	245 845	204	190 345	31 514	55 500	12.8	29.2	3 314	1.2
1123	33 017	Strafford	369	112 233	479	304.2	104 233	442	85 408	8 000	18 825	7.7	22.0	1 155	1.0
...	33 019	Sullivan	537	40 458	1 105	75.3	38 592	1 037	36 063	1 866	2 529	4.8	7.0	221	.5
	34 000	NEW JERSEY	7 417	8 414 350	X	1 134.5	7 747 750	X	7 365 011	666 600	382 739	8.6	5.2	1 117 191	13.3
6162	34 001	Atlantic	561	252 552	223	450.2	224 327	222	194 119	28 225	30 208	12.6	15.6	30 729	12.2
5602	34 003	Bergen	234	884 118	46	3 778.3	825 380	44	845 385	58 738	–20 005	7.1	–2.4	91 377	10.3
6162	34 005	Burlington	805	423 394	142	526.0	395 066	127	362 542	28 328	32 524	7.2	9.0	17 632	4.2
6162	34 007	Camden	222	508 932	110	2 292.5	502 824	96	471 650	6 108	31 174	1.2	6.6	49 166	9.7
6162	34 009	Cape May	255	102 326	519	401.3	95 089	488	82 266	7 237	12 823	7.6	15.6	3 378	3.3
6162	34 011	Cumberland	489	146 438	373	299.5	138 053	343	132 866	8 385	5 187	6.1	3.9	27 823	19.0
5602	34 013	Essex	126	793 633	59	6 298.7	777 964	50	851 304	15 669	–73 340	2.0	–8.6	122 347	15.4
6162	34 015	Gloucester	325	254 673	221	783.6	230 082	213	199 917	24 591	30 165	10.7	15.1	6 583	2.6
5602	34 017	Hudson	47	608 975	88	12 956.9	553 099	85	556 972	55 876	–3 873	10.1	–.7	242 123	39.8
5602	34 019	Hunterdon	430	121 989	445	283.7	107 852	427	87 361	14 137	20 491	13.1	23.5	3 371	2.8
5602	34 021	Mercer	226	350 761	167	1 552.0	325 759	157	307 863	25 002	17 896	7.7	5.8	33 898	9.7
5602	34 023	Middlesex	310	750 162	66	2 419.9	671 712	64	595 893	78 450	75 819	11.7	12.7	101 940	13.6
5602	34 025	Monmouth	472	615 301	87	1 303.6	553 192	84	503 173	62 109	50 019	11.2	9.9	38 175	6.2
5602	34 027	Morris	469	470 212	123	1 002.6	421 330	120	407 630	48 882	13 700	11.6	3.4	36 626	7.8
5602	34 029	Ocean	636	510 916	109	803.3	433 203	115	346 038	77 713	87 165	17.9	25.2	25 638	5.0
5602	34 031	Passaic	185	489 049	115	2 643.5	470 872	104	447 585	18 177	23 287	3.9	5.2	146 492	30.0
6162	34 033	Salem	338	64 285	758	190.2	65 294	671	64 676	–1 009	618	–1.5	1.0	2 498	3.9
5602	34 035	Somerset	305	297 490	190	975.4	240 222	207	203 129	57 268	37 093	23.8	18.3	25 811	8.7
5602	34 037	Sussex	521	144 166	379	276.7	130 936	354	116 119	13 230	14 817	10.1	12.8	4 822	3.3
5602	34 039	Union	103	522 541	106	5 073.2	493 819	99	504 094	28 722	–10 275	5.8	–2.0	103 011	19.7
5602	34 041	Warren	358	102 437	518	286.1	91 675	501	84 429	10 762	7 246	11.7	8.6	3 751	3.7
	35 000	NEW MEXICO	121 356	1 819 046	X	15.0	1 515 069	X	1 303 302	303 977	211 767	20.1	16.2	765 386	42.1
0200	35 001	Bernalillo	1 166	556 678	100	477.4	480 577	102	420 261	76 101	60 316	15.8	14.4	233 565	42.0
...	35 003	Catron	6 928	3 543	2 952	.5	2 563	3 019	2 720	980	–157	38.2	–5.8	679	19.2
...	35 005	Chaves	6 071	61 382	792	10.1	57 849	751	51 103	3 533	6 746	6.1	13.2	26 904	43.8
...	35 006	Cibola	4 539	25 595	1 532	5.6	23 794	1 500	[7]30 347	1 801	[7]–6 553	7.6	[7]–21.6	8 555	33.4
...	35 007	Colfax	3 757	14 189	2 148	3.8	12 925	2 143	13 667	1 264	–742	9.8	–5.4	6 739	47.5
...	35 009	Curry	1 406	45 044	998	32.0	42 207	954	42 019	2 837	188	6.7	.4	13 685	30.4
...	35 011	DeBaca	2 325	2 240	3 048	1.0	2 252	3 047	2 454	–12	–202	–.5	–8.2	790	35.3
4100	35 013	Dona Ana	3 807	174 682	313	45.9	135 510	346	96 340	39 172	39 170	28.9	40.7	110 665	63.4
...	35 015	Eddy	4 182	51 658	898	12.4	48 605	861	47 855	3 053	750	6.3	1.6	20 023	38.8
...	35 017	Grant	3 966	31 002	1 378	7.8	27 676	1 364	26 204	3 326	1 472	12.0	5.6	15 126	48.8
...	35 019	Guadalupe	3 030	4 680	2 868	1.5	4 156	2 900	4 496	524	–340	12.6	–7.6	3 801	81.2
...	35 021	Harding	2 125	810	3 123	.4	987	3 114	1 090	–177	–103	–17.9	–9.4	364	44.9
...	35 023	Hidalgo	3 446	5 932	2 790	1.7	5 958	2 763	6 049	–26	–91	–.4	–1.5	3 324	56.0
...	35 025	Lea	4 393	55 511	850	12.6	55 765	777	55 993	–254	–228	–.5	–.4	22 010	39.6
...	35 027	Lincoln	4 831	19 411	1 822	4.0	12 219	2 200	10 997	7 192	1 222	58.9	11.1	4 975	25.6
7490	35 028	Los Alamos	109	18 343	1 877	168.3	18 115	1 783	17 599	228	516	1.3	2.9	2 155	11.7
...	35 029	Luna	2 965	25 016	1 559	8.4	18 110	1 784	15 585	6 906	2 525	38.1	16.2	14 435	57.7
...	35 031	McKinley	5 449	74 798	667	13.7	60 686	716	56 536	14 112	4 150	23.3	7.3	9 276	12.4
...	35 033	Mora	1 931	5 180	2 838	2.7	4 264	2 893	4 205	916	59	21.5	1.4	4 229	81.6
...	35 035	Otero	6 627	62 298	781	9.4	51 928	814	44 665	10 370	7 263	20.0	16.3	20 033	32.2
...	35 037	Quay	2 875	10 155	2 431	3.5	10 823	2 309	10 577	–668	246	–6.2	2.3	3 857	38.0
...	35 039	Rio Arriba	5 858	41 190	1 074	7.0	34 365	1 158	29 282	6 825	5 083	19.9	17.4	30 025	72.9
...	35 041	Roosevelt	2 449	18 018	1 896	7.4	16 702	1 868	15 695	1 316	1 007	7.9	6.4	5 998	33.3
0200	35 043	Sandoval	3 709	89 908	575	24.2	63 319	689	34 400	26 589	28 919	42.0	84.1	26 437	29.4
...	35 045	San Juan	5 514	113 801	473	20.6	91 605	502	81 433	22 196	10 172	24.2	12.5	17 057	15.0
...	35 047	San Miguel	4 717	30 126	1 392	6.4	25 743	1 430	22 751	4 383	2 992	17.0	13.2	23 487	78.0
7490	35 049	Santa Fe	1 909	129 292	417	67.7	98 928	465	75 519	30 364	23 409	30.7	31.0	63 405	49.0
...	35 051	Sierra	4 180	13 270	2 205	3.2	9 912	2 395	8 454	3 358	1 458	33.9	17.2	3 488	26.3
...	35 053	Socorro	6 646	18 078	1 895	2.7	14 764	2 002	12 566	3 314	2 198	22.4	17.5	8 810	48.7
...	35 055	Taos	2 203	29 979	1 397	13.6	23 118	1 532	19 456	6 861	3 662	29.7	18.8	17 370	57.9
...	35 057	Torrance	3 345	16 911	1 958	5.1	10 285	2 361	7 491	6 626	2 794	64.4	37.3	6 283	37.2
...	35 059	Union	3 830	4 174	2 901	1.1	4 124	2 904	4 725	50	–601	1.2	–12.7	1 465	35.1
0200	35 061	Valencia	1 068	66 152	739	61.9	45 235	910	[7]30 768	20 917	[7]14 467	46.2	[7]47.0	36 371	55.0

[1] Federal Information Processing Standards (FIPS) codes for metropolitan areas defined as of June 30, 1999. [2] FIPS codes for states and counties/county equivalents. [3] Dry land and land temporarily or partially covered by water. [4] Based on 3,140 counties/county equivalents; excludes Yellowstone National Park in MT and South Boston independent city in VA which are no longer counties. When counties share the same rank, the next lower rank is omitted. [5] Includes count resolution corrections through 1997 and adjustments based on Census 2000 dress rehearsal results and boundary changes reported as legally effective as of January 1, 1998. [6] Persons of Hispanic or Latino origin may be of any race. [7] 1980 population based on 1990 county boundaries.

Sources: Land Area—U.S. Census Bureau, unpublished data file from Geography Division based on TIGER data base. 2000 Population—U.S. Census Bureau, Census of Population and Housing, Census 2000 Redistricting Data (Public Law 94-171) Summary Files (related Internet site <http://www.census.gov/dmd/www/2kresult.html>). 1990 Population—U.S. Census Bureau, "(CO-99-8) County Population Estimates and Demographic Components of Population Change: Annual Time Series, July 1, 1990 to July 1, 1999 (includes revised April 1, 1990 Population Estimates Base)"; published 9 March 2000; <http://www. census.gov/population/estimates/county/co-99-8/99C8_00.txt>. 1980 Population—U.S. Census Bureau, "1980–1990 Intercensal Population Estimates by County" on diskette (related Internet site <http://www.census.gov/population/www/estimates/countypop.html>).

Table B–1. Counties — **Area and Population**–Con.

[Includes U.S., states, and 3,142 counties/county equivalents defined as of January 1, 1992. For changes to these areas since January 1, 1992, see appendix B. Geographic Information]

Metro-politan area code[1]	State and county code[2]	County	Land area,[3] 2000 (sq. miles)	Population 2000 Number	Rank[4]	Per square mile	Population 1990[5] Number	Rank[4]	1980	Net change 1990–2000	Net change 1980–1990	Percent change 1990–2000	Percent change 1980–1990	Hispanic or Latino,[6] 2000 Number	Percent
	36 000	NEW YORK	47 214	18 976 457	X	401.9	17 990 778	X	17 558 165	985 679	432 613	5.5	2.5	2 867 583	15.1
0160	36 001	Albany.................	523	294 565	191	563.2	292 812	166	285 909	1 753	6 903	.6	2.4	9 079	3.1
...	36 003	Allegany...............	1 030	49 927	917	48.5	50 470	836	51 742	–543	–1 272	–1.1	–2.5	454	.9
5602	36 005	Bronx..................	42	1 332 650	27	31 729.8	1 203 789	24	1 168 972	128 861	34 817	10.7	3.0	644 705	48.4
0960	36 007	Broome.................	707	200 536	274	283.6	212 160	235	213 648	–11 624	–1 488	–5.5	–.7	3 986	2.0
...	36 009	Cattaraugus............	1 310	83 955	619	64.1	84 234	542	85 697	–279	–1 463	–.3	–1.7	791	.9
8160	36 011	Cayuga.................	693	81 963	633	118.3	82 313	551	79 894	–350	2 419	–.4	3.0	1 611	2.0
3610	36 013	Chautauqua............	1 062	139 750	391	131.6	141 895	336	146 925	–2 145	–5 030	–1.5	–3.4	5 901	4.2
2335	36 015	Chemung...............	408	91 070	565	223.2	95 195	486	97 656	–4 125	–2 461	–4.3	–2.5	1 609	1.8
...	36 017	Chenango..............	894	51 401	900	57.5	51 768	816	49 344	–367	2 424	–.7	4.9	548	1.1
...	36 019	Clinton................	1 039	79 894	643	76.9	85 969	533	80 750	–6 075	5 219	–7.1	6.5	1 964	2.5
...	36 021	Columbia...............	636	63 094	769	99.2	62 982	692	59 487	112	3 495	.2	5.9	1 598	2.5
...	36 023	Cortland...............	500	48 599	937	97.2	48 963	856	48 820	–364	143	–.7	.3	565	1.2
...	36 025	Delaware	1 446	48 055	952	33.2	47 352	886	46 824	703	528	1.5	1.1	983	2.0
5602	36 027	Dutchess...............	802	280 150	201	349.3	259 462	194	245 055	20 688	14 407	8.0	5.9	18 060	6.4
1280	36 029	Erie...................	1 044	950 265	37	910.2	968 584	32	1 015 472	–18 319	–46 888	–1.9	–4.6	31 054	3.3
...	36 031	Essex..................	1 797	38 851	1 145	21.6	37 152	1 069	36 176	1 699	976	4.6	2.7	851	2.2
...	36 033	Franklin...............	1 631	51 134	904	31.4	46 540	896	44 929	4 594	1 611	9.9	3.6	2 053	4.0
...	36 035	Fulton.................	496	55 073	858	111.0	54 191	793	55 153	882	–962	1.6	–1.7	884	1.6
6840	36 037	Genesee................	494	60 370	802	122.2	60 060	723	59 400	310	660	.5	1.1	904	1.5
...	36 039	Greene.................	648	48 195	944	74.4	44 739	915	40 861	3 456	3 878	7.7	9.5	2 075	4.3
...	36 041	Hamilton...............	1 720	5 379	2 822	3.1	5 279	2 822	5 034	100	245	1.9	4.9	57	1.1
8680	36 043	Herkimer...............	1 411	64 427	755	45.7	65 809	666	66 714	–1 382	–905	–2.1	–1.4	580	.9
...	36 045	Jefferson..............	1 272	111 738	482	87.8	110 943	416	88 151	795	22 792	.7	25.9	4 677	4.2
5602	36 047	Kings..................	71	2 465 326	7	34 722.9	2 300 664	6	2 231 028	164 662	69 636	7.2	3.1	487 878	19.8
...	36 049	Lewis..................	1 275	26 944	1 485	21.1	26 796	1 396	25 035	148	1 761	.6	7.0	172	.6
6840	36 051	Livingston.............	632	64 328	757	101.8	62 372	698	57 006	1 956	5 366	3.1	9.4	1 459	2.3
8160	36 053	Madison................	656	69 441	713	105.9	69 166	641	65 150	275	4 016	.4	6.2	734	1.1
6840	36 055	Monroe.................	659	735 343	68	1 115.8	713 968	58	702 238	21 375	11 730	3.0	1.7	39 065	5.3
0160	36 057	Montgomery.............	405	49 708	921	122.7	51 981	813	53 439	–2 273	–1 458	–4.4	–2.7	3 433	6.9
5602	36 059	Nassau.................	287	1 334 544	26	4 650.0	1 287 873	22	1 321 582	46 671	–33 709	3.6	–2.6	133 282	10.0
5602	36 061	New York...............	23	1 537 195	17	66 834.6	1 487 536	15	1 428 285	49 659	59 251	3.3	4.1	417 816	27.2
1280	36 063	Niagara................	523	219 846	257	420.4	220 756	225	227 354	–910	–6 598	–.4	–2.9	2 913	1.3
8680	36 065	Oneida.................	1 213	235 469	246	194.1	250 836	199	253 466	–15 367	–2 630	–6.1	–1.0	7 545	3.2
8160	36 067	Onondaga...............	780	458 336	126	587.6	468 973	105	463 920	–10 637	5 053	–2.3	1.1	11 175	2.4
6840	36 069	Ontario................	644	100 224	524	155.6	95 101	487	88 909	5 123	6 192	5.4	7.0	2 149	2.1
5602	36 071	Orange.................	816	341 367	171	418.3	307 571	162	259 603	33 796	47 968	11.0	18.5	39 738	11.6
6840	36 073	Orleans................	391	44 171	1 013	113.0	41 846	959	38 496	2 325	3 350	5.6	8.7	1 719	3.9
8160	36 075	Oswego.................	953	122 377	444	128.4	121 785	378	113 901	592	7 884	.5	6.9	1 592	1.3
...	36 077	Otsego.................	1 003	61 676	788	61.5	60 390	718	59 075	1 286	1 315	2.1	2.2	1 171	1.9
5602	36 079	Putnam.................	231	95 745	541	414.5	83 941	545	77 193	11 804	6 748	14.1	8.7	5 976	6.2
5602	36 081	Queens.................	109	2 229 379	9	20 453.0	1 951 598	9	1 891 325	277 781	60 273	14.2	3.2	556 605	25.0
0160	36 083	Rensselaer.............	654	152 538	349	233.2	154 429	301	151 966	–1 891	2 463	–1.2	1.6	3 225	2.1
5602	36 085	Richmond...............	58	443 728	134	7 650.5	378 977	133	352 029	64 751	26 948	17.1	7.7	53 550	12.1
5602	36 087	Rockland...............	174	286 753	195	1 648.0	265 475	185	259 530	21 278	5 945	8.0	2.3	29 182	10.2
...	36 089	St. Lawrence...........	2 686	111 931	481	41.7	111 974	410	114 347	–43	–2 373	Z	–2.1	2 008	1.8
0160	36 091	Saratoga...............	812	200 635	273	247.1	181 276	270	153 759	19 359	27 517	10.7	17.9	2 834	1.4
0160	36 093	Schenectady............	206	146 555	372	711.4	149 285	317	149 946	–2 730	–661	–1.8	–.4	4 639	3.2
0160	36 095	Schoharie..............	622	31 582	1 359	50.8	31 840	1 216	29 710	–258	2 130	–.8	7.2	588	1.9
...	36 097	Schuyler...............	329	19 224	1 831	58.4	18 662	1 754	17 686	562	976	3.0	5.5	235	1.2
...	36 099	Seneca.................	325	33 342	1 303	102.6	33 683	1 174	33 733	–341	–50	–1.0	–.1	659	2.0
...	36 101	Steuben	1 393	98 726	528	70.9	99 088	463	99 217	–362	–129	–.4	–.1	796	.8
5602	36 103	Suffolk................	912	1 419 369	22	1 556.3	1 321 339	20	1 284 231	98 030	37 108	7.4	2.9	149 411	10.5
...	36 105	Sullivan...............	970	73 966	675	76.3	69 277	640	65 155	4 689	4 122	6.8	6.3	6 839	9.2
0960	36 107	Tioga..................	519	51 784	896	99.8	52 337	809	49 812	–553	2 525	–1.1	5.1	509	1.0
...	36 109	Tompkins...............	476	96 501	535	202.7	94 097	491	87 085	2 404	7 012	2.6	8.1	2 968	3.1
...	36 111	Ulster.................	1 126	177 749	310	157.9	165 380	287	158 158	12 369	7 222	7.5	4.6	10 941	6.2
2975	36 113	Warren.................	869	63 303	766	72.8	59 209	736	54 854	4 094	4 355	6.9	7.9	663	1.0
2975	36 115	Washington	835	61 042	798	73.1	59 330	731	54 795	1 712	4 535	2.9	8.3	1 232	2.0
6840	36 117	Wayne..................	604	93 765	547	155.2	89 123	515	84 581	4 642	4 542	5.2	5.4	2 263	2.4
5602	36 119	Westchester............	433	923 459	40	2 132.7	874 866	35	866 599	48 593	8 267	5.6	1.0	144 124	15.6
...	36 121	Wyoming................	593	43 424	1 030	73.2	42 507	945	39 895	917	2 612	2.2	6.5	1 278	2.9
...	36 123	Yates..................	338	24 621	1 570	72.8	22 810	1 542	21 459	1 811	1 351	7.9	6.3	228	.9

[1] Federal Information Processing Standards (FIPS) codes for metropolitan areas defined as of June 30, 1999. [2] FIPS codes for states and counties/county equivalents. [3] Dry land and land temporarily or partially covered by water. [4] Based on 3,140 counties/county equivalents; excludes Yellowstone National Park in MT and South Boston independent city in VA which are no longer counties. When counties share the same rank, the next lower rank is omitted. [5] Includes count resolution corrections through 1997 and adjustments based on Census 2000 dress rehearsal results and boundary changes reported as legally effective as of January 1, 1998. [6] Persons of Hispanic or Latino origin may be of any race.

Sources: Land Area—U.S. Census Bureau, unpublished data file from Geography Division based on TIGER data base. 2000 Population—U.S. Census Bureau, Census of Population and Housing, Census 2000 Redistricting Data (Public Law 94-171) Summary Files (related Internet site <http://www.census.gov/dmd/www/2kresult.html>). 1990 Population—U.S. Census Bureau, "(CO-99-8) County Population Estimates and Demographic Components of Population Change: Annual Time Series, July 1, 1990 to July 1, 1999 (includes revised April 1, 1990 Population Estimates Base)"; published 9 March 2000; <http://www. census.gov/population/estimates/county/co-99-8/99C8_00.txt>. 1980 Population—U.S. Census Bureau, "1980–1990 Intercensal Population Estimates by County" on diskette (related Internet site <http://www.census.gov/population/www/estimates/countypop.html>).

Table B–1. Counties — **Area and Population**–Con.

[Includes U.S., states, and 3,142 counties/county equivalents defined as of January 1, 1992. For changes to these areas since January 1, 1992, see appendix B. Geographic Information]

Metro-politan area code[1]	State and county code[2]	County	Land area,[3] 2000 (sq. miles)	Population (April 1) 2000 Number	2000 Rank[4]	2000 Per square mile	1990[5] Number	1990[5] Rank[4]	1980	Net change 1990–2000	Net change 1980–1990	Percent change 1990–2000	Percent change 1980–1990	Hispanic or Latino,[6] 2000 Number	Hispanic or Latino,[6] 2000 Percent
	37 000	NORTH CAROLINA	48 711	8 049 313	X	165.2	6 632 448	X	5 880 095	1 416 865	752 353	21.4	12.8	378 963	4.7
3120	37 001	Alamance	430	130 800	410	304.2	108 213	426	99 319	22 587	8 894	20.9	9.0	8 835	6.8
3290	37 003	Alexander	260	33 603	1 297	129.2	27 544	1 372	24 999	6 059	2 545	22.0	10.2	841	2.5
...	37 005	Alleghany	235	10 677	2 387	45.4	9 590	2 424	9 587	1 087	3	11.3	Z	530	5.0
...	37 007	Anson	532	25 275	1 555	47.5	23 474	1 515	25 649	1 801	–2 175	7.7	–8.5	211	.8
...	37 009	Ashe	426	24 384	1 579	57.2	22 209	1 571	22 325	2 175	–116	9.8	–.5	590	2.4
...	37 011	Avery	247	17 167	1 943	69.5	14 867	1 997	14 409	2 300	458	15.5	3.2	413	2.4
...	37 013	Beaufort	828	44 958	1 000	54.3	42 283	953	40 355	2 675	1 928	6.3	4.8	1 455	3.2
...	37 015	Bertie	699	19 773	1 803	28.3	20 388	1 656	21 024	–615	–636	–3.0	–3.0	195	1.0
...	37 017	Bladen	875	32 278	1 340	36.9	28 663	1 341	30 491	3 615	–1 828	12.6	–6.0	1 198	3.7
9200	37 019	Brunswick	855	73 143	685	85.5	50 985	828	35 777	22 158	15 208	43.5	42.5	1 960	2.7
0480	37 021	Buncombe	656	206 330	269	314.5	174 357	276	160 934	31 973	13 423	18.3	8.3	5 730	2.8
3290	37 023	Burke	507	89 148	582	175.8	75 740	593	72 504	13 408	3 236	17.7	4.5	3 180	3.6
1520	37 025	Cabarrus	364	131 063	408	360.1	98 935	464	85 895	32 128	13 040	32.5	15.2	6 620	5.1
3290	37 027	Caldwell	472	77 415	655	164.0	70 709	627	67 746	6 706	2 963	9.5	4.4	1 927	2.5
...	37 029	Camden	241	6 885	2 696	28.6	5 904	2 771	5 829	981	75	16.6	1.3	49	.7
...	37 031	Carteret	520	59 383	809	114.2	52 407	807	41 092	6 976	11 315	13.3	27.5	1 035	1.7
...	37 033	Caswell	425	23 501	1 615	55.3	20 662	1 646	20 705	2 839	–43	13.7	–.2	415	1.8
3290	37 035	Catawba	400	141 685	386	354.2	118 412	393	105 208	23 273	13 204	19.7	12.6	7 886	5.6
6640	37 037	Chatham	683	49 329	927	72.2	38 979	1 023	33 415	10 350	5 564	26.6	16.7	4 743	9.6
...	37 039	Cherokee	455	24 298	1 584	53.4	20 170	1 666	18 933	4 128	1 237	20.5	6.5	303	1.2
...	37 041	Chowan	173	14 526	2 120	84.0	13 506	2 101	12 558	1 020	948	7.6	7.5	219	1.5
...	37 043	Clay	215	8 775	2 547	40.8	7 155	2 638	6 619	1 620	536	22.6	8.1	73	.8
...	37 045	Cleveland	465	96 287	538	207.1	84 958	540	83 435	11 329	1 523	13.3	1.8	1 433	1.5
...	37 047	Columbus	937	54 749	861	58.4	49 587	847	51 037	5 162	–1 450	10.4	–2.8	1 269	2.3
...	37 049	Craven	708	91 436	561	129.1	81 812	555	71 043	9 624	10 769	11.8	15.2	3 677	4.0
2560	37 051	Cumberland	653	302 963	187	464.0	274 713	181	247 160	28 250	27 553	10.3	11.1	20 919	6.9
5720	37 053	Currituck	262	18 190	1 888	69.4	13 736	2 079	11 089	4 454	2 647	32.4	23.9	261	1.4
...	37 055	Dare	384	29 967	1 398	78.0	22 746	1 547	13 377	7 221	9 369	31.7	70.0	666	2.2
3120	37 057	Davidson	552	147 246	369	266.8	126 688	366	113 162	20 558	13 526	16.2	12.0	4 765	3.2
3120	37 059	Davie	265	34 835	1 257	131.5	27 859	1 355	24 599	6 976	3 260	25.0	13.3	1 209	3.5
...	37 061	Duplin	818	49 063	929	60.0	39 995	999	40 952	9 068	–957	22.7	–2.3	7 426	15.1
6640	37 063	Durham	290	223 314	254	770.0	181 844	267	152 235	41 470	29 609	22.8	19.4	17 039	7.6
6895	37 065	Edgecombe	505	55 606	849	110.1	56 692	769	55 988	–1 086	704	–1.9	1.3	1 554	2.8
3120	37 067	Forsyth	410	306 067	186	746.5	265 855	184	243 704	40 212	22 151	15.1	9.1	19 577	6.4
6640	37 069	Franklin	492	47 260	963	96.1	36 414	1 092	30 055	10 846	6 359	29.8	21.2	2 100	4.4
1520	37 071	Gaston	356	190 365	289	534.7	174 769	275	162 568	15 596	12 201	8.9	7.5	5 719	3.0
...	37 073	Gates	341	10 516	2 396	30.8	9 305	2 443	8 875	1 211	430	13.0	4.8	81	.8
...	37 075	Graham	292	7 993	2 607	27.4	7 196	2 604	7 217	797	–21	11.1	–.3	60	.8
...	37 077	Granville	531	48 498	941	91.3	38 341	1 044	34 043	10 157	4 298	26.5	12.6	1 951	4.0
...	37 079	Greene	265	18 974	1 848	71.6	15 384	1 965	16 117	3 590	–733	23.3	–4.5	1 511	8.0
3120	37 081	Guilford	649	421 048	143	648.8	347 431	148	317 154	73 617	30 277	21.2	9.5	15 985	3.8
...	37 083	Halifax	725	57 370	832	79.1	55 516	780	55 076	1 854	440	3.3	.8	579	1.0
...	37 085	Harnett	595	91 025	566	153.0	67 833	653	59 570	23 192	8 263	34.2	13.9	5 336	5.9
...	37 087	Haywood	554	54 033	868	97.5	46 948	891	46 495	7 085	453	15.1	1.0	763	1.4
...	37 089	Henderson	374	89 173	581	238.4	69 747	637	58 580	19 426	11 167	27.9	19.1	4 880	5.5
...	37 091	Hertford	353	22 601	1 666	64.0	22 317	1 562	23 368	284	–1 051	1.3	–4.5	354	1.6
...	37 093	Hoke	391	33 646	1 293	86.1	22 856	1 539	20 383	10 790	2 473	47.2	12.1	2 415	7.2
...	37 095	Hyde	613	5 826	2 801	9.5	5 411	2 807	5 873	415	–462	7.7	–7.9	131	2.2
...	37 097	Iredell	576	122 660	442	213.0	93 205	496	82 538	29 455	10 667	31.6	12.9	4 182	3.4
...	37 099	Jackson	491	33 121	1 314	67.5	26 835	1 394	25 811	6 286	1 024	23.4	4.0	577	1.7
6640	37 101	Johnston	792	121 965	446	154.0	81 306	560	70 599	40 659	10 707	50.0	15.2	9 440	7.7
...	37 103	Jones	472	10 381	2 404	22.0	9 361	2 442	9 705	1 020	–344	10.9	–3.5	282	2.7
...	37 105	Lee	257	49 040	930	190.8	41 370	973	36 718	7 670	4 652	18.5	12.7	5 715	11.7
1520	37 107	Lenoir	400	59 648	805	149.1	57 274	762	59 819	2 374	–2 545	4.1	–4.3	1 891	3.2
1520	37 109	Lincoln	299	63 780	761	213.3	50 319	838	42 372	13 461	7 947	26.8	18.8	3 656	5.7
...	37 111	McDowell	442	42 151	1 055	95.4	35 681	1 108	35 135	6 470	546	18.1	1.6	1 214	2.9
...	37 113	Macon	516	29 811	1 403	57.8	23 504	1 513	20 178	6 307	3 326	26.8	16.5	454	1.5
0480	37 115	Madison	449	19 635	1 815	43.7	16 953	1 850	16 827	2 682	126	15.8	.7	266	1.4
...	37 117	Martin	461	25 593	1 534	55.5	25 078	1 458	25 948	515	–870	2.1	–3.4	528	2.1
1520	37 119	Mecklenburg	526	695 454	72	1 322.2	511 211	92	404 270	184 243	106 941	36.0	26.5	44 871	6.5
...	37 121	Mitchell	221	15 687	2 039	71.0	14 433	2 022	14 428	1 254	5	8.7	Z	311	2.0
...	37 123	Montgomery	492	26 822	1 490	54.5	23 359	1 524	22 469	3 463	890	14.8	4.0	2 797	10.4
...	37 125	Moore	698	74 769	668	107.1	59 000	737	50 505	15 769	8 495	26.7	16.8	2 981	4.0
6895	37 127	Nash	540	87 420	599	161.9	76 677	589	67 153	10 743	9 524	14.0	14.2	2 939	3.4
9200	37 129	New Hanover	199	160 307	332	805.6	120 284	384	103 471	40 023	16 813	33.3	16.2	3 276	2.0
...	37 131	Northampton	536	22 086	1 689	41.2	21 004	1 629	22 195	1 082	–1 191	5.2	–5.4	161	.7
3605	37 133	Onslow	767	150 355	358	196.0	149 838	315	112 784	517	37 054	.3	32.9	10 896	7.2

[1] Federal Information Processing Standards (FIPS) codes for metropolitan areas defined as of June 30, 1999.   [2] FIPS codes for states and counties/county equivalents.   [3] Dry land and land temporarily or partially covered by water.   [4] Based on 3,140 counties/county equivalents; excludes Yellowstone National Park in MT and South Boston independent city in VA which are no longer counties. When counties share the same rank, the next lower rank is omitted.   [5] Includes count resolution corrections through 1997 and adjustments based on Census 2000 dress rehearsal results and boundary changes reported as legally effective as of January 1, 1998.   [6] Persons of Hispanic or Latino origin may be of any race.

Sources: Land Area—U.S. Census Bureau, unpublished data file from Geography Division based on TIGER data base.   2000 Population—U.S. Census Bureau, Census of Population and Housing, Census 2000 Redistricting Data (Public Law 94-171) Summary Files (related Internet site <http://www.census.gov/dmd/www/2kresult.html>).   1990 Population—U.S. Census Bureau, "(CO-99-8) County Population Estimates and Demographic Components of Population Change: Annual Time Series, July 1, 1990 to July 1, 1999 (includes revised April 1, 1990 Population Estimates Base)," published 9 March 2000; <http://www. census.gov/population/estimates/county/co-99-8/99C8_00.txt>.   1980 Population—U.S. Census Bureau, "1980–1990 Intercensal Population Estimates by County" on diskette (related Internet site <http://www.census.gov/population/www/estimates/countypop.html>).

[Includes U.S., states, and 3,142 counties/county equivalents defined as of January 1, 1992. For changes to these areas since January 1, 1992, see appendix B. Geographic Information]

Metro-politan area code[1]	State and county code[2]	County	Land area,[3] 2000 (sq. miles)	Population (April 1) 2000 Number	2000 Rank[4]	Per square mile	1990[5] Number	1990 Rank[4]	1980	Net change 1990–2000	Net change 1980–1990	Percent change 1990–2000	Percent change 1980–1990	Hispanic or Latino,[6] 2000 Number	Percent
		NORTH CAROLINA–Con.													
6640	37 135	Orange	400	118 227	457	295.6	93 662	493	77 055	24 565	16 607	26.2	21.6	5 273	4.5
...	37 137	Pamlico	337	12 934	2 238	38.4	11 368	2 263	10 398	1 566	970	13.8	9.3	171	1.3
...	37 139	Pasquotank	227	34 897	1 254	153.7	31 298	1 236	28 462	3 599	2 836	11.5	10.0	429	1.2
...	37 141	Pender	871	41 082	1 080	47.2	28 855	1 334	22 262	12 227	6 593	42.4	29.6	1 496	3.6
...	37 143	Perquimans	247	11 368	2 344	46.0	10 447	2 342	9 486	921	961	8.8	10.1	68	.6
...	37 145	Person	392	35 623	1 228	90.9	30 180	1 290	29 164	5 443	1 016	18.0	3.5	746	2.1
3150	37 147	Pitt	652	133 798	401	205.2	108 480	424	90 146	25 318	18 334	23.3	20.3	4 216	3.2
...	37 149	Polk	238	18 324	1 879	77.0	14 458	2 020	12 984	3 866	1 474	26.7	11.4	551	3.0
3120	37 151	Randolph	787	130 454	411	165.8	106 546	434	91 300	23 908	15 246	22.4	16.7	8 646	6.6
...	37 153	Richmond	474	46 564	969	98.2	44 511	918	45 161	2 053	–650	4.6	–1.4	1 319	2.8
...	37 155	Robeson	949	123 339	437	130.0	105 170	439	101 610	18 169	3 560	17.3	3.5	5 994	4.9
...	37 157	Rockingham	566	91 928	556	162.4	86 064	532	83 426	5 864	2 638	6.8	3.2	2 825	3.1
1520	37 159	Rowan	511	130 340	413	255.1	110 605	418	99 186	19 735	11 419	17.8	11.5	5 369	4.1
...	37 161	Rutherford	564	62 899	773	111.5	56 956	765	53 787	5 943	3 169	10.4	5.9	1 136	1.8
...	37 163	Sampson	945	60 161	804	63.7	47 297	887	49 687	12 864	–2 390	27.2	–4.8	6 477	10.8
...	37 165	Scotland	319	35 998	1 218	112.8	33 763	1 171	32 273	2 235	1 490	6.6	4.6	423	1.2
...	37 167	Stanly	395	58 100	823	147.1	51 765	817	48 517	6 335	3 248	12.2	6.7	1 237	2.1
3120	37 169	Stokes	452	44 711	1 004	98.9	37 224	1 066	33 086	7 487	4 138	20.1	12.5	836	1.9
...	37 171	Surry	537	71 219	697	132.6	61 704	707	59 449	9 515	2 255	15.4	3.8	4 620	6.5
...	37 173	Swain	528	12 968	2 235	24.6	11 268	2 277	10 283	1 700	985	15.1	9.6	191	1.5
...	37 175	Transylvania	378	29 334	1 418	77.6	25 520	1 446	23 417	3 814	2 103	14.9	9.0	298	1.0
...	37 177	Tyrrell	390	4 149	2 904	10.6	3 856	2 928	3 975	293	–119	7.6	–3.0	150	3.6
1520	37 179	Union	637	123 677	435	194.2	84 210	543	70 436	39 467	13 774	46.9	19.6	7 637	6.2
...	37 181	Vance	254	42 954	1 038	169.1	38 892	1 025	36 748	4 062	2 144	10.4	5.8	1 957	4.6
6640	37 183	Wake	832	627 846	85	754.6	426 311	118	301 429	201 535	124 882	47.3	41.4	33 985	5.4
...	37 185	Warren	429	19 972	1 794	46.6	17 265	1 837	16 232	2 707	1 033	15.7	6.4	317	1.6
...	37 187	Washington	348	13 723	2 180	39.4	13 997	2 058	14 801	–274	–804	–2.0	–5.4	311	2.3
...	37 189	Watauga	313	42 695	1 044	136.4	36 952	1 074	31 666	5 743	5 286	15.5	16.7	622	1.5
2980	37 191	Wayne	553	113 329	475	204.9	104 666	441	97 054	8 663	7 612	8.3	7.8	5 604	4.9
...	37 193	Wilkes	757	65 632	743	86.7	59 393	728	58 657	6 239	736	10.5	1.3	2 262	3.4
...	37 195	Wilson	371	73 814	679	199.0	66 061	663	63 132	7 753	2 929	11.7	4.6	4 457	6.0
3120	37 197	Yadkin	336	36 348	1 204	108.2	30 488	1 269	28 439	5 860	2 049	19.2	7.2	2 357	6.5
...	37 199	Yancey	312	17 774	1 911	57.0	15 419	1 962	14 934	2 355	485	15.3	3.2	478	2.7
	38 000	**NORTH DAKOTA**	68 976	642 200	X	9.3	638 800	X	652 717	3 400	–13 917	.5	–2.1	7 786	1.2
...	38 001	Adams	988	2 593	3 021	2.6	3 174	2 986	3 584	–581	–410	–18.3	–11.4	7	.3
...	38 003	Barnes	1 492	11 775	2 309	7.9	12 545	2 179	13 960	–770	–1 415	–6.1	–10.1	64	.5
...	38 005	Benson	1 381	6 964	2 689	5.0	7 198	2 633	7 944	–234	–746	–3.3	–9.4	55	.8
...	38 007	Billings	1 151	888	3 115	.8	1 108	3 110	1 138	–220	–30	–19.9	–2.6	3	.3
...	38 009	Bottineau	1 669	7 149	2 672	4.3	8 011	2 564	9 239	–862	–1 228	–10.8	–13.3	35	.5
...	38 011	Bowman	1 162	3 242	2 977	2.8	3 596	2 950	4 229	–354	–633	–9.8	–15.0	22	.7
...	38 013	Burke	1 104	2 242	3 047	2.0	3 002	3 000	3 822	–760	–820	–25.3	–21.5	8	.4
1010	38 015	Burleigh	1 633	69 416	715	42.5	60 131	722	54 811	9 285	5 320	15.4	9.7	468	.7
2520	38 017	Cass	1 765	123 138	438	69.8	102 874	447	88 247	20 264	14 627	19.7	16.6	1 518	1.2
...	38 019	Cavalier	1 488	4 831	2 858	3.2	6 064	2 749	7 636	–1 233	–1 572	–20.3	–20.6	31	.6
...	38 021	Dickey	1 131	5 757	2 805	5.1	6 107	2 742	7 207	–350	–1 100	–5.7	–15.3	78	1.4
...	38 023	Divide	1 260	2 283	3 042	1.8	2 899	3 006	3 494	–616	–595	–21.2	–17.0	14	.6
...	38 025	Dunn	2 010	3 600	2 945	1.8	4 005	2 919	4 627	–405	–622	–10.1	–13.4	27	.8
...	38 027	Eddy	630	2 757	3 008	4.4	2 951	3 003	3 554	–194	–603	–6.6	–17.0	17	.6
...	38 029	Emmons	1 510	4 331	2 894	2.9	4 830	2 853	5 877	–499	–1 047	–10.3	–17.8	50	1.2
...	38 031	Foster	635	3 759	2 934	5.9	3 983	2 920	4 611	–224	–628	–5.6	–13.6	7	.2
...	38 033	Golden Valley	1 002	1 924	3 070	1.9	2 108	3 062	2 391	–184	–283	–8.7	–11.8	20	1.0
2985	38 035	Grand Forks	1 438	66 109	740	46.0	70 683	628	66 100	–4 574	4 583	–6.5	6.9	1 359	2.1
...	38 037	Grant	1 659	2 841	3 002	1.7	3 549	2 953	4 274	–708	–725	–19.9	–17.0	17	.6
...	38 039	Griggs	709	2 754	3 009	3.9	3 303	2 976	3 714	–549	–411	–16.6	–11.1	11	.4
...	38 041	Hettinger	1 132	2 715	3 012	2.4	3 445	2 959	4 275	–730	–830	–21.2	–19.4	6	.2
...	38 043	Kidder	1 351	2 753	3 010	2.0	3 332	2 967	3 833	–579	–501	–17.4	–13.1	16	.6
...	38 045	LaMoure	1 147	4 701	2 867	4.1	5 383	2 811	6 473	–682	–1 090	–12.7	–16.8	26	.6
...	38 047	Logan	993	2 308	3 037	2.3	2 847	3 008	3 493	–539	–646	–18.9	–18.5	16	.7
...	38 049	McHenry	1 874	5 987	2 782	3.2	6 528	2 705	7 858	–541	–1 330	–8.3	–16.9	24	.4
...	38 051	McIntosh	975	3 390	2 964	3.5	4 021	2 916	4 800	–631	–779	–15.7	–16.2	28	.8
...	38 053	McKenzie	2 742	5 737	2 808	2.1	6 383	2 718	7 132	–646	–749	–10.1	–10.5	58	1.0
...	38 055	McLean	2 110	9 311	2 505	4.4	10 457	2 341	12 383	–1 146	–1 926	–11.0	–15.6	81	.9
...	38 057	Mercer	1 045	8 644	2 555	8.3	9 808	2 402	9 404	–1 164	404	–11.9	4.3	32	.4
1010	38 059	Morton	1 926	25 303	1 553	13.1	23 700	1 503	25 177	1 603	–1 477	6.8	–5.9	164	.6
...	38 061	Mountrail	1 824	6 631	2 723	3.6	7 021	2 655	7 679	–390	–658	–5.6	–8.6	87	1.3
...	38 063	Nelson	982	3 715	2 942	3.8	4 410	2 879	5 233	–695	–823	–15.8	–15.7	6	.2
...	38 065	Oliver	724	2 065	3 062	2.9	2 381	3 033	2 495	–316	–114	–13.3	–4.6	13	.6
...	38 067	Pembina	1 119	8 585	2 558	7.7	9 238	2 450	10 399	–653	–1 161	–7.1	–11.2	264	3.1
...	38 069	Pierce	1 018	4 675	2 869	4.6	5 052	2 835	6 166	–377	–1 114	–7.5	–18.1	28	.6

[1] Federal Information Processing Standards (FIPS) codes for metropolitan areas defined as of June 30, 1999. [2] FIPS codes for states and counties/county equivalents. [3] Dry land and land temporarily or partially covered by water. [4] Based on 3,140 counties/county equivalents; excludes Yellowstone National Park in MT and South Boston independent city in VA which are no longer counties. When counties share the same rank, the next lower rank is omitted. [5] Includes count resolution corrections through 1997 and adjustments based on Census 2000 dress rehearsal results and boundary changes reported as legally effective as of January 1, 1998. [6] Persons of Hispanic or Latino origin may be of any race.

Sources: Land Area—U.S. Census Bureau, unpublished data file from Geography Division based on TIGER data base. 2000 Population—U.S. Census Bureau, Census of Population and Housing, Census 2000 Redistricting Data (Public Law 94-171) Summary Files (related Internet site <http://www.census.gov/dmd/www/2kresult.html>). 1990 Population—U.S. Census Bureau, "(CO-99-8) County Population Estimates and Demographic Components of Population Change: Annual Time Series, July 1, 1990 to July 1, 1999 (includes revised April 1, 1990 Population Estimates Base)"; published 9 March 2000; <http://www. census.gov/population/estimates/county/co-99-8/99C8_00.txt>. 1980 Population—U.S. Census Bureau, "1980–1990 Intercensal Population Estimates by County" on diskette (related Internet site <http://www.census.gov/population/www/estimates/countypop.html>).

[Includes U.S., states, and 3,142 counties/county equivalents defined as of January 1, 1992. For changes to these areas since January 1, 1992, see appendix B. Geographic Information]

Metro-politan area code[1]	State and county code[2]	County	Land area,[3] 2000 (sq. miles)	Population (April 1) 2000 Number	2000 Rank[4]	2000 Per square mile	1990[5] Number	1990 Rank[4]	1980	Net change 1990–2000	Net change 1980–1990	Percent change 1990–2000	Percent change 1980–1990	Hispanic or Latino,[6] 2000 Number	Hispanic or Latino,[6] 2000 Percent
		NORTH DAKOTA—Con.													
...	38 071	Ramsey................	1 185	12 066	2 291	10.2	12 681	2 168	13 048	−615	−367	−4.8	−2.8	63	.5
...	38 073	Ransom...............	863	5 890	2 794	6.8	5 921	2 768	6 698	−31	−777	−.5	−11.6	48	.8
...	38 075	Renville..............	875	2 610	3 019	3.0	3 160	2 987	3 608	−550	−448	−17.4	−12.4	19	.7
...	38 077	Richland..............	1 437	17 998	1 897	12.5	18 148	1 780	19 207	−150	−1 059	−.8	−5.5	123	.7
...	38 079	Rolette...............	902	13 674	2 186	15.2	12 772	2 160	12 177	902	595	7.1	4.9	110	.8
...	38 081	Sargent...............	859	4 366	2 889	5.1	4 549	2 868	5 512	−183	−963	−4.0	−17.5	32	.7
...	38 083	Sheridan..............	972	1 710	3 084	1.8	2 148	3 057	2 819	−438	−671	−20.4	−23.8	6	.4
...	38 085	Sioux.................	1 094	4 044	2 918	3.7	3 761	2 934	3 620	283	141	7.5	3.9	65	1.6
...	38 087	Slope.................	1 218	767	3 127	.6	907	3 117	1 157	−140	−250	−15.4	−21.6	1	.1
...	38 089	Stark.................	1 338	22 636	1 664	16.9	22 832	1 540	23 697	−196	−865	−.9	−3.7	236	1.0
...	38 091	Steele................	712	2 258	3 046	3.2	2 420	3 028	3 106	−162	−686	−6.7	−22.1	4	.2
...	38 093	Stutsman..............	2 221	21 908	1 697	9.9	22 241	1 567	24 154	−333	−1 913	−1.5	−7.9	204	.9
...	38 095	Towner................	1 025	2 876	3 001	2.8	3 627	2 948	4 052	−751	−425	−20.7	−10.5	5	.2
...	38 097	Traill................	862	8 477	2 567	9.8	8 752	2 490	9 624	−275	−872	−3.1	−9.1	185	2.2
...	38 099	Walsh.................	1 282	12 389	2 273	9.7	13 840	2 070	15 371	−1 451	−1 531	−10.5	−10.0	700	5.7
...	38 101	Ward..................	2 013	58 795	815	29.2	57 921	748	58 392	874	−471	1.5	−.8	1 125	1.9
...	38 103	Wells.................	1 271	5 102	2 843	4.0	5 864	2 774	6 979	−762	−1 115	−13.0	−16.0	15	.3
...	38 105	Williams..............	2 070	19 761	1 804	9.5	21 129	1 623	22 237	−1 368	−1 108	−6.5	−5.0	185	.9
	39 000	**OHIO**...............	40 948	11 353 140	X	277.3	10 847 115	X	10 797 603	506 025	49 512	4.7	.5	217 123	1.9
...	39 001	Adams.................	584	27 330	1 472	46.8	25 371	1 452	24 328	1 959	1 043	7.7	4.3	175	.6
4320	39 003	Allen.................	404	108 473	497	268.5	109 755	420	112 241	−1 282	−2 486	−1.2	−2.2	1 545	1.4
...	39 005	Ashland...............	424	52 523	889	123.9	47 507	882	46 178	5 016	1 329	10.6	2.9	339	.6
1692	39 007	Ashtabula.............	702	102 728	517	146.3	99 880	459	104 215	2 848	−4 335	2.9	−4.2	2 292	2.2
...	39 009	Athens................	507	62 223	782	122.7	59 549	727	56 399	2 674	3 150	4.5	5.6	639	1.0
4320	39 011	Auglaize..............	401	46 611	968	116.2	44 585	916	42 554	2 026	2 031	4.5	4.8	310	.7
9000	39 013	Belmont...............	537	70 226	706	130.8	71 074	623	82 569	−848	−11 495	−1.2	−13.9	274	.4
1642	39 015	Brown.................	492	42 285	1 050	85.9	34 966	1 134	31 920	7 319	3 046	20.9	9.5	185	.4
1642	39 017	Butler................	467	332 807	175	712.6	291 479	167	258 787	41 328	32 692	14.2	12.6	4 771	1.4
1320	39 019	Carroll...............	395	28 836	1 425	73.0	26 521	1 407	25 598	2 315	923	8.7	3.6	158	.5
...	39 021	Champaign.............	429	38 890	1 144	90.7	36 019	1 101	33 649	2 871	2 370	8.0	7.0	269	.7
2000	39 023	Clark.................	400	144 742	378	361.9	147 538	319	150 236	−2 796	−2 698	−1.9	−1.8	1 699	1.2
1642	39 025	Clermont..............	452	177 977	309	393.8	150 094	314	128 483	27 883	21 611	18.6	16.8	1 547	.9
...	39 027	Clinton...............	411	40 543	1 102	98.6	35 444	1 114	34 603	5 099	841	14.4	2.4	266	.7
9320	39 029	Columbiana............	532	112 075	480	210.7	108 276	425	113 572	3 799	−5 296	3.5	−4.7	1 309	1.2
...	39 031	Coshocton.............	564	36 655	1 197	65.0	35 427	1 116	36 024	1 228	−597	3.5	−1.7	216	.6
4800	39 033	Crawford..............	402	46 066	1 064	116.0	47 070	1 077	50 075	−904	−2 205	−1.9	−4.4	361	.8
1692	39 035	Cuyahoga..............	458	1 393 978	23	3 043.6	1 412 140	17	1 498 400	−18 162	−86 260	−1.3	−5.8	47 078	3.4
...	39 037	Darke.................	600	53 309	877	88.8	53 617	800	55 096	−308	−1 479	−.6	−2.7	457	.9
...	39 039	Defiance..............	411	39 500	1 126	96.1	39 350	1 016	39 987	150	−637	.4	−1.6	2 857	7.2
1840	39 041	Delaware..............	442	109 989	494	248.8	66 929	659	53 840	43 060	13 089	64.3	24.3	1 109	1.0
...	39 043	Erie..................	255	79 551	645	312.0	76 781	588	79 655	2 770	−2 874	3.6	−3.6	1 664	2.1
1840	39 045	Fairfield.............	505	122 759	441	243.1	103 468	445	93 678	19 291	9 790	18.6	10.5	993	.8
...	39 047	Fayette...............	407	28 433	1 433	69.9	27 466	1 376	27 467	967	−1	3.5	Z	352	1.2
1840	39 049	Franklin..............	540	1 068 978	33	1 979.6	961 437	33	869 126	107 541	92 311	11.2	10.6	24 279	2.3
8400	39 051	Fulton................	407	42 084	1 056	103.4	38 498	1 040	37 751	3 586	747	9.3	2.0	2 422	5.8
...	39 053	Gallia................	469	31 069	1 375	66.2	30 954	1 247	30 098	115	856	.4	2.8	191	.6
1692	39 055	Geauga................	404	90 895	568	225.0	81 087	562	74 474	9 808	6 613	12.1	8.9	538	.6
2000	39 057	Greene................	415	147 886	367	356.4	136 731	344	129 769	11 155	6 962	8.2	5.4	1 813	1.2
...	39 059	Guernsey..............	522	40 792	1 088	78.1	39 024	1 021	42 024	1 768	−3 000	4.5	−7.1	254	.6
1642	39 061	Hamilton..............	407	845 303	52	2 076.9	866 228	36	873 203	−20 925	−6 975	−2.4	−.8	9 514	1.1
...	39 063	Hancock...............	531	71 295	696	134.3	65 536	670	64 581	5 759	955	8.8	1.5	2 187	3.1
...	39 065	Hardin................	470	31 945	1 347	68.0	31 111	1 240	32 719	834	−1 608	2.7	−4.9	248	.8
...	39 067	Harrison..............	404	15 856	2 029	39.2	16 085	1 917	18 152	−229	−2 067	−1.4	−11.4	59	.4
...	39 069	Henry.................	417	29 210	1 422	70.0	29 108	1 326	28 383	102	725	.4	2.6	1 576	5.4
...	39 071	Highland..............	553	40 875	1 086	73.9	35 728	1 105	33 477	5 147	2 251	14.4	6.7	216	.5
...	39 073	Hocking...............	423	28 241	1 441	66.8	25 533	1 445	24 304	2 708	1 229	10.6	5.1	124	.4
...	39 075	Holmes................	423	38 943	1 142	92.1	32 849	1 194	29 416	6 094	3 433	18.6	11.7	292	.7
...	39 077	Huron.................	493	59 487	807	120.7	56 238	771	54 608	3 249	1 630	5.8	3.0	2 117	3.6
...	39 079	Jackson...............	420	32 641	1 327	77.7	30 230	1 286	30 592	2 411	−362	8.0	−1.2	197	.6
8080	39 081	Jefferson.............	410	73 894	677	180.2	80 298	571	91 564	−6 404	−11 266	−8.0	−12.3	459	.6
...	39 083	Knox..................	527	54 500	864	103.4	47 473	885	46 304	7 027	1 169	14.8	2.5	371	.7
1692	39 085	Lake..................	228	227 511	250	997.9	215 500	231	212 801	12 011	2 699	5.6	1.3	3 879	1.7
3400	39 087	Lawrence..............	455	62 319	779	137.0	61 834	706	63 849	485	−2 015	.8	−3.2	355	.6
1840	39 089	Licking...............	687	145 491	376	211.8	128 300	362	120 981	17 191	7 319	13.4	6.0	1 107	.8
...	39 091	Logan.................	458	46 005	983	100.4	42 310	951	39 155	3 695	3 155	8.7	8.1	332	.7
1692	39 093	Lorain................	493	284 664	197	577.4	271 126	183	274 909	13 538	−3 783	5.0	−1.4	19 676	6.9
8400	39 095	Lucas.................	340	455 054	129	1 338.4	462 361	108	471 741	−7 307	−9 380	−1.6	−2.0	20 670	4.5
1840	39 097	Madison...............	465	40 213	1 110	86.5	37 078	1 070	33 004	3 135	4 074	8.5	12.3	294	.7
9320	39 099	Mahoning..............	415	257 555	218	620.6	264 806	187	289 487	−7 251	−24 681	−2.7	−8.5	7 640	3.0

[1] Federal Information Processing Standards (FIPS) codes for metropolitan areas defined as of June 30, 1999. [2] FIPS codes for states and counties/county equivalents. [3] Dry land and land temporarily or partially covered by water. [4] Based on 3,140 counties/county equivalents; excludes Yellowstone National Park in MT and South Boston independent city in VA which are no longer counties. When counties share the same rank, the next lower rank is omitted. [5] Includes count resolution corrections through 1997 and adjustments based on Census 2000 dress rehearsal results and boundary changes reported as legally effective as of January 1, 1998. [6] Persons of Hispanic or Latino origin may be of any race.

Sources: Land Area—U.S. Census Bureau, unpublished data file from Geography Division based on TIGER data base. 2000 Population—U.S. Census Bureau, Census of Population and Housing, Census 2000 Redistricting Data (Public Law 94-171) Summary Files (related Internet site <http://www.census.gov/dmd/www/2kresult.html>). 1990 Population—U.S. Census Bureau, "(CO-99-8) County Population Estimates and Demographic Components of Population Change: Annual Time Series, July 1, 1990 to July 1, 1999 (includes revised April 1, 1990 Population Estimates Base)"; published 9 March 2000; <http://www. census.gov/population/estimates/county/co-99-8/99C8_00.txt>. 1980 Population—U.S. Census Bureau, "1980–1990 Intercensal Population Estimates by County" on diskette (related Internet site <http://www.census.gov/population/www/estimates/countypop.html>).

[Includes U.S., states, and 3,142 counties/county equivalents defined as of January 1, 1992. For changes to these areas since January 1, 1992, see appendix B. Geographic Information]

Metro-politan area code[1]	State and county code[2]	County	Land area,[3] 2000 (sq. miles)	Population (April 1) 2000 Number	2000 Rank[4]	Per square mile	1990[5] Number	1990 Rank[4]	1980	Net change 1990–2000	Net change 1980–1990	Percent change 1990–2000	Percent change 1980–1990	Hispanic or Latino,[6] 2000 Number	Percent
		OHIO—Con.													
...	39 101	Marion	404	66 217	737	163.9	64 274	681	67 974	1 943	-3 700	3.0	-5.4	723	1.1
1692	39 103	Medina	422	151 095	355	358.0	122 354	376	113 150	28 741	9 204	23.5	8.1	1 399	.9
...	39 105	Meigs	429	23 072	1 640	53.8	22 987	1 535	23 641	85	-654	.4	-2.8	138	.6
...	39 107	Mercer	463	40 924	1 083	88.4	39 443	1 013	38 334	1 481	1 109	3.8	2.9	470	1.1
2000	39 109	Miami	407	98 868	527	242.9	93 184	497	90 381	5 684	2 803	6.1	3.1	721	.7
...	39 111	Monroe	456	15 180	2 078	33.3	15 497	1 954	17 382	-317	-1 885	-2.0	-10.8	62	.4
2000	39 113	Montgomery	462	559 062	99	1 210.1	573 809	83	571 697	-14 747	2 112	-2.6	.4	7 096	1.3
...	39 115	Morgan	418	14 897	2 099	35.6	14 194	2 038	14 241	703	-47	5.0	-.3	61	.4
...	39 117	Morrow	406	31 628	1 355	77.9	27 749	1 362	26 480	3 879	1 269	14.0	4.8	183	.6
...	39 119	Muskingum	665	84 585	616	127.2	82 068	553	83 340	2 517	-1 272	3.1	-1.5	436	.5
...	39 121	Noble	399	14 058	2 159	35.2	11 336	2 271	11 310	2 722	26	24.0	.2	60	.4
...	39 123	Ottawa	255	40 985	1 081	160.7	40 029	997	40 076	956	-47	2.4	-.1	1 535	3.7
...	39 125	Paulding	416	20 293	1 774	48.8	20 488	1 654	21 302	-195	-814	-1.0	-3.8	612	3.0
...	39 127	Perry	410	34 078	1 278	83.1	31 557	1 229	31 032	2 521	525	8.0	1.7	152	.4
1840	39 129	Pickaway	502	52 727	883	105.0	48 248	865	43 662	4 479	4 586	9.3	10.5	333	.6
...	39 131	Pike	441	27 695	1 459	62.8	24 249	1 486	22 802	3 446	1 447	14.2	6.3	155	.6
1692	39 133	Portage	492	152 061	353	309.1	142 585	333	135 856	9 476	6 729	6.6	5.0	1 093	.7
...	39 135	Preble	425	42 337	1 049	99.6	40 113	996	38 223	2 224	1 890	5.5	4.9	181	.4
...	39 137	Putnam	484	34 726	1 260	71.7	33 819	1 169	32 991	907	828	2.7	2.5	1 521	4.4
4800	39 139	Richland	497	128 852	419	259.3	126 137	367	131 205	2 715	-5 068	2.2	-3.9	1 200	.9
...	39 141	Ross	688	73 345	682	106.6	69 330	639	65 004	4 015	4 326	5.8	6.7	429	.6
...	39 143	Sandusky	409	61 792	785	151.1	61 963	703	63 267	-171	-1 304	-.3	-2.1	4 298	7.0
...	39 145	Scioto	612	79 195	648	129.4	80 327	569	84 545	-1 132	-4 218	-1.4	-5.0	477	.6
...	39 147	Seneca	551	58 683	817	106.5	59 733	725	61 901	-1 050	-2 168	-1.8	-3.5	1 972	3.4
1320	39 149	Shelby	409	47 910	954	117.1	44 915	914	43 089	2 995	1 826	6.7	4.2	383	.8
1692	39 151	Stark	576	378 098	155	656.4	367 585	140	378 823	10 513	-11 238	2.9	-3.0	3 492	.9
9320	39 153	Summit	413	542 899	103	1 314.5	514 990	91	524 472	27 909	-9 482	5.4	-1.8	4 781	.9
...	39 155	Trumbull	616	225 116	252	365.4	227 795	216	241 863	-2 679	-14 068	-1.2	-5.8	1 794	.8
...	39 157	Tuscarawas	568	90 914	567	160.1	84 090	544	84 614	6 824	-524	8.1	-.6	650	.7
...	39 159	Union	437	40 909	1 084	93.6	31 969	1 213	29 536	8 940	2 433	28.0	8.2	309	.8
...	39 161	Van Wert	410	29 659	1 410	72.3	30 464	1 270	30 458	-805	6	-2.6	Z	462	1.6
...	39 163	Vinton	414	12 806	2 246	30.9	11 098	2 284	11 584	1 708	-486	15.4	-4.2	60	.5
1642	39 165	Warren	400	158 383	336	396.0	113 973	402	99 276	44 410	14 697	39.0	14.8	1 633	1.0
6020	39 167	Washington	635	63 251	767	99.6	62 254	700	64 266	997	-2 012	1.6	-3.1	324	.5
...	39 169	Wayne	555	111 564	483	201.0	101 461	451	97 408	10 103	4 053	10.0	4.2	837	.8
...	39 171	Williams	422	39 188	1 133	92.9	36 956	1 073	36 369	2 232	587	6.0	1.6	1 049	2.7
8400	39 173	Wood	617	121 065	448	196.2	113 269	406	107 372	7 796	5 897	6.9	5.5	4 033	3.3
...	39 175	Wyandot	406	22 908	1 648	56.4	22 254	1 566	22 651	654	-397	2.9	-1.8	334	1.5
	40 000	**OKLAHOMA**	68 667	3 450 654	X	50.3	3 145 576	X	3 025 487	305 078	120 089	9.7	4.0	179 304	5.2
...	40 001	Adair	576	21 038	1 733	36.5	18 421	1 768	18 575	2 617	-154	14.2	-.8	657	3.1
...	40 003	Alfalfa	867	6 105	2 769	7.0	6 416	2 715	7 077	-311	-661	-4.8	-9.3	177	2.9
...	40 005	Atoka	978	13 879	2 168	14.2	12 778	2 158	12 748	1 101	30	8.6	.2	196	1.4
...	40 007	Beaver	1 814	5 857	2 798	3.2	6 023	2 754	6 806	-166	-783	-2.8	-11.5	630	10.8
...	40 009	Beckham	902	19 799	1 800	22.0	18 812	1 746	19 243	987	-431	5.2	-2.2	1 079	5.4
...	40 011	Blaine	928	11 976	2 295	12.9	11 470	2 257	13 443	506	-1 973	4.4	-14.7	793	6.6
...	40 013	Bryan	909	36 534	1 201	40.2	32 089	1 209	30 535	4 445	1 554	13.9	5.1	967	2.6
...	40 015	Caddo	1 278	30 150	1 391	23.6	29 550	1 315	30 905	600	-1 355	2.0	-4.4	1 894	6.3
5880	40 017	Canadian	900	87 697	598	97.4	74 409	603	56 452	13 288	17 957	17.9	31.8	3 386	3.9
...	40 019	Carter	824	45 621	989	55.4	42 919	939	43 610	2 702	-691	6.3	-1.6	1 269	2.8
...	40 021	Cherokee	751	42 521	1 045	56.6	34 049	1 162	30 684	8 472	3 365	24.9	11.0	1 760	4.1
...	40 023	Choctaw	774	15 342	2 066	19.8	15 302	1 973	17 203	40	-1 901	.3	-11.1	246	1.6
...	40 025	Cimarron	1 835	3 148	2 982	1.7	3 301	2 977	3 648	-153	-347	-4.6	-9.5	485	15.4
5880	40 027	Cleveland	536	208 016	267	388.1	174 253	277	133 173	33 763	41 080	19.4	30.8	8 396	4.0
...	40 029	Coal	518	6 031	2 777	11.6	5 780	2 781	6 041	251	-261	4.3	-4.3	129	2.1
4200	40 031	Comanche	1 069	114 996	471	107.6	111 486	412	112 456	3 510	-970	3.1	-.9	9 675	8.4
...	40 033	Cotton	637	6 614	2 726	10.4	6 651	2 689	7 338	-37	-687	-.6	-9.4	321	4.9
...	40 035	Craig	761	14 950	2 095	19.6	14 104	2 047	15 014	846	-910	6.0	-6.1	179	1.2
8560	40 037	Creek	956	67 367	727	70.5	60 915	715	59 016	6 452	1 899	10.6	3.2	1 283	1.9
...	40 039	Custer	987	26 142	1 511	26.5	26 897	1 393	25 995	-755	902	-2.8	3.5	2 361	9.0
...	40 041	Delaware	741	37 077	1 187	50.0	28 070	1 350	23 946	9 007	4 124	32.1	17.2	649	1.8
...	40 043	Dewey	1 000	4 743	2 864	4.7	5 551	2 797	5 922	-808	-371	-14.6	-6.3	127	2.7
...	40 045	Ellis	1 229	4 075	2 913	3.3	4 497	2 875	5 596	-422	-1 099	-9.4	-19.6	106	2.6
2340	40 047	Garfield	1 058	57 813	826	54.6	56 735	768	62 820	1 078	-6 085	1.9	-9.7	2 387	4.1
...	40 049	Garvin	807	27 210	1 475	33.7	26 605	1 403	27 856	605	-1 251	2.3	-4.5	924	3.4
...	40 051	Grady	1 101	45 516	991	41.3	41 747	962	39 490	3 769	2 257	9.0	5.7	1 316	2.9
...	40 053	Grant	1 001	5 144	2 841	5.1	5 689	2 785	6 518	-545	-829	-9.6	-12.7	95	1.8
...	40 055	Greer	639	6 061	2 774	9.5	6 559	2 702	7 028	-498	-469	-7.6	-6.7	451	7.4
...	40 057	Harmon	538	3 283	2 974	6.1	3 793	2 931	4 519	-510	-726	-13.4	-16.1	748	22.8
...	40 059	Harper	1 039	3 562	2 949	3.4	4 063	2 912	4 715	-501	-652	-12.3	-13.8	201	5.6

[1] Federal Information Processing Standards (FIPS) codes for metropolitan areas defined as of June 30, 1999.   [2] FIPS codes for states and counties/county equivalents.   [3] Dry land and land temporarily or partially covered by water.   [4] Based on 3,140 counties/county equivalents; excludes Yellowstone National Park in MT and South Boston independent city in VA which are no longer counties. When counties share the same rank, the next lower rank is omitted.   [5] Includes count resolution corrections through 1997 and adjustments based on Census 2000 dress rehearsal results and boundary changes reported as legally effective as of January 1, 1998.   [6] Persons of Hispanic or Latino origin may be of any race.

Sources: Land Area—U.S. Census Bureau, unpublished data file from Geography Division based on TIGER data base.   2000 Population—U.S. Census Bureau, Census of Population and Housing, Census 2000 Redistricting Data (Public Law 94-171) Summary Files (related Internet site <http://www.census.gov/dmd/www/2kresult.html>).   1990 Population—U.S. Census Bureau, "(CO-99-8) County Population Estimates and Demographic Components of Population Change: Annual Time Series, July 1, 1990 to July 1, 1999 (includes revised April 1, 1990 Population Estimates Base)"; published 9 March 2000; <http://www.census.gov/population/estimates/county/co-99-8/99C8_00.txt>.   1980 Population—U.S. Census Bureau, "1980–1990 Intercensal Population Estimates by County" on diskette (related Internet site <http://www.census.gov/population/www/estimates/countypop.html>).

Table B–1. Counties — **Area and Population**–Con.

[Includes U.S., states, and 3,142 counties/county equivalents defined as of January 1, 1992. For changes to these areas since January 1, 1992, see appendix B. Geographic Information]

Metro-politan area code[1]	State and county code[2]	County	Land area,[3] 2000 (sq. miles)	Population (April 1)										
				2000			1990[5]		1980	Net change		Percent change		Hispanic or Latino,[6] 2000	
				Number	Rank[4]	Per square mile	Number	Rank[4]	1980	1990–2000	1980–1990	1990–2000	1980–1990	Number	Percent
		OKLAHOMA—Con.													
...	40 061	Haskell	577	11 792	2 308	20.4	10 940	2 298	11 010	852	−70	7.8	−.6	177	1.5
...	40 063	Hughes	807	14 154	2 150	17.5	13 014	2 140	14 338	1 140	−1 324	8.8	−9.2	353	2.5
...	40 065	Jackson	803	28 439	1 432	35.4	28 764	1 337	30 356	−325	−1 592	−1.1	−5.2	4 446	15.6
...	40 067	Jefferson	759	6 818	2 709	9.0	7 010	2 657	8 294	−192	−1 284	−2.7	−15.5	478	7.0
...	40 069	Johnston	645	10 513	2 397	16.3	10 032	2 384	10 356	481	−324	4.8	−3.1	260	2.5
...	40 071	Kay	919	48 080	949	52.3	48 056	869	49 852	24	−1 796	Z	−3.6	2 045	4.3
...	40 073	Kingfisher	903	13 926	2 166	15.4	13 212	2 121	14 187	714	−975	5.4	−6.9	961	6.9
...	40 075	Kiowa	1 015	10 227	2 423	10.1	11 347	2 268	12 711	−1 120	−1 364	−9.9	−10.7	689	6.7
...	40 077	Latimer	722	10 692	2 385	14.8	10 333	2 356	9 840	359	493	3.5	5.0	164	1.5
...	40 079	Le Flore	1 586	48 109	947	30.3	43 270	934	40 698	4 839	2 572	11.2	6.3	1 849	3.8
...	40 081	Lincoln	958	32 080	1 343	33.5	29 216	1 323	26 601	2 864	2 615	9.8	9.8	483	1.5
5880	40 083	Logan	744	33 924	1 283	45.6	29 011	1 328	26 881	4 913	2 130	16.9	7.9	987	2.9
...	40 085	Love	515	8 831	2 542	17.1	7 788	2 596	7 469	1 043	319	13.4	4.3	619	7.0
5880	40 087	McClain	570	27 740	1 457	48.7	22 795	1 543	20 291	4 945	2 504	21.7	12.3	1 349	4.9
...	40 089	McCurtain	1 852	34 402	1 267	18.6	33 433	1 179	36 151	969	−2 718	2.9	−7.5	1 064	3.1
...	40 091	McIntosh	620	19 456	1 820	31.4	16 779	1 861	15 562	2 677	1 217	16.0	7.8	248	1.3
...	40 093	Major	957	7 545	2 639	7.9	8 055	2 558	8 772	−510	−717	−6.3	−8.2	303	4.0
...	40 095	Marshall	371	13 184	2 211	35.5	10 829	2 308	10 550	2 355	279	21.7	2.6	1 134	8.6
...	40 097	Mayes	656	38 369	1 155	58.5	33 366	1 180	32 261	5 003	1 105	15.0	3.4	718	1.9
...	40 099	Murray	418	12 623	2 254	30.2	12 042	2 214	12 147	581	−105	4.8	−.9	397	3.1
...	40 101	Muskogee	814	69 451	712	85.3	68 078	650	67 033	1 373	1 045	2.0	1.6	1 857	2.7
...	40 103	Noble	732	11 411	2 340	15.6	11 045	2 288	11 573	366	−528	3.3	−4.6	205	1.8
...	40 105	Nowata	565	10 569	2 392	18.7	9 992	2 386	11 486	577	−1 494	5.8	−13.0	130	1.2
...	40 107	Okfuskee	625	11 814	2 304	18.9	11 551	2 252	11 125	263	426	2.3	3.8	194	1.6
5880	40 109	Oklahoma	709	660 448	80	931.5	599 611	77	568 933	60 837	30 678	10.1	5.4	57 336	8.7
...	40 111	Okmulgee	697	39 685	1 119	56.9	36 490	1 089	39 169	3 195	−2 679	8.8	−6.8	772	1.9
8560	40 113	Osage	2 251	44 437	1 009	19.7	41 645	965	39 327	2 792	2 318	6.7	5.9	940	2.1
...	40 115	Ottawa	471	33 194	1 309	70.5	30 561	1 263	32 870	2 633	−2 309	8.6	−7.0	1 061	3.2
...	40 117	Pawnee	569	16 612	1 983	29.2	15 575	1 948	15 310	1 037	265	6.7	1.7	192	1.2
...	40 119	Payne	686	68 190	722	99.4	61 507	710	62 435	6 683	−928	10.9	−1.5	1 463	2.1
...	40 121	Pittsburg	1 306	43 953	1 017	33.7	40 950	980	40 524	3 003	426	7.3	1.1	939	2.1
...	40 123	Pontotoc	720	35 143	1 243	48.8	34 119	1 161	32 598	1 024	1 521	3.0	4.7	808	2.3
5880	40 125	Pottawatomie	788	65 521	745	83.1	58 760	739	55 239	6 761	3 521	11.5	6.4	1 544	2.4
...	40 127	Pushmataha	1 397	11 667	2 320	8.4	10 997	2 295	11 773	670	−776	6.1	−6.6	191	1.6
...	40 129	Roger Mills	1 142	3 436	2 961	3.0	4 147	2 901	4 799	−711	−652	−17.1	−13.6	91	2.6
8560	40 131	Rogers	675	70 641	703	104.7	55 170	782	46 436	15 471	8 734	28.0	18.8	1 294	1.8
...	40 133	Seminole	633	24 894	1 561	39.3	25 412	1 451	27 465	−518	−2 053	−2.0	−7.5	552	2.2
2720	40 135	Sequoyah	674	38 972	1 139	57.8	33 828	1 168	30 740	5 144	3 070	15.2	10.0	790	2.0
...	40 137	Stephens	874	43 182	1 033	49.4	42 299	952	43 419	883	−1 120	2.1	−2.6	1 709	4.0
...	40 139	Texas	2 037	20 107	1 789	9.9	16 419	1 898	17 727	3 688	−1 308	22.5	−7.4	6 003	29.9
...	40 141	Tillman	872	9 287	2 507	10.7	10 384	2 349	12 398	−1 097	−2 014	−10.6	−16.2	1 641	17.7
8560	40 143	Tulsa	570	563 299	98	988.2	503 341	95	470 593	59 958	32 748	11.9	7.0	33 616	6.0
8560	40 145	Wagoner	563	57 491	830	102.1	47 883	875	41 801	9 608	6 082	20.1	14.5	1 437	2.5
...	40 147	Washington	417	48 996	933	117.5	48 066	868	48 113	930	−47	1.9	−.1	1 293	2.6
...	40 149	Washita	1 003	11 508	2 334	11.5	11 441	2 259	13 798	67	−2 357	.6	−17.1	516	4.5
...	40 151	Woods	1 287	9 089	2 522	7.1	9 103	2 461	10 923	−14	−1 820	−.2	−16.7	220	2.4
...	40 153	Woodward	1 242	18 486	1 870	14.9	18 976	1 736	21 172	−490	−2 196	−2.6	−10.4	896	4.8
	41 000	OREGON	95 997	3 421 399	X	35.6	2 842 337	X	2 633 156	579 062	209 181	20.4	7.9	275 314	8.0
...	41 001	Baker	3 068	16 741	1 973	5.5	15 317	1 971	16 134	1 424	−817	9.3	−5.1	392	2.3
1890	41 003	Benton	676	78 153	651	115.6	70 811	626	68 211	7 342	2 600	10.4	3.8	3 645	4.7
6442	41 005	Clackamas	1 868	338 391	173	181.2	278 850	177	241 911	59 541	36 939	21.4	15.3	16 744	4.9
...	41 007	Clatsop	827	35 630	1 227	43.1	33 301	1 183	32 489	2 329	812	7.0	2.5	1 597	4.5
6442	41 009	Columbia	657	43 560	1 028	66.3	37 557	1 058	35 646	6 003	1 911	16.0	5.4	1 093	2.5
...	41 011	Coos	1 600	62 779	775	39.2	60 273	719	64 047	2 506	−3 774	4.2	−5.9	2 133	3.4
...	41 013	Crook	2 979	19 182	1 834	6.4	14 111	2 045	13 091	5 071	1 020	35.9	7.8	1 082	5.6
...	41 015	Curry	1 627	21 137	1 728	13.0	19 327	1 713	16 992	1 810	2 335	9.4	13.7	761	3.6
...	41 017	Deschutes	3 018	115 367	466	38.2	74 976	599	62 142	40 391	12 834	53.9	20.7	4 304	3.7
...	41 019	Douglas	5 037	100 399	523	19.9	94 649	490	93 748	5 750	901	6.1	1.0	3 283	3.3
...	41 021	Gilliam	1 204	1 915	3 071	1.6	1 717	3 082	2 057	198	−340	11.5	−16.5	35	1.8
...	41 023	Grant	4 529	7 935	2 611	1.8	7 853	2 586	8 210	82	−357	1.0	−4.3	163	2.1
...	41 025	Harney	10 134	7 609	2 635	.8	7 060	2 653	8 314	549	−1 254	7.8	−15.1	316	4.2
...	41 027	Hood River	522	20 411	1 765	39.1	16 903	1 886	15 835	3 508	1 068	20.8	6.7	5 107	25.0
4890	41 029	Jackson	2 785	181 269	304	65.1	146 387	323	132 456	34 882	13 931	23.8	10.5	12 126	6.7
...	41 031	Jefferson	1 781	19 009	1 845	10.7	13 676	2 083	11 599	5 333	2 077	39.0	17.9	3 372	17.7
...	41 033	Josephine	1 640	75 726	662	46.2	62 649	694	58 855	13 077	3 794	20.9	6.4	3 229	4.3
...	41 035	Klamath	5 944	63 775	762	10.7	57 702	754	59 117	6 073	−1 415	10.5	−2.4	4 961	7.8
...	41 037	Lake	8 136	7 422	2 646	.9	7 186	2 635	7 532	236	−346	3.3	−4.6	404	5.4
2400	41 039	Lane	4 554	322 959	178	70.9	282 912	174	275 226	40 047	7 686	14.2	2.8	14 874	4.6
...	41 041	Lincoln	980	44 479	1 008	45.4	38 889	1 026	35 264	5 590	3 625	14.4	10.3	2 119	4.8

[1] Federal Information Processing Standards (FIPS) codes for metropolitan areas defined as of June 30, 1999. [2] FIPS codes for states and counties/county equivalents. [3] Dry land and land temporarily or partially covered by water. [4] Based on 3,140 counties/county equivalents; excludes Yellowstone National Park in MT and South Boston independent city in VA which are no longer counties. When counties share the same rank, the next lower rank is omitted. [5] Includes count resolution corrections through 1997 and adjustments based on Census 2000 dress rehearsal results and boundary changes reported as legally effective as of January 1, 1998. [6] Persons of Hispanic or Latino origin may be of any race.

Sources: Land Area—U.S. Census Bureau, unpublished data file from Geography Division based on TIGER data base. 2000 Population—U.S. Census Bureau, Census of Population and Housing, Census 2000 Redistricting Data (Public Law 94-171) Summary Files (related Internet site <http://www.census.gov/dmd/www/2kresult.html>). 1990 Population—U.S. Census Bureau, "(CO-99-8) County Population Estimates and Demographic Components of Population Change: Annual Time Series, July 1, 1990 to July 1, 1999 (includes revised April 1, 1990 Population Estimates Base)"; published 9 March 2000; <http://www.census.gov/population/estimates/county/co-99-8/99C8_00.txt>. 1980 Population—U.S. Census Bureau, "1980–1990 Intercensal Population Estimates by County" on diskette (related Internet site <http://www.census.gov/population/www/estimates/countypop.html>).

[Includes U.S., states, and 3,142 counties/county equivalents defined as of January 1, 1992. For changes to these areas since January 1, 1992, see appendix B. Geographic Information]

Metro-politan area code[1]	State and county code[2]	County	Land area,[3] 2000 (sq. miles)	Population (April 1)											
				2000			1990[5]		1980	Net change		Percent change		Hispanic or Latino,[6] 2000	
				Number	Rank[4]	Per square mile	Number	Rank[4]		1990–2000	1980–1990	1990–2000	1980–1990	Number	Percent
		OREGON—Con.													
...	41 043	Linn	2 292	103 069	515	45.0	91 227	504	89 495	11 842	1 732	13.0	1.9	4 514	4.4
...	41 045	Malheur	9 887	31 615	1 356	3.2	26 038	1 419	26 896	5 577	–858	21.4	–3.2	8 099	25.6
6442	41 047	Marion	1 184	284 834	196	240.6	228 483	215	204 692	56 351	23 791	24.7	11.6	48 714	17.1
...	41 049	Morrow	2 032	10 995	2 367	5.4	7 625	2 607	7 519	3 370	106	44.2	1.4	2 686	24.4
6442	41 051	Multnomah	435	660 486	79	1 518.4	583 887	81	562 647	76 599	21 240	13.1	3.8	49 607	7.5
6442	41 053	Polk	741	62 380	778	84.2	49 541	848	45 203	12 839	4 338	25.9	9.6	5 480	8.8
...	41 055	Sherman	823	1 934	3 068	2.3	1 918	3 072	2 172	16	–254	.8	–11.7	94	4.9
...	41 057	Tillamook	1 102	24 262	1 585	22.0	21 570	1 599	21 164	2 692	406	12.5	1.9	1 244	5.1
...	41 059	Umatilla	3 215	70 548	704	21.9	59 249	734	58 861	11 299	388	19.1	.7	11 366	16.1
...	41 061	Union	2 037	24 530	1 575	12.0	23 598	1 510	23 921	932	–323	3.9	–1.4	600	2.4
...	41 063	Wallowa	3 145	7 226	2 663	2.3	6 911	2 669	7 273	315	–362	4.6	–5.0	125	1.7
...	41 065	Wasco	2 381	23 791	1 599	10.0	21 683	1 594	21 732	2 108	–49	9.7	–.2	2 214	9.3
6442	41 067	Washington	724	445 342	133	615.1	311 554	161	245 860	133 788	65 694	42.9	26.7	49 735	11.2
...	41 069	Wheeler	1 715	1 547	3 092	.9	1 396	3 102	1 513	151	–117	10.8	–7.7	79	5.1
6442	41 071	Yamhill	716	84 992	612	118.7	65 551	669	55 332	19 441	10 219	29.7	18.5	9 017	10.6
	42 000	PENNSYLVANIA	44 817	12 281 054	X	274.0	11 882 842	X	11 864 720	398 212	18 122	3.4	.2	394 088	3.2
...	42 001	Adams	520	91 292	563	175.6	78 274	577	68 231	13 018	10 043	16.6	14.7	3 323	3.6
6280	42 003	Allegheny	730	1 281 666	28	1 755.7	1 336 449	19	1 450 195	–54 783	–113 746	–4.1	–7.8	11 166	.9
...	42 005	Armstrong	654	72 392	687	110.7	73 478	612	77 768	–1 086	–4 290	–1.5	–5.5	308	.4
6280	42 007	Beaver	434	181 412	303	418.0	186 093	261	204 441	–4 681	–18 348	–2.5	–9.0	1 315	.7
...	42 009	Bedford	1 015	49 984	916	49.2	47 919	873	46 784	2 065	1 135	4.3	2.4	263	.5
6680	42 011	Berks	859	373 638	157	435.0	336 523	151	312 509	37 115	24 014	11.0	7.7	36 357	9.7
0280	42 013	Blair	526	129 144	418	245.5	130 542	357	136 621	–1 398	–6 079	–1.1	–4.4	662	.5
...	42 015	Bradford	1 151	62 761	776	54.5	60 967	714	62 919	1 794	–1 952	2.9	–3.1	398	.6
6162	42 017	Bucks	607	597 635	91	984.6	541 174	89	479 180	56 461	61 994	10.4	12.9	14 005	2.3
6280	42 019	Butler	789	174 083	314	220.6	152 013	306	147 912	22 070	4 101	14.5	2.8	1 016	.6
3680	42 021	Cambria	688	152 598	348	221.8	163 062	292	183 263	–10 464	–20 201	–6.4	–11.0	1 352	.9
...	42 023	Cameron	397	5 974	2 784	15.0	5 913	2 770	6 674	61	–761	1.0	–11.4	34	.6
0240	42 025	Carbon	381	58 802	814	154.3	56 803	767	53 285	1 999	3 518	3.5	6.6	858	1.5
8050	42 027	Centre	1 108	135 758	397	122.5	124 812	369	112 760	10 946	12 052	8.8	10.7	2 243	1.7
6162	42 029	Chester	756	433 501	138	573.4	376 389	135	316 660	57 112	59 729	15.2	18.9	16 126	3.7
...	42 031	Clarion	602	41 765	1 060	69.4	41 699	964	43 362	66	–1 663	.2	–3.8	172	.4
...	42 033	Clearfield	1 147	83 382	624	72.7	78 097	579	83 578	5 285	–5 481	6.8	–6.6	471	.6
...	42 035	Clinton	891	37 914	1 168	42.6	37 182	1 067	38 971	732	–1 789	2.0	–4.6	205	.5
7560	42 037	Columbia	486	64 151	760	132.0	63 202	691	61 967	949	1 235	1.5	2.0	609	.9
...	42 039	Crawford	1 013	90 366	571	89.2	86 166	530	88 869	4 200	–2 703	4.9	–3.0	537	.6
3240	42 041	Cumberland	550	213 674	261	388.5	195 257	246	179 625	18 417	15 632	9.4	8.7	2 883	1.3
3240	42 043	Dauphin	525	251 798	226	479.6	237 813	211	232 317	13 985	5 496	5.9	2.4	10 404	4.1
6162	42 045	Delaware	184	550 864	102	2 993.8	547 658	86	555 029	3 206	–7 371	.6	–1.3	8 368	1.5
...	42 047	Elk	829	35 112	1 246	42.4	34 878	1 137	38 338	234	–3 460	.7	–9.0	142	.4
2360	42 049	Erie	802	280 843	199	350.2	275 575	179	279 780	5 268	–4 205	1.9	–1.5	6 126	2.2
6280	42 051	Fayette	790	148 644	364	188.2	145 351	326	159 417	3 293	–14 066	2.3	–8.8	564	.4
...	42 053	Forest	428	4 946	2 851	11.6	4 802	2 857	5 072	144	–270	3.0	–5.3	60	1.2
...	42 055	Franklin	772	129 313	416	167.5	121 082	380	113 629	8 231	7 453	6.8	6.6	2 268	1.8
...	42 057	Fulton	438	14 261	2 144	32.6	13 837	2 071	12 842	424	995	3.1	7.7	52	.4
...	42 059	Greene	576	40 672	1 093	70.6	39 550	1 010	40 476	1 122	–926	2.8	–2.3	357	.9
...	42 061	Huntingdon	874	45 586	990	52.2	44 164	922	42 253	1 422	1 911	3.2	4.5	524	1.1
...	42 063	Indiana	829	89 605	576	108.1	89 994	511	92 281	–389	–2 287	–.4	–2.5	457	.5
...	42 065	Jefferson	655	45 932	985	70.1	46 083	902	48 303	–151	–2 220	–.3	–4.6	188	.4
...	42 067	Juniata	392	22 821	1 652	58.2	20 625	1 649	19 188	2 196	1 437	10.6	7.5	369	1.6
7560	42 069	Lackawanna	459	213 295	263	464.7	219 097	226	227 908	–5 802	–8 811	–2.6	–3.9	2 958	1.4
4000	42 071	Lancaster	949	470 658	122	496.0	422 822	119	362 346	47 836	60 476	11.3	16.7	26 742	5.7
...	42 073	Lawrence	360	94 643	543	262.9	96 246	481	107 150	–1 603	–10 904	–1.7	–10.2	529	.6
3240	42 075	Lebanon	362	120 327	452	332.4	113 744	403	108 582	6 583	5 162	5.8	4.8	5 969	5.0
0240	42 077	Lehigh	347	312 090	183	899.4	291 130	169	272 349	20 960	18 781	7.2	6.9	31 881	10.2
7560	42 079	Luzerne	891	319 250	181	358.3	328 149	155	343 079	–8 899	–14 930	–2.7	–4.4	3 713	1.2
9140	42 081	Lycoming	1 235	120 044	454	97.2	118 710	391	118 416	1 334	294	1.1	.2	799	.7
...	42 083	McKean	982	45 936	984	46.8	47 131	889	50 635	–1 195	–3 504	–2.5	–6.9	485	1.1
7610	42 085	Mercer	672	120 293	453	179.0	121 003	381	128 299	–710	–7 296	–.6	–5.7	803	.7
...	42 087	Mifflin	412	46 486	973	112.8	46 197	899	46 908	289	–711	.6	–1.5	263	.6
...	42 089	Monroe	609	138 687	393	227.7	95 681	483	69 409	43 006	26 272	44.9	37.9	9 195	6.6
6162	42 091	Montgomery	483	750 097	67	1 553.0	678 193	61	643 371	71 904	34 822	10.6	5.4	15 300	2.0
...	42 093	Montour	131	18 236	1 884	139.2	17 735	1 801	16 675	501	1 060	2.8	6.4	167	.9
0240	42 095	Northampton	374	267 066	206	714.1	247 110	202	225 418	19 956	21 692	8.1	9.6	17 868	6.7
...	42 097	Northumberland	460	94 556	544	205.6	96 771	476	100 381	–2 215	–3 610	–2.3	–3.6	1 041	1.1
3240	42 099	Perry	554	43 602	1 027	78.7	41 172	976	35 718	2 430	5 454	5.9	15.3	301	.7
6162	42 101	Philadelphia	135	1 517 550	18	11 241.1	1 585 577	12	1 688 210	–68 027	–102 633	–4.3	–6.1	128 928	8.5
5602	42 103	Pike	547	46 302	976	84.6	28 032	1 351	18 271	18 270	9 761	65.2	53.4	2 315	5.0
...	42 105	Potter	1 081	18 080	1 894	16.7	16 717	1 867	17 726	1 363	–1 009	8.2	–5.7	103	.6

[1] Federal Information Processing Standards (FIPS) codes for metropolitan areas defined as of June 30, 1999.   [2] FIPS codes for states and counties/county equivalents.   [3] Dry land and land temporarily or partially covered by water.   [4] Based on 3,140 counties/county equivalents; excludes Yellowstone National Park in MT and South Boston independent city in VA which are no longer counties. When counties share the same rank, the next lower rank is omitted.   [5] Includes count resolution corrections through 1997 and adjustments based on Census 2000 dress rehearsal results and boundary changes reported as legally effective as of January 1, 1998.   [6] Persons of Hispanic or Latino origin may be of any race.

Sources: Land Area—U.S. Census Bureau, unpublished data file from Geography Division based on TIGER data base.   2000 Population—U.S. Census Bureau, Census of Population and Housing, Census 2000 Redistricting Data (Public Law 94-171) Summary Files (related Internet site <http://www.census.gov/dmd/www/2kresult.html>).   1990 Population—U.S. Census Bureau, "(CO-99-8) County Population Estimates and Demographic Components of Population Change: Annual Time Series, July 1, 1990 to July 1, 1999 (includes revised April 1, 1990 Population Estimates Base)"; published 9 March 2000; <http://www. census.gov/population/estimates/county/co-99-8/99C8_00.txt>.   1980 Population—U.S. Census Bureau, "1980–1990 Intercensal Population Estimates by County" on diskette (related Internet site <http://www.census.gov/population/www/estimates/countypop.html>).

Table B–1. Counties — Area and Population–Con.

[Includes U.S., states, and 3,142 counties/county equivalents defined as of January 1, 1992. For changes to these areas since January 1, 1992, see appendix B. Geographic Information]

Metro-politan area code[1]	State and county code[2]	County	Land area,[3] 2000 (sq. miles)	Population (April 1)										
				2000			1990[5]			Net change		Percent change		Hispanic or Latino,[6] 2000	
				Number	Rank[4]	Per square mile	Number	Rank[4]	1980	1990–2000	1980–1990	1990–2000	1980–1990	Number	Percent
		PENNSYLVANIA—Con.													
...	42 107	Schuylkill................	778	150 336	359	193.2	152 585	303	160 630	−2 249	−8 045	−1.5	−5.0	1 671	1.1
...	42 109	Snyder..................	331	37 546	1 175	113.4	36 680	1 083	33 584	866	3 096	2.4	9.2	368	1.0
3680	42 111	Somerset................	1 075	80 023	641	74.4	78 218	578	81 243	1 805	−3 025	2.3	−3.7	532	.7
...	42 113	Sullivan.................	450	6 556	2 732	14.6	6 104	2 744	6 349	452	−245	7.4	−3.9	72	1.1
...	42 115	Susquehanna.............	823	42 238	1 053	51.3	40 380	989	37 876	1 858	2 504	4.6	6.6	285	.7
...	42 117	Tioga...................	1 134	41 373	1 069	36.5	41 126	977	40 973	247	153	.6	.4	214	.5
...	42 119	Union...................	317	41 624	1 065	131.3	36 176	1 097	32 870	5 448	3 306	15.1	10.1	1 622	3.9
...	42 121	Venango.................	675	57 565	829	85.3	59 381	729	64 444	−1 816	−5 063	−3.1	−7.9	298	.5
...	42 123	Warren..................	883	43 863	1 020	49.7	45 050	912	47 449	−1 187	−2 399	−2.6	−5.1	151	.3
6280	42 125	Washington..............	857	202 897	271	236.8	204 584	243	217 074	−1 687	−12 490	−.8	−5.8	1 170	.6
...	42 127	Wayne..................	729	47 722	956	65.5	39 944	1 003	35 237	7 778	4 707	19.5	13.4	811	1.7
6280	42 129	Westmoreland............	1 025	369 993	158	361.0	370 321	138	392 184	−328	−21 863	−.1	−5.6	1 869	.5
7560	42 131	Wyoming................	397	28 080	1 449	70.7	28 076	1 348	26 433	4	1 643	Z	6.2	187	.7
9280	42 133	York....................	904	381 751	152	422.3	339 574	149	313 024	42 177	26 550	12.4	8.5	11 296	3.0
44 000		RHODE ISLAND........	1 045	1 048 319	X	1 003.2	1 003 464	X	947 154	44 855	56 310	4.5	5.9	90 820	8.7
6483	44 001	Bristol..................	25	50 648	913	2 025.9	48 859	859	46 942	1 789	1 917	3.7	4.1	572	1.1
6483	44 003	Kent....................	170	167 090	323	982.9	161 143	296	154 163	5 947	6 980	3.7	4.5	2 827	1.7
...	44 005	Newport................	104	85 433	611	821.5	87 194	521	81 383	−1 761	5 811	−2.0	7.1	2 409	2.8
6483	44 007	Providence..............	413	621 602	86	1 505.1	596 270	78	571 349	25 332	24 921	4.2	4.4	83 232	13.4
6483	44 009	Washington..............	333	123 546	436	371.0	109 998	419	93 317	13 548	16 681	12.3	17.9	1 780	1.4
45 000		SOUTH CAROLINA.....	30 110	4 012 012	X	133.2	3 486 310	X	3 120 729	525 702	365 581	15.1	11.7	95 076	2.4
0600	45 001	Abbeville................	508	26 167	1 510	51.5	23 862	1 498	22 627	2 305	1 235	9.7	5.5	217	.8
0600	45 003	Aiken...................	1 073	142 552	382	132.9	120 991	382	105 630	21 561	15 361	17.8	14.5	3 025	2.1
...	45 005	Allendale................	408	11 211	2 355	27.5	11 727	2 231	10 700	−516	1 027	−4.4	9.6	181	1.6
3160	45 007	Anderson................	718	165 740	325	230.8	145 177	327	133 235	20 563	11 942	14.2	9.0	1 832	1.1
...	45 009	Bamberg................	393	16 658	1 979	42.4	16 902	1 857	18 118	−244	−1 216	−1.4	−6.7	118	.7
...	45 011	Barnwell................	548	23 478	1 616	42.8	20 293	1 660	19 868	3 185	425	15.7	2.1	327	1.4
...	45 013	Beaufort................	587	120 937	444	206.0	86 425	527	65 364	34 512	21 061	39.9	32.2	8 208	6.8
1440	45 015	Berkeley................	1 098	142 651	381	129.9	128 658	361	94 745	13 993	33 913	10.9	35.8	3 935	2.8
...	45 017	Calhoun................	380	15 185	2 076	40.0	12 753	2 162	12 206	2 432	547	19.1	4.5	212	1.4
1440	45 019	Charleston..............	919	309 969	184	337.3	295 159	165	276 556	14 810	18 603	5.0	6.7	7 434	2.4
3160	45 021	Cherokee................	393	52 537	887	133.7	44 506	919	40 983	8 031	3 523	18.0	8.6	1 092	2.1
...	45 023	Chester.................	581	34 068	1 279	58.0	32 170	1 208	30 148	1 898	2 022	5.9	6.7	255	.7
...	45 025	Chesterfield.............	799	42 768	1 041	53.5	38 575	1 039	38 161	4 193	414	10.9	1.1	971	2.3
...	45 027	Clarendon...............	607	32 502	1 331	53.5	28 450	1 344	27 464	4 052	986	14.2	3.6	560	1.7
...	45 029	Colleton................	1 056	38 264	1 158	36.2	34 377	1 156	31 776	3 887	2 601	11.3	8.2	551	1.4
...	45 031	Darlington...............	561	67 394	726	120.1	61 851	705	62 717	5 543	−866	9.0	−1.4	658	1.0
...	45 033	Dillon..................	405	30 722	1 379	75.9	29 114	1 325	31 083	1 608	−1 969	5.5	−6.3	539	1.8
1440	45 035	Dorchester..............	575	96 413	537	167.7	83 060	549	59 045	13 353	24 015	16.1	40.7	1 722	1.8
0600	45 037	Edgefield...............	502	24 595	1 571	49.0	18 360	1 771	17 528	6 235	832	34.0	4.7	503	2.0
...	45 039	Fairfield................	687	23 454	1 619	34.1	22 295	1 563	20 700	1 159	1 595	5.2	7.7	250	1.1
2655	45 041	Florence................	800	125 761	432	157.2	114 344	401	110 163	11 417	4 181	10.0	3.8	1 383	1.1
...	45 043	Georgetown..............	815	55 797	846	68.5	46 302	898	42 461	9 495	3 841	20.5	9.0	919	1.6
3160	45 045	Greenville...............	790	379 616	154	480.5	320 127	158	287 895	59 489	32 232	18.6	11.2	14 283	3.8
...	45 047	Greenwood..............	456	66 271	736	145.3	59 567	726	55 859	6 704	3 708	11.3	6.6	1 902	2.9
...	45 049	Hampton................	560	21 386	1 719	38.2	18 186	1 778	18 159	3 200	27	17.6	.1	547	2.6
5330	45 051	Horry...................	1 134	196 629	281	173.4	144 053	329	101 419	52 576	42 634	36.5	42.0	5 057	2.6
...	45 053	Jasper..................	656	20 678	1 752	31.5	15 487	1 955	14 504	5 191	983	33.5	6.8	1 190	5.8
...	45 055	Kershaw................	726	52 647	885	72.5	43 599	929	39 015	9 048	4 584	20.8	11.7	886	1.7
...	45 057	Lancaster...............	549	61 351	793	111.8	54 516	791	53 361	6 835	1 155	12.5	2.2	978	1.6
...	45 059	Laurens.................	715	69 567	710	97.3	58 132	746	52 214	11 435	5 918	19.7	11.3	1 352	1.9
...	45 061	Lee.....................	410	20 119	1 787	49.1	18 437	1 765	18 929	1 682	−492	9.1	−2.6	264	1.3
1760	45 063	Lexington...............	699	216 014	260	309.0	167 526	286	140 353	48 488	27 173	28.9	19.4	4 146	1.9
...	45 065	McCormick..............	360	9 958	2 450	27.7	8 868	2 480	7 797	1 090	1 071	12.3	13.7	86	.9
...	45 067	Marion.................	489	35 466	1 235	72.5	33 899	1 167	34 179	1 567	−280	4.6	−.8	634	1.8
...	45 069	Marlboro................	480	28 818	1 426	60.0	29 716	1 307	31 634	−898	−1 918	−3.0	−6.1	205	.7
...	45 071	Newberry...............	631	36 108	1 210	57.2	33 172	1 186	31 242	2 936	1 930	8.9	6.2	1 533	4.2
...	45 073	Oconee.................	625	66 215	738	105.9	57 494	758	48 611	8 721	8 883	15.2	18.3	1 562	2.4
...	45 075	Orangeburg.............	1 106	91 582	559	82.8	84 804	541	82 276	6 778	2 528	8.0	3.1	875	1.0
3160	45 077	Pickens.................	497	110 757	490	222.9	93 896	492	79 292	16 861	14 604	18.0	18.4	1 879	1.7
1760	45 079	Richland................	756	320 677	180	424.2	286 321	171	269 600	34 356	16 721	12.0	6.2	8 713	2.7
...	45 081	Saluda..................	452	19 181	1 835	42.4	16 441	1 896	16 136	2 740	305	16.7	1.9	1 401	7.3
3160	45 083	Spartanburg.............	811	253 791	222	312.9	226 793	217	203 023	26 998	23 770	11.9	11.7	7 081	2.8
8140	45 085	Sumter.................	665	104 646	505	157.4	101 276	452	88 243	3 370	13 033	3.3	14.8	1 918	1.8
...	45 087	Union..................	514	29 881	1 399	58.1	30 337	1 278	30 764	−456	−427	−1.5	−1.4	199	.7
...	45 089	Williamsburg.............	934	37 217	1 185	39.8	36 815	1 080	38 226	402	−1 411	1.1	−3.7	273	.7
1520	45 091	York....................	682	164 614	327	241.4	131 497	353	106 720	33 117	24 777	25.2	23.2	3 220	2.0

[1] Federal Information Processing Standards (FIPS) codes for metropolitan areas defined as of June 30, 1999.   [2] FIPS codes for states and counties/county equivalents.   [3] Dry land and land temporarily or partially covered by water.   [4] Based on 3,140 counties/county equivalents; excludes Yellowstone National Park in MT and South Boston independent city in VA which are no longer counties. When counties share the same rank, the next lower rank is omitted.   [5] Includes count resolution corrections through 1997 and adjustments based on Census 2000 dress rehearsal results and boundary changes reported as legally effective as of January 1, 1998.   [6] Persons of Hispanic or Latino origin may be of any race.

Sources: Land Area—U.S. Census Bureau, unpublished data file from Geography Division based on TIGER data base.   2000 Population—U.S. Census Bureau, Census of Population and Housing, Census 2000 Redistricting Data (Public Law 94-171) Summary Files (related Internet site <http://www.census.gov/dmd/www/2kresult.html>).   1990 Population—U.S. Census Bureau, "(CO-99-8) County Population Estimates and Demographic Components of Population Change: Annual Time Series, July 1, 1990 to July 1, 1999 (includes revised April 1, 1990 Population Estimates Base)"; published 9 March 2000; <http://www. census.gov/population/estimates/county/co-99-8/99C8_00.txt>.   1980 Population—U.S. Census Bureau, "1980–1990 Intercensal Population Estimates by County" on diskette (related Internet site <http://www.census.gov/population/www/estimates/countypop.html>).

Table B–1. Counties — **Area and Population**–Con.

[Includes U.S., states, and 3,142 counties/county equivalents defined as of January 1, 1992. For changes to these areas since January 1, 1992, see appendix B. Geographic Information]

Metro-politan area code[1]	State and county code[2]	County	Land area,[3] 2000 (sq. miles)	Population (April 1) 2000 Number	Rank[4]	Per square mile	1990[5] Number	Rank[4]	1980	Net change 1990–2000	1980–1990	Percent change 1990–2000	1980–1990	Hispanic or Latino,[6] 2000 Number	Percent
	46 000	SOUTH DAKOTA	75 885	754 844	X	9.9	696 004	X	690 768	58 840	5 236	8.5	.8	10 903	1.4
...	46 003	Aurora..................	708	3 058	2 988	4.3	3 135	2 990	3 628	−77	−493	−2.5	−13.6	64	2.1
...	46 005	Beadle.................	1 259	17 023	1 951	13.5	18 253	1 776	19 195	−1 230	−942	−6.7	−4.9	155	.9
...	46 007	Bennett................	1 185	3 574	2 947	3.0	3 206	2 983	3 044	368	162	11.5	5.3	72	2.0
...	46 009	Bon Homme	563	7 260	2 658	12.9	7 089	2 647	8 059	171	−970	2.4	−12.0	42	.6
...	46 011	Brookings	794	28 220	1 444	35.5	25 207	1 454	24 332	3 013	875	12.0	3.6	247	.9
...	46 013	Brown	1 713	35 460	1 236	20.7	35 580	1 110	36 962	−120	−1 382	−.3	−3.7	237	.7
...	46 015	Brule	819	5 364	2 824	6.5	5 485	2 802	5 245	−121	240	−2.2	4.6	26	.5
...	46 017	Buffalo	471	2 032	3 063	4.3	1 759	3 080	1 795	273	−36	15.5	−2.0	18	.9
...	46 019	Butte	2 249	9 094	2 521	4.0	7 914	2 580	8 372	1 180	−458	14.9	−5.5	266	2.9
...	46 021	Campbell	736	1 782	3 080	2.4	1 965	3 068	2 243	−183	−278	−9.3	−12.4	4	.2
...	46 023	Charles Mix	1 098	9 350	2 502	8.5	9 131	2 458	9 680	219	−549	2.4	−5.7	177	1.9
...	46 025	Clark	958	4 143	2 905	4.3	4 403	2 882	4 894	−260	−491	−5.9	−10.0	20	.5
...	46 027	Clay	412	13 537	2 192	32.9	13 186	2 124	13 689	351	−503	2.7	−3.7	120	.9
...	46 029	Codington	688	25 897	1 521	37.6	22 698	1 548	20 885	3 199	1 813	14.1	8.7	274	1.1
...	46 031	Corson	2 473	4 181	2 900	1.7	4 195	2 898	5 196	−14	−1 001	−.3	−19.3	89	2.1
...	46 033	Custer	1 558	7 275	2 657	4.7	6 179	2 734	6 000	1 096	179	17.7	3.0	110	1.5
...	46 035	Davison	435	18 741	1 857	43.1	17 503	1 820	17 820	1 238	−317	7.1	−1.8	130	.7
...	46 037	Day	1 029	6 267	2 759	6.1	6 978	2 661	8 133	−711	−1 155	−10.2	−14.2	24	.4
...	46 039	Deuel..................	624	4 498	2 879	7.2	4 522	2 873	5 289	−24	−767	−.5	−14.5	34	.8
...	46 041	Dewey.................	2 303	5 972	2 786	2.6	5 523	2 800	5 366	449	157	8.1	2.9	51	.9
...	46 043	Douglas................	434	3 458	2 958	8.0	3 746	2 936	4 181	−288	−435	−7.7	−10.4	13	.4
...	46 045	Edmunds	1 146	4 367	2 888	3.8	4 356	2 888	5 159	11	−803	.3	−15.6	21	.5
...	46 047	Fall River	1 740	7 453	2 643	4.3	7 353	2 624	8 439	100	−1 086	1.4	−12.9	130	1.7
...	46 049	Faulk.................	1 000	2 640	3 018	2.6	2 744	3 013	3 327	−104	−583	−3.8	−17.5	6	.2
...	46 051	Grant..................	683	7 847	2 619	11.5	8 372	2 526	9 013	−525	−641	−6.3	−7.1	43	.5
...	46 053	Gregory................	1 016	4 792	2 860	4.7	5 359	2 814	6 015	−567	−656	−10.6	−10.9	41	.9
...	46 055	Haakon	1 813	2 196	3 051	1.2	2 624	3 016	2 794	−428	−170	−16.3	−6.1	13	.6
...	46 057	Hamlin	507	5 540	2 813	10.9	4 974	2 842	5 261	566	−287	11.4	−5.5	35	.6
...	46 059	Hand	1 437	3 741	2 939	2.6	4 272	2 892	4 948	−531	−676	−12.4	−13.7	11	.3
...	46 061	Hanson	435	3 139	2 983	7.2	2 994	3 001	3 415	145	−421	4.8	−12.3	3	.1
...	46 063	Harding	2 671	1 353	3 100	.5	1 669	3 087	1 700	−316	−31	−18.9	−1.8	22	1.6
...	46 065	Hughes	741	16 481	1 990	22.2	14 817	1 999	14 220	1 664	597	11.2	4.2	201	1.2
...	46 067	Hutchinson	813	8 075	2 600	9.9	8 262	2 541	9 350	−187	−1 088	−2.3	−11.6	42	.5
...	46 069	Hyde	861	1 671	3 086	1.9	1 696	3 084	2 069	−25	−373	−1.5	−18.0	8	.5
...	46 071	Jackson................	1 869	2 930	2 997	1.6	2 811	3 011	3 437	119	−626	4.2	−18.2	12	.4
...	46 073	Jerauld	530	2 295	3 039	4.3	2 425	3 027	2 929	−130	−504	−5.4	−17.2	7	.3
...	46 075	Jones..................	971	1 193	3 105	1.2	1 324	3 105	1 463	−131	−139	−9.9	−9.5	4	.3
...	46 077	Kingsbury	838	5 815	2 803	6.9	5 925	2 766	6 679	−110	−754	−1.9	−11.3	40	.7
...	46 079	Lake	563	11 276	2 351	20.0	10 550	2 331	10 724	726	−174	6.9	−1.6	89	.8
...	46 081	Lawrence	800	21 802	1 702	27.3	20 655	1 647	18 339	1 147	2 316	5.6	12.6	396	1.8
7760	46 083	Lincoln................	578	24 131	1 589	41.7	15 427	1 961	13 942	8 704	1 485	56.4	10.7	169	.7
...	46 085	Lyman	1 640	3 895	2 924	2.4	3 638	2 946	3 864	257	−226	7.1	−5.8	18	.5
...	46 087	McCook................	575	5 832	2 800	10.1	5 688	2 786	6 444	144	−756	2.5	−11.7	45	.8
...	46 089	McPherson	1 137	2 904	2 998	2.6	3 228	2 982	4 027	−324	−799	−10.0	−19.8	6	.2
...	46 091	Marshall	838	4 576	2 873	5.5	4 844	2 849	5 404	−268	−560	−5.5	−10.4	35	.8
...	46 093	Meade	3 471	24 253	1 586	7.0	21 878	1 585	20 717	2 375	1 161	10.9	5.6	509	2.1
...	46 095	Mellette...............	1 306	2 083	3 060	1.6	2 137	3 059	2 249	−54	−112	−2.5	−5.0	35	1.7
...	46 097	Miner	570	2 884	3 000	5.1	3 272	2 978	3 739	−388	−467	−11.9	−12.5	18	.6
7760	46 099	Minnehaha	810	148 281	365	183.1	123 809	370	109 435	24 472	14 374	19.8	13.1	3 187	2.1
...	46 101	Moody.................	520	6 595	2 727	12.7	6 507	2 709	6 692	88	−185	1.4	−2.8	50	.8
6660	46 103	Pennington	2 776	88 565	589	31.9	81 343	558	70 361	7 222	10 982	8.9	15.6	2 341	2.6
...	46 105	Perkins	2 872	3 363	2 966	1.2	3 932	2 924	4 700	−569	−768	−14.5	−16.3	25	.7
...	46 107	Potter	866	2 693	3 015	3.1	3 190	2 984	3 674	−497	−484	−15.6	−13.2	5	.2
...	46 109	Roberts	1 101	10 016	2 444	9.1	9 914	2 393	10 911	102	−997	1.0	−9.1	63	.6
...	46 111	Sanborn	569	2 675	3 016	4.7	2 833	3 010	3 213	−158	−380	−5.6	−11.8	27	1.0
...	46 113	Shannon	2 094	12 466	2 268	6.0	9 902	2 397	11 323	2 564	−1 421	25.9	−12.5	177	1.4
...	46 115	Spink	1 504	7 454	2 642	5.0	7 981	2 568	9 201	−527	−1 220	−6.6	−13.3	29	.4
...	46 117	Stanley	1 443	2 772	3 006	1.9	2 453	3 025	2 533	319	−80	13.0	−3.2	12	.4
...	46 119	Sully..................	1 007	1 556	3 091	1.5	1 589	3 091	1 990	−33	−401	−2.1	−20.2	12	.8
...	46 121	Todd..................	1 388	9 050	2 526	6.5	8 352	2 528	7 328	698	1 024	8.4	14.0	138	1.5
...	46 123	Tripp..................	1 614	6 430	2 745	4.0	6 924	2 668	7 268	−494	−344	−7.1	−4.7	55	.9
...	46 125	Turner	617	8 849	2 540	14.3	8 576	2 507	9 255	273	−679	3.2	−7.3	36	.4
...	46 127	Union	460	12 584	2 257	27.4	10 189	2 372	10 938	2 395	−749	23.5	−6.8	158	1.3
...	46 129	Walworth...............	708	5 974	2 784	8.4	6 087	2 746	7 011	−113	−924	−1.9	−13.2	36	.6
...	46 135	Yankton	522	21 652	1 710	41.5	19 252	1 715	18 952	2 400	300	12.5	1.6	395	1.8
...	46 137	Ziebach................	1 962	2 519	3 025	1.3	2 220	3 053	2 308	299	−88	13.5	−3.8	25	1.0

[1] Federal Information Processing Standards (FIPS) codes for metropolitan areas defined as of June 30, 1999.   [2] FIPS codes for states and counties/county equivalents.   [3] Dry land and land temporarily or partially covered by water.   [4] Based on 3,140 counties/county equivalents; excludes Yellowstone National Park in MT and South Boston independent city in VA which are no longer counties. When counties share the same rank, the next lower rank is omitted.   [5] Includes count resolution corrections through 1997 and adjustments based on Census 2000 dress rehearsal results and boundary changes reported as legally effective as of January 1, 1998.   [6] Persons of Hispanic or Latino origin may be of any race.

Sources: Land Area—U.S. Census Bureau, unpublished data file from Geography Division based on TIGER data base.   2000 Population—U.S. Census Bureau, Census of Population and Housing, Census 2000 Redistricting Data (Public Law 94-171) Summary Files (related Internet site <http://www.census.gov/dmd/www/2kresult.html>).   1990 Population—U.S. Census Bureau, "(CO-99-8) County Population Estimates and Demographic Components of Population Change: Annual Time Series, July 1, 1990 to July 1, 1999 (includes revised April 1, 1990 Population Estimates Base)"; published 9 March 2000; <http://www.census.gov/population/estimates/county/co-99-8/99C8_00.txt>.   1980 Population—U.S. Census Bureau, "1980–1990 Intercensal Population Estimates by County" on diskette (related Internet site <http://www.census.gov/population/www/estimates/countypop.html>).

[Includes U.S., states, and 3,142 counties/county equivalents defined as of January 1, 1992. For changes to these areas since January 1, 1992, see appendix B. Geographic Information]

Metro-politan area code[1]	State and county code[2]	County	Land area,[3] 2000 (sq. miles)	Population (April 1) 2000 Number	2000 Rank[4]	2000 Per square mile	1990[5] Number	1990[5] Rank[4]	1980	Net change 1990–2000	Net change 1980–1990	Percent change 1990–2000	Percent change 1980–1990	Hispanic or Latino,[6] 2000 Number	Hispanic or Latino,[6] 2000 Percent
	47 000	TENNESSEE	41 217	5 689 283	X	138.0	4 877 203	X	4 591 023	812 080	286 180	16.7	6.2	123 838	2.2
3840	47 001	Anderson	338	71 330	694	211.0	68 250	648	67 346	3 080	904	4.5	1.3	787	1.1
...	47 003	Bedford	474	37 586	1 174	79.3	30 411	1 273	27 916	7 175	2 495	23.6	8.9	2 811	7.5
...	47 005	Benton	395	16 537	1 987	41.9	14 524	2 017	14 901	2 013	−377	13.9	−2.5	157	.9
...	47 007	Bledsoe	406	12 367	2 276	30.5	9 669	2 416	9 478	2 698	191	27.9	2.0	138	1.1
3840	47 009	Blount	559	105 823	502	189.3	85 962	534	77 770	19 861	8 192	23.1	10.5	1 120	1.1
...	47 011	Bradley	329	87 965	594	267.4	73 712	610	67 547	14 253	6 165	19.3	9.1	1 822	2.1
...	47 013	Campbell	480	39 854	1 116	83.0	35 079	1 128	34 923	4 775	156	13.6	.4	269	.7
...	47 015	Cannon	266	12 826	2 245	48.2	10 467	2 339	10 234	2 359	233	22.5	2.3	157	1.2
...	47 017	Carroll	599	29 475	1 414	49.2	27 514	1 374	28 285	1 961	−771	7.1	−2.7	386	1.3
3660	47 019	Carter	341	56 742	835	166.4	51 505	820	50 205	5 237	1 300	10.2	2.6	504	.9
5360	47 021	Cheatham	303	35 912	1 221	118.5	27 140	1 387	21 616	8 772	5 524	32.3	25.6	437	1.2
3580	47 023	Chester	289	15 540	2 051	53.8	12 819	2 154	12 727	2 721	92	21.2	.7	150	1.0
...	47 025	Claiborne	434	29 862	1 400	68.8	26 137	1 417	24 595	3 725	1 542	14.3	6.3	192	.6
...	47 027	Clay	236	7 976	2 608	33.8	7 238	2 631	7 676	738	−438	10.2	−5.7	108	1.4
...	47 029	Cocke	434	33 565	1 298	77.3	29 141	1 324	28 792	4 424	349	15.2	1.2	354	1.1
...	47 031	Coffee	429	48 014	953	111.9	40 343	990	38 311	7 671	2 032	19.0	5.3	1 051	2.2
...	47 033	Crockett	265	14 532	2 119	54.8	13 378	2 107	14 941	1 154	−1 563	8.6	−10.5	793	5.5
...	47 035	Cumberland	682	46 802	965	68.6	34 736	1 143	28 676	12 066	6 060	34.7	21.1	578	1.2
5360	47 037	Davidson	502	569 891	95	1 135.2	510 786	93	477 811	59 105	32 975	11.6	6.9	26 091	4.6
...	47 039	Decatur	334	11 731	2 315	35.1	10 472	2 338	10 857	1 259	−385	12.0	−3.5	229	2.0
...	47 041	DeKalb	305	17 423	1 927	57.1	14 360	2 026	13 589	3 063	771	21.3	5.7	633	3.6
5360	47 043	Dickson	490	43 156	1 034	88.1	35 061	1 131	30 037	8 095	5 024	23.1	16.7	484	1.1
...	47 045	Dyer	511	37 279	1 183	73.0	34 854	1 138	34 663	2 425	191	7.0	.6	434	1.2
4920	47 047	Fayette	705	28 806	1 427	40.9	25 559	1 442	25 305	3 247	254	12.7	1.0	298	1.0
...	47 049	Fentress	499	16 625	1 982	33.3	14 669	2 007	14 826	1 956	−157	13.3	−1.1	90	.5
...	47 051	Franklin	555	39 270	1 131	70.8	34 923	1 136	31 983	4 347	2 940	12.4	9.2	620	1.6
...	47 053	Gibson	603	48 152	945	79.9	46 315	897	49 467	1 837	−3 152	4.0	−6.4	540	1.1
...	47 055	Giles	611	29 447	1 416	48.2	25 741	1 431	24 625	3 706	1 116	14.4	4.5	266	.9
...	47 057	Grainger	280	20 659	1 754	73.8	17 095	1 846	16 751	3 564	344	20.8	2.1	226	1.1
...	47 059	Greene	622	62 909	772	101.1	55 832	776	54 422	7 077	1 410	12.7	2.6	641	1.0
...	47 061	Grundy	361	14 332	2 138	39.7	13 362	2 109	13 787	970	−425	7.3	−3.1	141	1.0
...	47 063	Hamblen	161	58 128	822	361.0	50 480	835	49 300	7 648	1 180	15.2	2.4	3 299	5.7
1560	47 065	Hamilton	542	307 896	185	568.1	285 536	172	287 643	22 360	−2 107	7.8	−.7	5 481	1.8
...	47 067	Hancock	222	6 786	2 713	30.6	6 739	2 683	6 887	47	−148	.7	−2.1	25	.4
...	47 069	Hardeman	668	28 105	1 448	42.1	23 377	1 521	23 873	4 728	−496	20.2	−2.1	273	1.0
...	47 071	Hardin	578	25 578	1 536	44.3	22 633	1 552	22 280	2 945	353	13.0	1.6	260	1.0
3660	47 073	Hawkins	487	53 563	873	110.0	44 565	917	43 751	8 998	814	20.2	1.9	417	.8
...	47 075	Haywood	533	19 797	1 802	37.1	19 437	1 707	20 318	360	−881	1.9	−4.3	524	2.6
...	47 077	Henderson	520	25 522	1 539	49.1	21 844	1 586	21 390	3 678	454	16.8	2.1	247	1.0
...	47 079	Henry	562	31 115	1 374	55.4	27 888	1 353	28 656	3 227	−768	11.6	−2.7	311	1.0
...	47 081	Hickman	613	22 295	1 680	36.4	16 754	1 865	15 151	5 541	1 603	33.1	10.6	222	1.0
...	47 083	Houston	200	8 088	2 598	40.4	7 018	2 656	6 871	1 070	147	15.2	2.1	101	1.2
...	47 085	Humphreys	532	17 929	1 904	33.7	15 813	1 935	15 957	2 116	−144	13.4	−.9	148	.8
...	47 087	Jackson	309	10 984	2 368	35.5	9 297	2 444	9 398	1 687	−101	18.1	−1.1	89	.8
...	47 089	Jefferson	274	44 294	1 011	161.7	33 016	1 191	31 284	11 278	1 732	34.2	5.5	588	1.3
...	47 091	Johnson	298	17 499	1 923	58.7	13 766	2 075	13 745	3 733	21	27.1	.2	150	.9
3840	47 093	Knox	508	382 032	151	752.0	335 749	153	319 694	46 283	16 055	13.8	5.0	4 803	1.3
...	47 095	Lake	163	7 954	2 610	48.8	7 129	2 640	7 455	825	−326	11.6	−4.4	109	1.4
...	47 097	Lauderdale	470	27 101	1 478	57.7	23 491	1 514	24 555	3 610	−1 064	15.4	−4.3	314	1.2
...	47 099	Lawrence	617	39 926	1 114	64.7	35 303	1 122	34 110	4 623	1 193	13.1	3.5	399	1.0
...	47 101	Lewis	282	11 367	2 345	40.3	9 247	2 449	9 700	2 120	−453	22.9	−4.7	136	1.2
...	47 103	Lincoln	570	31 340	1 364	55.0	28 157	1 346	26 483	3 183	1 674	11.3	6.3	321	1.0
3840	47 105	Loudon	229	39 086	1 134	170.7	31 255	1 237	28 553	7 831	2 702	25.1	9.5	894	2.3
...	47 107	McMinn	430	49 015	932	114.0	42 383	950	41 878	6 632	505	15.6	1.2	884	1.8
...	47 109	McNairy	560	24 653	1 569	44.0	22 422	1 557	22 525	2 231	−103	10.0	−.5	229	.9
...	47 111	Macon	307	20 386	1 769	66.4	15 906	1 930	15 700	4 480	206	28.2	1.3	349	1.7
3580	47 113	Madison	557	91 837	557	164.9	77 982	581	74 546	13 855	3 436	17.8	4.6	1 572	1.7
1560	47 115	Marion	498	27 776	1 456	55.8	24 683	1 474	24 416	3 093	267	12.5	1.1	202	.7
...	47 117	Marshall	375	26 767	1 491	71.4	21 539	1 601	19 698	5 228	1 841	24.3	9.3	767	2.9
...	47 119	Maury	613	69 498	711	113.4	54 812	784	51 095	14 686	3 717	26.8	7.3	2 264	3.3
...	47 121	Meigs	195	11 086	2 358	56.9	8 033	2 561	7 431	3 053	602	38.0	8.1	63	.6
...	47 123	Monroe	635	38 961	1 140	61.4	30 541	1 265	28 700	8 420	1 841	27.6	6.4	684	1.8
1660	47 125	Montgomery	539	134 768	400	250.0	100 498	456	83 342	34 270	17 156	34.1	20.6	6 960	5.2
...	47 127	Moore	129	5 740	2 807	44.5	4 696	2 861	4 510	1 044	186	22.2	4.1	45	.8
...	47 129	Morgan	522	19 757	1 806	37.8	17 300	1 833	16 604	2 457	696	14.2	4.2	120	.6
...	47 131	Obion	545	32 450	1 335	59.5	31 717	1 221	32 781	733	−1 064	2.3	−3.2	616	1.9

[1] Federal Information Processing Standards (FIPS) codes for metropolitan areas defined as of June 30, 1999. [2] FIPS codes for states and counties/county equivalents. [3] Dry land and land temporarily or partially covered by water. [4] Based on 3,140 counties/county equivalents; excludes Yellowstone National Park in MT and South Boston independent city in VA which are no longer counties. When counties share the same rank, the next lower rank is omitted. [5] Includes count resolution corrections through 1997 and adjustments based on Census 2000 dress rehearsal results and boundary changes reported as legally effective as of January 1, 1998. [6] Persons of Hispanic or Latino origin may be of any race.

Sources: Land Area—U.S. Census Bureau, unpublished data file from Geography Division based on TIGER data base.   2000 Population—U.S. Census Bureau, Census of Population and Housing, Census 2000 Redistricting Data (Public Law 94-171) Summary Files (related Internet site <http://www.census.gov/dmd/www/2kresult.html>).   1990 Population—U.S. Census Bureau, "(CO-99-8) County Population Estimates and Demographic Components of Population Change: Annual Time Series, July 1, 1990 to July 1, 1999 (includes revised April 1, 1990 Population Estimates Base)"; published 9 March 2000; <http://www. census.gov/population/estimates/county/co-99-8/99C8_00.txt>.   1980 Population—U.S. Census Bureau, "1980–1990 Intercensal Population Estimates by County" on diskette (related Internet site <http://www.census.gov/population/www/estimates/countypop.html>).

[Includes U.S., states, and 3,142 counties/county equivalents defined as of January 1, 1992. For changes to these areas since January 1, 1992, see appendix B. Geographic Information]

Metro-politan area code[1]	State and county code[2]	County	Land area,[3] 2000 (sq. miles)	Population (April 1)											
				2000			1990[5]			Net change		Percent change		Hispanic or Latino,[6] 2000	
				Number	Rank[4]	Per square mile	Number	Rank[4]	1980	1990–2000	1980–1990	1990–2000	1980–1990	Number	Percent
		TENNESSEE—Con.													
...	47 133	Overton	433	20 118	1 788	46.5	17 636	1 809	17 575	2 482	61	14.1	.3	138	.7
...	47 135	Perry	415	7 631	2 634	18.4	6 612	2 697	6 111	1 019	501	15.4	8.2	61	.8
...	47 137	Pickett	163	4 945	2 852	30.3	4 548	2 869	4 358	397	190	8.7	4.4	41	.8
...	47 139	Polk	435	16 050	2 018	36.9	13 643	2 086	13 602	2 407	41	17.6	.3	117	.7
...	47 141	Putnam	401	62 315	780	155.4	51 373	821	47 690	10 942	3 683	21.3	7.7	1 891	3.0
...	47 143	Rhea	316	28 400	1 435	89.9	24 344	1 483	24 235	4 056	109	16.7	.4	474	1.7
...	47 145	Roane	361	51 910	894	143.8	47 227	888	48 425	4 683	−1 198	9.9	−2.5	359	.7
5360	47 147	Robertson	476	54 433	866	114.4	41 492	971	37 021	12 941	4 471	31.2	12.1	1 447	2.7
5360	47 149	Rutherford	619	182 023	302	294.1	118 570	392	84 058	63 453	34 512	53.5	41.1	5 065	2.8
...	47 151	Scott	532	21 127	1 729	39.7	18 358	1 772	19 259	2 769	−901	15.1	−4.7	120	.6
...	47 153	Sequatchie	266	11 370	2 343	42.7	8 863	2 482	8 605	2 507	258	28.3	3.0	93	.8
3840	47 155	Sevier	592	71 170	698	120.2	51 050	826	41 418	20 120	9 632	39.4	23.3	884	1.2
4920	47 157	Shelby	755	897 472	44	1 188.7	826 330	43	777 113	71 142	49 217	8.6	6.3	23 364	2.6
...	47 159	Smith	314	17 712	1 916	56.4	14 143	2 042	14 935	3 569	−792	25.2	−5.3	200	1.1
...	47 161	Stewart	458	12 370	2 274	27.0	9 479	2 435	8 665	2 891	814	30.5	9.4	124	1.0
3660	47 163	Sullivan	413	153 048	347	370.6	143 596	331	143 968	9 452	−372	6.6	−.3	1 090	.7
5360	47 165	Sumner	529	130 449	412	246.6	103 281	446	85 790	27 168	17 491	26.3	20.4	2 291	1.8
4920	47 167	Tipton	459	51 271	902	111.7	37 568	1 057	32 930	13 703	4 638	36.5	14.1	622	1.2
...	47 169	Trousdale	114	7 259	2 660	63.7	5 920	2 769	6 137	1 339	−217	22.6	−3.5	110	1.5
3660	47 171	Unicoi	186	17 667	1 918	95.0	16 549	1 885	16 362	1 118	187	6.8	1.1	342	1.9
3840	47 173	Union	224	17 808	1 909	79.5	13 694	2 081	11 707	4 114	1 987	30.0	17.0	140	.8
...	47 175	Van Buren	273	5 508	2 817	20.2	4 846	2 848	4 728	662	118	13.7	2.5	18	.3
...	47 177	Warren	433	38 276	1 157	88.4	32 992	1 192	32 653	5 284	339	16.0	1.0	1 885	4.9
3660	47 179	Washington	326	107 198	499	328.8	92 336	500	88 755	14 862	3 581	16.1	4.0	1 482	1.4
...	47 181	Wayne	734	16 842	1 965	22.9	13 935	2 062	13 946	2 907	−11	20.9	−.1	142	.8
...	47 183	Weakley	580	34 895	1 255	60.2	31 972	1 212	32 896	2 923	−924	9.1	−2.8	402	1.2
...	47 185	White	377	23 102	1 638	61.3	20 090	1 673	19 567	3 012	523	15.0	2.7	239	1.0
5360	47 187	Williamson	583	126 638	427	217.2	81 021	563	58 108	45 617	22 913	56.3	39.4	3 197	2.5
5360	47 189	Wilson	571	88 809	586	155.5	67 675	655	56 064	21 134	11 611	31.2	20.7	1 127	1.3
	48 000	TEXAS	261 797	20 851 820	X	79.6	16 986 335	X	14 225 513	3 865 485	2 760 822	22.8	19.4	6 669 666	32.0
...	48 001	Anderson	1 071	55 109	856	51.5	48 024	871	38 381	7 085	9 643	14.8	25.1	6 705	12.2
...	48 003	Andrews	1 501	13 004	2 233	8.7	14 338	2 029	13 323	−1 334	1 015	−9.3	7.6	5 202	40.0
...	48 005	Angelina	802	80 130	640	99.9	69 884	634	64 172	10 246	5 712	14.7	8.9	11 496	14.3
...	48 007	Aransas	252	22 497	1 671	89.3	17 892	1 794	14 260	4 605	3 632	25.7	25.5	4 571	20.3
9080	48 009	Archer	910	8 854	2 538	9.7	7 973	2 573	7 266	881	707	11.0	9.7	431	4.9
...	48 011	Armstrong	914	2 148	3 056	2.4	2 021	3 064	1 994	127	27	6.3	1.4	116	5.4
...	48 013	Atascosa	1 232	38 628	1 147	31.4	30 533	1 266	25 055	8 095	5 478	26.5	21.9	22 620	58.6
...	48 015	Austin	653	23 590	1 606	36.1	19 832	1 685	17 726	3 758	2 106	18.9	11.9	3 805	16.1
...	48 017	Bailey	827	6 594	2 728	8.0	7 064	2 652	8 168	−470	−1 104	−6.7	−13.5	3 119	47.3
...	48 019	Bandera	792	17 645	1 920	22.3	10 562	2 330	7 084	7 083	3 478	67.1	49.1	2 384	13.5
0640	48 021	Bastrop	888	57 733	827	65.0	38 263	1 047	24 726	19 470	13 537	50.9	54.7	13 845	24.0
...	48 023	Baylor	871	4 093	2 910	4.7	4 385	2 883	4 919	−292	−534	−6.7	−10.9	382	9.3
...	48 025	Bee	880	32 359	1 338	36.8	25 135	1 457	26 030	7 224	−895	28.7	−3.4	17 450	53.9
3810	48 027	Bell	1 060	237 974	244	224.5	191 073	251	157 820	46 901	33 253	24.5	21.1	39 701	16.7
7240	48 029	Bexar	1 247	1 392 931	24	1 117.0	1 185 394	25	988 971	207 537	196 423	17.5	19.9	757 033	54.3
...	48 031	Blanco	711	8 418	2 572	11.8	5 972	2 762	4 681	2 446	1 291	41.0	27.6	1 290	15.3
...	48 033	Borden	899	729	3 129	.8	799	3 123	859	−70	−60	−8.8	−7.0	87	11.9
...	48 035	Bosque	989	17 204	1 940	17.4	15 125	1 980	13 401	2 079	1 724	13.7	12.9	2 104	12.2
8360	48 037	Bowie	888	89 306	578	100.6	81 665	557	75 301	7 641	6 364	9.4	8.5	3 992	4.5
3362	48 039	Brazoria	1 386	241 767	238	174.4	191 707	250	169 587	50 060	22 120	26.1	13.0	55 063	22.8
1260	48 041	Brazos	586	152 415	350	260.1	121 862	377	93 588	30 553	28 274	25.1	30.2	27 253	17.9
...	48 043	Brewster	6 193	8 866	2 536	1.4	8 653	2 495	7 573	213	1 080	2.5	14.3	3 867	43.6
...	48 045	Briscoe	900	1 790	3 069	2.0	1 971	3 067	2 579	−181	−608	−9.2	−23.6	407	22.7
...	48 047	Brooks	943	7 976	2 608	8.5	8 204	2 547	8 428	−228	−224	−2.8	−2.7	7 304	91.6
...	48 049	Brown	944	37 674	1 170	39.9	34 371	1 157	33 057	3 303	1 314	9.6	4.0	5 793	15.4
...	48 051	Burleson	666	16 470	1 991	24.7	13 625	2 090	12 313	2 845	1 312	20.9	10.7	2 411	14.6
...	48 053	Burnet	996	34 147	1 277	34.3	22 677	1 549	17 803	11 470	4 874	50.6	27.4	5 044	14.8
0640	48 055	Caldwell	546	32 194	1 342	59.0	26 392	1 409	23 637	5 802	2 755	22.0	11.7	13 018	40.4
...	48 057	Calhoun	512	20 647	1 755	40.3	19 053	1 731	19 574	1 594	−521	8.4	−2.7	8 448	40.9
...	48 059	Callahan	899	12 905	2 240	14.4	11 859	2 226	10 992	1 046	867	8.8	7.9	812	6.3
1240	48 061	Cameron	906	335 227	174	370.0	260 120	193	209 727	75 107	50 393	28.9	24.0	282 736	84.3
...	48 063	Camp	198	11 549	2 330	58.3	9 904	2 396	9 275	1 645	629	16.6	6.8	1 707	14.8
...	48 065	Carson	923	6 516	2 738	7.1	6 576	2 701	6 672	−60	−96	−.9	−1.4	458	7.0
...	48 067	Cass	937	30 438	1 387	32.5	29 982	1 298	29 430	456	552	1.5	1.9	526	1.7
...	48 069	Castro	898	8 285	2 582	9.2	9 070	2 463	10 556	−785	−1 486	−8.7	−14.1	4 279	51.6

[1] Federal Information Processing Standards (FIPS) codes for metropolitan areas defined as of June 30, 1999. [2] FIPS codes for states and counties/county equivalents. [3] Dry land and land temporarily or partially covered by water. [4] Based on 3,140 counties/county equivalents; excludes Yellowstone National Park in MT and South Boston independent city in VA which are no longer counties. When counties share the same rank, the next lower rank is omitted. [5] Includes count resolution corrections through 1997 and adjustments based on Census 2000 dress rehearsal results and boundary changes reported as legally effective as of January 1, 1998. [6] Persons of Hispanic or Latino origin may be of any race.

Sources: Land Area—U.S. Census Bureau, unpublished data file from Geography Division based on TIGER data base. 2000 Population—U.S. Census Bureau, Census of Population and Housing, Census 2000 Redistricting Data (Public Law 94-171) Summary Files (related Internet site <http://www.census.gov/dmd/www/2kresult.html>). 1990 Population—U.S. Census Bureau, "(CO-99-8) County Population Estimates and Demographic Components of Population Change: Annual Time Series, July 1, 1990 to July 1, 1999 (includes revised April 1, 1990 Population Estimates Base)"; published 9 March 2000; <http://www. census.gov/population/estimates/county/co-99-8/99C8_00.txt>. 1980 Population—U.S. Census Bureau, "1980–1990 Intercensal Population Estimates by County" on diskette (related Internet site <http://www.census.gov/population/www/estimates/countypop.html>).

[Includes U.S., states, and 3,142 counties/county equivalents defined as of January 1, 1992. For changes to these areas since January 1, 1992, see appendix B. Geographic Information]

Metro-politan area code[1]	State and county code[2]	County	Land area,[3] 2000 (sq. miles)	Population (April 1)											
				2000			1990[5]			Net change		Percent change		Hispanic or Latino,[6] 2000	
				Number	Rank[4]	Per square mile	Number	Rank[4]	1980	1990–2000	1980–1990	1990–2000	1980–1990	Number	Percent
		TEXAS—Con.													
3362	48 071	Chambers	599	26 031	1 515	43.5	20 088	1 674	18 538	5 943	1 550	29.6	8.4	2 810	10.8
...	48 073	Cherokee	1 052	46 659	967	44.4	41 049	979	38 127	5 610	2 922	13.7	7.7	6 178	13.2
...	48 075	Childress	710	7 688	2 630	10.8	5 953	2 764	6 950	1 735	−997	29.1	−14.3	1 574	20.5
...	48 077	Clay	1 098	11 006	2 365	10.0	10 024	2 385	9 582	982	442	9.8	4.6	404	3.7
...	48 079	Cochran	775	3 730	2 941	4.8	4 377	2 885	4 825	−647	−448	−14.8	−9.3	1 646	44.1
...	48 081	Coke	899	3 864	2 926	4.3	3 424	2 961	3 196	440	228	12.9	7.1	653	16.9
...	48 083	Coleman	1 260	9 235	2 509	7.3	9 710	2 410	10 439	−475	−729	−4.9	−7.0	1 289	14.0
1922	48 085	Collin	848	491 675	113	579.8	264 036	188	144 576	227 639	119 460	86.2	82.6	50 510	10.3
...	48 087	Collingsworth	919	3 206	2 978	3.5	3 573	2 952	4 648	−367	−1 075	−10.3	−23.1	655	20.4
...	48 089	Colorado	963	20 390	1 768	21.2	18 383	1 770	18 823	2 007	−440	10.9	−2.3	4 024	19.7
7240	48 091	Comal	561	78 021	652	139.1	51 832	815	36 446	26 189	15 386	50.5	42.2	17 609	22.6
...	48 093	Comanche	938	14 026	2 161	15.0	13 381	2 106	12 617	645	764	4.8	6.1	2 928	20.9
...	48 095	Concho	991	3 966	2 922	4.0	3 044	2 996	2 915	922	129	30.3	4.4	1 639	41.3
...	48 097	Cooke	874	36 363	1 203	41.6	30 777	1 253	27 656	5 586	3 121	18.1	11.3	3 627	10.0
3810	48 099	Coryell	1 052	74 978	665	71.3	64 226	683	56 767	10 752	7 459	16.7	13.1	9 424	12.6
...	48 101	Cottle	901	1 904	3 072	2.1	2 247	3 050	2 947	−343	−700	−15.3	−23.8	360	18.9
...	48 103	Crane	786	3 996	2 921	5.1	4 652	2 864	4 600	−656	52	−14.1	1.1	1 753	43.9
...	48 105	Crockett	2 807	4 099	2 909	1.5	4 078	2 909	4 608	21	−530	.5	−11.5	2 242	54.7
...	48 107	Crosby	900	7 072	2 678	7.9	7 304	2 628	8 859	−232	−1 555	−3.2	−17.6	3 460	48.9
...	48 109	Culberson	3 812	2 975	2 993	.8	3 407	2 963	3 315	−432	92	−12.7	2.8	2 149	72.2
...	48 111	Dallam	1 505	6 222	2 761	4.1	5 461	2 803	6 531	761	−1 070	13.9	−16.4	1 766	28.4
1922	48 113	Dallas	880	2 218 899	10	2 521.5	1 852 691	11	1 556 419	366 208	296 272	19.8	19.0	662 729	29.9
...	48 115	Dawson	902	14 985	2 092	16.6	14 349	2 028	16 184	636	−1 835	4.4	−11.3	7 222	48.2
...	48 117	Deaf Smith	1 497	18 561	1 868	12.4	19 153	1 723	21 165	−592	−2 012	−3.1	−9.5	10 654	57.4
...	48 119	Delta	277	5 327	2 827	19.2	4 857	2 847	4 839	470	18	9.7	.4	165	3.1
1922	48 121	Denton	889	432 976	139	487.0	273 644	182	143 126	159 332	130 518	58.2	91.2	52 619	12.2
...	48 123	DeWitt	909	20 013	1 793	22.0	18 840	1 744	18 903	1 173	−63	6.2	−.3	5 452	27.2
...	48 125	Dickens	904	2 762	3 007	3.1	2 571	3 018	3 539	191	−968	7.4	−27.4	660	23.9
...	48 127	Dimmit	1 331	10 248	2 422	7.7	10 433	2 345	11 367	−185	−934	−1.8	−8.2	8 708	85.0
...	48 129	Donley	930	3 828	2 927	4.1	3 696	2 940	4 075	132	−379	3.6	−9.3	243	6.3
...	48 131	Duval	1 793	13 120	2 220	7.3	12 918	2 144	12 517	202	401	1.6	3.2	11 544	88.0
...	48 133	Eastland	926	18 297	1 880	19.8	18 488	1 762	19 480	−191	−992	−1.0	−5.1	1 976	10.8
5800	48 135	Ector	901	121 123	447	134.4	118 934	390	115 374	2 189	3 560	1.8	3.1	51 306	42.4
...	48 137	Edwards	2 120	2 162	3 053	1.0	2 266	3 044	2 033	−104	233	−4.6	11.5	974	45.1
1922	48 139	Ellis	940	111 360	486	118.5	85 167	539	59 743	26 193	25 424	30.8	42.6	20 508	18.4
2320	48 141	El Paso	1 013	679 622	75	670.9	591 610	79	479 899	88 012	111 711	14.9	23.3	531 654	78.2
...	48 143	Erath	1 086	33 001	1 319	30.4	27 991	1 352	22 560	5 010	5 431	17.9	24.1	4 959	15.0
...	48 145	Falls	769	18 576	1 866	24.2	17 712	1 803	17 946	864	−234	4.9	−1.3	2 941	15.8
...	48 147	Fannin	891	31 242	1 369	35.1	24 804	1 469	24 285	6 438	519	26.0	2.1	1 753	5.6
...	48 149	Fayette	950	21 804	1 701	23.0	20 095	1 672	18 832	1 709	1 263	8.5	6.7	2 786	12.8
...	48 151	Fisher	901	4 344	2 892	4.8	4 842	2 851	5 891	−498	−1 049	−10.3	−17.8	928	21.4
...	48 153	Floyd	992	7 771	2 628	7.8	8 497	2 512	9 834	−726	−1 337	−8.5	−13.6	3 569	45.9
...	48 155	Foard	707	1 622	3 088	2.3	1 794	3 078	2 158	−172	−364	−9.6	−16.9	265	16.3
3362	48 157	Fort Bend	875	354 452	166	405.1	225 421	219	130 962	129 031	94 459	57.2	72.1	74 871	21.1
...	48 159	Franklin	286	9 458	2 490	33.1	7 802	2 595	6 893	1 656	909	21.2	13.2	842	8.9
...	48 161	Freestone	877	17 867	1 907	20.4	15 818	1 934	14 830	2 049	988	13.0	6.7	1 465	8.2
...	48 163	Frio	1 133	16 252	2 004	14.3	13 472	2 103	13 785	2 780	−313	20.6	−2.3	11 987	73.8
...	48 165	Gaines	1 502	14 467	2 125	9.6	14 123	2 044	13 150	344	973	2.4	7.4	5 175	35.8
3362	48 167	Galveston	398	250 158	231	628.5	217 396	228	195 738	32 762	21 658	15.1	11.1	44 939	18.0
...	48 169	Garza	896	4 872	2 856	5.4	5 143	2 830	5 336	−271	−193	−5.3	−3.6	1 810	37.2
...	48 171	Gillespie	1 061	20 814	1 747	19.6	17 204	1 842	13 532	3 610	3 672	21.0	27.1	3 309	15.9
...	48 173	Glasscock	901	1 406	3 097	1.6	1 447	3 098	1 304	−41	143	−2.8	11.0	420	29.9
...	48 175	Goliad	854	6 928	2 693	8.1	5 980	2 761	5 193	948	787	15.9	15.2	2 439	35.2
...	48 177	Gonzales	1 068	18 628	1 865	17.4	17 205	1 841	16 949	1 423	256	8.3	1.5	7 381	39.6
...	48 179	Gray	928	22 744	1 661	24.5	23 967	1 494	26 386	−1 223	−2 419	−5.1	−9.2	2 959	13.0
7640	48 181	Grayson	934	110 595	491	118.4	95 019	489	89 796	15 576	5 223	16.4	5.8	7 519	6.8
4420	48 183	Gregg	274	111 379	485	406.5	104 948	440	99 495	6 431	5 453	6.1	5.5	10 183	9.1
...	48 185	Grimes	794	23 552	1 612	29.7	18 843	1 743	13 580	4 709	5 263	25.0	38.8	3 787	16.1
7240	48 187	Guadalupe	711	89 023	584	125.2	64 873	675	46 708	24 150	18 165	37.2	38.9	29 561	33.2
...	48 189	Hale	1 005	36 602	1 199	36.4	34 671	1 147	37 592	1 931	−2 921	5.6	−7.8	17 532	47.9
...	48 191	Hall	903	3 782	2 932	4.2	3 905	2 925	5 594	−123	−1 689	−3.1	−30.2	1 040	27.5
...	48 193	Hamilton	836	8 229	2 589	9.8	7 733	2 601	8 297	496	−564	6.4	−6.8	610	7.4
...	48 195	Hansford	920	5 369	2 823	5.8	5 848	2 775	6 209	−479	−361	−8.2	−5.8	1 690	31.5
...	48 197	Hardeman	695	4 724	2 866	6.8	5 283	2 821	6 368	−559	−1 085	−10.6	−17.0	685	14.5
0840	48 199	Hardin	894	48 073	950	53.8	41 320	974	40 721	6 753	599	16.3	1.5	1 223	2.5
3362	48 201	Harris	1 729	3 400 578	3	1 966.8	2 818 101	3	2 409 547	582 477	408 554	20.7	17.0	1 119 751	32.9

[1] Federal Information Processing Standards (FIPS) codes for metropolitan areas defined as of June 30, 1999.   [2] FIPS codes for states and counties/county equivalents.   [3] Dry land and land temporarily or partially covered by water.   [4] Based on 3,140 counties/county equivalents; excludes Yellowstone National Park in MT and South Boston independent city in VA which are no longer counties. When counties share the same rank, the next lower rank is omitted.   [5] Includes count resolution corrections through 1997 and adjustments based on Census 2000 dress rehearsal results and boundary changes reported as legally effective as of January 1, 1998.   [6] Persons of Hispanic or Latino origin may be of any race.

Sources: Land Area—U.S. Census Bureau, unpublished data file from Geography Division based on TIGER data base.   2000 Population—U.S. Census Bureau, Census of Population and Housing, Census 2000 Redistricting Data (Public Law 94-171) Summary Files (related Internet site <http://www.census.gov/dmd/www/2kresult.html>).   1990 Population—U.S. Census Bureau, "(CO-99-8) County Population Estimates and Demographic Components of Population Change: Annual Time Series, July 1, 1990 to July 1, 1999 (includes revised April 1, 1990 Population Estimates Base)"; published 9 March 2000; <http://www. census.gov/population/estimates/county/co-99-8/99C8_00.txt>.   1980 Population—U.S. Census Bureau, "1980–1990 Intercensal Population Estimates by County" on diskette (related Internet site <http://www.census.gov/population/www/estimates/countypop.html>).

[Includes U.S., states, and 3,142 counties/county equivalents defined as of January 1, 1992. For changes to these areas since January 1, 1992, see appendix B. Geographic Information]

Metro-politan area code[1]	State and county code[2]	County	Land area,[3] 2000 (sq. miles)	Population (April 1) 2000 Number	2000 Rank[4]	Per square mile	1990[5] Number	1990 Rank[4]	1980	Net change 1990–2000	Net change 1980–1990	Percent change 1990–2000	Percent change 1980–1990	Hispanic or Latino,[6] 2000 Number	Percent
		TEXAS—Con.													
4420	48 203	Harrison	899	62 110	783	69.1	57 483	759	52 265	4 627	5 218	8.0	10.0	3 316	5.3
...	48 205	Hartley	1 462	5 537	2 814	3.8	3 634	2 947	3 987	1 903	–353	52.4	–8.9	758	13.7
...	48 207	Haskell	903	6 093	2 771	6.7	6 820	2 674	7 725	–727	–905	–10.7	–11.7	1 249	20.5
0640	48 209	Hays	678	97 589	531	143.9	65 614	667	40 594	31 975	25 020	48.7	61.6	28 859	29.6
...	48 211	Hemphill	910	3 351	2 968	3.7	3 720	2 938	5 304	–369	–1 584	–9.9	–29.9	522	15.6
1922	48 213	Henderson	874	73 277	683	83.8	58 543	742	42 606	14 734	15 937	25.2	37.4	5 071	6.9
4880	48 215	Hidalgo	1 570	569 463	96	362.7	383 545	131	283 323	185 918	100 222	48.5	35.4	503 100	88.3
...	48 217	Hill	962	32 321	1 339	33.6	27 146	1 386	25 024	5 175	2 122	19.1	8.5	4 360	13.5
...	48 219	Hockley	908	22 716	1 662	25.0	24 199	1 487	23 230	–1 483	969	–6.1	4.2	8 459	37.2
1922	48 221	Hood	422	41 100	1 079	97.4	28 981	1 331	17 714	12 119	11 267	41.8	63.6	2 975	7.2
...	48 223	Hopkins	782	31 960	1 346	40.9	28 833	1 335	25 247	3 127	3 586	10.8	14.2	2 967	9.3
...	48 225	Houston	1 231	23 185	1 634	18.8	21 375	1 613	22 299	1 810	–924	8.5	–4.1	1 739	7.5
...	48 227	Howard	903	33 627	1 294	37.2	32 343	1 204	33 142	1 284	–799	4.0	–2.4	12 597	37.5
...	48 229	Hudspeth	4 571	3 344	2 969	.7	2 915	3 005	2 728	429	187	14.7	6.9	2 509	75.0
1922	48 231	Hunt	841	76 596	657	91.1	64 343	680	55 248	12 253	9 095	19.0	16.5	6 366	8.3
...	48 233	Hutchinson	887	23 857	1 596	26.9	25 689	1 434	26 304	–1 832	–615	–7.1	–2.3	3 506	14.7
...	48 235	Irion	1 051	1 771	3 081	1.7	1 629	3 089	1 386	142	243	8.7	17.5	436	24.6
...	48 237	Jack	917	8 763	2 549	9.6	6 981	2 660	7 408	1 782	–427	25.5	–5.8	691	7.9
...	48 239	Jackson	829	14 391	2 132	17.4	13 039	2 137	13 352	1 352	–313	10.4	–2.3	3 551	24.7
...	48 241	Jasper	937	35 604	1 229	38.0	31 102	1 242	30 781	4 502	321	14.5	1.0	1 384	3.9
...	48 243	Jeff Davis	2 264	2 207	3 050	1.0	1 946	3 069	1 647	261	299	13.4	18.2	783	35.5
0840	48 245	Jefferson	904	252 051	225	278.8	239 389	208	248 652	12 662	–9 263	5.3	–3.7	26 536	10.5
...	48 247	Jim Hogg	1 136	5 281	2 832	4.6	5 109	2 831	5 168	172	–59	3.4	–1.1	4 752	90.0
...	48 249	Jim Wells	865	39 326	1 128	45.5	37 679	1 055	36 498	1 647	1 181	4.4	3.2	29 772	75.7
1922	48 251	Johnson	729	126 811	424	174.0	97 165	473	67 649	29 646	29 516	30.5	43.6	15 375	12.1
...	48 253	Jones	931	20 785	1 749	22.3	16 490	1 895	17 268	4 295	–778	26.0	–4.5	4 346	20.9
...	48 255	Karnes	750	15 446	2 056	20.6	12 455	2 186	13 593	2 991	–1 138	24.0	–8.4	7 324	47.4
1922	48 257	Kaufman	786	71 313	695	90.7	52 220	811	39 038	19 093	13 182	36.6	33.8	7 925	11.1
...	48 259	Kendall	662	23 743	1 601	35.9	14 589	2 014	10 635	9 154	3 954	62.7	37.2	4 248	17.9
...	48 261	Kenedy	1 457	414	3 137	.3	460	3 137	543	–46	–83	–10.0	–15.3	327	79.0
...	48 263	Kent	902	859	3 119	1.0	1 010	3 113	1 145	–151	–135	–15.0	–11.8	78	9.1
...	48 265	Kerr	1 106	43 653	1 025	39.5	36 304	1 096	28 780	7 349	7 524	20.2	26.1	8 353	19.1
...	48 267	Kimble	1 251	4 468	2 884	3.6	4 122	2 905	4 063	346	59	8.4	1.5	926	20.7
...	48 269	King	912	356	3 138	.4	354	3 138	425	2	–71	.6	–16.7	34	9.6
...	48 271	Kinney	1 363	3 379	2 965	2.5	3 119	2 991	2 279	260	840	8.3	36.9	1 707	50.5
...	48 273	Kleberg	871	31 549	1 360	36.2	30 274	1 282	33 358	1 275	–3 084	4.2	–9.2	20 635	65.4
...	48 275	Knox	849	4 253	2 898	5.0	4 837	2 852	5 329	–584	–492	–12.1	–9.2	1 067	25.1
...	48 277	Lamar	917	48 499	940	52.9	43 949	926	42 156	4 550	1 793	10.4	4.3	1 614	3.3
...	48 279	Lamb	1 016	14 709	2 106	14.5	15 072	1 984	18 669	–363	–3 597	–2.4	–19.3	6 393	43.5
...	48 281	Lampasas	712	17 762	1 914	24.9	13 521	2 100	12 005	4 241	1 516	31.4	12.6	2 677	15.1
...	48 283	La Salle	1 489	5 866	2 797	3.9	5 254	2 823	5 514	612	–260	11.6	–4.7	4 524	77.1
...	48 285	Lavaca	970	19 210	1 832	19.8	18 690	1 750	19 004	520	–314	2.8	–1.7	2 183	11.4
...	48 287	Lee	629	15 657	2 044	24.9	12 854	2 150	10 952	2 803	1 902	21.8	17.4	2 848	18.2
...	48 289	Leon	1 072	15 335	2 069	14.3	12 665	2 169	9 594	2 670	3 071	21.1	32.0	1 213	7.9
3362	48 291	Liberty	1 160	70 154	708	60.5	52 726	805	47 088	17 428	5 638	33.1	12.0	7 660	10.9
...	48 293	Limestone	909	22 051	1 690	24.3	20 946	1 632	20 224	1 105	722	5.3	3.6	2 859	13.0
...	48 295	Lipscomb	932	3 057	2 989	3.3	3 143	2 989	3 766	–86	–623	–2.7	–16.5	633	20.7
...	48 297	Live Oak	1 036	12 309	2 279	11.9	9 556	2 428	9 606	2 753	–50	28.8	–.5	4 683	38.0
...	48 299	Llano	935	17 044	1 950	18.2	11 631	2 245	10 144	5 413	1 487	46.5	14.7	875	5.1
...	48 301	Loving	673	67	3 140	.1	107	3 140	91	–40	16	–37.4	17.6	7	10.4
4600	48 303	Lubbock	899	242 628	237	269.9	222 636	224	211 651	19 992	10 985	9.0	5.2	66 609	27.5
...	48 305	Lynn	892	6 550	2 735	7.3	6 758	2 679	8 605	–208	–1 847	–3.1	–21.5	2 923	44.6
...	48 307	McCulloch	1 069	8 205	2 591	7.7	8 778	2 487	8 735	–573	43	–6.5	.5	2 219	27.0
8800	48 309	McLennan	1 042	213 517	262	204.9	189 123	254	170 755	24 394	18 368	12.9	10.8	38 233	17.9
...	48 311	McMullen	1 113	851	3 120	.8	817	3 122	789	34	28	4.2	3.5	282	33.1
...	48 313	Madison	470	12 940	2 236	27.5	10 931	2 302	10 649	2 009	282	18.4	2.6	2 042	15.8
...	48 315	Marion	381	10 941	2 371	28.7	9 984	2 387	10 360	957	–376	9.6	–3.6	263	2.4
...	48 317	Martin	915	4 746	2 863	5.2	4 956	2 843	4 684	–210	272	–4.2	5.8	1 925	40.6
...	48 319	Mason	932	3 738	2 940	4.0	3 423	2 962	3 683	315	–260	9.2	–7.1	783	20.9
...	48 321	Matagorda	1 114	37 957	1 166	34.1	36 928	1 075	37 828	1 029	–900	2.8	–2.4	11 898	31.3
...	48 323	Maverick	1 280	47 297	961	37.0	36 378	1 094	31 398	10 919	4 980	30.0	15.9	44 938	95.0
...	48 325	Medina	1 328	39 304	1 130	29.6	27 312	1 380	23 164	11 992	4 148	43.9	17.9	17 873	45.5
...	48 327	Menard	902	2 360	3 035	2.6	2 252	3 047	2 346	108	–94	4.8	–4.0	748	31.7
5800	48 329	Midland	900	116 009	465	128.9	106 611	433	82 636	9 398	23 975	8.8	29.0	33 676	29.0
...	48 331	Milam	1 017	24 238	1 587	23.8	22 946	1 536	22 732	1 292	214	5.6	.9	4 516	18.6
...	48 333	Mills	748	5 151	2 840	6.9	4 531	2 870	4 477	620	54	13.7	1.2	671	13.0

[1] Federal Information Processing Standards (FIPS) codes for metropolitan areas defined as of June 30, 1999. [2] FIPS codes for states and counties/county equivalents. [3] Dry land and land temporarily or partially covered by water. [4] Based on 3,140 counties/county equivalents; excludes Yellowstone National Park in MT and South Boston independent city in VA which are no longer counties. When counties share the same rank, the next lower rank is omitted. [5] Includes count resolution corrections through 1997 and adjustments based on Census 2000 dress rehearsal results and boundary changes reported as legally effective as of January 1, 1998. [6] Persons of Hispanic or Latino origin may be of any race.

Sources: Land Area—U.S. Census Bureau, unpublished data file from Geography Division based on TIGER data base. 2000 Population—U.S. Census Bureau, Census of Population and Housing, Census 2000 Redistricting Data (Public Law 94-171) Summary Files (related Internet site <http://www.census.gov/dmd/www/2kresult.html>). 1990 Population—U.S. Census Bureau, "(CO-99-8) County Population Estimates and Demographic Components of Population Change: Annual Time Series, July 1, 1990 to July 1, 1999 (includes revised April 1, 1990 Population Estimates Base)"; published 9 March 2000; <http://www.census.gov/population/estimates/county/co-99-8/99C8_00.txt>. 1980 Population—U.S. Census Bureau, "1980–1990 Intercensal Population Estimates by County" on diskette (related Internet site <http://www.census.gov/population/www/estimates/countypop.html>).

Table B–1. Counties — **Area and Population**–Con.

[Includes U.S., states, and 3,142 counties/county equivalents defined as of January 1, 1992. For changes to these areas since January 1, 1992, see appendix B. Geographic Information]

Metro-politan area code[1]	State and county code[2]	County	Land area,[3] 2000 (sq. miles)	Population (April 1) 2000 Number	Rank[4]	Per square mile	1990[5] Number	Rank[4]	1980	Net change 1990–2000	1980–1990	Percent change 1990–2000	1980–1990	Hispanic or Latino,[6] 2000 Number	Percent
		TEXAS—Con.													
...	48 335	Mitchell	910	9 698	2 470	10.7	8 016	2 563	9 088	1 682	−1 072	21.0	−11.8	3 009	31.0
...	48 337	Montague	931	19 117	1 841	20.5	17 274	1 836	17 410	1 843	−136	10.7	−.8	1 035	5.4
3362	48 339	Montgomery	1 044	293 768	193	281.4	182 201	264	127 222	111 567	54 979	61.2	43.2	37 150	12.6
...	48 341	Moore	900	20 121	1 785	22.4	17 865	1 795	16 575	2 256	1 290	12.6	7.8	9 558	47.5
...	48 343	Morris	255	13 048	2 228	51.2	13 200	2 123	14 629	−152	−1 429	−1.2	−9.8	477	3.7
...	48 345	Motley	989	1 426	3 096	1.4	1 532	3 095	1 950	−106	−418	−6.9	−21.4	173	12.1
...	48 347	Nacogdoches	947	59 203	812	62.5	54 753	786	46 786	4 450	7 967	8.1	17.0	6 660	11.2
...	48 349	Navarro	1 008	45 124	995	44.8	39 926	1 005	35 323	5 198	4 603	13.0	13.0	7 113	15.8
...	48 351	Newton	933	15 072	2 085	16.2	13 569	2 094	13 254	1 503	315	11.1	2.4	571	3.8
...	48 353	Nolan	912	15 802	2 032	17.3	16 594	1 880	17 359	−792	−765	−4.8	−4.4	4 431	28.0
1880	48 355	Nueces	836	313 645	182	375.2	291 145	168	268 215	22 500	22 930	7.7	8.5	174 951	55.8
...	48 357	Ochiltree	918	9 006	2 520	9.8	9 128	2 459	9 588	−122	−400	−1.3	−4.8	2 803	31.0
...	48 359	Oldham	1 501	2 185	3 052	1.5	2 278	3 042	2 283	−93	−5	−4.1	−.2	241	11.0
0840	48 361	Orange	356	84 966	613	238.7	80 509	566	83 838	4 457	−3 329	5.5	−4.0	3 073	3.6
...	48 363	Palo Pinto	953	27 026	1 481	28.4	25 055	1 459	24 062	1 971	993	7.9	4.1	3 667	13.6
...	48 365	Panola	801	22 756	1 660	28.4	22 035	1 574	20 724	721	1 311	3.3	6.3	798	3.5
1922	48 367	Parker	904	88 495	590	97.9	64 785	676	44 609	23 710	20 176	36.6	45.2	6 211	7.0
...	48 369	Parmer	882	10 016	2 444	11.4	9 863	2 400	11 038	153	−1 175	1.6	−10.6	4 927	49.2
...	48 371	Pecos	4 764	16 809	1 967	3.5	14 675	2 006	14 618	2 134	57	14.5	.4	10 262	61.1
...	48 373	Polk	1 057	41 133	1 077	38.9	30 687	1 259	24 407	10 446	6 280	34.0	25.7	3 861	9.4
0320	48 375	Potter	909	113 546	474	124.9	97 841	470	98 637	15 705	−796	16.1	−.8	31 921	28.1
...	48 377	Presidio	3 856	7 304	2 655	1.9	6 637	2 690	5 188	667	1 449	10.0	27.9	6 162	84.4
...	48 379	Rains	232	9 139	2 518	39.4	6 715	2 686	4 839	2 424	1 876	36.1	38.8	505	5.5
0320	48 381	Randall	914	104 312	507	114.1	89 673	512	75 062	14 639	14 611	16.3	19.5	10 718	10.3
...	48 383	Reagan	1 175	3 326	2 970	2.8	4 514	2 874	4 135	−1 188	379	−26.3	9.2	1 646	49.5
...	48 385	Real	700	3 047	2 990	4.4	2 412	3 030	2 469	635	−57	26.3	−2.3	688	22.6
...	48 387	Red River	1 050	14 314	2 139	13.6	14 317	2 030	16 101	−3	−1 784	Z	−11.1	669	4.7
...	48 389	Reeves	2 636	13 137	2 219	5.0	15 852	1 933	15 801	−2 715	51	−17.1	.3	9 640	73.4
...	48 391	Refugio	770	7 828	2 621	10.2	7 976	2 570	9 289	−148	−1 313	−1.9	−14.1	3 490	44.6
...	48 393	Roberts	924	887	3 116	1.0	1 025	3 112	1 187	−138	−162	−13.5	−13.6	28	3.2
...	48 395	Robertson	855	16 000	2 022	18.7	15 511	1 952	14 653	489	858	3.2	5.9	2 359	14.7
1922	48 397	Rockwall	129	43 080	1 035	334.0	25 604	1 438	14 528	17 476	11 076	68.3	76.2	4 771	11.1
...	48 399	Runnels	1 051	11 495	2 336	10.9	11 294	2 276	11 872	201	−578	1.8	−4.9	3 372	29.3
...	48 401	Rusk	924	47 372	960	51.3	43 735	928	41 382	3 637	2 353	8.3	5.7	3 998	8.4
...	48 400	Sabine	400	10 469	2 400	21.4	9 500	2 425	8 702	969	804	9.2	10.2	189	1.8
...	48 405	San Augustine	528	8 946	2 530	16.9	7 999	2 566	8 785	947	−786	11.8	−8.9	320	3.6
...	48 407	San Jacinto	571	22 246	1 683	39.0	16 372	1 899	11 434	5 874	4 938	35.9	43.2	1 084	4.9
1880	48 409	San Patricio	692	67 138	732	97.0	58 749	740	58 013	8 389	736	14.3	1.3	33 181	49.4
...	48 411	San Saba	1 134	6 186	2 763	5.5	5 401	2 808	5 841	785	−440	14.5	−7.5	1 333	21.5
...	48 413	Schleicher	1 311	2 935	2 996	2.2	2 990	3 002	2 820	−55	170	−1.8	6.0	1 278	43.5
...	48 415	Scurry	903	16 361	2 000	18.1	18 634	1 757	18 192	−2 273	442	−12.2	2.4	4 544	27.8
...	48 417	Shackelford	914	3 302	2 973	3.6	3 316	2 973	3 915	−14	−599	−.4	−15.3	251	7.6
...	48 419	Shelby	794	25 224	1 557	31.8	22 034	1 575	23 084	3 190	−1 050	14.5	−4.5	2 489	9.9
...	48 421	Sherman	923	3 186	2 980	3.5	2 858	3 007	3 174	328	−316	11.5	−10.0	874	27.4
8640	48 423	Smith	928	174 706	312	188.3	151 309	308	128 366	23 397	22 943	15.5	17.9	19 521	11.2
...	48 425	Somervell	187	6 809	2 711	36.4	5 360	2 813	4 154	1 449	1 206	27.0	29.0	915	13.4
...	48 427	Starr	1 223	53 597	871	43.8	40 518	986	27 266	13 079	13 252	32.3	48.6	52 278	97.5
...	48 429	Stephens	895	9 674	2 491	10.8	9 010	2 468	9 926	664	−916	7.4	−9.2	1 418	14.7
...	48 431	Sterling	923	1 393	3 098	1.5	1 438	3 099	1 206	−45	232	−3.1	19.2	432	31.0
...	48 433	Stonewall	919	1 693	3 085	1.8	2 013	3 066	2 406	−320	−393	−15.9	−16.3	199	11.8
...	48 435	Sutton	1 454	4 077	2 912	2.8	4 135	2 902	5 130	−58	−995	−1.4	−19.4	2 106	51.7
...	48 437	Swisher	900	8 378	2 575	9.3	8 133	2 552	9 723	245	−1 590	3.0	−16.4	2 951	35.2
1922	48 439	Tarrant	863	1 446 219	20	1 675.8	1 170 103	27	860 880	276 116	309 223	23.6	35.9	285 290	19.7
0040	48 441	Taylor	916	126 555	428	138.2	119 655	387	110 932	6 900	8 723	5.8	7.9	22 328	17.6
...	48 443	Terrell	2 358	1 081	3 106	.5	1 410	3 100	1 595	−329	−185	−23.3	−11.6	525	48.6
...	48 445	Terry	890	12 761	2 247	14.3	13 218	2 120	14 581	−457	−1 363	−3.5	−9.3	5 626	44.1
...	48 447	Throckmorton	912	1 850	3 076	2.0	1 880	3 075	2 053	−30	−173	−1.6	−8.4	173	9.4
...	48 449	Titus	411	28 118	1 447	68.4	24 009	1 492	21 442	4 109	2 567	17.1	12.0	7 960	28.3
7200	48 451	Tom Green	1 522	104 010	509	68.3	98 458	466	84 784	5 552	13 674	5.6	16.1	31 946	30.7
0640	48 453	Travis	989	812 280	56	821.3	576 407	82	419 573	235 873	156 834	40.9	37.4	229 048	28.2
...	48 455	Trinity	693	13 779	2 174	19.9	11 445	2 258	9 450	2 334	1 995	20.4	21.1	668	4.8
...	48 457	Tyler	923	20 871	1 741	22.6	16 646	1 875	16 223	4 225	423	25.4	2.6	742	3.6
4420	48 459	Upshur	588	35 291	1 239	60.0	31 370	1 233	28 595	3 921	2 775	12.5	9.7	1 394	4.0
...	48 461	Upton	1 242	3 404	2 962	2.7	4 447	2 878	4 619	−1 043	−172	−23.5	−3.7	1 449	42.6
...	48 463	Uvalde	1 557	25 926	1 520	16.7	23 340	1 525	22 441	2 586	899	11.1	4.0	17 089	65.9
...	48 465	Val Verde	3 170	44 856	1 002	14.2	38 721	1 034	35 910	6 135	2 811	15.8	7.8	33 849	75.5

[1] Federal Information Processing Standards (FIPS) codes for metropolitan areas defined as of June 30, 1999.   [2] FIPS codes for states and counties/county equivalents.   [3] Dry land and land temporarily or partially covered by water.   [4] Based on 3,140 counties/county equivalents; excludes Yellowstone National Park in MT and South Boston independent city in VA which are no longer counties. When counties share the same rank, the next lower rank is omitted.   [5] Includes count resolution corrections through 1997 and adjustments based on Census 2000 dress rehearsal results and boundary changes reported as legally effective as of January 1, 1998.   [6] Persons of Hispanic or Latino origin may be of any race.

Sources: Land Area—U.S. Census Bureau, unpublished data file from Geography Division based on TIGER data base.   2000 Population—U.S. Census Bureau, Census of Population and Housing, Census 2000 Redistricting Data (Public Law 94-171) Summary Files (related Internet site <http://www.census.gov/dmd/www/2kresult.html>).   1990 Population—U.S. Census Bureau, "(CO-99-8) County Population Estimates and Demographic Components of Population Change: Annual Time Series, July 1, 1990 to July 1, 1999 (includes revised April 1, 1990 Population Estimates Base)"; published 9 March 2000; <http://www.census.gov/population/estimates/county/co-99-8/99C8_00.txt>.   1980 Population—U.S. Census Bureau, "1980–1990 Intercensal Population Estimates by County" on diskette (related Internet site <http://www.census.gov/population/www/estimates/countypop.html>).

[Includes U.S., states, and 3,142 counties/county equivalents defined as of January 1, 1992. For changes to these areas since January 1, 1992, see appendix B. Geographic Information]

Metro-politan area code[1]	State and county code[2]	County	Land area,[3] 2000 (sq. miles)	Population (April 1) 2000 Number	Rank[4]	Per square mile	1990[5] Number	Rank[4]	1980	Net change 1990–2000	1980–1990	Percent change 1990–2000	1980–1990	Hispanic or Latino,[6] 2000 Number	Percent
		TEXAS—Con.													
...	48 467	Van Zandt	849	48 140	946	56.7	37 944	1 051	31 426	10 196	6 518	26.9	20.7	3 201	6.6
8750	48 469	Victoria	883	84 088	618	95.2	74 361	604	68 807	9 727	5 554	13.1	8.1	32 959	39.2
...	48 471	Walker	787	61 758	786	78.5	50 917	829	41 789	10 841	9 128	21.3	21.8	8 712	14.1
3362	48 473	Waller	514	32 663	1 326	63.5	23 374	1 522	19 798	9 289	3 576	39.7	18.1	6 344	19.4
...	48 475	Ward	835	10 909	2 374	13.1	13 115	2 129	13 976	−2 206	−861	−16.8	−6.2	4 580	42.0
...	48 477	Washington	609	30 373	1 388	49.9	26 154	1 413	21 998	4 219	4 156	16.1	18.9	2 647	8.7
4080	48 479	Webb	3 357	193 117	284	57.5	133 239	349	99 258	59 878	33 981	44.9	34.2	182 070	94.3
...	48 481	Wharton	1 090	41 188	1 075	37.8	39 955	1 002	40 242	1 233	−287	3.1	−.7	12 888	31.3
...	48 483	Wheeler	914	5 284	2 831	5.8	5 879	2 772	7 137	−595	−1 258	−10.1	−17.6	664	12.6
9080	48 485	Wichita	628	131 664	405	209.7	122 378	375	121 082	9 286	1 296	7.6	1.1	16 097	12.2
...	48 487	Wilbarger	971	14 676	2 109	15.1	15 121	1 981	15 931	−445	−810	−2.9	−5.1	3 015	20.5
...	48 489	Willacy	597	20 082	1 790	33.6	17 705	1 805	17 495	2 377	210	13.4	1.2	17 209	85.7
0640	48 491	Williamson	1 123	249 967	232	222.6	139 551	340	76 521	110 416	63 030	79.1	82.4	42 990	17.2
7240	48 493	Wilson	807	32 408	1 336	40.2	22 650	1 550	16 756	9 758	5 894	43.1	35.2	11 834	36.5
...	48 495	Winkler	841	7 173	2 669	8.5	8 626	2 501	9 944	−1 453	−1 318	−16.8	−13.3	3 156	44.0
...	48 497	Wise	905	48 793	935	53.9	34 679	1 146	26 575	14 114	8 104	40.7	30.5	5 248	10.8
...	48 499	Wood	650	36 752	1 196	56.5	29 380	1 319	24 697	7 372	4 683	25.1	19.0	2 102	5.7
...	48 501	Yoakum	800	7 322	2 653	9.2	8 786	2 486	8 299	−1 464	487	−16.7	5.9	3 363	45.9
...	48 503	Young	922	17 943	1 903	19.5	18 126	1 782	19 083	−183	−957	−1.0	−5.0	1 906	10.6
...	48 505	Zapata	997	12 182	2 285	12.2	9 279	2 446	6 628	2 903	2 651	31.3	40.0	10 328	84.8
...	48 507	Zavala	1 298	11 600	2 324	8.9	12 162	2 202	11 666	−562	496	−4.6	4.3	10 582	91.2
	49 000	UTAH	82 144	2 233 169	X	27.2	1 722 850	X	1 461 037	510 319	261 813	29.6	17.9	201 559	9.0
...	49 001	Beaver	2 590	6 005	2 778	2.3	4 765	2 859	4 378	1 240	387	26.0	8.8	333	5.5
...	49 003	Box Elder	5 723	42 745	1 042	7.5	36 485	1 090	33 222	6 260	3 263	17.2	9.8	2 791	6.5
...	49 005	Cache	1 165	91 391	562	78.4	70 183	630	57 176	21 208	13 007	30.2	22.7	5 786	6.3
...	49 007	Carbon	1 478	20 422	1 764	13.8	20 228	1 664	22 179	194	−1 951	1.0	−8.8	2 097	10.3
...	49 009	Daggett	698	921	3 114	1.3	690	3 129	769	231	−79	33.5	−10.3	47	5.1
7160	49 011	Davis	304	238 994	241	786.2	187 941	256	146 540	51 053	41 401	27.2	28.3	12 955	5.4
...	49 013	Duchesne	3 238	14 371	2 135	4.4	12 645	2 173	12 565	1 726	80	13.6	.6	508	3.5
...	49 015	Emery	4 452	10 860	2 376	2.4	10 332	2 357	11 451	528	−1 119	5.1	−9.8	568	5.2
...	49 017	Garfield	5 174	4 735	2 865	.9	3 980	2 921	3 673	755	307	19.0	8.4	136	2.9
...	49 019	Grand	3 682	8 485	2 566	2.3	6 620	2 695	8 241	1 865	−1 621	28.2	−19.7	471	5.6
...	49 021	Iron	3 298	33 779	1 288	10.2	20 789	1 641	17 349	12 990	3 440	62.5	19.8	1 383	4.1
...	49 023	Juab	3 392	8 238	2 588	2.4	5 817	2 778	5 530	2 421	287	41.6	5.2	217	2.6
2620	49 025	Kane	3 992	6 046	2 776	1.5	5 169	2 827	4 024	877	1 145	17.0	28.5	140	2.3
...	49 027	Millard	6 589	12 405	2 271	1.9	11 333	2 272	8 970	1 072	2 363	9.5	26.3	891	7.2
...	49 029	Morgan	609	7 129	2 676	11.7	5 528	2 799	4 917	1 601	611	29.0	12.4	103	1.4
...	49 031	Piute	758	1 435	3 095	1.9	1 277	3 106	1 329	158	−52	12.4	−3.9	64	4.5
...	49 033	Rich	1 029	1 961	3 067	1.9	1 725	3 081	2 100	236	−375	13.7	−17.9	36	1.8
7160	49 035	Salt Lake	737	898 387	43	1 219.0	725 956	54	619 066	172 431	106 890	23.8	17.3	106 787	11.9
...	49 037	San Juan	7 820	14 413	2 129	1.8	12 621	2 176	12 253	1 792	368	14.2	3.0	540	3.7
...	49 039	Sanpete	1 588	22 763	1 658	14.3	16 259	1 908	14 620	6 504	1 639	40.0	11.2	1 510	6.6
...	49 041	Sevier	1 910	18 842	1 850	9.9	15 431	1 960	14 727	3 411	704	22.1	4.8	481	2.6
...	49 043	Summit	1 871	29 736	1 406	15.9	15 518	1 951	10 198	14 218	5 320	91.6	52.2	2 406	8.1
...	49 045	Tooele	6 930	40 735	1 092	5.9	26 601	1 404	26 033	14 134	568	53.1	2.2	4 214	10.3
...	49 047	Uintah	4 477	25 224	1 557	5.6	22 211	1 570	20 506	3 013	1 705	13.6	8.3	894	3.5
6520	49 049	Utah	1 998	368 536	159	184.5	263 590	189	218 106	104 946	45 484	39.8	20.9	25 791	7.0
...	49 051	Wasatch	1 177	15 215	2 074	12.9	10 089	2 378	8 523	5 126	1 566	50.8	18.4	775	5.1
...	49 053	Washington	2 427	90 354	572	37.2	48 560	862	26 065	41 794	22 495	86.1	86.3	4 727	5.2
...	49 055	Wayne	2 460	2 509	3 026	1.0	2 177	3 055	1 911	332	266	15.3	13.9	50	2.0
7160	49 057	Weber	576	196 533	282	341.2	158 330	299	144 616	38 203	13 714	24.1	9.5	24 858	12.6
	50 000	VERMONT	9 250	608 827	X	65.8	562 758	X	511 456	46 069	51 302	8.2	10.0	5 504	.9
...	50 001	Addison	770	35 974	1 219	46.7	32 953	1 193	29 406	3 021	3 547	9.2	12.1	397	1.1
...	50 003	Bennington	676	36 994	1 190	54.7	35 845	1 104	33 345	1 149	2 500	3.2	7.5	344	.9
...	50 005	Caledonia	651	29 702	1 409	45.6	27 846	1 356	25 808	1 856	2 038	6.7	7.9	201	.7
1303	50 007	Chittenden	539	146 571	371	271.9	131 761	351	115 534	14 810	16 227	11.2	14.0	1 561	1.1
...	50 009	Essex	665	6 459	2 741	9.7	6 405	2 717	6 313	54	92	.8	1.5	32	.5
1303	50 011	Franklin	637	45 417	992	71.3	39 980	1 001	34 788	5 437	5 192	13.6	14.9	270	.6
1303	50 013	Grand Isle	83	6 901	2 695	83.1	5 318	2 817	4 613	1 583	705	29.8	15.3	29	.4
...	50 015	Lamoille	461	23 233	1 631	50.4	19 735	1 690	16 767	3 498	2 968	17.7	17.7	180	.8
...	50 017	Orange	689	28 226	1 443	41.0	26 149	1 414	22 739	2 077	3 410	7.9	15.0	165	.6
...	50 019	Orleans	698	26 277	1 507	37.6	24 053	1 491	23 440	2 224	613	9.2	2.6	190	.7
...	50 021	Rutland	933	63 400	764	68.0	62 142	701	58 347	1 258	3 795	2.0	6.5	442	.7
...	50 023	Washington	689	58 039	824	84.2	54 928	783	52 393	3 111	2 535	5.7	4.8	732	1.3
...	50 025	Windham	789	44 216	1 012	56.0	41 588	968	36 933	2 628	4 655	6.3	12.6	493	1.1
...	50 027	Windsor	971	57 418	831	59.1	54 055	796	51 030	3 363	3 025	6.2	5.9	468	.8

[1] Federal Information Processing Standards (FIPS) codes for metropolitan areas defined as of June 30, 1999.   [2] FIPS codes for states and counties/county equivalents.   [3] Dry land and land temporarily or partially covered by water.   [4] Based on 3,140 counties/county equivalents; excludes Yellowstone National Park in MT and South Boston independent city in VA which are no longer counties. When counties share the same rank, the next lower rank is omitted.   [5] Includes count resolution corrections through 1997 and adjustments based on Census 2000 dress rehearsal results and boundary changes reported as legally effective as of January 1, 1998.   [6] Persons of Hispanic or Latino origin may be of any race.

Sources: Land Area—U.S. Census Bureau, unpublished data file from Geography Division based on TIGER data base.   2000 Population—U.S. Census Bureau, Census of Population and Housing, Census 2000 Redistricting Data (Public Law 94-171) Summary Files (related Internet site <http://www.census.gov/dmd/www/2kresult.html>).   1990 Population—U.S. Census Bureau, "(CO-99-8) County Population Estimates and Demographic Components of Population Change: Annual Time Series, July 1, 1990 to July 1, 1999 (includes revised April 1, 1990 Population Estimates Base)"; published 9 March 2000; <http://www. census.gov/population/estimates/county/co-99-8/99C8_00.txt>.   1980 Population—U.S. Census Bureau, "1980–1990 Intercensal Population Estimates by County" on diskette (related Internet site <http://www.census.gov/population/www/estimates/countypop.html>).

Table B-1. Counties — **Area and Population**–Con.

[Includes U.S., states, and 3,142 counties/county equivalents defined as of January 1, 1992. For changes to these areas since January 1, 1992, see appendix B. Geographic Information]

Metro-politan area code[1]	State and county code[2]	County	Land area,[3] 2000 (sq. miles)	Population (April 1)											
				2000			1990[5]			Net change		Percent change		Hispanic or Latino,[6] 2000	
				Number	Rank[4]	Per square mile	Number	Rank[4]	1980	1990–2000	1980–1990	1990–2000	1980–1990	Number	Percent
	51 000	VIRGINIA	39 594	7 078 515	X	178.8	6 189 197	X	5 346 797	889 318	842 400	14.4	15.8	329 540	4.7
...	51 001	Accomack	455	38 305	1 156	84.2	31 703	1 223	31 268	6 602	435	20.8	1.4	2 062	5.4
1540	51 003	Albemarle	723	79 236	646	109.6	68 177	649	55 783	11 059	12 394	16.2	22.2	2 029	2.6
...	51 005	Alleghany	445	12 926	2 239	29.0	12 815	2 155	14 333	111	–1 518	.9	–10.6	47	.4
...	51 007	Amelia	357	11 400	2 341	31.9	8 787	2 485	8 405	2 613	382	29.7	4.5	91	.8
4640	51 009	Amherst	475	31 894	1 348	67.1	28 578	1 342	29 122	3 316	–544	11.6	–1.9	306	1.0
...	51 011	Appomattox	334	13 705	2 183	41.0	12 300	2 195	11 971	1 405	329	11.4	2.7	65	.5
8872	51 013	Arlington	26	189 453	291	7 286.7	170 895	283	152 599	18 558	18 296	10.9	12.0	35 268	18.6
...	51 015	Augusta	970	65 615	744	67.6	54 557	790	[7]47 578	11 058	[7]6 979	20.3	[7]14.7	620	.9
...	51 017	Bath	532	5 048	2 849	9.5	4 799	2 858	5 860	249	–1 061	5.2	–18.1	18	.4
4640	51 019	Bedford	755	60 371	801	80.0	45 553	908	34 927	14 818	10 626	32.5	30.4	449	.7
...	51 021	Bland	359	6 871	2 700	19.1	6 514	2 708	6 349	357	165	5.5	2.6	32	.5
6800	51 023	Botetourt	543	30 496	1 385	56.2	24 992	1 463	23 270	5 504	1 722	22.0	7.4	181	.6
...	51 025	Brunswick	566	18 419	1 872	32.5	15 987	1 924	15 632	2 432	355	15.2	2.3	231	1.3
...	51 027	Buchanan	504	26 978	1 484	53.5	31 333	1 234	37 989	–4 355	–6 656	–13.9	–17.5	128	.5
...	51 029	Buckingham	581	15 623	2 048	26.9	12 873	2 149	11 751	2 750	1 122	21.4	9.5	126	.8
4640	51 031	Campbell	504	51 078	907	101.3	47 499	883	45 424	3 579	2 075	7.5	4.6	423	.8
...	51 033	Caroline	533	22 121	1 686	41.5	19 217	1 719	17 904	2 904	1 313	15.1	7.3	295	1.3
...	51 035	Carroll	476	29 245	1 421	61.4	26 519	1 408	27 270	2 726	–751	10.3	–2.8	479	1.6
6760	51 036	Charles City	183	6 926	2 694	37.8	6 282	2 724	6 692	644	–410	10.3	–6.1	45	.6
...	51 037	Charlotte	475	12 472	2 267	26.3	11 688	2 235	12 266	784	–578	6.7	–4.7	206	1.7
6760	51 041	Chesterfield	426	259 903	214	610.1	209 599	238	141 372	50 304	68 227	24.0	48.3	7 617	2.9
8872	51 043	Clarke	177	12 652	2 252	71.5	12 101	2 208	9 965	551	2 136	4.6	21.4	185	1.5
...	51 045	Craig	331	5 091	2 844	15.4	4 372	2 887	3 948	719	424	16.4	10.7	17	.3
8872	51 047	Culpeper	381	34 262	1 273	89.9	27 791	1 359	22 620	6 471	5 171	23.3	22.9	858	2.5
...	51 049	Cumberland	298	9 017	2 527	30.3	7 825	2 593	7 881	1 192	–56	15.2	–.7	150	1.7
...	51 051	Dickenson	332	16 395	1 998	49.4	17 620	1 810	19 806	–1 225	–2 186	–7.0	–11.0	70	.4
6760	51 053	Dinwiddie	504	24 533	1 574	48.7	22 279	1 564	22 602	2 254	–323	10.1	–1.4	237	1.0
...	51 057	Essex	258	9 989	2 447	38.7	8 689	2 493	8 864	1 300	–175	15.0	–2.0	72	.7
8872	51 059	Fairfax	395	969 749	36	2 455.1	818 310	45	[7]595 754	151 439	[7]222 556	18.5	[7]37.4	106 958	11.0
8872	51 061	Fauquier	650	55 139	855	84.8	48 700	860	35 889	6 439	12 811	13.2	35.7	1 114	2.0
...	51 063	Floyd	381	13 874	2 169	36.4	11 965	2 221	11 563	1 909	402	16.0	3.5	187	1.3
1540	51 065	Fluvanna	287	20 047	1 791	69.9	12 429	2 187	10 244	7 618	2 185	61.3	21.3	235	1.2
...	51 067	Franklin	692	47 286	962	68.3	39 549	1 011	35 740	7 737	3 809	19.6	10.7	573	1.2
...	51 069	Frederick	415	59 209	811	142.7	45 723	907	34 150	13 486	11 573	29.5	33.9	1 004	1.7
...	51 071	Giles	357	16 657	1 980	46.7	16 366	1 900	17 810	291	–1 444	1.8	–8.1	105	.6
5720	51 073	Gloucester	217	34 780	1 259	160.3	30 131	1 292	20 107	4 649	10 024	15.4	49.9	560	1.6
6760	51 075	Goochland	284	16 863	1 963	59.4	14 163	2 040	11 761	2 700	2 402	19.1	20.4	144	.9
...	51 077	Grayson	443	17 917	1 906	40.4	16 278	1 905	16 579	1 639	–301	10.1	–1.8	277	1.5
1540	51 079	Greene	157	15 244	2 073	97.1	10 297	2 359	7 625	4 947	2 672	48.0	35.0	201	1.3
...	51 081	Greensville	295	11 560	2 328	39.2	8 553	2 508	[7]9 669	3 007	[7]–1 116	35.2	[7]–11.5	108	.9
...	51 083	Halifax	819	37 355	1 181	45.6	36 030	1 099	[8]30 599	1 325	X	3.7	X	458	1.2
6760	51 085	Hanover	473	86 320	602	182.5	63 306	690	50 398	23 014	12 908	36.4	25.6	847	1.0
6760	51 087	Henrico	238	262 300	210	1 102.1	217 878	227	180 735	44 422	37 143	20.4	20.6	5 946	2.3
...	51 089	Henry	382	57 930	825	151.6	56 942	766	57 654	988	–712	1.7	–1.2	2 002	3.5
...	51 091	Highland	416	2 536	3 023	6.1	2 635	3 015	2 937	–99	–302	–3.8	–10.3	13	.5
5720	51 093	Isle of Wight	316	29 728	1 407	94.1	25 053	1 460	21 603	4 675	3 450	18.7	16.0	254	.9
5720	51 095	James City	143	48 102	948	336.4	34 779	1 141	[7]22 339	13 323	[7]12 440	38.3	[7]55.7	816	1.7
...	51 097	King and Queen	316	6 630	2 724	21.0	6 289	2 722	5 968	341	321	5.4	5.4	58	.9
8872	51 099	King George	180	16 803	1 968	93.4	13 527	2 099	10 543	3 276	2 984	24.2	28.3	301	1.8
...	51 101	King William	275	13 146	2 216	47.8	10 913	2 305	9 334	2 233	1 579	20.5	16.9	120	.9
...	51 103	Lancaster	133	11 567	2 326	87.0	10 896	2 306	10 129	671	767	6.2	7.6	71	.6
...	51 105	Lee	437	23 589	1 607	54.0	24 496	1 479	25 956	–907	–1 460	–3.7	–5.6	120	.5
8872	51 107	Loudoun	520	169 599	320	326.2	86 185	529	57 427	83 414	28 758	96.8	50.1	10 089	5.9
...	51 109	Louisa	497	25 627	1 529	51.6	20 325	1 659	17 825	5 302	2 500	26.1	14.0	182	.7
...	51 111	Lunenburg	432	13 146	2 216	30.4	11 419	2 260	12 124	1 727	–705	15.1	–5.8	235	1.8
...	51 113	Madison	321	12 520	2 263	39.0	11 949	2 224	10 232	571	1 717	4.8	16.8	96	.8
5720	51 115	Mathews	86	9 207	2 512	107.1	8 348	2 529	7 995	859	353	10.3	4.4	73	.8
...	51 117	Mecklenburg	624	32 380	1 337	51.9	29 241	1 322	29 444	3 139	–203	10.7	–.7	393	1.2
...	51 119	Middlesex	130	9 932	2 453	76.4	8 653	2 495	7 719	1 279	934	14.8	12.1	55	.6
...	51 121	Montgomery	388	83 629	621	215.5	73 913	609	[7]63 285	9 716	[7]10 628	13.1	[7]16.8	1 321	1.6
...	51 125	Nelson	472	14 445	2 126	30.6	12 778	2 158	12 204	1 667	574	13.0	4.7	305	2.1
6760	51 127	New Kent	210	13 462	2 196	64.1	10 466	2 340	8 781	2 996	1 685	28.6	19.2	176	1.3
...	51 131	Northampton	207	13 093	2 222	63.3	13 061	2 135	14 625	32	–1 564	.2	–10.7	454	3.5
...	51 133	Northumberland	192	12 259	2 281	63.8	10 524	2 334	9 828	1 735	696	16.5	7.1	114	.9
...	51 135	Nottoway	315	15 725	2 037	49.9	14 993	1 987	14 666	732	327	4.9	2.2	248	1.6
...	51 137	Orange	342	25 881	1 522	75.7	21 421	1 609	18 063	4 460	3 358	20.8	18.6	330	1.3
...	51 139	Page	311	23 177	1 635	74.5	21 690	1 593	19 401	1 487	2 289	6.9	11.8	251	1.1
...	51 141	Patrick	483	19 407	1 823	40.2	17 473	1 822	17 647	1 934	–174	11.1	–1.0	363	1.9
1950	51 143	Pittsylvania	971	61 745	787	63.6	55 672	778	[7]55 140	6 073	[7]532	10.9	[7]1.0	759	1.2
6760	51 145	Powhatan	261	22 377	1 675	85.7	15 328	1 969	13 062	7 049	2 266	46.0	17.3	184	.8

[1] Federal Information Processing Standards (FIPS) codes for metropolitan areas defined as of June 30, 1999. [2] FIPS codes for states and counties/county equivalents. [3] Dry land and land temporarily or partially covered by water. [4] Based on 3,140 counties/county equivalents; excludes Yellowstone National Park in MT and South Boston independent city in VA which are no longer counties. When counties share the same rank, the next lower rank is omitted. [5] Includes count resolution corrections through 1997 and adjustments based on Census 2000 dress rehearsal results and boundary changes reported as legally effective as of January 1, 1998. [6] Persons of Hispanic or Latino origin may be of any race. [7] 1980 population based on 1990 county boundaries. [8] Excludes South Boston independent city which is included with Halifax County in the 1990 and 2000 population data; for more information, see appendix B. Geographic Information.

Sources: Land Area—U.S. Census Bureau, unpublished data file from Geography Division based on TIGER data base. 2000 Population—U.S. Census Bureau, Census of Population and Housing, Census 2000 Redistricting Data (Public Law 94-171) Summary Files (related Internet site <http://www.census.gov/dmd/www/2kresult.html>). 1990 Population—U.S. Census Bureau, "(CO-99-8) County Population Estimates and Demographic Components of Population Change: Annual Time Series, July 1, 1990 to July 1, 1999 (includes revised April 1, 1990 Population Estimates Base)"; published 9 March 2000; <http://www. census.gov/population/estimates/county/co-99-8/99C8_00.txt>. 1980 Population—U.S. Census Bureau, "1980–1990 Intercensal Population Estimates by County" on diskette (related Internet site <http://www.census.gov/population/www/estimates/countypop.html>).

Table B-1. Counties — **Area and Population**–Con.

[Includes U.S., states, and 3,142 counties/county equivalents defined as of January 1, 1992. For changes to these areas since January 1, 1992, see appendix B. Geographic Information]

Metro-politan area code[1]	State and county code[2]	County	Land area,[3] 2000 (sq. miles)	2000 Number	2000 Rank[4]	2000 Per square mile	1990[5] Number	1990[5] Rank[4]	1980	Net change 1990–2000	Net change 1980–1990	Percent change 1990–2000	Percent change 1980–1990	Hispanic or Latino,[6] 2000 Number	Hispanic or Latino,[6] 2000 Percent
		VIRGINIA—Con.													
...	51 147	Prince Edward	353	19 720	1 808	55.9	17 320	1 831	16 456	2 400	864	13.9	5.3	186	.9
6760	51 149	Prince George	266	33 047	1 318	124.2	27 390	1 379	25 733	5 657	1 657	20.7	6.4	1 625	4.9
8872	51 153	Prince William	338	280 813	200	830.8	214 954	232	[7]144 636	65 859	[7]70 318	30.6	[7]48.6	27 338	9.7
...	51 155	Pulaski	321	35 127	1 245	109.4	34 496	1 151	35 229	631	−733	1.8	−2.1	336	1.0
...	51 157	Rappahannock	267	6 983	2 687	26.2	6 622	2 694	6 093	361	529	5.5	8.7	91	1.3
...	51 159	Richmond	191	8 809	2 545	46.1	7 273	2 629	6 952	1 536	321	21.1	4.6	185	2.1
6800	51 161	Roanoke	251	85 778	610	341.7	79 278	574	72 945	6 500	6 333	8.2	8.7	888	1.0
...	51 163	Rockbridge	600	20 808	1 748	34.7	18 350	1 773	[7]17 724	2 458	[7]626	13.4	[7]3.5	120	.6
...	51 165	Rockingham	851	67 725	724	79.6	57 482	760	[7]52 054	10 243	[7]5 428	17.8	[7]10.4	2 221	3.3
...	51 167	Russell	475	30 308	1 390	63.8	28 667	1 340	31 761	1 641	−3 094	5.7	−9.7	237	.8
3660	51 169	Scott	537	23 403	1 623	43.6	23 204	1 530	25 068	199	−1 864	.9	−7.4	99	.4
...	51 171	Shenandoah	512	35 075	1 248	68.5	31 636	1 227	27 559	3 439	4 077	10.9	14.8	1 194	3.4
...	51 173	Smyth	452	33 081	1 316	73.2	32 370	1 203	33 345	711	−975	2.2	−2.9	283	.9
...	51 175	Southampton	600	17 482	1 925	29.1	17 022	1 849	[7]18 316	460	[7]−1 294	2.7	[7]−7.1	115	.7
8872	51 177	Spotsylvania	401	90 395	570	225.4	57 397	761	[7]31 995	32 998	[7]25 402	57.5	[7]79.4	2 536	2.8
8872	51 179	Stafford	270	92 446	552	342.4	62 255	699	40 470	30 191	21 785	48.5	53.8	3 342	3.6
...	51 181	Surry	279	6 829	2 708	24.5	6 145	2 738	6 046	684	99	11.1	1.6	51	.7
...	51 183	Sussex	491	12 504	2 264	25.5	10 248	2 364	10 874	2 256	−626	22.0	−5.8	102	.8
...	51 185	Tazewell	520	44 598	1 006	85.8	45 960	903	50 511	−1 362	−4 551	−3.0	−9.0	228	.5
8872	51 187	Warren	214	31 584	1 358	147.6	26 142	1 416	21 200	5 442	4 942	20.8	23.3	494	1.6
3660	51 191	Washington	563	51 103	906	90.8	45 887	905	46 487	5 216	−600	11.4	−1.3	322	.6
...	51 193	Westmoreland	229	16 718	1 974	73.0	15 480	1 956	14 041	1 238	1 439	8.0	10.2	579	3.5
...	51 195	Wise	404	40 123	1 111	99.3	39 573	1 009	43 863	550	−4 290	1.4	−9.8	292	.7
...	51 197	Wythe	463	27 599	1 463	59.6	25 471	1 449	25 522	2 128	−51	8.4	−.2	157	.6
5720	51 199	York	106	56 297	840	531.1	42 434	949	35 463	13 863	6 971	32.7	19.7	1 509	2.7
		Independent Cities													
8872	51 510	Alexandria	15	128 283	421	8 552.2	111 183	413	103 217	17 100	7 966	15.4	7.7	18 882	14.7
4640	51 515	Bedford	7	6 299	2 757	899.9	6 176	2 735	5 991	123	185	2.0	3.1	56	.9
3660	51 520	Bristol	13	17 367	1 932	1 335.9	18 426	1 767	19 042	−1 059	−616	−5.7	−3.2	169	1.0
...	51 530	Buena Vista	7	6 349	2 751	907.0	6 406	2 716	[7]6 904	−57	[7]−498	−.9	[7]−7.2	64	1.0
1540	51 540	Charlottesville	10	45 049	997	4 504.9	40 470	987	39 916	4 579	554	11.3	1.4	1 102	2.4
5720	51 550	Chesapeake	341	199 184	278	584.1	151 982	307	114 486	47 202	37 496	31.1	32.8	4 076	2.0
...	51 560	Clifton Forge	3	4 289	2 897	1 429.7	4 679	2 862	5 046	−390	−367	−8.3	−7.3	38	.9
6760	51 570	Colonial Heights	7	16 897	1 960	2 413.9	16 064	1 920	16 509	833	−445	5.2	−2.7	274	1.6
...	51 580	Covington	6	6 303	2 756	1 050.5	7 352	2 625	9 063	−1 049	−1 711	−14.3	−18.9	40	.6
1950	51 590	Danville	43	48 411	942	1 125.8	53 056	803	[7]56 649	−4 645	[7]−3 593	−8.8	[7]−6.3	612	1.3
...	51 595	Emporia	7	5 665	2 810	809.3	5 556	2 795	[7]6 074	109	[7]−518	2.0	[7]−8.5	84	1.5
8872	51 600	Fairfax	6	21 498	1 715	3 583.0	19 945	1 682	[7]20 537	1 553	[7]−592	7.8	[7]−2.9	2 932	13.6
8872	51 610	Falls Church	2	10 377	2 406	5 188.5	9 464	2 438	9 515	913	−51	9.6	−.5	876	8.4
...	51 620	Franklin	8	8 346	2 577	1 043.3	8 392	2 521	[7]7 723	−46	[7]669	−.5	[7]8.7	46	.6
8872	51 630	Fredericksburg	11	19 279	1 829	1 752.6	19 033	1 733	[7]17 762	246	[7]1 271	1.3	[7]7.2	945	4.9
...	51 640	Galax	8	6 837	2 706	854.6	6 745	2 682	6 524	92	221	1.4	3.4	757	11.1
5720	51 650	Hampton	52	146 437	374	2 816.1	133 773	347	122 617	12 664	11 156	9.5	9.1	4 153	2.8
...	51 660	Harrisonburg	18	40 468	1 104	2 248.2	30 707	1 258	[7]24 655	9 761	[7]6 052	31.8	[7]24.5	3 580	8.8
6760	51 670	Hopewell	10	22 354	1 676	2 235.4	23 101	1 533	23 397	−747	−296	−3.2	−1.3	651	2.9
...	51 678	Lexington	2	6 867	2 701	3 433.5	6 959	2 664	7 292	−92	−333	−1.3	−4.6	109	1.6
4640	51 680	Lynchburg	49	65 269	747	1 332.0	66 120	661	66 743	−851	−623	−1.3	−.9	878	1.3
8872	51 683	Manassas	10	35 135	1 244	3 513.5	27 757	1 361	[7]15 505	7 378	[7]12 252	26.6	[7]79.0	5 316	15.1
8872	51 685	Manassas Park	2	10 290	2 417	5 145.0	6 798	2 676	6 524	3 492	274	51.4	4.2	1 544	15.0
...	51 690	Martinsville	11	15 416	2 058	1 401.5	16 162	1 914	18 149	−746	−1 987	−4.6	−10.9	358	2.3
5720	51 700	Newport News	68	180 150	306	2 649.3	171 477	281	144 903	8 673	26 574	5.1	18.3	7 595	4.2
5720	51 710	Norfolk	54	234 403	247	4 340.8	261 250	192	266 979	−26 847	−5 729	−10.3	−2.1	8 915	3.8
...	51 720	Norton	8	3 904	2 923	488.0	4 247	2 895	4 757	−343	−510	−8.1	−10.7	34	.9
6760	51 730	Petersburg	23	33 740	1 289	1 467.0	37 071	1 071	41 055	−3 331	−3 984	−9.0	−9.7	463	1.4
5720	51 735	Poquoson	16	11 566	2 327	722.9	11 005	2 292	8 726	561	2 279	5.1	26.1	122	1.1
5720	51 740	Portsmouth	33	100 565	522	3 047.4	103 910	443	104 577	−3 345	−667	−3.2	−.6	1 748	1.7
...	51 750	Radford	10	15 859	2 028	1 585.9	15 940	1 927	[7]13 456	−81	[7]2 484	−.5	[7]18.5	184	1.2
6760	51 760	Richmond	60	197 790	280	3 296.5	202 713	244	219 214	−4 923	−16 501	−2.4	−7.5	5 074	2.6
6800	51 770	Roanoke	43	94 911	542	2 207.2	96 487	478	100 220	−1 576	−3 733	−1.6	−3.7	1 405	1.5
6800	51 775	Salem	15	24 747	1 566	1 649.8	23 835	1 499	23 958	912	−123	3.8	−.5	205	.8
...	51 780	South Boston	X	X	X	X	X	X	7 093	X	X	X	X	X	X
...	51 790	Staunton	20	23 853	1 597	1 192.7	24 581	1 477	[7]24 777	−728	[7]−196	−3.0	[7]−.8	265	1.1
5720	51 800	Suffolk	400	63 677	763	159.2	52 143	812	47 621	11 534	4 522	22.1	9.5	809	1.3
5720	51 810	Virginia Beach	248	425 257	141	1 714.7	393 089	128	262 199	32 168	130 890	8.2	49.9	17 770	4.2
...	51 820	Waynesboro	15	19 520	1 819	1 301.3	18 549	1 760	[7]18 563	971	[7]−14	5.2	[7]−.1	643	3.3
5720	51 830	Williamsburg	9	11 998	2 294	1 333.1	11 600	2 248	[7]10 294	398	[7]1 306	3.4	[7]12.7	302	2.5
...	51 840	Winchester	9	23 585	1 609	2 620.6	21 947	1 579	20 217	1 638	1 730	7.5	8.6	1 527	6.5

[1] Federal Information Processing Standards (FIPS) codes for metropolitan areas defined as of June 30, 1999. [2] FIPS codes for states and counties/county equivalents. [3] Dry land and land temporarily or partially covered by water. [4] Based on 3,140 counties/county equivalents; excludes Yellowstone National Park in MT and South Boston independent city in VA which are no longer counties. When counties share the same rank, the next lower rank is omitted. [5] Includes count resolution corrections through 1997 and adjustments based on Census 2000 dress rehearsal results and boundary changes reported as legally effective as of January 1, 1998. [6] Persons of Hispanic or Latino origin may be of any race. [7] 1980 population based on 1990 county boundaries.

Sources: Land Area—U.S. Census Bureau, unpublished data file from Geography Division based on TIGER data base.   2000 Population—U.S. Census Bureau, Census of Population and Housing, Census 2000 Redistricting Data (Public Law 94-171) Summary Files (related Internet site <http://www.census.gov/dmd/www/2kresult.html>).   1990 Population—U.S. Census Bureau, "(CO-99-8) County Population Estimates and Demographic Components of Population Change: Annual Time Series, July 1, 1990 to July 1, 1999 (includes revised April 1, 1990 Population Estimates Base)"; published 9 March 2000; <http://www. census.gov/population/estimates/county/co-99-8/99C8_00.txt>.   1980 Population—U.S. Census Bureau, "1980–1990 Intercensal Population Estimates by County" on diskette (related Internet site <http://www.census.gov/population/www/estimates/countypop.html>).

Table B–1. Counties — **Area and Population**–Con.

[Includes U.S., states, and 3,142 counties/county equivalents defined as of January 1, 1992. For changes to these areas since January 1, 1992, see appendix B. Geographic Information]

Metro-politan area code[1]	State and county code[2]	County	Land area,[3] 2000 (sq. miles)	Population (April 1) 2000 Number	2000 Rank[4]	2000 Per square mile	1990[5] Number	1990[5] Rank[4]	1980	Net change 1990–2000	Net change 1980–1990	Percent change 1990–2000	Percent change 1980–1990	Hispanic or Latino,[6] 2000 Number	Hispanic or Latino,[6] 2000 Percent
	53 000	WASHINGTON	66 544	5 894 121	X	88.6	4 866 669	X	4 132 353	1 027 452	734 316	21.1	17.8	441 509	7.5
...	53 001	Adams.................	1 925	16 428	1 995	8.5	13 603	2 092	13 267	2 825	336	20.8	2.5	7 732	47.1
...	53 003	Asotin	635	20 551	1 758	32.4	17 605	1 814	16 823	2 946	782	16.7	4.6	401	2.0
6740	53 005	Benton................	1 703	142 475	383	83.7	112 560	408	109 444	29 915	3 116	26.6	2.8	17 806	12.5
...	53 007	Chelan................	2 921	66 616	734	22.8	52 250	810	45 061	14 366	7 189	27.5	16.0	12 831	19.3
...	53 009	Clallam...............	1 739	64 525	753	37.1	56 210	772	51 648	8 315	4 562	14.8	8.8	2 203	3.4
6442	53 011	Clark	628	345 238	169	549.7	238 053	210	192 227	107 185	45 826	45.0	23.8	16 248	4.7
...	53 013	Columbia	869	4 064	2 916	4.7	4 024	2 915	4 057	40	–33	1.0	–.8	258	6.3
...	53 015	Cowlitz	1 139	92 948	550	81.6	82 119	552	79 548	10 829	2 571	13.2	3.2	4 231	4.6
...	53 017	Douglas..............	1 821	32 603	1 328	17.9	26 205	1 412	22 144	6 398	4 061	24.4	18.3	6 433	19.7
...	53 019	Ferry	2 204	7 260	2 658	3.3	6 295	2 721	5 811	965	484	15.3	8.3	205	2.8
6740	53 021	Franklin..............	1 242	49 347	926	39.7	37 473	1 059	35 025	11 874	2 448	31.7	7.0	23 032	46.7
...	53 023	Garfield..............	711	2 397	3 030	3.4	2 248	3 049	2 468	149	–220	6.6	–8.9	47	2.0
...	53 025	Grant	2 681	74 698	669	27.9	54 798	785	48 522	19 900	6 276	36.3	12.9	22 476	30.1
...	53 027	Grays Harbor	1 917	67 194	729	35.1	64 175	685	66 314	3 019	–2 139	4.7	–3.2	3 258	4.8
7602	53 029	Island...............	208	71 558	690	344.0	60 195	720	44 048	11 363	16 147	18.9	36.7	2 843	4.0
...	53 031	Jefferson	1 814	25 953	1 518	14.3	20 406	1 655	15 965	5 547	4 441	27.2	27.8	535	2.1
7602	53 033	King	2 126	1 737 034	13	817.0	1 507 305	13	1 269 898	229 729	237 407	15.2	18.7	95 242	5.5
7602	53 035	Kitsap	396	231 969	249	585.8	189 731	252	147 152	42 238	42 579	22.3	28.9	9 609	4.1
...	53 037	Kittitas	2 297	33 362	1 302	14.5	26 725	1 400	24 877	6 637	1 848	24.8	7.4	1 668	5.0
...	53 039	Klickitat	1 872	19 161	1 838	10.2	16 616	1 876	15 822	2 545	794	15.3	5.0	1 496	7.8
...	53 041	Lewis	2 408	68 600	720	28.5	59 358	730	56 025	9 242	3 333	15.6	5.9	3 684	5.4
...	53 043	Lincoln...............	2 311	10 184	2 430	4.4	8 864	2 481	9 604	1 320	–740	14.9	–7.7	191	1.9
...	53 045	Mason	961	49 405	925	51.4	38 341	1 044	31 184	11 064	7 157	28.9	23.0	2 361	4.8
...	53 047	Okanogan	5 268	39 564	1 125	7.5	33 350	1 181	30 663	6 214	2 687	18.6	8.8	5 688	14.4
...	53 049	Pacific	933	20 984	1 736	22.5	18 882	1 741	17 237	2 102	1 645	11.1	9.5	1 052	5.0
...	53 051	Pend Oreille	1 400	11 732	2 314	8.4	8 915	2 478	8 580	2 817	335	31.6	3.9	241	2.1
7602	53 053	Pierce	1 679	700 820	71	417.4	586 203	80	485 667	114 617	100 536	19.6	20.7	38 621	5.5
...	53 055	San Juan	175	14 077	2 156	80.4	10 035	2 382	7 838	4 042	2 197	40.3	28.0	338	2.4
...	53 057	Skagit	1 735	102 979	516	59.4	79 545	573	64 138	23 434	15 407	29.5	24.0	11 536	11.2
...	53 059	Skamania	1 656	9 872	2 458	6.0	8 289	2 537	7 919	1 583	370	19.1	4.7	398	4.0
7602	53 061	Snohomish	2 089	606 024	90	290.1	465 628	107	337 720	140 396	127 908	30.2	37.9	28 590	4.7
7840	53 063	Spokane	1 764	417 939	144	236.9	361 333	142	341 835	56 606	19 498	15.7	5.7	11 561	2.8
...	53 065	Stevens	2 478	40 066	1 112	16.2	30 948	1 248	28 979	9 118	1 969	29.5	6.8	739	1.8
7602	53 067	Thurston	727	207 355	268	285.2	161 238	295	124 264	46 117	36 974	28.6	29.8	9 392	4.5
...	53 069	Wahkiakum	264	3 824	2 928	14.5	3 327	2 968	3 832	497	–505	14.9	–13.2	98	2.6
...	53 071	Walla Walla	1 271	55 180	854	43.4	48 439	864	47 435	6 741	1 004	13.9	2.1	8 654	15.7
0860	53 073	Whatcom	2 120	166 814	324	78.7	127 780	364	106 701	39 034	21 079	30.5	19.8	8 687	5.2
...	53 075	Whitman	2 159	40 740	1 091	18.9	38 775	1 031	40 103	1 965	–1 328	5.1	–3.3	1 219	3.0
9260	53 077	Yakima	4 296	222 581	255	51.8	188 823	255	172 508	33 758	16 315	17.9	9.5	79 905	35.9
	54 000	WEST VIRGINIA	24 078	1 808 344	X	75.1	1 793 477	X	1 950 186	14 867	–156 709	.8	–8.0	12 279	.7
...	54 001	Barbour..............	341	15 557	2 050	45.6	15 699	1 944	16 639	–142	–940	–.9	–5.6	73	.5
8872	54 003	Berkeley	321	75 905	660	236.5	59 253	733	46 775	16 652	12 478	28.1	26.7	1 156	1.5
...	54 005	Boone	503	25 535	1 538	50.8	25 870	1 427	30 447	–335	–4 577	–1.3	–15.0	117	.5
...	54 007	Braxton..............	513	14 702	2 107	28.7	12 998	2 142	13 894	1 704	–896	13.1	–6.4	65	.4
8080	54 009	Brooke...............	89	25 447	1 543	285.9	26 992	1 391	31 117	–1 545	–4 125	–5.7	–13.3	99	.4
3400	54 011	Cabell	282	96 784	534	343.2	96 827	475	106 835	–43	–10 008	Z	–9.4	654	.7
...	54 013	Calhoun	281	7 582	2 637	27.0	7 885	2 582	8 250	–303	–365	–3.8	–4.4	42	.6
...	54 015	Clay	342	10 330	2 412	30.2	9 983	2 388	11 265	347	–1 282	3.5	–11.4	42	.4
...	54 017	Doddridge............	320	7 403	2 648	23.1	6 994	2 659	7 433	409	–439	5.8	–5.9	42	.6
...	54 019	Fayette..............	664	47 579	958	71.7	47 952	872	57 863	–373	–9 911	–.8	–17.1	325	.7
...	54 021	Gilmer...............	340	7 160	2 671	21.1	7 669	2 604	8 334	–509	–665	–6.6	–8.0	50	.7
...	54 023	Grant	477	11 299	2 350	23.7	10 428	2 347	10 210	871	218	8.4	2.1	62	.5
...	54 025	Greenbrier	1 021	34 453	1 265	33.7	34 693	1 145	37 665	–240	–2 972	–.7	–7.9	236	.7
...	54 027	Hampshire	642	20 203	1 780	31.5	16 498	1 893	14 867	3 705	1 631	22.5	11.0	112	.6
8080	54 029	Hancock	83	32 667	1 325	393.6	35 233	1 125	41 053	–2 566	–5 820	–7.3	–14.2	243	.7
...	54 031	Hardy................	583	12 669	2 250	21.7	10 977	2 297	10 030	1 692	947	15.4	9.4	84	.7
...	54 033	Harrison..............	416	68 652	719	165.0	69 371	638	77 710	–719	–8 339	–1.0	–10.7	660	1.0
...	54 035	Jackson..............	466	28 000	1 451	60.1	25 938	1 424	25 794	2 062	144	7.9	.6	81	.3
8872	54 037	Jefferson	210	42 190	1 054	200.9	35 926	1 102	30 302	6 264	5 624	17.4	18.6	734	1.7
1480	54 039	Kanawha.............	903	200 073	276	221.6	207 619	241	231 414	–7 546	–23 795	–3.6	–10.3	1 172	.6
...	54 041	Lewis	382	16 919	1 957	44.3	17 223	1 840	18 813	–304	–1 590	–1.8	–8.5	85	.5
...	54 043	Lincoln...............	437	22 108	1 687	50.6	21 382	1 612	23 675	726	–2 293	3.4	–9.7	121	.5
...	54 045	Logan................	454	37 710	1 169	83.1	43 032	938	50 679	–5 322	–7 647	–12.4	–15.1	202	.5
...	54 047	McDowell	535	27 329	1 473	51.1	35 233	1 125	49 899	–7 904	–14 666	–22.4	–29.4	132	.5

[1] Federal Information Processing Standards (FIPS) codes for metropolitan areas defined as of June 30, 1999.   [2] FIPS codes for states and counties/county equivalents.   [3] Dry land and land temporarily or partially covered by water.   [4] Based on 3,140 counties/county equivalents; excludes Yellowstone National Park in MT and South Boston independent city in VA which are no longer counties. When counties share the same rank, the next lower rank is omitted.   [5] Includes count resolution corrections through 1997 and adjustments based on Census 2000 dress rehearsal results and boundary changes reported as legally effective as of January 1, 1998.   [6] Persons of Hispanic or Latino origin may be of any race.

Sources: Land Area—U.S. Census Bureau, unpublished data file from Geography Division based on TIGER data base.   2000 Population—U.S. Census Bureau, Census of Population and Housing, Census 2000 Redistricting Data (Public Law 94-171) Summary Files (related Internet site <http://www.census.gov/dmd/www/2kresult.html>).   1990 Population—U.S. Census Bureau, "(CO-99-8) County Population Estimates and Demographic Components of Population Change: Annual Time Series, July 1, 1990 to July 1, 1999 (includes revised April 1, 1990 Population Estimates Base)"; published 9 March 2000; <http://www. census.gov/population/estimates/county/co-99-8/99C8_00.txt>.   1980 Population—U.S. Census Bureau, "1980–1990 Intercensal Population Estimates by County" on diskette (related Internet site <http://www.census.gov/population/www/estimates/countypop.html>).

Table B–1. Counties — **Area and Population**–Con.

[Includes U.S., states, and 3,142 counties/county equivalents defined as of January 1, 1992. For changes to these areas since January 1, 1992, see appendix B. Geographic Information]

Metro-politan area code[1]	State and county code[2]	County	Land area,[3] 2000 (sq. miles)	2000 Number	2000 Rank[4]	2000 Per square mile	1990[5] Number	1990[5] Rank[4]	1980	Net change 1990–2000	Net change 1980–1990	Percent change 1990–2000	Percent change 1980–1990	Hispanic or Latino,[6] 2000 Number	Hispanic or Latino,[6] 2000 Percent
		WEST VIRGINIA—Con.													
...	54 049	Marion	310	56 598	1 837	182.6	57 249	763	65 789	−651	−8 540	−1.1	−13.0	394	.7
9000	54 051	Marshall	307	35 519	1 231	115.7	37 356	1 062	41 608	−1 837	−4 252	−4.9	−10.2	228	.6
...	54 053	Mason	432	25 957	1 517	60.1	25 178	1 456	27 045	779	−1 867	3.1	−6.9	121	.5
...	54 055	Mercer	420	62 980	770	150.0	64 980	674	73 870	−2 000	−8 890	−3.1	−12.0	285	.5
1900	54 057	Mineral	328	27 078	1 479	82.6	26 697	1 401	27 234	381	−537	1.4	−2.0	158	.6
...	54 059	Mingo	423	28 253	1 440	66.8	33 739	1 173	37 336	−5 486	−3 597	−16.3	−9.6	135	.5
...	54 061	Monongalia	361	81 866	634	226.8	75 509	597	75 024	6 357	485	8.4	.6	826	1.0
...	54 063	Monroe	473	14 583	2 113	30.8	12 406	2 189	12 873	2 177	−467	17.5	−3.6	72	.5
...	54 065	Morgan	229	14 943	2 096	65.3	12 128	2 205	10 711	2 815	1 417	23.2	13.2	124	.8
...	54 067	Nicholas	649	26 562	1 497	40.9	26 775	1 398	28 126	−213	−1 351	−.8	−4.8	127	.5
9000	54 069	Ohio	106	47 427	959	447.4	50 871	830	61 389	−3 444	−10 518	−6.8	−17.1	238	.5
...	54 071	Pendleton	698	8 196	2 593	11.7	8 054	2 559	7 910	142	144	1.8	1.8	73	.9
...	54 073	Pleasants	131	7 514	2 641	57.4	7 546	2 613	8 236	−32	−690	−.4	−8.4	28	.4
...	54 075	Pocahontas	940	9 131	2 520	9.7	9 008	2 470	9 919	123	−911	1.4	−9.2	39	.4
...	54 077	Preston	648	29 334	1 418	45.3	29 037	1 327	30 460	297	−1 423	1.0	−4.7	168	.6
1480	54 079	Putnam	346	51 589	899	149.1	42 835	941	38 181	8 754	4 654	20.4	12.2	262	.5
...	54 081	Raleigh	607	79 220	647	130.5	76 819	587	86 821	2 401	−10 002	3.1	−11.5	727	.9
...	54 083	Randolph	1 040	28 262	1 439	27.2	27 803	1 358	28 734	459	−931	1.7	−3.2	191	.7
...	54 085	Ritchie	454	10 343	2 410	22.8	10 233	2 365	11 442	110	−1 209	1.1	−10.6	49	.5
...	54 087	Roane	484	15 446	2 056	31.9	15 120	1 982	15 952	326	−832	2.2	−5.2	104	.7
...	54 089	Summers	361	12 999	2 234	36.0	14 204	2 036	15 875	−1 205	−1 671	−8.5	−10.5	71	.5
...	54 091	Taylor	173	16 089	2 017	93.0	15 144	1 977	16 584	945	−1 440	6.2	−8.7	95	.6
...	54 093	Tucker	419	7 321	2 654	17.5	7 728	2 602	8 675	−407	−947	−5.3	−10.9	18	.2
...	54 095	Tyler	258	9 592	2 479	37.2	9 796	2 406	11 320	−204	−1 524	−2.1	−13.5	41	.4
...	54 097	Upshur	355	23 404	1 622	65.9	22 867	1 538	23 427	537	−560	2.3	−2.4	137	.6
3400	54 099	Wayne	506	42 903	1 039	84.8	41 636	966	46 021	1 267	−4 385	3.0	−9.5	202	.5
...	54 101	Webster	556	9 719	2 469	17.5	10 729	2 315	12 245	−1 010	−1 516	−9.4	−12.4	36	.4
...	54 103	Wetzel	359	17 693	1 917	49.3	19 258	1 714	21 874	−1 565	−2 616	−8.1	−12.0	74	.4
...	54 105	Wirt	233	5 873	2 796	25.2	5 192	2 825	4 922	681	270	13.1	5.5	18	.3
6020	54 107	Wood	367	87 986	592	239.7	86 915	526	93 627	1 071	−6 712	1.2	−7.2	514	.6
...	54 109	Wyoming	501	25 708	1 527	51.3	28 990	1 330	35 993	−3 282	−7 003	−11.3	−19.5	135	.5
	55 000	**WISCONSIN**	54 310	5 363 675	X	98.8	4 891 954	X	4 705 642	471 721	186 312	9.6	4.0	192 921	3.6
...	55 001	Adams	648	18 643	1 864	28.8	15 682	1 945	13 457	2 961	2 225	18.9	16.5	268	1.4
...	55 003	Ashland	1 044	16 866	1 962	16.2	16 307	1 903	16 783	559	−476	3.4	−2.8	188	1.1
...	55 005	Barron	863	44 963	999	52.1	40 750	983	38 730	4 213	2 020	10.3	5.2	430	1.0
...	55 007	Bayfield	1 476	15 013	2 089	10.2	14 008	2 054	13 822	1 005	186	7.2	1.3	91	.6
3080	55 009	Brown	529	226 778	251	428.7	194 594	248	175 280	32 184	19 314	16.5	11.0	8 698	3.8
...	55 011	Buffalo	684	13 804	2 172	20.2	13 584	2 093	14 309	220	−725	1.6	−5.1	85	.6
...	55 013	Burnett	822	15 674	2 040	19.1	13 084	2 132	12 340	2 590	744	19.8	6.0	120	.8
0460	55 015	Calumet	320	40 631	1 097	127.0	34 291	1 159	30 867	6 340	3 424	18.5	11.1	435	1.1
2290	55 017	Chippewa	1 010	55 195	853	54.6	52 360	808	52 127	2 835	233	5.4	.4	289	.5
...	55 019	Clark	1 216	33 557	1 299	27.6	31 647	1 226	32 910	1 910	−1 263	6.0	−3.8	404	1.2
...	55 021	Columbia	774	52 468	890	67.8	45 088	911	43 222	7 380	1 866	16.4	4.3	827	1.6
...	55 023	Crawford	573	17 243	1 937	30.1	15 940	1 927	16 556	1 303	−616	8.2	−3.7	129	.7
4720	55 025	Dane	1 202	426 526	140	354.8	367 085	141	323 545	59 441	43 540	16.2	13.5	14 387	3.4
...	55 027	Dodge	882	85 897	609	97.4	76 559	590	75 064	9 338	1 495	12.2	2.0	2 188	2.5
...	55 029	Door	483	27 961	1 452	57.9	25 690	1 433	25 029	2 271	661	8.8	2.6	267	1.0
2240	55 031	Douglas	1 309	43 287	1 032	33.1	41 758	961	44 421	1 529	−2 663	3.7	−6.0	315	.7
...	55 033	Dunn	852	39 858	1 115	46.8	35 909	1 103	34 314	3 949	1 595	11.0	4.6	335	.8
2290	55 035	Eau Claire	638	93 142	549	146.0	85 183	538	78 805	7 959	6 378	9.3	8.1	879	.9
...	55 037	Florence	488	5 088	2 845	10.4	4 590	2 866	4 172	498	418	10.8	10.0	23	.5
...	55 039	Fond du Lac	723	97 296	533	134.6	90 083	509	88 964	7 213	1 119	8.0	1.3	1 987	2.0
...	55 041	Forest	1 014	10 024	2 442	9.9	8 776	2 488	9 044	1 248	−268	14.2	−3.0	108	1.1
...	55 043	Grant	1 148	49 597	924	43.2	49 266	852	51 736	331	−2 470	.7	−4.8	280	.6
...	55 045	Green	584	33 647	1 292	57.6	30 339	1 277	30 012	3 308	327	10.9	1.1	327	1.0
...	55 047	Green Lake	354	19 105	1 843	54.0	18 651	1 756	18 370	454	281	2.4	1.5	393	2.1
...	55 049	Iowa	763	22 780	1 656	29.9	20 150	1 667	19 802	2 630	348	13.1	1.8	75	.3
...	55 051	Iron	757	6 861	2 702	9.1	6 153	2 737	6 730	708	−577	11.5	−8.6	45	.7
...	55 053	Jackson	987	19 100	1 844	19.4	16 588	1 881	16 831	2 512	−243	15.1	−1.4	357	1.9
...	55 055	Jefferson	557	74 021	674	132.9	67 783	654	66 152	6 238	1 631	9.2	2.5	3 031	4.1
...	55 057	Juneau	768	24 316	1 583	31.7	21 650	1 596	21 037	2 666	613	12.3	2.9	347	1.4
1602	55 059	Kenosha	273	149 577	360	547.9	128 181	363	123 137	21 396	5 044	16.7	4.1	10 757	7.2
...	55 061	Kewaunee	343	20 187	1 781	58.9	18 878	1 742	19 539	1 309	−661	6.9	−3.4	153	.8
3870	55 063	La Crosse	453	107 120	500	236.5	97 904	469	91 056	9 216	6 848	9.4	7.5	990	.9

[1] Federal Information Processing Standards (FIPS) codes for metropolitan areas defined as of June 30, 1999.   [2] FIPS codes for states and counties/county equivalents.   [3] Dry land and land temporarily or partially covered by water.   [4] Based on 3,140 counties/county equivalents; excludes Yellowstone National Park in MT and South Boston independent city in VA which are no longer counties. When counties share the same rank, the next lower rank is omitted.   [5] Includes count resolution corrections through 1997 and adjustments based on Census 2000 dress rehearsal results and boundary changes reported as legally effective as of January 1, 1998.   [6] Persons of Hispanic or Latino origin may be of any race.

Sources: Land Area—U.S. Census Bureau, unpublished data file from Geography Division based on TIGER data base.   2000 Population—U.S. Census Bureau, Census of Population and Housing, Census 2000 Redistricting Data (Public Law 94-171) Summary Files (related Internet site <http://www.census.gov/dmd/www/2kresult.html>).   1990 Population—U.S. Census Bureau, "(CO-99-8) County Population Estimates and Demographic Components of Population Change: Annual Time Series, July 1, 1990 to July 1, 1999 (includes revised April 1, 1990 Population Estimates Base)"; published 9 March 2000; <http://www. census.gov/population/estimates/county/co-99-8/99C8_00.txt>.   1980 Population—U.S. Census Bureau, "1980–1990 Intercensal Population Estimates by County" on diskette (related Internet site <http://www.census.gov/population/www/estimates/countypop.html>).

[Includes U.S., states, and 3,142 counties/county equivalents defined as of January 1, 1992. For changes to these areas since January 1, 1992, see appendix B. Geographic Information]

Metro-politan area code[1]	State and county code[2]	County	Land area,[3] 2000 (sq. miles)	Population (April 1) 2000 Number	2000 Rank[4]	2000 Per square mile	1990[5] Number	1990[5] Rank[4]	1980	Net change 1990–2000	Net change 1980–1990	Percent change 1990–2000	Percent change 1980–1990	Hispanic or Latino,[6] 2000 Number	Hispanic or Latino,[6] 2000 Percent
		WISCONSIN—Con.													
...	55 065	Lafayette	634	16 137	2 014	25.5	16 074	1 918	17 412	63	−1 338	.4	−7.7	92	.6
...	55 067	Langlade	873	20 740	1 751	23.8	19 505	1 701	19 978	1 235	−473	6.3	−2.4	171	.8
...	55 069	Lincoln	883	29 641	1 411	33.6	26 993	1 390	26 555	2 648	438	9.8	1.6	243	.8
...	55 071	Manitowoc	592	82 887	625	140.0	80 421	567	82 918	2 466	−2 497	3.1	−3.0	1 343	1.6
8940	55 073	Marathon	1 545	125 834	431	81.4	115 400	399	111 270	10 434	4 130	9.0	3.7	979	.8
...	55 075	Marinette	1 402	43 384	1 031	30.9	40 548	985	39 314	2 836	1 234	7.0	3.1	325	.7
...	55 077	Marquette	455	15 832	2 030	34.8	12 321	2 193	11 672	3 511	649	28.5	5.6	421	2.7
...	55 078	Menominee	358	4 562	2 874	12.7	4 075	2 911	3 373	487	702	12.0	20.8	122	2.7
5082	55 079	Milwaukee	242	940 164	39	3 885.0	959 212	34	964 988	−19 048	−5 776	−2.0	−.6	82 406	8.8
...	55 081	Monroe	901	40 899	1 085	45.4	36 633	1 085	35 074	4 266	1 559	11.6	4.4	740	1.8
...	55 083	Oconto	998	35 634	1 226	35.7	30 226	1 287	28 947	5 408	1 279	17.9	4.4	240	.7
...	55 085	Oneida	1 125	36 776	1 195	32.7	31 679	1 224	31 216	5 097	463	16.1	1.5	244	.7
0460	55 087	Outagamie	640	160 971	331	251.5	140 510	338	128 730	20 461	11 780	14.6	9.2	3 207	2.0
5082	55 089	Ozaukee	232	82 317	629	354.8	72 894	615	66 981	9 423	5 913	12.9	8.8	1 073	1.3
...	55 091	Pepin	232	7 213	2 665	31.1	7 107	2 644	7 477	106	−370	1.5	−4.9	25	.3
5120	55 093	Pierce	576	36 804	1 194	63.9	32 765	1 196	31 149	4 039	1 616	12.3	5.2	301	.8
...	55 095	Polk	917	41 319	1 071	45.1	34 773	1 142	32 351	6 546	2 422	18.8	7.5	329	.8
...	55 097	Portage	806	67 182	730	83.4	61 405	711	57 420	5 777	3 985	9.4	6.9	967	1.4
...	55 099	Price	1 253	15 822	2 031	12.6	15 600	1 947	15 788	222	−188	1.4	−1.2	116	.7
5082	55 101	Racine	333	188 831	293	567.1	175 034	274	173 132	13 797	1 902	7.9	1.1	14 990	7.9
...	55 103	Richland	586	17 924	1 905	30.6	17 521	1 819	17 476	403	45	2.3	.3	167	.9
3620	55 105	Rock	720	152 307	351	211.5	139 510	341	139 420	12 797	90	9.2	.1	5 953	3.9
...	55 107	Rusk	913	15 347	2 065	16.8	15 079	1 983	15 589	268	−510	1.8	−3.3	116	.8
5120	55 109	St. Croix	722	63 155	768	87.5	50 251	839	43 262	12 904	6 989	25.7	16.2	483	.8
...	55 111	Sauk	838	55 225	852	65.9	46 975	890	43 469	8 250	3 506	17.6	8.1	938	1.7
...	55 113	Sawyer	1 256	16 196	2 007	12.9	14 181	2 039	12 843	2 015	1 338	14.2	10.4	145	.9
...	55 115	Shawano	893	40 664	1 095	45.5	37 157	1 068	35 928	3 507	1 229	9.4	3.4	407	1.0
7620	55 117	Sheboygan	514	112 646	477	219.2	103 877	444	100 935	8 769	2 942	8.4	2.9	3 789	3.4
...	55 119	Taylor	975	19 680	1 813	20.2	18 901	1 740	18 817	779	84	4.1	.4	127	.6
...	55 121	Trempealeau	734	27 010	1 482	36.8	25 263	1 453	26 158	1 747	−895	6.9	−3.4	240	.9
...	55 123	Vernon	795	28 056	1 450	35.3	25 617	1 437	25 642	2 439	−25	9.5	−.1	186	.7
...	55 125	Vilas	874	21 033	1 734	24.1	17 707	1 804	16 535	3 326	1 172	18.8	7.1	181	.9
...	55 127	Walworth	555	93 759	548	168.9	75 000	598	71 507	18 759	3 493	25.0	4.9	6 136	6.5
...	55 129	Washburn	810	16 036	2 020	19.8	13 772	2 073	13 174	2 264	598	16.4	4.5	143	.9
5082	55 131	Washington	431	117 493	461	272.6	95 328	485	84 848	22 165	10 480	23.3	12.4	1 529	1.3
5082	55 133	Waukesha	556	360 767	164	648.9	304 715	163	280 052	56 052	24 512	18.4	8.7	9 503	2.6
...	55 135	Waupaca	751	51 731	897	68.9	46 104	901	42 831	5 627	3 273	12.2	7.6	714	1.4
...	55 137	Waushara	626	23 154	1 636	37.0	19 385	1 711	18 526	3 769	859	19.4	4.6	848	3.7
0460	55 139	Winnebago	439	156 763	340	357.1	140 320	339	131 772	16 443	8 548	11.7	6.5	3 065	2.0
...	55 141	Wood	793	75 555	664	95.3	73 605	611	72 799	1 950	806	2.6	1.1	709	.9
	56 000	**WYOMING**	97 100	493 782	X	5.1	453 589	X	469 557	40 193	−15 968	8.9	−3.4	31 669	6.4
...	56 001	Albany	4 273	32 014	1 345	7.5	30 797	1 251	29 062	1 217	1 735	4.0	6.0	2 397	7.5
...	56 003	Big Horn	3 137	11 461	2 337	3.7	10 525	2 333	11 896	936	−1 371	8.9	−11.5	707	6.2
...	56 005	Campbell	4 797	33 698	1 290	7.0	29 370	1 320	24 367	4 328	5 003	14.7	20.5	1 191	3.5
...	56 007	Carbon	7 896	15 639	2 045	2.0	16 659	1 872	21 896	−1 020	−5 237	−6.1	−23.9	2 163	13.8
...	56 009	Converse	4 255	12 052	2 292	2.8	11 128	2 281	14 069	924	−2 941	8.3	−20.9	660	5.5
...	56 011	Crook	2 859	5 887	2 795	2.1	5 294	2 819	5 308	593	−14	11.2	−.3	54	.9
...	56 013	Fremont	9 182	35 804	1 225	3.9	33 662	1 175	38 992	2 142	−5 330	6.4	−13.7	1 566	4.4
...	56 015	Goshen	2 225	12 538	2 262	5.6	12 373	2 191	12 040	165	333	1.3	2.8	1 107	8.8
...	56 017	Hot Springs	2 004	4 882	2 855	2.4	4 809	2 856	5 710	73	−901	1.5	−15.8	116	2.4
...	56 019	Johnson	4 166	7 075	2 677	1.7	6 145	2 738	6 700	930	−555	15.1	−8.3	148	2.1
1580	56 021	Laramie	2 686	81 607	637	30.4	73 142	614	68 649	8 465	4 493	11.6	6.5	8 897	10.9
...	56 023	Lincoln	4 069	14 573	2 114	3.6	12 625	2 175	12 177	1 948	448	15.4	3.7	315	2.2
1350	56 025	Natrona	5 340	66 533	735	12.5	61 226	712	71 856	5 307	−10 630	8.7	−14.8	3 257	4.9
...	56 027	Niobrara	2 626	2 407	3 028	.9	2 499	3 022	2 924	−92	−425	−3.7	−14.5	36	1.5
...	56 029	Park	6 942	25 786	1 524	3.7	23 178	1 531	21 639	2 608	1 539	11.3	7.1	959	3.7
...	56 031	Platte	2 085	8 807	2 546	4.2	8 145	2 550	11 975	662	−3 830	8.1	−32.0	465	5.3
...	56 033	Sheridan	2 523	26 560	1 498	10.5	23 562	1 511	25 048	2 998	−1 486	12.7	−5.9	646	2.4
...	56 035	Sublette	4 883	5 920	2 791	1.2	4 843	2 850	4 548	1 077	295	22.2	6.5	112	1.9
...	56 037	Sweetwater	10 425	37 613	1 173	3.6	38 823	1 029	41 723	−1 210	−2 900	−3.1	−7.0	3 545	9.4
...	56 039	Teton	4 008	18 251	1 883	4.6	11 173	2 279	9 355	7 078	1 818	63.3	19.4	1 185	6.5
...	56 041	Uinta	2 082	19 742	1 807	9.5	18 705	1 749	13 021	1 037	5 684	5.5	43.7	1 055	5.3
...	56 043	Washakie	2 240	8 289	2 580	3.7	8 388	2 523	9 496	−99	−1 108	−1.2	−11.7	951	11.5
...	56 045	Weston	2 398	6 644	2 721	2.8	6 518	2 707	7 106	126	−588	1.9	−8.3	137	2.1

[1] Federal Information Processing Standards (FIPS) codes for metropolitan areas defined as of June 30, 1999. [2] FIPS codes for states and counties/county equivalents. [3] Dry land and land temporarily or partially covered by water. [4] Based on 3,140 counties/county equivalents; excludes Yellowstone National Park in MT and South Boston independent city in VA which are no longer counties. When counties share the same rank, the next lower rank is omitted. [5] Includes count resolution corrections through 1997 and adjustments based on Census 2000 dress rehearsal results and boundary changes reported as legally effective as of January 1, 1998. [6] Persons of Hispanic or Latino origin may be of any race.

Sources: Land Area—U.S. Census Bureau, unpublished data file from Geography Division based on TIGER data base. 2000 Population—U.S. Census Bureau, Census of Population and Housing, Census 2000 Redistricting Data (Public Law 94-171) Summary Files (related Internet site <http://www.census.gov/dmd/www/2kresult.html>). 1990 Population—U.S. Census Bureau, "(CO-99-8) County Population Estimates and Demographic Components of Population Change: Annual Time Series, July 1, 1990 to July 1, 1999 (includes revised April 1, 1990 Population Estimates Base)"; published 9 March 2000; <http://www. census.gov/population/estimates/county/co-99-8/99C8_00.txt>. 1980 Population—U.S. Census Bureau, "1980–1990 Intercensal Population Estimates by County" on diskette (related Internet site <http://www.census.gov/population/www/estimates/countypop.html>).

Table B–2. Counties — Population by Age, Sex, and Race

[Includes U.S., states, and 3,142 counties/county equivalents defined as of January 1, 1992. For changes to these areas since January 1, 1992, see appendix B. Geographic Information]

County	Population by age, 2000 (April 1) — Percent — Under 5 years	5 to 17 years	18 to 24 years	25 to 44 years	45 to 64 years	65 to 74 years	75 to 84 years	85 years and over	Median age (years)	Males per 100 females, 2000 (April 1)	White	Black or African American	American Indian and Alaska Native	Asian	Native Hawaiian and Other Pacific Islander	Some other race[1]	Two or more races[2]
UNITED STATES	6.8	18.9	9.6	30.2	22.0	6.5	4.4	1.5	35.3	96.3	211 460 626	34 658 190	2 475 956	10 242 998	398 835	15 359 073	6 826 228
ALABAMA	6.7	18.6	9.9	29.0	22.8	7.1	4.4	1.5	35.8	93.3	3 162 808	1 155 930	22 430	31 346	1 409	28 998	44 179
Autauga	6.9	21.7	8.0	30.7	22.5	6.1	3.1	1.0	35.1	94.5	35 221	7 473	194	200	13	165	405
Baldwin	6.1	18.3	7.5	27.7	24.9	8.8	5.1	1.5	39.0	96.2	122 366	14 444	809	537	38	755	1 466
Barbour	6.2	19.3	9.3	29.6	22.4	7.0	4.6	1.8	35.8	106.4	14 887	13 451	131	84	8	265	212
Bibb	7.0	18.4	9.5	30.9	22.7	6.4	3.6	1.6	34.7	106.6	15 966	4 624	49	17	2	61	107
Blount	6.9	18.5	8.4	29.2	24.1	7.4	4.1	1.4	36.4	99.7	48 512	606	250	71	12	1 054	519
Bullock	6.3	19.8	10.3	29.3	21.2	5.9	4.9	2.4	35.0	110.2	2 958	8 564	44	21	2	43	82
Butler	6.3	20.5	8.6	25.1	23.0	8.2	5.7	2.4	37.7	88.0	12 492	8 732	45	35	–	11	84
Calhoun	6.2	17.4	10.4	27.8	24.1	8.0	4.7	1.5	37.2	91.7	88 537	20 810	445	633	76	667	1 081
Chambers	6.6	18.0	8.6	27.0	23.5	8.2	5.8	2.2	37.7	89.6	22 271	13 943	49	68	–	43	209
Cherokee	6.0	16.2	7.6	27.6	26.7	9.4	4.8	1.6	40.0	96.7	22 268	1 330	75	34	–	83	198
Chilton	6.9	18.8	9.1	29.0	23.4	7.2	4.2	1.4	35.9	97.8	34 330	4 200	111	72	6	599	275
Choctaw	6.9	19.1	7.9	26.2	25.2	7.9	4.7	2.0	37.9	88.8	8 779	7 027	25	7	–	17	67
Clarke	7.5	20.6	8.5	27.5	22.5	7.3	4.4	1.8	35.5	89.7	15 589	11 989	62	45	1	45	136
Clay	6.2	17.7	8.0	27.4	24.2	8.6	5.5	2.5	38.7	95.2	11 776	2 238	45	14	3	66	112
Cleburne	6.1	18.2	8.2	28.5	25.3	7.8	4.4	1.4	37.5	99.3	13 380	523	42	20	1	48	109
Coffee	6.2	18.5	8.9	28.1	24.1	7.7	4.7	1.7	37.2	95.5	33 631	8 013	396	414	41	390	730
Colbert	6.1	17.7	8.1	27.8	24.9	8.3	5.4	1.7	38.7	91.8	44 825	9 137	205	131	12	187	487
Conecuh	6.2	19.7	8.3	25.8	24.3	8.5	5.2	2.1	38.0	89.8	7 806	6 136	28	16	7	12	84
Coosa	6.2	17.5	8.6	29.0	24.3	8.3	4.6	1.6	37.7	104.4	7 802	4 172	39	5	1	76	107
Covington	5.9	17.6	8.1	26.1	24.3	9.2	6.3	2.3	39.8	91.6	32 436	4 648	181	65	5	63	233
Crenshaw	5.9	18.8	7.9	26.3	23.9	8.5	6.3	2.3	38.8	89.8	10 088	3 388	51	15	1	27	95
Cullman	6.4	17.9	8.8	28.3	24.0	8.0	5.0	1.7	37.5	97.3	75 011	743	290	140	27	477	795
Dale	7.5	19.1	9.6	30.3	21.8	6.8	3.7	1.3	34.3	98.3	36 541	10 002	297	529	72	634	1 054
Dallas	7.4	21.2	9.4	26.2	21.9	7.4	4.8	1.7	35.3	83.5	16 496	29 332	50	160	5	67	255
DeKalb	6.8	17.9	9.2	29.1	23.2	7.5	4.6	1.7	36.3	95.6	59 652	1 083	518	124	36	1 998	1 041
Elmore	6.6	19.1	8.8	32.1	22.7	5.9	3.6	1.3	35.3	102.5	50 737	13 597	286	238	18	313	685
Escambia	6.2	17.9	9.7	28.9	23.7	7.3	4.6	1.7	36.9	102.7	24 754	11 837	1 157	94	10	154	434
Etowah	6.4	17.4	8.7	27.4	24.1	8.5	5.8	1.7	38.3	91.8	85 737	15 191	345	432	36	755	963
Fayette	6.0	17.9	8.2	26.5	25.3	8.3	5.4	2.3	39.0	93.5	16 075	2 207	38	28	2	50	95
Franklin	6.4	18.1	9.2	28.0	23.4	8.2	4.9	1.7	36.7	96.4	28 001	1 314	103	34	31	1 441	299
Geneva	5.6	18.4	7.5	26.8	25.3	8.7	5.5	2.1	39.3	94.7	22 442	2 743	197	32	6	159	185
Greene	7.7	21.5	8.9	25.1	22.1	7.8	4.4	2.5	35.9	88.4	1 904	8 013	12	8	–	10	27
Hale	8.2	21.4	9.1	26.7	21.1	6.9	4.6	2.0	34.4	89.4	6 844	10 131	30	27	4	50	99
Henry	6.2	17.8	8.4	25.7	25.5	8.5	5.5	2.3	39.3	90.6	10 710	5 268	34	10	4	163	121
Houston	6.8	19.1	8.2	28.7	23.5	7.4	4.6	1.7	36.7	90.5	64 886	21 840	329	551	14	347	820
Jackson	6.3	17.9	8.3	28.7	25.4	7.8	4.2	1.4	37.6	95.1	49 552	2 019	946	124	13	195	1 077
Jefferson	6.5	18.3	9.6	29.7	22.3	7.1	4.8	1.7	36.0	89.2	384 639	260 608	1 408	5 971	188	3 907	5 326
Lamar	5.8	17.8	8.7	27.7	24.1	8.6	5.2	2.2	38.2	93.4	13 816	1 906	18	10	–	73	81
Lauderdale	5.9	17.1	10.1	27.9	23.9	8.1	5.2	1.7	37.6	91.7	77 743	8 663	223	308	17	316	696
Lawrence	6.3	19.4	8.4	30.1	23.7	6.9	3.9	1.3	35.9	96.2	27 067	4 648	1 865	35	3	114	1 071
Lee	6.3	17.0	22.7	28.1	17.8	4.6	2.6	.9	27.5	96.9	85 247	26 071	273	1 875	25	532	1 069
Limestone	6.6	18.3	8.8	32.1	23.1	6.4	3.6	1.1	35.8	103.1	55 029	8 752	304	231	14	747	599
Lowndes	7.5	22.7	9.1	27.1	21.4	6.8	3.7	1.6	33.9	87.9	3 484	9 885	15	16	3	16	54
Macon	6.5	18.7	16.9	22.9	21.0	6.8	5.3	1.9	32.0	85.0	3 365	20 403	39	91	1	31	175
Madison	6.8	18.8	9.4	31.5	22.7	6.4	3.4	1.0	35.7	95.3	199 401	63 025	2 129	5 140	158	1 629	5 218
Marengo	6.8	21.7	8.0	26.0	22.9	7.8	4.8	2.0	36.4	88.3	10 657	11 655	19	41	3	57	107
Marion	6.0	16.5	8.2	28.2	25.2	8.4	5.3	2.0	38.9	98.0	29 579	1 134	91	62	10	121	217
Marshall	6.7	18.2	8.5	29.0	23.4	8.0	4.7	1.5	36.9	94.8	76 791	1 207	433	201	36	2 663	900
Mobile	7.3	20.1	10.0	28.7	21.9	6.5	4.1	1.3	34.4	91.5	252 199	133 465	2 682	5 628	101	1 600	4 168
Monroe	7.5	20.8	8.6	26.8	22.5	7.2	4.6	1.9	35.4	90.8	14 047	9 747	236	70	2	31	191
Montgomery	6.9	18.9	11.7	29.0	20.9	6.2	4.1	1.5	33.5	90.8	109 180	108 583	568	2 217	72	787	2 103
Morgan	6.6	18.8	8.4	30.1	23.8	7.0	4.1	1.3	36.6	96.2	94 485	12 485	747	495	75	1 391	1 386
Perry	7.6	22.2	11.1	23.6	20.7	7.8	4.7	2.4	33.3	83.9	3 660	8 111	9	4	3	10	64
Pickens	6.8	20.5	8.5	25.8	22.8	8.6	5.0	2.1	36.9	88.1	11 720	8 999	25	23	5	46	131
Pike	6.5	17.9	15.8	26.0	21.2	6.4	4.6	1.6	32.5	89.5	17 990	10 835	194	105	5	76	400
Randolph	6.6	18.5	8.7	26.8	23.5	8.5	5.3	2.1	37.7	93.4	17 094	4 977	45	50	1	75	138
Russell	7.1	19.5	9.1	28.8	22.4	7.5	4.3	1.3	35.4	91.0	28 209	20 319	182	181	37	295	533
St. Clair	6.6	18.8	7.9	30.7	24.3	7.0	3.7	1.1	36.4	101.8	58 288	5 263	242	112	17	267	553
Shelby	7.5	18.8	8.2	33.7	23.4	5.1	2.6	.7	34.9	96.2	128 671	10 606	473	1 477	26	1 013	1 027
Sumter	7.2	21.9	12.2	25.3	19.5	6.7	4.8	2.4	32.1	84.9	3 886	10 827	14	15	2	27	77
Talladega	6.3	18.6	9.0	28.8	23.9	7.4	4.5	1.4	36.6	95.7	53 830	25 339	184	162	20	216	570
Tallapoosa	6.2	18.0	7.6	26.7	24.9	8.7	5.7	2.2	39.3	90.5	30 474	10 518	109	75	3	70	226
Tuscaloosa	6.4	17.0	16.5	28.1	20.8	6.3	3.7	1.2	31.9	92.8	112 320	48 327	372	1 516	52	931	1 357
Walker	6.4	17.1	8.6	28.0	25.1	8.2	5.0	1.7	38.3	93.2	65 163	4 364	201	141	14	220	610
Washington	7.2	21.4	8.6	27.4	22.9	7.0	3.9	1.5	34.9	96.1	11 759	4 867	1 289	10	5	9	158
Wilcox	8.1	22.6	9.1	25.5	21.0	7.1	4.6	2.1	33.8	87.2	3 626	9 479	19	17	2	15	25
Winston	6.2	17.5	7.9	28.7	25.5	8.0	4.6	1.6	38.0	96.0	24 177	94	114	32	2	223	201

[1] Includes all other responses not included in the other five race categories shown. Also includes write-in entries such as multiracial, mixed, interracial, or a Hispanic/Latino group. [2] Refers to combinations of two or more of the six race categories shown under one race.

Source: Population by Age, Sex, and Race—U.S. Census Bureau; 2000 Census of Population and Housing, "Census 2000 Profiles of General Demographic Characteristics" data files, published May 2001 (related Internet site <http://www.census.gov/mp/www/pub/2000cen/mscen01.html>).

Table B–2. Counties — Population by Age, Sex, and Race–Con.

[Includes U.S., states, and 3,142 counties/county equivalents defined as of January 1, 1992. For changes to these areas since January 1, 1992, see appendix B. Geographic Information]

County	Population by age, 2000 (April 1) — Percent — Under 5 years	5 to 17 years	18 to 24 years	25 to 44 years	45 to 64 years	65 to 74 years	75 to 84 years	85 years and over	Median age (years)	Males per 100 females, 2000 (April 1)	Population by race, 2000 (April 1) — One race — White	Black or African American	American Indian and Alaska Native	Asian	Native Hawaiian and Other Pacific Islander	Some other race[1]	Two or more races[2]
ALASKA	7.6	22.8	9.1	32.5	22.3	3.6	1.7	.4	32.4	107.0	434 534	21 787	98 043	25 116	3 309	9 997	34 146
Aleutians East	4.3	12.5	10.2	42.3	28.1	1.9	.7	–	37.0	184.8	646	45	1 005	715	8	199	79
Aleutians West	4.7	12.5	7.8	47.6	25.1	1.7	.4	.1	36.1	180.0	2 188	165	1 145	1 344	34	400	189
Anchorage	7.7	21.5	9.6	33.9	21.9	3.4	1.6	.4	32.4	102.4	188 009	15 199	18 941	14 433	2 423	5 703	15 575
Bethel	10.0	29.8	9.7	28.9	16.4	3.2	1.6	.4	25.3	113.2	2 006	61	13 114	168	9	31	617
Bristol Bay	7.1	24.2	5.9	34.8	24.2	2.8	.9	.2	36.0	119.5	661	7	550	3	6	1	30
Denali	5.2	18.6	6.7	36.8	29.7	2.2	.5	.4	37.6	139.0	1 623	27	90	29	7	18	99
Dillingham	9.7	28.5	7.7	28.9	19.5	3.7	1.5	.5	28.9	109.0	1 065	18	3 452	30	1	27	329
Fairbanks North Star	8.1	22.0	12.2	33.3	19.8	2.9	1.4	.3	29.5	109.1	64 439	4 843	5 714	1 720	245	1 414	4 465
Haines	5.4	20.3	5.3	28.2	30.4	6.2	3.3	1.0	40.7	102.5	1 974	3	275	17	2	10	111
Juneau	6.5	20.9	8.1	32.8	25.7	3.5	2.0	.6	35.3	101.5	22 969	248	3 496	1 438	116	323	2 121
Kenai Peninsula	6.6	23.3	6.9	29.6	26.2	4.8	2.2	.4	36.3	108.5	42 841	229	3 713	480	86	415	1 927
Ketchikan Gateway	6.9	21.3	7.5	31.4	25.1	4.5	2.6	.8	36.0	104.5	10 460	70	2 109	603	22	62	744
Kodiak Island	8.9	23.5	8.3	34.0	20.4	3.2	1.3	.3	31.6	112.4	8 304	134	2 028	2 232	110	387	718
Lake and Peninsula	8.0	29.8	8.5	28.0	20.2	3.6	1.5	.3	29.2	113.5	342	1	1 340	4	3	6	127
Matanuska-Susitna	7.0	25.2	7.4	31.1	23.4	4.0	1.6	.3	34.1	108.2	51 938	411	3 264	414	74	509	2 712
Nome	8.6	28.6	9.3	29.0	18.6	3.5	1.7	.7	27.6	117.6	1 777	35	6 915	62	2	18	387
North Slope	9.5	28.6	9.5	30.1	18.1	2.7	1.2	.2	27.0	112.5	1 262	53	5 050	437	62	37	484
Northwest Arctic	10.7	30.8	10.0	28.1	15.5	3.4	1.2	.4	23.9	114.5	888	15	5 944	64	4	26	267
Prince of Wales-Outer Ketchikan	7.4	23.6	7.5	30.1	25.8	4.0	1.4	.3	34.7	119.8	3 265	9	2 377	22	3	31	439
Sitka	6.4	20.8	9.4	30.9	24.1	5.1	2.4	.9	35.2	104.0	6 052	28	1 641	335	31	83	665
Skagway-Yakutat-Angoon	5.1	21.9	6.8	30.1	29.2	4.4	2.0	.5	NA	121.4	2 405	6	1 523	23	11	33	243
Southeast Fairbanks	7.1	25.7	7.6	27.8	25.7	4.3	1.4	.3	33.7	107.2	4 877	122	785	42	9	45	294
Valdez-Cordova	6.7	23.0	7.0	30.9	26.5	3.9	1.7	.5	36.1	113.9	7 738	33	1 351	362	27	115	569
Wade Hampton	10.6	36.0	9.7	25.6	13.1	3.2	1.5	.3	20.0	109.0	333	4	6 503	7	2	2	177
Wrangell-Petersburg	6.7	23.0	5.7	29.0	26.0	5.0	3.4	1.1	37.2	108.4	4 882	15	1 074	108	9	74	522
Yukon-Koyukuk	7.1	27.9	8.7	26.9	22.1	4.8	1.9	.7	31.1	118.6	1 590	6	4 644	24	3	28	256
ARIZONA	7.5	19.2	10.0	29.5	20.9	7.1	4.6	1.3	34.2	99.7	3 873 611	158 873	255 879	92 236	6 733	596 774	146 526
Apache	9.1	29.4	9.4	25.1	18.7	5.0	2.4	.9	27.0	98.2	13 536	173	53 375	93	39	1 217	990
Cochise	6.8	19.6	9.3	26.0	23.7	8.7	4.8	1.3	36.9	101.6	90 269	5 321	1 350	1 942	301	14 193	4 379
Coconino	7.3	21.5	14.4	29.2	20.7	4.3	2.1	.6	29.6	99.7	73 381	1 215	33 161	910	108	4 801	2 744
Gila	6.1	19.0	6.4	22.3	26.4	11.2	6.7	1.9	42.3	96.8	39 951	197	6 630	220	28	3 385	924
Graham	7.8	22.3	12.0	27.3	18.7	6.5	4.1	1.3	30.0	112.5	22 470	685	5 005	100	13	4 470	715
Greenlee	8.3	23.4	7.5	28.2	22.6	5.9	3.2	.9	33.6	109.2	6 339	44	142	13	3	1 711	295
La Paz	4.9	16.2	6.1	20.4	26.6	16.6	7.8	1.4	46.8	105.5	14 619	155	2 470	80	19	1 844	528
Maricopa	7.9	19.1	10.2	31.4	19.8	6.1	4.2	1.3	33.0	100.1	2 376 359	114 551	56 706	66 445	4 406	364 213	89 469
Mohave	6.0	17.1	6.5	23.2	26.7	12.3	6.7	1.5	42.9	98.9	139 616	833	3 733	1 186	168	6 200	3 296
Navajo	8.6	26.9	8.8	25.3	20.4	6.2	3.0	.8	30.2	98.7	44 752	857	46 532	322	46	3 067	1 894
Pima	6.6	18.0	10.9	28.4	21.9	7.5	5.2	1.5	35.7	95.7	633 387	25 594	27 178	17 213	1 088	112 217	27 069
Pinal	6.7	18.4	8.7	27.3	22.7	10.0	5.1	1.1	37.1	114.2	126 559	4 958	14 034	1 086	146	28 149	4 795
Santa Cruz	8.7	25.0	8.2	26.6	20.8	6.3	3.6	.9	31.8	91.7	29 168	145	251	201	33	7 574	1 009
Yavapai	5.2	16.0	7.1	22.4	27.4	12.1	7.8	2.1	44.5	96.2	153 933	655	2 686	851	138	5 990	3 264
Yuma	7.9	21.0	10.0	25.6	18.9	10.0	5.5	1.1	33.9	102.0	109 269	3 550	2 626	1 486	197	37 743	5 155
ARKANSAS	6.8	18.7	9.8	28.1	22.7	7.4	4.8	1.7	36.0	95.3	2 138 598	418 950	17 808	20 220	1 668	40 412	35 744
Arkansas	6.6	18.3	8.3	26.3	24.4	8.2	5.8	2.2	38.7	90.9	15 602	4 848	44	74	1	44	136
Ashley	6.7	20.1	8.3	27.2	23.9	7.3	4.8	1.7	36.2	93.3	16 892	6 561	50	43	11	420	232
Baxter	4.5	14.5	5.8	21.1	27.4	14.2	9.2	3.3	48.1	92.3	37 547	43	201	131	9	83	372
Benton	7.6	19.0	8.6	29.4	21.1	8.0	5.0	1.4	35.3	97.4	139 399	629	2 531	1 673	130	6 253	2 791
Boone	6.3	17.7	8.2	26.5	24.7	8.8	5.7	2.2	38.9	93.1	33 132	39	240	108	8	114	307
Bradley	5.9	17.6	9.7	26.5	22.8	8.8	6.1	2.6	38.0	97.7	7 983	3 607	30	8	1	876	95
Calhoun	5.3	19.3	7.0	28.2	24.3	8.1	5.6	2.2	39.2	92.7	4 280	1 343	12	2	–	53	54
Carroll	6.4	17.5	8.1	26.2	26.0	8.8	5.2	1.8	39.4	97.4	23 741	27	222	105	20	848	394
Chicot	6.9	20.5	8.6	26.4	22.2	8.4	4.9	2.1	36.2	94.2	6 104	7 617	18	56	3	199	120
Clark	6.0	15.7	20.0	23.8	19.9	7.4	5.1	2.1	31.8	92.7	17 491	5 186	108	145	10	323	283
Clay	6.0	17.1	7.7	25.3	24.6	10.0	6.7	2.7	40.5	93.5	17 271	33	121	14	–	27	143
Cleburne	5.1	16.2	6.6	24.1	26.9	12.1	6.8	2.2	43.7	93.9	23 613	29	113	35	6	36	214
Cleveland	6.5	19.6	7.9	27.7	24.7	7.5	4.4	1.7	36.9	95.4	7 267	1 133	27	12	3	58	71
Columbia	6.1	19.0	12.3	25.3	21.4	8.0	5.6	2.3	35.7	90.9	15 894	9 232	67	88	7	118	197
Conway	6.5	19.0	8.3	26.7	23.5	8.5	5.7	1.9	37.9	94.4	17 137	2 654	101	47	7	150	240
Craighead	6.9	17.2	14.0	28.7	21.4	6.2	4.1	1.5	33.0	93.8	73 332	6 395	273	495	19	764	870
Crawford	7.4	20.8	8.4	29.3	22.8	6.5	3.6	1.1	35.1	97.7	49 087	465	1 069	634	11	787	1 194
Crittenden	8.4	22.7	9.4	29.1	20.5	5.3	3.5	1.1	32.0	91.0	25 896	23 934	124	240	11	335	326
Cross	6.7	21.1	8.5	27.4	22.6	7.2	4.8	1.7	35.9	94.0	14 606	4 628	44	61	1	41	145
Dallas	6.1	20.0	8.3	24.5	24.1	8.4	6.1	2.5	38.4	94.3	5 246	3 774	22	21	–	93	54
Desha	7.5	21.4	9.0	25.2	22.7	7.2	5.0	2.0	35.5	87.6	7 747	7 107	54	46	4	266	117

[1] Includes all other responses not included in the other five race categories shown. Also includes write-in entries such as multiracial, mixed, interracial, or a Hispanic/Latino group. [2] Refers to combinations of two or more of the six race categories shown under one race.

Source: Population by Age, Sex, and Race—U.S. Census Bureau; 2000 Census of Population and Housing, "Census 2000 Profiles of General Demographic Characteristics" data files, published May 2001 (related Internet site <http://www.census.gov/mp/www/pub/2000cen/mscen01.html>).

Table B–2. Counties — **Population by Age, Sex, and Race**–Con.

[Includes U.S., states, and 3,142 counties/county equivalents defined as of January 1, 1992. For changes to these areas since January 1, 1992, see appendix B. Geographic Information]

County	Population by age, 2000 (April 1) Percent— Under 5 years	5 to 17 years	18 to 24 years	25 to 44 years	45 to 64 years	65 to 74 years	75 to 84 years	85 years and over	Median age (years)	Males per 100 females, 2000 (April 1)	Population by race, 2000 (April 1) One race White	Black or African American	American Indian and Alaska Native	Asian	Native Hawaiian and Other Pacific Islander	Some other race[1]	Two or more races[2]
ARKANSAS—Con.																	
Drew	6.7	19.1	12.6	27.2	21.5	6.9	4.2	1.8	34.0	94.1	13 162	5 085	47	79	3	187	160
Faulkner	6.9	18.7	15.3	30.1	19.5	5.2	3.2	1.1	31.0	95.5	75 973	7 298	449	619	28	589	1 058
Franklin	6.5	19.4	8.5	26.7	23.2	8.0	5.5	2.2	37.6	98.0	17 091	110	142	46	10	132	240
Fulton	5.5	17.3	6.4	23.7	27.0	11.4	6.6	2.3	43.0	96.0	11 371	23	78	24	–	7	139
Garland	5.5	15.8	7.3	25.2	25.1	11.4	7.4	2.4	42.5	94.4	78 250	6 873	537	443	27	630	1 308
Grant	6.4	19.5	8.0	29.6	24.3	6.7	3.9	1.5	36.6	98.5	15 731	406	74	22	5	106	120
Greene	6.7	18.5	9.1	28.7	23.1	7.6	4.7	1.6	36.2	95.3	36 379	48	158	64	6	174	502
Hempstead	7.5	19.8	9.6	27.2	21.7	7.3	4.7	2.1	35.2	93.7	14 925	7 160	99	40	4	983	376
Hot Spring	6.3	18.8	8.2	26.5	24.5	8.6	5.4	1.8	38.4	95.5	26 508	3 115	136	67	13	133	381
Howard	6.7	20.1	8.6	27.8	21.6	7.3	5.4	2.4	36.1	95.1	10 525	3 126	58	71	2	395	123
Independence	6.4	18.1	9.2	27.7	24.1	7.7	4.9	1.9	37.7	96.3	32 490	697	155	222	10	220	439
Izard	5.1	15.8	7.1	25.0	25.8	11.0	7.8	2.3	42.6	102.9	12 773	191	83	15	3	34	150
Jackson	5.7	16.4	11.5	26.0	23.8	8.6	5.8	2.2	38.2	91.2	14 840	3 235	60	33	1	74	175
Jefferson	6.9	19.4	10.8	27.8	22.1	6.6	4.6	1.7	35.1	95.9	40 840	41 788	202	558	30	223	637
Johnson	6.7	18.5	9.7	27.6	22.7	7.8	5.0	1.9	36.4	99.0	21 344	313	141	58	2	598	325
Lafayette	6.0	19.4	8.1	24.4	24.4	8.8	6.1	2.9	39.3	93.6	5 313	3 123	32	19	1	17	54
Lawrence	6.3	17.6	9.6	25.9	23.2	8.8	6.1	2.5	38.2	93.6	17 379	79	102	9	2	22	181
Lee	6.4	19.6	10.2	28.7	21.1	7.1	4.8	2.1	34.6	111.4	5 209	7 201	20	34	–	66	50
Lincoln	5.7	16.5	12.4	33.2	20.4	5.9	4.1	1.9	34.7	142.3	9 402	4 771	58	9	1	143	108
Little River	6.9	18.3	8.4	25.7	25.6	7.9	5.1	2.0	38.2	94.7	10 155	2 899	198	27	4	117	228
Logan	6.5	19.4	7.5	26.7	23.9	8.2	5.7	2.1	38.0	98.4	21 690	236	147	33	5	88	287
Lonoke	7.1	21.6	8.0	30.9	21.9	5.6	3.4	1.4	34.7	96.8	48 089	3 404	259	222	17	267	570
Madison	6.4	20.4	7.5	27.0	24.3	7.6	4.8	1.9	37.7	99.7	13 665	16	174	9	13	210	156
Marion	5.0	17.1	6.0	23.3	28.5	11.2	6.6	2.2	44.1	97.9	15 740	20	122	32	8	21	197
Miller	7.4	19.1	9.7	28.6	22.1	6.9	4.7	1.6	34.9	95.0	29 935	9 297	255	150	8	219	579
Mississippi	8.1	21.5	9.9	27.5	20.8	6.6	4.1	1.5	33.1	91.8	33 499	16 997	134	196	15	557	581
Monroe	6.9	21.0	7.6	23.7	23.4	8.7	6.2	2.4	38.3	88.5	6 088	3 978	27	13	4	27	117
Montgomery	6.1	17.4	6.2	25.0	26.3	10.5	6.5	1.9	41.5	96.2	8 822	27	103	34	1	144	114
Nevada	6.4	18.8	8.7	26.1	23.8	7.9	6.0	2.3	37.7	94.4	6 660	3 104	38	6	–	85	62
Newton	5.8	19.1	7.6	25.0	27.6	7.8	5.3	1.7	40.1	102.3	8 385	12	48	14	1	35	113
Ouachita	6.1	19.7	8.0	25.6	23.6	8.7	5.9	2.4	38.7	89.8	17 200	11 125	73	70	8	76	238
Perry	6.3	19.0	7.4	28.0	24.5	8.2	4.7	1.8	38.0	98.3	9 762	177	100	15	2	40	113
Phillips	8.5	23.7	9.4	23.2	21.2	7.6	4.6	1.8	33.0	84.7	10 379	15 612	46	85	3	113	207
Pike	6.4	18.6	7.3	26.4	24.5	8.1	6.4	2.5	38.9	97.2	10 403	392	73	18	2	294	121
Poinsett	6.8	19.3	8.9	27.1	23.7	7.7	5.0	1.6	36.6	94.6	23 304	1 825	59	41	5	189	191
Polk	6.7	18.9	7.9	25.0	24.5	9.0	5.7	2.3	38.6	97.0	19 155	32	302	42	12	348	338
Pope	6.5	19.0	11.6	28.2	21.9	6.8	4.3	1.6	34.8	96.4	51 055	1 423	370	346	14	506	755
Prairie	6.0	18.0	7.5	26.1	25.1	8.7	6.3	2.3	40.1	97.0	8 092	1 308	34	17	–	27	61
Pulaski	7.2	18.1	9.6	31.1	22.6	6.0	4.1	1.4	35.0	92.0	231 211	115 197	1 409	4 510	149	3 935	5 063
Randolph	6.0	18.6	8.3	25.7	24.3	9.2	5.6	2.2	38.8	96.0	17 648	177	97	13	2	49	209
St. Francis	7.7	20.3	9.9	29.1	21.2	6.4	3.9	1.5	33.8	105.6	14 184	14 375	73	165	5	116	411
Saline	6.4	19.0	7.7	30.2	24.2	7.3	3.9	1.3	36.8	98.1	79 575	1 838	410	477	25	372	832
Scott	7.3	19.2	8.1	26.5	24.2	8.1	4.7	1.9	37.3	101.9	10 285	25	154	105	1	281	145
Searcy	5.5	17.1	6.9	24.5	26.7	10.3	6.7	2.3	42.3	98.0	8 035	3	62	12	1	37	111
Sebastian	7.4	18.7	9.2	29.5	22.3	6.6	4.7	1.7	35.5	95.3	94 745	7 086	1 810	4 039	53	4 266	3 072
Sevier	7.8	20.4	9.5	27.7	21.3	6.9	4.5	1.8	33.6	99.1	12 544	778	286	21	9	1 865	254
Sharp	5.5	16.4	6.3	22.8	25.5	13.1	7.8	2.7	44.3	92.4	16 630	84	116	21	3	27	238
Stone	5.5	16.8	7.1	23.6	28.5	10.9	5.7	2.0	43.1	96.9	11 185	9	89	6	4	17	189
Union	6.4	19.5	8.3	27.0	22.7	7.8	6.0	2.4	37.7	91.6	30 182	14 587	109	182	5	212	352
Van Buren	5.1	16.4	6.6	23.0	25.5	12.5	8.0	2.7	44.2	96.7	15 673	50	122	40	7	60	240
Washington	7.4	17.7	15.3	30.2	19.5	5.2	3.4	1.3	30.8	100.4	138 796	3 539	1 972	2 421	839	6 723	3 425
White	6.3	18.1	12.8	27.2	21.9	7.2	4.8	1.9	35.1	95.2	62 811	2 394	292	216	18	553	881
Woodruff	7.0	19.0	8.4	24.5	24.4	8.1	5.8	2.8	38.4	89.2	5 932	2 688	20	6	9	15	71
Yell	6.5	19.3	8.9	28.3	22.0	7.7	5.4	2.0	36.1	99.5	18 312	310	123	146	6	1 900	342
CALIFORNIA	7.3	20.0	9.9	31.6	20.5	5.6	3.8	1.3	33.3	99.3	20 170 059	2 263 882	333 346	3 697 513	116 961	5 682 241	1 607 646
Alameda	6.8	17.7	9.6	33.9	21.7	5.2	3.7	1.3	34.5	96.6	704 334	215 598	9 146	295 218	9 142	129 079	81 224
Alpine	5.0	17.8	10.4	27.5	29.3	6.2	2.6	1.1	39.3	110.8	890	7	228	4	1	17	61
Amador	4.2	16.4	6.9	26.2	28.3	9.8	6.4	1.8	42.7	122.5	30 113	1 359	626	350	36	1 769	847
Butte	5.7	18.3	13.6	24.8	21.8	7.5	6.2	2.1	35.8	96.1	171 728	2 816	3 866	6 752	296	9 790	7 923
Calaveras	4.4	18.4	5.5	22.4	31.1	10.7	5.9	1.6	44.6	98.5	36 982	304	705	345	38	839	1 341
Colusa	8.1	23.5	10.3	26.9	19.8	5.9	4.1	1.3	31.5	103.4	12 090	103	439	228	74	5 017	853
Contra Costa	7.0	19.6	7.7	30.6	23.9	5.8	4.1	1.4	36.4	95.4	621 490	88 813	5 830	103 993	3 466	76 510	48 714
Del Norte	5.5	19.5	8.0	32.2	22.3	6.7	4.4	1.4	36.4	123.3	21 693	1 184	1 770	637	23	1 079	1 121
El Dorado	5.7	20.4	6.8	27.8	26.9	7.0	4.2	1.1	39.4	99.5	140 209	813	1 566	3 328	209	5 547	4 627

[1] Includes all other responses not included in the other five race categories shown. Also includes write-in entries such as multiracial, mixed, interracial, or a Hispanic/Latino group. [2] Refers to combinations of two or more of the six race categories shown under one race.

Source: Population by Age, Sex, and Race—U.S. Census Bureau; 2000 Census of Population and Housing, "Census 2000 Profiles of General Demographic Characteristics" data files, published May 2001 (related Internet site <http://www.census.gov/mp/www/pub/2000cen/mscen01.html>).

Table B–2. Counties — **Population by Age, Sex, and Race**–Con.

[Includes U.S., states, and 3,142 counties/county equivalents defined as of January 1, 1992. For changes to these areas since January 1, 1992, see appendix B. Geographic Information]

County	Population by age, 2000 (April 1) Percent— Under 5 years	5 to 17 years	18 to 24 years	25 to 44 years	45 to 64 years	65 to 74 years	75 to 84 years	85 years and over	Median age (years)	Males per 100 females, 2000 (April 1)	White	Black or African American	American Indian and Alaska Native	Asian	Native Hawaiian and Other Pacific Islander	Some other race[1]	Two or more races[2]
CALIFORNIA—Con.																	
Fresno	8.5	23.6	11.1	28.5	18.5	5.2	3.5	1.2	29.9	100.4	434 045	42 337	12 790	64 362	1 000	207 061	37 812
Glenn	7.5	23.2	8.7	26.8	20.7	6.8	4.6	1.6	33.7	102.2	18 988	155	552	893	35	4 810	1 020
Humboldt	5.6	17.6	12.4	27.4	24.5	6.3	4.5	1.6	36.3	97.7	107 179	1 111	7 241	2 091	241	3 099	5 556
Imperial	7.7	23.8	9.9	30.4	18.2	5.9	3.3	.9	31.0	109.3	70 290	5 624	2 666	2 836	119	55 634	5 192
Inyo	5.4	19.0	5.8	23.4	27.3	10.0	6.8	2.3	42.8	95.4	14 367	29	1 802	163	15	825	744
Kern	8.4	23.5	10.2	29.8	18.7	5.2	3.2	1.0	30.6	105.3	407 581	39 798	9 999	22 268	972	153 610	27 417
Kings	8.1	20.9	11.8	35.0	16.8	4.1	2.5	.8	30.2	134.8	69 492	10 747	2 178	3 980	250	36 611	6 203
Lake	5.3	18.8	6.0	23.6	26.8	10.5	7.0	2.0	42.7	97.6	50 289	1 233	1 772	482	93	2 398	2 042
Lassen	5.0	16.9	10.8	36.9	21.4	5.0	3.1	.9	34.6	168.8	27 336	2 992	1 104	249	146	1 092	909
Los Angeles	7.7	20.3	10.3	32.6	19.4	5.2	3.4	1.1	32.0	97.7	4 637 062	930 957	76 988	1 137 500	27 053	2 239 997	469 781
Madera	7.7	22.0	9.9	29.1	20.4	6.2	3.7	1.1	32.7	91.8	76 612	5 072	3 212	1 566	210	29 979	6 458
Marin	5.4	14.9	5.5	31.0	29.7	6.8	4.9	1.9	41.3	98.2	207 800	7 142	1 061	11 203	388	11 116	8 579
Mariposa	4.4	17.2	6.9	25.1	29.2	9.8	5.8	1.6	42.9	104.7	15 234	114	602	122	22	457	579
Mendocino	6.0	19.6	8.1	25.6	27.1	6.9	4.9	1.7	38.9	98.9	69 671	536	4 103	1 038	126	7 427	3 364
Merced	8.9	25.6	10.3	27.9	17.8	5.3	3.2	1.0	29.0	99.3	118 350	8 064	2 510	14 321	396	55 013	11 900
Modoc	5.6	20.1	5.7	23.3	27.7	9.6	6.3	1.7	41.8	102.4	8 120	65	398	58	7	538	263
Mono	5.7	17.3	10.3	33.4	25.6	5.2	1.9	.5	36.0	121.8	10 818	61	309	143	11	1 222	289
Monterey	7.8	20.6	10.9	31.4	19.3	5.3	3.5	1.2	31.7	107.3	224 682	15 050	4 202	24 245	1 789	111 782	20 012
Napa	6.1	18.1	8.5	27.7	24.3	7.0	6.0	2.4	38.3	99.6	99 396	1 645	1 045	3 694	289	13 604	4 606
Nevada	4.7	18.4	6.1	24.1	29.3	9.1	6.5	1.9	43.1	98.3	85 948	259	814	715	81	1 782	2 434
Orange	7.6	19.4	9.4	33.2	20.6	5.2	3.4	1.2	33.3	99.0	1 844 652	47 649	19 906	386 785	8 938	421 208	117 151
Placer	6.4	20.1	6.9	29.0	24.5	7.0	4.7	1.5	38.0	96.4	220 053	2 031	2 199	7 317	386	8 432	7 981
Plumas	4.5	18.2	6.0	22.6	30.8	10.2	6.0	1.6	44.2	99.8	19 113	130	530	110	20	377	544
Riverside	7.9	22.5	9.2	28.9	18.9	6.7	4.6	1.4	33.1	99.1	1 013 478	96 421	18 168	56 954	3 902	288 868	67 596
Sacramento	7.3	20.3	9.5	31.0	20.9	5.8	4.0	1.3	33.8	95.9	783 240	121 804	13 359	134 899	7 264	91 541	71 392
San Benito	8.8	23.4	8.8	31.5	19.3	4.5	2.8	.9	31.4	102.5	34 695	573	616	1 277	99	13 237	2 737
San Bernardino	8.4	23.9	10.3	30.2	18.7	4.8	2.9	.9	30.3	99.6	1 006 960	155 348	19 915	80 217	5 110	355 843	86 041
San Diego	7.1	18.7	11.3	32.0	19.8	5.7	4.2	1.3	33.2	101.2	1 871 839	161 480	24 337	249 802	13 561	360 847	131 967
San Francisco	4.1	10.5	9.1	40.5	22.3	6.9	4.9	1.8	36.5	103.4	385 728	60 515	3 458	239 565	3 844	50 368	33 255
San Joaquin	8.0	23.0	10.0	28.8	19.6	5.4	3.8	1.3	31.9	99.9	327 607	37 689	6 377	64 283	1 955	91 613	34 074
San Luis Obispo	5.0	16.6	13.6	27.0	23.3	7.3	5.4	1.7	37.3	105.6	208 699	5 002	2 335	6 568	286	15 312	8 479
San Mateo	6.4	16.5	7.9	33.2	23.5	6.3	4.5	1.6	36.8	97.8	420 683	24 840	3 140	141 684	9 403	71 910	35 501
Santa Barbara	6.5	18.4	13.3	29.0	20.1	6.3	4.6	1.7	33.4	100.1	290 418	9 195	4 784	16 344	700	60 683	17 223
Santa Clara	7.1	17.7	9.3	35.4	21.0	5.2	3.3	1.1	34.0	102.8	905 660	47 182	11 350	430 095	5 773	204 088	78 437
Santa Cruz	6.1	17.7	11.9	30.8	23.5	4.8	3.6	1.5	35.0	99.7	191 931	2 477	2 461	8 789	382	38 301	11 171
Shasta	5.9	20.2	8.2	25.3	25.2	7.9	5.5	1.8	38.9	95.1	145 826	1 225	4 528	3 048	178	2 790	5 661
Sierra	4.1	19.2	4.8	24.0	30.2	9.5	5.9	2.4	43.7	102.0	3 348	7	67	6	3	37	87
Siskiyou	5.1	18.9	6.7	22.7	28.4	9.5	6.6	2.0	43.0	96.5	38 573	580	1 726	526	57	1 224	1 615
Solano	7.3	21.1	9.2	31.3	21.7	5.1	3.4	1.0	33.9	101.5	222 387	58 827	3 110	50 299	3 078	31 612	25 229
Sonoma	6.0	18.4	8.8	29.2	24.9	6.0	4.9	1.8	37.5	97.0	374 209	6 522	5 389	14 098	934	38 717	18 745
Stanislaus	8.0	23.2	9.8	29.0	19.5	5.5	3.7	1.3	31.7	96.8	309 901	11 521	5 676	18 848	1 529	75 187	24 335
Sutter	7.3	21.7	9.2	28.2	21.3	6.8	4.1	1.5	34.1	98.0	53 291	1 509	1 225	8 884	161	10 232	3 628
Tehama	6.3	21.1	7.8	25.7	23.2	8.4	5.7	1.8	37.8	97.7	47 518	318	1 178	440	55	4 631	1 899
Trinity	4.2	18.6	5.1	22.7	32.1	10.3	5.6	1.3	44.6	104.2	11 573	58	631	61	15	114	570
Tulare	8.9	24.8	10.6	27.6	18.2	5.2	3.4	1.2	29.2	100.0	213 751	5 852	5 737	12 018	408	113 317	16 938
Tuolumne	4.5	16.2	7.6	25.3	27.9	10.2	6.5	1.8	42.9	111.5	48 750	1 146	992	395	91	1 577	1 550
Ventura	7.5	21.0	9.0	30.7	21.7	5.3	3.6	1.2	34.2	99.7	526 721	14 664	7 106	40 284	1 671	133 178	29 573
Yolo	6.5	18.7	18.3	28.2	18.9	4.8	3.4	1.2	29.5	95.6	114 129	3 425	1 953	16 614	507	23 214	8 818
Yuba	8.2	22.8	10.7	28.0	19.6	6.0	3.6	1.0	31.4	101.6	42 537	1 904	1 569	4 519	123	5 989	3 578
COLORADO	6.9	18.7	10.0	32.6	22.2	5.3	3.3	1.1	34.3	101.4	3 560 005	165 063	44 241	95 213	4 621	309 931	122 187
Adams	8.4	20.1	10.3	34.0	19.4	4.7	2.4	.7	31.4	102.8	281 231	10 818	4 321	11 662	434	42 698	12 693
Alamosa	6.9	20.3	15.9	26.7	20.6	5.1	3.1	1.4	30.6	99.0	10 654	145	350	122	28	3 044	623
Arapahoe	6.9	19.8	8.6	33.1	23.0	4.6	3.0	1.0	34.5	97.1	390 048	37 428	3 234	19 259	586	22 001	15 411
Archuleta	5.4	20.0	6.3	26.1	30.4	8.1	3.0	.7	40.8	102.7	8 743	35	139	31	3	690	257
Baca	5.9	18.6	5.9	22.7	24.5	10.6	8.6	3.3	42.9	99.0	4 234	2	54	7	4	135	81
Bent	5.9	17.8	9.3	29.2	21.8	8.2	5.8	1.9	37.3	129.0	4 770	219	134	34	–	615	226
Boulder	6.0	16.9	13.4	33.6	22.3	4.2	2.6	1.0	33.4	102.2	257 909	2 559	1 787	8 915	171	13 596	6 351
Chaffee	4.4	15.3	7.7	28.0	27.5	9.9	5.5	1.7	41.8	113.6	14 771	257	177	71	8	684	274
Cheyenne	6.4	22.4	7.1	26.2	21.3	7.4	6.5	2.7	37.9	100.6	2 072	11	17	3	–	114	14
Clear Creek	5.7	16.8	5.6	32.6	32.2	4.4	2.1	.5	40.2	108.8	8 984	26	68	34	3	95	112
Conejos	7.9	24.3	8.5	23.6	20.8	8.3	4.9	1.8	34.2	98.5	6 112	18	142	13	6	1 806	303
Costilla	5.7	19.4	6.6	23.3	28.3	9.8	5.5	1.5	42.1	99.8	2 231	29	91	37	5	1 079	191
Crowley	4.4	14.4	9.9	39.6	20.8	5.7	3.6	1.5	36.6	205.4	4 577	389	143	45	1	263	100
Custer	5.5	17.0	4.5	23.3	35.0	10.1	3.9	.8	44.9	104.3	3 359	13	39	10	–	25	57

[1] Includes all other responses not included in the other five race categories shown. Also includes write-in entries such as multiracial, mixed, interracial, or a Hispanic/Latino group. [2] Refers to combinations of two or more of the six race categories shown under one race.

Source: Population by Age, Sex, and Race—U.S. Census Bureau; 2000 Census of Population and Housing, "Census 2000 Profiles of General Demographic Characteristics" data files, published May 2001 (related Internet site <http://www.census.gov/mp/www/pub/2000cen/mscen01.html>).

[Includes U.S., states, and 3,142 counties/county equivalents defined as of January 1, 1992. For changes to these areas since January 1, 1992, see appendix B. Geographic Information]

County	Population by age, 2000 (April 1) Percent— Under 5 years	5 to 17 years	18 to 24 years	25 to 44 years	45 to 64 years	65 to 74 years	75 to 84 years	85 years and over	Median age (years)	Males per 100 females, 2000 (April 1)	White	Black or African American	American Indian and Alaska Native	Asian	Native Hawaiian and Other Pacific Islander	Some other race[1]	Two or more races[2]
COLORADO—Con.																	
Delta	5.8	18.3	6.3	23.6	26.5	10.2	6.8	2.6	42.3	100.8	25 688	146	211	89	7	1 184	509
Denver	6.8	15.1	10.7	36.1	20.0	5.5	4.2	1.5	33.1	102.1	362 180	61 649	7 290	15 611	648	86 464	20 794
Dolores	5.0	16.9	6.8	26.3	27.8	9.4	5.9	1.8	42.4	107.2	1 757	1	36	7	1	11	31
Douglas	9.6	21.9	4.8	37.9	21.6	2.7	1.2	.3	33.7	99.7	163 064	1 676	716	4 404	97	2 513	3 296
Eagle	7.1	16.4	11.4	42.1	20.0	2.1	.7	.2	31.2	121.0	35 558	142	296	342	30	4 498	793
Elbert	6.6	23.6	5.5	32.8	25.5	3.7	1.7	.5	37.2	100.6	18 923	128	125	74	18	255	349
El Paso	7.6	20.0	10.5	32.5	20.7	4.9	2.9	.9	33.0	100.9	419 673	33 670	4 725	13 099	1 256	24 293	20 213
Fremont	4.8	15.8	7.5	33.4	24.0	7.7	4.9	1.9	38.8	133.9	41 311	2 464	706	232	26	564	842
Garfield	7.5	19.7	9.0	33.0	22.1	4.9	2.9	1.0	34.2	105.6	39 394	196	310	191	35	2 861	804
Gilpin	5.7	15.5	5.8	37.4	30.0	3.9	1.5	.3	38.3	112.7	4 489	25	39	33	9	73	89
Grand	5.8	16.0	9.0	34.7	26.8	5.4	1.8	.6	36.9	112.7	11 839	60	54	85	12	249	143
Gunnison	4.6	13.3	21.1	32.9	21.2	4.2	2.0	.7	30.4	118.3	13 269	68	98	75	5	201	240
Hinsdale	6.1	13.4	4.7	29.5	34.7	8.1	2.8	.8	43.9	105.7	769	–	12	2	–	3	4
Huerfano	4.4	16.6	7.3	27.4	27.4	8.3	6.5	2.2	41.7	118.8	6 365	216	212	31	6	740	292
Jackson	5.6	19.9	5.4	26.9	29.1	8.1	3.9	1.1	40.5	101.4	1 517	4	12	1	–	23	20
Jefferson	6.3	19.0	8.1	32.1	24.9	5.4	3.2	1.1	36.8	99.0	477 454	4 677	3 971	12 036	409	17 043	11 466
Kiowa	6.0	19.9	7.3	24.7	24.6	7.5	7.3	2.8	39.7	100.0	1 559	8	18	–	1	23	13
Kit Carson	6.1	20.6	7.5	29.0	22.2	7.1	5.2	2.3	37.4	112.2	6 992	139	41	26	3	737	73
Lake	7.8	19.0	12.8	33.1	20.6	4.1	1.8	.7	30.5	115.8	6 062	14	98	24	4	1 405	205
La Plata	5.1	17.6	13.9	29.0	25.1	5.3	3.0	1.0	35.6	103.6	38 364	136	2 539	177	24	1 712	989
Larimer	6.1	17.7	14.2	30.7	21.8	5.1	3.3	1.2	33.2	99.9	229 976	1 650	1 668	3 917	193	8 575	5 515
Las Animas	5.6	18.7	7.9	24.0	25.9	8.9	6.3	2.8	40.9	95.8	12 566	60	387	57	30	1 525	582
Lincoln	5.0	18.9	7.1	33.0	21.8	6.9	5.1	2.3	37.8	130.9	5 253	302	57	34	2	344	95
Logan	6.3	18.4	10.8	28.3	21.7	7.3	5.2	2.0	36.5	112.0	18 792	420	131	82	14	772	293
Mesa	6.3	18.8	9.4	26.7	23.7	7.9	5.4	1.8	38.1	96.0	107 349	537	1 059	618	112	4 261	2 319
Mineral	4.5	16.0	4.7	24.8	32.7	10.5	6.1	.7	45.0	104.2	805	–	7	–	–	1	18
Moffat	6.8	21.7	8.6	29.9	23.8	5.2	3.0	1.2	35.4	107.7	12 341	28	116	44	3	418	234
Montezuma	6.9	20.6	7.1	26.3	25.3	7.7	4.7	1.5	38.0	96.7	19 474	33	2 676	48	15	1 016	568
Montrose	6.8	20.0	7.2	25.8	25.0	7.8	5.3	2.1	38.8	97.0	30 074	102	340	140	23	1 920	833
Morgan	8.5	21.9	8.5	28.2	19.8	6.5	4.6	2.0	33.5	100.4	21 642	91	221	47	46	4 449	675
Otero	6.5	20.4	8.9	24.4	23.4	8.6	5.5	2.3	37.7	95.6	16 049	154	290	142	16	3 059	601
Ouray	4.8	17.7	4.1	27.2	34.1	8.0	3.3	.9	43.4	102.1	3 605	3	35	13	2	20	64
Park	5.7	17.8	5.1	33.4	30.6	5.2	1.7	.3	40.0	107.1	13 807	72	134	60	4	179	267
Phillips	6.9	20.0	6.3	25.3	22.2	9.1	6.5	3.8	39.8	93.4	4 168	9	13	18	1	211	60
Pitkin	4.1	12.5	7.7	38.3	30.5	4.7	1.7	.4	38.4	115.1	14 029	79	40	167	6	352	199
Prowers	7.9	22.2	10.7	26.5	20.2	6.4	4.4	1.8	32.4	101.0	11 379	43	177	54	4	2 487	339
Pueblo	6.7	19.1	9.4	27.2	22.4	8.0	5.3	1.8	36.7	95.8	112 430	2 685	2 251	926	94	18 298	4 788
Rio Blanco	5.7	20.8	9.2	27.5	25.6	6.3	3.5	1.4	37.5	101.9	5 687	11	46	17	–	121	104
Rio Grande	7.0	21.2	8.0	25.3	23.9	7.6	5.2	1.9	37.3	97.1	9 177	43	157	28	3	2 662	343
Routt	5.5	17.1	10.1	36.5	25.7	3.0	1.5	.5	35.0	116.6	19 079	25	96	76	18	144	252
Saguache	6.8	21.6	7.9	26.0	26.9	6.1	3.7	1.0	36.9	101.7	4 218	7	122	27	–	1 361	182
San Juan	4.7	15.4	4.3	28.1	40.5	4.3	2.7	–	43.7	110.6	542	–	4	1	2	4	5
San Miguel	4.5	13.1	9.9	43.3	25.8	2.3	.7	.3	34.2	120.8	6 170	19	56	49	5	222	73
Sedgwick	5.6	17.1	6.6	23.5	25.0	11.0	7.8	3.3	43.2	100.1	2 486	14	4	21	2	164	56
Summit	5.3	12.0	15.7	44.3	19.4	2.6	.6	.1	30.8	139.0	21 626	160	112	205	17	933	495
Teller	5.7	20.2	5.6	31.2	29.8	5.3	1.8	.4	39.4	102.7	19 510	113	200	120	16	185	411
Washington	6.2	20.3	6.3	24.8	24.2	9.7	6.5	2.0	40.2	103.4	4 748	2	28	5	1	100	42
Weld	7.8	20.4	13.2	29.7	20.0	4.8	3.0	1.1	30.9	100.6	147 834	1 022	1 581	1 508	150	24 044	4 797
Yuma	6.6	21.7	7.1	26.0	22.3	8.2	5.5	2.6	37.3	96.8	9 267	11	28	7	2	407	119
CONNECTICUT	6.6	18.2	8.0	30.3	23.2	6.8	5.1	1.9	37.4	93.9	2 780 355	309 843	9 639	82 313	1 366	147 201	74 848
Fairfield	7.3	18.4	7.0	30.9	23.3	6.8	4.7	1.8	37.3	93.4	699 992	88 362	1 736	28 689	366	41 471	21 951
Hartford	6.4	18.2	7.8	29.8	23.2	7.1	5.5	2.0	37.7	92.7	659 192	99 936	1 984	20 775	370	55 127	19 799
Litchfield	5.9	18.8	5.7	29.8	25.7	7.0	5.3	2.0	39.6	95.6	174 484	1 998	319	2 137	43	1 235	1 977
Middlesex	6.2	17.0	7.3	31.1	24.8	6.7	4.9	2.0	38.6	95.1	141 555	6 856	269	2 419	58	1 497	2 417
New Haven	6.4	18.0	8.7	30.0	22.4	6.8	5.6	2.1	37.0	92.5	654 244	93 239	2 035	19 220	290	37 160	17 820
New London	6.3	18.1	8.6	31.2	22.8	6.7	4.7	1.6	37.0	97.9	225 406	13 703	2 487	5 075	151	5 319	6 947
Tolland	5.9	17.2	12.9	30.7	23.2	5.4	3.6	1.1	35.7	100.6	125 915	3 708	290	3 090	43	1 477	1 841
Windham	6.1	19.0	9.6	30.3	22.7	6.1	4.5	1.8	36.3	97.3	99 567	2 041	519	908	45	3 915	2 096
DELAWARE	6.6	18.3	9.6	30.2	22.4	7.2	4.4	1.3	36.0	94.4	584 773	150 666	2 731	16 259	283	15 855	13 033
Kent	7.2	20.0	10.1	29.8	21.2	6.6	3.8	1.2	34.4	93.1	93 106	26 180	806	2 137	50	1 611	2 807
New Castle	6.7	18.3	10.3	31.5	21.7	6.2	4.1	1.3	35.0	94.4	365 810	101 167	979	12 950	165	11 087	8 107
Sussex	5.8	16.8	7.0	26.3	25.6	10.9	6.0	1.6	41.1	95.5	125 857	23 319	946	1 172	68	3 157	2 119
DISTRICT OF COLUMBIA	5.7	14.4	12.7	33.1	21.9	6.3	4.4	1.6	34.6	89.0	176 101	343 312	1 713	15 189	348	21 950	13 446
District of Columbia	5.7	14.4	12.7	33.1	21.9	6.3	4.4	1.6	34.6	89.0	176 101	343 312	1 713	15 189	348	21 950	13 446

[1] Includes all other responses not included in the other five race categories shown. Also includes write-in entries such as multiracial, mixed, interracial, or a Hispanic/Latino group.   [2] Refers to combinations of two or more of the six race categories shown under one race.

Source: Population by Age, Sex, and Race—U.S. Census Bureau; 2000 Census of Population and Housing, "Census 2000 Profiles of General Demographic Characteristics" data files, published May 2001 (related Internet site <http://www.census.gov/mp/www/pub/2000cen/mscen01.html>).

Table B–2. Counties — **Population by Age, Sex, and Race**–Con.

[Includes U.S., states, and 3,142 counties/county equivalents defined as of January 1, 1992. For changes to these areas since January 1, 1992, see appendix B. Geographic Information]

County	Under 5 years	5 to 17 years	18 to 24 years	25 to 44 years	45 to 64 years	65 to 74 years	75 to 84 years	85 years and over	Median age (years)	Males per 100 females, 2000 (April 1)	White	Black or African American	American Indian and Alaska Native	Asian	Native Hawaiian and Other Pacific Islander	Some other race[1]	Two or more races[2]
FLORIDA	5.9	16.9	8.3	28.6	22.7	9.1	6.4	2.1	38.7	95.3	12 465 029	2 335 505	53 541	266 256	8 625	477 107	376 315
Alachua	5.1	15.0	23.2	27.7	19.3	5.0	3.5	1.1	29.0	95.4	160 128	42 062	538	7 709	64	3 045	4 409
Baker	7.0	20.5	9.9	30.7	22.7	5.8	2.6	.8	34.0	110.6	18 707	3 098	85	89	7	55	218
Bay	6.1	18.0	8.7	30.2	23.7	7.9	4.3	1.2	37.4	98.1	124 761	15 772	1 159	2 561	115	980	2 869
Bradford	5.5	16.4	9.5	32.1	23.5	7.0	4.5	1.5	37.2	127.0	19 900	5 423	88	158	25	170	324
Brevard	5.2	16.8	6.8	27.1	24.3	10.9	7.1	1.9	41.4	95.9	413 411	40 000	1 765	7 152	305	5 168	8 429
Broward	6.3	17.2	7.2	31.4	21.7	7.2	6.2	2.7	37.8	93.3	1 145 287	333 304	3 867	36 581	916	48 642	54 421
Calhoun	5.9	17.3	9.0	31.5	22.3	7.3	4.6	2.0	36.2	117.2	10 397	2 056	164	69	7	135	189
Charlotte	3.7	12.0	4.5	18.8	26.4	18.4	12.7	3.6	54.3	91.4	131 125	6 219	312	1 207	40	1 116	1 608
Citrus	3.8	13.4	4.6	19.1	26.9	17.4	11.6	3.2	52.6	92.3	112 236	2 791	423	901	33	439	1 262
Clay	6.6	21.4	7.9	30.3	24.0	5.6	3.2	1.0	35.9	97.0	123 128	9 439	658	2 797	118	1 843	2 831
Collier	5.3	14.5	6.6	24.6	24.5	14.0	8.4	2.1	44.1	100.3	216 345	11 419	733	1 569	153	15 554	5 604
Columbia	6.4	18.9	9.0	27.7	24.0	8.0	4.7	1.3	37.3	102.9	45 053	9 623	302	378	20	337	800
Dade	6.5	18.3	9.1	31.0	21.7	7.2	4.4	1.7	35.6	93.5	1 570 558	457 214	4 365	31 753	799	103 251	85 422
DeSoto	5.8	16.9	11.2	26.7	20.5	10.6	6.7	1.7	36.5	128.3	23 619	4 098	511	131	13	3 378	459
Dixie	5.6	16.5	7.9	26.6	26.2	10.7	5.3	1.2	40.7	113.9	12 279	1 241	64	34	4	62	143
Duval	7.2	19.1	9.6	32.4	21.2	5.6	3.7	1.2	34.1	94.2	512 469	216 780	2 598	21 137	466	10 170	15 259
Escambia	6.1	17.4	12.2	29.0	22.0	7.3	4.6	1.4	35.4	98.6	213 008	63 010	2 660	6 519	339	2 506	6 368
Flagler	4.1	13.8	4.8	20.3	28.3	17.1	9.6	1.9	50.4	92.1	43 490	4 401	133	583	12	480	733
Franklin	4.6	13.4	7.6	30.8	27.8	8.9	5.0	1.9	40.8	129.6	8 983	1 804	50	22	2	48	148
Gadsden	6.7	19.7	9.5	28.9	20.3	6.8	4.0	1.5	35.5	90.7	17 448	25 763	105	117	9	1 243	402
Gilchrist	5.7	18.7	14.2	24.8	22.9	7.9	4.4	1.3	35.4	112.5	13 068	1 010	53	24	1	99	182
Glades	5.8	16.3	7.6	27.0	24.5	11.9	5.6	1.3	40.2	121.5	8 142	1 114	521	35	2	595	167
Gulf	5.1	16.7	6.8	29.4	26.0	9.6	5.1	1.5	40.3	114.6	10 651	2 259	86	53	6	70	207
Hamilton	6.3	17.2	10.8	31.8	22.8	6.4	3.5	1.3	35.1	135.0	7 835	5 027	56	26	2	225	156
Hardee	7.7	19.9	11.0	28.3	19.2	7.9	4.8	1.2	32.7	119.1	19 035	2 244	184	81	15	4 847	532
Hendry	7.8	22.2	13.3	28.3	18.3	5.9	3.2	.9	29.5	125.0	23 926	5 340	291	162	12	5 312	1 167
Hernando	4.5	14.4	5.4	20.4	24.4	16.3	11.9	2.6	49.5	90.5	121 453	5 330	391	840	29	1 285	1 474
Highlands	4.8	14.3	6.3	19.3	22.2	17.1	12.7	3.2	50.0	95.2	72 926	8 155	387	917	29	3 614	1 338
Hillsborough	6.9	18.5	9.3	31.7	21.7	6.4	4.3	1.3	35.1	95.8	750 903	149 423	3 879	21 947	727	46 539	25 530
Holmes	5.5	17.5	8.8	29.3	24.0	7.9	4.9	2.0	37.5	112.9	16 669	1 208	188	72	6	147	274
Indian River	4.7	14.6	6.0	22.3	23.3	14.6	11.5	3.1	47.0	93.7	98 754	9 253	277	838	30	2 428	1 367
Jackson	5.5	16.9	9.7	29.6	23.8	7.7	4.9	1.9	37.6	110.4	32 811	12 418	311	168	13	381	653
Jefferson	5.3	17.4	8.2	28.9	25.7	7.7	5.0	1.8	39.4	104.1	7 647	4 947	50	39	5	73	141
Lafayette	5.5	16.1	10.7	34.0	21.3	7.1	4.0	1.3	34.8	148.8	5 566	1 009	50	0	1	002	05
Lake	5.2	15.1	5.8	23.8	23.8	14.4	9.3	2.7	45.1	93.7	184 138	17 503	701	1 667	76	3 966	2 477
Lee	5.2	14.4	6.2	24.0	24.8	13.7	9.2	2.5	45.2	95.6	386 598	29 035	1 248	3 400	209	13 545	6 853
Leon	5.7	15.6	21.4	28.9	20.0	4.4	2.9	1.0	29.5	91.1	158 893	69 704	689	4 562	106	1 864	3 634
Levy	5.7	17.9	6.9	25.0	26.6	10.3	6.0	1.5	41.1	94.0	29 586	3 778	161	129	10	331	455
Liberty	5.5	16.3	9.4	37.7	21.0	6.2	3.2	.8	35.0	144.9	5 365	1 294	127	10	–	146	79
Madison	5.7	19.5	9.2	28.2	22.7	7.5	5.0	2.0	36.3	107.6	10 769	7 549	60	60	4	96	195
Manatee	5.6	15.1	6.5	24.6	23.3	12.5	9.4	2.9	43.6	93.5	227 981	21 611	728	2 365	134	7 506	3 677
Marion	5.2	16.2	6.4	23.8	23.9	13.6	8.8	2.1	43.8	93.3	217 909	29 900	1 158	1 806	57	4 363	3 723
Martin	4.4	14.2	5.3	22.9	24.9	14.2	11.0	3.1	47.3	96.4	113 912	6 673	382	756	121	3 445	1 442
Monroe	4.3	12.7	6.3	31.1	30.9	8.5	4.9	1.2	42.6	113.9	72 151	3 795	301	657	35	1 232	1 418
Nassau	6.2	18.9	7.2	28.8	26.3	7.9	3.7	.9	38.3	97.3	51 909	4 465	246	263	18	185	577
Okaloosa	6.4	18.4	9.6	31.1	22.4	7.4	3.8	.9	36.1	102.2	142 218	15 508	1 030	4 205	232	2 264	5 041
Okeechobee	6.3	18.9	9.5	27.1	21.9	9.5	5.4	1.4	36.7	115.5	28 468	2 844	193	240	16	3 434	715
Orange	6.8	18.4	10.9	33.8	20.0	5.5	3.5	1.1	33.3	98.0	614 830	162 899	3 079	30 033	843	53 889	30 771
Osceola	6.8	20.0	9.3	31.0	21.6	6.4	3.8	1.1	34.6	97.2	133 169	12 702	790	3 802	142	15 631	6 257
Palm Beach	5.6	15.7	6.6	27.0	22.0	10.8	9.2	3.1	41.8	93.5	894 207	156 055	2 466	17 127	692	33 709	26 928
Pasco	5.3	14.9	5.8	24.1	23.1	12.9	10.7	3.1	44.9	92.2	323 036	7 148	1 209	3 251	111	5 251	4 759
Pinellas	4.9	14.3	6.4	27.3	24.5	10.5	8.7	3.4	43.0	91.0	791 111	82 556	2 719	18 984	484	10 482	15 146
Polk	6.4	18.0	8.3	26.4	22.5	9.9	6.5	1.9	38.6	96.3	385 099	65 545	1 839	4 515	207	18 466	8 253
Putnam	6.1	18.4	7.7	24.2	25.1	10.8	6.2	1.5	40.5	97.6	54 868	12 003	297	311	29	2 071	844
St. Johns	5.4	17.7	7.0	27.6	26.4	8.8	5.6	1.6	40.6	94.5	111 955	7 744	326	1 172	67	675	1 196
St. Lucie	5.6	17.0	6.6	25.1	23.0	12.3	8.4	2.1	42.0	95.5	152 504	29 714	464	1 829	103	4 573	3 508
Santa Rosa	6.5	20.0	7.2	31.1	24.1	6.9	3.3	.8	36.8	100.6	106 822	5 000	1 185	1 525	100	785	2 326
Sarasota	3.9	12.3	5.0	21.7	25.6	15.2	12.2	4.0	50.5	90.0	301 985	13 621	717	2 522	92	3 708	3 312
Seminole	6.3	19.0	8.4	32.0	23.6	5.9	3.7	1.1	36.2	95.9	300 948	34 764	1 087	9 115	163	11 175	7 944
Sumter	4.0	12.1	5.9	23.3	27.3	17.8	8.0	1.6	49.2	113.1	44 061	7 351	270	220	28	621	794
Suwannee	6.0	18.0	8.5	25.1	25.4	9.4	5.5	2.0	39.7	95.4	29 455	4 221	137	179	13	391	448
Taylor	5.9	18.7	8.2	28.3	24.8	8.3	4.3	1.5	37.8	104.4	14 988	3 666	188	85	3	61	265
Union	5.5	16.4	8.7	39.8	22.2	4.7	2.1	.6	35.7	183.0	9 896	3 070	89	42	3	140	202
Volusia	4.9	15.4	8.2	25.3	24.2	11.3	8.2	2.6	42.4	94.5	381 760	41 198	1 373	4 430	164	8 071	6 347
Wakulla	5.9	19.7	7.6	31.7	24.7	6.4	3.0	.9	36.8	107.3	19 684	2 631	136	57	7	66	282
Walton	5.3	16.3	7.1	28.5	26.9	9.6	4.9	1.4	40.5	105.2	35 896	2 832	520	183	18	305	847
Washington	6.0	17.3	7.7	28.5	24.7	8.4	5.3	2.0	38.8	105.8	17 140	2 872	322	76	13	121	429

[1] Includes all other responses not included in the other five race categories shown. Also includes write-in entries such as multiracial, mixed, interracial, or a Hispanic/Latino group. [2] Refers to combinations of two or more of the six race categories shown under one race.

Source: Population by Age, Sex, and Race—U.S. Census Bureau; 2000 Census of Population and Housing, "Census 2000 Profiles of General Demographic Characteristics" data files, published May 2001 (related Internet site <http://www.census.gov/mp/www/pub/2000cen/mscen01.html>).

[Includes U.S., states, and 3,142 counties/county equivalents defined as of January 1, 1992. For changes to these areas since January 1, 1992, see appendix B. Geographic Information]

County	Population by age, 2000 (April 1) — Percent—								Median age (years)	Males per 100 females, 2000 (April 1)	Population by race, 2000 (April 1) — One race						Two or more races[2]
	Under 5 years	5 to 17 years	18 to 24 years	25 to 44 years	45 to 64 years	65 to 74 years	75 to 84 years	85 years and over			White	Black or African American	American Indian and Alaska Native	Asian	Native Hawaiian and Other Pacific Islander	Some other race[1]	
GEORGIA	7.3	19.2	10.2	32.4	21.3	5.3	3.2	1.1	33.4	96.8	5 327 281	2 349 542	21 737	173 170	4 246	196 289	114 188
Appling	7.3	19.8	9.0	28.5	23.5	6.6	4.0	1.3	35.4	97.1	13 376	3 412	36	52	2	434	107
Atkinson	9.5	20.9	10.9	29.6	19.9	5.1	3.0	1.1	30.7	98.0	5 082	1 492	28	9	2	915	81
Bacon	7.5	18.7	9.9	28.0	23.0	7.5	4.2	1.1	34.8	96.1	8 232	1 586	15	30	–	148	92
Baker	7.2	20.1	10.0	26.9	22.1	7.6	4.2	1.9	35.0	86.2	1 932	2 053	9	–	1	54	25
Baldwin	5.1	16.6	14.5	31.2	21.9	6.0	3.4	1.2	34.2	117.3	24 215	19 392	96	450	3	213	331
Banks	7.5	18.6	8.9	30.7	23.7	6.2	3.4	.9	35.2	102.0	13 435	464	43	87	9	282	102
Barrow	8.3	20.2	8.5	34.5	19.5	4.9	3.0	1.1	32.5	98.9	39 149	4 483	139	1 014	18	693	648
Bartow	7.8	20.1	8.3	33.0	21.4	5.5	3.0	1.0	33.7	97.7	66 734	6 600	214	386	21	1 228	836
Ben Hill	7.3	20.2	9.7	27.0	22.5	6.7	4.7	1.9	34.8	91.8	11 059	5 706	36	49	–	499	135
Berrien	7.1	20.2	8.6	28.7	22.9	6.9	4.1	1.5	35.2	96.5	13 877	1 856	43	48	13	249	149
Bibb	7.4	19.1	10.1	29.0	21.7	6.6	4.6	1.5	34.7	85.2	77 147	72 818	272	1 658	36	714	1 242
Bleckley	6.4	20.2	11.3	26.5	22.1	7.4	4.7	1.4	35.1	93.0	8 544	2 869	11	109	3	56	74
Brantley	7.4	21.0	8.5	29.9	23.2	6.4	2.9	.8	34.6	100.8	13 804	582	20	13	1	51	158
Brooks	6.5	20.4	8.9	26.9	22.3	7.4	5.2	2.4	36.3	92.2	9 436	6 472	50	43	4	290	155
Bryan	7.7	23.4	8.0	31.9	21.6	4.3	2.2	.8	33.3	98.2	19 386	3 311	74	181	16	135	314
Bulloch	5.8	16.5	26.2	24.8	17.4	5.0	3.2	1.1	26.1	94.9	38 460	16 101	72	461	15	446	428
Burke	8.0	23.3	9.1	27.3	21.4	5.8	3.6	1.5	33.0	90.3	10 433	11 343	51	57	3	141	215
Butts	6.3	17.8	9.2	33.0	23.5	5.9	3.1	1.2	35.9	114.1	13 514	5 627	76	50	4	66	185
Calhoun	6.0	16.0	11.3	33.3	20.8	6.2	4.5	1.8	35.6	130.1	2 418	3 830	9	4	–	28	31
Camden	8.7	23.0	12.9	33.9	16.3	3.2	1.5	.4	28.2	107.0	32 765	8 783	216	441	37	599	823
Candler	7.2	19.7	9.4	26.1	22.5	7.2	5.5	2.5	35.6	100.6	6 268	2 593	18	27	3	590	78
Carroll	7.1	18.9	12.9	29.9	21.2	5.5	3.3	1.2	32.5	95.1	70 265	14 241	232	538	16	980	996
Catoosa	6.8	19.0	8.1	30.8	23.4	7.1	3.7	1.1	35.8	93.8	51 356	669	163	379	10	210	495
Charlton	6.5	20.9	10.6	31.7	20.6	5.6	3.1	1.0	33.4	112.4	7 052	3 008	43	35	6	14	124
Chatham	6.7	18.3	11.2	29.5	21.4	6.8	4.6	1.5	34.4	93.0	128 279	93 971	580	4 013	151	2 073	2 981
Chattahoochee	8.4	20.0	27.9	36.4	5.5	1.2	.6	.1	23.2	171.7	8 643	4 453	119	268	67	771	561
Chattooga	6.5	16.4	10.0	30.0	22.8	7.8	5.0	1.4	36.5	106.6	22 084	2 856	20	31	5	214	260
Cherokee	8.2	20.0	7.7	35.8	21.7	3.9	2.1	.6	34.0	100.7	131 128	3 525	534	1 141	42	3 702	1 831
Clarke	5.2	12.6	31.3	27.4	15.4	4.1	2.9	1.0	25.4	95.3	65 852	27 656	214	3 173	45	3 123	1 426
Clay	6.6	19.2	8.0	21.0	25.7	10.1	7.0	2.4	41.9	83.3	1 290	2 030	4	9	2	–	22
Clayton	8.3	21.6	10.4	35.4	18.4	3.6	1.8	.5	30.2	94.5	89 741	121 927	751	10 629	155	8 392	4 922
Clinch	7.3	20.5	8.6	29.0	22.7	6.8	3.9	1.1	34.9	98.9	4 741	2 029	35	8	–	7	58
Cobb	7.2	18.8	9.0	36.5	21.5	4.0	2.3	.7	33.2	98.5	439 991	114 233	1 579	18 587	257	21 731	11 373
Coffee	7.8	20.4	11.0	30.3	20.5	5.5	3.3	1.2	32.1	98.6	25 528	9 684	120	210	14	1 513	344
Colquitt	7.6	19.9	10.3	28.0	21.4	6.7	4.7	1.5	33.7	98.1	28 503	9 869	124	105	15	2 966	471
Columbia	6.9	22.7	7.3	31.0	24.1	4.7	2.4	.9	35.4	95.6	73 814	10 011	285	2 997	80	710	1 391
Cook	7.7	20.5	9.1	27.9	21.8	7.1	4.3	1.6	34.3	92.1	10 714	4 587	34	66	5	242	123
Coweta	8.2	20.6	7.6	33.4	21.8	4.9	2.7	.9	33.6	98.0	70 353	16 032	208	610	13	1 089	910
Crawford	6.7	20.9	7.9	31.6	23.7	5.4	2.9	.9	35.2	100.5	9 103	2 974	46	21	2	226	123
Crisp	7.8	21.2	9.2	27.0	21.8	6.9	4.4	1.6	34.4	88.7	11 894	9 547	33	149	7	216	150
Dade	5.9	18.0	11.8	27.8	24.5	7.2	3.8	1.0	36.1	96.0	14 776	96	74	58	4	31	115
Dawson	7.0	18.0	7.6	32.5	25.5	6.3	2.5	.5	36.2	100.9	15 554	57	59	52	6	118	153
Decatur	7.7	20.9	9.1	28.0	21.1	7.2	4.4	1.6	34.4	91.0	16 126	11 270	68	92	11	464	209
De Kalb	7.1	17.5	10.9	36.7	19.7	4.3	2.7	1.0	32.3	94.1	238 521	361 111	1 548	26 718	329	23 517	14 121
Dodge	6.2	19.7	8.7	29.5	22.6	7.1	4.6	1.6	35.8	105.1	13 219	5 637	35	42	4	146	88
Dooly	6.8	18.8	10.3	29.8	22.5	6.1	4.2	1.6	35.1	109.5	5 298	5 709	19	49	13	332	105
Dougherty	7.6	20.0	12.2	27.6	20.9	6.4	3.9	1.3	32.2	87.4	36 315	57 762	225	552	30	470	711
Douglas	7.3	20.3	8.9	33.5	22.4	4.5	2.3	.7	33.8	96.5	71 235	17 065	324	1 080	21	1 122	1 327
Early	7.1	21.6	7.8	25.9	21.9	7.8	5.7	2.3	36.4	87.1	6 212	5 947	25	23	7	44	96
Echols	8.0	21.3	12.5	30.8	18.3	5.7	2.6	.8	29.7	116.1	2 896	260	43	3	1	514	37
Effingham	7.6	22.3	8.2	32.1	21.7	4.7	2.5	.8	33.6	98.7	31 776	4 876	119	170	9	195	390
Elbert	6.4	19.5	8.4	27.2	23.6	8.0	5.1	1.8	37.2	92.2	13 730	6 328	40	50	6	217	140
Emanuel	6.8	21.1	10.4	26.0	22.4	6.8	4.9	1.6	34.0	92.8	13 909	7 267	30	53	1	465	112
Evans	6.9	20.6	10.2	29.0	20.7	6.6	4.3	1.7	34.0	94.6	6 474	3 461	19	33	3	444	61
Fannin	5.4	15.6	7.0	24.9	28.2	11.1	6.1	1.8	43.1	93.5	19 398	24	93	47	1	31	204
Fayette	5.8	23.3	6.5	27.7	27.8	4.9	3.1	.9	38.2	95.8	76 541	10 465	194	2 208	22	694	1 139
Floyd	6.6	18.0	10.8	28.5	22.2	7.4	4.9	1.6	35.7	93.8	73 668	12 050	283	845	83	2 604	1 032
Forsyth	9.5	18.4	6.1	37.1	21.8	4.3	2.1	.7	34.6	102.7	93 531	684	247	785	13	2 236	911
Franklin	6.3	17.6	9.6	27.3	23.8	8.4	5.2	1.7	37.6	94.1	18 153	1 792	42	51	4	84	159
Fulton	7.0	17.5	11.0	35.5	20.7	4.4	2.9	1.2	32.7	97.0	392 598	363 656	1 514	24 823	346	21 216	11 853
Gilmer	7.2	17.2	8.5	28.5	25.6	8.3	3.7	1.2	37.3	103.0	21 963	63	107	55	60	883	325
Glascock	6.8	17.1	7.7	26.8	23.5	8.5	6.5	3.2	39.6	92.5	2 316	212	6	–	–	3	19
Glynn	6.5	18.8	8.2	27.6	24.5	7.8	5.1	1.6	37.9	91.7	47 746	17 874	177	408	32	595	736
Gordon	7.2	18.9	9.5	31.4	22.5	6.1	3.4	1.1	34.1	99.0	39 557	1 527	121	234	24	2 195	446
Grady	7.0	20.2	9.0	27.9	22.6	7.0	4.5	1.7	35.5	90.6	15 285	7 133	217	72	2	758	192
Greene	6.7	18.4	8.7	24.3	27.5	8.4	4.3	1.7	39.1	91.9	7 628	6 403	36	36	9	214	80

[1] Includes all other responses not included in the other five race categories shown. Also includes write-in entries such as multiracial, mixed, interracial, or a Hispanic/Latino group. [2] Refers to combinations of two or more of the six race categories shown under one race.

Source: Population by Age, Sex, and Race—U.S. Census Bureau; 2000 Census of Population and Housing, "Census 2000 Profiles of General Demographic Characteristics" data files, published May 2001 (related Internet site <http://www.census.gov/mp/www/pub/2000cen/mscen01.html>).

[Includes U.S., states, and 3,142 counties/county equivalents defined as of January 1, 1992. For changes to these areas since January 1, 1992, see appendix B. Geographic Information]

County	Population by age, 2000 (April 1) Percent— Under 5 years	5 to 17 years	18 to 24 years	25 to 44 years	45 to 64 years	65 to 74 years	75 to 84 years	85 years and over	Median age (years)	Males per 100 females, 2000 (April 1)	Population by race, 2000 (April 1) One race White	Black or African American	American Indian and Alaska Native	Asian	Native Hawaiian and Other Pacific Islander	Some other race[1]	Two or more races[2]
GEORGIA—Con.																	
Gwinnett	8.0	20.2	8.7	37.5	20.3	3.2	1.7	.5	32.5	101.7	427 883	78 224	1 638	42 360	263	25 407	12 673
Habersham	6.3	17.2	11.1	28.5	23.1	7.8	4.6	1.4	36.4	105.5	31 910	1 610	104	679	37	1 073	489
Hall	8.2	18.7	10.8	32.3	20.6	5.4	3.0	1.0	32.2	103.6	112 470	10 126	479	1 876	239	12 192	1 895
Hancock	5.8	18.3	9.9	31.0	23.0	7.0	3.7	1.3	35.8	114.6	2 162	7 835	16	11	–	14	38
Haralson	6.8	19.2	8.1	29.2	23.6	7.2	4.4	1.4	36.1	95.2	23 885	1 388	65	87	1	52	212
Harris	5.9	19.7	6.3	29.3	26.9	6.9	3.9	1.1	38.5	97.6	18 584	4 614	85	120	5	80	207
Hart	6.3	17.2	7.7	27.3	25.0	9.3	5.5	1.7	39.2	97.0	18 188	4 452	35	122	1	55	144
Heard	7.9	20.8	7.6	30.7	22.0	6.2	3.7	1.1	34.1	96.5	9 633	1 192	35	12	8	52	80
Henry	8.1	21.1	7.4	34.9	21.0	4.5	2.2	.7	33.4	97.3	97 116	17 523	269	2 096	46	945	1 346
Houston	7.0	21.2	9.5	31.8	21.3	5.7	2.9	.7	34.0	96.9	78 170	27 422	376	1 761	69	1 138	1 829
Irwin	6.8	22.0	9.2	26.1	21.9	7.4	4.7	1.9	34.6	96.6	7 148	2 570	6	32	1	124	50
Jackson	7.3	19.4	8.7	31.8	22.5	5.6	3.5	1.3	34.6	100.4	37 016	3 234	73	398	2	447	419
Jasper	7.0	20.3	7.9	28.6	24.5	6.8	3.9	1.1	36.3	96.2	8 107	3 115	24	18	2	70	90
Jeff Davis	7.7	19.5	9.3	28.2	23.3	6.9	3.8	1.2	35.0	96.5	10 300	1 920	30	56	5	303	70
Jefferson	7.2	21.2	9.0	27.1	21.9	6.8	5.1	1.8	34.9	88.9	7 267	9 717	21	27	1	144	89
Jenkins	7.1	21.4	9.2	26.4	22.3	7.3	4.7	1.5	35.4	92.0	4 827	3 472	13	18	8	177	60
Johnson	6.8	23.3	8.9	24.3	21.1	8.0	5.4	2.2	34.9	97.1	5 345	3 164	11	10	1	6	23
Jones	6.5	20.6	7.9	30.6	24.1	6.0	3.3	1.1	36.1	95.4	17 735	5 506	40	125	6	58	169
Lamar	6.1	18.4	11.4	27.9	23.6	7.0	4.1	1.4	35.7	91.9	10 785	4 836	44	59	2	44	142
Lanier	7.2	20.2	11.0	30.5	20.5	6.2	3.1	1.4	33.3	102.7	5 185	1 856	41	26	3	43	87
Laurens	6.9	19.9	9.1	28.0	22.8	6.9	4.7	1.6	35.8	92.6	28 469	15 494	89	361	13	178	270
Lee	7.3	23.4	8.5	33.2	21.3	3.8	1.9	.6	32.6	102.1	20 361	3 838	60	208	3	119	168
Liberty	10.4	21.6	17.9	33.9	12.2	2.4	1.2	.4	25.0	111.3	28 737	26 396	322	1 082	266	2 732	2 075
Lincoln	5.4	19.0	7.2	27.5	26.3	9.1	4.3	1.1	39.3	94.9	5 364	2 869	31	13	4	20	47
Long	11.0	22.1	14.2	31.0	15.9	3.5	1.9	.4	26.5	102.1	7 049	2 499	75	59	26	403	193
Lowndes	7.2	19.0	15.1	31.3	18.5	5.0	3.0	.9	30.2	98.9	57 112	31 309	343	1 101	42	991	1 217
Lumpkin	6.4	17.9	15.4	29.0	21.6	5.6	2.9	1.1	32.5	96.3	19 760	307	203	79	16	329	322
McDuffie	7.1	20.7	8.6	28.4	23.2	6.4	4.1	1.4	35.2	89.4	12 905	7 966	53	69	7	69	162
McIntosh	6.6	21.5	7.2	26.9	26.1	7.1	3.6	1.1	37.0	98.0	6 654	3 993	41	32	4	29	94
Macon	7.1	20.5	9.7	27.6	22.3	6.7	4.4	1.7	35.1	98.5	5 260	8 371	31	85	7	214	106
Madison	6.9	19.4	8.2	30.6	23.9	6.3	3.6	1.1	35.8	96.6	22 903	2 176	50	72	7	266	256
Marion	6.5	19.8	8.6	28.8	23.7	5.7	3.5	1.4	35.2	97.0	4 347	2 434	26	13	12	211	101
Meriwether	6.7	19.9	9.0	27.2	23.6	7.0	4.9	1.6	36.4	91.4	12 644	9 512	73	54	15	76	160
Miller	6.0	20.3	7.0	26.2	20.4	0.2	0.0	2.0	38.2	89.1	4 485	1 845	11	3	5	13	21
Mitchell	7.2	20.1	9.9	29.4	21.6	6.3	4.0	1.5	34.0	103.5	11 864	11 455	48	65	12	320	168
Monroe	6.3	19.9	8.3	30.4	24.7	6.0	3.2	1.1	36.4	99.4	15 309	6 077	76	74	6	54	161
Montgomery	6.8	18.2	12.8	30.2	21.4	6.1	3.5	1.0	33.6	105.1	5 766	2 253	6	16	2	176	51
Morgan	6.6	19.9	7.8	28.7	24.5	6.8	4.1	1.6	36.8	93.9	10 772	4 410	21	51	1	64	138
Murray	8.1	19.9	9.5	33.0	21.5	5.1	2.2	.7	32.6	99.9	34 789	226	107	92	5	964	323
Muscogee	7.3	19.5	11.9	29.8	19.7	6.5	3.9	1.3	32.6	94.7	93 936	81 488	716	2 864	270	3 533	3 484
Newton	7.9	19.7	8.9	32.1	21.5	5.7	3.1	1.0	33.3	94.7	46 666	13 771	139	449	10	359	607
Oconee	6.9	23.3	7.0	30.2	24.0	4.6	2.8	1.1	35.2	97.2	23 492	1 683	46	376	12	387	229
Oglethorpe	6.9	18.9	7.8	30.0	24.0	7.0	4.0	1.4	36.8	94.4	9 892	2 496	25	31	5	79	107
Paulding	9.4	21.3	7.6	38.4	17.4	3.6	1.8	.5	31.2	100.2	73 992	5 685	241	327	23	463	947
Peach	6.5	19.6	14.9	27.5	21.7	5.8	3.1	.9	31.8	93.6	12 135	10 738	77	78	8	433	199
Pickens	6.3	17.2	7.7	29.8	25.8	8.2	3.8	1.2	37.9	95.8	22 111	293	87	53	6	240	193
Pierce	6.7	20.0	8.5	28.1	24.5	6.8	4.0	1.4	36.2	96.9	13 588	1 706	40	28	8	152	114
Pike	7.0	20.6	8.0	30.2	23.3	6.2	3.6	1.0	35.7	100.2	11 448	2 025	29	51	–	57	78
Polk	7.2	18.9	9.7	28.8	22.3	7.2	4.5	1.5	35.1	99.2	30 700	5 085	84	119	17	1 761	361
Pulaski	6.4	16.7	9.3	31.0	23.3	7.0	4.4	1.8	36.7	74.1	6 041	3 287	25	33	12	111	79
Putnam	6.1	17.1	7.7	27.0	28.0	9.0	4.1	1.0	39.6	97.0	12 689	5 625	37	125	8	155	173
Quitman	6.1	17.9	7.2	23.6	25.4	11.7	6.6	1.6	42.0	88.9	1 354	1 218	6	1	–	5	14
Rabun	5.7	16.1	7.0	25.3	27.7	10.7	5.7	1.7	42.0	97.4	14 280	119	64	57	4	396	130
Randolph	7.1	20.2	11.0	24.2	21.9	7.5	5.8	2.2	36.1	85.9	3 034	4 633	27	14	9	40	34
Richmond	7.1	19.7	12.0	29.9	20.5	6.0	3.7	1.1	32.3	93.2	91 006	99 391	552	3 000	249	2 024	3 553
Rockdale	6.4	21.1	8.8	30.5	24.0	5.3	3.0	.9	35.4	98.8	53 100	12 771	181	1 340	57	1 776	886
Schley	8.5	20.8	8.2	27.5	24.0	6.3	3.7	1.1	34.5	91.8	2 477	1 178	8	3	6	51	43
Screven	6.6	21.3	8.9	26.5	22.7	7.4	5.0	1.7	36.2	91.4	8 234	6 963	22	40	8	31	76
Seminole	7.2	18.9	8.6	26.4	23.0	8.8	5.3	1.7	37.5	91.0	5 785	3 247	17	17	–	261	42
Spalding	7.5	19.8	9.2	29.4	22.5	6.3	4.0	1.4	34.6	93.2	38 846	18 141	133	390	11	380	516
Stephens	6.1	17.3	10.5	26.6	23.8	8.0	5.8	1.8	37.5	92.4	21 808	3 053	66	145	21	101	241
Stewart	6.4	18.5	8.0	25.3	23.3	8.6	6.8	3.1	38.8	91.5	1 949	3 232	13	9	–	6	43
Sumter	7.9	19.9	11.9	27.4	20.6	6.0	4.3	2.0	32.6	88.2	16 010	16 276	98	196	6	419	195
Talbot	5.9	18.2	7.7	26.9	26.8	8.7	4.0	1.8	39.5	87.5	2 391	4 002	15	18	1	17	54
Taliaferro	6.3	17.8	7.6	24.6	24.8	9.5	6.9	2.5	40.2	93.2	793	1 253	1	1	–	14	15
Tattnall	6.1	16.8	11.2	34.6	20.0	6.0	3.9	1.3	33.9	136.1	13 496	7 010	31	64	18	1 481	205

[1] Includes all other responses not included in the other five race categories shown. Also includes write-in entries such as multiracial, mixed, interracial, or a Hispanic/Latino group. [2] Refers to combinations of two or more of the six race categories shown under one race.

Source: Population by Age, Sex, and Race—U.S. Census Bureau; 2000 Census of Population and Housing, "Census 2000 Profiles of General Demographic Characteristics" data files, published May 2001 (related Internet site <http://www.census.gov/mp/www/pub/2000cen/mscen01.html>).

[Includes U.S., states, and 3,142 counties/county equivalents defined as of January 1, 1992. For changes to these areas since January 1, 1992, see appendix B. Geographic Information]

County	Population by age, 2000 (April 1) — Percent								Median age (years)	Males per 100 females, 2000 (April 1)	Population by race, 2000 (April 1) — One race						
	Under 5 years	5 to 17 years	18 to 24 years	25 to 44 years	45 to 64 years	65 to 74 years	75 to 84 years	85 years and over			White	Black or African American	American Indian and Alaska Native	Asian	Native Hawaiian and Other Pacific Islander	Some other race[1]	Two or more races[2]
GEORGIA—Con.																	
Taylor	7.1	19.8	9.0	28.1	22.8	6.6	5.0	1.6	35.7	95.4	4 883	3 752	10	16	–	82	72
Telfair	6.0	16.5	10.3	30.1	22.3	7.4	5.4	2.1	36.8	110.9	7 042	4 534	3	23	–	137	55
Terrell	7.7	20.6	9.5	26.0	23.2	6.6	4.7	1.7	35.4	88.3	4 163	6 658	22	38	3	10	76
Thomas	6.7	20.4	8.1	28.2	22.9	7.1	4.7	1.9	36.3	88.9	25 207	16 607	126	176	24	232	365
Tift	7.7	19.5	11.6	28.4	21.1	6.3	4.1	1.4	33.0	94.5	25 084	10 760	78	375	9	1 764	337
Toombs	7.7	20.8	9.2	27.8	22.3	6.5	4.0	1.7	34.2	91.3	18 029	6 296	54	122	2	1 392	172
Towns	4.4	11.9	9.1	20.5	28.3	14.9	8.2	2.7	48.6	89.9	9 207	12	16	29	–	17	38
Treutlen	7.4	18.6	11.9	27.2	21.7	6.8	4.8	1.6	33.9	98.7	4 501	2 269	4	18	–	22	40
Troup	7.2	20.6	9.2	28.4	21.9	6.5	4.5	1.6	34.6	91.0	38 676	18 734	95	342	33	438	461
Turner	7.7	21.7	10.2	26.4	21.1	6.8	4.6	1.6	33.3	92.6	5 357	3 895	14	31	1	172	34
Twiggs	6.7	20.3	9.4	29.0	23.3	6.6	3.6	1.1	35.4	91.8	5 812	4 623	22	12	3	26	92
Union	4.8	15.2	6.6	23.6	28.2	12.7	6.7	2.2	44.8	96.6	16 932	100	44	40	3	42	128
Upson	6.5	19.0	8.3	27.8	23.5	7.7	5.3	2.0	37.4	90.4	19 477	7 712	69	104	6	84	145
Walker	6.6	18.2	8.7	28.8	23.9	7.7	4.7	1.4	37.1	94.4	57 652	2 310	179	168	14	220	510
Walton	8.1	20.3	8.1	32.2	21.7	5.4	3.2	1.1	33.9	94.9	50 387	8 749	152	425	12	387	575
Ware	6.4	18.4	9.1	28.1	22.6	7.9	5.6	2.0	36.8	97.6	24 714	9 939	63	172	11	351	233
Warren	6.8	19.5	8.7	25.5	23.4	8.1	5.4	2.5	37.8	86.4	2 500	3 768	11	9	–	19	29
Washington	6.3	20.6	8.8	30.3	21.4	6.4	4.2	2.0	35.6	81.5	9 683	11 265	36	56	3	43	90
Wayne	6.6	19.3	8.6	30.7	23.4	6.8	3.4	1.1	35.5	108.4	20 382	5 398	60	118	5	349	253
Webster	7.1	18.2	8.2	27.7	24.1	7.9	4.9	1.9	37.5	101.0	1 207	1 124	2	–	–	38	19
Wheeler	5.9	16.4	10.2	31.6	23.1	5.9	5.0	1.7	36.1	128.1	3 989	2 050	8	6	–	77	49
White	6.2	16.9	9.2	27.8	25.2	8.5	4.8	1.3	38.3	98.2	18 979	432	80	102	36	101	214
Whitfield	8.2	19.2	10.0	30.8	21.5	5.9	3.3	1.1	33.0	101.3	67 602	3 214	293	766	28	10 031	1 591
Wilcox	6.2	16.5	9.6	31.2	22.8	6.9	4.7	1.9	36.7	123.7	5 370	3 106	8	14	1	41	37
Wilkes	5.8	18.1	8.0	26.7	24.1	8.6	6.3	2.2	39.0	91.5	5 891	4 601	21	25	4	54	91
Wilkinson	7.3	20.0	8.9	28.1	22.7	7.5	4.2	1.3	35.8	90.6	5 924	4 160	21	7	–	41	67
Worth	7.0	21.6	8.1	27.5	23.9	6.6	4.0	1.4	35.7	92.0	15 090	6 495	78	48	2	133	121
HAWAII	6.5	18.0	9.5	29.9	22.9	7.0	4.8	1.4	36.2	101.0	294 102	22 003	3 535	503 868	113 539	15 147	259 343
Hawaii	6.1	20.0	8.2	26.2	26.0	7.3	4.8	1.4	38.6	100.4	46 904	698	666	39 702	16 724	1 695	42 288
Honolulu	6.5	17.3	10.1	30.6	22.0	7.1	4.9	1.5	35.7	101.1	186 484	20 619	2 178	403 371	77 680	11 200	174 624
Kalawao	–	2.0	1.4	18.4	46.3	23.8	8.2	–	58.6	98.6	38	–	–	25	71	4	9
Kauai	6.2	20.2	7.1	27.2	25.5	7.0	5.0	1.8	38.4	100.1	17 255	177	212	21 042	5 334	505	13 938
Maui	6.7	18.8	7.7	30.9	24.4	6.0	4.1	1.3	36.8	100.9	43 421	509	479	39 728	13 730	1 743	28 484
IDAHO	7.5	21.0	10.7	28.0	21.5	5.9	4.0	1.4	33.2	100.5	1 177 304	5 456	17 645	11 889	1 308	54 742	25 609
Ada	7.7	19.6	10.3	32.5	20.8	4.6	3.3	1.2	32.8	100.6	279 427	1 942	2 085	5 223	448	5 025	6 754
Adams	4.0	19.9	4.6	22.6	32.7	9.9	4.6	1.6	44.4	105.4	3 347	2	49	5	1	32	40
Bannock	8.1	20.0	14.6	27.2	20.0	5.2	3.6	1.3	29.8	97.7	68 987	446	2 198	748	122	1 568	1 496
Bear Lake	6.9	26.0	7.4	22.4	21.7	8.1	5.7	1.8	35.8	98.4	6 261	6	34	5	3	69	33
Benewah	6.5	20.4	6.8	25.4	26.6	8.2	4.2	1.8	39.2	104.0	8 131	11	820	14	5	23	167
Bingham	8.8	26.2	9.7	25.3	19.7	5.7	3.5	1.1	29.7	100.0	34 403	70	2 798	236	13	3 320	895
Blaine	5.9	18.2	7.7	32.6	27.9	5.0	2.1	.7	37.4	107.9	17 231	25	62	139	13	1 222	299
Boise	6.6	20.3	4.7	27.1	30.3	7.0	3.3	.7	40.4	105.4	6 352	8	62	20	7	87	134
Bonner	5.7	19.8	6.7	25.4	29.3	7.6	4.2	1.3	40.8	100.3	35 574	40	322	101	17	155	626
Bonneville	8.2	23.9	9.5	27.2	21.0	5.4	3.6	1.1	31.8	99.4	76 574	403	535	675	56	3 073	1 206
Boundary	7.0	22.2	6.9	24.4	26.2	8.0	3.9	1.5	38.3	101.4	9 401	16	199	57	7	85	106
Butte	6.6	22.5	6.3	24.0	25.7	9.0	4.3	1.7	38.8	101.2	2 744	8	20	7	–	69	51
Camas	4.3	20.4	6.6	28.2	27.5	7.2	4.3	1.5	39.7	104.8	943	12	3	2	–	9	22
Canyon	9.1	21.8	10.7	28.3	19.1	5.5	4.1	1.5	30.5	98.7	109 225	421	1 120	1 056	176	15 997	3 446
Caribou	7.5	24.2	8.2	24.5	22.0	7.2	4.6	1.8	35.0	99.2	7 022	4	15	6	9	161	87
Cassia	8.7	25.4	9.0	24.5	19.6	6.3	4.7	1.8	31.1	101.2	18 137	36	171	79	11	2 582	400
Clark	8.9	26.3	8.0	27.5	20.1	5.4	2.9	.9	30.7	110.7	758	1	10	2	1	240	10
Clearwater	4.8	18.2	5.9	26.3	29.2	8.9	5.1	1.6	41.7	113.4	8 467	13	181	33	5	56	175
Custer	5.4	20.2	4.8	25.9	29.3	8.3	4.7	1.5	41.2	104.5	4 224	–	24	1	1	51	41
Elmore	8.4	19.6	13.9	36.0	15.0	4.1	2.3	.7	29.1	123.2	24 869	946	259	485	54	1 570	947
Franklin	10.0	27.4	9.3	24.2	17.5	5.5	4.4	1.8	27.7	99.4	10 775	12	33	16	5	387	101
Fremont	8.5	24.7	9.3	24.7	20.4	7.1	3.9	1.4	31.9	105.8	10 804	19	60	43	7	702	184
Gem	7.0	20.9	7.6	25.3	23.5	7.7	5.8	2.2	37.5	98.7	14 238	11	111	54	9	480	278
Gooding	7.8	21.9	8.7	25.1	21.2	7.8	5.5	2.1	35.1	104.2	12 399	33	119	33	8	1 166	397
Idaho	5.3	19.7	6.3	23.3	28.4	9.4	5.6	2.0	42.3	103.6	14 599	13	448	40	3	141	267
Jefferson	8.9	27.4	9.6	25.5	19.3	5.1	3.3	.9	28.8	102.2	17 406	53	89	44	15	1 294	254
Jerome	8.2	23.3	8.9	27.1	20.2	6.5	4.5	1.3	32.9	104.6	15 955	42	126	50	9	1 805	355

[1] Includes all other responses not included in the other five race categories shown. Also includes write-in entries such as multiracial, mixed, interracial, or a Hispanic/Latino group. [2] Refers to combinations of two or more of the six race categories shown under one race.

Source: Population by Age, Sex, and Race—U.S. Census Bureau; 2000 Census of Population and Housing, "Census 2000 Profiles of General Demographic Characteristics" data files, published May 2001 (related Internet site <http://www.census.gov/mp/www/pub/2000cen/mscen01.html>).

[Includes U.S., states, and 3,142 counties/county equivalents defined as of January 1, 1992. For changes to these areas since January 1, 1992, see appendix B. Geographic Information]

County	Population by age, 2000 (April 1) Percent—								Median age (years)	Males per 100 females, 2000 (April 1)	Population by race, 2000 (April 1) One race						Two or more races[2]
	Under 5 years	5 to 17 years	18 to 24 years	25 to 44 years	45 to 64 years	65 to 74 years	75 to 84 years	85 years and over			White	Black or African American	American Indian and Alaska Native	Asian	Native Hawaiian and Other Pacific Islander	Some other race[1]	
IDAHO—Con.																	
Kootenai	6.9	20.3	8.7	28.0	23.9	6.6	4.2	1.5	36.1	98.1	104 168	183	1 334	539	74	643	1 744
Latah	5.4	14.9	24.5	26.9	18.9	4.5	3.4	1.6	27.9	107.5	32 817	206	262	732	33	269	616
Lemhi	5.1	20.4	5.5	22.7	29.5	8.7	6.5	1.6	42.7	99.2	7 543	8	47	14	3	60	131
Lewis	4.8	20.6	5.3	23.8	27.1	9.6	6.6	2.2	42.5	101.9	3 455	13	144	16	3	35	81
Lincoln	7.5	22.8	9.0	25.5	22.0	7.1	4.4	1.5	34.3	106.5	3 497	19	49	18	2	381	78
Madison	7.1	19.0	39.9	16.0	11.9	3.1	2.2	.8	20.7	90.9	26 231	65	90	156	50	613	262
Minidoka	8.0	23.6	9.1	25.2	20.9	6.8	5.3	1.2	33.5	99.9	15 749	53	178	84	4	3 597	509
Nez Perce	6.0	17.7	10.0	26.7	23.0	8.0	6.3	2.3	38.1	96.7	34 260	105	1 988	245	27	188	597
Oneida	7.4	24.6	7.7	23.1	21.4	7.3	6.2	2.4	36.0	103.1	4 022	5	13	6	3	56	20
Owyhee	7.8	24.1	8.5	26.5	20.9	6.6	4.2	1.3	32.9	109.0	8 182	16	342	50	8	1 756	290
Payette	7.6	23.1	7.9	26.6	21.7	6.7	4.8	1.7	34.4	98.3	18 572	21	179	175	6	1 146	479
Power	8.4	25.4	8.4	25.4	22.0	5.6	3.6	1.2	31.6	101.0	6 315	7	248	24	3	837	104
Shoshone	5.6	17.3	6.7	25.5	27.4	9.1	6.3	2.0	41.8	99.4	13 198	15	209	32	10	68	239
Teton	8.5	23.3	8.1	33.8	18.9	4.2	2.8	.5	31.3	112.7	5 478	10	33	11	14	404	49
Twin Falls	7.3	20.6	10.4	26.0	21.5	6.9	5.3	2.1	34.9	96.5	59 445	124	457	487	53	2 421	1 297
Valley	4.3	19.3	4.4	24.9	32.2	9.1	4.4	1.4	43.5	105.9	7 378	3	53	23	3	84	107
Washington	6.7	20.7	7.2	23.4	24.3	9.0	6.2	2.5	39.2	95.8	8 741	10	66	103	7	815	235
ILLINOIS	7.1	19.1	9.8	30.6	21.5	6.2	4.3	1.5	34.7	95.9	9 125 471	1 876 875	31 006	423 603	4 610	722 712	235 016
Adams	6.2	18.7	8.8	26.4	22.4	8.2	6.6	2.8	38.3	92.7	64 932	2 094	109	272	8	212	650
Alexander	6.3	19.6	7.7	26.6	22.9	8.6	5.9	2.4	38.0	98.6	6 040	3 347	27	35	2	52	87
Bond	5.6	16.3	11.6	29.4	22.4	7.5	5.2	2.0	36.8	116.3	16 000	1 306	81	46	8	65	127
Boone	7.6	22.2	7.7	29.9	22.0	5.8	3.7	1.2	34.5	100.2	37 643	375	122	208	5	2 789	644
Brown	4.0	13.7	12.6	37.5	19.4	6.0	4.7	2.0	35.2	174.7	5 580	1 265	6	9	5	47	38
Bureau	5.9	18.8	7.4	26.2	23.8	8.2	6.9	2.6	39.6	94.4	34 365	116	61	182	10	455	314
Calhoun	5.3	17.6	7.6	25.9	24.4	10.0	6.5	2.7	40.5	100.8	5 023	2	16	9	–	8	26
Carroll	5.5	18.7	6.6	25.4	24.5	10.0	6.8	2.5	40.8	97.8	16 164	91	40	68	5	136	170
Cass	6.8	18.5	8.4	27.8	22.7	7.7	5.8	2.2	37.2	98.7	13 000	61	23	38	4	457	112
Champaign	5.8	15.3	23.1	28.2	18.0	5.1	3.4	1.3	28.6	101.1	141 536	20 045	433	11 592	72	2 416	3 575
Christian	6.1	18.0	7.6	28.1	23.0	8.3	6.2	2.8	38.9	99.6	34 077	758	57	132	11	167	170
Clark	6.0	18.9	7.4	26.6	23.1	8.6	6.6	2.8	39.2	94.7	16 801	34	30	23	5	14	101
Clay	5.9	18.0	8.0	25.9	23.0	8.7	7.2	3.3	39.7	92.3	14 345	16	33	76	2	30	58
Clinton	6.1	18.8	9.3	30.2	21.3	7.7	5.0	1.8	36.6	106.6	33 470	1 391	56	118	11	297	192
Coles	5.0	14.4	23.5	23.8	19.7	6.6	4.9	1.8	30.8	91.3	50 734	1 215	105	419	24	219	480
Cook	7.2	18.8	9.9	31.7	20.7	6.1	4.2	1.4	33.6	93.9	3 025 760	1 405 361	15 496	260 170	2 561	531 170	136 223
Crawford	5.5	17.3	8.6	28.9	23.0	8.5	5.8	2.3	38.6	107.3	19 139	927	56	71	2	112	145
Cumberland	6.3	20.1	8.0	27.5	22.2	7.7	5.9	2.2	37.2	95.9	11 123	12	22	17	2	26	51
DeKalb	6.2	16.9	22.0	27.6	17.4	4.8	3.6	1.4	28.4	98.2	78 704	4 084	197	2 087	58	2 440	1 399
De Witt	6.2	18.4	7.8	28.3	23.5	7.7	6.0	2.1	38.5	95.6	16 430	82	32	47	4	84	119
Douglas	6.9	20.1	8.0	26.8	22.1	8.1	5.8	2.1	37.4	94.4	19 375	60	32	51	2	263	139
DuPage	7.3	19.5	8.2	32.4	22.8	5.0	3.5	1.3	35.2	97.2	759 924	27 600	1 520	71 252	217	28 166	15 482
Edgar	5.7	18.1	8.3	27.0	23.2	8.3	6.6	2.9	39.3	95.1	19 137	362	37	37	2	50	79
Edwards	5.7	17.4	8.0	26.1	24.3	9.0	7.2	2.3	40.5	93.8	6 892	10	6	28	3	6	26
Effingham	7.2	21.4	8.2	28.2	21.1	6.9	4.9	2.1	35.7	98.2	33 804	56	61	108	4	75	156
Fayette	6.1	17.7	9.0	29.3	21.9	8.0	5.7	2.2	37.5	108.6	20 499	1 064	26	37	4	55	117
Ford	6.4	19.4	6.9	26.4	21.5	8.9	7.2	3.3	39.4	91.9	13 982	35	14	46	–	57	107
Franklin	5.6	17.3	7.9	26.2	24.3	8.9	7.2	2.6	40.3	91.9	38 485	59	85	70	5	56	258
Fulton	5.6	16.4	8.7	28.0	23.0	8.7	7.0	2.6	39.2	105.3	36 384	1 378	68	93	6	111	210
Gallatin	5.2	17.0	8.2	25.4	26.0	8.9	6.5	2.8	40.7	94.1	6 340	17	46	4	2	6	30
Greene	6.2	19.2	8.8	26.4	21.8	8.6	6.4	2.5	37.9	96.6	14 475	110	35	16	3	33	89
Grundy	6.6	20.0	8.3	30.2	22.5	6.1	4.5	1.6	36.3	98.9	36 442	71	90	114	4	487	327
Hamilton	5.9	18.0	7.9	24.7	24.2	9.3	7.1	2.8	40.6	93.3	8 470	58	22	11	1	12	47
Hancock	5.6	19.0	7.1	25.5	24.5	8.9	6.7	2.6	40.3	94.2	19 855	41	36	46	5	26	112
Hardin	5.5	15.0	7.8	26.2	26.9	9.9	6.5	2.3	42.1	100.6	4 580	132	2	24	6	23	33
Henderson	5.7	17.4	7.5	26.2	26.5	9.2	5.5	2.0	41.0	97.7	8 090	21	9	8	3	15	67
Henry	6.0	19.3	7.7	26.4	24.3	8.0	6.1	2.3	39.1	96.1	49 077	583	52	127	6	669	506
Iroquois	6.1	19.3	7.1	25.7	23.6	8.7	6.8	2.6	39.6	96.2	30 059	223	54	94	6	650	248
Jackson	5.0	14.2	26.0	25.9	17.9	5.5	3.9	1.6	27.5	104.3	48 158	7 759	184	1 806	35	596	1 074
Jasper	5.7	20.2	8.6	26.5	22.6	7.8	6.3	2.4	38.1	97.6	10 031	8	7	19	2	19	31
Jefferson	5.9	18.4	8.8	28.4	23.3	7.4	5.8	2.1	37.6	104.1	35 990	3 134	83	189	3	180	466
Jersey	5.9	19.5	9.9	27.6	22.8	7.5	4.9	1.9	37.3	95.6	21 263	114	44	55	7	33	152
Jo Daviess	5.6	17.6	6.7	25.3	26.8	9.6	6.3	2.1	41.6	100.5	21 991	44	23	36	1	75	119
Johnson	4.7	13.7	11.4	34.0	22.7	7.6	4.6	1.4	36.7	149.0	10 756	1 825	35	17	5	138	102
Kane	8.7	21.5	9.1	31.9	20.4	4.4	2.9	1.1	32.2	101.2	320 340	23 279	1 255	7 296	144	42 870	8 935

[1] Includes all other responses not included in the other five race categories shown. Also includes write-in entries such as multiracial, mixed, interracial, or a Hispanic/Latino group. [2] Refers to combinations of two or more of the six race categories shown under one race.

Source: Population by Age, Sex, and Race—U.S. Census Bureau; 2000 Census of Population and Housing, "Census 2000 Profiles of General Demographic Characteristics" data files, published May 2001 (related Internet site <http://www.census.gov/mp/www/pub/2000cen/mscen01.html>).

[Includes U.S., states, and 3,142 counties/county equivalents defined as of January 1, 1992. For changes to these areas since January 1, 1992, see appendix B. Geographic Information]

County	Population by age, 2000 (April 1) — Percent—									Males per 100 females, 2000 (April 1)	Population by race, 2000 (April 1) — One race					Some other race[1]	Two or more races[2]
	Under 5 years	5 to 17 years	18 to 24 years	25 to 44 years	45 to 64 years	65 to 74 years	75 to 84 years	85 years and over	Median age (years)		White	Black or African American	American Indian and Alaska Native	Asian	Native Hawaiian and Other Pacific Islander		
ILLINOIS—Con.																	
Kankakee	7.0	20.1	9.7	28.2	22.0	6.7	4.9	1.5	35.2	95.6	82 954	16 065	184	705	19	2 475	1 431
Kendall	8.0	21.5	7.5	32.4	22.1	4.5	3.0	1.0	34.1	98.7	50 658	718	105	480	12	1 842	729
Knox	5.8	16.3	9.8	26.5	24.1	8.5	6.4	2.7	39.4	99.2	50 175	3 512	105	383	8	876	777
Lake	8.2	21.2	8.9	31.6	21.6	4.8	2.8	.9	33.8	101.2	516 189	44 741	1 801	25 105	308	43 283	12 929
La Salle	6.3	18.8	8.1	28.0	22.3	7.9	6.1	2.4	38.1	97.9	105 896	1 723	191	598	26	1 908	1 167
Lawrence	5.5	17.2	7.6	26.2	23.4	9.3	7.1	3.7	40.8	91.0	15 139	118	21	18	–	41	115
Lee	5.5	18.7	7.8	30.3	23.1	7.5	5.2	2.0	37.9	105.2	36 629	1 772	41	202	8	277	340
Livingston	6.0	19.0	8.2	29.6	21.9	7.4	5.5	2.4	37.3	97.6	36 629	2 053	66	123	2	486	319
Logan	5.4	16.5	11.6	29.7	21.8	7.1	5.6	2.3	37.0	99.9	28 593	2 045	49	171	4	129	192
McDonough	4.4	13.3	27.6	21.5	19.1	6.7	5.3	2.2	29.0	95.3	30 568	1 138	47	664	12	154	330
McHenry	8.1	22.1	7.1	33.5	21.3	4.4	2.7	.9	34.2	100.7	244 240	1 523	445	3 782	55	7 211	2 821
McLean	6.5	17.0	18.6	29.2	19.0	5.0	3.4	1.3	30.5	93.6	134 170	9 305	245	3 087	49	1 524	2 053
Macon	6.4	18.2	9.8	26.4	24.0	7.9	5.5	1.9	38.0	91.2	95 760	16 130	199	657	23	379	1 558
Macoupin	5.7	18.9	8.3	26.7	22.9	8.4	6.3	2.8	38.9	94.9	48 034	400	109	89	14	72	301
Madison	6.3	18.6	9.4	28.9	22.5	7.4	5.1	1.8	36.9	93.0	233 645	18 935	700	1 542	54	1 269	2 796
Marion	6.4	19.1	8.1	26.3	23.3	7.8	6.1	2.7	38.4	93.0	39 209	1 598	90	237	16	93	448
Marshall	5.5	18.0	7.2	25.6	24.9	9.0	6.9	3.0	40.9	96.0	12 941	46	29	33	1	33	97
Mason	5.7	18.7	7.7	26.3	24.2	8.4	6.4	2.4	39.5	96.1	15 849	19	42	33	–	15	80
Massac	6.2	16.8	7.9	27.5	23.8	8.6	6.6	2.7	39.6	91.7	14 034	831	31	39	–	50	176
Menard	5.8	20.8	6.8	28.9	24.6	6.6	4.5	2.1	38.0	96.2	12 310	48	27	21	–	31	49
Mercer	5.7	19.1	7.3	26.6	25.4	7.9	5.9	2.2	39.5	96.9	16 680	50	21	29	1	60	116
Monroe	6.5	19.9	7.4	30.6	22.2	7.2	4.4	1.8	37.5	96.8	27 279	14	52	86	1	50	137
Montgomery	5.8	18.0	8.3	29.3	21.7	8.0	6.3	2.7	38.1	106.4	29 083	1 143	63	70	9	144	140
Morgan	5.4	17.3	11.1	27.2	23.3	7.6	5.7	2.3	37.8	98.6	33 811	1 961	67	170	3	256	348
Moultrie	6.5	19.2	7.9	26.0	22.8	8.2	6.3	3.1	38.7	93.0	14 131	28	24	14	7	16	67
Ogle	6.3	21.1	7.2	28.8	23.1	6.9	4.8	1.7	37.2	98.4	48 659	224	123	213	20	1 251	542
Peoria	6.9	18.3	10.4	27.6	22.8	7.0	5.2	1.9	36.0	92.6	145 602	29 532	411	3 041	51	1 734	3 062
Perry	5.3	16.7	10.3	29.2	22.5	7.8	5.9	2.3	37.6	113.1	20 681	1 851	53	64	10	252	183
Piatt	6.2	19.0	6.8	27.6	25.0	7.9	5.6	2.0	39.6	95.4	16 173	39	13	21	3	23	93
Pike	5.8	18.3	7.8	25.7	23.2	8.6	7.3	3.3	39.8	98.1	16 929	260	30	41	5	21	98
Pope	4.8	16.7	10.2	23.8	26.7	9.4	5.8	2.5	41.1	102.6	4 117	166	35	12	–	20	63
Pulaski	6.1	21.0	8.3	25.3	21.7	8.6	6.4	2.5	37.7	91.8	4 888	2 278	10	68	–	20	84
Putnam	5.9	19.2	7.0	26.7	25.3	8.2	5.7	1.9	39.6	97.7	5 941	38	21	16	–	38	32
Randolph	5.4	16.7	9.6	30.4	22.3	7.4	5.7	2.5	37.6	116.4	30 068	3 147	53	81	14	274	256
Richland	6.1	18.4	8.3	26.6	23.0	8.8	6.1	2.7	39.1	93.3	15 852	47	20	92	7	35	96
Rock Island	6.4	17.4	10.0	27.3	23.8	7.6	5.5	2.0	37.8	94.4	127 742	11 260	410	1 524	45	5 612	2 781
St. Clair	6.9	20.8	8.9	29.2	21.1	7.0	4.6	1.6	35.3	91.4	173 970	73 666	665	2 322	116	2 040	3 303
Saline	5.8	18.2	8.2	25.1	23.7	9.1	6.9	3.0	39.9	92.8	25 166	1 085	78	53	4	92	255
Sangamon	6.4	18.5	8.1	28.7	23.7	6.8	4.8	1.8	37.3	91.4	165 179	18 237	397	2 082	53	709	2 294
Schuyler	5.8	17.3	7.1	26.3	24.2	9.5	7.0	2.9	40.9	98.4	7 103	16	11	8	1	15	35
Scott	6.3	18.8	7.8	27.3	23.3	8.2	5.8	2.5	38.8	93.3	5 507	2	8	7	–	2	11
Shelby	5.8	19.2	7.6	26.2	23.4	8.9	6.5	2.4	39.3	97.5	22 651	35	31	49	1	31	95
Stark	6.3	18.8	6.8	25.2	23.7	8.7	7.3	3.1	39.9	93.2	6 245	4	12	12	–	9	50
Stephenson	6.1	19.1	7.6	27.5	23.3	8.0	5.9	2.4	38.5	93.1	43 733	3 761	74	334	22	307	748
Tazewell	6.2	18.2	8.1	28.6	24.0	8.0	5.0	1.9	38.1	96.8	125 142	1 131	322	665	10	341	874
Union	5.2	17.9	7.5	26.7	25.1	8.2	6.6	2.7	40.3	94.5	17 612	150	68	51	3	218	191
Vermilion	6.6	18.3	8.4	27.2	23.4	8.2	5.9	1.9	38.0	96.9	72 032	8 882	184	498	17	1 212	1 094
Wabash	5.7	18.5	7.9	26.4	23.3	8.4	6.1	2.5	39.0	95.3	12 660	51	22	58	6	33	107
Warren	5.6	17.5	12.4	24.5	23.6	8.0	5.9	2.4	37.8	93.8	17 910	298	33	63	19	206	206
Washington	5.7	19.7	7.6	27.3	23.0	7.9	6.5	2.3	38.8	97.6	14 933	50	34	28	4	20	79
Wayne	6.0	17.7	7.9	25.8	23.8	9.2	6.9	2.7	39.9	94.8	16 930	26	34	58	1	10	92
White	5.1	16.4	7.7	25.3	24.6	9.7	7.6	3.6	42.0	91.1	15 097	40	53	25	1	24	131
Whiteside	6.4	18.6	8.2	27.0	23.7	8.1	5.8	2.1	38.5	95.9	56 294	616	158	254	4	2 471	856
Will	8.4	21.6	8.1	32.4	20.6	4.5	2.8	.9	33.3	99.8	411 027	52 509	1 038	11 125	162	18 219	8 186
Williamson	6.0	17.0	8.6	27.9	24.1	8.1	6.2	2.2	38.8	93.9	58 441	1 527	167	308	19	233	601
Winnebago	7.1	19.3	8.4	29.8	22.7	6.6	4.6	1.6	35.9	95.8	229 595	29 317	797	4 780	101	8 648	5 180
Woodford	6.6	20.1	8.7	26.2	23.6	6.8	5.4	2.5	37.8	95.5	34 928	89	59	109	4	51	229
INDIANA	7.0	18.9	10.1	29.5	22.1	6.5	4.4	1.5	35.2	96.3	5 320 022	510 034	15 815	59 126	2 005	97 811	75 672
Adams	8.0	23.1	9.1	26.3	20.1	6.0	5.3	2.2	32.9	97.7	32 720	46	57	66	11	495	230
Allen	7.7	20.0	9.4	30.0	21.5	5.9	4.0	1.4	34.1	95.9	275 697	37 527	1 187	4 652	124	6 716	5 946
Bartholomew	7.4	19.2	7.7	29.7	24.0	6.4	4.2	1.3	36.2	96.6	67 271	1 310	105	1 358	28	683	680
Benton	6.6	21.2	7.1	27.8	21.5	7.3	6.0	2.3	36.7	98.6	9 129	20	13	8	–	121	130
Blackford	6.5	18.2	7.5	27.5	24.9	8.3	5.3	1.8	38.5	96.7	13 823	17	45	22	–	24	117
Boone	7.3	21.0	6.3	30.2	23.4	5.8	4.1	1.8	36.9	95.4	45 149	163	118	212	5	185	275
Brown	5.3	18.0	6.3	27.9	29.6	7.6	4.0	1.2	40.8	100.9	14 682	32	33	30	2	56	122
Carroll	6.8	19.5	7.4	28.7	23.6	7.2	5.2	1.5	37.2	99.6	19 691	40	33	12	1	280	108
Cass	7.0	18.9	8.7	28.4	22.6	7.3	5.4	1.7	36.7	101.0	38 352	527	127	221	17	1 320	366

[1] Includes all other responses not included in the other five race categories shown. Also includes write-in entries such as multiracial, mixed, interracial, or a Hispanic/Latino group. [2] Refers to combinations of two or more of the six race categories shown under one race.

Source: Population by Age, Sex, and Race—U.S. Census Bureau; 2000 Census of Population and Housing, "Census 2000 Profiles of General Demographic Characteristics" data files, published May 2001 (related Internet site <http://www.census.gov/mp/www/pub/2000cen/mscen01.html>).

[Includes U.S., states, and 3,142 counties/county equivalents defined as of January 1, 1992. For changes to these areas since January 1, 1992, see appendix B. Geographic Information]

County	Population by age, 2000 (April 1) Percent— Under 5 years	5 to 17 years	18 to 24 years	25 to 44 years	45 to 64 years	65 to 74 years	75 to 84 years	85 years and over	Median age (years)	Males per 100 females, 2000 (April 1)	White	Black or African American	American Indian and Alaska Native	Asian	Native Hawaiian and Other Pacific Islander	Some other race[1]	Two or more races[2]
INDIANA—Con.																	
Clark	6.7	17.5	9.0	30.6	23.8	6.8	4.2	1.4	36.5	94.7	87 110	6 393	247	569	41	763	1 349
Clay	6.6	19.5	8.6	27.8	22.5	7.6	5.4	2.0	37.1	94.3	26 127	88	65	29	4	62	181
Clinton	7.1	20.2	8.8	28.4	21.1	6.9	5.4	2.1	35.6	97.3	31 962	103	48	71	7	1 414	261
Crawford	6.3	19.2	8.4	28.4	25.0	7.2	3.9	1.5	37.3	101.4	10 557	17	41	14	16	32	66
Daviess	7.6	21.3	8.6	26.2	21.7	7.2	5.6	1.9	35.5	97.3	29 080	134	69	74	6	294	163
Dearborn	6.8	20.8	7.7	30.2	23.3	6.3	3.7	1.2	36.2	98.1	45 216	287	73	122	12	85	314
Decatur	7.5	18.8	8.9	29.3	22.3	7.0	4.6	1.7	35.8	97.6	24 186	12	26	177	3	24	127
De Kalb	7.6	20.4	8.6	30.3	21.7	5.9	4.0	1.5	34.7	99.2	39 381	101	87	134	20	269	293
Delaware	5.9	16.2	16.9	25.6	21.9	7.1	4.7	1.7	33.8	92.2	107 763	7 977	275	784	65	561	1 344
Dubois	7.2	20.2	7.9	29.8	22.1	6.7	4.4	1.7	36.1	97.8	38 698	56	40	79	14	601	186
Elkhart	8.1	20.8	9.5	29.8	20.9	5.6	3.9	1.4	33.0	98.8	157 931	9 551	495	1 681	78	9 805	3 250
Fayette	6.4	17.9	8.6	27.1	24.5	8.1	5.6	1.7	38.0	94.0	24 862	428	22	69	6	33	168
Floyd	6.5	19.3	8.4	29.9	23.6	6.5	4.4	1.5	36.8	93.0	66 026	3 126	151	325	25	356	814
Fountain	6.6	19.6	7.2	27.9	23.1	8.2	5.4	2.0	37.7	98.5	17 722	19	36	32	1	50	94
Franklin	7.0	21.2	7.6	29.2	22.6	6.8	4.1	1.5	35.9	99.7	21 934	7	35	48	4	19	104
Fulton	6.6	19.4	7.7	27.6	23.3	8.0	5.3	2.0	37.9	97.8	19 734	156	77	76	5	217	246
Gibson	6.4	18.4	8.4	28.2	23.1	8.0	5.4	2.1	38.0	95.9	31 350	622	61	168	1	73	225
Grant	5.9	17.7	11.8	25.8	23.8	8.0	5.2	1.7	37.4	92.2	65 495	5 281	322	412	27	746	1 120
Greene	6.2	18.5	7.7	28.3	24.0	7.8	5.5	1.9	38.1	96.8	32 691	26	104	72	5	57	202
Hamilton	9.1	21.7	5.6	34.9	21.2	4.2	2.5	.8	34.1	96.8	172 475	2 806	307	4 451	66	992	1 643
Hancock	6.8	19.8	6.8	30.0	25.4	6.4	3.7	1.1	37.4	97.5	54 527	74	95	206	15	128	346
Harrison	6.5	19.5	8.7	30.2	23.7	6.5	3.7	1.3	36.6	99.3	33 769	126	97	71	5	63	194
Hendricks	7.3	20.7	7.0	32.3	22.9	5.4	3.4	1.0	35.6	100.6	100 664	1 162	261	687	33	376	910
Henry	6.2	17.9	7.5	27.8	24.8	8.3	5.5	1.9	38.7	93.2	47 520	416	75	95	6	135	261
Howard	7.0	18.6	8.3	28.2	24.6	7.3	4.5	1.6	37.1	93.7	76 235	5 563	302	861	16	718	1 269
Huntington	6.7	19.5	9.9	28.1	21.8	6.6	5.2	2.3	36.2	94.9	37 371	69	157	118	4	99	257
Jackson	7.0	18.5	8.8	30.3	22.1	7.0	4.5	1.8	35.8	97.3	39 736	227	101	323	23	637	288
Jasper	6.9	20.5	10.1	27.7	22.3	6.8	4.1	1.6	35.0	98.2	29 434	104	54	56	–	190	205
Jay	7.3	19.7	7.7	27.3	23.3	7.5	5.4	1.7	36.7	96.3	21 291	55	36	74	5	185	160
Jefferson	6.2	18.2	10.6	28.5	23.4	7.1	4.6	1.5	36.6	98.1	30 498	461	75	187	5	124	355
Jennings	7.5	20.2	8.2	30.4	23.0	6.1	3.5	1.1	34.6	99.8	26 852	206	58	72	1	59	306
Johnson	7.5	19.7	8.7	30.8	22.3	5.7	3.8	1.5	34.9	96.0	111 796	914	207	962	32	548	750
Knox	5.9	17.1	13.6	25.4	22.7	7.6	5.5	2.2	36.7	98.5	37 830	728	82	203	19	122	272
Kosciusko	7.5	20.3	8.7	29.0	22.6	6.2	4.2	1.5	35.1	99.7	70 041	445	187	410	10	2 176	788
Lagrange	9.8	24.0	10.3	26.1	19.8	5.7	3.3	1.1	29.5	102.6	33 770	66	51	92	–	671	259
Lake	7.1	19.6	9.3	28.3	22.6	7.0	4.7	1.4	35.9	92.9	323 290	122 723	1 343	3 983	195	24 051	8 979
La Porte	6.5	10.1	0.0	29.7	23.0	7.1	4.9	1.5	37.1	105.5	94 972	11 156	342	498	23	1 441	1 674
Lawrence	6.5	18.1	7.7	28.1	25.0	8.1	5.0	1.7	38.2	95.1	44 969	178	129	129	4	154	359
Madison	6.4	17.4	9.1	28.3	23.9	7.8	5.4	1.7	37.4	97.1	119 892	10 511	310	469	21	803	1 352
Marion	7.4	18.4	10.0	32.9	20.2	5.8	3.9	1.3	33.6	93.6	606 502	207 964	2 181	12 325	365	16 998	14 119
Marshall	7.3	20.8	8.7	28.0	22.0	6.9	4.6	1.8	35.5	98.7	43 109	136	134	140	10	1 144	455
Martin	6.3	18.9	7.4	27.5	25.6	7.8	4.9	1.4	38.5	102.5	10 258	16	12	15	3	11	54
Miami	6.4	19.5	8.1	29.9	23.3	7.0	4.5	1.4	36.6	103.1	33 804	1 084	389	118	6	167	514
Monroe	5.1	12.9	27.7	31.7	17.9	4.9	3.2	1.1	27.6	96.3	109 510	3 615	317	4 067	56	1 031	1 967
Montgomery	6.7	19.3	9.0	28.6	22.6	7.2	4.9	1.8	36.6	99.6	36 414	288	73	159	13	413	269
Morgan	7.2	20.0	7.7	30.6	23.6	6.2	3.4	1.0	36.0	98.9	65 749	50	149	164	12	107	458
Newton	6.2	20.2	7.9	28.5	24.4	6.8	4.4	1.6	37.3	99.8	14 177	25	45	32	11	166	110
Noble	8.0	21.0	9.2	30.0	20.8	5.8	3.9	1.3	33.3	101.5	43 490	189	115	168	9	1 870	434
Ohio	5.9	19.0	7.8	28.6	25.0	7.6	4.6	1.5	38.4	97.0	5 550	27	7	8	1	3	27
Orange	6.7	19.0	8.0	28.0	23.5	7.9	5.1	1.8	37.5	96.7	18 900	122	60	33	2	48	141
Owen	6.3	20.3	7.2	28.8	24.5	7.6	3.8	1.4	37.6	99.0	21 397	55	81	36	4	34	179
Parke	5.5	18.4	7.3	28.7	25.4	8.1	5.0	1.6	38.9	91.2	16 625	370	43	31	4	39	129
Perry	5.4	17.5	9.8	29.2	23.3	7.7	5.4	1.8	38.0	107.0	18 447	274	33	22	3	25	95
Pike	6.1	17.8	7.7	28.2	24.9	8.1	5.2	1.9	38.8	99.9	12 722	13	16	18	5	13	50
Porter	6.5	19.3	9.8	28.8	24.6	5.9	3.8	1.2	36.3	96.4	139 946	1 344	326	1 341	42	1 855	1 944
Posey	6.3	21.0	7.4	29.0	23.9	6.8	4.3	1.3	37.4	99.1	26 511	234	72	42	1	44	157
Pulaski	6.1	20.8	7.4	27.3	23.0	7.8	5.5	2.0	37.8	101.8	13 415	127	30	28	3	48	104
Putnam	6.1	17.4	13.2	29.2	21.6	7.0	3.7	1.6	35.1	108.3	34 171	1 057	119	188	13	150	321
Randolph	6.7	18.5	7.9	27.3	23.8	8.3	5.5	2.0	38.2	96.2	26 869	70	50	42	9	162	199
Ripley	7.4	20.7	7.7	28.9	22.0	6.9	4.6	1.9	35.7	96.5	26 071	13	92	95	–	142	110
Rush	6.8	19.9	7.5	28.9	22.2	7.7	5.2	1.9	36.9	96.6	17 840	109	29	85	4	45	149
St. Joseph	7.0	18.7	11.8	28.0	20.9	6.7	5.1	1.8	34.4	93.2	218 706	30 422	938	3 557	133	6 580	5 223
Scott	7.4	18.9	9.2	30.3	23.2	6.3	3.5	1.2	35.1	98.6	22 648	11	36	42	–	99	124
Shelby	6.8	19.9	8.0	30.6	22.6	6.5	4.2	1.5	36.2	98.0	42 254	330	84	256	9	218	294
Spencer	6.3	20.2	7.3	29.1	24.1	7.2	4.3	1.4	37.3	100.4	19 923	123	45	39	2	150	109
Starke	6.5	20.3	8.0	27.8	23.5	7.8	4.6	1.5	37.0	98.0	22 971	53	57	47	6	175	247
Steuben	6.6	19.0	10.4	28.5	23.5	6.6	3.9	1.4	35.5	102.0	32 281	123	109	133	6	283	279
Sullivan	5.6	17.0	9.4	30.5	23.5	7.2	5.2	1.7	37.3	115.2	20 470	928	67	29	4	71	182
Switzerland	6.3	20.0	8.5	28.0	24.6	7.2	4.0	1.4	36.8	101.7	8 954	21	14	8	1	28	39
Tippecanoe	5.9	15.1	25.4	27.1	17.4	4.6	3.4	1.2	27.2	105.4	132 354	3 752	417	6 649	48	3 687	2 048

[1] Includes all other responses not included in the other five race categories shown. Also includes write-in entries such as multiracial, mixed, interracial, or a Hispanic/Latino group. [2] Refers to combinations of two or more of the six race categories shown under one race.

Source: Population by Age, Sex, and Race—U.S. Census Bureau; 2000 Census of Population and Housing, "Census 2000 Profiles of General Demographic Characteristics" data files, published May 2001 (related Internet site <http://www.census.gov/mp/www/pub/2000cen/mscen01.html>).

[Includes U.S., states, and 3,142 counties/county equivalents defined as of January 1, 1992. For changes to these areas since January 1, 1992, see appendix B. Geographic Information]

County	Population by age, 2000 (April 1)									Males per 100 females, 2000 (April 1)	Population by race, 2000 (April 1)						
	Percent—								Median age (years)		One race						Two or more races[2]
	Under 5 years	5 to 17 years	18 to 24 years	25 to 44 years	45 to 64 years	65 to 74 years	75 to 84 years	85 years and over			White	Black or African American	American Indian and Alaska Native	Asian	Native Hawaiian and Other Pacific Islander	Some other race[1]	
INDIANA—Con.																	
Tipton	6.1	18.9	7.2	28.1	25.1	7.1	5.4	2.0	38.4	95.7	16 303	23	37	50	2	54	108
Union	7.0	20.3	7.7	28.5	23.6	6.9	4.3	1.7	36.5	98.4	7 253	17	20	14	1	12	32
Vanderburgh	6.2	16.9	11.5	28.1	22.0	7.6	5.7	2.0	36.9	90.2	153 519	14 078	305	1 296	70	685	1 969
Vermillion	6.3	17.5	8.1	27.5	24.9	7.7	5.7	2.4	38.9	95.0	16 518	44	41	20	3	27	135
Vigo	6.1	16.8	14.3	27.3	21.3	6.9	5.5	1.9	34.9	96.6	95 965	6 392	290	1 293	38	414	1 456
Wabash	5.9	18.6	10.3	26.2	23.3	7.6	5.7	2.5	37.5	94.2	34 045	142	229	142	12	135	255
Warren	6.0	20.0	6.6	28.0	25.5	7.5	5.0	1.4	38.2	102.8	8 342	7	12	15	2	6	35
Warrick	6.6	20.3	7.2	29.7	25.5	5.8	3.6	1.4	37.3	96.6	51 053	525	78	330	25	86	286
Washington	6.7	19.8	8.7	29.7	23.0	6.4	4.3	1.3	35.8	100.1	26 884	36	36	44	2	64	157
Wayne	6.2	18.0	9.2	27.5	23.4	8.2	5.6	1.9	37.7	92.4	65 436	3 627	139	365	24	493	1 013
Wells	6.6	20.7	8.3	28.1	22.2	7.0	5.2	1.9	36.8	97.3	27 136	45	53	59	8	120	179
White	6.4	19.4	7.8	27.8	23.8	7.9	5.3	1.6	37.6	96.8	24 054	40	64	62	9	805	233
Whitley	6.8	19.9	8.1	28.9	23.2	6.7	4.6	1.7	36.9	98.5	30 205	57	110	55	13	91	176
IOWA	6.4	18.6	10.2	27.6	22.2	7.2	5.4	2.2	36.6	96.3	2 748 640	61 853	8 989	36 635	1 009	37 420	31 778
Adair	5.4	18.5	6.9	24.4	22.7	9.4	8.6	4.1	41.8	95.9	8 153	6	6	19	–	19	40
Adams	5.5	18.4	6.3	24.1	24.2	10.0	8.4	3.0	41.9	96.7	4 433	3	20	8	–	2	16
Allamakee	5.9	19.6	7.0	25.6	23.6	8.9	6.6	3.0	39.7	100.2	14 070	21	26	39	2	414	103
Appanoose	5.6	18.2	7.8	25.1	23.5	9.3	7.4	3.2	40.6	91.5	13 469	58	23	36	1	37	97
Audubon	5.8	20.1	5.0	22.7	22.9	10.6	8.9	3.9	42.4	92.0	6 773	10	6	13	–	2	26
Benton	6.5	20.9	6.8	29.3	21.1	7.5	5.6	2.4	37.2	100.0	25 015	51	37	43	4	27	131
Black Hawk	6.1	17.0	15.7	25.2	22.0	6.8	5.2	2.0	34.4	92.3	113 194	10 179	228	1 254	56	1 190	1 911
Boone	6.0	18.8	8.4	27.1	23.3	7.8	5.8	2.9	38.6	95.9	25 838	95	53	57	–	67	114
Bremer	5.5	18.6	12.0	23.9	23.9	7.3	6.1	2.6	38.1	93.6	22 909	112	15	121	5	24	139
Buchanan	6.9	21.7	8.1	26.3	22.5	7.0	5.5	2.0	36.4	98.7	20 757	57	45	85	1	34	114
Buena Vista	5.9	19.5	12.2	25.4	20.2	7.9	6.3	2.7	36.4	100.4	17 962	72	27	884	3	1 174	289
Butler	5.5	18.9	6.4	24.9	24.2	9.1	7.7	3.2	41.3	96.2	15 145	13	8	31	3	24	81
Calhoun	5.1	17.9	6.4	24.8	23.7	9.8	8.4	3.9	42.4	98.1	10 899	77	22	20	1	38	58
Carroll	6.0	20.9	7.4	25.9	21.0	8.7	7.1	2.8	38.7	95.1	21 178	38	22	73	1	43	66
Cass	5.4	18.3	6.8	24.8	23.8	9.6	7.5	3.6	41.6	94.3	14 513	31	18	20	6	46	50
Cedar	6.1	19.3	6.9	27.7	23.8	7.6	5.9	2.8	39.2	97.5	17 909	34	34	55	5	47	103
Cerro Gordo	5.9	17.8	9.0	26.4	23.2	8.7	6.4	2.6	39.3	92.8	44 711	373	79	324	9	410	541
Cherokee	5.5	19.1	6.8	24.0	24.3	10.0	7.4	3.0	41.7	97.4	12 817	41	21	56	–	48	52
Chickasaw	5.7	20.4	6.9	25.6	23.4	8.6	6.6	2.7	39.7	100.1	12 931	7	4	35	1	38	79
Clarke	6.4	19.9	7.6	26.5	22.5	8.2	5.9	3.0	38.6	97.0	8 826	10	30	32	3	179	53
Clay	6.1	18.6	8.0	26.9	22.5	8.5	6.7	2.8	39.4	93.3	17 039	30	17	142	5	44	95
Clayton	5.8	19.6	6.5	26.0	23.6	9.2	6.4	3.0	40.2	97.6	18 478	26	41	20	1	35	77
Clinton	6.4	19.2	8.2	27.0	23.3	7.7	6.0	2.1	38.2	94.3	48 079	946	120	283	9	172	540
Crawford	6.4	20.2	8.1	25.7	22.5	8.2	6.3	2.6	38.2	100.9	15 773	129	47	83	2	777	131
Dallas	8.3	19.9	6.9	32.1	21.6	5.5	4.0	1.6	35.1	97.7	38 609	300	62	282	18	1 135	344
Davis	7.1	20.1	7.4	25.2	22.9	8.4	5.9	3.1	38.5	97.9	8 400	15	18	17	4	18	69
Decatur	5.5	17.5	16.3	21.6	21.5	8.6	6.2	2.8	36.4	95.7	8 381	85	21	55	10	40	97
Delaware	6.4	22.6	7.0	27.6	21.5	7.5	5.5	2.0	37.1	98.4	18 271	13	18	26	2	19	55
Des Moines	6.3	18.1	8.5	26.1	24.3	7.9	6.4	2.4	38.9	93.5	39 679	1 511	104	251	16	289	501
Dickinson	5.3	16.6	6.6	23.9	26.9	10.7	7.1	2.8	43.3	95.0	16 244	29	34	30	1	16	70
Dubuque	6.6	18.9	10.2	27.2	22.3	7.3	5.2	2.2	36.5	94.4	86 531	767	131	514	76	447	677
Emmet	5.5	18.8	10.1	23.8	22.5	8.6	7.4	3.4	39.6	94.4	10 738	26	31	33	1	138	60
Fayette	6.0	19.0	8.6	24.9	22.4	9.0	7.1	2.9	39.4	97.5	21 505	116	29	87	7	94	170
Floyd	6.2	18.9	7.0	24.4	24.2	8.6	7.4	3.2	40.3	93.5	16 581	39	16	72	16	75	101
Franklin	5.6	18.6	7.3	24.0	23.9	9.8	7.8	2.9	41.3	96.4	10 160	9	25	17	2	434	57
Fremont	5.6	19.5	6.0	24.3	24.7	9.3	7.6	3.0	41.2	95.5	7 851	3	19	19	–	77	41
Greene	5.8	19.8	6.1	24.3	22.4	9.6	8.1	3.9	41.0	95.5	10 175	15	16	25	1	69	65
Grundy	5.4	19.8	6.3	25.1	24.1	8.8	7.3	3.2	40.8	95.7	12 242	10	3	36	–	19	59
Guthrie	5.5	18.0	6.3	24.8	24.9	10.2	7.2	3.1	41.9	97.6	11 195	14	6	16	5	48	69
Hamilton	6.4	19.0	7.1	27.1	22.4	8.7	6.7	2.6	39.1	98.0	15 898	38	33	240	1	100	128
Hancock	6.1	20.4	6.6	25.5	23.5	8.1	7.0	2.8	39.7	96.8	11 822	11	12	37	2	167	49
Hardin	5.7	19.0	8.4	23.8	22.4	9.0	8.0	3.6	40.6	95.7	18 274	116	24	60	9	234	95
Harrison	6.0	20.2	6.8	27.0	22.3	8.5	6.3	2.8	38.9	96.5	15 460	13	34	25	2	32	100
Henry	6.0	18.7	9.0	29.2	22.5	6.7	5.6	2.4	37.1	102.5	19 274	302	49	383	5	106	217
Howard	6.0	20.3	6.8	25.4	21.3	9.2	7.7	3.2	39.5	97.0	9 839	11	15	17	–	8	42
Humboldt	5.4	19.4	7.0	24.6	22.5	9.7	8.1	3.2	41.3	95.7	10 239	11	6	24	10	42	49
Ida	5.5	20.0	6.1	24.0	22.7	10.2	8.5	3.1	41.5	93.9	7 760	8	5	19	–	12	33
Iowa	6.2	20.2	6.3	27.8	22.4	7.9	6.1	3.1	38.8	95.0	15 467	27	10	47	4	56	60
Jackson	5.9	20.1	7.0	26.5	23.2	8.7	6.1	2.5	39.1	97.1	20 085	20	24	19	23	30	95
Jasper	6.2	18.4	7.4	28.6	23.4	8.2	5.7	2.2	38.5	101.6	36 313	309	81	162	19	98	231
Jefferson	5.4	19.0	7.6	24.4	29.8	6.3	5.2	2.3	41.1	95.9	15 537	104	27	275	6	85	147
Johnson	5.8	14.3	23.4	30.8	18.2	3.9	2.5	1.0	28.4	99.1	100 051	3 223	313	4 578	48	1 116	1 677
Jones	5.6	18.5	7.9	29.0	23.3	8.0	5.6	2.2	38.5	109.3	19 549	361	64	44	–	46	157
Keokuk	5.9	19.8	7.0	25.5	21.6	9.1	7.6	3.4	40.0	94.1	11 286	8	13	26	2	24	41

[1] Includes all other responses not included in the other five race categories shown. Also includes write-in entries such as multiracial, mixed, interracial, or a Hispanic/Latino group. [2] Refers to combinations of two or more of the six race categories shown under one race.

Source: Population by Age, Sex, and Race—U.S. Census Bureau; 2000 Census of Population and Housing, "Census 2000 Profiles of General Demographic Characteristics" data files, published May 2001 (related Internet site <http://www.census.gov/mp/www/pub/2000cen/mscen01.html>).

[Includes U.S., states, and 3,142 counties/county equivalents defined as of January 1, 1992. For changes to these areas since January 1, 1992, see appendix B. Geographic Information]

County	Under 5 years	5 to 17 years	18 to 24 years	25 to 44 years	45 to 64 years	65 to 74 years	75 to 84 years	85 years and over	Median age (years)	Males per 100 females, 2000 (April 1)	White	Black or African American	American Indian and Alaska Native	Asian	Native Hawaiian and Other Pacific Islander	Some other race[1]	Two or more races[2]
IOWA—Con.																	
Kossuth	5.4	20.4	6.1	24.3	23.6	9.6	7.4	3.1	41.3	95.3	16 950	19	25	60	1	50	58
Lee	6.0	18.4	7.8	26.7	24.6	8.0	6.1	2.4	39.5	97.9	35 862	1 066	99	150	22	392	461
Linn	7.0	18.3	10.1	30.3	22.1	6.2	4.4	1.6	35.2	96.1	179 999	4 919	418	2 634	91	881	2 759
Louisa	7.2	20.5	7.9	28.7	21.7	7.2	4.7	2.1	35.9	98.9	11 441	31	22	24	3	555	107
Lucas	6.0	19.3	7.3	24.6	23.4	9.1	6.8	3.5	39.9	94.5	9 275	12	10	28	1	35	61
Lyon	6.7	21.3	7.6	24.6	20.9	9.1	6.8	2.9	38.1	98.4	11 661	11	17	18	1	12	43
Madison	7.0	20.1	6.9	27.4	23.4	6.7	5.6	2.8	37.9	97.4	13 818	12	38	25	3	27	96
Mahaska	6.6	19.1	9.4	26.8	21.7	7.6	6.4	2.4	37.2	99.1	21 710	142	43	192	6	68	174
Marion	6.3	19.1	10.2	26.5	22.1	7.3	5.9	2.7	37.2	98.6	31 237	134	61	331	12	71	206
Marshall	6.5	18.8	8.1	26.3	23.9	8.0	6.1	2.3	38.6	99.2	35 551	365	136	308	22	2 371	558
Mills	6.3	20.4	7.0	28.1	25.5	6.5	4.4	1.7	38.1	100.6	14 251	41	39	42	2	52	120
Mitchell	6.1	20.4	6.1	24.2	21.7	9.8	7.8	4.0	40.6	95.7	10 795	19	8	19	2	8	23
Monona	5.3	17.9	6.2	23.3	23.3	10.7	8.8	4.4	43.0	94.2	9 854	8	76	12	4	8	58
Monroe	6.4	19.0	7.2	25.0	23.0	9.1	7.4	3.1	39.7	94.9	7 888	16	29	32	–	10	41
Montgomery	6.1	18.9	6.5	25.5	22.8	9.4	7.2	3.7	40.4	90.2	11 559	9	41	29	1	80	52
Muscatine	6.9	20.0	8.6	28.8	22.8	6.5	4.6	1.9	36.1	98.1	37 852	294	128	345	7	2 525	571
O'Brien	5.9	18.9	7.8	24.1	22.1	9.7	7.6	3.7	40.7	95.8	14 807	52	25	77	1	71	69
Osceola	5.9	20.2	7.2	26.2	21.6	9.0	6.9	3.0	39.7	95.0	6 866	8	18	14	1	59	37
Page	5.6	17.7	7.9	26.3	22.8	9.2	7.5	3.1	40.2	102.7	16 315	282	83	81	2	83	130
Palo Alto	5.4	18.6	9.5	23.2	21.9	10.3	7.4	3.6	40.7	94.7	10 007	9	19	31	4	19	58
Plymouth	6.6	21.7	7.2	26.4	22.0	7.9	5.7	2.3	37.8	98.8	24 393	72	36	66	14	115	153
Pocahontas	4.9	20.5	5.3	23.4	24.1	9.7	8.6	3.4	42.5	96.6	8 531	21	15	15	1	26	53
Polk	7.5	18.2	9.4	32.2	21.5	5.7	3.9	1.5	34.4	94.2	330 917	18 113	1 001	9 858	209	8 299	6 204
Pottawattamie	6.6	19.4	9.1	28.6	22.7	7.4	4.7	1.5	36.5	95.5	84 181	671	325	423	17	1 116	971
Poweshiek	5.5	17.1	12.8	24.4	22.5	8.1	6.5	3.0	38.4	92.5	18 202	103	44	202	9	92	163
Ringgold	5.9	18.2	6.9	21.4	23.6	11.3	8.6	4.1	43.2	94.1	5 418	6	12	9	–	1	23
Sac	5.6	18.5	6.9	23.5	22.8	10.2	8.6	3.9	42.1	95.5	11 359	30	10	16	2	46	66
Scott	6.9	19.6	9.3	29.4	23.0	6.1	4.2	1.5	35.4	95.8	140 481	9 689	500	2 502	32	2 606	2 858
Shelby	5.9	20.5	5.7	25.2	22.4	9.5	7.8	3.1	40.5	95.9	12 999	13	38	36	–	24	63
Sioux	6.6	20.5	15.2	23.5	19.1	7.1	5.7	2.2	32.8	96.3	30 746	64	40	186	4	380	169
Story	5.2	13.9	28.3	25.5	17.3	4.7	3.6	1.6	26.5	104.6	72 898	1 463	128	4 080	25	478	909
Tama	6.9	19.6	7.0	25.2	22.5	8.8	6.8	3.1	39.1	96.6	16 362	46	1 102	32	4	344	213
Taylor	5.5	18.4	7.5	23.4	22.8	9.7	8.8	3.9	41.6	94.1	6 799	2	7	21	4	79	46
Union	5.9	17.4	8.7	25.3	24.0	8.5	7.3	2.8	40.1	92.1	12 117	28	21	31	–	40	72
Van Buren	5.6	19.2	7.0	24.4	24.8	8.8	7.1	3.1	40.8	99.5	7 701	5	14	22	5	12	50
Wapello	5.9	17.3	9.7	26.0	23.3	8.7	6.4	2.6	39.2	94.8	34 709	337	102	233	7	379	284
Warren	6.8	20.2	9.7	28.2	23.2	6.0	4.1	1.7	36.0	94.6	39 889	108	71	156	18	118	311
Washington	6.7	19.4	7.0	26.8	22.3	7.8	6.9	3.2	38.8	93.0	20 059	60	40	51	7	312	141
Wayne	5.0	18.8	5.9	23.4	23.0	10.6	9.2	4.0	43.0	91.7	6 648	4	8	10	4	13	43
Webster	6.3	18.2	11.1	25.5	21.6	8.3	6.3	2.7	37.7	100.3	37 574	1 364	119	267	7	442	462
Winnebago	5.6	18.5	9.8	24.1	23.1	8.5	7.0	3.5	39.8	95.5	11 415	21	27	84	1	118	57
Winneshiek	5.1	17.9	16.7	24.2	20.4	7.4	5.8	2.5	35.7	96.8	20 852	108	16	174	1	52	107
Woodbury	7.6	19.7	10.2	28.3	20.8	6.7	4.9	1.8	34.2	96.1	90 875	2 097	1 753	2 501	43	4 538	2 070
Worth	5.7	18.6	6.5	26.3	23.5	8.8	7.0	3.6	40.7	98.5	7 780	22	7	11	1	33	55
Wright	5.7	18.8	6.5	24.5	23.3	9.2	8.1	3.9	41.4	96.2	13 750	24	26	28	–	415	91
KANSAS	7.0	19.5	10.3	28.6	21.4	6.5	4.8	1.9	35.2	97.7	2 313 944	154 198	24 936	46 806	1 313	90 725	56 496
Allen	5.9	19.3	9.8	24.1	22.9	8.4	6.7	2.9	38.8	95.6	13 637	234	112	38	–	123	241
Anderson	6.2	20.0	7.0	24.6	22.1	9.1	7.6	3.4	39.6	96.7	7 900	26	60	18	2	27	77
Atchison	6.4	20.3	11.3	24.5	21.4	7.9	5.9	2.5	36.2	93.3	15 369	893	93	57	10	86	266
Barber	5.0	19.9	5.8	23.2	24.5	10.4	8.5	2.6	42.6	92.4	5 151	20	31	5	–	47	53
Barton	6.4	19.6	9.0	25.1	22.0	8.8	6.4	2.7	38.6	93.8	26 225	323	145	66	3	991	452
Bourbon	6.1	19.6	9.5	24.2	22.3	8.5	6.7	3.0	38.0	93.0	14 466	474	129	56	7	43	204
Brown	6.4	20.0	7.4	24.0	22.7	8.4	7.5	3.5	39.8	93.5	9 316	167	946	22	1	78	194
Butler	6.9	21.7	8.3	28.8	21.7	6.3	4.5	1.8	35.9	100.9	56 471	819	541	239	19	390	1 003
Chase	6.0	18.1	6.5	26.6	24.1	8.8	7.0	2.9	40.3	103.9	2 936	31	17	4	–	17	25
Chautauqua	4.5	18.9	6.1	20.9	25.2	10.4	9.8	4.2	44.7	93.6	4 090	13	156	3	2	15	80
Cherokee	6.9	19.6	8.4	26.9	23.1	7.3	5.6	2.2	37.0	94.2	20 857	139	781	51	8	114	655
Cheyenne	4.7	19.1	5.1	22.7	21.8	12.7	10.2	3.7	44.2	97.3	3 099	4	3	10	1	31	17
Clark	6.1	20.5	4.9	23.1	23.6	9.6	7.9	4.4	42.1	95.6	2 289	6	27	2	–	45	21
Clay	5.4	19.6	6.7	23.9	23.7	9.3	8.0	3.4	41.3	99.1	8 621	50	36	13	–	23	79
Cloud	4.9	17.4	10.4	21.9	22.2	9.3	8.7	5.3	41.4	90.6	10 093	35	26	26	–	13	75
Coffey	5.9	20.9	6.5	26.4	24.0	7.1	5.9	3.2	39.2	96.2	8 595	22	46	30	1	44	127
Comanche	5.6	16.5	4.5	21.0	26.5	10.9	10.2	4.8	46.9	93.6	1 927	1	5	1	4	12	17
Cowley	6.4	19.7	9.9	26.0	22.2	7.7	5.7	2.5	37.0	95.7	32 708	979	713	557	5	493	836
Crawford	6.4	16.5	16.4	25.0	20.2	6.5	6.1	2.8	33.8	95.0	35 676	699	361	425	34	423	624
Decatur	4.5	19.1	4.7	22.9	22.6	12.6	9.2	4.3	44.3	97.5	3 398	18	3	5	4	13	31
Dickinson	5.7	20.0	6.3	26.3	23.1	9.1	6.5	3.1	40.0	95.1	18 655	113	94	58	2	158	264

[1] Includes all other responses not included in the other five race categories shown. Also includes write-in entries such as multiracial, mixed, interracial, or a Hispanic/Latino group.   [2] Refers to combinations of two or more of the six race categories shown under one race.

Source: Population by Age, Sex, and Race—U.S. Census Bureau; 2000 Census of Population and Housing, "Census 2000 Profiles of General Demographic Characteristics" data files, published May 2001 (related Internet site <http://www.census.gov/mp/www/pub/2000cen/mscen01.html>).

[Includes U.S., states, and 3,142 counties/county equivalents defined as of January 1, 1992. For changes to these areas since January 1, 1992, see appendix B. Geographic Information]

County	Population by age, 2000 (April 1) Percent— Under 5 years	5 to 17 years	18 to 24 years	25 to 44 years	45 to 64 years	65 to 74 years	75 to 84 years	85 years and over	Median age (years)	Males per 100 females, 2000 (April 1)	One race White	Black or African American	American Indian and Alaska Native	Asian	Native Hawaiian and Other Pacific Islander	Some other race[1]	Two or more races[2]
KANSAS—Con.																	
Doniphan	6.4	18.9	11.8	24.7	22.0	7.7	6.0	2.5	36.8	98.6	7 824	165	100	21	–	33	106
Douglas	5.6	14.8	26.4	28.3	16.9	4.1	2.9	1.0	26.6	98.7	86 060	4 238	2 561	3 119	62	1 197	2 725
Edwards	5.9	18.8	6.7	25.1	22.8	9.8	7.9	3.1	41.0	97.5	3 191	11	17	11	–	192	27
Elk	4.2	18.2	5.8	20.0	26.5	11.7	8.5	5.2	46.0	91.5	3 100	7	31	6	2	39	76
Ellis	5.8	16.7	18.4	25.2	19.6	7.1	5.1	2.2	32.7	95.8	26 433	183	57	225	5	359	245
Ellsworth	4.2	17.2	7.3	27.1	23.8	8.9	7.4	4.1	41.8	111.9	6 112	232	31	16	1	56	77
Finney	10.5	23.8	11.0	31.1	16.6	3.7	2.4	.8	28.1	104.2	27 982	508	389	1 163	32	9 316	1 133
Ford	9.4	21.7	11.2	29.4	17.3	5.2	4.1	1.7	29.9	107.2	24 295	527	204	666	38	5 896	832
Franklin	6.8	20.7	8.9	28.3	21.2	6.9	4.9	2.2	36.0	98.3	23 556	299	232	77	1	194	425
Geary	9.4	20.2	13.6	30.0	17.4	5.1	3.2	1.1	29.1	97.3	17 923	6 157	210	883	115	1 146	1 513
Gove	5.9	20.2	5.4	22.1	23.7	11.1	7.2	4.3	42.6	95.2	3 005	3	5	3	–	22	30
Graham	4.5	18.0	5.3	23.1	25.4	12.2	7.3	4.2	44.4	95.1	2 796	95	10	8	1	12	24
Grant	8.7	24.1	8.7	28.7	20.2	5.5	3.1	1.0	31.4	100.7	6 090	17	68	29	–	1 539	166
Gray	7.8	23.8	8.3	27.3	20.2	5.7	4.4	2.6	33.0	100.1	5 450	11	27	6	4	320	86
Greeley	6.7	21.5	6.8	27.3	19.9	9.3	5.9	2.5	38.6	98.4	1 428	3	4	1	2	80	16
Greenwood	5.5	18.2	6.5	23.2	23.7	11.0	8.0	3.8	42.6	95.5	7 407	11	64	8	–	62	121
Hamilton	6.9	21.5	7.2	25.3	20.9	9.0	6.3	3.1	37.6	97.6	2 180	13	13	15	–	404	45
Harper	5.6	19.0	6.6	22.0	23.5	9.9	8.9	4.4	42.9	93.7	6 355	15	54	9	1	25	77
Harvey	6.6	19.4	9.1	26.1	21.6	7.8	6.0	3.0	37.6	94.5	29 924	522	171	171	10	1 369	702
Haskell	9.1	23.8	9.1	27.8	19.5	5.9	3.4	1.3	30.8	103.3	3 664	8	25	27	–	493	90
Hodgeman	4.8	24.1	4.7	25.2	22.1	9.3	6.1	3.5	39.8	97.3	2 029	19	5	–	–	10	22
Jackson	6.9	21.3	6.8	26.7	23.4	7.4	5.1	2.4	37.4	96.8	11 418	67	866	21	3	49	233
Jefferson	6.4	21.0	7.0	28.0	24.9	6.6	4.4	1.8	38.0	102.6	17 818	69	170	31	2	77	259
Jewell	4.6	17.4	4.4	21.5	26.2	12.9	8.7	4.3	46.2	97.9	3 745	1	13	2	1	2	27
Johnson	7.5	19.6	7.6	32.3	22.5	5.1	3.6	1.3	35.2	95.5	410 990	11 780	1 481	12 768	156	6 976	6 935
Kearny	8.8	25.5	8.3	27.1	19.2	5.9	4.1	1.1	31.6	104.7	3 640	25	39	14	4	712	97
Kingman	6.1	21.3	5.8	24.7	22.5	8.8	7.4	3.4	40.2	96.3	8 452	18	50	21	2	30	100
Kiowa	5.5	18.5	8.2	21.8	24.6	10.6	7.7	3.1	42.1	96.3	3 186	7	20	9	–	32	24
Labette	6.2	19.5	8.7	25.8	22.5	7.9	6.5	2.9	37.9	95.7	20 386	1 064	445	73	3	274	590
Lane	5.3	20.1	5.4	24.6	24.1	9.3	7.3	3.9	41.6	100.3	2 106	–	1	2	1	11	34
Leavenworth	7.0	19.7	8.2	33.0	22.2	5.3	3.4	1.2	35.6	113.5	57 824	7 160	510	730	91	853	1 523
Lincoln	5.2	18.3	5.5	22.9	24.6	10.9	8.3	4.3	43.7	96.2	3 517	4	17	4	–	9	27
Linn	6.3	18.7	6.7	24.3	25.7	9.6	6.2	2.4	40.8	100.0	9 331	60	46	13	4	15	101
Logan	6.4	19.0	7.2	24.4	22.3	9.8	8.0	2.9	40.7	93.6	2 946	18	5	6	–	22	49
Lyon	6.9	18.9	16.2	27.2	19.1	5.4	4.2	2.0	30.9	97.4	29 924	815	168	733	2	3 518	775
McPherson	5.9	19.5	10.3	25.2	21.8	7.6	6.5	3.2	38.1	95.9	28 527	240	100	95	18	232	342
Marion	5.5	19.3	7.9	23.5	22.7	9.3	7.6	4.2	41.0	95.1	12 968	63	79	25	1	73	152
Marshall	5.0	20.0	6.6	23.6	22.8	10.0	8.1	3.9	41.7	96.8	10 761	25	40	21	2	28	88
Meade	7.9	21.6	6.9	26.5	19.2	8.9	5.9	3.2	36.1	98.2	4 219	18	25	10	–	289	70
Miami	6.9	21.1	7.3	29.7	23.1	6.3	3.8	1.7	36.7	97.8	27 206	436	147	49	3	124	386
Mitchell	5.1	19.4	8.5	22.5	23.1	9.8	7.4	4.2	41.1	97.4	6 766	36	28	21	2	16	63
Montgomery	6.0	19.0	8.6	24.7	23.3	8.4	7.1	2.9	39.1	93.2	31 095	2 199	1 157	172	7	410	1 212
Morris	5.7	19.6	5.6	23.9	24.3	10.1	7.5	3.5	42.0	97.0	5 951	21	20	14	1	43	54
Morton	8.1	21.3	8.0	27.2	21.5	7.5	4.9	1.6	36.2	94.4	3 090	7	40	37	–	263	59
Nemaha	7.1	21.4	6.0	24.1	19.4	9.2	7.8	5.0	39.1	97.0	10 540	53	25	11	6	18	64
Neosho	6.0	19.7	8.9	25.4	22.5	8.5	6.4	2.7	38.4	93.4	16 130	148	166	54	4	179	316
Ness	5.1	17.8	4.6	24.0	24.2	10.8	8.7	4.7	43.9	98.5	3 393	2	8	3	–	17	31
Norton	4.8	17.3	7.7	28.3	22.3	8.6	7.0	4.0	40.1	122.1	5 557	241	26	25	1	61	42
Osage	6.5	20.6	6.4	27.0	23.7	7.8	5.5	2.5	38.9	96.0	16 256	36	109	28	17	69	197
Osborne	4.6	19.2	5.5	22.3	22.6	10.6	9.8	5.3	44.0	96.8	4 390	3	10	9	1	3	36
Ottawa	5.7	20.0	5.8	26.7	24.2	8.5	5.6	3.5	40.1	99.9	6 011	33	23	8	1	20	67
Pawnee	5.6	18.5	7.3	25.4	24.6	8.4	7.0	3.1	40.5	112.0	6 579	362	69	41	–	88	94
Phillips	5.5	19.0	5.7	23.2	24.8	9.6	8.0	4.2	42.5	94.8	5 896	15	18	27	–	2	43
Pottawatomie	7.4	22.0	7.7	27.7	21.6	6.7	4.7	2.1	35.9	98.0	17 539	121	107	59	1	109	273
Pratt	5.9	18.6	9.4	24.0	22.8	8.9	7.3	3.1	40.2	94.0	9 192	95	34	53	3	167	103
Rawlins	4.5	19.5	3.8	21.5	25.1	12.1	9.3	4.1	45.4	99.9	2 922	9	9	3	–	2	21
Reno	6.4	18.1	9.3	26.9	22.9	7.9	6.0	2.4	38.2	100.9	59 320	1 865	379	291	23	1 740	1 172
Republic	4.5	17.8	4.5	22.1	25.0	11.4	10.2	4.5	45.7	93.2	5 751	15	12	11	–	19	27
Rice	5.8	18.8	13.3	22.8	21.3	8.8	6.5	2.8	37.6	92.2	10 188	124	61	36	4	198	150
Riley	5.7	13.1	34.5	25.9	13.3	3.6	2.7	1.2	23.9	114.3	53 281	4 325	395	2 022	105	1 186	1 529
Rooks	5.6	19.6	6.4	25.5	21.5	9.9	7.7	3.8	40.5	98.1	5 522	64	24	11	1	21	42
Rush	4.8	17.3	5.5	22.9	24.2	11.9	9.4	4.0	44.6	94.4	3 496	11	15	4	–	6	19
Russell	5.0	17.4	5.8	23.3	24.3	11.1	9.0	4.0	44.1	92.5	7 192	37	41	24	1	20	55
Saline	6.9	19.3	9.4	28.4	22.1	7.1	5.0	1.8	36.1	97.4	47 794	1 660	279	910	22	1 786	1 146
Scott	6.1	21.1	6.6	25.3	24.4	7.6	5.9	3.0	39.2	97.1	4 888	5	28	6	–	141	52
Sedgwick	7.9	20.3	9.5	30.3	20.6	5.9	4.1	1.3	33.6	97.8	359 489	41 367	5 041	15 137	265	18 867	12 703
Seward	9.6	22.4	11.7	30.5	16.9	4.6	2.9	1.4	29.0	105.3	14 730	852	174	644	14	5 359	737
Shawnee	6.8	18.5	8.8	28.4	23.7	7.1	4.9	1.8	37.1	93.8	140 811	15 337	1 980	1 618	61	5 438	4 626
Sheridan	5.0	21.4	5.8	23.7	23.9	10.6	6.6	3.0	41.5	100.1	2 775	4	2	2	4	10	16

[1] Includes all other responses not included in the other five race categories shown. Also includes write-in entries such as multiracial, mixed, interracial, or a Hispanic/Latino group. [2] Refers to combinations of two or more of the six race categories shown under one race.

Source: Population by Age, Sex, and Race—U.S. Census Bureau; 2000 Census of Population and Housing, "Census 2000 Profiles of General Demographic Characteristics" data files, published May 2001 (related Internet site <http://www.census.gov/mp/www/pub/2000cen/mscen01.html>).

Table B–2. Counties — **Population by Age, Sex, and Race**–Con.

[Includes U.S., states, and 3,142 counties/county equivalents defined as of January 1, 1992. For changes to these areas since January 1, 1992, see appendix B. Geographic Information]

County	Population by age, 2000 (April 1) Percent— Under 5 years	5 to 17 years	18 to 24 years	25 to 44 years	45 to 64 years	65 to 74 years	75 to 84 years	85 years and over	Median age (years)	Males per 100 females, 2000 (April 1)	Population by race, 2000 (April 1) One race White	Black or African American	American Indian and Alaska Native	Asian	Native Hawaiian and Other Pacific Islander	Some other race[1]	Two or more races[2]
KANSAS—Con.																	
Sherman	6.1	18.5	11.8	23.9	22.8	8.7	6.1	2.2	37.8	104.5	6 343	24	22	13	11	280	67
Smith	4.3	17.4	4.7	22.1	23.6	12.2	10.2	5.5	46.0	92.7	4 481	5	11	2	5	10	22
Stafford	5.7	20.6	5.4	24.6	22.5	10.0	7.7	3.5	41.0	95.2	4 548	7	18	6	–	142	68
Stanton	7.9	23.0	8.4	28.3	19.5	7.6	3.7	1.6	33.8	104.1	2 031	15	29	4	–	301	26
Stevens	8.2	23.0	8.3	27.8	19.4	6.4	5.1	1.8	33.6	95.3	4 535	51	51	13	1	724	88
Sumner	6.6	21.9	7.5	26.2	22.4	7.5	5.8	2.2	37.6	96.8	24 551	183	273	57	14	334	534
Thomas	6.7	19.6	13.5	24.4	21.2	7.1	5.5	2.1	35.3	94.6	7 946	35	27	22	2	78	70
Trego	5.1	18.8	5.5	23.5	23.2	11.0	8.7	4.3	43.5	91.1	3 245	6	13	16	2	5	32
Wabaunsee	6.2	20.5	6.2	26.7	24.8	8.4	5.3	1.9	39.5	102.5	6 695	32	34	10	4	41	69
Wallace	5.6	23.5	6.5	23.6	22.8	9.0	6.2	2.8	39.5	99.0	1 655	11	14	3	–	44	22
Washington	5.7	18.0	5.4	22.9	23.0	10.8	9.3	5.0	43.6	100.8	6 412	7	22	3	–	6	33
Wichita	8.3	20.4	7.3	25.7	22.3	8.0	4.9	3.1	36.7	104.4	2 183	2	18	2	–	266	60
Wilson	5.8	19.6	7.4	23.8	23.4	9.4	7.4	3.1	40.6	94.2	9 999	38	91	27	4	50	123
Woodson	5.0	16.7	7.4	22.1	23.9	11.5	9.3	4.0	44.1	96.8	3 673	31	33	2	–	9	40
Wyandotte	8.1	20.4	10.4	29.5	19.9	6.2	4.2	1.4	32.5	95.4	91 856	44 724	1 175	2 568	56	12 901	4 602
KENTUCKY	6.6	18.0	9.9	30.0	23.0	6.8	4.3	1.4	35.9	95.6	3 640 889	295 994	8 616	29 744	1 460	22 623	42 443
Adair	6.1	17.4	10.7	27.7	23.4	7.9	4.9	1.7	36.9	94.0	16 555	440	38	45	3	32	131
Allen	6.6	19.3	8.9	28.5	23.1	7.6	4.6	1.5	36.2	95.9	17 376	191	29	21	2	64	117
Anderson	7.5	19.1	7.4	32.4	22.7	5.8	3.6	1.4	35.5	95.6	18 448	449	23	23	1	33	134
Ballard	6.0	17.0	7.6	27.7	25.4	8.4	5.9	2.0	39.6	97.5	7 898	238	7	15	2	7	119
Barren	6.4	17.8	8.2	28.8	23.8	7.9	5.1	2.0	38.0	92.7	35 864	1 556	56	155	11	144	247
Bath	6.6	17.5	8.6	28.8	23.8	7.8	4.8	2.1	37.4	97.6	10 738	205	23	2	–	44	73
Bell	6.1	18.3	9.0	28.7	24.2	7.4	4.8	1.6	37.0	91.6	28 864	720	75	105	8	37	251
Boone	8.0	20.7	8.5	33.5	21.3	4.9	2.5	.8	33.4	97.7	81 822	1 306	200	1 108	29	641	885
Bourbon	6.5	18.6	8.1	28.6	24.7	7.2	4.7	1.7	37.6	94.6	17 497	1 343	29	27	2	264	198
Boyd	5.5	16.3	8.3	28.7	25.6	8.7	5.4	1.5	39.7	96.0	47 747	1 267	80	148	2	72	436
Boyle	5.6	17.1	11.0	28.6	23.7	7.4	5.0	1.7	36.9	98.3	24 311	2 680	52	156	7	180	311
Bracken	6.6	18.9	8.4	29.5	23.0	7.5	4.7	1.4	36.8	98.0	8 153	51	21	5	3	17	29
Breathitt	5.8	19.7	10.0	28.9	24.0	6.7	3.5	1.3	35.9	97.4	15 889	63	15	47	4	13	69
Breckinridge	6.3	18.6	8.2	26.7	26.0	8.2	4.5	1.6	38.5	98.6	17 872	534	42	14	3	16	167
Bullitt	7.2	19.9	8.6	32.7	23.7	5.1	2.2	.6	34.5	98.9	60 052	233	206	167	8	100	470
Butler	6.3	19.0	9.5	29.2	23.2	6.9	4.5	1.5	36.3	99.0	12 734	68	28	22	–	78	80
Caldwell	5.5	16.9	7.0	26.3	26.3	9.3	6.5	2.2	41.2	92.6	12 262	628	19	21	1	51	78
Calloway	4.9	13.8	19.8	24.6	21.9	7.3	5.6	2.1	34.5	93.2	31 950	1 218	67	456	10	157	319
Campbell	6.9	18.7	9.8	30.6	21.3	6.7	4.5	1.4	35.2	93.2	85 636	1 394	152	475	13	272	674
Carlisle	5.9	17.4	7.8	26.4	24.1	9.6	5.9	2.8	39.5	95.2	5 232	51	22	4	–	12	30
Carroll	6.7	18.7	9.1	29.9	23.2	7.0	4.1	1.3	35.9	101.2	9 663	197	23	17	5	144	106
Carter	6.4	18.1	10.8	28.4	23.8	7.1	4.0	1.4	35.8	95.9	26 625	35	67	29	1	22	110
Casey	6.3	18.2	8.2	27.5	24.7	8.3	4.9	1.9	37.8	95.6	15 184	51	44	10	8	48	102
Christian	9.9	18.4	15.8	30.1	16.0	5.2	3.3	1.2	27.9	106.6	50 529	17 148	376	660	228	1 613	1 711
Clark	6.5	18.3	8.1	30.3	24.3	6.9	4.3	1.2	36.8	93.6	31 023	1 582	58	65	3	177	236
Clay	5.7	19.7	9.2	32.6	22.5	5.9	3.3	1.2	34.6	111.7	23 063	1 178	51	29	4	56	175
Clinton	6.3	16.4	8.6	27.7	26.0	8.2	5.1	1.7	39.0	92.9	9 546	10	24	4	11	8	31
Crittenden	5.4	17.8	8.0	26.1	26.4	8.3	5.9	2.1	40.1	93.8	9 219	61	14	8	–	13	69
Cumberland	5.6	18.0	6.9	26.8	24.8	9.7	5.9	2.3	40.1	92.7	6 810	244	10	3	4	11	65
Daviess	6.7	19.1	9.0	28.4	23.0	7.3	4.8	1.7	36.8	92.6	85 772	3 982	120	393	17	405	856
Edmonson	6.0	17.6	9.0	27.8	25.3	8.3	4.6	1.5	38.0	97.5	11 457	67	51	8	–	7	54
Elliott	6.5	18.9	9.1	27.5	24.7	7.1	4.3	2.0	37.0	95.2	6 683	2	5	–	1	1	56
Estill	6.0	18.1	9.1	29.2	24.2	7.4	4.4	1.7	36.7	93.8	15 165	17	36	5	–	9	75
Fayette	6.2	15.1	14.6	33.2	20.9	5.3	3.5	1.2	33.0	96.5	211 120	35 116	507	6 407	83	3 165	4 114
Fleming	6.7	18.7	8.4	29.0	23.9	7.3	4.5	1.6	36.3	96.0	13 424	195	19	23	–	39	92
Floyd	5.9	17.7	9.4	30.3	24.5	6.8	4.1	1.3	36.7	96.7	41 478	546	49	102	34	52	180
Franklin	6.1	16.5	9.7	30.5	24.9	6.7	4.3	1.4	37.0	93.7	41 953	4 463	63	344	10	264	590
Fulton	6.5	18.4	8.9	25.5	23.2	8.5	6.5	2.6	38.5	87.7	5 823	1 798	9	24	–	25	73
Gallatin	7.5	21.0	7.7	31.0	22.5	5.4	3.5	1.4	34.6	98.9	7 612	125	14	17	–	20	82
Garrard	6.1	18.2	8.1	30.9	23.6	7.4	4.1	1.6	37.1	96.8	14 163	453	19	6	–	64	87
Grant	8.0	20.7	9.4	31.5	20.9	5.2	3.3	1.1	32.7	97.1	22 006	57	51	66	12	72	120
Graves	6.6	17.9	8.3	27.3	23.8	7.7	6.2	2.2	38.1	95.0	34 335	1 645	75	73	5	483	412
Grayson	6.3	18.2	9.0	28.0	24.6	8.0	4.6	1.5	37.5	98.1	23 634	120	40	34	2	53	170
Green	5.4	17.3	8.1	26.8	25.4	8.7	6.0	2.2	40.8	96.9	11 079	301	12	15	–	36	75
Greenup	5.8	17.8	7.9	27.9	26.0	8.5	4.8	1.3	39.2	92.8	36 179	212	69	139	1	55	236
Hancock	7.1	19.6	8.5	29.0	24.9	6.1	3.7	1.2	35.9	97.5	8 222	71	24	14	–	14	47
Hardin	7.2	20.4	10.6	31.5	20.6	5.6	3.0	1.0	33.5	102.0	77 217	11 178	392	1 693	209	1 270	2 215
Harlan	6.1	18.9	8.5	27.5	25.2	7.4	5.0	1.6	37.8	91.8	31 728	869	159	96	5	28	317
Harrison	6.3	18.7	8.2	29.8	23.6	7.0	4.6	1.8	37.1	95.0	17 200	454	50	24	3	113	139
Hart	6.6	19.2	8.6	28.2	23.5	7.7	4.7	1.5	36.9	96.9	16 150	1 081	38	19	6	31	120

[1] Includes all other responses not included in the other five race categories shown. Also includes write-in entries such as multiracial, mixed, interracial, or a Hispanic/Latino group. [2] Refers to combinations of two or more of the six race categories shown under one race.

Source: Population by Age, Sex, and Race—U.S. Census Bureau; 2000 Census of Population and Housing, "Census 2000 Profiles of General Demographic Characteristics" data files, published May 2001 (related Internet site <http://www.census.gov/mp/www/pub/2000cen/mscen01.html>).

[Includes U.S., states, and 3,142 counties/county equivalents defined as of January 1, 1992. For changes to these areas since January 1, 1992, see appendix B. Geographic Information]

County	Population by age, 2000 (April 1) Percent— Under 5 years	5 to 17 years	18 to 24 years	25 to 44 years	45 to 64 years	65 to 74 years	75 to 84 years	85 years and over	Median age (years)	Males per 100 females, 2000 (April 1)	White	Black or African American	American Indian and Alaska Native	Asian	Native Hawaiian and Other Pacific Islander	Some other race[1]	Two or more races[2]
KENTUCKY—Con.																	
Henderson	6.4	18.2	8.4	30.0	23.9	7.3	4.5	1.4	37.2	93.6	40 866	3 181	70	148	3	177	384
Henry	6.8	18.6	7.9	29.7	24.7	6.6	4.4	1.3	37.3	99.3	14 152	497	36	52	3	190	130
Hickman	5.4	16.7	6.9	26.7	25.9	8.7	6.7	3.0	40.9	91.3	4 649	521	15	3	–	9	65
Hopkins	6.1	18.0	8.3	28.2	24.6	7.5	5.3	1.9	38.3	91.0	42 808	2 887	89	157	9	170	399
Jackson	6.6	19.4	9.8	29.4	22.9	6.5	3.9	1.4	34.9	97.3	13 383	7	26	2	1	6	70
Jefferson	6.7	17.5	8.9	30.4	22.8	7.2	4.8	1.6	36.7	91.6	536 721	130 928	1 523	9 640	255	4 695	9 842
Jessamine	7.4	19.0	11.6	31.1	21.4	5.2	3.2	1.1	32.9	96.6	36 871	1 222	80	225	11	185	447
Johnson	6.1	17.9	8.8	28.9	25.7	7.1	4.1	1.5	37.4	93.1	23 126	59	30	68	5	21	136
Kenton	7.3	19.0	9.2	31.9	21.4	5.9	3.9	1.2	34.5	96.2	142 357	5 810	224	894	42	615	1 522
Knott	6.0	18.5	10.8	29.0	24.3	6.2	3.8	1.3	35.9	97.3	17 344	129	19	27	2	22	106
Knox	7.1	19.1	9.7	28.1	23.2	6.5	4.6	1.6	35.3	92.9	31 108	262	80	53	6	25	261
Larue	6.3	18.7	7.7	28.2	24.0	7.9	5.3	1.8	38.2	95.4	12 657	473	26	21	4	45	147
Laurel	7.1	18.3	9.2	30.4	23.5	6.7	3.6	1.2	35.5	95.6	51 484	331	193	182	5	44	476
Lawrence	5.9	19.4	8.8	28.7	24.7	7.0	4.1	1.4	36.5	97.3	15 403	15	44	11	1	8	87
Lee	5.2	17.5	9.0	30.3	23.6	7.9	4.5	1.9	37.4	109.4	7 528	300	22	8	1	5	52
Leslie	6.1	18.5	9.2	30.9	23.9	6.6	3.6	1.2	36.4	95.1	12 296	9	11	15	2	6	62
Letcher	5.7	18.0	9.2	28.7	25.8	7.1	4.2	1.4	37.9	95.8	24 952	129	25	70	4	8	89
Lewis	6.4	19.0	9.1	29.4	23.7	6.8	4.2	1.4	35.9	99.0	13 940	29	30	4	–	12	77
Lincoln	6.8	18.9	8.4	29.8	23.1	7.2	4.6	1.2	36.0	96.3	22 454	592	34	23	1	88	169
Livingston	5.3	17.1	7.5	28.2	27.0	8.2	5.0	1.7	39.8	97.8	9 656	14	41	3	1	27	62
Logan	6.8	18.8	8.4	28.5	23.6	7.2	4.8	1.8	37.0	93.1	24 101	2 025	55	45	3	88	256
Lyon	3.8	12.0	7.5	32.9	27.0	9.4	5.2	2.2	41.5	133.5	7 422	543	24	14	1	32	44
McCracken	6.1	17.3	7.9	28.1	24.7	8.1	5.7	2.2	39.2	90.5	56 841	7 128	142	337	34	260	772
McCreary	6.7	20.9	9.8	28.2	23.7	6.1	3.5	1.0	34.2	96.9	16 737	108	72	3	1	34	125
McLean	6.6	17.6	8.3	27.7	25.4	7.5	5.2	1.7	38.1	96.4	9 797	36	16	4	1	31	53
Madison	6.4	15.5	18.8	29.4	20.1	5.4	3.2	1.1	30.7	93.3	65 918	3 150	196	510	15	240	843
Magoffin	7.0	19.7	10.1	30.2	22.4	5.9	3.5	1.2	34.3	97.2	13 238	20	26	10	–	2	36
Marion	6.7	18.6	9.9	30.3	21.7	6.8	4.1	1.9	35.4	102.3	16 240	1 661	17	78	2	64	150
Marshall	5.1	16.7	7.5	27.0	26.2	9.4	5.9	2.3	40.9	96.1	29 694	37	51	45	3	66	229
Martin	7.0	21.1	9.5	29.3	23.3	5.8	3.1	.8	34.1	98.0	12 484	4	7	9	8	1	65
Mason	6.3	17.8	8.0	28.5	23.9	8.1	5.6	1.7	38.1	93.7	15 268	1 203	25	62	3	96	143
Meade	8.7	21.0	9.1	32.7	20.3	5.1	2.4	.6	32.2	100.4	24 339	1 088	156	139	33	218	376
Menifee	5.8	19.1	10.1	28.1	25.2	7.1	3.4	1.3	36.3	101.8	6 401	90	8	2	1	9	45
Mercer	6.4	18.0	7.4	29.1	24.5	7.7	5.1	1.7	38.2	94.0	19 568	769	44	97	7	132	200
Metcalfe	6.4	18.3	8.2	28.5	23.6	8.5	4.8	1.7	37.7	95.2	9 762	165	25	7	–	13	65
Monroe	6.3	17.6	8.9	27.7	24.3	8.3	5.0	1.9	38.2	94.2	11 235	324	15	1	3	109	69
Montgomery	7.0	17.9	8.7	30.2	23.4	6.9	4.5	1.5	36.0	94.6	21 442	784	34	24	7	78	185
Morgan	5.4	17.0	10.6	32.9	22.3	6.6	3.7	1.5	35.8	123.3	13 193	611	21	23	2	8	90
Muhlenberg	6.0	16.7	9.2	28.0	24.8	8.1	5.4	2.0	38.7	98.0	29 989	1 480	40	40	1	61	228
Nelson	7.4	20.3	8.7	30.8	22.2	5.9	3.6	1.1	34.9	96.7	34 792	2 064	48	193	7	138	235
Nicholas	6.2	17.4	8.3	28.2	24.5	7.7	5.4	2.3	38.4	93.7	6 698	57	17	8	–	16	17
Ohio	6.3	18.6	8.6	27.5	24.6	7.4	5.0	1.9	37.5	96.6	22 391	171	43	46	8	103	154
Oldham	6.6	20.8	6.9	33.1	25.6	4.2	2.1	.7	36.7	114.0	43 230	1 943	98	201	6	254	446
Owen	6.1	19.5	8.4	28.0	24.1	7.5	4.8	1.7	37.5	100.5	10 234	119	29	24	2	49	90
Owsley	5.5	19.1	8.9	27.0	24.5	8.1	4.9	2.0	38.2	101.8	4 820	5	3	2	1	1	26
Pendleton	6.7	21.6	8.5	31.2	21.5	6.0	3.3	1.2	34.4	100.3	14 159	71	28	16	1	51	64
Perry	5.8	18.5	9.1	30.7	24.6	6.4	3.7	1.1	36.3	94.6	28 609	482	15	143	4	12	125
Pike	6.1	17.6	9.2	30.0	24.7	7.1	4.1	1.1	37.1	95.5	67 599	312	74	280	20	69	382
Powell	6.8	19.8	9.5	30.0	23.3	6.3	3.2	1.1	34.8	99.4	13 046	82	16	7	–	9	77
Pulaski	5.9	17.5	8.0	28.6	24.9	8.5	5.0	1.6	38.5	95.6	54 798	604	123	208	9	97	378
Robertson	5.5	18.3	6.7	27.1	25.5	8.5	6.1	2.3	39.5	94.8	2 235	1	1	–	–	5	24
Rockcastle	6.0	18.5	8.8	30.3	23.6	7.5	4.1	1.7	36.3	97.9	16 385	23	40	21	1	7	105
Rowan	5.4	14.8	23.5	25.9	20.0	5.9	3.5	1.0	29.8	94.6	21 205	345	46	197	3	83	215
Russell	5.5	17.0	7.5	27.5	25.9	9.1	5.6	1.7	39.9	93.9	16 044	95	19	23	3	34	97
Scott	7.6	18.7	11.8	32.6	20.4	4.8	2.9	1.1	32.4	95.8	30 397	1 769	85	164	2	272	372
Shelby	6.9	18.3	8.7	31.4	24.0	5.9	3.6	1.3	35.9	94.9	28 874	2 942	101	133	41	798	448
Simpson	7.5	18.8	8.5	29.2	23.0	6.6	4.9	1.7	35.9	95.3	14 410	1 676	28	90	10	49	142
Spencer	7.3	19.7	7.7	33.5	22.7	5.2	2.9	1.0	35.1	101.8	11 472	133	26	10	–	32	93
Taylor	6.0	17.4	10.4	26.9	24.1	8.6	4.9	1.7	38.1	92.7	21 465	1 159	23	41	5	73	161
Todd	7.5	19.1	8.7	28.4	22.4	7.4	5.1	1.4	35.9	94.8	10 692	1 048	18	20	4	104	85
Trigg	5.9	17.1	6.8	26.7	27.0	9.7	5.4	1.6	40.5	96.9	11 128	1 233	26	32	1	23	154
Trimble	6.7	19.7	7.7	30.9	23.6	6.0	4.0	1.5	35.7	96.8	7 954	24	30	6	–	55	56
Union	6.2	19.1	13.8	25.5	22.5	6.8	4.4	1.7	34.5	101.8	13 297	2 015	26	23	–	61	215
Warren	6.4	16.7	16.2	29.1	21.1	5.6	3.6	1.3	32.3	96.2	80 474	7 934	223	1 251	70	1 229	1 341
Washington	5.8	19.4	8.8	27.9	23.1	7.6	5.4	2.0	37.1	96.6	9 892	820	17	31	–	67	89
Wayne	6.7	18.6	8.9	28.1	24.0	7.8	4.5	1.4	36.6	97.8	19 321	297	35	22	–	93	155
Webster	6.0	18.1	8.9	27.9	24.1	7.9	5.1	2.0	37.8	95.7	13 220	660	16	9	11	109	95
Whitley	6.3	19.4	10.8	27.3	23.2	7.0	4.4	1.6	35.4	93.3	35 280	123	81	71	5	31	274
Wolfe	6.7	19.3	9.4	28.5	23.5	6.8	4.0	1.8	36.4	98.5	7 011	17	6	2	2	4	23
Woodford	6.2	19.1	7.9	31.2	25.1	5.8	3.5	1.1	37.1	93.0	21 371	1 256	30	71	2	263	215

[1] Includes all other responses not included in the other five race categories shown. Also includes write-in entries such as multiracial, mixed, interracial, or a Hispanic/Latino group. [2] Refers to combinations of two or more of the six race categories shown under one race.

Source: Population by Age, Sex, and Race—U.S. Census Bureau; 2000 Census of Population and Housing, "Census 2000 Profiles of General Demographic Characteristics" data files, published May 2001 (related Internet site <http://www.census.gov/mp/www/pub/2000cen/mscen01.html>).

Table B–2. Counties — **Population by Age, Sex, and Race**–Con.

[Includes U.S., states, and 3,142 counties/county equivalents defined as of January 1, 1992. For changes to these areas since January 1, 1992, see appendix B. Geographic Information]

County	Population by age, 2000 (April 1) Percent— Under 5 years	5 to 17 years	18 to 24 years	25 to 44 years	45 to 64 years	65 to 74 years	75 to 84 years	85 years and over	Median age (years)	Males per 100 females, 2000 (April 1)	Population by race, 2000 (April 1) — One race White	Black or African American	American Indian and Alaska Native	Asian	Native Hawaiian and Other Pacific Islander	Some other race[1]	Two or more races[2]
LOUISIANA	7.1	20.2	10.6	28.9	21.6	6.3	3.9	1.3	34.0	93.8	2 856 161	1 451 944	25 477	54 758	1 240	31 131	48 265
Acadia	7.8	22.0	9.6	27.4	20.9	6.7	4.1	1.5	33.7	93.5	47 521	10 740	116	89	4	117	274
Allen	6.4	18.2	9.3	33.4	20.8	6.8	3.8	1.2	34.8	126.4	18 291	6 259	438	144	3	62	243
Ascension	8.2	21.9	9.5	32.6	20.2	4.4	2.5	.7	32.0	96.9	59 304	15 539	209	258	19	759	539
Assumption	7.0	21.5	9.8	28.7	22.2	6.0	3.7	1.2	34.2	93.9	15 710	7 371	72	55	2	40	138
Avoyelles	6.8	20.0	9.2	29.0	21.3	7.1	4.8	1.8	35.2	96.4	28 402	12 233	421	72	1	80	272
Beauregard	7.0	20.5	8.6	28.7	23.3	6.9	3.7	1.3	35.5	100.6	27 790	4 261	218	198	16	98	405
Bienville	6.5	20.8	8.0	24.6	22.5	8.7	5.8	3.1	38.0	91.2	8 651	6 897	42	24	–	51	87
Bossier	7.6	20.4	9.7	30.5	21.3	6.1	3.3	1.0	33.8	96.1	73 403	20 468	511	1 234	81	988	1 625
Caddo	6.9	19.9	10.2	27.4	22.0	7.0	4.8	1.8	35.1	89.7	133 424	112 483	978	1 732	76	1 056	2 412
Calcasieu	7.2	20.2	10.3	28.7	21.8	6.8	3.9	1.2	34.5	94.8	135 107	44 025	564	1 172	52	754	1 903
Caldwell	6.1	18.6	9.6	28.5	23.3	7.5	4.9	1.6	36.7	103.0	8 493	1 890	48	15	–	50	64
Cameron	6.7	21.7	9.4	29.6	21.9	6.6	2.9	1.1	35.0	100.9	9 357	388	37	44	2	94	69
Catahoula	6.5	19.3	10.0	26.8	23.0	7.9	4.7	1.7	36.7	100.6	7 888	2 962	21	14	–	21	64
Claiborne	6.0	19.6	8.0	26.9	22.3	8.7	6.0	2.6	37.7	99.8	8 728	7 982	24	17	5	14	81
Concordia	7.3	20.5	8.9	25.6	23.0	8.3	4.8	1.6	36.9	95.2	12 300	7 637	33	48	1	111	117
De Soto	7.0	21.4	8.3	26.3	23.0	7.5	4.6	1.9	36.3	90.8	14 269	10 748	129	29	14	137	168
East Baton Rouge	7.0	19.1	14.4	28.7	20.8	5.3	3.5	1.1	31.5	91.9	231 886	165 526	850	8 585	121	2 031	3 853
East Carroll	7.6	22.7	11.5	27.2	18.5	6.8	3.9	1.8	30.9	104.6	2 977	6 339	17	31	–	24	33
East Feliciana	6.5	19.2	9.3	30.7	23.7	5.9	3.4	1.3	35.8	116.5	11 063	10 057	35	49	1	39	116
Evangeline	7.9	21.6	9.6	27.6	20.4	7.0	4.3	1.5	33.7	99.4	24 951	10 122	81	51	3	63	163
Franklin	7.2	20.7	9.1	25.8	21.9	7.9	5.3	2.1	35.9	91.2	14 281	6 721	57	40	1	31	132
Grant	7.4	20.8	7.9	28.1	23.0	7.0	4.3	1.4	35.5	96.1	15 973	2 222	166	26	5	67	239
Iberia	8.0	22.0	9.6	28.4	20.6	6.1	3.9	1.3	33.3	92.8	47 682	22 574	228	1 414	15	438	915
Iberville	6.5	19.7	10.5	31.1	21.5	6.0	3.7	1.1	34.4	99.8	16 412	16 560	59	86	4	48	151
Jackson	6.5	18.8	9.3	25.7	23.6	8.1	5.6	2.4	37.6	91.4	10 934	4 291	44	33	1	37	57
Jefferson	6.6	18.7	9.1	30.2	23.4	6.6	4.2	1.2	35.9	92.4	318 002	104 121	2 032	14 065	154	9 239	7 853
Jefferson Davis	7.6	21.7	9.1	27.3	21.0	7.3	4.6	1.4	34.5	92.5	25 337	5 591	121	61	4	62	259
Lafayette	7.3	20.1	11.7	31.2	20.2	5.5	3.0	1.0	32.4	94.4	139 758	45 346	540	2 055	51	983	1 770
Lafourche	6.9	20.4	10.5	29.7	21.3	6.4	3.7	1.1	34.1	95.2	74 544	11 349	2 066	599	21	518	877
La Salle	6.1	20.0	9.4	27.2	22.6	8.0	5.1	1.7	36.4	100.3	12 301	1 742	92	25	1	29	92
Lincoln	6.0	16.1	25.7	23.2	17.6	5.6	4.0	1.7	26.5	94.2	24 409	16 934	76	543	6	221	320
Livingston	7.5	22.0	9.1	31.5	21.4	5.1	2.6	.7	32.8	98.5	86 625	3 874	335	163	14	175	628
Madison	8.2	24.4	11.2	25.5	19.1	6.2	3.9	1.6	29.8	103.3	5 197	8 283	21	22	2	48	155
Morehouse	7.0	20.5	9.5	26.4	21.4	8.1	5.3	1.8	35.6	91.4	17 297	13 451	40	57	2	37	137
Natchitoches	7.1	18.9	17.9	24.3	19.7	6.4	4.1	1.5	30.2	90.6	22 608	15 017	421	171	7	358	498
Orleans	6.9	19.8	11.4	29.3	20.9	6.0	4.2	1.5	33.1	88.2	135 956	325 947	991	10 972	109	4 498	6 201
Ouachita	7.2	20.7	12.0	27.9	20.3	6.5	4.0	1.3	32.3	89.3	94 947	49 526	337	940	37	480	983
Plaquemines	7.4	21.8	9.2	30.5	21.4	6.1	2.9	.8	33.7	99.4	18 668	6 258	553	700	4	194	380
Pointe Coupee	6.9	20.4	8.8	27.0	23.1	7.7	4.4	1.8	36.7	94.4	13 865	8 601	39	57	–	73	128
Rapides	7.1	20.2	9.5	27.9	22.4	7.1	4.5	1.5	35.5	91.7	84 024	38 445	930	1 087	45	529	1 277
Red River	7.5	22.6	9.3	24.8	21.5	7.3	5.3	1.8	34.6	90.8	5 568	3 936	27	9	2	21	59
Richland	7.4	19.9	9.9	26.8	21.0	7.6	5.3	2.1	35.8	88.7	12 791	7 974	28	37	–	42	109
Sabine	6.5	19.7	8.3	24.5	24.4	9.2	5.5	1.8	38.2	95.7	17 048	3 958	1 828	35	5	74	511
St. Bernard	6.3	18.9	9.2	29.2	22.6	7.9	4.8	1.2	36.6	93.6	59 356	5 122	329	889	14	494	1 025
St. Charles	7.3	23.0	8.3	31.4	21.0	5.4	2.7	.8	34.2	95.2	34 803	12 130	123	265	7	308	436
St. Helena	7.5	21.5	9.1	26.1	23.3	7.0	4.0	1.5	35.0	92.4	4 897	5 517	10	10	1	15	75
St. James	7.0	22.5	9.8	28.1	21.4	6.4	3.4	1.4	34.0	93.1	10 606	10 476	19	10	–	26	79
St. John the Baptist	8.0	23.1	9.7	30.2	21.1	4.5	2.5	.8	32.0	94.3	22 633	19 268	112	229	11	371	420
St. Landry	7.8	21.7	9.2	26.5	21.4	7.4	4.5	1.6	34.6	91.6	49 555	36 952	120	178	12	270	613
St. Martin	7.7	21.8	9.6	29.6	21.2	5.7	3.4	1.1	33.4	96.3	32 040	15 535	141	449	2	98	318
St. Mary	7.4	22.3	8.7	28.7	21.9	6.4	3.5	1.1	34.3	95.0	33 591	17 009	741	877	9	470	803
St. Tammany	7.1	21.4	7.3	29.9	24.3	5.7	3.3	1.0	36.3	96.1	166 458	18 929	825	1 420	57	1 164	2 415
Tangipahoa	7.2	20.5	12.7	27.7	21.2	6.0	3.4	1.2	32.3	93.0	70 175	28 519	242	395	8	461	788
Tensas	6.6	19.9	10.0	25.1	22.9	7.8	5.4	2.4	37.3	97.8	2 874	3 665	3	8	–	19	49
Terrebonne	7.4	21.8	10.1	29.8	21.1	5.7	3.1	.9	33.0	96.6	77 401	18 594	5 533	845	16	568	1 546
Union	7.0	18.7	9.1	26.5	23.8	8.1	5.0	1.9	37.3	94.5	15 914	6 373	43	59	11	288	115
Vermilion	7.1	20.9	9.4	28.2	20.8	7.1	4.6	1.8	35.1	93.4	44 488	7 624	161	977	6	141	410
Vernon	9.5	19.7	14.7	31.4	16.8	4.8	2.4	.8	28.3	109.3	38 717	8 962	768	828	160	1 311	1 785
Washington	7.2	19.6	9.5	26.7	22.6	7.6	5.1	1.6	36.1	95.4	29 614	13 851	100	73	1	48	239
Webster	6.5	19.1	8.6	26.0	23.6	8.6	5.6	2.1	38.1	91.8	27 405	13 735	143	80	16	94	358
West Baton Rouge	7.0	21.0	9.9	30.6	21.7	5.7	3.3	.8	34.0	96.6	13 561	7 666	44	40	5	114	171
West Carroll	6.0	19.6	9.7	26.5	22.6	7.9	5.4	2.3	37.2	102.1	9 838	2 325	31	16	1	53	50
West Feliciana	4.6	15.7	8.7	40.0	23.8	4.3	2.0	.9	36.6	191.1	7 348	7 633	30	25	3	5	67
Winn	6.3	18.5	9.6	28.9	22.7	7.1	5.1	1.8	36.2	110.8	11 195	5 411	84	27	9	22	146

[1] Includes all other responses not included in the other five race categories shown. Also includes write-in entries such as multiracial, mixed, interracial, or a Hispanic/Latino group. [2] Refers to combinations of two or more of the six race categories shown under one race.

Source: Population by Age, Sex, and Race—U.S. Census Bureau; 2000 Census of Population and Housing, "Census 2000 Profiles of General Demographic Characteristics" data files, published May 2001 (related Internet site <http://www.census.gov/mp/www/pub/2000cen/mscen01.html>).

[Includes U.S., states, and 3,142 counties/county equivalents defined as of January 1, 1992. For changes to these areas since January 1, 1992, see appendix B. Geographic Information]

County	Population by age, 2000 (April 1) Percent—								Median age (years)	Males per 100 females, 2000 (April 1)	Population by race, 2000 (April 1) One race						Two or more races[2]
	Under 5 years	5 to 17 years	18 to 24 years	25 to 44 years	45 to 64 years	65 to 74 years	75 to 84 years	85 years and over			White	Black or African American	American Indian and Alaska Native	Asian	Native Hawaiian and Other Pacific Islander	Some other race[1]	
MAINE	5.5	18.1	8.1	29.1	24.8	7.5	5.0	1.8	38.6	94.8	1 236 014	6 760	7 098	9 111	382	2 911	12 647
Androscoggin	5.9	18.0	9.1	29.7	22.9	7.1	5.2	2.1	37.2	94.3	100 658	683	282	572	40	294	1 264
Aroostook	5.0	17.6	7.9	26.3	26.2	9.2	5.7	2.1	40.7	95.4	71 572	281	1 005	351	19	122	588
Cumberland	5.8	17.5	8.4	31.3	23.6	6.6	4.9	1.8	37.6	93.8	254 291	2 815	763	3 707	99	923	3 014
Franklin	5.1	18.4	11.1	26.4	24.8	7.8	4.7	1.7	38.2	93.4	28 865	72	109	126	6	49	240
Hancock	4.9	17.4	7.4	27.5	26.8	8.6	5.4	2.1	40.7	95.7	50 554	130	193	196	18	105	595
Kennebec	5.5	18.4	8.5	28.6	24.9	7.4	5.0	1.8	38.7	94.0	114 129	404	469	690	24	206	1 192
Knox	5.3	17.1	6.3	27.4	26.7	8.5	6.3	2.4	41.4	95.2	38 935	94	87	141	4	49	308
Lincoln	4.8	17.9	5.5	25.6	28.1	9.6	6.1	2.4	42.6	95.1	33 099	57	88	124	8	34	206
Oxford	5.3	18.9	6.5	27.8	25.5	8.6	5.6	1.9	40.2	95.4	53 797	95	151	201	12	59	440
Penobscot	5.4	17.5	11.3	29.0	23.8	7.2	4.3	1.5	37.2	95.3	139 989	708	1 444	1 019	47	328	1 384
Piscataquis	4.8	18.6	5.7	26.0	27.5	9.0	6.0	2.4	42.1	96.4	16 862	36	89	47	4	24	173
Sagadahoc	6.1	19.7	6.6	30.5	24.9	6.4	4.2	1.7	38.0	96.3	33 977	323	110	222	22	133	427
Somerset	5.7	19.0	7.0	28.7	25.3	7.8	4.9	1.7	38.9	96.0	49 868	121	208	171	11	55	454
Waldo	5.6	18.6	7.5	27.8	26.8	7.6	4.5	1.5	39.3	96.6	35 513	68	144	76	5	57	417
Washington	5.1	17.8	8.0	26.3	25.6	9.1	6.1	2.1	40.5	95.5	31 728	88	1 505	101	4	151	364
York	5.9	18.9	6.9	30.0	24.8	7.3	4.7	1.6	38.5	94.5	182 177	785	451	1 367	59	322	1 581
MARYLAND	6.7	18.9	8.5	31.4	23.1	6.1	4.0	1.3	36.0	93.4	3 391 308	1 477 411	15 423	210 929	2 303	95 525	103 587
Allegany	5.0	15.5	11.2	26.8	23.5	9.0	6.7	2.2	39.1	99.2	69 702	4 006	114	390	19	140	559
Anne Arundel	6.8	18.5	8.1	32.8	23.9	5.7	3.4	.9	36.0	99.1	397 789	66 428	1 455	11 225	310	4 164	8 285
Baltimore	6.0	17.6	8.5	29.8	23.4	7.4	5.6	1.7	37.7	90.0	561 132	151 600	1 923	23 947	242	4 685	10 763
Calvert	6.8	22.8	6.4	31.7	23.4	4.9	3.1	.9	35.9	97.3	62 578	9 773	220	655	21	368	948
Caroline	6.2	20.6	7.7	28.9	23.1	7.1	4.8	1.7	37.0	95.9	24 322	4 398	110	163	5	376	398
Carroll	6.7	21.0	7.0	30.6	23.9	5.7	3.8	1.3	36.9	97.4	144 399	3 433	330	1 134	28	471	1 102
Cecil	6.9	20.7	7.5	31.2	23.2	6.0	3.6	.9	35.5	98.2	80 272	3 361	280	593	25	430	990
Charles	7.1	21.6	7.6	33.2	22.7	4.5	2.5	.7	34.6	95.5	82 587	31 411	907	2 192	70	869	2 510
Dorchester	5.4	17.9	6.7	26.8	25.5	9.4	6.3	2.1	40.7	89.8	21 302	8 708	70	202	1	119	272
Frederick	7.2	20.4	7.4	32.7	22.6	5.2	3.4	1.1	35.6	96.9	174 432	12 429	404	3 269	61	1 806	2 876
Garrett	6.1	19.0	7.8	27.6	24.6	8.0	5.1	1.9	38.3	97.2	29 496	128	22	57	7	26	110
Harford	7.2	20.7	6.8	31.6	23.7	5.9	3.4	.9	36.2	96.0	189 678	20 260	498	3 313	129	1 500	3 212
Howard	7.4	20.7	6.3	34.4	23.8	4.2	2.4	.9	35.5	96.6	184 215	35 730	583	19 037	87	2 755	5 435
Kent	4.6	16.1	10.9	23.7	25.3	9.9	7.0	2.4	41.3	91.9	15 288	3 343	28	103	9	199	227
Montgomery	6.9	18.5	6.9	32.3	24.2	5.7	4.0	1.5	36.8	92.1	565 719	132 256	2 544	98 651	412	43 642	30 117
Prince George's	7.2	19.5	10.4	33.0	22.1	4.6	2.4	.7	33.3	91.5	216 729	502 550	2 795	31 032	447	27 078	20 884
Queen Anne's	6.4	19.0	5.8	30.1	25.9	7.4	4.2	1.3	38.8	99.2	36 120	3 560	90	232	10	173	378
St. Mary's	7.2	20.7	8.9	32.6	21.5	5.0	3.1	.9	34.2	101.8	70 320	12 003	291	1 553	67	525	1 452
Somerset	4.8	13.7	15.7	29.5	22.2	7.8	4.8	1.6	36.5	114.6	13 949	10 172	92	116	4	118	296
Talbot	5.2	16.5	5.6	25.2	27.2	10.5	7.5	2.4	43.3	91.2	27 720	5 193	60	270	45	259	265
Washington	6.1	17.3	8.1	31.3	23.0	7.4	5.0	1.7	37.4	104.5	118 348	10 247	239	1 050	55	611	1 373
Wicomico	6.3	18.5	11.8	28.0	22.6	7.0	4.4	1.4	35.8	91.0	61 438	19 717	185	1 478	18	678	1 130
Worcester	4.9	15.7	6.2	26.4	26.9	11.9	6.4	1.8	43.0	95.2	37 791	7 754	86	282	9	170	451
Independent City																	
Baltimore city	6.4	18.4	10.9	29.9	21.2	6.9	4.8	1.5	35.0	87.4	205 982	418 951	2 097	9 985	222	4 363	9 554
MASSACHUSETTS	6.3	17.4	9.1	31.3	22.4	6.7	5.0	1.8	36.5	93.0	5 367 286	343 454	15 015	238 124	2 489	236 724	146 005
Barnstable	4.8	15.7	5.2	25.0	26.2	11.9	8.3	2.9	44.6	89.9	209 398	3 969	1 235	1 401	55	2 475	3 697
Berkshire	5.2	17.2	8.4	26.4	24.9	8.6	6.8	2.5	40.5	91.7	128 235	2 679	196	1 333	49	796	1 665
Bristol	6.4	18.2	8.5	30.5	22.2	6.9	5.4	1.9	36.7	92.4	486 434	10 856	1 308	6 728	145	16 695	12 512
Dukes	5.5	17.2	5.5	29.6	27.8	7.6	5.2	1.6	40.7	95.6	13 592	359	256	69	11	222	478
Essex	6.7	18.5	7.5	30.3	23.1	6.8	5.1	1.9	37.5	91.9	625 320	18 777	1 694	16 916	288	44 877	15 547
Franklin	5.2	18.3	7.8	28.5	25.9	6.7	5.6	1.9	39.5	93.8	68 244	637	205	741	19	534	1 155
Hampden	6.5	19.5	9.2	28.4	21.9	7.0	5.6	1.9	36.4	91.9	360 889	36 935	1 201	5 918	313	40 367	10 605
Hampshire	4.6	15.0	19.3	26.8	22.2	5.7	4.7	1.6	34.4	87.4	138 704	2 980	292	5 177	77	2 283	2 738
Middlesex	6.3	16.2	9.0	33.4	22.4	6.5	4.5	1.7	36.4	93.7	1 258 476	49 310	2 206	91 685	540	30 379	32 800
Nantucket	5.5	13.7	7.4	40.4	22.5	5.7	3.6	1.2	36.7	105.3	8 363	789	1	61	4	152	150
Norfolk	6.4	17.0	7.0	31.6	23.5	7.2	5.2	2.0	38.1	91.4	578 904	20 674	829	35 756	160	5 082	8 903
Plymouth	7.0	19.8	7.2	30.4	23.9	6.0	4.2	1.6	36.8	95.0	419 370	21 573	1 007	4 352	110	14 483	11 927
Suffolk	5.6	14.6	15.1	35.5	18.1	5.6	3.9	1.5	31.7	93.2	398 442	153 418	2 689	48 287	441	56 342	30 188
Worcester	6.7	19.0	8.4	31.1	21.8	6.3	5.0	1.8	36.3	95.5	672 915	20 498	1 896	19 700	277	22 037	13 640

[1] Includes all other responses not included in the other five race categories shown. Also includes write-in entries such as multiracial, mixed, interracial, or a Hispanic/Latino group. [2] Refers to combinations of two or more of the six race categories shown under one race.

Source: Population by Age, Sex, and Race—U.S. Census Bureau; 2000 Census of Population and Housing, "Census 2000 Profiles of General Demographic Characteristics" data files, published May 2001 (related Internet site <http://www.census.gov/mp/www/pub/2000cen/mscen01.html>).

Table B–2. Counties — **Population by Age, Sex, and Race**–Con.

[Includes U.S., states, and 3,142 counties/county equivalents defined as of January 1, 1992. For changes to these areas since January 1, 1992, see appendix B. Geographic Information]

County	Population by age, 2000 (April 1) Percent— Under 5 years	5 to 17 years	18 to 24 years	25 to 44 years	45 to 64 years	65 to 74 years	75 to 84 years	85 years and over	Median age (years)	Males per 100 females, 2000 (April 1)	Population by race, 2000 (April 1) — One race White	Black or African American	American Indian and Alaska Native	Asian	Native Hawaiian and Other Pacific Islander	Some other race[1]	Two or more races[2]
MICHIGAN	6.8	19.4	9.4	29.8	22.4	6.5	4.4	1.4	35.5	96.2	7 966 053	1 412 742	58 479	176 510	2 692	129 552	192 416
Alcona	4.3	14.7	4.6	20.9	31.0	14.0	8.0	2.4	49.0	102.2	11 489	19	73	21	1	7	109
Alger	4.6	16.0	7.3	28.7	26.3	8.9	6.3	1.9	41.2	116.6	8 660	603	325	32	4	38	200
Allegan	7.2	21.6	8.0	30.0	22.0	5.8	4.0	1.3	35.2	99.6	98 769	1 385	576	582	35	2 924	1 394
Alpena	5.5	18.2	7.8	26.5	24.9	9.0	5.9	2.2	40.4	94.6	30 753	77	123	103	1	39	218
Antrim	5.7	18.6	6.3	25.3	26.6	10.2	5.7	1.6	41.1	99.8	22 419	45	247	35	22	70	272
Arenac	5.3	18.0	7.8	26.8	25.5	9.6	5.4	1.6	40.1	105.4	16 472	315	164	50	2	36	230
Baraga	5.6	17.4	7.3	28.4	25.1	7.1	6.7	2.4	39.0	111.0	6 875	436	1 053	24	1	23	334
Barry	6.6	20.5	7.5	29.0	24.6	6.7	3.8	1.3	36.9	99.7	55 276	139	263	153	5	281	638
Bay	6.1	18.4	8.3	28.2	24.4	7.3	5.5	1.9	38.4	94.5	104 580	1 389	600	526	7	1 354	1 701
Benzie	5.9	17.5	6.2	27.1	25.8	9.9	5.7	1.9	40.8	98.1	15 420	45	254	25	1	62	191
Berrien	6.5	19.5	8.3	27.5	23.7	7.5	5.2	1.8	37.4	94.1	129 459	25 879	691	1 849	73	1 845	2 657
Branch	6.3	19.2	8.4	29.8	23.1	7.0	4.6	1.5	36.7	102.5	42 751	1 206	217	194	10	637	772
Calhoun	6.5	19.5	8.9	28.3	23.2	7.2	4.8	1.7	36.4	94.7	115 804	15 033	865	1 530	32	1 779	2 942
Cass	6.1	19.5	7.4	27.6	26.0	7.7	4.5	1.4	38.5	99.9	45 582	3 127	420	275	4	598	1 098
Charlevoix	6.5	19.4	6.5	27.4	25.2	8.2	5.0	1.7	39.1	97.9	25 128	45	403	59	23	107	325
Cheboygan	5.9	17.8	6.2	25.8	26.3	10.0	6.1	1.9	41.3	98.3	25 072	65	674	52	5	39	541
Chippewa	5.4	15.9	11.9	31.8	22.3	7.0	4.3	1.4	36.2	125.5	29 247	2 127	5 131	177	10	142	1 709
Clare	5.8	18.6	7.1	24.9	26.4	10.2	5.5	1.5	40.5	97.2	30 427	102	225	80	3	94	321
Clinton	6.9	21.2	7.3	29.2	24.5	6.0	3.6	1.3	36.7	98.9	62 420	405	282	337	28	523	758
Crawford	5.4	19.1	6.3	26.6	26.0	9.9	5.3	1.4	40.6	104.0	13 757	214	85	36	3	28	150
Delta	5.5	18.4	7.9	26.0	25.4	8.8	6.0	2.3	40.4	96.6	36 913	36	850	121	12	53	535
Dickinson	5.5	19.6	6.3	27.2	23.3	8.5	7.0	2.6	40.0	96.9	26 909	32	142	109	8	39	233
Eaton	6.4	19.8	9.1	28.8	24.6	6.0	3.9	1.4	36.4	94.6	93 549	5 481	453	1 173	31	1 209	1 759
Emmet	6.2	19.2	7.1	28.1	25.2	7.5	4.9	2.0	38.9	96.8	29 655	147	978	135	11	49	462
Genesee	7.3	20.2	8.9	29.7	22.4	6.6	3.8	1.2	35.0	92.6	328 350	88 843	2 414	3 515	92	3 408	9 519
Gladwin	5.5	17.7	6.5	24.2	27.8	11.1	5.5	1.7	42.3	98.5	25 411	35	145	69	5	81	277
Gogebic	4.6	15.9	8.3	24.4	24.2	10.1	8.9	3.6	42.9	101.0	16 370	305	382	40	1	60	212
Grand Traverse	6.1	19.3	7.9	29.7	24.0	6.6	4.7	1.7	37.7	95.2	74 945	307	724	383	22	423	850
Gratiot	5.9	17.9	11.6	29.5	21.6	6.5	4.9	2.1	35.6	108.3	38 908	1 572	232	145	7	746	675
Hillsdale	6.5	19.9	10.0	26.8	23.5	7.3	4.5	1.5	36.5	99.0	45 391	201	163	154	6	158	454
Houghton	5.4	16.4	19.1	22.6	20.9	7.0	5.9	2.6	34.0	113.7	34 402	339	194	646	8	60	367
Huron	5.5	18.7	6.5	25.1	24.8	9.9	7.2	2.3	41.2	97.9	35 363	69	102	128	3	117	297
Ingham	6.3	17.1	18.5	28.6	20.1	4.9	3.3	1.2	30.4	93.3	221 935	30 340	1 528	10 273	143	6 746	8 355
Ionia	6.9	20.0	11.5	31.0	20.5	5.4	3.4	1.2	32.9	115.2	56 572	2 807	344	198	7	638	952
Iosco	4.7	17.7	5.4	23.4	27.3	12.4	7.1	2.1	44.2	96.3	26 496	111	181	126	14	63	348
Iron	4.3	16.3	6.0	22.8	25.3	11.5	10.0	3.7	45.4	97.5	12 649	144	134	26	–	32	153
Isabella	5.2	15.1	29.4	23.8	17.4	4.9	3.1	1.0	25.1	91.4	57 970	1 224	1 745	886	29	433	1 064
Jackson	6.6	19.1	8.1	30.4	23.0	6.6	4.7	1.6	36.6	104.2	140 267	12 543	641	840	62	1 315	2 754
Kalamazoo	6.5	17.6	15.2	28.2	21.1	5.8	4.0	1.5	32.7	93.6	201 784	23 217	984	4 363	81	3 040	5 134
Kalkaska	6.4	19.1	7.6	28.6	24.5	8.1	4.4	1.2	38.0	101.3	16 163	35	129	37	8	16	183
Kent	7.8	20.5	10.5	31.2	19.7	5.3	3.8	1.4	32.5	96.9	477 421	51 287	2 999	10 667	349	19 200	12 412
Keweenaw	4.5	18.0	6.4	21.3	29.4	11.6	6.5	2.2	44.9	116.5	2 185	81	3	3	–	4	25
Lake	5.2	16.7	8.0	22.7	27.6	12.0	5.9	1.7	43.1	109.1	9 595	1 266	114	17	4	65	272
Lapeer	6.7	21.3	7.7	31.0	23.8	5.5	3.1	1.0	35.9	102.4	84 541	720	337	339	8	943	1 016
Leelanau	5.1	19.3	5.7	24.2	28.3	10.1	5.6	1.7	42.6	99.5	19 751	52	772	51	5	283	205
Lenawee	6.3	19.6	9.1	28.6	23.7	6.6	4.6	1.5	36.4	100.1	91 484	2 094	408	450	7	2 974	1 473
Livingston	7.2	21.5	6.6	31.7	24.6	4.7	2.8	.8	36.2	102.1	152 439	722	682	896	46	503	1 663
Luce	5.0	16.4	8.6	30.5	24.1	8.2	5.2	2.0	38.6	124.7	5 819	528	389	25	2	33	228
Mackinac	4.7	17.5	6.0	25.1	28.4	10.5	5.9	1.9	42.8	99.7	9 563	24	1 697	37	2	33	587
Macomb	6.5	17.6	8.0	31.5	22.8	7.1	5.0	1.5	36.9	96.0	730 270	21 326	2 478	16 843	178	3 106	13 948
Manistee	5.3	17.3	6.7	26.3	26.3	9.8	6.0	2.3	41.5	103.4	23 095	399	319	79	7	248	380
Marquette	5.1	16.3	13.6	26.9	24.6	6.8	5.0	1.7	37.5	100.9	61 478	853	964	319	14	160	846
Mason	5.4	18.8	7.1	26.2	25.8	8.3	6.3	2.2	40.4	97.5	27 098	206	220	78	6	232	434
Mecosta	6.0	16.5	19.8	23.0	21.5	7.6	4.3	1.3	31.9	102.8	37 586	1 460	261	354	15	152	725
Menominee	5.8	18.1	7.6	26.2	24.9	8.7	6.3	2.3	40.4	98.9	24 375	25	576	54	1	46	249
Midland	6.5	20.4	8.7	29.2	23.2	6.4	4.2	1.4	36.3	96.3	79 148	868	335	1 233	28	361	901
Missaukee	6.4	20.7	7.5	27.2	23.4	8.0	5.4	1.3	37.7	99.5	14 116	29	72	35	–	54	172
Monroe	6.6	20.8	8.1	29.8	23.5	6.2	3.7	1.2	36.0	98.4	139 264	2 766	405	679	13	907	1 911
Montcalm	6.5	20.5	8.3	30.2	22.3	6.7	4.1	1.4	35.6	105.5	58 101	1 330	366	159	28	390	892
Montmorency	4.4	15.9	5.9	20.9	29.1	13.9	7.5	2.5	47.0	96.6	10 146	25	37	10	–	10	87
Muskegon	6.9	20.7	8.7	29.0	21.9	6.6	4.7	1.5	35.5	98.3	138 291	24 166	1 402	718	21	2 184	3 418
Newaygo	6.9	22.2	7.4	27.5	23.2	7.2	4.3	1.3	36.4	99.6	45 386	535	311	140	14	779	709
Oakland	6.7	18.5	7.2	32.4	23.9	5.9	4.1	1.4	36.7	95.9	988 194	120 720	3 270	49 402	295	10 064	22 211

[1] Includes all other responses not included in the other five race categories shown. Also includes write-in entries such as multiracial, mixed, interracial, or a Hispanic/Latino group.   [2] Refers to combinations of two or more of the six race categories shown under one race.

Source: Population by Age, Sex, and Race—U.S. Census Bureau; 2000 Census of Population and Housing, "Census 2000 Profiles of General Demographic Characteristics" data files, published May 2001 (related Internet site <http://www.census.gov/mp/www/pub/2000cen/mscen01.html>).

[Includes U.S., states, and 3,142 counties/county equivalents defined as of January 1, 1992. For changes to these areas since January 1, 1992, see appendix B. Geographic Information]

County	Population by age, 2000 (April 1) Percent— Under 5 years	5 to 17 years	18 to 24 years	25 to 44 years	45 to 64 years	65 to 74 years	75 to 84 years	85 years and over	Median age (years)	Males per 100 females, 2000 (April 1)	Population by race, 2000 (April 1) One race White	Black or African American	American Indian and Alaska Native	Asian	Native Hawaiian and Other Pacific Islander	Some other race[1]	Two or more races[2]
MICHIGAN—Con.																	
Oceana	6.4	21.7	7.9	26.4	23.6	7.9	4.6	1.5	36.9	101.6	24 284	86	279	67	8	1 640	509
Ogemaw	5.2	18.3	6.4	24.4	27.0	10.9	6.1	1.7	42.3	98.4	21 100	29	129	82	7	28	270
Ontonagon	4.4	15.8	4.7	23.3	30.2	11.2	7.3	3.1	45.9	102.7	7 603	2	75	14	2	24	98
Osceola	6.2	21.0	8.0	26.5	24.2	8.1	4.6	1.4	37.6	97.7	22 620	81	116	50	4	46	280
Oscoda	5.2	18.1	5.6	22.8	28.0	11.8	6.6	1.8	43.7	96.4	9 213	8	67	7	1	13	109
Otsego	6.2	20.6	7.0	28.5	24.0	8.1	4.3	1.4	37.7	98.6	22 720	42	145	79	9	36	270
Ottawa	7.7	21.0	11.9	29.3	20.0	5.1	3.6	1.4	32.3	97.0	218 105	2 497	851	4 991	45	8 295	3 530
Presque Isle	4.8	16.1	6.5	22.4	27.8	12.2	7.7	2.4	45.1	99.2	14 133	38	85	23	1	13	118
Roscommon	4.3	15.7	5.5	21.4	29.3	14.0	7.6	2.1	47.2	96.9	24 956	82	162	49	11	25	184
Saginaw	6.8	19.8	9.0	27.6	23.2	6.9	4.8	1.8	36.3	92.5	158 220	39 112	863	1 671	28	6 039	4 106
St. Clair	6.7	20.1	7.9	30.0	23.1	6.4	4.4	1.5	36.4	97.1	155 962	3 451	829	650	32	1 052	2 259
St. Joseph	7.2	20.3	8.9	28.1	22.5	6.9	4.4	1.7	35.6	97.7	58 356	1 611	235	360	9	940	911
Sanilac	6.5	20.4	7.6	27.0	23.0	8.1	5.4	1.8	37.8	98.5	43 165	124	159	117	3	485	494
Schoolcraft	5.6	17.1	6.8	26.1	25.8	9.7	6.7	2.1	41.4	100.1	7 894	145	545	37	–	33	249
Shiawassee	6.8	20.1	8.3	29.2	23.6	6.4	4.2	1.4	36.4	96.5	69 818	139	334	201	8	349	838
Tuscola	6.0	20.7	8.2	28.1	24.1	6.6	4.7	1.5	37.0	99.8	55 963	622	334	182	11	419	735
Van Buren	6.8	21.3	7.9	28.1	23.7	6.7	4.1	1.5	36.6	98.5	67 051	4 001	705	229	9	2 614	1 654
Washtenaw	6.2	15.8	17.1	32.1	20.6	4.3	2.8	1.0	31.3	98.9	249 916	39 697	1 161	20 338	126	3 364	8 293
Wayne	7.4	20.6	8.7	30.3	20.9	6.3	4.5	1.3	34.0	92.2	1 065 607	868 992	7 627	35 141	506	32 020	51 269
Wexford	6.4	20.5	7.7	28.1	23.4	7.5	4.9	1.7	37.3	98.1	29 659	57	225	127	9	74	333
MINNESOTA	6.7	19.5	9.6	30.4	21.8	6.0	4.3	1.7	35.4	98.1	4 400 282	171 731	54 967	141 968	1 979	65 810	82 742
Aitkin	4.5	16.4	5.5	21.6	29.1	13.0	7.4	2.6	46.5	101.6	14 752	35	349	30	3	24	108
Anoka	7.6	21.3	8.3	34.1	21.6	4.2	2.2	.6	33.7	101.1	279 133	4 756	2 079	5 038	64	1 930	5 084
Becker	6.3	20.4	7.1	24.9	24.9	8.6	5.5	2.3	39.4	99.4	26 806	58	2 256	108	4	73	695
Beltrami	7.1	21.6	13.9	25.2	20.5	6.0	4.0	1.6	31.5	97.3	30 394	142	8 071	225	8	82	728
Benton	7.2	19.8	12.2	31.0	18.7	5.1	3.9	2.1	31.9	99.6	32 933	266	177	392	16	121	321
Big Stone	4.8	20.1	5.3	21.9	24.0	11.0	9.0	4.0	43.6	94.3	5 729	10	30	24	–	7	20
Blue Earth	5.6	15.8	22.1	25.6	18.8	5.5	4.6	2.0	29.9	99.1	53 121	666	155	1 000	35	386	578
Brown	5.4	19.9	9.7	25.6	21.9	8.3	6.6	2.7	38.4	98.2	26 325	27	31	111	4	244	169
Carlton	5.9	19.5	7.7	28.4	23.5	7.6	5.5	2.0	38.4	102.7	29 057	308	1 644	112	3	67	480
Carver	8.8	22.7	6.9	34.7	19.5	4.0	2.5	1.0	33.9	100.0	67 361	417	129	1 096	10	613	579
Cass	5.1	19.9	6.1	23.0	27.9	10.6	5.6	1.8	42.2	101.9	23 490	31	3 110	76	6	38	399
Chippewa	5.9	19.5	7.1	24.5	23.0	8.4	7.9	3.6	40.5	94.8	12 666	23	131	39	3	123	103
Chisago	7.6	22.6	7.1	32.2	20.7	5.1	3.4	1.4	34.3	103.9	39 953	210	187	287	11	126	327
Clay	6.2	18.8	17.1	25.7	19.3	6.2	4.6	2.0	32.3	93.7	48 149	268	740	449	14	857	752
Clearwater	5.8	20.2	7.6	24.6	24.3	8.1	6.3	3.0	39.7	101.1	7 518	16	723	21	1	20	124
Cook	4.5	15.9	5.4	25.8	31.2	9.4	5.4	2.4	44.0	99.7	4 623	15	392	17	2	13	106
Cottonwood	5.8	19.2	6.5	23.2	23.2	9.6	8.2	4.3	41.7	94.5	11 587	41	28	198	10	164	139
Crow Wing	6.1	18.8	8.1	25.6	24.4	9.2	5.9	2.1	39.4	96.8	53 801	170	429	152	7	112	428
Dakota	7.8	21.4	7.9	34.3	21.2	4.2	2.4	.8	33.7	97.6	325 166	8 091	1 347	10 285	165	4 606	6 244
Dodge	7.6	22.6	7.6	29.9	20.2	5.8	4.5	1.8	34.8	98.8	17 125	35	31	73	1	336	130
Douglas	5.5	18.5	9.2	25.0	23.8	8.8	6.3	2.8	39.7	99.0	32 326	60	78	132	9	58	158
Faribault	5.2	19.2	6.7	23.2	23.5	10.1	8.1	4.0	42.4	97.2	15 714	39	31	58	7	220	112
Fillmore	5.7	20.4	7.0	25.1	22.5	8.8	7.4	3.2	39.8	97.3	20 894	35	22	31	–	36	104
Freeborn	5.7	18.2	7.5	25.5	24.1	8.8	7.2	2.9	40.4	96.6	31 028	79	64	178	6	952	277
Goodhue	6.1	20.4	7.4	27.9	23.2	7.1	5.3	2.5	38.1	98.1	42 613	280	434	251	12	232	305
Grant	5.0	19.0	6.9	23.1	23.2	10.2	8.6	4.1	42.5	94.5	6 181	13	17	12	–	19	47
Hennepin	6.6	17.4	9.7	33.7	21.7	5.4	4.0	1.6	34.9	97.0	898 921	99 943	11 163	53 555	531	23 046	29 041
Houston	5.8	21.4	6.8	26.8	23.1	7.6	5.8	2.6	38.8	97.5	19 416	61	36	73	3	28	101
Hubbard	5.4	19.1	6.4	24.1	26.9	10.1	5.9	1.9	41.8	99.9	17 698	32	391	50	1	40	164
Isanti	6.6	22.1	7.8	30.4	22.2	5.3	3.7	1.8	35.7	100.5	30 551	80	182	120	7	53	294
Itasca	5.3	19.1	7.6	24.4	26.7	8.8	6.0	2.0	41.1	99.7	41 632	71	1 497	120	10	71	591
Jackson	5.2	19.3	7.0	25.3	22.6	9.1	7.9	3.4	40.8	100.6	10 938	10	13	155	–	109	43
Kanabec	6.0	21.5	6.9	27.5	23.9	7.9	4.8	1.5	38.0	102.0	14 587	26	121	66	5	25	166
Kandiyohi	6.2	20.4	9.5	26.5	22.5	7.1	5.6	2.3	36.9	98.0	38 576	209	138	158	27	1 719	376
Kittson	6.4	18.7	5.5	23.7	24.2	9.8	7.6	4.2	42.4	98.4	5 184	8	14	13	–	20	46
Koochiching	5.4	18.4	6.4	25.8	26.0	9.5	6.1	2.4	41.5	98.5	13 798	27	309	25	9	11	176
Lac qui Parle	5.0	19.5	5.7	22.7	23.9	10.0	8.7	4.5	43.4	98.6	7 974	13	18	26	–	5	31
Lake	5.1	17.2	6.6	24.5	26.7	11.2	6.3	2.5	42.9	99.7	10 836	11	77	20	1	16	97
Lake of the Woods	4.2	20.6	5.7	25.1	27.2	8.6	6.4	2.2	41.6	101.0	4 396	13	51	11	–	5	46
Le Sueur	6.2	21.1	7.5	27.8	23.2	6.9	5.1	2.0	37.3	100.3	24 551	38	66	77	10	513	171
Lincoln	5.5	18.2	6.1	23.0	22.7	10.2	9.8	4.5	43.0	97.3	6 353	3	18	13	–	27	15
Lyon	6.6	19.6	13.3	26.5	19.5	6.3	5.7	2.6	34.0	95.7	23 792	378	80	425	5	481	264
McLeod	7.0	20.8	7.8	29.3	21.3	6.5	5.3	2.1	35.6	98.4	33 717	76	63	194	23	623	202
Mahnomen	7.1	22.1	7.2	23.5	23.4	8.2	5.6	2.9	38.2	102.9	3 262	7	1 482	3	–	16	420
Marshall	5.7	19.7	6.7	24.7	24.7	9.0	7.3	2.3	40.5	103.2	9 873	10	29	17	–	165	61
Martin	5.5	19.4	6.4	24.9	24.0	8.9	7.7	3.3	41.5	95.3	21 195	55	22	91	5	274	160
Meeker	6.4	20.5	7.4	26.4	23.0	7.8	5.8	2.8	38.3	101.7	22 043	44	41	90	1	316	109

[1] Includes all other responses not included in the other five race categories shown. Also includes write-in entries such as multiracial, mixed, interracial, or a Hispanic/Latino group. [2] Refers to combinations of two or more of the six race categories shown under one race.

Source: Population by Age, Sex, and Race—U.S. Census Bureau; 2000 Census of Population and Housing, "Census 2000 Profiles of General Demographic Characteristics" data files, published May 2001 (related Internet site <http://www.census.gov/mp/www/pub/2000cen/mscen01.html>).

Table B–2. Counties — **Population by Age, Sex, and Race**–Con.

[Includes U.S., states, and 3,142 counties/county equivalents defined as of January 1, 1992. For changes to these areas since January 1, 1992, see appendix B. Geographic Information]

County	Population by age, 2000 (April 1) Percent— Under 5 years	5 to 17 years	18 to 24 years	25 to 44 years	45 to 64 years	65 to 74 years	75 to 84 years	85 years and over	Median age (years)	Males per 100 females, 2000 (April 1)	Population by race, 2000 (April 1) One race White	Black or African American	American Indian and Alaska Native	Asian	Native Hawaiian and Other Pacific Islander	Some other race[1]	Two or more races[2]
MINNESOTA—Con.																	
Mille Lacs	6.2	20.8	7.5	26.9	22.6	8.1	5.6	2.4	38.0	98.0	20 890	60	1 046	47	3	49	235
Morrison	6.6	21.4	8.0	26.7	21.7	7.8	5.6	2.2	36.9	101.2	31 230	66	102	80	11	49	174
Mower	6.1	19.0	8.2	25.7	21.4	9.0	7.6	3.0	38.9	97.0	36 571	215	66	568	6	843	334
Murray	5.3	19.7	5.9	23.3	24.7	10.3	7.6	3.3	42.4	98.5	9 013	9	20	19	2	41	61
Nicollet	6.0	18.8	16.4	26.9	21.2	5.7	3.7	1.5	32.6	99.3	28 691	239	78	339	7	194	223
Nobles	6.9	19.6	8.2	26.6	21.3	8.1	6.4	3.0	37.5	99.5	18 019	223	64	830	15	1 384	297
Norman	6.1	19.6	6.2	24.1	23.0	9.8	7.8	3.3	40.9	98.6	7 092	8	129	23	–	84	106
Olmsted	7.2	19.8	8.5	32.2	21.6	5.4	3.7	1.6	35.0	96.6	112 255	3 330	317	5 305	41	1 148	1 881
Otter Tail	5.5	19.4	7.2	24.2	24.7	9.5	6.5	3.0	41.1	100.4	55 505	163	291	251	27	479	443
Pennington	6.1	18.4	10.3	26.5	22.9	7.0	6.1	2.7	37.9	97.5	13 179	28	112	80	6	69	110
Pine	5.5	20.0	7.7	27.9	23.9	8.4	4.9	1.8	38.4	108.8	25 047	341	713	80	8	88	253
Pipestone	5.8	20.0	6.8	24.6	21.4	9.3	8.0	4.1	40.2	92.8	9 566	17	146	46	2	26	92
Polk	6.0	20.0	9.7	24.8	22.2	7.7	6.6	3.1	38.2	98.1	29 543	104	408	95	5	806	408
Pope	4.9	19.9	6.7	23.1	23.8	9.6	8.2	3.7	42.1	96.9	11 107	23	20	9	1	20	56
Ramsey	6.8	18.7	11.3	30.7	20.7	5.6	4.3	1.7	33.7	93.0	395 406	38 900	4 221	44 836	323	12 536	14 813
Red Lake	5.6	20.0	7.5	24.7	23.2	9.0	7.2	2.9	40.4	100.8	4 189	8	79	3	–	5	15
Redwood	6.1	20.4	6.6	24.8	22.7	8.4	7.4	3.5	39.5	99.7	15 969	22	544	53	11	73	143
Renville	6.0	20.5	6.6	25.3	21.7	9.1	7.5	3.3	39.7	99.3	16 419	10	87	35	3	475	125
Rice	6.1	19.1	15.8	27.4	20.2	5.6	4.0	1.8	32.9	101.8	53 032	741	244	826	24	1 060	738
Rock	5.9	20.4	7.2	24.1	22.0	8.8	8.4	3.2	39.9	97.6	9 456	52	42	60	2	52	57
Roseau	7.3	22.5	6.8	29.9	20.8	5.6	4.8	2.2	35.3	105.0	15 671	21	232	283	3	13	115
St. Louis	5.2	17.1	11.4	25.9	24.3	7.6	6.1	2.4	39.0	96.8	190 211	1 704	4 074	1 333	54	451	2 701
Scott	9.3	22.0	6.7	37.3	18.6	3.4	2.0	.7	32.7	101.9	83 813	824	693	1 946	27	1 114	1 081
Sherburne	8.4	22.5	9.6	33.9	18.4	3.6	2.4	1.1	31.4	104.3	62 308	550	287	372	14	276	610
Sibley	6.6	21.1	7.5	27.1	21.3	8.2	5.7	2.6	37.3	102.9	14 676	19	40	51	–	475	95
Stearns	6.4	19.3	16.1	28.0	19.1	5.9	3.8	1.3	31.6	101.2	127 832	1 110	350	2 104	45	632	1 093
Steele	6.9	21.0	8.2	29.0	21.6	6.5	4.9	1.9	35.7	97.5	32 061	360	35	286	7	555	376
Stevens	5.3	16.3	20.8	21.6	19.0	7.7	6.6	2.7	33.9	93.9	9 664	92	70	86	2	38	101
Swift	5.4	17.7	7.3	29.6	21.6	7.8	7.5	3.2	39.3	120.6	10 840	322	60	171	182	167	214
Todd	5.9	21.4	8.1	24.7	23.8	8.3	5.7	2.2	38.5	101.8	23 826	27	118	76	3	175	201
Traverse	5.4	19.9	5.6	21.7	21.2	12.0	9.0	5.2	42.9	96.7	3 986	1	116	11	3	2	15
Wabasha	5.7	21.4	7.2	27.0	23.8	7.2	5.6	2.2	38.0	100.0	21 171	54	59	94	–	135	97
Wadena	6.4	19.5	8.1	23.6	22.6	9.5	7.2	3.2	39.9	97.9	13 424	66	76	25	4	37	81
Waseca	6.7	19.1	8.7	30.0	21.3	6.6	5.3	2.2	36.3	109.3	18 482	441	116	90	6	252	139
Washington	7.6	21.8	6.8	32.9	23.2	4.4	2.4	.8	35.1	98.8	188 317	3 689	785	4 297	66	1 216	2 760
Watonwan	7.2	20.4	7.8	24.3	21.7	8.9	6.7	3.0	38.6	95.4	10 515	44	25	103	2	1 043	144
Wilkin	6.3	21.5	7.0	27.7	21.5	7.7	5.6	2.8	38.1	95.3	6 979	11	30	11	1	35	71
Winona	5.6	17.2	18.6	25.1	20.5	6.1	4.8	2.2	32.8	95.2	47 887	384	97	935	12	267	403
Wright	8.3	22.8	7.6	32.6	19.9	4.6	3.1	1.2	33.1	101.4	88 055	235	253	393	11	322	717
Yellow Medicine	5.7	20.0	7.4	24.2	22.2	8.9	7.8	3.8	40.4	98.2	10 647	12	226	19	1	102	73
MISSISSIPPI	7.2	20.1	10.9	28.4	21.4	6.5	4.0	1.5	33.8	93.4	1 746 099	1 033 809	11 652	18 626	667	13 784	20 021
Adams	6.8	20.0	8.6	25.6	23.5	8.5	5.2	1.8	38.1	86.1	15 809	18 117	49	85	4	72	204
Alcorn	6.5	17.4	9.1	27.9	24.4	7.8	5.2	1.9	37.6	93.9	30 193	3 827	33	73	22	203	207
Amite	5.9	20.1	8.5	25.6	24.6	8.4	5.4	1.6	38.3	93.3	7 673	5 800	17	11	2	29	67
Attala	6.4	19.5	9.2	25.2	22.4	9.0	5.9	2.4	37.3	91.5	11 470	7 864	34	53	–	127	113
Benton	7.4	19.5	10.0	25.8	22.0	8.5	5.1	1.7	35.6	94.6	4 954	2 950	47	4	1	23	47
Bolivar	7.4	22.2	14.0	25.7	19.6	5.5	4.0	1.6	29.8	87.8	13 507	26 458	40	200	6	196	226
Calhoun	6.5	18.7	8.4	27.0	22.7	8.4	5.9	2.4	37.4	90.7	10 460	4 318	20	9	5	168	89
Carroll	5.5	18.9	9.6	26.7	25.7	7.3	4.5	1.7	38.1	99.2	6 749	3 942	7	17	1	14	39
Chickasaw	7.6	21.0	9.3	27.6	21.0	6.9	4.7	2.0	34.4	92.6	11 060	8 020	37	34	8	192	89
Choctaw	6.8	21.0	8.8	24.9	23.5	7.8	4.8	2.3	36.9	91.9	6 638	2 994	30	13	1	41	41
Claiborne	6.8	19.5	23.1	22.3	17.9	5.0	3.7	1.8	25.6	85.7	1 796	9 951	6	17	–	12	49
Clarke	6.8	20.0	8.6	26.7	22.8	8.2	5.0	1.9	36.8	91.3	11 580	6 251	20	19	1	31	53
Clay	7.5	21.4	10.4	26.5	21.1	6.7	4.6	1.8	33.9	89.1	9 411	12 380	12	35	2	46	93
Coahoma	8.9	24.1	10.3	25.3	19.1	6.3	4.2	1.8	30.5	84.9	8 965	21 192	27	144	5	104	185
Copiah	6.6	20.3	12.5	26.8	21.1	6.8	4.3	1.5	34.0	92.9	13 747	14 653	21	45	3	133	155
Covington	7.5	21.3	9.6	27.3	21.2	6.9	4.5	1.5	33.8	92.6	12 307	6 910	26	23	3	30	108
DeSoto	7.8	20.4	8.2	32.7	22.1	5.5	2.7	.7	33.7	98.0	91 950	12 216	297	667	41	1 211	817
Forrest	6.9	17.6	18.2	27.6	18.3	5.9	3.9	1.6	29.7	89.3	46 717	24 360	140	536	13	292	546
Franklin	6.5	20.8	8.8	26.1	22.6	8.2	5.0	2.0	37.0	92.3	5 305	3 064	19	6	–	4	50
George	7.8	21.4	9.4	28.6	21.9	6.2	3.4	1.3	33.3	100.6	17 110	1 688	45	30	–	161	110
Greene	7.0	17.1	13.1	32.1	20.6	5.5	3.4	1.2	32.4	130.0	9 681	3 482	31	9	4	41	51
Grenada	6.9	20.3	9.0	27.5	22.0	7.4	4.9	2.1	35.7	87.8	13 474	9 522	33	80	4	30	120
Hancock	6.3	18.8	7.3	28.0	25.6	8.3	4.6	1.1	38.5	98.3	38 752	2 934	257	377	16	143	488
Harrison	7.1	18.9	11.1	30.5	21.2	6.5	3.6	1.0	33.9	99.1	138 692	39 984	861	4 934	163	1 697	3 270
Hinds	7.4	20.5	12.1	28.9	20.1	5.7	3.8	1.5	31.9	88.8	93 584	153 297	307	1 507	29	491	1 585
Holmes	7.7	24.4	12.4	24.8	18.3	6.4	4.2	1.8	29.7	87.3	4 424	16 997	26	33	–	16	113
Humphreys	7.8	24.9	10.7	25.8	18.8	6.0	3.8	2.1	30.5	87.5	3 045	8 013	11	30	–	72	35
Issaquena	5.7	21.9	10.9	30.9	19.9	6.2	3.5	1.0	33.1	113.5	826	1 427	2	–	–	5	14

[1] Includes all other responses not included in the other five race categories shown. Also includes write-in entries such as multiracial, mixed, interracial, or a Hispanic/Latino group.   [2] Refers to combinations of two or more of the six race categories shown under one race.

Source: Population by Age, Sex, and Race—U.S. Census Bureau; 2000 Census of Population and Housing, "Census 2000 Profiles of General Demographic Characteristics" data files, published May 2001 (related Internet site <http://www.census.gov/mp/www/pub/2000cen/mscen01.html>).

[Includes U.S., states, and 3,142 counties/county equivalents defined as of January 1, 1992. For changes to these areas since January 1, 1992, see appendix B. Geographic Information]

County	Population by age, 2000 (April 1) Percent— Under 5 years	5 to 17 years	18 to 24 years	25 to 44 years	45 to 64 years	65 to 74 years	75 to 84 years	85 years and over	Median age (years)	Males per 100 females, 2000 (April 1)	One race White	Black or African American	American Indian and Alaska Native	Asian	Native Hawaiian and Other Pacific Islander	Some other race[1]	Two or more races[2]
MISSISSIPPI—Con.																	
Itawamba	6.1	18.1	10.6	27.8	23.2	7.6	4.9	1.7	36.2	94.1	21 055	1 473	33	42	–	72	95
Jackson	7.0	20.6	9.3	29.8	22.9	6.1	3.2	1.0	34.7	98.2	99 026	27 432	440	2 059	52	941	1 470
Jasper	6.9	21.0	9.6	26.7	21.9	7.2	4.6	2.0	35.1	91.0	8 433	9 597	12	12	5	15	75
Jefferson	7.3	21.5	12.1	28.5	19.6	5.6	3.7	1.6	32.4	99.0	1 272	8 424	8	10	1	2	23
Jefferson Davis	7.2	21.2	9.9	25.4	22.5	7.1	4.9	1.8	35.0	89.9	5 816	8 011	19	25	1	11	79
Jones	7.0	18.8	10.5	27.3	22.2	7.9	4.7	1.6	35.8	93.7	46 192	17 107	252	174	6	913	314
Kemper	6.7	18.8	12.5	25.2	21.8	7.4	5.1	2.6	35.2	92.2	4 080	6 076	215	8	3	11	60
Lafayette	5.4	14.2	27.1	26.3	17.1	5.1	3.4	1.3	26.9	96.7	27 838	9 705	61	648	5	162	325
Lamar	7.4	20.6	10.9	30.4	21.0	5.7	3.1	1.0	32.6	93.3	33 342	5 040	65	254	4	116	249
Lauderdale	7.1	19.5	9.8	28.0	21.4	7.1	5.0	2.1	35.0	90.6	47 013	29 838	137	393	22	269	489
Lawrence	6.8	20.5	9.4	27.5	22.6	7.5	4.3	1.5	35.8	92.2	8 875	4 252	22	36	3	12	58
Leake	7.3	19.6	10.1	27.0	21.7	7.8	4.5	2.0	34.8	98.0	11 755	7 835	955	31	7	238	119
Lee	7.5	20.2	8.5	30.5	21.8	6.0	3.9	1.6	34.6	92.3	55 800	18 566	96	397	8	324	564
Leflore	7.8	21.9	13.1	27.0	18.2	5.8	4.1	2.0	30.1	92.5	11 384	25 701	43	245	15	370	189
Lincoln	7.1	19.6	9.5	27.6	22.3	7.6	4.6	1.8	35.8	92.2	23 010	9 839	57	81	3	54	122
Lowndes	7.7	20.9	10.6	29.2	20.4	5.9	3.7	1.6	32.7	89.9	34 775	25 594	102	333	17	239	526
Madison	7.8	20.8	8.9	32.4	20.3	4.9	3.2	1.6	33.4	90.2	45 021	27 987	83	973	16	200	394
Marion	6.9	20.9	9.5	26.9	21.5	7.6	4.7	1.9	35.1	93.7	17 138	8 156	58	55	2	28	158
Marshall	7.0	19.5	11.8	28.6	22.0	6.5	3.4	1.1	33.9	98.0	16 925	17 622	58	39	5	128	216
Monroe	6.6	20.6	8.7	27.6	22.5	7.2	4.8	1.9	35.7	89.7	25 991	11 698	37	66	4	41	177
Montgomery	6.6	20.1	8.9	25.3	22.4	8.6	5.8	2.2	37.3	86.4	6 613	5 479	10	31	3	8	45
Neshoba	7.8	20.5	9.0	27.0	21.6	7.5	4.7	1.9	34.7	91.1	18 788	5 546	3 959	55	6	97	233
Newton	7.1	19.0	11.2	26.0	21.7	7.8	5.2	2.0	35.1	92.4	14 197	6 632	803	39	–	72	95
Noxubee	8.1	22.6	10.3	26.7	19.5	6.8	4.2	1.8	32.3	90.5	3 700	8 696	19	14	–	46	73
Oktibbeha	6.0	15.1	29.6	24.8	16.0	4.6	2.9	1.1	24.8	99.9	25 167	16 059	70	1 086	12	202	306
Panola	7.7	21.7	10.4	27.4	20.8	6.6	4.0	1.5	33.0	91.8	17 302	16 575	56	63	4	140	134
Pearl River	7.0	19.9	9.4	27.1	23.9	7.5	3.9	1.2	35.9	94.4	41 596	5 924	242	131	13	166	549
Perry	7.7	21.0	10.0	28.0	22.2	6.4	3.6	1.0	33.5	95.6	9 245	2 742	40	14	6	34	57
Pike	7.4	20.3	10.1	26.0	22.1	7.3	5.0	1.9	35.2	88.0	19 955	18 507	74	127	4	77	196
Pontotoc	7.2	20.4	8.7	29.5	21.4	6.8	4.4	1.6	34.8	94.5	22 557	3 735	72	26	2	190	144
Prentiss	6.8	18.2	11.6	27.1	22.4	7.3	4.9	1.7	35.0	94.1	21 940	3 308	47	40	–	43	178
Quitman	8.1	23.9	9.6	25.7	19.5	6.7	4.7	1.7	31.8	86.5	3 083	6 942	13	17	1	8	53
Rankin	7.0	18.9	9.1	32.4	23.0	5.8	2.8	.9	34.6	95.6	93 450	19 743	189	763	24	469	689
Scott	7.4	21.2	9.6	27.9	21.4	6.7	4.0	1.7	33.8	94.4	16 258	11 052	88	50	6	715	254
Sharkey	8.6	24.4	10.4	24.8	20.4	5.5	3.9	1.9	30.8	88.7	1 932	4 561	12	18	–	18	39
Simpson	7.1	20.8	9.4	27.5	22.1	7.2	4.1	1.7	35.0	94.4	17 796	9 484	32	40	3	129	155
Smith	7.0	20.5	8.7	27.3	22.6	7.8	4.4	1.7	35.6	95.5	12 316	3 739	17	16	6	31	57
Stone	6.9	19.9	12.2	27.4	22.4	6.3	3.8	1.0	33.6	98.2	10 818	2 613	39	22	4	31	95
Sunflower	7.0	20.9	14.0	30.3	18.1	4.9	3.3	1.5	30.2	115.9	9 927	24 010	32	137	–	166	97
Tallahatchie	7.0	23.1	10.0	25.9	20.9	6.8	4.7	1.8	33.3	87.8	5 904	8 857	13	54	–	7	68
Tate	6.9	20.2	11.7	27.5	22.3	6.1	3.9	1.4	34.2	93.7	17 211	7 870	50	25	10	63	141
Tippah	6.3	18.6	10.1	27.9	22.5	7.4	5.1	2.0	35.9	93.7	17 046	3 316	42	22	3	269	128
Tishomingo	5.9	17.3	7.8	27.5	24.7	9.1	5.7	2.0	39.1	92.7	18 192	596	41	15	2	203	114
Tunica	8.4	23.1	10.9	27.4	20.2	5.4	3.5	1.2	30.6	91.1	2 541	6 473	10	39	6	89	69
Union	7.4	18.6	9.2	28.5	22.2	7.5	4.7	1.9	35.6	93.8	21 156	3 791	33	51	4	170	157
Walthall	7.1	21.3	9.9	25.4	22.3	7.4	4.8	1.8	35.1	91.5	8 277	6 682	18	37	2	40	100
Warren	7.6	21.0	9.1	28.4	22.4	6.0	4.1	1.6	34.8	88.3	27 288	21 439	112	307	8	164	326
Washington	8.4	23.1	10.1	26.5	20.5	6.0	3.8	1.6	31.5	87.7	21 393	40 667	57	332	10	156	362
Wayne	7.6	21.6	9.7	27.6	21.7	6.5	3.8	1.4	33.8	91.5	13 004	8 065	15	32	2	28	70
Webster	6.7	19.4	9.0	26.6	21.8	8.3	5.8	2.4	37.3	90.5	7 983	2 155	11	18	1	86	40
Wilkinson	5.8	20.0	10.7	29.0	20.6	6.9	5.0	2.0	35.0	108.0	3 219	7 034	10	3	–	7	39
Winston	6.7	20.0	9.2	26.1	22.5	8.3	5.0	2.1	36.3	93.7	11 141	8 719	134	17	–	56	93
Yalobusha	6.4	19.1	8.9	26.1	23.8	8.2	5.8	1.7	37.7	91.3	7 891	5 045	28	11	11	12	53
Yazoo	7.4	21.0	9.8	29.2	20.1	6.5	4.2	1.8	33.7	103.6	12 593	15 189	56	102	1	62	146
MISSOURI	6.6	18.9	9.6	29.1	22.3	7.0	4.7	1.8	36.1	94.6	4 748 083	629 391	25 076	61 595	3 178	45 827	82 061
Adair	5.3	13.9	27.4	22.8	18.4	5.8	4.5	2.0	27.9	88.2	23 932	299	64	347	12	103	220
Andrew	6.3	20.0	7.9	27.6	23.7	6.9	5.3	2.2	37.8	95.0	16 225	69	56	37	1	29	75
Atchison	4.5	19.6	6.5	24.2	24.2	9.4	7.9	3.7	41.7	99.3	6 237	132	12	9	–	20	20
Audrain	6.4	18.2	7.9	28.2	22.5	7.8	6.7	2.4	38.0	84.2	23 547	1 859	68	89	8	54	228
Barry	6.7	19.4	7.8	26.1	23.9	8.8	5.4	1.9	38.2	98.3	31 999	39	292	91	11	1 107	471
Barton	7.7	19.8	8.3	26.1	21.7	8.1	5.9	2.4	37.3	96.0	12 156	36	104	35	12	17	181
Bates	6.1	20.4	7.5	26.0	22.6	8.6	6.2	2.6	38.4	95.2	16 208	101	99	25	2	65	153
Benton	4.8	15.7	5.7	21.8	29.7	13.5	6.6	2.2	46.3	98.2	16 830	25	91	22	2	21	189
Bollinger	6.1	20.1	7.8	26.8	24.5	8.3	4.9	1.7	37.9	97.9	11 763	25	87	26	–	16	112
Boone	6.2	16.6	19.9	29.9	18.8	4.4	3.0	1.2	29.5	93.5	115 714	11 572	567	4 015	42	931	2 613
Buchanan	6.3	18.1	11.0	28.5	21.2	7.3	5.6	2.2	36.1	96.7	79 744	3 751	363	386	20	557	1 177
Butler	6.4	17.8	8.4	26.6	24.1	8.9	5.7	2.1	38.7	92.0	37 663	2 132	227	178	5	107	555
Caldwell	6.3	20.8	7.1	25.1	23.7	8.4	6.1	2.6	38.8	97.6	8 840	12	30	11	–	16	60
Callaway	6.2	19.2	11.1	31.0	21.5	6.0	3.6	1.3	34.7	107.6	37 420	2 307	210	210	5	121	493

[1] Includes all other responses not included in the other five race categories shown. Also includes write-in entries such as multiracial, mixed, interracial, or a Hispanic/Latino group.   [2] Refers to combinations of two or more of the six race categories shown under one race.

Source: Population by Age, Sex, and Race—U.S. Census Bureau; 2000 Census of Population and Housing, "Census 2000 Profiles of General Demographic Characteristics" data files, published May 2001 (related Internet site <http://www.census.gov/mp/www/pub/2000cen/mscen01.html>).

[Includes U.S., states, and 3,142 counties/county equivalents defined as of January 1, 1992. For changes to these areas since January 1, 1992, see appendix B. Geographic Information]

County	Population by age, 2000 (April 1) Percent—									Males per 100 females, 2000 (April 1)	Population by race, 2000 (April 1) One race						
	Under 5 years	5 to 17 years	18 to 24 years	25 to 44 years	45 to 64 years	65 to 74 years	75 to 84 years	85 years and over	Median age (years)		White	Black or African American	American Indian and Alaska Native	Asian	Native Hawaiian and Other Pacific Islander	Some other race[1]	Two or more races[2]
MISSOURI—Con.																	
Camden	4.6	15.6	6.1	23.3	31.4	12.2	5.5	1.3	45.2	100.0	36 190	95	181	107	14	82	382
Cape Girardeau	6.0	17.5	13.4	27.8	21.6	6.8	5.0	2.0	35.2	93.2	63 290	3 624	248	515	18	211	787
Carroll	6.4	18.8	7.4	24.5	22.9	9.0	7.7	3.3	40.0	94.2	9 971	177	28	13	1	14	81
Carter	6.2	18.9	8.0	25.9	25.0	9.4	4.9	1.6	38.9	96.5	5 739	5	80	6	–	2	109
Cass	7.4	21.0	7.3	30.2	22.3	6.4	3.7	1.6	35.8	95.9	78 499	1 166	476	397	30	413	1 111
Cedar	5.7	19.0	6.4	22.8	25.4	11.0	7.0	2.8	42.2	95.9	13 263	44	91	63	6	69	197
Chariton	5.1	18.6	6.5	23.7	23.8	10.6	8.0	3.7	42.5	91.9	8 100	269	14	11	–	9	35
Christian	7.7	20.2	8.1	31.7	21.8	5.9	3.5	1.1	34.5	94.7	52 824	145	302	157	16	230	611
Clark	6.1	18.8	7.8	25.5	25.0	8.2	5.9	2.6	39.2	97.6	7 329	5	15	5	1	16	45
Clay	7.2	18.6	8.7	32.3	22.3	5.9	3.7	1.2	35.0	94.6	170 129	4 894	890	2 479	164	2 173	3 277
Clinton	6.6	20.2	7.4	28.2	23.5	6.8	4.7	2.6	37.7	96.0	18 329	288	65	32	1	51	213
Cole	6.5	17.7	9.8	32.3	22.4	5.8	3.9	1.6	35.5	105.6	62 158	7 084	239	625	26	384	881
Cooper	5.8	17.0	14.0	27.4	20.6	7.0	5.8	2.4	35.2	117.4	14 844	1 493	60	39	3	46	185
Crawford	6.5	19.8	7.9	26.9	23.1	8.6	5.3	1.9	37.9	97.3	22 408	33	99	30	14	32	188
Dade	5.8	18.5	6.8	24.1	24.4	10.2	7.1	3.0	41.7	95.9	7 721	21	56	11	4	15	95
Dallas	6.7	20.8	7.4	26.4	23.5	8.3	5.0	1.8	37.9	98.3	15 262	19	119	11	5	31	214
Daviess	7.0	20.0	7.6	24.1	23.7	9.5	5.9	2.2	38.9	92.9	7 910	4	31	6	15	17	33
DeKalb	5.2	15.5	8.2	36.3	20.9	7.0	5.0	1.8	37.7	152.3	10 332	1 028	77	20	1	31	108
Dent	6.4	18.5	7.6	25.6	24.1	9.2	6.1	2.5	39.6	94.3	14 489	59	109	32	2	25	211
Douglas	6.0	19.8	7.0	24.5	25.6	9.5	5.4	2.2	40.1	96.6	12 673	14	124	28	2	22	221
Dunklin	7.1	18.8	8.1	26.0	23.5	8.1	6.2	2.2	37.8	89.6	29 388	2 879	104	90	4	340	350
Franklin	6.9	20.4	8.2	30.0	22.4	6.6	4.1	1.4	35.8	98.5	91 436	882	224	249	23	183	810
Gasconade	5.8	18.9	6.9	25.9	23.7	9.1	6.8	2.9	40.3	94.6	15 141	18	28	24	1	22	108
Gentry	6.2	19.8	7.0	23.7	21.6	9.7	8.2	3.7	40.2	95.1	6 763	8	21	12	11	7	39
Greene	6.1	16.1	13.8	28.6	21.8	6.8	4.9	1.9	35.1	94.4	224 859	5 426	1 583	2 720	145	1 617	4 041
Grundy	6.1	17.1	8.3	23.7	24.2	9.7	7.3	3.6	41.3	90.4	10 183	42	36	16	1	52	102
Harrison	6.4	17.3	7.2	23.9	23.2	10.4	7.6	4.0	41.7	94.2	8 700	12	22	13	5	8	90
Henry	6.0	17.8	7.8	25.8	24.4	9.0	6.7	2.6	40.0	95.5	21 251	225	155	54	5	75	232
Hickory	4.3	15.6	5.3	19.1	29.7	15.4	8.5	2.2	49.7	96.0	8 717	7	59	10	–	18	129
Holt	4.8	19.0	6.5	24.4	23.9	9.5	8.2	3.8	41.8	97.7	5 269	6	25	4	1	6	40
Howard	5.6	18.4	13.3	25.2	21.3	7.3	6.0	2.8	36.7	94.0	9 306	699	34	12	8	41	112
Howell	6.7	19.3	7.8	26.2	23.3	8.8	5.8	2.2	38.2	93.6	35 902	114	362	134	16	103	607
Iron	5.9	19.1	7.8	25.3	24.8	8.9	5.4	2.7	39.7	94.8	10 348	167	36	10	–	24	112
Jackson	7.0	18.8	9.1	31.1	21.5	6.5	4.4	1.6	35.2	92.9	459 061	152 391	3 168	8 412	1 168	15 914	14 766
Jasper	7.3	18.5	11.0	28.1	21.3	7.0	5.0	1.8	34.9	94.1	96 916	1 551	1 388	727	68	1 692	2 344
Jefferson	7.2	20.7	8.5	31.8	22.5	5.4	2.9	.9	34.9	98.9	193 102	1 354	577	708	28	479	1 851
Johnson	6.7	18.4	20.2	27.6	17.8	5.5	3.1	1.1	28.5	101.9	43 491	2 089	314	692	61	623	988
Knox	6.1	18.8	6.2	23.7	23.9	10.9	7.2	3.2	41.6	92.9	4 296	4	1	4	–	7	49
Laclede	6.9	19.8	8.4	27.8	22.9	7.6	4.9	1.6	36.6	96.4	31 552	138	160	95	15	109	444
Lafayette	6.1	20.1	7.6	27.5	23.3	7.6	5.3	2.5	37.9	95.9	31 485	749	96	82	9	169	370
Lawrence	7.1	20.1	7.9	26.9	22.4	7.7	5.7	2.2	36.9	97.0	33 682	95	267	79	8	589	484
Lewis	7.2	17.8	12.9	24.6	21.4	7.7	5.5	3.0	36.0	96.0	10 066	265	17	21	2	46	77
Lincoln	7.3	22.7	8.1	30.2	21.0	5.8	3.6	1.4	34.5	98.4	37 435	677	143	68	11	166	444
Linn	6.1	19.3	7.0	24.4	22.6	9.2	8.0	3.3	40.3	89.6	13 476	82	52	19	–	21	104
Livingston	6.1	18.3	7.4	26.2	23.0	8.5	7.3	3.2	39.7	84.8	13 962	339	49	39	2	35	132
McDonald	7.8	21.1	8.7	28.6	22.6	6.4	3.5	1.3	34.3	102.6	19 440	38	625	31	30	802	715
Macon	6.4	17.8	7.5	25.3	23.9	8.6	7.3	3.1	40.1	95.4	15 160	349	61	25	2	34	131
Madison	5.9	18.7	7.9	26.3	23.3	9.1	6.3	2.6	39.1	92.1	11 599	15	30	34	–	24	98
Maries	6.6	19.4	7.3	26.5	24.5	8.9	5.1	1.6	38.5	101.2	8 674	29	49	10	–	31	110
Marion	6.8	18.9	9.5	26.4	21.7	7.7	6.1	2.9	37.1	89.4	26 382	1 308	75	78	23	50	373
Mercer	5.6	17.4	6.7	24.2	24.0	10.9	7.6	3.6	42.4	95.7	3 709	7	21	–	2	1	17
Miller	6.8	19.5	8.4	27.4	22.7	8.1	5.1	2.1	37.2	97.3	23 090	65	108	30	5	68	198
Mississippi	7.2	19.2	8.8	25.4	20.8	8.0	5.7	2.2	37.3	87.6	10 463	2 757	33	15	1	39	119
Moniteau	6.7	19.2	8.2	31.1	20.9	6.5	5.3	2.1	35.9	113.3	13 752	561	59	46	2	219	188
Monroe	6.5	19.4	7.3	25.0	24.2	8.5	6.3	2.8	39.4	96.4	8 814	357	38	11	3	15	73
Montgomery	5.7	19.7	7.4	26.1	23.9	8.0	6.1	3.1	39.4	98.1	11 647	248	29	31	1	25	155
Morgan	6.0	17.8	6.2	23.1	27.3	11.8	5.6	2.2	42.6	97.2	18 796	98	122	23	4	30	236
New Madrid	6.6	19.8	8.5	26.4	23.2	8.1	5.5	1.9	37.4	92.4	16 442	3 035	37	27	1	63	155
Newton	7.0	19.2	8.7	27.1	23.8	7.6	4.8	1.7	37.1	95.6	49 086	312	1 175	169	145	589	1 160
Nodaway	4.7	14.7	25.1	23.1	18.6	6.5	5.0	2.4	30.2	99.7	21 162	295	51	190	5	46	163
Oregon	5.9	18.4	7.0	24.1	26.5	9.6	6.1	2.3	41.0	96.4	9 786	10	298	14	1	8	227
Osage	6.7	19.6	9.5	27.7	21.7	7.4	5.2	2.1	36.1	103.0	12 884	21	31	10	3	9	104
Ozark	5.4	16.7	6.9	22.8	28.7	11.5	6.2	1.9	43.6	98.1	9 310	14	62	8	–	18	130
Pemiscot	8.1	21.9	9.1	25.0	21.1	7.6	5.2	2.1	34.4	88.5	14 386	5 259	51	54	3	124	170
Perry	6.8	19.3	8.6	27.9	21.9	7.5	5.9	2.3	36.8	99.2	17 808	33	42	117	5	21	106
Pettis	7.0	19.3	9.3	27.9	21.1	7.8	5.5	2.1	36.4	94.4	36 275	1 197	148	154	21	970	638
Phelps	5.7	18.0	14.5	26.1	21.8	7.1	5.0	1.8	34.9	103.2	37 132	596	236	936	25	186	714
Pike	5.4	18.0	9.1	29.8	22.8	7.4	5.1	2.4	37.7	119.2	16 230	1 682	44	28	7	169	191
Platte	6.8	18.9	8.3	32.6	24.5	4.7	3.1	1.1	35.9	98.1	67 473	2 574	338	1 093	150	773	1 380
Polk	6.8	19.0	12.6	25.5	20.8	8.0	5.4	1.9	35.0	94.9	26 253	122	181	52	8	90	286

[1] Includes all other responses not included in the other five race categories shown. Also includes write-in entries such as multiracial, mixed, interracial, or a Hispanic/Latino group.   [2] Refers to combinations of two or more of the six race categories shown under one race.

Source: Population by Age, Sex, and Race—U.S. Census Bureau; 2000 Census of Population and Housing, "Census 2000 Profiles of General Demographic Characteristics" data files, published May 2001 (related Internet site <http://www.census.gov/mp/www/pub/2000cen/mscen01.html>).

Table B–2. Counties — **Population by Age, Sex, and Race**–Con.

[Includes U.S., states, and 3,142 counties/county equivalents defined as of January 1, 1992. For changes to these areas since January 1, 1992, see appendix B. Geographic Information]

County	Population by age, 2000 (April 1)									Population by race, 2000 (April 1)						
	Percent—								Males per 100 females, 2000 (April 1)	One race						Two or more races[2]
	Under 5 years	5 to 17 years	18 to 24 years	25 to 44 years	45 to 64 years	65 to 74 years	75 to 84 years	85 years and over	Median age (years)		White	Black or African American	American Indian and Alaska Native	Asian	Native Hawaiian and Other Pacific Islander	Some other race[1]	

County	Under 5 years	5 to 17 years	18 to 24 years	25 to 44 years	45 to 64 years	65 to 74 years	75 to 84 years	85 years and over	Median age (years)	Males per 100 females, 2000 (April 1)	White	Black or African American	American Indian and Alaska Native	Asian	Native Hawaiian and Other Pacific Islander	Some other race[1]	Two or more races[2]
MISSOURI—Con.																	
Pulaski	7.7	19.9	16.6	32.0	15.9	4.7	2.4	.8	28.5	112.1	32 254	4 935	413	936	130	1 028	1 469
Putnam	6.5	17.5	6.2	24.0	25.1	10.3	7.7	2.8	41.9	96.1	5 178	3	5	7	–	5	25
Ralls	5.7	19.6	7.1	26.9	26.5	7.5	5.1	1.7	39.3	100.9	9 427	107	19	8	1	4	60
Randolph	6.4	17.5	9.6	29.3	22.4	7.4	5.2	2.3	37.2	107.5	22 339	1 734	118	97	6	59	310
Ray	6.6	20.9	7.4	28.3	23.9	7.0	4.3	1.6	37.1	100.2	22 536	341	83	44	1	84	265
Reynolds	5.8	18.2	6.8	25.0	27.9	9.6	5.0	1.7	40.7	101.6	6 398	35	86	13	–	14	143
Ripley	6.0	18.8	7.9	25.3	24.7	9.6	5.6	2.1	39.4	94.3	13 127	6	179	30	2	7	158
St. Charles	7.6	21.3	8.2	32.6	21.6	5.1	2.8	.8	34.3	97.1	268 756	7 635	657	2 414	71	1 301	3 049
St. Clair	5.5	17.5	5.6	22.9	27.2	11.2	7.1	3.0	43.9	98.6	9 397	22	72	14	2	28	117
Ste. Genevieve	6.0	20.6	7.6	27.9	23.3	7.9	4.7	1.9	37.7	101.2	17 491	128	53	29	–	23	118
St. Francois	6.0	17.9	9.2	29.4	22.5	7.9	5.3	1.8	37.2	103.3	53 494	1 126	196	175	12	127	511
St. Louis	6.3	18.9	8.3	29.0	23.5	7.2	5.0	1.8	37.5	90.0	780 830	193 306	1 717	22 606	251	4 775	12 830
Saline	6.1	18.2	12.0	25.2	22.3	7.4	6.3	2.6	37.2	96.1	21 387	1 280	73	84	50	497	385
Schuyler	6.0	18.6	6.7	24.8	24.1	9.2	7.5	3.1	40.8	93.1	4 105	2	13	7	1	7	35
Scotland	7.2	21.4	7.6	24.1	20.8	8.1	7.5	3.4	37.4	94.3	4 924	10	7	4	1	8	29
Scott	7.0	20.4	8.5	27.5	22.9	7.0	5.0	1.7	36.0	91.6	35 442	4 246	113	93	3	160	365
Shannon	6.2	20.3	7.2	26.1	25.3	8.5	4.9	1.6	38.8	95.3	7 912	14	152	4	2	16	224
Shelby	5.7	19.7	7.2	24.4	23.3	8.7	7.0	4.0	40.4	91.6	6 654	66	19	7	–	13	40
Stoddard	5.7	18.2	8.5	26.3	24.1	8.6	6.4	2.3	39.1	92.6	28 915	270	118	28	3	72	299
Stone	5.5	16.0	6.2	23.8	29.7	12.1	5.2	1.6	44.1	96.2	27 983	21	175	52	10	73	344
Sullivan	7.1	17.9	7.5	26.3	22.7	8.3	7.0	3.2	38.9	100.1	6 855	10	18	10	5	256	65
Taney	6.1	16.3	10.2	26.2	25.0	9.3	5.2	1.7	38.8	94.0	38 202	138	347	136	21	294	565
Texas	5.8	19.2	7.1	24.9	25.3	9.7	5.9	2.2	40.4	93.5	22 190	49	221	78	4	44	417
Vernon	6.7	19.9	9.2	25.4	22.5	8.4	5.6	2.4	37.1	93.5	19 839	125	162	63	7	63	195
Warren	6.5	20.3	7.6	28.8	23.7	7.5	4.1	1.3	37.4	98.6	23 517	476	110	59	4	109	250
Washington	6.6	20.0	9.8	29.2	22.7	7.0	3.5	1.2	35.2	106.4	22 286	578	155	35	2	36	252
Wayne	5.3	17.9	6.7	23.5	26.8	11.7	5.8	2.3	42.5	98.3	12 951	22	77	15	4	10	180
Webster	7.5	21.3	8.3	29.7	21.7	6.2	3.7	1.5	34.6	101.4	29 866	359	203	81	8	96	432
Worth	5.5	18.8	6.8	23.5	23.1	10.5	7.2	4.6	41.9	96.0	2 358	4	8	2	–	–	10
Wright	7.0	20.2	8.2	25.3	22.8	8.8	5.6	2.1	37.7	94.3	17 526	50	118	25	1	48	187
Independent City																	
St. Louis city	6.7	19.0	10.6	30.9	19.1	6.6	5.0	2.1	33.7	88.6	152 666	178 266	950	6 891	94	2 783	6 539
MONTANA	6.1	19.4	9.5	27.2	24.4	6.9	4.8	1.7	37.5	99.3	817 229	2 692	56 068	4 691	470	5 315	15 730
Beaverhead	5.7	18.8	11.9	25.1	24.9	7.2	4.2	2.2	37.6	105.0	8 821	17	134	17	4	100	109
Big Horn	9.3	26.5	8.6	26.5	20.5	4.6	2.9	1.1	29.8	97.3	4 638	5	7 560	28	1	86	353
Blaine	8.1	24.5	8.0	24.8	21.6	6.9	4.4	1.6	34.4	97.5	3 685	12	3 180	6	2	16	108
Broadwater	5.3	19.9	4.8	26.2	27.4	9.0	5.4	2.0	41.3	104.0	4 255	12	51	5	3	15	44
Carbon	5.2	18.8	5.7	26.1	27.3	8.7	6.0	2.2	41.9	100.4	9 272	24	65	34	–	62	95
Carter	4.0	22.5	4.1	24.9	26.5	8.5	6.0	3.4	41.8	94.8	1 341	1	5	2	–	4	7
Cascade	6.6	19.4	9.1	28.1	22.8	7.2	5.0	1.8	36.7	97.9	72 897	900	3 394	652	67	547	1 900
Chouteau	6.5	22.4	6.5	24.1	23.1	8.5	6.6	2.4	39.3	100.8	5 015	5	873	14	6	14	43
Custer	5.9	19.2	8.4	25.6	23.8	8.5	6.5	2.2	39.3	95.8	11 347	11	149	30	6	40	113
Daniels	4.3	17.8	4.9	20.0	29.5	10.9	9.6	3.0	47.0	96.0	1 937	–	26	5	2	12	35
Dawson	5.1	18.0	8.8	24.9	25.4	9.0	6.2	2.5	41.0	98.3	8 826	23	111	12	1	28	58
Deer Lodge	4.6	17.9	7.9	24.0	26.8	9.6	6.8	2.4	42.3	99.8	9 028	16	167	34	1	17	154
Fallon	4.9	20.7	6.2	25.5	24.8	9.9	5.9	2.2	41.1	102.2	2 797	4	9	10	1	3	13
Fergus	5.2	19.4	6.1	23.6	25.8	9.5	7.1	3.3	42.4	94.8	11 548	10	140	23	–	34	138
Flathead	5.9	20.0	7.4	27.4	26.4	6.9	4.6	1.5	39.0	98.3	71 689	113	856	346	44	305	1 118
Gallatin	5.8	16.2	18.5	30.4	20.6	4.4	3.1	1.0	30.7	108.3	65 251	156	598	606	43	368	809
Garfield	6.7	17.7	7.1	23.3	25.8	8.4	8.2	2.7	41.6	106.6	1 268	1	5	1	1	–	3
Glacier	8.1	26.8	9.1	26.9	19.9	5.1	3.2	1.0	30.6	97.9	4 693	11	8 186	9	7	24	317
Golden Valley	5.2	22.5	5.9	23.0	27.0	10.6	4.7	1.2	41.5	107.2	1 033	–	6	1	–	–	2
Granite	4.8	19.4	5.7	23.3	30.8	8.5	5.8	1.6	42.8	105.1	2 724	1	36	4	1	13	52
Hill	7.1	21.1	11.6	26.0	21.4	6.6	4.6	1.7	34.5	99.3	13 263	15	2 884	62	3	59	387
Jefferson	5.2	22.6	5.2	26.8	29.9	6.1	3.1	1.1	40.2	100.8	9 654	14	127	42	7	38	167
Judith Basin	5.2	21.6	4.6	23.3	28.2	9.1	6.0	2.1	42.0	107.9	2 297	1	8	2	–	1	20
Lake	6.7	21.4	8.0	24.5	24.9	7.9	4.9	1.7	38.2	96.7	18 922	31	6 306	79	11	177	981
Lewis and Clark	6.2	19.4	8.5	27.9	26.2	6.2	4.2	1.4	38.0	96.5	53 046	111	1 137	287	28	209	898
Liberty	5.1	20.8	5.8	24.7	24.1	9.1	7.2	3.4	41.5	97.1	2 141	–	2	7	–	2	6
Lincoln	5.0	20.4	5.5	24.2	29.7	8.9	5.0	1.3	42.1	102.7	18 100	21	226	59	7	74	350
McCone	5.4	19.4	5.4	24.3	26.5	10.2	7.5	1.2	42.4	99.7	1 917	6	21	6	–	–	27
Madison	4.7	18.2	4.9	25.0	30.1	9.6	5.6	2.0	43.4	102.3	6 647	3	36	18	–	52	95
Meagher	5.0	20.0	6.1	22.7	28.1	9.7	7.0	1.5	42.8	100.4	1 878	–	20	3	1	11	19
Mineral	5.0	19.3	6.4	25.3	29.8	8.6	4.5	1.1	41.1	106.2	3 673	8	75	20	1	10	97
Missoula	5.7	17.2	15.4	29.2	22.6	5.0	3.7	1.3	33.2	99.9	90 073	261	2 193	978	80	431	1 786
Musselshell	4.9	18.4	5.7	24.0	29.4	8.5	6.4	2.6	43.2	95.4	4 358	3	57	7	2	17	53
Park	5.8	17.8	6.5	27.9	27.1	7.4	5.5	1.9	40.6	97.4	15 168	63	145	56	5	74	183
Petroleum	7.1	18.9	6.1	22.7	28.2	9.3	7.3	.4	41.1	110.7	489	–	1	–	–	1	2

[1] Includes all other responses not included in the other five race categories shown. Also includes write-in entries such as multiracial, mixed, interracial, or a Hispanic/Latino group. [2] Refers to combinations of two or more of the six race categories shown under one race.

Source: Population by Age, Sex, and Race—U.S. Census Bureau; 2000 Census of Population and Housing, "Census 2000 Profiles of General Demographic Characteristics" data files, published May 2001 (related Internet site <http://www.census.gov/mp/www/pub/2000cen/mscen01.html>).

Table B–2. Counties — **Population by Age, Sex, and Race**–Con.

[Includes U.S., states, and 3,142 counties/county equivalents defined as of January 1, 1992. For changes to these areas since January 1, 1992, see appendix B. Geographic Information]

| County | \
Population by age, 2000 (April 1) — Percent — Under 5 years | 5 to 17 years | 18 to 24 years | 25 to 44 years | 45 to 64 years | 65 to 74 years | 75 to 84 years | 85 years and over | Median age (years) | Males per 100 females, 2000 (April 1) | Population by race, 2000 (April 1) — One race — White | Black or African American | American Indian and Alaska Native | Asian | Native Hawaiian and Other Pacific Islander | Some other race[1] | Two or more races[2] |
|---|---|---|---|---|---|---|---|---|---|---|---|---|---|---|---|---|---|
| **MONTANA—Con.** | | | | | | | | | | | | | | | | | |
| Phillips | 4.9 | 22.4 | 5.5 | 24.5 | 25.1 | 8.2 | 6.7 | 2.7 | 40.8 | 100.4 | 4 115 | 7 | 350 | 15 | 1 | 17 | 96 |
| Pondera | 6.2 | 23.4 | 6.4 | 24.8 | 22.9 | 8.3 | 5.8 | 2.1 | 38.6 | 97.4 | 5 374 | 6 | 929 | 9 | 3 | 8 | 95 |
| Powder River | 5.9 | 20.7 | 4.8 | 23.3 | 26.8 | 10.1 | 6.0 | 2.4 | 42.1 | 97.2 | 1 810 | – | 33 | 2 | – | 4 | 9 |
| Powell | 4.6 | 16.6 | 7.8 | 30.8 | 26.2 | 7.2 | 4.9 | 1.8 | 39.7 | 143.2 | 6 643 | 36 | 252 | 31 | – | 53 | 165 |
| Prairie | 4.2 | 14.5 | 4.3 | 20.0 | 32.9 | 10.7 | 9.3 | 4.2 | 48.9 | 106.7 | 1 175 | – | 6 | 2 | – | 2 | 14 |
| Ravalli | 5.7 | 19.8 | 6.2 | 24.7 | 28.0 | 8.3 | 5.4 | 1.8 | 41.1 | 98.6 | 34 883 | 49 | 319 | 108 | 35 | 158 | 518 |
| Richland | 5.8 | 21.8 | 6.4 | 26.8 | 23.8 | 7.8 | 5.9 | 1.9 | 39.2 | 98.7 | 9 335 | 9 | 141 | 17 | 1 | 82 | 82 |
| Roosevelt | 8.1 | 26.5 | 7.9 | 25.8 | 20.2 | 5.8 | 4.2 | 1.6 | 32.3 | 98.3 | 4 347 | 5 | 5 921 | 46 | 5 | 27 | 269 |
| Rosebud | 7.7 | 25.8 | 7.2 | 25.7 | 24.8 | 5.1 | 2.8 | .9 | 34.5 | 100.9 | 6 043 | 22 | 3 041 | 27 | – | 61 | 189 |
| Sanders | 4.7 | 19.1 | 5.5 | 22.1 | 31.8 | 9.7 | 5.4 | 1.7 | 44.2 | 102.1 | 9 400 | 13 | 485 | 31 | 1 | 27 | 270 |
| Sheridan | 4.5 | 18.5 | 4.8 | 22.2 | 26.5 | 11.3 | 8.5 | 3.8 | 45.1 | 98.7 | 3 982 | 4 | 50 | 12 | 1 | 8 | 48 |
| Silver Bow | 5.8 | 17.9 | 9.6 | 26.7 | 24.0 | 7.7 | 6.1 | 2.2 | 38.9 | 97.8 | 32 998 | 54 | 704 | 149 | 21 | 205 | 475 |
| Stillwater | 5.5 | 19.8 | 5.7 | 26.9 | 27.6 | 7.9 | 4.8 | 1.8 | 40.8 | 104.0 | 7 934 | 11 | 57 | 17 | 2 | 77 | 97 |
| Sweet Grass | 5.8 | 20.1 | 5.3 | 24.7 | 26.4 | 8.1 | 6.3 | 3.1 | 41.1 | 99.5 | 3 500 | 2 | 20 | 12 | 1 | 27 | 47 |
| Teton | 6.2 | 21.1 | 6.1 | 24.6 | 25.4 | 7.8 | 6.4 | 2.4 | 40.0 | 97.0 | 6 207 | 12 | 98 | 6 | – | 27 | 95 |
| Toole | 5.4 | 20.2 | 6.8 | 28.2 | 23.6 | 7.8 | 6.1 | 2.0 | 39.1 | 106.5 | 4 945 | 8 | 168 | 16 | 1 | 17 | 112 |
| Treasure | 5.3 | 22.4 | 5.0 | 23.2 | 27.3 | 7.5 | 6.7 | 2.4 | 41.8 | 104.0 | 830 | 1 | 14 | 3 | – | 8 | 5 |
| Valley | 5.5 | 19.6 | 6.0 | 24.3 | 25.6 | 9.5 | 7.1 | 2.4 | 41.7 | 98.2 | 6 765 | 10 | 723 | 19 | 1 | 20 | 137 |
| Wheatland | 6.0 | 20.8 | 6.4 | 22.0 | 25.5 | 8.9 | 7.7 | 2.7 | 41.4 | 98.0 | 2 191 | 3 | 13 | 4 | 5 | 6 | 37 |
| Wibaux | 5.2 | 20.6 | 5.8 | 22.5 | 24.3 | 10.6 | 7.0 | 3.9 | 42.3 | 92.4 | 1 047 | 2 | 5 | 2 | – | 3 | 9 |
| Yellowstone | 6.6 | 18.9 | 9.3 | 28.7 | 23.2 | 6.8 | 4.8 | 1.7 | 36.9 | 95.2 | 120 014 | 580 | 3 950 | 698 | 57 | 1 634 | 2 419 |
| Yellowstone National Park | X | X | X | X | X | X | X | X | X | X | X | X | X | X | X | X | X |
| **NEBRASKA** | 6.8 | 19.5 | 10.2 | 28.5 | 21.5 | 6.8 | 4.8 | 2.0 | 35.3 | 97.2 | 1 533 261 | 68 541 | 14 896 | 21 931 | 836 | 47 845 | 23 953 |
| Adams | 6.4 | 18.1 | 11.9 | 26.2 | 21.7 | 7.2 | 6.1 | 2.6 | 36.5 | 96.1 | 29 451 | 200 | 112 | 498 | 11 | 620 | 259 |
| Antelope | 6.0 | 21.5 | 6.2 | 23.3 | 23.2 | 9.1 | 7.5 | 3.3 | 40.6 | 96.8 | 7 364 | 4 | 23 | 4 | – | 21 | 36 |
| Arthur | 5.2 | 18.7 | 5.4 | 29.5 | 24.8 | 9.7 | 4.5 | 2.3 | 40.3 | 101.8 | 428 | – | 1 | 3 | 1 | 4 | 7 |
| Banner | 4.8 | 24.1 | 3.7 | 24.3 | 27.2 | 10.9 | 4.0 | 1.1 | 39.9 | 108.4 | 785 | 1 | 2 | 1 | – | 25 | 5 |
| Blaine | 5.5 | 20.8 | 3.9 | 26.6 | 26.4 | 10.1 | 3.6 | 3.1 | 39.8 | 101.7 | 577 | – | 3 | – | – | – | 3 |
| Boone | 5.9 | 23.2 | 5.0 | 24.2 | 21.4 | 9.5 | 7.6 | 3.3 | 39.9 | 99.1 | 6 212 | 3 | 3 | 2 | 2 | 19 | 18 |
| Box Butte | 6.6 | 21.6 | 7.4 | 26.8 | 23.1 | 7.2 | 5.0 | 2.3 | 38.2 | 99.2 | 11 044 | 45 | 333 | 65 | 1 | 432 | 238 |
| Boyd | 5.0 | 19.9 | 5.4 | 21.2 | 24.1 | 11.0 | 8.8 | 4.5 | 43.8 | 93.3 | 2 411 | – | 14 | 4 | – | – | 9 |
| Brown | 5.3 | 19.5 | 5.2 | 22.8 | 24.7 | 10.2 | 8.4 | 3.9 | 43.1 | 96.5 | 3 477 | 1 | 7 | 9 | 1 | 8 | 22 |
| Buffalo | 6.6 | 18.4 | 17.8 | 26.6 | 19.0 | 5.4 | 4.2 | 2.0 | 30.0 | 96.0 | 40 221 | 232 | 140 | 289 | 13 | 929 | 435 |
| Burt | 5.7 | 20.0 | 5.4 | 23.4 | 23.8 | 11.0 | 7.3 | 3.5 | 42.2 | 93.8 | 7 606 | 14 | 83 | 15 | 2 | 17 | 54 |
| Butler | 6.8 | 21.0 | 6.6 | 25.3 | 22.5 | 8.9 | 6.5 | 2.4 | 38.8 | 104.1 | 8 625 | 9 | 11 | 11 | 5 | 71 | 35 |
| Cass | 7.0 | 20.9 | 7.0 | 29.0 | 23.8 | 6.6 | 4.0 | 1.7 | 36.9 | 97.7 | 23 821 | 43 | 72 | 85 | 4 | 86 | 223 |
| Cedar | 6.1 | 23.4 | 6.0 | 24.2 | 20.3 | 9.3 | 7.2 | 3.6 | 38.8 | 100.1 | 9 526 | 10 | 19 | 4 | 1 | 17 | 38 |
| Chase | 5.6 | 19.6 | 5.9 | 23.9 | 24.0 | 10.1 | 7.5 | 3.5 | 42.1 | 96.6 | 3 979 | 7 | 4 | 7 | 1 | 60 | 10 |
| Cherry | 6.2 | 20.8 | 6.2 | 25.5 | 24.0 | 8.7 | 6.1 | 2.5 | 39.4 | 98.8 | 5 791 | 4 | 200 | 26 | 1 | 20 | 106 |
| Cheyenne | 6.4 | 19.9 | 7.0 | 26.7 | 22.8 | 8.8 | 5.9 | 2.5 | 38.7 | 96.0 | 9 470 | 14 | 64 | 39 | 3 | 144 | 96 |
| Clay | 5.8 | 21.5 | 5.9 | 25.3 | 23.6 | 8.9 | 6.6 | 2.5 | 39.9 | 95.1 | 6 868 | 12 | 22 | 21 | – | 87 | 29 |
| Colfax | 7.2 | 21.7 | 8.5 | 27.9 | 18.7 | 7.5 | 5.8 | 2.7 | 35.0 | 106.4 | 8 533 | 7 | 20 | 21 | 15 | 1 664 | 181 |
| Cuming | 6.5 | 20.7 | 6.5 | 25.2 | 20.9 | 9.3 | 7.3 | 3.6 | 39.2 | 102.1 | 9 783 | 13 | 29 | 20 | 3 | 268 | 87 |
| Custer | 5.7 | 20.6 | 5.5 | 23.5 | 23.7 | 9.7 | 7.8 | 3.6 | 41.3 | 96.1 | 11 631 | 8 | 48 | 18 | – | 23 | 65 |
| Dakota | 8.7 | 21.7 | 10.1 | 29.4 | 20.1 | 5.1 | 3.5 | 1.4 | 31.4 | 99.7 | 15 968 | 126 | 377 | 624 | 12 | 2 615 | 531 |
| Dawes | 5.0 | 16.2 | 23.4 | 20.4 | 20.3 | 7.0 | 5.5 | 2.3 | 30.6 | 95.6 | 8 457 | 73 | 261 | 28 | 5 | 93 | 143 |
| Dawson | 8.4 | 20.8 | 8.4 | 27.6 | 20.7 | 6.8 | 5.2 | 2.1 | 34.3 | 101.7 | 20 058 | 76 | 164 | 161 | 3 | 3 530 | 373 |
| Deuel | 4.3 | 19.0 | 4.9 | 24.4 | 24.5 | 10.0 | 9.2 | 3.7 | 43.5 | 94.8 | 2 042 | 1 | 8 | 8 | – | 24 | 15 |
| Dixon | 6.4 | 21.1 | 7.1 | 24.9 | 22.4 | 8.3 | 6.6 | 3.2 | 38.7 | 98.5 | 5 999 | 2 | 31 | 17 | – | 240 | 50 |
| Dodge | 6.2 | 18.5 | 9.6 | 26.2 | 21.9 | 8.6 | 6.1 | 2.9 | 37.9 | 93.2 | 34 678 | 156 | 107 | 183 | 31 | 745 | 260 |
| Douglas | 7.4 | 19.2 | 10.3 | 31.2 | 21.0 | 5.7 | 3.8 | 1.4 | 33.6 | 95.7 | 375 317 | 53 330 | 2 809 | 7 944 | 250 | 15 760 | 8 175 |
| Dundy | 5.3 | 18.0 | 5.7 | 23.5 | 25.1 | 10.2 | 8.5 | 3.7 | 43.5 | 96.9 | 2 222 | 1 | 18 | 11 | 1 | 20 | 19 |
| Fillmore | 5.8 | 20.5 | 5.1 | 24.0 | 23.3 | 9.2 | 8.0 | 4.0 | 41.4 | 93.5 | 6 485 | 14 | 29 | 4 | 1 | 55 | 46 |
| Franklin | 5.2 | 19.3 | 4.5 | 23.6 | 23.5 | 10.9 | 9.1 | 4.0 | 42.8 | 92.8 | 3 547 | – | 10 | 2 | – | 3 | 12 |
| Frontier | 5.5 | 20.5 | 11.3 | 22.8 | 23.0 | 8.6 | 5.7 | 2.5 | 38.5 | 100.5 | 3 046 | 3 | 8 | 8 | – | 12 | 22 |
| Furnas | 5.6 | 18.5 | 5.3 | 22.8 | 23.9 | 10.9 | 8.5 | 4.3 | 43.5 | 92.3 | 5 229 | 4 | 22 | 12 | – | 17 | 40 |
| Gage | 5.9 | 18.1 | 7.7 | 26.3 | 22.8 | 8.9 | 7.2 | 3.2 | 39.9 | 94.1 | 22 463 | 73 | 133 | 65 | 7 | 59 | 193 |
| Garden | 3.6 | 18.2 | 4.6 | 22.7 | 27.0 | 11.8 | 8.2 | 4.0 | 45.6 | 94.9 | 2 254 | 3 | 6 | 6 | – | 12 | 11 |
| Garfield | 4.8 | 18.7 | 4.4 | 20.5 | 26.8 | 9.5 | 10.2 | 5.1 | 45.9 | 91.9 | 1 879 | – | 4 | 1 | 1 | 7 | 10 |
| Gosper | 5.2 | 18.6 | 5.4 | 24.0 | 26.0 | 10.1 | 7.1 | 3.5 | 43.4 | 102.0 | 2 117 | – | 3 | 5 | – | 9 | 9 |
| Grant | 5.0 | 24.2 | 5.2 | 24.4 | 27.6 | 8.6 | 4.1 | .9 | 39.9 | 114.0 | 738 | – | 1 | 2 | – | 6 | – |
| Greeley | 5.7 | 21.3 | 5.9 | 21.6 | 22.4 | 11.1 | 7.8 | 4.3 | 41.7 | 97.1 | 2 658 | 18 | 2 | 2 | – | 21 | 13 |
| Hall | 7.6 | 19.5 | 8.9 | 28.3 | 21.7 | 6.9 | 5.1 | 1.9 | 35.6 | 98.4 | 47 467 | 195 | 164 | 586 | 73 | 4 384 | 665 |
| Hamilton | 6.7 | 22.4 | 5.9 | 26.5 | 23.2 | 7.6 | 5.3 | 2.4 | 38.1 | 99.4 | 9 255 | 17 | 11 | 21 | – | 46 | 53 |
| Harlan | 4.8 | 19.4 | 5.0 | 21.6 | 26.2 | 11.2 | 8.2 | 3.6 | 44.5 | 98.0 | 3 743 | 5 | 4 | 3 | 1 | 6 | 24 |
| Hayes | 4.4 | 22.2 | 5.5 | 21.5 | 26.5 | 11.7 | 6.5 | 1.7 | 42.5 | 100.4 | 1 038 | 2 | – | 3 | – | 19 | 6 |
| Hitchcock | 4.3 | 19.4 | 5.9 | 22.6 | 25.4 | 10.7 | 7.6 | 4.0 | 43.6 | 95.0 | 3 060 | 3 | 9 | 4 | – | 9 | 26 |
| Holt | 5.8 | 21.4 | 5.7 | 24.5 | 22.7 | 9.4 | 7.3 | 3.1 | 40.5 | 96.9 | 11 419 | 4 | 33 | 21 | 6 | 27 | 41 |

[1] Includes all other responses not included in the other five race categories shown. Also includes write-in entries such as multiracial, mixed, interracial, or a Hispanic/Latino group. [2] Refers to combinations of two or more of the six race categories shown under one race.

Source: Population by Age, Sex, and Race—U.S. Census Bureau; 2000 Census of Population and Housing, "Census 2000 Profiles of General Demographic Characteristics" data files, published May 2001 (related Internet site <http://www.census.gov/mp/www/pub/2000cen/mscen01.html>).

[Includes U.S., states, and 3,142 counties/county equivalents defined as of January 1, 1992. For changes to these areas since January 1, 1992, see appendix B. Geographic Information]

County	Population by age, 2000 (April 1) Percent—								Median age (years)	Males per 100 females, 2000 (April 1)	Population by race, 2000 (April 1) One race						
	Under 5 years	5 to 17 years	18 to 24 years	25 to 44 years	45 to 64 years	65 to 74 years	75 to 84 years	85 years and over			White	Black or African American	American Indian and Alaska Native	Asian	Native Hawaiian and Other Pacific Islander	Some other race[1]	Two or more races[2]
NEBRASKA—Con.																	
Hooker	4.1	19.9	4.1	21.6	23.4	10.3	10.3	6.3	45.3	83.4	773	–	3	1	–	1	5
Howard	6.0	22.3	6.6	25.3	22.6	8.5	6.2	2.4	38.1	101.0	6 481	20	16	6	2	21	21
Jefferson	5.3	18.0	6.1	23.7	24.3	9.7	8.8	4.2	42.9	95.6	8 201	6	32	14	3	42	35
Johnson	5.5	18.7	5.7	24.4	23.6	9.8	8.2	4.1	42.4	91.9	4 198	5	18	120	1	88	58
Kearney	6.2	20.6	6.4	27.5	22.7	7.9	5.8	3.0	38.7	98.4	6 732	11	14	16	1	68	40
Keith	5.7	19.5	5.7	25.3	25.4	9.9	6.5	2.0	41.1	96.5	8 587	7	63	15	–	132	71
Keya Paha	6.1	17.7	6.7	23.4	25.4	10.5	7.5	2.6	41.9	101.4	977	–	2	–	–	–	4
Kimball	5.4	19.3	5.9	23.0	25.3	10.4	7.9	2.7	42.8	95.6	3 966	9	27	4	1	27	55
Knox	5.7	19.8	5.5	21.9	23.9	10.5	8.9	3.7	43.0	96.7	8 589	8	667	15	4	32	59
Lancaster	6.7	16.8	15.4	30.4	20.3	5.3	3.7	1.4	32.0	99.8	225 426	7 052	1 599	7 162	149	4 225	4 678
Lincoln	6.6	19.6	8.3	26.6	23.8	7.7	5.2	2.2	37.8	96.5	32 795	188	175	129	8	918	419
Logan	5.2	22.1	4.4	24.0	26.7	9.9	5.8	1.8	41.8	99.0	763	1	8	–	–	–	2
Loup	6.3	20.4	4.5	22.3	27.0	10.7	7.4	1.4	42.9	108.8	704	–	2	1	–	3	2
McPherson	7.3	20.3	5.3	26.1	22.9	8.8	6.9	2.4	40.6	99.6	522	–	2	–	–	9	–
Madison	6.9	19.9	11.6	27.1	20.1	6.6	5.3	2.5	35.0	98.5	32 179	330	419	142	11	1 783	362
Merrick	6.4	21.2	6.4	24.7	23.8	8.5	5.9	3.1	39.2	95.9	8 066	18	8	17	1	55	39
Morrill	5.9	21.3	7.2	24.4	24.2	8.8	5.9	2.3	39.5	97.9	5 096	4	39	12	–	224	65
Nance	6.2	21.7	6.8	23.6	22.0	10.3	6.9	2.5	40.1	104.2	3 973	–	15	2	–	18	30
Nemaha	4.6	18.5	11.9	23.9	22.7	8.1	7.1	3.2	39.4	93.3	7 394	27	23	45	3	28	56
Nuckolls	4.9	18.5	5.4	22.5	24.3	11.5	9.2	3.6	44.1	92.5	5 002	1	3	8	–	27	16
Otoe	6.4	19.9	6.4	26.1	22.8	8.4	6.8	3.2	39.5	96.2	14 999	44	34	38	5	176	100
Pawnee	4.9	17.8	5.1	21.0	24.2	12.0	10.4	4.7	45.9	92.5	3 052	–	6	8	–	1	20
Perkins	5.4	21.2	6.0	23.5	24.7	7.7	8.0	3.6	40.7	100.8	3 126	1	9	7	–	43	14
Phelps	6.2	20.3	6.1	25.8	23.6	8.6	6.2	3.3	39.4	96.1	9 532	11	27	27	–	77	73
Pierce	6.0	23.0	7.0	26.0	20.9	7.7	6.4	3.0	37.9	100.0	7 751	6	28	16	2	18	36
Platte	7.3	21.8	8.1	27.5	21.6	6.9	5.1	1.9	35.8	98.4	29 854	111	90	127	10	1 105	365
Polk	5.8	19.4	6.0	24.4	23.1	9.2	8.1	4.1	41.6	100.5	5 578	1	16	5	–	16	23
Red Willow	6.2	18.6	8.8	24.6	22.6	9.4	6.9	2.8	39.9	93.9	11 167	18	44	19	2	106	92
Richardson	5.2	20.3	5.9	23.8	23.3	9.5	8.4	3.6	41.4	93.5	9 116	18	221	14	–	21	141
Rock	5.5	17.5	6.5	23.6	24.6	10.6	7.2	4.4	43.5	92.3	1 739	–	8	3	–	1	5
Saline	6.2	18.9	12.3	25.0	20.3	7.4	6.3	3.5	36.4	97.8	12 872	50	52	236	4	470	159
Sarpy	8.2	22.2	9.4	33.8	19.7	4.1	1.9	.6	31.5	98.8	109 335	5 340	515	2 331	108	2 275	2 691
Saunders	6.4	21.5	6.3	27.6	22.9	8.0	5.0	2.3	38.0	99.1	19 530	21	57	43	1	69	109
Scotts Bluff	6.5	19.4	8.4	25.4	23.0	8.7	6.1	2.4	38.4	91.2	32 363	98	694	212	15	2 965	604
Seward	5.6	19.1	14.3	24.6	21.2	7.1	5.4	2.6	35.7	103.2	16 174	47	34	48	8	66	119
Sheridan	5.8	19.8	6.2	22.9	23.6	9.9	8.4	3.3	42.0	96.0	5 461	5	572	9	1	21	129
Sherman	5.2	19.3	4.5	23.7	24.1	11.3	8.0	3.9	43.3	97.0	3 268	2	7	8	1	14	18
Sioux	5.4	19.0	7.2	24.7	27.5	10.4	4.3	1.6	41.4	111.0	1 440	–	2	3	–	17	13
Stanton	6.7	23.1	7.6	27.4	21.8	6.7	4.5	2.3	35.9	98.4	6 243	27	31	8	–	89	57
Thayer	5.7	18.4	4.9	22.3	24.2	10.7	9.6	4.3	44.1	95.8	5 976	1	17	7	–	20	34
Thomas	5.9	17.7	4.4	23.9	27.8	9.9	7.3	3.2	44.2	99.7	725	–	2	–	–	–	2
Thurston	9.6	27.2	8.3	23.9	17.7	7.4	4.4	1.4	29.8	99.4	3 282	11	3 731	4	–	55	88
Valley	5.6	19.1	4.8	22.6	23.9	11.3	8.5	4.2	43.5	91.7	4 561	7	15	5	3	37	19
Washington	6.4	20.7	9.3	26.7	24.1	6.7	4.2	1.9	37.1	98.7	18 427	63	38	55	21	57	119
Wayne	5.3	16.3	25.4	21.2	18.0	6.9	4.5	2.4	27.9	92.3	9 534	93	34	34	1	84	71
Webster	5.2	18.4	4.6	22.9	24.6	10.6	9.5	4.2	44.2	92.7	3 984	6	11	19	3	9	29
Wheeler	7.8	21.3	6.4	21.9	25.7	10.0	5.3	1.5	40.4	96.0	878	–	2	–	–	5	1
York	5.6	19.7	9.0	25.4	23.0	8.2	6.3	2.9	38.8	91.5	14 128	140	42	71	12	93	112
NEVADA	7.3	18.3	9.0	31.5	23.0	6.6	3.5	.9	35.0	103.9	1 501 886	135 477	26 420	90 266	8 426	159 354	76 428
Churchill	8.0	20.9	8.1	28.7	22.3	6.7	4.1	1.2	34.7	100.6	20 192	383	1 146	649	54	773	785
Clark	7.5	18.1	9.2	32.2	22.3	6.6	3.4	.8	34.4	103.5	984 796	124 885	10 895	72 547	6 412	118 465	57 765
Douglas	5.2	18.9	5.5	26.4	28.9	9.3	4.8	1.0	41.7	102.1	37 908	129	692	517	63	1 048	902
Elko	8.5	24.0	8.8	31.5	21.3	3.5	1.8	.6	31.2	108.8	37 159	267	2 400	306	52	3 849	1 258
Esmeralda	4.3	16.2	6.0	23.4	33.0	10.3	5.3	1.6	45.1	123.7	796	1	50	–	2	74	48
Eureka	5.9	21.9	5.2	28.6	25.9	8.1	3.7	.6	38.3	106.6	1 474	7	26	13	1	72	58
Humboldt	8.0	23.4	7.5	31.2	22.3	4.4	2.5	.6	33.4	110.3	13 401	82	647	92	11	1 375	498
Lander	7.5	24.7	6.8	29.0	25.0	4.1	2.0	.8	34.1	105.5	4 891	12	231	20	2	502	136
Lincoln	6.3	23.8	6.0	21.9	25.9	9.0	5.5	1.7	38.8	107.9	3 811	74	73	14	1	112	80
Lyon	6.5	20.6	6.6	27.3	25.2	8.5	4.4	.9	38.2	102.5	30 576	225	844	210	47	1 585	1 014
Mineral	5.3	19.1	6.2	22.5	27.1	11.0	6.9	2.0	42.9	101.6	3 747	242	779	41	5	136	121
Nye	6.0	17.8	5.4	24.0	28.5	12.2	5.3	.9	42.9	105.1	29 117	383	636	253	105	969	1 022
Pershing	6.5	19.2	8.5	36.0	22.1	4.3	2.7	.8	34.4	158.8	5 200	358	229	42	15	628	221
Storey	4.4	15.3	4.7	26.8	35.7	8.4	3.7	.9	44.5	107.6	3 161	10	49	34	5	57	83
Washoe	7.0	17.9	9.8	31.0	23.8	6.0	3.6	1.0	35.6	102.8	272 985	7 093	6 162	14 526	1 553	26 034	11 133
White Pine	6.0	18.2	7.6	29.9	24.8	7.4	4.7	1.3	37.7	128.6	7 928	380	302	72	22	284	193
Independent City																	
Carson City city	6.3	17.1	7.9	28.9	24.9	7.8	5.6	1.5	38.7	106.9	44 744	946	1 259	930	76	3 391	1 111

[1] Includes all other responses not included in the other five race categories shown. Also includes write-in entries such as multiracial, mixed, interracial, or a Hispanic/Latino group. [2] Refers to combinations of two or more of the six race categories shown under one race.

Source: Population by Age, Sex, and Race—U.S. Census Bureau; 2000 Census of Population and Housing, "Census 2000 Profiles of General Demographic Characteristics" data files, published May 2001 (related Internet site <http://www.census.gov/mp/www/pub/2000cen/mscen01.html>).

Table B–2. Counties — Population by Age, Sex, and Race–Con.

[Includes U.S., states, and 3,142 counties/county equivalents defined as of January 1, 1992. For changes to these areas since January 1, 1992, see appendix B. Geographic Information]

County	Population by age, 2000 (April 1) Percent— Under 5 years	5 to 17 years	18 to 24 years	25 to 44 years	45 to 64 years	65 to 74 years	75 to 84 years	85 years and over	Median age (years)	Males per 100 females, 2000 (April 1)	Population by race, 2000 (April 1) One race White	Black or African American	American Indian and Alaska Native	Asian	Native Hawaiian and Other Pacific Islander	Some other race[1]	Two or more races[2]
NEW HAMPSHIRE	6.1	18.9	8.4	30.9	23.8	6.3	4.2	1.5	37.1	96.8	1 186 851	9 035	2 964	15 931	371	7 420	13 214
Belknap	5.3	18.3	6.7	28.1	26.4	8.0	5.4	1.7	40.1	97.1	54 979	165	170	311	13	92	595
Carroll	4.8	17.8	5.3	26.5	27.7	9.9	6.0	1.9	42.5	96.6	42 890	73	122	167	4	75	335
Cheshire	5.2	18.1	11.7	27.0	24.3	7.2	4.7	1.7	37.6	94.9	72 167	271	226	350	26	131	654
Coos	5.1	17.8	6.3	26.7	25.7	9.4	6.6	2.4	41.5	95.6	32 466	40	93	123	5	53	331
Grafton	5.2	16.7	13.5	27.0	24.2	7.0	4.8	1.7	37.0	96.7	78 276	435	255	1 414	22	315	1 026
Hillsborough	6.8	19.6	7.7	32.7	22.6	5.5	3.8	1.3	35.9	97.3	357 615	4 904	943	7 601	112	5 006	4 660
Merrimack	6.0	19.0	8.1	30.6	24.0	6.3	4.3	1.9	37.7	97.0	132 254	730	311	1 171	29	315	1 415
Rockingham	6.5	19.9	6.2	32.8	24.4	5.6	3.4	1.1	37.2	97.4	268 486	1 619	487	3 084	98	1 042	2 543
Strafford	5.9	17.7	13.6	30.6	20.9	6.0	3.9	1.3	34.4	94.3	108 073	702	238	1 560	53	333	1 274
Sullivan	5.6	18.3	6.4	28.0	25.9	8.5	5.5	1.8	40.0	97.1	39 645	96	119	150	9	58	381
NEW JERSEY	6.7	18.1	8.0	31.2	22.7	6.8	4.8	1.6	36.7	94.3	6 104 705	1 141 821	19 492	480 276	3 329	450 972	213 755
Atlantic	6.5	18.8	8.1	30.6	22.4	7.2	4.8	1.6	37.0	93.6	172 632	44 534	669	12 771	114	15 307	6 525
Bergen	6.3	16.7	6.6	30.6	24.5	7.8	5.5	1.9	39.1	92.8	693 236	46 568	1 336	94 324	193	28 503	19 958
Burlington	6.4	18.7	7.5	31.5	23.3	6.9	4.4	1.3	37.1	97.9	331 898	64 071	898	11 378	144	6 255	8 750
Camden	6.8	20.0	8.1	30.5	22.1	6.5	4.6	1.5	35.8	93.2	360 756	92 059	1 300	18 910	187	25 909	9 811
Cape May	5.1	17.2	6.4	25.5	25.6	10.4	7.2	2.6	42.3	92.6	93 700	5 178	186	661	40	1 379	1 182
Cumberland	6.3	19.1	8.5	31.2	21.9	6.6	4.8	1.6	35.6	104.2	96 478	29 585	1 419	1 397	82	13 300	4 177
Essex	7.3	18.8	9.4	31.1	21.5	6.2	4.2	1.6	34.7	90.7	352 859	327 324	1 861	29 429	417	54 588	27 155
Gloucester	6.6	19.8	8.9	30.4	22.6	6.3	4.1	1.2	36.1	93.7	221 742	23 084	487	3 805	75	2 173	3 307
Hudson	6.4	16.2	10.4	35.6	20.0	6.0	4.0	1.4	33.6	96.5	338 457	82 098	2 547	56 942	383	94 253	34 295
Hunterdon	6.6	19.1	5.8	31.3	27.1	5.6	3.3	1.1	38.8	97.6	114 563	2 743	169	2 348	35	921	1 210
Mercer	6.3	17.7	10.2	30.6	22.5	6.4	4.6	1.5	36.0	94.9	240 206	69 502	688	17 340	352	15 054	7 619
Middlesex	6.6	17.1	9.5	32.8	21.7	6.5	4.6	1.3	35.7	96.4	513 298	68 467	1 521	104 212	300	42 867	19 497
Monmouth	6.9	19.2	6.9	30.4	24.1	6.5	4.4	1.6	37.7	94.4	519 261	49 609	879	24 403	153	10 685	10 311
Morris	7.0	17.8	6.4	31.9	25.3	6.3	3.9	1.4	37.8	95.8	410 042	13 181	572	29 432	188	9 471	7 326
Ocean	6.3	17.0	6.6	26.0	21.9	10.6	8.6	2.9	41.0	90.4	475 391	15 268	702	6 550	103	6 333	6 569
Passaic	7.4	18.7	9.3	31.3	21.3	6.2	4.3	1.6	34.8	94.0	304 786	64 647	2 166	18 064	175	79 423	19 788
Salem	6.1	19.5	7.8	27.9	24.2	7.3	5.5	1.7	38.0	93.4	52 195	9 498	226	396	19	1 010	941
Somerset	7.5	18.1	5.9	33.8	23.5	6.0	3.9	1.4	37.2	95.4	236 042	22 396	375	24 941	121	8 158	5 457
Sussex	6.8	21.1	6.2	31.5	25.3	4.9	3.1	1.1	37.1	98.0	138 015	1 502	161	1 738	28	1 072	1 650
Union	7.0	17.9	7.9	31.3	22.1	6.8	5.2	1.8	36.6	92.7	342 302	108 593	1 215	19 993	201	33 277	16 960
Warren	6.9	19.2	6.3	31.3	23.5	6.6	4.7	1.7	37.6	94.9	96 846	1 914	115	1 242	19	1 034	1 267
NEW MEXICO	7.2	20.8	9.8	28.4	22.2	6.5	3.9	1.3	34.6	96.7	1 214 253	34 343	173 483	19 255	1 503	309 882	66 327
Bernalillo	6.9	18.4	10.3	30.4	22.4	6.1	4.1	1.3	35.0	95.5	393 851	15 401	23 175	10 751	574	89 446	23 480
Catron	4.2	16.9	4.2	19.5	36.4	11.8	5.5	1.5	47.8	104.7	3 109	10	78	24	2	192	128
Chaves	7.2	21.9	9.4	25.3	21.5	7.6	5.3	1.8	35.2	95.9	44 167	1 209	694	323	34	13 042	1 913
Cibola	7.9	22.7	9.6	27.5	21.5	6.7	3.0	1.0	33.1	95.5	10 138	246	10 319	98	14	3 952	828
Colfax	5.4	19.7	6.9	24.5	26.5	8.9	5.6	2.4	40.8	102.7	11 564	45	209	45	1	1 816	509
Curry	8.6	21.5	11.5	28.8	18.1	6.1	3.9	1.5	30.8	97.6	32 613	3 090	451	803	59	6 340	1 688
DeBaca	5.1	19.0	5.7	21.7	23.2	12.6	8.0	4.7	43.8	96.0	1 882	1	21	5	–	281	50
Dona Ana	7.8	21.9	13.3	27.1	19.3	6.2	3.4	1.0	30.2	96.5	118 478	2 723	2 580	1 330	117	43 209	6 245
Eddy	7.3	21.5	8.4	25.7	22.4	7.6	5.3	1.9	36.4	95.9	39 438	805	646	231	47	9 129	1 362
Grant	6.9	19.4	8.5	23.7	25.1	9.1	5.6	1.7	38.8	95.1	23 459	162	419	89	10	5 898	965
Guadalupe	5.3	19.0	9.2	30.7	21.9	7.8	4.0	2.0	37.5	121.5	2 530	62	53	25	2	1 828	180
Harding	3.1	17.2	4.6	18.8	28.1	15.9	8.5	3.8	48.7	102.5	683	3	11	–	–	86	27
Hidalgo	7.7	24.1	7.8	25.2	21.7	7.3	4.9	1.5	34.8	99.6	4 970	24	46	19	–	703	170
Lea	7.7	22.4	10.1	27.3	20.3	7.0	3.9	1.3	33.1	100.3	37 263	2 426	551	216	24	13 217	1 814
Lincoln	5.1	17.7	6.0	23.2	30.2	11.4	5.0	1.4	43.8	95.9	16 228	68	379	53	12	2 189	482
Los Alamos	5.6	20.2	4.4	27.7	30.0	6.7	4.5	.9	40.8	101.4	16 556	67	107	694	6	495	418
Luna	7.7	22.3	7.6	22.7	21.5	10.7	5.8	1.7	36.7	95.2	18 587	236	278	84	1	5 060	770
McKinley	9.1	28.8	9.7	27.8	17.6	4.1	2.0	.8	26.9	93.5	12 257	296	55 892	344	32	4 095	1 882
Mora	6.1	20.6	7.5	24.3	26.1	9.0	4.8	1.7	39.6	102.0	3 050	5	59	6	–	1 915	145
Otero	7.4	22.0	9.3	28.6	21.0	7.2	3.5	1.0	33.8	99.0	45 919	2 440	3 614	728	82	7 273	2 242
Quay	5.5	19.5	6.7	23.3	26.0	10.1	6.5	2.4	41.5	94.0	8 336	85	129	81	15	1 230	279
Rio Arriba	7.0	21.6	8.9	28.8	22.9	6.4	3.4	1.1	34.5	98.0	23 320	143	5 717	56	47	10 554	1 353
Roosevelt	7.5	20.6	16.0	25.5	18.3	6.3	4.3	1.5	29.5	96.5	13 359	298	199	111	12	3 561	478
Sandoval	7.3	22.2	7.5	30.1	22.2	5.7	3.8	1.1	35.1	95.2	58 512	1 535	14 634	894	98	11 118	3 117
San Juan	8.0	24.0	10.0	28.1	20.2	5.3	2.9	.9	31.0	98.3	60 118	499	41 968	303	55	7 699	3 159
San Miguel	6.5	20.9	10.9	27.0	22.9	6.4	3.8	1.5	35.1	96.7	16 938	236	549	163	25	10 910	1 305
Santa Fe	6.2	17.9	8.1	29.7	27.3	6.1	3.5	1.2	37.9	95.8	95 053	826	3 982	1 133	94	22 936	5 268
Sierra	4.8	15.3	5.4	19.5	27.4	14.9	9.7	3.1	48.9	100.0	11 541	64	197	23	11	1 097	337
Socorro	7.0	21.4	12.6	26.1	22.0	6.2	3.6	1.2	32.4	103.3	11 365	116	1 974	206	10	3 634	773
Taos	5.8	18.7	6.9	27.4	28.8	7.0	3.9	1.5	39.5	96.2	19 118	105	1 975	114	35	7 447	1 185
Torrance	6.9	23.4	7.5	29.2	23.2	5.8	3.2	.8	34.8	105.5	12 495	280	354	54	22	3 035	671
Union	6.0	21.3	6.3	24.6	24.1	9.7	6.3	1.8	39.9	97.0	3 355	–	40	14	5	668	92
Valencia	7.6	22.5	8.4	29.6	21.7	5.9	3.3	1.0	33.8	100.7	44 001	837	2 183	235	57	15 827	3 012

[1] Includes all other responses not included in the other five race categories shown. Also includes write-in entries such as multiracial, mixed, interracial, or a Hispanic/Latino group.   [2] Refers to combinations of two or more of the six race categories shown under one race.

Source: Population by Age, Sex, and Race—U.S. Census Bureau; 2000 Census of Population and Housing, "Census 2000 Profiles of General Demographic Characteristics" data files, published May 2001 (related Internet site <http://www.census.gov/mp/www/pub/2000cen/mscen01.html>).

[Includes U.S., states, and 3,142 counties/county equivalents defined as of January 1, 1992. For changes to these areas since January 1, 1992, see appendix B. Geographic Information]

County	Population by age, 2000 (April 1) — Percent								Median age (years)	Males per 100 females, 2000 (April 1)	Population by race, 2000 (April 1) — One race						Two or more races[2]
	Under 5 years	5 to 17 years	18 to 24 years	25 to 44 years	45 to 64 years	65 to 74 years	75 to 84 years	85 years and over			White	Black or African American	American Indian and Alaska Native	Asian	Native Hawaiian and Other Pacific Islander	Some other race[1]	
NEW YORK............	6.5	18.2	9.3	30.7	22.3	6.7	4.5	1.6	35.9	93.1	12 893 689	3 014 385	82 461	1 044 976	8 818	1 341 946	590 182
Albany..................	5.7	16.9	11.3	28.8	22.8	7.1	5.4	2.0	36.8	91.7	245 060	32 624	605	8 090	84	3 102	5 000
Allegany................	5.6	18.8	15.5	23.9	22.2	7.5	4.7	1.9	35.0	99.8	48 444	361	139	358	2	183	440
Bronx...................	8.2	21.6	10.6	30.7	18.8	5.3	3.3	1.4	31.2	87.0	398 003	475 007	11 371	40 120	1 383	329 724	77 042
Broome.................	5.6	17.4	11.0	26.8	22.8	8.0	6.1	2.3	38.2	93.2	183 153	6 575	384	5 585	53	1 593	3 193
Cattaraugus............	6.2	20.0	9.3	26.5	23.5	7.7	5.2	1.8	37.4	95.9	79 444	890	2 181	386	16	191	847
Cayuga.................	5.9	19.2	8.2	29.7	22.6	7.1	5.5	1.9	37.3	102.2	76 501	3 272	256	348	20	718	848
Chautauqua............	5.8	18.7	10.3	26.3	23.0	8.0	5.8	2.2	37.9	95.2	131 416	3 051	598	502	40	2 418	1 725
Chemung...............	6.0	18.4	8.8	28.3	22.9	7.8	5.9	1.9	37.9	97.7	82 840	5 303	210	709	16	681	1 311
Chenango..............	5.9	20.2	7.0	27.5	24.4	7.5	5.4	2.0	38.4	97.0	50 191	422	141	146	11	112	378
Clinton.................	5.1	17.8	12.4	30.6	22.1	6.8	3.7	1.4	35.7	104.9	74 562	2 863	291	537	17	878	746
Columbia...............	5.3	18.7	6.4	26.9	26.3	8.3	5.8	2.2	40.5	99.0	58 105	2 850	132	507	20	568	912
Cortland...............	5.9	17.8	15.5	26.5	21.8	6.2	4.6	1.6	34.2	93.5	47 115	416	133	201	5	154	575
Delaware...............	5.1	17.9	8.2	24.0	26.2	9.7	6.4	2.4	41.4	97.0	46 346	568	149	257	6	254	475
Dutchess...............	6.2	18.8	9.4	30.2	23.2	6.5	4.0	1.5	36.7	100.1	234 385	26 097	609	7 048	88	6 626	5 297
Erie....................	6.1	18.2	8.7	28.4	22.7	8.0	5.9	1.9	38.0	91.6	780 942	123 529	5 755	13 835	223	13 499	12 482
Essex..................	5.0	17.8	6.9	29.8	24.5	8.5	5.5	2.0	39.4	107.6	36 848	1 092	122	160	26	267	336
Franklin................	4.9	17.8	9.5	33.2	21.8	6.8	4.5	1.6	36.3	121.7	42 970	3 389	3 171	194	–	1 056	354
Fulton..................	5.7	19.2	7.2	28.1	23.6	7.9	6.2	2.3	38.6	97.1	52 863	992	105	293	9	308	503
Genesee................	6.1	20.0	7.5	29.5	22.6	7.1	5.4	1.8	37.4	96.9	57 167	1 284	470	292	14	430	713
Greene.................	5.4	17.6	9.5	27.0	24.8	8.4	5.4	1.9	39.1	106.5	43 740	2 664	135	260	8	734	654
Hamilton...............	4.3	15.4	5.2	24.2	30.9	11.1	7.0	1.9	45.4	100.0	5 257	24	14	8	3	36	37
Herkimer...............	5.6	18.8	8.3	26.6	24.0	7.9	6.7	2.2	39.0	94.2	63 031	329	139	263	11	113	541
Jefferson...............	7.3	19.1	11.8	31.3	19.1	5.8	4.0	1.5	32.5	107.3	99 118	6 517	589	1 027	156	2 296	2 035
Kings...................	7.4	19.5	10.3	30.8	20.6	6.1	4.0	1.4	33.1	88.4	1 015 728	898 350	10 117	185 818	1 465	248 557	105 291
Lewis..................	6.1	21.7	7.7	28.2	22.5	7.7	4.5	1.6	36.8	98.6	26 451	106	76	63	14	76	158
Livingston..............	5.4	18.0	14.2	28.9	22.1	6.1	3.9	1.4	35.3	100.7	60 494	1 938	172	492	20	545	667
Madison................	5.9	19.0	12.0	27.6	23.0	6.6	4.4	1.5	36.1	96.3	67 006	916	358	387	10	184	580
Monroe.................	6.4	19.2	9.5	29.3	22.6	6.3	4.9	1.9	36.1	93.0	581 961	101 078	1 950	17 922	220	17 925	14 287
Montgomery............	5.9	18.6	7.2	26.3	22.9	8.5	7.7	3.0	39.7	91.4	47 160	572	124	263	6	952	631
Nassau.................	6.5	18.2	7.3	28.9	24.0	7.9	5.4	1.7	38.5	92.8	1 058 285	134 673	2 112	63 140	400	47 638	28 296
New York...............	4.9	11.8	10.2	38.3	22.6	6.4	4.0	1.7	35.7	90.3	835 610	267 302	7 617	144 538	1 069	217 383	63 676
Niagara................	6.0	18.7	8.5	28.4	23.1	7.8	5.8	1.8	38.2	93.3	199 404	13 520	2 069	1 267	51	876	2 659
Oneida.................	5.7	18.2	8.6	28.2	22.9	7.8	6.4	2.3	38.2	98.6	212 414	13 521	549	2 722	55	2 625	3 583
Onondaga..............	6.5	19.2	9.5	28.8	22.1	7.0	5.1	1.7	36.3	91.7	388 555	43 011	3 945	9 569	147	4 076	9 033
Ontario.................	6.0	19.4	8.3	28.4	24.8	6.6	4.9	1.7	37.9	95.6	95 256	2 068	223	691	20	703	1 263
Orange.................	7.6	21.4	8.7	30.0	21.9	5.3	3.6	1.4	34.7	100.3	285 721	27 601	1 205	5 157	123	13 962	7 598
Orleans................	6.2	19.9	8.2	31.3	21.9	6.2	4.6	1.6	36.2	98.3	39 367	3 230	203	142	12	682	535
Oswego................	6.2	20.6	10.9	28.9	22.1	6.0	4.0	1.3	35.0	97.5	118 918	717	498	508	17	582	1 137
Otsego.................	4.8	17.9	14.4	24.3	23.6	7.5	5.5	2.0	37.1	93.1	59 083	1 079	141	390	31	306	646
Putnam.................	6.9	19.6	6.3	32.1	25.6	5.4	3.0	1.1	37.4	99.5	89 876	1 562	137	1 190	24	1 596	1 360
Queens.................	6.4	16.4	9.6	33.1	21.7	6.6	4.5	1.6	35.4	92.9	982 725	446 189	11 077	391 500	1 331	260 387	136 170
Rensselaer.............	6.1	18.2	10.1	29.1	23.0	6.9	4.9	1.7	36.7	95.9	139 002	7 147	347	2 606	31	1 360	2 045
Richmond..............	6.7	18.8	8.5	30.9	23.4	6.3	3.9	1.4	35.9	93.6	344 319	42 914	1 107	25 071	182	18 355	11 780
Rockland...............	7.6	20.4	7.9	28.0	24.3	6.7	3.6	1.5	36.2	95.3	220 538	31 472	676	15 826	205	10 838	7 198
St. Lawrence...........	5.4	18.0	13.8	27.4	22.4	7.1	4.4	1.5	35.4	103.3	105 782	2 664	977	800	32	773	903
Saratoga...............	6.5	18.6	7.8	31.5	24.2	6.1	4.1	1.3	36.9	97.2	192 579	2 725	361	2 077	44	846	2 003
Schenectady...........	6.1	18.2	7.9	28.1	23.0	7.8	6.5	2.4	38.6	92.6	128 631	9 953	341	2 888	43	1 769	2 930
Schoharie..............	5.6	18.4	10.6	26.2	24.4	7.9	5.1	1.9	38.0	99.0	30 514	403	96	120	7	149	293
Schuyler...............	5.8	19.5	7.9	26.6	25.4	7.6	5.3	1.8	38.8	100.5	18 548	279	77	56	5	69	190
Seneca.................	5.6	19.2	7.5	28.8	23.8	7.9	5.4	1.9	38.2	100.1	31 682	758	83	227	5	222	365
Steuben................	6.1	19.9	7.4	27.2	24.2	7.9	5.4	1.8	38.2	96.0	95 198	1 347	266	893	16	208	798
Suffolk	7.1	19.0	7.6	31.2	23.3	6.5	3.9	1.4	36.5	95.9	1 200 755	98 553	3 807	34 711	484	51 875	29 184
Sullivan................	5.9	19.1	7.3	28.1	25.4	7.9	4.9	1.5	38.8	103.6	63 103	6 292	197	825	29	2 139	1 381
Tioga..................	6.3	20.7	7.0	28.8	24.0	7.4	4.2	1.5	38.0	97.6	50 501	282	112	296	7	108	478
Tompkins...............	4.4	14.5	26.0	26.2	19.3	4.8	3.5	1.3	28.6	97.6	82 507	3 508	275	6 943	36	1 052	2 180
Ulster..................	5.5	18.0	8.7	29.7	24.7	7.1	4.6	1.7	38.2	99.1	158 042	9 646	472	2 199	51	3 826	3 513
Warren.................	5.4	18.6	7.5	28.2	25.1	8.1	5.2	1.9	39.0	94.2	61 705	395	130	347	7	145	574
Washington.............	5.6	19.0	8.3	29.4	23.7	7.5	4.8	1.7	37.5	105.2	57 973	1 785	125	172	9	510	468
Wayne.................	6.6	20.8	6.8	30.1	23.5	6.5	4.1	1.5	36.9	98.1	87 954	3 044	245	437	14	819	1 252
Westchester............	7.0	18.0	7.2	30.4	23.5	7.2	4.8	1.9	37.6	91.7	658 858	131 132	2 343	41 367	371	61 227	28 161
Wyoming...............	5.3	18.8	8.2	32.8	22.8	6.2	4.5	1.5	36.7	118.3	39 880	2 395	116	161	10	572	290
Yates..................	6.6	20.0	9.3	24.7	23.9	8.3	5.3	2.0	37.9	95.3	24 103	139	36	69	4	88	182

[1] Includes all other responses not included in the other five race categories shown. Also includes write-in entries such as multiracial, mixed, interracial, or a Hispanic/Latino group. [2] Refers to combinations of two or more of the six race categories shown under one race.

Source: Population by Age, Sex, and Race—U.S. Census Bureau; 2000 Census of Population and Housing, "Census 2000 Profiles of General Demographic Characteristics" data files, published May 2001 (related Internet site <http://www.census.gov/mp/www/pub/2000cen/mscen01.html>).

[Includes U.S., states, and 3,142 counties/county equivalents defined as of January 1, 1992. For changes to these areas since January 1, 1992, see appendix B. Geographic Information]

County	Population by age, 2000 (April 1) — Percent—								Median age (years)	Males per 100 females, 2000 (April 1)	Population by race, 2000 (April 1) — One race						Two or more races[2]
	Under 5 years	5 to 17 years	18 to 24 years	25 to 44 years	45 to 64 years	65 to 74 years	75 to 84 years	85 years and over			White	Black or African American	American Indian and Alaska Native	Asian	Native Hawaiian and Other Pacific Islander	Some other race[1]	
NORTH CAROLINA......	6.7	17.7	10.0	31.1	22.5	6.6	4.1	1.3	35.3	96.0	5 804 656	1 737 545	99 551	113 689	3 983	186 629	103 260
Alamance................	6.4	17.4	9.9	29.9	22.3	7.4	5.0	1.6	36.3	92.5	98 900	24 544	462	1 172	28	4 177	1 517
Alexander................	6.9	17.6	7.9	31.1	24.6	7.0	3.7	1.2	36.6	99.4	30 915	1 557	50	348	1	451	281
Alleghany................	5.2	14.2	7.4	26.3	27.7	10.8	5.9	2.5	43.0	97.1	10 217	131	28	21	1	187	92
Anson................	6.5	18.7	8.6	29.0	22.8	7.2	5.4	1.8	36.6	96.5	12 519	12 295	113	143	6	82	117
Ashe................	5.3	14.5	7.5	27.0	27.7	9.5	6.1	2.3	42.1	97.4	23 691	162	79	57	2	257	136
Avery................	4.8	14.6	10.3	30.1	24.4	8.7	5.4	1.7	38.4	111.8	16 129	598	58	33	7	220	122
Beaufort................	6.0	17.4	7.7	26.1	26.9	8.9	5.1	1.8	40.2	91.1	30 768	13 051	74	99	10	638	318
Bertie................	6.4	19.7	7.7	26.4	23.8	8.7	5.5	1.8	38.6	87.6	7 178	12 326	87	21	1	65	95
Bladen................	6.6	18.0	8.7	27.2	25.2	8.0	4.8	1.5	37.9	92.6	18 469	12 235	657	31	14	636	236
Brunswick	5.5	15.7	7.0	25.7	29.2	11.1	4.8	1.1	42.2	96.7	60 200	10 516	494	198	32	965	738
Buncombe	5.6	16.2	8.6	29.3	24.8	7.9	5.5	1.9	38.9	92.3	183 761	15 425	803	1 368	79	2 365	2 529
Burke................	6.2	17.8	8.9	29.6	24.0	7.5	4.4	1.5	36.9	100.0	76 678	5 984	270	3 106	185	1 931	994
Cabarrus	7.1	18.7	8.1	32.5	22.1	6.2	4.1	1.3	35.4	97.0	109 127	15 961	443	1 190	32	3 017	1 293
Caldwell	6.4	17.0	7.8	30.5	25.1	7.5	4.3	1.4	37.5	97.6	71 017	4 223	162	301	26	1 098	588
Camden	5.6	18.9	6.3	30.5	25.2	8.0	4.4	1.2	39.1	98.4	5 551	1 189	29	39	2	9	66
Carteret	4.9	15.8	6.4	27.2	28.4	10.1	5.6	1.6	42.3	96.5	53 611	4 151	258	323	35	357	648
Caswell................	5.7	17.5	7.7	30.1	26.0	7.1	4.6	1.3	38.2	102.5	14 352	8 583	45	36	6	276	203
Catawba	6.5	17.7	8.8	31.1	23.5	6.8	4.2	1.3	36.1	97.3	120 422	11 862	365	4 146	75	3 198	1 617
Chatham	6.3	16.2	7.3	30.4	24.6	8.0	5.5	1.7	38.8	96.8	36 969	8 422	201	292	18	2 868	559
Cherokee	5.4	15.1	6.5	24.4	28.8	10.7	6.7	2.3	44.0	94.2	23 040	387	396	69	3	109	294
Chowan	5.9	18.1	9.6	24.1	24.4	9.4	6.2	2.3	39.8	88.1	8 794	5 450	43	50	1	87	101
Clay................	4.2	14.3	6.2	22.8	29.8	12.1	7.7	2.9	46.7	94.9	8 600	70	29	8	6	13	49
Cleveland	6.7	18.5	8.8	28.8	23.7	7.3	4.6	1.5	36.5	92.6	73 955	20 155	145	669	10	657	696
Columbus	6.6	19.1	8.7	27.4	24.4	7.8	4.5	1.4	36.9	92.6	34 737	16 934	1 706	123	16	812	421
Craven	7.3	17.3	12.8	27.9	21.2	8.0	4.3	1.1	34.4	101.9	63 952	22 966	388	908	56	1 627	1 539
Cumberland	8.2	19.7	13.7	32.9	17.8	4.8	2.3	.6	29.6	102.3	167 093	105 731	4 691	5 694	902	9 477	9 375
Currituck................	6.1	19.3	6.7	30.5	25.4	7.2	3.7	1.1	38.3	98.6	16 445	1 318	83	71	6	91	176
Dare................	5.2	16.2	6.3	30.8	27.7	8.7	4.1	1.0	40.4	101.5	28 393	797	83	111	13	269	301
Davidson	6.5	17.8	7.6	31.2	24.1	7.1	4.3	1.3	37.1	96.0	128 184	13 463	545	1 204	18	2 446	1 386
Davie................	6.5	17.8	7.1	29.4	25.5	7.4	4.8	1.6	38.4	97.0	31 504	2 368	79	109	7	458	310
Duplin	7.4	18.7	9.6	29.3	22.1	7.1	4.4	1.3	34.9	98.3	28 785	14 198	113	75	36	5 334	522
Durham	6.9	16.0	12.8	34.8	19.8	4.9	3.5	1.2	32.2	93.0	113 698	88 109	660	7 350	79	9 404	4 014
Edgecombe	6.8	20.3	8.6	28.4	23.4	6.9	4.3	1.3	36.2	86.8	22 278	31 949	109	70	7	870	323
Forsyth	6.7	17.2	9.6	31.1	22.8	6.9	4.3	1.5	36.0	91.5	209 552	78 388	923	3 172	96	9 962	3 974
Franklin	7.0	18.3	8.4	32.4	22.9	6.0	3.7	1.3	35.8	97.4	31 190	14 193	208	140	17	1 082	430
Gaston	6.7	18.0	8.2	31.0	23.5	7.1	4.3	1.3	36.2	93.7	157 965	26 405	525	1 814	50	1 958	1 648
Gates	5.8	20.9	6.1	29.1	23.7	7.8	4.9	1.7	38.1	96.2	6 213	4 120	44	26	3	11	99
Graham	5.8	16.1	7.3	25.2	27.5	9.9	5.9	2.1	41.5	95.3	7 346	15	547	13	1	10	61
Granville	6.2	17.7	8.5	33.3	22.8	6.5	3.8	1.2	36.2	110.7	29 459	16 943	222	176	9	1 177	512
Greene	7.0	18.3	9.4	30.9	22.3	6.6	4.0	1.4	35.5	105.7	9 835	7 820	57	17	2	1 091	152
Guilford................	6.6	17.1	11.0	31.4	22.1	6.3	4.0	1.4	34.9	92.0	271 686	123 253	1 944	10 294	130	7 615	6 126
Halifax................	6.2	19.9	8.0	27.7	23.2	8.1	5.2	1.7	37.2	90.7	24 424	30 151	1 801	312	10	267	405
Harnett................	7.6	19.3	10.6	32.1	19.9	5.9	3.4	1.1	32.5	97.4	64 744	20 481	794	591	61	2 924	1 430
Haywood	5.3	15.5	6.2	26.9	27.1	10.4	6.6	2.0	42.3	92.0	52 330	684	266	114	20	237	382
Henderson	5.6	15.2	6.4	26.1	25.1	11.2	8.0	2.6	42.7	93.8	82 505	2 725	245	546	16	2 237	899
Hertford	5.5	19.9	7.8	26.3	24.8	8.5	5.5	1.8	39.2	85.0	8 464	13 459	269	71	5	147	186
Hoke................	9.2	20.6	10.7	34.1	17.6	4.7	2.4	.6	30.0	102.0	14 982	12 664	3 852	278	52	1 100	718
Hyde................	4.5	15.9	7.9	30.7	24.6	8.5	5.2	2.6	39.7	112.2	3 650	2 043	18	21	–	49	45
Iredell................	6.9	18.7	7.5	31.3	23.3	6.8	4.2	1.3	36.5	96.1	100 785	16 762	328	1 553	25	2 058	1 149
Jackson	5.1	13.9	17.9	24.4	25.0	7.9	4.5	1.4	36.2	98.4	28 378	552	3 379	169	6	181	456
Johnston	7.8	18.2	8.1	34.2	21.7	5.5	3.4	.9	34.2	98.7	95 237	19 090	494	368	43	5 530	1 203
Jones	6.0	19.6	6.8	26.9	25.2	8.4	5.4	1.6	39.1	93.0	6 329	3 724	37	16	4	176	95
Lee	6.9	18.7	9.0	29.7	22.7	7.2	4.4	1.3	35.9	97.5	34 343	10 032	206	328	19	3 593	519
Lenoir................	6.6	18.7	7.9	27.6	24.6	8.2	5.1	1.4	38.1	90.3	33 685	24 115	106	202	30	1 119	391
Lincoln	6.4	18.5	7.7	31.7	24.2	6.3	3.8	1.1	36.4	98.9	57 557	4 108	172	196	8	1 104	635
McDowell	6.1	16.7	8.2	29.9	24.9	7.9	4.8	1.6	38.0	99.3	38 853	1 753	122	388	5	678	352
Macon................	5.0	15.4	6.1	23.2	27.9	12.1	7.7	2.5	45.2	92.1	28 969	357	84	117	5	91	188
Madison	5.9	15.4	10.3	26.5	26.0	8.3	5.5	2.2	39.3	97.3	19 169	162	53	45	2	88	116
Martin	6.2	19.3	7.5	26.8	25.0	8.2	5.5	1.6	38.7	86.5	13 447	11 611	74	61	8	231	161
Mecklenburg	7.3	17.8	9.7	36.4	20.3	4.7	2.9	1.0	33.1	96.5	445 250	193 838	2 439	21 889	339	20 954	10 745
Mitchell	5.1	16.1	6.8	26.4	27.1	10.3	6.3	2.0	42.0	95.6	15 353	34	70	32	–	104	94
Montgomery	6.8	18.1	9.0	28.5	23.6	7.5	5.0	1.5	36.7	102.6	18 527	5 857	108	431	12	1 542	345
Moore................	5.6	16.5	6.6	25.8	23.5	11.5	8.1	2.3	41.8	93.0	60 002	11 589	506	332	38	1 642	660
Nash................	6.6	18.8	8.5	30.1	23.5	6.8	4.4	1.2	36.5	92.7	54 152	29 664	397	495	20	1 804	888
New Hanover	5.7	15.2	12.0	30.5	23.7	7.2	4.4	1.3	36.3	93.3	128 098	27 203	627	1 333	96	1 266	1 684
Northampton	5.7	18.6	6.9	26.5	24.9	9.2	6.1	2.1	40.0	92.0	8 633	13 125	71	20	12	86	139
Onslow................	8.8	17.3	23.8	29.2	14.4	4.0	1.8	.5	25.0	123.2	108 351	27 790	1 108	2 526	283	5 449	4 848

[1] Includes all other responses not included in the other five race categories shown. Also includes write-in entries such as multiracial, mixed, interracial, or a Hispanic/Latino group. [2] Refers to combinations of two or more of the six race categories shown under one race.

Source: Population by Age, Sex, and Race—U.S. Census Bureau; 2000 Census of Population and Housing, "Census 2000 Profiles of General Demographic Characteristics" data files, published May 2001 (related Internet site <http://www.census.gov/mp/www/pub/2000cen/mscen01.html>).

[Includes U.S., states, and 3,142 counties/county equivalents defined as of January 1, 1992. For changes to these areas since January 1, 1992, see appendix B. Geographic Information]

County	Population by age, 2000 (April 1) Percent— Under 5 years	5 to 17 years	18 to 24 years	25 to 44 years	45 to 64 years	65 to 74 years	75 to 84 years	85 years and over	Median age (years)	Males per 100 females, 2000 (April 1)	Population by race, 2000 (April 1) One race White	Black or African American	American Indian and Alaska Native	Asian	Native Hawaiian and Other Pacific Islander	Some other race[1]	Two or more races[2]
NORTH CAROLINA–Con.																	
Orange	5.0	15.3	21.0	29.9	20.4	4.5	2.9	1.0	30.4	90.1	92 272	16 298	457	4 845	20	2 312	2 023
Pamlico	5.0	16.1	6.4	25.8	28.0	11.2	5.6	1.9	42.9	101.4	9 464	3 178	68	49	3	76	96
Pasquotank	6.2	18.6	11.3	28.4	21.3	7.3	5.1	1.7	35.9	93.8	19 866	13 975	130	300	13	172	441
Pender	5.9	17.3	7.4	29.5	25.8	8.5	4.4	1.1	38.8	101.2	29 882	9 689	201	74	14	834	388
Perquimans	5.2	17.8	6.8	24.4	26.6	10.6	6.6	2.1	42.2	91.3	8 051	3 182	20	24	3	15	73
Person	6.3	17.7	7.4	30.6	24.2	7.5	4.8	1.4	38.0	93.2	24 504	10 049	218	53	5	487	307
Pitt	6.5	17.1	17.5	29.9	19.4	5.2	3.3	1.0	30.4	90.2	83 061	45 019	357	1 443	57	2 408	1 453
Polk	5.2	14.9	5.8	24.2	26.3	10.7	9.2	3.7	44.9	90.2	16 906	1 079	34	44	5	116	140
Randolph	6.8	18.2	8.0	31.3	23.5	6.7	4.1	1.3	36.2	97.8	116 370	7 342	582	830	21	3 932	1 377
Richmond	6.8	19.0	10.1	27.7	22.8	7.4	4.8	1.4	35.5	96.3	30 193	14 215	770	316	15	504	551
Robeson	8.0	21.1	10.6	29.3	21.1	5.6	3.3	1.0	32.0	94.7	40 460	30 973	46 896	404	77	2 787	1 742
Rockingham	6.2	17.2	7.6	29.4	24.8	7.9	5.1	1.8	38.5	93.3	71 087	17 987	250	254	33	1 550	767
Rowan	6.6	18.1	9.1	29.8	22.5	7.2	5.1	1.7	36.4	97.6	104 294	20 562	433	1 105	35	2 610	1 301
Rutherford	6.2	17.6	8.0	27.9	24.3	8.4	5.7	2.0	38.3	93.0	54 592	7 066	125	206	20	423	467
Sampson	7.3	18.5	9.4	29.7	22.3	7.0	4.3	1.5	35.0	98.2	35 955	18 018	1 086	186	54	4 183	679
Scotland	7.3	20.8	9.5	27.6	23.4	6.3	3.8	1.3	34.6	88.4	18 535	13 434	3 197	182	7	164	479
Stanly	6.2	18.8	8.4	29.0	23.4	7.6	5.1	1.5	36.9	97.4	49 196	6 657	144	1 049	11	584	459
Stokes	6.6	17.9	7.3	31.4	25.0	6.5	4.0	1.4	37.2	96.1	41 774	2 084	109	86	23	393	242
Surry	6.3	17.2	7.9	29.0	24.1	8.1	5.4	1.9	38.0	95.7	64 383	2 965	165	403	27	2 459	817
Swain	6.1	18.1	8.3	26.7	25.4	8.4	5.0	1.9	38.8	94.6	8 602	221	3 765	20	1	63	296
Transylvania	4.9	15.5	8.2	23.1	26.9	11.7	7.4	2.4	43.9	92.7	27 476	1 235	83	111	7	92	330
Tyrrell	4.9	17.7	8.2	30.3	22.7	8.3	5.8	2.1	38.7	114.1	2 343	1 636	8	31	–	85	46
Union	8.1	20.0	8.2	31.5	21.5	5.3	2.8	.9	34.0	99.7	102 441	15 480	475	720	30	3 264	1 267
Vance	7.0	20.0	8.9	28.8	22.6	7.0	4.2	1.4	35.0	89.7	20 709	20 749	85	167	13	871	360
Wake	7.2	17.9	10.7	36.5	20.4	4.1	2.5	.8	32.9	98.4	454 544	123 820	2 152	21 249	212	15 548	10 321
Warren	5.4	18.2	8.0	26.3	24.8	9.6	5.9	1.9	39.7	96.6	7 769	10 882	957	26	5	157	176
Washington	6.6	19.4	7.7	25.0	25.8	8.3	5.2	2.0	39.2	89.7	6 626	6 716	7	44	6	228	96
Watauga	3.9	12.4	27.8	23.4	21.5	6.1	3.7	1.3	29.9	99.3	41 181	680	108	251	16	194	265
Wayne	7.0	19.2	9.9	30.5	21.9	6.8	3.8	1.0	34.8	97.3	69 452	37 422	412	1 088	55	3 483	1 417
Wilkes	6.2	16.4	7.9	29.7	25.7	7.9	4.7	1.5	38.5	97.3	61 008	2 733	95	213	25	1 124	434
Wilson	6.9	18.7	9.1	28.8	21.6	7.1	4.5	1.3	36.2	91.3	41 210	29 032	199	310	16	2 367	680
Yadkin	6.6	17.3	7.5	30.2	24.2	7.9	4.7	1.6	37.6	96.4	33 638	1 246	59	62	7	1 057	279
Yancey	5.5	15.7	7.0	26.4	27.1	9.7	6.3	2.2	41.9	95.7	17 417	101	60	23	–	73	100
NORTH DAKOTA	6.1	18.9	11.4	27.2	21.6	7.1	5.3	2.3	36.2	99.6	593 181	3 916	31 329	3 606	230	2 540	7 398
Adams	4.5	18.7	4.1	21.7	27.0	10.8	8.9	4.4	45.6	91.5	2 554	14	8	4	1	3	9
Barnes	5.3	17.0	11.3	23.0	23.6	8.5	7.7	3.5	40.6	96.8	11 529	53	90	22	–	14	67
Benson	8.9	27.2	7.8	23.3	19.4	7.0	4.4	2.1	31.4	102.1	3 541	7	3 346	1	1	11	57
Billings	3.5	21.4	4.5	26.6	28.0	8.2	6.1	1.7	41.9	112.9	877	–	1	–	1	1	8
Bottineau	3.9	18.3	8.0	22.3	26.2	9.7	7.7	3.8	43.4	101.4	6 950	16	104	13	1	8	57
Bowman	4.6	19.5	5.3	24.6	24.2	10.4	7.5	3.9	43.0	94.6	3 209	1	5	1	–	5	21
Burke	3.7	17.2	3.5	22.3	28.3	13.4	8.8	2.9	47.5	101.6	2 225	3	5	3	–	1	5
Burleigh	6.2	18.5	11.0	29.3	22.5	6.5	4.2	1.7	35.9	95.5	65 966	182	2 276	275	19	109	589
Cass	6.6	16.8	16.0	31.3	19.6	4.9	3.3	1.4	31.3	100.3	117 106	996	1 325	1 551	43	530	1 587
Cavalier	4.3	20.3	3.7	21.3	27.5	11.3	7.9	3.7	45.2	98.9	4 739	7	25	5	–	5	50
Dickey	5.7	18.1	10.2	22.5	22.2	9.3	7.9	4.2	40.7	97.2	5 629	6	20	29	–	32	41
Divide	3.1	17.2	3.6	20.1	26.6	12.2	11.6	5.7	49.0	100.8	2 260	–	3	12	–	4	4
Dunn	5.7	21.7	5.8	23.6	25.9	8.4	6.4	2.5	40.9	104.2	3 117	1	448	3	–	–	31
Eddy	5.0	18.6	6.1	22.5	23.1	11.3	9.1	4.4	43.8	95.5	2 657	2	65	4	2	7	20
Emmons	5.3	19.5	3.7	22.3	23.6	12.7	8.8	4.0	44.5	101.7	4 290	2	6	7	8	13	5
Foster	5.3	20.9	5.5	25.9	21.0	10.9	7.4	3.1	40.5	98.8	3 722	5	16	–	–	2	14
Golden Valley	5.5	22.9	5.1	22.2	23.0	9.0	8.3	4.0	41.2	92.6	1 881	–	14	2	–	6	21
Grand Forks	6.4	17.4	19.6	28.8	18.2	4.7	3.5	1.4	29.2	103.7	61 479	904	1 525	646	44	475	1 036
Grant	4.3	19.1	4.3	20.5	27.1	11.6	8.4	4.8	46.5	104.1	2 753	–	49	10	–	10	19
Griggs	4.7	17.8	4.9	21.1	25.8	10.9	10.0	4.8	45.8	99.4	2 735	–	6	4	–	4	5
Hettinger	4.4	18.9	3.9	20.7	27.0	12.3	9.3	3.6	46.2	100.2	2 686	4	10	2	2	1	10
Kidder	5.0	18.2	5.0	22.9	24.9	12.1	8.5	3.5	44.5	103.2	2 739	5	3	2	–	–	4
LaMoure	4.4	19.8	5.4	23.0	24.0	11.5	8.3	3.6	44.3	102.4	4 665	1	8	6	–	5	16
Logan	5.5	17.1	3.6	21.8	25.0	13.6	9.5	3.9	46.4	98.3	2 289	2	3	4	–	3	7
McHenry	4.9	19.0	5.9	23.3	25.1	10.8	7.2	3.9	43.0	103.9	5 911	5	24	2	–	3	42
McIntosh	4.2	15.2	4.6	19.4	22.4	14.9	12.7	6.6	51.0	91.5	3 352	–	5	10	1	3	19
McKenzie	6.3	24.4	5.5	23.3	24.9	7.4	6.1	2.2	39.5	100.7	4 438	4	1 215	3	1	8	68
McLean	4.7	19.1	5.1	22.7	27.9	9.4	7.9	3.1	44.1	98.2	8 615	2	554	11	1	18	110
Mercer	4.6	24.5	4.2	27.5	24.9	6.9	5.3	2.1	40.1	101.2	8 302	4	173	22	33	10	100
Morton	6.5	20.5	7.8	28.2	22.4	7.6	5.0	2.0	37.4	99.3	24 246	40	604	77	2	40	294
Mountrail	6.5	21.6	6.8	23.2	24.2	8.0	6.5	3.2	39.6	96.8	4 376	6	1 988	14	3	17	227
Nelson	3.7	18.4	4.0	20.3	26.2	12.1	10.6	4.7	47.2	95.8	3 662	3	13	11	–	4	22
Oliver	4.5	22.9	4.7	23.5	30.1	7.8	5.0	1.4	42.0	107.5	2 015	3	26	2	–	–	19
Pembina	5.0	19.9	6.2	24.6	24.8	9.2	7.2	3.1	41.6	100.6	8 198	13	123	18	–	109	124
Pierce	5.3	18.6	5.5	23.9	22.7	10.7	8.9	4.6	42.9	96.6	4 605	5	32	12	–	2	19

[1] Includes all other responses not included in the other five race categories shown. Also includes write-in entries such as multiracial, mixed, interracial, or a Hispanic/Latino group. [2] Refers to combinations of two or more of the six race categories shown under one race.

Source: Population by Age, Sex, and Race—U.S. Census Bureau; 2000 Census of Population and Housing, "Census 2000 Profiles of General Demographic Characteristics" data files, published May 2001 (related Internet site <http://www.census.gov/mp/www/pub/2000cen/mscen01.html>).

[Includes U.S., states, and 3,142 counties/county equivalents defined as of January 1, 1992. For changes to these areas since January 1, 1992, see appendix B. Geographic Information]

County	Population by age, 2000 (April 1) Percent—								Median age (years)	Males per 100 females, 2000 (April 1)	Population by race, 2000 (April 1) One race					Some other race[1]	Two or more races[2]
	Under 5 years	5 to 17 years	18 to 24 years	25 to 44 years	45 to 64 years	65 to 74 years	75 to 84 years	85 years and over			White	Black or African American	American Indian and Alaska Native	Asian	Native Hawaiian and Other Pacific Islander		
NORTH DAKOTA—Con.																	
Ramsey	5.7	19.4	8.0	25.9	22.3	8.4	6.8	3.5	39.5	97.4	11 138	25	651	31	3	20	198
Ransom	5.9	19.1	5.9	25.4	22.4	9.8	7.6	3.9	40.7	106.2	5 768	11	19	15	–	22	55
Renville	4.3	19.0	4.9	24.4	25.3	10.5	7.4	4.2	43.6	100.3	2 551	6	17	12	–	3	21
Richland	6.0	18.7	14.5	25.6	20.0	7.0	5.5	2.7	35.4	107.7	17 428	62	299	44	6	25	134
Rolette	8.8	27.6	9.5	25.8	18.5	5.2	3.3	1.2	28.9	97.2	3 435	10	9 983	10	–	16	220
Sargent	5.7	20.8	5.3	25.7	25.7	8.1	6.9	1.9	40.3	110.6	4 289	2	20	2	–	24	29
Sheridan	3.2	18.2	3.8	19.9	28.3	13.7	9.9	3.0	48.1	105.8	1 697	2	7	–	–	1	3
Sioux	10.5	29.8	11.1	26.9	16.2	3.7	1.8	.1	23.9	104.2	580	1	3 421	1	2	3	36
Slope	4.7	20.6	4.2	25.0	27.6	11.3	5.2	1.3	42.5	116.7	765	–	1	–	–	–	1
Stark	5.8	19.8	11.6	26.0	21.4	7.5	5.7	2.3	36.9	97.0	22 074	51	212	52	6	64	177
Steele	5.6	22.0	4.7	23.1	25.0	10.8	7.0	1.8	41.4	107.2	2 220	1	14	1	–	5	17
Stutsman	5.4	17.5	10.5	25.7	23.3	8.6	6.3	2.7	39.6	96.5	21 367	61	206	80	9	45	140
Towner	4.8	19.9	3.6	24.0	24.5	9.8	8.9	4.6	44.0	97.0	2 799	2	59	2	–	1	13
Traill	6.0	18.8	9.7	24.8	21.6	8.4	7.4	3.4	39.0	100.8	8 249	9	80	13	1	81	44
Walsh	5.7	19.2	6.5	25.0	24.2	8.9	7.3	3.0	40.9	100.0	11 752	41	126	24	2	311	133
Ward	7.4	18.8	13.0	29.1	19.2	6.2	4.4	1.9	32.4	99.2	54 327	1 305	1 215	483	36	428	1 001
Wells	4.4	18.1	4.6	22.7	24.2	12.2	9.0	4.9	45.2	96.6	5 057	7	12	12	–	1	13
Williams	5.7	20.4	7.8	25.5	24.0	7.9	6.1	2.4	39.8	96.2	18 367	24	869	36	2	27	436
OHIO	6.6	18.8	9.3	29.3	22.7	7.0	4.8	1.6	36.2	94.4	9 645 453	1 301 307	24 486	132 633	2 749	88 627	157 885
Adams	6.4	19.9	8.7	28.2	23.4	7.4	4.4	1.5	36.3	96.1	26 721	48	187	34	9	31	300
Allen	6.7	19.2	9.9	27.6	22.4	7.3	5.1	1.8	36.3	100.0	92 147	13 225	224	601	13	686	1 577
Ashland	6.6	19.1	10.8	26.5	23.0	7.1	4.9	2.0	36.3	96.6	51 231	424	57	287	15	112	397
Ashtabula	6.5	19.6	7.6	28.0	23.6	7.6	5.3	1.8	37.6	95.1	96 635	3 247	195	346	25	878	1 402
Athens	4.8	13.6	30.7	23.7	18.0	4.9	3.2	1.1	25.7	95.6	58 166	1 485	177	1 184	14	224	973
Auglaize	6.8	20.8	7.8	28.2	22.0	7.0	5.3	2.0	36.5	96.5	45 735	110	86	189	13	93	385
Belmont	5.0	16.7	7.7	27.4	24.9	9.0	7.0	2.1	40.9	96.4	66 698	2 553	97	213	13	109	543
Brown	7.0	20.5	8.1	30.3	22.4	6.6	3.7	1.3	35.4	96.8	41 474	389	76	54	2	35	255
Butler	6.9	19.0	11.9	29.8	21.7	6.1	3.5	1.1	34.2	95.3	303 510	17 531	693	5 147	115	2 066	3 745
Carroll	6.0	19.1	7.5	27.5	25.7	8.0	4.8	1.4	38.8	98.0	28 316	155	93	33	7	26	206
Champaign	6.5	19.6	7.9	28.7	24.6	6.5	4.5	1.6	37.0	95.9	37 230	894	120	99	8	120	419
Clark	6.5	18.6	9.1	26.8	24.3	7.5	5.4	1.8	37.6	92.5	127 541	12 954	402	761	31	767	2 286
Clermont	7.6	20.3	8.4	31.7	22.6	5.4	3.1	1.0	34.8	96.4	172 866	1 621	333	1 129	33	467	1 528
Clinton	7.1	19.3	10.2	29.1	22.1	6.4	4.4	1.4	35.3	96.1	38 917	886	107	154	1	83	395
Columbiana	5.9	18.4	7.8	28.6	24.2	8.0	5.5	1.6	38.5	98.8	108 071	2 468	203	262	19	167	885
Coshocton	6.4	19.8	7.8	27.4	24.0	7.8	5.3	1.6	37.8	95.5	35 685	399	62	118	10	72	309
Crawford	6.6	18.4	8.0	27.6	24.3	7.9	5.6	1.8	38.2	93.4	46 022	279	93	145	9	113	305
Cuyahoga	6.5	18.4	8.0	29.3	22.2	7.7	5.9	2.0	37.3	89.5	938 863	382 634	2 529	25 245	338	20 962	23 407
Darke	6.7	19.6	7.8	27.5	23.2	7.5	5.6	2.2	37.4	96.1	52 290	208	89	132	12	182	396
Defiance	7.0	19.6	9.2	27.4	23.9	6.8	4.5	1.5	36.5	97.3	36 575	692	102	142	9	1 417	563
Delaware	7.9	20.3	7.6	32.6	23.3	4.8	2.6	.8	35.3	98.0	103 663	2 774	157	1 690	38	416	1 251
Erie	6.0	18.7	7.2	27.0	25.5	8.1	5.7	1.8	39.5	95.0	70 514	6 876	164	298	4	420	1 275
Fairfield	7.0	19.8	8.0	30.2	23.9	6.1	3.7	1.3	36.2	99.2	116 803	3 274	244	890	27	282	1 239
Fayette	6.7	18.6	8.0	28.3	24.0	7.6	5.1	1.6	37.5	97.3	27 182	589	44	130	2	157	329
Franklin	7.2	17.9	11.7	33.3	20.1	5.3	3.4	1.1	32.5	94.5	806 851	191 196	2 899	32 784	466	10 992	23 790
Fulton	7.2	21.1	7.7	28.7	22.6	6.4	4.6	1.7	36.1	95.6	40 254	103	110	175	15	973	454
Gallia	6.3	18.7	9.7	27.5	24.2	7.6	4.4	1.6	37.4	95.4	29 596	839	134	110	–	46	344
Geauga	6.8	21.6	6.4	26.6	26.7	6.5	4.1	1.4	38.7	96.8	88 553	1 110	69	385	10	123	645
Greene	5.9	18.0	13.7	27.0	23.6	6.7	4.0	1.2	35.6	94.8	131 975	9 414	434	2 995	51	565	2 452
Guernsey	6.7	19.4	7.9	27.5	24.0	7.9	4.9	1.7	37.7	94.5	39 275	623	125	122	2	91	554
Hamilton	6.7	19.1	9.6	29.7	21.5	6.9	4.8	1.8	35.5	91.1	616 487	198 061	1 481	13 602	242	4 301	11 129
Hancock	6.8	19.0	9.7	28.7	22.6	6.5	4.9	1.8	36.0	94.3	67 832	789	128	867	11	868	800
Hardin	6.4	17.9	15.4	26.0	21.3	6.6	4.7	1.6	33.3	95.9	31 159	224	81	138	1	72	270
Harrison	5.8	17.2	6.9	26.6	25.8	9.1	6.2	2.4	41.1	94.1	15 300	348	13	17	1	14	163
Henry	6.7	20.9	8.2	28.1	22.1	7.0	5.1	1.9	36.4	97.6	27 845	169	77	124	–	747	248
Highland	7.1	19.9	8.5	27.8	22.8	7.5	4.7	1.6	36.1	95.2	39 599	612	99	129	15	62	359
Hocking	6.7	18.8	8.1	28.3	25.0	7.5	4.2	1.5	37.7	99.3	27 547	259	82	22	–	22	309
Holmes	10.3	25.3	10.4	25.7	17.8	5.6	3.5	1.4	28.0	99.6	38 564	127	22	24	3	49	154
Huron	7.5	20.8	8.5	28.9	21.9	6.7	4.3	1.4	34.9	96.1	57 094	575	106	150	5	971	586
Jackson	6.6	19.4	8.7	28.7	23.0	7.2	4.8	1.6	36.3	93.2	31 953	193	111	56	8	53	267
Jefferson	5.2	16.2	8.5	25.6	25.9	9.6	7.0	2.1	41.6	91.2	68 341	4 200	147	247	14	187	758
Knox	6.2	18.6	11.7	26.7	23.0	7.3	4.9	1.7	36.5	94.7	53 226	367	112	188	9	112	486
Lake	6.1	18.1	7.3	29.7	24.7	7.5	5.1	1.5	38.6	94.5	217 041	4 527	251	2 048	41	1 505	2 098
Lawrence	6.2	18.3	8.6	28.0	24.5	8.1	4.9	1.4	37.6	92.2	60 169	1 302	112	117	4	66	549
Licking	6.9	19.1	8.8	29.4	23.9	6.6	4.0	1.3	36.6	94.8	139 147	2 990	435	849	29	434	1 607
Logan	6.9	19.8	8.2	27.9	23.3	7.6	4.8	1.5	36.9	96.1	44 233	786	94	185	13	123	571
Lorain	6.9	19.3	8.7	29.3	23.3	6.6	4.5	1.3	36.5	96.3	243 514	24 203	845	1 703	74	8 160	6 165
Lucas	6.9	19.4	9.8	29.1	21.7	6.7	4.8	1.6	35.0	92.6	352 678	77 268	1 179	5 527	92	8 468	9 842
Madison	6.2	18.4	9.1	32.8	22.6	6.0	3.6	1.2	35.8	117.0	36 896	2 511	80	175	6	139	406
Mahoning	6.0	17.8	8.4	26.4	23.7	8.8	6.9	2.0	39.7	91.4	208 727	40 884	445	1 220	62	2 656	3 561

[1] Includes all other responses not included in the other five race categories shown. Also includes write-in entries such as multiracial, mixed, interracial, or a Hispanic/Latino group.   [2] Refers to combinations of two or more of the six race categories shown under one race.

Source: Population by Age, Sex, and Race—U.S. Census Bureau; 2000 Census of Population and Housing, "Census 2000 Profiles of General Demographic Characteristics" data files, published May 2001 (related Internet site <http://www.census.gov/mp/www/pub/2000cen/mscen01.html>).

[Includes U.S., states, and 3,142 counties/county equivalents defined as of January 1, 1992. For changes to these areas since January 1, 1992, see appendix B. Geographic Information]

County	Under 5 years	5 to 17 years	18 to 24 years	25 to 44 years	45 to 64 years	65 to 74 years	75 to 84 years	85 years and over	Median age (years)	Males per 100 females, 2000 (April 1)	White	Black or African American	American Indian and Alaska Native	Asian	Native Hawaiian and Other Pacific Islander	Some other race[1]	Two or more races[2]
OHIO—Con.																	
Marion	6.0	18.4	8.3	30.3	23.5	7.2	4.7	1.5	37.2	106.9	60 987	3 805	126	344	6	323	626
Medina	7.0	20.5	7.0	30.6	24.4	5.7	3.7	1.1	36.6	97.1	146 956	1 323	232	969	25	375	1 215
Meigs	5.7	18.2	8.4	27.7	25.2	7.9	5.1	1.7	38.6	94.7	22 548	159	62	24	–	57	222
Mercer	7.3	22.3	7.9	26.7	21.2	7.5	5.3	1.6	35.7	99.8	40 286	39	105	117	9	138	230
Miami	6.4	19.5	7.6	28.4	24.8	7.1	4.7	1.5	37.7	96.2	94 694	1 932	190	780	9	273	990
Monroe	5.3	18.3	7.1	25.9	27.2	8.8	5.6	1.9	40.8	97.5	14 986	40	23	11	2	17	101
Montgomery	6.6	18.1	9.7	29.0	22.9	7.3	4.9	1.5	36.4	92.3	428 084	111 030	1 258	7 341	196	2 718	8 435
Morgan	6.1	19.2	7.8	26.3	25.0	8.6	5.3	1.7	38.9	96.5	13 952	508	52	12	–	39	334
Morrow	6.5	20.8	7.6	29.3	24.3	6.6	3.6	1.3	36.5	99.4	31 111	85	94	46	1	58	233
Muskingum	6.7	19.3	9.4	27.7	22.6	7.5	5.0	1.8	36.5	92.0	79 438	3 392	180	231	17	167	1 160
Noble	5.0	17.6	11.7	31.8	20.8	7.3	4.1	1.6	35.5	130.8	13 010	940	37	13	–	4	54
Ottawa	5.2	18.0	6.7	26.8	26.8	8.8	5.8	1.8	41.0	97.5	39 576	265	85	94	20	589	356
Paulding	6.6	20.2	8.6	28.0	24.0	6.7	4.4	1.4	36.5	96.7	19 451	194	58	31	3	286	270
Perry	7.4	20.8	8.5	29.1	22.3	6.6	4.2	1.3	35.0	98.9	33 581	74	95	33	4	31	260
Pickaway	5.9	18.3	9.0	32.6	23.4	6.2	3.6	1.1	36.0	122.2	48 482	3 391	148	117	17	80	492
Pike	6.9	20.3	8.9	28.9	21.5	7.1	4.7	1.7	35.3	95.4	26 786	246	204	51	10	20	378
Portage	6.1	17.6	14.3	28.6	22.3	6.2	3.6	1.1	34.4	95.4	143 545	4 840	277	1 246	20	328	1 805
Preble	6.3	19.7	7.7	28.7	24.4	7.2	4.6	1.3	37.5	99.3	41 691	136	91	111	7	47	254
Putnam	7.3	22.4	8.3	28.1	20.6	6.7	4.8	1.8	35.0	98.5	33 426	58	53	61	2	872	254
Richland	6.4	18.4	8.4	28.6	24.1	7.7	4.9	1.5	37.7	101.3	113 600	12 151	263	656	38	493	1 651
Ross	6.2	17.8	8.6	31.6	23.6	6.7	4.2	1.3	36.9	108.3	67 288	4 544	226	259	14	136	878
Sandusky	6.5	19.7	8.1	28.3	23.0	7.4	5.1	1.9	37.3	95.9	56 974	1 650	80	177	5	1 913	993
Scioto	6.3	18.1	9.6	28.3	22.7	8.0	5.1	1.8	36.7	95.3	75 139	2 163	502	189	19	144	1 039
Seneca	6.2	19.7	10.4	27.2	22.4	7.5	5.0	1.5	36.3	98.0	55 770	1 033	103	222	5	817	733
Shelby	7.6	21.0	8.2	29.3	21.7	6.2	4.3	1.7	34.8	98.6	46 011	714	80	464	25	113	503
Stark	6.4	18.5	8.3	27.8	24.0	7.7	5.6	1.8	38.2	92.4	341 342	27 219	920	2 059	57	1 098	5 403
Summit	6.6	18.4	8.2	29.6	23.0	7.3	5.2	1.6	37.2	92.9	453 336	71 608	1 086	7 641	100	1 590	7 538
Trumbull	6.1	18.2	7.7	27.3	24.8	8.2	5.9	1.7	39.0	93.8	203 084	17 778	333	1 014	34	472	2 401
Tuscarawas	6.6	18.8	8.0	28.1	23.6	7.7	5.4	1.9	37.9	95.1	88 976	663	154	220	43	195	663
Union	7.6	20.0	7.5	34.0	21.2	5.3	3.2	1.1	34.5	91.5	38 965	1 149	75	221	7	92	400
Van Wert	6.4	19.7	8.3	27.3	22.9	7.8	5.6	2.1	37.6	95.5	28 896	222	33	57	–	223	228
Vinton	7.2	19.7	8.8	29.0	23.1	7.1	3.8	1.2	35.5	99.1	12 560	45	58	11	–	10	122
Warren	7.8	19.9	7.1	34.0	21.8	5.4	3.0	1.0	35.2	102.6	149 919	4 327	282	1 991	47	485	1 332
Washington	5.8	17.7	8.8	27.5	25.1	8.0	5.2	1.7	39.1	94.6	61 563	585	151	274	29	85	564
Wayne	7.0	20.4	9.8	27.8	22.7	6.5	4.2	1.4	35.4	97.5	107 677	1 749	183	740	15	264	936
Williams	6.4	19.8	8.3	28.7	22.9	6.8	5.2	1.9	36.9	98.7	37 821	283	89	202	3	466	324
Wood	5.8	17.9	17.2	26.8	21.3	5.8	3.9	1.4	32.6	93.8	114 802	1 540	274	1 247	18	1 756	1 428
Wyandot	6.5	19.4	8.2	27.9	22.7	7.9	5.4	2.2	37.4	95.1	22 429	32	19	115	1	169	143
OKLAHOMA	6.8	19.0	10.3	28.3	22.3	7.0	4.5	1.7	35.5	96.6	2 628 434	260 968	273 230	46 767	2 372	82 898	155 985
Adair	7.5	22.7	8.9	27.2	21.6	6.7	4.0	1.3	33.2	97.2	10 207	38	8 938	20	5	262	1 568
Alfalfa	4.5	14.9	6.4	28.7	25.2	9.9	7.2	3.3	42.3	131.0	5 459	256	167	7	3	84	129
Atoka	5.9	17.7	8.2	29.1	24.3	7.8	5.1	1.9	38.3	117.8	10 528	814	1 578	32	2	80	845
Beaver	5.7	21.1	6.5	25.8	24.1	8.7	5.6	2.6	39.3	102.2	5 430	17	73	6	2	220	109
Beckham	6.2	17.9	9.8	29.6	21.1	7.6	5.4	2.4	36.6	109.6	17 236	1 098	510	81	4	443	427
Blaine	5.7	18.3	9.1	28.6	21.4	8.0	6.2	2.7	37.6	119.3	9 136	797	1 042	85	97	343	476
Bryan	6.5	18.3	11.7	25.7	22.3	8.0	5.3	2.2	35.8	95.1	29 236	520	4 443	159	13	394	1 769
Caddo	6.6	21.9	8.5	26.0	22.1	7.8	5.2	2.0	36.0	98.6	19 763	881	7 320	52	5	813	1 316
Canadian	6.8	21.3	8.2	30.7	23.5	5.5	3.0	1.1	35.4	99.4	76 301	1 892	3 745	2 146	42	1 186	2 385
Carter	6.9	19.3	7.9	26.7	23.2	8.4	5.4	2.2	38.0	92.9	35 550	3 467	3 770	276	14	516	2 028
Cherokee	7.0	19.3	14.6	25.7	21.5	6.8	3.9	1.3	32.3	96.3	23 985	509	13 787	116	17	893	3 214
Choctaw	6.4	19.6	7.8	24.7	24.1	8.7	6.3	2.4	38.7	90.4	10 517	1 678	2 295	24	3	73	752
Cimarron	6.6	21.0	6.4	23.4	24.0	8.4	7.4	2.8	39.3	97.4	2 700	18	32	5	–	313	80
Cleveland	6.3	18.2	14.7	30.7	21.7	4.9	2.7	.9	32.2	100.8	173 909	7 403	9 162	5 913	99	2 880	8 650
Coal	6.6	20.0	7.7	25.3	22.5	9.5	5.7	2.6	38.1	96.3	4 534	22	1 044	19	–	45	367
Comanche	7.9	19.8	13.9	30.7	17.8	5.6	3.1	1.1	30.1	107.7	74 988	21 847	5 904	2 405	455	4 001	5 396
Cotton	6.6	18.8	7.4	26.7	22.8	8.3	6.5	2.9	38.6	98.6	5 602	189	491	8	2	120	202
Craig	6.0	17.9	7.8	27.9	24.3	8.5	5.7	1.9	39.3	101.1	10 246	462	2 439	27	4	72	1 700
Creek	6.8	20.6	8.0	27.3	24.5	7.2	4.2	1.4	36.9	96.0	55 425	1 724	6 120	179	17	423	3 479
Custer	6.1	18.2	17.4	24.5	20.1	6.8	4.9	2.1	32.7	94.9	21 283	751	1 518	229	10	1 515	836
Delaware	6.1	18.3	6.9	24.4	26.7	10.1	5.7	1.8	40.8	96.5	26 037	50	8 273	64	14	217	2 422
Dewey	4.8	18.5	7.1	22.9	25.7	8.9	7.7	4.3	43.0	94.9	4 371	6	220	3	1	34	108
Ellis	4.9	16.8	6.0	21.6	28.6	9.7	8.0	4.3	45.3	97.7	3 924	2	49	4	–	30	66
Garfield	6.7	18.3	9.1	27.3	22.5	7.9	5.7	2.4	37.7	93.7	51 253	1 885	1 219	491	281	1 168	1 516
Garvin	6.5	18.4	8.1	26.0	23.1	8.9	6.2	2.8	39.0	92.7	23 109	695	2 004	62	10	420	910
Grady	6.8	19.8	9.3	27.7	23.2	7.0	4.3	1.8	36.5	95.3	39 742	1 391	2 206	155	19	509	1 494
Grant	5.1	20.1	6.5	24.1	22.8	10.8	7.5	3.2	41.4	94.4	4 903	4	126	7	1	36	67
Greer	4.7	15.3	9.1	28.4	22.4	9.3	7.2	3.5	40.0	123.8	4 937	532	150	16	1	242	183
Harmon	6.1	19.8	7.9	24.1	21.1	8.9	7.9	4.3	39.9	94.1	2 385	321	37	6	1	470	63
Harper	4.7	18.6	6.4	23.4	25.2	11.5	7.2	3.0	43.1	96.6	3 415	1	33	3	1	84	25

[1] Includes all other responses not included in the other five race categories shown. Also includes write-in entries such as multiracial, mixed, interracial, or a Hispanic/Latino group. [2] Refers to combinations of two or more of the six race categories shown under one race.

Source: Population by Age, Sex, and Race—U.S. Census Bureau; 2000 Census of Population and Housing, "Census 2000 Profiles of General Demographic Characteristics" data files, published May 2001 (related Internet site <http://www.census.gov/mp/www/pub/2000cen/mscen01.html>).

Table B–2. Counties — **Population by Age, Sex, and Race**–Con.

[Includes U.S., states, and 3,142 counties/county equivalents defined as of January 1, 1992. For changes to these areas since January 1, 1992, see appendix B. Geographic Information]

County	Under 5 years	5 to 17 years	18 to 24 years	25 to 44 years	45 to 64 years	65 to 74 years	75 to 84 years	85 years and over	Median age (years)	Males per 100 females, 2000 (April 1)	White	Black or African American	American Indian and Alaska Native	Asian	Native Hawaiian and Other Pacific Islander	Some other race[1]	Two or more races[2]
OKLAHOMA—Con.																	
Haskell	6.8	19.2	8.1	24.5	24.2	9.0	6.0	2.2	38.6	95.7	9 226	72	1 722	34	–	53	685
Hughes	5.8	17.4	8.0	27.2	23.2	9.3	6.2	3.0	39.3	105.8	10 300	634	2 290	30	3	139	758
Jackson	8.2	21.0	10.3	29.0	19.6	6.2	4.1	1.7	33.0	99.1	21 654	2 285	494	331	47	2 655	973
Jefferson	6.1	17.8	7.2	25.4	23.3	10.0	7.0	3.2	40.4	94.7	5 941	47	357	77	2	195	199
Johnston	6.3	19.2	9.7	25.0	24.3	8.2	5.2	2.0	38.0	96.8	7 999	174	1 611	28	5	130	566
Kay	6.8	19.6	8.8	25.0	22.8	8.4	6.2	2.4	38.1	93.7	40 463	860	3 621	253	12	950	1 921
Kingfisher	6.2	21.0	8.2	26.8	22.4	7.8	5.3	2.2	38.0	95.1	12 267	221	420	30	1	605	382
Kiowa	5.6	18.5	7.5	24.5	23.4	9.7	7.1	3.5	40.9	95.7	8 544	478	645	32	6	274	248
Latimer	6.8	19.0	11.4	24.2	22.5	8.6	5.6	1.9	36.8	97.5	7 806	103	2 076	19	1	55	632
Le Flore	6.8	19.3	9.7	27.0	23.3	7.3	4.6	1.8	36.1	99.3	38 657	1 065	5 157	103	14	694	2 419
Lincoln	6.5	20.9	7.8	26.7	24.1	7.6	4.5	1.8	37.5	97.3	27 726	790	2 109	80	6	143	1 226
Logan	6.1	19.3	12.0	26.5	23.7	6.7	3.8	1.8	36.1	97.6	27 676	3 739	985	115	16	406	987
Love	6.1	19.6	7.0	25.4	25.7	8.6	5.3	2.3	39.4	98.2	7 431	193	566	23	1	316	301
McClain	6.6	20.2	8.1	29.0	24.0	6.9	3.8	1.2	36.9	98.6	24 207	183	1 555	62	9	621	1 103
McCurtain	7.3	20.9	8.3	26.2	23.4	7.6	4.7	1.7	36.0	92.8	24 267	3 200	4 669	74	4	461	1 727
McIntosh	5.4	17.2	6.4	22.3	26.9	12.3	7.1	2.4	44.1	91.7	14 123	790	3 152	27	6	68	1 290
Major	5.7	18.9	6.7	24.4	24.9	9.5	6.9	3.0	41.6	95.4	7 165	14	68	7	1	181	109
Marshall	6.2	17.3	7.5	24.1	25.5	10.8	6.6	2.1	41.3	96.5	10 282	242	1 200	25	1	813	621
Mayes	6.8	19.8	8.6	26.2	23.8	8.2	5.0	1.7	37.2	98.4	27 679	115	7 330	108	4	237	2 896
Murray	6.6	17.6	8.0	25.1	24.3	9.5	6.5	2.5	39.8	97.4	10 194	240	1 460	41	4	146	538
Muskogee	7.0	18.9	9.5	26.7	22.6	7.6	5.5	2.2	37.0	93.3	44 261	9 142	10 331	404	22	828	4 463
Noble	6.4	19.1	7.9	27.5	23.9	8.1	5.1	2.0	38.3	97.4	9 864	180	864	38	3	74	388
Nowata	6.5	19.6	7.6	25.3	23.7	9.1	5.8	2.4	39.0	96.7	7 655	260	1 750	13	–	28	863
Okfuskee	6.2	18.5	8.2	26.7	24.2	8.3	5.8	2.2	38.6	106.5	7 734	1 230	2 150	10	–	67	623
Oklahoma	7.3	18.3	10.9	30.0	21.4	6.5	4.3	1.4	34.2	94.2	465 195	99 241	22 598	18 573	512	28 773	25 556
Okmulgee	6.8	20.1	9.5	25.3	23.3	7.8	5.3	2.0	36.9	95.2	27 674	4 046	5 099	77	7	244	2 538
Osage	6.2	20.2	7.7	27.5	25.4	7.5	4.1	1.4	38.1	102.1	29 779	4 817	6 410	103	14	279	3 035
Ottawa	6.6	19.1	9.7	24.8	22.9	8.9	6.2	1.7	37.3	94.3	24 612	192	5 488	97	45	510	2 250
Pawnee	6.3	20.3	7.3	26.2	25.2	7.9	5.1	1.8	38.5	97.4	13 667	114	2 015	34	8	40	734
Payne	5.4	14.1	25.9	26.2	17.6	5.2	3.9	1.7	27.6	103.3	57 508	2 476	3 126	2 044	29	526	2 481
Pittsburg	5.6	17.9	7.8	26.9	24.6	9.0	5.8	2.3	39.4	101.5	33 932	1 768	5 493	117	15	344	2 284
Pontotoc	6.3	18.4	12.5	26.0	21.9	7.7	5.1	2.1	35.7	93.3	26 638	725	5 451	160	6	278	1 885
Pottawatomie	6.8	19.0	11.2	26.9	22.3	7.5	4.5	1.8	35.5	93.4	52 336	1 893	7 337	395	72	425	3 063
Pushmataha	6.2	19.7	6.6	24.0	25.2	9.9	5.8	2.6	40.1	92.5	9 097	96	1 819	12	7	34	602
Roger Mills	5.5	18.3	6.7	24.7	26.0	9.4	6.5	2.8	41.7	100.5	3 153	10	188	3	–	18	64
Rogers	6.9	21.7	7.4	28.6	24.0	6.6	3.5	1.2	36.2	96.8	56 427	512	8 533	228	20	399	4 522
Seminole	6.7	19.6	9.0	24.4	23.4	8.7	5.7	2.3	38.1	93.2	17 610	1 391	4 328	54	12	184	1 315
Sequoyah	7.1	20.4	8.2	26.9	24.0	7.8	4.2	1.5	36.4	97.3	26 548	725	7 654	86	13	288	3 658
Stephens	6.3	18.3	7.8	25.1	24.0	9.8	6.3	2.4	40.1	93.7	38 158	950	2 123	130	15	623	1 183
Texas	8.5	20.3	12.7	29.1	19.2	5.5	3.6	1.1	30.4	105.9	15 429	142	249	112	21	3 641	513
Tillman	6.2	20.5	7.2	24.0	22.8	9.0	7.2	3.2	38.9	96.1	6 892	838	249	30	3	985	290
Tulsa	7.4	18.9	10.0	30.4	21.6	6.2	4.2	1.4	34.4	94.2	422 581	61 656	29 316	9 120	255	15 583	24 788
Wagoner	7.1	21.1	7.9	28.5	25.4	6.2	3.1	.8	36.2	97.7	46 032	2 158	5 393	296	12	490	3 110
Washington	6.0	19.1	7.7	25.0	24.5	9.1	6.5	2.1	40.1	92.1	39 771	1 221	4 214	365	6	445	2 974
Washita	6.1	20.1	7.6	25.2	22.2	8.9	7.0	2.8	39.2	93.9	10 623	50	342	30	3	251	209
Woods	4.4	14.7	16.8	23.2	20.9	8.8	7.5	3.5	37.8	103.9	8 490	216	146	48	3	51	135
Woodward	6.6	19.2	9.3	27.6	23.2	7.5	4.7	2.0	37.4	99.9	17 050	204	382	89	3	462	296
OREGON	6.5	18.2	9.6	29.1	23.7	6.4	4.7	1.7	36.3	98.4	2 961 623	55 662	45 211	101 350	7 976	144 832	104 745
Baker	5.3	18.9	5.8	23.6	27.3	9.7	6.7	2.6	42.7	98.1	16 018	39	182	64	7	154	277
Benton	5.1	16.2	20.2	26.7	21.4	5.1	3.8	1.4	31.1	99.1	69 678	658	619	3 506	188	1 503	2 001
Clackamas	6.5	19.7	8.0	28.7	26.0	5.6	4.0	1.4	37.5	97.5	308 852	2 233	2 416	8 292	569	7 699	8 330
Clatsop	5.6	18.0	8.9	25.3	26.6	8.0	5.6	2.0	40.0	97.8	33 185	185	367	430	60	585	818
Columbia	6.4	20.9	7.0	28.1	26.0	6.2	4.2	1.2	37.7	100.0	41 130	105	580	255	43	344	1 103
Coos	4.9	17.1	7.1	24.0	27.8	10.0	6.7	2.4	43.1	96.1	57 740	194	1 515	568	107	664	1 991
Crook	6.5	20.1	7.5	25.5	25.7	8.2	4.9	1.5	38.6	99.4	17 830	8	250	82	6	731	275
Curry	4.1	15.1	4.8	20.0	29.4	14.2	9.8	2.6	48.8	96.6	19 634	32	452	147	24	234	614
Deschutes	6.1	18.6	7.8	28.6	25.7	7.2	4.4	1.4	38.3	98.7	109 423	222	956	849	85	1 574	2 258
Douglas	5.6	18.4	7.5	24.2	26.4	9.6	6.3	1.9	41.2	96.8	94 234	177	1 530	628	93	1 025	2 712
Gilliam	4.5	18.7	5.4	25.6	26.7	9.6	7.0	2.5	42.8	102.2	1 853	3	16	3	–	22	18
Grant	5.7	20.1	5.6	24.0	27.9	8.6	5.7	2.5	41.7	99.3	6 995	10	127	15	3	54	135
Harney	5.7	20.3	6.4	26.6	26.1	8.3	5.1	1.6	39.8	102.9	6 999	117	302	39	5	99	159
Hood River	7.4	20.6	8.2	29.4	21.5	6.3	4.6	2.0	35.3	98.9	16 099	117	229	301	25	3 137	503
Jackson	6.0	18.4	8.7	25.5	25.4	7.9	6.0	2.0	39.2	94.6	166 125	724	1 980	1 631	322	5 218	5 269
Jefferson	7.7	22.1	7.7	26.9	23.2	7.6	3.7	1.2	34.8	101.9	13 113	50	2 981	57	42	2 152	614
Josephine	5.3	17.7	6.5	23.2	27.2	10.2	7.5	2.4	43.1	94.6	71 103	202	949	476	83	883	2 030
Klamath	6.4	19.4	8.6	25.5	25.2	8.1	5.1	1.7	38.2	100.1	55 695	404	2 672	512	79	2 200	2 213
Lake	5.0	19.9	5.1	24.3	28.1	9.8	6.0	1.9	42.7	100.5	6 752	10	176	53	10	237	184
Lane	5.8	17.1	12.0	27.5	24.4	6.6	5.0	1.7	36.6	96.9	292 728	2 506	3 642	6 470	599	6 292	10 722
Lincoln	4.9	16.6	6.5	23.5	29.0	10.7	6.9	1.9	44.1	94.0	40 292	132	1 397	413	70	737	1 438

[1] Includes all other responses not included in the other five race categories shown. Also includes write-in entries such as multiracial, mixed, interracial, or a Hispanic/Latino group. [2] Refers to combinations of two or more of the six race categories shown under one race.

Source: Population by Age, Sex, and Race—U.S. Census Bureau; 2000 Census of Population and Housing, "Census 2000 Profiles of General Demographic Characteristics" data files, published May 2001 (related Internet site <http://www.census.gov/mp/www/pub/2000cen/mscen01.html>).

[Includes U.S., states, and 3,142 counties/county equivalents defined as of January 1, 1992. For changes to these areas since January 1, 1992, see appendix B. Geographic Information]

County	Population by age, 2000 (April 1) Percent— Under 5 years	5 to 17 years	18 to 24 years	25 to 44 years	45 to 64 years	65 to 74 years	75 to 84 years	85 years and over	Median age (years)	Males per 100 females, 2000 (April 1)	Population by race, 2000 (April 1) One race White	Black or African American	American Indian and Alaska Native	Asian	Native Hawaiian and Other Pacific Islander	Some other race[1]	Two or more races[2]
OREGON—Con.																	
Linn	6.8	19.2	8.4	27.0	24.1	7.2	5.4	1.9	37.4	97.5	96 059	327	1 313	799	151	1 855	2 565
Malheur	7.6	20.1	10.6	27.2	21.0	6.8	5.0	1.9	34.0	116.0	23 959	387	322	619	24	5 496	808
Marion	7.7	19.7	10.3	28.7	21.2	6.0	4.6	1.7	33.7	101.1	232 469	2 539	4 111	4 997	1 022	30 148	9 548
Morrow	8.5	22.2	8.9	27.3	22.4	6.3	3.3	1.1	33.3	106.5	8 386	15	156	46	9	2 148	235
Multnomah	6.4	15.9	10.3	33.8	22.5	5.2	4.3	1.6	34.9	98.0	522 825	37 434	6 785	37 638	2 320	26 620	26 864
Polk	6.3	19.1	11.7	24.7	23.4	6.8	5.5	2.5	36.5	94.0	55 639	263	1 151	683	153	2 792	1 699
Sherman	5.1	21.4	5.8	23.4	26.1	10.1	6.1	2.0	41.8	102.9	1 810	4	27	9	–	54	30
Tillamook	4.8	17.4	6.5	23.5	28.0	11.2	6.6	2.0	43.5	100.4	22 772	54	289	157	50	459	481
Umatilla	7.5	20.3	9.4	28.3	22.2	6.2	4.5	1.5	34.6	104.8	57 852	582	2 375	530	124	7 529	1 556
Union	5.9	18.7	12.1	23.5	25.0	7.3	5.1	2.3	37.7	95.1	23 129	124	208	209	151	299	410
Wallowa	4.9	19.4	4.9	21.9	30.0	10.0	6.6	2.2	44.4	100.1	6 973	2	51	17	3	69	111
Wasco	6.5	18.8	7.4	25.2	25.4	8.2	6.3	2.2	39.9	97.9	20 599	71	906	191	119	1 344	561
Washington	7.9	19.0	9.3	34.1	20.9	4.3	3.3	1.2	33.0	99.1	366 007	5 119	2 913	29 752	1 325	26 100	14 126
Wheeler	4.7	18.0	3.4	19.3	31.4	13.8	7.2	2.3	48.1	102.2	1 444	1	13	4	1	54	30
Yamhill	7.0	19.9	11.4	28.5	21.4	5.8	4.4	1.6	34.1	102.2	75 628	721	1 253	908	104	4 321	2 057
PENNSYLVANIA	5.9	17.9	8.9	28.6	23.1	7.9	5.8	1.9	38.0	93.4	10 484 203	1 224 612	18 348	219 813	3 417	188 437	142 224
Adams	5.9	19.0	9.2	28.9	23.0	7.3	4.9	1.7	37.0	96.3	87 088	1 105	184	448	21	1 559	887
Allegheny	5.5	16.4	8.5	28.3	23.4	8.8	6.8	2.2	39.6	90.0	1 080 800	159 058	1 593	21 716	335	4 399	13 765
Armstrong	5.4	17.5	7.2	27.6	24.2	9.1	6.8	2.1	40.4	94.7	71 173	592	66	89	13	97	362
Beaver	5.4	17.2	7.4	27.3	24.2	9.6	6.9	1.9	40.7	91.9	167 890	10 811	190	458	24	362	1 677
Bedford	6.0	17.5	7.2	28.1	24.6	9.1	5.7	1.7	39.5	97.2	49 253	178	54	143	7	78	271
Berks	6.2	18.4	8.8	28.9	22.6	7.7	5.4	1.9	37.4	95.9	329 460	13 778	611	3 785	77	20 317	5 610
Blair	5.6	17.1	8.9	27.0	24.0	8.6	6.6	2.2	39.5	92.1	126 059	1 535	109	463	19	180	779
Bradford	6.1	19.5	6.8	27.2	24.7	8.1	5.7	1.9	38.9	95.1	61 471	251	193	285	4	121	436
Bucks	6.4	19.3	7.0	30.7	24.3	6.7	4.3	1.4	37.7	96.3	552 588	19 495	765	13 627	164	4 932	6 064
Butler	6.4	18.2	8.8	29.4	23.0	6.9	5.3	2.0	37.6	95.4	170 302	1 367	149	978	54	293	940
Cambria	5.0	16.0	9.0	26.2	24.1	9.6	7.7	2.4	41.2	94.2	146 183	4 322	132	573	37	374	977
Cameron	4.8	19.7	6.0	24.9	24.8	9.5	7.5	2.7	41.3	96.6	5 904	21	8	7	3	3	28
Carbon	5.1	17.0	6.9	28.3	24.2	9.6	6.9	2.0	40.6	94.9	57 520	353	96	183	20	186	444
Centre	4.6	13.4	26.8	26.4	18.4	5.6	3.6	1.2	28.7	104.3	124 134	3 544	184	5 373	94	1 003	1 426
Chester	6.8	19.4	7.9	30.4	23.8	6.3	4.1	1.3	36.9	96.4	386 745	27 040	645	8 468	140	5 852	4 611
Clarion	5.4	16.2	15.4	25.2	22.7	8.0	5.4	1.8	36.3	93.3	40 998	329	45	142	2	32	217
Clearfield	5.5	17.2	7.7	28.8	23.9	8.5	6.3	2.1	39.3	99.5	81 218	1 239	97	220	10	216	382
Clinton	5.4	16.1	13.6	25.5	22.7	8.8	6.1	1.8	37.8	94.2	37 264	197	42	151	9	55	196
Columbia	4.9	15.9	14.3	25.9	23.1	8.0	6.1	1.8	37.5	90.8	62 602	516	94	334	21	213	371
Crawford	5.9	18.8	9.2	26.6	23.9	7.9	5.6	2.0	38.1	94.8	87 653	1 437	184	254	23	117	698
Cumberland	5.5	16.5	10.6	28.5	24.1	7.6	5.4	1.8	38.1	95.2	201 716	5 048	272	3 578	77	915	2 068
Dauphin	6.2	18.1	7.6	30.1	23.8	7.4	5.1	1.7	37.9	92.3	194 158	42 580	415	4 931	82	4 972	4 660
Delaware	6.2	18.6	8.9	28.8	21.9	7.6	5.9	2.0	37.4	91.2	442 449	79 981	609	18 103	100	3 066	6 556
Elk	5.7	18.3	6.8	28.6	23.3	9.1	6.1	2.1	39.4	98.0	34 746	52	33	122	15	36	108
Erie	6.2	18.8	10.8	27.7	22.2	7.1	5.5	1.7	36.2	95.2	255 282	17 202	464	1 929	61	2 406	3 499
Fayette	5.7	17.0	7.7	27.2	24.2	9.0	6.9	2.2	40.2	91.8	141 657	5 223	168	323	18	170	1 085
Forest	3.6	19.1	5.9	22.6	28.9	11.0	7.2	1.7	44.2	111.2	4 745	110	20	7	–	34	30
Franklin	6.3	17.8	7.9	28.2	23.7	8.3	5.8	1.9	38.3	94.8	123 279	3 016	192	717	40	960	1 109
Fulton	6.3	18.3	7.6	28.4	25.0	8.4	4.7	1.5	38.2	100.1	14 012	94	29	15	2	6	103
Greene	5.2	16.9	9.7	29.0	24.0	7.5	5.7	2.0	38.2	106.2	38 665	1 585	61	87	9	21	244
Huntingdon	5.4	16.3	10.1	29.4	24.0	8.3	4.9	1.7	37.7	109.6	42 544	2 342	48	94	4	205	349
Indiana	4.9	16.1	16.6	24.8	22.7	7.4	5.7	1.8	36.2	94.0	86 796	1 407	71	665	8	142	516
Jefferson	5.5	18.0	7.7	27.2	23.6	8.9	6.7	2.3	39.8	95.7	45 457	59	75	97	5	32	207
Juniata	6.5	18.5	8.0	28.1	23.8	8.2	5.0	2.0	37.7	99.0	22 376	85	32	57	39	115	117
Lackawanna	5.3	16.5	8.9	26.4	23.5	9.3	7.5	2.7	40.3	89.3	206 160	2 793	185	1 602	22	1 120	1 413
Lancaster	6.9	19.7	9.2	28.3	21.9	6.9	5.2	1.9	36.1	95.1	430 456	12 993	681	6 802	158	13 669	5 899
Lawrence	5.6	17.5	8.3	25.7	23.6	9.3	7.6	2.4	40.5	90.6	89 894	3 416	95	258	9	176	795
Lebanon	6.1	17.6	8.2	28.0	23.7	8.3	5.9	2.2	38.7	95.0	113 662	1 548	157	1 067	43	2 716	1 134
Lehigh	6.0	17.9	8.1	29.2	23.0	7.8	5.8	2.2	38.3	93.2	271 590	11 097	553	6 552	116	16 474	5 708
Luzerne	5.0	16.1	8.1	27.2	24.0	9.4	7.5	2.7	40.8	93.0	308 476	5 408	285	1 860	47	1 359	1 815
Lycoming	5.5	17.8	9.7	27.5	23.4	8.2	5.8	2.0	38.4	95.6	112 737	5 189	258	509	12	312	1 027
McKean	5.7	18.0	7.9	28.5	23.2	8.4	6.0	2.3	38.7	100.4	44 312	860	149	139	11	186	279
Mercer	5.7	17.7	8.9	26.1	23.5	9.1	6.8	2.2	39.6	94.7	112 031	6 318	127	486	27	204	1 100
Mifflin	6.3	18.3	7.0	27.4	23.9	8.8	6.1	2.1	38.8	93.2	45 803	226	38	135	2	83	199
Monroe	6.0	20.8	8.6	28.8	23.5	7.1	4.0	1.1	37.2	97.6	122 342	8 343	298	1 545	40	3 353	2 766
Montgomery	6.3	17.8	7.1	30.5	23.4	7.4	5.5	2.0	38.2	93.6	648 510	55 969	848	30 191	255	5 598	8 726
Montour	5.7	18.7	6.4	28.2	24.0	8.2	6.2	2.6	39.8	90.5	17 628	185	12	234	–	69	108
Northampton	5.6	17.8	9.2	28.3	23.4	7.8	6.0	2.0	38.5	94.8	243 639	7 400	408	3 657	80	8 176	3 706
Northumberland	5.1	16.8	7.0	27.7	24.4	9.3	7.3	2.5	40.8	96.3	91 803	1 439	90	211	16	444	553
Perry	6.1	19.4	7.4	29.8	25.1	6.9	4.1	1.2	37.5	98.4	42 964	189	53	65	5	92	234
Philadelphia	6.5	18.8	11.1	29.3	20.3	7.1	5.2	1.8	34.2	86.8	683 267	655 824	4 073	67 654	729	72 429	33 574
Pike	5.9	20.8	5.3	27.7	25.1	9.6	4.4	1.2	39.6	99.3	43 109	1 513	111	285	3	602	679
Potter	6.2	19.8	6.9	26.1	24.3	8.6	6.1	2.0	39.1	97.4	17 729	52	40	90	5	35	129

[1] Includes all other responses not included in the other five race categories shown. Also includes write-in entries such as multiracial, mixed, interracial, or a Hispanic/Latino group. [2] Refers to combinations of two or more of the six race categories shown under one race.

Source: Population by Age, Sex, and Race—U.S. Census Bureau; 2000 Census of Population and Housing, "Census 2000 Profiles of General Demographic Characteristics" data files, published May 2001 (related Internet site <http://www.census.gov/mp/www/pub/2000cen/mscen01.html>).

Table B–2. Counties — Population by Age, Sex, and Race–Con.

[Includes U.S., states, and 3,142 counties/county equivalents defined as of January 1, 1992. For changes to these areas since January 1, 1992, see appendix B. Geographic Information]

County	Population by age, 2000 (April 1) Percent— Under 5 years	5 to 17 years	18 to 24 years	25 to 44 years	45 to 64 years	65 to 74 years	75 to 84 years	85 years and over	Median age (years)	Males per 100 females, 2000 (April 1)	Population by race, 2000 (April 1) One race White	Black or African American	American Indian and Alaska Native	Asian	Native Hawaiian and Other Pacific Islander	Some other race[1]	Two or more races[2]
PENNSYLVANIA—Con.																	
Schuylkill	4.9	16.0	7.2	28.3	23.8	9.7	7.6	2.6	40.9	99.1	145 249	3 147	114	625	19	531	651
Snyder	5.6	18.4	11.2	27.4	23.3	7.7	4.8	1.6	36.7	95.6	36 768	307	18	156	2	113	182
Somerset	5.2	17.0	7.6	27.8	24.3	8.9	6.9	2.2	40.2	99.8	77 938	1 275	65	172	6	250	317
Sullivan	4.3	16.5	7.9	24.1	25.3	11.3	7.7	2.9	43.0	102.1	6 266	144	50	10	–	30	56
Susquehanna	5.7	19.8	6.7	27.1	25.2	8.2	5.5	1.8	39.5	98.9	41 621	128	63	92	6	73	255
Tioga	5.4	18.3	10.6	25.4	24.2	8.4	5.7	1.9	38.5	95.9	40 589	250	96	124	4	56	254
Union	4.8	15.3	13.9	30.9	21.7	6.6	4.8	2.0	35.8	123.9	37 496	2 878	67	443	17	152	571
Venango	5.7	18.6	7.2	26.7	25.1	9.2	5.8	1.9	40.2	95.4	56 208	626	105	132	11	98	385
Warren	5.7	18.5	6.4	27.0	25.9	8.8	5.9	1.9	40.5	96.2	43 286	90	82	118	8	52	227
Washington	5.5	16.6	7.7	27.2	25.0	8.9	7.0	2.1	40.8	92.4	193 297	6 606	175	725	44	381	1 669
Wayne	5.6	18.4	6.1	26.8	25.6	9.5	5.9	2.1	40.8	100.7	46 160	757	69	182	1	249	304
Westmoreland	5.2	16.8	6.8	27.5	25.4	9.3	6.9	2.1	41.3	93.1	357 325	7 446	327	1 920	64	548	2 363
Wyoming	5.8	19.7	8.0	28.1	25.2	7.0	4.7	1.5	37.8	98.6	27 598	149	47	77	2	41	166
York	6.1	18.5	7.5	30.3	24.0	7.1	4.8	1.6	37.8	96.7	354 103	14 095	679	3 273	116	5 297	4 188
RHODE ISLAND	6.1	17.5	10.2	29.6	22.0	7.0	5.5	2.0	36.7	92.5	891 191	46 908	5 121	23 665	567	52 616	28 251
Bristol	5.4	17.5	9.5	27.4	23.4	8.1	6.5	2.1	39.3	93.1	49 034	349	82	505	14	150	514
Kent	5.9	17.3	7.0	30.5	24.2	7.5	5.7	1.8	38.9	92.3	159 645	1 558	388	2 241	32	1 086	2 140
Newport	5.8	16.7	8.4	29.9	24.8	7.3	5.2	1.9	38.6	94.6	78 136	3 184	365	1 054	56	935	1 703
Providence	6.3	17.7	11.1	29.8	20.5	6.9	5.6	2.1	35.4	91.8	487 235	40 685	3 143	18 007	435	49 871	22 226
Washington	5.9	17.5	11.2	28.3	24.4	6.5	4.6	1.6	37.4	94.2	117 141	1 132	1 143	1 858	30	574	1 668
SOUTH CAROLINA	6.6	18.6	10.2	29.6	23.0	6.7	4.1	1.3	35.4	94.5	2 695 560	1 185 216	13 718	36 014	1 628	39 926	39 950
Abbeville	6.7	18.6	9.5	26.7	23.8	7.9	5.0	1.9	36.9	92.1	17 881	7 926	27	59	7	81	186
Aiken	6.7	19.5	8.8	28.9	23.3	7.3	4.3	1.3	36.4	92.9	101 745	36 442	566	905	36	1 181	1 677
Allendale	6.9	19.7	9.8	28.2	22.8	6.4	4.6	1.7	35.1	108.6	3 068	7 960	10	14	7	95	57
Anderson	6.7	17.9	8.4	29.1	24.3	7.4	4.8	1.4	37.3	93.5	135 177	27 491	362	703	27	670	1 310
Bamberg	6.2	19.2	12.9	24.6	23.2	7.3	5.1	1.4	35.2	88.7	6 075	10 411	27	32	1	23	89
Barnwell	7.1	21.0	8.7	27.9	22.6	6.9	4.4	1.3	35.5	92.7	12 956	9 990	81	91	8	182	170
Beaufort	6.7	16.6	12.0	27.2	22.1	9.4	4.9	1.3	35.8	102.4	85 451	29 005	321	953	63	3 438	1 706
Berkeley	7.2	20.8	11.7	31.2	21.2	4.9	2.4	.6	32.0	103.2	96 997	37 985	748	2 671	114	1 718	2 418
Calhoun	6.3	18.7	7.4	27.0	26.7	7.6	4.7	1.6	38.9	90.1	7 597	7 393	29	21	4	36	105
Charleston	6.4	17.3	12.0	30.3	22.0	6.5	4.2	1.2	34.5	93.5	191 928	106 918	813	3 463	172	3 071	3 604
Cherokee	7.2	18.7	9.0	29.6	23.2	6.8	4.2	1.4	35.3	93.8	40 409	10 801	103	163	11	610	440
Chester	6.7	20.2	8.4	28.2	23.8	6.9	4.4	1.3	36.0	92.5	20 416	13 168	112	96	2	85	189
Chesterfield	6.8	19.9	8.5	29.0	23.9	6.8	3.9	1.2	35.7	93.2	27 515	14 206	145	128	9	443	322
Clarendon	6.1	19.7	10.5	25.1	24.7	8.2	4.4	1.3	37.0	96.4	14 602	17 273	78	84	10	286	169
Colleton	6.9	20.6	8.0	26.9	24.7	7.3	4.3	1.3	36.5	91.9	21 245	16 140	242	97	15	213	312
Darlington	6.9	19.4	9.0	28.2	24.4	6.6	4.2	1.3	36.0	89.8	38 402	28 104	127	142	6	260	353
Dillon	7.4	21.7	9.5	27.5	22.4	6.3	4.1	1.1	34.2	87.4	15 481	13 932	679	103	8	303	216
Dorchester	6.7	22.2	7.7	31.6	22.6	5.2	3.0	.9	34.7	95.8	68 498	24 176	703	1 086	66	570	1 314
Edgefield	6.0	18.1	9.8	32.1	23.2	6.0	3.7	1.2	35.6	112.8	13 962	10 209	81	59	–	107	169
Fairfield	6.7	19.4	8.6	27.8	24.3	7.2	4.5	1.5	36.9	90.9	9 282	13 859	36	44	–	104	129
Florence	6.5	19.4	9.7	28.9	23.6	6.3	4.1	1.4	35.5	88.7	73 760	49 474	282	881	21	491	852
Georgetown	6.2	18.9	7.7	25.9	26.2	8.7	5.1	1.2	39.1	91.8	33 307	21 541	77	130	17	453	272
Greenville	6.8	17.8	9.6	31.2	22.8	6.3	4.1	1.3	35.5	94.8	294 324	69 455	726	5 242	171	5 387	4 311
Greenwood	6.9	18.6	10.4	28.2	22.2	7.3	4.8	1.6	35.2	88.4	43 455	21 036	116	470	24	681	489
Hampton	6.7	20.9	8.5	29.7	22.1	6.8	4.1	1.3	34.8	103.8	9 173	11 906	43	36	2	133	93
Horry	5.7	15.6	9.4	29.3	25.0	9.4	4.6	1.0	38.3	96.4	159 363	30 468	793	1 498	121	2 281	2 105
Jasper	7.2	19.5	10.3	30.7	21.2	6.2	3.6	1.2	33.8	111.0	8 766	10 895	76	92	10	700	139
Kershaw	6.6	19.6	7.6	28.8	24.5	7.3	4.3	1.3	37.4	93.4	37 701	13 840	154	164	18	328	442
Lancaster	6.5	18.9	8.6	30.3	23.6	6.7	4.1	1.2	35.9	98.2	43 577	16 479	133	164	12	548	438
Laurens	6.6	18.7	9.2	28.5	23.8	7.1	4.4	1.6	36.2	93.6	49 789	18 245	192	101	36	662	542
Lee	6.3	19.4	10.0	29.2	22.6	6.6	4.4	1.4	35.7	101.4	7 048	12 787	27	39	1	118	99
Lexington	6.8	19.2	8.3	31.6	23.8	5.7	3.4	1.1	35.7	94.5	181 844	27 274	725	2 259	83	1 706	2 123
McCormick	4.2	15.3	8.3	27.6	28.1	9.7	5.1	1.8	41.1	113.7	4 459	5 365	7	29	3	38	57
Marion	7.0	20.7	9.7	26.8	23.8	6.6	4.2	1.3	35.1	85.9	14 787	19 984	90	99	2	320	184
Marlboro	6.6	19.5	9.3	29.4	22.8	6.8	4.2	1.4	35.4	96.3	12 820	14 618	968	70	1	68	273
Newberry	6.4	17.7	9.8	27.6	23.7	7.4	5.4	2.0	37.1	93.2	23 115	11 958	102	106	33	470	324
Oconee	6.0	16.8	8.0	27.4	26.2	9.4	4.9	1.3	39.5	96.7	59 025	5 550	145	235	13	702	545
Orangeburg	6.5	19.4	11.9	26.1	22.8	7.2	4.6	1.5	35.3	87.0	34 045	55 736	423	396	15	330	637
Pickens	6.1	16.2	17.5	27.6	21.2	6.1	3.9	1.4	32.7	99.6	99 978	7 559	179	1 312	13	772	944
Richland	6.3	17.9	13.8	31.6	20.6	5.3	3.5	1.1	32.6	93.2	161 276	144 809	782	5 501	263	3 724	4 322
Saluda	6.5	18.4	9.2	27.6	23.8	7.7	5.0	1.8	37.0	98.6	12 622	5 753	44	7	1	631	123
Spartanburg	6.6	18.2	9.2	29.9	23.6	6.7	4.3	1.4	36.1	94.5	190 569	52 775	555	3 738	86	3 437	2 631
Sumter	7.5	20.6	10.5	29.4	20.7	6.1	3.9	1.2	33.4	93.9	52 462	48 850	282	944	58	833	1 217
Union	6.3	17.5	8.2	27.9	24.4	8.3	5.6	1.7	38.6	89.0	20 262	9 278	44	55	11	49	182
Williamsburg	6.9	21.7	9.0	25.7	23.6	7.3	4.4	1.3	35.5	87.9	12 184	24 660	60	73	–	61	179
York	6.8	19.5	9.5	31.1	22.8	5.8	3.5	1.1	34.9	94.0	127 162	31 532	1 403	1 459	39	1 527	1 492

[1] Includes all other responses not included in the other five race categories shown. Also includes write-in entries such as multiracial, mixed, interracial, or a Hispanic/Latino group. [2] Refers to combinations of two or more of the six race categories shown under one race.

Source: Population by Age, Sex, and Race—U.S. Census Bureau; 2000 Census of Population and Housing, "Census 2000 Profiles of General Demographic Characteristics" data files, published May 2001 (related Internet site <http://www.census.gov/mp/www/pub/2000cen/mscen01.html>).

[Includes U.S., states, and 3,142 counties/county equivalents defined as of January 1, 1992. For changes to these areas since January 1, 1992, see appendix B. Geographic Information]

County	Population by age, 2000 (April 1) Percent— Under 5 years	5 to 17 years	18 to 24 years	25 to 44 years	45 to 64 years	65 to 74 years	75 to 84 years	85 years and over	Median age (years)	Males per 100 females, 2000 (April 1)	Population by race, 2000 (April 1) One race White	Black or African American	American Indian and Alaska Native	Asian	Native Hawaiian and Other Pacific Islander	Some other race[1]	Two or more races[2]
SOUTH DAKOTA	6.8	20.1	10.3	27.3	21.2	7.0	5.2	2.1	35.6	98.5	669 404	4 685	62 283	4 378	261	3 677	10 156
Aurora	5.7	21.9	6.5	22.1	22.2	10.0	7.6	4.0	40.6	104.3	2 926	9	59	3	–	44	17
Beadle	5.7	19.0	8.3	24.7	23.0	9.1	7.3	2.9	40.1	96.6	16 501	118	161	52	3	44	144
Bennett	8.9	27.4	9.2	25.3	18.0	6.0	3.6	1.6	29.2	98.3	1 462	10	1 861	2	5	6	228
Bon Homme	4.9	18.1	7.6	26.8	21.7	9.4	8.0	3.5	40.3	123.0	6 934	45	217	6	–	13	45
Brookings	5.7	15.1	26.8	24.3	17.3	4.9	4.1	1.8	26.6	102.1	27 194	87	254	377	11	86	211
Brown	6.4	17.2	11.6	26.7	21.9	7.6	6.1	2.5	37.2	93.3	33 854	100	964	142	31	63	306
Brule	5.7	24.8	6.8	24.7	21.2	7.6	6.3	3.0	36.9	93.2	4 823	14	444	26	1	3	53
Buffalo	10.6	30.7	11.0	25.0	16.1	3.5	2.6	.4	23.3	105.5	332	2	1 658	–	–	6	34
Butte	6.1	22.2	7.2	26.0	23.4	7.9	5.3	2.0	38.0	96.9	8 687	9	150	22	–	99	127
Campbell	5.2	21.2	3.5	24.5	23.5	11.2	8.2	2.7	41.9	100.7	1 770	–	6	1	–	–	5
Charles Mix	8.6	23.4	7.1	23.2	20.4	8.3	5.8	3.2	35.7	96.6	6 512	12	2 644	9	1	44	128
Clark	5.4	21.6	5.8	22.0	23.0	10.5	8.6	3.2	41.6	97.4	4 087	3	25	4	1	8	15
Clay	5.4	13.4	31.5	23.8	15.8	4.7	3.7	1.6	24.9	94.3	12 560	135	360	264	2	39	177
Codington	7.1	19.7	10.4	28.0	20.7	6.7	5.4	2.0	35.3	98.5	25 054	35	365	73	4	148	218
Corson	9.1	27.9	9.8	24.3	18.5	6.4	3.3	.8	28.3	102.0	1 555	4	2 542	2	–	9	69
Custer	4.6	19.4	6.3	22.4	31.1	8.9	4.9	2.2	43.2	104.4	6 851	20	227	13	1	26	137
Davison	6.5	18.8	12.0	25.9	20.4	7.5	6.1	2.7	36.0	94.1	18 034	51	371	80	4	56	145
Day	5.5	20.0	5.2	22.4	23.4	10.8	9.0	3.7	42.9	96.5	5 719	8	464	4	3	10	59
Deuel	5.5	19.9	5.9	25.4	22.6	10.5	6.8	3.3	40.8	99.6	4 431	4	13	8	1	11	30
Dewey	9.2	29.7	9.0	27.2	16.6	5.2	2.3	.8	26.5	95.9	1 442	2	4 429	7	3	4	85
Douglas	5.8	21.9	4.9	22.4	22.4	9.9	8.4	4.2	41.8	95.1	3 391	2	34	5	–	4	22
Edmunds	5.7	21.0	5.1	23.3	22.7	10.6	7.9	3.7	41.6	97.2	4 332	3	11	4	1	2	14
Fall River	4.8	18.0	5.8	20.6	28.3	11.5	8.2	2.8	45.5	109.8	6 746	24	451	17	4	22	189
Faulk	5.5	21.1	5.4	23.1	22.0	11.9	7.8	3.1	41.5	99.8	2 626	2	4	1	–	–	7
Grant	5.9	20.7	5.7	25.1	23.5	8.5	7.3	3.3	40.3	97.7	7 738	1	34	18	–	31	25
Gregory	4.9	19.4	5.1	22.0	23.8	10.3	9.5	5.0	44.3	94.5	4 465	2	268	11	–	5	41
Haakon	5.3	20.4	7.0	25.2	24.1	7.5	7.1	3.4	41.3	96.6	2 117	–	55	2	–	–	22
Hamlin	6.5	22.9	6.9	24.0	20.5	8.3	7.4	3.5	37.9	98.9	5 456	7	32	10	–	6	29
Hand	5.2	19.4	5.1	22.3	23.8	12.2	9.0	3.0	43.6	96.2	3 715	1	5	3	–	5	12
Hanson	7.5	22.0	7.7	26.1	21.8	8.4	4.9	1.5	36.0	100.3	3 124	–	3	4	1	1	6
Harding	4.2	28.3	4.4	24.8	24.8	6.5	5.2	1.6	37.6	104.7	1 321	4	10	8	–	5	5
Hughes	6.6	21.2	6.2	28.6	23.7	6.7	4.6	2.4	37.5	92.6	14 654	31	1 434	66	3	51	242
Hutchinson	5.9	18.9	5.6	22.1	21.2	11.1	10.1	5.1	43.1	94.9	7 980	7	46	8	–	5	29
Hyde	7.6	18.0	5.8	23.5	22.7	10.4	7.9	4.0	42.2	102.1	1 522	2	133	–	2	2	10
Jackson	8.3	28.2	8.0	23.6	20.3	6.0	4.0	1.6	30.6	98.8	1 467	1	1 402	1	1	4	54
Jerauld	3.7	17.7	6.9	19.8	26.2	11.0	10.3	4.4	46.3	98.4	2 272	–	13	3	–	–	7
Jones	4.9	21.4	6.2	25.5	23.9	10.1	6.0	2.2	41.1	103.9	1 143	–	29	4	1	2	18
Kingsbury	5.4	19.1	6.1	22.9	22.4	11.0	9.0	4.2	42.7	96.3	5 730	3	23	17	–	11	31
Lake	5.5	18.2	15.0	23.4	21.4	7.7	6.1	2.5	36.5	99.8	11 023	23	74	61	1	37	57
Lawrence	4.8	18.3	13.7	25.4	23.1	7.4	5.1	2.1	37.2	96.8	20 884	51	476	72	11	73	235
Lincoln	8.0	21.6	7.6	31.9	20.4	5.0	3.7	1.7	34.0	99.8	23 539	82	128	112	4	70	196
Lyman	8.6	23.5	7.6	25.9	20.9	7.5	4.4	1.7	34.5	104.6	2 522	3	1 296	9	–	2	63
McCook	6.7	21.7	6.2	25.5	20.4	8.7	7.0	3.7	38.6	99.5	5 766	3	21	12	–	9	21
McPherson	5.5	16.7	4.5	20.1	23.6	14.0	10.8	4.7	47.6	93.7	2 885	–	8	4	–	1	6
Marshall	5.9	21.1	5.1	22.8	23.8	9.6	7.8	3.9	41.6	100.0	4 237	4	289	4	–	10	32
Meade	7.7	20.7	10.6	29.6	21.0	5.6	3.5	1.3	33.4	102.2	22 471	360	495	153	16	147	611
Mellette	9.0	26.3	7.5	24.6	19.4	7.2	4.1	1.9	32.1	101.3	932	–	1 092	2	–	5	52
Miner	5.1	20.4	5.6	22.7	22.3	10.4	9.1	4.4	42.5	99.6	2 848	15	9	3	–	3	6
Minnehaha	7.3	18.9	10.8	32.0	20.0	5.6	3.9	1.5	33.5	98.1	137 941	2 246	2 748	1 493	76	1 536	2 241
Moody	6.2	22.9	7.2	26.4	22.3	6.2	6.2	2.5	37.0	99.8	5 600	19	792	37	–	4	143
Pennington	7.1	19.5	10.5	29.2	21.9	6.4	4.0	1.4	35.0	98.3	76 789	755	7 162	776	54	605	2 424
Perkins	5.8	18.3	5.6	23.4	23.2	11.1	9.0	3.5	43.1	96.3	3 250	5	55	8	–	17	28
Potter	4.5	18.5	3.9	22.3	25.7	11.6	9.0	4.5	45.8	96.7	2 643	–	22	5	–	2	21
Roberts	6.7	23.3	7.2	23.6	22.2	8.5	5.7	2.8	37.1	98.8	6 840	10	2 991	21	–	3	151
Sanborn	5.8	19.9	7.7	23.7	23.4	10.5	7.2	1.8	40.8	107.2	2 645	1	8	10	1	3	7
Shannon	10.9	34.4	10.6	25.6	13.8	3.2	1.3	.3	20.6	99.6	562	10	11 743	3	6	28	114
Spink	5.6	19.9	6.7	26.1	22.6	9.5	7.0	2.4	39.9	107.2	7 272	16	110	7	1	9	39
Stanley	5.6	21.5	7.1	28.2	26.6	6.5	3.3	1.2	37.6	101.6	2 579	5	136	8	–	4	40
Sully	5.7	19.9	6.1	26.5	24.4	9.8	5.5	2.2	40.0	105.5	1 522	–	12	2	–	2	18
Todd	12.0	31.9	10.4	25.1	14.8	3.8	1.6	.4	21.7	97.9	1 138	8	7 747	13	–	19	125
Tripp	6.3	21.4	6.2	24.4	21.9	9.2	7.6	2.9	39.5	97.4	5 625	2	720	4	–	5	74
Turner	5.7	20.1	6.2	24.8	22.8	9.1	8.0	3.3	40.5	97.2	8 748	13	24	15	–	11	38
Union	6.9	20.1	7.3	28.4	23.7	6.8	4.9	1.8	36.9	99.2	12 187	42	46	168	1	30	110
Walworth	6.3	17.8	6.5	22.4	25.0	11.0	7.6	3.3	42.8	94.2	5 172	2	703	9	2	4	82
Yankton	6.3	19.4	8.7	29.0	22.0	7.0	5.2	2.4	37.0	101.9	20 592	252	354	92	4	160	198
Ziebach	10.8	29.9	10.8	24.7	16.5	4.7	2.4	.3	23.8	97.0	665	–	1 821	2	–	3	28

[1] Includes all other responses not included in the other five race categories shown. Also includes write-in entries such as multiracial, mixed, interracial, or a Hispanic/Latino group. [2] Refers to combinations of two or more of the six race categories shown under one race.

Source: Population by Age, Sex, and Race—U.S. Census Bureau; 2000 Census of Population and Housing, "Census 2000 Profiles of General Demographic Characteristics" data files, published May 2001 (related Internet site <http://www.census.gov/mp/www/pub/2000cen/mscen01.html>).

[Includes U.S., states, and 3,142 counties/county equivalents defined as of January 1, 1992. For changes to these areas since January 1, 1992, see appendix B. Geographic Information]

County	Population by age, 2000 (April 1) Percent—								Median age (years)	Males per 100 females, 2000 (April 1)	Population by race, 2000 (April 1) One race						
	Under 5 years	5 to 17 years	18 to 24 years	25 to 44 years	45 to 64 years	65 to 74 years	75 to 84 years	85 years and over			White	Black or African American	American Indian and Alaska Native	Asian	Native Hawaiian and Other Pacific Islander	Some other race[1]	Two or more races[2]
TENNESSEE	6.6	18.0	9.6	30.2	23.2	6.7	4.2	1.4	35.9	94.9	4 563 310	932 809	15 152	56 662	2 205	56 036	63 109
Anderson	5.6	17.6	7.5	27.3	25.5	8.4	6.2	1.9	39.9	91.1	66 593	2 766	226	593	9	274	869
Bedford...............	7.4	18.4	9.9	29.7	22.0	6.8	4.3	1.5	34.9	98.4	32 640	3 189	105	170	20	1 025	437
Benton	5.2	16.8	7.0	26.2	27.0	9.7	5.9	2.1	41.6	93.8	15 948	348	54	40	–	33	114
Bledsoe	5.9	17.2	8.4	31.3	25.8	6.8	3.7	.9	37.4	121.0	11 680	458	47	14	3	23	142
Blount	5.8	17.0	8.3	29.4	25.4	7.4	5.1	1.6	38.4	93.8	100 241	3 077	308	759	27	363	1 048
Bradley...............	6.6	17.1	11.3	29.8	23.5	6.8	3.8	1.2	35.5	95.1	81 792	3 511	250	501	14	784	1 113
Campbell	5.9	17.0	8.5	28.0	25.5	8.5	5.0	1.6	38.3	93.0	39 109	120	123	62	15	62	363
Cannon...............	6.7	18.7	8.3	28.9	23.7	7.7	4.5	1.5	36.8	96.3	12 424	187	42	15	3	51	104
Carroll...............	5.9	17.3	8.4	26.7	24.4	8.8	6.2	2.4	39.0	92.3	25 843	3 050	72	47	6	134	323
Carter	5.6	15.8	9.2	29.0	25.4	8.0	5.3	1.7	38.5	94.5	55 316	566	112	146	5	153	444
Cheatham	7.1	20.5	7.3	33.5	23.0	5.1	2.5	1.0	35.3	100.3	34 783	532	135	63	17	130	252
Chester...............	6.7	17.5	14.4	26.4	21.4	7.2	4.6	1.8	34.1	94.5	13 696	1 558	35	36	–	48	167
Claiborne	5.7	17.9	8.9	28.7	25.4	7.5	4.5	1.5	37.4	93.3	29 202	224	72	85	3	56	220
Clay.................	5.1	16.4	7.9	27.4	27.6	8.6	5.2	1.8	39.9	94.6	7 717	115	26	11	9	19	79
Cocke	5.9	16.9	8.3	28.8	26.4	8.1	4.1	1.4	38.6	94.6	32 277	669	135	52	5	106	321
Coffee	6.6	18.5	8.3	28.4	23.6	8.2	4.9	1.5	37.5	95.1	44 858	1 724	146	353	15	438	480
Crockett..............	6.4	18.7	8.1	28.3	22.7	7.4	5.9	2.4	37.4	93.3	11 910	2 088	29	8	–	406	91
Cumberland...........	5.5	15.9	6.7	25.1	26.3	12.7	6.2	1.7	42.5	94.4	45 917	59	118	113	12	211	372
Davidson	6.6	15.6	11.6	34.0	21.1	5.9	3.9	1.4	34.1	93.8	381 783	147 696	1 679	13 275	403	13 816	11 239
Decatur	5.6	16.1	7.9	25.9	26.3	9.6	5.9	2.7	41.2	94.5	11 041	407	27	23	3	141	89
DeKalb	6.1	17.2	8.5	29.3	24.6	7.8	4.7	1.8	37.7	97.7	16 653	250	48	24	3	282	163
Dickson	6.9	19.7	8.1	30.7	22.9	6.5	3.9	1.3	35.7	96.2	40 243	1 978	172	116	5	204	438
Dyer	6.6	19.1	8.7	28.6	23.5	6.9	4.7	1.8	36.5	92.0	31 835	4 795	82	124	9	160	274
Fayette	6.7	19.0	8.2	27.4	25.6	7.3	4.1	1.6	38.1	96.5	17 997	10 355	56	63	2	113	220
Fentress	6.2	18.0	8.0	28.1	26.1	7.6	4.4	1.6	38.0	96.2	16 499	18	25	16	–	5	62
Franklin	6.0	17.1	10.9	26.4	24.4	8.6	4.9	1.7	38.1	94.8	36 206	2 157	78	162	13	237	417
Gibson	6.2	17.7	8.1	26.9	23.3	8.8	6.4	2.5	38.8	89.5	37 878	9 497	94	67	8	240	368
Giles	6.2	18.4	8.3	27.9	24.8	7.3	5.3	1.9	38.0	94.4	25 454	3 476	87	103	3	62	262
Grainger	6.1	16.8	8.2	30.5	25.8	7.6	3.6	1.3	37.7	99.0	20 330	67	32	18	5	82	125
Greene	5.8	16.5	8.1	28.7	26.1	8.5	4.7	1.6	38.9	95.1	60 659	1 329	112	169	15	272	353
Grundy	6.8	18.3	9.0	27.8	24.1	7.3	5.2	1.5	36.6	96.7	14 093	20	43	24	–	50	102
Hamblen	6.6	16.7	8.9	29.6	24.9	7.7	4.2	1.4	37.1	97.1	52 732	2 396	130	335	33	1 927	575
Hamilton	6.0	17.2	9.6	29.0	24.3	7.4	4.8	1.7	37.4	91.7	235 000	62 005	900	3 924	196	2 356	3 515
Hancock	5.0	17.8	8.8	26.0	25.5	8.6	6.5	1.7	39.2	95.1	6 644	33	16	5	1	23	64
Hardeman	5.9	18.0	9.8	31.3	22.4	6.8	4.2	1.5	36.0	116.9	16 116	11 516	74	88	5	85	221
Hardin	5.9	17.2	7.9	26.6	26.4	9.0	5.3	1.8	39.8	96.7	24 277	944	50	42	4	77	184
Hawkins	6.2	17.1	7.5	30.0	25.9	7.4	4.3	1.5	37.8	94.7	52 086	830	90	124	8	124	301
Haywood	7.2	20.0	9.8	27.3	21.9	7.2	4.6	2.0	35.3	87.8	9 252	10 106	24	18	10	273	114
Henderson	6.5	17.9	8.7	28.8	23.9	7.9	4.7	1.6	37.3	92.9	23 085	2 042	33	35	3	84	240
Henry	5.7	16.5	7.6	26.3	25.7	9.8	6.3	2.1	40.9	93.4	27 757	2 787	59	86	9	122	295
Hickman	6.5	18.1	8.5	31.0	23.8	6.6	4.2	1.2	36.3	112.5	20 893	1 009	108	18	3	64	200
Houston	6.7	17.7	7.3	26.1	25.6	9.0	5.6	2.1	39.5	97.8	7 650	268	15	10	5	63	77
Humphreys	6.0	17.9	7.6	27.5	26.2	8.5	4.8	1.5	39.0	96.8	17 125	527	48	46	2	29	152
Jackson	5.7	16.5	7.8	28.2	26.8	8.3	4.8	1.8	39.8	97.8	10 834	16	37	7	3	13	74
Jefferson	6.1	16.7	10.6	29.1	24.5	7.5	4.0	1.4	36.5	97.5	42 370	1 027	138	118	18	280	343
Johnson	4.9	14.8	7.4	30.8	27.1	8.1	5.0	1.8	40.0	114.6	16 869	424	60	21	4	40	81
Knox	6.1	16.2	11.6	30.4	23.1	6.8	4.4	1.5	36.0	93.5	336 571	32 987	1 007	4 937	111	1 902	4 517
Lake	5.0	12.7	13.7	33.8	21.5	6.7	4.9	1.7	35.8	151.0	5 300	2 481	31	11	–	49	82
Lauderdale...........	6.8	18.0	10.3	31.2	21.7	6.0	4.4	1.6	34.9	108.1	17 295	9 236	169	43	5	142	211
Lawrence	6.7	19.5	8.4	28.1	23.0	7.7	5.0	1.6	36.2	94.3	38 660	587	128	96	9	156	290
Lewis	6.5	19.3	8.3	27.4	24.8	7.5	4.3	1.8	37.3	96.9	11 034	165	23	21	–	33	91
Lincoln	6.1	17.8	8.0	27.7	24.9	8.4	5.3	1.9	38.9	93.9	28 289	2 304	155	100	10	108	374
Loudon	5.8	16.1	6.7	27.5	27.7	9.5	5.0	1.7	41.0	95.1	37 482	447	126	84	6	558	383
McMinn..............	6.3	17.6	8.4	28.5	24.8	7.8	4.9	1.6	37.9	93.4	45 445	2 195	133	344	12	367	519
McNairy	6.2	17.5	8.1	26.7	25.6	8.8	5.2	2.0	39.1	94.2	22 734	1 537	50	32	–	59	241
Macon...............	7.1	19.0	8.5	29.4	23.3	6.8	4.4	1.5	35.5	97.4	19 949	44	85	48	14	157	89
Madison	6.9	18.9	11.0	29.1	21.7	6.3	4.4	1.6	34.7	92.1	59 877	29 810	150	578	13	616	793
Marion	5.9	17.8	8.5	28.6	26.3	7.6	4.0	1.2	38.2	95.9	26 201	1 149	72	58	3	76	217
Marshall	6.5	19.0	8.7	29.9	23.2	6.5	4.6	1.4	36.3	95.4	23 935	2 081	66	84	4	392	205
Maury	6.9	19.4	8.7	29.8	23.2	6.5	4.1	1.4	36.3	94.6	57 262	9 904	214	232	14	1 003	869
Meigs	6.9	18.2	8.1	28.9	26.3	6.8	3.7	1.0	36.7	100.0	10 826	138	23	20	–	12	67
Monroe	6.4	18.4	8.7	28.6	24.8	7.2	4.5	1.4	36.8	97.2	36 962	884	142	140	6	335	492
Montgomery	8.5	19.9	12.3	34.3	17.2	4.6	2.4	.8	30.0	101.2	98 611	25 848	709	2 455	287	2 939	3 919
Moore	5.8	17.6	8.4	26.5	26.3	8.5	5.0	2.0	39.7	98.1	5 501	156	11	8	–	29	35
Morgan	5.8	17.4	8.8	31.9	24.5	6.5	3.7	1.3	36.5	114.3	19 109	440	40	23	1	27	117
Obion	6.4	17.0	8.4	27.7	25.4	7.8	5.3	2.0	38.7	93.4	28 607	3 196	44	61	15	296	231

[1] Includes all other responses not included in the other five race categories shown. Also includes write-in entries such as multiracial, mixed, interracial, or a Hispanic/Latino group. [2] Refers to combinations of two or more of the six race categories shown under one race.

Source: Population by Age, Sex, and Race—U.S. Census Bureau; 2000 Census of Population and Housing, "Census 2000 Profiles of General Demographic Characteristics" data files, published May 2001 (related Internet site <http://www.census.gov/mp/www/pub/2000cen/mscen01.html>).

[Includes U.S., states, and 3,142 counties/county equivalents defined as of January 1, 1992. For changes to these areas since January 1, 1992, see appendix B. Geographic Information]

County	Population by age, 2000 (April 1) — Percent								Median age (years)	Males per 100 females, 2000 (April 1)	Population by race, 2000 (April 1) — One race						Two or more races[2]
	Under 5 years	5 to 17 years	18 to 24 years	25 to 44 years	45 to 64 years	65 to 74 years	75 to 84 years	85 years and over			White	Black or African American	American Indian and Alaska Native	Asian	Native Hawaiian and Other Pacific Islander	Some other race[1]	
TENNESSEE—Con.																	
Overton	6.2	16.9	8.4	27.7	25.9	8.3	4.9	1.8	38.8	96.2	19 834	56	56	19	10	45	98
Perry	6.1	18.3	7.5	25.4	26.3	9.5	4.9	2.0	39.8	99.0	7 368	130	26	7	11	25	64
Pickett	5.8	15.6	8.6	24.7	27.7	10.2	5.3	2.2	41.6	96.8	4 903	5	8	2	–	5	22
Polk	6.4	16.2	8.2	28.5	26.4	8.2	4.6	1.6	38.6	98.3	15 785	22	44	19	3	15	162
Putnam	6.0	16.2	14.7	27.9	21.9	7.2	4.6	1.5	34.4	98.4	58 903	1 064	127	581	56	996	588
Rhea	6.2	17.6	10.0	27.5	25.0	7.4	4.6	1.8	37.2	94.3	27 097	580	111	83	10	213	306
Roane	5.9	16.5	7.5	26.9	27.2	8.9	5.5	1.6	40.7	94.0	49 440	1 409	112	210	15	87	637
Robertson	6.8	20.0	8.5	31.4	22.5	6.2	3.5	1.1	35.4	98.8	48 518	4 691	154	169	12	451	438
Rutherford	7.5	18.9	13.2	33.5	19.4	4.3	2.4	.8	31.2	99.1	156 050	17 312	522	3 467	74	2 408	2 190
Scott	7.0	19.1	10.3	28.7	23.6	6.2	3.9	1.2	34.7	97.4	20 817	19	52	25	–	22	192
Sequatchie	6.9	17.7	8.4	30.0	24.8	7.0	3.8	1.4	36.7	98.3	11 218	22	38	15	3	19	55
Sevier	6.0	17.0	8.3	29.8	26.3	7.5	4.0	1.2	38.1	95.9	69 230	396	229	394	14	299	608
Shelby	7.6	20.6	9.7	31.1	21.0	5.3	3.5	1.2	32.9	91.4	424 834	435 824	1 789	14 694	334	10 802	9 195
Smith	6.5	19.0	8.0	30.0	23.1	7.0	4.6	1.8	36.8	97.0	16 900	448	65	30	1	104	164
Stewart	5.9	18.1	7.5	28.4	25.4	8.5	4.7	1.7	38.7	99.1	11 785	159	75	180	6	29	136
Sullivan	5.6	16.2	7.3	28.4	26.5	8.7	5.6	1.6	40.1	93.3	147 771	2 888	334	652	21	319	1 063
Sumner	6.8	19.6	8.0	30.7	24.3	5.9	3.5	1.3	36.1	95.9	119 344	7 540	373	856	38	1 047	1 251
Tipton	7.0	22.3	8.6	30.4	21.8	5.6	3.2	1.1	34.4	97.0	39 920	10 202	197	190	31	197	534
Trousdale	6.0	18.2	8.5	28.1	24.9	7.3	5.2	1.8	38.1	96.9	6 284	824	17	8	2	72	52
Unicoi	5.5	15.0	7.5	27.5	26.5	9.4	6.5	2.1	41.5	95.1	17 307	12	44	15	5	167	117
Union	6.7	19.0	8.9	31.0	23.6	6.5	3.3	1.0	35.8	98.8	17 534	18	41	29	3	30	153
Van Buren	5.9	17.0	9.2	27.5	26.3	8.3	4.2	1.4	38.7	99.3	5 454	7	10	4	–	5	28
Warren	6.6	17.7	9.1	29.4	23.4	7.6	4.7	1.6	36.6	96.5	35 083	1 211	79	160	18	1 364	361
Washington	5.9	15.4	10.8	30.0	24.0	7.3	4.8	1.8	37.1	94.8	100 466	4 091	252	782	20	545	1 042
Wayne	5.1	16.3	9.1	31.7	24.2	7.5	4.6	1.5	37.3	121.7	15 482	1 145	33	42	2	32	106
Weakley	5.8	15.9	15.9	26.1	21.9	7.1	5.2	2.1	34.8	94.2	31 501	2 424	52	462	2	182	272
White	6.0	17.5	7.9	27.9	25.4	8.5	5.1	1.7	38.8	96.2	22 323	378	46	54	12	106	183
Williamson	7.2	22.3	6.2	31.6	24.9	4.5	2.5	.8	36.2	97.0	115 941	6 564	248	1 583	32	1 226	1 044
Wilson	6.8	19.4	7.7	31.7	24.7	5.5	3.1	1.1	36.3	97.4	81 261	5 563	288	426	24	428	819
TEXAS	7.8	20.4	10.5	31.1	20.2	5.5	3.3	1.1	32.3	98.6	14 799 505	2 404 566	118 362	562 319	14 434	2 438 001	514 633
Anderson	5.5	15.2	9.3	37.7	20.6	6.1	3.9	1.7	35.8	155.8	36 617	12 941	350	246	15	4 410	530
Andrews	7.4	24.2	8.1	27.3	20.5	7.2	4.2	1.1	34.1	96.3	10 024	214	115	92	3	2 183	373
Angelina	7.7	20.0	9.7	28.6	21.5	6.7	4.3	1.6	34.2	96.4	60 174	11 792	240	538	15	6 230	1 141
Aransas	5.5	18.3	6.2	23.2	27.1	11.8	6.3	1.7	42.7	98.9	19 672	322	131	623	11	1 200	538
Archer	6.3	21.9	7.0	27.4	23.5	7.9	4.3	1.7	38.1	100.2	8 459	7	55	11	3	202	117
Armstrong	5.6	20.4	6.1	24.8	23.8	8.8	6.4	4.0	40.7	93.2	2 050	6	14	–	–	60	18
Atascosa	8.3	23.5	8.9	27.6	21.0	6.0	3.7	1.1	32.3	96.6	28 286	230	310	121	25	8 315	1 341
Austin	6.6	20.4	8.1	26.4	23.7	7.4	5.2	2.2	37.6	96.5	18 924	2 509	66	69	1	1 649	372
Bailey	8.1	22.2	8.6	24.7	21.2	8.2	5.1	1.9	34.9	96.0	4 397	84	43	9	–	1 886	175
Bandera	5.5	19.1	5.8	25.7	27.6	9.9	4.9	1.3	41.3	99.0	16 590	58	159	49	10	450	329
Bastrop	7.6	20.4	7.6	31.3	22.9	5.8	3.3	1.1	35.4	105.5	46 327	5 072	404	268	33	4 385	1 244
Baylor	4.9	18.5	5.5	21.4	25.6	11.5	9.0	3.5	44.8	89.5	3 723	137	24	21	5	136	47
Bee	6.1	17.3	13.3	35.4	17.8	5.6	3.3	1.2	31.8	148.4	21 957	3 203	137	164	11	6 198	689
Bell	8.9	20.0	13.4	31.9	17.0	4.7	3.0	1.1	29.2	100.8	150 900	48 624	1 719	6 097	1 141	20 324	9 169
Bexar	7.9	20.6	10.7	30.6	19.9	5.6	3.6	1.1	32.1	94.7	959 122	100 025	11 193	22 437	1 452	247 979	50 723
Blanco	6.2	18.2	6.2	25.6	27.1	8.2	6.1	2.3	41.2	97.7	7 658	62	50	16	1	495	136
Borden	3.7	20.9	6.7	27.4	25.0	10.7	4.4	1.2	40.5	103.1	660	1	2	–	–	46	20
Bosque	5.7	18.7	6.2	23.8	25.0	9.6	7.5	3.4	41.7	95.9	15 613	330	94	19	6	889	253
Bowie	6.4	18.4	9.4	29.6	22.4	7.1	4.9	1.8	36.3	101.8	65 424	20 913	521	384	36	1 003	1 025
Brazoria	7.7	20.8	8.6	32.4	21.5	5.3	2.8	.8	34.0	106.8	186 383	20 540	1 280	4 842	73	23 281	5 368
Brazos	6.2	15.3	32.0	26.0	13.8	3.5	2.3	.9	23.6	102.1	113 479	16 333	548	6 110	104	12 835	3 006
Brewster	5.4	16.7	14.8	24.5	23.9	8.1	5.1	1.4	36.2	99.0	7 189	108	75	33	5	1 192	264
Briscoe	6.4	20.7	6.8	22.0	24.8	10.1	7.0	2.2	39.9	95.0	1 492	41	7	1	–	205	44
Brooks	8.3	23.3	8.9	23.4	21.7	8.3	4.5	1.6	34.4	94.2	6 049	15	37	7	6	1 721	141
Brown	6.2	19.6	10.1	24.7	22.9	8.4	5.7	2.4	37.2	97.4	32 910	1 509	198	140	2	2 288	627
Burleson	6.7	20.2	8.0	25.8	23.2	8.9	5.3	1.8	37.9	94.7	12 199	2 481	83	28	4	1 359	316
Burnet	6.5	18.0	7.0	26.0	24.5	10.0	5.8	2.1	40.2	93.8	30 610	519	232	95	20	2 131	540
Caldwell	7.4	21.0	8.5	29.8	20.8	6.4	4.2	1.9	34.4	97.5	22 577	2 735	196	108	11	5 685	882
Calhoun	7.8	20.7	8.7	27.3	22.3	8.3	3.9	1.1	35.3	100.9	16 112	542	102	675	14	2 723	479
Callahan	5.5	20.7	6.6	24.9	25.3	9.3	5.7	1.9	39.8	94.4	12 231	29	81	34	7	349	174
Cameron	9.5	24.3	10.5	26.8	17.8	6.3	3.7	1.1	29.0	91.9	269 139	1 617	1 471	1 607	114	53 581	7 698
Camp	7.3	19.5	8.5	25.5	22.8	8.9	5.3	2.1	36.9	96.2	8 030	2 217	40	20	6	1 112	124
Carson	6.1	21.7	6.2	26.3	23.9	8.3	5.7	1.7	38.9	95.8	6 113	38	65	9	1	198	92
Cass	6.0	18.9	7.6	24.5	25.4	8.9	6.2	2.5	40.0	92.2	23 801	5 927	143	44	5	199	319
Castro	8.5	24.6	9.0	24.3	20.9	7.6	3.9	1.2	32.3	100.5	6 243	188	97	2	1	1 584	170

[1] Includes all other responses not included in the other five race categories shown. Also includes write-in entries such as multiracial, mixed, interracial, or a Hispanic/Latino group. [2] Refers to combinations of two or more of the six race categories shown under one race.

Source: Population by Age, Sex, and Race—U.S. Census Bureau; 2000 Census of Population and Housing, "Census 2000 Profiles of General Demographic Characteristics" data files, published May 2001 (related Internet site <http://www.census.gov/mp/www/pub/2000cen/mscen01.html>).

Table B–2. Counties — **Population by Age, Sex, and Race**–Con.

[Includes U.S., states, and 3,142 counties/county equivalents defined as of January 1, 1992. For changes to these areas since January 1, 1992, see appendix B. Geographic Information]

County	Population by age, 2000 (April 1) — Percent— Under 5 years	5 to 17 years	18 to 24 years	25 to 44 years	45 to 64 years	65 to 74 years	75 to 84 years	85 years and over	Median age (years)	Males per 100 females, 2000 (April 1)	Population by race, 2000 (April 1) — One race — White	Black or African American	American Indian and Alaska Native	Asian	Native Hawaiian and Other Pacific Islander	Some other race[1]	Two or more races[2]
TEXAS—Con.																	
Chambers	6.9	22.0	8.2	29.9	24.0	5.4	2.8	.8	35.1	100.6	21 315	2 542	124	175	–	1 568	307
Cherokee	7.0	19.3	9.3	27.4	21.9	7.6	5.3	2.1	36.0	101.0	34 685	7 446	220	188	28	3 466	626
Childress	5.7	16.4	12.1	30.6	19.4	8.5	4.8	2.5	36.6	142.4	5 205	1 083	25	23	4	1 207	141
Clay	5.8	19.0	6.8	26.4	25.9	9.3	4.8	2.0	40.2	94.0	10 494	46	113	11	1	185	156
Cochran	6.5	25.0	8.0	24.9	21.2	8.0	4.6	1.9	35.1	92.1	2 405	169	31	8	2	1 020	95
Coke	4.3	20.1	7.5	20.5	23.6	13.3	7.1	3.7	43.3	100.0	3 433	75	30	3	1	268	54
Coleman	5.8	17.9	6.6	22.7	24.0	11.1	8.3	3.7	43.0	92.2	8 176	202	57	20	1	603	176
Collin	8.6	20.1	7.4	37.9	20.7	3.1	1.6	.5	32.9	99.8	400 181	23 561	2 323	34 047	230	20 957	10 376
Collingsworth	5.9	20.5	6.6	22.6	22.5	10.3	8.3	3.4	40.6	93.0	2 559	171	52	6	–	349	69
Colorado	6.0	19.6	8.9	23.8	23.1	9.4	6.4	2.8	39.3	95.3	14 841	3 017	75	42	4	2 048	363
Comal	6.2	19.3	7.0	27.5	25.2	8.0	5.1	1.8	39.0	96.0	69 501	741	414	360	23	5 449	1 533
Comanche	6.3	19.0	7.1	23.3	24.0	10.0	7.0	3.3	40.3	95.8	12 245	62	85	18	1	1 360	255
Concho	3.7	12.4	10.4	38.2	21.5	6.4	5.3	2.1	36.0	181.3	3 498	39	19	3	4	354	49
Cooke	6.7	20.6	8.7	26.1	23.0	7.7	5.2	2.0	36.7	97.4	32 305	1 112	362	122	3	1 875	584
Coryell	7.8	18.4	17.9	36.3	13.8	3.3	1.7	.7	27.8	105.3	48 946	16 344	659	1 313	365	4 696	2 655
Cottle	5.1	18.9	5.7	21.5	23.3	11.1	10.2	4.3	43.9	87.2	1 551	188	–	–	–	137	28
Crane	7.7	24.2	7.7	26.9	22.6	5.7	3.9	1.3	34.2	94.8	2 945	116	39	14	–	779	103
Crockett	6.7	22.2	7.1	26.4	24.7	7.0	3.9	2.0	37.2	98.2	3 129	28	24	11	1	808	98
Crosby	7.8	22.9	8.5	24.0	21.1	8.2	5.4	2.1	34.3	91.1	4 510	275	38	2	5	2 114	128
Culberson	7.5	24.6	7.8	25.8	23.0	7.5	3.0	.7	32.8	102.7	2 051	21	14	17	–	807	65
Dallam	8.6	23.2	8.6	28.8	20.6	5.8	3.3	1.2	31.4	102.0	5 142	102	56	13	–	772	137
Dallas	8.2	19.7	10.7	34.4	18.9	4.4	2.7	.9	31.1	99.8	1 294 769	450 557	12 499	88 369	1 277	311 504	59 924
Dawson	6.3	19.3	8.9	30.7	20.5	7.3	5.0	1.9	35.6	124.3	10 859	1 297	45	37	–	2 482	265
Deaf Smith	9.0	24.3	9.6	25.5	19.4	6.4	4.1	1.6	30.6	95.5	13 415	280	148	47	25	4 255	391
Delta	5.6	20.0	7.5	25.5	23.8	8.1	6.4	3.2	38.8	94.5	4 684	441	41	6	2	63	90
Denton	8.2	19.6	11.3	37.0	19.0	2.9	1.6	.6	31.0	99.0	353 855	25 369	2 533	17 444	221	24 072	9 482
DeWitt	5.5	18.3	7.0	27.1	23.3	9.4	6.6	2.9	40.1	105.5	15 293	2 209	109	42	5	2 004	351
Dickens	4.2	14.3	10.4	29.7	22.4	8.3	7.5	3.2	39.2	130.7	2 144	226	10	3	7	341	31
Dimmit	8.3	24.9	8.8	24.7	20.7	6.5	4.8	1.4	31.6	94.3	7 886	90	72	68	7	1 868	257
Donley	4.7	17.6	9.8	20.6	25.5	11.2	7.6	2.9	42.8	94.4	3 499	151	34	4	–	104	36
Duval	7.4	22.1	9.5	26.4	20.6	7.5	4.7	1.7	33.8	100.7	10 525	71	70	14	4	2 028	408
Eastland	5.9	17.4	9.8	22.3	23.9	10.4	7.5	2.9	41.3	94.1	16 656	399	87	38	4	884	229
Ector	8.0	22.4	10.5	27.9	20.2	6.4	3.5	1.0	32.0	94.7	89 257	5 583	1 002	775	49	21 051	3 406
Edwards	5.0	20.7	6.5	20.2	25.7	10.0	4.0	1.4	40.0	102.6	1 800	17	17	3	–	275	60
Ellis	7.6	22.6	9.3	29.8	21.5	5.1	3.0	1.2	33.2	98.3	89 789	9 626	662	392	18	8 797	2 076
El Paso	8.7	23.3	10.6	29.3	18.4	5.7	3.1	.9	30.0	93.2	502 579	20 809	5 559	6 633	669	121 721	21 652
Erath	6.5	18.1	17.0	25.9	19.1	6.6	4.6	2.2	31.4	97.8	29 610	269	218	120	10	2 237	537
Falls	6.0	21.7	7.8	27.0	20.8	8.3	6.1	2.5	36.5	85.8	11 424	5 100	92	20	7	1 637	296
Fannin	5.8	17.4	8.9	28.6	23.2	8.1	5.6	2.4	38.0	113.8	27 043	2 488	288	81	8	867	467
Fayette	5.4	17.8	7.0	23.6	24.2	9.7	8.3	3.9	42.6	93.7	18 442	1 528	79	49	12	1 452	242
Fisher	5.7	18.2	6.3	23.0	24.1	11.6	7.8	3.3	42.9	92.9	3 638	120	16	6	–	503	61
Floyd	8.2	23.2	7.4	24.4	20.7	8.2	5.5	2.4	34.8	93.8	5 763	263	59	13	4	1 528	141
Foard	5.7	20.1	5.8	22.3	22.9	9.7	8.3	5.2	41.7	86.4	1 365	53	10	3	–	166	25
Fort Bend	7.7	24.3	7.6	32.3	22.4	3.4	1.7	.5	33.3	99.1	201 896	70 356	1 046	39 706	130	32 240	9 078
Franklin	5.7	18.6	7.3	24.8	25.0	10.5	5.8	2.3	40.3	94.3	8 436	373	60	20	–	486	83
Freestone	5.6	18.1	8.9	28.1	23.0	8.3	5.5	2.6	37.8	110.5	13 501	3 378	67	48	3	696	174
Frio	7.7	21.0	11.2	30.8	18.7	5.9	3.4	1.3	30.7	121.4	11 679	792	94	67	3	3 211	406
Gaines	8.4	26.7	9.5	26.8	18.4	6.1	3.1	1.2	29.7	97.0	11 614	330	110	22	1	2 050	340
Galveston	7.0	19.7	8.7	30.2	23.3	6.3	3.7	1.1	35.9	95.9	181 830	38 625	1 181	5 254	112	17 957	5 199
Garza	6.5	21.6	7.9	28.6	21.3	6.9	5.1	2.1	35.1	112.3	3 642	234	12	4	–	834	146
Gillespie	5.0	16.5	5.5	21.2	26.2	12.7	9.1	3.8	46.3	89.7	19 320	43	68	37	5	1 096	245
Glasscock	8.0	25.5	7.1	28.4	22.0	6.0	2.1	.9	33.5	108.9	1 090	7	2	–	3	269	35
Goliad	5.8	20.1	6.5	25.0	25.2	9.5	5.8	2.2	40.2	98.9	5 724	334	38	15	1	696	120
Gonzales	7.0	21.0	8.7	25.7	20.9	8.5	5.7	2.5	36.3	98.4	13 458	1 563	99	49	16	3 069	374
Gray	5.9	18.2	8.4	27.2	22.3	9.1	6.3	2.7	38.9	104.0	18 685	1 330	214	88	5	1 871	551
Grayson	6.5	18.8	9.3	27.6	22.8	7.7	5.4	2.0	37.2	94.0	96 443	6 471	1 446	625	53	3 206	2 351
Gregg	7.0	19.7	10.3	28.2	21.5	7.0	4.6	1.7	35.0	93.8	81 184	22 115	579	752	21	5 070	1 658
Grimes	6.1	18.6	7.7	29.8	24.0	7.6	4.3	1.8	38.1	117.5	16 909	4 700	76	71	11	1 397	388
Guadalupe	7.3	21.2	9.0	29.1	22.2	6.3	3.8	1.2	34.9	97.0	69 122	4 460	486	772	87	11 360	2 736
Hale	8.3	21.9	11.4	27.2	18.3	6.9	4.3	1.7	31.4	102.4	24 438	2 121	335	110	14	8 697	887
Hall	7.3	19.9	6.8	22.1	22.4	10.3	7.6	3.6	40.2	91.7	2 722	311	20	6	–	677	46
Hamilton	5.6	18.2	6.0	22.9	23.8	11.0	8.0	4.5	43.1	93.5	7 720	12	36	12	4	359	86
Hansford	6.8	22.5	6.8	26.3	22.3	8.0	5.1	2.1	36.5	96.5	4 289	2	40	12	–	938	88
Hardeman	6.5	18.8	7.5	22.6	24.3	9.4	7.6	3.2	41.2	89.4	4 035	228	36	14	–	335	76
Hardin	6.9	20.8	8.5	28.3	23.2	7.0	4.0	1.2	36.0	96.7	43 677	3 324	154	112	6	355	445
Harris	8.3	20.7	10.3	33.4	19.8	4.3	2.4	.8	31.2	99.2	1 997 123	628 619	15 180	174 626	2 095	482 283	100 652

[1] Includes all other responses not included in the other five race categories shown. Also includes write-in entries such as multiracial, mixed, interracial, or a Hispanic/Latino group. [2] Refers to combinations of two or more of the six race categories shown under one race.

Source: Population by Age, Sex, and Race—U.S. Census Bureau; 2000 Census of Population and Housing, "Census 2000 Profiles of General Demographic Characteristics" data files, published May 2001 (related Internet site <http://www.census.gov/mp/www/pub/2000cen/mscen01.html>).

Table B–2. Counties — Population by Age, Sex, and Race–Con.

[Includes U.S., states, and 3,142 counties/county equivalents defined as of January 1, 1992. For changes to these areas since January 1, 1992, see appendix B. Geographic Information]

County	Population by age, 2000 (April 1) Percent— Under 5 years	5 to 17 years	18 to 24 years	25 to 44 years	45 to 64 years	65 to 74 years	75 to 84 years	85 years and over	Median age (years)	Males per 100 females, 2000 (April 1)	White	Black or African American	American Indian and Alaska Native	Asian	Native Hawaiian and Other Pacific Islander	Some other race[1]	Two or more races[2]
TEXAS—Con.																	
Harrison	6.5	20.4	10.0	27.1	23.0	7.1	4.4	1.6	36.1	94.1	44 313	14 926	217	192	24	1 777	661
Hartley	5.7	15.1	4.7	35.7	26.9	6.3	3.5	2.1	39.6	154.1	4 489	451	24	15	3	476	79
Haskell	5.0	18.8	5.7	22.1	22.9	12.7	9.0	3.7	43.9	88.9	5 044	170	33	9	1	711	125
Hays	6.3	18.2	20.5	28.2	19.1	4.2	2.5	.9	28.4	101.3	77 014	3 588	678	772	69	13 038	2 430
Hemphill	5.7	22.3	6.5	25.3	25.4	7.5	4.9	2.3	38.6	101.3	2 937	52	24	9	1	284	44
Henderson	6.4	17.9	7.6	25.0	24.8	10.5	5.9	1.8	40.2	96.2	64 850	4 842	399	221	24	1 992	949
Hidalgo	10.2	25.1	11.3	27.6	16.0	5.5	3.3	.9	27.2	94.4	442 525	2 807	2 402	3 375	131	106 164	12 059
Hill	6.9	19.0	8.5	24.9	23.4	9.0	5.9	2.4	38.3	96.7	27 200	2 391	141	82	8	1 946	553
Hockley	7.2	21.9	11.8	25.9	20.6	6.8	4.2	1.7	33.3	96.3	16 897	846	187	30	8	4 244	504
Hood	5.8	17.8	6.7	25.2	26.6	10.6	5.7	1.7	41.5	96.2	38 952	134	339	126	18	987	544
Hopkins	6.5	19.6	8.4	27.3	23.0	7.6	5.4	2.2	36.9	96.1	27 200	2 554	218	79	18	1 455	436
Houston	5.2	18.0	6.8	27.7	24.3	9.0	6.2	2.8	40.3	114.1	15 899	6 476	61	57	13	502	177
Howard	5.9	18.3	9.0	30.9	21.3	7.9	5.0	1.7	36.4	118.0	26 950	1 390	197	199	4	4 180	707
Hudspeth	8.6	25.5	8.9	26.7	20.4	6.7	2.3	.9	30.2	102.9	2 917	11	47	6	–	293	70
Hunt	6.7	19.8	10.0	28.0	22.8	6.8	4.2	1.5	35.5	98.1	64 013	7 242	559	416	56	3 009	1 301
Hutchinson	6.9	20.6	8.7	25.5	22.7	8.4	5.7	1.5	37.5	97.0	20 756	574	323	83	4	1 589	528
Irion	5.7	21.0	4.7	26.9	26.1	9.4	4.9	1.4	39.9	100.3	1 606	7	14	–	–	116	28
Jack	5.7	17.7	10.0	29.8	21.6	8.3	5.0	2.0	37.0	120.4	7 771	486	59	24	2	336	85
Jackson	7.1	20.3	8.2	26.1	22.3	8.3	5.4	2.2	37.3	96.7	11 008	1 099	56	56	8	1 820	344
Jasper	6.8	19.7	8.0	26.8	23.4	8.7	4.9	1.7	37.3	94.6	27 855	6 341	148	113	9	727	411
Jeff Davis	4.1	20.3	5.3	24.1	30.0	8.6	6.2	1.5	42.5	104.5	1 998	20	7	2	–	114	66
Jefferson	6.7	19.2	10.0	29.3	21.1	7.1	4.9	1.6	35.3	101.1	144 274	85 046	857	7 274	81	10 733	3 786
Jim Hogg	7.9	23.7	8.1	24.6	21.1	7.8	4.8	2.1	33.9	96.7	4 248	24	41	11	–	836	121
Jim Wells	8.2	23.2	9.0	26.5	20.6	6.8	4.1	1.5	32.8	95.2	30 634	237	243	171	35	7 050	956
Johnson	7.4	21.4	8.8	30.2	22.3	5.7	3.1	1.1	34.3	99.7	114 142	3 166	809	664	230	5 728	2 072
Jones	4.9	17.6	11.1	31.5	21.0	7.2	4.8	2.0	36.0	150.1	16 378	2 392	102	97	2	1 551	263
Karnes	5.4	16.4	11.5	34.2	18.2	7.1	5.2	2.1	34.1	146.2	10 588	1 667	105	66	9	2 662	349
Kaufman	7.2	22.0	8.2	29.5	22.4	5.8	3.5	1.4	34.9	97.4	57 837	7 511	437	333	15	4 035	1 145
Kendall	6.3	20.9	6.1	26.4	26.4	7.2	4.6	2.0	39.3	95.0	22 047	83	133	55	11	1 046	368
Kenedy	8.9	20.3	9.7	26.3	24.2	7.0	2.9	.7	34.2	110.2	267	3	3	2	–	132	7
Kent	3.5	17.1	5.4	21.8	26.8	12.6	8.3	4.7	47.1	91.7	820	2	3	–	–	32	2
Kerr	5.3	17.3	6.7	22.3	23.5	12.3	9.2	3.4	43.8	92.0	38 802	776	244	221	24	2 879	707
Kimble	6.1	17.6	6.0	22.6	26.9	11.2	7.1	2.6	43.1	92.7	4 034	4	15	20	1	334	60
King	6.7	27.0	3.7	29.5	22.8	7.9	2.0	.6	37.0	95.6	335	–	4	–	–	11	6
Kinney	6.2	19.5	5.3	21.5	23.1	14.7	8.0	1.5	43.2	99.8	2 562	57	11	4	–	629	116
Kleberg	7.6	19.7	15.7	27.4	19.0	5.9	3.3	1.4	29.2	101.0	22 675	1 167	192	464	31	5 995	1 025
Knox	6.4	21.3	5.6	22.9	21.0	10.5	8.4	3.7	40.5	89.4	3 162	294	46	10	4	628	109
Lamar	7.1	19.1	8.6	26.8	22.9	7.6	5.7	2.4	36.9	91.3	39 990	6 534	522	192	11	567	683
Lamb	7.4	22.2	8.1	24.2	20.8	8.7	5.9	2.8	36.2	94.2	11 193	632	100	15	3	2 493	273
Lampasas	6.8	20.8	7.7	27.2	23.0	7.7	4.6	2.2	36.9	96.3	15 409	550	124	134	11	1 153	381
La Salle	7.3	22.0	10.0	27.7	21.3	6.6	3.8	1.3	33.0	113.5	4 779	208	20	18	–	716	125
Lavaca	5.9	18.3	6.9	23.5	23.6	9.5	8.6	3.7	41.9	93.1	16 686	1 305	36	31	3	930	219
Lee	6.9	21.9	9.2	26.3	21.4	7.5	4.7	2.2	35.6	101.6	11 992	1 892	72	38	5	1 388	270
Leon	5.6	18.7	6.7	23.4	25.6	11.9	6.0	2.2	42.1	96.4	12 809	1 593	52	27	1	690	163
Liberty	7.1	20.5	9.2	31.6	21.4	5.9	3.3	1.0	34.0	95.7	55 355	8 996	327	224	22	4 230	1 000
Limestone	6.4	18.9	9.1	26.4	22.7	8.4	5.7	2.4	37.4	103.2	15 602	4 205	100	26	3	1 786	329
Lipscomb	6.2	21.3	5.9	24.7	23.4	9.2	6.1	3.1	39.5	94.6	2 533	16	42	2	–	397	67
Live Oak	4.9	17.3	9.5	27.1	25.1	8.8	5.3	1.8	39.2	122.2	10 743	301	50	24	2	950	239
Llano	3.8	12.1	4.5	18.4	30.5	17.0	10.3	3.4	53.0	94.4	16 408	51	71	64	5	302	143
Loving	3.0	16.4	1.5	26.9	35.8	13.4	3.0	–	45.8	116.1	60	–	–	–	–	6	1
Lubbock	7.2	18.5	16.3	27.9	19.2	6.0	3.7	1.3	30.5	95.8	180 269	18 602	1 420	3 168	85	34 329	4 755
Lynn	7.3	23.9	7.8	26.0	21.0	7.8	4.7	1.5	35.2	99.6	4 947	186	67	10	–	1 195	145
McCulloch	6.8	19.9	6.6	22.9	24.3	9.7	6.9	2.9	40.4	90.1	6 945	129	21	14	1	961	134
McLennan	7.1	19.5	14.6	26.4	19.5	6.5	4.6	1.7	31.9	94.1	154 087	32 428	1 056	2 284	100	19 657	3 905
McMullen	4.0	19.4	6.3	23.7	28.7	10.5	4.6	2.8	43.1	101.2	752	10	2	–	–	76	11
Madison	5.4	15.7	13.0	31.9	20.0	6.8	4.8	2.3	33.4	142.6	8 642	2 959	41	50	4	1 022	222
Marion	5.6	16.8	6.4	23.6	28.4	10.9	6.2	2.1	43.3	95.4	7 958	2 616	87	24	1	86	169
Martin	8.6	25.3	6.7	26.4	19.7	7.2	4.2	1.9	32.5	95.6	3 750	75	39	8	–	762	112
Mason	5.1	17.3	4.7	20.7	28.8	12.0	8.0	3.5	46.7	92.4	3 424	5	23	2	1	215	68
Matagorda	7.4	22.6	8.9	26.9	21.8	6.9	4.1	1.4	34.8	98.6	25 745	4 829	256	903	16	5 305	903
Maverick	10.0	27.0	9.2	26.7	17.7	5.7	2.9	.9	27.8	91.9	33 529	146	635	184	20	11 389	1 394
Medina	7.2	21.8	8.4	28.7	21.5	6.8	4.1	1.5	34.4	105.6	31 200	866	269	130	19	5 690	1 130
Menard	4.7	19.6	5.3	21.9	26.6	10.8	7.5	3.7	44.1	99.7	2 066	12	15	8	1	231	27
Midland	7.5	22.7	8.8	28.4	20.9	6.5	3.8	1.3	34.1	93.4	89 702	8 101	741	1 074	36	14 124	2 231
Milam	6.8	20.6	7.7	24.7	22.9	8.3	6.4	2.5	38.0	96.1	19 121	2 678	122	53	2	1 867	395
Mills	5.4	20.2	4.7	20.5	26.1	10.6	8.2	4.3	44.4	102.4	4 597	65	14	4	4	398	69

[1] Includes all other responses not included in the other five race categories shown. Also includes write-in entries such as multiracial, mixed, interracial, or a Hispanic/Latino group. [2] Refers to combinations of two or more of the six race categories shown under one race.

Source: Population by Age, Sex, and Race—U.S. Census Bureau; 2000 Census of Population and Housing, "Census 2000 Profiles of General Demographic Characteristics" data files, published May 2001 (related Internet site <http://www.census.gov/mp/www/pub/2000cen/mscen01.html>).

Table B–2. Counties — Population by Age, Sex, and Race–Con.

[Includes U.S., states, and 3,142 counties/county equivalents defined as of January 1, 1992. For changes to these areas since January 1, 1992, see appendix B. Geographic Information]

| | Population by age, 2000 (April 1) | | | | | | | | | Males per 100 females, 2000 (April 1) | Population by race, 2000 (April 1) | | | | | | |
| | Percent— | | | | | | | | | | One race | | | | | | |
County	Under 5 years	5 to 17 years	18 to 24 years	25 to 44 years	45 to 64 years	65 to 74 years	75 to 84 years	85 years and over	Median age (years)		White	Black or African American	American Indian and Alaska Native	Asian	Native Hawaiian and Other Pacific Islander	Some other race[1]	Two or more races[2]
TEXAS—Con.																	
Mitchell	4.7	15.1	11.5	30.7	22.9	7.6	5.5	2.1	38.6	159.3	7 227	1 242	40	35	2	988	164
Montague	6.0	18.0	6.8	24.3	25.1	10.4	6.8	2.6	41.3	92.5	18 343	34	141	49	5	313	232
Montgomery	7.7	21.8	8.0	30.6	23.1	5.2	2.7	.8	34.4	98.4	259 258	10 258	1 374	3 261	102	14 271	5 244
Moore	9.3	24.3	9.2	28.4	18.3	6.0	3.4	1.1	30.4	100.6	12 864	139	134	173	6	6 278	527
Morris	5.9	19.3	7.8	24.3	24.5	10.0	6.2	2.1	40.2	92.7	9 357	3 148	69	23	8	297	146
Motley	5.9	18.1	6.0	21.1	25.2	12.6	8.1	2.9	44.4	101.7	1 246	50	9	2	2	90	27
Nacogdoches	6.5	17.5	20.0	24.7	19.2	6.3	4.2	1.6	29.7	93.0	44 405	9 908	229	412	40	3 375	834
Navarro	7.2	20.1	9.9	26.9	21.5	7.1	5.0	2.3	35.2	97.0	31 966	7 577	209	214	150	4 263	745
Newton	6.5	19.7	9.0	26.6	24.1	8.4	4.4	1.4	36.9	104.1	11 431	3 118	95	40	5	235	148
Nolan	6.7	20.4	8.5	25.4	22.6	8.5	5.6	2.3	37.4	94.7	12 397	739	77	38	9	2 215	327
Nueces	7.7	20.7	10.5	28.9	21.1	6.2	3.8	1.2	33.3	95.8	225 912	13 307	1 994	3 632	230	58 762	9 808
Ochiltree	8.1	22.5	8.4	28.7	20.7	6.7	3.7	1.3	33.7	99.8	7 763	12	85	35	1	926	184
Oldham	6.5	28.5	7.2	23.3	23.2	6.8	3.4	1.1	32.9	108.1	1 981	41	28	8	–	101	26
Orange	6.7	20.6	8.7	28.1	23.2	7.3	4.2	1.2	36.1	96.4	74 749	7 124	473	664	25	950	981
Palo Pinto	6.7	19.3	8.2	25.9	23.6	8.7	5.5	2.2	38.3	96.7	23 835	626	182	142	8	1 772	461
Panola	6.2	19.0	9.2	25.1	24.6	8.3	5.4	2.2	38.8	92.3	17 927	4 021	82	55	1	426	244
Parker	6.3	21.2	7.9	29.8	24.2	6.1	3.3	1.1	36.5	104.1	81 955	1 586	596	306	21	2 808	1 223
Parmer	8.6	24.3	8.5	26.2	19.6	6.1	4.6	2.0	32.1	97.9	6 612	101	76	32	4	2 956	235
Pecos	6.6	21.1	13.8	27.2	20.5	6.3	3.4	1.1	31.2	123.1	12 749	738	71	86	1	2 711	453
Polk	5.9	17.0	8.1	26.8	24.2	10.5	5.7	1.8	39.3	108.7	32 760	5 416	717	156	3	1 538	543
Potter	8.3	19.7	11.1	30.1	19.1	5.9	4.1	1.7	32.1	100.9	77 890	11 308	993	2 832	43	17 528	2 952
Presidio	7.8	24.9	8.3	24.9	20.2	7.8	4.7	1.5	32.8	94.3	6 205	20	20	6	1	984	68
Rains	5.6	18.2	7.4	25.1	27.7	9.5	4.9	1.6	41.0	99.8	8 400	267	75	31	4	233	129
Randall	6.8	19.2	11.2	28.4	22.4	6.9	3.9	1.1	34.9	94.7	94 340	1 564	674	1 073	31	4 915	1 715
Reagan	8.2	26.0	7.6	28.1	19.9	5.8	3.5	1.0	32.4	100.5	2 150	100	18	9	–	983	66
Real	4.9	18.6	5.4	21.5	28.8	12.2	6.5	2.1	44.6	97.9	2 785	6	19	6	1	183	47
Red River	5.8	18.0	7.8	24.4	24.3	9.6	7.1	3.0	40.4	92.9	11 170	2 548	85	17	1	328	165
Reeves	7.0	22.9	11.3	25.2	21.0	7.2	4.1	1.3	32.1	112.0	10 421	276	67	46	1	1 974	352
Refugio	6.0	20.2	7.4	25.9	24.0	8.8	5.6	2.2	38.6	95.8	6 280	530	44	23	4	816	131
Roberts	5.0	20.1	4.8	24.8	30.9	8.5	4.4	1.6	42.0	100.2	856	3	5	1	–	12	10
Robertson	7.2	21.0	7.5	24.2	23.1	8.4	6.0	2.5	37.6	91.0	10 592	3 871	68	26	8	1 148	287
Rockwall	7.5	22.6	7.0	31.1	23.3	4.8	2.6	1.1	35.3	100.8	38 414	1 396	173	568	23	1 915	591
Runnels	6.3	20.6	6.4	24.2	22.9	9.3	6.9	3.3	39.4	92.9	9 361	161	61	37	2	1 645	228
Rusk	6.1	18.8	8.3	27.8	23.3	8.0	5.3	2.3	38.1	104.0	35 477	9 102	165	113	3	1 997	515
Sabine	5.2	15.9	5.6	21.1	27.2	14.3	8.0	2.7	47.0	93.4	9 197	1 039	43	9	3	86	92
San Augustine	5.7	18.0	6.8	23.0	25.1	11.3	6.9	3.1	42.1	92.1	6 196	2 500	18	18	–	147	67
San Jacinto	6.0	19.1	7.4	24.9	26.6	10.2	4.4	1.4	40.0	100.5	18 606	2 813	102	63	16	362	284
San Patricio	8.1	23.0	10.0	28.2	20.2	6.2	3.3	1.0	32.0	100.5	51 533	1 885	472	426	76	10 699	2 047
San Saba	5.3	22.6	8.2	20.8	22.8	9.6	7.2	3.5	39.4	107.4	5 227	169	66	7	–	651	66
Schleicher	6.2	21.8	7.3	24.0	24.4	8.1	5.6	2.7	38.8	98.8	2 248	45	2	5	1	557	77
Scurry	6.3	18.9	10.7	26.2	22.4	8.2	5.1	2.1	37.0	107.8	13 296	991	87	37	–	1 720	230
Shackelford	5.4	21.3	6.0	24.8	24.3	9.5	6.1	2.7	40.1	90.1	3 111	16	14	–	–	140	21
Shelby	7.0	19.6	8.8	25.8	22.2	8.5	5.8	2.2	36.9	92.4	18 324	4 903	92	57	6	1 480	362
Sherman	6.9	24.5	7.0	26.5	21.5	7.2	4.6	1.9	34.4	102.5	2 628	17	21	1	–	466	53
Smith	7.1	19.5	9.8	27.4	22.1	7.5	4.8	1.8	35.5	92.1	126 853	33 298	746	1 218	47	10 031	2 513
Somervell	6.4	22.0	7.7	26.8	23.7	6.6	4.4	2.3	36.8	99.6	6 277	19	47	18	1	348	99
Starr	10.4	27.0	11.0	27.1	16.3	4.9	2.5	.8	26.1	94.2	47 120	79	133	151	22	5 309	783
Stephens	5.6	18.8	9.1	25.6	23.2	9.3	6.2	2.2	38.9	103.3	8 406	282	34	28	2	788	134
Sterling	5.1	23.6	6.1	29.7	20.8	7.4	5.2	2.1	37.9	96.5	1 194	1	4	–	1	165	28
Stonewall	5.1	17.7	6.2	22.6	24.5	12.0	7.1	4.8	43.7	90.0	1 494	50	6	6	–	109	28
Sutton	7.2	21.6	6.7	27.7	24.4	7.6	3.8	1.0	36.5	99.5	3 069	10	17	7	–	908	66
Swisher	7.4	20.5	10.3	25.5	20.4	8.7	5.4	1.8	34.6	109.2	6 011	490	45	13	2	1 626	191
Tarrant	8.0	20.1	10.0	33.5	20.1	4.6	2.8	.9	32.3	98.1	1 030 208	185 143	8 300	52 594	2 252	131 393	36 329
Taylor	7.2	19.4	13.8	27.8	19.3	6.5	4.3	1.6	32.2	94.1	102 016	8 517	733	1 577	85	10 562	3 065
Terrell	5.6	21.0	5.0	23.4	27.5	10.5	5.3	1.8	42.0	103.2	955	–	18	7	–	90	11
Terry	7.3	21.0	9.5	27.0	20.6	7.9	5.0	1.7	35.0	108.0	9 769	638	67	28	3	1 822	434
Throckmorton	5.5	19.7	5.7	22.9	25.7	9.9	7.3	3.3	41.8	97.2	1 704	1	8	1	–	103	33
Titus	8.6	21.7	9.8	28.0	19.5	6.2	4.5	1.8	31.8	97.8	19 724	3 008	162	122	5	4 616	481
Tom Green	6.9	19.2	12.8	27.1	20.6	6.9	4.7	1.8	33.8	93.7	82 246	4 298	679	893	73	13 331	2 490
Travis	7.2	16.5	14.7	36.5	18.2	3.7	2.3	.8	30.4	104.9	554 058	75 247	4 684	36 286	559	118 294	23 152
Trinity	5.9	17.0	7.0	22.3	25.8	12.7	7.1	2.1	43.3	93.6	11 540	1 642	57	32	2	367	139
Tyler	5.8	17.4	8.0	27.2	23.8	10.1	5.9	1.8	38.9	106.9	17 487	2 497	90	41	4	520	232
Upshur	6.6	20.4	8.0	26.6	24.1	8.0	4.6	1.7	37.7	95.5	30 246	3 582	224	65	20	740	414
Upton	5.5	23.8	7.9	24.9	23.8	8.0	4.4	1.8	38.1	95.9	2 648	55	41	1	2	611	46
Uvalde	8.4	23.0	9.8	25.3	20.0	7.1	4.5	2.0	32.2	95.0	19 621	93	176	101	22	5 095	818
Val Verde	8.9	23.1	9.4	27.9	19.6	6.3	3.6	1.1	30.8	97.0	34 251	690	306	248	23	8 172	1 166

[1] Includes all other responses not included in the other five race categories shown. Also includes write-in entries such as multiracial, mixed, interracial, or a Hispanic/Latino group. [2] Refers to combinations of two or more of the six race categories shown under one race.

Source: Population by Age, Sex, and Race—U.S. Census Bureau; 2000 Census of Population and Housing, "Census 2000 Profiles of General Demographic Characteristics" data files, published May 2001 (related Internet site <http://www.census.gov/mp/www/pub/2000cen/mscen01.html>).

[Includes U.S., states, and 3,142 counties/county equivalents defined as of January 1, 1992. For changes to these areas since January 1, 1992, see appendix B. Geographic Information]

County	Population by age, 2000 (April 1) Percent— Under 5 years	5 to 17 years	18 to 24 years	25 to 44 years	45 to 64 years	65 to 74 years	75 to 84 years	85 years and over	Median age (years)	Males per 100 females, 2000 (April 1)	White	Black or African American	American Indian and Alaska Native	Asian	Native Hawaiian and Other Pacific Islander	Some other race[1]	Two or more races[2]
TEXAS—Con.																	
Van Zandt	6.3	19.2	7.3	25.2	24.9	9.3	5.6	2.2	39.5	97.0	44 268	1 416	298	88	14	1 303	753
Victoria	7.6	21.5	9.2	28.1	21.5	6.6	4.0	1.4	34.2	94.9	62 406	5 297	444	651	34	13 390	1 866
Walker	4.9	13.1	23.0	31.1	18.9	5.1	2.8	1.0	31.0	151.1	42 686	14 747	219	475	31	2 728	872
Waller	6.9	18.8	18.1	26.4	20.5	5.1	3.2	1.0	30.1	98.7	18 889	9 553	159	124	6	3 357	575
Ward	6.6	24.0	7.8	25.1	22.2	8.2	4.6	1.5	36.0	99.8	8 704	503	72	31	3	1 366	230
Washington	6.0	18.7	11.1	25.3	22.1	8.3	5.8	2.7	37.4	94.7	22 682	5 669	81	367	1	1 221	352
Webb	10.6	25.6	11.4	29.3	15.6	4.3	2.4	.8	26.5	92.9	158 670	713	912	833	48	27 030	4 911
Wharton	7.0	21.7	9.3	26.5	21.5	7.1	5.0	1.9	35.3	96.9	28 423	6 159	153	129	26	5 621	677
Wheeler	6.0	18.9	6.5	22.5	25.2	10.3	6.7	3.8	42.5	92.0	4 641	147	41	29	4	351	71
Wichita	7.0	18.2	13.7	29.0	19.5	6.9	4.3	1.5	33.2	103.8	103 705	13 466	1 176	2 418	114	7 259	3 526
Wilbarger	6.6	21.3	9.5	24.8	21.6	7.4	5.9	2.8	36.3	98.0	11 472	1 301	97	93	4	1 428	281
Willacy	8.2	23.4	11.9	26.6	18.3	6.7	3.7	1.1	29.8	105.2	14 132	439	101	22	6	4 912	470
Williamson	8.5	21.4	8.1	35.6	19.1	4.0	2.4	.9	32.3	99.3	205 994	12 790	1 130	6 595	198	17 976	5 284
Wilson	6.9	22.3	7.6	28.6	23.2	6.3	3.6	1.5	35.9	99.7	26 311	392	188	98	13	4 618	788
Winkler	7.0	22.8	8.7	26.1	21.0	7.7	5.1	1.6	35.2	96.4	5 366	133	32	14	–	1 460	168
Wise	6.8	21.5	7.8	30.2	23.0	6.1	3.3	1.2	35.5	101.5	44 407	600	366	107	21	2 456	836
Wood	5.2	16.6	7.9	22.9	26.4	11.6	6.9	2.3	43.0	97.1	32 749	2 250	203	73	8	1 070	399
Yoakum	7.5	24.6	8.3	26.8	21.3	6.5	3.8	1.2	34.1	94.5	5 171	102	52	9	1	1 866	121
Young	6.0	19.0	7.0	24.7	23.6	9.9	6.9	2.9	40.7	91.6	16 325	218	115	46	8	948	283
Zapata	9.2	23.9	10.0	24.1	18.6	8.0	5.1	1.3	30.7	96.8	10 241	50	39	23	5	1 540	284
Zavala	8.9	25.2	10.2	25.6	18.7	6.2	3.9	1.2	29.0	97.5	7 547	57	69	10	4	3 605	308
UTAH	9.4	22.8	14.2	28.1	17.0	4.5	3.0	1.0	27.1	100.4	1 992 975	17 657	29 684	37 108	15 145	93 405	47 195
Beaver	9.3	24.2	9.4	24.0	19.2	7.2	5.1	1.7	30.8	106.0	5 599	16	54	37	5	188	106
Box Elder	9.3	26.8	10.5	25.4	17.7	5.7	3.4	1.2	28.0	101.7	39 699	71	375	409	34	1 473	684
Cache	9.9	21.4	22.2	25.7	13.7	3.5	2.5	1.1	23.9	97.0	84 286	348	529	1 814	181	3 026	1 207
Carbon	7.2	21.5	12.3	24.4	21.3	6.6	4.9	1.7	33.6	95.6	18 601	56	216	71	9	971	498
Daggett	6.6	16.6	8.9	27.4	27.0	10.0	2.4	1.1	39.2	125.2	871	6	7	1	–	22	14
Davis	9.8	25.4	12.2	28.2	17.1	4.2	2.5	.7	26.8	100.9	220 486	2 615	1 379	3 665	639	5 501	4 709
Duchesne	9.1	27.7	9.4	24.7	19.8	5.7	2.9	.7	28.3	102.8	12 956	21	769	30	8	228	359
Emery	8.1	27.2	9.6	24.1	20.9	5.5	3.2	1.3	30.1	100.8	10 386	20	71	34	11	203	135
Garfield	8.6	24.1	7.8	23.1	22.4	8.0	4.7	1.4	33.8	104.6	4 496	8	87	19	2	53	70
Grand	7.0	19.9	8.2	27.9	24.5	7.2	4.1	1.3	36.9	96.3	7 861	21	327	19	4	141	112
Iron	9.4	21.9	20.6	23.6	16.1	4.8	2.8	.9	24.2	98.4	31 416	119	737	251	92	600	564
Juab	11.2	27.4	9.4	25.2	16.9	4.8	3.7	1.3	26.5	100.3	7 955	12	84	28	4	71	84
Kane	6.6	22.8	6.8	21.2	25.9	9.3	5.8	1.6	39.1	98.3	5 804	2	94	13	3	45	85
Millard	8.1	29.2	8.0	22.9	19.4	6.6	4.3	1.4	29.9	104.9	11 653	13	163	59	25	342	150
Morgan	8.1	28.9	9.7	24.3	20.2	5.3	2.6	.8	28.5	102.9	6 994	3	13	11	–	32	76
Piute	8.2	22.5	6.6	19.7	26.0	9.1	5.4	2.6	38.9	104.4	1 372	2	17	3	1	27	13
Rich	7.2	27.4	7.2	22.2	21.9	7.5	4.6	1.9	34.3	103.6	1 925	–	1	8	–	18	9
Salt Lake	8.9	21.6	12.9	30.6	18.0	4.2	2.9	1.0	28.9	101.7	775 666	9 495	7 892	22 991	11 075	48 166	23 102
San Juan	9.7	29.6	10.0	25.2	17.1	4.8	2.7	1.0	25.5	99.5	5 876	18	8 026	25	5	245	218
Sanpete	8.3	24.9	16.4	21.8	17.8	5.8	3.6	1.4	25.3	102.4	21 040	71	199	109	81	924	339
Sevier	8.8	25.7	10.1	22.9	19.7	6.7	4.6	1.5	30.3	99.2	18 014	51	376	49	17	149	186
Summit	7.1	22.7	8.4	34.0	22.9	3.1	1.4	.4	33.3	108.3	27 299	72	91	285	13	1 615	361
Tooele	11.0	24.0	11.5	29.5	16.6	4.2	2.5	.6	27.1	97.0	36 330	521	694	244	72	1 835	1 039
Uintah	8.4	26.3	10.7	25.4	19.3	5.7	3.2	1.0	29.0	99.3	22 130	29	2 365	56	20	264	360
Utah	11.0	23.1	21.0	25.9	12.7	3.4	2.2	.8	23.3	98.3	340 388	1 096	2 206	3 917	2 122	11 974	6 833
Wasatch	9.2	25.0	9.9	29.0	18.5	4.9	2.7	.9	29.5	103.3	14 549	33	65	45	15	298	210
Washington	9.1	22.1	11.6	24.7	17.8	9.1	6.2	1.7	31.0	97.3	84 543	186	1 328	405	384	2 020	1 488
Wayne	8.8	23.6	8.1	22.5	22.6	7.5	5.2	1.8	34.1	103.5	2 441	4	9	2	4	31	18
Weber	9.0	22.0	12.6	27.9	18.1	5.4	3.8	1.1	29.3	100.6	172 339	2 748	1 510	2 508	319	12 943	4 166
VERMONT	5.6	18.6	9.3	29.0	24.8	6.7	4.4	1.6	37.7	96.1	589 208	3 063	2 420	5 217	141	1 443	7 335
Addison	5.7	19.2	12.5	26.9	24.3	6.0	4.0	1.4	36.1	97.7	34 844	196	93	264	10	104	463
Bennington	5.2	18.5	7.7	26.3	25.7	8.8	5.6	2.3	40.3	92.2	36 161	155	74	228	5	76	295
Caledonia	5.5	19.8	8.8	26.3	25.3	7.4	5.2	1.8	38.5	97.5	28 954	87	163	111	3	67	317
Chittenden	5.8	17.8	13.1	32.0	21.9	5.0	3.1	1.3	34.2	95.1	139 446	1 328	403	2 914	32	498	1 950
Essex	5.4	20.2	6.5	27.2	25.5	8.9	5.1	1.2	39.0	100.1	6 237	11	41	17	–	15	138
Franklin	7.1	21.0	7.0	31.4	22.5	6.1	3.7	1.2	35.7	98.5	43 627	138	684	118	11	95	744
Grand Isle	5.5	19.3	5.6	28.7	28.5	7.5	3.9	.9	40.1	99.9	6 722	10	60	16	3	2	88
Lamoille	5.5	18.8	10.0	29.9	24.5	6.0	3.9	1.5	36.5	100.1	22 608	76	104	87	7	29	322
Orange	5.6	20.0	7.8	28.2	25.6	7.1	4.3	1.4	38.6	99.2	27 666	68	76	99	10	38	269
Orleans	5.7	19.5	7.1	26.8	25.9	7.7	5.5	1.9	39.3	98.6	25 532	97	172	78	4	34	360
Rutland	5.2	18.1	8.3	27.7	25.8	7.6	5.4	1.9	39.5	94.7	62 214	209	144	245	16	107	465
Washington	5.4	18.1	8.9	28.7	26.0	6.5	4.4	1.9	38.5	96.1	56 326	274	175	330	7	152	775
Windham	5.3	18.3	7.1	28.1	27.2	7.2	4.8	2.0	40.0	95.0	42 764	223	97	348	16	141	627
Windsor	5.0	18.4	5.9	27.3	27.6	8.1	5.7	2.0	41.3	94.8	56 107	191	134	362	17	85	522

[1] Includes all other responses not included in the other five race categories shown. Also includes write-in entries such as multiracial, mixed, interracial, or a Hispanic/Latino group. [2] Refers to combinations of two or more of the six race categories shown under one race.

Source: Population by Age, Sex, and Race—U.S. Census Bureau; 2000 Census of Population and Housing, "Census 2000 Profiles of General Demographic Characteristics" data files, published May 2001 (related Internet site <http://www.census.gov/mp/www/pub/2000cen/mscen01.html>).

Table B–2. Counties — **Population by Age, Sex, and Race**–Con.

[Includes U.S., states, and 3,142 counties/county equivalents defined as of January 1, 1992. For changes to these areas since January 1, 1992, see appendix B. Geographic Information]

County	Population by age, 2000 (April 1) — Percent — Under 5 years	5 to 17 years	18 to 24 years	25 to 44 years	45 to 64 years	65 to 74 years	75 to 84 years	85 years and over	Median age (years)	Males per 100 females, 2000 (April 1)	White	Black or African American	American Indian and Alaska Native	Asian	Native Hawaiian and Other Pacific Islander	Some other race[1]	Two or more races[2]
VIRGINIA	6.5	18.0	9.6	31.6	23.0	6.1	3.9	1.2	35.7	96.3	5 120 110	1 390 293	21 172	261 025	3 946	138 900	143 069
Accomack	6.1	18.2	8.2	26.2	24.7	9.2	5.6	2.0	39.4	94.3	24 276	12 089	125	86	23	1 367	339
Albemarle	6.3	18.6	7.3	30.9	24.5	6.7	4.3	1.5	37.4	92.2	67 474	7 650	135	2 268	9	681	1 019
Alleghany	5.6	17.3	6.2	26.8	28.5	8.5	5.5	1.6	41.1	99.6	12 454	317	27	31	2	26	69
Amelia	6.3	19.1	6.7	29.2	25.4	7.2	4.2	1.9	38.5	97.3	8 045	3 198	32	19	2	28	76
Amherst	5.7	17.8	9.7	27.7	25.3	7.9	4.4	1.4	38.0	91.1	24 772	6 311	259	113	6	132	301
Appomattox	6.1	18.5	7.1	27.8	25.6	8.2	5.0	1.6	39.1	94.8	10 408	3 140	18	23	3	36	77
Arlington	5.5	11.0	10.4	42.4	21.3	4.4	3.6	1.3	34.0	101.5	130 601	17 705	662	16 327	143	15 786	8 229
Augusta	5.7	18.1	6.9	29.8	26.8	7.4	4.1	1.3	39.0	101.1	62 347	2 360	101	185	15	210	397
Bath	4.4	16.6	5.5	28.2	28.5	10.2	5.0	1.6	41.8	100.6	4 659	317	11	19	3	5	34
Bedford	5.8	18.2	5.8	29.9	27.5	7.8	3.9	1.1	39.7	99.5	55 649	3 767	119	261	9	121	445
Bland	4.5	14.9	7.6	30.6	27.9	8.2	4.7	1.6	40.3	119.9	6 515	288	6	8	1	6	47
Botetourt	5.7	17.7	5.8	28.9	28.8	8.1	4.0	1.1	40.7	99.7	28 944	1 073	66	144	1	59	209
Brunswick	5.0	15.5	9.9	30.7	24.4	8.3	4.7	1.5	38.1	113.1	7 734	10 472	16	40	1	62	94
Buchanan	4.8	16.6	8.5	31.2	27.5	6.9	3.5	1.1	38.8	102.9	26 101	708	16	37	1	26	89
Buckingham	5.0	17.4	7.5	31.9	24.6	7.4	4.6	1.5	38.2	121.6	9 235	6 102	32	27	1	57	169
Campbell	5.8	18.1	7.7	29.3	25.6	7.9	4.4	1.2	38.3	95.3	42 516	7 516	99	315	3	170	459
Caroline	6.2	18.5	7.4	29.9	25.0	7.1	4.3	1.5	37.7	99.1	13 842	7 604	172	79	6	116	302
Carroll	5.6	15.5	7.2	28.0	26.7	9.5	5.6	1.8	40.7	97.2	28 651	129	40	29	–	240	156
Charles City	5.6	16.5	7.5	28.9	28.8	8.0	3.6	1.0	39.9	96.3	2 470	3 799	543	7	–	12	95
Charlotte	5.5	18.8	7.2	26.2	24.9	9.3	6.4	1.8	40.0	92.0	8 171	4 102	18	20	–	87	74
Chesterfield	6.7	21.5	7.7	31.2	24.9	4.8	2.6	.7	35.7	95.0	199 447	46 195	851	6 154	111	3 472	3 673
Clarke	5.2	18.2	5.8	29.1	27.1	8.1	4.8	1.7	40.6	98.0	11 532	852	24	62	4	70	108
Craig	5.7	17.9	6.4	29.7	26.7	7.7	4.4	1.5	39.6	103.4	5 037	10	11	8	–	7	18
Culpeper	6.4	19.3	8.1	31.1	23.3	6.7	3.9	1.2	36.5	103.3	26 816	6 220	112	225	5	394	490
Cumberland	6.3	18.5	7.3	28.0	25.1	8.6	4.6	1.6	38.4	91.0	5 444	3 376	16	32	–	53	96
Dickenson	5.3	16.7	8.9	27.6	26.9	8.2	4.7	1.5	39.7	95.7	16 224	58	19	12	–	9	73
Dinwiddie	5.6	18.4	6.7	30.9	26.2	7.0	4.2	1.0	38.5	98.8	15 837	8 257	55	76	10	97	201
Essex	5.2	17.7	7.0	27.0	25.7	9.0	6.0	2.3	40.3	89.9	5 790	3 900	55	81	3	32	128
Fairfax	7.0	18.4	7.5	33.9	25.3	4.6	2.6	.7	35.9	98.6	677 904	83 098	2 561	126 038	691	44 019	35 438
Fauquier	6.4	20.4	6.4	30.3	26.0	5.9	3.4	1.2	37.8	97.7	48 740	4 844	146	324	19	331	735
Floyd	5.6	16.6	6.9	27.6	27.4	8.0	5.7	2.2	40.5	97.5	13 418	277	12	13	2	50	102
Fluvanna	6.5	17.1	6.4	31.7	24.4	9.2	3.8	1.0	38.3	86.6	15 925	3 690	38	77	8	59	250
Franklin	5.4	16.8	8.1	28.2	27.2	8.4	4.6	1.4	39.7	97.2	42 063	4 420	89	169	11	198	336
Frederick	6.5	19.9	7.0	31.9	24.1	6.2	3.4	1.1	36.7	100.1	56 240	1 550	92	388	10	329	600
Giles	5.7	16.4	6.8	28.4	26.1	8.7	6.3	1.7	40.2	95.6	16 226	263	23	31	–	26	88
Gloucester	5.8	20.4	6.8	30.4	24.8	6.6	3.8	1.5	38.0	96.5	30 148	3 585	146	240	18	140	503
Goochland	5.2	16.1	5.3	32.1	28.9	7.7	3.5	1.3	40.5	101.5	12 261	4 324	33	80	2	33	130
Grayson	4.8	14.7	7.6	29.8	26.2	9.5	5.6	1.8	40.5	107.7	16 429	1 217	21	12	5	125	108
Greene	7.5	19.8	6.7	33.2	23.0	5.4	3.2	1.2	35.5	98.4	13 871	983	29	68	5	98	190
Greensville	3.8	14.4	7.4	38.7	24.2	6.7	3.6	1.2	38.1	160.9	4 502	6 907	12	46	2	54	37
Halifax	5.9	17.5	6.9	26.3	26.3	8.7	6.2	2.1	40.7	90.8	22 531	14 204	74	91	2	166	287
Hanover	6.5	20.6	6.9	30.7	24.8	6.1	3.6	1.0	37.4	96.9	76 242	8 065	289	686	7	316	715
Henrico	6.8	17.8	7.8	32.9	22.2	6.2	4.6	1.7	36.0	88.2	180 761	64 805	920	9 451	82	2 562	3 719
Henry	5.5	16.8	7.5	29.0	26.1	8.7	4.9	1.4	39.3	95.1	43 118	13 127	93	236	19	804	533
Highland	3.7	16.2	4.1	24.5	31.2	10.4	8.2	1.8	46.0	97.8	2 517	2	3	3	–	2	9
Isle of Wight	6.0	19.4	6.6	29.6	26.2	7.2	3.9	1.1	38.9	95.7	21 130	8 071	78	101	8	83	257
James City	5.6	17.7	6.4	27.3	26.1	9.5	5.5	1.8	40.8	93.9	39 467	6 910	134	702	22	213	654
King and Queen	5.4	17.4	7.0	26.8	27.0	8.8	5.8	1.8	40.9	95.2	4 059	2 365	94	18	1	10	83
King George	7.6	20.2	8.2	31.7	22.7	5.3	3.2	1.1	35.1	101.0	13 055	3 148	80	169	12	76	263
King William	6.9	19.2	5.9	31.5	24.8	6.6	3.8	1.3	37.0	96.9	9 703	2 999	202	48	–	43	151
Lancaster	4.2	14.8	5.0	19.6	28.0	14.1	10.5	3.9	49.8	86.8	8 091	3 340	16	39	7	11	63
Lee	5.8	16.9	8.0	27.5	26.3	8.2	5.5	1.8	39.7	94.2	23 221	103	53	42	1	19	150
Loudoun	9.7	20.1	5.7	38.9	20.0	3.2	1.9	.6	33.6	97.8	140 419	11 683	358	9 067	105	3 837	4 130
Louisa	5.9	18.5	6.6	29.9	26.2	7.5	4.1	1.3	38.8	96.9	19 617	5 530	108	64	3	46	259
Lunenburg	4.9	16.4	8.0	28.1	25.8	9.2	6.1	1.5	40.5	113.8	7 772	5 072	21	27	6	98	150
Madison	5.8	18.3	6.9	27.6	26.4	8.2	4.8	2.1	40.0	95.0	10 856	1 429	17	63	3	36	116
Mathews	4.6	15.3	5.2	23.1	30.1	11.4	7.4	2.9	46.2	93.2	8 038	1 036	23	17	–	29	64
Mecklenburg	5.4	16.2	7.2	27.4	26.0	10.2	6.0	1.6	40.9	97.3	19 181	12 654	67	98	4	157	219
Middlesex	3.8	15.4	5.1	22.9	30.3	12.5	7.5	2.5	46.8	92.5	7 797	1 999	25	12	–	41	58
Montgomery	4.8	12.4	31.3	25.6	17.3	4.7	2.9	1.0	25.9	110.0	75 270	3 055	151	3 320	30	526	1 277
Nelson	5.3	16.4	6.4	25.6	29.6	9.8	5.4	1.6	42.8	94.8	11 939	2 151	27	34	9	90	195
New Kent	5.6	19.3	5.9	32.0	27.7	5.8	2.9	.7	38.4	102.6	10 805	2 181	173	72	2	71	158
Northampton	5.5	17.7	7.1	23.6	24.8	11.5	7.0	2.7	42.4	87.9	6 977	5 634	22	26	3	278	153
Northumberland	4.3	14.3	4.8	20.2	30.1	15.0	8.8	2.3	50.1	91.2	8 849	3 259	18	24	–	40	69
Nottoway	5.6	17.3	8.1	29.3	22.6	8.8	6.1	2.2	38.6	106.6	8 988	6 378	21	61	5	159	113
Orange	6.0	17.0	6.5	27.8	25.6	9.9	5.6	1.6	40.4	93.8	21 833	3 566	53	88	5	102	234
Page	5.5	17.4	7.7	28.3	25.3	8.7	5.3	1.7	39.0	96.2	22 311	501	34	55	6	112	158
Patrick	5.7	16.0	7.1	28.0	26.7	8.9	5.6	2.0	40.5	96.9	17 805	1 203	41	32	7	182	137
Pittsylvania	5.7	17.4	7.2	28.8	26.6	8.1	4.8	1.4	39.6	95.4	46 311	14 606	88	117	3	230	390
Powhatan	5.8	18.1	7.3	34.7	25.6	5.2	2.6	.6	36.8	122.3	18 237	3 784	46	46	1	74	189

[1] Includes all other responses not included in the other five race categories shown. Also includes write-in entries such as multiracial, mixed, interracial, or a Hispanic/Latino group.   [2] Refers to combinations of two or more of the six race categories shown under one race.

Source: Population by Age, Sex, and Race—U.S. Census Bureau; 2000 Census of Population and Housing, "Census 2000 Profiles of General Demographic Characteristics" data files, published May 2001 (related Internet site <http://www.census.gov/mp/www/pub/2000cen/mscen01.html>).

Table B–2. Counties — **Population by Age, Sex, and Race**–Con.

[Includes U.S., states, and 3,142 counties/county equivalents defined as of January 1, 1992. For changes to these areas since January 1, 1992, see appendix B. Geographic Information]

County	Under 5 years	5 to 17 years	18 to 24 years	25 to 44 years	45 to 64 years	65 to 74 years	75 to 84 years	85 years and over	Median age (years)	Males per 100 females, 2000 (April 1)	White	Black or African American	American Indian and Alaska Native	Asian	Native Hawaiian and Other Pacific Islander	Some other race[1]	Two or more races[2]
VIRGINIA—Con.																	
Prince Edward	5.0	15.3	23.5	22.5	19.6	6.9	5.0	2.3	31.5	95.7	12 260	7 063	36	108	20	45	188
Prince George	6.0	19.1	13.6	33.3	20.8	4.5	2.2	.5	32.1	117.0	20 135	10 753	140	573	51	723	672
Prince William	8.5	21.9	8.8	35.2	20.8	3.0	1.4	.4	31.9	99.5	193 574	52 691	1 094	10 701	368	12 207	10 178
Pulaski	5.5	15.1	7.3	29.2	27.7	8.2	5.3	1.6	40.3	97.4	32 529	1 957	54	114	13	131	329
Rappahannock	5.1	17.2	5.6	26.4	31.8	8.1	4.4	1.2	42.6	98.8	6 469	380	11	15	–	28	80
Richmond	4.1	14.3	8.0	31.8	24.1	8.6	6.2	2.9	40.3	127.6	5 706	2 922	8	28	6	75	64
Roanoke	5.3	17.4	6.6	27.5	27.2	8.4	5.5	2.0	40.9	89.6	80 312	2 876	105	1 377	14	334	760
Rockbridge	5.4	16.8	7.9	27.2	27.1	9.3	4.9	1.4	40.4	100.4	19 856	617	54	92	1	25	163
Rockingham	6.3	18.4	8.7	28.9	23.8	7.5	4.8	1.7	37.5	97.0	65 406	924	85	199	7	610	494
Russell	5.4	15.8	8.6	30.9	26.0	7.6	4.2	1.5	38.7	102.7	29 118	934	34	15	1	86	120
Scott	5.1	15.5	7.5	27.3	26.8	9.6	6.0	2.2	41.4	93.3	23 055	139	32	17	4	35	121
Shenandoah	5.6	16.7	6.6	27.6	26.2	9.4	6.0	1.9	40.9	94.9	33 533	412	62	122	6	628	312
Smyth	5.3	16.3	8.0	28.1	26.0	8.9	5.6	1.8	40.0	93.8	32 043	619	51	61	1	107	199
Southampton	5.1	17.6	8.8	29.2	25.0	7.4	5.4	1.4	38.6	111.7	9 783	7 495	35	32	1	44	92
Spotsylvania	7.6	22.4	7.3	32.2	22.2	4.8	2.7	.8	34.3	97.1	74 924	11 255	288	1 243	45	941	1 699
Stafford	7.8	23.8	7.8	33.7	21.1	3.5	1.8	.6	33.1	101.1	75 807	11 211	417	1 512	93	1 123	2 283
Surry	5.6	19.6	7.2	27.8	25.7	7.7	5.0	1.3	39.4	93.7	3 201	3 524	17	9	2	17	59
Sussex	4.6	15.0	9.0	34.4	23.6	7.1	4.6	1.7	37.6	135.1	4 550	7 769	16	15	2	68	84
Tazewell	5.3	16.2	8.4	27.2	27.5	8.6	5.3	1.7	40.7	92.0	42 886	1 020	74	272	–	70	276
Warren	6.6	18.9	7.6	30.6	23.9	6.8	4.3	1.3	37.1	96.7	29 280	1 526	84	136	7	145	406
Washington	5.1	15.7	8.7	28.3	26.9	8.7	5.0	1.6	40.3	94.2	49 854	676	58	137	13	69	296
Westmoreland	5.2	17.8	6.3	23.9	27.8	10.6	6.5	1.9	42.8	92.3	10 936	5 164	47	61	2	292	216
Wise	5.8	17.2	10.2	28.0	24.8	7.6	4.9	1.5	37.8	95.0	38 870	713	64	121	4	106	245
Wythe	5.5	16.4	7.6	28.9	25.9	8.7	5.2	2.0	39.4	91.4	26 429	791	44	105	4	65	161
York	6.3	22.8	6.6	30.7	24.4	5.6	2.8	.7	36.5	96.5	45 038	7 533	195	1 829	65	509	1 128
Independent Cities																	
Alexandria	6.2	10.6	9.2	43.5	21.5	4.4	3.3	1.3	34.4	93.5	76 702	28 915	355	7 249	112	9 467	5 483
Bedford	5.6	16.0	7.2	27.8	20.7	9.7	9.0	3.9	40.9	90.6	4 745	1 410	15	36	5	15	73
Bristol	5.3	15.0	8.6	26.2	24.4	10.2	7.7	2.6	41.3	82.0	16 072	967	43	64	2	32	187
Buena Vista	6.2	16.3	10.6	26.0	24.6	8.5	5.5	2.2	37.9	86.5	5 940	305	19	27	1	5	52
Charlottesville	4.4	10.8	33.8	25.8	15.2	5.1	3.6	1.3	25.6	87.5	31 337	10 009	49	2 223	15	458	958
Chesapeake	7.2	21.6	8.2	32.3	21.7	5.1	3.1	.8	34.7	94.4	133 193	56 823	770	3 673	101	1 400	3 224
Clifton Forge	5.3	15.8	6.7	25.4	23.2	10.6	9.0	4.1	42.9	78.9	3 558	627	4	2	–	21	77
Colonial Heights	5.3	17.3	8.3	26.8	23.7	9.6	7.0	2.0	39.9	87.8	15 052	1 059	32	459	14	108	173
Covington	6.3	15.2	8.2	26.3	23.9	9.9	7.3	3.0	40.5	91.6	5 298	828	22	41	1	13	100
Danville	6.0	17.3	8.0	25.5	23.6	9.7	7.4	2.5	40.5	83.5	26 075	21 352	81	291	14	219	379
Emporia	6.2	19.0	8.1	25.6	20.6	8.9	8.0	3.7	38.8	83.4	2 405	3 181	4	30	4	17	24
Fairfax	6.0	14.5	9.2	33.7	23.8	6.8	4.4	1.6	37.0	95.2	15 675	1 090	73	2 617	16	1 326	701
Falls Church	5.5	17.9	5.1	31.1	28.1	5.1	5.1	2.0	39.7	94.8	8 817	340	25	675	7	261	252
Franklin	5.1	20.1	7.7	24.9	23.9	8.6	6.6	3.2	39.9	79.2	3 816	4 366	12	65	1	16	70
Fredericksburg	5.8	11.9	23.8	27.2	18.4	6.3	4.8	1.7	30.3	81.8	14 108	3 935	65	291	11	494	375
Galax	6.4	16.6	7.9	26.4	23.5	9.8	6.7	2.6	39.8	90.6	5 887	428	31	48	1	377	65
Hampton	6.3	17.9	12.6	32.5	20.4	5.8	3.6	.9	34.0	98.3	72 556	65 428	616	2 694	136	1 505	3 502
Harrisonburg	4.7	10.7	40.9	21.2	13.2	4.3	3.6	1.4	22.6	90.0	34 334	2 394	76	1 257	10	1 355	1 042
Hopewell	7.5	19.2	9.1	28.6	21.0	7.8	5.1	1.7	35.0	87.7	13 924	7 484	79	180	16	275	396
Lexington	3.0	8.0	41.4	14.5	16.7	7.7	6.1	2.6	23.3	123.2	5 906	713	18	132	1	33	64
Lynchburg	5.8	16.3	15.5	25.3	20.8	7.5	6.1	2.7	35.1	84.2	43 487	19 382	169	838	28	413	952
Manassas	8.6	21.0	9.8	35.8	19.4	3.1	1.7	.6	31.3	103.5	25 316	4 535	128	1 206	31	2 773	1 146
Manassas Park	10.0	21.1	8.7	40.1	15.9	3.0	1.0	.2	30.3	103.8	7 490	1 149	45	418	7	838	343
Martinsville	5.6	16.9	7.0	26.7	23.2	9.7	7.8	3.2	40.8	82.4	8 537	6 559	16	72	–	107	125
Newport News	7.9	19.6	11.5	32.2	18.8	5.4	3.6	1.0	32.0	93.8	96 383	70 388	752	4 195	214	3 225	4 993
Norfolk	7.1	17.0	18.2	29.9	16.9	5.5	4.1	1.2	29.6	104.6	113 358	103 387	1 071	6 593	251	3 923	5 820
Norton	5.1	16.6	10.2	27.3	25.4	8.1	5.2	1.9	39.0	81.8	3 575	240	3	39	5	7	35
Petersburg	6.4	18.7	8.9	27.5	22.9	8.0	5.6	2.0	36.9	84.2	6 249	26 643	67	236	9	198	338
Poquoson	5.1	21.7	6.4	26.7	28.7	6.6	3.4	1.3	39.5	100.2	11 134	78	27	182	4	31	110
Portsmouth	7.1	18.6	11.1	29.1	20.3	6.8	5.4	1.5	34.5	93.5	46 096	50 899	478	775	67	618	1 632
Radford	3.5	9.4	44.0	19.6	14.3	4.9	3.4	1.0	22.8	83.5	13 990	1 284	39	226	4	77	239
Richmond	6.3	15.6	13.1	31.7	20.1	6.5	4.9	1.8	33.9	87.1	75 744	113 108	479	2 471	157	2 948	2 883
Roanoke	6.5	16.1	8.2	30.5	22.3	7.8	6.3	2.3	37.6	88.3	65 848	25 380	190	1 096	23	685	1 689
Salem	4.9	16.0	11.7	26.7	24.0	8.8	6.0	2.0	39.2	89.3	22 738	1 455	32	241	6	61	214
South Boston	X	X	X	X	X	X	X	X	X	X	X	X	X	X	X	X	X
Staunton	5.2	14.6	10.2	27.8	24.1	8.9	6.7	2.5	39.8	89.1	19 866	3 328	52	110	2	125	370
Suffolk	7.3	20.6	7.1	31.1	22.5	6.3	3.9	1.2	36.0	91.4	34 271	27 718	191	491	15	233	758
Virginia Beach	7.2	20.3	10.0	34.3	19.8	4.9	2.7	.8	32.7	98.0	303 681	80 593	1 619	20 869	416	6 402	11 677
Waynesboro	6.6	17.3	7.9	27.4	23.2	8.9	6.6	2.1	38.9	88.1	16 877	1 945	61	112	6	213	306
Williamsburg	2.7	6.9	46.0	17.7	15.0	5.9	4.3	1.4	22.6	81.3	9 543	1 601	32	549	6	90	176
Winchester	6.1	15.6	13.1	29.8	20.9	7.7	5.2	1.6	35.2	94.1	19 355	2 470	56	375	8	817	504

[1] Includes all other responses not included in the other five race categories shown. Also includes write-in entries such as multiracial, mixed, interracial, or a Hispanic/Latino group. [2] Refers to combinations of two or more of the six race categories shown under one race.

Source: Population by Age, Sex, and Race—U.S. Census Bureau; 2000 Census of Population and Housing, "Census 2000 Profiles of General Demographic Characteristics" data files, published May 2001 (related Internet site <http://www.census.gov/mp/www/pub/2000cen/mscen01.html>).

Table B–2. Counties — **Population by Age, Sex, and Race**–Con.

[Includes U.S., states, and 3,142 counties/county equivalents defined as of January 1, 1992. For changes to these areas since January 1, 1992, see appendix B. Geographic Information]

County	Population by age, 2000 (April 1) Percent— Under 5 years	5 to 17 years	18 to 24 years	25 to 44 years	45 to 64 years	65 to 74 years	75 to 84 years	85 years and over	Median age (years)	Males per 100 females, 2000 (April 1)	Population by race, 2000 (April 1) One race White	Black or African American	American Indian and Alaska Native	Asian	Native Hawaiian and Other Pacific Islander	Some other race[1]	Two or more races[2]
WASHINGTON..........	6.7	19.0	9.5	30.8	22.8	5.7	4.1	1.4	35.3	99.1	4 821 823	190 267	93 301	322 335	23 953	228 923	213 519
Adams	9.4	24.7	9.8	26.3	19.4	5.7	3.5	1.2	29.6	104.5	10 672	46	112	99	6	5 042	451
Asotin	6.8	18.7	8.1	26.1	24.0	8.0	5.8	2.5	38.8	91.1	19 650	39	260	105	5	129	363
Benton	7.6	22.2	8.6	28.5	22.9	5.5	3.7	1.1	34.4	98.7	122 879	1 319	1 165	3 134	163	9 986	3 829
Chelan	7.1	20.8	8.3	27.2	22.7	6.9	5.0	1.9	36.3	99.1	55 711	172	661	451	77	8 121	1 423
Clallam	5.1	16.8	7.1	22.8	26.9	10.8	8.0	2.4	43.8	98.7	57 505	545	3 303	731	104	761	1 576
Clark	7.8	20.9	8.4	30.8	22.6	5.0	3.4	1.1	34.2	98.5	306 648	5 813	2 910	11 095	1 274	6 857	10 641
Columbia	5.3	18.6	7.0	22.8	27.7	9.2	7.3	2.0	42.4	95.2	3 809	9	39	17	2	111	77
Cowlitz	6.7	20.1	8.3	27.5	24.1	6.8	4.7	1.8	36.9	98.2	85 326	482	1 417	1 206	124	1 958	2 435
Douglas	7.6	21.9	8.2	27.3	22.4	6.8	4.5	1.4	35.7	98.2	27 599	101	355	178	31	3 530	809
Ferry	5.4	21.4	7.6	23.4	29.5	7.7	4.0	1.0	40.0	107.7	5 480	15	1 327	21	4	162	251
Franklin	10.0	24.6	10.9	28.1	17.9	4.7	3.0	.8	28.0	109.1	30 553	1 230	362	800	57	14 300	2 045
Garfield...............	4.6	21.4	5.4	21.9	25.9	10.2	7.8	2.9	43.0	97.9	2 312	–	9	16	1	33	26
Grant	8.7	23.3	9.8	27.0	19.7	6.3	4.1	1.2	31.1	104.5	57 174	742	863	652	53	12 967	2 247
Grays Harbor	6.2	19.4	7.9	26.0	25.0	8.0	5.6	1.8	38.8	98.8	59 335	226	3 132	818	73	1 527	2 083
Island	6.7	18.8	8.5	28.0	23.7	7.7	5.2	1.3	37.0	100.4	62 374	1 691	693	3 001	314	1 025	2 460
Jefferson	4.1	15.7	5.0	21.6	32.5	11.7	7.3	2.1	47.1	95.8	23 920	110	599	309	34	197	784
King	6.1	16.4	9.3	34.7	23.1	5.1	3.9	1.4	35.7	99.1	1 315 507	93 875	15 922	187 745	9 013	44 473	70 499
Kitsap	6.7	20.1	9.2	29.6	23.8	5.4	3.8	1.3	35.8	102.7	195 481	6 648	3 760	10 192	1 805	3 309	10 774
Kittitas...............	5.1	15.5	21.6	24.6	21.6	5.9	4.0	1.7	31.4	98.7	30 617	236	303	731	49	768	658
Klickitat..............	6.4	20.7	6.5	25.7	27.0	7.5	4.6	1.7	39.5	99.5	16 778	51	665	139	41	961	526
Lewis	6.4	20.1	8.2	25.2	24.5	7.9	5.6	2.0	38.4	98.3	63 772	259	840	475	122	1 751	1 381
Lincoln	5.7	19.5	5.2	23.2	27.4	9.7	6.5	2.8	42.8	98.4	9 740	23	166	25	7	59	164
Mason..................	5.4	18.1	7.7	26.5	25.8	9.5	5.4	1.5	40.3	107.0	43 705	587	1 840	519	221	1 036	1 497
Okanogan	6.3	21.4	7.3	25.5	25.5	7.8	4.6	1.7	38.2	99.2	29 799	109	4 537	176	28	3 791	1 124
Pacific................	4.6	16.9	6.0	21.2	28.9	12.4	7.8	2.4	45.8	98.3	18 998	42	513	436	19	384	592
Pend Oreille...........	5.4	20.9	5.5	23.8	29.5	8.9	4.9	1.1	41.9	100.5	10 973	17	338	74	24	67	239
Pierce.................	7.1	20.1	9.8	31.3	21.5	5.4	3.6	1.2	34.1	98.9	549 369	48 730	9 963	35 583	5 922	15 410	35 843
San Juan	3.7	15.4	4.5	21.7	35.7	10.1	6.9	2.0	47.4	95.1	13 372	36	117	125	12	128	287
Skagit	6.5	19.8	8.6	26.9	23.6	7.3	5.4	1.9	37.2	98.0	89 070	450	1 909	1 538	163	7 381	2 468
Skamania..............	6.4	20.2	6.7	28.6	27.1	6.4	3.5	1.1	38.7	101.3	9 093	30	217	53	17	240	222
Snohomish.............	7.2	20.2	8.5	33.0	22.0	4.7	3.3	1.1	34.7	100.1	518 948	10 113	8 250	35 030	1 705	11 629	20 349
Spokane...............	6.6	19.1	10.6	28.9	22.4	6.0	4.6	1.8	35.4	96.4	381 934	6 659	5 847	7 870	666	3 410	11 553
Stevens...............	6.1	22.6	6.4	24.9	27.1	7.1	4.2	1.6	39.2	99.1	36 078	111	2 266	193	66	271	1 081
Thurston..............	6.2	19.1	9.3	29.3	24.6	5.8	4.2	1.4	36.5	96.0	177 617	4 881	3 143	9 145	1 078	3 506	7 985
Wahkiakum.............	5.3	18.1	5.3	22.2	30.6	9.9	6.7	1.8	44.4	100.1	3 574	10	60	18	3	63	96
Walla Walla	6.3	18.3	13.4	26.5	20.8	6.6	5.7	2.4	34.9	103.8	47 081	930	465	614	123	4 548	1 419
Whatcom	6.1	18.0	14.2	27.5	22.5	5.9	4.2	1.5	34.0	97.1	147 485	1 150	4 709	4 637	235	4 159	4 439
Whitman	4.8	13.2	32.6	24.0	16.0	4.4	3.5	1.3	24.7	102.5	35 880	623	298	2 260	109	498	1 072
Yakima	8.7	23.1	9.8	27.5	19.7	5.6	4.0	1.6	31.2	99.6	146 005	2 157	9 966	2 124	203	54 375	7 751
WEST VIRGINIA	5.6	16.6	9.5	27.7	25.2	8.2	5.3	1.8	38.9	94.6	1 718 777	57 232	3 606	9 434	400	3 107	15 788
Barbour	5.3	17.7	9.4	26.8	25.2	8.2	5.3	2.2	38.7	96.7	15 147	77	111	40	3	19	160
Berkeley..............	6.6	19.1	8.3	31.3	23.6	6.6	3.6	1.0	35.8	99.1	70 392	3 558	186	350	17	428	974
Boone.................	6.3	16.9	9.0	28.0	26.3	7.5	4.7	1.4	38.8	95.5	25 160	167	31	18	4	17	138
Braxton...............	5.3	17.5	7.5	28.1	25.8	8.2	5.5	2.2	39.6	102.6	14 411	101	51	16	7	12	104
Brooke................	5.0	15.4	9.4	25.8	26.0	9.6	6.7	2.0	41.2	91.8	24 913	216	25	87	9	22	175
Cabell................	5.4	14.6	13.5	26.8	23.6	8.4	5.8	1.8	37.5	91.4	90 370	4 150	174	749	38	196	1 107
Calhoun	5.1	17.3	8.0	25.9	27.1	9.0	5.4	2.3	41.3	99.7	7 499	8	23	8	1	10	33
Clay..................	6.1	19.5	9.0	27.5	24.2	8.0	4.0	1.6	36.8	97.9	10 146	8	73	2	–	9	92
Doddridge.............	5.9	19.1	8.4	26.6	25.1	8.4	4.8	1.6	38.7	101.9	7 278	20	23	11	–	10	61
Fayette...............	5.6	16.1	9.6	27.1	25.1	8.6	5.8	2.1	39.6	98.2	44 125	2 650	130	144	17	70	443
Gilmer................	4.9	15.4	16.4	24.5	23.5	8.2	4.9	2.3	36.8	101.1	6 969	65	14	41	1	7	63
Grant	6.3	16.4	7.8	27.5	26.8	8.2	5.2	1.9	39.3	97.7	11 110	76	29	16	2	15	51
Greenbrier	5.5	16.1	7.7	26.1	26.9	9.5	6.0	2.3	41.6	92.5	32 810	1 048	116	64	2	53	360
Hampshire	6.1	19.0	7.1	27.6	25.6	8.4	4.7	1.5	38.5	99.7	19 807	167	48	33	4	25	119
Hancock	5.3	15.5	7.2	27.1	26.4	9.9	6.6	1.9	41.7	92.4	31 497	752	39	114	3	38	224
Hardy	6.0	17.4	7.6	28.8	25.4	8.5	4.9	1.5	38.8	97.5	12 273	244	20	18	–	29	85
Harrison	5.7	17.4	8.3	27.5	24.5	8.3	6.1	2.1	39.2	91.8	66 282	1 105	102	408	19	145	591
Jackson	6.1	18.1	7.9	27.7	24.9	8.9	4.8	1.7	38.8	94.8	27 649	23	58	64	4	29	173
Jefferson	6.3	17.6	10.0	29.9	25.1	6.3	3.8	1.1	36.8	97.9	38 400	2 571	120	252	17	254	576
Kanawha	5.7	15.6	8.4	28.1	25.6	8.7	5.9	1.9	40.2	90.7	180 989	13 955	420	1 697	42	425	2 545
Lewis	5.3	16.8	7.7	28.0	25.9	8.6	5.6	2.2	40.1	94.2	16 681	22	34	49	–	14	119
Lincoln	6.0	17.6	9.3	29.1	24.9	7.7	4.0	1.4	37.4	97.2	21 895	13	37	13	2	13	135
Logan	5.7	16.4	9.3	28.0	26.1	8.4	4.8	1.3	39.3	94.2	36 325	975	44	113	8	22	223
McDowell...............	5.1	18.0	7.9	26.8	26.1	8.5	5.8	1.8	40.5	90.4	23 792	3 250	46	16	2	20	203

[1] Includes all other responses not included in the other five race categories shown. Also includes write-in entries such as multiracial, mixed, interracial, or a Hispanic/Latino group. [2] Refers to combinations of two or more of the six race categories shown under one race.

Source: Population by Age, Sex, and Race—U.S. Census Bureau; 2000 Census of Population and Housing, "Census 2000 Profiles of General Demographic Characteristics" data files, published May 2001 (related Internet site <http://www.census.gov/mp/www/pub/2000cen/mscen01.html>).

[Includes U.S., states, and 3,142 counties/county equivalents defined as of January 1, 1992. For changes to these areas since January 1, 1992, see appendix B. Geographic Information]

County	Under 5 years	5 to 17 years	18 to 24 years	25 to 44 years	45 to 64 years	65 to 74 years	75 to 84 years	85 years and over	Median age (years)	Males per 100 females, 2000 (April 1)	White	Black or African American	American Indian and Alaska Native	Asian	Native Hawaiian and Other Pacific Islander	Some other race[1]	Two or more races[2]
WEST VIRGINIA—Con.																	
Marion	5.1	15.5	10.5	26.4	24.7	8.7	6.8	2.3	39.9	90.6	53 823	1 823	114	231	5	74	528
Marshall	5.3	17.5	7.3	27.1	26.4	8.8	5.8	1.7	40.4	94.8	34 949	153	38	90	9	41	239
Mason	5.9	16.9	8.3	27.7	26.1	8.7	5.0	1.5	39.7	96.2	25 533	130	47	71	2	28	146
Mercer	5.8	15.3	9.8	26.2	25.5	9.0	6.3	2.0	40.2	91.1	58 295	3 668	122	288	8	66	533
Mineral	5.5	17.8	8.6	27.1	25.9	8.1	5.3	1.7	39.1	95.8	26 037	690	31	54	2	57	207
Mingo	5.8	18.4	9.2	29.1	25.0	7.2	4.1	1.1	37.2	93.7	27 233	661	68	58	6	17	210
Monongalia	4.9	13.3	23.4	27.7	20.0	5.6	3.8	1.3	30.4	101.8	75 500	2 763	162	2 009	34	264	1 134
Monroe	5.0	15.2	8.1	30.3	26.1	8.4	5.4	1.6	39.7	79.7	13 514	872	33	23	2	5	134
Morgan	6.1	16.3	6.8	27.3	26.9	9.8	5.2	1.6	40.7	96.6	14 689	89	26	18	2	34	85
Nicholas	5.4	17.9	8.1	27.6	26.0	8.3	5.0	1.7	39.4	95.6	26 255	14	65	50	6	27	145
Ohio	5.2	16.1	10.5	25.1	24.4	9.3	7.2	2.3	40.6	87.8	44 820	1 691	42	369	14	61	430
Pendleton	5.4	16.5	7.3	27.0	26.1	9.5	6.0	2.3	41.1	101.3	7 896	174	22	15	3	23	63
Pleasants	5.9	17.9	7.8	28.7	24.8	7.9	5.4	1.6	38.9	100.2	7 386	36	35	15	–	5	37
Pocahontas	5.0	15.9	7.0	27.5	27.4	9.3	5.6	2.4	41.9	106.2	8 983	71	6	13	–	5	53
Preston	5.6	18.1	8.0	27.8	25.6	8.1	5.1	1.7	39.1	98.2	28 995	86	32	43	5	14	159
Putnam	6.5	18.4	7.6	30.4	25.5	6.7	3.8	1.1	37.7	96.7	50 542	287	80	298	11	67	304
Raleigh	5.5	16.0	8.7	28.6	25.7	8.3	5.4	1.7	39.5	96.8	71 006	6 753	147	568	13	99	634
Randolph	5.2	17.1	8.7	28.5	25.4	7.6	5.5	2.0	38.8	101.3	27 609	302	46	106	4	45	150
Ritchie	5.5	17.5	7.7	28.0	26.1	8.0	5.2	2.0	39.9	96.2	10 206	14	28	13	–	11	71
Roane	5.7	17.7	8.7	26.6	26.5	8.1	5.0	1.7	39.5	98.0	15 223	34	32	35	–	29	93
Summers	4.6	15.9	7.5	24.7	27.3	10.7	6.7	2.5	43.4	95.6	12 553	280	33	12	5	13	103
Taylor	5.4	17.5	7.9	28.5	24.9	8.3	5.6	2.0	39.1	95.7	15 779	134	31	27	6	10	102
Tucker	4.8	16.4	6.7	26.4	27.7	9.5	6.1	2.3	42.0	95.2	7 237	5	14	1	9	7	48
Tyler	5.2	18.0	6.5	26.9	26.9	9.2	5.3	1.9	40.8	95.5	9 530	2	5	8	1	3	43
Upshur	5.3	17.2	12.6	25.7	24.5	7.6	5.0	2.2	37.4	94.2	22 981	144	39	72	3	30	135
Wayne	5.8	17.6	8.7	27.7	25.3	8.6	5.0	1.3	38.4	95.8	42 382	54	99	86	8	35	239
Webster	5.1	17.8	8.0	26.7	27.1	8.2	5.2	1.9	40.4	96.9	9 639	1	7	6	1	1	64
Wetzel	5.7	18.1	6.8	26.5	26.8	9.0	5.1	2.0	40.4	94.3	17 502	15	17	57	4	5	93
Wirt	5.6	19.8	7.6	29.6	24.4	7.3	4.2	1.5	37.9	100.2	5 788	17	12	6	–	6	44
Wood	5.8	17.2	8.0	27.9	25.6	8.1	5.5	1.9	39.3	92.4	85 627	887	188	448	35	124	677
Wyoming	5.7	16.7	8.7	27.5	27.4	8.4	4.3	1.2	40.1	96.9	25 345	161	31	21	–	19	131
WISCONSIN	6.4	19.1	9.7	29.5	22.2	6.6	4.7	1.8	36.0	97.6	4 769 857	304 460	47 228	88 763	1 630	84 842	66 895
Adams	4.8	16.0	5.6	24.3	28.4	12.9	6.3	1.8	44.5	102.9	18 201	50	110	62	3	62	155
Ashland	6.3	19.1	11.2	25.8	21.7	7.3	6.0	2.7	36.9	97.1	14 690	36	1 745	53	8	49	285
Barron	5.7	19.7	8.1	26.8	23.4	8.1	5.9	2.4	38.9	98.2	43 924	63	363	145	18	142	308
Bayfield	5.3	19.4	5.3	25.2	28.5	8.9	5.6	1.9	42.1	102.2	13 280	20	1 409	41	1	39	223
Brown	6.9	19.2	10.5	31.9	20.9	5.4	3.8	1.5	34.2	98.9	206 688	2 641	5 191	4 935	64	4 300	2 959
Buffalo	5.8	19.3	6.9	27.6	23.7	8.9	5.7	2.2	39.2	100.7	13 623	16	42	45	3	11	64
Burnett	4.9	17.2	6.0	23.2	28.4	11.8	6.2	2.3	44.1	101.5	14 616	56	698	37	11	33	223
Calumet	7.0	21.6	7.2	32.0	21.4	5.7	3.9	1.2	35.2	100.0	39 282	124	139	629	3	154	300
Chippewa	6.3	20.2	7.7	28.2	23.1	7.4	5.1	2.1	37.6	99.1	54 006	89	176	492	8	93	331
Clark	7.6	22.3	7.7	26.2	20.2	7.6	5.9	2.5	35.9	100.5	32 904	43	161	101	3	188	157
Columbia	6.1	19.1	7.1	29.9	23.4	7.2	5.1	2.1	38.0	101.6	50 990	460	185	175	12	232	414
Crawford	5.9	20.2	8.1	25.0	24.8	8.1	5.8	2.1	38.9	102.2	16 780	233	37	45	2	29	117
Dane	6.1	16.5	14.3	32.5	21.3	4.7	3.3	1.3	33.2	97.9	379 447	17 069	1 404	14 735	133	6 118	7 620
Dodge	5.9	18.8	8.3	31.2	21.9	6.8	5.1	2.1	37.0	109.7	81 843	2 142	345	296	25	744	502
Door	4.6	17.5	6.1	25.4	27.7	9.9	6.4	2.5	42.9	97.1	27 356	53	183	81	3	91	194
Douglas	5.9	17.7	10.3	28.0	23.6	7.0	5.5	2.0	37.7	97.2	41 273	246	786	273	12	85	612
Dunn	5.7	17.6	19.8	25.7	19.8	5.6	3.9	1.7	30.6	101.7	38 294	135	107	849	5	148	320
Eau Claire	6.0	17.5	17.1	26.7	20.5	5.9	4.6	1.7	32.4	93.8	88 443	482	500	2 344	31	305	1 037
Florence	4.5	18.4	5.3	27.1	27.3	9.4	5.7	2.4	41.9	104.3	4 995	8	22	14	1	7	41
Fond du Lac	6.0	19.2	9.4	28.7	22.4	7.0	5.2	2.2	36.9	95.3	93 562	876	371	845	28	814	800
Forest	5.7	19.6	7.8	23.9	23.8	10.7	6.2	2.4	39.9	100.2	8 607	118	1 133	17	4	23	122
Grant	5.2	18.5	14.6	24.8	21.6	7.6	5.4	2.3	35.9	103.0	48 719	259	64	230	4	71	250
Green	6.4	20.1	6.7	29.2	22.9	7.0	5.5	2.2	37.9	96.9	33 021	86	70	97	–	120	253
Green Lake	5.6	18.5	6.6	26.2	24.2	9.3	6.7	2.8	40.9	97.0	18 687	29	38	59	7	170	115
Iowa	6.4	20.6	6.6	30.4	22.5	6.9	4.8	1.6	37.1	99.3	22 484	38	25	78	3	26	126
Iron	4.0	15.4	5.9	24.7	26.8	11.7	8.4	3.1	45.0	96.1	6 743	6	41	9	3	4	55
Jackson	5.6	18.5	8.8	29.4	22.8	7.5	5.3	2.1	37.6	114.6	17 109	433	1 176	31	8	193	150
Jefferson	6.3	18.9	8.5	30.4	23.2	6.4	4.5	1.7	36.6	98.4	71 309	210	249	333	14	1 220	686
Juneau	5.9	19.5	6.9	26.6	24.3	8.8	5.9	2.1	39.4	100.1	23 491	81	316	106	4	138	180
Kenosha	6.9	20.1	9.4	31.3	20.7	5.9	4.2	1.5	34.8	98.3	132 193	7 600	564	1 381	57	4 924	2 858
Kewaunee	5.9	19.9	8.0	28.2	22.8	7.1	5.9	2.3	37.5	100.6	19 897	31	55	27	1	61	115
La Crosse	5.9	17.6	15.6	27.5	20.8	6.2	4.6	1.8	33.5	94.1	100 883	1 016	440	3 376	21	286	1 098

[1] Includes all other responses not included in the other five race categories shown. Also includes write-in entries such as multiracial, mixed, interracial, or a Hispanic/Latino group. [2] Refers to combinations of two or more of the six race categories shown under one race.

Source: Population by Age, Sex, and Race—U.S. Census Bureau; 2000 Census of Population and Housing, "Census 2000 Profiles of General Demographic Characteristics" data files, published May 2001 (related Internet site <http://www.census.gov/mp/www/pub/2000cen/mscen01.html>).

[Includes U.S., states, and 3,142 counties/county equivalents defined as of January 1, 1992. For changes to these areas since January 1, 1992, see appendix B. Geographic Information]

County	Population by age, 2000 (April 1) Percent—								Median age (years)	Males per 100 females, 2000 (April 1)	Population by race, 2000 (April 1) One race						Two or more races[2]
	Under 5 years	5 to 17 years	18 to 24 years	25 to 44 years	45 to 64 years	65 to 74 years	75 to 84 years	85 years and over			White	Black or African American	American Indian and Alaska Native	Asian	Native Hawaiian and Other Pacific Islander	Some other race[1]	
WISCONSIN—Con.																	
Lafayette	5.9	21.3	7.6	27.2	22.1	8.3	5.4	2.1	38.1	99.8	15 980	17	18	36	6	23	57
Langlade	5.4	19.0	6.5	26.0	24.3	9.4	6.8	2.6	40.5	98.5	20 311	31	113	57	5	42	181
Lincoln	5.7	19.7	6.9	28.0	23.3	8.2	5.6	2.6	38.9	99.9	28 977	123	130	116	8	86	201
Manitowoc	5.8	19.6	7.6	28.2	23.0	7.7	5.8	2.2	38.3	98.2	79 485	245	356	1 644	34	494	629
Marathon	6.4	20.4	8.2	29.5	22.5	6.4	4.8	1.7	36.3	99.5	118 079	347	435	5 715	26	324	908
Marinette	5.1	18.4	8.1	25.9	25.0	8.7	6.2	2.7	40.5	97.5	42 550	100	215	119	9	91	300
Marquette	4.8	16.2	6.7	28.9	25.0	10.8	5.9	1.7	40.9	118.9	14 828	545	165	42	16	60	176
Menominee	9.5	29.4	8.4	24.7	19.5	6.0	2.1	.3	27.7	97.3	528	3	3 981	–	1	15	34
Milwaukee	7.1	19.2	10.5	30.3	20.0	6.4	4.8	1.8	33.7	92.0	616 973	231 157	6 794	24 145	422	39 931	20 742
Monroe	6.7	21.4	7.7	27.5	22.8	6.9	5.2	1.9	36.8	101.5	39 474	188	376	195	15	347	304
Oconto	5.7	20.0	6.4	28.7	24.0	8.0	5.3	1.8	38.8	101.3	34 836	48	277	72	5	84	312
Oneida	4.7	17.6	5.7	26.5	26.8	10.7	5.9	2.1	42.4	99.2	35 934	121	242	109	17	77	276
Outagamie	6.9	20.8	8.9	31.9	20.7	5.5	3.9	1.5	34.4	99.5	151 101	867	2 471	3 595	56	1 311	1 570
Ozaukee	6.2	20.5	6.8	28.0	25.9	6.9	4.3	1.4	38.9	97.3	79 621	765	162	882	14	276	597
Pepin	5.9	20.6	7.9	25.9	22.8	7.8	6.2	2.9	38.7	101.1	7 134	6	14	15	3	6	35
Pierce	5.7	18.7	17.0	28.1	20.8	4.8	3.5	1.3	32.1	97.3	36 071	91	105	158	10	104	265
Polk	5.9	20.3	6.7	27.7	24.3	7.5	5.4	2.2	38.7	99.9	40 342	63	436	109	9	82	278
Portage	5.9	18.2	16.2	27.7	21.1	5.6	3.8	1.5	33.0	99.4	64 316	215	242	1 511	29	288	581
Price	4.9	19.0	5.8	25.8	25.7	9.2	6.6	3.0	41.7	101.0	15 541	16	95	47	5	23	95
Racine	7.0	20.0	8.3	29.9	22.5	6.4	4.4	1.5	36.1	98.0	156 796	19 777	687	1 363	77	6 972	3 159
Richland	5.6	19.6	8.4	25.5	23.7	8.4	6.3	2.5	39.2	98.2	17 636	27	46	38	5	51	121
Rock	6.7	19.8	8.6	29.8	22.3	6.7	4.4	1.7	35.9	97.0	138 610	7 048	422	1 191	61	2 691	2 284
Rusk	5.4	19.4	7.9	24.8	24.1	9.1	6.7	2.7	40.0	98.5	14 992	79	65	40	15	54	102
St. Croix	7.0	20.9	8.2	32.2	21.9	5.0	3.3	1.5	35.0	100.2	61 796	177	159	389	14	141	479
Sauk	6.5	19.6	7.4	29.3	22.8	7.0	5.3	2.1	37.3	97.7	53 775	142	479	144	9	324	352
Sawyer	5.5	18.6	6.0	24.6	27.4	10.2	5.6	2.1	42.1	101.8	13 236	51	2 603	48	3	56	199
Shawano	6.1	19.5	6.9	27.5	23.1	8.4	6.1	2.3	38.5	99.8	37 251	91	2 545	136	18	128	495
Sheboygan	6.4	19.1	8.4	29.8	22.3	6.7	5.2	2.0	36.8	100.6	104 438	1 224	409	3 698	28	1 642	1 207
Taylor	5.8	21.3	7.6	28.3	21.8	7.3	5.5	2.4	37.4	102.6	19 427	17	37	46	–	37	116
Trempealeau	6.2	19.2	6.9	28.2	23.1	7.5	6.3	2.6	38.3	100.3	26 688	35	45	36	3	77	126
Vernon	6.5	20.9	6.8	25.3	23.5	8.2	6.3	2.5	39.1	97.7	27 723	18	42	60	2	75	136
Vilas	4.3	16.4	5.0	23.1	28.5	13.1	7.4	2.3	45.8	99.1	18 865	43	1 909	38	2	39	137
Walworth	5.9	18.3	13.8	27.6	21.8	6.4	4.4	1.8	35.1	98.9	88 597	790	219	612	24	2 452	1 065
Washburn	5.1	18.7	5.8	24.7	27.1	9.7	6.5	2.3	42.1	101.3	15 599	27	162	30	4	19	195
Washington	6.8	19.9	7.2	31.5	23.4	5.9	4.0	1.4	36.6	99.5	114 778	465	296	674	35	474	771
Waukesha	0.4	19.9	0.0	29.8	25.1	0.5	4.0	1.5	38.1	96.8	345 506	2 646	788	5 381	87	3 128	3 231
Waupaca	6.0	19.6	7.1	27.8	22.7	7.8	6.3	2.6	38.5	100.3	50 660	87	217	139	7	280	341
Waushara	5.0	18.5	6.0	24.9	26.3	10.7	6.3	2.2	42.1	101.6	22 413	62	72	80	7	314	206
Winnebago	6.0	17.8	11.8	30.4	21.5	6.3	4.5	1.8	35.4	99.4	148 795	1 756	726	2 892	32	1 121	1 441
Wood	6.1	19.5	7.7	28.4	22.9	7.3	5.7	2.3	38.0	96.1	72 855	201	528	1 220	7	223	521
WYOMING	6.3	19.8	10.1	28.1	24.0	6.3	4.0	1.4	36.2	101.2	454 670	3 722	11 133	2 771	302	12 301	8 883
Albany	5.1	13.3	28.2	26.1	19.1	4.4	2.9	.9	26.7	106.7	29 235	354	305	545	18	847	710
Big Horn	6.8	21.9	7.3	22.6	24.6	8.4	5.9	2.5	38.7	100.2	10 777	13	86	24	8	386	167
Campbell	7.4	23.7	9.5	32.3	21.9	3.2	1.5	.5	32.2	105.6	32 369	51	313	108	29	378	450
Carbon	5.7	18.4	8.6	28.4	26.7	6.8	4.0	1.4	38.9	115.3	14 092	105	199	105	9	808	321
Converse	6.4	22.1	7.0	28.1	25.4	6.5	3.4	1.1	37.5	99.4	11 416	18	110	32	3	296	177
Crook	5.2	21.7	6.6	24.6	27.2	8.4	4.4	2.0	40.2	102.4	5 761	3	60	4	–	15	44
Fremont	6.5	20.9	8.3	25.9	25.0	7.6	4.2	1.5	37.7	98.2	27 388	44	7 047	106	9	417	793
Goshen	5.8	18.4	9.4	24.3	24.8	8.4	6.4	2.4	40.0	98.9	11 764	25	108	25	15	458	143
Hot Springs	4.8	17.2	5.9	23.3	28.7	10.1	7.2	2.7	44.2	92.7	4 685	17	74	12	–	31	63
Johnson	5.2	19.0	5.6	23.5	28.7	9.7	6.2	2.2	43.0	96.6	6 865	6	45	8	–	39	112
Laramie	6.6	19.2	9.6	30.5	22.7	6.1	3.9	1.4	35.3	100.9	72 563	2 124	693	777	89	3 267	2 094
Lincoln	6.8	24.1	7.2	25.4	24.2	6.9	4.4	1.0	36.8	102.0	14 157	15	83	33	8	103	174
Natrona	6.5	19.5	10.1	27.9	23.3	7.1	4.3	1.3	36.4	97.7	62 644	505	686	277	25	1 275	1 121
Niobrara	4.8	17.8	6.1	26.0	26.6	10.3	5.9	2.5	42.8	95.2	2 360	3	12	3	–	12	17
Park	5.5	18.9	9.1	25.6	26.7	7.6	5.0	1.9	39.8	95.0	24 872	23	122	114	13	364	278
Platte	5.2	20.2	6.6	24.3	27.3	8.5	5.8	2.2	41.2	97.4	8 471	14	44	15	2	149	112
Sheridan	5.3	18.8	8.0	25.3	27.1	7.8	5.6	2.1	40.6	95.9	25 465	49	338	102	33	217	356
Sublette	5.9	19.9	6.0	27.5	28.7	7.2	3.6	1.2	39.8	104.3	5 771	12	29	14	5	31	58
Sweetwater	6.9	22.0	10.1	29.3	23.7	4.3	2.9	.9	34.2	102.4	34 461	275	380	240	16	1 349	892
Teton	5.2	14.7	9.8	38.3	25.0	4.4	1.8	.7	35.0	114.3	17 081	27	97	99	6	718	223
Uinta	8.2	25.2	9.0	29.2	21.4	4.0	2.3	.7	31.4	103.8	18 621	22	172	54	13	564	296
Washakie	5.9	21.4	6.4	25.2	25.3	8.3	5.5	2.1	39.4	99.4	7 478	9	46	61	–	515	180
Weston	5.2	18.8	7.4	26.3	26.7	7.9	5.6	2.0	40.7	103.1	6 374	8	84	13	1	62	102

[1] Includes all other responses not included in the other five race categories shown. Also includes write-in entries such as multiracial, mixed, interracial, or a Hispanic/Latino group. [2] Refers to combinations of two or more of the six race categories shown under one race.

Source: Population by Age, Sex, and Race—U.S. Census Bureau; 2000 Census of Population and Housing, "Census 2000 Profiles of General Demographic Characteristics" data files, published May 2001 (related Internet site <http://www.census.gov/mp/www/pub/2000cen/mscen01.html>).

Table B–3. Counties — Group Quarters Population and Households

[Includes U.S., states, and 3,142 counties or county equivalents defined as of January 1, 1992. For changes to these areas since then, see appendix B. Geographic Information]

County	Group quarters population, 2000[1] Number	Institutionalized population[2]	Households, 2000 (April 1) Number	Percent change, 1990–2000	Persons per household	Percent— One-person	With 1 or more persons under 18 years	With 1 or more persons 65 years and over	Family households (families) Number	Percent with own children under 18 years	Married-couple Number	Percent with own children[3]	Female householder[4] Number	Percent with own children[3]	Nonfamily households Number	Percent change, 1990–2000
UNITED STATES......	7 778 633	4 059 039	105 480 101	14.7	2.59	25.8	36.0	23.4	71 787 347	48.2	54 493 232	45.6	12 900 103	58.6	33 692 754	22.8
ALABAMA	114 720	65 363	1 737 080	15.3	2.49	26.1	36.1	24.1	1 215 968	46.2	906 916	43.1	246 466	57.2	521 112	29.3
Autauga	260	181	16 003	35.3	2.71	19.9	43.0	20.7	12 353	50.7	9 653	48.9	2 098	57.1	3 650	57.0
Baldwin...............	2 274	1 654	55 336	49.4	2.50	23.3	34.5	27.3	40 260	43.2	32 839	40.4	5 670	57.4	15 076	69.4
Barbour...............	2 718	2 711	10 409	12.9	2.53	26.5	38.1	27.7	7 393	46.9	4 986	42.0	1 983	59.1	3 016	19.2
Bibb..................	1 239	1 024	7 421	29.2	2.64	22.1	38.5	24.0	5 581	45.8	4 331	44.1	939	53.8	1 840	45.2
Blount...............	610	440	19 265	31.6	2.62	20.8	37.6	24.1	14 807	44.6	12 616	43.2	1 514	53.2	4 458	49.1
Bullock...............	1 511	1 511	3 986	5.3	2.56	28.9	39.4	28.4	2 731	48.9	1 415	39.4	1 124	61.5	1 255	16.7
Butler...............	265	243	8 398	5.8	2.52	27.5	37.1	30.1	5 872	46.4	4 009	41.9	1 528	59.0	2 526	19.7
Calhoun...............	2 428	859	45 307	5.4	2.42	26.9	33.5	25.8	31 300	42.7	23 647	39.6	6 055	53.4	14 007	24.3
Chambers	518	476	14 522	5.3	2.48	27.0	34.9	29.4	10 197	41.7	7 043	38.3	2 523	52.2	4 325	21.3
Cherokee	360	348	9 719	30.2	2.43	23.9	32.2	27.4	7 202	39.0	5 970	36.9	894	46.9	2 517	56.7
Chilton	351	302	15 287	26.2	2.57	22.9	38.0	24.7	11 339	46.4	9 185	44.5	1 598	56.3	3 948	42.9
Choctaw...............	133	133	6 363	10.7	2.48	26.5	37.0	27.4	4 573	45.2	3 310	41.1	1 021	57.1	1 790	24.8
Clarke...............	387	348	10 578	11.3	2.60	25.5	39.8	26.4	7 699	48.6	5 697	45.4	1 662	59.5	2 879	24.4
Clay..................	266	246	5 765	15.2	2.43	26.7	34.1	29.1	4 098	43.3	3 271	40.4	603	56.1	1 667	37.9
Cleburne	113	100	5 590	17.0	2.51	23.0	36.2	25.3	4 128	44.5	3 430	42.8	485	51.3	1 462	42.2
Coffee	780	738	17 421	14.2	2.46	24.9	35.2	25.2	12 485	44.8	9 822	41.2	2 100	60.5	4 936	33.8
Colbert	592	462	22 461	11.8	2.42	26.1	33.9	27.3	16 038	42.7	12 584	40.0	2 707	54.3	6 423	30.5
Conecuh...............	79	79	5 792	10.1	2.42	30.1	35.0	29.3	3 941	45.4	2 763	40.3	941	60.7	1 851	36.0
Coosa	392	392	4 682	16.6	2.52	24.3	34.8	27.6	3 407	41.2	2 568	38.6	633	50.7	1 275	38.3
Covington.............	523	456	15 640	8.3	2.37	28.6	32.7	31.3	10 788	42.8	8 462	39.7	1 768	56.1	4 852	22.2
Crenshaw.............	160	160	5 577	6.0	2.42	28.2	34.5	31.3	3 891	44.4	2 828	41.3	858	53.3	1 686	14.2
Cullman	998	729	30 706	19.9	2.49	24.0	34.9	25.9	22 487	43.9	18 665	41.9	2 664	53.8	8 219	44.4
Dale	1 665	426	18 878	7.4	2.51	24.3	39.0	21.9	13 637	49.9	10 386	45.2	2 564	66.3	5 241	23.6
Dallas	539	187	17 841	4.7	2.57	27.8	39.6	27.6	12 494	47.8	7 214	41.8	4 526	58.3	5 347	15.5
DeKalb	864	600	25 113	19.8	2.53	23.8	36.3	25.2	18 440	45.3	14 944	43.2	2 497	55.5	6 673	36.9
Elmore	5 341	5 333	22 737	37.5	2.66	20.0	40.9	21.4	17 542	48.4	13 952	46.1	2 734	59.4	5 195	47.1
Escambia	3 005	1 821	14 297	10.8	2.48	26.4	36.5	26.7	10 088	45.4	7 386	42.0	2 160	56.3	4 209	24.1
Etowah	2 043	1 401	41 615	7.6	2.44	26.3	33.6	28.8	29 467	42.2	22 543	39.2	5 449	54.1	12 148	20.4
Fayette	340	215	7 493	9.2	2.42	26.6	34.0	28.9	5 342	43.2	4 293	40.5	794	53.8	2 151	27.0
Franklin	402	344	12 259	13.0	2.51	24.5	35.7	27.0	8 954	44.5	7 257	42.0	1 269	57.3	3 305	23.0
Geneva................	274	224	10 477	13.5	2.43	26.3	34.0	28.9	7 457	42.9	5 907	39.9	1 156	55.6	3 020	27.9
Greene	78	78	3 931	11.9	2.52	30.8	38.8	29.0	2 651	48.5	1 430	40.6	1 067	61.2	1 280	30.6
Hale	290	290	6 415	18.9	2.63	26.4	41.8	26.4	4 606	50.8	2 925	46.2	1 412	62.0	1 809	27.9
Henry	179	164	6 525	13.1	2.47	25.3	34.8	29.6	4 728	42.0	3 516	39.1	959	52.2	1 797	24.0
Houston	1 148	1 036	35 834	16.2	2.45	26.4	36.2	24.3	25 113	47.0	18 821	42.7	5 047	62.7	10 721	30.5
Jackson	579	501	21 615	20.0	2.47	24.3	34.9	24.6	15 830	43.0	12 753	40.5	2 269	54.6	5 785	45.4
Jefferson	16 113	8 371	263 265	4.7	2.45	28.7	34.8	24.7	175 950	46.1	121 478	43.5	45 205	54.4	87 315	16.6
Lamar	199	192	6 468	7.7	2.43	25.4	34.1	27.9	4 715	43.0	3 789	40.0	704	58.0	1 753	17.4
Lauderdale.............	1 707	905	36 088	16.8	2.39	26.4	32.9	25.9	25 163	43.6	20 150	40.7	3 911	58.0	10 925	37.6
Lawrence	231	222	13 538	18.7	2.55	22.6	38.4	22.9	10 197	46.1	8 186	44.4	1 521	54.0	3 341	40.5
Lee	4 467	751	45 702	38.1	2.42	27.8	32.8	14.9	27 270	49.8	20 159	47.4	5 397	60.3	18 432	42.0
Limestone	2 643	2 523	24 688	25.4	2.55	23.4	37.8	21.4	18 231	47.1	14 815	45.2	2 571	56.7	6 457	46.5
Lowndes...............	47	30	4 909	21.0	2.73	24.6	43.0	26.4	3 588	48.5	2 104	43.4	1 262	57.7	1 321	44.7
Macon.................	2 285	472	8 950	5.5	2.44	33.0	34.9	27.4	5 543	45.8	2 836	38.5	2 312	55.8	3 407	15.6
Madison	7 258	1 959	109 955	20.6	2.45	27.2	35.9	19.6	75 342	48.2	58 679	45.2	13 008	61.1	34 613	34.5
Marengo	193	171	8 767	7.5	2.55	26.5	39.3	28.1	6 280	48.4	4 247	44.1	1 704	59.9	2 487	20.3
Marion	907	861	12 697	10.2	2.39	26.5	33.2	27.8	9 040	42.6	7 417	40.0	1 206	56.1	3 657	29.6
Marshall	972	799	32 547	17.2	2.50	24.6	35.8	25.8	23 527	44.8	18 802	42.0	3 489	58.6	9 020	32.0
Mobile................	8 068	4 003	150 179	9.7	2.61	24.8	39.1	23.2	106 745	48.4	74 335	45.0	26 561	58.6	43 434	20.4
Monroe	241	241	9 383	11.5	2.57	25.7	40.3	25.9	6 774	49.3	4 911	46.3	1 515	58.6	2 609	26.8
Montgomery	12 043	4 280	86 068	11.5	2.46	29.5	36.2	22.3	56 807	48.7	37 683	44.0	15 976	60.5	29 261	24.0
Morgan	1 707	1 357	43 602	15.4	2.51	24.8	36.3	22.6	31 445	46.5	25 040	43.6	4 881	59.4	12 157	32.9
Perry	471	154	4 333	3.1	2.63	27.9	39.6	29.4	3 046	48.0	1 752	40.9	1 089	59.8	1 287	17.1
Pickens...............	211	202	8 086	6.8	2.56	26.4	37.6	29.3	5 790	45.6	4 029	41.2	1 471	57.8	2 296	20.2
Pike..................	1 198	84	11 933	15.7	2.38	29.8	33.9	24.2	7 646	46.4	5 198	41.7	2 006	59.4	4 287	27.4
Randolph	574	450	8 642	14.4	2.52	25.6	35.2	28.3	6 225	43.1	4 853	40.5	1 054	54.5	2 417	26.3
Russell	687	609	19 741	12.8	2.49	28.0	36.9	24.9	13 424	47.0	8 763	42.1	3 732	57.9	6 317	32.6
St. Clair	1 903	1 857	24 143	36.7	2.60	20.8	38.7	22.3	18 437	45.9	15 166	44.0	2 403	56.1	5 706	59.7
Shelby	1 675	642	54 631	51.8	2.59	21.7	39.0	15.9	40 617	49.4	34 769	48.7	4 422	55.9	14 014	70.5
Sumter	253	145	5 708	2.9	2.55	31.2	37.8	27.3	3 665	49.7	2 093	45.0	1 341	58.3	2 043	25.3
Talladega.............	3 701	3 152	30 674	16.0	2.50	25.9	36.7	25.3	21 911	44.9	16 061	41.2	4 648	56.6	8 763	40.1
Tallapoosa.............	859	819	16 656	13.3	2.44	26.5	33.1	28.3	11 807	42.2	8 835	38.3	2 381	55.7	4 849	30.8
Tuscaloosa.............	8 691	2 447	64 517	16.6	2.42	28.4	33.6	20.5	41 689	46.9	30 473	43.5	9 036	59.1	22 828	26.8
Walker	1 021	845	28 364	11.0	2.46	25.3	34.8	26.8	20 469	42.6	15 979	40.7	3 364	48.9	7 895	31.1
Washington	84	69	6 705	17.4	2.69	22.8	42.4	25.0	5 042	50.4	3 964	49.2	839	56.5	1 663	43.2
Wilcox................	301	253	4 776	8.2	2.70	27.5	42.3	28.7	3 378	50.8	1 903	45.2	1 264	59.7	1 398	24.2
Winston	306	286	10 107	18.3	2.43	25.6	34.5	25.5	7 286	44.0	6 026	41.2	922	57.7	2 821	44.7

[1] As of April 1. [2] Includes people under formally authorized, supervised care or custody in institutions at the time of enumeration (such as correctional institutions, nursing homes, and juvenile institutions). [3] Under 18 years. [4] No husband present.

Sources: Group Quarters Population—U.S. Census Bureau, 2000 Census of Population and Housing, "Census 2000 Profiles of General Demographic Characteristics" data files, published May 2001 (related Internet site <http://www.census.gov/mp/www/pub/2000cen/mscen01.html>). Households, 2000—U.S. Census Bureau, 2000 Census of Population and Housing, "Census 2000 Profiles of General Demographic Characteristics" data files, published May 2001 (related Internet site <http://www.census.gov/mp/www/pub/2000cen/mscen01.html>). Households, 1990—U.S. Census Bureau, 1990 Census of Population and Housing, Summary Tape File (STF) 1C on CD-ROM (related Internet site <http://homer.ssd.census.gov/cdrom/lookup>).

[Includes U.S., states, and 3,142 counties or county equivalents defined as of January 1, 1992. For changes to these areas since then, see appendix B. Geographic Information]

County	Group quarters population, 2000[1] Number	Institutionalized population[2]	Households, 2000 (April 1) Number	Percent change, 1990–2000	Persons per household	Percent— One-person	With 1 or more persons under 18 years	With 1 or more persons 65 years and over	Family households (families) Number	Percent with own children under 18 years	Married-couple Number	Percent with own children[3]	Female householder[4] Number	Percent with own children[3]	Nonfamily households Number	Percent change, 1990–2000
ALASKA	19 349	4 824	221 600	17.3	2.74	23.5	42.9	11.9	152 337	58.1	116 318	54.4	23 937	72.0	69 263	23.5
Aleutians East	1 283	–	526	–1.3	2.69	27.4	41.4	9.7	344	59.9	232	53.4	76	76.3	182	16.7
Aleutians West	2 267	–	1 270	–31.2	2.52	32.0	37.4	6.9	736	61.0	559	60.1	97	61.9	534	31.9
Anchorage	7 014	1 915	94 822	14.7	2.67	23.4	41.6	11.0	64 131	57.5	48 421	53.6	10 884	72.0	30 691	17.1
Bethel	241	194	4 226	17.2	3.73	19.9	58.5	15.8	3 175	67.9	2 123	72.1	642	60.0	1 051	26.3
Bristol Bay	–	–	490	20.4	2.57	31.2	39.6	8.0	301	62.1	241	58.9	30	70.0	189	40.0
Denali	104	–	785	X	2.28	35.0	32.0	6.1	453	53.6	380	50.5	35	82.9	332	X
Dillingham	33	7	1 529	25.8	3.20	23.3	50.9	13.7	1 106	62.7	781	61.6	229	65.1	423	44.4
Fairbanks North Star	3 080	407	29 777	11.6	2.68	23.6	43.6	9.5	20 502	60.0	16 274	56.3	2 756	76.7	9 275	21.1
Haines	5	–	991	25.3	2.41	27.1	33.5	18.6	654	47.9	535	42.8	72	75.0	337	32.2
Juneau	678	229	11 543	16.6	2.60	24.4	39.6	12.1	7 638	55.5	5 910	51.4	1 213	69.2	3 905	19.3
Kenai Peninsula	1 328	935	18 438	29.4	2.62	24.7	40.4	14.1	12 716	55.1	10 218	50.2	1 654	77.1	5 722	41.8
Ketchikan Gateway	230	116	5 399	7.3	2.56	26.1	39.4	15.0	3 634	54.7	2 778	49.9	609	71.6	1 765	11.7
Kodiak Island	338	24	4 424	8.4	3.07	19.9	49.2	11.5	3 257	62.4	2 639	60.6	389	71.7	1 167	6.0
Lake and Peninsula	–	–	588	15.5	3.10	24.7	51.5	14.1	418	62.9	285	61.8	57	63.2	170	33.9
Matanuska-Susitna	985	695	20 556	53.5	2.84	20.3	45.2	12.6	15 057	57.7	12 109	53.7	1 868	75.4	5 499	66.0
Nome	223	121	2 693	13.6	3.33	23.2	53.3	14.9	1 899	64.9	1 141	66.6	412	62.6	794	22.5
North Slope	103	–	2 109	26.1	3.45	21.4	54.6	10.9	1 524	66.5	914	68.2	387	65.1	585	26.1
Northwest Arctic	319	17	1 780	16.6	3.87	16.6	63.2	14.9	1 405	70.0	853	70.6	350	70.9	375	11.6
Prince of Wales- Outer Ketchikan	76	–	2 262	9.8	2.68	26.0	41.7	12.7	1 537	55.3	1 150	50.6	227	70.5	725	25.9
Sitka	271	124	3 278	11.5	2.61	24.5	39.5	15.1	2 218	53.4	1 736	49.9	339	66.1	1 060	26.6
Skagway-Yakutat-Angoon	142	–	1 634	14.9	2.51	30.4	34.7	14.3	1 026	49.6	777	45.8	147	61.2	608	47.6
Southeast Fairbanks	299	–	2 098	9.9	2.80	23.5	42.0	14.3	1 506	54.8	1 221	52.3	181	67.4	592	35.8
Valdez-Cordova	182	14	3 884	13.4	2.58	27.0	39.4	12.3	2 559	56.6	2 023	52.6	329	73.6	1 325	19.0
Wade Hampton	10	–	1 602	17.1	4.38	16.0	69.5	17.5	1 296	73.8	759	78.4	326	68.1	306	8.5
Wrangell-Petersburg	70	26	2 587	2.9	2.56	26.3	39.4	17.7	1 765	53.8	1 406	49.2	238	73.5	822	13.2
Yukon-Koyukuk	68	–	2 309	X	2.81	30.5	43.9	16.8	1 480	60.7	853	58.6	390	67.7	829	X
ARIZONA	109 850	63 768	1 901 327	38.9	2.64	24.8	35.4	24.5	1 287 367	47.2	986 303	43.5	210 781	61.4	613 960	43.2
Apache	1 273	851	19 971	25.0	3.41	21.2	52.4	21.9	15 266	57.3	9 839	57.9	4 280	57.0	4 705	58.6
Cochise	5 667	2 895	43 893	27.1	2.55	25.3	35.6	28.3	30 786	45.6	24 193	40.8	4 857	64.0	13 107	42.2
Coconino	3 090	313	40 448	35.2	2.80	22.1	39.0	15.0	26 946	52.4	20 108	48.7	4 937	64.1	13 502	54.1
Gila	931	828	20 140	30.5	2.50	25.8	30.7	34.8	14 090	37.7	11 103	32.4	2 174	58.2	6 050	42.9
Graham	3 232	2 930	10 116	27.6	2.99	20.9	44.1	27.6	7 614	51.8	5 789	48.7	1 360	62.3	2 502	40.8
Greenlee	27	27	3 117	11.0	2.73	24.5	43.2	19.9	2 266	53.9	1 818	51.0	279	65.2	851	21.7
La Paz	280	255	8 362	56.4	2.32	26.6	24.2	41.9	5 616	31.6	4 535	25.2	686	62.1	2 746	78.4
Maricopa	44 783	23 982	1 132 886	40.3	2.67	24.5	36.2	22.0	763 110	49.0	584 928	45.9	121 637	61.7	369 776	42.0
Mohave	1 231	1 004	62 809	70.7	2.45	24.1	28.5	35.3	43 372	36.4	34 585	30.5	5 838	60.1	19 437	91.5
Navajo	2 240	1 962	30 043	35.4	3.17	19.9	47.3	23.6	23 069	52.7	16 666	49.9	4 907	60.2	6 974	63.7
Pima	22 034	9 168	332 350	27.0	2.47	28.5	32.5	25.3	212 092	45.8	158 471	41.3	39 217	60.4	120 258	30.5
Pinal	15 230	13 876	61 364	56.7	2.68	21.1	34.2	32.0	45 211	40.4	34 909	34.3	7 060	61.7	16 153	72.4
Santa Cruz	205	99	11 809	34.1	3.23	16.5	51.8	25.6	9 511	56.6	7 237	56.4	1 823	58.0	2 298	38.6
Yavapai	3 764	2 139	70 171	56.7	2.33	26.7	26.3	35.6	46 754	35.7	38 563	30.7	5 683	59.6	23 417	73.3
Yuma	5 863	3 439	53 848	50.5	2.86	18.5	40.6	32.8	41 664	47.7	33 559	43.3	6 043	67.9	12 184	50.0
ARKANSAS	73 908	45 152	1 042 696	17.0	2.49	25.6	35.6	25.3	732 261	45.7	566 401	41.9	126 561	60.7	310 435	29.6
Arkansas	363	315	8 457	.8	2.41	26.1	35.4	28.0	5 967	44.5	4 481	39.7	1 179	61.9	2 490	6.5
Ashley	240	240	9 384	5.6	2.55	23.9	38.4	26.0	6 910	45.7	5 329	42.2	1 218	58.9	2 474	19.3
Baxter	710	601	17 052	26.4	2.21	27.5	24.0	40.6	11 792	31.8	10 066	27.4	1 315	59.0	5 260	47.3
Benton	2 131	1 152	58 212	55.0	2.60	21.1	37.1	25.4	43 474	46.1	36 675	43.0	4 778	64.2	14 738	72.3
Boone	600	444	13 851	24.4	2.41	25.6	33.1	28.0	9 859	43.2	8 246	39.3	1 222	63.2	3 992	40.1
Bradley	754	346	4 834	6.4	2.45	27.6	34.1	30.8	3 389	42.1	2 521	38.4	702	55.0	1 445	19.2
Calhoun	117	117	2 317	6.0	2.43	27.3	34.8	27.9	1 629	44.4	1 288	41.8	262	61.5	688	20.9
Carroll	235	198	10 189	35.0	2.47	25.2	32.3	27.4	7 107	41.9	5 820	37.6	879	64.3	3 082	45.8
Chicot	714	690	5 205	–6.3	2.58	26.9	38.6	30.6	3 642	45.3	2 273	39.7	1 144	57.4	1 563	–2.3
Clark	2 328	291	8 912	12.7	2.38	27.6	33.0	27.2	5 820	45.6	4 438	41.4	1 085	62.3	3 092	27.2
Clay	179	172	7 417	–1.2	2.35	28.4	31.3	33.8	5 070	41.4	4 196	38.7	635	54.5	2 347	10.6
Cleburne	268	223	10 190	28.6	2.33	24.4	28.8	34.2	7 405	36.2	6 289	32.5	800	59.3	2 785	46.7
Cleveland	69	3	3 273	14.1	2.60	21.4	39.2	25.4	2 515	45.4	2 053	42.9	325	59.4	758	26.1
Columbia	1 119	299	9 981	3.6	2.45	29.2	34.5	29.8	6 746	44.6	4 882	41.0	1 510	55.8	3 235	16.3
Conway	349	215	7 967	11.0	2.51	25.4	35.3	29.3	5 733	43.7	4 519	41.0	915	53.7	2 234	22.7
Craighead	2 783	887	32 301	22.9	2.46	25.2	35.1	21.0	22 100	47.2	17 230	44.4	3 692	60.8	10 201	37.7
Crawford	457	346	19 702	29.2	2.68	20.0	41.1	21.8	15 160	48.7	12 258	45.5	2 141	63.4	4 542	50.3
Crittenden	628	549	18 471	7.9	2.72	23.7	43.4	20.4	13 373	51.7	8 457	46.7	3 929	62.4	5 098	23.3
Cross	300	234	7 391	9.4	2.60	23.5	39.7	25.8	5 447	47.1	4 077	43.8	1 042	59.4	1 944	28.6
Dallas	486	325	3 519	–2.3	2.48	28.3	35.3	30.4	2 430	42.9	1 796	39.9	487	56.3	1 089	11.6
Desha	135	132	5 922	–.6	2.57	26.9	39.9	27.4	4 192	48.8	2 751	41.9	1 181	65.1	1 730	10.1

[1] As of April 1. [2] Includes people under formally authorized, supervised care or custody in institutions at the time of enumeration (such as correctional institutions, nursing homes, and juvenile institutions). [3] Under 18 years. [4] No husband present.

Sources: Group Quarters Population—U.S. Census Bureau, 2000 Census of Population and Housing, "Census 2000 Profiles of General Demographic Characteristics" data files, published May 2001 (related Internet site <http://www.census.gov/mp/www/pub/2000cen/mscen01.html>). Households, 2000—U.S. Census Bureau, 2000 Census of Population and Housing, "Census 2000 Profiles of General Demographic Characteristics" data files, published May 2001 (related Internet site <http://www.census.gov/mp/www/pub/2000cen/mscen01.html>). Households, 1990—U.S. Census Bureau, 1990 Census of Population and Housing, Summary Tape File (STF) 1C on CD-ROM (related Internet site <http://homer.ssd.census.gov/cdrom/lookup>).

[Includes U.S., states, and 3,142 counties or county equivalents defined as of January 1, 1992. For changes to these areas since then, see appendix B. Geographic Information]

County	Group quarters population, 2000[1] Number	Group quarters population, 2000[1] Institutionalized population[2]	Households, 2000 (April 1) Number	Households, 2000 (April 1) Percent change, 1990–2000	Households, 2000 (April 1) Persons per household	Percent— One-person	Percent— With 1 or more persons under 18 years	Percent— With 1 or more persons 65 years and over	By type— Family households (families) Number	By type— Family households (families) Percent with own children under 18 years	By type— Married-couple Number	By type— Married-couple Percent with own children[3]	By type— Female householder[4] Number	By type— Female householder[4] Percent with own children[3]	Nonfamily households Number	Nonfamily households Percent change, 1990–2000
ARKANSAS—Con.																
Drew	660	127	7 337	15.7	2.46	26.0	37.3	23.7	5 092	48.2	3 764	44.4	1 044	61.1	2 245	36.6
Faulkner	4 072	555	31 882	49.5	2.57	22.5	38.4	17.9	22 454	50.7	18 085	47.9	3 250	63.9	9 428	69.1
Franklin	483	222	6 882	23.4	2.51	24.6	35.8	28.6	4 965	44.9	4 072	42.4	604	56.8	1 917	44.6
Fulton	130	120	4 810	20.0	2.39	24.4	29.9	34.1	3 511	37.6	3 001	34.3	377	57.8	1 299	31.1
Garland	1 861	1 299	37 813	22.6	2.28	28.8	28.0	34.2	25 250	37.7	20 113	32.7	3 809	59.3	12 563	33.2
Grant	181	165	6 241	21.9	2.61	20.4	39.0	22.8	4 780	46.4	4 035	44.9	531	57.6	1 461	38.7
Greene	588	441	14 750	19.7	2.49	24.0	36.2	24.9	10 703	45.5	8 730	42.8	1 428	57.8	4 047	35.5
Hempstead	271	241	8 959	9.1	2.60	25.5	38.0	27.0	6 378	46.9	4 608	43.2	1 372	59.4	2 581	16.7
Hot Spring	356	280	12 004	18.7	2.50	23.5	35.5	28.1	8 840	43.2	7 109	39.6	1 267	58.6	3 164	27.6
Howard	371	320	5 471	10.0	2.55	25.7	37.7	27.4	3 920	47.5	3 022	44.8	697	59.3	1 551	25.4
Independence	937	467	13 467	13.7	2.47	25.5	35.2	26.2	9 670	44.7	7 944	42.3	1 244	55.6	3 797	28.8
Izard	758	758	5 440	16.1	2.30	27.8	28.1	36.1	3 772	36.7	3 193	33.3	410	57.3	1 668	39.2
Jackson	1 666	1 622	6 971	-5.3	2.40	27.9	32.3	30.7	4 830	40.0	3 641	36.3	914	53.8	2 141	7.5
Jefferson	5 289	4 097	30 555	1.8	2.59	26.2	38.5	25.5	21 508	47.0	14 486	41.9	5 742	59.6	9 047	12.7
Johnson	582	180	8 738	23.8	2.54	24.6	35.9	27.6	6 235	45.4	5 079	42.5	829	59.1	2 503	30.6
Lafayette	121	121	3 434	–4.2	2.46	28.4	33.5	32.7	2 375	42.1	1 736	36.9	494	50.6	1 059	6.1
Lawrence	551	290	7 108	3.7	2.42	26.7	33.7	30.4	5 009	43.7	4 101	40.5	685	58.2	2 099	15.7
Lee	1 748	1 728	4 182	–8.7	2.59	27.2	38.2	31.6	2 962	44.0	1 805	36.2	964	58.4	1 220	–2.6
Lincoln	3 274	3 270	4 265	12.4	2.63	23.5	39.9	26.0	3 129	47.4	2 314	43.7	632	57.8	1 136	20.3
Little River	176	140	5 465	6.1	2.46	26.3	35.9	26.9	3 912	43.8	3 037	39.8	670	56.7	1 553	27.2
Logan	481	377	8 693	14.0	2.53	24.4	36.5	29.3	6 303	45.3	5 101	42.3	877	58.4	2 390	25.1
Lonoke	621	592	19 262	38.9	2.71	19.0	44.1	19.7	15 018	51.8	12 194	49.6	2 048	63.4	4 244	49.6
Madison	83	83	5 463	24.4	2.59	22.4	36.9	26.7	4 079	45.5	3 442	43.0	434	59.9	1 384	38.4
Marion	153	136	6 776	36.3	2.36	24.9	28.6	33.5	4 869	36.1	4 153	32.0	503	64.2	1 907	51.7
Miller	1 082	902	15 637	9.6	2.52	25.6	38.1	24.6	11 080	48.0	7 963	43.2	1 500	61.9	4 557	22.7
Mississippi	841	760	19 349	–5.2	2.64	24.7	41.4	24.2	13 908	50.1	9 668	45.2	3 363	63.1	5 441	7.7
Monroe	135	135	4 105	–5.9	2.47	30.1	34.6	32.0	2 733	44.1	1 894	38.2	684	58.5	1 372	3.8
Montgomery	109	96	3 785	23.6	2.41	24.5	31.3	32.2	2 749	38.5	2 370	36.7	266	49.6	1 036	35.2
Nevada	294	182	3 893	2.5	2.48	27.8	35.7	29.3	2 723	45.0	2 021	41.9	545	56.0	1 170	12.9
Newton	66	52	3 500	24.2	2.44	26.0	34.3	26.7	2 495	45.2	2 099	42.3	270	61.1	1 005	58.0
Ouachita	393	226	11 613	–.8	2.45	28.0	35.3	30.2	8 070	44.3	5 809	40.2	1 806	56.5	3 543	8.9
Perry	157	122	3 989	30.6	2.52	23.2	35.5	26.5	2 940	44.3	2 438	41.8	349	58.7	1 049	35.7
Phillips	314	234	9 711	–4.6	2.69	27.6	41.3	29.1	6 767	49.2	3 909	40.8	2 441	62.5	2 944	1.2
Pike	182	182	4 504	16.8	2.47	25.2	35.1	29.8	3 266	44.3	2 745	41.6	374	57.2	1 238	35.0
Poinsett	395	395	10 026	7.0	2.52	24.8	37.3	26.4	7 232	45.2	5 479	41.8	1 327	56.7	2 794	21.3
Polk	193	183	8 047	17.9	2.49	25.0	34.8	30.5	5 796	44.3	4 862	41.5	677	59.4	2 251	28.6
Pope	1 725	558	20 701	23.0	2.55	23.0	37.2	23.1	14 998	47.3	12 135	44.5	2 103	61.4	5 703	37.5
Prairie	140	140	3 894	6.4	2.41	25.6	34.7	30.0	2 794	42.6	2 205	39.4	433	55.4	1 100	16.4
Pulaski	8 253	4 590	147 942	7.8	2.39	30.0	33.8	20.4	95 679	47.1	67 960	42.1	22 322	61.9	52 263	19.6
Randolph	311	300	7 265	12.7	2.46	24.7	33.8	29.5	5 242	42.6	4 246	39.5	722	56.8	2 023	25.5
St. Francis	2 688	2 605	10 043	.9	2.65	25.1	40.9	25.9	7 227	49.0	4 708	42.8	2 085	63.8	2 816	11.1
Saline	1 787	1 297	31 778	37.9	2.57	19.6	38.2	22.1	24 489	45.9	20 279	42.7	3 073	61.5	7 289	60.6
Scott	102	102	4 323	9.2	2.52	24.8	36.2	26.8	3 123	45.1	2 571	42.2	369	60.4	1 200	29.4
Searcy	52	52	3 523	13.0	2.33	28.0	29.8	32.8	2 466	39.8	2 062	36.8	273	58.6	1 057	34.8
Sebastian	2 324	1 752	45 300	15.3	2.49	27.5	35.9	22.8	30 723	48.4	23 745	44.6	5 119	63.3	14 577	25.0
Sevier	169	140	5 708	11.5	2.73	22.8	40.7	25.7	4 226	49.1	3 384	46.8	572	61.4	1 482	14.6
Sharp	226	200	7 211	23.9	2.34	25.6	28.4	38.3	5 142	36.2	4 321	32.6	582	56.4	2 069	39.0
Stone	141	135	4 768	23.3	2.38	24.8	29.6	31.1	3 463	37.0	2 972	34.3	338	53.8	1 305	41.5
Union	983	871	17 989	1.0	2.48	26.9	36.5	28.1	12 652	45.8	9 221	41.9	2 740	57.1	5 337	8.1
Van Buren	276	262	6 825	19.8	2.33	26.4	28.2	37.4	4 804	35.8	4 031	32.3	525	53.7	2 021	42.0
Washington	6 060	2 021	60 151	38.7	2.52	25.8	35.1	17.7	39 483	49.6	31 468	46.9	5 645	63.3	20 668	54.1
White	3 557	811	25 148	26.9	2.53	23.4	36.2	25.4	18 412	45.1	15 076	42.3	2 400	59.1	6 736	44.0
Woodruff	142	125	3 531	–2.7	2.44	28.2	35.6	29.8	2 439	44.8	1 716	40.7	589	55.0	1 092	5.3
Yell	433	312	7 922	14.7	2.61	23.2	37.7	27.6	5 816	45.8	4 634	42.9	803	60.3	2 106	20.8
CALIFORNIA	819 754	413 656	11 502 870	10.8	2.87	23.5	39.7	22.3	7 920 049	52.0	5 877 084	50.9	1 448 510	57.6	3 582 821	10.5
Alameda	27 735	13 214	523 366	9.1	2.71	26.0	36.5	20.5	339 096	50.4	245 766	50.1	67 886	54.0	184 270	8.0
Alpine	1	–	483	7.3	2.50	27.7	31.3	17.8	295	41.7	212	37.7	53	47.2	188	2.2
Amador	4 581	4 477	12 759	21.3	2.39	23.9	28.9	33.8	9 069	36.8	7 519	31.7	1 110	62.5	3 690	30.2
Butte	5 844	1 630	79 566	11.0	2.48	27.2	31.2	27.8	49 386	45.7	37 130	40.2	8 879	63.3	30 180	18.2
Calaveras	425	349	16 469	30.2	2.44	23.3	29.9	31.5	11 747	37.4	9 694	32.8	1 416	60.1	4 722	46.1
Colusa	447	275	6 097	8.6	3.01	21.5	45.3	24.9	4 576	55.1	3 631	54.2	584	62.7	1 521	5.5
Contra Costa	11 337	5 292	344 129	14.6	2.72	22.9	38.8	22.2	242 233	50.3	187 613	49.0	39 683	56.4	101 896	16.3
Del Norte	3 833	3 697	9 170	14.8	2.58	25.3	37.3	26.8	6 293	48.8	4 586	41.5	1 250	68.8	2 877	27.9
El Dorado	1 052	633	58 939	25.8	2.63	20.1	36.8	23.0	43 029	46.8	35 415	43.3	5 242	64.3	15 910	34.3

[1] As of April 1.   [2] Includes people under formally authorized, supervised care or custody in institutions at the time of enumeration (such as correctional institutions, nursing homes, and juvenile institutions).   [3] Under 18 years.   [4] No husband present.

Sources: Group Quarters Population—U.S. Census Bureau, 2000 Census of Population and Housing, "Census 2000 Profiles of General Demographic Characteristics" data files, published May 2001 (related Internet site <http://www.census.gov/mp/www/pub/2000cen/mscen01.html>).   Households, 2000—U.S. Census Bureau, 2000 Census of Population and Housing, "Census 2000 Profiles of General Demographic Characteristics" data files, published May 2001 (related Internet site <http://www.census.gov/mp/www/pub/2000cen/mscen01.html>).   Households, 1990—U.S. Census Bureau, 1990 Census of Population and Housing, Summary Tape File (STF) 1C on CD-ROM (related Internet site <http://homer.ssd.census.gov/cdrom/lookup>).

[Includes U.S., states, and 3,142 counties or county equivalents defined as of January 1, 1992. For changes to these areas since then, see appendix B. Geographic Information]

County	Group quarters population, 2000[1] Number	Group quarters population, 2000[1] Institutionalized population[2]	Households, 2000 (April 1) Number	Percent change, 1990–2000	Persons per household	Percent— One-person	Percent— With 1 or more persons under 18 years	Percent— With 1 or more persons 65 years and over	Family households Number	Family households Percent with own children under 18 years	Married-couple Number	Married-couple Percent with own children[3]	Female householder[4] Number	Female householder[4] Percent with own children[3]	Nonfamily Number	Nonfamily Percent change, 1990–2000
CALIFORNIA—Con.																
Fresno	17 667	11 230	252 940	14.5	3.09	20.6	45.8	22.3	186 736	55.8	132 874	53.7	38 569	63.1	66 204	11.9
Glenn	388	310	9 172	4.0	2.84	22.0	41.5	27.0	6 733	51.9	5 197	48.5	1 003	65.8	2 439	2.4
Humboldt	4 073	1 131	51 238	10.4	2.39	28.9	31.4	22.1	30 645	47.6	22 074	40.9	6 022	65.6	20 593	26.1
Imperial	11 044	10 423	39 384	19.9	3.33	17.1	53.4	26.6	31 465	58.5	22 719	57.9	6 726	61.8	7 919	15.8
Inyo	157	141	7 703	1.8	2.31	31.4	30.3	31.4	4 937	43.5	3 835	36.9	762	67.7	2 766	10.6
Kern	29 970	26 278	208 652	15.0	3.03	20.3	46.8	21.6	156 401	56.4	114 025	53.3	30 262	66.6	52 251	14.7
Kings	20 129	18 578	34 418	18.3	3.18	17.0	51.0	19.5	26 989	59.2	19 948	56.7	4 929	68.3	7 429	19.9
Lake	1 089	592	23 974	15.2	2.39	29.0	30.0	33.9	15 370	41.4	11 447	33.9	2 715	64.4	8 604	31.4
Lassen	8 910	8 748	9 625	12.7	2.59	24.5	38.8	22.7	6 777	50.9	5 366	45.7	990	71.2	2 848	28.6
Los Angeles	175 252	77 712	3 133 774	4.8	2.98	24.6	41.3	21.5	2 136 977	53.9	1 491 327	54.4	459 392	56.1	996 797	2.2
Madera	8 100	7 574	36 155	27.4	3.18	16.5	45.2	26.2	28 610	50.8	22 016	48.3	4 401	61.5	7 545	29.3
Marin	11 486	8 467	100 650	5.9	2.34	29.8	28.9	23.5	60 679	45.6	48 709	43.2	8 580	57.4	39 971	8.3
Mariposa	1 426	199	6 613	18.0	2.37	26.5	28.4	31.6	4 490	37.7	3 691	33.3	527	57.2	2 123	34.5
Mendocino	2 141	792	33 266	9.4	2.53	27.0	35.0	25.4	21 864	47.8	16 255	42.1	3 894	65.7	11 402	21.7
Merced	2 855	1 071	63 815	15.3	3.25	17.7	50.0	22.6	49 760	58.2	36 854	56.3	9 013	65.2	14 055	16.3
Modoc	412	246	3 784	2.0	2.39	28.1	32.0	30.9	2 551	43.2	2 065	37.6	332	71.4	1 233	16.5
Mono	358	36	5 137	29.7	2.43	26.6	30.9	13.9	3 145	46.8	2 597	43.1	334	68.3	1 992	31.8
Monterey	20 976	13 361	121 236	7.3	3.14	21.2	43.5	23.9	87 931	53.9	67 843	53.0	14 094	59.2	33 305	11.2
Napa	5 233	3 054	45 402	9.9	2.62	25.8	34.4	27.9	30 694	46.4	24 153	43.9	4 496	57.1	14 708	15.2
Nevada	866	692	36 894	19.9	2.47	22.8	31.3	29.8	25 930	40.9	21 254	36.4	3 265	61.1	10 964	35.9
Orange	42 365	16 464	935 287	13.1	3.00	21.1	40.5	21.4	667 917	51.8	522 514	52.0	99 652	53.4	267 370	9.6
Placer	2 888	1 819	93 382	45.7	2.63	21.3	37.7	23.7	67 742	48.6	55 494	45.8	8 565	62.3	25 640	57.2
Plumas	188	169	9 000	10.8	2.29	27.5	28.5	28.3	6 051	39.3	4 990	32.8	724	71.7	2 949	28.1
Riverside	34 353	21 947	506 218	25.9	2.98	20.7	43.2	27.1	372 386	52.9	285 808	50.7	60 692	61.8	133 832	26.2
Sacramento	25 495	13 625	453 602	15.0	2.64	26.7	37.3	21.3	297 596	51.4	210 378	47.9	63 910	61.8	156 006	18.5
San Benito	507	217	15 885	39.1	3.32	14.1	51.3	19.2	12 893	57.1	10 429	56.7	1 667	58.7	2 992	27.7
San Bernardino	45 032	26 852	528 594	13.7	3.15	18.4	48.8	20.1	404 327	57.1	294 701	55.5	78 189	63.1	124 267	9.9
San Diego	97 013	23 447	994 677	12.1	2.73	24.2	37.2	22.3	663 170	50.8	503 876	49.0	114 970	58.9	331 507	15.1
San Francisco	19 757	4 200	329 700	7.9	2.30	38.6	19.4	23.9	145 186	37.7	104 310	38.6	29 202	38.6	184 514	12.7
San Joaquin	18 771	11 312	181 629	14.8	3.00	20.7	45.3	23.2	134 708	54.7	98 604	52.5	25 467	62.7	46 921	13.7
San Luis Obispo	15 571	10 287	92 739	15.5	2.49	26.0	30.5	26.8	58 654	44.5	46 769	41.0	8 460	59.8	34 085	21.9
San Mateo	10 450	6 234	254 103	5.0	2.74	24.6	34.3	24.5	171 249	46.1	134 739	46.5	25 611	46.5	82 854	4.1
Santa Barbara	16 617	6 128	136 622	5.3	2.80	24.3	35.6	25.7	89 555	49.4	70 179	47.7	13 668	57.0	47 067	7.6
Santa Clara	29 714	10 975	565 863	8.8	2.92	21.4	38.6	20.0	395 561	49.9	310 778	50.6	56 793	50.5	170 302	6.1
Santa Cruz	9 028	2 174	91 139	9.1	2.71	25.1	34.7	19.9	57 132	51.0	43 790	48.4	9 270	60.5	34 007	14.1
Shasta	3 359	1 668	63 426	13.3	2.52	24.7	35.0	27.3	44 002	45.7	33 644	39.8	7 546	64.7	19 424	25.4
Sierra	36	34	1 520	13.8	2.32	29.0	29.5	29.1	986	42.6	807	36.8	120	70.8	534	30.9
Siskiyou	690	372	18 556	7.2	2.35	28.6	30.3	31.0	12 231	41.9	9 598	35.4	1 873	67.1	6 325	20.9
Solano	15 974	12 090	130 403	15.0	2.90	19.6	44.6	20.2	97 375	53.4	72 596	51.1	17 947	61.6	33 028	21.0
Sonoma	11 102	3 408	172 403	15.7	2.60	25.7	34.7	24.0	112 397	49.0	86 712	46.3	17 908	59.2	60 006	22.1
Stanislaus	7 489	3 440	145 146	15.8	3.03	19.4	45.8	22.5	109 517	54.6	81 323	52.9	19 859	61.3	35 629	14.7
Sutter	1 383	1 042	27 033	17.0	2.87	21.2	41.9	24.7	19 946	51.3	15 418	48.4	3 151	63.4	7 087	16.6
Tehama	1 005	616	21 013	12.3	2.62	24.0	36.5	30.1	14 897	46.3	11 466	41.2	2 441	63.1	6 116	24.9
Trinity	242	193	5 587	8.4	2.29	29.5	28.1	29.4	3 625	39.1	2 819	31.6	565	68.0	1 962	28.8
Tulare	6 041	3 884	110 385	12.8	3.28	17.1	50.0	22.8	87 061	56.9	64 123	54.8	15 985	65.2	23 324	9.3
Tuolumne	4 836	4 471	21 004	17.0	2.36	26.0	28.9	32.9	14 249	38.4	11 425	32.5	2 018	62.2	6 755	36.9
Ventura	13 212	4 668	243 234	11.9	3.04	18.9	43.6	22.4	182 959	52.8	144 778	52.1	26 528	56.9	60 275	14.8
Yolo	7 515	1 235	59 375	16.5	2.71	23.3	36.5	18.9	37 468	53.2	28 275	51.3	6 580	61.9	21 907	16.6
Yuba	1 334	483	20 535	3.8	2.87	21.7	42.7	22.9	14 801	52.8	10 926	49.1	2 740	64.8	5 734	17.1
COLORADO	102 955	52 741	1 658 238	29.3	2.53	26.3	35.3	17.7	1 084 461	50.1	858 671	47.2	158 979	64.2	573 777	34.0
Adams	3 414	2 720	128 156	33.0	2.81	21.2	42.0	16.0	92 081	52.6	68 998	50.4	15 524	62.1	36 075	36.6
Alamosa	995	193	5 467	15.8	2.56	27.3	38.0	18.7	3 654	52.8	2 762	48.6	637	67.8	1 813	24.9
Arapahoe	4 847	3 769	190 909	23.4	2.53	27.0	37.2	15.4	125 791	53.0	97 830	50.3	20 319	65.8	65 118	29.8
Archuleta	84	61	3 980	98.0	2.47	22.1	33.8	20.8	2 872	43.8	2 381	38.6	325	71.7	1 108	139.3
Baca	85	85	1 905	1.8	2.33	30.4	30.6	35.7	1 269	42.6	1 082	40.2	143	55.9	636	13.2
Bent	926	911	2 003	7.4	2.53	27.2	35.5	28.7	1 388	46.9	1 072	41.4	229	68.1	615	6.2
Boulder	8 513	1 737	114 680	29.7	2.47	26.3	32.3	13.9	68 787	51.2	56 087	48.4	8 831	66.3	45 893	34.9
Chaffee	1 363	1 347	6 584	35.8	2.26	28.4	26.9	29.1	4 362	38.0	3 730	33.8	451	64.3	2 222	50.7
Cheyenne	30	30	880	-2.7	2.50	29.0	35.2	28.4	603	49.8	522	48.7	50	52.0	277	-1.8
Clear Creek	42	42	4 019	27.5	2.31	27.2	29.7	12.4	2 608	43.4	2 193	39.0	277	65.3	1 411	33.5
Conejos	53	48	2 980	19.6	2.80	23.7	42.4	30.2	2 211	51.8	1 677	49.4	378	61.4	769	34.4
Costilla	–	–	1 503	26.1	2.44	28.1	32.6	31.3	1 030	41.6	790	38.0	170	51.2	473	51.1
Crowley	1 996	1 994	1 358	16.6	2.59	25.7	37.3	29.4	958	48.9	748	44.4	150	68.7	400	14.6
Custer	16	7	1 480	92.2	2.36	23.8	27.7	25.2	1 078	35.0	956	31.2	80	68.8	402	100.0

[1] As of April 1. [2] Includes people under formally authorized, supervised care or custody in institutions at the time of enumeration (such as correctional institutions, nursing homes, and juvenile institutions). [3] Under 18 years. [4] No husband present.

Sources: Group Quarters Population—U.S. Census Bureau, 2000 Census of Population and Housing, "Census 2000 Profiles of General Demographic Characteristics" data files, published May 2001 (related Internet site <http://www.census.gov/mp/www/pub/2000cen/mscen01.html>). Households, 2000—U.S. Census Bureau, 2000 Census of Population and Housing, "Census 2000 Profiles of General Demographic Characteristics" data files, published May 2001 (related Internet site <http://www.census.gov/mp/www/pub/2000cen/mscen01.html>). Households, 1990—U.S. Census Bureau, 1990 Census of Population and Housing, Summary Tape File (STF) 1C on CD-ROM (related Internet site <http://homer.ssd.census.gov/cdrom/lookup>).

[Includes U.S., states, and 3,142 counties or county equivalents defined as of January 1, 1992. For changes to these areas since then, see appendix B. Geographic Information]

County	Group quarters population, 2000[1]		Households, 2000 (April 1)													
						Percent—			By type—						Nonfamily households	
									Family households (families)							
											Married-couple		Female householder[4]			
	Number	Institutionalized population[2]	Number	Percent change, 1990–2000	Persons per household	One-person	With 1 or more persons under 18 years	With 1 or more persons 65 years and over	Number	Percent with own children under 18 years	Number	Percent with own children[3]	Number	Percent with own children[3]	Number	Percent change, 1990–2000
COLORADO—Con.																
Delta	916	634	11 058	32.1	2.43	24.8	31.1	33.5	7 940	40.4	6 672	36.4	870	62.2	3 118	38.0
Denver	12 719	6 216	239 235	13.4	2.27	39.3	26.3	19.3	119 300	46.6	83 016	43.2	25 923	58.7	119 935	17.7
Dolores	–	–	785	35.1	2.35	26.2	27.1	28.7	542	35.4	453	31.1	67	55.2	243	55.8
Douglas	466	349	60 924	192.3	2.88	13.3	48.5	8.3	49 850	57.7	44 951	56.3	3 494	72.2	11 074	222.4
Eagle	353	57	15 148	81.3	2.73	20.9	34.7	6.4	9 020	54.8	7 581	53.1	841	72.8	6 128	87.2
Elbert	35	35	6 770	100.5	2.93	12.2	45.2	12.5	5 655	51.2	5 081	49.8	383	67.4	1 115	81.6
El Paso	15 396	3 852	192 409	30.9	2.61	23.9	39.3	16.4	133 829	52.8	107 064	49.5	19 655	67.9	58 580	36.6
Fremont	9 143	9 024	15 232	30.0	2.43	26.9	32.7	29.5	10 501	43.5	8 570	38.7	1 399	64.7	4 731	38.1
Garfield	849	572	16 229	44.1	2.65	22.8	39.6	15.9	11 286	53.5	9 340	50.4	1 265	71.6	4 943	49.8
Gilpin	24	24	2 043	56.2	2.32	26.8	28.4	10.2	1 264	43.4	1 082	38.6	117	77.8	779	69.3
Grand	393	63	5 075	60.2	2.37	24.8	29.5	13.1	3 217	44.4	2 774	40.4	264	75.4	1 858	66.2
Gunnison	975	39	5 649	46.5	2.30	27.2	24.9	12.1	2 968	45.9	2 496	41.9	306	73.2	2 681	63.8
Hinsdale	–	–	359	67.8	2.20	24.8	24.0	17.3	247	34.0	219	28.8	17	76.5	112	41.8
Huerfano	919	915	3 082	26.0	2.25	32.8	27.7	30.5	1 920	40.1	1 492	34.5	319	59.9	1 162	45.8
Jackson	10	4	661	4.6	2.37	28.4	31.5	23.9	443	43.6	363	39.1	52	73.1	218	22.5
Jefferson	7 730	4 632	206 067	23.7	2.52	24.5	35.5	17.1	140 439	49.0	113 607	46.1	18 818	63.0	65 628	39.4
Kiowa	24	19	665	1.2	2.40	29.8	32.0	29.6	452	42.5	383	38.9	44	68.2	213	15.8
Kit Carson	531	503	2 990	7.4	2.50	27.2	35.5	27.5	2 081	48.3	1 776	46.2	188	66.5	909	17.0
Lake	99	25	2 977	25.0	2.59	26.3	36.7	12.9	1 915	52.6	1 508	50.3	250	66.8	1 062	29.5
La Plata	1 825	383	17 342	44.8	2.43	24.8	31.6	16.9	10 892	47.2	8 656	42.9	1 502	66.3	6 450	62.6
Larimer	7 120	1 448	97 164	37.9	2.52	23.4	33.4	16.8	63 197	48.7	52 121	45.6	7 651	66.8	33 967	46.3
Las Animas	391	201	6 173	13.9	2.40	29.7	32.2	31.9	4 095	43.4	3 081	39.0	719	58.4	2 078	20.3
Lincoln	1 056	1 056	2 058	13.3	2.44	29.0	35.7	27.8	1 389	50.0	1 139	45.9	172	70.9	669	17.8
Logan	1 988	1 617	7 551	8.2	2.45	28.5	34.1	27.0	5 064	47.6	4 140	44.2	646	65.5	2 487	13.7
Mesa	3 284	1 085	45 823	26.4	2.47	25.1	33.9	26.1	31 563	45.6	25 337	41.1	4 482	64.6	14 260	31.7
Mineral	1	–	377	52.6	2.20	28.1	24.9	27.9	251	33.5	215	31.6	22	40.9	126	43.2
Moffat	311	53	4 983	19.3	2.58	23.6	40.4	17.6	3 576	53.2	2 924	48.4	407	79.1	1 407	26.0
Montezuma	438	285	9 201	36.1	2.54	24.6	36.5	24.6	6 518	47.0	5 190	42.9	972	64.9	2 683	65.3
Montrose	550	211	13 043	38.7	2.52	24.3	35.0	27.1	9 311	45.6	7 696	41.5	1 133	64.8	3 732	53.5
Morgan	484	455	9 539	17.2	2.80	23.0	41.5	25.0	6 969	51.9	5 695	49.5	856	64.8	2 570	14.3
Otero	568	352	7 920	4.3	2.49	27.8	35.4	29.3	5 473	46.7	4 170	41.6	947	64.5	2 447	14.1
Ouray	18	8	1 576	66.4	2.36	23.5	30.2	20.1	1 123	40.1	967	36.0	103	67.0	453	67.8
Park	70	70	5 894	112.4	2.45	21.1	31.7	12.9	4 223	42.2	3 776	39.2	262	69.1	1 671	137.4
Phillips	89	83	1 781	4.0	2.47	27.5	34.7	31.3	1 239	47.3	1 090	44.8	99	61.6	542	2.3
Pitkin	328	18	6 807	15.8	2.14	35.8	21.8	11.2	3 185	45.0	2 631	40.7	362	70.2	3 622	13.5
Prowers	300	163	5 307	6.5	2.67	25.4	40.8	24.2	3 728	53.2	2 900	50.0	581	65.9	1 579	11.2
Pueblo	4 135	3 034	54 579	16.0	2.52	26.6	35.2	27.4	37 332	46.1	27 355	41.3	7 278	60.6	17 247	24.9
Rio Blanco	232	28	2 306	5.7	2.50	24.8	37.3	20.4	1 646	49.8	1 385	45.7	180	73.9	660	15.4
Rio Grande	251	179	4 701	19.6	2.59	24.1	38.5	25.6	3 417	48.3	2 719	43.8	525	65.7	1 284	35.0
Routt	257	95	7 953	45.0	2.44	24.4	32.3	9.1	4 778	51.8	4 024	47.9	460	76.7	3 175	56.3
Saguache	36	17	2 300	40.0	2.56	26.9	36.7	21.0	1 556	49.4	1 211	45.7	253	67.2	744	73.4
San Juan	5	–	269	–6.3	2.06	36.8	25.3	11.2	158	40.5	118	29.7	24	87.5	111	26.1
San Miguel	17	17	3 015	102.5	2.18	32.7	23.9	6.0	1 424	48.2	1 156	43.0	164	79.9	1 591	147.4
Sedgwick	57	49	1 165	2.1	2.31	29.4	28.4	34.0	803	38.4	689	35.0	77	63.6	362	4.6
Summit	927	52	9 120	72.2	2.48	21.6	25.3	6.1	4 768	45.9	4 013	43.4	398	71.9	4 352	77.8
Teller	120	104	7 993	69.3	2.56	19.6	36.2	13.7	5 925	45.4	5 135	42.3	524	65.1	2 068	85.0
Washington	39	37	1 989	3.9	2.46	26.2	33.1	30.2	1 408	44.2	1 208	41.6	128	59.4	581	7.4
Weld	4 977	1 615	63 247	33.2	2.78	21.0	40.5	18.0	45 245	52.1	36 411	49.7	5 959	64.8	18 002	31.3
Yuma	135	119	3 800	9.4	2.55	27.4	35.6	28.6	2 644	47.9	2 263	45.9	257	65.4	1 156	14.2
CONNECTICUT	107 939	55 256	1 301 670	5.8	2.53	26.4	34.7	25.1	881 170	47.6	676 467	45.4	157 411	57.9	420 500	14.9
Fairfield	17 976	9 847	324 232	6.3	2.67	24.0	36.8	25.3	228 399	48.6	179 800	48.4	37 399	53.0	95 833	11.5
Hartford	26 845	16 828	335 098	3.2	2.48	27.9	33.8	25.7	222 356	47.1	164 796	48.4	45 404	59.8	112 742	12.4
Litchfield	2 511	1 838	71 551	7.8	2.51	25.3	34.0	25.2	49 598	46.3	40 925	44.7	6 166	55.6	21 953	18.1
Middlesex	6 227	2 701	61 341	12.2	2.43	27.2	32.2	23.6	40 580	45.8	33 346	44.1	5 385	56.0	20 761	24.4
New Haven	27 674	13 098	319 040	4.7	2.50	28.2	33.8	26.1	210 687	47.2	155 005	44.4	43 313	58.3	108 353	14.2
New London	11 880	6 018	99 835	7.1	2.48	26.4	34.7	23.5	67 193	48.1	52 427	44.6	10 935	63.2	32 642	21.5
Tolland	11 053	3 329	49 431	11.6	2.54	23.5	34.9	19.8	34 134	48.2	28 659	45.9	3 933	62.1	15 297	24.9
Windham	3 773	1 597	41 142	9.8	2.56	24.3	36.2	22.6	28 223	48.9	21 509	44.8	4 876	64.0	12 919	23.8
DELAWARE	24 583	11 510	298 736	20.7	2.54	25.0	35.4	23.9	204 590	46.5	153 136	42.8	38 986	58.9	94 146	31.4
Kent	3 630	1 296	47 224	19.1	2.61	23.0	39.3	22.0	33 615	49.9	24 994	45.1	6 530	64.4	13 609	32.0
New Castle	17 514	7 345	188 935	15.1	2.56	25.7	36.0	21.8	127 106	48.3	93 789	45.6	25 356	57.5	61 829	24.5
Sussex	3 439	2 869	62 577	43.3	2.45	24.3	30.8	31.8	43 869	38.7	34 353	33.5	7 100	58.9	18 708	60.4
DISTRICT OF COLUMBIA	35 562	7 964	248 338	–.5	2.16	43.8	24.6	21.5	114 166	43.0	56 631	36.6	47 032	52.2	134 172	5.2
District of Columbia	35 562	7 964	248 338	–.5	2.16	43.8	24.6	21.5	114 166	43.0	56 631	36.6	47 032	52.2	134 172	5.2

[1] As of April 1. [2] Includes people under formally authorized, supervised care or custody in institutions at the time of enumeration (such as correctional institutions, nursing homes, and juvenile institutions). [3] Under 18 years. [4] No husband present.

Sources: Group Quarters Population—U.S. Census Bureau, 2000 Census of Population and Housing, "Census 2000 Profiles of General Demographic Characteristics" data files, published May 2001 (related Internet site <http://www.census.gov/mp/www/pub/2000cen/mscen01.html>). Households, 2000—U.S. Census Bureau, 2000 Census of Population and Housing, "Census 2000 Profiles of General Demographic Characteristics" data files, published May 2001 (related Internet site <http://www.census.gov/mp/www/pub/2000cen/mscen01.html>). Households, 1990—U.S. Census Bureau, 1990 Census of Population and Housing, Summary Tape File (STF) 1C on CD-ROM (related Internet site <http://homer.ssd.census.gov/cdrom/lookup>).

Table B–3. Counties — Group Quarters Population and Households–Con.

[Includes U.S., states, and 3,142 counties or county equivalents defined as of January 1, 1992. For changes to these areas since then, see appendix B. Geographic Information]

County	Group quarters population, 2000[1] Number	Institutionalized population[2]	Households 2000 Number	Percent change, 1990–2000	Persons per household	Percent— One-person	With 1 or more persons under 18 years	With 1 or more persons 65 years and over	Family households (families) Number	Percent with own children under 18 years	Married-couple Number	Married-couple Percent with own children[3]	Female householder[4] Number	Female householder Percent with own children[3]	Nonfamily households Number	Nonfamily Percent change, 1990–2000
FLORIDA	388 945	248 350	6 337 929	23.4	2.46	26.6	31.3	30.7	4 210 760	42.3	3 192 266	38.1	759 000	57.7	2 127 169	31.1
Alachua	12 848	2 457	87 509	22.8	2.34	29.1	27.8	16.8	47 819	46.2	33 967	42.0	10 768	60.4	39 690	31.8
Baker	2 105	2 031	7 043	26.8	2.86	17.1	46.2	20.0	5 599	51.8	4 347	49.1	920	61.5	1 444	38.4
Bay	3 344	2 440	59 597	21.8	2.43	26.0	33.8	23.7	40 480	45.0	30 968	40.0	7 152	62.8	19 117	43.4
Bradford	4 155	4 063	8 497	18.1	2.58	22.9	36.6	27.0	6 196	43.8	4 708	39.7	1 133	57.8	2 301	33.5
Brevard	9 695	6 303	198 195	22.8	2.35	26.9	29.2	32.7	132 480	39.6	104 964	34.4	20 215	58.4	65 715	36.3
Broward	19 924	13 063	654 445	23.8	2.45	29.6	32.2	28.8	411 403	46.6	301 745	43.6	81 818	57.7	243 042	25.7
Calhoun	1 720	1 679	4 468	17.8	2.53	26.5	36.5	28.1	3 130	46.4	2 335	43.5	602	54.5	1 338	32.6
Charlotte	2 592	2 446	63 864	31.9	2.18	26.0	19.5	50.9	44 123	25.1	37 823	20.6	4 624	52.5	19 741	50.6
Citrus	2 161	1 634	52 634	29.7	2.20	26.1	21.3	47.6	36 339	27.5	30 690	22.4	4 009	55.8	16 295	49.6
Clay	1 567	989	50 243	37.0	2.77	16.9	43.1	18.4	39 389	50.5	32 032	47.5	5 380	64.2	10 854	54.6
Collier	4 790	2 294	102 973	66.9	2.39	24.5	25.2	39.4	71 264	32.8	59 871	28.4	7 445	60.2	31 709	77.1
Columbia	2 927	2 614	20 925	34.0	2.56	23.8	36.5	26.6	14 919	45.1	11 244	40.7	2 702	58.8	6 006	46.7
Dade	45 971	29 577	776 774	12.2	2.84	23.3	39.0	27.8	548 493	47.9	370 898	47.3	133 671	52.6	228 281	8.1
DeSoto	3 229	2 194	10 746	30.7	2.70	21.0	31.4	37.5	7 676	37.2	5 966	32.4	1 110	58.9	3 070	41.1
Dixie	1 107	1 078	5 205	32.9	2.44	23.9	32.2	32.8	3 660	38.9	2 858	34.3	552	56.0	1 545	51.2
Duval	15 675	6 874	303 747	18.1	2.51	26.5	37.2	19.8	201 678	50.1	141 177	46.0	47 503	61.7	102 069	24.6
Escambia	21 966	10 825	111 049	12.6	2.45	26.9	33.8	24.9	74 163	44.7	53 096	39.6	16 815	59.3	36 886	29.2
Flagler	462	428	21 294	79.2	2.32	21.6	23.6	44.0	15 683	28.6	13 378	24.5	1 729	53.8	5 611	106.9
Franklin	1 718	1 705	4 096	12.9	2.28	28.7	27.8	29.7	2 727	37.2	2 149	31.9	403	58.3	1 369	31.4
Gadsden	2 422	2 195	15 867	18.4	2.69	23.9	39.8	25.5	11 429	45.3	7 055	40.8	3 567	54.4	4 438	35.9
Gilchrist	1 321	1 311	5 021	52.9	2.61	21.1	36.7	26.6	3 715	44.5	2 964	40.7	560	63.2	1 306	77.9
Glades	910	720	3 852	33.5	2.51	22.7	30.0	37.1	2 764	36.0	2 244	30.8	333	59.2	1 088	42.0
Gulf	1 397	1 352	4 931	14.0	2.42	25.5	33.0	31.1	3 537	39.6	2 737	36.1	585	51.6	1 394	28.8
Hamilton	2 501	2 464	4 161	19.3	2.60	24.1	39.2	25.2	2 995	45.7	2 094	41.6	700	55.6	1 166	36.9
Hardee	1 919	1 463	8 166	27.8	3.06	18.0	41.1	31.0	6 253	45.5	4 903	43.1	908	54.5	1 913	45.5
Hendry	2 722	1 572	10 850	29.1	3.09	18.6	46.5	23.2	8 141	53.6	6 046	51.0	1 351	67.0	2 709	44.9
Hernando	2 109	1 632	55 425	31.0	2.32	23.3	24.4	47.8	40 019	30.1	33 471	25.4	4 802	54.8	15 406	58.3
Highlands	1 319	1 091	37 471	26.8	2.30	26.3	23.0	50.3	25 794	29.0	21 427	23.7	3 190	57.0	11 677	43.3
Hillsborough	17 427	7 377	391 357	20.5	2.51	26.9	34.8	21.8	255 222	48.1	186 613	44.2	51 541	60.7	136 135	29.3
Holmes	1 719	1 674	6 921	19.3	2.43	26.1	34.1	28.7	4 893	43.7	3 848	40.1	749	57.1	2 028	36.7
Indian River	2 297	1 361	49 137	29.1	2.25	28.2	24.3	44.9	32 708	32.6	26 804	27.6	4 390	57.1	16 429	51.1
Jackson	6 194	5 690	16 620	14.9	2.44	27.0	34.6	28.9	11 607	44.2	8 551	39.6	2 398	58.5	5 013	26.6
Jefferson	1 034	958	4 695	17.9	2.53	25.2	34.5	27.8	3 307	41.5	2 395	38.9	711	48.9	1 388	38.5
Lafayette	1 322	1 287	2 142	24.5	2.66	22.0	38.7	27.6	1 591	45.8	1 269	42.9	198	59.1	551	46.2
Lake	3 767	3 071	88 413	39.0	2.34	24.6	26.1	41.7	62 468	33.1	52 105	28.4	7 518	57.7	25 945	49.5
Lee	5 617	4 188	188 599	34.6	2.31	25.8	24.8	39.6	127 611	33.1	104 693	27.8	16 327	59.2	60 988	50.9
Leon	13 594	3 958	96 521	29.0	2.34	29.7	30.3	14.7	54 305	49.2	38 376	45.2	12 553	61.7	42 216	42.1
Levy	617	541	13 867	37.6	2.44	24.9	31.5	32.1	9 674	39.3	7 406	33.6	1 636	59.0	4 193	57.8
Liberty	1 443	1 370	2 222	30.2	2.51	25.9	37.6	24.2	1 554	48.8	1 150	43.9	293	67.2	668	59.0
Madison	1 701	1 701	6 629	20.0	2.57	25.4	37.5	29.3	4 683	45.1	3 241	40.2	1 159	57.3	1 946	37.1
Manatee	6 005	3 679	112 460	23.5	2.29	28.4	25.6	39.9	73 726	35.0	59 296	29.7	10 568	58.2	38 734	31.7
Marion	6 881	5 644	106 755	36.6	2.36	25.0	28.4	39.9	74 637	35.4	59 339	29.7	11 426	58.5	32 118	51.9
Martin	3 356	2 686	55 288	28.5	2.23	29.0	23.3	43.4	36 194	32.8	30 424	28.5	4 088	56.9	19 094	47.3
Monroe	1 362	849	35 086	4.5	2.23	28.8	23.0	23.8	20 387	35.9	16 416	31.5	2 558	58.5	14 699	13.2
Nassau	687	513	21 980	35.7	2.59	20.1	36.7	23.5	16 532	43.6	13 457	40.8	2 166	57.6	5 448	35.1
Okaloosa	5 507	3 656	66 269	24.3	2.49	23.5	35.9	21.7	46 499	47.1	37 250	43.2	6 749	64.8	19 770	45.3
Okeechobee	2 095	2 048	12 593	23.3	2.69	21.5	34.9	31.8	9 022	42.4	6 986	37.8	1 353	60.4	3 571	41.8
Orange	18 831	11 987	336 286	32.0	2.61	24.2	36.2	19.0	220 258	49.5	157 937	46.5	45 981	60.0	116 028	38.6
Osceola	2 400	1 921	60 977	55.8	2.79	19.1	40.7	22.8	45 077	49.3	34 207	45.9	7 798	61.9	15 900	58.3
Palm Beach	19 328	11 653	474 175	29.7	2.34	29.2	27.3	37.6	303 772	38.9	240 646	34.5	45 939	58.4	170 403	38.2
Pasco	5 372	3 430	147 566	21.3	2.30	27.3	26.0	42.2	99 073	35.1	80 642	30.5	13 135	55.0	48 493	34.7
Pinellas	22 911	13 561	414 968	9.0	2.17	34.1	24.4	34.6	243 339	37.7	185 707	32.4	43 573	56.6	171 629	19.1
Polk	12 546	8 388	187 233	20.0	2.52	24.1	33.0	32.2	132 305	41.0	101 862	36.1	22 528	58.7	54 928	32.6
Putnam	1 398	946	27 839	11.0	2.48	25.1	32.2	33.2	19 464	40.1	14 689	34.6	3 590	58.3	8 375	25.0
St. Johns	2 193	1 132	49 614	48.4	2.44	24.3	31.7	27.2	34 103	42.5	28 176	39.3	4 420	57.9	15 511	52.6
St. Lucie	2 712	1 586	76 933	32.2	2.47	23.5	29.7	38.1	54 258	37.3	42 511	31.9	8 524	58.8	22 675	52.6
Santa Rosa	2 552	2 166	43 793	46.5	2.63	19.3	39.8	20.9	33 321	48.0	27 225	44.7	4 479	63.6	10 472	59.5
Sarasota	6 473	4 883	149 937	19.5	2.13	30.4	20.1	45.3	94 528	29.0	79 001	24.4	11 565	53.4	55 409	32.7
Seminole	3 606	2 260	139 572	29.6	2.59	22.9	37.0	19.8	97 249	48.7	75 718	46.5	16 033	58.3	42 323	39.7
Sumter	6 267	6 246	20 779	71.5	2.27	23.5	21.8	47.2	15 035	25.9	12 650	20.6	1 745	54.4	5 744	78.1
Suwannee	665	543	13 460	34.1	2.54	23.3	33.9	30.3	9 687	41.0	7 606	37.4	1 509	55.4	3 773	44.8
Taylor	1 217	1 211	7 176	12.1	2.51	24.2	36.6	27.6	5 129	44.3	3 768	38.4	1 035	61.0	2 047	31.0
Union	4 148	4 087	3 367	26.7	2.76	19.5	46.2	20.0	2 606	54.0	1 943	49.7	504	67.3	761	37.9
Volusia	14 737	7 391	184 723	20.4	2.32	27.9	27.0	36.2	120 064	37.0	93 161	32.1	20 098	55.4	64 659	27.9
Wakulla	1 144	1 114	8 450	62.2	2.57	22.0	39.1	20.1	6 237	48.3	4 823	43.9	1 048	63.5	2 213	89.1
Walton	1 795	1 759	16 548	46.5	2.35	27.1	29.7	27.5	11 119	39.3	8 763	34.4	1 667	57.7	5 429	72.2
Washington	1 449	1 341	7 931	23.1	2.46	25.1	33.8	29.2	5 648	42.5	4 455	38.6	901	58.3	2 283	41.4

[1] As of April 1. [2] Includes people under formally authorized, supervised care or custody in institutions at the time of enumeration (such as correctional institutions, nursing homes, and juvenile institutions). [3] Under 18 years. [4] No husband present.

Sources: Group Quarters Population—U.S. Census Bureau, 2000 Census of Population and Housing, "Census 2000 Profiles of General Demographic Characteristics" data files, published May 2001 (related Internet site <http://www.census.gov/mp/www/pub/2000cen/mscen01.html>). Households, 2000—U.S. Census Bureau, 2000 Census of Population and Housing, "Census 2000 Profiles of General Demographic Characteristics" data files, published May 2001 (related Internet site <http://www.census.gov/mp/www/pub/2000cen/mscen01.html>). Households, 1990—U.S. Census Bureau, 1990 Census of Population and Housing, Summary Tape File (STF) 1C on CD-ROM (related Internet site <http://homer.ssd.census.gov/cdrom/lookup>).

[Includes U.S., states, and 3,142 counties or county equivalents defined as of January 1, 1992. For changes to these areas since then, see appendix B. Geographic Information]

County	Group quarters population, 2000[1] Number	Institutionalized population[2]	Households, 2000 (April 1) Number	Percent change, 1990–2000	Persons per household	Percent— One-person	Percent— With 1 or more persons under 18 years	Percent— With 1 or more persons 65 years and over	Family households (families) Number	Percent with own children under 18 years	Married-couple Number	Percent with own children[3]	Female householder[4] Number	Percent with own children[3]	Nonfamily households Number	Percent change, 1990–2000
GEORGIA	233 822	126 023	3 006 369	27.0	2.65	23.6	39.1	18.8	2 111 647	49.8	1 548 800	47.3	435 410	59.3	894 722	36.9
Appling	242	237	6 606	13.2	2.60	23.2	39.5	23.5	4 856	47.0	3 738	44.4	825	57.9	1 750	12.3
Atkinson	46	16	2 717	22.9	2.78	23.3	43.9	20.3	1 981	53.2	1 497	50.9	347	61.4	736	30.7
Bacon	155	141	3 833	11.4	2.60	23.6	38.3	23.7	2 815	44.9	2 115	41.9	540	55.0	1 018	27.7
Baker	12	4	1 514	16.5	2.68	25.1	39.0	28.4	1 094	45.4	722	43.5	295	52.2	420	19.7
Baldwin	7 811	6 693	14 758	21.3	2.50	25.6	35.4	20.0	9 843	46.4	6 484	41.1	2 688	58.6	4 915	43.3
Banks	–	–	5 364	42.1	2.69	19.2	39.3	21.1	4 160	45.9	3 510	44.9	426	50.5	1 204	50.1
Barrow	457	275	16 354	53.2	2.79	18.6	43.8	18.2	12 542	52.0	9 864	50.8	1 894	58.6	3 812	64.7
Bartow	901	796	27 176	35.3	2.76	18.7	42.6	18.9	21 028	49.4	16 829	48.0	3 007	56.3	6 148	38.9
Ben Hill	367	330	6 673	11.7	2.57	26.7	38.1	25.9	4 629	47.9	3 150	43.1	1 161	60.1	2 044	25.5
Berrien	153	153	6 261	21.6	2.57	23.6	39.1	23.6	4 541	48.2	3 519	45.1	734	60.6	1 720	43.5
Bibb	5 310	3 280	59 667	6.0	2.49	28.2	36.5	23.7	39 824	47.7	25 215	41.8	12 263	60.4	19 843	16.7
Bleckley	637	240	4 372	14.6	2.52	25.5	37.1	25.8	3 122	46.1	2 263	41.5	679	60.1	1 250	31.3
Brantley	81	81	5 436	42.6	2.68	20.4	42.3	20.3	4 153	50.0	3 308	47.3	574	59.9	1 283	82.8
Brooks	399	290	6 155	14.2	2.61	25.2	37.4	27.6	4 371	44.5	2 973	41.1	1 113	53.4	1 784	32.0
Bryan	130	130	8 089	59.5	2.88	16.4	48.8	15.7	6 510	55.9	5 210	53.5	962	67.8	1 579	87.1
Bulloch	3 590	257	20 743	38.4	2.53	24.6	32.9	17.5	12 341	49.9	9 149	47.1	2 452	60.7	8 402	58.6
Burke	280	63	7 934	12.7	2.77	23.6	44.7	22.6	5 803	52.5	3 604	47.4	1 810	63.2	2 131	21.8
Butts	1 915	1 890	6 455	37.5	2.73	20.9	40.2	22.3	4 867	45.8	3 677	43.2	899	53.8	1 588	59.0
Calhoun	1 315	1 300	1 962	9.4	2.55	28.7	37.3	28.8	1 347	45.4	818	41.0	455	54.7	615	17.1
Camden	1 850	175	14 705	55.5	2.84	17.7	49.9	11.5	11 375	60.5	9 141	57.5	1 715	74.3	3 330	67.6
Candler	412	400	3 375	19.3	2.72	23.9	39.9	26.8	2 426	46.9	1 783	44.2	484	56.0	949	20.7
Carroll	3 229	944	31 568	24.4	2.66	21.2	39.3	19.7	23 026	48.3	17 760	46.0	3 876	58.3	8 542	33.4
Catoosa	415	334	20 425	29.7	2.59	21.3	38.8	22.3	15 391	47.0	12 386	44.4	2 251	58.4	5 034	49.0
Charlton	1 126	1 126	3 342	14.8	2.74	21.8	42.9	22.4	2 499	50.3	1 853	47.1	502	60.0	843	28.9
Chatham	8 050	3 709	89 865	10.8	2.49	27.1	35.0	24.0	59 431	46.0	40 603	41.4	15 276	58.0	30 434	24.0
Chattahoochee	4 876	–	2 932	1.7	3.41	8.9	67.1	7.4	2 623	72.5	2 236	72.0	296	76.0	309	25.1
Chattooga	1 670	1 638	9 577	13.1	2.49	25.2	35.3	28.0	6 836	43.2	5 141	40.2	1 208	51.7	2 741	32.2
Cherokee	983	520	49 495	58.1	2.85	16.0	44.3	13.6	39 194	52.3	33 238	51.7	4 117	59.6	10 301	85.6
Clarke	8 180	1 179	39 706	19.7	2.35	29.7	25.4	14.7	19 678	45.3	12 940	41.0	5 289	59.1	20 028	33.6
Clay	57	57	1 347	11.3	2.45	27.8	32.1	33.3	928	37.3	548	28.5	315	54.0	419	24.7
Clayton	3 258	1 964	82 243	25.5	2.84	21.8	45.8	12.4	59 190	56.5	37 554	52.7	16 719	67.0	23 053	37.3
Clinch	359	295	2 512	15.6	2.60	24.6	42.3	22.9	1 823	50.4	1 298	46.1	425	62.6	689	33.0
Cobb	7 294	4 098	227 487	32.8	2.64	23.2	38.4	13.0	156 579	52.1	123 587	50.7	24 447	60.9	70 908	38.6
Coffee	1 459	1 236	13 354	26.7	2.69	22.6	42.5	20.7	9 791	50.8	7 146	48.4	2 036	59.0	3 563	39.2
Colquitt	1 265	645	15 495	19.4	2.63	24.9	39.4	25.6	11 066	48.5	7 910	44.3	2 404	61.9	4 429	36.5
Columbia	691	241	31 120	42.5	2.85	15.4	47.5	15.9	25 348	54.5	21 018	53.0	3 311	63.6	5 772	63.7
Cook	240	130	5 882	21.9	2.64	24.0	39.6	25.3	4 280	47.8	3 138	44.6	900	58.0	1 602	31.5
Coweta	787	765	31 442	66.1	2.81	17.6	44.3	17.4	24 699	50.8	19 656	49.5	3 842	59.0	6 743	72.5
Crawford	114	114	4 461	45.4	2.78	18.8	42.6	18.6	3 457	48.3	2 697	46.7	562	55.0	1 004	52.8
Crisp	463	394	8 337	14.4	2.58	26.1	39.5	24.7	5 872	49.4	3 731	41.2	1 797	65.7	2 465	24.1
Dade	770	104	5 633	20.9	2.55	21.7	36.1	22.8	4 264	44.0	3 531	43.2	537	48.4	1 369	47.8
Dawson	97	78	6 069	80.6	2.62	18.6	36.8	18.1	4 687	43.7	3 989	41.6	497	58.8	1 382	120.8
Decatur	701	610	10 380	15.8	2.65	24.3	40.6	26.0	7 543	48.7	5 091	44.9	2 020	57.2	2 837	24.0
De Kalb	13 671	6 487	249 339	19.5	2.62	26.9	35.7	15.2	156 670	49.3	99 987	46.7	43 947	57.7	92 669	30.4
Dodge	1 689	1 573	7 062	10.6	2.48	27.8	36.3	25.7	4 885	46.5	3 534	43.1	1 071	55.9	2 177	28.1
Dooly	1 271	1 253	3 909	9.9	2.62	25.9	38.9	25.5	2 767	47.5	1 763	41.6	803	60.4	1 142	17.1
Dougherty	4 481	1 614	35 552	4.1	2.58	26.8	38.2	22.9	24 293	48.1	14 541	41.0	8 234	60.7	11 259	24.2
Douglas	849	817	32 822	35.2	2.78	18.4	42.9	15.3	24 912	50.9	19 317	48.5	4 164	60.3	7 910	74.3
Early	258	248	4 695	10.1	2.58	26.9	37.8	29.6	3 294	45.6	2 115	39.2	977	58.3	1 401	21.8
Echols	–	–	1 264	54.9	2.97	18.7	43.7	21.4	937	51.4	741	49.1	137	62.0	327	101.9
Effingham	248	242	13 151	50.1	2.84	16.9	46.8	17.0	10 490	54.0	8 454	52.5	1 459	61.2	2 661	65.3
Elbert	268	238	8 004	12.5	2.53	25.0	36.6	27.3	5 768	44.4	4 154	40.5	1 256	55.7	2 236	24.2
Emanuel	808	590	8 045	8.4	2.61	25.0	39.1	25.8	5 749	48.0	4 030	43.4	1 376	62.1	2 296	19.6
Evans	584	544	3 778	20.2	2.62	25.0	40.4	24.5	2 680	49.2	1 851	45.6	618	59.4	1 098	27.7
Fannin	144	144	8 369	32.1	2.35	25.6	29.1	32.4	6 011	36.1	5 008	33.5	747	48.3	2 358	58.3
Fayette	578	537	31 524	49.7	2.88	15.0	45.6	18.0	25 990	52.3	22 525	51.2	2 629	60.5	5 534	82.3
Floyd	3 756	1 903	34 028	11.5	2.55	24.5	36.3	26.0	24 214	45.1	18 250	42.8	4 414	53.8	9 814	22.7
Forsyth	729	463	34 565	116.9	2.83	14.8	44.0	14.0	28 106	51.3	24 835	50.9	2 294	56.3	6 459	105.0
Franklin	590	250	7 888	23.9	2.50	24.6	34.9	27.6	5 696	43.1	4 510	40.7	831	52.8	2 192	38.9
Fulton	31 384	9 801	321 242	24.9	2.44	32.2	32.5	15.9	185 721	49.7	119 714	46.8	52 923	58.8	135 521	33.8
Gilmer	166	164	9 071	78.8	2.57	22.2	34.6	24.6	6 692	41.9	5 541	39.6	766	54.2	2 379	110.2
Glascock	104	–	1 004	15.8	2.44	26.3	36.7	28.4	716	45.9	589	44.0	96	53.1	288	32.1
Glynn	1 262	475	27 208	13.6	2.44	27.2	34.4	25.7	18 401	44.7	13 460	39.4	3 973	60.8	8 807	32.7
Gordon	429	375	16 173	26.6	2.70	20.3	40.5	20.8	12 261	47.2	9 767	45.3	1 793	55.6	3 912	37.8
Grady	278	201	8 797	19.6	2.66	22.4	39.4	25.9	6 508	46.0	4 675	42.7	1 425	56.5	2 289	28.4
Greene	197	171	5 477	34.1	2.59	23.0	34.8	27.4	4 040	39.7	2 794	32.6	1 003	58.5	1 437	34.2

[1] As of April 1. [2] Includes people under formally authorized, supervised care or custody in institutions at the time of enumeration (such as correctional institutions, nursing homes, and juvenile institutions). [3] Under 18 years. [4] No husband present.

Sources: Group Quarters Population—U.S. Census Bureau, 2000 Census of Population and Housing, "Census 2000 Profiles of General Demographic Characteristics" data files, published May 2001 (related Internet site <http://www.census.gov/mp/www/pub/2000cen/mscen01.html>). Households, 2000—U.S. Census Bureau, 2000 Census of Population and Housing, "Census 2000 Profiles of General Demographic Characteristics" data files, published May 2001 (related Internet site <http://www.census.gov/mp/www/pub/2000cen/mscen01.html>). Households, 1990—U.S. Census Bureau, 1990 Census of Population and Housing, Summary Tape File (STF) 1C on CD-ROM (related Internet site <http://homer.ssd.census.gov/cdrom/lookup>).

[Includes U.S., states, and 3,142 counties or county equivalents defined as of January 1, 1992. For changes to these areas since then, see appendix B. Geographic Information]

County	Group quarters population, 2000[1]		Households, 2000 (April 1)			Percent—			By type—							
									Family households (families)		Married-couple		Female householder[4]		Nonfamily households	
	Number	Institutionalized population[2]	Number	Percent change, 1990–2000	Persons per household	One-person	With 1 or more persons under 18 years	With 1 or more persons 65 years and over	Number	Percent with own children under 18 years	Number	Percent with own children[3]	Number	Percent with own children[3]	Number	Percent change, 1990–2000
GEORGIA—Con.																
Gwinnett	6 385	3 913	202 317	59.3	2.88	18.4	45.0	11.2	152 296	56.1	123 729	55.8	20 319	62.3	50 021	63.6
Habersham	1 867	1 362	13 259	33.0	2.57	22.4	35.4	26.1	9 854	43.1	8 069	40.8	1 231	56.1	3 405	48.4
Hall	2 297	1 536	47 381	36.5	2.89	19.2	41.5	19.6	36 021	48.8	28 500	47.9	5 102	55.6	11 360	38.6
Hancock	1 463	1 451	3 237	9.0	2.66	26.1	38.7	28.0	2 311	43.9	1 231	37.0	913	54.2	926	20.6
Haralson	338	280	9 826	19.1	2.58	23.0	37.7	24.4	7 196	45.7	5 669	43.1	1 113	54.6	2 630	31.8
Harris	209	187	8 822	36.7	2.66	17.9	38.6	23.1	6 986	43.9	5 715	42.2	945	52.1	1 836	34.8
Hart	534	379	9 106	22.1	2.47	24.4	33.0	28.7	6 615	39.9	5 168	36.8	1 094	51.2	2 491	39.9
Heard	109	99	4 043	30.7	2.70	21.3	43.0	21.9	3 042	50.1	2 342	47.6	489	57.3	1 001	44.0
Henry	755	475	41 373	106.7	2.87	15.4	46.9	15.0	33 323	53.3	27 492	52.2	4 268	59.7	8 050	149.4
Houston	2 393	733	40 911	26.1	2.65	22.1	42.0	17.9	30 221	52.0	22 913	48.3	5 732	64.9	10 690	38.1
Irwin	369	360	3 644	16.0	2.62	23.1	39.8	26.6	2 698	47.6	2 022	44.3	523	57.2	946	19.4
Jackson	809	690	15 057	40.4	2.71	19.7	40.4	20.4	11 488	47.6	9 113	45.9	1 631	54.1	3 569	50.7
Jasper	83	83	4 175	37.5	2.72	21.4	40.1	23.7	3 122	46.3	2 371	43.8	556	54.1	1 053	44.4
Jeff Davis	96	96	4 828	10.8	2.61	22.3	40.1	23.2	3 591	48.0	2 728	45.4	658	55.3	1 237	26.4
Jefferson	460	277	6 339	4.0	2.65	25.7	40.7	26.8	4 548	47.8	2 802	44.0	1 466	55.9	1 791	11.7
Jenkins	126	13	3 214	8.9	2.63	25.6	39.7	26.7	2 270	47.7	1 476	45.1	632	54.7	944	23.4
Johnson	627	618	3 130	4.0	2.53	26.6	36.3	29.3	2 240	45.1	1 555	39.8	571	58.5	890	12.8
Jones	352	336	8 659	18.6	2.69	20.2	41.8	19.7	6 665	48.8	5 086	47.1	1 148	54.8	1 994	33.0
Lamar	830	293	5 712	22.3	2.64	21.6	37.7	25.1	4 286	42.9	3 086	39.5	932	54.4	1 426	29.5
Lanier	278	278	2 593	32.0	2.69	21.8	42.0	21.7	1 932	50.4	1 427	48.1	356	59.6	661	43.7
Laurens	1 244	1 131	17 083	17.7	2.55	25.7	37.9	24.3	12 177	47.4	8 586	42.8	2 922	60.2	4 906	32.9
Lee	798	784	8 229	58.3	2.91	14.3	52.1	13.8	6 796	58.5	5 413	56.2	1 072	68.8	1 433	58.2
Liberty	4 784	169	19 383	28.1	2.93	16.6	54.1	9.4	15 145	64.6	11 554	61.8	2 873	74.9	4 238	55.1
Lincoln	72	72	3 251	20.3	2.55	23.7	35.8	28.9	2 379	41.8	1 731	40.4	504	46.8	872	35.6
Long	–	–	3 574	62.8	2.88	19.6	50.1	13.4	2 678	60.8	1 965	58.1	519	70.5	896	74.7
Lowndes	6 824	4 765	32 654	24.1	2.61	24.2	39.3	18.9	22 242	51.8	15 826	48.2	5 182	62.4	10 412	44.9
Lumpkin	1 352	284	7 537	51.5	2.61	22.0	36.2	19.2	5 363	46.2	4 337	44.3	706	55.0	2 174	96.9
McDuffie	332	125	7 970	9.6	2.62	23.2	40.9	23.3	5 857	49.4	3 964	44.4	1 529	61.4	2 113	19.9
McIntosh	164	164	4 202	31.9	2.54	24.2	36.5	24.0	3 014	43.3	2 194	39.4	616	53.1	1 188	45.8
Macon	983	983	4 834	10.2	2.71	25.2	40.9	25.8	3 483	47.8	2 063	44.3	1 178	55.4	1 351	26.7
Madison	158	146	9 800	26.6	2.61	21.5	38.4	21.1	7 332	46.2	5 934	43.9	1 040	56.0	2 468	47.0
Marion	85	85	2 668	36.0	2.65	24.3	39.5	21.2	1 912	49.2	1 378	44.7	404	64.1	756	72.6
Meriwether	429	404	8 248	8.0	2.68	23.8	38.3	27.1	6 012	43.2	4 043	40.5	1 519	48.7	2 236	21.7
Miller	133	120	2 487	6.5	2.51	26.7	36.0	30.3	1 766	44.4	1 262	40.9	385	55.1	721	21.2
Mitchell	1 972	1 913	8 063	18.6	2.72	23.3	41.3	25.0	5 937	46.7	3 757	40.9	1 814	58.3	2 126	37.7
Monroe	626	620	7 719	32.2	2.74	18.9	40.7	20.9	6 009	46.0	4 602	44.5	1 062	51.3	1 710	32.5
Montgomery	754	478	2 919	17.1	2.57	25.6	38.3	23.5	2 063	48.1	1 551	45.4	395	57.0	856	31.5
Morgan	169	169	5 558	26.3	2.75	19.4	40.1	24.4	4 302	45.0	3 271	43.2	811	50.9	1 256	31.2
Murray	204	193	13 286	41.9	2.73	18.8	43.5	16.6	10 261	50.5	8 076	48.0	1 469	60.7	3 025	62.3
Muscogee	9 107	3 249	69 819	6.0	2.54	26.7	39.1	22.7	47 678	50.7	31 177	46.3	13 663	60.5	22 141	18.9
Newton	1 070	494	21 997	52.7	2.77	18.3	42.7	19.9	17 113	48.5	13 026	46.2	3 092	57.4	4 884	59.4
Oconee	240	95	9 051	47.0	2.87	15.5	47.1	16.4	7 326	55.2	6 228	53.8	847	65.4	1 725	44.2
Oglethorpe	116	44	4 849	35.4	2.58	23.0	38.0	23.3	3 541	46.0	2 780	43.6	558	54.5	1 308	57.0
Paulding	512	475	28 089	96.1	2.89	14.6	49.5	12.4	22 893	56.6	19 185	55.7	2 531	62.5	5 196	123.3
Peach	1 074	86	8 436	18.1	2.68	22.6	39.0	21.2	6 002	47.2	3 961	42.8	1 652	59.3	2 434	45.1
Pickens	212	212	8 960	66.4	2.54	20.5	34.2	23.5	6 795	41.0	5 686	38.3	784	54.7	2 165	88.8
Pierce	115	110	5 958	23.9	2.61	23.1	38.4	23.8	4 439	46.0	3 517	44.5	689	56.9	1 519	44.9
Pike	315	308	4 755	34.9	2.81	17.5	42.1	22.6	3 785	46.5	3 108	46.3	500	46.6	970	38.2
Polk	840	804	14 012	11.9	2.66	22.7	38.2	25.9	10 338	44.6	7 838	42.8	1 830	52.6	3 674	19.9
Pulaski	1 106	1 106	3 407	10.0	2.49	27.9	35.0	27.8	2 339	44.2	1 665	39.6	535	57.8	1 068	17.0
Putnam	270	262	7 402	41.6	2.50	22.0	32.6	25.8	5 474	38.5	4 204	33.4	949	56.5	1 928	49.3
Quitman	–	–	1 047	22.2	2.48	24.9	31.3	36.7	756	36.0	526	30.2	196	50.0	291	26.0
Rabun	284	153	6 279	35.6	2.35	26.8	29.3	30.8	4 353	38.2	3 605	35.4	507	50.5	1 926	67.0
Randolph	303	107	2 909	3.3	2.57	30.0	37.1	31.5	1 971	44.7	1 189	39.9	657	54.6	938	15.5
Richmond	10 911	3 193	73 920	7.6	2.55	27.7	38.7	21.1	49 509	50.2	30 900	44.7	15 356	61.4	24 411	16.3
Rockdale	1 102	708	24 052	31.2	2.87	16.9	43.3	18.4	18 883	49.8	14 826	47.9	2 986	60.7	5 169	60.7
Schley	11	7	1 435	9.1	2.62	24.8	40.8	23.2	1 042	50.0	747	47.5	225	58.2	393	12.0
Screven	309	158	5 797	14.8	2.60	26.5	39.2	26.9	4 103	47.7	2 780	43.7	1 060	57.5	1 694	25.5
Seminole	304	84	3 573	13.9	2.54	24.3	35.5	30.1	2 597	41.2	1 826	36.2	639	53.4	976	21.8
Spalding	873	790	21 519	10.8	2.67	22.3	39.7	23.0	15 783	46.3	10 822	42.2	3 916	57.0	5 736	26.8
Stephens	941	325	9 951	11.2	2.46	25.5	33.6	27.5	7 070	42.9	5 633	39.9	1 104	55.8	2 881	24.4
Stewart	269	269	2 007	1.3	2.48	29.5	35.7	32.3	1 349	41.2	793	35.4	464	51.9	658	21.2
Sumter	1 512	931	12 025	14.7	2.64	25.0	39.9	22.2	8 498	48.8	5 348	43.5	2 649	60.3	3 527	22.7
Talbot	17	17	2 538	8.2	2.55	25.4	34.8	28.9	1 824	39.3	1 188	34.2	513	50.3	714	23.1
Taliaferro	23	23	870	19.7	2.36	33.3	32.4	34.7	559	41.7	342	34.2	174	55.2	311	32.3
Tattnall	3 938	3 922	7 057	20.7	2.60	26.7	37.6	25.1	4 874	47.8	3 608	44.3	943	59.8	2 183	38.8

[1] As of April 1. [2] Includes people under formally authorized, supervised care or custody in institutions at the time of enumeration (such as correctional institutions, nursing homes, and juvenile institutions). [3] Under 18 years. [4] No husband present.

Sources: Group Quarters Population—U.S. Census Bureau, 2000 Census of Population and Housing, "Census 2000 Profiles of General Demographic Characteristics" data files, published May 2001 (related Internet site <http://www.census.gov/mp/www/pub/2000cen/mscen01.html>). Households, 2000—U.S. Census Bureau, 2000 Census of Population and Housing, "Census 2000 Profiles of General Demographic Characteristics" data files, published May 2001 (related Internet site <http://www.census.gov/mp/www/pub/2000cen/mscen01.html>). Households, 1990—U.S. Census Bureau, 1990 Census of Population and Housing, Summary Tape File (STF) 1C on CD-ROM (related Internet site <http://homer.ssd.census.gov/cdrom/lookup>).

[Includes U.S., states, and 3,142 counties or county equivalents defined as of January 1, 1992. For changes to these areas since then, see appendix B. Geographic Information]

County	Group quarters population, 2000[1] Number	Institutionalized population[2]	Households 2000 Number	Percent change, 1990–2000	Persons per household	Percent— One-person	With 1 or more persons under 18 years	With 1 or more persons 65 years and over	Family households (families) Percent with own children under 18 years	Married-couple Number	Percent with own children[3]	Female householder[4] Number	Percent with own children[3]	Nonfamily households Number	Percent change, 1990–2000
GEORGIA—Con.															
Taylor	418	279	3 281	17.0	2.56	27.6	36.8	26.3	2 285	44.2	1 494	41.0	658	53.2	996	35.7
Telfair	1 547	1 547	4 110	3.1	2.48	28.4	36.4	29.7	2 872	44.9	2 002	41.9	692	51.6	1 268	13.6
Terrell	208	185	4 002	7.1	2.69	24.3	39.6	26.3	2 912	45.8	1 764	38.9	959	58.4	1 090	12.8
Thomas	1 149	898	16 309	13.9	2.55	25.8	37.8	25.7	11 466	46.5	7 819	42.3	3 000	58.2	4 843	31.6
Tift	1 509	626	13 919	14.2	2.65	23.3	40.0	22.3	10 105	48.8	7 152	44.3	2 351	61.1	3 814	23.7
Toombs	474	440	9 877	12.2	2.59	27.0	39.6	23.1	6 825	50.3	4 815	46.5	1 536	62.2	3 052	26.2
Towns	507	112	3 998	42.2	2.20	26.0	22.1	39.7	2 825	29.4	2 476	26.2	253	47.8	1 173	55.2
Treutlen	388	374	2 531	17.3	2.55	25.3	38.0	26.5	1 825	46.1	1 270	42.4	438	56.6	706	28.1
Troup	1 517	945	21 920	7.6	2.61	24.9	39.7	24.5	15 615	48.5	10 757	45.3	3 919	58.0	6 305	17.0
Turner	161	137	3 435	12.9	2.72	23.2	42.0	26.0	2 538	48.3	1 719	43.6	640	60.6	897	26.0
Twiggs	140	140	3 832	16.3	2.73	22.3	39.9	23.2	2 861	44.2	1 991	42.6	671	50.4	971	33.7
Union	443	396	7 159	52.0	2.35	24.2	27.1	35.4	5 209	34.1	4 501	31.2	505	53.7	1 950	84.7
Upson	452	413	10 722	8.2	2.53	25.2	37.0	27.4	7 690	44.2	5 434	40.7	1 811	53.2	3 032	17.7
Walker	1 005	987	23 605	8.8	2.54	22.9	36.6	25.7	17 472	44.0	13 645	41.9	2 836	51.8	6 133	27.5
Walton	542	530	21 307	58.6	2.82	16.6	43.9	19.2	16 995	49.2	13 360	47.0	2 735	58.5	4 312	60.7
Ware	2 251	2 105	13 475	3.3	2.47	27.9	35.2	28.1	9 299	44.4	6 774	40.8	1 993	55.9	4 176	15.0
Warren	117	105	2 435	14.3	2.55	27.4	36.6	29.6	1 692	44.0	1 026	36.8	539	57.3	743	41.0
Washington	1 452	1 222	7 435	10.3	2.65	24.8	40.6	26.0	5 384	47.8	3 475	44.5	1 595	54.9	2 051	16.9
Wayne	2 148	2 096	9 324	17.7	2.62	22.6	39.9	23.8	6 937	48.2	5 271	44.7	1 308	60.6	2 387	32.0
Webster	2	2	911	14.2	2.62	23.5	37.9	30.1	675	43.1	464	42.9	153	43.8	236	25.5
Wheeler	1 080	1 075	2 011	12.6	2.54	27.8	36.8	28.7	1 395	47.0	1 047	43.7	262	59.5	616	35.4
White	515	200	7 731	57.6	2.51	21.7	34.0	25.7	5 784	41.6	4 847	39.1	673	54.4	1 947	75.6
Whitfield	768	538	29 385	9.4	2.82	20.6	41.3	21.2	22 149	48.8	17 481	48.2	3 161	52.2	7 236	13.9
Wilcox	1 475	1 433	2 785	10.9	2.55	26.7	37.3	28.8	1 976	45.9	1 452	42.8	419	55.8	809	19.3
Wilkes	135	117	4 314	7.3	2.45	28.1	34.0	31.8	2 970	42.3	2 033	39.2	745	51.5	1 344	23.3
Wilkinson	83	76	3 827	5.7	2.65	24.1	40.2	25.7	2 806	45.9	1 935	42.2	704	55.4	1 021	18.2
Worth	208	27	8 106	17.6	2.68	21.5	41.1	23.5	6 124	48.1	4 512	44.1	1 270	61.7	1 982	35.1
HAWAII	35 782	7 690	403 240	13.2	2.92	21.9	37.9	27.4	287 068	45.0	216 077	44.8	49 923	47.3	116 172	25.2
Hawaii	2 804	931	52 985	27.8	2.75	23.1	37.5	26.7	36 903	46.3	26 828	42.1	7 000	58.5	16 082	43.3
Honolulu	30 945	5 809	286 450	8.0	2.95	21.6	37.8	28.1	205 672	44.3	156 195	45.1	35 138	43.4	80 778	18.8
Kalawao	–	–	115	85.5	1.28	79.1	1.7	39.1	22	9.1	19	5.3	3	33.3	93	138.5
Kauai	632	345	20 183	23.9	2.87	21.4	39.8	27.7	14 572	47.1	10 881	44.5	2 582	55.2	5 611	42.8
Maui	1 401	605	43 507	31.3	2.91	21.9	38.8	23.5	29 899	48.0	22 154	45.9	5 200	55.1	13 608	41.6
IDAHO	31 496	17 717	469 645	30.2	2.69	22.4	38.7	21.5	335 588	50.8	276 511	47.8	40 849	66.3	134 057	37.5
Ada	7 118	5 329	113 408	46.4	2.59	23.8	38.2	16.7	77 361	53.1	62 514	50.2	10 604	66.8	36 047	55.4
Adams	38	32	1 421	13.6	2.42	23.2	30.6	28.0	1 031	38.6	900	33.7	81	72.8	390	32.2
Bannock	2 285	872	27 192	16.1	2.69	22.8	39.0	19.5	19 213	51.7	15 413	49.0	2 724	64.8	7 979	20.6
Bear Lake	56	35	2 259	12.7	2.81	22.2	40.2	30.1	1 710	51.3	1 512	49.5	144	69.4	549	17.8
Benewah	142	129	3 580	19.7	2.52	24.0	34.4	25.6	2 537	44.1	2 091	39.7	277	62.1	1 043	35.8
Bingham	403	281	13 317	15.7	3.10	17.1	48.1	22.5	10 713	55.4	8 876	53.7	1 300	63.8	2 604	23.1
Blaine	353	97	7 780	41.3	2.40	27.3	33.1	14.0	4 841	51.2	3 986	47.1	561	72.9	2 939	34.9
Boise	76	33	2 616	92.8	2.52	21.8	33.2	20.0	1 899	42.2	1 636	37.9	151	67.5	717	92.7
Bonner	310	213	14 693	43.1	2.49	24.0	33.1	23.4	10 264	43.7	8 603	38.9	1 098	68.0	4 429	59.5
Bonneville	1 126	760	28 753	18.4	2.83	21.4	42.9	20.3	21 463	54.4	17 818	51.9	2 666	68.3	7 290	24.3
Boundary	212	67	3 707	29.8	2.61	23.1	36.5	24.4	2 698	46.9	2 275	42.7	277	71.1	1 009	46.0
Butte	21	21	1 089	9.2	2.64	23.6	34.7	28.7	803	44.5	688	42.4	81	66.7	286	21.7
Camas	3	3	396	44.0	2.49	22.2	32.1	23.0	287	42.5	258	39.9	18	72.2	109	65.2
Canyon	2 940	1 282	45 018	43.9	2.85	19.8	43.0	21.9	33 954	52.8	27 326	50.0	4 549	65.8	11 064	44.2
Caribou	63	36	2 560	13.2	2.83	20.4	41.8	26.3	1 978	51.2	1 773	49.4	134	71.6	582	23.6
Cassia	322	227	7 060	10.8	2.99	19.5	45.0	25.6	5 489	54.5	4 605	52.3	621	67.1	1 571	8.9
Clark	–	–	340	22.7	3.01	20.0	47.4	21.5	257	59.5	210	56.7	24	75.0	83	1.2
Clearwater	599	564	3 456	7.6	2.41	24.0	31.1	28.5	2 483	40.2	2 090	35.1	240	67.1	973	18.5
Custer	71	4	1 770	13.4	2.41	27.7	31.4	25.8	1 197	44.3	1 063	40.7	77	70.1	573	34.8
Elmore	4 060	3 268	9 092	27.4	2.76	20.7	45.4	16.2	6 848	57.1	5 826	54.4	685	75.5	2 244	45.7
Franklin	76	49	3 476	23.1	3.24	16.0	50.2	25.1	2 873	58.0	2 558	57.7	200	59.5	603	8.6
Fremont	316	288	3 885	12.5	2.96	19.5	42.2	25.9	3 029	50.7	2 637	49.4	270	58.5	856	14.7
Gem	199	144	5 539	25.2	2.70	20.8	37.3	28.7	4 175	45.1	3 509	42.8	465	56.6	1 364	26.3
Gooding	203	174	5 046	16.8	2.76	22.0	39.1	29.6	3 719	49.0	3 123	47.2	386	61.4	1 327	11.3
Idaho	539	401	6 084	17.3	2.46	25.3	31.5	30.1	4 294	41.4	3 699	37.8	385	63.6	1 790	29.3
Jefferson	81	20	5 901	21.1	3.23	15.2	49.7	21.0	4 880	57.5	4 285	56.7	404	66.3	1 021	22.0
Jerome	113	46	6 298	18.3	2.89	19.5	42.5	24.7	4 806	51.3	4 018	49.0	479	68.3	1 492	20.1

[1] As of April 1. [2] Includes people under formally authorized, supervised care or custody in institutions at the time of enumeration (such as correctional institutions, nursing homes, and juvenile institutions). [3] Under 18 years. [4] No husband present.

Sources: Group Quarters Population—U.S. Census Bureau, 2000 Census of Population and Housing, "Census 2000 Profiles of General Demographic Characteristics" data files, published May 2001 (related Internet site <http://www.census.gov/mp/www/pub/2000cen/mscen01.html>). Households, 2000—U.S. Census Bureau, 2000 Census of Population and Housing, "Census 2000 Profiles of General Demographic Characteristics" data files, published May 2001 (related Internet site <http://www.census.gov/mp/www/pub/2000cen/mscen01.html>). Households, 1990—U.S. Census Bureau, 1990 Census of Population and Housing, Summary Tape File (STF) 1C on CD-ROM (related Internet site <http://homer.ssd.census.gov/cdrom/lookup>).

[Includes U.S., states, and 3,142 counties or county equivalents defined as of January 1, 1992. For changes to these areas since then, see appendix B. Geographic Information]

County	Group quarters population, 2000[1] Number	Institutionalized population[2]	Households Number	Percent change, 1990–2000	Persons per household	One-person	With 1 or more persons under 18 years	With 1 or more persons 65 years and over	Family households Number	Percent with own children under 18 years	Married-couple Number	Percent with own children[3]	Female householder[4] Number	Percent with own children[3]	Nonfamily households Number	Percent change, 1990–2000
IDAHO—Con.																
Kootenai	1 400	928	41 308	53.3	2.60	21.9	37.4	22.3	29 668	48.5	24 213	44.3	3 784	67.8	11 640	55.3
Latah	3 914	344	13 059	16.3	2.38	26.3	29.1	16.3	7 764	47.0	6 592	44.0	794	66.4	5 295	27.8
Lemhi	27	14	3 275	18.3	2.38	27.7	30.7	29.4	2 217	42.3	1 892	38.7	227	66.5	1 058	28.4
Lewis	34	8	1 554	11.6	2.39	28.1	30.1	32.8	1 050	40.8	898	36.5	100	71.0	504	26.6
Lincoln	36	32	1 447	21.5	2.77	22.9	40.8	25.2	1 050	52.0	890	50.3	80	61.3	397	21.8
Madison	1 396	170	7 129	22.9	3.66	12.7	40.9	15.8	4 855	57.3	4 287	56.7	403	65.8	2 274	37.5
Minidoka	144	122	6 973	7.7	2.87	20.0	42.2	26.2	5 360	50.6	4 492	48.7	571	60.9	1 613	15.9
Nez Perce	662	405	15 286	12.2	2.40	26.7	31.7	27.4	10 151	43.7	8 077	38.9	1 416	63.3	5 135	20.6
Oneida	46	28	1 430	23.4	2.85	22.5	40.6	31.0	1 093	50.2	980	48.4	65	66.2	337	22.1
Owyhee	74	65	3 710	31.6	2.85	21.8	41.0	24.6	2 756	50.9	2 272	48.1	322	68.6	954	29.1
Payette	117	66	7 371	22.0	2.78	20.6	40.9	26.3	5 576	49.9	4 568	46.5	689	65.7	1 795	17.8
Power	54	52	2 560	8.0	2.92	20.3	44.6	22.0	1 968	53.2	1 624	49.8	226	72.1	592	13.4
Shoshone	197	187	5 906	3.8	2.30	29.4	29.2	29.2	3 858	40.8	3 113	34.5	478	65.7	2 048	18.2
Teton	31	6	2 078	85.0	2.87	21.3	41.8	15.6	1 465	56.2	1 254	56.3	120	60.0	613	112.1
Twin Falls	1 420	730	23 853	20.9	2.64	23.6	37.4	25.7	16 967	48.8	13 828	45.4	2 190	64.6	6 886	29.7
Valley	72	65	3 208	33.4	2.36	24.8	30.0	24.3	2 251	40.1	1 955	35.1	173	72.8	957	50.2
Washington	147	120	3 762	15.5	2.61	23.5	35.8	32.6	2 737	45.0	2 284	42.8	310	59.4	1 025	15.2
ILLINOIS	321 781	174 727	4 591 779	9.3	2.63	26.8	36.2	23.2	3 105 513	48.8	2 353 892	47.3	563 718	56.0	1 486 266	16.4
Adams	2 750	2 003	26 860	5.3	2.44	28.5	33.4	28.5	18 003	46.4	14 554	42.6	2 644	64.0	8 857	13.1
Alexander	595	549	3 808	−10.1	2.36	32.3	34.0	31.3	2 475	46.2	1 681	38.7	665	63.9	1 333	−2.3
Bond	2 414	1 781	6 155	8.9	2.47	25.6	34.7	29.0	4 348	45.5	3 636	42.3	497	62.4	1 807	17.8
Boone	319	308	14 597	33.3	2.84	19.0	42.9	21.2	11 260	52.0	9 373	50.1	1 277	65.1	3 337	35.5
Brown	1 972	1 972	2 108	5.9	2.36	30.8	31.2	29.1	1 380	44.5	1 165	40.6	144	64.6	728	16.5
Bureau	500	370	14 182	2.8	2.47	27.0	32.7	30.4	9 890	44.1	8 242	41.0	1 129	60.1	4 292	10.8
Calhoun	55	55	2 046	−.1	2.46	26.5	30.7	33.0	1 439	41.3	1 244	40.4	116	46.6	607	13.0
Carroll	248	220	6 794	2.4	2.42	27.3	31.2	32.0	4 081	42.0	3 905	38.4	502	62.9	2 113	14.0
Cass	212	177	5 347	2.9	2.52	26.1	34.9	27.8	3 692	46.4	2 985	43.1	490	62.0	1 655	11.3
Champaign	14 838	1 479	70 597	10.5	2.33	31.4	29.1	17.4	39 308	48.9	30 766	44.8	6 489	66.8	31 289	23.7
Christian	1 810	1 719	13 921	2.4	2.41	28.4	33.0	30.4	9 477	44.6	7 697	40.9	1 270	60.9	4 444	11.6
Clark	247	241	6 971	9.0	2.40	28.1	33.4	30.0	4 808	45.2	3 969	41.5	604	62.4	2 163	18.8
Clay	477	360	5 839	2.3	2.41	27.9	32.7	31.4	4 003	44.6	3 291	41.0	502	60.6	1 836	15.3
Clinton	2 366	2 280	12 754	10.1	2.60	24.2	37.0	27.4	9 226	48.6	7 671	46.9	1 074	58.5	3 528	25.2
Coles	4 554	825	21 043	11.0	2.31	31.2	27.9	23.1	12 071	45.5	9 722	41.7	1 737	62.6	8 972	28.0
Cook	93 617	47 532	1 974 181	5.0	2.68	29.4	35.2	23.5	1 269 592	48.0	868 244	47.9	307 079	51.7	704 589	11.7
Crawford	1 568	1 446	7 842	.6	2.41	26.8	32.9	30.2	5 447	44.1	4 533	40.8	677	61.0	2 395	8.6
Cumberland	135	135	4 368	8.4	2.55	25.5	35.7	28.4	3 085	46.9	2 601	44.0	332	62.3	1 283	20.4
DeKalb	7 785	700	31 674	19.9	2.56	25.5	34.4	18.7	19 964	51.6	16 113	49.1	2 686	66.0	11 710	24.9
De Witt	266	235	6 770	4.3	2.44	26.8	33.3	27.4	4 683	44.7	3 843	40.8	574	62.4	2 087	13.7
Douglas	300	256	7 574	5.1	2.59	24.7	35.4	28.6	5 476	46.3	4 631	43.8	602	59.6	2 098	14.4
DuPage	15 113	8 125	325 601	16.6	2.73	22.9	38.9	18.6	234 354	51.4	198 240	51.8	25 882	52.8	91 247	29.4
Edgar	788	747	7 874	.2	2.40	28.5	32.6	30.3	5 326	44.2	4 249	39.5	756	62.2	2 548	8.4
Edwards	72	42	2 905	−3.7	2.37	27.5	31.6	31.1	2 027	42.8	1 715	39.7	237	58.6	878	2.7
Effingham	467	368	13 001	13.4	2.60	26.1	37.9	25.2	9 182	51.4	7 511	48.7	1 183	66.4	3 819	28.0
Fayette	1 774	1 717	8 146	5.5	2.46	27.2	34.5	29.5	5 657	45.9	4 613	42.7	689	60.5	2 489	13.7
Ford	403	403	5 639	.7	2.45	28.0	33.9	31.9	3 903	45.9	3 260	42.5	453	63.8	1 736	8.2
Franklin	565	480	16 408	−.9	2.34	29.8	30.9	32.0	10 971	42.2	8 689	38.3	1 657	57.3	5 437	5.4
Fulton	2 562	2 521	14 877	−.1	2.40	27.5	31.1	32.0	10 252	41.5	8 409	37.5	1 311	59.3	4 625	6.0
Gallatin	71	52	2 726	−2.1	2.34	29.4	30.3	32.0	1 838	42.0	1 493	38.4	266	59.0	888	9.4
Greene	325	324	5 757	−2.6	2.51	25.7	35.4	31.3	4 078	45.9	3 284	43.3	532	55.3	1 679	2.4
Grundy	347	334	14 293	19.3	2.60	23.5	37.6	22.2	10 278	46.3	8 514	46.3	1 228	63.4	4 015	29.2
Hamilton	205	164	3 462	−.4	2.43	27.3	32.6	33.4	2 436	42.6	2 043	39.8	274	56.6	1 026	1.8
Hancock	360	269	8 069	−4.0	2.45	26.9	32.4	30.8	5 606	44.0	4 754	41.2	613	58.1	2 463	4.9
Hardin	237	223	1 987	−3.0	2.30	28.6	30.6	32.8	1 367	41.3	1 136	38.9	175	59.3	620	3.7
Henderson	77	64	3 365	4.0	2.42	25.3	31.3	28.8	2 377	40.5	2 004	37.1	240	57.1	988	6.2
Henry	587	527	20 056	2.8	2.51	25.1	34.0	28.8	14 309	44.6	12 028	41.5	1 614	62.0	5 747	11.8
Iroquois	686	640	12 220	3.7	2.51	25.2	33.7	30.9	8 712	43.9	7 234	41.0	1 042	58.6	3 508	11.5
Jackson	6 208	965	24 215	3.2	2.21	34.9	26.2	19.4	12 653	46.7	9 509	41.4	2 354	66.9	11 562	8.9
Jasper	78	78	3 930	−.8	2.55	24.7	34.9	29.5	2 850	45.4	2 450	43.3	277	57.8	1 080	9.5
Jefferson	2 570	2 449	15 374	5.3	2.44	27.6	33.6	27.8	10 559	45.3	8 497	41.0	1 517	63.0	4 815	14.1
Jersey	897	375	8 096	10.2	2.57	23.9	36.8	26.3	5 861	47.8	4 865	45.2	737	61.7	2 235	24.0
Jo Daviess	203	162	9 218	10.1	2.40	27.5	28.9	30.4	6 287	40.1	5 368	37.5	599	59.1	2 931	29.4
Johnson	2 724	2 689	4 183	12.3	2.43	24.2	33.0	29.3	3 052	41.9	2 607	39.5	299	58.5	1 131	19.3
Kane	6 503	4 631	133 901	24.9	2.97	19.6	44.6	17.8	101 454	54.9	81 968	54.4	13 406	61.1	32 447	25.0

[1] As of April 1. [2] Includes people under formally authorized, supervised care or custody in institutions at the time of enumeration (such as correctional institutions, nursing homes, and juvenile institutions). [3] Under 18 years. [4] No husband present.

Sources: Group Quarters Population—U.S. Census Bureau, 2000 Census of Population and Housing, "Census 2000 Profiles of General Demographic Characteristics" data files, published May 2001 (related Internet site <http://www.census.gov/mp/www/pub/2000cen/mscen01.html>). Households, 2000—U.S. Census Bureau, 2000 Census of Population and Housing, "Census 2000 Profiles of General Demographic Characteristics" data files, published May 2001 (related Internet site <http://www.census.gov/mp/www/pub/2000cen/mscen01.html>). Households, 1990—U.S. Census Bureau, 1990 Census of Population and Housing, Summary Tape File (STF) 1C on CD-ROM (related Internet site <http://homer.ssd.census.gov/cdrom/lookup>).

[Includes U.S., states, and 3,142 counties or county equivalents defined as of January 1, 1992. For changes to these areas since then, see appendix B. Geographic Information]

County	Group quarters population, 2000[1] Number	Institutionalized population[2]	Households, 2000 (April 1) Number	Percent change, 1990–2000	Persons per house-hold	Percent— One-person	With 1 or more persons under 18 years	With 1 or more persons 65 years and over	Family households (families) Number	Percent with own children under 18 years	Married-couple Number	Percent with own children[3]	Female householder[4] Number	Percent with own children[3]	Nonfamily households Number	Percent change 1990–2000
ILLINOIS—Con.																
Kankakee	4 096	2 339	38 182	10.3	2.61	24.9	37.8	24.3	26 759	49.1	20 145	45.1	5 000	62.7	11 423	17.8
Kendall	192	190	18 798	41.3	2.89	16.4	44.2	17.5	14 969	52.3	12 938	51.6	1 407	59.4	3 829	50.3
Knox	4 370	2 836	22 056	.7	2.33	29.6	30.3	30.0	14 429	42.3	11 328	36.6	2 342	65.2	7 627	9.7
Lake	20 978	5 642	216 297	24.3	2.88	19.7	44.4	17.7	163 978	55.5	136 686	54.9	19 861	62.3	52 319	32.8
La Salle	3 208	2 871	43 417	5.2	2.49	27.4	33.9	29.0	29 840	46.1	24 166	43.2	4 011	59.8	13 577	13.4
Lawrence	588	483	6 309	–.2	2.36	29.2	31.3	31.3	4 254	42.6	3 462	38.9	568	57.6	2 055	9.8
Lee	3 006	2 744	13 253	6.2	2.49	26.5	34.5	26.9	9 138	46.6	7 410	42.6	1 235	64.3	4 115	16.3
Livingston	3 623	3 214	14 374	4.6	2.51	26.8	35.1	27.7	9 948	47.5	8 163	43.6	1 265	65.4	4 426	17.8
Logan	4 275	3 234	11 113	.7	2.42	27.8	33.5	28.7	7 583	45.7	6 142	41.5	1 035	63.3	3 530	7.8
McDonough	4 776	382	12 360	.9	2.28	31.8	25.8	25.5	7 096	42.4	5 816	38.5	922	62.1	5 264	12.8
McHenry	1 519	1 106	89 403	42.0	2.89	16.4	44.9	16.8	69 303	55.3	59 453	55.0	6 760	59.9	20 100	52.7
McLean	11 293	1 222	56 746	21.3	2.45	27.6	33.1	18.0	35 470	50.3	28 911	47.2	4 995	66.5	21 276	29.0
Macon	3 573	1 690	46 561	1.2	2.39	28.8	32.4	26.3	30 960	44.5	23 626	38.8	5 664	65.3	15 601	14.2
Macoupin	1 190	820	19 253	5.9	2.48	25.6	34.0	30.1	13 629	44.4	11 183	40.7	1 712	61.3	5 624	16.4
Madison	5 779	2 754	101 953	7.5	2.48	26.3	34.9	25.5	70 070	46.8	54 078	43.1	12 031	60.4	31 883	20.6
Marion	969	905	16 619	2.1	2.45	27.2	34.2	28.8	11 487	45.4	8 852	40.3	1 925	62.1	5 132	8.2
Marshall	277	260	5 225	6.6	2.47	25.0	31.3	30.6	3 718	41.6	3 177	38.9	348	59.5	1 507	19.5
Mason	219	179	6 389	.7	2.48	24.9	33.4	29.8	4 563	42.7	3 728	38.9	574	58.7	1 826	7.5
Massac	334	306	6 261	6.0	2.37	28.0	32.6	29.6	4 318	43.4	3 476	39.9	626	59.3	1 943	16.1
Menard	182	182	4 873	16.1	2.52	23.8	37.6	23.2	3 550	49.6	2 958	45.6	442	69.2	1 323	31.5
Mercer	213	213	6 624	.8	2.53	22.8	34.8	27.7	4 914	43.2	4 209	40.3	479	61.0	1 710	4.1
Monroe	384	364	10 275	25.5	2.65	21.3	39.5	23.9	7 780	49.8	6 710	48.6	748	56.6	2 495	28.1
Montgomery	2 559	2 516	11 507	.2	2.44	27.8	34.4	30.7	7 927	46.4	6 456	42.3	1 023	63.7	3 580	11.3
Morgan	3 370	2 127	14 039	2.6	2.37	29.3	32.3	27.5	9 251	45.6	7 396	41.2	1 401	64.6	4 788	8.9
Moultrie	469	390	5 405	5.5	2.56	23.6	35.2	28.3	3 976	44.9	3 423	42.4	385	60.5	1 429	13.4
Ogle	614	565	19 278	12.5	2.62	22.5	37.8	24.1	14 168	48.3	11 811	45.2	1 608	65.2	5 110	17.3
Peoria	6 880	2 928	72 733	2.7	2.43	29.7	32.7	24.6	47 133	46.1	35 343	40.5	9 347	65.1	25 600	11.4
Perry	2 443	2 407	8 504	2.4	2.43	27.9	32.8	30.7	5 843	43.8	4 700	40.2	829	58.7	2 661	16.4
Piatt	192	172	6 475	9.1	2.50	23.7	34.5	26.6	4 727	44.7	4 099	42.3	442	64.0	1 748	21.9
Pike	722	681	6 876	–2.0	2.42	27.8	32.6	33.4	4 780	43.9	4 023	41.2	534	58.4	2 096	3.9
Pope	287	55	1 769	9.8	2.33	27.9	29.7	31.1	1 220	39.9	1 023	36.4	134	64.2	549	21.2
Pulaski	291	235	2 893	–2.2	2.44	30.0	35.4	32.9	1 942	46.5	1 372	41.5	458	60.0	951	2.0
Putnam	11	10	2 415	9.6	2.52	24.6	32.7	28.8	1 749	42.1	1 499	40.0	168	58.9	666	21.8
Randolph	4 115	3 996	12 084	1.1	2.46	26.9	33.7	29.3	8 363	45.3	6 768	41.9	1 116	61.1	3 721	12.8
Richland	150	128	6 660	2.4	2.40	27.7	32.1	30.1	4 534	44.9	3 714	40.2	588	66.3	2 126	16.2
Rock Island	4 645	2 660	60 712	2.4	2.38	30.2	31.7	26.5	39 162	44.9	29 826	39.5	7 054	64.4	21 550	11.2
St. Clair	4 869	3 508	96 810	1.5	2.59	25.9	38.4	24.6	67 323	49.6	46 557	45.5	16 551	60.3	29 487	10.9
Saline	1 183	1 177	10 992	1.4	2.32	31.3	31.5	32.0	7 229	44.0	5 708	40.7	1 126	58.1	3 763	8.3
Sangamon	3 334	1 762	78 722	9.1	2.36	31.0	32.8	22.9	49 898	48.2	37 974	43.6	9 203	63.9	28 824	17.2
Schuyler	105	87	2 975	–.9	2.38	27.3	30.9	31.5	2 070	41.3	1 775	38.8	211	55.5	905	8.5
Scott	56	56	2 222	1.5	2.47	26.1	36.0	29.0	1 562	48.1	1 295	45.4	185	61.6	660	13.6
Shelby	293	249	9 056	5.8	2.50	25.4	33.1	30.6	6 502	43.2	5 546	40.1	644	61.5	2 554	20.0
Stark	117	115	2 525	.5	2.46	27.1	32.4	32.4	1 765	43.3	1 515	41.8	177	53.1	760	11.6
Stephenson	820	638	19 785	4.6	2.43	27.6	32.8	27.7	13 471	45.1	10 962	40.5	1 878	67.6	6 314	12.3
Tazewell	3 302	2 872	50 327	6.7	2.49	24.8	34.2	25.7	35 859	44.6	29 817	41.2	4 363	63.0	14 468	18.5
Union	915	320	7 290	6.6	2.38	28.4	32.4	30.0	4 973	44.4	4 053	41.0	690	61.0	2 317	16.8
Vermilion	3 109	2 931	33 406	–2.0	2.42	28.9	33.3	28.5	22 313	45.1	16 914	39.3	4 074	63.5	11 093	9.1
Wabash	177	158	5 192	3.2	2.46	27.0	33.5	29.4	3 588	44.8	2 972	42.0	454	57.5	1 604	12.2
Warren	1 223	280	7 166	–3.1	2.44	26.7	32.1	28.7	4 968	43.0	4 049	38.8	632	62.7	2 198	–.8
Washington	262	222	5 848	3.4	2.55	24.3	35.3	29.8	4 242	46.2	3 607	41.4	418	58.6	1 606	5.4
Wayne	207	169	7 143	3.0	2.37	27.6	32.1	31.7	4 973	42.8	4 167	39.4	596	61.6	2 170	15.8
White	427	399	6 534	–4.5	2.29	29.8	29.2	33.3	4 376	40.0	3 697	36.5	495	58.8	2 158	6.1
Whiteside	1 254	872	23 684	4.2	2.51	25.1	34.4	27.7	16 759	44.5	13 630	40.4	2 261	63.5	6 925	15.4
Will	9 661	7 294	167 542	43.3	2.94	17.8	45.6	17.5	130 972	54.6	108 630	54.5	16 093	57.4	36 570	50.5
Williamson	1 653	1 550	25 358	9.7	2.35	28.9	31.7	28.0	16 969	44.0	13 531	40.3	2 598	60.2	8 389	19.7
Winnebago	5 074	3 600	107 980	11.6	2.53	26.3	36.0	22.7	73 666	48.2	56 423	43.9	12 751	64.4	34 314	22.4
Woodford	1 098	670	12 797	12.3	2.69	20.5	37.2	25.7	9 807	46.2	8 634	44.4	850	61.5	2 990	22.3
INDIANA	178 154	90 885	2 336 306	13.1	2.53	25.9	35.7	22.5	1 602 501	47.9	1 251 458	44.4	259 372	61.8	733 805	25.4
Adams	427	368	11 818	12.9	2.81	24.0	39.2	25.7	8 668	51.1	7 288	48.9	982	64.9	3 150	31.5
Allen	5 580	3 317	128 745	13.6	2.53	27.4	36.6	20.4	86 235	50.9	66 251	46.9	15 105	66.4	42 510	26.1
Bartholomew	900	863	27 936	15.5	2.52	24.0	36.5	21.4	20 067	47.2	16 377	44.0	2 721	62.9	7 869	30.0
Benton	203	203	3 558	1.0	2.59	24.5	37.9	27.3	2 549	49.1	2 118	45.5	304	66.1	1 009	9.0
Blackford	183	177	5 690	4.7	2.44	25.9	33.5	26.9	4 029	43.5	3 231	39.1	569	61.9	1 661	19.2
Boone	829	719	17 081	22.7	2.65	21.1	40.1	20.9	12 810	50.7	11 008	48.7	1 332	62.9	4 271	37.5
Brown	139	127	5 897	9.8	2.51	20.6	32.2	22.5	4 435	39.7	3 820	37.2	383	54.0	1 462	13.0
Carroll	212	202	7 718	9.2	2.59	22.8	35.3	24.7	5 686	45.0	4 901	42.5	503	58.4	2 032	21.1
Cass	1 162	989	15 715	7.2	2.53	25.9	34.4	26.7	10 928	45.5	8 791	42.4	1 477	60.4	4 787	18.2

[1] As of April 1. [2] Includes people under formally authorized, supervised care or custody in institutions at the time of enumeration (such as correctional institutions, nursing homes, and juvenile institutions). [3] Under 18 years. [4] No husband present.

Sources: Group Quarters Population—U.S. Census Bureau, 2000 Census of Population and Housing, "Census 2000 Profiles of General Demographic Characteristics" data files, published May 2001 (related Internet site <http://www.census.gov/mp/www/pub/2000cen/mscen01.html>).   Households, 2000—U.S. Census Bureau, 2000 Census of Population and Housing, "Census 2000 Profiles of General Demographic Characteristics" data files, published May 2001 (related Internet site <http://www.census.gov/mp/www/pub/2000cen/mscen01.html>).   Households, 1990—U.S. Census Bureau, 1990 Census of Population and Housing, Summary Tape File (STF) 1C on CD-ROM (related Internet site <http://homer.ssd.census.gov/cdrom/lookup>).

Table B–3. Counties — Group Quarters Population and Households–Con.

[Includes U.S., states, and 3,142 counties or county equivalents defined as of January 1, 1992. For changes to these areas since then, see appendix B. Geographic Information]

County	Group quarters population, 2000[1] Number	Institutionalized population[2]	Households, 2000 (April 1) Number	Percent change, 1990–2000	Persons per household	Percent— One-person	With 1 or more persons under 18 years	With 1 or more persons 65 years and over	Family households (families) Number	Percent with own children under 18 years	Married-couple Number	Percent with own children[3]	Female householder[4] Number	Percent with own children[3]	Nonfamily households Number	Percent change, 1990–2000
INDIANA—Con.																
Clark	1 578	1 286	38 751	16.4	2.45	26.3	34.7	21.8	26 541	45.9	20 170	42.1	4 832	59.4	12 210	36.6
Clay	314	286	10 216	8.9	2.57	23.8	36.5	27.5	7 435	46.2	6 102	43.2	958	59.8	2 781	13.5
Clinton	854	834	12 545	9.6	2.63	23.6	37.8	24.9	9 059	48.7	7 390	45.6	1 123	64.2	3 486	22.7
Crawford	101	90	4 181	14.2	2.55	22.5	35.8	23.1	3 057	44.4	2 471	40.6	397	61.2	1 124	24.1
Daviess	544	496	10 094	8.0	2.69	25.0	37.8	26.9	7 023	49.4	6 511	47.1	945	61.4	3 071	17.8
Dearborn	513	430	16 832	23.4	2.71	20.1	40.3	21.3	12 768	49.3	10 523	46.7	1 618	62.7	4 064	37.8
Decatur	295	267	9 389	11.4	2.58	22.8	36.8	23.6	6 878	46.5	5 644	43.6	867	58.9	2 511	27.3
De Kalb	454	405	15 134	18.9	2.63	23.4	39.1	21.2	10 915	50.3	8 968	47.3	1 334	64.9	4 219	35.7
Delaware	6 933	1 609	47 131	4.3	2.37	28.2	30.4	23.6	29 686	44.2	22 881	39.2	5 150	62.9	17 445	16.4
Dubois	779	537	14 813	13.7	2.63	23.5	38.7	22.7	10 743	51.2	9 156	49.5	1 091	62.7	4 070	28.1
Elkhart	2 782	1 692	66 154	16.6	2.72	22.6	39.6	20.8	47 659	50.5	37 573	46.8	6 955	66.7	18 495	23.6
Fayette	500	434	10 199	2.6	2.46	25.8	34.0	27.2	7 151	44.0	5 672	39.6	1 043	61.0	3 048	15.8
Floyd	1 039	953	27 511	14.2	2.54	23.5	37.5	21.6	19 707	48.5	15 231	45.0	3 424	61.6	7 804	29.5
Fountain	184	183	7 041	2.7	2.52	24.8	35.4	28.2	5 038	45.6	4 158	42.8	566	59.0	2 003	10.4
Franklin	360	195	7 868	18.6	2.77	19.0	40.2	23.4	6 130	48.2	5 193	47.0	630	56.2	1 738	30.4
Fulton	153	153	8 082	10.0	2.52	24.9	34.4	27.6	5 739	44.8	4 807	41.3	607	61.1	2 343	17.5
Gibson	683	440	12 847	4.5	2.48	25.7	34.5	27.1	9 092	45.3	7 462	41.9	1 178	61.8	3 755	13.9
Grant	4 515	1 277	28 319	2.2	2.43	26.7	32.9	26.8	19 578	42.6	15 194	39.7	3 266	62.2	8 741	16.5
Greene	546	488	13 372	12.3	2.44	26.5	34.2	26.4	9 366	45.3	7 752	41.8	1 127	62.6	4 006	24.5
Hamilton	1 617	1 316	65 933	69.8	2.75	18.6	45.0	14.1	50 849	56.6	44 507	55.2	4 639	67.1	15 084	89.0
Hancock	458	414	20 718	29.8	2.65	18.8	39.0	20.8	16 156	47.0	13 990	45.0	1 535	60.1	4 562	48.5
Harrison	360	306	12 917	21.7	2.63	20.7	38.8	21.4	9 712	47.9	8 058	45.2	1 140	61.6	3 205	47.0
Hendricks	3 218	3 058	37 275	42.8	2.71	18.3	41.8	18.4	29 084	50.8	25 009	48.7	2 879	64.0	8 191	67.5
Henry	692	610	19 486	4.5	2.45	24.8	33.4	27.4	13 975	42.8	11 379	39.3	1 926	57.7	5 511	18.1
Howard	1 157	993	34 800	10.4	2.41	28.2	33.8	23.0	23 572	46.2	18 344	41.2	3 989	65.3	11 228	27.7
Huntington	1 435	749	14 242	11.0	2.57	23.6	33.8	23.7	10 280	47.6	8 458	44.4	1 297	62.4	3 962	24.3
Jackson	556	500	16 052	14.4	2.54	23.5	36.7	23.5	11 573	46.7	9 329	44.2	1 597	57.3	4 479	34.5
Jasper	988	329	10 686	25.3	2.72	19.9	39.4	24.1	8 213	47.4	6 992	45.6	818	57.0	2 473	37.3
Jay	227	170	8 405	3.0	2.57	24.8	34.9	27.1	6 016	45.1	4 946	42.2	763	57.9	2 389	12.4
Jefferson	1 044	639	12 140	11.5	2.46	25.7	35.0	20.9	8 435	46.1	6 877	42.0	1 292	60.1	3 710	29.2
Jennings	530	178	10 134	21.4	2.67	20.6	40.2	20.5	7 604	48.6	6 156	45.4	960	61.6	2 530	31.7
Johnson	3 603	1 432	42 434	35.3	2.63	21.2	39.8	19.0	31 660	50.2	26 309	47.6	3 817	64.4	10 834	52.7
Knox	2 496	658	15 552	2.7	2.36	29.7	32.1	27.1	10 136	46.0	8 019	42.0	1 586	62.7	5 416	10.6
Kosciusko	1 371	1 124	27 283	16.4	2.66	21.9	38.3	21.1	19 997	48.6	16 604	45.4	2 263	63.6	7 286	31.9
Lagrange	205	156	11 225	21.9	3.09	18.0	42.8	21.2	8 856	51.4	7 650	50.6	776	55.9	2 369	31.1
Lake	5 648	3 686	181 633	6.4	2.64	25.8	37.1	25.3	127 036	46.9	88 473	44.1	30 202	55.9	54 597	21.4
La Porte	6 490	6 256	41 050	6.7	2.52	25.2	35.1	25.6	28 597	45.7	22 093	41.9	4 787	60.5	12 453	17.7
Lawrence	717	659	18 535	14.2	2.44	25.5	34.2	25.5	13 139	44.3	10 839	41.1	1 659	60.3	5 396	32.8
Madison	5 326	3 980	53 052	6.5	2.41	27.2	33.1	26.6	36 211	43.8	27 835	38.7	6 234	61.9	16 841	20.3
Marion	18 696	11 963	352 164	10.2	2.39	31.8	33.6	19.6	213 454	49.8	145 161	44.7	52 302	62.8	138 710	21.9
Marshall	681	401	16 519	9.1	2.69	22.3	38.3	24.5	12 188	48.5	10 127	46.1	1 369	62.2	4 331	19.0
Martin	108	104	4 183	9.0	2.45	27.6	33.9	26.4	2 876	46.0	2 363	43.4	343	59.5	1 307	31.2
Miami	1 490	1 455	13 716	1.7	2.52	24.6	36.3	23.9	9 803	47.1	7 921	43.1	1 350	64.5	3 913	22.3
Monroe	14 331	1 140	46 898	19.2	2.27	32.4	25.9	16.6	24 737	46.0	19 584	41.9	3 788	63.8	22 161	35.1
Montgomery	1 205	491	14 595	10.3	2.50	25.3	35.7	24.5	10 246	47.6	8 413	43.4	1 258	68.9	4 349	18.9
Morgan	696	609	24 437	24.7	2.70	18.4	40.2	20.3	19 025	47.4	15 927	45.1	2 090	58.9	5 412	45.7
Newton	190	190	5 340	10.4	2.69	20.9	37.4	24.1	4 000	45.7	3 368	43.5	414	56.0	1 340	18.7
Noble	662	623	16 696	24.4	2.73	21.9	40.5	21.0	12 294	50.8	10 044	48.1	1 501	65.8	4 402	41.5
Ohio	46	46	2 201	11.2	2.53	23.2	34.8	24.8	1 588	44.3	1 318	40.7	187	61.0	613	26.9
Orange	314	306	7 621	9.7	2.49	26.2	34.8	26.3	5 340	46.3	4 392	43.3	653	61.1	2 281	28.1
Owen	287	243	8 282	29.5	2.60	21.3	36.8	23.4	6 192	44.9	5 160	41.6	704	61.4	2 090	43.3
Parke	1 168	1 114	6 415	9.8	2.51	24.1	33.0	27.7	4 627	42.3	3 843	38.6	531	61.4	1 788	19.0
Perry	1 111	1 071	7 270	6.2	2.45	26.7	33.0	27.6	5 071	43.9	4 123	41.0	657	55.6	2 199	28.7
Pike	172	156	5 119	3.9	2.47	24.9	32.8	27.2	3 682	42.6	3 059	39.5	429	57.1	1 437	13.4
Porter	3 530	1 257	54 649	21.0	2.62	22.2	37.5	20.4	39 709	48.2	32 667	46.2	5 041	58.4	14 940	41.9
Posey	272	260	10 205	7.3	2.63	22.1	38.8	23.0	7 613	48.8	6 484	46.4	799	62.2	2 592	19.1
Pulaski	368	339	5 170	9.5	2.59	23.5	36.6	27.5	3 780	46.4	3 175	43.6	379	63.1	1 390	12.4
Putnam	4 373	2 447	12 374	23.8	2.56	22.4	36.5	24.4	9 121	46.1	7 727	42.9	953	65.0	3 253	32.9
Randolph	311	273	10 937	4.7	2.48	25.0	34.0	27.5	7 798	44.2	6 444	40.7	951	59.4	3 139	17.9
Ripley	353	268	9 842	12.1	2.66	22.7	39.3	24.7	7 272	49.7	6 029	47.6	853	60.5	2 570	20.5
Rush	279	259	6 923	6.4	2.60	23.3	37.0	26.5	5 047	47.0	4 210	44.6	584	59.2	1 876	23.5
St. Joseph	13 414	2 948	100 743	9.1	2.50	27.9	34.9	24.6	66 802	48.3	50 369	44.2	12 507	62.9	33 941	18.1
Scott	208	172	8 832	16.3	2.58	22.5	38.8	21.4	6 495	47.6	5 087	44.3	1 002	59.3	2 337	36.5
Shelby	668	438	16 561	12.2	2.58	22.7	37.9	22.1	12 057	47.7	9 800	44.1	1 541	63.1	4 504	25.4
Spencer	363	200	7 569	8.7	2.65	20.8	37.7	24.3	5 755	46.5	4 923	45.0	545	53.8	1 814	15.2
Starke	310	309	8 740	7.4	2.66	22.4	37.2	26.0	6 447	45.7	5 192	42.6	866	59.1	2 293	17.3
Steuben	924	259	12 738	25.0	2.53	24.3	35.2	21.8	8 911	46.5	7 265	42.1	1 088	65.7	3 827	39.3
Sullivan	2 292	2 244	7 819	6.2	2.49	25.3	34.9	27.7	5 573	44.8	4 545	42.2	731	58.0	2 246	10.9
Switzerland	92	79	3 435	21.0	2.61	21.7	36.3	23.4	2 540	44.6	2 018	40.5	349	60.2	895	20.9
Tippecanoe	15 126	1 629	55 226	21.1	2.42	28.0	30.4	16.7	32 403	48.6	25 918	45.5	4 603	65.4	22 823	35.2

[1] As of April 1.　[2] Includes people under formally authorized, supervised care or custody in institutions at the time of enumeration (such as correctional institutions, nursing homes, and juvenile institutions).　[3] Under 18 years.　[4] No husband present.

Sources: Group Quarters Population—U.S. Census Bureau, 2000 Census of Population and Housing, "Census 2000 Profiles of General Demographic Characteristics" data files, published May 2001 (related Internet site <http://www.census.gov/mp/www/pub/2000cen/mscen01.html>). Households, 2000—U.S. Census Bureau, 2000 Census of Population and Housing, "Census 2000 Profiles of General Demographic Characteristics" data files, published May 2001 (related Internet site <http://www.census.gov/mp/www/pub/2000cen/mscen01.html>). Households, 1990—U.S. Census Bureau, 1990 Census of Population and Housing, Summary Tape File (STF) 1C on CD-ROM (related Internet site <http://homer.ssd.census.gov/cdrom/lookup>).

[Includes U.S., states, and 3,142 counties or county equivalents defined as of January 1, 1992. For changes to these areas since then, see appendix B. Geographic Information]

County	Group quarters population, 2000[1] Number	Institutionalized population[2]	Households, 2000 (April 1) Number	Percent change, 1990–2000	Persons per household	Percent— One-person	With 1 or more persons under 18 years	With 1 or more persons 65 years and over	By type— Family households (families) Percent with own children under 18	Married-couple Number	Percent with own children[3]	Female householder[4] Number	Percent with own children[3]	Nonfamily households Number	Percent change, 1990–2000
INDIANA—Con.															
Tipton	201	176	6 469	7.4	2.53	23.1	34.8	25.8	4 750 44.3	4 033	42.1	500	55.8	1 719	16.8
Union	79	66	2 793	8.4	2.60	22.4	38.0	23.7	2 072 47.6	1 749	45.2	229	61.1	721	16.7
Vanderburgh	7 099	2 825	70 623	5.8	2.33	31.0	31.2	25.9	44 442 45.6	33 563	41.1	8 426	61.2	26 181	16.5
Vermillion	306	294	6 762	1.9	2.44	26.6	33.0	27.1	4 715 44.2	3 874	41.1	609	59.8	2 047	3.0
Vigo	8 182	3 381	40 998	3.0	2.38	30.0	32.4	25.4	26 058 46.5	19 678	41.7	4 810	62.2	14 940	13.2
Wabash	1 965	1 050	13 215	4.6	2.50	24.9	33.9	26.3	9 393 44.1	7 803	40.8	1 128	60.2	3 822	20.2
Warren	113	113	3 219	6.8	2.58	21.2	36.1	25.3	2 423 44.3	2 088	41.4	219	58.9	796	25.0
Warrick	683	636	19 438	22.9	2.66	18.6	39.9	19.6	15 176 48.2	13 005	46.2	1 585	61.5	4 262	39.5
Washington	334	304	10 264	18.5	2.62	22.2	37.8	22.1	7 582 47.3	6 179	44.7	947	58.8	2 682	29.8
Wayne	2 245	1 221	28 469	3.2	2.42	27.4	33.2	27.1	19 308 44.4	15 038	39.4	3 254	62.4	9 161	17.1
Wells	463	447	10 402	10.2	2.61	23.3	37.1	24.4	7 625 47.8	6 435	45.2	860	62.4	2 777	26.9
White	293	269	9 727	9.0	2.57	22.6	35.1	26.8	7 093 44.4	5 872	41.0	816	60.3	2 634	11.7
Whitley	451	377	11 711	17.0	2.58	22.4	36.9	23.3	8 605 46.9	7 175	43.9	975	62.6	3 106	33.1
IOWA	104 169	50 256	1 149 276	8.0	2.46	27.2	33.3	25.4	769 684 46.9	633 254	43.4	98 270	65.5	379 592	17.3
Adair	197	179	3 398	−.6	2.37	28.1	30.5	34.7	2 324 42.7	2 021	38.8	195	72.3	1 074	6.2
Adams	120	65	1 867	−6.9	2.34	30.0	29.7	35.6	1 236 42.2	1 083	39.2	102	63.7	631	2.3
Allamakee	412	346	5 722	8.6	2.49	27.5	32.0	31.4	3 929 44.6	3 339	42.2	375	58.9	1 793	15.8
Appanoose	219	191	5 779	3.0	2.34	29.9	30.6	32.8	3 803 43.2	3 070	38.6	507	63.1	1 976	10.9
Audubon	180	180	2 773	−5.6	2.40	28.2	31.3	36.5	1 926 43.3	1 703	40.3	155	69.0	847	1.6
Benton	311	280	9 746	14.4	2.56	23.4	36.7	26.9	7 053 48.2	6 109	45.3	635	67.6	2 693	19.8
Black Hawk	6 477	1 548	49 683	5.9	2.45	27.1	31.7	24.2	31 963 45.8	24 960	41.0	5 384	66.0	17 720	19.8
Boone	960	634	10 374	5.6	2.44	26.7	32.8	26.3	7 135 45.4	6 021	42.2	814	65.0	3 239	12.7
Bremer	1 460	361	8 860	5.6	2.47	24.7	33.0	28.0	6 324 44.9	5 540	41.6	550	71.3	2 536	13.8
Buchanan	407	342	7 933	5.7	2.61	24.7	36.1	26.6	5 675 48.2	4 815	45.3	587	66.4	2 258	16.3
Buena Vista	1 381	368	7 499	−.2	2.54	27.0	33.6	29.7	5 125 46.7	4 310	43.3	543	68.5	2 374	3.3
Butler	289	288	6 175	2.3	2.43	25.0	32.1	32.5	4 470 42.7	3 880	39.8	388	64.2	1 705	10.3
Calhoun	677	621	4 513	−3.7	2.31	30.5	29.2	36.1	3 015 41.6	2 612	38.2	299	64.9	1 498	−1.1
Carroll	528	507	8 486	6.6	2.46	29.6	33.8	31.4	5 669 49.3	4 833	46.5	581	69.0	2 817	20.5
Cass	463	237	6 120	−.9	2.32	29.8	30.6	32.3	4 094 43.8	3 465	39.0	440	71.6	2 026	2.8
Cedar	283	252	7 147	6.9	2.51	23.7	34.8	27.1	5 136 46.4	4 399	43.3	478	63.8	2 011	13.3
Cerro Gordo	1 461	742	19 374	1.6	2.32	30.9	30.6	28.6	12 398 45.5	10 052	40.8	1 768	65.4	6 976	9.0
Cherokee	380	377	5 378	−2.5	2.35	29.5	30.5	32.4	3 598 43.5	3 081	39.7	352	66.5	1 780	6.0
Chickasaw	225	176	5 192	3.0	2.48	26.1	33.2	30.3	3 646 45.4	3 151	41.9	326	70.9	1 546	11.8
Clarke	156	115	3 584	7.2	2.50	25.9	34.4	29.2	2 498 46.1	2 072	42.1	298	68.1	1 086	7.5
Clay	293	283	7 259	2.6	2.35	29.8	32.0	28.6	4 774 46.7	4 039	42.5	495	72.5	2 485	11.0
Clayton	481	326	7 375	2.2	2.47	26.3	32.2	30.3	5 134 44.4	4 400	41.3	451	64.7	2 241	11.5
Clinton	1 023	446	20 105	1.8	2.44	27.4	33.9	26.9	13 676 46.7	10 973	42.7	1 979	64.8	6 429	12.8
Crawford	642	329	6 441	.7	2.53	26.2	33.7	29.5	4 488 45.4	3 768	42.1	448	68.8	1 953	2.2
Dallas	459	452	15 584	39.1	2.59	23.6	38.8	19.4	11 166 51.9	9 441	49.0	1 240	68.7	4 418	52.0
Davis	184	175	3 207	3.7	2.61	25.0	33.8	30.1	2 286 44.8	2 012	42.4	166	60.2	921	19.0
Decatur	769	106	3 337	4.1	2.37	30.3	29.8	31.5	2 150 43.4	1 812	39.0	239	72.4	1 187	11.9
Delaware	254	242	6 834	7.0	2.66	23.0	38.1	26.6	5 030 49.9	4 380	47.9	422	66.4	1 804	17.3
Des Moines	920	688	17 270	2.3	2.40	28.6	31.9	27.5	11 535 44.3	9 103	39.0	1 808	65.4	5 735	11.6
Dickinson	285	266	7 103	15.3	2.27	28.6	27.3	31.7	4 760 39.0	4 103	35.1	475	66.3	2 343	24.0
Dubuque	4 546	1 251	33 690	9.4	2.51	26.7	34.5	24.6	23 111 48.2	19 136	45.6	2 916	63.8	10 579	22.3
Emmet	537	358	4 450	−.2	2.36	30.3	29.3	31.6	2 909 42.7	2 447	39.2	346	61.6	1 541	14.3
Fayette	832	372	8 778	3.4	2.41	28.2	31.9	32.3	5 952 44.9	4 987	41.3	652	66.1	2 826	12.0
Floyd	495	385	6 828	1.6	2.40	28.0	32.0	31.0	4 708 44.3	3 938	39.6	528	72.2	2 120	9.7
Franklin	211	200	4 356	−4.9	2.41	27.6	30.8	32.9	2 985 42.8	2 567	39.3	277	66.4	1 371	−.1
Fremont	175	160	3 199	−.6	2.45	26.3	32.2	33.2	2 243 43.0	1 884	39.2	261	64.0	956	5.3
Greene	246	233	4 205	.2	2.41	29.1	32.0	35.2	2 859 45.1	2 411	40.9	302	67.9	1 346	–
Grundy	173	166	4 984	4.4	2.45	25.5	32.1	31.6	3 584 42.7	3 180	40.2	272	62.5	1 400	10.6
Guthrie	265	264	4 641	5.3	2.39	26.1	29.7	32.4	3 251 39.8	2 785	36.2	304	59.2	1 390	11.3
Hamilton	206	194	6 692	5.3	2.43	27.5	32.1	29.8	4 600 44.5	3 874	41.4	510	62.2	2 092	20.0
Hancock	201	201	4 795	−1.5	2.48	26.5	33.9	30.0	3 376 46.2	2 919	43.5	286	69.6	1 419	6.9
Hardin	860	545	7 628	.2	2.35	29.4	30.9	32.9	5 085 44.2	4 359	40.2	498	68.7	2 543	9.1
Harrison	319	311	6 115	8.1	2.51	26.1	34.0	29.8	4 305 45.8	3 628	42.8	462	66.2	1 810	13.8
Henry	1 589	1 319	7 626	7.6	2.46	26.8	34.5	26.2	5 268 47.5	4 397	43.4	622	68.8	2 358	17.1
Howard	272	161	3 974	3.1	2.43	29.5	32.3	32.9	2 650 46.7	2 257	44.0	261	66.3	1 324	13.0
Humboldt	160	158	4 295	−1.0	2.38	29.8	31.0	34.3	2 884 44.2	2 465	40.7	274	64.6	1 411	14.0
Ida	157	101	3 213	−.3	2.39	29.3	30.8	34.5	2 186 43.2	1 911	40.9	189	61.4	1 027	13.5
Iowa	282	257	6 163	7.9	2.50	25.9	34.2	28.4	4 300 47.1	3 706	44.5	406	65.3	1 863	17.4
Jackson	310	252	8 078	7.3	2.47	27.0	33.5	29.6	5 587 46.3	4 699	43.2	619	64.3	2 491	21.6
Jasper	1 670	1 479	14 689	7.8	2.42	26.1	33.3	26.9	10 265 45.3	8 712	41.6	1 087	66.3	4 424	22.0
Jefferson	628	241	6 649	5.4	2.34	30.4	32.9	23.7	4 279 48.3	3 533	43.3	531	74.6	2 370	17.3
Johnson	8 006	1 547	44 080	22.2	2.34	30.2	27.5	13.1	23 578 49.5	19 335	47.1	2 995	64.8	20 502	30.2
Jones	1 565	1 523	7 560	9.3	2.47	25.3	33.0	28.6	5 301 44.2	4 461	40.6	594	66.5	2 259	23.0
Keokuk	180	179	4 586	.3	2.45	27.8	32.3	33.5	3 153 44.4	2 704	41.3	298	62.1	1 433	13.2

[1] As of April 1. [2] Includes people under formally authorized, supervised care or custody in institutions at the time of enumeration (such as correctional institutions, nursing homes, and juvenile institutions). [3] Under 18 years. [4] No husband present.

Sources: Group Quarters Population—U.S. Census Bureau, 2000 Census of Population and Housing, "Census 2000 Profiles of General Demographic Characteristics" data files, published May 2001 (related Internet site <http://www.census.gov/mp/www/pub/2000cen/mscen01.html>). Households, 2000—U.S. Census Bureau, 2000 Census of Population and Housing, "Census 2000 Profiles of General Demographic Characteristics" data files, published May 2001 (related Internet site <http://www.census.gov/mp/www/pub/2000cen/mscen01.html>). Households, 1990—U.S. Census Bureau, 1990 Census of Population and Housing, Summary Tape File (STF) 1C on CD-ROM (related Internet site <http://homer.ssd.census.gov/cdrom/lookup>).

Table B–3. Counties — Group Quarters Population and Households–Con.

[Includes U.S., states, and 3,142 counties or county equivalents defined as of January 1, 1992. For changes to these areas since then, see appendix B. Geographic Information]

County	Group quarters population, 2000[1] Number	Institutionalized population[2]	Households, 2000 (April 1) Number	Percent change, 1990–2000	Persons per household	Percent— One-person	With 1 or more persons under 18 years	With 1 or more persons 65 years and over	Family households (families) Number	Percent with own children under 18 years	Married-couple Number	Percent with own children[3]	Female householder[4] Number	Percent with own children[3]	Nonfamily households Number	Percent change, 1990–2000
IOWA—Con.																
Kossuth	311	263	6 974	−3.1	2.42	28.7	31.7	33.3	4 792	44.9	4 214	42.6	406	64.8	2 182	4.3
Lee	1 583	1 460	15 161	1.5	2.41	28.3	32.8	28.5	10 248	45.0	8 138	40.0	1 569	64.8	4 913	10.3
Linn	5 053	1 857	76 753	17.2	2.43	27.5	33.7	20.8	50 335	48.5	40 828	44.8	6 942	66.4	26 418	29.1
Louisa	167	143	4 519	5.2	2.66	22.5	37.9	25.1	3 319	47.6	2 770	44.4	371	63.1	1 200	8.9
Lucas	206	167	3 811	1.2	2.42	28.7	30.4	32.0	2 561	42.1	2 162	38.6	267	60.7	1 250	1.7
Lyon	202	201	4 428	3.2	2.61	24.3	35.8	32.0	3 264	47.2	2 970	46.0	193	62.7	1 164	15.8
Madison	299	289	5 326	13.0	2.58	22.7	36.6	25.9	3 923	47.3	3 403	44.7	373	67.3	1 403	14.7
Mahaska	578	257	8 880	6.9	2.45	26.6	34.2	27.7	6 147	46.8	5 208	42.9	665	68.6	2 733	19.4
Marion	1 955	585	12 017	11.1	2.50	25.6	34.6	26.7	8 527	46.5	7 351	43.4	825	66.1	3 490	18.9
Marshall	1 270	1 182	15 338	3.0	2.48	26.9	33.3	26.5	10 456	45.6	8 494	40.8	1 429	67.3	4 882	10.7
Mills	700	524	5 324	14.1	2.60	22.3	37.2	23.5	3 938	47.0	3 283	43.2	472	68.9	1 386	15.9
Mitchell	281	254	4 294	1.0	2.47	27.6	31.1	34.9	2 984	43.4	2 612	40.4	245	64.9	1 310	7.2
Monona	273	272	4 211	2.8	2.31	31.0	28.8	37.1	2 738	41.1	2 296	38.0	298	54.4	1 473	15.2
Monroe	178	169	3 228	1.0	2.43	28.0	32.8	32.3	2 210	44.5	1 814	40.8	276	64.5	1 018	6.3
Montgomery	253	245	4 886	−1.4	2.36	29.5	31.5	31.9	3 259	44.6	2 656	39.9	426	66.9	1 627	3.4
Muscatine	724	521	15 847	7.0	2.59	24.1	37.4	23.1	11 290	48.9	9 168	45.1	1 466	66.2	4 557	16.4
O'Brien	591	553	6 001	.4	2.42	28.0	31.3	32.7	4 125	44.2	3 661	41.8	293	63.5	1 876	7.6
Osceola	122	113	2 778	−1.4	2.48	27.6	32.8	31.5	1 942	45.4	1 722	43.3	143	65.0	836	3.9
Page	1 392	1 149	6 708	.3	2.32	29.9	29.9	32.8	4 459	42.5	3 723	38.3	545	65.1	2 249	8.2
Palo Alto	402	271	4 119	−1.5	2.37	30.4	29.5	34.5	2 674	43.9	2 317	41.6	241	58.9	1 445	4.9
Plymouth	379	355	9 372	11.3	2.61	24.0	37.1	27.9	6 806	49.1	5 930	46.6	580	66.9	2 566	18.8
Pocahontas	162	161	3 617	−5.3	2.35	30.2	30.7	35.2	2 431	43.9	2 109	40.5	215	69.3	1 186	4.0
Polk	8 930	4 480	149 112	15.4	2.45	28.1	34.5	19.5	96 601	49.8	76 055	46.7	15 334	63.5	52 511	21.0
Pottawattamie	1 676	1 148	33 844	8.3	2.54	24.9	35.5	24.3	23 619	46.3	18 135	42.2	3 999	61.4	10 225	21.2
Poweshiek	1 458	339	7 398	3.4	2.35	29.2	30.4	29.4	4 880	44.0	4 128	39.6	551	70.1	2 518	18.7
Ringgold	151	143	2 245	1.2	2.37	28.6	29.2	38.2	1 537	40.5	1 340	36.9	124	69.4	708	7.9
Sac	287	273	4 746	−3.4	2.37	29.4	29.7	35.9	3 199	42.4	2 769	39.1	295	64.7	1 547	6.0
Scott	3 276	1 702	62 334	8.5	2.49	26.9	35.7	20.9	41 895	49.4	32 580	44.8	7 079	67.7	20 439	19.9
Shelby	299	285	5 173	3.0	2.49	25.2	33.6	32.7	3 705	45.5	3 224	42.6	354	68.1	1 468	11.0
Sioux	2 648	477	10 693	7.7	2.71	22.2	37.6	27.8	8 064	48.8	7 426	47.6	444	66.0	2 629	12.3
Story	9 612	623	29 383	13.3	2.39	26.7	28.2	17.6	17 056	47.0	14 581	44.9	1 737	63.4	12 327	22.6
Tama	494	462	7 018	3.7	2.51	25.3	33.9	31.4	4 971	44.7	4 154	41.2	563	63.6	2 047	8.3
Taylor	182	128	2 824	−1.2	2.40	27.8	29.8	35.6	1 913	41.4	1 667	38.3	168	60.1	911	7.7
Union	292	167	5 242	1.3	2.29	31.3	29.2	29.7	3 354	43.0	2 784	37.7	420	69.8	1 888	13.0
Van Buren	127	87	3 181	4.1	2.41	28.0	30.4	32.7	2 164	42.1	1 854	38.5	191	65.4	1 017	14.4
Wapello	1 037	508	14 784	1.6	2.37	28.2	31.4	29.6	9 797	43.5	7 789	38.7	1 470	64.4	4 987	12.8
Warren	1 715	618	14 708	16.2	2.65	19.9	39.9	21.0	11 214	49.6	9 482	46.5	1 288	67.5	3 494	29.0
Washington	503	446	8 056	8.1	2.50	26.4	33.1	28.8	5 628	45.0	4 856	42.8	543	58.0	2 428	12.1
Wayne	132	128	2 821	−4.5	2.34	29.8	29.0	38.3	1 919	40.1	1 641	36.0	181	68.0	902	1.2
Webster	2 472	2 122	15 878	−.5	2.38	30.3	32.1	28.6	10 300	46.5	8 221	41.8	1 510	67.2	5 578	10.8
Winnebago	529	199	4 749	1.0	2.36	29.4	31.6	31.0	3 182	45.6	2 702	41.9	340	71.2	1 567	9.4
Winneshiek	2 293	336	7 734	6.6	2.46	27.6	31.9	27.9	5 188	46.1	4 553	44.3	428	62.9	2 546	19.3
Woodbury	2 762	1 208	39 151	6.1	2.58	26.6	36.6	24.5	26 432	50.3	20 332	46.2	4 412	66.2	12 719	13.9
Worth	120	119	3 278	1.2	2.38	27.6	31.7	31.1	2 264	44.0	1 905	41.0	240	61.7	1 014	7.5
Wright	312	288	5 940	.7	2.36	30.2	29.9	33.5	3 939	42.9	3 405	39.2	369	67.5	2 001	10.1
KANSAS	81 950	45 396	1 037 891	9.9	2.51	27.0	35.5	23.3	701 547	49.2	567 924	45.9	96 661	64.9	336 344	17.6
Allen	357	189	5 775	1.2	2.43	28.5	32.6	30.6	3 895	44.2	3 156	39.4	512	64.5	1 880	10.9
Anderson	127	118	3 221	5.0	2.48	26.8	32.9	34.1	2 265	44.2	1 928	41.7	221	57.9	956	8.5
Atchison	1 053	313	6 275	2.4	2.51	27.6	35.2	28.3	4 278	47.6	3 410	43.6	628	66.1	1 997	12.1
Barber	65	65	2 235	−5.2	2.35	29.9	30.3	35.5	1 511	42.4	1 312	39.5	146	63.0	724	4.5
Barton	772	439	11 393	−1.5	2.41	30.2	32.9	30.0	7 530	47.4	6 280	43.4	887	68.0	3 863	13.1
Bourbon	324	205	6 161	4.5	2.44	29.0	33.0	31.1	4 126	45.5	3 360	41.3	567	63.8	2 035	12.1
Brown	202	202	4 318	−.7	2.44	28.8	33.1	32.4	2 949	45.9	2 408	40.8	396	70.2	1 369	1.0
Butler	2 010	1 754	21 527	16.4	2.67	21.9	40.5	22.8	16 049	50.9	13 469	47.9	1 797	67.1	5 478	27.8
Chase	113	113	1 246	2.6	2.34	31.1	30.9	31.6	817	43.2	680	40.6	95	49.5	429	25.8
Chautauqua	154	154	1 796	−2.1	2.34	29.4	28.0	37.7	1 235	38.1	1 029	34.2	141	58.2	561	−5.4
Cherokee	335	264	8 875	5.7	2.51	26.3	36.0	26.9	6 242	46.1	5 025	42.6	862	59.4	2 633	10.2
Cheyenne	54	54	1 360	−2.1	2.29	30.8	28.6	40.1	920	40.8	817	37.2	69	69.6	440	−.5
Clark	46	46	979	−2.7	2.39	29.6	32.3	35.1	676	43.8	590	40.8	61	62.3	303	−7.9
Clay	165	165	3 617	−.7	2.39	27.7	31.9	33.6	2 516	43.8	2 166	40.0	221	71.0	1 101	5.3
Cloud	662	346	4 163	−7.1	2.31	30.8	28.6	34.5	2 698	41.8	2 293	38.2	276	64.1	1 465	−4.7
Coffey	170	126	3 489	5.4	2.49	26.0	35.1	27.8	2 477	46.8	2 118	43.2	240	68.3	1 012	5.1
Comanche	70	70	872	−8.2	2.18	35.9	26.1	38.6	541	39.4	474	36.5	54	59.3	331	10.3
Cowley	1 808	946	14 039	−.1	2.46	27.9	34.8	28.3	9 616	47.1	7 747	42.4	1 350	67.0	4 423	9.4
Crawford	1 814	698	15 504	6.1	2.35	30.6	30.4	26.1	9 436	46.8	7 426	42.7	1 440	62.8	6 068	11.1
Decatur	121	120	1 494	−9.5	2.24	32.8	26.6	38.7	982	39.2	851	36.5	84	58.3	512	−1.3
Dickinson	338	330	7 903	4.8	2.40	28.1	33.2	30.4	5 424	45.3	4 573	40.9	611	71.0	2 479	11.7

[1] As of April 1.   [2] Includes people under formally authorized, supervised care or custody in institutions at the time of enumeration (such as correctional institutions, nursing homes, and juvenile institutions).   [3] Under 18 years.   [4] No husband present.

Sources: Group Quarters Population—U.S. Census Bureau, 2000 Census of Population and Housing, "Census 2000 Profiles of General Demographic Characteristics" data files, published May 2001 (related Internet site <http://www.census.gov/mp/www/pub/2000cen/mscen01.html>).   Households, 2000—U.S. Census Bureau, 2000 Census of Population and Housing, "Census 2000 Profiles of General Demographic Characteristics" data files, published May 2001 (related Internet site <http://www.census.gov/mp/www/pub/2000cen/mscen01.html>).   Households, 1990—U.S. Census Bureau, 1990 Census of Population and Housing, Summary Tape File (STF) 1C on CD-ROM (related Internet site <http://homer.ssd.census.gov/cdrom/lookup>).

[Includes U.S., states, and 3,142 counties or county equivalents defined as of January 1, 1992. For changes to these areas since then, see appendix B. Geographic Information]

County	Group quarters population, 2000[1] Number	Institu- tionalized population[2]	Households, 2000 (April 1) Number	Percent change, 1990– 2000	Per- sons per house- hold	Percent— One- person	With 1 or more per- sons under 18 years	With 1 or more per- sons 65 years and over	Family households (families) Number	Per- cent with own chil- dren under 18 years	Married-couple Number	Per- cent with own chil- dren[3]	Female householder[4] Number	Per- cent with own chil- dren[3]	Nonfamily households Number	Percent change, 1990– 2000
KANSAS—Con.																
Doniphan	391	94	3 173	3.2	2.48	27.6	34.7	29.5	2 184	47.3	1 789	44.3	277	64.3	989	15.7
Douglas	8 714	583	38 486	27.7	2.37	28.5	28.9	14.1	21 159	49.8	16 590	46.3	3 265	66.5	17 327	34.9
Edwards	61	59	1 455	-8.2	2.33	32.0	30.0	34.0	956	43.6	819	39.9	87	66.7	499	-4.0
Elk	86	86	1 412	-1.7	2.25	32.9	26.5	39.3	924	37.2	791	39.9	86	54.7	488	3.8
Ellis	1 259	323	11 193	10.9	2.35	30.1	30.3	23.6	6 773	47.7	5 594	45.0	874	61.9	4 420	24.5
Ellsworth	826	810	2 481	-1.6	2.30	31.4	29.5	34.9	1 639	42.2	1 420	38.4	154	68.8	842	.8
Finney	572	237	12 948	19.5	3.09	19.6	49.3	15.2	9 750	61.1	7 739	58.9	1 355	74.2	3 198	22.8
Ford	782	502	10 852	9.9	2.92	22.7	44.1	21.6	7 856	56.4	6 282	54.7	997	70.6	2 996	4.5
Franklin	592	315	9 452	13.8	2.56	24.8	37.5	24.9	6 722	48.8	5 492	44.8	841	68.0	2 730	21.2
Geary	611	228	10 458	-2.0	2.61	22.5	42.7	18.0	7 578	54.6	5 950	50.1	1 291	72.8	2 880	15.9
Gove	53	53	1 245	-3.0	2.42	29.7	29.4	37.4	861	41.1	790	39.4	43	58.1	384	5.5
Graham	69	45	1 263	-12.0	2.28	30.1	28.1	37.1	848	40.8	751	38.5	75	65.3	415	-4.8
Grant	71	71	2 742	14.6	2.86	21.0	45.9	19.1	2 099	57.0	1 822	55.0	194	71.6	643	34.0
Gray	141	136	2 045	6.9	2.82	21.2	43.2	22.0	1 556	55.2	1 384	53.6	114	67.5	489	2.5
Greeley	27	27	602	-8.2	2.50	28.6	36.5	28.9	414	49.8	368	49.5	27	59.3	188	10.6
Greenwood	191	163	3 234	-1.6	2.31	30.3	29.2	36.3	2 153	40.8	1 826	36.7	214	63.6	1 081	-.6
Hamilton	43	43	1 054	6.9	2.49	29.4	36.1	31.1	716	49.9	600	46.7	80	67.5	338	-.3
Harper	168	168	2 773	-7.8	2.30	32.1	29.8	36.3	1 807	42.6	1 533	39.3	191	62.8	966	-2.3
Harvey	1 440	791	12 581	8.6	2.50	25.8	34.9	27.6	8 930	46.2	7 579	43.1	966	66.3	3 651	13.2
Haskell	35	35	1 481	7.9	2.88	20.1	45.4	21.0	1 154	56.0	1 028	55.1	87	64.4	327	1.9
Hodgeman	35	35	796	-3.6	2.58	24.7	36.4	32.7	581	47.5	518	45.2	35	62.9	215	4.9
Jackson	231	214	4 727	10.5	2.63	22.7	37.4	27.1	3 506	47.5	2 947	44.6	388	62.4	1 221	14.3
Jefferson	259	248	6 830	18.2	2.66	20.1	38.3	23.5	5 194	46.9	4 456	44.4	481	62.6	1 636	24.7
Jewell	45	41	1 695	-6.1	2.21	32.4	25.0	39.6	1 098	36.6	985	34.6	82	57.3	597	10.4
Johnson	4 978	3 775	174 570	28.0	2.56	24.5	37.5	17.3	121 618	51.7	103 274	50.2	13 669	62.5	52 952	38.3
Kearny	45	45	1 542	11.8	2.91	20.2	46.4	21.9	1 200	55.9	1 004	53.3	128	72.7	342	13.2
Kingman	198	198	3 371	6.2	2.51	26.0	34.4	32.2	2 421	45.1	2 086	42.5	240	61.7	950	12.7
Kiowa	108	60	1 365	-6.9	2.32	30.5	28.8	35.2	924	40.9	814	37.8	73	63.0	441	-2.6
Labette	857	591	9 194	-2.0	2.39	29.8	33.4	29.1	6 118	46.8	4 791	41.8	935	67.0	3 076	3.1
Lane	23	23	910	-5.8	2.34	30.3	31.9	34.4	613	43.7	538	40.1	46	67.4	297	-1.3
Leavenworth	6 635	5 989	23 071	17.0	2.69	21.7	41.8	19.9	17 206	52.1	14 174	49.4	2 187	67.3	5 865	30.5
Lincoln	76	76	1 529	-.1	2.29	29.6	28.7	36.2	1 040	39.9	888	36.1	98	62.2	489	2.5
Linn	131	109	3 807	18.4	2.48	24.0	31.9	31.5	2 747	40.0	2 386	37.5	235	59.1	1 060	27.4
Logan	57	57	1 243	1.8	2.40	28.6	30.5	34.4	857	42.8	737	41.7	78	50.0	386	5.8
Lyon	1 613	426	13 691	4.8	2.51	28.5	34.9	20.9	8 642	51.7	6 949	47.6	1 153	70.5	5 049	10.2
McPherson	1 637	658	11 205	9.5	2.49	25.5	34.5	27.6	7 968	46.4	7 003	43.7	667	67.2	3 237	14.4
Marion	765	331	5 114	2.8	2.46	25.2	32.2	34.2	3 689	42.3	3 263	40.0	283	62.2	1 425	2.0
Marshall	244	233	4 458	-4.9	2.40	29.5	31.4	35.9	3 027	44.5	2 662	42.3	240	62.9	1 431	-2.7
Meade	114	114	1 728	3.7	2.61	25.6	37.8	31.1	1 252	50.2	1 118	48.7	85	61.2	476	-.6
Miami	746	606	10 365	23.4	2.66	21.0	39.3	22.0	7 798	49.2	6 578	46.0	832	67.2	2 567	26.3
Mitchell	345	240	2 850	.1	2.31	31.2	28.7	33.7	1 863	42.6	1 632	39.9	151	63.6	987	6.5
Montgomery	900	557	14 903	-4.9	2.37	29.7	32.5	30.6	9 954	44.6	7 899	39.5	1 505	64.9	4 949	1.2
Morris	75	75	2 539	.4	2.37	28.0	31.7	34.2	1 777	43.1	1 542	40.2	168	64.9	762	7.8
Morton	57	57	1 306	1.2	2.63	24.3	38.5	23.7	961	49.7	839	48.2	89	67.4	345	5.8
Nemaha	498	454	3 959	-.9	2.58	28.0	35.0	34.6	2 765	48.6	2 449	48.3	201	61.7	1 194	1.8
Neosho	478	297	6 739	-.1	2.45	27.1	33.4	29.8	4 684	45.3	3 867	41.3	571	63.4	2 055	2.0
Ness	79	76	1 516	-9.2	2.23	33.5	27.4	36.9	978	40.5	865	37.6	72	56.9	538	2.1
Norton	790	774	2 266	-2.7	2.28	32.3	29.6	35.2	1 471	43.4	1 257	39.3	158	68.4	795	2.8
Osage	233	219	6 490	11.8	2.54	23.5	36.3	27.3	4 737	46.3	3 959	42.1	527	65.8	1 753	18.7
Osborne	119	113	1 940	-5.7	2.23	35.2	26.6	37.9	1 208	41.6	1 057	38.8	101	64.4	732	9.6
Ottawa	191	172	2 430	7.2	2.46	25.7	33.6	28.6	1 717	44.7	1 493	40.1	154	77.9	713	11.2
Pawnee	904	648	2 739	-6.3	2.31	32.2	30.8	31.9	1 787	44.8	1 502	40.8	199	64.8	952	-3.8
Phillips	143	143	2 496	-7.4	2.35	28.6	29.5	34.1	1 723	41.0	1 535	39.0	138	58.7	773	-4.9
Pottawatomie	282	142	6 771	14.0	2.65	23.2	38.2	24.1	4 931	49.9	4 228	47.6	488	66.4	1 840	18.9
Pratt	325	144	3 963	.7	2.35	30.4	31.4	31.5	2 641	45.1	2 247	40.3	299	72.2	1 322	6.7
Rawlins	56	50	1 269	-6.8	2.29	31.4	28.2	40.1	847	41.2	755	39.2	62	51.6	422	.2
Reno	3 253	2 953	25 498	5.2	2.41	27.9	32.4	27.7	17 309	44.6	14 244	40.1	2 209	66.2	8 189	13.3
Republic	140	140	2 557	-7.7	2.23	31.8	26.2	38.4	1 685	38.8	1 503	35.4	124	66.9	872	-3.0
Rice	879	153	4 050	-2.8	2.44	27.8	33.1	32.7	2 832	44.7	2 395	41.0	292	68.2	1 218	-1.0
Riley	9 314	427	22 137	4.0	2.42	27.5	29.0	14.3	12 262	50.3	10 217	48.5	1 495	65.5	9 875	26.1
Rooks	197	197	2 362	-3.4	2.32	31.8	30.4	35.7	1 556	44.2	1 309	40.4	170	66.5	806	5.9
Rush	88	88	1 548	-5.7	2.24	31.7	27.5	38.0	1 014	40.5	868	36.6	90	66.7	534	2.9
Russell	209	172	3 207	-4.9	2.23	32.8	26.9	36.7	2 021	40.4	1 712	35.1	227	70.9	1 186	3.3
Saline	1 443	710	21 436	8.1	2.43	28.3	34.4	23.9	14 211	48.5	11 336	44.0	2 078	66.7	7 225	14.4
Scott	86	86	2 045	1.1	2.46	27.3	35.2	27.7	1 435	47.4	1 248	43.6	137	73.0	610	15.7
Sedgwick	6 278	3 937	176 444	12.7	2.53	28.2	37.0	20.6	117 770	51.5	91 278	48.1	19 244	64.8	58 674	19.2
Seward	414	226	7 419	12.2	2.98	20.6	47.1	18.5	5 503	58.7	4 419	57.0	739	71.7	1 916	13.5
Shawnee	4 896	4 077	68 920	8.1	2.39	29.8	33.4	23.1	44 685	47.4	34 161	42.3	8 003	65.4	24 235	17.0
Sheridan	44	44	1 124	-4.0	2.46	27.6	31.3	33.0	796	43.0	717	40.9	51	64.7	328	5.1

[1] As of April 1.   [2] Includes people under formally authorized, supervised care or custody in institutions at the time of enumeration (such as correctional institutions, nursing homes, and juvenile institutions).   [3] Under 18 years.   [4] No husband present.

Sources: Group Quarters Population—U.S. Census Bureau, 2000 Census of Population and Housing, "Census 2000 Profiles of General Demographic Characteristics" data files, published May 2001 (related Internet site <http://www.census.gov/mp/www/pub/2000cen/mscen01.html>).   Households, 2000—U.S. Census Bureau, 2000 Census of Population and Housing, "Census 2000 Profiles of General Demographic Characteristics" data files, published May 2001 (related Internet site <http://www.census.gov/mp/www/pub/2000cen/mscen01.html>).   Households, 1990—U.S. Census Bureau, 1990 Census of Population and Housing, Summary Tape File (STF) 1C on CD-ROM (related Internet site <http://homer.ssd.census.gov/cdrom/lookup>).

Table B–3. Counties — Group Quarters Population and Households–Con.

[Includes U.S., states, and 3,142 counties or county equivalents defined as of January 1, 1992. For changes to these areas since then, see appendix B. Geographic Information]

County	Group quarters population, 2000[1] Number	Institutionalized population[2]	Households 2000 Number	Percent change, 1990–2000	Persons per household	Percent One-person	With 1 or more persons under 18 years	With 1 or more persons 65 years and over	Family households Number	Percent with own children under 18 years	Married-couple Number	Percent with own children[3]	Female householder[4] Number	Percent with own children[3]	Nonfamily households Number	Percent change, 1990–2000
KANSAS—Con.																
Sherman	134	72	2 758	.9	2.40	29.2	30.3	29.5	1 783	45.2	1 538	42.0	166	68.7	975	19.9
Smith	109	104	1 953	-9.8	2.27	30.2	26.8	41.6	1 323	37.8	1 183	34.6	92	63.0	630	-8.2
Stafford	79	70	2 010	-8.8	2.34	33.0	31.3	34.6	1 295	46.4	1 124	42.9	118	71.2	715	3.8
Stanton	55	55	858	3.2	2.74	22.6	43.0	23.9	638	54.1	545	52.7	58	65.5	220	15.2
Stevens	60	60	1 988	5.5	2.72	24.3	41.1	25.3	1 457	52.0	1 264	61.0	142	64.8	531	8.8
Sumner	408	382	9 888	2.1	2.58	25.6	37.1	27.3	7 092	48.1	5 924	45.0	792	65.5	2 796	9.4
Thomas	281	118	3 226	3.3	2.45	28.4	34.2	25.3	2 126	49.9	1 811	47.0	221	69.7	1 100	16.6
Trego	109	109	1 412	-3.6	2.27	31.4	28.8	37.3	936	41.2	821	38.7	89	55.1	476	14.4
Wabaunsee	112	112	2 633	6.1	2.57	23.0	35.4	27.2	1 958	45.0	1 693	42.2	167	67.1	675	9.9
Wallace	25	25	674	-.4	2.56	27.6	35.8	30.7	477	47.8	429	45.2	27	77.8	197	3.1
Washington	204	181	2 673	-6.6	2.35	31.2	27.8	39.0	1 781	39.9	1 589	39.1	111	55.0	892	.7
Wichita	25	25	967	-2.9	2.59	23.7	37.1	27.6	723	46.9	631	43.9	56	76.8	244	1.7
Wilson	238	167	4 203	.2	2.40	29.1	31.8	32.9	2 848	43.8	2 398	39.8	329	66.6	1 355	5.7
Woodson	114	114	1 642	-3.4	2.24	33.3	27.7	40.4	1 052	40.2	883	35.2	121	66.1	590	6.5
Wyandotte	1 592	1 116	59 700	-2.9	2.62	28.9	37.6	22.9	39 174	49.7	25 138	44.8	10 619	61.2	20 526	5.1
KENTUCKY	114 804	62 057	1 590 647	15.3	2.47	26.0	35.5	22.8	1 104 398	46.8	857 944	43.7	187 957	58.8	486 249	33.7
Adair	752	192	6 747	16.3	2.44	26.2	34.0	27.7	4 801	44.3	3 886	41.7	686	54.7	1 946	40.4
Allen	205	201	6 910	23.5	2.55	23.1	36.7	25.2	5 110	46.0	4 188	43.7	679	58.2	1 800	35.8
Anderson	141	112	7 320	34.6	2.59	20.5	39.8	20.2	5 526	46.0	4 595	46.5	672	61.9	1 794	48.4
Ballard	160	147	3 395	6.4	2.39	25.8	33.5	27.6	2 415	43.1	2 022	40.7	273	56.4	980	13.0
Barren	634	623	15 346	16.8	2.44	25.6	34.3	25.7	10 953	44.4	8 953	41.6	1 506	58.8	4 407	36.2
Bath	115	115	4 445	21.5	2.47	25.3	35.3	26.2	3 194	45.0	2 565	41.7	456	61.2	1 251	44.1
Bell	776	628	12 004	4.3	2.44	26.8	35.9	26.0	8 522	45.0	6 126	43.3	1 882	51.8	3 482	28.2
Boone	588	546	31 258	55.3	2.73	20.2	42.4	16.2	23 435	53.1	19 241	51.5	3 062	61.7	7 823	77.6
Bourbon	199	189	7 681	5.9	2.49	24.8	36.1	25.3	5 448	46.3	4 198	42.0	941	61.8	2 233	27.4
Boyd	2 077	1 754	20 010	.7	2.38	26.5	31.8	28.4	14 111	41.0	11 144	37.4	2 326	55.7	5 899	14.8
Boyle	2 526	1 592	10 574	11.5	2.00	27.1	34.2	26.0	7 045	44.7	5 670	40.4	1 322	61.1	3 229	28.7
Bracken	54	54	3 228	12.4	2.55	23.9	37.1	26.1	2 346	46.1	1 850	43.6	346	58.4	882	27.3
Breathitt	400	230	6 170	11.1	2.54	23.8	37.9	22.3	4 541	46.4	3 391	44.6	876	53.8	1 629	39.2
Breckinridge	273	203	7 324	18.9	2.51	24.6	34.3	26.8	5 307	42.8	4 366	40.1	650	57.5	2 017	34.6
Bullitt	231	170	22 171	38.9	2.75	16.4	43.0	16.0	17 745	48.8	14 495	46.1	2 307	62.2	4 426	76.2
Butler	238	238	5 059	21.0	2.52	23.7	37.6	23.4	3 709	47.0	3 049	45.0	470	58.7	1 350	38.6
Caldwell	233	233	5 431	3.0	2.36	27.5	31.3	31.0	3 801	40.8	3 099	37.9	533	53.8	1 630	13.9
Calloway	2 996	558	13 862	19.4	2.25	29.7	27.6	25.3	8 594	41.5	7 069	37.7	1 121	62.4	5 268	43.5
Campbell	2 041	981	34 742	11.5	2.49	28.6	35.4	22.8	23 093	48.9	17 458	46.1	4 272	59.6	11 649	30.4
Carlisle	59	59	2 208	4.8	2.40	26.3	32.5	30.3	1 575	42.9	1 292	39.2	206	59.7	633	13.0
Carroll	250	178	3 940	12.4	2.51	25.3	37.5	22.9	2 723	47.9	2 063	43.3	462	63.6	1 217	25.7
Carter	625	153	10 342	19.2	2.54	22.3	36.6	24.0	7 741	44.7	6 259	42.7	1 110	53.6	2 601	44.9
Casey	197	187	6 260	15.2	2.44	26.8	34.0	28.0	4 421	43.9	3 511	42.1	678	50.3	1 839	45.5
Christian	6 083	1 218	24 857	14.9	2.66	22.5	44.0	19.7	18 350	55.7	14 158	52.7	3 378	67.1	6 507	30.5
Clark	423	364	13 015	18.6	2.51	22.8	36.6	23.1	9 548	45.5	7 531	42.6	1 571	57.7	3 467	40.0
Clay	2 179	2 159	8 556	16.1	2.62	22.5	40.7	22.0	6 440	49.0	5 016	47.7	1 061	55.0	2 116	67.1
Clinton	63	62	4 086	13.8	2.34	28.4	31.8	26.4	2 811	43.3	2 267	40.7	396	54.3	1 275	38.9
Crittenden	131	131	3 829	5.0	2.42	27.0	32.0	29.1	2 706	41.9	2 251	39.2	340	58.2	1 123	13.5
Cumberland	108	103	2 976	9.7	2.37	28.9	33.0	30.9	2 040	42.9	1 576	40.4	332	52.1	936	33.5
Daviess	2 595	1 337	36 033	9.1	2.47	27.1	35.7	24.5	24 828	47.7	19 330	44.3	4 247	61.1	11 205	23.7
Edmonson	160	89	4 648	20.9	2.47	22.4	35.0	25.6	3 461	42.7	2 893	40.8	413	55.7	1 187	57.4
Elliott	57	57	2 638	13.5	2.54	24.7	35.9	25.1	1 926	45.7	1 583	44.3	256	54.7	712	46.8
Estill	139	117	6 108	14.0	2.48	24.6	35.7	24.8	4 432	44.1	3 386	41.6	787	55.5	1 676	43.0
Fayette	12 723	4 722	108 288	21.0	2.29	31.7	29.6	17.3	62 955	46.9	47 074	43.4	12 477	60.3	45 333	36.9
Fleming	121	101	5 367	16.0	2.55	23.3	37.7	24.9	3 965	47.1	3 234	45.1	517	55.7	1 402	25.6
Floyd	1 043	868	16 881	7.8	2.45	25.2	35.7	23.3	12 267	45.4	9 537	43.4	2 078	54.9	4 614	41.7
Franklin	1 825	605	19 907	14.5	2.30	30.4	32.4	22.7	12 839	45.8	9 695	41.7	2 432	59.7	7 068	33.4
Fulton	258	250	3 237	-4.2	2.32	32.3	33.8	31.5	2 115	44.8	1 437	37.0	583	63.5	1 122	5.6
Gallatin	106	106	2 902	49.5	2.68	22.0	40.8	19.4	2 136	50.2	1 682	48.2	310	57.1	766	71.0
Garrard	98	92	5 741	29.4	2.56	21.1	36.5	24.0	4 336	44.2	3 594	42.0	541	57.7	1 405	43.8
Grant	179	174	8 175	46.4	2.72	19.8	43.3	19.1	6 219	52.0	4 916	49.1	907	65.2	1 956	64.4
Graves	765	597	14 841	10.9	2.44	26.2	34.2	28.2	10 562	44.2	8 587	40.8	1 486	61.6	4 279	21.4
Grayson	324	318	9 596	20.1	2.47	24.1	35.0	25.2	6 966	44.3	5 650	40.7	962	61.6	2 630	40.1
Green	161	142	4 706	15.1	2.41	25.4	32.6	29.3	3 379	41.6	2 809	38.6	402	57.0	1 327	37.5
Greenup	447	438	14 536	8.4	2.51	21.7	34.9	26.1	11 026	42.2	9 061	39.7	1 514	54.5	3 510	34.7
Hancock	72	52	3 215	15.0	2.59	21.2	38.7	20.6	2 436	48.0	2 071	45.4	267	63.7	779	47.5
Hardin	3 923	1 156	34 497	17.5	2.62	22.8	41.2	19.0	25 347	52.3	19 942	48.6	4 113	67.3	9 150	47.2
Harlan	377	365	13 291	.2	2.47	27.0	35.9	26.6	9 446	45.3	7 221	44.2	1 749	50.8	3 845	25.2
Harrison	236	234	7 012	15.2	2.53	24.0	36.9	24.6	5 065	46.3	4 064	43.4	724	59.4	1 947	28.8
Hart	244	244	6 769	17.9	2.54	25.3	36.0	26.7	4 811	45.9	3 843	43.5	703	55.8	1 958	39.3

[1] As of April 1. [2] Includes people under formally authorized, supervised care or custody in institutions at the time of enumeration (such as correctional institutions, nursing homes, and juvenile institutions). [3] Under 18 years. [4] No husband present.

Sources: Group Quarters Population—U.S. Census Bureau, 2000 Census of Population and Housing, "Census 2000 Profiles of General Demographic Characteristics" data files, published May 2001 (related Internet site <http://www.census.gov/mp/www/pub/2000cen/mscen01.html>). Households, 2000—U.S. Census Bureau, 2000 Census of Population and Housing, "Census 2000 Profiles of General Demographic Characteristics" data files, published May 2001 (related Internet site <http://www.census.gov/mp/www/pub/2000cen/mscen01.html>). Households, 1990—U.S. Census Bureau, 1990 Census of Population and Housing, Summary Tape File (STF) 1C on CD-ROM (related Internet site <http://homer.ssd.census.gov/cdrom/lookup>).

[Includes U.S., states, and 3,142 counties or county equivalents defined as of January 1, 1992. For changes to these areas since then, see appendix B. Geographic Information]

County	Group quarters population, 2000[1] Number	Institutionalized population[2]	Households, 2000 (April 1) Number	Percent change, 1990–2000	Persons per household	One-person	With 1 or more persons under 18 years	With 1 or more persons 65 years and over	Family households Number	Percent with own children under 18 years	Married-couple Number	Percent with own children[3]	Female householder[4] Number	Percent with own children[3]	Nonfamily households Number	Percent change, 1990–2000
KENTUCKY—Con.																
Henderson	822	677	18 095	9.3	2.43	26.4	35.5	23.4	12 570	46.7	9 843	42.8	2 100	61.4	5 525	27.0
Henry	61	58	5 844	19.4	2.57	22.0	37.7	23.6	4 333	45.5	3 432	42.1	607	59.8	1 511	26.5
Hickman	151	151	2 188	–	2.34	27.6	30.9	29.9	1 542	40.0	1 237	36.1	237	58.6	646	15.6
Hopkins	805	692	18 820	6.0	2.43	25.8	34.6	25.7	13 400	44.4	10 588	40.9	2 241	58.6	5 420	22.5
Jackson	111	86	5 307	21.1	2.52	23.0	38.7	22.8	3 953	47.7	3 193	46.0	547	55.0	1 354	46.5
Jefferson	12 795	7 699	287 012	8.7	2.37	30.5	32.8	23.5	182 971	46.4	129 651	42.1	42 271	58.7	104 041	23.2
Jessamine	1 796	439	13 867	30.8	2.69	18.5	42.0	18.1	10 657	50.5	8 579	47.8	1 539	63.4	3 210	50.9
Johnson	516	235	9 103	7.5	2.52	22.3	37.3	23.2	6 867	45.2	5 510	43.1	1 029	55.5	2 236	21.5
Kenton	1 866	1 170	59 444	12.8	2.52	27.8	36.3	20.6	39 444	50.4	29 774	48.2	7 188	59.0	20 000	31.0
Knott	573	89	6 717	10.4	2.54	23.6	37.9	22.3	4 992	46.3	3 868	44.7	847	52.1	1 725	46.1
Knox	645	403	12 416	15.8	2.51	25.7	38.2	23.6	8 936	47.8	6 736	45.7	1 684	54.6	3 480	45.7
Larue	214	194	5 275	17.1	2.49	23.7	35.4	26.7	3 866	44.4	3 125	41.2	555	58.6	1 409	30.6
Laurel	669	648	20 353	30.6	2.56	21.7	38.6	21.6	15 364	46.7	12 341	44.2	2 330	58.1	4 989	65.3
Lawrence	144	1	5 954	18.9	2.59	22.4	38.3	24.3	4 478	46.6	3 648	45.0	627	54.7	1 476	37.9
Lee	713	711	2 985	8.2	2.41	26.6	35.8	27.2	2 122	45.9	1 636	43.1	381	54.9	863	36.6
Leslie	110	107	4 885	3.7	2.52	22.4	38.8	21.8	3 668	47.2	2 850	45.8	631	51.3	1 217	48.6
Letcher	225	221	10 085	3.6	2.48	24.1	35.7	23.7	7 461	43.7	5 894	42.6	1 159	47.5	2 624	29.3
Lewis	212	169	5 422	15.0	2.56	22.5	37.9	23.6	4 049	47.0	3 274	44.7	527	55.4	1 373	34.2
Lincoln	241	210	9 206	23.9	2.51	23.6	36.5	24.5	6 732	46.1	5 397	43.2	949	57.4	2 474	50.4
Livingston	137	124	3 996	11.2	2.42	24.4	32.5	26.0	2 893	40.7	2 414	39.1	315	50.8	1 103	25.1
Logan	315	275	10 506	12.9	2.50	25.0	36.6	25.6	7 577	46.1	6 006	43.2	1 176	57.6	2 929	26.8
Lyon	1 543	1 543	2 898	23.1	2.26	26.8	27.2	30.3	2 043	35.6	1 734	31.5	234	59.4	855	27.0
McCracken	1 334	1 196	27 736	8.2	2.31	29.7	32.1	26.4	18 457	44.4	14 181	39.6	3 389	61.6	9 279	23.1
McCreary	429	135	6 520	19.0	2.55	24.7	39.6	20.8	4 756	48.9	3 555	45.8	899	58.2	1 764	50.3
McLean	117	115	3 984	8.5	2.47	24.7	35.1	25.7	2 881	44.7	2 391	41.6	348	59.5	1 103	26.8
Madison	5 299	535	27 152	35.7	2.42	25.2	34.1	18.4	18 218	47.0	14 420	43.5	2 916	62.7	8 934	64.1
Magoffin	175	170	5 024	13.2	2.62	21.4	40.6	20.0	3 857	48.8	3 108	48.0	562	52.8	1 167	47.9
Marion	1 151	1 100	6 613	16.3	2.58	24.4	38.5	23.6	4 755	49.5	3 559	46.5	909	59.8	1 858	39.5
Marshall	572	537	12 412	15.0	2.38	25.0	31.2	28.9	8 993	40.3	7 623	37.2	976	59.5	3 419	37.2
Martin	84	–	4 776	11.1	2.62	21.8	42.7	19.5	3 621	51.7	2 843	49.5	598	60.2	1 155	51.8
Mason	332	304	6 847	4.7	2.41	27.6	34.1	27.4	4 698	45.6	3 711	43.1	759	56.5	2 149	20.0
Meade	108	89	9 470	17.2	2.77	18.4	45.6	16.8	7 393	54.0	6 066	51.9	923	64.1	2 077	54.5
Menifee	243	75	2 537	37.7	2.49	22.1	35.7	21.8	1 900	42.7	1 584	39.6	222	59.5	637	61.7
Mercer	146	113	8 423	13.6	2.45	25.1	34.8	26.4	6 039	44.4	4 870	41.7	878	56.6	2 384	33.3
Metcalfe	127	100	4 016	17.0	2.47	25.2	35.2	27.4	2 883	45.0	2 332	42.3	400	54.5	1 133	40.6
Monroe	131	129	4 741	5.2	2.45	26.3	34.1	27.5	3 380	43.6	2 722	42.0	491	51.5	1 361	19.7
Montgomery	400	335	8 902	21.7	2.49	23.9	36.8	23.4	6 435	46.5	5 133	43.1	997	60.6	2 467	47.5
Morgan	1 843	1 814	4 752	16.2	2.55	22.6	37.4	25.1	3 570	46.3	2 966	44.6	438	54.6	1 182	39.2
Muhlenberg	1 533	1 269	12 357	5.8	2.45	24.3	34.1	28.3	9 056	42.0	7 381	40.0	1 280	51.4	3 301	22.3
Nelson	705	447	13 953	33.9	2.64	22.3	40.8	19.1	10 267	51.6	7 941	48.3	1 695	63.1	3 686	59.3
Nicholas	103	103	2 710	3.4	2.48	24.6	35.1	26.7	1 952	43.7	1 557	41.0	272	51.5	758	12.1
Ohio	340	324	8 899	13.9	2.54	23.2	35.5	26.5	6 587	44.6	5 443	42.7	820	54.4	2 312	33.7
Oldham	3 880	3 789	14 856	39.2	2.85	14.9	46.5	14.6	12 199	53.7	10 618	52.6	1 159	61.1	2 657	54.0
Owen	110	110	4 086	19.8	2.55	23.1	36.7	25.5	2 996	45.6	2 479	42.7	327	56.9	1 090	31.8
Owsley	96	94	1 894	2.5	2.51	24.5	37.2	26.5	1 388	44.5	1 037	42.4	240	56.3	506	28.8
Pendleton	179	81	5 170	19.3	2.75	20.1	42.4	20.9	3 971	50.7	3 247	48.6	496	58.3	1 199	23.1
Perry	383	319	11 460	8.1	2.53	23.3	38.1	21.9	8 493	46.2	6 500	44.8	1 518	51.6	2 967	37.9
Pike	946	579	27 612	5.6	2.46	24.1	36.6	22.8	20 364	45.6	16 224	44.1	3 159	53.4	7 248	39.7
Powell	115	97	5 044	24.3	2.60	21.8	40.3	21.1	3 784	48.1	2 934	45.5	625	56.5	1 260	56.3
Pulaski	1 220	1 061	22 719	20.4	2.42	24.9	33.9	26.4	16 339	43.4	13 299	39.9	2 300	59.9	6 380	43.3
Robertson	70	62	866	5.6	2.54	24.7	35.0	28.9	622	43.2	499	41.3	79	48.1	244	-.4
Rockcastle	310	273	6 544	19.8	2.49	24.4	36.6	24.6	4 763	46.1	3 788	43.6	744	57.1	1 781	47.4
Rowan	3 156	307	7 927	17.4	2.39	27.0	32.7	21.2	5 216	46.3	4 156	43.6	806	58.1	2 711	36.6
Russell	171	145	6 941	17.7	2.33	28.0	32.0	28.4	4 796	42.0	3 836	38.7	706	53.8	2 145	44.7
Scott	1 468	333	12 110	42.5	2.61	21.0	41.3	17.1	8 990	51.8	7 126	48.6	1 396	66.0	3 120	63.9
Shelby	1 488	1 089	12 104	33.8	2.63	20.2	38.0	20.6	9 121	46.1	7 382	43.4	1 282	59.0	2 983	48.0
Simpson	236	217	6 415	11.2	2.52	24.2	37.1	24.3	4 637	46.8	3 645	43.3	735	61.0	1 778	24.9
Spencer	119	111	4 251	73.4	2.74	17.1	41.9	16.9	3 357	48.6	2 888	46.9	322	59.0	894	77.4
Taylor	672	136	9 233	12.4	2.41	26.0	33.7	27.7	6 559	43.5	5 211	39.5	1 059	59.8	2 674	34.2
Todd	126	126	4 569	11.3	2.59	23.0	36.8	26.7	3 369	45.4	2 684	43.2	528	54.4	1 200	20.2
Trigg	111	111	5 215	27.1	2.39	25.0	31.5	28.7	3 767	40.2	3 138	36.8	436	60.8	1 448	45.1
Trimble	55	55	3 137	39.7	2.57	22.0	38.8	21.4	2 297	43.3	1 900	45.7	268	61.6	840	86.3
Union	1 389	197	5 710	2.3	2.50	26.1	35.7	25.7	4 081	44.9	3 224	42.0	650	58.0	1 629	16.9
Warren	5 559	1 158	35 365	22.7	2.46	26.1	34.3	19.4	23 427	47.4	18 170	44.0	3 971	61.8	11 938	35.6
Washington	335	181	4 121	11.1	2.57	24.0	36.1	26.5	3 020	45.2	2 454	42.7	413	55.9	1 101	37.3
Wayne	184	181	7 913	21.4	2.49	23.9	36.1	25.4	5 812	45.5	4 664	43.1	837	56.2	2 101	51.6
Webster	257	250	5 560	3.5	2.49	24.3	35.3	26.7	4 054	43.8	3 277	41.1	574	56.6	1 506	12.1
Whitley	1 205	455	13 780	13.4	2.52	25.2	37.2	24.3	9 888	46.9	7 568	44.5	1 785	56.1	3 892	35.8
Wolfe	152	101	2 816	14.9	2.45	27.0	36.8	22.8	1 977	47.9	1 472	44.8	352	56.0	839	41.7
Woodford	366	203	8 893	23.1	2.57	21.0	37.5	19.7	6 641	46.9	5 501	44.9	862	59.0	2 252	48.8

[1] As of April 1. [2] Includes people under formally authorized, supervised care or custody in institutions at the time of enumeration (such as correctional institutions, nursing homes, and juvenile institutions). [3] Under 18 years. [4] No husband present.

Sources: Group Quarters Population—U.S. Census Bureau, 2000 Census of Population and Housing, "Census 2000 Profiles of General Demographic Characteristics" data files, published May 2001 (related Internet site <http://www.census.gov/mp/www/pub/2000cen/mscen01.html>). Households, 2000—U.S. Census Bureau, 2000 Census of Population and Housing, "Census 2000 Profiles of General Demographic Characteristics" data files, published May 2001 (related Internet site <http://www.census.gov/mp/www/pub/2000cen/mscen01.html>). Households, 1990—U.S. Census Bureau, 1990 Census of Population and Housing, Summary Tape File (STF) 1C on CD-ROM (related Internet site <http://homer.ssd.census.gov/cdrom/lookup>).

[Includes U.S., states, and 3,142 counties or county equivalents defined as of January 1, 1992. For changes to these areas since then, see appendix B. Geographic Information]

County	Group quarters population, 2000[1] Number	Institutionalized population[2]	Households, 2000 (April 1) Number	Percent change, 1990–2000	Persons per household	Percent— One-person	With 1 or more persons under 18 years	With 1 or more persons 65 years and over	Family households (families) Number	Percent with own children under 18 years	Married-couple Number	Percent with own children[3]	Female householder[4] Number	Percent with own children[3]	Nonfamily households Number	Percent change, 1990–2000
LOUISIANA	135 965	90 002	1 656 053	10.5	2.62	25.3	39.2	22.5	1 156 438	49.5	809 498	46.2	275 075	58.7	499 615	22.0
Acadia	982	901	21 142	9.6	2.74	22.6	42.6	24.0	15 676	51.9	11 531	49.1	3 147	60.6	5 466	22.6
Allen	4 182	4 166	8 102	14.4	2.62	24.3	41.4	26.4	5 927	50.4	4 379	47.5	1 233	59.1	2 175	35.1
Ascension	646	577	26 691	38.0	2.85	18.3	46.7	16.0	20 789	54.6	16 052	52.6	3 554	62.5	5 902	57.5
Assumption	200	163	8 239	11.4	2.81	20.3	43.7	23.2	6 312	49.5	4 680	47.5	1 224	56.3	1 927	28.6
Avoyelles	3 102	3 074	14 736	9.3	2.60	25.0	40.1	26.2	10 584	50.5	7 618	46.4	2 316	62.3	4 152	27.3
Beauregard	1 190	1 166	12 104	16.8	2.63	22.2	39.9	23.0	9 080	48.3	7 329	45.7	1 320	59.9	3 024	29.3
Bienville	373	367	6 108	4.4	2.52	28.8	36.6	31.8	4 216	44.9	2 853	40.5	1 079	55.6	1 892	15.9
Bossier	2 085	1 222	36 628	19.2	2.63	22.9	40.9	20.0	26 627	50.7	19 989	47.0	5 172	63.3	10 001	35.4
Caddo	6 397	4 460	97 974	5.1	2.51	28.9	36.1	25.2	64 980	46.6	41 391	40.9	19 350	58.1	32 994	17.3
Calcasieu	4 547	3 015	68 613	13.7	2.61	24.0	39.7	22.6	49 034	49.8	36 119	46.3	10 089	61.5	19 579	28.0
Caldwell	708	654	3 941	10.2	2.50	25.4	37.2	26.8	2 819	44.9	2 184	42.3	497	57.1	1 122	29.6
Cameron	65	36	3 592	13.9	2.76	20.9	43.2	22.1	2 703	51.8	2 236	50.7	324	58.3	889	45.0
Catahoula	508	508	4 082	3.9	2.55	24.3	37.5	27.7	2 994	44.6	2 231	40.4	592	57.4	1 088	14.5
Claiborne	1 165	1 151	6 270	3.4	2.50	28.5	35.0	32.7	4 336	43.0	2 953	37.7	1 105	55.7	1 934	10.5
Concordia	689	689	7 521	2.5	2.60	25.3	39.1	28.9	5 433	45.7	3 683	41.4	1 426	55.2	2 088	18.9
De Soto	322	301	9 691	6.2	2.60	25.4	39.2	27.7	6 999	46.6	4 723	42.0	1 802	56.9	2 722	17.8
East Baton Rouge	14 584	5 246	156 365	12.8	2.55	26.9	36.9	18.7	102 581	49.9	69 854	46.5	26 336	59.7	53 784	25.9
East Carroll	1 057	1 051	2 969	–5.1	2.82	25.6	44.2	27.7	2 140	50.7	1 189	42.1	821	63.9	829	–1.3
East Feliciana	2 852	2 213	6 699	19.9	2.76	22.5	42.6	22.0	5 032	47.5	3 510	45.1	1 206	54.8	1 667	41.0
Evangeline	1 772	1 709	12 736	8.0	2.64	25.8	41.6	25.0	9 151	52.8	6 657	49.0	1 972	65.7	3 585	22.2
Franklin	789	755	7 754	–.3	2.64	23.9	39.5	28.6	5 705	46.0	4 136	42.8	1 277	55.2	2 049	7.1
Grant	219	195	7 073	13.0	2.61	22.6	41.2	24.2	5 274	48.9	4 045	45.1	909	63.6	1 799	24.0
Iberia	1 615	1 052	25 381	11.1	2.82	21.1	44.8	23.0	19 165	52.3	13 515	49.0	4 355	61.7	6 216	23.3
Iberville	3 354	3 333	10 674	8.1	2.81	21.9	43.2	24.4	8 012	48.3	5 296	46.7	2 175	53.7	2 662	17.2
Jackson	278	271	6 086	4.6	2.48	27.0	35.8	29.1	4 300	44.8	3 216	42.0	874	54.7	1 786	15.1
Jefferson	4 357	3 040	176 234	5.9	2.56	26.7	36.2	22.6	120 183	46.8	84 997	44.1	27 060	55.1	56 051	16.6
Jefferson Davis	415	370	11 480	7.6	2.70	22.6	41.4	25.7	8 525	50.1	6 518	46.9	1 576	60.9	2 955	21.2
Lafayette	4 849	2 262	72 372	19.8	2.57	25.4	39.3	17.4	48 839	53.0	35 605	50.0	10 168	65.4	23 533	29.3
Lafourche	1 716	802	32 057	11.2	2.75	19.6	41.9	22.0	24 296	49.9	18 945	47.7	3 981	58.3	7 761	29.9
La Salle	924	924	5 291	4.0	2.52	25.7	38.0	28.4	3 798	46.8	3 120	46.3	518	50.8	1 493	14.4
Lincoln	5 309	767	15 235	11.5	2.44	27.0	33.6	21.6	9 686	47.3	6 774	42.9	2 335	60.6	5 549	19.3
Livingston	584	504	32 630	37.0	2.80	18.2	45.6	17.7	25 545	53.1	20 575	50.9	3 476	61.9	7 085	57.0
Madison	1 467	1 238	4 469	5.1	2.74	26.6	42.0	25.8	3 140	50.4	1 841	43.8	1 082	61.7	1 329	11.4
Morehouse	955	929	11 382	3.8	2.64	24.4	39.8	28.4	8 319	45.6	5 593	40.9	2 249	56.6	3 063	16.0
Natchitoches	2 604	612	14 263	12.8	2.56	27.1	37.5	24.8	9 503	49.5	6 467	45.8	2 523	60.8	4 760	34.1
Orleans	17 641	9 772	188 251	Z	2.48	33.2	35.3	22.6	112 997	48.7	58 013	43.0	46 171	57.2	75 274	7.2
Ouachita	4 965	2 467	55 216	9.3	2.58	25.8	38.8	22.6	38 319	49.2	26 319	44.4	9 897	61.6	16 897	20.4
Plaquemines	728	646	9 021	9.8	2.89	18.6	45.3	21.5	6 999	50.9	5 183	49.9	1 313	54.4	2 022	23.4
Pointe Coupee	337	330	8 397	8.5	2.67	23.4	40.4	27.0	6 171	47.9	4 512	46.0	1 283	54.9	2 226	22.8
Rapides	5 504	3 457	47 120	2.6	2.56	26.0	39.2	24.5	33 133	49.2	23 396	45.2	7 913	60.4	13 987	19.1
Red River	283	283	3 414	2.8	2.74	23.1	41.4	28.2	2 527	48.2	1 759	44.9	635	59.1	887	8.7
Richland	1 169	1 019	7 490	5.8	2.65	24.0	40.2	27.5	5 481	46.9	3 757	42.6	1 411	56.5	2 009	17.6
Sabine	417	387	9 221	10.3	2.50	26.0	35.7	29.8	6 596	43.9	5 132	39.9	1 109	60.1	2 625	22.9
St. Bernard	788	727	25 123	8.5	2.64	22.9	38.2	26.6	18 301	46.2	13 411	45.1	3 677	50.2	6 822	40.2
St. Charles	430	372	16 422	14.6	2.90	16.7	47.9	18.3	13 094	54.4	9 924	52.8	2 422	59.9	3 328	14.3
St. Helena	72	66	3 873	16.4	2.70	25.4	41.1	25.8	2 784	47.3	1 892	45.5	711	51.3	1 089	31.0
St. James	265	258	6 992	8.7	3.00	18.4	46.0	24.4	5 550	49.0	3 869	48.3	1 349	52.9	1 442	34.9
St. John the Baptist	443	424	14 283	12.4	2.98	17.5	49.0	17.7	11 314	54.3	8 011	52.3	2 586	60.2	2 969	24.5
St. Landry	1 528	1 338	32 328	17.7	2.67	25.4	40.6	26.2	23 205	50.2	15 934	46.7	5 791	59.9	9 123	40.7
St. Martin	792	753	17 164	17.3	2.78	20.7	44.3	20.7	12 983	52.5	9 368	49.1	2 733	63.0	4 181	36.0
St. Mary	629	506	19 317	–.7	2.74	23.2	42.7	22.7	14 090	50.3	9 859	47.2	3 187	58.7	5 227	14.4
St. Tammany	2 346	1 965	69 253	37.6	2.73	19.7	42.7	19.6	52 727	51.6	42 534	49.8	7 594	59.4	16 526	50.4
Tangipahoa	3 275	1 388	36 558	23.2	2.66	24.0	40.1	21.2	25 768	50.1	18 257	47.2	5 931	59.1	10 790	35.2
Tensas	491	491	2 416	–3.9	2.54	29.3	36.8	32.1	1 635	44.3	1 041	39.4	488	52.3	781	14.2
Terrebonne	1 413	1 242	35 997	13.1	2.86	19.3	44.6	20.4	27 409	51.5	20 525	49.4	5 084	58.2	8 588	30.4
Union	450	440	8 857	17.7	2.52	24.9	35.8	26.9	6 412	43.3	4 897	40.1	1 213	55.8	2 445	42.4
Vermilion	767	738	19 832	11.7	2.67	23.1	40.8	25.6	14 453	50.9	11 016	48.0	2 584	61.6	5 379	24.1
Vernon	3 370	531	18 260	–4.5	2.69	22.0	45.4	17.1	13 706	56.4	11 178	54.1	1 945	67.3	4 554	20.2
Washington	1 787	1 750	16 467	6.4	2.56	26.6	38.4	28.3	11 646	46.2	8 113	43.1	2 813	54.7	4 821	21.8
Webster	936	745	16 501	4.1	2.48	27.0	35.2	29.9	11 559	43.4	8 198	39.0	2 690	55.5	4 942	15.1
West Baton Rouge	570	552	7 663	16.0	2.74	21.5	43.5	20.8	5 736	50.3	3 950	48.5	1 397	53.8	1 927	32.9
West Carroll	790	772	4 458	1.5	2.59	24.8	38.1	30.1	3 250	45.7	2 576	43.6	548	53.1	1 208	10.7
West Feliciana	5 146	5 138	3 645	33.0	2.73	23.1	43.1	20.8	2 705	52.4	1 971	49.6	567	61.7	940	42.2
Winn	1 772	1 722	5 930	2.5	2.55	26.2	38.0	28.8	4 235	45.6	3 069	42.7	910	54.3	1 695	11.4

[1] As of April 1.   [2] Includes people under formally authorized, supervised care or custody in institutions at the time of enumeration (such as correctional institutions, nursing homes, and juvenile institutions).   [3] Under 18 years.   [4] No husband present.

Sources: Group Quarters Population—U.S. Census Bureau, 2000 Census of Population and Housing, "Census 2000 Profiles of General Demographic Characteristics" data files, published May 2001 (related Internet site <http://www.census.gov/mp/www/pub/2000cen/mscen01.html>).   Households, 2000—U.S. Census Bureau, 2000 Census of Population and Housing, "Census 2000 Profiles of General Demographic Characteristics" data files, published May 2001 (related Internet site <http://www.census.gov/mp/www/pub/2000cen/mscen01.html>).   Households, 1990—U.S. Census Bureau, 1990 Census of Population and Housing, Summary Tape File (STF) 1C on CD-ROM (related Internet site <http://homer.ssd.census.gov/cdrom/lookup>).

Table B–3. Counties — Group Quarters Population and Households–Con.

[Includes U.S., states, and 3,142 counties or county equivalents defined as of January 1, 1992. For changes to these areas since then, see appendix B. Geographic Information]

County	Group quarters population, 2000[1] Number	Institutionalized population[2]	Households Number	Percent change, 1990–2000	Persons per household	One-person	With 1 or more persons under 18 years	With 1 or more persons 65 years and over	Family households Number	Family Percent with own children under 18 years	Married-couple Number	Married-couple Percent with own children[3]	Female householder[4] Number	Female householder Percent with own children[3]	Nonfamily Number	Nonfamily Percent change, 1990–2000
MAINE	34 912	13 091	518 200	11.4	2.39	27.0	32.4	24.7	340 685	46.2	272 152	41.4	49 022	66.0	177 515	29.9
Androscoggin	3 668	1 528	42 028	5.0	2.38	28.3	32.9	24.1	27 183	47.7	20 851	41.6	4 533	69.7	14 845	24.0
Aroostook	2 312	908	30 356	-3.2	2.36	27.6	30.3	28.9	20 436	42.2	16 865	38.3	2 452	61.9	9 920	25.1
Cumberland	8 627	2 838	107 989	14.3	2.38	28.4	31.8	22.8	67 699	48.0	54 109	44.5	10 213	63.4	40 290	28.2
Franklin	1 124	257	11 806	9.5	2.40	25.8	31.7	24.7	7 748	45.0	6 186	39.2	1 084	68.1	4 058	27.7
Hancock	1 307	415	21 864	19.2	2.31	27.9	30.1	26.9	14 238	43.4	11 692	38.3	1 766	66.6	7 626	38.5
Kennebec	3 686	1 290	47 683	8.6	2.38	27.6	33.1	24.1	31 328	47.5	24 603	41.9	4 788	69.0	16 355	25.6
Knox	1 257	1 115	16 608	15.8	2.31	29.0	30.1	28.9	10 728	43.8	8 676	38.7	1 495	65.2	5 880	30.8
Lincoln	391	149	14 158	18.3	2.35	26.7	30.2	29.8	9 545	41.9	7 938	37.2	1 089	65.7	4 613	36.4
Oxford	809	635	22 314	11.2	2.42	25.6	32.6	27.1	15 180	44.8	12 065	39.4	2 124	66.3	7 134	29.9
Penobscot	6 463	1 421	58 096	7.5	2.38	26.7	32.2	23.1	37 813	46.3	29 913	41.3	5 733	66.0	20 283	27.3
Piscataquis	182	130	7 278	1.2	2.34	27.8	30.8	30.0	4 858	42.8	3 934	37.2	612	66.8	2 420	22.0
Sagadahoc	294	157	14 117	12.2	2.47	25.2	35.3	21.7	9 636	48.6	7 709	44.0	1 355	69.0	4 481	30.3
Somerset	895	428	20 496	10.7	2.44	24.6	34.0	24.9	14 117	45.8	11 102	39.8	2 060	67.6	6 379	27.5
Waldo	522	169	14 726	18.6	2.43	24.9	32.9	24.1	10 053	44.9	8 124	39.4	1 328	68.7	4 673	38.7
Washington	916	471	14 118	5.2	2.34	28.3	30.4	29.7	9 304	42.5	7 356	37.1	1 338	62.7	4 814	28.3
York	2 459	1 180	74 563	20.6	2.47	24.9	34.3	23.8	50 819	47.2	41 029	43.2	7 052	65.4	23 744	41.8
MARYLAND	134 056	69 318	1 980 859	13.3	2.61	25.0	37.3	21.7	1 359 318	48.7	994 549	46.4	279 876	56.9	621 541	23.5
Allegany	6 158	4 443	29 322	-1.1	2.35	30.1	29.0	32.2	18 896	41.2	14 835	37.5	3 016	56.2	10 426	12.9
Anne Arundel	15 990	8 862	178 670	19.8	2.65	21.3	38.3	19.5	129 193	48.2	102 197	46.2	19 749	57.0	49 477	38.6
Baltimore	17 640	6 961	299 877	11.8	2.46	27.3	33.4	26.0	198 605	45.7	148 099	42.6	38 398	56.5	101 272	29.1
Calvert	581	459	25 447	49.8	2.91	16.3	45.6	18.5	20 149	52.7	16 478	51.5	2 530	58.2	5 298	70.7
Caroline	453	331	11 097	11.2	2.64	21.5	39.2	25.2	8 156	47.3	6 030	43.1	1 509	59.9	2 941	14.4
Carroll	3 581	2 054	52 503	24.3	2.81	17.5	42.4	21.3	41 094	50.8	34 936	49.5	4 350	58.1	11 409	36.8
Cecil	1 221	780	31 223	26.3	2.71	19.9	40.9	20.0	23 290	49.6	18 295	46.4	3 474	62.2	7 933	45.3
Charles	1 369	969	41 668	26.5	2.86	17.2	45.5	16.4	32 277	53.0	24 174	50.3	6 052	62.8	9 391	51.9
Dorchester	670	490	12 706	4.9	2.36	28.2	31.7	30.9	8 506	40.8	6 030	34.7	1 969	57.5	4 200	15.8
Frederick	4 655	1 963	70 060	33.3	2.72	20.1	41.2	18.5	51 949	52.0	42 815	50.5	6 557	61.0	18 111	46.6
Garrett	617	497	11 476	13.5	2.55	23.5	35.0	26.6	8 356	44.8	6 971	42.3	960	57.4	3 120	34.0
Harford	1 562	966	79 667	26.1	2.72	19.7	41.4	20.1	60 403	51.1	49 285	49.1	8 128	60.2	19 264	47.8
Howard	3 618	1 876	90 043	31.8	2.71	20.8	42.1	14.3	65 790	54.8	54 441	53.7	8 551	62.3	24 253	37.4
Kent	1 348	338	7 666	14.4	2.33	27.8	29.4	33.3	5 136	39.2	3 962	33.5	850	57.2	2 530	25.7
Montgomery	9 431	5 436	324 565	15.0	2.66	24.4	37.2	21.2	224 225	50.7	179 192	50.2	33 919	56.1	100 340	19.5
Prince George's	17 357	4 897	286 610	11.1	2.74	24.1	41.0	16.0	198 066	51.1	126 012	48.7	56 077	57.8	88 544	17.2
Queen Anne's	509	437	15 315	22.6	2.62	19.6	36.6	24.1	11 542	44.2	9 530	41.5	1 450	57.0	3 773	36.8
St. Mary's	2 782	766	30 642	20.2	2.72	21.3	41.9	17.3	22 306	52.7	17 714	50.2	3 233	62.6	8 336	39.4
Somerset	4 904	3 399	8 361	4.8	2.37	29.4	30.7	30.2	5 444	39.8	3 852	35.3	1 259	51.7	2 917	21.7
Talbot	612	442	14 307	12.9	2.32	27.8	29.2	33.4	9 630	39.1	7 779	35.2	1 405	56.4	4 677	23.1
Washington	9 420	8 609	49 726	11.1	2.46	26.0	34.0	25.9	34 092	45.6	26 828	41.1	5 314	63.1	15 634	25.9
Wicomico	3 144	1 070	32 218	16.0	2.53	24.8	36.1	24.0	21 781	47.7	15 854	42.8	4 558	62.0	10 437	26.4
Worcester	681	639	19 694	39.3	2.33	26.3	27.7	32.8	13 278	36.3	10 469	31.3	2 120	56.8	6 416	47.7
Independent City																
Baltimore city	25 753	12 634	257 996	-6.7	2.42	34.9	32.7	25.5	147 154	44.7	68 771	37.4	64 448	53.3	110 842	6.9
MASSACHUSETTS	221 216	88 453	2 443 580	8.7	2.51	28.0	32.9	24.7	1 576 696	47.5	1 197 917	45.8	289 944	56.4	866 884	18.4
Barnstable	5 677	2 609	94 822	22.2	2.28	29.5	26.1	36.7	61 041	37.8	49 457	34.0	8 939	55.9	33 781	32.1
Berkshire	6 132	2 275	56 006	3.1	2.30	31.6	29.4	30.1	35 110	43.8	26 887	39.2	6 156	61.4	20 896	18.1
Bristol	13 674	6 566	205 411	9.5	2.54	26.5	35.6	25.8	140 610	48.1	105 958	45.1	26 733	60.0	64 801	24.6
Dukes	193	137	6 421	28.3	2.30	32.0	30.2	24.6	3 791	48.1	2 915	44.4	627	61.2	2 630	33.0
Essex	16 889	8 894	275 419	9.6	2.57	27.1	35.2	25.6	185 094	48.4	140 631	46.9	34 025	58.6	90 325	18.9
Franklin	1 406	942	29 466	6.6	2.38	29.0	31.4	24.1	18 415	47.2	14 119	42.5	3 129	64.9	11 051	19.0
Hampden	14 429	7 432	175 288	3.2	2.52	28.4	34.8	26.7	115 773	48.4	80 359	43.3	27 911	63.4	59 515	16.3
Hampshire	18 245	1 589	55 991	11.9	2.39	28.6	29.9	23.1	33 819	46.7	26 566	43.6	5 488	61.1	22 172	25.1
Middlesex	52 890	16 580	561 220	8.0	2.52	27.1	32.1	23.5	361 076	46.9	287 632	47.2	55 308	49.7	200 144	16.2
Nantucket	760	43	3 699	42.4	2.37	29.8	28.3	19.5	2 106	47.2	1 690	45.1	297	59.9	1 593	43.6
Norfolk	17 432	10 238	248 827	9.2	2.54	26.8	33.0	26.4	165 858	46.8	134 985	47.9	23 526	45.6	82 969	19.5
Plymouth	11 724	8 593	168 361	12.6	2.74	22.2	39.1	23.2	122 421	49.9	95 906	49.0	20 092	55.6	45 940	25.3
Suffolk	36 593	9 803	278 722	5.6	2.34	36.3	26.5	20.0	139 159	47.0	81 651	43.2	45 362	57.5	139 563	10.9
Worcester	25 172	12 752	283 927	9.1	2.56	26.2	35.9	23.9	192 423	49.6	149 161	47.3	32 351	60.9	91 504	20.9

[1] As of April 1.   [2] Includes people under formally authorized, supervised care or custody in institutions at the time of enumeration (such as correctional institutions, nursing homes, and juvenile institutions).   [3] Under 18 years.   [4] No husband present.

Sources: Group Quarters Population—U.S. Census Bureau, 2000 Census of Population and Housing, "Census 2000 Profiles of General Demographic Characteristics" data files, published May 2001 (related Internet site <http://www.census.gov/mp/www/pub/2000cen/mscen01.html>).   Households, 2000—U.S. Census Bureau, 2000 Census of Population and Housing, "Census 2000 Profiles of General Demographic Characteristics" data files, published May 2001 (related Internet site <http://www.census.gov/mp/www/pub/2000cen/mscen01.html>).   Households, 1990—U.S. Census Bureau, 1990 Census of Population and Housing, Summary Tape File (STF) 1C on CD-ROM (related Internet site <http://homer.ssd.census.gov/cdrom/lookup>).

[Includes U.S., states, and 3,142 counties or county equivalents defined as of January 1, 1992. For changes to these areas since then, see appendix B. Geographic Information]

County	Group quarters population, 2000[1]		Households, 2000 (April 1)													
						Percent—			By type—						Nonfamily households	
									Family households (families)							
											Married-couple		Female householder[4]			
	Number	Institutionalized population[2]	Number	Percent change, 1990–2000	Persons per household	One-person	With 1 or more persons under 18 years	With 1 or more persons 65 years and over	Number	Percent with own children under 18 years	Number	Percent with own children[3]	Number	Percent with own children[3]	Number	Percent change, 1990–2000
MICHIGAN	249 889	126 132	3 785 661	10.7	2.56	26.2	35.6	22.8	2 575 699	48.0	1 947 710	44.8	473 802	59.9	1 209 962	23.4
Alcona	199	129	5 132	20.4	2.24	26.6	22.8	38.1	3 568	29.4	3 085	25.3	299	51.5	1 564	33.2
Alger	986	912	3 785	13.4	2.35	26.8	28.8	30.3	2 587	39.5	2 157	35.3	287	58.9	1 198	32.8
Allegan	1 917	799	38 165	20.4	2.72	20.7	40.1	20.6	28 405	50.3	23 438	47.3	3 474	65.1	9 760	32.6
Alpena	567	219	12 818	8.3	2.40	27.8	31.2	29.3	8 694	43.3	7 093	39.3	1 151	60.6	4 124	25.9
Antrim	286	182	9 222	32.1	2.47	23.4	31.9	29.6	6 712	40.9	5 627	36.7	724	61.9	2 510	41.2
Arenac	804	680	6 710	18.9	2.45	25.5	31.4	29.7	4 719	41.2	3 824	35.8	605	64.1	1 991	35.7
Baraga	783	685	3 353	9.4	2.37	29.5	31.1	29.2	2 223	43.9	1 727	38.7	340	62.4	1 130	17.3
Barry	435	278	21 035	18.4	2.68	19.5	37.9	21.9	15 994	46.3	13 481	43.0	1 612	64.3	5 041	32.9
Bay	1 773	814	43 930	4.1	2.47	27.2	33.0	25.7	30 039	44.9	23 586	41.0	4 803	60.0	13 891	19.3
Benzie	264	164	6 500	36.2	2.42	24.1	31.0	29.4	4 593	40.8	3 846	36.9	500	63.2	1 907	50.5
Berrien	4 367	1 468	63 569	4.2	2.49	27.1	34.5	25.9	43 336	45.8	32 550	40.8	8 419	62.8	20 233	17.8
Branch	3 126	2 735	16 349	9.6	2.61	24.2	36.2	25.3	11 570	46.9	9 150	42.7	1 613	63.1	4 779	22.2
Calhoun	4 132	1 892	54 100	4.4	2.47	28.8	35.0	24.4	36 249	47.4	26 840	41.8	7 033	64.0	17 851	15.8
Cass	744	337	19 676	7.9	2.56	22.6	34.6	24.8	14 298	42.7	11 447	38.7	1 955	58.4	5 378	22.5
Charlevoix	288	163	10 400	26.2	2.48	25.2	33.9	26.2	7 306	45.3	6 072	41.0	840	66.1	3 094	37.6
Cheboygan	361	232	10 835	32.1	2.41	25.8	30.8	30.3	7 579	40.9	6 284	36.2	930	65.1	3 256	56.7
Chippewa	5 966	4 994	13 474	16.7	2.42	27.5	32.3	25.2	8 962	45.7	6 938	39.6	1 446	68.9	4 512	27.6
Clare	501	359	12 686	30.8	2.42	26.2	30.8	29.9	8 749	40.4	7 010	34.1	1 191	65.5	3 937	52.3
Clinton	805	597	23 653	17.0	2.70	19.8	39.4	19.9	17 976	49.3	15 203	46.7	1 977	65.4	5 677	32.2
Crawford	467	383	5 625	26.7	2.45	24.0	32.5	29.0	4 037	41.9	3 242	35.9	545	66.1	1 588	42.9
Delta	569	435	15 836	9.0	2.40	28.0	31.5	28.7	10 684	44.1	8 834	40.2	1 317	64.8	5 152	22.0
Dickinson	467	309	11 386	7.1	2.37	29.4	32.5	30.3	7 579	46.5	6 246	42.5	951	67.2	3 807	21.4
Eaton	1 734	694	40 167	18.0	2.54	24.5	36.2	20.4	28 251	48.1	22 622	44.1	4 123	65.3	11 916	36.1
Emmet	712	413	12 577	32.2	2.44	26.9	33.5	24.1	8 527	46.7	7 030	42.9	1 067	65.8	4 050	48.5
Genesee	5 347	2 550	169 825	5.3	2.54	26.6	37.3	21.6	115 956	49.4	80 574	43.7	27 702	64.1	53 869	18.5
Gladwin	338	234	10 561	26.4	2.43	24.0	29.3	31.1	7 616	37.6	6 387	32.7	847	62.9	2 945	41.6
Gogebic	1 017	725	7 425	–.3	2.20	34.2	25.9	36.9	4 581	39.6	3 644	35.1	688	57.8	2 844	10.5
Grand Traverse	1 823	838	30 396	26.8	2.49	25.0	34.6	22.2	20 726	48.1	16 917	44.6	2 799	63.7	9 670	40.2
Gratiot	5 057	3 753	14 501	6.2	2.57	23.7	36.4	25.0	10 401	47.4	8 356	42.9	1 478	65.7	4 100	21.1
Hillsdale	1 481	319	17 335	10.9	2.60	22.9	35.6	24.4	12 544	45.5	10 392	41.6	1 462	63.6	4 791	23.5
Houghton	3 106	645	13 793	4.7	2.39	32.6	27.2	28.2	8 143	44.3	6 553	40.8	1 109	60.1	5 650	11.3
Huron	682	317	14 597	10.0	2.42	27.3	30.8	33.1	10 141	41.8	8 554	38.9	1 086	56.7	4 456	24.2
Ingham	16 827	1 783	108 593	5.8	2.42	30.2	32.2	17.3	63 767	50.7	46 660	46.1	13 098	65.4	44 826	18.6
Ionia	5 789	5 536	20 606	11.7	2.70	21.9	40.6	20.9	15 151	51.8	12 095	47.8	2 084	67.8	5 455	21.8
Iosco	395	319	11 727	1.2	2.30	28.6	27.1	34.6	7 855	37.2	6 471	31.6	986	63.0	3 872	24.2
Iron	575	502	5 748	1.6	2.19	33.7	25.1	39.7	3 614	37.7	2 899	32.3	483	61.9	2 134	12.4
Isabella	6 103	634	22 425	27.5	2.55	23.8	30.2	17.7	13 014	48.9	10 179	44.7	2 000	66.0	9 411	55.2
Jackson	10 039	8 484	58 168	8.4	2.55	24.6	36.6	23.9	40 840	47.7	31 314	42.6	6 969	65.3	17 328	17.2
Kalamazoo	11 140	2 169	93 479	11.7	2.43	28.0	32.5	19.8	57 936	49.0	44 548	44.3	10 260	67.2	35 543	25.6
Kalkaska	194	131	6 428	30.3	2.55	22.3	34.5	24.1	4 636	43.9	3 770	39.0	580	66.7	1 792	48.7
Kent	12 789	6 036	212 890	17.1	2.64	25.6	38.3	19.0	144 123	52.9	111 354	49.9	24 653	66.0	68 767	30.5
Keweenaw	178	133	998	28.4	2.13	35.8	21.6	35.3	605	34.5	515	30.5	57	66.7	393	31.0
Lake	603	585	4 704	33.0	2.28	29.6	25.8	34.0	3 055	35.4	2 467	29.4	410	61.7	1 649	47.0
Lapeer	1 869	1 327	30 729	24.6	2.80	18.5	41.0	19.0	23 889	49.2	20 183	47.4	2 483	59.6	6 840	46.9
Leelanau	220	126	8 436	34.5	2.48	22.3	31.3	28.6	6 216	40.6	5 362	37.0	600	64.3	2 220	47.3
Lenawee	5 146	3 194	35 930	13.6	2.61	22.9	37.0	23.7	26 052	47.1	21 074	43.9	3 594	61.8	9 878	32.1
Livingston	1 681	1 107	55 384	42.4	2.80	17.1	41.8	16.4	43 506	50.7	37 939	49.7	3 778	58.5	11 878	61.5
Luce	1 059	996	2 481	15.2	2.40	26.3	32.0	29.6	1 740	42.1	1 436	36.8	211	65.4	741	19.9
Mackinac	197	138	5 067	19.5	2.32	28.0	28.5	29.6	3 408	39.4	2 817	35.0	411	58.6	1 659	34.3
Macomb	8 861	6 752	309 203	16.7	2.52	26.9	33.2	24.9	210 867	45.6	167 806	44.9	31 194	50.3	98 336	41.6
Manistee	1 164	960	9 880	14.9	2.37	27.3	29.6	31.5	6 715	40.2	5 428	35.5	893	61.4	3 145	25.0
Marquette	4 036	1 870	25 767	1.3	2.35	28.9	30.2	23.4	16 480	44.7	13 225	40.3	2 290	65.9	9 287	25.8
Mason	535	382	11 406	14.2	2.43	26.5	31.9	28.4	7 878	43.0	6 428	37.9	1 054	66.8	3 528	26.2
Mecosta	3 383	221	14 915	21.7	2.49	24.5	31.2	24.6	9 893	43.9	7 946	38.0	1 385	70.1	5 022	26.8
Menominee	435	331	10 529	7.8	2.36	29.2	30.9	28.5	7 006	43.4	5 660	39.0	927	64.8	3 523	21.0
Midland	1 458	563	31 769	14.3	2.56	23.5	36.5	21.6	22 691	48.8	19 098	45.8	2 561	65.2	9 078	31.4
Missaukee	206	104	5 450	24.2	2.62	21.5	36.5	26.6	4 046	45.8	3 424	42.3	405	65.2	1 404	41.5
Monroe	1 543	843	53 772	15.6	2.69	21.7	39.1	21.3	39 933	48.5	32 241	46.2	5 426	58.8	13 839	34.3
Montcalm	2 717	2 497	22 079	18.9	2.65	21.9	38.2	23.4	16 176	48.2	12 972	43.4	2 148	67.0	5 903	33.6
Montmorency	127	83	4 455	23.8	2.29	27.5	24.7	38.7	3 047	32.9	2 587	28.6	318	55.7	1 408	45.9
Muskegon	6 059	5 112	63 330	9.6	2.59	25.2	37.8	24.2	44 298	49.4	32 692	44.2	8 810	65.7	19 032	22.0
Newaygo	681	497	17 599	27.8	2.68	22.2	38.1	24.1	12 941	47.9	10 597	43.8	1 587	66.4	4 658	49.3
Oakland	13 748	6 919	471 115	14.8	2.51	27.3	34.5	20.5	315 392	48.4	255 361	47.5	44 598	55.0	155 723	31.0

[1] As of April 1.   [2] Includes people under formally authorized, supervised care or custody in institutions at the time of enumeration (such as correctional institutions, nursing homes, and juvenile institutions).   [3] Under 18 years.   [4] No husband present.

Sources: Group Quarters Population—U.S. Census Bureau, 2000 Census of Population and Housing, "Census 2000 Profiles of General Demographic Characteristics" data files, published May 2001 (related Internet site <http://www.census.gov/mp/www/pub/2000cen/mscen01.html>).   Households, 2000—U.S. Census Bureau, 2000 Census of Population and Housing, "Census 2000 Profiles of General Demographic Characteristics" data files, published May 2001 (related Internet site <http://www.census.gov/mp/www/pub/2000cen/mscen01.html>).   Households, 1990—U.S. Census Bureau, 1990 Census of Population and Housing, Summary Tape File (STF) 1C on CD-ROM (related Internet site <http://homer.ssd.census.gov/cdrom/lookup>).

[Includes U.S., states, and 3,142 counties or county equivalents defined as of January 1, 1992. For changes to these areas since then, see appendix B. Geographic Information]

County	Group quarters population, 2000[1] Number	Institutionalized population[2]	Households, 2000 (April 1) Number	Percent change, 1990–2000	Persons per household	One-person	With 1 or more persons under 18 years	With 1 or more persons 65 years and over	Family households (families) Percent with own children under 18 years	Married-couple Number	Married-couple Percent with own children[3]	Female householder[4] Number	Female householder Percent with own children[3]	Nonfamily households Number	Nonfamily households Percent change, 1990–2000
MICHIGAN—Con.															
Oceana	765	323	9 778	21.1	2.67	21.6	36.8	26.4	7 265	45.7	5 918	41.7	903	64.7	2 513	36.0
Ogemaw	304	252	8 842	23.0	2.41	25.7	29.6	31.6	6 189	38.7	5 075	33.9	775	62.2	2 653	43.9
Ontonagon	177	130	3 456	−5.1	2.21	31.5	24.7	34.5	2 225	36.6	1 854	32.1	216	62.0	1 231	9.2
Osceola	360	191	8 861	20.6	2.58	22.6	35.7	26.0	6 413	45.4	5 152	40.0	859	69.7	2 448	35.6
Oscoda	60	60	3 921	24.1	2.39	26.0	28.2	33.8	2 719	36.5	2 280	31.2	295	61.7	1 202	36.7
Otsego	231	122	8 995	37.9	2.56	22.5	36.2	24.5	6 539	46.9	5 437	43.4	751	65.8	2 456	60.1
Ottawa	8 778	1 939	81 662	30.3	2.81	19.6	41.2	19.1	61 360	52.3	52 744	50.4	6 119	66.1	20 302	53.9
Presque Isle	221	105	6 155	14.5	2.31	28.4	26.0	35.6	4 201	35.9	3 617	32.1	390	58.7	1 954	34.7
Roscommon	333	270	11 250	32.1	2.23	28.1	23.9	37.0	7 619	32.3	6 380	26.5	869	62.3	3 631	46.5
Saginaw	5 600	3 109	80 430	2.8	2.54	26.0	35.9	24.5	55 790	47.1	40 364	41.4	12 402	64.5	24 640	17.5
St. Clair	1 677	852	62 072	17.4	2.62	23.4	37.2	22.9	44 631	48.1	35 615	45.0	6 456	62.0	17 441	31.8
St. Joseph	996	685	23 381	8.4	2.63	23.6	37.4	24.1	16 603	48.0	13 059	43.1	2 429	66.4	6 778	23.0
Sanilac	756	455	16 871	15.1	2.60	24.3	35.0	28.2	12 169	45.4	10 094	42.6	1 445	58.8	4 702	27.2
Schoolcraft	381	329	3 606	9.5	2.36	27.4	30.0	31.3	2 498	40.5	2 078	35.1	293	70.3	1 108	20.4
Shiawassee	721	471	26 896	8.2	2.64	21.7	38.1	22.5	19 862	47.7	15 906	44.2	2 783	61.3	7 034	22.7
Tuscola	1 461	1 069	21 454	10.2	2.65	21.9	37.2	24.1	15 981	46.2	13 120	43.1	1 982	59.7	5 473	26.2
Van Buren	1 916	712	27 982	10.2	2.66	22.5	38.3	23.2	20 327	48.2	15 878	44.3	3 136	62.7	7 655	20.2
Washtenaw	21 302	5 182	125 327	19.9	2.41	29.5	31.1	14.9	73 690	49.7	58 211	47.4	11 677	61.6	51 637	26.8
Wayne	32 618	20 067	768 440	−1.5	2.64	28.3	37.7	24.1	511 717	49.2	313 028	46.2	158 179	56.8	256 723	5.7
Wexford	371	221	11 824	19.2	2.55	24.2	36.1	24.9	8 386	47.3	6 643	42.1	1 217	66.6	3 438	29.7
MINNESOTA	135 883	63 058	1 895 127	15.0	2.52	26.9	34.8	21.3	1 255 141	49.9	1 018 245	46.9	168 782	66.0	639 986	23.7
Aitkin	174	174	6 644	29.6	2.28	28.7	24.6	36.4	4 457	33.7	3 817	29.5	416	57.7	2 187	45.2
Anoka	2 978	2 285	106 428	29.1	2.77	19.3	42.3	14.3	79 413	53.5	64 650	51.5	10 419	65.4	27 015	56.1
Becker	483	440	11 844	13.0	2.49	26.9	33.1	28.4	8 190	45.2	6 766	40.8	940	68.6	3 654	25.1
Beltrami	1 898	532	14 337	20.8	2.63	24.8	38.2	22.4	9 752	50.9	7 062	44.3	1 953	70.5	4 585	31.8
Benton	769	518	13 065	19.5	2.56	25.8	37.0	18.5	8 518	54.2	6 801	50.8	1 156	70.5	4 547	34.8
Big Stone	173	155	2 377	−3.5	2.38	30.2	29.4	37.0	1 611	42.8	1 416	39.8	125	73.6	766	4.1
Blue Earth	4 116	556	21 062	9.3	2.46	27.1	30.3	21.0	12 621	48.6	10 229	45.4	1 637	67.7	8 441	15.9
Brown	1 161	110	10 598	2.7	2.43	29.0	32.5	30.5	7 164	46.6	6 075	43.9	736	65.9	3 434	8.9
Carlton	1 472	1 341	12 064	11.3	2.50	26.1	34.7	27.0	8 406	46.8	6 813	42.3	1 090	68.0	3 658	22.5
Carver	1 019	339	24 356	46.7	2.84	18.1	46.6	14.7	18 774	58.7	16 184	57.5	1 775	68.5	5 582	49.4
Cass	433	128	10 893	31.2	2.45	25.0	30.2	30.7	7 730	39.1	6 360	33.6	871	67.6	3 163	43.4
Chippewa	297	216	5 361	2.2	2.39	29.5	32.1	31.9	3 599	46.5	3 054	42.8	356	68.5	1 762	12.9
Chisago	755	649	14 454	37.0	2.79	18.4	43.2	19.0	11 082	53.4	9 324	50.0	1 157	73.7	3 372	42.4
Clay	4 061	727	18 670	6.7	2.53	26.1	35.2	23.3	12 347	51.2	10 054	47.6	1 652	71.8	6 323	13.5
Clearwater	180	164	3 330	8.7	2.48	27.9	33.0	30.6	2 288	44.5	1 890	40.7	249	64.7	1 042	26.5
Cook	57	57	2 350	44.0	2.17	32.5	25.3	25.8	1 438	39.9	1 221	34.1	143	76.9	912	62.9
Cottonwood	406	251	4 917	−2.8	2.39	28.9	30.0	34.8	3 341	42.1	2 856	38.8	341	65.1	1 576	6.8
Crow Wing	1 041	706	22 250	29.3	2.43	26.4	32.0	28.4	15 183	44.3	12 615	39.6	1 781	68.6	7 067	40.1
Dakota	2 321	1 070	131 151	33.4	2.70	21.7	41.6	14.0	94 011	55.8	77 648	53.9	11 981	68.0	37 140	50.6
Dodge	192	152	6 420	15.9	2.73	20.2	42.3	22.3	4 853	53.9	4 153	51.0	461	72.7	1 567	24.3
Douglas	676	502	13 276	20.8	2.42	26.5	30.9	28.9	9 030	43.9	7 829	40.9	847	67.7	4 246	32.4
Faribault	450	415	6 652	−1.8	2.36	29.7	29.6	35.5	4 477	42.4	3 844	38.9	406	64.5	2 175	5.5
Fillmore	520	487	8 228	5.2	2.50	26.6	32.2	31.5	5 721	44.5	4 986	41.9	502	64.9	2 507	15.6
Freeborn	590	420	13 356	2.5	2.40	28.2	30.9	30.8	9 013	43.2	7 547	39.1	1 007	67.6	4 343	16.1
Goodhue	1 100	928	16 983	11.7	2.53	25.2	35.3	25.6	11 900	48.2	10 049	45.0	1 231	68.7	5 083	18.3
Grant	199	157	2 534	3.3	2.40	28.0	30.5	36.3	1 741	42.6	1 495	39.5	164	65.2	793	10.6
Hennepin	28 216	12 006	456 129	8.8	2.39	31.8	30.5	18.5	267 303	49.1	206 487	46.2	44 992	62.9	188 826	16.8
Houston	375	300	7 633	11.5	2.53	25.4	35.7	27.4	5 408	48.5	4 580	45.2	567	71.3	2 225	24.2
Hubbard	169	144	7 435	28.6	2.45	24.2	31.3	30.2	5 347	40.7	4 540	36.4	529	66.7	2 088	38.6
Isanti	470	378	11 236	27.5	2.74	20.1	40.7	20.1	8 420	50.9	6 973	47.5	940	68.9	2 816	41.2
Itasca	710	508	17 789	15.1	2.43	26.0	31.0	28.7	12 385	41.9	10 370	37.5	1 348	66.4	5 404	33.9
Jackson	313	214	4 556	−.1	2.40	28.5	30.9	31.7	3 117	43.5	2 734	40.3	244	68.0	1 439	11.7
Kanabec	122	109	5 759	21.2	2.58	23.8	36.2	25.9	4 146	47.4	3 386	42.4	484	71.7	1 613	27.2
Kandiyohi	865	701	15 936	11.5	2.53	25.7	34.4	25.4	10 972	48.1	9 198	44.4	1 200	72.4	4 964	19.5
Kittson	147	138	2 167	−4.7	2.37	30.5	30.1	34.1	1 448	43.6	1 243	42.0	131	54.2	719	4.5
Koochiching	288	214	6 040	.2	2.33	30.4	30.0	30.1	3 962	43.3	3 221	38.7	511	65.4	2 078	18.9
Lac qui Parle	213	204	3 316	−5.4	2.37	30.2	29.0	36.6	2 225	41.6	1 984	39.5	137	59.9	1 091	7.2
Lake	270	212	4 646	9.5	2.32	28.0	28.4	31.3	3 141	40.1	2 685	35.8	306	67.6	1 505	23.1
Lake of the Woods	47	47	1 903	20.7	2.35	29.7	30.5	28.6	1 267	43.9	1 093	41.0	101	61.4	636	56.3
Le Sueur	293	227	9 630	13.7	2.61	23.7	36.1	25.2	6 922	47.8	5 912	45.6	652	65.5	2 708	21.9
Lincoln	205	178	2 653	−1.9	2.35	30.5	27.6	37.4	1 786	40.1	1 585	38.3	122	54.9	867	8.4
Lyon	1 256	364	9 715	7.1	2.49	27.9	34.2	25.3	6 331	50.7	5 355	47.8	686	70.7	3 384	19.9
McLeod	477	327	13 449	13.8	2.56	25.0	36.4	24.3	9 433	49.8	7 964	46.8	977	68.9	4 016	25.3
Mahnomen	75	45	1 969	9.1	2.60	27.0	35.8	31.7	1 367	46.7	1 016	40.6	229	65.5	602	29.2
Marshall	123	112	4 101	−2.2	2.45	28.7	31.0	32.1	2 836	43.7	2 467	41.3	221	62.4	1 265	7.5
Martin	480	376	9 067	−.7	2.35	30.0	30.9	32.0	6 045	44.7	5 135	40.8	657	68.8	3 022	9.9
Meeker	515	470	8 590	12.3	2.58	24.4	35.1	27.4	6 132	47.2	5 287	44.1	537	68.0	2 458	21.5

[1] As of April 1. [2] Includes people under formally authorized, supervised care or custody in institutions at the time of enumeration (such as correctional institutions, nursing homes, and juvenile institutions). [3] Under 18 years. [4] No husband present.

Sources: Group Quarters Population—U.S. Census Bureau, 2000 Census of Population and Housing, "Census 2000 Profiles of General Demographic Characteristics" data files, published May 2001 (related Internet site <http://www.census.gov/mp/www/pub/2000cen/mscen01.html>). Households, 2000—U.S. Census Bureau, 2000 Census of Population and Housing, "Census 2000 Profiles of General Demographic Characteristics" data files, published May 2001 (related Internet site <http://www.census.gov/mp/www/pub/2000cen/mscen01.html>). Households, 1990—U.S. Census Bureau, 1990 Census of Population and Housing, Summary Tape File (STF) 1C on CD-ROM (related Internet site <http://homer.ssd.census.gov/cdrom/lookup>).

[Includes U.S., states, and 3,142 counties or county equivalents defined as of January 1, 1992. For changes to these areas since then, see appendix B. Geographic Information]

County	Group quarters population, 2000[1]		Households, 2000 (April 1)													
						Percent—			By type—							
									Family households (families)						Nonfamily households	
											Married-couple		Female householder[4]			
	Number	Institu-tionalized population[2]	Number	Percent change, 1990–2000	Per-sons per house-hold	One-person	With 1 or more per-sons under 18 years	With 1 or more per-sons 65 years and over	Number	Per-cent with own chil-dren under 18 years	Number	Per-cent with own chil-dren[3]	Number	Per-cent with own chil-dren[3]	Number	Percent change, 1990–2000
MINNESOTA—Con.																
Mille Lacs	515	457	8 638	25.0	2.53	25.9	34.4	28.0	6 006	46.4	4 797	41.3	821	67.5	2 632	40.0
Morrison	557	204	11 816	13.6	2.64	24.9	36.1	27.7	8 461	48.2	7 019	45.1	920	65.7	3 355	25.0
Mower	856	583	15 582	3.7	2.42	29.1	31.3	32.3	10 318	44.9	8 519	40.8	1 248	67.2	5 264	13.1
Murray	161	121	3 722	-1.0	2.42	27.1	30.0	34.8	2 602	41.5	2 326	38.9	172	65.1	1 120	7.4
Nicollet	2 552	620	10 642	12.3	2.56	24.6	36.4	20.3	7 309	51.4	6 123	48.2	842	72.1	3 333	23.0
Nobles	389	255	7 939	3.3	2.58	26.5	33.8	30.8	5 520	46.2	4 671	43.7	546	63.6	2 419	12.1
Norman	185	166	3 010	-3.5	2.41	31.3	31.0	34.8	2 008	45.1	1 741	43.1	178	62.9	1 002	4.0
Olmsted	3 110	1 716	47 807	19.3	2.53	25.8	36.6	18.3	32 308	52.0	27 093	49.3	3 808	68.1	15 499	25.8
Otter Tail	1 397	1 194	22 671	16.2	2.46	26.6	31.5	31.2	15 768	43.0	13 636	40.5	1 374	65.9	6 903	23.9
Pennington	441	221	5 525	6.8	2.38	29.5	32.2	25.7	3 555	47.5	2 859	43.3	502	68.1	1 970	15.2
Pine	1 337	1 262	9 939	31.2	2.53	25.1	33.6	27.8	6 918	44.8	5 620	40.3	864	65.5	3 021	46.4
Pipestone	231	213	4 069	-.2	2.38	30.1	32.1	34.4	2 727	46.3	2 344	42.4	266	69.9	1 342	6.8
Polk	1 500	730	12 070	.7	2.47	28.9	34.0	28.9	8 045	48.5	6 628	45.0	1 026	66.8	4 025	15.7
Pope	309	287	4 513	9.1	2.42	28.7	30.6	34.3	3 064	43.7	2 663	41.5	267	64.0	1 449	26.1
Ramsey	17 526	5 270	201 236	5.6	2.45	32.0	31.9	20.5	120 016	50.0	88 473	46.1	23 923	64.5	81 220	15.5
Red Lake	163	93	1 727	-.2	2.39	30.5	31.7	30.7	1 132	46.8	957	43.9	118	73.7	595	6.4
Redwood	500	383	6 674	1.8	2.44	28.8	32.6	31.4	4 526	46.4	3 825	42.6	473	70.6	2 148	12.4
Renville	369	284	6 779	-.2	2.48	28.5	32.8	33.1	4 622	46.2	4 008	43.7	378	68.6	2 157	11.1
Rice	6 690	1 966	18 888	15.5	2.65	23.9	38.3	21.6	13 347	51.7	10 968	48.5	1 617	67.5	5 541	17.8
Rock	232	195	3 843	2.4	2.47	27.0	32.3	33.5	2 707	44.4	2 386	42.0	213	64.8	1 136	11.3
Roseau	241	215	6 190	14.3	2.60	24.6	39.6	22.3	4 439	53.5	3 717	50.4	424	73.6	1 751	25.2
St. Louis	8 966	3 691	82 619	4.7	2.32	31.2	29.3	26.8	51 374	44.4	40 706	39.5	7 731	66.0	31 245	15.7
Scott	906	844	30 692	58.5	2.89	16.0	47.0	12.2	23 977	58.2	20 521	56.7	2 256	70.1	6 715	70.9
Sherburne	1 620	1 419	21 581	58.2	2.91	15.7	46.8	13.5	16 743	57.8	14 294	55.6	1 615	74.1	4 838	65.2
Sibley	324	168	5 772	8.4	2.60	25.4	35.4	29.5	4 089	47.5	3 525	45.8	332	63.3	1 683	21.9
Stearns	7 335	1 088	47 604	19.7	2.64	23.6	36.3	20.5	32 129	51.8	26 822	49.7	3 592	66.5	15 475	28.9
Steele	629	294	12 846	13.3	2.57	24.6	37.0	23.5	9 077	50.2	7 640	46.9	953	70.4	3 769	25.0
Stevens	955	105	3 751	-1.9	2.43	29.1	29.8	30.4	2 367	45.3	2 079	43.5	193	62.2	1 384	2.9
Swift	1 538	1 491	4 353	2.0	2.39	30.9	31.2	34.8	2 882	45.3	2 479	42.7	266	65.0	1 471	11.6
Todd	302	219	9 342	8.8	2.58	26.3	33.4	29.5	6 510	45.6	5 585	43.1	568	65.1	2 832	19.0
Traverse	108	108	1 717	-3.4	2.34	32.0	29.0	41.0	1 129	43.0	978	39.3	103	70.9	588	12.0
Wabasha	359	257	8 277	13.6	2.57	24.3	35.3	25.8	5 878	47.6	5 036	44.4	541	70.1	2 399	26.3
Wadena	445	348	5 426	9.0	2.45	29.2	31.7	32.5	3 609	45.1	2 998	41.3	412	66.5	1 817	20.3
Waseca	1 440	1 386	7 059	6.2	2.56	25.1	36.3	25.2	4 990	49.1	4 164	46.2	554	64.8	2 069	9.3
Washington	3 191	2 585	71 462	45.1	2.77	18.7	43.2	14.8	54 665	54.4	46 318	52.5	6 044	67.7	16 797	68.5
Watonwan	170	158	4 627	2.1	2.53	28.7	34.1	32.3	3 143	47.8	2 620	43.7	340	71.8	1 484	6.2
Wilkin	147	128	2 752	-1.9	2.54	25.9	36.7	28.0	1 927	50.2	1 638	49.0	194	60.3	825	5.4
Winona	3 806	668	18 744	10.7	2.46	28.2	31.6	22.8	11 704	48.3	9 625	45.2	1 457	65.1	7 040	25.7
Wright	894	658	31 465	36.7	2.83	18.8	43.7	17.1	23 923	55.3	20 289	53.2	2 430	70.2	7 542	52.6
Yellow Medicine	337	255	4 439	-3.6	2.42	29.3	31.6	32.7	2 974	45.3	2 602	42.4	254	71.7	1 465	4.7
MISSISSIPPI	95 414	50 826	1 046 434	14.8	2.63	24.6	39.6	23.7	747 159	48.6	520 844	45.0	180 705	58.8	299 275	26.3
Adams	487	389	13 677	3.1	2.48	28.0	37.1	28.7	9 403	46.2	5 858	40.1	2 943	58.3	4 274	19.7
Alcorn	514	449	14 224	14.3	2.39	27.6	33.9	26.1	9 921	44.3	7 754	41.2	1 635	57.3	4 303	30.4
Amite	24	24	5 271	9.1	2.58	24.5	36.2	30.1	3 878	42.4	2 800	40.2	860	51.0	1 393	12.7
Attala	382	341	7 567	9.0	2.55	26.4	37.2	31.6	5 383	45.1	3 804	42.0	1 260	54.4	2 184	13.9
Benton	116	116	2 999	5.5	2.64	23.8	38.8	29.5	2 216	45.2	1 626	42.9	443	52.6	783	20.5
Bolivar	2 192	655	13 776	3.6	2.79	25.3	43.2	24.2	9 719	49.9	5 258	43.6	3 764	59.4	4 057	12.7
Calhoun	248	196	6 019	6.3	2.46	27.1	36.5	30.4	4 258	44.7	3 067	40.4	925	57.5	1 761	19.4
Carroll	302	302	4 071	21.4	2.57	22.4	37.1	27.6	3 068	42.5	2 288	40.0	618	51.5	1 003	26.0
Chickasaw	208	189	7 253	11.9	2.65	24.9	41.2	26.7	5 289	49.8	3 684	46.7	1 308	57.7	1 964	24.5
Choctaw	316	83	3 686	14.6	2.56	25.0	37.7	28.5	2 668	45.0	1 966	42.1	537	56.6	1 018	30.3
Claiborne	1 804	85	3 685	10.3	2.72	28.0	42.3	25.6	2 532	50.7	1 344	44.1	993	58.4	1 153	17.3
Clarke	179	179	6 978	10.2	2.55	25.5	37.6	27.9	5 025	46.0	3 631	42.3	1 109	58.2	1 953	25.7
Clay	426	262	8 152	12.4	2.64	25.5	40.9	25.6	5 888	49.5	3 733	44.4	1 826	61.0	2 264	25.8
Coahoma	774	471	10 553	.2	2.83	26.2	44.9	26.5	7 479	51.9	3 924	45.4	3 032	60.6	3 074	2.7
Copiah	1 246	190	10 142	9.0	2.71	23.6	40.8	26.8	7 498	46.6	4 939	44.1	2 039	53.2	2 644	14.4
Covington	294	294	7 126	23.2	2.68	23.6	41.6	25.0	5 281	49.4	3 669	46.0	1 227	58.3	1 845	37.2
DeSoto	578	516	38 792	66.7	2.75	18.1	43.1	17.7	30 112	50.8	23 929	48.4	4 504	61.5	8 680	120.7
Forrest	5 410	1 523	27 183	8.1	2.47	28.5	35.2	21.4	17 305	48.8	11 569	44.5	4 687	59.5	9 878	17.3
Franklin	93	79	3 211	4.1	2.60	25.6	39.4	28.9	2 337	47.5	1 739	45.8	469	54.6	874	9.0
George	403	222	6 742	16.7	2.78	19.1	43.1	22.3	5 308	49.2	4 315	47.7	703	55.8	1 434	22.7
Greene	2 229	2 170	4 148	24.7	2.67	22.0	41.1	23.0	3 152	49.0	2 539	46.9	493	58.2	996	43.9
Grenada	526	451	8 820	14.5	2.58	25.3	39.3	26.2	6 301	47.4	4 310	42.6	1 644	60.1	2 519	28.3
Hancock	452	353	16 897	43.0	2.52	24.7	35.5	25.8	11 822	45.1	9 106	41.3	1 917	57.4	5 075	63.7
Harrison	7 281	2 592	71 538	20.1	2.55	25.8	37.7	21.4	48 605	49.3	34 410	44.9	10 805	62.1	22 933	37.9
Hinds	10 193	3 343	91 030	Z	2.64	26.7	39.8	21.7	62 315	50.2	37 439	45.7	20 678	59.1	28 715	6.4
Holmes	672	186	7 314	2.5	2.86	26.3	44.5	28.5	5 231	50.4	2 554	45.1	2 284	58.1	2 083	7.8
Humphreys	95	95	3 765	-4.1	2.95	24.9	46.0	27.4	2 697	51.1	1 441	47.4	1 042	56.5	1 068	1.9
Issaquena	263	263	726	14.7	2.77	26.2	41.7	27.4	510	48.6	331	46.5	116	54.3	216	37.6

[1] As of April 1. [2] Includes people under formally authorized, supervised care or custody in institutions at the time of enumeration (such as correctional institutions, nursing homes, and juvenile institutions). [3] Under 18 years. [4] No husband present.

Sources: Group Quarters Population—U.S. Census Bureau, 2000 Census of Population and Housing, "Census 2000 Profiles of General Demographic Characteristics" data files, published May 2001 (related Internet site <http://www.census.gov/mp/www/pub/2000cen/mscen01.html>). Households, 2000—U.S. Census Bureau, 2000 Census of Population and Housing, "Census 2000 Profiles of General Demographic Characteristics" data files, published May 2001 (related Internet site <http://www.census.gov/mp/www/pub/2000cen/mscen01.html>). Households, 1990—U.S. Census Bureau, 1990 Census of Population and Housing, Summary Tape File (STF) 1C on CD-ROM (related Internet site <http://homer.ssd.census.gov/cdrom/lookup>).

[Includes U.S., states, and 3,142 counties or county equivalents defined as of January 1, 1992. For changes to these areas since then, see appendix B. Geographic Information]

County	Group quarters population, 2000[1] Number	Institutionalized population[2] Number	Households, 2000 (April 1) Number	Percent change, 1990–2000	Persons per household	Percent— One-person	Percent— With 1 or more persons under 18 years	Percent— With 1 or more persons 65 years and over	Family households (families) Number	Percent with own children under 18 years	Married-couple Number	Percent with own children[3]	Female householder[4] Number	Percent with own children[3]	Nonfamily households Number	Nonfamily Percent change, 1990–2000
MISSISSIPPI—Con.																
Itawamba	768	188	8 773	17.0	2.51	23.4	36.4	26.5	6 501	44.8	5 291	42.8	869	52.9	2 272	33.1
Jackson	1 966	723	47 676	17.9	2.72	20.8	41.7	20.8	35 724	49.4	26 566	45.9	6 930	61.2	11 952	34.7
Jasper	162	152	6 708	12.6	2.68	24.2	40.7	27.7	4 956	47.3	3 416	44.9	1 224	54.1	1 752	29.8
Jefferson	636	636	3 308	17.6	2.75	27.1	44.1	24.8	2 339	51.8	1 191	47.3	942	58.7	969	38.4
Jefferson Davis	104	104	5 177	8.1	2.68	25.0	40.2	28.4	3 770	45.2	2 364	41.1	1 118	54.2	1 407	26.4
Jones	1 708	393	24 275	7.9	2.61	24.4	37.4	27.4	17 555	45.1	12 874	41.9	3 664	55.1	6 720	21.5
Kemper	397	88	3 909	7.8	2.57	26.4	37.0	29.6	2 786	45.2	1 825	40.4	789	56.7	1 123	14.1
Lafayette	4 822	451	14 373	29.6	2.36	29.1	29.7	18.4	8 318	46.5	6 211	43.6	1 640	59.7	6 055	46.9
Lamar	465	323	14 396	32.3	2.68	20.4	41.5	18.8	10 721	51.6	8 584	49.6	1 655	61.1	3 675	54.0
Lauderdale	3 412	2 273	29 990	6.2	2.49	28.0	37.5	25.5	20 569	49.4	14 003	44.5	5 474	61.8	9 421	14.9
Lawrence	94	94	5 040	11.9	2.61	24.1	40.2	26.4	3 751	47.6	2 819	45.4	725	54.6	1 289	18.3
Leake	755	755	7 611	12.1	2.65	24.3	39.6	28.2	5 566	46.9	3 971	44.5	1 255	54.7	2 045	17.9
Lee	1 350	1 033	29 200	19.4	2.55	25.0	39.7	20.6	20 810	50.7	15 363	46.9	4 258	63.1	8 390	32.5
Leflore	2 960	1 674	12 956	1.6	2.70	28.2	42.5	25.7	8 890	51.6	4 662	44.3	3 572	61.7	4 066	7.8
Lincoln	645	558	12 538	13.1	2.59	24.4	39.2	26.2	9 191	47.6	6 880	45.5	1 839	56.4	3 347	20.8
Lowndes	1 909	960	22 849	6.8	2.61	24.6	41.0	21.3	16 405	50.8	11 239	46.0	4 279	63.5	6 444	13.0
Madison	2 059	1 470	27 219	41.2	2.67	25.0	41.6	17.8	19 332	52.7	14 139	51.2	4 238	58.9	7 887	39.9
Marion	930	921	9 336	2.5	2.64	24.2	39.9	28.4	6 882	47.3	5 045	45.0	1 453	54.4	2 454	10.9
Marshall	1 699	1 143	12 163	20.7	2.74	22.0	41.0	23.7	9 115	45.8	6 038	41.9	2 440	54.9	3 048	33.3
Monroe	415	365	14 603	9.4	2.57	24.7	39.4	26.7	10 667	47.5	7 593	44.1	2 506	57.5	3 936	20.3
Montgomery	150	150	4 690	3.5	2.57	26.1	37.8	31.3	3 369	45.4	2 276	41.7	884	55.9	1 321	11.7
Neshoba	608	550	10 694	20.9	2.63	24.7	39.8	26.6	7 746	48.2	5 618	44.2	1 664	59.6	2 948	40.8
Newton	736	212	8 221	11.7	2.57	24.6	38.4	27.8	6 004	45.9	4 360	42.8	1 318	55.6	2 217	24.6
Noxubee	178	178	4 470	8.0	2.77	25.9	42.3	27.0	3 225	49.6	1 920	46.3	1 104	56.5	1 245	18.8
Oktibbeha	4 380	366	15 945	23.5	2.42	27.7	31.3	16.7	9 265	48.5	6 361	43.9	2 357	62.4	6 680	43.5
Panola	597	313	12 232	20.8	2.75	23.2	42.2	25.2	9 019	48.9	5 984	45.1	2 440	58.6	3 213	29.7
Pearl River	788	416	18 078	31.4	2.65	21.7	39.2	24.5	13 583	46.4	10 548	43.4	2 261	57.1	4 495	46.8
Perry	118	91	4 420	16.3	2.72	21.9	43.0	22.4	3 333	49.8	2 568	48.1	582	56.9	1 087	27.7
Pike	859	581	14 792	10.3	2.57	26.5	39.4	27.0	10 502	48.2	6 921	43.3	2 939	60.2	4 290	16.0
Pontotoc	243	194	10 097	21.0	2.62	22.7	40.9	24.4	7 563	49.6	5 978	47.7	1 199	58.2	2 534	28.8
Prentiss	853	189	9 821	13.6	2.52	24.9	37.4	26.7	7 166	46.2	5 534	44.3	1 235	54.3	2 655	27.8
Quitman	129	129	3 565	1.2	2.80	26.9	43.6	28.7	2 507	48.9	1 339	43.0	955	57.2	1 058	11.1
Rankin	4 869	4 393	42 089	41.0	2.62	21.9	40.2	13.4	31 136	49.6	24 447	47.6	5 136	57.6	10 953	83.5
Scott	324	290	10 183	19.6	2.76	22.2	42.3	25.4	7 534	49.0	5 073	45.9	1 915	58.0	2 649	30.4
Sharkey	105	80	2 163	3.8	2.99	23.5	46.3	25.4	1 589	49.2	865	45.2	580	52.9	574	18.8
Simpson	964	624	10 076	20.6	2.65	24.0	39.9	26.0	7 381	47.6	5 458	44.9	1 488	56.0	2 695	34.1
Smith	131	22	6 046	14.6	2.65	23.0	40.2	27.3	4 556	47.7	3 601	46.5	717	52.3	1 490	27.2
Stone	704	146	4 747	28.8	2.72	20.6	41.8	23.3	3 628	48.8	2 790	46.1	632	57.6	1 119	25.9
Sunflower	5 340	4 900	9 637	-.1	3.01	21.2	48.1	25.4	7 312	50.6	4 081	46.4	2 738	57.4	2 325	-11.0
Tallahatchie	103	101	5 263	4.5	2.81	24.6	42.0	28.7	3 828	46.7	2 287	42.5	1 235	54.3	1 435	9.0
Tate	1 153	181	8 850	26.0	2.74	21.3	41.4	23.9	6 714	47.6	4 959	45.5	1 372	55.2	2 136	47.5
Tippah	380	248	8 108	13.3	2.52	24.9	37.4	26.5	5 907	46.3	4 639	43.8	954	57.9	2 201	31.7
Tishomingo	276	276	7 917	12.2	2.39	27.5	33.0	28.5	5 575	42.9	4 519	40.8	799	54.3	2 342	34.2
Tunica	110	105	3 258	29.0	2.80	26.9	42.0	23.1	2 192	49.5	1 106	43.4	877	57.6	1 066	64.0
Union	245	163	9 786	17.0	2.57	23.4	38.1	26.2	7 245	46.8	5 767	44.3	1 083	59.1	2 541	25.3
Walthall	178	165	5 571	13.0	2.69	24.0	39.4	27.6	4 114	46.0	2 951	42.8	944	56.6	1 457	25.8
Warren	601	502	18 756	7.7	2.61	25.8	40.5	22.7	13 220	50.4	8 785	46.0	3 585	60.5	5 536	16.9
Washington	860	686	22 158	-1.9	2.80	24.6	44.0	24.4	15 937	50.5	9 007	44.5	5 770	59.8	6 221	6.7
Wayne	201	156	7 857	14.6	2.67	23.1	42.7	23.2	5 857	50.6	4 164	47.3	1 352	60.9	2 000	31.4
Webster	194	160	3 905	2.1	2.59	24.0	37.7	30.2	2 877	46.1	2 193	44.1	512	55.3	1 028	1.6
Wilkinson	1 039	1 039	3 578	6.9	2.59	27.9	40.7	29.5	2 510	46.9	1 446	42.1	877	54.6	1 068	29.1
Winston	561	485	7 578	7.3	2.59	25.2	38.0	29.5	5 473	46.4	3 784	42.2	1 373	57.5	2 105	16.3
Yalobusha	99	89	5 260	14.0	2.46	28.7	35.0	30.0	3 599	43.4	2 449	39.4	924	53.4	1 661	21.2
Yazoo	2 375	2 324	9 178	4.1	2.81	24.5	42.3	27.7	6 644	49.2	3 965	43.5	2 173	58.7	2 534	7.8
MISSOURI	162 058	90 430	2 194 594	11.9	2.48	27.3	34.7	24.0	1 476 516	47.4	1 140 866	43.6	253 760	61.7	718 078	21.1
Adair	2 790	300	9 669	6.7	2.29	31.5	26.8	21.6	5 343	45.6	4 404	42.3	693	63.9	4 326	18.5
Andrew	264	245	6 273	15.5	2.59	22.3	37.1	25.0	4 636	46.7	3 933	43.6	467	63.4	1 637	31.6
Atchison	297	290	2 722	-8.1	2.25	31.5	28.5	34.2	1 778	40.7	1 518	37.1	166	62.0	944	1.7
Audrain	1 933	1 839	9 844	6.9	2.43	27.8	33.6	29.4	6 758	45.7	5 434	40.8	970	67.7	3 086	21.6
Barry	355	319	13 398	23.4	2.51	24.7	34.1	28.6	9 584	43.6	7 942	39.9	1 129	61.1	3 814	35.6
Barton	172	150	4 895	8.2	2.53	26.4	36.6	29.0	3 440	48.3	2 845	45.2	417	63.1	1 455	8.9
Bates	279	279	6 511	10.0	2.51	26.1	35.0	30.4	4 556	46.1	3 830	42.6	498	64.1	1 955	21.1
Benton	248	192	7 420	28.7	2.28	26.3	25.8	35.8	5 176	33.3	4 425	28.7	504	62.5	2 244	44.6
Bollinger	164	75	4 576	16.0	2.59	21.6	37.0	27.6	3 463	45.3	2 921	42.6	385	61.8	1 113	25.2
Boone	8 935	982	53 094	26.6	2.38	28.7	32.2	15.1	31 391	51.3	24 177	46.8	5 529	69.5	21 703	32.6
Buchanan	4 625	3 159	33 557	3.3	2.42	28.9	33.6	26.8	21 928	46.9	16 556	42.2	4 013	62.2	11 629	14.4
Butler	928	698	16 718	9.0	2.39	28.0	32.9	28.4	11 313	43.9	8 772	39.1	1 932	61.3	5 405	23.9
Caldwell	119	119	3 523	9.3	2.51	25.5	34.7	29.4	2 503	45.5	2 085	41.5	282	68.4	1 020	19.6
Callaway	3 834	2 837	14 416	24.8	2.56	23.0	38.8	21.3	10 338	49.9	8 228	45.1	1 502	68.3	4 078	40.0

[1] As of April 1. [2] Includes people under formally authorized, supervised care or custody in institutions at the time of enumeration (such as correctional institutions, nursing homes, and juvenile institutions). [3] Under 18 years. [4] No husband present.

Sources: Group Quarters Population—U.S. Census Bureau, 2000 Census of Population and Housing, "Census 2000 Profiles of General Demographic Characteristics" data files, published May 2001 (related Internet site <http://www.census.gov/mp/www/pub/2000cen/mscen01.html>).   Households, 2000—U.S. Census Bureau, 2000 Census of Population and Housing, "Census 2000 Profiles of General Demographic Characteristics" data files, published May 2001 (related Internet site <http://www.census.gov/mp/www/pub/2000cen/mscen01.html>).   Households, 1990—U.S. Census Bureau, 1990 Census of Population and Housing, Summary Tape File (STF) 1C on CD-ROM (related Internet site <http://homer.ssd.census.gov/cdrom/lookup>).

[Includes U.S., states, and 3,142 counties or county equivalents defined as of January 1, 1992. For changes to these areas since then, see appendix B. Geographic Information]

County	Group quarters population, 2000[1]		Households, 2000 (April 1)			Percent—			By type—							
									Family households (families)		Married-couple		Female householder[4]		Nonfamily households	
	Number	Institutionalized population[2]	Number	Percent change, 1990–2000	Persons per household	One-person	With 1 or more persons under 18 years	With 1 or more persons 65 years and over	Number	Percent with own children under 18 years	Number	Percent with own children[3]	Number	Percent with own children[3]	Number	Percent change, 1990–2000

MISSOURI—Con.

County	Number	Inst.	Number	% chg	PPH	1-person	<18	65+	Fam Num	Fam %	MC Num	MC %	FH Num	FH %	Nonfam Num	Nonfam % chg
Camden	622	392	15 779	39.6	2.31	23.3	26.1	30.4	11 298	33.3	9 751	28.3	1 038	65.1	4 481	65.4
Cape Girardeau	3 406	1 178	26 980	15.3	2.42	27.3	33.3	23.2	17 941	46.9	14 517	43.7	2 633	62.5	9 039	25.0
Carroll	194	180	4 169	-3.8	2.42	27.8	32.3	33.5	2 879	43.7	2 395	40.5	333	58.6	1 290	-2.0
Carter	85	45	2 378	11.7	2.46	26.7	33.7	28.6	1 673	43.8	1 365	40.6	211	60.2	705	16.0
Cass	966	880	30 168	31.8	2.69	20.0	40.8	21.7	22 978	50.0	19 181	47.1	2 744	65.8	7 190	42.3
Cedar	350	206	5 685	13.6	2.35	28.1	30.1	34.7	3 892	40.5	3 267	36.1	447	63.5	1 793	21.3
Chariton	196	184	3 469	-5.2	2.38	29.8	30.0	36.3	2 344	42.0	2 024	39.9	227	58.6	1 125	5.7
Christian	603	405	20 425	71.1	2.63	19.1	41.0	19.0	15 652	50.3	13 064	46.8	1 909	68.6	4 773	96.7
Clark	122	122	2 966	3.7	2.46	26.4	32.8	28.6	2 079	43.3	1 742	39.3	209	65.1	887	18.1
Clay	2 920	1 527	72 558	23.2	2.50	25.2	36.3	18.9	50 120	48.9	40 192	45.9	7 392	63.1	22 438	36.3
Clinton	430	356	7 152	17.0	2.59	22.0	37.4	24.0	5 301	47.1	4 394	43.6	627	63.3	1 851	25.7
Cole	5 744	4 992	27 040	17.7	2.43	28.7	35.4	20.6	17 940	50.6	14 333	46.7	2 705	67.5	9 100	28.4
Cooper	2 071	1 945	5 932	10.7	2.46	26.1	34.2	28.3	4 139	45.6	3 404	42.0	535	63.2	1 793	23.1
Crawford	380	293	8 858	21.4	2.53	24.3	35.7	27.6	6 354	45.7	5 196	41.5	799	65.8	2 504	35.8
Dade	120	120	3 202	7.6	2.44	26.5	30.9	34.1	2 276	41.0	1 962	38.4	207	53.6	926	5.5
Dallas	144	108	6 030	23.1	2.57	23.7	35.9	28.0	4 381	45.3	3 668	41.7	507	64.5	1 649	31.8
Daviess	56	56	3 178	4.5	2.50	25.7	33.5	31.3	2 265	44.2	1 932	40.6	237	66.2	913	10.1
DeKalb	2 769	2 759	3 528	15.5	2.50	26.9	34.4	30.4	2 472	46.2	2 101	42.9	261	67.4	1 056	30.7
Dent	269	173	5 982	12.3	2.45	25.0	33.2	30.6	4 278	42.7	3 531	38.7	545	62.6	1 704	22.7
Douglas	125	59	5 201	13.4	2.49	26.1	32.8	30.6	3 672	42.6	3 119	38.9	376	62.0	1 529	29.8
Dunklin	712	629	13 411	2.2	2.42	28.1	35.1	28.5	9 166	45.7	6 914	40.6	1 766	62.5	4 245	10.7
Franklin	1 004	887	34 945	21.1	2.66	22.1	38.9	22.4	25 689	49.1	21 101	46.5	3 151	61.3	9 256	40.0
Gasconade	307	287	6 171	11.3	2.44	27.0	33.2	31.7	4 291	44.6	3 582	41.0	472	62.3	1 880	18.7
Gentry	202	143	2 747	-.3	2.42	29.3	32.4	35.7	1 884	45.3	1 592	41.7	198	67.7	863	1.9
Greene	11 831	3 649	97 859	20.1	2.34	29.1	30.5	22.7	61 837	44.8	48 961	40.5	9 569	62.4	36 022	33.7
Grundy	353	186	4 382	.8	2.30	30.8	29.5	32.9	2 888	41.1	2 401	36.2	352	66.5	1 494	10.5
Harrison	228	194	3 658	2.6	2.36	28.8	30.3	34.8	2 489	41.7	2 083	37.9	283	61.5	1 169	4.9
Henry	359	265	9 133	11.5	2.37	27.7	31.1	30.3	6 245	41.6	5 055	36.4	853	64.8	2 888	15.5
Hickory	107	98	3 911	22.9	2.26	26.5	24.7	41.0	2 737	31.4	2 344	26.9	262	57.3	1 174	40.8
Holt	101	101	2 237	-8.3	2.35	29.7	30.0	35.0	1 503	41.9	1 282	38.5	137	66.4	734	-2.3
Howard	793	102	3 836	7.4	2.46	27.3	33.8	29.1	2 633	45.9	2 123	42.2	365	64.4	1 203	14.2
Howell	761	553	14 762	20.2	2.47	25.0	35.2	28.7	10 611	45.5	8 683	41.3	1 455	65.0	4 151	27.5
Iron	381	290	4 197	5.1	2.46	25.8	34.7	27.8	2 962	45.3	2 383	39.4	394	71.6	1 235	20.5
Jackson	11 710	6 877	266 294	5.4	2.42	31.2	33.4	22.2	166 143	48.0	115 602	43.1	39 248	61.2	100 151	13.5
Jasper	2 632	971	41 412	14.6	2.46	27.2	35.0	24.7	27 943	47.4	21 723	42.8	4 614	64.6	13 469	19.8
Jefferson	2 030	1 424	71 499	20.8	2.74	18.9	42.4	17.6	54 528	51.0	43 605	48.3	7 454	61.9	16 971	41.6
Johnson	3 344	336	17 410	19.4	2.58	22.7	37.3	17.8	11 814	51.7	9 731	48.4	1 487	70.5	5 596	28.2
Knox	90	62	1 791	-1.5	2.38	29.3	29.7	35.2	1 217	41.0	1 029	38.9	123	49.6	574	5.1
Laclede	377	353	12 760	22.5	2.52	24.0	37.1	25.6	9 190	47.0	7 519	42.9	1 198	65.7	3 570	33.7
Lafayette	937	903	12 569	7.1	2.55	24.0	36.6	26.1	9 095	46.9	7 456	43.2	1 177	62.8	3 474	9.9
Lawrence	628	610	13 568	15.7	2.55	24.5	36.4	27.5	9 735	46.9	7 989	43.8	1 219	61.7	3 833	18.4
Lewis	748	190	3 956	5.6	2.46	27.4	34.0	28.5	2 710	46.8	2 245	42.4	327	69.7	1 246	14.3
Lincoln	577	434	13 851	34.3	2.77	19.7	43.2	20.6	10 555	52.5	8 512	48.7	1 403	69.9	3 296	37.2
Linn	239	217	5 697	-.1	2.37	30.3	31.8	34.2	3 761	44.8	3 056	40.5	508	64.0	1 936	3.7
Livingston	928	927	5 736	1.6	2.38	30.5	32.4	31.2	3 800	45.9	3 127	41.8	481	64.4	1 936	11.6
McDonald	164	110	8 113	27.0	2.65	23.3	39.3	22.0	5 867	49.3	4 677	45.3	777	65.6	2 246	40.2
Macon	311	292	6 501	5.5	2.38	29.0	31.7	31.1	4 384	43.2	3 619	38.9	545	64.2	2 117	18.7
Madison	230	213	4 711	8.4	2.46	25.9	34.1	31.3	3 333	44.1	2 704	40.8	475	60.2	1 378	21.0
Maries	85	85	3 519	16.2	2.51	25.7	34.1	28.3	2 502	44.5	2 076	41.0	270	58.5	1 017	34.3
Marion	1 258	680	11 066	3.2	2.44	28.1	35.7	28.2	7 523	49.0	5 915	44.1	1 263	67.1	3 543	6.8
Mercer	60	39	1 600	1.5	2.31	29.3	29.4	36.0	1 089	41.6	921	37.5	107	68.2	511	2.6
Miller	396	302	9 284	16.4	2.50	26.1	35.5	27.2	6 443	47.0	5 198	43.1	852	62.8	2 841	27.0
Mississippi	270	270	5 383	-.5	2.44	28.5	36.0	28.9	3 673	45.7	2 565	38.9	932	62.7	1 710	18.5
Moniteau	1 346	1 287	5 259	14.8	2.56	25.6	37.5	26.9	3 731	49.8	3 049	45.8	453	68.2	1 528	21.8
Monroe	186	165	3 656	5.3	2.50	26.5	33.8	30.2	2 567	45.1	2 161	42.5	283	57.6	1 089	8.4
Montgomery	323	321	4 775	10.0	2.47	26.3	33.9	29.3	3 336	44.8	2 719	41.4	413	59.3	1 439	17.3
Morgan	287	158	7 850	25.2	2.42	25.1	29.1	32.0	5 547	37.7	4 750	33.7	556	60.6	2 303	40.4
New Madrid	350	349	7 824	.4	2.48	26.5	36.8	27.7	5 505	46.6	4 065	41.2	1 146	62.3	2 319	12.1
Newton	968	620	20 140	19.3	2.57	22.7	36.0	24.7	14 733	45.3	12 192	41.8	1 776	62.8	5 407	28.5
Nodaway	2 912	784	8 138	6.8	2.33	30.0	28.3	24.9	4 818	46.1	4 069	43.5	506	64.0	3 320	26.5
Oregon	110	100	4 263	10.7	2.40	26.2	32.0	31.4	3 018	41.5	2 505	38.0	358	57.8	1 245	20.8
Osage	202	163	4 922	15.5	2.61	23.8	36.7	26.3	3 580	47.9	3 038	46.3	330	59.1	1 342	24.1
Ozark	74	74	3 950	13.3	2.40	24.4	29.3	33.3	2 857	36.3	2 455	33.3	271	53.1	1 093	25.6
Pemiscot	278	238	7 855	-4.3	2.52	28.8	38.1	28.3	5 317	49.7	3 532	41.6	1 456	67.4	2 538	3.5
Perry	379	307	6 904	13.0	2.57	24.5	36.5	27.0	4 955	47.7	4 177	44.9	544	64.7	1 949	23.8
Pettis	687	450	15 568	10.8	2.49	27.0	35.4	26.7	10 568	47.8	8 301	43.8	1 629	64.3	5 000	21.7
Phelps	2 432	605	15 683	18.1	2.38	28.6	32.5	24.2	10 235	46.4	8 262	42.0	1 484	65.4	5 448	31.2
Pike	2 253	2 152	6 451	6.0	2.50	26.7	33.9	29.7	4 477	45.1	3 596	40.8	620	62.7	1 974	15.9
Platte	844	530	29 278	32.2	2.49	24.9	36.1	15.6	20 222	49.3	16 680	46.0	2 562	66.2	9 056	49.3
Polk	1 600	515	9 917	23.5	2.56	23.2	35.6	27.2	7 140	45.9	5 996	42.2	816	65.1	2 777	30.3

[1] As of April 1. [2] Includes people under formally authorized, supervised care or custody in institutions at the time of enumeration (such as correctional institutions, nursing homes, and juvenile institutions). [3] Under 18 years. [4] No husband present.

Sources: Group Quarters Population—U.S. Census Bureau, 2000 Census of Population and Housing, "Census 2000 Profiles of General Demographic Characteristics" data files, published May 2001 (related Internet site <http://www.census.gov/mp/www/pub/2000cen/mscen01.html>). Households, 2000—U.S. Census Bureau, 2000 Census of Population and Housing, "Census 2000 Profiles of General Demographic Characteristics" data files, published May 2001 (related Internet site <http://www.census.gov/mp/www/pub/2000cen/mscen01.html>). Households, 1990—U.S. Census Bureau, 1990 Census of Population and Housing, Summary Tape File (STF) 1C on CD-ROM (related Internet site <http://homer.ssd.census.gov/cdrom/lookup>).

[Includes U.S., states, and 3,142 counties or county equivalents defined as of January 1, 1992. For changes to these areas since then, see appendix B. Geographic Information]

County	Group quarters population, 2000[1] Number	Institutionalized population[2]	Households, 2000 (April 1) Number	Percent change, 1990–2000	Persons per household	Percent— One-person	With 1 or more persons under 18 years	With 1 or more persons 65 years and over	Family households (families) Number	Percent with own children under 18 years	Married-couple Number	Percent with own children[3]	Female householder[4] Number	Percent with own children[3]	Nonfamily households Number	Percent change, 1990–2000
MISSOURI—Con.																
Pulaski	5 209	280	13 433	8.4	2.68	21.6	44.9	17.6	9 949	57.1	8 137	54.0	1 302	72.1	3 484	38.5
Putnam	57	53	2 228	2.9	2.32	28.7	29.7	34.2	1 517	40.9	1 274	36.8	160	60.0	711	2.4
Ralls	105	81	3 736	15.8	2.55	21.2	35.9	24.9	2 784	45.6	2 399	42.4	241	63.9	952	26.6
Randolph	2 297	2 145	9 199	2.9	2.43	27.9	34.2	27.2	6 234	46.3	4 849	41.0	1 023	66.5	2 965	9.5
Ray	324	316	8 743	9.0	2.63	22.1	38.2	24.0	6 540	47.0	5 517	43.6	699	64.5	2 203	22.0
Reynolds	156	43	2 721	7.0	2.40	26.0	31.1	29.0	1 915	39.5	1 611	36.1	211	60.2	806	36.1
Ripley	159	139	5 416	13.1	2.46	25.9	33.7	30.9	3 848	42.6	3 110	39.8	518	54.1	1 568	23.9
St. Charles	3 788	1 360	101 663	36.8	2.76	19.4	42.9	16.8	77 104	53.4	64 244	51.4	9 388	64.8	24 559	48.7
St. Clair	182	176	4 040	15.5	2.34	27.4	29.4	35.1	2 790	38.0	2 327	33.7	311	58.5	1 250	18.1
Ste. Genevieve	354	308	6 586	15.4	2.66	21.8	37.6	26.6	4 926	46.9	4 189	43.9	499	62.3	1 660	28.6
St. Francois	3 979	3 711	20 793	17.7	2.48	24.9	35.8	26.5	14 669	46.2	11 421	41.4	2 355	63.3	6 124	34.0
St. Louis	19 286	12 080	404 312	6.4	2.47	28.0	34.3	24.4	270 810	47.2	206 240	44.5	51 493	57.8	133 502	21.7
Saline	1 655	716	9 015	1.3	2.45	28.2	34.2	29.3	6 017	45.9	4 681	41.1	930	63.2	2 998	7.8
Schuyler	54	54	1 725	−.2	2.39	28.2	30.9	32.8	1 193	42.7	1 020	38.8	125	65.6	532	7.5
Scotland	124	124	1 902	−2.8	2.55	28.2	34.0	32.7	1 302	47.4	1 107	45.0	134	65.7	600	−4.9
Scott	570	437	15 626	5.9	2.55	25.0	38.8	25.3	11 223	49.3	8 535	44.7	2 097	66.5	4 403	15.5
Shannon	70	61	3 319	13.8	2.49	25.8	35.6	27.8	2 358	45.7	1 952	42.3	272	62.1	961	33.8
Shelby	256	127	2 745	−2.3	2.38	30.3	32.2	32.7	1 848	45.5	1 562	41.7	201	67.7	897	.8
Stoddard	813	349	12 064	6.0	2.39	26.6	33.3	29.5	8 481	43.4	6 930	39.6	1 139	61.1	3 583	18.8
Stone	261	190	11 822	49.9	2.40	21.4	28.5	31.5	8 843	34.2	7 647	30.2	847	59.5	2 979	56.0
Sullivan	151	113	2 925	11.9	2.42	29.1	31.7	31.8	1 961	44.2	1 560	40.2	266	62.0	964	19.6
Taney	1 461	359	16 158	56.6	2.37	25.7	30.5	27.6	11 053	40.7	9 141	36.0	1 393	64.2	5 105	80.8
Texas	342	281	9 378	11.1	2.42	26.0	33.2	30.7	6 647	43.4	5 452	39.0	838	64.6	2 731	21.6
Vernon	1 054	763	7 966	9.1	2.44	28.1	34.6	28.1	5 436	47.1	4 404	42.7	767	67.1	2 530	14.2
Warren	270	129	9 185	29.9	2.64	20.8	37.3	24.1	6 892	46.2	5 713	42.7	821	64.4	2 293	39.2
Washington	1 175	1 121	8 406	20.4	2.64	22.0	40.2	23.1	6 237	49.0	4 930	45.0	890	64.9	2 169	38.9
Wayne	142	127	5 551	20.5	2.36	27.2	31.1	34.0	3 839	39.6	3 119	34.5	508	61.0	1 712	43.9
Webster	966	926	11 073	32.0	2.72	20.4	40.4	22.5	8 437	49.8	7 084	46.8	920	65.9	2 636	44.7
Worth	49	38	1 009	−2.7	2.31	30.0	30.3	35.9	677	43.1	569	39.0	78	66.7	332	−7.3
Wright	218	195	7 081	8.8	2.50	26.3	35.4	29.6	5 023	46.6	4 144	42.4	626	66.0	2 058	15.3
Independent City																
St. Louis city	10 632	4 667	147 076	−10.8	2.30	40.3	30.1	24.9	76 976	48.6	38 470	41.5	31 359	58.3	70 100	−5.3
MONTANA	24 762	12 068	358 667	17.1	2.45	27.4	33.3	23.4	237 407	47.1	192 067	42.9	32 016	66.2	121 260	28.3
Beaverhead	494	78	3 684	14.7	2.36	29.7	32.0	24.0	2 355	47.1	2 017	45.0	228	60.1	1 329	26.0
Big Horn	216	126	3 924	13.8	3.17	19.3	51.5	19.8	3 033	54.8	2 119	52.9	690	59.3	891	25.7
Blaine	66	43	2 501	5.1	2.78	26.0	42.3	26.3	1 794	50.2	1 308	47.9	361	60.4	707	4.4
Broadwater	60	57	1 752	36.9	2.47	24.1	31.7	28.1	1 270	41.5	1 076	38.8	121	55.4	482	34.3
Carbon	101	78	4 065	24.3	2.32	28.8	29.8	28.0	2 706	42.7	2 303	39.7	274	60.9	1 359	38.5
Carter	17	17	543	−7.8	2.47	27.1	32.2	32.2	383	43.3	329	41.3	38	50.0	160	−11.1
Cascade	1 941	1 272	32 547	8.0	2.41	28.8	34.2	24.3	21 450	44.8	17 025	43.9	3 220	69.1	11 097	22.0
Chouteau	199	151	2 226	7.8	2.59	24.9	36.3	28.5	1 614	46.9	1 356	43.9	186	65.1	612	12.1
Custer	421	299	4 768	3.0	2.36	29.9	32.3	27.5	3 092	46.9	2 435	41.1	475	70.5	1 676	9.1
Daniels	37	35	892	−2.9	2.22	33.6	24.9	36.3	561	37.6	490	34.1	49	63.3	331	16.5
Dawson	482	328	3 625	−1.8	2.37	28.4	30.4	28.3	2 477	43.4	2 121	39.7	246	67.1	1 148	6.9
Deer Lodge	371	218	3 995	−1.6	2.26	33.4	27.4	32.4	2 526	40.8	1 999	35.7	375	60.0	1 469	4.5
Fallon	46	42	1 140	−2.2	2.45	26.6	33.6	30.6	804	45.5	690	43.3	68	58.8	336	11.3
Fergus	557	296	4 860	5.6	2.33	30.5	30.5	30.9	3 197	43.7	2 728	40.3	324	62.0	1 663	19.5
Flathead	1 145	765	29 588	29.6	2.48	25.2	34.5	22.2	20 425	47.1	16 841	42.5	2 450	68.7	9 163	42.1
Gallatin	3 116	323	26 323	38.4	2.46	24.1	30.9	14.9	16 196	48.3	13 643	45.5	1 736	68.1	10 127	51.5
Garfield	12	11	532	−7.8	2.38	28.2	29.3	31.4	366	41.8	321	39.6	24	70.8	166	16.1
Glacier	186	148	4 304	12.8	3.03	21.6	50.0	20.5	3 246	56.8	2 295	55.1	699	61.4	1 058	13.8
Golden Valley	162	–	365	10.6	2.41	24.4	27.9	32.3	263	57.3	244	36.1	12	58.3	102	2.0
Granite	32	21	1 200	14.2	2.33	30.1	29.3	26.8	785	41.4	656	37.8	89	61.8	415	21.0
Hill	344	142	6 457	.5	2.53	28.6	37.1	23.7	4 255	52.0	3 261	47.8	706	69.5	2 202	13.7
Jefferson	221	204	3 747	30.7	2.62	20.2	37.4	19.6	2 846	46.8	2 515	44.6	222	62.2	901	28.9
Judith Basin	–	–	951	4.7	2.45	27.5	30.9	29.8	662	43.1	596	42.1	41	56.1	289	15.1
Lake	616	238	10 192	30.4	2.54	24.5	36.0	26.3	7 217	46.6	5 584	40.5	1 172	68.9	2 975	39.8
Lewis and Clark	1 246	329	22 850	22.5	2.38	29.1	34.0	20.0	14 958	49.2	11 983	44.3	2 107	70.9	7 892	30.7
Liberty	64	60	833	5.7	2.51	27.9	31.3	31.7	584	43.3	522	41.2	47	68.1	249	8.3
Lincoln	191	173	7 764	16.4	2.40	26.7	31.6	26.2	5 335	42.4	4 434	37.1	603	68.0	2 429	37.8
McCone	–	–	810	−4.0	2.44	26.6	31.6	32.2	597	41.0	542	40.2	31	45.2	213	6.5
Madison	74	65	2 956	23.8	2.29	29.3	27.3	27.7	1 921	40.2	1 708	37.6	131	64.9	1 035	38.7
Meagher	26	26	803	13.3	2.37	31.0	28.8	31.6	529	41.4	456	37.7	49	61.2	274	18.6
Mineral	63	62	1 584	23.6	2.41	26.6	30.4	23.9	1 068	41.1	914	35.9	95	72.6	516	36.1
Missoula	3 619	791	38 439	24.9	2.40	28.0	31.0	17.6	23 145	48.5	18 237	44.2	3 524	66.1	15 294	39.9
Musselshell	115	34	1 878	13.1	2.33	30.1	28.9	30.4	1 235	41.4	1 045	37.6	124	61.3	643	16.7
Park	214	102	6 828	21.5	2.27	32.4	29.4	24.7	4 223	45.5	3 483	41.1	497	64.4	2 605	40.2
Petroleum	–	–	211	1.0	2.34	31.3	32.7	31.8	137	48.2	118	44.9	12	75.0	74	37.0

[1] As of April 1.   [2] Includes people under formally authorized, supervised care or custody in institutions at the time of enumeration (such as correctional institutions, nursing homes, and juvenile institutions).   [3] Under 18 years.   [4] No husband present.

Sources: Group Quarters Population—U.S. Census Bureau, 2000 Census of Population and Housing, "Census 2000 Profiles of General Demographic Characteristics" data files, published May 2001 (related Internet site <http://www.census.gov/mp/www/pub/2000cen/mscen01.html>).   Households, 2000—U.S. Census Bureau, 2000 Census of Population and Housing, "Census 2000 Profiles of General Demographic Characteristics" data files, published May 2001 (related Internet site <http://www.census.gov/mp/www/pub/2000cen/mscen01.html>).   Households, 1990—U.S. Census Bureau, 1990 Census of Population and Housing, Summary Tape File (STF) 1C on CD-ROM (related Internet site <http://homer.ssd.census.gov/cdrom/lookup>).

[Includes U.S., states, and 3,142 counties or county equivalents defined as of January 1, 1992. For changes to these areas since then, see appendix B. Geographic Information]

County	Group quarters population, 2000[1] Number	Group quarters population, 2000 Institutionalized population[2]	Households, 2000 (April 1) Number	Percent change, 1990–2000	Persons per house-hold	Percent— One-person	Percent— With 1 or more persons under 18 years	Percent— With 1 or more persons 65 years and over	Family households (families) Number	Family households Per-cent with own children under 18 years	Married-couple Number	Married-couple Per-cent with own chil-dren[3]	Female householder[4] Number	Female householder Per-cent with own chil-dren[3]	Nonfamily households Number	Nonfamily households Percent change, 1990–2000
MONTANA—Con.																
Phillips	79	50	1 848	–4.3	2.45	29.1	34.7	30.8	1 241	47.5	1 057	44.7	126	65.9	607	5.2
Pondera	77	58	2 410	7.3	2.63	25.5	37.8	29.6	1 739	48.9	1 447	45.5	202	65.8	671	9.3
Powder River	33	33	737	–8.4	2.48	24.8	32.6	29.9	525	43.0	478	41.2	30	60.0	212	–3.2
Powell	1 403	1 403	2 422	8.4	2.39	28.6	31.3	28.8	1 634	43.7	1 344	38.5	187	71.7	788	11.5
Prairie	24	19	537	–5.5	2.19	31.3	24.0	36.5	355	33.8	328	32.3	13	61.5	182	14.5
Ravalli	587	323	14 289	47.3	2.48	24.1	32.3	27.0	10 182	42.4	8 616	37.9	1 065	68.5	4 107	54.8
Richland	114	89	3 878	–2.0	2.46	28.8	35.2	32.7	2 653	49.1	2 224	45.2	286	70.6	1 225	17.0
Roosevelt	268	168	3 581	–3.1	2.89	23.6	47.1	23.8	2 615	55.5	1 692	49.9	676	64.8	966	5.0
Rosebud	96	96	3 307	–4.9	2.81	24.3	44.1	18.9	2 417	52.9	1 852	47.7	391	69.3	890	4.7
Sanders	194	74	4 273	25.8	2.35	28.0	28.1	28.8	2 897	38.6	2 450	33.8	302	67.5	1 376	34.9
Sheridan	121	89	1 741	–8.3	2.29	32.3	28.0	36.2	1 140	41.2	1 001	39.4	83	54.2	601	7.3
Silver Bow	1 092	715	14 432	3.8	2.32	32.8	30.1	27.6	8 931	45.2	6 893	41.3	1 514	59.4	5 501	12.9
Stillwater	172	77	3 234	28.2	2.48	24.1	34.5	25.0	2 348	44.8	2 089	42.4	162	67.9	886	32.4
Sweet Grass	57	52	1 476	15.2	2.41	28.9	32.0	29.5	987	46.0	885	44.9	67	56.7	489	19.6
Teton	66	54	2 538	9.0	2.51	27.3	33.1	29.9	1 762	45.6	1 550	42.6	149	67.8	776	16.9
Toole	423	408	1 962	2.1	2.47	30.2	34.0	28.6	1 309	48.4	1 115	45.7	127	63.8	653	7.6
Treasure	–	–	357	5.3	2.41	30.0	33.1	30.5	242	45.5	211	45.0	15	40.0	115	38.6
Valley	184	69	3 150	–3.6	2.38	29.3	31.6	30.5	2 128	43.9	1 748	39.6	258	63.6	1 022	3.5
Wheatland	352	80	853	.5	2.24	34.5	27.2	33.2	541	40.7	459	37.9	42	61.9	312	4.3
Wibaux	37	37	421	–7.3	2.45	29.0	29.7	35.6	287	42.9	245	41.2	25	52.0	134	–2.9
Yellowstone	2 929	1 640	52 084	16.5	2.43	27.9	33.7	23.0	34 219	48.0	26 989	43.7	5 270	65.3	17 865	25.9
Yellowstone National Park	X	X	X	X	X	X	X	X	X	X	X	X	X	X	X	X
NEBRASKA	50 818	26 011	666 184	10.6	2.49	27.6	34.5	23.7	443 411	49.1	360 996	45.9	60 343	65.8	222 773	19.2
Adams	1 642	689	12 141	4.7	2.43	28.6	32.6	27.1	7 969	47.0	6 606	43.6	1 002	65.2	4 172	9.4
Antelope	104	99	2 953	–3.0	2.49	27.8	33.2	33.9	2 072	45.8	1 846	43.5	161	66.5	881	2.9
Arthur	–	–	185	–1.1	2.40	21.6	30.3	29.2	138	37.0	117	35.9	14	28.6	47	–2.1
Banner	–	–	311	2.0	2.63	19.9	33.1	29.3	238	39.5	218	38.5	13	46.2	73	69.8
Blaine	–	–	238	–11.2	2.45	26.9	30.7	30.3	169	42.6	157	41.4	6	83.3	69	–13.8
Boone	112	110	2 454	–4.1	2.50	29.1	34.6	34.5	1 700	48.9	1 492	47.4	134	63.4	754	–.5
Box Butte	227	181	4 780	–2.4	2.50	27.5	37.4	24.4	3 299	51.6	2 760	47.4	397	75.6	1 481	5.3
Boyd	46	46	1 014	–11.7	2.36	32.0	30.2	39.4	670	43.9	602	42.2	38	63.2	344	–5.2
Brown	49	49	1 530	2.1	2.27	31.6	28.1	35.6	996	40.9	872	37.5	91	67.0	534	14.8
Buffalo	2 788	750	15 930	16.0	2.48	26.1	34.1	20.3	10 222	50.9	8 420	47.5	1 316	70.6	5 708	18.6
Burt	113	102	3 155	.5	2.43	26.5	31.3	36.0	2 241	41.6	1 935	38.2	197	62.9	914	–4.7
Butler	102	72	3 426	5.3	2.53	28.3	34.3	31.4	2 351	48.1	2 052	46.5	194	61.3	1 075	12.9
Cass	251	246	9 161	17.5	2.63	21.6	38.0	22.4	6 806	48.2	5 799	45.1	697	67.9	2 355	24.7
Cedar	186	186	3 623	–.8	2.60	27.0	35.7	34.4	2 564	49.2	2 303	48.5	157	58.6	1 059	5.9
Chase	100	100	1 662	–2.5	2.39	27.3	31.6	32.3	1 164	43.6	1 032	40.2	91	70.3	498	3.5
Cherry	80	73	2 508	2.9	2.42	28.9	33.1	28.8	1 711	46.5	1 451	43.1	174	66.7	797	17.6
Cheyenne	126	119	4 071	5.7	2.38	30.1	32.6	28.9	2 685	47.2	2 230	42.6	324	68.5	1 386	16.4
Clay	102	102	2 756	.5	2.52	25.7	34.3	30.2	1 981	45.8	1 756	43.0	151	72.2	775	5.9
Colfax	132	123	3 682	3.4	2.80	25.7	37.8	31.6	2 593	50.6	2 169	49.2	261	62.1	1 089	–2.2
Cuming	241	236	3 945	2.4	2.53	27.1	33.6	33.0	2 757	46.7	2 434	44.9	208	66.3	1 188	7.0
Custer	238	218	4 826	–2.6	2.39	28.9	32.0	33.5	3 320	44.0	2 939	41.6	263	60.8	1 506	.3
Dakota	291	227	7 095	17.6	2.81	22.9	43.1	19.7	5 089	55.6	3 873	52.2	842	71.4	2 006	24.0
Dawes	1 046	91	3 512	5.6	2.28	31.0	27.7	26.9	2 085	44.1	1 703	39.3	276	68.8	1 427	23.1
Dawson	473	337	8 824	12.7	2.71	24.6	38.0	26.4	6 275	50.4	5 191	46.8	700	70.4	2 549	15.7
Deuel	23	23	908	–.8	2.29	31.2	27.2	36.3	601	38.6	523	35.6	54	59.3	307	8.9
Dixon	111	111	2 413	3.2	2.58	25.9	34.7	31.5	1 706	47.1	1 484	44.7	158	67.7	707	8.3
Dodge	1 173	602	14 433	7.3	2.42	27.6	32.7	28.9	9 750	46.0	8 060	41.8	1 224	67.2	4 683	15.4
Douglas	11 707	6 769	182 194	13.1	2.48	29.8	34.4	19.6	115 083	50.7	86 454	47.6	22 070	63.0	67 111	22.7
Dundy	87	56	961	–11.4	2.29	30.9	29.6	35.4	637	41.9	576	40.3	37	64.9	324	–9.7
Fillmore	264	263	2 689	–4.9	2.37	30.2	31.4	33.7	1 802	45.1	1 588	42.6	135	61.5	887	1.0
Franklin	106	82	1 485	–10.3	2.34	29.2	29.5	36.7	1 021	41.5	882	38.2	89	66.3	464	–10.1
Frontier	144	40	1 192	–1.2	2.48	26.3	32.7	29.4	829	45.1	745	41.7	57	82.5	363	5.8
Furnas	134	125	2 278	–2.4	2.28	32.5	29.1	37.6	1 490	42.8	1 302	39.5	134	63.4	788	–4.1
Gage	1 036	884	9 316	3.3	2.36	29.2	31.6	31.3	6 208	45.4	5 283	41.7	657	68.8	3 108	10.0
Garden	60	60	1 020	–1.9	2.19	32.5	25.9	35.5	659	38.4	570	34.9	61	60.7	361	7.8
Garfield	57	57	813	–5.9	2.27	32.7	27.3	38.4	529	40.1	485	37.3	29	69.0	284	8.0
Gosper	51	51	863	13.0	2.42	22.8	30.4	31.3	655	39.4	596	37.2	34	61.8	208	20.9
Grant	–	–	292	–3.6	2.56	22.3	37.7	25.3	226	47.8	197	44.2	19	57.9	66	–13.2
Greeley	62	62	1 077	–4.9	2.46	30.5	30.6	39.4	734	43.1	635	42.7	69	49.3	343	–2.6
Hall	1 253	913	20 356	9.0	2.57	25.5	37.1	23.7	14 085	50.3	11 371	46.3	1 973	70.0	6 271	11.5
Hamilton	148	148	3 503	8.3	2.64	21.1	38.8	25.8	2 677	48.7	2 360	45.8	206	70.4	826	7.4
Harlan	55	52	1 597	.8	2.34	30.8	27.5	36.8	1 050	39.1	943	36.5	69	68.1	547	12.8
Hayes	–	–	430	–10.4	2.48	26.5	28.8	35.1	312	38.8	288	41.0	11	27.3	118	3.5
Hitchcock	61	61	1 287	–12.3	2.37	27.4	29.1	35.7	900	40.0	786	36.5	82	67.1	387	–13.2
Holt	225	215	4 608	–2.9	2.46	28.7	32.6	32.9	3 171	45.9	2 799	44.5	258	58.1	1 437	3.5

[1] As of April 1. [2] Includes people under formally authorized, supervised care or custody in institutions at the time of enumeration (such as correctional institutions, nursing homes, and juvenile institutions). [3] Under 18 years. [4] No husband present.

Sources: Group Quarters Population—U.S. Census Bureau, 2000 Census of Population and Housing, "Census 2000 Profiles of General Demographic Characteristics" data files, published May 2001 (related Internet site <http://www.census.gov/mp/www/pub/2000cen/mscen01.html>). Households, 2000—U.S. Census Bureau, 2000 Census of Population and Housing, "Census 2000 Profiles of General Demographic Characteristics" data files, published May 2001 (related Internet site <http://www.census.gov/mp/www/pub/2000cen/mscen01.html>). Households, 1990—U.S. Census Bureau, 1990 Census of Population and Housing, Summary Tape File (STF) 1C on CD-ROM (related Internet site <http://homer.ssd.census.gov/cdrom/lookup>).

[Includes U.S., states, and 3,142 counties or county equivalents defined as of January 1, 1992. For changes to these areas since then, see appendix B. Geographic Information]

County	Group quarters population, 2000[1]		Households, 2000 (April 1)			Percent—			By type—							
									Family households (families)		Married-couple		Female householder[4]		Nonfamily households	
	Number	Institutionalized population[2]	Number	Percent change, 1990–2000	Persons per household	One-person	With 1 or more persons under 18 years	With 1 or more persons 65 years and over	Number	Percent with own children under 18 years	Number	Percent with own children[3]	Number	Percent with own children[3]	Number	Percent change, 1990–2000
NEBRASKA—Con.																
Hooker	26	26	335	.9	2.26	33.1	27.5	40.0	220	40.9	202	40.1	13	53.8	115	1.8
Howard	42	42	2 546	10.3	2.56	26.0	35.3	31.4	1 798	47.9	1 552	44.5	157	66.9	748	20.8
Jefferson	166	139	3 527	-2.9	2.32	29.6	29.3	36.2	2 354	42.0	2 043	39.4	205	61.5	1 173	3.4
Johnson	62	62	1 887	-2.7	2.35	29.9	31.0	36.1	1 255	44.5	1 097	42.1	104	61.5	632	2.1
Kearney	262	145	2 643	4.8	2.50	24.3	35.9	26.9	1 902	47.7	1 663	44.1	170	73.5	741	9.1
Keith	100	79	3 707	8.1	2.37	27.9	32.0	30.5	2 535	44.2	2 174	40.3	259	67.2	1 172	16.7
Keya Paha	–	–	409	-2.4	2.40	26.2	26.2	35.0	292	34.9	263	33.5	18	44.4	117	9.3
Kimball	60	60	1 727	4.7	2.33	30.5	28.5	34.3	1 136	40.0	968	36.7	115	62.6	591	23.1
Knox	244	225	3 811	-.2	2.40	29.9	30.6	37.2	2 594	43.0	2 250	40.4	229	63.8	1 217	3.0
Lancaster	12 197	4 061	99 187	19.9	2.40	29.1	31.8	18.4	60 702	49.5	48 393	46.2	9 018	65.9	38 485	29.3
Lincoln	670	391	14 076	11.0	2.41	28.3	33.9	25.1	9 445	47.8	7 873	43.6	1 124	69.7	4 631	22.7
Logan	–	–	316	-1.3	2.45	25.0	31.3	30.1	229	41.0	210	38.6	12	75.0	87	20.8
Loup	–	–	289	4.7	2.46	27.0	32.2	34.9	207	44.4	187	43.9	12	50.0	82	5.1
McPherson	–	–	202	-4.7	2.64	19.8	36.1	34.7	158	43.7	149	42.3	7	71.4	44	-17.0
Madison	1 326	780	13 436	9.4	2.52	27.9	34.8	25.0	8 895	50.2	7 353	46.7	1 127	71.1	4 541	17.8
Merrick	135	118	3 209	4.8	2.51	25.0	35.2	29.6	2 308	46.3	1 960	43.1	207	67.1	901	8.2
Morrill	108	82	2 138	2.6	2.49	26.9	34.2	29.2	1 494	46.0	1 273	42.8	138	62.3	644	11.8
Nance	112	72	1 577	-.5	2.49	27.6	33.8	33.1	1 107	46.7	954	44.0	89	69.7	470	4.9
Nemaha	494	109	3 047	-1.0	2.32	30.5	30.7	31.4	1 981	45.3	1 676	41.9	220	66.8	1 066	8.6
Nuckolls	44	44	2 218	-6.0	2.26	32.3	27.5	38.1	1 445	40.6	1 304	37.7	102	72.5	773	7.1
Otoe	360	315	6 060	7.1	2.48	26.4	34.4	30.0	4 232	46.5	3 618	43.8	434	62.2	1 828	6.0
Pawnee	54	54	1 339	-4.9	2.27	32.9	26.1	42.4	850	38.5	734	35.7	75	53.3	489	6.1
Perkins	54	54	1 275	-.6	2.47	27.5	34.0	32.2	894	46.3	802	43.4	59	74.6	381	10.8
Phelps	259	255	3 844	2.0	2.47	26.7	34.2	28.6	2 682	47.5	2 367	44.7	222	69.4	1 162	8.1
Pierce	131	131	2 979	1.7	2.59	25.7	36.6	29.8	2 142	49.1	1 889	47.4	169	62.1	837	6.6
Platte	328	223	12 076	10.2	2.59	25.9	37.4	25.1	8 461	51.5	7 151	48.8	920	70.8	3 615	19.1
Polk	159	159	2 259	1.6	2.43	27.6	31.3	33.1	1 569	43.1	1 421	41.4	93	61.3	690	9.0
Red Willow	262	142	4 710	-.3	2.37	28.6	31.4	31.0	3 190	44.6	2 706	41.1	340	66.2	1 520	.1
Richardson	204	203	3 993	-3.1	2.34	32.2	31.5	34.7	2 568	45.9	2 132	41.1	296	69.3	1 425	3.8
Rock	30	30	763	-4.4	2.26	31.3	27.7	34.5	501	40.9	438	38.8	49	57.1	262	14.9
Saline	887	263	5 188	7.4	2.50	27.5	34.4	29.9	3 507	48.6	2 930	44.4	373	72.4	1 681	10.7
Sarpy	1 301	571	43 426	27.9	2.79	18.4	45.0	13.2	33 238	56.1	27 690	53.9	4 160	69.3	10 188	58.5
Saunders	255	227	7 498	10.1	2.61	23.6	35.7	27.6	5 443	47.1	4 696	45.4	503	59.0	2 055	15.4
Scotts Bluff	652	480	14 887	5.9	2.44	27.8	34.0	28.9	10 170	46.2	8 063	40.9	1 589	67.8	4 717	13.0
Seward	1 291	261	6 013	10.7	2.53	24.9	33.8	27.2	4 215	46.7	3 701	44.3	337	67.4	1 798	25.3
Sheridan	136	131	2 549	-2.6	2.38	29.6	31.6	35.3	1 729	44.2	1 447	40.1	203	68.5	820	4.2
Sherman	55	55	1 394	-2.6	2.34	30.4	29.3	37.2	935	41.2	825	39.3	79	55.7	459	9.8
Sioux	–	–	605	-1.1	2.44	23.6	31.1	27.9	444	38.3	395	37.2	31	58.1	161	9.5
Stanton	120	119	2 297	6.0	2.76	19.2	40.6	22.8	1 784	50.1	1 550	48.3	166	65.1	513	8.0
Thayer	180	180	2 541	-4.8	2.31	31.5	28.8	37.4	1 691	41.6	1 495	38.5	126	69.0	850	8.3
Thomas	–	–	325	2.8	2.24	31.4	26.8	34.2	216	40.3	197	37.1	14	78.6	109	62.7
Thurston	100	88	2 255	-1.4	3.14	21.3	47.4	28.6	1 724	52.4	1 140	48.0	431	64.3	531	-7.3
Valley	85	70	1 965	-8.2	2.32	31.0	29.1	37.7	1 299	42.4	1 153	39.8	101	69.3	666	-5.8
Washington	550	229	6 940	15.3	2.63	21.8	38.1	23.5	5 149	49.0	4 444	46.9	485	65.4	1 791	23.2
Wayne	1 225	61	3 437	6.3	2.51	25.1	31.6	25.1	2 205	47.6	1 931	45.1	186	68.8	1 232	20.7
Webster	161	121	1 708	-2.7	2.28	32.6	27.9	37.0	1 119	40.8	986	37.6	86	72.1	589	6.7
Wheeler	–	–	352	.6	2.52	29.0	33.5	31.5	244	45.9	221	43.9	11	45.5	108	22.7
York	725	424	5 722	4.7	2.42	27.5	32.0	29.7	3 933	45.2	3 446	42.1	346	67.6	1 789	15.3
NEVADA	33 675	22 173	751 165	61.1	2.62	24.9	35.3	21.3	498 333	47.9	373 201	44.5	83 482	60.7	252 832	59.1
Churchill	414	164	8 912	33.7	2.64	22.5	40.4	23.1	6 465	51.3	5 144	47.0	926	69.4	2 447	30.5
Clark	19 415	11 919	512 253	78.5	2.65	24.5	35.4	21.0	339 693	47.8	249 720	44.5	60 351	59.7	172 560	75.6
Douglas	236	170	16 401	55.2	2.50	20.7	33.2	25.9	11 894	42.3	9 930	37.9	1 319	66.0	4 507	66.2
Elko	794	660	15 638	32.8	2.85	20.9	46.2	12.8	11 493	58.5	9 266	56.3	1 317	69.7	4 145	25.9
Esmeralda	6	6	455	-22.6	2.12	36.0	23.7	28.8	260	36.9	211	32.7	29	65.5	195	-18.8
Eureka	9	9	666	7.9	2.47	29.1	35.1	24.2	440	50.0	376	49.5	33	60.6	226	-2.2
Humboldt	223	189	5 733	26.3	2.77	22.8	44.1	15.8	4 136	56.7	3 417	54.3	435	72.4	1 597	21.5
Lander	86	26	2 093	-5.4	2.73	22.3	42.8	14.2	1 523	54.6	1 250	50.9	170	71.2	570	-3.9
Lincoln	351	351	1 540	16.2	2.48	31.3	31.8	33.8	1 011	44.1	865	42.0	121	58.7	529	26.6
Lyon	509	450	13 007	69.4	2.61	21.4	36.5	26.3	9 449	45.7	7 602	42.1	1 178	60.4	3 558	73.8
Mineral	109	44	2 197	-13.1	2.26	31.6	29.2	34.3	1 380	40.4	994	31.9	252	61.9	817	1.4
Nye	231	197	13 309	99.7	2.42	25.7	29.4	32.4	9 068	38.8	7 493	34.1	984	62.4	4 241	110.4
Pershing	1 414	1 403	1 962	21.6	2.69	24.3	41.4	19.1	1 383	54.5	1 122	50.7	144	75.0	579	21.4
Storey	4	4	1 462	45.3	2.32	25.6	25.2	23.1	969	32.9	798	28.6	110	50.0	493	56.5
Washoe	5 410	2 245	132 084	29.1	2.53	27.0	34.0	19.9	83 752	49.0	63 233	45.5	13 591	62.4	48 332	27.2
White Pine	1 241	1 234	3 282	-.4	2.42	29.6	33.9	26.9	2 161	47.4	1 700	41.8	305	68.2	1 121	11.1
Independent City																
Carson City city	3 223	3 102	20 171	26.9	2.44	27.8	32.7	27.6	13 256	45.4	10 080	40.6	2 217	60.8	6 915	31.1

[1] As of April 1. [2] Includes people under formally authorized, supervised care or custody in institutions at the time of enumeration (such as correctional institutions, nursing homes, and juvenile institutions). [3] Under 18 years. [4] No husband present.

Sources: Group Quarters Population—U.S. Census Bureau, 2000 Census of Population and Housing, "Census 2000 Profiles of General Demographic Characteristics" data files, published May 2001 (related Internet site <http://www.census.gov/mp/www/pub/2000cen/mscen01.html>). Households, 2000—U.S. Census Bureau, 2000 Census of Population and Housing, "Census 2000 Profiles of General Demographic Characteristics" data files, published May 2001 (related Internet site <http://www.census.gov/mp/www/pub/2000cen/mscen01.html>). Households, 1990—U.S. Census Bureau, 1990 Census of Population and Housing, Summary Tape File (STF) 1C on CD-ROM (related Internet site <http://homer.ssd.census.gov/cdrom/lookup>).

[Includes U.S., states, and 3,142 counties or county equivalents defined as of January 1, 1992. For changes to these areas since then, see appendix B. Geographic Information]

County	Group quarters population, 2000[1] Number	Institutionalized population[2]	Households, 2000 (April 1) Number	Percent change, 1990–2000	Persons per household	One-person	With 1 or more persons under 18 years	With 1 or more persons 65 years and over	Family households (families) Number	Percent with own children under 18 years	Married-couple Number	Percent with own children[3]	Female householder[4] Number	Percent with own children[3]	Nonfamily households Number	Percent change, 1990–2000
NEW HAMPSHIRE	35 539	13 784	474 606	15.4	2.53	24.4	35.5	21.5	323 651	48.9	262 438	45.9	42 952	63.5	150 955	27.3
Belknap	1 213	1 068	22 459	19.2	2.45	24.4	32.5	25.5	15 501	44.0	12 499	39.4	2 074	65.0	6 958	26.4
Carroll	569	338	18 351	28.8	2.35	26.6	29.3	29.2	12 312	40.9	10 145	36.1	1 435	64.2	6 039	37.7
Cheshire	4 030	797	28 299	9.4	2.47	25.5	32.7	24.4	18 784	46.1	15 129	42.4	2 550	62.1	9 515	23.6
Coos	646	467	13 961	1.2	2.33	28.8	30.1	30.3	9 164	42.8	7 302	37.4	1 227	65.3	4 797	14.5
Grafton	6 388	941	31 598	14.7	2.38	27.4	31.4	23.2	20 266	46.0	16 543	41.7	2 624	64.9	11 332	25.9
Hillsborough	7 669	3 609	144 455	16.0	2.58	24.3	37.2	19.4	98 855	51.4	79 432	48.9	13 727	63.1	45 600	26.3
Merrimack	6 293	3 672	51 843	16.3	2.51	24.6	36.0	21.8	35 473	49.6	28 446	45.6	5 060	66.6	16 370	28.0
Rockingham	2 409	1 633	104 529	17.3	2.63	22.0	38.1	18.9	74 358	50.5	62 165	49.1	8 549	59.2	30 171	30.2
Strafford	5 765	893	42 581	12.8	2.50	24.8	34.8	20.4	27 759	50.0	21 743	45.6	4 278	67.3	14 822	28.7
Sullivan	557	366	16 530	11.1	2.41	25.7	31.9	26.7	11 179	43.5	9 034	38.4	1 428	65.0	5 351	26.7
NEW JERSEY	194 821	110 169	3 064 645	9.7	2.68	24.5	36.6	25.9	2 154 539	47.6	1 638 322	47.4	387 012	50.9	910 106	17.7
Atlantic	6 494	2 687	95 024	11.6	2.59	27.0	35.7	26.3	63 151	47.7	44 148	45.0	14 099	55.9	31 873	11.7
Bergen	11 349	5 939	330 817	7.1	2.64	24.7	34.2	28.9	235 070	45.2	191 678	46.9	32 099	40.6	95 747	14.4
Burlington	14 172	11 860	154 371	13.0	2.65	22.9	37.5	24.0	111 581	47.5	89 052	46.7	16 785	51.3	42 790	32.2
Camden	10 406	7 602	185 744	3.9	2.68	25.1	38.5	24.8	129 844	49.5	92 536	47.8	28 534	55.7	55 900	13.6
Cape May	2 656	1 775	42 148	11.3	2.36	30.2	28.6	34.4	27 372	40.1	21 296	36.7	4 579	53.5	14 776	21.2
Cumberland	12 265	10 442	49 143	4.3	2.73	23.6	39.3	27.4	35 185	47.7	23 917	43.2	8 511	58.3	13 958	14.9
Essex	22 789	13 046	283 736	1.8	2.72	26.7	38.9	24.2	193 498	49.6	120 031	48.5	57 750	54.5	90 238	3.3
Gloucester	5 201	1 526	90 717	15.1	2.75	21.2	39.9	23.3	67 197	49.5	52 918	48.8	10 547	52.7	23 520	30.4
Hudson	9 450	5 728	230 546	10.4	2.60	29.5	33.3	22.9	143 532	47.5	91 772	46.9	38 326	52.7	87 014	19.9
Hunterdon	4 346	3 962	43 678	15.2	2.69	20.0	38.5	19.5	32 837	49.3	28 953	49.3	2 755	51.5	10 841	25.9
Mercer	21 092	7 148	125 807	7.6	2.62	25.6	36.2	25.2	86 288	47.8	63 604	46.9	17 418	53.2	39 519	14.6
Middlesex	20 820	7 688	265 815	11.3	2.74	22.4	37.0	24.9	190 930	47.6	151 461	48.4	28 812	47.2	74 885	18.1
Monmouth	10 036	4 899	224 236	13.5	2.70	23.8	38.0	24.6	160 233	49.6	130 530	50.1	22 456	50.2	64 003	23.8
Morris	9 186	4 462	169 711	14.1	2.72	21.5	37.3	22.3	124 907	48.1	106 544	48.9	13 354	45.8	44 804	25.6
Ocean	7 891	5 741	200 402	19.2	2.51	27.0	30.3	39.0	137 803	40.8	112 966	39.7	18 386	46.9	62 599	32.2
Passaic	9 076	4 080	160 056	5.5	2.92	22.2	40.1	20.1	119 009	40.0	84 091	40.0	26 222	51.5	44 107	10.0
Salem	1 222	803	24 295	2.1	2.60	24.3	36.2	26.8	17 371	45.4	13 070	41.8	3 238	58.1	6 924	12.6
Somerset	4 509	3 333	108 984	23.4	2.69	22.8	38.0	20.7	78 409	50.3	66 004	51.0	8 988	49.4	30 575	33.1
Sussex	1 687	1 240	50 831	14.3	2.80	18.9	42.0	18.3	38 805	52.2	33 024	52.2	4 072	52.9	12 026	34.5
Union	7 808	5 007	186 124	3.4	2.77	23.6	37.8	27.7	133 352	47.4	97 916	48.3	26 512	47.4	52 772	8.1
Warren	1 466	898	38 660	13.7	2.61	24.0	36.9	24.4	27 485	48.8	22 481	48.0	3 569	53.7	11 175	24.4
NEW MEXICO	36 307	19 178	677 971	24.9	2.63	25.4	38.6	22.4	466 515	50.4	341 818	46.1	89 622	62.6	211 456	39.8
Bernalillo	10 627	4 401	220 936	19.1	2.47	28.5	34.8	20.6	141 237	49.2	101 523	44.9	28 393	61.3	79 699	31.1
Catron	10	9	1 584	56.8	2.23	30.1	24.6	30.9	1 041	34.0	877	29.9	120	59.2	543	88.5
Chaves	1 296	658	22 561	9.6	2.66	24.8	39.8	28.7	16 077	50.0	11 895	45.0	3 080	65.0	6 484	19.5
Cibola	1 066	997	8 327	14.2	2.95	21.1	45.5	23.8	6 281	50.4	4 216	45.8	1 524	59.1	2 046	36.8
Colfax	421	399	5 821	17.4	2.37	27.7	33.2	28.5	3 977	44.3	3 074	37.9	599	65.9	1 844	31.6
Curry	1 181	501	16 766	10.9	2.62	25.5	41.3	21.6	11 869	53.7	9 054	49.0	2 142	69.8	4 897	34.3
DeBaca	71	71	922	1.0	2.35	30.8	29.8	39.6	615	40.8	522	38.7	67	53.7	307	13.7
Dona Ana	5 019	2 109	59 556	32.3	2.85	21.3	43.0	22.1	42 912	53.4	31 211	49.5	8 776	65.0	16 644	41.0
Eddy	750	579	19 379	10.9	2.63	24.2	39.7	27.2	14 060	49.1	10 869	44.5	2 299	64.8	5 319	26.6
Grant	604	351	12 146	24.3	2.50	25.7	35.1	29.3	8 511	44.7	6 396	38.6	1 569	63.8	3 635	55.0
Guadalupe	525	506	1 655	8.9	2.51	27.9	37.9	28.6	1 145	48.9	819	44.2	237	59.5	510	32.8
Harding	–	–	371	-6.3	2.18	35.3	24.8	45.6	232	35.3	195	35.4	28	35.7	139	13.0
Hidalgo	85	84	2 152	7.4	2.72	25.3	41.5	26.3	1 543	52.2	1 157	48.5	293	66.6	609	32.7
Lea	1 800	1 545	19 699	2.0	2.73	22.5	43.1	24.5	14 714	52.6	11 390	48.8	2 408	66.7	4 985	14.0
Lincoln	219	197	8 202	71.3	2.34	26.7	29.3	29.8	5 631	38.2	4 562	32.1	761	65.8	2 571	90.7
Los Alamos	92	75	7 497	3.9	2.43	24.9	34.5	20.0	5 341	47.0	4 703	43.6	426	73.2	2 156	13.8
Luna	253	253	9 397	38.3	2.64	26.4	37.9	35.0	6 592	48.3	5 040	43.0	1 163	66.8	2 805	47.5
McKinley	859	569	21 476	29.5	3.44	19.5	54.9	18.3	16 679	59.3	10 239	59.8	4 866	57.7	4 797	48.8
Mora	56	–	2 017	32.8	2.54	26.9	35.0	29.2	1 398	45.0	1 019	40.5	241	56.4	619	57.9
Otero	1 228	366	22 984	26.6	2.66	23.3	40.5	22.7	16 802	50.8	13 205	46.2	2 703	68.9	6 182	46.9
Quay	188	176	4 201	-.9	2.37	28.9	32.4	32.1	2 845	42.7	2 188	36.8	503	62.8	1 356	15.2
Rio Arriba	465	222	15 044	31.3	2.71	23.5	41.7	22.4	10 815	51.4	7 339	47.1	2 390	58.5	4 229	61.0
Roosevelt	765	135	6 639	10.8	2.60	24.7	38.7	23.2	4 544	51.8	3 517	48.6	775	64.6	2 095	14.2
Sandoval	695	257	31 411	50.5	2.84	19.9	43.4	21.3	23 632	51.3	18 136	49.1	3 817	59.0	7 779	82.9
San Juan	1 214	972	37 711	31.2	2.99	19.3	47.1	19.7	28 930	54.7	21 012	51.7	5 558	61.8	8 781	46.0
San Miguel	1 391	227	11 134	28.0	2.58	26.6	38.9	22.6	7 533	51.2	4 950	45.2	1 830	61.5	3 601	56.8
Santa Fe	2 376	1 209	52 482	38.7	2.42	29.4	33.2	19.5	32 787	48.7	23 900	43.7	6 159	62.7	19 695	53.9
Sierra	266	249	6 113	38.1	2.13	35.9	22.7	42.2	3 617	34.4	2 904	28.6	523	57.4	2 496	56.6
Socorro	574	85	6 675	27.9	2.62	26.8	38.3	21.8	4 491	50.3	3 232	44.9	886	65.1	2 184	44.4
Taos	300	167	12 675	44.8	2.34	32.1	32.8	21.8	7 755	48.8	5 415	42.2	1 614	63.3	4 920	87.7
Torrance	524	524	6 024	64.1	2.72	23.2	41.7	20.8	4 392	51.8	3 335	48.2	740	62.4	1 632	84.4
Union	16	7	1 733	7.3	2.40	30.0	33.8	32.4	1 177	45.8	948	42.9	157	58.0	556	19.6
Valencia	1 371	1 278	22 681	49.5	2.86	18.8	44.2	21.3	17 340	51.8	12 976	48.1	2 975	62.5	5 341	68.1

[1] As of April 1.　[2] Includes people under formally authorized, supervised care or custody in institutions at the time of enumeration (such as correctional institutions, nursing homes, and juvenile institutions).　[3] Under 18 years.　[4] No husband present.

Sources: Group Quarters Population—U.S. Census Bureau, 2000 Census of Population and Housing, "Census 2000 Profiles of General Demographic Characteristics" data files, published May 2001 (related Internet site <http://www.census.gov/mp/www/pub/2000cen/mscen01.html>). Households, 2000—U.S. Census Bureau, 2000 Census of Population and Housing, "Census 2000 Profiles of General Demographic Characteristics" data files, published May 2001 (related Internet site <http://www.census.gov/mp/www/pub/2000cen/mscen01.html>). Households, 1990—U.S. Census Bureau, 1990 Census of Population and Housing, Summary Tape File (STF) 1C on CD-ROM (related Internet site <http://homer.ssd.census.gov/cdrom/lookup>).

Table B–3. Counties — Group Quarters Population and Households–Con.

[Includes U.S., states, and 3,142 counties or county equivalents defined as of January 1, 1992. For changes to these areas since then, see appendix B. Geographic Information]

County	Group quarters population, 2000[1] — Number	Institutionalized population[2]	Households 2000 — Number	Percent change, 1990–2000	Persons per household	Percent — One-person	Percent — With 1 or more persons under 18 years	Percent — With 1 or more persons 65 years and over	Family households — Number	Family — Percent with own children under 18 years	Married-couple — Number	Married-couple — Percent with own children[3]	Female householder[4] — Number	Female householder — Percent with own children[3]	Nonfamily — Number	Nonfamily — Percent change, 1990–2000
NEW YORK	580 461	262 262	7 056 860	6.3	2.61	28.1	35.0	25.0	4 639 387	48.1	3 289 514	46.4	1 038 176	55.2	2 417 473	12.4
Albany	15 557	4 495	120 512	4.0	2.32	33.0	29.9	24.7	70 973	47.5	52 050	43.4	14 659	61.2	49 539	11.7
Allegany	4 304	401	18 009	5.9	2.53	26.0	34.0	26.9	12 189	46.6	9 761	42.4	1 619	64.6	5 820	24.0
Bronx	47 235	27 904	463 212	9.2	2.78	27.4	43.8	21.6	315 090	56.0	145 537	51.7	140 620	63.2	148 122	9.3
Broome	9 115	3 338	80 749	–1.3	2.37	31.0	30.3	28.0	50 231	45.4	38 408	41.2	8 724	60.4	30 518	12.9
Cattaraugus	3 236	1 050	32 023	5.1	2.52	26.8	34.8	26.6	21 662	47.5	16 739	43.1	3 463	62.7	10 361	17.8
Cayuga	4 801	3 971	30 558	5.1	2.53	26.2	35.1	26.9	20 829	47.9	15 896	43.6	3 371	62.2	9 729	19.4
Chautauqua	6 387	2 983	54 515	1.5	2.45	28.1	32.8	28.2	35 966	46.2	27 765	41.3	5 907	64.3	18 549	12.5
Chemung	5 513	4 141	35 049	–.6	2.44	27.9	33.9	27.9	23 280	46.7	17 466	41.2	4 360	64.8	11 769	12.4
Chenango	1 258	972	19 926	4.1	2.52	26.1	35.2	26.2	13 546	47.8	10 571	42.4	1 954	67.2	6 380	19.9
Clinton	7 097	4 486	29 423	1.0	2.47	26.3	34.5	22.9	19 261	48.8	15 008	44.1	2 987	65.3	10 162	22.7
Columbia	2 723	2 223	24 796	4.6	2.43	27.1	32.2	28.3	16 580	44.7	12 939	40.5	2 560	61.0	8 216	20.6
Cortland	3 120	474	18 210	5.6	2.50	26.5	33.5	23.1	11 619	48.6	8 966	43.6	1 877	64.8	6 591	21.0
Delaware	2 018	677	19 270	9.2	2.39	28.3	30.2	31.6	12 735	42.5	10 171	37.8	1 730	60.6	6 535	24.0
Dutchess	18 163	9 175	99 536	11.1	2.63	24.6	37.1	23.6	69 201	49.6	55 209	48.0	10 237	58.2	30 335	22.3
Erie	30 791	16 420	380 873	1.0	2.41	30.5	31.9	28.0	243 359	46.4	177 089	43.0	52 284	58.2	137 514	12.2
Essex	2 908	2 576	15 028	9.5	2.39	28.3	31.5	29.1	9 832	44.6	7 843	40.4	1 339	60.5	5 196	23.0
Franklin	6 979	5 907	17 931	10.1	2.46	28.2	34.6	26.0	11 805	49.0	8 878	43.6	1 987	66.0	6 126	22.1
Fulton	1 927	1 507	21 884	4.2	2.43	27.7	33.3	28.7	14 520	46.0	10 947	40.4	2 470	62.8	7 364	15.2
Genesee	1 439	1 189	22 770	5.3	2.59	24.8	35.8	26.2	15 823	47.9	12 611	45.1	2 241	60.7	6 947	24.9
Greene	3 943	3 280	18 256	10.0	2.42	27.9	31.4	29.2	12 073	44.2	9 343	39.8	1 888	61.3	6 183	24.8
Hamilton	95	3	2 362	9.7	2.24	29.6	25.7	33.1	1 558	35.8	1 315	32.1	158	55.7	804	24.7
Herkimer	1 108	646	25 734	3.2	2.46	27.6	32.8	29.7	17 101	46.0	13 183	41.8	2 648	60.4	8 633	17.3
Jefferson	8 202	3 097	40 068	5.9	2.58	24.4	39.4	22.3	28 142	52.9	22 284	49.3	4 152	67.8	11 926	23.1
Kings	39 299	15 582	880 727	6.3	2.75	27.8	38.2	24.4	584 120	50.1	339 957	49.5	195 988	55.0	296 607	8.7
Lewis	264	175	10 040	8.5	2.66	22.6	37.7	26.1	7 307	48.6	5 964	46.1	846	60.4	2 733	24.4
Livingston	6 749	2 889	22 150	4.5	2.60	23.1	36.3	22.9	15 346	49.1	12 149	45.2	2 222	64.2	6 804	13.0
Madison	4 674	829	25 368	7.6	2.55	24.5	36.0	24.3	17 577	48.5	13 968	44.9	2 467	62.7	7 791	21.6
Monroe	26 509	8 401	286 512	5.4	2.47	28.6	34.3	23.1	184 479	49.4	135 937	45.0	38 376	64.5	102 033	14.5
Montgomery	1 210	1 001	20 038	–.7	2.42	29.5	31.9	32.3	13 111	44.9	9 824	40.2	2 332	59.7	6 927	12.5
Nassau	21 658	9 568	447 387	3.7	2.93	18.8	38.6	31.1	347 026	45.5	282 126	47.5	48 942	38.9	100 361	15.3
New York	59 837	12 422	738 644	3.1	2.00	48.0	19.7	20.4	301 970	41.8	186 023	38.2	92 994	51.4	436 674	5.1
Niagara	4 218	2 225	87 846	3.6	2.45	28.6	33.3	27.4	58 582	46.3	44 173	42.6	10 819	59.7	29 264	16.7
Oneida	15 414	10 866	90 496	–2.2	2.43	29.5	32.7	29.2	59 170	46.6	44 474	42.3	10 889	61.3	31 326	8.7
Onondaga	13 506	4 009	181 153	1.8	2.46	29.4	34.2	24.6	115 320	50.1	85 022	45.8	23 386	64.4	65 833	11.0
Ontario	3 091	1 027	38 370	9.9	2.53	24.7	35.2	23.9	26 354	47.7	21 121	44.2	3 804	62.2	12 016	22.8
Orange	13 692	6 152	114 788	13.1	2.85	21.5	42.5	21.8	84 457	53.8	66 478	52.2	13 039	58.8	30 331	24.3
Orleans	3 486	3 271	15 363	6.5	2.65	23.7	38.4	25.1	10 839	49.6	8 343	45.2	1 719	64.1	4 524	20.9
Oswego	4 005	864	45 522	7.3	2.60	24.3	37.7	22.0	31 233	51.0	24 058	46.4	4 918	66.6	14 289	23.9
Otsego	5 012	627	23 291	7.2	2.43	27.0	31.7	27.7	15 120	45.5	11 913	41.0	2 210	61.6	8 171	17.5
Putnam	2 164	477	32 703	16.4	2.86	18.1	41.4	20.1	25 179	50.6	21 391	51.2	2 706	50.6	7 524	35.7
Queens	26 873	14 928	782 664	8.7	2.81	25.6	35.9	26.8	537 991	45.8	366 876	47.8	125 089	45.5	244 673	6.7
Rensselaer	5 192	1 827	59 894	4.0	2.46	27.9	33.6	24.3	39 028	48.1	29 246	44.1	7 161	61.4	20 866	14.3
Richmond	9 186	5 034	156 341	19.8	2.78	23.2	38.5	23.5	114 052	49.1	85 912	49.6	21 663	51.5	42 289	34.4
Rockland	7 649	3 382	92 675	9.2	3.01	19.3	40.5	24.9	70 944	49.2	58 177	50.0	9 502	48.3	21 731	18.8
St. Lawrence	11 166	4 421	40 506	6.7	2.49	26.5	34.1	25.3	26 939	47.8	20 871	42.6	4 176	66.4	13 567	21.4
Saratoga	4 309	1 949	78 165	17.7	2.51	24.5	35.7	21.0	53 738	48.9	43 915	46.3	7 007	61.8	24 427	35.2
Schenectady	4 662	2 171	59 684	.8	2.38	30.6	32.1	28.3	38 037	47.1	28 349	42.5	7 340	62.2	21 647	11.1
Schoharie	1 741	475	11 991	6.5	2.49	25.8	33.5	28.0	8 175	45.7	6 497	41.8	1 120	62.0	3 816	21.9
Schuyler	622	544	7 374	8.2	2.52	23.6	35.3	26.4	5 189	45.9	4 110	40.9	716	64.9	2 185	21.9
Seneca	1 625	1 185	12 630	2.8	2.51	25.3	34.4	27.6	8 632	46.6	6 765	41.9	1 300	63.8	3 998	21.6
Steuben	1 529	1 159	39 071	4.8	2.49	27.2	34.5	26.8	26 212	47.4	20 182	42.4	4 132	63.9	12 859	18.5
Suffolk	28 578	11 252	469 299	10.5	2.96	18.3	40.5	24.9	360 422	48.2	291 098	49.1	50 659	46.3	108 877	29.4
Sullivan	4 825	2 718	27 661	12.6	2.50	27.9	34.2	27.2	18 324	47.2	13 861	42.3	3 152	63.6	9 337	24.7
Tioga	511	304	19 725	4.7	2.60	22.4	37.3	24.1	14 326	47.8	11 578	44.0	1 941	63.8	5 399	23.6
Tompkins	11 955	1 028	36 420	9.2	2.32	32.5	27.4	18.1	19 120	49.1	15 014	44.4	2 992	67.7	17 300	21.1
Ulster	11 294	5 006	67 499	11.0	2.47	27.9	33.3	24.8	43 563	47.6	33 185	44.3	7 356	60.0	23 936	28.7
Warren	1 293	554	25 726	14.0	2.41	27.3	32.8	26.5	17 068	46.2	13 361	42.2	2 671	61.2	8 658	27.9
Washington	3 748	3 328	22 458	10.9	2.55	24.0	36.2	26.3	15 798	47.2	12 394	43.2	2 335	61.3	6 660	27.3
Wayne	1 729	1 262	34 908	9.2	2.64	22.4	38.8	23.0	25 066	50.3	19 792	46.1	3 607	66.0	9 842	22.8
Westchester	23 653	13 656	337 142	5.3	2.67	25.7	36.6	26.8	235 201	48.8	181 690	49.0	41 145	51.5	101 941	10.6
Wyoming	4 421	4 303	14 906	7.3	2.62	23.2	36.6	24.7	10 713	47.5	8 687	44.3	1 368	61.3	4 193	24.5
Yates	1 193	476	9 029	7.2	2.59	24.6	34.2	28.3	6 284	45.3	5 054	40.5	852	64.0	2 745	18.4

[1] As of April 1.   [2] Includes people under formally authorized, supervised care or custody in institutions at the time of enumeration (such as correctional institutions, nursing homes, and juvenile institutions).   [3] Under 18 years.   [4] No husband present.

Sources: Group Quarters Population—U.S. Census Bureau, 2000 Census of Population and Housing, "Census 2000 Profiles of General Demographic Characteristics" data files, published May 2001 (related Internet site <http://www.census.gov/mp/www/pub/2000cen/mscen01.html>).   Households, 2000—U.S. Census Bureau, 2000 Census of Population and Housing, "Census 2000 Profiles of General Demographic Characteristics" data files, published May 2001 (related Internet site <http://www.census.gov/mp/www/pub/2000cen/mscen01.html>).   Households, 1990—U.S. Census Bureau, 1990 Census of Population and Housing, Summary Tape File (STF) 1C on CD-ROM (related Internet site <http://homer.ssd.census.gov/cdrom/lookup>).

[Includes U.S., states, and 3,142 counties or county equivalents defined as of January 1, 1992. For changes to these areas since then, see appendix B. Geographic Information]

County	Group quarters population, 2000[1]		Households, 2000 (April 1)													
						Percent—			By type—							
									Family households (families)						Nonfamily households	
							With 1 or more persons under 18 years	With 1 or more persons 65 years and over		Per-cent with own children under 18 years	Married-couple		Female householder[4]			
	Number	Institu-tionalized population[2]	Number	Percent change, 1990–2000	Per-sons per house-hold	One-person			Number		Number	Per-cent with own chil-dren[3]	Number	Per-cent with own chil-dren[3]	Number	Percent change, 1990–2000
NORTH CAROLINA......	253 881	106 659	3 132 013	24.4	2.49	25.4	35.3	21.8	2 158 869	46.1	1 645 346	43.0	389 997	58.3	973 144	38.0
Alamance.................	3 751	1 142	51 584	20.9	2.46	26.0	34.4	24.8	35 526	45.1	26 851	41.7	6 526	58.0	16 058	34.9
Alexander................	235	186	13 137	27.2	2.54	21.9	35.9	21.8	9 744	44.2	7 945	41.6	1 238	57.4	3 393	48.7
Alleghany................	209	148	4 593	18.0	2.28	27.8	26.9	32.2	3 169	35.9	2 676	33.6	345	49.6	1 424	33.7
Anson	1 427	1 401	9 204	7.9	2.59	25.1	37.4	28.4	6 667	42.8	4 402	38.6	1 819	51.2	2 537	16.8
Ashe	301	235	10 411	17.7	2.31	25.8	28.4	30.1	7 422	36.7	6 184	34.2	877	48.9	2 989	42.3
Avery	1 874	1 405	6 532	18.3	2.34	26.6	29.7	28.7	4 546	39.0	3 732	36.9	595	48.2	1 986	46.2
Beaufort................	577	459	18 319	13.4	2.42	25.7	32.7	28.0	12 954	40.8	9 823	36.3	2 438	57.1	5 365	24.3
Bertie	198	153	7 743	4.5	2.53	27.0	36.2	30.6	5 424	42.5	3 563	38.9	1 554	50.4	2 319	21.4
Bladen	698	516	12 897	19.9	2.45	27.7	35.3	26.2	8 935	43.8	6 305	40.4	2 031	53.6	3 962	44.4
Brunswick	724	309	30 438	51.7	2.38	22.9	29.2	28.4	22 028	35.5	17 695	30.4	3 105	56.9	8 410	76.0
Buncombe	6 765	3 444	85 776	21.1	2.33	28.9	30.2	25.7	55 661	42.4	43 280	38.8	9 227	56.5	30 115	40.3
Burke	3 610	3 089	34 528	18.3	2.48	25.5	34.4	24.2	24 331	44.0	18 940	41.1	3 787	54.4	10 197	36.5
Cabarrus	2 169	1 400	49 519	32.0	2.60	21.8	38.2	21.2	36 526	47.2	29 310	45.3	5 216	57.1	12 993	42.0
Caldwell	1 149	902	30 768	13.2	2.48	23.1	35.0	23.6	22 399	42.7	17 622	39.5	3 389	54.9	8 369	28.4
Camden	4	4	2 662	22.1	2.58	20.7	35.8	26.7	2 024	41.6	1 656	41.0	251	42.2	638	30.7
Carteret	1 084	675	25 204	18.7	2.31	26.1	29.1	27.9	17 376	38.4	14 116	34.0	2 407	58.7	7 828	31.3
Caswell.................	1 299	1 151	8 670	16.1	2.56	23.2	35.8	25.6	6 401	42.0	4 786	40.3	1 233	49.1	2 269	34.5
Catawba	2 142	1 000	55 533	21.5	2.51	24.6	35.0	22.5	39 111	44.7	30 622	42.1	6 042	55.6	16 422	37.7
Chatham	603	557	19 741	29.1	2.47	24.5	31.9	26.2	13 855	41.1	11 110	39.1	1 967	51.0	5 886	44.8
Cherokee	284	231	10 336	29.8	2.32	25.7	28.4	32.8	7 373	35.9	6 081	33.1	965	49.2	2 963	56.2
Chowan	699	301	5 580	9.1	2.48	25.3	34.8	31.2	4 007	42.2	2 955	36.8	875	60.0	1 573	17.6
Clay....................	124	104	3 847	31.4	2.25	26.3	25.9	35.8	2 727	33.2	2 299	30.1	289	52.6	1 120	49.1
Cleveland...............	2 480	1 060	37 046	15.6	2.53	23.6	36.7	24.4	27 001	44.1	20 359	40.7	5 085	55.5	10 045	29.5
Columbus................	1 379	831	21 308	15.4	2.50	26.5	36.5	26.4	15 048	44.6	10 823	41.1	3 366	54.7	6 260	33.0
Craven	5 137	1 474	34 582	17.1	2.50	23.4	36.7	24.8	25 060	45.9	19 643	41.8	4 306	63.0	9 522	34.9
Cumberland..............	18 466	1 795	107 358	17.3	2.65	22.4	43.5	15.9	77 656	54.5	56 740	51.1	16 688	65.0	29 702	37.9
Currituck...............	163	163	6 902	37.0	2.61	19.4	37.4	22.6	5 203	44.5	4 255	41.8	638	57.5	1 699	43.5
Dare	232	163	12 690	35.7	2.34	25.0	29.5	23.1	8 451	41.0	6 981	36.8	1 026	61.4	4 239	45.0
Davidson................	1 896	1 430	58 156	18.8	2.50	22.9	36.0	22.7	42 535	44.7	33 713	41.8	6 295	56.0	15 621	32.7
Davie...................	376	302	13 750	27.5	2.51	22.2	35.3	24.3	10 261	43.8	8 443	41.6	1 260	53.8	3 489	38.7
Duplin	982	339	18 267	22.4	2.63	24.5	38.0	25.3	13 067	46.4	9 543	44.5	2 601	53.9	5 200	33.7
Durham	9 810	2 734	89 015	23.1	2.40	30.0	32.6	17.0	54 045	47.9	37 410	43.9	13 193	61.0	34 970	32.9
Edgecombe..............	1 122	915	20 392	.4	2.67	24.0	39.8	25.4	14 812	45.2	9 423	41.3	4 375	54.1	5 580	6.6
Forsyth.................	9 949	3 799	123 851	15.3	2.39	28.9	33.6	21.9	81 693	46.2	60 569	42.0	16 718	60.5	42 158	21.2
Franklin................	1 251	860	17 843	32.1	2.58	23.5	37.6	20.9	12 875	46.4	9 722	44.7	2 345	52.5	4 968	43.8
Gaston	3 091	2 176	73 936	13.1	2.53	23.3	36.5	22.9	53 327	44.4	40 066	41.6	9 784	53.9	20 609	32.2
Gates	157	88	3 901	16.4	2.66	21.7	39.6	28.6	2 933	45.5	2 233	43.9	519	51.6	968	27.5
Graham	117	89	3 354	21.0	2.35	26.0	30.1	30.1	2 411	37.7	2 038	35.7	282	48.2	943	55.6
Granville...............	5 491	5 371	16 654	26.8	2.58	23.9	38.2	23.2	12 048	46.0	8 840	44.0	2 490	53.2	4 606	41.7
Greene	1 223	1 183	6 696	24.1	2.65	22.6	39.6	25.0	4 958	46.3	3 490	44.0	1 157	53.4	1 738	30.8
Guilford................	13 977	3 132	168 667	22.5	2.41	27.9	33.5	20.6	109 819	46.7	80 910	43.2	22 537	59.8	58 848	31.3
Halifax.................	1 760	1 568	22 122	8.8	2.51	27.7	36.9	28.5	15 302	45.1	9 766	40.5	4 510	55.7	6 820	24.9
Harnett	2 887	1 407	33 800	34.4	2.61	23.3	40.2	20.0	24 107	50.4	17 985	47.2	4 573	61.8	9 693	46.4
Haywood	961	643	23 100	20.2	2.30	26.7	28.8	30.8	16 043	37.7	13 093	34.3	2 200	53.2	7 057	38.6
Henderson	1 841	1 269	37 414	30.3	2.33	25.7	28.3	33.8	26 357	36.9	21 943	33.7	3 160	54.2	11 057	46.6
Hertford	420	300	8 953	9.9	2.48	26.9	35.9	28.5	6 237	43.0	4 103	38.0	1 748	54.2	2 716	21.8
Hoke	1 126	1 053	11 373	53.6	2.86	19.0	47.7	16.7	8 746	53.9	5 992	51.6	2 068	61.7	2 627	63.1
Hyde	666	659	2 185	4.3	2.36	30.6	30.8	31.7	1 434	40.2	1 064	39.8	287	42.2	751	33.9
Iredell	1 583	1 054	47 360	33.1	2.56	22.7	36.9	22.2	34 658	45.8	27 396	43.1	5 334	57.4	12 702	45.9
Jackson	2 752	196	13 191	36.2	2.30	27.0	28.3	24.7	8 586	39.2	6 774	35.0	1 317	55.7	4 605	69.7
Johnston	1 717	1 445	46 595	47.6	2.58	23.1	38.8	19.0	33 692	49.0	26 916	46.6	4 918	61.7	12 903	54.5
Jones	119	103	4 061	16.3	2.53	24.5	36.4	28.7	2 938	43.8	2 121	40.3	619	54.9	1 123	31.7
Lee	896	757	18 466	17.7	2.61	23.5	37.6	23.8	13 361	46.0	10 019	42.3	2 472	59.4	5 105	29.2
Lenoir	1 769	1 378	23 862	8.8	2.43	28.4	35.5	26.7	16 182	46.1	11 066	40.7	4 139	60.1	7 680	21.4
Lincoln	891	668	24 041	28.1	2.62	20.1	37.7	21.4	18 181	45.2	14 713	43.2	2 407	54.0	5 860	42.8
McDowell	1 394	1 253	16 604	21.4	2.45	24.3	33.9	25.7	11 962	42.1	9 550	39.3	1 690	52.1	4 642	40.1
Macon	533	273	12 828	30.4	2.28	27.0	27.1	36.0	8 908	35.7	7 506	32.3	1 021	53.5	3 920	50.8
Madison	895	199	8 000	23.3	2.34	26.3	30.8	27.7	5 595	40.6	4 601	37.6	714	55.0	2 405	43.0
Martin	291	4	10 020	7.5	2.53	25.7	36.3	28.6	7 198	44.0	5 038	40.6	1 764	53.9	2 822	16.8
Mecklenburg.............	15 412	6 114	273 416	36.6	2.49	27.6	35.2	15.3	175 063	50.1	130 511	47.8	33 926	61.0	98 353	49.3
Mitchell	187	140	6 551	13.4	2.37	25.2	29.7	31.0	4 737	37.8	3 990	35.7	533	49.3	1 814	33.5
Montgomery	1 081	1 008	9 848	18.8	2.61	24.1	35.7	26.9	7 187	42.5	5 475	40.2	1 225	50.5	2 661	32.0
Moore	1 662	1 014	30 713	28.9	2.38	24.9	29.7	33.9	21 950	37.3	17 836	33.1	3 125	57.2	8 763	38.1
Nash	2 127	1 338	33 644	15.9	2.54	25.0	36.9	23.3	23 931	46.0	17 733	43.3	4 882	55.7	9 713	24.3
New Hanover	4 266	1 169	68 183	41.6	2.29	28.9	28.6	21.5	41 599	42.8	31 722	38.3	7 831	60.1	26 584	68.9
Northampton	881	842	8 691	14.5	2.44	28.4	33.7	31.5	5 952	40.5	3 953	35.7	1 589	51.4	2 739	40.7
Onslow..................	19 415	411	48 122	18.4	2.72	18.6	45.7	14.4	36 594	56.1	29 354	53.2	5 569	68.8	11 528	50.0

[1] As of April 1.   [2] Includes people under formally authorized, supervised care or custody in institutions at the time of enumeration (such as correctional institutions, nursing homes, and juvenile institutions).   [3] Under 18 years.   [4] No husband present.

Sources: Group Quarters Population—U.S. Census Bureau, 2000 Census of Population and Housing, "Census 2000 Profiles of General Demographic Characteristics" data files, published May 2001 (related Internet site <http://www.census.gov/mp/www/pub/2000cen/mscen01.html>).   Households, 2000—U.S. Census Bureau, 2000 Census of Population and Housing, "Census 2000 Profiles of General Demographic Characteristics" data files, published May 2001 (related Internet site <http://www.census.gov/mp/www/pub/2000cen/mscen01.html>).   Households, 1990—U.S. Census Bureau, 1990 Census of Population and Housing, Summary Tape File (STF) 1C on CD-ROM (related Internet site <http://homer.ssd.census.gov/cdrom/lookup>).

[Includes U.S., states, and 3,142 counties or county equivalents defined as of January 1, 1992. For changes to these areas since then, see appendix B. Geographic Information]

County	Group quarters population, 2000[1] Number	Institutionalized population[2]	Households, 2000 (April 1) Number	Percent change, 1990–2000	Persons per household	Percent— One-person	With 1 or more persons under 18 years	With 1 or more persons 65 years and over	Family households (families) Number	Percent with own children under 18	Married-couple Number	Percent with own children[3]	Female householder[4] Number	Percent with own children[3]	Nonfamily households Number	Percent change, 1990–2000
NORTH CAROLINA–Con.																
Orange	9 943	990	45 863	27.0	2.36	28.1	30.3	15.3	26 126	49.7	20 446	47.3	4 316	62.0	19 737	31.7
Pamlico	628	616	5 178	14.5	2.38	25.0	30.2	33.7	3 718	35.2	2 933	32.3	596	46.5	1 460	28.0
Pasquotank	2 434	1 250	12 907	13.4	2.52	25.4	37.6	26.4	9 094	47.4	6 503	42.0	2 098	63.5	3 813	24.7
Pender	1 164	1 011	16 054	44.5	2.49	22.9	33.5	25.2	11 712	40.3	9 288	37.1	1 795	53.4	4 342	61.3
Perquimans	120	108	4 645	16.5	2.42	24.1	31.9	33.0	3 378	38.8	2 624	35.1	584	52.6	1 267	33.4
Person	394	361	14 085	23.3	2.50	24.2	35.4	25.0	10 115	43.9	7 580	40.9	1 940	54.7	3 970	39.2
Pitt	6 333	988	52 559	29.8	2.43	28.3	33.4	17.6	32 237	48.7	22 794	45.0	7 558	60.7	20 302	44.4
Polk	328	301	7 908	29.4	2.28	28.9	26.2	36.7	5 338	34.9	4 456	32.0	625	48.8	2 570	45.7
Randolph	1 345	934	50 659	23.3	2.55	22.5	37.0	22.0	37 348	45.7	29 956	43.1	5 148	57.8	13 311	36.8
Richmond	1 702	1 194	17 873	6.4	2.51	26.3	36.9	25.8	12 574	45.6	8 628	40.7	3 042	58.1	5 299	17.2
Robeson	3 330	2 362	43 677	20.8	2.75	22.7	43.8	21.1	32 015	50.5	20 367	46.4	9 018	59.1	11 662	33.7
Rockingham	1 186	735	36 989	10.6	2.45	25.7	34.2	26.3	26 194	42.5	19 830	39.9	4 725	51.9	10 795	23.0
Rowan	4 696	2 744	49 940	17.5	2.52	24.7	36.1	24.7	35 495	45.6	27 356	42.2	5 922	58.7	14 445	26.1
Rutherford	1 532	1 374	25 191	13.5	2.44	25.5	33.7	27.2	17 938	42.2	13 967	38.8	2 949	55.1	7 253	26.8
Sampson	1 349	569	22 273	27.1	2.64	23.7	38.2	25.1	16 222	45.9	11 940	43.8	3 188	53.5	6 051	39.6
Scotland	977	384	13 399	13.2	2.61	24.4	40.4	22.1	9 673	47.6	6 308	42.1	2 734	59.5	3 726	30.0
Stanly	1 788	1 242	22 223	12.5	2.53	24.3	35.8	25.9	16 156	44.8	12 953	42.1	2 332	57.2	6 067	26.9
Stokes	573	403	17 579	24.5	2.51	22.8	36.8	21.0	13 035	45.5	10 652	43.2	1 709	57.0	4 544	46.5
Surry	1 270	1 032	28 408	17.1	2.46	25.0	33.7	26.7	20 484	42.7	16 585	40.9	2 758	52.2	7 924	32.1
Swain	415	226	5 137	23.1	2.44	25.8	33.9	27.2	3 631	42.4	2 686	37.3	714	54.5	1 506	38.2
Transylvania	1 044	273	12 320	24.1	2.30	26.1	27.3	34.0	8 666	35.7	7 219	31.5	1 066	56.4	3 654	50.5
Tyrrell	437	427	1 537	4.5	2.42	28.2	34.0	33.4	1 056	41.6	729	37.6	255	52.9	481	22.4
Union	1 666	931	43 390	48.1	2.81	17.0	43.0	17.9	34 280	50.0	28 338	49.2	4 249	55.4	9 110	57.7
Vance	829	484	16 199	14.4	2.60	24.2	38.9	24.2	11 643	46.6	7 613	41.6	3 304	57.5	4 556	24.3
Wake	19 192	6 201	242 040	46.0	2.51	25.7	36.2	13.5	158 765	51.9	127 114	50.2	23 755	62.6	83 275	48.2
Warren	853	766	7 708	22.3	2.48	26.2	33.5	31.5	5 448	39.9	3 794	35.8	1 336	50.8	2 260	46.5
Washington	174	152	5 367	6.2	2.52	24.7	36.2	28.9	3 906	43.6	2 690	37.8	1 010	59.4	1 461	20.4
Watauga	5 392	214	16 540	20.8	2.26	28.6	24.7	20.1	9 410	40.7	7 845	38.1	1 129	55.9	7 130	35.1
Wayne	4 635	3 096	42 612	15.5	2.55	24.5	38.7	22.0	30 244	48.8	21 975	45.1	6 552	60.2	12 368	32.8
Wilkes	906	765	26 650	15.8	2.43	24.5	33.0	24.9	19 311	41.7	15 746	39.3	2 501	52.8	7 339	35.0
Wilson	1 865	1 116	28 613	14.0	2.51	26.4	36.5	23.8	19 782	46.2	13 775	42.3	4 733	58.1	8 831	25.0
Yadkin	473	310	14 505	20.2	2.47	24.0	34.8	25.1	10 593	43.9	8 710	41.8	1 311	53.8	3 912	35.1
Yancey	151	119	7 472	22.0	2.36	25.4	29.5	30.9	5 373	38.0	4 572	36.4	583	47.2	2 099	45.7
NORTH DAKOTA	23 631	9 688	257 152	6.8	2.41	29.3	32.7	24.7	166 150	48.4	137 433	45.1	20 148	67.7	91 002	22.0
Adams	79	71	1 121	−11.5	2.24	32.6	27.5	36.7	725	41.1	635	37.0	62	72.6	396	−.5
Barnes	571	213	4 884	−1.8	2.29	31.5	28.4	32.7	3 118	43.0	2 631	39.8	333	62.5	1 766	8.1
Benson	52	42	2 328	−3.6	2.97	24.5	44.0	28.6	1 701	52.0	1 128	45.2	387	66.1	627	6.6
Billings	–	–	366	−5.4	2.43	26.8	30.3	27.6	256	41.8	229	43.7	16	31.3	110	34.1
Bottineau	327	135	2 962	−4.6	2.30	31.5	28.3	34.2	1 954	41.5	1 739	39.5	126	61.1	1 008	8.2
Bowman	90	82	1 358	−4.4	2.32	31.5	30.3	34.4	891	45.0	808	43.4	55	61.8	467	8.4
Burke	1	–	1 013	−19.1	2.21	31.6	23.6	40.4	681	34.2	590	32.2	54	53.7	332	−14.7
Burleigh	2 526	1 398	27 670	22.0	2.42	28.1	33.8	21.2	18 198	49.6	14 954	46.4	2 415	67.1	9 472	37.8
Cass	4 087	889	51 315	27.4	2.32	31.2	30.9	16.0	29 825	51.4	24 251	48.4	3 920	68.8	21 490	42.7
Cavalier	119	98	2 017	−15.1	2.34	30.8	28.1	36.7	1 361	40.8	1 227	39.7	77	53.2	656	−6.6
Dickey	374	182	2 283	−.7	2.36	32.0	29.0	34.6	1 500	42.4	1 325	39.8	111	65.8	783	15.0
Divide	90	90	1 005	−15.8	2.18	33.4	23.5	42.1	649	34.8	571	32.9	42	54.8	356	−1.4
Dunn	53	53	1 378	−3.8	2.57	25.3	33.5	30.6	987	44.7	831	43.1	99	52.5	391	8.9
Eddy	78	78	1 164	−2.5	2.30	34.2	28.1	39.1	744	43.3	657	40.5	58	69.0	420	6.9
Emmons	85	70	1 786	−3.4	2.38	28.4	28.3	40.4	1 241	39.1	1 090	37.4	79	54.4	545	15.5
Foster	83	77	1 540	−.1	2.39	30.6	32.1	34.7	1 032	46.2	885	44.4	99	59.6	508	15.7
Golden Valley	115	114	761	−6.2	2.38	31.5	30.5	34.7	507	43.8	444	40.1	37	75.7	254	−3.8
Grand Forks	4 405	678	25 435	.4	2.43	28.3	33.5	17.2	15 623	52.7	12 584	49.1	2 237	71.8	9 812	15.7
Grant	89	54	1 195	−13.0	2.30	31.8	26.0	39.3	801	37.5	726	36.5	46	56.5	394	5.3
Griggs	57	57	1 178	−9.0	2.29	31.6	27.4	39.8	781	40.3	699	40.3	55	45.5	397	15.7
Hettinger	65	59	1 152	−14.1	2.30	31.2	27.2	39.6	779	39.0	705	37.0	44	63.6	373	4.2
Kidder	45	45	1 158	−7.1	2.34	29.9	28.0	38.9	788	40.0	703	38.3	47	55.3	370	27.1
LaMoure	79	76	1 942	−6.4	2.38	30.8	28.6	37.4	1 308	40.9	1 174	38.8	78	59.0	634	7.1
Logan	72	36	963	−12.1	2.32	29.2	26.3	40.7	660	37.6	608	37.0	30	56.7	303	9.4
McHenry	63	47	2 526	−1.0	2.35	29.8	29.8	35.6	1 701	42.0	1 469	39.8	142	61.3	825	15.5
McIntosh	174	162	1 467	−13.0	2.19	32.0	22.6	47.0	975	33.5	885	31.6	51	62.7	492	.2
McKenzie	61	61	2 151	−6.5	2.64	25.8	37.7	29.4	1 549	47.9	1 245	43.9	199	62.3	602	−2.4
McLean	168	154	3 815	−3.0	2.40	26.6	30.6	32.6	2 711	41.2	2 376	38.5	214	65.4	1 104	5.7
Mercer	121	86	3 346	−6.0	2.55	24.8	38.3	24.6	2 445	50.7	2 182	48.4	172	70.9	901	5.6
Morton	480	418	9 889	14.0	2.51	25.7	36.3	25.1	6 931	49.8	5 758	45.7	845	74.3	2 958	28.2
Mountrail	164	151	2 560	−1.0	2.53	28.5	35.4	30.3	1 753	46.4	1 326	41.7	301	60.5	807	9.6
Nelson	160	146	1 628	−11.1	2.18	36.3	25.3	41.6	1 005	39.2	876	37.6	85	52.9	623	3.7
Oliver	1	–	791	−2.2	2.61	21.0	36.4	26.7	604	46.5	547	44.4	31	64.5	187	13.3
Pembina	187	152	3 535	−.6	2.38	30.5	30.6	32.3	2 365	44.6	2 057	42.1	189	61.4	1 170	12.5
Pierce	134	93	1 964	−.5	2.31	32.0	29.2	36.4	1 277	43.4	1 107	39.7	124	74.2	687	12.4

[1] As of April 1. [2] Includes people under formally authorized, supervised care or custody in institutions at the time of enumeration (such as correctional institutions, nursing homes, and juvenile institutions). [3] Under 18 years. [4] No husband present.

Sources: Group Quarters Population—U.S. Census Bureau, 2000 Census of Population and Housing, "Census 2000 Profiles of General Demographic Characteristics" data files, published May 2001 (related Internet site <http://www.census.gov/mp/www/pub/2000cen/mscen01.html>). Households, 2000—U.S. Census Bureau, 2000 Census of Population and Housing, "Census 2000 Profiles of General Demographic Characteristics" data files, published May 2001 (related Internet site <http://www.census.gov/mp/www/pub/2000cen/mscen01.html>). Households, 1990—U.S. Census Bureau, 1990 Census of Population and Housing, Summary Tape File (STF) 1C on CD-ROM (related Internet site <http://homer.ssd.census.gov/cdrom/lookup>).

[Includes U.S., states, and 3,142 counties or county equivalents defined as of January 1, 1992. For changes to these areas since then, see appendix B. Geographic Information]

County	Group quarters population, 2000[1] — Number	Institutionalized population[2]	Households, 2000 (April 1) — Number	Percent change, 1990–2000	Persons per household	Percent — One-person	With 1 or more persons under 18 years	With 1 or more persons 65 years and over	Family households (families) — Number	Percent with own children under 18 years	Married-couple — Number	Percent with own children[3]	Female householder[4] — Number	Percent with own children[3]	Nonfamily households — Number	Percent change, 1990–2000
NORTH DAKOTA—Con.																
Ramsey	442	289	4 957	−.4	2.34	31.1	31.5	30.1	3 187	46.5	2 566	41.9	422	69.0	1 770	9.1
Ransom	266	266	2 350	2.9	2.39	30.7	29.3	32.1	1 560	46.7	1 366	44.9	120	64.2	790	16.7
Renville	57	57	1 085	−10.3	2.35	28.5	29.3	34.2	749	41.5	655	39.2	61	55.7	336	4.3
Richland	1 295	317	6 885	5.6	2.43	29.4	33.6	25.6	4 427	50.4	3 733	48.4	446	65.7	2 458	22.3
Rolette	162	121	4 556	9.8	2.97	22.6	50.0	21.7	3 367	59.3	2 003	51.9	1 032	71.0	1 189	15.5
Sargent	29	29	1 786	1.3	2.43	27.7	31.2	29.3	1 243	43.6	1 089	42.1	70	60.0	543	9.7
Sheridan	20	20	731	−14.8	2.31	27.5	26.0	42.0	515	35.5	459	34.0	32	62.5	216	2.9
Sioux	64	42	1 095	7.1	3.63	16.6	61.1	16.1	872	61.5	428	58.9	319	64.9	223	14.9
Slope	–	–	313	−6.0	2.45	27.2	31.6	31.0	223	42.2	202	41.1	12	41.7	90	7.1
Stark	871	316	8 932	5.3	2.44	29.1	33.6	26.1	5 874	48.9	4 900	46.1	705	66.2	3 058	22.2
Steele	–	–	923	−6.9	2.45	28.3	31.0	33.3	635	43.1	575	40.7	41	70.7	288	−.7
Stutsman	1 523	789	8 954	3.4	2.28	32.7	29.8	29.3	5 648	45.7	4 699	41.8	670	66.6	3 306	16.6
Towner	68	68	1 218	−15.0	2.31	33.6	28.7	36.4	786	42.4	693	39.7	56	66.1	432	−6.5
Traill	429	196	3 341	.4	2.41	29.3	32.0	31.1	2 232	46.2	1 939	44.4	182	63.7	1 109	9.0
Walsh	382	202	5 029	−3.8	2.39	31.3	31.6	31.9	3 321	46.3	2 769	43.2	377	64.2	1 708	10.3
Ward	2 171	646	23 041	7.2	2.46	27.2	35.7	21.6	15 370	51.5	12 724	48.2	1 927	69.4	7 671	23.2
Wells	118	99	2 215	−7.9	2.25	32.6	26.5	39.9	1 454	38.7	1 298	37.0	106	58.5	761	4.8
Williams	479	164	8 095	.7	2.38	30.9	33.0	27.4	5 261	48.1	4 313	43.4	710	71.7	2 834	18.1
OHIO	299 121	172 368	4 445 773	8.8	2.49	27.3	34.5	23.8	2 993 023	47.1	2 285 798	43.6	536 878	60.2	1 452 750	21.8
Adams	342	214	10 501	14.2	2.57	24.0	37.1	25.0	7 616	46.9	6 000	43.6	1 095	60.7	2 885	35.1
Allen	6 113	4 560	40 646	3.1	2.52	26.3	35.8	25.7	28 213	47.4	21 562	42.6	5 043	65.1	12 433	19.1
Ashland	2 228	742	19 524	14.2	2.58	24.0	35.0	25.3	14 015	45.2	11 616	41.8	1 652	63.0	5 509	25.7
Ashtabula	1 765	1 351	39 397	7.2	2.56	24.8	35.6	26.3	27 768	46.0	21 581	42.0	4 478	60.9	11 629	20.8
Athens	8 238	677	22 501	11.7	2.40	28.3	28.5	18.6	12 710	46.7	9 797	42.4	2 067	61.7	9 791	28.3
Auglaize	1 101	721	17 376	8.8	2.62	23.3	37.1	25.0	12 776	48.0	10 792	45.4	1 359	62.5	4 600	23.8
Belmont	3 148	3 038	28 309	.5	2.37	28.7	30.7	32.3	19 263	41.6	15 038	38.4	3 165	54.6	9 046	13.9
Brown	453	373	15 555	25.7	2.69	20.2	40.7	22.2	11 785	48.9	9 535	45.9	1 552	61.6	3 770	43.7
Butler	11 247	2 956	123 082	17.7	2.61	22.7	38.3	20.1	87 892	49.6	70 152	47.0	13 150	61.4	35 190	32.3
Carroll	366	254	11 126	15.1	2.56	22.9	34.7	25.6	8 156	43.5	6 885	40.7	852	60.1	2 970	32.9
Champaign	680	427	14 952	12.8	2.56	23.5	36.4	22.7	10 868	46.7	8 924	43.5	1 369	60.0	4 084	26.6
Clark	3 917	2 001	56 648	2.6	2.49	26.0	34.6	25.7	39 383	45.1	29 786	40.3	7 271	61.2	17 265	16.8
Clermont	1 465	1 184	66 013	25.2	2.67	21.0	40.9	18.4	49 077	51.2	39 842	48.8	6 601	62.2	16 936	48.8
Clinton	1 002	292	15 416	18.2	2.56	23.7	37.5	22.8	11 075	48.3	8 846	44.3	1 556	65.8	4 341	32.4
Columbiana	3 764	3 320	42 973	5.4	2.52	24.8	34.5	27.9	30 688	44.4	24 527	41.5	4 446	56.6	12 285	18.9
Coshocton	464	326	14 356	6.9	2.52	25.4	34.8	26.6	10 168	46.0	8 291	42.1	1 323	63.6	4 188	18.5
Crawford	609	459	18 957	3.1	2.45	26.3	33.7	26.3	13 173	44.9	10 448	40.4	1 982	63.8	5 784	17.8
Cuyahoga	30 178	17 186	571 457	1.5	2.39	32.8	31.7	27.3	354 615	46.0	242 389	42.2	89 793	56.9	216 842	12.3
Darke	954	490	20 419	4.9	2.56	23.5	35.5	26.0	14 898	45.6	12 450	42.6	1 634	60.5	5 521	21.0
Defiance	605	313	15 138	7.6	2.57	23.0	36.9	23.0	11 016	47.2	8 923	42.8	1 456	66.8	4 122	20.0
Delaware	2 727	1 137	39 674	71.6	2.70	18.1	41.8	15.5	30 658	51.9	26 876	50.5	2 667	63.0	9 016	90.2
Erie	1 868	1 584	31 727	9.7	2.45	27.0	33.3	25.8	21 750	44.4	17 027	40.0	3 561	61.9	9 977	25.1
Fairfield	2 591	2 512	45 425	23.4	2.65	20.7	39.4	21.1	34 149	49.0	28 465	46.6	4 117	61.6	11 276	40.6
Fayette	650	447	11 054	8.1	2.51	24.5	36.0	25.4	7 841	45.7	6 059	40.9	1 268	62.2	3 213	26.5
Franklin	22 106	7 674	438 778	15.9	2.39	30.9	33.1	17.2	263 601	50.7	188 793	46.6	57 195	63.4	175 177	28.0
Fulton	430	376	15 480	14.6	2.69	21.1	39.5	23.3	11 693	49.2	9 783	46.5	1 277	62.5	3 787	28.6
Gallia	945	484	12 060	6.1	2.50	25.2	35.8	24.8	8 592	46.4	6 809	42.7	1 323	61.1	3 468	22.8
Geauga	1 047	771	31 630	17.6	2.84	17.6	39.0	22.8	24 997	47.0	21 782	46.5	2 279	53.0	6 633	39.9
Greene	7 781	1 338	55 312	14.4	2.53	23.0	35.0	21.2	39 159	46.3	32 090	43.3	5 323	62.1	16 153	38.9
Guernsey	507	418	16 094	8.1	2.50	26.1	35.4	26.1	11 234	46.4	8 674	41.9	1 827	61.7	4 860	18.4
Hamilton	18 974	11 055	346 790	2.3	2.38	32.9	33.0	23.3	212 459	49.3	150 483	44.8	49 609	62.6	134 331	14.3
Hancock	1 728	859	27 898	13.2	2.49	26.0	34.9	22.6	19 127	47.5	15 734	44.0	2 435	65.0	8 771	32.8
Hardin	1 915	229	11 963	6.3	2.51	26.5	34.1	24.2	8 129	46.2	6 581	42.4	1 066	64.0	3 834	20.3
Harrison	271	268	6 398	4.7	2.44	25.6	31.5	29.8	4 517	41.2	3 742	38.0	564	58.3	1 881	21.6
Henry	579	415	10 935	5.1	2.62	23.5	37.3	25.1	7 966	48.4	6 677	45.5	890	63.3	2 969	18.9
Highland	426	323	15 587	17.8	2.60	23.2	37.5	25.9	11 395	46.5	9 102	43.4	1 606	58.5	4 192	29.2
Hocking	725	670	10 843	16.0	2.54	23.7	36.3	23.4	7 824	46.5	6 319	42.6	1 032	62.4	3 019	34.6
Holmes	911	891	11 337	21.7	3.35	16.1	46.0	21.2	9 190	54.6	8 109	55.0	736	52.2	2 147	32.4
Huron	579	532	22 307	10.2	2.64	23.1	38.9	23.2	16 225	49.9	13 053	46.4	2 316	65.6	6 082	24.9
Jackson	438	408	12 619	12.1	2.55	24.0	38.2	24.5	9 130	47.7	6 987	44.5	1 520	58.6	3 489	26.0
Jefferson	2 104	839	30 411	−2.9	2.36	28.5	29.3	32.5	20 596	39.4	15 922	36.0	3 541	52.3	9 821	12.8
Knox	3 462	926	19 975	15.9	2.56	23.9	34.7	25.6	14 364	45.2	11 913	42.1	1 701	61.1	5 611	26.1
Lake	2 900	1 894	89 700	11.5	2.50	25.6	33.2	25.1	62 564	44.5	50 292	42.9	8 978	52.2	27 136	30.5
Lawrence	618	534	24 732	8.0	2.49	24.9	35.3	23.9	17 809	44.4	13 843	41.0	2 948	57.3	6 923	30.0
Licking	3 255	1 172	55 609	17.7	2.56	23.1	37.1	22.1	40 126	47.7	32 557	44.1	5 582	63.0	15 483	32.6
Logan	585	561	17 956	12.6	2.53	24.8	36.0	24.2	12 731	46.9	10 242	42.6	1 707	65.3	5 225	24.4
Lorain	8 484	6 058	105 836	10.2	2.61	23.6	37.1	23.8	76 192	46.7	58 469	43.0	13 324	60.9	29 644	28.2
Lucas	8 896	4 268	182 847	3.0	2.44	30.1	34.1	23.1	116 330	48.9	81 807	43.8	26 838	63.4	66 517	15.1
Madison	4 426	4 273	13 672	14.0	2.62	22.3	38.4	22.6	10 034	47.9	8 096	44.9	1 354	61.1	3 638	33.2
Mahoning	7 247	5 321	102 587	1.4	2.44	29.1	31.5	31.2	68 865	42.3	50 285	39.2	14 476	53.6	33 722	18.4

[1] As of April 1. [2] Includes people under formally authorized, supervised care or custody in institutions at the time of enumeration (such as correctional institutions, nursing homes, and juvenile institutions). [3] Under 18 years. [4] No husband present.

Sources: Group Quarters Population–U.S. Census Bureau, 2000 Census of Population and Housing, "Census 2000 Profiles of General Demographic Characteristics" data files, published May 2001 (related Internet site <http://www.census.gov/mp/www/pub/2000cen/mscen01.html>). Households, 2000–U.S. Census Bureau, 2000 Census of Population and Housing, "Census 2000 Profiles of General Demographic Characteristics" data files, published May 2001 (related Internet site <http://www.census.gov/mp/www/pub/2000cen/mscen01.html>). Households, 1990–U.S. Census Bureau, 1990 Census of Population and Housing, Summary Tape File (STF) 1C on CD-ROM (related Internet site <http://homer.ssd.census.gov/cdrom/lookup>).

[Includes U.S., states, and 3,142 counties or county equivalents defined as of January 1, 1992. For changes to these areas since then, see appendix B. Geographic Information]

County	Group quarters population, 2000[1] Number	Institutionalized population[2]	Households, 2000 (April 1) Number	Percent change, 1990–2000	Persons per household	Percent— One-person	With 1 or more persons under 18 years	With 1 or more persons 65 years and over	Family households (families) Number	Percent with own children under 18 years	Married-couple Number	Married-couple Percent with own children[3]	Female householder[4] Number	Female householder Percent with own children[3]	Nonfamily households Number	Nonfamily households Percent change, 1990–2000
OHIO—Con.																
Marion	4 658	4 512	24 578	4.7	2.50	25.1	35.5	25.4	17 252	46.0	13 401	41.2	2 805	62.2	7 326	19.5
Medina	1 519	1 256	54 542	30.5	2.74	18.9	39.9	20.0	42 202	48.7	36 255	47.5	4 261	57.6	12 340	54.9
Meigs	232	203	9 234	6.6	2.47	25.0	34.2	26.6	6 572	43.9	5 256	40.2	923	58.2	2 662	22.3
Mercer	519	404	14 756	10.1	2.74	22.7	38.7	26.6	11 017	49.7	9 461	48.1	1 099	60.0	3 739	26.0
Miami	1 399	1 255	38 437	11.2	2.54	23.2	35.8	23.4	27 943	45.8	22 852	42.2	3 718	62.6	10 494	29.2
Monroe	144	128	6 021	4.6	2.50	24.0	31.8	28.8	4 411	40.3	3 716	38.9	488	49.6	1 610	21.0
Montgomery	15 607	7 412	229 229	1.3	2.37	30.4	32.7	23.6	146 843	46.3	106 201	41.2	31 721	61.0	82 386	14.7
Morgan	185	180	5 890	13.9	2.50	25.5	33.8	27.7	4 178	43.6	3 349	39.3	581	60.4	1 712	35.2
Morrow	371	328	11 499	19.1	2.72	19.0	39.3	21.9	8 852	46.2	7 433	43.4	934	58.6	2 647	42.0
Muskingum	2 474	1 241	32 518	5.7	2.53	24.9	36.3	25.5	22 873	47.3	17 663	42.7	3 896	63.2	9 645	16.8
Noble	2 214	2 209	4 546	9.9	2.61	24.3	35.9	28.5	3 318	45.9	2 794	44.0	350	59.7	1 228	22.7
Ottawa	637	584	16 474	8.6	2.45	25.0	31.4	27.9	11 733	40.9	9 703	38.0	1 394	55.5	4 741	24.9
Paulding	125	90	7 773	7.2	2.59	23.0	36.8	23.5	5 693	46.6	4 730	43.5	626	62.3	2 080	29.9
Perry	293	185	12 500	11.0	2.70	21.4	39.9	23.4	9 352	49.1	7 517	46.1	1 226	61.3	3 148	21.3
Pickaway	6 497	6 244	17 599	12.8	2.63	20.6	38.5	22.5	13 287	46.9	10 829	43.5	1 728	62.3	4 312	28.4
Pike	484	416	10 444	18.6	2.61	22.8	38.9	24.7	7 667	48.4	5 933	44.4	1 247	62.4	2 777	34.6
Portage	7 552	1 062	56 449	14.7	2.56	23.3	34.8	20.7	39 201	46.5	31 388	43.5	5 711	60.4	17 248	28.1
Preble	489	384	16 001	11.5	2.62	20.6	37.0	24.2	12 138	45.1	10 153	42.4	1 356	58.1	3 863	33.3
Putnam	460	317	12 200	10.1	2.81	21.3	41.0	25.4	9 303	51.5	7 919	50.8	907	55.5	2 897	32.8
Richland	6 460	5 805	49 534	4.1	2.47	26.5	33.9	25.9	34 297	44.6	26 898	40.2	5 630	61.5	15 237	17.7
Ross	5 429	5 193	27 136	11.6	2.50	24.9	35.9	23.7	19 174	46.3	14 979	42.5	3 022	60.1	7 962	27.0
Sandusky	1 017	704	23 717	5.6	2.56	24.1	36.3	25.4	16 960	46.5	13 402	43.0	2 489	60.7	6 757	20.8
Scioto	3 425	3 039	30 871	3.6	2.45	26.9	35.3	27.0	21 372	46.0	16 151	42.4	4 031	57.6	9 499	17.1
Seneca	1 658	390	22 292	4.8	2.56	24.7	35.9	25.5	15 741	47.2	12 510	43.3	2 284	62.8	6 551	19.1
Shelby	665	641	17 636	12.9	2.68	22.0	39.3	22.1	13 083	49.7	10 704	46.8	1 636	65.3	4 553	30.5
Stark	8 933	5 087	148 316	6.3	2.49	26.1	33.8	26.4	102 739	44.7	80 342	41.3	16 996	58.6	45 577	19.8
Summit	9 144	5 775	217 788	8.9	2.45	28.0	33.3	24.8	144 601	46.2	109 183	42.7	27 540	58.7	73 187	20.4
Trumbull	4 088	3 833	89 020	3.4	2.48	26.9	33.0	28.1	61 648	43.2	47 064	39.7	11 107	56.3	27 372	21.4
Tuscarawas	1 163	1 007	35 653	11.5	2.52	24.9	34.8	26.4	25 315	45.5	20 701	42.6	3 312	58.9	10 338	24.0
Union	2 181	2 180	14 346	30.0	2.70	19.9	41.0	18.9	10 884	50.8	9 238	48.6	1 151	62.5	3 462	40.8
Van Wert	464	385	11 587	2.8	2.52	24.7	34.9	26.6	8 358	45.6	6 973	42.6	981	60.4	3 229	19.5
Vinton	140	94	4 892	20.2	2.59	23.6	37.8	23.1	3 552	46.8	2 797	42.7	499	59.9	1 340	40.8
Warren	6 384	6 164	55 966	43.0	2.72	18.9	42.1	18.1	43 261	51.4	37 035	49.9	4 505	60.8	12 705	69.7
Washington	1 727	816	25 137	6.4	2.45	25.4	33.3	26.0	17 683	43.9	14 562	40.7	2 275	59.0	7 454	19.9
Wayne	3 261	1 285	40 445	13.5	2.68	22.7	37.2	22.7	29 488	48.0	24 600	45.7	3 521	60.0	10 957	26.4
Williams	1 083	1 024	15 105	9.4	2.52	24.9	35.8	24.5	10 666	47.1	8 680	42.9	1 354	65.5	4 439	27.3
Wood	7 781	1 015	45 172	13.8	2.51	25.8	33.9	20.5	29 695	48.6	24 332	45.7	3 857	63.4	15 477	27.0
Wyandot	445	400	8 882	8.7	2.53	25.4	35.6	26.4	6 269	46.9	5 139	43.2	813	61.1	2 613	28.2
OKLAHOMA	112 375	66 746	1 342 293	11.3	2.49	26.7	35.7	23.8	921 750	47.2	717 611	43.4	152 575	61.9	420 543	19.9
Adair	384	327	7 471	17.0	2.76	22.8	42.6	24.2	5 567	50.1	4 266	48.3	965	55.3	1 904	31.5
Alfalfa	1 063	1 063	2 199	-10.9	2.29	31.0	28.4	37.8	1 482	39.9	1 305	37.5	125	59.2	717	-1.5
Atoka	1 556	1 556	4 964	10.4	2.48	27.1	35.3	30.3	3 503	44.3	2 825	41.5	504	56.3	1 461	28.9
Beaver	96	96	2 245	-3.5	2.57	22.0	35.8	30.4	1 706	44.0	1 489	41.7	138	66.7	539	-3.6
Beckham	1 874	1 868	7 356	.1	2.44	28.5	35.0	28.7	5 002	47.5	3 956	43.4	767	62.1	2 354	9.7
Blaine	1 592	1 578	4 159	-5.9	2.50	29.0	34.0	32.5	2 867	44.2	2 336	42.0	359	56.0	1 292	.3
Bryan	956	354	14 422	15.2	2.47	26.6	34.3	27.3	9 943	44.1	7 793	40.8	1 563	57.9	4 479	23.2
Caddo	1 421	1 044	10 957	.7	2.62	24.8	38.5	29.5	7 961	45.9	6 043	42.7	1 427	57.9	2 996	7.5
Canadian	2 470	2 305	31 484	23.0	2.71	19.2	42.8	18.6	24 432	51.3	20 236	48.4	3 056	65.7	7 052	35.3
Carter	1 097	993	17 992	8.4	2.47	26.6	36.3	27.8	12 642	46.2	9 798	42.4	2 162	59.9	5 350	18.6
Cherokee	1 699	327	16 175	27.8	2.52	25.3	36.4	22.7	11 077	47.7	8 491	43.6	1 922	62.8	5 098	47.2
Choctaw	230	216	6 220	4.5	2.43	28.3	34.6	31.7	4 286	43.6	3 190	39.0	898	57.5	1 934	13.7
Cimarron	41	41	1 257	-3.3	2.47	29.3	33.5	32.9	868	43.9	759	43.9	75	49.3	389	7.2
Cleveland	9 487	4 092	79 186	23.7	2.51	24.4	36.2	15.5	53 833	49.4	43 068	46.6	7 910	62.5	25 353	34.0
Coal	76	76	2 373	4.1	2.51	27.3	34.7	32.8	1 654	44.0	1 309	41.6	252	52.8	719	4.8
Comanche	10 320	3 082	39 808	6.0	2.63	23.4	42.8	19.9	28 858	53.8	21 722	49.9	5 601	67.0	10 950	23.8
Cotton	175	175	2 614	.2	2.46	27.3	34.7	31.9	1 840	44.5	1 506	41.4	254	59.8	774	12.2
Craig	1 137	902	5 620	6.6	2.46	27.0	34.4	30.1	3 948	44.0	3 219	40.3	546	59.9	1 672	7.7
Creek	675	660	25 289	12.5	2.64	21.6	38.8	24.0	19 024	46.2	15 195	43.2	2 748	58.4	6 265	22.0
Custer	1 264	520	10 136	2.2	2.45	27.8	33.2	23.7	6 581	46.5	5 231	43.9	962	59.9	3 555	15.9
Delaware	531	259	14 838	34.9	2.46	24.0	32.7	30.1	10 767	39.9	8 830	35.5	1 323	59.3	4 071	50.9
Dewey	134	134	1 962	-11.7	2.35	30.0	29.2	33.3	1 336	39.2	1 173	38.4	99	49.5	626	-2.0
Ellis	63	63	1 769	-3.1	2.27	29.2	27.1	34.7	1 219	36.8	1 060	34.1	107	59.8	550	6.0
Garfield	1 725	1 221	23 175	3.2	2.42	27.7	34.1	26.9	15 799	46.1	12 570	41.7	2 437	63.4	7 376	9.7
Garvin	580	360	10 865	4.3	2.45	26.9	34.0	31.7	7 608	43.8	6 127	40.9	1 099	56.9	3 257	13.5
Grady	834	461	17 341	11.6	2.58	22.9	38.2	24.4	12 799	47.0	10 490	43.7	1 680	62.5	4 542	22.2
Grant	99	99	2 089	-10.2	2.42	28.4	32.3	35.2	1 455	44.1	1 262	40.5	132	66.7	634	-4.9
Greer	982	972	2 237	-12.3	2.27	33.4	29.1	38.9	1 442	39.7	1 140	34.9	214	59.3	795	-10.3
Harmon	154	115	1 266	-14.8	2.47	29.0	33.3	36.0	863	44.3	705	39.4	117	65.8	403	-15.5
Harper	45	45	1 509	-8.3	2.33	29.2	29.8	34.8	1 030	41.0	884	38.6	98	54.1	479	1.5

[1] As of April 1. [2] Includes people under formally authorized, supervised care or custody in institutions at the time of enumeration (such as correctional institutions, nursing homes, and juvenile institutions). [3] Under 18 years. [4] No husband present.

Sources: Group Quarters Population—U.S. Census Bureau, 2000 Census of Population and Housing, "Census 2000 Profiles of General Demographic Characteristics" data files, published May 2001 (related Internet site <http://www.census.gov/mp/www/pub/2000cen/mscen01.html>). Households, 2000—U.S. Census Bureau, 2000 Census of Population and Housing, "Census 2000 Profiles of General Demographic Characteristics" data files, published May 2001 (related Internet site <http://www.census.gov/mp/www/pub/2000cen/mscen01.html>). Households, 1990—U.S. Census Bureau, 1990 Census of Population and Housing, Summary Tape File (STF) 1C on CD-ROM (related Internet site <http://homer.ssd.census.gov/cdrom/lookup>).

Table B–3. Counties — **Group Quarters Population and Households**–Con.

[Includes U.S., states, and 3,142 counties or county equivalents defined as of January 1, 1992. For changes to these areas since then, see appendix B. Geographic Information]

County	Group quarters population, 2000[1]		Households, 2000 (April 1)			Percent—			By type—							
									Family households (families)						Nonfamily households	
											Married-couple		Female householder[4]			
	Number	Institu- tionalized population[2]	Number	Percent change, 1990– 2000	Per- sons per house- hold	One- person	With 1 or more per- sons under 18 years	With 1 or more per- sons 65 years and over	Number	Per- cent with own chil- dren under 18 years	Number	Per- cent with own chil- dren[3]	Number	Per- cent with own chil- dren[3]	Number	Percent change, 1990– 2000
OKLAHOMA—Con.																
Haskell	139	139	4 624	7.1	2.52	24.7	35.4	30.9	3 379	43.4	2 801	41.5	421	52.3	1 245	7.0
Hughes	1 305	1 218	5 319	1.8	2.42	28.6	32.8	34.3	3 677	41.7	2 847	38.8	600	52.2	1 642	11.1
Jackson	770	406	10 590	1.3	2.61	24.2	41.3	22.2	7 666	52.6	6 125	48.5	1 130	69.7	2 924	13.5
Jefferson	342	342	2 716	-4.5	2.38	28.8	32.1	33.7	1 864	42.5	1 511	38.6	249	59.8	852	-3.5
Johnston	254	135	4 057	7.2	2.53	25.2	35.9	29.0	2 899	43.8	2 297	42.1	435	51.0	1 158	14.8
Kay	1 166	630	19 157	.4	2.45	27.9	34.6	29.2	13 136	46.5	10 478	42.0	1 947	64.6	6 021	6.3
Kingfisher	275	275	5 247	6.4	2.60	23.5	38.3	27.6	3 894	47.8	3 262	45.9	418	58.4	1 353	8.8
Kiowa	336	330	4 208	-7.5	2.35	30.6	31.1	34.2	2 814	41.6	2 187	37.9	436	54.1	1 394	1.3
Latimer	659	273	3 951	7.0	2.54	24.9	36.6	29.0	2 869	44.3	2 248	40.1	455	60.2	1 082	20.5
Le Flore	1 510	1 221	17 861	12.1	2.61	23.1	38.2	26.4	13 201	45.2	10 448	43.0	1 972	54.3	4 660	20.5
Lincoln	480	255	12 178	12.4	2.59	22.4	37.8	25.8	9 122	45.5	7 494	42.3	1 115	61.3	3 056	22.5
Logan	2 077	117	12 389	21.7	2.57	23.7	36.9	23.1	8 994	46.4	7 331	43.6	1 219	59.1	3 395	31.8
Love	98	86	3 442	15.0	2.54	22.9	35.3	29.7	2 556	42.6	2 079	39.8	343	54.5	886	17.7
McClain	222	198	10 331	24.0	2.66	19.4	39.1	22.6	8 042	46.3	6 744	43.5	929	62.4	2 289	35.8
McCurtain	510	506	13 216	8.0	2.56	25.4	38.9	26.1	9 536	47.2	7 042	43.0	1 925	61.4	3 680	21.3
McIntosh	324	324	8 085	19.1	2.37	26.7	29.4	36.5	5 685	36.4	4 577	31.5	837	57.0	2 400	33.7
Major	120	120	3 046	-2.4	2.44	25.2	32.9	31.9	2 209	42.8	1 940	39.3	184	68.5	837	7.3
Marshall	275	228	5 371	23.5	2.40	26.4	31.3	34.3	3 800	38.6	3 122	35.4	475	54.1	1 571	34.2
Mayes	535	472	14 823	17.0	2.55	23.8	36.2	27.2	10 818	44.7	8 929	41.4	1 335	60.5	4 005	32.7
Murray	356	346	5 003	7.6	2.45	25.2	34.3	30.6	3 589	43.1	2 886	39.6	512	58.0	1 414	8.0
Muskogee	3 172	2 637	26 458	5.1	2.51	26.7	36.0	28.0	18 463	45.6	13 979	41.7	3 516	59.0	7 995	14.5
Noble	274	274	4 504	6.6	2.47	25.5	35.2	26.4	3 213	44.9	2 659	42.4	380	56.3	1 291	8.3
Nowata	203	203	4 147	3.8	2.50	25.5	35.2	30.5	2 991	44.1	2 440	39.8	405	62.2	1 156	2.5
Okfuskee	1 067	843	4 270	2.5	2.52	27.8	34.1	31.7	2 972	42.0	2 309	39.2	477	51.6	1 298	13.1
Oklahoma	16 994	10 161	266 834	12.2	2.41	30.2	34.2	21.4	170 663	48.4	123 551	43.7	36 045	63.2	96 171	21.7
Okmulgee	1 035	531	15 300	8.9	2.53	27.1	36.7	28.2	10 701	45.8	8 082	42.0	1 998	58.2	4 599	14.4
Osage	1 535	1 524	16 617	8.0	2.58	23.3	37.1	25.3	12 214	45.1	9 872	41.8	1 707	57.7	4 403	13.5
Ottawa	1 012	450	12 984	7.1	2.48	26.6	34.5	30.6	9 121	44.0	7 220	40.2	1 391	58.4	3 863	8.0
Pawnee	164	157	6 383	6.3	2.58	22.8	36.0	27.4	4 747	43.8	3 931	41.4	574	56.6	1 636	10.4
Payne	6 993	1 341	26 680	11.9	2.29	30.1	27.8	18.8	15 316	45.0	12 178	41.8	2 216	60.6	11 364	18.0
Pittsburg	2 815	2 763	17 157	7.8	2.40	27.7	33.0	30.8	11 944	41.6	9 420	37.5	1 922	57.2	5 213	16.3
Pontotoc	1 097	576	13 978	5.0	2.44	28.1	34.0	27.0	9 426	45.7	7 393	42.1	1 507	60.2	4 552	14.1
Pottawatomie	2 958	1 567	24 540	12.6	2.55	24.0	36.8	25.8	17 730	45.3	13 862	41.4	2 886	60.0	6 810	17.8
Pushmataha	184	179	4 739	8.4	2.42	27.9	34.2	32.3	3 290	43.4	2 622	39.3	512	60.5	1 449	18.3
Roger Mills	38	38	1 428	-10.0	2.38	28.6	32.2	34.0	988	42.5	840	40.1	97	53.6	440	12.2
Rogers	853	725	25 724	29.5	2.71	19.0	41.6	20.9	20 091	49.2	16 882	46.5	2 287	63.8	5 633	43.0
Seminole	547	485	9 575	-.9	2.54	25.9	36.1	30.7	6 793	43.3	5 104	40.0	1 274	54.3	2 782	4.6
Sequoyah	490	369	14 761	19.7	2.61	22.4	38.9	25.5	10 989	46.0	8 597	42.5	1 763	59.0	3 772	35.5
Stephens	614	540	17 463	4.2	2.44	25.3	33.7	31.2	12 591	42.2	10 398	38.9	1 608	60.1	4 872	11.6
Texas	433	132	7 153	15.1	2.75	21.2	41.6	20.2	5 248	53.1	4 397	50.8	534	68.4	1 905	18.6
Tillman	387	327	3 594	-8.6	2.48	28.8	34.4	35.1	2 486	44.1	1 981	41.3	386	54.1	1 108	2.0
Tulsa	12 088	6 157	226 892	12.0	2.43	29.6	35.0	20.6	147 316	49.5	111 329	45.6	27 431	64.2	79 576	18.3
Wagoner	214	185	21 010	24.0	2.73	17.7	41.0	20.0	16 698	47.0	13 855	44.2	2 053	61.2	4 312	32.7
Washington	660	393	20 179	4.9	2.40	27.5	32.9	30.1	14 031	43.8	11 539	39.8	1 875	63.9	6 148	18.1
Washita	231	231	4 506	1.9	2.50	25.3	36.2	31.0	3 265	46.3	2 748	43.2	382	64.9	1 241	9.8
Woods	997	605	3 684	-3.1	2.20	33.4	26.8	33.2	2 243	39.6	1 874	36.0	269	56.9	1 441	4.9
Woodward	807	728	7 141	.8	2.48	25.4	36.0	25.5	5 078	46.5	4 223	42.5	603	67.2	2 063	9.9
OREGON	**77 491**	**37 901**	**1 333 723**	**20.9**	**2.51**	**26.1**	**33.4**	**22.9**	**877 671**	**46.8**	**692 532**	**42.8**	**130 782**	**63.6**	**456 052**	**29.4**
Baker	422	274	6 883	12.5	2.37	27.8	30.1	32.0	4 681	41.2	3 870	35.8	589	66.9	2 202	21.6
Benton	5 005	386	30 145	15.4	2.43	26.1	29.9	18.0	18 244	46.9	15 183	44.0	2 182	64.4	11 901	21.8
Clackamas	2 878	1 927	128 201	23.8	2.62	22.0	36.8	20.6	91 670	47.8	75 126	45.1	11 547	61.2	36 531	36.2
Clatsop	1 121	357	14 703	9.9	2.35	29.5	30.8	26.9	9 450	44.3	7 436	38.6	1 432	66.2	5 253	17.9
Columbia	248	143	16 375	17.7	2.65	21.1	37.3	22.2	12 034	46.8	9 912	42.6	1 421	66.0	4 341	23.2
Coos	1 430	761	26 213	6.6	2.34	27.2	28.9	32.0	17 448	39.1	13 858	33.5	2 597	61.0	8 765	23.1
Crook	273	197	7 354	34.8	2.57	21.3	35.2	26.8	5 425	43.8	4 524	39.5	603	64.8	1 929	34.1
Curry	277	122	9 543	14.8	2.19	29.7	23.0	40.8	6 180	32.2	5 205	26.6	683	63.4	3 363	39.0
Deschutes	1 221	575	45 595	56.1	2.50	22.0	34.3	22.5	31 953	45.8	26 438	40.9	3 853	70.4	13 642	70.2
Douglas	1 524	932	39 821	11.0	2.48	23.9	32.4	30.8	28 218	41.0	22 789	35.8	3 821	63.9	11 603	25.4
Gilliam	26	–	819	17.7	2.31	29.5	30.0	30.8	544	41.5	474	38.8	48	66.7	275	39.6
Grant	172	74	3 246	5.0	2.39	27.1	32.8	27.1	2 233	43.8	1 880	38.3	255	74.9	1 013	14.9
Harney	169	136	3 036	10.0	2.45	25.9	32.0	25.9	2 094	42.7	1 760	39.1	206	60.2	942	22.3
Hood River	870	325	7 248	12.8	2.70	22.7	38.3	24.6	5 175	50.0	4 247	47.5	636	63.4	2 073	13.1
Jackson	3 677	1 587	71 532	25.0	2.48	25.1	30.0	28.4	48 423	44.7	38 053	39.5	7 530	64.6	23 109	35.2
Jefferson	150	108	6 727	41.8	2.80	18.6	39.6	24.5	5 166	46.3	4 070	41.4	707	65.9	1 561	43.9
Josephine	1 010	704	31 000	23.6	2.41	25.4	29.8	33.8	21 364	39.0	16 865	33.4	3 220	61.2	9 636	33.8
Klamath	1 013	394	25 205	12.8	2.49	25.3	33.4	26.6	17 293	44.2	13 654	38.3	2 516	67.1	7 912	20.5
Lake	55	43	3 084	11.5	2.39	26.2	31.4	29.5	2 152	41.5	1 808	36.2	232	68.1	932	32.8
Lane	7 418	2 054	130 453	17.7	2.42	26.6	31.0	22.9	82 180	45.3	63 833	40.0	13 093	65.0	48 273	29.4
Lincoln	642	276	19 296	17.3	2.27	29.3	27.2	31.9	12 244	38.5	9 554	30.9	1 939	65.2	7 052	31.2

[1] As of April 1. [2] Includes people under formally authorized, supervised care or custody in institutions at the time of enumeration (such as correctional institutions, nursing homes, and juvenile institutions). [3] Under 18 years. [4] No husband present.

Sources: Group Quarters Population—U.S. Census Bureau, 2000 Census of Population and Housing, "Census 2000 Profiles of General Demographic Characteristics" data files, published May 2001 (related Internet site <http://www.census.gov/mp/www/pub/2000cen/mscen01.html>). Households, 2000—U.S. Census Bureau, 2000 Census of Population and Housing, "Census 2000 Profiles of General Demographic Characteristics" data files, published May 2001 (related Internet site <http://www.census.gov/mp/www/pub/2000cen/mscen01.html>). Households, 1990—U.S. Census Bureau, 1990 Census of Population and Housing, Summary Tape File (STF) 1C on CD-ROM (related Internet site <http://homer.ssd.census.gov/cdrom/lookup>).

[Includes U.S., states, and 3,142 counties or county equivalents defined as of January 1, 1992. For changes to these areas since then, see appendix B. Geographic Information]

County	Group quarters population, 2000[1]		Households, 2000 (April 1)													
	Number	Institutionalized population[2]	Number	Percent change, 1990–2000	Persons per household	Percent—			By type—						Nonfamily households	
						One-person	With 1 or more persons under 18 years	With 1 or more persons 65 years and over	Family households (families)		Married-couple		Female householder[4]			
									Number	Percent with own children under 18 years	Number	Percent with own children[3]	Number	Percent with own children[3]	Number	Percent change, 1990–2000
OREGON—Con.																
Linn	994	737	39 541	13.9	2.58	23.0	35.1	26.4	28 232	44.8	22 506	40.4	3 952	63.0	11 309	20.7
Malheur	3 321	3 122	10 221	8.1	2.77	23.7	39.3	28.8	7 346	50.3	5 853	46.5	1 066	68.3	2 875	12.5
Marion	10 588	7 113	101 641	21.7	2.70	24.0	37.6	23.8	70 458	49.8	54 570	46.0	11 156	65.3	31 183	24.3
Morrow	40	21	3 776	34.7	2.90	18.1	42.5	22.0	2 920	50.2	2 364	46.2	334	72.5	856	23.0
Multnomah	16 688	6 458	272 098	12.4	2.37	32.5	29.1	19.3	152 232	47.4	111 400	43.7	29 485	59.7	119 866	21.1
Polk	2 032	850	23 058	26.9	2.62	22.3	34.6	25.6	16 130	45.8	13 170	42.1	2 131	65.0	6 928	33.3
Sherman	–	–	797	1.7	2.43	28.7	31.6	32.7	546	43.6	466	40.8	52	55.8	251	12.6
Tillamook	466	383	10 200	15.3	2.33	27.9	27.0	32.9	6 798	36.9	5 589	32.0	784	62.1	3 402	25.9
Umatilla	3 300	2 797	25 195	14.4	2.67	23.7	38.4	24.2	17 846	49.5	13 876	45.0	2 677	66.5	7 349	14.4
Union	669	204	9 740	7.8	2.45	26.1	32.5	25.6	6 514	44.8	5 363	39.9	824	70.1	3 226	20.0
Wallowa	109	63	3 029	8.3	2.35	27.1	30.4	30.3	2 084	41.5	1 779	36.6	210	72.9	945	15.8
Wasco	527	366	9 401	9.2	2.47	26.1	33.1	28.5	6 503	43.6	5 149	38.5	930	64.1	2 898	11.8
Washington	4 101	1 519	169 162	42.2	2.61	24.7	37.7	16.5	114 074	52.8	92 254	50.6	15 211	65.0	55 088	53.5
Wheeler	31	–	653	11.8	2.32	27.4	24.3	37.5	445	31.2	406	28.1	26	69.2	208	23.8
Yamhill	5 024	2 893	28 732	28.1	2.78	19.7	40.4	23.1	21 372	50.2	17 248	47.0	2 834	65.9	7 360	36.1
PENNSYLVANIA	433 301	213 790	4 777 003	6.3	2.48	27.7	32.6	27.8	3 208 388	44.6	2 467 673	42.3	554 693	53.7	1 568 615	17.1
Adams	3 611	1 326	33 652	19.9	2.61	21.3	36.2	24.9	24 777	45.8	20 551	42.9	2 876	59.4	8 875	29.1
Allegheny	40 617	18 451	537 150	-.8	2.31	32.7	28.5	29.8	332 237	42.6	247 549	40.3	66 541	51.9	204 913	12.0
Armstrong	1 175	462	29 005	2.5	2.46	25.9	31.6	31.2	20 548	41.6	16 794	39.2	2 604	52.2	8 457	13.4
Beaver	4 407	2 139	72 576	.9	2.44	26.9	31.1	32.0	50 521	41.1	39 581	38.7	8 266	51.8	22 055	14.6
Bedford	468	357	19 768	9.6	2.50	23.5	33.1	29.3	14 493	41.8	12 206	39.9	1 532	50.8	5 275	23.0
Berks	12 419	5 204	141 570	10.9	2.55	24.6	34.3	26.9	98 463	45.6	78 517	42.5	14 038	58.5	43 107	18.5
Blair	4 107	2 480	51 518	2.4	2.43	27.8	31.9	29.5	34 895	43.2	27 080	40.0	5 769	53.9	16 623	14.3
Bradford	1 040	682	24 453	8.7	2.52	24.7	34.4	27.8	17 308	45.0	14 032	41.3	2 182	60.4	7 145	23.2
Bucks	9 024	5 795	218 725	14.8	2.69	21.5	37.7	23.3	160 946	48.0	133 878	47.7	19 312	50.8	57 779	29.6
Butler	6 415	2 999	65 862	19.0	2.55	24.2	34.7	24.7	46 839	46.3	39 384	44.7	5 323	56.2	19 023	33.3
Cambria	8 308	4 568	60 531	-2.4	2.38	29.8	29.2	34.7	40 615	40.3	31 967	38.4	6 318	48.3	19 916	11.7
Cameron	81	45	2 465	2.9	2.39	30.1	30.2	33.8	1 624	42.1	1 292	38.1	228	56.1	841	9.9
Carbon	918	703	23 701	7.8	2.44	26.0	31.2	32.1	16 416	41.5	12 986	38.8	2 357	51.9	7 285	21.2
Centre	14 777	3 029	49 323	15.6	2.45	26.6	27.0	19.2	28 501	44.1	24 138	42.3	3 025	56.2	20 822	27.6
Chester	14 744	5 922	157 905	18.5	2.65	22.6	37.1	21.5	113 303	49.0	95 491	48.3	12 846	54.1	44 602	31.4
Clarion	2 317	517	16 052	7.1	2.46	26.0	30.5	27.3	10 735	42.8	8 820	39.9	1 351	58.3	5 317	20.4
Clearfield	3 235	2 952	32 785	10.0	2.44	26.3	32.1	29.8	22 926	42.4	18 556	39.9	3 049	52.8	9 859	23.1
Clinton	2 195	569	14 773	6.7	2.42	26.6	30.3	30.1	9 934	41.2	7 972	36.7	1 388	60.8	4 839	22.0
Columbia	3 758	892	24 915	6.1	2.42	26.6	29.8	27.9	16 564	41.6	13 393	38.4	2 177	55.6	8 351	21.5
Crawford	3 702	1 917	34 678	7.7	2.50	26.2	32.9	27.6	23 871	44.2	19 270	40.8	3 177	59.1	10 807	18.1
Cumberland	13 952	7 219	83 015	13.0	2.41	26.7	31.3	24.9	56 077	43.6	46 937	40.8	6 667	58.7	26 938	25.4
Dauphin	6 787	4 876	102 670	7.8	2.39	30.0	32.5	24.2	66 132	46.1	48 916	41.4	13 287	61.0	36 538	13.8
Delaware	21 741	8 808	206 320	2.5	2.56	27.6	34.4	28.8	139 453	46.6	104 911	46.1	26 542	50.0	66 867	13.7
Elk	466	341	14 124	7.6	2.45	27.3	33.0	30.3	9 748	44.9	7 916	43.2	1 231	55.1	4 376	27.0
Erie	13 953	6 365	106 507	4.9	2.51	27.6	34.3	25.9	71 039	47.4	53 792	43.6	12 890	61.1	35 468	16.5
Fayette	3 011	1 046	59 969	6.9	2.43	28.0	31.6	32.1	41 170	41.7	31 046	39.0	7 466	51.5	18 799	23.9
Forest	376	95	2 000	4.8	2.29	29.1	25.5	34.6	1 328	34.9	1 113	32.9	134	45.5	672	17.5
Franklin	3 029	2 186	50 633	10.9	2.49	23.7	33.2	27.2	36 410	42.8	30 358	39.6	4 169	58.4	14 223	23.9
Fulton	102	57	5 660	10.1	2.50	24.0	34.4	25.9	4 097	43.8	3 369	40.1	466	56.7	1 563	28.9
Greene	3 267	2 529	15 060	3.0	2.48	25.7	33.6	28.9	10 588	43.5	8 342	41.0	1 635	52.5	4 472	13.7
Huntingdon	4 683	3 605	16 759	7.9	2.44	25.8	32.5	28.4	11 798	42.8	9 741	39.5	1 397	57.1	4 961	17.3
Indiana	5 280	599	34 123	7.6	2.47	26.5	29.8	26.9	22 517	42.3	18 528	40.4	2 800	51.6	11 606	26.1
Jefferson	929	550	18 375	4.4	2.45	26.6	32.3	30.6	12 861	43.2	10 444	40.8	1 669	54.9	5 514	17.6
Juniata	487	448	8 584	13.0	2.60	21.1	35.1	26.3	6 467	43.7	5 549	41.4	537	56.1	2 117	18.0
Lackawanna	7 835	3 396	86 218	2.0	2.38	31.3	29.1	33.8	55 758	42.0	42 150	41.1	10 173	47.4	30 460	16.5
Lancaster	14 356	6 893	172 560	14.3	2.64	23.1	35.9	24.6	124 129	46.9	103 320	44.4	14 900	60.4	48 431	24.7
Lawrence	2 972	1 512	37 091	2.0	2.47	27.0	31.4	33.8	25 886	41.3	20 199	38.8	4 269	51.5	11 205	17.1
Lebanon	4 363	2 431	46 551	9.0	2.49	25.2	32.8	27.5	32 761	43.2	26 708	40.1	4 273	57.9	13 790	19.7
Lehigh	10 251	5 980	121 906	8.0	2.48	27.1	32.9	27.2	82 106	45.4	64 558	42.2	12 780	58.4	39 800	18.1
Luzerne	12 863	8 556	130 687	1.7	2.34	31.3	28.6	33.9	84 304	41.1	63 725	39.6	15 039	47.2	46 383	15.8
Lycoming	5 513	3 228	47 003	4.6	2.44	26.9	32.3	28.2	31 703	44.3	24 966	39.6	4 826	61.4	15 300	19.7
McKean	2 640	2 000	18 024	1.0	2.40	28.3	32.7	29.2	12 098	45.4	9 468	40.9	1 815	60.9	5 926	12.9
Mercer	6 362	3 065	46 712	2.5	2.44	27.0	31.9	31.4	32 387	42.3	25 609	39.0	5 094	55.9	14 325	16.3
Mifflin	690	625	18 413	4.0	2.49	26.0	32.6	29.7	12 905	43.1	10 604	40.3	1 563	55.5	5 508	13.5
Monroe	3 840	987	49 454	44.6	2.73	20.2	38.8	23.8	36 459	49.1	30 021	47.0	4 339	60.0	12 995	53.7
Montgomery	23 257	13 988	286 098	12.2	2.54	25.6	34.0	26.1	197 640	46.3	163 746	45.9	25 290	50.0	88 458	19.7
Montour	1 003	733	7 085	8.3	2.43	28.0	31.9	26.8	4 817	44.1	3 991	41.0	628	60.8	2 268	17.1
Northampton	10 537	3 480	101 541	11.6	2.53	24.7	33.6	28.0	71 074	44.5	57 295	42.4	9 988	54.7	30 467	28.2
Northumberland	3 719	3 134	38 835	.3	2.34	30.2	29.3	32.4	25 589	41.5	20 332	38.1	3 728	55.0	13 246	12.8
Perry	502	470	16 695	11.7	2.58	21.7	35.8	22.7	12 320	45.0	10 290	42.4	1 302	57.5	4 375	31.7
Philadelphia	54 731	20 411	590 071	-2.2	2.48	33.8	33.1	27.0	352 331	46.2	189 291	42.2	131 332	53.1	237 740	5.6
Pike	392	263	17 433	65.5	2.63	20.7	36.7	27.8	13 026	46.1	11 066	43.6	1 333	62.6	4 407	74.1
Potter	299	222	7 005	12.2	2.54	24.7	34.0	29.0	4 999	44.2	4 165	41.2	534	56.2	2 006	21.9

[1] As of April 1. [2] Includes people under formally authorized, supervised care or custody in institutions at the time of enumeration (such as correctional institutions, nursing homes, and juvenile institutions). [3] Under 18 years. [4] No husband present.

Sources: Group Quarters Population—U.S. Census Bureau, 2000 Census of Population and Housing, "Census 2000 Profiles of General Demographic Characteristics" data files, published May 2001 (related Internet site <http://www.census.gov/mp/www/pub/2000cen/mscen01.html>). Households, 2000—U.S. Census Bureau, 2000 Census of Population and Housing, "Census 2000 Profiles of General Demographic Characteristics" data files, published May 2001 (related Internet site <http://www.census.gov/mp/www/pub/2000cen/mscen01.html>). Households, 1990—U.S. Census Bureau, 1990 Census of Population and Housing, Summary Tape File (STF) 1C on CD-ROM (related Internet site <http://homer.ssd.census.gov/cdrom/lookup>).

[Includes U.S., states, and 3,142 counties or county equivalents defined as of January 1, 1992. For changes to these areas since then, see appendix B. Geographic Information]

County	Group quarters population, 2000[1] Number	Institutionalized population[2]	Households, 2000 (April 1) Number	Percent change, 1990–2000	Persons per household	Percent— One-person	With 1 or more persons under 18 years	With 1 or more persons 65 years and over	Family households (families) Number	Percent with own children under 18 years	Married-couple Number	Married-couple Percent with own children[3]	Female householder[4] Number	Female householder Percent with own children[3]	Nonfamily households Number	Nonfamily Percent change, 1990–2000
PENNSYLVANIA—Con.																
Schuylkill	7 226	6 637	60 530	-.4	2.36	29.9	29.2	34.8	40 116	40.5	31 133	38.7	6 177	46.7	20 414	10.4
Snyder	2 289	897	13 654	7.0	2.58	22.4	34.2	26.4	9 979	43.9	8 461	41.7	1 010	55.0	3 675	19.8
Somerset	3 494	3 065	31 222	5.6	2.45	26.1	31.5	31.5	22 044	41.7	18 214	39.7	2 640	50.3	9 178	22.1
Sullivan	443	145	2 660	16.7	2.30	29.3	26.6	36.3	1 754	36.8	1 454	33.3	181	53.6	906	33.4
Susquehanna	434	355	16 529	10.9	2.53	24.3	34.3	28.0	11 777	44.7	9 539	41.5	1 427	58.7	4 752	29.8
Tioga	1 887	357	15 925	6.4	2.48	24.4	33.0	28.7	11 191	43.3	9 211	39.3	1 365	63.4	4 734	22.3
Union	8 693	5 793	13 178	12.7	2.50	25.3	32.7	27.7	9 205	44.5	7 891	41.2	915	65.6	3 973	30.2
Venango	1 830	1 154	22 747	1.5	2.45	26.2	32.8	29.2	15 926	43.5	12 693	39.2	2 248	59.9	6 821	14.9
Warren	1 069	884	17 696	2.6	2.42	27.2	32.1	28.0	12 122	43.5	9 926	39.8	1 495	59.7	5 574	18.0
Washington	5 341	1 994	81 130	3.3	2.44	27.0	30.8	31.3	56 052	41.1	44 811	39.5	8 390	48.2	25 078	17.8
Wayne	1 901	1 617	18 350	25.4	2.50	25.2	32.8	31.3	12 942	43.0	10 488	40.0	1 641	56.9	5 408	44.8
Westmoreland	8 496	5 015	149 813	4.0	2.41	26.9	30.3	31.4	104 597	40.7	85 326	39.2	14 335	48.7	45 216	18.8
Wyoming	690	341	10 762	7.6	2.55	24.1	35.7	24.1	7 704	46.4	6 248	43.8	1 004	58.0	3 058	20.5
York	8 002	4 429	148 219	15.2	2.52	23.3	34.9	23.6	105 486	45.6	86 355	42.2	13 410	61.3	42 733	26.6
RHODE ISLAND	38 816	13 801	408 424	8.1	2.47	28.6	32.9	26.3	265 398	47.0	196 757	43.6	52 609	60.3	143 026	20.1
Bristol	2 774	769	19 033	8.4	2.52	25.1	33.7	29.4	13 359	45.3	10 908	44.2	1 888	53.4	5 674	26.8
Kent	1 871	1 289	67 320	8.5	2.45	27.6	32.1	26.6	44 964	44.8	35 492	42.9	7 049	53.5	22 356	21.9
Newport	2 472	531	35 228	7.8	2.35	29.9	30.4	25.1	22 232	45.3	17 565	42.2	3 622	60.1	12 996	25.5
Providence	26 454	10 352	239 936	6.0	2.48	29.8	33.2	26.7	152 823	48.2	106 778	43.8	35 637	62.2	87 113	16.7
Washington	5 245	860	46 907	19.3	2.52	24.1	33.9	23.5	32 020	46.6	26 014	44.5	4 413	58.6	14 887	32.0
SOUTH CAROLINA	135 037	60 533	1 533 854	21.9	2.53	25.0	36.5	22.6	1 072 822	46.2	783 142	42.6	226 958	57.7	461 032	39.8
Abbeville	710	229	10 131	15.4	2.51	25.3	36.5	27.1	7 288	44.1	5 289	40.7	1 548	55.0	2 843	28.1
Aiken	2 073	1 297	55 587	23.8	2.53	25.2	37.0	23.4	39 434	46.7	29 625	43.0	7 668	59.8	16 153	41.3
Allendale	1 178	1 164	3 915	3.3	2.56	30.0	38.5	27.3	2 617	45.3	1 401	37.6	1 012	56.6	1 298	21.2
Anderson	2 676	1 577	65 649	18.3	2.48	24.3	35.3	24.4	47 276	43.9	36 109	40.5	8 377	55.0	10 373	31.4
Bamberg	1 065	131	6 123	9.6	2.55	27.8	37.3	27.7	4 253	44.8	2 670	41.0	1 306	54.1	1 870	27.3
Barnwell	277	232	9 021	27.1	2.57	25.6	39.5	24.0	6 433	48.9	4 273	44.0	1 745	60.8	2 588	49.5
Beaufort	6 609	618	45 532	48.3	2.51	21.5	33.4	27.8	33 060	41.8	26 485	37.1	4 998	63.6	12 472	58.7
Berkeley	5 442	2 412	49 922	17.8	2.75	19.4	43.8	16.9	37 696	51.9	28 305	48.9	7 110	62.0	12 226	47.2
Calhoun	161	121	5 917	31.9	2.54	24.5	35.4	25.7	4 270	41.9	3 079	39.3	934	48.7	1 647	51.0
Charleston	11 398	3 306	123 326	15.2	2.42	28.3	32.7	21.4	77 416	45.7	53 230	41.5	19 556	57.8	45 910	36.3
Cherokee	729	364	20 495	24.5	2.53	25.0	37.7	23.2	14 614	45.9	10 506	42.3	3 159	57.5	5 881	43.3
Chester	316	291	12 880	12.5	2.62	24.2	38.8	24.8	9 343	45.4	6 285	41.1	2 402	56.4	3 537	26.8
Chesterfield	659	466	16 557	17.9	2.54	25.9	38.4	23.2	11 703	47.3	8 213	43.9	2 698	57.4	4 854	39.6
Clarendon	1 526	1 406	11 812	23.8	2.62	24.6	37.7	28.5	8 598	43.1	5 730	39.2	2 338	53.8	3 214	50.9
Colleton	333	198	14 470	20.2	2.62	24.0	39.1	25.8	10 494	45.7	7 390	42.3	2 432	55.2	3 976	41.0
Darlington	1 231	765	25 793	17.2	2.57	25.1	38.0	23.0	18 444	45.0	12 453	41.2	4 823	55.0	7 349	38.3
Dillon	427	332	11 199	13.3	2.71	25.1	41.8	23.7	8 065	48.1	5 022	45.9	2 492	53.2	3 134	27.2
Dorchester	2 089	1 708	34 709	23.0	2.72	20.2	44.0	18.2	26 293	52.9	19 855	49.7	5 073	64.2	8 416	42.7
Edgefield	2 593	2 529	8 270	28.7	2.66	22.4	39.4	23.5	6 214	46.3	4 596	43.7	1 285	55.6	2 056	35.3
Fairfield	421	341	8 774	17.5	2.63	24.4	38.8	25.2	6 387	44.5	4 204	39.8	1 751	54.8	2 387	34.9
Florence	3 866	2 100	47 147	17.2	2.59	24.5	38.7	21.9	33 798	47.2	23 449	44.4	8 513	55.3	13 349	32.9
Georgetown	581	399	21 659	33.1	2.55	23.3	35.3	27.5	15 844	41.3	11 720	37.0	3 274	55.3	5 815	55.5
Greenville	10 825	3 863	149 556	21.7	2.47	26.8	35.1	21.2	102 012	46.7	78 215	43.8	18 332	58.8	47 544	35.9
Greenwood	2 311	1 034	25 729	13.2	2.49	26.3	36.2	25.2	17 754	46.0	12 525	41.8	4 130	58.8	7 975	24.0
Hampton	1 712	1 688	7 444	17.7	2.64	25.8	41.0	26.2	5 312	48.5	3 563	45.7	1 396	56.6	2 132	37.0
Horry	2 505	1 317	81 800	46.7	2.37	25.8	29.5	25.4	54 515	39.4	42 027	34.5	9 418	57.7	27 285	78.2
Jasper	1 347	1 330	7 042	32.9	2.75	23.2	41.7	23.9	5 092	47.7	3 388	44.9	1 283	56.2	1 950	54.2
Kershaw	520	382	20 188	27.7	2.58	22.6	38.4	24.1	14 918	45.7	11 261	43.1	2 751	54.8	5 270	46.6
Lancaster	1 984	1 783	23 178	17.2	2.56	23.7	38.2	23.2	16 840	46.0	12 195	42.0	3 591	58.2	6 338	41.9
Laurens	2 628	1 095	26 290	27.3	2.55	24.6	37.5	24.2	18 870	45.2	13 432	41.3	4 108	56.4	7 420	46.2
Lee	1 686	1 627	6 886	13.7	2.68	25.9	40.1	27.1	4 916	45.9	2 960	42.3	1 636	53.2	1 970	43.7
Lexington	2 883	1 896	83 240	35.1	2.56	22.5	38.4	18.2	59 830	49.3	47 143	46.2	9 675	62.7	23 410	63.0
McCormick	1 446	1 303	3 558	30.3	2.39	24.4	29.8	31.0	2 604	33.9	1 843	27.0	626	54.2	954	40.9
Marion	334	309	13 301	13.0	2.64	25.4	39.8	24.7	9 511	45.1	5 758	44.1	3 144	53.2	3 790	32.2
Marlboro	1 635	1 628	10 478	3.1	2.59	26.9	39.3	26.1	7 338	45.7	4 464	41.8	2 330	52.7	3 140	18.5
Newberry	1 029	331	14 026	13.9	2.50	26.5	34.6	27.4	9 809	43.5	6 895	38.7	2 253	57.8	4 217	27.4
Oconee	640	304	27 283	22.0	2.40	24.7	31.6	26.7	19 589	39.7	15 756	36.0	2 761	56.5	7 694	40.3
Orangeburg	3 657	1 037	34 118	18.0	2.58	26.0	38.1	25.9	23 876	45.8	15 374	42.0	6 922	54.9	10 242	39.5
Pickens	7 409	571	41 306	23.6	2.50	23.3	34.1	21.2	28 453	45.3	22 984	42.8	3 868	57.3	12 853	38.8
Richland	28 012	9 754	120 101	18.2	2.44	29.1	35.3	18.5	76 378	49.5	52 505	45.8	19 575	60.3	43 723	28.7
Saluda	262	218	7 127	22.4	2.65	22.5	36.7	27.2	5 295	42.8	3 866	40.5	1 033	55.1	1 832	36.8
Spartanburg	7 439	3 503	97 735	15.7	2.52	24.8	36.4	23.0	69 299	45.4	51 638	42.3	13 529	56.3	28 436	30.2
Sumter	3 445	1 460	37 728	15.3	2.68	23.2	41.7	22.7	27 611	49.9	18 958	47.3	6 897	57.3	10 117	43.5
Union	426	260	12 087	6.0	2.44	26.8	34.6	27.8	8 495	41.8	5 902	37.9	2 029	52.0	3 592	24.4
Williamsburg	335	279	13 714	13.3	2.69	24.9	41.3	26.7	10 050	47.1	6 343	44.4	3 071	53.9	3 664	34.3
York	4 207	1 575	61 051	29.9	2.63	21.3	39.5	19.6	44 915	48.2	34 258	45.6	8 116	58.2	16 136	45.4

[1] As of April 1. [2] Includes people under formally authorized, supervised care or custody in institutions at the time of enumeration (such as correctional institutions, nursing homes, and juvenile institutions). [3] Under 18 years. [4] No husband present.

Sources: Group Quarters Population—U.S. Census Bureau, 2000 Census of Population and Housing, "Census 2000 Profiles of General Demographic Characteristics" data files, published May 2001 (related Internet site <http://www.census.gov/mp/www/pub/2000cen/mscen01.html>). Households, 2000—U.S. Census Bureau, 2000 Census of Population and Housing, "Census 2000 Profiles of General Demographic Characteristics" data files, published May 2001 (related Internet site <http://www.census.gov/mp/www/pub/2000cen/mscen01.html>). Households, 1990—U.S. Census Bureau, 1990 Census of Population and Housing, Summary Tape File (STF) 1C on CD-ROM (related Internet site <http://homer.ssd.census.gov/cdrom/lookup>).

[Includes U.S., states, and 3,142 counties or county equivalents defined as of January 1, 1992. For changes to these areas since then, see appendix B. Geographic Information]

County	Group quarters population, 2000[1]		Households, 2000 (April 1)			Percent—			By type—							
									Family households (families)		Married-couple		Female householder[4]		Nonfamily households	
	Number	Institutionalized population[2]	Number	Percent change, 1990–2000	Persons per household	One-person	With 1 or more persons under 18 years	With 1 or more persons 65 years and over	Number	Percent with own children under 18 years	Number	Percent with own children[3]	Number	Percent with own children[3]	Number	Percent change, 1990–2000
SOUTH DAKOTA	28 418	14 387	290 245	12.0	2.50	27.6	34.8	25.0	194 330	49.0	157 391	45.2	26 205	67.3	95 915	21.8
Aurora	201	196	1 165	1.7	2.45	28.2	30.9	34.3	817	42.4	714	40.9	58	58.6	348	5.1
Beadle	443	279	7 210	-1.8	2.30	33.1	29.6	31.2	4 532	41.4	3 788	41.3	532	64.5	2 678	11.5
Bennett	48	48	1 123	9.0	3.14	23.3	45.5	25.4	819	54.5	546	49.1	196	64.8	304	8.2
Bon Homme	997	993	2 635	-.5	2.38	29.5	29.7	36.9	1 786	42.3	1 577	40.1	135	60.7	849	6.8
Brookings	2 824	260	10 665	19.7	2.38	29.6	29.4	19.1	6 219	49.1	5 230	46.2	705	68.2	4 446	34.4
Brown	1 452	503	14 638	5.6	2.32	30.8	31.0	25.9	9 322	46.5	7 735	42.8	1 153	67.0	5 316	17.0
Brule	382	87	1 998	.1	2.49	29.9	32.4	29.7	1 328	46.6	1 122	43.9	144	64.6	670	4.4
Buffalo	15	–	526	17.9	3.83	16.0	59.9	19.2	422	58.8	198	58.1	165	58.8	104	76.3
Butte	131	96	3 516	15.9	2.55	25.6	37.1	27.0	2 467	49.9	2 019	46.3	315	69.8	1 049	17.6
Campbell	19	–	725	-5.5	2.43	28.6	30.9	37.2	508	43.3	477	43.6	19	52.6	217	11.9
Charles Mix	189	177	3 343	3.4	2.74	28.3	38.1	32.6	2 328	49.1	1 775	45.3	392	63.8	1 015	8.2
Clark	81	48	1 598	-6.0	2.54	28.1	30.3	37.7	1 111	42.1	984	41.0	75	60.0	487	1.0
Clay	2 216	191	4 878	10.0	2.32	31.0	28.7	17.8	2 720	50.1	2 195	44.7	395	78.0	2 158	18.1
Codington	417	107	10 357	18.5	2.46	27.9	34.8	23.8	6 872	50.6	5 648	47.2	837	70.1	3 485	25.1
Corson	3	–	1 271	-2.5	3.29	22.1	47.9	27.3	950	51.3	595	50.3	251	54.6	321	7.4
Custer	300	254	2 970	26.3	2.35	25.9	29.1	27.4	2 068	38.7	1 788	35.2	196	61.2	902	43.4
Davison	677	332	7 585	9.2	2.38	30.8	32.6	26.9	4 773	49.4	3 902	45.2	620	69.2	2 812	13.2
Day	153	146	2 586	-5.3	2.36	31.8	29.2	37.9	1 688	41.9	1 406	39.0	176	56.3	898	8.8
Deuel	68	–	1 843	4.3	2.40	28.6	30.1	33.9	1 259	42.7	1 113	41.2	90	62.2	584	26.1
Dewey	107	50	1 863	8.3	3.15	22.1	52.2	21.8	1 387	58.8	800	57.4	416	59.6	476	13.3
Douglas	108	108	1 321	-2.3	2.54	26.8	33.0	36.0	947	45.0	864	44.2	47	57.4	374	4.8
Edmunds	134	133	1 681	.7	2.52	25.6	32.5	35.5	1 211	43.7	1 091	42.3	81	60.5	470	3.8
Fall River	466	428	3 127	9.2	2.23	32.7	25.9	33.4	1 976	37.6	1 592	31.7	265	61.1	1 151	17.7
Faulk	48	43	1 014	-4.1	2.56	29.1	29.9	38.7	709	41.3	643	40.7	34	50.0	305	–
Grant	232	127	3 116	-1.2	2.44	28.6	34.3	30.9	2 156	48.3	1 889	46.5	163	62.6	960	7.9
Gregory	92	78	2 022	-5.5	2.32	33.9	28.0	40.2	1 290	41.4	1 117	39.6	115	53.0	732	2.1
Haakon	49	49	870	-6.0	2.47	26.0	33.7	29.0	620	45.8	553	43.6	42	73.8	250	-8.1
Hamlin	168	59	2 048	10.5	2.62	27.0	34.7	31.3	1 452	47.7	1 300	46.2	98	63.3	596	11.8
Hand	70	70	1 543	-5.0	2.38	30.2	28.8	39.0	1 051	41.3	940	40.0	68	51.5	492	12.8
Hanson	–	–	1 115	4.0	2.82	21.7	35.2	29.5	848	45.3	785	44.8	41	56.1	267	2.7
Harding	42	42	525	-11.3	2.50	31.0	35.8	27.8	353	52.1	307	51.1	28	64.3	172	12.4
Hughes	775	708	6 512	12.7	2.41	29.8	35.3	22.1	4 310	51.1	3 516	46.5	582	73.0	2 202	19.7
Hutchinson	328	327	3 190	-1.0	2.43	29.6	29.1	40.9	2 193	40.8	1 963	39.7	139	51.1	997	6.2
Hyde	37	37	679	-.1	2.41	30.3	31.5	36.4	456	44.1	378	39.9	41	75.6	223	.5
Jackson	23	23	945	4.7	3.08	25.2	45.2	25.7	676	54.0	486	50.4	139	66.2	269	20.6
Jerauld	40	40	987	2.2	2.28	31.3	25.5	40.0	651	36.9	557	33.0	62	61.3	336	18.7
Jones	–	–	509	-1.9	2.34	33.2	31.4	32.0	328	45.4	271	42.4	38	52.6	181	32.1
Kingsbury	179	169	2 406	2.1	2.34	31.5	29.2	37.2	1 592	42.2	1 419	39.2	106	62.3	814	11.8
Lake	732	141	4 372	8.5	2.41	29.2	31.0	28.3	2 830	46.0	2 446	42.7	260	71.2	1 542	19.5
Lawrence	1 147	242	8 881	12.0	2.33	29.6	30.4	24.5	5 560	46.0	4 530	40.6	754	71.1	3 321	25.8
Lincoln	263	227	8 782	60.8	2.72	19.5	42.3	19.0	6 669	54.0	5 843	52.2	591	69.2	2 113	71.8
Lyman	15	10	1 400	10.4	2.77	24.6	39.9	26.6	1 010	50.1	720	43.8	193	66.8	390	18.9
McCook	154	154	2 204	2.8	2.58	26.8	35.3	32.8	1 559	48.2	1 368	46.7	113	65.5	645	7.3
McPherson	68	68	1 227	-7.9	2.31	31.1	24.2	45.5	822	35.2	762	34.6	33	48.5	405	12.8
Marshall	89	89	1 844	-3.9	2.43	30.1	31.5	35.0	1 252	43.8	1 054	42.0	119	52.9	592	2.1
Meade	863	235	8 805	24.3	2.66	19.9	42.1	19.2	6 700	52.5	5 668	49.4	727	69.7	2 105	40.0
Mellette	45	45	694	1.9	2.94	24.2	45.0	26.5	499	54.1	325	49.8	116	59.5	195	12.1
Miner	55	55	1 212	-5.0	2.33	32.3	29.2	37.6	789	43.3	685	40.3	66	63.6	423	9.0
Minnehaha	5 331	3 114	57 996	21.6	2.46	27.8	35.4	19.2	37 573	52.1	30 014	48.5	5 508	69.9	20 423	29.6
Moody	77	59	2 526	5.3	2.58	26.4	37.7	26.6	1 762	51.1	1 431	46.8	214	66.8	764	18.8
Pennington	2 425	998	34 641	13.4	2.49	26.1	35.8	20.8	23 271	49.9	17 787	44.2	4 069	71.0	11 370	29.3
Perkins	68	40	1 429	-9.9	2.31	32.9	27.9	37.3	937	41.6	826	39.2	75	61.3	492	3.8
Potter	68	55	1 145	-8.3	2.29	31.3	27.2	38.0	767	39.6	678	37.9	56	50.0	378	1.1
Roberts	213	133	3 683	1.8	2.66	26.8	37.7	30.6	2 619	47.5	1 971	43.7	436	59.4	1 064	2.0
Sanborn	37	37	1 043	-1.5	2.53	25.4	32.4	32.8	732	43.2	641	41.7	51	58.8	311	9.5
Shannon	310	56	2 785	26.3	4.36	13.2	68.8	17.3	2 354	61.1	987	64.9	1 013	58.9	431	33.9
Spink	485	479	2 847	-5.8	2.45	29.3	31.9	33.6	1 933	45.1	1 667	42.2	175	69.7	914	-2.1
Stanley	9	–	1 111	20.6	2.49	25.2	35.4	20.2	775	48.1	618	44.0	112	67.0	336	33.3
Sully	–	–	630	1.4	2.47	25.7	32.9	29.8	443	44.0	394	42.9	27	40.7	187	17.6
Todd	126	73	2 462	11.4	3.62	18.9	60.7	16.6	1 917	62.8	866	58.7	782	64.5	545	25.6
Tripp	97	90	2 550	-.9	2.48	29.6	32.8	34.1	1 720	45.1	1 451	43.1	169	58.6	830	17.1
Turner	203	203	3 510	5.3	2.46	26.5	33.1	33.0	2 478	44.8	2 172	42.8	197	63.5	1 032	12.1
Union	122	122	4 927	27.7	2.53	24.2	36.3	23.5	3 520	48.8	3 055	45.6	311	68.8	1 407	31.5
Walworth	176	169	2 506	2.4	2.31	31.4	28.9	35.0	1 643	41.0	1 338	35.8	223	65.5	863	18.7
Yankton	1 726	1 285	8 187	15.2	2.43	29.3	34.3	25.3	5 407	50.0	4 456	46.2	680	71.5	2 780	21.8
Ziebach	–	–	741	17.6	3.40	17.4	55.6	19.0	594	58.9	355	52.4	176	71.6	147	6.5

[1] As of April 1. [2] Includes people under formally authorized, supervised care or custody in institutions at the time of enumeration (such as correctional institutions, nursing homes, and juvenile institutions). [3] Under 18 years. [4] No husband present.

Sources: Group Quarters Population—U.S. Census Bureau, 2000 Census of Population and Housing, "Census 2000 Profiles of General Demographic Characteristics" data files, published May 2001 (related Internet site <http://www.census.gov/mp/www/pub/2000cen/mscen01.html>). Households, 2000—U.S. Census Bureau, 2000 Census of Population and Housing, "Census 2000 Profiles of General Demographic Characteristics" data files, published May 2001 (related Internet site <http://www.census.gov/mp/www/pub/2000cen/mscen01.html>). Households, 1990—U.S. Census Bureau, 1990 Census of Population and Housing, Summary Tape File (STF) 1C on CD-ROM (related Internet site <http://homer.ssd.census.gov/cdrom/lookup>).

[Includes U.S., states, and 3,142 counties or county equivalents defined as of January 1, 1992. For changes to these areas since then, see appendix B. Geographic Information]

County	Group quarters population, 2000[1] Number	Institutionalized population[2]	Households, 2000 (April 1) Number	Percent change, 1990–2000	Persons per household	Percent— One-person	With 1 or more persons under 18 years	With 1 or more persons 65 years and over	Family households (families) Number	Percent with own children under 18 years	Married-couple Number	Married-couple Percent with own children[3]	Female householder[4] Number	Female householder Percent with own children[3]	Nonfamily households Number	Nonfamily Percent change, 1990–2000
TENNESSEE	147 946	83 397	2 232 905	20.5	2.48	25.8	35.2	22.5	1 547 835	45.7	1 173 960	42.5	287 899	57.6	685 070	35.5
Anderson	877	717	29 780	8.7	2.37	27.7	32.4	27.9	20 513	43.0	16 024	39.4	3 426	56.9	9 267	22.9
Bedford	513	352	13 905	19.8	2.67	21.5	38.2	24.1	10 350	45.6	7 968	42.7	1 658	57.4	3 555	25.2
Benton	273	218	6 863	18.7	2.37	25.7	30.9	29.9	4 888	38.3	3 987	34.9	651	54.5	1 975	36.1
Bledsoe	1 173	1 159	4 430	35.8	2.53	22.1	35.5	23.5	3 312	41.9	2 726	39.3	404	51.0	1 118	51.3
Blount	2 098	1 179	42 667	26.9	2.43	24.4	33.3	24.6	30 642	42.4	24 936	39.8	4 264	54.7	12 025	45.2
Bradley	2 215	656	34 281	24.2	2.50	23.4	35.4	21.5	24 660	44.4	19 644	41.8	3 733	56.9	9 621	49.2
Campbell	499	462	16 125	22.6	2.44	25.4	33.2	27.3	11 575	41.5	8 911	39.1	2 027	50.6	4 550	52.1
Cannon	165	154	4 998	25.6	2.53	24.3	36.3	25.3	3 644	45.4	2 931	43.3	497	54.9	1 354	44.3
Carroll	919	519	11 779	9.8	2.42	25.8	33.6	29.4	8 394	42.1	6 635	38.8	1 357	55.7	3 385	24.7
Carter	1 453	887	23 486	16.3	2.35	26.5	31.4	26.0	16 351	40.9	12 902	38.1	2 592	52.9	7 135	36.9
Cheatham	401	373	12 878	35.3	2.76	16.9	43.6	16.7	10 162	50.2	8 356	48.2	1 242	57.5	2 716	53.7
Chester	1 121	161	5 660	24.2	2.55	22.6	37.1	26.6	4 198	45.3	3 340	42.6	650	57.7	1 462	38.8
Claiborne	647	357	11 799	22.5	2.48	23.4	35.1	24.8	8 680	43.5	6 936	41.6	1 297	51.1	3 119	52.1
Clay	89	81	3 379	18.4	2.33	27.6	30.5	27.3	2 333	40.1	1 848	36.7	329	53.2	1 046	47.1
Cocke	364	346	13 762	23.0	2.41	25.7	33.7	25.0	9 720	41.8	7 314	38.9	1 789	50.2	4 042	49.3
Coffee	784	458	18 885	21.8	2.50	24.3	35.8	26.0	13 589	45.1	10 745	41.2	2 089	60.7	5 296	40.4
Crockett	298	297	5 632	8.7	2.53	25.3	36.7	27.4	4 065	45.3	3 176	43.3	663	52.8	1 567	18.1
Cumberland	540	469	19 508	45.3	2.37	22.4	29.4	33.4	14 518	35.7	12 047	31.6	1 864	56.1	4 990	67.7
Davidson	24 165	10 298	237 405	14.4	2.30	33.4	30.0	19.3	138 106	45.8	94 784	41.3	34 039	58.7	99 299	30.4
Decatur	230	230	4 908	16.4	2.34	27.6	30.6	30.2	3 415	39.2	2 785	36.5	444	50.9	1 493	34.9
DeKalb	315	166	6 984	22.6	2.45	25.5	33.6	25.6	4 989	42.1	3 920	39.3	778	54.8	1 995	44.6
Dickson	536	481	16 473	26.5	2.59	22.3	39.1	22.1	12 175	48.2	9 604	45.0	1 901	61.1	4 298	47.2
Dyer	609	485	14 751	8.3	2.49	25.3	36.8	24.3	10 459	46.4	7 854	42.4	2 008	60.5	4 292	16.2
Fayette	392	385	10 467	23.8	2.71	20.5	37.1	26.2	8 020	40.5	6 118	39.1	1 462	47.3	2 447	41.0
Fentress	153	143	6 693	21.4	2.46	25.5	34.5	25.3	4 819	43.8	3 832	42.5	757	49.8	1 874	49.6
Franklin	1 660	287	15 003	18.5	2.51	22.6	34.6	28.0	11 160	41.6	9 010	39.2	1 567	52.6	3 843	38.4
Gibson	1 068	1 024	19 518	6.3	2.41	27.4	33.9	30.1	13 578	43.4	10 198	39.6	2 660	55.9	5 940	21.5
Giles	547	338	11 713	19.1	2.47	25.7	35.0	26.4	8 360	44.0	6 541	41.5	1 392	53.8	3 353	41.0
Grainger	178	154	8 270	29.3	2.48	22.5	34.3	23.0	6 158	42.1	5 118	40.7	728	48.6	2 112	60.2
Greene	1 610	1 088	25 756	19.9	2.38	25.8	32.6	25.8	18 130	41.5	14 347	38.1	2 790	53.9	7 626	46.6
Grundy	205	149	5 562	16.3	2.54	24.0	37.8	25.7	4 056	45.8	3 148	43.5	669	55.5	1 506	44.7
Hamblen	790	653	23 211	19.5	2.47	24.7	34.3	23.8	16 604	42.6	13 022	39.8	2 616	54.9	6 607	42.6
Hamilton	7 790	3 385	124 444	11.3	2.41	27.9	32.4	24.4	83 692	42.9	62 429	39.6	16 797	54.8	40 752	24.1
Hancock	162	162	2 769	11.5	2.39	27.7	33.4	28.9	1 938	44.3	1 527	42.6	305	50.8	831	48.4
Hardeman	3 964	3 861	9 412	13.7	2.56	25.1	38.4	26.9	6 764	45.4	4 705	41.4	1 661	56.7	2 648	26.9
Hardin	464	399	10 426	19.5	2.41	25.5	32.8	27.7	7 442	41.6	5 975	38.9	1 055	53.2	2 984	42.6
Hawkins	463	463	21 936	27.8	2.42	24.4	34.1	23.2	15 932	43.1	13 014	40.3	2 160	56.2	6 004	52.2
Haywood	253	224	7 558	7.8	2.59	25.4	39.1	26.8	5 418	46.5	3 462	41.9	1 659	57.0	2 140	14.8
Henderson	352	271	10 306	20.9	2.44	24.9	35.8	25.3	7 451	44.6	5 863	41.2	1 201	58.5	2 855	38.5
Henry	524	440	13 019	14.6	2.35	27.0	30.7	30.5	9 006	39.7	7 084	35.6	1 462	56.6	4 013	27.6
Hickman	1 386	1 373	8 081	35.2	2.59	22.6	37.1	23.8	5 952	46.0	4 803	43.6	776	55.0	2 129	55.6
Houston	190	177	3 216	19.9	2.46	25.3	34.5	28.9	2 300	43.4	1 833	40.7	333	58.3	916	42.2
Humphreys	233	174	7 238	19.4	2.44	25.0	33.7	26.3	5 145	42.7	4 144	39.0	735	60.0	2 093	42.4
Jackson	136	134	4 466	22.6	2.43	25.5	32.1	26.2	3 141	41.0	2 468	38.6	459	48.1	1 325	54.1
Jefferson	1 662	638	17 155	39.1	2.49	22.5	34.2	23.1	12 612	42.2	10 283	39.3	1 682	54.5	4 543	61.2
Johnson	1 484	1 462	6 827	26.3	2.35	26.4	30.4	28.1	4 754	37.9	3 783	35.6	681	47.1	2 073	56.5
Knox	12 864	3 558	157 872	18.1	2.34	29.6	31.0	21.9	100 726	44.6	78 571	41.7	17 211	57.2	57 146	32.7
Lake	2 278	2 278	2 410	-.3	2.36	30.0	33.6	30.5	1 615	43.0	1 137	39.1	392	55.1	795	16.4
Lauderdale	2 688	2 678	9 567	13.6	2.55	25.6	38.6	25.3	6 816	46.1	4 754	41.8	1 681	58.0	2 751	32.8
Lawrence	367	365	15 480	16.1	2.56	23.7	36.7	26.5	11 369	45.9	9 155	43.2	1 641	57.7	4 111	33.8
Lewis	233	226	4 381	24.0	2.54	23.5	37.0	25.1	3 216	45.2	2 579	42.9	467	55.7	1 165	25.7
Lincoln	468	372	12 503	14.9	2.47	24.6	34.4	27.6	9 083	43.5	7 279	40.6	1 366	56.1	3 420	29.0
Loudon	433	406	15 944	31.2	2.42	22.8	31.3	27.8	11 802	38.3	9 838	35.4	1 423	52.8	4 142	44.5
McMinn	712	500	19 721	20.6	2.45	24.4	34.7	25.4	14 318	43.2	11 580	40.1	2 087	57.6	5 403	38.8
McNairy	528	358	9 980	13.0	2.42	25.9	33.4	28.2	7 133	41.9	5 785	39.2	988	53.3	2 847	32.1
Macon	213	210	7 916	28.5	2.55	23.8	37.9	23.8	5 806	47.8	4 802	45.9	697	59.0	2 110	45.7
Madison	3 302	1 278	35 552	20.1	2.49	26.2	37.1	22.3	24 652	48.3	17 709	44.0	5 659	62.1	10 900	31.2
Marion	249	224	11 037	19.8	2.49	23.6	35.3	24.6	8 131	42.2	6 395	40.2	1 278	49.2	2 906	42.2
Marshall	348	229	10 307	24.7	2.56	23.9	37.6	23.4	7 475	46.6	5 857	43.7	1 196	58.6	2 832	31.8
Maury	1 238	1 120	26 444	28.3	2.58	23.2	38.7	22.0	19 274	47.8	14 792	45.0	3 407	58.5	7 170	41.8
Meigs	114	114	4 304	43.7	2.55	20.8	36.6	21.2	3 264	43.3	2 656	40.9	425	53.6	1 040	56.9
Monroe	546	359	15 329	34.9	2.51	23.3	35.7	24.1	11 243	43.8	9 098	41.2	1 539	54.6	4 086	58.2
Montgomery	4 324	935	48 330	40.7	2.70	20.2	43.9	15.5	35 964	54.7	28 371	51.8	5 892	67.1	12 366	66.4
Moore	112	89	2 211	27.5	2.55	21.4	34.5	27.5	1 687	40.2	1 439	38.4	167	49.1	524	52.8
Morgan	1 723	1 723	6 990	19.7	2.58	22.1	37.6	23.7	5 237	44.7	4 243	43.3	718	52.2	1 753	43.7
Obion	522	357	13 182	6.2	2.42	25.7	34.3	26.5	9 404	43.4	7 440	39.8	1 463	57.5	3 778	18.3

[1] As of April 1. [2] Includes people under formally authorized, supervised care or custody in institutions at the time of enumeration (such as correctional institutions, nursing homes, and juvenile institutions). [3] Under 18 years. [4] No husband present.

Sources: Group Quarters Population—U.S. Census Bureau, 2000 Census of Population and Housing, "Census 2000 Profiles of General Demographic Characteristics" data files, published May 2001 (related Internet site <http://www.census.gov/mp/www/pub/2000cen/mscen01.html>). Households, 2000—U.S. Census Bureau, 2000 Census of Population and Housing, "Census 2000 Profiles of General Demographic Characteristics" data files, published May 2001 (related Internet site <http://www.census.gov/mp/www/pub/2000cen/mscen01.html>). Households, 1990—U.S. Census Bureau, 1990 Census of Population and Housing, Summary Tape File (STF) 1C on CD-ROM (related Internet site <http://homer.ssd.census.gov/cdrom/lookup>).

[Includes U.S., states, and 3,142 counties or county equivalents defined as of January 1, 1992. For changes to these areas since then, see appendix B. Geographic Information]

County	Group quarters population, 2000[1] Number	Institutionalized population[2]	Households, 2000 Number	Percent change, 1990–2000	Persons per household	Percent One-person	With 1 or more persons under 18 years	With 1 or more persons 65 years and over	Family Percent with own children under 18 years	Married-couple Number	Married-couple Percent with own children[3]	Female householder[4] Number	Female householder Percent with own children[3]	Nonfamily Number	Nonfamily Percent change, 1990–2000
TENNESSEE—Con.															
Overton	177	165	8 110	20.4	2.46	24.1	32.6	27.0	5 924	40.0	4 798	38.5	802	46.8	2 186	48.9
Perry	141	116	3 023	20.3	2.48	25.2	33.8	29.5	2 163	42.8	1 792	40.5	265	54.7	860	41.7
Pickett	70	70	2 091	17.1	2.33	27.2	29.3	30.0	1 461	39.2	1 219	37.0	164	50.6	630	38.2
Polk	194	186	6 448	26.6	2.46	23.3	33.8	25.8	4 750	40.4	3 885	39.6	582	45.0	1 698	56.9
Putnam	2 547	606	24 865	25.9	2.40	27.1	31.8	23.3	16 417	43.9	13 108	41.3	2 429	57.1	8 448	46.7
Rhea	855	388	11 184	21.8	2.46	23.8	34.6	24.6	8 104	43.0	6 421	39.3	1 254	58.5	3 080	40.0
Roane	695	478	21 200	14.9	2.42	25.0	32.0	27.8	15 242	39.8	12 367	37.0	2 145	52.3	5 958	32.8
Robertson	516	461	19 906	34.5	2.71	18.6	41.3	21.0	15 442	48.2	12 327	46.0	2 233	59.8	4 464	53.1
Rutherford	5 772	2 117	66 443	57.8	2.65	20.8	40.9	14.2	47 457	52.9	37 394	50.6	7 422	64.1	18 986	74.3
Scott	200	189	8 203	25.5	2.55	24.3	39.1	21.9	6 016	48.6	4 690	47.0	972	55.8	2 187	55.5
Sequatchie	125	125	4 463	35.8	2.52	22.4	36.7	22.2	3 311	44.5	2 623	40.8	498	57.8	1 152	57.4
Sevier	637	476	28 467	45.8	2.48	22.0	33.9	22.8	20 836	41.9	16 884	38.7	2 883	56.1	7 631	72.3
Shelby	18 997	12 092	338 366	11.5	2.60	27.0	39.0	19.5	228 644	50.6	144 924	46.9	67 932	59.8	109 722	19.9
Smith	148	139	6 878	28.4	2.55	23.4	37.3	25.1	5 070	46.2	4 136	43.5	676	59.6	1 808	49.8
Stewart	100	95	4 930	34.0	2.49	23.1	34.5	27.0	3 652	42.5	3 071	39.3	398	60.6	1 278	47.6
Sullivan	2 762	1 655	63 556	12.0	2.36	26.4	31.2	27.2	44 802	40.4	36 267	38.0	6 456	51.7	18 754	31.9
Sumner	1 391	1 240	48 941	32.8	2.64	20.3	39.8	19.8	37 054	48.0	29 897	45.7	5 272	58.6	11 887	62.0
Tipton	889	864	18 106	38.9	2.78	18.7	44.3	20.2	14 173	50.6	10 899	47.9	2 508	61.8	3 933	46.3
Trousdale	164	121	2 780	23.0	2.55	23.0	36.0	25.4	2 036	43.5	1 621	41.4	314	49.7	744	36.3
Unicoi	292	271	7 516	13.5	2.31	27.5	29.6	30.2	5 222	38.4	4 239	36.4	711	46.8	2 294	36.3
Union	138	120	6 742	36.7	2.62	19.8	39.4	20.7	5 194	46.0	4 192	44.2	711	52.5	1 548	64.7
Van Buren	78	78	2 180	21.2	2.49	21.9	34.0	24.3	1 620	41.0	1 297	37.8	240	55.4	560	60.9
Warren	723	437	15 181	19.7	2.47	25.0	35.4	24.9	10 821	44.8	8 527	41.6	1 695	58.9	4 360	41.6
Washington	4 013	1 795	44 195	23.4	2.33	27.8	30.8	23.6	29 466	42.3	23 268	39.3	4 641	55.8	14 729	41.0
Wayne	2 167	2 100	5 936	14.7	2.47	24.4	34.1	26.7	4 324	42.6	3 509	40.7	597	50.4	1 612	47.2
Weakley	2 499	564	13 599	13.4	2.38	27.0	32.2	25.6	9 125	43.8	7 366	40.9	1 289	56.9	4 474	31.5
White	305	246	9 229	19.5	2.47	23.4	33.8	27.4	6 771	41.5	5 399	38.7	997	52.7	2 458	41.6
Williamson	991	598	44 725	60.1	2.81	16.6	45.1	15.1	35 758	53.8	31 211	53.3	3 493	59.4	8 967	85.6
Wilson	1 148	337	32 798	36.3	2.67	18.1	40.7	18.3	25 595	47.6	21 069	45.3	3 314	58.6	7 203	61.5
TEXAS	561 109	374 704	7 393 354	21.8	2.74	23.7	40.9	19.9	5 247 794	51.9	3 989 741	50.2	937 589	60.2	2 145 560	24.2
Anderson	14 628	14 551	15 678	10.2	2.58	24.8	38.3	28.3	11 343	47.1	8 698	43.6	2 070	59.9	4 335	24.6
Andrews	79	79	4 601	-3.3	2.81	21.8	44.5	25.0	3 519	53.2	2 932	51.1	439	62.0	1 082	16.6
Angelina	2 707	2 326	28 685	14.7	2.70	22.8	40.7	24.7	21 263	48.6	16 577	46.4	3 532	57.6	7 422	21.8
Aransas	268	233	9 132	31.6	2.43	25.3	30.2	33.5	6 397	38.5	5 204	33.6	862	60.8	2 735	49.9
Archer	55	41	3 345	13.1	2.63	21.9	39.9	25.9	2 517	49.5	2 174	47.6	242	62.8	828	27.0
Armstrong	77	77	802	4.4	2.58	21.4	36.3	31.0	613	44.4	539	42.3	49	61.2	189	-3.6
Atascosa	355	327	12 816	28.9	2.99	18.9	46.6	23.5	10 016	53.3	7 731	51.2	1 668	60.8	2 800	36.4
Austin	276	236	8 747	17.0	2.67	22.8	37.9	28.1	6 479	46.9	5 297	44.8	837	58.7	2 268	10.1
Bailey	60	60	2 348	-4.3	2.78	22.3	40.8	30.3	1 778	49.0	1 525	46.8	175	62.3	570	5.9
Bandera	181	53	7 010	67.7	2.49	23.2	32.4	29.2	5 060	40.3	4 259	36.9	515	59.2	1 950	77.0
Bastrop	2 005	1 950	20 097	50.2	2.77	21.5	40.2	21.0	14 776	48.8	11 761	46.4	2 112	58.9	5 321	62.2
Baylor	49	49	1 791	-6.0	2.26	33.3	27.9	39.4	1 157	39.1	959	34.9	147	59.9	634	-.5
Bee	7 556	7 328	9 061	5.5	2.74	23.7	42.5	26.3	6 580	52.1	4 793	48.3	1 345	63.4	2 481	15.7
Bell	9 137	2 960	85 507	27.2	2.68	22.3	43.4	16.8	61 971	55.3	48 414	51.7	10 525	70.8	23 536	39.7
Bexar	34 511	14 655	488 942	19.5	2.78	24.0	41.4	21.1	345 717	51.7	247 095	49.9	75 868	58.5	143 225	28.0
Blanco	153	140	3 303	41.3	2.50	24.0	32.9	28.3	2 390	42.0	2 032	39.0	238	60.1	913	41.3
Borden	–	–	292	-.7	2.50	22.6	31.5	28.4	217	40.6	190	36.8	18	77.8	75	44.2
Bosque	534	461	6 726	12.3	2.48	25.4	32.5	33.5	4 854	40.8	4 079	37.6	551	57.5	1 872	13.8
Bowie	6 779	6 420	33 058	8.1	2.50	26.0	37.3	25.8	23 426	46.6	17 203	42.3	4 964	60.7	9 632	16.4
Brazoria	10 961	10 531	81 954	28.0	2.82	19.1	44.7	18.5	63 128	52.9	50 990	51.0	8 523	62.2	18 826	34.7
Brazos	13 345	2 458	55 202	26.2	2.52	25.5	30.3	13.1	30 390	50.6	22 821	49.4	5 528	60.7	24 812	31.8
Brewster	400	74	3 669	9.5	2.31	32.8	29.8	25.8	2 216	44.0	1 713	39.5	367	64.9	1 453	22.3
Briscoe	–	–	724	-8.2	2.47	27.9	33.0	35.4	511	41.5	429	38.5	55	58.2	213	-4.1
Brooks	72	72	2 711	1.4	2.92	21.4	44.7	30.9	2 080	50.7	1 415	48.9	519	57.4	631	6.2
Brown	2 223	1 650	14 306	9.2	2.48	26.5	34.9	29.2	10 013	44.8	7 993	40.6	1 555	61.4	4 293	15.7
Burleson	105	105	6 363	22.9	2.57	24.9	35.6	30.7	4 572	44.4	3 591	41.4	725	55.0	1 791	20.1
Burnet	892	806	13 133	45.0	2.53	22.5	33.3	31.5	9 661	40.9	8 076	37.3	1 126	60.1	3 472	45.0
Caldwell	1 681	1 645	10 816	23.7	2.82	21.2	42.1	24.9	8 075	49.6	6 056	47.2	1 439	58.2	2 741	24.8
Calhoun	174	141	7 442	9.8	2.75	21.3	40.2	26.0	5 572	47.3	4 403	44.6	819	59.7	1 870	14.1
Callahan	122	122	5 061	10.9	2.53	23.3	35.4	30.3	3 752	43.0	3 116	39.8	473	60.9	1 309	15.6
Cameron	4 089	3 273	97 267	32.7	3.40	15.4	52.7	27.2	79 944	55.7	59 105	55.9	16 915	56.7	17 323	32.2
Camp	175	153	4 336	14.9	2.62	24.2	36.2	29.8	3 158	43.2	2 435	39.8	541	56.7	1 178	15.9
Carson	99	70	2 470	2.8	2.60	22.3	38.4	28.3	1 884	46.9	1 614	44.9	201	61.2	586	11.4
Cass	479	467	12 190	7.7	2.46	26.4	34.4	30.9	8 658	42.6	6 694	38.4	1 485	58.9	3 532	22.9
Castro	65	64	2 761	-4.0	2.98	20.5	45.3	26.6	2 160	52.3	1 797	50.9	240	60.4	601	2.9

[1] As of April 1. [2] Includes people under formally authorized, supervised care or custody in institutions at the time of enumeration (such as correctional institutions, nursing homes, and juvenile institutions). [3] Under 18 years. [4] No husband present.

Sources: Group Quarters Population—U.S. Census Bureau, 2000 Census of Population and Housing, "Census 2000 Profiles of General Demographic Characteristics" data files, published May 2001 (related Internet site <http://www.census.gov/mp/www/pub/2000cen/mscen01.html>). Households, 2000—U.S. Census Bureau, 2000 Census of Population and Housing, "Census 2000 Profiles of General Demographic Characteristics" data files, published May 2001 (related Internet site <http://www.census.gov/mp/www/pub/2000cen/mscen01.html>). Households, 1990—U.S. Census Bureau, 1990 Census of Population and Housing, Summary Tape File (STF) 1C on CD-ROM (related Internet site <http://homer.ssd.census.gov/cdrom/lookup>).

[Includes U.S., states, and 3,142 counties or county equivalents defined as of January 1, 1992. For changes to these areas since then, see appendix B. Geographic Information]

County	Group quarters population, 2000[1] Number	Institutionalized population[2]	Households, 2000 (April 1) Number	Percent change, 1990–2000	Persons per household	Percent— One-person	With 1 or more persons under 18 years	With 1 or more persons 65 years and over	Family households (families) Number	Percent with own children under 18 years	Married-couple Number	Percent with own children[3]	Female householder[4] Number	Percent with own children[3]	Nonfamily households Number	Percent change, 1990–2000
TEXAS—Con.																
Chambers	234	221	9 139	31.9	2.82	17.8	44.9	18.6	7 216	51.5	6 005	50.5	818	56.5	1 923	32.7
Cherokee	2 824	2 419	16 651	11.1	2.63	24.2	37.5	28.9	12 098	46.0	9 272	43.0	2 131	57.6	4 553	11.2
Childress	1 754	1 754	2 474	1.6	2.40	30.8	34.4	33.3	1 651	46.9	1 296	42.1	281	66.9	823	8.7
Clay	94	86	4 323	13.5	2.52	23.5	34.6	29.2	3 181	41.7	2 732	39.8	317	53.0	1 142	28.0
Cochran	75	74	1 309	-8.5	2.79	20.9	42.4	29.7	1 017	49.1	835	48.1	130	51.5	292	-1.7
Coke	293	293	1 544	12.4	2.31	29.0	29.6	40.1	1 068	39.2	902	36.4	125	55.2	476	25.3
Coleman	163	163	3 889	-3.4	2.33	30.2	30.4	37.9	2 608	40.6	2 091	36.8	361	59.0	1 281	–
Collin	3 332	1 839	181 970	89.9	2.68	22.1	42.5	10.1	132 268	55.8	113 089	54.9	13 576	65.0	49 702	107.9
Collingsworth	53	53	1 294	-10.6	2.44	27.8	32.6	37.6	916	42.1	744	38.8	127	52.8	378	-16.6
Colorado	849	393	7 641	8.8	2.56	26.2	34.9	33.7	5 406	43.9	4 301	41.6	833	55.0	2 235	11.7
Comal	1 267	858	29 066	50.5	2.64	20.6	36.6	26.7	21 881	44.3	18 252	41.9	2 615	57.6	7 185	54.3
Comanche	342	333	5 522	3.8	2.48	26.3	32.6	35.1	3 925	42.0	3 267	39.0	445	60.0	1 597	7.0
Concho	1 370	1 370	1 058	-.5	2.45	26.6	32.8	34.0	758	41.6	628	39.0	103	52.4	300	-2.6
Cooke	842	707	13 643	18.2	2.60	23.3	37.2	27.3	10 004	46.2	8 137	43.5	1 354	60.9	3 639	20.1
Coryell	16 932	9 275	19 950	19.6	2.91	16.9	50.7	14.9	15 782	60.3	12 922	57.6	2 193	75.1	4 168	34.5
Cottle	37	35	820	-10.4	2.28	32.0	30.2	42.0	550	41.8	442	37.1	87	59.8	270	-7.5
Crane	45	43	1 360	-11.5	2.91	18.8	46.5	22.6	1 083	54.5	922	52.3	108	69.4	277	-9.2
Crockett	55	52	1 524	5.2	2.65	24.7	41.7	25.1	1 114	49.9	919	47.8	141	60.3	410	14.5
Crosby	92	89	2 512	-.2	2.78	23.8	41.0	30.5	1 866	47.9	1 483	45.4	287	56.4	646	7.1
Culberson	9	3	1 052	-2.2	2.82	21.5	44.8	24.6	797	51.6	612	49.8	142	54.2	255	19.2
Dallam	16	12	2 317	9.2	2.68	26.2	42.9	21.5	1 628	55.5	1 276	52.9	225	68.0	689	11.7
Dallas	33 470	23 633	807 621	15.1	2.71	27.3	39.4	16.0	533 613	53.1	378 411	51.9	113 881	60.4	274 008	14.9
Dawson	2 272	2 269	4 726	-7.0	2.69	23.9	39.8	32.1	3 503	47.3	2 809	45.1	521	54.9	1 223	-3.4
Deaf Smith	254	242	6 180	Z	2.96	19.7	46.1	25.2	4 834	52.4	3 772	49.4	778	65.9	1 346	6.6
Delta	115	102	2 094	10.2	2.49	27.5	33.9	31.5	1 462	43.3	1 180	40.0	209	57.9	632	17.7
Denton	9 150	3 204	158 903	55.8	2.67	22.2	41.4	9.6	111 324	55.8	92 047	54.4	13 668	66.2	47 579	47.0
DeWitt	1 784	1 748	7 207	.2	2.53	26.4	35.2	35.0	5 132	43.6	3 970	40.2	854	55.9	2 075	-2.8
Dickens	519	515	980	-8.7	2.29	32.4	27.1	37.3	639	35.4	535	33.8	77	44.2	341	-6.8
Dimmit	122	95	3 308	7.7	3.06	18.0	48.0	28.3	2 645	52.6	1 898	51.2	568	56.5	663	26.5
Donley	203	48	1 578	4.2	2.30	31.4	27.5	37.6	1 057	37.0	895	33.2	119	57.1	521	16.0
Duval	584	572	4 350	4.6	2.88	22.9	43.7	31.6	3 268	49.0	2 315	48.9	729	48.3	1 082	22.3
Eastland	787	282	7 321	-.4	2.39	28.6	30.8	36.0	5 036	40.2	4 053	36.7	698	55.4	2 285	-.7
Ector	1 711	1 397	43 846	3.6	2.72	24.0	43.4	22.0	31 716	53.7	23 738	50.3	6 004	65.0	12 130	12.6
Edwards	28	27	801	.8	2.66	24.7	36.6	33.1	586	43.3	487	40.0	71	57.7	215	7.0
Ellis	1 933	917	37 020	29.5	2.96	16.6	46.7	19.4	29 660	52.5	23 972	51.4	4 054	59.6	7 360	30.5
El Paso	12 744	7 875	210 022	17.7	3.18	17.8	51.3	23.1	166 226	56.7	118 999	56.9	37 841	58.4	43 796	23.3
Erath	1 808	558	12 568	15.5	2.48	27.7	33.6	23.1	8 108	48.1	6 747	46.2	909	60.0	4 460	15.5
Falls	2 086	2 043	6 496	.1	2.54	29.4	35.2	33.9	4 410	45.1	3 134	44.1	1 015	55.0	2 086	3.5
Fannin	3 377	3 363	11 105	14.6	2.51	25.2	34.8	30.3	7 990	43.3	6 435	40.5	1 142	55.9	3 115	14.8
Fayette	560	499	8 722	7.7	2.44	28.0	31.0	36.2	6 047	41.2	5 059	39.0	677	54.5	2 675	8.9
Fisher	76	63	1 785	-5.7	2.39	28.3	30.3	38.7	1 245	39.5	1 052	36.5	145	57.2	540	6.1
Floyd	141	141	2 730	-8.5	2.79	21.3	42.5	29.8	2 111	50.9	1 745	48.0	266	66.2	619	-11.8
Foard	42	41	664	-10.1	2.38	31.8	31.0	38.4	438	44.1	359	39.8	63	60.3	226	-5.8
Fort Bend	6 298	4 843	110 915	57.5	3.14	13.5	53.5	13.0	93 040	59.4	76 277	59.3	12 655	62.4	17 875	55.4
Franklin	163	163	3 754	24.4	2.48	24.6	33.3	32.0	2 733	41.3	2 325	38.3	317	61.2	1 021	33.1
Freestone	1 543	1 537	6 588	8.7	2.48	26.4	33.8	31.4	4 664	42.9	3 732	39.4	702	56.1	1 924	11.5
Frio	2 140	2 121	4 743	14.9	2.98	20.6	46.8	25.3	3 643	53.0	2 617	50.4	758	60.2	1 100	32.7
Gaines	95	93	4 681	4.0	3.07	18.2	49.2	22.5	3 756	56.4	3 168	55.7	414	63.5	925	4.4
Galveston	4 156	2 803	94 782	16.4	2.60	25.1	37.9	21.2	66 156	48.5	49 664	45.8	12 415	58.5	28 626	23.0
Garza	457	457	1 663	-8.7	2.65	23.8	39.4	28.7	1 218	49.1	973	47.7	186	52.7	445	2.3
Gillespie	557	496	8 521	27.0	2.38	25.8	27.9	39.2	6 081	36.2	5 292	33.8	595	52.6	2 440	39.7
Glasscock	–	–	483	5.9	2.91	23.8	43.7	19.5	355	57.2	326	56.7	14	71.4	128	64.1
Goliad	123	109	2 644	19.7	2.57	22.8	36.6	31.5	1 975	44.3	1 641	42.2	231	55.8	669	23.0
Gonzales	363	328	6 782	8.8	2.69	25.2	38.7	32.3	4 873	47.7	3 663	44.7	831	58.4	1 909	9.3
Gray	1 711	1 710	8 793	-7.9	2.39	28.7	33.2	32.5	6 052	43.6	5 009	39.7	791	63.6	2 741	4.8
Grayson	2 973	1 928	42 849	16.3	2.51	25.5	35.7	26.9	30 191	45.6	23 671	42.1	4 864	58.8	12 658	22.7
Gregg	3 094	1 838	42 687	6.6	2.54	26.1	37.5	24.6	29 677	48.2	22 181	44.4	5 784	60.8	13 010	11.0
Grimes	2 731	2 725	7 753	28.4	2.69	23.8	38.9	26.5	5 630	47.7	4 297	45.9	978	54.7	2 123	34.7
Guadalupe	1 612	710	30 900	36.3	2.83	18.9	42.6	22.6	23 831	49.6	19 043	47.2	3 452	61.5	7 069	41.9
Hale	2 404	2 010	11 975	2.3	2.86	21.0	45.2	26.8	9 142	52.9	7 226	49.9	1 394	66.3	2 833	1.7
Hall	41	41	1 548	-7.2	2.42	32.4	31.4	38.9	1 014	43.1	831	40.3	139	54.0	534	-8.7
Hamilton	235	235	3 374	3.8	2.37	28.4	30.4	38.2	2 323	39.8	1 963	37.4	260	55.8	1 051	1.3
Hansford	86	77	2 005	-5.1	2.63	24.0	40.2	27.6	1 489	49.6	1 304	47.8	119	63.0	516	6.2
Hardeman	67	55	1 943	-7.5	2.40	29.5	32.9	36.4	1 319	44.0	1 063	41.4	202	55.4	624	-5.9
Hardin	426	404	17 805	21.2	2.68	20.7	40.9	23.5	13 644	48.6	11 141	46.0	1 824	60.5	4 161	35.9
Harris	42 134	25 631	1 205 516	17.4	2.79	25.1	41.9	15.5	834 290	54.5	609 446	54.0	165 497	60.1	371 226	14.2

[1] As of April 1. [2] Includes people under formally authorized, supervised care or custody in institutions at the time of enumeration (such as correctional institutions, nursing homes, and juvenile institutions). [3] Under 18 years. [4] No husband present.

Sources: Group Quarters Population—U.S. Census Bureau, 2000 Census of Population and Housing, "Census 2000 Profiles of General Demographic Characteristics" data files, published May 2001 (related Internet site <http://www.census.gov/mp/www/pub/2000cen/mscen01.html>). Households, 2000—U.S. Census Bureau, 2000 Census of Population and Housing, "Census 2000 Profiles of General Demographic Characteristics" data files, published May 2001 (related Internet site <http://www.census.gov/mp/www/pub/2000cen/mscen01.html>). Households, 1990—U.S. Census Bureau, 1990 Census of Population and Housing, Summary Tape File (STF) 1C on CD-ROM (related Internet site <http://homer.ssd.census.gov/cdrom/lookup>).

[Includes U.S., states, and 3,142 counties or county equivalents defined as of January 1, 1992. For changes to these areas since then, see appendix B. Geographic Information]

County	Group quarters population, 2000[1] — Number	Institutionalized population[2]	Households, 2000 (April 1) — Number	Percent change, 1990-2000	Persons per household	Percent — One person	Percent — With 1 or more persons under 18 years	Percent — With 1 or more persons 65 years and over	Family households — Number	Family households — Percent with own children under 18 years	Married-couple — Number	Married-couple — Percent with own children[3]	Female householder[4] — Number	Female householder[4] — Percent with own children[3]	Nonfamily households — Number	Nonfamily households — Percent change, 1990-2000
TEXAS—Con.																
Harrison	1 679	582	23 087	11.5	2.62	23.7	38.8	25.7	16 952	46.9	12 930	44.4	3 144	55.8	6 135	18.7
Hartley	1 425	1 421	1 604	20.4	2.56	21.6	35.1	26.6	1 221	46.6	1 105	44.9	76	63.2	383	27.2
Haskell	104	100	2 569	-6.7	2.33	29.4	29.8	41.3	1 775	39.7	1 481	35.9	226	59.3	794	.3
Hays	7 639	1 490	33 410	50.4	2.69	21.0	37.1	15.4	22 135	51.3	17 746	50.1	3 012	59.9	11 275	45.7
Hemphill	145	145	1 280	-5.0	2.50	24.4	34.8	26.6	948	44.2	835	42.3	75	61.3	332	5.7
Henderson	1 140	812	28 804	25.5	2.50	23.7	33.3	32.1	20 982	39.8	16 903	36.1	2 985	55.6	7 822	36.5
Hidalgo	5 662	5 088	156 824	51.6	3.60	13.1	56.5	24.7	132 859	58.7	101 884	59.6	24 682	58.2	23 965	53.9
Hill	820	520	12 204	18.9	2.58	24.8	35.1	30.7	8 731	43.0	7 018	40.1	1 237	57.4	3 473	22.5
Hockley	610	255	7 994	.1	2.77	21.2	42.5	25.0	6 088	50.0	4 829	47.4	916	61.2	1 906	14.4
Hood	601	416	16 176	45.2	2.50	21.6	32.3	30.7	12 103	38.5	10 287	35.1	1 261	58.0	4 073	67.8
Hopkins	472	433	12 286	12.0	2.56	24.1	36.3	27.6	8 885	45.0	7 186	42.6	1 226	56.0	3 401	16.3
Houston	2 999	2 999	8 259	6.0	2.44	27.9	32.9	35.4	5 756	41.1	4 288	36.2	1 169	58.0	2 503	14.2
Howard	4 787	4 392	11 389	-.8	2.53	26.8	36.8	30.1	7 946	47.0	6 070	42.9	1 393	61.0	3 443	15.3
Hudspeth	32	32	1 092	15.4	3.03	21.1	51.0	23.4	842	58.8	688	58.0	124	64.5	250	9.2
Hunt	1 896	705	28 742	19.4	2.60	24.1	37.2	23.9	20 519	46.1	16 141	42.8	3 161	59.1	8 223	27.2
Hutchinson	297	112	9 283	-3.7	2.54	23.9	37.6	28.3	6 869	47.0	5 701	43.6	848	63.0	2 414	2.3
Irion	–	–	694	15.5	2.55	21.8	39.2	29.1	524	42.9	450	40.7	46	50.0	170	38.2
Jack	1 081	1 081	3 047	11.8	2.52	24.5	35.7	30.2	2 228	44.7	1 836	42.7	280	51.1	819	8.5
Jackson	255	243	5 336	10.4	2.65	24.2	38.6	29.9	3 891	47.5	3 105	45.7	562	57.8	1 445	17.8
Jasper	937	927	13 450	17.7	2.58	23.3	37.9	28.9	9 970	45.1	7 822	41.7	1 687	59.0	3 480	29.9
Jeff Davis	68	68	896	15.0	2.39	26.3	30.4	28.5	633	38.7	545	37.1	62	48.4	263	10.5
Jefferson	15 099	13 793	92 880	2.6	2.55	27.3	37.2	26.6	63 806	48.1	44 918	44.2	15 015	60.1	29 074	10.2
Jim Hogg	44	37	1 815	8.4	2.89	24.4	35.1	30.8	1 360	51.3	1 002	50.4	265	54.7	455	27.1
Jim Wells	508	449	12 961	8.2	2.99	19.7	46.6	26.7	10 102	51.6	7 513	50.1	1 967	56.8	2 859	19.7
Johnson	2 490	2 067	43 636	30.4	2.85	17.3	44.0	20.3	34 440	50.0	28 222	48.2	4 343	59.0	9 196	39.1
Jones	4 965	4 896	6 140	-.6	2.58	24.1	37.4	31.7	4 525	45.4	3 662	42.5	618	59.5	1 615	.8
Karnes	3 614	3 607	4 454	2.7	2.66	24.4	38.4	33.8	3 246	46.6	2 388	43.7	608	54.9	1 208	12.1
Kaufman	1 438	1 248	24 367	36.7	2.87	17.8	44.5	21.6	19 228	50.1	15 371	48.5	2 751	57.2	5 139	33.2
Kendall	479	338	8 613	61.2	2.70	19.2	38.7	25.0	6 694	46.7	5 791	45.3	682	58.4	1 919	60.5
Kenedy	4	–	138	-4.8	2.97	18.8	45.7	23.9	111	44.1	81	44.4	15	26.7	27	-3.6
Kent	38	38	353	-11.5	2.33	28.0	27.8	36.8	247	37.2	216	36.1	21	38.1	106	-5.4
Kerr	1 771	1 213	17 813	23.8	2.35	27.5	28.5	39.9	12 300	36.9	10 119	32.5	1 641	56.1	5 513	27.1
Kimble	51	51	1 866	14.9	2.37	28.6	30.9	35.8	1 286	40.9	1 068	37.2	160	60.0	580	33.9
King	57	18	108	-12.9	2.77	16.7	41.7	18.5	89	50.6	86	50.0	2	100.0	19	-9.5
Kinney	23	23	1 314	10.7	2.55	26.6	30.5	44.5	941	38.0	812	36.1	84	51.2	373	8.4
Kleberg	1 311	279	10 896	8.3	2.78	22.3	45.8	22.0	7 684	49.4	5 672	47.2	1 512	58.9	3 212	18.3
Knox	132	130	1 690	-10.4	2.44	29.6	33.8	37.8	1 166	44.4	947	40.7	167	61.1	524	-6.9
Lamar	1 117	799	19 077	13.6	2.48	26.1	36.3	27.7	13 473	45.7	10 296	41.8	2 511	60.6	5 604	22.1
Lamb	287	287	5 360	-2.3	2.69	23.7	39.8	31.7	3 991	47.5	3 191	45.5	547	56.1	1 369	-.9
Lampasas	357	291	6 554	29.6	2.66	21.9	38.9	26.6	4 877	47.2	3 980	44.2	622	61.3	1 677	31.7
La Salle	603	601	1 819	6.9	2.89	22.9	43.4	28.6	1 352	50.7	995	51.7	281	46.3	467	17.0
Lavaca	472	451	7 669	4.4	2.44	27.6	32.3	36.3	5 389	42.7	4 423	40.0	711	57.2	2 280	7.5
Lee	622	604	5 663	20.3	2.65	23.8	38.7	27.4	4 149	48.7	3 395	47.1	501	54.9	1 514	23.4
Leon	111	111	6 189	23.6	2.46	24.8	31.6	35.3	4 510	38.6	3 726	35.5	569	54.5	1 679	20.5
Liberty	5 041	5 013	23 242	25.4	2.80	20.4	43.0	22.7	17 755	49.9	14 071	48.1	2 646	57.0	5 487	25.9
Limestone	1 855	1 833	7 906	2.4	2.55	25.6	36.0	31.5	5 649	44.7	4 266	41.2	1 067	58.9	2 257	-.2
Lipscomb	46	46	1 205	-2.0	2.50	28.0	35.0	32.6	846	46.3	748	44.3	71	69.0	359	10.8
Live Oak	1 598	1 573	4 230	19.2	2.53	23.9	34.9	31.6	3 073	42.5	2 543	39.8	366	57.7	1 157	33.4
Llano	248	233	7 879	49.3	2.13	28.3	18.8	44.5	5 363	24.9	4 691	21.8	465	48.0	2 516	59.0
Loving	–	–	31	-26.2	2.16	32.3	19.4	25.8	20	25.0	17	23.5	2	50.0	11	-21.4
Lubbock	9 606	3 695	92 516	13.5	2.52	26.9	35.5	20.2	60 090	48.9	44 576	45.7	11 635	60.8	32 426	24.4
Lynn	44	41	2 354	-1.2	2.76	23.1	42.6	28.4	1 778	51.5	1 435	49.4	261	57.1	576	6.7
McCulloch	122	122	3 277	-3.9	2.47	28.2	34.5	34.4	2 267	44.3	1 811	41.0	334	57.5	1 010	.1
McLennan	9 225	4 119	78 859	12.3	2.59	26.0	37.0	23.7	52 892	49.3	39 219	45.9	10 686	61.2	25 967	16.2
McMullen	–	–	355	11.3	2.40	30.7	28.7	32.4	239	38.5	212	38.2	20	45.0	116	36.5
Madison	2 871	2 861	3 914	16.9	2.57	24.5	35.9	32.0	2 839	43.5	2 235	41.4	458	53.7	1 075	12.9
Marion	89	89	4 610	13.9	2.35	28.8	29.0	33.8	3 119	36.2	2 382	32.5	548	50.2	1 491	23.5
Martin	85	66	1 624	-.5	2.87	21.7	46.3	26.7	1 257	55.1	1 044	51.5	154	74.7	367	12.6
Mason	33	33	1 607	12.0	2.31	29.2	27.6	38.6	1 111	37.5	950	33.7	123	60.2	496	15.1
Matagorda	475	442	13 901	5.6	2.70	25.1	40.9	24.4	9 922	51.4	7 484	48.8	1 772	60.9	3 979	16.9
Maverick	115	56	13 089	34.2	3.60	12.9	59.5	25.2	11 231	60.1	8 707	62.1	2 088	55.1	1 858	20.5
Medina	1 782	1 618	12 880	41.4	2.91	18.2	43.8	25.8	10 136	49.7	8 145	47.9	1 429	57.2	2 744	47.3
Menard	41	41	990	5.7	2.34	30.4	31.5	36.8	665	42.4	535	37.8	87	69.0	325	3.8
Midland	1 594	1 214	42 745	9.8	2.68	24.2	42.4	21.7	30 935	53.8	24 541	51.3	4 887	64.7	11 810	14.1
Milam	432	431	9 199	5.9	2.59	25.9	36.2	31.8	6 595	45.3	5 196	42.3	1 035	56.7	2 604	4.4
Mills	291	139	2 001	12.3	2.43	27.8	30.2	38.4	1 398	39.3	1 204	35.4	141	66.0	603	16.4

[1] As of April 1. [2] Includes people under formally authorized, supervised care or custody in institutions at the time of enumeration (such as correctional institutions, nursing homes, and juvenile institutions). [3] Under 18 years. [4] No husband present.

Sources: Group Quarters Population—U.S. Census Bureau, 2000 Census of Population and Housing, "Census 2000 Profiles of General Demographic Characteristics" data files, published May 2001 (related Internet site <http://www.census.gov/mp/www/pub/2000cen/mscen01.html>). Households, 2000—U.S. Census Bureau, 2000 Census of Population and Housing, "Census 2000 Profiles of General Demographic Characteristics" data files, published May 2001 (related Internet site <http://www.census.gov/mp/www/pub/2000cen/mscen01.html>). Households, 1990—U.S. Census Bureau, 1990 Census of Population and Housing, Summary Tape File (STF) 1C on CD-ROM (related Internet site <http://homer.ssd.census.gov/cdrom/lookup>).

[Includes U.S., states, and 3,142 counties or county equivalents defined as of January 1, 1992. For changes to these areas since then, see appendix B. Geographic Information]

County	Group quarters population, 2000[1] Number	Institutionalized population[2]	Households, 2000 Number	Percent change, 1990–2000	Persons per house-hold	One-person	With 1 or more persons under 18 years	With 1 or more persons 65 years and over	Family households Number	Percent with own children under 18 years	Married-couple Number	Percent with own children[3]	Female householder[4] Number	Percent with own children[3]	Nonfamily households Number	Percent change, 1990–2000
TEXAS—Con.																
Mitchell	2 671	2 671	2 837	−7.1	2.48	27.5	34.2	35.1	1 996	43.4	1 576	40.4	324	54.9	841	−3.4
Montague	404	370	7 770	13.3	2.41	27.1	32.1	33.5	5 484	40.7	4 513	37.2	682	56.7	2 286	19.8
Montgomery	1 691	1 453	103 296	62.5	2.83	18.3	44.1	17.9	80 175	52.3	66 287	50.6	9 837	61.5	23 121	71.4
Moore	210	197	6 774	11.0	2.94	18.2	48.3	21.5	5 328	57.0	4 408	54.2	611	71.8	1 446	10.6
Morris	166	166	5 215	4.6	2.47	25.8	34.0	32.5	3 747	41.1	2 813	35.9	734	56.8	1 468	18.7
Motley	–	–	606	−6.3	2.35	25.7	29.9	38.8	435	37.0	365	34.2	53	50.9	171	−15.8
Nacogdoches	4 512	859	22 006	9.4	2.49	27.6	33.9	22.4	14 039	47.8	10 636	44.9	2 605	60.3	7 967	8.6
Navarro	1 430	500	16 491	10.9	2.65	24.1	38.5	27.9	11 908	47.0	9 189	44.1	2 011	58.0	4 583	11.3
Newton	600	600	5 583	13.7	2.59	24.1	37.4	27.8	4 092	44.1	3 241	41.1	641	55.5	1 491	30.4
Nolan	500	338	6 170	−.2	2.48	27.1	35.8	29.6	4 288	46.3	3 268	40.6	776	67.4	1 882	12.4
Nueces	5 761	2 613	110 365	10.7	2.79	22.6	41.8	22.7	79 693	50.3	57 191	47.9	16 928	57.5	30 672	19.4
Ochiltree	73	72	3 261	−2.0	2.74	21.0	43.6	22.4	2 487	53.6	2 086	51.1	256	72.3	774	4.9
Oldham	270	5	735	7.9	2.61	21.0	37.0	25.0	566	45.6	490	43.7	65	61.5	169	17.4
Orange	981	854	31 642	9.0	2.65	21.7	39.5	24.4	23 798	46.9	18 595	43.5	3 820	60.3	7 844	24.8
Palo Pinto	312	303	10 594	11.2	2.52	26.2	34.7	30.1	7 443	43.3	5 893	39.6	1 100	56.3	3 151	22.1
Panola	452	305	8 821	7.0	2.53	25.1	36.0	28.9	6 397	44.2	5 111	41.7	994	55.8	2 424	13.2
Parker	2 921	2 703	31 131	35.1	2.75	18.3	41.8	21.0	24 310	48.7	20 416	46.3	2 707	61.4	6 821	45.2
Parmer	153	153	3 322	2.5	2.97	19.3	46.4	25.7	2 616	54.5	2 226	53.2	277	65.3	706	6.2
Pecos	2 067	2 063	5 153	9.4	2.86	19.6	46.2	24.5	4 029	52.4	3 200	50.1	597	63.1	1 124	19.6
Polk	3 349	3 286	15 119	27.5	2.50	24.6	32.9	34.3	10 920	39.9	8 752	36.2	1 628	55.1	4 199	37.4
Potter	7 024	6 455	40 760	9.1	2.61	26.9	39.3	22.6	27 475	51.5	19 303	47.5	6 099	63.1	13 285	10.3
Presidio	96	89	2 530	12.2	2.85	24.2	45.3	30.9	1 864	54.8	1 430	52.7	343	63.6	666	16.6
Rains	72	71	3 617	38.6	2.51	22.3	32.4	29.6	2 682	38.8	2 239	35.1	328	62.8	935	40.2
Randall	1 766	424	41 240	19.4	2.49	25.4	36.3	21.4	28 777	48.5	23 714	45.6	3 810	63.9	12 463	31.6
Reagan	45	45	1 107	−18.5	2.96	19.8	51.9	20.9	872	59.4	754	58.6	80	66.3	235	2.2
Real	78	71	1 245	34.7	2.38	28.2	30.0	35.1	869	38.0	727	34.5	94	55.3	376	61.4
Red River	273	273	5 827	2.4	2.41	27.7	32.4	33.4	4 065	40.2	3 120	36.6	686	52.5	1 762	5.7
Reeves	1 155	1 149	4 091	−15.4	2.93	21.6	45.4	28.7	3 130	50.8	2 438	50.2	507	56.4	961	−1.5
Refugio	111	111	2 985	1.6	2.59	24.6	36.3	30.6	2 175	43.3	1 646	41.5	383	48.0	810	8.4
Roberts	–	–	362	−7.4	2.45	23.8	33.7	25.7	275	41.8	256	40.2	14	57.1	87	−1.1
Robertson	272	269	6 179	6.7	2.55	26.9	36.9	31.3	4 355	45.4	3 156	40.6	957	59.4	1 824	9.2
Rockwall	617	598	14 530	64.4	2.92	14.4	47.1	15.8	11 977	53.9	10 320	52.8	1 168	61.6	2 553	59.2
Runnels	293	282	4 428	1.9	2.53	26.7	34.8	34.5	3 159	44.0	2 543	40.3	427	58.8	1 269	4.4
Rusk	2 731	2 707	17 364	6.4	2.57	24.2	36.6	30.1	12 720	44.3	10 108	42.3	1 942	53.3	4 644	10.4
Sabine	124	118	4 485	12.5	2.31	27.0	26.9	40.3	3 156	33.5	2 642	29.4	388	56.4	1 329	27.9
San Augustine	267	266	3 575	16.3	2.43	27.0	31.4	35.9	2 521	38.0	1 912	34.7	481	50.5	1 054	30.3
San Jacinto	143	139	8 651	38.5	2.55	22.6	34.2	29.5	6 399	40.5	5 212	37.3	843	54.0	2 252	49.6
San Patricio	1 555	678	22 093	17.7	2.97	18.7	46.8	23.1	17 237	53.3	13 396	51.9	2 808	57.4	4 856	32.0
San Saba	569	522	2 289	7.9	2.45	27.5	32.3	37.0	1 617	41.2	1 348	38.7	192	53.6	672	8.6
Schleicher	47	46	1 115	6.1	2.59	25.4	37.5	30.0	817	46.8	698	45.1	84	56.0	298	25.7
Scurry	1 662	1 498	5 756	−9.6	2.55	25.1	37.4	30.2	4 163	46.8	3 363	43.1	601	61.4	1 593	5.2
Shackelford	62	47	1 300	−2.7	2.49	26.2	35.1	33.3	941	45.3	792	43.4	113	56.6	359	−13.7
Shelby	380	351	9 595	13.2	2.59	25.4	36.8	30.9	6 907	45.0	5 284	42.2	1 234	54.6	2 688	16.4
Sherman	79	56	1 124	6.7	2.76	21.5	43.0	24.1	865	52.8	764	50.4	67	70.1	259	6.6
Smith	4 674	2 292	65 692	15.7	2.59	24.7	37.0	25.7	46 901	46.4	36 462	43.4	8 054	58.8	18 791	20.3
Somervell	158	151	2 438	28.2	2.73	21.3	41.3	23.5	1 840	49.6	1 504	48.1	235	61.3	598	28.3
Starr	397	364	14 410	39.5	3.69	11.3	62.7	22.9	12 663	62.3	9 580	64.8	2 513	56.5	1 747	53.4
Stephens	649	649	3 661	3.0	2.47	26.4	34.7	32.2	2 592	44.1	2 098	40.1	362	61.0	1 069	3.8
Sterling	25	25	513	3.8	2.67	23.2	40.2	26.1	386	49.0	329	47.1	36	63.9	127	29.6
Stonewall	41	41	713	−11.5	2.32	29.0	30.6	36.6	493	38.1	403	36.5	63	47.6	220	−7.9
Sutton	31	30	1 515	3.3	2.67	22.6	42.4	24.0	1 145	50.5	964	48.8	117	57.3	370	5.4
Swisher	640	631	2 925	−2.3	2.65	24.1	38.9	31.9	2 154	48.5	1 760	45.3	279	65.9	771	−.5
Tarrant	22 970	15 761	533 864	21.7	2.67	24.9	40.4	16.0	369 306	53.3	280 611	51.4	64 968	62.2	164 558	24.6
Taylor	6 354	1 232	47 274	9.2	2.54	25.7	38.0	23.1	32 537	50.4	25 419	46.4	5 420	61.0	14 737	20.1
Terrell	–	–	443	−15.5	2.44	31.8	33.0	33.6	295	44.7	241	42.3	33	63.6	148	.7
Terry	972	971	4 278	−4.5	2.76	22.1	40.3	30.5	3 246	47.2	2 556	44.8	510	58.0	1 032	11.6
Throckmorton	22	22	765	−3.2	2.39	28.0	30.5	35.7	535	41.7	450	39.1	63	49.2	230	−10.9
Titus	652	514	9 552	12.3	2.88	22.1	43.4	25.7	7 150	52.3	5 639	50.5	1 086	61.4	2 402	16.3
Tom Green	4 268	1 123	39 503	11.6	2.52	27.2	36.6	25.0	26 802	48.6	20 571	44.8	4 700	62.1	12 701	24.6
Travis	20 706	7 053	320 766	37.7	2.47	30.1	32.1	12.1	183 832	51.1	136 632	49.5	33 333	61.5	136 934	40.5
Trinity	180	180	5 723	23.2	2.38	26.8	29.6	37.4	4 000	36.8	3 153	31.5	643	58.2	1 723	32.5
Tyler	1 584	1 584	7 775	20.4	2.48	24.3	33.8	33.1	5 674	40.7	4 671	37.8	777	54.6	2 101	31.7
Upshur	449	449	13 290	17.0	2.62	21.8	38.2	27.1	10 035	44.4	8 070	42.0	1 468	54.6	3 255	24.7
Upton	33	32	1 256	−14.7	2.68	23.5	40.9	28.4	934	48.8	767	45.1	114	64.9	322	1.3
Uvalde	619	397	8 559	13.3	2.96	19.9	45.5	28.4	6 645	51.8	5 086	50.1	1 174	58.0	1 914	19.3
Val Verde	805	433	14 151	19.5	3.11	17.5	49.3	25.2	11 323	53.6	8 843	52.7	1 963	58.2	2 828	28.1

[1] As of April 1. [2] Includes people under formally authorized, supervised care or custody in institutions at the time of enumeration (such as correctional institutions, nursing homes, and juvenile institutions). [3] Under 18 years. [4] No husband present.

Sources: Group Quarters Population—U.S. Census Bureau, 2000 Census of Population and Housing, "Census 2000 Profiles of General Demographic Characteristics" data files, published May 2001 (related Internet site <http://www.census.gov/mp/www/pub/2000cen/mscen01.html>). Households, 2000—U.S. Census Bureau, 2000 Census of Population and Housing, "Census 2000 Profiles of General Demographic Characteristics" data files, published May 2001 (related Internet site <http://www.census.gov/mp/www/pub/2000cen/mscen01.html>). Households, 1990—U.S. Census Bureau, 1990 Census of Population and Housing, Summary Tape File (STF) 1C on CD-ROM (related Internet site <http://homer.ssd.census.gov/cdrom/lookup>).

[Includes U.S., states, and 3,142 counties or county equivalents defined as of January 1, 1992. For changes to these areas since then, see appendix B. Geographic Information]

County	Group quarters population, 2000[1] Number	Institutionalized population[2]	Households, 2000 (April 1) Number	Percent change, 1990–2000	Persons per household	Percent— One-person	With 1 or more persons under 18 years	With 1 or more persons 65 years and over	Family households (families) Number	Percent with own children under 18 years	Married-couple Number	Percent with own children[3]	Female householder[4] Number	Percent with own children[3]	Nonfamily households Number	Percent change, 1990–2000
TEXAS—Con.																
Van Zandt	946	716	18 195	26.8	2.59	22.0	35.7	30.5	13 657	42.3	11 398	39.8	1 585	53.9	4 538	34.2
Victoria	1 507	1 210	30 071	14.7	2.75	22.4	41.6	23.6	22 201	50.4	17 059	47.2	3 810	63.2	7 870	22.8
Walker	17 091	14 305	18 303	22.7	2.44	27.0	31.9	20.6	11 389	46.1	8 565	42.3	2 134	60.8	6 914	28.1
Waller	3 209	378	10 557	42.6	2.79	21.0	39.8	21.0	7 747	47.8	5 875	46.3	1 369	53.3	2 810	37.6
Ward	369	358	3 964	–10.8	2.66	23.6	41.1	28.8	2 931	45.2	2 329	46.5	459	63.4	1 033	2.6
Washington	1 733	947	11 322	17.7	2.53	25.7	34.6	30.4	7 934	45.1	6 208	42.4	1 292	59.1	3 388	21.1
Webb	3 078	1 929	50 740	47.3	3.75	12.4	60.8	21.2	43 436	62.1	31 778	65.5	9 290	55.6	7 304	47.0
Wharton	747	358	14 799	4.1	2.73	24.4	40.0	28.1	10 744	49.2	8 219	47.4	1 847	56.8	4 055	10.0
Wheeler	134	134	2 152	–8.4	2.39	29.1	32.4	34.5	1 486	42.3	1 249	39.7	165	62.4	666	–4.4
Wichita	11 120	5 424	48 441	7.0	2.49	27.2	37.0	24.4	32 902	49.4	25 340	45.6	5 747	64.2	15 539	19.3
Wilbarger	921	798	5 537	–3.6	2.48	29.0	35.9	30.4	3 746	47.6	2 942	44.0	596	61.1	1 791	2.8
Willacy	1 072	1 063	5 584	10.6	3.40	16.5	50.6	31.3	4 586	52.2	3 466	53.7	901	48.7	998	11.4
Williamson	4 926	3 467	86 766	77.8	2.82	17.6	46.5	14.1	66 991	56.9	55 519	55.3	8 340	67.6	19 775	74.2
Wilson	518	498	11 038	47.5	2.89	17.1	44.0	23.0	8 826	50.0	7 341	48.8	1 020	56.6	2 212	64.0
Winkler	135	135	2 584	–12.1	2.72	21.7	42.7	28.6	1 970	51.4	1 598	49.3	261	62.8	614	–.2
Wise	1 153	1 100	17 178	41.1	2.77	18.3	41.9	21.0	13 465	48.8	11 347	46.8	1 411	58.5	3 713	43.1
Wood	1 459	1 044	14 583	27.6	2.42	24.1	29.9	35.7	10 651	36.6	8 974	33.3	1 197	58.0	3 932	31.8
Yoakum	48	48	2 469	–13.0	2.95	17.3	46.9	23.8	2 008	53.4	1 699	51.6	210	67.6	461	–3.4
Young	402	303	7 167	.9	2.45	26.3	34.1	32.9	5 084	43.5	4 160	40.2	675	59.7	2 083	9.6
Zapata	25	25	3 921	37.0	3.10	17.5	48.2	31.5	3 164	53.5	2 518	52.7	508	58.3	757	53.2
Zavala	363	340	3 428	2.1	3.28	16.6	52.2	29.1	2 806	53.5	1 889	54.7	748	52.9	622	8.6
UTAH	40 480	19 467	701 281	30.5	3.13	17.8	45.8	18.6	535 294	56.0	442 931	55.5	65 941	61.2	165 987	31.3
Beaver	202	202	1 982	24.3	2.93	20.5	43.6	28.5	1 531	53.5	1 329	51.6	138	68.1	451	23.2
Box Elder	371	299	13 144	20.0	3.22	16.0	49.8	22.7	10 809	57.3	9 338	56.1	1 044	65.9	2 335	18.2
Cache	2 189	423	27 543	31.0	3.24	14.5	45.6	15.8	21 018	57.1	18 294	57.0	1 973	61.9	6 525	27.4
Carbon	536	184	7 413	7.3	2.68	23.8	39.8	25.6	5 379	50.9	4 312	48.5	741	62.1	2 034	25.0
Daggett	78	77	340	34.4	2.48	25.9	30.0	25.3	240	38.3	214	36.4	15	73.3	100	44.9
Davis	3 481	1 262	71 201	32.8	3.31	13.6	52.3	16.5	59 273	59.4	50 441	58.8	6 548	64.7	11 928	44.7
Duchesne	210	209	4 559	23.0	3.11	16.8	49.6	21.5	3 669	57.6	3 094	55.2	408	70.8	890	36.7
Emery	93	93	3 468	15.7	3.10	17.6	48.5	21.3	2 799	56.9	2 422	55.4	251	68.9	669	32.7
Garfield	128	121	1 576	19.3	2.92	20.5	40.9	28.6	1 199	50.5	1 047	48.5	107	62.6	377	39.1
Grand	106	55	3 434	38.0	2.44	29.5	32.8	22.4	2 170	47.2	1 669	41.1	368	69.6	1 264	67.4
Iron	693	247	10 627	69.5	3.11	15.9	43.4	18.6	8 073	54.0	6 822	52.9	901	63.7	2 554	83.6
Juab	101	80	2 456	36.4	3.31	17.5	51.9	22.5	1 983	61.1	1 696	59.9	195	71.8	473	20.1
Kane	67	36	2 237	29.8	2.67	23.3	34.7	31.2	1 629	44.3	1 446	42.3	134	63.4	608	53.9
Millard	152	143	3 840	14.7	3.19	18.3	48.5	26.8	3 093	57.2	2 710	57.3	272	61.8	747	12.2
Morgan	–	–	2 046	31.6	3.48	11.7	52.2	20.9	1 782	57.0	1 628	56.7	114	64.0	264	33.3
Piute	16	–	509	13.4	2.79	22.4	37.3	34.2	390	43.1	344	40.7	29	72.4	119	20.2
Rich	18	18	645	23.8	3.01	17.1	43.7	28.2	522	52.1	480	51.5	24	62.5	123	21.8
Salt Lake	14 380	9 124	295 141	22.6	3.00	20.8	43.4	17.3	214 102	55.2	170 666	54.8	30 648	59.8	81 039	23.5
San Juan	254	177	4 089	21.2	3.46	18.7	53.1	20.8	3 233	59.4	2 468	59.0	576	59.9	856	42.2
Sanpete	1 380	861	6 547	34.7	3.27	17.8	46.1	26.6	5 065	56.1	4 388	55.4	471	62.6	1 482	28.8
Sevier	427	342	6 081	24.7	3.03	17.6	45.4	26.7	4 907	53.3	4 260	51.5	474	67.3	1 174	18.1
Summit	56	43	10 332	96.0	2.87	18.4	42.6	10.2	7 502	56.1	6 562	54.7	638	70.7	2 830	89.3
Tooele	1 328	186	12 677	47.7	3.11	16.8	51.0	16.9	10 126	59.4	8 372	58.4	1 200	65.8	2 551	41.9
Uintah	248	231	8 187	22.7	3.05	17.2	48.1	21.2	6 543	55.7	5 378	54.0	871	65.0	1 644	37.9
Utah	9 545	2 556	99 937	42.4	3.59	11.2	51.3	15.8	80 738	59.8	69 790	60.8	8 005	56.9	19 199	40.6
Wasatch	124	122	4 743	54.3	3.18	14.3	48.6	18.3	3 872	56.5	3 368	56.1	356	61.0	871	46.1
Washington	1 359	832	29 939	96.2	2.97	17.5	39.5	32.6	23 429	47.4	20 230	45.0	2 386	64.8	6 510	107.1
Wayne	7	7	890	27.3	2.81	21.5	37.6	27.6	669	48.1	592	45.8	47	78.7	221	52.4
Weber	2 931	1 537	65 698	23.4	2.95	20.0	43.6	21.2	49 549	53.4	39 571	51.8	7 007	61.5	16 149	22.7
VERMONT	20 760	5 663	240 634	14.2	2.44	26.2	33.6	22.5	157 763	48.4	126 413	44.2	22 272	66.4	82 871	26.0
Addison	2 605	164	13 068	14.5	2.55	23.4	36.4	22.2	9 105	49.3	7 495	46.1	1 086	64.6	3 963	28.3
Bennington	1 273	614	14 846	9.2	2.41	26.8	32.5	27.7	9 914	45.7	7 885	41.1	1 497	63.3	4 932	21.2
Caledonia	958	398	11 663	12.5	2.46	25.6	34.4	25.8	7 901	47.9	6 246	42.6	1 210	68.1	3 762	23.5
Chittenden	7 397	930	56 452	16.5	2.47	26.1	33.7	17.1	35 168	51.5	28 403	48.3	4 901	66.8	21 284	24.4
Essex	27	–	2 602	11.0	2.47	24.1	34.0	27.7	1 807	45.8	1 460	41.8	215	64.2	795	31.2
Franklin	601	444	16 765	17.0	2.67	20.6	40.1	20.7	12 194	51.8	9 784	48.0	1 655	67.8	4 571	26.2
Grand Isle	–	–	2 761	36.8	2.50	22.2	33.6	22.5	1 954	44.1	1 658	41.0	195	58.5	807	51.1
Lamoille	597	124	9 221	24.7	2.45	25.0	33.8	20.3	5 980	49.4	4 741	44.4	820	67.4	3 241	32.0
Orange	646	106	10 936	15.7	2.52	23.4	35.6	23.8	7 614	48.0	6 139	43.5	978	68.0	3 322	35.1
Orleans	707	633	10 446	17.7	2.45	25.2	34.1	25.6	7 153	46.9	5 683	41.4	1 008	69.3	3 293	39.6
Rutland	2 012	746	25 678	8.4	2.39	27.9	31.7	25.8	16 740	45.7	13 182	41.6	2 591	61.6	8 938	21.1
Washington	2 117	615	23 659	12.9	2.36	28.5	32.6	22.1	15 053	48.7	11 968	43.9	2 183	69.1	8 606	25.9
Windham	1 126	378	18 375	13.0	2.35	29.7	31.9	23.3	11 456	48.0	9 039	42.4	1 770	69.5	6 919	28.2
Windsor	694	511	24 162	12.3	2.35	28.1	30.9	26.4	15 724	44.9	12 730	40.3	2 163	65.3	8 438	24.1

[1] As of April 1. [2] Includes people under formally authorized, supervised care or custody in institutions at the time of enumeration (such as correctional institutions, nursing homes, and juvenile institutions). [3] Under 18 years. [4] No husband present.

Sources: Group Quarters Population—U.S. Census Bureau, 2000 Census of Population and Housing, "Census 2000 Profiles of General Demographic Characteristics" data files, published May 2001 (related Internet site <http://www.census.gov/mp/www/pub/2000cen/mscen01.html>). Households, 2000—U.S. Census Bureau, 2000 Census of Population and Housing, "Census 2000 Profiles of General Demographic Characteristics" data files, published May 2001 (related Internet site <http://www.census.gov/mp/www/pub/2000cen/mscen01.html>). Households, 1990—U.S. Census Bureau, 1990 Census of Population and Housing, Summary Tape File (STF) 1C on CD-ROM (related Internet site <http://homer.ssd.census.gov/cdrom/lookup>).

[Includes U.S., states, and 3,142 counties or county equivalents defined as of January 1, 1992. For changes to these areas since then, see appendix B. Geographic Information]

County	Group quarters population, 2000[1] Number	Institutionalized population[2]	Households, 2000 (April 1) Number	Percent change, 1990–2000	Persons per household	Percent— One-person	With 1 or more persons under 18 years	With 1 or more persons 65 years and over	Family households (families) Number	Percent with own children under 18 years	Married-couple Number	Percent with own children[3]	Female householder[4] Number	Percent with own children[3]	Nonfamily households Number	Percent change, 1990–2000
VIRGINIA	231 398	111 484	2 699 173	17.8	2.54	25.1	35.9	20.9	1 847 796	47.7	1 426 044	45.3	320 290	58.3	851 377	28.5
Accomack	864	409	15 299	20.9	2.45	27.7	34.4	29.9	10 387	42.6	7 520	37.5	2 210	55.8	4 912	26.8
Albemarle	1 535	1 321	31 876	30.5	2.44	27.0	34.1	21.2	21 069	48.4	17 284	45.7	2 890	62.4	10 807	46.0
Alleghany	249	139	5 149	4.2	2.46	22.2	33.0	27.1	3 868	39.9	3 255	37.5	419	51.1	1 281	17.2
Amelia	106	106	4 240	35.4	2.66	20.7	38.1	25.0	3 177	43.8	2 504	42.9	485	45.4	1 063	51.2
Amherst	1 972	797	11 941	21.5	2.51	24.0	35.6	26.3	8 648	43.7	6 685	40.4	1 483	56.6	3 293	53.1
Appomattox	135	83	5 322	17.5	2.55	21.3	36.2	27.3	4 013	42.7	3 178	40.0	613	54.0	1 309	35.8
Arlington	4 158	1 459	86 352	10.0	2.15	40.8	20.9	15.4	39 322	42.3	30 522	41.9	6 029	48.8	47 030	14.2
Augusta	1 999	1 883	24 818	25.5	2.56	20.1	36.1	23.8	18 903	43.4	15 809	41.1	2 134	55.3	5 915	41.5
Bath	234	59	2 053	8.3	2.34	26.3	29.9	29.0	1 452	39.6	1 204	36.7	160	52.5	601	18.8
Bedford	376	181	23 838	37.9	2.52	20.2	35.0	22.8	18 158	42.6	15 584	40.5	1 788	55.3	5 680	57.2
Bland	638	638	2 568	14.4	2.43	23.3	30.8	27.8	1 907	38.2	1 603	36.5	224	47.3	661	31.2
Botetourt	528	388	11 700	27.9	2.56	19.2	35.3	24.2	9 117	41.5	7 935	40.7	823	46.1	2 583	39.6
Brunswick	2 901	2 531	6 277	14.1	2.47	27.6	32.7	31.7	4 310	39.9	2 947	36.0	1 042	50.0	1 967	27.7
Buchanan	1 205	1 038	10 464	-5.4	2.46	22.5	33.9	22.8	7 899	40.5	6 375	40.0	1 111	43.9	2 565	31.3
Buckingham	2 199	2 163	5 324	22.6	2.52	25.1	35.0	29.3	3 760	43.0	2 718	38.9	758	56.3	1 564	40.6
Campbell	504	497	20 639	15.0	2.45	24.6	34.2	24.1	14 702	43.3	11 555	40.1	2 358	56.3	5 937	43.4
Caroline	578	554	8 021	21.0	2.69	20.5	38.0	25.4	6 009	42.3	4 519	40.0	1 061	48.2	2 012	39.4
Carroll	509	114	12 186	16.5	2.36	25.4	30.4	29.0	8 786	38.6	7 281	36.2	1 054	50.9	3 400	41.9
Charles City	–	–	2 670	23.6	2.59	22.5	34.4	25.5	1 977	37.1	1 431	35.2	405	40.0	693	62.7
Charlotte	231	139	4 951	14.8	2.47	27.4	33.4	32.2	3 437	40.5	2 600	38.4	643	47.7	1 514	41.6
Chesterfield	4 239	2 197	93 772	27.7	2.73	18.5	43.6	15.8	72 139	53.0	58 363	50.8	10 479	63.8	21 633	43.8
Clarke	312	284	4 942	16.7	2.50	24.1	32.9	26.1	3 514	41.4	2 874	39.6	439	46.7	1 428	45.7
Craig	42	20	2 060	22.9	2.45	23.9	33.6	25.2	1 507	42.1	1 276	40.9	144	45.8	553	49.1
Culpeper	1 715	1 638	12 141	24.4	2.68	20.6	39.4	23.5	9 050	46.9	7 099	44.5	1 371	55.2	3 091	32.9
Cumberland	36	14	3 528	25.4	2.55	24.8	35.3	28.5	2 488	42.5	1 819	39.5	503	54.3	1 040	46.5
Dickenson	137	132	6 732	4.3	2.42	25.3	33.6	26.5	4 887	41.9	3 907	40.5	715	49.0	1 845	38.7
Dinwiddie	998	939	9 107	21.6	2.58	22.2	37.7	24.4	6 722	43.5	4 992	41.1	1 267	50.2	2 385	47.0
Essex	160	143	3 995	22.6	2.46	26.1	32.3	29.8	2 741	40.9	2 027	37.5	561	50.3	1 254	39.5
Fairfax	10 297	6 392	350 714	20.0	2.74	21.4	38.4	15.8	250 281	50.8	208 393	50.7	30 166	55.9	100 433	27.5
Fauquier	568	394	19 842	20.2	2.75	18.7	39.7	20.4	15 140	47.3	12 657	46.6	1 702	51.6	4 702	45.0
Floyd	55	54	5 791	21.6	2.39	24.7	31.0	27.3	4 160	40.5	3 468	37.8	468	54.7	1 631	34.3
Fluvanna	931	929	7 387	63.5	2.59	18.8	35.8	25.8	5 706	42.1	4 697	39.7	733	54.6	1 681	75.1
Franklin	1 046	329	18 963	29.4	2.44	22.6	32.2	25.2	13 928	39.7	11 405	36.6	1 778	54.4	5 035	50.4
Frederick	786	671	22 097	34.2	2.64	19.2	39.5	20.1	16 718	48.3	13 806	45.8	1 948	60.1	5 379	56.5
Giles	95	59	6 994	8.2	2.37	26.6	31.0	29.3	4 890	40.2	3 923	38.1	675	49.5	2 104	31.5
Gloucester	334	272	13 127	19.7	2.62	20.3	38.7	22.1	9 883	46.8	8 059	44.5	1 305	57.2	3 244	31.8
Goochland	1 388	1 272	6 158	26.2	2.51	19.9	33.0	24.4	4 712	39.0	3 978	37.7	520	46.3	1 446	45.0
Grayson	1 163	1 163	7 259	12.2	2.31	26.8	28.8	30.5	5 087	37.7	4 179	35.9	619	44.4	2 172	36.3
Greene	147	102	5 574	48.7	2.71	18.0	41.8	18.2	4 291	49.7	3 448	47.3	582	58.4	1 283	60.4
Greensville...........	3 075	3 027	3 375	7.1	2.51	25.4	35.7	29.4	2 397	41.3	1 682	37.6	541	49.2	978	36.6
Halifax	924	796	15 018	40.0	2.43	27.4	33.1	30.5	10 514	40.9	7 685	38.2	2 226	49.1	4 504	78.1
Hanover	2 123	1 008	31 121	37.5	2.71	17.7	42.1	20.7	24 463	50.2	20 670	49.3	2 888	56.6	6 658	46.7
Henrico..............	3 812	3 462	108 121	21.3	2.39	28.9	34.6	20.6	69 834	49.5	52 177	46.2	14 166	61.5	38 287	30.2
Henry	437	382	23 910	9.8	2.40	25.8	32.7	26.6	16 953	40.3	12 977	36.6	2 911	53.1	6 957	37.2
Highland.............	–	–	1 131	4.6	2.24	29.1	26.3	34.8	764	35.6	643	34.4	80	45.0	367	23.6
Isle of Wight	180	125	11 319	25.3	2.61	20.0	38.3	23.6	8 672	44.4	6 832	42.2	1 384	53.9	2 647	36.1
James City	1 245	994	19 003	46.5	2.47	21.4	32.9	28.1	13 989	41.4	11 735	37.8	1 699	60.3	5 014	49.4
King and Queen	–	–	2 673	14.3	2.48	24.6	32.7	31.3	1 897	37.8	1 407	37.0	360	40.0	776	31.7
King George	355	125	6 091	28.6	2.70	20.4	41.4	18.4	4 524	51.2	3 622	48.6	641	63.7	1 567	40.7
King William..........	99	54	4 846	26.4	2.69	18.3	40.6	22.8	3 786	46.6	3 099	45.7	495	52.1	1 060	27.6
Lancaster	421	364	5 004	9.6	2.23	28.7	24.4	42.1	3 412	31.0	2 735	25.4	553	56.8	1 592	21.4
Lee	235	93	9 706	5.1	2.41	27.0	32.5	28.4	6 856	41.0	5 337	39.5	1 136	45.8	2 850	29.4
Loudoun	851	700	59 900	96.5	2.82	18.4	45.1	11.5	45 020	57.3	38 501	56.9	4 675	63.4	14 880	106.3
Louisa	185	106	9 945	33.9	2.56	22.1	36.0	24.6	7 264	42.7	5 702	39.8	1 078	51.2	2 681	49.0
Lunenburg	1 191	1 173	4 998	13.0	2.39	28.7	31.5	33.4	3 385	40.3	2 474	36.3	664	52.4	1 613	33.6
Madison	219	139	4 739	14.4	2.60	21.8	34.5	27.3	3 521	41.6	2 909	40.7	419	45.8	1 218	29.2
Mathews.............	69	60	3 932	11.4	2.32	24.9	26.6	35.7	2 822	33.7	2 408	31.6	310	44.8	1 110	7.9
Mecklenburg	1 569	1 433	12 951	15.2	2.38	27.2	30.7	32.5	8 962	38.3	6 605	33.7	1 829	52.5	3 989	29.5
Middlesex	259	251	4 253	20.5	2.27	27.1	25.7	37.2	2 912	32.7	2 387	29.2	404	46.8	1 341	40.9
Montgomery	9 160	576	30 997	18.1	2.40	25.5	27.1	16.2	17 212	45.6	13 872	43.0	2 371	60.1	13 785	32.7
Nelson	206	65	5 887	22.5	2.42	25.0	30.4	29.4	4 147	38.4	3 277	36.1	628	46.5	1 740	41.9
New Kent	396	396	4 925	32.5	2.65	16.6	38.4	19.3	3 897	43.8	3 282	42.6	442	51.1	1 028	55.3
Northampton	367	190	5 321	3.7	2.39	29.4	31.3	37.8	3 546	38.6	2 412	34.3	929	49.7	1 775	10.0
Northumberland	12	12	5 470	21.8	2.24	27.7	23.5	42.1	3 785	29.1	3 135	25.5	478	48.1	1 685	33.4
Nottoway	1 656	1 595	5 664	8.0	2.48	27.6	34.8	32.1	3 888	43.6	2 754	39.4	870	54.6	1 776	21.4
Orange	487	435	10 150	28.0	2.50	22.1	33.2	30.1	7 471	40.2	5 962	36.6	1 084	52.2	2 679	46.6
Page	260	227	9 305	15.5	2.46	24.4	33.2	28.0	6 632	41.5	5 191	38.3	973	52.9	2 673	37.9
Patrick	229	165	8 141	17.8	2.36	25.8	30.9	27.7	5 814	40.0	4 796	36.7	698	58.6	2 327	42.4
Pittsylvania	395	318	24 684	19.7	2.49	23.4	34.3	26.4	18 218	41.4	14 392	39.3	2 898	48.2	6 466	45.2
Powhatan.............	2 479	2 451	7 258	55.4	2.74	14.6	41.0	18.6	5 901	46.2	5 059	45.1	590	53.9	1 357	74.9

[1] As of April 1. [2] Includes people under formally authorized, supervised care or custody in institutions at the time of enumeration (such as correctional institutions, nursing homes, and juvenile institutions). [3] Under 18 years. [4] No husband present.

Sources: Group Quarters Population—U.S. Census Bureau, 2000 Census of Population and Housing, "Census 2000 Profiles of General Demographic Characteristics" data files, published May 2001 (related Internet site <http://www.census.gov/mp/www/pub/2000cen/mscen01.html>). Households, 2000—U.S. Census Bureau, 2000 Census of Population and Housing, "Census 2000 Profiles of General Demographic Characteristics" data files, published May 2001 (related Internet site <http://www.census.gov/mp/www/pub/2000cen/mscen01.html>). Households, 1990—U.S. Census Bureau, 1990 Census of Population and Housing, Summary Tape File (STF) 1C on CD-ROM (related Internet site <http://homer.ssd.census.gov/cdrom/lookup>).

[Includes U.S., states, and 3,142 counties or county equivalents defined as of January 1, 1992. For changes to these areas since then, see appendix B. Geographic Information]

County	Group quarters population, 2000[1]		Households, 2000 (April 1)													
						Percent—			By type—							
									Family households (families)						Nonfamily households	
											Married-couple		Female householder[4]			
	Number	Institutionalized population[2]	Number	Percent change, 1990–2000	Persons per household	One-person	With 1 or more persons under 18 years	With 1 or more persons 65 years and over	Number	Percent with own children under 18 years	Number	Percent with own children[3]	Number	Percent with own children[3]	Number	Percent change, 1990–2000
VIRGINIA—Con.																
Prince Edward	3 753	539	6 561	22.1	2.43	28.9	33.9	29.1	4 272	44.6	3 050	40.7	977	55.3	2 289	38.0
Prince George	4 968	2 277	10 159	23.1	2.76	17.2	45.7	17.5	8 097	52.5	6 454	49.4	1 243	66.1	2 062	56.9
Prince William	2 389	679	94 570	35.7	2.94	17.1	47.6	10.6	72 737	57.4	57 957	55.7	10 626	67.1	21 833	62.7
Pulaski	1 112	1 023	14 643	9.7	2.32	27.0	30.2	26.1	10 141	38.8	8 034	35.5	1 541	51.6	4 502	30.6
Rappahannock	10	10	2 788	11.7	2.50	23.4	30.7	25.4	2 004	38.1	1 687	36.3	199	45.2	784	33.3
Richmond	1 752	1 725	2 937	11.0	2.40	28.3	30.9	32.8	2 000	39.9	1 536	37.2	348	47.7	937	37.6
Roanoke	2 256	1 325	34 686	14.3	2.41	25.1	32.7	25.9	24 690	43.0	20 762	40.9	2 942	54.2	9 996	34.7
Rockbridge	204	194	8 486	17.8	2.43	23.9	32.0	27.9	6 072	40.8	4 879	38.1	806	51.0	2 414	32.3
Rockingham	1 563	301	25 355	22.2	2.61	21.2	36.0	25.4	18 899	44.1	15 819	42.5	1 996	51.6	6 456	38.2
Russell	1 490	1 390	11 789	10.8	2.44	23.1	34.1	24.7	8 818	41.5	7 184	40.3	1 189	47.0	2 971	34.6
Scott	343	204	9 795	9.2	2.35	26.1	30.2	30.0	7 023	38.5	5 821	37.4	884	45.0	2 772	38.9
Shenandoah	513	366	14 296	14.8	2.42	25.1	30.9	29.5	10 066	39.9	8 148	36.4	1 331	53.3	4 230	26.4
Smyth	1 085	679	13 493	10.3	2.37	26.0	32.3	28.5	9 601	41.1	7 509	38.1	1 516	51.1	3 892	38.4
Southampton	1 565	1 565	6 279	4.5	2.53	24.9	35.6	28.5	4 505	42.9	3 395	40.7	848	52.1	1 774	19.6
Spotsylvania	554	421	31 308	65.3	2.87	16.4	46.0	16.8	24 635	53.9	20 294	52.4	3 099	60.7	6 673	102.8
Stafford	1 494	510	30 187	55.5	3.01	13.8	50.4	12.7	24 493	57.8	20 534	56.2	2 807	67.5	5 694	77.4
Surry	–	–	2 619	14.7	2.61	23.7	36.8	27.7	1 916	41.6	1 453	40.3	368	45.1	703	23.8
Sussex	2 543	2 524	4 126	8.7	2.41	28.2	33.4	29.9	2 808	41.9	1 857	36.9	781	52.9	1 318	29.7
Tazewell	819	517	18 277	5.6	2.40	25.2	31.9	27.9	13 228	39.7	10 638	37.6	1 980	48.9	5 049	27.6
Warren	546	273	12 087	22.4	2.57	24.0	36.3	23.0	8 526	46.6	6 721	43.6	1 207	57.3	3 561	37.0
Washington	1 342	414	21 056	20.4	2.36	25.8	30.9	26.5	14 949	39.5	12 437	38.2	1 823	46.5	6 107	52.8
Westmoreland	105	83	6 846	13.0	2.43	26.9	30.4	34.2	4 687	37.5	3 470	32.6	921	52.2	2 159	29.7
Wise	1 111	435	16 013	10.3	2.44	25.5	34.3	26.0	11 517	43.1	8 992	41.3	1 918	50.4	4 496	38.6
Wythe	410	354	11 511	16.8	2.36	26.3	31.8	26.7	8 103	41.0	6 473	38.3	1 208	50.7	3 408	37.9
York	627	118	20 000	38.2	2.78	16.7	44.9	18.0	15 887	53.2	13 458	51.5	1 871	63.1	4 113	56.8
Independent Cities																
Alexandria	1 901	1 439	61 889	16.2	2.04	43.4	20.5	13.8	27 749	41.4	19 905	38.5	5 700	54.4	34 140	17.2
Bedford	609	405	2 519	1.8	2.26	33.0	30.5	33.2	1 593	43.8	1 083	35.9	434	63.1	926	11.3
Bristol	632	298	7 678	1.1	2.18	34.3	27.5	34.7	4 795	39.7	3 538	35.4	1 046	52.6	2 883	16.5
Buena Vista	291	89	2 547	5.9	2.38	27.6	33.3	29.3	1 749	43.7	1 262	38.9	365	57.3	798	27.7
Charlottesville	6 832	374	16 851	5.3	2.27	34.9	23.0	18.7	7 626	45.3	4 927	37.3	2 215	62.9	9 225	18.6
Chesapeake	4 114	3 205	69 900	34.5	2.79	18.0	45.3	18.1	54 158	52.9	41 702	50.8	9 797	61.8	15 742	50.1
Clifton Forge	206	206	1 841	–4.6	2.22	34.4	29.4	36.2	1 147	41.9	799	36.9	274	54.7	694	–1.1
Colonial Heights	234	192	7 027	10.4	2.37	27.6	32.0	30.8	4 720	43.3	3 534	38.5	914	59.4	2 307	38.6
Covington	11	–	2 835	–5.4	2.22	34.0	27.9	34.1	1 742	38.5	1 272	34.9	355	47.6	1 093	10.5
Danville	1 679	1 078	20 607	–5.1	2.27	33.9	30.6	33.0	12 931	41.7	8 083	34.0	4 036	56.9	7 676	6.7
Emporia	258	181	2 226	9.6	2.43	32.2	34.1	33.8	1 406	46.3	835	39.8	468	59.4	820	32.5
Fairfax	528	360	8 035	9.1	2.61	23.4	30.5	21.8	5 407	41.6	4 382	42.0	744	44.5	2 628	11.2
Falls Church	71	67	4 471	6.6	2.31	33.8	31.5	21.0	2 622	51.3	2 107	50.0	383	58.0	1 849	8.1
Franklin	274	274	3 384	12.6	2.39	28.9	34.5	29.3	2 279	44.7	1 415	38.0	741	59.5	1 105	29.8
Fredericksburg	2 319	93	8 102	8.8	2.09	39.2	24.1	23.7	3 925	44.6	2 575	36.2	1 065	63.9	4 177	26.1
Galax	139	135	2 950	7.3	2.27	34.2	30.2	30.4	1 845	44.2	1 356	39.7	374	60.7	1 105	24.7
Hampton	12 468	9 341	53 887	8.5	2.49	26.6	36.8	20.5	35 911	48.8	24 907	43.6	8 834	62.6	17 976	24.1
Harrisonburg	7 194	898	13 133	27.4	2.53	28.3	25.3	18.1	6 442	47.5	4 778	43.4	1 217	61.8	6 691	44.4
Hopewell	328	328	9 055	.5	2.43	27.6	36.5	25.7	6 073	47.8	3 680	37.6	1 918	65.7	2 982	13.0
Lexington	2 269	142	2 232	2.8	2.06	41.0	20.0	33.6	1 080	37.8	823	36.2	197	44.2	1 152	13.8
Lynchburg	6 551	1 703	25 477	1.3	2.30	32.7	30.9	28.1	15 588	45.4	10 597	39.1	4 066	60.6	9 889	12.8
Manassas	861	747	11 757	24.0	2.92	21.1	45.5	11.3	8 437	58.9	6 556	58.0	1 324	64.8	3 320	39.6
Manassas Park	2	–	3 254	49.1	3.16	14.4	50.2	11.0	2 558	57.7	1 950	58.3	394	58.9	696	60.0
Martinsville	688	593	6 498	–5.0	2.27	34.2	30.8	32.9	4 025	42.5	2 533	36.2	1 243	55.8	2 473	6.6
Newport News	5 833	2 064	69 686	9.0	2.50	27.0	39.3	19.0	46 358	53.6	31 084	48.0	12 473	67.5	23 328	24.7
Norfolk	23 289	3 000	86 210	–3.7	2.45	30.2	34.9	21.9	51 915	50.3	31 813	44.4	16 218	62.2	34 295	7.7
Norton	49	49	1 730	1.9	2.23	34.9	29.8	26.4	1 067	42.3	744	37.0	271	56.5	663	29.5
Petersburg	906	589	13 799	–6.3	2.38	32.2	33.8	27.4	8 508	44.7	4 150	34.0	3 604	57.4	5 291	–1.9
Poquoson	98	58	4 166	10.5	2.75	15.9	41.8	21.8	3 370	44.7	2 892	46.6	351	57.8	796	34.7
Portsmouth	4 814	1 798	38 170	–1.5	2.51	27.5	36.6	26.6	25 482	45.9	15 704	39.9	7 977	57.6	12 688	12.8
Radford	2 813	20	5 809	11.6	2.25	32.0	20.7	18.9	2 644	41.3	1 972	37.1	515	58.1	3 165	21.4
Richmond	11 236	3 179	84 549	–.9	2.21	37.6	27.7	23.0	43 649	44.8	22 898	35.5	17 269	58.2	40 900	6.1
Roanoke	2 538	1 698	42 003	2.4	2.20	35.9	29.1	26.6	24 255	44.1	15 574	37.3	6 939	58.5	17 748	15.0
Salem	1 696	683	9 954	8.7	2.32	29.0	30.4	28.2	6 544	42.9	5 070	39.3	1 146	55.9	3 410	21.8
South Boston	X	X	X	X	X	X	X	X	X	X	X	X	X	X	X	X
Staunton	2 637	1 853	9 676	2.6	2.19	34.7	27.5	30.4	5 766	41.8	4 297	36.4	1 134	58.8	3 910	18.5
Suffolk	979	874	23 283	25.7	2.69	20.2	41.7	22.7	17 730	48.1	12 833	45.4	3 908	57.3	5 553	27.7
Virginia Beach	7 683	2 794	154 455	13.9	2.70	20.4	42.1	16.4	110 953	54.0	85 982	51.4	19 135	64.9	43 502	30.4
Waynesboro	265	242	8 332	10.1	2.31	30.1	32.4	28.4	5 434	44.4	3 878	37.4	1 209	63.9	2 898	25.7
Williamsburg	4 498	136	3 619	4.4	2.07	35.9	18.4	26.3	1 787	33.4	1 348	27.8	348	53.4	1 832	–1.8
Winchester	785	148	10 001	10.1	2.28	34.4	28.7	25.3	5 649	45.3	4 046	41.1	1 175	58.2	4 352	21.3

[1] As of April 1. [2] Includes people under formally authorized, supervised care or custody in institutions at the time of enumeration (such as correctional institutions, nursing homes, and juvenile institutions). [3] Under 18 years. [4] No husband present.

Sources: Group Quarters Population—U.S. Census Bureau, 2000 Census of Population and Housing, "Census 2000 Profiles of General Demographic Characteristics" data files, published May 2001 (related Internet site <http://www.census.gov/mp/www/pub/2000cen/mscen01.html>). Households, 2000—U.S. Census Bureau, 2000 Census of Population and Housing, "Census 2000 Profiles of General Demographic Characteristics" data files, published May 2001 (related Internet site <http://www.census.gov/mp/www/pub/2000cen/mscen01.html>). Households, 1990—U.S. Census Bureau, 1990 Census of Population and Housing, Summary Tape File (STF) 1C on CD-ROM (related Internet site <http://homer.ssd.census.gov/cdrom/lookup>).

Table B–3. Counties — Group Quarters Population and Households–Con.

[Includes U.S., states, and 3,142 counties or county equivalents defined as of January 1, 1992. For changes to these areas since then, see appendix B. Geographic Information]

County	Group quarters population, 2000[1] Number	Institutionalized population[2]	Households, 2000 (April 1) Number	Percent change, 1990–2000	Persons per household	Percent— One-person	With 1 or more persons under 18 years	With 1 or more persons 65 years and over	Family households (families) Number	Percent with own children under 18 years	Married-couple Number	Percent with own children[3]	Female householder[4] Number	Percent with own children[3]	Nonfamily households Number	Percent change, 1990–2000
WASHINGTON	136 382	57 218	2 271 398	21.3	2.53	26.2	35.2	20.4	1 499 127	49.5	1 181 995	45.8	224 618	65.4	772 271	27.1
Adams	245	112	5 229	14.0	3.09	18.7	47.3	22.3	4 094	56.2	3 320	53.9	527	69.6	1 135	6.3
Asotin	342	171	8 364	19.4	2.42	27.0	33.7	27.3	5 650	45.9	4 303	38.7	999	71.4	2 714	28.6
Benton	823	622	52 866	25.2	2.68	23.2	40.7	19.8	38 075	53.0	30 437	48.8	5 376	71.0	14 791	26.2
Chelan	1 082	616	25 021	21.2	2.62	25.1	36.9	25.8	17 356	49.7	14 110	46.0	2 172	67.6	7 665	17.3
Clallam	1 868	1 624	27 164	18.9	2.31	28.1	27.8	34.9	18 068	36.6	14 648	32.2	2 439	66.2	9 096	31.2
Clark	3 044	2 181	127 208	43.8	2.69	21.8	40.0	18.2	90 958	52.0	72 256	48.6	13 140	66.8	36 250	47.7
Columbia	78	48	1 687	6.6	2.36	29.0	30.1	30.6	1 139	41.0	944	35.7	144	68.1	548	7.0
Cowlitz	1 420	952	35 850	13.3	2.55	24.3	36.0	23.8	25 056	47.0	19 563	41.2	3 833	69.2	10 794	19.5
Douglas	293	195	11 726	21.0	2.76	20.0	41.2	23.9	8 871	50.8	7 229	47.3	1 132	68.5	2 855	20.4
Ferry	220	24	2 823	25.6	2.49	24.8	33.6	24.3	1 988	42.7	1 545	36.1	289	69.9	835	36.4
Franklin	914	794	14 840	21.7	3.26	17.8	49.1	20.1	11 603	57.5	9 029	55.4	1 688	69.2	3 237	12.0
Garfield	37	37	987	7.0	2.39	28.3	32.1	33.9	670	42.4	563	39.3	66	60.6	317	15.3
Grant	1 093	564	25 204	27.6	2.92	21.2	43.2	23.7	18 674	53.9	14 955	50.6	2 473	71.1	6 530	23.7
Grays Harbor	640	442	26 808	5.1	2.48	26.7	33.9	27.6	17 914	45.6	13 597	39.6	2 973	66.4	8 894	9.9
Island	1 479	219	27 784	27.5	2.52	21.5	35.2	25.2	20 241	45.7	17 285	41.8	2 161	70.5	7 543	45.6
Jefferson	192	72	11 645	35.0	2.21	28.5	24.8	32.7	7 578	35.6	6 242	28.7	952	69.5	4 067	48.4
King	37 619	12 525	710 916	15.4	2.39	30.5	30.4	18.0	419 959	48.1	329 768	45.7	64 184	60.1	290 957	22.5
Kitsap	7 225	3 833	86 416	24.8	2.60	22.6	38.5	19.7	61 344	50.7	49 839	46.7	8 232	69.0	25 072	30.8
Kittitas	2 163	205	13 382	27.9	2.33	28.4	27.9	20.6	7 787	45.0	6 400	40.7	963	70.4	5 595	33.5
Klickitat	209	107	7 473	20.3	2.54	23.8	35.3	25.0	5 305	45.6	4 314	39.7	681	71.1	2 168	29.4
Lewis	1 019	845	26 306	17.0	2.57	24.0	34.8	28.1	18 559	44.7	14 705	39.5	2 615	64.8	7 747	23.9
Lincoln	125	90	4 151	15.1	2.42	26.0	31.1	31.2	2 914	41.7	2 528	37.8	265	64.9	1 237	23.5
Mason	2 331	2 147	18 912	29.8	2.49	23.3	32.3	29.3	13 391	40.8	10 769	34.8	1 731	66.6	5 521	42.4
Okanogan	851	367	15 027	18.8	2.58	24.5	36.3	25.6	10 585	47.1	8 180	40.8	1 647	70.8	4 442	23.7
Pacific	326	230	9 096	15.2	2.27	29.5	25.8	36.7	5 886	35.7	4 832	30.3	716	62.2	3 210	29.2
Pend Oreille	100	70	4 639	36.6	2.51	25.0	32.3	27.2	3 260	42.1	2 666	36.4	391	68.3	1 379	57.2
Pierce	21 510	8 013	260 800	21.5	2.60	24.3	38.9	19.3	180 199	52.0	137 673	47.8	30 679	66.9	80 601	28.0
San Juan	110	70	6 466	47.2	2.10	30.0	24.1	20.5	4 014	30.0	3 349	29.5	440	72.4	2 452	66.0
Skagit	1 841	893	38 852	27.1	2.60	23.3	35.6	26.2	27 343	46.6	21 993	42.2	3 761	67.0	11 509	30.7
Skamania	64	56	3 755	25.2	2.61	21.1	37.0	20.2	2 758	46.3	2 271	42.4	307	65.5	997	30.8
Snohomish	9 112	3 485	224 852	30.9	2.65	22.6	39.7	17.2	157 820	53.1	125 957	50.2	22 085	66.4	67 032	40.9
Spokane	14 699	6 591	163 611	15.5	2.46	28.1	34.7	22.0	106 017	49.9	81 649	45.0	17 956	67.1	57 594	20.9
Stevens	362	245	15 017	33.6	2.64	22.0	37.5	23.8	11 018	46.8	9 064	42.4	1 308	68.0	3 999	46.4
Thurston	3 398	1 898	81 625	31.3	2.50	25.1	35.4	20.3	54 951	48.9	43 352	44.3	8 429	67.8	26 674	41.8
Wahkiakum	59	58	1 553	17.6	2.42	24.4	29.3	30.8	1 109	37.7	954	32.9	98	68.4	444	27.2
Walla Walla	5 301	3 036	19 647	11.5	2.54	27.1	34.6	28.1	13 238	47.7	10 610	43.6	1 871	66.5	6 409	13.8
Whatcom	4 969	1 129	64 446	32.8	2.51	25.6	32.5	20.9	41 094	47.7	33 025	43.7	5 669	67.1	23 352	42.9
Whitman	5 473	235	15 257	12.6	2.31	29.4	25.5	16.9	8 057	46.5	6 750	43.1	944	70.0	7 200	20.1
Yakima	3 737	2 417	73 993	12.1	2.96	21.5	43.9	23.7	54 584	53.9	41 321	50.0	9 276	68.2	19 409	8.6
WEST VIRGINIA	43 147	24 009	736 481	7.0	2.40	27.1	31.8	27.3	504 055	42.3	397 499	39.5	79 120	53.5	232 426	23.4
Barbour	430	118	6 123	4.9	2.47	25.1	32.9	29.0	4 367	42.2	3 500	40.0	631	50.7	1 756	13.9
Berkeley	1 216	960	29 569	32.3	2.53	24.2	36.8	20.7	20 702	47.8	16 153	43.6	3 151	62.2	8 867	44.6
Boone	107	81	10 291	6.6	2.47	24.6	34.4	25.4	7 464	42.9	5 914	40.9	1 079	50.1	2 827	26.9
Braxton	531	525	5 771	16.6	2.46	25.2	33.4	29.9	4 099	42.6	3 305	40.1	530	54.5	1 672	31.5
Brooke	871	223	10 396	2.6	2.36	27.9	29.5	32.0	7 156	39.1	5 751	37.0	1 033	48.8	3 240	26.0
Cabell	3 325	1 321	41 180	5.2	2.27	31.3	27.8	27.3	25 474	40.8	19 377	37.3	4 776	53.1	15 706	21.8
Calhoun	31	24	3 071	3.1	2.46	24.9	32.0	31.1	2 202	40.4	1 751	39.5	316	44.3	869	17.4
Clay	70	65	4 020	10.8	2.55	24.3	36.3	26.2	2 942	45.8	2 341	43.2	420	57.1	1 078	29.3
Doddridge	109	109	2 845	8.5	2.56	22.5	35.8	29.0	2 102	44.0	1 686	41.8	294	50.7	743	11.4
Fayette	1 977	1 464	18 945	3.6	2.41	26.9	32.7	30.2	13 121	41.8	9 862	39.1	2 497	50.7	5 824	14.1
Gilmer	435	64	2 768	1.9	2.43	25.5	31.0	29.2	1 862	41.9	1 506	38.7	239	57.7	906	22.1
Grant	144	124	4 591	17.0	2.43	24.5	32.4	27.0	3 274	42.4	2 733	40.0	376	56.1	1 317	40.1
Greenbrier	583	489	14 571	5.8	2.32	28.6	30.3	30.2	9 927	40.5	7 891	37.6	1 560	51.7	4 644	19.7
Hampshire	421	336	7 955	28.7	2.49	24.6	34.1	27.1	5 641	44.1	4 513	40.1	758	59.2	2 314	47.0
Hancock	351	337	13 678	–.7	2.36	26.6	29.2	30.7	9 507	37.9	7 481	34.9	1 465	49.8	4 171	17.1
Hardy	75	59	5 204	21.4	2.42	27.0	32.8	27.1	3 564	43.2	2 922	40.3	447	56.2	1 640	49.0
Harrison	1 197	711	27 867	3.2	2.42	27.7	32.5	29.6	19 085	43.3	14 848	40.6	3 186	53.2	8 782	15.6
Jackson	328	282	11 061	14.7	2.50	22.7	34.6	26.7	8 207	43.0	6 810	39.9	1 040	60.4	2 854	41.9
Jefferson	1 145	177	16 165	25.2	2.54	23.2	35.5	21.5	11 319	45.6	9 034	42.5	1 610	57.8	4 846	41.4
Kanawha	3 159	1 553	86 226	1.8	2.28	30.8	29.3	28.0	55 922	40.9	42 256	37.3	10 569	53.4	30 304	17.7
Lewis	226	226	6 946	5.0	2.40	26.9	31.3	29.8	4 805	41.4	3 793	38.2	732	54.2	2 141	13.9
Lincoln	70	58	8 664	13.3	2.54	22.2	36.2	25.5	6 536	43.7	5 235	41.8	932	53.4	2 128	37.6
Logan	552	521	14 880	–3.5	2.50	24.0	34.8	27.6	10 935	41.5	8 476	40.3	1 878	46.0	3 945	18.2
McDowell	303	259	11 169	–13.3	2.42	27.3	33.7	30.2	7 841	41.5	5 710	39.2	1 667	48.3	3 328	7.1

[1] As of April 1. [2] Includes people under formally authorized, supervised care or custody in institutions at the time of enumeration (such as correctional institutions, nursing homes, and juvenile institutions). [3] Under 18 years. [4] No husband present.

Sources: Group Quarters Population—U.S. Census Bureau, 2000 Census of Population and Housing, "Census 2000 Profiles of General Demographic Characteristics" data files, published May 2001 (related Internet site <http://www.census.gov/mp/www/pub/2000cen/mscen01.html>). Households, 2000—U.S. Census Bureau, 2000 Census of Population and Housing, "Census 2000 Profiles of General Demographic Characteristics" data files, published May 2001 (related Internet site <http://www.census.gov/mp/www/pub/2000cen/mscen01.html>). Households, 1990—U.S. Census Bureau, 1990 Census of Population and Housing, Summary Tape File (STF) 1C on CD-ROM (related Internet site <http://homer.ssd.census.gov/cdrom/lookup>).

Table B–3. Counties — Group Quarters Population and Households–Con.

[Includes U.S., states, and 3,142 counties or county equivalents defined as of January 1, 1992. For changes to these areas since then, see appendix B. Geographic Information]

County	Group quarters population, 2000[1] Number	Institutionalized population[2]	Households, 2000 (April 1) Number	Percent change, 1990–2000	Persons per household	Percent— One-person	With 1 or more persons under 18 years	With 1 or more persons 65 years and over	Family households (families) Number	Percent with own children under 18 years	Married-couple Number	Percent with own children[3]	Female householder[4] Number	Percent with own children[3]	Nonfamily households Number	Percent change, 1990–2000
WEST VIRGINIA—Con.																
Marion	1 247	682	23 652	4.3	2.34	28.9	28.6	30.4	15 510	39.7	12 161	37.3	2 529	49.3	8 142	19.3
Marshall	857	581	14 207	1.1	2.44	25.6	32.1	29.4	10 108	41.5	8 064	38.4	1 534	54.4	4 099	14.8
Mason	293	270	10 587	10.2	2.42	25.5	33.2	26.8	7 571	42.8	6 099	39.5	1 069	56.3	3 016	28.8
Mercer	1 261	473	26 509	4.4	2.33	28.7	29.9	30.3	17 943	39.5	14 051	36.7	2 976	50.9	8 566	23.0
Mineral	517	200	10 784	8.0	2.46	25.0	33.2	27.1	7 708	42.5	6 247	39.2	1 042	57.7	3 076	23.8
Mingo	127	109	11 303	−4.5	2.49	25.2	37.1	24.1	8 218	46.1	6 348	45.4	1 430	50.6	3 085	22.5
Monongalia	5 688	1 504	33 446	15.0	2.28	31.3	25.9	19.0	18 504	43.8	14 651	42.1	2 771	53.6	14 942	30.5
Monroe	1 467	1 465	5 447	14.7	2.41	25.8	31.3	30.3	3 885	40.6	3 258	38.9	432	49.1	1 562	31.0
Morgan	171	163	6 145	29.9	2.40	24.5	31.1	27.3	4 345	40.6	3 560	36.4	504	55.6	1 800	52.9
Nicholas	193	176	10 722	7.5	2.46	24.8	33.3	27.3	7 761	42.5	6 297	40.5	1 077	51.6	2 961	30.4
Ohio	2 670	584	19 733	−4.4	2.27	33.7	28.1	32.1	12 147	42.1	9 325	38.8	2 201	53.6	7 586	5.9
Pendleton	168	97	3 350	9.4	2.40	25.8	30.4	31.0	2 354	39.8	1 922	38.1	270	49.3	996	34.6
Pleasants	256	256	2 887	4.3	2.51	22.9	35.5	27.5	2 135	44.2	1 735	41.2	300	58.7	752	8.4
Pocahontas	298	288	3 835	5.7	2.30	29.6	28.5	30.5	2 526	39.2	2 066	36.4	302	51.0	1 309	22.1
Preston	429	271	11 544	8.7	2.50	23.7	34.4	27.5	8 353	43.5	6 861	41.4	1 055	51.4	3 191	29.0
Putnam	301	123	20 028	27.6	2.56	20.6	37.7	20.9	15 291	46.3	12 865	44.4	1 790	57.6	4 737	54.3
Raleigh	3 661	3 125	31 793	7.8	2.38	27.1	31.6	28.6	22 103	41.2	17 253	38.3	3 793	52.6	9 690	26.6
Randolph	1 538	1 218	11 072	6.8	2.41	26.3	32.6	27.3	7 663	43.0	6 058	40.0	1 086	53.8	3 409	19.6
Ritchie	76	76	4 184	6.5	2.45	25.0	32.9	28.4	3 001	42.1	2 437	40.5	407	49.1	1 183	18.8
Roane	112	94	6 161	7.3	2.49	23.5	33.6	27.5	4 479	42.3	3 644	39.7	576	54.2	1 682	17.5
Summers	157	154	5 530	5.5	2.32	29.1	28.6	33.6	3 756	37.8	2 975	35.3	553	47.4	1 774	23.8
Taylor	463	446	6 320	10.1	2.47	25.5	33.3	28.8	4 486	43.6	3 565	41.1	688	51.6	1 834	22.9
Tucker	134	134	3 052	1.2	2.35	27.2	29.1	31.0	2 121	38.9	1 769	37.1	237	48.5	931	11.5
Tyler	107	77	3 836	3.4	2.47	23.1	32.8	29.7	2 833	41.0	2 354	38.4	331	55.9	1 003	16.2
Upshur	1 381	141	8 972	8.8	2.45	25.2	33.4	27.7	6 353	44.0	5 218	40.8	818	58.4	2 619	20.4
Wayne	195	69	17 239	10.3	2.48	24.1	34.0	27.4	12 648	42.5	10 202	40.1	1 854	53.8	4 591	30.2
Webster	60	60	4 010	.4	2.41	26.5	32.5	27.6	2 816	42.5	2 221	39.0	425	56.2	1 194	29.8
Wetzel	170	118	7 164	−1.9	2.45	25.7	33.0	29.0	5 080	42.7	4 134	39.7	665	55.9	2 084	11.7
Wirt	24	24	2 284	17.6	2.56	22.2	37.8	26.1	1 700	47.2	1 404	44.4	204	60.3	584	26.4
Wood	1 351	885	36 275	6.2	2.39	27.1	31.9	26.5	24 898	42.7	19 704	39.0	3 921	58.0	11 377	23.6
Wyoming	119	60	10 454	−.2	2.45	24.4	34.2	26.3	7 705	42.0	6 203	40.2	1 094	49.8	2 749	28.2
WISCONSIN	155 958	79 073	2 084 544	14.4	2.50	26.8	33.9	23.0	1 386 815	48.0	1 108 597	44.5	200 300	64.4	697 729	27.6
Adams	246	167	7 900	32.3	2.33	25.5	26.0	33.8	5 464	34.2	4 620	29.4	528	60.2	2 436	52.3
Ashland	795	300	6 718	7.4	2.39	30.8	32.5	28.0	4 281	47.6	3 263	43.0	732	64.3	2 437	12.2
Barron	692	563	17 851	15.7	2.48	25.4	33.4	28.0	12 349	45.2	10 161	41.3	1 456	65.9	5 502	25.5
Bayfield	120	99	6 207	12.5	2.40	26.4	30.8	28.4	4 275	42.0	3 472	36.4	483	67.5	1 932	17.5
Brown	7 785	3 826	87 295	20.8	2.51	26.5	35.6	18.8	57 539	51.5	46 469	48.0	7 797	69.5	29 756	36.6
Buffalo	172	147	5 511	7.6	2.47	27.1	32.5	29.0	3 783	44.9	3 245	43.2	344	57.8	1 728	25.1
Burnett	260	210	6 613	26.2	2.33	26.9	27.1	32.8	4 503	36.9	3 715	31.5	494	62.1	2 110	38.2
Calumet	360	306	14 910	26.7	2.70	20.4	39.9	19.6	11 164	51.5	9 689	49.6	972	67.3	3 746	49.7
Chippewa	1 077	932	21 356	11.9	2.53	24.7	35.5	25.3	15 006	48.0	12 450	44.6	1 714	66.6	6 350	24.9
Clark	623	520	12 047	7.5	2.73	23.8	36.6	29.6	8 678	48.6	7 377	46.7	787	61.8	3 369	12.1
Columbia	1 555	1 418	20 439	21.2	2.49	25.5	34.0	25.0	14 160	46.5	11 878	43.5	1 520	63.2	6 279	35.0
Crawford	675	599	6 677	12.9	2.48	26.7	33.3	28.7	4 611	45.7	3 786	42.2	559	63.0	2 066	24.3
Dane	15 807	4 674	173 484	21.5	2.37	29.4	30.3	15.8	100 856	49.9	81 649	46.6	13 741	67.4	72 628	31.0
Dodge	5 562	5 297	31 417	17.0	2.56	24.1	35.5	25.2	22 313	47.7	18 737	45.1	2 357	63.3	9 104	34.4
Door	381	323	11 828	17.5	2.33	28.1	28.2	30.0	7 997	39.8	6 867	36.6	763	63.6	3 831	33.3
Douglas	1 293	585	17 808	8.8	2.36	29.8	31.2	24.7	11 280	46.1	8 745	40.6	1 800	67.4	6 528	21.8
Dunn	3 007	422	14 337	17.0	2.57	24.4	32.9	21.1	9 265	48.5	7 754	45.5	993	67.1	5 072	28.0
Eau Claire	5 105	1 142	35 822	14.5	2.46	27.1	31.4	21.8	22 270	48.2	18 111	44.6	3 098	65.7	13 552	27.6
Florence	75	70	2 133	21.5	2.35	27.9	29.1	28.6	1 441	40.7	1 250	37.7	128	63.3	692	50.8
Fond du Lac	4 256	2 305	36 931	13.1	2.52	25.4	34.5	24.4	25 467	47.5	21 321	44.8	2 863	64.4	11 464	27.7
Forest	362	182	4 043	22.9	2.39	28.2	31.0	32.5	2 768	42.6	2 183	36.1	398	69.6	1 275	40.6
Grant	3 274	812	18 465	7.5	2.51	26.0	31.9	27.2	12 399	45.5	10 361	42.5	1 376	62.6	6 066	23.3
Green	508	332	13 212	14.5	2.51	25.0	35.3	25.1	9 215	48.3	7 708	44.8	995	66.6	3 997	21.4
Green Lake	359	263	7 703	7.1	2.43	27.0	31.0	31.3	5 322	42.6	4 510	40.2	533	54.8	2 381	18.3
Iowa	322	190	8 764	18.3	2.56	24.3	36.4	23.7	6 210	48.9	5 212	46.8	666	59.6	2 554	27.1
Iron	111	110	3 083	18.5	2.19	32.0	24.0	35.9	1 960	34.8	1 634	31.8	217	51.2	1 123	31.3
Jackson	1 463	1 138	7 070	13.1	2.49	26.2	33.7	27.8	4 835	45.3	3 917	41.4	611	63.0	2 235	23.2
Jefferson	2 026	995	28 205	17.4	2.55	23.6	35.0	22.9	19 894	47.1	16 510	44.3	2 313	62.9	8 311	29.5
Juneau	369	215	9 696	17.3	2.47	26.0	32.8	29.2	6 701	43.9	5 382	39.8	853	63.2	2 995	27.6
Kenosha	4 024	1 612	56 057	19.2	2.60	25.5	37.6	21.5	38 451	50.8	29 561	47.5	6 468	64.4	17 606	34.4
Kewaunee	258	155	7 623	12.8	2.61	23.5	35.0	27.4	5 548	46.0	4 753	44.5	504	56.7	2 075	21.8
La Crosse	5 349	1 493	41 599	13.5	2.45	28.4	31.4	21.6	25 599	48.5	20 807	45.0	3 486	66.3	16 000	25.4

[1] As of April 1. [2] Includes people under formally authorized, supervised care or custody in institutions at the time of enumeration (such as correctional institutions, nursing homes, and juvenile institutions). [3] Under 18 years. [4] No husband present.

Sources: Group Quarters Population—U.S. Census Bureau, 2000 Census of Population and Housing, "Census 2000 Profiles of General Demographic Characteristics" data files, published May 2001 (related Internet site <http://www.census.gov/mp/www/pub/2000cen/mscen01.html>). Households, 2000—U.S. Census Bureau, 2000 Census of Population and Housing, "Census 2000 Profiles of General Demographic Characteristics" data files, published May 2001 (related Internet site <http://www.census.gov/mp/www/pub/2000cen/mscen01.html>). Households, 1990—U.S. Census Bureau, 1990 Census of Population and Housing, Summary Tape File (STF) 1C on CD-ROM (related Internet site <http://homer.ssd.census.gov/cdrom/lookup>).

[Includes U.S., states, and 3,142 counties or county equivalents defined as of January 1, 1992. For changes to these areas since then, see appendix B. Geographic Information]

County	Group quarters population, 2000[1] Number	Institutionalized population[2]	Households 2000 (April 1) Number	Percent change, 1990–2000	Persons per household	Percent— One-person	With 1 or more persons under 18 years	With 1 or more persons 65 years and over	Family households (families) Number	Percent with own children under 18 years	Married-couple Number	Percent with own children[3]	Female householder[4] Number	Percent with own children[3]	Nonfamily households Number	Percent change, 1990–2000
WISCONSIN—Con.																
Lafayette	154	105	6 211	5.7	2.57	25.4	34.9	29.3	4 378	47.3	3 663	45.5	470	57.2	1 833	14.3
Langlade	256	223	8 452	11.8	2.42	26.7	31.3	32.1	5 819	42.7	4 792	39.2	689	62.7	2 633	18.5
Lincoln	853	688	11 721	15.4	2.46	25.5	33.2	27.8	8 230	44.7	6 842	40.9	949	62.6	3 491	29.6
Manitowoc	1 438	874	32 721	8.7	2.49	26.8	33.0	26.7	22 364	46.1	18 683	43.2	2 440	63.4	10 357	21.1
Marathon	1 743	1 069	47 702	14.8	2.60	23.6	35.5	23.3	33 849	47.9	28 580	45.6	3 513	63.2	13 853	31.4
Marinette	1 468	540	17 585	13.1	2.38	28.3	30.4	29.3	11 840	42.7	9 922	39.1	1 300	63.0	5 745	28.8
Marquette	1 435	1 366	5 986	23.9	2.41	25.4	29.0	33.3	4 167	38.7	3 516	35.2	404	60.1	1 819	41.6
Menominee	52	35	1 345	24.7	3.35	16.5	52.6	21.8	1 065	53.3	572	44.1	358	63.7	280	60.9
Milwaukee	24 110	12 169	377 729	1.3	2.43	33.0	32.6	23.0	225 046	49.5	147 500	43.7	61 497	64.0	152 683	14.1
Monroe	899	680	15 399	17.2	2.60	25.0	36.7	24.7	10 790	49.2	8 734	45.7	1 349	67.2	4 609	30.2
Oconto	358	290	13 979	23.9	2.52	23.5	34.1	26.5	10 046	44.8	8 479	41.3	958	64.4	3 933	34.9
Oneida	908	782	15 333	21.1	2.34	26.4	28.7	30.4	10 493	39.5	8 867	35.6	1 086	62.2	4 840	33.8
Outagamie	3 253	1 626	60 530	19.8	2.61	24.2	37.4	19.6	42 219	51.6	35 622	49.5	4 588	64.6	18 311	37.7
Ozaukee	1 759	648	30 857	20.0	2.61	21.4	37.1	22.5	23 014	48.2	20 244	46.8	1 994	60.4	7 843	50.2
Pepin	119	114	2 759	5.6	2.57	26.1	33.5	29.8	1 934	46.2	1 653	43.9	188	60.1	825	15.9
Pierce	2 348	291	13 015	18.2	2.65	21.3	36.7	18.4	9 030	50.4	7 566	48.1	970	66.4	3 985	30.5
Polk	585	538	16 254	24.5	2.51	25.2	34.1	25.7	11 325	46.1	9 454	42.2	1 206	67.7	4 929	41.3
Portage	3 541	444	25 040	17.5	2.54	24.5	33.5	20.4	16 496	48.7	13 808	46.3	1 827	63.4	8 544	33.0
Price	273	254	6 564	8.4	2.37	28.5	30.4	31.4	4 416	43.0	3 710	40.0	430	59.1	2 148	21.9
Racine	5 471	3 658	70 819	11.1	2.59	24.5	37.3	22.5	49 861	49.0	38 253	44.9	8 682	65.2	20 958	25.3
Richland	302	165	7 118	8.0	2.48	27.2	32.2	29.6	4 833	45.0	4 009	41.3	546	64.7	2 285	24.7
Rock	3 470	1 802	58 617	12.2	2.54	25.1	36.3	22.6	40 403	48.7	31 381	44.1	6 411	67.3	18 214	23.6
Rusk	405	185	6 095	7.1	2.45	27.0	30.7	32.3	4 158	41.9	3 407	39.1	479	53.0	1 937	19.6
St. Croix	936	815	23 410	32.7	2.66	21.2	39.6	17.4	16 946	52.5	14 410	50.0	1 647	69.5	6 464	49.6
Sauk	881	607	21 644	22.3	2.51	25.2	34.5	24.8	14 863	47.4	12 284	43.9	1 745	67.0	6 781	35.6
Sawyer	295	265	6 640	19.2	2.39	26.2	29.7	30.3	4 581	39.8	3 600	32.9	663	67.0	2 059	30.9
Shawano	900	777	15 815	14.8	2.51	24.9	33.4	29.1	11 154	44.6	9 220	41.3	1 258	61.2	4 661	30.0
Sheboygan	3 566	2 714	43 545	12.8	2.50	26.1	33.8	24.0	29 936	46.9	25 273	44.1	3 197	65.5	13 609	28.6
Taylor	271	211	7 529	12.5	2.58	24.7	35.6	27.0	5 343	47.6	4 468	45.4	533	63.4	2 186	30.3
Trempealeau	636	465	10 747	13.2	2.45	27.6	33.5	27.9	7 239	47.1	5 937	43.7	792	64.3	3 508	28.7
Vernon	473	371	10 825	11.3	2.55	26.7	33.2	29.9	7 502	45.5	6 357	43.0	739	60.4	3 323	17.4
Vilas	288	214	9 066	24.3	2.29	26.0	25.2	35.7	6 297	33.7	5 294	29.0	682	59.2	2 769	40.2
Walworth	5 149	1 039	34 522	25.0	2.57	24.7	33.9	23.1	23 271	47.2	19 111	44.7	2 817	61.0	11 251	29.6
Washburn	239	213	6 604	21.0	2.39	26.7	29.6	30.8	4 531	42.0	3 801	35.8	459	64.1	2 073	25.3
Washington	1 298	898	43 842	32.9	2.65	20.3	38.0	20.1	32 757	48.8	28 167	47.0	3 143	62.1	11 085	57.7
Waukesha	5 753	3 930	135 229	27.6	2.63	20.9	36.8	21.5	100 502	47.7	87 606	46.4	9 159	58.2	34 727	58.5
Waupaca	1 801	1 639	19 863	16.6	2.51	25.2	34.5	26.4	13 877	46.7	11 593	43.8	1 475	64.3	5 986	27.7
Waushara	470	216	9 336	22.6	2.43	24.9	29.5	31.8	6 583	39.1	5 602	35.6	624	59.8	2 753	34.4
Winnebago	8 325	4 011	61 157	14.9	2.43	27.6	32.4	21.9	39 547	47.9	32 422	44.4	5 068	66.5	21 610	27.7
Wood	1 206	740	30 135	9.7	2.47	27.2	33.7	25.7	20 506	47.3	17 098	44.1	2 416	65.6	9 629	28.1
WYOMING	14 083	7 861	193 608	14.7	2.48	26.3	35.0	20.8	130 497	48.5	106 179	44.3	16 837	68.9	63 111	28.8
Albany	2 411	133	13 269	11.0	2.23	31.4	25.3	14.1	7 001	45.3	5 573	41.5	994	64.9	6 268	22.9
Big Horn	247	218	4 312	10.4	2.60	25.0	35.3	29.3	3 087	45.4	2 630	42.3	292	64.7	1 225	17.8
Campbell	321	118	12 207	22.5	2.73	20.2	45.4	10.1	9 004	58.5	7 302	54.5	1 070	77.5	3 203	35.9
Carbon	973	962	6 129	2.1	2.39	27.5	33.5	22.4	4 134	46.2	3 377	41.5	506	72.3	1 995	19.7
Converse	94	84	4 694	16.0	2.55	23.4	38.5	20.5	3 410	50.3	2 844	45.7	394	75.4	1 284	29.0
Crook	100	95	2 308	22.0	2.51	24.9	33.8	25.7	1 646	45.3	1 437	42.4	124	70.2	662	50.8
Fremont	820	544	13 545	12.9	2.58	25.5	36.2	24.7	9 484	46.0	7 353	41.4	1 479	63.8	4 061	32.5
Goshen	491	197	5 061	5.7	2.38	27.6	31.0	30.0	3 426	42.3	2 868	38.2	390	64.9	1 635	20.8
Hot Springs	145	145	2 108	8.5	2.25	31.7	27.7	31.3	1 353	39.7	1 145	35.4	157	63.1	755	22.4
Johnson	95	66	2 959	23.4	2.36	28.5	30.4	29.4	2 005	42.4	1 688	38.0	210	67.1	954	40.3
Laramie	3 300	2 313	31 927	13.7	2.45	27.2	35.6	20.6	21 600	49.0	17 210	44.7	3 174	68.0	10 327	24.8
Lincoln	76	71	5 266	27.3	2.75	21.0	38.7	23.2	3 948	48.7	3 514	46.9	270	65.9	1 318	45.6
Natrona	1 560	877	26 819	12.5	2.42	27.5	34.8	21.9	17 747	48.7	13 785	43.0	2 856	69.9	9 072	26.4
Niobrara	101	100	1 011	-2.0	2.28	29.5	28.7	33.1	679	40.4	582	36.9	61	68.9	332	-4.0
Park	867	285	10 312	17.8	2.42	26.2	31.7	24.9	7 092	43.7	6 069	40.1	735	68.2	3 220	30.6
Platte	93	87	3 625	14.0	2.40	27.3	32.0	28.8	2 495	43.6	2 134	40.1	247	65.6	1 130	25.8
Sheridan	715	492	11 167	18.5	2.31	30.9	30.3	26.0	7 079	44.8	5 803	40.0	917	67.6	4 088	33.6
Sublette	72	70	2 371	29.3	2.47	23.6	34.5	19.9	1 707	45.4	1 502	41.9	125	72.8	664	32.0
Sweetwater	613	194	14 105	3.6	2.62	23.6	41.1	15.6	10 096	53.4	8 158	49.5	1 292	71.0	4 009	13.3
Teton	136	80	7 688	68.3	2.36	27.3	27.1	11.5	4 177	47.0	3 484	44.3	436	69.3	3 511	98.9
Uinta	358	298	6 823	15.9	2.84	20.9	46.9	14.1	5 147	59.2	4 173	55.4	677	76.2	1 676	28.8
Washakie	198	190	3 278	3.9	2.47	26.5	34.3	27.5	2 311	46.0	1 962	42.8	240	63.3	967	13.0
Weston	297	242	2 624	8.5	2.42	25.0	33.0	26.9	1 869	43.7	1 586	41.1	191	63.4	755	25.0

[1] As of April 1. [2] Includes people under formally authorized, supervised care or custody in institutions at the time of enumeration (such as correctional institutions, nursing homes, and juvenile institutions). [3] Under 18 years. [4] No husband present.

Sources: Group Quarters Population—U.S. Census Bureau, 2000 Census of Population and Housing, "Census 2000 Profiles of General Demographic Characteristics" data files, published May 2001 (related Internet site <http://www.census.gov/mp/www/pub/2000cen/mscen01.html>). Households, 2000—U.S. Census Bureau, 2000 Census of Population and Housing, "Census 2000 Profiles of General Demographic Characteristics" data files, published May 2001 (related Internet site <http://www.census.gov/mp/www/pub/2000cen/mscen01.html>). Households, 1990—U.S. Census Bureau, 1990 Census of Population and Housing, Summary Tape File (STF) 1C on CD-ROM (related Internet site <http://homer.ssd.census.gov/cdrom/lookup>).

Table B–4. Counties — Vital Statistics and Health

[Includes U.S., states, and 3,142 counties or county equivalents defined as of January 1, 1992. For changes to these areas since then, see appendix B. Geographic Information]

| County | Births, 1997 | | Deaths, 1997 | | | | Physicians,[4] 1999 | | Community hospitals,[6] 1998 | Beds | | Nursing and personal care facilities,[7] 1997 | | Medicare program enrollment,[9] 1999 | |
| | | | Total | | Infant[2] | | | | | | | | | | |
	Number	Rate[1]	Number	Rate[1]	Number	Rate[3]	Number	Rate[5]	Number	Number	Rate[5]	Estab-lishments	Em-ployees[8]	Total[10]	Aged
UNITED STATES......	3 880 894	14.5	2 314 245	8.6	28 045	7.2	693 345	254	5 015	839 988	311	33 140	2 013 278	[11]38 299 382	[11]33 237 188
ALABAMA	60 914	14.1	43 258	10.0	581	9.5	8 733	200	110	16 998	391	349	27 346	676 569	553 223
Autauga	575	13.9	328	7.9	3	5.2	21	49	1	51	121	2	[12]	5 192	4 232
Baldwin.................	1 724	13.4	1 214	9.4	25	14.5	247	182	4	455	342	9	617	22 449	19 583
Barbour	353	13.2	284	10.6	–	–	18	67	1	74	275	1	[12]	4 389	3 451
Bibb....................	275	14.8	186	10.0	1	3.6	13	66	1	138	727	1	[13]	3 050	2 274
Blount	593	13.2	436	9.7	3	5.1	20	42	1	56	121	3	230	5 605	4 609
Bullock	170	15.0	140	12.4	1	5.9	9	79	1	30	265	1	[12]	1 945	1 529
Butler	294	13.5	262	12.0	1	3.4	17	79	2	89	411	2	[12]	4 015	3 269
Calhoun	1 588	13.6	1 244	10.6	20	12.6	184	158	3	387	331	10	618	20 378	16 168
Chambers	495	13.5	470	12.8	3	6.1	35	96	1	200	545	3	244	6 877	5 721
Cherokee	268	12.4	248	11.5	1	3.7	10	46	1	45	206	–	–	3 682	2 955
Chilton	490	13.5	361	9.9	2	4.1	14	37	1	45	122	1	[12]	5 500	4 420
Choctaw.................	211	13.3	178	11.2	–	–	7	45	–	–	–	2	[12]	2 775	2 159
Clarke	492	17.2	297	10.4	3	6.1	17	59	3	103	361	2	[12]	4 750	3 785
Clay....................	180	13.0	157	11.3	2	11.1	5	36	1	119	852	1	[12]	2 693	2 161
Cleburne	168	11.9	160	11.4	1	6.0	3	21	–	–	–	1	[13]	2 335	1 789
Coffee	566	13.5	432	10.3	8	14.1	44	104	2	238	564	2	[14]	6 899	5 842
Colbert	689	13.0	561	10.6	7	10.2	87	166	2	280	529	4	[14]	9 891	8 048
Conecuh.................	160	11.4	188	13.4	5	31.3	7	51	–	–	–	1	[15]	2 642	2 055
Coosa	146	12.6	113	9.8	1	6.8	2	17	–	–	–	2	[15]	2 041	1 543
Covington	504	13.5	464	12.4	2	4.0	34	90	3	167	446	3	376	7 755	6 444
Crenshaw	172	12.6	186	13.6	3	17.4	4	29	1	52	382	1	[12]	2 783	2 321
Cullman	896	12.1	767	10.4	4	4.5	92	122	2	215	287	5	512	12 788	10 850
Dale	749	15.3	403	8.2	7	9.3	35	71	1	85	174	2	[14]	9 130	7 380
Dallas	841	17.9	560	11.9	7	8.3	96	206	2	304	650	5	360	8 534	6 639
DeKalb	791	13.7	657	11.4	7	8.8	39	66	1	91	156	5	532	10 005	8 085
Elmore	900	14.9	538	8.9	5	5.6	32	50	2	114	184	4	389	8 668	7 063
Escambia	492	13.4	411	11.2	8	16.3	31	85	2	118	321	2	[12]	6 207	5 034
Etowah	1 318	12.7	1 331	12.8	13	9.9	184	178	2	514	495	12	999	19 168	15 475
Fayette	212	11.7	229	12.6	2	9.4	12	66	1	183	1 011	1	[13]	3 133	2 558
Franklin	443	15.0	360	12.2	6	13.5	25	84	2	133	448	7	310	5 935	4 739
Geneva	280	11.3	286	11.5	1	3.6	11	44	1	151	607	1	[12]	4 987	4 112
Greene	165	16.6	128	12.9	1	6.1	6	62	1	72	731	–	–	1 743	1 361
Hale	269	16.4	191	11.6	1	3.7	5	30	1	30	179	2	[12]	3 039	2 416
Henry	185	11.8	178	11.3	2	10.8	2	13	–	–	–	2	[12]	2 972	2 531
Houston	1 158	13.6	764	9.0	13	11.2	261	303	2	568	663	2	[14]	11 377	9 435
Jackson	645	12.7	571	11.3	6	9.3	45	87	2	221	430	4	[12]	8 904	7 176
Jefferson	9 351	14.2	7 323	11.1	101	10.8	3 309	503	14	4 077	618	47	4 818	110 187	91 905
Lamar	197	12.3	196	12.3	4	20.3	3	19	–	–	–	2	[12]	3 249	2 663
Lauderdale...............	1 019	12.1	852	10.2	6	5.9	158	187	2	610	724	8	480	15 255	12 732
Lawrence	430	12.9	311	9.3	3	7.0	9	27	1	30	90	3	[12]	4 287	3 410
Lee	1 392	14.1	699	7.1	10	7.2	150	147	1	280	279	2	[14]	10 319	8 386
Limestone	838	13.7	538	8.8	4	4.8	48	76	1	101	162	8	373	7 777	6 365
Lowndes.................	223	17.3	128	9.9	5	22.4	4	31	–	–	–	–	–	1 718	1 273
Macon...................	370	16.0	280	12.1	4	10.8	23	100	–	–	–	2	[12]	3 541	2 871
Madison	3 914	14.4	1 968	7.2	21	5.4	613	219	3	709	255	25	1 109	32 777	28 404
Marengo.................	345	14.7	246	10.5	1	2.9	15	65	1	99	424	1	[15]	3 532	2 854
Marion	332	10.7	382	12.4	5	15.1	29	95	2	175	567	3	202	5 528	4 470
Marshall	1 205	15.1	838	10.5	10	8.3	84	104	2	192	239	9	665	15 322	12 592
Mobile..................	6 219	15.6	3 894	9.8	86	13.8	1 042	261	6	1 633	409	32	2 336	56 706	46 501
Monroe	387	16.0	229	9.5	3	7.8	18	75	1	59	246	1	[12]	3 785	3 058
Montgomery	3 424	15.7	1 956	9.0	36	10.5	558	259	4	804	370	20	1 514	30 826	25 417
Morgan	1 487	13.7	969	8.9	11	7.4	174	159	3	444	407	17	565	16 700	13 930
Perry	182	14.4	166	13.2	4	22.0	4	32	1	76	599	1	[15]	2 033	1 621
Pickens.................	265	12.7	248	11.8	–	–	13	62	1	50	238	2	[12]	3 878	3 145
Pike....................	370	13.0	334	11.7	4	10.8	28	98	1	97	339	1	[12]	4 819	3 904
Randolph	299	15.0	206	10.3	5	16.7	12	59	2	105	524	2	[12]	4 038	3 298
Russell	708	14.0	542	10.7	8	11.3	29	58	1	114	226	4	362	8 213	6 634
St. Clair	763	12.6	513	8.5	5	6.6	32	50	1	51	82	6	457	7 486	5 926
Shelby	2 072	15.3	838	6.2	22	10.6	129	88	1	228	162	2	[14]	11 043	8 979
Sumter	243	15.3	177	11.1	–	–	6	38	–	–	–	1	[12]	2 447	1 977
Talladega	1 087	14.2	867	11.3	8	7.4	62	80	2	273	354	4	422	13 661	9 979
Tallapoosa	542	13.5	510	12.7	6	11.1	49	122	2	109	270	9	562	7 201	5 858
Tuscaloosa	2 124	13.3	1 302	8.1	20	9.4	374	232	2	641	399	15	1 071	22 174	17 572
Walker	933	13.2	855	12.1	9	9.6	64	90	1	245	345	11	761	14 047	10 720
Washington	235	13.4	168	9.6	2	8.5	7	39	1	103	583	1	[13]	2 739	2 119
Wilcox..................	208	15.5	181	13.5	–	–	3	22	1	322	2 394	1	[15]	2 467	1 837
Winston	293	12.2	259	10.8	3	10.2	10	41	1	43	178	3	253	4 475	3 537

[1] Per 1,000 resident population estimated as of July 1, 1997. [2] Deaths of infants under 1 year old. [3] Infant deaths per 1,000 live births. [4] Active, nonfederal physicians as of December 31. Data subject to copyright; see below for source citation. [5] Per 100,000 resident population estimated as of July 1 of the year shown. [6] Nonfederal, short-stay (average length of stay less than 30 days) hospitals except hospital units of institutions. Data subject to copyright; see below for source citation. [7] SIC 805 includes skilled nursing care facilities; intermediate care facilities; and nursing and personal care, not elsewhere classified. [8] Full- and part-time employees on the payroll in the pay period including March 12. [9] Unduplicated count of persons enrolled in either hospital and/or supplemental medical insurance as of July 1. State totals include data not distributed by county. [10] Includes disabled, not shown separately. [11] Includes data not distributed by State. [12] 100 to 249 employees. [13] 0 to 19 employees. [14] 250 to 499 employees. [15] 20 to 99 employees.

Sources: Births—U.S. National Center for Health Statistics, "Vital Statistics of the United States, Vol. I, Natality," annual, and unpublished data. Deaths—U.S. National Center for Health Statistics, "Vital Statistics of the United States, Vol. II, Mortality," annual, and unpublished data. Physicians—American Medical Association, Chicago, IL, "Physician Characteristics and Distribution in the U.S.," annual (copyright). Community Hospitals—Health Forum, LLC, an American Hospital Association Company, Chicago, IL, "Hospital Statistics" 2000 edition and unpublished data (copyright). Nursing and Personal Care Facilities—U.S. Census Bureau, County Business Patterns 1997 on CD-ROM (related Internet site <http://www.census.gov/epcd/cbp/view/cbpview.html>). Medicare—U.S. Health Care Financing Administration; "Medicare County Enrollment as of July 1, 1999 - Aged and Disabled 3/2000 update," <http://www.hcfa.gov/stats/enroll/default.htm>.

[Includes U.S., states, and 3,142 counties or county equivalents defined as of January 1, 1992. For changes to these areas since then, see appendix B. Geographic Information]

County	Births, 1997		Deaths, 1997				Physicians,[4] 1999		Community hospitals,[6] 1998			Nursing and personal care facilities,[7] 1997		Medicare program enrollment,[9] 1999	
			Total		Infant[2]					Beds					
	Number	Rate[1]	Number	Rate[1]	Number	Rate[3]	Number	Rate[5]	Number	Number	Rate[5]	Estab-lishments	Em-ployees[8]	Total[10]	Aged
ALASKA	9 947	16.3	2 575	4.2	75	7.5	1 054	170	17	1 240	202	21	694	40 062	33 338
Aleutians East	29	12.7	11	4.8	–	–	–	–	–	–	–	–	–	(11)	(11)
Aleutians West	47	11.5	19	4.6	–	–	–	–	–	–	–	–	–	[11]190	[11]163
Anchorage	4 167	16.6	953	3.8	29	7.0	602	234	2	530	207	7	(12)	16 091	13 081
Bethel	418	26.5	74	4.7	6	14.4	16	99	–	–	–	–	–	[13]692	[13]601
Bristol Bay	24	22.0	5	4.6	–	–	–	–	–	–	–	–	–	221	180
Denali	(14)	(14)	(14)	(14)	–	–	–	–	–	–	–	–	–	(14)	(14)
Dillingham	101	22.7	21	4.7	–	–	10	219	–	–	–	2	(15)	[16]374	[16]331
Fairbanks North Star	1 424	17.1	306	3.7	10	7.0	151	179	1	198	235	–	–	4 631	3 857
Haines	19	8.2	13	5.6	–	–	–	–	–	–	–	–	–	297	267
Juneau	403	13.3	117	3.9	2	5.0	57	189	1	64	212	1	(17)	2 414	2 062
Kenai Peninsula	651	13.6	255	5.3	3	4.6	56	114	3	103	213	3	221	4 193	3 528
Ketchikan Gateway	193	13.2	84	5.7	3	15.5	–	–	1	64	450	–	–	1 233	1 060
Kodiak Island	263	17.9	45	3.1	1	3.8	14	98	1	44	304	1	(15)	413	379
Lake and Peninsula	37	21.4	16	9.3	–	–	–	–	–	–	–	–	–	(16)	(16)
Matanuska-Susitna	694	12.9	221	4.1	8	11.5	47	81	1	36	65	1	(15)	3 744	3 022
Nome	201	22.5	60	6.7	6	29.9	12	135	1	34	378	–	–	536	472
North Slope	153	21.2	43	6.0	–	–	8	113	–	–	–	–	–	306	255
Northwest Arctic	176	26.4	28	4.2	–	–	4	60	–	–	–	–	–	366	310
Prince of Wales-Outer Ketchikan	94	13.5	33	4.7	2	21.3	27	403	–	–	–	–	–	384	327
Sitka	110	13.0	48	5.7	–	–	28	342	2	82	987	–	–	724	636
Skagway-Yakutat-Angoon	40	8.6	25	5.4	–	–	–	–	–	–	–	–	–	328	278
Southeast Fairbanks	105	17.9	29	4.9	1	9.5	3	51	–	–	–	–	–	437	356
Valdez-Cordova	130	12.6	47	4.5	–	–	9	88	2	38	371	5	(15)	656	561
Wade Hampton	226	33.3	33	4.9	3	13.3	–	–	–	–	–	–	–	384	343
Wrangell-Petersburg	98	14.2	44	6.4	1	10.2	9	132	2	47	690	1	(15)	662	592
Yukon-Koyukuk	[14]144	[14]17.4	[14]45	[14]5.4	–	–	1	16	–	–	–	–	–	[18]658	[18]578
ARIZONA	75 699	16.6	37 066	8.1	536	7.1	9 714	203	64	10 857	233	355	22 514	658 193	576 916
Apache	1 333	19.2	406	5.8	9	6.8	60	88	2	109	159	2	(17)	6 250	5 218
Cochise	1 648	14.8	985	8.8	10	6.1	98	87	5	275	245	12	522	17 627	15 262
Coconino	1 815	16.0	472	4.2	17	9.4	268	234	2	181	159	10	273	12 388	10 703
Gila	665	13.8	583	12.1	7	10.5	63	128	2	90	184	3	393	10 930	9 508
Graham	490	15.7	234	7.5	4	8.2	20	63	1	44	139	3	(19)	4 170	3 598
Greenlee	166	17.6	60	6.4	–	–	7	78	–	–	–	–	–	1 049	941
La Paz	226	15.3	185	12.5	6	26.5	–	–	1	39	263	–	–	3 455	3 053
Maricopa	47 135	17.5	20 466	7.6	345	7.3	6 048	211	29	6 656	239	210	14 931	355 749	313 595
Mohave	1 842	14.4	1 668	13.0	16	8.7	150	112	4	457	350	6	224	31 913	27 766
Navajo	1 654	17.5	662	7.0	12	7.3	90	92	2	88	91	2	(19)	10 686	8 918
Pima	11 377	14.6	7 021	9.0	70	6.2	2 454	305	10	2 101	266	63	3 743	123 255	107 649
Pinal	2 150	15.0	1 349	9.4	21	9.8	76	50	2	321	218	8	241	24 042	20 367
Santa Cruz	780	21.0	216	5.8	2	2.6	29	74	1	80	210	1	(15)	4 600	4 121
Yavapai	1 544	10.7	1 817	12.6	8	5.2	190	124	2	159	107	28	1 219	34 156	30 276
Yuma	2 874	22.3	942	7.3	9	3.1	161	119	1	257	195	7	576	17 758	15 810
ARKANSAS	36 478	14.5	27 844	11.0	316	8.7	4 906	192	82	9 876	389	332	21 305	435 880	357 554
Arkansas	252	12.1	283	13.6	3	11.9	19	92	2	154	746	3	(19)	3 906	3 353
Ashley	340	14.0	288	11.8	6	17.6	14	58	1	37	152	2	(19)	4 186	3 388
Baxter	309	8.5	581	16.1	–	–	81	221	1	191	526	5	319	11 184	9 868
Benton	2 071	15.9	1 194	9.2	10	4.8	169	122	3	212	158	16	755	23 410	20 513
Boone	465	14.7	382	12.0	2	4.3	58	182	1	125	393	3	(12)	6 993	5 599
Bradley	145	12.6	176	15.3	1	6.9	8	70	1	56	491	2	(19)	2 489	2 044
Calhoun	61	10.7	84	14.7	1	16.4	1	18	–	–	–	1	(17)	893	707
Carroll	314	14.0	227	10.1	3	9.6	23	102	2	55	245	2	(19)	4 234	3 621
Chicot	216	14.2	194	12.7	4	18.5	16	108	1	42	280	1	(17)	2 688	2 170
Clark	278	12.5	253	11.4	2	7.2	16	75	1	57	264	2	(19)	4 079	3 471
Clay	192	11.0	298	17.1	2	10.4	7	41	1	35	204	2	(19)	4 033	3 429
Cleburne	233	10.3	283	12.6	–	–	20	86	1	24	105	4	259	5 493	4 728
Cleveland	94	11.3	106	12.7	–	–	1	12	–	–	–	1	(17)	1 358	1 090
Columbia	339	13.4	348	13.8	1	2.9	15	61	1	62	247	4	245	4 933	4 085
Conway	268	13.4	260	13.0	1	3.7	14	71	–	–	–	8	621	4 628	3 657
Craighead	1 116	14.6	714	9.4	10	9.0	237	305	3	470	609	13	578	11 220	9 132
Crawford	758	15.3	460	9.3	8	10.6	35	68	1	103	205	6	364	7 815	5 798
Crittenden	882	17.8	513	10.4	10	11.3	43	86	1	95	191	6	274	6 108	4 759
Cross	277	14.3	242	12.5	3	10.8	10	52	1	53	273	1	(19)	3 111	2 545
Dallas	123	13.4	151	16.5	4	32.5	5	56	1	26	287	5	400	1 912	1 544
Desha	250	16.4	154	10.1	1	4.0	16	108	2	69	458	2	(19)	2 579	2 145

[1] Per 1,000 resident population estimated as of July 1, 1997. [2] Deaths of infants under 1 year old. [3] Infant deaths per 1,000 live births. [4] Active, nonfederal physicians as of December 31. Data subject to copyright; see below for source citation. [5] Per 100,000 resident population estimated as of July 1 of the year shown. [6] Nonfederal, short-stay (average length of stay less than 30 days) hospitals except hospital units of institutions. Data subject to copyright; see below for source citation. [7] SIC 805 includes skilled nursing care facilities; intermediate care facilities; and nursing and personal care, not elsewhere classified. [8] Full- and part-time employees on the payroll in the pay period including March 12. [9] Unduplicated count of persons enrolled in either hospital and/or supplemental medical insurance as of July 1. State totals include data not distributed by county. [10] Includes disabled, not shown separately. [11] Aleutians East Borough included with Aleutians West Census Area; data not available separately. [12] 250 to 499 employees. [13] Bethel Census Area excludes part of old Kuskokwim Census Division not available separately from Yukon-Koyukuk Census Area. [14] Denali Borough included with Yukon-Koyukuk Census Area; data not available separately. [15] 0 to 19 employees. [16] Lake and Peninsula Borough included with Dillingham Census Area;data not available separately. [17] 20 to 99 employees. [18] Yukon-Koyukuk Census Area includes part of old Kuskokwim Census Division now in Bethel Census Area as well as Denali Borough. [19] 100 to 249 employees.

Sources: Births—U.S. National Center for Health Statistics, "Vital Statistics of the United States, Vol. I, Natality," annual, and unpublished data. Deaths—U.S. National Center for Health Statistics, "Vital Statistics of the United States, Vol. II, Mortality," annual, and unpublished data. Physicians—American Medical Association, Chicago, IL, "Physician Characteristics and Distribution in the U.S.," annual (copyright). Community Hospitals—Health Forum, LLC, an American Hospital Association Company, Chicago, IL, "Hospital Statistics" 2000 edition and unpublished data (copyright). Nursing and Personal Care Facilities—U.S. Census Bureau, County Business Patterns 1997 on CD-ROM (related Internet site <http://www.census.gov/epcd/cbp/view/cbpview.html>). Medicare—U.S. Health Care Financing Administration; "Medicare County Enrollment as of July 1, 1999 - Aged and Disabled 3/2000 update," <http://www.hcfa.gov/stats/enroll/default.htm>.

[Includes U.S., states, and 3,142 counties or county equivalents defined as of January 1, 1992. For changes to these areas since then, see appendix B. Geographic Information]

County	Births, 1997 Number	Births, 1997 Rate[1]	Deaths, 1997 Total Number	Deaths, 1997 Total Rate[1]	Deaths, 1997 Infant[2] Number	Deaths, 1997 Infant[2] Rate[3]	Physicians,[4] 1999 Number	Physicians,[4] 1999 Rate[5]	Community hospitals,[6] 1998 Number	Community hospitals,[6] 1998 Beds Number	Community hospitals,[6] 1998 Beds Rate[5]	Nursing and personal care facilities,[7] 1997 Establishments	Nursing and personal care facilities,[7] 1997 Employees[8]	Medicare program enrollment,[9] 1999 Total[10]	Medicare program enrollment,[9] 1999 Aged
ARKANSAS—Con.															
Drew	277	15.7	186	10.6	3	10.8	8	46	1	50	286	1	(11)	2 589	2 119
Faulkner	1 075	14.0	563	7.4	8	7.4	89	111	1	116	148	11	343	9 379	7 746
Franklin	220	13.3	179	10.8	1	4.5	5	30	1	39	232	2	(12)	3 135	2 417
Fulton	123	11.4	159	14.7	1	8.1	8	73	1	30	274	1	(12)	2 713	2 155
Garland	1 015	12.3	1 235	14.9	4	3.9	216	256	2	432	516	12	863	22 373	19 801
Grant	181	11.6	136	8.7	3	16.6	6	38	–	–	–	1	(11)	2 219	1 827
Greene	467	13.2	418	11.8	6	12.8	40	110	1	129	358	2	(13)	6 078	4 963
Hempstead	357	16.2	271	12.3	5	14.0	20	91	2	129	585	10	262	3 600	3 003
Hot Spring	367	12.8	319	11.1	3	8.2	12	41	1	74	256	3	155	5 266	4 378
Howard	206	15.0	195	14.2	2	9.7	10	73	–	–	–	6	370	2 653	2 241
Independence	417	12.8	373	11.4	1	2.4	57	172	1	174	529	4	377	6 107	4 848
Izard	141	10.8	192	14.7	–	–	8	61	1	26	198	5	331	3 311	2 709
Jackson	218	12.2	267	14.9	2	9.2	20	114	2	174	982	5	308	5 201	4 076
Jefferson	1 300	15.8	977	11.9	18	13.8	162	201	1	535	656	7	484	12 901	10 461
Johnson	319	15.1	238	11.2	3	9.4	19	89	1	68	317	2	(12)	3 941	3 113
Lafayette	125	13.9	118	13.1	–	–	2	23	–	–	–	1	(11)	1 642	1 322
Lawrence	207	11.9	256	14.7	4	19.3	10	58	1	205	1 191	1	(11)	4 035	3 306
Lee	155	12.2	158	12.4	3	19.4	6	47	–	–	–	1	(11)	2 043	1 657
Lincoln	167	11.7	140	9.8	2	12.0	2	14	–	–	–	2	(12)	1 819	1 447
Little River	186	14.1	143	10.8	1	5.4	5	38	1	42	319	2	(12)	2 283	1 916
Logan	286	13.5	257	12.1	–	–	13	62	2	42	199	3	214	4 498	3 527
Lonoke	661	13.4	402	8.2	6	9.1	17	33	–	–	–	7	474	6 266	5 089
Madison	181	13.9	154	11.8	–	–	6	45	–	–	–	1	(11)	2 392	1 890
Marion	128	8.9	188	13.0	1	7.8	4	27	–	–	–	2	(12)	3 270	2 626
Miller	596	15.1	388	9.8	4	6.7	26	66	–	–	–	4	323	5 809	4 845
Mississippi	935	18.6	613	12.2	11	11.8	39	78	2	254	503	5	261	7 728	6 087
Monroe	157	15.2	156	15.1	1	6.4	4	40	–	–	–	2	(12)	2 025	1 674
Montgomery	110	12.9	116	13.6	–	–	2	23	–	–	–	–	–	1 790	1 511
Nevada	127	12.6	143	14.2	2	15.7	3	30	–	–	–	2	(12)	1 853	1 515
Newton	95	11.6	86	10.5	1	10.5	3	36	–	–	–	–	–	1 547	1 130
Ouachita	362	12.9	392	14.0	4	11.0	19	69	1	118	425	4	240	5 997	4 872
Perry	109	11.6	130	13.8	3	27.5	1	10	–	–	–	1	(11)	1 894	1 446
Phillips	514	18.6	367	13.3	8	15.6	20	74	1	115	421	5	262	4 783	3 818
Pike	151	14.4	121	11.6	1	6.6	7	67	1	32	303	2	(12)	2 048	1 744
Poinsett	341	13.9	337	13.7	3	8.8	6	24	–	–	–	3	227	4 623	3 624
Polk	306	15.7	267	13.7	–	–	22	112	1	48	244	2	(12)	3 949	3 368
Pope	756	14.7	466	9.1	5	6.6	86	164	1	157	302	7	350	7 815	6 060
Prairie	114	12.3	131	14.1	1	8.8	2	22	–	–	–	2	(12)	1 753	1 419
Pulaski	5 484	15.7	3 205	9.2	56	10.2	2 099	601	10	2 602	746	38	2 517	50 088	40 836
Randolph	229	13.0	209	11.8	2	8.7	12	67	1	50	281	2	(11)	3 528	2 855
St. Francis	509	17.9	327	11.5	4	7.9	18	65	1	86	306	2	(12)	4 606	3 706
Saline	982	12.9	701	9.2	5	5.1	71	91	1	77	100	4	(12)	7 712	6 328
Scott	126	11.6	138	12.7	3	23.8	5	47	1	129	1 219	1	(12)	2 067	1 604
Searcy	77	9.9	119	15.3	–	–	4	51	–	–	–	2	(12)	2 046	1 586
Sebastian	1 770	16.7	1 119	10.6	15	8.5	340	320	3	714	674	31	1 700	17 274	13 925
Sevier	250	17.2	189	13.0	2	8.0	13	89	1	75	513	2	(11)	2 379	2 015
Sharp	167	10.0	236	14.2	3	18.0	12	70	1	40	237	3	235	4 752	3 998
Stone	109	9.9	140	12.8	–	–	10	89	1	30	270	2	(11)	2 436	1 889
Union	611	13.5	558	12.3	4	6.5	99	220	1	167	369	5	426	8 795	7 141
Van Buren	152	9.8	216	13.9	2	13.2	4	26	2	217	1 397	1	(11)	3 904	3 372
Washington	2 355	16.4	1 166	8.1	20	8.5	321	219	3	475	328	11	851	18 676	15 012
White	832	13.2	737	11.7	5	6.0	81	124	2	274	424	6	573	11 054	9 201
Woodruff	126	14.1	125	13.9	1	7.9	6	69	–	–	–	–	–	1 794	1 466
Yell	264	13.9	231	12.1	1	3.8	18	95	2	85	448	3	244	4 083	3 147
CALIFORNIA	524 840	16.3	224 592	7.0	3 104	5.9	82 176	248	405	74 482	228	2 949	138 273	3 837 080	3 385 486
Alameda	20 789	15.2	9 624	7.0	126	6.1	3 638	257	14	3 177	227	143	7 107	156 177	136 086
Alpine	10	8.3	10	8.3	–	–	–	–	–	–	–	–	–	124	106
Amador	271	8.1	358	10.7	–	–	52	152	1	85	254	1	(12)	6 660	6 018
Butte	2 254	11.7	2 199	11.4	15	6.7	372	191	5	594	306	38	1 185	35 957	31 157
Calaveras	327	8.4	386	9.9	–	–	32	80	1	30	76	3	(12)	7 838	6 905
Colusa	308	16.7	133	7.2	2	6.5	12	64	1	38	204	1	(12)	2 486	2 183
Contra Costa	12 300	13.7	6 380	7.1	63	5.1	2 117	227	7	1 875	204	86	3 305	114 456	101 428
Del Norte	324	11.9	268	9.9	5	15.4	42	159	1	47	174	1	(11)	4 231	3 371
El Dorado	1 668	10.8	1 053	6.8	3	1.8	229	142	2	184	116	7	(12)	24 293	21 381

[1] Per 1,000 resident population estimated as of July 1, 1997. [2] Deaths of infants under 1 year old. [3] Infant deaths per 1,000 live births. [4] Active, nonfederal physicians as of December 31. Data subject to copyright; see below for source citation. [5] Per 100,000 resident population estimated as of July 1 of the year shown. [6] Nonfederal, short-stay (average length of stay less than 30 days) hospitals except hospital units of institutions. Data subject to copyright; see below for source citation. [7] SIC 805 includes skilled nursing care facilities; intermediate care facilities; and nursing and personal care, not elsewhere classified. [8] Full- and part-time employees on the payroll in the pay period including March 12. [9] Unduplicated count of persons enrolled in either hospital and/or supplemental medical insurance as of July 1. State totals include data not distributed by county. [10] Includes disabled, not shown separately. [11] 20 to 99 employees. [12] 100 to 249 employees. [13] 250 to 499 employees.

Sources: Births—U.S. National Center for Health Statistics, "Vital Statistics of the United States, Vol. I, Natality," annual, and unpublished data. Deaths—U.S. National Center for Health Statistics, "Vital Statistics of the United States, Vol. II, Mortality," annual, and unpublished data. Physicians—American Medical Association, Chicago, IL, "Physician Characteristics and Distribution in the U.S.," annual (copyright). Community Hospitals—Health Forum, LLC, an American Hospital Association Company, Chicago, IL, "Hospital Statistics" 2000 edition and unpublished data (copyright). Nursing and Personal Care Facilities—U.S. Census Bureau, County Business Patterns 1997 on CD-ROM (related Internet site <http://www.census.gov/epcd/cbp/view/cbpview.html>). Medicare—U.S. Health Care Financing Administration; "Medicare County Enrollment as of July 1, 1999 - Aged and Disabled 3/2000 update," <http://www.hcfa.gov/stats/enroll/default.htm>.

Table B–4. Counties — **Vital Statistics and Health**–Con.

[Includes U.S., states, and 3,142 counties or county equivalents defined as of January 1, 1992. For changes to these areas since then, see appendix B. Geographic Information]

County	Births, 1997 Number	Rate[1]	Deaths, 1997 Total Number	Rate[1]	Infant[2] Number	Rate[3]	Physicians,[4] 1999 Number	Rate[5]	Community hospitals,[6] 1998 Number	Beds Number	Rate[5]	Nursing and personal care facilities,[7] 1997 Establishments	Employees[8]	Medicare program enrollment,[9] 1999 Total[10]	Aged
CALIFORNIA—Con.															
Fresno	14 122	18.8	5 143	6.9	118	8.4	1 438	188	12	1 602	212	98	3 814	88 668	76 022
Glenn	427	16.3	206	7.9	3	7.0	9	34	1	27	103	2	(11)	4 024	3 504
Humboldt	1 484	12.1	1 139	9.3	6	4.0	264	218	5	291	238	19	616	19 004	15 453
Imperial	2 458	17.3	913	6.4	6	2.4	105	72	2	187	130	5	155	17 201	14 842
Inyo	191	10.5	215	11.8	2	10.5	38	212	2	67	371	1	(11)	3 832	3 470
Kern..................	11 288	18.1	4 438	7.1	78	6.9	896	139	12	1 586	251	41	2 058	72 391	59 407
Kings..................	2 084	18.2	716	6.3	12	5.8	100	81	3	131	110	6	286	10 468	8 764
Lake	566	10.3	760	13.9	6	10.6	68	123	2	87	158	8	334	12 988	10 862
Lassen..................	368	11.0	196	5.9	1	2.7	30	91	1	58	174	1	(11)	3 792	3 192
Los Angeles..............	162 149	17.8	60 332	6.6	951	5.9	25 221	270	105	24 619	267	777	40 965	975 304	871 318
Madera	1 989	17.7	748	6.7	8	4.0	106	91	4	497	434	13	332	17 437	14 876
Marin..................	2 653	11.3	1 885	8.0	12	4.5	1 265	534	4	377	159	44	2 218	34 192	31 549
Mariposa..................	136	8.7	163	10.5	–	–	10	64	1	32	203	–	–	3 035	2 661
Mendocino..................	1 025	12.3	797	9.6	5	4.9	175	208	3	164	196	14	385	13 747	11 479
Merced	3 610	18.6	1 348	7.0	25	6.9	213	106	3	296	150	18	762	19 515	16 800
Modoc..................	103	10.7	120	12.5	1	9.7	4	43	2	113	1 210	–	–	1 716	1 465
Mono..................	131	12.6	51	4.9	–	–	20	190	1	15	146	–	–	807	728
Monterey	6 732	18.8	2 176	6.1	39	5.8	663	178	4	613	167	21	1 155	42 526	37 976
Napa	1 500	12.7	1 308	11.1	5	3.3	365	302	3	871	729	19	771	21 676	18 906
Nevada	815	9.1	824	9.2	3	3.7	190	206	2	130	143	6	403	16 213	14 587
Orange	47 513	17.8	16 198	6.1	210	4.4	7 504	272	32	5 796	213	209	12 326	282 452	257 837
Placer	2 631	11.9	1 643	7.5	5	1.9	562	235	2	265	116	23	1 182	30 818	27 765
Plumas	183	9.0	206	10.1	–	–	22	108	4	108	530	2	(11)	3 873	3 355
Riverside	23 338	16.2	11 311	7.9	140	6.0	1 893	124	15	2 618	177	154	5 435	196 148	175 014
Sacramento	17 325	15.0	8 653	7.5	121	7.0	2 896	244	9	2 636	226	104	3 994	147 960	124 952
San Benito	889	19.1	253	5.4	6	6.7	34	66	1	71	145	1	(11)	4 468	3 977
San Bernardino...........	28 392	17.6	10 694	6.6	236	8.3	2 988	179	18	3 402	208	170	6 638	164 919	139 241
San Diego	43 308	15.9	18 735	6.9	240	5.5	7 456	264	24	5 973	216	203	10 919	336 516	302 487
San Francisco	8 204	11.1	6 822	9.2	39	4.8	5 085	681	9	2 606	349	48	2 716	117 217	103 316
San Joaquin	8 723	16.2	4 057	7.5	63	7.2	759	135	7	1 050	191	87	3 075	66 446	56 056
San Luis Obispo	2 493	10.8	1 929	8.3	15	6.0	580	245	5	459	196	15	604	38 602	34 058
San Mateo	10 058	14.5	4 901	7.0	51	5.1	2 351	335	7	1 365	195	67	2 708	91 684	84 114
Santa Barbara...........	5 791	15.0	2 782	7.2	26	4.5	1 011	259	7	964	248	37	2 582	54 627	48 591
Santa Clara	26 426	16.3	8 852	5.5	149	5.6	5 171	314	13	3 098	189	119	6 246	164 906	149 121
Santa Cruz..............	3 561	14.9	1 643	6.9	17	4.8	533	217	3	422	174	22	1 047	28 364	24 845
Shasta	2 001	12.3	1 661	10.2	17	8.5	399	243	3	475	289	19	882	30 619	25 072
Sierra	23	6.8	37	11.0	–	–	2	60	1	40	1 185	–	–	706	627
Siskiyou	424	9.6	490	11.1	3	7.1	66	151	2	100	227	2	(12)	9 467	8 166
Solano	5 480	14.8	2 305	6.2	36	6.6	645	167	4	511	136	52	1 188	37 967	32 675
Sonoma	5 414	12.7	3 780	8.9	22	4.1	1 075	244	9	892	206	58	2 059	62 630	55 124
Stanislaus	6 794	16.2	3 263	7.8	48	7.1	661	151	4	1 076	252	34	2 354	53 593	44 768
Sutter	1 210	15.8	623	8.1	8	6.6	154	196	1	78	101	10	590	10 665	9 007
Tehama	627	11.7	547	10.2	4	6.4	49	91	1	53	98	4	69	9 265	7 817
Trinity	100	7.6	157	11.9	–	–	9	70	1	65	498	–	–	2 587	2 096
Tulare	6 938	19.8	2 642	7.5	42	6.1	407	114	6	684	193	50	1 484	40 519	34 103
Tuolumne	467	8.9	493	9.4	4	8.6	98	182	2	195	368	4	43	10 849	9 608
Ventura	11 291	15.6	4 521	6.3	85	7.5	1 422	191	8	1 439	197	61	2 037	82 821	73 551
Yolo	2 107	13.9	1 009	6.7	13	6.2	607	390	2	151	99	16	821	17 016	14 722
Yuba	1 047	17.4	496	8.2	9	8.6	63	106	1	97	162	5	(12)	8 076	6 497
COLORADO	56 533	14.5	25 626	6.6	397	7.0	9 914	244	69	9 179	231	333	23 669	458 380	394 517
Adams	4 995	15.8	1 835	5.8	34	6.8	583	176	4	429	133	20	1 566	37 603	30 947
Alamosa	250	17.3	118	8.2	3	12.0	40	274	1	85	584	7	(12)	1 690	1 370
Arapahoe	6 181	13.4	2 394	5.2	44	7.1	1 076	223	3	801	169	47	2 517	41 533	36 801
Archuleta	98	11.5	40	4.7	2	20.4	16	167	–	–	–	1	(13)	1 268	1 104
Baca	33	7.5	69	15.8	–	–	4	93	1	81	1 872	–	–	1 059	965
Bent	62	11.5	73	13.5	–	–	1	17	–	–	–	–	–	976	795
Boulder..................	3 257	12.5	1 307	5.0	20	6.1	771	282	3	376	141	12	1 254	27 015	23 664
Chaffee..................	131	8.7	157	10.5	–	–	26	167	1	33	217	2	(12)	2 997	2 672
Cheyenne	24	10.6	26	11.5	–	–	2	90	1	12	517	–	–	371	347
Clear Creek	74	8.3	33	3.7	–	–	2	22	–	–	–	–	–	560	471
Conejos	129	16.4	60	7.6	1	7.8	5	62	1	49	614	–	–	1 389	1 159
Costilla	40	11.1	49	13.6	–	–	1	28	–	–	–	–	–	784	592
Crowley	46	10.7	37	8.6	1	21.7	1	23	–	–	–	–	(11)	694	557
Custer..................	32	9.7	13	3.9	–	–	2	56	–	–	–	–	–	550	470

[1] Per 1,000 resident population estimated as of July 1, 1997. [2] Deaths of infants under 1 year old. [3] Infant deaths per 1,000 live births. [4] Active, nonfederal physicians as of December 31. Data subject to copyright; see below for source citation. [5] Per 100,000 resident population estimated as of July 1 of the year shown. [6] Nonfederal, short-stay (average length of stay less than 30 days) hospitals except hospital units of institutions. Data subject to copyright; see below for source citation. [7] SIC 805 includes skilled nursing care facilities; intermediate care facilities; and nursing and personal care, not elsewhere classified. [8] Full- and part-time employees on the payroll in the pay period including March 12. [9] Unduplicated count of persons enrolled in either hospital and/or supplemental medical insurance as of July 1. State totals include data not distributed by county. [10] Includes disabled, not shown separately. [11] 20 to 99 employees. [12] 100 to 249 employees. [13] 0 to 19 employees.

Sources: Births—U.S. National Center for Health Statistics, "Vital Statistics of the United States, Vol. I, Natality," annual, and unpublished data. Deaths—U.S. National Center for Health Statistics, "Vital Statistics of the United States, Vol. II, Mortality," annual, and unpublished data. Physicians—American Medical Association, Chicago, IL, "Physician Characteristics and Distribution in the U.S.," annual (copyright). Community Hospitals—Health Forum, LLC, an American Hospital Association Company, Chicago, IL, "Hospital Statistics" 2000 edition and unpublished data (copyright). Nursing and Personal Care Facilities—U.S. Census Bureau, County Business Patterns 1997 on CD-ROM (related Internet site <http://www.census.gov/epcd/cbp/view/cbpview.html>). Medicare—U.S. Health Care Financing Administration; "Medicare County Enrollment as of July 1, 1999 - Aged and Disabled 3/2000 update," <http://www.hcfa.gov/stats/enroll/default.htm>.

[Includes U.S., states, and 3,142 counties or county equivalents defined as of January 1, 1992. For changes to these areas since then, see appendix B. Geographic Information]

County	Births, 1997		Deaths, 1997				Physicians,[4] 1999		Community hospitals,[6] 1998			Nursing and personal care facilities,[7] 1997		Medicare program enrollment,[9] 1999	
			Total		Infant[2]					Beds					
	Number	Rate[1]	Number	Rate[1]	Number	Rate[3]	Number	Rate[5]	Number	Number	Rate[5]	Establishments	Employees[8]	Total[10]	Aged
COLORADO—Con.															
Delta	306	11.8	312	12.0	6	19.6	28	103	1	44	165	5	245	5 900	5 237
Denver	9 310	18.6	4 704	9.4	72	7.7	3 305	661	10	2 669	536	51	4 146	71 414	60 309
Dolores	16	9.3	14	8.2	–	–	–	–	–	–	–	–	–	378	321
Douglas	2 360	18.6	334	2.6	6	2.5	165	105	–	–	–	2	(11)	4 600	4 151
Eagle	600	18.8	53	1.7	5	8.3	101	289	1	49	145	1	(12)	1 225	1 089
Elbert	200	11.5	65	3.7	–	–	6	30	–	–	–	2	(11)	1 116	958
El Paso	7 700	16.0	2 710	5.6	58	7.5	888	178	2	757	154	42	2 623	50 821	43 185
Fremont	410	9.5	459	10.6	2	4.9	46	103	1	40	90	9	505	7 322	6 200
Garfield	595	15.8	240	6.4	5	8.4	71	175	2	129	328	2	(13)	4 254	3 679
Gilpin	39	9.8	13	3.3	–	–	2	45	–	–	–	–	–	165	128
Grand	111	11.3	41	4.2	–	–	10	95	1	19	188	–	–	1 017	923
Gunnison	121	9.9	51	4.2	1	8.3	17	135	1	22	177	–	–	997	897
Hinsdale	5	7.1	2	2.8	–	–	1	135	–	–	–	–	–	86	D
Huerfano	61	9.1	100	14.9	–	–	9	132	1	24	354	1	(11)	1 514	1 268
Jackson	21	13.9	15	9.9	–	–	–	–	–	–	–	–	–	228	200
Jefferson	6 387	12.9	2 981	6.0	36	5.6	767	151	2	607	121	31	2 948	52 499	46 718
Kiowa	18	11.0	18	11.0	–	–	1	61	1	42	2 550	–	–	320	292
Kit Carson	73	10.2	73	10.2	1	13.7	5	67	1	24	328	2	(11)	1 283	1 163
Lake	100	15.8	28	4.4	1	10.0	4	63	1	31	488	–	–	567	467
La Plata	413	10.3	224	5.6	3	7.3	136	331	1	81	200	2	(13)	4 433	3 912
Larimer	2 807	12.4	1 304	5.8	14	5.0	486	205	3	409	177	24	1 792	25 902	22 953
Las Animas	150	10.4	168	11.6	1	6.7	14	95	1	31	213	–	–	3 095	2 568
Lincoln	54	9.6	50	8.8	–	–	3	53	1	56	985	1	(11)	841	760
Logan	252	13.9	185	10.2	3	11.9	26	145	1	36	201	1	(11)	3 379	2 992
Mesa	1 396	12.6	1 025	9.3	12	8.6	273	237	3	695	616	13	927	19 622	17 039
Mineral	4	6.0	7	10.5	–	–	–	–	–	–	–	–	–	115	D
Moffat	160	13.0	86	7.0	–	–	10	79	1	29	231	5	(11)	1 524	1 291
Montezuma	274	12.3	193	8.7	2	7.3	38	168	1	42	188	2	(13)	3 658	3 147
Montrose	431	14.3	270	8.9	3	7.0	51	162	1	63	205	4	336	5 466	4 846
Morgan	472	18.8	217	8.7	2	4.2	24	95	2	64	255	5	417	3 675	3 235
Otero	281	13.5	236	11.3	2	7.1	31	150	1	182	881	2	(11)	4 073	3 355
Ouray	26	8.1	15	4.7	–	–	8	230	–	–	–	–	–	426	403
Park	134	10.6	48	3.8	3	22.4	3	21	–	–	–	–	–	1 035	810
Phillips	60	13.9	72	16.7	1	16.7	7	166	2	66	1 535	1	(11)	955	882
Pitkin	143	10.5	34	2.5	–	–	58	435	1	41	307	–	–	816	769
Prowers	214	15.7	110	8.1	2	9.3	10	73	1	40	292	2	(13)	2 092	1 804
Pueblo	1 775	13.4	1 368	10.3	20	11.3	342	250	2	521	386	15	1 410	24 749	20 221
Rio Blanco	62	9.8	40	6.3	1	16.1	5	81	2	71	1 134	–	–	752	667
Rio Grande	137	12.0	108	9.5	–	–	12	104	–	–	–	3	137	1 958	1 677
Routt	176	10.2	60	3.5	1	5.7	50	279	1	74	423	3	(12)	1 079	946
Saguache	91	15.4	36	6.1	–	–	2	32	–	–	–	–	–	750	637
San Juan	3	5.5	5	9.2	–	–	1	192	–	–	–	–	–	62	49
San Miguel	55	10.4	13	2.4	–	–	11	201	–	–	–	–	–	250	222
Sedgwick	29	11.1	36	13.8	–	–	1	39	1	66	2 585	–	–	695	628
Summit	220	11.9	39	2.1	3	13.6	50	255	–	–	–	–	–	836	747
Teller	220	11.1	71	3.6	2	9.1	18	85	–	–	–	–	–	1 821	1 487
Washington	44	9.6	47	10.2	1	22.7	3	69	–	–	–	–	–	881	815
Weld	2 531	16.3	1 027	6.6	22	8.7	273	165	1	262	164	9	931	17 509	14 792
Yuma	134	14.3	108	11.5	1	7.5	12	127	2	27	286	3	137	1 644	1 534
CONNECTICUT	43 109	13.2	29 415	9.0	310	7.2	11 859	361	33	6 949	212	470	45 140	511 611	455 570
Fairfield	12 400	14.9	7 064	8.5	74	6.0	3 049	362	6	1 590	190	97	8 695	123 398	112 476
Hartford	11 342	13.7	8 132	9.8	105	9.3	3 173	382	8	2 179	263	119	14 463	138 705	122 552
Litchfield	1 929	10.7	1 695	9.4	9	4.7	362	198	3	209	115	30	2 596	28 108	25 180
Middlesex	1 927	12.9	1 254	8.4	14	7.3	411	271	1	119	79	34	2 305	22 400	20 092
New Haven	10 363	13.1	7 602	9.6	58	5.6	3 975	501	9	2 090	264	128	11 674	130 932	115 593
New London	2 491	10.0	1 892	7.6	20	8.0	546	222	2	392	159	36	3 317	37 856	33 399
Tolland	1 402	10.7	875	6.7	18	12.8	195	147	2	191	145	12	777	14 553	12 947
Windham	1 255	12.0	901	8.6	12	9.6	148	141	2	179	171	14	1 313	15 589	13 275
DELAWARE	10 253	13.9	6 510	8.9	80	7.8	1 791	238	6	1 977	266	56	5 130	109 575	95 615
Kent	1 715	14.0	989	8.1	14	8.2	173	137	1	345	278	10	860	15 837	13 383
New Castle	6 705	14.0	3 947	8.2	48	7.2	1 332	273	3	1 220	253	35	2 752	63 288	55 275
Sussex	1 833	13.7	1 574	11.8	18	9.8	286	204	2	412	300	11	1 518	30 338	26 868
DISTRICT OF COLUMBIA	7 927	15.0	6 129	11.6	105	13.2	3 935	758	12	3 552	681	115	4 839	75 619	66 219
District of Columbia	7 927	15.0	6 129	11.6	105	13.2	3 935	758	12	3 552	681	115	4 839	75 619	66 219

[1] Per 1,000 resident population estimated as of July 1, 1997. [2] Deaths of infants under 1 year old. [3] Infant deaths per 1,000 live births. [4] Active, nonfederal physicians as of December 31. Data subject to copyright; see below for source citation. [5] Per 100,000 resident population estimated as of July 1 of the year shown. [6] Nonfederal, short-stay (average length of stay less than 30 days) hospitals except hospital units of institutions. Data subject to copyright; see below for source citation. [7] SIC 805 includes skilled nursing care facilities; intermediate care facilities; and nursing and personal care, not elsewhere classified. [8] Full- and part-time employees on the payroll in the pay period including March 12. [9] Unduplicated count of persons enrolled in either hospital and/or supplemental medical insurance as of July 1. State totals include data not distributed by county. [10] Includes disabled, not shown separately. [11] 20 to 99 employees. [12] 0 to 19 employees. [13] 100 to 249 employees.

Sources: Births—U.S. National Center for Health Statistics, "Vital Statistics of the United States, Vol. I, Natality," annual, and unpublished data. Deaths—U.S. National Center for Health Statistics, "Vital Statistics of the United States, Vol. II, Mortality," annual, and unpublished data. Physicians—American Medical Association, Chicago, IL, "Physician Characteristics and Distribution in the U.S.," annual (copyright). Community Hospitals—Health Forum, LLC, an American Hospital Association Company, Chicago, IL, "Hospital Statistics" 2000 edition and unpublished data (copyright). Nursing and Personal Care Facilities—U.S. Census Bureau, County Business Patterns 1997 on CD-ROM (related Internet site <http://www.census.gov/epcd/cbp/view/cbpview.html>). Medicare—U.S. Health Care Financing Administration; "Medicare County Enrollment as of July 1, 1999 - Aged and Disabled 3/2000 update," <http://www.hcfa.gov/stats/enroll/default.htm>.

Table B–4. Counties — **Vital Statistics and Health**–Con.

[Includes U.S., states, and 3,142 counties or county equivalents defined as of January 1, 1992. For changes to these areas since then, see appendix B. Geographic Information]

| County | Births, 1997 | | Deaths, 1997 | | | | Physicians,[4] 1999 | | Community hospitals,[6] 1998 | | | Nursing and personal care facilities,[7] 1997 | | Medicare program enrollment,[9] 1999 | |
| | | | Total | | Infant[2] | | | | | Beds | | | | | |
	Number	Rate[1]	Number	Rate[1]	Number	Rate[3]	Number	Rate[5]	Number	Number	Rate[5]	Establishments	Employees[8]	Total[10]	Aged
FLORIDA	192 383	13.1	154 497	10.5	1 366	7.1	36 760	243	204	49 231	330	1 222	98 391	2 770 576	2 472 896
Alachua	2 504	12.7	1 523	7.7	20	8.0	1 635	824	4	1 151	581	13	883	25 051	20 929
Baker	314	15.1	148	7.1	4	12.7	15	71	1	68	323	3	190	2 481	1 799
Bay	2 005	13.7	1 293	8.8	18	9.0	271	183	2	491	335	16	946	22 484	18 957
Bradford	326	13.3	267	10.9	6	18.4	10	40	1	23	93	6	414	3 309	2 663
Brevard	4 795	10.4	4 563	9.9	25	5.2	849	180	5	1 158	249	33	3 444	93 639	83 464
Broward	20 419	13.8	15 661	10.6	140	6.9	3 508	228	17	4 898	325	89	5 594	251 056	227 983
Calhoun	156	12.6	125	10.1	1	6.4	11	88	1	32	258	1	(11)	1 949	1 566
Charlotte	982	7.4	2 033	15.4	6	6.1	285	208	3	713	529	9	1 039	38 452	35 643
Citrus	842	7.6	1 816	16.3	4	4.8	191	164	2	299	263	10	913	35 083	31 915
Clay	1 790	13.4	948	7.1	15	8.4	228	161	1	196	142	14	1 292	14 621	12 525
Collier	2 511	13.0	2 057	10.7	27	10.8	544	263	1	458	229	10	858	47 572	44 828
Columbia	754	14.6	554	10.7	5	6.6	84	156	2	203	384	6	280	8 816	7 065
Dade	31 301	14.7	18 355	8.6	176	5.6	7 628	351	27	8 156	379	166	10 152	304 339	273 764
DeSoto	351	14.2	281	11.4	5	14.2	30	122	1	58	235	2	(12)	5 084	4 316
Dixie	158	12.5	134	10.6	2	12.7	2	15	–	–	–	1	(13)	2 514	1 975
Duval	11 972	16.4	6 182	8.5	115	9.6	2 127	288	9	2 553	348	56	4 789	92 737	78 547
Escambia	3 990	14.2	2 604	9.3	37	9.3	743	263	3	1 543	543	27	1 993	42 825	36 450
Flagler	336	7.5	535	11.9	2	6.0	41	83	1	81	172	7	122	13 493	12 274
Franklin	112	11.1	147	14.6	4	35.7	9	90	1	29	287	3	(11)	1 833	1 565
Gadsden	687	15.6	427	9.7	9	13.1	38	86	1	51	116	3	(14)	6 808	5 268
Gilchrist	174	13.0	132	9.9	1	5.7	6	43	–	–	–	3	(11)	2 042	1 658
Glades	97	11.5	101	12.0	2	20.6	–	–	–	–	–	–	–	900	763
Gulf	141	10.4	155	11.5	2	14.2	13	96	1	45	334	1	(11)	2 457	2 090
Hamilton	157	12.6	119	9.5	1	6.4	6	47	1	20	158	2	(12)	1 848	1 429
Hardee	441	20.9	178	8.5	1	2.3	9	43	–	–	–	3	84	3 373	2 813
Hendry	612	20.9	235	8.0	4	6.5	21	71	1	45	153	2	(11)	3 575	3 039
Hernando	1 045	8.4	1 883	15.2	11	10.5	175	136	3	370	292	11	651	41 011	36 682
Highlands	877	11.7	1 251	16.7	6	6.8	131	175	2	321	428	16	763	25 438	23 413
Hillsborough	13 890	15.3	7 941	8.7	108	7.8	2 745	292	11	3 058	330	73	6 200	132 602	111 927
Holmes	219	11.9	218	11.9	2	9.1	8	43	1	34	183	1	(11)	3 304	2 650
Indian River	984	10.1	1 316	13.4	4	4.1	276	275	3	483	487	10	774	31 587	29 614
Jackson	571	12.8	493	11.1	2	3.5	49	110	2	120	270	4	233	8 267	6 619
Jefferson	160	12.2	145	11.1	3	18.8	4	31	–	–	–	3	(11)	2 062	1 718
Lafayette	87	14.0	43	6.9	2	23.0	2	31	–	–	–	–	–	686	578
Lake	2 038	10.5	2 509	12.9	15	7.4	315	150	3	659	326	16	1 154	58 936	54 103
Lee	4 540	11.8	4 640	12.0	32	7.0	821	205	5	1 758	447	29	2 175	99 107	90 886
Leon	2 851	13.3	1 339	6.2	23	8.1	569	264	3	864	402	16	1 513	21 392	18 723
Levy	353	11.4	353	11.4	2	5.7	19	59	1	40	126	1	(11)	6 550	5 399
Liberty	76	11.3	54	8.0	2	26.3	–	–	–	–	–	2	(11)	883	675
Madison	216	12.3	146	8.3	2	9.3	9	50	1	26	147	2	(11)	3 070	2 511
Manatee	2 857	12.2	3 156	13.4	12	4.2	470	193	2	796	332	21	2 426	53 829	49 352
Marion	2 718	11.5	2 953	12.5	22	8.1	397	161	2	528	219	14	1 358	66 595	59 448
Martin	1 106	9.7	1 496	13.1	7	6.3	330	279	1	310	267	7	658	33 507	31 427
Monroe	809	10.0	710	8.8	4	4.9	163	204	3	258	319	4	(14)	11 092	9 901
Nassau	693	12.8	445	8.2	2	2.9	51	90	1	24	43	3	491	7 730	6 478
Okaloosa	2 288	13.6	1 152	6.9	18	7.9	340	200	3	405	240	10	791	23 429	20 520
Okeechobee	515	16.7	380	12.3	5	9.7	45	139	1	101	316	2	(11)	6 715	5 721
Orange	12 378	15.8	5 846	7.4	70	5.7	2 013	246	6	3 525	438	52	4 410	103 228	87 224
Osceola	2 135	15.2	1 212	8.6	22	10.3	164	109	2	224	154	10	1 186	21 110	17 447
Palm Beach	12 555	12.4	12 574	12.4	88	7.0	2 838	270	15	3 363	326	97	7 663	239 091	223 827
Pasco	3 363	10.6	5 005	15.7	21	6.2	496	150	5	1 032	317	22	1 713	84 944	75 986
Pinellas	9 255	10.6	12 671	14.5	66	7.1	2 133	243	14	3 277	374	119	11 068	205 973	185 448
Polk	6 470	14.5	4 828	10.8	53	8.2	708	155	4	1 292	285	34	2 873	88 530	77 195
Putnam	911	13.0	840	12.0	10	11.0	58	83	1	141	201	5	384	13 759	11 421
St. Johns	1 211	10.9	1 053	9.4	14	11.6	304	254	1	260	224	14	1 105	20 484	18 286
St. Lucie	2 177	12.3	2 042	11.5	22	10.1	254	140	2	513	286	13	1 155	39 972	35 144
Santa Rosa	1 488	13.1	758	6.7	12	8.1	157	130	3	203	173	4	508	14 316	12 008
Sarasota	2 537	8.4	4 628	15.4	10	3.9	975	318	5	1 111	366	38	3 851	103 102	96 894
Seminole	4 444	12.9	2 336	6.8	20	4.5	586	164	2	432	123	21	1 836	37 978	33 084
Sumter	412	10.2	482	11.9	4	9.7	9	21	–	–	–	3	(11)	8 367	7 138
Suwannee	412	12.9	405	12.7	4	9.7	14	42	1	17	52	4	628	6 812	5 622
Taylor	232	12.4	209	11.2	2	8.6	15	79	1	48	254	1	(11)	3 142	2 592
Union	129	10.4	150	12.1	2	15.5	14	110	–	–	–	–	–	1 159	898
Volusia	4 557	11.0	5 503	13.2	23	5.0	765	180	6	1 262	300	48	4 510	100 263	89 050
Wakulla	227	12.3	130	7.1	2	8.8	11	57	–	–	–	2	(11)	2 520	2 093
Walton	418	11.4	408	11.2	3	7.2	10	26	1	34	91	1	(11)	5 358	4 396
Washington	252	12.4	221	10.9	2	7.9	13	63	1	71	351	3	(11)	3 805	3 072

[1] Per 1,000 resident population estimated as of July 1, 1997.   [2] Deaths of infants under 1 year old.   [3] Infant deaths per 1,000 live births.   [4] Active, nonfederal physicians as of December 31. Data subject to copyright; see below for source citation.   [5] Per 100,000 resident population estimated as of July 1 of the year shown.   [6] Nonfederal, short-stay (average length of stay less than 30 days) hospitals except hospital units of institutions. Data subject to copyright; see below for source citation.   [7] SIC 805 includes skilled nursing care facilities; intermediate care facilities; and nursing and personal care, not elsewhere classified.   [8] Full- and part-time employees on the payroll in the pay period including March 12.   [9] Unduplicated count of persons enrolled in either hospital and/or supplemental medical insurance as of July 1. State totals include data not distributed by county.   [10] Includes disabled, not shown separately.   [11] 100 to 249 employees.   [12] 20 to 99 employees. [13] 0 to 19 employees.   [14] 250 to 499 employees.

Sources: Births—U.S. National Center for Health Statistics, "Vital Statistics of the United States, Vol. I, Natality," annual, and unpublished data.   Deaths—U.S. National Center for Health Statistics, "Vital Statistics of the United States, Vol. II, Mortality," annual, and unpublished data.   Physicians—American Medical Association, Chicago, IL, "Physician Characteristics and Distribution in the U.S.," annual (copyright).   Community Hospitals—Health Forum, LLC, an American Hospital Association Company, Chicago, IL, "Hospital Statistics" 2000 edition and unpublished data (copyright).   Nursing and Personal Care Facilities—U.S. Census Bureau, County Business Patterns 1997 on CD-ROM (related Internet site <http://www.census.gov/epcd/cbp/view/cbpview.html>).   Medicare—U.S. Health Care Financing Administration; "Medicare County Enrollment as of July 1, 1999 - Aged and Disabled 3/2000 update," <http://www.hcfa.gov/stats/enroll/default.htm>.

[Includes U.S., states, and 3,142 counties or county equivalents defined as of January 1, 1992. For changes to these areas since then, see appendix B. Geographic Information]

County	Births, 1997		Deaths, 1997				Physicians,[4] 1999		Community hospitals,[6] 1998			Nursing and personal care facilities,[7] 1997		Medicare program enrollment,[9] 1999	
			Total		Infant[2]					Beds					
	Number	Rate[1]	Number	Rate[1]	Number	Rate[3]	Number	Rate[5]	Number	Number	Rate[5]	Establishments	Employees[8]	Total[10]	Aged
GEORGIA	118 221	15.8	59 351	7.9	1 022	8.6	16 470	211	156	25 236	330	530	36 512	897 503	736 497
Appling	293	17.9	159	9.7	3	10.2	14	84	1	137	828	1	(11)	2 371	1 858
Atkinson	181	25.4	78	10.9	–	–	–	–	–	–	–	–	–	1 028	773
Bacon	144	14.0	104	10.1	1	6.9	10	96	1	126	1 216	–	–	1 480	1 114
Baker	34	9.1	27	7.3	–	–	–	–	–	–	–	–	–	447	358
Baldwin	476	11.4	338	8.1	7	14.7	112	266	1	143	341	7	566	5 760	4 208
Banks	162	13.0	105	8.4	1	6.2	4	30	–	–	–	–	–	1 410	1 117
Barrow	733	18.8	307	7.9	2	2.7	24	57	1	56	138	2	(12)	4 998	3 963
Bartow	1 225	17.7	574	8.3	8	6.5	58	78	1	80	111	7	343	8 475	6 762
Ben Hill	264	15.2	191	11.0	4	15.2	8	46	1	60	343	1	(13)	2 959	2 392
Berrien	244	15.3	163	10.2	1	4.1	10	60	1	179	1 097	1	(12)	2 464	1 930
Bibb	2 542	16.3	1 613	10.3	33	13.0	668	430	5	961	616	19	1 416	25 953	20 536
Bleckley	151	13.6	114	10.3	1	6.6	6	53	1	45	403	2	(13)	1 897	1 540
Brantley	102	7.7	126	9.5	4	39.2	–	–	–	–	–	1	(13)	1 747	1 220
Brooks	194	12.3	201	12.7	1	5.2	5	31	1	35	220	3	(14)	2 318	1 891
Bryan	368	15.9	132	5.7	1	2.7	20	82	–	–	–	2	(12)	2 378	1 877
Bulloch	633	12.7	391	7.8	8	12.6	79	156	1	158	313	5	(12)	5 305	4 380
Burke	368	16.4	227	10.1	4	10.9	11	47	1	40	175	5	201	2 937	2 293
Butts	229	13.3	154	8.9	3	13.1	7	38	1	28	157	1	(12)	2 699	2 144
Calhoun	86	17.0	93	18.4	–	–	1	20	1	24	480	–	–	1 150	955
Camden	791	17.4	192	4.2	3	3.8	38	81	1	40	85	–	–	2 619	1 995
Candler	138	15.6	119	13.4	3	21.7	9	101	1	42	462	2	(12)	1 518	1 209
Carroll	1 261	15.5	658	8.1	7	5.6	113	133	3	262	316	7	488	11 201	8 866
Catoosa	621	12.6	388	7.9	5	8.1	45	86	1	288	568	2	(12)	4 898	4 109
Charlton	159	17.2	97	10.5	2	12.6	6	63	1	36	382	1	(11)	1 292	956
Chatham	3 485	15.5	2 152	9.5	30	8.6	710	315	3	1 103	490	17	1 011	33 435	28 413
Chattahoochee	235	14.4	20	1.2	3	12.8	11	66	–	–	–	–	–	315	249
Chattooga	308	13.5	283	12.4	2	6.5	7	31	–	–	–	1	(13)	4 344	3 526
Cherokee	2 039	16.0	682	5.4	14	6.9	83	59	1	60	45	5	175	9 286	7 881
Clarke	1 195	13.2	591	6.5	12	10.0	267	295	2	598	661	4	301	9 990	8 187
Clay	71	20.5	49	14.2	–	–	3	85	–	–	–	1	(13)	636	537
Clayton	3 841	18.8	1 243	6.1	39	10.2	269	126	1	324	155	6	508	17 193	13 501
Clinch	103	15.6	68	10.3	1	9.7	6	90	1	36	541	2	(13)	1 023	728
Cobb	8 511	15.4	2 795	5.1	62	7.3	1 000	171	3	773	137	21	2 217	48 046	41 821
Coffee	600	17.8	278	8.2	4	6.7	43	123	1	88	257	2	(12)	4 521	3 458
Colquitt	611	15.4	424	10.7	8	13.1	45	110	1	101	251	7	279	6 180	5 147
Columbia	1 133	12.8	447	5.0	8	7.1	377	404	–	–	–	5	483	7 905	6 770
Cook	263	18.0	180	12.3	3	11.4	10	66	1	155	1 034	2	(12)	2 321	1 872
Coweta	1 379	17.1	534	6.6	6	4.4	82	92	2	349	410	3	(12)	8 690	7 178
Crawford	136	12.7	62	5.8	2	14.7	2	19	–	–	–	1	(13)	860	636
Crisp	347	16.9	241	11.7	6	17.3	29	141	1	208	1 005	4	252	3 302	2 669
Dade	199	13.6	125	8.6	1	5.0	7	46	1	13	86	1	(13)	2 226	1 845
Dawson	222	15.9	67	4.8	1	4.5	10	63	–	–	–	–	–	1 697	1 379
Decatur	428	16.0	259	9.7	2	4.7	30	111	1	187	692	3	(13)	4 167	3 437
De Kalb	9 931	16.8	3 928	6.7	97	9.8	1 386	232	4	1 248	211	49	2 967	58 382	48 818
Dodge	236	13.0	232	12.8	3	12.7	23	127	1	87	480	2	(12)	2 816	2 195
Dooly	190	18.1	134	12.8	5	26.3	6	58	1	32	307	2	(13)	1 664	1 361
Dougherty	1 686	17.6	858	9.0	25	14.8	261	277	2	617	649	10	489	13 562	11 014
Douglas	1 260	14.5	538	6.2	9	7.1	87	95	2	312	349	9	(14)	8 074	6 634
Early	196	16.2	156	12.9	3	15.3	8	66	1	164	1 347	–	–	2 040	1 711
Echols	22	9.1	18	7.5	–	–	–	–	–	–	–	–	–	162	128
Effingham	510	14.5	229	6.5	1	2.0	10	26	1	150	410	–	–	3 142	2 481
Elbert	231	12.0	226	11.8	–	–	12	62	1	42	217	3	205	3 817	3 015
Emanuel	309	14.7	264	12.6	2	6.5	15	71	1	91	433	6	236	3 788	2 925
Evans	131	13.5	117	12.1	2	15.3	12	119	1	195	1 965	1	(13)	1 576	1 239
Fannin	228	12.6	204	11.2	1	4.4	10	53	1	46	248	1	(13)	4 042	3 384
Fayette	835	9.8	449	5.3	8	9.6	164	178	–	–	–	2	(12)	8 017	7 279
Floyd	1 129	13.3	957	11.3	8	7.1	285	333	2	415	487	10	793	14 631	11 936
Forsyth	1 401	18.4	423	5.5	9	6.4	51	53	1	30	35	2	(14)	5 903	5 162
Franklin	242	13.1	224	12.1	3	12.4	16	83	1	331	1 737	1	(13)	4 009	3 307
Fulton	12 522	17.3	6 161	8.5	106	8.5	4 895	657	13	4 400	597	52	3 879	80 069	66 483
Gilmer	297	16.5	168	9.3	2	6.7	10	51	1	150	800	–	–	3 709	2 995
Glascock	36	14.5	32	12.9	–	–	–	–	–	–	–	1	(12)	543	461
Glynn	856	12.9	684	10.3	12	14.0	178	262	1	337	502	8	507	10 937	9 197
Gordon	634	15.7	373	9.3	4	6.3	40	95	1	54	131	3	(12)	5 707	4 500
Grady	310	14.4	242	11.3	5	16.1	12	56	1	45	210	1	(12)	3 368	2 696
Greene	200	15.0	137	10.3	2	10.0	17	121	1	58	425	1	(13)	2 369	1 897

[1] Per 1,000 resident population estimated as of July 1, 1997. [2] Deaths of infants under 1 year old. [3] Infant deaths per 1,000 live births. [4] Active, nonfederal physicians as of December 31. Data subject to copyright; see below for source citation. [5] Per 100,000 resident population estimated as of July 1 of the year shown. [6] Nonfederal, short-stay (average length of stay less than 30 days) hospitals except hospital units of institutions. Data subject to copyright; see below for source citation. [7] SIC 805 includes skilled nursing care facilities; intermediate care facilities; and nursing and personal care, not elsewhere classified. [8] Full- and part-time employees on the payroll in the pay period including March 12. [9] Unduplicated count of persons enrolled in either hospital and/or supplemental medical insurance as of July 1. State totals include data not distributed by county. [10] Includes disabled, not shown separately. [11] 0 to 19 employees. [12] 100 to 249 employees. [13] 20 to 99 employees. [14] 250 to 499 employees.

Sources: Births—U.S. National Center for Health Statistics, "Vital Statistics of the United States, Vol. I, Natality," annual, and unpublished data. Deaths—U.S. National Center for Health Statistics, "Vital Statistics of the United States, Vol. II, Mortality," annual, and unpublished data. Physicians—American Medical Association, Chicago, IL, "Physician Characteristics and Distribution in the U.S.," annual (copyright). Community Hospitals—Health Forum, LLC, an American Hospital Association Company, Chicago, IL, "Hospital Statistics" 2000 edition and unpublished data (copyright). Nursing and Personal Care Facilities—U.S. Census Bureau, County Business Patterns 1997 on CD-ROM (related Internet site <http://www.census.gov/epcd/cbp/view/cbpview.html>). Medicare—U.S. Health Care Financing Administration; "Medicare County Enrollment as of July 1, 1999 - Aged and Disabled 3/2000 update," <http://www.hcfa.gov/stats/enroll/default.htm>.

Table B–4. Counties — **Vital Statistics and Health**–Con.

[Includes U.S., states, and 3,142 counties or county equivalents defined as of January 1, 1992. For changes to these areas since then, see appendix B. Geographic Information]

County	Births, 1997		Deaths, 1997				Physicians,[4] 1999		Community hospitals,[6] 1998			Nursing and personal care facilities,[7] 1997		Medicare program enrollment,[9] 1999	
			Total		Infant[2]					Beds					
	Number	Rate[1]	Number	Rate[1]	Number	Rate[3]	Number	Rate[5]	Number	Number	Rate[5]	Estab-lishments	Em-ployees[8]	Total[10]	Aged
GEORGIA—Con.															
Gwinnett	8 115	16.2	1 989	4.0	54	6.7	685	126	2	504	96	14	1 117	30 227	25 973
Habersham	449	14.4	346	11.1	5	11.1	37	114	1	159	501	2	(11)	5 463	4 639
Hall	2 230	19.3	897	7.7	10	4.5	257	208	2	457	383	4	331	15 261	12 782
Hancock	135	15.0	100	11.1	2	14.8	5	55	1	35	383	2	(11)	1 519	1 191
Haralson	326	13.5	275	11.4	–	–	16	64	1	39	159	3	196	3 935	3 114
Harris	286	12.9	194	8.7	1	3.5	14	62	–	–	–	2	(11)	2 679	2 290
Hart	239	11.1	212	9.9	4	16.7	13	59	1	175	803	2	(11)	3 309	2 849
Heard	155	15.5	97	9.7	3	19.4	2	19	–	–	–	1	(12)	1 236	918
Henry	1 673	17.1	614	6.3	13	7.8	126	111	1	118	112	2	(11)	9 744	8 080
Houston	1 463	14.1	719	6.9	11	7.5	138	128	2	231	219	6	421	11 274	9 429
Irwin	122	13.6	101	11.3	–	–	2	22	1	64	707	1	(12)	1 301	1 048
Jackson	614	16.9	350	9.6	2	3.3	16	41	1	233	618	1	(12)	5 390	4 259
Jasper	100	10.1	97	9.8	–	–	3	28	1	67	659	–	–	1 332	1 105
Jeff Davis	199	15.7	127	10.0	2	10.1	9	71	1	50	393	1	(13)	1 964	1 462
Jefferson	279	15.7	190	10.7	–	–	12	67	1	37	208	3	(11)	3 122	2 493
Jenkins	117	13.8	86	10.2	–	–	4	48	1	33	391	2	(11)	1 408	1 133
Johnson	144	17.2	91	10.9	–	–	3	36	–	–	–	1	(12)	1 417	1 147
Jones	258	11.4	172	7.6	5	19.4	5	21	–	–	–	3	(11)	1 754	1 334
Lamar	201	13.9	153	10.6	2	10.0	6	40	–	–	–	1	(11)	2 323	1 872
Lanier	78	11.5	72	10.6	1	12.8	3	43	1	102	1 460	2	(12)	805	622
Laurens	605	14.0	441	10.2	9	14.9	84	191	1	190	435	5	400	6 929	5 540
Lee	279	12.7	102	4.7	3	10.8	6	26	–	–	–	1	(12)	1 556	1 257
Liberty	1 489	24.8	234	3.9	14	9.4	30	50	1	32	54	2	(11)	2 972	2 297
Lincoln	86	10.6	93	11.5	–	–	2	24	–	–	–	1	–	1 368	1 134
Long	168	20.2	64	7.7	1	6.0	1	11	–	–	–	–	–	567	450
Lowndes	1 442	17.0	620	7.3	16	11.1	156	183	2	359	422	5	302	10 354	8 409
Lumpkin	218	12.0	158	8.7	1	4.6	13	66	1	49	258	3	(11)	2 097	1 684
McDuffie	308	14.3	214	9.9	1	3.2	21	96	1	33	152	1	(11)	3 017	2 412
McIntosh	144	14.5	93	9.4	1	6.9	1	10	–	–	–	–	–	1 499	1 138
Macon	200	15.1	159	12.0	–	–	5	38	1	49	371	2	(11)	1 844	1 454
Madison	341	14.1	209	8.6	1	2.9	5	20	–	–	–	2	(12)	3 606	2 763
Marion	92	14.1	67	10.3	3	32.6	5	74	–	–	–	1	(12)	727	577
Meriwether	306	13.4	266	11.6	2	6.5	11	48	2	176	763	1	(11)	3 322	2 699
Miller	77	12.2	56	8.8	–	–	4	63	1	135	2 123	1	(13)	1 107	952
Mitchell	329	15.6	247	11.7	0	0.1	12	57	1	24	113	1	(10)	3 219	2 608
Monroe	233	12.0	193	10.0	1	4.3	12	60	1	37	189	4	(11)	2 358	1 819
Montgomery	99	12.8	69	8.9	1	10.1	–	–	–	–	–	–	–	1 165	867
Morgan	195	13.4	128	8.8	1	5.1	5	32	1	20	133	1	(12)	2 172	1 816
Murray	550	17.2	243	7.6	9	16.4	17	50	1	33	101	–	–	3 538	2 525
Muscogee	3 024	16.5	1 718	9.4	43	14.2	447	246	4	1 025	562	7	1 015	25 378	21 463
Newton	936	17.0	449	8.1	8	8.5	32	53	1	90	156	2	(11)	7 469	6 035
Oconee	270	11.6	162	7.0	2	7.4	57	232	–	–	–	2	(11)	2 387	2 024
Oglethorpe	129	11.5	96	8.6	–	–	2	17	–	–	–	1	(12)	1 131	899
Paulding	1 082	15.7	350	5.1	5	4.6	12	15	1	38	51	–	–	4 276	3 399
Peach	368	15.4	172	7.2	1	2.7	15	60	1	36	147	–	–	3 453	2 705
Pickens	236	12.7	152	8.2	1	4.2	22	105	–	–	–	3	(11)	2 888	2 509
Pierce	223	14.4	136	8.8	2	9.0	7	44	–	–	–	2	–	2 504	1 904
Pike	175	14.3	121	9.9	1	5.7	4	31	–	–	–	1	(12)	1 786	1 453
Polk	613	17.1	439	12.2	4	6.5	20	55	1	35	96	4	(14)	6 500	5 099
Pulaski	108	13.0	101	12.2	4	37.0	14	167	1	55	654	4	84	1 512	1 260
Putnam	215	12.7	159	9.4	1	4.7	12	66	1	50	285	1	(11)	2 620	2 213
Quitman	30	12.1	37	15.0	–	–	–	–	–	–	–	–	–	615	508
Rabun	172	13.0	185	14.0	1	5.8	21	153	2	70	523	3	136	2 817	2 418
Randolph	130	16.4	104	13.1	1	7.7	3	37	1	120	1 509	1	(12)	1 419	1 197
Richmond	3 150	16.4	1 802	9.4	25	7.9	1 221	642	5	1 460	763	18	1 007	25 910	20 399
Rockdale	862	12.9	480	7.2	11	12.8	114	165	1	107	157	1	(11)	6 979	5 947
Schley	77	20.1	38	9.9	1	13.0	1	25	–	–	–	–	–	495	404
Screven	227	15.8	177	12.3	1	4.4	5	35	1	40	277	3	(11)	2 445	1 999
Seminole	117	12.2	94	9.8	–	–	7	71	1	140	1 434	2	(12)	1 719	1 437
Spalding	858	14.9	532	9.3	16	18.6	77	133	1	158	274	4	389	8 516	6 661
Stephens	358	14.2	268	10.6	3	8.4	40	158	1	178	702	3	(11)	5 273	4 344
Stewart	75	13.8	73	13.5	–	–	4	74	1	25	462	1	(12)	980	835
Sumter	519	16.5	343	10.9	9	17.3	46	147	1	221	706	4	(14)	4 525	3 685
Talbot	85	12.3	85	12.3	1	11.8	1	14	–	–	–	–	–	1 071	851
Taliaferro	24	12.8	30	15.9	–	–	–	–	–	–	–	–	–	423	347
Tattnall	349	18.3	213	11.2	3	8.6	9	47	1	40	210	2	(11)	3 085	2 484

[1] Per 1,000 resident population estimated as of July 1, 1997.   [2] Deaths of infants under 1 year old.   [3] Infant deaths per 1,000 live births.   [4] Active, nonfederal physicians as of December 31. Data subject to copyright; see below for source citation.   [5] Per 100,000 resident population estimated as of July 1 of the year shown.   [6] Nonfederal, short-stay (average length of stay less than 30 days) hospitals except hospital units of institutions. Data subject to copyright; see below for source citation.   [7] SIC 805 includes skilled nursing care facilities; intermediate care facilities; and nursing and personal care, not elsewhere classified.   [8] Full- and part-time employees on the payroll in the pay period including March 12.   [9] Unduplicated count of persons enrolled in either hospital and/or supplemental medical insurance as of July 1. State totals include data not distributed by county.   [10] Includes disabled, not shown separately.   [11] 100 to 249 employees.   [12] 20 to 99 employees. [13] 0 to 19 employees.   [14] 250 to 499 employees.

Sources: Births—U.S. National Center for Health Statistics, "Vital Statistics of the United States, Vol. I, Natality," annual, and unpublished data.   Deaths—U.S. National Center for Health Statistics, "Vital Statistics of the United States, Vol. II, Mortality," annual, and unpublished data.   Physicians—American Medical Association, Chicago, IL, "Physician Characteristics and Distribution in the U.S.," annual (copyright).   Community Hospitals—Health Forum, LLC, an American Hospital Association Company, Chicago, IL, "Hospital Statistics," 2000 edition and unpublished data (copyright).   Nursing and Personal Care Facilities—U.S. Census Bureau, County Business Patterns 1997 on CD-ROM (related Internet site <http://www.census.gov/epcd/cbp/view/cbpview.html>).   Medicare—U.S. Health Care Financing Administration; "Medicare County Enrollment as of July 1, 1999 - Aged and Disabled 3/2000 update," <http://www.hcfa.gov/stats/enroll/default.htm>.

[Includes U.S., states, and 3,142 counties or county equivalents defined as of January 1, 1992. For changes to these areas since then, see appendix B. Geographic Information]

County	Births, 1997 Number	Births, 1997 Rate[1]	Deaths, 1997 Total Number	Deaths, 1997 Total Rate[1]	Deaths, 1997 Infant[2] Number	Deaths, 1997 Infant[2] Rate[3]	Physicians,[4] 1999 Number	Physicians,[4] 1999 Rate[5]	Community hospitals,[6] 1998 Number	Community hospitals,[6] 1998 Beds Number	Community hospitals,[6] 1998 Beds Rate[5]	Nursing and personal care facilities,[7] 1997 Establishments	Nursing and personal care facilities,[7] 1997 Employees[8]	Medicare program enrollment,[9] 1999 Total[10]	Medicare program enrollment,[9] 1999 Aged
GEORGIA—Con.															
Taylor	113	13.8	101	12.4	2	17.7	2	24	–	–	–	1	(11)	1 490	1 169
Telfair	142	12.4	175	15.3	–	–	6	53	1	52	451	2	(12)	2 240	1 770
Terrell	198	17.9	124	11.2	2	10.1	6	54	–	–	–	1	(11)	1 707	1 427
Thomas	657	15.4	451	10.6	8	12.2	128	298	1	264	616	4	258	7 640	6 069
Tift	656	17.9	330	9.0	12	18.3	88	238	1	181	492	3	250	5 371	4 380
Toombs	430	16.8	265	10.3	4	9.3	35	135	1	108	418	4	339	4 107	3 138
Towns	79	9.6	102	12.4	–	–	9	102	1	142	1 675	1	(13)	2 465	2 207
Treutlen	97	16.3	85	14.3	1	10.3	3	51	–	–	–	1	(11)	974	763
Troup	901	15.4	709	12.2	8	8.9	102	173	1	460	785	4	(12)	9 343	7 645
Turner	166	18.2	113	12.4	1	6.0	5	54	–	–	–	1	(11)	1 564	1 301
Twiggs	126	12.9	104	10.6	2	15.9	2	20	–	–	–	1	(12)	1 358	1 004
Union	151	9.6	172	10.9	–	–	15	87	1	192	1 163	1	(13)	3 784	3 321
Upson	346	12.8	327	12.1	1	2.9	38	140	1	115	425	2	(12)	4 726	3 817
Walker	810	13.0	670	10.8	6	7.4	22	35	–	–	–	5	396	11 069	9 184
Walton	931	18.1	408	7.9	4	4.3	32	55	1	113	207	2	(12)	6 956	5 686
Ware	532	14.9	436	12.2	7	13.2	71	202	1	116	328	4	(14)	7 018	5 468
Warren	74	12.3	76	12.7	1	13.5	2	33	–	–	–	1	(12)	1 087	890
Washington	272	13.6	218	10.9	2	7.4	21	104	1	116	578	6	204	3 129	2 545
Wayne	332	13.3	256	10.2	3	9.0	33	129	1	110	434	7	273	3 712	2 915
Webster	33	14.6	22	9.7	–	–	–	–	–	–	–	–	–	317	270
Wheeler	76	15.3	57	11.4	–	–	–	–	1	30	612	1	(11)	906	692
White	220	13.1	132	7.8	1	4.5	8	44	–	–	–	2	(12)	3 149	2 712
Whitfield	1 514	18.7	604	7.4	8	5.3	145	174	1	282	344	4	(14)	10 693	8 641
Wilcox	121	16.5	90	12.3	2	16.5	3	40	–	–	–	2	(12)	1 356	1 094
Wilkes	150	14.1	158	14.9	2	13.3	8	76	1	38	358	1	(11)	2 163	1 804
Wilkinson	156	14.5	106	9.8	5	32.1	1	9	–	–	–	1	(11)	1 701	1 317
Worth	285	12.8	201	9.0	1	3.5	9	40	1	49	218	1	(11)	2 449	1 997
HAWAII	17 393	14.6	7 892	6.6	114	6.6	3 184	269	20	2 791	234	37	3 303	161 787	148 077
Hawaii	2 244	15.9	1 198	8.5	16	7.1	267	188	2	349	246	5	(12)	20 924	18 433
Honolulu	12 614	14.4	5 594	6.4	83	6.6	2 573	298	12	1 874	215	25	2 540	117 980	108 943
Kalawao	2	26.3	5	65.8	–	–	–	–	–	–	–	–	–	70	D
Kauai	737	13.1	419	7.4	5	6.8	111	196	2	226	402	1	(11)	8 101	7 452
Maui	1 796	15.1	681	5.7	10	5.6	233	191	4	342	284	6	(14)	14 623	13 116
IDAHO	18 582	15.3	8 976	7.4	127	6.8	1 944	155	42	3 414	277	143	7 570	161 362	141 679
Ada	4 070	15.2	1 624	6.1	18	4.4	682	241	3	670	243	33	1 623	29 756	26 399
Adams	24	6.3	45	11.8	1	41.7	12	317	1	26	687	–	–	698	610
Bannock	1 298	17.6	549	7.4	9	6.9	150	200	2	324	436	6	262	8 935	7 622
Bear Lake	73	11.2	68	10.4	–	–	6	91	1	58	891	–	–	1 090	998
Benewah	117	13.0	97	10.8	–	–	8	88	1	25	275	1	(12)	1 535	1 259
Bingham	713	17.2	296	7.1	5	7.0	22	52	1	100	239	1	(13)	4 912	4 277
Blaine	242	14.1	65	3.8	1	4.1	73	421	1	64	372	–	–	1 457	1 352
Boise	77	15.3	33	6.5	–	–	–	–	–	–	–	–	–	673	566
Bonner	354	10.2	272	7.8	2	5.6	40	111	1	48	136	2	(12)	5 314	4 552
Bonneville	1 354	16.9	507	6.3	12	8.9	166	204	2	304	377	12	681	9 500	8 203
Boundary	122	12.4	80	8.1	–	–	9	90	1	62	631	1	(13)	1 581	1 349
Butte	40	12.9	31	10.0	2	50.0	2	66	1	43	1 414	–	–	514	447
Camas	11	13.2	2	2.4	–	–	–	–	–	–	–	–	–	134	118
Canyon	2 092	17.9	893	7.7	13	6.2	144	116	2	271	225	14	683	15 984	13 943
Caribou	88	12.1	58	8.0	1	11.4	4	55	1	65	878	1	(11)	1 071	984
Cassia	397	18.5	154	7.2	2	5.0	26	121	1	38	178	4	159	2 881	2 607
Clark	19	22.6	5	6.0	–	–	–	–	–	–	–	–	–	99	D
Clearwater	93	9.9	88	9.4	–	–	12	128	1	18	193	1	(11)	1 583	1 310
Custer	50	11.8	42	9.9	2	40.0	2	49	–	–	–	–	–	678	598
Elmore	538	21.8	153	6.2	4	7.4	19	74	1	80	315	–	–	2 225	1 968
Franklin	228	21.1	109	10.1	6	26.3	4	35	1	65	585	1	(11)	1 438	1 344
Fremont	198	16.9	73	6.2	2	10.1	3	25	–	–	–	2	(11)	1 700	1 513
Gem	180	12.5	134	9.3	–	–	6	40	1	24	162	4	188	2 516	2 266
Gooding	226	16.7	114	8.4	–	–	3	22	1	14	103	3	(12)	2 314	2 124
Idaho	161	10.7	165	11.0	1	6.2	15	100	2	44	293	1	(11)	2 730	2 356
Jefferson	355	18.6	103	5.4	4	11.3	1	5	–	–	–	1	(13)	2 086	1 845
Jerome	276	15.7	134	7.6	2	7.2	9	50	1	65	362	1	(11)	2 455	2 211

[1] Per 1,000 resident population estimated as of July 1, 1997.   [2] Deaths of infants under 1 year old.   [3] Infant deaths per 1,000 live births.   [4] Active, nonfederal physicians as of December 31. Data subject to copyright; see below for source citation.   [5] Per 100,000 resident population estimated as of July 1 of the year shown.   [6] Nonfederal, short-stay (average length of stay less than 30 days) hospitals except hospital units of institutions. Data subject to copyright; see below for source citation.   [7] SIC 805 includes skilled nursing care facilities; intermediate care facilities; and nursing and personal care, not elsewhere classified.   [8] Full- and part-time employees on the payroll in the pay period including March 12.   [9] Unduplicated count of persons enrolled in either hospital and/or supplemental medical insurance as of July 1. State totals include data not distributed by county.   [10] Includes disabled, not shown separately.   [11] 20 to 99 employees.   [12] 100 to 249 employees. [13] 0 to 19 employees.   [14] 250 to 499 employees.

Sources: Births—U.S. National Center for Health Statistics, "Vital Statistics of the United States, Vol. I, Natality," annual, and unpublished data.   Deaths—U.S. National Center for Health Statistics, "Vital Statistics of the United States, Vol. II, Mortality," annual, and unpublished data.   Physicians—American Medical Association, Chicago, IL, "Physician Characteristics and Distribution in the U.S.," annual (copyright).   Community Hospitals—Health Forum, LLC, an American Hospital Association Company, Chicago, IL, "Hospital Statistics" 2000 edition and unpublished data (copyright). Nursing and Personal Care Facilities—U.S. Census Bureau, County Business Patterns 1997 on CD-ROM (related Internet site <http://www.census.gov/epcd/cbp/view/cbpview.html>).   Medicare—U.S. Health Care Financing Administration; "Medicare County Enrollment as of July 1, 1999 - Aged and Disabled 3/2000 update," <http://www.hcfa.gov/stats/enroll/default.htm>.

[Includes U.S., states, and 3,142 counties or county equivalents defined as of January 1, 1992. For changes to these areas since then, see appendix B. Geographic Information]

| County | Births, 1997 | | Deaths, 1997 | | | | Physicians,[4] 1999 | | Community hospitals,[6] 1998 | | | Nursing and personal care facilities,[7] 1997 | | Medicare program enrollment,[9] 1999 | |
| | | | Total | | Infant[2] | | | | | Beds | | | | | |
	Number	Rate[1]	Number	Rate[1]	Number	Rate[3]	Number	Rate[5]	Number	Number	Rate[5]	Estab-lishments	Em-ployees[8]	Total[10]	Aged
IDAHO—Con.															
Kootenai	1 296	13.1	757	7.7	9	6.9	169	161	1	225	222	12	769	14 906	12 819
Latah	426	12.8	217	6.5	3	7.0	42	129	1	35	107	7	572	3 627	3 193
Lemhi	91	11.3	74	9.2	–	–	3	38	1	28	348	1	(11)	1 536	1 335
Lewis	35	8.7	51	12.7	2	57.1	1	25	–	–	–	–	–	1 166	994
Lincoln	51	13.4	36	9.5	–	–	1	26	–	–	–	1	(11)	534	499
Madison	415	16.7	131	5.3	4	9.6	32	129	1	42	167	4	(12)	1 748	1 607
Minidoka	357	17.4	154	7.5	3	8.4	8	39	1	101	500	–	–	2 968	2 653
Nez Perce	443	12.0	366	9.9	3	6.8	85	230	1	156	423	4	311	6 715	5 898
Oneida	52	13.0	33	8.3	–	–	1	25	1	52	1 290	–	–	676	617
Owyhee	164	16.2	83	8.2	3	18.3	1	10	–	–	–	1	(11)	1 214	1 061
Payette	275	13.6	189	9.4	3	10.9	8	38	–	–	–	4	263	3 032	2 671
Power	157	19.1	57	6.9	–	–	2	24	1	41	487	–	–	814	724
Shoshone	166	11.9	164	11.8	1	6.0	14	103	1	44	317	2	(12)	2 940	2 378
Teton	92	17.4	13	2.5	–	–	5	88	1	13	237	1	(13)	547	498
Twin Falls	936	15.2	582	9.5	9	9.6	133	211	2	217	349	14	769	9 732	8 859
Valley	91	11.3	65	8.0	–	–	17	216	2	25	312	1	(11)	1 369	1 203
Washington	139	13.8	110	10.9	–	–	4	39	1	27	264	2	(11)	1 930	1 720
ILLINOIS	180 803	15.1	102 914	8.6	1 523	8.4	31 928	263	203	39 218	325	1 336	97 115	1 628 744	1 436 573
Adams	812	12.0	731	10.8	7	8.6	137	205	1	240	356	15	1 067	12 659	11 415
Alexander	131	13.1	145	14.5	1	7.6	2	20	–	–	–	2	(12)	1 962	1 578
Bond	191	11.2	193	11.3	2	10.5	9	52	1	192	1 111	3	89	2 810	2 495
Boone	533	14.1	273	7.2	2	3.8	51	129	2	119	307	3	140	4 551	4 102
Brown	64	9.5	64	9.5	–	–	1	14	–	–	–	1	(12)	972	876
Bureau	388	10.9	383	10.7	3	7.7	39	110	2	210	592	3	234	6 741	6 199
Calhoun	37	7.4	65	13.0	1	27.0	3	62	–	–	–	1	(13)	1 031	913
Carroll	164	9.7	205	12.1	2	12.2	7	42	–	–	–	4	200	3 478	3 179
Cass	186	14.0	171	12.9	1	5.4	3	23	–	–	–	8	288	2 465	2 189
Champaign	2 180	12.8	1 042	6.1	24	11.0	565	332	2	748	440	15	1 114	18 628	16 525
Christian	439	12.2	406	11.3	5	11.4	26	73	2	181	506	8	572	6 708	5 978
Clark	180	11.0	194	11.8	1	5.6	7	42	–	–	–	3	258	3 350	3 031
Clay	168	11.7	195	13.5	–	–	8	56	1	31	214	5	237	2 996	2 629
Clinton	424	12.0	302	8.6	1	2.4	20	56	1	57	160	12	528	4 864	4 338
Coles	563	10.8	481	9.2	4	7.1	75	145	1	174	335	12	760	7 880	6 896
Cook	85 696	16.5	45 832	8.8	858	10.0	18 707	360	65	19 322	372	385	35 028	673 286	590 286
Crawford	214	10.2	247	11.8	1	4.7	14	67	1	93	444	5	178	3 900	3 480
Cumberland	135	12.1	121	10.9	2	14.8	1	9	–	–	–	2	(12)	1 835	1 644
DeKalb	1 060	12.5	564	6.6	8	7.5	81	93	3	199	232	9	572	9 923	8 967
De Witt	191	11.4	174	10.4	–	–	14	84	1	33	197	3	132	3 003	2 658
Douglas	287	14.4	193	9.7	1	3.5	11	55	–	–	–	4	266	2 869	2 642
DuPage	13 447	15.5	5 083	5.8	78	5.8	3 427	384	8	1 769	201	56	5 659	92 890	85 784
Edgar	215	10.8	263	13.2	2	9.3	12	61	1	49	248	4	242	3 757	3 309
Edwards	80	11.4	80	11.4	1	12.5	–	–	–	–	–	1	(11)	1 319	1 220
Effingham	480	14.4	292	8.7	2	4.2	64	189	1	146	435	8	414	5 474	4 866
Fayette	268	12.1	217	9.8	2	7.5	11	50	1	142	642	5	177	3 725	3 291
Ford	180	12.7	183	12.9	2	11.1	12	85	1	82	583	4	249	2 756	2 561
Franklin	471	11.6	549	13.5	3	6.4	24	59	2	137	339	5	157	8 672	7 411
Fulton	420	10.8	424	10.9	2	4.8	26	67	1	124	320	7	626	7 996	7 017
Gallatin	65	9.8	92	13.8	–	–	4	61	–	–	–	2	(12)	1 380	1 167
Greene	195	12.4	188	12.0	1	5.1	9	57	1	60	381	1	(11)	3 040	2 684
Grundy	458	12.6	284	7.8	3	6.6	29	78	1	82	223	3	110	5 105	4 646
Hamilton	91	10.6	117	13.6	–	–	7	82	1	91	1 056	3	(11)	1 822	1 616
Hancock	212	10.0	221	10.4	1	4.7	11	52	1	59	279	4	177	4 175	3 837
Hardin	59	11.9	61	12.3	–	–	3	61	1	48	973	4	81	959	800
Henderson	89	10.3	97	11.2	–	–	5	58	–	–	–	1	(11)	1 372	1 235
Henry	547	10.6	556	10.8	2	3.7	31	60	2	168	326	3	316	8 832	8 153
Iroquois	352	11.2	371	11.8	1	2.8	21	67	1	112	358	7	498	6 228	5 546
Jackson	665	10.9	455	7.4	6	9.0	188	310	2	192	316	7	502	7 642	6 430
Jasper	113	10.6	94	8.9	–	–	2	19	–	–	–	1	(11)	1 767	1 639
Jefferson	447	11.4	438	11.2	2	4.5	60	153	2	164	420	5	205	6 612	5 754
Jersey	260	12.2	214	10.1	–	–	12	56	1	67	311	5	299	2 895	2 531
Jo Daviess	251	11.6	223	10.3	–	–	11	51	1	85	395	3	146	4 271	3 955
Johnson	98	7.4	138	10.5	2	20.4	3	22	–	–	–	3	(11)	2 219	1 921
Kane	6 981	18.3	2 345	6.1	55	7.9	598	149	4	779	199	31	2 129	39 171	34 587

[1] Per 1,000 resident population estimated as of July 1, 1997. [2] Deaths of infants under 1 year old. [3] Infant deaths per 1,000 live births. [4] Active, nonfederal physicians as of December 31. Data subject to copyright; see below for source citation. [5] Per 100,000 resident population estimated as of July 1 of the year shown. [6] Nonfederal, short-stay (average length of stay less than 30 days) hospitals except hospital units of institutions. Data subject to copyright; see below for source citation. [7] SIC 805 includes skilled nursing care facilities; intermediate care facilities; and nursing and personal care, not elsewhere classified. [8] Full- and part-time employees on the payroll in the pay period including March 12. [9] Unduplicated count of persons enrolled in either hospital and/or supplemental medical insurance as of July 1. State totals include data not distributed by county. [10] Includes disabled, not shown separately. [11] 20 to 99 employees. [12] 100 to 249 employees. [13] 0 to 19 employees.

Sources: Births—U.S. National Center for Health Statistics, "Vital Statistics of the United States, Vol. I, Natality," annual, and unpublished data. Deaths—U.S. National Center for Health Statistics, "Vital Statistics of the United States, Vol. II, Mortality," annual, and unpublished data. Physicians—American Medical Association, Chicago, IL, "Physician Characteristics and Distribution in the U.S.," annual (copyright). Community Hospitals—Health Forum, LLC, an American Hospital Association Company, Chicago, IL, "Hospital Statistics" 2000 edition and unpublished data (copyright). Nursing and Personal Care Facilities—U.S. Census Bureau, County Business Patterns 1997 on CD-ROM (related Internet site <http://www.census.gov/epcd/cbp/view/cbpview.html>). Medicare—U.S. Health Care Financing Administration; "Medicare County Enrollment as of July 1, 1999 - Aged and Disabled 3/2000 update," <http://www.hcfa.gov/stats/enroll/default.htm>.

[Includes U.S., states, and 3,142 counties or county equivalents defined as of January 1, 1992. For changes to these areas since then, see appendix B. Geographic Information]

County	Births, 1997		Deaths, 1997				Physicians,[4] 1999		Community hospitals,[6] 1998			Nursing and personal care facilities,[7] 1997		Medicare program enrollment,[9] 1999	
			Total		Infant[2]					Beds					
	Number	Rate[1]	Number	Rate[1]	Number	Rate[3]	Number	Rate[5]	Number	Number	Rate[5]	Establishments	Employees[8]	Total[10]	Aged
ILLINOIS—Con.															
Kankakee	1 511	14.8	1 082	10.6	12	7.9	146	142	2	562	549	17	879	16 174	13 292
Kendall	685	13.7	280	5.6	6	8.8	20	37	–	–	–	2	(11)	3 903	3 564
Knox	620	11.1	646	11.6	3	4.8	94	170	2	323	581	19	1 102	10 856	9 582
Lake	10 184	17.0	3 371	5.6	57	5.6	1 717	278	7	1 164	191	48	3 442	58 885	52 603
La Salle	1 362	12.4	1 185	10.8	10	7.3	115	104	4	440	399	20	1 269	20 214	18 256
Lawrence	164	10.6	253	16.3	2	12.2	11	73	1	58	378	8	639	3 337	2 936
Lee	424	11.8	375	10.4	4	9.4	39	109	1	100	278	3	286	6 053	5 337
Livingston	462	11.6	413	10.4	2	4.3	29	73	1	81	204	10	670	6 178	5 520
Logan	316	10.1	319	10.1	2	6.3	23	72	1	60	188	16	1 456	5 346	4 631
McDonough	284	8.0	294	8.3	2	7.0	48	136	1	120	338	6	389	4 989	4 561
McHenry	3 839	16.3	1 448	6.1	25	6.5	260	105	3	352	146	19	1 056	23 204	20 826
McLean	1 997	14.1	923	6.5	15	7.5	271	186	2	440	307	25	1 317	16 265	14 520
Macon	1 491	13.1	1 229	10.8	18	12.1	204	180	2	413	363	21	1 492	20 007	17 430
Macoupin	513	10.5	565	11.6	2	3.9	17	35	2	77	158	11	791	9 723	8 654
Madison	3 315	12.8	2 584	10.0	28	8.4	306	118	6	925	357	40	2 793	42 267	36 391
Marion	561	13.3	471	11.2	4	7.1	59	141	2	307	732	11	738	8 755	7 408
Marshall	150	11.7	163	12.7	2	13.3	6	46	–	–	–	3	265	2 406	2 257
Mason	179	10.6	190	11.3	2	11.2	10	60	1	36	214	2	(11)	3 319	2 960
Massac	172	11.1	204	13.2	–	–	11	71	1	38	245	5	348	2 998	2 545
Menard	150	12.1	115	9.2	1	6.7	11	86	–	–	–	1	(12)	1 777	1 603
Mercer	191	10.9	177	10.1	2	10.5	6	34	1	45	255	–	–	2 774	2 538
Monroe	308	11.9	223	8.6	2	6.5	19	70	–	–	–	3	180	3 818	3 495
Montgomery	319	10.2	353	11.2	3	9.4	17	54	2	192	611	6	462	5 916	5 315
Morgan	393	11.0	415	11.6	5	12.7	47	134	1	116	328	11	537	6 475	5 511
Moultrie	178	12.3	191	13.2	–	–	9	62	–	–	–	6	582	3 017	2 747
Ogle	569	11.3	458	9.1	5	8.8	32	63	1	42	83	7	604	7 137	6 450
Peoria	2 575	14.1	1 630	8.9	20	7.8	734	405	3	992	547	25	1 915	29 533	25 888
Perry	240	11.2	262	12.3	1	4.2	14	66	2	95	447	6	201	4 181	3 667
Piatt	207	12.6	145	8.8	–	–	10	60	1	16	97	2	(12)	2 891	2 638
Pike	191	11.0	225	13.0	1	5.2	11	64	1	45	260	5	274	3 676	3 311
Pope	50	10.6	45	9.5	–	–	–	–	–	–	–	–	–	745	641
Pulaski	92	12.8	107	14.8	–	–	–	–	–	–	–	1	(13)	1 524	1 311
Putnam	55	9.5	61	10.5	–	–	1	17	–	–	–	–	–	1 052	961
Randolph	369	10.9	347	10.3	2	5.4	27	80	3	190	564	6	353	5 943	5 261
Richland	218	12.9	208	12.3	1	4.6	37	222	1	90	536	4	272	3 211	2 856
Rock Island	2 015	13.6	1 506	10.2	21	10.4	256	174	2	455	308	19	1 139	25 303	22 479
St. Clair	3 689	14.0	2 562	9.7	29	7.9	396	152	4	992	379	34	2 646	38 345	32 646
Saline	315	12.0	399	15.2	–	–	26	100	1	51	195	11	559	5 786	4 861
Sangamon	2 488	13.0	1 746	9.1	28	11.3	846	442	3	1 160	606	21	1 298	28 798	25 072
Schuyler	83	10.8	96	12.5	–	–	5	67	1	58	766	1	(12)	1 392	1 270
Scott	72	12.8	67	12.0	–	–	1	18	–	–	–	–	–	923	834
Shelby	262	11.6	243	10.7	–	–	12	53	1	52	229	5	212	4 291	3 854
Stark	78	12.3	90	14.2	1	12.8	4	64	–	–	–	1	(11)	1 297	1 210
Stephenson	605	12.3	482	9.8	2	3.3	65	133	1	174	356	5	299	9 041	8 159
Tazewell	1 572	12.2	1 152	8.9	12	7.6	129	99	2	245	189	24	1 431	21 219	19 204
Union	195	10.8	238	13.2	–	–	29	161	1	58	322	12	485	3 587	2 951
Vermilion	1 139	13.4	937	11.1	5	4.4	122	146	2	405	479	6	480	15 699	13 175
Wabash	113	8.9	128	10.1	2	17.7	10	80	1	56	446	5	273	2 377	2 138
Warren	230	12.2	204	10.8	1	4.3	10	53	1	58	307	4	253	3 326	2 975
Washington	154	10.0	159	10.4	1	6.5	4	26	1	53	346	2	(11)	2 691	2 452
Wayne	197	11.6	203	11.9	1	5.1	10	59	1	185	1 091	2	(12)	3 382	3 058
White	163	10.4	239	15.2	–	–	12	77	1	112	718	3	249	3 793	3 385
Whiteside	771	10.8	612	10.2	4	5.2	71	119	2	203	339	17	835	11 059	9 737
Will	6 936	15.6	2 527	5.7	52	7.5	416	87	2	639	139	40	2 488	42 570	37 177
Williamson	698	11.4	762	12.4	8	11.5	100	162	2	176	287	14	767	10 772	9 278
Winnebago	3 814	14.3	2 296	8.6	24	6.3	669	250	3	812	303	57	2 942	39 761	34 440
Woodford	393	11.3	343	9.8	4	10.2	23	65	–	–	–	8	874	4 769	4 496
INDIANA	83 436	14.2	53 130	9.0	682	8.2	11 753	198	111	19 401	328	1 010	56 307	844 835	731 685
Adams	535	16.3	272	8.3	8	15.0	16	48	1	87	263	6	292	4 563	4 190
Allen	5 029	16.1	2 545	8.2	40	8.0	747	236	3	1 149	365	37	2 624	42 156	36 714
Bartholomew	997	14.5	602	8.7	10	10.0	153	219	1	239	344	8	572	9 684	8 327
Benton	150	15.5	83	8.6	1	6.7	6	61	–	–	–	4	(11)	1 740	1 592
Blackford	177	12.6	141	10.1	2	11.3	9	65	1	36	258	2	(11)	2 412	2 151
Boone	582	13.5	423	9.8	4	6.9	180	401	1	60	137	9	317	5 468	4 968
Brown	119	7.6	120	7.7	3	25.2	7	44	–	–	–	2	(11)	1 302	1 149
Carroll	254	12.8	193	9.7	2	7.9	6	30	–	–	–	2	(11)	2 596	2 372
Cass	571	14.7	383	9.9	4	7.0	43	110	1	104	268	6	509	6 689	5 701

[1] Per 1,000 resident population estimated as of July 1, 1997.   [2] Deaths of infants under 1 year old.   [3] Infant deaths per 1,000 live births.   [4] Active, nonfederal physicians as of December 31. Data subject to copyright; see below for source citation.   [5] Per 100,000 resident population estimated as of July 1 of the year shown.   [6] Nonfederal, short-stay (average length of stay less than 30 days) hospitals except hospital units of institutions. Data subject to copyright; see below for source citation.   [7] SIC 805 includes skilled nursing care facilities; intermediate care facilities; and nursing and personal care, not elsewhere classified.   [8] Full- and part-time employees on the payroll in the pay period including March 12.   [9] Unduplicated count of persons enrolled in either hospital and/or supplemental medical insurance as of July 1. State totals include data not distributed by county.   [10] Includes disabled, not shown separately.   [11] 100 to 249 employees.   [12] 20 to 99 employees.   [13] 0 to 19 employees.

Sources: Births—U.S. National Center for Health Statistics, "Vital Statistics of the United States, Vol. I, Natality," annual, and unpublished data.   Deaths—U.S. National Center for Health Statistics, "Vital Statistics of the United States, Vol. II, Mortality," annual, and unpublished data.   Physicians—American Medical Association, Chicago, IL, "Physician Characteristics and Distribution in the U.S.," annual (copyright).   Community Hospitals—Health Forum, LLC, an American Hospital Association Company, Chicago, IL, "Hospital Statistics" 2000 edition and unpublished data (copyright). Nursing and Personal Care Facilities—U.S. Census Bureau, County Business Patterns 1997 on CD-ROM (related Internet site <http://www.census.gov/epcd/cbp/view/cbpview.html>).   Medicare—U.S. Health Care Financing Administration; "Medicare County Enrollment as of July 1, 1999 - Aged and Disabled 3/2000 update," <http://www.hcfa.gov/stats/enroll/default.htm>.

Table B–4. Counties — **Vital Statistics and Health**–Con.

[Includes U.S., states, and 3,142 counties or county equivalents defined as of January 1, 1992. For changes to these areas since then, see appendix B. Geographic Information]

County	Births, 1997 Number	Births, 1997 Rate[1]	Deaths, 1997 Total Number	Deaths, 1997 Total Rate[1]	Deaths, 1997 Infant[2] Number	Deaths, 1997 Infant[2] Rate[3]	Physicians,[4] 1999 Number	Physicians,[4] 1999 Rate[5]	Community hospitals,[6] 1998 Number	Community hospitals,[6] 1998 Beds Number	Community hospitals,[6] 1998 Beds Rate[5]	Nursing and personal care facilities,[7] 1997 Estab-lishments	Nursing and personal care facilities,[7] 1997 Em-ployees[8]	Medicare program enrollment,[9] 1999 Total[10]	Medicare program enrollment,[9] 1999 Aged
INDIANA—Con.															
Clark	1 242	13.3	939	10.1	13	10.5	139	146	2	323	344	14	865	14 185	11 597
Clay	337	12.7	269	10.1	3	8.9	17	63	1	33	123	5	205	4 952	4 335
Clinton	451	13.6	367	11.1	5	11.1	22	67	1	53	160	7	666	5 231	4 693
Crawford	118	11.3	110	10.5	–	–	–	–	–	–	–	2	(11)	1 848	1 468
Daviess	417	14.5	292	10.1	3	7.2	13	45	1	85	294	8	433	4 435	3 897
Dearborn	633	13.6	372	8.0	3	4.7	38	79	1	87	184	10	482	6 042	5 137
Decatur	380	15.0	231	9.1	1	2.6	23	89	1	70	274	5	248	3 763	3 365
De Kalb	566	14.5	341	8.8	4	7.1	34	86	1	45	114	13	449	5 085	4 517
Delaware	1 420	12.1	1 150	9.8	13	9.2	325	281	1	400	344	31	1 478	18 131	15 435
Dubois	561	14.4	346	8.9	3	5.3	55	137	2	184	464	11	693	5 553	5 019
Elkhart	2 920	17.1	1 325	7.8	20	6.8	213	122	2	434	251	26	1 989	21 856	19 276
Fayette	373	14.3	275	10.5	3	8.0	24	93	1	111	427	12	371	4 619	3 906
Floyd	902	12.6	617	8.6	4	4.4	143	198	2	238	331	14	680	10 054	8 435
Fountain	233	12.8	232	12.7	3	12.9	4	22	–	–	–	3	214	3 503	3 082
Franklin	244	11.4	169	7.9	3	12.3	5	23	–	–	–	3	118	2 747	2 381
Fulton	292	14.3	205	10.1	2	6.8	15	72	1	35	169	2	(12)	3 409	3 030
Gibson	382	11.9	310	9.7	3	7.9	22	68	2	120	373	6	317	5 599	4 994
Grant	856	11.8	777	10.7	7	8.2	106	147	1	212	292	9	850	12 581	10 614
Greene	372	11.3	332	10.0	3	8.1	22	66	1	56	168	8	460	5 598	4 813
Hamilton	2 427	15.7	787	5.1	18	7.4	725	421	1	111	68	22	1 336	13 100	11 788
Hancock	716	13.5	427	8.0	3	4.2	68	122	1	102	187	13	334	6 537	5 739
Harrison	384	11.3	239	7.0	4	10.4	21	59	1	47	136	7	208	4 752	3 976
Hendricks	1 213	13.2	652	7.1	6	4.9	123	124	1	127	133	14	722	10 005	9 071
Henry	581	11.9	512	10.5	6	10.3	41	85	1	107	220	14	538	8 818	7 644
Howard	1 193	14.2	766	9.1	3	2.5	137	164	3	332	398	8	690	13 208	11 363
Huntington	496	13.3	390	10.5	2	4.0	38	102	1	37	99	11	659	6 092	5 507
Jackson	619	15.1	402	9.8	6	9.7	39	94	1	107	261	7	515	6 544	5 525
Jasper	361	12.6	217	7.6	3	8.3	17	58	1	69	237	1	(13)	4 240	3 726
Jay	344	15.9	251	11.6	1	2.9	13	60	1	65	299	3	(12)	3 819	3 354
Jefferson	388	12.4	323	10.3	4	10.3	46	145	1	115	366	7	335	4 946	3 995
Jennings	409	15.1	239	8.8	8	19.6	9	32	1	34	123	3	77	3 802	2 812
Johnson	1 450	13.6	830	7.8	3	2.1	184	163	1	160	146	17	1 339	13 651	12 142
Knox	441	11.1	472	11.9	4	9.1	69	177	1	289	736	8	665	7 034	6 001
Kosciusko	1 140	16.2	622	8.8	10	8.8	57	80	1	161	226	12	748	9 657	8 567
Lagrange	673	20.5	195	5.9	2	3.0	12	35	1	53	159	3	255	3 402	2 980
Lake	6 911	14.4	4 571	9.5	65	9.4	801	167	6	2 085	433	38	3 077	71 745	61 514
La Porte	1 496	13.6	980	8.9	12	8.0	163	148	2	389	354	13	706	16 247	14 239
Lawrence	615	13.5	494	10.9	4	6.6	52	114	2	164	359	9	522	7 459	6 377
Madison	1 699	12.9	1 392	10.5	26	15.3	161	123	2	299	228	23	1 246	22 359	19 472
Marion	13 890	17.0	7 554	9.3	147	10.6	3 573	441	9	4 458	549	172	8 436	112 170	94 777
Marshall	703	15.5	400	8.8	5	7.1	40	87	2	64	140	12	495	6 504	5 890
Martin	158	15.0	103	9.8	–	–	3	29	–	–	–	3	111	1 851	1 573
Miami	464	14.0	334	10.1	1	2.2	29	86	1	74	221	2	(12)	5 274	4 623
Monroe	1 268	10.9	692	6.0	8	6.3	274	234	1	856	734	13	856	12 352	10 736
Montgomery	507	14.0	384	10.6	4	7.9	39	107	1	98	269	10	467	5 768	5 133
Morgan	898	13.9	515	8.0	5	5.6	60	90	2	146	223	11	477	7 907	6 857
Newton	162	11.0	131	8.9	1	6.2	2	13	–	–	–	2	(11)	1 852	1 645
Noble	707	16.9	367	8.8	1	1.4	26	60	1	43	101	9	366	5 552	4 803
Ohio	55	10.1	72	13.2	3	54.5	1	18	–	–	–	2	(11)	758	652
Orange	246	12.7	219	11.3	4	16.3	14	71	1	37	189	6	315	3 196	2 700
Owen	250	12.3	189	9.3	–	–	5	24	–	–	–	5	178	2 736	2 349
Parke	178	10.7	153	9.2	–	–	13	77	–	–	–	3	168	2 772	2 369
Perry	194	10.0	184	9.5	2	10.3	9	47	1	38	197	4	(12)	3 184	2 815
Pike	149	11.6	132	10.3	1	6.7	3	23	–	–	–	2	(12)	2 178	1 863
Porter	1 727	12.0	1 095	7.6	15	8.7	238	161	1	352	241	13	878	16 740	14 691
Posey	268	10.1	236	8.9	1	3.7	10	38	–	–	–	4	182	3 605	3 136
Pulaski	160	12.0	119	8.9	1	6.3	7	52	1	19	141	2	(12)	2 285	2 011
Putnam	412	12.1	285	8.4	1	2.4	19	55	1	85	246	10	346	4 673	4 109
Randolph	350	12.7	301	10.9	4	11.4	16	58	1	27	98	4	206	4 872	4 337
Ripley	405	14.9	243	8.9	3	7.4	36	130	1	82	301	7	309	4 411	3 812
Rush	253	13.8	219	11.9	1	4.0	8	44	1	52	285	5	238	2 914	2 569
St. Joseph	3 766	14.6	2 342	9.1	40	10.6	569	220	3	762	295	39	2 182	40 741	36 628
Scott	357	15.6	218	9.5	4	11.2	12	51	1	45	195	3	166	3 598	2 736
Shelby	582	13.5	369	8.5	2	3.4	28	64	1	49	113	11	439	5 563	4 895
Spencer	289	13.9	193	9.3	–	–	6	28	–	–	–	3	172	2 996	2 623
Starke	276	11.7	251	10.6	–	–	9	38	1	35	146	5	338	3 598	2 916
Steuben	440	14.2	288	9.3	3	6.8	25	79	1	30	95	5	176	4 691	4 172
Sullivan	239	11.2	279	13.0	3	12.6	8	37	1	46	215	2	(12)	3 646	3 074
Switzerland	103	11.9	90	10.4	1	9.7	2	22	–	–	–	1	(11)	1 219	993
Tippecanoe	1 803	13.0	948	6.8	6	3.3	312	219	2	462	327	18	842	14 876	13 138

[1] Per 1,000 resident population estimated as of July 1, 1997. [2] Deaths of infants under 1 year old. [3] Infant deaths per 1,000 live births. [4] Active, nonfederal physicians as of December 31. Data subject to copyright; see below for source citation. [5] Per 100,000 resident population estimated as of July 1 of the year shown. [6] Nonfederal, short-stay (average length of stay less than 30 days) hospitals except hospital units of institutions. Data subject to copyright; see below for source citation. [7] SIC 805 includes skilled nursing care facilities; intermediate care facilities; and nursing and personal care, not elsewhere classified. [8] Full- and part-time employees on the payroll in the pay period including March 12. [9] Unduplicated count of persons enrolled in either hospital and/or supplemental medical insurance as of July 1. State totals include data not distributed by county. [10] Includes disabled, not shown separately. [11] 20 to 99 employees. [12] 100 to 249 employees. [13] 0 to 19 employees.

Sources: Births—U.S. National Center for Health Statistics, "Vital Statistics of the United States, Vol. I, Natality," annual, and unpublished data. Deaths—U.S. National Center for Health Statistics, "Vital Statistics of the United States, Vol. II, Mortality," annual, and unpublished data. Physicians—American Medical Association, Chicago, IL, "Physician Characteristics and Distribution in the U.S.," annual (copyright). Community Hospitals—Health Forum, LLC, an American Hospital Association Company, Chicago, IL, "Hospital Statistics" 2000 edition and unpublished data (copyright). Nursing and Personal Care Facilities—U.S. Census Bureau, County Business Patterns 1997 on CD-ROM (related Internet site <http://www.census.gov/epcd/cbp/view/cbpview.html>). Medicare—U.S. Health Care Financing Administration; "Medicare County Enrollment as of July 1, 1999 - Aged and Disabled 3/2000 update," <http://www.hcfa.gov/stats/enroll/default.htm>.

Table B–4. Counties — **Vital Statistics and Health**–Con.

[Includes U.S., states, and 3,142 counties or county equivalents defined as of January 1, 1992. For changes to these areas since then, see appendix B. Geographic Information]

County	Births, 1997 Number	Births, 1997 Rate[1]	Deaths, 1997 Total Number	Deaths, 1997 Total Rate[1]	Deaths, 1997 Infant[2] Number	Deaths, 1997 Infant[2] Rate[3]	Physicians,[4] 1999 Number	Physicians,[4] 1999 Rate[5]	Community hospitals,[6] 1998 Number	Community hospitals,[6] 1998 Beds Number	Community hospitals,[6] 1998 Beds Rate[5]	Nursing and personal care facilities,[7] 1997 Establishments	Nursing and personal care facilities,[7] 1997 Employees[8]	Medicare program enrollment,[9] 1999 Total[10]	Medicare program enrollment,[9] 1999 Aged
INDIANA—Con.															
Tipton	179	10.9	146	8.9	–	–	14	84	1	100	600	2	(11)	2 475	2 242
Union	93	12.7	63	8.6	–	–	1	14	–	–	–	4	(12)	1 087	941
Vanderburgh	2 166	12.9	1 860	11.1	18	8.3	527	314	4	1 181	704	38	2 493	30 275	26 102
Vermillion	224	13.2	194	11.4	1	4.5	7	41	1	27	159	3	224	2 924	2 552
Vigo	1 358	12.8	1 152	10.9	14	10.3	266	255	2	515	491	21	845	17 229	14 776
Wabash	413	11.9	355	10.2	4	9.7	34	98	1	75	217	11	815	6 061	5 319
Warren	96	11.7	79	9.6	–	–	3	36	1	16	192	1	(12)	1 021	900
Warrick	660	13.0	371	7.3	4	6.1	129	245	1	28	54	12	613	5 986	5 238
Washington	343	12.7	252	9.3	1	2.9	15	53	1	58	209	4	(11)	3 745	3 004
Wayne	857	11.9	783	10.9	6	7.0	118	166	1	212	297	10	891	13 179	11 205
Wells	382	14.3	291	10.9	1	2.6	43	160	2	125	466	8	308	3 759	3 395
White	328	13.1	225	9.0	3	9.1	19	74	1	59	233	1	(11)	4 673	4 179
Whitley	409	13.6	272	9.1	3	7.3	18	58	1	131	432	9	272	4 644	4 205
IOWA	36 659	12.8	27 694	9.7	229	6.2	5 009	175	116	12 219	427	779	41 340	475 854	427 230
Adair	68	8.3	117	14.4	–	–	1	12	1	22	272	4	264	1 609	1 531
Adams	33	7.5	56	12.7	–	–	4	91	1	22	502	3	192	D	D
Allamakee	166	11.9	155	11.1	2	12.0	12	85	1	25	178	6	425	2 855	2 653
Appanoose	142	10.5	187	13.8	2	14.1	10	74	1	54	398	3	157	3 082	2 712
Audubon	82	12.0	64	9.4	–	–	1	15	1	29	426	2	(11)	1 647	1 546
Benton	281	11.2	228	9.1	3	10.7	6	23	1	89	350	6	256	4 010	3 665
Black Hawk	1 587	13.1	1 158	9.5	15	9.5	246	205	3	581	480	56	1 807	19 923	17 238
Boone	289	11.0	300	11.5	1	3.5	13	49	1	57	218	4	407	4 417	3 999
Bremer	219	9.4	204	8.8	–	–	18	77	2	61	261	4	403	4 108	3 826
Buchanan	284	13.4	221	10.4	1	3.5	14	66	1	109	515	4	166	3 403	3 111
Buena Vista	260	13.2	212	10.8	2	7.7	15	77	1	30	155	6	452	3 846	3 598
Butler	160	10.2	192	12.2	–	–	2	13	–	–	–	5	249	3 387	3 159
Calhoun	97	8.5	178	15.5	–	–	9	80	1	53	466	5	499	2 650	2 440
Carroll	238	11.0	242	11.2	2	8.4	21	98	2	229	1 059	23	264	4 399	4 005
Cass	160	10.9	197	13.4	1	6.3	12	83	1	72	492	8	344	3 368	3 072
Cedar	198	11.0	199	11.1	1	5.1	6	33	–	–	–	5	257	2 930	2 723
Cerro Gordo	525	11.3	493	10.6	6	11.4	135	296	1	255	553	9	1 021	9 214	8 178
Cherokee	142	10.6	164	12.3	1	7.0	11	84	1	40	303	5	244	2 828	2 595
Chickasaw	157	11.7	135	10.1	1	6.4	4	30	1	55	410	4	190	2 536	2 350
Clarke	83	10.1	80	9.7	–	–	2	24	1	48	578	2	(11)	1 580	1 427
Clay	197	11.2	169	9.6	1	5.1	27	157	1	86	492	2	(13)	3 268	2 993
Clayton	194	10.3	188	10.0	–	–	9	48	2	36	192	7	536	3 766	3 459
Clinton	629	12.6	576	11.5	3	4.8	63	127	2	465	931	4	337	8 877	7 884
Crawford	209	12.7	178	10.8	2	9.6	8	49	1	72	437	3	263	3 176	2 859
Dallas	482	13.5	317	8.9	3	6.2	16	42	1	49	133	7	469	5 129	4 542
Davis	119	14.1	79	9.3	–	–	6	70	1	67	792	1	(12)	1 534	1 386
Decatur	98	12.0	132	16.2	–	–	4	48	1	49	595	3	141	1 746	1 575
Delaware	208	11.3	152	8.2	1	4.8	6	32	1	35	189	3	(11)	2 757	2 514
Des Moines	550	13.1	445	10.6	2	3.6	66	157	1	366	870	14	674	7 722	6 879
Dickinson	170	10.6	174	10.8	–	–	18	111	1	49	302	3	169	3 629	3 390
Dubuque	1 144	13.0	791	9.0	3	2.6	198	225	2	524	596	25	1 094	14 454	13 011
Emmet	119	10.9	143	13.0	–	–	9	85	1	36	332	3	270	2 332	2 142
Fayette	260	11.9	259	11.8	2	7.7	11	51	2	94	431	7	451	4 310	3 955
Floyd	210	12.7	200	12.1	2	9.5	8	49	1	31	189	12	560	3 537	3 086
Franklin	130	11.9	135	12.4	–	–	2	19	1	82	755	7	195	2 134	1 977
Fremont	94	12.0	114	14.6	1	10.6	2	26	1	49	631	4	171	1 670	1 502
Greene	110	10.9	131	13.0	1	9.1	7	70	1	115	1 141	1	(12)	2 369	2 182
Grundy	128	10.4	135	11.0	1	7.8	5	41	1	75	613	3	140	2 426	2 290
Guthrie	127	11.1	118	10.3	–	–	6	52	1	26	226	4	219	2 564	2 366
Hamilton	210	13.1	194	12.1	2	9.5	12	75	1	40	250	4	210	3 118	2 878
Hancock	128	10.7	128	10.7	–	–	3	25	1	26	216	3	(11)	2 266	2 096
Hardin	189	10.2	247	13.4	1	5.3	16	88	2	58	316	9	407	4 331	4 053
Harrison	179	11.7	173	11.3	2	11.2	9	59	1	39	254	5	371	2 967	2 692
Henry	241	12.2	196	9.9	3	12.4	16	79	1	99	494	5	320	3 369	3 060
Howard	125	12.9	140	14.4	–	–	7	73	1	32	331	5	223	2 025	1 879
Humboldt	120	11.6	117	11.3	–	–	7	68	1	49	474	2	(11)	2 258	2 080
Ida	99	12.4	85	10.6	–	–	–	–	1	36	455	4	244	1 748	1 641
Iowa	156	10.1	157	10.2	1	6.4	10	64	–	–	–	4	191	2 760	2 569
Jackson	242	12.1	234	11.7	–	–	11	55	1	61	303	4	247	3 761	3 430
Jasper	435	12.2	340	9.5	5	11.5	16	44	1	52	142	17	533	6 246	5 615
Jefferson	161	9.4	157	9.2	–	–	21	125	1	83	487	2	(11)	2 322	2 095
Johnson	1 275	12.5	479	4.7	10	7.8	1 371	1 321	2	1 060	1 034	36	777	9 007	7 748
Jones	210	10.3	163	8.0	–	–	5	25	1	17	84	3	191	3 327	3 063
Keokuk	127	11.0	152	13.2	–	–	3	26	1	26	227	3	166	2 653	2 443

[1] Per 1,000 resident population estimated as of July 1, 1997. [2] Deaths of infants under 1 year old. [3] Infant deaths per 1,000 live births. [4] Active, nonfederal physicians as of December 31. Data subject to copyright; see below for source citation. [5] Per 100,000 resident population estimated as of July 1 of the year shown. [6] Nonfederal, short-stay (average length of stay less than 30 days) hospitals except hospital units of institutions. Data subject to copyright; see below for source citation. [7] SIC 805 includes skilled nursing care facilities; intermediate care facilities; and nursing and personal care, not elsewhere classified. [8] Full- and part-time employees on the payroll in the pay period including March 12. [9] Unduplicated count of persons enrolled in either hospital and/or supplemental medical insurance as of July 1. State totals include data not distributed by county. [10] Includes disabled, not shown separately. [11] 100 to 249 employees. [12] 20 to 99 employees. [13] 250 to 499 employees.

Sources: Births—U.S. National Center for Health Statistics, "Vital Statistics of the United States, Vol. I, Natality," annual, and unpublished data. Deaths—U.S. National Center for Health Statistics, "Vital Statistics of the United States, Vol. II, Mortality," annual, and unpublished data. Physicians—American Medical Association, Chicago, IL, "Physician Characteristics and Distribution in the U.S.," annual (copyright). Community Hospitals—Health Forum, LLC, an American Hospital Association Company, Chicago, IL, "Hospital Statistics" 2000 edition and unpublished data (copyright). Nursing and Personal Care Facilities—U.S. Census Bureau, County Business Patterns 1997 on CD-ROM (related Internet site <http://www.census.gov/epcd/cbp/view/cbpview.html>). Medicare—U.S. Health Care Financing Administration; "Medicare County Enrollment as of July 1, 1999 - Aged and Disabled 3/2000 update," <http://www.hcfa.gov/stats/enroll/default.htm>.

[Includes U.S., states, and 3,142 counties or county equivalents defined as of January 1, 1992. For changes to these areas since then, see appendix B. Geographic Information]

County	Births, 1997		Deaths, 1997				Physicians,[4] 1999		Community hospitals,[6] 1998			Nursing and personal care facilities,[7] 1997		Medicare program enrollment,[9] 1999	
			Total		Infant[2]					Beds					
	Number	Rate[1]	Number	Rate[1]	Number	Rate[3]	Number	Rate[5]	Number	Number	Rate[5]	Establishments	Employees[8]	Total[10]	Aged
IOWA—Con.															
Kossuth	180	10.1	210	11.7	3	16.7	8	45	1	29	164	8	436	3 616	3 330
Lee	446	11.5	424	11.0	3	6.7	45	117	2	163	424	7	330	6 787	6 028
Linn	2 584	14.2	1 340	7.4	15	5.8	357	193	2	798	437	48	1 434	26 037	23 244
Louisa	190	16.0	101	8.5	2	10.5	2	17	–	–	–	4	159	1 821	1 634
Lucas	95	10.4	119	13.1	–	–	3	33	1	22	242	3	130	2 040	1 822
Lyon	139	11.6	118	9.9	1	7.2	3	25	1	16	133	4	267	2 284	2 163
Madison	169	12.3	173	12.6	1	5.9	2	14	1	31	223	5	266	2 213	2 003
Mahaska	258	11.8	204	9.4	–	–	13	59	1	53	242	7	243	3 905	3 549
Marion	333	10.7	314	10.1	3	9.0	24	76	2	208	664	9	324	5 356	4 777
Marshall	472	12.2	511	13.2	2	4.2	49	126	1	111	287	13	364	7 145	6 432
Mills	159	11.1	139	9.7	–	–	11	75	–	–	–	7	1 308	2 312	1 821
Mitchell	133	12.0	151	13.6	2	15.0	4	36	1	28	254	6	372	2 554	2 392
Monona	108	10.7	156	15.4	–	–	11	109	1	48	477	3	342	2 410	2 223
Monroe	95	11.8	99	12.2	1	10.5	1	12	1	38	473	3	160	1 670	1 478
Montgomery	112	9.5	177	14.9	2	17.9	9	77	1	40	338	6	361	2 605	2 335
Muscatine	570	13.9	358	8.8	–	–	35	85	1	66	161	6	491	6 260	5 491
O'Brien	192	12.8	181	12.1	2	10.4	10	68	2	155	1 041	7	638	3 415	3 141
Osceola	82	11.6	79	11.2	1	12.2	3	43	1	32	460	3	155	1 415	1 327
Page	172	9.9	253	14.6	3	17.4	14	82	2	114	660	6	278	3 714	3 331
Palo Alto	123	12.2	140	13.9	–	–	4	40	1	54	537	10	337	2 345	2 139
Plymouth	328	13.3	248	10.0	–	–	13	52	1	44	179	8	377	4 228	3 880
Pocahontas	77	8.7	129	14.6	–	–	3	34	1	25	284	4	209	2 074	1 944
Polk	5 687	16.0	2 706	7.6	35	6.2	811	222	5	1 529	425	59	3 880	46 194	40 423
Pottawattamie	1 185	13.9	805	9.4	9	7.6	108	125	2	312	362	15	853	13 755	11 916
Poweshiek	192	10.1	204	10.8	–	–	20	107	1	46	245	7	417	3 484	3 227
Ringgold	67	12.5	91	17.0	–	–	4	75	1	36	672	4	(11)	1 313	1 211
Sac	131	11.0	170	14.3	–	–	6	51	1	54	454	4	244	2 727	2 560
Scott	2 175	13.8	1 270	8.1	12	5.5	332	208	2	566	357	16	1 574	21 039	18 381
Shelby	140	10.7	188	14.4	1	7.1	5	39	1	52	402	8	445	2 740	2 526
Sioux	413	13.2	270	8.6	3	7.3	21	67	4	343	1 091	2	(11)	5 034	4 725
Story	846	11.3	453	6.0	5	5.9	132	175	2	316	422	12	650	8 538	7 831
Tama	248	14.0	194	11.0	4	16.1	3	17	–	–	–	5	237	3 632	3 384
Taylor	79	11.1	108	15.2	1	12.7	–	–	–	–	–	4	157	1 664	1 530
Union	136	10.9	152	12.2	–	–	8	63	1	49	391	5	247	2 687	2 397
Van Buren	79	10.1	96	12.3	2	25.3	3	38	1	40	509	1	(11)	1 776	1 620
Wapello	417	11.8	444	12.5	5	12.0	66	186	1	82	232	6	396	7 498	6 443
Warren	514	12.9	297	7.5	3	5.8	7	17	–	–	–	12	560	4 775	4 263
Washington	254	12.2	231	11.1	3	11.8	14	66	1	83	396	8	506	4 035	3 730
Wayne	57	8.4	127	18.7	–	–	3	46	1	28	419	2	(11)	1 729	1 587
Webster	520	13.4	491	12.7	3	5.8	70	180	1	175	449	9	675	7 869	6 933
Winnebago	134	11.1	135	11.2	2	14.9	3	25	–	–	–	4	278	2 496	2 339
Winneshiek	202	9.7	178	8.5	1	5.0	21	100	1	83	396	4	394	3 409	3 162
Woodbury	1 692	16.6	964	9.5	15	8.9	216	213	2	480	473	26	1 366	16 024	13 978
Worth	76	9.8	98	12.6	–	–	2	26	–	–	–	2	(11)	1 555	1 436
Wright	152	10.8	218	15.4	–	–	10	72	2	55	392	4	259	3 279	3 048
KANSAS	37 289	14.3	23 750	9.1	276	7.4	5 424	204	129	10 923	414	505	29 755	389 103	346 757
Allen	186	12.8	186	12.8	–	–	5	35	1	41	282	7	267	2 839	2 512
Anderson	79	9.8	99	12.3	–	–	6	74	1	56	696	3	89	1 795	1 625
Atchison	209	12.4	182	10.8	–	–	19	113	1	121	718	5	102	2 925	2 639
Barber	57	10.6	89	16.5	–	–	3	57	2	66	1 237	3	(12)	1 268	1 160
Barton	375	12.9	306	10.5	4	10.7	37	129	3	227	784	4	301	5 415	4 985
Bourbon	187	12.3	209	13.7	1	5.3	22	147	1	108	712	5	253	3 097	2 750
Brown	131	11.9	160	14.5	1	7.6	13	119	2	78	707	4	207	2 271	2 059
Butler	742	12.2	475	7.8	3	4.0	50	80	2	242	391	10	573	7 664	6 921
Chase	56	19.2	39	13.4	1	17.9	–	–	–	–	–	1	(12)	565	511
Chautauqua	29	6.6	89	20.3	3	103.4	4	94	2	63	1 451	2	(11)	1 054	926
Cherokee	319	14.1	279	12.4	2	6.3	7	31	1	30	133	5	277	3 838	3 277
Cheyenne	31	9.7	41	12.8	1	32.3	2	62	1	16	506	2	(12)	836	798
Clark	24	9.9	42	17.4	–	–	3	128	2	63	2 677	–	–	547	515
Clay	83	9.0	145	15.8	1	12.0	7	78	1	35	385	4	209	1 919	1 772
Cloud	95	9.3	147	14.4	–	–	15	150	1	40	398	7	378	2 576	2 376
Coffey	105	12.0	97	11.1	2	19.0	6	69	1	62	714	4	106	1 564	1 437
Comanche	19	9.4	49	24.3	–	–	–	–	1	14	699	2	(12)	531	499
Cowley	468	12.5	409	10.9	1	2.1	30	81	2	126	340	9	1 347	6 493	5 700
Crawford	495	13.6	470	12.9	2	4.0	38	105	2	164	451	9	639	6 784	5 937
Decatur	31	8.8	64	18.2	–	–	4	119	1	74	2 147	2	(12)	921	875
Dickinson	207	10.5	232	11.7	1	4.8	10	51	2	85	434	6	303	3 937	3 618

[1] Per 1,000 resident population estimated as of July 1, 1997. [2] Deaths of infants under 1 year old. [3] Infant deaths per 1,000 live births. [4] Active, nonfederal physicians as of December 31. Data subject to copyright; see below for source citation. [5] Per 100,000 resident population estimated as of July 1 of the year shown. [6] Nonfederal, short-stay (average length of stay less than 30 days) hospitals except hospital units of institutions. Data subject to copyright; see below for source citation. [7] SIC 805 includes skilled nursing care facilities; intermediate care facilities; and nursing and personal care, not elsewhere classified. [8] Full- and part-time employees on the payroll in the pay period including March 12. [9] Unduplicated count of persons enrolled in either hospital and/or supplemental medical insurance as of July 1. State totals include data not distributed by county. [10] Includes disabled, not shown separately. [11] 100 to 249 employees. [12] 20 to 99 employees.

Sources: Births—U.S. National Center for Health Statistics, "Vital Statistics of the United States, Vol. I, Natality," annual, and unpublished data.   Deaths—U.S. National Center for Health Statistics, "Vital Statistics of the United States, Vol. II, Mortality," annual, and unpublished data.   Physicians—American Medical Association, Chicago, IL, "Physician Characteristics and Distribution in the U.S.," annual (copyright).   Community Hospitals—Health Forum, LLC, an American Hospital Association Company, Chicago, IL, "Hospital Statistics" 2000 edition and unpublished data (copyright).   Nursing and Personal Care Facilities—U.S. Census Bureau, County Business Patterns 1997 on CD-ROM (related Internet site <http://www.census.gov/epcd/cbp/view/cbpview.html>).   Medicare—U.S. Health Care Financing Administration; "Medicare County Enrollment as of July 1, 1999 - Aged and Disabled 3/2000 update," <http://www.hcfa.gov/stats/enroll/default.htm>.

Table B–4. Counties — Vital Statistics and Health–Con.

[Includes U.S., states, and 3,142 counties or county equivalents defined as of January 1, 1992. For changes to these areas since then, see appendix B. Geographic Information]

County	Births, 1997 Number	Births, 1997 Rate[1]	Deaths, 1997 Total Number	Deaths, 1997 Total Rate[1]	Deaths, 1997 Infant[2] Number	Deaths, 1997 Infant[2] Rate[3]	Physicians,[4] 1999 Number	Physicians,[4] 1999 Rate[5]	Community hospitals,[6] 1998 Number	Beds Number	Beds Rate[5]	Nursing and personal care facilities,[7] 1997 Establishments	Nursing and personal care facilities,[7] 1997 Employees[8]	Medicare program enrollment,[9] 1999 Total[10]	Medicare program enrollment,[9] 1999 Aged
KANSAS—Con.															
Doniphan	101	12.9	85	10.9	–	–	2	25	–	–	–	2	(11)	1 432	1 301
Douglas	1 020	10.7	440	4.6	4	3.9	151	154	1	105	109	15	693	8 802	7 598
Edwards	30	8.8	46	13.5	–	–	–	–	–	–	–	1	(12)	788	736
Elk	31	9.2	38	11.3	–	–	–	–	–	–	–	–	–	859	772
Ellis	335	12.6	226	8.5	2	6.0	65	247	1	168	632	6	(13)	4 244	3 793
Ellsworth	41	6.5	100	15.8	1	24.4	5	80	1	25	398	2	(11)	1 351	1 257
Finney	917	25.5	196	5.5	7	7.6	46	123	1	100	273	3	(11)	3 536	3 054
Ford	625	21.5	259	8.9	8	12.8	41	139	1	101	343	9	268	3 790	3 441
Franklin	342	13.9	297	12.1	4	11.7	15	60	1	48	193	8	210	3 937	3 437
Geary	637	25.4	184	7.3	9	14.1	18	72	1	49	194	2	(11)	2 919	2 529
Gove	32	10.4	46	14.9	–	–	3	99	1	80	2 627	–	–	717	689
Graham	16	5.0	36	11.1	–	–	3	96	1	26	815	1	(12)	714	656
Grant	147	18.7	60	7.6	2	13.6	3	38	1	42	525	–	–	820	750
Gray	80	14.6	48	8.7	–	–	1	18	–	–	–	2	(11)	824	758
Greeley	17	9.8	25	14.5	–	–	1	61	1	48	2 834	–	–	290	271
Greenwood	79	9.8	130	16.2	1	12.7	2	25	1	46	568	3	189	1 988	1 776
Hamilton	29	12.7	29	12.7	1	34.5	2	84	1	26	1 098	–	–	523	484
Harper	63	9.7	119	18.3	–	–	5	79	1	38	593	1	(12)	1 556	1 465
Harvey	413	12.2	341	10.0	3	7.3	75	219	2	203	594	6	658	5 963	5 455
Haskell	80	19.9	25	6.2	–	–	2	49	1	45	1 136	–	–	466	434
Hodgeman	16	7.2	24	10.8	–	–	1	45	1	52	2 348	–	–	396	370
Jackson	156	13.0	154	12.8	–	–	4	33	1	13	107	3	138	2 026	1 819
Jefferson	202	11.3	164	9.1	3	14.9	4	22	1	95	523	3	124	2 657	2 338
Jewell	30	7.6	53	13.5	–	–	2	53	1	51	1 317	–	–	1 036	966
Johnson	6 224	14.9	2 337	5.6	32	5.1	1 835	417	5	977	227	45	3 053	46 546	42 683
Kearny	77	18.4	46	11.0	–	–	2	48	1	25	604	–	–	526	481
Kingman	94	11.0	101	11.8	2	21.3	6	69	1	40	467	4	228	1 719	1 594
Kiowa	37	10.7	35	10.1	–	–	4	119	1	46	1 345	1	(12)	785	714
Labette	287	12.4	293	12.7	–	–	30	131	1	76	330	11	728	4 462	3 832
Lane	20	9.1	16	7.3	–	–	1	46	1	31	1 381	–	–	490	460
Leavenworth	870	12.3	491	7.0	6	6.9	55	77	2	113	159	7	305	6 827	5 967
Lincoln	30	8.9	48	14.3	–	–	1	30	1	34	1 021	1	(12)	858	805
Linn	97	10.7	120	13.2	–	–	2	22	–	–	–	4	135	1 951	1 717
Logan	30	9.9	46	15.2	1	33.3	–	–	1	51	1 706	1	(12)	720	677
Lyon	515	15.2	294	8.6	3	5.8	36	107	1	110	326	9	545	4 686	4 120
McPherson	349	12.2	309	10.8	3	8.6	25	87	3	77	270	14	812	5 364	5 051
Marion	130	9.5	168	12.3	1	7.7	8	59	2	132	970	5	323	2 929	2 697
Marshall	98	8.8	175	15.7	1	10.2	6	55	1	109	991	8	230	2 592	2 403
Meade	67	15.3	66	15.0	2	29.9	3	68	1	20	451	1	(12)	863	830
Miami	301	11.5	253	9.6	2	6.6	26	96	1	18	68	7	653	3 547	3 015
Mitchell	77	11.0	107	15.3	1	13.0	6	86	1	89	1 281	1	(11)	1 594	1 499
Montgomery	449	12.1	493	13.3	3	6.7	44	120	2	181	489	15	915	7 678	6 800
Morris	69	11.1	83	13.3	–	–	5	81	1	28	455	1	(12)	1 328	1 219
Morton	57	16.7	30	8.8	–	–	8	229	1	100	2 917	–	–	515	479
Nemaha	145	14.2	144	14.1	3	20.7	3	29	2	51	500	7	473	2 315	2 176
Neosho	206	12.2	195	11.6	–	–	13	78	1	60	359	4	181	3 382	2 988
Ness	31	8.6	55	15.3	–	–	2	56	2	111	3 060	–	–	912	870
Norton	57	9.8	71	12.2	–	–	6	106	1	24	418	1	(12)	1 289	1 191
Osage	201	11.8	187	11.0	1	5.0	6	35	–	–	–	5	165	2 909	2 592
Osborne	41	8.7	75	16.0	–	–	1	22	1	29	620	2	(11)	1 217	1 153
Ottawa	63	10.8	84	14.4	–	–	3	51	1	53	901	3	153	1 096	1 014
Pawnee	66	9.0	91	12.5	–	–	18	250	–	–	–	1	(12)	1 430	1 284
Phillips	57	9.4	93	15.3	–	–	5	84	1	62	1 027	2	(12)	1 408	1 300
Pottawatomie	254	13.9	166	9.1	1	3.9	16	84	3	255	1 368	4	234	2 520	2 318
Pratt	119	12.3	116	12.0	1	8.4	11	116	1	132	1 363	1	(12)	1 914	1 782
Rawlins	30	9.4	39	12.2	–	–	2	66	1	24	767	1	(12)	789	740
Reno	816	13.0	635	10.1	5	6.1	110	173	1	163	258	17	1 053	11 516	10 385
Republic	48	7.8	97	15.8	–	–	5	84	1	86	1 410	2	(11)	1 577	1 484
Rice	115	11.0	128	12.2	2	17.4	5	49	1	44	422	2	(11)	2 186	1 982
Riley	864	13.4	260	4.0	1	1.2	91	143	1	99	155	16	482	5 075	4 607
Rooks	68	11.9	92	16.1	1	14.7	3	53	1	25	440	–	–	1 313	1 219
Rush	30	8.7	69	20.1	–	–	2	59	1	50	1 468	1	(12)	990	922
Russell	66	8.6	108	14.1	–	–	4	54	1	57	756	3	(11)	1 969	1 806
Saline	695	13.5	531	10.3	8	11.5	113	220	1	257	500	7	599	8 305	7 417
Scott	68	13.6	51	10.2	–	–	4	81	1	27	538	1	(12)	497	474
Sedgwick	7 217	16.4	3 446	7.8	71	9.8	1 131	250	5	1 624	363	52	2 751	57 277	50 182
Seward	422	21.1	141	7.0	3	7.1	34	169	1	87	433	3	(11)	2 115	1 859
Shawnee	2 367	14.0	1 588	9.4	23	9.7	463	271	3	648	380	28	2 589	27 122	22 894
Sheridan	25	9.1	34	12.4	–	–	3	112	1	66	2 426	–	–	545	521

[1] Per 1,000 resident population estimated as of July 1, 1997.   [2] Deaths of infants under 1 year old.   [3] Infant deaths per 1,000 live births.   [4] Active, nonfederal physicians as of December 31. Data subject to copyright; see below for source citation.   [5] Per 100,000 resident population estimated as of July 1 of the year shown.   [6] Nonfederal, short-stay (average length of stay less than 30 days) hospitals except hospital units of institutions. Data subject to copyright; see below for source citation.   [7] SIC 805 includes skilled nursing care facilities; intermediate care facilities; and nursing and personal care, not elsewhere classified.   [8] Full- and part-time employees on the payroll in the pay period including March 12.   [9] Unduplicated count of persons enrolled in either hospital and/or supplemental medical insurance as of July 1. State totals include data not distributed by county.   [10] Includes disabled, not shown separately.   [11] 100 to 249 employees.   [12] 20 to 99 employees. [13] 250 to 499 employees.

Sources: Births—U.S. National Center for Health Statistics, "Vital Statistics of the United States, Vol. I, Natality," annual, and unpublished data.   Deaths—U.S. National Center for Health Statistics, "Vital Statistics of the United States, Vol. II, Mortality," annual, and unpublished data.   Physicians—American Medical Association, Chicago, IL, "Physician Characteristics and Distribution in the U.S.," annual (copyright).   Community Hospitals—Health Forum, LLC, an American Hospital Association Company, Chicago, IL, "Hospital Statistics" 2000 edition and unpublished data (copyright). Nursing and Personal Care Facilities—U.S. Census Bureau, County Business Patterns 1997 on CD-ROM (related Internet site <http://www.census.gov/epcd/cbp/view/cbpview.html>).   Medicare—U.S. Health Care Financing Administration; "Medicare County Enrollment as of July 1, 1999 - Aged and Disabled 3/2000 update," <http://www.hcfa.gov/stats/enroll/default.htm>.

[Includes U.S., states, and 3,142 counties or county equivalents defined as of January 1, 1992. For changes to these areas since then, see appendix B. Geographic Information]

County	Births, 1997 Number	Rate1	Deaths, 1997 Total Number	Rate1	Infant2 Number	Rate3	Physicians,4 1999 Number	Rate5	Community hospitals,6 1998 Number	Beds Number	Rate5	Nursing and personal care facilities,7 1997 Establishments	Employees8	Medicare program enrollment,9 1999 Total10	Aged
KANSAS—Con.															
Sherman	90	13.7	70	10.6	–	–	6	92	1	49	747	1	(11)	1 265	1 145
Smith	37	8.0	85	18.4	–	–	5	109	1	54	1 175	2	(11)	1 287	1 218
Stafford	55	10.8	93	18.3	2	36.4	1	20	1	25	495	2	(11)	1 094	1 009
Stanton	46	20.0	18	7.8	–	–	2	90	1	43	1 916	–	–	334	308
Stevens	98	18.3	57	10.6	–	–	4	74	1	17	314	–	–	792	742
Sumner	328	12.2	301	11.2	2	6.1	11	40	2	102	375	14	518	4 700	4 218
Thomas	113	13.8	83	10.2	1	8.8	7	88	1	120	1 494	2	(12)	1 245	1 136
Trego	33	9.9	51	15.3	–	–	5	153	1	73	2 217	–	–	807	747
Wabaunsee	70	10.5	61	9.1	–	–	2	30	–	–	–	2	(12)	1 157	1 038
Wallace	26	14.4	21	11.6	–	–	–	–	–	–	–	1	(11)	346	328
Washington	72	10.9	102	15.4	–	–	3	46	2	72	1 106	6	150	1 772	1 668
Wichita	41	15.1	13	4.8	1	24.4	1	39	1	38	1 436	–	–	427	399
Wilson	117	11.4	152	14.8	–	–	7	68	2	89	867	3	(12)	2 156	1 931
Woodson	30	7.5	55	13.8	–	–	2	51	–	–	–	1	(11)	1 039	932
Wyandotte	2 817	18.4	1 647	10.8	25	8.9	479	316	3	878	576	12	1 072	22 512	18 658
KENTUCKY	53 203	13.6	37 998	9.7	387	7.3	8 382	212	106	15 240	387	375	31 174	615 436	487 877
Adair	198	12.0	189	11.5	2	10.1	17	103	1	80	486	2	(11)	2 963	2 315
Allen	222	13.7	188	11.6	1	4.5	7	42	–	–	–	1	(11)	2 780	2 253
Anderson	237	13.1	153	8.5	1	4.2	13	69	–	–	–	1	(11)	2 277	1 915
Ballard	109	13.0	111	13.2	–	–	3	35	–	–	–	1	(12)	1 913	1 588
Barren	455	12.4	385	10.5	3	6.6	64	171	1	196	530	4	537	6 440	5 186
Bath	140	13.5	132	12.7	1	7.1	9	84	–	–	–	3	87	1 936	1 539
Bell	387	13.0	364	12.2	4	10.3	53	183	2	246	844	2	(12)	6 106	4 001
Boone	1 180	15.5	426	5.6	4	3.4	109	131	1	136	171	6	384	8 133	6 738
Bourbon	249	12.9	206	10.7	2	8.0	25	129	1	58	300	1	(12)	2 928	2 487
Boyd	635	12.8	644	12.9	6	9.4	158	323	1	341	689	4	(13)	9 964	8 123
Boyle	313	11.6	290	10.8	3	9.6	75	274	1	177	653	2	(12)	4 676	3 940
Bracken	90	10.8	79	9.5	–	–	3	35	–	–	–	–	–	1 349	1 129
Breathitt	219	14.0	190	12.1	2	9.1	20	127	1	55	350	1	(12)	2 762	1 633
Breckinridge	214	12.4	176	10.2	2	9.3	9	51	1	45	258	3	(11)	3 164	2 617
Bullitt	835	14.4	333	5.8	3	3.6	14	23	–	–	–	2	(12)	4 971	3 786
Butler	141	12.0	156	13.2	1	7.1	3	25	–	–	–	1	(12)	1 859	1 427
Caldwell	160	12.0	192	14.4	1	6.3	10	75	1	40	300	1	(12)	2 732	2 303
Calloway	327	9.9	339	10.2	3	9.2	42	126	1	333	996	1	(12)	5 651	4 897
Campbell	1 329	15.2	838	9.6	7	5.0	137	157	1	167	191	7	898	12 542	10 717
Carlisle	55	10.2	84	15.7	1	18.2	2	37	–	–	–	1	(11)	1 132	959
Carroll	135	14.1	113	11.8	1	7.4	8	82	1	37	384	3	(11)	1 627	1 301
Carter	377	14.2	246	9.3	4	10.6	5	18	–	–	–	2	(12)	4 387	3 289
Casey	182	12.5	166	11.4	–	–	6	40	–	–	–	1	(14)	2 494	1 959
Christian	1 483	20.2	564	7.7	11	7.4	87	121	1	139	192	9	636	8 031	6 629
Clark	414	13.1	301	9.5	1	2.4	46	142	1	75	235	1	(12)	4 861	3 927
Clay	298	13.2	233	10.3	1	3.4	8	35	1	61	268	1	(11)	3 592	2 243
Clinton	103	11.1	101	10.9	–	–	5	53	1	42	449	1	(11)	2 006	1 432
Crittenden	107	11.4	126	13.4	–	–	6	63	1	50	522	1	(12)	1 730	1 374
Cumberland	74	10.8	105	15.3	–	–	2	29	1	31	453	–	–	1 542	1 218
Daviess	1 258	13.8	879	9.7	5	4.0	179	196	1	377	414	6	686	14 918	12 611
Edmonson	127	11.4	115	10.3	–	–	4	34	–	–	–	1	(11)	1 602	1 193
Elliott	75	11.4	77	11.7	–	–	3	46	–	–	–	1	(11)	825	607
Estill	174	11.3	168	10.9	1	5.7	7	45	1	26	167	1	(11)	3 345	2 412
Fayette	3 342	14.0	1 949	8.1	30	9.0	1 659	681	7	1 638	678	19	2 869	29 568	25 029
Fleming	160	12.1	145	11.0	–	–	8	59	1	52	386	1	(12)	2 278	1 878
Floyd	613	14.1	483	11.1	9	14.7	66	153	3	297	686	3	211	7 908	4 870
Franklin	608	13.1	439	9.5	4	6.6	68	146	1	147	316	2	(12)	8 655	6 836
Fulton	96	12.6	98	12.9	1	10.4	16	215	1	70	927	1	(11)	1 873	1 512
Gallatin	105	15.5	68	10.0	–	–	1	13	–	–	–	1	(11)	902	713
Garrard	176	12.9	119	8.7	3	17.0	7	49	1	131	941	–	–	2 190	1 782
Grant	350	17.7	166	8.4	1	2.9	8	38	1	20	98	1	(11)	2 926	2 267
Graves	493	13.8	464	13.0	4	8.1	33	91	1	106	295	3	315	7 301	6 041
Grayson	273	11.7	235	10.1	1	3.7	18	76	1	75	316	3	184	4 217	3 314
Green	103	9.8	132	12.5	–	–	7	66	1	64	606	1	(12)	2 074	1 682
Greenup	405	10.9	364	9.8	2	4.9	33	90	1	194	525	4	(13)	6 311	4 828
Hancock	129	14.5	75	8.5	2	15.5	1	11	–	–	–	1	(11)	1 080	909
Hardin	1 565	17.4	607	6.8	13	8.3	167	182	2	310	342	11	609	10 874	8 925
Harlan	460	13.0	392	11.1	5	10.9	45	131	1	125	359	3	169	7 170	4 528
Harrison	196	11.4	207	12.0	3	15.3	15	85	1	77	439	2	(12)	2 853	2 411
Hart	232	14.0	205	12.4	1	4.3	10	59	1	28	167	1	(12)	2 793	2 270

[1] Per 1,000 resident population estimated as of July 1, 1997.   [2] Deaths of infants under 1 year old.   [3] Infant deaths per 1,000 live births.   [4] Active, nonfederal physicians as of December 31. Data subject to copyright; see below for source citation.   [5] Per 100,000 resident population estimated as of July 1 of the year shown.   [6] Nonfederal, short-stay (average length of stay less than 30 days) hospitals except hospital units of institutions. Data subject to copyright; see below for source citation.   [7] SIC 805 includes skilled nursing care facilities; intermediate care facilities; and nursing and personal care, not elsewhere classified.   [8] Full- and part-time employees on the payroll in the pay period including March 12.   [9] Unduplicated count of persons enrolled in either hospital and/or supplemental medical insurance as of July 1. State totals include data not distributed by county.   [10] Includes disabled, not shown separately.   [11] 20 to 99 employees.   [12] 100 to 249 employees.   [13] 250 to 499 employees.   [14] 0 to 19 employees.

Table B–4. Counties — **Vital Statistics and Health**–Con.

[Includes U.S., states, and 3,142 counties or county equivalents defined as of January 1, 1992. For changes to these areas since then, see appendix B. Geographic Information]

County	Births, 1997		Deaths, 1997				Physicians,[4] 1999		Community hospitals,[6] 1998			Nursing and personal care facilities,[7] 1997		Medicare program enrollment,[9] 1999	
			Total		Infant[2]					Beds					
	Number	Rate[1]	Number	Rate[1]	Number	Rate[3]	Number	Rate[5]	Number	Number	Rate[5]	Establishments	Employees[8]	Total[10]	Aged
KENTUCKY—Con.															
Henderson	579	13.0	426	9.6	2	3.5	66	149	1	193	434	2	(11)	6 949	5 737
Henry	184	12.5	151	10.3	2	10.9	7	47	–	–	–	1	(12)	2 436	2 019
Hickman	54	10.3	77	14.7	–	–	2	39	–	–	–	2	(13)	869	697
Hopkins	584	12.6	509	11.0	7	12.0	137	297	1	327	705	7	696	8 391	6 681
Jackson	161	12.5	112	8.7	–	–	4	31	–	–	–	1	(12)	2 152	1 504
Jefferson	9 586	14.3	6 940	10.3	72	7.5	2 774	412	10	3 129	466	69	7 012	110 333	93 383
Jessamine	581	16.1	247	6.8	3	5.2	62	166	–	–	–	–	–	4 084	3 348
Johnson	289	12.0	243	10.1	2	6.9	37	154	1	72	300	1	(12)	4 329	2 972
Kenton	2 267	15.5	1 227	8.4	12	5.3	361	245	2	506	345	11	1 053	19 311	16 184
Knott	199	11.1	144	8.0	3	15.1	6	33	–	–	–	1	(12)	2 579	1 565
Knox	457	14.5	306	9.7	5	10.9	18	56	1	58	182	1	(12)	4 449	2 917
Larue	148	11.5	149	11.6	1	6.8	4	30	–	–	–	1	(13)	2 221	1 847
Laurel	703	14.0	403	8.0	9	12.8	66	127	1	70	138	–	–	7 149	5 109
Lawrence	147	9.5	165	10.7	1	6.8	14	89	1	90	577	1	(13)	2 611	1 833
Lee	89	11.2	96	12.0	2	22.5	3	38	–	–	–	3	(13)	1 475	1 027
Leslie	158	11.7	115	8.5	4	25.3	10	74	1	40	294	1	(12)	2 339	1 352
Letcher	320	12.1	286	10.8	1	3.1	40	153	2	136	518	2	(13)	4 882	3 099
Lewis	187	13.8	158	11.7	4	21.4	4	30	–	–	–	1	(13)	2 237	1 681
Lincoln	300	13.6	242	11.0	–	–	8	35	1	73	326	2	(13)	3 989	3 107
Livingston	105	11.2	123	13.1	–	–	6	63	1	26	275	2	(13)	1 895	1 472
Logan	345	13.2	293	11.2	2	5.8	19	72	1	63	241	3	(13)	4 446	3 689
Lyon	67	8.4	108	13.5	1	14.9	2	25	–	–	–	2	(13)	1 489	1 241
McCracken	835	12.9	785	12.1	10	12.0	198	307	2	656	1 019	8	661	11 979	10 026
McCreary	252	15.2	193	11.6	3	11.9	6	36	–	–	–	2	(12)	2 686	1 691
McLean	113	11.6	123	12.6	3	26.5	4	40	–	–	–	2	(13)	1 812	1 480
Madison	858	13.1	496	7.6	5	5.8	96	142	2	230	346	5	(11)	8 463	6 722
Magoffin	193	13.9	132	9.5	1	5.2	2	14	–	–	–	1	(13)	2 016	1 312
Marion	239	14.1	167	9.8	–	–	17	99	1	86	505	5	250	3 058	2 435
Marshall	310	10.4	333	11.1	2	6.5	18	60	1	80	265	4	412	5 910	5 042
Martin	159	13.0	109	8.9	2	12.6	6	50	–	–	–	1	(12)	2 041	1 094
Mason	205	12.1	187	11.0	3	14.6	30	178	1	65	384	4	(13)	2 910	2 508
Meade	284	10.1	172	6.1	6	21.1	5	17	–	–	–	2	(12)	2 201	1 751
Menifee	79	14.0	52	9.2	–	–	–	–	–	–	–	1	(12)	1 018	699
Mercer	270	13.2	224	11.0	–	–	15	72	1	64	310	1	(13)	3 565	3 030
Metcalfe	137	14.4	112	11.8	–	–	2	21	–	–	–	1	(14)	1 927	1 518
Monroe	154	13.6	162	14.4	1	6.5	7	63	1	49	440	1	(13)	2 453	1 819
Montgomery	308	14.8	218	10.5	2	6.5	33	153	1	103	490	2	(13)	3 490	2 700
Morgan	159	11.8	127	9.4	1	6.3	9	66	1	45	331	1	(12)	2 094	1 523
Muhlenberg	366	11.5	376	11.8	1	2.7	21	66	1	135	421	4	333	5 949	4 665
Nelson	544	15.5	275	7.8	2	3.7	28	76	1	36	100	5	194	5 156	4 236
Nicholas	83	11.8	78	11.1	–	–	3	42	1	122	1 741	–	–	1 289	1 058
Ohio	280	12.8	286	13.0	2	7.1	16	72	1	54	245	3	279	3 848	3 044
Oldham	519	12.0	239	5.5	3	5.8	61	133	1	105	236	5	242	3 364	2 760
Owen	118	11.7	94	9.3	–	–	5	48	1	50	483	1	(13)	1 282	1 068
Owsley	63	11.8	73	13.6	–	–	1	19	–	–	–	1	(13)	1 071	778
Pendleton	174	12.6	150	10.8	1	5.7	3	21	–	–	–	3	(12)	1 753	1 410
Perry	465	14.9	303	9.7	5	10.8	78	253	1	288	929	1	(13)	5 688	3 552
Pike	852	11.8	744	10.3	7	8.2	121	169	2	329	457	4	438	13 010	7 880
Powell	189	14.9	106	8.4	1	5.3	5	38	–	–	–	1	(12)	1 252	840
Pulaski	662	11.9	515	9.2	4	6.0	102	179	1	227	403	10	425	11 065	8 276
Robertson	31	14.2	34	15.5	–	–	1	44	–	–	–	1	(12)	373	314
Rockcastle	173	11.0	160	10.2	3	17.3	9	56	1	86	540	2	(12)	2 442	1 836
Rowan	222	10.1	163	7.4	–	–	62	280	1	133	601	1	(13)	2 823	2 146
Russell	176	10.8	186	11.4	–	–	8	49	1	45	278	2	(13)	3 344	2 521
Scott	428	14.5	208	7.1	4	9.3	36	112	1	61	198	4	168	3 418	2 872
Shelby	401	13.9	261	9.1	3	7.5	25	82	1	58	196	2	(13)	3 772	3 176
Simpson	220	13.7	169	10.5	3	13.6	10	60	1	28	170	2	(12)	2 423	2 053
Spencer	124	13.5	82	8.9	–	–	4	38	–	–	–	1	(12)	1 220	977
Taylor	259	11.3	230	10.1	1	3.9	28	122	1	90	392	2	(13)	4 461	3 476
Todd	161	14.4	140	12.5	–	–	4	35	–	–	–	1	(12)	1 838	1 554
Trigg	151	12.4	123	10.1	1	6.6	3	24	1	29	234	2	(12)	2 509	2 097
Trimble	111	15.2	62	8.5	–	–	4	50	–	–	–	1	(12)	1 057	859
Union	198	12.0	147	8.9	1	5.1	7	42	1	53	320	2	(12)	2 489	2 032
Warren	1 187	13.7	684	7.9	13	11.0	209	238	3	753	862	11	975	12 144	9 866
Washington	133	12.3	131	12.1	1	7.5	4	36	–	–	–	2	(13)	1 879	1 587
Wayne	241	12.8	193	10.3	1	4.1	9	47	1	30	157	2	(12)	3 345	2 440
Webster	175	12.9	171	12.6	1	5.7	2	15	–	–	–	2	(13)	2 527	2 084
Whitley	453	12.7	397	11.2	5	11.0	73	202	1	240	670	10	416	8 045	5 759
Wolfe	95	13.0	100	13.7	2	–	2	27	–	–	–	1	(12)	1 318	901
Woodford	276	12.4	189	8.5	2	7.2	39	171	1	81	356	2	(12)	2 731	2 354

[1] Per 1,000 resident population estimated as of July 1, 1997.   [2] Deaths of infants under 1 year old.   [3] Infant deaths per 1,000 live births.   [4] Active, nonfederal physicians as of December 31. Data subject to copyright; see below for source citation.   [5] Per 100,000 resident population estimated as of July 1 of the year shown.   [6] Nonfederal, short-stay (average length of stay less than 30 days) hospitals except hospital units of institutions. Data subject to copyright; see below for source citation.   [7] SIC 805 includes skilled nursing care facilities; intermediate care facilities; and nursing and personal care, not elsewhere classified.   [8] Full- and part-time employees on the payroll in the pay period including March 12.   [9] Unduplicated count of persons enrolled in either hospital and/or supplemental medical insurance as of July 1. State totals include data not distributed by county.   [10] Includes disabled, not shown separately.   [11] 250 to 499 employees.   [12] 20 to 99 employees. [13] 100 to 249 employees.   [14] 0 to 19 employees.

Sources: Births—U.S. National Center for Health Statistics, "Vital Statistics of the United States, Vol. I, Natality," annual, and unpublished data.   Deaths—U.S. National Center for Health Statistics, "Vital Statistics of the United States, Vol. II, Mortality," annual, and unpublished data.   Physicians—American Medical Association, Chicago, IL, "Physician Characteristics and Distribution in the U.S.," annual (copyright).   Community Hospitals—Health Forum, LLC, an American Hospital Association Company, Chicago, IL, "Hospital Statistics" 2000 edition and unpublished data (copyright).   Nursing and Personal Care Facilities—U.S. Census Bureau, County Business Patterns 1997 on CD-ROM (related Internet site <http://www.census.gov/epcd/cbp/view/cbpview.html>).   Medicare—U.S. Health Care Financing Administration; "Medicare County Enrollment as of July 1, 1999 - Aged and Disabled 3/2000 update," <http://www.hcfa.gov/stats/enroll/default.htm>.

[Includes U.S., states, and 3,142 counties or county equivalents defined as of January 1, 1992. For changes to these areas since then, see appendix B. Geographic Information]

County	Births, 1997 Number	Births, 1997 Rate[1]	Deaths, 1997 Total Number	Deaths, 1997 Total Rate[1]	Deaths, 1997 Infant[2] Number	Deaths, 1997 Infant[2] Rate[3]	Physicians,[4] 1999 Number	Physicians,[4] 1999 Rate[5]	Community hospitals,[6] 1998 Number	Community hospitals,[6] 1998 Beds Number	Community hospitals,[6] 1998 Beds Rate[5]	Nursing and personal care facilities,[7] 1997 Estab- lishments	Nursing and personal care facilities,[7] 1997 Em- ployees[8]	Medicare program enrollment,[9] 1999 Total[10]	Medicare program enrollment,[9] 1999 Aged
LOUISIANA	66 025	15.2	40 006	9.2	630	9.5	10 975	251	126	17 820	408	610	35 225	597 485	494 949
Acadia	970	16.8	603	10.5	14	14.4	48	83	2	217	375	8	577	8 676	6 740
Allen	325	13.7	232	9.7	–	–	18	74	2	103	426	1	(11)	3 328	2 658
Ascension	1 166	16.7	468	6.7	5	4.3	42	57	2	110	153	4	312	6 778	5 583
Assumption	298	13.0	198	8.7	2	6.7	8	34	–	–	–	2	(11)	3 014	2 325
Avoyelles	586	14.4	497	12.2	3	5.1	27	66	2	88	216	9	720	6 947	5 601
Beauregard	477	15.0	286	9.0	3	6.3	22	68	1	93	291	4	(11)	4 647	3 895
Bienville	216	13.6	229	14.4	2	9.3	6	38	–	–	–	3	311	3 122	2 701
Bossier	1 384	14.8	683	7.3	19	13.7	150	161	1	152	165	16	674	10 827	9 341
Caddo..................	3 700	15.2	2 622	10.8	47	12.7	1 223	506	7	1 731	714	37	2 607	38 368	33 216
Calcasieu	2 776	15.5	1 638	9.1	26	9.4	341	189	6	873	485	31	1 480	25 334	21 359
Caldwell	138	13.3	161	15.6	2	14.5	10	96	1	25	241	1	(11)	1 787	1 472
Cameron	107	12.0	70	7.8	–	–	1	11	1	33	365	–	–	850	749
Catahoula	133	12.1	122	11.1	5	37.6	6	55	–	–	–	1	(12)	1 968	1 605
Claiborne	213	12.5	207	12.2	4	18.8	15	89	1	50	294	2	(12)	2 961	2 620
Concordia	333	16.1	255	12.3	4	12.0	16	78	2	77	371	1	(12)	3 448	2 875
De Soto	349	13.9	288	11.5	2	5.7	7	28	1	49	196	3	(12)	4 232	3 573
East Baton Rouge	6 094	15.5	3 062	7.8	69	11.3	1 199	305	9	1 929	490	37	2 721	44 853	38 903
East Carroll	146	16.3	102	11.4	1	6.8	6	69	1	29	327	2	(12)	1 458	1 223
East Feliciana	307	14.8	213	10.2	2	6.5	21	99	–	–	–	2	(11)	2 780	2 196
Evangeline..............	587	17.2	360	10.6	6	10.2	43	125	2	410	1 200	6	509	5 955	4 300
Franklin	289	13.1	268	12.1	2	6.9	7	32	1	53	240	13	558	3 652	3 175
Grant	261	14.0	191	10.3	2	7.7	5	26	–	–	–	3	85	2 820	2 224
Iberia	1 224	17.0	665	9.2	15	12.3	89	121	2	161	221	14	559	9 897	8 028
Iberville	445	14.3	273	8.8	5	11.2	23	73	1	80	254	2	(11)	4 352	3 619
Jackson	209	13.4	200	12.8	–	–	3	19	1	49	316	4	290	2 899	2 526
Jefferson	6 329	14.0	3 904	8.7	52	8.2	1 664	372	7	1 872	416	55	2 645	61 739	52 301
Jefferson Davis...........	516	16.3	345	10.9	5	9.7	26	83	1	49	155	3	214	4 870	3 957
Lafayette	2 870	15.6	1 235	6.7	25	8.7	527	281	5	909	488	28	1 458	20 695	17 294
Lafourche	1 178	13.3	651	7.4	10	8.5	116	130	3	273	307	9	621	11 453	9 196
La Salle	190	13.8	172	12.5	–	–	11	80	2	101	738	2	(11)	2 482	2 017
Lincoln	534	12.8	316	7.6	4	7.5	60	146	1	124	301	6	457	5 270	4 652
Livingston..............	1 329	15.5	608	7.1	8	6.0	17	19	–	–	–	8	332	8 801	7 015
Madison	233	17.9	140	10.7	3	12.9	5	39	1	47	363	9	224	1 821	1 545
Morehouse..............	500	15.8	390	12.3	5	10.0	33	106	1	106	337	5	573	5 637	4 812
Natchitoches	593	16.0	399	10.7	5	8.4	37	99	1	175	472	6	264	5 536	4 663
Orleans	7 738	16.5	5 131	10.9	95	12.3	3 010	653	11	3 069	661	49	3 079	67 155	54 263
Ouachita................	2 220	15.1	1 317	9.0	18	8.1	394	269	6	875	596	15	1 189	19 459	16 981
Plaquemines	425	16.4	200	7.7	3	7.1	16	61	–	–	–	3	(12)	3 052	2 506
Pointe Coupee	331	14.0	227	9.6	2	6.0	14	60	1	29	123	1	(11)	3 327	2 854
Rapides	1 851	14.6	1 261	10.0	18	9.7	340	268	3	710	561	48	3 009	19 949	15 972
Red River...............	134	13.9	123	12.8	–	–	5	53	1	74	770	2	(12)	1 542	1 289
Richland	323	15.4	254	12.1	2	6.2	17	81	2	91	433	15	687	3 785	3 272
Sabine	334	14.1	288	12.1	6	18.0	12	50	1	48	202	8	(11)	4 179	3 476
St. Bernard	885	13.3	700	10.6	3	3.4	64	98	1	106	161	13	459	10 829	9 102
St. Charles.............	715	15.0	320	6.7	4	5.6	34	70	1	56	116	3	(13)	4 872	4 016
St. Helena	102	10.6	91	9.4	2	19.6	4	42	1	99	1 034	–	–	1 002	815
St. James..............	303	14.5	170	8.1	3	9.9	14	66	1	26	124	1	(11)	2 815	2 370
St. John the Baptist	674	16.1	305	7.3	8	11.9	42	99	1	79	187	4	136	4 091	3 218
St. Landry	1 352	16.2	856	10.3	15	11.1	123	146	3	317	378	8	571	14 294	10 899
St. Martin	755	16.1	370	7.9	4	5.3	14	29	1	12	25	3	275	5 676	4 356
St. Mary	889	15.6	489	8.6	5	5.6	52	92	2	182	318	5	315	7 478	5 858
St. Tammany	2 533	13.7	1 288	7.0	14	5.5	519	269	4	620	329	22	1 000	21 547	18 017
Tangipahoa	1 652	17.3	930	9.8	14	8.5	105	107	3	362	373	18	636	13 585	10 521
Tensas	89	13.3	77	11.5	1	11.2	1	15	–	–	–	1	(12)	1 193	1 068
Terrebonne	1 701	16.5	779	7.6	18	10.6	156	148	2	384	367	8	583	13 508	9 884
Union	307	14.1	280	12.8	7	22.8	14	63	2	38	172	4	362	3 765	3 208
Vermilion	711	13.8	502	9.7	7	9.8	42	80	2	101	194	7	526	8 157	6 913
Vernon	964	18.6	356	6.9	7	7.3	41	80	1	59	115	3	177	4 697	3 903
Washington	663	15.4	513	11.9	5	7.5	46	107	3	204	473	8	446	7 821	6 217
Webster	555	13.0	483	11.3	5	9.0	36	84	2	164	384	15	563	8 062	6 971
West Baton Rouge	345	16.9	189	9.3	4	11.6	5	24	–	–	–	2	(11)	2 486	2 066
West Carroll............	130	10.7	148	12.1	–	–	4	33	1	21	173	3	212	2 270	1 947
West Feliciana	108	8.1	80	6.0	2	18.5	8	58	1	23	168	2	(12)	1 022	855
Winn	231	13.0	226	12.7	1	4.3	11	63	1	103	582	2	(11)	2 482	2 080

[1] Per 1,000 resident population estimated as of July 1, 1997. [2] Deaths of infants under 1 year old. [3] Infant deaths per 1,000 live births. [4] Active, nonfederal physicians as of December 31. Data subject to copyright; see below for source citation. [5] Per 100,000 resident population estimated as of July 1 of the year shown. [6] Nonfederal, short-stay (average length of stay less than 30 days) hospitals except hospital units of institutions. Data subject to copyright; see below for source citation. [7] SIC 805 includes skilled nursing care facilities; intermediate care facilities; and nursing and personal care, not elsewhere classified. [8] Full- and part-time employees on the payroll in the pay period including March 12. [9] Unduplicated count of persons enrolled in either hospital and/or supplemental medical insurance as of July 1. State totals include data not distributed by county. [10] Includes disabled, not shown separately. [11] 100 to 249 employees. [12] 20 to 99 employees. [13] 250 to 499 employees.

Sources: Births—U.S. National Center for Health Statistics, "Vital Statistics of the United States, Vol. I, Natality," annual, and unpublished data. Deaths—U.S. National Center for Health Statistics, "Vital Statistics of the United States, Vol. II, Mortality," annual, and unpublished data. Physicians—American Medical Association, Chicago, IL, "Physician Characteristics and Distribution in the U.S.," annual (copyright). Community Hospitals—Health Forum, LLC, an American Hospital Association Company, Chicago, IL, "Hospital Statistics" 2000 edition and unpublished data (copyright). Nursing and Personal Care Facilities—U.S. Census Bureau, County Business Patterns 1997 on CD-ROM (related Internet site <http://www.census.gov/epcd/cbp/view/cbpview.html>). Medicare—U.S. Health Care Financing Administration; "Medicare County Enrollment as of July 1, 1999 - Aged and Disabled 3/2000 update," <http://www.hcfa.gov/stats/enroll/default.htm>.

[Includes U.S., states, and 3,142 counties or county equivalents defined as of January 1, 1992. For changes to these areas since then, see appendix B. Geographic Information]

| County | Births, 1997 | | Deaths, 1997 | | | | Physicians,[4] 1999 | | Community hospitals,[6] 1998 | | | Nursing and personal care facilities,[7] 1997 | | Medicare program enrollment,[9] 1999 | |
| | | | Total | | Infant[2] | | | | | Beds | | | | | |
	Number	Rate[1]	Number	Rate[1]	Number	Rate[3]	Number	Rate[5]	Number	Number	Rate[5]	Estab-lishments	Em-ployees[8]	Total[10]	Aged
MAINE	13 669	11.0	11 993	9.6	70	5.1	2 913	232	38	3 768	302	271	14 851	213 210	178 598
Androscoggin	1 135	11.2	974	9.7	9	7.9	242	239	2	293	289	30	1 824	17 884	14 346
Aroostook	722	9.3	836	10.7	2	2.8	127	167	4	398	519	28	1 342	15 355	12 401
Cumberland	3 037	12.0	2 281	9.0	15	4.9	1 083	422	6	956	376	60	3 112	40 254	34 388
Franklin	297	10.2	272	9.4	–	–	46	160	1	60	208	8	425	4 919	4 105
Hancock	436	8.8	573	11.6	2	4.6	106	213	3	113	227	9	619	9 098	8 089
Kennebec	1 214	10.5	1 164	10.1	7	5.8	291	253	2	390	339	29	1 335	20 004	16 265
Knox	418	11.0	428	11.3	2	4.8	96	251	1	145	382	4	381	7 444	6 583
Lincoln	322	10.2	330	10.4	3	9.3	63	197	2	86	271	6	370	6 599	5 958
Oxford	580	10.8	573	10.7	4	6.9	65	120	2	77	143	12	765	10 082	8 340
Penobscot	1 592	11.0	1 293	8.9	5	3.1	355	246	4	474	328	27	1 119	23 525	18 933
Piscataquis	170	9.3	238	13.0	4	23.5	17	94	2	96	528	4	475	3 782	3 172
Sagadahoc	367	10.4	275	7.8	1	2.7	51	141	1	88	247	4	(11)	4 675	4 007
Somerset	592	11.3	490	9.4	3	5.1	50	95	2	91	174	13	837	8 664	6 989
Waldo	377	10.4	287	8.0	–	–	63	170	1	45	123	3	(12)	5 795	4 877
Washington	354	9.9	447	12.4	–	–	43	122	2	95	267	10	492	7 120	6 055
York	2 056	11.8	1 532	8.8	13	6.3	215	121	3	361	206	24	1 285	27 890	23 989
MARYLAND	70 215	13.8	41 794	8.2	616	8.8	19 592	379	51	12 670	247	593	39 982	634 527	562 188
Allegany	771	10.6	1 014	14.0	–	–	156	219	2	491	681	17	808	15 306	13 488
Anne Arundel	6 353	13.5	3 207	6.8	47	7.4	982	204	3	781	165	30	2 619	53 407	47 341
Baltimore	8 870	12.3	6 856	9.5	74	8.3	1 984	274	5	1 293	179	100	9 081	114 589	103 745
Calvert	935	13.5	411	5.9	3	3.2	105	142	1	125	174	4	481	7 062	6 248
Caroline	366	12.4	309	10.5	6	16.4	13	44	–	–	–	2	(11)	4 517	3 957
Carroll	1 941	13.2	1 057	7.2	13	6.7	204	134	1	158	106	34	1 197	19 242	17 386
Cecil	1 106	13.7	675	8.4	14	12.7	87	103	1	104	126	7	663	9 782	8 285
Charles	1 568	13.6	616	5.3	7	4.5	129	107	1	104	88	11	706	9 701	8 279
Dorchester	371	12.4	383	12.8	1	2.7	44	148	1	60	203	5	(11)	5 675	5 047
Frederick	2 533	13.8	1 121	6.1	14	5.5	276	145	1	166	89	32	1 080	18 914	16 908
Garrett	336	11.4	284	9.7	3	8.9	20	68	1	76	260	3	(11)	4 473	3 852
Harford	2 830	13.3	1 374	6.5	16	5.7	318	146	2	270	126	11	453	22 826	20 331
Howard	3 301	14.4	1 052	4.6	22	6.7	1 310	539	1	160	68	20	1 276	15 068	13 066
Kent	197	10.4	206	10.9	–	–	47	246	1	64	337	4	356	4 485	4 117
Montgomery	11 854	14.3	5 110	6.2	74	6.2	6 036	708	5	1 393	166	106	6 564	94 403	88 256
Prince George's	11 730	15.2	5 064	6.6	147	12.5	1 580	202	5	1 172	151	49	2 945	66 001	56 780
Queen Anne's	432	11.1	340	8.7	6	13.9	27	66	–	–	–	1	(12)	4 682	4 232
St. Mary's	1 237	14.5	594	7.0	12	9.7	101	114	1	100	114	3	473	8 018	7 057
Somerset	234	9.6	276	11.3	2	8.5	21	87	1	45	186	2	(12)	3 901	3 402
Talbot	322	9.8	370	11.3	1	3.1	137	408	1	164	495	3	504	7 101	6 573
Washington	1 572	12.4	1 187	9.3	7	4.5	218	171	1	333	261	73	1 916	19 944	17 715
Wicomico	1 094	13.8	827	10.5	4	3.7	255	321	2	382	481	5	916	11 681	10 278
Worcester	495	11.7	533	12.6	6	12.1	43	98	1	62	145	3	359	9 632	8 847
Independent City															
Baltimore city	9 767	14.9	8 928	13.6	137	14.0	5 499	869	13	5 167	800	68	6 310	103 995	86 305
MASSACHUSETTS	80 364	13.1	54 685	8.9	421	5.2	26 062	422	82	16 493	268	1 311	78 804	954 180	825 864
Barnstable	2 073	10.1	2 549	12.4	11	5.3	523	246	2	332	159	57	2 866	55 123	50 575
Berkshire	1 352	10.1	1 510	11.3	9	6.7	417	315	3	441	332	55	3 069	26 555	23 344
Bristol	6 483	12.6	4 800	9.3	32	4.9	693	133	4	1 170	226	130	6 913	87 194	73 368
Dukes	154	11.3	141	10.4	–	–	43	306	1	22	159	3	(12)	2 405	2 192
Essex	9 467	13.6	6 310	9.1	67	7.1	1 547	220	10	1 671	239	151	8 710	110 320	95 732
Franklin	741	10.5	675	9.5	5	6.7	97	137	1	85	120	10	1 148	11 452	9 855
Hampden	5 745	13.0	4 537	10.3	40	7.0	1 119	255	6	1 237	282	87	6 401	75 696	64 333
Hampshire	1 356	9.0	1 176	7.8	1	.7	501	332	2	161	107	17	(13)	20 019	17 506
Middlesex	19 274	13.6	11 368	8.0	78	4.0	7 204	505	16	3 389	238	262	14 992	204 598	180 262
Nantucket	112	15.0	86	11.5	1	8.9	18	219	1	19	241	1	(14)	1 060	993
Norfolk	8 353	13.1	5 704	8.9	34	4.1	3 830	595	6	926	144	159	8 865	97 747	87 555
Plymouth	6 376	13.8	3 785	8.2	28	4.4	712	151	3	588	126	84	6 130	62 971	53 485
Suffolk	9 252	14.4	5 547	8.6	68	7.3	6 924	1 079	17	4 684	730	90	7 072	87 737	71 601
Worcester	9 626	13.3	6 497	9.0	47	4.9	2 434	330	10	1 768	242	205	11 373	111 133	94 935

[1] Per 1,000 resident population estimated as of July 1, 1997. [2] Deaths of infants under 1 year old. [3] Infant deaths per 1,000 live births. [4] Active, nonfederal physicians as of December 31. Data subject to copyright; see below for source citation. [5] Per 100,000 resident population estimated as of July 1 of the year shown. [6] Nonfederal, short-stay (average length of stay less than 30 days) hospitals except hospital units of institutions. Data subject to copyright; see below for source citation. [7] SIC 805 includes skilled nursing care facilities; intermediate care facilities; and nursing and personal care, not elsewhere classified. [8] Full- and part-time employees on the payroll in the pay period including March 12. [9] Unduplicated count of persons enrolled in either hospital and/or supplemental medical insurance as of July 1. State totals include data not distributed by county. [10] Includes disabled, not shown separately. [11] 250 to 499 employees. [12] 100 to 249 employees. [13] 1,000 to 2,499 employees. [14] 0 to 19 employees.

Sources: Births—U.S. National Center for Health Statistics, "Vital Statistics of the United States, Vol. I, Natality," annual, and unpublished data. Deaths—U.S. National Center for Health Statistics, "Vital Statistics of the United States, Vol. II, Mortality," annual, and unpublished data. Physicians—American Medical Association, Chicago, IL, "Physician Characteristics and Distribution in the U.S.," annual (copyright). Community Hospitals—Health Forum, LLC, an American Hospital Association Company, Chicago, IL, "Hospital Statistics" 2000 edition and unpublished data (copyright). Nursing and Personal Care Facilities—U.S. Census Bureau, County Business Patterns 1997 on CD-ROM (related Internet site <http://www.census.gov/epcd/cbp/view/cbpview.html>). Medicare—U.S. Health Care Financing Administration; "Medicare County Enrollment as of July 1, 1999 - Aged and Disabled 3/2000 update," <http://www.hcfa.gov/stats/enroll/default.htm>.

Table B–4. Counties — **Vital Statistics and Health**–Con.

[Includes U.S., states, and 3,142 counties or county equivalents defined as of January 1, 1992. For changes to these areas since then, see appendix B. Geographic Information]

County	Births, 1997 Number	Births, 1997 Rate[1]	Deaths, 1997 Total Number	Deaths, 1997 Total Rate[1]	Deaths, 1997 Infant[2] Number	Deaths, 1997 Infant[2] Rate[3]	Physicians,[4] 1999 Number	Physicians,[4] 1999 Rate[5]	Community hospitals,[6] 1998 Number	Community hospitals,[6] 1998 Beds Number	Community hospitals,[6] 1998 Beds Rate[5]	Nursing and personal care facilities,[7] 1997 Establishments	Nursing and personal care facilities,[7] 1997 Employees[8]	Medicare program enrollment,[9] 1999 Total[10]	Medicare program enrollment,[9] 1999 Aged
MICHIGAN	133 714	13.7	83 301	8.5	1 092	8.2	22 246	226	151	27 168	277	1 706	64 579	1 389 107	1 193 930
Alcona	92	8.4	174	16.0	–	–	3	27	–	–	–	2	(11)	3 046	2 668
Alger	96	9.6	91	9.1	1	10.4	10	99	1	40	401	1	(12)	1 976	1 734
Allegan	1 418	14.1	783	7.8	9	6.3	48	46	1	63	62	21	861	11 400	9 799
Alpena	353	11.5	334	10.9	2	5.7	58	189	1	121	397	4	(11)	6 500	5 547
Antrim	250	11.9	228	10.9	3	12.0	9	41	–	–	–	9	255	4 144	3 664
Arenac	165	10.1	176	10.8	1	6.1	14	85	1	70	427	4	118	3 627	3 056
Baraga	108	12.8	139	16.5	2	18.5	5	58	1	40	465	–	–	1 677	1 452
Barry	682	12.6	432	8.0	9	13.2	42	77	1	88	162	3	(11)	6 505	5 759
Bay	1 341	12.1	1 031	9.3	10	7.5	137	125	2	362	329	35	787	17 914	15 642
Benzie	190	13.2	136	9.5	1	5.3	17	111	1	48	326	6	48	2 960	2 615
Berrien	2 171	13.5	1 500	9.4	22	10.1	256	160	2	663	415	34	976	28 086	24 322
Branch	511	11.7	441	10.1	4	7.8	39	89	1	96	220	9	266	6 569	5 623
Calhoun	1 824	13.1	1 522	10.9	17	9.3	196	139	4	562	399	21	906	22 299	18 642
Cass	570	11.4	455	9.1	8	14.0	10	20	1	47	94	5	(11)	6 759	5 795
Charlevoix	320	13.3	217	9.0	5	15.6	33	132	1	33	135	9	157	4 379	3 950
Cheboygan	276	11.8	323	13.8	3	10.9	13	54	1	92	386	4	(11)	4 711	4 183
Chippewa	429	11.4	282	7.5	3	7.0	25	66	1	86	227	2	(11)	5 616	4 895
Clare	358	12.4	372	12.8	1	2.8	15	50	1	64	217	9	248	6 745	5 520
Clinton	793	12.6	399	6.3	3	3.8	29	45	1	28	44	11	442	6 048	5 462
Crawford	150	10.8	128	9.2	1	6.7	19	133	1	98	694	2	(12)	2 250	1 894
Delta	394	10.1	412	10.6	2	5.1	48	124	1	66	170	5	306	7 585	6 584
Dickinson	300	11.1	319	11.8	–	–	51	189	1	96	355	4	250	5 384	4 820
Eaton	1 200	12.0	674	6.7	2	1.7	22	22	2	56	55	19	498	9 769	8 631
Emmet	345	12.2	246	8.7	–	–	128	441	1	202	705	1	(11)	5 025	4 491
Genesee	6 317	14.5	3 727	8.6	81	12.8	876	200	3	1 322	303	96	3 095	61 020	50 844
Gladwin	252	10.1	281	11.3	3	11.9	12	47	1	42	166	5	189	5 440	4 693
Gogebic	179	10.2	290	16.6	6	33.5	21	123	1	35	203	2	(11)	4 730	4 129
Grand Traverse	894	12.3	627	8.6	4	4.5	261	346	1	368	496	13	494	12 542	11 090
Gratiot	512	12.8	423	10.6	5	9.8	54	135	1	127	316	21	950	6 437	5 671
Hillsdale	566	12.2	424	9.1	5	8.8	36	77	1	47	101	10	155	6 847	5 880
Houghton	387	10.8	391	10.9	2	5.2	49	138	2	123	345	3	160	6 264	5 494
Huron	390	11.0	397	11.2	1	2.6	40	113	3	167	473	6	164	7 819	7 051
Ingham	3 990	13.9	1 725	6.0	28	7.0	853	299	2	1 059	370	23	1 375	35 951	30 239
Ionia	780	11.8	434	6.6	7	9.0	18	27	1	77	115	7	(13)	6 984	6 023
Iosco	251	9.8	346	13.5	–	–	18	69	1	49	191	4	311	6 743	5 903
Iron	107	8.2	215	10.5	–	–	11	86	1	82	637	4	320	3 733	3 374
Isabella	633	11.0	364	6.3	1	1.6	57	96	1	118	202	19	467	6 162	5 108
Jackson	2 073	13.3	1 398	9.0	18	8.7	166	106	2	477	306	30	903	23 609	20 299
Kalamazoo	3 125	13.6	1 743	7.6	27	8.6	813	354	3	753	328	44	1 953	30 734	26 416
Kalkaska	196	12.7	141	9.1	2	10.2	2	13	1	76	489	4	(12)	2 174	1 843
Kent	8 998	16.6	3 956	7.3	64	7.1	1 395	253	6	1 811	332	75	4 506	67 897	58 978
Keweenaw	18	8.8	33	16.1	–	–	3	140	–	–	–	–	–	503	452
Lake	114	11.2	141	13.9	–	–	1	9	–	–	–	1	(12)	2 468	2 042
Lapeer	1 097	12.6	596	6.9	10	9.1	37	41	1	222	252	16	180	8 695	7 501
Leelanau	197	10.5	169	9.0	1	5.1	18	93	1	91	475	2	(12)	3 051	2 829
Lenawee	1 198	12.2	805	8.2	4	3.3	86	86	3	201	204	18	675	14 895	12 781
Livingston	1 900	13.4	858	6.0	9	4.7	124	82	1	45	31	10	528	11 840	10 396
Luce	72	10.9	67	10.1	2	27.8	7	104	1	86	1 266	2	(12)	1 327	1 107
Mackinac	114	10.3	136	12.3	1	8.8	6	54	1	107	969	2	(12)	2 281	1 987
Macomb	9 782	12.5	6 629	8.5	57	5.8	932	118	5	1 030	131	91	4 815	117 132	104 821
Manistee	248	10.7	270	11.6	1	4.0	24	101	1	54	230	10	317	5 009	4 351
Marquette	638	10.3	603	9.7	3	4.7	182	290	2	350	559	4	437	10 017	8 575
Mason	288	10.4	306	11.0	5	17.4	31	111	1	85	305	3	(11)	5 190	4 583
Mecosta	444	11.3	316	8.0	3	6.8	38	93	1	52	129	7	168	5 914	5 094
Menominee	252	10.3	274	11.2	2	7.9	9	37	–	–	–	2	(11)	4 736	4 179
Midland	988	12.2	585	7.2	7	7.1	189	231	1	250	307	13	643	10 798	9 562
Missaukee	173	12.7	133	9.8	–	–	4	28	–	–	–	4	103	2 227	1 921
Monroe	1 839	12.9	1 182	8.3	12	6.5	106	73	1	143	100	18	790	18 341	15 605
Montcalm	847	14.2	520	8.7	4	4.7	32	52	3	231	381	3	206	9 383	7 966
Montmorency	91	9.1	154	15.4	–	–	2	20	–	–	–	1	117	3 144	2 724
Muskegon	2 386	14.4	1 539	9.3	22	9.2	204	121	2	370	222	31	962	27 012	21 919
Newaygo	633	14.1	447	9.9	3	4.7	26	56	1	73	159	6	199	6 423	5 394
Oakland	15 994	13.7	8 425	7.2	97	6.1	5 536	469	12	3 080	262	246	6 824	148 289	131 689

[1] Per 1,000 resident population estimated as of July 1, 1997. [2] Deaths of infants under 1 year old. [3] Infant deaths per 1,000 live births. [4] Active, nonfederal physicians as of December 31. Data subject to copyright; see below for source citation. [5] Per 100,000 resident population estimated as of July 1 of the year shown. [6] Nonfederal, short-stay (average length of stay less than 30 days) hospitals except hospital units of institutions. Data subject to copyright; see below for source citation. [7] SIC 805 includes skilled nursing care facilities; intermediate care facilities; and nursing and personal care, not elsewhere classified. [8] Full- and part-time employees on the payroll in the pay period including March 12. [9] Unduplicated count of persons enrolled in either hospital and/or supplemental medical insurance as of July 1. State totals include data not distributed by county. [10] Includes disabled, not shown separately. [11] 100 to 249 employees. [12] 20 to 99 employees. [13] 250 to 499 employees.

Sources: Births—U.S. National Center for Health Statistics, "Vital Statistics of the United States, Vol. I, Natality," annual, and unpublished data. Deaths—U.S. National Center for Health Statistics, "Vital Statistics of the United States, Vol. II, Mortality," annual, and unpublished data. Physicians—American Medical Association, Chicago, IL, "Physician Characteristics and Distribution in the U.S.," annual (copyright). Community Hospitals—Health Forum, LLC, an American Hospital Association Company, Chicago, IL, "Hospital Statistics" 2000 edition and unpublished data (copyright). Nursing and Personal Care Facilities—U.S. Census Bureau, County Business Patterns 1997 on CD-ROM (related Internet site <http://www.census.gov/epcd/cbp/view/cbpview.html>). Medicare—U.S. Health Care Financing Administration; "Medicare County Enrollment as of July 1, 1999 - Aged and Disabled 3/2000 update," <http://www.hcfa.gov/stats/enroll/default.htm>.

[Includes U.S., states, and 3,142 counties or county equivalents defined as of January 1, 1992. For changes to these areas since then, see appendix B. Geographic Information]

County	Births, 1997		Deaths, 1997				Physicians,[4] 1999		Community hospitals,[6] 1998			Nursing and personal care facilities,[7] 1997		Medicare program enrollment,[9] 1999	
			Total		Infant[2]					Beds					
	Number	Rate[1]	Number	Rate[1]	Number	Rate[3]	Number	Rate[5]	Number	Number	Rate[5]	Establishments	Employees[8]	Total[10]	Aged
MICHIGAN—Con.															
Oceana	324	13.1	216	8.8	1	3.1	9	36	1	24	97	3	(11)	4 626	3 883
Ogemaw	238	11.4	256	12.2	1	4.2	28	132	1	92	436	2	(12)	4 345	3 670
Ontonagon	66	8.2	137	16.9	–	–	6	78	1	72	918	1	(11)	1 912	1 649
Osceola	278	12.6	232	10.5	–	–	7	32	1	83	375	2	(13)	4 280	3 632
Oscoda	105	11.9	105	11.9	1	9.5	1	11	–	–	–	2	(12)	1 699	1 399
Otsego	273	12.5	183	8.4	2	7.3	19	84	1	73	328	7	166	3 714	3 255
Ottawa	3 356	15.2	1 344	6.1	20	6.0	253	110	3	301	134	32	1 756	26 719	24 041
Presque Isle	144	10.0	189	13.2	–	–	4	27	1	17	117	1	(11)	3 712	3 317
Roscommon	202	8.7	349	15.0	1	5.0	14	59	–	–	–	4	196	7 210	6 284
Saginaw	2 905	13.8	1 900	9.0	27	9.3	441	211	3	1 126	536	33	1 442	32 905	27 964
St. Clair	2 058	13.1	1 362	8.6	16	7.8	185	114	3	373	234	12	978	22 687	19 726
St. Joseph	837	13.7	580	9.5	5	6.0	52	85	2	127	208	11	522	9 181	7 974
Sanilac	604	14.1	497	11.6	–	–	29	67	3	133	309	20	302	7 613	6 748
Schoolcraft	94	10.8	126	14.5	–	–	7	80	1	20	228	1	(13)	1 947	1 713
Shiawassee	943	13.0	567	7.8	8	8.5	51	70	1	137	189	11	477	10 338	8 914
Tuscola	684	11.8	540	9.3	10	14.6	32	55	2	62	107	6	386	8 828	7 533
Van Buren	1 054	14.0	636	8.4	12	11.4	55	72	2	178	235	7	429	11 197	9 460
Washtenaw	4 048	13.5	1 626	5.4	25	6.2	2 935	959	5	1 406	464	48	1 990	29 531	24 860
Wayne	31 864	15.0	20 275	9.5	353	11.1	4 563	217	22	6 642	314	424	14 872	296 587	246 156
Wexford	338	11.6	297	10.2	4	11.8	49	166	1	78	268	3	(12)	5 164	4 362
MINNESOTA	64 499	13.8	36 913	7.9	382	5.9	12 125	254	136	16 486	349	1 350	62 598	648 272	578 935
Aitkin	153	11.1	201	14.5	2	13.1	10	70	1	68	479	2	(12)	3 666	3 309
Anoka	4 235	14.8	1 217	4.2	25	5.9	271	91	2	411	141	35	1 177	21 507	18 301
Becker	389	13.3	319	10.9	1	2.6	30	101	1	163	553	5	402	5 172	4 649
Beltrami	560	14.5	323	8.3	7	12.5	53	135	1	163	422	13	555	5 371	4 640
Benton	484	14.4	293	8.7	4	8.3	12	34	–	–	–	10	582	3 143	2 785
Big Stone	60	10.6	93	16.4	–	–	6	108	2	197	3 485	2	(11)	1 517	1 395
Blue Earth	580	10.8	412	7.7	6	10.3	110	204	1	147	274	24	1 101	8 606	7 527
Brown	290	10.6	277	10.2	3	10.3	32	119	3	89	329	7	681	5 345	4 947
Carlton	350	11.3	289	9.4	2	5.7	29	92	2	242	773	7	229	5 486	4 837
Carver	1 029	16.3	347	5.5	5	4.9	90	134	1	90	139	8	771	5 197	4 689
Cass	260	10.0	294	11.4	1	3.8	17	63	–	–	–	5	306	5 281	4 709
Chippewa	160	12.2	166	12.7	2	12.5	10	77	1	29	222	2	(12)	2 562	2 407
Chisago	600	15.2	273	6.9	5	8.3	29	69	1	78	190	6	413	5 030	4 459
Clay	619	12.0	376	7.3	5	8.1	19	37	–	–	–	9	697	7 072	6 272
Clearwater	95	11.5	104	12.6	–	–	5	61	1	92	1 116	2	(12)	1 551	1 399
Cook	43	9.1	30	6.3	–	–	6	126	1	63	1 326	–	–	922	861
Cottonwood	144	11.9	166	13.7	2	13.9	9	76	2	43	357	9	541	2 840	2 651
Crow Wing	582	11.4	481	9.4	3	5.2	93	177	2	313	605	18	728	10 568	9 502
Dakota	5 129	15.3	1 559	4.7	23	4.5	335	96	3	309	90	59	1 923	23 018	20 375
Dodge	248	14.5	128	7.5	1	4.0	11	63	–	–	–	4	31	2 258	2 073
Douglas	339	11.0	319	10.4	1	2.9	48	153	1	110	354	12	457	6 372	5 839
Faribault	160	9.8	228	13.9	2	12.5	9	55	1	24	148	9	425	3 902	3 691
Fillmore	230	11.1	238	11.5	2	8.7	13	63	1	53	255	6	479	4 498	4 233
Freeborn	344	10.9	383	12.1	1	2.9	38	121	1	72	228	9	860	6 556	5 907
Goodhue	504	11.8	417	9.8	6	11.9	76	175	3	179	415	25	1 094	6 986	6 409
Grant	61	9.9	106	17.2	–	–	3	49	1	15	246	6	268	1 559	1 450
Hennepin	15 467	14.7	8 025	7.6	114	7.4	4 311	405	9	3 179	300	274	15 567	137 044	121 213
Houston	202	10.5	154	8.0	1	5.0	17	87	1	81	420	8	616	3 351	3 092
Hubbard	176	10.6	172	10.3	–	–	19	112	1	40	237	1	(11)	3 470	3 115
Isanti	339	11.5	227	7.7	5	14.7	40	130	1	81	270	9	524	3 316	2 935
Itasca	451	10.3	419	9.6	1	2.2	47	106	3	210	478	5	243	8 345	7 360
Jackson	116	10.0	150	12.9	–	–	5	44	1	41	357	2	(12)	2 160	2 034
Kanabec	151	10.8	137	9.8	2	13.2	12	83	1	35	247	4	121	2 187	1 900
Kandiyohi	552	13.5	366	8.9	2	3.6	105	257	1	198	484	12	1 073	6 708	5 951
Kittson	62	11.6	75	14.0	–	–	6	116	1	108	2 037	2	(12)	1 215	1 126
Koochiching	148	9.7	152	10.0	1	6.8	11	74	1	35	232	4	250	2 969	2 599
Lac qui Parle	94	11.6	128	15.8	–	–	6	77	2	105	1 313	4	42	1 884	1 777
Lake	115	10.8	121	11.3	–	–	20	186	1	66	619	3	(11)	2 209	2 046
Lake of the Woods	31	6.9	36	8.0	–	–	3	65	1	64	1 403	–	–	828	761
Le Sueur	318	12.7	190	7.6	–	–	21	82	1	133	525	10	298	4 348	4 021
Lincoln	61	9.3	93	14.1	–	–	4	62	3	202	3 114	1	(11)	1 570	1 478
Lyon	340	13.9	227	9.3	1	2.9	25	103	2	143	586	7	468	4 318	3 911
McLeod	509	15.1	293	8.7	3	5.9	33	96	2	342	1 002	16	227	5 229	4 853
Mahnomen	76	14.9	56	11.0	2	26.3	3	59	1	67	1 326	1	(12)	993	891
Marshall	112	10.7	123	11.7	2	17.9	1	10	1	20	195	7	216	2 077	1 935
Martin	239	10.8	247	11.1	–	–	23	106	1	92	418	10	466	4 694	4 300
Meeker	265	12.3	231	10.7	2	7.5	12	55	1	38	175	6	389	3 695	3 351

[1] Per 1,000 resident population estimated as of July 1, 1997. [2] Deaths of infants under 1 year old. [3] Infant deaths per 1,000 live births. [4] Active, nonfederal physicians as of December 31. Data subject to copyright; see below for source citation. [5] Per 100,000 resident population estimated as of July 1 of the year shown. [6] Nonfederal, short-stay (average length of stay less than 30 days) hospitals except hospital units of institutions. Data subject to copyright; see below for source citation. [7] SIC 805 includes skilled nursing care facilities; intermediate care facilities; and nursing and personal care, not elsewhere classified. [8] Full- and part-time employees on the payroll in the pay period including March 12. [9] Unduplicated count of persons enrolled in either hospital and/or supplemental medical insurance as of July 1. State totals include data not distributed by county. [10] Includes disabled, not shown separately. [11] 20 to 99 employees. [12] 100 to 249 employees. [13] 0 to 19 employees.

Sources: Births—U.S. National Center for Health Statistics, "Vital Statistics of the United States, Vol. I, Natality," annual, and unpublished data. Deaths—U.S. National Center for Health Statistics, "Vital Statistics of the United States, Vol. II, Mortality," annual, and unpublished data. Physicians—American Medical Association, Chicago, IL, "Physician Characteristics and Distribution in the U.S.," annual (copyright). Community Hospitals—Health Forum, LLC, an American Hospital Association Company, Chicago, IL, "Hospital Statistics" 2000 edition and unpublished data (copyright). Nursing and Personal Care Facilities—U.S. Census Bureau, County Business Patterns 1997 on CD-ROM (related Internet site <http://www.census.gov/epcd/cbp/view/cbpview.html>). Medicare—U.S. Health Care Financing Administration; "Medicare County Enrollment as of July 1, 1999 - Aged and Disabled 3/2000 update," <http://www.hcfa.gov/stats/enroll/default.htm>.

[Includes U.S., states, and 3,142 counties or county equivalents defined as of January 1, 1992. For changes to these areas since then, see appendix B. Geographic Information]

County	Births, 1997 Number	Births, 1997 Rate[1]	Deaths, 1997 Total Number	Deaths, 1997 Total Rate[1]	Deaths, 1997 Infant[2] Number	Deaths, 1997 Infant[2] Rate[3]	Physicians,[4] 1999 Number	Physicians,[4] 1999 Rate[5]	Community hospitals,[6] 1998 Number	Community hospitals,[6] 1998 Beds Number	Community hospitals,[6] 1998 Beds Rate[5]	Nursing and personal care facilities,[7] 1997 Estab-lishments	Nursing and personal care facilities,[7] 1997 Em-ployees[8]	Medicare program enrollment,[9] 1999 Total[10]	Medicare program enrollment,[9] 1999 Aged
MINNESOTA—Con.															
Mille Lacs	250	12.1	238	11.5	2	8.0	27	126	2	138	655	4	(11)	4 530	3 999
Morrison	408	13.4	315	10.3	2	4.9	29	95	1	205	672	13	694	5 369	4 781
Mower	430	11.6	422	11.4	4	9.3	48	129	–	–	–	22	826	8 353	7 551
Murray	104	10.9	100	10.5	–	–	4	42	1	25	262	8	251	1 976	1 868
Nicollet	334	11.2	171	5.7	2	6.0	31	106	1	118	400	3	(12)	2 673	2 438
Nobles	298	15.1	197	10.0	3	10.1	24	126	2	116	602	14	299	3 955	3 653
Norman	82	10.7	110	14.4	–	–	4	53	1	8	106	5	(11)	1 647	1 535
Olmsted	1 784	15.6	695	6.1	10	5.6	2 286	1 920	3	1 179	1 008	48	1 471	13 725	12 380
Otter Tail	588	10.8	596	11.0	–	–	68	122	2	259	473	19	914	10 997	10 079
Pennington	168	12.3	118	8.7	1	6.0	16	118	1	130	960	4	40	2 335	2 102
Pine	262	11.1	217	9.2	2	7.6	12	49	1	106	440	9	381	4 360	3 814
Pipestone	113	11.2	112	11.1	–	–	7	70	1	87	865	3	293	2 232	2 085
Polk	391	12.2	415	13.0	3	7.7	18	58	2	305	981	18	829	5 784	5 239
Pope	120	11.0	169	15.4	–	–	8	73	2	38	348	6	372	2 429	2 260
Ramsey	7 434	15.3	4 091	8.4	48	6.5	1 886	388	6	1 407	290	178	7 985	76 070	66 741
Red Lake	36	8.3	60	13.9	–	–	1	24	–	–	–	1	(13)	854	789
Redwood	207	12.5	215	12.9	1	4.8	8	49	1	30	182	8	351	3 541	3 270
Renville	203	11.9	203	11.9	–	–	5	30	1	30	177	7	464	3 500	3 285
Rice	691	12.9	421	7.9	2	2.9	73	133	2	115	212	26	1 068	6 842	6 156
Rock	117	11.9	106	10.7	2	17.1	12	125	1	28	288	3	210	2 026	1 896
Roseau	272	16.7	146	9.0	2	7.4	12	75	1	161	1 001	2	(12)	2 207	2 053
St. Louis	2 004	10.3	2 186	11.2	6	3.0	556	287	8	1 219	630	81	2 458	36 169	31 883
Scott	1 342	17.6	337	4.4	3	2.2	63	76	1	63	80	18	743	5 215	4 663
Sherburne	958	16.5	339	5.8	4	4.2	28	44	–	–	–	14	868	4 560	3 962
Sibley	217	14.8	155	10.6	2	9.2	3	20	1	17	116	3	(12)	2 617	2 410
Stearns	1 624	12.7	714	5.6	8	4.9	292	224	4	812	631	37	883	17 886	15 777
Steele	419	13.3	253	8.0	2	4.8	44	137	1	55	173	12	283	4 855	4 467
Stevens	104	10.3	93	9.2	1	9.6	7	70	1	39	389	2	(11)	1 831	1 714
Swift	140	12.9	140	12.9	–	–	6	53	2	135	1 174	4	141	2 436	2 267
Todd	287	12.0	242	10.1	–	–	9	37	1	141	587	3	(12)	4 132	3 704
Traverse	54	12.7	67	15.7	–	–	4	96	1	25	589	1	(13)	1 079	1 024
Wabasha	225	10.9	219	10.6	3	13.3	22	104	2	319	1 527	4	205	3 737	3 447
Wadena	156	12.0	147	11.3	–	–	11	83	2	170	1 296	2	(13)	3 043	2 708
Waseca	249	13.5	167	9.0	–	–	22	119	1	24	129	17	486	3 016	2 799
Washington	2 685	14.0	850	4.4	7	2.6	278	137	1	25	13	30	1 209	11 654	10 396
Watonwan	185	15.9	129	11.1	–	–	6	52	2	49	425	4	264	2 386	2 222
Wilkin	107	14.5	79	10.7	3	28.0	1	14	1	171	2 320	2	(12)	1 263	1 119
Winona	587	12.2	405	8.4	6	10.2	50	105	1	186	387	7	469	6 944	6 209
Wright	1 258	15.1	467	5.6	7	5.6	47	53	2	133	156	27	836	8 771	7 766
Yellow Medicine	134	11.5	146	12.6	1	7.5	9	80	2	188	1 647	1	(13)	2 622	2 446
MISSISSIPPI	41 533	15.2	27 503	10.1	442	10.6	4 533	164	96	13 005	473	206	15 218	413 900	327 980
Adams	479	13.9	434	12.6	8	16.7	73	217	2	222	650	3	209	6 213	5 164
Alcorn	446	13.6	419	12.8	4	9.0	39	118	1	163	498	3	243	6 542	4 796
Amite	167	12.2	132	9.7	1	6.0	4	29	–	–	–	–	–	2 277	1 830
Attala	251	13.6	261	14.2	5	19.9	12	65	1	72	393	2	(12)	3 921	3 169
Benton	111	13.8	80	10.0	2	18.0	–	–	–	–	–	1	(13)	1 496	1 149
Bolivar	682	16.8	458	11.3	8	11.7	31	78	1	144	358	4	373	6 126	4 651
Calhoun	226	15.1	186	12.4	–	–	5	34	1	30	201	1	(13)	2 954	2 291
Carroll	91	9.1	83	8.3	–	–	6	60	–	–	–	–	–	1 510	1 217
Chickasaw	315	17.3	194	10.6	–	–	7	39	2	160	887	1	(13)	3 634	2 759
Choctaw	113	12.1	98	10.5	1	8.8	3	32	1	88	936	–	–	1 369	1 080
Claiborne	205	17.7	118	10.2	3	14.6	4	34	1	32	278	1	(13)	1 469	1 143
Clarke	229	12.7	196	10.9	1	4.4	7	38	1	43	236	–	–	3 200	2 578
Clay	346	16.0	239	11.1	4	11.6	17	78	1	60	277	3	(12)	3 299	2 613
Coahoma	609	19.4	379	12.0	8	13.1	48	154	1	195	623	5	385	4 942	3 833
Copiah	386	13.4	308	10.7	6	15.5	17	59	1	49	170	1	(12)	5 232	4 108
Covington	287	16.4	221	12.6	2	7.0	5	28	1	82	463	3	(12)	3 094	2 378
DeSoto	1 468	15.9	632	6.8	17	11.6	57	56	1	260	268	1	(12)	10 503	8 770
Forrest	1 122	15.2	743	10.1	9	8.0	300	400	2	748	1 004	4	653	11 344	9 123
Franklin	110	13.3	113	13.6	–	–	3	37	1	41	495	2	(13)	1 417	1 133
George	345	18.2	179	9.4	–	–	12	59	1	53	270	1	(13)	2 958	2 308
Greene	124	10.0	116	9.4	–	–	2	16	–	–	–	2	(13)	1 415	1 060
Grenada	312	13.9	300	13.4	4	12.8	27	120	1	127	567	2	(12)	4 029	3 204
Hancock	448	11.4	394	10.0	4	8.9	49	118	1	66	164	–	–	6 021	4 930
Harrison	2 762	15.7	1 710	9.7	23	8.3	410	230	4	752	424	14	701	25 765	20 700
Hinds	4 060	16.4	2 410	9.7	41	10.1	1 057	430	5	2 224	899	29	1 497	32 957	26 640
Holmes	363	16.9	233	10.9	3	8.3	10	46	2	109	507	1	(13)	3 842	2 920
Humphreys	180	15.9	132	11.6	3	16.7	4	36	1	28	247	1	(13)	1 785	1 381
Issaquena	19	11.6	22	13.4	–	–	–	–	–	–	–	–	–	154	112

[1] Per 1,000 resident population estimated as of July 1, 1997. [2] Deaths of infants under 1 year old. [3] Infant deaths per 1,000 live births. [4] Active, nonfederal physicians as of December 31. Data subject to copyright; see below for source citation. [5] Per 100,000 resident population estimated as of July 1 of the year shown. [6] Nonfederal, short-stay (average length of stay less than 30 days) hospitals except hospital units of institutions. Data subject to copyright; see below for source citation. [7] SIC 805 includes skilled nursing care facilities; intermediate care facilities; and nursing and personal care, not elsewhere classified. [8] Full- and part-time employees on the payroll in the pay period including March 12. [9] Unduplicated count of persons enrolled in either hospital and/or supplemental medical insurance as of July 1. State totals include data not distributed by county. [10] Includes disabled, not shown separately. [11] 250 to 499 employees. [12] 100 to 249 employees. [13] 20 to 99 employees.

Sources: Births—U.S. National Center for Health Statistics, "Vital Statistics of the United States, Vol. I, Natality," annual, and unpublished data. Deaths—U.S. National Center for Health Statistics, "Vital Statistics of the United States, Vol. II, Mortality," annual, and unpublished data. Physicians—American Medical Association, Chicago, IL, "Physician Characteristics and Distribution in the U.S.," annual (copyright). Community Hospitals—Health Forum, LLC, an American Hospital Association Company, Chicago, IL, "Hospital Statistics" 2000 edition and unpublished data (copyright). Nursing and Personal Care Facilities—U.S. Census Bureau, County Business Patterns 1997 on CD-ROM (related Internet site <http://www.census.gov/epcd/cbp/view/cbpview.html>). Medicare—U.S. Health Care Financing Administration; "Medicare County Enrollment as of July 1, 1999 - Aged and Disabled 3/2000 update," <http://www.hcfa.gov/stats/enroll/default.htm>.

[Includes U.S., states, and 3,142 counties or county equivalents defined as of January 1, 1992. For changes to these areas since then, see appendix B. Geographic Information]

County	Births, 1997		Deaths, 1997				Physicians,[4] 1999		Community hospitals,[6] 1998			Nursing and personal care facilities,[7] 1997		Medicare program enrollment,[9] 1999	
			Total		Infant[2]					Beds					
	Number	Rate[1]	Number	Rate[1]	Number	Rate[3]	Number	Rate[5]	Number	Number	Rate[5]	Estab-lishments	Em-ployees[8]	Total[10]	Aged
MISSISSIPPI—Con.															
Itawamba	263	12.5	242	11.5	2	7.6	8	38	–	406	310	2	(11)	3 130	2 503
Jackson	1 771	13.7	1 005	7.8	20	11.3	242	182	2	406	310	5	487	15 174	12 287
Jasper	292	16.6	177	10.1	2	6.8	2	11	1	124	702	–	–	3 140	2 371
Jefferson	142	16.7	98	11.5	1	7.0	4	48	1	27	319	1	(12)	1 379	948
Jefferson Davis	187	13.4	181	13.0	4	21.4	8	58	1	101	731	–	–	2 071	1 568
Jones	964	15.2	708	11.2	13	13.5	80	127	1	266	418	5	363	11 570	8 985
Kemper	117	11.2	104	10.0	2	17.1	–	–	1	29	274	1	(12)	1 755	1 422
Lafayette	430	12.5	289	8.4	5	11.6	74	212	1	204	587	2	(11)	3 763	2 967
Lamar	579	16.2	252	7.0	5	8.6	13	34	–	–	–	1	(11)	3 700	2 919
Lauderdale	1 131	14.8	791	10.3	12	10.6	214	282	3	635	834	10	565	12 821	10 626
Lawrence	156	12.1	121	9.4	1	6.4	5	38	1	53	408	1	(12)	2 888	2 196
Leake	329	17.0	269	13.9	1	3.0	10	51	1	76	391	2	(13)	3 789	2 989
Lee	1 153	15.6	707	9.6	18	15.6	233	310	1	724	970	3	(13)	11 417	9 050
Leflore	670	17.9	438	11.7	7	10.4	55	149	1	207	556	5	498	5 734	4 576
Lincoln	453	14.3	332	10.5	7	15.5	31	97	1	109	342	5	472	5 284	4 189
Lowndes	1 044	17.0	610	10.0	14	13.4	99	164	1	328	537	4	190	8 145	6 640
Madison	1 144	16.1	479	6.8	12	10.5	299	401	1	127	174	4	409	7 720	6 292
Marion	397	15.1	313	11.9	3	7.6	16	60	1	79	299	4	181	4 823	3 797
Marshall	529	16.5	330	10.3	5	9.5	8	25	1	40	124	1	(12)	4 935	3 766
Monroe	456	12.0	360	9.5	6	13.2	42	110	2	122	320	2	(13)	5 956	4 731
Montgomery	185	14.9	203	16.3	3	16.2	4	32	2	68	548	1	(11)	2 524	2 090
Neshoba	423	15.6	293	10.8	5	11.8	16	58	1	192	698	–	–	3 872	3 093
Newton	317	14.8	246	11.5	6	18.9	13	60	1	50	232	2	(11)	4 545	3 645
Noxubee	235	19.0	131	10.6	7	29.8	5	40	1	109	878	–	–	2 067	1 590
Oktibbeha	536	13.5	290	7.3	6	11.2	47	118	1	96	242	3	248	4 647	3 714
Panola	548	16.7	351	10.7	9	16.4	22	65	1	70	210	2	(11)	5 368	4 098
Pearl River	611	13.4	438	9.6	4	6.5	21	44	2	161	344	2	(12)	7 217	5 598
Perry	200	16.9	100	8.4	–	–	3	25	1	88	742	–	–	1 587	1 192
Pike	580	15.3	512	13.5	6	10.3	65	171	2	167	441	2	(13)	6 970	5 552
Pontotoc	347	14.0	237	9.6	3	8.6	10	39	1	71	281	1	(12)	3 858	3 061
Prentiss	321	13.2	244	10.1	4	12.5	18	73	1	99	406	4	(11)	4 871	3 705
Quitman	171	17.4	108	11.0	1	5.8	4	41	1	96	974	–	–	1 865	1 367
Rankin	1 535	14.4	748	7.0	11	7.2	300	267	3	290	265	3	(13)	12 364	9 780
Scott	421	16.8	249	9.9	2	4.8	10	40	1	74	296	1	(11)	4 461	3 558
Sharkey	122	18.4	75	11.3	1	8.2	2	31	–	–	–	1	(12)	993	788
Simpson	335	13.3	284	11.3	4	11.9	12	47	2	113	447	4	607	4 221	3 216
Smith	190	12.5	154	10.1	5	26.3	5	32	–	–	–	1	(11)	2 312	1 768
Stone	209	16.3	155	12.1	3	14.4	8	59	1	50	378	1	(11)	2 193	1 689
Sunflower	529	15.4	362	10.5	5	9.5	18	54	2	155	462	2	(11)	4 078	3 145
Tallahatchie	222	14.9	155	10.4	7	31.5	3	21	1	77	521	–	–	2 396	1 781
Tate	340	14.4	218	9.2	5	14.7	10	41	1	52	217	1	(11)	3 458	2 766
Tippah	306	14.6	257	12.3	4	13.1	8	38	1	110	523	2	(11)	4 376	3 218
Tishomingo	206	11.1	242	13.0	1	4.9	11	59	1	48	257	2	(11)	4 454	3 436
Tunica	156	19.3	100	12.4	1	6.4	2	25	–	–	–	1	(12)	1 187	891
Union	360	15.3	208	8.8	1	2.8	23	95	1	153	641	4	(11)	4 187	3 304
Walthall	221	15.4	169	11.8	5	22.6	9	63	1	49	340	2	(11)	2 194	1 687
Warren	839	17.0	512	10.4	12	14.3	84	171	2	351	711	5	319	6 781	5 657
Washington	1 159	17.7	724	11.0	14	12.1	93	145	2	262	402	9	451	9 134	7 186
Wayne	313	14.1	204	10.1	5	16.0	11	53	1	80	394	2	(12)	2 747	2 005
Webster	160	15.3	144	13.8	–	–	4	38	1	76	718	1	(11)	1 986	1 599
Wilkinson	110	11.9	118	12.8	–	–	11	122	1	66	721	1	(11)	1 678	1 343
Winston	241	12.4	212	10.9	–	–	7	36	1	185	959	1	(12)	3 425	2 833
Yalobusha	171	13.9	137	11.1	–	–	4	32	1	91	733	–	–	2 959	2 278
Yazoo	451	17.8	327	12.9	5	11.1	18	71	1	51	200	2	(11)	4 215	3 454
MISSOURI	74 037	13.7	54 322	10.0	564	7.6	12 695	232	122	20 685	380	952	54 694	854 472	734 440
Adair	256	10.5	190	7.8	2	7.8	8	33	1	164	677	6	219	3 391	2 860
Andrew	182	11.8	144	9.4	–	–	4	26	1	504	3 241	4	(13)	2 034	1 864
Atchison	54	7.6	84	11.8	–	–	3	43	1	42	597	2	(11)	1 426	1 326
Audrain	308	13.1	305	13.0	1	3.2	37	158	1	154	654	5	225	4 656	4 164
Barry	457	14.0	395	12.1	4	8.8	18	54	2	71	214	11	389	6 649	5 712
Barton	177	14.9	156	13.1	1	5.6	3	25	1	42	348	2	(12)	2 157	1 951
Bates	194	12.3	224	14.2	1	5.2	7	44	1	52	329	4	237	3 221	2 836
Benton	149	9.0	207	12.5	2	13.4	3	17	–	–	–	1	(12)	4 434	3 672
Bollinger	117	10.2	108	9.4	1	8.5	–	–	–	–	–	1	(14)	1 963	1 599
Boone	1 762	13.8	746	5.8	6	3.4	1 022	785	3	975	756	14	803	13 703	11 371
Buchanan	1 078	13.2	1 011	12.4	7	6.5	148	181	–	–	–	16	885	15 118	13 138
Butler	514	12.7	532	13.2	5	9.7	90	223	2	359	888	14	576	8 170	6 433
Caldwell	98	11.2	117	13.4	–	–	2	22	–	–	–	2	(11)	1 758	1 569
Callaway	484	13.1	335	9.1	4	8.3	25	66	1	31	83	6	297	5 333	4 329

[1] Per 1,000 resident population estimated as of July 1, 1997. [2] Deaths of infants under 1 year old. [3] Infant deaths per 1,000 live births. [4] Active, nonfederal physicians as of December 31. Data subject to copyright; see below for source citation. [5] Per 100,000 resident population estimated as of July 1 of the year shown. [6] Nonfederal, short-stay (average length of stay less than 30 days) hospitals except hospital units of institutions. Data subject to copyright; see below for source citation. [7] SIC 805 includes skilled nursing care facilities; intermediate care facilities; and nursing and personal care, not elsewhere classified. [8] Full- and part-time employees on the payroll in the pay period including March 12. [9] Unduplicated count of persons enrolled in either hospital and/or supplemental medical insurance as of July 1. State totals include data not distributed by county. [10] Includes disabled, not shown separately. [11] 100 to 249 employees. [12] 20 to 99 employees. [13] 250 to 499 employees. [14] 0 to 19 employees.

Sources: Births—U.S. National Center for Health Statistics, "Vital Statistics of the United States, Vol. I, Natality," annual, and unpublished data. Deaths—U.S. National Center for Health Statistics, "Vital Statistics of the United States, Vol. II, Mortality," annual, and unpublished data. Physicians—American Medical Association, Chicago, IL, "Physician Characteristics and Distribution in the U.S.," annual (copyright). Community Hospitals—Health Forum, LLC, an American Hospital Association Company, Chicago, IL, "Hospital Statistics" 2000 edition and unpublished data (copyright). Nursing and Personal Care Facilities—U.S. Census Bureau, County Business Patterns 1997 on CD-ROM (related Internet site <http://www.census.gov/epcd/cbp/view/cbpview.html>). Medicare—U.S. Health Care Financing Administration; "Medicare County Enrollment as of July 1, 1999 - Aged and Disabled 3/2000 update," <http://www.hcfa.gov/stats/enroll/default.htm>.

[Includes U.S., states, and 3,142 counties or county equivalents defined as of January 1, 1992. For changes to these areas since then, see appendix B. Geographic Information]

County	Births, 1997		Deaths, 1997				Physicians,[4] 1999		Community hospitals,[6] 1998			Nursing and personal care facilities,[7] 1997		Medicare program enrollment,[9] 1999	
			Total		Infant[2]					Beds					
	Number	Rate[1]	Number	Rate[1]	Number	Rate[3]	Number	Rate[5]	Number	Number	Rate[5]	Establishments	Employees[8]	Total[10]	Aged
MISSOURI—Con.															
Camden	299	9.0	345	10.4	2	6.7	24	69	1	94	277	5	218	6 387	5 604
Cape Girardeau	774	11.7	650	9.8	4	5.2	188	280	2	508	767	8	751	10 120	8 935
Carroll	122	11.9	142	13.9	–	–	2	20	–	–	–	4	(11)	2 268	2 062
Carter	87	13.7	96	15.2	1	11.5	–	–	–	–	–	3	(12)	1 288	1 017
Cass	930	11.9	627	8.0	7	7.5	33	40	2	82	102	17	772	10 003	8 786
Cedar	153	11.7	209	16.0	–	–	5	37	1	34	258	2	(11)	3 303	2 872
Chariton	79	9.0	133	15.1	–	–	1	12	–	–	–	2	(11)	1 790	1 633
Christian	682	14.5	372	7.9	7	10.3	24	47	–	–	–	8	353	6 473	5 504
Clark	83	11.1	101	13.5	2	24.1	–	–	–	–	–	–	–	1 291	1 148
Clay	2 459	14.1	1 299	7.5	11	4.5	151	84	4	681	386	28	1 077	22 391	19 841
Clinton	225	12.1	213	11.4	2	8.9	6	31	1	48	252	5	265	2 978	2 655
Cole	876	12.7	587	8.5	6	6.8	131	188	2	301	435	15	628	9 285	8 102
Cooper	197	12.3	173	10.8	1	5.1	6	37	1	49	305	5	221	2 746	2 443
Crawford	333	15.2	246	11.2	1	3.0	3	13	–	–	–	7	348	3 839	3 167
Dade	75	9.5	117	14.8	–	–	2	25	–	–	–	–	–	1 807	1 583
Dallas	208	13.8	145	9.6	–	–	–	–	–	–	–	3	181	2 628	2 181
Daviess	120	15.4	109	14.0	–	–	–	–	–	–	–	2	(11)	1 552	1 393
DeKalb	105	9.5	123	11.1	2	19.0	1	9	–	–	–	5	187	1 420	1 293
Dent	183	13.0	194	13.8	–	–	7	49	1	46	325	3	(11)	3 064	2 539
Douglas	149	12.1	147	12.0	1	6.7	1	8	–	–	–	4	84	2 270	1 863
Dunklin	495	15.1	489	14.9	2	4.0	27	83	1	116	355	9	532	6 747	5 367
Franklin	1 292	14.2	829	9.1	2	1.5	89	96	1	46	50	13	890	13 784	11 787
Gasconade	180	12.1	206	13.8	1	5.6	7	47	1	41	277	4	182	3 227	2 899
Gentry	79	11.5	106	15.4	–	–	2	29	1	35	506	10	231	1 832	1 514
Greene	3 014	13.4	2 146	9.5	19	6.3	688	303	3	1 395	616	26	2 261	36 349	31 125
Grundy	128	12.5	162	15.9	–	–	5	49	1	38	373	1	(12)	2 359	2 103
Harrison	79	9.4	136	16.1	–	–	5	59	1	21	248	7	246	2 116	1 930
Henry	251	11.9	306	14.5	1	4.0	13	61	1	106	499	4	220	4 872	4 167
Hickory	73	8.5	157	18.3	4	54.8	1	11	–	–	–	1	(11)	2 304	1 965
Holt	48	8.5	64	11.4	1	20.8	2	36	–	–	–	2	(11)	1 234	1 123
Howard	115	11.8	116	11.9	1	8.7	6	62	–	–	–	6	236	1 781	1 605
Howell	476	13.4	422	11.9	2	4.2	44	122	2	140	392	8	672	7 570	6 163
Iron	130	11.8	158	14.4	–	–	9	82	1	50	458	2	(11)	2 323	1 846
Jackson	10 041	15.3	6 246	9.5	89	8.9	1 918	293	14	3 334	509	79	5 789	94 515	80 810
Jasper	1 556	15.7	1 101	11.1	4	2.6	220	219	3	690	693	21	934	19 116	16 133
Jefferson	2 705	14.0	1 450	7.5	12	4.4	87	44	1	393	201	33	1 787	19 626	16 129
Johnson	599	12.7	326	6.9	4	6.7	36	75	1	69	145	8	328	4 902	4 224
Knox	52	11.9	73	16.8	–	–	–	–	–	–	–	1	(13)	992	880
Laclede	404	13.3	312	10.2	4	9.9	19	60	1	35	113	5	(11)	5 400	4 522
Lafayette	376	11.6	397	12.2	5	13.3	11	34	1	37	113	8	627	5 705	4 923
Lawrence	497	15.2	413	12.6	–	–	17	51	1	31	94	4	208	5 800	4 931
Lewis	150	14.8	137	13.5	1	6.7	2	20	–	–	–	1	(12)	1 905	1 709
Lincoln	507	14.4	263	7.5	1	2.0	11	29	1	36	98	5	226	4 536	3 895
Linn	183	13.1	230	16.5	2	10.9	5	36	1	34	246	4	296	3 283	2 945
Livingston	176	12.4	203	14.3	2	11.4	10	71	1	80	566	6	447	2 948	2 607
McDonald	342	17.4	199	10.1	1	2.9	2	10	–	–	–	3	92	2 852	2 261
Macon	199	13.0	225	14.7	3	15.1	2	7	1	28	183	3	163	3 279	2 933
Madison	149	13.0	160	13.9	4	26.8	13	112	1	143	1 238	1	(12)	2 474	2 058
Maries	89	10.7	86	10.3	1	11.2	1	12	–	–	–	1	(12)	1 293	1 100
Marion	409	14.7	386	13.9	6	14.7	43	155	1	105	377	14	454	5 396	4 561
Mercer	35	8.8	56	14.0	–	–	1	25	–	–	–	2	(12)	825	749
Miller	324	14.4	255	11.3	1	3.1	8	35	–	–	–	3	162	4 352	3 762
Mississippi	197	14.6	178	13.2	–	–	3	22	–	–	–	3	217	2 704	2 198
Moniteau	199	15.0	155	11.7	–	–	3	23	–	–	–	3	189	2 250	2 021
Monroe	110	12.2	97	10.8	1	9.1	2	22	–	–	–	4	37	1 810	1 622
Montgomery	135	11.4	174	14.7	–	–	3	25	–	–	–	4	292	2 354	2 063
Morgan	224	12.4	272	15.1	2	8.9	6	32	–	–	–	1	(13)	4 169	3 574
New Madrid	286	13.9	266	13.0	2	7.0	6	30	–	–	–	5	348	3 387	2 733
Newton	683	14.1	443	9.2	3	4.4	23	46	1	54	110	9	448	6 193	5 314
Nodaway	193	9.2	195	9.3	1	5.2	22	107	1	54	261	11	329	3 245	2 981
Oregon	113	11.3	124	12.4	–	–	–	–	–	–	–	2	(11)	2 229	1 796
Osage	178	14.3	128	10.3	1	5.6	2	16	–	–	–	2	(11)	1 856	1 668
Ozark	110	11.4	136	14.1	–	–	–	–	–	–	–	1	(12)	2 152	1 764
Pemiscot	411	19.1	306	14.2	6	14.6	19	90	1	179	835	1	(12)	3 787	2 936
Perry	244	13.9	180	10.3	1	4.1	11	63	1	47	269	6	251	2 898	2 593
Pettis	552	15.0	452	12.3	7	12.7	47	127	1	147	396	13	486	6 725	5 828
Phelps	430	11.2	383	10.0	3	7.0	58	149	1	214	555	13	496	6 501	5 392
Pike	195	12.1	207	12.9	3	15.4	7	43	1	31	189	4	(11)	3 034	2 671
Platte	921	13.4	384	5.6	8	8.7	35	49	1	58	83	9	592	6 812	6 038
Polk	329	13.0	290	11.4	3	9.1	21	82	1	74	290	14	545	4 926	4 221

[1] Per 1,000 resident population estimated as of July 1, 1997.   [2] Deaths of infants under 1 year old.   [3] Infant deaths per 1,000 live births.   [4] Active, nonfederal physicians as of December 31. Data subject to copyright; see below for source citation.   [5] Per 100,000 resident population estimated as of July 1 of the year shown.   [6] Nonfederal, short-stay (average length of stay less than 30 days) hospitals except hospital units of institutions. Data subject to copyright; see below for source citation.   [7] SIC 805 includes skilled nursing care facilities; intermediate care facilities; and nursing and personal care, not elsewhere classified.   [8] Full- and part-time employees on the payroll in the pay period including March 12.   [9] Unduplicated count of persons enrolled in either hospital and/or supplemental medical insurance as of July 1. State totals include data not distributed by county.   [10] Includes disabled, not shown separately.   [11] 100 to 249 employees.   [12] 20 to 99 employees.   [13] 0 to 19 employees.

Sources: Births—U.S. National Center for Health Statistics, "Vital Statistics of the United States, Vol. I, Natality," annual, and unpublished data.   Deaths—U.S. National Center for Health Statistics, "Vital Statistics of the United States, Vol. II, Mortality," annual, and unpublished data.   Physicians—American Medical Association, Chicago, IL, "Physician Characteristics and Distribution in the U.S.," annual (copyright).   Community Hospitals—Health Forum, LLC, an American Hospital Association Company, Chicago, IL, "Hospital Statistics" 2000 edition and unpublished data (copyright).   Nursing and Personal Care Facilities—U.S. Census Bureau, County Business Patterns 1997 on CD-ROM (related Internet site <http://www.census.gov/epcd/cbp/view/cbpview.html>).   Medicare—U.S. Health Care Financing Administration; "Medicare County Enrollment as of July 1, 1999 - Aged and Disabled 3/2000 update," <http://www.hcfa.gov/stats/enroll/default.htm>.

[Includes U.S., states, and 3,142 counties or county equivalents defined as of January 1, 1992. For changes to these areas since then, **see** appendix B. Geographic Information]

County	Births, 1997		Deaths, 1997				Physicians,[4] 1999		Community hospitals,[6] 1998			Nursing and personal care facilities,[7] 1997		Medicare program enrollment,[9] 1999	
			Total		Infant[2]					Beds					
	Number	Rate[1]	Number	Rate[1]	Number	Rate[3]	Number	Rate[5]	Number	Number	Rate[5]	Establishments	Employees[8]	Total[10]	Aged
MISSOURI—Con.															
Pulaski	609	16.1	243	6.4	6	9.9	22	58	–	–	–	4	245	4 274	3 543
Putnam	62	12.5	70	14.1	–	–	2	–	–	–	–	–	–	1 169	1 029
Ralls	90	10.3	100	11.4	–	–	2	22	–	–	–	4	233	1 166	1 043
Randolph	333	13.9	297	12.4	1	3.0	12	50	1	92	385	6	446	4 206	3 611
Ray	288	12.4	224	9.6	2	6.9	2	8	1	50	211	3	80	2 935	2 517
Reynolds	70	10.5	73	10.9	–	–	3	45	–	–	–	2	(11)	1 260	961
Ripley	147	10.6	168	12.1	2	13.6	7	49	1	26	185	3	(12)	2 921	2 298
St. Charles	3 907	14.8	1 533	5.8	27	6.9	251	89	4	409	150	30	1 588	26 841	23 570
St. Clair	94	10.3	159	17.4	–	–	8	86	2	72	794	2	(12)	2 097	1 765
Ste. Genevieve	173	10.1	145	8.5	3	17.3	11	63	1	34	196	5	102	2 734	2 397
St. Francois	670	12.3	606	11.1	4	6.0	39	70	2	214	387	19	793	10 392	8 298
St. Louis	12 905	12.9	9 597	9.6	112	8.7	1 654	166	13	4 358	437	134	10 150	158 038	142 409
Saline	251	11.0	299	13.1	3	12.0	22	97	1	57	251	8	342	4 544	3 823
Schuyler	64	14.6	65	14.8	–	–	–	–	–	–	–	–	–	1 056	919
Scotland	75	15.4	59	12.1	–	–	–	–	1	32	664	–	–	1 037	928
Scott	584	14.5	417	10.3	4	6.8	56	138	1	154	382	12	528	7 216	5 788
Shannon	100	12.3	67	8.2	2	20.0	2	24	–	–	–	–	–	1 380	1 060
Shelby	74	10.9	110	16.2	1	13.5	2	30	–	–	–	–	–	1 550	1 423
Stoddard	303	10.3	378	12.8	2	6.6	10	34	1	48	162	9	340	6 081	5 059
Stone	331	12.5	279	10.5	1	3.0	11	40	–	–	–	2	(12)	5 239	4 598
Sullivan	80	11.9	92	13.7	1	12.5	1	15	1	38	543	2	(12)	1 470	1 282
Taney	494	14.5	388	11.4	3	6.1	46	130	1	99	287	3	248	7 221	6 307
Texas	255	11.4	255	11.4	2	7.8	7	31	1	66	295	5	285	4 551	3 772
Vernon	266	13.8	259	13.4	5	18.8	23	118	1	85	436	5	196	3 776	3 176
Warren	277	11.7	183	7.7	1	3.6	4	16	–	–	–	2	(13)	3 371	2 965
Washington	292	12.9	206	9.1	–	–	4	17	1	42	182	1	(14)	3 100	2 331
Wayne	140	10.9	164	12.8	1	7.1	5	38	–	–	–	4	(12)	3 538	2 755
Webster	449	15.8	251	8.8	2	4.5	12	40	–	–	–	5	274	4 848	4 047
Worth	23	9.8	41	17.5	–	–	1	44	–	–	–	1	(14)	568	517
Wright	234	12.0	231	11.9	2	8.5	4	20	–	–	–	5	187	3 889	3 235
Independent City															
St. Louis city	5 765	16.7	4 596	13.3	82	14.2	4 942	1 480	9	2 711	800	62	4 305	58 283	47 383
MONTANA	10 849	12.3	7 769	8.8	75	6.9	1 683	191	53	4 413	502	149	7 235	135 415	117 593
Beaverhead	99	11.1	94	10.5	–	–	19	216	1	22	250	3	(12)	1 339	1 173
Big Horn	252	20.0	106	8.4	4	15.9	15	119	1	53	421	3	(11)	1 167	1 002
Blaine	112	15.7	54	7.6	1	8.9	4	57	1	53	748	1	(11)	942	847
Broadwater	48	11.7	40	9.8	–	–	4	96	1	44	1 065	1	(14)	759	650
Carbon	80	8.5	100	10.6	–	–	9	94	1	56	596	3	(12)	1 713	1 567
Carter	14	9.3	17	11.3	–	–	–	–	–	–	–	1	(11)	263	246
Cascade	1 072	13.6	747	9.5	9	8.4	185	236	1	444	565	7	827	12 698	10 914
Chouteau	45	8.6	56	10.7	–	–	2	39	2	82	1 581	2	(11)	1 048	969
Custer	132	10.9	153	12.6	–	–	21	177	1	151	1 254	4	(12)	2 259	1 986
Daniels	13	6.3	30	14.6	1	76.9	2	102	1	54	2 705	–	–	487	455
Dawson	77	8.6	99	11.0	1	13.0	9	104	1	101	1 146	–	–	1 688	1 527
Deer Lodge	105	10.5	125	12.5	–	–	13	134	1	92	924	1	(11)	2 164	1 803
Fallon	29	9.7	33	11.0	–	–	1	35	1	52	1 759	–	–	543	501
Fergus	119	9.5	172	13.8	1	8.4	11	90	1	124	1 010	3	(12)	2 521	2 279
Flathead	902	12.6	594	8.3	7	7.8	166	228	2	241	335	5	569	11 425	9 790
Gallatin	743	12.1	295	4.8	2	2.7	137	214	1	70	112	9	305	6 246	5 658
Garfield	22	15.3	12	8.3	–	–	–	–	–	–	–	1	(11)	251	239
Glacier	243	19.3	123	9.7	5	20.6	10	79	–	–	–	–	–	1 356	1 163
Golden Valley	11	10.6	9	8.7	–	–	–	–	–	–	–	–	–	217	183
Granite	42	15.8	35	13.2	–	–	–	–	1	35	1 313	–	–	429	378
Hill	264	15.1	156	8.9	1	3.8	22	129	1	259	1 492	5	(11)	2 444	2 148
Jefferson	98	10.0	58	5.9	1	10.2	12	116	–	–	–	2	(11)	1 256	1 016
Judith Basin	24	10.4	23	10.0	–	–	–	–	–	–	–	–	–	426	393
Lake	305	12.0	226	8.9	2	6.6	32	124	2	121	473	4	267	4 038	3 510
Lewis and Clark	652	12.2	377	7.1	3	4.6	124	229	1	54	101	11	339	7 559	6 390
Liberty	28	12.0	26	11.1	–	–	5	222	1	64	2 767	–	–	625	579
Lincoln	189	10.1	165	8.8	1	5.3	19	101	1	26	139	2	(12)	3 456	2 697
McCone	19	9.4	21	10.4	–	–	1	52	1	38	1 938	1	(11)	373	355
Madison	71	10.3	64	9.3	1	14.1	7	101	2	17	247	–	–	1 189	1 084
Meagher	26	14.5	16	8.9	–	–	4	225	1	37	2 062	1	(11)	383	340
Mineral	39	10.5	29	7.8	–	–	2	52	1	30	793	–	–	766	611
Missoula	995	11.2	631	7.1	8	8.0	256	287	2	330	371	13	634	10 947	9 189
Musselshell	51	11.1	61	13.3	2	39.2	2	44	1	54	1 181	–	–	891	771
Park	177	11.0	143	8.9	–	–	22	138	1	32	203	5	225	2 598	2 295
Petroleum	7	13.5	5	9.6	–	–	–	–	–	–	–	–	–	83	D

[1] Per 1,000 resident population estimated as of July 1, 1997. [2] Deaths of infants under 1 year old. [3] Infant deaths per 1,000 live births. [4] Active, nonfederal physicians as of December 31. Data subject to copyright; see below for source citation. [5] Per 100,000 resident population estimated as of July 1 of the year shown. [6] Nonfederal, short-stay (average length of stay less than 30 days) hospitals except hospital units of institutions. Data subject to copyright; see below for source citation. [7] SIC 805 includes skilled nursing care facilities; intermediate care facilities; and nursing and personal care, not elsewhere classified. [8] Full- and part-time employees on the payroll in the pay period including March 12. [9] Unduplicated count of persons enrolled in either hospital and/or supplemental medical insurance as of July 1. State totals include data not distributed by county. [10] Includes disabled, not shown separately. [11] 20 to 99 employees. [12] 100 to 249 employees. [13] 250 to 499 employees. [14] 0 to 19 employees.

Sources: Births—U.S. National Center for Health Statistics, "Vital Statistics of the United States, Vol. I, Natality," annual, and unpublished data. Deaths—U.S. National Center for Health Statistics, "Vital Statistics of the United States, Vol. II, Mortality," annual, and unpublished data. Physicians—American Medical Association, Chicago, IL, "Physician Characteristics and Distribution in the U.S.," annual (copyright). Community Hospitals—Health Forum, LLC, an American Hospital Association Company, Chicago, IL, "Hospital Statistics" 2000 edition and unpublished data (copyright). Nursing and Personal Care Facilities—U.S. Census Bureau, County Business Patterns 1997 on CD-ROM (related Internet site <http://www.census.gov/epcd/cbp/view/cbpview.html>). Medicare—U.S. Health Care Financing Administration; "Medicare County Enrollment as of July 1, 1999 - Aged and Disabled 3/2000 update," <http://www.hcfa.gov/stats/enroll/default.htm>.

[Includes U.S., states, and 3,142 counties or county equivalents defined as of January 1, 1992. For changes to these areas since then, see appendix B. Geographic Information]

County	Births, 1997 Number	Rate[1]	Deaths, 1997 Total Number	Rate[1]	Infant[2] Number	Rate[3]	Physicians[4] 1999 Number	Rate[5]	Community hospitals[6] 1998 Number	Beds Number	Beds Rate[5]	Nursing and personal care facilities[7] 1997 Establishments	Employees[8]	Medicare program enrollment[9] 1999 Total[10]	Aged
MONTANA—Con.															
Phillips	47	9.5	46	9.3	–	–	2	43	1	14	292	1	(11)	894	796
Pondera	77	12.0	77	12.0	2	26.0	4	64	1	79	1 244	1	(12)	1 205	1 115
Powder River	14	7.4	27	14.3	–	–	–	–	–	–	–	–	–	306	287
Powell	57	8.1	61	8.7	–	–	4	58	1	35	500	1	(11)	1 119	962
Prairie	12	9.0	18	13.5	–	–	1	74	1	21	1 553	–	–	311	288
Ravalli	384	11.1	313	9.1	1	2.6	46	128	1	48	137	6	302	6 128	5 319
Richland	136	13.3	115	11.3	1	7.4	13	129	1	135	1 329	–	–	1 715	1 536
Roosevelt	212	19.1	86	7.7	2	9.4	9	82	2	171	1 555	2	(13)	1 472	1 318
Rosebud	178	17.5	80	7.9	3	16.9	7	71	1	75	749	–	–	995	848
Sanders	106	10.4	125	12.2	1	9.4	8	78	1	44	432	2	(12)	1 989	1 655
Sheridan	29	6.8	68	15.9	–	–	3	73	1	93	2 191	2	(13)	1 062	996
Silver Bow	402	11.7	438	12.7	3	7.5	72	212	1	100	290	12	427	6 459	5 446
Stillwater	85	10.8	61	7.8	–	–	5	60	1	23	285	2	(13)	1 278	1 151
Sweet Grass	34	10.0	44	13.0	–	–	1	28	1	60	1 769	–	–	637	592
Teton	65	10.3	74	11.7	–	–	1	16	1	46	725	–	–	1 104	1 005
Toole	67	13.9	57	11.8	–	–	5	108	1	84	1 773	1	(12)	578	534
Treasure	7	8.3	6	7.1	–	–	1	116	–	–	–	–	–	173	D
Valley	100	12.0	88	10.6	–	–	10	123	1	32	389	1	(13)	1 648	1 493
Wheatland	21	9.0	27	11.5	2	95.2	2	88	1	54	2 303	–	–	490	441
Wibaux	13	11.4	17	15.0	–	–	–	–	–	–	–	1	(11)	215	200
Yellowstone	1 698	13.5	1 046	8.3	10	5.9	373	293	2	563	446	29	1 218	19 040	16 627
Yellowstone National Park	–	X	–	X	–	–	–	X	–	–	X	–	–	–	–
NEBRASKA	23 319	14.1	15 282	9.2	173	7.4	3 679	221	86	8 133	490	269	19 097	252 231	226 916
Adams	372	12.6	357	12.1	4	10.8	72	246	1	125	425	3	563	5 208	4 721
Antelope	88	12.0	76	10.3	–	–	6	83	3	84	1 153	1	(11)	1 436	1 342
Arthur	3	7.0	2	4.7	–	–	–	–	–	–	–	–	–	98	D
Banner	4	4.6	8	9.2	–	–	–	–	–	–	–	–	–	90	D
Blaine	9	14.4	6	9.6	–	–	–	–	–	–	–	–	–	89	D
Boone	86	13.4	74	11.5	1	11.6	8	126	1	20	314	2	(13)	1 370	1 305
Box Butte	169	13.0	105	8.1	–	–	7	55	1	44	345	3	192	1 956	1 771
Boyd	26	9.8	40	15.0	1	38.5	3	119	1	20	780	1	(11)	694	652
Brown	33	9.2	56	15.6	–	–	3	86	1	25	708	1	(11)	824	768
Buffalo	568	14.2	288	7.2	3	5.3	114	283	1	267	662	7	545	5 373	4 879
Burt	69	8.7	126	15.9	–	–	5	63	1	23	290	2	(13)	1 825	1 697
Butler	122	14.1	94	10.9	1	8.2	5	58	1	31	357	2	(13)	1 701	1 569
Cass	333	13.9	198	8.3	3	9.0	16	64	–	–	–	3	271	3 251	2 940
Cedar	122	12.5	114	11.6	2	16.4	5	52	–	–	–	2	(13)	1 915	1 831
Chase	57	13.4	52	12.2	1	17.5	3	71	1	12	281	1	(11)	934	886
Cherry	76	11.8	59	9.2	1	13.2	5	79	1	28	445	1	(11)	1 233	1 136
Cheyenne	131	13.7	106	11.1	–	–	8	85	1	102	1 076	1	(11)	1 903	1 725
Clay	67	9.4	91	12.8	–	–	3	42	–	–	–	2	(13)	1 487	1 386
Colfax	140	13.3	105	10.0	2	14.3	7	65	1	50	469	3	(13)	3 686	3 434
Cuming	145	14.5	108	10.8	–	–	5	50	1	102	1 021	1	(11)	1 984	1 898
Custer	129	10.7	181	14.9	2	15.5	12	101	3	146	1 221	3	(13)	2 618	2 408
Dakota	354	19.0	165	8.9	1	2.8	5	26	–	–	–	1	(11)	2 390	2 053
Dawes	86	9.6	94	10.5	–	–	8	91	1	32	361	1	(11)	1 511	1 382
Dawson	426	18.4	240	10.4	5	11.7	21	90	3	107	462	8	234	3 642	3 350
Deuel	20	9.9	29	14.3	–	–	2	101	–	–	–	–	–	532	500
Dixon	73	11.5	73	11.5	–	–	1	16	–	–	–	3	184	1 227	1 138
Dodge	423	12.0	383	10.9	2	4.7	42	119	1	262	742	7	551	6 740	6 169
Douglas	7 136	16.2	3 577	8.1	61	8.5	2 092	469	8	2 652	598	29	3 328	58 505	50 925
Dundy	22	9.6	34	14.8	–	–	3	138	1	14	614	1	(11)	501	482
Fillmore	78	11.3	80	11.6	–	–	6	87	1	53	764	3	170	1 450	1 364
Franklin	34	8.9	59	15.5	–	–	3	82	1	20	538	2	(13)	928	864
Frontier	26	8.2	24	7.6	–	–	–	–	–	–	–	1	(11)	526	485
Furnas	62	11.4	95	17.5	1	16.1	4	74	1	56	1 031	2	(13)	1 504	1 373
Gage	254	11.1	302	13.2	1	3.9	23	101	1	108	474	8	791	5 039	4 270
Garden	14	6.3	49	22.2	–	–	5	241	1	46	2 161	–	–	630	581
Garfield	24	11.6	44	21.3	1	41.7	–	–	–	–	–	1	(11)	560	523
Gosper	21	9.3	26	11.5	–	–	–	–	–	–	–	–	–	501	465
Grant	7	9.4	5	6.7	1	142.9	–	–	–	–	–	–	–	145	D
Greeley	36	12.4	37	12.8	–	–	–	–	1	–	–	1	(11)	645	612
Hall	834	16.2	509	9.9	9	10.8	84	162	1	198	383	8	610	8 080	7 185
Hamilton	110	11.7	100	10.6	–	–	10	105	1	78	825	–	–	1 496	1 400
Harlan	35	9.3	58	15.4	1	28.6	–	–	1	25	675	1	(11)	836	774
Hayes	3	2.8	14	12.9	–	–	–	–	–	–	–	–	–	119	107
Hitchcock	36	10.6	42	12.3	–	–	–	–	–	–	–	–	–	778	725
Holt	138	11.4	123	10.1	2	14.5	12	101	2	47	391	3	239	2 403	2 217

[1] Per 1,000 resident population estimated as of July 1, 1997.   [2] Deaths of infants under 1 year old.   [3] Infant deaths per 1,000 live births.   [4] Active, nonfederal physicians as of December 31. Data subject to copyright; see below for source citation.   [5] Per 100,000 resident population estimated as of July 1 of the year shown.   [6] Nonfederal, short-stay (average length of stay less than 30 days) hospitals except hospital units of institutions. Data subject to copyright; see below for source citation.   [7] SIC 805 includes skilled nursing care facilities; intermediate care facilities; and nursing and personal care, not elsewhere classified.   [8] Full- and part-time employees on the payroll in the pay period including March 12.   [9] Unduplicated count of persons enrolled in either hospital and/or supplemental medical insurance as of July 1. State totals include data not distributed by county.   [10] Includes disabled, not shown separately.   [11] 20 to 99 employees.   [12] 0 to 19 employees.   [13] 100 to 249 employees.

Sources: Births—U.S. National Center for Health Statistics, "Vital Statistics of the United States, Vol. I, Natality," annual, and unpublished data.   Deaths—U.S. National Center for Health Statistics, "Vital Statistics of the United States, Vol. II, Mortality," annual, and unpublished data.   Physicians—American Medical Association, Chicago, IL, "Physician Characteristics and Distribution in the U.S.," annual (copyright).   Community Hospitals—Health Forum, LLC, an American Hospital Association Company, Chicago, IL, "Hospital Statistics" 2000 edition and unpublished data (copyright).   Nursing and Personal Care Facilities—U.S. Census Bureau, County Business Patterns 1997 on CD-ROM (related Internet site <http://www.census.gov/epcd/cbp/view/cbpview.html>).   Medicare—U.S. Health Care Financing Administration; "Medicare County Enrollment as of July 1, 1999 - Aged and Disabled 3/2000 update," <http://www.hcfa.gov/stats/enroll/default.htm>.

[Includes U.S., states, and 3,142 counties or county equivalents defined as of January 1, 1992. For changes to these areas since then, see appendix B. Geographic Information]

County	Births, 1997 Number	Births, 1997 Rate[1]	Deaths, 1997 Total Number	Deaths, 1997 Total Rate[1]	Deaths, 1997 Infant[2] Number	Deaths, 1997 Infant[2] Rate[3]	Physicians,[4] 1999 Number	Physicians,[4] 1999 Rate[5]	Community hospitals,[6] 1998 Number	Community hospitals,[6] 1998 Beds Number	Community hospitals,[6] 1998 Beds Rate[5]	Nursing and personal care facilities,[7] 1997 Estab-lishments	Nursing and personal care facilities,[7] 1997 Em-ployees[8]	Medicare program enrollment,[9] 1999 Total[10]	Medicare program enrollment,[9] 1999 Age
NEBRASKA—Con.															
Hooker	10	14.1	18	25.4	–	–	1	145	–	–	–	1	[11]	223	20
Howard	74	11.5	60	9.3	1	13.5	1	15	1	36	554	1	[11]	1 203	1 12
Jefferson	70	8.3	109	12.9	–	–	4	48	1	65	779	1	[11]	2 024	1 86
Johnson	59	12.8	62	13.5	–	–	4	88	1	22	481	2	[11]	1 083	1 01
Kearney	76	11.3	88	13.1	–	–	5	73	1	72	1 051	2	[12]	1 174	1 05
Keith	102	11.8	89	10.3	–	–	7	79	1	29	334	3	[11]	1 655	1 47
Keya Paha	10	10.2	12	12.3	–	–	–	–	–	–	–	–	–	189	
Kimball	35	8.7	46	11.4	–	–	2	50	1	20	491	–	–	926	84
Knox	125	13.4	140	15.0	–	–	5	55	1	76	827	2	[13]	2 345	2 18
Lancaster	3 223	13.8	1 562	6.7	18	5.6	527	222	3	945	401	55	2 352	29 038	25 68
Lincoln	432	12.9	319	9.5	8	18.5	55	162	1	99	296	8	395	5 759	5 08
Logan	9	10.0	6	6.7	–	–	–	–	–	–	–	–	–	163	
Loup	7	10.4	9	13.4	–	–	–	–	–	–	–	–	–	97	
McPherson	4	7.1	4	7.1	–	–	–	–	–	–	–	–	–	125	
Madison	572	16.4	362	10.4	6	10.5	63	184	1	225	651	9	553	5 857	5 27
Merrick	97	11.9	105	12.9	1	10.3	1	12	1	64	794	3	[13]	1 485	1 37
Morrill	56	10.4	74	13.7	1	17.9	2	38	1	20	369	1	[11]	1 039	94
Nance	42	10.0	62	14.7	1	23.8	1	25	1	79	1 926	2	[11]	817	76
Nemaha	71	9.1	112	14.3	1	14.1	6	79	1	30	391	1	[13]	1 446	1 31
Nuckolls	45	8.4	70	13.1	–	–	5	98	1	49	942	2	[13]	1 372	1 27
Otoe	175	12.1	227	15.6	4	22.9	12	81	2	46	313	4	398	2 891	2 63
Pawnee	25	7.9	56	17.6	–	–	3	97	1	14	447	1	[11]	888	83
Perkins	21	6.5	39	12.0	–	–	1	31	1	84	2 632	–	–	628	60
Phelps	125	12.6	131	13.2	–	–	13	132	1	28	283	3	439	1 812	1 64
Pierce	94	11.9	85	10.7	1	10.6	5	63	1	30	377	2	[13]	1 412	1 32
Platte	454	14.8	240	7.8	2	4.4	27	89	1	73	238	2	[13]	3 073	2 90
Polk	57	10.1	78	13.9	–	–	2	36	1	21	374	2	[13]	1 120	1 07
Red Willow	145	12.8	129	11.4	2	13.8	11	97	1	44	391	6	[13]	2 409	2 19
Richardson	82	8.7	167	17.7	–	–	5	54	1	35	371	2	[13]	2 287	2 07
Rock	16	9.1	22	12.5	–	–	1	59	1	47	2 717	–	–	416	39
Saline	138	10.6	175	13.4	1	7.2	10	76	2	130	1 003	2	[13]	2 534	2 32
Sarpy	1 957	16.5	536	4.5	11	5.6	135	110	1	160	133	5	381	7 019	6 26
Saunders	242	12.6	169	8.8	–	–	5	26	1	103	536	3	[13]	3 127	2 87
Scotts Bluff	488	13.4	386	10.6	2	4.1	83	230	1	202	561	5	406	7 216	6 26
Seward	173	10.7	143	8.8	–	–	9	55	1	154	940	4	266	2 502	2 33
Sheridan	61	9.2	95	14.4	–	–	6	93	1	40	620	1	[11]	1 418	1 32
Sherman	32	9.1	62	17.5	–	–	2	58	–	–	–	1	[11]	801	74
Sioux	8	5.3	8	5.3	–	–	–	–	–	–	–	–	–	131	[
Stanton	97	15.7	50	8.1	–	–	–	–	–	–	–	–	–	615	57
Thayer	58	9.2	101	16.1	–	–	5	81	1	14	224	3	[12]	1 601	1 51
Thomas	10	12.4	4	4.9	–	–	–	–	–	–	–	–	–	142	12
Thurston	149	20.7	76	10.5	1	6.7	2	28	1	30	418	2	[11]	1 005	88
Valley	50	10.5	78	16.4	1	20.0	6	133	1	87	1 878	–	–	1 155	1 07
Washington	206	11.2	166	9.0	4	19.4	18	96	1	33	177	2	[12]	2 362	2 19
Wayne	103	10.9	65	6.9	–	–	5	54	1	34	364	1	[13]	1 398	1 30
Webster	40	10.0	96	23.9	–	–	3	76	1	16	398	3	115	1 044	95
Wheeler	12	12.7	7	7.4	–	–	–	–	–	–	–	–	–	152	[
York	181	12.4	174	11.9	1	5.5	13	90	2	100	687	3	[12]	2 650	2 47
NEVADA	26 911	16.1	13 380	8.0	175	6.5	3 209	177	20	3 528	202	66	4 237	228 631	199 81
Churchill	391	17.1	211	9.3	3	7.7	19	81	1	40	173	1	[13]	3 069	2 755
Clark	18 565	16.8	8 780	7.9	122	6.6	2 093	172	8	2 298	198	46	2 593	150 920	131 134
Douglas	330	9.1	274	7.6	3	9.1	50	133	–	–	–	–	–	5 502	5 07
Elko	775	17.0	195	4.3	3	3.9	37	81	1	50	109	1	[11]	2 828	2 47
Esmeralda	10	8.8	11	9.6	–	–	–	–	–	–	–	–	–	139	11
Eureka	21	11.3	16	8.6	–	–	–	–	–	–	–	–	–	227	19
Humboldt	298	17.1	105	6.0	3	10.1	12	67	1	52	288	–	–	1 433	1 22
Lander	130	18.0	39	5.4	–	–	3	45	1	23	330	–	–	447	37
Lincoln	49	11.9	43	10.4	1	20.4	3	71	–	–	–	–	–	747	66
Lyon	344	11.9	296	10.3	1	2.9	10	32	1	44	146	1	[11]	5 477	4 79
Mineral	70	12.4	63	11.1	–	–	6	116	–	–	–	–	–	1 071	94
Nye	299	11.1	284	10.5	3	10.0	14	47	1	45	157	–	–	6 342	5 45
Pershing	77	16.1	25	5.2	1	13.0	2	42	1	34	703	–	–	517	46
Storey	9	3.1	21	7.2	–	–	–	–	–	–	–	–	–	157	14
Washoe	4 700	15.3	2 407	7.9	30	6.4	842	263	3	774	247	11	1 016	38 743	34 035
White Pine	129	12.6	85	8.3	–	–	11	112	1	40	397	1	[11]	1 382	1 223
Independent City															
Carson City city	714	14.7	525	10.8	5	7.0	107	214	1	128	260	5	341	9 488	8 625

[1] Per 1,000 resident population estimated as of July 1, 1997. [2] Deaths of infants under 1 year old. [3] Infant deaths per 1,000 live births. [4] Active, nonfederal physicians as of December 31. Data subject to copyright; see below for source citation. [5] Per 100,000 resident population estimated as of July 1 of the year shown. [6] Nonfederal, short-stay (average length of stay less than 30 days) hospitals except hospital units of institutions. Data subject to copyright; see below for source citation. [7] SIC 805 includes skilled nursing care facilities; intermediate care facilities; and nursing and personal care, not elsewhere classified. [8] Full- and part-time employees on the payroll in the pay period including March 12. [9] Unduplicated count of persons enrolled in either hospital and/or supplemental medical insurance as of July 1. State totals include data not distributed by county. [10] Includes disabled, not shown separately. [11] 20 to 99 employees. [12] 250 to 499 employees. [13] 100 to 249 employees.

Sources: Births—U.S. National Center for Health Statistics, "Vital Statistics of the United States, Vol. I, Natality," annual, and unpublished data. Deaths—U.S. National Center for Health Statistics, "Vital Statistics of the United States, Vol. II, Mortality," annual, and unpublished data. Physicians—American Medical Association, Chicago, IL, "Physician Characteristics and Distribution in the U.S.," annual (copyright). Community Hospitals—Health Forum, LLC, an American Hospital Association Company, Chicago, IL, "Hospital Statistics" 2000 edition and unpublished data (copyright). Nursing and Personal Care Facilities—U.S. Census Bureau, County Business Patterns 1997 on CD-ROM (related Internet site <http://www.census.gov/epcd/cbp/view/cbpview.html>). Medicare—U.S. Health Care Financing Administration; "Medicare County Enrollment as of July 1, 1999 - Aged and Disabled 3/2000 update," <http://www.hcfa.gov/stats/enroll/default.htm>.

Table B–4. Counties — **Vital Statistics and Health**–Con.

[Includes U.S., states, and 3,142 counties or county equivalents defined as of January 1, 1992. For changes to these areas since then, see appendix B. Geographic Information]

County	Births, 1997 Number	Births, 1997 Rate[1]	Deaths, 1997 Total Number	Deaths, 1997 Total Rate[1]	Deaths, 1997 Infant[2] Number	Deaths, 1997 Infant Rate[3]	Physicians,[4] 1999 Number	Physicians Rate[5]	Community hospitals,[6] 1998 Number	Beds Number	Beds Rate[5]	Nursing and personal care facilities,[7] 1997 Establishments	Nursing Employees[8]	Medicare program enrollment,[9] 1999 Total[10]	Medicare Aged
NEW HAMPSHIRE	14 313	12.2	9 458	8.1	62	4.3	2 813	234	28	2 841	240	139	8 869	166 751	144 530
Belknap	538	10.3	521	10.0	3	5.6	117	218	1	117	221	6	633	10 313	9 012
Carroll....................	410	10.6	427	11.0	2	4.9	69	172	2	162	411	6	(11)	8 355	7 452
Cheshire.................	770	10.7	629	8.8	7	9.1	115	159	1	141	196	11	737	11 105	9 783
Coos	337	10.2	416	12.5	2	5.9	63	193	3	122	371	3	320	7 273	6 273
Grafton..................	807	10.4	693	8.9	1	1.2	715	910	5	505	645	7	599	12 247	10 890
Hillsborough	4 938	13.8	2 671	7.5	22	4.5	700	191	5	806	222	62	2 913	45 536	38 956
Merrimack	1 373	10.8	1 109	8.8	4	2.9	352	271	4	368	288	14	1 034	18 940	16 303
Rockingham	3 364	12.6	1 785	6.7	7	2.1	434	158	4	392	145	19	1 601	31 658	27 523
Strafford	1 327	12.2	800	7.4	11	8.3	174	157	2	185	169	8	640	14 256	12 221
Sullivan	449	11.3	407	10.2	3	6.7	74	184	1	43	108	3	(11)	6 890	5 975
NEW JERSEY	113 279	14.1	72 137	9.0	710	6.3	24 525	301	83	26 050	320	629	52 372	1 194 539	1 064 754
Atlantic	3 490	14.8	2 403	10.2	26	7.4	483	202	4	749	315	27	1 878	37 333	32 834
Bergen	10 697	12.6	7 537	8.9	50	4.7	4 298	501	6	2 896	339	68	4 306	140 168	129 762
Burlington	5 178	12.3	3 220	7.7	28	5.4	1 014	239	4	923	219	23	3 116	56 371	50 286
Camden..................	7 180	14.2	4 665	9.2	60	8.4	1 556	309	6	1 767	350	24	3 427	72 152	63 113
Cape May	1 145	11.7	1 242	12.7	11	9.6	112	114	1	206	210	17	943	21 847	19 617
Cumberland.............	1 875	13.3	1 356	9.6	21	11.2	201	143	2	491	350	14	1 407	22 159	18 534
Essex	12 326	16.4	7 395	9.9	114	9.2	3 130	419	11	3 731	499	62	5 469	102 848	87 999
Gloucester	3 189	13.0	2 011	8.2	14	4.4	255	102	1	239	96	24	1 510	30 868	26 918
Hudson	8 719	15.7	4 775	8.6	73	8.4	1 154	209	9	2 512	454	14	1 773	72 790	63 029
Hunterdon	1 444	12.0	727	6.0	7	4.8	297	238	1	176	144	12	547	13 318	11 855
Mercer	4 453	13.5	3 004	9.1	38	8.5	1 197	359	5	1 373	414	30	2 108	51 102	44 060
Middlesex...............	9 854	13.9	5 552	7.8	45	4.6	2 410	336	6	1 829	257	29	2 806	96 143	86 041
Monmouth	8 152	13.7	5 146	8.6	51	6.3	1 937	317	4	2 126	352	57	3 553	86 022	77 126
Morris	6 262	13.8	3 263	7.2	25	4.0	1 580	341	3	2 317	505	32	3 225	57 136	52 261
Ocean	6 162	12.8	6 511	13.5	35	5.7	708	142	4	958	195	47	4 615	116 856	108 066
Passaic	7 758	16.1	4 257	8.8	42	5.4	1 100	227	5	1 467	304	28	3 067	65 020	56 787
Salem	776	11.9	702	10.8	3	3.9	67	104	1	122	188	6	313	10 512	9 241
Somerset	4 234	15.3	1 953	7.1	12	2.8	1 240	430	1	297	105	35	2 698	31 666	28 935
Sussex	1 868	13.2	969	6.8	5	2.7	179	124	1	162	113	19	1 001	15 056	12 979
Union	7 251	14.6	4 563	9.2	52	7.2	1 469	295	6	1 713	343	49	3 743	79 780	71 539
Warren	1 266	12.9	886	9.0	7	5.5	138	138	2	299	303	12	867	15 204	13 630
NEW MEXICO	26 871	15.6	12 653	7.3	164	6.1	3 717	214	36	3 409	201	147	9 033	229 124	196 179
Bernalillo	7 933	15.1	3 872	7.4	41	5.2	2 081	398	10	1 454	277	65	4 184	69 080	59 880
Catron....................	23	8.2	22	7.9	–	–	4	140	–	–	–	–	647	566	
Chaves...................	903	14.4	566	9.0	13	14.4	98	157	2	197	315	5	412	10 041	8 636
Cibola....................	431	16.5	199	7.6	3	7.0	13	48	1	22	83	3	206	2 329	1 890
Colfax....................	167	12.2	141	10.3	2	12.0	21	154	1	68	501	3	(11)	2 540	2 216
Curry.....................	890	19.1	364	7.8	11	12.4	50	115	1	74	165	8	331	5 848	4 958
DeBaca...................	23	9.8	29	12.4	1	43.5	1	42	1	17	720	1	(12)	583	525
Dona Ana................	2 968	17.8	966	5.8	15	5.1	231	136	1	228	135	5	473	19 601	17 089
Eddy......................	791	14.9	554	10.4	9	11.4	45	85	2	151	283	7	710	8 686	7 439
Grant	459	14.6	307	9.8	1	2.2	57	182	1	59	187	2	(13)	5 421	4 700
Guadalupe	54	13.2	36	8.8	–	–	2	50	–	–	–	–	790	616	
Harding...................	7	7.8	12	13.4	–	–	–	–	–	–	–	–	251	234	
Hidalgo...................	78	12.5	49	7.8	–	–	1	17	–	–	–	1	(12)	842	702
Lea........................	933	16.6	515	9.2	4	4.3	48	87	2	169	299	5	331	7 692	6 566
Lincoln	186	11.6	138	8.6	–	–	25	149	1	31	189	2	(11)	3 318	2 981
Los Alamos	203	11.1	83	4.6	–	–	44	241	1	47	257	2	(12)	2 112	2 015
Luna	385	16.3	267	11.3	5	13.0	17	70	1	119	496	–	–	4 598	4 047
McKinley	1 357	20.2	389	5.8	8	5.9	118	176	1	113	168	2	(11)	5 786	4 860
Mora	54	11.3	27	5.6	1	18.5	1	20	–	–	–	–	–	908	739
Otero	899	16.2	389	7.0	3	3.3	56	103	1	73	134	2	(11)	7 266	6 325
Quay......................	113	11.2	129	12.8	–	–	7	71	1	37	370	3	(12)	2 098	1 788
Rio Arriba	653	17.4	304	8.1	5	7.7	29	76	1	80	211	1	(12)	5 277	4 085
Roosevelt................	276	15.2	115	6.3	1	3.6	7	40	–	–	–	–	–	2 562	2 229
Sandoval	1 309	15.2	500	5.8	11	8.4	121	134	–	–	–	5	(11)	10 004	8 718
San Juan	1 856	17.9	607	5.9	11	5.9	149	136	1	168	158	4	289	11 422	9 607
San Miguel..............	373	12.9	251	8.7	4	10.7	36	126	1	54	188	2	(11)	4 271	3 300
Santa Fe	1 586	13.0	722	5.9	5	3.2	351	283	1	202	164	13	755	14 644	12 522
Sierra	128	11.7	226	20.7	1	7.8	16	145	1	32	291	1	(11)	3 521	3 095
Socorro...................	249	15.3	121	7.4	2	8.0	12	73	1	30	184	1	(12)	2 006	1 655
Taos	352	13.3	202	7.6	2	5.7	40	148	1	34	127	2	(11)	4 012	3 270
Torrance..................	212	14.4	89	6.0	1	4.7	1	6	–	–	–	–	–	1 742	1 390
Union	50	12.4	46	11.4	–	–	5	128	1	30	753	–	–	877	790
Valencia	970	15.6	416	6.7	4	4.1	30	46	–	–	–	1	(11)	8 165	6 598

[1] Per 1,000 resident population estimated as of July 1, 1997.   [2] Deaths of infants under 1 year old.   [3] Infant deaths per 1,000 live births.   [4] Active, nonfederal physicians as of December 31. Data subject to copyright; see below for source citation.   [5] Per 100,000 resident population estimated as of July 1 of the year shown.   [6] Nonfederal, short-stay (average length of stay less than 30 days) hospitals except hospital units of institutions. Data subject to copyright; see below for source citation.   [7] SIC 805 includes skilled nursing care facilities; intermediate care facilities; and nursing and personal care, not elsewhere classified.   [8] Full- and part-time employees on the payroll in the pay period including March 12.   [9] Unduplicated count of persons enrolled in either hospital and/or supplemental medical insurance as of July 1. State totals include data not distributed by county.   [10] Includes disabled, not shown separately.   [11] 100 to 249 employees.   [12] 20 to 99 employees.   [13] 250 to 499 employees.

Sources: Births—U.S. National Center for Health Statistics, "Vital Statistics of the United States, Vol. I, Natality," annual, and unpublished data.   Deaths—U.S. National Center for Health Statistics, "Vital Statistics of the United States, Vol. II, Mortality," annual, and unpublished data.   Physicians—American Medical Association, Chicago, IL, "Physician Characteristics and Distribution in the U.S.," annual (copyright).   Community Hospitals—Health Forum, LLC, an American Hospital Association Company, Chicago, IL, "Hospital Statistics" 2000 edition and unpublished data (copyright).   Nursing and Personal Care Facilities—U.S. Census Bureau, County Business Patterns 1997 on CD-ROM (related Internet site <http://www.census.gov/epcd/cbp/view/cbpview.html>).   Medicare—U.S. Health Care Financing Administration; "Medicare County Enrollment as of July 1, 1999 - Aged and Disabled 3/2000 update," <http://www.hcfa.gov/stats/enroll/default.htm>.

[Includes U.S., states, and 3,142 counties or county equivalents defined as of January 1, 1992. For changes to these areas since then, see appendix B. Geographic Information]

County	Births, 1997 Number	Births, 1997 Rate[1]	Deaths, 1997 Total Number	Deaths, 1997 Total Rate[1]	Deaths, 1997 Infant[2] Number	Deaths, 1997 Infant[2] Rate[3]	Physicians,[4] 1999 Number	Physicians,[4] 1999 Rate[5]	Community hospitals,[6] 1998 Number	Community hospitals,[6] 1998 Beds Number	Community hospitals,[6] 1998 Beds Rate[5]	Nursing and personal care facilities,[7] 1997 Estab-lishments	Nursing and personal care facilities,[7] 1997 Em-ployees[8]	Medicare program enrollment,[9] 1999 Total[10]	Medicare program enrollment,[9] 1999 Aged
NEW YORK	257 238	14.2	158 653	8.7	1 727	6.7	71 840	395	222	68 511	377	2 005	145 728	2 694 015	2 333 581
Albany	3 260	11.1	2 844	9.7	20	6.1	1 572	538	4	1 196	408	55	4 213	45 195	39 287
Allegany	556	10.9	479	9.4	3	5.4	46	91	1	70	138	13	546	7 888	6 721
Bronx	22 451	18.9	10 726	9.0	176	7.8	3 216	269	10	4 280	359	95	14 940	145 145	121 479
Broome	2 210	11.2	2 093	10.6	18	8.1	529	271	2	700	356	8	1 660	38 140	32 964
Cattaraugus	1 042	12.2	888	10.4	10	9.6	124	147	2	274	323	4	355	14 541	12 414
Cayuga	939	11.4	809	9.8	6	6.4	97	119	1	306	372	5	582	12 701	11 084
Chautauqua	1 627	11.7	1 504	10.8	13	8.0	197	143	4	642	464	12	1 325	25 821	22 544
Chemung	1 030	11.1	985	10.6	5	4.9	240	262	2	471	511	16	811	16 581	14 130
Chenango	609	11.8	528	10.2	3	4.9	56	110	1	138	271	11	404	8 823	7 443
Clinton	790	9.9	653	8.2	12	15.2	156	196	1	400	501	26	599	10 703	8 823
Columbia	666	10.5	694	11.0	4	6.0	95	151	1	244	387	9	1 053	11 084	9 569
Cortland	560	11.6	436	9.1	2	3.6	56	117	1	193	400	10	524	6 955	5 863
Delaware	497	10.7	554	11.9	4	8.0	47	101	3	151	326	8	346	9 158	7 910
Dutchess	3 405	12.9	2 137	8.1	17	5.0	659	246	3	634	239	76	3 057	39 721	33 068
Erie	11 662	12.4	10 135	10.7	96	8.2	3 501	378	12	4 634	496	131	9 478	168 739	146 781
Essex	388	10.3	442	11.7	2	5.2	39	104	2	64	170	25	455	7 269	6 330
Franklin	466	9.5	449	9.1	5	10.7	84	173	2	228	468	28	443	7 714	6 193
Fulton	647	12.1	595	11.1	3	4.6	59	112	1	208	392	27	(11)	9 255	7 830
Genesee	755	12.4	568	9.3	11	14.6	76	126	2	152	250	5	327	9 791	8 530
Greene	489	10.3	486	10.2	2	4.1	33	68	–	–	–	3	(12)	8 567	7 364
Hamilton	46	8.9	54	10.4	–	–	5	96	–	–	–	–	–	1 248	1 157
Herkimer	699	10.8	723	11.1	6	8.6	42	66	2	348	544	20	1 050	11 886	10 342
Jefferson	1 734	15.4	904	8.0	9	5.2	167	152	3	308	277	9	1 067	15 149	12 768
Kings	39 758	17.5	19 243	8.5	345	8.7	6 566	289	15	7 667	338	185	12 456	291 465	252 305
Lewis	335	12.1	218	7.9	3	9.0	26	95	–	–	–	–	–	4 012	3 477
Livingston	704	10.7	492	7.5	6	8.5	62	94	1	49	75	7	(13)	8 725	7 566
Madison	826	11.7	522	7.4	4	4.8	96	135	2	345	486	12	397	10 055	8 658
Monroe	9 648	13.4	6 163	8.6	79	8.2	3 197	449	7	2 073	290	109	7 425	107 977	93 373
Montgomery	597	11.7	601	11.7	2	3.4	70	139	2	385	758	11	786	11 480	10 084
Nassau	17 139	13.2	11 026	8.5	83	4.8	7 976	611	15	6 556	504	83	8 962	219 926	198 632
New York	19 378	12.6	12 277	8.0	99	5.1	17 252	1 112	21	10 980	710	61	8 325	209 874	184 205
Niagara	2 641	12.0	2 296	10.5	28	10.6	288	133	5	722	332	23	1 956	39 463	33 945
Oneida	2 703	11.6	2 576	11.1	16	5.9	512	223	4	933	404	50	3 529	45 090	37 733
Onondaga	5 969	13.0	4 043	8.8	40	6.7	2 089	458	4	1 516	331	34	4 041	71 885	62 538
Ontario	1 171	11.8	909	9.1	8	6.8	199	199	3	1 042	1 047	10	259	14 939	12 938
Orange	4 917	15.1	2 470	7.6	32	6.5	607	182	6	907	275	42	1 869	41 060	33 786
Orleans	551	12.3	382	8.5	3	5.4	33	73	1	101	225	2	(12)	6 159	5 195
Oswego	1 447	11.6	1 013	8.1	7	4.8	90	73	2	275	222	5	710	17 331	14 119
Otsego	586	9.7	606	10.0	3	5.1	250	412	2	426	703	21	584	10 631	9 188
Putnam	1 226	13.3	588	6.4	10	8.2	153	161	1	164	176	1	(12)	10 200	8 665
Queens	31 599	15.9	16 710	8.4	183	5.8	6 012	301	10	4 019	202	129	12 139	282 485	251 394
Rensselaer	1 784	11.7	1 484	9.7	19	10.7	244	161	2	616	405	33	1 558	23 641	20 502
Richmond	5 717	14.2	3 430	8.5	34	5.9	1 623	393	3	1 302	320	26	4 504	57 651	47 331
Rockland	4 422	15.9	1 958	7.0	19	4.3	1 108	390	3	780	278	42	1 916	38 885	33 223
St. Lawrence	1 183	10.4	1 049	9.2	8	6.8	150	133	5	360	318	30	1 233	18 018	14 978
Saratoga	2 485	12.7	1 399	7.2	12	4.8	315	158	1	191	97	37	1 977	25 919	22 284
Schenectady	1 783	12.2	1 628	11.1	11	6.2	450	313	4	809	558	40	1 977	29 040	25 600
Schoharie	336	10.4	316	9.8	5	14.9	23	72	1	40	125	8	(12)	5 224	4 443
Schuyler	216	11.3	177	9.3	1	4.6	15	78	1	169	880	6	(12)	2 944	2 510
Seneca	371	11.5	311	9.7	2	5.4	21	66	–	–	–	8	395	5 468	4 639
Steuben	1 186	12.1	966	9.8	7	5.9	125	128	3	650	663	7	582	17 142	14 734
Suffolk	19 848	14.6	10 795	7.9	123	6.2	3 969	287	13	3 852	281	130	9 886	193 418	162 410
Sullivan	842	12.1	717	10.3	4	4.8	96	138	1	257	370	33	1 194	12 642	10 351
Tioga	640	12.2	437	8.3	3	4.7	34	65	–	–	–	3	(11)	7 337	6 387
Tompkins	855	8.8	594	6.1	7	8.2	215	220	1	145	149	12	1 052	10 344	9 010
Ulster	1 918	11.5	1 564	9.4	7	3.6	325	194	3	393	236	40	905	26 867	22 535
Warren	689	11.2	611	10.0	4	5.8	193	314	1	410	669	22	537	11 017	9 361
Washington	611	10.1	531	8.8	2	3.3	39	65	1	114	189	17	534	9 520	8 148
Wayne	1 266	13.4	725	7.7	13	10.3	73	76	1	267	281	4	331	14 801	11 871
Westchester	12 586	14.0	7 525	8.4	62	4.9	6 183	683	15	3 876	430	117	9 242	138 356	125 326
Wyoming	443	10.0	342	7.7	5	11.3	38	86	1	262	593	5	288	6 100	5 252
Yates	334	13.8	273	11.3	1	3.0	27	110	1	217	894	4	88	4 467	3 915

[1] Per 1,000 resident population estimated as of July 1, 1997.   [2] Deaths of infants under 1 year old.   [3] Infant deaths per 1,000 live births.   [4] Active, nonfederal physicians as of December 31. Data subject to copyright; see below for source citation.   [5] Per 100,000 resident population estimated as of July 1 of the year shown.   [6] Nonfederal, short-stay (average length of stay less than 30 days) hospitals except hospital units of institutions. Data subject to copyright; see below for source citation.   [7] SIC 805 includes skilled nursing care facilities; intermediate care facilities; and nursing and personal care, not elsewhere classified.   [8] Full- and part-time employees on the payroll in the pay period including March 12.   [9] Unduplicated count of persons enrolled in either hospital and/or supplemental medical insurance as of July 1. State totals include data not distributed by county.   [10] Includes disabled, not shown separately.   [11] 250 to 499 employees.   [12] 100 to 249 employees.   [13] 20 to 99 employees.

Sources: Births—U.S. National Center for Health Statistics, "Vital Statistics of the United States, Vol. I, Natality," annual, and unpublished data.   Deaths—U.S. National Center for Health Statistics, "Vital Statistics of the United States, Vol. II, Mortality," annual, and unpublished data.   Physicians—American Medical Association, Chicago, IL, "Physician Characteristics and Distribution in the U.S.," annual (copyright).   Community Hospitals—Health Forum, LLC, an American Hospital Association Company, Chicago, IL, "Hospital Statistics" 2000 edition and unpublished data (copyright).   Nursing and Personal Care Facilities—U.S. Census Bureau, County Business Patterns 1997 on CD-ROM (related Internet site <http://www.census.gov/epcd/cbp/view/cbpview.html>).   Medicare—U.S. Health Care Financing Administration; "Medicare County Enrollment as of July 1, 1999 - Aged and Disabled 3/2000 update," <http://www.hcfa.gov/stats/enroll/default.htm>.

[Includes U.S., states, and 3,142 counties or county equivalents defined as of January 1, 1992. For changes to these areas since then, see appendix B. Geographic Information]

County	Births, 1997		Deaths, 1997				Physicians,[4] 1999		Community hospitals,[6] 1998			Nursing and personal care facilities,[7] 1997		Medicare program enrollment,[9] 1999	
			Total		Infant[2]					Beds					
	Number	Rate[1]	Number	Rate[1]	Number	Rate[3]	Number	Rate[5]	Number	Number	Rate[5]	Estab- lishments	Em- ployees[8]	Total[10]	Aged
NORTH CAROLINA......	107 015	14.4	66 022	8.9	985	9.2	18 166	237	116	23 297	309	977	57 239	1 111 273	925 041
Alamance...............	1 728	14.6	1 209	10.2	18	10.4	184	152	1	319	267	20	939	21 429	18 473
Alexander...............	432	14.1	261	8.5	1	2.3	12	38	1	39	125	3	277	4 391	3 670
Alleghany...............	103	10.6	111	11.4	1	9.7	20	203	1	46	469	2	(11)	2 426	2 053
Anson..................	336	13.8	284	11.7	3	8.9	11	45	1	125	513	4	(12)	4 250	3 389
Ashe...................	261	10.9	267	11.2	2	7.7	22	91	1	115	478	2	(11)	4 907	4 155
Avery..................	174	11.1	172	11.0	–	–	31	196	1	90	573	3	(11)	3 269	2 781
Beaufort...............	553	12.5	514	11.6	5	9.0	68	151	2	145	326	7	329	8 430	6 865
Bertie.................	268	13.1	263	12.8	2	7.5	12	59	1	16	78	3	240	4 213	3 236
Bladen.................	460	15.0	340	11.1	3	6.5	17	55	1	58	188	10	186	5 361	4 032
Brunswick..............	752	11.4	644	9.8	7	9.3	50	70	2	96	140	5	335	13 352	11 073
Buncombe..............	2 249	11.7	2 055	10.7	19	8.4	703	358	2	789	406	43	3 028	35 895	30 548
Burke..................	1 055	12.9	751	9.2	11	10.4	151	182	2	468	568	11	694	13 083	10 618
Cabarrus...............	1 699	14.6	1 015	8.7	8	4.7	270	216	1	338	281	14	795	19 243	16 369
Caldwell...............	952	12.6	713	9.4	10	10.5	73	96	1	68	90	7	451	11 563	9 698
Camden................	30	4.5	62	9.3	1	33.3	4	58	–	–	–	–	–	1 031	882
Carteret...............	626	10.5	613	10.3	4	6.4	85	142	1	225	376	8	485	10 126	8 780
Caswell................	243	11.0	219	9.9	1	4.1	5	22	–	–	–	7	(11)	3 214	2 548
Catawba...............	1 799	13.8	1 190	9.1	11	6.1	311	232	2	538	406	12	1 084	20 180	17 422
Chatham...............	593	13.2	431	9.6	5	8.4	38	82	1	35	77	6	563	6 612	5 732
Cherokee..............	278	12.5	263	11.8	1	3.6	35	151	2	220	967	3	(12)	5 479	4 514
Chowan................	205	14.5	182	12.9	2	9.8	23	161	1	111	781	5	(11)	2 914	2 507
Clay...................	74	8.9	90	10.8	–	–	10	114	–	–	–	2	(11)	2 109	1 808
Cleveland..............	1 255	13.6	930	10.1	16	12.7	140	149	2	380	408	9	577	16 042	13 009
Columbus..............	780	14.9	570	10.9	5	6.4	45	85	1	117	222	8	596	9 890	7 267
Craven.................	1 620	18.4	751	8.5	10	6.2	209	234	1	258	290	8	806	14 626	12 421
Cumberland............	5 558	19.5	1 773	6.2	58	10.4	482	170	2	557	196	35	1 520	28 345	22 398
Currituck..............	165	9.6	157	9.1	1	6.1	3	16	–	–	–	1	(11)	2 399	2 052
Dare..................	310	11.1	212	7.6	3	9.7	26	88	–	–	–	1	(11)	4 229	3 777
Davidson..............	1 735	12.5	1 260	9.1	14	8.1	97	68	2	210	149	15	1 083	18 926	15 839
Davie.................	383	12.3	306	9.8	4	10.4	39	119	1	32	100	4	243	5 154	4 476
Duplin.................	760	17.7	543	12.7	8	10.5	31	71	1	80	186	9	324	7 116	5 678
Durham................	3 250	16.3	1 706	8.5	32	9.8	2 267	1 111	3	1 087	537	26	2 003	25 014	20 510
Edgecombe............	817	14.7	599	10.8	4	4.9	179	327	1	127	231	4	368	9 665	7 542
Forsyth................	4 280	15.0	2 586	9.0	61	14.3	1 575	545	3	1 560	542	29	2 758	44 787	39 053
Franklin...............	577	13.2	395	9.1	2	3.5	25	55	1	85	191	3	298	5 619	4 422
Gaston................	2 614	14.3	1 749	9.6	18	6.9	281	152	1	348	189	35	1 631	28 298	23 247
Gates.................	127	12.8	130	13.1	–	–	–	–	–	–	–	1	(12)	1 792	1 504
Graham................	95	12.4	103	13.5	–	–	5	66	–	–	–	1	(12)	1 639	1 313
Granville..............	563	13.4	384	9.1	5	8.9	44	99	1	128	292	4	(13)	6 600	4 930
Greene................	233	12.9	156	8.7	2	8.6	1	5	–	–	–	2	(11)	2 252	1 821
Guilford...............	5 320	13.9	3 352	8.8	53	10.0	1 013	259	2	1 418	366	59	3 356	55 746	48 450
Halifax................	772	13.7	641	11.3	11	14.2	62	111	2	257	456	6	326	11 560	8 669
Harnett................	1 376	17.1	689	8.5	13	9.4	46	54	2	144	175	6	394	9 611	7 717
Haywood...............	555	10.9	602	11.8	4	7.2	96	185	1	111	216	10	604	11 394	9 790
Henderson.............	926	11.6	1 016	12.7	7	7.6	199	242	2	315	388	13	695	20 651	18 548
Hertford...............	246	11.1	256	11.6	3	12.2	34	155	1	118	537	5	157	4 272	3 423
Hoke..................	530	18.1	198	6.8	4	7.5	8	26	–	–	–	2	(11)	2 465	1 815
Hyde..................	42	7.7	70	12.8	1	23.8	2	34	–	–	–	–	–	1 008	837
Iredell................	1 565	14.3	984	9.0	15	9.6	212	180	3	437	385	13	785	16 950	14 441
Jackson................	311	10.5	270	9.1	2	6.4	74	245	1	175	584	4	194	4 903	4 129
Johnston..............	1 719	16.8	886	8.7	13	7.6	67	60	1	127	119	10	698	13 859	10 668
Jones.................	93	9.9	98	10.4	1	10.8	8	86	–	–	–	1	(12)	1 789	1 441
Lee...................	728	15.1	441	9.2	7	9.6	81	164	1	137	278	10	355	8 411	7 002
Lenoir.................	796	13.5	696	11.8	14	17.6	96	163	1	245	416	11	814	11 344	8 899
Lincoln................	777	13.6	492	8.6	3	3.9	57	97	1	75	129	8	380	8 534	7 121
McDowell..............	391	9.9	324	8.2	8	20.5	32	79	1	65	162	8	427	7 020	5 782
Macon.................	290	10.5	389	14.0	–	–	52	180	2	155	548	2	(13)	7 074	6 284
Madison...............	221	12.0	205	11.1	4	18.1	11	58	–	–	–	3	(11)	3 489	2 913
Martin.................	430	16.3	324	12.3	3	7.0	17	65	1	49	187	6	215	4 733	3 834
Mecklenburg...........	9 665	15.7	4 116	6.7	72	7.4	1 972	304	8	2 310	366	80	4 231	67 832	58 411
Mitchell...............	155	10.5	217	14.7	1	6.5	14	95	1	45	304	1	(11)	3 310	2 728
Montgomery............	407	17.0	229	9.6	4	9.8	10	41	1	66	274	5	167	4 209	3 402
Moore.................	864	12.3	792	11.3	7	8.1	211	289	1	371	520	12	836	17 220	15 503
Nash..................	1 162	13.0	787	8.8	7	6.0	17	18	1	273	300	11	851	12 673	10 117
New Hanover...........	1 875	12.8	1 277	8.7	14	7.5	549	364	2	655	437	17	1 184	23 593	19 956
Northampton...........	241	11.3	287	13.5	–	–	5	24	–	–	–	3	204	4 565	3 580
Onslow................	3 218	22.8	697	4.9	25	7.8	157	110	1	133	93	10	(14)	11 422	9 396

[1] Per 1,000 resident population estimated as of July 1, 1997.   [2] Deaths of infants under 1 year old.   [3] Infant deaths per 1,000 live births.   [4] Active, nonfederal physicians as of December 31. Data subject to copyright; see below for source citation.   [5] Per 100,000 resident population estimated as of July 1 of the year shown.   [6] Nonfederal, short-stay (average length of stay less than 30 days) hospitals except hospital units of institutions. Data subject to copyright; see below for source citation.   [7] SIC 805 includes skilled nursing care facilities; intermediate care facilities; and nursing and personal care, not elsewhere classified.   [8] Full- and part-time employees on the payroll in the pay period including March 12.   [9] Unduplicated count of persons enrolled in either hospital and/or supplemental medical insurance as of July 1. State totals include data not distributed by county.   [10] Includes disabled, not shown separately.   [11] 100 to 249 employees.   [12] 20 to 99 employees. [13] 250 to 499 employees.   [14] 500 to 999 employees.

Sources: Births—U.S. National Center for Health Statistics, "Vital Statistics of the United States, Vol. I, Natality," annual, and unpublished data.   Deaths—U.S. National Center for Health Statistics, "Vital Statistics of the United States, Vol. II, Mortality," annual, and unpublished data.   Physicians—American Medical Association, Chicago, IL, "Physician Characteristics and Distribution in the U.S.," annual (copyright).   Community Hospitals—Health Forum, LLC, an American Hospital Association Company, Chicago, IL, "Hospital Statistics" 2000 edition and unpublished data (copyright).   Nursing and Personal Care Facilities—U.S. Census Bureau, County Business Patterns 1997 on CD-ROM (related Internet site <http://www.census.gov/epcd/cbp/view/cbpview.html>).   Medicare—U.S. Health Care Financing Administration; "Medicare County Enrollment as of July 1, 1999 - Aged and Disabled 3/2000 update," <http://www.hcfa.gov/stats/enroll/default.htm>.

[Includes U.S., states, and 3,142 counties or county equivalents defined as of January 1, 1992. For changes to these areas since then, see appendix B. Geographic Information]

County	Births, 1997 Number	Births, 1997 Rate[1]	Deaths, 1997 Total Number	Deaths, 1997 Total Rate[1]	Deaths, 1997 Infant[2] Number	Deaths, 1997 Infant[2] Rate[3]	Physicians,[4] 1999 Number	Physicians,[4] 1999 Rate[5]	Community hospitals,[6] 1998 Number	Community hospitals,[6] 1998 Beds Number	Community hospitals,[6] 1998 Beds Rate[5]	Nursing and personal care facilities,[7] 1997 Establishments	Nursing and personal care facilities,[7] 1997 Employees[8]	Medicare program enrollment,[9] 1999 Total[10]	Medicare program enrollment,[9] 1999 Aged
NORTH CAROLINA–Con.															
Orange	1 168	10.8	613	5.7	11	9.4	1 631	1 462	1	670	610	19	880	11 200	9 882
Pamlico	115	9.5	153	12.6	1	8.7	7	57	–	–	–	1	(11)	2 371	2 035
Pasquotank	445	12.6	342	9.7	9	20.2	82	230	1	147	413	4	335	5 541	4 712
Pender	455	12.0	358	9.4	4	8.8	22	55	1	86	218	4	215	6 115	4 904
Perquimans	103	9.3	149	13.5	3	29.1	5	44	–	–	–	1	(12)	2 429	2 092
Person	418	12.6	346	10.4	7	16.7	24	71	1	110	327	2	(11)	5 418	4 410
Pitt	1 791	14.4	1 028	8.3	25	14.0	789	617	1	684	540	16	719	15 761	12 480
Polk	145	8.7	229	13.7	2	13.8	27	160	1	73	436	3	331	4 464	4 040
Randolph	1 717	14.4	1 030	8.6	9	5.2	112	91	1	105	87	13	640	17 925	15 296
Richmond	647	14.1	514	11.2	2	3.1	40	87	2	215	468	5	286	8 357	6 163
Robeson	2 000	17.5	1 116	9.8	30	15.0	110	94	1	281	243	12	646	17 186	12 348
Rockingham	1 077	12.0	963	10.7	11	10.2	89	99	2	388	431	17	520	15 983	13 213
Rowan	1 545	12.5	1 356	11.0	14	9.1	146	115	1	222	178	15	1 274	18 139	15 309
Rutherford	773	12.8	702	11.7	7	9.1	80	130	1	261	428	10	524	11 215	9 341
Sampson	804	15.6	575	11.1	7	8.7	49	93	1	146	279	5	(13)	8 507	6 636
Scotland	564	15.9	391	11.0	10	17.7	57	159	1	174	487	4	256	5 145	3 783
Stanly	690	12.4	580	10.5	7	10.1	56	99	1	119	213	10	655	9 748	8 201
Stokes	522	12.2	377	8.8	4	7.7	18	41	1	93	215	4	348	5 328	4 383
Surry	910	13.7	709	10.7	10	11.0	74	109	2	304	452	13	497	13 219	11 135
Swain	157	12.9	140	11.5	1	6.4	14	113	1	42	342	2	(11)	2 379	1 898
Transylvania	259	9.3	325	11.7	7	27.0	52	180	1	90	316	3	(11)	6 744	5 992
Tyrrell	41	10.9	49	13.0	–	–	–	–	–	–	–	–	727	620
Union	1 912	18.0	775	7.3	15	7.8	91	79	1	223	202	7	357	10 986	9 281
Vance	648	15.6	452	10.9	12	18.5	47	111	1	102	243	6	347	7 196	5 470
Wake	8 639	15.7	3 040	5.5	75	8.7	1 414	241	3	1 394	244	52	2 776	54 809	46 353
Warren	188	10.4	226	12.5	1	5.3	6	32	–	–	–	1	(14)	3 413	2 706
Washington	190	13.9	142	10.4	3	15.8	5	37	1	33	244	2	(12)	2 549	2 079
Watauga	345	8.5	263	6.5	1	2.9	90	217	2	205	501	10	353	4 955	4 362
Wayne	1 649	14.7	984	8.8	22	13.3	166	149	1	262	234	17	822	16 621	12 840
Wilkes	760	12.2	609	9.8	5	6.6	53	83	1	130	207	9	494	10 255	8 422
Wilson	1 054	15.5	719	10.6	10	9.5	91	132	1	221	324	15	631	11 387	9 196
Yadkin	430	12.5	314	9.1	4	9.3	15	43	1	26	75	4	225	5 961	5 038
Yancey	187	11.4	159	9.7	2	10.7	18	107	–	–	–	3	(11)	3 619	3 074
NORTH DAKOTA	8 353	13.0	5 893	9.2	52	6.2	1 420	224	43	3 978	624	152	10 185	103 066	93 029
Adams	26	9.4	42	15.2	–	–	13	492	1	43	1 588	2	(12)	582	545
Barnes	117	9.7	160	13.3	–	–	9	76	1	50	418	5	(13)	2 565	2 341
Benson	130	19.0	69	10.1	1	7.7	1	15	–	–	–	1	(14)	1 085	986
Billings	10	9.1	3	2.7	–	–	–	–	–	–	–	–	–	85	D
Bottineau	73	9.8	97	13.1	1	13.7	5	69	1	67	918	3	(11)	1 603	1 509
Bowman	35	10.6	48	14.5	–	–	2	61	1	34	1 029	2	(11)	763	720
Burke	17	7.3	39	16.7	–	–	–	–	–	–	–	–	–	648	618
Burleigh	878	13.2	441	6.6	9	10.3	263	390	2	499	746	7	929	9 466	8 258
Cass	1 632	14.2	729	6.3	9	5.5	490	414	2	514	440	24	1 361	13 421	11 702
Cavalier	50	9.8	70	13.7	–	–	4	83	1	28	557	2	(11)	1 147	1 098
Dickey	54	9.6	65	11.5	–	–	5	88	1	30	531	2	(11)	1 217	1 149
Divide	15	6.2	48	19.8	–	–	2	87	1	29	1 225	1	(11)	580	564
Dunn	34	9.4	49	13.5	–	–	1	29	–	–	–	1	(11)	581	540
Eddy	21	7.4	41	14.4	–	–	–	–	–	–	–	3	(11)	684	610
Emmons	48	11.0	50	11.4	–	–	1	23	1	25	577	1	(12)	1 126	1 070
Foster	38	10.1	58	15.4	–	–	5	132	1	70	1 838	2	(12)	861	820
Golden Valley	21	11.0	16	8.4	–	–	1	56	–	–	–	–	–	451	432
Grand Forks	1 006	14.5	411	5.9	5	5.0	208	322	2	383	574	16	790	7 033	6 198
Grant	25	8.2	32	10.6	1	40.0	2	70	1	68	2 297	1	(12)	710	678
Griggs	28	9.8	46	16.1	–	–	2	72	1	69	2 424	–	–	711	679
Hettinger	20	6.8	33	11.2	–	–	–	–	–	–	–	1	(12)	780	735
Kidder	29	9.9	38	13.0	–	–	–	–	–	–	–	1	(12)	659	630
LaMoure	42	8.6	65	13.3	1	23.8	–	–	–	–	–	1	(12)	1 188	1 137
Logan	23	9.6	41	17.1	1	43.5	–	–	–	–	–	2	(12)	596	569
McHenry	61	9.9	71	11.5	–	–	1	17	–	–	–	1	(12)	1 522	1 399
McIntosh	31	8.7	74	20.7	–	–	2	59	2	92	2 660	1	(11)	1 211	1 170
McKenzie	84	14.6	66	11.5	–	–	2	36	1	24	422	1	(12)	844	772
McLean	90	9.2	132	13.5	–	–	4	42	2	77	793	2	(11)	2 170	1 988
Mercer	80	8.4	69	7.3	–	–	6	65	1	32	340	2	(11)	1 369	1 264
Morton	309	12.7	213	8.7	–	–	15	61	–	–	–	7	434	4 170	3 722
Mountrail	98	14.7	100	15.0	2	20.4	5	77	1	25	379	4	314	1 292	1 162
Nelson	38	9.9	70	18.2	–	–	3	82	1	19	510	3	254	1 151	1 092
Oliver	17	7.7	11	5.0	–	–	–	–	–	–	–	–	–	239	223
Pembina	92	10.7	126	14.6	4	43.5	5	60	1	89	1 049	2	(11)	1 794	1 676
Pierce	58	12.5	57	12.3	–	–	9	196	1	218	4 692	–	–	1 064	1 013

[1] Per 1,000 resident population estimated as of July 1, 1997. [2] Deaths of infants under 1 year old. [3] Infant deaths per 1,000 live births. [4] Active, nonfederal physicians as of December 31. Data subject to copyright; see below for source citation. [5] Per 100,000 resident population estimated as of July 1 of the year shown. [6] Nonfederal, short-stay (average length of stay less than 30 days) hospitals except hospital units of institutions. Data subject to copyright; see below for source citation. [7] SIC 805 includes skilled nursing care facilities; intermediate care facilities; and nursing and personal care, not elsewhere classified. [8] Full- and part-time employees on the payroll in the pay period including March 12. [9] Unduplicated count of persons enrolled in either hospital and/or supplemental medical insurance as of July 1. State totals include data not distributed by county. [10] Includes disabled, not shown separately. [11] 100 to 249 employees. [12] 20 to 99 employees. [13] 250 to 499 employees. [14] 0 to 19 employees.

Sources: Births—U.S. National Center for Health Statistics, "Vital Statistics of the United States, Vol. I, Natality," annual, and unpublished data. Deaths—U.S. National Center for Health Statistics, "Vital Statistics of the United States, Vol. II, Mortality," annual, and unpublished data. Physicians—American Medical Association, Chicago, IL, "Physician Characteristics and Distribution in the U.S.," annual (copyright). Community Hospitals—Health Forum, LLC, an American Hospital Association Company, Chicago, IL, "Hospital Statistics" 2000 edition and unpublished data (copyright). Nursing and Personal Care Facilities—U.S. Census Bureau, County Business Patterns 1997 on CD-ROM (related Internet site <http://www.census.gov/epcd/cbp/view/cbpview.html>). Medicare—U.S. Health Care Financing Administration; "Medicare County Enrollment as of July 1, 1999 - Aged and Disabled 3/2000 update," <http://www.hcfa.gov/stats/enroll/default.htm>.

Table B–4. Counties — **Vital Statistics and Health**–Con.

[Includes U.S., states, and 3,142 counties or county equivalents defined as of January 1, 1992. For changes to these areas since then, see appendix B. Geographic Information]

County	Births, 1997 Number	Rate¹	Deaths, 1997 Total Number	Rate¹	Infant² Number	Rate³	Physicians,⁴ 1999 Number	Rate⁵	Community hospitals,⁶ 1998 Number	Beds Number	Rate⁵	Nursing and personal care facilities,⁷ 1997 Establishments	Employees⁸	Medicare program enrollment,⁹ 1999 Total¹⁰	Aged
NORTH DAKOTA—Con.															
Ramsey	156	12.6	158	12.8	1	6.4	16	134	1	35	289	6	344	2 527	2 298
Ransom	55	9.4	93	16.0	–	–	5	87	1	64	1 107	2	(11)	1 245	1 156
Renville	26	9.2	29	10.2	–	–	2	71	–	–	–	1	(12)	568	537
Richland	230	12.6	177	9.7	1	4.3	21	117	–	–	–	10	362	2 807	2 599
Rolette	291	20.6	100	7.1	1	3.4	16	112	1	102	721	1	(12)	1 579	1 299
Sargent	47	10.6	52	11.8	1	21.3	–	–	–	–	–	1	(11)	838	782
Sheridan	15	8.5	19	10.8	1	66.7	–	–	–	–	–	–	–	462	436
Sioux	99	24.1	31	7.6	–	–	2	48	–	–	–	–	–	272	202
Slope	11	12.9	4	4.7	–	–	–	–	–	–	–	–	–	97	D
Stark	267	11.8	198	8.7	3	11.2	36	160	2	116	511	8	455	4 010	3 540
Steele	20	8.8	24	10.6	–	–	–	–	–	–	–	–	–	456	D
Stutsman	234	11.1	235	11.2	2	8.5	38	180	1	56	267	2	(13)	4 321	3 836
Towner	32	10.4	51	16.6	–	–	3	102	1	32	1 062	1	–	673	639
Traill	114	13.2	111	12.9	2	17.5	6	70	2	102	1 195	2	(11)	1 695	1 614
Walsh	130	9.5	189	13.8	1	7.7	14	105	2	37	273	7	413	2 678	2 408
Ward	1 025	17.4	435	7.4	5	4.9	147	252	2	632	1 080	9	470	8 207	7 257
Wells	38	7.3	89	17.0	–	–	6	118	1	165	3 168	1	(14)	1 441	1 353
Williams	233	11.5	218	10.7	–	–	42	213	2	152	754	1	(11)	3 712	3 296
OHIO	152 033	13.6	105 345	9.4	1 189	7.8	26 731	237	172	35 187	313	1 756	119 587	1 692 072	1 473 557
Adams	374	13.2	288	10.2	–	–	17	59	1	49	172	4	217	4 904	3 891
Allen	1 507	14.0	1 028	9.5	8	5.3	222	208	2	648	604	19	1 541	16 993	14 972
Ashland	630	12.3	466	9.1	2	3.2	48	92	1	70	136	6	525	7 520	6 826
Ashtabula	1 350	13.1	1 075	10.4	6	4.4	85	82	3	329	319	21	1 530	17 311	15 012
Athens	625	10.2	492	8.0	4	6.4	32	52	2	145	235	11	478	7 397	6 136
Auglaize	597	12.7	439	9.4	3	5.0	32	68	1	91	193	7	651	8 092	7 301
Belmont	765	10.7	909	12.7	6	7.8	79	111	3	299	416	13	1 113	14 188	12 494
Brown	525	13.1	391	9.7	3	5.7	25	60	1	53	130	13	591	5 441	4 460
Butler	4 492	13.7	2 495	7.6	36	8.0	410	123	4	656	198	46	2 540	40 559	34 333
Carroll	332	11.5	245	8.5	–	–	10	34	–	–	–	3	(11)	3 267	2 877
Champaign	500	13.1	358	9.4	3	6.0	20	52	1	20	52	3	212	5 353	4 545
Clark	1 923	13.2	1 608	11.0	15	7.8	199	137	2	418	288	21	1 833	24 229	20 628
Clermont	2 623	15.2	1 243	7.2	19	7.2	172	96	1	133	76	17	1 209	15 626	12 864
Clinton	572	14.5	348	8.8	2	3.5	66	162	1	93	232	7	340	5 976	5 147
Columbiana	1 332	12.0	1 143	10.3	16	12.0	85	76	2	321	288	36	1 175	19 577	17 188
Coshocton	443	12.3	397	11.0	4	9.0	21	58	1	151	418	8	422	6 009	5 105
Crawford	579	12.3	497	10.5	3	5.2	36	77	2	156	331	7	445	8 262	7 250
Cuyahoga	19 498	14.0	15 235	11.0	208	10.7	6 793	495	21	6 470	469	181	16 604	238 811	212 947
Darke	640	11.8	564	10.4	6	9.4	35	65	1	92	170	10	871	8 483	7 599
Defiance	540	13.5	324	8.1	2	3.7	52	131	2	104	261	4	265	5 712	4 991
Delaware	1 284	13.9	580	6.3	7	5.5	198	191	1	84	86	11	638	8 390	7 360
Erie	1 017	12.9	783	10.0	6	5.9	125	160	2	402	514	9	661	13 324	11 809
Fairfield	1 618	13.3	900	7.4	8	4.9	149	118	1	196	158	24	1 094	15 033	13 087
Fayette	390	13.7	345	12.1	3	7.7	16	56	–	–	–	6	417	4 309	3 740
Franklin	16 178	15.9	7 799	7.7	138	8.5	3 436	334	9	3 757	368	127	9 639	121 170	103 234
Fulton	573	13.8	370	8.9	2	3.5	27	64	1	172	411	6	337	6 390	5 739
Gallia	365	11.0	319	9.6	7	19.2	91	274	1	269	810	11	454	5 291	4 233
Geauga	1 231	14.1	612	7.0	7	5.7	109	122	2	376	424	7	828	9 141	8 405
Greene	1 615	11.1	1 069	7.3	4	2.5	232	156	1	150	101	17	1 219	14 701	12 863
Guernsey	569	14.0	479	11.8	2	3.5	49	120	1	113	276	7	300	7 196	5 982
Hamilton	12 027	14.1	8 435	9.9	111	9.2	3 785	450	12	3 006	355	167	11 177	134 956	117 138
Hancock	949	13.8	614	9.0	3	3.2	96	138	1	192	278	9	681	9 282	8 366
Hardin	412	13.0	294	9.3	2	4.9	18	57	1	51	161	5	127	4 738	4 144
Harrison	179	11.1	197	12.2	1	5.6	10	62	1	48	298	3	355	3 260	2 811
Henry	367	12.3	282	9.4	3	8.2	18	60	1	34	114	5	608	4 555	4 109
Highland	565	14.2	377	9.5	2	3.5	30	73	2	87	215	6	427	6 420	5 376
Hocking	328	11.4	261	9.1	3	9.1	15	51	1	92	318	7	236	4 060	3 361
Holmes	870	23.3	254	6.8	4	4.6	24	63	1	38	100	7	774	2 932	2 613
Huron	931	15.5	476	7.9	3	3.2	68	112	2	173	287	6	568	9 716	8 546
Jackson	428	13.2	312	9.6	2	4.7	11	34	1	58	178	9	309	5 251	4 092
Jefferson	824	10.8	999	13.1	8	9.7	92	125	1	364	488	18	831	16 324	14 198
Knox	607	11.5	503	9.6	8	13.2	57	106	1	75	140	13	735	8 372	7 250
Lake	2 755	12.2	1 898	8.4	15	5.4	322	142	1	374	165	23	1 941	35 298	31 877
Lawrence	811	12.6	682	10.6	6	7.4	46	71	1	219	340	7	663	11 115	8 720
Licking	1 795	13.8	1 239	9.5	13	7.2	129	95	1	239	177	22	1 569	18 470	16 131
Logan	605	13.2	419	9.1	2	3.3	45	96	1	72	155	11	469	7 218	6 411
Lorain	3 886	13.8	2 433	8.6	32	8.2	383	136	4	730	259	30	2 306	38 920	34 265
Lucas	6 590	14.6	4 438	9.8	44	6.7	1 645	368	8	2 441	544	58	4 415	67 781	57 687
Madison	493	12.1	351	8.6	10	20.3	32	77	1	46	112	2	(11)	5 393	4 651
Mahoning	3 017	11.7	3 145	12.2	35	11.6	710	281	3	821	322	46	3 849	52 028	46 271

¹ Per 1,000 resident population estimated as of July 1, 1997. ² Deaths of infants under 1 year old. ³ Infant deaths per 1,000 live births. ⁴ Active, nonfederal physicians as of December 31. Data subject to copyright; see below for source citation. ⁵ Per 100,000 resident population estimated as of July 1 of the year shown. ⁶ Nonfederal, short-stay (average length of stay less than 30 days) hospitals except hospital units of institutions. Data subject to copyright; see below for source citation. ⁷ SIC 805 includes skilled nursing care facilities; intermediate care facilities; and nursing and personal care, not elsewhere classified. ⁸ Full- and part-time employees on the payroll in the pay period including March 12. ⁹ Unduplicated count of persons enrolled in either hospital and/or supplemental medical insurance as of July 1. State totals include data not distributed by county. ¹⁰ Includes disabled, not shown separately. ¹¹ 100 to 249 employees. ¹² 20 to 99 employees. ¹³ 250 to 499 employees. ¹⁴ 0 to 19 employees.

Sources: Births—U.S. National Center for Health Statistics, "Vital Statistics of the United States, Vol. I, Natality," annual, and unpublished data. Deaths—U.S. National Center for Health Statistics, "Vital Statistics of the United States, Vol. II, Mortality," annual, and unpublished data. Physicians—American Medical Association, Chicago, IL, "Physician Characteristics and Distribution in the U.S.," annual (copyright). Community Hospitals—Health Forum, LLC, an American Hospital Association Company, Chicago, IL, "Hospital Statistics" 2000 edition and unpublished data (copyright). Nursing and Personal Care Facilities—U.S. Census Bureau, County Business Patterns 1997 on CD-ROM (related Internet site <http://www.census.gov/epcd/cbp/view/cbpview.html>). Medicare—U.S. Health Care Financing Administration; "Medicare County Enrollment as of July 1, 1999 - Aged and Disabled 3/2000 update," <http://www.hcfa.gov/stats/enroll/default.htm>.

Table B–4. Counties — Vital Statistics and Health–Con.

[Includes U.S., states, and 3,142 counties or county equivalents defined as of January 1, 1992. For changes to these areas since then, see appendix B. Geographic Information]

County	Births, 1997 Number	Births, 1997 Rate[1]	Deaths, 1997 Total Number	Deaths, 1997 Total Rate[1]	Deaths, 1997 Infant[2] Number	Deaths, 1997 Infant[2] Rate[3]	Physicians,[4] 1999 Number	Physicians,[4] 1999 Rate[5]	Community hospitals,[6] 1998 Number	Community hospitals,[6] 1998 Beds Number	Community hospitals,[6] 1998 Beds Rate[5]	Nursing and personal care facilities,[7] 1997 Establishments	Nursing and personal care facilities,[7] 1997 Employees[8]	Medicare program enrollment,[9] 1999 Total[10]	Medicare program enrollment,[9] 1999 Aged
OHIO—Con.															
Marion	844	12.5	637	9.5	7	8.3	116	173	2	216	322	14	469	10 610	8 842
Medina	1 832	12.9	993	7.0	5	2.7	198	134	3	203	141	32	1 642	16 842	15 245
Meigs	271	11.3	299	12.5	3	11.1	6	25	1	69	288	10	268	3 804	3 132
Mercer	575	14.0	353	8.6	5	8.7	37	90	1	58	141	9	494	6 508	5 897
Miami	1 256	12.9	851	8.7	4	3.2	119	121	1	214	218	4	471	14 873	13 006
Monroe	154	10.1	168	11.0	1	6.5	9	58	–	–	–	1	(11)	2 722	2 353
Montgomery	7 800	13.6	5 481	9.6	63	8.1	1 655	292	6	2 168	380	67	5 664	92 510	78 914
Morgan	151	10.4	166	11.4	1	6.6	1	7	1	178	1 225	4	259	2 272	1 900
Morrow	372	12.0	227	7.3	3	8.1	10	31	1	75	238	8	274	3 440	2 828
Muskingum	1 168	13.8	880	10.4	9	7.7	135	159	1	467	552	13	958	14 490	12 074
Noble	127	8.8	118	8.2	1	7.9	1	7	–	–	–	1	(11)	1 673	1 440
Ottawa	426	10.5	380	9.3	5	11.7	39	94	1	33	80	6	573	7 839	7 029
Paulding	275	13.6	186	9.2	3	10.9	7	35	1	51	254	2	(11)	2 844	2 451
Perry	468	13.7	323	9.4	3	6.4	6	18	–	–	–	19	342	5 301	4 304
Pickaway	580	11.0	443	8.4	4	6.9	28	52	1	86	161	4	370	6 274	5 297
Pike	357	13.0	312	11.3	2	5.6	20	71	1	40	144	15	502	4 233	3 409
Portage	1 838	12.2	1 040	6.9	9	4.9	131	86	1	131	87	19	1 179	18 107	16 056
Preble	498	11.6	364	8.5	1	2.0	11	25	–	–	–	6	354	6 121	5 217
Putnam	505	14.4	290	8.3	3	5.9	8	23	–	–	–	5	382	5 016	4 617
Richland	1 678	12.9	1 204	9.3	10	6.0	187	144	1	309	238	22	1 107	21 022	18 166
Ross	962	12.8	715	9.5	4	4.2	92	121	1	161	213	17	529	10 758	8 869
Sandusky	860	13.8	553	8.9	7	8.1	44	71	3	348	561	23	644	8 818	7 748
Scioto	1 074	13.2	970	11.9	8	7.4	100	124	1	281	348	23	1 215	14 841	11 660
Seneca	737	12.2	547	9.1	10	13.6	61	102	2	110	183	18	1 076	10 978	9 404
Shelby	705	14.9	366	7.7	4	5.7	42	88	1	142	299	2	(12)	6 213	5 420
Stark	4 819	12.9	3 847	10.3	36	7.5	775	208	5	1 623	435	68	4 724	66 417	59 354
Summit	7 230	13.5	5 135	9.6	45	6.2	1 478	275	6	1 846	344	105	5 274	83 638	74 227
Trumbull	2 731	12.0	2 344	10.3	31	11.4	253	112	3	462	204	24	2 168	38 330	33 618
Tuscarawas	1 194	13.6	911	10.3	10	8.4	84	95	2	134	151	19	1 407	14 987	13 443
Union	529	13.6	303	7.8	6	11.3	25	61	1	145	364	3	168	3 800	3 306
Van Wert	334	11.0	324	10.7	2	6.0	21	70	1	100	332	4	383	4 453	4 028
Vinton	185	15.4	150	12.5	1	5.4	–	–	–	–	–	3	(11)	1 761	1 380
Warren	2 037	14.6	928	6.6	9	4.4	184	120	–	–	–	22	1 949	15 370	13 181
Washington	727	11.4	682	10.7	4	5.5	69	109	2	182	287	6	581	10 690	9 251
Wayne	1 558	14.2	955	8.7	16	10.3	117	105	2	128	116	25	1 074	15 471	13 647
Williams	477	12.6	334	8.8	4	8.4	43	114	1	121	320	4	389	5 997	5 421
Wood	1 305	11.0	914	7.7	9	6.9	197	164	1	98	82	7	803	14 258	12 787
Wyandot	268	11.8	242	10.7	4	14.9	15	65	1	31	136	6	345	3 904	3 495
OKLAHOMA	48 269	14.6	33 944	10.2	361	7.5	5 614	167	109	11 022	330	517	29 694	503 506	436 048
Adair	383	19.0	201	10.0	2	5.2	14	68	–	–	–	2	(11)	3 149	2 491
Alfalfa	54	8.9	76	12.6	1	18.5	1	17	–	–	–	3	62	1 367	1 272
Atoka	172	12.9	166	12.4	1	5.8	4	30	1	25	188	2	(11)	2 153	1 821
Beaver	37	6.2	55	9.3	2	54.1	2	33	1	24	397	–	–	1 007	958
Beckham	276	14.3	280	14.5	2	7.2	30	152	2	128	642	7	298	3 256	2 858
Blaine	123	11.6	184	17.3	2	16.3	7	68	2	79	758	5	300	2 049	1 842
Bryan	467	13.6	429	12.5	6	12.8	28	80	1	103	297	6	397	6 536	5 505
Caddo	400	13.0	387	12.5	4	10.0	11	36	2	58	188	8	285	5 368	4 754
Canadian	1 068	12.7	543	6.4	10	9.4	45	52	1	54	63	8	427	8 153	7 221
Carter	601	13.6	578	13.0	3	5.0	58	130	1	199	449	9	497	8 713	7 482
Cherokee	575	15.0	413	10.7	3	5.2	38	96	1	86	220	4	273	5 404	4 546
Choctaw	216	14.2	206	13.6	–	–	5	33	1	38	252	3	215	3 334	2 733
Cimarron	47	15.3	39	12.7	–	–	1	34	1	61	2 040	–	–	613	574
Cleveland	2 371	12.0	1 102	5.6	10	4.2	257	126	1	271	135	19	1 067	16 084	13 734
Coal	78	12.8	81	13.3	–	–	4	65	1	95	1 575	1	(13)	1 203	1 006
Comanche	2 165	19.9	858	7.9	20	9.2	165	155	2	482	446	8	570	12 333	10 609
Cotton	82	12.2	102	15.2	1	12.2	2	30	–	–	–	2	(13)	1 253	1 117
Craig	175	12.1	172	11.9	–	–	15	104	1	36	249	9	(11)	3 202	2 610
Creek	897	13.5	690	10.4	6	6.7	30	44	3	144	215	7	376	8 699	7 210
Custer	358	14.0	290	11.3	4	11.2	27	106	2	95	372	5	365	3 847	3 425
Delaware	406	12.0	424	12.5	1	2.5	18	51	1	72	210	6	386	5 779	4 907
Dewey	36	7.2	106	21.3	2	55.6	4	82	1	18	366	–	–	1 096	1 005
Ellis	44	10.5	58	13.8	–	–	7	167	1	27	636	1	(13)	956	885
Garfield	767	13.5	681	12.0	6	7.8	113	198	2	344	604	10	816	10 223	9 006
Garvin	332	12.4	403	15.0	–	–	15	56	1	50	187	14	344	5 933	5 121
Grady	574	12.6	470	10.3	6	10.5	43	93	1	147	321	6	257	6 186	5 354
Grant	44	8.1	73	13.5	–	–	2	38	1			1	(13)	1 183	1 111
Greer	45	7.0	99	15.4	–	–	7	110	1	24	378	1	(13)	1 419	1 292
Harmon	41	11.6	51	14.5	1	24.4	1	30	1	11	316	–	–	732	654
Harper	26	7.2	51	14.1	–	–	2	56	1	25	696	1	(13)	873	815

[1] Per 1,000 resident population estimated as of July 1, 1997. [2] Deaths of infants under 1 year old. [3] Infant deaths per 1,000 live births. [4] Active, nonfederal physicians as of December 31. Data subject to copyright; see below for source citation. [5] Per 100,000 resident population estimated as of July 1 of the year shown. [6] Nonfederal, short-stay (average length of stay less than 30 days) hospitals except hospital units of institutions. Data subject to copyright; see below for source citation. [7] SIC 805 includes skilled nursing care facilities; intermediate care facilities; and nursing and personal care, not elsewhere classified. [8] Full- and part-time employees on the payroll in the pay period including March 12. [9] Unduplicated count of persons enrolled in either hospital and/or supplemental medical insurance as of July 1. State totals include data not distributed by county. [10] Includes disabled, not shown separately. [11] 100 to 249 employees. [12] 250 to 499 employees. [13] 20 to 99 employees.

Sources: Births—U.S. National Center for Health Statistics, "Vital Statistics of the United States, Vol. I, Natality," annual, and unpublished data. Deaths—U.S. National Center for Health Statistics, "Vital Statistics of the United States, Vol. II, Mortality," annual, and unpublished data. Physicians—American Medical Association, Chicago, IL, "Physician Characteristics and Distribution in the U.S.," annual (copyright). Community Hospitals—Health Forum, LLC, an American Hospital Association Company, Chicago, IL, "Hospital Statistics" 2000 edition and unpublished data (copyright). Nursing and Personal Care Facilities—U.S. Census Bureau, County Business Patterns 1997 on CD-ROM (related Internet site <http://www.census.gov/epcd/cbp/view/cbpview.html>). Medicare—U.S. Health Care Financing Administration; "Medicare County Enrollment as of July 1, 1999 - Aged and Disabled 3/2000 update," <http://www.hcfa.gov/stats/enroll/default.htm>.

[Includes U.S., states, and 3,142 counties or county equivalents defined as of January 1, 1992. For changes to these areas since then, see appendix B. Geographic Information]

County	Births, 1997 Number	Rate[1]	Deaths, 1997 Total Number	Rate[1]	Infant[2] Number	Rate[3]	Physicians,[4] 1999 Number	Rate[5]	Community hospitals,[6] 1998 Number	Beds Number	Rate[5]	Nursing and personal care facilities,[7] 1997 Establishments	Employees[8]	Medicare program enrollment,[9] 1999 Total[10]	Aged
OKLAHOMA—Con.															
Haskell	161	14.2	143	12.6	1	6.2	3	26	1	31	273	2	(11)	2 469	2 064
Hughes	166	11.8	199	14.2	1	6.0	5	36	1	27	191	2	(11)	3 071	2 616
Jackson	548	19.3	272	9.6	2	3.6	33	116	1	101	354	3	246	3 744	3 317
Jefferson	66	9.9	114	17.1	1	15.2	1	15	1	30	456	3	127	1 626	1 430
Johnston	125	12.1	149	14.4	–	–	5	48	1	27	262	2	(11)	1 855	1 527
Kay	665	14.2	635	13.6	4	6.0	61	131	2	124	266	8	403	9 280	8 350
Kingfisher	173	12.8	150	11.1	1	5.8	2	15	1	38	282	8	291	2 380	2 162
Kiowa	151	13.9	159	14.7	2	13.2	6	57	1	40	375	5	239	2 368	2 099
Latimer	121	11.8	135	13.1	1	8.3	6	59	1	33	321	3	79	1 452	1 209
Le Flore	674	14.5	540	11.6	4	5.9	26	56	1	72	154	8	485	8 248	6 505
Lincoln	386	12.4	349	11.2	5	13.0	10	31	2	39	125	5	233	4 764	4 106
Logan	355	11.9	282	9.4	1	2.8	13	43	1	32	106	10	463	3 786	3 338
Love	101	11.8	101	11.8	–	–	1	12	1	30	351	1	(12)	1 492	1 274
McClain	320	12.4	224	8.7	2	6.3	16	60	1	20	76	3	148	3 760	3 187
McCurtain	547	15.8	392	11.3	7	12.8	8	23	1	89	256	6	396	5 847	4 713
McIntosh	211	11.2	272	14.5	1	4.7	7	36	1	33	174	6	258	4 680	4 002
Major	91	11.7	99	12.7	–	–	3	39	1	31	397	1	(11)	1 473	1 351
Marshall	162	13.4	144	11.9	2	12.3	2	16	1	25	204	2	(12)	2 787	2 399
Mayes	518	14.0	396	10.7	3	5.8	12	31	1	34	90	9	231	5 956	5 123
Murray	146	11.8	182	14.7	2	13.7	11	88	1	35	284	3	191	2 381	2 054
Muskogee	1 047	15.0	871	12.5	13	12.4	109	156	1	222	317	16	850	12 537	10 585
Noble	155	13.7	143	12.7	1	6.5	4	35	1	28	246	5	287	1 888	1 628
Nowata	134	13.6	126	12.7	–	–	3	30	1	34	341	3	(11)	2 035	1 764
Okfuskee	161	14.2	139	12.2	1	6.2	4	36	–	–	–	3	316	2 259	1 865
Oklahoma	10 624	16.8	6 259	9.9	94	8.8	2 338	367	14	3 049	482	71	5 033	89 648	78 673
Okmulgee	498	12.9	493	12.8	3	6.0	20	52	3	145	375	8	519	6 798	5 786
Osage	422	9.9	398	9.4	2	4.7	10	23	3	295	688	5	(13)	3 622	3 143
Ottawa	451	14.7	447	14.6	4	8.9	28	91	1	123	398	7	344	7 183	6 191
Pawnee	221	13.6	179	11.0	1	4.5	4	24	2	49	299	2	(11)	2 751	2 316
Payne	825	12.7	482	7.4	5	6.1	88	135	2	168	257	9	433	7 963	6 978
Pittsburg	509	11.8	537	12.5	3	5.9	53	122	1	197	458	9	481	7 922	6 729
Pontotoc	485	14.0	424	12.2	3	6.2	62	179	1	139	401	13	397	6 352	5 330
Pottawatomie	870	14.2	732	12.0	8	9.2	69	110	2	175	281	12	745	9 734	8 378
Pushmataha	130	11.3	182	15.8	–	–	4	35	1	46	401	2	(11)	2 444	2 059
Roger Mills	32	9.0	44	12.3	1	31.3	4	111	1	15	419	1	(12)	709	658
Rogers	834	12.7	522	8.0	8	9.6	44	62	1	68	100	6	404	7 412	6 393
Seminole	369	14.8	331	13.2	5	13.6	10	41	1	32	129	7	501	4 958	4 089
Sequoyah	540	14.6	395	10.7	5	9.3	11	29	1	41	109	9	501	6 219	4 874
Stephens	585	13.5	561	12.9	1	1.7	34	79	1	100	230	9	457	8 308	7 439
Texas	286	15.9	155	8.6	–	–	12	65	1	35	189	1	(12)	2 230	2 042
Tillman	118	12.3	138	14.3	1	8.5	5	53	1	30	315	2	(11)	1 920	1 701
Tulsa	8 737	16.3	4 788	8.9	61	7.0	1 404	256	8	1 912	352	56	4 153	81 941	71 926
Wagoner	656	12.1	337	6.2	5	7.6	8	14	1	100	181	2	(11)	4 417	3 728
Washington	534	11.2	564	11.9	1	1.9	76	159	1	219	461	7	416	9 657	8 679
Washita	151	13.0	171	14.7	–	–	3	26	1	28	236	3	233	2 321	2 056
Woods	83	10.0	130	15.7	1	12.0	5	61	1	117	1 410	2	(11)	1 892	1 778
Woodward	265	14.2	191	10.3	1	3.8	15	81	1	68	365	9	157	2 801	2 469
OREGON	43 809	13.5	28 771	8.9	256	5.8	7 519	227	60	6 809	207	561	22 470	483 898	428 641
Baker	177	10.8	225	13.7	1	5.6	21	129	1	134	817	–	–	3 447	3 044
Benton	838	10.8	435	5.6	3	3.6	177	229	1	127	163	16	475	7 996	7 282
Clackamas	4 082	12.4	2 527	7.6	30	7.3	669	198	4	441	132	45	1 226	38 834	35 020
Clatsop	416	11.7	365	10.3	1	2.4	42	119	2	87	246	11	127	6 124	5 326
Columbia	508	11.7	355	8.2	2	3.9	10	22	–	–	–	6	160	5 913	5 175
Coos	673	10.8	815	13.0	4	5.9	114	185	3	152	245	12	562	13 239	11 543
Crook	223	13.2	172	10.2	1	4.5	9	51	1	30	173	3	72	3 039	2 682
Curry	158	7.5	286	13.6	–	–	22	104	1	24	114	7	149	6 282	5 676
Deschutes	1 316	12.9	763	7.5	6	4.6	228	206	2	229	217	8	278	16 209	14 590
Douglas	1 129	11.1	1 176	11.6	12	10.6	133	131	3	252	247	19	580	20 045	17 668
Gilliam	19	9.7	16	8.1	–	–	2	96	–	–	–	1	(14)	416	391
Grant	95	11.9	88	11.0	1	10.5	6	76	1	73	908	1	(14)	1 473	1 323
Harney	72	10.3	78	11.1	–	–	6	82	1	36	500	1	(12)	1 276	1 124
Hood River	300	15.6	167	8.7	1	3.3	48	241	1	31	158	4	159	2 737	2 512
Jackson	2 088	12.2	1 707	10.0	11	5.3	376	214	3	415	240	21	1 012	31 590	28 117
Jefferson	311	18.8	143	8.6	1	3.2	10	59	1	102	609	2	(14)	2 875	2 559
Josephine	718	9.8	916	12.5	1	1.4	102	136	1	150	202	9	824	16 934	15 003
Klamath	807	10.8	665	10.6	8	9.9	119	188	1	238	377	13	294	10 491	9 188
Lake	74	10.2	72	9.9	–	–	5	70	1	68	950	–	–	1 512	1 347
Lane	3 573	11.5	2 686	8.6	17	4.8	660	210	3	522	167	52	2 207	47 785	42 229
Lincoln	450	9.9	502	11.0	2	4.4	58	129	2	71	157	11	138	9 737	8 702

[1] Per 1,000 resident population estimated as of July 1, 1997. [2] Deaths of infants under 1 year old. [3] Infant deaths per 1,000 live births. [4] Active, nonfederal physicians as of December 31. Data subject to copyright; see below for source citation. [5] Per 100,000 resident population estimated as of July 1 of the year shown. [6] Nonfederal, short-stay (average length of stay less than 30 days) hospitals except hospital units of institutions. Data subject to copyright; see below for source citation. [7] SIC 805 includes skilled nursing care facilities; intermediate care facilities; and nursing and personal care, not elsewhere classified. [8] Full- and part-time employees on the payroll in the pay period including March 12. [9] Unduplicated count of persons enrolled in either hospital and/or supplemental medical insurance as of July 1. State totals include data not distributed by county. [10] Includes disabled, not shown separately. [11] 100 to 249 employees. [12] 20 to 99 employees. [13] 250 to 499 employees. [14] 0 to 19 employees.

Sources: Births—U.S. National Center for Health Statistics, "Vital Statistics of the United States, Vol. I, Natality," annual, and unpublished data. Deaths—U.S. National Center for Health Statistics, "Vital Statistics of the United States, Vol. II, Mortality," annual, and unpublished data. Physicians—American Medical Association, Chicago, IL, "Physician Characteristics and Distribution in the U.S.," annual (copyright). Community Hospitals—Health Forum, LLC, an American Hospital Association Company, Chicago, IL, "Hospital Statistics" 2000 edition and unpublished data (copyright). Nursing and Personal Care Facilities—U.S. Census Bureau, County Business Patterns 1997 on CD-ROM (related Internet site <http://www.census.gov/epcd/cbp/view/cbpview.html>). Medicare—U.S. Health Care Financing Administration; "Medicare County Enrollment as of July 1, 1999 - Aged and Disabled 3/2000 update," <http://www.hcfa.gov/stats/enroll/default.htm>.

[Includes U.S., states, and 3,142 counties or county equivalents defined as of January 1, 1992. For changes to these areas since then, see appendix B. Geographic Information]

County	Births, 1997 Number	Rate[1]	Deaths, 1997 Total Number	Rate[1]	Infant[2] Number	Rate[3]	Physicians,[4] 1999 Number	Rate[5]	Community hospitals,[6] 1998 Number	Beds Number	Rate[5]	Nursing and personal care facilities,[7] 1997 Establishments	Employees[8]	Medicare program enrollment,[9] 1999 Total[10]	Aged
OREGON—Con.															
Linn	1 427	13.8	1 011	9.8	10	7.0	114	108	2	120	115	10	659	16 976	14 897
Malheur	478	16.9	293	10.3	4	8.4	45	158	1	74	259	3	(11)	4 746	4 197
Marion	4 430	16.7	2 412	9.1	35	7.9	487	179	3	473	176	65	1 944	40 408	35 689
Morrow	147	15.4	77	8.1	1	6.8	1	10	1	43	432	1	(12)	1 261	1 097
Multnomah	9 012	14.4	5 699	9.1	45	5.0	3 256	514	9	1 910	303	101	5 662	88 920	77 285
Polk	699	11.7	483	8.1	4	5.7	20	32	1	44	72	8	609	8 566	7 711
Sherman	15	8.3	18	10.0	–	–	–	–	–	–	–	1	(12)	411	375
Tillamook	244	10.0	277	11.4	–	–	33	135	1	30	124	3	161	5 323	4 756
Umatilla	1 032	16.0	603	9.4	7	6.8	85	127	2	94	143	12	618	9 712	8 525
Union	299	11.9	252	10.1	4	13.4	42	169	1	62	249	7	153	4 073	3 633
Wallowa	63	8.4	90	12.0	–	–	6	83	1	55	750	–	–	1 510	1 365
Wasco	296	12.8	264	11.4	2	6.8	41	176	1	49	212	6	63	4 325	3 861
Washington	6 541	16.7	2 435	6.2	32	4.9	487	119	2	571	142	85	3 287	38 374	34 551
Wheeler	14	8.7	21	13.1	–	–	–	–	–	–	–	–	–	378	343
Yamhill	1 085	13.6	677	8.5	10	9.2	85	102	2	102	124	17	788	10 850	9 772
PENNSYLVANIA	144 224	12.0	127 925	10.6	1 098	7.6	35 148	293	212	44 739	373	2 027	119 728	2 088 116	1 864 828
Adams	977	11.4	813	9.5	2	2.0	77	88	1	99	114	8	1 186	12 543	11 428
Allegheny	14 715	11.5	15 169	11.8	104	7.1	6 474	515	28	7 831	618	242	11 380	244 854	222 382
Armstrong	791	10.8	851	11.6	3	3.8	58	79	1	210	286	20	236	15 850	14 024
Beaver	1 974	10.6	2 015	10.9	12	6.1	233	128	2	475	258	16	987	36 009	32 272
Bedford	566	11.5	506	10.3	2	3.5	35	70	1	59	119	6	(11)	9 064	8 109
Berks	4 343	12.3	3 718	10.5	41	9.4	671	187	3	903	254	22	2 673	60 126	54 844
Blair	1 406	10.7	1 545	11.8	11	7.8	272	209	5	519	398	18	1 371	24 773	22 090
Bradford	703	11.3	697	11.2	4	5.7	234	377	3	371	595	13	394	11 092	9 541
Bucks	7 161	12.3	4 732	8.1	42	5.9	1 330	224	5	1 209	206	109	5 526	77 746	69 804
Butler	2 090	12.4	1 624	9.6	13	6.2	207	120	1	239	140	14	1 983	26 668	23 648
Cambria	1 502	9.5	1 892	12.0	11	7.3	399	259	3	714	459	32	926	33 850	30 030
Cameron	69	12.2	55	9.7	1	14.5	3	54	–	–	–	1	(13)	1 305	1 182
Carbon	566	9.6	728	12.4	6	10.6	43	73	2	272	463	6	204	12 113	10 666
Centre	1 231	9.3	798	6.0	4	3.2	234	177	2	274	208	22	793	15 106	13 562
Chester	5 369	12.9	3 021	7.3	34	6.3	949	221	6	870	206	92	4 834	49 477	45 067
Clarion	413	9.9	416	10.0	3	7.3	16	38	1	86	206	14	432	6 895	5 926
Clearfield	855	10.6	883	10.9	4	4.7	119	147	2	304	377	8	1 217	14 828	13 002
Clinton	399	10.8	412	11.1	1	2.5	37	101	2	245	663	1	(11)	6 739	5 950
Columbia	627	9.8	643	10.0	2	3.2	92	144	2	457	715	10	749	11 792	10 508
Crawford	1 079	12.1	1 000	11.2	9	8.3	113	127	2	349	391	16	857	15 928	13 770
Cumberland	2 174	10.5	1 852	8.9	11	5.1	485	230	4	568	271	34	2 530	34 113	31 816
Dauphin	3 240	13.2	2 451	10.0	22	6.8	1 139	464	2	1 312	535	66	2 364	38 447	34 602
Delaware	6 804	12.5	5 662	10.4	37	5.4	1 951	360	4	1 094	202	110	8 421	91 421	83 200
Elk	403	11.6	366	10.5	1	2.5	44	128	2	255	737	16	257	6 588	5 979
Erie	3 476	12.4	2 689	9.6	28	8.1	532	192	8	1 254	451	79	2 670	44 902	39 667
Fayette	1 682	11.6	1 829	12.6	11	6.5	149	104	3	408	283	20	1 078	31 329	26 755
Forest	33	6.7	87	17.5	–	–	1	20	–	–	–	1	(13)	1 327	1 110
Franklin	1 604	12.6	1 171	9.2	7	4.4	163	127	2	267	208	8	1 208	20 828	19 044
Fulton	165	11.4	110	7.6	2	12.1	3	21	1	100	688	–	–	2 239	1 972
Greene	414	9.8	489	11.6	5	12.1	26	62	1	60	142	7	267	7 202	6 094
Huntingdon	469	10.5	407	9.1	2	4.3	47	105	1	104	232	8	358	7 432	6 583
Indiana	840	9.4	855	9.6	12	14.3	113	129	1	148	167	17	621	14 804	12 911
Jefferson	489	10.5	513	11.0	3	6.1	49	106	2	128	277	9	525	9 179	8 155
Juniata	301	13.7	214	9.8	3	10.0	5	23	–	–	–	6	276	3 468	3 128
Lackawanna	2 142	10.2	2 942	14.0	13	6.1	516	250	6	1 050	504	60	3 278	45 259	40 067
Lancaster	6 445	14.2	4 028	8.9	45	7.0	720	157	5	1 126	247	72	7 312	68 534	62 837
Lawrence	1 090	11.4	1 108	11.6	9	8.3	116	123	3	465	490	9	898	21 494	19 191
Lebanon	1 447	12.4	1 158	9.9	2	1.4	239	203	1	175	149	13	1 462	20 799	18 961
Lehigh	3 629	12.2	3 022	10.1	43	11.8	831	277	4	1 069	358	51	2 927	51 836	46 511
Luzerne	3 064	9.7	4 407	13.9	23	7.5	664	213	6	1 123	357	59	3 295	69 133	61 336
Lycoming	1 295	11.0	1 201	10.2	13	10.0	240	206	2	544	463	12	1 205	21 386	18 870
McKean	496	10.6	584	12.5	1	2.0	60	130	2	241	520	17	513	8 679	7 547
Mercer	1 352	11.1	1 418	11.6	12	8.9	176	145	3	571	469	13	1 163	24 230	21 513
Mifflin	574	12.2	511	10.9	3	5.2	63	135	1	179	381	4	543	8 336	7 272
Monroe	1 414	11.5	1 042	8.5	7	5.0	169	131	2	215	171	8	706	18 857	16 077
Montgomery	8 980	12.6	6 665	9.3	51	5.7	4 660	644	11	2 673	371	134	10 773	123 967	114 159
Montour	219	12.3	242	13.6	2	9.1	368	2 094	1	515	2 929	4	(14)	3 461	3 025
Northampton	2 803	10.9	2 364	9.2	17	6.1	655	252	2	797	308	31	1 816	46 507	41 924
Northumberland	939	9.9	1 266	13.3	9	9.6	73	78	2	161	171	28	1 113	20 035	17 589
Perry	508	11.5	346	7.8	3	5.9	18	41	–	–	–	6	333	6 012	5 329
Philadelphia	22 078	15.2	18 356	12.6	291	13.2	7 012	495	31	8 496	592	255	12 962	241 843	207 390
Pike	407	10.4	349	8.9	4	9.8	21	51	–	–	–	1	(13)	5 967	5 160
Potter	209	12.2	208	12.1	1	4.8	24	140	1	125	730	3	(11)	3 344	2 942

[1] Per 1,000 resident population estimated as of July 1, 1997. [2] Deaths of infants under 1 year old. [3] Infant deaths per 1,000 live births. [4] Active, nonfederal physicians as of December 31. Data subject to copyright; see below for source citation. [5] Per 100,000 resident population estimated as of July 1 of the year shown. [6] Nonfederal, short-stay (average length of stay less than 30 days) hospitals except hospital units of institutions. Data subject to copyright; see below for source citation. [7] SIC 805 includes skilled nursing care facilities; intermediate care facilities; and nursing and personal care, not elsewhere classified. [8] Full- and part-time employees on the payroll in the pay period including March 12. [9] Unduplicated count of persons enrolled in either hospital and/or supplemental medical insurance as of July 1. State totals include data not distributed by county. [10] Includes disabled, not shown separately. [11] 100 to 249 employees. [12] 0 to 19 employees. [13] 20 to 99 employees. [14] 250 to 499 employees.

Sources: Births—U.S. National Center for Health Statistics, "Vital Statistics of the United States, Vol. I, Natality," annual, and unpublished data. Deaths—U.S. National Center for Health Statistics, "Vital Statistics of the United States, Vol. II, Mortality," annual, and unpublished data. Physicians—American Medical Association, Chicago, IL, "Physician Characteristics and Distribution in the U.S.," annual (copyright). Community Hospitals—Health Forum, LLC, an American Hospital Association Company, Chicago, IL, "Hospital Statistics" 2000 edition and unpublished data (copyright). Nursing and Personal Care Facilities—U.S. Census Bureau, County Business Patterns 1997 on CD-ROM (related Internet site <http://www.census.gov/epcd/cbp/view/cbpview.html>). Medicare—U.S. Health Care Financing Administration; "Medicare County Enrollment as of July 1, 1999 - Aged and Disabled 3/2000 update," <http://www.hcfa.gov/stats/enroll/default.htm>.

Table B–4. Counties — **Vital Statistics and Health**–Con.

[Includes U.S., states, and 3,142 counties or county equivalents defined as of January 1, 1992. For changes to these areas since then, see appendix B. Geographic Information]

| County | Births, 1997 | | Deaths, 1997 | | | | Physicians,[4] 1999 | | Community hospitals,[6] 1998 | | | Nursing and personal care facilities,[7] 1997 | | Medicare program enrollment,[9] 1999 | |
| | | | Total | | Infant[2] | | | | | Beds | | | | | |
	Number	Rate[1]	Number	Rate[1]	Number	Rate[3]	Number	Rate[5]	Number	Number	Rate[5]	Estab-lishments	Em-ployees[8]	Total[10]	Aged
PENNSYLVANIA—Con.															
Schuylkill	1 420	9.4	2 047	13.5	11	7.7	152	102	4	575	383	12	1 402	32 620	29 149
Snyder	413	10.8	310	8.1	4	9.7	32	84	–	–	–	4	(11)	6 023	5 058
Somerset	803	10.0	880	10.9	3	3.7	89	111	3	219	273	6	737	15 577	13 887
Sullivan	37	6.1	109	17.9	–	–	1	17	–	–	–	2	(12)	1 499	1 320
Susquehanna	410	9.8	456	10.8	3	7.3	34	81	2	137	326	4	241	7 276	6 416
Tioga	382	9.2	413	10.0	2	5.2	49	118	1	97	234	5	359	7 519	6 507
Union	347	8.5	339	8.3	5	14.4	90	222	1	115	286	4	560	5 829	5 333
Venango	623	10.7	646	11.1	2	3.2	95	165	1	176	305	16	435	11 150	9 208
Warren	481	10.9	495	11.2	3	6.2	67	154	1	109	249	5	521	8 035	6 970
Washington	2 173	10.6	2 499	12.1	14	6.4	304	148	3	628	306	32	1 337	40 969	36 494
Wayne	544	12.0	561	12.4	2	3.7	66	143	1	95	209	9	686	10 837	9 498
Westmoreland	3 758	10.1	4 349	11.6	26	6.9	619	167	6	1 158	311	48	2 389	71 849	65 082
Wyoming	367	12.5	282	9.6	1	2.7	25	85	1	60	205	4	(12)	4 424	3 843
York	4 445	12.0	3 109	8.4	20	4.5	597	159	3	661	177	45	2 802	54 564	49 361
RHODE ISLAND	12 455	12.6	9 820	9.9	87	7.0	3 362	339	12	2 581	261	209	13 892	170 331	147 537
Bristol	518	10.6	464	9.5	2	3.9	200	407	–	–	–	15	678	8 822	7 899
Kent	1 814	11.2	1 670	10.4	11	6.1	413	255	1	326	202	33	2 414	28 806	24 932
Newport	970	11.7	779	9.4	5	5.2	175	211	1	110	133	29	1 030	13 470	12 036
Providence	7 786	13.6	5 961	10.4	64	8.2	2 309	402	8	1 920	335	103	8 477	102 381	87 587
Washington	1 367	11.5	946	7.9	5	3.7	265	216	2	225	186	29	1 293	16 760	15 016
SOUTH CAROLINA	52 214	13.8	33 690	8.9	501	9.6	8 294	213	65	11 518	300	397	19 085	555 082	454 448
Abbeville	326	13.3	221	9.0	–	–	17	69	1	42	170	2	(12)	3 818	3 185
Aiken	1 878	14.1	1 186	8.9	16	8.5	177	131	1	269	201	10	707	20 035	16 896
Allendale	160	13.9	129	11.2	2	12.5	7	62	1	80	701	–	–	1 581	1 291
Anderson	2 104	13.3	1 521	9.6	21	10.0	286	176	1	364	226	19	957	26 351	20 965
Bamberg	216	13.0	189	11.4	3	13.9	12	74	1	84	511	3	(13)	2 502	2 067
Barnwell	355	16.3	222	10.2	1	2.8	10	46	1	33	151	2	(12)	3 419	2 708
Beaufort	1 610	15.0	854	8.0	13	8.1	266	235	2	264	240	7	549	18 044	16 408
Berkeley	1 959	14.6	817	6.1	17	8.7	32	22	–	–	–	14	439	11 099	8 600
Calhoun	174	12.6	133	9.6	1	5.7	6	42	–	–	–	1	(13)	1 766	1 452
Charleston	4 187	13.4	2 482	7.9	64	15.3	2 063	645	7	1 700	537	21	1 512	42 505	35 398
Cherokee	744	15.3	450	9.3	8	10.8	42	84	1	125	254	4	243	7 198	5 669
Chester	479	14.2	329	9.7	6	12.5	24	69	1	70	204	–	–	5 420	4 324
Chesterfield	567	13.9	420	10.3	2	3.5	26	63	1	66	161	3	285	6 222	4 790
Clarendon	370	12.0	309	10.1	3	8.1	18	58	1	56	182	4	(12)	4 900	3 842
Colleton	536	14.5	342	9.2	5	9.3	42	112	1	131	351	1	(12)	5 764	4 423
Darlington	955	14.5	732	11.1	10	10.5	64	96	1	100	151	4	(11)	9 488	7 484
Dillon	467	15.8	322	10.9	3	6.4	21	71	1	117	394	6	380	4 510	3 406
Dorchester	1 144	13.2	688	8.0	12	10.5	64	71	1	99	112	4	(12)	10 540	8 368
Edgefield	282	14.3	192	9.7	4	14.2	9	45	1	40	200	3	120	2 542	2 028
Fairfield	314	14.1	285	12.8	2	6.4	10	44	1	33	147	3	231	3 517	2 868
Florence	1 730	13.9	1 311	10.5	18	10.4	359	287	4	879	705	26	901	18 410	14 621
Georgetown	770	14.7	521	9.9	15	19.5	93	169	1	131	244	4	244	11 462	9 718
Greenville	4 919	14.1	2 900	8.3	32	6.5	1 026	286	5	1 317	372	56	1 283	52 429	43 819
Greenwood	915	14.5	676	10.7	12	13.1	196	308	1	363	571	3	429	10 887	9 188
Hampton	288	15.1	171	9.0	–	–	10	52	1	36	188	1	(14)	3 658	2 840
Horry	2 064	12.2	1 564	9.2	21	10.2	305	171	3	606	347	9	444	28 923	24 487
Jasper	289	17.0	157	9.2	3	10.4	13	75	1	31	182	1	(13)	2 213	1 737
Kershaw	676	14.1	435	9.1	6	8.9	62	126	1	100	206	3	252	8 251	6 817
Lancaster	765	13.2	562	9.7	7	9.2	48	81	1	169	287	5	269	8 486	6 719
Laurens	840	13.5	682	10.9	7	8.3	49	77	1	85	135	2	(11)	9 906	7 446
Lee	246	12.2	180	8.9	3	12.2	4	20	–	–	–	3	(13)	2 749	2 214
Lexington	2 934	14.6	1 437	7.2	23	7.8	243	116	1	273	133	27	1 018	23 687	20 055
McCormick	90	9.4	97	10.2	–	–	4	42	–	–	–	1	–	1 806	1 509
Marion	497	14.3	373	10.7	5	10.1	39	113	1	216	625	4	(12)	5 753	4 487
Marlboro	424	14.3	333	11.2	4	9.4	25	85	1	105	355	1	(12)	4 704	3 504
Newberry	445	13.0	322	9.4	3	6.7	35	102	1	65	189	3	434	6 311	5 337
Oconee	753	11.9	556	8.8	5	6.6	114	175	1	190	296	3	(11)	11 940	9 826
Orangeburg	1 194	13.6	931	10.6	18	15.1	126	144	1	295	336	25	814	14 403	11 704
Pickens	1 301	12.4	818	7.8	16	12.3	114	105	2	148	138	14	390	15 184	12 393
Richland	4 159	13.8	2 397	7.9	42	10.1	1 352	440	4	1 286	422	46	2 009	37 254	30 863
Saluda	255	15.1	178	10.5	1	3.9	3	18	–	–	–	1	(12)	2 432	2 023
Spartanburg	3 222	13.1	2 382	9.7	26	8.1	501	201	4	758	307	29	1 312	38 460	30 659
Sumter	1 641	14.7	829	7.4	17	10.4	123	109	1	239	213	8	589	13 265	10 868
Union	380	12.4	420	13.7	3	7.9	33	109	2	230	754	2	(12)	5 738	4 416
Williamsburg	490	13.2	386	10.4	4	8.2	17	46	1	47	127	2	(14)	5 576	4 246
York	2 100	14.0	1 249	8.3	17	8.1	204	129	1	276	179	8	595	19 888	16 714

[1] Per 1,000 resident population estimated as of July 1, 1997. [2] Deaths of infants under 1 year old. [3] Infant deaths per 1,000 live births. [4] Active, nonfederal physicians as of December 31. Data subject to copyright; see below for source citation. [5] Per 100,000 resident population estimated as of July 1 of the year shown. [6] Nonfederal, short-stay (average length of stay less than 30 days) hospitals except hospital units of institutions. Data subject to copyright; see below for source citation. [7] SIC 805 includes skilled nursing care facilities; intermediate care facilities; and nursing and personal care, not elsewhere classified. [8] Full- and part-time employees on the payroll in the pay period including March 12. [9] Unduplicated count of persons enrolled in either hospital and/or supplemental medical insurance as of July 1. State totals include data not distributed by county. [10] Includes disabled, not shown separately. [11] 250 to 499 employees. [12] 100 to 249 employees. [13] 20 to 99 employees. [14] 0 to 19 employees.

Sources: Births—U.S. National Center for Health Statistics, "Vital Statistics of the United States, Vol. I, Natality," annual, and unpublished data. Deaths—U.S. National Center for Health Statistics, "Vital Statistics of the United States, Vol. II, Mortality," annual, and unpublished data. Physicians—American Medical Association, Chicago, IL, "Physician Characteristics and Distribution in the U.S.," annual (copyright). Community Hospitals—Health Forum, LLC, an American Hospital Association Company, Chicago, IL, "Hospital Statistics" 2000 edition and unpublished data (copyright). Nursing and Personal Care Facilities—U.S. Census Bureau, County Business Patterns 1997 on CD-ROM (related Internet site <http://www.census.gov/epcd/cbp/view/cbpview.html>). Medicare—U.S. Health Care Financing Administration; "Medicare County Enrollment as of July 1, 1999 - Aged and Disabled 3/2000 update," <http://www.hcfa.gov/stats/enroll/default.htm>.

Table B–4. Counties — **Vital Statistics and Health**–Con.

[Includes U.S., states, and 3,142 counties or county equivalents defined as of January 1, 1992. For changes to these areas since then, see appendix B. Geographic Information]

| County | Births, 1997 | | Deaths, 1997 | | | | Physicians,[4] 1999 | | Community hospitals,[6] 1998 | | | Nursing and personal care facilities,[7] 1997 | | Medicare program enrollment,[9] 1999 | |
| | | | Total | | Infant[2] | | | | | Beds | | | | | |
	Number	Rate[1]	Number	Rate[1]	Number	Rate[3]	Number	Rate[5]	Number	Number	Rate[5]	Estab-lishments	Em-ployees[8]	Total[10]	Aged
SOUTH DAKOTA	10 173	13.9	6 865	9.4	78	7.7	1 379	188	49	4 401	602	138	9 604	118 979	106 219
Aurora	33	10.9	39	12.9	–	–	–	–	–	–	–	1	(11)	623	584
Beadle	199	11.1	213	11.9	1	5.0	25	150	1	61	356	3	416	3 636	3 258
Bennett	62	18.7	30	9.0	1	16.1	2	60	1	68	2 009	–	–	427	372
Bon Homme	63	8.5	78	10.6	–	–	5	70	2	53	730	2	(12)	1 585	1 506
Brookings	327	12.5	188	7.2	1	3.1	21	81	1	140	539	12	278	3 218	2 924
Brown	488	13.7	354	9.9	6	12.3	74	210	1	224	633	4	377	6 279	5 631
Brule	67	12.1	58	10.5	–	–	9	164	1	54	976	2	(12)	1 014	915
Buffalo	41	23.3	26	14.8	–	–	–	–	–	–	–	–	–	129	100
Butte	120	13.4	100	11.2	–	–	4	46	–	–	–	3	(12)	1 592	1 375
Campbell	15	7.7	16	8.2	–	–	–	–	–	–	–	–	–	679	637
Charles Mix	156	16.5	108	11.4	1	6.4	7	76	2	83	892	2	(12)	1 717	1 594
Clark	45	10.3	59	13.5	–	–	–	–	–	–	–	1	(11)	983	926
Clay	152	11.5	102	7.7	1	6.6	14	107	1	95	720	6	155	1 494	1 343
Codington	389	15.3	249	9.8	2	5.1	56	221	1	119	468	1	(12)	4 104	3 665
Corson	67	15.6	35	8.2	–	–	–	–	–	–	–	–	–	935	835
Custer	67	9.7	77	11.1	–	–	9	128	1	10	144	1	(11)	1 326	1 131
Davison	247	13.9	186	10.5	2	8.1	34	190	1	183	1 032	1	(12)	3 471	3 084
Day	68	10.5	112	17.4	2	29.4	4	65	1	26	406	3	219	1 587	1 481
Deuel	48	10.6	50	11.0	1	20.8	3	67	1	16	355	1	(11)	989	926
Dewey	132	23.1	36	6.3	1	7.6	2	33	–	–	–	–	–	604	523
Douglas	41	11.5	52	14.6	–	–	3	86	1	9	256	2	(12)	806	760
Edmunds	49	11.6	45	10.6	–	–	5	119	1	61	1 447	1	(11)	1 005	963
Fall River	77	11.1	117	16.9	–	–	11	161	1	60	874	2	(11)	1 951	1 598
Faulk	34	13.4	22	8.6	–	–	–	–	1	19	755	1	(11)	717	683
Grant	85	10.5	88	10.9	3	35.3	6	75	1	117	1 453	1	(11)	1 603	1 477
Gregory	51	10.2	71	14.2	–	–	5	102	2	100	2 019	1	(13)	1 324	1 255
Haakon	29	11.8	30	12.2	–	–	2	86	1	66	2 798	1	(11)	435	415
Hamlin	77	14.4	74	13.8	–	–	1	18	–	–	–	2	(12)	1 097	1 032
Hand	48	11.5	38	9.1	–	–	2	48	1	21	505	1	(11)	802	754
Hanson	51	17.4	22	7.5	–	–	–	–	–	–	–	–	–	463	436
Harding	15	10.1	12	8.1	–	–	–	–	–	–	–	–	–	204	188
Hughes	230	15.0	133	8.7	1	4.3	24	155	1	191	1 244	1	(11)	2 246	2 019
Hutchinson	94	11.6	137	16.9	–	–	9	112	2	165	2 050	1	(11)	2 125	2 026
Hyde	20	12.3	28	17.2	–	–	–	–	–	–	–	2	(11)	380	356
Jackson	55	19.3	30	10.5	–	–	1	34	–	–	–	1	(11)	361	325
Jerauld	13	5.8	39	17.3	–	–	2	94	1	28	1 268	1	(11)	610	593
Jones	11	8.7	15	11.9	–	–	–	–	–	–	–	–	–	232	218
Kingsbury	66	11.3	79	13.6	–	–	3	52	1	13	226	3	252	1 573	1 478
Lake	106	9.9	112	10.5	–	–	7	66	1	49	459	6	154	2 000	1 840
Lawrence	201	9.1	196	8.8	1	5.0	36	168	2	50	228	2	(12)	3 504	3 084
Lincoln	269	13.8	137	7.0	–	–	10	46	1	25	122	4	341	1 894	1 733
Lyman	66	17.0	44	11.4	–	–	1	26	–	–	–	–	–	572	511
McCook	73	12.9	83	14.7	1	13.7	3	54	–	–	–	3	220	1 184	1 097
McPherson	16	5.7	43	15.4	–	–	3	111	1	6	219	1	(11)	607	581
Marshall	44	9.5	60	13.0	–	–	2	44	1	20	439	1	(11)	1 045	983
Meade	393	18.0	177	8.1	2	5.1	18	84	1	114	527	–	–	3 257	2 649
Mellette	36	18.0	20	10.0	1	27.8	–	–	–	–	–	1	(11)	273	246
Miner	22	7.6	49	16.9	–	–	–	–	–	–	–	1	(12)	719	682
Minnehaha	2 125	15.3	975	7.0	17	8.0	578	405	3	1 103	786	19	1 999	19 073	16 609
Moody	69	10.6	74	11.3	–	–	1	16	1	18	277	–	–	970	905
Pennington	1 265	14.5	637	7.3	11	8.7	242	275	1	360	412	9	1 097	11 859	10 075
Perkins	34	9.6	47	13.3	1	29.4	–	–	1	56	1 604	1	(11)	889	821
Potter	24	8.2	52	17.7	–	–	2	70	1	61	2 128	1	(11)	776	738
Roberts	172	17.3	122	12.2	4	23.3	5	51	1	31	314	3	230	1 812	1 676
Sanborn	25	9.1	35	12.7	–	–	1	37	–	–	–	3	(12)	636	587
Shannon	299	24.8	113	9.4	10	33.4	2	16	–	–	–	–	–	783	551
Spink	84	11.0	90	11.8	–	–	6	81	1	25	331	2	(12)	1 761	1 500
Stanley	29	9.9	22	7.5	1	34.5	1	35	–	–	–	–	–	369	322
Sully	19	12.3	9	5.8	–	–	–	–	–	–	–	–	–	259	241
Todd	247	26.7	66	7.1	2	8.1	4	42	–	–	–	–	–	544	415
Tripp	83	12.1	65	9.5	1	12.0	5	76	1	116	1 725	1	(11)	1 317	1 222
Turner	94	10.9	112	13.0	1	10.6	6	69	1	64	742	3	211	1 871	1 773
Union	148	12.4	105	8.8	–	–	20	160	–	–	–	2	(12)	2 109	1 927
Walworth	67	11.8	83	14.7	1	14.9	4	71	1	64	1 144	2	(12)	902	848
Yankton	293	14.1	182	8.7	1	3.4	79	373	1	257	1 224	9	164	3 486	3 056
Ziebach	38	16.9	7	3.1	–	–	–	–	–	–	–	–	–	148	133

[1] Per 1,000 resident population estimated as of July 1, 1997.   [2] Deaths of infants under 1 year old.   [3] Infant deaths per 1,000 live births.   [4] Active, nonfederal physicians as of December 31. Data subject to copyright; see below for source citation.   [5] Per 100,000 resident population estimated as of July 1 of the year shown.   [6] Nonfederal, short-stay (average length of stay less than 30 days) hospitals except hospital units of institutions. Data subject to copyright; see below for source citation.   [7] SIC 805 includes skilled nursing care facilities; intermediate care facilities; and nursing and personal care, not elsewhere classified.   [8] Full- and part-time employees on the payroll in the pay period including March 12.   [9] Unduplicated count of persons enrolled in either hospital and/or supplemental medical insurance as of July 1. State totals include data not distributed by county.   [10] Includes disabled, not shown separately.   [11] 20 to 99 employees.   [12] 100 to 249 employees. [13] 0 to 19 employees.

Sources: Births—U.S. National Center for Health Statistics, "Vital Statistics of the United States, Vol. I, Natality," annual, and unpublished data.   Deaths—U.S. National Center for Health Statistics, "Vital Statistics of the United States, Vol. II, Mortality," annual, and unpublished data.   Physicians—American Medical Association, Chicago, IL, "Physician Characteristics and Distribution in the U.S.," annual (copyright).   Community Hospitals—Health Forum, LLC, an American Hospital Association Company, Chicago, IL, "Hospital Statistics" 2000 edition and unpublished data (copyright).   Nursing and Personal Care Facilities—U.S. Census Bureau, County Business Patterns 1997 on CD-ROM (related Internet site <http://www.census.gov/epcd/cbp/view/cbpview.html>).   Medicare—U.S. Health Care Financing Administration; "Medicare County Enrollment as of July 1, 1999 - Aged and Disabled 3/2000 update," <http://www.hcfa.gov/stats/enroll/default.htm>.

Table B–4. Counties — **Vital Statistics and Health**–Con.

[Includes U.S., states, and 3,142 counties or county equivalents defined as of January 1, 1992. For changes to these areas since then, see appendix B. Geographic Information]

County	Births, 1997		Deaths, 1997				Physicians,[4] 1999		Community hospitals,[6] 1998			Nursing and personal care facilities,[7] 1997		Medicare program enrollment,[9] 1999	
			Total		Infant[2]					Beds					
	Number	Rate[1]	Number	Rate[1]	Number	Rate[3]	Number	Rate[5]	Number	Number	Rate[5]	Estab-lishments	Em-ployees[8]	Total[10]	Aged
TENNESSEE	74 478	13.8	52 665	9.8	637	8.6	13 626	248	122	20 682	381	554	37 081	815 231	672 228
Anderson	754	10.6	799	11.2	2	2.7	193	272	1	295	416	13	641	13 184	11 115
Bedford.................	513	15.0	374	10.9	4	7.8	25	72	1	180	521	7	(11)	5 409	4 618
Benton	167	10.3	193	11.9	1	6.0	10	61	1	34	209	1	(11)	3 392	2 839
Bledsoe	132	12.5	122	11.5	1	7.6	1	9	1	26	242	–	–	1 405	1 124
Blount	1 156	11.6	1 021	10.2	7	6.1	156	152	1	173	171	11	655	16 245	13 829
Bradley	1 143	13.9	710	8.6	7	6.1	133	158	2	244	293	25	1 354	11 788	9 627
Campbell	418	11.0	418	11.0	3	7.2	32	83	2	215	563	4	(12)	7 924	5 486
Cannon.................	141	11.7	137	11.4	2	14.2	7	57	1	55	453	2	(13)	1 965	1 670
Carroll.................	376	13.0	354	12.3	1	2.7	26	88	2	97	332	5	290	6 382	5 317
Carter	543	10.2	560	10.5	2	3.7	34	64	1	112	210	8	435	8 542	6 897
Cheatham	461	13.4	242	7.0	5	10.8	13	36	1	29	82	1	(11)	3 335	2 666
Chester	194	13.4	158	10.9	–	–	3	20	–	–	–	1	(13)	2 043	1 706
Claiborne	340	11.8	309	10.7	2	5.9	16	54	1	110	373	3	247	5 725	3 999
Clay...................	82	11.2	107	14.6	1	12.2	3	41	1	77	1 059	1	(13)	1 172	903
Cocke..................	437	13.8	368	11.6	5	11.4	20	62	1	109	341	6	(11)	5 791	4 405
Coffee.................	624	13.8	466	10.3	2	3.2	79	170	3	294	642	9	223	8 179	6 978
Crockett	174	12.6	184	13.3	–	–	6	43	–	–	–	2	(11)	2 699	2 273
Cumberland	470	10.9	476	11.0	2	4.3	68	150	1	177	401	7	508	9 940	8 559
Davidson	8 360	15.6	5 103	9.5	72	8.6	3 039	573	9	3 325	624	39	3 721	72 553	61 822
Decatur.................	126	11.7	157	14.5	–	–	6	56	1	40	372	2	(11)	2 140	1 794
DeKalb	208	13.2	189	12.0	5	24.0	13	80	1	52	325	3	(11)	2 970	2 378
Dickson	590	14.4	387	9.5	5	8.5	45	105	1	176	416	2	(12)	5 940	4 977
Dyer	463	12.7	442	12.1	1	2.2	57	155	1	105	287	5	286	6 152	4 845
Fayette	339	11.5	291	9.9	3	8.8	14	45	1	38	125	1	(11)	3 226	2 585
Fentress	217	13.7	187	11.8	–	–	9	55	1	73	452	1	(11)	3 188	2 255
Franklin	417	11.2	378	10.1	3	7.2	40	106	1	211	561	5	256	6 443	5 476
Gibson	505	10.5	673	14.0	10	19.8	33	69	3	150	312	9	792	9 917	8 340
Giles	353	12.4	356	12.5	2	5.7	25	86	1	80	277	4	299	4 869	4 129
Grainger	257	13.2	198	10.2	1	3.9	2	10	–	–	–	1	(11)	3 452	2 539
Greene	710	12.0	687	11.6	4	5.6	87	143	2	310	514	7	676	11 514	9 091
Grundy	174	12.5	170	12.2	–	–	4	28	–	–	–	3	199	2 587	1 949
Hamblen................	765	14.3	547	10.2	3	3.9	80	148	2	278	515	3	(12)	8 869	6 981
Hamilton	3 774	12.8	3 040	10.3	27	7.2	1 066	362	6	1 672	568	57	1 895	48 809	41 820
Hancock................	81	11.9	71	10.5	–	–	3	44	–	–	–	2	(13)	1 161	903
Hardeman	319	13.2	288	11.9	8	25.1	12	49	1	47	194	7	(11)	4 131	3 460
Hardin.................	284	11.4	299	12.1	2	7.0	18	71	1	123	494	3	100	4 522	3 527
Hawkins	517	10.6	496	10.2	6	11.6	30	60	1	50	101	3	355	8 115	6 318
Haywood	293	14.9	219	11.1	7	23.9	9	46	1	44	225	1	(11)	2 870	2 355
Henderson	352	14.7	261	10.9	1	2.8	12	48	1	32	131	1	(11)	4 557	3 700
Henry	318	10.7	387	13.0	–	–	31	103	1	269	898	5	345	6 557	5 492
Hickman	277	13.8	222	11.1	–	–	7	33	1	65	315	2	(11)	3 198	2 568
Houston	100	12.9	100	12.9	–	–	4	51	1	28	357	1	(11)	1 528	1 263
Humphreys	214	12.7	173	10.3	2	9.3	15	87	1	46	270	1	(13)	3 026	2 569
Jackson	110	11.5	129	13.5	–	–	4	41	–	–	–	1	(11)	1 578	1 231
Jefferson	476	11.3	398	9.4	4	8.4	34	75	1	22	50	3	(12)	7 878	6 347
Johnson	166	10.0	200	12.1	1	6.0	9	54	–	–	–	1	–	3 330	2 589
Knox	4 683	12.5	3 492	9.4	35	7.5	1 445	384	6	1 827	488	19	2 317	55 675	46 720
Lake	87	10.5	96	11.6	–	–	1	12	–	–	–	1	(13)	1 285	1 020
Lauderdale	350	14.5	326	13.6	4	11.4	7	29	1	70	290	1	(11)	4 234	3 340
Lawrence	551	14.1	458	11.7	7	12.7	31	78	1	98	249	3	(12)	7 280	6 073
Lewis	123	11.4	105	9.7	–	–	9	81	–	–	–	1	(11)	1 683	1 368
Lincoln	349	11.9	375	12.8	4	11.5	24	81	1	51	172	8	(13)	5 362	4 669
Loudon	441	11.5	398	10.4	6	13.6	43	108	1	30	77	15	361	7 649	6 459
McMinn	566	12.3	506	11.0	4	7.1	62	134	2	251	543	3	323	7 997	6 524
McNairy	287	12.1	317	13.4	5	17.4	16	66	1	48	200	2	(12)	5 216	4 100
Macon..................	245	13.7	186	10.4	1	4.1	9	49	1	43	238	2	(11)	2 842	2 298
Madison	1 162	13.7	833	9.8	12	10.3	351	405	2	806	939	15	520	13 115	10 837
Marion	352	13.3	283	10.7	1	2.8	21	78	1	47	176	1	(11)	4 161	3 225
Marshall	313	12.2	261	10.2	–	–	17	64	1	77	293	4	(11)	3 877	3 251
Maury	935	13.7	610	8.9	10	10.7	146	207	1	255	366	17	770	9 946	8 352
Meigs	134	13.8	85	8.8	2	14.9	3	30	–	–	–	1	(13)	1 674	1 266
Monroe	450	13.3	385	11.3	6	13.3	21	59	1	59	169	4	240	6 071	4 805
Montgomery	2 400	19.3	774	6.2	20	8.3	169	131	1	199	157	5	456	11 463	9 551
Moore..................	49	9.5	57	11.0	–	–	1	19	–	–	–	1	(11)	573	499
Morgan.................	200	10.8	193	10.5	–	–	5	27	–	–	–	1	(11)	2 417	1 763
Obion..................	393	12.3	405	12.6	2	5.1	40	124	1	133	413	5	258	6 059	5 034

[1] Per 1,000 resident population estimated as of July 1, 1997.   [2] Deaths of infants under 1 year old.   [3] Infant deaths per 1,000 live births.   [4] Active, nonfederal physicians as of December 31. Data subject to copyright; see below for source citation.   [5] Per 100,000 resident population estimated as of July 1 of the year shown.   [6] Nonfederal, short-stay (average length of stay less than 30 days) hospitals except hospital units of institutions. Data subject to copyright; see below for source citation.   [7] SIC 805 includes skilled nursing care facilities; intermediate care facilities; and nursing and personal care, not elsewhere classified.   [8] Full- and part-time employees on the payroll in the pay period including March 12.   [9] Unduplicated count of persons enrolled in either hospital and/or supplemental medical insurance as of July 1. State totals include data not distributed by county.   [10] Includes disabled, not shown separately.   [11] 100 to 249 employees.   [12] 250 to 499 employees.   [13] 20 to 99 employees.

Sources: Births—U.S. National Center for Health Statistics, "Vital Statistics of the United States, Vol. I, Natality," annual, and unpublished data.   Deaths—U.S. National Center for Health Statistics, "Vital Statistics of the United States, Vol. II, Mortality," annual, and unpublished data.   Physicians—American Medical Association, Chicago, IL, "Physician Characteristics and Distribution in the U.S.," annual (copyright).   Community Hospitals—Health Forum, LLC, an American Hospital Association Company, Chicago, IL, "Hospital Statistics" 2000 edition and unpublished data (copyright). Nursing and Personal Care Facilities—U.S. Census Bureau, County Business Patterns 1997 on CD-ROM (related Internet site <http://www.census.gov/epcd/cbp/view/cbpview.html>).   Medicare—U.S. Health Care Financing Administration; "Medicare County Enrollment as of July 1, 1999 - Aged and Disabled 3/2000 update," <http://www.hcfa.gov/stats/enroll/default.htm>.

[Includes U.S., states, and 3,142 counties or county equivalents defined as of January 1, 1992. For changes to these areas since then, see appendix B. Geographic Information]

County	Births, 1997		Deaths, 1997				Physicians,[4] 1999		Community hospitals,[6] 1998			Nursing and personal care facilities,[7] 1997		Medicare program enrollment,[9] 1999	
			Total		Infant[2]					Beds					
	Number	Rate[1]	Number	Rate[1]	Number	Rate[3]	Number	Rate[5]	Number	Number	Rate[5]	Estab-lishments	Em-ployees[8]	Total[10]	Aged
TENNESSEE—Con.															
Overton	232	12.1	239	12.5	1	4.3	19	97	1	88	451	–	–	3 508	2 708
Perry	95	12.7	92	12.3	2	21.1	2	26	1	53	704	1	(11)	1 418	1 144
Pickett	60	13.0	44	9.5	–	–	–	–	–	–	–	2	(11)	808	622
Polk	203	13.8	185	12.6	3	14.8	10	66	1	40	268	1	(12)	3 092	2 403
Putnam	794	13.6	603	10.3	2	2.5	124	208	1	158	268	5	437	10 878	8 826
Rhea	371	13.4	300	10.8	2	5.4	10	36	1	131	471	2	(11)	4 855	3 953
Roane	557	11.2	552	11.1	5	9.0	30	60	1	85	170	10	381	10 138	8 105
Robertson	791	15.4	448	8.7	8	10.1	34	62	1	100	188	5	309	6 888	5 722
Rutherford	2 490	15.6	979	6.1	20	8.0	220	128	1	193	116	11	887	14 773	12 160
Scott	309	15.6	209	10.5	1	3.2	13	64	1	77	384	4	160	3 392	2 177
Sequatchie	143	14.1	100	9.9	–	–	4	37	–	–	–	1	(11)	1 431	1 069
Sevier	840	13.4	542	8.6	7	8.3	67	102	1	100	155	7	317	10 297	8 442
Shelby	14 747	17.1	7 885	9.1	184	12.5	3 035	348	9	3 660	422	46	4 037	105 525	87 220
Smith	214	13.3	202	12.6	–	–	11	66	2	94	575	3	(12)	2 822	2 348
Stewart	123	11.0	130	11.6	–	–	4	34	–	–	–	1	(11)	2 184	1 800
Sullivan	1 667	11.1	1 633	10.9	15	9.0	542	361	4	901	599	8	911	29 021	24 155
Sumner	1 623	13.3	979	8.0	8	4.9	148	117	2	223	180	11	725	14 884	12 484
Tipton	695	15.1	435	9.5	9	12.9	34	70	1	48	101	2	(13)	5 857	4 756
Trousdale	77	11.4	82	12.2	–	–	4	57	–	–	–	1	(11)	1 069	867
Unicoi	210	12.2	195	11.3	2	9.5	13	75	1	84	488	1	(12)	3 881	3 104
Union	192	12.0	153	9.6	3	15.6	3	18	–	–	–	1	(11)	2 057	1 445
Van Buren	51	10.1	44	8.7	–	–	1	20	–	–	–	1	(11)	698	551
Warren	458	12.8	365	10.2	6	13.1	36	99	1	86	238	3	(13)	6 482	5 362
Washington	1 237	12.2	1 040	10.3	6	4.9	658	640	4	643	629	8	888	18 006	14 854
Wayne	158	9.6	168	10.2	1	6.3	8	49	1	32	195	5	(11)	2 485	1 955
Weakley	406	12.4	360	11.0	6	14.8	35	106	1	65	198	5	222	5 414	4 672
White	259	11.7	268	12.1	4	15.4	20	87	1	18	79	1	(12)	4 419	3 593
Williamson	1 435	12.9	570	5.1	7	4.9	498	402	1	121	103	13	974	10 612	9 541
Wilson	1 081	13.3	672	8.3	2	1.9	89	103	1	225	268	8	495	9 165	7 661
TEXAS	333 974	17.3	142 776	7.4	2 150	6.4	41 084	205	400	56 573	287	1 992	111 222	2 223 175	1 942 812
Anderson	624	12.0	569	10.9	6	9.6	60	115	2	234	449	13	629	7 463	6 415
Andrews	230	16.5	112	8.0	4	17.4	9	66	1	71	505	1	(11)	1 790	1 560
Angelina	1 277	16.7	751	9.8	12	9.4	113	146	2	343	444	17	990	11 980	9 756
Aransas	213	9.5	224	10.0	1	4.7	21	91	–	–	–	5	173	3 938	3 551
Archer	100	12.2	61	7.4	–	–	–	–	–	–	–	2	(11)	1 062	972
Armstrong	21	9.6	33	15.1	–	–	–	–	–	–	–	1	(11)	378	349
Atascosa	549	15.5	259	7.3	4	7.3	19	51	1	30	82	6	291	4 147	3 456
Austin	307	13.4	228	9.9	1	3.3	15	63	1	32	137	7	324	3 882	3 567
Bailey	124	18.3	65	9.6	–	–	3	45	1	25	365	1	(11)	1 115	1 039
Bandera	159	10.6	134	9.0	2	12.6	5	30	–	–	–	1	(11)	2 640	2 359
Bastrop	764	15.6	381	7.8	5	6.5	20	38	1	24	48	5	249	6 448	5 581
Baylor	42	10.1	66	15.9	–	–	3	73	1	34	818	1	(11)	1 104	1 014
Bee	416	14.9	244	8.7	2	4.8	20	73	1	69	249	3	205	3 420	2 913
Bell	5 101	23.0	1 458	6.6	32	6.3	766	344	3	792	355	20	1 567	21 679	18 998
Bexar	22 958	17.2	9 568	7.2	176	7.7	4 404	321	17	4 431	327	129	7 219	158 899	136 602
Blanco	96	11.7	91	11.1	2	20.8	5	59	–	–	–	3	(12)	3 511	3 184
Borden	4	5.2	2	2.6	–	–	–	–	–	–	–	–	–	50	D
Bosque	203	12.2	273	16.4	4	19.7	12	72	1	70	423	3	(13)	3 648	3 323
Bowie	1 130	13.5	914	10.9	13	11.5	251	301	3	721	866	20	1 131	13 845	11 773
Brazoria	3 546	15.9	1 507	6.7	23	6.5	418	178	3	199	87	16	971	22 988	20 328
Brazos	1 994	15.1	614	4.6	14	7.0	342	255	2	402	302	7	448	10 788	9 604
Brewster	107	12.1	85	9.6	1	9.3	7	80	1	25	283	2	(11)	1 380	1 263
Briscoe	22	11.4	28	14.5	–	–	–	–	–	–	–	–	–	411	385
Brooks	146	17.4	81	9.7	–	–	3	36	–	–	–	1	(11)	1 328	1 154
Brown	483	13.1	463	12.6	11	22.8	52	141	1	164	445	11	433	6 865	5 903
Burleson	215	14.0	163	10.6	2	9.3	5	32	1	30	193	2	(12)	2 852	2 525
Burnet	429	13.9	340	11.0	–	–	33	97	1	26	81	11	304	4 850	4 480
Caldwell	426	13.6	260	8.3	2	4.7	19	58	1	21	66	7	422	4 125	3 618
Calhoun	354	17.2	168	8.1	1	2.8	18	88	1	35	170	1	(12)	2 871	2 560
Callahan	148	11.6	127	10.0	–	–	2	15	–	–	–	3	82	2 297	2 050
Cameron	7 641	24.0	1 905	6.0	31	4.1	419	127	5	852	263	26	1 364	35 311	31 259
Camp	185	16.9	142	13.0	–	–	4	37	1	42	384	4	127	2 251	1 955
Carson	69	10.3	64	9.6	1	14.5	–	–	–	–	–	2	(11)	1 033	953
Cass	372	12.1	431	14.1	3	8.1	15	49	3	113	368	7	342	6 001	5 078
Castro	139	16.8	62	7.5	1	7.2	4	48	1	36	433	1	(11)	1 018	942

[1] Per 1,000 resident population estimated as of July 1, 1997. [2] Deaths of infants under 1 year old. [3] Infant deaths per 1,000 live births. [4] Active, nonfederal physicians as of December 31. Data subject to copyright; see below for source citation. [5] Per 100,000 resident population estimated as of July 1 of the year shown. [6] Nonfederal, short-stay (average length of stay less than 30 days) hospitals except hospital units of institutions. Data subject to copyright; see below for source citation. [7] SIC 805 includes skilled nursing care facilities; intermediate care facilities; and nursing and personal care, not elsewhere classified. [8] Full- and part-time employees on the payroll in the pay period including March 12. [9] Unduplicated count of persons enrolled in either hospital and/or supplemental medical insurance as of July 1. State totals include data not distributed by county. [10] Includes disabled, not shown separately. [11] 20 to 99 employees. [12] 100 to 249 employees. [13] 250 to 499 employees.

Sources: Births—U.S. National Center for Health Statistics, "Vital Statistics of the United States, Vol. I, Natality," annual, and unpublished data. Deaths—U.S. National Center for Health Statistics, "Vital Statistics of the United States, Vol. II, Mortality," annual, and unpublished data. Physicians—American Medical Association, Chicago, IL, "Physician Characteristics and Distribution in the U.S.," annual (copyright). Community Hospitals—Health Forum, LLC, an American Hospital Association Company, Chicago, IL, "Hospital Statistics" 2000 edition and unpublished data (copyright). Nursing and Personal Care Facilities—U.S. Census Bureau, County Business Patterns 1997 on CD-ROM (related Internet site <http://www.census.gov/epcd/cbp/view/cbpview.html>). Medicare—U.S. Health Care Financing Administration; "Medicare County Enrollment as of July 1, 1999 - Aged and Disabled 3/2000 update," <http://www.hcfa.gov/stats/enroll/default.htm>.

Table B–4. Counties — **Vital Statistics and Health**–Con.

[Includes U.S., states, and 3,142 counties or county equivalents defined as of January 1, 1992. For changes to these areas since then, see appendix B. Geographic Information]

County	Births, 1997 Number	Rate[1]	Deaths, 1997 Total Number	Rate[1]	Infant[2] Number	Rate[3]	Physicians,[4] 1999 Number	Rate[5]	Community hospitals,[6] 1998 Number	Beds Number	Rate[5]	Nursing and personal care facilities,[7] 1997 Establishments	Employees[8]	Medicare program enrollment,[9] 1999 Total[10]	Aged
TEXAS—Con.															
Chambers	306	13.2	152	6.5	3	9.8	4	17	2	61	256	1	(11)	2 019	1 747
Cherokee	675	15.8	514	12.0	4	5.9	56	128	2	108	249	15	806	6 729	5 798
Childress	93	12.1	109	14.2	–	–	6	80	1	35	461	2	(11)	1 259	1 151
Clay	109	10.4	104	10.0	–	–	5	48	1	25	237	1	(11)	1 492	1 363
Cochran	42	10.7	39	9.9	–	–	3	79	1	15	383	1	(11)	606	536
Coke	30	8.8	60	17.7	1	33.3	1	30	–	–	–	–	–	806	732
Coleman	116	12.0	175	18.0	2	17.2	4	42	1	27	284	3	163	2 387	2 165
Collin	6 817	17.0	1 453	3.6	30	4.4	760	166	4	633	148	22	1 066	22 778	20 151
Collingsworth	38	11.5	52	15.7	–	–	3	95	1	20	612	1	(11)	721	673
Colorado	263	13.9	261	13.8	–	–	23	121	3	106	561	4	258	3 811	3 520
Comal	959	13.6	661	9.4	9	9.4	106	138	1	89	121	13	723	12 223	11 088
Comanche	167	12.3	192	14.2	–	–	6	44	2	30	222	3	230	2 881	2 604
Concho	26	8.4	55	17.8	–	–	1	33	1	20	646	1	(11)	565	488
Cooke	465	14.2	350	10.7	2	4.3	20	60	2	68	207	7	292	5 385	4 847
Coryell	932	12.7	317	4.3	11	11.8	19	26	1	48	65	3	(12)	4 782	4 189
Cottle	16	8.2	36	18.5	–	–	1	53	–	–	–	1	(11)	510	475
Crane	53	11.9	34	7.6	–	–	1	23	1	28	630	–	–	479	418
Crockett	70	15.5	33	7.3	–	–	1	23	–	–	–	–	–	539	485
Crosby	119	16.2	103	14.0	–	–	2	28	1	35	484	2	(11)	1 154	1 042
Culberson	36	11.6	18	5.8	–	–	1	33	1	25	832	–	–	331	291
Dallam	98	15.3	65	10.2	3	30.6	5	75	1	23	351	–	–	1 256	1 159
Dallas	38 695	19.2	13 408	6.6	248	6.4	6 127	297	28	6 233	305	126	9 185	202 451	175 156
Dawson	191	13.0	144	9.8	1	5.2	7	48	1	44	301	2	(11)	2 348	2 109
Deaf Smith	396	20.6	156	8.1	3	7.6	13	69	1	36	189	4	240	2 411	2 156
Delta	54	10.9	82	16.6	3	55.6	–	–	–	–	–	3	(12)	1 018	897
Denton	5 914	16.3	1 444	4.0	22	3.7	394	98	4	641	167	23	1 396	20 533	17 338
DeWitt	220	11.2	306	15.6	–	–	9	47	1	49	250	5	314	3 463	3 110
Dickens	25	11.0	46	20.3	–	–	1	46	–	–	–	1	(11)	605	547
Dimmit	198	19.0	88	8.4	3	15.2	7	68	1	35	336	1	(11)	1 501	1 281
Donley	43	11.3	63	16.6	2	46.5	2	52	–	–	–	–	–	871	793
Duval	207	15.3	122	9.0	–	–	1	7	–	–	–	1	(11)	2 034	1 763
Eastland	209	11.8	273	15.4	2	9.6	7	40	1	38	216	7	247	4 287	3 830
Ector	2 263	18.4	957	7.8	18	8.0	216	175	2	368	295	6	314	15 075	13 029
Edwards	20	5.5	23	6.4	–	–	2	55	–	–	–	–	–	2 008	1 769
Ellis	1 592	15.8	802	8.0	10	6.3	72	67	1	00	00	7	570	11 780	10 244
El Paso	14 482	21.1	3 773	5.5	65	4.5	1 148	164	8	1 736	250	38	1 302	72 503	63 599
Erath	445	14.2	298	9.5	4	9.0	32	102	1	75	239	5	171	4 804	4 250
Falls	235	13.3	261	14.8	2	8.5	11	64	1	36	206	4	255	3 023	2 630
Fannin	361	13.0	419	15.0	–	–	10	35	1	46	162	7	420	5 447	4 739
Fayette	263	12.5	295	14.0	2	7.6	17	79	1	45	212	6	423	5 025	4 693
Fisher	45	10.4	82	19.0	–	–	3	72	1	23	538	2	(11)	956	870
Floyd	140	17.1	74	9.0	1	7.1	6	74	1	27	329	2	(11)	1 269	1 170
Foard	18	10.6	22	12.9	–	–	–	–	–	–	–	2	(11)	392	363
Fort Bend	4 451	13.9	1 272	4.0	18	4.0	646	183	4	319	95	18	860	17 219	14 868
Franklin	88	9.2	103	10.8	–	–	8	80	1	30	308	2	(12)	1 360	1 234
Freestone	193	11.0	201	11.5	–	–	6	34	1	19	108	4	222	2 850	2 534
Frio	293	18.5	132	8.4	–	–	9	57	1	22	139	4	(12)	1 737	1 442
Gaines	240	16.3	108	7.3	2	8.3	3	20	1	33	222	1	(13)	1 497	1 331
Galveston	3 567	14.7	1 979	8.2	21	5.9	1 248	502	3	1 106	451	18	1 549	30 422	26 636
Garza	77	16.4	58	12.4	1	13.0	–	–	–	–	–	2	(11)	772	680
Gillespie	209	10.6	278	14.1	2	9.6	53	260	1	59	295	5	(14)	4 959	4 691
Glasscock	13	9.2	4	2.8	–	–	–	–	–	–	–	–	–	96	D
Goliad	71	10.4	77	11.3	–	–	1	14	–	–	–	2	(11)	1 109	990
Gonzales	234	13.4	192	11.0	–	–	11	63	2	102	583	4	133	3 367	2 968
Gray	302	12.8	289	12.2	2	6.6	26	112	1	107	454	4	234	4 417	4 065
Grayson	1 447	14.4	1 174	11.7	9	6.2	196	189	3	555	544	18	1 340	18 340	16 014
Gregg	1 751	15.6	1 134	10.1	15	8.6	238	210	3	535	474	35	1 478	19 030	16 675
Grimes	294	12.9	198	8.7	1	3.4	12	50	1	30	129	1	(11)	3 110	2 762
Guadalupe	1 046	13.5	639	8.2	7	6.7	60	72	1	94	117	11	630	9 588	8 425
Hale	643	17.6	287	7.9	2	3.1	39	107	2	118	322	6	359	5 288	4 723
Hall	57	15.5	68	18.5	–	–	3	83	1	20	551	–	(11)	846	785
Hamilton	120	15.7	139	18.2	2	16.7	6	79	–	–	–	5	208	1 675	1 541
Hansford	79	14.8	56	10.5	–	–	1	19	1	28	523	–	–	852	799
Hardeman	61	13.1	78	16.7	–	–	4	91	2	35	767	1	(11)	1 038	955
Hardin	630	13.0	444	9.1	3	4.8	20	40	1	59	120	8	428	6 581	5 730
Harris	59 190	18.8	18 966	6.0	366	6.2	9 773	301	40	10 551	330	189	9 759	273 424	238 294

[1] Per 1,000 resident population estimated as of July 1, 1997. [2] Deaths of infants under 1 year old. [3] Infant deaths per 1,000 live births. [4] Active, nonfederal physicians as of December 31. Data subject to copyright; see below for source citation. [5] Per 100,000 resident population estimated as of July 1 of the year shown. [6] Nonfederal, short-stay (average length of stay less than 30 days) hospitals except hospital units of institutions. Data subject to copyright; see below for source citation. [7] SIC 805 includes skilled nursing care facilities; intermediate care facilities; and nursing and personal care, not elsewhere classified. [8] Full- and part-time employees on the payroll in the pay period including March 12. [9] Unduplicated count of persons enrolled in either hospital and/or supplemental medical insurance as of July 1. State totals include data not distributed by county. [10] Includes disabled, not shown separately. [11] 20 to 99 employees. [12] 100 to 249 employees. [13] 0 to 19 employees. [14] 250 to 499 employees.

Sources: Births—U.S. National Center for Health Statistics, "Vital Statistics of the United States, Vol. I, Natality," annual, and unpublished data. Deaths—U.S. National Center for Health Statistics, "Vital Statistics of the United States, Vol. II, Mortality," annual, and unpublished data. Physicians—American Medical Association, Chicago, IL, "Physician Characteristics and Distribution in the U.S.," annual (copyright). Community Hospitals—Health Forum, LLC, an American Hospital Association Company, Chicago, IL, "Hospital Statistics," 2000 edition and unpublished data (copyright). Nursing and Personal Care Facilities—U.S. Census Bureau, County Business Patterns 1997 on CD-ROM (related Internet site <http://www.census.gov/epcd/cbp/view/cbpview.html>). Medicare—U.S. Health Care Financing Administration; "Medicare County Enrollment as of July 1, 1999 - Aged and Disabled 3/2000 update," <http://www.hcfa.gov/stats/enroll/default.htm>.

[Includes U.S., states, and 3,142 counties or county equivalents defined as of January 1, 1992. For changes to these areas since then, see appendix B. Geographic Information]

| County | Births, 1997 | | Deaths, 1997 | | | | Physicians,[4] 1999 | | Community hospitals,[6] 1998 | | | Nursing and personal care facilities,[7] 1997 | | Medicare program enrollment,[9] 1999 | |
| | | | Total | | Infant[2] | | | | | Beds | | | | | |
	Number	Rate[1]	Number	Rate[1]	Number	Rate[3]	Number	Rate[5]	Number	Number	Rate[5]	Estab-lishments	Em-ployees[8]	Total[10]	Aged
TEXAS—Con.															
Harrison	739	12.4	611	10.3	7	9.5	51	85	1	101	169	8	595	8 067	6 859
Hartley	60	11.7	22	4.3	–	–	–	–	–	–	–	–	–	160	148
Haskell	55	9.0	105	17.1	1	18.2	1	17	1	30	490	2	(11)	1 580	1 479
Hays	1 206	14.1	440	5.1	5	4.1	91	98	1	113	127	7	463	7 929	6 966
Hemphill	29	8.1	39	10.8	–	–	5	144	1	19	539	1	(11)	466	430
Henderson	929	13.8	837	12.4	5	5.4	46	65	1	108	157	8	543	9 944	8 692
Hidalgo	13 084	26.0	2 690	5.3	71	5.4	589	110	5	1 177	226	22	1 394	52 177	45 887
Hill	403	13.4	408	13.6	4	9.9	19	61	2	124	406	6	396	6 024	5 269
Hockley	324	13.6	212	8.9	–	–	12	51	1	44	186	5	208	3 004	2 650
Hood	407	11.3	440	12.2	3	7.4	23	59	1	49	132	11	373	7 736	7 048
Hopkins	383	12.7	413	13.7	1	2.6	29	95	1	90	297	7	382	5 244	4 631
Houston	279	12.8	346	15.8	4	14.3	13	58	1	68	309	4	343	4 534	3 974
Howard	455	14.2	398	12.4	3	6.6	54	170	1	128	399	5	314	5 342	4 643
Hudspeth	31	9.7	23	7.2	–	–	–	–	–	–	–	–	–	340	297
Hunt	1 030	15.0	762	11.1	10	9.7	56	78	1	147	209	18	606	10 751	9 080
Hutchinson	338	14.1	251	10.5	4	11.8	16	67	1	48	200	2	(12)	4 147	3 817
Irion	11	6.5	14	8.2	–	–	–	–	–	–	–	–	–	267	236
Jack	92	12.6	78	10.7	1	10.9	4	53	1	18	242	2	(11)	1 268	1 151
Jackson	199	14.5	160	11.7	2	10.1	5	37	1	31	227	3	(12)	2 289	2 042
Jasper	528	15.9	409	12.3	5	9.5	32	96	1	54	161	3	221	5 704	4 917
Jeff Davis	18	8.1	15	6.7	1	55.6	3	124	–	–	–	–	–	364	327
Jefferson	3 411	14.1	2 591	10.7	19	5.6	563	233	8	1 765	732	25	1 723	38 347	33 405
Jim Hogg	71	14.5	41	8.4	–	–	3	60	–	–	–	–	–	799	709
Jim Wells	662	16.6	317	8.0	7	10.6	29	72	1	120	300	5	356	5 822	4 964
Johnson	1 656	14.5	940	8.3	9	5.4	81	66	2	281	238	16	961	14 898	12 788
Jones	162	8.7	202	10.8	1	6.2	5	27	3	88	472	5	302	2 861	2 523
Karnes	166	10.9	179	11.7	–	–	6	40	1	30	198	5	221	2 495	2 205
Kaufman	870	13.7	554	8.7	2	2.3	42	62	2	199	304	8	520	12 479	10 744
Kendall	285	14.0	203	10.0	1	3.5	76	348	–	–	–	5	247	3 857	3 597
Kenedy	10	23.3	3	7.0	–	–	–	–	–	–	–	–	–	52	D
Kent	11	12.6	16	18.3	–	–	–	–	–	–	–	–	–	213	200
Kerr	480	11.4	579	13.8	1	2.1	119	275	1	130	305	6	447	11 170	10 365
Kimble	49	11.8	54	13.0	–	–	4	94	1	15	362	1	(11)	855	785
King	1	2.9	1	2.9	–	–	–	–	–	–	–	–	–	35	D
Kinney	35	10.4	40	11.9	–	–	2	58	–	–	–	–	–	734	670
Kleberg	530	17.6	222	7.4	5	9.4	20	67	1	100	332	3	112	3 516	3 082
Knox	46	10.7	62	14.4	1	21.7	3	73	–	–	–	4	122	988	907
Lamar	612	13.4	572	12.5	3	4.9	109	237	2	333	726	8	582	8 347	7 196
Lamb	244	16.5	165	11.1	–	–	5	34	1	41	278	3	109	2 713	2 477
Lampasas	251	14.4	189	10.8	1	4.0	8	45	–	–	–	4	193	2 660	2 387
La Salle	92	15.4	48	8.0	–	–	–	–	–	–	–	–	–	761	666
Lavaca	220	11.7	307	16.4	1	4.5	20	106	2	64	340	5	359	4 964	4 535
Lee	204	13.9	168	11.4	2	9.8	4	27	–	–	–	3	171	2 092	1 895
Leon	178	12.3	211	14.6	–	–	4	27	–	–	–	2	(11)	3 688	3 294
Liberty	1 012	15.7	614	9.5	8	7.9	31	46	2	128	196	5	295	8 917	7 551
Limestone	264	12.8	317	15.3	1	3.8	9	44	2	59	284	5	309	4 230	3 383
Lipscomb	42	14.0	37	12.3	–	–	–	–	–	–	–	–	–	611	575
Live Oak	104	10.3	120	11.9	–	–	2	20	–	–	–	2	(12)	1 337	1 194
Llano	130	9.9	246	18.7	3	23.1	28	202	1	30	223	5	259	4 497	4 159
Loving	–	–	–	–	–	–	–	–	–	–	–	–	–	18	D
Lubbock	3 654	15.9	1 838	8.0	34	9.3	882	387	6	1 474	646	41	1 648	29 062	25 133
Lynn	88	13.3	58	8.8	–	–	4	60	1	24	357	1	(11)	1 010	907
McCulloch	119	13.6	127	14.5	1	8.4	4	45	1	27	310	2	(12)	1 813	1 639
McLennan	3 089	15.3	1 931	9.5	20	6.5	408	200	3	708	348	21	1 975	30 158	26 321
McMullen	11	13.9	9	11.3	–	–	–	–	–	–	–	–	–	134	D
Madison	142	12.1	140	11.9	–	–	8	67	1	35	295	2	(12)	1 733	1 560
Marion	135	12.7	171	16.1	2	14.8	5	45	–	–	–	2	(12)	1 800	1 518
Martin	80	16.0	46	9.2	–	–	2	40	1	21	418	1	(11)	634	563
Mason	35	9.6	57	15.6	–	–	1	27	–	–	–	1	(11)	884	828
Matagorda	621	16.4	347	9.2	9	14.5	31	82	2	73	192	4	247	5 059	4 504
Maverick	1 033	22.1	251	5.4	7	6.8	39	80	1	69	145	1	(11)	5 622	4 816
Medina	529	14.7	312	8.7	3	5.7	13	34	1	27	73	4	279	4 578	3 974
Menard	23	9.8	35	14.9	1	43.5	–	–	–	–	–	–	–	547	504
Midland	1 922	16.4	823	7.0	26	13.5	213	180	2	362	304	23	593	13 669	12 192
Milam	329	13.7	295	12.2	1	3.0	10	41	2	74	306	5	331	4 443	3 992
Mills	57	12.1	74	15.7	–	–	1	21	–	–	–	3	118	1 184	1 059

¹ Per 1,000 resident population estimated as of July 1, 1997.   ² Deaths of infants under 1 year old.   ³ Infant deaths per 1,000 live births.   ⁴ Active, nonfederal physicians as of December 31. Data subject to copyright; see below for source citation.   ⁵ Per 100,000 resident population estimated as of July 1 of the year shown.   ⁶ Nonfederal, short-stay (average length of stay less than 30 days) hospitals except hospital units of institutions. Data subject to copyright; see below for source citation.   ⁷ SIC 805 includes skilled nursing care facilities; intermediate care facilities; and nursing and personal care, not elsewhere classified.   ⁸ Full- and part-time employees on the payroll in the pay period including March 12.   ⁹ Unduplicated count of persons enrolled in either hospital and/or supplemental medical insurance as of July 1. State totals include data not distributed by county.   ¹⁰ Includes disabled, not shown separately.   ¹¹ 20 to 99 employees.   ¹² 100 to 249 employees.

Sources: Births—U.S. National Center for Health Statistics, "Vital Statistics of the United States, Vol. I, Natality," annual, and unpublished data.   Deaths—U.S. National Center for Health Statistics, "Vital Statistics of the United States, Vol. II, Mortality," annual, and unpublished data.   Physicians—American Medical Association, Chicago, IL, "Physician Characteristics and Distribution in the U.S.," annual (copyright).   Community Hospitals—Health Forum, LLC, an American Hospital Association Company, Chicago, IL, "Hospital Statistics" 2000 edition and unpublished data (copyright).   Nursing and Personal Care Facilities—U.S. Census Bureau, County Business Patterns 1997 on CD-ROM (related Internet site <http://www.census.gov/epcd/cbp/view/cbpview.html>).   Medicare—U.S. Health Care Financing Administration; "Medicare County Enrollment as of July 1, 1999 - Aged and Disabled 3/2000 update," <http://www.hcfa.gov/stats/enroll/default.htm>.

[Includes U.S., states, and 3,142 counties or county equivalents defined as of January 1, 1992. For changes to these areas since then, see appendix B. Geographic Information]

County	Births, 1997		Deaths, 1997				Physicians,[4] 1999		Community hospitals,[6] 1998			Nursing and personal care facilities,[7] 1997		Medicare program enrollment,[9] 1999	
			Total		Infant[2]					Beds					
	Number	Rate[1]	Number	Rate[1]	Number	Rate[3]	Number	Rate[5]	Number	Number	Rate[5]	Estab-lishments	Em-ployees[8]	Total[10]	Aged
TEXAS—Con.															
Mitchell	92	10.6	117	13.4	–	–	5	57	1	25	283	2	(11)	1 643	1 454
Montague	227	12.3	308	16.7	–	–	11	59	2	82	442	6	342	4 201	3 712
Montgomery	3 859	15.0	1 718	6.7	28	7.3	162	56	3	470	173	8	564	26 084	22 871
Moore	403	20.9	139	7.2	5	12.4	13	66	1	118	603	3	(11)	2 132	1 970
Morris	179	13.5	162	12.2	–	–	4	30	–	–	–	3	191	2 795	2 461
Motley	22	16.8	25	19.1	–	–	1	76	–	–	–	–	–	347	326
Nacogdoches	809	14.3	576	10.2	8	9.9	115	205	2	305	542	12	595	8 111	6 910
Navarro	619	15.1	507	12.3	8	12.9	52	124	1	144	346	13	723	7 382	6 259
Newton	179	12.4	132	9.2	2	11.2	3	21	–	–	–	1	(12)	2 113	1 733
Nolan	237	14.4	193	11.8	–	–	6	37	1	54	329	6	177	3 054	2 702
Nueces	5 397	17.1	2 421	7.7	36	6.7	797	253	7	1 768	560	33	2 181	38 548	33 064
Ochiltree	125	14.2	72	8.2	1	8.0	3	35	1	45	512	1	(12)	1 095	1 005
Oldham	22	9.9	19	8.5	–	–	1	45	–	–	–	–	–	345	324
Orange	1 177	13.9	807	9.5	7	5.9	44	52	1	120	142	18	514	12 246	10 495
Palo Pinto	376	14.7	342	13.4	7	18.6	20	76	1	44	170	5	236	4 557	4 022
Panola	292	12.7	242	10.5	1	3.4	8	35	1	30	130	8	267	3 643	3 173
Parker	938	11.9	580	7.4	8	8.5	48	56	1	67	81	9	381	9 372	8 309
Parmer	179	17.3	101	9.8	5	27.9	2	19	1	34	330	–	–	1 270	1 162
Pecos	210	12.9	110	6.8	8	38.1	8	50	2	44	274	1	(12)	1 827	1 623
Polk	471	9.9	474	10.0	4	8.5	24	46	1	28	56	4	180	11 751	10 395
Potter	2 026	18.7	1 170	10.8	23	11.4	504	462	2	830	766	13	1 041	22 329	19 678
Presidio	128	15.5	49	5.9	–	–	3	34	–	–	–	1	(13)	1 280	1 164
Rains	83	10.1	86	10.5	–	–	1	11	–	–	–	2	(11)	1 304	1 128
Randall	1 344	13.8	635	6.5	8	6.0	17	17	–	–	–	5	178	4 713	4 417
Reagan	73	17.3	33	7.8	–	–	3	78	1	62	1 465	–	–	366	319
Real	31	11.7	52	19.6	–	–	2	73	–	–	–	1	(12)	741	658
Red River	170	12.3	207	15.0	–	–	8	58	1	36	262	1	298	3 098	2 708
Reeves	213	14.6	119	8.2	–	–	4	29	1	44	308	1	(12)	1 829	1 580
Refugio	98	12.4	79	10.0	–	–	1	13	1	20	253	1	(11)	1 486	1 319
Roberts	3	3.0	9	9.1	–	–	–	–	–	–	–	–	–	126	113
Robertson	243	15.7	195	12.6	–	–	2	13	–	–	–	4	226	2 884	2 565
Rockwall	563	15.8	232	6.5	4	7.1	82	208	–	–	–	3	280	3 450	3 077
Runnels	166	14.5	150	13.1	2	12.0	9	79	2	37	321	4	124	2 449	2 211
Rusk	537	11.8	558	12.3	6	11.2	25	55	1	96	210	8	547	6 770	5 990
Sabine	103	9.8	157	14.9	1	9.7	5	47	1	36	342	1	(12)	3 210	2 808
San Augustine	117	14.4	127	15.6	1	8.5	4	50	1	16	198	3	211	1 911	1 623
San Jacinto	222	10.7	191	9.2	1	4.5	1	4	–	–	–	1	(13)	2 839	2 416
San Patricio	1 145	16.5	505	7.3	9	7.9	29	40	1	69	98	6	284	8 540	7 292
San Saba	55	9.3	83	14.0	–	–	–	–	–	–	–	2	(11)	1 214	1 125
Schleicher	38	12.6	34	11.2	–	–	2	68	1	16	539	–	–	470	428
Scurry	197	10.9	157	8.7	–	–	12	68	1	64	356	2	(11)	2 805	2 538
Shackelford	31	9.4	36	10.9	–	–	2	62	–	–	–	2	(12)	617	563
Shelby	354	15.7	356	15.8	4	11.3	13	57	1	46	201	3	289	4 579	3 935
Sherman	51	17.6	27	9.3	–	–	–	–	–	–	–	–	–	446	422
Smith	2 496	15.1	1 660	10.0	9	3.6	542	319	6	971	578	17	1 483	26 726	23 560
Somervell	84	13.6	62	10.0	–	–	6	91	1	16	251	2	(12)	809	717
Starr	1 382	25.4	234	4.3	6	4.3	14	25	1	44	79	1	(12)	5 013	4 325
Stephens	142	14.3	124	12.5	1	7.0	6	62	1	33	339	1	(12)	1 752	1 559
Sterling	20	14.6	12	8.8	–	–	–	–	–	–	–	–	–	179	164
Stonewall	20	11.0	27	14.9	–	–	2	117	1	16	891	1	(12)	426	402
Sutton	62	14.0	32	7.2	–	–	2	46	1	13	291	–	–	544	490
Swisher	124	14.9	80	9.6	–	–	3	36	1	26	314	1	(12)	1 528	1 401
Tarrant	22 607	17.1	8 921	6.7	165	7.3	2 189	158	17	3 028	224	140	7 641	129 679	112 955
Taylor	2 028	16.7	1 069	8.8	17	8.4	264	216	2	567	465	32	1 329	18 142	15 740
Terrell	12	10.1	13	11.0	–	–	–	–	–	–	–	–	–	230	209
Terry	196	15.1	119	9.2	1	5.1	6	47	1	42	326	2	(11)	2 018	1 807
Throckmorton	16	9.4	23	13.5	–	–	1	59	1	25	1 467	1	(12)	371	345
Titus	500	19.9	287	11.4	5	10.0	39	154	1	92	362	9	433	3 749	3 314
Tom Green	1 543	15.1	955	9.3	14	9.1	203	198	2	403	392	19	1 058	15 679	13 704
Travis	11 939	17.3	3 736	5.4	76	6.4	2 068	284	9	1 666	235	80	4 104	60 139	51 728
Trinity	165	13.2	184	14.8	5	30.3	4	31	1	22	174	1	(12)	3 124	2 774
Tyler	206	10.2	248	12.3	3	14.6	9	44	1	26	128	4	248	3 809	3 278
Upshur	428	12.1	406	11.4	1	2.3	16	44	–	–	–	3	292	5 863	5 075
Upton	59	15.5	21	5.5	–	–	2	56	2	66	1 752	–	–	524	460
Uvalde	427	16.8	239	9.4	3	7.0	22	85	1	51	200	2	(11)	3 788	3 343
Val Verde	913	21.3	272	6.3	6	6.6	40	91	1	76	174	1	142	3 734	3 360

[1] Per 1,000 resident population estimated as of July 1, 1997.   [2] Deaths of infants under 1 year old.   [3] Infant deaths per 1,000 live births.   [4] Active, nonfederal physicians as of December 31. Data subject to copyright; see below for source citation.   [5] Per 100,000 resident population estimated as of July 1 of the year shown.   [6] Nonfederal, short-stay (average length of stay less than 30 days) hospitals except hospital units of institutions. Data subject to copyright; see below for source citation.   [7] SIC 805 includes skilled nursing care facilities; intermediate care facilities; and nursing and personal care, not elsewhere classified.   [8] Full- and part-time employees on the payroll in the pay period including March 12.   [9] Unduplicated count of persons enrolled in either hospital and/or supplemental medical insurance as of July 1. State totals include data not distributed by county.   [10] Includes disabled, not shown separately.   [11] 100 to 249 employees.   [12] 20 to 99 employees. [13] 0 to 19 employees.

Sources: Births—U.S. National Center for Health Statistics, "Vital Statistics of the United States, Vol. I, Natality," annual, and unpublished data.   Deaths—U.S. National Center for Health Statistics, "Vital Statistics of the United States, Vol. II, Mortality," annual, and unpublished data.   Physicians—American Medical Association, Chicago, IL, "Physician Characteristics and Distribution in the U.S.," annual (copyright).   Community Hospitals—Health Forum, LLC, an American Hospital Association Company, Chicago, IL, "Hospital Statistics," annual (copyright). Nursing and Personal Care Facilities—U.S. Census Bureau, County Business Patterns 1997 on CD-ROM (related Internet site <http://www.census.gov/epcd/cbp/view/cbpview.html>).   Medicare—U.S. Health Care Financing Administration; "Medicare County Enrollment as of July 1, 1999 - Aged and Disabled 3/2000 update," <http://www.hcfa.gov/stats/enroll/default.htm>.

[Includes U.S., states, and 3,142 counties or county equivalents defined as of January 1, 1992. For changes to these areas since then, see appendix B. Geographic Information]

County	Births, 1997		Deaths, 1997				Physicians,[4] 1999		Community hospitals,[6] 1998			Nursing and personal care facilities,[7] 1997		Medicare program enrollment,[9] 1999	
			Total		Infant[2]					Beds					
	Number	Rate[1]	Number	Rate[1]	Number	Rate[3]	Number	Rate[5]	Number	Number	Rate[5]	Estab-lishments	Em-ployees[8]	Total[10]	Aged
TEXAS—Con.															
Van Zandt	581	13.5	541	12.6	2	3.4	14	31	1	16	36	7	458	8 148	7 118
Victoria	1 297	16.1	664	8.2	12	9.3	193	235	3	590	722	7	547	11 171	9 737
Walker	598	11.0	447	8.2	4	6.7	48	87	1	130	237	3	272	5 687	5 071
Waller	456	17.1	239	8.9	3	6.6	8	29	–	–	–	2	(11)	2 936	2 570
Ward	174	14.8	112	9.5	3	17.2	4	35	1	36	305	1	(12)	1 739	1 502
Washington	362	12.6	336	11.7	3	8.3	35	120	1	60	206	4	412	5 526	4 845
Webb	5 145	28.5	905	5.0	26	5.1	193	100	2	437	234	5	417	16 260	14 312
Wharton	582	14.5	380	9.5	4	6.9	50	124	2	203	506	4	279	6 256	5 638
Wheeler	49	9.2	79	14.8	2	40.8	4	75	2	55	1 040	2	(11)	1 245	1 141
Wichita	1 878	14.6	1 197	9.3	12	6.4	320	250	2	426	332	24	1 503	18 975	16 732
Wilbarger	188	13.2	170	12.0	–	–	24	171	1	49	348	4	188	2 705	2 404
Willacy	404	20.7	116	5.9	2	5.0	5	25	–	–	–	1	(12)	2 591	2 266
Williamson	3 414	16.2	1 026	4.9	17	5.0	237	98	3	177	79	22	1 061	17 234	15 545
Wilson	378	12.5	237	7.8	1	2.6	11	34	1	30	96	4	246	3 551	3 041
Winkler	115	14.6	69	8.8	1	8.7	3	39	1	16	201	1	(12)	1 113	977
Wise	607	14.3	394	9.3	2	3.3	14	30	1	69	156	7	366	5 245	4 566
Wood	424	12.5	484	14.2	3	7.1	20	58	2	63	184	8	418	7 963	7 065
Yoakum	128	16.0	61	7.6	–	–	3	38	1	24	301	1	(13)	934	843
Young	229	13.0	261	14.8	1	4.4	15	85	2	79	450	5	(11)	3 814	3 436
Zapata	221	19.8	95	8.5	1	4.5	2	17	–	–	–	1	(12)	1 355	1 201
Zavala	210	17.8	92	7.8	–	–	1	8	–	–	–	–	–	1 590	1 330
UTAH	43 059	20.8	11 578	5.6	249	5.8	4 312	202	41	4 010	191	203	10 238	201 217	178 271
Beaver	114	19.4	65	11.1	–	–	6	100	2	70	1 186	–	–	915	825
Box Elder	722	17.6	273	6.6	–	–	30	70	2	107	255	5	182	4 725	4 331
Cache	2 055	24.0	395	4.6	6	2.9	124	142	1	112	128	4	457	6 812	6 272
Carbon	325	15.5	205	9.8	3	9.2	27	129	1	60	285	2	(12)	3 301	2 751
Daggett	4	5.3	6	8.0	–	–	–	–	–	–	–	–	–	121	109
Davis	4 517	19.9	917	4.0	17	3.8	260	109	2	216	92	11	670	17 674	15 941
Duchesne	248	17.4	100	7.0	1	4.0	15	102	1	42	289	1	(12)	1 751	1 463
Emery	195	17.9	81	7.4	2	10.3	1	9	–	–	–	–	–	1 234	1 032
Garfield	73	17.3	32	7.6	–	–	1	23	1	44	1 025	–	–	760	697
Grand	129	15.9	62	7.7	2	15.5	8	98	1	38	471	–	–	1 126	982
Iron	679	24.4	168	6.0	3	4.4	31	105	1	36	125	3	110	3 344	2 951
Juab	168	23.2	60	8.3	–	–	6	77	1	22	289	1	(11)	866	752
Kane	101	16.6	42	6.9	–	–	8	130	1	38	611	–	–	1 061	966
Millard	209	17.0	99	8.1	1	4.8	7	56	2	40	326	1	(12)	1 574	1 432
Morgan	96	13.9	34	4.9	–	–	6	83	–	–	–	–	–	641	606
Piute	20	14.3	17	12.1	–	–	–	–	–	–	–	–	–	280	251
Rich	30	16.5	17	9.3	1	33.3	–	–	–	–	–	–	–	272	D
Salt Lake	16 730	19.9	4 814	5.7	103	6.2	2 679	315	11	1 806	213	80	4 686	78 471	68 772
San Juan	252	18.6	56	4.1	2	7.9	5	37	1	35	257	1	(11)	1 215	1 035
Sanpete	411	19.7	158	7.6	1	2.4	19	86	2	41	190	1	(12)	2 621	2 323
Sevier	306	17.0	141	7.8	3	9.8	10	54	1	27	146	2	(11)	2 760	2 449
Summit	402	15.7	59	2.3	3	7.5	105	379	–	–	–	3	(12)	1 448	1 309
Tooele	671	21.3	199	6.3	1	1.5	15	42	1	107	320	–	–	3 000	2 675
Uintah	412	16.2	164	6.4	1	2.4	19	73	1	29	113	1	(13)	2 629	2 245
Utah	8 715	26.5	1 435	4.4	61	7.0	455	131	4	532	157	43	1 752	25 494	22 390
Wasatch	241	18.9	80	6.3	2	8.3	17	123	1	20	151	3	(12)	1 316	1 183
Washington	1 624	20.5	567	7.1	12	7.4	124	145	1	116	141	13	538	13 358	12 338
Wayne	40	16.7	21	8.8	–	–	1	42	–	–	–	–	–	368	338
Weber	3 570	19.6	1 311	7.2	24	6.7	333	180	2	472	257	28	1 141	21 956	19 494
VERMONT	6 607	11.2	5 053	8.6	40	6.1	1 860	313	14	1 671	283	95	4 925	87 644	74 923
Addison	368	10.6	250	7.2	2	5.4	73	206	1	163	464	13	225	4 390	3 838
Bennington	366	10.1	431	12.0	3	8.2	97	270	1	84	234	11	525	6 554	5 669
Caledonia	309	10.8	278	9.7	2	6.5	47	163	1	28	98	2	(11)	4 817	4 133
Chittenden	1 738	12.3	856	6.0	9	5.2	920	639	1	481	338	14	937	15 667	13 467
Essex	57	8.8	63	9.7	1	17.5	3	45	–	–	–	–	–	1 262	1 040
Franklin	586	13.5	346	7.9	2	3.4	47	106	1	70	159	6	278	5 563	4 629
Grand Isle	67	10.9	34	5.5	1	14.9	11	173	–	–	–	–	–	D	D
Lamoille	283	13.2	165	7.7	2	7.1	52	237	1	41	189	3	(11)	3 015	2 553
Orange	287	10.3	240	8.6	2	7.0	51	183	1	93	334	2	(11)	3 956	3 394
Orleans	314	12.4	255	10.1	–	–	30	118	1	27	106	7	329	4 575	3 823
Rutland	643	10.3	654	10.5	5	7.8	126	202	1	132	211	13	645	11 204	9 384
Washington	588	10.5	547	9.7	6	10.2	123	219	1	294	523	7	657	8 885	7 493
Windham	456	10.6	386	9.0	3	6.6	104	244	2	109	255	8	449	6 863	5 903
Windsor	545	9.9	548	9.9	2	3.7	176	317	2	149	269	9	392	9 879	8 717

[1] Per 1,000 resident population estimated as of July 1, 1997. [2] Deaths of infants under 1 year old. [3] Infant deaths per 1,000 live births. [4] Active, nonfederal physicians as of December 31. Data subject to copyright; see below for source citation. [5] Per 100,000 resident population estimated as of July 1 of the year shown. [6] Nonfederal, short-stay (average length of stay less than 30 days) hospitals except hospital units of institutions. Data subject to copyright; see below for source citation. [7] SIC 805 includes skilled nursing care facilities; intermediate care facilities; and nursing and personal care, not elsewhere classified. [8] Full- and part-time employees on the payroll in the pay period including March 12. [9] Unduplicated count of persons enrolled in either hospital and/or supplemental medical insurance as of July 1. State totals include data not distributed by county. [10] Includes disabled, not shown separately. [11] 100 to 249 employees. [12] 20 to 99 employees. [13] 0 to 19 employees.

Sources: Births—U.S. National Center for Health Statistics, "Vital Statistics of the United States, Vol. I, Natality," annual, and unpublished data. Deaths—U.S. National Center for Health Statistics, "Vital Statistics of the United States, Vol. II, Mortality," annual, and unpublished data. Physicians—American Medical Association, Chicago, IL, "Physician Characteristics and Distribution in the U.S.," annual (copyright). Community Hospitals—Health Forum, LLC, an American Hospital Association Company, Chicago, IL, "Hospital Statistics" 2000 edition and unpublished data (copyright). Nursing and Personal Care Facilities—U.S. Census Bureau, County Business Patterns 1997 on CD-ROM (related Internet site <http://www.census.gov/epcd/cbp/view/cbpview.html>). Medicare—U.S. Health Care Financing Administration; "Medicare County Enrollment as of July 1, 1999 - Aged and Disabled 3/2000 update," <http://www.hcfa.gov/stats/enroll/default.htm>.

[Includes U.S., states, and 3,142 counties or county equivalents defined as of January 1, 1992. For changes to these areas since then, see appendix B. Geographic Information]

County	Births, 1997 Number	Births, 1997 Rate[1]	Deaths, 1997 Total Number	Deaths, 1997 Total Rate[1]	Deaths, 1997 Infant[2] Number	Deaths, 1997 Infant[2] Rate[3]	Physicians,[4] 1999 Number	Physicians,[4] 1999 Rate[5]	Community hospitals,[6] 1998 Number	Community hospitals,[6] 1998 Beds Number	Community hospitals,[6] 1998 Beds Rate[5]	Nursing and personal care facilities,[7] 1997 Establishments	Nursing and personal care facilities,[7] 1997 Employees[8]	Medicare program enrollment,[9] 1999 Total[10]	Medicare program enrollment,[9] 1999 Aged
VIRGINIA	91 862	13.6	53 852	8.0	714	7.8	16 717	243	93	17 890	264	440	39 276	875 799	747 960
Accomack	391	12.2	442	13.8	3	7.7	23	72	–	–	–	4	240	6 706	5 943
Albemarle	915	11.8	493	6.4	3	3.3	107	134	–	–	–	5	543	8 146	7 372
Alleghany	159	13.0	123	10.1	–	–	10	82	1	156	1 279	1	(11)	424	342
Amelia	118	11.6	96	9.4	–	–	2	19	–	–	–	1	(11)	1 593	1 340
Amherst	348	11.6	253	8.5	3	8.6	15	49	–	–	–	2	(12)	4 835	4 030
Appomattox	176	13.6	126	9.7	2	11.4	6	45	–	–	–	1	(11)	2 084	1 779
Arlington	2 676	15.4	1 102	6.3	16	6.0	758	434	4	574	329	14	817	17 665	16 414
Augusta	694	11.6	497	8.3	5	7.2	75	123	2	251	416	1	(11)	6 451	5 449
Bath	44	9.0	62	12.7	–	–	8	162	1	25	509	–	–	1 044	909
Bedford	629	11.3	448	8.1	3	4.8	48	83	1	322	568	1	(11)	8 620	7 307
Bland	62	9.1	60	8.8	–	–	6	88	–	–	–	1	(11)	1 239	963
Botetourt	294	10.4	221	7.8	–	–	24	82	–	–	–	2	(11)	4 352	3 710
Brunswick	177	10.6	193	11.6	1	5.6	6	33	–	–	–	3	(11)	3 063	2 530
Buchanan	288	9.8	291	9.9	1	3.5	21	74	1	144	497	1	(13)	6 461	3 113
Buckingham	135	9.3	128	8.8	1	7.4	6	41	–	–	–	1	(11)	2 009	1 680
Campbell	611	12.2	406	8.1	10	16.4	8	16	1	350	699	2	(13)	6 452	5 320
Caroline	298	13.7	182	8.4	3	10.1	3	14	–	–	–	1	(11)	3 032	2 524
Carroll	309	11.1	327	11.7	–	–	10	36	–	–	–	3	240	4 455	3 615
Charles City	86	12.4	62	8.9	4	46.5	4	55	–	–	–	–	–	812	683
Charlotte	137	11.2	182	14.9	–	–	11	89	–	–	–	1	(11)	3 035	2 536
Chesterfield	3 123	12.6	1 340	5.4	16	5.1	347	137	–	–	–	6	338	20 277	17 788
Clarke	97	7.6	122	9.6	–	–	20	156	–	–	–	1	(13)	1 743	1 590
Craig	43	8.8	41	8.4	–	–	–	–	–	–	–	–	–	733	587
Culpeper	434	13.4	286	8.8	8	18.4	43	128	1	70	211	2	(14)	4 623	3 986
Cumberland	113	14.5	95	12.2	1	8.8	3	38	–	–	–	–	–	947	796
Dickenson	174	10.1	185	10.8	3	17.2	12	72	1	41	243	1	(11)	3 699	2 116
Dinwiddie	253	10.1	236	9.4	2	7.9	8	31	–	–	–	2	(15)	2 776	2 029
Essex	106	11.5	113	12.3	1	9.4	19	208	1	100	1 101	1	(11)	1 779	1 556
Fairfax	12 850	14.0	3 831	4.2	54	4.2	1 967	208	4	1 139	123	38	2 419	57 092	53 050
Fauquier	641	12.1	384	7.3	5	7.8	78	141	1	83	154	2	(14)	5 835	5 204
Floyd	132	10.2	144	11.1	–	–	7	53	–	–	–	1	(11)	2 208	1 914
Fluvanna	249	14.0	138	7.7	–	–	26	133	–	–	–	1	(13)	2 935	2 643
Franklin	469	10.7	450	10.2	2	4.3	36	80	1	37	83	4	313	6 865	5 646
Frederick	694	12.7	378	6.9	5	7.2	9	16	1	376	675	5	429	5 827	5 046
Giles	182	11.3	208	12.9	1	5.5	13	80	1	53	326	1	(11)	3 568	2 930
Gloucester	330	9.6	269	7.8	–	–	46	130	1	71	203	2	(13)	4 360	3 772
Goochland	157	9.2	111	6.5	2	12.7	26	147	–	–	–	1	(10)	1 930	1 705
Grayson	156	9.5	192	11.7	–	–	8	49	–	–	–	–	–	2 974	2 474
Greene	210	15.7	92	6.9	4	19.0	9	61	–	–	–	2	(11)	1 595	1 321
Greensville	113	10.2	99	9.0	–	–	–	–	–	–	–	1	(15)	737	597
Halifax	434	11.8	502	13.6	2	4.6	65	176	1	157	427	5	243	6 249	5 049
Hanover	938	11.8	541	6.8	7	7.5	109	128	1	252	306	8	265	11 525	10 281
Henrico	3 223	13.4	2 232	9.3	27	8.4	137	56	5	915	378	16	1 930	28 337	25 444
Henry	650	11.6	585	10.4	5	7.7	9	16	–	–	–	2	(13)	8 087	6 447
Highland	20	7.9	34	13.4	–	–	4	161	–	–	–	–	–	532	471
Isle of Wight	311	10.9	259	9.1	3	9.6	16	54	–	–	–	4	191	3 966	3 313
James City	400	9.2	297	6.9	2	5.0	–	–	–	–	–	1	(11)	1 925	1 733
King and Queen	76	11.7	83	12.8	–	–	3	46	–	–	–	–	–	1 063	938
King George	220	13.0	134	7.9	2	9.1	11	62	–	–	–	1	(13)	1 707	1 484
King William	180	14.4	105	8.4	–	–	5	38	–	–	–	1	(11)	1 761	1 555
Lancaster	97	8.6	186	16.5	1	10.3	50	441	1	76	670	2	(14)	3 602	3 365
Lee	281	11.7	278	11.6	1	3.6	22	92	1	80	335	4	112	5 128	3 487
Loudoun	2 601	19.4	541	4.0	8	3.1	205	131	1	92	64	3	455	9 203	8 332
Louisa	284	11.9	242	10.1	2	7.0	12	48	–	–	–	3	(11)	3 590	2 981
Lunenburg	127	10.5	161	13.3	1	7.9	4	34	–	–	–	–	–	2 055	1 742
Madison	120	9.6	117	9.4	1	8.3	8	63	–	–	–	2	(13)	1 784	1 567
Mathews	92	10.1	147	16.2	–	–	6	65	–	–	–	1	(11)	2 059	1 892
Mecklenburg	379	12.2	394	12.7	2	5.3	43	139	1	284	915	–	–	6 621	5 562
Middlesex	62	6.5	122	12.7	–	–	11	113	–	–	–	2	(13)	2 384	2 142
Montgomery	837	11.1	476	6.3	4	4.8	110	143	1	115	150	2	(14)	8 217	6 833
Nelson	181	13.1	173	12.6	1	5.5	26	183	–	–	–	2	(11)	2 957	2 561
New Kent	149	11.9	88	7.0	2	13.4	13	98	–	–	–	–	–	1 728	1 462
Northampton	155	12.1	182	14.2	4	25.8	40	312	1	123	967	1	(13)	2 958	2 617
Northumberland	87	7.6	159	14.0	1	11.5	12	103	–	–	–	–	–	2 865	2 606
Nottoway	180	12.0	217	14.4	1	5.6	41	268	–	–	–	1	(13)	3 091	2 661
Orange	305	12.2	302	12.1	3	9.8	19	74	–	–	–	1	(11)	5 258	4 654
Page	252	11.0	247	10.8	1	4.0	12	52	1	54	234	1	(13)	4 002	3 395
Patrick	192	10.5	218	11.9	2	10.4	15	81	1	59	320	1	(13)	3 485	2 887
Pittsylvania	662	11.7	594	10.5	10	15.1	9	16	–	–	–	3	(11)	7 949	6 593
Powhatan	229	11.1	123	6.0	1	4.4	20	89	–	–	–	1	(15)	2 163	1 871

[1] Per 1,000 resident population estimated as of July 1, 1997.   [2] Deaths of infants under 1 year old.   [3] Infant deaths per 1,000 live births.   [4] Active, nonfederal physicians as of December 31. Data subject to copyright; see below for source citation.   [5] Per 100,000 resident population estimated as of July 1 of the year shown.   [6] Nonfederal, short-stay (average length of stay less than 30 days) hospitals except hospital units of institutions. Data subject to copyright; see below for source citation.   [7] SIC 805 includes skilled nursing care facilities; intermediate care facilities; and nursing and personal care, not elsewhere classified.   [8] Full- and part-time employees on the payroll in the pay period including March 12.   [9] Unduplicated count of persons enrolled in either hospital and/or supplemental medical insurance as of July 1. State totals include data not distributed by county.   [10] Includes disabled, not shown separately.   [11] 20 to 99 employees.   [12] 1,000 to 2,499 employees.   [13] 100 to 249 employees.   [14] 250 to 499 employees.   [15] 0 to 19 employees.

Sources: Births—U.S. National Center for Health Statistics, "Vital Statistics of the United States, Vol. I, Natality," annual, and unpublished data.   Deaths—U.S. National Center for Health Statistics, "Vital Statistics of the United States, Vol. II, Mortality," annual, and unpublished data.   Physicians—American Medical Association, Chicago, IL, "Physician Characteristics and Distribution in the U.S.," annual (copyright).   Community Hospitals—Health Forum, LLC, an American Hospital Association Company, Chicago, IL, "Hospital Statistics" 2000 edition and unpublished data (copyright).   Nursing and Personal Care Facilities—U.S. Census Bureau, County Business Patterns 1997 on CD-ROM (related Internet site <http://www.census.gov/epcd/cbp/view/cbpview.html>).   Medicare—U.S. Health Care Financing Administration; "Medicare County Enrollment as of July 1, 1999 - Aged and Disabled 3/2000 update," <http://www.hcfa.gov/stats/enroll/default.htm>.

[Includes U.S., states, and 3,142 counties or county equivalents defined as of January 1, 1992. For changes to these areas since then, see appendix B. Geographic Information]

| County | Births, 1997 | | Deaths, 1997 | | | | Physicians,[4] 1999 | | Community hospitals,[6] 1998 | | | Nursing and personal care facilities,[7] 1997 | | Medicare program enrollment,[9] 1999 | |
| | | | Total | | Infant[2] | | | | | Beds | | | | | |
	Number	Rate[1]	Number	Rate[1]	Number	Rate[3]	Number	Rate[5]	Number	Number	Rate[5]	Estab-lishments	Em-ployees[8]	Total[10]	Aged
VIRGINIA—Con.															
Prince Edward	214	11.3	212	11.2	1	4.7	48	249	1	88	458	3	(11)	3 590	3 002
Prince George	350	12.4	138	4.9	–	–	11	38	–	–	–	1	(12)	1 933	1 620
Prince William	4 445	17.4	977	3.8	40	9.0	152	56	1	153	58	5	756	10 743	9 164
Pulaski	367	10.7	397	11.5	4	10.9	39	113	1	62	180	4	214	6 116	4 825
Rappahannock	65	9.0	53	7.4	–	–	7	91	–	–	–	–	–	1 265	1 102
Richmond	77	8.9	128	14.8	1	13.0	1	11	–	–	–	2	(13)	1 547	1 347
Roanoke	562	6.9	815	10.0	2	3.6	12	15	1	677	833	3	(14)	5 671	5 027
Rockbridge	210	11.0	182	9.5	1	4.8	4	20	–	–	–	–	–	2 225	1 879
Rockingham	798	12.6	573	9.0	9	11.3	24	38	–	–	–	6	778	8 613	7 552
Russell	318	11.0	310	10.7	2	6.3	14	49	1	78	270	3	(15)	5 145	3 349
Scott	235	10.3	285	12.5	–	–	5	22	–	–	–	2	(13)	4 995	3 916
Shenandoah	385	11.3	384	11.2	4	10.4	34	97	1	129	372	7	435	6 453	5 838
Smyth	370	11.3	413	12.6	3	8.1	47	144	1	279	851	2	(11)	6 645	5 239
Southampton	177	10.0	178	10.1	1	5.6	2	11	–	–	–	1	(15)	2 291	1 954
Spotsylvania	1 179	14.6	442	5.5	8	6.8	15	17	1	328	391	3	(11)	3 947	3 312
Stafford	1 194	13.9	380	4.4	7	5.9	16	17	–	–	–	1	(12)	4 003	3 469
Surry	68	10.6	73	11.4	1	14.7	2	31	–	–	–	1	(12)	962	823
Sussex	110	10.9	128	12.7	1	9.1	1	8	–	–	–	3	(13)	2 247	1 873
Tazewell	492	10.5	521	11.1	2	4.1	120	259	2	238	510	3	238	10 344	7 159
Warren	409	13.7	274	9.1	2	4.9	27	88	1	95	316	4	142	4 066	3 566
Washington	495	10.1	540	11.0	5	10.1	91	183	1	135	272	3	101	7 475	5 982
Westmoreland	188	11.6	205	12.6	2	10.6	6	37	–	–	–	2	(15)	3 308	2 933
Wise	514	13.1	450	11.5	5	9.7	48	119	2	112	286	3	(11)	8 396	5 601
Wythe	281	10.7	317	12.0	–	–	34	128	1	90	343	3	(11)	5 659	4 493
York	489	8.6	288	5.1	1	2.0	101	173	–	–	–	2	(13)	6 629	6 018
Independent Cities															
Alexandria	2 270	20.0	768	6.8	9	4.0	648	552	1	316	275	9	1 523	19 467	17 969
Bedford	65	10.3	114	18.1	–	–	19	285	1	161	2 443	1	(12)	3 182	2 778
Bristol	154	9.0	255	14.8	1	6.5	11	66	–	–	–	1	(13)	5 716	4 768
Buena Vista	72	11.0	98	15.0	–	–	3	46	–	–	–	1	(15)	1 430	1 190
Charlottesville	488	12.9	381	10.1	6	12.3	1 298	3 526	2	751	2 030	4	491	7 174	6 225
Chesapeake	2 718	13.9	1 248	6.4	28	10.3	435	215	1	260	130	8	580	19 357	16 396
Clifton Forge	59	13.6	100	23.0	–	–	16	380	–	–	–	3	(13)	1 543	1 322
Colonial Heights	169	10.4	215	13.2	2	11.8	39	240	–	–	–	1	(13)	3 685	3 312
Covington	61	8.6	123	17.4	1	16.4	11	161	–	–	–	–	–	2 990	2 499
Danville	577	11.0	816	15.6	10	17.3	160	315	1	312	603	6	697	13 339	11 263
Emporia	70	11.9	125	21.2	2	28.6	20	353	1	144	2 506	–	–	2 060	1 694
Fairfax	297	14.5	207	10.1	2	6.7	481	2 324	–	–	–	6	486	8 856	8 150
Falls Church	127	13.3	85	8.9	3	23.6	414	4 163	–	–	–	–	–	3 801	3 620
Franklin	88	10.0	117	13.3	2	22.7	35	430	1	203	2 396	–	–	2 350	1 979
Fredericksburg	316	15.1	221	10.5	4	12.7	219	1 163	1	–	–	3	(13)	8 259	7 196
Galax	98	14.7	101	15.1	–	–	42	648	1	89	1 338	1	(13)	3 241	2 676
Hampton	2 044	14.7	1 088	7.8	16	7.8	199	145	1	178	130	5	473	17 277	14 810
Harrisonburg	381	11.3	266	7.9	5	13.1	134	393	1	266	784	5	772	4 604	4 170
Hopewell	326	14.5	268	11.9	3	9.2	37	163	1	222	967	2	(13)	4 042	3 465
Lexington	45	6.2	72	9.9	–	–	31	421	1	130	1 770	1	(15)	2 532	2 253
Lynchburg	811	12.5	787	12.1	11	13.6	257	402	2	–	–	13	1 301	14 464	12 031
Manassas	687	21.3	184	5.7	3	4.4	130	388	1	130	398	2	(11)	5 591	4 709
Manassas Park	169	22.7	39	5.2	2	11.8	1	13	–	–	–	–	–	12	D
Martinsville	185	11.9	272	17.5	–	–	69	460	1	152	995	4	(11)	6 783	5 628
Newport News	3 052	17.5	1 357	7.8	37	12.1	351	196	3	812	456	10	1 458	20 706	17 518
Norfolk	3 927	16.7	2 193	9.3	74	18.8	858	380	5	1 135	500	10	1 354	28 999	24 680
Norton	28	6.9	49	12.0	1	35.7	37	923	1	98	2 416	–	–	1 329	899
Petersburg	525	14.9	517	14.7	5	9.5	90	262	1	268	769	4	(11)	8 346	6 688
Poquoson	91	8.0	79	7.0	–	–	21	181	–	–	–	1	(15)	685	648
Portsmouth	1 674	16.8	1 133	11.4	20	11.9	178	181	1	441	445	8	950	16 120	13 665
Radford	127	8.1	99	6.3	2	15.7	71	453	1	158	1 015	–	–	2 281	1 942
Richmond	3 280	17.2	2 471	13.0	30	9.1	2 267	1 195	8	2 011	1 053	34	2 014	38 202	32 455
Roanoke	1 616	17.0	1 271	13.4	9	5.6	665	712	–	–	–	14	1 451	24 442	20 850
Salem	256	10.6	287	11.9	–	–	128	533	1	521	2 151	2	(13)	6 105	5 384
South Boston	X	X	X	X	X	X	X	X	X	X	X	X	X	980	828
Staunton	248	10.1	298	12.2	1	4.0	63	257	–	–	–	1	(13)	6 293	5 350
Suffolk	860	14.1	528	8.6	8	9.3	121	187	1	160	255	5	348	8 745	7 030
Virginia Beach	6 414	14.9	2 226	5.2	58	9.0	945	218	2	390	91	18	1 778	37 838	33 262
Waynesboro	252	13.1	202	10.5	–	–	43	223	–	–	–	2	(13)	5 009	4 322
Williamsburg	136	11.2	127	10.4	3	22.1	223	1 785	1	119	963	1	(13)	6 209	5 763
Winchester	310	13.8	255	11.4	1	3.2	221	983	–	–	–	3	(13)	4 893	4 420

[1] Per 1,000 resident population estimated as of July 1, 1997. [2] Deaths of infants under 1 year old. [3] Infant deaths per 1,000 live births. [4] Active, nonfederal physicians as of December 31. Data subject to copyright; see below for source citation. [5] Per 100,000 resident population estimated as of July 1 of the year shown. [6] Nonfederal, short-stay (average length of stay less than 30 days) hospitals except hospital units of institutions. Data subject to copyright; see below for source citation. [7] SIC 805 includes skilled nursing care facilities; intermediate care facilities; and nursing and personal care, not elsewhere classified. [8] Full- and part-time employees on the payroll in the pay period including March 12. [9] Unduplicated count of persons enrolled in either hospital and/or supplemental medical insurance as of July 1. State totals include data not distributed by county. [10] Includes disabled, not shown separately. [11] 250 to 499 employess. [12] 0 to 19 employees. [13] 100 to 249 employees. [14] 500 to 999 employees. [15] 20 to 99 employees.

Sources: Births—U.S. National Center for Health Statistics, "Vital Statistics of the United States, Vol. I, Natality," annual, and unpublished data. Deaths—U.S. National Center for Health Statistics, "Vital Statistics of the United States, Vol. II, Mortality," annual, and unpublished data. Physicians—American Medical Association, Chicago, IL, "Physician Characteristics and Distribution in the U.S.," annual (copyright). Community Hospitals—Health Forum, LLC, an American Hospital Association Company, Chicago, IL, "Hospital Statistics" 2000 edition and unpublished data (copyright). Nursing and Personal Care Facilities—U.S. Census Bureau, County Business Patterns 1997 on CD-ROM (related Internet site <http://www.census.gov/epcd/cbp/view/cbpview.html>). Medicare—U.S. Health Care Financing Administration; "Medicare County Enrollment as of July 1, 1999 - Aged and Disabled 3/2000 update," <http://www.hcfa.gov/stats/enroll/default.htm>.

Table B–4. Counties — **Vital Statistics and Health**–Con.

[Includes U.S., states, and 3,142 counties or county equivalents defined as of January 1, 1992. For changes to these areas since then, see appendix B. Geographic Information]

County	Births, 1997		Deaths, 1997				Physicians,[4] 1999		Community hospitals,[6] 1998			Nursing and personal care facilities,[7] 1997		Medicare program enrollment,[9] 1999	
			Total		Infant[2]					Beds					
	Number	Rate[1]	Number	Rate[1]	Number	Rate[3]	Number	Rate[5]	Number	Number	Rate[5]	Estab-lishments	Em-ployees[8]	Total[10]	Aged
WASHINGTON	78 190	14.0	41 463	7.4	440	5.6	13 616	237	86	10 739	189	545	36 772	725 018	635 190
Adams	294	19.2	100	6.5	1	3.4	11	72	2	49	319	2	(11)	1 530	1 358
Asotin	287	13.7	219	10.4	2	7.0	23	108	1	41	193	4	264	3 745	3 206
Benton	2 024	15.0	833	6.2	14	6.9	232	168	3	244	179	8	555	15 808	13 806
Chelan	979	16.5	561	9.4	3	3.1	202	332	2	163	271	7	538	7 452	6 726
Clallam	647	10.2	769	12.1	3	4.6	123	190	2	256	398	11	452	15 182	13 689
Clark	4 951	15.6	2 120	6.7	21	4.2	441	131	1	310	95	30	1 397	35 921	31 185
Columbia	41	9.8	50	11.9	–	–	2	48	1	18	433	–	–	816	703
Cowlitz	1 172	12.9	872	9.6	10	8.5	158	172	1	171	187	18	731	14 477	12 421
Douglas	436	13.2	230	7.0	–	–	8	23	–	–	–	2	(11)	6 688	5 955
Ferry	79	10.9	71	9.8	1	12.7	4	56	1	25	349	–	–	974	784
Franklin	974	21.3	277	6.1	5	5.1	45	96	1	132	284	3	(11)	4 627	4 004
Garfield	12	5.2	28	12.2	–	–	–	–	1	54	2 331	–	–	524	482
Grant	1 390	20.1	492	7.1	9	6.5	58	81	4	194	275	4	(12)	9 977	8 626
Grays Harbor	850	12.5	793	11.7	5	5.9	52	77	2	178	264	8	437	12 474	10 515
Island	953	13.4	500	7.0	9	9.4	78	106	1	51	71	3	(11)	8 503	7 825
Jefferson	214	8.3	257	10.0	2	9.3	47	176	1	35	133	4	111	5 768	5 257
King	21 660	13.3	11 312	6.9	113	5.2	6 774	407	15	3 209	194	151	12 030	197 865	176 202
Kitsap	3 257	14.0	1 597	6.9	19	5.8	369	156	1	252	108	15	1 384	26 495	23 261
Kittitas	306	9.8	241	7.7	1	3.3	37	116	1	37	118	3	190	4 189	3 703
Klickitat	237	12.5	139	7.3	2	8.4	16	82	2	39	201	2	(13)	3 015	2 632
Lewis	878	13.0	709	10.5	4	4.6	74	108	2	190	279	6	410	12 348	10 604
Lincoln	131	13.5	97	10.0	2	15.3	8	82	2	137	1 403	–	–	2 077	1 875
Mason	522	10.5	447	9.0	3	5.7	40	79	1	51	102	4	(11)	9 145	8 041
Okanogan	523	13.7	365	9.5	3	5.7	47	122	3	167	436	4	(11)	6 259	5 322
Pacific	219	10.4	259	12.3	–	–	24	116	2	40	192	3	(13)	5 146	4 564
Pend Oreille	124	11.0	116	10.3	–	–	5	43	1	74	642	1	(14)	2 062	1 647
Pierce	9 739	14.7	4 718	7.1	61	6.3	1 266	184	6	1 125	166	60	4 329	79 956	68 283
San Juan	113	9.3	100	8.2	–	–	34	264	–	–	–	–	–	2 466	2 339
Skagit	1 338	13.8	863	8.9	7	5.2	214	212	2	237	238	10	503	16 458	14 697
Skamania	88	9.1	69	7.1	–	–	2	20	–	–	–	–	–	946	809
Snohomish	8 110	14.3	3 443	6.1	49	6.0	797	134	4	503	86	46	2 874	59 825	52 345
Spokane	5 503	13.6	3 518	8.7	35	6.4	1 051	257	7	1 368	335	62	4 043	58 435	50 215
Stevens	477	12.1	298	7.6	4	8.4	41	102	2	97	245	2	(11)	5 556	4 649
Thurston	2 420	12.1	1 428	7.1	10	4.1	462	225	2	425	210	11	1 078	26 187	22 762
Wahkiakum	37	9.6	42	10.8	1	27.0	2	52	–	–	–	1	(13)	737	653
Walla Walla	677	12.6	500	9.3	4	5.9	136	253	2	149	278	7	648	8 607	7 648
Whatcom	1 948	12.6	1 103	7.1	6	3.1	330	206	1	189	120	25	1 274	20 976	18 531
Whitman	392	10.2	221	5.7	3	7.7	48	125	2	68	176	6	290	4 102	3 697
Yakima	4 188	19.4	1 706	7.9	28	6.7	355	161	4	461	211	22	1 618	27 567	24 063
WEST VIRGINIA	20 730	11.4	20 881	11.5	198	9.6	3 962	219	58	8 117	448	286	14 416	335 529	270 449
Barbour	157	9.8	207	12.9	1	6.4	9	56	1	72	447	3	118	2 855	2 306
Berkeley	965	14.0	644	9.3	7	7.3	86	118	1	143	201	9	733	9 896	8 091
Boone	358	13.6	278	10.5	–	–	11	42	1	38	145	2	(11)	4 695	3 358
Braxton	157	11.9	184	13.9	3	19.1	4	30	1	30	227	1	(13)	2 630	2 121
Brooke	255	9.7	327	12.5	4	15.7	10	39	1	240	923	5	266	4 276	3 769
Cabell	1 106	11.6	1 267	13.3	16	14.5	543	580	3	736	782	25	1 075	19 795	16 325
Calhoun	79	10.0	82	10.4	1	12.7	4	50	1	49	617	–	–	1 575	1 228
Clay	112	10.6	130	12.4	1	8.9	4	38	–	–	–	1	(13)	1 917	1 386
Doddridge	76	10.3	68	9.2	1	13.2	2	27	–	–	–	–	–	947	792
Fayette	562	11.8	643	13.5	3	5.3	47	100	2	178	378	7	512	10 225	7 911
Gilmer	76	10.7	89	12.5	–	–	3	42	–	–	–	1	(13)	1 297	1 038
Grant	131	11.8	115	10.4	2	15.3	10	90	1	61	549	5	(13)	1 920	1 633
Greenbrier	387	10.9	448	12.6	3	7.8	54	153	1	122	345	8	397	7 376	5 920
Hampshire	228	12.1	189	10.0	–	–	10	51	1	47	245	8	241	3 139	2 619
Hancock	321	9.3	381	11.1	1	3.1	69	205	–	–	–	7	284	7 529	6 744
Hardy	131	11.2	127	10.8	–	–	5	42	–	–	–	3	(13)	2 110	1 811
Harrison	808	11.4	904	12.7	12	14.9	133	189	1	360	508	17	817	14 013	11 681
Jackson	324	11.7	271	9.8	2	6.2	17	60	1	82	293	3	(11)	4 961	4 126
Jefferson	467	11.4	329	8.1	4	8.6	52	123	1	58	140	5	238	5 334	4 571
Kanawha	2 497	12.3	2 454	12.1	12	4.8	734	368	4	1 181	586	44	1 599	39 720	33 326
Lewis	195	11.1	216	12.3	3	15.4	20	115	1	70	398	–	–	3 629	2 930
Lincoln	306	13.8	272	12.3	3	9.8	4	18	–	–	–	1	(13)	3 882	2 653
Logan	479	11.6	453	11.0	7	14.6	66	164	3	193	470	4	305	8 187	5 604
McDowell	345	11.3	420	13.7	7	20.3	19	65	–	–	–	1	(11)	7 353	4 578

[1] Per 1,000 resident population estimated as of July 1, 1997. [2] Deaths of infants under 1 year old. [3] Infant deaths per 1,000 live births. [4] Active, nonfederal physicians as of December 31. Data subject to copyright; see below for source citation. [5] Per 100,000 resident population estimated as of July 1 of the year shown. [6] Nonfederal, short-stay (average length of stay less than 30 days) hospitals except hospital units of institutions. Data subject to copyright; see below for source citation. [7] SIC 805 includes skilled nursing care facilities; intermediate care facilities; and nursing and personal care, not elsewhere classified. [8] Full- and part-time employees on the payroll in the pay period including March 12. [9] Unduplicated count of persons enrolled in either hospital and/or supplemental medical insurance as of July 1. State totals include data not distributed by county. [10] Includes disabled, not shown separately. [11] 100 to 249 employees. [12] 250 to 499 employees. [13] 20 to 99 employees. [14] 0 to 19 employees.

Sources: Births—U.S. National Center for Health Statistics, "Vital Statistics of the United States, Vol. I, Natality," annual, and unpublished data. Deaths—U.S. National Center for Health Statistics, "Vital Statistics of the United States, Vol. II, Mortality," annual, and unpublished data. Physicians—American Medical Association, Chicago, IL, "Physician Characteristics and Distribution in the U.S.," annual (copyright). Community Hospitals—Health Forum, LLC, an American Hospital Association Company, Chicago, IL, "Hospital Statistics" 2000 edition and unpublished data (copyright). Nursing and Personal Care Facilities—U.S. Census Bureau, County Business Patterns 1997 on CD-ROM (related Internet site <http://www.census.gov/epcd/cbp/view/cbpview.html>). Medicare—U.S. Health Care Financing Administration; "Medicare County Enrollment as of July 1, 1999 - Aged and Disabled 3/2000 update," <http://www.hcfa.gov/stats/enroll/default.htm>.

[Includes U.S., states, and 3,142 counties or county equivalents defined as of January 1, 1992. For changes to these areas since then, see appendix B. Geographic Information]

County	Births, 1997 Number	Births, 1997 Rate[1]	Deaths, 1997 Total Number	Deaths, 1997 Total Rate[1]	Deaths, 1997 Infant[2] Number	Deaths, 1997 Infant[2] Rate[3]	Physicians,[4] 1999 Number	Physicians,[4] 1999 Rate[5]	Community hospitals,[6] 1998 Number	Community hospitals,[6] 1998 Beds Number	Community hospitals,[6] 1998 Beds Rate[5]	Nursing and personal care facilities,[7] 1997 Establishments	Nursing and personal care facilities,[7] 1997 Employees[8]	Medicare program enrollment,[9] 1999 Total[10]	Medicare program enrollment,[9] 1999 Aged
WEST VIRGINIA—Con.															
Marion	643	11.3	723	12.7	3	4.7	92	164	1	211	374	6	444	11 858	10 209
Marshall	373	10.5	416	11.7	6	16.1	31	89	1	140	397	9	374	5 875	5 133
Mason	285	11.0	305	11.8	3	10.5	27	104	1	201	775	1	(11)	4 578	3 732
Mercer	832	12.9	833	12.9	10	12.0	149	232	4	603	937	12	593	13 940	10 753
Mineral	287	10.6	330	12.2	4	13.9	23	85	1	42	155	4	243	4 713	4 067
Mingo	439	13.5	372	11.4	5	11.4	35	111	1	76	238	1	(12)	5 950	3 674
Monongalia	795	10.2	582	7.5	7	8.8	746	969	3	663	856	8	512	9 503	8 125
Monroe	135	10.3	141	10.7	3	22.2	6	45	–	–	–	1	(11)	2 943	2 369
Morgan	158	11.6	148	10.9	2	12.7	11	79	1	44	321	1	(12)	2 599	2 258
Nicholas	257	9.3	268	9.7	3	11.7	31	113	2	134	486	5	113	5 141	3 815
Ohio	535	11.0	690	14.2	3	5.6	251	526	2	661	1 370	15	751	10 561	9 383
Pendleton	82	10.2	105	13.1	–	–	5	62	–	–	–	2	(12)	1 620	1 410
Pleasants	72	9.6	83	11.1	1	13.9	3	40	–	–	–	2	(12)	1 326	1 123
Pocahontas	85	9.4	104	11.5	1	11.8	5	55	1	27	297	2	(11)	1 888	1 525
Preston	298	10.0	314	10.5	3	10.1	27	91	1	60	201	1	(12)	5 177	4 276
Putnam	588	11.7	430	8.5	3	5.1	62	119	1	64	125	3	(13)	6 367	5 288
Raleigh	891	11.3	872	11.0	7	7.9	194	246	2	448	565	12	539	15 467	11 547
Randolph	314	10.9	332	11.6	3	9.6	56	195	1	115	401	5	273	5 406	4 374
Ritchie	95	9.3	130	12.7	–	–	3	29	–	–	–	2	(12)	1 909	1 546
Roane	153	10.0	198	12.9	3	19.6	15	97	1	55	359	1	(11)	2 686	2 086
Summers	133	9.6	191	13.8	4	30.1	6	43	1	50	359	2	(12)	2 811	2 230
Taylor	169	11.0	193	12.6	2	11.8	6	39	1	106	690	3	124	2 658	2 194
Tucker	62	8.0	100	13.0	–	–	4	53	–	–	–	1	(12)	1 478	1 251
Tyler	93	9.3	106	10.6	–	–	2	21	1	12	123	1	(11)	1 571	1 333
Upshur	258	10.9	269	11.3	4	15.5	27	115	1	95	403	5	(12)	3 955	3 255
Wayne	469	11.1	444	10.5	7	14.9	13	31	–	–	–	3	90	6 289	4 728
Webster	91	8.8	125	12.1	1	11.0	4	40	1	15	147	1	(11)	2 065	1 450
Wetzel	209	11.3	220	11.9	2	9.6	16	88	1	63	344	3	179	3 812	3 208
Wirt	64	11.3	57	10.1	–	–	3	52	–	–	–	–	–	949	749
Wood	1 023	11.7	1 027	11.8	10	9.8	186	215	3	572	660	12	741	15 645	13 398
Wyoming	320	11.6	275	9.9	5	15.6	7	26	–	–	–	2	(11)	5 475	3 407
WISCONSIN	66 557	12.8	44 891	8.6	431	6.5	12 167	232	123	16 693	320	944	51 644	777 273	689 270
Adams	157	8.6	184	10.1	2	12.7	7	37	1	58	315	3	(12)	2 831	2 421
Ashland	202	12.2	194	11.7	1	5.0	48	293	1	101	614	3	310	3 296	2 884
Barron	464	10.6	445	10.2	2	4.3	63	143	3	292	666	10	522	8 132	7 159
Bayfield	153	10.1	161	10.6	1	6.5	13	85	–	–	–	1	(11)	2 563	2 281
Brown	3 050	14.2	1 476	6.9	20	6.6	434	200	3	591	275	42	1 682	26 605	23 643
Buffalo	144	10.1	159	11.2	–	–	5	35	–	–	–	4	241	2 637	2 380
Burnett	134	9.2	172	11.8	1	7.5	7	47	1	70	478	2	(12)	3 162	2 807
Calumet	452	11.9	231	6.1	3	6.6	11	28	1	53	138	4	198	3 608	3 282
Chippewa	638	11.8	500	9.2	1	1.6	64	117	3	355	651	14	861	9 079	7 894
Clark	471	14.3	318	9.6	2	4.2	21	63	1	169	510	7	123	5 953	5 432
Columbia	633	12.6	495	9.8	4	6.3	55	106	2	220	430	5	569	9 279	8 413
Crawford	181	11.0	172	10.4	3	16.6	14	85	1	43	259	3	345	2 997	2 626
Dane	5 024	11.9	2 441	5.8	24	4.8	2 081	486	4	1 192	281	121	3 361	44 320	38 579
Dodge	924	11.2	797	9.7	5	5.4	51	61	2	261	314	9	885	9 707	8 799
Door	218	8.1	305	11.3	–	–	36	133	1	75	277	6	(13)	5 554	5 152
Douglas	534	12.4	501	11.6	2	3.7	24	56	1	42	97	14	784	7 429	6 339
Dunn	468	12.1	246	6.4	1	2.1	30	77	1	55	141	7	362	4 968	4 387
Eau Claire	1 105	12.4	658	7.4	8	7.2	321	358	2	440	493	23	709	12 830	11 172
Florence	48	9.2	47	9.0	–	–	1	19	–	–	–	1	(11)	856	749
Fond du Lac	1 118	11.8	785	8.3	7	6.3	148	156	3	257	272	27	863	15 813	14 194
Forest	117	12.3	109	11.4	–	–	3	31	–	–	–	2	(12)	2 024	1 781
Grant	530	10.8	482	9.8	2	3.8	37	75	3	316	641	7	505	9 012	8 209
Green	370	11.2	309	9.3	2	5.4	73	216	1	117	350	2	(12)	5 306	4 841
Green Lake	216	11.2	246	12.7	1	4.6	23	118	1	187	959	10	320	4 019	3 659
Iowa	259	11.7	182	8.2	1	3.9	16	70	1	84	376	4	89	3 040	2 745
Iron	63	9.8	101	15.7	–	–	4	64	–	–	–	3	(12)	1 580	1 406
Jackson	211	10.2	178	10.1	2	9.5	18	101	1	38	214	5	17	3 068	2 713
Jefferson	914	12.5	603	8.2	5	5.5	80	108	1	102	139	28	1 239	12 007	10 284
Juneau	272	11.4	263	11.0	–	–	17	71	1	97	408	1	(11)	4 759	4 178
Kenosha	2 175	15.2	1 128	7.9	11	5.1	186	127	2	264	183	19	1 035	18 393	15 779
Kewaunee	228	11.6	172	8.7	2	8.8	9	45	1	18	91	2	(11)	3 347	3 100
La Crosse	1 327	13.0	888	8.7	14	10.6	443	432	2	499	487	17	1 396	14 788	13 084

[1] Per 1,000 resident population estimated as of July 1, 1997. [2] Deaths of infants under 1 year old. [3] Infant deaths per 1,000 live births. [4] Active, nonfederal physicians as of December 31. Data subject to copyright; see below for source citation. [5] Per 100,000 resident population estimated as of July 1 of the year shown. [6] Nonfederal, short-stay (average length of stay less than 30 days) hospitals except hospital units of institutions. Data subject to copyright; see below for source citation. [7] SIC 805 includes skilled nursing care facilities; intermediate care facilities; and nursing and personal care, not elsewhere classified. [8] Full- and part-time employees on the payroll in the pay period including March 12. [9] Unduplicated count of persons enrolled in either hospital and/or supplemental medical insurance as of July 1. State totals include data not distributed by county. [10] Includes disabled, not shown separately. [11] 20 to 99 employees. [12] 100 to 249 employees. [13] 250 to 499 employees.

Sources: Births—U.S. National Center for Health Statistics, "Vital Statistics of the United States, Vol. I, Natality," annual, and unpublished data. Deaths—U.S. National Center for Health Statistics, "Vital Statistics of the United States, Vol. II, Mortality," annual, and unpublished data. Physicians—American Medical Association, Chicago, IL, "Physician Characteristics and Distribution in the U.S.," annual (copyright). Community Hospitals—Health Forum, LLC, an American Hospital Association Company, Chicago, IL, "Hospital Statistics" 2000 edition and unpublished data (copyright). Nursing and Personal Care Facilities—U.S. Census Bureau, County Business Patterns 1997 on CD-ROM (related Internet site <http://www.census.gov/epcd/cbp/view/cbpview.html>). Medicare—U.S. Health Care Financing Administration; "Medicare County Enrollment as of July 1, 1999 - Aged and Disabled 3/2000 update," <http://www.hcfa.gov/stats/enroll/default.htm>.

[Includes U.S., states, and 3,142 counties or county equivalents defined as of January 1, 1992. For changes to these areas since then, see appendix B. Geographic Information]

County	Births, 1997		Deaths, 1997				Physicians,[4] 1999		Community hospitals,[6] 1998				Nursing and personal care facilities,[7] 1997		Medicare program enrollment,[9] 1999	
			Total		Infant[2]						Beds					
	Number	Rate[1]	Number	Rate[1]	Number	Rate[3]	Number	Rate[5]	Number	Number	Rate[5]	Estab- lishments	Em- ployees[8]		Total[10]	Aged
WISCONSIN—Con.																
Lafayette	160	9.8	167	10.2	1	6.3	6	37	1	28	173	–	–		2 678	2 475
Langlade	229	11.1	228	11.1	2	8.7	22	107	1	43	210	2	(11)		4 169	3 739
Lincoln	329	11.1	296	10.0	1	3.0	35	117	1	63	212	4	237		5 708	5 107
Manitowoc	902	11.0	813	9.9	12	13.3	113	137	2	314	381	19	709		14 530	13 196
Marathon	1 580	12.9	877	7.2	4	2.5	247	200	1	212	172	16	667		16 844	15 145
Marinette	414	9.6	504	11.7	4	9.7	47	109	1	115	267	6	756		8 832	7 849
Marquette	179	12.0	152	10.2	–	–	6	39	–	–	–	3	(12)		3 742	3 376
Menominee	95	19.1	35	7.1	1	10.5	1	20	–	–	–	–	–		480	381
Milwaukee	14 339	15.6	8 844	9.6	132	9.2	3 114	344	13	3 815	419	123	11 948		140 462	120 365
Monroe	511	13.0	355	9.1	8	15.7	33	83	2	104	263	4	280		6 061	5 313
Oconto	347	10.4	326	9.8	2	5.8	16	47	2	43	127	6	353		5 429	4 871
Oneida	346	9.7	387	10.9	1	2.9	123	341	2	117	327	5	(13)		8 112	7 315
Outagamie	2 029	13.1	1 197	7.8	15	7.4	307	194	3	340	217	18	1 456		19 657	17 678
Ozaukee	862	10.7	565	7.0	4	4.6	279	340	1	90	111	9	493		11 023	10 225
Pepin	88	12.3	87	12.2	1	11.4	6	82	1	83	1 162	1	(12)		1 388	1 262
Pierce	351	10.0	244	6.9	1	2.8	25	69	1	36	101	11	239		4 611	4 154
Polk	414	10.8	398	10.4	2	4.8	50	127	3	137	353	5	401		6 429	5 842
Portage	759	11.7	468	7.2	4	5.3	91	140	1	114	176	1	(14)		8 168	7 312
Price	150	9.5	206	13.1	1	6.7	15	96	1	42	267	4	(12)		3 241	2 924
Racine	2 567	13.9	1 552	8.4	27	10.5	287	154	3	453	244	27	1 347		27 583	23 775
Richland	192	10.7	201	11.2	–	–	16	90	1	38	213	2	(12)		2 986	2 681
Rock	1 990	13.3	1 369	9.1	14	7.0	260	172	3	548	364	27	1 057		21 678	19 045
Rusk	162	10.6	175	11.4	1	6.2	10	66	1	134	882	1	(12)		3 069	2 722
St. Croix	771	13.4	453	7.9	2	2.6	59	98	3	86	146	11	615		5 949	5 365
Sauk	697	13.1	455	8.6	2	2.9	83	153	3	200	375	8	453		8 713	7 869
Sawyer	175	10.9	169	10.5	–	–	19	117	1	117	727	1	(12)		3 078	2 714
Shawano	438	11.4	421	10.9	1	2.3	28	71	1	46	119	8	732		7 057	6 395
Sheboygan	1 348	12.3	997	9.1	8	5.9	142	129	3	502	456	20	885		17 373	15 839
Taylor	198	10.3	197	10.2	2	10.1	14	73	1	153	795	3	258		3 069	2 779
Trempealeau	327	12.4	290	11.0	1	3.1	20	75	3	269	1 015	9	343		5 137	4 638
Vernon	347	12.7	322	11.8	–	–	27	97	2	117	428	5	377		5 229	4 743
Vilas	172	8.2	264	12.5	–	–	18	83	1	9	42	–	–		4 948	4 557
Walworth	1 018	12.1	748	8.9	2	2.0	83	96	1	78	91	25	837		12 242	11 018
Washburn	143	9.4	193	12.7	–	–	20	127	2	185	1 199	4	112		3 960	3 540
Washington	1 416	12.6	746	6.6	6	4.2	115	99	2	192	169	25	1 003		14 209	12 925
Waukesha	4 156	11.9	2 443	7.0	22	5.3	1 263	352	4	645	183	82	3 303		46 113	42 451
Waupaca	573	11.4	618	12.3	4	7.0	51	100	1	40	79	12	950		10 359	9 411
Waushara	236	11.0	234	10.9	4	16.9	11	50	1	26	120	5	260		4 385	3 883
Winnebago	1 824	12.2	1 259	8.4	10	5.5	345	229	2	442	295	17	1 714		21 770	19 474
Wood	923	12.2	688	9.1	2	2.2	417	547	2	721	948	9	(11)		13 714	12 446
WYOMING	6 387	13.3	3 745	7.8	37	5.8	825	172	25	1 935	403	27	2 721		64 448	56 549
Albany	387	13.0	159	5.4	3	7.8	60	206	1	74	253	1	(11)		3 018	2 627
Big Horn	149	13.4	124	11.2	–	–	7	62	1	112	988	–	–		2 063	1 834
Campbell	467	14.6	156	4.9	4	8.6	44	134	1	86	266	1	(11)		2 073	1 721
Carbon	157	10.0	118	7.5	2	12.7	18	117	1	45	290	2	(11)		2 171	1 892
Converse	156	12.7	77	6.2	–	–	7	56	1	34	277	1	(12)		1 464	1 292
Crook	52	9.0	36	6.2	–	–	2	35	1	48	830	–	–		866	777
Fremont	487	13.5	372	10.3	5	10.3	72	199	2	161	446	3	229		5 392	4 644
Goshen	154	11.9	116	9.0	–	–	10	79	1	36	281	1	(12)		2 327	2 109
Hot Springs	44	9.4	65	13.9	–	–	8	179	1	49	1 055	1	(15)		1 048	923
Johnson	75	11.1	80	11.8	–	–	10	146	1	65	956	–	–		1 363	1 233
Laramie	1 185	15.1	603	7.7	7	5.9	183	232	1	163	207	3	535		10 500	9 108
Lincoln	183	13.2	90	6.5	1	5.5	12	86	2	55	398	–	–		1 886	1 764
Natrona	847	13.3	537	8.4	6	7.1	142	225	1	154	244	5	633		9 592	8 260
Niobrara	26	9.8	33	12.5	–	–	2	75	1	46	1 704	–	–		510	461
Park	312	12.2	243	9.5	4	12.8	55	216	2	319	1 239	1	(15)		4 010	3 675
Platte	97	11.3	97	11.3	1	10.3	6	70	1	86	998	–	–		1 656	1 489
Sheridan	285	11.3	249	9.9	1	3.5	51	203	1	60	239	2	(14)		4 501	3 965
Sublette	64	11.3	59	10.4	–	–	10	172	–	–	–	1	(12)		781	714
Sweetwater	556	14.0	229	5.8	1	1.8	35	89	1	99	249	2	(11)		3 554	3 028
Teton	189	13.6	61	4.4	–	–	55	378	1	102	719	–	–		1 331	1 237
Uinta	347	17.1	109	5.4	1	2.9	25	123	1	38	186	2	(12)		1 613	1 340
Washakie	104	12.1	72	8.4	–	–	7	82	1	30	345	1	(12)		1 448	1 324
Weston	64	9.8	60	9.2	1	15.6	4	62	1	73	1 123	–	–		1 144	1 015

[1] Per 1,000 resident population estimated as of July 1, 1997. [2] Deaths of infants under 1 year old. [3] Infant deaths per 1,000 live births. [4] Active, nonfederal physicians as of December 31. Data subject to copyright; see below for source citation. [5] Per 100,000 resident population estimated as of July 1 of the year shown. [6] Nonfederal, short-stay (average length of stay less than 30 days) hospitals except hospital units of institutions. Data subject to copyright; see below for source citation. [7] SIC 805 includes skilled nursing care facilities; intermediate care facilities; and nursing and personal care, not elsewhere classified. [8] Full- and part-time employees on the payroll in the pay period including March 12. [9] Unduplicated count of persons enrolled in either hospital and/or supplemental medical insurance as of July 1. State totals include data not distributed by county. [10] Includes disabled, not shown separately. [11] 100 to 249 employees. [12] 20 to 99 employees. [13] 500 to 999 employees. [14] 250 to 499 employees. [15] 0 to 19 employees.

Sources: Births—U.S. National Center for Health Statistics, "Vital Statistics of the United States, Vol. I, Natality," annual, and unpublished data. Deaths—U.S. National Center for Health Statistics, "Vital Statistics of the United States, Vol. II, Mortality," annual, and unpublished data. Physicians—American Medical Association, Chicago, IL, "Physician Characteristics and Distribution in the U.S.," annual (copyright). Community Hospitals—Health Forum, LLC, an American Hospital Association Company, Chicago, IL, "Hospital Statistics" 2000 edition and unpublished data (copyright). Nursing and Personal Care Facilities—U.S. Census Bureau, County Business Patterns 1997 on CD-ROM (related Internet site <http://www.census.gov/epcd/cbp/view/cbpview.html>). Medicare—U.S. Health Care Financing Administration; "Medicare County Enrollment as of July 1, 1999 - Aged and Disabled 3/2000 update," <http://www.hcfa.gov/stats/enroll/default.htm>.

Table B–5. Counties — Education, Income, and Poverty

[Includes U.S., states, and 3,142 counties or county equivalents defined as of January 1, 1992. For changes to these areas since January 1, 1992, see appendix B. Geographic Information]

County	Public school enrollment Fall 1998–1999	Public school enrollment Fall 1994–1995[1]	1990	Educational attainment, 1990 Persons 25 years and over	Percent— High school graduate or higher	Percent— Bachelor's degree or higher	Median household income[2] 1997 (dollars)	Median household income[2] 1989 (dollars)	Percent change, 1989–1997	Persons below poverty level,[2] 1997 Number Persons of all ages Total	Net change, 1989–1997	Persons under 18 years	Percent Persons of all ages	Percent Persons under 18 years
UNITED STATES......	46 368 903	43 993 459	41 058 718	158 868 436	75.2	20.3	37 005	30 056	23.1	35 573 858	3 830 994	14 113 067	13.3	19.9
ALABAMA	737 639	727 989	716 155	2 545 969	66.9	15.7	30 790	23 597	30.5	700 944	−22 670	260 970	16.2	23.8
Autauga	8 489	7 568	6 829	20 861	70.0	14.5	36 803	28 337	29.9	5 034	−290	2 091	11.8	17.4
Baldwin.................	22 176	19 961	16 507	64 623	73.2	16.8	35 438	25 712	37.8	14 907	960	5 614	11.1	16.7
Barbour	4 906	5 017	5 198	15 702	55.6	11.8	25 925	19 389	33.7	6 119	−125	2 340	23.8	32.8
Bibb...........	3 689	3 539	3 536	10 065	51.8	4.7	28 039	19 775	41.8	3 306	−148	1 312	17.4	24.8
Blount	8 135	7 421	7 042	25 241	60.5	7.0	32 676	22 382	46.0	6 203	265	2 323	13.3	20.1
Bullock	1 945	1 972	2 139	6 727	49.0	10.0	20 401	14 745	38.4	3 051	−725	1 114	29.2	34.2
Butler	3 850	4 300	4 423	13 490	52.8	8.0	22 813	16 054	42.1	5 106	−1 709	1 953	23.4	30.8
Calhoun	19 267	19 619	20 198	72 445	67.4	14.2	30 432	23 802	27.9	18 593	1 208	6 937	16.2	24.5
Chambers	5 686	5 750	6 744	23 681	54.3	8.9	28 093	21 256	32.2	6 192	−657	2 285	16.8	24.7
Cherokee.................	3 933	3 714	3 429	12 954	53.5	6.7	28 922	21 368	35.4	3 506	82	1 265	15.8	25.0
Chilton.................	6 562	6 228	6 256	20 781	56.6	7.5	30 539	21 627	41.2	6 062	567	2 344	16.3	24.2
Choctaw.................	2 431	2 929	3 117	9 806	54.3	8.5	24 714	17 115	44.4	3 568	−1 241	1 316	22.3	29.6
Clarke.................	5 391	5 677	5 818	16 285	60.3	10.8	26 898	19 067	41.1	6 256	−704	2 457	21.8	29.9
Clay.................	2 553	2 616	2 488	8 659	53.8	7.3	26 809	19 252	39.3	2 061	−211	727	14.8	21.8
Cleburne	2 564	2 446	2 351	8 101	49.8	6.5	29 104	21 158	37.6	2 123	187	782	14.7	21.4
Coffee.................	8 370	8 424	7 619	25 974	67.2	16.5	31 316	23 905	31.0	6 332	152	2 391	14.9	23.1
Colbert	8 571	8 646	9 032	34 311	65.2	11.5	31 413	22 378	40.4	7 217	−260	2 590	13.5	21.0
Conecuh.................	2 159	2 382	2 681	8 962	52.7	6.4	22 643	15 992	41.6	3 833	−312	1 479	27.4	39.2
Coosa.................	1 817	1 855	2 044	7 184	53.9	6.3	26 531	20 279	30.8	1 847	−137	667	16.1	23.7
Covington.................	6 730	6 904	6 797	24 090	57.3	9.1	25 691	18 394	39.7	7 356	−615	2 612	19.5	28.3
Crenshaw.................	2 300	2 382	2 553	8 797	51.3	8.4	23 472	16 602	42.6	2 837	−442	1 064	20.7	29.9
Cullman.................	12 242	11 927	11 754	43 909	58.8	7.8	30 705	21 672	41.7	9 809	−405	3 470	13.0	18.9
Dale	7 599	7 899	9 375	29 258	74.2	13.5	30 476	24 091	26.5	8 357	1 386	3 446	17.3	26.2
Dallas.................	9 437	10 151	10 873	28 420	59.6	12.2	23 379	16 493	41.8	13 902	−3 197	5 467	29.7	39.2
DeKalb.................	10 240	9 889	10 000	35 484	53.0	7.1	27 948	20 135	38.8	9 096	−286	3 383	15.5	23.4
Elmore.................	11 791	10 352	9 074	31 432	66.5	12.8	35 305	26 341	34.0	7 688	1 045	3 067	13.1	19.3
Escambia.................	6 460	6 443	6 912	22 527	59.9	7.6	25 712	18 472	39.2	7 401	−2 183	2 586	20.8	27.8
Etowah.................	16 391	16 548	17 453	65 672	64.1	10.2	28 747	22 314	28.8	17 664	1 422	6 312	16.9	25.5
Fayette.................	2 840	2 879	3 529	11 672	56.6	8.5	28 717	19 844	44.7	2 851	−764	1 006	15.6	22.3
Franklin.................	5 651	5 552	4 895	18 292	55.1	6.9	26 592	17 907	48.5	4 965	−726	1 767	16.6	24.5
Geneva.................	4 293	4 322	4 200	15 475	55.4	6.8	26 009	20 027	29.9	4 699	116	1 737	18.7	28.5
Greene.................	1 976	2 244	2 581	5 917	53.8	10.4	17 602	11 990	46.8	3 521	−1 054	1 366	35.5	44.6
Hale	3 407	3 511	3 476	9 244	54.4	8.9	20 704	14 508	42.8	4 448	−972	1 761	26.6	34.1
Henry	2 820	2 823	2 959	9 932	58.5	8.2	28 276	22 130	27.8	2 882	246	1 133	18.1	28.6
Houston	15 376	15 395	15 420	51 154	68.3	15.0	32 086	24 813	29.3	14 134	859	5 628	16.4	24.4
Jackson	9 194	9 204	9 455	30 847	58.1	8.0	30 791	21 910	40.5	7 632	−269	2 756	14.7	21.7
Jefferson	111 903	111 362	106 664	425 708	73.8	19.9	35 464	25 858	37.1	95 276	−7 000	33 805	14.5	21.5
Lamar.................	2 837	2 991	2 930	10 195	52.9	6.2	26 867	20 618	30.3	2 902	104	1 066	18.0	27.2
Lauderdale.................	13 341	13 448	12 877	51 436	67.9	16.4	33 204	23 690	40.2	11 222	−384	3 820	13.3	19.6
Lawrence	6 258	6 176	6 161	19 498	55.6	6.2	31 609	21 519	46.9	5 326	−875	1 925	15.7	22.2
Lee	17 124	15 279	13 376	45 484	73.2	25.3	31 821	21 227	49.9	14 671	−5 863	4 335	15.0	19.8
Limestone	10 912	10 229	9 236	34 872	63.1	13.8	35 981	26 875	33.9	8 231	906	3 040	15.3	20.0
Lowndes.................	2 800	2 931	2 920	6 942	56.7	8.2	20 285	15 584	30.2	4 152	−706	1 724	31.5	39.4
Macon.................	4 062	4 265	4 771	13 759	61.9	18.0	21 469	15 642	37.3	6 792	−1 020	2 293	31.9	40.4
Madison.................	44 208	41 375	37 559	152 864	80.2	30.1	43 239	33 048	30.8	30 571	5 282	11 453	11.0	17.6
Marengo.................	4 867	4 880	4 412	14 050	61.4	11.5	25 504	18 663	36.7	5 630	−1 221	2 217	23.9	32.6
Marion	5 287	5 503	5 354	19 465	50.0	6.7	26 919	18 455	45.9	4 896	−687	1 652	16.0	22.5
Marshall.................	14 696	13 952	12 227	46 678	61.5	11.5	29 604	21 458	38.0	12 108	36	4 410	15.0	23.0
Mobile.................	65 324	64 645	67 092	232 254	70.1	15.5	29 943	22 994	30.2	80 068	755	31 547	20.1	28.8
Monroe	4 726	5 256	5 156	14 228	59.2	10.8	28 061	21 140	32.7	5 239	−147	2 153	21.6	30.5
Montgomery	33 994	35 255	35 924	128 365	75.3	24.2	34 569	26 551	30.2	37 506	1 462	14 853	17.6	26.2
Morgan.................	19 315	18 935	18 163	64 715	69.4	15.5	36 984	28 364	30.4	12 460	635	4 621	11.4	16.9
Perry.................	2 293	2 420	2 615	7 153	51.0	11.5	18 069	13 769	31.2	4 509	−645	1 746	36.6	45.2
Pickens.................	3 844	3 951	4 183	12 963	56.2	6.6	24 567	17 879	37.4	4 962	−943	1 921	23.4	32.9
Pike.................	4 562	4 833	4 819	15 717	59.0	14.3	23 915	17 312	38.1	6 778	−265	2 439	24.6	34.4
Randolph.................	3 775	3 824	3 814	12 800	50.3	7.7	25 882	19 440	33.1	3 747	37	1 416	18.6	27.9
Russell.................	8 936	8 590	8 248	29 672	57.0	8.2	28 141	20 995	34.0	9 444	4	3 609	18.6	28.0
St. Clair	10 670	9 714	9 238	31 921	61.0	8.5	33 812	24 106	40.3	8 476	1 330	3 245	13.9	20.2
Shelby.................	19 211	17 773	16 145	61 938	78.2	29.0	52 450	36 852	42.3	9 616	694	3 683	6.8	9.8
Sumter.................	2 864	2 866	3 282	8 954	52.4	11.1	19 199	12 811	49.9	5 090	−1 041	1 906	33.1	40.1
Talladega.................	13 726	14 034	14 885	46 091	60.7	10.2	27 147	21 378	27.0	14 776	341	5 582	19.4	27.6
Tallapoosa.................	7 030	7 088	7 502	25 161	57.8	11.5	27 804	22 020	26.3	6 817	701	2 587	16.9	26.0
Tuscaloosa.................	25 771	25 099	24 956	88 962	69.6	20.0	31 029	23 056	34.6	26 524	−1 776	9 051	17.0	24.2
Walker.................	11 142	11 763	12 471	44 020	56.0	7.2	28 254	20 464	38.1	10 270	−1 302	3 710	14.4	21.2
Washington.................	3 708	3 755	3 580	9 960	58.2	6.7	28 549	20 082	42.2	3 395	−725	1 290	19.0	25.4
Wilcox.................	2 618	2 803	3 029	7 715	51.1	10.3	17 822	12 437	43.3	4 858	−1 176	1 968	36.1	44.0
Winston.................	4 594	4 505	3 809	14 446	48.8	5.4	25 418	17 936	41.7	4 074	−244	1 356	16.8	23.5

[1] Revised. [2] 1997 data are model-based estimates; 1989 data are census estimates. For more information on these estimates, see appendix A. Source Notes and Explanations or <http://www.census.gov/hhes/www/saipe.html>.

Sources: Public School Enrollment, 1998-1999 and 1994-1995—U.S. National Center for Education Statistics, <http://nces.ed.gov/ccd/pubagency.html> (accessed: 16 March 2001). Public School Enrollment and Educational Attainment, 1990—U.S. Census Bureau, "1990 Census of Population and Housing, Summary Tape File (STF) 3C" on CD-ROM (related Internet site <http://homer.ssd.census.gov/cdrom/lookup>). Income and Poverty, 1997—U.S. Census Bureau, "State and County Income and Poverty Estimates - 1997," published 22 November 2000, <http://www.census.gov/housing/saipe/estmod97/est97ALL.dat>. Income and Poverty, 1989—U.S. Census Bureau, "1990 Census of Population and Housing, Summary Tape File (STF) 3C" on CD-ROM (related Internet site <http://homer.ssd.census.gov/cdrom/lookup>).

[Includes U.S., states, and 3,142 counties or county equivalents defined as of January 1, 1992. For changes to these areas since January 1, 1992, see appendix B. Geographic Information]

County	Public school enrollment Fall			Educational attainment, 1990			Median household income[2]			Persons below poverty level,[2] 1997				
					Percent—					Number			Percent	
										Persons of all ages				
	1998–1999	1994–1995[1]	1990	Persons 25 years and over	High school graduate or higher	Bachelor's degree or higher	1997 (dollars)	1989 (dollars)	Percent change, 1989–1997	Total	Net change, 1989–1997	Persons under 18 years	Persons of all ages	Persons under 18 years
ALASKA	135 374	126 348	108 967	323 429	86.6	23.0	43 657	41 408	5.4	68 409	20 503	31 968	11.2	16.2
Aleutians East	366	367	389	1 531	66.4	12.9	42 714	42 384	.8	322	30	125	14.2	20.8
Aleutians West	608	236	1 044	5 467	85.8	14.8	44 745	35 187	27.2	269	−393	62	6.7	8.2
Anchorage	49 587	47 655	40 784	136 655	90.4	26.9	54 245	43 946	23.4	23 244	7 630	9 862	9.1	13.2
Bethel	4 586	4 169	3 686	6 854	62.3	13.1	29 628	25 402	16.6	5 290	1 268	2 832	33.1	40.5
Bristol Bay	1 110	965	272	889	89.8	18.9	56 570	51 112	10.7	92	33	51	8.4	12.8
Denali	(3)	(3)	(3)	(3)	(3)	(3)	44 065	(3)	NA	107	107	50	6.1	10.1
Dillingham	567	507	974	2 159	69.8	15.3	35 094	28 779	21.9	1 284	300	726	28.1	38.0
Fairbanks North Star	17 669	17 202	14 463	43 288	89.8	25.2	46 944	37 468	25.3	7 507	1 933	3 397	9.1	12.5
Haines	440	414	421	1 393	78.5	17.6	37 631	36 048	4.4	263	76	107	11.5	17.2
Juneau	7 348	6 729	5 004	16 769	89.9	30.7	57 809	47 924	20.6	1 952	484	774	6.5	8.7
Kenai Peninsula	10 300	10 142	8 732	24 423	87.2	17.9	47 189	42 403	11.3	5 481	2 405	2 599	11.4	16.6
Ketchikan Gateway	2 757	2 873	2 564	8 551	85.4	20.2	53 502	45 172	18.4	1 160	594	519	8.2	12.3
Kodiak Island	2 804	2 826	2 486	7 788	84.7	21.5	46 673	44 815	4.1	1 323	620	673	9.2	14.0
Lake and Peninsula	578	565	436	904	60.7	14.4	27 016	25 231	7.1	479	149	251	27.4	33.9
Matanuska-Susitna	12 942	12 077	9 190	23 440	87.8	18.1	50 273	40 745	23.4	6 478	2 817	3 170	11.6	16.0
Nome	2 674	2 444	2 276	4 351	65.0	13.8	36 633	30 144	21.5	2 170	361	1 149	24.2	29.7
North Slope	2 101	2 075	1 585	3 183	68.5	14.1	56 915	50 473	12.8	406	−100	180	5.8	6.2
Northwest Arctic	2 232	1 954	1 776	2 844	63.8	11.9	39 119	33 313	17.4	1 434	319	826	21.0	25.0
Prince of Wales-Outer Ketchikan	1 395	1 475	1 443	3 726	77.5	11.4	42 226	39 495	6.9	983	413	421	14.1	17.4
Sitka	2 021	2 094	1 748	5 225	87.0	21.4	50 166	43 337	15.8	686	288	298	8.5	11.6
Skagway-Yakutat-Angoon	831	935	1 033	2 655	79.3	15.8	NA	38 583	NA	376	−14	216	8.3	13.6
Southeast Fairbanks	517	533	1 314	3 298	85.9	19.0	36 982	30 222	22.4	1 092	285	579	18.4	27.3
Valdez-Cordova	2 211	2 200	1 953	6 282	83.9	18.5	50 526	47 500	6.4	1 005	140	394	9.8	12.9
Wade Hampton	2 603	2 269	1 821	2 494	57.8	10.2	23 796	20 586	15.6	2 762	968	1 682	39.4	48.3
Wrangell-Petersburg	1 474	1 514	1 493	4 359	81.0	19.8	44 826	42 020	6.7	703	308	321	10.2	14.8
Yukon-Koyukuk	35 653	32 128	32 080	34 901	373.2	313.8	30 532	323 945	NA	1 542	−517	704	24.2	27.1
ARIZONA	847 416	735 752	635 900	2 301 177	78.7	20.3	34 751	27 540	26.2	720 713	156 351	305 109	15.5	23.2
Apache	16 037	15 407	17 833	29 660	54.7	8.5	20 260	14 100	43.7	27 436	−1 204	13 080	39.7	45.4
Cochise	20 924	21 270	18 951	61 230	75.7	16.1	29 295	22 425	30.6	23 611	4 890	10 333	21.7	31.8
Coconino	21 084	20 432	20 563	50 478	79.0	24.6	33 747	26 112	29.2	21 855	1 050	9 452	20.0	25.7
Gila	9 484	9 058	7 352	26 996	68.1	9.7	27 960	20 964	33.4	9 885	2 651	4 263	20.2	32.8
Graham	6 368	6 056	6 386	14 913	67.6	11.3	27 564	18 455	49.4	6 885	362	2 923	22.8	26.4
Greenlee	2 056	2 274	2 184	4 743	74.2	10.4	43 696	27 491	58.9	972	−38	427	10.3	12.6
La Paz	3 033	3 104	2 599	8 991	63.0	8.5	23 534	16 555	42.2	3 633	−242	1 328	24.3	36.3
Maricopa	502 835	418 249	350 285	1 344 654	81.5	22.1	40 134	30 797	30.3	355 924	98 565	148 482	12.7	19.1
Mohave	22 795	20 260	13 915	66 039	72.8	10.3	28 250	24 002	17.7	23 184	10 135	9 703	17.6	32.5
Navajo	23 758	19 421	21 127	40 768	64.6	10.0	25 913	19 452	33.2	27 546	1 088	12 800	28.4	34.1
Pima	129 785	119 210	105 948	424 032	80.5	23.3	32 544	25 401	28.1	127 496	15 616	50 547	16.2	24.4
Pinal	26 689	24 804	24 221	71 721	65.5	8.2	28 000	21 301	31.5	28 695	2 543	12 384	20.0	27.9
Santa Cruz	9 500	8 643	7 042	16 650	57.2	10.8	26 515	22 066	20.2	9 961	2 165	5 031	25.8	36.4
Yavapai	23 970	20 254	15 523	77 278	78.9	17.7	30 230	22 060	37.0	20 549	6 241	7 707	13.8	23.2
Yuma	29 098	27 310	21 971	63 024	64.9	12.7	27 227	23 635	15.2	33 080	12 528	16 651	25.3	40.3
ARKANSAS	452 267	448 109	425 717	1 496 150	66.3	13.3	27 875	21 147	31.8	442 856	5 767	169 089	17.5	25.0
Arkansas	3 818	3 875	4 514	14 059	61.1	10.3	28 742	19 516	47.3	3 906	−449	1 528	18.9	26.8
Ashley	4 622	4 965	5 123	15 222	62.8	9.3	30 040	20 609	45.8	4 892	−130	1 963	20.0	28.3
Baxter	5 078	4 912	4 415	23 364	67.9	10.4	26 352	18 826	40.0	5 356	342	1 828	14.6	25.2
Benton	23 509	20 251	16 027	64 675	74.8	14.4	36 004	26 021	38.4	13 601	4 365	5 705	10.1	16.3
Boone	5 808	5 792	4 899	18 765	67.6	10.7	28 336	20 656	37.2	5 296	1 433	2 048	16.6	25.6
Bradley	2 238	2 368	2 204	7 731	56.1	9.8	24 482	17 259	41.9	2 424	−438	905	21.4	30.1
Calhoun	852	935	1 175	3 770	63.3	7.4	27 092	21 198	27.8	943	53	368	16.5	23.8
Carroll	3 572	3 593	3 127	12 678	68.4	11.6	26 411	20 623	28.1	3 896	1 091	1 499	17.2	26.7
Chicot	2 901	3 178	3 697	9 278	51.2	8.3	19 604	12 682	54.6	4 956	−1 343	1 897	33.8	40.8
Clark	3 170	3 560	3 601	12 805	64.9	17.9	26 783	18 068	48.2	3 794	−825	1 220	18.9	24.6
Clay	2 923	3 017	2 974	12 450	47.9	5.2	24 735	16 219	52.5	3 087	−697	1 028	18.0	25.9
Cleburne	3 520	3 327	2 905	13 848	61.0	9.4	27 223	19 438	40.1	3 644	332	1 258	15.8	25.4
Cleveland	1 535	1 523	1 558	5 017	59.9	7.8	29 956	19 703	52.0	1 429	−38	527	16.8	23.5
Columbia	4 719	5 017	4 846	16 102	64.3	13.1	26 826	18 470	45.2	5 367	−654	1 996	21.9	30.7
Conway	3 571	3 535	3 559	12 317	64.5	9.8	28 503	20 538	38.8	3 396	294	1 238	17.1	24.0
Craighead	12 815	12 380	11 586	42 031	67.5	16.4	31 515	22 150	42.3	12 626	1 307	4 463	16.6	22.9
Crawford	10 352	9 774	8 554	26 414	63.8	7.6	30 400	21 574	40.9	8 183	1 340	3 475	16.1	23.0
Crittenden	10 792	10 701	10 852	29 107	57.6	9.8	27 549	20 948	31.5	12 521	−839	5 259	24.9	33.0
Cross	4 072	4 226	4 261	11 619	55.8	8.0	26 344	19 049	38.3	4 356	−433	1 749	22.4	29.4
Dallas	1 766	1 920	1 893	6 376	59.2	8.8	24 786	17 651	40.4	1 879	−222	670	20.9	28.1
Desha	3 638	4 087	3 876	9 953	56.5	10.4	23 361	15 719	48.6	4 151	−1 470	1 628	27.5	34.5

[1] Revised. [2] 1997 data are model-based estimates; 1989 data are census estimates. For more information on these estimates, see appendix A. Source Notes and Explanations or <http://www.census.gov/hhes/www/saipe.html>. [3] Denali Borough included with Yukon-Koyukuk Census Area; data not available separately.

Sources: Public School Enrollment, 1998-1999 and 1994-1995—U.S. National Center for Education Statistics, <http://nces.ed.gov/ccd/pubagency.html> (accessed: 16 March 2001). Public School Enrollment and Educational Attainment, 1990—U.S. Census Bureau, "1990 Census of Population and Housing, Summary Tape File (STF) 3C" on CD-ROM (related Internet site <http://homer.ssd.census.gov/cdrom/lookup>). Income and Poverty, 1997—U.S. Census Bureau, "State and County Income and Poverty Estimates - 1997," published 22 November 2000, <http://www.census.gov/housing/saipe/estmod97/est97ALL.dat>. Income and Poverty, 1989—U.S. Census Bureau, "1990 Census of Population and Housing, Summary Tape File (STF) 3C" on CD-ROM (related Internet site <http://homer.ssd.census.gov/cdrom/lookup>).

[Includes U.S., states, and 3,142 counties or county equivalents defined as of January 1, 1992. For changes to these areas since January 1, 1992, see appendix B. Geographic Information]

County	Public school enrollment Fall			Educational attainment, 1990			Median household income[2]			Persons below poverty level,[2] 1997				
					Percent—					Number			Percent	
										Persons of all ages				
	1998–1999	1994–1995[1]	1990	Persons 25 years and over	High school graduate or higher	Bachelor's degree or higher	1997 (dollars)	1989 (dollars)	Percent change, 1989–1997	Total	Net change, 1989–1997	Persons under 18 years	Persons of all ages	Persons under 18 years
ARKANSAS—Con.														
Drew	3 298	3 271	3 570	10 405	63.1	13.9	27 738	18 906	46.7	3 419	–606	1 291	19.9	26.4
Faulkner	14 020	12 652	10 330	34 794	72.4	17.9	35 722	23 663	51.0	8 304	489	3 136	10.9	15.1
Franklin	3 634	3 470	2 780	9 638	60.1	8.8	27 300	18 408	48.3	2 917	–58	1 080	17.3	23.4
Fulton	1 712	1 740	1 723	6 960	54.9	5.4	20 848	14 950	39.5	2 763	170	917	25.2	36.6
Garland	12 773	12 056	10 877	51 901	70.2	14.2	28 140	20 260	38.9	13 632	661	4 874	16.3	27.2
Grant	4 546	4 154	2 725	8 989	68.9	9.3	35 486	24 278	46.2	1 843	–219	716	11.5	16.6
Greene	6 410	6 266	5 508	20 743	58.5	9.1	29 904	19 940	50.0	5 373	–216	2 000	14.9	21.7
Hempstead	4 123	4 458	4 074	13 881	62.0	9.3	24 690	16 986	45.4	4 717	–107	1 806	21.4	29.3
Hot Spring	5 603	5 672	4 864	17 199	64.5	9.0	27 757	19 355	43.4	4 909	117	1 783	16.9	23.6
Howard	3 105	3 100	2 615	8 567	61.8	8.3	27 782	21 277	30.6	2 515	67	965	18.6	25.3
Independence	5 902	5 962	5 930	20 123	63.1	10.3	28 864	20 208	42.8	5 484	242	2 070	16.7	23.7
Izard	2 021	1 930	1 743	8 180	61.1	9.4	22 868	16 910	35.2	2 841	494	986	22.4	34.1
Jackson	2 794	3 094	3 603	12 651	51.6	6.7	23 942	16 641	43.9	4 187	–777	1 489	23.6	33.8
Jefferson	15 449	16 716	17 190	51 741	65.9	14.6	27 363	21 322	28.3	19 564	154	7 548	24.9	33.3
Johnson	4 067	3 679	3 206	11 767	63.3	12.0	25 612	18 225	40.5	4 022	480	1 559	19.0	28.6
Lafayette	1 671	1 729	2 130	6 098	51.6	6.9	21 324	13 849	54.0	2 539	–766	842	28.2	33.7
Lawrence	3 353	3 416	3 191	11 470	53.3	6.1	23 133	15 337	50.8	3 775	–485	1 341	22.1	31.3
Lee	1 998	2 284	3 100	7 625	44.2	7.4	19 194	11 949	60.6	4 456	–1 663	1 698	38.0	43.6
Lincoln	2 203	2 188	2 407	9 040	58.5	5.6	26 071	18 457	41.3	3 165	404	1 071	27.9	30.9
Little River	2 164	2 419	2 814	8 710	64.6	8.1	28 739	21 791	31.9	2 408	–253	887	18.2	24.3
Logan	3 686	3 720	3 806	13 246	58.1	6.8	26 233	18 992	38.1	3 831	4	1 436	18.4	25.3
Lonoke	10 531	9 602	8 381	24 400	67.1	10.0	35 825	23 831	50.3	6 194	428	2 496	12.3	16.5
Madison	2 632	2 580	2 075	7 553	59.6	8.2	26 499	18 392	44.1	2 526	219	966	18.9	26.7
Marion	2 385	2 218	1 895	8 663	64.2	8.0	23 450	17 220	36.2	2 909	669	1 069	19.4	31.8
Miller	6 930	7 569	7 626	23 846	63.9	9.5	28 034	20 232	38.6	8 439	–4	3 361	21.3	29.6
Mississippi	10 216	10 649	12 656	33 340	60.0	10.5	26 528	18 522	43.2	11 955	–2 758	4 960	23.5	30.9
Monroe	2 050	2 212	2 368	7 094	52.9	8.4	20 702	13 633	51.9	3 110	–912	1 213	30.6	40.1
Montgomery	1 424	1 450	1 327	5 418	60.1	7.0	23 928	16 503	45.0	1 858	26	619	21.3	30.5
Nevada	1 985	1 992	2 086	6 501	60.6	9.8	25 561	18 919	35.1	1 962	–45	728	19.7	26.2
Newton	1 420	1 469	1 668	4 929	58.1	6.8	21 621	15 139	42.8	2 081	–161	790	25.2	34.5
Ouachita	5 673	6 168	6 113	19 999	64.8	12.2	27 593	21 056	31.0	5 880	–523	2 243	21.1	30.4
Perry	1 868	1 734	1 377	5 226	61.1	6.2	26 507	17 626	50.4	1 490	–110	553	15.3	22.1
Phillips	6 084	6 478	6 735	16 474	51.5	9.2	18 898	13 071	44.6	10 273	–1 956	4 340	37.5	45.8
Pike	2 216	1 947	1 829	6 590	61.1	8.5	26 974	19 240	40.2	1 916	138	731	18.1	26.0
Poinsett	4 869	5 072	4 851	15 815	48.9	5.6	25 052	16 858	48.6	5 594	–629	2 066	22.6	31.1
Polk	3 694	3 635	3 182	11 509	62.4	9.9	23 934	17 789	34.5	4 179	1 010	1 648	21.1	31.5
Pope	9 650	9 375	8 303	27 976	66.5	14.7	31 290	22 326	40.2	8 037	1 287	3 102	15.7	22.0
Prairie	1 577	1 617	1 739	6 236	56.3	7.2	26 039	17 044	52.8	1 731	–410	614	18.4	25.3
Pulaski	53 427	54 397	54 927	223 000	79.0	23.5	34 727	26 883	29.2	50 110	1 907	19 551	14.3	21.3
Randolph	2 984	2 947	2 943	10 892	54.4	7.9	24 454	16 719	46.3	3 660	353	1 345	20.5	30.1
St. Francis	6 024	6 581	6 929	16 653	55.1	8.5	22 001	15 029	46.4	8 642	–1 660	3 540	30.5	37.8
Saline	12 051	11 706	12 084	41 032	72.9	11.9	39 001	28 262	38.0	7 429	1 584	2 786	9.6	13.2
Scott	1 672	1 685	1 779	6 730	53.8	5.9	24 049	16 470	46.0	2 387	186	918	22.4	33.4
Searcy	1 401	1 431	1 526	5 352	52.6	7.5	19 091	13 221	44.4	2 130	–186	734	27.4	38.7
Sebastian	18 494	18 061	16 706	64 319	71.7	14.6	32 360	24 037	34.6	15 292	2 489	6 140	14.4	21.6
Sevier	3 036	2 837	2 623	8 855	59.0	7.2	26 121	19 208	36.0	2 757	270	1 092	18.9	27.4
Sharp	3 069	3 066	2 320	10 060	64.5	8.7	22 433	17 362	29.2	3 614	588	1 269	21.2	32.5
Stone	1 793	1 850	1 724	6 759	59.6	9.4	21 846	15 655	39.5	2 603	94	899	23.2	33.6
Union	8 790	9 262	8 742	30 202	65.9	12.7	29 359	21 041	39.5	8 475	–1 612	3 208	18.7	25.6
Van Buren	2 422	2 385	2 373	9 918	62.6	10.5	23 828	17 103	39.3	3 150	79	1 091	20.1	31.3
Washington	25 112	22 782	18 270	68 196	73.2	20.0	32 188	23 124	39.2	19 298	3 384	7 097	13.5	19.1
White	11 440	10 924	9 413	33 760	62.6	10.9	28 513	19 722	44.6	10 842	1 159	3 936	17.4	23.7
Woodruff	1 615	1 808	2 128	5 917	48.7	7.5	20 623	14 024	47.1	2 733	–506	1 010	30.9	39.2
Yell	3 930	3 708	3 187	11 627	57.2	7.4	25 751	19 647	31.1	3 229	214	1 230	16.8	25.0
CALIFORNIA	5 844 111	5 342 071	5 002 596	18 695 499	76.2	23.4	39 595	35 798	10.6	5 195 477	1 567 892	2 223 674	16.0	24.6
Alameda	214 301	195 716	187 557	838 304	81.4	28.8	46 795	37 544	24.6	164 225	32 214	61 864	11.8	17.6
Alpine	125	175	214	739	87.6	24.0	31 080	24 929	24.7	210	10	90	17.5	30.6
Amador	5 691	4 760	4 559	20 632	82.5	14.0	37 829	30 265	25.0	3 380	1 241	1 153	11.4	17.1
Butte	35 290	33 955	28 342	114 908	77.6	19.5	29 367	22 776	28.9	40 224	6 771	15 351	20.9	30.9
Calaveras	6 876	7 295	5 647	22 470	81.6	14.4	34 672	27 645	25.4	5 163	1 983	2 093	13.0	20.8
Colusa	4 288	4 087	3 733	9 854	62.9	11.1	30 464	24 912	22.3	3 380	1 259	1 812	18.1	29.4
Contra Costa	154 019	139 573	128 542	532 716	86.5	31.6	54 275	45 087	20.4	80 691	22 824	32 488	8.7	13.6
Del Norte	5 274	5 281	4 262	15 091	70.9	10.0	29 044	22 917	26.7	5 523	2 226	2 368	22.9	31.8
El Dorado	28 864	28 422	22 892	84 412	85.9	20.8	44 954	35 058	28.2	14 074	4 527	5 742	8.8	13.2

[1] Revised. [2] 1997 data are model-based estimates; 1989 data are census estimates. For more information on these estimates, see appendix A. Source Notes and Explanations or <http://www.census.gov/hhes/www/saipe.html>.

Sources: Public School Enrollment, 1998-1999 and 1994-1995—U.S. National Center for Education Statistics, <http://nces.ed.gov/ccd/pubagency.html> (accessed: 16 March 2001). Public School Enrollment and Educational Attainment, 1990—U.S. Census Bureau, "1990 Census of Population and Housing, Summary Tape File (STF) 3C" on CD-ROM (related Internet site <http://homer.ssd.census.gov/cdrom/lookup>). Income and Poverty, 1997—U.S. Census Bureau, "State and County Income and Poverty Estimates - 1997," published 22 November 2000, <http://www.census.gov/housing/saipe/estmod97/est97ALL.dat>. Income and Poverty, 1989—U.S. Census Bureau, "1990 Census of Population and Housing, Summary Tape File (STF) 3C" on CD-ROM (related Internet site <http://homer.ssd.census.gov/cdrom/lookup>).

Table B–5. Counties — Education, Income, and Poverty–Con.

[Includes U.S., states, and 3,142 counties or county equivalents defined as of January 1, 1992. For changes to these areas since January 1, 1992, see appendix B. Geographic Information]

County	Public school enrollment — Fall 1998–1999	Public school enrollment — Fall 1994–1995[1]	Public school enrollment — Fall 1990	Educational attainment, 1990 — Persons 25 years and over	Percent — High school graduate or higher	Percent — Bachelor's degree or higher	Median household income[2] 1997 (dollars)	Median household income[2] 1989 (dollars)	Percent change, 1989–1997	Persons below poverty level,[2] 1997 — Number — Persons of all ages — Total	Net change, 1989–1997	Persons under 18 years	Percent — Persons of all ages	Percent — Persons under 18 years
CALIFORNIA—Con.														
Fresno	177 213	167 371	144 149	385 736	66.2	16.9	31 587	26 377	19.8	191 614	51 167	95 511	25.6	38.0
Glenn	6 215	6 232	5 119	15 205	66.9	9.4	28 649	22 831	25.5	5 200	956	2 485	19.9	29.2
Humboldt	22 209	21 796	21 217	75 580	80.5	20.0	30 426	23 586	29.0	22 332	1 975	8 555	18.5	26.0
Imperial	32 898	32 025	28 103	60 910	53.2	9.7	23 359	22 442	4.1	41 065	15 548	21 408	30.3	43.8
Inyo	3 426	3 481	3 215	12 901	81.7	13.5	32 871	24 386	34.8	2 514	386	970	14.0	21.5
Kern	143 671	133 702	112 676	319 209	67.6	13.3	32 359	28 634	13.0	128 669	39 357	62 711	21.0	30.2
Kings	25 018	23 491	21 009	58 427	65.6	9.0	30 577	25 507	19.9	24 724	8 506	11 883	23.6	31.3
Lake	9 911	10 272	8 382	35 961	70.9	10.7	27 295	21 794	25.2	11 092	3 478	4 677	20.1	33.2
Lassen	5 518	5 470	5 002	17 655	72.8	11.7	36 819	26 764	37.6	4 813	1 806	1 773	19.4	22.9
Los Angeles	1 617 764	1 473 717	1 504 666	5 481 222	70.0	22.3	36 441	34 965	4.2	1 886 639	578 384	779 303	20.5	30.5
Madera	24 343	22 011	19 434	52 992	63.4	11.7	30 804	27 370	12.5	24 741	9 581	12 423	22.8	35.5
Marin	28 793	26 925	24 400	169 493	91.9	44.0	60 967	48 544	25.6	16 099	4 557	4 370	7.0	9.5
Mariposa	2 807	2 745	2 189	10 185	77.8	16.8	31 178	25 272	23.4	2 425	643	999	15.3	27.1
Mendocino	15 800	15 877	15 387	52 489	78.7	17.8	32 306	26 443	22.2	15 071	3 926	6 731	18.1	28.5
Merced	49 732	46 957	41 561	98 819	63.1	12.0	29 178	25 548	14.2	50 275	15 462	26 975	25.4	37.4
Modoc	2 098	2 404	1 955	6 447	72.2	11.2	28 174	22 029	27.9	1 919	523	842	21.1	33.3
Mono	2 109	1 799	1 541	6 583	87.8	21.9	36 276	31 924	13.6	1 167	200	475	11.2	17.8
Monterey	69 534	61 844	64 072	212 004	72.9	21.5	38 341	33 520	14.4	54 559	15 741	25 986	15.4	24.1
Napa	19 303	18 067	16 685	75 205	80.7	22.3	44 667	36 773	21.5	10 283	3 054	4 218	8.8	14.4
Nevada	13 280	13 377	13 111	55 233	86.3	22.1	40 347	32 200	25.3	8 761	2 787	3 487	9.6	15.3
Orange	471 404	412 266	375 646	1 528 199	81.2	27.8	49 583	45 922	8.0	299 636	98 776	123 692	11.0	17.4
Placer	52 306	42 527	29 413	114 422	85.1	22.7	49 638	37 601	32.0	17 812	5 695	6 919	7.7	11.0
Plumas	3 540	3 851	3 777	13 806	82.7	15.1	35 154	24 299	44.7	2 687	364	1 073	13.1	20.1
Riverside	295 229	260 571	214 379	724 705	74.1	14.6	36 368	33 081	9.9	221 430	89 740	103 143	15.0	22.7
Sacramento	209 598	190 085	173 974	661 727	82.2	23.0	39 461	32 297	22.2	200 479	73 696	88 593	17.2	27.3
San Benito	10 912	9 204	7 708	21 905	68.4	14.4	42 578	36 473	16.7	5 634	2 181	2 949	11.4	17.9
San Bernardino	364 942	327 528	278 852	824 828	75.4	14.9	36 876	33 443	10.3	291 422	116 695	138 568	17.9	25.7
San Diego	470 494	428 360	393 483	1 558 082	81.9	25.3	39 427	35 022	12.6	386 232	114 842	160 744	14.2	22.0
San Francisco	62 101	62 293	69 571	536 015	78.0	35.0	43 405	33 414	29.9	94 142	4 123	27 810	12.6	21.7
San Joaquin	114 141	103 635	93 586	289 533	68.6	13.2	35 629	30 635	16.3	101 876	28 713	47 244	18.8	27.3
San Luis Obispo	37 126	34 013	31 507	138 986	83.3	22.9	38 597	31 164	23.9	28 888	2 519	10 133	12.9	18.5
San Mateo	92 901	88 064	83 510	448 853	84.1	31.3	57 267	46 437	23.3	46 164	5 759	15 354	6.6	9.5
Santa Barbara	64 500	58 533	54 725	231 347	80.0	26.6	40 232	35 677	12.8	55 429	10 205	21 915	14.6	22.5
Santa Clara	253 367	237 335	227 841	974 783	82.0	32.6	59 639	48 115	24.0	146 523	36 717	56 294	9.0	13.6
Santa Cruz	40 512	37 640	35 411	147 964	81.9	29.7	44 607	37 112	20.2	31 272	7 502	13 295	13.1	21.3
Shasta	30 484	30 039	26 605	94 844	78.4	13.7	32 109	25 581	25.5	29 709	9 869	13 107	18.1	28.2
Sierra	2 995	870	524	2 521	75.5	15.9	34 941	23 657	47.7	392	90	140	11.6	15.2
Siskiyou	7 939	8 910	8 347	28 991	77.4	14.2	28 178	21 921	28.5	8 337	2 355	3 635	19.0	30.1
Solano	71 610	67 022	62 724	208 813	82.7	18.7	46 115	39 113	17.9	41 722	17 288	19 198	11.3	17.0
Sonoma	71 644	67 233	60 845	258 705	84.4	24.5	43 770	36 299	20.6	39 585	10 544	15 370	9.1	13.6
Stanislaus	93 426	87 132	74 498	221 702	68.4	13.0	35 913	29 793	20.5	78 638	27 301	38 071	18.4	27.2
Sutter	15 724	14 630	12 740	39 854	72.3	15.4	33 775	27 096	24.6	13 275	3 493	6 127	17.2	26.5
Tehama	10 952	10 927	9 608	32 527	72.2	10.2	28 030	22 436	24.9	10 774	3 323	4 765	20.0	30.9
Trinity	2 298	2 530	2 615	8 893	74.2	12.9	27 042	20 494	32.0	2 525	160	987	19.4	28.2
Tulare	84 723	81 126	72 130	177 655	60.2	11.8	27 622	24 450	13.0	98 816	29 691	50 568	27.9	39.9
Tuolumne	8 219	8 084	7 659	34 033	80.0	14.7	33 810	27 030	25.1	7 246	3 258	2 879	14.8	23.6
Ventura	134 535	120 733	117 580	415 551	79.4	23.0	49 763	45 612	9.1	75 183	27 441	35 178	10.3	16.6
Yolo	26 946	24 524	21 456	81 045	79.1	30.3	38 751	28 866	34.2	23 632	263	9 488	15.8	23.6
Yuba	13 173	13 579	12 261	33 828	68.5	9.5	26 842	21 523	24.7	15 181	4 193	7 690	25.5	38.1
COLORADO	699 135	640 521	567 007	2 107 072	84.4	27.0	40 853	30 140	35.5	403 410	28 196	155 960	10.2	14.6
Adams	57 067	51 794	51 052	162 662	78.8	13.0	40 802	30 522	33.7	33 794	6 527	15 180	10.4	15.7
Alamosa	2 824	2 813	2 805	7 491	76.9	24.1	28 204	20 265	39.2	3 207	80	1 328	23.0	29.4
Arapahoe	93 168	85 357	69 034	251 916	91.5	35.2	50 748	37 234	36.3	30 749	7 776	12 318	6.4	9.6
Archuleta	1 552	1 331	1 111	3 484	80.9	19.7	30 518	22 894	33.3	1 273	370	552	13.7	20.1
Baca	908	928	891	3 152	72.0	13.6	26 731	18 602	43.7	824	−29	296	19.1	28.1
Bent	1 035	1 022	974	3 486	72.7	14.6	26 427	18 977	39.3	1 209	252	501	24.5	36.5
Boulder	45 409	41 140	33 801	141 125	91.3	42.1	50 245	35 322	42.2	20 591	−3 147	6 234	7.8	9.9
Chaffee	2 199	2 206	2 392	8 722	81.0	15.2	30 881	21 174	45.8	1 854	205	637	13.1	18.4
Cheyenne	463	511	552	1 501	80.8	11.9	34 746	24 341	42.7	250	−23	101	10.8	13.6
Clear Creek	1 438	1 393	1 415	5 250	91.8	31.2	56 537	33 149	70.6	470	−248	184	5.2	7.9
Conejos	2 014	2 002	1 963	4 353	63.7	10.7	20 708	14 188	46.0	2 315	−195	1 013	28.6	35.8
Costilla	670	714	690	2 050	60.5	10.5	18 700	13 057	43.2	1 241	140	512	33.5	46.8
Crowley	616	614	649	2 758	70.3	8.0	23 524	16 088	46.2	1 070	377	399	32.2	40.0
Custer	423	410	377	1 345	83.8	19.2	29 797	20 000	49.0	505	153	207	14.5	22.7

[1] Revised. [2] 1997 data are model-based estimates; 1989 data are census estimates. For more information on these estimates, see appendix A. Source Notes and Explanations or <http://www.census.gov/hhes/www/saipe.html>.

Sources: Public School Enrollment, 1998-1999 and 1994-1995—U.S. National Center for Education Statistics, <http://nces.ed.gov/ccd/pubagency.html> (accessed: 16 March 2001). Public School Enrollment and Educational Attainment, 1990—U.S. Census Bureau, "1990 Census of Population and Housing, Summary Tape File (STF) 3C" on CD-ROM (related Internet site <http://homer.ssd.census.gov/cdrom/lookup>). Income and Poverty, 1997—U.S. Census Bureau, "State and County Income and Poverty Estimates - 1997," published 22 November 2000, <http://www.census.gov/housing/saipe/estmod97/est97ALL.dat>. Income and Poverty, 1989—U.S. Census Bureau, "1990 Census of Population and Housing, Summary Tape File (STF) 3C" on CD-ROM (related Internet site <http://homer.ssd.census.gov/cdrom/lookup>).

Table B–5. Counties — Education, Income, and Poverty–Con.

[Includes U.S., states, and 3,142 counties or county equivalents defined as of January 1, 1992. For changes to these areas since January 1, 1992, see appendix B. Geographic Information]

County	Public school enrollment Fall 1998–1999	Public school enrollment Fall 1994–1995[1]	Public school enrollment 1990	Educational attainment, 1990 Persons 25 years and over	Percent High school graduate or higher	Percent Bachelor's degree or higher	Median household income[2] 1997 (dollars)	Median household income[2] 1989 (dollars)	Percent change, 1989–1997	Persons below poverty level,[2] 1997 Number Persons of all ages Total	Net change, 1989–1997	Persons under 18 years	Percent Persons of all ages	Percent Persons under 18 years
COLORADO—Con.														
Delta	4 665	4 564	3 749	14 588	73.0	13.6	27 418	18 532	47.9	4 261	614	1 588	16.2	23.9
Denver	68 790	62 773	59 967	321 186	79.2	29.0	35 616	25 106	41.9	81 561	3 046	31 572	16.4	26.6
Dolores	344	332	295	994	71.8	9.8	25 826	19 952	29.4	259	42	99	14.0	19.8
Douglas	29 847	20 041	12 100	38 338	94.8	40.7	77 513	51 718	49.9	2 785	890	998	1.9	2.2
Eagle	4 344	3 515	3 422	14 189	89.8	33.0	50 000	36 931	35.4	1 454	–189	562	4.3	6.1
Elbert	3 592	2 734	2 198	6 151	84.2	19.8	52 636	36 273	45.1	1 050	396	430	5.6	7.4
El Paso	89 117	82 382	68 704	240 251	88.3	25.8	42 023	29 604	42.0	45 856	6 337	18 880	9.5	13.8
Fremont	6 609	6 092	5 301	22 562	75.4	11.8	29 939	19 988	49.8	6 343	1 766	2 152	17.2	22.5
Garfield	9 146	8 055	5 439	19 299	85.2	21.6	40 923	29 176	40.3	3 508	788	1 444	8.9	12.9
Gilpin	384	349	529	2 214	93.0	29.5	51 044	31 898	60.0	221	–100	82	5.2	8.0
Grand	1 793	1 632	1 457	5 335	87.4	30.2	38 865	29 991	29.6	676	–59	238	6.6	9.1
Gunnison	1 672	1 676	1 372	5 737	90.6	36.9	32 300	23 013	40.4	1 367	–130	359	11.8	13.4
Hinsdale	66	38	62	356	93.0	32.0	32 993	26 250	25.7	81	16	28	10.8	20.8
Huerfano	1 217	1 139	1 029	4 105	65.0	12.6	21 389	14 730	45.2	1 584	73	618	23.4	34.3
Jackson	306	325	346	1 089	82.1	15.3	29 031	20 938	38.7	206	46	79	13.3	21.0
Jefferson	88 654	84 018	76 423	286 391	89.8	30.7	54 175	39 084	38.6	27 365	2 439	9 484	5.4	7.3
Kiowa	394	392	399	1 128	69.8	9.1	32 455	21 417	51.5	230	2	93	14.0	19.1
Kit Carson	1 727	1 658	1 512	4 620	73.5	15.8	32 964	23 125	42.5	949	–127	370	12.9	17.0
Lake	1 438	1 248	1 259	3 736	81.7	16.2	34 986	24 708	41.6	610	–127	239	9.5	12.8
La Plata	6 977	6 590	5 879	19 375	85.7	28.1	36 822	25 759	42.9	4 533	–271	1 557	11.5	14.6
Larimer	38 683	35 719	31 531	112 991	88.6	32.3	43 853	29 686	47.7	19 507	–1 959	6 188	8.5	10.3
Las Animas	2 351	2 481	2 449	9 085	67.6	12.7	22 682	16 286	39.3	3 433	–65	1 315	23.8	33.9
Lincoln	1 053	940	829	3 072	74.5	12.9	29 117	20 595	41.4	823	34	272	17.4	21.7
Logan	3 401	3 372	3 552	11 385	79.1	14.2	33 076	22 065	49.9	2 366	–189	887	13.4	18.8
Mesa	19 877	19 103	17 210	60 358	79.5	17.4	33 519	23 698	41.4	14 674	882	5 571	13.0	18.3
Mineral	158	116	88	414	84.8	17.9	29 810	19 830	50.3	92	19	30	12.9	21.2
Moffat	2 697	2 847	2 633	6 910	79.9	16.4	42 476	31 615	34.4	1 441	205	625	11.4	15.5
Montezuma	4 844	4 706	4 160	11 714	74.8	15.9	30 882	22 491	37.3	4 007	272	1 696	17.8	24.7
Montrose	5 882	5 692	4 762	16 227	74.5	15.4	32 312	22 610	42.9	4 088	676	1 696	13.2	19.8
Morgan	5 518	5 182	4 819	13 588	67.6	11.7	31 197	22 849	36.5	3 583	169	1 506	14.4	19.5
Otero	4 292	4 552	4 516	12 857	69.4	13.0	25 143	18 178	38.3	4 658	–40	1 974	22.8	32.1
Ouray	559	509	446	1 626	87.5	27.9	38 465	27 500	39.9	244	24	87	7.2	10.7
Park	2 209	2 045	1 335	4 921	91.1	22.4	46 090	32 102	43.6	919	250	350	6.8	9.5
Phillips	965	952	819	2 861	79.0	14.2	32 863	21 484	53.0	454	–125	155	10.5	13.4
Pitkin	1 289	1 197	1 310	9 487	94.7	49.8	52 744	39 991	31.9	707	–87	169	5.2	7.7
Prowers	2 958	3 172	3 001	8 094	70.2	12.2	28 881	20 625	40.0	2 801	45	1 229	20.4	27.9
Pueblo	24 245	22 750	23 025	79 524	73.9	14.0	29 112	21 553	35.1	24 269	–49	9 455	18.1	25.8
Rio Blanco	1 497	1 617	1 389	3 634	81.2	15.4	40 921	29 243	39.9	630	–157	229	10.3	12.4
Rio Grande	2 588	2 580	2 488	6 719	69.7	17.5	25 808	19 193	34.5	2 684	168	1 264	23.4	35.1
Routt	2 962	2 856	2 593	9 138	91.7	34.7	42 799	31 409	36.3	1 194	–168	358	6.8	7.8
Saguache	1 115	1 116	1 116	2 804	65.9	14.4	22 419	15 853	41.4	1 591	192	733	26.1	35.9
San Juan	86	93	168	463	82.7	24.0	27 635	26 167	5.6	106	10	45	19.8	27.1
San Miguel	817	786	557	2 531	93.5	40.3	42 160	30 578	37.9	471	55	161	8.5	12.7
Sedgwick	495	498	519	1 903	70.9	8.6	28 209	19 335	45.9	365	60	142	14.2	23.2
Summit	2 526	2 157	1 653	8 673	95.5	39.7	45 857	35 229	30.2	863	–141	241	4.5	5.9
Teller	3 886	3 392	2 427	8 312	92.1	26.4	45 552	32 209	41.4	1 747	496	721	8.4	12.2
Washington	1 022	1 021	955	3 210	75.9	11.8	29 870	20 637	44.7	560	–188	191	12.2	15.8
Weld	28 203	25 372	25 482	77 777	74.9	18.4	35 351	25 642	37.9	19 746	152	7 899	12.5	16.8
Yuma	2 089	1 910	2 027	5 855	78.5	13.4	31 639	22 249	42.2	1 131	–40	439	12.0	16.1
CONNECTICUT	544 698	506 824	473 898	2 198 963	79.2	27.2	46 648	41 721	11.8	291 242	73 895	121 256	8.9	14.7
Fairfield	133 532	120 932	114 700	564 538	81.0	34.2	56 872	49 891	14.0	67 095	17 616	26 912	7.9	12.9
Hartford	141 622	133 075	125 921	572 676	77.7	25.8	46 011	40 609	13.3	86 299	20 778	36 156	10.4	17.5
Litchfield	28 906	27 216	26 798	118 556	80.9	25.0	50 589	42 565	18.9	9 700	2 877	3 897	5.3	8.3
Middlesex	32 512	30 013	20 155	97 312	82.6	28.2	53 624	43 212	24.1	7 673	2 238	3 118	5.2	8.6
New Haven	126 042	117 175	112 089	536 686	77.5	24.2	44 412	38 471	15.4	83 789	22 501	35 880	10.6	18.0
New London	41 941	39 781	37 701	164 959	80.9	21.8	44 566	37 488	18.9	19 724	4 382	7 991	8.1	12.4
Tolland	21 945	20 513	19 482	79 077	84.7	29.2	55 223	45 019	22.7	6 773	1 297	2 474	5.4	7.5
Windham	18 198	18 119	17 052	65 159	71.1	16.8	41 108	33 851	21.4	10 188	2 205	4 828	9.8	16.1
DELAWARE	113 735	107 228	96 156	428 499	77.5	21.4	41 315	34 875	18.5	73 868	17 645	28 193	10.0	15.4
Kent	25 040	24 314	19 540	67 716	73.1	15.0	36 555	29 497	23.9	14 822	2 751	5 980	12.1	17.7
New Castle	67 375	62 772	58 331	283 809	80.6	25.2	47 819	38 617	23.8	41 658	9 390	15 303	8.7	13.1
Sussex	21 320	20 142	18 285	76 974	69.7	13.0	33 281	26 904	23.7	17 388	5 504	6 910	12.7	21.5
DISTRICT OF COLUMBIA	71 889	80 450	72 810	409 131	73.1	33.3	34 980	30 727	13.8	96 253	–25	33 503	19.3	33.7
District of Columbia	71 889	80 450	72 810	409 131	73.1	33.3	34 980	30 727	13.8	96 253	–25	33 503	19.3	33.7

[1] Revised. [2] 1997 data are model-based estimates; 1989 data are census estimates. For more information on these estimates, see appendix A. Source Notes and Explanations or <http://www.census.gov/hhes/www/saipe.html>.

Sources: Public School Enrollment, 1998-1999 and 1994-1995—U.S. National Center for Education Statistics, <http://nces.ed.gov/ccd/pubagency.html> (accessed: 16 March 2001). Public School Enrollment and Educational Attainment, 1990—U.S. Census Bureau, "1990 Census of Population and Housing, Summary Tape File (STF) 3C" on CD-ROM (related Internet site <http://homer.ssd.census.gov/cdrom/lookup>). Income and Poverty, 1997—U.S. Census Bureau, "State and County Income and Poverty Estimates - 1997," published 22 November 2000, <http://www.census.gov/housing/saipe/estmod97/est97ALL.dat>. Income and Poverty, 1989—U.S. Census Bureau, "1990 Census of Population and Housing, Summary Tape File (STF) 3C" on CD-ROM (related Internet site <http://homer.ssd.census.gov/cdrom/lookup>).

Table B–5. Counties — Education, Income, and Poverty–Con.

[Includes U.S., states, and 3,142 counties or county equivalents defined as of January 1, 1992. For changes to these areas since January 1, 1992, see appendix B. Geographic Information]

County	Public school enrollment Fall 1998–1999	Public school enrollment Fall 1994–1995[1]	Public school enrollment 1990	Educational attainment, 1990 Persons 25 years and over	Percent High school graduate or higher	Percent Bachelor's degree or higher	Median household income 1997 (dollars)	Median household income 1989 (dollars)	Percent change, 1989–1997	Persons below poverty level, 1997 Number Persons of all ages Total	Net change, 1989–1997	Persons under 18 years	Percent Persons of all ages	Percent Persons under 18 years
FLORIDA	2 337 757	2 108 968	1 812 155	8 887 168	74.4	18.3	32 877	27 483	19.6	2 129 825	525 639	775 812	14.4	21.8
Alachua	30 703	28 812	25 263	102 647	82.7	34.6	31 382	22 084	42.1	34 670	–5 403	10 864	18.3	23.0
Baker	4 731	4 647	4 055	10 957	64.1	5.7	32 377	25 816	25.4	3 255	617	1 410	16.9	20.7
Bay	25 936	24 802	21 660	82 448	74.7	15.7	32 047	24 684	29.8	21 975	4 065	8 971	15.1	22.4
Bradford	4 162	4 116	3 933	15 088	65.0	8.1	30 033	24 625	22.0	4 710	1 687	1 753	22.2	28.0
Brevard	68 681	64 595	54 820	277 346	82.3	20.4	36 353	30 534	19.1	52 556	16 741	18 644	11.3	17.6
Broward	231 187	199 255	156 193	898 829	76.8	18.8	37 832	30 571	23.8	176 882	50 571	61 197	11.7	17.5
Calhoun	2 268	2 288	2 284	7 005	55.9	8.2	25 362	18 615	36.2	2 567	694	974	23.0	28.2
Charlotte	16 557	15 092	11 597	87 427	75.7	13.4	32 211	25 746	25.1	12 782	4 628	4 067	9.5	17.8
Citrus	14 627	13 566	11 339	72 054	68.6	10.4	26 883	21 285	26.3	16 523	4 973	5 496	14.5	25.6
Clay	27 342	23 839	20 529	65 390	81.2	17.9	42 729	34 860	22.6	10 656	3 250	4 499	7.7	10.6
Collier	30 790	25 157	20 131	110 308	79.0	22.3	41 000	34 001	20.6	22 518	6 756	8 761	11.2	20.5
Columbia	9 418	8 878	8 151	26 839	69.0	11.0	28 521	21 961	29.9	10 076	1 496	4 235	19.7	28.0
Dade	352 536	321 615	296 622	1 281 295	65.0	18.8	30 000	26 909	11.5	453 238	111 977	160 665	21.1	29.6
DeSoto	4 640	4 381	3 944	16 171	54.5	7.6	25 525	20 962	21.8	5 427	1 230	2 208	23.4	35.1
Dixie	2 388	2 227	1 633	7 175	57.7	6.2	21 982	15 380	42.9	2 988	245	1 094	23.9	32.9
Duval	127 411	121 362	104 998	424 040	76.9	18.4	35 883	28 513	25.8	98 139	14 324	39 029	13.4	18.8
Escambia	45 667	44 765	42 041	165 094	76.2	18.2	31 069	25 158	23.5	48 916	5 906	18 855	17.8	24.9
Flagler	6 074	4 924	3 801	21 411	78.7	17.3	34 675	28 628	21.1	5 014	2 356	1 842	10.5	20.2
Franklin	1 510	1 631	1 488	6 107	59.5	12.4	24 088	17 247	39.7	1 880	–452	628	19.0	25.2
Gadsden	8 360	8 625	8 461	24 654	59.9	11.2	24 881	19 985	24.5	10 793	–169	4 401	25.9	32.3
Gilchrist	2 719	2 373	1 619	5 956	63.0	7.4	27 483	20 632	33.2	2 348	821	909	18.4	25.0
Glades	1 173	1 091	1 276	5 198	57.4	7.1	26 336	20 687	27.3	1 430	383	566	18.1	28.0
Gulf	2 308	2 264	2 056	7 641	66.4	9.2	26 865	21 866	30.8	2 402	507	879	19.8	27.4
Hamilton	2 250	2 380	2 384	6 562	58.4	7.0	24 174	18 709	29.2	2 932	207	1 156	26.2	30.5
Hardee	5 168	4 692	3 988	11 868	54.8	8.6	25 482	22 065	15.5	5 495	1 101	2 415	27.8	38.6
Hendry	7 464	6 754	5 544	15 027	56.6	10.0	28 325	24 904	13.7	6 599	1 830	3 166	22.8	33.0
Hernando	16 421	14 842	12 556	76 525	70.5	9.7	27 740	22 741	22.0	17 512	6 542	5 903	13.8	23.9
Highlands	11 090	10 462	8 185	51 747	68.2	10.9	26 006	21 146	23.0	12 305	2 040	4 207	16.4	29.0
Hillsborough	156 452	138 575	121 335	545 020	75.6	20.2	35 994	28 477	26.4	139 088	30 316	53 420	15.0	22.0
Holmes	3 735	3 699	2 942	10 389	57.1	7.4	23 416	17 241	35.8	4 328	670	1 682	24.7	33.6
Indian River	14 617	13 165	11 295	66 798	76.5	19.1	35 895	28 961	23.9	11 106	3 358	4 047	11.2	20.3
Jackson	7 828	8 060	7 977	26 740	61.6	10.9	25 953	19 471	33.3	8 439	–94	3 063	20.8	27.0
Jefferson	1 964	2 141	2 222	7 054	64.1	14.7	27 788	21 782	27.6	2 710	215	1 107	22.0	28.9
Lafayette	1 067	1 033	1 057	3 595	58.2	5.2	27 354	20 744	31.9	1 251	111	401	24.1	25.7
Lake	27 817	23 617	19 006	111 982	70.6	12.7	30 768	23 395	31.5	25 887	9 370	9 795	12.8	22.7
Lee	54 779	49 413	41 202	245 559	76.9	16.4	34 117	28 448	19.9	45 160	14 893	16 403	11.5	19.9
Leon	33 284	31 069	27 139	110 187	84.9	37.1	37 832	27 323	38.5	28 848	–1 990	9 300	13.8	17.4
Levy	6 234	5 450	4 381	17 612	62.8	8.3	24 838	18 807	32.1	6 249	1 002	2 353	19.8	29.0
Liberty	1 222	1 194	975	3 598	56.7	7.3	27 178	22 253	22.1	1 194	441	452	22.3	27.0
Madison	3 477	3 359	3 084	10 244	56.5	9.7	24 980	18 153	37.6	3 765	–155	1 411	23.2	27.9
Manatee	34 083	30 864	26 156	156 377	75.6	15.5	35 063	25 951	35.1	28 117	6 876	9 777	11.7	18.9
Marion	37 915	34 020	27 559	137 001	69.6	11.5	28 244	22 452	25.8	39 399	11 605	14 873	16.4	26.7
Martin	15 938	13 654	10 821	76 596	79.7	20.3	40 161	31 760	26.5	11 547	3 393	3 887	10.1	17.9
Monroe	9 463	9 380	8 209	58 585	79.7	20.3	36 353	29 351	23.9	9 314	1 112	2 749	11.5	18.3
Nassau	10 301	9 406	7 934	28 031	71.2	12.5	40 128	30 233	32.7	5 408	346	2 123	9.7	13.7
Okaloosa	30 414	29 029	25 037	90 946	83.8	21.0	36 788	27 941	31.7	17 425	3 242	6 854	10.5	14.7
Okeechobee	6 786	6 305	5 461	18 889	59.1	9.8	26 129	21 427	21.9	6 079	81	2 481	20.0	28.5
Orange	138 866	118 666	99 198	432 193	78.8	21.2	36 979	30 252	22.2	105 950	32 320	42 319	13.4	20.2
Osceola	30 127	24 231	17 749	70 244	73.7	11.2	32 552	27 260	19.4	19 570	9 656	8 774	13.4	21.8
Palm Beach	147 041	127 519	100 037	632 078	78.8	22.1	37 045	32 524	13.9	118 247	39 338	41 093	11.5	18.6
Pasco	46 065	40 114	33 391	212 612	66.9	9.1	28 202	21 480	31.3	43 756	11 770	14 841	13.5	21.8
Pinellas	110 582	102 170	94 982	637 871	78.1	18.5	32 816	26 296	24.8	105 737	26 743	34 129	12.2	19.4
Polk	77 300	71 297	63 716	271 411	68.0	12.9	31 030	25 216	23.1	74 345	23 144	29 777	16.6	25.4
Putnam	12 822	12 792	12 106	43 273	64.3	8.3	25 318	20 155	25.6	15 431	2 661	5 925	22.1	31.5
St. Johns	19 006	15 180	11 563	57 696	79.9	23.6	42 857	29 926	43.2	10 797	2 356	3 860	9.4	14.1
St. Lucie	28 877	26 214	22 047	104 680	71.7	13.1	30 788	27 710	11.1	27 105	7 832	10 418	15.1	23.9
Santa Rosa	22 021	18 972	14 899	51 922	78.5	18.6	37 201	27 584	34.9	13 912	2 537	5 475	11.8	16.1
Sarasota	33 958	30 431	27 748	217 375	81.3	21.9	37 660	29 919	25.9	26 344	7 409	7 929	8.7	15.3
Seminole	58 156	53 366	47 185	187 891	84.6	26.3	43 061	35 637	20.8	34 512	13 999	13 998	9.8	14.2
Sumter	5 901	5 632	5 194	21 867	64.3	7.8	25 601	19 584	30.7	7 922	2 003	3 076	21.4	32.6
Suwannee	5 802	5 577	5 289	17 444	63.8	8.2	26 070	19 775	31.8	5 893	735	2 327	18.2	25.6
Taylor	3 880	3 755	3 365	10 865	62.1	9.8	27 354	21 380	27.9	3 956	420	1 540	22.0	28.7
Union	2 339	2 094	1 923	6 701	67.7	7.9	29 968	22 831	31.3	2 054	835	735	23.2	23.2
Volusia	59 851	55 530	46 636	263 263	75.4	14.8	29 843	24 818	20.2	58 694	15 126	19 897	14.2	22.3
Wakulla	4 640	4 059	2 942	9 050	71.6	10.1	34 492	25 019	37.9	2 559	646	1 104	13.7	19.8
Walton	5 824	5 130	4 535	19 510	66.5	11.9	27 211	21 297	27.8	6 880	1 717	2 560	18.8	27.2
Washington	3 742	3 371	3 307	11 210	60.9	7.4	25 224	18 266	38.1	4 257	675	1 573	22.5	30.0

[1] Revised.   [2] 1997 data are model-based estimates; 1989 data are census estimates. For more information on these estimates, see appendix A. Source Notes and Explanations or <http://www.census.gov/hhes/www/saipe.html>.

Sources: Public School Enrollment, 1998-1999 and 1994-1995—U.S. National Center for Education Statistics, <http://nces.ed.gov/ccd/pubagency.html> (accessed: 16 March 2001). Public School Enrollment and Educational Attainment, 1990—U.S. Census Bureau, "1990 Census of Population and Housing, Summary Tape File (STF) 3C" on CD-ROM (related Internet site <http://homer.ssd.census.gov/cdrom/lookup>). Income and Poverty, 1997—U.S. Census Bureau, "State and County Income and Poverty Estimates - 1997," published 22 November 2000, <http://www.census.gov/housing/saipe/estmod97/est97ALL.dat>. Income and Poverty, 1989—U.S. Census Bureau, "1990 Census of Population and Housing, Summary Tape File (STF) 3C" on CD-ROM (related Internet site <http://homer.ssd.census.gov/cdrom/lookup>).

[Includes U.S., states, and 3,142 counties or county equivalents defined as of January 1, 1992. For changes to these areas since January 1, 1992, see appendix B. Geographic Information]

County	Public school enrollment Fall			Educational attainment, 1990	Percent—		Median household income[2]			Persons below poverty level,[2] 1997 Number Persons of all ages			Percent	
	1998–1999	1994–1995[1]	1990	Persons 25 years and over	High school graduate or higher	Bachelor's degree or higher	1997 (dollars)	1989 (dollars)	Percent change, 1989–1997	Total	Net change, 1989–1997	Persons under 18 years	Persons of all ages	Persons under 18 years
GEORGIA	1 401 291	1 270 948	1 134 100	4 023 420	70.9	19.3	36 372	29 021	25.3	1 113 562	190 477	470 440	14.7	22.8
Appling	3 474	3 470	3 627	9 646	57.2	8.2	28 620	22 271	28.5	3 320	233	1 418	19.9	29.2
Atkinson	1 574	1 469	1 334	3 679	51.5	6.4	24 493	17 685	38.5	1 655	43	735	22.8	32.7
Bacon	1 997	2 166	2 060	5 730	58.1	6.6	25 594	19 118	33.9	2 336	73	1 010	22.5	32.3
Baker	440	391	729	2 166	53.6	9.4	25 261	18 489	36.6	908	12	393	24.6	36.6
Baldwin	6 386	6 491	6 519	25 193	64.7	13.3	31 153	25 513	22.1	6 491	858	2 373	18.4	25.2
Banks	2 262	1 751	2 137	6 474	56.6	6.4	33 061	24 220	36.5	1 874	321	816	14.4	23.7
Barrow	7 844	6 601	5 249	18 280	58.8	9.2	37 258	27 538	35.3	5 056	742	2 168	12.4	18.6
Bartow	14 688	12 286	10 346	34 522	58.7	9.0	37 469	27 554	36.0	8 320	2 420	3 742	11.5	18.7
Ben Hill	3 588	3 670	3 608	9 810	56.8	7.6	26 126	19 106	36.7	3 699	197	1 663	21.2	30.7
Berrien	3 172	2 866	2 666	8 782	57.5	7.5	27 848	20 979	32.7	3 181	507	1 361	19.5	30.6
Bibb	24 620	24 878	24 641	94 391	68.2	17.0	32 553	25 813	26.1	32 185	4 253	13 668	20.9	33.0
Bleckley	2 374	2 159	2 028	6 390	60.3	10.3	31 756	22 690	40.0	1 948	118	834	17.9	28.0
Brantley	3 134	2 674	2 495	6 609	64.1	5.8	29 430	22 087	33.2	2 568	574	1 205	18.8	30.1
Brooks	2 753	2 683	3 152	9 363	58.7	9.1	26 002	19 474	33.5	3 753	–142	1 773	23.7	36.6
Bryan	5 127	4 842	3 526	9 048	68.5	11.8	39 198	28 623	36.9	2 877	857	1 397	12.2	18.2
Bulloch	8 372	8 014	6 800	22 331	67.6	19.9	30 483	20 640	47.7	9 896	–924	3 472	20.7	28.2
Burke	4 888	4 791	4 375	11 834	55.3	9.6	23 787	17 667	34.6	5 802	–345	2 667	25.3	34.4
Butts	3 175	3 000	2 865	9 748	58.4	7.2	32 153	24 420	31.7	2 680	548	1 126	16.3	24.0
Calhoun	805	1 195	1 149	3 137	52.2	10.1	21 573	15 640	37.9	1 414	–144	630	28.4	42.3
Camden	9 698	8 109	5 685	16 900	79.5	13.5	37 797	28 212	34.0	4 768	1 645	2 229	11.1	15.1
Candler	1 933	1 635	1 426	4 881	53.2	9.9	25 017	19 375	29.1	2 055	263	899	23.0	34.9
Carroll	15 212	14 218	13 243	42 311	60.5	12.0	34 061	25 607	33.0	11 966	2 076	5 255	14.7	23.4
Catoosa	9 165	8 276	7 511	27 287	63.8	8.1	35 597	25 581	39.2	5 916	889	2 299	11.6	17.7
Charlton	2 067	1 998	1 759	5 002	56.2	6.4	27 357	22 328	22.5	1 946	415	878	20.6	29.5
Chatham	36 729	35 442	34 139	135 851	73.7	18.6	33 639	26 721	25.9	42 117	6 131	17 805	19.0	29.8
Chattahoochee	509	426	2 982	6 873	88.5	20.2	36 899	25 305	45.8	1 489	403	712	14.2	14.7
Chattooga	4 177	4 136	3 892	14 281	50.1	5.9	27 909	20 335	37.2	3 400	192	1 316	14.9	22.9
Cherokee	24 341	19 701	14 823	56 489	75.2	18.4	54 423	39 052	39.4	7 972	2 551	3 442	5.9	9.0
Clarke	11 222	11 094	11 143	44 819	77.1	37.5	30 664	20 806	47.4	16 301	–5 159	5 125	19.4	26.7
Clay	390	389	661	2 079	51.4	11.2	20 277	13 709	47.9	1 120	–50	479	32.3	47.2
Clayton	44 068	39 149	33 317	110 326	77.2	14.7	38 366	33 472	14.6	28 455	13 060	13 465	13.5	22.8
Clinch	1 520	1 425	1 484	3 652	46.2	6.7	25 828	18 098	42.7	1 538	–62	661	23.1	32.3
Cobb	97 938	86 442	71 438	288 528	85.8	33.0	52 924	41 297	28.2	37 995	12 934	15 287	6.6	10.6
Coffee	7 474	6 890	6 012	17 427	58.0	11.1	28 484	20 651	37.9	7 075	511	3 086	20.6	29.4
Colquitt	8 330	7 973	7 531	22 546	57.0	10.0	26 039	20 331	28.1	9 460	1 301	4 112	23.5	34.9
Columbia	18 617	16 928	13 477	40 113	81.1	23.9	50 345	40 122	25.5	7 056	2 801	3 197	7.7	11.7
Cook	3 130	2 858	2 846	8 231	55.2	6.5	26 448	19 858	33.2	3 090	117	1 339	20.6	30.8
Coweta	15 792	12 694	10 072	33 373	67.4	13.3	44 493	31 925	39.4	8 904	2 825	4 027	10.4	16.2
Crawford	2 140	1 868	1 815	5 583	60.2	5.7	33 827	25 799	31.1	1 607	373	678	15.0	22.4
Crisp	4 610	4 600	4 026	12 169	56.2	10.0	23 859	17 797	34.1	5 882	220	2 657	28.6	42.4
Dade	2 589	2 353	2 297	8 139	55.3	8.0	30 079	20 176	49.1	2 210	375	857	15.0	22.2
Dawson	2 471	2 025	1 774	5 938	60.1	8.6	40 128	28 380	41.4	1 663	462	724	11.0	17.5
Decatur	5 844	5 970	5 625	15 358	59.8	11.7	26 377	20 854	26.5	6 694	885	2 983	24.9	36.7
De Kalb	95 875	86 405	82 245	353 321	83.9	32.7	42 767	35 721	19.7	78 171	25 392	33 004	13.2	22.9
Dodge	3 522	3 355	3 277	11 160	56.8	8.0	25 409	18 244	39.3	3 944	320	1 554	22.7	32.7
Dooly	1 809	1 731	1 837	5 973	54.7	9.5	22 555	16 326	38.2	2 902	–289	1 254	27.9	39.2
Dougherty	17 310	18 085	19 985	55 627	67.5	17.0	29 658	23 587	25.7	23 418	416	10 468	24.8	36.4
Douglas	16 770	15 011	13 487	43 407	72.3	12.0	46 284	37 138	24.6	8 159	3 530	3 722	9.1	14.7
Early	2 863	2 662	2 338	7 202	54.1	9.4	22 525	16 421	37.2	3 622	–13	1 597	29.9	43.5
Echols	706	660	493	1 396	61.0	4.7	30 080	21 574	39.4	480	139	231	20.0	31.6
Effingham	8 054	6 762	5 620	15 161	66.0	7.6	41 511	29 443	41.0	4 279	1 023	1 884	11.5	16.4
Elbert	3 883	3 949	3 720	12 311	54.3	8.0	27 555	20 501	34.4	3 688	19	1 487	19.1	28.9
Emanuel	4 991	4 952	4 479	12 419	52.6	9.1	22 876	17 891	27.9	5 535	359	2 530	26.4	39.1
Evans	2 026	1 885	1 758	5 376	58.5	8.6	25 659	19 972	28.5	2 401	277	1 074	24.6	36.6
Fannin	3 071	3 002	2 583	11 013	55.8	7.8	26 062	19 023	37.0	3 088	358	1 133	16.5	26.9
Fayette	18 911	16 016	12 757	39 171	86.5	25.8	69 309	50 167	38.2	3 620	1 997	1 511	4.0	6.0
Floyd	15 278	14 330	13 073	52 583	63.9	13.7	33 584	25 536	31.5	13 000	2 394	5 186	15.7	25.3
Forsyth	14 299	9 237	7 619	28 366	67.6	15.6	60 250	36 642	64.4	4 437	1 483	1 865	5.1	8.2
Franklin	3 513	3 254	2 646	10 891	54.1	9.5	28 909	21 663	33.4	3 150	469	1 174	16.6	25.9
Fulton	126 183	112 703	96 088	415 191	77.8	31.6	39 047	29 978	30.3	133 562	18 051	54 114	18.3	29.8
Gilmer	3 526	2 995	2 323	8 727	52.3	8.6	28 607	21 410	33.6	2 737	559	1 141	14.5	24.7
Glascock	531	496	416	1 602	50.3	5.3	28 625	21 806	31.3	362	–13	139	15.0	23.8
Glynn	11 915	11 133	10 742	40 432	74.3	19.9	35 077	27 887	25.8	10 842	2 048	4 564	16.1	26.5
Gordon	8 259	7 038	6 496	21 849	58.4	9.2	33 828	26 981	25.4	5 258	1 406	2 305	12.7	20.7
Grady	4 713	4 645	4 149	12 691	54.9	7.7	25 527	19 507	30.9	4 681	235	2 092	21.8	34.2
Greene	2 465	2 545	2 557	7 110	51.2	8.8	27 011	20 264	33.3	2 971	44	1 372	21.6	32.4

[1] Revised. [2] 1997 data are model-based estimates; 1989 data are census estimates. For more information on these estimates, see appendix A. Source Notes and Explanations or <http://www.census.gov/hhes/www/saipe.html>.

Sources: Public School Enrollment, 1998-1999 and 1994-1995—U.S. National Center for Education Statistics, <http://nces.ed.gov/ccd/pubagency.html> (accessed: 16 March 2001). Public School Enrollment and Educational Attainment, 1990—U.S. Census Bureau, "1990 Census of Population and Housing, Summary Tape File (STF) 3C" on CD-ROM (related Internet site <http://homer.ssd.census.gov/cdrom/lookup>). Income and Poverty, 1997—U.S. Census Bureau, "State and County Income and Poverty Estimates - 1997," published 22 November 2000, <http://www.census.gov/housing/saipe/estmod97/est97ALL.dat>. Income and Poverty, 1989—U.S. Census Bureau, "1990 Census of Population and Housing, Summary Tape File (STF) 3C" on CD-ROM (related Internet site <http://homer.ssd.census.gov/cdrom/lookup>).

[Includes U.S., states, and 3,142 counties or county equivalents defined as of January 1, 1992. For changes to these areas since January 1, 1992, see appendix B. Geographic Information]

County	Public school enrollment			Educational attainment, 1990			Median household income[2]			Persons below poverty level,[2] 1997				
	Fall				Percent—					Number			Percent	
										Persons of all ages				
	1998–1999	1994–1995[1]	1990	Persons 25 years and over	High school graduate or higher	Bachelor's degree or higher	1997 (dollars)	1989 (dollars)	Percent change, 1989–1997	Total	Net change, 1989–1997	Persons under 18 years	Persons of all ages	Persons under 18 years
GEORGIA—Con.														
Gwinnett	100 721	81 885	63 114	220 449	86.7	29.6	56 082	43 518	28.9	29 473	15 522	13 027	5.6	8.8
Habersham	5 540	5 355	4 776	17 327	59.0	12.0	33 582	24 386	37.7	3 418	436	1 301	11.2	17.2
Hall	22 360	19 185	16 374	60 321	65.1	15.4	38 435	29 774	29.1	14 244	4 287	6 316	11.9	20.0
Hancock	1 769	1 995	1 935	5 248	49.5	6.8	23 230	17 825	30.3	2 575	−53	1 076	28.3	38.5
Haralson	5 126	4 412	4 035	13 897	56.0	7.5	30 043	22 775	31.9	4 107	990	1 727	16.7	26.6
Harris	4 068	3 352	2 927	11 781	65.0	13.6	40 645	27 616	47.2	2 389	−18	920	10.6	16.2
Hart	3 452	3 263	3 483	12 951	56.9	9.1	30 794	24 333	26.6	3 456	714	1 354	15.9	25.2
Heard	2 068	1 818	1 720	5 292	49.1	5.7	30 441	21 513	41.5	1 752	133	734	17.3	25.0
Henry	20 300	14 306	10 515	36 993	72.9	10.7	49 548	37 550	32.0	6 811	3 297	3 077	6.4	10.5
Houston	20 825	18 391	16 608	55 396	79.5	16.0	41 188	31 229	31.9	12 507	3 235	5 667	11.8	19.0
Irwin	1 984	1 862	1 902	5 350	53.1	8.3	26 957	20 169	33.7	1 990	−326	781	21.9	29.2
Jackson	7 456	6 448	5 508	18 997	54.5	9.0	34 033	25 418	33.9	5 414	1 257	2 287	14.4	22.5
Jasper	1 999	1 775	1 594	5 327	64.6	10.8	34 164	25 736	32.7	1 699	246	760	16.6	26.5
Jeff Davis	2 669	2 632	2 340	7 309	55.2	8.3	28 010	21 470	30.5	2 445	203	1 037	19.1	28.8
Jefferson	3 838	3 752	3 604	10 310	49.7	6.2	23 243	17 076	36.1	4 715	−597	2 024	26.6	37.0
Jenkins	1 813	1 736	1 800	5 130	49.9	7.7	22 686	16 967	33.7	2 194	−53	896	26.0	36.6
Johnson	1 419	1 529	1 632	5 184	52.0	4.9	24 315	18 064	34.6	2 044	235	890	24.8	36.4
Jones	4 747	4 193	3 834	13 040	70.2	12.0	39 176	31 934	22.7	2 816	614	1 118	12.2	17.6
Lamar	2 634	2 394	2 323	8 153	58.0	10.0	30 332	23 336	30.0	2 493	414	1 024	17.0	26.5
Lanier	1 367	1 335	1 166	3 332	51.2	5.4	24 428	17 618	38.7	1 575	163	696	22.4	32.7
Laurens	9 146	8 837	7 862	24 964	61.0	12.0	28 950	21 788	32.9	8 712	771	3 794	20.1	30.4
Lee	5 255	4 666	3 847	9 485	69.8	13.7	44 326	30 974	43.1	2 439	485	1 087	10.8	14.4
Liberty	11 411	10 442	9 215	24 659	82.1	13.4	29 508	21 596	36.6	9 942	2 197	4 915	18.8	25.6
Lincoln	1 582	1 482	1 429	4 758	59.2	8.2	27 034	21 472	25.9	1 572	251	640	18.8	29.1
Long	1 841	1 446	1 179	3 367	63.6	5.2	27 388	18 802	45.7	1 869	420	882	21.7	33.3
Lowndes	16 098	15 582	14 305	43 540	69.8	16.3	30 296	23 295	30.1	16 818	2 573	7 143	20.5	29.4
Lumpkin	3 205	2 794	2 411	8 628	60.2	11.1	35 598	26 116	36.3	2 599	569	1 032	14.4	21.5
McDuffie	4 476	4 514	3 838	12 352	56.1	10.4	28 268	21 292	32.8	4 437	144	1 903	20.3	29.7
McIntosh	1 917	1 721	1 622	5 415	56.9	8.7	24 357	19 182	27.0	2 251	341	978	22.2	35.1
Macon	2 426	2 593	2 916	7 742	53.7	10.1	24 175	17 526	37.9	3 778	61	1 602	29.0	38.7
Madison	4 509	4 138	3 617	13 332	59.7	9.7	33 855	25 092	34.9	3 546	253	1 417	14.4	21.6
Marion	1 853	1 668	1 175	3 448	54.5	4.6	25 355	18 343	38.2	1 479	−71	634	22.0	32.1
Meriwether	4 164	4 202	4 393	13 030	51.0	0.7	27 049	20 212	35.0	4 007	48	2 024	21.1	30.1
Miller	1 283	1 258	1 229	3 989	57.4	8.2	26 289	20 488	28.3	1 483	126	612	23.4	35.1
Mitchell	4 645	4 760	4 458	11 942	54.9	7.8	24 688	18 926	30.4	5 573	−139	2 448	26.3	36.6
Monroe	3 747	3 546	2 981	10 799	66.2	12.9	34 310	27 770	23.6	2 858	588	1 181	14.8	22.6
Montgomery	1 352	1 237	1 348	4 304	57.4	10.1	24 936	20 054	24.3	1 674	29	669	23.3	33.4
Morgan	2 915	2 640	2 662	8 137	59.6	11.0	33 165	26 018	27.5	2 449	553	1 034	16.2	24.8
Murray	6 396	5 763	5 109	15 763	52.1	5.5	33 173	26 517	25.1	4 005	1 065	1 810	12.1	19.2
Muscogee	33 349	32 513	30 513	108 954	71.5	16.6	31 349	24 056	30.3	34 293	2 352	14 557	19.3	29.5
Newton	10 615	8 785	7 766	25 213	59.7	9.5	37 415	27 992	33.7	7 622	1 749	3 465	13.1	21.0
Oconee	5 060	4 375	3 365	10 981	77.1	28.4	47 059	34 566	37.9	1 961	584	790	8.2	11.5
Oglethorpe	2 054	1 937	1 799	6 245	61.8	12.8	33 398	24 667	35.4	1 730	172	670	15.0	22.1
Paulding	14 328	10 282	7 267	24 989	64.1	7.6	44 575	33 085	34.7	5 769	2 163	2 703	7.7	12.1
Peach	4 450	4 474	3 935	12 223	67.5	15.2	29 557	25 604	15.4	6 075	1 274	2 480	25.6	37.6
Pickens	3 551	3 107	2 447	9 367	56.8	9.0	36 883	25 248	46.1	2 423	609	1 062	12.2	21.2
Pierce	3 214	3 025	2 715	8 266	60.0	6.3	28 318	20 499	38.1	3 164	357	1 343	19.9	30.3
Pike	2 511	2 202	1 760	6 491	64.9	9.3	35 062	27 733	26.4	1 491	152	615	11.8	18.2
Polk	6 896	6 742	6 361	21 411	51.8	6.8	29 437	22 326	31.9	6 202	765	2 539	17.0	26.1
Pulaski	1 654	1 686	1 613	5 179	60.6	10.7	29 139	21 376	36.3	1 722	−212	701	20.4	30.4
Putnam	2 533	2 323	2 542	9 189	61.8	11.7	32 956	24 325	35.5	2 856	585	1 197	16.3	26.5
Quitman	273	237	423	1 424	49.5	7.3	20 838	15 972	30.5	712	−15	287	28.2	44.2
Rabun	2 049	1 834	1 680	8 099	62.7	11.6	29 803	21 177	40.7	1 859	298	662	13.9	23.0
Randolph	1 800	1 809	1 630	4 779	49.3	6.0	20 461	13 972	46.4	2 485	−255	1 022	32.2	43.2
Richmond	36 326	35 918	32 765	114 690	70.9	17.3	30 339	25 265	20.1	40 010	7 420	16 593	21.9	32.5
Rockdale	13 268	12 369	10 275	33 497	77.7	18.1	48 632	39 389	23.5	5 987	2 698	2 744	8.7	14.3
Schley	632	468	676	2 160	56.4	8.0	28 479	21 417	33.0	793	83	338	19.8	28.7
Screven	3 263	3 168	2 902	8 602	58.9	8.6	26 631	20 531	29.7	3 231	119	1 378	22.3	32.4
Seminole	1 920	2 046	1 619	5 637	52.7	7.8	24 521	18 438	33.0	2 599	22	1 045	26.6	39.8
Spalding	10 562	10 367	10 532	33 651	60.0	11.1	33 073	25 634	29.0	9 591	1 239	4 165	16.6	25.4
Stephens	4 370	4 205	3 838	15 013	60.1	13.1	29 980	22 204	35.0	4 136	292	1 591	16.5	26.2
Stewart	919	856	1 067	3 572	51.4	8.0	21 518	15 606	37.9	1 468	−273	558	27.2	37.4
Sumter	5 868	5 937	5 616	17 752	62.8	15.9	28 247	20 957	34.8	7 576	429	3 275	25.0	35.1
Talbot	914	924	1 214	4 147	56.2	7.1	25 356	20 489	23.8	1 569	−50	599	22.2	32.0
Taliaferro	156	164	371	1 222	48.6	5.6	20 700	14 700	40.8	562	−44	228	29.0	43.4
Tattnall	3 392	3 211	3 104	11 654	57.4	6.5	26 649	20 293	31.3	4 375	979	1 792	25.6	37.3

[1] Revised.   [2] 1997 data are model-based estimates; 1989 data are census estimates. For more information on these estimates, see appendix A. Source Notes and Explanations or <http://www.census.gov/hhes/www/saipe.html>.

Sources: Public School Enrollment, 1998-1999 and 1994-1995—U.S. National Center for Education Statistics, <http://nces.ed.gov/ccd/pubagency.html> (accessed: 16 March 2001). Public School Enrollment and Educational Attainment, 1990—U.S. Census Bureau, "1990 Census of Population and Housing, Summary Tape File (STF) 3C" on CD-ROM (related Internet site <http://homer.ssd.census.gov/cdrom/lookup>). Income and Poverty, 1997—U.S. Census Bureau, "State and County Income and Poverty Estimates - 1997," published 22 November 2000, <http://www.census.gov/housing/saipe/estmod97/est97ALL.dat>. Income and Poverty, 1989—U.S. Census Bureau, "1990 Census of Population and Housing, Summary Tape File (STF) 3C" on CD-ROM (related Internet site <http://homer.ssd.census.gov/cdrom/lookup>).

Table B–5. Counties — Education, Income, and Poverty–Con.

[Includes U.S., states, and 3,142 counties or county equivalents defined as of January 1, 1992. For changes to these areas since January 1, 1992, see appendix B. Geographic Information]

County	Public school enrollment Fall 1998–1999	Public school enrollment Fall 1994–1995[1]	Public school enrollment 1990	Educational attainment, 1990 Persons 25 years and over	Percent High school graduate or higher	Percent Bachelor's degree or higher	Median household income 1997 (dollars)	Median household income 1989 (dollars)	Percent change, 1989–1997	Persons below poverty level, 1997 Number Persons of all ages Total	Net change, 1989–1997	Persons under 18 years	Percent Persons of all ages	Percent Persons under 18 years
GEORGIA—Con.														
Taylor	1 827	1 723	1 607	4 678	51.2	7.1	22 906	16 210	41.3	2 189	–55	888	26.3	38.4
Telfair	1 962	2 233	2 248	7 043	52.1	8.6	22 159	16 573	33.7	2 919	1	1 191	25.7	35.8
Terrell	1 877	2 055	1 989	6 538	52.4	9.2	23 292	18 036	29.1	3 057	15	1 312	27.5	39.3
Thomas	8 873	8 788	7 888	24 219	63.3	13.4	27 741	20 901	32.7	9 101	419	3 707	21.2	29.9
Tift	7 489	7 605	7 131	20 829	61.3	14.0	29 926	22 421	33.5	7 713	–38	3 328	21.3	31.0
Toombs	5 161	5 162	4 690	14 712	59.0	11.4	24 964	19 473	28.2	6 422	769	2 855	24.9	36.3
Towns	1 057	852	908	4 813	58.2	11.4	28 170	19 356	45.5	1 124	232	355	13.7	25.2
Treutlen	1 278	1 328	1 164	3 674	52.7	6.3	23 362	17 391	34.3	1 574	–37	670	26.3	38.8
Troup	11 182	11 078	10 248	34 332	60.8	13.6	32 523	24 788	31.2	9 536	672	4 009	16.3	24.2
Turner	2 009	2 043	2 042	5 170	55.3	7.2	22 686	17 766	27.7	2 526	–168	1 119	27.4	38.0
Twiggs	2 030	1 992	1 953	5 835	48.4	4.8	26 941	19 213	40.2	2 246	–259	899	22.2	29.3
Union	2 687	2 198	1 923	8 275	58.7	10.1	28 294	20 275	39.6	2 329	177	813	14.1	22.5
Upson	4 958	4 986	4 786	17 139	54.6	9.0	28 680	22 747	26.1	4 463	669	1 736	16.5	24.8
Walker	9 919	9 985	10 372	37 846	58.3	8.4	30 675	24 068	27.5	8 549	1 223	3 324	13.6	20.6
Walton	10 424	8 878	7 255	23 776	57.9	9.4	36 324	28 198	28.8	7 476	2 452	3 221	13.6	20.8
Ware	6 486	6 782	7 111	22 611	61.1	10.4	25 866	20 426	26.6	8 187	1 068	3 274	23.9	34.9
Warren	1 036	1 170	1 111	3 792	42.8	4.2	22 520	17 284	30.3	1 642	–301	654	27.1	38.3
Washington	3 997	3 852	3 695	11 721	58.1	9.8	28 092	21 460	30.9	4 589	560	1 992	23.0	34.2
Wayne	5 267	4 895	4 566	13 870	62.9	9.6	30 376	23 311	30.3	5 417	819	2 343	21.6	31.7
Webster	398	324	406	1 416	50.4	5.5	26 651	19 028	40.1	414	–93	158	18.5	26.7
Wheeler	1 072	1 026	1 072	3 040	56.7	8.6	22 855	16 585	37.8	1 290	–173	525	26.3	36.1
White	3 084	2 670	2 042	8 671	62.9	13.6	32 377	24 234	33.6	2 153	578	828	12.4	20.6
Whitfield	15 912	14 548	12 734	45 411	59.8	12.0	35 754	27 797	28.6	9 846	1 878	4 254	11.9	19.4
Wilcox	1 340	1 374	1 432	4 407	52.8	7.6	23 291	16 333	42.6	1 931	–13	825	26.6	39.0
Wilkes	1 998	2 171	1 882	6 902	56.6	10.4	26 224	18 629	40.8	2 202	–163	855	20.7	31.2
Wilkinson	1 875	1 993	1 973	6 141	62.0	8.8	30 950	25 166	23.0	1 906	352	826	17.4	25.6
Worth	4 678	4 519	4 319	11 837	58.1	6.3	28 921	21 312	35.7	5 112	–30	2 187	22.5	31.6
HAWAII	188 069	183 869	167 841	709 820	80.1	22.9	43 627	38 829	12.4	130 644	42 236	48 849	11.1	16.2
Hawaii	NA	NA	23 207	77 099	77.7	18.5	34 557	29 712	16.3	23 475	6 699	9 449	16.6	23.4
Honolulu	NA	NA	118 547	534 187	81.2	24.6	44 310	40 581	9.2	87 155	27 062	31 308	10.2	14.8
Kalawao	NA	NA	–	130	51.5	4.6	9 213	10 000	–7.9	–	–48	–	–	–
Kauai	NA	NA	9 460	33 045	73.1	16.3	38 877	37 425	3.9	6 847	3 207	2 916	12.1	18.6
Maui	NA	NA	16 627	65 359	77.0	17.8	40 647	38 771	4.8	13 167	5 316	5 176	10.8	15.8
IDAHO	244 722	240 601	214 664	601 292	79.7	17.7	33 612	25 257	33.1	159 237	28 649	61 496	13.0	17.3
Ada	51 440	46 428	38 055	127 588	87.2	24.9	43 321	30 246	43.2	24 489	6 710	8 853	8.9	12.0
Adams	623	675	657	2 143	75.3	10.8	28 944	22 455	28.9	559	206	208	14.6	21.2
Bannock	14 504	15 614	15 335	37 391	82.9	19.8	35 382	26 275	34.7	10 254	1 310	3 871	13.9	17.1
Bear Lake	1 664	1 837	1 737	3 454	79.8	11.4	32 181	21 646	48.7	874	13	366	13.4	15.8
Benewah	1 824	1 336	1 691	4 982	74.2	8.8	31 728	21 508	47.5	1 310	31	479	14.4	19.1
Bingham	10 719	11 664	10 643	20 242	76.8	13.1	34 488	25 158	37.1	6 178	374	2 793	14.7	18.1
Blaine	2 836	2 798	2 335	8 962	91.7	33.0	45 504	31 199	45.9	1 300	266	461	7.5	10.9
Boise	1 137	928	687	2 295	80.0	14.4	34 807	26 048	33.6	585	123	217	11.3	15.8
Bonner	5 816	6 139	5 031	17 689	78.2	15.2	30 311	21 465	41.2	5 399	1 296	2 009	15.2	21.2
Bonneville	18 623	19 038	17 585	40 392	84.0	23.2	39 962	30 462	31.2	9 906	2 850	4 155	12.2	15.7
Boundary	1 661	1 807	1 763	4 986	74.6	13.3	29 732	21 662	37.3	1 600	475	657	16.5	23.1
Butte	617	710	762	1 751	80.4	13.5	31 780	26 292	20.9	472	80	192	15.4	19.0
Camas	200	209	167	473	81.8	15.0	35 445	24 440	45.0	63	–23	19	7.4	7.5
Canyon	23 407	20 980	18 975	53 308	71.0	12.0	31 558	22 979	37.3	19 042	5 810	7 879	16.0	21.6
Caribou	1 963	2 232	2 132	3 924	84.3	11.8	42 574	29 979	42.0	714	222	315	9.6	12.0
Cassia	5 242	5 515	5 248	10 765	72.7	14.0	32 175	23 381	37.6	3 302	507	1 525	15.4	20.4
Clark	223	227	193	475	74.7	14.1	30 827	24 583	25.4	112	41	47	12.4	18.1
Clearwater	1 589	1 761	1 652	5 845	73.4	11.4	32 881	23 925	37.4	1 324	344	448	14.9	20.8
Custer	923	966	930	2 652	81.7	15.6	34 460	24 393	41.3	500	–111	169	12.1	14.9
Elmore	5 187	4 952	4 350	11 963	83.1	15.8	32 486	23 750	36.8	3 139	572	1 340	12.7	17.6
Franklin	2 971	2 939	2 825	4 879	82.2	14.3	33 892	25 446	33.2	1 400	423	656	12.5	15.4
Fremont	2 529	2 673	2 998	5 907	75.6	11.1	30 579	23 498	30.1	1 701	95	736	14.4	17.9
Gem	2 991	2 760	2 498	7 698	70.1	8.6	30 132	21 495	40.2	2 295	322	837	15.4	21.0
Gooding	3 107	3 023	2 668	7 375	72.5	13.3	28 957	19 823	46.1	2 021	83	770	14.8	19.6
Idaho	2 392	2 644	2 863	9 142	75.1	12.7	29 642	22 093	34.3	2 590	752	972	17.6	25.2
Jefferson	5 515	5 800	4 848	8 569	77.6	11.8	34 390	24 421	40.8	2 590	237	1 194	13.1	15.8
Jerome	3 758	3 842	3 437	9 218	72.4	11.0	30 938	21 209	45.9	2 784	392	1 154	15.4	20.5

[1] Revised.   [2] 1997 data are model-based estimates; 1989 data are census estimates. For more information on these estimates, see appendix A. Source Notes and Explanations or <http://www.census.gov/hhes/www/saipe.html>.

Sources: Public School Enrollment, 1998-1999 and 1994-1995—U.S. National Center for Education Statistics, <http://nces.ed.gov/ccd/pubagency.html> (accessed: 16 March 2001). Public School Enrollment and Educational Attainment, 1990—U.S. Census Bureau, "1990 Census of Population and Housing, Summary Tape File (STF) 3C" on CD-ROM (related Internet site <http://homer.ssd.census.gov/cdrom/lookup>). Income and Poverty, 1997—U.S. Census Bureau, "State and County Income and Poverty Estimates - 1997," published 22 November 2000, <http://www.census.gov/housing/saipe/estmod97/est97ALL.dat>. Income and Poverty, 1989—U.S. Census Bureau, "1990 Census of Population and Housing, Summary Tape File (STF) 3C" on CD-ROM (related Internet site <http://homer.ssd.census.gov/cdrom/lookup>).

[Includes U.S., states, and 3,142 counties or county equivalents defined as of January 1, 1992. For changes to these areas since January 1, 1992, see appendix B. Geographic Information]

County	Public school enrollment Fall 1998–1999	1994–1995[1]	1990	Educational attainment, 1990 Persons 25 years and over	Percent— High school graduate or higher	Bachelor's degree or higher	Median household income[2] 1997 (dollars)	1989 (dollars)	Percent change, 1989–1997	Persons below poverty level,[2] 1997 Number, Persons of all ages Total	Net change, 1989–1997	Persons under 18 years	Percent Persons of all ages	Persons under 18 years
IDAHO—Con.														
Kootenai	17 531	16 327	12 699	45 083	81.1	16.0	36 123	25 593	41.1	11 735	3 423	4 280	11.5	16.6
Latah	4 576	4 779	4 490	16 616	86.6	35.8	35 005	22 635	54.6	4 070	-1 012	1 055	13.5	15.1
Lemhi	1 478	1 479	1 372	4 613	73.9	11.8	28 159	19 697	43.0	1 278	-104	437	15.8	20.7
Lewis	1 129	1 209	705	2 325	78.8	13.2	28 202	20 926	34.8	611	68	232	15.2	22.2
Lincoln	875	900	789	2 040	79.8	11.9	30 036	21 640	38.8	493	49	212	13.0	18.7
Madison	5 524	5 957	5 427	7 936	87.6	19.2	35 718	23 000	55.3	3 699	-2 687	1 063	15.3	14.4
Minidoka	4 864	5 361	4 995	11 158	68.5	9.0	30 598	23 327	31.2	3 299	747	1 409	16.3	20.6
Nez Perce	5 914	5 882	5 961	22 232	79.9	15.6	34 963	25 219	38.6	4 687	690	1 524	12.8	18.3
Oneida	1 011	993	951	2 009	78.7	12.9	33 141	22 582	46.8	517	33	218	12.8	15.3
Owyhee	2 569	2 543	1 939	4 858	62.0	8.7	26 702	18 595	43.6	2 210	158	933	21.4	28.2
Payette	4 334	4 106	3 455	10 210	67.4	9.8	29 849	20 367	46.6	3 532	643	1 399	17.2	23.4
Power	1 864	1 923	1 912	4 016	72.1	11.1	32 719	24 771	32.1	1 508	579	692	17.8	23.9
Shoshone	2 480	2 768	2 790	9 313	70.1	9.0	27 555	20 980	31.3	2 791	563	990	20.1	29.5
Teton	1 280	1 172	799	1 981	80.2	17.4	31 680	22 799	39.0	541	-80	214	9.7	11.7
Twin Falls	12 349	11 924	11 163	33 144	75.4	13.3	32 169	23 520	36.8	8 770	1 604	3 381	14.1	18.9
Valley	1 484	1 687	1 251	4 113	83.8	19.4	33 587	24 232	38.6	1 111	343	427	13.8	20.6
Washington	1 999	2 094	1 901	5 577	72.7	10.3	26 134	17 917	45.9	1 880	230	708	18.4	24.4
ILLINOIS	2 011 530	1 929 153	1 824 313	7 293 930	76.2	21.0	41 179	32 252	27.7	1 353 506	26 775	564 675	11.3	17.5
Adams	10 554	11 848	10 096	43 298	75.1	13.7	34 425	23 317	47.6	8 054	-314	3 068	12.2	17.3
Alexander	1 744	2 037	2 161	6 724	59.7	7.8	20 807	14 786	40.7	2 952	-443	1 300	30.1	43.9
Bond	2 387	2 499	2 566	9 669	69.3	12.7	33 762	23 756	42.1	1 888	170	665	12.5	17.0
Boone	7 328	6 344	5 397	19 272	75.5	12.0	49 782	35 103	41.8	2 391	204	1 047	6.1	9.4
Brown	797	806	879	3 979	68.9	9.8	31 633	20 445	54.7	757	106	232	14.8	16.7
Bureau	6 340	6 584	6 507	23 444	76.6	12.5	36 572	26 248	39.3	3 107	-544	1 171	8.7	12.2
Calhoun	766	753	727	3 583	62.8	7.0	32 469	21 163	53.4	594	-200	198	12.1	16.3
Carroll	3 233	3 368	3 124	11 323	76.0	10.6	34 934	25 758	35.6	1 734	-193	667	10.3	15.7
Cass	2 330	2 272	2 565	8 825	72.3	10.6	32 897	23 642	39.1	1 475	-340	576	11.2	16.4
Champaign	24 193	23 687	23 661	95 971	87.5	34.1	38 245	26 541	44.1	18 901	-5 226	6 413	12.1	16.8
Christian	5 618	5 841	5 822	22 945	73.1	9.3	34 836	24 506	42.2	3 710	-246	1 437	10.7	16.1
Clark	3 169	3 082	2 829	10 734	71.3	9.2	32 800	23 281	40.9	1 822	-53	728	11.0	17.3
Clay	2 794	2 719	2 587	9 647	65.6	7.6	29 330	20 006	46.6	1 819	-571	668	12.5	17.5
Clinton	5 953	5 714	5 851	21 563	67.2	9.2	39 651	29 890	32.7	2 940	-351	1 155	8.0	12.0
Coles	7 812	8 209	7 692	29 136	76.1	18.7	35 093	24 153	45.3	6 387	-1 266	2 077	13.7	18.8
Cook	796 419	752 777	750 756	3 291 995	73.4	22.8	40 181	32 673	23.0	730 426	17 171	311 294	14.0	22.7
Crawford	3 651	3 821	3 462	13 317	76.0	9.5	32 516	23 912	36.0	2 377	362	913	12.0	18.0
Cumberland	2 079	2 069	2 101	6 727	72.2	8.2	33 612	23 623	42.3	1 279	3	550	11.4	17.2
DeKalb	14 942	14 212	10 848	41 817	83.9	26.1	44 758	30 864	45.0	6 347	-3 016	1 937	8.1	10.1
De Witt	3 389	3 358	3 092	10 941	74.6	11.8	38 385	27 196	41.1	1 746	71	712	10.4	16.1
Douglas	3 172	3 266	3 631	12 550	74.0	11.1	36 640	26 758	36.9	1 881	38	857	9.4	15.0
DuPage	150 361	138 914	123 147	502 321	88.6	36.0	62 825	48 876	28.5	32 379	11 431	13 334	3.6	5.6
Edgar	3 771	3 852	3 504	13 082	73.5	11.0	31 089	21 657	43.6	2 637	-445	1 042	13.4	20.1
Edwards	1 058	1 147	1 417	5 019	69.7	8.4	30 874	21 238	45.4	772	-125	285	11.0	16.2
Effingham	6 540	6 324	5 737	19 477	75.0	13.0	37 864	27 245	39.0	2 999	190	1 288	8.9	12.5
Fayette	3 396	3 552	3 621	13 894	68.8	8.5	30 256	22 029	37.3	2 946	297	1 183	14.3	21.0
Ford	2 480	2 600	2 700	9 592	77.2	12.1	36 681	25 801	42.2	1 193	-91	477	8.6	12.9
Franklin	6 658	6 853	7 066	27 214	66.7	8.2	25 665	18 698	37.3	7 291	-953	2 839	17.9	28.2
Fulton	6 046	7 873	7 033	25 592	73.8	9.5	30 723	21 701	41.6	4 884	-755	1 871	13.2	20.0
Gallatin	1 009	1 032	1 132	4 680	58.4	7.4	26 278	19 105	37.5	1 257	-187	474	19.1	29.6
Greene	2 550	2 657	2 690	10 031	69.0	9.0	29 129	20 752	40.4	2 174	-171	877	13.9	20.6
Grundy	8 190	8 007	6 044	20 541	79.0	12.5	50 255	35 728	40.7	2 053	-63	819	5.5	7.8
Hamilton	1 425	1 448	1 452	5 859	60.0	7.6	27 994	18 274	53.2	1 277	-387	474	14.7	21.9
Hancock	4 239	4 373	3 885	14 322	77.5	14.4	35 162	24 036	46.3	2 172	-296	792	10.3	14.4
Hardin	752	914	990	3 492	59.7	7.0	24 285	15 498	56.7	953	-372	334	20.0	28.5
Henderson	1 297	1 306	1 489	5 467	73.3	9.5	33 363	22 165	50.5	965	-74	371	11.0	16.5
Henry	9 742	10 210	9 879	33 423	77.2	11.8	38 644	26 198	47.5	4 420	-869	1 798	8.5	12.7
Iroquois	5 851	5 886	5 511	20 578	73.4	10.1	34 287	25 435	34.8	2 982	205	1 253	9.5	15.2
Jackson	8 091	8 239	8 044	32 172	78.8	29.5	27 109	17 567	54.3	11 610	-3 776	3 474	21.0	28.3
Jasper	1 900	2 083	1 989	6 835	69.7	8.2	32 578	22 751	43.2	1 283	-94	555	11.9	17.7
Jefferson	6 913	7 244	6 940	24 023	69.9	11.3	31 850	22 397	42.2	6 378	518	2 594	17.0	25.1
Jersey	3 309	3 242	3 276	12 847	71.9	9.3	37 772	27 126	39.2	2 115	204	879	10.1	15.1
Jo Daviess	3 683	4 183	3 781	14 409	74.1	12.1	37 575	26 882	39.8	1 703	-88	648	7.8	11.6
Johnson	1 810	1 808	1 884	7 922	66.2	9.1	30 621	21 953	39.5	1 767	339	602	16.5	22.5
Kane	94 821	83 659	57 309	191 807	77.7	21.4	53 337	40 080	33.1	26 537	5 262	11 896	6.8	9.8

[1] Revised. [2] 1997 data are model-based estimates; 1989 data are census estimates. For more information on these estimates, see appendix A. Source Notes and Explanations or <http://www.census.gov/hhes/www/saipe.html>.

Sources: Public School Enrollment, 1998-1999 and 1994-1995—U.S. National Center for Education Statistics, <http://nces.ed.gov/ccd/pubagency.html> (accessed: 16 March 2001). Public School Enrollment and Educational Attainment, 1990—U.S. Census Bureau, "1990 Census of Population and Housing, Summary Tape File (STF) 3C" on CD-ROM (related Internet site <http://homer.ssd.census.gov/cdrom/lookup>). Income and Poverty, 1997—U.S. Census Bureau, "State and County Income and Poverty Estimates - 1997," published 22 November 2000, <http://www.census.gov/housing/saipe/estmod97/est97ALL.dat>. Income and Poverty, 1989—U.S. Census Bureau, "1990 Census of Population and Housing, Summary Tape File (STF) 3C" on CD-ROM (related Internet site <http://homer.ssd.census.gov/cdrom/lookup>).

[Includes U.S., states, and 3,142 counties or county equivalents defined as of January 1, 1992. For changes to these areas since January 1, 1992, see appendix B. Geographic Information]

County	Public school enrollment Fall 1998–1999	1994–1995[1]	1990	Educational attainment, 1990 Persons 25 years and over	Percent— High school graduate or higher	Bachelor's degree or higher	Median household income 1997 (dollars)	1989 (dollars)	Percent change, 1989–1997	Persons below poverty level, 1997 Number - Persons of all ages Total	Net change, 1989–1997	Persons under 18 years	Percent Persons of all ages	Persons under 18 years
ILLINOIS—Con.														
Kankakee	18 691	18 801	17 387	59 821	73.1	11.9	37 436	28 284	32.4	12 938	626	5 820	12.9	19.5
Kendall	9 788	8 713	8 136	24 175	83.7	17.8	58 694	42 834	37.0	2 018	691	833	3.8	5.3
Knox	8 455	9 044	9 765	37 723	76.6	12.7	33 536	24 523	36.8	6 692	–673	2 512	12.7	19.0
Lake	118 525	104 134	86 843	318 475	84.7	32.0	63 354	46 047	37.6	35 205	9 648	15 344	5.9	8.9
La Salle	17 671	17 619	17 939	70 357	73.1	10.5	37 439	27 093	38.2	10 825	–773	4 121	9.9	14.3
Lawrence	2 541	2 807	2 750	10 950	69.2	6.3	28 505	19 688	44.8	2 195	–851	805	14.7	21.3
Lee	5 658	5 765	6 065	22 661	76.3	11.8	38 947	28 284	37.7	2 942	104	1 150	8.7	12.4
Livingston	7 877	8 264	6 886	26 084	74.1	9.4	41 414	29 848	38.7	3 584	280	1 382	9.7	13.5
Logan	4 057	4 432	4 796	20 324	75.9	12.5	37 223	27 528	35.2	3 290	260	1 183	11.6	16.1
McDonough	4 320	4 618	4 709	18 784	80.3	23.2	32 790	21 774	50.6	4 599	–892	1 306	15.6	19.6
McHenry	41 684	36 615	33 752	114 721	84.5	21.0	59 162	43 471	36.1	8 645	2 303	3 441	3.5	4.8
McLean	24 204	23 136	19 456	72 957	84.7	29.0	46 615	31 366	48.6	11 807	–2 166	4 230	8.8	12.2
Macon	19 242	20 743	20 478	76 297	76.2	14.8	38 653	28 598	35.2	15 707	1 176	6 845	14.0	23.2
Macoupin	9 940	10 102	8 788	31 217	72.8	9.2	33 934	23 913	41.9	5 857	–272	2 313	12.1	17.9
Madison	43 667	44 365	40 294	161 517	75.8	14.4	39 405	29 861	32.0	28 676	854	11 665	11.0	17.3
Marion	8 246	8 712	7 705	27 077	70.1	9.6	30 867	22 813	35.3	6 466	–212	2 627	15.4	23.0
Marshall	1 703	1 740	2 461	8 600	77.8	10.3	38 347	26 450	45.0	1 159	–20	438	9.0	13.3
Mason	3 550	3 633	3 218	10 729	72.6	8.8	33 274	22 434	48.3	2 039	–446	815	12.1	18.3
Massac	2 707	2 670	2 573	10 068	65.3	8.0	29 159	19 632	48.5	2 330	–72	955	15.1	24.9
Menard	2 833	2 712	2 234	7 390	77.3	13.8	42 678	29 326	45.5	1 130	82	498	9.0	14.1
Mercer	3 659	3 757	3 351	11 357	77.4	11.3	38 584	26 606	45.0	1 653	–70	672	9.3	14.1
Monroe	4 509	4 377	3 389	14 613	75.9	13.7	49 620	35 086	41.4	1 272	210	494	4.7	6.8
Montgomery	5 537	5 508	5 443	20 386	72.2	8.1	33 368	23 879	39.7	4 046	–23	1 590	13.7	19.7
Morgan	5 745	6 089	5 918	23 605	75.9	16.0	36 018	26 403	36.4	3 970	192	1 532	11.9	18.1
Moultrie	1 886	1 991	2 435	9 282	70.3	9.5	37 859	26 852	41.0	1 173	–342	452	8.3	11.5
Ogle	10 433	9 944	9 039	29 575	77.6	12.1	42 064	30 958	35.9	3 556	279	1 398	7.0	9.9
Peoria	29 204	28 619	29 824	115 963	77.9	19.5	39 579	28 193	40.4	24 209	–1 454	10 661	13.5	22.1
Perry	3 183	3 104	3 626	13 921	67.8	7.3	30 674	22 979	33.5	2 941	–399	1 151	13.9	20.5
Piatt	3 465	3 377	2 934	10 458	83.0	15.9	43 109	31 369	37.4	1 102	163	409	6.7	9.6
Pike	3 166	3 193	3 159	11 820	69.9	8.1	29 308	20 527	42.8	2 476	–638	905	14.2	20.4
Pope	668		675	928	2 821	65.2	6.3	28 308	19 031	48.7	791	–256	272	17.3	24.0
Pulaski	1 642	1 833	1 744	4 816	59.8	6.1	22 768	15 625	45.7	1 903	–343	877	25.9	39.8
Putnam	1 027	1 046	1 042	3 783	75.8	9.8	42 300	30 136	40.4	414	–18	148	7.0	9.7
Randolph	4 878	5 198	5 727	22 847	64.2	8.3	33 754	25 859	30.5	3 669	293	1 410	12.0	16.7
Richland	2 901	2 909	2 762	10 917	73.5	11.9	31 468	23 013	36.7	2 163	–105	868	12.9	19.6
Rock Island	23 335	25 040	25 154	96 715	77.4	15.0	37 213	26 803	38.8	17 353	–1 720	7 387	11.8	19.2
St. Clair	46 167	47 271	48 002	162 550	72.6	14.7	35 439	26 813	32.2	42 241	–2 635	18 905	16.1	24.7
Saline	4 557	4 639	4 681	18 020	63.2	9.4	25 876	18 349	41.0	4 796	–360	1 876	18.7	29.5
Sangamon	41 678	41 453	27 132	117 686	81.8	22.4	40 851	30 350	34.6	19 288	1 905	8 412	10.0	16.8
Schuyler	1 242	1 196	1 406	5 090	69.4	10.7	30 794	21 080	46.1	866	–349	304	11.4	15.7
Scott	1 063	1 080	995	3 732	73.6	9.2	33 609	23 642	42.2	628	–15	247	11.1	16.2
Shelby	4 397	4 516	4 140	14 745	72.7	9.8	34 827	26 040	33.7	2 294	92	878	10.0	14.6
Stark	1 250	1 330	1 314	4 396	77.0	10.8	35 747	25 130	42.2	616	–182	232	9.8	14.1
Stephenson	8 045	8 156	8 140	31 555	76.7	13.6	38 935	28 340	37.4	4 631	–48	1 851	9.5	14.5
Tazewell	20 470	21 093	22 324	80 310	78.6	13.6	42 860	30 933	38.6	10 808	–331	4 237	8.4	12.6
Union	3 559	3 548	3 082	12 092	64.2	10.9	28 982	20 173	43.7	2 944	–513	1 162	16.8	26.8
Vermilion	14 440	15 629	15 663	58 087	72.8	11.1	31 903	23 841	33.8	12 459	–512	5 108	15.1	23.0
Wabash	2 231	2 306	2 335	8 520	74.9	12.6	32 639	26 021	25.4	1 542	–121	614	12.3	18.7
Warren	3 097	3 484	3 460	12 220	76.3	14.5	31 412	22 259	41.1	2 406	–202	898	13.3	18.3
Washington	2 342	2 395	2 448	9 906	65.7	8.7	36 681	25 387	44.5	1 233	–124	454	8.1	11.0
Wayne	3 019	3 087	3 068	11 613	63.1	8.7	30 246	20 659	46.4	2 045	–410	722	12.0	17.0
White	2 879	3 100	2 842	11 451	66.2	9.5	29 569	20 662	43.1	2 378	–700	878	15.3	23.7
Whiteside	10 566	11 498	11 060	39 020	73.3	9.9	37 453	27 085	38.3	5 514	–945	2 187	9.2	13.6
Will	74 111	65 587	65 988	215 823	80.4	18.0	54 061	41 195	31.2	29 709	8 885	13 044	6.5	9.3
Williamson	9 472	9 683	9 636	38 733	71.8	14.2	31 147	22 043	41.3	9 021	122	3 563	14.9	23.7
Winnebago	44 040	42 309	40 449	163 047	76.3	16.7	41 004	31 336	30.9	27 780	2 638	11 941	10.4	16.7
Woodford	7 746	7 836	6 564	20 469	80.0	15.4	49 396	34 375	43.7	2 180	–98	830	6.3	8.1
INDIANA	989 015	969 419	947 784	3 489 470	75.6	15.6	37 909	28 797	31.6	583 055	9 423	228 246	9.9	14.8
Adams	5 230	5 185	5 595	18 119	74.4	10.7	38 587	28 792	34.0	3 142	–406	1 518	9.5	14.4
Allen	51 591	49 082	48 309	187 856	81.2	19.0	42 631	31 835	33.9	28 259	4 850	12 234	8.9	14.1
Bartholomew	12 308	11 172	11 038	41 218	76.9	16.9	43 444	30 971	40.3	5 395	30	2 061	7.7	11.7
Benton	2 141	2 193	1 821	6 053	77.1	9.2	36 927	26 860	37.5	803	55	347	8.2	12.6
Blackford	2 439	2 390	2 524	9 259	73.0	8.9	35 048	25 523	37.3	1 403	33	567	10.0	16.3
Boone	8 272	7 476	7 266	24 915	82.5	22.2	51 856	34 652	49.6	2 253	–102	827	5.1	7.0
Brown	2 529	2 420	2 141	9 510	76.4	15.2	42 891	29 425	45.8	1 228	270	501	7.6	13.1
Carroll	2 921	2 873	3 536	12 241	76.2	10.0	40 352	28 506	41.6	1 394	8	578	6.9	11.0
Cass	6 778	7 018	7 064	25 123	75.9	9.0	35 029	25 963	34.9	3 840	–20	1 492	9.9	14.7

[1] Revised. [2] 1997 data are model-based estimates; 1989 data are census estimates. For more information on these estimates, see appendix A. Source Notes and Explanations or <http://www.census.gov/hhes/www/saipe.html>.

Sources: Public School Enrollment, 1998-1999 and 1994-1995—U.S. National Center for Education Statistics, <http://nces.ed.gov/ccd/pubagency.html> (accessed: 16 March 2001). Public School Enrollment and Educational Attainment, 1990—U.S. Census Bureau, "1990 Census of Population and Housing, Summary Tape File (STF) 3C" on CD-ROM (related Internet site <http://homer.ssd.census.gov/cdrom/lookup>). Income and Poverty, 1997—U.S. Census Bureau, "State and County Income and Poverty Estimates - 1997," published 22 November 2000, <http://www.census.gov/housing/saipe/estmod97/est97ALL.dat>. Income and Poverty, 1989—U.S. Census Bureau, "1990 Census of Population and Housing, Summary Tape File (STF) 3C" on CD-ROM (related Internet site <http://homer.ssd.census.gov/cdrom/lookup>).

[Includes U.S., states, and 3,142 counties or county equivalents defined as of January 1, 1992. For changes to these areas since January 1, 1992, see appendix B. Geographic Information]

County	Public school enrollment Fall 1998–1999	Public school enrollment Fall 1994–1995[1]	Public school enrollment 1990	Educational attainment, 1990 Persons 25 years and over	Percent— High school graduate or higher	Percent— Bachelor's degree or higher	Median household income[2] 1997 (dollars)	Median household income[2] 1989 (dollars)	Percent change, 1989–1997	Persons below poverty level,[2] 1997 Number — Persons of all ages Total	Net change, 1989–1997	Persons under 18 years	Percent Persons of all ages	Percent Persons under 18 years
INDIANA—Con.														
Clark	14 292	14 367	15 412	56 970	72.8	11.2	36 729	27 386	34.1	9 168	485	3 679	9.7	15.5
Clay	4 709	4 701	4 505	16 197	75.9	9.8	32 919	23 470	40.3	2 822	−61	1 130	10.5	15.9
Clinton	6 479	6 327	5 827	19 875	76.2	11.0	38 044	26 148	45.5	2 932	97	1 189	8.9	13.1
Crawford	1 901	1 884	1 879	6 297	59.6	5.7	28 679	20 367	40.8	1 646	−160	674	15.4	23.4
Daviess	4 518	4 372	4 495	17 267	66.2	7.6	31 238	22 801	37.0	3 863	−317	1 701	13.3	20.1
Dearborn	8 812	8 355	7 563	24 335	73.5	10.7	43 559	31 398	38.7	3 402	158	1 354	7.1	10.0
Decatur	4 342	4 500	4 745	14 625	72.3	9.7	39 954	27 701	44.2	2 153	46	888	8.4	12.1
De Kalb	7 457	7 352	6 912	21 801	77.5	9.9	42 612	30 970	37.6	2 234	−15	875	5.6	7.7
Delaware	17 719	18 057	18 249	70 609	74.5	16.5	34 155	24 436	39.8	15 403	−3 295	5 056	13.8	20.0
Dubois	7 458	7 129	6 791	22 921	72.2	10.9	44 242	31 227	41.7	1 836	−366	621	4.6	5.6
Elkhart	31 981	29 615	27 284	96 003	72.8	14.2	40 332	30 973	30.2	15 151	4 380	6 892	8.7	14.1
Fayette	4 553	4 594	4 965	16 744	63.9	8.1	34 737	25 565	35.9	2 882	124	1 041	11.0	15.3
Floyd	11 544	11 119	11 449	41 499	73.2	15.1	38 808	28 460	36.4	6 988	19	2 740	9.6	14.4
Fountain	3 409	3 272	3 302	11 700	73.0	7.6	34 593	24 772	39.6	1 645	−84	606	8.9	12.8
Franklin	2 976	2 776	3 737	12 029	65.3	8.2	39 604	27 734	42.8	1 683	−376	700	7.6	11.0
Fulton	2 848	2 719	3 592	12 405	75.3	9.4	35 666	26 141	36.4	1 945	21	779	9.3	14.1
Gibson	5 291	5 427	5 600	20 949	72.8	9.1	35 762	25 985	37.6	2 773	−250	982	8.6	11.9
Grant	11 759	11 960	13 190	47 541	71.8	11.2	34 274	26 248	30.6	9 235	−3	3 527	13.2	20.6
Greene	5 934	5 953	5 843	20 124	71.6	9.9	32 293	23 139	39.6	3 625	−323	1 350	10.8	15.9
Hamilton	31 058	25 777	20 263	69 127	88.7	36.2	68 017	45 748	48.7	5 310	1 433	2 024	3.2	4.3
Hancock	9 966	9 351	9 146	29 024	80.1	14.9	52 055	37 333	39.4	2 594	586	992	4.7	6.7
Harrison	6 162	5 996	5 908	18 829	71.1	8.4	38 204	27 238	40.3	3 233	327	1 268	9.2	13.1
Hendricks	17 860	15 650	14 155	48 047	84.1	18.2	55 548	39 892	39.2	4 039	1 353	1 629	4.3	6.4
Henry	8 629	8 635	8 780	31 989	71.4	9.2	35 458	25 668	38.1	5 115	−732	1 814	10.4	15.4
Howard	13 991	14 300	14 950	52 042	78.5	14.3	43 491	31 511	38.0	8 164	−1 018	3 258	9.7	15.1
Huntington	6 711	6 930	6 347	22 188	78.6	11.8	39 793	29 681	34.1	2 633	375	1 058	7.1	10.2
Jackson	6 566	6 509	6 721	24 151	69.3	8.7	35 440	25 767	37.5	3 904	−2	1 485	9.4	13.4
Jasper	4 914	4 724	4 828	14 984	75.5	10.8	40 978	28 546	43.6	2 185	284	888	7.6	10.6
Jay	3 981	4 045	3 994	13 843	68.9	8.2	32 147	23 705	35.6	2 277	214	920	10.4	16.2
Jefferson	4 936	4 882	5 137	18 876	70.3	13.3	33 630	24 820	35.5	3 506	266	1 376	11.6	17.6
Jennings	4 827	4 554	4 332	14 942	64.1	6.5	32 121	24 617	30.5	2 729	−197	1 043	9.8	13.8
Johnson	19 952	18 266	16 223	55 137	80.4	16.7	48 879	35 035	39.5	6 304	399	2 346	5.8	8.0
Knox	6 166	6 411	6 246	24 740	74.5	11.1	30 709	21 550	42.5	5 477	−332	1 881	14.5	20.6
Kosciusko	14 182	14 281	12 167	40 321	77.5	14.4	41 989	31 666	32.6	2 708	−624	1 357	8.0	11.8
Lagrange	6 415	6 309	5 057	16 100	56.7	7.3	38 566	27 296	41.3	2 708	−624	1 357	8.0	11.8
Lake	84 212	86 792	88 400	298 552	73.5	12.8	38 205	30 439	25.5	63 292	−1 561	26 654	13.0	20.0
La Porte	18 047	18 257	18 504	70 102	73.9	11.7	38 753	28 469	36.1	10 950	838	4 228	10.4	15.5
Lawrence	7 514	7 483	7 499	28 005	69.7	9.4	35 933	25 764	39.5	4 319	221	1 641	9.4	14.2
Madison	20 365	21 058	22 535	84 886	73.5	11.7	36 035	27 435	31.3	14 291	−1 635	5 408	11.1	17.0
Marion	126 110	123 873	118 211	511 309	76.8	21.4	37 686	29 152	29.3	98 254	4 123	40 506	12.0	19.5
Marshall	7 975	7 932	8 208	26 511	74.0	12.3	39 179	28 311	38.4	3 352	221	1 328	7.3	10.3
Martin	1 919	1 964	1 966	6 625	64.4	8.6	33 765	23 344	44.6	1 190	−224	463	11.3	16.9
Miami	7 661	7 689	7 032	22 509	76.4	9.7	34 795	24 441	42.4	3 695	−240	1 536	10.9	16.2
Monroe	13 303	13 236	13 240	57 368	82.1	32.9	35 366	24 781	42.7	12 424	−5 789	3 035	12.0	14.1
Montgomery	6 638	6 238	6 034	22 174	80.0	12.8	38 831	28 020	38.6	3 163	47	1 132	8.8	12.5
Morgan	11 436	11 025	10 887	35 089	73.6	10.0	44 120	32 762	34.7	5 169	1 479	2 054	7.8	11.4
Newton	2 917	2 837	2 676	8 567	72.4	8.1	36 875	28 624	28.8	1 458	279	600	9.8	14.0
Noble	7 893	7 632	7 575	23 151	72.1	8.0	40 449	29 845	35.5	2 758	−236	1 137	6.4	9.1
Ohio	1 016	1 016	1 052	3 457	67.7	6.0	38 937	26 237	48.4	361	−160	127	6.5	8.9
Orange	3 421	3 452	3 487	11 902	64.9	6.0	29 491	21 015	40.3	2 598	−180	996	13.2	19.0
Owen	3 139	3 012	3 249	11 151	66.3	7.1	32 835	23 404	40.3	2 435	125	915	11.8	16.9
Parke	2 768	2 674	2 624	10 217	76.7	10.1	33 022	24 514	34.7	2 023	212	796	12.4	19.4
Perry	3 365	3 513	3 443	12 271	65.4	6.8	34 365	24 158	42.3	1 753	−358	562	9.4	11.3
Pike	2 233	2 073	2 182	8 387	65.5	8.5	32 424	23 096	40.4	1 449	−190	510	11.1	16.3
Porter	25 926	25 321	24 247	79 625	82.4	18.5	50 493	37 142	35.9	9 030	1 377	3 297	6.2	8.3
Posey	4 719	4 843	4 671	16 513	76.3	11.0	45 011	31 530	42.8	2 135	177	819	8.0	11.1
Pulaski	2 588	2 616	2 653	7 974	71.9	8.9	35 837	25 418	41.0	1 412	62	565	10.5	14.9
Putnam	6 711	6 523	5 123	18 437	76.1	11.3	37 804	27 708	36.4	2 800	643	1 004	9.0	12.4
Randolph	4 952	5 103	5 103	17 694	71.9	8.6	33 264	24 773	34.3	3 365	324	1 257	12.1	17.9
Ripley	5 437	5 104	4 588	15 331	68.8	9.8	36 854	26 608	38.5	2 659	100	935	9.7	11.9
Rush	2 744	2 909	3 578	11 404	73.6	8.7	35 434	25 111	41.1	1 677	−289	598	9.3	12.3
St. Joseph	39 207	38 771	36 675	154 443	76.1	19.2	37 482	28 235	32.8	27 524	4 876	11 017	11.0	16.9
Scott	4 096	4 053	4 165	13 060	60.0	6.6	31 306	21 723	44.1	3 281	−636	1 296	14.1	20.4
Shelby	7 849	7 839	7 589	25 585	74.1	9.9	40 915	30 366	34.7	3 281	407	1 227	7.5	10.5
Spencer	3 929	3 803	3 659	12 509	71.9	9.2	38 960	28 777	35.4	1 857	−26	713	8.8	12.4
Starke	4 463	4 459	4 416	14 260	59.9	6.0	29 349	22 784	28.8	3 337	344	1 460	13.9	22.0
Steuben	5 053	4 752	5 029	17 256	79.0	12.5	39 664	29 203	35.8	2 219	724	906	7.1	11.0
Sullivan	3 642	3 613	3 425	12 602	74.1	10.0	31 067	22 940	35.4	2 734	397	993	14.1	19.9
Switzerland	1 652	1 603	1 497	5 015	65.8	5.6	31 355	23 871	31.4	1 148	−7	443	12.9	18.5
Tippecanoe	18 754	17 857	17 047	69 148	85.2	30.7	40 042	27 630	44.9	12 786	−3 618	3 665	10.1	12.2

[1] Revised. [2] 1997 data are model-based estimates; 1989 data are census estimates. For more information on these estimates, see appendix A. Source Notes and Explanations or <http://www.census.gov/hhes/www/saipe.html>.

Sources: Public School Enrollment, 1998-1999 and 1994-1995—U.S. National Center for Education Statistics, <http://nces.ed.gov/ccd/pubagency.html> (accessed: 16 March 2001). Public School Enrollment and Educational Attainment, 1990—U.S. Census Bureau, "1990 Census of Population and Housing, Summary Tape File (STF) 3C" on CD-ROM (related Internet site <http://homer.ssd.census.gov/cdrom/lookup>). Income and Poverty, 1997—U.S. Census Bureau, "State and County Income and Poverty Estimates - 1997," published 22 November 2000, <http://www.census.gov/housing/saipe/estmod97/est97ALL.dat>. Income and Poverty, 1989—U.S. Census Bureau, "1990 Census of Population and Housing, Summary Tape File (STF) 3C" on CD-ROM (related Internet site <http://homer.ssd.census.gov/cdrom/lookup>).

[Includes U.S., states, and 3,142 counties or county equivalents defined as of January 1, 1992. For changes to these areas since January 1, 1992, see appendix B. Geographic Information]

County	Public school enrollment Fall			Educational attainment, 1990			Median household income[2]			Persons below poverty level,[2] 1997				
					Percent—					Number			Percent	
										Persons of all ages				
	1998–1999	1994–1995[1]	1990	Persons 25 years and over	High school graduate or higher	Bachelor's degree or higher	1997 (dollars)	1989 (dollars)	Percent change, 1989–1997	Total	Net change, 1989–1997	Persons under 18 years	Persons of all ages	Persons under 18 years
INDIANA—Con.														
Tipton	2 948	2 963	3 044	10 511	77.0	9.8	43 258	31 198	38.7	1 189	163	418	7.0	9.7
Union	1 572	1 473	1 420	4 397	71.3	8.4	35 644	24 635	44.7	763	115	284	10.5	14.5
Vanderburgh	23 328	23 679	22 987	109 217	75.2	16.0	35 327	25 798	36.9	19 822	−194	7 367	12.0	18.7
Vermillion	2 941	3 057	3 124	11 163	72.1	7.8	33 002	22 339	47.7	1 765	−160	663	10.4	15.5
Vigo	16 867	16 885	16 745	66 140	76.0	18.1	32 007	23 505	36.2	14 481	194	5 126	14.6	21.1
Wabash	6 192	6 449	6 365	22 008	74.4	11.7	36 878	26 724	38.0	2 791	−244	984	8.4	11.2
Warren	1 359	1 296	1 566	5 403	71.6	9.4	36 143	25 680	40.7	644	−96	234	7.6	10.7
Warrick	9 110	9 013	8 683	28 368	80.1	16.2	47 588	34 069	39.7	3 413	507	1 326	6.6	9.2
Washington	4 789	4 591	4 629	14 989	66.2	6.8	31 668	22 897	38.3	3 341	−3	1 343	11.9	17.4
Wayne	11 831	12 330	13 017	46 603	71.2	11.3	33 379	23 475	42.2	9 535	−796	3 534	13.5	20.2
Wells	5 285	5 292	5 021	16 396	79.0	12.1	42 291	31 261	35.3	1 559	140	610	5.8	8.0
White	5 616	5 575	4 632	15 292	77.9	10.7	35 583	26 610	33.7	2 370	600	929	9.2	13.6
Whitley	5 016	4 983	5 394	17 369	78.9	8.8	43 494	31 128	39.7	1 618	194	617	5.3	7.2
IOWA	499 819	500 414	479 505	1 776 798	80.1	16.9	35 427	26 229	35.1	280 797	−26 623	100 262	9.9	13.7
Adair	1 232	1 289	1 583	5 769	77.5	9.8	32 245	21 426	50.5	875	−228	279	10.8	13.6
Adams	735	773	857	3 438	77.1	9.4	29 334	20 570	42.6	633	−163	221	14.5	21.2
Allamakee	2 758	2 841	2 648	9 185	75.9	8.9	30 475	21 098	44.4	1 554	−240	587	11.1	15.4
Appanoose	2 399	2 492	2 492	9 244	72.1	11.5	26 547	17 833	48.9	2 404	−331	844	17.7	24.9
Audubon	1 150	1 205	1 296	5 058	71.7	9.8	31 376	21 501	45.9	754	−105	277	11.2	16.5
Benton	4 384	4 188	4 420	14 547	78.2	9.6	39 886	25 959	53.6	1 930	−572	677	7.6	9.7
Black Hawk	18 566	19 272	19 958	75 401	80.4	17.3	35 644	25 683	38.8	15 080	−2 852	5 413	12.8	18.0
Boone	4 164	4 131	4 255	17 075	80.8	13.7	37 774	26 110	44.7	2 037	−82	730	7.9	11.5
Bremer	5 317	5 870	4 219	14 390	78.5	15.1	41 445	27 326	51.7	1 604	−358	505	7.2	8.8
Buchanan	3 388	3 481	4 258	12 927	78.4	11.2	35 939	23 386	53.7	2 240	−1 155	924	10.6	14.3
Buena Vista	3 900	3 928	3 441	12 528	82.1	15.2	35 545	25 311	40.4	1 794	161	679	9.8	13.9
Butler	2 147	2 756	3 199	10 567	71.8	9.4	35 469	23 292	52.3	1 303	−346	456	8.3	11.2
Calhoun	2 545	2 792	2 142	8 037	78.9	11.6	32 924	22 496	46.4	1 216	−101	422	11.2	15.3
Carroll	3 447	3 269	2 992	13 537	74.6	11.3	36 859	24 391	51.1	1 912	−308	720	8.8	11.3
Cass	3 061	3 254	2 828	10 383	80.7	12.5	31 513	21 801	44.5	1 629	−64	555	11.2	15.0
Cedar	3 647	3 650	3 449	11 557	79.3	12.8	40 666	27 713	46.7	1 410	−341	496	7.8	10.5
Cerro Gordo	7 243	7 464	7 726	30 988	81.3	15.5	35 631	25 116	41.9	4 366	316	1 524	9.5	13.8
Cherokee	2 372	2 839	2 815	9 425	81.3	10.8	34 690	22 967	51.0	1 175	−353	402	8.9	11.6
Chickasaw	2 678	2 364	2 630	8 704	75.2	9.9	36 314	24 656	47.3	1 186	−216	424	8.7	11.2
Clarke	1 875	1 763	1 612	5 561	77.6	8.8	30 831	21 735	41.8	1 102	−20	419	13.1	19.4
Clay	2 963	3 115	3 439	11 470	84.8	14.5	37 019	25 028	47.9	1 484	−238	513	8.4	11.0
Clayton	3 604	3 760	3 720	12 463	74.5	9.0	31 594	21 406	47.6	1 873	−823	667	10.0	12.9
Clinton	8 881	9 317	9 694	33 363	77.4	12.9	35 978	25 410	41.6	5 558	147	2 081	11.1	15.9
Crawford	2 643	2 777	3 165	10 878	72.5	9.8	32 555	22 209	46.6	2 027	−579	743	12.3	16.6
Dallas	8 134	7 300	5 842	19 388	83.6	16.3	45 825	28 874	58.7	2 213	−9	838	5.9	8.1
Davis	1 241	1 367	1 467	5 444	71.9	10.5	30 349	20 054	51.3	1 174	−266	446	13.9	19.2
Decatur	1 470	1 468	1 394	5 230	71.8	12.3	25 535	18 105	41.0	1 480	−118	490	19.5	25.6
Delaware	3 686	3 765	3 670	11 154	78.3	11.0	36 963	25 757	43.5	1 922	−350	760	10.3	13.6
Des Moines	7 133	7 664	7 791	28 106	78.9	12.7	37 294	26 536	40.5	4 848	100	1 830	11.4	17.2
Dickinson	2 882	2 874	2 719	10 513	84.1	17.5	36 739	25 211	45.7	1 310	−28	438	8.0	11.7
Dubuque	12 350	12 447	11 930	53 689	77.7	16.8	38 276	28 276	37.9	7 862	−666	2 811	9.1	12.1
Emmet	2 033	2 258	2 305	7 442	78.3	11.0	32 841	22 790	44.1	1 148	−299	422	10.8	15.4
Fayette	4 390	4 527	3 968	14 351	76.6	11.8	31 301	21 109	48.3	2 659	−361	949	12.3	16.6
Floyd	3 035	3 212	3 252	11 371	79.0	12.2	32 486	23 344	39.2	1 961	−239	723	12.1	17.6
Franklin	1 988	1 983	2 110	7 783	79.4	12.3	34 741	23 741	46.3	1 068	−191	386	9.8	13.9
Fremont	1 659	1 691	1 629	5 589	77.7	11.3	33 074	22 948	44.1	915	−57	344	11.8	17.2
Greene	2 119	2 045	1 897	6 990	81.2	13.7	33 384	22 320	49.6	1 064	−139	375	10.5	15.3
Grundy	2 539	2 747	2 280	8 259	79.5	12.3	40 457	26 314	53.7	847	−133	281	6.9	9.0
Guthrie	2 339	2 366	2 060	7 549	78.0	9.9	33 467	23 356	43.3	1 151	−44	398	10.0	14.0
Hamilton	3 033	3 123	2 964	10 930	79.5	12.8	37 073	25 847	43.4	1 372	76	503	8.5	12.4
Hancock	2 102	2 151	2 582	8 252	78.4	10.3	36 048	25 445	41.7	963	−136	345	8.0	10.3
Hardin	3 694	3 916	3 562	12 808	78.5	12.4	34 846	23 457	48.6	1 824	−137	599	10.2	13.9
Harrison	3 413	3 347	2 778	9 755	76.2	9.1	33 746	22 258	51.6	1 720	−255	622	11.2	15.0
Henry	3 888	3 993	3 453	12 453	79.1	14.5	37 047	24 952	48.5	1 892	108	660	10.1	13.2
Howard	2 120	2 286	1 707	6 627	72.9	8.2	32 052	21 913	46.3	1 075	−246	391	11.2	15.1
Humboldt	1 928	1 942	1 996	7 382	80.0	11.6	37 018	24 557	50.7	838	−95	286	8.1	11.0
Ida	1 484	1 635	1 718	5 546	75.9	11.0	34 459	22 859	50.7	816	−129	300	10.3	13.8
Iowa	2 908	3 129	2 589	9 904	76.4	11.1	40 002	26 579	50.5	1 103	−73	364	7.1	9.1
Jackson	3 602	3 700	3 644	12 841	72.2	10.0	32 214	22 487	43.3	2 300	−511	781	11.3	14.1
Jasper	6 518	6 378	6 420	23 226	77.6	12.7	41 892	28 702	46.0	2 655	288	917	7.4	10.4
Jefferson	2 197	2 036	2 369	11 209	82.3	26.5	34 196	22 630	51.1	2 084	−31	672	12.7	16.1
Johnson	13 101	12 171	11 880	53 053	90.6	44.0	41 678	27 862	49.6	8 842	−6 057	1 966	9.2	9.5
Jones	3 489	3 747	3 369	12 851	78.7	10.6	34 772	24 480	42.0	1 895	−148	634	9.9	12.6
Keokuk	2 455	2 502	2 196	7 845	76.8	9.4	31 979	22 234	43.8	1 464	−26	532	12.7	18.0

[1] Revised.　[2] 1997 data are model-based estimates; 1989 data are census estimates. For more information on these estimates, see appendix A. Source Notes and Explanations or <http://www.census.gov/hhes/www/saipe.html>.

Sources: Public School Enrollment, 1998-1999 and 1994-1995—U.S. National Center for Education Statistics, <http://nces.ed.gov/ccd/pubagency.html> (accessed: 16 March 2001). Public School Enrollment and Educational Attainment, 1990—U.S. Census Bureau, "1990 Census of Population and Housing, Summary Tape File (STF) 3C" on CD-ROM (related Internet site <http://homer.ssd.census.gov/cdrom/lookup>). Income and Poverty, 1997—U.S. Census Bureau, "State and County Income and Poverty Estimates - 1997," published 22 November 2000, <http://www.census.gov/housing/saipe/estmod97/est97ALL.dat>. Income and Poverty, 1989—U.S. Census Bureau, "1990 Census of Population and Housing, Summary Tape File (STF) 3C" on CD-ROM (related Internet site <http://homer.ssd.census.gov/cdrom/lookup>).

[Includes U.S., states, and 3,142 counties or county equivalents defined as of January 1, 1992. For changes to these areas since January 1, 1992, see appendix B. Geographic Information]

County	Public school enrollment			Educational attainment, 1990			Median household income[2]			Persons below poverty level,[2] 1997				
	Fall				Percent—					Number			Percent	
										Persons of all ages				
	1998–1999	1994–1995[1]	1990	Persons 25 years and over	High school graduate or higher	Bachelor's degree or higher	1997 (dollars)	1989 (dollars)	Percent change, 1989–1997	Total	Net change, 1989–1997	Persons under 18 years	Persons of all ages	Persons under 18 years
IOWA—Con.														
Kossuth	2 633	2 722	3 196	12 372	79.1	11.8	34 492	23 321	47.9	1 681	–316	614	9.5	12.6
Lee	6 255	6 612	6 173	25 792	77.5	10.7	34 966	24 671	41.7	4 652	–131	1 712	12.3	17.5
Linn	32 337	30 902	27 728	107 886	84.9	21.5	44 748	32 137	39.2	14 229	43	5 051	7.8	11.2
Louisa	2 884	2 919	2 342	7 427	76.3	9.2	35 652	25 590	39.3	1 346	18	572	11.2	17.6
Lucas	1 569	1 605	1 609	6 193	77.1	9.5	30 683	21 316	43.9	1 247	91	417	13.7	18.9
Lyon	2 104	2 331	2 268	7 520	70.4	10.2	35 180	22 676	55.1	1 085	–479	422	8.9	11.7
Madison	3 025	2 848	2 463	8 174	81.6	12.0	39 187	26 644	47.1	1 076	–278	350	7.7	9.0
Mahaska	3 357	3 396	3 638	13 858	74.8	13.1	35 589	23 115	54.0	2 490	–228	851	11.4	14.8
Marion	5 924	5 629	5 054	18 789	73.7	12.9	41 988	27 991	50.0	2 443	–319	818	8.2	10.1
Marshall	6 663	6 530	6 954	25 635	81.8	15.8	37 314	28 333	31.7	3 997	809	1 566	10.5	16.2
Mills	2 744	2 617	2 798	8 608	76.1	12.6	37 113	27 420	35.4	1 301	31	509	9.1	12.8
Mitchell	1 863	1 899	1 940	7 365	76.0	11.1	35 524	24 519	44.9	947	–145	352	8.7	12.3
Monona	1 704	1 808	1 866	7 046	73.0	10.3	30 266	20 714	46.1	1 262	–174	427	12.6	17.5
Monroe	1 363	1 386	1 540	5 467	75.6	8.0	29 870	20 745	44.0	1 112	–123	376	13.9	18.2
Montgomery	2 105	2 133	2 184	8 300	80.0	12.8	32 264	23 312	38.4	1 359	171	515	11.5	17.6
Muscatine	7 551	7 911	8 058	25 240	75.0	13.0	40 800	29 786	37.0	4 628	661	1 779	11.2	15.5
O'Brien	2 873	3 022	2 536	10 290	73.5	12.6	35 048	23 125	51.6	1 261	–554	427	8.5	10.9
Osceola	1 069	1 042	1 314	4 797	72.1	10.0	34 804	23 037	51.1	619	–80	238	8.9	12.7
Page	3 244	3 113	3 312	11 454	78.2	13.5	33 729	22 050	53.0	1 985	–237	623	12.3	15.4
Palo Alto	1 952	2 071	1 928	7 024	76.9	12.8	32 669	21 223	53.9	1 048	–534	343	10.5	13.1
Plymouth	4 565	4 472	3 989	14 593	78.0	15.0	40 109	26 796	49.7	1 772	–273	616	7.2	8.6
Pocahontas	1 417	1 389	1 684	6 590	80.1	12.8	34 867	23 517	48.3	833	–136	297	9.5	13.2
Polk	60 615	57 404	52 397	209 165	85.4	23.9	42 975	31 221	37.6	31 417	2 053	11 630	8.7	13.0
Pottawattamie	17 378	16 530	15 460	52 964	77.1	11.0	35 851	26 639	34.6	9 743	1 219	3 917	11.2	17.1
Poweshiek	3 106	3 213	3 391	11 992	81.6	16.2	38 079	26 063	46.1	1 648	–191	544	9.2	12.0
Ringgold	956	1 079	1 071	3 840	78.0	10.3	27 802	20 761	33.9	851	–55	284	16.0	22.6
Sac	2 281	2 444	2 462	8 339	77.3	12.7	32 612	21 818	49.5	1 254	–165	460	10.5	14.7
Scott	28 044	28 362	27 740	94 114	81.4	21.9	40 920	29 979	36.5	18 260	346	7 218	11.5	16.6
Shelby	2 553	2 765	2 426	8 846	79.0	12.8	34 588	22 702	52.4	1 162	–43	427	9.0	12.4
Sioux	4 370	4 383	4 100	17 175	71.7	14.4	40 895	25 692	59.2	2 062	–178	780	7.0	8.5
Story	11 102	11 118	10 026	38 328	91.0	38.4	40 851	26 668	53.2	6 080	–4 435	1 339	9.1	8.9
Tama	3 751	3 354	3 398	11 606	75.8	11.2	34 794	24 297	43.2	1 630	–159	557	9.2	12.4
Taylor	1 339	1 330	1 386	4 872	75.0	8.7	27 341	18 641	46.7	1 115	–150	397	15.7	21.5
Union	2 251	2 266	2 408	8 378	79.0	12.8	29 928	21 550	38.9	1 607	–323	552	12.8	16.9
Van Buren	1 429	1 501	1 370	5 140	74.7	9.0	29 000	19 244	50.7	1 067	204	401	13.4	19.5
Wapello	6 633	6 667	6 033	24 026	74.2	11.0	29 856	21 060	41.8	5 145	–199	1 820	14.5	21.5
Warren	7 690	7 708	7 504	22 163	87.0	16.2	46 404	32 452	43.0	2 510	336	849	6.3	7.7
Washington	3 551	3 590	3 309	12 949	76.9	11.7	36 470	25 822	41.2	1 924	127	790	9.3	14.2
Wayne	1 169	1 230	1 214	5 002	71.7	8.4	25 699	17 599	46.0	1 042	–281	353	15.6	22.3
Webster	5 857	6 083	6 312	26 493	78.4	13.7	34 353	23 692	45.0	4 638	38	1 700	12.2	17.3
Winnebago	2 916	3 005	2 222	7 895	78.6	14.0	34 048	23 480	45.0	1 094	–252	364	9.5	12.1
Winneshiek	2 844	2 915	3 124	12 385	76.4	17.1	35 955	24 383	47.5	1 848	–629	509	9.7	10.1
Woodbury	18 520	18 249	17 097	61 309	78.4	16.7	36 357	25 186	44.4	10 823	–2 035	4 226	10.7	14.9
Worth	1 194	1 231	1 468	5 471	77.9	10.9	34 024	22 902	48.6	658	–119	220	8.5	11.4
Wright	3 040	3 270	2 634	9 891	77.6	11.3	35 533	24 582	44.5	1 236	–117	426	8.8	12.5
KANSAS	469 758	460 905	430 595	1 565 936	81.3	21.1	36 488	27 291	33.7	283 038	8 415	109 324	10.9	15.4
Allen	2 718	2 922	2 881	9 445	74.2	12.4	30 171	20 774	45.2	2 152	–46	848	15.0	21.4
Anderson	1 484	1 455	1 230	5 196	70.2	8.1	30 776	21 956	40.2	1 039	43	414	12.9	18.9
Atchison	2 533	2 556	2 894	10 442	77.5	13.3	32 515	22 339	45.6	2 367	–157	945	14.6	21.4
Barber	1 133	1 172	1 200	3 996	79.4	12.9	30 317	21 476	41.2	662	34	248	12.4	17.3
Barton	5 020	5 323	5 415	19 121	78.0	13.6	33 079	23 432	41.2	3 613	221	1 384	12.5	17.8
Bourbon	2 723	2 677	2 621	9 847	73.9	14.0	28 362	20 367	39.3	2 626	–225	1 019	17.6	25.7
Brown	1 899	1 999	2 274	7 347	78.4	12.5	30 260	20 392	48.4	1 677	–127	678	15.3	22.0
Butler	13 425	12 505	9 883	32 125	81.0	17.0	44 998	31 012	45.1	4 957	941	1 978	8.1	11.2
Chase	510	591	595	2 084	77.9	13.6	29 129	20 128	44.7	469	–70	182	16.0	23.5
Chautauqua	757	719	762	3 162	70.5	10.6	24 358	17 067	42.7	793	–88	290	18.6	28.1
Cherokee	4 057	3 973	4 043	13 847	70.2	10.3	27 729	19 001	45.9	3 894	–360	1 523	17.2	25.0
Cheyenne	654	678	603	2 307	74.2	13.3	29 484	21 750	35.6	359	–125	117	11.4	15.4
Clark	542	553	438	1 717	83.5	17.5	33 987	24 003	41.6	225	94	97	9.7	16.0
Clay	1 641	1 765	1 680	6 309	77.8	13.3	33 910	21 896	54.9	1 026	–93	402	11.4	16.8
Cloud	1 641	1 681	1 946	7 494	76.0	13.8	29 851	20 782	43.6	1 322	–339	438	13.4	18.9
Coffey	1 928	2 008	1 692	5 589	76.9	13.5	34 411	24 435	40.8	937	201	372	10.8	15.2
Comanche	371	435	412	1 626	78.0	14.9	27 139	19 421	39.7	243	–137	75	12.6	15.5
Cowley	6 774	7 022	6 777	23 837	76.9	14.9	33 933	25 047	35.5	4 619	899	1 811	12.8	18.5
Crawford	6 032	6 261	5 653	22 641	74.7	18.7	28 442	19 616	45.0	5 973	–426	1 975	16.9	22.9
Decatur	674	739	772	2 822	78.5	13.6	28 427	20 131	41.2	445	–114	164	13.3	18.9
Dickinson	4 342	4 388	3 578	12 731	79.7	11.9	33 975	22 953	48.0	1 923	–160	688	9.9	13.4

[1] Revised. [2] 1997 data are model-based estimates; 1989 data are census estimates. For more information on these estimates, see appendix A. Source Notes and Explanations or <http://www.census.gov/hhes/www/saipe.html>.

Sources: Public School Enrollment, 1998-1999 and 1994-1995—U.S. National Center for Education Statistics, <http://nces.ed.gov/ccd/pubagency.html> (accessed: 16 March 2001). Public School Enrollment and Educational Attainment, 1990—U.S. Census Bureau, "1990 Census of Population and Housing, Summary Tape File (STF) 3C" on CD-ROM (related Internet site <http://homer.ssd.census.gov/cdrom/lookup>). Income and Poverty, 1997—U.S. Census Bureau, "State and County Income and Poverty Estimates - 1997," published 22 November 2000, <http://www.census.gov/housing/saipe/estmod97/est97ALL.dat>. Income and Poverty, 1989—U.S. Census Bureau, "1990 Census of Population and Housing, Summary Tape File (STF) 3C" on CD-ROM (related Internet site <http://homer.ssd.census.gov/cdrom/lookup>).

[Includes U.S., states, and 3,142 counties or county equivalents defined as of January 1, 1992. For changes to these areas since January 1, 1992, see appendix B. Geographic Information]

County	Public school enrollment — Fall			Educational attainment, 1990 — Percent—			Median household income[2]			Persons below poverty level,[2] 1997 — Number — Persons of all ages			Percent	
	1998–1999	1994–1995[1]	1990	Persons 25 years and over	High school graduate or higher	Bachelor's degree or higher	1997 (dollars)	1989 (dollars)	Percent change, 1989–1997	Total	Net change, 1989–1997	Persons under 18 years	Persons of all ages	Persons under 18 years
KANSAS—Con.														
Doniphan	1 688	1 662	1 462	5 167	73.0	9.7	32 077	22 102	45.1	1 152	−94	401	15.1	19.7
Douglas	12 880	11 870	11 177	42 308	88.8	38.4	37 248	25 244	47.6	10 632	−4 380	2 843	11.9	14.1
Edwards	578	658	705	2 649	76.3	13.1	31 082	21 904	41.9	392	−74	141	12.1	17.1
Elk	787	822	485	2 421	67.3	10.5	23 604	17 730	33.1	673	105	241	20.1	31.0
Ellis	4 288	4 335	4 401	15 396	80.6	23.4	33 279	22 466	48.1	2 900	−804	929	11.2	13.7
Ellsworth	1 352	1 469	1 048	4 568	76.6	12.8	31 314	20 064	56.1	645	−80	199	11.5	13.8
Finney	8 562	8 092	7 458	18 051	70.9	14.4	36 823	27 645	33.2	3 968	521	1 975	10.8	15.4
Ford	6 004	5 662	4 801	16 197	76.6	18.1	34 434	25 041	37.5	3 503	360	1 565	12.0	17.8
Franklin	4 867	4 784	4 224	13 922	77.1	12.9	34 879	24 981	39.6	2 930	390	1 190	11.8	16.7
Geary	6 462	7 170	5 265	16 214	83.4	14.6	28 857	21 905	31.7	4 009	−603	1 865	16.7	26.2
Gove	759	729	617	2 215	79.1	13.6	30 725	23 377	31.4	290	−66	102	9.5	12.7
Graham	536	643	748	2 456	77.5	14.2	29 829	22 047	35.3	431	−101	156	13.5	19.2
Grant	1 842	1 752	1 801	4 116	75.1	13.6	43 557	30 173	44.4	795	−288	354	9.9	12.6
Gray	1 311	1 234	1 160	3 266	69.4	12.6	39 728	25 872	53.6	480	−56	206	8.6	11.3
Greeley	330	371	378	1 128	82.4	16.8	34 125	25 709	32.7	135	−25	51	8.0	10.1
Greenwood	1 247	1 328	1 300	5 490	75.1	10.4	27 401	19 481	40.7	1 247	129	458	15.5	22.8
Hamilton	528	436	411	1 639	73.4	12.9	33 413	22 500	48.5	291	28	119	12.4	19.6
Harper	1 299	1 301	1 330	4 964	78.2	10.9	30 760	21 226	44.9	821	−10	295	12.9	18.6
Harvey	6 034	5 987	5 430	19 969	81.2	20.3	39 525	27 539	43.5	3 064	578	1 153	9.3	12.9
Haskell	980	882	821	2 318	76.1	13.4	42 696	26 761	59.5	376	84	176	9.4	13.4
Hodgeman	483	459	431	1 475	84.9	17.3	34 381	23 788	44.5	202	−9	71	9.2	11.5
Jackson	2 455	2 336	2 386	7 389	80.8	10.4	35 498	25 398	39.8	1 421	53	572	11.7	16.7
Jefferson	4 393	4 361	3 215	10 399	81.0	13.5	41 130	29 048	41.6	1 514	182	560	8.4	11.2
Jewell	686	725	762	3 055	80.8	11.7	28 555	18 839	51.6	478	−146	163	12.2	17.6
Johnson	73 522	67 124	56 810	230 732	92.9	40.5	59 870	42 741	40.1	17 701	5 034	6 209	4.1	5.4
Kearny	1 141	1 165	908	2 397	73.8	12.5	38 950	29 303	32.9	480	71	230	11.5	16.5
Kingman	1 640	1 607	1 512	5 545	77.5	11.9	35 312	22 763	55.1	905	−39	349	10.6	14.8
Kiowa	605	685	661	2 481	78.0	14.6	32 148	22 628	42.1	346	−141	119	10.4	13.4
Labette	4 451	4 580	4 430	15 347	74.2	12.1	29 369	21 871	34.3	3 537	215	1 356	15.6	22.2
Lane	461	523	499	1 604	81.1	17.8	31 953	23 532	35.8	243	−24	91	10.9	14.8
Leavenworth	12 023	12 396	11 593	42 005	84.5	23.9	44 056	32 500	35.6	5 950	1 648	2 343	9.5	12.1
Lincoln	648	617	652	2 637	77.6	11.6	28 563	18 652	53.1	392	−171	129	11.8	15.7
Linn	2 008	1 948	1 564	5 594	73.9	10.4	29 802	21 287	40.0	1 283	61	493	14.0	20.2
Logan	614	682	554	2 089	78.3	15.9	32 148	22 126	45.3	353	2	139	11.8	17.5
Lyon	6 237	6 198	6 314	19 815	81.9	21.4	33 688	24 050	40.1	4 383	−216	1 653	13.5	17.8
McPherson	5 271	5 244	4 711	17 413	78.2	17.4	40 361	27 003	49.5	1 755	−51	597	6.4	8.1
Marion	2 661	2 546	2 110	8 808	73.8	14.9	32 643	21 725	50.3	1 368	29	454	10.5	14.1
Marshall	2 561	2 636	2 035	8 001	77.5	10.2	32 432	20 597	57.5	1 507	−38	571	13.8	19.5
Meade	639	598	795	2 840	79.5	17.1	34 411	23 403	47.0	362	−121	134	8.2	10.8
Miami	4 802	4 405	4 292	15 144	78.5	13.2	40 625	29 259	38.8	2 373	550	896	9.1	12.2
Mitchell	1 410	1 468	1 221	4 804	82.6	15.8	33 611	22 159	51.7	672	−97	226	10.0	12.8
Montgomery	6 338	6 510	6 726	25 490	73.0	13.6	29 277	20 864	40.3	5 847	−90	2 216	15.9	23.2
Morris	1 071	1 151	1 157	4 258	80.8	12.5	31 810	22 202	43.3	699	−125	244	11.4	15.6
Morton	805	762	785	2 148	75.8	16.2	38 752	25 659	51.0	393	−159	168	11.5	15.9
Nemaha	1 930	1 966	1 966	6 777	75.7	12.3	34 266	22 144	54.7	1 036	−481	365	10.0	12.3
Neosho	3 241	3 274	3 149	11 258	77.2	11.5	30 890	22 299	38.5	2 283	12	831	13.8	19.0
Ness	682	760	697	2 808	78.0	12.3	33 244	23 594	40.9	338	−97	117	9.3	12.3
Norton	1 081	1 131	959	4 216	76.9	12.8	31 013	21 259	45.9	693	−42	238	13.3	18.5
Osage	3 351	3 295	3 100	10 137	76.9	9.3	35 499	24 867	42.8	1 735	110	665	10.1	13.9
Osborne	518	539	812	3 468	76.1	11.0	27 601	18 365	50.3	589	−69	206	12.8	18.0
Ottawa	1 357	1 342	1 068	3 887	81.0	14.0	37 087	21 852	69.7	494	−10	199	8.4	12.8
Pawnee	1 276	1 444	1 423	5 116	82.1	16.7	33 528	23 898	40.3	835	102	317	12.4	18.1
Phillips	1 139	1 181	1 174	4 610	73.9	10.9	32 418	20 918	55.0	720	−127	253	12.1	16.8
Pottawatomie	3 817	3 829	3 248	10 068	81.8	15.6	38 587	25 305	52.5	1 575	−10	697	8.4	12.5
Pratt	1 770	1 826	1 784	6 472	82.4	19.5	34 857	23 865	46.1	1 104	177	419	11.5	16.7
Rawlins	549	597	707	2 333	80.4	14.4	29 655	21 332	39.0	373	−56	137	11.9	17.1
Reno	10 820	11 144	10 761	41 151	77.4	14.9	35 475	24 665	43.8	7 556	1 145	2 946	12.3	18.5
Republic	1 093	1 150	1 126	4 776	78.3	10.3	28 994	20 224	43.4	748	−24	262	12.5	18.3
Rice	2 001	1 989	2 044	6 988	81.2	18.7	32 195	21 088	52.7	1 318	−315	466	13.3	17.2
Riley	7 016	7 747	8 920	30 565	91.7	34.3	33 744	21 700	55.5	7 572	−3 985	1 888	14.1	13.4
Rooks	1 109	1 170	1 150	4 084	74.1	11.0	29 792	20 113	48.1	744	−150	278	13.2	18.1
Rush	715	750	654	2 793	72.6	11.5	28 395	19 356	46.7	446	−6	141	13.2	18.6
Russell	1 356	1 413	1 373	5 650	74.5	14.1	28 214	20 843	35.4	1 060	23	340	14.1	19.7
Saline	8 803	8 625	8 335	31 778	82.4	17.7	36 682	25 728	42.6	5 778	−23	2 196	11.2	16.2
Scott	1 168	1 162	1 069	3 405	77.2	13.8	38 781	25 474	52.2	396	−75	160	7.9	10.1
Sedgwick	75 716	70 611	67 056	252 868	82.4	22.2	40 875	30 216	35.3	50 949	7 491	21 223	11.3	17.0
Seward	4 990	4 860	3 926	10 810	72.2	11.6	35 710	26 055	37.1	2 816	97	1 326	14.0	20.1
Shawnee	26 969	27 172	26 888	104 795	84.4	22.3	40 122	29 879	34.3	18 195	2 460	7 312	10.7	16.7
Sheridan	458	497	644	2 030	81.5	13.3	34 183	21 540	58.7	311	−182	110	11.4	14.4

[1] Revised.   [2] 1997 data are model-based estimates; 1989 data are census estimates. For more information on these estimates, see appendix A. Source Notes and Explanations or <http://www.census.gov/hhes/www/saipe.html>.

Sources: Public School Enrollment, 1998-1999 and 1994-1995—U.S. National Center for Education Statistics, <http://nces.ed.gov/ccd/pubagency.html> (accessed: 16 March 2001). Public School Enrollment and Educational Attainment, 1990—U.S. Census Bureau, "1990 Census of Population and Housing, Summary Tape File (STF) 3C" on CD-ROM (related Internet site <http://homer.ssd.census.gov/cdrom/lookup>).   Income and Poverty, 1997—U.S. Census Bureau, "State and County Income and Poverty Estimates - 1997," published 22 November 2000, <http://www.census.gov/housing/saipe/estmod97/est97ALL.dat>.   Income and Poverty, 1989—U.S. Census Bureau, "1990 Census of Population and Housing, Summary Tape File (STF) 3C" on CD-ROM (related Internet site <http://homer.ssd.census.gov/cdrom/lookup>).

Table B–5. Counties — Education, Income, and Poverty–Con.

[Includes U.S., states, and 3,142 counties or county equivalents defined as of January 1, 1992. For changes to these areas since January 1, 1992, see appendix B. Geographic Information]

County	Public school enrollment Fall 1998–1999	1994–1995[1]	1990	Educational attainment, 1990 Persons 25 years and over	Percent— High school graduate or higher	Bachelor's degree or higher	Median household income[2] 1997 (dollars)	1989 (dollars)	Percent change, 1989–1997	Persons below poverty level[2] 1997 Number Persons of all ages Total	Net change, 1989–1997	Persons under 18 years	Percent Persons of all ages	Persons under 18 years
KANSAS—Con.														
Sherman	1 202	1 261	1 275	4 442	75.0	12.5	30 801	21 138	45.7	995	−107	380	15.3	21.9
Smith	803	869	865	3 769	74.0	10.0	28 257	18 834	50.0	594	−160	173	13.2	16.8
Stafford	1 105	1 138	1 053	3 640	78.7	16.5	29 419	19 778	48.7	717	11	277	14.4	20.4
Stanton	584	569	526	1 406	76.9	16.9	39 024	24 545	59.0	209	−131	86	9.2	11.8
Stevens	1 209	1 273	1 138	3 155	78.4	14.1	40 593	27 549	47.3	563	−22	256	10.3	15.0
Sumner	4 907	4 777	5 197	16 820	77.1	11.3	38 987	26 885	45.0	2 568	584	1 021	9.5	12.8
Thomas	1 510	1 711	1 652	4 988	85.4	15.7	34 654	22 247	55.8	937	−203	341	11.9	14.9
Trego	592	663	718	2 564	72.9	11.2	28 421	19 921	42.7	365	−70	112	11.2	12.9
Wabaunsee	1 253	1 296	1 269	4 359	83.8	12.6	36 802	27 727	32.7	513	−81	178	7.8	9.9
Wallace	447	429	372	1 147	77.8	12.5	28 082	20 417	40.5	230	120	61	13.1	17.1
Washington	1 456	1 363	1 207	4 939	69.6	11.2	28 557	19 424	47.0	817	−211	274	12.6	16.7
Wichita	497	611	626	1 723	71.7	12.5	35 341	23 395	51.1	321	45	144	12.2	17.5
Wilson	2 086	2 181	1 905	7 087	74.6	11.4	28 111	18 776	49.7	1 579	25	598	15.3	22.3
Woodson	638	659	735	2 912	70.6	8.4	26 400	19 637	34.4	594	119	221	15.4	22.8
Wyandotte	28 427	29 296	29 530	100 533	69.9	10.3	30 056	23 780	26.4	28 141	770	12 028	18.3	27.6
KENTUCKY	653 128	639 708	632 679	2 333 833	64.6	13.6	31 730	22 534	40.8	624 219	−57 608	229 043	16.0	23.1
Adair	2 650	2 597	2 605	9 885	46.3	7.4	21 914	15 809	38.6	3 627	−117	1 338	22.3	33.8
Allen	3 049	2 821	2 556	9 463	51.1	4.6	28 798	17 915	60.7	2 314	−1 234	860	13.9	20.0
Anderson	3 504	3 045	2 764	9 421	66.7	9.9	39 913	27 747	43.8	1 407	68	570	7.5	11.8
Ballard	1 496	1 448	1 464	5 328	64.2	8.7	30 629	19 371	58.1	1 131	−312	373	13.3	19.0
Barren	6 849	6 531	6 114	22 627	54.5	8.3	29 580	19 546	51.3	5 859	−1 301	2 051	15.8	22.8
Bath	1 930	1 864	1 738	6 341	46.3	6.2	24 020	15 940	50.7	2 410	−188	911	22.7	35.0
Bell	5 809	6 023	6 373	19 644	46.7	9.3	19 896	13 078	52.1	8 611	−2 598	3 029	29.5	39.3
Boone	13 758	12 143	10 093	35 347	76.4	15.3	48 999	34 485	42.1	5 067	846	2 165	6.3	9.5
Bourbon	3 561	3 615	3 725	12 332	64.0	11.8	33 314	22 445	48.4	2 713	−617	1 021	13.9	20.9
Boyd	7 956	8 302	9 061	34 809	68.9	11.9	32 239	23 835	35.3	8 056	−147	2 863	16.5	25.9
Boyle	4 591	4 462	4 600	16 693	65.4	14.4	33 521	23 125	45.0	3 483	−560	1 194	13.6	19.6
Bracken	1 497	1 530	1 437	5 016	56.0	6.5	29 242	19 684	48.6	1 336	−307	482	15.8	22.2
Breathitt	3 123	3 040	3 165	9 455	47.8	8.6	18 404	12 383	48.6	5 159	−913	1 967	32.9	44.9
Breckinridge	3 161	3 101	2 639	10 615	56.7	6.3	27 050	17 687	52.9	3 105	−638	1 173	17.6	26.5
Bullitt	10 767	9 939	9 740	28 596	64.7	6.3	41 199	29 455	39.9	5 714	797	2 346	9.5	14.0
Butler	2 330	2 419	2 123	7 252	46.6	5.1	25 578	17 514	46.0	2 281	−335	852	19.1	27.8
Caldwell	2 138	2 136	2 300	8 928	61.9	8.2	27 050	17 997	50.7	2 225	354	803	16.7	25.8
Calloway	4 682	4 616	4 343	18 542	69.1	19.4	29 853	19 408	53.8	4 413	−402	1 294	14.5	20.0
Campbell	12 544	13 034	12 727	52 731	71.0	14.9	39 201	29 228	34.1	8 756	−331	3 326	10.0	14.6
Carlisle	880	875	917	3 508	62.3	6.6	28 450	19 404	46.6	790	−131	299	14.6	24.4
Carroll	1 794	1 843	1 784	5 938	59.6	10.7	29 535	20 179	46.4	1 624	−384	629	16.9	25.0
Carter	4 770	5 130	4 798	15 035	51.3	7.6	23 986	17 083	40.4	6 395	18	2 428	23.8	34.6
Casey	2 451	2 540	2 478	9 152	43.1	6.5	22 182	14 993	47.9	3 287	−853	1 218	22.0	32.6
Christian	9 166	9 158	11 339	38 693	72.2	10.4	27 968	21 032	33.0	11 276	606	4 737	17.3	24.7
Clark	5 266	5 315	5 183	19 172	65.1	13.0	35 343	25 323	39.6	4 373	−769	1 626	13.6	20.5
Clay	4 382	4 560	4 627	12 818	38.9	7.4	19 231	12 732	51.0	7 760	−896	2 979	33.7	43.8
Clinton	1 566	1 594	1 670	5 987	44.4	6.6	17 104	11 348	50.7	2 801	−646	963	29.7	42.5
Crittenden	1 535	1 591	1 511	6 102	59.6	5.1	20 105	18 566	51.8	1 653	−33	603	17.3	25.8
Cumberland	1 239	1 176	1 153	4 583	39.5	6.1	18 217	12 989	40.2	1 849	−263	636	26.9	40.4
Daviess	14 532	14 647	14 058	55 048	72.3	14.1	34 335	24 399	40.7	11 965	−1 214	4 460	13.2	18.8
Edmonson	1 965	1 869	2 202	6 570	48.6	5.4	24 568	15 134	62.3	2 212	−571	813	19.2	28.2
Elliott	1 249	1 347	1 364	3 912	44.0	5.6	20 660	13 890	48.7	1 826	−630	752	27.2	39.4
Estill	2 796	2 788	2 754	9 170	46.5	5.4	23 937	16 056	49.1	3 577	−622	1 357	22.7	33.7
Fayette	33 124	33 039	31 292	142 116	80.2	30.6	39 295	28 056	40.1	26 900	−3 208	8 974	11.5	16.9
Fleming	2 429	2 413	2 379	7 946	53.8	8.7	25 240	18 014	40.1	2 731	−355	971	20.1	28.8
Floyd	7 628	8 246	8 934	26 566	50.8	7.4	22 748	15 661	45.3	12 139	−1 382	4 561	27.7	37.2
Franklin	6 931	6 930	7 065	28 819	76.0	21.3	37 284	27 484	35.7	4 989	372	1 839	11.0	17.1
Fulton	1 471	1 527	1 504	5 512	54.4	10.3	23 741	16 087	47.6	1 855	−612	708	24.5	38.0
Gallatin	1 497	1 168	940	3 349	59.8	5.0	29 996	21 454	39.8	1 151	388	472	15.9	23.6
Garrard	2 428	2 105	1 981	7 776	54.3	6.3	30 355	21 057	44.2	2 080	4	765	14.8	22.9
Grant	4 252	3 705	3 321	9 635	61.6	7.2	32 879	24 502	34.2	2 674	329	1 138	13.1	19.7
Graves	5 923	5 726	5 701	22 682	62.0	8.8	29 677	20 647	43.7	5 109	−484	1 814	14.1	21.1
Grayson	4 128	4 025	3 962	13 615	48.3	6.1	25 009	17 306	44.5	4 749	−186	1 722	19.9	28.6
Green	1 700	1 762	1 789	7 093	49.0	6.8	24 470	18 432	32.8	1 992	−196	690	19.0	29.7
Greenup	6 495	6 863	7 105	24 051	64.7	11.1	31 235	24 527	27.3	6 054	−331	2 153	16.3	24.2
Hancock	1 527	1 558	1 578	4 844	69.3	6.9	38 734	26 080	48.5	1 114	−191	414	12.3	16.1
Hardin	15 767	15 695	16 650	49 643	75.3	12.9	35 603	24 431	45.7	10 428	−589	4 195	12.2	16.9
Harlan	6 260	6 963	7 490	22 506	49.5	6.4	21 442	14 774	45.1	10 520	−1 475	3 830	29.9	39.1
Harrison	3 255	3 158	3 197	10 490	62.4	8.6	31 971	21 787	46.7	2 433	−260	905	13.9	19.6
Hart	2 369	2 279	2 683	9 659	45.3	5.2	23 194	15 671	48.0	3 988	−36	1 482	23.5	34.5

[1] Revised. [2] 1997 data are model-based estimates; 1989 data are census estimates. For more information on these estimates, see appendix A. Source Notes and Explanations or <http://www.census.gov/hhes/www/saipe.html>.

Sources: Public School Enrollment, 1998-1999 and 1994-1995—U.S. National Center for Education Statistics, <http://nces.ed.gov/ccd/pubagency.html> (accessed: 16 March 2001). Public School Enrollment and Educational Attainment, 1990—U.S. Census Bureau, "1990 Census of Population and Housing, Summary Tape File (STF) 3C" on CD-ROM (related Internet site <http://homer.ssd.census.gov/cdrom/lookup>). Income and Poverty, 1997—U.S. Census Bureau, "State and County Income and Poverty Estimates - 1997," published 22 November 2000, <http://www.census.gov/housing/saipe/estmod97/est97ALL.dat>. Income and Poverty, 1989—U.S. Census Bureau, "1990 Census of Population and Housing, Summary Tape File (STF) 3C" on CD-ROM (related Internet site <http://homer.ssd.census.gov/cdrom/lookup>).

Table B–5. Counties — Education, Income, and Poverty–Con.

[Includes U.S., states, and 3,142 counties or county equivalents defined as of January 1, 1992. For changes to these areas since January 1, 1992, see appendix B. Geographic Information]

County	Public school enrollment Fall 1998–1999	Public school enrollment Fall 1994–1995[1]	Public school enrollment 1990	Educational attainment, 1990 Persons 25 years and over	Percent High school graduate or higher	Percent Bachelor's degree or higher	Median household income 1997 (dollars)	Median household income 1989 (dollars)	Percent change, 1989–1997	Persons below poverty level, 1997 Number Persons of all ages Total	Net change, 1989–1997	Persons under 18 years	Percent Persons of all ages	Percent Persons under 18 years
KENTUCKY—Con.														
Henderson	7 431	7 702	7 585	27 643	68.5	11.1	35 263	25 556	38.0	5 863	−343	2 156	13.1	18.9
Henry	2 692	2 554	2 268	8 389	60.9	8.2	31 846	22 528	41.4	2 285	−228	830	15.3	22.4
Hickman	825	869	926	3 852	56.8	7.6	28 542	20 347	40.3	846	−241	292	16.5	24.3
Hopkins	8 056	8 238	8 291	29 896	62.5	9.6	29 936	22 155	35.1	7 721	−68	2 912	16.6	24.8
Jackson	2 442	2 453	2 304	7 324	38.3	4.9	18 503	11 885	55.7	4 030	−514	1 570	30.8	42.5
Jefferson	101 888	93 770	92 113	439 055	74.1	19.3	38 733	27 092	43.0	82 360	−7 395	30 490	12.2	19.4
Jessamine	6 461	6 108	5 416	18 458	69.0	19.1	36 726	27 059	35.7	4 482	634	1 734	12.4	17.8
Johnson	4 678	4 951	4 765	14 571	54.7	8.2	24 052	15 782	52.4	6 098	−475	2 211	25.3	34.9
Kenton	21 406	21 418	20 919	88 454	74.4	17.0	41 581	30 516	36.3	14 830	1 038	5 734	10.1	14.5
Knott	3 371	3 446	3 856	10 619	45.1	8.2	22 470	13 329	68.6	5 227	−1 808	1 852	29.4	35.9
Knox	5 646	5 492	5 961	17 934	46.6	8.0	19 780	12 697	55.8	9 949	−1 340	3 837	31.3	43.1
Larue	2 398	2 289	1 936	7 814	59.0	8.1	30 479	22 405	36.0	2 080	−217	716	15.8	22.3
Laurel	8 934	8 958	8 597	27 037	52.7	8.2	27 146	18 584	46.1	10 629	−1	4 156	20.7	30.2
Lawrence	2 861	2 746	3 005	8 677	46.4	6.2	22 608	15 273	48.0	4 318	−662	1 565	27.5	36.5
Lee	1 411	1 494	1 531	4 654	43.4	5.8	18 326	12 461	47.1	2 609	−95	935	34.6	47.0
Leslie	2 510	2 698	2 783	8 048	40.4	6.6	20 757	13 692	51.6	4 196	−612	1 530	30.6	38.3
Letcher	4 600	5 334	5 841	16 645	45.6	6.7	22 893	15 112	51.5	6 949	−1 575	2 475	26.1	33.6
Lewis	2 510	2 514	2 822	8 127	45.4	6.7	22 270	15 775	41.2	3 466	−480	1 317	25.5	36.1
Lincoln	4 172	3 887	3 863	12 759	50.4	6.2	25 282	17 169	47.3	4 637	−738	1 724	20.5	29.5
Livingston	1 538	1 499	1 435	6 200	63.1	5.4	30 822	20 892	47.5	1 387	11	470	14.6	22.8
Logan	4 874	4 656	4 450	15 856	57.7	8.1	30 547	21 279	43.6	3 727	−154	1 387	14.1	20.7
Lyon	1 002	973	975	4 959	61.0	8.1	29 466	20 239	45.6	983	209	267	14.7	21.2
McCracken	10 315	10 229	10 897	42 531	73.1	14.3	33 538	22 606	48.4	9 297	−501	3 402	14.4	22.5
McCreary	3 495	3 511	3 395	9 118	40.2	4.6	16 433	10 598	55.1	5 968	−1 094	2 332	35.3	46.6
McLean	1 688	1 718	1 770	6 316	58.6	6.6	28 841	20 474	40.9	1 508	−316	520	15.3	21.8
Madison	10 339	9 589	8 738	32 274	64.8	19.1	31 963	21 388	49.4	9 968	−891	3 137	16.2	21.2
Magoffin	2 714	2 909	2 978	7 567	38.2	4.6	19 292	12 160	58.7	4 670	−809	1 779	33.6	41.9
Marion	3 016	2 915	2 865	10 339	58.9	6.4	27 284	18 181	50.1	3 050	−1 011	1 059	18.2	23.1
Marshall	4 939	5 081	4 448	18 824	67.6	9.6	33 061	22 413	47.5	3 481	−284	1 159	11.5	17.2
Martin	2 745	2 962	2 963	7 208	44.4	6.0	22 497	15 142	48.6	3 790	−632	1 473	30.8	39.7
Mason	2 758	2 814	2 946	10 895	60.7	10.2	29 347	20 582	42.6	3 094	−247	1 125	13.2	26.5
Meade	4 636	4 175	5 217	13 790	74.3	11.0	34 885	23 676	47.3	3 352	267	1 362	11.5	14.4
Menifee	1 111	1 003	985	3 122	46.0	4.9	21 481	14 650	46.6	1 583	−193	594	27.0	37.8
Mercer	3 533	3 394	3 371	12 757	62.8	8.9	32 522	22 774	42.8	2 906	−261	998	13.9	20.2
Metcalfe	1 689	1 626	1 550	5 873	45.2	5.0	22 178	14 815	49.7	2 264	−197	768	23.6	33.3
Monroe	2 107	2 101	1 960	7 553	47.1	6.9	23 348	15 214	53.5	2 518	−507	866	22.5	32.6
Montgomery	3 959	3 678	3 822	12 460	56.1	9.2	28 579	20 025	42.7	3 658	−385	1 313	17.3	24.5
Morgan	2 385	2 414	2 333	7 325	44.1	6.7	20 627	13 229	55.9	4 003	−325	1 375	32.3	41.0
Muhlenberg	5 322	5 583	5 950	20 133	54.9	6.2	26 698	18 679	42.9	5 572	−809	2 025	17.3	25.4
Nelson	6 393	5 792	5 491	18 159	67.4	9.3	35 234	24 220	45.5	4 375	−33	1 722	12.1	16.7
Nicholas	1 205	1 292	1 307	4 420	55.4	6.0	25 311	18 070	40.1	1 443	−57	482	20.5	28.1
Ohio	4 120	4 041	4 105	13 562	53.1	6.2	26 333	18 196	44.7	4 175	−736	1 559	18.9	26.5
Oldham	8 255	7 395	6 909	21 049	80.2	22.9	54 599	38 416	42.1	2 216	246	809	5.1	6.5
Owen	1 929	1 853	1 726	5 887	55.2	7.4	29 976	21 067	42.3	1 857	129	720	17.9	26.4
Owsley	895	1 003	1 053	3 187	35.5	9.8	14 392	8 595	67.4	2 202	−368	717	40.9	50.0
Pendleton	2 964	2 697	2 407	7 336	60.1	6.8	32 811	22 500	45.8	2 000	−250	771	14.4	19.7
Perry	6 158	6 745	6 442	18 362	47.6	6.7	23 768	16 202	46.7	8 571	−1 065	3 153	27.4	36.7
Pike	12 391	13 943	15 315	44 941	50.2	7.7	26 026	17 468	49.0	16 413	−1 821	5 754	22.6	29.6
Powell	2 660	2 643	2 477	7 012	50.1	5.3	24 233	16 828	44.0	2 948	−84	1 190	22.6	31.1
Pulaski	9 714	9 260	8 918	32 512	56.2	9.2	25 488	18 198	40.1	10 537	−417	3 650	18.8	27.6
Robertson	404	366	371	1 408	50.8	7.7	26 181	19 756	32.5	450	−71	152	20.3	29.8
Rockcastle	3 036	2 922	2 944	9 249	44.9	5.9	22 915	14 967	53.1	3 706	−792	1 341	23.1	32.1
Rowan	3 183	3 124	2 935	10 476	57.9	17.3	25 553	15 922	60.5	4 353	−503	1 268	23.0	28.1
Russell	2 837	2 799	2 442	9 839	50.2	6.2	22 997	16 788	37.0	3 622	−118	1 245	22.1	33.3
Scott	5 667	4 982	4 501	14 554	69.1	15.2	42 465	27 563	54.1	3 513	190	1 337	11.6	16.2
Shelby	4 861	4 619	4 288	16 318	69.9	12.9	40 134	28 500	40.8	2 993	−471	1 060	10.1	14.3
Simpson	2 994	2 880	2 791	9 730	58.9	8.8	33 233	21 793	52.5	1 947	−371	742	11.8	17.2
Spencer	1 986	1 560	1 291	4 343	57.5	9.9	33 958	22 680	49.7	1 147	−145	428	11.7	16.6
Taylor	3 914	4 013	3 661	13 792	57.4	10.1	28 552	21 083	35.4	3 789	−232	1 315	16.6	23.9
Todd	2 152	1 916	1 922	7 028	50.6	7.1	29 247	20 309	44.0	1 839	−190	727	16.2	25.0
Trigg	1 980	1 857	1 765	7 223	58.9	11.4	29 190	19 860	47.0	1 766	−80	621	14.1	22.3
Trimble	1 386	1 289	1 115	3 931	61.6	7.3	30 948	22 372	38.3	1 149	169	448	14.8	22.2
Union	2 595	2 814	3 033	9 408	68.1	8.9	31 197	23 798	31.1	2 414	−1 201	836	14.5	18.0
Warren	14 216	13 611	13 081	46 161	70.9	19.2	34 891	24 175	44.3	12 078	−610	4 255	14.4	20.8
Washington	1 860	1 776	1 903	6 669	57.8	7.5	29 266	20 606	42.0	1 699	−230	585	15.6	20.2
Wayne	3 617	3 548	3 472	11 030	44.6	5.5	20 242	12 560	61.2	5 286	−1 160	1 956	27.5	39.0
Webster	2 521	2 676	2 737	9 089	60.7	6.0	30 325	21 189	43.1	1 973	−293	733	14.6	21.1
Whitley	7 420	7 036	6 600	20 195	53.0	11.3	21 553	14 979	43.9	9 877	−745	3 607	27.9	38.2
Wolfe	1 363	1 380	1 397	4 052	42.8	7.7	16 323	11 000	48.4	2 722	−113	960	36.6	46.4
Woodford	3 825	3 864	3 474	12 840	73.5	19.5	45 269	32 858	37.8	1 847	309	700	8.1	12.1

[1] Revised. [2] 1997 data are model-based estimates; 1989 data are census estimates. For more information on these estimates, see appendix A. Source Notes and Explanations or <http://www.census.gov/hhes/www/saipe.html>.

Sources: Public School Enrollment, 1998-1999 and 1994-1995—U.S. National Center for Education Statistics, <http://nces.ed.gov/ccd/pubagency.html> (accessed: 16 March 2001). Public School Enrollment and Educational Attainment, 1990—U.S. Census Bureau, "1990 Census of Population and Housing, Summary Tape File (STF) 3C" on CD-ROM (related Internet site <http://homer.ssd.census.gov/cdrom/lookup>). Income and Poverty, 1997—U.S. Census Bureau, "State and County Income and Poverty Estimates - 1997," published 22 November 2000, <http://www.census.gov/housing/saipe/estmod97/est97ALL.dat>. Income and Poverty, 1989—U.S. Census Bureau, "1990 Census of Population and Housing, Summary Tape File (STF) 3C" on CD-ROM (related Internet site <http://homer.ssd.census.gov/cdrom/lookup>).

Table B–5. Counties — **Education, Income, and Poverty**–Con.

[Includes U.S., states, and 3,142 counties or county equivalents defined as of January 1, 1992. For changes to these areas since January 1, 1992, see appendix B. Geographic Information]

County	Public school enrollment Fall			Educational attainment, 1990	Percent—		Median household income[2]			Persons below poverty level,[2] 1997			Percent	
										Number Persons of all ages				
	1998–1999	1994–1995[1]	1990	Persons 25 years and over	High school graduate or higher	Bachelor's degree or higher	1997 (dollars)	1989 (dollars)	Percent change, 1989–1997	Total	Net change, 1989–1997	Persons under 18 years	Persons of all ages	Persons under 18 years
LOUISIANA	768 734	799 237	765 022	2 536 994	68.3	16.1	30 466	21 949	38.8	793 472	–173 530	316 991	18.4	26.0
Acadia	10 492	10 948	10 957	32 919	54.6	8.4	24 975	16 022	55.9	11 838	–4 994	4 881	20.4	27.3
Allen	4 463	4 568	4 529	13 262	57.1	6.7	24 755	15 838	56.3	4 712	–1 204	1 644	22.8	26.8
Ascension	14 705	14 122	12 664	33 455	68.5	9.3	39 248	27 435	43.1	8 737	–1 467	3 735	12.1	16.6
Assumption	4 702	5 066	4 849	13 152	50.4	6.7	29 993	20 021	49.8	4 254	–2 100	1 799	18.3	25.5
Avoyelles	7 478	7 793	7 655	24 123	50.5	7.4	21 449	13 451	59.5	9 806	–4 011	3 741	25.4	32.8
Beauregard	6 134	6 557	6 287	18 301	70.6	13.0	31 486	22 442	40.3	4 924	–333	1 969	15.8	22.1
Bienville	2 860	3 216	3 056	10 046	62.6	9.3	22 995	16 043	43.3	3 811	–1 013	1 497	24.5	35.4
Bossier	18 674	18 537	17 024	52 171	78.9	15.5	35 521	26 058	36.3	11 806	–1 786	4 933	12.8	19.2
Caddo..................	47 089	49 609	49 477	153 972	73.4	18.2	29 667	22 395	32.5	49 296	–9 243	19 604	20.4	29.5
Calcasieu..............	33 115	34 487	32 710	102 341	70.3	14.7	34 175	24 375	40.2	25 313	–5 177	10 011	14.1	20.0
Caldwell...............	2 014	2 077	1 953	6 144	57.1	9.3	23 563	16 069	46.6	2 052	–698	810	19.9	27.8
Cameron	2 074	2 069	1 943	5 584	61.1	7.9	36 665	25 164	45.7	1 018	–472	373	11.2	14.3
Catahoula	2 079	2 403	2 468	6 736	53.9	8.7	21 091	14 956	41.0	2 784	–1 205	1 092	25.2	34.0
Claiborne	2 959	3 024	3 090	11 320	60.9	10.1	23 676	16 073	47.3	4 051	–1 045	1 450	25.8	35.0
Concordia	4 109	4 337	4 372	12 605	56.9	9.1	23 271	17 265	34.8	5 101	–1 167	2 096	24.5	34.5
De Soto	5 210	5 492	5 174	15 466	64.0	9.5	24 767	16 315	51.8	5 646	–1 808	2 274	22.5	31.8
East Baton Rouge	60 143	63 200	59 386	223 392	80.5	27.5	35 644	27 224	30.9	62 253	–10 174	24 031	16.0	23.2
East Carroll	2 022	2 139	2 303	5 234	49.1	10.3	14 910	9 791	52.3	3 686	–1 607	1 620	42.7	52.9
East Feliciana	2 861	3 289	3 636	11 649	58.2	8.9	26 864	20 139	33.4	3 817	–436	1 543	20.6	26.0
Evangeline..............	6 815	7 188	6 653	19 673	48.2	8.3	22 310	13 797	61.7	8 735	–2 736	3 510	25.6	33.5
Franklin	4 183	4 671	5 146	13 393	53.7	10.3	20 339	15 159	34.2	5 971	–1 529	2 472	27.3	37.8
Grant	3 692	3 774	3 743	10 654	62.8	9.6	26 425	17 711	49.2	3 500	–897	1 451	18.4	26.2
Iberia	15 072	15 912	14 415	39 332	59.3	9.0	29 951	20 838	43.7	13 556	–3 873	5 723	18.5	25.1
Iberville...............	5 294	5 455	5 597	18 556	59.0	8.9	27 838	20 371	36.7	6 406	–1 753	2 524	21.8	28.7
Jackson	2 737	3 060	3 341	9 768	63.9	9.2	26 631	18 804	41.6	2 719	–948	1 161	17.6	27.6
Jefferson	53 615	56 790	56 709	283 003	76.0	18.8	37 312	27 916	33.7	59 409	–3 418	23 754	13.1	20.6
Jefferson Davis	6 124	6 816	6 781	18 517	59.9	8.0	26 645	18 467	44.3	5 971	–2 292	2 362	18.9	25.0
Lafayette	30 618	30 843	29 284	97 171	73.3	22.5	35 554	24 339	46.1	25 498	–6 887	9 709	13.8	18.6
Lafourche..............	15 741	16 544	16 615	49 724	56.2	10.0	32 795	21 416	53.1	13 078	–6 176	5 021	14.7	19.7
La Salle	3 036	2 956	2 778	8 752	61.0	7.9	27 398	18 597	47.3	2 133	–698	799	15.6	21.9
Lincoln	6 826	7 189	6 592	20 573	74.5	26.2	28 038	19 254	45.6	7 890	–1 420	2 581	21.5	27.3
Livingston	19 184	17 982	15 466	41 417	66.7	8.7	35 875	25 470	40.9	10 586	367	4 558	11.9	17.0
Madison................	3 232	3 290	3 091	6 992	53.3	9.2	18 965	12 792	48.3	3 988	–1 428	1 741	32.6	41.9
Morehouse..............	5 648	6 161	6 524	19 248	57.8	10.5	22 387	17 309	29.3	7 752	–1 893	3 204	24.8	34.3
Natchitoches	7 186	8 096	7 693	20 351	65.0	16.4	23 874	15 778	51.3	8 786	–2 808	3 520	24.9	33.5
Orleans................	82 176	86 028	80 964	305 065	68.1	22.4	25 200	18 477	36.4	127 476	–24 566	49 993	27.9	40.1
Ouachita...............	28 263	28 917	27 697	82 648	71.6	18.9	28 651	21 129	35.6	28 615	–5 161	12 056	19.8	29.1
Plaquemines	5 141	5 190	4 953	14 888	58.0	7.5	31 908	24 076	32.5	4 058	–1 598	1 639	15.6	21.0
Pointe Coupee	3 633	3 731	3 859	13 669	58.6	9.7	27 541	18 772	46.7	4 766	–1 983	1 876	20.1	27.1
Rapides	23 990	24 800	25 004	79 953	69.0	14.6	27 231	20 811	30.8	24 769	–3 507	10 178	20.0	29.1
Red River..............	2 055	2 067	1 934	5 616	57.4	8.7	21 928	14 831	47.9	2 488	–728	1 032	26.0	35.6
Richland	3 906	4 427	4 363	12 514	52.0	10.7	20 515	15 298	34.1	5 701	–937	2 396	27.5	37.8
Sabine	4 549	4 690	4 575	14 297	61.9	8.3	25 824	16 790	53.8	4 538	–1 503	1 733	19.0	26.3
St. Bernard	8 946	9 511	8 674	41 894	67.2	7.3	32 478	25 482	27.5	8 757	–1 066	3 317	13.2	19.7
St. Charles	10 128	9 819	8 292	25 442	74.0	14.8	41 905	31 777	31.9	5 926	–448	2 546	12.2	17.4
St. Helena	1 535	1 706	1 893	5 733	57.6	7.7	22 255	15 475	43.8	2 365	–993	1 078	24.6	37.1
St. James	4 590	4 540	4 133	12 019	61.1	8.1	30 830	23 105	33.4	3 570	–1 705	1 453	16.8	22.7
St. John the Baptist	6 626	7 140	6 794	22 773	71.5	11.4	35 588	29 035	22.6	6 789	–328	3 048	15.9	22.2
St. Landry	16 301	17 663	16 666	47 386	55.3	9.7	22 364	14 670	52.4	21 243	–7 422	8 562	25.3	33.5
St. Martin	8 697	9 180	9 264	25 216	53.7	6.7	27 427	19 116	43.5	8 683	–3 178	3 707	18.2	25.3
St. Mary	11 324	11 922	12 597	33 562	58.1	8.3	29 528	20 980	40.7	11 379	–4 072	4 695	19.8	26.6
St. Tammany...........	32 553	31 405	27 188	89 425	76.9	23.1	43 653	30 656	42.4	18 880	–666	7 830	9.9	14.3
Tangipahoa	18 728	18 009	16 849	49 559	60.7	12.9	24 164	16 849	43.4	22 096	–3 854	8 877	23.1	30.8
Tensas	1 285	1 583	1 405	4 291	58.1	11.7	17 824	11 931	49.4	2 232	–1 003	927	33.8	44.4
Terrebonne	20 610	22 089	20 380	55 636	59.6	9.4	31 744	21 765	45.8	17 704	–5 499	7 203	16.8	22.3
Union	3 746	3 940	4 050	13 054	64.3	11.0	26 478	18 083	46.4	3 887	–971	1 511	17.7	25.2
Vermilion	9 417	9 849	10 281	30 263	58.3	8.8	27 680	18 202	52.1	9 120	–3 970	3 568	17.4	23.1
Vernon	10 466	11 576	11 224	30 493	76.9	10.3	28 836	19 147	50.6	7 147	–2 906	2 775	16.5	20.5
Washington	7 927	8 847	9 027	27 176	61.5	8.6	22 584	16 246	39.0	10 400	–2 717	4 138	24.7	34.8
Webster	7 950	8 573	8 003	26 934	63.9	10.0	26 388	18 716	41.0	8 143	–2 193	3 240	19.1	29.0
West Baton Rouge	3 936	4 078	3 365	11 554	66.0	9.9	33 251	24 852	33.8	3 241	–652	1 353	15.6	22.8
West Carroll	2 592	2 740	2 502	7 546	52.0	8.7	19 942	14 924	33.6	2 978	–280	1 208	24.4	35.6
West Feliciana	2 371	2 225	1 953	9 226	57.2	7.8	30 796	19 402	58.7	1 958	–710	539	22.1	19.5
Winn	3 107	3 332	3 172	10 146	58.0	9.0	24 807	16 967	46.2	3 683	–582	1 320	22.5	29.1

[1] Revised.   [2] 1997 data are model-based estimates; 1989 data are census estimates. For more information on these estimates, see appendix A. Source Notes and Explanations or <http://www.census.gov/hhes/www/saipe.html>.

Sources: Public School Enrollment, 1998-1999 and 1994-1995—U.S. National Center for Education Statistics, <http://nces.ed.gov/ccd/pubagency.html> (accessed: 16 March 2001). Public School Enrollment and Educational Attainment, 1990—U.S. Census Bureau, "1990 Census of Population and Housing, Summary Tape File (STF) 3C" on CD-ROM (related Internet site <http://homer.ssd.census.gov/cdrom/lookup>). Income and Poverty, 1997—U.S. Census Bureau, "State and County Income and Poverty Estimates - 1997," published 22 November 2000, <http://www.census.gov/housing/saipe/estmod97/est97ALL.dat>. Income and Poverty, 1989—U.S. Census Bureau, "1990 Census of Population and Housing, Summary Tape File (STF) 3C" on CD-ROM (related Internet site <http://homer.ssd.census.gov/cdrom/lookup>).

[Includes U.S., states, and 3,142 counties or county equivalents defined as of January 1, 1992. For changes to these areas since January 1, 1992, see appendix B. Geographic Information]

County	Public school enrollment — Fall			Educational attainment, 1990			Median household income[2]			Persons below poverty level,[2] 1997				
					Percent—					Number			Percent	
										Persons of all ages				
	1998–1999	1994–1995[1]	1990	Persons 25 years and over	High school graduate or higher	Bachelor's degree or higher	1997 (dollars)	1989 (dollars)	Percent change, 1989–1997	Total	Net change, 1989–1997	Persons under 18 years	Persons of all ages	Persons under 18 years
MAINE	210 080	212 225	212 465	795 613	78.8	18.8	33 140	27 854	19.0	132 809	4 343	44 122	10.7	14.9
Androscoggin	16 472	17 438	17 664	66 785	71.8	12.6	34 242	26 979	26.9	10 732	–840	3 575	10.7	14.5
Aroostook..................	13 349	14 653	16 509	55 738	70.9	12.5	29 124	22 230	31.0	11 152	–724	3 562	15.0	19.6
Cumberland...............	39 693	37 475	37 559	159 876	85.0	27.6	41 393	32 286	28.2	20 432	1 660	6 366	8.1	11.3
Franklin	5 348	5 471	5 575	17 980	79.7	17.7	30 712	24 432	25.7	3 643	163	1 247	12.7	17.6
Hancock..................	8 198	8 354	7 565	31 475	83.3	21.4	33 397	25 247	32.3	4 974	428	1 626	10.1	14.5
Kennebec.................	18 361	18 735	20 441	74 858	78.9	18.1	35 559	28 616	24.3	12 040	576	4 046	10.6	14.7
Knox	4 744	4 842	5 837	24 778	80.8	19.8	33 478	25 405	31.8	4 050	–149	1 347	10.8	15.5
Lincoln	6 236	6 353	5 037	20 674	81.4	22.2	35 696	28 373	25.8	3 067	184	1 117	9.6	15.3
Oxford	10 673	10 585	9 814	34 779	76.9	12.7	30 688	24 535	25.1	6 663	219	2 313	12.3	17.4
Penobscot	24 571	25 473	24 756	91 410	79.1	17.7	33 574	26 631	26.1	17 229	–866	5 486	12.1	16.4
Piscataquis	3 173	3 473	4 057	12 248	75.4	12.3	28 599	22 132	29.2	2 488	–312	850	13.6	19.1
Sagadahoc	6 952	6 991	5 885	21 573	81.1	21.6	39 991	31 948	25.2	2 795	410	980	7.8	11.0
Somerset	9 316	9 821	10 066	31 726	71.9	10.5	28 300	22 829	24.0	7 840	768	2 806	14.9	20.6
Waldo	5 240	5 226	6 404	21 295	77.4	16.8	29 812	23 148	28.8	5 279	80	1 820	14.3	19.5
Washington	5 428	6 059	6 777	23 087	73.2	12.7	25 673	19 993	28.4	6 252	–348	2 106	17.7	24.5
York	32 326	31 276	28 519	107 331	79.5	19.0	39 288	32 432	21.1	14 173	3 094	4 875	8.0	11.3
MARYLAND	841 671	790 938	703 379	3 122 665	78.4	26.5	45 289	39 386	15.0	484 987	99 691	194 703	9.5	14.9
Allegany	10 978	11 303	10 872	49 857	71.0	11.8	28 794	21 546	33.6	11 209	–656	4 011	15.9	24.2
Anne Arundel	74 079	70 588	63 918	276 130	81.1	24.6	56 147	45 147	24.4	24 894	6 503	11 893	5.3	9.7
Baltimore.................	105 914	99 231	85 386	473 574	78.4	25.0	44 715	38 837	15.1	54 891	17 737	20 936	7.6	12.8
Calvert	15 241	12 819	9 659	32 408	79.3	17.6	57 017	47 608	19.8	4 815	2 161	2 212	6.6	10.4
Caroline..................	5 685	5 290	4 616	17 510	66.8	10.8	32 902	27 758	18.5	3 772	652	1 649	12.8	20.4
Carroll...................	27 224	24 515	21 115	79 153	78.5	19.6	55 906	42 378	31.9	7 320	2 792	2 996	4.9	7.2
Cecil	15 550	14 258	12 628	44 944	72.2	12.1	44 650	36 019	24.0	7 375	2 169	3 359	9.0	14.2
Charles..................	22 263	20 419	18 228	60 821	81.0	16.2	54 110	46 415	16.6	8 757	3 750	4 407	7.4	12.2
Dorchester...............	5 143	5 165	4 821	20 861	64.7	10.9	29 361	24 922	17.8	4 629	414	1 825	15.5	25.3
Frederick	35 383	31 655	26 088	94 994	80.4	22.0	53 415	41 382	29.1	10 695	3 640	4 448	5.8	8.6
Garrett	5 082	5 104	5 306	17 908	68.4	9.5	30 197	22 733	32.8	4 605	563	1 957	15.8	24.2
Harford..................	38 909	35 956	30 153	115 199	81.6	21.5	52 231	41 680	25.3	13 841	4 719	5 813	6.4	9.6
Howard...................	41 858	36 125	29 545	122 454	91.1	46.9	68 024	54 348	25.2	10 503	4 719	4 187	4.4	6.6
Kent	2 891	2 794	2 595	11 822	71.4	16.9	36 391	30 104	20.9	1 949	6	703	10.7	17.1
Montgomery	127 933	117 082	101 083	512 839	90.6	49.9	62 130	54 089	14.9	47 141	15 490	18 201	5.6	8.8
Prince George's	130 259	118 478	106 064	458 296	83.2	25.5	47 882	43 127	11.0	71 557	30 275	30 164	9.3	15.1
Queen Anne's	6 888	6 020	5 498	22 993	76.8	19.9	48 226	39 190	23.1	3 016	781	1 151	7.5	11.3
St. Mary's................	14 743	13 428	12 800	45 592	77.1	16.8	49 495	37 158	33.2	7 628	2 235	3 528	8.8	13.2
Somerset	3 113	3 339	3 698	15 901	61.2	9.6	26 867	23 379	14.9	4 344	1 179	1 453	21.8	29.1
Talbot	4 590	4 340	3 829	21 903	76.5	23.0	39 663	31 885	24.4	3 224	660	1 208	9.7	16.7
Washington	20 159	19 510	18 459	81 140	69.3	11.4	37 327	29 632	26.0	12 284	1 710	4 762	10.1	15.7
Wicomico	14 330	13 652	11 738	47 231	72.1	18.5	34 827	28 512	22.1	10 493	2 214	4 431	13.5	21.6
Worcester	6 916	6 439	5 241	24 828	70.8	14.8	32 815	27 586	19.0	5 106	1 323	2 119	11.9	21.8
Independent City														
Baltimore city.............	106 540	113 428	110 039	474 307	60.7	15.5	27 713	24 045	15.3	150 937	–5 347	57 290	23.7	34.4
MASSACHUSETTS......	937 647	893 727	830 138	3 962 223	80.0	27.2	43 015	36 952	16.4	649 293	129 954	250 244	10.7	17.0
Barnstable	28 788	30 964	26 042	133 951	88.4	28.1	40 791	31 766	28.4	18 547	4 751	6 912	8.9	15.5
Berkshire	15 802	21 204	20 346	92 609	77.9	20.9	37 284	30 470	22.4	14 783	3 223	5 577	11.3	18.2
Bristol	84 296	82 475	80 028	327 994	65.0	15.9	38 866	31 520	23.3	61 556	16 389	25 043	11.9	18.8
Dukes	2 543	2 182	1 796	8 245	90.4	32.1	40 852	31 994	27.7	931	162	319	6.7	10.1
Essex	116 844	105 625	94 592	445 994	80.2	25.9	44 187	37 913	16.5	74 648	13 877	29 994	10.6	17.0
Franklin	11 907	11 813	10 925	46 559	82.4	24.2	38 330	30 350	26.3	7 461	838	2 922	10.5	16.5
Hampden	77 037	71 919	69 898	292 806	73.6	17.6	36 746	31 100	18.2	72 537	15 200	31 647	16.6	26.9
Hampshire	20 100	20 772	18 531	85 463	83.0	31.9	42 287	34 154	23.8	12 798	–886	3 500	9.4	11.3
Middlesex................	206 094	189 963	177 247	941 201	84.3	35.4	53 268	43 847	21.5	103 324	20 385	33 979	7.3	10.9
Nantucket................	1 238	1 042	764	4 316	89.4	32.9	48 151	40 331	19.4	340	...	106	4.2	6.0
Norfolk	95 758	88 154	77 929	421 102	88.0	34.4	54 528	46 215	18.0	32 148	5 013	9 828	5.0	7.0
Plymouth	78 989	77 360	73 465	276 957	83.8	22.2	49 165	40 905	20.2	40 461	12 608	16 935	8.6	13.2
Suffolk	79 258	73 551	72 355	427 138	75.4	27.7	36 260	29 399	23.3	129 133	14 385	51 621	20.7	35.4
Worcester	118 993	116 703	106 220	457 888	77.4	22.2	40 489	35 774	13.2	80 628	24 011	31 862	11.1	16.8

[1] Revised. [2] 1997 data are model-based estimates; 1989 data are census estimates. For more information on these estimates, see appendix A. Source Notes and Explanations or <http://www.census.gov/hhes/www/saipe.html>.

Sources: Public School Enrollment, 1998-1999 and 1994-1995—U.S. National Center for Education Statistics, <http://nces.ed.gov/ccd/pubagency.html> (accessed: 16 March 2001). Public School Enrollment and Educational Attainment, 1990—U.S. Census Bureau, "1990 Census of Population and Housing, Summary Tape File (STF) 3C" on CD-ROM (related Internet site <http://homer.ssd.census.gov/cdrom/lookup>). Income and Poverty, 1997—U.S. Census Bureau, "State and County Income and Poverty Estimates - 1997," published 22 November 2000, <http://www.census.gov/housing/saipe/estmod97/est97ALL.dat>. Income and Poverty, 1989—U.S. Census Bureau, "1990 Census of Population and Housing, Summary Tape File (STF) 3C" on CD-ROM (related Internet site <http://homer.ssd.census.gov/cdrom/lookup>).

[Includes U.S., states, and 3,142 counties or county equivalents defined as of January 1, 1992. For changes to these areas since January 1, 1992, see appendix B. Geographic Information]

County	Public school enrollment Fall 1998–1999	Public school enrollment Fall 1994–1995[1]	Public school enrollment 1990	Educational attainment, 1990 Persons 25 years and over	Percent— High school graduate or higher	Percent— Bachelor's degree or higher	Median household income[2] 1997 (dollars)	Median household income[2] 1989 (dollars)	Percent change, 1989–1997	Persons below poverty level,[2] 1997 Number Persons of all ages Total	Net change, 1989–1997	Persons under 18 years	Percent Persons of all ages	Percent Persons under 18 years
MICHIGAN.............	1 698 501	1 604 141	1 636 182	5 842 642	76.8	17.4	38 883	31 020	25.3	1 127 886	−62 812	468 947	11.5	18.0
Alcona	1 050	995	1 640	7 368	68.6	9.0	25 466	18 013	41.4	1 534	−198	630	13.7	26.5
Alger	1 609	1 731	1 699	6 009	73.0	11.5	31 877	21 569	47.8	1 081	−143	387	11.8	16.2
Allegan	18 189	17 300	17 790	55 740	74.4	12.0	43 128	30 596	41.0	8 405	−37	3 728	8.2	12.1
Alpena	5 552	5 751	5 851	20 165	73.6	11.4	31 836	22 598	40.9	3 981	−106	1 661	12.9	20.6
Antrim	4 129	4 022	3 439	12 185	76.4	13.7	34 015	22 636	50.3	2 043	−328	894	9.4	16.0
Arenac	3 009	3 266	3 210	9 782	65.4	7.1	27 758	19 489	42.4	2 713	−315	1 215	16.6	27.6
Baraga	1 492	1 532	1 505	5 166	70.5	8.3	29 412	19 424	51.4	1 063	−232	412	13.3	19.0
Barry	8 205	7 873	10 057	31 892	78.3	10.8	43 955	30 516	44.0	4 751	296	2 015	8.7	13.4
Bay	17 485	16 927	18 850	71 684	74.0	11.0	36 836	27 940	31.8	13 633	−207	5 693	12.3	19.7
Benzie	2 402	2 349	2 096	8 333	76.6	15.1	31 666	21 577	46.8	1 404	−149	571	9.4	16.0
Berrien	29 350	29 194	28 657	102 485	74.7	16.7	35 846	27 245	31.6	22 636	−645	9 957	14.1	23.0
Branch	6 436	6 515	8 195	26 446	73.8	10.3	33 824	25 332	33.5	5 134	−466	2 250	12.2	18.7
Calhoun	25 064	24 830	25 016	86 623	76.8	13.8	37 295	27 476	35.7	18 787	−45	8 159	13.5	21.7
Cass	7 529	7 367	9 437	31 841	72.3	9.2	36 600	28 002	30.7	6 183	367	2 560	12.2	19.3
Charlevoix	4 432	4 410	4 242	13 963	79.7	16.0	36 885	24 738	49.1	2 234	25	881	9.0	13.3
Cheboygan	4 025	3 946	4 056	14 207	73.5	10.0	29 623	21 006	41.0	3 007	−276	1 310	12.5	21.2
Chippewa	6 028	5 724	6 480	21 848	73.6	10.8	30 477	21 449	42.1	4 854	−181	1 828	14.7	20.8
Clare	5 643	5 324	4 706	16 401	66.9	6.8	25 237	17 163	47.0	5 055	−760	2 247	17.0	28.6
Clinton	9 923	9 459	10 968	35 745	83.7	14.6	50 538	36 180	39.7	3 783	325	1 687	5.9	9.3
Crawford	2 264	2 195	2 286	8 057	73.2	12.6	29 587	21 497	37.6	2 011	323	946	14.6	25.8
Delta	7 222	7 780	7 795	24 476	76.9	11.3	33 301	22 791	46.1	4 764	−678	1 873	12.2	18.0
Dickinson	5 287	5 174	5 074	17 972	78.5	13.0	35 854	24 809	44.5	2 499	−120	958	9.2	13.5
Eaton	16 783	16 336	17 766	58 205	85.5	18.5	46 527	35 734	30.2	7 196	956	3 159	7.1	11.4
Emmet	5 211	5 126	4 239	16 448	81.5	19.2	36 641	26 015	40.8	2 541	447	1 080	8.8	14.0
Genesee	83 153	81 375	85 285	265 430	76.8	12.8	40 153	31 030	29.4	62 559	−7 464	28 592	14.2	23.5
Gladwin	3 949	3 885	4 036	14 388	64.8	6.5	27 911	18 587	50.2	3 931	−900	1 631	15.4	24.5
Gogebic	2 613	2 902	3 016	12 497	76.3	11.4	26 003	17 343	49.9	2 645	58	964	15.7	24.8
Grand Traverse	12 816	12 613	11 609	41 094	84.9	22.1	39 841	29 034	37.2	5 656	281	2 349	7.6	11.6
Gratiot	8 216	8 188	7 860	23 966	77.1	10.9	33 952	24 530	38.4	4 599	−562	1 994	12.0	18.2
Hillsdale	7 781	7 857	8 337	26 657	75.2	11.3	35 694	26 019	37.2	5 100	−295	2 169	11.1	16.5
Houghton	5 995	6 023	6 035	20 646	73.9	18.0	28 170	17 650	59.6	5 032	−1 794	1 662	15.0	19.8
Huron	7 299	6 459	6 492	22 798	68.0	8.9	33 362	21 852	52.7	4 279	−897	1 686	12.0	17.6
Ingham	50 295	49 139	45 220	158 966	83.9	29.2	40 626	30 162	34.7	36 432	−7 023	13 644	13.4	19.3
Ionia	12 407	11 968	10 975	33 466	77.2	8.9	38 443	29 430	30.6	6 397	540	2 461	11.1	14.0
Iosco	6 446	6 155	5 431	19 194	76.3	10.4	27 140	20 091	35.1	3 503	−618	1 443	13.6	21.9
Iron	12 318	2 300	2 307	9 554	73.0	10.0	25 527	16 307	56.5	1 713	−493	568	13.6	19.8
Isabella	7 057	6 511	8 068	26 492	79.7	21.5	33 561	22 659	48.1	7 406	−4 648	2 396	13.9	17.3
Jackson	25 836	24 533	25 427	97 049	77.7	12.9	38 253	29 156	31.2	17 415	534	6 939	11.6	17.3
Kalamazoo	33 893	33 374	34 880	134 684	83.4	27.1	41 517	31 060	33.7	24 216	−4 441	9 126	10.8	16.2
Kalkaska	2 882	2 961	2 957	8 485	69.6	7.1	30 783	22 078	39.4	2 026	131	868	12.9	18.7
Kent	95 797	89 671	83 048	305 356	80.3	20.7	44 512	32 358	37.6	47 114	2 335	21 035	8.7	13.4
Keweenaw	6	11	278	1 287	64.3	11.1	24 887	13 821	80.1	241	−108	78	11.3	16.5
Lake	756	876	1 652	5 931	61.3	6.6	22 291	14 562	53.1	2 112	−103	926	20.3	34.5
Lapeer	15 057	14 315	16 078	45 437	77.6	9.3	47 774	35 874	33.2	6 078	69	2 549	6.9	9.8
Leelanau	2 785	2 505	2 677	11 127	85.1	24.1	41 624	28 589	45.6	1 609	130	641	8.3	13.0
Lenawee	18 605	18 154	18 344	56 323	76.3	12.9	40 778	31 012	31.5	8 989	−116	3 753	9.4	13.7
Livingston	25 701	22 375	22 911	72 343	85.6	19.6	61 915	45 439	36.3	5 678	962	2 174	3.8	5.2
Luce	1 202	1 230	1 233	3 811	69.6	9.6	28 252	20 370	38.7	966	−18	369	16.4	22.7
Mackinac	1 854	1 900	2 110	7 156	71.4	10.4	28 367	19 397	46.2	1 323	−411	544	11.8	19.2
Macomb	123 871	114 333	115 170	472 323	76.9	13.5	49 601	38 931	27.4	47 088	10 206	17 557	5.9	9.4
Manistee	3 550	3 791	3 753	14 619	73.3	10.5	28 889	19 977	44.6	3 318	−383	1 287	14.5	23.3
Marquette	10 736	12 129	13 352	42 386	81.8	20.3	35 478	25 137	41.1	6 753	−1 619	2 349	11.3	14.5
Mason	5 211	5 158	4 930	16 796	76.1	11.8	31 189	21 701	43.7	3 697	161	1 567	13.2	21.3
Mecosta	7 888	6 327	5 733	19 005	77.7	17.9	31 055	20 784	49.4	5 877	−2 302	2 211	15.4	23.3
Menominee	4 116	4 343	4 807	16 514	74.3	9.3	32 472	21 586	50.4	2 712	−420	1 038	11.1	16.0
Midland	14 671	13 762	14 501	47 213	83.2	27.4	48 093	33 948	41.7	7 335	−883	2 868	9.0	13.0
Missaukee	2 407	2 419	2 415	7 628	69.4	8.0	30 571	20 932	46.0	1 937	−133	875	13.9	21.0
Monroe	24 634	23 936	25 744	82 291	74.1	10.5	48 607	35 462	37.1	10 986	−443	4 605	7.6	11.2
Montcalm	13 742	13 399	11 065	32 959	73.4	8.2	33 522	23 880	40.4	7 861	61	3 209	13.3	18.4
Montmorency	1 206	1 185	1 566	6 279	67.6	8.7	25 297	17 819	42.0	1 514	−28	632	15.1	26.9
Muskegon	33 202	32 058	31 163	99 720	74.2	11.1	34 951	25 617	36.4	23 655	149	10 375	14.4	21.9
Newaygo	9 967	9 071	7 995	23 989	71.1	10.5	33 631	23 468	43.3	5 813	−178	2 632	12.6	19.2
Oakland	191 144	175 447	173 119	717 210	84.6	30.2	59 677	43 407	37.5	71 312	6 594	27 784	6.0	9.6

[1] Revised. [2] 1997 data are model-based estimates; 1989 data are census estimates. For more information on these estimates, see appendix A. Source Notes and Explanations or <http://www.census.gov/hhes/www/saipe.html>.

Sources: Public School Enrollment, 1998-1999 and 1994-1995—U.S. National Center for Education Statistics, <http://nces.ed.gov/ccd/pubagency.html> (accessed: 16 March 2001). Public School Enrollment and Educational Attainment, 1990—U.S. Census Bureau, "1990 Census of Population and Housing, Summary Tape File (STF) 3C" on CD-ROM (related Internet site <http://homer.ssd.census.gov/cdrom/lookup>). Income and Poverty, 1997—U.S. Census Bureau, "State and County Income and Poverty Estimates - 1997," published 22 November 2000, <http://www.census.gov/housing/saipe/estmod97/est97ALL.dat>. Income and Poverty, 1989—U.S. Census Bureau, "1990 Census of Population and Housing, Summary Tape File (STF) 3C" on CD-ROM (related Internet site <http://homer.ssd.census.gov/cdrom/lookup>).

[Includes U.S., states, and 3,142 counties or county equivalents defined as of January 1, 1992. For changes to these areas since January 1, 1992, see appendix B. Geographic Information]

County	Public school enrollment Fall			Educational attainment, 1990 Percent—			Median household income[2]			Persons below poverty level,[2] 1997				
										Number — Persons of all ages			Percent	
	1998–1999	1994–1995[1]	1990	Persons 25 years and over	High school graduate or higher	Bachelor's degree or higher	1997 (dollars)	1989 (dollars)	Percent change, 1989–1997	Total	Net change, 1989–1997	Persons under 18 years	Persons of all ages	Persons under 18 years
MICHIGAN—Con.														
Oceana	4 139	4 030	4 956	14 069	73.3	10.4	31 324	22 383	39.9	4 179	216	1 869	16.8	25.2
Ogemaw	2 914	2 851	3 602	12 379	63.0	7.2	25 383	17 665	43.7	3 689	–306	1 506	17.4	26.8
Ontonagon	1 284	1 500	1 660	6 198	74.6	9.2	27 811	21 147	31.5	1 069	–80	412	13.6	22.4
Osceola	5 804	5 575	4 470	12 491	72.1	8.7	29 712	20 880	42.3	3 449	–233	1 500	15.5	23.1
Oscoda	1 406	1 411	1 219	5 433	66.6	7.9	25 044	17 772	40.9	1 528	154	592	17.1	27.8
Otsego	4 665	4 411	3 356	11 358	79.5	13.7	37 938	26 356	43.9	1 917	243	828	8.6	13.0
Ottawa	44 491	35 157	32 807	110 737	79.8	18.7	51 677	36 507	41.6	10 815	–77	4 224	4.9	6.3
Presque Isle	2 145	2 258	2 278	9 285	65.7	8.7	28 886	20 941	37.9	1 781	–222	675	12.1	18.8
Roscommon	4 278	4 040	3 073	14 435	69.4	7.9	24 172	17 047	41.8	3 933	394	1 539	16.6	31.1
Saginaw	37 679	36 301	40 877	131 154	74.8	13.0	36 318	27 980	29.8	32 154	–3 860	14 380	15.3	24.6
St. Clair	27 978	26 479	28 671	91 241	74.8	10.7	42 617	30 692	38.9	14 301	–1 453	5 951	8.9	13.3
St. Joseph	12 064	11 898	11 271	36 757	73.8	10.9	36 779	27 510	33.7	6 853	184	2 937	11.1	16.6
Sanilac	8 861	8 730	8 531	25 404	72.1	8.4	32 199	23 107	39.3	5 322	–323	2 315	12.2	18.7
Schoolcraft	1 273	1 296	1 620	5 643	71.6	8.9	28 681	20 112	42.6	1 356	–9	546	15.6	25.0
Shiawassee	14 359	14 591	14 272	43 097	78.7	10.3	38 430	30 283	26.9	7 366	58	2 973	10.1	14.3
Tuscola	12 330	12 169	11 194	34 607	73.0	8.1	36 568	27 374	33.6	6 401	–565	2 641	11.0	16.0
Van Buren	17 646	16 867	14 747	43 758	71.8	12.1	33 852	25 491	32.8	11 345	889	4 932	14.9	22.2
Washtenaw	45 043	39 986	38 789	167 214	87.2	41.9	51 286	36 307	41.3	25 107	–6 670	7 960	8.7	12.0
Wayne	354 874	339 120	366 707	1 324 635	70.0	13.7	35 357	27 997	26.3	383 172	–35 095	163 749	18.0	28.5
Wexford	5 775	5 707	5 449	16 597	74.6	12.6	31 841	22 915	39.0	3 975	163	1 768	13.5	21.0
MINNESOTA	856 410	821 404	747 713	2 770 562	82.4	21.8	41 591	30 909	34.6	417 797	–17 534	167 853	8.9	13.1
Aitkin	2 361	2 400	2 290	8 891	70.5	9.5	26 746	17 564	52.3	2 125	–164	876	14.9	25.9
Anoka	63 683	59 258	48 509	145 367	86.7	15.5	53 308	40 076	33.0	15 472	2 657	6 971	5.3	8.1
Becker	5 006	5 173	5 750	17 832	72.9	12.0	30 323	20 920	44.9	4 309	–557	1 852	14.6	21.5
Beltrami	8 336	8 115	6 981	19 231	75.9	20.4	29 851	20 925	42.7	7 113	–657	3 129	18.9	26.8
Benton	5 155	5 105	5 289	17 612	77.3	14.8	38 241	26 619	43.7	2 918	–110	1 295	8.5	12.4
Big Stone	1 340	1 432	1 208	4 312	72.3	10.1	27 919	19 408	43.9	755	–159	309	13.7	21.9
Blue Earth	10 407	10 704	7 993	29 251	82.7	22.7	37 135	25 366	46.4	5 365	–3 916	1 601	10.5	12.9
Brown	4 496	4 595	3 864	17 308	71.7	12.3	36 938	25 032	47.6	1 959	–218	734	7.4	10.0
Carlton	6 560	6 599	6 004	18 964	75.1	12.2	36 871	24 900	48.1	3 123	–361	1 258	10.3	14.6
Carver	11 379	9 604	8 075	29 247	84.6	21.4	58 797	39 188	50.0	2 421	133	980	3.7	4.9
Cass	3 610	3 270	4 231	14 648	72.5	11.4	27 704	18 732	47.9	4 014	–607	1 777	15.3	24.5
Chippewa	2 723	2 893	2 618	8 866	73.7	10.9	34 301	22 227	54.3	1 259	–402	493	9.7	13.8
Chisago	7 990	7 209	6 572	18 804	80.1	11.9	46 563	31 281	48.9	2 517	181	1 115	6.1	8.7
Clay	9 295	9 448	8 497	27 817	80.5	21.5	37 711	25 891	45.7	6 088	–1 267	2 165	12.5	16.6
Clearwater	1 803	1 892	1 775	5 362	64.9	9.8	26 177	17 752	47.5	1 562	–279	689	19.1	28.0
Cook	748		710	684	2 760	84.9	20.7	33 460	22 908	46.1	367	–47	131	7.7	11.8
Cottonwood	2 690	2 976	2 377	8 644	71.7	12.3	31 272	21 661	44.4	1 306	–395	518	11.0	16.7
Crow Wing	10 213	9 954	8 455	28 901	75.7	13.5	32 616	22 250	46.6	6 134	–384	2 491	11.8	18.0
Dakota	71 138	64 546	51 248	168 000	90.7	27.6	57 802	42 218	36.9	15 765	4 035	6 701	4.6	6.6
Dodge	2 761	2 695	3 430	9 550	78.7	11.7	42 511	29 071	46.2	1 196	18	489	6.9	8.9
Douglas	7 485	7 897	5 423	18 488	76.1	12.7	34 444	22 067	56.1	2 903	–850	1 095	9.4	13.0
Faribault	2 710	2 947	3 324	11 496	74.4	12.0	31 670	22 421	41.3	1 697	–296	669	10.5	15.6
Fillmore	3 471	3 604	3 989	13 561	70.2	10.5	31 850	22 155	43.8	2 181	–823	842	10.6	14.5
Freeborn	5 141	5 341	6 322	22 152	75.5	11.5	33 893	24 764	36.9	3 249	–71	1 290	10.3	16.2
Goodhue	8 052	8 014	8 187	26 242	78.0	14.1	43 192	29 237	47.7	2 909	–307	1 115	6.8	9.2
Grant	1 570	1 424	1 222	4 341	71.9	11.4	30 909	19 773	56.3	722	–193	278	12.0	17.5
Hennepin	169 430	159 130	142 980	686 381	88.2	31.6	48 054	35 659	34.8	99 321	5 933	38 669	9.4	15.5
Houston	3 652	3 472	3 346	11 874	75.9	14.4	38 078	25 846	47.3	1 541	–63	614	8.0	11.1
Hubbard	2 893	2 878	3 041	9 984	76.4	14.7	28 457	20 151	41.2	2 352	–187	943	13.9	20.6
Isanti	6 069	5 857	5 761	15 856	78.2	11.5	43 409	31 308	38.7	2 194	4	989	7.3	10.5
Itasca	8 122	8 486	8 480	26 470	77.5	12.5	32 769	22 442	46.0	5 428	–934	2 173	12.3	17.9
Jackson	1 947	2 104	2 269	7 750	74.2	10.0	33 304	23 157	43.8	1 083	–259	414	9.5	13.2
Kanabec	2 836	2 821	2 875	8 021	69.9	8.9	31 555	22 495	40.3	1 789	–171	787	12.5	18.2
Kandiyohi	7 617	7 259	7 652	24 026	76.3	15.7	36 767	25 368	44.9	4 542	–622	1 910	11.2	16.2
Kittson	1 099	1 218	1 144	3 953	71.0	12.5	31 221	23 518	32.8	640	–37	257	12.2	18.8
Koochiching	2 531	2 625	2 972	10 849	73.0	10.4	34 633	23 411	47.9	1 760	–307	685	11.7	18.1
Lac qui Parle	2 080	1 906	1 751	6 160	72.2	10.9	32 011	21 646	47.9	732	–397	247	9.3	11.8
Lake	2 139	2 246	1 948	7 303	80.2	12.2	35 598	23 478	51.6	866	–104	315	8.1	12.7
Lake of the Woods	867	853	821	2 687	75.2	11.0	32 302	24 383	32.5	417	–10	176	9.1	13.8
Le Sueur	3 922	3 753	4 510	14 595	76.3	13.1	40 833	27 706	47.4	1 827	–200	744	7.2	10.0
Lincoln	1 036	1 122	1 401	4 753	67.7	8.4	27 341	19 211	42.3	765	–287	276	12.0	16.4
Lyon	4 824	6 505	4 355	14 755	75.9	16.8	37 367	24 689	51.4	2 170	–567	836	9.2	12.3
McLeod	6 361	6 397	5 572	20 077	75.5	11.7	43 010	29 549	45.6	2 167	–208	864	6.3	8.7
Mahnomen	1 451	1 542	1 205	3 162	64.7	10.5	24 664	16 924	45.7	1 035	–251	490	20.5	30.4
Marshall	1 869	2 300	2 451	7 177	68.5	10.2	30 975	21 707	42.7	1 200	–294	491	11.6	16.6
Martin	2 759	2 947	4 181	15 472	75.2	13.0	34 839	24 414	42.7	2 269	–391	866	10.4	14.9
Meeker	5 323	5 824	4 273	13 367	73.4	10.0	36 119	24 516	47.3	1 863	–336	769	8.6	11.9

[1] Revised. [2] 1997 data are model-based estimates; 1989 data are census estimates. For more information on these estimates, see appendix A. Source Notes and Explanations or <http://www.census.gov/hhes/www/saipe.html>.

Sources: Public School Enrollment, 1998-1999 and 1994-1995—U.S. National Center for Education Statistics, <http://nces.ed.gov/ccd/pubagency.html> (accessed: 16 March 2001). Public School Enrollment and Educational Attainment, 1990—U.S. Census Bureau, "1990 Census of Population and Housing, Summary Tape File (STF) 3C" on CD-ROM (related Internet site <http://homer.ssd.census.gov/cdrom/lookup>). Income and Poverty, 1997—U.S. Census Bureau, "State and County Income and Poverty Estimates - 1997," published 22 November 2000, <http://www.census.gov/housing/saipe/estmod97/est97ALL.dat>. Income and Poverty, 1989—U.S. Census Bureau, "1990 Census of Population and Housing, Summary Tape File (STF) 3C" on CD-ROM (related Internet site <http://homer.ssd.census.gov/cdrom/lookup>).

Table B–5. Counties — Education, Income, and Poverty–Con.

[Includes U.S., states, and 3,142 counties or county equivalents defined as of January 1, 1992. For changes to these areas since January 1, 1992, see appendix B. Geographic Information]

County	Public school enrollment Fall 1998–1999	Public school enrollment Fall 1994–1995[1]	Public school enrollment 1990	Educational attainment, 1990 Persons 25 years and over	Percent— High school graduate or higher	Percent— Bachelor's degree or higher	Median household income[2] 1997 (dollars)	Median household income[2] 1989 (dollars)	Percent change, 1989–1997	Persons below poverty level,[2] 1997 Number Persons of all ages Total	Net change, 1989–1997	Persons under 18 years	Percent Persons of all ages	Percent Persons under 18 years
MINNESOTA—Con.														
Mille Lacs	6 276	6 095	3 912	11 869	70.1	9.4	31 218	22 689	37.6	2 647	107	1 165	12.6	19.1
Morrison	6 237	6 357	6 177	18 106	67.7	9.0	31 100	22 102	40.7	4 067	–600	1 790	13.3	18.6
Mower	6 113	6 052	6 530	25 099	75.8	12.9	34 330	23 763	44.5	3 730	59	1 446	10.1	15.4
Murray	1 536	1 591	1 828	6 461	69.7	8.5	31 594	22 673	39.3	934	–419	350	9.8	13.4
Nicollet	2 346	2 470	4 532	16 232	81.5	22.4	42 786	30 491	40.3	2 048	–209	722	7.4	9.1
Nobles	3 634	3 707	3 790	13 163	70.4	11.1	32 516	22 942	41.7	2 089	–202	828	10.9	16.3
Norman	1 441	1 602	1 689	5 421	69.7	9.7	29 518	21 238	39.0	1 029	–91	415	13.9	20.2
Olmsted	21 171	20 136	17 644	67 315	88.0	29.5	49 000	35 789	36.9	8 144	989	3 262	7.0	10.1
Otter Tail	11 146	10 977	9 118	33 883	71.6	13.0	31 721	21 909	44.8	6 201	–796	2 450	11.4	16.8
Pennington	2 535	2 642	2 603	8 374	72.3	13.7	31 848	21 571	47.6	1 504	–610	586	11.2	15.8
Pine	3 469	3 514	4 481	13 813	69.2	9.5	30 820	21 191	45.4	3 073	90	1 327	13.3	19.6
Pipestone	2 200	2 239	1 893	6 806	70.4	9.4	31 021	20 737	49.6	1 080	–426	425	10.9	14.9
Polk	6 088	6 602	6 259	20 677	73.0	12.9	32 126	22 559	42.4	4 339	–159	1 776	14.3	20.1
Pope	103	106	2 194	7 216	72.1	10.2	31 165	20 131	54.8	1 167	–284	468	10.8	15.4
Ramsey	88 986	80 387	67 359	310 366	85.0	28.8	42 284	32 043	32.0	55 092	1 195	23 613	11.5	19.2
Red Lake	1 478	1 014	900	2 917	64.3	9.3	29 033	19 926	45.7	515	–160	199	12.1	15.4
Redwood	3 062	3 166	3 137	11 396	71.3	11.1	34 606	22 827	51.6	1 497	–670	583	9.1	12.4
Renville	1 581	2 045	3 296	11 709	71.7	10.2	34 940	23 278	50.1	1 839	–394	751	10.9	15.9
Rice	8 393	8 055	8 111	28 207	78.7	19.3	42 685	29 596	44.2	3 898	107	1 436	7.9	10.1
Rock	1 779	1 898	1 998	6 432	69.8	10.8	34 775	24 483	42.0	766	–406	285	7.9	10.4
Roseau	3 867	3 656	3 177	9 063	71.8	10.2	36 832	25 910	42.2	1 246	–421	507	7.7	9.9
St. Louis	31 819	31 779	34 552	129 893	80.3	17.3	36 254	24 093	50.5	22 568	–4 633	7 936	11.7	16.8
Scott	12 697	11 255	10 744	34 888	84.8	17.2	59 412	40 798	45.6	3 091	741	1 367	3.9	5.5
Sherburne	12 893	10 609	8 477	23 976	84.2	16.7	51 450	35 585	44.6	3 351	138	1 391	5.6	7.1
Sibley	1 455	1 454	2 718	9 320	68.2	8.9	33 692	24 957	35.0	1 336	–140	552	9.1	13.1
Stearns	24 936	25 488	20 936	65 025	78.3	17.5	38 806	27 512	41.1	10 645	–3 179	4 198	8.5	11.6
Steele	6 422	6 216	5 714	19 253	79.4	16.0	43 657	30 571	42.8	2 318	295	978	7.3	10.6
Stevens	1 704	1 888	1 801	5 903	77.0	17.0	36 408	21 921	66.1	928	–1 088	271	9.8	11.5
Swift	1 229	1 481	2 045	7 364	68.2	11.2	30 259	18 740	61.5	1 256	–221	446	12.3	15.7
Todd	4 805	5 048	5 104	14 632	68.4	7.8	27 846	18 836	47.8	3 625	–754	1 554	15.0	20.9
Traverse	709	756	873	3 086	71.2	9.8	29 980	20 746	44.5	578	–76	232	13.8	20.9
Wabasha	4 157	4 103	3 837	12 597	76.4	12.4	38 159	26 998	41.3	1 565	–70	655	7.5	10.8
Wadena	1 787	1 856	2 618	8 498	70.6	11.6	27 036	17 333	56.0	2 104	–679	762	16.2	20.9
Waseca	4 089	4 420	3 554	11 260	77.5	13.6	38 187	26 992	41.5	1 536	–110	615	8.5	11.5
Washington	34 329	32 459	29 364	89 896	90.0	26.2	61 994	44 122	40.5	7 839	1 627	3 118	4.0	5.2
Watonwan	2 194	2 218	2 204	7 614	72.2	10.1	31 722	22 496	41.0	1 182	–205	508	10.3	15.9
Wilkin	1 469	1 611	1 375	4 831	73.8	11.6	35 206	23 081	52.5	836	31	345	11.4	16.6
Winona	6 686	6 549	6 907	27 444	77.7	19.7	36 450	25 937	40.5	4 553	–1 068	1 616	10.1	13.6
Wright	18 421	16 598	14 733	40 413	80.1	12.1	47 713	33 456	42.6	5 091	476	2 189	5.9	7.8
Yellow Medicine	2 218	2 255	2 224	7 825	72.6	9.9	32 582	21 537	51.3	1 099	–593	359	9.7	11.5
MISSISSIPPI	503 742	505 962	509 252	1 538 997	64.3	14.7	28 527	20 136	41.7	494 044	–136 985	188 272	18.1	24.5
Adams	5 391	5 561	6 377	22 376	67.3	14.8	23 444	17 214	36.2	7 797	–2 837	2 869	22.6	30.8
Alcorn	5 587	5 814	5 963	20 746	56.3	9.6	28 057	18 538	51.3	5 020	–1 492	1 740	15.2	21.7
Amite	1 729	2 038	2 355	8 224	57.1	8.7	24 072	15 669	53.6	2 595	–1 505	980	18.4	24.8
Attala	3 577	3 592	3 437	11 741	51.4	10.0	21 854	15 380	42.1	3 979	–1 533	1 498	21.5	30.9
Benton	1 292	1 408	1 695	4 843	46.4	7.8	23 458	15 794	48.5	1 598	–783	601	19.5	26.3
Bolivar	8 866	9 568	10 035	21 777	54.9	15.2	21 110	14 020	50.6	11 505	–5 653	4 566	29.4	34.9
Calhoun	2 573	2 720	2 707	9 453	52.8	8.2	24 965	18 182	37.3	2 518	–634	941	16.8	24.8
Carroll	1 266	1 220	1 472	5 775	54.0	10.3	24 421	16 639	46.8	1 837	–786	715	18.0	25.9
Chickasaw	3 500	3 894	3 638	10 861	52.9	9.5	24 926	18 259	36.5	3 036	–778	1 208	16.6	23.0
Choctaw	1 927	1 896	1 871	5 558	57.6	10.8	23 367	17 313	35.0	2 016	–196	774	21.5	29.2
Claiborne	2 018	2 195	2 238	5 432	58.7	16.1	20 137	12 876	56.4	2 854	–1 233	990	28.6	31.4
Clarke	3 517	3 390	3 711	10 624	61.6	8.2	26 236	19 055	37.7	2 732	–1 263	1 057	14.8	20.9
Clay	4 190	4 421	4 333	12 282	60.4	12.9	25 464	18 337	38.9	4 553	–761	1 842	21.2	28.3
Coahoma	6 648	7 266	7 633	17 510	54.0	14.7	19 895	13 780	44.4	9 338	–4 659	3 790	30.0	36.4
Copiah	4 956	5 226	5 401	15 962	61.1	9.4	23 107	16 583	39.3	5 908	–2 620	2 265	20.7	27.4
Covington	3 608	3 704	3 668	9 687	55.5	8.6	23 798	17 589	35.3	3 504	–1 633	1 379	19.4	25.8
DeSoto	18 180	15 293	12 262	41 533	71.2	9.5	43 386	31 756	36.6	7 495	199	2 999	7.6	11.1
Forrest	11 874	11 889	12 399	38 761	72.1	19.8	27 652	17 986	53.7	13 031	–4 530	4 702	18.3	24.9
Franklin	1 778	1 857	1 713	5 233	58.1	7.4	22 749	14 341	58.6	1 645	–1 115	594	19.7	24.9
George	3 967	3 779	3 778	9 846	58.8	8.3	28 656	18 397	55.8	3 086	–950	1 223	15.5	20.9
Greene	1 884	2 002	2 246	6 137	62.4	6.0	24 753	17 958	37.8	2 418	–167	842	22.3	25.4
Grenada	4 637	4 152	4 191	13 252	56.5	10.8	26 468	19 955	32.6	4 096	–645	1 608	18.1	25.4
Hancock	6 359	5 811	5 152	20 398	68.0	14.3	29 168	20 720	40.8	6 172	–889	2 324	15.3	22.5
Harrison	30 446	29 951	29 532	99 878	74.7	16.3	30 706	22 157	38.6	26 059	–3 969	10 283	14.9	21.4
Hinds	43 954	44 570	45 683	153 310	75.2	26.4	32 033	24 676	29.8	45 188	–7 147	16 911	18.5	25.8
Holmes	4 812	4 853	5 358	11 623	48.0	9.7	15 307	9 809	56.1	7 728	–3 538	2 983	36.0	41.1
Humphreys	2 475	2 523	2 784	6 605	46.4	10.4	18 014	12 696	41.9	3 631	–1 848	1 526	32.0	40.2
Issaquena	X	X	386	1 099	43.7	5.6	19 249	13 005	48.0	554	–385	219	33.2	41.8

[1] Revised.   [2] 1997 data are model-based estimates; 1989 data are census estimates. For more information on these estimates, see appendix A. Source Notes and Explanations or <http://www.census.gov/hhes/www/saipe.html>.

Sources: Public School Enrollment, 1998-1999 and 1994-1995—U.S. National Center for Education Statistics, <http://nces.ed.gov/ccd/pubagency.html> (accessed: 16 March 2001). Public School Enrollment and Educational Attainment, 1990—U.S. Census Bureau, "1990 Census of Population and Housing, Summary Tape File (STF) 3C" on CD-ROM (related Internet site <http://homer.ssd.census.gov/cdrom/lookup>). Income and Poverty, 1997—U.S. Census Bureau, "State and County Income and Poverty Estimates - 1997," published 22 November 2000, <http://www.census.gov/housing/saipe/estmod97/est97ALL.dat>. Income and Poverty, 1989—U.S. Census Bureau, "1990 Census of Population and Housing, Summary Tape File (STF) 3C" on CD-ROM (related Internet site <http://homer.ssd.census.gov/cdrom/lookup>).

[Includes U.S., states, and 3,142 counties or county equivalents defined as of January 1, 1992. For changes to these areas since January 1, 1992, see appendix B. Geographic Information]

County	Public school enrollment — Fall 1998–1999	Public school enrollment — Fall 1994–1995[1]	Public school enrollment — 1990	Educational attainment, 1990 — Persons 25 years and over	Percent — High school graduate or higher	Percent — Bachelor's degree or higher	Median household income[2] 1997 (dollars)	Median household income[2] 1989 (dollars)	Percent change, 1989–1997	Persons below poverty level,[2] 1997 — Number — Persons of all ages — Total	Net change, 1989–1997	Persons under 18 years	Percent — Persons of all ages	Percent — Persons under 18 years
MISSISSIPPI—Con.														
Itawamba	3 803	3 562	3 660	12 807	49.0	6.7	30 194	20 770	45.4	2 408	−629	878	11.6	17.3
Jackson	25 448	25 035	24 095	69 935	74.4	14.4	34 411	26 444	30.1	17 844	−623	7 057	13.6	19.0
Jasper	3 242	3 253	3 727	10 292	60.0	9.8	23 612	16 130	46.4	3 535	−1 669	1 304	19.8	25.0
Jefferson	1 733	1 954	2 173	4 729	53.0	10.3	16 349	10 267	59.2	2 430	−1 618	898	28.3	32.3
Jefferson Davis	2 462	2 803	3 159	8 267	57.4	8.9	21 064	15 442	36.4	3 402	−1 231	1 406	24.3	33.8
Jones	11 310	12 003	12 466	39 024	64.3	12.2	26 639	19 239	38.5	10 490	−3 322	3 743	16.5	22.1
Kemper	1 481	1 649	2 162	6 182	56.3	7.9	21 670	14 315	51.4	2 089	−1 433	767	20.2	25.8
Lafayette	5 181	5 064	4 875	16 387	70.2	29.2	27 958	18 186	53.7	4 460	−2 392	1 278	14.3	17.7
Lamar	7 469	6 966	6 218	18 151	73.3	20.9	32 363	23 263	39.1	5 625	−83	2 126	14.9	19.3
Lauderdale	14 072	14 414	14 632	46 312	69.7	13.3	28 225	20 414	38.3	13 119	−3 533	5 065	17.5	24.8
Lawrence	2 494	2 653	2 888	7 564	61.9	9.2	24 574	17 519	40.3	2 312	−1 140	888	17.5	23.6
Leake	3 203	3 202	3 471	11 543	54.3	9.2	23 054	15 975	44.3	3 842	−1 563	1 447	19.5	26.8
Lee	14 797	14 162	12 919	40 775	67.8	15.0	33 160	24 647	34.5	9 060	−911	3 551	12.0	17.4
Leflore	7 062	7 585	8 617	20 941	55.3	15.7	21 027	15 219	38.2	10 376	−3 611	3 967	29.1	35.0
Lincoln	6 123	5 983	6 225	19 095	63.0	11.6	25 922	18 193	42.5	5 664	−1 423	2 091	17.7	23.8
Lowndes	11 331	11 571	11 618	34 439	69.0	18.6	30 068	22 985	30.8	10 777	−2 039	4 287	17.7	24.6
Madison	12 229	10 948	9 339	32 164	71.5	29.3	37 445	25 887	44.6	10 463	−2 328	3 984	14.3	19.0
Marion	4 796	4 944	5 617	15 450	58.8	8.4	22 516	16 084	40.0	5 894	−1 512	2 375	22.3	31.1
Marshall	5 233	5 418	5 382	17 629	51.7	9.4	26 328	18 492	42.4	6 158	−2 691	2 359	19.1	25.4
Monroe	6 617	6 620	7 648	22 351	55.6	8.4	27 782	20 047	38.6	5 733	−1 928	2 220	14.9	20.7
Montgomery	2 191	2 282	2 497	7 718	56.6	9.5	21 715	15 396	41.1	2 799	−1 354	1 024	22.4	30.2
Neshoba	4 073	5 594	5 373	15 137	60.9	10.1	27 149	18 237	48.9	4 681	−1 798	1 804	16.9	22.6
Newton	3 688	3 784	3 875	12 426	60.1	9.7	25 659	19 302	32.9	3 490	−597	1 323	16.4	23.0
Noxubee	2 413	2 488	2 586	7 064	49.6	7.9	20 005	14 205	40.8	3 557	−1 636	1 418	28.3	35.5
Oktibbeha	5 583	5 681	5 546	18 826	73.0	31.7	27 224	18 507	47.1	7 125	−2 944	2 148	20.0	24.2
Panola	6 716	6 671	6 711	17 281	54.3	8.7	23 572	17 686	33.3	7 290	−2 741	2 887	21.6	27.8
Pearl River	8 459	8 095	7 650	23 589	68.4	11.4	27 091	20 133	34.6	8 259	104	3 247	17.5	24.9
Perry	2 346	2 526	2 510	6 419	61.8	7.1	24 328	16 230	49.9	2 305	−837	883	19.2	24.6
Pike	7 283	7 449	8 394	22 164	60.6	12.8	21 689	15 149	43.2	8 852	−3 052	3 273	23.2	29.6
Pontotoc	5 122	4 751	4 235	13 954	57.4	8.1	28 991	20 223	43.4	3 266	−539	1 166	12.7	17.1
Prentiss	4 910	4 864	4 431	14 374	52.9	8.4	25 784	17 736	45.4	3 772	−1 105	1 196	15.6	19.8
Quitman	1 722	1 850	2 250	5 948	45.5	9.0	18 118	13 730	32.0	3 142	−1 173	1 228	31.5	38.1
Rankin	18 841	17 755	16 214	55 365	73.8	19.0	41 627	31 668	31.4	10 370	1 465	4 040	9.7	14.0
Scott	5 714	5 634	4 951	14 444	53.1	9.4	23 642	17 040	38.7	4 846	−1 708	1 858	19.1	25.5
Sharkey	1 628	1 809	1 869	3 672	51.3	12.4	17 245	13 304	29.6	2 375	−930	1 003	35.9	43.7
Simpson	4 419	4 421	4 946	14 782	58.0	8.7	25 392	19 053	33.3	4 875	−391	1 827	19.5	25.6
Smith	3 119	3 078	2 974	9 164	57.0	7.6	26 406	19 111	38.2	2 657	−903	973	17.2	22.8
Stone	2 666	2 561	2 200	6 324	68.1	12.4	25 433	19 045	33.5	2 667	58	955	20.7	25.7
Sunflower	6 439	6 966	7 529	18 299	49.2	12.4	19 878	14 431	37.7	9 832	−2 470	3 613	34.3	37.7
Tallahatchie	3 092	3 147	3 340	8 575	48.2	7.9	18 628	13 593	37.0	4 144	−2 184	1 647	27.6	34.5
Tate	4 675	4 735	4 186	12 553	61.0	11.7	30 911	22 207	39.2	3 496	−1 136	1 331	14.9	19.7
Tippah	4 097	4 228	3 922	12 156	54.4	9.0	26 316	17 991	46.3	3 109	−1 219	1 099	14.8	19.9
Tishomingo	3 211	3 153	3 011	11 803	55.0	6.6	25 993	17 500	48.5	2 627	−930	881	13.9	20.5
Tunica	1 999	1 986	2 031	4 110	45.9	8.5	19 322	10 965	76.2	2 169	−2 428	888	26.6	30.5
Union	4 537	4 473	4 226	14 114	57.3	10.1	29 875	21 128	41.4	3 051	−522	1 116	12.6	18.1
Walthall	2 768	3 029	3 382	8 466	55.0	10.1	20 201	14 135	42.9	3 948	−1 153	1 465	27.2	33.2
Warren	9 402	9 597	10 190	29 311	67.7	19.1	31 459	22 804	38.0	8 435	−2 169	3 414	16.9	23.7
Washington	12 970	13 721	15 272	37 954	58.8	14.3	24 001	17 492	37.2	17 067	−5 604	7 013	26.0	32.9
Wayne	4 211	4 157	4 476	11 588	56.1	8.9	24 508	16 095	52.3	4 264	−1 455	1 581	20.7	25.4
Webster	2 035	2 087	2 082	6 464	58.6	10.8	23 856	17 094	39.6	1 840	−616	723	17.4	26.1
Wilkinson	1 777	1 788	1 726	5 811	48.3	8.9	18 282	11 910	53.5	2 654	−1 379	940	28.8	35.2
Winston	3 427	3 754	4 066	11 937	59.1	10.8	26 181	18 320	42.9	3 691	−1 417	1 364	18.9	25.0
Yalobusha	2 234	2 397	2 312	7 666	55.7	9.9	23 057	15 885	45.1	2 754	−393	976	21.9	29.0
Yazoo	4 878	5 069	5 380	14 976	53.4	12.0	20 670	14 234	45.2	7 065	−2 796	2 850	27.5	35.5
MISSOURI	913 689	864 301	808 221	3 291 579	73.9	17.8	34 502	26 362	30.9	658 159	−4 916	252 485	12.2	17.7
Adair	2 947	3 020	3 319	13 091	74.3	22.7	28 246	17 285	63.4	3 287	−2 031	899	15.4	18.2
Andrew	2 881	2 869	2 780	9 492	78.6	13.5	37 621	26 103	44.1	1 352	−496	501	8.7	11.6
Atchison	1 277	1 211	1 208	4 970	76.8	14.2	31 287	20 126	55.5	823	−432	241	12.4	15.0
Audrain	3 781	3 755	4 090	15 722	68.0	10.9	32 606	23 424	39.2	2 922	−516	1 144	12.5	18.1
Barry	6 637	6 137	4 830	18 539	67.4	8.5	26 543	19 169	38.5	5 171	659	2 118	15.5	24.1
Barton	2 179	2 218	2 008	7 530	68.2	8.2	28 536	19 951	43.0	1 649	58	653	13.6	19.6
Bates	2 993	2 933	2 809	10 089	66.9	8.4	28 735	20 085	43.1	2 259	−344	860	14.2	20.2
Benton	2 768	2 412	2 213	10 013	64.5	7.7	23 451	16 925	38.6	2 955	207	1 020	17.3	27.8
Bollinger	2 101	2 007	1 895	6 930	52.7	6.9	26 068	19 430	34.2	1 913	−155	733	16.4	23.0
Boone	20 649	18 721	16 120	62 424	84.8	36.5	38 421	25 647	49.8	13 817	−3 063	4 343	11.4	14.3
Buchanan	14 368	14 081	14 349	53 549	72.1	13.5	31 544	23 019	37.0	11 698	−849	4 289	14.4	19.8
Butler	6 797	6 914	7 031	25 486	56.8	8.6	24 073	16 285	47.8	8 120	−1 377	3 056	20.0	29.0
Caldwell	1 905	1 781	1 549	5 580	75.4	8.1	28 742	19 448	47.8	1 183	−304	434	13.5	17.9
Callaway	6 085	4 729	5 660	20 493	70.1	13.9	35 105	26 663	31.7	3 747	586	1 476	10.6	14.7

[1] Revised. [2] 1997 data are model-based estimates; 1989 data are census estimates. For more information on these estimates, see appendix A. Source Notes and Explanations or <http://www.census.gov/hhes/www/saipe.html>.

Sources: Public School Enrollment, 1998-1999 and 1994-1995—U.S. National Center for Education Statistics, <http://nces.ed.gov/ccd/pubagency.html> (accessed: 16 March 2001). Public School Enrollment and Educational Attainment, 1990—U.S. Census Bureau, "1990 Census of Population and Housing, Summary Tape File (STF) 3C" on CD-ROM (related Internet site <http://homer.ssd.census.gov/cdrom/lookup>). Income and Poverty, 1997—U.S. Census Bureau, "State and County Income and Poverty Estimates - 1997," published 22 November 2000, <http://www.census.gov/housing/saipe/estmod97/est97ALL.dat>. Income and Poverty, 1989—U.S. Census Bureau, "1990 Census of Population and Housing, Summary Tape File (STF) 3C" on CD-ROM (related Internet site <http://homer.ssd.census.gov/cdrom/lookup>).

Table B–5. Counties — Education, Income, and Poverty-Con.

[Includes U.S., states, and 3,142 counties or county equivalents defined as of January 1, 1992. For changes to these areas since January 1, 1992, see appendix B. Geographic Information]

County	Public school enrollment Fall 1998–1999	Public school enrollment Fall 1994–1995[1]	Public school enrollment 1990	Educational attainment, 1990 Persons 25 years and over	Percent High school graduate or higher	Percent Bachelor's degree or higher	Median household income[2] 1997 (dollars)	Median household income[2] 1989 (dollars)	Percent change, 1989–1997	Persons below poverty level,[2] 1997 Number Persons of all ages Total	Net change, 1989–1997	Persons under 18 years	Percent Persons of all ages	Percent Persons under 18 years
MISSOURI—Con.														
Camden	5 269	4 666	4 165	19 732	73.6	12.4	30 225	22 564	34.0	4 131	708	1 586	12.1	21.6
Cape Girardeau	9 622	9 190	8 917	37 822	74.4	19.2	36 264	24 510	48.0	7 476	−649	2 585	11.6	16.1
Carroll	1 919	1 929	2 130	7 185	70.3	11.7	27 937	19 697	41.8	1 495	1	574	14.6	20.8
Carter	1 423	1 445	1 146	3 544	56.0	8.8	20 808	15 357	35.5	1 599	95	662	24.8	36.3
Cass	15 436	13 958	11 923	39 787	80.0	13.0	43 100	31 373	37.4	5 830	666	2 392	7.2	10.1
Cedar	2 455	2 191	1 976	8 472	63.9	7.6	23 423	16 939	38.3	2 406	−60	873	18.3	27.4
Chariton	1 465	1 471	1 579	6 216	71.3	10.4	28 790	20 829	38.2	1 092	−206	389	12.6	16.9
Christian	9 436	8 082	6 459	20 518	76.6	12.5	36 236	25 995	39.4	4 518	1 254	1 952	9.1	13.8
Clark	1 413	1 431	1 423	4 867	67.4	7.9	29 168	19 674	48.3	1 087	−430	400	14.5	19.4
Clay	31 377	28 660	25 148	98 948	84.7	20.0	46 602	34 370	35.6	9 808	990	3 764	5.5	8.3
Clinton	3 438	3 152	3 248	10 737	77.1	10.3	37 405	26 306	42.2	1 785	−164	662	9.4	12.2
Cole	12 077	12 422	9 106	41 262	77.3	22.3	42 486	30 362	39.9	5 301	683	1 906	8.2	10.8
Cooper	2 589	2 540	2 366	9 232	70.9	11.5	31 567	22 785	38.5	1 682	−32	586	11.6	15.0
Crawford	3 462	3 457	3 793	12 559	58.6	7.1	27 143	19 711	37.7	3 550	506	1 446	15.8	23.3
Dade	1 418	1 446	1 210	5 078	71.8	9.0	26 142	18 724	39.6	1 200	−41	448	15.5	22.4
Dallas	2 200	2 027	2 108	8 328	63.0	6.5	24 307	16 673	45.8	2 540	−363	972	16.4	22.6
Daviess	1 375	1 320	1 296	5 196	70.6	8.9	27 477	18 351	49.7	1 286	−510	511	16.2	22.9
DeKalb	1 410	1 431	1 557	6 811	73.1	8.3	30 996	22 771	36.1	1 429	359	398	16.7	17.0
Dent	2 583	2 581	2 667	9 070	53.9	7.9	24 695	16 594	48.8	2 765	−624	1 024	19.5	27.0
Douglas	1 933	1 882	2 166	7 876	59.8	7.5	21 955	16 187	35.6	2 704	−261	1 033	21.5	30.8
Dunklin	6 229	6 059	6 428	21 522	51.2	8.0	23 341	15 388	51.7	7 827	−1 876	3 054	23.9	33.8
Franklin	17 042	15 696	13 831	50 038	67.5	9.3	39 611	28 622	38.4	7 778	1 210	3 154	8.4	11.8
Gasconade	3 226	2 999	2 364	9 518	61.1	8.0	31 080	22 328	39.2	1 581	107	576	10.7	15.3
Gentry	1 414	1 346	1 220	4 725	71.0	10.3	26 553	17 594	50.9	884	−364	293	13.0	16.5
Greene	36 127	34 784	31 048	129 726	78.9	20.7	33 087	24 285	36.2	26 959	−808	9 731	12.2	18.5
Grundy	1 792	1 774	1 760	7 315	71.3	10.1	28 036	18 084	55.0	1 492	−594	512	14.8	20.9
Harrison	1 603	1 547	1 434	5 989	71.6	8.3	24 936	17 460	42.8	1 312	−240	462	15.6	23.0
Henry	3 344	3 322	3 414	13 607	67.6	10.3	27 021	18 476	46.2	3 091	−469	1 141	14.5	21.3
Hickory	1 921	1 811	1 002	5 547	60.4	6.4	20 755	16 010	29.6	1 682	105	557	19.4	32.1
Holt	992	951	1 124	4 072	75.4	12.2	28 075	18 729	49.9	777	−253	277	14.1	18.9
Howard	1 658	1 602	1 500	6 153	69.9	16.8	28 827	21 378	34.8	1 285	13	473	13.9	18.7
Howell	7 311	6 609	5 456	20 594	61.2	8.7	23 423	16 564	41.4	7 022	−804	2 740	19.6	28.6
Iron	2 459	2 490	2 090	7 034	56.3	6.8	23 782	17 303	37.4	2 222	−217	897	20.8	30.2
Jackson	107 949	101 466	106 577	411 005	79.5	20.0	37 732	27 853	35.5	80 422	−720	31 412	12.2	18.4
Jasper	18 167	17 055	15 476	58 533	71.4	13.4	29 877	20 924	42.8	13 943	413	5 326	14.0	20.5
Jefferson	35 556	34 357	31 477	104 226	71.6	9.0	43 172	32 281	33.7	15 310	2 624	6 450	7.8	11.0
Johnson	8 056	7 675	6 785	22 252	80.7	21.4	33 270	23 044	44.4	5 303	−519	1 837	12.1	15.1
Knox	731	661	733	3 116	72.2	8.1	23 041	17 293	33.2	796	−202	287	18.2	26.7
Laclede	5 939	5 269	5 113	17 456	64.4	8.0	28 136	20 122	39.8	4 675	188	1 836	15.0	21.7
Lafayette	5 940	5 862	5 381	20 215	71.1	11.5	33 304	24 669	35.0	3 483	−214	1 317	10.8	14.9
Lawrence	5 877	5 710	5 348	19 670	68.9	9.7	27 968	20 643	35.5	4 856	115	1 843	14.7	20.2
Lewis	1 713	1 762	1 687	6 385	71.7	10.3	29 314	20 575	42.5	1 376	−275	454	14.6	18.5
Lincoln	6 873	6 069	5 269	17 875	66.8	8.0	38 449	28 054	37.1	3 725	366	1 561	10.1	14.1
Linn	2 967	2 895	2 440	9 502	70.8	10.6	26 477	17 367	52.5	1 939	−428	683	14.2	19.1
Livingston	2 509	2 463	2 546	9 827	71.7	12.5	31 104	21 647	43.7	1 769	−304	631	13.1	17.8
McDonald	3 562	2 937	2 970	10 770	61.1	6.6	24 802	17 312	43.3	3 844	400	1 603	19.0	28.1
Macon	2 526	2 645	2 765	10 391	70.3	11.5	28 263	20 271	39.4	1 812	−350	663	11.9	16.9
Madison	2 173	2 136	2 004	7 371	54.4	6.7	24 462	17 100	43.1	2 044	−343	759	17.7	25.1
Maries	1 507	1 509	1 334	5 237	61.2	8.3	27 017	19 041	41.9	1 207	−90	447	14.3	20.1
Marion	5 274	5 353	4 990	17 891	70.9	12.9	31 109	21 420	45.2	3 803	−712	1 457	13.8	18.6
Mercer	672	666	721	2 686	71.0	8.2	25 537	16 629	53.6	575	−98	178	14.4	18.6
Miller	5 020	4 939	3 940	13 204	63.0	7.5	26 659	18 985	40.4	3 441	−116	1 316	15.3	21.3
Mississippi	2 699	2 771	3 172	9 042	49.2	7.2	22 987	16 159	42.3	3 509	−699	1 515	26.1	37.6
Moniteau	2 451	2 429	2 020	7 862	67.8	8.7	31 941	22 110	44.5	1 257	−123	495	9.6	13.0
Monroe	1 904	1 895	1 613	5 965	69.8	8.1	29 763	19 804	50.3	1 093	−532	397	12.1	15.4
Montgomery	2 110	2 097	2 112	7 559	62.6	7.8	30 011	21 726	38.1	1 532	1	594	12.8	18.1
Morgan	2 249	2 009	2 187	10 837	64.3	7.2	25 603	19 158	33.6	2 934	361	1 091	15.8	25.0
New Madrid	3 696	3 816	4 435	13 020	52.0	6.7	24 772	17 491	41.6	4 541	−993	1 900	22.3	30.7
Newton	8 386	7 510	7 684	28 517	72.8	12.1	31 236	22 263	40.3	6 387	257	2 424	12.9	18.2
Nodaway	3 136	3 302	3 338	11 798	80.7	17.5	32 332	20 347	58.9	2 256	−1 877	586	12.3	12.3
Oregon	1 954	1 876	1 647	6 495	59.3	7.8	19 847	13 705	44.8	2 443	−119	873	23.8	34.6
Osage	1 707	1 651	1 776	7 377	65.0	7.1	36 171	24 983	44.8	993	−160	351	7.9	9.8
Ozark	1 840	1 813	1 505	6 072	60.9	8.0	21 345	16 417	30.0	2 128	249	783	21.2	33.3
Pemiscot	4 592	4 666	4 811	13 204	49.5	6.8	20 938	13 911	50.5	6 106	−1 622	2 654	28.4	37.6
Perry	2 523	2 464	2 550	10 602	56.4	6.4	33 561	23 803	41.0	1 723	−157	617	9.9	12.1
Pettis	6 258	6 187	5 950	23 146	72.2	12.5	30 831	22 101	39.5	4 924	78	1 952	13.1	19.7
Phelps	6 677	6 303	5 689	21 343	70.1	18.3	29 529	20 885	41.4	5 721	−325	2 047	15.5	22.1
Pike	3 069	2 974	2 900	10 394	67.5	10.6	29 673	21 178	40.1	2 198	−629	822	13.5	18.2
Platte	12 061	11 238	10 088	37 465	87.8	25.6	52 960	38 173	38.7	3 453	227	1 247	4.9	6.8
Polk	4 993	4 573	3 427	13 381	67.0	12.0	26 487	18 672	41.9	4 089	−56	1 456	16.6	22.6

[1] Revised. [2] 1997 data are model-based estimates; 1989 data are census estimates. For more information on these estimates, see appendix A. Source Notes and Explanations or <http://www.census.gov/hhes/www/saipe.html>.

Sources: Public School Enrollment, 1998-1999 and 1994-1995—U.S. National Center for Education Statistics, <http://nces.ed.gov/ccd/pubagency.html> (accessed: 16 March 2001). Public School Enrollment and Educational Attainment, 1990—U.S. Census Bureau, "1990 Census of Population and Housing, Summary Tape File (STF) 3C" on CD-ROM (related Internet site <http://homer.ssd.census.gov/cdrom/lookup>). Income and Poverty, 1997—U.S. Census Bureau, "State and County Income and Poverty Estimates - 1997," published 22 November 2000, <http://www.census.gov/housing/saipe/estmod97/est97ALL.dat>. Income and Poverty, 1989—U.S. Census Bureau, "1990 Census of Population and Housing, Summary Tape File (STF) 3C" on CD-ROM (related Internet site <http://homer.ssd.census.gov/cdrom/lookup>).

[Includes U.S., states, and 3,142 counties or county equivalents defined as of January 1, 1992. For changes to these areas since January 1, 1992, see appendix B. Geographic Information]

County	Public school enrollment — Fall			Educational attainment, 1990			Median household income[2]			Persons below poverty level,[2] 1997				
					Percent—					Number — Persons of all ages			Percent	
	1998–1999	1994–1995[1]	1990	Persons 25 years and over	High school graduate or higher	Bachelor's degree or higher	1997 (dollars)	1989 (dollars)	Percent change, 1989–1997	Total	Net change, 1989–1997	Persons under 18 years	Persons of all ages	Persons under 18 years
MISSOURI—Con.														
Pulaski	7 915	7 752	7 737	22 343	78.5	12.8	31 701	21 559	47.0	4 956	–266	1 945	14.3	16.6
Putnam	864	871	833	3 579	64.5	8.7	23 135	15 549	48.8	866	–135	298	17.5	26.0
Ralls	957	918	1 591	5 606	70.2	7.8	31 825	22 070	44.2	1 080	134	374	12.0	15.3
Randolph	3 840	4 005	4 436	15 976	68.4	10.8	27 987	21 425	30.6	3 712	8	1 264	16.8	20.9
Ray	3 856	3 784	4 303	14 023	71.2	8.4	36 927	27 124	36.1	2 323	61	905	9.7	13.1
Reynolds	1 313	1 338	1 303	4 414	53.1	6.5	22 584	17 008	32.8	1 558	–30	583	23.3	33.3
Ripley	2 359	2 448	2 257	8 033	48.5	6.1	19 671	13 740	43.2	3 684	–130	1 421	26.0	36.6
St. Charles	47 081	41 149	34 897	129 996	83.3	21.2	54 759	40 307	35.9	12 804	2 995	5 215	4.7	6.4
St. Clair	1 668	1 549	1 353	5 933	60.8	7.9	23 256	17 265	34.7	1 730	–113	599	19.2	27.8
Ste. Genevieve	2 206	2 164	2 339	10 251	62.8	7.4	37 170	26 712	39.2	1 649	–255	625	9.4	12.8
St. Francois	10 479	10 045	8 400	31 916	62.5	9.1	28 589	20 745	37.8	8 587	828	3 274	16.3	23.0
St. Louis	155 395	149 655	129 819	660 909	82.3	29.2	47 825	38 127	25.4	72 453	17 850	27 597	7.2	11.2
Saline	4 003	3 944	4 185	15 299	67.3	11.9	28 818	21 685	32.9	2 804	–148	1 017	13.1	17.7
Schuyler	787	801	734	2 884	68.0	8.0	23 895	16 729	42.8	740	–136	261	16.5	22.2
Scotland	764	804	716	3 276	69.5	8.5	24 060	15 944	50.9	864	–331	316	18.0	24.5
Scott	7 887	7 792	7 691	24 664	62.4	9.5	28 760	20 764	38.5	7 055	–62	2 951	17.4	25.0
Shannon	908	896	1 383	4 985	54.0	6.0	19 753	14 910	32.5	2 122	316	842	25.4	37.0
Shelby	1 284	1 320	1 228	4 734	74.2	8.0	27 598	18 316	50.7	929	–283	342	14.0	18.9
Stoddard	5 717	5 697	5 379	19 189	55.9	8.2	26 222	18 259	43.6	5 063	–946	1 836	17.0	24.5
Stone	4 374	3 977	2 925	13 639	70.6	11.1	28 623	21 049	36.0	3 547	769	1 370	13.1	23.0
Sullivan	1 084	923	1 055	4 453	65.8	6.8	23 817	15 826	50.5	1 180	–117	406	17.0	24.2
Taney	5 806	5 244	3 661	17 710	70.8	14.3	27 001	20 260	33.3	4 446	1 117	1 687	13.1	22.2
Texas	4 425	4 576	4 134	14 113	60.9	7.0	22 773	16 757	35.9	4 665	–186	1 750	20.7	28.8
Vernon	3 486	3 392	3 449	12 304	67.8	13.1	26 489	19 641	34.9	3 121	–131	1 186	16.4	22.4
Warren	3 793	3 463	3 045	12 515	68.0	9.1	38 839	28 944	34.2	2 104	25	822	8.5	11.6
Washington	4 106	3 946	4 223	12 397	50.8	5.7	24 649	17 117	44.0	5 269	–93	2 099	23.3	30.4
Wayne	2 169	2 134	1 996	7 873	48.9	5.9	18 786	13 815	36.0	3 338	36	1 190	25.4	37.9
Webster	4 591	4 193	4 600	14 801	66.8	8.5	28 577	20 525	39.2	4 492	89	1 861	15.5	21.7
Worth	453	466	420	1 703	74.3	8.7	23 440	14 568	60.9	431	–99	148	19.1	25.5
Wright	4 036	3 939	3 379	10 737	59.7	7.4	22 330	15 770	41.6	4 043	–145	1 553	20.5	27.1
Independent City														
St. Louis city	45 981	41 054	53 375	255 785	62.8	15.3	26 364	19 458	35.5	86 448	–8 823	35 090	25.7	38.4
MONTANA	159 988	164 341	153 344	507 851	81.0	19.8	29 672	22 988	29.1	135 691	10 838	49 055	15.5	21.3
Beaverhead	1 636	1 802	1 695	5 131	83.9	20.6	29 796	20 925	42.4	1 439	–56	481	16.7	21.0
Big Horn	2 496	2 520	2 704	6 183	69.2	12.8	24 317	19 101	27.3	3 768	–181	1 657	29.6	34.8
Blaine	1 576	1 641	1 682	3 970	70.4	14.4	23 670	18 512	27.9	1 904	79	775	26.8	32.9
Broadwater	797	791	718	2 184	73.9	13.5	29 034	20 257	43.3	675	145	257	16.2	22.9
Carbon	1 671	1 692	1 732	5 609	78.1	19.2	29 010	19 042	52.3	1 230	–107	399	12.9	16.2
Carter	219	214	262	1 032	76.0	10.8	23 505	16 458	42.8	294	–112	88	19.3	23.6
Cascade	14 455	15 156	14 232	49 198	82.9	18.4	31 489	23 700	32.9	11 269	937	4 101	14.4	20.1
Chouteau	1 035	1 128	1 120	3 631	83.4	16.8	30 365	22 362	35.8	676	–191	226	13.2	16.5
Custer	2 195	2 357	2 440	7 644	77.1	16.0	29 451	21 348	38.0	2 022	159	738	17.0	24.4
Daniels	397	462	468	1 587	74.4	11.5	30 409	21 433	41.9	272	–72	91	13.6	19.2
Dawson	1 626	1 824	1 956	6 185	74.5	13.2	31 964	23 414	36.5	1 089	–257	354	12.3	15.9
Deer Lodge	1 648	1 734	1 833	7 007	74.5	11.5	26 692	20 281	31.6	1 852	64	595	19.4	26.7
Fallon	700	733	674	2 013	75.3	10.6	33 260	23 162	43.6	328	–8	103	11.0	12.4
Fergus	2 301	2 389	2 295	8 199	77.4	14.5	28 446	21 398	32.9	1 733	71	581	14.4	18.9
Flathead	13 587	13 317	11 400	38 684	82.1	17.2	32 387	24 145	34.1	10 278	1 849	3 906	14.2	20.4
Gallatin	9 508	9 156	7 724	29 276	90.4	33.8	35 710	23 345	53.0	7 059	–1 076	2 001	11.6	13.9
Garfield	246	290	367	1 026	72.6	8.8	24 808	17 201	44.2	205	–68	73	14.4	18.0
Glacier	3 187	3 256	3 226	6 685	72.0	14.5	22 491	18 598	20.9	4 198	–26	1 850	33.6	40.2
Golden Valley	226	215	156	606	72.4	14.7	20 453	18 062	13.2	216	–26	63	21.2	25.5
Granite	511	548	485	1 729	75.9	16.9	26 063	18 278	42.6	485	–63	163	18.1	24.5
Hill	3 478	3 696	3 690	10 629	78.4	18.1	30 736	25 467	20.7	3 314	235	1 299	19.2	25.3
Jefferson	1 995	1 889	1 708	5 139	81.3	20.8	41 820	31 400	33.2	1 045	477	414	10.4	14.5
Judith Basin	463	488	439	1 583	80.4	19.8	26 198	22 558	16.0	414	68	133	17.6	24.1
Lake	4 772	4 787	4 547	13 194	77.3	15.7	27 169	19 755	37.5	5 475	1 070	2 162	21.4	28.9
Lewis and Clark	10 092	10 425	9 211	30 351	87.4	27.8	36 409	26 409	37.9	6 701	1 244	2 404	12.6	17.6
Liberty	476	564	435	1 462	77.2	16.9	27 412	24 969	9.8	320	–70	86	14.4	16.1
Lincoln	3 569	3 911	3 748	11 218	73.3	12.5	27 934	20 898	33.7	3 549	1 099	1 427	18.7	27.9
McCone	314	1 111	522	1 484	79.5	14.3	28 974	20 487	41.4	283	–133	88	14.4	17.2
Madison	1 134	348	1 126	4 093	85.0	19.7	28 831	22 066	30.7	905	–181	285	13.0	17.0
Meagher	282	328	324	1 236	73.9	14.4	22 471	18 936	18.7	350	–5	110	19.7	25.9
Mineral	828	901	749	2 197	74.0	13.1	26 068	20 938	24.5	771	199	301	20.3	29.4
Missoula	14 032	14 511	13 780	48 247	85.4	27.7	33 248	23 388	42.2	13 365	501	4 295	15.3	20.0
Musselshell	801	885	787	2 826	70.9	11.4	22 923	16 661	37.6	893	–49	290	19.4	26.2
Park	2 435	2 560	2 180	10 093	81.7	19.3	29 845	22 658	31.7	2 196	34	725	13.8	19.1
Petroleum	98	118	94	337	81.9	17.5	24 234	19 219	26.1	102	–31	34	19.5	24.9

[1] Revised. [2] 1997 data are model-based estimates; 1989 data are census estimates. For more information on these estimates, see appendix A. Source Notes and Explanations or <http://www.census.gov/hhes/www/saipe.html>.

Sources: Public School Enrollment, 1998-1999 and 1994-1995—U.S. National Center for Education Statistics, <http://nces.ed.gov/ccd/pubagency.html> (accessed: 16 March 2001). Public School Enrollment and Educational Attainment, 1990—U.S. Census Bureau, "1990 Census of Population and Housing, Summary Tape File (STF) 3C" on CD-ROM (related Internet site <http://homer.ssd.census.gov/cdrom/lookup>). Income and Poverty, 1997—U.S. Census Bureau, "State and County Income and Poverty Estimates - 1997," published 22 November 2000, <http://www.census.gov/housing/saipe/estmod97/est97ALL.dat>. Income and Poverty, 1989—U.S. Census Bureau, "1990 Census of Population and Housing, Summary Tape File (STF) 3C" on CD-ROM (related Internet site <http://homer.ssd.census.gov/cdrom/lookup>).

[Includes U.S., states, and 3,142 counties or county equivalents defined as of January 1, 1992. For changes to these areas since January 1, 1992, see appendix B. Geographic Information]

County	Public school enrollment Fall 1998–1999	Public school enrollment Fall 1994–1995[1]	Public school enrollment 1990	Educational attainment, 1990 Persons 25 years and over	Percent— High school graduate or higher	Percent— Bachelor's degree or higher	Median household income[2] 1997 (dollars)	Median household income[2] 1989 (dollars)	Median household income[2] Percent change, 1989–1997	Persons below poverty level,[2] 1997 Number Persons of all ages Total	Persons below poverty level,[2] 1997 Number Persons of all ages Net change, 1989–1997	Persons below poverty level,[2] 1997 Number Persons under 18 years	Persons below poverty level,[2] 1997 Percent Persons of all ages	Persons below poverty level,[2] 1997 Percent Persons under 18 years
MONTANA—Con.														
Phillips	1 050	1 104	1 100	3 283	74.1	13.1	26 699	22 245	20.0	924	53	341	19.3	24.7
Pondera	1 479	1 531	1 479	4 068	73.7	15.0	28 198	23 533	19.8	1 253	171	477	20.1	26.5
Powder River	390	429	397	1 378	75.2	15.3	29 283	22 354	31.0	277	–99	83	15.3	18.5
Powell	1 122	1 165	1 216	4 476	76.5	16.6	29 595	21 621	36.9	1 138	225	355	19.7	24.4
Prairie	221	254	273	994	71.1	13.2	24 999	16 694	49.7	172	–36	53	12.7	17.2
Ravalli	6 238	6 024	4 868	16 632	79.1	18.2	28 589	21 113	35.4	5 536	1 514	2 129	15.6	23.3
Richland	2 156	2 353	2 386	6 655	75.4	13.4	31 885	23 264	37.1	1 488	6	563	14.5	18.7
Roosevelt	2 915	2 908	2 729	6 292	70.1	11.3	23 953	19 445	23.2	3 415	440	1 535	31.1	39.8
Rosebud	2 293	2 757	2 656	5 890	78.3	13.4	34 889	27 192	28.3	1 999	–104	900	19.9	24.8
Sanders	1 949	2 004	1 777	5 692	75.2	14.8	24 183	18 616	29.9	2 034	354	755	19.8	27.4
Sheridan	773	917	956	3 291	74.5	11.7	29 761	20 728	43.6	528	–223	160	12.5	15.6
Silver Bow	5 643	5 877	5 463	22 443	78.3	17.9	30 795	21 216	45.1	5 581	692	1 887	16.1	23.2
Stillwater	1 556	1 541	1 336	4 341	78.2	16.9	33 897	23 582	43.7	860	178	312	10.6	14.2
Sweet Grass	589	591	621	2 182	78.9	20.0	29 456	20 867	41.2	418	95	145	12.3	16.6
Teton	1 417	1 375	1 246	4 076	76.8	17.8	27 944	22 072	26.6	995	–26	334	15.9	20.4
Toole	1 021	1 148	1 055	3 289	77.4	14.0	30 673	25 108	22.2	745	13	259	15.9	19.7
Treasure	183	185	197	569	85.1	13.2	24 321	18 152	34.0	141	3	54	15.8	22.8
Valley	1 497	1 607	1 691	5 479	78.6	13.2	29 581	21 781	35.8	1 492	144	542	18.0	25.3
Wheatland	392	465	457	1 492	72.2	10.6	21 293	16 946	25.7	453	–3	150	19.8	27.9
Wibaux	224	251	250	799	68.3	10.9	25 010	19 375	29.1	202	–8	71	18.1	23.8
Yellowstone	22 094	22 108	20 669	72 856	83.7	21.5	35 680	25 942	37.5	15 363	1 928	5 394	12.1	16.8
Yellowstone National Park	X	X	13	26	100.0	–	X	31 250	X	X	X	X	X	X
NEBRASKA	291 140	287 100	272 985	996 049	81.8	18.9	35 337	26 016	35.8	158 962	–11 654	57 013	9.6	12.6
Adams	5 017	4 903	4 717	19 138	81.2	15.6	35 771	24 399	46.6	2 737	–45	914	9.7	12.5
Antelope	1 230	1 340	1 581	5 122	77.5	9.9	30 271	18 447	64.1	958	–567	337	13.0	15.1
Arthur	90	103	83	319	83.7	13.8	19 468	19 038	2.3	59	6	16	13.5	15.4
Banner	192	204	185	559	87.7	12.0	29 688	22 176	33.9	62	–124	18	6.9	7.1
Blaine	153	174	132	448	85.3	15.8	22 144	19 716	12.3	87	–68	31	14.6	18.2
Boone	1 317	1 299	1 232	4 367	76.1	9.4	31 324	21 653	44.7	765	–164	272	12.0	14.8
Box Butte	2 741	2 965	2 797	8 207	84.0	13.0	39 126	26 493	47.7	1 450	–65	597	11.3	14.3
Boyd	578	597	561	1 965	72.1	9.9	23 212	16 329	42.2	337	–206	104	13.2	14.0
Brown	652	691	710	2 487	79.8	11.3	25 684	17 067	50.5	535	–140	191	15.1	20.4
Buffalo	7 307	7 217	6 542	20 731	83.3	23.7	36 296	23 999	51.2	3 960	–908	1 267	10.3	12.3
Burt	1 661	1 683	1 539	5 399	77.6	13.5	31 585	21 061	50.0	820	–328	264	10.4	12.6
Butler	1 336	1 308	1 318	5 672	72.5	8.0	34 451	23 267	48.1	738	–226	255	8.5	10.4
Cass	3 812	3 468	4 207	13 504	82.1	13.6	42 623	28 490	49.6	1 891	269	728	7.7	10.3
Cedar	1 726	1 864	1 705	6 378	75.2	10.3	33 078	21 014	57.4	872	–434	323	9.1	11.0
Chase	1 010	1 117	936	2 895	79.0	15.1	32 125	21 488	49.5	502	–102	180	11.8	14.7
Cherry	1 092	1 155	1 131	4 201	75.2	13.1	27 326	18 962	44.1	1 010	–376	345	15.9	19.7
Cheyenne	2 061	2 080	1 799	6 234	80.3	15.1	33 886	23 400	44.8	1 110	154	432	11.6	16.5
Clay	1 522	1 592	1 446	4 781	76.9	11.7	34 467	22 949	50.2	754	–17	281	10.6	14.6
Colfax	2 162	2 110	1 651	6 001	70.4	8.5	31 357	22 140	41.6	851	–96	286	8.0	10.5
Cuming	1 702	1 628	1 443	6 690	71.5	11.8	33 874	21 623	56.7	883	–78	324	8.9	11.5
Custer	2 255	2 446	2 345	8 338	80.5	10.8	29 595	21 440	38.0	1 654	31	612	13.9	18.7
Dakota	3 640	3 383	3 109	10 152	74.9	11.7	35 037	25 397	38.0	1 934	18	818	10.3	14.1
Dawes	1 568	1 662	1 669	5 099	80.0	23.1	26 992	17 784	51.8	1 438	–406	457	17.7	20.7
Dawson	5 028	4 890	4 263	13 032	78.8	12.3	32 285	22 420	44.0	2 464	383	1 000	10.6	15.1
Deuel	512	463	475	1 533	79.2	12.9	31 843	21 272	49.7	155	–115	51	7.6	9.3
Dixon	826	796	1 210	4 033	76.1	11.0	32 331	20 047	61.3	565	–318	188	8.9	10.4
Dodge	6 363	6 361	5 953	22 442	78.3	13.5	36 298	24 817	46.3	2 952	–22	1 024	8.5	11.3
Douglas	76 765	73 393	65 715	261 876	84.5	24.9	42 260	29 857	41.5	44 506	542	16 702	10.0	14.1
Dundy	364	402	501	1 781	71.3	13.0	30 745	21 271	44.5	252	–21	88	11.1	15.4
Fillmore	1 380	1 368	1 339	4 868	81.4	11.9	35 954	23 219	54.8	622	13	228	9.2	12.8
Franklin	518	574	629	2 843	71.1	11.8	27 938	20 553	35.9	438	–72	146	11.9	16.5
Frontier	865	709	663	2 053	81.0	10.5	30 504	20 364	49.8	402	–151	148	12.9	16.9
Furnas	1 275	1 352	1 039	3 986	75.3	12.0	27 410	17 949	52.7	637	–177	206	12.0	15.5
Gage	3 427	3 392	3 686	15 639	73.7	11.3	32 052	22 876	40.1	2 212	–941	671	9.8	12.0
Garden	408	475	441	1 756	76.4	13.9	26 114	18 614	40.3	192	–169	54	9.1	11.5
Garfield	403	425	395	1 483	73.8	12.9	26 029	17 308	50.4	279	–82	89	13.8	17.0
Gosper	293	257	364	1 367	79.1	13.9	33 076	25 669	28.9	133	–26	45	5.7	8.1
Grant	245	247	154	507	89.5	14.6	26 679	19 063	40.0	66	–20	27	8.7	12.9
Greeley	652	723	595	1 939	78.9	11.5	25 604	18 248	40.3	343	–98	127	12.1	14.8
Hall	9 411	9 411	8 976	30 976	79.3	14.6	35 764	25 546	40.0	5 233	116	2 052	10.2	13.9
Hamilton	1 747	1 685	1 742	5 752	79.9	13.0	38 914	25 026	55.5	649	–107	235	6.9	8.6
Harlan	407	395	670	2 713	80.9	12.9	27 747	18 478	50.2	412	–108	136	11.1	15.0
Hayes	177	166	240	840	80.6	10.7	29 356	20 531	43.0	109	–105	36	10.0	12.2
Hitchcock	500	569	762	2 480	80.4	12.1	26 894	19 735	36.3	437	–148	150	12.8	15.9
Holt	2 183	2 335	2 272	8 057	76.1	12.8	29 517	20 059	47.2	1 561	–324	569	12.9	16.0

[1] Revised. [2] 1997 data are model-based estimates; 1989 data are census estimates. For more information on these estimates, see appendix A. Source Notes and Explanations or <http://www.census.gov/hhes/www/saipe.html>.

Sources: Public School Enrollment, 1998-1999 and 1994-1995—U.S. National Center for Education Statistics, <http://nces.ed.gov/ccd/pubagency.html> (accessed: 16 March 2001). Public School Enrollment and Educational Attainment, 1990—U.S. Census Bureau, "1990 Census of Population and Housing, Summary Tape File (STF) 3C" on CD-ROM (related Internet site <http://homer.ssd.census.gov/cdrom/lookup>). Income and Poverty, 1997—U.S. Census Bureau, "State and County Income and Poverty Estimates - 1997," published 22 November 2000, <http://www.census.gov/housing/saipe/estmod97/est97ALL.dat>. Income and Poverty, 1989—U.S. Census Bureau, "1990 Census of Population and Housing, Summary Tape File (STF) 3C" on CD-ROM (related Internet site <http://homer.ssd.census.gov/cdrom/lookup>).

Table B–5. Counties — Education, Income, and Poverty–Con.

[Includes U.S., states, and 3,142 counties or county equivalents defined as of January 1, 1992. For changes to these areas since January 1, 1992, see appendix B. Geographic Information]

County	Public school enrollment — Fall			Educational attainment, 1990			Median household income[2]			Persons below poverty level,[2] 1997				
					Percent—					Number — Persons of all ages			Percent	
	1998–1999	1994–1995[1]	1990	Persons 25 years and over	High school graduate or higher	Bachelor's degree or higher	1997 (dollars)	1989 (dollars)	Percent change, 1989–1997	Total	Net change, 1989–1997	Persons under 18 years	Persons of all ages	Persons under 18 years
NEBRASKA—Con.														
Hooker	196	247	153	561	79.5	13.5	24 862	18 682	33.1	103	17	39	15.3	23.2
Howard	1 600	1 531	1 173	3 945	75.2	8.6	30 893	21 688	42.4	663	−69	240	10.1	13.0
Jefferson	1 950	2 025	1 513	6 101	75.1	12.7	31 028	21 740	42.7	870	−146	277	10.4	13.3
Johnson	939	1 007	790	3 303	73.6	8.5	29 246	19 925	46.8	524	−31	171	11.5	14.8
Kearney	1 478	1 336	1 138	4 436	80.3	17.9	38 847	27 207	42.8	542	−138	181	7.9	9.7
Keith	1 643	1 763	1 689	5 688	81.5	13.1	32 269	22 909	40.9	900	55	321	10.3	13.3
Keya Paha	147	178	207	720	76.8	8.1	20 756	17 202	20.7	190	−74	66	19.1	25.8
Kimball	714	743	797	2 829	73.8	12.7	31 373	23 232	35.0	299	−166	101	7.3	9.4
Knox	2 030	2 061	1 747	6 575	71.1	8.8	26 711	17 877	49.4	1 427	−430	481	15.6	20.1
Lancaster	35 495	34 734	31 351	129 320	88.1	27.6	39 478	28 909	36.6	20 542	−798	6 503	9.0	11.5
Lincoln	6 069	6 233	6 404	20 676	81.4	14.2	35 907	25 915	38.6	3 969	109	1 541	11.8	15.7
Logan	216	204	207	538	82.9	13.4	30 037	21 250	41.4	110	−8	46	12.2	15.6
Loup	126	144	125	471	78.3	9.8	18 136	17 933	1.1	110	−1	41	16.2	23.1
McPherson	115	101	113	368	78.0	9.0	20 856	17 500	19.2	86	−95	29	15.2	17.9
Madison	6 530	6 708	5 259	20 426	78.3	13.2	36 880	24 461	50.8	3 075	−123	1 181	9.0	12.0
Merrick	1 561	1 567	1 610	5 317	77.0	11.7	32 345	22 518	43.6	753	−132	273	9.4	12.1
Morrill	1 129	1 197	1 102	3 632	74.1	12.7	27 932	19 398	44.0	788	3	305	14.6	19.6
Nance	818	894	871	2 854	71.0	10.7	29 499	20 742	42.2	437	−77	178	10.9	15.0
Nemaha	1 319	1 385	1 453	5 058	77.2	18.5	34 185	22 383	52.7	809	−133	258	10.9	13.6
Nuckolls	868	942	1 019	4 038	74.2	10.1	28 679	20 250	41.6	593	−326	180	11.4	13.7
Otoe	2 723	2 715	2 538	9 665	77.4	13.1	35 458	23 189	52.9	1 299	−305	416	8.9	10.7
Pawnee	699	656	544	2 367	75.0	11.1	26 157	18 286	43.0	423	−91	127	13.6	17.9
Perkins	595	674	766	2 233	79.0	16.7	32 473	23 132	40.4	322	−161	110	10.1	11.6
Phelps	2 056	1 954	1 824	6 446	85.0	15.5	37 595	26 693	40.8	874	45	322	8.9	11.9
Pierce	1 584	1 542	1 290	5 049	73.8	9.1	34 408	22 293	54.3	752	−66	258	9.4	10.9
Platte	4 750	4 972	4 887	18 222	79.5	12.8	39 189	26 123	50.0	2 339	−244	918	7.5	9.3
Polk	1 178	1 219	1 143	3 893	81.0	12.4	39 269	25 959	43.7	384	−72	127	6.9	8.2
Red Willow	2 162	2 160	2 162	7 551	82.2	14.9	31 965	22 336	43.1	1 463	−19	523	13.0	17.5
Richardson	1 806	1 755	1 544	6 916	73.3	11.7	28 765	19 521	47.4	1 211	−37	380	13.0	16.3
Rock	316	395	449	1 336	79.4	10.1	27 051	18 974	42.6	254	−55	94	14.5	19.5
Saline	2 702	2 608	2 214	8 176	76.0	12.6	35 541	24 455	45.3	971	−317	300	7.9	9.1
Sarpy	19 442	17 878	20 762	59 009	91.0	25.4	49 644	35 575	39.5	4 981	458	1 875	4.1	4.9
Saunders	3 013	3 054	3 234	11 922	79.1	12.0	37 441	26 058	43.7	1 456	−275	486	7.5	8.9
Scotts Bluff	6 878	7 107	7 409	23 315	74.3	13.9	30 152	21 369	41.1	5 638	164	2 237	15.6	21.5
Seward	2 788	2 865	2 352	9 341	80.5	14.8	40 984	27 200	50.7	1 108	−201	340	7.2	8.1
Sheridan	1 237	1 423	1 412	4 477	74.4	15.5	27 075	19 237	40.7	1 035	−157	384	16.1	21.3
Sherman	588	678	822	2 438	72.2	11.4	25 454	17 025	49.5	399	−306	127	11.5	13.2
Sioux	161	181	315	1 062	77.1	17.8	26 965	18 810	43.4	139	−115	38	9.2	9.8
Stanton	516	513	1 346	3 768	79.4	7.6	35 443	24 375	45.4	625	−201	218	10.0	10.8
Thayer	1 159	1 200	1 134	4 676	72.7	10.2	31 115	20 298	53.3	698	−192	226	11.2	14.6
Thomas	133	135	209	543	78.8	11.4	24 909	17 273	44.2	103	−74	39	12.7	15.3
Thurston	2 029	1 961	1 608	3 948	70.6	8.8	25 623	18 588	37.8	1 656	−451	715	23.0	27.5
Valley	784	805	952	3 537	75.7	11.6	28 202	19 201	46.9	573	−104	192	12.4	16.4
Washington	3 497	3 317	3 334	10 585	82.7	15.4	45 194	29 805	51.6	937	31	302	5.1	6.0
Wayne	1 832	1 772	1 543	5 127	80.4	19.8	33 981	20 956	62.2	801	−443	212	9.6	9.6
Webster	697	784	788	3 058	74.0	10.3	27 807	18 349	51.5	458	−201	148	11.7	14.9
Wheeler	151	165	197	594	79.0	12.1	31 594	22 604	39.8	93	−42	36	9.7	12.2
York	2 148	2 235	2 564	9 296	81.8	13.0	38 051	25 722	47.9	1 152	240	432	8.2	11.1
NEVADA	311 236	250 910	190 335	789 638	78.8	15.3	39 280	31 011	26.7	186 345	66 685	74 006	10.7	15.4
Churchill	4 834	4 350	3 478	11 318	79.5	13.1	38 009	29 007	31.0	2 469	549	1 004	10.7	13.7
Clark	203 777	156 348	114 869	486 908	77.3	13.8	39 586	30 746	28.8	129 276	52 539	52 257	11.1	16.4
Douglas	7 322	7 031	4 847	18 882	87.3	20.0	46 026	35 209	30.7	2 698	850	1 079	7.3	10.8
Elko	10 616	9 647	7 176	19 516	78.5	13.3	49 822	33 715	47.8	3 365	276	1 414	7.3	8.4
Esmeralda	114	117	229	912	71.5	11.1	33 366	25 577	30.5	176	−30	52	15.2	17.8
Eureka	358	276	285	1 003	75.2	13.6	45 572	31 047	46.8	165	8	52	8.2	8.9
Humboldt	4 288	3 702	2 696	7 745	75.5	12.2	47 512	33 269	42.8	1 442	148	594	8.0	9.4
Lander	1 703	1 523	1 420	3 556	73.2	10.8	49 667	33 988	46.1	623	−45	258	8.8	9.6
Lincoln	1 052	1 128	936	2 287	77.6	13.1	32 993	20 872	58.1	571	76	231	14.8	17.7
Lyon	6 351	5 134	3 721	13 333	75.2	9.4	33 684	25 065	34.4	3 436	1 055	1 398	11.4	15.8
Mineral	1 039	1 192	1 194	4 109	73.1	9.1	33 738	26 278	28.4	858	54	348	16.3	23.1
Nye	5 265	4 170	2 924	12 263	75.1	9.5	36 580	30 211	21.1	3 652	1 812	1 465	12.7	20.7
Pershing	985	886	895	2 644	73.1	7.2	40 197	27 519	46.1	529	−31	211	10.9	12.5
Storey	507	501	392	1 787	84.4	17.6	55 008	32 457	69.5	127	−113	42	4.2	5.4
Washoe	52 813	45 752	37 176	169 341	82.5	20.7	42 070	31 891	31.9	30 791	7 334	11 307	9.8	13.8
White Pine	1 854	1 784	1 987	5 971	73.1	11.4	39 026	27 427	42.3	1 201	277	441	13.4	15.3
Independent City														
Carson City city	8 358	7 369	6 110	28 063	82.7	16.3	40 712	31 570	29.0	4 964	1 924	1 853	10.6	15.4

[1] Revised. [2] 1997 data are model-based estimates; 1989 data are census estimates. For more information on these estimates, see appendix A. Source Notes and Explanations or <http://www.census.gov/hhes/www/saipe.html>.

Sources: Public School Enrollment, 1998-1999 and 1994-1995—U.S. National Center for Education Statistics, <http://nces.ed.gov/ccd/pubagency.html> (accessed: 16 March 2001). Public School Enrollment and Educational Attainment, 1990—U.S. Census Bureau, "1990 Census of Population and Housing, Summary Tape File (STF) 3C" on CD-ROM (related Internet site <http://homer.ssd.census.gov/cdrom/lookup>). Income and Poverty, 1997—U.S. Census Bureau, "State and County Income and Poverty Estimates - 1997," published 22 November 2000, <http://www.census.gov/housing/saipe/estmod97/est97ALL.dat>. Income and Poverty, 1989—U.S. Census Bureau, "1990 Census of Population and Housing, Summary Tape File (STF) 3C" on CD-ROM (related Internet site <http://homer.ssd.census.gov/cdrom/lookup>).

Table B–5. Counties — Education, Income, and Poverty-Con.

[Includes U.S., states, and 3,142 counties or county equivalents defined as of January 1, 1992. For changes to these areas since January 1, 1992, see appendix B. Geographic Information]

County	Public school enrollment Fall 1998–1999	Public school enrollment Fall 1994–1995[1]	Public school enrollment 1990	Educational attainment, 1990 Persons 25 years and over	Educational attainment, 1990 Percent High school graduate or higher	Educational attainment, 1990 Percent Bachelor's degree or higher	Median household income[2] 1997 (dollars)	Median household income[2] 1989 (dollars)	Median household income[2] Percent change, 1989–1997	Persons below poverty level,[2] 1997 Number Persons of all ages Total	Persons below poverty level,[2] 1997 Number Persons of all ages Net change, 1989–1997	Persons below poverty level,[2] 1997 Number Persons under 18 years	Persons below poverty level,[2] 1997 Percent Persons of all ages	Persons below poverty level,[2] 1997 Percent Persons under 18 years
NEW HAMPSHIRE	204 713	189 286	171 104	713 894	82.2	24.4	42 023	36 329	15.7	87 975	18 871	30 356	7.5	10.0
Belknap	9 324	8 993	8 312	32 809	80.4	20.5	38 787	31 474	23.2	4 553	1 404	1 750	8.7	13.1
Carroll	8 845	8 378	5 690	24 618	83.5	23.4	35 001	28 145	24.4	4 040	903	1 491	10.2	15.8
Cheshire	9 213	9 130	11 331	44 193	80.8	23.9	39 730	31 648	25.5	5 703	1 031	1 868	8.2	10.5
Coos	4 252	4 269	6 074	23 406	70.0	11.0	31 735	25 897	22.5	3 988	527	1 406	12.1	17.2
Grafton	14 717	14 408	11 481	45 960	81.4	26.4	38 469	30 065	28.0	6 978	341	2 254	9.4	12.3
Hillsborough	70 916	63 734	50 321	215 914	82.2	26.4	46 650	40 404	15.5	25 314	6 053	8 795	6.9	9.2
Merrimack	19 021	18 058	19 055	78 633	83.2	25.4	43 679	35 801	22.0	9 139	2 740	3 177	7.3	9.6
Rockingham	41 464	36 858	37 614	159 886	86.2	25.9	54 161	41 881	29.3	14 073	3 380	4 665	5.1	6.5
Strafford	17 917	16 666	14 578	62 963	79.8	21.7	39 969	32 812	21.8	10 225	2 245	3 501	9.7	13.2
Sullivan	9 044	8 792	6 648	25 512	75.0	16.5	37 006	29 053	27.4	3 961	246	1 449	9.8	14.1
NEW JERSEY	1 259 166	1 173 960	1 097 317	5 166 233	76.7	24.9	47 903	40 927	17.0	749 198	176 046	302 459	9.3	14.8
Atlantic	41 143	37 380	30 718	149 789	72.9	16.4	38 124	33 716	13.1	25 502	5 033	10 769	10.8	18.1
Bergen	116 835	108 412	99 824	583 985	81.6	31.7	59 557	49 249	20.9	45 668	13 737	15 219	5.3	8.1
Burlington	69 065	64 426	61 512	255 060	81.9	23.6	52 543	42 373	24.0	24 020	7 936	9 908	5.8	9.0
Camden	87 978	85 730	80 525	321 621	75.5	21.0	41 441	36 190	14.5	64 508	13 876	28 949	10.0	20.0
Cape May	15 201	14 797	13 096	65 916	74.0	17.2	36 211	30 435	19.0	10 677	3 012	4 298	12.8	20.0
Cumberland	25 189	24 848	23 937	88 609	63.4	10.8	34 935	29 985	16.5	21 445	4 359	9 689	15.8	24.7
Essex	118 820	117 295	117 232	506 226	70.1	24.0	39 823	34 518	15.4	128 780	19 840	52 285	17.3	27.0
Gloucester	43 886	41 547	38 937	145 019	77.5	18.1	49 279	39 387	25.1	18 399	4 463	7 816	7.4	11.0
Hudson	77 770	73 598	69 137	372 106	64.1	19.7	34 848	30 917	12.7	95 753	14 582	38 401	17.1	28.6
Hunterdon	20 796	18 445	17 501	72 699	85.9	34.6	72 398	54 628	32.5	3 750	984	1 209	3.1	3.9
Mercer	52 481	49 597	43 009	214 314	77.1	29.5	49 251	41 227	19.5	30 417	7 333	11 973	9.4	14.8
Middlesex	102 847	94 072	88 112	447 679	79.4	26.5	52 646	45 623	15.4	47 775	14 606	17 905	6.8	10.7
Monmouth	98 813	90 061	81 989	368 859	82.8	28.4	57 985	45 912	26.3	39 877	12 647	15 797	6.6	9.9
Morris	69 582	62 840	60 371	284 434	87.0	36.7	67 919	56 273	20.7	15 847	4 388	5 385	3.4	4.8
Ocean	71 710	65 844	61 911	301 185	74.9	15.3	42 053	33 110	27.0	38 692	13 092	16 093	7.8	13.3
Passaic	72 290	66 894	62 994	294 620	68.8	18.7	39 783	37 596	5.8	60 390	15 834	26 222	12.5	20.2
Salem	11 880	12 085	11 665	42 815	72.6	11.8	42 378	33 155	27.8	6 789	53	2 834	10.5	16.1
Somerset	42 306	35 214	31 632	167 616	86.3	38.3	74 586	55 519	34.3	11 492	5 431	4 424	4.1	6.6
Sussex	26 819	25 261	23 647	83 589	85.1	24.9	59 626	48 823	22.1	5 941	1 497	2 380	4.1	5.6
Union	76 447	69 687	65 055	339 266	75.2	25.0	50 254	41 791	20.3	46 766	11 546	18 225	9.3	15.4
Warren	17 308	15 927	14 513	60 826	77.6	19.6	50 002	39 929	25.2	6 709	1 796	2 676	6.7	10.1
NEW MEXICO	328 715	327 253	301 380	922 590	75.1	20.4	30 836	24 087	28.0	333 913	27 979	139 854	19.3	27.5
Bernalillo	85 847	89 001	80 173	306 632	82.1	26.7	36 853	27 382	34.6	76 836	7 991	29 259	14.6	21.5
Catron	482	512	499	1 717	73.3	18.7	22 661	18 460	22.8	714	57	262	24.9	35.8
Chaves	12 610	13 080	12 150	34 723	67.3	14.3	27 531	21 764	26.5	14 300	1 679	6 141	23.1	32.4
Cibola	3 768	3 945	5 866	13 583	66.7	8.8	23 722	16 848	40.8	6 437	-1 316	2 484	24.8	29.1
Colfax	2 696	2 776	2 791	8 329	71.1	14.7	27 382	20 800	31.6	2 697	376	1 132	20.1	30.8
Curry	9 700	10 606	8 698	24 597	75.8	13.7	28 297	21 303	32.8	9 141	1 269	4 021	20.5	29.0
DeBaca	446	493	406	1 559	63.0	11.4	21 721	15 686	38.5	515	32	189	22.0	31.8
Dona Ana	36 541	34 789	28 158	75 367	70.4	21.9	26 379	21 859	20.7	44 490	9 814	19 460	26.6	37.7
Eddy	11 288	11 979	10 967	30 216	67.3	10.9	31 228	23 418	33.4	9 953	198	4 093	18.6	25.3
Grant	5 947	6 216	6 296	16 811	70.5	16.4	28 882	21 350	35.3	6 317	586	2 527	20.3	27.3
Guadalupe	1 006	1 081	926	2 564	57.8	6.1	18 820	13 350	41.0	1 217	-372	450	29.7	37.0
Harding	179	175	221	645	65.9	15.7	27 213	19 020	43.1	127	-24	37	13.8	15.2
Hidalgo	1 471	1 391	1 379	3 462	71.6	11.7	28 400	23 504	20.8	1 393	181	602	22.6	29.1
Lea	12 902	13 383	13 091	32 383	63.8	11.5	31 337	23 352	34.2	11 685	-624	5 003	20.7	27.1
Lincoln	3 675	3 452	2 257	8 321	77.1	16.1	25 831	19 489	32.5	3 132	748	1 257	19.3	31.0
Los Alamos	3 674	3 691	3 378	12 543	94.7	53.4	74 253	54 801	35.5	504	71	153	2.7	3.4
Luna	5 569	5 354	4 014	11 603	58.8	11.1	19 349	15 684	23.4	7 219	1 574	3 274	29.8	44.9
McKinley	16 091	15 656	15 708	30 888	58.5	11.1	21 681	17 468	24.1	23 563	-2 555	11 915	34.7	45.4
Mora	898	1 074	950	2 655	59.7	14.2	18 160	12 993	39.8	1 471	-69	560	29.9	39.2
Otero	9 831	10 264	10 558	30 239	81.6	15.0	29 412	22 624	30.0	9 567	1 163	4 201	17.7	25.8
Quay	2 166	2 256	2 185	7 097	70.3	9.9	23 105	18 711	23.5	2 674	-7	1 012	26.5	37.7
Rio Arriba	6 917	7 170	7 182	20 014	65.9	10.3	25 036	18 373	36.3	8 604	-768	3 654	22.5	29.7
Roosevelt	3 552	3 894	3 182	9 517	66.1	18.1	24 368	18 699	30.3	4 593	428	1 817	26.5	36.1
Sandoval	14 700	10 978	13 056	38 464	79.3	19.1	40 139	28 950	38.6	11 552	1 700	5 025	12.9	17.7
San Juan	24 760	24 519	23 362	50 692	69.2	12.3	30 160	22 300	35.2	22 194	-3 458	9 925	20.7	25.9
San Miguel	5 751	6 278	5 521	15 434	68.4	16.2	22 772	17 885	27.3	8 010	653	3 187	29.3	37.7
Santa Fe	15 699	15 026	16 533	65 016	82.6	32.3	37 882	29 403	28.8	14 544	1 980	5 410	11.9	17.2
Sierra	1 874	1 797	1 364	7 482	63.7	8.5	20 724	15 612	32.7	2 547	665	897	23.4	40.9
Socorro	2 750	2 662	3 241	8 619	67.2	17.1	24 025	19 165	25.4	5 056	774	2 133	31.4	43.1
Taos	5 404	5 339	4 671	14 630	71.8	18.5	22 777	16 966	34.3	6 632	297	2 578	24.4	33.7
Torrance	6 171	5 337	2 487	6 334	72.6	10.9	26 334	19 619	34.2	3 787	1 634	1 669	24.6	33.3
Union	909	1 002	706	2 720	63.6	12.0	26 320	18 227	44.4	827	-25	327	20.7	29.2
Valencia	13 441	12 077	9 404	27 734	73.3	12.1	30 092	24 312	23.8	11 612	3 324	5 202	18.3	26.1

[1] Revised. [2] 1997 data are model-based estimates; 1989 data are census estimates. For more information on these estimates, see appendix A. Source Notes and Explanations or <http://www.census.gov/hhes/www/saipe.html>.

Sources: Public School Enrollment, 1998-1999 and 1994-1995—U.S. National Center for Education Statistics, <http://nces.ed.gov/ccd/pubagency.html> (accessed: 16 March 2001). Public School Enrollment and Educational Attainment, 1990—U.S. Census Bureau, "1990 Census of Population and Housing, Summary Tape File (STF) 3C" on CD-ROM (related Internet site <http://homer.ssd.census.gov/cdrom/lookup>). Income and Poverty, 1997—U.S. Census Bureau, "State and County Income and Poverty Estimates - 1997," published 22 November 2000, <http://www.census.gov/housing/saipe/estmod97/est97ALL.dat>. Income and Poverty, 1989—U.S. Census Bureau, "1990 Census of Population and Housing, Summary Tape File (STF) 3C" on CD-ROM (related Internet site <http://homer.ssd.census.gov/cdrom/lookup>).

Table B–5. Counties — Education, Income, and Poverty–Con.

[Includes U.S., states, and 3,142 counties or county equivalents defined as of January 1, 1992. For changes to these areas since January 1, 1992, see appendix B. Geographic Information]

County	Public school enrollment Fall 1998–1999	Public school enrollment Fall 1994–1995[1]	Public school enrollment 1990	Educational attainment, 1990 Persons 25 years and over	Percent High school graduate or higher	Percent Bachelor's degree or higher	Median household income 1997 (dollars)	Median household income 1989 (dollars)	Percent change, 1989–1997	Persons below poverty level, 1997 Number Persons of all ages Total	Net change, 1989–1997	Persons under 18 years (Number)	Percent Persons of all ages	Percent Persons under 18 years
NEW YORK	2 877 142	2 766 208	2 650 601	11 818 569	74.8	23.1	36 369	32 965	10.3	2 814 460	537 164	1 121 585	15.6	24.7
Albany	41 902	39 653	38 311	191 118	80.9	28.3	40 490	33 358	21.4	31 352	4 321	11 542	10.9	17.4
Allegany	8 763	9 363	9 336	29 095	76.9	15.6	31 291	24 164	29.5	8 522	1 796	3 677	18.1	27.0
Bronx	(3)	(3)	206 321	735 022	58.5	12.2	24 031	21 944	9.5	355 768	21 631	148 767	30.2	41.9
Broome	34 108	34 900	31 427	138 549	78.9	20.7	35 340	28 743	23.0	26 587	5 057	10 455	13.8	22.5
Cattaraugus	18 251	18 772	16 018	51 927	74.5	12.8	31 348	23 421	33.8	13 206	1 812	5 620	15.7	22.9
Cayuga	13 198	13 939	14 933	52 621	73.3	13.0	35 508	27 568	28.8	10 153	2 221	4 334	12.9	19.3
Chautauqua	25 243	26 209	25 450	90 582	74.4	14.2	31 051	24 183	28.4	22 554	3 736	9 313	16.7	25.4
Chemung	14 550	15 494	16 433	61 336	77.2	15.4	33 988	26 135	30.0	12 315	2 068	5 074	13.8	21.0
Chenango	10 509	10 632	10 233	33 069	75.5	13.1	31 757	26 032	22.0	7 899	1 957	3 623	15.5	24.7
Clinton	13 925	14 446	13 661	51 585	74.2	16.5	34 918	26 903	29.8	11 265	971	4 403	15.2	21.2
Columbia	10 131	9 928	10 499	42 371	73.6	18.5	36 697	29 785	23.2	7 422	1 587	3 082	11.9	19.5
Cortland	7 987	8 255	8 378	28 497	76.8	18.2	33 758	26 791	26.0	6 657	847	2 688	14.5	21.3
Delaware	7 977	8 613	8 540	30 350	74.0	13.2	30 362	24 132	25.8	6 623	855	2 724	14.6	23.1
Dutchess	45 175	42 580	40 076	168 446	79.8	24.8	47 828	42 250	13.2	21 384	8 387	8 503	8.4	12.9
Erie	145 788	142 892	140 216	640 137	76.4	20.0	36 711	28 005	31.1	129 553	13 940	49 075	13.9	21.5
Essex	5 010	5 057	6 031	24 853	74.2	15.8	32 051	25 002	28.2	5 146	883	2 024	14.4	21.8
Franklin	9 512	9 970	8 769	29 657	69.5	11.7	29 235	21 791	34.2	8 296	942	3 293	18.7	26.1
Fulton	10 267	10 468	10 424	35 369	70.5	11.4	30 502	23 862	27.8	8 027	1 138	3 515	15.2	25.0
Genesee	11 258	11 203	10 413	38 267	77.4	14.0	37 859	30 955	22.3	5 973	1 673	2 554	9.8	15.3
Greene	7 568	7 242	7 679	30 028	72.8	13.4	34 408	27 469	25.3	6 182	2 101	2 465	13.6	21.4
Hamilton	713	721	913	3 745	77.3	15.1	31 015	23 195	33.7	572	122	217	11.0	19.6
Herkimer	12 501	12 680	12 188	42 657	72.6	12.9	30 321	23 075	31.4	8 909	456	3 716	13.9	21.6
Jefferson	20 272	20 861	19 442	64 967	76.4	13.6	31 515	25 929	21.5	16 414	4 162	7 351	15.9	23.2
Kings	[3]1 072 628	[3]1 022 534	358 474	1 457 904	63.7	16.6	26 108	25 684	1.7	605 959	91 796	251 033	26.5	39.7
Lewis	5 104	5 412	5 813	16 261	73.6	10.5	32 416	25 599	26.6	3 978	483	1 796	14.4	20.7
Livingston	11 020	11 075	10 583	37 638	77.5	18.1	39 354	30 981	27.0	6 707	1 881	2 670	11.1	16.1
Madison	13 259	13 404	12 204	41 081	79.2	18.2	38 293	29 547	29.6	7 543	1 671	3 045	11.2	16.3
Monroe	125 758	118 896	107 773	457 919	80.1	26.3	41 954	35 337	18.7	88 707	16 973	36 890	12.5	19.9
Montgomery	8 098	8 424	8 904	34 782	70.1	10.8	30 482	24 068	26.6	7 502	1 512	3 266	14.8	24.5
Nassau	199 942	185 063	172 123	881 037	84.2	30.0	61 026	54 283	12.4	75 486	28 294	28 527	5.8	9.6
New York	(3)	(3)	139 304	1 095 317	75.3	42.2	38 224	32 262	18.5	318 778	21 161	109 591	20.7	38.4
Niagara	36 508	36 349	35 797	144 612	75.8	13.6	36 218	28 408	27.5	26 448	3 172	10 796	12.1	19.0
Oneida	38 930	40 173	41 619	161 944	75.1	16.7	34 668	26 710	29.8	33 339	5 136	13 485	15.1	23.4
Onondaga	79 893	79 198	75 228	297 702	80.7	24.4	38 447	31 783	21.0	57 522	11 060	22 716	12.7	19.4
Ontario	18 817	18 407	15 877	61 394	81.0	19.5	41 266	33 133	24.5	9 068	2 284	3 887	9.2	14.9
Orange	62 148	58 342	52 092	189 949	77.2	19.5	46 446	39 198	18.5	37 042	9 571	16 063	11.4	16.7
Orleans	8 984	9 455	8 227	26 554	71.5	10.7	34 942	28 359	23.2	5 315	1 494	2 273	12.6	18.4
Oswego	26 237	26 464	23 635	71 872	74.7	12.9	35 809	29 083	23.1	17 157	3 543	7 685	14.1	21.1
Otsego	10 178	10 167	10 076	36 679	77.7	19.9	32 474	25 099	29.4	7 961	203	2 902	13.9	19.7
Putnam	15 035	14 084	13 232	54 701	86.5	27.8	62 646	53 634	16.8	4 181	1 136	1 463	4.4	5.9
Queens	(3)	(3)	234 659	1 350 456	71.1	20.6	35 820	34 186	4.8	341 587	131 530	132 195	17.0	29.3
Rensselaer	23 990	23 639	23 346	97 670	77.7	19.5	39 550	31 958	23.8	17 481	3 702	7 087	11.7	18.6
Richmond	(3)	(3)	50 273	245 575	78.6	20.7	51 141	43 861	16.6	39 492	10 472	16 531	9.7	15.5
Rockland	40 571	38 254	37 554	169 897	83.3	33.0	58 362	52 731	10.7	27 248	10 716	13 108	9.7	17.4
St. Lawrence	19 734	20 139	20 584	65 413	73.1	15.1	31 169	23 799	31.0	19 149	1 735	7 415	18.5	25.4
Saratoga	34 825	33 749	30 988	115 939	83.0	25.2	46 290	36 635	26.4	14 450	3 941	5 765	7.3	11.0
Schenectady	22 082	21 383	21 451	100 422	80.7	23.0	41 079	31 569	30.1	15 905	3 771	6 638	11.0	19.0
Schoharie	5 778	5 752	5 809	19 697	73.7	14.4	33 209	26 077	27.3	4 216	801	1 634	13.6	19.8
Schuyler	2 373	2 426	3 550	12 034	74.2	13.6	32 241	25 712	25.4	2 439	413	1 060	12.9	20.1
Seneca	5 429	5 429	5 530	21 960	76.2	14.2	35 650	28 604	24.6	3 842	459	1 656	11.9	19.1
Steuben	20 035	20 325	18 878	63 573	75.0	14.4	33 732	25 312	33.3	15 214	2 127	6 459	15.5	23.4
Suffolk	241 832	225 906	218 908	855 043	82.2	23.0	53 560	49 128	9.0	105 078	43 689	42 124	7.6	11.9
Sullivan	11 595	11 803	11 644	46 108	71.2	14.4	33 123	27 582	20.1	10 885	2 080	4 631	16.2	25.6
Tioga	9 879	10 096	10 279	33 160	80.6	18.0	38 503	31 497	22.2	5 908	1 085	2 630	11.1	17.3
Tompkins	13 716	13 766	12 460	50 667	87.2	41.7	36 822	27 742	32.7	11 884	-3 804	3 311	13.7	16.8
Ulster	28 884	27 763	24 726	110 058	76.6	21.6	38 162	34 033	12.1	19 938	6 488	7 963	12.3	20.0
Warren	11 271	11 111	10 402	38 518	78.3	19.4	37 096	30 434	21.9	7 185	1 878	3 007	11.7	18.9
Washington	11 406	11 729	11 220	38 003	74.0	11.6	33 905	28 660	18.3	7 451	2 118	3 130	12.9	19.3
Wayne	18 996	18 767	17 009	56 329	74.3	14.0	40 181	32 469	23.8	10 126	2 853	4 332	10.6	15.7
Westchester	138 337	123 388	112 752	604 544	81.0	35.3	55 040	48 405	13.7	83 131	24 967	31 295	9.3	15.2
Wyoming	6 027	6 224	8 173	27 208	70.3	9.7	35 915	27 515	30.5	4 685	1 385	1 853	11.6	15.4
Yates	3 235	3 234	3 754	14 701	73.7	15.0	31 926	24 874	28.4	3 696	727	1 656	15.3	24.7

[1] Revised. [2] 1997 data are model-based estimates; 1989 data are census estimates. For more information on these estimates, see appendix A. Source Notes and Explanations or <http://www.census.gov/hhes/www/saipe.html>. [3] Bronx, New York, Queens, and Richmond Counties included with Kings County; data not available separately.

Sources: Public School Enrollment, 1998-1999 and 1994-1995—U.S. National Center for Education Statistics, <http://nces.ed.gov/ccd/pubagency.html> (accessed: 16 March 2001). Public School Enrollment and Educational Attainment, 1990—U.S. Census Bureau, "1990 Census of Population and Housing, Summary Tape File (STF) 3C" on CD-ROM (related Internet site <http://homer.ssd.census.gov/cdrom/lookup>). Income and Poverty, 1997—U.S. Census Bureau, "State and County Income and Poverty Estimates - 1997," published 22 November 2000, <http://www.census.gov/housing/saipe/estmod97/est97ALL.dat>. Income and Poverty, 1989—U.S. Census Bureau, "1990 Census of Population and Housing, Summary Tape File (STF) 3C" on CD-ROM (related Internet site <http://homer.ssd.census.gov/cdrom/lookup>).

[Includes U.S., states, and 3,142 counties or county equivalents defined as of January 1, 1992. For changes to these areas since January 1, 1992, see appendix B. Geographic Information]

County	Public school enrollment			Educational attainment, 1990			Median household income[2]			Persons below poverty level,[2] 1997				
	Fall				Percent—					Number			Percent	
										Persons of all ages				
	1998–1999	1994–1995[1]	1990	Persons 25 years and over	High school graduate or higher	Bach-elor's degree or higher	1997 (dollars)	1989 (dollars)	Percent change, 1989–1997	Total	Net change, 1989–1997	Persons under 18 years	Persons of all ages	Persons under 18 years
NORTH CAROLINA......	1 254 821	1 156 786	1 091 659	4 253 494	70.0	17.4	35 320	26 647	32.5	940 547	110 689	361 170	12.6	18.6
Alamance..............	20 066	17 918	15 764	72 412	67.9	14.6	35 281	27 231	29.6	10 443	1 107	3 849	8.8	13.8
Alexander.............	5 291	4 965	4 888	17 865	59.0	7.9	35 302	26 539	33.0	3 190	519	1 280	10.1	15.6
Alleghany.............	1 500	1 488	1 596	6 785	52.6	9.0	27 730	18 476	50.1	1 385	−495	438	14.2	20.2
Anson.................	4 539	4 443	4 578	14 914	60.8	7.3	27 703	21 836	26.9	4 291	221	1 630	18.3	24.7
Ashe.................	3 303	3 509	3 652	15 486	55.6	8.1	26 968	18 951	42.3	3 754	−286	1 233	15.5	22.5
Avery.................	2 595	2 463	2 487	9 452	62.2	12.4	28 407	20 403	39.2	2 356	332	878	15.3	23.5
Beaufort..............	7 634	7 929	7 705	27 827	65.9	10.8	28 614	21 738	31.6	7 804	−326	3 077	17.4	25.6
Bertie.................	3 861	4 028	4 065	12 848	54.9	8.0	22 816	17 795	28.2	4 702	−541	1 858	22.9	31.5
Bladen................	5 906	5 579	5 801	18 389	56.4	7.7	26 984	19 015	41.9	5 792	−372	2 346	18.8	27.5
Brunswick	10 029	9 019	8 529	34 755	69.2	10.7	30 689	23 480	30.7	9 682	1 907	3 750	14.0	22.7
Buncombe.............	29 254	28 853	25 398	119 815	74.5	19.1	35 159	25 847	36.0	23 603	4 240	8 759	12.3	19.1
Burke.................	14 244	13 008	12 302	50 223	60.1	10.6	32 113	25 879	24.1	9 509	2 110	3 758	11.8	18.6
Cabarrus	21 782	19 163	15 931	65 139	67.4	12.3	41 781	30 133	38.7	9 669	1 776	3 940	8.0	12.7
Caldwell	12 267	11 657	11 402	46 597	56.8	8.9	32 838	25 691	27.8	8 549	1 056	3 246	11.2	17.3
Camden...............	1 282	1 218	1 017	4 011	66.2	10.1	35 423	26 699	32.7	850	−95	325	12.2	18.8
Carteret	8 623	8 202	7 931	35 796	75.5	16.2	34 348	25 811	33.1	7 088	1 111	2 634	11.8	18.7
Caswell...............	3 559	3 445	3 706	13 940	55.0	6.6	31 152	22 736	37.0	3 050	−197	1 084	14.3	20.3
Catawba	22 644	20 767	19 945	77 710	66.7	14.2	38 456	29 228	31.6	12 365	4 108	5 226	9.3	15.5
Chatham	7 020	6 393	5 847	26 827	70.0	19.5	41 632	28 539	45.9	3 539	−163	1 400	7.7	13.1
Cherokee	3 660	3 483	3 381	13 824	59.9	8.0	25 489	19 625	29.9	3 905	−166	1 357	17.0	24.6
Chowan	2 597	2 642	2 610	9 048	63.3	12.2	27 900	20 397	36.8	2 651	310	1 069	18.7	27.3
Clay..................	1 302	1 219	1 299	5 003	62.9	12.6	26 800	18 532	44.6	1 311	32	455	15.2	23.0
Cleveland	17 260	15 894	14 775	55 121	63.5	11.1	33 552	26 476	26.7	12 274	3 168	4 949	13.2	20.5
Columbus.............	10 277	10 558	9 977	31 889	59.4	9.1	25 504	18 468	38.1	10 756	−943	4 138	20.5	27.8
Craven	14 824	14 562	14 039	48 900	75.9	15.1	33 214	25 619	29.6	11 834	1 249	4 980	13.8	20.0
Cumberland	51 297	49 995	49 777	151 424	80.3	16.6	33 836	25 462	32.9	41 885	5 390	18 308	15.5	21.2
Currituck	3 122	2 971	2 518	9 117	67.7	8.2	36 287	27 905	30.0	1 933	580	805	10.8	16.4
Dare	4 539	3 960	3 254	15 823	81.0	21.4	35 258	29 322	20.2	2 378	517	857	8.1	12.5
Davidson	24 223	22 446	21 287	83 737	64.2	10.0	36 099	27 913	29.3	14 387	2 097	5 484	10.1	15.3
Davie	5 360	4 768	4 943	18 997	69.6	14.7	39 871	29 659	34.4	2 512	212	932	7.8	11.8
Duplin	8 507	8 255	7 687	25 712	56.4	6.6	27 384	19 695	39.0	7 943	413	3 029	18.4	24.9
Durham	31 180	29 407	26 664	116 509	78.9	33.4	40 007	30 526	31.1	24 477	3 826	9 535	12.4	19.4
Edgecombe	7 994	8 127	11 422	35 259	58.5	8.1	27 464	21 390	28.4	12 031	402	4 976	21.9	30.6
Forsyth	43 876	39 554	38 847	176 502	77.6	24.1	39 536	30 449	29.8	30 641	3 539	11 114	10.8	16.2
Franklin	7 362	6 610	6 001	23 681	62.4	9.2	33 713	25 049	34.6	5 956	850	2 405	13.5	20.7
Gaston	30 424	29 215	29 917	112 130	60.9	10.8	36 590	28 126	30.1	22 118	3 841	8 899	12.0	18.0
Gates	2 072	1 906	1 731	6 085	60.9	7.4	30 087	23 408	28.5	1 568	126	610	15.4	22.9
Graham	1 237	1 244	1 274	4 781	56.9	10.0	24 355	16 754	45.4	1 403	−387	492	18.3	26.1
Granville	7 814	6 926	6 314	25 577	62.0	9.6	34 779	26 488	31.3	5 042	304	1 869	12.3	17.4
Greene	2 966	2 781	2 798	10 092	59.2	8.9	29 993	22 703	32.1	2 806	17	1 142	16.1	23.2
Guilford...............	61 250	55 688	51 803	225 647	76.1	24.8	39 721	30 148	31.8	42 953	9 098	15 895	11.2	17.3
Halifax................	10 765	10 892	10 679	35 145	53.9	8.6	24 741	18 932	30.7	13 156	−646	5 066	23.6	31.5
Harnett...............	15 662	13 322	11 460	41 569	64.0	9.5	31 941	21 743	46.9	11 870	474	4 728	14.7	20.7
Haywood	7 714	7 245	7 095	33 107	68.0	12.8	31 013	22 462	38.1	7 040	1 185	2 472	13.7	22.3
Henderson	11 484	10 658	10 058	49 650	76.2	19.5	35 260	26 967	30.8	9 286	2 141	3 388	11.4	18.6
Hertford..............	4 272	4 435	4 449	14 105	58.1	10.7	23 724	18 180	30.5	5 024	−357	1 932	23.1	31.3
Hoke	6 211	5 704	5 205	13 267	55.7	8.4	27 525	22 770	20.9	5 350	819	2 469	18.1	24.7
Hyde.................	792	793	970	3 605	60.0	7.7	23 568	17 665	33.4	1 315	34	445	24.8	32.6
Iredell	19 972	17 055	15 681	61 494	66.5	11.8	38 086	28 627	33.0	10 626	1 979	3 888	9.2	13.2
Jackson	3 773	3 456	3 936	16 169	68.7	19.7	29 776	21 520	38.4	4 437	468	1 441	16.1	21.7
Johnston	19 314	16 083	14 159	53 439	64.6	11.1	36 406	25 169	44.6	13 213	1 786	5 251	12.3	18.2
Jones	1 657	1 621	1 695	6 112	62.4	8.1	27 219	19 392	40.4	1 700	−202	667	18.0	26.6
Lee	8 761	8 113	7 541	26 875	72.4	14.3	34 864	26 419	32.0	6 343	389	2 597	12.9	19.0
Lenoir	10 514	10 394	10 936	37 269	62.9	11.5	27 982	21 207	31.9	10 894	−226	4 214	18.6	26.6
Lincoln	10 354	9 136	8 643	32 617	62.0	10.5	35 811	28 662	24.9	6 180	1 414	2 218	10.6	14.5
McDowell.............	6 392	6 128	6 255	23 887	58.5	8.1	30 957	22 562	37.2	4 566	541	1 650	11.6	16.4
Macon................	3 980	3 626	3 411	17 068	66.7	13.2	28 696	20 450	40.3	3 761	−76	1 218	13.2	20.2
Madison	2 592	2 536	2 616	11 167	56.4	11.3	27 466	18 956	44.9	3 071	−205	1 020	16.7	23.0
Martin	5 024	5 027	4 975	16 170	58.3	9.5	26 053	19 995	30.3	5 310	−199	2 010	20.1	27.8
Mecklenburg	99 141	86 023	76 426	330 603	81.6	28.3	45 350	33 830	34.1	61 069	13 159	24 226	9.7	14.7
Mitchell	2 401	2 376	2 354	10 016	55.3	9.2	29 238	20 554	42.2	1 999	−282	648	13.4	19.2
Montgomery	4 373	4 215	4 331	14 947	55.3	7.8	28 832	22 682	27.1	3 746	541	1 518	16.0	23.3
Moore	10 965	10 002	9 318	41 048	74.3	19.9	36 688	28 053	30.8	7 761	1 361	3 021	10.9	18.2
Nash	18 738	17 647	13 332	49 831	65.1	13.7	34 079	25 834	31.9	12 415	2 184	4 829	13.7	20.3
New Hanover	21 492	20 839	18 849	77 970	78.1	21.2	38 480	27 320	40.8	19 342	2 973	7 184	13.0	19.8
Northampton	3 979	3 946	3 910	13 754	52.8	8.8	24 218	18 029	34.3	4 862	144	1 810	23.1	32.8
Onslow	21 538	20 223	21 725	72 824	83.0	13.4	30 682	23 386	31.2	17 200	3 250	7 147	14.6	18.0

[1] Revised.   [2] 1997 data are model-based estimates; 1989 data are census estimates. For more information on these estimates, see appendix A. Source Notes and Explanations or <http://www.census.gov/hhes/www/saipe.html>.

Sources: Public School Enrollment, 1998-1999 and 1994-1995—U.S. National Center for Education Statistics, <http://nces.ed.gov/ccd/pubagency.html> (accessed: 16 March 2001). Public School Enrollment and Educational Attainment, 1990—U.S. Census Bureau, "1990 Census of Population and Housing, Summary Tape File (STF) 3C" on CD-ROM (related Internet site <http://homer.ssd.census.gov/cdrom/lookup>). Income and Poverty, 1997—U.S. Census Bureau, "State and County Income and Poverty Estimates - 1997," published 22 November 2000, <http://www.census.gov/housing/saipe/estmod97/est97ALL.dat>. Income and Poverty, 1989—U.S. Census Bureau, "1990 Census of Population and Housing, Summary Tape File (STF) 3C" on CD-ROM (related Internet site <http://homer.ssd.census.gov/cdrom/lookup>).

[Includes U.S., states, and 3,142 counties or county equivalents defined as of January 1, 1992. For changes to these areas since January 1, 1992, see appendix B. Geographic Information]

County	Public school enrollment Fall 1998–1999	Public school enrollment Fall 1994–1995[1]	Public school enrollment 1990	Educational attainment, 1990 Persons 25 years and over	Percent High school graduate or higher	Percent Bachelor's degree or higher	Median household income 1997 (dollars)	Median household income 1989 (dollars)	Percent change, 1989–1997	Persons below poverty level, 1997 Number, Persons of all ages Total	Net change, 1989–1997	Persons under 18 years	Percent Persons of all ages	Percent Persons under 18 years
NORTH CAROLINA–Con.														
Orange	15 007	13 337	11 075	54 779	83.6	46.1	39 410	29 968	31.5	10 845	–897	2 904	10.5	12.5
Pamlico	2 136	2 170	2 080	7 834	65.9	11.6	28 629	21 060	35.9	2 081	–38	773	16.8	25.9
Pasquotank	6 262	6 233	5 837	19 262	67.4	14.4	29 305	21 816	34.3	6 375	487	2 496	19.0	25.3
Pender	6 353	5 409	5 013	19 329	64.6	11.6	30 705	23 270	32.0	5 880	987	2 234	15.0	22.0
Perquimans	1 919	1 948	1 720	7 058	61.2	8.8	26 489	20 022	32.3	2 195	–19	839	19.5	29.4
Person	5 799	5 373	5 305	20 053	63.2	7.6	33 501	25 625	30.7	3 928	72	1 450	11.6	16.5
Pitt	20 162	19 136	17 787	62 325	71.0	21.9	31 987	23 324	37.1	21 830	–821	7 691	17.7	23.2
Polk	2 371	2 094	1 879	10 565	69.6	20.1	34 909	26 801	30.3	1 448	87	496	8.7	14.7
Randolph	20 627	18 706	17 153	70 226	62.0	9.1	35 453	27 130	30.7	10 767	1 990	4 128	8.8	13.3
Richmond	8 344	8 263	8 714	28 330	60.4	7.9	27 349	21 953	24.6	8 298	986	3 377	18.2	26.3
Robeson	24 167	23 479	23 679	61 514	57.0	11.0	25 518	19 716	29.4	26 227	1 488	10 663	22.8	28.8
Rockingham	14 731	14 383	14 572	57 494	59.2	8.8	32 305	25 402	27.2	10 996	648	3 959	12.1	17.3
Rowan	19 865	18 251	17 781	73 374	66.0	11.7	35 112	26 354	33.2	14 546	4 459	5 596	11.8	17.6
Rutherford	10 298	10 006	10 077	37 401	59.4	9.8	30 981	23 828	30.0	8 381	1 498	3 198	13.7	20.2
Sampson	10 160	9 481	9 437	30 496	61.3	8.1	28 199	19 709	43.1	9 182	–470	3 452	17.5	23.8
Scotland	7 263	7 364	7 272	20 051	60.7	13.6	29 323	22 561	30.0	6 657	590	2 843	18.8	25.6
Stanly	10 113	9 225	8 717	33 734	62.1	9.4	34 437	25 374	35.7	6 060	488	2 268	10.8	15.5
Stokes	7 139	6 598	6 701	24 438	62.8	7.3	35 618	27 945	27.5	4 499	885	1 725	10.3	15.3
Surry	11 420	10 676	10 067	41 502	57.3	9.4	30 848	23 444	31.6	7 996	1 040	2 871	11.8	17.5
Swain	1 687	1 673	2 025	7 389	59.0	9.9	21 858	16 068	36.0	2 568	–452	989	20.9	29.8
Transylvania	4 058	3 973	3 838	17 344	72.1	17.9	34 547	25 179	37.2	3 511	183	1 297	12.4	20.3
Tyrrell	800	777	696	2 521	58.0	7.6	21 616	16 363	32.1	982	18	375	25.7	33.9
Union	20 821	17 591	15 575	51 926	69.0	13.2	41 145	30 957	32.9	9 894	2 936	4 464	8.9	13.7
Vance	8 193	7 342	7 362	24 370	57.1	9.5	26 499	21 555	22.9	8 181	675	3 284	19.3	27.4
Wake	93 809	76 922	62 815	271 387	85.4	35.3	51 391	36 222	41.9	44 103	9 854	16 282	7.8	11.3
Warren	3 239	3 120	3 040	11 599	53.7	7.1	23 025	16 937	35.9	4 267	–500	1 392	23.4	29.6
Washington	2 631	2 710	2 912	8 827	60.6	8.7	27 726	21 840	27.0	2 798	–6	1 138	20.5	29.3
Watauga	4 808	4 825	4 420	19 905	72.0	27.4	31 013	20 252	53.1	5 321	–1 673	1 258	14.5	16.1
Wayne	19 520	18 516	19 185	66 158	71.2	12.7	31 410	23 560	33.3	17 557	2 741	6 733	16.6	22.1
Wilkes	10 138	9 887	10 192	39 535	54.1	8.8	30 700	22 261	37.9	8 366	569	3 018	13.3	19.4
Wilson	12 351	12 002	12 381	41 950	62.2	14.4	30 191	24 021	25.7	12 727	20	4 785	18.7	26.0
Yadkin	5 702	5 134	4 872	20 872	58.9	7.1	33 929	25 062	35.4	3 555	–36	1 232	10.1	14.6
Yancey	2 526	2 421	2 549	10 589	60.7	10.0	27 797	19 401	43.3	2 607	–234	892	15.6	22.7
NORTH DAKOTA	114 927	120 900	120 680	396 550	76.7	18.1	31 764	23 213	36.8	78 461	–9 815	27 807	12.5	16.8
Adams	495	545	615	2 180	72.5	11.2	27 346	20 722	32.0	354	–68	119	13.2	18.1
Barnes	1 968	2 167	2 222	8 181	75.4	15.4	29 588	20 419	44.9	1 621	–420	520	13.9	18.6
Benson	1 061	1 569	1 788	4 130	65.4	9.2	21 833	16 917	29.1	1 989	–262	932	28.7	38.5
Billings	107	126	238	684	71.5	12.6	29 541	22 639	30.5	133	–194	46	12.1	14.0
Bottineau	1 271	1 400	1 573	5 348	74.9	14.3	30 156	22 294	35.3	905	–83	305	12.6	17.2
Bowman	783	762	772	2 397	74.3	13.9	31 058	21 478	44.6	354	–195	117	10.7	13.7
Burke	399	512	602	2 146	66.9	8.7	28 783	19 160	50.2	282	–269	85	12.1	17.0
Burleigh	11 085	11 361	11 232	37 463	83.0	25.1	39 664	28 450	39.4	6 129	278	2 148	9.2	12.3
Cass	19 269	18 278	16 595	61 530	87.1	26.5	38 871	26 806	45.0	10 383	–1 238	3 178	9.0	11.5
Cavalier	878	925	1 136	4 158	68.4	12.6	31 223	21 250	46.9	649	–189	222	12.9	18.3
Dickey	967	996	1 079	3 979	68.8	16.0	28 090	20 248	38.7	814	–193	267	15.3	19.7
Divide	391	460	523	2 097	69.4	12.8	29 291	21 507	36.2	291	–59	93	12.6	18.3
Dunn	609	676	834	2 537	70.5	10.1	25 257	19 824	27.4	600	–390	218	16.7	21.2
Eddy	582	591	589	2 068	66.5	11.0	26 181	19 310	35.6	368	73	137	13.0	19.8
Emmons	825	819	953	3 317	57.3	9.0	23 504	16 892	39.1	686	–445	215	15.7	21.5
Foster	767	724	827	2 665	69.4	12.1	30 687	20 760	47.8	469	–208	157	12.4	16.1
Golden Valley	462	508	513	1 333	74.6	15.7	26 669	20 281	31.5	263	–59	96	14.5	20.0
Grand Forks	11 001	12 261	11 604	39 091	85.6	25.8	35 959	25 162	42.9	7 101	–894	2 353	11.2	14.1
Grant	434	510	736	2 454	62.6	8.9	20 257	17 368	16.6	673	–187	239	22.5	33.7
Griggs	630	728	666	2 285	67.9	12.1	28 108	19 417	44.8	412	–93	142	14.4	20.7
Hettinger	627	661	546	2 377	69.5	12.2	28 249	19 601	44.1	396	–231	130	13.6	18.9
Kidder	532	643	726	2 235	60.5	11.3	23 779	17 378	36.8	500	–292	174	17.2	23.7
LaMoure	1 054	1 197	1 071	3 665	66.4	12.4	28 985	19 710	47.1	577	–441	188	12.0	15.5
Logan	477	483	526	2 036	51.9	9.3	23 910	19 490	22.7	376	–138	123	16.2	22.4
McHenry	1 209	1 346	1 362	4 439	66.7	9.7	24 851	18 275	36.0	1 044	–180	368	16.9	24.0
McIntosh	568	666	784	2 987	48.8	9.5	23 018	17 798	29.3	576	–79	179	17.0	27.8
McKenzie	1 157	1 221	1 536	3 929	72.7	14.2	32 034	24 662	29.9	1 124	–33	464	19.6	25.8
McLean	2 154	2 438	2 278	6 892	68.2	11.9	32 129	21 853	47.0	1 235	–383	425	12.7	15.9
Mercer	2 141	2 355	2 324	6 113	71.2	11.2	47 215	31 969	47.7	738	–136	246	7.8	8.5
Morton	5 227	5 136	5 062	14 763	70.4	13.8	32 755	23 685	38.3	3 225	374	1 240	13.0	18.3
Mountrail	1 607	1 712	1 654	4 490	73.0	12.9	27 543	19 399	42.0	1 149	–287	463	17.6	24.0
Nelson	749	882	809	3 202	69.4	10.6	25 831	19 360	33.4	404	–188	120	11.1	15.1
Oliver	334	408	567	1 460	68.2	10.8	34 989	23 000	52.1	275	–182	97	12.2	14.1
Pembina	1 876	2 006	1 985	6 150	73.1	13.1	34 875	23 256	50.0	882	49	329	10.4	14.7
Pierce	815	877	969	3 477	65.9	13.4	26 796	20 216	32.5	652	–116	233	14.4	20.4

[1] Revised. [2] 1997 data are model-based estimates; 1989 data are census estimates. For more information on these estimates, see appendix A. Source Notes and Explanations or <http://www.census.gov/hhes/www/saipe.html>.

Sources: Public School Enrollment, 1998-1999 and 1994-1995—U.S. National Center for Education Statistics, <http://nces.ed.gov/ccd/pubagency.html> (accessed: 16 March 2001). Public School Enrollment and Educational Attainment, 1990—U.S. Census Bureau, "1990 Census of Population and Housing, Summary Tape File (STF) 3C" on CD-ROM (related Internet site <http://homer.ssd.census.gov/cdrom/lookup>). Income and Poverty, 1997—U.S. Census Bureau, "State and County Income and Poverty Estimates - 1997," published 22 November 2000, <http://www.census.gov/housing/saipe/estmod97/est97ALL.dat>. Income and Poverty, 1989—U.S. Census Bureau, "1990 Census of Population and Housing, Summary Tape File (STF) 3C" on CD-ROM (related Internet site <http://homer.ssd.census.gov/cdrom/lookup>).

Table B-5. Counties — **Education, Income, and Poverty**–Con.

[Includes U.S., states, and 3,142 counties or county equivalents defined as of January 1, 1992. For changes to these areas since January 1, 1992, see appendix B. Geographic Information]

County	Public school enrollment Fall 1998–1999	1994–1995[1]	1990	Educational attainment, 1990 Percent— Persons 25 years and over	High school graduate or higher	Bachelor's degree or higher	Median household income[2] 1997 (dollars)	1989 (dollars)	Percent change, 1989–1997	Persons below poverty level,[2] 1997 Number Persons of all ages Total	Net change, 1989–1997	Persons under 18 years	Percent Persons of all ages	Persons under 18 years
NORTH DAKOTA—Con.														
Ramsey	2 368	2 565	2 431	8 305	74.5	16.3	30 355	21 780	39.4	1 744	137	658	14.8	22.0
Ransom	1 191	1 254	1 144	4 081	73.1	11.1	32 823	23 017	42.6	537	−96	157	9.6	11.1
Renville	775	810	683	2 129	74.2	9.8	30 684	22 659	35.4	295	−63	102	10.5	13.8
Richland	3 130	3 414	3 244	11 025	75.9	13.0	36 591	24 248	50.9	1 922	−120	649	11.4	14.6
Rolette	3 345	3 483	3 460	6 660	59.4	11.7	21 831	15 163	44.0	4 380	−723	2 012	30.7	36.2
Sargent	866	823	963	3 050	72.7	9.7	36 041	23 838	51.2	401	−116	123	8.9	10.9
Sheridan	223	269	372	1 545	49.5	8.2	23 067	17 145	34.5	383	−107	122	22.4	32.8
Sioux	561	1 163	1 186	1 794	68.3	9.9	19 120	14 838	28.9	1 580	−189	753	37.4	40.8
Slope	41	41	179	585	71.5	10.4	22 759	18 355	24.0	114	−76	34	12.6	14.1
Stark	4 066	4 117	3 875	14 009	73.1	14.8	32 028	22 048	45.3	3 088	−78	1 051	13.7	17.0
Steele	366	387	478	1 678	71.9	13.7	32 659	23 307	40.1	295	−7	113	12.9	20.3
Stutsman	3 448	3 670	3 867	14 524	73.5	16.7	32 213	22 415	43.7	2 581	15	854	12.7	17.3
Towner	577	654	701	2 449	71.9	12.7	27 205	18 608	46.2	443	−315	146	14.8	19.3
Traill	1 816	1 847	1 664	5 652	76.6	17.7	35 162	22 050	59.5	907	−113	299	10.9	14.1
Walsh	2 400	2 547	2 738	9 142	68.0	13.0	29 847	21 973	35.8	1 951	163	719	14.5	20.4
Ward	10 257	10 444	10 810	33 917	82.8	19.0	33 095	22 996	43.9	6 829	−224	2 451	11.8	15.7
Wells	1 035	1 084	1 095	4 173	63.2	11.3	27 798	18 568	49.7	740	−295	225	14.2	19.1
Williams	3 951	4 369	4 494	13 514	76.8	14.3	33 249	23 249	43.0	2 641	−251	976	13.1	17.5
OHIO	1 849 182	1 829 761	1 779 522	6 924 764	75.7	17.0	36 029	28 706	25.5	1 223 791	−101 977	465 752	11.0	16.0
Adams	5 461	5 352	5 426	15 569	58.4	5.2	24 708	16 318	51.4	5 279	−1 861	2 117	18.3	25.3
Allen	19 223	19 777	19 803	68 893	76.1	11.4	35 411	27 166	30.4	11 783	−1 459	4 584	11.4	15.8
Ashland	7 982	8 148	8 479	29 403	76.0	13.0	36 428	26 668	36.6	4 113	−1 047	1 588	8.1	11.5
Ashtabula	18 717	18 467	18 380	63 850	72.4	9.0	32 318	24 126	34.0	13 812	−1 909	5 552	13.4	19.9
Athens	9 256	9 604	9 172	30 179	74.6	23.4	28 965	19 169	51.1	10 376	−4 248	3 053	19.1	23.6
Auglaize	9 393	9 303	8 700	27 676	76.5	9.8	39 705	30 090	32.0	2 888	135	1 075	6.1	7.9
Belmont	10 127	10 480	11 948	48 645	72.3	9.0	27 061	20 987	28.9	11 291	−894	3 808	16.3	23.3
Brown	8 326	7 985	6 871	21 769	64.9	7.4	33 138	25 286	31.1	4 925	50	2 072	12.0	17.5
Butler	54 023	52 902	48 139	176 989	76.0	18.7	43 534	32 440	34.2	26 292	−3 495	9 664	8.1	11.1
Carroll	4 081	4 105	5 156	17 124	71.5	7.9	34 161	25 787	32.5	3 145	82	1 298	10.8	16.3
Champaign	7 627	7 514	6 749	23 023	75.4	9.7	40 807	31 198	30.8	2 877	−248	1 112	7.5	10.9
Clark	25 623	26 188	26 126	93 950	73.4	12.2	36 145	27 743	30.3	18 051	−1 141	7 134	12.5	19.4
Clermont	28 900	28 732	28 085	91 613	72.8	14.5	44 605	32 465	37.4	11 940	−963	5 038	6.7	9.0
Clinton	8 546	8 320	8 943	21 969	74.3	11.6	37 516	27 157	38.1	3 608	−621	1 449	9.0	13.1
Columbiana	18 604	18 818	20 505	70 249	71.8	8.5	32 222	23 368	37.9	14 901	−2 094	5 609	13.3	19.1
Coshocton	6 528	6 625	6 626	22 878	71.3	8.1	31 900	23 617	35.1	4 163	−431	1 723	11.5	17.7
Crawford	8 421	8 606	8 774	30 958	73.8	9.3	33 105	24 981	32.5	4 786	−684	1 885	10.1	15.2
Cuyahoga	203 432	198 483	192 475	943 924	74.0	20.1	36 754	28 595	28.5	188 102	−3 047	72 017	13.6	21.4
Darke	9 394	9 822	10 445	34 048	73.5	8.8	37 160	27 640	34.4	3 973	−750	1 435	7.4	9.7
Defiance	7 492	7 731	7 823	24 362	76.8	12.5	41 686	31 505	32.3	2 838	−524	1 118	7.1	9.9
Delaware	13 428	11 847	11 871	41 799	84.4	26.4	56 641	37 896	49.5	4 343	713	1 698	4.5	6.4
Erie	14 564	14 532	13 223	50 112	76.2	13.8	39 321	30 470	29.0	7 281	505	2 860	9.3	14.2
Fairfield	21 477	20 503	19 110	65 269	78.8	15.5	42 060	31 284	34.4	8 553	−325	3 435	6.9	10.3
Fayette	5 323	5 483	5 217	17 854	65.3	8.5	32 477	22 704	43.0	3 408	−953	1 265	12.0	16.8
Franklin	166 595	160 384	144 777	597 303	81.0	26.6	39 498	30 375	30.0	113 115	−8 360	43 580	11.1	17.1
Fulton	9 382	9 209	7 881	23 846	78.3	10.3	41 290	31 890	29.5	2 361	−6	924	5.6	7.5
Gallia	5 692	5 741	5 988	19 586	64.2	10.9	28 349	20 972	35.2	6 057	−650	2 371	18.4	27.0
Geauga	12 859	12 221	12 417	51 290	82.0	25.9	52 425	41 113	27.5	4 511	46	1 774	5.0	7.3
Greene	24 072	24 170	23 320	83 757	82.4	26.0	46 768	35 116	33.2	10 516	−1 835	3 824	7.3	10.3
Guernsey	6 522	6 595	7 571	25 188	71.4	9.2	28 306	21 143	33.9	6 287	−372	2 562	15.4	23.1
Hamilton	128 997	129 323	122 712	551 233	75.6	23.7	38 763	29 498	31.4	96 461	−16 114	37 012	11.4	16.6
Hancock	11 771	11 450	11 406	41 492	82.9	18.7	40 758	31 897	27.8	5 062	390	1 853	7.3	10.0
Hardin	6 313	6 377	5 823	18 589	74.0	11.6	33 666	24 589	36.9	3 495	−1 274	1 231	11.5	15.1
Harrison	2 958	3 093	3 238	10 726	69.8	7.0	27 254	19 943	36.7	2 368	−746	860	14.7	21.2
Henry	5 505	5 384	5 531	18 245	75.4	10.3	41 032	31 032	31.0	1 921	−63	748	6.4	8.8
Highland	8 289	8 013	7 263	22 784	66.5	8.2	29 740	21 505	38.3	5 118	−703	1 910	12.5	17.0
Hocking	4 328	4 092	4 701	16 368	67.8	8.1	30 865	22 727	35.8	3 710	−195	1 448	12.9	18.9
Holmes	4 714	4 815	5 233	17 780	46.9	6.6	33 441	25 448	31.4	3 737	−1 752	1 756	10.0	12.8
Huron	11 926	11 833	10 594	34 521	74.1	9.4	36 500	27 401	33.2	5 363	85	2 247	8.8	12.8
Jackson	6 020	6 024	6 244	19 136	60.9	7.9	27 774	18 298	51.8	5 401	−1 825	2 080	16.4	22.8
Jefferson	12 033	12 744	12 964	54 294	71.9	8.8	28 443	22 142	28.5	11 515	−1 949	3 962	15.5	23.0
Knox	8 422	8 248	8 193	29 992	75.2	12.8	34 027	24 701	37.8	5 128	−384	1 968	10.1	14.7
Lake	35 254	35 020	32 721	142 348	81.1	17.5	43 115	35 605	21.1	13 084	2 651	4 589	5.7	8.3
Lawrence	11 835	12 060	12 137	39 219	65.9	8.2	26 075	19 454	34.0	13 056	−1 305	5 051	20.1	29.2
Licking	24 061	23 736	22 393	81 642	76.4	13.0	39 845	29 606	34.6	12 227	−864	4 563	9.1	13.0
Logan	8 043	8 048	8 306	26 780	74.5	8.9	37 531	26 857	39.7	4 416	65	1 756	9.5	13.7
Lorain	45 738	46 130	48 991	169 492	75.3	12.3	40 496	31 098	30.2	28 999	−1 460	11 607	10.4	15.1
Lucas	70 235	69 069	69 775	289 965	76.2	17.0	37 064	28 245	31.2	61 023	−8 351	24 376	13.6	20.3
Madison	7 086	6 958	6 506	23 896	69.5	9.0	39 761	29 935	32.8	3 204	431	1 175	8.7	11.8
Mahoning	41 142	41 019	42 530	176 658	74.6	14.0	31 236	24 062	29.8	36 743	−4 690	13 182	14.4	21.1

[1] Revised. [2] 1997 data are model-based estimates; 1989 data are census estimates. For more information on these estimates, see appendix A. Source Notes and Explanations or <http://www.census.gov/hhes/www/saipe.html>.

Sources: Public School Enrollment, 1998-1999 and 1994-1995—U.S. National Center for Education Statistics, <http://nces.ed.gov/ccd/pubagency.html> (accessed: 16 March 2001). Public School Enrollment and Educational Attainment, 1990—U.S. Census Bureau, "1990 Census of Population and Housing, Summary Tape File (STF) 3C" on CD-ROM (related Internet site <http://homer.ssd.census.gov/cdrom/lookup>). Income and Poverty, 1997—U.S. Census Bureau, "State and County Income and Poverty Estimates - 1997," published 22 November 2000, <http://www.census.gov/housing/saipe/estmod97/est97ALL.dat>. Income and Poverty, 1989—U.S. Census Bureau, "1990 Census of Population and Housing, Summary Tape File (STF) 3C" on CD-ROM (related Internet site <http://homer.ssd.census.gov/cdrom/lookup>).

[Includes U.S., states, and 3,142 counties or county equivalents defined as of January 1, 1992. For changes to these areas since January 1, 1992, see appendix B. Geographic Information]

County	Public school enrollment Fall			Educational attainment, 1990 Percent—			Median household income[2]			Persons below poverty level,[2] 1997 Number — Persons of all ages			Percent	
	1998–1999	1994–1995[1]	1990	Persons 25 years and over	High school graduate or higher	Bachelor's degree or higher	1997 (dollars)	1989 (dollars)	Percent change, 1989–1997	Total	Net change, 1989–1997	Persons under 18 years	Persons of all ages	Persons under 18 years
OHIO—Con.														
Marion	12 237	12 119	11 886	41 239	73.8	9.9	34 456	26 330	30.9	7 493	–329	2 821	11.9	16.6
Medina	27 454	26 132	23 698	76 962	82.4	18.0	49 194	38 083	29.2	7 170	487	2 596	4.9	6.4
Meigs	4 172	4 295	4 574	14 772	64.0	7.3	25 223	17 707	42.4	4 925	–970	1 834	20.4	28.3
Mercer	10 168	9 839	8 135	23 780	75.5	8.6	38 887	29 618	31.3	2 689	77	1 081	6.5	8.5
Miami	18 015	18 105	17 099	59 893	76.6	14.1	41 678	31 425	32.6	6 922	–772	2 704	7.0	10.4
Monroe	3 000	3 211	2 883	10 196	69.4	6.8	27 923	20 413	36.8	2 614	–669	930	16.9	24.1
Montgomery	85 901	87 033	88 606	371 530	77.8	20.0	37 174	30 111	23.5	63 281	–7 686	23 533	11.1	16.7
Morgan	2 649	2 687	2 961	8 980	71.6	7.4	29 443	21 396	37.6	2 216	–737	904	15.3	21.9
Morrow	5 510	5 509	5 981	17 158	71.3	7.2	36 005	27 318	31.8	3 207	168	1 233	10.1	13.5
Muskingum	16 697	16 584	14 944	51 692	71.1	10.1	31 000	23 967	29.3	12 116	338	4 931	14.4	21.8
Noble	2 565	2 530	2 310	7 235	69.9	5.6	29 206	21 617	35.1	1 963	133	643	15.8	17.7
Ottawa	6 691	6 851	6 958	26 931	75.9	13.5	39 823	31 360	27.0	2 845	240	1 011	6.9	10.2
Paulding	4 224	4 304	4 402	12 456	72.2	6.9	37 556	28 345	32.5	1 569	–418	615	7.7	10.3
Perry	6 784	6 657	6 345	19 411	68.6	5.8	29 116	21 517	35.3	5 320	–639	2 067	15.4	20.6
Pickaway	9 634	9 290	8 503	31 380	69.7	9.0	37 886	28 403	33.4	5 403	283	1 938	11.3	15.3
Pike	5 861	5 855	5 088	15 099	60.8	8.0	27 989	19 486	43.6	5 072	–1 261	2 171	18.2	27.0
Portage	24 574	24 279	24 424	82 726	79.3	17.6	40 060	30 253	32.4	12 759	–3 133	4 373	8.7	11.8
Preble	8 103	8 156	8 065	25 469	72.5	7.0	37 214	27 582	34.9	3 498	–538	1 289	8.0	11.0
Putnam	7 620	7 677	6 895	20 028	77.5	8.8	42 741	32 492	31.5	1 953	31	740	5.5	6.6
Richland	22 109	22 494	21 809	81 363	73.5	11.6	34 413	27 329	25.9	14 498	734	5 416	11.5	16.5
Ross	12 444	12 364	13 167	45 531	67.6	9.2	33 580	24 286	38.3	10 257	–1 005	3 639	14.6	19.5
Sandusky	11 549	11 800	11 427	38 993	76.6	10.7	36 864	29 060	26.9	5 908	437	2 320	9.5	13.4
Scioto	14 549	14 961	15 902	51 585	63.8	8.5	25 807	17 595	46.7	16 628	–3 164	6 165	21.0	28.1
Seneca	9 888	10 323	11 297	36 666	75.3	10.1	34 234	26 988	26.8	5 659	–540	2 177	9.6	12.8
Shelby	9 160	9 054	8 822	27 365	72.9	11.2	40 543	30 929	31.1	3 631	213	1 470	7.6	10.5
Stark	65 336	64 715	61 040	241 153	76.0	14.3	38 323	27 852	37.6	38 979	–754	14 681	10.5	15.8
Summit	85 796	84 270	80 703	337 442	78.3	19.7	38 996	28 996	33.7	58 744	–2 747	22 134	10.9	16.8
Trumbull	37 364	37 419	37 642	149 822	75.2	11.4	36 410	28 186	29.2	25 322	–365	9 743	11.2	17.4
Tuscarawas	15 697	15 737	14 713	55 192	71.9	9.0	32 877	24 773	32.7	9 125	–90	3 516	10.2	15.2
Union	5 999	5 440	5 887	20 527	76.2	12.0	43 392	33 244	30.5	2 579	341	956	6.7	8.8
Van Wert	4 503	4 564	5 752	19 497	79.2	9.3	37 296	28 642	30.2	1 925	–203	692	6.4	8.4
Vinton	2 538	2 454	2 277	6 963	58.7	4.8	26 697	19 066	40.0	2 291	–291	877	18.7	25.6
Warren	24 283	21 808	20 194	73 151	75.5	18.0	50 152	36 728	36.5	8 067	1 118	2 860	5.6	7.4
Washington	10 989	11 311	11 194	40 411	77.5	13.2	33 426	24 456	36.7	7 720	–570	2 789	12.3	17.4
Wayne	19 264	19 121	18 220	62 178	73.6	13.9	37 947	29 190	30.0	9 583	–1 873	3 889	8.8	12.6
Williams	7 351	7 353	7 511	23 340	76.1	8.9	37 571	28 451	32.1	2 600	–157	987	6.8	9.2
Wood	18 664	18 303	18 731	64 052	83.8	21.9	42 790	31 197	37.2	8 073	–2 981	2 477	7.1	8.4
Wyandot	4 101	4 071	4 216	14 361	76.5	8.7	35 245	27 454	28.4	1 603	–244	547	7.0	8.8
OKLAHOMA	628 522	609 743	571 787	1 995 424	74.6	17.8	30 002	23 577	27.3	536 804	26 950	210 470	16.3	23.7
Adair	5 023	4 936	4 029	10 964	56.1	9.6	23 123	16 886	36.9	4 842	–4	2 063	23.7	33.3
Alfalfa	978	886	1 055	4 597	77.3	17.3	25 826	18 407	40.3	887	–66	265	16.4	20.4
Atoka	2 292	2 287	2 598	8 363	59.8	10.2	21 062	13 898	51.5	3 412	–210	1 225	27.5	35.4
Beaver	1 305	1 296	1 260	3 962	75.3	15.4	34 960	27 372	27.7	606	74	228	10.0	13.2
Beckham	3 765	3 841	3 869	12 185	66.5	12.3	26 701	19 154	39.4	3 959	187	1 555	20.3	27.0
Blaine	2 223	2 357	2 254	7 492	71.2	12.4	27 252	20 395	33.6	2 082	–159	851	20.3	29.0
Bryan	6 933	6 407	5 652	20 211	67.3	16.9	24 270	16 610	46.1	7 261	–347	2 569	21.2	29.3
Caddo	6 663	6 751	6 107	18 700	66.2	11.6	25 045	17 857	40.3	7 107	–925	2 788	23.8	32.2
Canadian	17 712	17 054	15 974	46 349	82.3	16.7	44 610	33 855	31.8	7 529	1 449	3 128	8.9	12.2
Carter	9 101	9 027	8 392	28 252	70.3	13.4	28 017	21 800	28.5	8 474	202	3 293	19.2	27.2
Cherokee	7 153	6 524	6 461	20 653	69.9	21.1	24 399	17 513	39.3	9 118	–376	3 491	23.6	33.0
Choctaw	2 985	3 134	3 128	9 815	57.9	7.1	19 213	12 451	54.3	4 468	–451	1 685	29.6	40.0
Cimarron	621	707	707	2 194	71.0	15.1	27 257	19 173	42.2	433	–142	171	14.4	20.0
Cleveland	36 122	35 488	31 800	102 913	83.9	25.9	41 085	29 975	37.1	21 264	2 828	8 038	10.9	15.2
Coal	1 258	1 191	1 128	3 824	60.4	9.1	20 617	14 177	45.4	1 511	–45	573	25.1	35.5
Comanche	23 067	23 086	21 163	62 977	81.1	18.4	31 132	24 378	27.7	18 524	2 258	8 093	17.6	25.6
Cotton	1 254	1 263	1 273	4 446	62.8	8.9	27 095	18 978	42.8	1 192	–171	429	18.0	24.3
Craig	3 145	2 788	2 475	9 789	66.8	10.0	25 754	18 986	35.6	2 237	–207	744	16.2	22.3
Creek	13 443	12 863	12 253	38 689	68.9	10.6	31 800	23 795	33.6	9 585	863	3 853	14.2	21.1
Custer	5 079	5 117	5 164	15 487	75.1	20.4	30 093	22 592	33.2	4 262	–551	1 582	17.3	22.8
Delaware	6 609	5 858	4 926	19 357	66.2	10.8	25 455	18 681	36.3	6 642	1 876	2 559	19.3	31.0
Dewey	1 127	1 253	1 109	3 770	68.2	12.1	26 943	18 968	42.0	741	–218	263	15.1	19.8
Ellis	777	888	925	3 096	73.8	14.0	26 892	20 017	34.3	614	–9	228	14.5	20.3
Garfield	10 145	10 320	10 363	37 294	76.5	17.3	31 256	23 243	34.5	8 347	600	3 310	14.9	22.4
Garvin	5 583	5 674	4 923	17 799	63.4	10.1	25 109	18 659	34.6	5 010	–79	1 932	18.9	28.0
Grady	8 586	8 513	8 570	26 360	69.0	13.2	31 241	21 885	42.8	7 661	145	3 069	16.8	23.4
Grant	1 098	1 061	1 018	3 948	77.9	15.6	28 870	21 659	33.3	759	–5	274	14.3	19.7
Greer	1 010	1 018	989	4 634	64.7	10.0	23 992	17 010	41.0	1 492	164	478	27.1	37.1
Harmon	694	796	802	2 467	58.0	10.5	20 799	13 880	49.8	1 057	–179	430	31.5	43.8
Harper	746	823	805	2 821	76.1	13.6	32 818	22 813	43.9	340	–86	118	9.5	12.8

[1] Revised. [2] 1997 data are model-based estimates; 1989 data are census estimates. For more information on these estimates, see appendix A. Source Notes and Explanations or <http://www.census.gov/hhes/www/saipe.html>.

Sources: Public School Enrollment, 1998-1999 and 1994-1995—U.S. National Center for Education Statistics, <http://nces.ed.gov/ccd/pubagency.html> (accessed: 16 March 2001). Public School Enrollment and Educational Attainment, 1990—U.S. Census Bureau, "1990 Census of Population and Housing, Summary Tape File (STF) 3C" on CD-ROM (related Internet site <http://homer.ssd.census.gov/cdrom/lookup>). Income and Poverty, 1997—U.S. Census Bureau, "State and County Income and Poverty Estimates - 1997," published 22 November 2000, <http://www.census.gov/housing/saipe/estmod97/est97ALL.dat>. Income and Poverty, 1989—U.S. Census Bureau, "1990 Census of Population and Housing, Summary Tape File (STF) 3C" on CD-ROM (related Internet site <http://homer.ssd.census.gov/cdrom/lookup>).

Table B–5. Counties — **Education, Income, and Poverty**–Con.

[Includes U.S., states, and 3,142 counties or county equivalents defined as of January 1, 1992. For changes to these areas since January 1, 1992, see appendix B. Geographic Information]

County	Public school enrollment — Fall			Educational attainment, 1990	Percent—		Median household income[2]			Persons below poverty level,[2] 1997 — Number — Persons of all ages			Percent	
	1998–1999	1994–1995[1]	1990	Persons 25 years and over	High school graduate or higher	Bachelor's degree or higher	1997 (dollars)	1989 (dollars)	Percent change, 1989–1997	Total	Net change, 1989–1997	Persons under 18 years	Persons of all ages	Persons under 18 years
OKLAHOMA—Con.														
Haskell	2 401	2 158	2 166	7 272	56.4	7.7	22 419	15 592	43.8	2 644	−286	963	23.2	32.8
Hughes	2 584	2 548	2 391	8 946	58.7	7.7	21 394	15 168	41.0	3 322	−93	1 129	25.5	34.1
Jackson	6 145	6 108	5 960	16 871	74.1	16.5	30 330	21 715	39.7	4 749	−325	2 055	16.8	23.2
Jefferson	1 418	1 375	1 353	4 777	58.7	6.6	22 347	15 553	43.7	1 453	−131	523	22.4	31.5
Johnston	2 066	2 077	2 180	6 335	61.0	9.3	21 713	15 264	42.2	2 479	−280	927	24.2	33.0
Kay	9 480	9 219	8 668	31 413	76.8	18.5	31 732	24 295	30.6	6 764	681	2 690	14.6	22.1
Kingfisher	3 257	3 204	2 673	8 513	76.2	13.4	34 556	25 367	36.2	1 559	160	615	11.6	15.8
Kiowa	2 046	2 216	2 199	7 567	65.0	11.1	22 095	16 322	35.4	2 449	−591	897	23.2	30.4
Latimer	1 930	1 985	2 068	6 438	63.1	11.0	23 720	17 477	35.7	2 351	94	977	24.1	35.5
Le Flore	9 842	9 543	8 587	27 527	61.2	9.6	26 057	18 832	38.4	10 026	578	3 957	21.7	30.7
Lincoln	5 926	5 746	6 000	18 854	68.8	10.1	31 148	21 515	44.8	4 778	−223	2 020	15.2	23.1
Logan	4 488	4 583	5 472	17 567	72.0	14.8	35 771	24 050	48.7	4 036	−899	1 601	13.8	19.3
Love	1 640	1 573	1 591	5 377	66.5	9.3	27 775	20 320	36.7	1 434	210	575	16.7	25.1
McClain	5 424	5 220	4 617	14 583	72.2	13.3	34 208	25 437	34.5	3 668	455	1 450	13.9	20.0
McCurtain	7 609	7 732	7 237	20 551	59.2	9.6	23 132	16 413	40.9	9 209	−728	3 700	26.5	36.0
McIntosh	3 333	3 420	2 863	11 709	61.5	10.7	22 904	17 738	29.1	4 240	325	1 547	22.3	36.0
Major	1 732	1 776	1 603	5 362	70.9	13.1	31 859	23 568	35.2	1 083	−176	396	13.9	18.7
Marshall	2 365	2 117	1 707	7 531	60.7	9.7	23 597	16 292	44.8	2 299	106	833	18.9	29.6
Mayes	7 298	6 852	6 339	21 664	67.9	10.8	29 381	21 209	38.5	6 524	359	2 545	17.2	25.7
Murray	2 281	2 345	2 338	8 118	64.0	13.5	25 266	18 321	37.9	2 357	−175	857	19.5	27.2
Muskogee	14 131	14 053	13 123	43 554	68.3	14.1	27 432	20 407	34.4	13 713	−545	5 320	20.0	27.8
Noble	2 281	2 358	2 238	7 243	72.8	12.7	31 827	23 227	37.0	1 567	−248	579	14.0	18.8
Nowata	1 956	1 955	2 020	6 792	67.4	7.4	26 073	18 274	42.7	1 705	−332	587	17.2	23.9
Okfuskee	2 353	2 261	2 300	7 595	60.7	8.2	21 202	15 738	34.7	2 956	−194	1 092	27.6	37.1
Oklahoma	108 136	104 969	97 694	382 705	79.1	22.6	34 513	26 129	32.1	99 769	12 635	40 497	15.8	24.4
Okmulgee	7 557	7 129	6 994	23 452	66.3	8.8	24 039	17 368	38.4	8 589	102	3 277	22.5	31.5
Osage	4 645	4 822	8 408	27 183	73.0	13.1	32 421	24 617	31.7	6 456	94	2 713	15.2	22.8
Ottawa	6 356	5 768	5 266	19 926	67.8	10.4	25 013	17 716	41.2	6 020	117	2 199	19.7	29.5
Pawnee	2 779	2 612	3 000	10 201	73.0	10.4	29 496	21 199	39.1	2 755	81	1 063	16.7	23.9
Payne	10 106	10 165	9 353	33 024	82.2	30.1	30 444	19 591	55.4	9 911	−2 133	2 886	16.6	20.8
Pittsburg	8 402	8 216	7 648	27 427	64.3	10.3	26 665	18 906	41.0	8 075	451	2 957	19.8	29.0
Pontotoc	6 991	6 991	6 138	21 483	69.3	18.0	25 859	17 945	44.1	7 050	−74	2 647	20.8	30.4
Pottawatomie	12 335	12 088	11 134	36 723	70.3	12.2	30 409	21 914	38.8	11 867	2 108	4 840	19.5	29.0
Pushmataha	2 472	2 474	2 017	7 370	57.8	7.8	19 362	13 613	42.2	3 363	85	1 234	29.2	42.1
Roger Mills	708	812	847	2 702	72.1	0.5	27 240	20 100	35.5	807	−115	229	10.9	23.0
Rogers	13 261	11 575	10 382	34 882	78.1	13.0	41 466	29 389	41.1	6 238	493	2 622	9.1	14.1
Seminole	5 151	5 200	5 090	16 558	62.1	9.6	22 426	17 007	31.9	6 561	608	2 563	26.7	39.0
Sequoyah	8 349	7 980	7 012	21 019	59.6	8.8	26 044	18 441	41.2	7 899	−373	3 139	21.0	29.7
Stephens	8 421	8 506	8 128	28 392	70.8	14.7	30 175	22 647	33.2	7 184	−284	2 709	16.5	23.6
Texas	3 809	3 346	3 307	10 122	75.5	15.1	36 041	23 587	52.8	2 100	−43	884	11.3	15.9
Tillman	1 972	2 067	2 227	6 643	61.7	11.4	22 989	17 799	29.2	2 215	−101	887	23.6	32.6
Tulsa	104 191	97 325	82 163	322 632	81.7	23.7	35 280	27 228	29.6	72 130	7 171	28 358	13.3	20.0
Wagoner	5 930	5 730	9 774	29 685	74.7	12.0	37 904	28 544	32.8	7 116	1 298	3 024	12.8	18.3
Washington	9 043	8 745	8 792	32 050	79.6	25.8	37 346	28 857	29.4	5 852	714	2 295	12.3	19.1
Washita	2 278	2 228	2 244	7 630	66.6	11.0	25 395	18 385	38.1	2 335	33	900	19.9	27.7
Woods	1 467	1 555	1 474	5 971	76.1	23.5	28 010	19 762	41.7	1 225	−129	397	15.5	22.0
Woodward	3 680	3 809	3 830	12 077	73.4	13.0	32 809	23 796	38.3	2 650	58	1 031	14.6	19.6
OREGON	542 809	519 945	471 013	1 855 369	81.5	20.6	37 284	27 250	36.8	379 506	34 639	134 932	11.6	16.3
Baker	2 892	3 108	2 881	10 430	75.0	13.3	29 203	22 150	31.8	2 734	545	1 012	16.8	24.4
Benton	10 223	10 305	10 517	40 193	89.3	41.3	43 632	27 295	59.9	6 711	−3 294	1 741	9.1	10.0
Clackamas	54 055	51 974	49 378	182 372	85.7	23.6	49 455	35 419	39.6	21 688	2 585	7 513	6.4	8.6
Clatsop	5 736	5 351	5 830	22 090	81.8	16.7	33 502	25 135	33.3	4 727	−	1 633	13.3	18.3
Columbia	8 534	8 723	7 449	24 064	78.0	11.0	42 924	29 507	45.5	3 872	59	1 405	8.6	11.1
Coos	10 039	11 056	10 762	41 031	75.5	12.3	29 933	22 146	35.2	10 341	600	3 520	16.7	23.6
Crook	3 132	3 059	2 667	9 151	71.8	10.1	33 188	24 275	36.7	2 226	689	854	12.8	18.6
Curry	3 294	3 314	2 734	14 343	78.1	12.8	28 463	22 579	26.1	2 951	582	918	13.9	22.9
Deschutes	18 983	16 864	13 266	50 121	83.2	18.9	37 046	27 317	35.6	11 331	3 231	4 291	10.6	15.9
Douglas	17 227	17 957	17 178	61 986	74.5	11.7	32 005	23 693	35.1	14 854	1 026	5 274	14.6	20.5
Gilliam	385	365	358	1 184	85.4	18.7	34 685	24 020	44.4	192	−12	62	9.4	11.5
Grant	1 491	1 602	1 603	5 223	77.2	12.5	32 939	24 640	33.7	1 169	186	407	14.5	19.7
Harney	1 483	1 484	1 400	4 646	78.0	14.1	29 809	22 334	33.5	1 072	334	418	14.8	21.9
Hood River	3 788	3 550	3 089	11 008	71.3	18.0	34 380	25 242	36.2	2 552	−58	1 030	13.0	18.8
Jackson	28 814	27 680	23 818	97 604	80.1	17.6	32 807	25 069	30.9	23 924	4 999	8 679	13.8	20.3
Jefferson	3 536	3 395	2 883	8 258	73.9	12.2	31 915	23 532	35.6	2 785	282	1 127	16.6	23.0
Josephine	11 784	11 539	9 594	43 448	75.2	12.0	26 988	20 936	28.9	13 907	2 646	5 034	18.7	28.5
Klamath	11 085	11 379	10 661	36 914	76.2	12.4	30 781	23 054	33.5	10 091	597	3 763	15.9	22.8
Lake	1 453	1 595	1 409	4 720	75.0	14.5	30 427	24 659	23.4	1 060	68	387	14.7	20.1
Lane	49 093	48 355	45 710	180 913	83.0	22.2	34 672	25 268	37.2	41 460	1 622	13 433	13.3	18.0
Lincoln	7 041	6 979	6 365	27 491	80.5	16.7	30 294	22 883	32.4	6 691	1 167	2 356	14.7	23.0

[1] Revised. [2] 1997 data are model-based estimates; 1989 data are census estimates. For more information on these estimates, see appendix A. Source Notes and Explanations or <http://www.census.gov/hhes/www/saipe.html>.

Sources: Public School Enrollment, 1998-1999 and 1994-1995—U.S. National Center for Education Statistics, <http://nces.ed.gov/ccd/pubagency.html> (accessed: 16 March 2001). Public School Enrollment and Educational Attainment, 1990—U.S. Census Bureau, "1990 Census of Population and Housing, Summary Tape File (STF) 3C" on CD-ROM (related Internet site <http://homer.ssd.census.gov/cdrom/lookup>). Income and Poverty, 1997—U.S. Census Bureau, "State and County Income and Poverty Estimates - 1997," published 22 November 2000, <http://www.census.gov/housing/saipe/estmod97/est97ALL.dat>. Income and Poverty, 1989—U.S. Census Bureau, "1990 Census of Population and Housing, Summary Tape File (STF) 3C" on CD-ROM (related Internet site <http://homer.ssd.census.gov/cdrom/lookup>).

[Includes U.S., states, and 3,142 counties or county equivalents defined as of January 1, 1992. For changes to these areas since January 1, 1992, see appendix B. Geographic Information]

County	Public school enrollment Fall			Educational attainment, 1990			Median household income[2]			Persons below poverty level,[2] 1997				
					Percent—					Number			Percent	
										Persons of all ages				
	1998–1999	1994–1995[1]	1990	Persons 25 years and over	High school graduate or higher	Bachelor's degree or higher	1997 (dollars)	1989 (dollars)	Percent change, 1989–1997	Total	Net change, 1989–1997	Persons under 18 years	Persons of all ages	Persons under 18 years
OREGON—Con.														
Linn	17 864	17 873	15 587	58 878	76.2	11.0	36 107	25 209	43.2	12 883	705	4 727	12.3	17.2
Malheur	5 861	5 750	5 631	16 009	69.9	13.1	28 204	20 242	39.3	5 547	602	2 316	19.6	26.0
Marion	51 714	44 349	38 192	146 583	78.7	17.5	36 853	26 876	37.1	34 724	6 086	13 820	13.2	19.0
Morrow	2 227	2 030	1 649	4 731	73.9	11.8	33 181	23 969	38.4	700	−441	247	7.0	8.3
Multnomah	93 113	90 843	81 908	391 422	82.9	23.7	38 225	26 928	42.0	76 286	1 401	25 640	12.2	17.6
Polk	6 379	6 143	8 871	30 864	80.0	21.2	38 415	26 292	46.1	6 390	−85	2 272	10.5	14.3
Sherman	396	420	392	1 311	83.1	18.9	31 298	25 030	25.0	220	30	76	12.0	15.8
Tillamook	3 827	3 867	3 562	15 265	76.3	13.1	30 713	21 965	39.8	3 301	133	1 144	13.6	20.7
Umatilla	12 967	12 575	11 548	37 316	75.1	13.3	31 454	22 791	38.0	10 071	652	3 909	15.6	21.0
Union	4 365	4 735	4 561	14 589	80.2	17.0	32 912	22 484	46.4	3 437	−190	1 167	13.9	17.3
Wallowa	1 315	1 525	1 335	4 703	81.2	15.7	30 361	21 300	42.5	967	−111	317	13.1	16.8
Wasco	3 802	4 004	4 106	14 484	77.4	14.5	34 540	24 908	38.7	2 971	120	1 119	12.9	18.3
Washington	69 328	61 450	51 820	200 510	88.2	29.8	49 753	35 554	39.9	27 045	6 847	10 010	6.7	9.3
Wheeler	267	276	251	1 015	69.4	10.7	23 385	15 224	53.6	200	−91	61	12.5	18.2
Yamhill	15 316	14 471	12 048	40 499	79.1	17.1	40 252	28 303	42.2	8 424	1 125	3 251	10.5	13.8
PENNSYLVANIA	1 816 414	1 764 946	1 666 743	7 872 932	74.7	17.9	37 267	29 069	28.2	1 297 614	13 985	482 596	10.9	16.6
Adams	14 552	13 563	12 242	49 898	70.0	13.2	40 958	30 304	35.2	5 490	409	2 209	6.4	9.9
Allegheny	173 819	167 882	164 362	926 826	79.0	22.6	38 893	28 136	38.2	137 730	−12 983	47 491	10.9	17.1
Armstrong	12 009	12 114	12 403	49 575	71.1	8.1	31 017	22 554	37.5	9 067	−238	3 414	12.2	18.7
Beaver	28 782	28 856	28 924	127 047	74.9	11.9	33 583	24 276	38.3	21 141	−2 904	7 261	11.4	16.5
Bedford	8 525	8 544	8 387	31 555	68.5	7.8	30 173	21 622	39.5	5 904	−554	2 248	11.8	17.8
Berks	63 211	58 561	48 705	224 754	70.0	15.1	40 587	32 048	26.6	31 020	4 800	12 062	8.8	14.1
Blair	20 782	21 263	21 192	86 870	75.0	10.5	30 881	23 271	32.7	17 795	−220	6 317	13.7	19.3
Bradford	11 970	12 172	11 555	39 290	75.7	12.9	32 185	23 970	34.3	8 283	320	3 273	13.2	19.1
Bucks	89 396	83 877	77 248	353 129	82.9	24.8	54 664	43 347	26.1	28 181	7 105	10 241	4.7	6.7
Butler	27 816	26 573	25 415	97 671	78.6	15.6	39 390	29 358	34.2	14 312	98	5 275	8.4	12.1
Cambria	20 915	21 940	24 674	110 251	71.2	10.8	28 786	21 462	34.1	19 331	−2 597	6 771	12.7	18.4
Cameron	1 204	1 111	1 089	3 947	73.1	9.8	31 084	20 839	49.2	614	−43	232	10.8	16.4
Carbon	8 693	8 879	8 217	39 049	69.4	8.4	33 551	25 501	31.6	5 500	247	2 031	9.3	14.8
Centre	14 515	13 789	14 839	66 356	83.6	32.3	38 108	26 060	46.2	11 675	−8 073	2 957	9.9	11.8
Chester	63 201	57 556	52 924	245 407	84.9	34.7	59 569	45 642	30.5	20 915	3 755	7 752	5.0	7.2
Clarion	7 773	8 040	6 783	24 969	73.1	11.7	30 562	21 602	41.5	5 759	−1 226	1 854	14.5	18.7
Clearfield	15 828	15 975	13 431	51 464	70.2	8.6	30 176	21 773	38.6	10 654	−60	3 943	13.4	19.3
Clinton	5 273	5 599	5 888	23 485	72.5	11.7	30 139	22 128	36.2	4 918	−458	1 829	13.7	20.8
Columbia	11 583	11 679	9 454	39 589	73.1	12.5	33 201	24 211	37.1	6 388	82	2 210	10.5	15.5
Crawford	12 219	12 230	15 052	54 755	74.1	11.8	31 749	23 083	37.5	11 807	−1 083	4 601	13.5	19.6
Cumberland	52 208	51 115	28 288	127 451	81.0	22.9	45 284	34 493	31.3	10 141	358	3 519	5.0	7.6
Dauphin	38 637	37 778	34 022	160 436	77.6	18.6	41 140	30 985	32.8	23 577	−103	9 693	9.5	16.0
Delaware	70 981	66 892	60 889	362 470	81.4	24.8	44 913	37 337	20.3	45 513	8 342	16 760	8.5	13.0
Elk	4 694	4 718	5 168	22 980	74.9	9.5	37 483	24 866	50.7	2 745	−529	963	7.8	10.7
Erie	42 860	42 961	42 300	171 369	77.5	16.2	35 341	26 581	33.0	34 565	342	13 783	12.7	18.7
Fayette	21 550	21 853	23 572	97 760	67.8	9.3	25 878	19 195	34.8	27 847	−2 214	10 739	19.1	29.8
Forest	789	787	765	3 326	70.5	7.9	25 702	19 170	34.1	721	184	298	15.4	29.6
Franklin	18 354	18 220	19 133	79 728	69.4	12.4	37 843	28 806	31.4	10 271	466	4 020	8.0	12.6
Fulton	2 574	2 652	2 562	8 823	64.0	7.4	33 127	23 736	39.6	1 532	−143	628	10.4	15.9
Greene	6 634	6 960	7 428	25 473	68.0	11.3	27 444	19 903	37.9	7 470	−683	2 780	18.6	25.6
Huntingdon	6 551	6 627	7 419	28 598	71.2	9.4	31 879	22 967	38.2	5 214	−125	1 872	12.6	17.8
Indiana	13 213	13 951	14 706	53 384	74.0	14.4	31 510	22 966	37.2	13 027	−2 669	4 599	15.4	21.5
Jefferson	7 064	7 536	8 431	30 439	72.6	8.9	30 457	22 063	38.0	5 954	−188	2 288	12.8	19.0
Juniata	3 446	3 457	3 486	13 418	65.2	7.3	33 092	25 359	30.5	1 923	−51	791	8.7	13.6
Lackawanna	27 812	27 106	28 519	148 840	73.3	14.8	32 536	24 816	31.1	22 611	−99	7 671	10.9	16.3
Lancaster	68 164	65 343	61 497	266 024	70.5	16.7	43 119	33 255	29.7	34 367	1 730	14 619	7.6	11.8
Lawrence	16 037	16 142	15 807	64 760	73.0	11.8	30 367	22 317	36.1	13 139	130	4 939	13.9	21.7
Lebanon	18 034	17 632	17 653	75 181	70.0	11.8	38 657	29 469	31.2	9 222	1 251	3 599	7.9	12.4
Lehigh	44 569	41 751	40 211	198 134	74.6	19.6	41 477	32 455	27.8	25 553	4 974	9 893	8.6	14.2
Luzerne	40 959	41 589	42 211	226 563	72.0	13.1	32 463	23 600	37.6	33 876	−1 866	11 367	10.8	16.4
Lycoming	19 780	20 442	20 045	77 533	74.5	12.3	32 767	25 552	28.2	13 790	610	5 447	11.9	18.2
McKean	7 771	8 069	7 958	31 196	75.4	12.2	32 517	23 106	40.7	6 115	−545	2 276	13.7	19.4
Mercer	19 495	19 466	19 147	80 181	75.1	13.6	32 005	24 599	30.1	15 662	853	5 893	13.2	20.4
Mifflin	6 313	6 319	7 411	30 339	68.2	8.7	30 416	22 778	33.5	6 075	−4	2 428	12.8	20.5
Monroe	26 215	22 264	15 056	62 178	78.0	17.6	40 120	32 465	23.6	10 651	3 943	4 379	8.5	13.4
Montgomery	96 870	88 928	78 519	465 684	83.8	32.1	55 580	43 720	27.1	34 758	10 979	11 781	4.8	7.1
Montour	2 964	2 913	2 685	11 967	75.2	18.7	36 113	27 260	32.5	1 762	344	681	10.3	15.5
Northampton	41 187	38 614	35 728	162 397	73.1	16.7	43 437	32 890	32.1	18 248	867	6 644	7.1	10.7
Northumberland	14 417	14 503	13 880	66 177	68.5	8.6	30 951	22 124	39.9	10 622	−414	3 754	11.5	17.1
Perry	7 892	7 799	7 262	26 354	72.3	8.9	39 305	29 539	33.1	3 462	410	1 450	7.7	12.0
Philadelphia	210 480	208 710	193 042	1 024 833	64.3	15.2	28 897	24 603	17.5	311 263	−2 111	121 716	21.7	32.8
Pike	4 620	3 808	4 456	19 125	79.2	14.7	39 790	30 314	31.3	3 139	1 175	1 331	7.7	12.7
Potter	3 335	3 470	3 254	10 847	73.8	9.8	30 554	21 377	42.9	2 486	51	1 059	14.5	22.3

[1] Revised.   [2] 1997 data are model-based estimates; 1989 data are census estimates. For more information on these estimates, see appendix A. Source Notes and Explanations or <http://www.census.gov/hhes/www/saipe.html>.

Sources: Public School Enrollment, 1998-1999 and 1994-1995—U.S. National Center for Education Statistics, <http://nces.ed.gov/ccd/pubagency.html> (accessed: 16 March 2001). Public School Enrollment and Educational Attainment, 1990—U.S. Census Bureau, "1990 Census of Population and Housing, Summary Tape File (STF) 3C" on CD-ROM (related Internet site <http://homer.ssd.census.gov/cdrom/lookup>). Income and Poverty, 1997—U.S. Census Bureau, "State and County Income and Poverty Estimates - 1997," published 22 November 2000, <http://www.census.gov/housing/saipe/estmod97/est97ALL.dat>. Income and Poverty, 1989—U.S. Census Bureau, "1990 Census of Population and Housing, Summary Tape File (STF) 3C" on CD-ROM (related Internet site <http://homer.ssd.census.gov/cdrom/lookup>).

[Includes U.S., states, and 3,142 counties or county equivalents defined as of January 1, 1992. For changes to these areas since January 1, 1992, see appendix B. Geographic Information]

County	Public school enrollment			Educational attainment, 1990			Median household income[2]			Persons below poverty level,[2] 1997				
	Fall				Percent—					Number			Percent	
										Persons of all ages				
	1998– 1999	1994– 1995[1]	1990	Persons 25 years and over	High school gradu- ate or higher	Bach- elor's degree or higher	1997 (dollars)	1989 (dollars)	Percent change, 1989– 1997	Total	Net change, 1989– 1997	Persons under 18 years	Persons of all ages	Persons under 18 years
PENNSYLVANIA—Con.														
Schuylkill	20 613	20 553	21 341	105 805	68.4	8.1	31 675	23 028	37.5	15 379	−589	5 122	10.4	15.3
Snyder	5 688	5 650	5 373	22 638	64.4	10.6	32 807	25 864	26.8	3 606	−183	1 403	9.9	14.3
Somerset	12 796	13 397	13 508	52 252	68.9	8.9	28 665	21 674	32.3	10 787	−239	3 893	13.7	19.5
Sullivan	923	995	988	4 122	70.2	8.6	28 046	20 107	39.5	767	−295	241	12.8	16.7
Susquehanna	8 726	8 878	7 657	26 329	76.0	11.1	32 383	24 736	30.9	5 316	484	2 187	12.5	18.9
Tioga	7 105	7 237	7 316	25 750	72.9	12.6	31 160	22 571	38.1	5 418	−289	2 047	13.3	19.2
Union	4 484	4 373	5 130	22 019	73.1	17.5	36 528	27 622	32.2	3 690	504	1 289	11.2	14.8
Venango	10 870	11 461	10 526	39 356	74.2	10.8	29 474	22 593	30.5	7 985	−703	2 999	13.9	20.0
Warren	6 974	7 120	7 834	30 156	76.6	10.7	33 863	26 351	28.5	4 649	441	1 784	10.6	16.0
Washington	30 773	30 609	31 729	139 715	73.2	13.6	34 998	25 469	37.4	24 044	−1 368	8 100	11.7	17.0
Wayne	9 430	8 941	7 091	26 727	74.2	13.1	30 529	24 912	26.5	5 352	969	2 132	12.0	18.8
Westmoreland	57 599	56 986	54 656	255 717	77.7	15.4	34 073	25 736	32.4	38 026	−966	12 557	10.2	14.8
Wyoming	4 914	5 021	5 295	17 370	77.6	13.2	35 110	27 207	29.0	3 188	158	1 247	11.1	15.8
York	56 984	53 147	53 005	225 121	72.8	13.9	43 488	32 605	33.4	25 617	4 414	9 965	6.8	10.7
RHODE ISLAND	154 785	147 493	138 054	658 956	72.0	21.3	36 699	32 181	14.0	108 836	16 166	41 893	11.2	17.3
Bristol	9 068	6 838	6 188	32 678	73.9	27.4	47 141	37 539	25.6	3 320	1 096	1 122	6.9	9.9
Kent	23 551	23 641	22 760	110 174	76.8	20.5	44 089	36 070	22.2	11 237	2 407	4 039	6.9	10.4
Newport	11 798	11 630	12 213	57 136	82.8	30.1	43 684	35 829	21.9	6 528	329	2 375	7.9	11.7
Providence	92 053	86 293	80 432	390 104	67.0	18.3	34 311	29 580	16.0	80 136	11 763	31 775	14.2	22.5
Washington	18 315	19 091	16 461	68 864	82.8	29.1	47 467	36 948	28.5	7 616	572	2 582	6.5	8.6
SOUTH CAROLINA	655 650	640 756	633 545	2 167 590	68.3	16.6	33 325	26 256	26.9	569 045	51 252	224 380	14.9	23.0
Abbeville	3 861	3 780	4 703	15 061	58.9	10.8	31 037	23 170	34.0	3 437	327	1 331	14.1	21.9
Aiken	24 451	24 683	22 448	76 260	70.7	17.2	38 084	29 994	27.0	18 512	1 841	7 631	13.7	21.6
Allendale	2 107	2 299	2 683	6 890	52.3	9.5	20 942	15 013	39.5	3 617	−220	1 393	35.1	44.4
Anderson	26 397	25 848	25 085	95 330	64.0	12.9	34 662	25 748	34.6	17 611	432	6 552	10.8	16.7
Bamberg	2 948	3 166	3 694	9 522	59.2	11.2	23 858	17 496	36.4	4 230	−317	1 649	26.4	36.3
Barnwell	4 954	5 024	4 551	12 160	59.9	11.9	29 085	23 501	23.8	4 729	362	1 973	21.5	30.5
Beaufort	15 531	14 135	12 942	52 125	83.4	26.5	38 867	30 450	27.6	13 586	2 785	5 799	13.0	22.0
Berkeley	26 384	27 410	27 642	73 054	75.4	11.6	36 249	29 106	24.5	19 428	3 756	8 891	14.1	20.6
Calhoun	2 093	2 103	2 235	8 157	61.9	11.7	29 479	23 750	24.1	2 746	200	1 072	19.2	29.0
Charleston	43 934	44 669	44 879	179 358	75.5	22.4	35 150	26 875	30.8	53 275	4 767	20 707	16.0	20.7
Cherokee	8 586	8 350	8 420	28 178	57.2	9.3	31 489	24 655	27.7	7 007	484	2 808	14.1	22.2
Chester	6 715	6 693	6 639	20 071	56.9	9.1	29 110	23 054	26.3	6 006	625	2 438	17.2	26.1
Chesterfield	8 039	7 910	8 101	24 100	53.9	7.7	28 422	21 069	34.9	7 812	458	3 162	18.8	28.6
Clarendon	6 093	6 250	5 831	17 467	54.9	10.2	23 906	17 645	35.5	8 053	−107	3 163	26.8	38.2
Colleton	6 966	7 049	7 298	21 362	61.7	9.6	25 682	20 617	24.6	8 546	596	3 564	22.6	33.9
Darlington	10 924	11 448	12 566	38 488	62.3	12.4	28 844	22 642	26.5	13 390	1 347	5 588	20.2	31.4
Dillon	6 266	6 593	6 773	17 148	52.5	8.5	23 572	18 365	28.4	7 725	−389	3 361	25.7	36.6
Dorchester	18 977	17 585	15 849	49 610	76.7	17.3	36 590	30 764	18.9	11 511	2 151	4 905	13.1	19.4
Edgefield	4 142	4 108	3 769	11 453	62.6	12.2	29 031	23 021	26.1	3 714	688	1 421	18.8	26.2
Fairfield	3 679	3 812	4 703	13 642	58.1	9.6	27 752	21 484	29.2	4 375	−126	1 746	19.5	28.8
Florence	22 460	23 472	23 498	70 001	64.3	14.8	30 557	24 264	25.9	24 237	1 737	9 805	19.4	28.7
Georgetown	10 420	10 843	10 460	28 431	63.9	15.6	30 915	23 981	28.9	10 161	854	4 419	18.6	29.9
Greenville	57 884	54 064	51 117	207 093	71.6	21.0	38 807	29 088	33.4	36 925	4 273	13 816	10.5	16.2
Greenwood	11 337	11 373	10 751	37 559	64.1	16.0	32 937	23 584	39.7	8 647	−226	3 167	13.8	20.5
Hampton	4 281	4 395	4 374	10 659	58.9	8.8	25 108	18 615	34.9	4 639	−350	2 002	23.9	34.8
Horry	26 837	25 253	24 210	94 908	74.3	16.0	31 312	24 959	25.5	25 278	3 920	10 095	14.4	25.1
Jasper	2 866	3 028	3 158	9 155	54.5	4.8	25 154	18 071	39.2	4 306	440	1 594	25.5	31.4
Kershaw	9 505	9 271	8 707	28 123	67.8	12.5	34 077	28 282	20.5	6 113	554	2 551	12.4	20.4
Lancaster	10 924	10 662	10 387	34 417	60.0	9.6	32 656	25 320	29.0	8 847	869	3 526	14.8	23.1
Laurens	9 373	9 030	10 652	36 822	57.4	11.3	30 159	24 905	21.1	8 869	1 610	3 516	14.3	22.4
Lee	3 204	3 455	4 151	10 948	53.5	7.5	23 160	18 174	27.4	5 405	−5	2 097	28.3	38.2
Lexington	44 486	39 848	31 246	106 563	77.3	21.0	42 697	32 914	29.7	19 500	5 519	8 214	9.4	15.4
McCormick	1 225	1 370	1 426	5 641	52.5	7.1	27 056	19 226	40.7	1 628	−77	559	19.6	28.7
Marion	6 776	7 390	8 292	20 362	55.3	9.1	23 302	17 825	30.7	8 424	−1 189	3 382	24.1	32.7
Marlboro	5 431	5 793	6 398	17 874	50.9	7.9	23 589	18 068	30.3	6 716	−924	2 545	23.2	31.6
Newberry	5 858	5 846	6 216	21 275	62.1	12.5	30 637	23 405	30.9	4 966	18	1 891	14.4	22.3
Oconee	10 030	9 799	10 051	38 114	63.4	13.3	34 286	25 723	33.3	7 246	754	2 739	11.1	18.2
Orangeburg	16 524	16 891	16 389	50 212	62.4	13.7	26 554	20 216	31.4	19 895	−276	7 436	23.3	32.0
Pickens	15 778	15 146	14 344	54 715	65.4	16.9	35 825	26 336	36.0	11 312	577	3 634	11.1	15.3
Richland	45 760	43 172	46 343	174 489	79.4	28.0	35 903	28 848	24.5	42 162	6 379	15 450	14.8	22.1
Saluda	2 161	2 243	3 188	10 487	59.8	8.0	29 005	22 176	30.8	2 856	−69	1 065	16.8	25.4
Spartanburg	40 880	38 897	39 483	146 403	63.0	14.3	35 713	26 941	32.6	28 666	2 613	10 585	11.6	17.9
Sumter	18 953	19 371	19 733	61 056	69.8	15.0	29 005	22 387	29.6	21 078	1 528	8 377	19.7	26.9
Union	4 866	5 322	5 831	19 895	55.0	7.2	28 716	21 526	33.4	4 378	−724	1 562	14.2	21.4
Williamsburg	6 619	7 088	8 833	21 199	55.6	9.9	22 448	18 409	21.9	10 606	119	4 423	28.3	39.0
York	28 165	24 819	23 496	81 753	67.5	16.9	39 728	31 288	27.0	16 877	3 670	6 686	11.0	17.0

[1] Revised. [2] 1997 data are model-based estimates; 1989 data are census estimates. For more information on these estimates, see appendix A. Source Notes and Explanations or <http://www.census.gov/hhes/www/saipe.html>.

Sources: Public School Enrollment, 1998-1999 and 1994-1995—U.S. National Center for Education Statistics, <http://nces.ed.gov/ccd/pubagency.html> (accessed: 16 March 2001). Public School Enrollment and Educational Attainment, 1990—U.S. Census Bureau, "1990 Census of Population and Housing, Summary Tape File (STF) 3C" on CD-ROM (related Internet site <http://homer.ssd.census.gov/cdrom/lookup>). Income and Poverty, 1997—U.S. Census Bureau, "State and County Income and Poverty Estimates - 1997," published 22 November 2000, <http://www.census.gov/housing/saipe/estmod97/est97ALL.dat>. Income and Poverty, 1989—U.S. Census Bureau, "1990 Census of Population and Housing, Summary Tape File (STF) 3C" on CD-ROM (related Internet site <http://homer.ssd.census.gov/cdrom/lookup>).

Table B-5. Counties — **Education, Income, and Poverty**-Con.

[Includes U.S., states, and 3,142 counties or county equivalents defined as of January 1, 1992. For changes to these areas since January 1, 1992, see appendix B. Geographic Information]

County	Public school enrollment Fall 1998–1999	Public school enrollment Fall 1994–1995[1]	Public school enrollment Fall 1990	Educational attainment, 1990 Persons 25 years and over	Percent— High school graduate or higher	Percent— Bachelor's degree or higher	Median household income 1997 (dollars)	Median household income 1989 (dollars)	Percent change, 1989–1997	Persons below poverty level, 1997 Number, Persons of all ages Total	Number, Net change, 1989–1997	Persons under 18 years	Percent, Persons of all ages	Percent, Persons under 18 years
SOUTH DAKOTA	132 495	143 482	132 431	430 500	77.1	17.2	31 354	22 503	39.3	100 537	-5 768	38 270	14.0	19.0
Aurora	737	730	676	2 083	70.2	11.0	26 723	16 497	62.0	427	-6	173	15.1	22.6
Beadle	3 202	3 479	3 306	12 076	75.7	15.1	32 620	22 425	45.5	1 975	-389	641	11.5	14.8
Bennett	591	772	735	1 807	67.7	10.4	22 345	16 864	32.5	1 224	45	593	36.1	46.5
Bon Homme	1 463	1 554	1 205	4 844	68.0	11.3	28 703	17 778	61.5	877	-111	277	13.7	17.1
Brookings	4 312	4 382	3 972	13 094	82.2	27.3	35 097	21 807	60.9	2 625	-1 315	656	11.1	11.4
Brown	5 321	5 640	6 085	22 231	77.9	20.7	35 046	22 967	52.6	3 679	-356	1 170	10.6	13.5
Brule	1 250	1 388	1 112	3 348	73.4	14.9	30 971	21 184	46.2	845	-117	343	15.8	21.8
Buffalo	X	X	558	814	61.2	4.2	18 444	14 566	26.6	690	-95	341	38.9	43.2
Butte	1 891	1 968	1 623	5 076	74.5	12.3	28 585	19 811	44.3	1 630	107	652	18.2	26.0
Campbell	315	312	314	1 360	65.5	10.7	24 400	17 202	41.8	322	-34	102	17.0	25.6
Charles Mix	1 855	2 188	1 807	5 616	67.5	9.9	26 551	16 541	60.5	2 203	-582	902	23.9	30.5
Clark	892	857	812	2 939	70.4	9.8	28 449	19 035	49.5	624	-197	210	14.2	17.6
Clay	1 631	1 681	1 721	6 181	84.4	36.3	31 147	19 392	60.6	2 140	-485	562	19.1	21.3
Codington	4 753	4 807	4 513	14 106	76.0	12.9	34 621	21 816	58.7	2 785	-16	995	10.9	14.0
Corson	764	970	1 169	2 315	63.3	10.5	19 878	14 324	38.8	1 594	-185	711	37.4	45.8
Custer	1 353	1 310	1 279	4 138	80.4	17.5	31 095	22 662	37.2	923	183	348	13.5	19.7
Davison	3 219	3 388	3 066	10 992	75.9	14.8	33 409	20 733	61.1	2 221	-312	755	12.7	16.3
Day	1 211	1 440	1 347	4 685	69.2	11.3	26 542	18 760	41.5	1 147	-334	409	18.0	24.0
Deuel	612	666	879	3 073	69.2	9.7	28 800	17 784	61.9	551	-188	183	12.2	15.8
Dewey	789	1 919	1 580	2 851	67.1	10.4	22 027	14 599	50.9	1 963	-475	905	32.9	36.7
Douglas	495	522	667	2 412	58.0	11.2	29 365	17 067	72.1	468	-324	170	13.5	16.9
Edmunds	793	746	767	3 010	64.2	11.3	30 611	20 569	48.8	487	-489	148	11.7	13.9
Fall River	1 292	1 376	1 400	5 306	74.1	16.3	28 440	20 483	38.8	1 041	72	357	16.5	22.8
Faulk	527	482	489	1 882	67.1	10.6	27 522	18 709	47.1	378	-277	117	15.0	18.9
Grant	1 548	1 650	1 718	5 415	74.0	9.3	34 381	23 431	46.7	838	-47	308	10.4	13.4
Gregory	1 019	1 163	1 200	3 600	70.3	11.8	24 383	16 848	44.7	1 050	-89	390	21.1	29.2
Haakon	541	694	708	1 555	83.6	12.7	31 256	21 166	47.7	313	-38	139	13.2	17.4
Hamlin	1 316	1 302	1 034	3 241	69.5	11.2	30 161	19 949	51.2	667	-115	250	12.7	16.8
Hand	637	706	754	2 852	73.4	12.8	28 776	19 310	49.0	603	-125	207	14.7	19.4
Hanson	559	551	566	1 959	73.1	15.3	33 830	21 920	54.3	358	-144	131	11.8	14.8
Harding	323	357	360	1 014	82.8	16.2	27 927	20 217	38.1	204	-104	75	13.7	17.6
Hughes	3 060	3 289	2 961	9 294	84.5	25.6	40 724	27 058	50.5	1 607	90	630	10.4	14.5
Hutchinson	1 795	1 852	1 486	5 773	62.6	11.3	30 293	18 832	60.9	1 039	-489	310	13.2	16.0
Hyde	319	844	325	1 186	71.2	14.5	29 022	19 907	45.8	267	-4	101	16.7	24.5
Jackson	434	799	679	1 600	68.9	10.9	23 783	17 246	37.9	981	-96	439	33.5	40.7
Jerauld	480	576	477	1 668	68.0	11.3	28 026	18 588	50.8	308	-126	100	13.9	18.3
Jones	276	276	263	869	75.7	14.4	30 038	21 202	41.7	180	-20	68	14.3	20.4
Kingsbury	966	1 062	1 126	4 089	74.0	11.6	30 938	20 290	52.5	602	-174	193	10.6	13.3
Lake	2 244	2 236	1 974	6 630	79.6	18.5	34 130	23 674	44.2	1 132	82	380	10.9	13.9
Lawrence	3 550	4 045	3 798	12 613	81.7	19.2	31 934	24 815	28.7	2 744	-55	900	12.7	15.9
Lincoln	3 338	3 196	3 439	9 727	79.5	16.4	45 830	28 543	60.6	1 175	244	469	5.7	7.5
Lyman	430	744	800	2 167	71.0	10.5	27 283	21 993	24.1	933	39	424	24.3	32.7
McCook	1 104	1 088	1 086	3 788	71.6	11.9	32 417	20 764	56.1	661	14	241	12.0	15.8
McPherson	527	564	529	2 352	46.0	10.0	23 815	15 345	55.2	395	-285	118	14.5	18.6
Marshall	898	875	895	3 281	65.7	10.2	28 428	18 305	55.3	626	-213	212	13.7	18.6
Meade	3 241	3 321	4 929	12 719	81.8	16.4	34 655	24 672	40.5	2 388	273	1 039	11.4	15.6
Mellette	512	486	543	1 224	68.0	12.3	20 688	14 539	42.3	677	-187	300	33.4	39.0
Miner	558	635	639	2 207	71.3	10.3	28 085	18 750	49.8	445	-81	151	16.1	20.6
Minnehaha	24 626	23 874	20 322	77 339	83.1	21.3	39 992	27 764	44.0	12 024	2 413	4 380	8.7	12.1
Moody	1 238	1 906	1 376	4 103	74.6	13.9	35 199	23 926	47.1	713	-140	273	10.9	13.8
Pennington	17 578	18 621	14 955	48 782	84.8	21.2	34 507	25 340	36.2	12 570	2 285	4 986	14.3	20.6
Perkins	699	800	769	2 716	72.5	12.7	26 543	19 862	33.6	575	-15	201	16.4	23.3
Potter	543	584	579	2 153	71.1	12.3	31 174	20 674	50.8	364	-230	123	12.8	16.8
Roberts	1 928	2 367	2 027	6 224	63.5	10.4	25 808	17 480	47.6	2 141	-392	858	21.9	29.0
Sanborn	553	659	588	1 855	73.9	16.4	28 842	19 818	45.5	372	-215	118	13.6	15.9
Shannon	1 107	3 371	2 700	4 251	59.4	10.7	17 814	11 105	60.4	5 241	-877	2 590	42.9	46.2
Spink	1 618	1 612	1 473	5 286	72.8	12.7	28 412	19 398	46.5	1 050	-365	343	14.3	17.6
Stanley	611	601	576	1 496	77.5	14.6	33 630	22 321	50.7	323	20	132	10.9	15.0
Sully	389	421	363	1 062	78.9	12.9	34 072	23 601	44.4	151	-57	48	10.1	12.4
Todd	2 138	2 804	2 576	3 686	67.2	11.8	18 032	13 327	35.3	4 332	189	2 152	46.1	49.7
Tripp	1 293	1 363	1 496	4 404	71.5	9.6	28 631	20 082	42.6	1 363	-43	539	20.2	27.4
Turner	1 565	1 620	1 751	5 866	72.8	12.5	32 510	19 926	63.2	942	-257	294	11.0	13.2
Union	2 649	2 585	2 125	6 516	74.2	13.9	40 373	22 274	81.3	1 017	-290	366	8.2	10.5
Walworth	1 029	1 094	1 126	4 222	71.5	14.5	28 178	19 513	44.4	959	-79	363	17.6	25.5
Yankton	3 724	3 705	3 542	12 372	77.2	18.6	32 997	21 798	51.4	2 367	-75	770	11.8	14.5
Ziebach	264	607	716	1 105	62.5	8.5	20 139	14 129	42.5	1 020	-111	442	46.4	46.0

[1] Revised. [2] 1997 data are model-based estimates; 1989 data are census estimates. For more information on these estimates, see appendix A. Source Notes and Explanations or <http://www.census.gov/hhes/www/saipe.html>.

Sources: Public School Enrollment, 1998-1999 and 1994-1995—U.S. National Center for Education Statistics, <http://nces.ed.gov/ccd/pubagency.html> (accessed: 16 March 2001). Public School Enrollment and Educational Attainment, 1990—U.S. Census Bureau, "1990 Census of Population and Housing, Summary Tape File (STF) 3C" on CD-ROM (related Internet site <http://homer.ssd.census.gov/cdrom/lookup>). Income and Poverty, 1997—U.S. Census Bureau, "State and County Income and Poverty Estimates - 1997," published 22 November 2000, <http://www.census.gov/housing/saipe/estmod97/est97ALL.dat>. Income and Poverty, 1989—U.S. Census Bureau, "1990 Census of Population and Housing, Summary Tape File (STF) 3C" on CD-ROM (related Internet site <http://homer.ssd.census.gov/cdrom/lookup>).

Table B–5. Counties — **Education, Income, and Poverty**–Con.

[Includes U.S., states, and 3,142 counties or county equivalents defined as of January 1, 1992. For changes to these areas since January 1, 1992, see appendix B. Geographic Information]

County	Public school enrollment — Fall 1998–1999	Public school enrollment — Fall 1994–1995[1]	Public school enrollment — Fall 1990	Educational attainment, 1990 — Persons 25 years and over	Educational attainment, 1990 — Percent — High school graduate or higher	Educational attainment, 1990 — Percent — Bachelor's degree or higher	Median household income[2] — 1997 (dollars)	Median household income[2] — 1989 (dollars)	Median household income[2] — Percent change, 1989–1997	Persons below poverty level,[2] 1997 — Number — Persons of all ages — Total	Persons below poverty level,[2] 1997 — Number — Persons of all ages — Net change, 1989–1997	Persons below poverty level,[2] 1997 — Number — Persons under 18 years	Persons below poverty level,[2] 1997 — Percent — Persons of all ages	Persons below poverty level,[2] 1997 — Percent — Persons under 18 years
TENNESSEE	892 936	870 594	806 796	3 139 066	67.1	16.0	32 047	24 807	29.2	734 108	−10 833	258 288	13.6	18.9
Anderson	12 647	12 819	11 752	46 176	72.4	18.6	36 006	26 496	35.9	9 414	−250	3 277	13.1	19.5
Bedford..................	5 998	5 893	5 632	19 807	57.6	10.5	32 347	23 613	37.0	4 142	−656	1 464	11.9	16.4
Benton	2 553	2 543	2 443	9 943	56.3	7.4	26 579	20 382	30.4	2 663	205	897	16.3	24.1
Bledsoe	1 749	1 652	1 660	6 378	52.1	5.4	25 815	18 250	41.5	1 984	336	685	20.2	27.4
Blount	16 076	15 253	14 318	57 983	68.5	14.3	35 571	25 575	39.1	11 135	711	3 770	10.9	16.1
Bradley	13 365	13 324	12 227	46 833	64.4	11.9	34 368	25 678	33.8	9 951	5	3 347	12.2	16.6
Campbell	6 379	6 479	6 411	22 563	47.5	6.6	23 314	16 450	41.7	8 200	−1 113	2 787	21.3	28.6
Cannon..................	2 052	1 911	1 834	6 844	54.6	6.9	30 078	22 847	31.6	1 524	30	574	12.4	18.7
Carroll	5 189	5 120	4 796	18 434	55.5	7.3	29 615	20 763	42.6	3 899	−361	1 372	13.4	19.9
Carter	7 900	8 408	8 060	34 457	57.5	10.8	26 736	19 140	39.7	8 684	343	2 781	16.4	23.0
Cheatham	6 740	6 125	4 880	17 135	65.0	10.5	41 036	30 778	33.3	3 064	159	1 166	8.6	11.8
Chester.................	2 463	2 366	1 950	7 753	54.6	8.7	29 196	19 413	50.4	2 059	−164	693	14.8	19.5
Claiborne	4 733	4 609	4 859	16 574	50.8	8.0	23 622	17 132	37.9	6 171	−370	2 146	20.9	28.8
Clay....................	1 238	1 258	1 313	4 875	48.5	7.8	22 055	17 799	23.9	1 498	−146	485	20.4	28.6
Cocke	5 435	5 231	5 054	19 186	50.4	5.5	23 408	16 818	39.2	6 736	−537	2 286	20.9	30.2
Coffee	8 719	8 376	7 201	26 355	65.1	15.3	32 889	24 802	32.6	5 931	−134	2 134	12.8	18.2
Crockett................	2 628	2 522	2 302	9 003	57.2	6.4	28 276	20 296	39.3	2 042	−254	732	14.6	21.0
Cumberland..............	6 707	6 264	5 807	23 588	59.8	10.2	27 132	20 474	32.5	6 551	364	2 307	14.7	23.0
Davidson	67 016	71 574	66 621	335 805	75.9	24.4	39 112	28 377	37.8	64 997	1 517	22 714	12.5	18.6
Decatur.................	1 848	1 866	1 718	7 154	52.9	4.8	26 581	17 925	48.3	1 609	−441	509	14.9	20.8
DeKalb	2 638	2 643	2 529	9 557	50.3	8.4	28 036	19 388	44.6	2 583	−305	909	16.0	23.3
Dickson	7 870	7 457	6 641	22 161	61.5	9.2	34 086	24 419	39.6	5 120	−192	1 912	12.0	16.3
Dyer	6 877	6 745	6 381	22 534	55.3	9.4	31 092	22 105	40.7	5 494	−548	1 956	14.9	20.5
Fayette	3 811	4 475	4 624	15 630	55.5	8.0	33 062	22 199	48.9	4 141	−1 890	1 594	13.6	17.6
Fentress	2 354	2 257	2 786	9 349	44.9	6.6	20 332	13 924	46.0	3 910	−785	1 364	23.9	32.5
Franklin	5 880	5 901	5 988	22 461	63.5	13.1	32 015	23 438	36.6	4 771	−17	1 614	12.9	17.9
Gibson	8 568	8 599	7 943	31 181	57.5	8.0	29 587	20 938	41.3	6 838	−540	2 343	14.2	20.2
Giles	4 733	4 765	4 583	16 761	60.1	8.9	31 855	22 078	44.3	3 671	−490	1 276	12.6	17.3
Grainger	3 205	3 129	3 012	11 128	46.3	4.8	26 848	19 097	40.6	3 431	−33	1 175	17.2	24.6
Greene	9 481	9 045	8 929	37 588	58.1	10.3	27 791	21 513	29.2	8 891	−388	2 889	14.8	21.4
Grundy	2 378	2 484	2 605	8 308	44.7	5.4	22 502	16 425	37.0	3 293	156	1 247	23.4	32.0
Hamblen	8 919	8 882	8 294	33 214	61.6	11.2	32 221	23 853	35.1	7 130	197	2 476	13.1	19.5
Hamilton................	42 292	44 365	42 321	187 566	72.5	19.7	34 364	26 523	31.3	37 514	051	10 200	12.0	18.0
Hancock.................	1 151	1 251	1 264	4 389	42.4	5.1	18 529	11 822	56.7	1 969	−658	634	29.1	36.4
Hardeman	4 734	4 850	4 578	14 565	53.0	7.6	25 337	19 128	32.5	4 823	−439	1 777	20.0	25.5
Hardin	3 974	4 077	3 908	14 892	54.8	6.1	25 852	17 719	45.9	4 588	97	1 591	18.3	25.7
Hawkins	7 636	7 152	7 552	29 549	58.0	8.4	31 286	21 960	42.5	7 453	−454	2 479	14.8	21.3
Haywood	3 667	3 973	4 272	12 043	53.0	8.7	25 064	17 376	44.2	4 136	−1 162	1 522	20.9	26.2
Henderson	4 324	4 228	3 920	14 433	55.2	6.8	30 665	21 099	45.3	3 373	−29	1 127	13.7	18.4
Henry	4 821	4 873	4 642	19 266	60.0	8.5	27 141	18 891	43.7	4 558	−636	1 490	15.1	21.5
Hickman	3 561	3 166	2 714	11 216	55.6	7.2	30 097	21 567	39.6	2 946	119	987	15.0	19.9
Houston	1 362	1 351	1 278	4 722	52.8	6.3	25 979	20 112	29.2	1 162	−116	391	14.9	20.6
Humphreys	3 062	3 001	2 968	10 429	63.5	9.2	30 574	22 256	37.4	2 152	−98	732	12.5	17.4
Jackson	1 610	1 492	1 620	6 328	45.2	6.8	25 871	18 081	43.1	1 535	308	523	15.8	23.4
Jefferson	6 395	5 673	5 047	21 504	60.5	11.7	29 128	22 219	31.1	5 856	1 114	2 013	13.7	21.1
Johnson	2 325	2 332	2 322	9 330	47.2	5.0	21 932	14 967	46.5	3 442	−436	1 048	22.1	29.1
Knox	51 667	52 285	49 803	218 321	74.6	23.9	35 408	26 010	36.1	43 537	−2 071	13 727	11.7	16.2
Lake	894	1 001	1 284	4 700	49.6	5.0	21 682	16 804	29.0	1 758	100	483	30.2	32.8
Lauderdale..............	4 707	5 106	4 609	14 762	52.1	6.0	26 065	18 972	37.4	4 398	−648	1 604	18.8	23.7
Lawrence	6 934	6 771	6 158	22 533	53.7	6.7	29 364	20 842	40.9	5 445	87	1 916	13.7	18.5
Lewis	1 929	1 964	1 761	5 906	51.5	5.0	25 354	17 362	46.0	1 878	−21	679	17.3	23.2
Lincoln	5 313	5 290	4 918	18 592	57.5	9.1	30 178	21 996	37.2	4 091	150	1 387	13.6	18.9
Loudon	6 497	6 116	4 989	21 047	63.8	9.6	34 382	24 258	41.7	4 513	321	1 613	11.4	18.0
McMinn.................	7 872	7 827	7 193	27 830	57.1	10.5	30 352	21 901	38.6	6 439	−713	2 202	13.9	19.5
McNairy	4 142	4 015	3 977	15 105	57.4	5.2	26 757	18 715	43.0	4 110	−378	1 373	17.0	23.4
Macon..................	3 510	3 158	2 933	10 279	49.2	5.5	27 332	19 147	42.7	2 863	−176	1 006	15.6	21.9
Madison	13 683	13 579	13 669	48 976	68.3	16.6	32 909	23 716	38.8	12 573	−275	4 485	14.8	19.6
Marion	4 580	4 861	4 727	15 993	51.9	6.4	28 563	20 045	42.5	4 183	−576	1 473	15.5	21.1
Marshall	4 720	4 487	3 946	14 087	60.0	7.7	33 399	23 855	40.0	2 930	148	1 025	11.0	15.0
Maury	11 684	11 692	9 737	35 515	65.2	12.1	36 966	26 238	40.9	7 670	535	2 782	10.9	15.1
Meigs	1 720	1 636	1 484	5 185	52.7	6.6	26 931	20 181	33.4	1 882	121	673	18.7	27.0
Monroe	6 247	5 910	5 710	19 521	49.9	7.6	27 511	19 932	38.0	6 025	722	2 181	17.2	24.6
Montgomery	23 337	20 560	17 219	58 067	77.9	16.5	35 728	25 568	39.7	14 231	2 267	5 570	11.5	15.5
Moore	970	1 003	887	3 092	66.7	11.7	36 958	28 056	31.7	510	204	192	9.7	14.8
Morgan	3 275	3 284	3 345	11 086	56.7	3.7	25 982	19 280	34.8	3 293	72	1 241	18.9	25.8
Obion	5 581	5 536	5 993	20 903	61.3	8.5	31 911	22 344	42.8	4 360	−398	1 512	13.4	18.8

[1] Revised. [2] 1997 data are model-based estimates; 1989 data are census estimates. For more information on these estimates, see appendix A. Source Notes and Explanations or <http://www.census.gov/hhes/www/saipe.html>.

Sources: Public School Enrollment, 1998-1999 and 1994-1995—U.S. National Center for Education Statistics, <http://nces.ed.gov/ccd/pubagency.html> (accessed: 16 March 2001). Public School Enrollment and Educational Attainment, 1990—U.S. Census Bureau, "1990 Census of Population and Housing, Summary Tape File (STF) 3C" on CD-ROM (related Internet site <http://homer.ssd.census.gov/cdrom/lookup>). Income and Poverty, 1997—U.S. Census Bureau, "State and County Income and Poverty Estimates - 1997," published 22 November 2000, <http://www.census.gov/housing/saipe/estmod97/est97ALL.dat>. Income and Poverty, 1989—U.S. Census Bureau, "1990 Census of Population and Housing, Summary Tape File (STF) 3C" on CD-ROM (related Internet site <http://homer.ssd.census.gov/cdrom/lookup>).

[Includes U.S., states, and 3,142 counties or county equivalents defined as of January 1, 1992. For changes to these areas since January 1, 1992, see appendix B. Geographic Information]

County	Public school enrollment Fall			Educational attainment, 1990			Median household income[2]			Persons below poverty level,[2] 1997				
					Percent—					Number Persons of all ages			Percent	
	1998–1999	1994–1995[1]	1990	Persons 25 years and over	High school graduate or higher	Bachelor's degree or higher	1997 (dollars)	1989 (dollars)	Percent change, 1989–1997	Total	Net change, 1989–1997	Persons under 18 years	Persons of all ages	Persons under 18 years
TENNESSEE—Con.														
Overton	3 148	3 006	3 114	11 670	44.1	6.9	25 216	18 293	37.8	3 256	130	1 124	16.5	23.6
Perry	1 170	1 167	1 115	4 432	52.7	6.9	27 209	19 039	42.9	1 178	–23	406	15.7	22.0
Pickett	767	837	805	3 055	45.8	9.1	22 027	14 993	46.9	1 000	–115	333	21.4	29.4
Polk	2 319	2 236	2 426	8 980	51.3	5.8	27 703	21 663	27.9	2 204	–270	739	14.6	20.6
Putnam	9 495	9 030	8 037	31 470	63.2	16.8	30 570	21 693	40.9	7 993	–10	2 529	13.7	19.1
Rhea	4 680	4 643	4 468	15 592	56.0	8.5	27 479	19 915	38.0	4 635	159	1 667	16.8	23.7
Roane	7 343	7 653	7 998	31 943	66.7	13.2	31 448	24 210	29.9	7 378	–89	2 359	14.6	20.7
Robertson	9 741	9 227	7 568	26 549	65.5	9.6	38 432	28 687	34.0	5 223	896	2 086	9.7	14.1
Rutherford	30 325	26 017	21 589	70 105	73.9	18.7	43 488	30 878	40.8	12 339	54	4 427	7.5	9.6
Scott	3 989	4 136	3 976	11 094	51.2	6.6	21 635	15 858	36.4	4 774	–256	1 797	23.6	30.6
Sequatchie	1 803	1 617	1 599	5 660	51.4	7.6	27 542	19 223	43.3	1 743	–259	595	16.5	22.4
Sevier	11 909	10 481	8 799	34 071	63.0	10.8	30 189	23 042	31.0	9 029	2 406	3 182	13.9	21.1
Shelby	159 867	152 486	138 958	508 251	75.1	20.8	34 583	27 132	27.5	140 104	–6 749	53 142	16.3	22.1
Smith	3 144	2 912	2 551	9 363	54.2	6.1	32 077	23 255	37.9	2 075	49	722	12.6	17.5
Stewart	2 025	1 715	1 606	6 550	58.9	7.7	28 473	20 802	36.9	1 529	–15	502	13.2	19.7
Sullivan	23 165	23 312	22 754	97 517	66.8	15.6	33 199	25 089	32.3	19 763	522	6 483	13.0	19.7
Sumner	22 165	21 028	19 467	65 477	70.6	14.4	42 571	31 795	33.9	10 964	1 601	3 969	8.7	11.7
Tipton	10 636	9 687	7 899	22 479	61.8	6.7	32 845	23 860	37.7	6 737	–709	2 612	14.1	17.9
Trousdale	1 228	1 156	1 043	3 956	47.7	7.0	27 319	20 127	35.7	1 082	56	375	15.7	22.0
Unicoi	2 483	2 582	2 792	11 479	59.6	9.5	28 650	20 536	39.5	2 502	–285	786	14.4	21.2
Union	3 078	2 775	2 600	8 583	45.6	4.5	26 692	19 595	36.2	2 800	–95	1 034	17.1	23.8
Van Buren	796	773	875	3 098	48.0	4.1	28 361	20 676	37.2	807	–124	272	15.7	20.6
Warren	6 314	6 284	5 628	21 552	57.0	8.1	30 135	21 019	43.4	5 334	–150	1 835	14.6	20.2
Washington	14 923	14 647	14 090	60 572	68.4	18.9	32 651	23 698	37.8	12 807	–849	3 873	12.8	17.2
Wayne	2 686	2 661	2 487	8 987	51.0	5.0	25 053	18 429	35.9	2 969	399	966	19.8	25.2
Weakley	5 126	5 147	4 995	19 677	56.9	10.3	30 401	21 004	44.7	4 132	–414	1 260	13.3	17.1
White	3 867	3 672	3 402	13 486	53.2	7.6	27 224	19 874	37.0	3 635	267	1 204	15.8	22.0
Williamson	21 984	18 449	14 267	51 652	81.8	34.2	63 959	43 615	46.6	5 744	1 121	1 933	4.8	5.7
Wilson	14 435	13 323	11 987	43 316	71.4	15.6	45 250	32 852	37.7	6 653	784	2 471	7.8	10.7
TEXAS	3 945 367	3 670 193	3 303 198	10 310 605	72.1	20.3	34 478	27 016	27.6	3 259 559	259 044	1 350 837	16.7	23.6
Anderson	8 819	8 696	8 193	31 240	67.7	9.5	29 760	22 737	30.9	8 302	1 352	2 913	20.4	24.0
Andrews	3 468	3 633	3 686	8 192	61.2	9.8	34 638	26 434	31.0	2 225	–153	994	15.8	20.1
Angelina	15 977	15 340	14 066	43 065	65.3	13.2	30 276	22 986	31.7	13 190	440	5 421	17.3	24.1
Aransas	3 468	3 272	3 258	12 105	67.2	14.5	27 664	21 315	29.8	5 180	730	2 056	22.7	36.0
Archer	2 043	1 893	1 714	5 152	72.5	12.3	36 394	25 131	44.8	778	–139	307	9.3	13.2
Armstrong	387	417	405	1 351	77.4	14.1	31 091	23 081	34.7	238	6	86	11.2	13.7
Atascosa	8 205	7 760	7 331	17 648	58.8	8.4	26 832	20 048	33.8	8 373	–600	3 821	23.0	31.2
Austin	5 228	5 040	3 988	13 021	62.6	13.8	33 945	25 043	35.5	3 080	–132	1 159	13.1	17.7
Bailey	1 492	1 635	1 564	4 390	55.4	7.4	27 005	19 873	35.9	1 667	–17	750	24.2	33.7
Bandera	2 795	2 239	1 768	7 516	76.7	16.9	33 306	24 671	35.0	2 070	600	792	13.0	21.6
Bastrop	10 453	9 087	8 091	24 437	68.3	13.3	34 006	23 967	41.9	6 924	322	2 940	13.9	19.4
Baylor	751	806	635	3 137	63.6	10.3	23 287	17 228	35.2	854	–162	284	20.6	29.6
Bee	5 450	5 560	5 627	14 588	65.0	12.7	26 840	20 614	30.2	6 582	–128	2 588	26.5	32.3
Bell	48 878	46 769	35 301	108 410	79.1	17.2	31 431	23 755	32.3	31 852	4 223	14 141	14.7	21.3
Bexar	255 330	241 906	231 388	705 629	72.7	19.7	32 374	25 926	24.9	247 843	18 075	106 133	18.5	26.4
Blanco	1 546	1 390	1 030	4 062	68.9	13.0	29 285	22 297	31.3	751	–237	244	9.1	12.7
Borden	207	192	172	532	71.2	17.3	36 730	29 375	25.0	91	–29	31	11.7	14.0
Bosque	3 159	3 103	2 526	10 547	64.0	10.8	28 633	21 411	33.7	2 643	267	1 028	16.2	24.8
Bowie	16 517	16 523	16 127	52 405	72.1	14.3	32 433	24 237	33.8	13 901	325	5 675	16.9	25.1
Brazoria	47 399	44 544	40 648	117 871	75.5	15.1	43 688	34 418	26.9	24 530	5 621	10 336	11.0	15.1
Brazos	20 858	19 255	16 648	56 864	79.8	35.8	32 045	20 411	57.0	22 075	–7 124	6 715	18.0	22.1
Brewster	1 572	1 520	1 389	5 303	73.2	28.0	24 952	17 586	41.9	1 950	–299	678	22.7	31.5
Briscoe	274	287	410	1 324	63.0	11.6	23 777	17 696	34.4	444	–71	186	23.1	33.3
Brooks	1 969	1 979	2 000	4 729	45.6	6.6	17 701	13 509	31.0	3 246	257	1 397	38.4	50.5
Brown	7 212	7 106	6 733	21 795	67.1	13.7	26 963	19 291	39.8	6 902	118	2 635	19.5	27.0
Burleson	3 238	3 174	2 480	8 815	58.2	9.5	27 802	19 785	40.5	2 588	–382	1 025	16.6	23.4
Burnet	6 239	5 332	3 975	15 683	69.1	14.0	31 146	21 420	45.4	4 151	203	1 553	13.0	18.3
Caldwell	6 059	5 527	5 619	15 560	60.3	10.9	28 004	20 169	38.8	6 260	–1 750	2 495	19.9	25.3
Calhoun	4 324	4 314	4 180	11 846	64.2	10.1	30 625	22 706	34.9	3 745	230	1 571	18.1	25.7
Callahan	2 994	3 034	2 424	7 866	68.7	9.8	28 427	20 712	37.2	2 111	–241	804	16.4	22.5
Cameron	82 139	80 254	70 685	139 703	50.0	12.0	21 699	17 336	25.2	114 709	13 347	52 661	35.3	45.2
Camp	2 083	2 085	1 881	6 543	63.8	10.0	27 269	19 673	38.6	1 938	–261	811	17.7	27.9
Carson	1 414	1 414	1 496	4 176	76.2	13.9	38 076	26 765	42.3	586	3	228	8.7	11.0
Cass	6 194	6 242	6 099	19 397	66.5	9.0	27 929	19 886	40.4	5 622	–1 161	2 204	18.3	26.2
Castro	2 110	2 303	2 467	4 999	58.2	10.5	28 315	17 838	58.7	2 167	–462	999	26.0	32.6

[1] Revised. [2] 1997 data are model-based estimates; 1989 data are census estimates. For more information on these estimates, see appendix A. Source Notes and Explanations or <http://www.census.gov/hhes/www/saipe.html>.

Sources: Public School Enrollment, 1998-1999 and 1994-1995—U.S. National Center for Education Statistics, <http://nces.ed.gov/ccd/pubagency.html> (accessed: 16 March 2001). Public School Enrollment and Educational Attainment, 1990—U.S. Census Bureau, "1990 Census of Population and Housing, Summary Tape File (STF) 3C" on CD-ROM (related Internet site <http://homer.ssd.census.gov/cdrom/lookup>). Income and Poverty, 1997—U.S. Census Bureau, "State and County Income and Poverty Estimates - 1997," published 22 November 2000, <http://www.census.gov/housing/saipe/estmod97/est97ALL.dat>. Income and Poverty, 1989—U.S. Census Bureau, "1990 Census of Population and Housing, Summary Tape File (STF) 3C" on CD-ROM (related Internet site <http://homer.ssd.census.gov/cdrom/lookup>).

[Includes U.S., states, and 3,142 counties or county equivalents defined as of January 1, 1992. For changes to these areas since January 1, 1992, see appendix B. Geographic Information]

County	Public school enrollment Fall			Educational attainment, 1990	Percent—		Median household income[2]			Persons below poverty level,[2] 1997 Number			Percent	
										Persons of all ages				
	1998–1999	1994–1995[1]	1990	Persons 25 years and over	High school graduate or higher	Bachelor's degree or higher	1997 (dollars)	1989 (dollars)	Percent change, 1989–1997	Total	Net change, 1989–1997	Persons under 18 years	Persons of all ages	Persons under 18 years
TEXAS—Con.														
Chambers	5 065	4 508	4 537	12 406	68.1	11.5	43 345	31 671	36.9	2 589	119	1 188	10.8	16.5
Cherokee	7 902	7 556	7 403	26 363	62.7	10.2	26 928	19 296	39.6	8 584	176	3 415	20.9	29.8
Childress	1 232	1 291	1 351	4 047	61.1	10.5	24 904	16 091	54.8	1 638	−160	533	26.6	30.7
Clay	2 032	2 004	1 905	6 795	68.9	11.1	32 368	23 721	36.5	1 229	121	425	11.6	15.0
Cochran	1 143	1 305	1 051	2 519	57.3	10.6	26 258	19 301	36.0	1 006	−196	445	26.1	35.5
Coke	724	707	589	2 441	64.6	11.7	25 700	19 220	33.7	571	−30	213	17.2	25.6
Coleman	1 746	1 860	1 700	6 798	59.0	9.6	21 718	15 519	39.9	2 258	−108	831	23.9	34.7
Collin	80 634	62 427	48 292	164 351	88.3	39.1	65 814	46 020	43.0	20 447	5 323	8 305	4.7	6.5
Collingsworth	758	843	702	2 383	62.0	12.0	23 092	15 421	49.7	813	−186	323	25.1	35.4
Colorado	3 823	3 686	3 350	12 261	57.9	10.6	28 966	20 795	39.3	3 226	−627	1 232	17.1	23.9
Comal	16 135	13 557	8 953	34 784	75.7	20.3	39 600	29 457	34.4	7 642	1 066	2 981	10.4	15.5
Comanche	2 545	2 357	2 133	9 180	57.8	9.2	23 687	17 504	35.3	2 909	91	1 137	21.8	33.6
Concho	539	548	512	2 082	54.2	10.3	23 050	15 942	44.6	604	−85	209	21.9	27.2
Cooke	6 078	5 734	5 677	19 556	71.5	11.9	32 975	24 525	34.5	4 817	−97	1 985	14.8	21.8
Coryell	10 430	10 541	12 379	33 105	80.3	11.0	33 259	23 504	41.5	8 614	2 996	3 556	14.4	17.0
Cottle	389	407	465	1 537	51.8	10.7	21 187	15 583	36.0	529	−127	193	27.8	38.8
Crane	1 101	1 219	1 372	2 643	71.5	9.4	38 169	30 659	24.5	582	−109	254	13.1	16.1
Crockett	977	952	958	2 550	57.8	15.2	28 647	19 087	50.1	765	−248	309	16.9	21.7
Crosby	1 620	1 910	1 757	4 431	53.1	10.0	23 177	17 162	35.0	1 967	−154	880	27.3	37.5
Culberson	795	784	891	1 951	53.3	12.1	20 416	16 559	23.3	994	−22	429	32.6	41.5
Dallam	1 754	1 636	1 149	3 464	66.0	7.2	30 099	19 764	52.3	1 078	97	494	16.3	23.7
Dallas	390 801	353 674	310 494	1 158 253	77.1	26.3	40 960	31 605	29.6	276 124	30 729	112 011	13.5	19.9
Dawson	3 219	3 433	3 390	8 695	54.0	9.0	25 738	18 920	36.0	3 582	−761	1 439	26.7	33.0
Deaf Smith	4 441	4 511	4 601	10 711	57.5	11.0	28 490	21 177	34.5	4 615	−602	2 146	24.2	30.9
Delta	1 198	1 161	807	3 265	64.2	12.5	26 362	20 208	30.5	1 001	−42	378	20.8	30.2
Denton	63 690	50 987	45 690	162 602	86.8	32.3	52 242	36 914	41.5	23 463	1 602	8 216	6.1	7.6
DeWitt	4 664	4 702	3 623	12 543	55.2	9.2	25 625	18 041	42.0	3 890	−765	1 378	21.5	27.3
Dickens	462	526	479	1 773	60.3	11.2	21 408	14 484	47.8	538	−253	192	24.2	34.3
Dimmit	2 618	2 749	2 894	5 608	39.8	7.8	16 958	12 222	38.7	4 219	−843	1 842	40.2	49.0
Donley	687	653	616	2 519	67.8	11.1	24 046	16 747	43.6	779	29	257	21.2	29.5
Duval	3 264	3 400	3 391	7 475	47.9	6.4	19 837	13 602	45.8	4 252	−769	1 690	31.9	38.9
Eastland	3 294	3 449	3 096	12 381	63.1	11.0	22 645	15 774	43.6	3 658	−334	1 273	21.5	29.5
Ector	28 389	28 161	26 283	70 055	66.9	11.4	31 039	23 801	30.4	23 523	−569	10 197	18.7	25.1
Edwards	820	826	587	1 352	58.3	13.8	19 254	14 639	31.5	1 139	200	303	30.8	46.3
Ellis	23 315	20 092	17 248	51 154	71.7	13.4	39 855	30 553	30.4	11 570	1 002	5 207	11.2	15.9
El Paso	153 480	148 028	141 062	327 999	63.7	15.2	25 866	22 644	14.2	193 843	38 545	88 863	27.8	38.6
Erath	5 602	5 351	4 611	16 474	71.3	20.3	27 882	19 881	40.2	5 060	−487	1 829	16.7	23.2
Falls	3 209	3 292	3 214	11 597	58.9	8.5	24 285	17 227	41.0	3 966	−553	1 440	25.0	32.6
Fannin	5 252	4 705	4 232	17 014	64.6	11.2	28 595	20 669	38.3	4 441	−76	1 523	16.5	22.2
Fayette	3 731	3 692	3 417	14 005	57.6	9.1	29 487	19 963	47.7	2 926	−725	985	13.8	18.6
Fisher	729	804	976	3 273	63.0	11.5	26 288	19 368	35.7	861	−392	298	20.2	26.4
Floyd	1 963	2 041	1 877	5 188	60.7	11.2	26 587	19 186	38.6	2 142	−132	985	26.1	36.2
Foard	347	383	325	1 237	62.2	11.2	23 185	18 713	23.9	393	41	161	23.8	38.0
Fort Bend	70 875	61 094	50 518	133 052	80.9	30.2	55 164	42 809	28.9	27 020	7 360	11 832	8.0	10.6
Franklin	1 544	1 396	1 449	5 242	64.9	11.3	29 822	23 103	29.1	1 380	76	540	14.2	21.2
Freestone	3 144	3 292	3 096	10 386	65.5	9.2	28 845	21 561	33.8	2 960	−39	1 052	18.3	23.2
Frio	3 336	3 372	3 497	7 425	50.1	7.5	20 094	14 059	42.9	5 061	−97	2 122	35.0	41.0
Gaines	3 281	3 290	3 204	7 751	53.2	9.9	29 484	22 333	32.0	3 096	−742	1 439	20.6	26.0
Galveston	65 219	61 855	41 670	138 490	75.8	19.3	39 119	29 466	32.8	32 958	−207	13 011	13.4	19.2
Garza	1 174	1 198	1 094	3 136	57.6	9.8	26 361	18 994	38.8	1 090	−84	459	23.6	30.5
Gillespie	3 241	3 063	2 545	12 192	68.6	17.1	31 497	23 722	32.8	2 322	−31	840	11.8	18.6
Glasscock	399	419	347	813	64.8	9.8	35 799	29 306	22.2	158	−165	76	11.3	15.1
Goliad	1 407	1 340	1 194	3 995	62.6	9.9	28 037	21 411	30.9	1 326	268	549	18.9	27.8
Gonzales	3 846	3 852	3 655	10 841	55.5	8.5	23 826	17 500	36.1	4 504	−398	1 848	25.9	35.7
Gray	4 223	4 338	4 547	15 910	71.1	11.9	32 709	24 118	35.6	3 434	223	1 277	15.2	21.3
Grayson	19 915	18 650	16 836	62 069	72.1	14.0	33 145	25 241	31.3	14 175	1 404	5 421	13.9	20.4
Gregg	23 623	23 356	19 387	65 986	75.8	17.7	33 594	25 484	31.8	17 325	157	7 126	15.4	22.8
Grimes	4 346	4 049	3 773	12 034	59.6	8.6	27 891	20 623	35.2	4 389	393	1 584	21.1	24.6
Guadalupe	15 497	13 486	12 936	40 307	69.8	13.9	34 874	26 801	30.1	12 311	994	5 135	15.3	21.7
Hale	8 499	8 513	7 777	20 037	61.1	12.7	28 369	21 183	33.9	7 880	137	3 496	22.0	29.1
Hall	853	907	682	2 718	61.3	8.7	20 045	13 987	43.3	992	−129	370	27.4	40.6
Hamilton	1 577	1 440	1 194	5 533	62.9	12.4	25 321	18 161	39.4	1 463	137	532	19.6	27.9
Hansford	1 327	1 332	1 427	3 620	71.7	15.3	36 272	25 787	40.7	567	−154	226	10.6	13.4
Hardeman	925	1 100	1 105	3 568	62.8	11.0	25 513	18 657	36.7	870	−173	336	19.4	27.0
Hardin	10 981	10 997	8 982	25 629	70.6	9.7	35 279	25 289	39.5	6 635	506	2 683	13.6	19.0
Harris	635 350	579 064	539 025	1 713 593	74.9	25.4	39 037	30 970	26.0	488 199	51 483	194 588	15.2	20.9

[1] Revised. [2] 1997 data are model-based estimates; 1989 data are census estimates. For more information on these estimates, see appendix A. Source Notes and Explanations or <http://www.census.gov/hhes/www/saipe.html>.

Sources: Public School Enrollment, 1998-1999 and 1994-1995—U.S. National Center for Education Statistics, <http://nces.ed.gov/ccd/pubagency.html> (accessed: 16 March 2001). Public School Enrollment and Educational Attainment, 1990—U.S. Census Bureau, "1990 Census of Population and Housing, Summary Tape File (STF) 3C" on CD-ROM (related Internet site <http://homer.ssd.census.gov/cdrom/lookup>). Income and Poverty, 1997—U.S. Census Bureau, "State and County Income and Poverty Estimates - 1997," published 22 November 2000, <http://www.census.gov/housing/saipe/estmod97/est97ALL.dat>. Income and Poverty, 1989—U.S. Census Bureau, "1990 Census of Population and Housing, Summary Tape File (STF) 3C" on CD-ROM (related Internet site <http://homer.ssd.census.gov/cdrom/lookup>).

[Includes U.S., states, and 3,142 counties or county equivalents defined as of January 1, 1992. For changes to these areas since January 1, 1992, see appendix B. Geographic Information]

County	Public school enrollment Fall 1998–1999	Public school enrollment Fall 1994–1995[1]	Public school enrollment 1990	Educational attainment, 1990 Persons 25 years and over	Educational attainment, 1990 Percent— High school graduate or higher	Educational attainment, 1990 Percent— Bachelor's degree or higher	Median household income[2] 1997 (dollars)	Median household income[2] 1989 (dollars)	Median household income[2] Percent change, 1989–1997	Persons below poverty level,[2] 1997 Number Persons of all ages Total	Persons below poverty level,[2] 1997 Number Persons of all ages Net change, 1989–1997	Persons below poverty level,[2] 1997 Number Persons under 18 years	Persons below poverty level,[2] 1997 Percent Persons of all ages	Persons below poverty level,[2] 1997 Percent Persons under 18 years
TEXAS—Con.														
Harrison	13 440	12 639	12 359	35 781	70.4	12.7	29 805	22 625	31.7	10 944	−540	4 237	18.6	24.6
Hartley	328	271	794	2 382	84.6	19.7	43 504	28 826	50.9	260	−106	66	6.9	5.9
Haskell	1 209	1 284	1 258	4 755	58.4	9.0	23 824	19 386	22.9	1 455	65	570	23.9	36.1
Hays	17 874	15 265	11 221	34 529	76.9	26.4	37 341	25 492	46.5	10 971	−1 458	3 789	13.1	16.6
Hemphill	824	820	823	2 359	72.9	12.3	42 393	28 697	47.7	292	−60	107	8.3	9.5
Henderson	10 014	9 470	10 169	39 738	64.7	10.3	28 383	20 747	36.8	11 284	874	4 148	16.3	24.9
Hidalgo	136 005	127 406	109 611	199 262	46.6	11.5	20 034	16 703	19.9	196 989	37 773	93 043	37.6	47.9
Hill	5 911	5 597	4 861	18 028	61.5	10.7	27 481	20 067	36.9	5 678	−63	2 175	18.8	27.1
Hockley	5 362	5 652	5 739	13 761	64.0	12.4	31 256	23 713	31.8	4 575	−160	2 006	19.5	25.5
Hood	6 920	6 333	5 148	19 856	74.7	15.2	38 973	31 627	23.2	3 946	1 164	1 594	10.5	17.4
Hopkins	5 970	5 936	5 479	18 593	62.9	11.2	28 126	20 771	35.4	4 771	−465	1 826	15.7	22.1
Houston	4 054	4 134	3 928	14 454	64.0	10.1	25 157	18 138	38.7	4 893	−118	1 790	24.1	32.6
Howard	6 001	6 217	6 328	20 839	65.2	11.8	29 347	23 145	26.8	5 889	−266	2 350	19.4	26.4
Hudspeth	815	821	728	1 707	48.1	8.0	19 987	15 401	29.8	1 033	−56	461	32.9	44.2
Hunt	13 862	13 128	11 499	40 939	69.1	15.9	31 542	25 317	24.6	10 790	1 215	4 333	15.5	23.0
Hutchinson	5 156	5 592	5 502	16 318	71.9	13.0	36 739	26 717	37.5	2 962	−464	1 163	12.3	16.6
Irion	344	340	327	1 030	70.5	13.8	31 533	24 280	29.9	227	7	92	13.0	18.6
Jack	1 820	1 708	1 335	4 652	62.2	11.0	28 349	21 627	31.1	1 236	−14	464	16.6	22.4
Jackson	3 339	3 349	2 492	8 519	56.6	10.2	30 345	20 687	46.7	2 189	−524	854	16.0	22.0
Jasper	7 489	7 526	6 666	19 869	64.4	8.3	28 930	20 451	41.5	6 428	224	2 641	19.2	27.6
Jeff Davis	416	436	418	1 293	69.5	25.1	25 895	18 995	36.3	389	15	153	16.6	25.5
Jefferson	45 088	45 321	43 521	152 608	74.4	15.5	32 362	25 132	28.8	45 130	−638	17 472	19.1	27.3
Jim Hogg	1 245	1 346	1 294	2 959	48.9	11.2	21 817	14 704	48.4	1 549	−249	653	30.5	40.1
Jim Wells	8 895	8 837	9 131	21 880	55.3	9.4	24 586	18 315	34.2	10 859	−403	4 562	27.0	34.7
Johnson	23 961	21 711	19 787	59 921	71.9	11.5	37 768	30 612	23.4	13 240	2 193	5 573	11.3	16.0
Jones	3 251	3 293	3 522	10 772	60.8	10.9	25 380	19 270	31.7	3 637	254	1 239	23.4	27.5
Karnes	2 725	2 854	2 829	7 671	51.3	8.9	23 226	16 155	43.8	3 732	−718	1 257	30.4	31.8
Kaufman	16 527	14 955	10 660	32 427	67.9	10.9	35 477	27 280	30.0	8 990	975	3 722	13.8	19.0
Kendall	5 786	4 560	2 734	9 702	80.2	19.9	39 212	27 433	42.9	2 254	64	853	10.6	15.1
Kenedy	58	43	101	281	43.1	7.8	23 134	16 500	40.2	92	−6	37	20.1	26.8
Kent	185	191	187	697	63.4	10.3	28 148	19 508	44.3	98	−115	34	11.4	15.4
Kerr	7 019	6 382	5 722	25 375	75.9	20.2	30 766	23 205	32.6	6 049	818	2 616	14.5	26.5
Kimble	756	789	785	2 853	64.7	12.4	23 530	17 553	34.1	778	−11	305	18.8	28.3
King	90	84	93	216	78.2	24.5	32 386	27 625	17.2	35	9	16	9.6	13.1
Kinney	648	584	639	2 111	56.2	11.0	21 850	15 750	38.7	913	29	353	26.0	41.4
Kleberg	6 449	6 557	6 311	16 542	63.3	18.9	27 915	21 887	27.5	7 479	−450	3 044	25.5	34.0
Knox	984	1 098	965	3 218	58.6	10.9	23 780	17 370	36.9	993	−126	433	23.9	35.6
Lamar	9 062	8 705	8 258	28 247	67.3	13.0	29 578	21 551	37.2	8 917	286	3 462	19.6	28.5
Lamb	3 465	3 697	3 530	9 408	56.7	11.1	26 129	19 000	37.5	3 423	−610	1 405	23.1	30.7
Lampasas	3 589	3 252	2 534	8 677	70.7	12.8	28 058	22 572	24.3	3 103	441	1 230	17.4	24.2
La Salle	1 429	1 330	1 270	3 215	45.3	10.8	20 054	15 615	28.4	1 938	20	775	35.4	42.2
Lavaca	2 257	2 233	2 783	12 794	55.7	8.4	27 956	19 945	40.2	2 717	−622	927	14.6	19.6
Lee	2 932	2 866	2 624	8 088	61.1	11.3	30 438	21 553	41.2	1 913	−282	742	13.2	17.6
Leon	2 960	2 926	2 342	8 477	67.4	10.2	27 657	20 152	37.2	2 402	−269	882	16.5	23.2
Liberty	13 650	12 861	11 459	32 682	62.4	7.9	31 683	22 637	40.0	10 628	1 263	4 199	17.2	22.9
Limestone	4 042	4 146	3 985	14 006	60.2	10.6	25 239	19 620	28.6	4 421	−519	1 683	21.4	29.8
Lipscomb	715	729	669	2 057	73.8	14.9	34 795	24 648	41.2	341	−83	141	11.4	16.2
Live Oak	2 048	2 189	2 038	6 249	60.9	12.0	29 403	20 898	40.7	1 842	−292	723	18.0	25.5
Llano	1 578	1 388	1 309	9 225	71.6	13.3	26 798	19 042	40.7	1 942	55	607	14.5	27.2
Loving	X	X	24	75	56.0	4.0	32 152	26 563	21.0	27	27	8	22.9	23.0
Lubbock	42 177	42 907	40 610	127 820	74.2	23.4	31 961	24 328	31.4	42 849	2 438	16 877	19.3	27.1
Lynn	1 683	1 638	1 450	4 150	54.2	7.5	26 361	17 823	47.9	1 640	−539	709	24.3	32.9
McCulloch	1 718	1 751	1 815	5 780	62.5	13.8	23 532	16 544	42.2	1 959	−409	762	22.7	30.6
McLennan	39 389	37 620	33 026	112 797	71.6	16.6	31 877	22 665	40.6	36 501	−795	14 361	18.3	26.3
McMullen	189	200	148	560	64.6	14.6	34 300	29 205	17.4	112	−35	40	13.9	20.2
Madison	2 382	2 180	1 839	6 691	58.8	10.1	25 564	17 838	43.3	2 608	268	857	27.4	32.5
Marion	1 523	1 677	1 796	6 901	60.2	7.6	21 444	15 288	40.3	3 044	20	1 004	27.7	36.9
Martin	1 050	1 095	1 204	2 833	54.3	6.7	29 194	20 596	41.7	1 008	−164	456	20.0	25.8
Mason	596	704	563	2 402	65.1	12.9	22 164	15 366	44.2	730	−204	253	19.9	27.9
Matagorda	8 243	8 691	8 077	22 442	67.4	12.6	31 446	25 368	24.0	6 941	−656	3 046	18.1	24.9
Maverick	12 207	11 682	10 362	18 537	35.7	7.3	16 626	12 262	35.6	19 111	894	9 198	39.7	50.7
Medina	8 156	7 271	5 888	16 902	61.7	11.0	29 605	22 455	31.8	6 933	588	2 798	19.7	26.2
Menard	499	446	393	1 569	58.0	11.3	19 458	14 271	36.3	649	−41	244	28.1	41.8
Midland	24 575	24 556	21 525	64 196	76.8	26.4	38 529	31 164	23.6	17 203	1 926	7 484	14.3	19.8
Milam	4 700	4 250	4 858	14 741	61.0	10.0	26 537	18 355	44.6	4 902	−434	1 911	20.2	27.4
Mills	1 009	944	815	3 222	61.6	12.8	24 013	17 558	36.8	896	−93	319	19.4	28.1

[1] Revised. [2] 1997 data are model-based estimates; 1989 data are census estimates. For more information on these estimates, see appendix A. Source Notes and Explanations or <http://www.census.gov/hhes/www/saipe.html>.

Sources: Public School Enrollment, 1998-1999 and 1994-1995—U.S. National Center for Education Statistics, <http://nces.ed.gov/ccd/pubagency.html> (accessed: 16 March 2001). Public School Enrollment and Educational Attainment, 1990—U.S. Census Bureau, "1990 Census of Population and Housing, Summary Tape File (STF) 3C" on CD-ROM (related Internet site <http://homer.ssd.census.gov/cdrom/lookup>). Income and Poverty, 1997—U.S. Census Bureau, "State and County Income and Poverty Estimates - 1997," published 22 November 2000, <http://www.census.gov/housing/saipe/estmod97/est97ALL.dat>. Income and Poverty, 1989—U.S. Census Bureau, "1990 Census of Population and Housing, Summary Tape File (STF) 3C" on CD-ROM (related Internet site <http://homer.ssd.census.gov/cdrom/lookup>).

Table B-5. Counties — **Education, Income, and Poverty**-Con.

[Includes U.S., states, and 3,142 counties or county equivalents defined as of January 1, 1992. For changes to these areas since January 1, 1992, see appendix B. Geographic Information]

County	Public school enrollment Fall 1998–1999	1994–1995[1]	1990	Educational attainment, 1990 Persons 25 years and over	Percent— High school graduate or higher	Bachelor's degree or higher	Median household income[2] 1997 (dollars)	1989 (dollars)	Percent change, 1989–1997	Persons below poverty level,[2] 1997 Number, Persons of all ages Total	Net change, 1989–1997	Persons under 18 years	Percent Persons of all ages	Persons under 18 years
TEXAS—Con.														
Mitchell	1 539	1 647	1 691	5 284	59.3	10.6	24 925	17 600	41.6	1 761	−64	605	23.6	28.1
Montague	3 310	3 398	2 982	11 771	63.6	10.2	26 117	19 054	37.1	3 115	−1	1 117	16.9	23.5
Montgomery	54 588	45 709	36 967	112 214	75.5	19.4	46 292	32 254	43.5	28 249	6 404	11 866	10.3	14.6
Moore	4 694	4 509	4 033	10 263	61.9	10.8	35 372	27 466	28.8	2 496	183	1 171	12.7	17.4
Morris	2 690	2 925	2 608	8 657	68.6	10.5	27 513	19 895	38.3	2 467	−548	947	18.6	25.9
Motley	233	275	259	1 088	62.2	10.8	22 391	16 780	33.4	271	−81	96	20.1	29.8
Nacogdoches	10 099	9 654	8 834	29 589	69.7	20.0	27 741	19 340	43.4	10 969	−1 662	3 789	20.5	27.9
Navarro	8 514	7 880	7 812	25 376	64.6	12.7	28 217	21 479	31.4	7 780	201	2 994	19.0	26.2
Newton	2 735	2 803	3 043	8 399	59.1	5.5	25 358	16 656	52.2	3 269	−290	1 218	22.8	29.5
Nolan	3 525	3 689	3 340	10 486	62.3	12.0	26 369	20 350	29.6	3 495	102	1 457	21.8	31.4
Nueces	63 152	64 722	62 949	174 396	68.9	17.0	29 198	25 337	15.2	67 638	8 110	28 526	21.5	29.2
Ochiltree	2 062	2 000	2 050	5 637	71.2	13.8	36 685	26 352	39.2	1 107	−132	462	12.6	17.0
Oldham	789	972	807	1 228	73.7	18.6	35 241	28 167	25.1	243	−64	109	13.3	19.2
Orange	17 276	17 604	16 582	50 076	72.6	10.4	35 712	26 563	34.4	12 993	828	5 262	15.2	21.9
Palo Pinto	4 911	4 788	4 700	16 414	65.0	11.1	27 083	20 389	32.8	4 827	66	1 883	18.8	27.1
Panola	3 999	4 084	4 555	14 002	67.6	12.0	30 124	21 027	43.3	3 766	−721	1 418	16.4	21.8
Parker	15 329	12 982	12 745	41 144	74.5	13.9	40 492	30 592	32.4	7 437	642	3 005	9.0	13.1
Parmer	2 570	2 596	2 331	5 802	55.7	8.9	29 764	19 742	50.8	1 683	−671	715	16.3	20.2
Pecos	3 455	3 735	3 934	8 426	58.0	12.1	27 309	21 170	29.0	3 566	−725	1 369	25.2	28.7
Polk	6 556	6 365	5 582	20 808	59.7	8.6	27 404	18 968	44.5	8 090	1 594	3 244	17.0	28.0
Potter	31 944	32 061	18 390	59 877	67.8	11.5	27 848	20 472	36.0	21 704	85	9 082	20.5	29.3
Presidio	1 869	1 650	1 678	3 851	43.9	11.8	17 753	13 016	36.4	3 079	−93	1 352	35.6	48.1
Rains	1 444	1 328	1 206	4 547	62.4	7.5	28 152	21 741	29.5	1 236	242	471	14.3	21.6
Randall	7 312	6 595	16 659	55 881	85.7	26.4	44 405	31 472	41.1	8 391	572	3 190	8.5	11.2
Reagan	996	1 152	1 316	2 387	64.1	10.4	36 158	28 586	26.5	547	47	263	12.9	15.7
Real	263	276	416	1 657	60.2	10.0	22 319	17 428	28.1	779	55	304	29.1	49.9
Red River	2 868	2 846	2 585	9 676	57.0	7.3	22 035	16 217	35.9	3 187	−609	1 128	23.4	33.4
Reeves	3 268	3 550	3 957	8 979	45.3	6.9	22 930	17 952	27.7	3 817	−567	1 588	27.5	33.4
Refugio	1 704	1 646	1 691	5 067	61.9	11.3	28 459	20 733	37.3	1 570	−339	594	19.7	27.2
Roberts	182	199	235	671	81.4	17.4	34 334	30 203	13.7	88	24	37	9.3	13.1
Robertson	3 295	3 230	2 983	9 864	57.2	9.5	23 600	17 206	37.2	3 798	−527	1 507	24.4	33.0
Rockwall	9 080	7 253	5 089	16 121	84.1	28.5	57 397	42 417	35.3	2 523	867	1 011	6.7	9.5
Runnels	2 593	2 611	2 417	7 361	56.8	10.0	24 707	19 348	27.7	2 171	279	912	19.0	27.9
Rusk	7 690	7 720	8 929	28 238	66.6	10.7	29 418	22 211	32.4	7 892	−765	2 922	17.4	22.8
Sabine	1 603	1 578	1 459	6 985	60.8	9.5	25 064	17 512	43.1	1 935	118	666	18.5	30.9
San Augustine	1 517	1 585	1 522	5 423	57.2	8.3	21 658	15 134	43.1	1 887	−415	668	23.7	33.6
San Jacinto	3 583	3 294	3 243	10 853	58.9	7.7	28 337	19 867	42.6	4 349	504	1 633	19.7	28.4
San Patricio	15 746	15 407	14 291	34 297	60.6	11.0	28 765	22 864	25.8	15 891	1 205	6 733	23.1	29.7
San Saba	1 158	1 148	973	3 662	61.7	11.9	21 722	14 462	50.2	1 310	−452	510	24.4	35.5
Schleicher	727	790	742	1 841	62.4	13.4	29 721	21 696	37.0	503	−82	218	17.0	22.2
Scurry	3 451	3 831	4 081	11 381	64.3	10.0	32 307	24 046	34.4	3 011	−108	1 175	18.2	23.2
Shackelford	687	663	687	2 247	66.1	15.0	28 198	18 773	50.2	478	−100	168	14.7	18.5
Shelby	4 861	4 838	4 236	14 456	57.3	8.8	24 560	17 446	40.8	4 919	−465	1 843	21.6	30.0
Sherman	999	818	601	1 792	70.5	13.2	35 140	23 005	52.7	322	−84	119	11.2	14.5
Smith	30 202	29 508	27 831	95 585	75.7	19.8	34 336	25 769	33.2	24 994	566	9 768	14.9	21.7
Somervell	1 555	1 443	1 171	3 228	66.9	13.8	38 415	29 539	30.0	905	16	404	14.3	20.4
Starr	14 429	13 828	12 774	19 616	31.6	6.7	14 178	10 182	39.2	26 183	2 033	12 399	46.7	56.4
Stephens	1 883	1 982	1 860	5 955	67.5	11.8	26 079	19 203	35.8	1 861	−61	707	20.3	27.4
Sterling	349	371	342	867	68.3	13.5	32 781	25 208	30.0	165	−38	72	12.0	14.9
Stonewall	346	377	371	1 371	65.1	9.8	26 494	21 210	24.9	314	−7	118	17.8	25.3
Sutton	994	1 077	989	2 519	62.0	20.4	31 567	20 933	50.8	658	−114	281	14.7	20.3
Swisher	1 933	2 043	1 795	5 135	61.8	11.5	28 250	19 569	44.4	1 795	−167	718	23.0	30.4
Tarrant	255 992	228 990	197 978	725 554	79.9	24.0	42 927	32 335	32.8	155 595	29 042	63 273	11.5	16.8
Taylor	24 425	24 614	21 993	71 420	75.4	20.7	31 606	24 661	28.2	19 614	2 194	7 933	16.8	23.4
Terrell	230	284	347	909	66.3	12.0	24 682	21 213	16.4	248	−136	88	20.9	26.2
Terry	2 874	3 148	3 328	7 814	59.7	9.7	29 117	22 392	30.0	3 000	−325	1 300	24.1	31.3
Throckmorton	387	392	321	1 331	69.8	15.3	25 922	18 844	37.6	277	−56	96	16.4	22.2
Titus	5 721	5 165	4 815	14 900	65.4	12.3	28 873	22 173	30.2	4 277	−352	1 733	17.0	23.2
Tom Green	19 664	19 750	19 109	59 600	71.0	17.0	31 084	24 349	27.7	17 045	945	6 933	17.2	24.2
Travis	112 596	98 022	88 138	349 209	83.4	34.7	40 250	27 488	46.4	82 300	−6 790	30 490	11.7	17.0
Trinity	2 361	2 388	1 959	7 935	60.7	9.0	24 087	16 963	42.0	2 711	−152	968	21.5	33.6
Tyler	3 836	3 862	3 184	11 297	62.2	8.5	27 208	20 647	31.8	3 708	708	1 303	20.3	28.2
Upshur	6 763	6 533	6 163	19 838	67.1	8.8	29 591	21 889	35.2	5 997	566	2 298	16.9	23.4
Upton	976	1 164	1 182	2 530	62.5	10.3	31 754	24 342	30.4	652	−128	305	17.2	22.7
Uvalde	6 421	6 231	5 524	13 273	56.1	13.5	22 617	18 001	25.6	7 627	525	3 441	30.0	41.2
Val Verde	10 171	10 372	9 039	21 502	56.1	13.0	23 774	18 042	31.8	12 846	−944	5 853	29.5	38.6

[1] Revised.   [2] 1997 data are model-based estimates; 1989 data are census estimates. For more information on these estimates, see appendix A. Source Notes and Explanations or <http://www.census.gov/hhes/www/saipe.html>.

Sources: Public School Enrollment, 1998-1999 and 1994-1995—U.S. National Center for Education Statistics, <http://nces.ed.gov/ccd/pubagency.html> (accessed: 16 March 2001). Public School Enrollment and Educational Attainment, 1990—U.S. Census Bureau, "1990 Census of Population and Housing, Summary Tape File (STF) 3C" on CD-ROM (related Internet site <http://homer.ssd.census.gov/cdrom/lookup>). Income and Poverty, 1997—U.S. Census Bureau, "State and County Income and Poverty Estimates - 1997," published 22 November 2000, <http://www.census.gov/housing/saipe/estmod97/est97ALL.dat>. Income and Poverty, 1989—U.S. Census Bureau, "1990 Census of Population and Housing, Summary Tape File (STF) 3C" on CD-ROM (related Internet site <http://homer.ssd.census.gov/cdrom/lookup>).

[Includes U.S., states, and 3,142 counties or county equivalents defined as of January 1, 1992. For changes to these areas since January 1, 1992, see appendix B. Geographic Information]

County	Public school enrollment Fall 1998–1999	Public school enrollment Fall 1994–1995[1]	Public school enrollment 1990	Educational attainment, 1990 Persons 25 years and over	Percent High school graduate or higher	Percent Bachelor's degree or higher	Median household income[2] 1997 (dollars)	Median household income[2] 1989 (dollars)	Percent change, 1989–1997	Persons below poverty level,[2] 1997 Number, Persons of all ages Total	Net change, 1989–1997	Persons under 18 years	Percent Persons of all ages	Percent Persons under 18 years
TEXAS—Con.														
Van Zandt	9 178	8 512	6 958	25 380	62.1	8.7	28 901	21 072	37.2	6 910	410	2 501	15.7	22.0
Victoria	16 193	15 617	15 683	45 206	70.2	14.1	36 466	26 945	35.3	13 100	175	5 672	16.0	22.7
Walker	7 769	7 779	7 528	31 362	73.3	19.0	30 971	21 631	43.2	8 193	–32	2 406	19.9	22.5
Waller	6 666	5 851	4 192	12 735	69.6	16.2	29 832	22 334	33.6	5 218	817	1 943	20.9	26.9
Ward	2 614	2 777	3 307	7 613	63.2	10.4	29 524	22 270	32.6	2 247	–327	962	19.4	25.8
Washington	5 194	5 197	4 823	16 523	62.9	15.1	32 973	23 052	43.0	4 312	–118	1 618	15.5	21.7
Webb	47 239	42 634	36 807	68 167	47.8	11.1	23 386	18 074	29.4	61 235	11 119	29 538	32.6	42.3
Wharton	8 682	8 686	8 595	24 585	61.2	11.8	30 531	23 896	27.8	6 970	–1 407	2 808	17.4	23.0
Wheeler	1 052	1 076	1 225	3 969	65.2	12.7	28 839	20 108	43.4	868	–118	331	16.6	22.5
Wichita	22 769	23 238	21 307	75 376	75.1	16.5	32 301	23 899	35.2	19 065	756	6 972	15.9	21.0
Wilbarger	2 856	2 919	2 753	9 817	62.9	12.7	27 028	20 886	29.4	2 632	–136	1 039	19.4	26.9
Willacy	4 984	5 197	5 179	9 494	42.9	8.8	18 616	14 590	27.6	7 849	1	3 587	39.7	50.3
Williamson	55 429	44 568	29 155	83 641	81.4	24.6	50 102	33 695	48.7	15 011	1 200	6 180	6.7	8.6
Wilson	6 675	5 881	4 837	13 743	61.2	8.8	33 182	23 184	43.1	4 797	157	1 980	15.2	19.8
Winkler	1 894	2 029	2 223	5 090	57.5	10.1	31 590	22 366	41.2	1 347	–495	559	16.8	20.3
Wise	7 871	6 768	6 621	21 962	67.1	10.0	36 125	25 885	39.6	4 871	157	1 873	11.2	14.6
Wood	6 037	6 025	5 060	20 049	65.7	9.6	27 395	20 927	30.9	5 856	723	2 044	17.5	24.8
Yoakum	2 170	2 398	2 163	5 005	64.0	10.4	35 414	26 442	33.9	1 244	–473	549	15.4	19.5
Young	3 592	3 735	3 455	12 071	60.7	11.2	28 514	21 710	31.3	3 136	260	1 190	18.0	25.2
Zapata	2 925	2 882	2 517	5 144	50.1	6.9	20 905	14 926	40.1	3 722	–68	1 691	32.1	40.6
Zavala	2 531	2 525	3 264	6 423	38.6	6.9	15 439	11 822	30.6	5 340	–664	2 295	45.2	53.5
UTAH	479 854	473 308	438 499	897 321	85.1	22.3	38 884	29 470	31.9	210 783	18 368	89 867	10.0	12.5
Beaver	1 456	1 426	1 364	2 731	83.4	9.0	30 352	21 092	43.9	727	96	326	12.2	15.7
Box Elder	11 204	11 290	10 712	19 230	83.6	17.6	44 570	33 468	33.2	3 406	777	1 597	8.0	9.9
Cache	19 076	18 865	17 571	32 982	89.3	30.0	37 084	26 949	37.6	9 160	–193	3 525	10.5	11.7
Carbon	4 639	5 160	5 063	11 547	74.3	12.5	35 526	25 555	39.0	3 284	426	1 400	15.7	20.4
Daggett	183	212	194	410	75.4	11.7	35 584	22 941	55.1	79	–23	30	10.8	12.6
Davis	59 285	58 122	53 150	93 502	89.9	23.5	48 690	35 108	38.7	15 666	2 375	6 918	6.6	7.9
Duchesne	4 324	4 648	4 050	6 323	74.8	11.8	31 768	23 653	34.3	2 839	489	1 428	19.3	24.3
Emery	3 101	3 347	3 426	5 215	82.4	10.4	39 838	30 525	30.5	1 396	316	681	12.5	15.4
Garfield	1 112	1 129	1 060	2 305	79.9	15.0	30 149	21 160	42.5	589	6	251	13.5	17.8
Grand	1 626	1 625	1 603	4 124	79.9	15.4	28 881	21 695	33.1	1 452	496	624	17.8	26.0
Iron	6 948	6 148	5 273	10 209	85.8	21.9	32 911	23 185	41.9	4 477	1 097	2 009	15.7	21.3
Juab	2 160	2 035	1 759	3 233	77.3	8.8	35 251	23 569	49.6	841	237	407	11.0	14.1
Kane	1 444	1 479	1 405	2 935	82.5	11.8	30 498	21 134	44.3	1 052	216	471	16.7	22.4
Millard	3 606	3 861	3 607	5 818	84.9	15.9	35 315	26 376	33.9	1 758	189	849	14.2	16.9
Morgan	2 047	2 052	1 783	2 859	90.1	19.0	49 084	33 274	47.5	358	–116	149	5.0	5.5
Piute	418	420	359	778	79.8	12.5	25 746	19 125	34.6	275	7	111	19.2	25.6
Rich	506	574	540	900	81.8	15.1	36 627	24 940	46.9	204	–34	93	11.0	12.4
Salt Lake	179 069	182 006	173 186	398 673	85.3	23.8	44 118	30 149	46.3	77 360	6 735	32 501	9.1	11.7
San Juan	3 430	3 452	3 979	6 184	59.7	13.1	26 723	17 289	54.6	4 107	–416	1 754	30.0	32.0
Sanpete	5 471	5 459	4 861	8 014	82.0	15.6	30 460	20 197	50.8	3 273	97	1 454	15.7	18.7
Sevier	4 776	4 972	4 608	8 369	81.9	12.6	32 749	23 300	40.6	2 810	551	1 303	15.2	19.3
Summit	6 092	5 173	3 766	9 106	91.6	32.9	56 472	36 756	53.6	1 482	375	569	5.5	6.7
Tooele	8 169	7 488	7 245	14 518	77.3	11.3	42 277	30 178	40.1	3 027	15	1 371	9.0	11.9
Uintah	6 472	6 831	6 735	11 426	73.7	11.2	32 706	23 968	36.5	4 505	378	2 041	17.4	20.7
Utah	78 754	74 023	68 045	114 438	87.9	26.2	41 509	27 432	51.3	34 817	–4 283	13 580	10.3	11.3
Wasatch	3 581	3 288	2 772	5 378	83.2	18.5	42 998	27 981	53.7	1 034	244	492	7.7	10.0
Washington	18 513	16 550	12 473	26 072	84.5	17.7	34 710	24 602	41.1	10 533	4 143	5 006	12.7	17.9
Wayne	554	602	652	1 237	82.0	20.0	28 100	20 000	40.5	388	35	187	16.4	22.4
Weber	41 838	41 071	37 258	88 805	82.5	18.0	42 764	30 125	42.0	19 883	4 132	8 742	10.8	14.9
VERMONT	105 120	104 593	95 243	357 245	80.8	24.3	35 210	29 792	18.2	56 967	3 598	18 244	9.7	12.7
Addison	5 713	5 638	5 797	19 874	82.0	25.1	37 520	30 112	24.6	3 333	369	1 037	9.8	11.8
Bennington	7 675	7 816	6 084	23 452	77.8	23.5	35 779	28 485	25.6	3 762	–133	1 192	10.5	13.9
Caledonia	4 448	4 781	4 621	17 465	77.4	19.0	31 581	25 356	24.6	3 694	436	1 281	13.0	17.1
Chittenden	23 461	22 365	19 541	79 369	86.7	34.0	46 747	36 877	26.8	9 910	–914	2 802	7.1	8.7
Essex	1 312	1 248	1 232	4 285	68.0	8.5	29 014	22 358	29.8	935	55	342	13.9	21.1
Franklin	9 120	8 987	8 490	24 743	74.8	14.3	35 720	28 401	25.8	4 982	979	1 814	11.2	14.4
Grand Isle	829	847	949	3 508	79.0	20.3	39 362	30 536	28.9	572	–36	190	8.9	12.0
Lamoille	4 019	3 816	3 509	12 285	80.2	23.9	33 418	27 315	22.3	2 221	132	716	10.3	13.3
Orange	5 928	6 137	4 898	16 557	80.4	21.9	35 844	28 004	28.0	2 692	301	916	9.6	12.4
Orleans	4 699	4 914	4 816	15 232	70.7	14.2	29 184	22 809	27.9	3 787	286	1 413	14.8	20.5
Rutland	10 602	10 345	9 714	40 525	79.4	20.6	34 304	28 229	21.5	6 512	722	2 044	10.5	14.1
Washington	10 125	10 070	9 322	35 603	81.3	24.4	36 926	29 623	24.7	5 104	755	1 611	9.2	11.8
Windham	7 135	7 378	6 748	27 490	81.7	25.2	35 590	27 767	28.2	4 159	324	1 300	9.8	12.6
Windsor	10 054	10 251	9 522	36 857	81.3	23.6	36 407	29 258	24.4	5 303	321	1 587	9.4	12.1

[1] Revised. [2] 1997 data are model-based estimates; 1989 data are census estimates. For more information on these estimates, see appendix A. Source Notes and Explanations or <http://www.census.gov/hhes/www/saipe.html>.

Sources: Public School Enrollment, 1998-1999 and 1994-1995—U.S. National Center for Education Statistics, <http://nces.ed.gov/ccd/pubagency.html> (accessed: 16 March 2001). Public School Enrollment and Educational Attainment, 1990—U.S. Census Bureau, "1990 Census of Population and Housing, Summary Tape File (STF) 3C" on CD-ROM (related Internet site <http://homer.ssd.census.gov/cdrom/lookup>). Income and Poverty, 1997—U.S. Census Bureau, "State and County Income and Poverty Estimates - 1997," published 22 November 2000, <http://www.census.gov/housing/saipe/estmod97/est97ALL.dat>. Income and Poverty, 1989—U.S. Census Bureau, "1990 Census of Population and Housing, Summary Tape File (STF) 3C" on CD-ROM (related Internet site <http://homer.ssd.census.gov/cdrom/lookup>).

Table B–5. Counties — Education, Income, and Poverty–Con.

[Includes U.S., states, and 3,142 counties or county equivalents defined as of January 1, 1992. For changes to these areas since January 1, 1992, see appendix B. Geographic Information]

County	Public school enrollment Fall			Educational attainment, 1990			Median household income[2]			Persons below poverty level,[2] 1997				
					Percent—					Number			Percent	
										Persons of all ages				
	1998–1999	1994–1995[1]	1990	Persons 25 years and over	High school graduate or higher	Bach-elor's degree or higher	1997 (dollars)	1989 (dollars)	Percent change, 1989–1997	Total	Net change, 1989–1997	Persons under 18 years	Persons of all ages	Persons under 18 years
VIRGINIA	1 120 819	1 060 809	985 675	3 974 814	75.2	24.5	40 209	33 328	20.6	782 827	171 216	286 182	11.6	17.0
Accomack	5 434	5 500	4 969	21 643	59.5	9.2	25 309	20 431	23.9	7 090	983	2 620	21.9	34.0
Albemarle	11 981	10 889	9 337	42 102	81.5	39.4	46 371	36 886	25.7	6 238	1 562	2 239	8.5	12.6
Alleghany	[3]2 956	[3]3 080	2 340	8 866	67.4	9.3	36 774	26 486	38.8	1 399	138	531	11.4	18.2
Amelia	1 804	1 697	1 540	5 788	56.3	7.2	33 121	26 612	24.5	1 297	356	521	12.3	19.3
Amherst	4 662	4 603	4 649	18 745	58.9	10.7	34 745	27 771	25.1	3 579	985	1 317	12.5	18.9
Appomattox	2 383	2 332	2 225	8 176	61.1	8.7	32 582	25 612	27.2	1 820	319	679	13.7	20.4
Arlington	18 121	16 854	15 051	125 776	87.5	52.3	57 244	44 600	28.3	14 172	2 277	4 655	8.1	15.9
Augusta	10 901	10 468	9 330	36 461	69.0	11.7	38 934	29 474	32.1	5 062	1 263	1 892	8.4	12.6
Bath	892	885	774	3 355	67.3	12.8	32 768	24 203	35.4	492	–187	148	9.8	14.3
Bedford	[4]10 303	[4]9 489	7 455	31 129	68.8	15.6	42 540	30 712	38.5	4 451	1 289	1 668	7.7	12.1
Bland	962	1 045	1 163	4 514	62.6	4.6	32 199	23 587	36.5	725	132	228	11.4	14.9
Botetourt	4 621	4 352	4 188	17 113	72.9	13.6	45 370	33 079	37.2	1 872	361	621	6.5	9.4
Brunswick	2 582	2 576	2 874	10 210	50.5	7.0	25 652	19 424	32.1	3 579	–38	1 174	23.1	29.8
Buchanan	4 487	5 427	6 505	19 467	42.5	6.4	25 812	19 851	30.0	7 014	244	2 329	24.7	31.1
Buckingham	2 247	2 153	2 135	8 752	53.6	7.9	27 712	22 661	22.3	2 871	578	916	22.3	28.5
Campbell	8 498	8 203	7 903	30 977	66.1	12.9	34 895	27 212	28.2	5 606	843	2 256	11.0	18.4
Caroline	3 804	3 641	3 381	12 350	58.8	8.3	34 799	28 934	20.3	3 167	924	1 200	14.3	20.7
Carroll	4 000	3 914	4 285	18 294	49.7	6.5	28 375	21 564	31.6	4 041	347	1 427	14.4	23.3
Charles City	1 025	1 066	1 033	4 247	56.4	8.4	37 173	29 544	25.8	901	–90	326	12.3	19.1
Charlotte	2 260	2 138	2 156	7 746	52.1	6.5	26 422	20 481	29.0	2 325	82	813	18.7	27.0
Chesterfield	50 621	48 050	42 221	130 006	84.2	29.2	55 324	43 604	26.9	16 167	7 223	6 959	6.4	9.4
Clarke	1 891	1 766	1 785	8 348	75.0	18.6	43 442	34 636	25.4	1 148	127	341	9.2	12.3
Craig	726	714	696	2 984	68.4	7.7	34 900	25 106	39.0	439	14	147	8.9	12.9
Culpeper	5 522	5 067	4 872	17 837	66.7	14.9	41 324	33 523	23.3	3 756	1 401	1 531	11.7	17.6
Cumberland	1 283	1 141	1 341	5 126	57.6	11.2	28 177	22 115	27.4	1 440	212	580	18.0	27.8
Dickenson	2 971	3 292	3 656	11 189	47.1	6.0	22 941	16 292	40.8	4 366	–152	1 518	25.5	32.9
Dinwiddie	4 267	3 807	3 492	14 002	59.2	8.4	34 830	29 388	18.5	3 139	776	1 116	12.7	18.7
Essex	1 666	1 564	1 408	5 937	64.7	16.4	31 385	26 074	20.4	1 347	201	484	14.8	22.6
Fairfax	[5]149 029	[5]137 646	126 355	540 230	91.4	49.0	71 057	59 284	19.9	49 529	21 319	18 367	5.3	8.0
Fauquier	9 309	8 685	8 240	31 462	78.9	21.5	56 691	45 222	25.4	3 848	1 869	1 516	7.1	10.5
Floyd	1 915	1 867	2 007	8 240	60.2	10.4	31 297	22 968	36.3	1 776	103	602	13.4	19.9
Fluvanna	2 895	2 452	2 162	8 232	68.5	16.3	40 134	31 378	27.9	1 577	290	580	8.3	12.2
Franklin	6 962	6 593	6 249	26 044	59.9	10.1	33 693	26 357	27.8	5 442	1 214	1 999	12.3	19.4
Frederick	10 376	9 248	7 970	29 402	70.1	14.7	42 545	32 806	29.7	4 382	1 185	1 720	7.8	11.6
Giles	2 567	2 560	2 622	11 199	64.5	8.9	32 519	24 125	34.8	2 089	115	692	12.7	19.2
Gloucester	6 656	6 370	5 557	19 695	74.0	14.7	39 889	31 591	26.3	3 861	1 351	1 574	10.9	16.3
Goochland	1 981	1 749	1 807	10 011	66.7	19.3	50 104	36 239	38.3	1 311	298	435	8.0	12.2
Grayson	2 315	2 220	2 480	11 267	51.1	4.2	26 608	19 324	37.7	2 735	274	855	16.5	24.1
Greene	2 540	2 205	1 834	6 650	63.5	12.7	37 714	29 799	26.6	1 607	347	625	11.2	16.3
Greensville	[6]2 747	[6]2 771	1 816	5 641	50.0	5.3	27 923	22 116	26.3	1 710	260	560	20.7	25.6
Halifax	6 221	5 821	5 377	19 471	51.6	6.4	28 485	[7]22 296	X	6 325	X	2 155	17.2	24.0
Hanover	15 831	13 412	10 755	41 385	77.5	18.9	53 618	40 683	31.8	4 159	1 496	1 401	5.0	6.9
Henrico	39 995	35 934	32 511	147 243	81.3	28.0	44 122	35 604	23.9	19 261	7 568	7 484	7.9	13.2
Henry	9 230	9 062	8 895	38 082	53.9	6.7	30 843	25 834	19.4	7 298	2 057	2 762	13.0	21.5
Highland	350	390	427	1 919	61.8	13.0	28 609	20 903	36.9	348	–10	114	13.7	21.0
Isle of Wight	5 014	4 557	4 196	16 398	65.4	10.4	39 331	29 168	34.8	3 452	538	1 334	11.6	17.5
James City	[8]8 025	[8]7 013	5 153	23 223	82.5	32.9	51 424	39 785	29.3	3 508	1 248	1 429	7.8	13.4
King and Queen	923	886	1 003	4 185	57.6	7.5	32 563	25 755	26.4	1 062	118	400	16.2	25.4
King George	2 973	2 733	2 543	8 468	73.1	20.4	45 575	35 556	28.2	1 582	792	688	9.2	14.1
King William	1 748	2 252	2 142	7 145	68.5	13.0	43 037	33 676	27.8	1 152	150	446	8.9	12.8
Lancaster	1 616	1 617	1 486	8 018	64.8	18.9	32 085	27 275	17.6	1 875	423	697	16.5	30.2
Lee	3 977	4 303	4 851	15 983	48.0	6.5	21 574	14 618	47.6	6 900	–74	2 424	28.5	38.0
Loudoun	26 080	18 131	14 507	55 021	86.6	32.7	67 455	52 064	29.6	5 739	3 114	2 191	3.9	5.5
Louisa	4 118	3 840	3 639	13 483	59.8	8.7	34 609	26 169	32.3	3 127	668	1 182	12.6	18.8
Lunenburg	1 918	2 195	2 182	7 666	52.2	6.6	25 500	19 459	31.0	2 423	260	822	21.9	29.9
Madison	1 863	1 909	1 871	7 975	62.7	15.4	34 947	26 662	31.1	1 599	35	579	12.7	18.2
Mathews	1 318	1 282	1 211	6 154	70.0	15.5	36 385	27 428	32.7	1 061	258	344	11.5	18.1
Mecklenburg	5 042	5 103	4 898	19 959	58.1	10.0	27 752	20 901	32.8	4 949	279	1 743	16.2	24.0
Middlesex	1 379	1 340	1 072	6 347	66.6	14.7	32 671	25 167	29.8	1 336	322	457	13.9	23.4
Montgomery	9 227	8 859	8 720	37 940	73.6	31.6	34 498	22 949	50.3	10 617	–3 764	2 583	15.2	17.9
Nelson	2 087	2 122	2 121	8 739	57.0	13.4	31 817	23 705	34.2	1 925	1	662	13.7	19.7
New Kent	2 301	2 043	1 850	6 970	72.8	13.4	49 908	38 403	30.0	806	299	295	6.3	9.4
Northampton	2 393	2 499	2 336	8 813	57.3	12.4	22 912	18 117	26.5	3 423	18	1 225	26.9	37.9
Northumberland	1 542	1 545	1 419	7 811	63.9	13.5	30 888	23 065	33.9	1 669	244	567	14.3	25.3
Nottoway	2 477	2 461	2 325	10 296	53.2	8.8	27 544	21 774	26.5	2 901	505	1 016	21.2	30.3
Orange	3 823	3 858	3 743	14 483	65.9	16.1	39 156	31 782	23.2	2 704	1 156	1 077	10.6	17.6
Page	3 616	3 505	3 415	14 636	55.4	7.9	31 157	24 971	24.8	2 997	468	1 076	12.8	19.5
Patrick	2 738	2 608	2 872	12 016	54.1	7.0	29 726	22 287	33.4	2 767	415	934	14.8	22.8
Pittsylvania	9 310	9 311	9 711	37 301	56.1	7.4	32 384	25 585	26.6	7 228	475	2 749	12.6	19.8
Powhatan	3 344	2 657	2 162	10 406	66.3	12.2	49 009	37 394	31.1	1 272	510	437	6.6	9.0

[1] Revised. [2] 1997 data are model-based estimates; 1989 data are census estimates. For more information on these estimates, see appendix A. Source Notes and Explanations or <http://www.census.gov/hhes/www/saipe.html>. [3] Independent city of Clifton Forge included with Alleghany County; data not available separately. [4] Independent city of Bedford included with Bedford County; data not available separately. [5] Independent city of Fairfax included with Fairfax County; data not available separately. [6] Independent city of Emporia included with Greensville County; data not available separately. [7] Excludes South Boston independent city which is included in the 1997 data; for more information, see appendix B. Geographic Information. [8] Independent city of Williamsburg included with James City County; data not available separately.

Sources: Public School Enrollment, 1998-1999 and 1994-1995—U.S. National Center for Education Statistics, <http://nces.ed.gov/ccd/pubagency.html> (accessed: 16 March 2001). Public School Enrollment and Educational Attainment, 1990—U.S. Census Bureau, "1990 Census of Population and Housing, Summary Tape File (STF) 3C" on CD-ROM (related Internet site <http://homer.ssd.census.gov/cdrom/lookup>). Income and Poverty, 1997—U.S. Census Bureau, "State and County Income and Poverty Estimates - 1997," published 22 November 2000, <http://www.census.gov/housing/saipe/estmod97/est97ALL.dat>. Income and Poverty, 1989—U.S. Census Bureau, "1990 Census of Population and Housing, Summary Tape File (STF) 3C" on CD-ROM (related Internet site <http://homer.ssd.census.gov/cdrom/lookup>).

[Includes U.S., states, and 3,142 counties or county equivalents defined as of January 1, 1992. For changes to these areas since January 1, 1992, see appendix B. Geographic Information]

County	Public school enrollment Fall 1998–1999	Public school enrollment Fall 1994–1995[1]	1990	Educational attainment, 1990 Persons 25 years and over	High school graduate or higher (Percent)	Bachelor's degree or higher (Percent)	Median household income[2] 1997 (dollars)	Median household income[2] 1989 (dollars)	Percent change, 1989–1997	Persons below poverty level,[2] 1997 Number Persons of all ages Total	Net change, 1989–1997	Persons under 18 years	Percent Persons of all ages	Percent Persons under 18 years
VIRGINIA—Con.														
Prince Edward	2 686	2 622	2 453	9 451	60.5	14.2	27 854	21 395	30.2	3 775	719	1 170	24.0	28.8
Prince George	5 669	5 320	5 005	16 395	77.9	16.2	44 845	34 825	28.8	2 353	1 212	1 016	9.1	13.1
Prince William	51 111	45 675	41 325	126 523	87.8	27.6	59 080	49 370	19.7	16 874	10 020	7 822	6.4	9.6
Pulaski	5 038	5 194	5 484	23 270	59.6	11.5	31 806	23 319	36.4	4 814	334	1 594	14.1	21.0
Rappahannock	1 052	1 008	997	4 610	67.2	18.9	40 172	32 377	24.1	767	55	246	10.4	15.1
Richmond	1 303	1 288	1 230	5 010	56.8	11.8	29 444	24 583	19.8	1 352	261	414	18.9	23.9
Roanoke	13 895	13 691	12 789	54 407	79.4	22.6	47 838	36 886	29.7	4 476	1 312	1 633	5.5	8.8
Rockbridge	3 199	3 168	2 805	12 404	62.1	12.9	33 687	24 955	35.0	2 367	–93	804	12.1	18.5
Rockingham	10 589	9 998	8 974	37 579	64.7	14.6	37 759	29 637	27.4	5 910	2 057	2 381	9.4	15.2
Russell	4 410	4 737	5 377	18 842	50.6	6.7	25 956	17 853	45.4	6 053	–317	2 048	20.7	27.6
Scott	3 741	3 883	3 999	15 904	51.2	5.9	26 888	18 346	46.6	4 204	–595	1 307	18.3	25.8
Shenandoah	5 399	5 192	4 611	21 803	65.2	11.2	34 377	26 527	29.6	3 857	443	1 292	11.0	16.6
Smyth	5 333	5 330	5 612	21 716	53.3	7.8	28 367	20 912	35.6	5 606	387	1 894	17.3	25.1
Southampton	2 884	2 792	2 914	11 523	58.4	11.4	33 943	26 376	28.7	2 791	31	948	17.1	23.5
Spotsylvania	17 270	14 724	11 676	34 901	76.6	19.0	51 218	41 342	23.9	5 766	2 957	2 544	6.8	9.8
Stafford	19 009	15 459	12 245	36 273	80.9	21.6	58 005	44 661	29.9	5 076	2 677	2 180	5.7	7.9
Surry	1 222	1 235	1 044	4 037	58.0	11.0	31 097	25 027	24.3	1 060	219	410	16.0	23.2
Sussex	1 498	1 506	1 556	6 734	54.2	8.6	27 489	20 833	31.9	2 091	68	746	21.0	30.8
Tazewell	7 735	8 288	8 754	30 096	57.3	9.1	27 573	19 670	40.2	9 244	635	3 149	19.6	26.5
Warren	4 745	4 599	3 839	17 244	64.6	11.8	39 400	31 062	26.8	3 275	1 310	1 281	10.9	17.1
Washington	7 447	7 479	7 485	31 082	60.4	12.2	31 387	22 179	41.5	7 050	299	2 309	14.3	20.7
Westmoreland	2 114	2 665	2 369	10 687	59.0	10.9	30 597	24 654	24.1	2 671	722	980	16.1	25.3
Wise	7 346	8 046	8 037	24 931	52.1	8.6	26 593	19 594	35.7	9 094	655	3 211	23.1	30.4
Wythe	4 379	4 399	4 470	17 109	61.8	10.0	29 355	20 964	40.0	4 294	–81	1 451	16.2	23.6
York	11 454	10 710	8 958	26 468	88.3	28.9	51 898	40 363	28.6	3 586	1 595	1 395	6.1	8.2
Independent Cities														
Alexandria	10 803	9 792	9 189	82 034	86.9	48.5	51 052	41 472	23.1	11 784	4 052	3 993	10.2	21.6
Bedford	(3)	(3)	826	4 345	60.1	15.0	29 777	22 787	30.7	1 190	263	426	19.0	29.7
Bristol	2 380	2 528	2 832	12 519	60.9	13.8	27 506	19 226	43.1	3 512	–124	1 085	21.1	30.7
Buena Vista	1 102	1 078	1 085	4 195	55.5	8.7	31 374	23 929	31.1	977	107	284	15.4	20.3
Charlottesville	4 396	4 478	4 542	23 674	75.5	34.1	32 597	24 190	34.8	7 714	–1 311	1 998	21.6	29.6
Chesapeake	36 724	34 130	28 360	93 946	77.1	16.9	45 427	35 737	27.1	20 102	6 773	8 221	10.1	14.2
Clifton Forge	(4)	(4)	796	3 343	69.0	8.9	27 604	20 659	33.6	774	55	250	19.0	27.2
Colonial Heights	2 745	2 694	2 533	11 086	77.8	16.7	40 923	34 472	18.7	1 241	336	407	7.5	11.3
Covington	946	972	1 029	4 856	64.5	7.0	27 748	20 913	32.7	1 210	301	368	17.2	25.5
Danville	7 867	8 299	8 011	36 157	57.4	12.4	26 481	20 413	29.7	11 538	1 743	3 625	22.4	31.0
Emporia	(5)	(5)	892	3 559	58.1	13.4	24 255	21 009	15.5	1 512	596	523	26.9	36.7
Fairfax	(6)	(6)	2 301	13 177	87.5	43.1	61 099	50 913	20.0	1 131	–30	294	5.4	7.4
Falls Church	1 541	1 356	1 181	7 047	91.4	52.8	64 420	51 011	26.3	345	–148	83	3.5	4.4
Franklin	1 693	1 759	1 462	5 160	61.9	14.4	27 348	20 357	34.3	1 990	396	790	23.4	34.4
Fredericksburg	2 180	2 163	2 083	11 118	73.8	26.1	35 484	26 614	33.3	3 046	997	981	17.8	27.9
Galax	1 280	1 207	950	4 612	56.2	11.3	25 767	20 263	27.2	1 435	235	521	22.1	36.2
Hampton	23 541	23 434	21 174	82 670	79.7	19.1	36 297	30 144	20.4	19 657	5 826	7 687	14.6	22.4
Harrisonburg	3 575	3 509	3 033	14 531	76.8	28.7	35 283	25 312	39.4	5 074	–203	1 243	18.3	22.5
Hopewell	4 005	4 099	4 082	14 692	67.4	10.0	32 781	26 934	21.7	4 126	862	1 692	18.4	28.9
Lexington	NA	476	599	3 217	72.8	32.1	29 490	21 361	38.1	1 013	160	181	20.1	21.0
Lynchburg	9 387	9 403	9 593	40 823	69.5	21.7	29 105	23 726	22.7	12 862	2 973	4 294	21.4	30.2
Manassas	6 193	5 437	4 621	16 697	84.2	25.8	54 608	46 674	17.0	2 255	1 227	978	7.0	10.4
Manassas Park	1 788	1 490	1 356	3 865	70.4	7.9	44 835	39 076	14.7	773	514	401	9.9	16.5
Martinsville	2 723	2 830	2 399	11 308	62.9	15.8	28 344	22 446	26.3	2 681	177	885	17.3	26.8
Newport News	33 335	32 324	29 588	102 848	79.3	18.4	34 306	27 469	24.9	29 430	6 261	12 202	16.7	24.4
Norfolk	37 852	36 479	35 322	144 773	72.7	16.8	28 350	23 563	20.3	50 713	6 769	18 698	24.4	34.0
Norton	766	829	892	2 690	54.3	11.6	23 171	15 460	49.9	968	–164	343	23.3	31.9
Petersburg	6 341	6 218	6 065	24 935	62.2	13.5	25 428	21 309	19.3	8 894	1 535	3 264	25.6	39.6
Poquoson	2 436	2 452	2 326	7 054	84.4	29.4	58 371	43 236	35.0	545	236	212	4.7	6.6
Portsmouth	17 508	17 778	18 555	64 726	66.6	11.6	29 815	24 601	21.2	20 105	2 185	8 365	20.5	31.5
Radford	1 564	1 497	1 389	6 319	75.4	29.1	30 571	19 487	56.9	2 479	–1 673	445	18.9	20.9
Richmond	27 621	27 736	26 248	134 576	68.1	24.2	29 234	23 551	24.1	46 036	5 933	15 001	24.9	38.1
Roanoke	13 511	12 925	14 030	65 855	68.0	15.6	27 492	22 591	21.7	19 323	4 085	6 600	20.6	31.7
Salem	3 948	3 758	3 282	16 174	76.1	17.8	37 133	29 047	27.8	2 392	1 276	687	10.5	14.4
South Boston	X	748	1 137	4 773	59.6	14.5	X	20 401	X	X	X	X	X	X
Staunton	2 908	2 959	3 310	16 892	71.4	17.8	32 833	25 366	29.4	3 384	850	981	15.3	21.1
Suffolk	11 241	9 622	8 964	33 584	63.9	12.3	34 560	26 125	32.3	10 323	1 459	4 101	16.4	23.6
Virginia Beach	77 442	75 926	67 849	233 138	88.0	25.5	44 714	36 271	23.3	38 897	16 590	16 343	9.0	13.2
Waynesboro	2 981	2 865	2 875	12 587	71.2	18.2	33 118	26 668	24.2	3 014	955	1 111	15.9	26.2
Williamsburg	(7)	(7)	602	5 005	83.7	42.9	34 657	25 393	36.5	1 714	308	257	22.0	23.9
Winchester	3 327	3 224	3 048	14 506	68.8	18.8	33 538	26 086	28.6	3 431	1 067	1 096	15.8	23.1

[1] Revised. [2] 1997 data are model-based estimates; 1989 data are census estimates. For more information on these estimates, see appendix A. Source Notes and Explanations or <http://www.census.gov/hhes/www/saipe.html>. [3] Independent city of Bedford included with Bedford County; data not available separately. [4] Independent city of Clifton Forge included with Alleghany County; data not available separately. [5] Independent city of Emporia included with Greensville County; data not available separately. [6] Independent city of Fairfax included with Fairfax County; data not available separately. [7] Independent city of Williamsburg included with James City County; data not available separately.

Sources: Public School Enrollment, 1998-1999 and 1994-1995—U.S. National Center for Education Statistics, <http://nces.ed.gov/ccd/pubagency.html> (accessed: 16 March 2001). Public School Enrollment and Educational Attainment, 1990—U.S. Census Bureau, "1990 Census of Population and Housing, Summary Tape File (STF) 3C" on CD-ROM (related Internet site <http://homer.ssd.census.gov/cdrom/lookup>). Income and Poverty, 1997—U.S. Census Bureau, "State and County Income and Poverty Estimates - 1997," published 22 November 2000, <http://www.census.gov/housing/saipe/estmod97/est97ALL.dat>. Income and Poverty, 1989—U.S. Census Bureau, "1990 Census of Population and Housing, Summary Tape File (STF) 3C" on CD-ROM (related Internet site <http://homer.ssd.census.gov/cdrom/lookup>).

[Includes U.S., states, and 3,142 counties or county equivalents defined as of January 1, 1992. For changes to these areas since January 1, 1992, see appendix B. Geographic Information]

County	Public school enrollment			Educational attainment, 1990			Median household income[2]			Persons below poverty level,[2] 1997				
	Fall				Percent—					Number			Percent	
										Persons of all ages				
	1998–1999	1994–1995[1]	1990	Persons 25 years and over	High school graduate or higher	Bachelor's degree or higher	1997 (dollars)	1989 (dollars)	Percent change, 1989–1997	Total	Net change, 1989–1997	Persons under 18 years	Persons of all ages	Persons under 18 years
WASHINGTON..........	999 616	938 314	814 938	3 126 390	83.8	22.9	41 715	31 183	33.8	579 789	61 856	227 904	10.2	15.2
Adams	3 777	3 751	3 330	7 905	66.4	12.3	32 250	24 604	31.1	2 388	28	1 217	15.4	21.4
Asotin	3 651	3 662	3 317	11 425	77.2	12.4	31 753	22 897	38.7	3 308	–23	1 369	15.6	22.9
Benton	28 415	27 179	22 539	69 511	83.9	23.3	46 002	32 593	41.1	12 859	457	5 457	9.3	13.1
Chelan	13 122	11 982	9 459	34 219	74.3	16.7	33 882	24 312	39.4	8 230	386	3 637	13.6	21.0
Clallam	10 632	10 572	9 349	38 864	79.7	16.1	34 376	25 434	35.2	7 812	960	2 976	12.3	19.4
Clark	63 299	55 268	45 180	149 683	83.9	16.8	45 890	31 800	44.3	29 806	7 896	12 716	9.0	13.5
Columbia	720	827	804	2 782	71.8	15.1	32 009	22 418	42.8	514	–243	181	12.5	17.7
Cowlitz	17 931	17 269	15 285	52 654	77.3	11.3	37 189	27 866	33.5	11 701	954	4 554	12.8	18.4
Douglas	6 513	5 912	5 389	16 487	75.9	13.8	35 999	27 054	33.1	3 397	227	1 352	10.0	14.6
Ferry	1 262	1 410	1 489	3 775	72.6	12.0	30 427	25 170	20.9	1 373	–111	548	19.0	24.4
Franklin	10 436	9 836	9 035	20 795	68.1	13.4	32 276	24 604	31.2	8 212	–279	4 050	17.7	24.0
Garfield	474	455	422	1 582	81.8	13.7	32 363	25 156	28.6	251	20	81	10.9	13.4
Grant	15 629	14 155	11 883	32 992	71.6	11.9	32 405	22 372	44.8	10 638	7	4 714	14.9	20.6
Grays Harbor	13 327	13 975	12 120	41 822	74.0	11.0	31 091	23 042	34.9	10 948	642	4 323	16.2	23.9
Island	10 075	9 583	9 505	38 379	88.3	20.0	41 294	29 161	41.6	4 719	563	1 995	6.6	10.4
Jefferson	3 739	3 765	3 128	14 584	82.7	21.8	35 373	25 197	40.4	2 989	305	1 055	11.4	18.2
King	251 261	235 190	207 220	1 017 973	88.2	32.8	51 300	36 179	41.8	131 804	14 215	46 391	8.0	12.3
Kitsap	42 431	40 539	34 765	117 021	86.6	19.8	43 492	32 043	35.7	20 471	3 352	8 329	8.9	12.6
Kittitas	4 909	4 757	4 042	15 234	81.2	22.2	32 375	20 489	58.0	3 974	–939	1 190	13.3	17.1
Klickitat	3 849	3 874	3 476	10 568	70.4	10.9	33 208	23 012	44.3	3 011	225	1 323	15.5	23.0
Lewis	13 093	12 992	11 662	37 795	75.4	11.8	32 557	24 410	33.4	9 686	1 301	3 964	14.2	20.4
Lincoln	2 331	2 324	1 667	6 142	81.9	16.0	34 888	24 617	41.7	1 125	54	411	11.5	15.9
Mason	8 528	8 318	6 889	25 967	79.2	13.6	35 419	26 304	34.7	5 913	1 096	2 349	12.2	18.8
Okanogan	8 790	9 029	6 449	21 427	71.3	12.0	27 453	20 303	35.2	7 121	44	2 970	18.5	26.9
Pacific	3 594	3 743	3 078	13 227	74.2	11.3	28 131	20 029	40.5	3 254	88	1 224	15.6	25.2
Pend Oreille..........	2 174	2 362	1 901	5 814	74.8	12.0	29 599	20 808	42.2	2 059	283	950	17.7	27.8
Pierce	125 170	116 099	103 249	361 037	83.2	17.5	41 853	30 412	37.6	73 016	8 948	29 084	11.0	15.6
San Juan	1 933	1 837	1 329	7 612	91.2	33.5	41 610	31 278	33.0	1 026	298	369	8.1	14.3
Skagit	18 466	17 051	13 901	52 588	81.0	16.3	38 148	28 389	34.4	11 129	2 117	4 703	11.1	17.7
Skamania.............	1 355	1 461	1 739	5 263	77.4	11.7	38 915	28 778	35.2	997	223	418	10.1	14.5
Snohomish............	102 481	90 654	80 686	296 401	85.7	19.3	49 439	36 847	34.2	42 106	11 933	16 828	7.2	10.4
Spokane	73 302	71 248	61 870	228 353	84.4	20.6	35 691	25 769	38.5	49 340	1 313	18 613	12.2	17.1
Stevens	6 637	6 708	7 205	19 301	80.9	12.1	32 387	24 440	32.5	6 016	767	2 604	15.1	21.0
Thurston	38 031	36 343	29 843	103 094	86.5	24.7	42 360	30 976	36.8	18 263	2 356	7 012	9.0	12.8
Wahkiakum	551	544	628	2 295	77.8	10.4	35 446	26 969	31.4	393	52	144	10.2	14.6
Walla Walla	9 181	9 179	7 834	30 400	79.1	18.8	34 471	24 414	41.2	7 220	76	2 681	14.5	19.8
Whatcom	25 736	23 572	20 336	79 410	83.2	22.0	37 896	28 367	33.6	17 650	2 508	6 546	11.4	16.3
Whitman	5 033	5 057	4 767	18 517	91.0	42.6	33 952	21 674	56.6	4 878	–2 949	1 116	14.5	15.5
Yakima	47 778	45 832	38 168	113 492	66.1	13.7	30 822	23 612	30.5	40 192	2 706	18 458	18.3	26.2
WEST VIRGINIA	297 129	310 511	320 282	1 171 766	66.0	12.3	27 432	20 795	31.9	302 521	–42 572	102 253	16.8	24.7
Barbour	2 828	2 787	3 074	10 001	59.8	10.1	23 259	15 607	49.0	3 437	–886	1 152	21.4	29.7
Berkeley	12 612	11 341	10 037	38 025	68.4	11.9	35 715	27 412	30.3	7 943	1 002	3 032	11.2	17.6
Boone................	4 685	5 037	5 509	16 534	54.1	6.4	26 808	17 073	57.0	5 237	–1 720	1 837	19.7	27.9
Braxton	2 770	2 669	2 458	8 582	56.8	8.1	23 427	16 359	43.2	2 872	–454	1 031	21.5	32.2
Brooke	3 921	4 071	4 424	18 004	71.6	12.2	32 466	26 500	22.5	2 971	–177	1 005	11.6	18.7
Cabell	13 240	14 290	14 792	63 333	71.9	18.9	29 404	21 255	38.3	14 989	–2 866	4 656	16.2	24.6
Calhoun	1 476	1 640	1 597	5 160	56.3	6.8	22 282	14 496	53.7	1 945	–569	669	24.2	33.2
Clay..................	2 159	2 156	2 221	6 096	49.4	6.2	21 172	12 855	64.7	2 872	–1 029	1 035	26.8	35.2
Doddridge	1 325	1 399	1 346	4 593	64.6	10.3	26 265	17 159	53.1	1 463	–136	570	19.2	29.9
Fayette	7 778	8 846	9 367	31 343	57.1	8.8	23 578	16 774	40.6	9 981	–1 367	3 484	21.2	31.2
Gilmer	1 188	1 280	1 356	4 720	56.6	14.2	22 686	14 539	56.0	1 713	–665	531	25.0	34.0
Grant	1 971	1 899	1 962	6 820	60.2	8.6	27 808	20 923	32.9	1 507	–85	530	13.6	20.7
Greenbrier	5 841	6 146	5 906	23 592	63.0	11.5	26 800	19 411	38.1	5 755	–370	1 872	16.2	24.3
Hampshire	3 741	3 630	3 228	10 564	61.8	9.0	27 976	20 753	34.8	3 072	121	1 170	16.0	26.0
Hancock..............	4 682	4 984	5 845	24 218	72.5	8.9	32 037	26 031	23.1	4 047	–102	1 305	11.8	18.4
Hardy	2 141	1 976	1 886	7 381	55.3	7.3	29 355	20 745	41.5	1 548	–42	530	12.9	20.3
Harrison	11 962	12 263	12 168	46 448	70.6	13.5	28 989	20 367	42.3	11 571	–281	4 020	16.4	24.9
Jackson	5 091	5 114	5 051	17 017	65.4	8.7	30 739	21 655	41.9	4 308	–816	1 439	15.3	21.8
Jefferson	6 972	6 579	6 152	22 307	68.2	16.2	39 607	30 941	28.0	4 058	389	1 443	10.0	14.8
Kanawha	31 095	33 409	34 057	141 944	72.4	17.6	32 546	23 999	35.6	29 057	–2 366	9 786	14.3	22.8
Lewis	2 851	2 927	3 056	11 547	62.1	8.2	24 837	17 972	38.2	3 551	–421	1 201	20.2	29.9
Lincoln	4 109	4 382	4 459	13 401	49.1	4.7	22 744	14 659	55.2	5 604	–1 593	1 952	24.9	33.7
Logan	6 772	7 884	9 128	27 192	53.4	6.3	24 600	17 942	37.1	9 552	–2 293	3 205	23.0	30.3
McDowell	5 400	6 578	8 079	22 135	42.3	4.6	18 592	13 141	41.5	9 509	–3 686	3 199	31.4	39.3

[1] Revised.   [2] 1997 data are model-based estimates; 1989 data are census estimates. For more information on these estimates, see appendix A. Source Notes and Explanations or <http://www.census.gov/hhes/www/saipe.html>.

Sources: Public School Enrollment, 1998-1999 and 1994-1995—U.S. National Center for Education Statistics, <http://nces.ed.gov/ccd/pubagency.html> (accessed: 16 March 2001). Public School Enrollment and Educational Attainment, 1990—U.S. Census Bureau, "1990 Census of Population and Housing, Summary Tape File (STF) 3C" on CD-ROM (related Internet site <http://homer.ssd.census.gov/cdrom/lookup>). Income and Poverty, 1997—U.S. Census Bureau, "State and County Income and Poverty Estimates - 1997," published 22 November 2000, <http://www.census.gov/housing/saipe/estmod97/est97ALL.dat>. Income and Poverty, 1989—U.S. Census Bureau, "1990 Census of Population and Housing, Summary Tape File (STF) 3C" on CD-ROM (related Internet site <http://homer.ssd.census.gov/cdrom/lookup>).

[Includes U.S., states, and 3,142 counties or county equivalents defined as of January 1, 1992. For changes to these areas since January 1, 1992, see appendix B. Geographic Information]

County	Public school enrollment Fall			Educational attainment, 1990 Percent—			Median household income[2]			Persons below poverty level,[2] 1997				
										Number			Percent	
										Persons of all ages				
	1998–1999	1994–1995[1]	1990	Persons 25 years and over	High school graduate or higher	Bachelor's degree or higher	1997 (dollars)	1989 (dollars)	Percent change, 1989–1997	Total	Net change, 1989–1997	Persons under 18 years	Persons of all ages	Persons under 18 years
WEST VIRGINIA—Con.														
Marion	8 929	9 057	9 125	38 105	71.4	12.5	27 987	20 386	37.3	8 833	−1 825	2 805	15.7	23.5
Marshall	5 791	5 993	6 165	25 045	70.9	9.7	29 284	22 687	29.1	5 428	−408	1 842	15.3	23.1
Mason	4 397	4 635	4 845	16 694	61.1	6.8	28 695	20 135	42.5	4 482	−1 003	1 497	17.2	24.3
Mercer	9 849	10 481	11 563	42 781	63.1	11.6	26 279	19 365	35.7	12 060	−854	4 116	19.0	29.3
Mineral	4 793	4 791	4 634	17 122	72.8	10.4	29 672	22 036	34.7	3 867	−4	1 401	14.3	22.6
Mingo	5 654	6 763	7 701	20 040	50.4	6.6	24 462	16 066	52.3	8 030	−2 340	2 847	24.9	31.3
Monongalia	10 378	10 158	10 111	42 959	75.4	28.1	32 365	22 183	45.9	10 470	−3 895	2 562	14.4	18.0
Monroe	2 049	1 969	2 228	8 295	62.1	8.0	26 592	18 217	46.0	2 108	−450	680	15.9	22.3
Morgan	2 291	2 172	1 915	8 336	64.8	11.8	30 915	24 372	26.8	1 683	366	605	12.2	21.2
Nicholas	4 763	5 077	5 480	17 099	61.2	8.0	25 872	18 116	42.8	5 594	−877	1 968	20.1	28.0
Ohio	6 178	6 317	6 496	34 472	75.1	18.4	31 941	22 489	42.0	6 326	−1 006	1 981	13.5	20.3
Pendleton	1 352	1 442	1 384	5 435	60.6	8.2	27 366	19 565	39.9	1 081	−258	332	13.4	18.7
Pleasants	1 431	1 456	1 447	4 950	68.7	8.5	29 723	20 910	42.1	1 066	−340	348	14.3	19.3
Pocahontas	1 480	1 534	1 468	6 241	60.6	9.7	24 035	17 237	39.4	1 585	−285	519	17.5	26.4
Preston	5 093	5 383	5 913	18 628	62.7	8.3	26 097	19 940	30.9	5 324	−86	1 899	17.8	25.4
Putnam	8 781	8 569	8 117	27 824	73.8	13.3	40 649	27 405	48.3	4 902	−212	1 628	9.5	12.8
Raleigh	12 523	13 708	15 079	50 466	63.2	10.7	27 864	19 566	42.4	13 852	−1 197	4 958	17.4	25.7
Randolph	4 900	4 987	4 858	18 282	65.9	11.9	25 577	18 278	39.9	5 025	−740	1 718	18.3	27.4
Ritchie	1 847	1 866	1 929	6 834	61.5	6.0	25 126	17 333	45.0	1 908	−708	656	18.3	27.2
Roane	2 896	3 068	3 076	9 853	57.2	6.6	23 846	15 375	55.1	3 386	−822	1 199	21.9	31.5
Summers	1 740	1 941	2 411	9 815	58.0	8.5	21 664	16 457	31.6	3 190	−23	1 019	24.2	34.1
Taylor	2 711	2 747	2 772	10 006	66.0	8.1	25 195	17 963	40.3	2 942	−448	969	19.4	27.1
Tucker	1 277	1 391	1 395	5 178	64.0	8.6	25 359	17 949	41.3	1 159	−128	385	15.3	23.7
Tyler	1 604	1 731	1 908	6 451	68.7	9.0	28 958	20 360	42.2	1 512	−274	517	15.3	22.4
Upshur	4 095	4 337	4 216	14 099	64.3	12.0	27 150	18 739	44.9	4 487	−70	1 526	19.9	27.5
Wayne	7 867	7 939	8 186	26 911	63.1	9.0	28 560	19 688	45.1	7 906	−1 103	2 644	18.6	26.8
Webster	1 834	2 051	2 221	6 894	46.5	5.6	19 533	13 371	46.1	2 943	−757	1 024	28.5	38.9
Wetzel	3 703	3 792	3 713	12 545	70.1	10.4	29 719	21 545	37.9	3 228	−671	1 101	17.6	25.8
Wirt	1 187	1 183	972	3 383	66.2	8.0	26 155	16 951	54.3	1 098	−45	431	18.9	29.5
Wood	14 439	14 932	15 131	57 988	73.2	13.5	33 410	25 161	32.8	12 112	−24	4 244	13.9	21.8
Wyoming	4 687	5 754	6 665	18 078	53.0	6.2	23 994	17 248	39.1	6 370	−1 675	2 178	23.0	30.3
WISCONSIN	879 542	860 686	800 466	3 094 226	78.6	17.7	39 800	29 442	35.2	478 698	−29 847	196 327	9.2	14.3
Adams	2 032	2 000	2 398	11 378	67.0	7.4	30 299	21 548	40.6	2 258	160	810	12.9	21.1
Ashland	3 313	3 441	2 993	10 262	75.3	12.8	29 185	19 012	53.5	2 460	−66	1 065	15.4	23.5
Barron	8 650	8 652	7 812	26 198	73.0	11.7	32 040	22 570	42.0	4 676	63	1 957	10.6	16.1
Bayfield	2 229	2 263	2 689	9 418	78.5	18.3	30 043	20 666	45.4	2 139	−155	900	13.9	22.2
Brown	37 303	35 074	30 406	120 575	82.6	17.7	46 319	31 303	48.0	16 072	−1 285	6 677	7.5	11.4
Buffalo	2 598	2 510	2 513	8 918	72.6	10.8	32 665	23 573	38.6	1 564	−24	674	10.9	17.5
Burnett	2 278	2 251	2 440	9 045	72.3	8.9	29 356	20 153	45.7	1 689	−296	677	11.5	18.9
Calumet	4 357	4 392	6 502	20 940	79.7	12.9	48 827	34 050	43.4	1 707	53	693	4.4	5.8
Chippewa	9 199	9 296	9 191	33 195	74.9	10.8	36 052	25 858	39.4	5 254	−87	2 212	9.6	14.4
Clark	6 037	6 475	5 895	19 702	67.5	8.6	30 875	22 177	39.2	3 813	−449	1 761	11.5	17.5
Columbia	9 671	9 213	7 777	29 637	78.3	12.9	39 936	28 360	40.8	3 252	−26	1 260	6.4	9.4
Crawford	2 827	2 847	2 928	10 169	72.4	10.8	29 849	21 436	39.2	1 829	−449	740	11.0	15.7
Dane	62 905	59 200	52 259	225 973	88.9	34.2	47 607	32 703	45.6	30 278	−6 611	10 106	7.2	10.4
Dodge	8 756	8 708	12 274	49 694	72.3	10.2	42 443	29 166	45.5	4 888	48	1 836	6.1	8.2
Door	4 308	4 467	4 402	17 369	79.6	16.4	36 611	26 259	39.4	2 210	−277	848	8.1	12.3
Douglas	7 114	7 353	7 534	27 060	77.2	14.8	31 510	22 122	42.4	5 702	−330	2 406	13.4	21.2
Dunn	6 164	5 946	6 274	19 755	77.7	19.4	35 947	24 452	47.0	4 405	−1 057	1 624	11.9	16.3
Eau Claire	14 387	14 408	13 552	49 336	82.8	20.9	37 404	25 886	44.5	9 484	−3 344	3 373	11.0	15.2
Florence	920	1 002	964	3 057	75.2	8.9	31 303	22 416	39.6	554	−39	210	10.7	15.2
Fond du Lac	15 980	16 411	15 067	56 764	77.5	13.3	42 700	29 441	45.0	6 164	−502	2 323	6.6	9.1
Forest	2 134	1 961	1 755	5 608	64.1	7.6	27 400	16 907	62.1	1 301	−568	506	13.4	19.0
Grant	8 897	9 237	8 613	29 160	77.9	14.7	33 757	24 505	37.8	4 578	−1 774	1 738	9.7	13.2
Green	6 000	5 787	5 859	19 708	76.8	12.0	38 771	28 435	36.3	2 339	2	924	6.9	10.2
Green Lake	3 882	3 911	3 175	12 453	74.6	11.4	36 015	25 708	40.1	1 551	−279	599	7.9	11.7
Iowa	3 978	3 806	3 952	12 747	80.6	13.3	37 079	25 914	43.1	1 908	−80	792	8.5	12.4
Iron	1 051	1 076	922	4 447	74.7	10.5	26 438	17 537	50.8	741	−46	268	11.7	19.7
Jackson	3 375	3 298	3 304	10 800	68.8	8.8	31 374	21 409	46.5	2 062	−319	864	11.6	17.8
Jefferson	12 171	11 824	10 488	42 214	77.0	15.1	42 567	30 749	38.4	3 785	−870	1 318	5.3	6.9
Juneau	4 457	4 614	3 796	14 210	70.6	8.6	31 461	22 073	42.5	2 533	−195	1 038	10.5	16.1
Kenosha	26 203	24 176	21 454	80 794	75.1	12.7	42 529	30 638	38.8	13 156	338	5 468	9.1	13.9
Kewaunee	3 675	3 634	3 214	11 945	73.5	8.2	37 356	26 927	38.7	1 373	−161	504	6.8	8.9
La Crosse	15 630	15 366	14 513	58 586	82.6	21.1	38 523	26 857	43.4	9 943	−2 561	3 667	10.0	14.4

[1] Revised. [2] 1997 data are model-based estimates; 1989 data are census estimates. For more information on these estimates, see appendix A. Source Notes and Explanations or <http://www.census.gov/hhes/www/saipe.html>.

Sources: Public School Enrollment, 1998-1999 and 1994-1995—U.S. National Center for Education Statistics, <http://nces.ed.gov/ccd/pubagency.html> (accessed: 16 March 2001). Public School Enrollment and Educational Attainment, 1990—U.S. Census Bureau, "1990 Census of Population and Housing, Summary Tape File (STF) 3C" on CD-ROM (related Internet site <http://homer.ssd.census.gov/cdrom/lookup>). Income and Poverty, 1997—U.S. Census Bureau, "State and County Income and Poverty Estimates - 1997," published 22 November 2000, <http://www.census.gov/housing/saipe/estmod97/est97ALL.dat>. Income and Poverty, 1989—U.S. Census Bureau, "1990 Census of Population and Housing, Summary Tape File (STF) 3C" on CD-ROM (related Internet site <http://homer.ssd.census.gov/cdrom/lookup>).

Table B–5. Counties — Education, Income, and Poverty–Con.

[Includes U.S., states, and 3,142 counties or county equivalents defined as of January 1, 1992. For changes to these areas since January 1, 1992, see appendix B. Geographic Information]

County	Public school enrollment Fall			Educational attainment, 1990	Percent—		Median household income[2]			Persons below poverty level,[2] 1997				
										Number			Percent	
										Persons of all ages				
	1998–1999	1994–1995[1]	1990	Persons 25 years and over	High school graduate or higher	Bachelor's degree or higher	1997 (dollars)	1989 (dollars)	Percent change, 1989–1997	Total	Net change, 1989–1997	Persons under 18 years	Persons of all ages	Persons under 18 years
WISCONSIN—Con.														
Lafayette	3 721	3 770	3 348	10 181	77.0	10.1	32 886	24 479	34.3	1 445	−309	579	8.8	12.5
Langlade	3 857	3 941	3 480	12 933	71.5	8.8	30 671	20 703	48.1	2 460	−353	974	11.9	17.8
Lincoln	5 257	5 163	4 853	17 567	71.1	10.8	36 694	25 175	45.8	2 400	−337	907	8.1	11.7
Manitowoc	12 539	12 053	12 162	52 215	75.4	12.1	40 097	27 467	46.0	5 620	−977	2 124	6.8	9.6
Marathon	19 845	19 355	20 661	72 367	75.9	13.5	42 120	30 143	39.7	9 700	664	4 367	7.8	12.5
Marinette	7 577	8 013	7 450	26 699	73.6	10.1	33 457	22 396	49.4	4 189	−407	1 643	9.8	14.4
Marquette	2 326	2 293	1 973	8 499	69.7	8.8	29 958	22 234	34.7	1 519	105	591	9.9	16.1
Menominee	1 089	1 088	1 152	1 922	62.7	3.7	21 412	14 122	51.6	1 292	−568	679	25.8	32.9
Milwaukee	151 365	149 515	142 508	610 538	76.3	19.3	37 229	27 867	33.6	149 477	1 293	68 169	16.5	28.4
Monroe	7 061	6 779	6 674	23 025	75.7	10.0	34 392	24 799	38.7	4 392	−222	2 012	11.2	17.3
Oconto	5 289	5 245	5 626	19 760	69.4	8.5	33 910	22 927	47.9	2 993	−605	1 148	8.8	12.3
Oneida	6 486	6 222	5 205	22 153	77.6	14.9	34 713	23 901	45.2	3 170	199	1 170	8.9	14.2
Outagamie	29 501	27 748	23 505	86 689	81.5	16.7	47 845	33 770	41.7	8 487	−41	3 358	5.4	7.5
Ozaukee	12 744	12 459	11 389	47 058	86.9	29.7	62 427	42 695	46.2	2 180	619	706	2.7	3.3
Pepin	1 666	1 744	1 271	4 578	71.0	9.6	32 663	22 992	42.1	682	−194	258	9.6	12.3
Pierce	7 474	7 470	5 723	18 623	81.1	17.8	43 666	30 520	43.1	2 230	−953	779	6.5	8.0
Polk	8 233	8 071	7 134	22 515	78.0	11.4	36 282	24 267	49.5	3 441	−591	1 374	8.9	12.5
Portage	10 543	10 918	9 835	35 004	79.7	19.1	41 782	28 686	45.7	5 833	−1 621	2 161	9.3	12.9
Price	2 805	2 950	2 881	10 414	73.3	10.6	33 942	22 662	49.8	1 631	−32	642	10.4	15.3
Racine	30 111	30 269	29 440	110 593	76.4	16.5	44 675	32 751	36.4	16 905	−595	7 195	9.1	14.2
Richland	2 115	2 211	3 174	11 309	73.7	10.8	31 988	21 946	45.8	2 002	−317	817	11.1	16.7
Rock	27 372	27 090	25 234	88 072	78.2	13.3	41 802	30 632	36.5	13 239	−186	5 492	8.6	13.7
Rusk	2 815	3 008	2 977	9 704	70.3	10.9	27 772	19 617	41.6	2 210	−235	911	14.6	21.9
St. Croix	10 548	9 964	10 102	30 873	84.4	20.3	51 680	36 716	40.8	2 804	−358	1 040	4.7	5.9
Sauk	11 861	11 398	7 874	30 347	74.7	12.9	37 657	26 217	43.6	4 342	−135	1 782	8.1	12.2
Sawyer	2 473	2 567	2 648	9 600	73.7	12.9	27 130	18 094	49.9	2 474	−381	1 032	15.4	23.9
Shawano	6 393	6 157	6 328	24 271	69.5	9.4	33 849	23 841	42.0	3 726	−385	1 462	9.6	14.0
Sheboygan	19 675	19 455	17 655	66 938	77.4	13.8	44 323	31 603	40.2	6 221	−336	2 360	5.7	8.0
Taylor	3 753	3 870	3 678	11 676	68.8	9.2	33 844	24 304	39.3	2 052	−304	833	10.6	14.5
Trempealeau............	5 796	5 699	4 439	16 648	71.7	10.1	31 799	23 864	33.3	2 749	130	1 090	10.5	15.6
Vernon	4 709	4 858	4 522	16 883	69.2	11.2	29 853	21 548	38.5	3 562	−408	1 464	13.0	19.6
Vilas	2 591	2 511	2 785	12 815	76.1	13.7	29 422	20 352	44.6	2 515	−56	925	11.7	19.7
Walworth	14 533	13 241	11 657	46 742	79.0	17.5	41 584	30 345	37.0	5 535	−1 364	1 910	6.6	9.3
Washburn	3 076	3 054	2 684	0 207	74.9	12.0	20 903	19 902	44.9	1 820	−327	700	11.7	17.6
Washington	19 377	18 770	16 077	59 583	81.3	15.9	53 937	38 431	40.3	4 057	1 009	1 507	3.5	4.7
Waukesha	58 504	56 475	50 299	195 837	88.0	27.1	61 562	44 565	38.1	10 993	1 636	3 674	3.1	4.0
Waupaca	10 632	10 453	8 371	30 109	72.1	11.0	36 842	26 083	41.2	3 658	−112	1 393	7.3	10.2
Waushara	3 302	3 265	3 250	13 316	70.0	10.0	30 836	21 888	40.9	2 703	61	1 055	12.3	19.8
Winnebago	23 910	22 762	20 947	88 960	80.6	18.2	43 937	30 007	46.4	10 082	−1 711	3 677	6.9	10.2
Wood	14 137	14 213	12 680	46 796	78.3	13.5	41 762	29 735	40.4	6 242	45	2 524	8.1	12.0
WYOMING	94 988	100 369	95 907	277 769	83.0	18.8	33 197	27 096	22.5	57 421	4 968	20 080	12.0	15.3
Albany	4 063	4 170	4 227	16 297	89.3	38.5	32 374	20 715	56.3	4 143	−1 389	971	15.1	17.6
Big Horn	2 533	2 574	2 402	6 687	77.1	15.0	31 792	21 454	48.2	1 405	−291	494	12.4	15.5
Campbell	7 729	8 029	7 456	16 740	86.5	15.7	49 042	37 055	32.3	2 546	107	967	7.8	9.0
Carbon	2 903	3 354	3 736	10 471	81.7	14.2	36 124	27 109	33.3	1 842	263	609	12.5	14.6
Converse	2 626	2 715	2 686	6 746	83.4	12.7	37 978	27 713	37.0	1 562	251	597	12.6	16.3
Crook	1 269	1 285	1 115	3 317	79.7	15.6	35 003	23 440	49.3	547	−160	187	9.4	11.2
Fremont	7 196	7 657	7 553	20 645	77.5	16.5	29 765	22 260	33.7	6 766	498	2 515	18.7	24.1
Goshen	2 150	2 262	2 474	7 885	76.5	14.5	29 446	21 750	35.4	2 124	47	707	16.7	22.0
Hot Springs	871	901	1 054	3 302	76.1	14.3	29 963	24 500	22.3	620	127	211	13.6	19.3
Johnson	1 336	1 305	1 176	4 127	79.8	17.9	31 832	22 157	43.7	877	107	287	13.0	17.9
Laramie	14 598	14 862	13 581	45 754	84.2	20.7	37 168	27 571	34.8	8 915	1 349	3 144	11.3	15.8
Lincoln	3 430	3 800	3 653	7 058	83.2	15.2	40 589	28 488	42.5	1 413	59	593	10.1	12.3
Natrona	12 284	13 144	12 373	38 433	85.3	20.4	34 685	27 586	25.7	8 318	1 339	2 917	13.1	17.7
Niobrara	493	484	484	1 760	75.7	13.0	28 740	20 947	37.2	463	59	139	17.8	22.9
Park	4 629	4 834	4 607	14 705	82.6	18.8	35 150	25 942	35.5	3 245	1 118	1 169	12.7	17.8
Platte	1 740	1 824	1 778	5 321	79.7	11.4	31 717	21 822	45.3	1 164	−103	388	13.4	17.2
Sheridan	4 623	4 649	4 658	15 630	81.6	17.6	33 000	24 772	33.2	3 114	738	1 074	12.5	17.7
Sublette	1 292	1 378	1 015	3 187	84.2	21.4	38 194	26 825	42.4	497	99	177	8.6	12.1
Sweetwater	8 440	9 773	9 435	22 533	81.5	13.3	49 255	36 210	36.0	3 389	309	1 248	8.5	9.9
Teton	2 348	2 155	1 678	7 637	91.9	30.0	46 385	31 586	46.9	711	−194	191	4.9	6.0
Uinta	5 232	5 790	5 548	9 931	84.1	14.3	43 939	33 259	32.1	2 099	516	918	10.3	12.0
Washakie	1 908	1 912	1 775	5 432	78.8	18.4	36 386	25 172	44.5	950	36	346	11.0	15.0
Weston	1 295	1 512	1 443	4 171	83.2	12.7	35 667	26 213	36.1	711	83	230	11.0	13.3

[1] Revised. [2] 1997 data are model-based estimates; 1989 data are census estimates. For more information on these estimates, see appendix A. Source Notes and Explanations or <http://www.census.gov/hhes/www/saipe.html>.

Sources: Public School Enrollment, 1998-1999 and 1994-1995—U.S. National Center for Education Statistics, <http://nces.ed.gov/ccd/pubagency.html> (accessed: 16 March 2001). Public School Enrollment and Educational Attainment, 1990—U.S. Census Bureau, "1990 Census of Population and Housing, Summary Tape File (STF) 3C" on CD-ROM (related Internet site <http://homer.ssd.census.gov/cdrom/lookup>). Income and Poverty, 1997—U.S. Census Bureau, "State and County Income and Poverty Estimates - 1997," published 22 November 2000, <http://www.census.gov/housing/saipe/estmod97/est97ALL.dat>. Income and Poverty, 1989—U.S. Census Bureau, "1990 Census of Population and Housing, Summary Tape File (STF) 3C" on CD-ROM (related Internet site <http://homer.ssd.census.gov/cdrom/lookup>).

Table B–6. Counties — Crime, Housing, and Building Permits

[Includes U.S., states, and 3,142 counties or county equivalents defined as of January 1, 1992. For changes to these areas since January 1, 1992, see appendix B. Geographic Information]

County	Serious crimes known to police (as reported to the FBI)[1] Number 1999 Total	Violent[2]	Property[3]	Number 1990	Rate[4] 1999	Rate[4] 1990	Housing, 2000 Total units	Percent change 1990–2000	Occupied units Number	Percent owner-occupied	New private housing units authorized by building permits, 2000 Number	Percent in structures with— One unit	Five units or more	Valuation ($1,000)
UNITED STATES	10 674 012	1 328 303	9 345 709	13 900 249	4 347	5 826	115 904 641	13.3	105 480 101	66.2	1 592 267	75.2	20.7	185 743 965
ALABAMA	184 492	20 432	164 060	189 406	4 433	5 181	1 963 711	17.6	1 737 080	72.5	17 406	78.5	19.1	1 718 032
Autauga	1 665	200	1 465	1 295	3 939	6 612	17 662	38.7	16 003	80.8	181	100.0	–	9 855
Baldwin	4 805	343	4 462	2 884	3 603	3 232	74 285	45.8	55 336	79.5	2 472	74.5	24.6	310 388
Barbour	708	53	655	591	2 622	2 325	12 461	16.4	10 409	73.1	67	40.3	59.7	4 236
Bibb	NA	NA	NA	1	NA	10	8 345	30.3	7 421	80.2	4	100.0	–	310
Blount	864	75	789	659	1 902	1 707	21 158	34.0	19 265	83.4	71	83.1	16.9	9 071
Bullock	29	6	23	267	682	6 717	4 727	6.0	3 986	74.5	1	100.0	–	53
Butler	835	132	703	796	3 833	8 446	9 957	13.9	8 398	76.2	104	7.7	92.3	4 196
Calhoun	7 210	907	6 303	6 026	6 136	5 193	51 322	9.8	45 307	72.5	336	75.0	13.4	43 645
Chambers	1 264	193	1 071	1 005	3 429	2 725	16 256	9.0	14 522	75.7	26	100.0	–	2 081
Cherokee	184	15	169	492	5 714	2 678	14 025	49.5	9 719	81.7	14	100.0	–	1 358
Chilton	732	148	584	810	1 975	2 553	17 651	27.1	15 287	82.3	45	100.0	–	4 480
Choctaw	26	4	22	NA	190	NA	7 839	15.5	6 363	86.3	1	100.0	–	75
Clarke	367	25	342	386	1 358	3 814	12 631	16.4	10 578	81.2	11	100.0	–	1 568
Clay	173	15	158	26	1 454	587	6 612	17.9	5 765	77.2	5	100.0	–	662
Cleburne	217	12	205	35	1 564	1 204	6 189	18.3	5 590	80.4	27	40.7	59.3	2 290
Coffee	795	90	705	1 170	1 866	4 621	19 837	17.0	17 421	71.4	108	100.0	–	10 054
Colbert	1 797	97	1 700	1 613	3 380	3 183	24 980	14.5	22 461	75.7	144	66.7	33.3	9 854
Conecuh	145	19	126	159	1 033	1 131	7 265	17.0	5 792	81.0	5	100.0	–	387
Coosa	286	30	256	139	2 443	1 256	6 142	20.1	4 682	84.8	–	–	–	–
Covington	1 044	186	858	1 001	2 933	2 744	18 578	14.8	15 640	77.7	21	100.0	–	2 269
Crenshaw	304	69	235	197	2 220	1 561	6 644	11.9	5 577	76.7	2	100.0	–	320
Cullman	1 829	101	1 728	647	2 429	4 144	35 233	24.2	30 706	78.0	66	63.6	36.4	5 242
Dale	1 102	178	924	721	2 297	3 147	21 779	12.1	18 878	64.3	46	95.7	–	4 073
Dallas	2 989	504	2 485	2 876	6 365	12 107	20 450	7.4	17 841	65.7	65	13.8	–	4 237
DeKalb	558	23	535	39	3 059	248	28 051	22.3	25 113	78.7	77	74.0	–	7 591
Elmore	1 653	140	1 513	1 357	2 656	2 810	25 733	32.0	22 737	81.3	248	88.7	–	20 785
Escambia	1 366	215	1 151	575	3 703	1 940	16 544	15.2	14 297	77.1	16	100.0	–	1 583
Etowah	4 925	839	4 086	5 367	4 786	5 376	45 959	10.0	41 615	74.4	263	68.4	31.6	22 940
Fayette	352	48	304	239	1 933	1 331	8 472	12.1	7 493	77.3	6	100.0	–	720
Franklin	282	28	254	169	955	694	13 749	16.8	12 259	74.3	21	100.0	–	1 124
Geneva	338	47	291	321	1 350	1 496	12 115	16.3	10 477	80.6	22	100.0	–	1 301
Greene	315	64	251	355	3 175	3 497	5 117	22.9	3 931	75.6	7	100.0	–	402
Hale	347	58	289	198	2 532	1 278	7 756	21.8	6 415	80.2	32	100.0	–	3 840
Henry	398	46	352	413	2 585	2 686	8 037	13.9	6 525	80.9	17	100.0	–	2 346
Houston	3 881	398	3 483	7 376	4 591	9 226	39 571	19.2	35 834	69.5	652	50.9	45.7	30 368
Jackson	1 257	134	1 123	1 143	2 513	2 670	24 168	22.3	21 615	77.9	103	45.6	54.4	7 562
Jefferson	38 575	4 470	34 105	50 775	5 836	7 946	288 162	5.5	263 265	66.5	3 057	76.8	23.1	381 358
Lamar	75	4	71	NA	475	NA	7 517	13.6	6 468	76.8	2	100.0	–	160
Lauderdale	1 997	152	1 845	2 881	2 398	3 617	40 424	20.6	36 088	73.2	180	68.9	26.7	15 880
Lawrence	136	12	124	355	479	1 179	15 009	22.9	13 538	83.0	32	25.0	–	1 835
Lee	5 850	909	4 941	5 133	5 800	5 890	50 329	37.4	45 702	62.1	574	57.5	16.4	59 567
Limestone	1 210	79	1 131	1 018	1 936	1 880	26 897	25.4	24 688	77.3	109	100.0	–	15 895
Lowndes	290	59	231	247	2 224	1 951	5 801	21.1	4 909	83.3	3	100.0	–	290
Macon	1 184	108	1 076	2 041	5 138	8 188	10 627	8.2	8 950	67.3	70	100.0	–	2 930
Madison	15 794	1 753	14 041	14 966	5 673	6 324	120 288	22.9	109 955	69.9	1 101	86.2	13.1	51 866
Marengo	463	62	401	255	2 274	1 638	10 127	10.8	8 767	79.2	8	100.0	–	923
Marion	471	29	442	239	1 827	849	14 416	14.4	12 697	77.8	65	38.5	61.5	4 789
Marshall	2 129	138	1 991	1 739	2 639	2 455	36 331	20.2	32 547	74.7	153	100.0	–	17 175
Mobile	23 916	2 542	21 374	27 861	5 980	7 368	165 101	9.2	150 179	68.8	2 158	80.9	19.0	164 464
Monroe	765	202	563	594	3 179	2 478	11 343	17.8	9 383	80.4	61	21.3	78.7	3 770
Montgomery	16 533	1 711	14 822	13 190	7 564	6 308	95 437	12.9	86 068	64.1	835	97.1	2.4	89 088
Morgan	4 500	315	4 185	4 425	4 172	4 530	47 388	17.2	43 602	73.1	367	100.0	–	39 007
Perry	77	5	72	303	1 150	2 375	5 406	12.5	4 333	74.0	3	100.0	–	165
Pickens	200	29	171	386	944	1 865	9 520	13.6	8 086	79.3	14	100.0	–	968
Pike	1 295	127	1 168	276	4 502	1 898	13 981	21.5	11 933	67.2	25	100.0	–	3 222
Randolph	538	58	480	322	2 758	1 620	10 285	17.8	8 642	79.2	2	100.0	–	218
Russell	1 650	179	1 471	2 618	3 261	5 587	22 831	16.3	19 741	62.5	358	30.2	69.3	21 807
St. Clair	1 247	120	1 127	682	2 184	1 670	27 303	34.0	24 143	83.7	207	98.6	–	19 841
Shelby	1 590	138	1 452	1 152	1 125	1 203	59 302	51.3	54 631	81.0	1 798	96.9	3.1	201 478
Sumter	314	24	290	154	5 014	1 218	6 953	6.2	5 708	72.3	7	100.0	–	255
Talladega	1 586	150	1 436	2 325	4 088	3 137	34 469	15.4	30 674	76.3	101	76.2	23.8	8 322
Tallapoosa	1 262	145	1 117	939	3 095	4 312	20 510	18.5	16 656	76.3	87	44.8	55.2	5 820
Tuscaloosa	14 009	1 285	12 724	11 165	8 678	7 418	71 429	21.6	64 517	63.5	703	81.9	17.2	70 926
Walker	1 456	131	1 325	1 675	2 193	2 636	32 417	14.0	28 364	80.0	32	100.0	–	4 038
Washington	121	21	100	NA	5 699	NA	8 123	22.6	6 705	88.1	5	100.0	–	485
Wilcox	54	12	42	72	483	646	6 183	20.8	4 776	83.3	–	–	–	–
Winston	163	21	142	270	691	1 260	12 502	21.9	10 107	80.1	3	100.0	–	224

[1] Data on serious crimes have not been adjusted for underreporting; this may affect comparability over time or among geographic areas. [2] Includes murder and nonnegligent manslaughter, forcible rape, robbery, and aggravated assault. [3] Includes burglary, larceny-theft, and motor vehicle theft. [4] Per 100,000 resident population provided by the U.S. Federal Bureau of Investigation.

Sources: Serious Crimes Known to Police—U.S. Federal Bureau of Investigation, Uniform Crime Reporting Program, unpublished data, annual (related Internet site <http://www.fbi.gov/ucr/ucr.htm>). Housing, 2000—U.S. Census Bureau, 2000 Census of Population and Housing, "Census 2000 Profiles of General Demographic Characteristics" data files, published May 2001 (related Internet site <http://www.census.gov/mp/www/pub/2000cen/mscen01.html>). Housing, 1990—U.S. Census Bureau, 1990 Census of Population and Housing, Summary Tape File (STF) 1C on CD-ROM (related Internet site <http://homer.ssd.census.gov/cdrom/lookup>). Building Permits—U.S. Census Bureau, "New Residential Construction–Building Permits," e-mail from Manufacturing and Construction Division/Residential Construction Branch, subject: building permits by place 2000, 22 May 2001 (related Internet site <http://www.census.gov/const/www/permitsindex.html>).

[Includes U.S., states, and 3,142 counties or county equivalents defined as of January 1, 1992. For changes to these areas since January 1, 1992, see appendix B. Geographic Information]

County	Serious crimes known to police (as reported to the FBI)[1] Number 1999 Total	Violent[2]	Property[3]	1990	Rate[4] 1999	1990	Housing, 2000 Total units	Percent change, 1990–2000	Occupied units Number	Percent owner–occupied	New private housing units authorized by building permits, 2000 Number	Percent in structures with— One unit	Five units or more	Valuation ($1,000)
ALASKA	[5]24 280	[5]3 497	[5]20 783	[5]27 115	[5]4 281	[5]5 104	260 978	12.2	221 600	62.5	[5]2 147	[5]74.8	[5]10.9	[5]332 576
Aleutians East	NA	NA	NA	NA	NA	NA	724	4.5	526	58.2	1	100.0	–	85
Aleutians West	12	2	10	NA	3 390	NA	2 234	8.9	1 270	27.8	51	37.3	62.7	7 317
Anchorage	13 223	1 689	11 534	13 162	5 130	5 815	100 368	6.6	94 822	60.1	1 190	69.0	11.2	202 855
Bethel	398	63	335	140	6 220	2 995	5 188	18.9	4 226	61.1	50	100.0	–	6 321
Bristol Bay	54	18	36	45	3 947	3 191	979	64.3	490	50.0	–	–	–	–
Denali	NA	NA	NA	NA	NA	NA	1 351	NA	785	65.1	X	X	X	X
Dillingham	193	80	113	NA	7 763	NA	2 332	37.9	1 529	60.4	X	X	X	X
Fairbanks North Star	1 768	381	1 387	2 314	5 008	7 164	33 291	4.6	29 777	54.0	124	100.0	–	12 700
Haines	52	7	45	50	3 889	4 039	1 419	27.6	991	70.0	9	100.0	–	824
Juneau	NA	NA	NA	1 008	NA	3 768	12 282	15.5	11 543	63.7	98	87.8	–	19 313
Kenai Peninsula	1 115	119	996	1 133	5 375	6 873	24 871	28.4	18 438	73.7	109	83.5	5.5	12 488
Ketchikan Gateway	606	44	562	880	7 963	10 650	6 218	13.8	5 399	60.7	39	79.5	–	4 990
Kodiak Island	342	47	295	703	4 391	11 045	5 159	5.6	4 424	54.8	54	85.2	–	7 157
Lake and Peninsula	NA	NA	NA	NA	NA	NA	1 557	57.1	588	68.2	X	X	X	X
Matanuska-Susitna	812	91	721	248	8 047	8 653	27 329	30.4	20 556	78.9	120	50.8	40.0	12 837
Nome	NA	NA	NA	247	NA	7 057	3 649	-1.0	2 693	58.1	3	100.0	–	612
North Slope	428	100	328	426	5 931	7 125	2 538	17.9	2 109	48.9	11	100.0	–	1 526
Northwest Arctic	NA	NA	NA	313	NA	11 378	2 540	27.1	1 780	56.0	X	X	X	X
Prince of Wales- Outer Ketchikan	120	22	98	188	4 736	9 485	3 055	20.1	2 262	69.8	1	100.0	–	129
Sitka	NA	NA	NA	NA	NA	NA	3 650	13.3	3 278	58.1	38	73.7	–	3 281
Skagway-Yakutat-Angoon	NA	NA	NA	19	NA	2 746	2 607	24.0	1 634	62.4	38	73.7	26.3	3 282
Southeast Fairbanks	NA	NA	NA	NA	NA	NA	3 225	2.4	2 098	68.5	X	X	X	X
Valdez-Cordova	198	13	185	23	2 812	1 090	5 148	-.9	3 884	67.9	35	100.0	–	4 836
Wade Hampton	NA	NA	NA	NA	NA	NA	2 063	9.6	1 602	66.7	X	X	X	X
Wrangell-Petersburg	296	45	251	249	5 225	4 379	3 284	9.3	2 587	70.4	9	100.0	–	715
Yukon-Koyukuk	NA	NA	NA	NA	NA	NA	3 917	NA	2 309	67.3	X	X	X	X
ARIZONA	278 661	25 931	252 730	[5]286 187	5 870	[5]7 933	2 189 189	31.9	1 901 327	68.0	61 485	79.4	18.3	7 157 587
Apache	608	66	542	461	864	748	31 621	18.3	19 971	74.3	104	100.0	–	11 141
Cochise	4 298	431	3 867	4 522	3 731	4 632	51 126	27.1	43 893	67.3	686	100.0	–	53 630
Coconino	6 108	429	5 679	5 935	5 417	6 392	53 443	24.5	40 448	61.4	683	85.1	13.5	99 010
Gila	1 075	113	962	1 415	3 881	3 519	28 189	22.8	20 140	78.7	339	98.8	–	39 106
Graham	806	50	756	581	2 485	2 188	11 430	25.4	10 116	73.2	70	100.0	–	5 800
Greenlee	86	5	81	104	1 382	2 308	3 744	4.5	3 117	50.6	5	100.0	–	721
La Paz	730	60	670	622	4 793	4 493	15 133	48.6	8 362	78.0	32	100.0	–	2 711
Maricopa	181 451	16 578	164 873	184 270	6 369	8 683	1 250 231	31.3	1 132 886	67.5	43 056	74.4	23.8	5 056 808
Mohave	6 009	470	5 539	6 853	4 495	7 330	80 062	57.5	62 809	73.6	1 938	97.4	–	174 318
Navajo	2 887	290	2 597	2 683	2 908	3 455	47 413	21.7	30 043	75.4	584	95.0	5.0	72 197
Pima	56 050	5 315	50 735	62 875	6 925	9 428	366 737	23.0	332 350	64.3	7 779	87.6	8.0	995 003
Pinal	6 803	878	5 925	5 962	4 524	5 461	81 154	53.9	61 364	77.4	2 254	96.9	2.0	241 011
Santa Cruz	1 018	95	923	1 544	2 678	5 363	13 036	35.9	11 809	68.0	440	74.8	11.4	36 609
Yavapai	6 731	698	6 033	3 688	4 428	3 424	81 730	49.1	70 171	73.4	2 227	91.2	2.9	273 227
Yuma	4 001	453	3 548	4 650	2 956	7 219	74 140	59.3	53 848	72.3	1 288	91.6	8.1	96 295
ARKANSAS	102 269	10 731	91 538	113 661	4 016	4 839	1 173 043	17.2	1 042 696	69.4	9 203	75.3	15.0	858 621
Arkansas	647	67	580	946	3 097	4 369	9 672	1.0	8 457	67.9	13	100.0	–	1 031
Ashley	600	55	545	926	2 442	3 808	10 615	8.1	9 384	76.0	25	20.0	80.0	1 865
Baxter	567	42	525	381	1 550	1 222	19 891	27.9	17 052	79.7	131	44.3	31.3	9 594
Benton	3 263	254	3 009	2 702	2 420	2 771	64 281	55.1	58 212	72.2	1 159	91.4	2.7	122 997
Boone	768	73	695	578	2 397	2 043	15 426	24.6	13 851	73.3	151	91.4	8.6	15 107
Bradley	208	14	194	280	1 810	2 374	5 930	16.5	4 834	72.7	3	100.0	–	185
Calhoun	68	6	62	85	1 181	1 459	3 012	23.6	2 317	82.3	2	100.0	–	218
Carroll	591	75	516	606	2 609	3 249	11 828	35.3	10 189	73.0	39	89.7	–	2 526
Chicot	704	97	607	744	4 719	4 735	5 974	-3.5	5 205	69.8	12	100.0	–	544
Clark	520	28	492	224	2 359	1 045	10 166	15.4	8 912	65.7	29	100.0	–	1 978
Clay	308	14	294	287	1 779	1 585	8 498	1.6	7 417	74.9	14	57.1	42.9	792
Cleburne	592	28	564	424	2 569	2 184	13 732	27.1	10 190	80.4	46	78.3	–	3 062
Cleveland	108	10	98	67	1 271	861	3 834	15.4	3 273	82.2	–	–	–	–
Columbia	1 034	147	887	314	4 105	1 222	11 566	8.2	9 981	71.4	12	100.0	–	2 115
Conway	333	6	327	237	1 663	1 238	9 028	12.7	7 967	78.1	9	100.0	–	774
Craighead	3 127	236	2 891	3 434	4 014	4 980	35 133	23.6	32 301	63.9	320	85.6	5.0	30 695
Crawford	1 344	136	1 208	1 120	2 656	2 636	21 315	27.6	19 702	75.9	149	77.2	18.8	13 286
Crittenden	2 609	414	2 195	3 205	5 201	6 418	20 507	8.6	18 471	60.3	405	53.6	11.9	27 299
Cross	460	73	387	501	2 339	2 606	8 030	10.7	7 391	70.8	31	87.1	–	1 655
Dallas	396	101	295	327	4 348	3 401	4 401	8.7	3 519	73.8	3	100.0	–	488
Desha	803	135	668	857	5 287	5 102	6 663	-.6	5 922	63.5	31	48.4	–	1 678

[1] Data on serious crimes have not been adjusted for underreporting; this may affect comparability over time or among geographic areas. [2] Includes murder and nonnegligent manslaughter, forcible rape, robbery, and aggravated assault. [3] Includes burglary, larceny-theft, and motor vehicle theft. [4] Per 100,000 resident population provided by the U.S. Federal Bureau of Investigation. [5] Includes data not distributed by county.

Sources: Serious Crimes Known to Police—U.S. Federal Bureau of Investigation, Uniform Crime Reporting Program, unpublished data, annual (related Internet site <http://www.fbi.gov/ucr/ucr.htm>). Housing, 2000—U.S. Census Bureau, 2000 Census of Population and Housing, "Census 2000 Profiles of General Demographic Characteristics" data files, published May 2001 (related Internet site <http://www.census.gov/mp/www/pub/2000cen/mscen01.html>). Housing, 1990—U.S. Census Bureau, 1990 Census of Population and Housing, Summary Tape File (STF) 1C on CD-ROM (related Internet site <http://homer.ssd.census.gov/cdrom/lookup>). Building Permits—U.S. Census Bureau, "New Residential Construction–Building Permits," e-mail from Manufacturing and Construction Division/Residential Construction Branch, subject: building permits by place 2000, 22 May 2001 (related Internet site <http://www.census.gov/const/www/permitsindex.html>).

[Includes U.S., states, and 3,142 counties or county equivalents defined as of January 1, 1992. For changes to these areas since January 1, 1992, see appendix B. Geographic Information]

County	Serious crimes known to police (as reported to the FBI)[1]						Housing, 2000				New private housing units authorized by building permits, 2000			
	Number				Rate[4]							Percent in structures with—		
	1999							Percent change, 1990–2000	Occupied units					
	Total	Violent[2]	Property[3]	1990	1999	1990	Total units		Number	Percent owner-occupied	Number	One unit	Five units or more	Valuation ($1,000)
ARKANSAS—Con.														
Drew	287	23	264	176	1 625	1 013	8 287	15.8	7 337	69.0	69	56.5	34.8	4 458
Faulkner	2 726	160	2 566	2 270	3 460	3 783	34 546	47.7	31 882	68.6	523	87.8	–	59 557
Franklin	179	17	162	253	1 052	1 698	7 673	23.2	6 882	78.1	15	100.0	–	689
Fulton	167	24	143	113	1 524	1 126	5 973	23.4	4 810	81.1	9	100.0	–	981
Garland	3 883	303	3 580	4 528	4 600	6 169	44 953	18.4	37 813	71.1	105	100.0	–	11 500
Grant	161	9	152	309	1 008	2 215	6 960	25.6	6 241	80.4	8	100.0	–	663
Greene	850	89	761	1 121	2 337	3 525	16 161	22.3	14 750	71.3	204	98.0	–	13 544
Hempstead	924	68	856	876	4 157	4 052	10 166	4.9	8 959	69.3	16	100.0	–	1 434
Hot Spring	909	109	800	669	3 115	2 562	13 384	17.6	12 004	77.9	7	71.4	–	850
Howard	353	19	334	282	2 559	2 078	6 297	12.4	5 471	72.2	17	100.0	–	1 141
Independence	1 239	58	1 181	827	3 729	2 651	14 841	15.6	13 467	74.4	34	29.4	–	2 351
Izard	127	8	119	44	965	387	6 591	19.1	5 440	80.2	16	100.0	–	1 204
Jackson	601	113	488	396	3 362	2 090	7 956	-1.6	6 971	69.6	22	100.0	–	1 417
Jefferson	5 601	1 186	4 415	6 233	6 832	7 291	34 350	3.1	30 555	66.2	139	78.4	8.6	8 539
Johnson	470	6	464	505	2 185	2 772	9 926	24.3	8 738	73.1	26	100.0	–	2 553
Lafayette	53	3	50	105	788	1 089	4 560	.8	3 434	78.6	18	11.1	88.9	860
Lawrence	278	34	244	120	1 598	687	8 085	5.1	7 108	71.1	20	80.0	–	2 119
Lee	466	31	435	528	3 737	4 045	4 768	-6.2	4 182	63.7	33	36.4	57.6	1 094
Lincoln	91	6	85	122	634	891	4 955	15.4	4 265	76.1	9	100.0	–	865
Little River	241	15	226	450	1 816	3 222	6 435	4.3	5 465	76.5	2	100.0	–	205
Logan	251	33	218	269	1 179	1 309	9 942	16.4	8 693	77.1	8	100.0	–	626
Lonoke	1 411	209	1 202	691	2 799	1 760	20 749	38.2	19 262	75.9	356	93.5	–	32 950
Madison	145	22	123	122	1 091	1 050	6 537	26.1	5 463	79.1	5	100.0	–	318
Marion	218	55	163	158	1 454	1 317	8 235	34.1	6 776	80.1	179	96.6	–	10 319
Miller	2 207	324	1 883	3 663	5 509	9 522	17 727	9.6	15 637	68.0	161	100.0	–	10 736
Mississippi	3 146	391	2 755	3 751	6 181	6 521	22 310	.4	19 349	58.9	40	100.0	–	3 053
Monroe	120	21	99	416	1 170	3 671	5 067	.1	4 105	65.0	32	21.9	78.1	968
Montgomery	109	24	85	109	1 253	1 390	5 048	18.2	3 785	82.9	X	X	X	X
Nevada	111	5	106	177	1 101	1 752	4 751	10.8	3 893	74.8	4	100.0	–	192
Newton	92	11	81	73	1 119	952	4 316	25.5	3 500	81.5	3	100.0	–	327
Ouachita	1 063	97	966	1 217	3 788	3 981	13 450	1.9	11 613	71.4	8	100.0	–	952
Perry	136	28	108	137	1 404	1 719	4 702	27.0	3 989	82.2	–	–	–	–
Phillips	1 149	125	1 024	1 574	4 178	5 458	10 859	-2.1	9 711	56.2	9	100.0	–	928
Pike	46	8	38	55	432	545	5 536	21.7	4 504	78.9	X	X	X	X
Poinsett	460	16	444	647	1 849	2 623	11 051	7.6	10 026	66.8	57	100.0	–	4 306
Polk	293	32	261	242	1 483	1 395	9 236	19.5	8 047	78.4	23	82.6	–	1 374
Pope	2 056	106	1 950	1 516	3 929	3 304	22 851	24.0	20 701	71.2	135	65.9	11.9	8 147
Prairie	163	12	151	116	1 723	1 219	4 790	10.4	3 894	73.1	6	100.0	–	335
Pulaski	28 796	2 738	26 058	39 444	8 186	11 281	161 135	6.3	147 942	60.9	1 415	72.9	13.4	187 152
Randolph	446	57	389	162	2 492	978	8 268	12.6	7 265	74.4	42	59.5	–	1 221
St. Francis	2 102	290	1 812	2 047	7 426	7 183	11 242	2.6	10 043	63.2	80	20.0	80.0	3 607
Saline	2 743	151	2 592	2 292	3 525	3 571	33 825	37.5	31 778	80.7	444	92.1	1.8	54 222
Scott	187	6	181	154	1 741	1 509	4 924	9.8	4 323	74.3	23	13.0	87.0	420
Searcy	48	11	37	73	615	931	4 292	14.8	3 523	77.7	3	100.0	–	500
Sebastian	5 383	512	4 871	6 433	5 044	6 459	49 311	13.0	45 300	63.5	419	63.2	19.6	39 518
Sevier	382	32	350	383	2 599	2 809	6 434	9.4	5 708	74.1	7	100.0	–	531
Sharp	194	9	185	204	1 136	1 446	9 342	22.6	7 211	80.3	–	–	–	–
Stone	159	11	148	43	1 418	440	5 715	25.7	4 768	78.1	10	100.0	–	632
Union	2 099	377	1 722	1 726	4 609	3 694	20 676	2.0	17 989	72.9	7	100.0	–	892
Van Buren	177	16	161	264	1 132	1 885	9 164	20.9	6 825	81.1	–	–	–	–
Washington	5 254	479	4 775	5 319	3 775	4 690	64 330	35.9	60 151	59.5	1 683	56.1	40.5	130 020
White	1 930	163	1 767	1 485	3 067	2 716	27 613	27.5	25 148	72.9	122	78.7	–	9 046
Woodruff	55	1	54	53	616	702	4 089	-1.9	3 531	65.4	6	100.0	–	341
Yell	482	67	415	474	2 509	2 669	9 157	16.4	7 922	72.9	40	40.0	60.0	1 075
CALIFORNIA	1 260 684	207 900	1 052 784	1 955 842	3 805	6 572	12 214 549	9.2	11 502 870	56.9	145 575	72.1	24.9	23 343 968
Alameda	76 680	10 233	66 447	95 300	5 397	7 450	540 183	7.2	523 366	54.7	4 054	75.8	21.1	933 252
Alpine	129	15	114	149	10 513	13 387	1 514	14.8	483	68.3	25	100.0	–	13 346
Amador	812	107	705	718	2 462	2 457	15 035	17.3	12 759	75.5	253	96.8	–	33 165
Butte	7 450	678	6 772	8 684	3 773	4 768	85 523	12.4	79 566	60.7	1 134	85.1	14.9	130 381
Calaveras	1 148	112	1 036	1 072	2 841	3 350	22 946	19.8	16 469	78.7	425	100.0	–	84 327
Colusa	458	66	392	570	2 430	3 502	6 774	7.6	6 097	63.2	46	95.7	–	6 812
Contra Costa	37 703	4 453	33 250	48 122	4 047	5 987	354 577	12.1	344 129	69.3	5 479	76.4	23.4	965 154
Del Norte	1 007	134	873	1 032	3 676	4 399	10 434	14.8	9 170	63.8	45	100.0	–	5 392
El Dorado	3 090	550	2 540	4 902	1 921	3 891	71 278	16.0	58 939	74.7	1 476	94.1	5.5	341 283

[1] Data on serious crimes have not been adjusted for underreporting; this may affect comparability over time or among geographic areas.   [2] Includes murder and nonnegligent manslaughter, forcible rape, robbery, and aggravated assault.   [3] Includes burglary, larceny-theft, and motor vehicle theft.   [4] Per 100,000 resident population provided by the U.S. Federal Bureau of Investigation.

Sources: Serious Crimes Known to Police—U.S. Federal Bureau of Investigation, Uniform Crime Reporting Program, unpublished data, annual (related Internet site <http://www.fbi.gov/ucr/ucr.htm>).   Housing, 2000—U.S. Census Bureau, 2000 Census of Population and Housing, "Census 2000 Profiles of General Demographic Characteristics" data files, published May 2001 (related Internet site <http://www.census.gov/mp/www/pub/2000cen/mscen01.html>).   Housing, 1990—U.S. Census Bureau, 1990 Census of Population and Housing, Summary Tape File (STF) 1C on CD-ROM (related Internet site <http://homer.ssd.census.gov/cdrom/lookup>).   Building Permits—U.S. Census Bureau, "New Residential Construction–Building Permits," e-mail from Manufacturing and Construction Division/Residential Construction Branch, subject: building permits by place 2000, 22 May 2001 (related Internet site <http://www.census.gov/const/www/permitsindex.html>).

[Includes U.S., states, and 3,142 counties or county equivalents defined as of January 1, 1992. For changes to these areas since January 1, 1992, see appendix B. Geographic Information]

County	Serious crimes known to police (as reported to the FBI)[1] Number 1999 Total	Violent[2]	Property[3]	Number 1990	Rate[4] 1999	Rate[4] 1990	Housing, 2000 Total units	Percent change, 1990–2000	Occupied units Number	Percent owner-occupied	New private housing units authorized by building permits, 2000 Number	Percent in structures with— One unit	Five units or more	Valuation ($1,000)
CALIFORNIA—Con.														
Fresno	42 846	6 344	36 502	55 032	5 588	8 245	270 767	14.9	252 940	56.5	3 156	92.2	5.3	426 594
Glenn	949	99	850	849	3 565	3 424	9 982	7.0	9 172	63.8	41	100.0	–	4 596
Humboldt	5 682	481	5 201	5 916	4 580	4 967	55 912	9.3	51 238	57.6	532	73.3	18.4	41 739
Imperial	6 586	766	5 820	8 199	4 506	7 501	43 891	20.1	39 384	58.3	773	76.8	22.9	77 291
Inyo	515	58	457	716	2 800	3 917	9 042	3.8	7 703	65.9	18	100.0	–	3 637
Kern	26 379	3 418	22 961	34 850	4 169	6 412	231 564	16.6	208 652	62.1	3 070	93.2	4.9	371 102
Kings	3 597	412	3 185	3 891	2 982	3 835	36 563	18.5	34 418	55.9	445	100.0		44 709
Lake	2 093	245	1 848	2 639	3 741	5 212	32 528	12.9	23 974	70.6	132	100.0	–	31 673
Lassen	495	76	419	739	1 466	2 678	12 000	15.9	9 625	68.3	106	96.2	–	11 234
Los Angeles	362 967	86 220	276 747	661 767	3 883	7 466	3 270 909	3.4	3 133 774	47.9	16 968	49.3	46.0	2 364 386
Madera	4 427	713	3 714	4 293	3 802	4 873	40 387	31.0	36 155	66.2	648	84.7	8.8	64 176
Marin	6 035	767	5 268	8 569	2 512	3 724	104 990	5.2	100 650	63.6	593	73.7	19.1	165 780
Mariposa	516	152	364	359	3 203	2 510	8 826	14.6	6 613	69.8	87	100.0	–	12 060
Mendocino	2 414	399	2 015	3 611	2 841	4 494	36 937	9.8	33 266	61.3	284	95.1	4.2	23 587
Merced	9 260	1 385	7 875	8 264	4 616	4 632	68 373	17.1	63 815	58.7	1 380	97.4	–	184 033
Modoc	170	32	138	243	1 783	2 511	4 807	2.9	3 784	70.7	–	–	–	–
Mono	570	37	533	696	5 460	6 991	11 757	10.2	5 137	60.0	237	41.8	34.6	36 274
Monterey	12 921	2 160	10 761	18 077	3 483	5 083	131 708	8.6	121 236	54.6	1 714	87.8	3.9	375 398
Napa	3 021	331	2 690	4 841	2 496	4 371	48 554	9.9	45 402	65.1	542	99.3	–	170 427
Nevada	2 178	292	1 886	2 571	2 350	3 275	44 282	18.6	36 894	75.8	831	88.9	8.7	129 807
Orange	76 502	8 794	67 708	143 775	2 770	5 964	969 484	10.8	935 287	61.4	12 520	54.4	40.5	1 981 284
Placer	6 564	628	5 936	7 990	2 822	4 624	107 302	37.8	93 382	73.2	6 443	73.6	25.8	1 060 856
Plumas	629	71	558	967	3 043	4 899	13 386	12.1	9 000	70.0	178	100.0	–	21 877
Riverside	56 956	9 348	47 608	83 321	3 796	7 119	584 674	20.8	506 218	68.9	15 025	88.7	10.3	2 583 928
Sacramento	58 164	6 992	51 172	75 887	5 010	7 288	474 814	13.7	453 602	58.2	7 672	82.0	16.8	1 090 940
San Benito	1 689	315	1 374	1 750	3 536	4 769	16 499	34.9	15 885	68.2	538	100.0	–	79 181
San Bernardino	65 290	8 998	56 292	92 465	3 935	6 519	601 369	10.9	528 594	64.5	6 471	89.1	10.0	1 043 021
San Diego	97 717	14 300	83 417	178 595	3 464	7 149	1 040 149	9.9	994 677	55.4	15 592	59.6	36.4	2 732 528
San Francisco	44 541	6 630	37 911	71 592	5 886	9 889	346 527	5.5	329 700	35.0	2 766	2.9	90.3	413 414
San Joaquin	29 590	4 188	25 402	39 978	5 298	8 318	189 160	13.8	181 629	60.4	5 392	99.2	.4	828 298
San Luis Obispo	6 764	659	6 105	8 296	2 844	3 820	102 275	13.4	92 739	61.5	1 673	92.1	5.6	269 987
San Mateo	19 225	1 933	17 292	29 364	2 704	4 520	260 576	3.5	254 103	61.4	2 221	51.5	46.5	361 875
Santa Barbara	10 372	1 426	8 946	17 299	2 621	4 680	142 901	3.4	136 622	66.1	867	87.6	6.2	171 683
Santa Clara	48 248	7 445	40 803	69 524	2 897	4 642	579 329	7.2	565 863	59.8	6 639	42.8	54.0	936 631
Santa Cruz	8 620	1 065	7 555	13 719	3 496	5 972	98 873	7.6	91 139	60.0	545	71.6	22.9	115 221
Shasta	5 786	796	4 990	7 332	3 470	4 987	68 810	13.6	63 426	66.1	970	81.5	–	125 541
Sierra	84	4	80	116	2 449	3 496	2 202	1.7	1 520	70.7	19	100.0	–	1 992
Siskiyou	1 125	115	1 010	1 563	2 517	3 676	21 947	9.0	18 556	67.2	148	97.3	–	23 131
Solano	16 466	2 385	14 081	20 691	4 300	6 078	134 513	12.5	130 403	65.2	2 233	91.7	7.7	393 921
Sonoma	13 682	1 304	12 378	16 811	3 112	4 330	183 153	13.7	172 403	64.1	2 505	80.4	11.7	369 134
Stanislaus	22 339	3 076	19 263	24 201	5 163	6 532	150 807	14.2	145 146	61.9	3 023	92.6	6.5	400 923
Sutter	2 956	234	2 722	3 415	3 785	5 302	28 319	17.2	27 033	61.5	240	99.2	–	37 304
Tehama	1 927	311	1 616	2 252	3 512	4 538	23 547	15.4	21 013	67.6	217	62.2	33.2	32 308
Trinity	220	23	197	478	1 653	3 659	7 980	5.8	5 587	71.3	34	100.0	–	4 404
Tulare	15 424	2 291	13 133	16 755	4 279	5 372	119 639	13.9	110 385	61.5	1 627	94.6	.7	162 800
Tuolumne	1 645	300	1 345	1 625	3 045	3 354	28 336	12.6	21 004	71.3	279	98.6	–	37 254
Ventura	17 351	2 143	15 208	26 476	2 336	3 957	251 712	10.2	243 234	67.6	3 960	75.4	22.9	815 295
Yolo	5 952	1 036	4 916	9 305	3 813	6 595	61 587	16.2	59 375	53.1	1 202	86.6	13.1	184 065
Yuba	2 758	355	2 403	3 629	4 525	6 232	22 636	6.5	20 535	54.1	82	100.0	–	10 557
COLORADO	157 843	13 268	144 575	[5]198 540	3 939	[5]6 027	1 808 037	22.4	1 658 238	67.3	54 596	70.7	26.2	6 822 090
Adams	16 415	1 282	15 133	19 692	4 962	7 430	132 594	24.0	128 156	70.6	5 479	52.9	44.0	512 902
Alamosa	619	56	563	564	4 194	4 142	6 088	15.9	5 467	64.0	54	100.0	–	4 625
Arapahoe	20 126	1 850	18 276	25 604	4 170	6 540	196 835	16.7	190 909	68.0	8 140	52.1	46.6	748 565
Archuleta	213	2	211	195	2 288	3 648	6 212	57.2	3 980	76.8	360	99.4	–	71 820
Baca	11	4	7	74	247	1 624	2 364	-2.9	1 905	76.1	7	100.0	–	320
Bent	134	19	115	89	2 386	1 763	2 366	1.5	2 003	68.0	17	100.0	–	1 564
Boulder	8 479	507	7 972	13 192	3 106	5 854	119 900	26.7	114 680	64.7	2 780	89.0	6.2	372 871
Chaffee	494	29	465	452	3 208	3 564	8 392	28.2	6 584	73.4	230	98.7	–	20 861
Cheyenne	37	5	32	39	1 544	1 627	1 105	2.0	880	74.3	3	100.0	–	215
Clear Creek	282	26	256	443	3 067	5 814	5 128	6.6	4 019	76.1	58	100.0	–	10 171
Conejos	52	9	43	101	785	1 355	3 886	8.7	2 980	78.8	193	100.0	–	4 936
Costilla	51	11	40	41	1 371	1 285	2 202	26.3	1 503	78.2	X	X	X	X
Crowley	21	18	3	10	477	253	1 542	9.0	1 358	72.5	20	100.0	–	1 110
Custer	34	–	34	46	965	2 388	2 989	34.9	1 480	79.2	143	90.9	–	18 345

[1] Data on serious crimes have not been adjusted for underreporting; this may affect comparability over time or among geographic areas. [2] Includes murder and nonnegligent manslaughter, forcible rape, robbery, and aggravated assault. [3] Includes burglary, larceny-theft, and motor vehicle theft. [4] Per 100,000 resident population provided by the U.S. Federal Bureau of Investigation. [5] Includes data not distributed by county.

Sources: Serious Crimes Known to Police—U.S. Federal Bureau of Investigation, Uniform Crime Reporting Program, unpublished data, annual (related Internet site <http://www.fbi.gov/ucr/ucr.htm>). Housing, 2000—U.S. Census Bureau, 2000 Census of Population and Housing, "Census 2000 Profiles of General Demographic Characteristics" data files, published May 2001 (related Internet site <http://www.census.gov/mp/www/pub/2000cen/mscen01.html>). Housing, 1990—U.S. Census Bureau, 1990 Census of Population and Housing, Summary Tape File (STF) 1C on CD-ROM (related Internet site <http://homer.ssd.census.gov/cdrom/lookup>). Building Permits—U.S. Census Bureau, "New Residential Construction–Building Permits," e-mail from Manufacturing and Construction Division/Residential Construction Branch, subject: building permits by place 2000, 22 May 2001 (related Internet site <http://www.census.gov/const/www/permitsindex.html>).

[Includes U.S., states, and 3,142 counties or county equivalents defined as of January 1, 1992. For changes to these areas since January 1, 1992, see appendix B. Geographic Information]

County	Serious crimes known to police (as reported to the FBI)[1]						Housing, 2000				New private housing units authorized by building permits, 2000			
	Number				Rate[4]				Occupied units			Percent in structures with—		
	1999			1990	1999	1990	Total units	Percent change, 1990–2000	Number	Percent owner-occupied	Number	One unit	Five units or more	Valuation ($1,000)
	Total	Violent[2]	Property[3]											
COLORADO—Con.														
Delta	492	39	453	638	1 927	3 041	12 374	22.7	11 058	77.5	94	97.9	–	7 219
Denver	27 381	2 934	24 447	37 051	5 373	7 923	251 435	4.9	239 235	52.5	3 649	39.4	52.0	314 704
Dolores	42	3	39	44	2 257	2 926	1 193	26.0	785	76.8	7	100.0	–	822
Douglas	2 166	98	2 068	1 553	1 504	2 572	63 333	184.1	60 924	87.9	6 395	74.4	25.6	961 042
Eagle	1 121	55	1 066	2 027	3 531	9 244	22 111	45.2	15 148	63.7	701	63.9	32.0	308 344
Elbert	4	–	4	164	664	1 700	7 113	78.0	6 770	89.6	317	100.0	–	47 492
El Paso	21 725	2 254	19 471	24 601	4 343	6 197	202 428	22.6	192 409	64.7	6 264	81.2	17.8	710 779
Fremont	1 079	72	1 007	1 273	2 406	3 944	17 145	25.3	15 232	75.9	385	97.9	–	28 553
Garfield	1 305	88	1 217	1 333	3 251	4 447	17 336	38.5	16 229	65.2	674	76.6	18.8	106 381
Gilpin	269	9	260	127	6 288	4 137	2 929	20.1	2 043	78.4	83	100.0	–	9 300
Grand	60	23	37	613	584	7 695	10 894	9.1	5 075	68.2	544	63.6	31.6	104 131
Gunnison	552	11	541	861	4 339	8 381	9 135	25.2	5 649	58.3	330	63.0	21.2	52 254
Hinsdale	17	1	16	4	2 258	857	1 304	4.0	359	64.9	15	73.3	–	1 953
Huerfano	182	16	166	168	2 615	2 796	4 599	17.5	3 082	70.7	96	100.0	–	8 820
Jackson	23	2	21	37	1 467	2 305	1 145	-13.7	661	67.6	24	100.0	–	6 310
Jefferson	17 554	721	16 833	22 913	3 428	5 226	212 488	19.0	206 067	72.5	3 016	63.7	34.7	313 755
Kiowa	1	–	1	6	60	355	817	-6.9	665	71.3	–	–	–	
Kit Carson	203	23	180	216	2 718	3 025	3 430	6.4	2 990	71.9	32	75.0	–	3 770
Lake	130	4	126	238	1 991	3 962	3 913	10.9	2 977	68.2	61	100.0	–	6 471
La Plata	1 553	101	1 452	1 439	3 762	4 457	20 765	34.7	17 342	68.4	433	90.8	2.5	54 454
Larimer	7 666	576	7 090	8 354	3 246	4 488	105 392	35.4	97 164	67.7	3 524	77.3	19.8	427 366
Las Animas	386	50	336	568	2 593	4 126	7 629	9.4	6 173	70.6	83	100.0	–	8 023
Lincoln	57	15	42	80	974	1 766	2 406	9.2	2 058	69.0	13	100.0	–	1 376
Logan	722	30	692	566	3 951	3 222	8 424	7.7	7 551	69.9	73	94.5	–	6 556
Mesa	4 123	234	3 889	4 672	3 576	5 016	48 427	23.5	45 823	72.7	1 316	86.0	6.3	128 285
Mineral	7	–	7	21	987	3 763	1 119	-6.8	377	74.0	14	100.0	–	152
Moffat	354	29	325	490	2 850	4 315	5 635	7.6	4 983	72.1	41	100.0	–	4 156
Montezuma	585	9	576	840	2 549	4 499	10 497	30.4	9 201	74.8	41	70.7	–	3 564
Montrose	918	50	868	854	2 921	3 497	14 202	37.2	13 043	74.9	309	92.6	–	28 963
Morgan	710	28	682	902	2 861	4 111	10 410	12.8	9 539	68.4	116	94.8	–	12 145
Otero	387	47	340	832	3 144	4 122	8 813	.8	7 920	69.1	42	81.0	19.0	4 310
Ouray	13	3	10	6	863	261	2 146	42.4	1 576	73.4	66	89.4	–	19 020
Park	208	17	191	266	1 520	3 708	10 697	47.6	5 894	87.6	434	100.0	–	45 744
Phillips	47	3	44	13	1 064	310	2 014	2.8	1 781	75.6	9	77.8	–	785
Pitkin	898	51	847	1 140	6 549	9 004	10 096	2.6	6 807	59.2	274	72.6	8.8	138 515
Prowers	266	16	250	568	1 897	4 256	5 977	2.1	5 307	66.2	18	100.0	–	1 269
Pueblo	7 732	1 128	6 604	8 722	5 613	7 088	58 926	15.8	54 579	70.4	1 098	93.6	.9	106 645
Rio Blanco	121	11	110	206	1 891	3 449	2 855	1.9	2 306	70.6	17	88.2	–	1 434
Rio Grande	390	35	355	343	3 334	3 185	6 003	13.8	4 701	70.7	123	97.6	–	14 418
Routt	497	20	477	760	3 396	5 395	11 217	21.2	7 953	69.2	527	55.4	14.0	116 785
Saguache	98	19	79	147	1 579	3 183	3 087	33.9	2 300	69.3	134	100.0	–	6 933
San Juan	26	2	24	89	4 806	11 946	632	31.4	269	67.7	5	100.0	–	215
San Miguel	234	11	223	108	4 213	2 956	5 197	97.2	3 015	51.6	142	92.3	–	122 972
Sedgwick	35	1	34	35	1 345	1 301	1 387	-1.9	1 165	73.0	4	100.0	–	620
Summit	2 046	92	1 954	2 692	10 684	20 899	24 201	41.6	9 120	58.9	799	48.1	46.9	180 899
Teller	390	33	357	375	1 882	3 008	10 362	37.0	7 993	80.9	368	98.4	–	44 292
Washington	7	–	7	41	150	852	2 307	–	1 989	73.6	16	100.0	–	1 269
Weld	5 946	483	5 463	8 624	3 826	6 542	66 194	29.4	63 247	68.6	4 369	90.0	7.9	579 176
Yuma	147	3	144	207	1 533	2 312	4 295	5.2	3 800	70.8	17	100.0	–	1 344
CONNECTICUT	[5]111 084	[5]11 366	[5]99 718	[5]176 751	[5]3 385	[5]6 266	1 385 975	4.9	1 301 670	66.8	9 376	87.0	10.4	1 425 048
Fairfield	25 875	2 859	23 016	45 864	3 172	5 704	339 466	4.7	324 232	69.2	2 278	70.3	24.4	535 924
Hartford	31 038	2 841	28 197	49 790	3 831	5 977	353 022	3.3	335 098	64.2	1 705	95.0	.7	215 160
Litchfield	2 198	128	2 070	3 267	1 952	3 112	79 267	6.7	71 551	75.2	725	99.0	.7	118 515
Middlesex	2 301	90	2 211	3 728	2 320	4 246	67 285	9.2	61 341	72.1	867	88.2	9.5	100 570
New Haven	34 364	3 586	30 778	54 013	4 575	7 086	340 732	4.2	319 040	63.1	1 918	83.3	15.4	215 085
New London	4 632	530	4 102	7 366	3 435	4 906	110 674	5.9	99 835	66.7	814	100.0	–	108 777
Tolland	1 311	53	1 258	1 647	3 242	4 127	51 570	10.5	49 431	73.5	693	100.0	–	94 071
Windham	1 529	192	1 337	1 645	3 916	4 257	43 959	8.3	41 142	67.4	376	93.1	6.4	36 946
DELAWARE	35 927	5 005	30 922	35 431	4 765	5 319	343 072	18.3	298 736	72.3	4 611	84.9	15.1	414 089
Kent	5 583	738	4 845	4 692	4 440	4 227	50 481	19.9	47 224	70.0	858	99.4	.6	75 131
New Castle	24 710	3 349	21 361	25 153	5 046	5 691	199 521	15.0	188 935	70.1	2 331	70.4	29.6	164 782
Sussex	5 634	918	4 716	5 586	4 067	4 933	93 070	25.3	62 577	80.7	1 422	100.0	–	174 176
DISTRICT OF COLUMBIA	41 868	8 448	33 420	65 435	8 067	10 782	274 845	-1.3	248 338	40.8	806	23.2	74.9	53 993
District of Columbia	41 868	8 448	33 420	65 435	8 067	10 782	274 845	-1.3	248 338	40.8	806	23.2	74.9	53 993

[1] Data on serious crimes have not been adjusted for underreporting; this may affect comparability over time or among geographic areas. [2] Includes murder and nonnegligent manslaughter, forcible rape, robbery, and aggravated assault. [3] Includes burglary, larceny-theft, and motor vehicle theft. [4] Per 100,000 resident population provided by the U.S. Federal Bureau of Investigation. [5] Includes data not distributed by county.

Sources: Serious Crimes Known to Police—U.S. Federal Bureau of Investigation, Uniform Crime Reporting Program, unpublished data, annual (related Internet site <http://www.fbi.gov/ucr/ucr.htm>). Housing, 2000—U.S. Census Bureau, 2000 Census of Population and Housing, "Census 2000 Profiles of General Demographic Characteristics" data files, published May 2001 (related Internet site <http://www.census.gov/mp/www/pub/2000cen/mscen01.html>). Housing, 1990—U.S. Census Bureau, 1990 Census of Population and Housing, Summary Tape File (STF) 1C on CD-ROM (related Internet site <http://homer.ssd.census.gov/cdrom/lookup>). Building Permits—U.S. Census Bureau, "New Residential Construction–Building Permits," e-mail from Manufacturing and Construction Division/Residential Construction Branch, subject: building permits by place 2000, 22 May 2001 (related Internet site <http://www.census.gov/const/www/permitsindex.html>).

Table B–6. Counties — Crime, Housing, and Building Permits–Con.

[Includes U.S., states, and 3,142 counties or county equivalents defined as of January 1, 1992. For changes to these areas since January 1, 1992, see appendix B. Geographic Information]

County	Serious crimes known to police (as reported to the FBI)[1]						Housing, 2000				New private housing units authorized by building permits, 2000			
	Number				Rate[4]				Occupied units			Percent in structures with—		
	1999							Percent change, 1990–2000		Percent owner-occupied		One unit	Five units or more	Valuation ($1,000)
	Total	Violent[2]	Property[3]	1990	1999	1990	Total units		Number		Number			
FLORIDA	931 961	128 332	803 629	1 095 149	6 204	8 477	7 302 947	19.7	6 337 929	70.1	155 269	68.6	28.0	17 462 405
Alachua	16 023	2 055	13 968	17 261	7 961	9 505	95 113	20.4	87 509	54.9	1 973	54.3	42.1	164 574
Baker	543	81	462	463	2 540	2 505	7 592	27.1	7 043	81.2	111	98.2	–	10 284
Bay	7 195	742	6 453	8 051	4 831	6 390	78 435	18.8	59 597	68.6	1 452	52.3	42.8	167 155
Bradford	977	174	803	1 290	3 939	5 730	9 605	18.6	8 497	79.0	59	100.0	–	3 971
Brevard	22 702	3 670	19 032	29 063	4 808	7 284	222 072	19.9	198 195	74.6	4 284	80.3	18.9	509 725
Broward	84 612	9 704	74 908	109 980	5 555	8 760	741 043	17.9	654 445	69.5	11 970	76.5	21.3	1 486 623
Calhoun	114	16	98	85	4 517	808	5 250	17.5	4 468	80.2	23	100.0	–	1 316
Charlotte	3 218	212	3 006	2 645	2 355	2 383	79 758	23.4	63 864	83.7	1 670	72.5	22.3	182 298
Citrus	2 903	416	2 487	2 794	2 512	2 988	62 204	24.8	52 634	85.6	1 190	98.8	–	78 697
Clay	4 768	459	4 309	5 060	3 424	4 774	53 748	33.5	50 243	77.9	1 528	99.5	.5	162 963
Collier	9 967	1 357	8 610	9 526	5 260	6 263	144 536	53.5	102 973	75.6	7 970	51.0	39.0	1 188 311
Columbia	3 306	582	2 724	2 471	6 162	5 799	23 579	32.3	20 925	77.2	289	100.0	–	16 745
Dade	190 689	27 289	163 400	255 653	8 745	13 198	852 278	10.5	776 774	57.8	12 475	48.1	45.3	1 221 757
DeSoto	1 323	296	1 027	1 026	5 261	4 299	13 608	32.0	10 746	74.7	121	37.2	59.5	14 884
Dixie	497	70	427	377	3 786	3 562	7 362	14.2	5 205	86.4	53	96.2	–	5 781
Duval	52 956	7 560	45 396	67 636	7 107	10 227	329 778	15.8	303 747	63.1	5 801	62.6	37.1	552 245
Escambia	14 425	2 288	12 137	17 893	5 044	6 809	124 647	11.1	111 049	67.3	1 455	93.7	2.3	136 707
Flagler	1 172	116	1 056	1 162	2 566	4 049	24 452	60.7	21 294	84.0	1 445	92.4	6.5	108 656
Franklin	385	25	360	51	6 219	569	7 180	21.9	4 096	79.2	131	100.0	–	23 184
Gadsden	1 886	406	1 480	1 798	4 653	4 374	17 703	19.1	15 867	78.0	80	100.0	–	10 197
Gilchrist	394	54	340	47	2 820	486	5 906	45.1	5 021	86.3	70	100.0	–	5 656
Glades	407	52	355	276	4 731	3 636	5 790	25.2	3 852	81.7	25	100.0	–	2 385
Gulf	444	107	337	210	3 252	2 159	7 587	19.7	4 931	81.0	188	100.0	–	21 898
Hamilton	419	76	343	348	3 704	3 403	4 966	20.6	4 161	77.4	36	100.0	–	3 649
Hardee	1 094	101	993	1 074	5 131	5 508	9 820	23.7	8 166	73.4	56	92.9	–	4 928
Hendry	1 595	210	1 385	1 375	5 363	5 335	12 294	23.6	10 850	72.4	75	100.0	–	6 501
Hernando	5 113	749	4 364	5 222	3 967	5 164	62 727	25.4	55 425	86.5	1 326	86.7	7.8	137 923
Highlands	3 737	387	3 350	3 979	4 905	5 815	48 846	21.8	37 471	79.7	450	95.1	–	39 580
Hillsborough	74 015	11 257	62 758	83 538	7 896	10 016	425 962	15.8	391 357	64.1	11 656	62.9	34.5	995 237
Holmes	196	41	155	195	1 039	1 236	7 998	17.9	6 921	81.5	41	100.0	–	3 141
Indian River	5 042	519	4 523	4 968	5 019	5 507	57 902	22.9	49 137	77.6	2 059	59.0	39.2	362 733
Jackson	1 100	360	1 121	1 055	3 221	2 550	10 400	10.4	16 620	77.9	209	72.1	27.9	10 000
Jefferson	344	101	243	567	2 622	5 019	5 251	19.5	4 695	80.9	70	100.0	–	7 653
Lafayette	26	17	9	29	406	520	2 660	17.4	2 142	80.6	30	100.0	–	2 624
Lake	8 667	2 014	6 653	7 236	4 260	4 757	102 830	35.8	88 413	81.5	5 231	70.7	26.2	437 956
Lee	20 648	2 633	18 015	16 336	5 187	4 875	245 405	29.8	188 599	76.5	9 120	56.5	32.1	1 283 813
Leon	16 950	2 614	14 336	17 741	7 711	9 216	103 974	27.8	96 521	57.0	2 200	61.2	35.0	200 211
Levy	1 894	401	1 493	1 273	5 880	4 911	16 570	34.6	13 867	83.6	156	83.3	15.4	15 521
Liberty	123	27	96	40	1 796	718	3 156	46.3	2 222	81.8	6	100.0	–	648
Madison	1 133	134	999	500	6 336	3 201	7 886	24.9	6 629	78.4	45	100.0	–	3 757
Manatee	13 826	2 060	11 766	16 322	5 694	7 710	138 128	19.9	112 460	73.8	3 452	82.5	15.5	411 875
Marion	11 864	1 952	9 912	14 218	4 849	7 298	122 663	29.7	106 755	79.8	2 354	99.1	–	363 775
Martin	4 550	489	4 061	4 800	3 874	4 757	65 471	20.8	55 288	79.8	1 384	74.1	21.4	248 290
Monroe	3 117	352	2 765	10 456	5 543	13 401	51 617	11.7	35 086	62.4	203	96.1	–	26 658
Nassau	2 680	383	2 297	1 709	4 779	3 889	25 917	38.4	21 980	80.6	758	81.8	2.9	147 037
Okaloosa	5 000	563	4 437	5 181	2 991	3 604	78 593	25.6	66 269	66.4	1 489	71.0	27.5	177 457
Okeechobee	1 437	268	1 169	1 510	4 552	5 097	15 504	16.9	12 593	74.8	131	97.7	–	10 829
Orange	70 624	9 974	60 650	62 109	8 651	9 177	361 349	27.8	336 286	60.7	10 239	60.3	39.3	907 846
Osceola	10 575	1 169	9 406	10 086	7 166	9 362	72 293	50.7	60 977	67.7	5 035	60.8	37.3	487 061
Palm Beach	75 295	8 795	66 500	83 457	7 197	9 669	556 428	20.5	474 175	74.7	10 504	64.4	33.9	1 331 562
Pasco	13 944	1 597	12 347	12 469	4 224	4 451	173 717	16.6	147 566	82.4	3 486	86.7	7.3	337 383
Pinellas	52 029	7 606	44 423	65 908	5 848	7 739	481 573	5.1	414 968	70.8	2 776	64.6	32.6	410 941
Polk	27 230	3 008	24 222	36 396	5 997	8 978	226 376	21.6	187 233	73.4	4 746	74.2	24.4	330 680
Putnam	4 392	748	3 644	5 503	6 156	8 457	33 870	6.4	27 839	80.0	180	98.9	–	14 913
St. Johns	4 476	560	3 916	5 579	3 804	6 655	58 008	42.5	49 614	76.4	2 484	84.0	15.4	450 117
St. Lucie	8 488	1 475	7 013	11 308	4 676	7 530	91 262	23.6	76 933	78.0	2 093	82.1	16.5	193 997
Santa Rosa	2 843	415	2 428	3 000	2 392	3 676	49 119	49.6	43 793	80.4	1 056	99.4	–	114 447
Sarasota	12 677	1 327	11 350	19 439	4 359	6 998	182 461	16.2	149 937	79.1	3 658	83.1	16.0	480 274
Seminole	15 344	1 913	13 431	16 331	4 317	5 680	147 079	24.8	139 572	69.5	4 419	55.8	43.2	569 205
Sumter	1 288	294	994	1 209	3 230	3 829	25 195	64.7	20 779	86.5	1 909	99.9	–	121 107
Suwannee	1 400	229	1 171	931	4 231	3 476	15 679	34.0	13 460	80.9	125	100.0	–	11 459
Taylor	874	153	721	596	4 577	3 483	9 646	22.0	7 176	79.8	47	95.7	–	2 700
Union	147	55	92	91	1 168	888	3 736	25.6	3 367	74.6	28	100.0	–	1 997
Volusia	22 568	3 276	19 292	25 445	5 275	6 864	211 938	17.1	184 723	75.3	3 587	86.1	10.1	413 094
Wakulla	700	160	540	245	3 704	1 725	9 820	49.1	8 450	84.2	394	99.2	–	24 143
Walton	1 003	102	901	455	2 646	1 639	29 083	55.3	16 548	79.0	1 464	61.7	35.4	269 865
Washington	198	28	170	102	963	632	9 503	23.4	7 931	81.9	79	100.0	–	5 438

[1] Data on serious crimes have not been adjusted for underreporting; this may affect comparability over time or among geographic areas. [2] Includes murder and nonnegligent manslaughter, forcible rape, robbery, and aggravated assault. [3] Includes burglary, larceny-theft, and motor vehicle theft. [4] Per 100,000 resident population provided by the U.S. Federal Bureau of Investigation.

Sources: Serious Crimes Known to Police—U.S. Federal Bureau of Investigation, Uniform Crime Reporting Program, unpublished data, annual (related Internet site <http://www.fbi.gov/ucr/ucr.htm>). Housing, 2000—U.S. Census Bureau, 2000 Census of Population and Housing, "Census 2000 Profiles of General Demographic Characteristics" data files, published May 2001 (related Internet site <http://www.census.gov/mp/www/pub/2000cen/mscen01.html>). Housing, 1990—U.S. Census Bureau, 1990 Census of Population and Housing, Summary Tape File (STF) 1C on CD-ROM (related Internet site <http://homer.ssd.census.gov/cdrom/lookup>). Building Permits—U.S. Census Bureau, "New Residential Construction–Building Permits," e-mail from Manufacturing and Construction Division/Residential Construction Branch, subject: building permits by place 2000, 22 May 2001 (related Internet site <http://www.census.gov/const/www/permitsindex.html>).

Table B–6. Counties — Crime, Housing, and Building Permits–Con.

[Includes U.S., states, and 3,142 counties or county equivalents defined as of January 1, 1992. For changes to these areas since January 1, 1992, see appendix B. Geographic Information]

County	Serious crimes known to police (as reported to the FBI)[1] Number 1999 Total	Violent[2]	Property[3]	Number 1990	Rate[4] 1999	Rate[4] 1990	Housing, 2000 Total units	Percent change, 1990–2000	Occupied units Number	Percent owner-occupied	New private housing units Number	One unit	Five units or more	Valuation ($1,000)
GEORGIA	384 791	39 799	344 992	[5]417 321	5 053	[5]6 551	3 281 737	24.4	3 006 369	67.5	91 820	75.0	23.3	8 722 256
Appling	289	68	221	591	7 495	3 754	7 854	18.5	6 606	79.1	3	100.0	–	305
Atkinson	32	11	21	69	605	1 111	3 171	29.5	2 717	74.4	X	X	X	X
Bacon	170	7	163	255	1 608	2 666	4 464	15.7	3 833	74.9	3	100.0	–	423
Baker	10	2	8	64	267	1 770	1 740	16.1	1 514	77.7	X	X	X	X
Baldwin	1 592	172	1 420	2 076	3 722	5 252	17 173	20.9	14 758	66.5	151	73.5	15.9	13 210
Banks	528	43	485	87	4 048	844	5 808	38.5	5 364	80.9	128	100.0	–	12 698
Barrow	1 617	106	1 511	1 044	3 933	3 513	17 304	46.5	16 354	75.5	855	100.0	–	59 536
Bartow	1 683	126	1 557	1 883	2 340	3 405	28 751	32.1	27 176	75.3	1 355	90.2	6.3	142 655
Ben Hill	1 333	168	1 165	967	7 476	5 953	7 623	10.9	6 673	66.7	29	93.1	–	2 368
Berrien	281	48	233	443	1 686	3 269	7 100	21.2	6 261	75.4	16	100.0	–	834
Bibb	15 351	1 202	14 149	13 781	9 669	9 201	67 194	9.3	59 667	58.8	794	69.6	30.4	68 194
Bleckley	225	21	204	183	1 974	1 755	4 866	14.0	4 372	76.1	46	80.4	19.6	4 069
Brantley	265	25	240	194	1 916	1 751	6 490	47.4	5 436	86.9	3	100.0	–	295
Brooks	643	120	523	460	4 092	3 009	7 118	19.2	6 115	76.9	41	100.0	–	3 001
Bryan	515	36	479	580	2 152	3 757	8 675	56.3	8 089	77.9	341	100.0	–	47 511
Bulloch	1 703	64	1 639	1 669	3 345	3 918	22 742	37.5	20 743	58.1	526	48.7	50.2	39 746
Burke	1 216	270	946	941	5 358	4 715	8 842	6.2	7 934	76.0	42	90.5	–	5 246
Butts	677	41	636	213	3 724	1 447	7 380	33.3	6 455	76.6	305	91.5	7.9	24 412
Calhoun	163	31	132	68	3 165	1 356	2 305	11.8	1 962	71.8	2	100.0	–	185
Camden	1 764	185	1 579	894	3 648	2 964	16 958	55.8	14 705	63.3	512	88.3	4.3	36 328
Candler	160	16	144	91	3 286	1 175	3 893	21.5	3 375	73.1	2	100.0	–	322
Carroll	3 668	292	3 376	4 687	4 335	6 864	34 067	22.8	31 568	70.5	1 856	88.9	4.5	140 130
Catoosa	1 635	95	1 540	1 609	3 174	3 789	21 794	30.0	20 425	77.1	500	82.0	13.2	49 954
Charlton	211	29	182	154	2 193	2 049	3 859	19.8	3 342	80.8	17	100.0	–	1 400
Chatham	16 369	1 887	14 482	18 455	7 122	8 507	99 683	9.3	89 865	60.4	1 922	64.3	32.9	182 701
Chattahoochee	71	17	54	74	418	437	3 316	6.7	2 932	27.0	4	100.0	–	500
Chattooga	197	5	192	641	886	3 022	10 677	16.8	9 577	75.3	9	100.0	–	521
Cherokee	2 309	173	2 136	3 512	1 685	4 000	51 937	53.5	49 495	83.9	3 776	76.3	23.4	372 334
Clarke	7 323	468	6 855	3 232	7 929	3 727	42 126	17.1	39 706	42.0	963	55.7	31.3	69 890
Clay	32	9	23	28	909	832	1 925	21.4	1 347	74.5	–	–	–	–
Clayton	15 449	1 012	14 437	15 978	7 253	8 777	86 461	20.2	82 243	60.6	3 347	69.4	30.6	294 519
Clinch	305	139	166	86	4 494	1 396	2 837	17.1	2 512	72.6	–	–	–	–
Cobb	19 838	1 411	18 427	28 662	3 438	6 401	237 522	25.1	227 487	68.2	6 642	82.1	17.4	736 201
Coffee	2 568	293	2 275	1 801	7 347	6 086	15 610	34.0	13 354	74.4	126	93.7	–	10 649
Colquitt	2 279	325	1 954	2 114	5 605	6 001	17 554	22.3	15 495	66.7	9	100.0	–	926
Columbia	2 034	91	1 943	1 280	2 190	1 938	33 321	40.3	31 120	82.1	943	99.6	–	120 213
Cook	342	26	316	369	2 236	2 912	6 558	22.8	5 882	74.9	37	100.0	–	3 062
Coweta	2 653	200	2 453	864	3 106	5 846	33 182	62.6	31 442	78.0	1 279	97.0	.7	159 638
Crawford	221	13	208	178	2 033	1 980	4 872	48.6	4 461	84.6	96	56.3	41.7	8 120
Crisp	1 345	183	1 162	1 974	6 515	10 083	9 559	14.9	8 337	60.5	88	79.5	–	7 688
Dade	172	18	154	244	1 121	1 856	6 224	24.5	5 633	80.3	9	100.0	–	1 080
Dawson	312	24	288	435	2 136	4 854	7 163	65.8	6 069	81.4	282	100.0	–	43 994
Decatur	1 655	189	1 466	1 434	6 155	5 758	11 968	18.3	10 380	72.5	94	89.4	10.6	7 731
De Kalb	43 813	3 687	40 126	56 222	7 343	10 300	261 231	12.8	249 339	58.5	6 145	69.4	30.6	696 193
Dodge	648	107	541	354	3 678	2 104	8 186	15.4	7 062	73.7	41	100.0	–	2 602
Dooly	235	31	204	196	2 220	1 980	4 499	12.4	3 909	71.3	–	–	–	–
Dougherty	7 055	615	6 440	10 428	7 263	10 827	39 656	6.1	35 552	53.5	396	47.2	48.7	27 321
Douglas	4 210	285	3 925	3 398	4 598	4 778	34 825	31.4	32 822	74.8	901	98.8	–	57 004
Early	117	23	94	274	941	2 369	5 338	13.2	4 695	72.4	5	100.0	–	339
Echols	13	2	11	11	531	471	1 482	57.3	1 264	75.7	X	X	X	X
Effingham	404	29	375	487	1 087	1 896	14 169	49.3	13 151	82.6	445	89.7	–	45 613
Elbert	606	79	527	666	3 076	3 515	9 136	15.8	8 004	75.9	14	28.6	71.4	501
Emanuel	741	139	602	633	3 719	3 425	9 419	12.9	8 045	71.1	–	–	–	–
Evans	14	5	9	122	1 400	1 398	4 381	24.7	3 778	71.5	12	100.0	–	1 175
Fannin	178	10	168	350	938	2 189	11 134	33.1	8 369	82.6	797	100.0	–	86 878
Fayette	1 834	61	1 773	1 147	2 031	1 838	32 726	45.9	31 524	86.4	938	100.0	–	161 267
Floyd	4 832	691	4 141	5 278	5 566	6 496	36 615	11.6	34 028	66.8	382	80.4	–	39 215
Forsyth	2 835	228	2 607	1 968	3 230	4 464	36 505	104.3	34 565	88.0	3 389	93.9	6.1	381 054
Franklin	711	99	612	431	3 656	2 589	9 303	22.2	7 888	79.3	22	100.0	–	2 121
Fulton	73 329	12 140	61 189	93 976	9 735	14 481	348 632	17.2	321 242	52.0	9 621	35.8	62.0	839 136
Gilmer	216	12	204	286	1 156	2 139	11 924	70.7	9 071	78.1	534	89.5	10.5	41 045
Glascock	13	5	8	NA	508	NA	1 192	15.1	1 004	80.0	–	–	–	–
Glynn	5 643	1 137	4 506	4 770	8 225	7 632	32 636	17.7	27 208	65.5	613	86.8	8.6	112 822
Gordon	1 754	64	1 690	1 394	4 193	4 051	17 145	24.4	16 173	71.8	549	68.3	29.7	38 259
Grady	816	114	702	621	3 724	3 156	9 991	22.9	8 797	73.4	64	100.0	–	7 329
Greene	480	38	442	281	3 633	2 451	6 653	41.6	5 477	76.4	194	99.0	–	52 552

[1] Data on serious crimes have not been adjusted for underreporting; this may affect comparability over time or among geographic areas. [2] Includes murder and nonnegligent manslaughter, forcible rape, robbery, and aggravated assault. [3] Includes burglary, larceny-theft, and motor vehicle theft. [4] Per 100,000 resident population provided by the U.S. Federal Bureau of Investigation. [5] Includes data not distributed by county.

Sources: Serious Crimes Known to Police—U.S. Federal Bureau of Investigation, Uniform Crime Reporting Program, unpublished data, annual (related Internet site <http://www.fbi.gov/ucr/ucr.htm>). Housing, 2000—U.S. Census Bureau, 2000 Census of Population and Housing, "Census 2000 Profiles of General Demographic Characteristics" data files, published May 2001 (related Internet site <http://www.census.gov/mp/www/pub/2000cen/mscen01.html>). Housing, 1990—U.S. Census Bureau, 1990 Census of Population and Housing, Summary Tape File (STF) 1C on CD-ROM (related Internet site <http://homer.ssd.census.gov/cdrom/lookup>). Building Permits—U.S. Census Bureau, "New Residential Construction–Building Permits," e-mail from Manufacturing and Construction Division/Residential Construction Branch, subject: building permits by place 2000, 22 May 2001 (related Internet site <http://www.census.gov/const/www/permitsindex.html>).

[Includes U.S., states, and 3,142 counties or county equivalents defined as of January 1, 1992. For changes to these areas since January 1, 1992, see appendix B. Geographic Information]

County	Serious crimes known to police (as reported to the FBI)[1] Number 1999 Total	Violent[2]	Property[3]	Number 1990	Rate[4] 1999	Rate[4] 1990	Housing, 2000 Total units	Percent change, 1990–2000	Occupied units Number	Percent owner-occupied	New private housing units authorized by building permits, 2000 Number	Percent in structures with— One unit	Five units or more	Valuation ($1,000)
GEORGIA—Con.														
Gwinnett	23 247	1 635	21 612	17 684	4 489	5 172	209 682	52.4	202 317	72.4	12 372	71.5	27.6	1 044 856
Habersham	765	86	679	386	2 356	1 397	14 634	32.1	13 259	76.2	376	99.5	–	35 848
Hall	5 080	409	4 671	5 200	4 183	5 450	51 046	33.2	47 381	71.1	2 121	77.0	22.3	204 172
Hancock	103	29	74	22	1 106	247	4 287	26.2	3 237	76.4	37	100.0	–	3 106
Haralson	453	35	418	445	1 803	2 527	10 719	18.9	9 826	75.1	106	96.2	–	11 067
Harris	188	26	162	558	827	3 281	10 288	31.7	8 822	86.1	301	100.0	–	53 619
Hart	290	57	233	543	1 303	2 755	11 111	24.3	9 106	80.8	15	46.7	–	1 347
Heard	126	10	116	235	1 339	2 724	4 512	27.6	4 043	77.4	56	100.0	–	6 041
Henry	3 915	267	3 648	1 700	3 006	3 240	43 100	102.9	41 373	85.2	4 130	82.3	16.9	348 869
Houston	4 632	402	4 230	5 562	4 296	6 235	44 509	28.0	40 911	68.5	1 505	75.1	24.1	101 021
Irwin	227	24	203	258	2 480	2 983	4 149	19.3	3 644	76.8	–	–	–	–
Jackson	1 300	108	1 192	1 010	3 389	3 489	16 226	37.8	15 057	74.9	864	88.7	3.7	109 811
Jasper	195	5	190	157	1 884	1 857	4 806	32.1	4 175	79.0	153	100.0	–	13 674
Jeff Davis	414	45	369	295	3 186	2 452	5 581	16.5	4 828	77.4	1	100.0	–	52
Jefferson	234	33	201	304	1 292	1 776	7 221	2.2	6 339	72.2	28	100.0	–	2 771
Jenkins	238	66	172	206	2 765	2 498	3 907	16.1	3 214	73.3	–	–	–	–
Johnson	120	9	111	43	1 416	554	3 634	7.2	3 130	79.8	–	–	–	–
Jones	791	105	686	423	3 372	2 040	9 272	20.1	8 659	85.8	240	91.7	–	26 523
Lamar	461	73	388	289	3 076	2 217	6 145	21.3	5 712	72.4	90	73.3	11.1	5 765
Lanier	75	20	55	194	1 054	3 508	3 011	36.7	2 593	76.2	39	59.0	41.0	1 611
Laurens	1 872	198	1 674	2 024	4 197	5 062	19 687	19.3	17 083	71.3	45	100.0	–	3 011
Lee	595	60	535	416	2 564	2 560	8 813	59.2	8 229	78.3	285	97.9	–	32 245
Liberty	1 804	129	1 675	1 283	3 042	2 432	21 977	31.0	19 383	50.7	221	80.1	18.1	17 667
Lincoln	70	8	62	127	830	1 707	4 514	16.6	3 251	81.7	43	100.0	–	5 134
Long	198	6	192	66	2 263	1 064	4 232	60.4	3 574	66.2	X	X	X	X
Lowndes	1 377	40	1 337	3 744	3 082	4 928	36 551	26.4	32 654	60.8	886	56.5	42.1	46 074
Lumpkin	352	34	318	414	1 820	2 841	8 263	44.2	7 537	72.3	354	98.0	–	46 917
McDuffie	783	43	740	433	3 529	2 152	8 916	10.9	7 970	71.3	55	100.0	–	5 603
McIntosh	444	31	413	237	4 349	2 745	5 735	34.1	4 202	83.6	91	100.0	–	12 401
Macon	327	36	291	268	2 531	2 044	5 495	13.3	4 834	73.0	14	100.0	–	777
Madison	35	5	30	319	2 533	1 537	10 520	24.8	9 800	80.2	154	100.0	–	17 531
Marion	110	9	101	20	1 000	519	3 130	45.4	2 668	78.1	X	X	X	X
Meriwether	759	72	687	490	3 222	2 525	9 211	9.5	8 248	74.2	158	100.0	–	16 063
Miller	140	17	123	22	2 144	350	2 770	6.5	2 487	77.0	3	100.0	–	100
Mitchell	520	33	487	708	2 410	3 492	8 880	19.3	8 063	72.0	99	79.8	–	8 071
Monroe	772	31	741	775	3 856	4 529	8 425	31.6	7 719	79.5	146	100.0	–	18 649
Montgomery	6	1	5	55	229	768	3 492	21.0	2 919	77.9	37	94.6	–	4 485
Morgan	355	25	330	553	2 417	4 524	6 128	27.3	5 558	77.5	189	88.9	2.6	21 336
Murray	703	11	692	450	2 111	1 742	14 320	40.3	13 286	73.7	223	89.7	8.5	21 258
Muscogee	12 418	991	11 427	12 020	6 687	6 705	76 182	7.4	69 819	56.4	975	57.0	40.4	72 220
Newton	1 937	160	1 777	2 494	3 286	5 965	23 033	48.7	21 997	77.7	1 918	78.0	21.3	179 239
Oconee	474	29	445	381	1 959	2 163	9 528	45.2	9 051	80.2	241	100.0	–	48 588
Oglethorpe	277	120	157	227	2 381	2 325	5 368	36.4	4 849	82.6	X	X	X	X
Paulding	1 533	145	1 388	1 255	2 046	3 120	29 274	92.1	28 089	86.8	2 845	76.3	23.7	180 510
Peach	818	124	694	589	3 281	2 780	9 093	20.6	8 436	68.4	131	87.8	7.6	11 925
Pickens	257	8	249	265	1 281	1 836	10 687	66.9	8 960	82.1	410	99.5	–	55 686
Pierce	134	19	115	301	3 166	2 258	6 719	27.5	5 958	80.6	66	100.0	–	6 268
Pike	129	3	126	118	1 001	1 349	5 068	33.5	4 755	81.6	212	100.0	–	21 237
Polk	1 519	100	1 419	1 084	4 105	3 206	15 059	10.9	14 012	71.3	266	96.2	3.8	19 519
Pulaski	110	28	82	224	1 285	2 763	3 944	13.7	3 407	73.6	73	100.0	–	4 433
Putnam	666	105	561	170	3 722	1 809	10 319	45.1	7 402	79.3	186	98.9	–	27 282
Quitman	84	9	75	2	3 315	154	1 773	31.7	1 047	81.1	1	100.0	–	200
Rabun	287	46	241	259	2 101	2 330	10 210	29.5	6 279	79.5	299	95.3	1.7	19 344
Randolph	131	24	107	97	1 631	1 414	3 402	5.5	2 909	68.9	–	–	–	–
Richmond	12 854	813	12 041	17 519	6 592	9 234	82 312	6.5	73 920	58.0	525	92.0	8.0	56 865
Rockdale	2 968	340	2 628	3 088	4 264	5 709	25 082	25.6	24 052	74.5	766	59.3	40.7	62 166
Schley	57	8	49	19	1 418	530	1 612	11.4	1 435	76.4	4	100.0	–	350
Screven	367	106	261	189	2 495	1 440	6 853	16.9	5 797	77.9	6	100.0	–	360
Seminole	292	104	188	143	2 927	1 587	4 742	16.9	3 573	80.5	–	–	–	–
Spalding	4 025	432	3 593	3 716	6 854	6 824	23 001	11.1	21 519	62.8	430	98.1	1.9	35 300
Stephens	699	34	665	944	2 698	4 059	11 652	13.6	9 951	72.7	91	95.6	–	10 182
Stewart	70	16	54	104	1 282	1 839	2 354	9.2	2 007	72.9	–	–	–	–
Sumter	1 297	121	1 176	1 671	4 063	5 528	13 700	16.8	12 025	64.0	72	68.1	29.2	3 403
Talbot	78	9	69	61	1 104	1 021	2 871	8.5	2 538	82.6	–	–	–	–
Taliaferro	35	3	32	41	1 800	3 358	1 085	22.5	870	76.9	X	X	X	X
Tattnall	713	134	579	428	3 755	2 462	8 578	27.0	7 057	70.6	4	100.0	–	343

[1] Data on serious crimes have not been adjusted for underreporting; this may affect comparability over time or among geographic areas. [2] Includes murder and nonnegligent manslaughter, forcible rape, robbery, and aggravated assault. [3] Includes burglary, larceny-theft, and motor vehicle theft. [4] Per 100,000 resident population provided by the U.S. Federal Bureau of Investigation.

Sources: Serious Crimes Known to Police—U.S. Federal Bureau of Investigation, Uniform Crime Reporting Program, unpublished data, annual (related Internet site <http://www.fbi.gov/ucr/ucr.htm>). Housing, 2000—U.S. Census Bureau, 2000 Census of Population and Housing, "Census 2000 Profiles of General Demographic Characteristics" data files, published May 2001 (related Internet site <http://www.census.gov/mp/www/pub/2000cen/mscen01.html>). Housing, 1990—U.S. Census Bureau, 1990 Census of Population and Housing, Summary Tape File (STF) 1C on CD-ROM (related Internet site <http://homer.ssd.census.gov/cdrom/lookup>). Building Permits—U.S. Census Bureau, "New Residential Construction-Building Permits," e-mail from Manufacturing and Construction Division/Residential Construction Branch, subject: building permits by place 2000, 22 May 2001 (related Internet site <http://www.census.gov/const/www/permitsindex.html>).

[Includes U.S., states, and 3,142 counties or county equivalents defined as of January 1, 1992. For changes to these areas since January 1, 1992, see appendix B. Geographic Information]

County	Serious crimes known to police (as reported to the FBI)[1]						Housing, 2000				New private housing units authorized by building permits, 2000			
	Number				Rate[4]				Occupied units			Percent in structures with—		
	1999							Percent change, 1990–2000		Percent owner–occupied		One unit	Five units or more	Valuation ($1,000)
	Total	Violent[2]	Property[3]	1990	1999	1990	Total units		Number		Number			
GEORGIA—Con.														
Taylor	113	23	90	101	1 335	1 322	3 978	25.8	3 281	76.9	14	100.0	–	782
Telfair	306	55	251	148	2 598	1 780	5 083	6.9	4 140	78.4	1	100.0	–	300
Terrell	415	70	345	293	3 832	2 890	4 460	9.6	4 002	66.3	48	93.8	–	1 945
Thomas	2 040	195	1 845	2 274	4 819	5 965	18 285	14.7	16 309	70.0	192	100.0	–	17 787
Tift	2 121	297	1 824	2 712	5 675	7 879	15 411	15.4	13 919	67.3	116	100.0	–	9 723
Toombs	920	93	827	596	4 272	2 476	11 371	14.3	9 877	65.5	24	91.7	–	1 963
Towns	11	1	10	38	1 558	678	6 282	37.3	3 998	85.2	181	100.0	–	19 465
Treutlen	49	5	44	165	801	2 753	2 865	17.6	2 531	74.8	–	–	–	–
Troup	4 725	264	4 461	3 430	7 887	6 176	23 824	6.2	21 920	64.5	590	54.9	44.4	43 685
Turner	289	57	232	196	3 096	2 365	3 916	14.3	3 435	71.6	4	25.0	–	130
Twiggs	77	9	68	100	746	1 020	4 291	17.6	3 832	82.6	22	100.0	–	2 234
Union	276	13	263	169	1 639	1 409	10 001	51.0	7 159	82.3	401	99.5	–	42 409
Upson	1 005	122	883	666	3 642	2 532	11 616	8.9	10 722	69.8	138	96.4	–	12 010
Walker	1 931	75	1 856	2 202	3 023	3 774	25 577	9.6	23 605	76.9	334	88.0	1.8	27 134
Walton	1 567	166	1 401	1 205	2 822	3 123	22 500	55.0	21 307	76.5	1 241	96.3	–	125 698
Ware	2 205	165	2 040	2 205	6 118	6 216	15 831	8.2	13 475	70.3	67	100.0	–	6 557
Warren	161	22	139	50	2 607	823	2 767	13.3	2 435	77.0	–	–	–	–
Washington	481	43	438	664	2 435	3 551	8 327	12.3	7 435	74.0	13	100.0	–	1 070
Wayne	675	59	616	746	2 604	3 396	10 827	22.9	9 324	76.5	13	69.2	–	1 246
Webster	4	–	4	8	216	427	1 115	24.2	911	81.7	X	X	X	X
Wheeler	45	11	34	57	906	1 163	2 447	13.9	2 011	77.5	–	–	–	–
White	507	33	474	323	2 850	2 483	9 454	55.4	7 731	79.2	315	99.0	–	33 296
Whitfield	3 756	304	3 452	4 346	4 514	6 042	30 722	6.6	29 385	67.6	876	41.9	48.7	41 433
Wilcox	17	6	11	49	226	764	3 320	15.9	2 785	79.9	–	–	–	–
Wilkes	210	36	174	198	1 950	1 868	5 022	10.4	4 314	75.5	13	100.0	–	1 123
Wilkinson	385	133	252	165	3 668	1 613	4 449	7.2	3 827	82.5	X	X	X	X
Worth	493	16	477	506	2 175	2 563	9 086	19.6	8 106	76.2	44	100.0	–	4 356
HAWAII	57 324	2 785	54 539	67 676	4 837	6 107	460 542	18.1	403 240	56.5	4 905	86.7	10.4	823 362
Hawaii	5 815	257	5 558	7 460	4 088	6 200	62 674	29.9	52 985	64.5	1 503	90.2	7.7	231 366
Honolulu	42 678	2 198	40 480	51 028	4 925	6 102	315 988	12.2	286 450	54.6	1 969	88.0	11.8	288 748
Kalawao	NA	NA	NA	NA	NA	NA	172	70.3	115	–	X	X	X	X
Kauai	2 076	62	2 014	2 596	3 691	5 073	25 331	43.8	20 183	61.4	290	90.7	9.3	94 392
Maui	6 755	268	6 487	6 592	5 631	6 559	56 377	33.7	43 507	57.6	1 143	79.1	11.7	208 856
IDAHO	39 684	3 112	36 572	40 552	3 190	4 075	527 824	27.7	469 645	72.4	10 915	88.7	5.5	1 358 936
Ada	11 208	743	10 465	9 727	3 986	4 727	118 516	46.6	113 408	70.7	3 925	90.5	3.1	560 941
Adams	122	13	109	43	3 148	1 321	1 982	11.5	1 421	79.1	43	100.0	–	7 612
Bannock	2 364	209	2 155	3 151	3 100	4 772	29 102	13.3	27 192	70.7	235	96.6	–	23 348
Bear Lake	40	5	35	131	601	2 153	3 268	11.4	2 259	83.1	71	100.0	–	7 398
Benewah	165	12	153	275	1 776	3 465	4 238	13.6	3 580	78.5	18	100.0	–	1 969
Bingham	867	61	806	831	2 035	2 211	14 303	12.9	13 317	79.3	112	92.9	–	11 475
Blaine	495	33	462	670	2 825	4 944	12 186	28.3	7 780	68.9	397	60.7	33.5	122 551
Boise	79	10	69	88	1 516	2 508	4 349	50.3	2 616	83.4	88	100.0	–	8 894
Bonner	944	68	876	998	2 631	3 749	19 646	29.7	14 693	77.9	23	82.6	–	2 182
Bonneville	3 190	255	2 935	3 640	3 882	5 041	30 484	17.0	28 753	74.7	563	84.7	5.0	48 657
Boundary	154	11	143	189	1 542	2 268	4 095	26.3	3 707	78.3	31	100.0	–	4 175
Butte	32	–	32	42	1 036	1 439	1 290	2.0	1 089	77.0	–	–	–	–
Camas	3	–	3	8	348	1 100	601	24.9	396	77.5	21	90.5	–	2 744
Canyon	4 980	376	4 604	5 398	4 065	5 993	47 965	44.7	45 018	73.3	2 043	92.8	3.4	209 920
Caribou	98	2	96	109	1 295	1 565	3 188	11.2	2 560	79.5	24	100.0	–	2 427
Cassia	857	81	776	934	3 939	4 782	7 862	9.0	7 060	72.6	43	90.7	–	5 990
Clark	18	1	17	19	2 025	2 493	521	3.8	340	67.9	–	–	–	–
Clearwater	111	8	103	240	1 170	2 822	4 144	8.9	3 456	78.0	52	26.9	73.1	3 407
Custer	42	3	39	70	1 004	1 694	2 983	22.4	1 770	74.9	3	100.0	–	133
Elmore	699	78	621	528	2 726	2 490	10 527	24.9	9 092	57.4	195	70.3	22.6	14 411
Franklin	155	6	149	293	1 370	3 174	3 872	19.5	3 476	80.8	81	100.0	–	8 186
Fremont	82	9	73	168	677	1 536	6 890	15.6	3 885	84.4	85	100.0	–	13 241
Gem	210	31	179	265	1 391	2 237	5 888	24.6	5 539	79.8	113	68.1	31.9	10 055
Gooding	266	23	243	194	1 916	1 668	5 505	14.7	5 046	72.3	83	90.4	–	8 167
Idaho	229	20	209	200	1 492	1 451	7 537	18.8	6 084	77.2	11	100.0	–	1 266
Jefferson	304	47	257	400	1 561	2 418	6 287	17.4	5 901	84.9	102	100.0	–	10 997
Jerome	514	63	451	523	2 809	3 455	6 713	14.1	6 298	70.0	53	96.2	–	5 413

[1] Data on serious crimes have not been adjusted for underreporting; this may affect comparability over time or among geographic areas.   [2] Includes murder and nonnegligent manslaughter, forcible rape, robbery, and aggravated assault.   [3] Includes burglary, larceny-theft, and motor vehicle theft.   [4] Per 100,000 resident population provided by the U.S. Federal Bureau of Investigation.

Sources: Serious Crimes Known to Police—U.S. Federal Bureau of Investigation, Uniform Crime Reporting Program, unpublished data, annual (related Internet site <http://www.fbi.gov/ucr/ucr.htm>).   Housing, 2000—U.S. Census Bureau, 2000 Census of Population and Housing, "Census 2000 Profiles of General Demographic Characteristics" data files, published May 2001 (related Internet site <http://www.census.gov/mp/www/pub/2000cen/mscen01.html>).   Housing, 1990—U.S. Census Bureau, 1990 Census of Population and Housing, Summary Tape File (STF) 1C on CD-ROM (related Internet site <http://homer.ssd.census.gov/cdrom/lookup>).   Building Permits—U.S. Census Bureau, "New Residential Construction–Building Permits," e-mail from Manufacturing and Construction Division/Residential Construction Branch, subject: building permits by place 2000, 22 May 2001 (related Internet site <http://www.census.gov/const/www/permitsindex.html>).

[Includes U.S., states, and 3,142 counties or county equivalents defined as of January 1, 1992. For changes to these areas since January 1, 1992, see appendix B. Geographic Information]

County	Serious crimes known to police (as reported to the FBI)[1]						Housing, 2000				New private housing units authorized by building permits, 2000			
	Number				Rate[4]				Occupied units			Percent in structures with—		
	1999			1990	1999	1990	Total units	Percent change, 1990–2000	Number	Percent owner-occupied	Number	One unit	Five units or more	Valuation ($1,000)
	Total	Violent[2]	Property[3]											
IDAHO—Con.														
Kootenai	3 884	446	3 438	3 328	3 760	4 768	46 607	45.8	41 308	74.5	1 174	90.1	6.6	135 730
Latah	685	35	650	768	2 098	2 508	13 838	16.6	13 059	58.7	127	58.3	9.4	12 586
Lemhi	NA	NA	NA	55	NA	1 870	4 154	10.7	3 275	76.2	45	100.0	–	2 497
Lewis	43	–	43	87	1 053	2 474	1 795	6.8	1 554	74.6	5	100.0	–	384
Lincoln	16	3	13	NA	414	NA	1 651	19.1	1 447	74.8	19	100.0	–	2 184
Madison	352	17	335	798	1 466	3 371	7 630	24.4	7 129	59.1	83	92.8	7.2	9 121
Minidoka	475	44	431	510	2 307	2 634	7 498	6.4	6 973	76.9	21	100.0	–	2 505
Nez Perce	1 386	39	1 347	1 113	3 692	3 297	16 203	12.0	15 286	68.8	129	72.9	22.5	10 808
Oneida	70	12	58	NA	1 696	NA	1 755	17.3	1 430	82.4	33	100.0	–	2 791
Owyhee	205	19	186	204	1 958	2 431	4 452	33.6	3 710	69.6	46	91.3	–	4 362
Payette	481	37	444	630	2 301	3 834	7 949	21.9	7 371	74.1	112	93.8	–	8 300
Power	245	22	223	304	2 894	4 290	2 844	5.3	2 560	74.6	12	100.0	–	1 126
Shoshone	387	51	336	583	2 739	4 185	7 057	1.9	5 906	72.6	13	100.0	–	1 395
Teton	110	8	102	30	1 967	872	2 632	60.0	2 078	73.5	216	79.6	3.7	17 892
Twin Falls	2 697	192	2 505	2 501	4 252	4 668	25 595	21.0	23 853	68.3	288	90.3	–	25 160
Valley	303	12	291	264	3 716	5 046	8 084	21.7	3 208	78.9	159	94.3	–	23 755
Washington	117	7	110	243	1 129	2 842	4 138	12.3	3 762	73.7	18	100.0	–	2 781
ILLINOIS	[5]267 004	[5]53 068	213 936	[5]671 512	[5]7 750	[5]5 886	4 885 615	8.4	4 591 779	67.3	51 944	72.8	21.2	6 527 982
Adams	NA	NA	NA	[5]2 352	NA	[5]3 559	29 386	4.9	26 860	73.7	100	66.0	7.0	12 433
Alexander	NA	NA	NA	[5]510	NA	[5]4 800	4 591	-6.3	3 808	71.8	2	100.0	–	60
Bond	NA	NA	NA	[5]290	NA	[5]1 934	6 690	9.0	6 155	79.7	106	49.1	50.9	8 312
Boone	NA	NA	NA	[5]904	NA	[5]2 934	15 414	34.3	14 597	78.6	365	98.9	–	48 781
Brown	NA	NA	NA	[5]75	NA	[5]1 285	2 456	4.2	2 108	74.1	17	11.8	88.2	1 180
Bureau	NA	NA	NA	[5]488	NA	[5]1 367	15 331	3.9	14 182	76.0	99	57.6	42.4	9 280
Calhoun	NA	NA	NA	[5]46	NA	[5]864	2 681	-9.1	2 046	80.7	13	76.9	–	1 251
Carroll	NA	NA	NA	[5]367	NA	[5]2 184	7 945	6.2	6 794	76.7	70	94.3	–	10 782
Cass	NA	NA	NA	[5]157	NA	[5]1 168	5 784	1.5	5 347	74.9	11	100.0	–	767
Champaign	NA	NA	NA	[5]9 847	NA	[5]5 702	75 280	10.0	70 597	55.7	1 049	56.6	39.3	105 874
Christian	NA	NA	NA	[5]378	NA	[5]1 098	14 992	2.4	13 921	76.2	99	86.9	5.1	8 485
Clark	NA	NA	NA	[5]340	NA	[5]2 136	7 816	9.9	6 971	77.5	14	85.7	–	1 158
Clay	NA	NA	NA	[5]379	NA	[5]2 681	6 394	2.0	5 839	79.9	11	100.0	–	1 116
Clinton	NA	NA	NA	[5]539	NA	[5]1 621	13 805	8.3	12 754	80.2	98	82.7	–	12 770
Coles	NA	NA	NA	[5]1 236	NA	[5]2 393	22 768	12.0	21 043	61.9	101	37.6	47.5	5 542
Cook	[5]227 529	[5]48 878	178 651	[5]420 139	[5]8 065	[5]8 230	2 096 121	3.7	1 974 181	57.9	11 877	45.2	43.6	1 400 300
Crawford	NA	NA	NA	[5]198	NA	[5]1 051	8 785	3.8	7 842	80.3	5	100.0	–	545
Cumberland	NA	NA	NA	[5]124	NA	[5]1 162	4 876	9.6	4 368	82.1	11	81.8	–	1 109
DeKalb	NA	NA	NA	[5]2 863	NA	[5]3 674	32 988	20.6	31 674	59.5	576	55.4	29.0	60 237
De Witt	NA	NA	NA	[5]411	NA	[5]2 488	7 282	4.9	6 770	75.0	53	100.0	–	6 845
Douglas	NA	NA	NA	[5]293	NA	[5]1 505	8 005	5.2	7 574	76.9	32	100.0	–	4 111
DuPage	[5]1 924	[5]60	1 864	[5]29 562	[5]1 834	[5]3 782	335 601	14.7	325 601	76.4	3 931	83.7	15.5	694 047
Edgar	NA	NA	NA	[5]488	NA	[5]2 644	8 611	-1.4	7 874	74.6	68	32.4	67.6	3 939
Edwards	NA	NA	NA	[5]535	NA	[5]470	3 199	-1.9	2 905	81.2	X	X	X	X
Effingham	NA	NA	NA	[5]942	NA	[5]2 971	13 959	14.5	13 001	76.0	57	86.0	14.0	6 851
Fayette	NA	NA	NA	[5]274	NA	[5]1 311	9 053	5.9	8 146	79.8	11	100.0	–	994
Ford	NA	NA	NA	[5]318	NA	[5]2 228	6 060	-.9	5 639	76.2	37	83.8	–	3 431
Franklin	NA	NA	NA	[5]434	NA	[5]1 076	18 105	-1.8	16 408	77.7	29	93.1	–	2 480
Fulton	NA	NA	NA	[5]977	NA	[5]2 566	16 240	-1.5	14 877	76.4	73	100.0	–	6 685
Gallatin	NA	NA	NA	[5]545	NA	[5]651	3 071	-3.9	2 726	81.1	–			536
Greene	NA	NA	NA	[5]311	NA	[5]2 197	6 332	-3.7	5 757	76.2	6	100.0	–	
Grundy	NA	NA	NA	[5]898	NA	[5]2 777	15 040	18.9	14 293	72.4	227	74.9	4.0	30 855
Hamilton	NA	NA	NA	[5]106	NA	[5]1 247	3 983	-.7	3 462	81.4	X	X	X	X
Hancock	NA	NA	NA	[5]282	NA	[5]1 452	8 909	-8.1	8 069	80.4	22	90.9	–	1 546
Hardin	NA	NA	NA	[5]44	NA	[5]1 155	2 494	3.8	1 987	80.4	–			
Henderson	NA	NA	NA	[5]556	NA	[5]709	4 126	.9	3 365	78.8	18	100.0	–	850
Henry	NA	NA	NA	[5]1 227	NA	[5]2 398	21 270	1.9	20 056	78.7	107	87.9	–	13 568
Iroquois	NA	NA	NA	[5]440	NA	[5]1 429	13 362	4.2	12 220	76.4	69	94.2	–	6 365
Jackson	NA	NA	NA	[5]3 476	NA	[5]5 692	26 844	5.1	24 215	53.3	112	40.2	59.8	5 914
Jasper	NA	NA	NA	[5]195	NA	[5]1 838	4 294	-.1	3 930	83.2	2	100.0	–	140
Jefferson	NA	NA	NA	[5]1 706	NA	[5]4 608	16 990	5.7	15 374	74.6	87	33.3	66.7	6 361
Jersey	NA	NA	NA	[5]590	NA	[5]2 873	8 918	8.5	8 096	77.7	103	100.0	–	11 966
Jo Daviess	NA	NA	NA	[5]367	NA	[5]1 682	12 003	11.6	9 218	77.3	134	100.0	–	21 413
Johnson	NA	NA	NA	[5]532	NA	[5]282	5 046	8.0	4 183	84.7	X	X	X	X
Kane	[5]5 692	[5]778	4 914	[5]16 318	[5]4 532	[5]5 140	138 998	24.7	133 901	76.0	5 784	75.2	21.7	847 887

[1] Data on serious crimes have not been adjusted for underreporting; this may affect comparability over time or among geographic areas. [2] Includes murder and nonnegligent manslaughter, forcible rape, robbery, and aggravated assault. [3] Includes burglary, larceny-theft, and motor vehicle theft. [4] Per 100,000 resident population provided by the U.S. Federal Bureau of Investigation. [5] Excludes rape.

Sources: Serious Crimes Known to Police—U.S. Federal Bureau of Investigation, Uniform Crime Reporting Program, unpublished data, annual (related Internet site <http://www.fbi.gov/ucr/ucr.htm>). Housing, 2000—U.S. Census Bureau, 2000 Census of Population and Housing, "Census 2000 Profiles of General Demographic Characteristics" data files, published May 2001 (related Internet site <http://www.census.gov/mp/www/pub/2000cen/mscen01.html>). Housing, 1990—U.S. Census Bureau, 1990 Census of Population and Housing, Summary Tape File (STF) 1C on CD-ROM (related Internet site <http://homer.ssd.census.gov/cdrom/lookup>). Building Permits—U.S. Census Bureau, "New Residential Construction–Building Permits," e-mail from Manufacturing and Construction Division/Residential Construction Branch, subject: building permits by place 2000, 22 May 2001 (related Internet site <http://www.census.gov/const/www/permitsindex.html>).

[Includes U.S., states, and 3,142 counties or county equivalents defined as of January 1, 1992. For changes to these areas since January 1, 1992, see appendix B. Geographic Information]

County	Serious crimes known to police (as reported to the FBI)[1] Number 1999 Total	Violent[2]	Property[3]	Number 1990	Rate[4] 1999	Rate[4] 1990	Housing, 2000 Total units	Percent change, 1990–2000	Occupied units Number	Percent owner-occupied	New private housing units authorized by building permits, 2000 Number	Percent in structures with— One unit	Five units or more	Valuation ($1,000)
ILLINOIS—Con.														
Kankakee	NA	NA	NA	[5]6 375	NA	[5]6 623	40 610	9.8	38 182	69.4	389	80.5	5.4	50 466
Kendall	NA	NA	NA	[5]1 021	NA	[5]2 591	19 519	42.0	18 798	84.1	863	88.9	1.4	113 691
Knox	NA	NA	NA	[5]2 531	NA	[5]4 534	23 717	Z	22 056	71.6	110	100.0	–	11 599
Lake	NA	NA	NA	[5]21 276	NA	[5]4 120	225 919	23.3	216 297	77.8	4 134	76.6	20.4	638 453
La Salle	NA	NA	NA	[5]2 474	NA	[5]2 314	46 438	6.0	43 417	75.0	494	65.6	10.9	45 186
Lawrence	NA	NA	NA	[5]237	NA	[5]1 484	7 014	.5	6 309	77.0	3	100.0	–	400
Lee	NA	NA	NA	[5]814	NA	[5]2 367	14 310	7.5	13 253	73.9	118	76.3	10.2	12 093
Livingston	NA	NA	NA	[5]921	NA	[5]2 343	15 297	6.5	14 374	74.1	95	87.4	8.4	9 136
Logan	NA	NA	NA	[5]916	NA	[5]2 974	11 872	2.0	11 113	71.3	27	92.6	–	2 548
McDonough	NA	NA	NA	[5]1 237	NA	[5]3 510	13 289	.2	12 360	63.1	152	12.5	87.5	7 958
McHenry	NA	NA	NA	[5]5 041	NA	[5]2 774	92 908	40.8	89 403	83.2	3 522	92.8	4.9	473 431
McLean	NA	NA	NA	[5]5 436	NA	[5]4 208	59 972	22.0	56 746	66.5	909	71.5	23.0	78 743
Macon	NA	NA	NA	[5]6 401	NA	[5]5 505	50 241	.4	46 561	71.6	361	66.8	31.0	38 744
Macoupin	NA	NA	NA	[5]514	NA	[5]1 078	21 097	5.1	19 253	79.0	59	79.7	–	5 474
Madison	NA	NA	NA	[5]11 063	NA	[5]4 439	108 942	7.8	101 953	73.8	1 165	78.1	11.8	136 640
Marion	NA	NA	NA	[5]1 542	NA	[5]3 773	18 022	-.6	16 619	76.6	17	88.2	–	1 158
Marshall	NA	NA	NA	[5]108	NA	[5]841	5 914	11.2	5 225	80.1	17	100.0	–	1 718
Mason	NA	NA	NA	[5]218	NA	[5]1 340	7 033	-8.5	6 389	76.8	15	100.0	–	1 369
Massac	NA	NA	NA	[5]408	NA	[5]2 766	6 951	7.8	6 261	78.6	5	100.0	–	412
Menard	NA	NA	NA	[5]98	NA	[5]950	5 285	13.7	4 873	78.9	79	100.0	–	9 028
Mercer	NA	NA	NA	[5]141	NA	[5]816	7 109	-1.9	6 624	79.7	41	95.1	–	4 212
Monroe	NA	NA	NA	[5]263	NA	[5]1 173	10 749	22.5	10 275	80.2	268	94.0	–	38 213
Montgomery	NA	NA	NA	[5]374	NA	[5]1 217	12 525	.6	11 507	78.4	17	100.0	–	1 561
Morgan	NA	NA	NA	[5]1 777	NA	[5]4 882	15 291	3.9	14 039	70.4	22	63.6	–	2 005
Moultrie	NA	NA	NA	[5]152	NA	[5]1 091	5 743	6.7	5 405	78.5	47	95.7	–	4 739
Ogle	NA	NA	NA	[5]1 071	NA	[5]2 330	20 420	13.1	19 278	74.5	207	100.0	–	24 679
Peoria	[5]10 266	[5]972	9 294	[5]12 127	[5]9 173	[5]6 651	78 204	4.0	72 733	67.7	938	64.4	31.8	88 417
Perry	NA	NA	NA	[5]469	NA	[5]2 190	9 457	2.4	8 504	78.6	X	X	X	X
Piatt	NA	NA	NA	[5]294	NA	[5]1 891	6 798	9.2	6 475	80.2	69	100.0	–	9 951
Pike	NA	NA	NA	[5]261	NA	[5]1 485	8 011	-.6	6 876	77.1	46	100.0	–	2 955
Pope	NA	NA	NA	[5]29	NA	[5]663	2 351	9.1	1 769	82.2	2	100.0	–	185
Pulaski	NA	NA	NA	[5]33	NA	[5]439	3 353	-1.7	2 893	75.6	3	100.0	–	140
Putnam	NA	NA	NA	[5]36	NA	[5]628	2 888	11.1	2 415	82.6	40	100.0	–	4 002
Randolph	NA	NA	NA	[5]479	NA	[5]1 385	13 328	1.1	12 084	79.4	64	79.7	10.9	5 686
Richland	NA	NA	NA	[5]505	NA	[5]3 052	7 468	4.6	6 660	76.5	45	33.3	66.7	4 519
Rock Island	NA	NA	NA	[5]6 677	NA	[5]4 490	64 489	1.8	60 712	69.7	220	93.6	–	32 131
St. Clair	NA	NA	NA	[5]14 050	NA	[5]5 394	104 446	1.0	96 810	67.0	1 102	82.5	14.1	122 793
Saline	NA	NA	NA	[5]779	NA	[5]2 934	12 360	.1	10 992	76.5	–	–	–	–
Sangamon	[5]8 207	[5]1 087	7 120	[5]9 710	[5]6 961	[5]5 559	85 459	11.2	78 722	70.0	850	80.0	5.2	86 629
Schuyler	NA	NA	NA	[5]81	NA	[5]1 080	3 304	-.8	2 975	78.8	X	X	X	X
Scott	NA	NA	NA	[5]24	NA	[5]619	2 464	.9	2 222	77.6	–	–	–	–
Shelby	NA	NA	NA	[5]211	NA	[5]948	10 060	7.8	9 056	81.0	60	85.0	–	5 951
Stark	NA	NA	NA	[5]67	NA	[5]1 025	2 725	.3	2 525	77.2	17	100.0	–	1 609
Stephenson	NA	NA	NA	[5]1 695	NA	[5]3 527	21 713	6.6	19 785	74.8	141	57.4	34.0	16 317
Tazewell	NA	NA	NA	[5]3 170	NA	[5]2 578	52 973	7.4	50 327	76.1	445	88.5	4.0	57 557
Union	NA	NA	NA	[5]250	NA	[5]1 419	7 894	6.6	7 290	75.4	48	100.0	–	4 444
Vermilion	NA	NA	NA	[5]4 022	NA	[5]4 557	36 349	-1.9	33 406	71.7	70	91.4	–	6 587
Wabash	NA	NA	NA	[5]328	NA	[5]2 502	5 758	3.3	5 192	75.3	13	100.0	–	1 567
Warren	NA	NA	NA	[5]565	NA	[5]2 946	7 787	-5.4	7 166	74.6	38	100.0	–	3 872
Washington	NA	NA	NA	[5]195	NA	[5]1 314	6 385	2.0	5 848	81.1	71	94.4	–	7 438
Wayne	NA	NA	NA	[5]190	NA	[5]1 102	7 950	4.3	7 143	79.4	54	14.8	85.2	2 544
White	NA	NA	NA	[5]208	NA	[5]1 259	7 393	-5.2	6 534	78.0	2	100.0	–	216
Whiteside	NA	NA	NA	[5]1 790	NA	[5]3 016	25 025	4.3	23 684	74.5	136	92.6	–	16 523
Will	[5]355	[5]11	344	[5]16 608	[5]1 829	[5]4 648	175 524	42.9	167 542	83.1	7 159	90.5	8.5	838 315
Williamson	NA	NA	NA	[5]1 947	NA	[5]3 372	27 703	10.0	25 358	73.6	145	93.1	–	14 227
Winnebago	[5]13 031	[5]1 282	11 749	[5]20 978	[5]9 009	[5]8 295	114 404	12.5	107 980	70.0	1 263	80.2	4.8	92 529
Woodford	NA	NA	NA	[5]266	NA	[5]815	13 487	13.0	12 797	82.8	181	85.6	–	20 456
INDIANA	177 355	17 954	159 401	195 840	4 069	4 823	2 532 319	12.7	2 336 306	71.4	37 903	80.2	15.3	4 414 450
Adams	213	15	198	464	1 653	1 492	12 404	13.5	11 818	77.0	121	85.1	9.9	11 565
Allen	15 065	1 027	14 038	18 898	4 759	6 282	138 905	13.0	128 745	71.0	1 791	92.1	3.9	272 687
Bartholomew	2 166	74	2 092	2 141	3 109	3 363	29 853	17.4	27 936	74.3	212	99.1	–	29 614
Benton	55	5	50	80	735	1 125	3 818	-.4	3 558	75.8	28	92.9	–	1 545
Blackford	277	10	267	286	1 977	2 033	6 155	5.1	5 690	78.7	96	29.2	66.7	5 661
Boone	18	5	13	282	2 609	2 339	17 929	23.5	17 081	78.7	678	60.5	39.5	96 430
Brown	10	4	6	55	NA	391	7 163	2.4	5 897	85.0	140	97.1	–	8 184
Carroll	82	14	68	265	3 113	1 628	8 675	2.9	7 718	79.7	92	100.0	–	6 525
Cass	967	73	894	994	6 063	5 912	16 620	6.3	15 715	73.7	87	100.0	–	10 225

[1] Data on serious crimes have not been adjusted for underreporting; this may affect comparability over time or among geographic areas. [2] Includes murder and nonnegligent manslaughter, forcible rape, robbery, and aggravated assault. [3] Includes burglary, larceny-theft, and motor vehicle theft. [4] Per 100,000 resident population provided by the U.S. Federal Bureau of Investigation. [5] Excludes rape.

Sources: Serious Crimes Known to Police—U.S. Federal Bureau of Investigation, Uniform Crime Reporting Program, unpublished data, annual (related Internet site <http://www.fbi.gov/ucr/ucr.htm>). Housing, 2000—U.S. Census Bureau, 2000 Census of Population and Housing, "Census 2000 Profiles of General Demographic Characteristics" data files, published May 2001 (related Internet site <http://www.census.gov/mp/www/pub/2000cen/mscen01.html>). Housing, 1990—U.S. Census Bureau, 1990 Census of Population and Housing, Summary Tape File (STF) 1C on CD-ROM (related Internet site <http://homer.ssd.census.gov/cdrom/lookup>). Building Permits—U.S. Census Bureau, "New Residential Construction–Building Permits," e-mail from Manufacturing and Construction Division/Residential Construction Branch, subject: building permits by place 2000, 22 May 2001 (related Internet site <http://www.census.gov/const/www/permitsindex.html>).

Table B–6. Counties — **Crime, Housing, and Building Permits**–Con.

[Includes U.S., states, and 3,142 counties or county equivalents defined as of January 1, 1992. For changes to these areas since January 1, 1992, see appendix B. Geographic Information]

County	Serious crimes known to police (as reported to the FBI)[1] — Number 1999 Total	Violent[2]	Property[3]	Number 1990	Rate[4] 1999	Rate[4] 1990	Housing, 2000 Total units	Percent change, 1990–2000	Occupied units Number	Percent owner-occupied	New private housing units authorized by building permits, 2000 Number	Percent in structures with— One unit	Five units or more	Valuation ($1,000)
INDIANA—Con.														
Clark	3 115	192	2 923	3 396	4 561	3 869	41 176	16.6	38 751	70.0	793	92.2	4.7	77 341
Clay	252	24	228	200	3 104	2 618	11 097	4.6	10 216	79.1	62	95.2	–	4 368
Clinton	164	31	133	27	908	NA	13 267	9.6	12 545	72.9	77	94.8	–	8 673
Crawford	34	10	24	125	319	NA	5 138	17.5	4 181	82.9	6	100.0	–	425
Daviess	21	6	15	171	NA	1 024	11 898	8.3	10 894	78.6	22	100.0	–	4 137
Dearborn	565	78	487	112	1 306	NA	17 791	22.4	16 832	78.6	374	90.9	1.6	44 774
Decatur	23	14	9	179	NA	1 247	9 992	9.8	9 389	73.2	100	100.0	–	10 887
De Kalb	19	4	15	501	365	1 418	16 144	18.7	15 134	81.5	192	99.0	–	24 664
Delaware	1 192	171	1 021	2 713	2 398	3 819	51 032	4.6	47 131	67.2	402	67.2	27.9	51 957
Dubois	373	17	356	364	2 254	3 629	15 511	11.1	14 813	78.0	250	83.2	11.2	31 302
Elkhart	8 270	607	7 663	7 387	4 764	4 729	69 791	16.0	66 154	72.2	1 296	69.1	25.6	125 684
Fayette	25	11	14	963	NA	6 193	10 981	4.3	10 199	71.5	88	100.0	–	6 249
Floyd	2 515	182	2 333	2 328	6 126	6 060	29 087	15.3	27 511	72.5	425	83.1	16.9	55 056
Fountain	31	5	26	46	NA	396	7 692	4.7	7 041	77.9	8	100.0	–	1 042
Franklin	56	16	40	95	5 091	11 890	8 596	19.8	7 868	81.4	88	100.0	–	11 601
Fulton	17	4	13	13	NA	NA	9 123	5.4	8 082	78.4	32	100.0	–	3 536
Gibson	168	24	144	54	756	NA	14 125	5.0	12 847	77.9	179	10.1	86.6	8 234
Grant	1 821	93	1 728	3 292	2 491	4 439	30 560	2.2	28 319	73.2	237	90.7	4.2	21 549
Greene	58	14	44	157	NA	1 959	15 053	12.9	13 372	80.0	–	–	–	–
Hamilton	3 029	119	2 910	2 115	1 849	1 942	69 478	69.2	65 933	80.9	4 282	82.1	16.8	649 860
Hancock	605	20	585	1 062	1 101	2 333	21 750	31.9	20 718	81.4	699	86.3	1.1	89 929
Harrison	690	14	676	639	1 972	2 347	13 699	19.6	12 917	84.1	204	100.0	–	26 271
Hendricks	709	32	677	499	3 968	4 783	39 229	45.5	37 275	83.0	1 901	90.8	6.1	225 910
Henry	2 034	46	1 988	1 435	4 139	8 083	20 592	3.8	19 486	77.0	209	83.7	16.3	20 130
Howard	3 245	237	3 008	3 324	3 860	4 112	37 604	11.2	34 800	71.7	408	91.7	2.0	54 298
Huntington	648	105	543	681	1 726	4 155	15 269	12.0	14 242	77.1	153	100.0	–	16 656
Jackson	1 222	131	1 091	194	7 125	876	17 137	15.6	16 052	74.3	203	76.8	16.3	19 358
Jasper	247	15	232	43	4 659	852	11 236	25.1	10 686	77.5	270	87.4	6.7	22 353
Jay	235	3	232	344	2 716	3 786	9 074	1.9	8 405	77.7	65	100.0	–	5 349
Jefferson	604	76	528	254	1 905	1 428	13 386	12.3	12 148	74.6	169	90.5	–	14 185
Jennings	520	79	441	358	1 857	1 513	11 469	25.6	10 134	79.1	208	100.0	–	16 302
Johnson	2 120	72	2 048	1 419	4 152	4 521	45 095	35.5	42 434	76.5	1 480	98.0	–	203 451
Knox	1 196	49	1 147	698	3 280	3 515	17 305	3.4	15 552	69.0	64	75.0	–	5 901
Kosciusko	1 025	64	961	763	1 516	5 080	32 188	5.5	27 283	79.0	433	93.1	2.8	53 389
Lagrange	57	13	44	328	NA	1 113	11 225	5.9	11 225	81.5	217	99.1	–	16 818
Lake	19 166	2 276	16 890	29 150	4 819	6 385	194 992	6.5	181 633	69.0	1 928	80.3	14.5	248 413
La Porte	4 688	281	4 407	5 156	4 546	5 190	45 621	7.9	41 050	75.2	440	95.0	–	44 613
Lawrence	900	19	881	931	2 205	2 439	20 560	16.9	18 535	78.9	41	100.0	–	3 217
Madison	882	38	844	5 115	5 119	6 609	56 939	6.7	53 052	74.2	356	93.8	2.8	43 902
Marion	43 356	7 844	35 512	56 649	5 290	7 106	387 183	10.8	352 164	59.3	5 216	75.8	18.8	614 580
Marshall	477	16	461	139	3 122	1 067	18 099	7.6	16 519	76.8	286	78.3	12.6	19 755
Martin	111	5	106	159	1 421	1 533	4 729	14.9	4 183	81.2	7	100.0	–	632
Miami	67	20	47	125	NA	NA	15 299	4.5	13 716	76.0	115	100.0	–	11 359
Monroe	4 042	339	3 703	2 961	3 485	2 717	50 846	21.2	46 898	54.0	620	77.4	7.4	73 296
Montgomery	980	46	934	980	2 677	2 846	15 678	12.3	14 595	73.4	116	100.0	–	11 549
Morgan	1 152	46	1 106	871	5 504	5 059	25 908	26.4	24 437	79.7	583	94.5	2.4	63 742
Newton	164	7	157	270	1 105	1 992	5 726	8.5	5 340	79.9	98	88.8	11.2	8 028
Noble	518	40	478	624	3 413	5 563	18 233	17.5	16 696	78.0	244	90.6	4.9	25 060
Ohio	16	5	11	17	NA	NA	2 424	12.2	2 201	77.6	23	100.0	–	2 152
Orange	43	8	35	52	NA	NA	8 348	8.0	7 621	79.1	5	100.0	–	327
Owen	38	9	29	52	NA	NA	9 853	23.0	8 282	81.6	5	20.0	–	397
Parke	31	10	21	34	NA	NA	7 539	4.9	6 415	80.2	43	100.0	–	3 533
Perry	281	38	243	191	3 467	2 362	8 223	11.1	7 270	79.3	56	89.3	–	5 961
Pike	16	7	9	50	NA	2 042	5 611	2.3	5 119	82.5	73	83.6	11.0	6 203
Porter	3 711	152	3 559	3 401	2 528	2 839	57 616	22.0	54 649	76.7	1 107	76.4	15.8	142 002
Posey	160	14	146	45	2 422	NA	11 076	6.5	10 205	81.8	97	100.0	–	13 287
Pulaski	46	9	37	117	344	925	5 918	6.8	5 170	80.6	70	94.3	–	6 911
Putnam	665	191	474	188	2 647	NA	13 505	23.0	12 374	78.6	40	95.0	–	3 731
Randolph	407	13	394	409	1 462	4 697	11 775	4.0	10 937	75.9	60	100.0	–	5 381
Ripley	175	35	140	234	4 031	951	10 482	9.3	9 842	76.8	210	74.8	21.4	15 473
Rush	215	9	206	276	3 894	1 522	7 337	4.6	6 923	74.1	77	97.4	–	6 737
St. Joseph	15 561	1 075	14 486	5 777	5 985	4 082	107 013	9.2	100 743	71.7	1 665	53.4	38.9	162 876
Scott	86	32	54	218	497	4 087	9 737	20.5	8 832	75.9	205	57.1	40.0	9 746
Shelby	28	9	19	90	NA	NA	17 633	12.6	16 561	73.4	161	90.1	–	20 104
Spencer	56	14	42	62	NA	NA	8 333	9.1	7 569	83.2	147	98.6	–	12 915
Starke	292	82	210	311	1 454	1 633	10 201	3.2	8 740	80.9	111	100.0	–	8 361
Steuben	1 078	64	1 014	500	3 402	8 585	17 337	10.0	12 738	78.1	275	87.3	12.7	35 051
Sullivan	120	38	82	68	2 610	NA	8 804	3.7	7 819	79.8	21	90.5	–	1 700
Switzerland	24	7	17	27	NA	NA	4 226	13.2	3 435	77.9	122	100.0	–	7 108
Tippecanoe	4 070	186	3 884	4 766	3 639	3 649	58 343	21.2	55 226	55.9	1 710	45.0	46.6	140 085

[1] Data on serious crimes have not been adjusted for underreporting; this may affect comparability over time or among geographic areas. [2] Includes murder and nonnegligent manslaughter, forcible rape, robbery, and aggravated assault. [3] Includes burglary, larceny-theft, and motor vehicle theft. [4] Per 100,000 resident population provided by the U.S. Federal Bureau of Investigation.

Sources: Serious Crimes Known to Police—U.S. Federal Bureau of Investigation, Uniform Crime Reporting Program, unpublished data, annual (related Internet site <http://www.fbi.gov/ucr/ucr.htm>). Housing, 2000—U.S. Census Bureau, 2000 Census of Population and Housing, "Census 2000 Profiles of General Demographic Characteristics" data files, published May 2001 (related Internet site <http://www.census.gov/mp/www/pub/2000cen/mscen01.html>). Housing, 1990—U.S. Census Bureau, 1990 Census of Population and Housing, Summary Tape File (STF) 1C on CD-ROM (related Internet site <http://homer.ssd.census.gov/cdrom/lookup>). Building Permits—U.S. Census Bureau, "New Residential Construction–Building Permits," e-mail from Manufacturing and Construction Division/Residential Construction Branch, subject: building permits by place 2000, 22 May 2001 (related Internet site <http://www.census.gov/const/www/permitsindex.html>).

[Includes U.S., states, and 3,142 counties or county equivalents defined as of January 1, 1992. For changes to these areas since January 1, 1992, see appendix B. Geographic Information]

County	Serious crimes known to police (as reported to the FBI)[1]						Housing, 2000				New private housing units authorized by building permits, 2000			
	Number				Rate[4]				Occupied units			Percent in structures with—		
	1999							Percent change, 1990–2000		Percent owner-occupied				
	Total	Violent[2]	Property[3]	1990	1999	1990	Total units		Number		Number	One unit	Five units or more	Valuation ($1,000)
INDIANA—Con.														
Tipton	154	24	130	16	3 197	141	6 848	6.6	6 469	79.9	53	100.0	–	8 099
Union	27	3	24	53	NA	NA	3 077	9.4	2 793	75.3	39	100.0	–	3 878
Vanderburgh	7 541	616	6 925	8 352	4 451	5 060	76 300	5.0	70 623	66.8	1 040	54.4	42.9	66 090
Vermillion	20	6	14	48	NA	NA	7 405	1.6	6 762	79.5	41	100.0	–	4 494
Vigo	5 444	249	5 195	3 360	9 650	5 602	45 203	2.3	40 998	67.5	312	90.1	3.8	34 257
Wabash	320	5	315	547	1 812	1 560	14 034	4.8	13 215	75.9	88	100.0	–	10 157
Warren	7	3	4	44	NA	NA	3 477	6.2	3 219	81.1	67	94.0	–	4 470
Warrick	854	12	842	159	1 643	2 365	20 546	21.4	19 438	83.3	439	83.4	11.6	58 804
Washington	95	23	72	85	1 477	470	11 191	17.6	10 264	81.1	35	100.0	–	2 830
Wayne	3 048	193	2 855	2 681	4 243	3 726	30 468	3.0	28 469	68.7	146	97.3	–	15 124
Wells	374	9	365	317	1 383	3 514	10 970	10.5	10 402	80.9	123	90.2	9.8	15 854
White	51	16	35	382	919	7 294	12 083	1.8	9 727	76.6	134	94.0	–	12 490
Whitley	40	6	34	37	NA	NA	12 545	15.6	11 711	83.3	212	99.1	–	25 641
IOWA	87 021	7 513	79 508	112 339	3 262	4 078	1 232 511	7.8	1 149 276	72.3	12 500	67.8	25.3	1 333 198
Adair	67	3	64	114	829	1 356	3 690	–.6	3 398	75.0	61	41.0	59.0	4 459
Adams	59	3	56	61	1 352	1 254	2 109	–5.6	1 867	74.7	2	100.0	–	275
Allamakee	NA	NA	NA	177	NA	1 278	7 142	8.2	5 722	76.4	75	84.0	16.0	4 768
Appanoose	579	49	530	536	4 249	3 900	6 697	4.6	5 779	74.0	16	100.0	–	938
Audubon	69	5	64	118	2 926	1 609	2 995	–7.8	2 773	79.2	2	100.0	–	210
Benton	117	3	114	364	521	1 623	10 377	13.7	9 746	79.4	95	89.5	–	12 249
Black Hawk	5 722	438	5 284	6 340	4 713	5 121	51 759	4.2	49 683	68.9	379	66.2	29.6	39 574
Boone	429	16	413	571	1 631	2 267	10 968	5.8	10 374	75.8	55	89.1	–	6 054
Bremer	253	25	228	397	1 078	1 740	9 337	5.5	8 860	78.2	138	79.7	15.9	17 079
Buchanan	431	9	422	551	2 029	2 643	8 697	5.1	7 933	78.2	42	90.5	–	4 250
Buena Vista	498	31	467	522	2 554	2 615	8 145	.1	7 499	70.4	22	90.9	–	2 858
Butler	23	1	22	172	146	1 093	6 578	1.5	6 175	80.4	21	100.0	–	2 233
Calhoun	178	5	173	127	1 561	1 104	5 219	–2.7	4 513	77.4	11	100.0	–	1 365
Carroll	397	5	392	381	1 825	1 778	9 019	7.9	8 486	74.4	41	100.0	–	6 075
Cass	369	20	349	286	2 523	1 891	6 590	–2.9	6 120	74.6	31	100.0	–	2 894
Cedar	182	11	171	277	1 010	1 594	7 570	5.9	7 147	76.8	76	86.8	–	9 233
Cerro Gordo	2 644	146	2 498	3 061	5 714	6 550	21 488	2.5	19 374	71.5	80	82.5	–	9 994
Cherokee	188	4	184	327	1 422	2 319	5 850	–2.1	5 378	73.7	17	100.0	–	1 959
Chickasaw	6	1	5	217	45	1 632	5 593	2.0	5 192	80.2	9	55.6	–	1 303
Clarke	189	6	183	214	2 255	2 582	3 934	9.3	3 584	72.4	20	100.0	–	2 488
Clay	307	5	302	662	1 747	3 765	7 828	2.2	7 259	69.1	45	100.0	–	4 480
Clayton	19	–	19	212	101	1 113	8 619	3.3	7 375	76.5	96	50.0	27.1	6 867
Clinton	170	3	167	2 237	1 826	4 383	21 585	1.4	20 105	72.9	136	76.5	23.5	14 474
Crawford	146	9	137	299	886	1 782	6 958	.5	6 441	73.0	35	71.4	–	3 460
Dallas	342	33	309	709	2 183	2 383	16 529	39.9	15 584	76.3	283	86.6	4.2	47 023
Davis	43	–	43	127	511	1 528	3 530	4.9	3 207	79.7	8	100.0	–	510
Decatur	9	–	9	156	109	1 871	3 833	3.8	3 337	71.1	10	70.0	–	1 158
Delaware	145	32	113	303	779	1 680	7 682	3.7	6 834	77.8	17	100.0	–	1 853
Des Moines	1 781	197	1 584	2 102	4 236	4 933	18 643	2.2	17 270	74.2	49	71.4	–	5 897
Dickinson	NA	NA	NA	332	NA	2 227	11 375	17.0	7 103	78.0	138	79.7	10.1	18 205
Dubuque	2 264	145	2 119	3 124	2 572	3 616	35 505	10.8	33 690	73.5	341	76.8	3.5	44 983
Emmet	250	10	240	279	2 291	2 412	4 889	–.5	4 450	75.1	33	54.5	36.4	2 888
Fayette	178	3	175	462	816	2 115	9 505	2.6	8 778	75.7	32	78.1	15.6	3 051
Floyd	240	16	224	323	1 464	1 894	7 317	1.2	6 828	74.1	9	100.0	–	1 095
Franklin	120	5	115	331	1 102	2 913	4 763	–5.1	4 356	75.0	8	100.0	–	888
Fremont	NA	NA	NA	273	NA	3 319	3 514	–2.6	3 199	74.5	23	100.0	–	2 083
Greene	82	–	82	201	813	2 001	4 623	–1.8	4 205	75.6	15	100.0	–	2 080
Grundy	88	5	83	117	721	973	5 304	2.8	4 984	79.9	60	60.0	40.0	6 457
Guthrie	74	–	74	165	638	1 509	5 467	5.6	4 641	79.6	59	100.0	–	9 416
Hamilton	332	7	325	482	2 069	2 999	7 082	3.0	6 692	72.8	35	94.3	–	4 567
Hancock	127	7	120	246	1 052	1 947	5 164	–1.4	4 795	78.2	42	66.7	33.3	4 624
Hardin	325	24	301	518	1 756	2 713	8 318	–1.2	7 628	74.6	23	56.5	43.5	2 240
Harrison	256	16	240	218	1 662	1 480	6 602	6.9	6 115	76.6	73	94.5	–	7 203
Henry	354	36	318	518	1 767	2 694	8 246	9.8	7 626	73.0	55	92.7	–	6 850
Howard	160	9	151	142	1 647	1 448	4 327	4.1	3 974	79.2	16	100.0	–	1 365
Humboldt	171	3	168	111	1 652	1 032	4 645	–.5	4 295	76.0	61	27.9	72.1	5 292
Ida	68	–	68	178	857	2 128	3 506	1.0	3 213	73.2	8	100.0	–	1 198
Iowa	43	3	40	128	276	875	6 545	9.0	6 163	77.9	37	67.6	32.4	3 105
Jackson	310	3	307	427	1 540	2 140	8 949	6.2	8 078	76.0	67	73.1	26.9	5 387
Jasper	198	14	184	1 070	959	3 075	15 659	9.2	14 689	75.7	80	82.5	17.5	9 967
Jefferson	575	28	547	436	3 352	2 673	7 241	7.4	6 649	67.2	18	33.3	–	1 958
Johnson	3 531	525	3 006	4 642	3 429	4 829	45 831	23.2	44 080	56.6	1 151	46.0	46.8	122 604
Jones	311	7	304	253	1 525	1 301	8 126	10.3	7 560	75.9	35	82.9	–	2 945
Keokuk	104	5	99	153	902	1 316	5 013	–.2	4 586	78.7	13	100.0	–	1 038

[1] Data on serious crimes have not been adjusted for underreporting; this may affect comparability over time or among geographic areas. [2] Includes murder and nonnegligent manslaughter, forcible rape, robbery, and aggravated assault. [3] Includes burglary, larceny-theft, and motor vehicle theft. [4] Per 100,000 resident population provided by the U.S. Federal Bureau of Investigation.

Sources: Serious Crimes Known to Police—U.S. Federal Bureau of Investigation, Uniform Crime Reporting Program, unpublished data, annual (related Internet site <http://www.fbi.gov/ucr/ucr.htm>). Housing, 2000—U.S. Census Bureau, 2000 Census of Population and Housing, "Census 2000 Profiles of General Demographic Characteristics" data files, published May 2001 (related Internet site <http://www.census.gov/mp/www/pub/2000cen/mscen01.html>). Housing, 1990—U.S. Census Bureau, 1990 Census of Population and Housing, Summary Tape File (STF) 1C on CD-ROM (related Internet site <http://homer.ssd.census.gov/cdrom/lookup>). Building Permits—U.S. Census Bureau, "New Residential Construction–Building Permits," e-mail from Manufacturing and Construction Division/Residential Construction Branch, subject: building permits by place 2000, 22 May 2001 (related Internet site <http://www.census.gov/const/www/permitsindex.html>).

Table B–6. Counties — Crime, Housing, and Building Permits–Con.

[Includes U.S., states, and 3,142 counties or county equivalents defined as of January 1, 1992. For changes to these areas since January 1, 1992, see appendix B. Geographic Information]

County	Serious crimes known to police (as reported to the FBI)[1] Number 1999 Total	Violent[2]	Property[3]	1990	Rate[4] 1999	1990	Housing, 2000 Total units	Percent change, 1990-2000	Occupied units Number	Percent owner-occupied	New private housing units authorized by building permits, 2000 Number	Percent in structures with— One unit	Five units or more	Valuation ($1,000)
IOWA—Con.														
Kossuth	222	22	200	312	1 249	1 678	7 605	-2.1	6 974	77.8	11	81.8	–	1 531
Lee	1 219	143	1 076	1 450	3 161	3 748	16 612	1.0	15 161	75.5	44	31.8	54.5	3 134
Linn	8 100	446	7 654	8 948	4 625	5 302	80 551	17.8	76 753	72.7	1 679	50.6	37.9	131 869
Louisa	141	4	137	347	1 178	2 993	5 133	1.8	4 519	77.3	17	100.0	–	2 321
Lucas	239	7	232	358	2 605	3 947	4 239	1.4	3 811	78.3	1	100.0	–	120
Lyon	128	15	113	102	1 063	853	4 758	4.3	4 428	81.8	21	100.0	–	2 190
Madison	43	4	39	267	467	2 139	5 661	13.3	5 326	78.0	103	89.3	–	10 649
Mahaska	547	34	513	501	2 492	2 328	9 551	6.4	8 880	71.1	32	93.8	–	4 007
Marion	537	59	478	648	1 708	2 160	12 755	11.7	12 017	75.6	238	79.0	16.8	24 047
Marshall	1 464	219	1 245	1 708	3 771	4 462	16 324	2.9	15 338	73.7	61	73.8	–	7 702
Mills	NA	NA	NA	318	NA	2 409	5 671	13.3	5 324	79.5	20	60.0	–	1 345
Mitchell	85	3	82	133	770	1 217	4 594	1.8	4 294	81.6	6	100.0	–	578
Monona	262	16	246	254	2 585	2 531	4 660	2.3	4 211	76.0	41	78.0	–	4 318
Monroe	113	28	85	187	1 402	2 305	3 588	-4.1	3 228	78.4	5	100.0	–	441
Montgomery	124	13	111	493	1 987	4 082	5 399	.7	4 886	73.1	9	100.0	–	899
Muscatine	1 226	182	1 044	1 110	2 974	4 851	16 786	4.6	15 847	75.4	108	100.0	–	11 193
O'Brien	174	6	168	329	1 164	2 130	6 509	.5	6 001	76.9	40	57.5	30.0	4 235
Osceola	69	1	68	69	986	949	3 012	.5	2 778	77.5	4	100.0	–	518
Page	364	12	352	541	2 103	3 207	7 302	-.5	6 708	71.6	22	90.9	–	1 950
Palo Alto	177	7	170	285	1 763	2 671	4 631	-4.0	4 119	74.1	16	87.5	–	2 090
Plymouth	361	17	344	338	1 451	1 445	9 880	12.2	9 372	77.5	101	90.1	5.9	13 771
Pocahontas	35	–	35	63	398	661	3 988	-4.9	3 617	79.3	–	–	–	–
Polk	17 161	1 070	16 091	24 073	4 763	7 359	156 447	15.1	149 112	68.8	2 370	85.6	9.6	310 704
Pottawattamie	5 334	547	4 787	5 405	6 175	6 541	35 761	8.9	33 844	71.1	663	44.5	52.2	57 682
Poweshiek	324	11	313	203	1 713	1 067	8 556	4.4	7 398	71.9	87	69.0	9.2	8 148
Ringgold	3	–	3	42	56	775	2 789	2.8	2 245	75.7	3	100.0	–	255
Sac	135	17	118	119	1 129	966	5 460	-3.3	4 746	76.8	14	100.0	–	1 315
Scott	8 987	1 506	7 481	10 515	5 653	6 965	65 649	7.0	62 334	70.6	701	67.6	30.7	74 421
Shelby	90	8	82	295	1 751	2 230	5 459	.5	5 173	77.0	29	100.0	–	3 644
Sioux	146	8	138	182	641	733	11 260	9.0	10 693	80.5	133	58.6	34.6	14 612
Story	2 528	77	2 451	2 703	3 351	3 640	30 630	14.1	29 383	58.3	674	37.7	59.6	45 561
Tama	291	84	207	336	1 944	1 929	7 583	2.2	7 018	77.5	53	75.5	9.4	5 649
Taylor	41	–	41	104	572	1 462	3 199	-3.3	2 824	76.4	7	100.0	–	672
Union	186	9	177	222	2 427	1 741	5 657	.6	5 242	72.1	17	100.0	–	1 765
Van Buren	80	3	77	136	1 012	1 772	3 581	1.5	3 181	79.7	6	100.0	–	415
Wapello	1 298	134	1 164	1 742	3 654	4 881	15 873	1.5	14 784	75.6	53	100.0	–	4 570
Warren	739	33	706	957	1 834	2 656	15 289	16.2	14 708	79.9	364	42.3	52.7	36 256
Washington	NA	NA	NA	207	NA	1 055	8 543	8.6	8 056	75.3	54	100.0	–	6 696
Wayne	99	7	92	155	1 483	2 193	3 357	.7	2 821	79.3	4	50.0	–	277
Webster	2 165	155	2 010	2 220	5 580	5 503	16 969	-.6	15 878	71.3	82	87.8	–	9 167
Winnebago	82	9	73	166	686	1 369	5 065	.7	4 749	76.1	32	50.0	50.0	2 684
Winneshiek	190	9	181	391	905	1 876	8 208	6.2	7 734	73.5	49	59.2	36.7	5 000
Woodbury	5 710	649	5 061	6 290	5 602	6 400	41 394	5.9	39 151	68.6	203	91.1	–	24 954
Worth	102	4	98	146	1 308	1 827	3 534	2.6	3 278	79.0	7	100.0	–	795
Wright	177	4	173	220	1 261	1 542	6 559	-1.2	5 940	74.2	12	100.0	–	1 579
KANSAS	34 327	3 035	31 292	128 415	7 588	5 195	1 131 200	8.3	1 037 891	69.2	12 542	74.1	19.9	1 397 050
Allen	NA	NA	NA	355	NA	2 425	6 449	-1	5 775	75.0	14	100.0	–	1 216
Anderson	NA	NA	NA	96	NA	1 230	3 596	2.3	3 221	80.0	5	100.0	–	687
Atchison	NA	NA	NA	574	NA	3 390	6 818	1.9	6 275	73.3	11	100.0	–	1 337
Barber	NA	NA	NA	74	NA	1 260	2 740	-12.2	2 235	75.3	1	100.0	–	92
Barton	NA	NA	NA	1 277	NA	4 346	12 888	-1.9	11 393	72.1	12	100.0	–	1 396
Bourbon	NA	NA	NA	433	NA	2 893	7 135	3.1	6 161	74.0	17	64.7	35.3	821
Brown	NA	NA	NA	188	NA	1 689	4 815	-1.5	4 318	71.4	32	25.0	43.8	1 811
Butler	NA	NA	NA	1 582	NA	3 128	23 176	15.5	21 527	77.7	522	72.6	24.5	57 730
Chase	NA	NA	NA	9	NA	298	1 529	-1.2	1 246	73.3	–	–	–	–
Chautauqua	NA	NA	NA	62	NA	1 407	2 169	-3.6	1 796	82.1	X	X	X	X
Cherokee	NA	NA	NA	508	NA	2 377	10 031	6.4	8 875	76.1	18	61.1	38.9	924
Cheyenne	NA	NA	NA	1	NA	31	1 636	-3.0	1 360	77.2	1	100.0	–	240
Clark	NA	NA	NA	13	NA	538	1 111	-16.3	979	76.4	7	100.0	–	908
Clay	NA	NA	NA	115	NA	1 256	4 084	-1.3	3 617	76.7	25	76.0	–	1 930
Cloud	NA	NA	NA	176	NA	1 597	4 838	-6.9	4 163	74.3	–	–	–	–
Coffey	NA	NA	NA	122	NA	1 452	3 876	4.4	3 489	78.3	34	88.2	–	3 088
Comanche	NA	NA	NA	3	NA	130	1 088	-13.4	872	73.9	–	–	–	–
Cowley	NA	NA	NA	1 596	NA	4 323	15 673	.7	14 039	70.8	77	35.1	62.3	5 751
Crawford	NA	NA	NA	1 656	NA	4 656	17 221	4.2	15 504	64.4	146	51.4	40.4	10 708
Decatur	NA	NA	NA	33	NA	821	1 821	-11.7	1 494	76.0	–	–	–	–
Dickinson	NA	NA	NA	231	NA	1 218	8 686	3.2	7 903	74.8	48	100.0	–	4 692

[1] Data on serious crimes have not been adjusted for underreporting; this may affect comparability over time or among geographic areas. [2] Includes murder and nonnegligent manslaughter, forcible rape, robbery, and aggravated assault. [3] Includes burglary, larceny-theft, and motor vehicle theft. [4] Per 100,000 resident population provided by the U.S. Federal Bureau of Investigation.

Sources: Serious Crimes Known to Police—U.S. Federal Bureau of Investigation, Uniform Crime Reporting Program, unpublished data, annual (related Internet site <http://www.fbi.gov/ucr/ucr.htm>). Housing, 2000—U.S. Census Bureau, 2000 Census of Population and Housing, "Census 2000 Profiles of General Demographic Characteristics" data files, published May 2001 (related Internet site <http://www.census.gov/mp/www/pub/2000cen/mscen01.html>). Housing, 1990—U.S. Census Bureau, 1990 Census of Population and Housing, Summary Tape File (STF) 1C on CD-ROM (related Internet site <http://homer.ssd.census.gov/cdrom/lookup>). Building Permits—U.S. Census Bureau, "New Residential Construction–Building Permits," e-mail from Manufacturing and Construction Division/Residential Construction Branch, subject: building permits by place 2000, 22 May 2001 (related Internet site <http://www.census.gov/const/www/permitsindex.html>).

Table B–6. Counties — Crime, Housing, and Building Permits–Con.

[Includes U.S., states, and 3,142 counties or county equivalents defined as of January 1, 1992. For changes to these areas since January 1, 1992, see appendix B. Geographic Information]

County	Serious crimes known to police (as reported to the FBI)[1] Number 1999 Total	Violent[2]	Property[3]	1990	Rate[4] 1999	1990	Housing, 2000 Total units	Percent change, 1990–2000	Occupied units Number	Percent owner-occupied	New private housing units authorized by building permits, 2000 Number	Percent in structures with— One unit	Five units or more	Valuation ($1,000)
KANSAS—Con.														
Doniphan	NA	NA	NA	122	NA	1 500	3 489	4.6	3 173	74.5	15	86.7	–	1 337
Douglas	NA	NA	NA	6 011	NA	7 349	40 250	26.6	38 486	51.9	803	59.5	20.0	83 869
Edwards	NA	NA	NA	16	NA	422	1 754	-6.1	1 455	77.7	–	–	–	–
Elk	NA	NA	NA	85	NA	2 555	1 860	6.7	1 412	81.1	X	X	X	X
Ellis	NA	NA	NA	877	NA	3 373	12 078	8.7	11 193	63.3	35	94.3	–	3 457
Ellsworth	NA	NA	NA	41	NA	623	3 228	-2.7	2 481	79.6	10	80.0	–	746
Finney	NA	NA	NA	2 538	NA	7 675	13 763	17.7	12 948	64.8	62	58.1	–	4 355
Ford	NA	NA	NA	2 018	NA	7 348	11 650	7.5	10 852	64.8	66	90.9	–	6 722
Franklin	NA	NA	NA	547	NA	2 487	10 229	14.6	9 452	73.5	149	93.3	–	17 164
Geary	NA	NA	NA	2 362	NA	7 756	11 959	.1	10 458	50.5	43	95.3	–	4 322
Gove	NA	NA	NA	76	NA	2 352	1 423	-4.8	1 245	79.8	–	–	–	–
Graham	NA	NA	NA	25	NA	706	1 553	-11.4	1 263	79.5	–	–	–	–
Grant	NA	NA	NA	203	NA	2 836	3 027	16.5	2 742	74.6	7	100.0	–	772
Gray	NA	NA	NA	10	NA	185	2 181	3.2	2 045	72.7	10	100.0	–	806
Greeley	NA	NA	NA	4	NA	225	712	-11.1	602	74.4	1	100.0	–	70
Greenwood	NA	NA	NA	67	NA	854	4 273	.7	3 234	75.2	2	100.0	–	147
Hamilton	NA	NA	NA	15	NA	628	1 211	-.2	1 054	69.4	3	100.0	–	376
Harper	NA	NA	NA	110	NA	1 544	3 270	-6.1	2 773	74.3	6	100.0	–	605
Harvey	NA	NA	NA	806	NA	2 598	13 378	8.9	12 581	71.9	124	100.0	–	14 778
Haskell	NA	NA	NA	24	NA	618	1 639	3.3	1 481	72.2	–	–	–	–
Hodgeman	NA	NA	NA	1	NA	46	945	-7.5	796	78.5	X	X	X	X
Jackson	NA	NA	NA	170	NA	2 041	5 094	11.6	4 727	80.6	58	100.0	–	4 708
Jefferson	NA	NA	NA	407	NA	2 559	7 491	18.6	6 830	84.8	121	100.0	–	11 411
Jewell	NA	NA	NA	21	NA	494	2 103	-12.7	1 695	79.4	–	–	–	–
Johnson	NA	NA	NA	15 811	NA	4 453	181 612	26.0	174 570	72.3	5 468	64.1	33.4	656 480
Kearny	NA	NA	NA	127	NA	3 154	1 657	6.1	1 542	73.3	19	100.0	–	1 165
Kingman	NA	NA	NA	64	NA	772	3 852	5.7	3 371	77.8	25	100.0	–	2 768
Kiowa	NA	NA	NA	124	NA	3 388	1 643	-5.5	1 365	71.8	–	–	–	–
Labette	NA	NA	NA	832	NA	3 512	10 306	-3.1	9 194	73.2	66	100.0	–	3 832
Lane	NA	NA	NA	26	NA	1 095	1 065	-4.7	910	77.3	–	–	–	–
Leavenworth	NA	NA	NA	2 452	NA	3 809	24 401	14.8	23 071	67.0	431	82.8	2.3	44 124
Lincoln	NA	NA	NA	24	NA	657	1 853	-.6	1 529	78.3	2	–	–	85
Linn	NA	NA	NA	159	NA	1 926	4 720	-1.9	3 807	82.6	26	100.0	–	3 569
Logan	NA	NA	NA	72	NA	2 337	1 423	-2.9	1 243	76.3	–	–	–	–
Lyon	NA	NA	NA	2 154	NA	6 202	14 757	2.9	13 691	61.0	34	70.6	–	2 735
McPherson	NA	NA	NA	563	NA	2 065	11 830	8.1	11 205	74.0	107	96.3	–	13 193
Marion	NA	NA	NA	157	NA	1 218	5 882	3.9	5 114	79.9	52	92.3	–	4 463
Marshall	NA	NA	NA	188	NA	1 606	4 999	-5.1	4 458	79.5	3	100.0	–	337
Meade	NA	NA	NA	1	NA	24	1 968	-4.0	1 728	74.4	2	100.0	–	200
Miami	NA	NA	NA	545	NA	2 323	10 984	22.4	10 365	78.6	156	94.9	–	23 811
Mitchell	NA	NA	NA	116	NA	1 610	3 340	-.6	2 850	74.6	2	100.0	–	258
Montgomery	NA	NA	NA	2 160	NA	5 565	17 207	-4.0	14 903	71.6	14	100.0	–	814
Morris	NA	NA	NA	117	NA	1 888	3 160	.3	2 539	78.0	9	11.1	–	565
Morton	NA	NA	NA	88	NA	2 529	1 519	.3	1 306	71.3	–	–	–	–
Nemaha	NA	NA	NA	105	NA	1 291	4 340	.5	3 959	80.8	28	35.7	42.9	3 235
Neosho	NA	NA	NA	471	NA	2 765	7 461	-3.4	6 739	74.6	16	50.0	50.0	1 477
Ness	NA	NA	NA	11	NA	273	1 835	-10.4	1 516	76.0	3	100.0	–	136
Norton	NA	NA	NA	66	NA	1 110	2 673	-4.5	2 266	77.8	2	100.0	–	216
Osage	NA	NA	NA	275	NA	1 804	7 018	11.0	6 490	79.8	75	89.3	8.0	8 669
Osborne	NA	NA	NA	6	NA	123	2 419	-3.1	1 940	78.8	3	100.0	–	595
Ottawa	NA	NA	NA	32	NA	568	2 755	6.3	2 430	82.1	5	100.0	–	857
Pawnee	NA	NA	NA	165	NA	2 184	3 114	-8.7	2 739	74.2	3	100.0	–	180
Phillips	NA	NA	NA	32	NA	486	3 088	-5.4	2 496	77.9	3	100.0	–	281
Pottawatomie	NA	NA	NA	190	NA	1 178	7 311	13.0	6 771	78.4	95	97.9	–	12 921
Pratt	NA	NA	NA	435	NA	4 484	4 633	.3	3 963	73.4	26	23.1	38.5	1 945
Rawlins	NA	NA	NA	34	NA	999	1 565	-10.3	1 269	76.8	2	100.0	–	280
Reno	NA	NA	NA	3 369	NA	5 400	27 625	3.8	25 498	70.7	128	87.5	–	14 431
Republic	NA	NA	NA	25	NA	386	3 113	-5.2	2 557	79.0	1	100.0	–	45
Rice	NA	NA	NA	205	NA	1 932	4 609	-5.3	4 050	76.6	5	100.0	–	393
Riley	NA	NA	NA	2 567	NA	3 823	23 397	2.3	22 137	47.2	169	56.8	13.0	20 200
Rooks	NA	NA	NA	82	NA	1 358	2 758	-7.4	2 362	77.1	–	–	–	–
Rush	NA	NA	NA	21	NA	547	1 928	-3.6	1 548	82.0	–	–	–	–
Russell	NA	NA	NA	172	NA	2 195	3 871	-5.1	3 207	75.2	2	100.0	–	230
Saline	NA	NA	NA	2 555	NA	5 182	22 695	7.4	21 436	69.0	139	100.0	–	17 049
Scott	NA	NA	NA	123	NA	2 326	2 291	-.6	2 045	74.4	4	100.0	–	740
Sedgwick	20 977	1 927	19 050	30 578	6 313	7 575	191 133	12.3	176 444	66.2	1 949	88.4	6.6	183 501
Seward	NA	NA	NA	1 330	NA	7 096	8 027	6.0	7 419	64.1	15	100.0	–	1 543
Shawnee	13 350	1 108	12 242	12 687	11 115	7 881	73 768	6.9	68 920	67.4	591	91.0	–	83 668
Sheridan	NA	NA	NA	13	NA	427	1 263	-4.6	1 124	82.3	X	X	X	X

[1] Data on serious crimes have not been adjusted for underreporting; this may affect comparability over time or among geographic areas. [2] Includes murder and nonnegligent manslaughter, forcible rape, robbery, and aggravated assault. [3] Includes burglary, larceny-theft, and motor vehicle theft. [4] Per 100,000 resident population provided by the U.S. Federal Bureau of Investigation.

Sources: Serious Crimes Known to Police—U.S. Federal Bureau of Investigation, Uniform Crime Reporting Program, unpublished data, annual (related Internet site <http://www.fbi.gov/ucr/ucr.htm>). Housing, 2000—U.S. Census Bureau, 2000 Census of Population and Housing, "Census 2000 Profiles of General Demographic Characteristics" data files, published May 2001 (related Internet site <http://www.census.gov/mp/www/pub/2000cen/mscen01.html>). Housing, 1990—U.S. Census Bureau, 1990 Census of Population and Housing, Summary Tape File (STF) 1C on CD-ROM (related Internet site <http://homer.ssd.census.gov/cdrom/lookup>). Building Permits—U.S. Census Bureau, "New Residential Construction–Building Permits," e-mail from Manufacturing and Construction Division/Residential Construction Branch, subject: building permits by place 2000, 22 May 2001 (related Internet site <http://www.census.gov/const/www/permitsindex.html>).

Table B–6. Counties — **Crime, Housing, and Building Permits**–Con.

[Includes U.S., states, and 3,142 counties or county equivalents defined as of January 1, 1992. For changes to these areas since January 1, 1992, see appendix B. Geographic Information]

County	Serious crimes known to police (as reported to the FBI)[1]						Housing, 2000				New private housing units authorized by building permits, 2000			
	Number				Rate[4]				Occupied units			Percent in structures with—		
	1999			1990	1999	1990	Total units	Percent change, 1990–2000	Number	Percent owner–occupied	Number	One unit	Five units or more	Valuation ($1,000)
	Total	Violent[2]	Property[3]											
KANSAS—Con.														
Sherman	NA	NA	NA	348	NA	5 025	3 184	.2	2 758	68.9	11	27.3	–	980
Smith	NA	NA	NA	13	NA	256	2 326	-11.1	1 953	79.6	5	100.0	–	517
Stafford	NA	NA	NA	57	NA	1 062	2 458	-7.8	2 010	77.8	–	–	–	–
Stanton	NA	NA	NA	15	NA	643	1 007	5.3	858	67.8	–	–	–	–
Stevens	NA	NA	NA	80	NA	1 585	2 265	7.0	1 988	75.6	11	45.5	54.5	918
Sumner	NA	NA	NA	596	NA	2 306	10 877	1.0	9 888	76.6	64	100.0	–	7 370
Thomas	NA	NA	NA	296	NA	3 584	3 562	.8	3 226	69.0	3	100.0	–	411
Trego	NA	NA	NA	32	NA	866	1 723	-6.9	1 412	81.1	1	100.0	–	210
Wabaunsee	NA	NA	NA	100	NA	1 514	3 033	6.3	2 633	83.1	32	100.0	–	2 610
Wallace	NA	NA	NA	4	NA	220	791	-5.8	674	77.3	–	–	–	–
Washington	NA	NA	NA	98	NA	1 386	3 142	-6.3	2 673	79.5	–	–	–	–
Wichita	NA	NA	NA	21	NA	761	1 119	-6.0	967	74.0	2	100.0	–	140
Wilson	NA	NA	NA	252	NA	2 449	4 937	-3.0	4 203	78.1	2	100.0	–	182
Woodson	NA	NA	NA	84	NA	2 041	2 076	-5.6	1 642	81.4	7	71.4	–	400
Wyandotte	NA	NA	NA	19 430	NA	11 994	65 892	-4.6	59 700	62.9	239	79.1	20.1	23 345
KENTUCKY	56 767	7 938	48 829	5121 043	4 846	53 286	1 750 927	16.2	1 590 647	70.8	18 460	80.3	14.8	1 767 186
Adair	NA	NA	NA	177	NA	1 152	7 792	21.1	6 747	80.2	–	X	X	X
Allen	NA	NA	NA	104	NA	711	8 057	26.3	6 910	79.0	X	X	X	X
Anderson	NA	NA	NA	297	NA	2 038	7 752	33.6	7 320	79.7	167	90.4	–	5 460
Ballard	NA	NA	NA	140	NA	1 772	3 837	8.0	3 395	81.9	X	X	X	X
Barren	NA	NA	NA	329	NA	968	17 095	20.4	15 346	72.3	61	73.8	–	3 708
Bath	NA	NA	NA	119	NA	1 228	4 994	24.2	4 445	79.8	4	100.0	–	436
Bell	NA	NA	NA	999	NA	3 171	13 341	6.2	12 004	67.6	69	94.2	–	3 615
Boone	2 587	160	2 427	2 382	3 227	4 136	33 351	55.3	31 258	74.3	1 452	87.1	11.6	122 576
Bourbon	NA	NA	NA	538	NA	2 797	8 349	7.3	7 681	65.5	157	100.0	–	16 372
Boyd	1 149	102	1 047	1 246	5 098	2 436	21 976	2.9	20 010	72.9	18	100.0	–	1 842
Boyle	NA	NA	NA	862	NA	3 362	11 418	12.0	10 574	69.3	146	88.4	8.9	15 234
Bracken	NA	NA	NA	26	NA	335	3 715	17.3	3 228	76.9	X	X	X	X
Breathitt	NA	NA	NA	180	NA	1 146	6 812	11.2	6 170	76.5	–	–	–	–
Breckinridge	NA	NA	NA	120	NA	736	9 890	19.7	7 324	81.7	14	100.0	–	704
Bullitt	NA	NA	NA	746	NA	1 568	23 160	39.3	22 171	83.9	689	91.9	6.1	76 181
Butler	NA	NA	NA	105	NA	934	5 815	23.8	5 059	79.6	1	100.0	–	75
Caldwell	NA	NA	NA	373	NA	2 819	6 126	5.7	5 431	77.4	27	100.0	–	1 749
Calloway	NA	NA	NA	740	NA	2 408	16 069	21.3	13 862	68.4	65	33.8	18.5	3 582
Campbell	348	85	263	2 467	1 962	2 942	36 898	12.1	34 742	69.0	299	79.9	20.1	32 083
Carlisle	NA	NA	NA	36	NA	687	2 490	8.5	2 208	83.8	X	X	X	X
Carroll	NA	NA	NA	239	NA	2 572	4 439	14.7	3 940	66.7	4	100.0	–	294
Carter	NA	NA	NA	260	NA	1 068	11 534	24.2	10 342	81.0	15	46.7	–	508
Casey	NA	NA	NA	107	NA	753	7 242	19.8	6 260	80.9	2	100.0	–	219
Christian	NA	NA	NA	2 133	NA	3 094	27 182	16.0	24 857	55.3	329	75.7	17.0	15 513
Clark	NA	NA	NA	1 014	NA	3 438	13 749	18.2	13 015	68.7	390	89.0	9.0	38 267
Clay	NA	NA	NA	377	NA	1 734	9 439	19.0	8 556	74.7	–	–	–	–
Clinton	NA	NA	NA	35	NA	383	4 888	16.7	4 086	77.1	6	–	–	147
Crittenden	NA	NA	NA	114	NA	1 240	4 410	9.2	3 829	80.5	X	X	X	X
Cumberland	NA	NA	NA	45	NA	663	3 567	16.9	2 976	77.6	3	33.3	–	141
Daviess	3 047	148	2 899	3 052	3 323	3 500	38 432	9.7	36 033	70.3	835	84.7	9.6	53 720
Edmonson	NA	NA	NA	184	NA	1 777	6 104	21.9	4 648	85.6	X	X	X	X
Elliott	NA	NA	NA	108	NA	1 673	3 107	17.7	2 638	82.3	X	X	X	X
Estill	NA	NA	NA	110	NA	753	6 824	16.4	6 108	74.0	1	100.0	–	120
Fayette	14 842	1 913	12 929	17 270	6 102	7 663	116 167	18.9	108 288	55.3	2 544	74.6	23.0	243 912
Fleming	NA	NA	NA	63	NA	513	6 120	18.5	5 367	78.9	2	100.0	–	150
Floyd	NA	NA	NA	576	NA	1 322	18 551	8.0	16 881	76.3	6	33.3	–	269
Franklin	NA	NA	NA	1 681	NA	3 840	21 409	15.5	19 907	64.8	230	60.0	31.3	21 800
Fulton	NA	NA	NA	275	NA	3 325	3 697	.4	3 237	64.3	5	100.0	–	283
Gallatin	NA	NA	NA	106	NA	1 966	3 362	46.8	2 902	76.8	–	–	–	–
Garrard	NA	NA	NA	158	NA	1 365	6 414	30.1	5 741	76.4	17	52.9	–	1 143
Grant	NA	NA	NA	326	NA	2 072	9 306	42.2	8 175	74.2	219	71.7	–	19 787
Graves	NA	NA	NA	613	NA	1 827	16 340	12.5	14 841	77.9	15	73.3	–	814
Grayson	NA	NA	NA	257	NA	1 221	12 802	22.6	9 596	77.3	3	–	–	150
Green	NA	NA	NA	86	NA	829	5 420	19.8	4 706	78.2	–	–	–	–
Greenup	NA	NA	NA	510	NA	1 388	15 977	9.0	14 536	81.6	52	92.3	–	6 587
Hancock	NA	NA	NA	46	NA	585	3 600	16.9	3 215	82.4	–	–	–	–
Hardin	700	67	633	2 333	3 573	2 614	37 673	16.4	34 497	66.9	440	92.0	2.7	42 315
Harlan	NA	NA	NA	437	NA	1 234	15 017	1.9	13 291	73.5	–	–	–	–
Harrison	NA	NA	NA	252	NA	1 551	7 660	18.1	7 012	70.5	73	82.2	–	4 544
Hart	NA	NA	NA	158	NA	1 061	8 045	23.8	6 769	77.3	37	94.6	–	1 992

[1] Data on serious crimes have not been adjusted for underreporting; this may affect comparability over time or among geographic areas.   [2] Includes murder and nonnegligent manslaughter, forcible rape, robbery, and aggravated assault.   [3] Includes burglary, larceny-theft, and motor vehicle theft.   [4] Per 100,000 resident population provided by the U.S. Federal Bureau of Investigation.   [5] Includes data not distributed by county.

Sources: Serious Crimes Known to Police—U.S. Federal Bureau of Investigation, Uniform Crime Reporting Program, unpublished data, annual (related Internet site <http://www.fbi.gov/ucr/ucr.htm>).   Housing, 2000—U.S. Census Bureau, 2000 Census of Population and Housing, "Census 2000 Profiles of General Demographic Characteristics" data files, published May 2001 (related Internet site <http://www.census.gov/mp/www/pub/2000cen/mscen01.html>).   Housing, 1990—U.S. Census Bureau, 1990 Census of Population and Housing, Summary Tape File (STF) 1C on CD-ROM (related Internet site <http://homer.ssd.census.gov/cdrom/lookup>).   Building Permits—U.S. Census Bureau, "New Residential Construction–Building Permits," e-mail from Manufacturing and Construction Division/Residential Construction Branch, subject: building permits by place 2000, 22 May 2001 (related Internet site <http://www.census.gov/const/www/permitsindex.html>).

[Includes U.S., states, and 3,142 counties or county equivalents defined as of January 1, 1992. For changes to these areas since January 1, 1992, see appendix B. Geographic Information]

County	Serious crimes known to police (as reported to the FBI)[1] Number 1999 Total	Violent[2]	Property[3]	1990	Rate[4] 1999	1990	Housing, 2000 Total units	Percent change, 1990–2000	Occupied units Number	Percent owner-occupied	New private housing units authorized by building permits, 2000 Number	Percent in structures with— One unit	Five units or more	Valuation ($1,000)
KENTUCKY—Con.														
Henderson	NA	NA	NA	2 772	NA	6 560	19 466	8.6	18 095	67.3	171	81.3	3.5	16 582
Henry	NA	NA	NA	101	NA	788	6 381	17.1	5 844	77.6	127	100.0	–	11 981
Hickman	NA	NA	NA	14	NA	252	2 436	2.6	2 188	81.4	X	X	X	X
Hopkins	1 356	322	1 034	1 870	7 080	4 054	20 668	6.9	18 820	74.7	40	90.0	–	3 823
Jackson	NA	NA	NA	83	NA	694	6 065	23.9	5 307	80.1	–	–	–	–
Jefferson	27 570	4 566	23 004	35 853	4 612	5 392	305 835	8.2	287 012	64.9	3 809	73.4	25.6	381 256
Jessamine	NA	NA	NA	1 097	NA	3 596	14 646	30.7	13 867	67.1	452	75.2	–	44 015
Johnson	NA	NA	NA	273	NA	1 174	10 236	9.1	9 103	76.5	4	100.0	–	609
Kenton	NA	NA	NA	6 100	NA	4 295	63 571	13.3	59 444	66.4	743	73.1	25.6	63 361
Knott	NA	NA	NA	194	NA	1 083	7 579	12.8	6 717	79.6	X	X	X	X
Knox	NA	NA	NA	391	NA	1 318	13 999	19.3	12 416	71.4	2	100.0	–	148
Larue	NA	NA	NA	150	NA	1 284	5 860	21.5	5 275	80.2	109	98.2	–	4 353
Laurel	NA	NA	NA	884	NA	2 035	22 317	31.9	20 353	77.0	17	58.8	29.4	1 266
Lawrence	NA	NA	NA	87	NA	622	7 040	23.9	5 954	78.1	–	–	–	–
Lee	NA	NA	NA	37	NA	499	3 321	9.8	2 985	76.6	X	X	X	X
Leslie	NA	NA	NA	104	NA	762	5 502	9.2	4 885	82.3	X	X	X	X
Letcher	NA	NA	NA	233	NA	863	11 405	5.5	10 085	80.9	–	–	–	–
Lewis	NA	NA	NA	147	NA	1 128	6 173	15.9	5 422	81.2	–	–	–	–
Lincoln	NA	NA	NA	168	NA	838	10 127	26.8	9 206	78.9	206	95.1	–	21 670
Livingston	NA	NA	NA	118	NA	1 302	4 772	14.2	3 996	85.2	X	X	X	X
Logan	NA	NA	NA	526	NA	2 154	11 875	15.3	10 506	75.2	50	22.0	26.0	2 210
Lyon	NA	NA	NA	101	NA	1 525	4 189	21.1	2 898	81.8	11	100.0	–	942
McCracken	1 960	185	1 775	3 128	7 526	4 975	30 361	10.1	27 736	68.7	171	95.3	–	21 193
McCreary	NA	NA	NA	155	NA	993	7 405	22.6	6 520	75.7	X	X	X	X
McLean	NA	NA	NA	78	NA	810	4 392	8.7	3 984	80.3	4	100.0	–	436
Madison	NA	NA	NA	2 003	NA	3 483	29 595	37.9	27 152	59.7	351	65.0	15.7	23 918
Magoffin	NA	NA	NA	126	NA	964	5 447	13.5	5 024	82.0	X	X	X	X
Marion	NA	NA	NA	382	NA	2 315	7 277	19.0	6 613	78.1	7	100.0	–	773
Marshall	NA	NA	NA	446	NA	1 639	14 730	17.6	12 412	82.6	130	96.2	–	13 106
Martin	NA	NA	NA	178	NA	1 421	5 551	18.2	4 776	79.4	X	X	X	X
Mason	NA	NA	NA	386	NA	2 316	7 754	9.4	6 847	67.4	17	100.0	–	2 305
Meade	NA	NA	NA	217	NA	898	10 293	15.6	9 470	73.8	27	33.3	–	2 119
Menifee	NA	NA	NA	86	NA	1 689	3 710	53.2	2 537	81.4	X	X	X	X
Mercer	NA	NA	NA	208	NA	1 086	9 289	13.1	8 423	74.6	117	93.2	–	9 915
Metcalfe	NA	NA	NA	84	NA	937	4 592	21.1	4 016	79.3	X	X	X	X
Monroe	NA	NA	NA	51	NA	447	5 288	8.3	4 741	75.2	X	X	X	X
Montgomery	NA	NA	NA	608	NA	3 108	9 682	24.8	8 902	71.4	134	94.0	–	10 757
Morgan	NA	NA	NA	151	NA	1 296	5 487	20.3	4 752	79.8	X	X	X	X
Muhlenberg	NA	NA	NA	523	NA	1 670	13 675	7.2	12 357	82.8	18	72.2	27.8	975
Nelson	NA	NA	NA	584	NA	1 966	14 934	34.8	13 953	78.0	468	93.8	2.4	40 516
Nicholas	NA	NA	NA	43	NA	639	3 051	4.1	2 710	74.7	3	100.0	–	327
Ohio	NA	NA	NA	419	NA	1 985	9 909	14.2	8 899	80.3	12	83.3	–	1 061
Oldham	NA	NA	NA	603	NA	1 813	15 541	38.7	14 856	86.9	626	89.6	10.4	114 370
Owen	NA	NA	NA	142	NA	1 572	5 345	13.2	4 086	78.3	8	12.5	87.5	269
Owsley	NA	NA	NA	56	NA	1 112	2 247	5.1	1 894	78.5	X	X	X	X
Pendleton	NA	NA	NA	107	NA	889	5 756	20.4	5 170	77.9	–	–	–	–
Perry	NA	NA	NA	949	NA	3 134	12 741	10.2	11 460	77.4	20	50.0	50.0	1 630
Pike	NA	NA	NA	1 202	NA	1 656	30 923	7.5	27 612	78.7	38	73.7	–	2 645
Powell	NA	NA	NA	127	NA	1 087	5 526	24.0	5 044	74.0	X	X	X	X
Pulaski	NA	NA	NA	1 121	NA	2 265	27 181	21.7	22 719	76.0	34	88.2	–	3 570
Robertson	NA	NA	NA	10	NA	471	1 034	8.3	866	78.1	X	X	X	X
Rockcastle	NA	NA	NA	223	NA	1 506	7 353	23.4	6 544	79.5	X	X	X	X
Rowan	NA	NA	NA	727	NA	3 572	8 985	21.8	7 927	69.8	16	100.0	–	574
Russell	NA	NA	NA	231	NA	1 570	9 064	22.9	6 941	79.5	3	100.0	–	150
Scott	NA	NA	NA	1 091	NA	4 571	12 977	41.5	12 110	69.8	186	98.9	–	23 846
Shelby	NA	NA	NA	658	NA	2 651	12 857	33.7	12 104	72.8	422	74.9	19.4	50 436
Simpson	NA	NA	NA	381	NA	2 516	7 016	13.7	6 415	71.8	134	73.1	–	12 121
Spencer	NA	NA	NA	74	NA	1 088	4 555	72.5	4 251	82.6	317	89.6	7.9	31 039
Taylor	NA	NA	NA	275	NA	1 300	10 180	15.7	9 233	72.3	8	100.0	–	755
Todd	NA	NA	NA	104	NA	951	5 121	16.0	4 569	76.6	–	–	–	–
Trigg	NA	NA	NA	191	NA	1 843	6 698	26.8	5 215	81.5	12	100.0	–	1 175
Trimble	NA	NA	NA	73	NA	1 199	3 437	36.9	3 137	80.7	X	X	X	X
Union	NA	NA	NA	471	NA	2 845	6 234	2.3	5 710	77.9	42	100.0	–	4 578
Warren	2 898	363	2 535	4 571	6 426	5 962	38 350	23.5	35 365	64.0	801	78.3	19.7	75 112
Washington	NA	NA	NA	161	NA	1 542	4 542	13.3	4 121	80.0	5	60.0	–	621
Wayne	NA	NA	NA	206	NA	1 179	9 789	25.6	7 913	76.5	–	–	–	–
Webster	NA	NA	NA	92	NA	659	6 250	5.7	5 560	78.1	5	100.0	–	545
Whitley	NA	NA	NA	424	NA	1 272	15 288	14.1	13 780	72.6	25	28.0	–	1 278
Wolfe	NA	NA	NA	139	NA	2 137	3 264	17.5	2 816	73.9	X	X	X	X
Woodford	310	27	283	561	3 742	2 811	9 374	21.9	8 893	72.4	161	97.5	–	26 563

[1] Data on serious crimes have not been adjusted for underreporting; this may affect comparability over time or among geographic areas. [2] Includes murder and nonnegligent manslaughter, forcible rape, robbery, and aggravated assault. [3] Includes burglary, larceny-theft, and motor vehicle theft. [4] Per 100,000 resident population provided by the U.S. Federal Bureau of Investigation.

Sources: Serious Crimes Known to Police—U.S. Federal Bureau of Investigation, Uniform Crime Reporting Program, unpublished data, annual (related Internet site <http://www.fbi.gov/ucr/ucr.htm>). Housing, 2000—U.S. Census Bureau, 2000 Census of Population and Housing, "Census 2000 Profiles of General Demographic Characteristics" data files, published May 2001 (related Internet site <http://www.census.gov/mp/www/pub/2000cen/mscen01.html>). Housing, 1990—U.S. Census Bureau, 1990 Census of Population and Housing, Summary Tape File (STF) 1C on CD-ROM (related Internet site <http://homer.ssd.census.gov/cdrom/lookup>). Building Permits—U.S. Census Bureau, "New Residential Construction–Building Permits," e-mail from Manufacturing and Construction Division/Residential Construction Branch, subject: building permits by place 2000, 22 May 2001 (related Internet site <http://www.census.gov/const/www/permitsindex.html>).

[Includes U.S., states, and 3,142 counties or county equivalents defined as of January 1, 1992. For changes to these areas since January 1, 1992, see appendix B. Geographic Information]

County	Serious crimes known to police (as reported to the FBI)[1]						Housing, 2000				New private housing units authorized by building permits, 2000			
	Number				Rate[4]				Occupied units			Percent in structures with—		
	1999							Percent change, 1990–2000		Percent owner-occupied		One unit	Five units or more	Valuation ($1,000)
	Total	Violent[2]	Property[3]	1990	1999	1990	Total units		Number		Number			
LOUISIANA	241 847	30 579	211 268	241 822	5 737	6 827	1 847 181	7.6	1 656 053	67.9	14 720	89.1	7.3	1 552 997
Acadia	2 090	227	1 863	1 078	3 618	2 284	23 209	8.2	21 142	72.2	152	100.0	–	14 321
Allen	722	139	583	272	3 020	1 890	9 157	10.7	8 102	76.1	17	100.0	–	1 234
Ascension	2 818	241	2 577	1 406	3 931	2 415	29 172	37.8	26 691	82.3	800	99.5	–	73 740
Assumption	417	80	337	331	1 811	1 455	9 635	11.5	8 239	84.0	81	100.0	–	8 706
Avoyelles	446	80	366	298	5 928	1 042	16 576	7.4	14 736	74.4	208	100.0	–	21 422
Beauregard	712	108	604	443	2 225	2 191	14 501	14.5	12 104	79.8	3	100.0	–	220
Bienville	94	24	70	NA	804	NA	7 830	10.5	6 108	77.9	–	–	–	–
Bossier	5 050	667	4 383	4 627	5 399	5 375	40 286	15.1	36 628	69.5	438	100.0	–	52 931
Caddo	20 124	2 234	17 890	23 006	8 294	9 267	108 296	.6	07 074	63.8	505	100.0	–	70 970
Calcasieu	12 570	1 144	11 426	10 551	7 111	6 275	75 995	14.4	68 613	71.6	959	93.1	–	70 748
Caldwell	100	13	87	74	964	754	5 035	11.1	3 941	79.2	12	100.0	–	1 233
Cameron	289	47	242	NA	3 187	NA	5 336	6.1	3 592	85.1	42	100.0	–	3 054
Catahoula	176	61	115	NA	1 590	NA	5 351	4.1	4 082	83.1	24	100.0	–	1 813
Claiborne	393	63	330	296	2 321	2 233	7 815	4.0	6 270	75.8	–	–	–	–
Concordia	557	108	449	116	2 683	2 342	9 148	1.2	7 521	76.1	33	100.0	–	2 914
De Soto	1 366	529	837	1	5 477	19	11 204	2.6	9 691	76.7	–	–	–	–
East Baton Rouge	35 701	3 005	32 696	39 453	9 346	10 754	169 073	7.8	156 365	61.6	1 493	74.3	25.1	110 916
East Carroll	226	46	180	NA	2 536	NA	3 303	–7.3	2 969	62.1	–	–	–	–
East Feliciana	748	267	481	NA	3 585	NA	7 915	22.2	6 699	82.4	1	100.0	–	50
Evangeline	660	102	558	594	2 146	1 785	14 258	7.1	12 736	69.4	112	92.9	–	6 872
Franklin	324	52	272	266	1 461	1 623	8 623	–1.1	7 754	76.3	34	100.0	–	3 247
Grant	642	131	511	272	3 378	1 552	8 531	13.8	7 073	81.7	1	100.0	–	90
Iberia	1 820	178	1 642	1 458	2 486	3 834	27 844	9.3	25 381	73.4	181	100.0	–	22 456
Iberville	960	313	647	366	7 494	5 093	11 953	5.3	10 674	77.4	79	100.0	–	8 419
Jackson	211	59	152	154	1 355	981	7 338	4.2	6 086	77.2	2	100.0	–	212
Jefferson	30 521	3 300	27 221	39 532	6 764	8 818	187 907	1.5	176 234	63.9	817	85.6	13.0	102 487
Jefferson Davis	1 318	295	1 023	838	4 167	5 738	12 824	7.2	11 480	74.9	73	91.8	–	5 870
Lafayette	11 234	1 171	10 063	9 945	6 206	6 036	78 122	15.9	72 372	66.0	898	95.1	–	102 940
Lafourche	3 372	425	2 947	822	3 881	1 178	35 045	11.9	32 057	78.0	285	100.0	–	34 398
La Salle	121	50	71	139	1 092	1 017	6 273	5.1	5 291	83.3	3	100.0	–	327
Lincoln	1 931	193	1 738	2 082	4 740	5 878	17 000	11.2	15 235	60.0	120	87.5	9.2	8 532
Livingston	2 455	387	2 068	917	2 785	1 476	36 212	34.0	32 630	80.7	040	100.0	–	98 306
Madison	298	120	178	367	7 641	2 945	4 979	3.2	4 469	61.9	20	85.0	–	2 427
Morehouse	386	62	324	217	2 780	1 248	12 711	3.2	11 382	71.5	45	15.6	71.1	1 931
Natchitoches	1 660	260	1 400	725	4 481	3 611	16 890	11.0	14 263	64.5	123	55.3	31.7	10 089
Orleans	36 058	5 936	30 122	61 799	7 741	12 436	215 091	–4.6	188 251	46.5	679	51.3	33.7	93 433
Ouachita	11 470	1 414	10 056	9 176	7 858	6 453	60 154	6.8	55 216	64.1	395	92.7	4.3	48 742
Plaquemines	490	79	411	639	1 862	2 499	10 481	11.1	9 021	78.9	118	100.0	–	11 059
Pointe Coupee	535	125	410	NA	2 269	NA	10 297	6.2	8 397	77.7	101	66.3	–	8 924
Rapides	7 766	804	6 962	6 422	6 276	4 910	52 038	1.6	47 120	68.0	440	85.5	13.9	44 877
Red River	288	58	230	NA	2 998	NA	3 988	3.9	3 414	76.3	1	100.0	–	100
Richland	195	2	193	NA	1 510	NA	8 335	3.8	7 490	72.2	33	93.9	–	4 127
Sabine	386	79	307	NA	1 756	NA	13 671	6.9	9 221	81.0	–	–	–	–
St. Bernard	2 080	261	1 819	NA	3 146	NA	26 790	6.5	25 123	74.6	108	88.9	–	6 310
St. Charles	2 036	375	1 661	2 007	4 214	4 729	17 430	8.8	16 422	81.4	176	98.9	–	25 839
St. Helena	224	25	199	NA	2 336	NA	5 034	31.1	3 873	84.9	11	100.0	–	659
St. James	890	293	597	NA	4 209	NA	7 605	9.7	6 992	85.6	16	87.5	–	1 841
St. John the Baptist	1 353	98	1 255	1 287	3 199	3 218	15 532	9.0	14 283	81.0	250	96.8	–	28 804
St. Landry	3 669	650	3 019	800	4 525	1 562	36 216	16.3	32 328	70.7	237	98.3	–	24 692
St. Martin	902	102	800	607	1 896	1 393	20 245	15.1	17 164	81.7	171	100.0	–	16 266
St. Mary	3 180	444	2 736	2 664	5 558	4 586	21 650	–1.1	19 317	73.9	102	88.2	–	9 461
St. Tammany	7 115	672	6 443	4 467	3 763	3 964	75 398	30.0	69 253	80.5	2 019	89.1	7.5	247 548
Tangipahoa	4 786	709	4 077	1 041	5 951	13 189	40 794	21.3	36 558	73.3	552	85.0	–	51 382
Tensas	115	26	89	NA	2 776	NA	3 359	.7	2 416	69.1	28	100.0	–	3 036
Terrebonne	6 998	910	6 088	4 567	6 690	4 709	39 928	12.7	35 997	75.6	411	99.0	–	33 919
Union	592	63	529	167	2 690	5 009	10 873	16.9	8 857	81.2	2	100.0	–	200
Vermilion	1 601	245	1 356	763	3 071	1 963	22 461	10.3	19 832	77.1	125	100.0	–	13 436
Vernon	1 403	235	1 168	1 445	2 831	2 332	21 030	–2.7	18 260	56.7	1	100.0	–	51
Washington	2 038	273	1 765	1 778	4 730	4 117	19 106	8.5	16 467	76.4	116	98.3	–	7 202
Webster	915	236	679	874	2 141	2 406	18 991	3.4	16 501	74.5	77	22.1	77.9	3 809
West Baton Rouge	1 397	146	1 251	617	7 469	4 695	8 370	14.7	7 663	78.8	86	100.0	–	10 529
West Carroll	257	67	190	35	2 503	351	4 980	3.1	4 458	78.9	2	100.0	–	70
West Feliciana	194	11	183	NA	1 442	NA	4 485	32.2	3 645	74.5	59	100.0	–	7 746
Winn	402	60	342	21	2 268	342	7 502	7.1	5 930	74.8	–	–	–	–

[1] Data on serious crimes have not been adjusted for underreporting; this may affect comparability over time or among geographic areas. [2] Includes murder and nonnegligent manslaughter, forcible rape, robbery, and aggravated assault. [3] Includes burglary, larceny-theft, and motor vehicle theft. [4] Per 100,000 resident population provided by the U.S. Federal Bureau of Investigation.

Sources: Serious Crimes Known to Police—U.S. Federal Bureau of Investigation, Uniform Crime Reporting Program, unpublished data, annual (related Internet site <http://www.fbi.gov/ucr/ucr.htm>). Housing, 2000—U.S. Census Bureau, 2000 Census of Population and Housing, "Census 2000 Profiles of General Demographic Characteristics" data files, published May 2001 (related Internet site <http://www.census.gov/mp/www/pub/2000cen/mscen01.html>). Housing, 1990—U.S. Census Bureau, 1990 Census of Population and Housing, Summary Tape File (STF) 1C on CD-ROM (related Internet site <http://homer.ssd.census.gov/cdrom/lookup>). Building Permits—U.S. Census Bureau, "New Residential Construction-Building Permits," e-mail from Manufacturing and Construction Division/Residential Construction Branch, subject: building permits by place 2000, 22 May 2001 (related Internet site <http://www.census.gov/const/www/permitsindex.html>).

[Includes U.S., states, and 3,142 counties or county equivalents defined as of January 1, 1992. For changes to these areas since January 1, 1992, see appendix B. Geographic Information]

County	Serious crimes known to police (as reported to the FBI)[1]						Housing, 2000				New private housing units authorized by building permits, 2000			
	Number				Rate[4]				Occupied units			Percent in structures with—		
	1999			1990	1999	1990	Total units	Percent change, 1990–2000	Number	Percent owner-occupied	Number	One unit	Five units or more	Valuation ($1,000)
	Total	Violent[2]	Property[3]											
MAINE	35 460	1 243	34 217	45 394	2 845	3 697	651 901	11.0	518 200	71.6	⁵6 177	⁵93.1	⁵4.1	⁵722 989
Androscoggin	3 705	169	3 536	4 451	3 633	4 229	45 960	4.9	42 028	63.4	321	96.6	–	34 698
Aroostook	1 623	44	1 579	1 905	2 118	2 191	38 719	.8	30 356	73.0	129	93.8	–	10 414
Cumberland	8 118	309	7 809	13 733	3 179	5 648	122 600	11.6	107 989	66.8	1 678	94.5	2.4	220 974
Franklin	942	18	924	1 311	3 233	4 519	19 159	10.9	11 806	76.1	109	100.0	–	13 915
Hancock	1 316	35	1 281	1 202	2 617	2 560	33 945	11.7	21 864	75.7	378	94.2	–	48 696
Kennebec	3 524	131	3 393	3 862	3 129	3 332	56 364	9.1	47 683	71.2	389	89.5	7.7	33 299
Knox	773	26	747	1 394	2 028	3 839	21 612	13.7	16 608	74.0	236	92.8	2.1	32 499
Lincoln	551	18	533	648	1 720	2 135	20 849	18.9	14 158	83.0	204	100.0	–	23 191
Oxford	1 271	29	1 242	1 549	2 351	2 945	32 295	8.8	22 314	77.0	272	91.2	–	23 042
Penobscot	3 907	133	3 774	4 867	2 735	3 320	66 847	8.9	58 096	69.8	482	73.9	25.5	38 477
Piscataquis	344	30	314	421	1 868	2 257	13 783	4.5	7 278	79.5	43	95.3	–	2 817
Sagadahoc	1 086	31	1 055	1 008	3 014	3 006	16 489	12.7	14 117	72.1	157	100.0	–	18 174
Somerset	1 730	57	1 673	1 450	3 280	2 914	28 222	13.2	20 496	77.8	82	100.0	–	6 211
Waldo	489	18	471	492	1 332	1 490	18 904	16.8	14 726	79.8	219	82.6	14.6	34 072
Washington	861	29	832	775	2 612	2 195	21 919	14.6	14 118	77.7	86	97.7	–	6 715
York	5 220	166	5 054	6 326	2 959	3 844	94 234	17.9	74 563	72.6	1 302	96.5	1.7	166 640
MARYLAND	186 989	23 561	163 428	278 747	4 136	5 830	2 145 283	13.4	1 980 859	67.7	30 358	82.8	16.1	3 232 130
Allegany	2 379	283	2 096	2 388	3 311	3 186	32 984	1.4	29 322	70.2	79	100.0	–	8 094
Anne Arundel	21 368	2 834	18 534	21 184	4 457	4 958	186 937	18.9	178 670	75.5	3 078	80.2	17.9	329 303
Baltimore	36 221	6 099	30 122	42 991	4 982	6 211	313 734	11.4	299 877	67.6	2 707	76.4	22.5	270 037
Calvert	1 676	279	1 397	1 136	2 315	2 211	27 576	45.3	25 447	85.2	931	97.3	2.7	108 425
Caroline	1 142	249	893	574	3 845	2 123	12 028	11.9	11 097	74.1	154	100.0	–	16 387
Carroll	3 373	281	3 092	2 925	2 237	2 371	54 260	24.6	52 503	82.0	1 459	92.3	6.2	169 731
Cecil	2 966	453	2 513	2 812	3 569	3 941	34 461	24.6	31 223	75.0	768	88.9	10.8	74 368
Charles	4 395	700	3 695	4 641	3 699	4 588	43 903	27.3	41 668	78.2	1 233	92.7	7.3	146 861
Dorchester	1 168	199	969	1 235	3 931	4 085	14 681	2.9	12 706	70.1	109	100.0	–	11 120
Frederick	4 761	715	4 046	5 190	2 531	3 455	73 017	33.1	70 060	75.9	2 747	98.1	1.7	306 995
Garrett	517	30	487	625	1 756	2 221	16 761	18.7	11 476	77.9	253	100.0	–	38 741
Harford	5 440	563	4 877	5 751	2 516	3 158	83 146	25.1	79 667	78.0	1 702	90.8	9.2	193 126
Howard	7 772	490	7 282	8 305	3 264	4 433	92 818	27.9	90 043	73.8	2 182	74.7	25.3	240 337
Kent	368	43	325	540	1 931	3 027	9 410	15.0	7 666	70.4	334	100.0	–	34 774
Montgomery	27 249	1 692	25 557	30 489	3 217	4 027	334 632	13.2	324 565	68.7	4 950	59.2	38.7	505 398
Prince George's	49 019	6 660	42 359	52 736	6 257	7 231	302 378	12.0	286 610	61.8	3 456	92.0	8.0	335 676
Queen Anne's	1 221	78	1 143	977	3 056	2 878	16 674	19.6	15 315	83.4	419	100.0	–	54 873
St. Mary's	2 108	276	1 832	2 626	2 387	3 456	34 081	22.3	30 642	71.8	1 163	89.7	9.5	111 987
Somerset	832	143	689	640	3 400	2 730	10 092	7.4	8 361	69.6	27	100.0	–	2 331
Talbot	1 145	114	1 031	1 075	3 438	3 519	16 500	12.3	14 307	71.6	339	100.0	–	47 181
Washington	3 298	413	2 885	3 180	2 571	2 620	52 972	11.6	49 726	65.6	721	77.5	19.7	67 537
Wicomico	4 219	640	3 579	4 182	5 278	5 626	34 401	14.3	32 218	66.5	480	77.3	9.4	45 043
Worcester	2 658	275	2 383	3 267	6 168	9 327	47 360	13.3	19 694	75.0	810	77.4	18.8	92 581
Independent City														
Baltimore city	1 694	52	1 642	79 278	NA	10 771	300 477	−1.1	257 996	50.3	257	85.2	14.8	21 224
MASSACHUSETTS	195 639	33 256	162 383	238 901	3 236	5 044	2 621 989	6.0	2 443 580	61.7	18 000	78.9	15.4	2 741 246
Barnstable	6 893	1 300	5 593	7 815	3 292	4 975	147 083	8.8	94 822	77.8	1 882	94.7	.3	363 417
Berkshire	3 100	365	2 735	1 360	2 688	2 825	66 301	3.1	56 006	66.9	314	84.4	14.0	50 249
Bristol	17 177	2 960	14 217	23 680	3 304	5 426	216 918	7.8	205 411	61.6	1 650	92.5	1.9	210 805
Dukes	369	27	342	437	3 542	6 306	14 836	27.9	6 421	71.3	246	89.0	11.0	33 350
Essex	21 558	2 918	18 640	32 869	3 132	5 271	287 144	5.6	275 419	63.5	1 937	65.9	28.7	288 440
Franklin	2 002	575	1 427	791	2 823	2 017	31 939	5.1	29 466	66.9	207	97.1	–	25 491
Hampden	23 624	5 470	18 154	21 134	5 470	6 045	185 876	3.3	175 288	61.9	750	88.7	6.7	108 645
Hampshire	2 624	305	2 319	2 520	1 974	2 045	58 644	10.5	55 991	65.0	370	96.2	3.2	51 887
Middlesex	30 767	3 634	27 133	39 460	2 162	3 391	576 681	6.0	561 220	61.7	3 617	64.4	29.0	561 733
Nantucket	668	39	629	756	8 477	12 575	9 210	31.2	3 699	63.1	217	85.3	–	63 581
Norfolk	11 199	945	10 254	17 094	1 735	3 376	255 154	7.7	248 827	69.7	1 542	68.0	28.1	278 322
Plymouth	12 345	2 038	10 307	6 044	2 876	2 607	181 524	7.7	168 361	75.6	1 815	88.8	8.0	243 874
Suffolk	40 050	8 166	31 884	75 403	6 214	12 220	292 520	1.1	278 722	33.9	652	16.9	52.8	79 148
Worcester	23 263	4 514	18 749	9 538	3 246	2 237	298 159	6.7	283 927	64.1	2 801	93.7	2.6	382 304

[1] Data on serious crimes have not been adjusted for underreporting; this may affect comparability over time or among geographic areas. [2] Includes murder and nonnegligent manslaughter, forcible rape, robbery, and aggravated assault. [3] Includes burglary, larceny-theft, and motor vehicle theft. [4] Per 100,000 resident population provided by the U.S. Federal Bureau of Investigation. [5] Includes data not distributed by county.

Sources: Serious Crimes Known to Police—U.S. Federal Bureau of Investigation, Uniform Crime Reporting Program, unpublished data, annual (related Internet site <http://www.fbi.gov/ucr/ucr.htm>). Housing, 2000—U.S. Census Bureau, 2000 Census of Population and Housing, "Census 2000 Profiles of General Demographic Characteristics" data files, published May 2001 (related Internet site <http://www.census.gov/mp/www/pub/2000cen/mscen01.html>). Housing, 1990—U.S. Census Bureau, 1990 Census of Population and Housing, Summary Tape File (STF) 1C on CD-ROM (related Internet site <http://homer.ssd.census.gov/cdrom/lookup>). Building Permits—U.S. Census Bureau, "New Residential Construction–Building Permits," e-mail from Manufacturing and Construction Division/Residential Construction Branch, subject: building permits by place 2000, 22 May 2001 (related Internet site <http://www.census.gov/const/www/permitsindex.html>).

[Includes U.S., states, and 3,142 counties or county equivalents defined as of January 1, 1992. For changes to these areas since January 1, 1992, see appendix B. Geographic Information]

County	Serious crimes known to police (as reported to the FBI)[1]						Housing, 2000				New private housing units authorized by building permits, 2000			
	Number				Rate[4]				Occupied units			Percent in structures with—		
	1999			1990	1999	1990	Total units	Percent change, 1990–2000	Number	Percent owner-occupied	Number	One unit	Five units or more	Valuation ($1,000)
	Total	Violent[2]	Property[3]											
MICHIGAN	406 393	54 885	351 508	545 020	4 281	5 961	4 234 279	10.0	3 785 661	73.8	[5]52 489	[5]81.8	[5]15.0	[5]6 255 876
Alcona	203	12	191	317	1 819	3 125	10 584	1.6	5 132	89.9	135	100.0	–	13 424
Alger	141	24	117	201	1 419	2 240	5 964	3.3	3 785	82.5	91	100.0	–	3 960
Allegan	2 185	258	1 927	2 996	2 242	3 310	43 292	19.0	38 165	82.9	689	93.2	3.5	80 529
Alpena	689	65	624	1 109	2 255	3 624	15 289	5.9	12 818	79.1	90	100.0	–	8 328
Antrim	364	30	334	341	1 683	1 919	15 090	14.8	9 222	84.9	308	100.0	–	44 147
Arenac	366	37	329	433	2 219	2 900	9 563	7.6	6 710	84.6	81	100.0	–	6 341
Baraga	76	14	62	247	1 201	3 105	4 631	-1.1	3 353	77.7	58	87.9	–	4 403
Barry	1 054	106	948	1 359	2 171	2 715	23 876	14.3	21 035	85.8	331	96.4	–	43 234
Bay	3 754	331	3 423	5 083	3 395	4 550	46 423	4.9	43 930	79.3	274	90.5	–	36 906
Benzie	282	33	249	507	1 977	4 156	10 312	20.5	6 500	85.7	250	100.0	–	27 157
Berrien	7 058	778	6 280	11 975	4 400	7 420	73 445	5.6	63 569	72.3	507	95.7	2.4	84 030
Branch	1 121	99	1 022	987	2 823	2 518	19 822	7.4	16 349	78.9	123	100.0	–	18 130
Calhoun	8 021	1 021	7 000	6 136	5 662	4 512	58 691	5.5	54 100	73.0	483	76.2	23.8	47 035
Cass	1 286	81	1 205	2 041	2 576	4 125	23 884	5.5	19 676	81.9	322	97.5	–	38 776
Charlevoix	145	31	114	605	846	2 818	15 370	17.2	10 400	81.1	371	100.0	–	55 298
Cheboygan	621	41	580	618	2 604	2 888	16 583	17.7	10 835	82.8	254	94.5	–	27 861
Chippewa	718	66	652	1 183	1 905	3 419	19 430	7.8	13 474	74.0	199	100.0	–	12 919
Clare	725	40	685	1 464	2 440	5 867	22 229	16.2	12 686	82.3	160	91.3	6.3	11 879
Clinton	863	62	801	1 323	1 551	2 313	24 630	17.5	23 653	85.3	680	63.2	32.9	77 309
Crawford	393	27	366	472	2 764	3 850	10 042	15.1	5 625	82.8	100	100.0	–	7 410
Delta	262	33	229	1 186	5 658	3 139	19 223	7.2	15 836	79.6	237	75.9	24.1	23 537
Dickinson	577	33	544	661	2 121	2 464	13 702	6.2	11 386	80.2	106	98.1	–	9 539
Eaton	3 126	227	2 899	4 361	3 198	4 695	42 118	18.6	40 167	74.2	649	80.0	18.5	74 361
Emmet	335	25	310	1 135	3 397	4 533	18 554	26.0	12 577	75.6	492	76.8	15.4	66 494
Genesee	27 870	4 161	23 709	33 322	6 485	7 826	183 630	7.5	169 825	73.2	2 324	75.1	19.4	268 677
Gladwin	515	58	457	652	2 137	2 978	16 828	13.1	10 561	85.7	266	100.0	–	28 368
Gogebic	337	15	322	383	2 071	2 122	10 839	-1.4	7 425	78.8	46	100.0	–	5 368
Grand Traverse	2 244	129	2 115	2 156	3 013	3 354	34 842	21.2	30 396	77.4	979	61.7	36.3	83 748
Gratiot	842	53	789	1 202	2 089	3 083	15 516	5.6	14 501	77.7	112	55.4	42.9	9 062
Hillsdale	1 017	105	912	1 107	2 381	2 549	20 189	8.9	17 335	79.9	331	79.5	18.1	26 422
Houghton	555	30	525	658	1 546	1 856	17 748	2.6	13 793	71.4	122	95.1	–	11 269
Huron	620	42	578	813	1 892	2 326	20 430	3.4	14 597	83.4	206	100.0	–	24 799
Ingham	12 167	1 416	10 751	17 349	5 272	7 045	115 056	6.0	108 593	60.8	987	72.1	21.7	109 003
Ionia	1 171	120	1 051	1 592	1 889	2 792	22 006	11.9	20 606	80.0	424	87.3	12.3	39 514
Iosco	696	47	649	968	2 759	3 204	20 432	4.7	11 727	82.0	161	100.0	–	19 813
Iron	281	22	259	402	2 171	3 051	8 772	-3.0	5 748	82.4	50	100.0	–	4 929
Isabella	1 694	113	1 581	2 345	2 906	4 293	24 528	22.9	22 425	63.2	1 210	24.7	72.3	61 346
Jackson	6 340	704	5 636	7 425	4 292	4 958	62 906	8.5	58 168	76.5	919	74.9	23.6	85 631
Kalamazoo	10 737	1 080	9 657	14 796	4 818	6 623	99 250	11.6	93 479	65.7	1 487	61.0	35.5	181 805
Kalkaska	510	33	477	539	3 260	3 993	10 822	18.3	6 428	85.1	132	98.5	–	11 252
Kent	24 081	2 942	21 139	29 741	4 401	5 941	224 000	16.2	212 890	70.3	3 050	88.4	8.0	376 703
Keweenaw	31	2	29	59	1 485	3 469	2 327	3.1	998	88.8	25	100.0	–	2 704
Lake	509	66	443	666	4 836	7 760	13 498	11.4	4 704	83.0	113	100.0	–	3 361
Lapeer	1 327	112	1 215	2 126	1 583	2 861	32 732	23.8	30 729	84.9	566	100.0	–	81 037
Leelanau	262	15	247	285	1 407	1 724	13 297	19.0	8 436	84.6	329	83.9	15.5	42 004
Lenawee	1 652	197	1 455	2 962	1 932	3 238	39 769	13.3	35 930	78.2	498	95.4	–	55 862
Livingston	2 503	152	2 351	3 754	1 704	3 246	58 919	40.7	55 384	88.0	2 167	86.6	13.4	269 736
Luce	114	12	102	220	1 709	3 817	4 008	11.5	2 481	80.3	30	100.0	–	2 388
Mackinac	585	15	570	797	5 247	7 467	9 413	1.7	5 067	79.2	114	98.2	–	11 731
Macomb	21 310	2 652	18 658	40 428	2 710	5 635	320 276	16.5	309 203	78.9	5 963	85.4	10.4	725 962
Manistee	468	34	434	632	1 997	2 972	14 272	7.1	9 860	81.3	52	65.4	11.5	4 249
Marquette	1 656	137	1 519	2 240	2 768	3 160	32 877	5.9	25 767	69.8	267	89.5	10.5	21 419
Mason	958	82	876	1 089	3 411	4 264	16 063	13.8	11 406	78.4	191	75.9	24.1	15 848
Mecosta	1 292	174	1 118	1 682	3 214	4 508	19 593	13.4	14 915	73.7	263	100.0	–	17 926
Menominee	495	41	454	815	2 014	3 270	13 639	9.0	10 529	79.5	138	100.0	–	10 881
Midland	1 396	113	1 283	2 309	1 750	3 052	33 796	15.2	31 769	78.4	299	78.3	13.4	32 985
Missaukee	329	22	307	228	2 357	1 877	8 621	21.2	5 450	83.7	93	93.5	6.5	9 570
Monroe	3 947	353	3 594	6 212	2 843	4 650	56 471	16.9	53 772	81.0	1 202	59.9	39.1	115 787
Montcalm	1 473	136	1 337	1 930	2 618	3 715	25 900	13.5	22 079	81.6	272	88.2	4.4	20 946
Montmorency	171	11	160	342	1 700	3 827	9 238	5.1	4 455	86.1	99	100.0	–	10 063
Muskegon	9 840	897	8 943	10 776	6 019	6 778	68 556	10.6	63 330	77.7	836	96.1	1.8	103 753
Newaygo	1 302	97	1 205	1 099	2 851	2 981	23 202	15.4	17 599	84.4	210	100.0	–	18 390
Oakland	36 804	3 807	32 997	49 142	3 324	4 854	492 006	13.7	471 115	74.7	5 459	85.3	11.2	929 499

[1] Data on serious crimes have not been adjusted for underreporting; this may affect comparability over time or among geographic areas. [2] Includes murder and nonnegligent manslaughter, forcible rape, robbery, and aggravated assault. [3] Includes burglary, larceny-theft, and motor vehicle theft. [4] Per 100,000 resident population provided by the U.S. Federal Bureau of Investigation. [5] Includes data not distributed by county.

Sources: Serious Crimes Known to Police—U.S. Federal Bureau of Investigation, Uniform Crime Reporting Program, unpublished data, annual (related Internet site <http://www.fbi.gov/ucr/ucr.htm>). Housing, 2000—U.S. Census Bureau, 2000 Census of Population and Housing, "Census 2000 Profiles of General Demographic Characteristics" data files, published May 2001 (related Internet site <http://www.census.gov/mp/www/pub/2000cen/mscen01.html>). Housing, 1990—U.S. Census Bureau, 1990 Census of Population and Housing, Summary Tape File (STF) 1C on CD-ROM (related Internet site <http://homer.ssd.census.gov/cdrom/lookup>). Building Permits—U.S. Census Bureau, "New Residential Construction–Building Permits," e-mail from Manufacturing and Construction Division/Residential Construction Branch, subject: building permits by place 2000, 22 May 2001 (related Internet site <http://www.census.gov/const/www/permitsindex.html>).

[Includes U.S., states, and 3,142 counties or county equivalents defined as of January 1, 1992. For changes to these areas since January 1, 1992, see appendix B. Geographic Information]

County	Serious crimes known to police (as reported to the FBI)[1]						Housing, 2000				New private housing units authorized by building permits, 2000			
	Number				Rate[4]				Occupied units			Percent in structures with—		
	1999			1990	1999	1990	Total units	Percent change, 1990–2000	Number	Percent owner-occupied	Number	One unit	Five units or more	Valuation ($1,000)
	Total	Violent[2]	Property[3]											
MICHIGAN—Con.														
Oceana	461	53	408	490	2 302	2 182	15 009	16.7	9 778	82.7	153	84.3	13.1	15 593
Ogemaw	587	48	539	741	2 757	3 967	15 404	10.2	8 842	84.6	135	100.0	–	7 413
Ontonagon	110	15	95	175	1 782	1 977	5 404	1.4	3 456	85.0	18	100.0	–	1 200
Osceola	435	45	390	678	1 958	3 365	12 853	12.3	8 861	81.4	204	100.0	–	15 984
Oscoda	130	9	121	319	1 457	4 068	8 690	7.1	3 921	85.8	92	100.0	–	7 375
Otsego	484	44	440	622	2 177	3 464	13 375	25.4	8 995	81.7	317	93.7	2.5	39 230
Ottawa	5 734	467	5 267	5 575	2 588	2 969	86 856	30.4	81 662	80.7	2 039	74.5	22.5	239 683
Presque Isle	147	12	135	254	1 014	1 848	9 910	11.1	6 155	85.6	134	100.0	–	12 948
Roscommon	883	65	818	1 398	3 745	7 069	23 109	16.2	11 250	85.9	373	100.0	–	26 558
Saginaw	10 339	1 538	8 801	15 724	5 138	7 419	85 505	4.4	80 430	73.8	972	64.8	30.7	86 072
St. Clair	4 661	456	4 205	5 662	2 904	3 889	67 107	16.7	62 072	79.6	1 076	87.0	10.0	117 949
St. Joseph	2 095	225	1 870	2 419	3 498	4 261	26 503	9.3	23 381	76.9	240	96.7	–	26 151
Sanilac	804	99	705	658	1 910	1 671	21 314	9.5	16 871	81.9	226	100.0	–	15 247
Schoolcraft	104	4	100	202	1 932	2 433	5 700	3.9	3 606	82.0	59	100.0	–	2 854
Shiawassee	1 446	114	1 332	1 861	2 050	2 667	29 087	12.6	26 896	80.1	342	82.2	17.3	30 890
Tuscola	948	96	852	1 220	1 705	2 215	23 378	10.1	21 454	84.1	172	97.7	–	15 384
Van Buren	2 859	312	2 547	4 014	3 801	5 729	33 975	7.8	27 982	79.6	447	92.2	7.4	38 469
Washtenaw	11 974	1 184	10 790	19 206	3 984	6 788	131 069	17.8	125 327	59.7	1 980	94.1	5.1	319 641
Wayne	146 358	26 346	120 012	190 620	6 990	9 160	826 145	–.8	768 440	66.6	4 082	72.0	20.8	529 123
Wexford	1 368	82	1 286	1 199	4 665	4 549	14 872	15.6	11 824	79.3	226	72.6	25.2	19 587
MINNESOTA	169 982	13 061	156 921	5159 526	3 559	53 646	2 065 946	11.8	1 895 127	74.6	32 814	77.9	17.2	4 203 938
Aitkin	549	21	528	692	3 839	5 569	14 168	9.5	6 644	85.4	183	85.8	13.1	17 985
Anoka	11 496	563	10 933	12 111	3 893	4 971	108 091	26.4	106 428	83.4	2 047	96.9	.5	282 243
Becker	385	17	368	1 090	1 297	3 909	16 612	6.7	11 844	80.5	199	96.0	–	21 148
Beltrami	1 773	65	1 708	1 794	4 530	5 218	16 989	15.8	14 337	74.5	85	90.6	–	7 750
Benton	546	19	527	901	1 583	2 985	13 460	16.8	13 065	67.3	396	69.7	29.3	34 354
Big Stone	102	8	94	81	1 785	1 289	3 171	–.7	2 377	85.1	10	100.0	–	1 129
Blue Earth	2 190	65	2 125	2 171	4 030	4 017	21 971	7.9	21 062	66.4	331	64.0	10.3	36 824
Brown	418	12	406	547	1 530	2 027	11 163	3.2	10 598	80.0	39	94.9	–	4 394
Carlton	801	42	759	1 008	2 572	3 445	13 721	11.2	12 064	82.1	301	74.1	25.2	23 406
Carver	1 214	47	1 167	969	1 857	2 022	24 883	42.6	24 356	83.5	1 375	65.5	33.1	193 612
Cass	1 417	105	1 312	1 372	5 298	6 296	21 286	12.8	10 893	85.9	392	97.7	1.8	42 447
Chippewa	149	12	137	145	1 130	1 096	5 855	1.7	5 361	76.6	45	88.9	11.1	2 819
Chisago	945	45	900	998	2 289	3 270	15 533	30.0	14 454	87.1	659	96.4	1.2	72 370
Clay	1 184	82	1 102	2 090	2 271	4 145	19 746	6.5	18 670	71.6	225	80.4	–	22 383
Clearwater	183	23	160	270	2 186	3 249	4 114	2.6	3 330	81.6	5	100.0	–	470
Cook	140	10	130	209	2 891	5 403	4 708	9.2	2 350	78.3	117	90.6	–	11 457
Cottonwood	251	16	235	162	2 062	1 276	5 376	–2.2	4 917	80.4	17	76.5	–	1 587
Crow Wing	2 086	92	1 994	2 510	3 994	5 672	33 483	11.9	22 250	79.7	817	97.1	–	87 242
Dakota	10 333	457	9 876	10 588	2 985	3 847	133 750	30.2	131 151	78.2	3 166	75.3	22.5	427 044
Dodge	279	7	272	291	1 604	1 850	6 642	15.1	6 420	84.0	181	96.7	–	18 231
Douglas	893	27	866	835	2 846	2 912	16 694	14.4	13 276	77.2	356	91.6	8.4	38 114
Faribault	274	15	259	412	1 669	2 433	7 247	–2.3	6 652	80.7	18	100.0	–	1 821
Fillmore	158	9	149	140	752	674	8 908	6.6	8 228	80.9	128	84.4	–	13 870
Freeborn	678	28	650	730	2 124	2 208	13 996	1.5	13 356	78.7	106	60.4	22.6	11 703
Goodhue	1 221	62	1 159	1 290	2 801	3 170	17 879	12.2	16 983	79.0	307	77.5	5.9	39 680
Grant	121	5	116	133	1 938	2 129	3 098	–2.5	2 534	82.1	11	100.0	–	1 097
Hennepin	58 833	6 266	52 567	34 101	5 491	3 303	468 824	5.7	456 129	66.2	4 924	55.0	41.8	728 830
Houston	338	23	315	292	1 736	1 579	8 168	12.6	7 633	81.0	73	97.3	–	10 436
Hubbard	581	22	559	539	3 395	3 608	12 229	21.8	7 435	83.3	55	52.7	47.3	4 326
Isanti	671	30	641	723	2 204	2 789	12 062	24.4	11 236	85.7	330	98.8	–	34 011
Itasca	986	40	946	918	2 225	2 247	24 528	9.0	17 789	83.0	348	100.0	–	37 606
Jackson	160	8	152	230	1 373	1 970	5 092	–.6	4 556	79.0	26	100.0	–	1 805
Kanabec	448	35	413	278	3 128	2 172	6 846	12.3	5 759	84.6	85	97.6	–	8 272
Kandiyohi	1 117	77	1 040	1 422	2 690	3 669	18 415	10.5	15 936	75.6	212	71.7	11.3	22 443
Kittson	77	4	73	92	1 432	1 595	2 719	–5.1	2 167	82.8	10	100.0	–	945
Koochiching	430	22	408	717	2 738	4 399	7 719	–1.4	6 040	80.4	50	96.0	–	4 146
Lac qui Parle	136	7	129	184	1 678	2 062	3 774	–4.6	3 316	80.9	12	100.0	–	1 431
Lake	203	12	191	178	1 901	1 709	6 840	.9	4 646	84.0	131	96.2	3.8	13 819
Lake of the Woods	93	5	88	124	2 017	3 042	3 238	6.2	1 903	85.3	3	100.0	–	216
Le Sueur	275	7	268	224	1 075	964	10 858	11.0	9 630	83.3	204	77.9	11.8	16 854
Lincoln	8	8	–	69	123	1 001	3 043	–.2	2 653	80.3	13	23.1	76.9	843
Lyon	410	35	375	445	1 667	1 795	10 298	6.4	9 715	68.4	97	69.1	10.3	9 920
McLeod	865	63	802	927	2 516	2 894	14 087	13.7	13 449	78.2	190	87.4	8.4	22 926
Mahnomen	317	56	261	140	6 178	2 776	2 700	7.8	1 969	77.2	3	100.0	–	108
Marshall	148	2	146	177	1 420	1 610	4 791	–5.1	4 101	83.6	6	100.0	–	534
Martin	571	18	553	719	2 570	3 138	9 800	–.5	9 067	77.4	92	39.1	58.7	8 573
Meeker	572	43	529	561	2 604	2 691	9 821	7.5	8 590	81.7	147	95.9	–	16 287

[1] Data on serious crimes have not been adjusted for underreporting; this may affect comparability over time or among geographic areas. [2] Includes murder and nonnegligent manslaughter, forcible rape, robbery, and aggravated assault. [3] Includes burglary, larceny-theft, and motor vehicle theft. [4] Per 100,000 resident population provided by the U.S. Federal Bureau of Investigation. [5] Includes data not distributed by county.

Sources: Serious Crimes Known to Police—U.S. Federal Bureau of Investigation, Uniform Crime Reporting Program, unpublished data, annual (related Internet site <http://www.fbi.gov/ucr/ucr.htm>). Housing, 2000—U.S. Census Bureau, 2000 Census of Population and Housing, "Census 2000 Profiles of General Demographic Characteristics" data files, published May 2001 (related Internet site <http://www.census.gov/mp/www/pub/2000cen/mscen01.html>). Housing, 1990—U.S. Census Bureau, 1990 Census of Population and Housing, Summary Tape File (STF) 1C on CD-ROM (related Internet site <http://homer.ssd.census.gov/cdrom/lookup>). Building Permits—U.S. Census Bureau, "New Residential Construction–Building Permits," e-mail from Manufacturing and Construction Division/Residential Construction Branch, subject: building permits by place 2000, 22 May 2001 (related Internet site <http://www.census.gov/const/www/permitsindex.html>).

[Includes U.S., states, and 3,142 counties or county equivalents defined as of January 1, 1992. For changes to these areas since January 1, 1992, see appendix B. Geographic Information]

County	Serious crimes known to police (as reported to the FBI)[1]				Rate[4]		Housing, 2000				New private housing units authorized by building permits, 2000			
	Number								Occupied units			Percent in structures with—		
	1999			1990	1999	1990	Total units	Percent change, 1990–2000	Number	Percent owner–occupied	Number	One unit	Five units or more	Valuation ($1,000)
	Total	Violent[2]	Property[3]											
MINNESOTA—Con.														
Mille Lacs	887	60	827	805	4 171	4 312	10 467	15.5	8 638	80.1	193	96.9	–	20 426
Morrison	761	27	734	770	2 465	2 601	13 870	11.5	11 816	81.9	296	80.4	19.6	29 403
Mower	1 144	68	1 076	1 255	3 056	3 357	16 251	2.7	15 582	78.2	120	89.2	4.2	15 458
Murray	163	8	155	101	1 695	1 046	4 357	–5.5	3 722	84.2	44	95.5	–	3 779
Nicollet	764	29	735	755	2 554	2 689	11 240	12.8	10 642	75.8	139	66.2	13.7	14 365
Nobles	454	34	420	436	2 326	2 169	8 465	4.6	7 939	75.0	24	58.3	–	2 405
Norman	88	3	85	152	1 156	1 906	3 455	–5.3	3 010	81.0	12	100.0	–	823
Olmsted	3 153	208	2 945	3 906	2 673	3 669	49 422	18.8	47 807	75.9	1 552	57.5	30.7	167 560
Otter Tail	1 176	50	1 126	1 195	2 119	2 356	33 862	15.6	22 671	80.0	127	88.2	7.1	12 816
Pennington	440	19	421	580	3 210	4 359	6 033	6.2	5 525	74.4	40	55.0	15.0	3 176
Pine	1 007	36	971	920	4 166	4 327	15 353	20.5	9 939	83.7	82	87.8	–	6 933
Pipestone	180	2	178	76	1 765	724	4 434	1.1	4 069	78.0	34	88.2	–	2 977
Polk	784	65	719	1 008	2 506	3 102	14 008	–1.9	12 070	74.1	92	97.8	–	8 472
Pope	183	7	176	161	1 663	1 498	5 827	–.2	4 513	81.0	75	92.0	–	7 760
Ramsey	25 992	2 483	23 509	30 940	5 296	6 369	206 448	2.7	201 236	63.5	1 105	46.8	33.7	160 494
Red Lake	71	–	71	63	1 645	1 392	1 883	–.8	1 727	80.1	4	50.0	–	275
Redwood	360	30	330	344	2 160	1 994	7 230	1.2	6 674	79.8	36	94.4	–	3 520
Renville	346	24	322	227	2 023	1 284	7 413	–.4	6 779	80.9	29	100.0	–	3 318
Rice	1 640	91	1 549	1 618	2 999	3 290	20 061	14.5	18 888	77.9	427	85.0	6.6	55 846
Rock	173	20	153	NA	1 757	NA	4 137	4.4	3 843	77.9	30	46.7	40.0	2 634
Roseau	428	11	417	334	2 627	2 223	7 101	13.9	6 190	83.8	24	83.3	–	2 023
St. Louis	6 516	438	6 078	7 002	3 333	3 533	95 800	.4	82 619	74.7	581	86.1	4.0	54 705
Scott	2 223	112	2 111	2 132	2 783	3 686	31 609	55.7	30 692	86.5	2 202	89.7	8.4	345 229
Sherburne	1 064	54	1 010	1 302	1 743	3 104	22 827	52.5	21 581	84.1	1 287	86.1	8.5	145 068
Sibley	62	4	58	69	421	480	6 024	7.1	5 772	80.9	64	90.6	–	7 194
Stearns	1 059	50	1 009	4 044	818	3 404	50 291	14.8	47 604	73.8	958	88.6	7.3	106 681
Steele	996	38	958	947	3 106	3 082	13 306	12.4	12 846	80.1	199	86.9	6.0	18 682
Stevens	160	10	150	173	1 562	1 627	4 074	–.8	3 751	70.4	28	100.0	–	2 424
Swift	200	13	187	220	1 832	2 051	4 821	.5	4 353	77.0	22	72.7	–	2 340
Todd	464	28	436	574	1 911	2 457	11 900	5.9	9 342	83.2	146	98.6	–	15 409
Traverse	50	3	47	69	1 165	1 546	2 199	–.9	1 717	80.5	6	100.0	–	794
Wabasha	311	20	291	440	1 469	2 229	9 066	10.5	8 277	82.4	121	98.3	–	15 402
Wadena	314	19	295	425	2 364	3 231	6 334	9.2	5 426	77.6	65	93.8	–	4 540
Waseca	414	26	388	216	2 254	1 195	7 427	7.1	7 059	80.1	96	63.6	34.4	8 123
Washington	5 014	198	4 816	5 259	2 525	3 605	73 635	42.6	71 462	85.7	2 231	80.5	15.1	364 406
Watonwan	294	16	278	245	2 536	2 097	5 036	3.1	4 627	77.1	15	100.0	–	1 326
Wilkin	204	10	194	271	2 760	3 606	3 105	–1.1	2 752	80.8	14	100.0	–	1 650
Winona	1 292	37	1 255	1 758	2 659	3 676	19 551	10.9	18 744	70.8	169	89.9	7.7	19 750
Wright	2 070	69	2 001	1 882	2 406	2 739	34 355	30.4	31 465	84.4	1 572	90.7	8.1	203 411
Yellow Medicine	56	4	52	123	485	1 053	4 873	–2.2	4 439	79.5	26	92.3	–	2 830
MISSISSIPPI	90 385	8 063	82 322	71 574	5 106	4 590	1 161 953	15.0	1 046 434	72.3	11 270	67.6	29.5	917 766
Adams	2 138	138	2 000	1 848	6 210	9 496	15 175	3.1	13 677	70.3	12	100.0	–	675
Alcorn	777	76	701	409	6 329	3 460	15 818	15.4	14 224	73.5	36	80.6	–	3 698
Amite	9	3	6	NA	65	NA	6 446	13.2	5 271	86.0	4	100.0	–	251
Attala	278	18	260	223	1 501	3 192	8 639	12.6	7 567	77.7	63	17.5	63.5	2 207
Benton	NA	NA	NA	NA	NA	NA	3 456	2.3	2 999	84.3	3	33.3	–	68
Bolivar	1 437	89	1 348	NA	8 345	NA	14 939	2.9	13 776	61.1	77	61.0	39.0	5 883
Calhoun	97	23	74	5	873	272	6 902	10.3	6 019	76.3	1	100.0	–	103
Carroll	NA	NA	NA	NA	NA	NA	4 888	23.8	4 071	84.8	X	X	X	X
Chickasaw	98	29	69	25	651	349	7 981	14.1	7 253	77.9	6	100.0	–	407
Choctaw	17	–	17	7	991	445	4 249	20.1	3 686	81.3	2	100.0	–	130
Claiborne	172	26	146	79	1 725	826	4 252	3.7	3 685	80.2	–	–	–	–
Clarke	NA	NA	NA	161	NA	1 104	8 100	14.6	6 978	84.3	7	100.0	–	466
Clay	NA	NA	NA	176	NA	1 393	8 810	13.9	8 152	73.6	25	100.0	–	2 288
Coahoma	299	25	274	942	2 796	2 975	11 490	Z	10 553	57.3	22	100.0	–	1 495
Copiah	NA	NA	NA	178	NA	4 217	11 101	8.2	10 142	79.9	10	100.0	–	348
Covington	304	84	220	19	1 697	748	8 083	23.7	7 126	84.9	2	100.0	–	90
DeSoto	2 558	169	2 389	70	4 755	2 240	40 795	66.7	38 792	79.2	2 475	65.1	34.9	200 907
Forrest	3 705	183	3 522	3 554	6 384	7 142	29 913	7.8	27 183	60.2	317	42.6	54.3	24 340
Franklin	NA	NA	NA	34	NA	411	4 119	15.9	3 211	86.1	2	100.0	–	450
George	27	5	22	NA	883	NA	7 513	12.8	6 742	86.2	2	100.0	–	163
Greene	NA	NA	NA	40	NA	413	4 947	28.0	4 148	87.1	–	–	–	–
Grenada	1 219	121	1 098	535	5 403	4 925	9 973	14.5	8 820	69.2	34	94.1	–	3 054
Hancock	897	43	854	797	5 299	5 934	21 072	27.2	16 897	79.6	105	100.0	–	10 715
Harrison	12 909	690	12 219	7 354	7 210	6 177	79 636	17.4	71 538	62.7	2 222	49.0	49.3	178 633
Hinds	21 277	2 145	19 132	22 574	9 534	8 893	100 287	.4	91 030	63.9	873	69.4	30.6	75 054
Holmes	120	47	73	NA	826	NA	8 439	5.9	7 314	73.3	11	100.0	–	842
Humphreys	243	20	223	29	10 206	239	4 138	–2.2	3 765	61.4	9	100.0	–	423
Issaquena	NA	NA	NA	NA	NA	NA	877	25.6	726	66.9	–	–	–	–

[1] Data on serious crimes have not been adjusted for underreporting; this may affect comparability over time or among geographic areas. [2] Includes murder and nonnegligent manslaughter, forcible rape, robbery, and aggravated assault. [3] Includes burglary, larceny-theft, and motor vehicle theft. [4] Per 100,000 resident population provided by the U.S. Federal Bureau of Investigation.

Sources: Serious Crimes Known to Police—U.S. Federal Bureau of Investigation, Uniform Crime Reporting Program, unpublished data, annual (related Internet site <http://www.fbi.gov/ucr/ucr.htm>). Housing, 2000—U.S. Census Bureau, 2000 Census of Population and Housing, "Census 2000 Profiles of General Demographic Characteristics" data files, published May 2001 (related Internet site <http://www.census.gov/mp/www/pub/2000cen/mscen01.html>). Housing, 1990—U.S. Census Bureau, 1990 Census of Population and Housing, Summary Tape File (STF) 1C on CD-ROM (related Internet site <http://homer.ssd.census.gov/cdrom/lookup>). Building Permits—U.S. Census Bureau, "New Residential Construction–Building Permits," e-mail from Manufacturing and Construction Division/Residential Construction Branch, subject: building permits by place 2000, 22 May 2001 (related Internet site <http://www.census.gov/const/www/permitsindex.html>).

[Includes U.S., states, and 3,142 counties or county equivalents defined as of January 1, 1992. For changes to these areas since January 1, 1992, see appendix B. Geographic Information]

County	Serious crimes known to police (as reported to the FBI)[1] Number 1999 Total	Violent[2]	Property[3]	1990	Rate[4] 1999	1990	Housing, 2000 Total units	Percent change, 1990–2000	Occupied units Number	Percent owner-occupied	New private housing units authorized by building permits, 2000 Number	Percent in structures with— One unit	Five units or more	Valuation ($1,000)
MISSISSIPPI—Con.														
Itawamba	109	4	105	107	2 954	3 159	9 804	20.8	8 773	82.4	36	33.3	66.7	1 042
Jackson	8 107	1 239	6 868	4 094	6 156	7 011	51 678	13.5	47 676	74.6	977	87.5	11.0	66 490
Jasper	17	2	15	49	1 803	340	7 671	14.5	6 708	86.7	19	68.4	–	512
Jefferson	9	2	7	NA	135	NA	3 819	20.6	3 308	80.4	6	100.0	–	116
Jefferson Davis	NA	NA	NA	149	NA	1 060	5 891	10.4	5 177	84.5	–	–	–	
Jones	2 338	166	2 172	2 480	3 953	4 247	26 921	7.5	24 275	76.8	12	100.0	–	2 473
Kemper	NA	NA	NA	3	NA	280	4 533	9.2	3 909	83.8	–	–	–	
Lafayette	532	35	497	921	4 372	9 225	16 587	32.9	14 373	60.6	259	31.3	68.7	21 105
Lamar	NA	NA	NA	7	NA	327	15 433	30.2	14 396	75.8	9	100.0	–	570
Lauderdale	2 624	282	2 342	2 015	3 426	2 667	33 418	7.0	29 990	67.8	98	59.2	40.8	5 448
Lawrence	NA	NA	NA	NA	NA	NA	5 688	10.2	5 040	84.2	4	100.0	–	350
Leake	26	4	22	NA	633	NA	8 585	12.8	7 611	82.0	8	100.0	–	590
Lee	3 494	274	3 220	1 959	4 754	3 049	31 887	22.8	29 200	69.2	112	82.1	–	10 319
Leflore	2 081	138	1 943	1 621	5 964	8 574	14 097	2.2	12 956	53.4	20	100.0	–	2 330
Lincoln	657	88	569	NA	2 056	NA	14 052	15.8	12 538	78.1	8	100.0	–	770
Lowndes	2 431	217	2 214	1 978	3 948	3 335	25 104	8.6	22 849	66.5	170	100.0	–	16 817
Madison	1 901	101	1 800	1 545	3 116	3 533	28 781	38.6	27 219	70.9	606	98.0	–	84 353
Marion	303	24	279	NA	4 343	NA	10 395	2.6	9 336	80.4	3	100.0	–	265
Marshall	NA	NA	NA	NA	NA	NA	13 252	20.6	12 163	80.5	76	100.0	–	3 982
Monroe	589	40	549	453	4 164	3 252	16 236	13.7	14 603	79.0	19	89.5	–	1 243
Montgomery	52	10	42	62	915	500	5 402	8.3	4 690	77.0	84	4.8	95.2	2 182
Neshoba	NA	NA	NA	262	NA	1 056	11 980	22.6	10 694	79.5	14	100.0	–	1 383
Newton	120	17	103	62	2 338	326	9 259	14.4	8 221	81.9	16	43.8	–	860
Noxubee	NA	NA	NA	NA	NA	NA	5 228	12.6	4 470	79.5	3	100.0	–	200
Oktibbeha	1 389	68	1 321	1 792	6 841	4 670	17 344	25.1	15 945	55.6	356	28.7	57.0	14 845
Panola	594	55	539	289	1 894	3 710	13 736	19.6	12 232	77.9	18	100.0	–	1 058
Pearl River	770	63	707	610	5 140	5 737	20 610	30.5	18 078	79.8	340	97.1	–	29 110
Perry	NA	NA	NA	30	NA	276	5 107	19.0	4 420	84.5	4	100.0	–	465
Pike	727	78	649	1 028	5 160	8 869	16 720	11.5	14 792	74.4	12	100.0	–	1 090
Pontotoc	NA	NA	NA	NA	NA	NA	10 816	20.2	10 097	77.9	80	45.0	–	4 688
Prentiss	493	30	463	206	5 843	2 590	10 681	16.7	9 821	77.9	24	100.0	–	2 129
Quitman	NA	NA	NA	NA	NA	NA	3 923	1.1	3 565	68.5	1	100.0	–	41
Rankin	2 439	127	2 312	1 711	2 261	2 005	45 070	41.4	42 089	77.1	791	99.5	–	75 112
Scott	58	5	53	137	1 768	1 656	11 116	17.2	10 183	78.3	17	100.0	–	1 818
Sharkey	NA	NA	NA	32	NA	1 309	2 416	5.5	2 163	65.5	4	100.0	–	120
Simpson	369	28	341	56	1 608	313	11 307	20.6	10 076	81.1	32	100.0	–	2 684
Smith	NA	NA	NA	NA	NA	NA	7 005	19.7	6 046	86.9	4	100.0	–	352
Stone	NA	NA	NA	212	NA	6 656	5 343	28.8	4 747	81.2	10	100.0	–	605
Sunflower	1 438	124	1 314	943	10 663	4 884	10 338	1.7	9 637	61.8	35	100.0	–	1 971
Tallahatchie	NA	NA	NA	NA	NA	NA	5 711	4.0	5 263	76.2	3	100.0	–	179
Tate	201	16	185	101	3 681	666	9 354	25.2	8 850	78.3	157	98.7	–	13 902
Tippah	NA	NA	NA	NA	NA	NA	8 868	13.0	8 108	78.2	20	100.0	–	1 400
Tishomingo	42	8	34	21	1 337	144	9 553	13.0	7 917	78.9	3	100.0	–	220
Tunica	38	2	36	NA	470	NA	3 705	23.9	3 258	51.7	244	11.9	80.7	11 902
Union	90	5	85	NA	539	NA	10 693	17.5	9 786	77.6	16	100.0	–	1 379
Walthall	NA	NA	NA	9	NA	72	6 418	13.7	5 571	83.3	4	100.0	–	105
Warren	2 568	333	2 235	2 104	5 167	4 394	20 789	6.5	18 756	68.2	42	42.9	57.1	2 729
Washington	4 721	499	4 222	4 434	7 601	7 646	24 381	-8	22 158	59.5	126	54.0	–	10 022
Wayne	176	9	167	165	1 169	1 148	9 049	17.2	7 857	85.0	4	100.0	–	364
Webster	NA	NA	NA	62	NA	607	4 344	.4	3 905	78.4	7	71.4	–	485
Wilkinson	NA	NA	NA	NA	NA	NA	5 106	20.4	3 578	83.3	–	–	–	
Winston	141	17	124	4	1 978	21	8 472	11.3	7 578	79.7	16	100.0	–	2 124
Yalobusha	39	10	29	106	445	881	6 224	15.0	5 260	79.0	19	100.0	–	643
Yazoo	121	9	112	696	1 007	5 601	10 015	4.9	9 178	68.8	2	100.0	–	134
MISSOURI	234 794	25 496	209 298	249 123	4 909	5 369	2 442 017	11.0	2 194 594	70.3	24 321	73.7	17.8	2 569 413
Adair	752	27	725	734	4 405	4 279	10 826	7.2	9 669	60.3	111	27.0	53.2	6 369
Andrew	116	9	107	251	1 047	1 715	6 662	14.1	6 273	80.0	39	43.6	30.8	3 030
Atchison	18	3	15	49	256	657	3 103	-5.9	2 722	69.0	6	100.0	–	541
Audrain	568	16	552	456	2 396	1 932	10 881	8.4	9 844	74.1	20	85.0	–	1 584
Barry	290	37	253	440	871	1 923	15 964	23.7	13 398	75.7	83	78.3	–	6 341
Barton	213	15	198	194	1 754	1 715	5 409	7.9	4 895	73.5	13	100.0	–	656
Bates	227	28	199	213	1 901	5 196	7 247	6.9	6 511	75.1	–	–	–	
Benton	280	19	261	310	1 634	2 237	12 691	23.5	7 420	82.2	5	100.0	–	423
Bollinger	NA	NA	NA	46	NA	433	5 522	21.6	4 576	81.3	2	100.0	–	217
Boone	5 325	413	4 912	5 998	4 102	5 337	56 678	26.8	53 094	57.5	1 263	71.2	21.9	118 678
Buchanan	4 708	279	4 429	4 515	5 726	5 434	36 574	2.6	33 557	67.6	247	83.8	16.2	25 287
Butler	2 100	400	1 700	1 821	5 149	4 698	18 707	9.7	16 718	68.9	22	100.0	–	1 860
Caldwell	37	4	33	66	416	788	4 493	23.1	3 523	77.3	2	100.0	–	71
Callaway	399	39	360	431	3 502	4 296	16 167	24.3	14 416	76.8	124	30.6	38.7	12 108

[1] Data on serious crimes have not been adjusted for underreporting; this may affect comparability over time or among geographic areas. [2] Includes murder and nonnegligent manslaughter, forcible rape, robbery, and aggravated assault. [3] Includes burglary, larceny-theft, and motor vehicle theft. [4] Per 100,000 resident population provided by the U.S. Federal Bureau of Investigation.

Sources: Serious Crimes Known to Police—U.S. Federal Bureau of Investigation, Uniform Crime Reporting Program, unpublished data, annual (related Internet site <http://www.fbi.gov/ucr/ucr.htm>). Housing, 2000—U.S. Census Bureau, 2000 Census of Population and Housing, "Census 2000 Profiles of General Demographic Characteristics" data files, published May 2001 (related Internet site <http://www.census.gov/mp/www/pub/2000cen/mscen01.html>). Housing, 1990—U.S. Census Bureau, 1990 Census of Population and Housing, Summary Tape File (STF) 1C on CD-ROM (related Internet site <http://homer.ssd.census.gov/cdrom/lookup>). Building Permits—U.S. Census Bureau, "New Residential Construction–Building Permits," e-mail from Manufacturing and Construction Division/Residential Construction Branch, subject: building permits by place 2000, 22 May 2001 (related Internet site <http://www.census.gov/const/www/permitsindex.html>).

Table B–6. Counties — Crime, Housing, and Building Permits–Con.

[Includes U.S., states, and 3,142 counties or county equivalents defined as of January 1, 1992. For changes to these areas since January 1, 1992, see appendix B. Geographic Information]

County	Serious crimes known to police (as reported to the FBI)[1]						Housing, 2000				New private housing units authorized by building permits, 2000			
	Number				Rate[4]				Occupied units			Percent in structures with—		
	1999			1990	1999	1990	Total units	Percent change, 1990–2000	Number	Percent owner-occupied	Number	One unit	Five units or more	Valuation ($1,000)
	Total	Violent[2]	Property[3]											
MISSOURI—Con.														
Camden	1 071	163	908	496	3 137	1 804	33 470	30.4	15 779	82.2	122	20.5	43.4	7 292
Cape Girardeau	3 207	107	3 100	2 567	4 810	4 165	29 434	16.3	26 980	68.4	330	45.5	45.5	29 083
Carroll	73	8	65	99	1 140	921	4 897	-2.1	4 169	74.0	6	100.0	–	649
Carter	NA	NA	NA	NA	NA	NA	3 028	12.4	2 378	76.8	1	100.0	–	100
Cass	1 821	223	1 598	1 214	2 327	4 093	31 677	30.2	30 168	79.5	811	78.5	1.7	83 389
Cedar	203	17	186	37	1 528	306	6 813	12.9	5 685	78.3	12	83.3	–	1 147
Chariton	19	–	19	65	219	706	4 250	-5.1	3 469	80.6	4	100.0	–	433
Christian	393	8	385	414	798	1 268	21 827	70.4	20 425	75.9	545	86.6	2.9	47 724
Clark	NA	NA	NA	NA	NA	NA	3 483	2.5	2 966	78.5	4	100.0	–	433
Clay	12 191	1 540	10 651	10 720	6 881	8 063	76 230	21.0	72 558	70.7	653	99.5	–	80 884
Clinton	107	20	87	85	2 567	3 518	7 877	20.1	7 152	78.9	180	92.2	4.4	17 407
Cole	2 197	165	2 032	2 162	3 153	3 400	28 915	15.9	27 040	67.8	631	70.8	2.5	76 948
Cooper	273	10	263	207	3 576	1 395	6 676	11.2	5 932	74.1	75	26.7	64.0	6 188
Crawford	355	22	333	282	1 593	1 471	10 850	20.2	8 858	76.6	19	100.0	–	1 462
Dade	83	20	63	NA	1 046	NA	3 758	6.1	3 202	78.5	–	–	–	–
Dallas	NA	NA	NA	164	NA	1 297	6 914	26.1	6 030	79.2	X	X	X	X
Daviess	89	12	77	94	1 129	1 195	3 853	6.6	3 178	76.6	2	100.0	–	180
DeKalb	156	23	133	160	1 394	1 605	3 839	14.3	3 528	73.6	–	–	–	–
Dent	149	2	147	NA	3 147	NA	6 994	14.4	5 982	74.2	3	100.0	–	220
Douglas	NA	NA	NA	126	NA	1 061	5 919	15.9	5 201	79.0	12	100.0	–	1 221
Dunklin	1 013	172	841	497	3 081	1 776	14 682	4.1	13 411	66.0	48	70.8	–	3 933
Franklin	2 019	160	1 859	2 401	2 188	2 979	38 295	18.0	34 945	78.1	575	92.0	1.7	91 384
Gasconade	NA	NA	NA	99	NA	880	7 813	9.2	6 171	80.4	11	100.0	–	787
Gentry	6	2	4	NA	86	NA	3 214	-.6	2 747	75.5	4	100.0	–	275
Greene	13 318	671	12 647	14 273	5 841	6 864	104 517	18.9	97 859	63.6	1 914	68.5	28.0	201 683
Grundy	292	29	263	201	2 859	1 908	5 102	-.2	4 382	71.8	20	100.0	–	1 592
Harrison	NA	NA	NA	81	NA	956	4 316	1.7	3 658	74.8	11	100.0	–	1 183
Henry	743	35	708	686	3 480	3 422	10 261	10.1	9 133	72.9	53	43.4	45.3	3 475
Hickory	NA	NA	NA	150	NA	2 045	6 184	12.8	3 911	84.5	–	–	–	–
Holt	NA	NA	NA	45	NA	746	2 931	-8.1	2 237	74.5	4	100.0	–	378
Howard	42	5	37	79	1 481	2 735	4 346	8.0	3 836	75.3	3	100.0	–	260
Howell	963	117	846	545	2 677	6 115	16 340	22.6	14 762	73.6	63	96.8	–	5 676
Iron	48	5	43	40	2 152	373	4 907	4.4	4 197	75.9	2	100.0	–	280
Jackson	54 778	6 988	47 790	59 694	8 318	9 495	288 231	2.7	266 294	62.9	4 347	71.0	16.7	461 250
Jasper	4 622	177	4 445	5 045	4 721	5 577	45 571	15.2	41 412	67.0	444	81.8	10.8	36 559
Jefferson	4 614	502	4 112	5 240	2 345	3 058	75 586	19.2	71 499	83.4	1 272	97.6	.8	137 783
Johnson	644	35	609	1 074	3 675	2 526	18 886	18.0	17 410	61.7	73	67.1	8.2	5 981
Knox	NA	NA	NA	NA	NA	NA	2 317	2.8	1 791	77.4	2	100.0	–	180
Laclede	758	67	691	719	6 441	2 647	14 320	23.8	12 760	72.8	106	71.7	–	8 042
Lafayette	413	9	404	259	1 258	833	13 707	6.9	12 569	75.4	16	100.0	–	2 042
Lawrence	242	50	192	212	916	3 282	14 789	15.6	13 568	74.3	38	52.6	42.1	2 358
Lewis	104	23	81	53	1 014	2 021	4 602	8.4	3 956	76.5	8	25.0	75.0	360
Lincoln	NA	NA	NA	NA	NA	NA	15 511	26.3	13 851	80.7	114	98.2	–	11 005
Linn	109	7	102	292	785	2 103	6 554	-.2	5 697	76.9	10	60.0	–	902
Livingston	314	32	282	148	3 760	2 557	6 467	2.7	5 736	70.7	34	100.0	–	2 789
McDonald	NA	NA	NA	110	NA	649	9 287	26.8	8 113	71.4	7	42.9	–	388
Macon	14	4	10	70	141	1 257	7 502	7.9	6 501	76.2	11	100.0	–	1 190
Madison	NA	NA	NA	25	NA	225	5 656	7.1	4 711	76.2	8	100.0	–	470
Maries	NA	NA	NA	84	NA	1 053	4 149	11.7	3 519	81.7	X	X	X	X
Marion	1 056	146	910	995	3 782	3 594	12 443	3.5	11 066	70.3	107	51.4	–	8 791
Mercer	48	8	40	7	1 193	188	2 125	-4.5	1 600	76.8	–	–	–	–
Miller	528	120	408	NA	2 342	NA	11 263	15.3	9 284	75.0	55	20.0	80.0	3 115
Mississippi	497	160	337	109	10 890	1 165	5 840	1.4	5 383	63.6	23	65.2	–	1 136
Moniteau	NA	NA	NA	NA	NA	NA	5 742	13.9	5 259	77.7	4	100.0	–	517
Monroe	NA	NA	NA	25	NA	275	4 565	11.0	3 656	78.7	34	100.0	–	2 071
Montgomery	126	8	118	NA	1 038	NA	5 726	9.3	4 775	78.5	23	82.6	–	2 169
Morgan	327	43	284	407	1 764	2 613	13 898	9.9	7 850	82.8	X	X	X	X
New Madrid	NA	NA	NA	145	NA	825	8 600	.5	7 824	66.0	15	100.0	–	1 185
Newton	1 086	51	1 035	886	7 683	7 094	21 897	19.1	20 140	76.6	37	100.0	–	3 300
Nodaway	380	16	364	523	1 819	2 409	8 909	6.7	8 138	63.7	59	39.0	27.1	4 824
Oregon	NA	NA	NA	34	NA	359	4 997	11.4	4 263	78.2	–	–	–	–
Osage	NA	NA	NA	88	NA	732	5 904	9.1	4 922	82.9	X	X	X	X
Ozark	130	5	125	124	1 306	1 442	5 114	14.9	3 950	81.3	5	100.0	–	188
Pemiscot	249	52	197	114	1 151	520	8 793	-.1	7 855	58.3	36	72.2	27.8	1 888
Perry	99	3	96	129	566	775	7 815	13.8	6 904	80.1	57	100.0	–	4 688
Pettis	1 409	153	1 256	1 084	6 853	5 475	16 963	9.8	15 568	72.5	16	87.5	–	1 505
Phelps	1 180	74	1 106	656	3 041	4 656	17 501	18.9	15 683	65.5	166	41.0	39.8	10 208
Pike	72	2	70	89	762	986	7 493	5.1	6 451	74.0	13	100.0	–	975
Platte	4 275	584	3 691	3 494	6 068	6 038	30 902	26.8	29 278	67.5	467	81.2	5.1	72 858
Polk	555	19	536	389	2 162	1 782	11 183	24.5	9 917	72.8	66	60.6	–	5 363

[1] Data on serious crimes have not been adjusted for underreporting; this may affect comparability over time or among geographic areas. [2] Includes murder and nonnegligent manslaughter, forcible rape, robbery, and aggravated assault. [3] Includes burglary, larceny-theft, and motor vehicle theft. [4] Per 100,000 resident population provided by the U.S. Federal Bureau of Investigation.

Sources: Serious Crimes Known to Police—U.S. Federal Bureau of Investigation, Uniform Crime Reporting Program, unpublished data, annual (related Internet site <http://www.fbi.gov/ucr/ucr.htm>). Housing, 2000—U.S. Census Bureau, 2000 Census of Population and Housing, "Census 2000 Profiles of General Demographic Characteristics" data files, published May 2001 (related Internet site <http://www.census.gov/mp/www/pub/2000cen/mscen01.html>). Housing, 1990—U.S. Census Bureau, 1990 Census of Population and Housing, Summary Tape File (STF) 1C on CD-ROM (related Internet site <http://homer.ssd.census.gov/cdrom/lookup>). Building Permits—U.S. Census Bureau, "New Residential Construction–Building Permits," e-mail from Manufacturing and Construction Division/Residential Construction Branch, subject: building permits by place 2000, 22 May 2001 (related Internet site <http://www.census.gov/const/www/permitsindex.html>).

[Includes U.S., states, and 3,142 counties or county equivalents defined as of January 1, 1992. For changes to these areas since January 1, 1992, see appendix B. Geographic Information]

County	Serious crimes known to police (as reported to the FBI)[1]						Housing, 2000				New private housing units authorized by building permits, 2000			
	Number				Rate[4]				Occupied units			Percent in structures with—		
	1999							Percent change, 1990–2000					Five units or more	
	Total	Violent[2]	Property[3]	1990	1999	1990	Total units		Number	Percent owner–occupied	Number	One unit		Valuation ($1,000)
MISSOURI—Con.														
Pulaski	213	26	187	350	577	847	15 408	11.3	13 433	58.1	7	71.4	–	613
Putnam	18	2	16	NA	5 505	NA	2 914	12.5	2 228	77.0	4	100.0	–	330
Ralls	NA	NA	NA	10	NA	4 630	4 564	21.2	3 736	82.2	2	100.0	–	135
Randolph	862	67	795	582	3 568	4 533	10 740	6.0	9 199	72.1	21	100.0	–	2 348
Ray	391	55	336	452	1 640	2 057	9 371	8.8	8 743	79.5	99	96.0	–	10 094
Reynolds	NA	NA	NA	78	NA	1 171	3 759	6.3	2 721	77.3	X	X	X	X
Ripley	141	7	134	7	997	57	6 392	14.2	5 416	77.9	3	100.0	–	325
St. Charles	7 668	529	7 139	7 529	2 800	3 536	105 514	33.4	101 663	82.0	4 001	74.1	25.0	392 862
St. Clair	NA	NA	NA	213	NA	2 519	5 205	12.1	4 040	79.4	X	X	X	X
Ste. Genevieve	199	23	176	244	1 131	1 521	8 018	18.5	6 586	82.3	9	100.0	–	1 432
St. Francois	300	34	266	1 021	2 479	2 088	24 449	20.3	20 793	73.1	240	50.8	40.0	19 147
St. Louis	36 668	2 337	34 331	39 702	3 695	4 043	423 749	5.5	404 312	74.1	2 691	74.1	17.6	370 200
Saline	495	14	481	574	2 168	2 440	10 019	-.1	9 015	69.1	23	65.2	–	1 933
Schuyler	67	1	66	48	1 500	1 133	2 027	2.1	1 725	75.5	20	100.0	–	2 163
Scotland	NA	NA	NA	24	NA	498	2 292	-.4	1 902	76.6	6	100.0	–	423
Scott	1 236	163	1 073	1 365	5 916	3 467	16 951	6.7	15 626	69.4	59	89.8	–	5 473
Shannon	59	19	40	5	711	66	3 862	16.6	3 319	79.2	13	7.7	–	15
Shelby	47	4	43	69	687	994	3 245	-1.0	2 745	74.7	–	–	–	–
Stoddard	230	56	174	110	3 008	381	13 221	7.6	12 064	72.4	33	100.0	–	2 483
Stone	621	61	560	111	2 304	582	16 241	43.8	11 822	81.2	24	91.7	–	1 881
Sullivan	NA	NA	NA	42	NA	664	3 364	8.8	2 925	71.5	6	100.0	–	643
Taney	1 052	104	948	831	20 965	3 251	19 688	48.3	16 158	68.9	475	48.2	51.4	34 918
Texas	NA	NA	NA	NA	NA	NA	10 764	13.0	9 378	76.6	9	100.0	–	620
Vernon	910	45	865	718	4 657	3 771	8 872	8.4	7 966	72.2	15	100.0	–	1 318
Warren	658	55	603	466	2 660	2 386	11 046	24.9	9 185	83.1	321	78.2	17.4	35 971
Washington	422	41	381	365	1 827	1 791	9 894	22.5	8 406	80.0	1	100.0	–	100
Wayne	83	3	80	138	632	1 196	7 496	17.0	5 551	78.2	X	X	X	X
Webster	243	75	168	32	830	135	12 052	32.9	11 073	77.9	99	65.7	24.2	6 567
Worth	7	1	6	2	303	82	1 245	-1.9	1 009	76.6	–	–	–	–
Wright	NA	NA	NA	NA	NA	NA	7 957	10.3	7 081	73.1	15	100.0	–	1 243
Independent City														
St. Louis city	47 711	7 611	40 100	58 199	13 998	14 671	176 354	-9.5	147 076	46.9	397	40.8	38.0	37 265
MONTANA	18 674	974	17 700	31 834	3 699	4 289	412 633	14.3	358 667	69.1	2 572	60.8	19.0	235 126
Beaverhead	NA	NA	NA	3	NA	68	4 571	10.7	3 684	63.4	9	77.8	–	1 167
Big Horn	NA	NA	NA	388	NA	3 422	4 655	8.2	3 924	64.6	5	–	100.0	156
Blaine	47	3	44	31	656	461	2 947	.6	2 501	61.1	2	100.0	–	175
Broadwater	NA	NA	NA	137	NA	4 129	2 002	25.7	1 752	79.4	6	100.0	–	345
Carbon	82	4	78	143	949	1 770	5 494	13.8	4 065	74.4	27	100.0	–	2 810
Carter	NA	NA	NA	NA	NA	NA	811	-.6	543	74.8	–	–	–	–
Cascade	3 820	126	3 694	5 301	6 687	6 823	35 225	6.5	32 547	64.9	99	81.8	12.1	11 989
Chouteau	97	9	88	100	1 865	1 834	2 776	4.0	2 226	68.8	2	100.0	–	170
Custer	NA	NA	NA	329	NA	2 813	5 360	-.8	4 768	70.2	8	100.0	–	676
Daniels	NA	NA	NA	10	NA	899	1 154	-5.4	892	78.4	1	100.0	–	65
Dawson	NA	NA	NA	23	NA	242	4 168	-7.1	3 625	74.0	1	100.0	–	220
Deer Lodge	242	12	230	436	2 414	4 242	4 958	2.7	3 995	73.6	11	100.0	–	793
Fallon	NA	NA	NA	12	NA	387	1 410	-7.5	1 140	77.4	–	–	–	–
Fergus	251	26	225	384	2 040	3 178	5 558	-3.0	4 860	73.5	5	100.0	–	464
Flathead	1 280	90	1 190	3 330	2 477	5 623	34 773	28.9	29 588	73.3	234	80.3	–	27 323
Gallatin	357	14	343	492	986	1 770	29 489	38.1	26 323	62.4	723	43.8	20.1	60 308
Garfield	NA	NA	NA	NA	NA	NA	961	4.0	532	73.7	–	–	–	–
Glacier	NA	NA	NA	NA	NA	NA	5 243	9.3	4 304	62.0	1	100.0	–	70
Golden Valley	NA	NA	NA	NA	NA	NA	450	4.2	365	77.3	–	–	–	–
Granite	103	25	78	57	3 852	2 237	2 074	7.8	1 200	74.4	–	–	–	–
Hill	961	27	934	813	5 517	4 605	7 453	1.5	6 457	64.3	5	100.0	–	592
Jefferson	NA	NA	NA	6	NA	76	4 199	27.2	3 747	83.2	3	100.0	–	105
Judith Basin	NA	NA	NA	NA	NA	NA	1 325	-1.6	951	77.1	–	–	–	–
Lake	NA	NA	NA	795	NA	3 778	13 605	24.0	10 192	71.4	65	52.3	41.5	5 622
Lewis and Clark	NA	NA	NA	2 480	NA	5 222	25 672	19.9	22 850	70.1	99	40.4	–	8 078
Liberty	33	1	32	37	1 417	1 612	1 070	6.3	833	71.3	–	–	–	–
Lincoln	34	3	31	574	3 320	3 473	9 319	16.5	7 764	76.6	22	9.1	81.8	275
McCone	10	4	6	3	508	132	1 087	-6.4	810	78.0	–	–	–	–
Madison	40	3	37	103	580	1 720	4 671	19.7	2 956	70.4	2	100.0	–	905
Meagher	21	4	17	2	1 165	110	1 363	8.3	803	73.2	–	–	–	–
Mineral	NA	NA	NA	27	NA	814	1 961	19.9	1 584	73.4	5	100.0	–	645
Missoula	4 052	258	3 794	4 582	7 736	5 823	41 319	23.5	38 439	61.9	571	52.4	38.5	40 178
Musselshell	20	3	17	49	433	1 193	2 317	6.1	1 878	76.9	1	100.0	–	77
Park	213	2	211	437	2 891	3 001	8 247	19.1	6 828	66.4	15	33.3	–	518
Petroleum	NA	NA	NA	NA	NA	NA	292	-.3	211	74.4	–	–	–	–

[1] Data on serious crimes have not been adjusted for underreporting; this may affect comparability over time or among geographic areas. [2] Includes murder and nonnegligent manslaughter, forcible rape, robbery, and aggravated assault. [3] Includes burglary, larceny-theft, and motor vehicle theft. [4] Per 100,000 resident population provided by the U.S. Federal Bureau of Investigation.

Sources: Serious Crimes Known to Police—U.S. Federal Bureau of Investigation, Uniform Crime Reporting Program, unpublished data, annual (related Internet site <http://www.fbi.gov/ucr/ ucr.htm>). Housing, 2000—U.S. Census Bureau, 2000 Census of Population and Housing, "Census 2000 Profiles of General Demographic Characteristics" data files, published May 2001 (related Internet site <http://www.census.gov/mp/www/pub/2000cen/mscen01.html>). Housing, 1990—U.S. Census Bureau, 1990 Census of Population and Housing, Summary Tape File (STF) 1C on CD-ROM (related Internet site <http://homer.ssd.census.gov/cdrom/lookup>). Building Permits—U.S. Census Bureau, "New Residential Construction–Building Permits," e-mail from Manufacturing and Construction Division/Residential Construction Branch, subject: building permits by place 2000, 22 May 2001 (related Internet site <http://www.census.gov/const/www/permitsindex.html>).

[Includes U.S., states, and 3,142 counties or county equivalents defined as of January 1, 1992. For changes to these areas since January 1, 1992, see appendix B. Geographic Information]

County	Serious crimes known to police (as reported to the FBI)[1]				Rate[4]		Housing, 2000		Occupied units		New private housing units authorized by building permits, 2000			
	Number											Percent in structures with—		
	1999							Percent change, 1990–2000		Percent owner-occupied		One unit	Five units or more	Valuation ($1,000)
	Total	Violent[2]	Property[3]	1990	1999	1990	Total units		Number		Number			
MONTANA—Con.														
Phillips	78	12	66	99	1 614	1 917	2 502	–9.5	1 848	70.6	1	100.0	–	84
Pondera	41	4	37	68	1 408	1 057	2 834	8.3	2 410	70.5	1	100.0	–	75
Powder River	17	1	16	44	928	2 105	1 007	–8.1	737	73.8	–	–	–	–
Powell	NA	NA	NA	NA	NA	NA	2 930	3.4	2 422	71.3	–	–	–	–
Prairie	NA	NA	NA	NA	NA	NA	718	–4.1	537	77.5	–	–	–	–
Ravalli	655	39	616	509	1 858	2 035	15 946	43.7	14 289	75.7	74	47.3	16.2	7 883
Richland	137	11	126	289	2 809	2 697	4 557	–5.6	3 878	72.4	7	100.0	–	641
Roosevelt	33	8	25	334	300	3 037	4 044	–5.2	3 581	65.1	1	100.0	–	65
Rosebud	164	40	124	137	1 627	1 304	3 912	–8.0	3 307	67.1	2	100.0	–	350
Sanders	59	6	53	86	3 782	992	5 271	21.6	4 273	76.4	14	14.3	–	224
Sheridan	102	8	94	78	2 383	1 648	2 167	–10.3	1 741	80.2	–	–	–	–
Silver Bow	NA	NA	NA	1 994	NA	5 875	16 176	4.5	14 432	70.4	31	93.5	–	3 195
Stillwater	4	2	2	100	49	1 530	3 947	19.9	3 234	76.0	24	87.5	–	2 304
Sweet Grass	76	6	70	69	2 225	2 188	1 860	13.5	1 476	74.1	25	4.0	84.0	1 822
Teton	NA	NA	NA	25	NA	399	2 910	6.8	2 538	75.4	4	50.0	–	211
Toole	NA	NA	NA	69	NA	1 367	2 300	–2.3	1 962	71.2	2	100.0	–	165
Treasure	6	1	5	2	688	229	422	–5.8	357	71.4	–	–	–	–
Valley	139	2	137	223	1 692	2 707	4 847	–8.6	3 150	75.8	–	–	–	–
Wheatland	NA	NA	NA	28	NA	1 247	1 154	2.2	853	72.6	–	–	–	–
Wibaux	NA	NA	NA	NA	NA	NA	587	4.3	421	73.4	–	–	–	–
Yellowstone	5 500	220	5 280	6 596	4 556	5 813	54 563	11.9	52 084	69.2	464	87.9	6.0	54 381
Yellowstone National Park	NA	NA	NA	NA	NA	NA	X	X	X	X	X	X	X	X
NEBRASKA	67 049	7 030	60 019	65 847	4 049	4 189	722 668	9.4	666 184	67.4	9 105	71.5	23.9	830 398
Adams	1 149	30	1 119	949	3 892	3 203	13 014	4.2	12 141	66.8	85	95.3	–	8 399
Antelope	60	1	59	50	834	803	3 346	–3.8	2 953	76.4	16	100.0	–	1 730
Arthur	1	–	1	2	233	433	273	12.8	185	63.2	X	X	X	X
Banner	NA	NA	NA	5	NA	587	375	2.5	311	64.6	X	X	X	X
Blaine	NA	NA	NA	4	NA	593	333	–12.6	238	65.5	X	X	X	X
Boone	63	–	63	32	986	1 670	2 733	–5.0	2 454	75.1	3	100.0	–	305
Box Butte	254	20	234	460	1 975	3 503	5 488	–.8	4 780	70.1	2	100.0	–	154
Boyd	28	1	27	13	1 089	459	1 406	–8.6	1 014	80.2	–	–	–	–
Brown	39	3	36	56	1 096	1 531	1 916	–1.7	1 530	74.2	4	100.0	–	390
Buffalo	1 781	102	1 679	1 537	4 378	4 104	16 830	15.8	15 930	63.6	214	74.8	19.2	29 872
Burt	104	11	93	185	1 298	2 351	3 723	–.5	3 155	75.8	7	100.0	–	755
Butler	132	–	132	187	1 518	2 174	3 901	2.6	3 426	75.8	15	46.7	40.0	1 219
Cass	417	20	397	621	1 700	2 913	10 179	13.7	9 161	79.5	171	86.5	9.9	14 299
Cedar	29	2	27	72	300	711	4 200	1.2	3 623	80.6	23	100.0	–	2 774
Chase	27	2	25	30	634	685	1 927	–4.2	1 662	76.9	12	100.0	–	1 098
Cherry	213	17	196	85	3 360	1 348	3 220	6.5	2 508	62.4	7	100.0	–	713
Cheyenne	306	14	292	263	3 223	2 770	4 569	5.2	4 071	72.8	36	88.9	–	3 212
Clay	63	1	62	55	880	772	3 066	–3.4	2 756	77.8	19	100.0	–	1 609
Colfax	161	7	154	179	1 499	1 959	4 088	2.9	3 682	75.2	7	100.0	–	660
Cuming	99	9	90	60	989	593	4 283	3.7	3 945	71.4	21	61.9	–	2 150
Custer	133	3	130	208	1 104	1 695	5 585	–2.5	4 826	73.0	6	100.0	–	754
Dakota	483	18	465	554	2 565	3 309	7 528	16.1	7 095	67.4	76	78.9	15.8	6 433
Dawes	174	6	168	413	1 934	4 578	4 004	2.4	3 512	62.7	7	100.0	–	304
Dawson	798	47	751	828	3 435	4 152	9 805	8.7	8 824	69.2	22	81.8	–	1 558
Deuel	34	2	32	15	1 672	671	1 032	–4.0	908	78.0	3	100.0	–	310
Dixon	93	1	92	92	1 473	1 498	2 673	2.3	2 413	76.3	11	100.0	–	1 140
Dodge	1 095	52	1 043	1 227	3 093	3 557	15 468	5.9	14 433	67.8	141	66.0	25.5	12 076
Douglas	27 801	4 756	23 045	25 645	6 247	6 158	192 672	11.8	182 194	63.3	2 888	72.3	20.3	230 886
Dundy	20	1	19	50	867	1 936	1 196	–9.8	961	72.7	–	–	–	–
Fillmore	111	6	105	54	1 599	760	2 990	–3.6	2 689	74.5	10	100.0	–	1 133
Franklin	54	2	52	53	1 445	1 346	1 746	–10.5	1 485	81.3	4	100.0	–	733
Frontier	60	–	60	30	1 943	967	1 543	–1.4	1 192	72.5	2	100.0	–	70
Furnas	70	3	67	53	1 298	954	2 730	–6.0	2 278	76.6	6	100.0	–	966
Gage	937	16	921	862	4 126	3 782	10 030	3.0	9 316	71.2	148	18.2	63.5	8 646
Garden	43	–	43	47	2 007	1 911	1 298	–3.4	1 020	70.1	2	100.0	–	165
Garfield	2	–	2	8	98	374	1 021	–	813	72.6	3	100.0	–	234
Gosper	3	1	2	60	129	3 112	1 281	5.7	863	75.9	8	100.0	–	700
Grant	7	1	6	NA	915	NA	449	5.6	292	68.8	X	X	X	X
Greeley	19	–	19	2	665	67	1 199	–6.6	1 077	78.6	–	–	–	–
Hall	3 100	143	2 957	2 950	6 008	6 030	21 574	10.5	20 356	65.9	147	75.5	24.5	15 190
Hamilton	191	1	190	148	2 013	1 670	3 850	7.3	3 503	75.1	33	100.0	–	2 836
Harlan	10	2	8	38	266	997	2 327	–3.4	1 597	80.3	2	100.0	–	243
Hayes	NA	NA	NA	8	NA	655	526	–9.8	430	71.9	2	100.0	–	110
Hitchcock	15	2	13	34	435	907	1 675	–10.6	1 287	78.2	–	–	–	–
Holt	152	4	148	82	1 260	651	5 281	–3.5	4 608	73.6	44	81.8	18.2	3 383

[1] Data on serious crimes have not been adjusted for underreporting; this may affect comparability over time or among geographic areas. [2] Includes murder and nonnegligent manslaughter, forcible rape, robbery, and aggravated assault. [3] Includes burglary, larceny-theft, and motor vehicle theft. [4] Per 100,000 resident population provided by the U.S. Federal Bureau of Investigation.

Sources: Serious Crimes Known to Police—U.S. Federal Bureau of Investigation, Uniform Crime Reporting Program, unpublished data, annual (related Internet site <http://www.fbi.gov/ucr/ucr.htm>). Housing, 2000—U.S. Census Bureau, 2000 Census of Population and Housing, "Census 2000 Profiles of General Demographic Characteristics" data files, published May 2001 (related Internet site <http://www.census.gov/mp/www/pub/2000cen/mscen01.html>). Housing, 1990—U.S. Census Bureau, 1990 Census of Population and Housing, Summary Tape File (STF) 1C on CD-ROM (related Internet site <http://homer.ssd.census.gov/cdrom/lookup>). Building Permits—U.S. Census Bureau, "New Residential Construction–Building Permits," e-mail from Manufacturing and Construction Division/Residential Construction Branch, subject: building permits by place 2000, 22 May 2001 (related Internet site <http://www.census.gov/const/www/permitsindex.html>).

[Includes U.S., states, and 3,142 counties or county equivalents defined as of January 1, 1992. For changes to these areas since January 1, 1992, see appendix B. Geographic Information]

County	Serious crimes known to police (as reported to the FBI)[1]						Housing, 2000				New private housing units authorized by building permits, 2000			
	Number			Rate[4]					Occupied units			Percent in structures with—		
	1999						Total units	Percent change, 1990–2000						
	Total	Violent[2]	Property[3]	1990	1999	1990			Number	Percent owner–occupied	Number	One unit	Five units or more	Valuation ($1,000)
NEBRASKA—Con.														
Hooker	7	–	7	5	996	631	440	1.6	335	74.3	–	–	–	–
Howard	112	10	102	109	1 731	1 800	2 782	7.1	2 546	76.9	56	35.7	64.3	3 999
Jefferson	220	2	218	78	2 621	891	3 942	–3.4	3 527	76.1	5	100.0	–	620
Johnson	56	1	55	58	1 945	1 241	2 116	–1.7	1 887	75.3	6	100.0	–	362
Kearney	176	10	166	120	2 563	1 810	2 846	3.3	2 643	74.3	7	100.0	–	540
Keith	224	8	216	255	2 580	2 971	5 178	4.9	3 707	72.9	140	82.9	17.1	4 733
Keya Paha	NA	NA	NA	6	NA	583	548	–6.2	409	72.1	X	X	X	X
Kimball	67	5	62	107	1 638	2 605	1 972	.3	1 727	76.3	–	–	–	–
Knox	94	5	89	87	1 018	913	4 773	–.5	3 811	75.0	6	100.0	–	618
Lancaster	14 504	1 248	13 256	14 862	6 144	6 957	104 217	20.2	99 187	60.5	1 697	77.3	20.2	187 802
Lincoln	527	69	458	1 722	1 569	5 297	15 438	8.6	14 076	69.2	161	67.7	29.8	12 640
Logan	1	–	1	2	NA	228	386	–.3	316	71.5	X	X	X	X
Loup	2	2	–	NA	300	NA	377	–5.5	289	78.2	–	–	–	–
McPherson	4	1	3	NA	709	NA	283	10.1	202	67.3	X	X	X	X
Madison	1 120	42	1 078	1 239	3 232	3 794	14 432	10.4	13 436	65.6	95	78.9	–	10 613
Merrick	174	1	173	159	2 157	1 977	3 649	3.3	3 209	74.1	18	100.0	–	1 542
Morrill	130	2	128	17	2 378	313	2 460	–2.8	2 138	71.4	3	100.0	–	233
Nance	29	–	29	26	706	608	1 787	–1.1	1 577	74.7	2	100.0	–	200
Nemaha	131	5	126	69	1 699	865	3 439	.2	3 047	72.5	9	100.0	–	868
Nuckolls	10	–	10	22	191	380	2 530	–6.3	2 218	80.0	3	100.0	–	290
Otoe	288	7	281	279	1 944	1 958	6 567	7.0	6 060	74.0	128	100.0	–	11 741
Pawnee	53	1	52	29	1 690	874	1 587	–5.2	1 339	80.7	2	100.0	–	67
Perkins	42	1	41	40	1 322	1 188	1 444	–6.1	1 275	75.7	1	100.0	–	85
Phelps	300	16	284	209	3 022	2 151	4 191	2.6	3 844	73.4	8	37.5	62.5	722
Pierce	59	2	57	71	941	907	3 247	2.2	2 979	77.6	20	100.0	–	1 960
Platte	826	25	801	785	2 682	2 632	12 916	10.2	12 076	73.3	116	51.7	41.4	12 225
Polk	84	–	84	74	1 489	1 304	2 717	–.9	2 259	77.2	10	20.0	–	739
Red Willow	438	23	415	246	3 884	2 102	5 278	Z	4 710	70.6	32	25.0	75.0	2 058
Richardson	156	8	148	168	1 653	1 691	4 560	–3.1	3 993	74.9	–	–	–	–
Rock	29	1	28	30	1 661	1 486	935	–6.6	763	73.0	2	100.0	–	145
Saline	259	6	253	264	1 994	2 076	5 611	5.9	5 188	70.7	41	56.1	39.0	3 147
Sarpy	3 232	73	3 159	2 788	2 671	2 718	44 981	25.0	43 426	69.2	1 893	59.5	40.2	160 565
Saunders	253	6	247	311	1 312	1 701	8 266	8.8	7 498	79.7	105	81.9	8.6	11 383
Scotts Bluff	1 314	47	1 267	1 601	3 632	4 444	16 119	3.9	14 887	66.2	70	94.3	–	6 914
Seward	366	26	340	344	2 241	2 227	6 428	8.8	6 013	72.0	74	67.6	32.4	8 451
Sheridan	248	29	219	202	3 835	2 993	3 013	–6.2	2 549	70.2	1	100.0	–	125
Sherman	47	–	47	70	1 367	1 883	1 839	–1.9	1 394	80.0	2	100.0	–	111
Sioux	9	–	9	3	604	194	780	–10.2	605	66.6	X	X	X	X
Stanton	21	4	17	48	337	769	2 452	4.1	2 297	80.0	15	100.0	–	1 708
Thayer	92	3	89	83	1 463	1 251	2 828	–6.3	2 541	80.0	7	42.9	–	528
Thomas	NA	NA	NA	8	NA	940	446	10.4	325	73.2	X	X	X	X
Thurston	10	6	4	20	139	288	2 467	–3.2	2 255	60.8	12	100.0	–	1 684
Valley	49	1	48	102	2 186	1 973	2 273	–7.9	1 965	75.7	3	33.3	–	134
Washington	354	12	342	273	1 893	1 644	7 408	16.1	6 940	77.2	112	91.1	–	19 245
Wayne	143	5	138	150	1 518	1 602	3 662	4.1	3 437	64.9	13	100.0	–	1 834
Webster	70	2	68	75	1 738	1 753	1 972	–3.7	1 708	78.6	2	100.0	–	175
Wheeler	6	–	6	7	647	738	561	–	352	69.3	–	–	–	–
York	382	8	374	318	2 627	2 204	6 172	5.3	5 722	69.5	21	100.0	–	2 383
NEVADA	84 185	10 311	73 874	67 611	4 654	6 081	827 457	59.5	751 165	60.9	32 285	79.7	19.4	3 312 244
Churchill	681	75	606	441	2 823	2 458	9 732	33.5	8 912	65.8	117	94.0	–	11 020
Clark	61 841	8 019	53 822	47 071	5 139	6 785	559 799	76.5	512 253	59.1	26 224	81.2	17.9	2 666 696
Douglas	713	50	663	NA	1 858	NA	19 006	34.6	16 401	74.3	646	83.9	16.1	97 909
Elko	1 550	157	1 393	538	3 248	2 863	18 456	37.1	15 638	69.9	144	70.8	29.2	13 338
Esmeralda	13	4	9	29	1 105	2 158	833	–13.8	455	67.0	X	X	X	X
Eureka	34	12	22	58	1 646	3 749	1 025	25.5	666	73.7	X	X	X	X
Humboldt	388	34	354	440	2 065	3 426	6 954	37.9	5 733	72.9	48	12.5	87.5	3 274
Lander	187	51	136	183	2 584	2 921	2 780	7.5	2 093	77.2	4	100.0	–	337
Lincoln	48	7	41	45	1 098	1 192	2 178	21.0	1 540	75.1	12	100.0	–	805
Lyon	764	68	696	147	2 453	735	14 279	63.7	13 007	75.8	227	75.8	24.2	18 978
Mineral	153	16	137	218	2 704	3 367	2 866	–4.3	2 197	72.5	3	100.0	–	104
Nye	836	74	762	223	2 803	1 254	15 934	97.4	13 309	76.4	–	–	–	–
Pershing	218	57	161	138	3 873	3 183	2 389	25.2	1 962	69.5	4	100.0	–	411
Storey	48	3	45	77	1 518	3 048	1 596	47.1	1 462	79.8	30	90.0	–	2 611
Washoe	14 868	1 460	13 408	17 540	4 577	6 887	143 908	28.3	132 084	59.3	4 544	69.9	29.4	463 002
White Pine	234	18	216	304	2 242	3 282	4 439	11.5	3 282	76.6	6	100.0	–	875
Independent City														
Carson City city	1 609	206	1 403	159	3 151	393	21 283	28.0	20 171	63.1	276	100.0	–	32 884

[1] Data on serious crimes have not been adjusted for underreporting; this may affect comparability over time or among geographic areas. [2] Includes murder and nonnegligent manslaughter, forcible rape, robbery, and aggravated assault. [3] Includes burglary, larceny-theft, and motor vehicle theft. [4] Per 100,000 resident population provided by the U.S. Federal Bureau of Investigation.

Sources: Serious Crimes Known to Police—U.S. Federal Bureau of Investigation, Uniform Crime Reporting Program, unpublished data, annual (related Internet site <http://www.fbi.gov/ucr/ucr.htm>). Housing, 2000—U.S. Census Bureau, 2000 Census of Population and Housing, "Census 2000 Profiles of General Demographic Characteristics" data files, published May 2001 (related Internet site <http://www.census.gov/mp/www/pub/2000cen/mscen01.html>). Housing, 1990—U.S. Census Bureau, 1990 Census of Population and Housing, Summary Tape File (STF) 1C on CD-ROM (related Internet site <http://homer.ssd.census.gov/cdrom/lookup>). Building Permits—U.S. Census Bureau, "New Residential Construction–Building Permits," e-mail from Manufacturing and Construction Division/Residential Construction Branch, subject: building permits by place 2000, 22 May 2001 (related Internet site <http://www.census.gov/const/www/permitsindex.html>).

[Includes U.S., states, and 3,142 counties or county equivalents defined as of January 1, 1992. For changes to these areas since January 1, 1992, see appendix B. Geographic Information]

County	Serious crimes known to police (as reported to the FBI)[1]						Housing, 2000				New private housing units authorized by building permits, 2000			
	Number				Rate[4]				Occupied units			Percent in structures with—		
	1999			1990	1999	1990	Total units	Percent change, 1990–2000	Number	Percent owner–occupied	Number	One unit	Five units or more	Valuation ($1,000)
	Total	Violent[2]	Property[3]											
NEW HAMPSHIRE	13 194	694	12 500	39 045	2 705	3 651	547 024	8.6	474 606	69.7	6 680	91.3	5.8	936 637
Belknap	1 178	76	1 102	1 968	2 836	4 540	32 121	6.0	22 459	74.1	458	95.2	–	59 116
Carroll	414	18	396	1 091	2 005	3 885	34 750	8.1	18 351	77.8	418	98.1	–	63 662
Cheshire	776	50	726	1 681	2 167	2 590	31 876	5.0	28 299	70.8	284	89.8	8.5	29 783
Coos	295	13	282	511	1 727	1 490	19 623	4.9	13 961	71.2	77	94.8	–	8 065
Grafton	1 201	32	1 169	2 308	3 707	3 261	43 729	3.6	31 598	68.6	367	89.1	7.6	46 883
Hillsborough	4 939	284	4 655	14 166	3 170	4 337	149 961	10.6	144 455	64.9	1 843	84.9	11.9	273 662
Merrimack	415	42	373	3 853	1 522	3 345	56 244	10.6	51 843	69.5	692	99.4	–	99 118
Rockingham	2 188	103	2 085	8 126	2 145	3 305	113 023	11.1	104 529	75.6	1 729	91.3	5.4	257 670
Strafford	1 555	63	1 492	4 127	3 530	3 959	45 539	7.4	42 581	64.5	598	94.0	2.3	73 555
Sullivan	233	13	220	1 214	2 090	3 369	20 158	3.2	16 530	72.0	214	94.4	3.7	25 123
NEW JERSEY	[5]277 000	[5]33 539	[5]243 461	421 079	[5]3 402	5 447	3 310 275	7.6	3 064 645	65.6	34 585	73.0	20.7	3 375 991
Atlantic	16 166	1 358	14 808	25 220	6 767	11 243	114 090	6.7	95 024	66.4	1 625	88.2	11.2	119 767
Bergen	18 071	1 136	16 935	29 388	2 098	3 561	339 820	4.6	330 817	67.2	2 847	37.8	51.1	369 406
Burlington	10 260	839	9 421	12 108	2 432	3 065	161 311	12.6	154 371	77.4	2 775	82.2	15.7	240 294
Camden	21 789	3 171	18 618	31 652	4 298	6 295	199 679	5.0	185 744	70.0	796	86.2	13.6	64 543
Cape May	5 238	338	4 900	7 159	5 323	7 529	91 047	6.4	42 148	74.2	1 242	63.7	4.9	134 861
Cumberland	6 674	991	5 683	8 708	4 739	6 308	52 863	5.1	49 143	67.9	255	88.6	6.7	22 448
Essex	45 869	8 996	36 873	81 342	6 096	10 453	301 011	.8	283 736	45.6	1 491	46.0	15.8	135 104
Gloucester	8 563	579	7 984	8 753	3 442	3 804	95 054	15.3	90 717	79.9	1 337	96.8	3.0	112 132
Hudson	25 515	4 495	21 020	42 228	4 564	7 635	240 618	4.8	230 546	30.7	1 338	7.3	72.1	83 483
Hunterdon	1 403	74	1 329	1 764	1 142	1 637	45 032	12.6	43 678	83.6	616	100.0	–	104 764
Mercer	13 295	1 684	11 611	19 066	3 995	4 386	133 280	7.8	125 807	67.0	1 283	94.3	5.4	135 036
Middlesex	19 910	1 818	18 092	29 462	2 770	4 386	273 637	9.4	265 815	66.7	2 460	75.2	23.6	227 026
Monmouth	14 221	1 209	13 012	21 604	2 348	3 906	240 884	10.3	224 236	74.6	2 912	77.9	22.1	322 127
Morris	7 905	511	7 394	12 601	1 713	2 991	174 379	12.0	169 711	76.0	2 684	79.1	20.7	277 076
Ocean	12 720	966	11 754	16 857	2 588	3 891	248 711	13.1	200 402	83.2	5 633	89.3	8.0	494 014
Passaic	17 208	2 230	14 978	29 451	3 530	6 500	170 048	4.6	163 856	55.6	457	74.6	19.7	50 368
Salem	1 794	203	1 591	2 087	2 754	3 196	26 158	3.2	24 295	73.0	161	100.0	–	17 249
Somerset	5 696	340	5 356	7 597	2 006	3 162	112 023	20.9	108 984	77.2	2 282	53.8	46.2	229 839
Sussex	1 690	104	1 586	2 854	1 177	2 180	56 528	9.6	50 831	82.7	719	100.0	–	98 248
Union	19 897	2 316	17 581	29 217	3 961	5 917	192 945	3.2	186 124	61.6	776	49.9	15.6	54 488
Warren	1 668	00	1 668	1 061	1 676	2 141	41 157	12.6	38 660	72.7	806	84.0	12.2	80 710
NEW MEXICO	[5]92 600	[5]12 733	[5]79 867	[5]78 703	[5]6 055	[5]6 853	780 579	23.5	677 971	70.0	[5]8 869	[5]92.3	[5]6.8	[5]1 072 810
Bernalillo	47 103	6 234	40 869	39 590	8 938	10 290	239 074	18.8	220 936	63.7	3 847	97.1	1.8	389 116
Catron	15	7	8	25	526	975	2 548	64.2	1 584	80.6	X	X	X	X
Chaves	NA	NA	NA	2 816	NA	4 868	25 647	9.7	22 561	70.9	30	100.0	–	3 682
Cibola	832	200	632	675	3 164	2 837	10 328	6.6	8 327	77.0	X	X	X	X
Colfax	384	52	332	380	5 069	5 155	8 959	8.4	5 821	72.6	X	X	X	X
Curry	2 733	597	2 136	1 867	6 024	4 423	19 212	13.6	16 766	59.4	39	100.0	–	4 261
DeBaca	32	3	29	NA	1 337	NA	1 307	-1.7	922	78.0	X	X	X	X
Dona Ana	8 389	718	7 671	8 475	5 052	6 254	65 210	32.7	59 556	67.5	982	76.8	22.1	95 920
Eddy	2 759	232	2 527	2 750	5 144	5 658	22 249	10.5	19 379	74.3	31	100.0	–	3 745
Grant	667	52	615	1 365	2 319	5 282	14 066	23.9	12 146	74.4	X	X	X	X
Guadalupe	7	1	6	27	1 153	4 265	2 160	.3	1 655	73.8	X	X	X	X
Harding	11	3	8	2	1 221	243	545	-11.2	371	75.2	X	X	X	X
Hidalgo	55	17	38	NA	884	NA	2 848	18.0	2 152	67.9	X	X	X	X
Lea	2 081	400	1 681	3 050	4 838	5 469	23 405	.3	19 699	72.6	2	100.0	–	312
Lincoln	740	147	593	545	8 459	4 790	15 298	21.2	8 202	77.2	180	93.3	–	27 523
Los Alamos	319	79	240	378	1 736	2 087	7 937	4.9	7 497	78.6	196	38.8	61.2	28 405
Luna	1 137	128	1 009	1 058	4 716	5 842	11 291	45.4	9 397	74.9	25	100.0	–	2 187
McKinley	3 141	402	2 739	2 666	4 642	13 919	26 718	27.6	21 476	72.4	144	20.1	79.9	11 591
Mora	34	10	24	43	698	1 008	2 973	19.6	2 017	82.4	X	X	X	X
Otero	1 195	113	1 082	1 467	3 761	2 860	29 272	26.3	22 984	66.9	144	66.7	31.9	14 948
Quay	95	42	53	642	1 628	5 932	5 664	1.6	4 201	70.6	X	X	X	X
Rio Arriba	1 215	336	879	NA	5 233	NA	18 016	25.5	15 044	81.6	9	100.0	–	1 573
Roosevelt	702	40	662	563	3 854	3 371	7 746	12.2	6 639	62.7	15	86.7	–	1 317
Sandoval	2 121	315	1 806	1 423	2 419	2 481	34 866	47.3	31 411	83.6	576	100.0	–	50 634
San Juan	3 704	585	3 119	3 920	3 488	4 279	43 221	26.2	37 711	75.4	172	98.3	–	23 418
San Miguel	1 197	179	1 018	NA	4 293	NA	14 254	28.8	11 134	73.1	X	X	X	X
Santa Fe	6 061	694	5 367	2	4 979	NA	57 701	39.2	52 482	68.6	395	89.6	9.4	49 056
Sierra	126	27	99	362	2 820	3 652	8 727	35.2	6 113	74.9	X	X	X	X
Socorro	881	222	659	49	5 385	742	7 808	24.2	6 675	71.1	8	100.0	–	1 265
Taos	998	250	748	1 003	5 170	4 412	17 404	44.8	12 675	75.5	234	100.0	–	24 186
Torrance	75	6	69	111	2 398	1 371	7 257	48.8	6 024	83.9	X	X	X	X
Union	57	11	46	138	2 381	5 556	2 225	-3.2	1 733	73.0	X	X	X	X
Valencia	1 455	116	1 339	1 284	5 437	10 223	24 643	46.9	22 681	83.9	350	100.0	–	34 241

[1] Data on serious crimes have not been adjusted for underreporting; this may affect comparability over time or among geographic areas. [2] Includes murder and nonnegligent manslaughter, forcible rape, robbery, and aggravated assault. [3] Includes burglary, larceny-theft, and motor vehicle theft. [4] Per 100,000 resident population provided by the U.S. Federal Bureau of Investigation. [5] Includes data not distributed by county.

Sources: Serious Crimes Known to Police—U.S. Federal Bureau of Investigation, Uniform Crime Reporting Program, unpublished data, annual (related Internet site <http://www.fbi.gov/ucr/ucr.htm>). Housing, 2000—U.S. Census Bureau, 2000 Census of Population and Housing, "Census 2000 Profiles of General Demographic Characteristics" data files, published May 2001 (related Internet site <http://www.census.gov/mp/www/pub/2000cen/mscen01.html>). Housing, 1990—U.S. Census Bureau, 1990 Census of Population and Housing, Summary Tape File (STF) 1C on CD-ROM (related Internet site <http://homer.ssd.census.gov/cdrom/lookup>). Building Permits—U.S. Census Bureau, "New Residential Construction–Building Permits," e-mail from Manufacturing and Construction Division/Residential Construction Branch, subject: building permits by place 2000, 22 May 2001 (related Internet site <http://www.census.gov/const/www/permitsindex.html>).

Table B–6. Counties — Crime, Housing, and Building Permits–Con.

[Includes U.S., states, and 3,142 counties or county equivalents defined as of January 1, 1992. For changes to these areas since January 1, 1992, see appendix B. Geographic Information]

County	Serious crimes known to police (as reported to the FBI)[1] Number 1999 Total	Violent[2]	Property[3]	1990	Rate[4] 1999	1990	Housing, 2000 Total units	Percent change, 1990–2000	Occupied units Number	Percent owner-occupied	New private housing units authorized by building permits, 2000 Number	Percent in structures with— One unit	Five units or more	Valuation ($1,000)
NEW YORK	537 078	101 781	435 297	1 137 857	3 401	6 346	7 679 307	6.3	7 056 860	53.0	44 105	54.1	30.1	4 991 541
Albany	13 756	1 128	12 628	14 014	4 696	4 978	129 972	4.6	120 512	57.7	735	80.4	17.4	99 605
Allegany	747	92	655	1 280	1 527	2 536	24 505	11.6	18 009	73.8	99	100.0	–	6 802
Bronx	(5)	(5)	(5)	(5)	(5)	(5)	490 659	11.3	463 212	19.6	1 646	2.2	40.2	110 146
Broome	5 414	355	5 059	7 471	2 751	3 521	88 817	1.0	80 749	65.1	158	98.7	–	22 604
Cattaraugus	1 664	175	1 489	2 569	1 993	3 050	39 839	8.1	32 023	74.4	162	90.7	6.8	10 426
Cayuga	1 976	177	1 799	2 327	2 429	2 827	35 477	6.6	30 558	72.1	148	95.9	–	13 970
Chautauqua	3 779	308	3 471	5 713	2 733	4 026	64 900	3.5	54 515	69.2	236	88.1	–	28 983
Chemung	2 458	239	2 219	3 816	2 668	4 009	37 745	1.2	35 049	68.9	178	79.8	11.8	22 603
Chenango	1 163	153	1 010	1 139	2 275	2 200	23 890	7.8	19 926	75.3	81	81.5	18.5	4 174
Clinton	1 204	192	1 012	2 221	1 525	2 583	33 091	2.8	29 423	68.5	241	78.4	–	24 905
Columbia	1 357	198	1 159	1 953	2 144	3 101	30 207	3.7	24 796	70.6	190	97.9	–	29 782
Cortland	1 626	82	1 544	2 123	3 381	4 336	20 116	7.7	18 210	64.3	63	100.0	–	5 506
Delaware	837	106	731	1 087	1 814	2 302	28 952	5.8	19 270	75.7	135	98.5	–	12 576
Dutchess	6 500	585	5 915	8 915	2 492	3 436	106 103	8.7	99 536	69.0	1 003	98.0	–	172 168
Erie	35 032	4 114	30 918	52 265	3 744	5 396	415 868	3.4	380 873	65.3	2 183	66.2	32.8	255 672
Essex	686	121	565	996	1 825	2 681	23 115	7.5	15 028	73.8	148	91.9	8.1	18 509
Franklin	875	164	711	1 131	1 799	2 430	23 936	9.0	17 931	70.5	93	100.0	–	7 195
Fulton	1 424	140	1 284	2 021	2 688	3 738	27 787	5.8	21 884	72.1	114	83.3	16.7	10 652
Genesee	1 024	73	951	1 647	1 686	2 742	24 190	7.1	22 770	73.0	106	98.1	–	12 184
Greene	1 086	213	873	1 333	2 580	2 980	26 544	6.2	18 256	72.1	185	100.0	–	20 975
Hamilton	132	7	125	61	2 539	17 784	7 965	-3.3	2 362	79.3	52	100.0	–	4 102
Herkimer	1 248	137	1 111	1 276	1 946	2 099	32 026	4.0	25 734	71.2	124	100.0	–	12 590
Jefferson	2 225	165	2 060	3 135	2 013	2 826	54 070	7.0	40 068	59.7	164	100.0	–	15 323
Kings	[5]302 962	[5]79 258	[5]223 704	[5]711 295	[5]4 078	[5]9 714	930 866	6.5	880 727	27.1	2 904	4.6	45.2	198 210
Lewis	284	29	255	322	1 032	1 202	15 134	14.8	10 040	77.2	150	100.0	–	7 328
Livingston	1 548	111	1 437	1 915	2 343	3 070	24 023	4.1	22 150	74.5	293	45.4	46.4	21 737
Madison	1 086	65	1 021	1 909	1 526	2 762	28 646	7.5	25 368	75.0	127	96.9	–	14 114
Monroe	30 397	1 934	28 463	42 322	4 240	6 001	304 388	6.6	286 512	65.1	2 160	73.8	25.8	283 997
Montgomery	816	101	715	861	1 606	1 656	22 522	3.1	20 038	67.3	53	100.0	–	4 415
Nassau	6 283	1 046	5 237	42 066	2 292	3 268	458 151	2.7	447 387	80.3	1 506	50.0	40.2	270 130
New York	(5)	(5)	(5)	(5)	(5)	(5)	798 144	1.7	738 644	20.1	5 110	–	96.6	310 901
Niagara	3 339	151	3 188	9 785	2 068	4 432	95 715	5.9	87 846	69.9	489	93.5	4.9	56 330
Oneida	6 378	519	5 859	7 748	2 762	3 089	102 803	1.5	90 496	67.2	281	90.0	8.5	29 037
Onondaga	16 135	1 870	14 265	21 797	3 516	4 648	196 633	3.0	181 153	64.5	1 223	76.2	16.9	149 629
Ontario	2 185	127	2 058	2 588	2 190	2 721	42 647	9.5	38 370	73.6	447	83.2	12.1	61 735
Orange	8 571	964	7 607	10 946	2 665	3 558	122 754	10.8	114 788	67.0	2 000	79.9	17.5	227 119
Orleans	893	94	799	1 104	2 093	2 638	17 347	6.1	15 363	75.6	65	100.0	–	6 360
Oswego	2 751	126	2 625	3 370	2 216	2 767	52 831	8.8	45 522	72.8	241	94.2	–	19 247
Otsego	1 315	156	1 159	1 214	2 161	2 006	28 481	7.9	23 291	73.0	577	24.4	–	14 983
Putnam	1 220	66	1 154	1 899	1 305	2 262	35 030	9.8	32 703	82.2	359	95.8	4.2	67 412
Queens	(5)	(5)	(5)	(5)	(5)	(5)	817 250	8.6	782 664	42.8	2 723	3.2	39.7	184 381
Rensselaer	2 282	166	2 116	5 386	2 249	3 488	66 120	5.6	59 894	64.9	380	87.4	10.5	42 877
Richmond	(5)	(5)	(5)	(5)	(5)	(5)	163 993	17.4	156 341	63.8	2 667	51.0	9.4	260 142
Rockland	6 670	724	5 946	7 536	2 368	2 839	94 973	7.6	92 675	71.7	542	63.8	21.2	66 595
St. Lawrence	2 756	194	2 562	3 541	2 421	3 162	49 721	4.6	40 506	70.6	242	94.2	3.3	17 143
Saratoga	2 909	217	2 692	5 143	1 470	2 901	86 701	15.4	78 165	72.0	1 131	85.9	10.8	151 986
Schenectady	4 407	434	3 973	5 924	3 025	3 968	65 032	3.6	59 684	65.4	250	80.0	17.6	30 247
Schoharie	425	42	383	749	1 309	2 351	15 915	10.3	11 991	75.2	80	85.0	15.0	7 102
Schuyler	372	18	354	646	1 943	3 462	9 181	8.4	7 374	77.1	38	100.0	–	3 593
Seneca	649	39	610	793	2 071	2 403	14 794	3.4	12 630	73.8	46	100.0	–	5 121
Steuben	2 279	181	2 098	3 410	2 344	3 441	46 132	7.2	39 071	73.2	245	96.7	–	27 069
Suffolk	5 620	458	5 162	65 551	4 084	4 959	522 323	8.5	469 299	79.8	4 896	79.1	13.5	814 305
Sullivan	2 102	232	1 870	3 041	3 038	4 390	44 730	7.0	27 661	68.1	283	97.9	–	27 237
Tioga	592	40	552	851	1 127	1 626	21 410	5.7	19 725	77.8	95	81.1	18.9	8 459
Tompkins	2 645	158	2 487	4 459	2 796	4 739	38 625	9.3	36 420	53.7	556	29.7	66.9	52 293
Ulster	4 014	382	3 632	5 193	2 410	3 221	77 656	8.3	67 499	68.0	548	93.1	3.5	72 668
Warren	1 702	107	1 595	2 506	2 775	4 232	34 852	9.8	25 726	69.8	378	84.9	6.3	51 225
Washington	1 121	193	928	1 392	1 944	2 346	26 794	10.6	22 458	74.4	172	95.3	4.7	19 292
Wayne	1 951	109	1 842	2 603	2 089	2 921	38 767	10.2	34 908	77.6	320	79.7	17.8	32 726
Westchester	20 742	2 409	18 333	37 658	2 307	4 409	349 445	3.8	337 142	60.1	2 126	60.5	29.7	438 763
Wyoming	1 023	105	918	1 354	2 320	3 185	16 940	6.9	14 906	76.7	92	89.1	8.7	8 599
Yates	441	32	409	487	1 820	2 135	12 064	3.7	9 029	77.1	66	100.0	–	5 582

[1] Data on serious crimes have not been adjusted for underreporting; this may affect comparability over time or among geographic areas. [2] Includes murder and nonnegligent manslaughter, forcible rape, robbery, and aggravated assault. [3] Includes burglary, larceny-theft, and motor vehicle theft. [4] Per 100,000 resident population provided by the U.S. Federal Bureau of Investigation. [5] Bronx, New York, Queens, and Richmond Counties included with Kings County; data not available separately.

Sources: Serious Crimes Known to Police—U.S. Federal Bureau of Investigation, Uniform Crime Reporting Program, unpublished data, annual (related Internet site <http://www.fbi.gov/ucr/ucr.htm>). Housing, 2000—U.S. Census Bureau, 2000 Census of Population and Housing, "Census 2000 Profiles of General Demographic Characteristics" data files, published May 2001 (related Internet site <http://www.census.gov/mp/www/pub/2000cen/mscen01.html>). Housing, 1990—U.S. Census Bureau, 1990 Census of Population and Housing, Summary Tape File (STF) 1C on CD-ROM (related Internet site <http://homer.ssd.census.gov/cdrom/lookup>). Building Permits—U.S. Census Bureau, "New Residential Construction–Building Permits," e-mail from Manufacturing and Construction Division/Residential Construction Branch, subject: building permits by place 2000, 22 May 2001 (related Internet site <http://www.census.gov/const/www/permitsindex.html>).

Crime, Housing, and Building Permits–Con.

[Includes U.S., states, and 3,142 counties or county equivalents defined as of January 1, 1992. For changes to these areas since January 1, 1992, see appendix B. Geographic Information]

County	Serious crimes known to police (as reported to the FBI)[1] Number 1999 Total	Violent[2]	Property[3]	1990	Rate[4] 1999	1990	Housing, 2000 Total units	Percent change, 1990-2000	Occupied units Number	Percent owner-occupied	New private housing units authorized by building permits, 2000 Number	Percent in structures with— One unit	Five units or more	Valuation ($1,000)
NORTH CAROLINA......	384 312	40 401	343 911	[5]353 425	5 105	[5]5 397	3 523 944	25.0	3 132 013	69.4	78 376	75.4	22.3	8 643 196
Alamance.............	5 537	463	5 074	4 461	4 574	4 194	55 463	22.4	51 584	70.1	945	92.3	5.1	101 109
Alexander............	733	32	701	634	2 311	2 302	14 098	25.9	13 137	80.5	166	94.0	–	29 875
Alleghany............	48	7	41	192	2 377	2 002	6 412	20.0	4 593	78.9	151	100.0	–	14 815
Anson...............	932	84	848	822	4 060	3 679	10 221	10.4	9 204	75.9	31	100.0	–	3 371
Ashe................	332	31	301	306	1 444	1 378	13 268	19.3	10 411	81.0	239	100.0	–	29 162
Avery...............	233	21	212	250	1 472	1 682	11 911	33.5	6 532	80.6	148	95.9	–	40 537
Beaufort............	1 588	174	1 414	1 693	3 517	4 064	22 139	13.0	18 319	75.0	190	100.0	–	30 608
Bertie..............	503	84	419	443	2 425	2 173	9 050	8.6	7 743	74.9	28	100.0	–	1 093
Bladen..............	1 257	244	1 013	933	4 036	3 255	15 316	20.7	12 897	77.8	63	100.0	–	7 582
Brunswick...........	2 898	188	2 710	981	4 178	1 924	51 431	38.6	30 438	82.2	1 449	92.0	5.6	161 462
Buncombe...........	8 292	834	7 458	9 060	4 197	5 222	93 973	20.6	85 776	70.3	1 327	74.7	19.2	158 996
Burke...............	2 519	300	2 219	2 172	3 014	2 868	37 427	18.5	34 528	74.1	302	98.0	–	34 532
Cabarrus............	3 529	262	3 267	3 564	2 899	3 602	52 848	33.1	49 519	74.7	1 724	84.2	14.2	156 062
Caldwell............	2 547	272	2 275	3 099	3 320	4 383	33 430	13.5	30 768	74.9	442	90.5	9.5	51 410
Camden.............	75	11	64	63	1 076	1 067	2 973	20.6	2 662	83.4	63	100.0	–	7 515
Carteret............	2 019	123	1 896	2 547	3 316	4 846	40 947	18.4	25 204	76.6	459	96.7	1.3	72 743
Caswell.............	508	65	443	481	2 256	2 324	9 601	16.3	8 670	79.3	89	100.0	–	10 250
Catawba............	6 260	420	5 840	6 720	4 674	5 675	59 919	21.8	55 533	72.5	1 280	90.0	7.8	152 036
Chatham............	1 743	146	1 597	1 296	3 786	3 344	21 358	28.3	19 741	77.2	418	100.0	–	83 820
Cherokee...........	603	36	567	432	2 613	2 142	13 499	30.8	10 336	82.2	271	100.0	–	23 102
Chowan.............	455	54	401	551	3 163	4 080	6 443	9.0	5 580	72.2	42	100.0	–	5 356
Clay................	102	5	97	85	1 173	1 188	5 425	30.5	3 847	84.5	151	100.0	–	18 488
Cleveland...........	3 257	390	2 867	4 292	3 553	5 132	40 317	17.8	37 046	72.8	370	95.1	–	42 346
Columbus...........	2 763	252	2 511	1 999	5 280	4 257	24 060	17.3	21 308	76.4	99	93.9	–	9 483
Craven.............	2 894	328	2 566	2 912	3 276	3 568	38 150	18.1	34 582	66.7	490	90.2	–	52 808
Cumberland.........	17 390	1 594	15 796	24 470	6 026	8 912	118 425	20.4	107 358	59.4	1 544	52.7	45.3	104 663
Currituck...........	593	51	542	335	3 266	2 439	10 687	45.1	6 902	81.6	340	98.8	–	67 464
Dare...............	1 724	85	1 639	1 806	5 874	7 940	26 671	23.7	12 690	74.5	920	97.7	1.8	182 289
Davidson...........	4 271	331	3 940	5 172	2 984	4 083	62 432	17.2	58 156	74.2	893	84.7	10.0	88 062
Davie..............	633	53	580	723	1 945	2 595	14 953	30.1	13 750	83.3	328	100.0	–	45 564
Duplin.............	1 905	188	1 717	1 405	4 424	3 556	20 520	25.2	18 267	74.9	167	58.1	–	14 690
Durham............	20 181	2 184	17 997	14 768	9 834	8 122	95 452	22.8	89 015	54.3	2 863	53.8	44.9	296 014
Edgecombe.........	2 907	313	2 594	3 393	5 195	6 013	24 002	10.0	20 392	64.1	95	100.0	–	7 486
Forsyth............	21 900	2 566	19 334	19 047	7 508	7 164	133 093	15.0	123 851	65.6	2 875	76.2	23.8	285 217
Franklin............	1 370	01	1 200	950	3 040	2 856	20 364	36.2	17 843	77.8	374	99.5	–	42 631
Gaston.............	11 123	1 375	9 748	12 227	6 111	7 123	78 842	14.0	73 936	68.8	1 213	88.6	11.4	118 555
Gates..............	197	15	182	155	1 930	1 666	4 389	18.8	3 901	82.1	18	100.0	–	3 382
Graham............	44	18	26	17	568	236	5 084	23.0	3 354	82.7	58	100.0	–	4 489
Granville...........	1 904	203	1 701	1 589	4 377	4 144	17 896	26.3	16 654	75.0	414	94.7	3.9	46 818
Greene............	669	70	599	365	3 604	2 373	7 368	24.0	6 696	74.7	31	100.0	–	5 844
Guilford............	25 924	2 970	22 954	24 698	6 595	7 109	180 391	22.9	168 667	62.7	3 529	86.7	10.9	373 766
Halifax.............	3 032	321	2 711	2 722	5 299	4 965	25 309	12.6	22 122	67.0	94	100.0	–	10 515
Harnett............	4 268	435	3 833	3 784	5 254	5 579	38 605	38.4	33 800	70.3	692	88.4	6.8	49 281
Haywood...........	1 442	146	1 296	1 681	2 766	3 581	28 640	19.5	23 100	77.4	393	100.0	–	54 792
Henderson..........	1 928	105	1 823	2 127	2 353	3 070	42 996	26.0	37 414	78.8	720	93.1	5.4	120 851
Hertford...........	1 002	107	895	872	4 434	3 872	9 724	9.0	8 953	70.0	31	83.9	–	2 317
Hoke..............	296	17	279	938	7 574	4 104	12 518	56.5	11 373	75.0	261	100.0	–	27 950
Hyde..............	64	3	61	32	1 125	591	3 302	13.7	2 185	78.4	20	100.0	–	2 209
Iredell.............	4 512	511	4 001	1 862	3 930	2 471	51 918	32.5	47 360	75.4	1 830	73.3	26.4	235 947
Jackson............	747	58	689	617	2 439	2 298	19 291	37.3	13 191	72.5	745	56.9	38.7	92 495
Johnston...........	5 410	485	4 925	3 655	5 007	4 569	50 196	46.9	46 595	73.4	1 635	72.2	22.2	142 852
Jones..............	147	18	129	NA	1 533	NA	4 679	22.2	4 061	79.8	5	100.0	–	545
Lee................	3 239	227	3 012	2 888	6 477	6 980	19 909	17.4	18 466	71.7	231	100.0	–	24 996
Lenoir.............	3 284	367	2 917	2 494	5 540	4 355	27 184	14.5	23 862	67.0	242	80.2	18.2	21 732
Lincoln............	2 121	148	1 973	1 637	3 601	3 253	25 717	27.4	24 041	78.5	833	79.5	19.8	88 508
McDowell..........	895	74	821	1 232	2 204	3 453	18 377	21.8	16 604	77.2	132	92.4	–	13 586
Macon.............	534	17	517	279	1 859	1 187	20 746	20.8	12 828	81.3	359	100.0	–	69 833
Madison...........	71	5	66	NA	405	NA	9 722	26.8	8 000	76.6	143	100.0	–	15 667
Martin.............	1 137	145	992	1 158	4 282	4 618	10 930	8.2	10 020	71.8	50	100.0	–	5 691
Mecklenburg........	56 406	8 289	48 117	56 832	8 883	11 112	292 780	35.3	273 416	62.3	13 960	61.3	37.0	1 402 702
Mitchell...........	20	1	19	34	947	1 692	7 919	13.4	6 551	80.8	70	100.0	–	7 530
Montgomery........	1 033	94	939	745	4 518	3 385	14 145	35.7	9 848	76.7	102	100.0	–	18 843
Moore.............	2 439	164	2 275	2 021	3 387	3 482	35 151	25.5	30 713	78.7	672	89.4	10.6	105 806
Nash..............	4 950	504	4 446	4 132	5 421	5 454	37 051	19.4	33 644	67.7	695	75.3	19.6	52 840
New Hanover........	10 875	983	9 892	10 419	7 201	8 707	79 616	39.5	68 183	64.7	1 860	75.4	22.8	207 885
Northampton........	572	88	484	381	2 663	2 069	10 455	16.5	8 691	77.0	45	100.0	–	4 767
Onslow.............	5 335	378	4 957	5 637	3 697	3 762	55 726	17.3	48 122	58.1	915	69.3	27.2	67 461

[1] Data on serious crimes have not been adjusted for underreporting; this may affect comparability over time or among geographic areas. [2] Includes murder and nonnegligent manslaughter, forcible rape, robbery, and aggravated assault. [3] Includes burglary, larceny-theft, and motor vehicle theft. [4] Per 100,000 resident population provided by the U.S. Federal Bureau of Investigation. [5] Includes data not distributed by county.

Sources: Serious Crimes Known to Police—U.S. Federal Bureau of Investigation, Uniform Crime Reporting Program, unpublished data, annual (related Internet site <http://www.fbi.gov/ucr/ucr.htm>). Housing, 2000—U.S. Census Bureau, 2000 Census of Population and Housing, "Census 2000 Profiles of General Demographic Characteristics" data files, published May 2001 (related Internet site <http://www.census.gov/mp/www/pub/2000cen/mscen01.html>). Housing, 1990—U.S. Census Bureau, 1990 Census of Population and Housing, Summary Tape File (STF) 1C on CD-ROM (related Internet site <http://homer.ssd.census.gov/cdrom/lookup>). Building Permits—U.S. Census Bureau, "New Residential Construction–Building Permits," e-mail from Manufacturing and Construction Division/Residential Construction Branch, subject: building permits by place 2000, 22 May 2001 (related Internet site <http://www.census.gov/const/www/permitsindex.html>).

[Includes U.S., states, and 3,142 counties or county equivalents defined as of January 1, 1992. For changes to these areas since January 1, 1992, see appendix B. Geographic Information]

County	Serious crimes known to police (as reported to the FBI)[1]						Housing, 2000				New private housing units authorized by building permits, 2000			
	Number				Rate[4]				Occupied units			Percent in structures with—		
	1999			1990	1999	1990	Total units	Percent change, 1990–2000	Number	Percent owner-occupied	Number	One unit	Five units or more	Valuation ($1,000)
	Total	Violent[2]	Property[3]											
NORTH CAROLINA–Con.														
Orange	6 147	398	5 749	5 663	5 506	6 034	49 289	27.4	45 863	57.6	1 070	95.8	1.7	169 134
Pamlico	218	23	195	184	1 742	1 618	6 781	12.1	5 178	82.2	56	100.0	–	9 191
Pasquotank	1 272	166	1 106	1 365	3 537	4 361	14 289	16.2	12 907	65.7	108	100.0	–	9 807
Pender	1 054	84	970	368	2 631	1 275	20 798	34.7	16 054	82.6	348	84.2	14.1	53 955
Perquimans	189	22	167	213	1 652	2 039	6 043	21.5	4 645	78.6	63	100.0	–	11 909
Person	979	106	873	1 175	2 870	3 893	15 504	23.6	14 085	74.6	180	95.6	–	31 209
Pitt	8 484	877	7 607	6 499	6 609	6 047	58 408	35.6	52 539	58.1	1 766	40.9	53.8	123 846
Polk	80	8	72	207	3 507	1 436	9 192	26.4	7 908	78.7	121	100.0	–	15 002
Randolph	4 796	215	4 581	3 102	3 900	2 911	54 422	24.7	50 659	76.6	915	62.8	29.1	67 232
Richmond	2 524	209	2 315	1 943	5 528	4 365	19 886	9.2	17 873	71.9	274	100.0	–	14 734
Robeson	7 192	825	6 367	4 092	6 157	3 891	47 779	22.4	43 677	72.8	413	97.1	–	48 780
Rockingham	3 814	402	3 412	2 865	4 229	3 329	40 208	12.8	36 989	73.7	342	84.8	14.0	34 680
Rowan	3 947	404	3 543	4 441	3 102	4 015	53 980	16.7	49 940	73.6	764	82.5	6.5	91 828
Rutherford	1 990	136	1 854	1 976	3 262	3 513	29 535	17.1	25 191	74.5	290	96.6	–	29 818
Sampson	2 232	232	2 000	1 596	4 232	3 374	25 142	31.1	22 273	73.5	134	100.0	–	14 688
Scotland	1 971	177	1 794	1 859	5 503	5 587	14 693	15.2	13 399	69.2	144	61.1	11.1	11 771
Stanly	2 633	165	2 468	552	4 732	1 066	24 582	12.7	22 223	76.3	287	95.8	–	29 268
Stokes	1 107	135	972	976	2 522	2 622	19 262	27.1	17 579	82.1	183	77.0	–	21 659
Surry	2 259	262	1 997	1 813	3 323	2 938	31 033	19.3	28 408	76.3	222	96.4	3.6	26 828
Swain	217	30	187	90	4 046	1 739	7 105	25.4	5 137	76.8	155	67.7	25.8	11 601
Transylvania	616	94	522	464	2 133	1 818	15 553	20.6	12 320	79.4	238	100.0	–	55 863
Tyrrell	55	7	48	81	1 453	2 101	2 032	6.6	1 537	74.9	9	100.0	–	2 383
Union	4 875	400	4 475	3 279	4 437	4 029	45 695	48.6	43 390	80.5	2 457	93.2	6.8	286 646
Vance	2 773	253	2 520	2 312	6 488	5 945	18 196	15.6	16 199	66.3	138	98.6	–	14 732
Wake	28 234	2 615	25 619	21 440	5 002	5 064	258 953	46.2	242 040	65.9	12 193	65.3	34.3	1 368 381
Warren	510	69	441	227	2 893	1 315	10 548	21.0	7 708	77.4	89	100.0	–	11 064
Washington	291	81	210	683	2 108	4 880	6 174	9.4	5 367	73.6	17	100.0	–	2 226
Watauga	1 426	64	1 362	1 179	3 434	3 191	23 155	18.5	16 540	62.9	573	86.7	10.5	101 199
Wayne	5 469	598	4 871	6 157	4 807	5 883	47 313	19.8	42 612	65.4	428	83.4	–	40 778
Wilkes	1 550	158	1 392	1 443	2 433	2 445	29 261	17.2	26 650	77.9	242	97.1	2.1	32 464
Wilson	4 318	483	3 835	5 175	6 246	7 906	30 729	15.3	28 613	61.2	598	65.6	8.0	44 460
Yadkin	874	72	802	575	2 670	1 925	15 821	22.4	14 505	80.3	138	97.1	–	18 053
Yancey	86	8	78	15	565	108	9 729	21.7	7 472	80.2	87	93.1	–	4 911
NORTH DAKOTA	14 608	467	14 141	14 583	2 443	3 024	289 677	4.8	257 152	66.6	2 128	59.1	31.2	190 198
Adams	32	1	31	NA	1 187	NA	1 416	–5.9	1 121	71.1	10	100.0	–	333
Barnes	117	1	116	129	986	1 028	5 599	–3.5	4 884	71.2	11	81.8	–	727
Benson	NA	NA	NA	129	NA	1 792	2 932	–7.3	2 328	68.3	–	–	–	–
Billings	NA	NA	NA	16	NA	1 444	529	–.8	366	76.8	–	–	–	–
Bottineau	46	–	46	17	641	212	4 409	–5.4	2 962	80.0	1	100.0	–	124
Bowman	8	1	7	NA	503	NA	1 596	–5.6	1 358	79.4	4	100.0	–	480
Burke	9	–	9	NA	463	NA	1 412	–16.5	1 013	84.4	3	100.0	–	173
Burleigh	2 063	43	2 020	2 208	3 108	3 672	29 003	21.8	27 670	68.0	409	73.6	–	54 026
Cass	3 654	150	3 504	3 904	3 185	3 795	53 790	26.8	51 315	54.3	1 079	43.3	50.1	77 640
Cavalier	87	–	87	59	1 749	973	2 725	–10.3	2 017	81.5	–	–	–	–
Dickey	57	4	53	15	1 017	346	2 656	–3.9	2 283	71.5	1	100.0	–	75
Divide	2	–	2	NA	151	NA	1 469	–11.9	1 005	82.1	–	–	–	–
Dunn	1	–	1	NA	28	NA	1 965	–4.5	1 378	80.0	2	100.0	–	180
Eddy	25	–	25	NA	884	NA	1 418	–3.5	1 164	75.4	3	100.0	–	415
Emmons	46	–	46	6	1 075	124	2 168	–1.5	1 786	83.4	12	100.0	–	854
Foster	7	–	7	NA	417	NA	1 793	–4.4	1 540	74.4	3	100.0	–	310
Golden Valley	NA	NA	NA	36	NA	1 708	973	–6.0	761	78.1	–	–	–	–
Grand Forks	2 805	86	2 719	2 962	4 225	4 445	27 373	1.1	25 435	53.9	63	96.8	–	8 529
Grant	21	–	21	NA	712	NA	1 722	–14.4	1 195	79.3	1	100.0	–	130
Griggs	7	–	7	NA	407	NA	1 521	–8.4	1 178	78.3	–	–	–	–
Hettinger	1	–	1	NA	34	NA	1 419	–13.3	1 152	83.6	–	–	–	–
Kidder	17	1	16	3	595	90	1 610	–3.7	1 158	81.7	4	100.0	–	210
LaMoure	4	–	4	NA	122	NA	2 271	–6.7	1 942	80.6	6	100.0	–	550
Logan	13	–	13	NA	916	NA	1 193	–10.6	963	85.8	–	–	–	–
McHenry	74	4	70	NA	1 227	NA	2 983	–10.2	2 526	81.4	5	100.0	–	420
McIntosh	13	–	13	NA	535	NA	1 853	–8.8	1 467	83.1	5	100.0	–	357
McKenzie	32	–	32	NA	567	NA	2 719	–14.4	2 151	73.9	–	–	–	–
McLean	161	1	160	NA	1 671	NA	5 264	–4.6	3 815	82.2	9	100.0	–	650
Mercer	114	5	109	NA	1 219	NA	4 402	–2.1	3 346	84.5	8	100.0	–	612
Morton	669	19	650	815	2 742	3 576	10 587	11.8	9 889	75.5	93	91.4	8.6	9 661
Mountrail	68	2	66	1	1 033	14	3 438	–6.4	2 560	72.6	8	100.0	–	609
Nelson	NA	NA	NA	NA	NA	NA	2 014	–10.9	1 628	80.2	4	50.0	–	465
Oliver	11	–	11	32	500	1 344	903	–6.7	791	85.7	1	100.0	–	70
Pembina	97	7	90	NA	1 151	NA	4 115	–4.2	3 535	78.4	5	100.0	–	543
Pierce	53	–	53	83	1 155	1 643	2 269	–3.7	1 964	72.9	5	60.0	–	550

[1] Data on serious crimes have not been adjusted for underreporting; this may affect comparability over time or among geographic areas. [2] Includes murder and nonnegligent manslaughter, forcible rape, robbery, and aggravated assault. [3] Includes burglary, larceny-theft, and motor vehicle theft. [4] Per 100,000 resident population provided by the U.S. Federal Bureau of Investigation.

Sources: Serious Crimes Known to Police—U.S. Federal Bureau of Investigation, Uniform Crime Reporting Program, unpublished data, annual (related Internet site <http://www.fbi.gov/ucr/ucr.htm>). Housing, 2000—U.S. Census Bureau, 2000 Census of Population and Housing, "Census 2000 Profiles of General Demographic Characteristics" data files, published May 2001 (related Internet site <http://www.census.gov/mp/www/pub/2000cen/mscen01.html>). Housing, 1990—U.S. Census Bureau, 1990 Census of Population and Housing, Summary Tape File (STF) 1C on CD-ROM (related Internet site <http://homer.ssd.census.gov/cdrom/lookup>). Building Permits—U.S. Census Bureau, "New Residential Construction–Building Permits," e-mail from Manufacturing and Construction Division/Residential Construction Branch, subject: building permits by place 2000, 22 May 2001 (related Internet site <http://www.census.gov/const/www/permitsindex.html>).

Table B–6. Counties — Crime, Housing, and Building Permits-Con.

[Includes U.S., states, and 3,142 counties or county equivalents defined as of January 1, 1992. For changes to these areas since January 1, 1992, see appendix B. Geographic Information]

County	Serious crimes known to police (as reported to the FBI)[1]						Housing, 2000				New private housing units authorized by building permits, 2000			
	Number				Rate[4]				Occupied units			Percent in structures with—		
	1999			1990	1999	1990	Total units	Percent change, 1990–2000	Number	Percent owner–occupied	Number	One unit	Five units or more	Valuation ($1,000)
	Total	Violent[2]	Property[3]											
NORTH DAKOTA—Con.														
Ramsey	545	17	528	495	4 529	3 903	5 729	2.0	4 957	65.0	18	100.0	–	1 927
Ransom	83	4	79	NA	2 318	NA	2 604	1.4	2 350	75.3	46	13.0	78.3	3 076
Renville	19	–	19	NA	681	NA	1 413	-9.3	1 085	77.8	4	100.0	–	100
Richland	467	14	453	261	2 574	1 438	7 575	2.4	6 885	69.6	22	100.0	–	1 775
Rolette	82	1	81	NA	581	NA	5 027	6.0	4 556	67.4	3	100.0	–	260
Sargent	71	–	71	NA	1 883	NA	2 016	-2.0	1 786	79.8	6	100.0	–	663
Sheridan	24	–	24	NA	1 427	NA	924	-12.9	731	84.5	–	–	–	–
Sioux	NA	NA	NA	NA	NA	NA	1 216	3.5	1 095	46.3	–	–	–	–
Slope	1	–	1	NA	116	NA	451	-6.2	313	86.9	–	–	–	–
Stark	522	17	505	476	2 341	2 115	9 722	1.4	8 932	70.3	34	100.0	–	4 655
Steele	NA	NA	NA	NA	NA	NA	1 231	-6.1	923	77.2	–	–	–	–
Stutsman	406	20	386	648	1 951	2 914	9 817	.5	8 954	67.2	50	46.0	54.0	4 533
Towner	17	–	17	NA	567	NA	1 558	-12.0	1 218	73.9	–	–	–	–
Traill	62	1	61	NA	878	NA	3 708	-1.6	3 341	72.6	7	100.0	–	721
Walsh	319	11	308	NA	2 374	NA	5 757	-5.5	5 029	76.8	8	50.0	–	1 026
Ward	1 317	44	1 273	1 616	2 261	2 790	25 097	6.4	23 041	62.6	149	57.0	34.9	10 737
Wells	45	–	45	48	977	819	2 643	-7.9	2 215	76.5	1	100.0	–	108
Williams	314	13	301	624	1 570	2 953	9 680	-4.9	8 095	71.4	25	100.0	–	1 924
OHIO	354 710	30 181	324 529	468 698	4 151	5 028	4 783 051	9.4	4 445 773	69.1	49 745	76.4	17.8	6 153 635
Adams	539	41	498	NA	2 629	NA	11 822	15.5	10 501	73.9	1	100.0	–	50
Allen	4 699	487	4 212	4 540	4 529	8 752	44 245	3.5	40 646	72.1	231	93.1	–	32 684
Ashland	188	9	179	636	674	1 339	20 832	14.8	19 524	75.6	185	92.4	–	19 578
Ashtabula	1 729	40	1 689	3 854	2 445	3 861	43 792	6.3	39 397	74.1	449	99.1	–	47 650
Athens	996	57	939	967	3 762	4 547	24 901	14.6	22 501	60.5	41	92.7	–	2 983
Auglaize	225	35	190	1 012	768	2 282	18 470	9.2	17 376	77.9	164	93.9	–	21 184
Belmont	769	57	712	584	1 241	926	31 236	2.2	28 309	75.0	25	100.0	–	2 596
Brown	1	–	1	NA	64	NA	17 193	25.3	15 555	79.6	111	78.4	21.6	11 622
Butler	14 670	1 079	13 591	12 588	4 421	5 567	129 793	17.6	123 082	71.6	2 385	79.1	16.9	253 381
Carroll	474	82	392	77	1 837	3 552	13 016	12.8	11 126	80.0	24	50.0	–	2 407
Champaign	1 044	50	994	768	2 849	2 245	15 890	13.3	14 952	75.9	175	100.0	–	19 112
Clark	8 200	991	7 209	10 085	5 629	6 848	61 056	4.6	56 648	71.5	284	96.5	–	29 932
Clermont	2 862	164	2 698	5 036	2 175	3 464	69 226	25.1	66 013	74.7	1 657	69.8	24.0	184 620
Clinton	719	54	665	966	1 701	2 607	16 577	20.0	15 416	68.9	206	96.1	–	25 459
Columbiana	697	28	669	761	714	817	46 083	4.7	42 973	76.0	140	39.3	20.0	11 692
Coshocton	482	27	455	377	1 329	1 064	16 107	7.6	14 356	76.0	8	62.5	–	1 085
Crawford	1 284	27	1 257	1 749	2 708	3 654	20 178	3.4	18 957	72.6	93	100.0	–	11 291
Cuyahoga	46 162	6 682	39 480	73 035	4 863	5 551	616 903	2.0	571 457	63.2	2 209	80.4	16.3	365 739
Darke	864	52	812	1 270	1 684	2 426	21 583	6.1	20 419	76.6	177	96.0	–	19 532
Defiance	422	11	411	1 397	1 798	3 550	16 040	8.8	15 138	79.6	142	94.4	–	14 076
Delaware	1 929	80	1 849	1 710	2 083	2 555	42 374	73.8	39 674	80.4	3 093	99.0	.7	421 393
Erie	3 152	152	3 000	3 879	4 010	5 052	35 909	9.4	31 727	72.0	309	89.6	–	40 029
Fairfield	2 045	43	2 002	2 434	4 367	7 054	47 922	22.8	45 425	76.3	914	89.4	9.7	138 298
Fayette	1 197	32	1 165	919	4 183	3 346	11 904	10.1	11 054	66.6	105	100.0	–	13 210
Franklin	77 048	6 644	70 404	80 004	7 782	8 560	471 016	16.2	438 778	56.9	9 321	52.4	39.1	964 305
Fulton	814	36	778	983	1 935	2 590	16 232	15.2	15 480	80.1	163	90.2	–	21 068
Gallia	62	6	56	224	218	4 637	13 498	7.4	12 060	74.9	7	71.4	–	465
Geauga	470	14	456	849	2 170	1 097	32 805	17.5	31 630	87.2	519	100.0	–	106 308
Greene	5 425	194	5 231	5 052	3 685	3 695	58 224	15.9	55 312	69.7	860	60.7	35.6	96 110
Guernsey	1 164	58	1 106	991	2 828	8 435	18 771	8.7	16 094	73.4	84	100.0	–	5 868
Hamilton	36 331	3 219	33 112	46 946	4 753	5 693	373 393	3.3	346 790	59.9	1 940	68.1	29.6	299 985
Hancock	NA	NA	NA	NA	NA	NA	29 785	14.1	27 898	73.1	305	79.7	–	40 242
Hardin	224	6	218	412	1 249	1 947	12 907	7.8	11 963	73.0	67	92.5	7.5	5 211
Harrison	162	19	143	440	1 002	2 735	7 680	5.2	6 398	77.6	–	–	–	–
Henry	577	24	553	347	2 113	3 361	11 622	5.7	10 935	80.5	72	100.0	–	8 988
Highland	419	89	330	518	7 469	1 450	17 583	18.5	15 587	75.3	59	100.0	–	4 702
Hocking	443	12	431	528	1 521	2 068	12 141	15.8	10 843	75.7	4	100.0	–	415
Holmes	NA	NA	NA	184	NA	617	12 280	22.7	11 337	77.0	19	15.8	84.2	964
Huron	1 081	34	1 047	1 114	1 785	1 981	23 594	10.3	22 307	72.2	160	91.9	–	16 272
Jackson	442	22	420	5	1 744	28	13 909	11.7	12 619	73.9	186	80.6	19.4	16 161
Jefferson	230	60	170	2 192	2 385	2 730	33 291	-1.8	30 417	74.3	112	28.6	53.6	5 994
Knox	NA	NA	NA	NA	NA	NA	21 793	17.7	19 975	75.7	325	89.2	5.8	32 220
Lake	2 977	149	2 828	5 642	2 119	3 158	93 487	12.4	89 700	77.5	761	88.6	1.6	119 799
Lawrence	NA	NA	NA	83	NA	651	27 189	9.7	24 732	74.8	103	68.9	–	5 833
Licking	1 470	28	1 442	1 726	1 197	2 344	58 760	17.4	55 609	74.4	1 135	89.3	4.1	156 166
Logan	1 072	86	986	NA	2 310	NA	21 571	10.8	17 956	75.6	260	94.6	2.3	25 957
Lorain	3 950	289	3 661	8 982	1 938	3 524	111 368	11.4	105 836	74.2	1 783	74.3	15.2	268 172
Lucas	27 706	2 345	25 361	38 210	6 381	8 286	196 259	2.5	182 847	65.4	1 227	80.0	15.7	156 915
Madison	518	53	465	473	3 410	1 337	14 399	14.1	13 672	72.3	185	98.9	–	20 963
Mahoning	7 346	926	6 420	10 422	5 884	6 592	111 762	3.6	102 587	72.8	716	85.5	6.1	91 391

[1] Data on serious crimes have not been adjusted for underreporting; this may affect comparability over time or among geographic areas. [2] Includes murder and nonnegligent manslaughter, forcible rape, robbery, and aggravated assault. [3] Includes burglary, larceny-theft, and motor vehicle theft. [4] Per 100,000 resident population provided by the U.S. Federal Bureau of Investigation.

Sources: Serious Crimes Known to Police—U.S. Federal Bureau of Investigation, Uniform Crime Reporting Program, unpublished data, annual (related Internet site <http://www.fbi.gov/ucr/ucr.htm>). Housing, 2000—U.S. Census Bureau, 2000 Census of Population and Housing, "Census 2000 Profiles of General Demographic Characteristics" data files, published May 2001 (related Internet site <http://www.census.gov/mp/www/pub/2000cen/mscen01.html>). Housing, 1990—U.S. Census Bureau, 1990 Census of Population and Housing, Summary Tape File (STF) 1C on CD-ROM (related Internet site <http://homer.ssd.census.gov/cdrom/lookup>). Building Permits—U.S. Census Bureau, "New Residential Construction–Building Permits," e-mail from Manufacturing and Construction Division/Residential Construction Branch, subject: building permits by place 2000, 22 May 2001 (related Internet site <http://www.census.gov/const/www/permitsindex.html>).

[Includes U.S., states, and 3,142 counties or county equivalents defined as of January 1, 1992. For changes to these areas since January 1, 1992, see appendix B. Geographic Information]

County	Serious crimes known to police (as reported to the FBI)[1]						Housing, 2000				New private housing units authorized by building permits, 2000			
	Number				Rate[4]				Occupied units			Percent in structures with—		
	1999			1990	1999	1990	Total units	Percent change, 1990–2000	Number	Percent owner-occupied	Number	One unit	Five units or more	Valuation ($1,000)
	Total	Violent[2]	Property[3]											
OHIO—Con.														
Marion	2 010	57	1 953	3 137	3 120	4 930	26 298	4.6	24 578	72.9	134	96.3	–	12 536
Medina	429	13	416	793	2 432	1 708	56 793	31.1	54 542	81.3	1 681	85.8	12.5	251 522
Meigs	NA	NA	NA	NA	NA	NA	10 782	10.1	9 234	79.4	12	100.0	–	764
Mercer	66	2	64	194	1 107	2 010	15 875	6.1	14 756	80.1	149	69.1	20.8	17 636
Miami	1 726	81	1 645	1 676	2 194	3 366	40 554	12.7	38 437	72.3	265	100.0	–	43 250
Monroe	23	1	22	174	149	1 153	7 212	9.8	6 021	80.8	–	–	–	–
Montgomery	27 658	2 433	25 225	37 495	6 169	6 743	248 443	3.2	229 229	64.7	1 384	76.2	14.9	177 310
Morgan	62	–	62	97	425	683	7 771	16.3	5 890	78.3	1	100.0	–	104
Morrow	12	–	12	50	574	201	12 132	17.6	11 499	82.2	51	100.0	–	4 955
Muskingum	1 426	37	1 389	2 696	2 464	3 321	35 163	6.5	32 518	73.5	186	11.8	75.3	8 480
Noble	107	3	104	NA	863	NA	5 480	9.6	4 546	79.8	32	100.0	–	2 546
Ottawa	339	7	332	988	4 739	2 616	25 532	9.4	16 474	80.6	243	98.4	–	20 302
Paulding	6	2	4	127	244	710	8 478	6.6	7 773	83.8	143	54.5	39.9	10 727
Perry	590	27	563	253	1 894	4 944	13 655	11.4	12 500	79.4	34	100.0	–	3 699
Pickaway	169	26	143	1 070	313	2 217	18 596	13.5	17 599	74.6	205	100.0	–	28 715
Pike	295	7	288	183	6 701	4 088	11 602	19.3	10 444	70.0	96	14.6	81.3	5 206
Portage	2 744	142	2 602	2 507	1 813	4 779	60 096	14.9	56 449	71.3	737	98.4	1.6	133 868
Preble	948	61	887	861	2 184	2 247	17 186	13.3	16 001	78.9	176	94.9	2.8	16 756
Putnam	NA	NA	NA	249	NA	736	12 753	9.9	12 200	84.1	92	84.8	–	11 120
Richland	5 382	220	5 162	6 982	4 209	5 718	53 062	5.4	49 534	71.5	538	57.6	19.1	52 003
Ross	3 013	93	2 920	2 494	3 975	3 597	29 461	12.6	27 136	73.5	68	77.9	22.1	6 911
Sandusky	1 674	77	1 597	1 999	5 294	3 226	25 253	6.3	23 717	75.3	149	94.6	–	16 709
Scioto	4 352	192	4 160	2 915	5 393	3 629	34 054	5.1	30 871	70.1	6	66.7	–	265
Seneca	1 001	31	970	653	1 659	1 093	23 692	5.4	22 292	75.1	203	92.1	–	11 992
Shelby	282	20	262	1 316	994	2 930	18 682	13.2	17 636	74.3	210	88.6	–	27 792
Stark	4 209	233	3 976	16 271	2 068	4 499	157 024	6.9	148 316	72.4	1 255	94.7	.8	188 773
Summit	19 484	1 213	18 271	25 333	3 869	6 203	230 980	9.2	217 788	70.2	2 605	71.1	25.0	325 320
Trumbull	1 436	115	1 321	6 868	1 654	3 282	95 117	5.1	89 020	74.3	468	78.0	1.3	49 913
Tuscarawas	1 129	102	1 027	1 902	1 269	2 262	38 113	12.2	35 653	74.9	173	82.7	–	21 631
Union	97	15	82	643	380	2 230	15 217	31.2	14 346	77.5	450	100.0	–	67 599
Van Wert	729	37	692	864	2 404	2 836	12 363	3.0	11 587	81.7	84	97.6	–	7 881
Vinton	NA	NA	NA	215	NA	1 937	5 653	16.4	4 892	77.8	–	–	–	–
Warren	2 508	61	2 447	3 707	1 964	3 254	58 692	44.4	55 966	78.5	2 906	81.0	15.8	307 380
Washington	1 279	126	1 153	1 234	2 079	2 050	27 760	7.8	25 137	76.3	19	100.0	–	2 868
Wayne	404	29	375	2 074	2 276	2 099	42 324	14.3	40 445	73.3	497	82.1	2.2	55 807
Williams	448	14	434	1 003	1 326	2 714	16 140	9.5	15 105	76.8	170	82.9	–	18 559
Wood	3 016	98	2 918	4 204	2 715	3 743	47 468	13.7	45 172	70.7	754	57.4	37.0	74 891
Wyandot	377	13	364	511	1 965	2 296	9 324	8.5	8 882	74.7	68	91.2	–	7 768
OKLAHOMA	157 263	17 064	140 199	176 026	4 685	5 599	1 514 400	7.7	1 342 293	68.4	11 148	80.5	17.1	1 204 001
Adair	550	77	473	280	2 694	1 520	8 348	17.2	7 471	73.4	10	60.0	–	680
Alfalfa	71	2	69	99	1 171	1 543	2 832	–15.6	2 199	81.6	–	–	–	–
Atoka	318	51	267	194	2 394	1 518	5 673	11.0	4 964	76.2	1	100.0	–	140
Beaver	123	1	122	121	2 024	2 009	2 719	–7.0	2 245	79.1	1	100.0	–	80
Beckham	593	20	573	876	3 018	4 657	8 796	–3.5	7 356	71.0	96	37.5	62.5	5 326
Blaine	271	44	227	379	2 569	3 304	5 208	–9.1	4 159	76.8	1	100.0	–	65
Bryan	1 017	106	911	1 312	2 922	4 089	16 715	12.4	14 422	69.4	21	100.0	–	1 738
Caddo	679	97	582	791	2 184	2 677	13 096	–.7	10 957	73.4	28	92.9	–	1 266
Canadian	3 961	284	3 677	3 536	4 619	4 752	33 969	18.9	31 484	79.0	259	91.5	–	28 828
Carter	2 389	237	2 152	2 463	5 350	5 967	20 577	7.2	17 992	71.2	148	50.0	50.0	12 030
Cherokee	1 341	143	1 198	1 250	3 415	3 671	19 499	22.4	16 175	66.8	158	3.8	96.2	4 004
Choctaw	484	146	338	343	3 199	2 242	7 539	10.2	6 220	70.9	7	100.0	–	385
Cimarron	30	9	21	55	1 010	1 666	1 583	–6.3	1 257	72.2	–	–	–	–
Cleveland	9 617	681	8 936	12 710	4 766	7 294	84 844	19.4	79 186	67.0	811	98.0	–	94 055
Coal	141	32	109	72	2 339	1 246	2 744	.7	2 373	75.1	1	100.0	–	100
Comanche	5 242	537	4 705	4 874	4 603	4 372	45 416	4.2	39 808	60.3	138	92.8	7.2	15 161
Cotton	148	21	127	131	2 200	1 970	3 085	–2.1	2 614	76.6	2	100.0	–	132
Craig	407	35	372	375	2 807	2 659	6 459	6.9	5 620	75.1	2	100.0	–	140
Creek	1 731	202	1 529	2 197	2 609	3 607	27 986	11.3	25 289	78.0	99	73.7	18.2	11 908
Custer	861	82	779	1 032	3 366	3 837	11 675	.3	10 136	63.6	45	77.8	22.2	4 201
Delaware	777	102	675	645	2 267	2 298	22 290	32.6	14 838	79.2	115	100.0	–	14 096
Dewey	99	8	91	108	2 002	1 946	2 425	–11.3	1 962	79.2	–	–	–	–
Ellis	36	3	33	56	836	1 245	2 146	–12.4	1 769	80.7	2	100.0	–	175
Garfield	3 226	272	2 954	3 442	5 654	6 067	26 047	–1.7	23 175	70.3	59	93.2	–	9 770
Garvin	759	69	690	839	2 797	3 154	12 641	5.9	10 865	73.8	8	100.0	–	752
Grady	1 570	210	1 360	1 959	3 406	4 693	19 444	9.3	17 341	75.7	65	100.0	–	8 467
Grant	78	5	73	68	1 456	1 195	2 622	–11.3	2 089	78.7	1	100.0	–	34
Greer	164	13	151	69	2 567	1 052	2 788	–10.8	2 237	75.0	1	100.0	–	80
Harmon	122	11	111	53	3 495	1 397	1 647	–8.1	1 266	77.0	X	X	X	X
Harper	47	12	35	57	1 303	1 403	1 863	–10.3	1 509	79.2	2	100.0	–	211

[1] Data on serious crimes have not been adjusted for underreporting; this may affect comparability over time or among geographic areas. [2] Includes murder and nonnegligent manslaughter, forcible rape, robbery, and aggravated assault. [3] Includes burglary, larceny-theft, and motor vehicle theft. [4] Per 100,000 resident population provided by the U.S. Federal Bureau of Investigation.

Sources: Serious Crimes Known to Police—U.S. Federal Bureau of Investigation, Uniform Crime Reporting Program, unpublished data, annual (related Internet site <http://www.fbi.gov/ucr/ucr.htm>). Housing, 2000—U.S. Census Bureau, 2000 Census of Population and Housing, "Census 2000 Profiles of General Demographic Characteristics" data files, published May 2001 (related Internet site <http://www.census.gov/mp/www/pub/2000cen/mscen01.html>). Housing, 1990—U.S. Census Bureau, 1990 Census of Population and Housing, Summary Tape File (STF) 1C on CD-ROM (related Internet site <http://homer.ssd.census.gov/cdrom/lookup>). Building Permits—U.S. Census Bureau, "New Residential Construction–Building Permits," e-mail from Manufacturing and Construction Division/Residential Construction Branch, subject: building permits by place 2000, 22 May 2001 (related Internet site <http://www.census.gov/const/www/permitsindex.html>).

[Includes U.S., states, and 3,142 counties or county equivalents defined as of January 1, 1992. For changes to these areas since January 1, 1992, see appendix B. Geographic Information]

County	Serious crimes known to police (as reported to the FBI)[1] Number 1999 Total	Violent[2]	Property[3]	1990	Rate[4] 1999	1990	Housing, 2000 Total units	Percent change, 1990–2000	Occupied units Number	Percent owner–occupied	New private housing units authorized by building permits, 2000 Number	Percent in structures with— One unit	Five units or more	Valuation ($1,000)
OKLAHOMA—Con.														
Haskell	315	52	263	239	2 762	2 185	5 573	8.5	4 624	77.5	3	100.0	–	182
Hughes	356	37	319	292	2 520	2 242	6 237	3.6	5 319	75.8	9	100.0	–	524
Jackson	1 354	87	1 267	1 501	4 690	5 218	12 377	2.1	10 590	60.2	14	100.0	–	1 551
Jefferson	112	17	95	117	1 696	1 669	3 373	-4.2	2 716	74.2	1	100.0	–	192
Johnston	98	17	81	306	944	3 050	4 782	6.8	4 057	73.9	27	11.1	88.9	1 294
Kay	2 323	173	2 150	2 148	4 958	4 470	21 804	-2.9	19 157	71.7	78	55.1	44.9	9 025
Kingfisher	270	8	262	321	1 989	2 430	5 879	1.5	5 247	78.2	27	100.0	–	3 697
Kiowa	273	39	234	331	2 564	2 917	5 304	-6.0	4 208	75.3	3	100.0	–	186
Latimer	233	44	189	210	2 250	2 032	4 709	9.4	3 951	74.6	7	100.0	–	224
Le Flore	1 277	204	1 073	791	2 733	1 828	20 142	11.7	17 861	75.2	46	100.0	–	3 214
Lincoln	601	89	512	541	1 910	1 852	13 712	11.5	12 178	80.0	24	100.0	–	2 315
Logan	643	78	565	1 108	2 069	3 819	13 906	13.3	12 389	78.4	16	100.0	–	1 631
Love	232	44	188	303	2 709	3 715	4 066	13.5	3 442	81.6	–	–	–	–
McClain	727	131	596	758	2 763	3 325	11 189	20.3	10 331	81.4	123	95.9	4.1	12 129
McCurtain	1 304	266	1 038	1 254	3 736	3 751	15 427	11.6	13 216	73.3	28	100.0	–	1 631
McIntosh	751	79	672	478	3 929	2 849	12 640	18.0	8 085	79.0	67	25.4	–	2 215
Major	182	25	157	196	2 317	2 433	3 540	-8.2	3 046	81.1	2	100.0	–	155
Marshall	243	32	211	321	1 965	2 964	8 517	15.3	5 371	79.3	1	100.0	–	76
Mayes	1 066	94	972	889	2 823	2 664	17 423	12.6	14 823	77.0	39	84.6	–	3 370
Murray	358	58	300	379	2 892	3 147	6 479	12.8	5 003	74.2	15	100.0	–	1 268
Muskogee	3 407	427	2 980	3 806	4 850	5 591	29 575	2.4	26 458	69.6	76	100.0	–	7 719
Noble	239	26	213	271	2 085	2 454	5 082	3.8	4 504	75.3	10	100.0	–	785
Nowata	372	45	327	329	3 719	3 293	4 705	3.8	4 147	77.8	6	16.7	83.3	440
Okfuskee	350	42	308	297	3 059	2 571	5 114	4.5	4 270	76.2	1	100.0	–	25
Oklahoma	47 153	4 174	42 979	54 118	7 425	9 026	295 020	5.6	266 834	60.4	4 092	70.8	27.9	428 842
Okmulgee	1 407	179	1 228	1 766	3 608	4 840	17 316	5.4	15 300	72.5	35	94.3	–	2 531
Osage	1 478	205	1 273	1 225	3 439	2 942	18 826	3.5	16 617	80.6	46	100.0	–	4 252
Ottawa	1 259	78	1 181	1 130	4 055	3 698	14 842	5.5	12 984	73.9	15	46.7	–	1 140
Pawnee	365	33	332	348	2 213	2 234	7 464	.8	6 383	80.1	–	–	–	–
Payne	2 370	246	2 124	2 579	3 628	4 193	29 326	7.1	26 680	55.9	220	61.8	27.3	17 293
Pittsburg	1 473	154	1 319	1 378	3 430	3 396	21 520	10.7	17 157	76.0	43	86.0	–	4 536
Pontotoc	1 106	131	975	1 243	3 187	3 643	15 575	3.2	13 978	67.0	32	56.3	–	1 978
Pottawatomie	2 788	270	2 518	3 074	4 464	5 231	27 302	11.3	24 540	72.1	100	100.0	–	10 663
Pushmataha	325	89	236	339	2 796	3 083	5 795	11.7	4 739	77.7	1	100.0	–	43
Roger Mills	43	5	38	81	1 107	1 950	1 749	-14.0	1 428	78.7	–	–	–	–
Rogers	1 677	139	1 538	1 489	2 453	2 699	27 476	28.1	25 724	81.1	448	99.1	–	49 648
Seminole	840	91	749	1 102	3 380	4 337	11 146	-2.3	9 575	72.5	6	100.0	–	581
Sequoyah	1 267	184	1 083	582	3 364	1 720	16 940	18.3	14 761	75.2	96	53.1	32.3	6 235
Stephens	1 589	98	1 491	1 737	3 648	4 106	19 854	.9	17 463	75.5	43	100.0	–	4 148
Texas	663	56	607	405	3 545	2 467	8 014	9.4	7 153	66.8	75	14.7	85.3	5 161
Tillman	256	20	236	362	2 685	3 486	4 342	-7.7	3 594	77.3	–	–	–	–
Tulsa	33 119	4 937	28 182	41 651	6 073	8 275	243 953	7.1	226 892	61.8	2 715	91.5	8.0	349 144
Wagoner	1 198	110	1 088	946	2 161	1 976	23 174	20.3	21 010	81.1	428	97.4	–	41 456
Washington	1 911	159	1 752	1 766	4 008	3 674	22 250	2.5	20 179	74.0	37	100.0	–	6 663
Washita	128	17	111	215	1 081	1 879	5 452	-10.6	4 506	74.7	1	100.0	–	80
Woods	182	25	157	180	2 168	1 977	4 492	-6.1	3 684	69.8	5	100.0	–	620
Woodward	728	38	690	738	3 911	3 889	8 341	-2.0	7 141	72.0	6	100.0	–	1 315
OREGON	165 062	12 418	152 644	159 755	4 991	5 635	1 452 709	21.7	1 333 723	64.3	[5]19 877	[5]78.6	[5]16.0	[5]2 533 336
Baker	763	42	721	560	4 591	3 656	8 402	11.7	6 883	70.1	28	100.0	–	3 155
Benton	3 051	189	2 862	3 169	3 883	4 475	31 980	18.3	30 145	57.3	264	85.6	9.8	43 104
Clackamas	15 033	568	14 465	11 567	4 445	4 148	136 954	25.6	128 201	71.1	2 311	76.6	20.5	388 547
Clatsop	1 491	86	1 405	1 478	4 166	4 438	19 685	13.3	14 703	64.2	154	89.0	–	22 469
Columbia	909	23	886	952	2 025	2 535	17 572	20.6	16 375	76.1	278	91.7	–	36 151
Coos	2 165	67	2 098	2 981	3 486	4 946	29 247	9.7	26 213	68.1	36	94.4	–	4 146
Crook	481	10	471	513	2 762	3 635	8 264	36.2	7 354	74.3	205	98.0	–	24 925
Curry	441	25	416	650	2 063	3 363	11 406	15.4	9 543	73.0	122	68.0	28.7	16 500
Deschutes	5 206	232	4 974	3 744	4 877	4 995	54 583	51.9	45 595	72.3	2 099	90.4	1.2	325 687
Douglas	3 204	136	3 068	3 576	3 114	3 778	43 284	13.0	39 821	71.7	363	84.0	6.6	46 313
Gilliam	24	3	21	31	1 174	1 805	1 043	11.9	819	70.2	1	100.0	–	67
Grant	95	2	93	226	1 164	2 878	4 004	6.1	3 246	73.5	X	X	X	X
Harney	213	9	204	149	2 929	2 110	3 533	6.9	3 036	72.7	11	100.0	–	987
Hood River	657	20	637	681	3 325	4 029	7 818	3.3	7 248	64.9	109	80.7	–	15 137
Jackson	7 873	460	7 413	7 752	4 528	5 295	75 737	25.4	71 532	66.5	1 351	84.4	9.4	160 010
Jefferson	623	19	604	289	3 708	2 113	8 319	31.8	6 727	71.3	209	98.1	–	14 457
Josephine	3 241	182	3 059	3 197	4 313	5 103	33 239	23.5	31 000	70.1	424	86.6	12.5	46 705
Klamath	1 783	208	1 575	2 743	2 793	4 814	28 883	11.3	25 205	68.0	150	98.7	–	26 028
Lake	132	27	105	116	1 827	1 614	3 999	16.5	3 084	68.9	16	100.0	–	2 021
Lane	18 693	1 067	17 626	15 398	5 891	5 443	138 946	19.1	130 453	62.3	1 330	86.7	5.8	183 160
Lincoln	2 456	155	2 301	2 054	5 358	5 282	26 889	20.1	19 296	65.7	314	56.4	37.9	33 233

[1] Data on serious crimes have not been adjusted for underreporting; this may affect comparability over time or among geographic areas. [2] Includes murder and nonnegligent manslaughter, forcible rape, robbery, and aggravated assault. [3] Includes burglary, larceny-theft, and motor vehicle theft. [4] Per 100,000 resident population provided by the U.S. Federal Bureau of Investigation. [5] Includes data not distributed by county.

Sources: Serious Crimes Known to Police—U.S. Federal Bureau of Investigation, Uniform Crime Reporting Program, unpublished data, annual (related Internet site <http://www.fbi.gov/ucr/ucr.htm>). Housing, 2000—U.S. Census Bureau, 2000 Census of Population and Housing, "Census 2000 Profiles of General Demographic Characteristics" data files, published May 2001 (related Internet site <http://www.census.gov/mp/www/pub/2000cen/mscen01.html>). Housing, 1990—U.S. Census Bureau, 1990 Census of Population and Housing, Summary Tape File (STF) 1C on CD-ROM (related Internet site <http://homer.ssd.census.gov/cdrom/lookup>). Building Permits—U.S. Census Bureau, "New Residential Construction–Building Permits," e-mail from Manufacturing and Construction Division/Residential Construction Branch, subject: building permits by place 2000, 22 May 2001 (related Internet site <http://www.census.gov/const/www/permitsindex.html>).

Table B–6. Counties — **Crime, Housing, and Building Permits**–Con.

[Includes U.S., states, and 3,142 counties or county equivalents defined as of January 1, 1992. For changes to these areas since January 1, 1992, see appendix B. Geographic Information]

County	Serious crimes known to police (as reported to the FBI)[1] Number 1999 Total	Violent[2]	Property[3]	1990	Rate[4] 1999	1990	Housing, 2000 Total units	Percent change, 1990-2000	Occupied units Number	Percent owner-occupied	New private housing units authorized by building permits, 2000 Number	Percent in structures with— One unit	Five units or more	Valuation ($1,000)
OREGON—Con.														
Linn	5 240	194	5 046	5 400	4 964	5 919	42 521	16.6	39 541	67.9	512	72.1	21.9	55 156
Malheur	898	42	856	1 104	3 114	4 240	11 233	5.5	10 221	63.8	56	100.0	–	6 227
Marion	15 384	543	14 841	13 593	5 670	5 999	108 174	24.5	101 641	62.9	1 424	83.8	10.6	160 444
Morrow	409	70	339	274	4 054	3 593	4 276	25.3	3 776	73.1	X	X	X	X
Multnomah	48 598	6 755	41 843	55 953	7 623	9 583	288 561	12.8	272 098	56.9	2 591	54.8	36.6	266 446
Polk	2 572	97	2 475	2 370	4 135	4 784	24 461	28.9	23 058	68.4	260	64.2	32.3	29 098
Sherman	46	4	42	47	2 544	2 450	935	3.9	797	70.5	4	100.0	–	600
Tillamook	628	30	598	576	2 552	2 670	15 906	19.4	10 200	71.8	179	95.5	–	25 128
Umatilla	2 597	67	2 530	2 537	3 924	4 282	27 676	13.7	25 195	64.9	144	75.0	13.9	16 028
Union	571	28	543	987	2 470	4 183	10 603	6.3	9 740	66.5	46	100.0	–	5 118
Wallowa	77	2	75	116	1 429	1 678	3 900	3.9	3 029	71.8	X	X	X	X
Wasco	985	41	944	1 143	4 228	5 280	10 651	1.7	9 401	68.4	31	87.1	–	4 265
Washington	15 505	840	14 665	11 436	3 855	3 677	178 913	43.5	169 162	60.6	3 827	84.4	13.6	466 146
Wheeler	23	5	18	37	1 454	2 650	842	7.7	653	72.1	4	100.0	–	536
Yamhill	2 995	170	2 825	2 356	3 670	3 826	30 270	30.5	28 732	69.6	750	54.1	41.6	82 565
PENNSYLVANIA	345 405	47 614	297 791	356 245	3 030	3 126	5 249 750	6.3	4 777 003	71.3	41 076	84.0	12.1	4 616 212
Adams	1 261	153	1 108	1 396	1 531	1 783	35 831	18.9	33 652	76.8	639	93.9	6.1	67 123
Allegheny	39 840	5 047	34 793	17 903	3 244	1 884	583 646	.5	537 150	67.0	2 706	68.9	26.8	329 955
Armstrong	717	63	654	994	1 192	1 389	32 387	2.0	29 005	77.3	151	64.2	5.3	12 171
Beaver	2 910	468	2 442	3 908	1 854	2 100	77 765	1.9	72 576	74.9	467	97.9	–	49 596
Bedford	738	46	692	661	1 569	1 379	23 529	8.2	19 768	80.1	175	87.4	10.3	15 884
Berks	11 248	1 316	9 932	11 392	3 327	3 401	150 222	11.7	141 570	74.0	1 809	87.5	10.6	192 356
Blair	3 488	260	3 228	3 052	2 672	2 338	55 061	1.3	51 518	72.9	226	93.8	–	20 948
Bradford	1 149	107	1 042	1 316	1 841	2 159	28 664	5.9	24 453	75.5	159	100.0	–	12 757
Bucks	12 069	663	11 406	15 474	2 297	2 859	225 498	12.8	218 725	77.4	2 768	85.5	6.1	354 824
Butler	2 956	229	2 727	2 824	1 775	1 858	69 868	18.3	65 862	77.9	1 030	83.2	13.6	131 658
Cambria	2 094	302	1 792	2 871	1 470	1 761	65 796	-2.3	60 531	74.8	220	95.9	2.3	19 453
Cameron	167	15	152	152	2 973	2 571	4 592	4.4	2 465	74.8	9	100.0	–	1 075
Carbon	1 075	107	968	1 202	2 099	2 114	30 492	11.4	23 701	78.2	207	99.0	–	26 577
Centre	3 046	140	2 906	4 201	2 408	3 394	53 161	15.1	49 323	60.2	653	84.8	11.3	67 780
Chester	8 105	889	7 216	8 321	1 923	2 211	163 773	17.3	157 905	76.3	3 051	95.4	3.2	431 765
Clarion	611	32	579	714	1 843	1 762	19 426	7.8	16 052	72.3	120	95.0	–	9 186
Clearfield	1 676	195	1 481	1 474	2 310	2 063	37 855	10.4	32 785	79.2	186	100.0	–	15 119
Clinton	874	24	850	1 052	3 049	2 934	18 166	10.2	14 773	72.9	137	92.7	7.3	11 131
Columbia	1 001	47	954	1 106	1 910	1 823	27 733	8.3	24 915	72.4	259	79.5	18.9	19 566
Crawford	1 740	105	1 635	1 910	1 970	2 217	42 416	4.8	34 678	75.5	240	94.6	2.5	18 659
Cumberland	4 727	305	4 422	4 497	2 282	2 303	86 951	12.8	83 015	73.1	1 008	91.9	7.0	121 076
Dauphin	8 601	1 066	7 535	11 829	3 630	4 992	111 133	8.2	102 670	65.4	780	83.1	13.1	76 676
Delaware	15 396	2 623	12 773	18 189	2 871	3 321	216 978	2.8	206 320	71.9	1 142	77.6	20.3	154 675
Elk	788	54	734	867	2 283	2 486	18 115	5.0	14 124	79.4	99	100.0	–	9 517
Erie	7 527	682	6 845	9 914	2 725	3 598	114 322	5.3	106 507	69.2	704	81.5	15.1	72 804
Fayette	2 399	280	2 119	3 155	1 991	2 287	66 490	8.3	59 969	73.2	352	83.0	17.0	22 041
Forest	224	13	211	295	4 481	6 143	8 701	3.0	2 000	82.7	47	100.0	–	2 992
Franklin	3 089	421	2 668	3 237	2 415	2 673	53 803	10.6	50 633	74.0	714	83.2	3.4	67 235
Fulton	203	18	185	286	1 401	2 067	6 790	9.8	5 660	78.8	49	100.0	–	4 010
Greene	572	67	505	714	1 695	1 805	16 678	4.4	15 060	74.1	106	77.4	22.6	7 139
Huntingdon	648	88	560	770	1 454	1 744	21 058	9.2	16 759	77.5	180	98.9	–	15 492
Indiana	1 384	97	1 287	1 660	1 604	1 845	37 250	7.1	34 123	71.7	335	40.3	50.7	21 130
Jefferson	632	39	593	785	1 506	1 743	22 104	4.1	18 375	77.1	143	100.0	–	9 497
Juniata	147	9	138	163	713	816	10 031	17.9	8 584	77.7	49	100.0	–	4 334
Lackawanna	1 733	194	1 539	4 429	1 574	2 200	95 362	4.0	86 218	67.6	520	71.2	20.0	55 180
Lancaster	10 088	730	9 358	11 545	2 245	2 730	179 990	15.0	172 560	70.8	2 016	84.5	10.2	250 472
Lawrence	2 043	226	1 817	2 074	2 388	2 411	39 635	2.0	37 091	77.3	270	65.6	–	26 890
Lebanon	2 734	213	2 521	2 617	2 330	2 301	49 320	10.5	46 551	72.7	514	100.0	–	51 504
Lehigh	10 496	960	9 536	11 254	3 509	3 866	128 910	8.9	121 906	68.8	1 344	89.9	9.2	165 633
Luzerne	6 108	609	5 499	5 025	2 145	1 587	144 686	4.3	130 687	70.3	603	94.2	2.7	67 491
Lycoming	2 975	201	2 774	3 545	2 761	2 986	52 464	5.8	47 003	69.4	313	90.4	9.6	31 727
McKean	495	41	454	811	1 079	1 721	21 644	.9	18 024	74.7	88	100.0	–	7 061
Mercer	2 725	188	2 537	2 321	2 300	1 918	49 859	2.4	46 712	76.3	432	70.1	28.2	38 375
Mifflin	822	95	727	852	1 906	1 844	20 745	5.6	18 413	74.0	120	100.0	–	9 760
Monroe	3 057	233	2 824	3 454	2 947	3 609	67 581	23.3	49 454	78.3	1 630	90.9	8.1	220 696
Montgomery	18 626	1 469	17 157	16 794	2 590	2 573	297 434	11.9	286 098	73.5	3 058	90.9	5.4	324 100
Montour	333	48	285	302	1 879	1 703	7 627	10.8	7 085	73.0	62	100.0	–	8 606
Northampton	6 186	591	5 595	6 051	2 605	2 449	106 710	11.9	101 541	73.3	1 312	83.2	10.5	143 961
Northumberland	1 701	275	1 426	1 698	2 077	1 805	43 164	3.0	38 835	73.5	169	96.4	–	15 558
Perry	580	76	504	634	1 353	1 540	18 941	11.0	16 695	79.8	165	94.5	–	16 332
Philadelphia	104 673	23 035	81 638	114 080	7 292	7 195	661 958	-1.9	590 071	59.3	1 333	7.1	90.5	87 571
Pike	845	77	768	1 175	2 184	4 202	34 681	12.4	17 433	84.8	475	98.7	1.3	64 093
Potter	304	27	277	368	1 918	2 201	12 159	7.3	7 005	77.3	105	100.0	–	9 779

[1] Data on serious crimes have not been adjusted for underreporting; this may affect comparability over time or among geographic areas. [2] Includes murder and nonnegligent manslaughter, forcible rape, robbery, and aggravated assault. [3] Includes burglary, larceny-theft, and motor vehicle theft. [4] Per 100,000 resident population provided by the U.S. Federal Bureau of Investigation.

Sources: Serious Crimes Known to Police—U.S. Federal Bureau of Investigation, Uniform Crime Reporting Program, unpublished data, annual (related Internet site <http://www.fbi.gov/ucr/ucr.htm>). Housing, 2000—U.S. Census Bureau, 2000 Census of Population and Housing, "Census 2000 Profiles of General Demographic Characteristics" data files, published May 2001 (related Internet site <http://www.census.gov/mp/www/pub/2000cen/mscen01.html>). Housing, 1990—U.S. Census Bureau, 1990 Census of Population and Housing, Summary Tape File (STF) 1C on CD-ROM (related Internet site <http://homer.ssd.census.gov/cdrom/lookup>). Building Permits—U.S. Census Bureau, "New Residential Construction–Building Permits," e-mail from Manufacturing and Construction Division/Residential Construction Branch, subject: building permits by place 2000, 22 May 2001 (related Internet site <http://www.census.gov/const/www/permitsindex.html>).

[Includes U.S., states, and 3,142 counties or county equivalents defined as of January 1, 1992. For changes to these areas since January 1, 1992, see appendix B. Geographic Information]

County	Serious crimes known to police (as reported to the FBI)[1] Number 1999 Total	Violent[2]	Property[3]	1990	Rate[4] 1999	1990	Housing, 2000 Total units	Percent change, 1990–2000	Occupied units Number	Percent owner-occupied	New private housing units authorized by building permits, 2000 Number	Percent in structures with— One unit	Five units or more	Valuation ($1,000)
PENNSYLVANIA—Con.														
Schuylkill	2 272	288	1 984	1 991	1 840	1 315	67 806	2.0	60 530	78.0	352	82.1	17.9	32 629
Snyder	596	104	492	553	1 620	1 508	14 890	9.3	13 654	76.5	121	90.9	–	11 051
Somerset	754	58	696	1 038	995	1 339	37 163	4.1	31 222	78.1	240	87.5	2.5	21 898
Sullivan	157	3	154	223	2 573	3 653	6 017	10.2	2 660	80.8	25	100.0	–	2 361
Susquehanna	627	66	561	424	1 604	1 050	21 893	7.5	16 529	79.5	130	100.0	–	10 966
Tioga	517	26	491	563	1 295	1 493	19 893	9.3	15 925	76.2	196	87.8	12.2	14 545
Union	302	15	287	458	943	1 266	14 684	14.0	13 178	73.3	111	100.0	–	10 797
Venango	1 204	85	1 119	1 530	2 083	2 577	26 904	-.2	22 747	76.4	129	78.3	18.6	9 533
Warren	811	55	756	904	1 993	2 007	23 058	3.7	17 696	78.2	88	100.0	–	6 121
Washington	3 727	345	3 382	4 053	1 904	1 991	87 267	3.7	81 130	77.1	876	90.6	5.9	127 623
Wayne	912	97	815	741	2 076	1 911	30 593	7.4	18 350	80.4	253	100.0	–	25 184
Westmoreland	5 888	676	5 212	6 391	1 590	1 728	161 058	4.9	149 813	78.0	999	86.6	4.0	127 227
Wyoming	383	24	359	302	1 421	1 076	12 713	7.2	10 762	78.9	98	100.0	–	8 815
York	7 629	514	7 115	9 761	2 136	2 874	156 720	16.3	148 219	76.1	2 009	85.3	8.6	216 472
RHODE ISLAND	[5]35 498	[5]2 839	[5]32 659	53 712	[5]3 582	5 381	439 837	6.1	408 424	60.0	2 596	86.9	7.3	296 394
Bristol	1 046	56	990	1 187	2 125	2 429	19 881	7.1	19 033	71.3	85	100.0	–	10 428
Kent	4 695	270	4 425	7 733	2 895	4 799	70 365	7.5	67 320	71.5	453	89.6	–	47 544
Newport	2 865	221	2 644	4 047	3 449	4 641	39 561	5.6	35 228	61.6	307	82.7	16.6	41 965
Providence	24 162	2 114	22 048	36 905	4 198	6 189	253 214	4.1	239 936	53.2	1 002	76.2	13.8	97 014
Washington	2 682	141	2 541	3 840	2 218	3 669	56 816	14.0	46 907	72.8	749	99.7	–	99 443
SOUTH CAROLINA	208 987	33 360	175 627	209 842	5 383	6 023	1 753 670	23.1	1 533 854	72.2	32 812	75.8	21.6	3 532 670
Abbeville	1 027	183	844	653	4 116	2 737	11 656	18.4	10 131	80.5	48	100.0	–	4 361
Aiken	5 492	804	4 688	6 309	4 053	5 217	61 987	25.8	55 587	75.6	678	100.0	–	74 145
Allendale	458	115	343	335	3 945	2 858	4 568	7.7	3 915	72.7	20	–	–	1 001
Anderson	6 715	947	5 768	7 585	4 152	5 260	73 213	20.5	65 649	76.3	1 110	85.8	8.6	112 511
Bamberg	511	121	390	372	3 058	2 201	7 130	11.3	6 123	74.7	21	81.0	–	1 485
Barnwell	811	166	645	595	3 678	2 932	10 191	29.8	9 021	75.5	4	100.0	–	546
Beaufort	6 571	829	5 742	6 541	5 953	7 568	60 509	31.6	45 532	73.2	2 689	73.9	25.5	438 370
Berkeley	5 548	1 026	4 522	5 435	4 014	4 221	54 717	19.7	49 922	74.2	556	100.0	–	56 001
Calhoun	434	102	332	267	3 049	2 094	6 864	31.4	5 917	84.4	84	100.0	–	4 725
Charleston	22 509	3 153	19 356	26 114	7 021	8 051	141 031	14.1	123 326	61.0	4 086	67.9	28.0	608 561
Cherokee	2 667	510	2 157	1 259	5 355	2 829	22 400	27.2	20 495	73.9	151	97.4	–	11 280
Chester	1 975	426	1 549	1 365	5 668	4 243	14 374	16.9	12 880	78.4	88	100.0	–	9 750
Chesterfield	1 985	395	1 590	1 165	4 770	3 079	18 818	24.6	16 557	76.3	268	91.0	–	22 530
Clarendon	1 216	273	943	278	3 896	977	15 303	26.5	11 812	79.1	109	100.0	–	10 389
Colleton	2 177	379	1 798	1 755	5 752	5 105	18 129	21.5	14 470	80.3	130	86.2	–	17 633
Darlington	3 649	466	3 183	3 665	5 428	5 926	28 942	22.6	25 793	77.0	169	100.0	–	15 328
Dillon	1 898	384	1 514	1 786	6 317	6 135	12 679	19.7	11 199	72.0	42	95.2	–	4 108
Dorchester	3 366	537	2 829	3 806	3 770	4 582	37 237	21.6	34 709	75.0	745	77.0	22.1	79 609
Edgefield	618	113	505	686	3 050	3 733	9 223	26.5	8 270	80.5	76	100.0	–	7 255
Fairfield	1 077	346	731	1 347	4 748	6 154	10 383	18.9	8 774	77.4	71	100.0	–	8 297
Florence	8 673	1 441	7 232	7 592	6 855	6 640	51 836	20.0	47 147	73.0	645	80.0	14.1	50 243
Georgetown	2 881	472	2 409	2 661	5 294	5 747	28 282	33.8	21 659	81.4	647	74.7	14.7	106 296
Greenville	18 849	3 016	15 833	20 385	5 259	6 367	162 803	23.7	149 556	68.2	3 411	82.7	16.1	281 807
Greenwood	3 884	917	2 967	3 383	6 026	5 679	28 243	14.2	25 729	69.2	384	51.0	33.6	24 509
Hampton	650	127	523	257	3 342	1 413	8 582	21.6	7 444	78.1	22	100.0	–	2 223
Horry	16 855	1 908	14 947	12 966	9 521	9 001	122 085	35.7	81 800	73.0	4 492	42.5	53.3	406 482
Jasper	1 421	178	1 243	911	8 254	5 882	7 928	30.6	7 042	77.7	72	100.0	–	7 589
Kershaw	1 604	253	1 351	1 493	3 259	3 474	22 683	29.8	20 188	82.0	314	100.0	–	33 217
Lancaster	3 442	617	2 825	2 663	5 770	4 885	24 962	19.3	23 178	75.0	367	98.6	1.4	46 653
Laurens	3 229	661	2 568	2 175	5 040	3 744	30 239	30.3	26 290	77.5	326	96.3	–	29 828
Lee	740	182	558	439	3 581	2 381	7 670	17.3	6 886	79.4	51	47.1	52.9	3 552
Lexington	8 774	1 159	7 615	9 731	4 220	5 806	90 978	34.7	83 240	77.2	1 383	100.0	–	146 112
McCormick	236	68	168	215	2 441	2 424	4 459	33.2	3 558	81.0	91	100.0	–	15 643
Marion	1 624	279	1 345	1 544	4 671	4 555	15 143	18.5	13 301	73.5	77	53.2	40.3	4 889
Marlboro	1 947	440	1 507	1 603	6 496	5 460	11 894	8.6	10 478	70.8	21	100.0	–	1 985
Newberry	747	187	560	992	2 140	2 990	16 805	16.3	14 026	76.8	128	100.0	–	15 651
Oconee	1 977	260	1 717	1 588	3 047	2 762	32 383	24.6	27 283	78.4	473	100.0	–	83 041
Orangeburg	7 227	1 429	5 798	5 493	8 189	6 477	39 304	21.5	34 118	75.6	234	84.2	–	18 848
Pickens	3 135	366	2 769	3 795	2 890	4 042	46 000	28.3	41 306	73.5	611	100.0	–	92 489
Richland	20 922	3 030	17 892	22 488	6 721	7 871	129 793	18.5	120 101	61.4	2 936	84.9	14.9	227 627
Saluda	507	103	404	259	2 940	1 583	8 543	25.8	7 127	80.6	47	100.0	–	5 169
Spartanburg	15 006	2 507	12 499	18 602	5 986	8 202	106 986	19.0	97 735	72.0	1 567	96.7	1.3	133 817
Sumter	4 442	830	3 612	6 063	4 121	5 907	41 751	19.2	37 728	69.5	294	100.0	–	28 197
Union	1 063	204	859	722	3 441	2 380	13 351	9.2	12 087	76.7	47	100.0	–	4 917
Williamsburg	635	152	483	974	1 689	2 646	15 552	17.2	13 714	80.5	50	100.0	–	717
York	7 813	1 299	6 514	9 530	4 998	7 247	66 061	31.0	61 051	73.1	2 977	57.4	41.3	273 284

[1] Data on serious crimes have not been adjusted for underreporting; this may affect comparability over time or among geographic areas. [2] Includes murder and nonnegligent manslaughter, forcible rape, robbery, and aggravated assault. [3] Includes burglary, larceny-theft, and motor vehicle theft. [4] Per 100,000 resident population provided by the U.S. Federal Bureau of Investigation. [5] Includes data not distributed by county.

Sources: Serious Crimes Known to Police—U.S. Federal Bureau of Investigation, Uniform Crime Reporting Program, unpublished data, annual (related Internet site <http://www.fbi.gov/ucr/ucr.htm>). Housing, 2000—U.S. Census Bureau, 2000 Census of Population and Housing, "Census 2000 Profiles of General Demographic Characteristics" data files, published May 2001 (related Internet site <http://www.census.gov/mp/www/pub/2000cen/mscen01.html>). Housing, 1990—U.S. Census Bureau, 1990 Census of Population and Housing, Summary Tape File (STF) 1C on CD-ROM (related Internet site <http://homer.ssd.census.gov/cdrom/lookup>). Building Permits—U.S. Census Bureau, "New Residential Construction–Building Permits," e-mail from Manufacturing and Construction Division/Residential Construction Branch, subject: building permits by place 2000, 22 May 2001 (related Internet site <http://www.census.gov/const/www/permitsindex.html>).

Table B–6. Counties — Crime, Housing, and Building Permits–Con.

[Includes U.S., states, and 3,142 counties or county equivalents defined as of January 1, 1992. For changes to these areas since January 1, 1992, see appendix B. Geographic Information]

County	Serious crimes known to police (as reported to the FBI)[1]						Housing, 2000				New private housing units authorized by building permits, 2000			
	Number				Rate[4]				Occupied units			Percent in structures with—		
	1999			1990	1999	1990	Total units	Percent change, 1990–2000	Number	Percent owner-occupied	Number	One unit	Five units or more	Valuation ($1,000)
	Total	Violent[2]	Property[3]											
SOUTH DAKOTA	16 182	1 041	15 141	18 486	2 933	3 052	323 208	10.5	290 245	68.2	4 196	74.9	20.9	369 138
Aurora	2	1	1	56	68	1 786	1 298	–3.3	1 165	76.7	2	100.0	–	93
Beadle	385	11	374	558	2 256	3 057	8 206	1.4	7 210	67.8	29	100.0	–	2 994
Bennett	NA	NA	NA	48	NA	1 497	1 278	–1.1	1 123	59.1	1	100.0	–	50
Bon Homme	8	2	6	37	105	522	3 007	–2.6	2 635	75.9	5	100.0	–	472
Brookings	575	24	551	707	2 228	2 805	11 576	17.8	10 665	58.2	101	70.3	23.8	7 904
Brown	792	51	741	1 142	2 251	3 210	15 861	5.0	14 638	66.3	111	49.5	44.1	6 240
Brule	NA	NA	NA	87	NA	1 586	2 272	–.1	1 998	71.2	13	69.2	–	911
Buffalo	NA	NA	NA	NA	NA	NA	602	12.5	526	42.8	X	X	X	X
Butte	13	–	13	186	318	2 350	4 059	15.9	3 516	73.2	12	66.7	–	665
Campbell	NA	NA	NA	1	NA	51	962	1.9	725	82.2	–	–	–	–
Charles Mix	61	6	55	30	658	329	3 853	2.7	3 343	68.4	7	100.0	–	662
Clark	NA	NA	NA	NA	NA	NA	1 880	–7.2	1 598	80.3	2	100.0	–	136
Clay	449	23	426	583	2 981	4 421	5 438	11.2	4 878	54.4	49	83.7	–	5 090
Codington	NA	NA	NA	843	NA	3 714	11 324	18.7	10 357	70.2	109	94.5	–	10 873
Corson	8	–	8	37	237	4 744	1 536	–1.3	1 271	59.4	–	–	–	–
Custer	NA	NA	NA	231	NA	3 738	3 624	20.7	2 970	77.0	70	100.0	–	5 264
Davison	493	24	469	752	2 757	4 296	8 093	8.1	7 585	61.9	70	80.0	11.4	5 147
Day	NA	NA	NA	28	NA	564	3 618	–7.6	2 586	76.0	21	100.0	–	1 444
Deuel	35	2	33	80	781	1 769	2 172	–1.6	1 843	80.1	22	100.0	–	2 120
Dewey	35	8	27	8	709	1 636	2 133	.5	1 863	55.2	16	–	100.0	1 066
Douglas	1	1	–	11	28	294	1 453	–4.2	1 321	80.8	5	20.0	–	145
Edmunds	2	–	2	17	48	390	2 022	.9	1 681	81.9	6	100.0	–	503
Fall River	16	3	13	[5]122	390	[5]707	3 812	3.3	3 127	69.7	5	100.0	–	371
Faulk	22	–	22	NA	879	NA	1 235	–4.0	1 014	81.9	4	100.0	–	270
Grant	36	2	34	27	990	696	3 456	–2.6	3 116	77.6	19	100.0	–	2 093
Gregory	18	1	17	6	489	794	2 405	–7.3	2 022	75.0	–	–	–	–
Haakon	NA	NA	NA	27	NA	1 029	1 002	–6.4	870	76.8	–	–	–	–
Hamlin	NA	NA	NA	NA	NA	NA	2 626	5.0	2 048	81.9	23	82.6	–	2 229
Hand	46	3	43	32	1 118	749	1 840	–10.4	1 543	73.8	3	100.0	–	410
Hanson	NA	NA	NA	36	NA	1 202	1 218	–1.1	1 115	79.1	X	X	X	X
Harding	NA	NA	NA	1	NA	60	804	3.6	525	73.5	–	–	–	–
Hughes	522	17	505	738	3 419	4 981	7 055	12.8	6 512	66.1	49	83.7	–	6 055
Hutchinson	17	–	17	46	1 119	389	3 517	–3.8	3 190	78.8	15	73.3	–	1 045
Hyde	6	3	3	3	376	177	769	–5.8	679	71.7	–	–	–	–
Jackson	25	2	23	53	3 383	1 885	1 173	2.3	945	63.4	–	–	–	–
Jerauld	5	–	5	30	227	1 237	1 167	–1.3	987	72.2	3	100.0	–	106
Jones	NA	NA	NA	26	NA	1 964	614	–12.2	509	72.5	4	100.0	–	320
Kingsbury	NA	NA	NA	NA	NA	NA	2 724	–1.5	2 406	75.6	21	81.0	–	2 218
Lake	193	6	187	299	2 922	2 834	5 282	2.6	4 372	70.5	81	70.4	29.6	5 698
Lawrence	543	31	512	285	2 632	1 380	10 427	14.7	8 881	64.8	136	80.9	19.1	16 183
Lincoln	37	1	36	77	1 040	499	9 131	56.8	8 782	79.7	168	97.0	–	19 033
Lyman	38	1	37	41	1 015	1 127	1 636	7.4	1 400	69.4	5	100.0	–	300
McCook	26	4	22	NA	468	NA	2 383	.5	2 204	78.9	45	82.2	–	4 389
McPherson	NA	NA	NA	4	NA	124	1 465	–6.4	1 227	83.1	–	–	–	162
Marshall	61	2	59	74	1 346	1 528	2 562	–3.0	1 844	77.8	24	70.8	20.8	1 252
Meade	515	30	485	280	2 367	5 253	10 149	33.7	8 805	68.2	101	91.1	–	12 549
Mellette	NA	NA	NA	NA	NA	NA	824	–9.5	694	64.7	–	–	–	–
Miner	55	2	53	91	1 978	2 781	1 408	–4.5	1 212	76.7	2	100.0	–	260
Minnehaha	4 772	399	4 373	4 959	3 363	4 005	60 237	21.0	57 996	64.7	2 137	65.2	31.7	168 099
Moody	NA	NA	NA	142	NA	2 182	2 745	3.0	2 526	72.6	2	100.0	–	162
Pennington	5 318	308	5 010	4 164	6 105	5 119	37 249	10.4	34 641	66.2	427	96.7	1.9	44 883
Perkins	14	–	14	33	660	839	1 854	–7.6	1 429	76.6	–	–	–	–
Potter	49	–	49	23	1 727	721	1 760	5.8	1 145	79.5	4	100.0	–	270
Roberts	131	8	123	NA	6 244	NA	4 734	.1	3 683	69.1	38	100.0	–	4 097
Sanborn	44	8	36	1	1 617	35	1 220	–8.0	1 043	77.9	6	100.0	–	348
Shannon	NA	NA	NA	(5)	NA	(5)	3 123	15.7	2 785	49.6	X	X	X	X
Spink	37	–	37	83	492	1 040	3 352	–5.4	2 847	73.8	8	62.5	–	402
Stanley	52	7	45	26	1 788	1 402	1 277	20.9	1 111	76.4	18	100.0	–	1 853
Sully	2	–	2	5	137	315	844	4.1	630	75.9	7	100.0	–	645
Todd	NA	NA	NA	NA	NA	NA	2 766	7.5	2 462	45.1	–	–	–	–
Tripp	131	5	126	363	3 977	10 823	3 036	.4	2 550	74.7	13	7.7	61.5	642
Turner	NA	NA	NA	1	NA	102	3 852	1.4	3 510	77.5	25	84.0	–	2 616
Union	142	1	141	174	2 166	1 708	5 345	24.7	4 927	74.4	71	100.0	–	10 672
Walworth	18	2	16	168	1 138	2 760	3 144	7.4	2 506	71.3	2	100.0	–	236
Yankton	408	40	368	604	1 951	3 137	8 840	16.8	8 187	69.1	79	54.4	38.0	7 653
Ziebach	24	2	22	NA	1 111	NA	879	9.9	741	59.4	X	X	X	X

[1] Data on serious crimes have not been adjusted for underreporting; this may affect comparability over time or among geographic areas. [2] Includes murder and nonnegligent manslaughter, forcible rape, robbery, and aggravated assault. [3] Includes burglary, larceny-theft, and motor vehicle theft. [4] Per 100,000 resident population provided by the U.S. Federal Bureau of Investigation. [5] Shannon County included with Fall River County; data not available separately.

Sources: Serious Crimes Known to Police—U.S. Federal Bureau of Investigation, Uniform Crime Reporting Program, unpublished data, annual (related Internet site <http://www.fbi.gov/ucr/ucr.htm>). Housing, 2000—U.S. Census Bureau, 2000 Census of Population and Housing, "Census 2000 Profiles of General Demographic Characteristics" data files, published May 2001 (related Internet site <http://www.census.gov/mp/www/pub/2000cen/mscen01.html>). Housing, 1990—U.S. Census Bureau, 1990 Census of Population and Housing, Summary Tape File (STF) 1C on CD-ROM (related Internet site <http://homer.ssd.census.gov/cdrom/lookup>). Building Permits—U.S. Census Bureau, "New Residential Construction–Building Permits," e-mail from Manufacturing and Construction Division/Residential Construction Branch, subject: building permits by place 2000, 22 May 2001 (related Internet site <http://www.census.gov/const/www/permitsindex.html>).

[Includes U.S., states, and 3,142 counties or county equivalents defined as of January 1, 1992. For changes to these areas since January 1, 1992, see appendix B. Geographic Information]

County	Serious crimes known to police (as reported to the FBI)[1] Number 1999 Total	Violent[2]	Property[3]	1990	Rate[4] 1999	1990	Housing, 2000 Total units	Percent change, 1990–2000	Occupied units Number	Percent owner–occupied	New private housing units authorized by building permits, 2000 Number	Percent in structures with— One unit	Five units or more	Valuation ($1,000)
TENNESSEE	248 849	37 037	211 812	218 433	4 680	5 445	2 439 443	20.4	2 232 905	69.9	32 203	75.9	21.0	3 377 637
Anderson	2 465	223	2 242	1 439	3 433	4 606	32 451	10.7	29 780	72.5	212	98.1	–	25 841
Bedford	882	123	759	614	2 529	4 370	14 990	18.6	13 905	73.5	61	100.0	–	3 722
Benton	364	27	337	NA	2 208	NA	8 595	20.9	6 863	80.5	5	100.0	–	656
Bledsoe	77	8	69	NA	706	NA	5 142	36.4	4 430	81.8	X	X	X	X
Blount	3 348	449	2 899	1 271	3 273	4 814	47 059	28.8	42 667	75.9	188	79.3	17.0	20 685
Bradley	3 208	418	2 790	2 440	3 814	3 310	36 820	24.6	34 281	68.6	510	84.7	8.0	37 193
Campbell	1 132	189	943	406	2 932	4 212	18 527	25.0	16 125	73.4	46	78.3	–	2 028
Cannon	170	18	152	38	1 387	1 662	5 420	24.1	4 998	78.6	8	75.0	–	850
Carroll	597	78	519	339	2 031	2 919	13 057	10.8	11 779	78.9	13	100.0	–	1 040
Carter	1 525	76	1 449	557	2 856	1 407	25 920	19.0	23 486	74.9	17	100.0	–	1 951
Cheatham	520	51	469	60	1 457	2 351	13 508	31.2	12 878	83.7	203	80.3	19.7	17 414
Chester	293	42	251	17	1 974	133	6 178	25.0	5 660	77.3	63	100.0	–	5 040
Claiborne	533	68	465	156	1 788	597	13 262	23.8	11 799	78.6	254	100.0	–	15 558
Clay	119	12	107	NA	1 624	NA	3 959	18.5	3 379	80.1	X	X	X	X
Cocke	1 163	156	1 007	848	3 603	2 910	15 844	29.0	13 762	75.5	6	100.0	–	385
Coffee	1 459	70	1 389	772	3 157	4 700	20 746	23.6	18 885	71.5	224	32.6	53.1	12 674
Crockett	193	23	170	388	1 369	3 306	6 138	11.2	5 632	74.9	7	100.0	–	590
Cumberland	1 329	79	1 250	250	2 972	3 608	22 442	41.5	19 508	80.6	101	53.5	–	7 759
Davidson	49 114	8 579	40 535	40 368	9 109	7 903	252 977	10.4	237 405	55.3	3 087	77.0	19.0	469 116
Decatur	151	15	136	1	1 411	114	6 448	20.6	4 908	80.1	6	33.3	–	238
DeKalb	451	59	392	NA	2 941	NA	8 409	25.6	6 984	74.9	10	100.0	–	645
Dickson	1 424	280	1 144	225	3 338	2 559	17 614	24.5	16 473	76.1	314	90.4	–	36 339
Dyer	1 629	274	1 355	1 584	4 386	8 114	16 123	12.1	14 751	65.7	274	54.4	40.9	14 004
Fayette	934	222	712	139	3 037	4 948	11 224	23.0	10 467	80.3	162	100.0	–	22 563
Fentress	415	40	375	170	2 539	1 159	7 598	24.2	6 693	79.1	4	–	–	50
Franklin	1 111	123	988	453	2 937	3 443	16 813	22.6	15 003	78.5	306	87.6	–	24 147
Gibson	1 552	207	1 345	1 405	3 190	3 034	21 059	7.3	19 518	72.2	151	100.0	–	14 036
Giles	889	138	751	663	3 044	2 576	13 113	21.1	11 713	75.3	49	100.0	–	1 147
Grainger	540	90	450	364	2 697	2 129	9 732	29.7	8 270	83.7	–	–	–	–
Greene	1 958	170	1 788	1 573	3 205	2 832	28 116	20.8	25 756	76.6	282	95.4	–	22 947
Grundy	251	27	224	NA	1 836	NA	6 282	21.9	5 562	82.2	X	X	X	X
Hamblen	2 414	362	2 052	1 843	4 423	3 651	24 693	20.4	23 211	72.6	308	71.8	27.6	24 232
Hamilton	10 468	3 023	10 445	23 509	6 541	8 233	134 692	9.9	124 444	65.9	1 426	84.8	13.8	174 580
Hancock	89	9	80	NA	1 300	NA	3 280	13.5	2 769	78.9	3	100.0	–	93
Hardeman	984	124	860	619	3 914	2 841	10 694	16.6	9 412	74.2	97	100.0	–	9 826
Hardin	356	29	327	303	1 412	1 339	12 807	24.6	10 426	77.2	10	100.0	–	441
Hawkins	927	164	763	221	1 911	567	24 416	30.0	21 936	78.8	138	89.9	–	10 033
Haywood	946	203	743	503	4 798	2 588	8 086	8.2	7 558	65.9	59	42.4	13.6	3 707
Henderson	736	100	636	280	3 034	1 306	11 446	23.4	10 306	79.3	27	77.8	22.2	2 633
Henry	1 055	137	918	403	3 475	2 172	15 783	14.6	13 019	77.4	17	88.2	–	1 876
Hickman	441	77	364	90	2 125	2 489	8 904	33.7	8 081	80.2	–	–	–	–
Houston	138	21	117	64	1 740	1 178	3 901	26.5	3 216	77.0	2	100.0	–	139
Humphreys	354	37	317	166	2 055	1 157	8 482	18.9	7 238	77.9	20	90.0	–	1 771
Jackson	76	17	59	NA	782	NA	5 163	22.4	4 466	80.7	–	–	–	–
Jefferson	1 486	127	1 359	572	3 371	1 831	19 319	36.3	17 155	77.9	320	96.3	–	30 126
Johnson	223	46	177	NA	1 318	NA	7 879	29.4	6 827	79.7	82	39.0	61.0	3 679
Knox	15 550	2 163	13 387	19 904	4 198	5 928	171 439	19.4	157 872	66.9	2 814	81.4	15.6	259 943
Lake	26	6	20	NA	315	NA	2 716	4.1	2 410	60.0	7	100.0	–	410
Lauderdale	1 127	174	953	97	4 611	1 051	10 563	13.1	9 567	64.8	104	96.2	–	7 392
Lawrence	1 622	224	1 398	649	4 081	1 860	16 821	18.2	15 480	77.1	15	26.7	53.3	524
Lewis	195	18	177	103	1 777	2 739	4 821	22.3	4 381	79.6	9	100.0	–	454
Lincoln	886	138	748	811	2 948	2 880	13 999	17.6	12 503	76.3	6	66.7	–	670
Loudon	1 245	151	1 094	109	3 157	349	17 277	33.0	15 944	79.1	197	94.9	–	20 975
McMinn	1 913	253	1 660	166	4 093	578	21 626	22.8	19 721	75.7	65	93.8	–	4 700
McNairy	559	93	466	235	2 382	1 318	11 219	15.3	9 980	80.0	23	100.0	–	1 067
Macon	344	37	307	40	1 874	1 099	8 894	29.3	7 916	78.6	18	27.8	72.2	748
Madison	6 353	1 017	5 336	5 997	7 320	7 690	38 205	20.1	35 552	67.0	593	100.0	–	61 300
Marion	630	127	503	1	2 638	25	12 140	21.3	11 037	80.7	241	96.7	–	21 108
Marshall	732	124	608	1	2 756	146	11 181	25.5	10 307	73.1	152	96.1	3.9	10 442
Maury	3 507	519	2 988	2 405	4 988	4 388	28 674	28.7	26 444	72.8	754	100.0	–	60 498
Meigs	197	6	191	21	1 960	315	5 188	40.6	4 304	81.9	7	100.0	–	505
Monroe	1 429	198	1 231	210	4 063	688	17 287	35.0	15 329	78.3	136	100.0	–	7 232
Montgomery	4 465	647	3 818	5 623	3 475	5 595	52 167	40.1	48 330	63.5	1 343	71.9	23.9	81 818
Moore	86	18	68	NA	1 639	NA	2 515	31.5	2 211	83.7	70	100.0	–	5 911
Morgan	175	31	144	2	923	3 077	7 714	20.9	6 990	82.9	1	100.0	–	55
Obion	1 516	148	1 368	1 133	4 970	7 545	14 489	8.5	13 182	71.5	87	95.4	–	8 075

[1] Data on serious crimes have not been adjusted for underreporting; this may affect comparability over time or among geographic areas. [2] Includes murder and nonnegligent manslaughter, forcible rape, robbery, and aggravated assault. [3] Includes burglary, larceny-theft, and motor vehicle theft. [4] Per 100,000 resident population provided by the U.S. Federal Bureau of Investigation.

Sources: Serious Crimes Known to Police—U.S. Federal Bureau of Investigation, Uniform Crime Reporting Program, unpublished data, annual (related Internet site <http://www.fbi.gov/ucr/ucr.htm>). Housing, 2000—U.S. Census Bureau, 2000 Census of Population and Housing, "Census 2000 Profiles of General Demographic Characteristics" data files, published May 2001 (related Internet site <http://www.census.gov/mp/www/pub/2000cen/mscen01.html>). Housing, 1990—U.S. Census Bureau, 1990 Census of Population and Housing, Summary Tape File (STF) 1C on CD-ROM (related Internet site <http://homer.ssd.census.gov/cdrom/lookup>). Building Permits—U.S. Census Bureau, "New Residential Construction–Building Permits," e-mail from Manufacturing and Construction Division/Residential Construction Branch, subject: building permits by place 2000, 22 May 2001 (related Internet site <http://www.census.gov/const/www/permitsindex.html>).

[Includes U.S., states, and 3,142 counties or county equivalents defined as of January 1, 1992. For changes to these areas since January 1, 1992, see appendix B. Geographic Information]

County	Serious crimes known to police (as reported to the FBI)[1]						Housing, 2000				New private housing units authorized by building permits, 2000			
	Number				Rate[4]				Occupied units			Percent in structures with—		
	1999							Percent change, 1990– 2000		Percent owner– occupied		One unit	Five units or more	Valuation ($1,000)
	Total	Violent[2]	Property[3]	1990	1999	1990	Total units		Number		Number			
TENNESSEE—Con.														
Overton	140	30	110	248	709	1 406	9 168	24.1	8 110	80.9	3	100.0	–	410
Perry	132	2	130	14	1 741	212	4 115	27.6	3 023	86.0	1	100.0	–	100
Pickett	59	9	50	NA	1 262	NA	2 956	31.2	2 091	84.3	X	X	X	X
Polk	339	67	272	7	2 256	706	7 369	30.2	6 448	80.8	–	–	–	–
Putnam	2 177	177	2 000	1 237	3 645	2 603	26 916	25.7	24 865	65.6	243	35.8	26.3	16 266
Rhea	758	136	622	324	2 697	4 117	12 565	21.3	11 184	75.5	122	100.0	–	12 929
Roane	1 518	186	1 332	933	3 005	1 976	23 369	14.9	21 200	77.6	34	100.0	–	2 645
Robertson	2 488	381	2 107	1 605	4 642	4 156	20 995	32.7	19 906	76.5	610	97.7	1.6	56 893
Rutherford	7 073	895	6 178	4 869	4 219	4 106	70 616	54.3	66 443	69.8	3 486	70.5	28.5	248 436
Scott	495	88	407	NA	2 446	NA	8 909	25.1	8 203	76.4	4	100.0	–	270
Sequatchie	316	50	266	NA	3 019	NA	4 916	37.7	4 463	76.4	23	100.0	–	1 522
Sevier	3 302	201	3 101	1 669	5 070	3 270	37 252	54.2	28 467	73.4	485	44.9	49.5	42 847
Shelby	53 665	8 779	44 886	67 544	7 388	8 174	362 954	10.7	338 366	63.1	6 734	53.2	45.5	791 644
Smith	234	19	215	24	1 416	741	7 665	26.7	6 878	78.7	55	100.0	–	5 873
Stewart	170	42	128	89	1 458	939	5 977	36.3	4 930	79.2	3	100.0	–	240
Sullivan	4 945	789	4 156	5 822	3 251	4 054	69 052	13.9	63 556	75.7	457	98.0	1.5	46 031
Sumner	4 020	445	3 575	3 145	3 209	3 045	51 657	29.8	48 941	75.6	878	96.4	2.7	75 711
Tipton	1 046	142	904	NA	2 188	NA	19 064	35.5	18 106	76.1	483	99.2	–	44 979
Trousdale	208	26	182	135	3 010	2 280	3 095	22.0	2 780	76.4	19	100.0	–	1 486
Unicoi	332	26	306	137	1 910	2 732	8 214	16.1	7 516	76.4	8	100.0	–	1 013
Union	281	29	252	207	1 884	1 512	7 916	39.0	6 742	81.0	94	100.0	–	7 415
Van Buren	64	22	42	54	1 250	1 114	2 453	22.6	2 180	85.3	X	X	X	X
Warren	1 251	98	1 153	915	3 426	2 773	16 689	20.9	15 181	72.8	59	100.0	–	2 689
Washington	4 327	529	3 798	4 408	4 193	4 775	47 779	24.5	44 195	68.2	483	45.8	49.7	40 802
Wayne	122	16	106	2	782	197	6 701	16.7	5 936	82.9	2	100.0	–	170
Weakley	1 020	127	893	672	3 066	2 279	14 928	16.1	13 599	69.0	136	47.8	11.0	8 474
White	629	62	567	132	2 743	2 820	10 191	21.8	9 229	79.8	38	50.0	50.0	1 879
Williamson	2 946	360	2 586	1 426	2 530	3 504	47 005	57.3	44 725	81.5	1 205	100.0	–	287 027
Wilson	2 746	402	2 344	195	3 240	3 618	34 921	33.3	32 798	81.4	824	92.0	1.9	104 305
TEXAS	1 002 171	111 635	890 536	1 328 954	5 010	7 830	8 157 575	16.4	7 393 354	63.8	141 231	76.9	20.1	15 418 421
Anderson	1 709	241	1 468	2 301	3 218	4 791	18 436	9.0	15 678	74.0	68	50.0	20.6	4 039
Andrews	339	17	322	521	2 391	3 634	5 400	-1.1	4 601	79.7	24	100.0	–	1 669
Angelina	3 775	552	3 223	3 718	4 811	5 320	32 435	12.6	28 685	72.4	141	93.6	–	14 638
Aransas	1 336	48	1 288	1 269	5 749	7 093	12 848	18.0	9 132	75.2	213	47.4	31.9	18 742
Archer	104	10	94	65	1 230	815	3 871	5.2	3 345	81.3	10	100.0	–	1 245
Armstrong	42	5	37	26	1 913	1 286	920	.4	802	78.9	2	100.0	–	162
Atascosa	756	90	666	626	2 043	2 050	14 883	28.1	12 816	78.4	66	100.0	–	4 247
Austin	555	59	496	443	2 334	2 234	10 205	14.9	8 747	77.2	114	100.0	–	6 200
Bailey	112	10	102	235	1 599	3 327	2 738	-11.9	2 348	71.4	1	100.0	–	305
Bandera	357	33	324	407	2 234	3 853	9 503	46.5	7 010	82.9	3	100.0	–	181
Bastrop	1 562	118	1 444	1 263	3 056	3 301	22 254	36.5	20 097	80.4	148	98.6	–	11 349
Baylor	118	21	97	57	2 802	1 300	2 820	-6.2	1 791	72.4	–	–	–	–
Bee	880	60	820	1 135	3 130	4 516	10 939	7.2	9 061	65.5	4	100.0	–	145
Bell	10 366	955	9 411	9 657	4 599	5 054	92 782	22.2	85 507	55.7	1 795	73.6	1.7	165 675
Bexar	86 391	7 426	78 965	131 294	6 294	11 076	521 359	14.4	488 942	61.2	8 978	76.6	22.2	683 594
Blanco	109	8	101	48	1 279	804	4 031	28.6	3 303	78.8	12	100.0	–	1 150
Borden	11	–	11	17	1 430	2 128	435	-9.0	292	74.0	X	X	X	X
Bosque	208	19	189	301	1 238	1 990	8 644	7.1	6 726	77.7	6	100.0	–	421
Bowie	3 296	388	2 908	4 159	3 891	5 093	36 463	6.5	33 058	71.0	258	39.5	–	12 273
Brazoria	6 815	474	6 341	7 744	2 928	4 039	90 628	21.6	81 954	74.0	2 085	91.3	8.6	292 169
Brazos	7 580	557	7 023	7 834	5 601	6 429	59 023	21.0	55 202	45.6	1 372	54.8	36.4	101 964
Brewster	193	17	176	266	2 139	3 064	4 614	2.9	3 669	59.5	35	37.1	–	2 216
Briscoe	15	4	11	34	783	1 725	1 006	-6.3	724	77.1	X	X	X	X
Brooks	247	12	235	220	2 864	2 682	3 203	3.2	2 711	73.0	3	100.0	–	111
Brown	1 799	171	1 628	1 944	4 786	5 656	17 889	5.8	14 306	72.2	33	93.9	–	3 112
Burleson	336	33	303	447	2 116	3 281	8 197	16.4	6 363	79.7	2	100.0	–	158
Burnet	680	61	619	774	2 130	3 413	15 933	24.5	13 133	78.3	444	95.0	–	50 900
Caldwell	772	99	673	1 088	2 346	4 122	11 901	17.6	10 816	69.7	57	100.0	–	2 826
Calhoun	761	90	671	686	3 642	3 600	10 238	7.1	7 442	72.8	68	94.1	–	5 856
Callahan	117	11	106	100	901	843	5 925	7.7	5 061	80.7	7	100.0	–	655
Cameron	17 360	1 536	15 824	17 250	5 242	6 632	119 654	34.8	97 267	67.7	3 111	87.0	5.2	194 471
Camp	267	63	204	370	2 401	3 736	5 228	15.4	4 336	74.7	3	100.0	–	192
Carson	56	6	50	61	824	928	2 815	-1.4	2 470	83.7	1	100.0	–	291
Cass	657	112	545	548	2 101	1 828	13 890	5.3	12 190	78.6	15	100.0	–	1 108
Castro	167	29	138	244	1 970	2 690	3 198	-4.7	2 761	71.1	–	–	–	–

[1] Data on serious crimes have not been adjusted for underreporting; this may affect comparability over time or among geographic areas. [2] Includes murder and nonnegligent manslaughter, forcible rape, robbery, and aggravated assault. [3] Includes burglary, larceny-theft, and motor vehicle theft. [4] Per 100,000 resident population provided by the U.S. Federal Bureau of Investigation.

Sources: Serious Crimes Known to Police—U.S. Federal Bureau of Investigation, Uniform Crime Reporting Program, unpublished data, annual (related Internet site <http://www.fbi.gov/ucr/ ucr.htm>). Housing, 2000—U.S. Census Bureau, 2000 Census of Population and Housing, "Census 2000 Profiles of General Demographic Characteristics" data files, published May 2001 (related Internet site <http://www.census.gov/mp/www/pub/2000cen/mscen01.html>). Housing, 1990—U.S. Census Bureau, 1990 Census of Population and Housing, Summary Tape File (STF) 1C on CD-ROM (related Internet site <http://homer.ssd.census.gov/cdrom/lookup>). Building Permits—U.S. Census Bureau, "New Residential Construction–Building Permits," e-mail from Manufacturing and Construction Division/Residential Construction Branch, subject: building permits by place 2000, 22 May 2001 (related Internet site <http://www.census.gov/const/www/permitsindex.html>).

[Includes U.S., states, and 3,142 counties or county equivalents defined as of January 1, 1992. For changes to these areas since January 1, 1992, see appendix B. Geographic Information]

County	Serious crimes known to police (as reported to the FBI)[1]						Housing, 2000				New private housing units authorized by building permits, 2000			
	Number				Rate[4]				Occupied units			Percent in structures with—		
	1999							Percent change, 1990– 2000		Percent owner– occupied			Five units or more	Valuation ($1,000)
	Total	Violent[2]	Property[3]	1990	1999	1990	Total units		Number		Number	One unit		
TEXAS—Con.														
Chambers	641	45	596	641	2 661	3 191	10 336	28.2	9 139	83.6	309	100.0	–	28 788
Cherokee	1 474	259	1 215	1 726	3 400	4 205	19 173	8.8	16 651	73.8	45	95.6	–	3 780
Childress	263	38	225	180	3 442	3 024	3 059	.4	2 474	70.5	1	100.0	–	34
Clay	187	25	162	241	1 745	2 404	4 992	6.0	4 323	83.0	12	100.0	–	886
Cochran	81	3	78	143	2 020	3 267	1 587	–10.0	1 309	73.6	–	–	–	–
Coke	58	2	56	31	1 698	905	2 843	1.8	1 544	78.9	–	–	–	–
Coleman	281	7	274	199	2 903	2 049	5 248	–2.5	3 889	74.4	2	100.0	–	60
Collin	15 282	1 618	13 664	16 540	3 513	6 264	194 892	87.7	181 970	68.6	10 111	95.2	4.6	1 723 896
Collingsworth	61	4	57	84	1 830	2 351	1 723	–11.7	1 294	78.8	–	–	–	–
Colorado	565	67	498	715	2 928	3 889	9 431	10.5	7 641	76.7	12	100.0	–	1 320
Comal	3 415	161	3 254	2 197	4 587	4 239	32 718	42.3	29 066	77.2	1 132	92.8	6.0	126 862
Comanche	220	22	198	173	1 598	1 293	7 105	5.7	5 522	76.2	1	100.0	–	46
Concho	13	3	10	95	411	3 121	1 488	–1.7	1 058	75.0	X	X	X	X
Cooke	1 009	64	945	1 234	3 029	4 009	15 061	13.1	13 643	72.1	50	76.0	–	4 805
Coryell	1 599	227	1 372	1 691	2 021	2 633	21 776	14.8	19 950	54.9	90	86.7	–	10 396
Cottle	25	5	20	37	1 282	1 647	1 088	–15.4	820	71.6	–	–	–	–
Crane	66	7	59	147	1 443	3 160	1 596	–11.1	1 360	85.1	–	–	–	–
Crockett	64	7	57	96	1 371	2 354	2 049	8.0	1 524	71.3	X	X	X	X
Crosby	42	5	37	24	574	329	3 202	–3.3	2 512	69.3	2	100.0	–	91
Culberson	27	7	20	32	873	939	1 321	2.7	1 052	70.8	–	–	–	–
Dallam	147	13	134	83	2 195	1 520	2 697	4.7	2 317	63.1	30	100.0	–	1 710
Dallas	149 390	18 237	131 153	216 416	7 181	11 680	854 119	7.4	807 621	52.6	13 745	64.4	34.0	1 794 049
Dawson	390	75	315	612	2 615	4 265	5 500	–7.9	4 726	73.5	4	100.0	–	359
Deaf Smith	537	107	430	955	2 777	4 986	6 914	–3.3	6 180	67.4	3	100.0	–	360
Delta	103	14	89	74	1 933	1 524	2 410	4.6	2 094	77.3	2	100.0	–	218
Denton	13 296	1 169	12 127	20 384	3 441	7 452	168 069	49.7	158 903	64.4	5 789	90.6	9.2	903 577
DeWitt	532	55	477	226	2 667	1 200	8 756	2.2	7 207	76.5	10	100.0	–	499
Dickens	22	4	18	68	967	2 645	1 368	–12.5	980	77.7	X	X	X	X
Dimmit	337	58	279	50	3 206	479	4 112	3.0	3 308	73.9	–	–	–	–
Donley	67	11	56	66	1 728	1 786	2 378	3.2	1 578	74.7	–	–	–	–
Duval	312	60	252	425	2 251	3 290	5 543	8.1	4 350	80.9	X	X	X	X
Eastland	460	30	430	621	2 578	3 611	9 547	–2.3	7 321	76.7	1	100.0	–	55
Ector	6 488	636	5 852	14 242	5 087	11 975	49 500	1.5	43 846	68.6	238	43.7	56.3	20 621
Edwards	51	11	40	41	1 331	1 809	1 217	–21.5	801	79.9	X	X	X	X
Ellis	3 567	304	3 263	4 552	3 393	5 345	39 071	24.8	37 020	76.2	975	68.5	20.6	93 825
El Paso	39 230	4 723	34 507	60 858	5 500	10 287	224 447	19.7	210 022	63.6	3 203	89.9	2.9	166 594
Erath	677	39	638	929	2 115	3 319	14 422	13.0	12 568	63.2	23	100.0	–	1 782
Falls	643	108	535	535	3 636	6 667	7 658	–1.0	6 496	71.5	9	100.0	–	394
Fannin	751	100	651	622	2 632	2 508	12 887	12.0	11 105	74.8	50	72.0	20.0	3 088
Fayette	241	13	228	229	1 109	1 140	11 113	3.3	8 722	78.3	15	100.0	–	1 484
Fisher	45	4	41	63	1 046	1 301	2 277	–5.6	1 785	76.8	–	–	–	–
Floyd	182	27	155	193	2 190	2 271	3 221	–8.9	2 730	73.9	3	100.0	–	406
Foard	13	7	6	18	754	1 003	850	–4.5	664	75.2	–	–	–	–
Fort Bend	8 997	998	7 999	9 191	2 626	4 077	115 991	50.5	110 915	80.8	1 313	81.0	19.0	144 963
Franklin	188	30	158	134	1 915	1 718	5 132	21.6	3 754	79.0	3	100.0	–	149
Freestone	286	36	250	451	1 595	2 851	8 138	4.2	6 588	78.8	49	42.9	–	3 065
Frio	492	47	445	531	3 078	4 899	5 660	16.0	4 743	69.0	15	100.0	–	418
Gaines	221	19	202	522	1 453	3 696	5 410	3.6	4 681	78.6	1	100.0	–	250
Galveston	14 671	1 384	13 287	16 590	5 890	7 678	111 733	12.3	94 782	66.2	2 931	76.3	23.4	338 069
Garza	92	10	82	173	1 968	3 364	1 928	–11.7	1 663	70.7	3	100.0	–	150
Gillespie	360	5	355	314	1 770	1 825	9 902	19.8	8 521	77.5	61	100.0	–	8 568
Glasscock	6	1	5	12	424	829	660	10.0	483	67.3	X	X	X	X
Goliad	38	1	37	24	535	401	3 426	20.8	2 644	80.0	X	X	X	X
Gonzales	398	99	299	458	2 235	2 662	8 194	4.9	6 782	69.1	3	100.0	–	484
Gray	880	125	755	1 496	3 675	6 242	10 567	–8.4	8 793	77.4	–	–	–	–
Grayson	4 671	333	4 338	6 465	4 479	6 804	48 315	9.3	42 849	70.6	200	85.5	2.5	20 605
Gregg	6 547	515	6 032	8 390	5 695	7 994	46 349	3.7	42 687	64.1	160	100.0	–	20 798
Grimes	623	63	560	661	2 637	3 511	9 490	22.5	7 753	77.7	13	100.0	–	941
Guadalupe	3 005	210	2 795	2 966	3 681	4 572	33 585	31.2	30 900	77.0	473	100.0	–	56 907
Hale	1 432	103	1 329	1 684	3 849	4 857	13 526	2.7	11 975	64.8	124	19.4	–	6 075
Hall	63	3	60	38	1 705	973	1 988	–9.2	1 548	74.1	–	–	–	–
Hamilton	124	10	114	208	1 608	2 690	4 455	4.4	3 374	78.1	8	50.0	–	460
Hansford	59	6	53	116	1 088	1 984	2 329	–7.8	2 005	74.7	2	100.0	–	193
Hardeman	51	12	39	138	1 095	2 612	2 358	–11.9	1 943	73.3	–	–	–	–
Hardin	1 010	79	931	943	2 042	2 282	19 836	20.3	17 805	82.7	21	100.0	–	1 384
Harris	185 053	27 668	157 385	258 037	5 690	9 156	1 298 130	10.6	1 205 516	55.3	24 565	74.3	25.3	2 745 797

[1] Data on serious crimes have not been adjusted for underreporting; this may affect comparability over time or among geographic areas. [2] Includes murder and nonnegligent manslaughter, forcible rape, robbery, and aggravated assault. [3] Includes burglary, larceny-theft, and motor vehicle theft. [4] Per 100,000 resident population provided by the U.S. Federal Bureau of Investigation.

Sources: Serious Crimes Known to Police—U.S. Federal Bureau of Investigation, Uniform Crime Reporting Program, unpublished data, annual (related Internet site <http://www.fbi.gov/ucr/ucr.htm>). Housing, 2000—U.S. Census Bureau, 2000 Census of Population and Housing, "Census 2000 Profiles of General Demographic Characteristics" data files, published May 2001 (related Internet site <http://www.census.gov/mp/www/pub/2000cen/mscen01.html>). Housing, 1990—U.S. Census Bureau, 1990 Census of Population and Housing, Summary Tape File (STF) 1C on CD-ROM (related Internet site <http://homer.ssd.census.gov/cdrom/lookup>). Building Permits—U.S. Census Bureau, "New Residential Construction–Building Permits," e-mail from Manufacturing and Construction Division/Residential Construction Branch, subject: building permits by place 2000, 22 May 2001 (related Internet site <http://www.census.gov/const/www/permitsindex.html>).

[Includes U.S., states, and 3,142 counties or county equivalents defined as of January 1, 1992. For changes to these areas since January 1, 1992, see appendix B. Geographic Information]

County	Serious crimes known to police (as reported to the FBI)[1] Number 1999 Total	Violent[2]	Property[3]	1990	Rate[4] 1999	1990	Housing, 2000 Total units	Percent change, 1990–2000	Occupied units Number	Percent owner-occupied	New private housing units authorized by building permits, 2000 Number	Percent in structures with— One unit	Five units or more	Valuation ($1,000)
TEXAS—Con.														
Harrison	2 146	226	1 920	2 302	3 539	4 005	26 271	11.9	23 087	77.2	28	100.0	–	2 295
Hartley	92	9	83	45	1 778	1 238	1 760	14.2	1 604	76.4	X	X	X	X
Haskell	60	8	52	80	1 092	1 173	3 555	-7.5	2 569	78.9	1	100.0	–	100
Hays	3 343	307	3 036	3 382	3 722	5 154	35 643	41.2	33 410	64.8	1 724	42.2	42.8	126 118
Hemphill	51	6	45	44	1 425	1 183	1 548	-9.6	1 280	77.0	–	–	–	–
Henderson	2 257	238	2 019	2 445	3 236	4 176	35 935	13.1	28 804	80.0	115	96.5	–	11 956
Hidalgo	30 257	2 569	27 688	25 276	5 730	6 590	192 658	50.2	156 824	73.1	5 640	89.0	4.4	310 379
Hill	929	57	872	915	2 999	3 371	14 624	13.4	12 204	74.9	16	100.0	–	1 160
Hockley	610	127	483	771	2 528	3 186	9 148	-1.4	7 994	74.4	16	100.0	–	1 173
Hood	1 149	59	1 090	838	3 045	2 892	19 105	27.7	16 176	81.2	33	87.9	–	3 891
Hopkins	807	87	720	1 391	2 607	4 824	14 020	10.6	12 286	71.3	33	100.0	–	3 204
Houston	413	57	356	572	1 859	2 676	10 730	4.5	8 259	76.1	5	100.0	–	433
Howard	1 287	115	1 172	1 893	3 958	5 853	13 589	-.5	11 389	69.4	15	100.0	–	964
Hudspeth	27	4	23	28	819	961	1 471	14.2	1 092	81.0	X	X	X	X
Hunt	3 715	676	3 039	5 510	5 166	8 563	32 490	12.2	28 742	71.5	58	100.0	–	4 972
Hutchinson	794	63	731	914	3 251	3 558	10 871	-4.8	9 283	78.9	1	100.0	–	380
Irion	27	8	19	29	1 531	1 780	914	8.6	694	77.7	X	X	X	X
Jack	151	12	139	139	2 003	1 991	3 668	4.9	3 047	76.7	–	–	–	–
Jackson	209	23	186	273	1 506	2 094	6 545	12.1	5 336	73.8	25	100.0	–	2 361
Jasper	844	118	726	771	2 488	2 479	16 576	19.9	13 450	80.7	9	100.0	–	613
Jeff Davis	10	2	8	16	418	822	1 420	5.3	896	70.1	X	X	X	X
Jefferson	16 139	1 891	14 248	21 687	6 577	9 059	102 080	.8	92 880	66.0	615	96.9	.8	73 177
Jim Hogg	64	12	52	40	1 260	783	2 308	9.7	1 815	77.6	X	X	X	X
Jim Wells	2 035	193	1 842	2 292	5 012	6 083	14 819	6.2	12 961	76.5	24	100.0	–	2 199
Johnson	3 958	284	3 674	3 610	3 303	3 715	46 269	25.0	43 636	78.9	665	96.1	–	65 138
Jones	308	33	275	443	1 626	2 686	7 236	-5.3	6 140	79.3	–	–	–	–
Karnes	37	7	30	79	1 287	634	5 479	7.1	4 454	74.2	2	100.0	–	17
Kaufman	2 660	320	2 340	2 690	3 989	5 151	26 133	30.0	24 367	79.2	330	61.2	33.0	21 813
Kendall	346	13	333	610	1 607	4 181	9 609	56.6	8 613	79.5	278	100.0	–	57 801
Kenedy	9	–	9	25	2 027	5 435	281	31.9	138	34.8	X	X	X	X
Kent	6	1	5	7	672	693	551	-8.6	353	79.3	X	X	X	X
Kerr	1 151	89	1 062	1 386	2 624	3 818	20 228	17.9	17 813	73.3	167	47.3	4.8	14 990
Kimble	30	1	35	37	861	898	2 996	15.5	1 866	73.5	–	–	–	–
King	1	–	1	9	272	2 542	174	-8.9	108	34.3	X	X	X	X
Kinney	2	1	1	14	57	449	1 907	4.7	1 314	77.4	3	100.0	–	327
Kleberg	1 914	168	1 746	2 151	6 256	7 105	12 743	6.1	10 896	58.6	11	100.0	–	848
Knox	99	29	70	15	2 295	310	2 129	-13.4	1 690	75.4	X	X	X	X
Lamar	3 473	439	3 034	3 472	7 436	7 900	21 113	11.3	19 077	67.2	117	82.1	6.0	8 521
Lamb	221	44	177	397	1 476	2 634	6 294	-3.6	5 360	75.6	4	25.0	–	215
Lampasas	344	11	333	473	1 908	3 498	7 601	22.7	6 554	73.9	12	100.0	–	392
La Salle	116	21	95	67	1 895	1 275	2 436	8.6	1 819	74.7	1	100.0	–	62
Lavaca	256	14	242	280	1 341	1 498	9 657	1.1	7 669	78.5	10	100.0	–	973
Lee	226	38	188	293	1 494	2 279	6 851	18.7	5 663	79.3	10	100.0	–	1 127
Leon	301	70	231	184	2 048	1 453	8 299	18.2	6 189	82.8	X	X	X	X
Liberty	1 881	156	1 725	1 993	2 849	3 780	26 359	18.5	23 242	79.0	213	100.0	–	14 407
Limestone	928	131	797	817	4 371	3 901	7 906	-2.0	7 906	74.9	11	100.0	–	1 105
Lipscomb	33	3	30	71	1 094	2 259	1 541	-8.4	1 205	77.8	–	–	–	–
Live Oak	126	2	124	123	1 225	1 287	6 196	12.3	4 230	81.4	4	100.0	–	147
Llano	268	19	249	300	1 960	2 579	11 829	21.0	7 879	80.9	24	100.0	–	2 268
Loving	NA	NA	NA	2	NA	1 869	70	18.6	31	83.9	X	X	X	X
Lubbock	14 353	2 513	11 840	14 264	6 166	6 407	100 595	9.6	92 516	59.2	924	87.0	2.2	94 120
Lynn	107	13	94	165	1 573	2 442	2 671	-10.3	2 354	74.3	3	100.0	–	313
McCulloch	240	42	198	250	2 704	2 848	4 184	-5.4	3 277	72.8	6	66.7	–	275
McLennan	13 246	1 306	11 940	14 591	6 418	7 715	84 795	7.5	78 859	60.2	691	74.2	9.0	74 672
McMullen	NA	NA	NA	26	NA	3 182	587	3.9	355	80.6	X	X	X	X
Madison	369	37	332	492	3 060	4 501	4 797	10.9	3 914	77.0	6	100.0	–	535
Marion	411	54	357	391	3 722	3 916	6 384	11.4	4 610	82.1	–	–	–	–
Martin	52	1	51	59	1 016	1 190	1 898	-6.9	1 624	74.1	1	100.0	–	20
Mason	20	2	18	22	534	643	2 372	.7	1 607	80.2	3	100.0	–	321
Matagorda	1 975	243	1 732	2 582	5 128	6 992	18 611	.4	13 901	66.8	118	76.3	23.7	9 842
Maverick	1 768	120	1 648	1 452	3 621	3 991	14 889	33.6	13 089	69.6	179	82.7	10.1	9 012
Medina	1 073	101	972	952	2 807	3 486	14 826	36.5	12 880	79.8	35	100.0	–	2 617
Menard	41	6	35	38	1 730	1 687	1 607	2.9	990	74.6	X	X	X	X
Midland	4 149	404	3 745	6 413	3 418	6 015	48 060	6.4	42 745	69.6	158	100.0	–	17 182
Milam	478	73	405	581	1 940	2 532	10 866	3.4	9 199	73.0	10	60.0	–	770
Mills	15	1	14	11	313	243	2 691	4.2	2 001	80.5	X	X	X	X

[1] Data on serious crimes have not been adjusted for underreporting; this may affect comparability over time or among geographic areas. [2] Includes murder and nonnegligent manslaughter, forcible rape, robbery, and aggravated assault. [3] Includes burglary, larceny-theft, and motor vehicle theft. [4] Per 100,000 resident population provided by the U.S. Federal Bureau of Investigation.

Sources: Serious Crimes Known to Police—U.S. Federal Bureau of Investigation, Uniform Crime Reporting Program, unpublished data, annual (related Internet site <http://www.fbi.gov/ucr/ucr.htm>). Housing, 2000—U.S. Census Bureau, 2000 Census of Population and Housing, "Census 2000 Profiles of General Demographic Characteristics" data files, published May 2001 (related Internet site <http://www.census.gov/mp/www/pub/2000cen/mscen01.html>). Housing, 1990—U.S. Census Bureau, 1990 Census of Population and Housing, Summary Tape File (STF) 1C on CD-ROM (related Internet site <http://homer.ssd.census.gov/cdrom/lookup>). Building Permits—U.S. Census Bureau, "New Residential Construction–Building Permits," e-mail from Manufacturing and Construction Division/Residential Construction Branch, subject: building permits by place 2000, 22 May 2001 (related Internet site <http://www.census.gov/const/www/permitsindex.html>).

Table B–6. Counties — Crime, Housing, and Building Permits–Con.

[Includes U.S., states, and 3,142 counties or county equivalents defined as of January 1, 1992. For changes to these areas since January 1, 1992, see appendix B. Geographic Information]

County	Serious crimes known to police (as reported to the FBI)[1]						Housing, 2000				New private housing units authorized by building permits, 2000			
	Number				Rate[4]							Percent in structures with—		
	1999			1990	1999	1990	Total units	Percent change, 1990–2000	Number	Percent owner–occupied	Number	One unit	Five units or more	Valuation ($1,000)
	Total	Violent[2]	Property[3]						(Occupied units)					
TEXAS—Con.														
Mitchell	215	12	203	263	2 183	3 281	4 168	–8.6	2 837	75.9	–	–	–	–
Montague	592	46	546	591	3 322	3 421	9 862	6.5	7 770	78.8	8	100.0	–	360
Montgomery	8 749	1 021	7 728	9 854	3 173	5 408	112 770	52.7	103 296	78.1	4 197	96.9	1.2	636 114
Moore	646	33	613	599	3 235	3 353	7 478	9.4	6 774	70.5	14	100.0	–	1 931
Morris	352	48	304	413	2 926	3 129	6 017	3.7	5 215	77.9	2	100.0	–	115
Motley	7	1	6	16	529	1 044	839	–18.2	606	76.7	–	–	–	–
Nacogdoches	2 458	207	2 251	2 681	4 310	4 897	25 051	10.0	22 006	61.6	100	42.0	54.0	5 100
Navarro	1 862	116	1 746	2 455	4 398	6 149	18 449	7.1	16 491	70.8	39	89.7	–	4 246
Newton	166	11	155	186	1 149	1 371	7 331	14.9	5 583	84.5	–	–	–	–
Nolan	513	35	478	790	3 065	4 761	7 112	–4.7	6 170	67.4	2	100.0	–	154
Nueces	22 261	2 634	19 627	27 840	6 937	9 562	123 041	7.6	110 365	61.3	939	78.5	10.0	93 483
Ochiltree	257	35	222	317	2 870	3 473	3 769	–5.7	3 261	72.5	3	100.0	–	470
Oldham	14	2	12	49	641	2 151	815	–5.3	735	66.4	–	–	–	–
Orange	3 400	389	3 011	4 594	3 948	5 706	34 781	8.6	31 642	77.2	174	100.0	–	23 945
Palo Pinto	941	96	845	1 212	3 602	4 837	14 102	5.6	10 594	72.0	4	100.0	–	289
Panola	599	75	524	415	2 560	1 883	10 524	8.5	8 821	80.8	6	100.0	–	428
Parker	1 730	157	1 573	2 258	2 080	3 485	34 084	30.9	31 131	80.6	282	100.0	–	29 702
Parmer	165	12	153	215	1 836	2 180	3 732	1.3	3 322	72.3	5	100.0	–	620
Pecos	444	40	404	501	2 735	3 414	6 338	8.5	5 153	74.1	4	100.0	–	262
Polk	1 089	73	1 016	1 181	2 134	3 849	21 177	13.5	15 119	81.7	117	6.0	80.3	3 143
Potter	8 211	760	7 451	8 288	7 430	8 468	44 598	3.9	40 760	60.1	520	99.6	–	66 601
Presidio	82	5	77	51	936	768	3 299	14.2	2 530	70.3	67	100.0	–	5 911
Rains	183	12	171	146	2 093	2 174	4 523	28.0	3 617	82.8	9	100.0	–	368
Randall	6 254	567	5 687	6 311	6 186	7 038	43 261	14.4	41 240	70.3	37	78.4	16.2	5 191
Reagan	47	10	37	70	1 102	1 551	1 452	–13.8	1 107	78.4	3	100.0	–	38
Real	22	1	21	20	807	829	2 007	–2.0	1 245	76.9	31	100.0	–	3 028
Red River	311	25	286	574	2 233	4 009	6 916	4.0	5 827	74.9	5	100.0	–	420
Reeves	382	48	334	577	2 601	3 640	5 043	–16.6	4 091	77.7	1	100.0	–	180
Refugio	78	8	70	167	972	2 094	3 669	–1.9	2 985	74.9	1	100.0	–	135
Roberts	21	2	19	12	2 204	1 171	449	–8.7	362	79.0	X	X	X	X
Robertson	337	82	255	803	2 140	5 177	7 874	7.3	6 179	71.5	9	100.0	–	660
Rockwall	905	73	892	1 023	2 559	3 995	15 351	50.4	14 530	82.7	955	100.0	–	185 615
Runnels	245	28	217	189	2 099	1 673	5 400	1.0	4 428	77.4	1	100.0	–	36
Rusk	1 793	285	1 508	2 275	3 853	5 202	19 867	4.1	17 364	79.9	13	100.0	–	1 401
Sabine	109	13	96	174	1 018	1 815	7 659	9.5	4 485	86.2	–	–	–	–
San Augustine	205	25	180	197	2 499	2 463	5 356	28.5	3 575	81.4	–	–	–	–
San Jacinto	472	42	430	484	2 138	2 956	11 520	17.3	8 651	87.7	11	100.0	–	935
San Patricio	1 847	107	1 740	2 569	2 550	4 373	24 864	12.4	22 093	68.2	495	47.1	45.7	29 400
San Saba	117	14	103	115	2 054	2 129	2 951	–4.1	2 289	75.8	23	100.0	–	1 528
Schleicher	31	–	31	85	1 024	2 843	1 371	6.4	1 115	75.7	–	–	–	–
Scurry	391	41	350	520	2 133	2 791	7 112	–7.7	5 756	73.8	8	100.0	–	268
Shackelford	12	–	12	28	358	844	1 613	–8.1	1 300	79.0	X	X	X	X
Shelby	631	69	562	831	2 734	3 771	11 955	12.6	9 595	78.3	1	100.0	–	80
Sherman	27	–	27	20	929	700	1 275	–1.4	1 124	73.6	16	87.5	–	1 623
Smith	6 817	754	6 063	11 271	4 022	7 449	71 701	11.4	65 692	69.7	543	86.0	12.3	71 031
Somervell	124	3	121	180	1 904	3 358	2 750	13.2	2 438	74.9	40	15.0	85.0	1 980
Starr	1 465	156	1 309	920	2 583	2 271	17 589	44.1	14 410	79.5	–	–	–	–
Stephens	142	5	137	242	1 427	2 686	4 893	–1.8	3 661	72.4	1	100.0	–	120
Sterling	16	4	12	24	1 156	1 669	633	1.6	513	75.6	X	X	X	X
Stonewall	22	9	13	29	1 216	1 441	936	–13.7	713	78.7	X	X	X	X
Sutton	126	8	118	142	2 783	3 434	1 998	3.8	1 515	72.3	–	–	–	–
Swisher	138	11	127	209	1 639	2 570	3 315	–5.2	2 925	70.4	–	–	–	–
Tarrant	77 617	7 667	69 950	119 497	5 646	10 213	565 830	15.2	533 864	60.8	11 685	81.3	17.7	1 321 012
Taylor	5 354	518	4 836	6 038	4 326	5 046	52 056	4.1	47 274	61.6	374	43.9	51.3	33 646
Terrell	3	1	2	23	250	1 631	991	22.3	443	77.0	X	X	X	X
Terry	267	27	240	695	2 041	5 258	5 087	–3.9	4 278	71.2	3	100.0	–	435
Throckmorton	14	2	12	19	799	1 011	1 066	–3.6	765	77.0	X	X	X	X
Titus	1 128	150	978	1 107	4 374	4 611	10 675	14.1	9 552	72.4	28	100.0	–	1 768
Tom Green	4 492	364	4 128	6 421	5 019	6 522	43 916	9.4	39 503	64.1	247	96.8	–	25 994
Travis	43 663	3 295	40 368	61 181	6 057	10 614	335 881	27.1	320 766	51.4	14 154	51.8	44.9	1 351 035
Trinity	420	54	366	322	3 283	2 813	8 141	13.1	5 723	80.8	–	–	–	–
Tyler	314	49	265	392	1 517	2 355	10 419	15.2	7 775	84.1	1	100.0	–	30
Upshur	827	69	758	891	2 272	2 840	14 930	15.9	13 290	81.8	13	100.0	–	1 478
Upton	36	7	29	80	947	1 799	1 609	–13.9	1 256	75.2	–	–	–	–
Uvalde	1 072	92	980	635	4 134	2 721	10 166	4.9	8 559	72.2	31	100.0	–	1 705
Val Verde	2 005	138	1 867	1 847	4 509	4 770	16 288	17.1	14 151	66.0	127	92.1	7.9	6 951

[1] Data on serious crimes have not been adjusted for underreporting; this may affect comparability over time or among geographic areas. [2] Includes murder and nonnegligent manslaughter, forcible rape, robbery, and aggravated assault. [3] Includes burglary, larceny-theft, and motor vehicle theft. [4] Per 100,000 resident population provided by the U.S. Federal Bureau of Investigation.

Sources: Serious Crimes Known to Police—U.S. Federal Bureau of Investigation, Uniform Crime Reporting Program, unpublished data, annual (related Internet site <http://www.fbi.gov/ucr/ucr.htm>). Housing, 2000—U.S. Census Bureau, 2000 Census of Population and Housing, "Census 2000 Profiles of General Demographic Characteristics" data files, published May 2001 (related Internet site <http://www.census.gov/mp/www/pub/2000cen/mscen01.html>). Housing, 1990—U.S. Census Bureau, 1990 Census of Population and Housing, Summary Tape File (STF) 1C on CD-ROM (related Internet site <http://homer.ssd.census.gov/cdrom/lookup>). Building Permits—U.S. Census Bureau, "New Residential Construction–Building Permits," e-mail from Manufacturing and Construction Division/Residential Construction Branch, subject: building permits by place 2000, 22 May 2001 (related Internet site <http://www.census.gov/const/www/permitsindex.html>).

[Includes U.S., states, and 3,142 counties or county equivalents defined as of January 1, 1992. For changes to these areas since January 1, 1992, see appendix B. Geographic Information]

County	Serious crimes known to police (as reported to the FBI)[1]						Housing, 2000				New private housing units authorized by building permits, 2000			
	Number				Rate[4]				Occupied units			Percent in structures with—		
	1999							Percent change, 1990–2000		Percent owner–occupied		One unit	Five units or more	Valuation ($1,000)
	Total	Violent[2]	Property[3]	1990	1999	1990	Total units		Number		Number			
TEXAS—Con.														
Van Zandt	1 458	150	1 308	940	3 264	2 477	20 896	22.8	18 195	80.8	32	100.0	–	3 866
Victoria	3 960	476	3 484	4 891	4 723	6 577	32 945	13.0	30 071	67.4	167	100.0	–	18 335
Walker	1 954	224	1 730	2 545	3 504	4 998	21 099	15.0	18 303	59.8	56	100.0	–	6 681
Waller	951	105	846	1 441	4 444	6 161	11 955	35.5	10 557	72.5	287	7.3	90.6	6 785
Ward	229	29	200	498	1 913	3 797	4 832	-9.9	3 964	78.1	2	100.0	–	289
Washington	933	124	809	707	3 158	2 703	13 241	13.0	11 322	73.5	26	100.0	–	3 133
Webb	13 698	872	12 826	11 289	7 176	8 473	55 206	48.4	50 740	65.7	1 863	76.4	20.0	111 755
Wharton	1 646	213	1 433	1 997	4 043	4 998	16 606	2.0	14 799	68.8	132	24.2	–	6 984
Wheeler	75	16	59	120	1 397	2 041	2 687	-12.5	2 152	78.0	1	100.0	–	204
Wichita	6 579	664	5 915	11 599	5 031	9 478	53 304	3.7	48 441	62.3	221	95.5	3.6	25 118
Wilbarger	657	115	542	574	4 724	3 796	6 371	-6.5	5 537	66.3	3	100.0	–	173
Willacy	581	91	490	836	2 919	4 722	6 727	10.8	5 584	77.3	42	100.0	–	1 929
Williamson	4 232	348	3 884	5 148	1 863	3 689	90 325	65.8	86 766	74.2	5 691	82.0	17.1	534 010
Wilson	406	37	369	516	1 274	2 278	12 110	42.2	11 038	85.0	11	100.0	–	845
Winkler	152	17	135	187	1 881	2 168	3 214	-13.3	2 584	83.2	–	–	–	X
Wise	782	98	684	866	1 747	2 497	19 242	35.3	17 178	81.4	78	97.4	–	8 582
Wood	913	145	768	849	2 622	2 890	17 939	23.4	14 583	81.4	13	100.0	–	1 168
Yoakum	117	14	103	212	1 440	2 413	2 974	-11.8	2 469	78.1	1	100.0	–	72
Young	558	45	513	603	3 108	3 327	8 504	-.2	7 167	73.9	7	100.0	–	761
Zapata	218	19	199	114	1 870	1 229	6 167	46.0	3 921	81.9	X	X	X	X
Zavala	395	40	355	226	3 265	1 858	4 075	-2.5	3 428	73.1	4	100.0	–	250
UTAH	104 315	5 840	98 475	95 937	4 950	5 612	768 594	28.4	701 281	71.5	17 638	83.4	10.4	2 137 948
Beaver	107	8	99	99	2 036	2 078	2 660	20.9	1 982	79.0	37	100.0	–	4 115
Box Elder	1 363	62	1 301	925	3 415	2 535	14 209	19.5	13 144	80.2	287	78.4	–	31 023
Cache	2 061	80	1 981	2 157	2 337	3 073	29 035	31.7	27 543	64.6	644	74.7	20.7	70 514
Carbon	808	44	764	472	3 799	2 808	8 741	.3	7 413	77.3	116	27.6	72.4	7 074
Daggett	20	–	20	40	2 674	5 797	1 084	31.4	340	70.9	8	100.0	–	709
Davis	6 480	361	6 119	6 858	2 742	3 649	74 114	32.9	71 201	77.5	1 788	94.4	.7	230 955
Duchesne	435	18	417	393	2 962	3 108	6 988	19.2	4 559	80.8	141	100.0	–	8 512
Emery	257	9	248	528	2 306	5 110	4 093	4.2	3 468	82.0	40	100.0	–	2 681
Garfield	8	–	8	NA	185	NA	2 767	11.2	1 576	79.1	66	100.0	–	5 491
Grand	569	24	545	416	6 953	6 284	4 062	35.8	3 434	71.0	91	79.1	–	7 330
Iron	930	43	887	898	3 210	4 320	13 618	60.2	10 627	66.2	452	63.3	19.0	37 600
Juab	109	8	101	209	2 378	3 593	2 810	21.6	2 456	79.8	85	100.0	–	9 304
Kane	87	6	81	125	2 202	2 418	3 767	16.4	2 237	77.9	85	97.6	–	7 132
Millard	415	15	400	214	3 340	2 567	4 522	9.6	3 840	79.7	51	100.0	–	3 172
Morgan	82	10	72	91	1 151	1 646	2 158	28.4	2 046	88.3	58	100.0	–	9 006
Piute	54	9	45	17	3 797	1 331	745	5.8	509	87.0	6	100.0	–	435
Rich	51	4	47	37	2 742	2 145	2 408	29.5	645	83.9	95	90.5	–	8 032
Salt Lake	60 832	3 624	57 208	57 327	7 052	7 897	310 988	20.8	295 141	69.0	4 435	77.8	15.3	543 645
San Juan	194	32	162	120	1 395	951	5 449	17.2	4 089	79.3	52	100.0	–	4 130
Sanpete	274	13	261	357	3 006	2 333	7 879	19.9	6 547	78.8	162	46.9	43.2	9 235
Sevier	758	32	726	374	4 050	2 773	7 016	15.8	6 081	82.0	92	100.0	–	9 808
Summit	1 090	29	1 061	826	4 018	5 323	17 489	55.4	10 332	75.6	539	73.8	21.9	98 018
Tooele	1 048	88	960	1 007	3 145	3 786	13 812	45.2	12 677	78.4	849	91.5	5.7	88 790
Uintah	683	40	643	719	2 624	3 237	9 040	11.0	8 187	77.0	121	98.3	–	16 658
Utah	13 300	436	12 864	10 565	3 907	4 008	104 315	43.3	99 937	66.8	3 731	85.6	8.2	509 145
Wasatch	222	10	212	263	1 650	2 607	6 564	47.0	4 743	80.7	318	100.0	–	62 324
Washington	2 399	165	2 234	1 522	2 880	3 134	36 478	86.8	29 939	73.9	1 551	87.5	5.7	173 834
Wayne	53	9	44	20	2 196	919	1 329	25.3	890	77.8	–	–	–	X
Weber	9 626	661	8 965	9 358	5 156	5 910	70 454	21.8	65 698	74.9	1 738	82.7	12.0	179 276
VERMONT	16 078	653	15 425	[5]22 794	2 795	[5]4 173	294 382	8.5	240 634	70.6	2 506	88.3	7.5	319 491
Addison	780	20	760	649	2 207	4 515	15 312	9.2	13 068	74.9	185	98.9	–	21 871
Bennington	846	31	815	804	2 341	3 911	19 403	4.9	14 846	71.4	213	91.5	–	25 083
Caledonia	699	22	677	483	2 554	4 084	14 504	7.8	11 663	72.9	111	100.0	–	11 654
Chittenden	5 541	285	5 256	6 144	3 859	6 728	58 864	13.0	56 452	66.1	661	85.3	4.5	91 409
Essex	NA	NA	NA	NA	NA	NA	4 762	8.2	2 602	79.5	16	100.0	–	1 056
Franklin	1 046	38	1 008	495	2 365	5 104	19 191	11.3	16 765	75.0	225	89.3	8.9	22 310
Grand Isle	81	–	81	NA	1 293	NA	4 663	12.8	2 761	81.4	38	100.0	–	4 504
Lamoille	583	25	558	696	2 687	5 093	11 009	11.5	9 221	70.9	121	93.4	–	19 561
Orange	295	13	282	97	1 154	2 036	13 386	8.5	10 936	78.3	52	96.2	–	5 758
Orleans	799	26	773	428	3 143	5 969	14 673	12.9	10 446	74.1	77	100.0	–	6 829
Rutland	1 736	49	1 687	1 602	2 763	5 409	32 311	3.6	25 678	69.7	135	98.5	–	16 516
Washington	1 568	52	1 516	1 289	2 771	3 648	27 644	9.1	23 659	68.5	211	100.0	–	23 915
Windham	1 395	69	1 326	2 033	3 255	8 466	27 039	4.8	18 375	67.9	208	69.2	29.8	35 475
Windsor	709	23	686	1 294	1 497	3 515	31 621	5.9	24 162	71.5	253	69.6	29.6	33 550

[1] Data on serious crimes have not been adjusted for underreporting; this may affect comparability over time or among geographic areas. [2] Includes murder and nonnegligent manslaughter, forcible rape, robbery, and aggravated assault. [3] Includes burglary, larceny-theft, and motor vehicle theft. [4] Per 100,000 resident population provided by the U.S. Federal Bureau of Investigation. [5] Includes data not distributed by county.

Sources: Serious Crimes Known to Police—U.S. Federal Bureau of Investigation, Uniform Crime Reporting Program, unpublished data, annual (related Internet site <http://www.fbi.gov/ucr/ucr.htm>). Housing, 2000—U.S. Census Bureau, 2000 Census of Population and Housing, "Census 2000 Profiles of General Demographic Characteristics" data files, published May 2001 (related Internet site <http://www.census.gov/mp/www/pub/2000cen/mscen01.html>). Housing, 1990—U.S. Census Bureau, 1990 Census of Population and Housing, Summary Tape File (STF) 1C on CD-ROM (related Internet site <http://homer.ssd.census.gov/cdrom/lookup>). Building Permits—U.S. Census Bureau, "New Residential Construction–Building Permits," e-mail from Manufacturing and Construction Division/Residential Construction Branch, subject: building permits by place 2000, 22 May 2001 (related Internet site <http://www.census.gov/const/www/permitsindex.html>).

[Includes U.S., states, and 3,142 counties or county equivalents defined as of January 1, 1992. For changes to these areas since January 1, 1992, see appendix B. Geographic Information]

County	Serious crimes known to police (as reported to the FBI)[1]						Housing, 2000				New private housing units authorized by building permits, 2000			
	Number				Rate[4]			Percent change, 1990–2000	Occupied units			Percent in structures with—		
	1999			1990	1999	1990	Total units		Number	Percent owner-occupied	Number	One unit	Five units or more	Valuation ($1,000)
	Total	Violent[2]	Property[3]											
VIRGINIA	215 373	20 350	195 023	275 475	3 138	4 452	2 904 192	16.3	2 699 173	68.1	48 402	82.1	16.4	5 051 607
Accomack	772	71	701	606	2 366	1 911	19 550	23.4	15 299	75.1	132	90.2	–	14 138
Albemarle	1 848	155	1 693	1 693	2 329	2 488	33 720	29.9	31 876	65.9	587	93.5	1.0	108 958
Alleghany	137	14	123	203	1 115	1 541	5 812	6.0	5 149	84.9	27	100.0	–	2 368
Amelia	115	11	104	131	1 096	1 491	4 609	34.0	4 240	81.9	69	100.0	–	8 485
Amherst	457	28	429	713	1 503	2 495	12 958	22.3	11 941	78.1	106	87.7	–	9 831
Appomattox	149	9	140	144	1 121	1 171	5 828	18.6	5 322	81.1	65	100.0	–	5 797
Arlington	6 590	409	6 181	11 976	3 673	7 006	90 426	6.6	86 352	43.3	811	7.3	90.0	46 246
Augusta	1 081	49	1 032	1 025	1 729	1 875	26 738	26.1	24 818	83.1	467	100.0	–	52 100
Bath	36	3	33	68	727	1 417	2 896	11.6	2 053	79.9	51	100.0	–	8 130
Bedford	617	51	566	633	1 091	1 386	26 841	36.7	23 838	86.6	468	100.0	–	76 474
Bland	83	6	77	116	1 215	1 781	3 161	16.8	2 568	86.1	54	100.0	–	2 508
Botetourt	332	37	295	414	1 149	1 657	12 571	28.5	11 700	87.8	203	100.0	–	27 483
Brunswick	215	17	198	268	1 271	1 676	7 541	16.8	6 277	77.6	47	100.0	–	5 504
Buchanan	433	56	377	433	1 479	1 382	11 887	-2.7	10 464	82.9	21	81.0	–	1 638
Buckingham	188	31	157	252	1 269	1 958	6 290	25.5	5 324	77.8	55	96.4	–	5 322
Campbell	935	76	859	1 038	1 835	2 182	22 088	16.2	20 639	77.3	187	100.0	–	23 658
Caroline	364	96	268	504	1 631	2 623	8 889	21.9	8 021	81.9	97	100.0	–	10 418
Carroll	472	47	425	313	1 673	1 177	14 680	20.2	12 186	81.7	166	81.9	18.1	14 980
Charles City	13	4	9	77	181	1 226	2 895	25.1	2 670	84.9	44	100.0	–	4 279
Charlotte	202	31	171	138	1 628	1 181	5 734	15.9	4 951	77.6	94	95.7	–	5 290
Chesterfield	7 867	477	7 390	8 514	3 161	4 068	97 707	26.4	93 772	80.9	1 958	98.1	–	227 037
Clarke	193	24	169	252	1 492	2 082	5 388	18.9	4 942	75.6	101	100.0	–	15 674
Craig	45	2	43	24	911	549	2 554	28.1	2 060	81.2	42	100.0	–	3 459
Culpeper	766	79	687	669	2 288	2 407	12 871	22.9	12 141	70.5	334	90.1	8.4	35 653
Cumberland	110	15	95	53	1 385	677	4 085	28.9	3 528	77.2	34	100.0	–	3 202
Dickenson	59	8	51	141	349	800	7 684	8.0	6 732	82.1	24	100.0	–	1 187
Dinwiddie	608	40	568	383	2 437	1 827	9 707	21.0	9 107	79.2	144	97.2	–	14 973
Essex	272	24	248	305	2 945	3 510	4 926	20.9	3 995	77.3	41	100.0	–	5 754
Fairfax	15 196	654	14 542	28 408	1 616	3 470	359 411	16.7	350 714	70.9	5 816	65.6	34.4	554 483
Fauquier	891	68	823	888	1 627	1 822	21 046	18.8	19 842	76.2	533	100.0	–	97 038
Floyd	158	3	155	82	1 193	683	6 763	22.9	5 791	81.9	97	97.9	–	7 859
Fluvanna	154	7	147	105	819	845	8 018	59.2	7 387	85.2	336	100.0	–	40 337
Franklin	875	77	798	607	1 941	1 535	22 717	29.6	18 963	81.1	392	96.9	2.6	58 069
Frederick	1 209	53	1 156	1 066	2 163	2 331	23 319	30.5	22 097	80.3	500	100.0	–	59 906
Giles	198	22	176	179	1 267	1 094	7 732	8.9	6 994	79.1	53	100.0	–	4 796
Gloucester	684	56	628	626	1 927	2 078	14 494	16.4	13 127	81.4	182	100.0	–	19 822
Goochland	239	40	199	237	1 325	1 673	6 555	26.0	6 158	86.6	223	100.0	–	36 043
Grayson	150	12	138	106	920	651	9 123	21.2	7 259	81.4	122	100.0	–	8 152
Greene	202	22	180	162	1 427	1 573	5 986	44.1	5 574	81.4	201	100.0	–	16 969
Greensville	106	26	80	264	929	2 982	3 765	11.0	3 375	78.3	72	44.4	55.6	4 516
Halifax	839	134	705	5378	2 249	51 302	16 953	43.8	15 018	76.1	72	100.0	–	6 523
Hanover	1 647	101	1 546	1 678	1 985	2 651	32 196	35.7	31 121	84.3	966	92.2	7.8	94 618
Henrico	11 928	643	11 285	10 128	4 790	4 648	112 570	19.1	108 121	65.7	1 566	100.0	–	179 316
Henry	1 815	180	1 635	1 917	3 224	3 367	25 921	11.9	23 910	76.9	112	82.1	14.3	12 735
Highland	13	–	13	33	514	1 252	1 822	3.6	1 131	83.8	20	100.0	–	1 219
Isle of Wight	760	47	713	567	2 567	2 263	12 066	23.7	11 319	80.8	257	98.8	–	32 057
James City	1 154	106	1 048	1 198	2 578	3 437	20 772	45.0	19 003	77.0	1 071	72.9	25.7	203 376
King and Queen	55	8	47	50	832	795	3 010	11.6	2 673	82.5	24	100.0	–	3 220
King George	397	38	359	162	2 276	1 198	6 820	29.2	6 091	71.8	129	96.9	–	14 628
King William	135	10	125	174	1 045	1 594	5 189	23.8	4 846	85.0	117	100.0	–	9 559
Lancaster	165	16	149	118	1 434	1 083	6 498	9.8	5 004	83.0	91	91.2	8.8	14 373
Lee	386	33	353	202	1 664	825	11 086	8.0	9 706	74.4	65	96.9	–	4 426
Loudoun	3 636	285	3 351	2 307	2 496	2 679	62 160	88.8	59 900	79.4	6 300	81.4	18.6	525 130
Louisa	344	35	309	179	1 378	881	11 855	30.6	9 945	81.5	262	100.0	–	27 136
Lunenburg	151	24	127	124	1 239	1 086	5 736	13.2	4 998	77.7	18	100.0	–	1 764
Madison	108	3	105	136	841	1 138	5 239	15.2	4 739	76.8	106	100.0	–	11 728
Mathews	48	2	46	103	523	1 234	5 333	12.9	3 932	84.7	45	100.0	–	6 808
Mecklenburg	1 003	128	875	925	3 192	3 163	17 403	19.3	12 951	74.4	186	65.6	34.4	16 862
Middlesex	159	7	152	153	1 631	1 768	6 362	16.0	4 253	83.1	74	95.9	–	11 038
Montgomery	2 548	239	2 309	2 980	3 318	4 032	32 527	17.1	30 997	55.1	330	80.0	16.4	36 079
Nelson	271	17	254	97	1 924	759	8 554	21.1	5 887	80.8	112	100.0	–	17 629
New Kent	253	29	224	269	1 915	2 575	5 203	31.1	4 925	88.7	157	100.0	–	18 427
Northampton	363	30	333	393	2 822	3 009	6 547	5.9	5 321	68.6	109	57.8	42.2	10 720
Northumberland	145	11	134	141	1 245	1 340	8 057	17.8	5 470	87.4	124	100.0	–	19 907
Nottoway	293	38	255	369	2 001	2 461	6 373	11.2	5 664	70.9	51	87.9	–	4 843
Orange	332	47	285	293	1 291	1 368	11 354	25.6	10 150	77.1	247	87.9	9.7	31 264
Page	298	25	273	256	1 281	1 180	10 557	18.0	9 305	73.9	80	97.5	–	6 436
Patrick	361	30	331	474	1 934	2 713	9 823	20.9	8 141	80.3	87	100.0	–	9 186
Pittsylvania	577	69	508	901	994	1 619	28 011	22.5	24 684	80.1	269	97.0	–	25 544
Powhatan	263	52	211	156	1 184	1 018	7 509	52.9	7 258	88.8	260	100.0	–	30 481

[1] Data on serious crimes have not been adjusted for underreporting; this may affect comparability over time or among geographic areas.   [2] Includes murder and nonnegligent manslaughter, forcible rape, robbery, and aggravated assault.   [3] Includes burglary, larceny-theft, and motor vehicle theft.   [4] Per 100,000 resident population provided by the U.S. Federal Bureau of Investigation.
[5] Excludes South Boston independent city which is included in the 1999 data; for more information, see appendix B. Geographic Information.

Sources: Serious Crimes Known to Police—U.S. Federal Bureau of Investigation, Uniform Crime Reporting Program, unpublished data, annual (related Internet site <http://www.fbi.gov/ucr/ucr.htm>).   Housing, 2000—U.S. Census Bureau, 2000 Census of Population and Housing, "Census 2000 Profiles of General Demographic Characteristics" data files, published May 2001 (related Internet site <http://www.census.gov/mp/www/pub/2000cen/mscen01.html>).   Housing, 1990—U.S. Census Bureau, 1990 Census of Population and Housing, Summary Tape File (STF) 1C on CD-ROM (related Internet site <http://homer.ssd.census.gov/cdrom/lookup>).   Building Permits—U.S. Census Bureau, "New Residential Construction–Building Permits," e-mail from Manufacturing and Construction Division/Residential Construction Branch, subject: building permits by place 2000, 22 May 2001 (related Internet site <http://www.census.gov/const/www/permitsindex.html>).

Table B–6. Counties — Crime, Housing, and Building Permits–Con.

[Includes U.S., states, and 3,142 counties or county equivalents defined as of January 1, 1992. For changes to these areas since January 1, 1992, see appendix B. Geographic Information]

County	Serious crimes known to police (as reported to the FBI)[1]						Housing, 2000				New private housing units authorized by building permits, 2000			
	Number				Rate[4]				Occupied units			Percent in structures with—		
	1999							Percent change, 1990– 2000		Percent owner– occupied		One unit	Five units or more	Valuation ($1,000)
	Total	Violent[2]	Property[3]	1990	1999	1990	Total units		Number		Number			
VIRGINIA—Con.														
Prince Edward	217	29	188	401	1 127	2 315	7 527	23.9	6 561	68.4	67	76.1	–	6 855
Prince George	478	25	453	566	1 567	2 066	10 726	24.1	10 159	73.0	181	100.0	–	20 467
Prince William	8 183	640	7 543	8 099	3 122	3 755	98 052	31.2	94 570	71.7	4 758	80.2	19.8	445 644
Pulaski	1 044	95	949	1 370	2 987	3 971	16 325	10.8	14 643	73.7	145	100.0	–	13 980
Rappahannock	88	3	85	92	1 196	1 389	3 303	11.4	2 788	75.2	44	100.0	–	4 691
Richmond	76	14	62	82	867	1 127	3 512	10.5	2 937	77.4	38	89.5	–	4 441
Roanoke	1 264	163	1 101	3 060	1 545	3 857	36 121	14.0	34 686	77.2	580	82.4	16.6	29 167
Rockbridge	326	19	307	531	1 647	2 894	9 550	19.7	8 486	77.7	219	97.3	–	18 245
Rockingham	453	37	416	436	708	758	27 328	20.8	25 355	78.0	438	94.3	1.8	54 384
Russell	350	31	319	251	1 191	876	13 191	14.1	11 789	81.1	58	100.0	–	4 437
Scott	389	25	364	284	1 875	1 224	11 355	13.5	9 795	78.2	67	100.0	–	4 564
Shenandoah	597	97	500	508	1 702	1 606	16 709	10.2	14 296	73.2	270	88.9	8.9	23 302
Smyth	519	58	461	496	1 566	1 532	15 111	15.1	13 493	74.1	71	91.5	8.5	7 265
Southampton	369	67	302	221	2 166	1 259	7 058	7.6	6 279	74.3	68	97.1	–	6 311
Spotsylvania	2 249	175	2 074	2 097	2 655	3 653	33 329	62.7	31 308	82.2	1 460	100.0	–	208 554
Stafford	1 873	112	1 761	1 263	2 126	2 063	31 405	53.0	30 187	80.6	1 694	65.0	34.7	188 937
Surry	136	33	103	179	2 077	2 913	3 294	10.5	2 619	77.2	53	100.0	–	3 048
Sussex	261	53	208	230	2 599	2 244	4 653	9.4	4 126	69.5	13	100.0	–	1 100
Tazewell	1 572	535	1 037	750	3 322	1 632	20 390	7.9	18 277	77.3	94	84.0	6.4	8 841
Warren	925	32	893	841	3 034	3 217	13 299	18.5	12 087	74.2	201	98.0	–	22 512
Washington	887	50	837	817	1 818	1 780	22 985	19.8	21 056	77.2	294	96.9	1.7	19 677
Westmoreland	286	31	255	308	1 736	1 990	9 286	10.8	6 846	79.2	58	100.0	–	6 389
Wise	828	92	736	565	2 172	1 428	17 792	11.7	16 013	75.3	49	100.0	–	3 818
Wythe	664	42	622	438	2 593	1 720	12 744	19.6	11 511	77.3	108	94.4	–	10 054
York	1 691	360	1 331	1 227	2 842	2 892	20 701	35.4	20 000	75.8	783	82.1	16.9	77 143
Independent Cities														
Alexandria	5 690	390	5 300	7 422	4 753	6 675	64 251	10.3	61 889	40.0	1 100	35.1	64.9	109 267
Bedford	261	23	238	139	4 083	2 289	2 702	2.9	2 519	60.3	15	73.3	–	1 417
Bristol	523	70	453	1 130	2 955	6 133	8 469	3.6	7 678	65.1	37	83.8	–	2 821
Buena Vista	70	20	50	90	1 100	1 405	2 716	8.9	2 547	70.7	20	100.0	–	1 295
Charlottesville	2 770	380	2 390	3 102	7 161	7 689	17 591	4.8	16 851	40.8	64	75.0	25.0	5 331
Chesapeake	8 263	1 062	7 201	7 360	4 091	4 843	72 672	30.4	69 900	74.9	1 081	100.0	–	125 057
Clifton Forge	120	30	90	169	2 731	3 612	2 069	-2.9	1 841	62.6	1	100.0	–	65
Colonial Heights	1 131	41	1 090	759	6 591	4 725	7 340	11.3	7 027	69.3	41	100.0	–	4 844
Covington	225	10	215	242	3 243	3 462	3 195	-2.3	2 835	69.7	3	100.0	–	150
Danville	2 633	230	2 403	2 149	5 115	4 050	23 108	-.8	20 607	58.1	89	32.6	62.9	6 473
Emporia	433	77	356	467	7 816	8 801	2 412	10.7	2 226	52.2	58	12.1	81.0	2 140
Fairfax	1 280	51	1 229	1 713	6 111	8 730	8 204	6.9	8 035	69.1	166	100.0	–	17 915
Falls Church	480	56	424	684	4 723	7 141	4 725	1.2	4 471	60.6	1	100.0	–	187
Franklin	385	25	360	416	4 380	5 290	3 767	19.0	3 384	53.7	6	100.0	–	808
Fredericksburg	930	78	852	833	4 238	4 378	8 888	10.2	8 102	35.6	41	100.0	–	4 520
Galax	301	36	265	134	4 333	2 009	3 217	9.3	2 950	66.2	15	86.7	–	1 322
Hampton	6 058	490	5 568	8 139	4 370	6 083	57 311	6.9	53 887	58.6	324	100.0	–	21 041
Harrisonburg	1 702	162	1 540	1 700	5 030	5 536	13 689	25.6	13 133	39.0	193	74.6	21.2	13 343
Hopewell	1 132	152	980	1 331	4 965	5 762	9 749	1.3	9 055	56.0	66	100.0	–	4 931
Lexington	122	17	105	227	1 638	3 262	2 376	2.8	2 232	54.9	17	88.2	–	1 562
Lynchburg	2 784	298	2 486	3 858	4 202	5 841	27 640	1.5	25 477	58.5	364	41.8	54.4	35 314
Manassas	1 192	83	1 109	1 221	3 333	4 367	12 114	18.4	11 757	69.8	54	100.0	–	3 529
Manassas Park	298	14	284	269	3 380	3 995	3 365	49.4	3 254	78.7	207	100.0	–	22 770
Martinsville	908	78	830	1 158	5 727	7 165	7 249	-.8	6 498	60.2	56	14.3	85.7	1 863
Newport News	10 339	1 496	8 843	10 289	5 925	6 051	74 117	6.3	69 686	52.4	407	100.0	–	25 035
Norfolk	8 410	892	7 518	27 485	3 861	10 521	94 416	-4.4	86 210	45.5	287	61.7	33.1	26 356
Norton	248	29	219	163	5 898	3 838	1 946	5.5	1 730	55.9	3	100.0	–	193
Petersburg	2 805	371	2 434	3 030	7 982	7 894	15 955	-1.5	13 799	51.5	11	100.0	–	510
Poquoson	90	13	77	187	776	1 699	4 300	10.5	4 166	84.1	20	100.0	–	3 054
Portsmouth	6 924	887	6 037	9 841	6 915	9 471	41 605	-1.6	38 170	58.6	213	100.0	–	15 660
Radford	444	50	394	588	2 788	3 689	6 137	11.7	5 809	44.6	15	100.0	–	2 494
Richmond	16 557	2 262	14 295	24 269	8 426	11 952	92 282	-2.0	84 549	46.1	270	63.0	–	21 230
Roanoke	5 125	661	4 464	7 793	5 402	8 084	45 257	2.0	42 003	56.3	310	54.2	42.6	21 002
Salem	648	26	622	1 036	2 595	4 361	10 403	8.3	9 954	67.6	73	94.5	–	8 859
South Boston	NA	NA	NA	136	NA	1 944	X	X	X	X	X	X	X	X
Staunton	970	39	931	852	4 106	3 483	10 427	4.2	9 676	61.4	65	90.8	9.2	3 817
Suffolk	3 038	385	2 653	3 011	4 788	5 775	24 704	23.5	23 283	72.2	773	82.7	–	83 013
Virginia Beach	16 099	1 050	15 049	22 736	3 678	5 784	162 277	10.4	154 455	65.6	1 464	89.6	7.7	181 594
Waynesboro	707	61	646	897	3 764	4 836	8 863	12.2	8 332	61.2	100	50.0	–	7 964
Williamsburg	696	37	659	765	5 745	6 635	3 880	-2.0	3 619	44.3	182	46.7	38.5	21 533
Winchester	1 389	103	1 286	1 896	6 057	8 639	10 587	7.9	10 001	45.7	116	87.9	12.1	11 914

[1] Data on serious crimes have not been adjusted for underreporting; this may affect comparability over time or among geographic areas. [2] Includes murder and nonnegligent manslaughter, forcible rape, robbery, and aggravated assault. [3] Includes burglary, larceny-theft, and motor vehicle theft. [4] Per 100,000 resident population provided by the U.S. Federal Bureau of Investigation.

Sources: Serious Crimes Known to Police—U.S. Federal Bureau of Investigation, Uniform Crime Reporting Program, unpublished data, annual (related Internet site <http://www.fbi.gov/ucr/ucr.htm>). Housing, 2000—U.S. Census Bureau, 2000 Census of Population and Housing, "Census 2000 Profiles of General Demographic Characteristics" data files, published May 2001 (related Internet site <http://www.census.gov/mp/www/pub/2000cen/mscen01.html>). Housing, 1990—U.S. Census Bureau, 1990 Census of Population and Housing, Summary Tape File (STF) 1C on CD-ROM (related Internet site <http://homer.ssd.census.gov/cdrom/lookup>). Building Permits—U.S. Census Bureau, "New Residential Construction-Building Permits," e-mail from Manufacturing and Construction Division/Residential Construction Branch, subject: building permits by place 2000, 22 May 2001 (related Internet site <http://www.census.gov/const/www/permitsindex.html>).

Table B–6. Counties — Crime, Housing, and Building Permits–Con.

[Includes U.S., states, and 3,142 counties or county equivalents defined as of January 1, 1992. For changes to these areas since January 1, 1992, see appendix B. Geographic Information]

County	Serious crimes known to police (as reported to the FBI)[1]						Housing, 2000				New private housing units authorized by building permits, 2000			
	Number			Rate[4]					Occupied units			Percent in structures with—		
	1999			1990	1999	1990	Total units	Percent change, 1990–2000	Number	Percent owner-occupied	Number	One unit	Five units or more	Valuation ($1,000)
	Total	Violent[2]	Property[3]											
WASHINGTON	295 660	21 344	274 316	298 711	5 214	6 186	2 451 075	20.6	2 271 398	64.6	39 021	65.3	28.5	4 426 088
Adams	656	51	605	667	4 231	4 903	5 773	9.7	5 229	68.4	27	100.0	–	3 098
Asotin	900	38	862	777	4 183	4 414	9 111	21.2	8 364	67.1	50	92.0	–	5 369
Benton	5 290	340	4 950	6 081	3 837	5 402	55 963	24.7	52 866	68.7	737	92.9	1.6	121 500
Chelan	3 550	157	3 393	3 285	5 843	6 287	30 407	21.4	25 021	64.7	266	94.7	4.5	36 185
Clallam	1 942	83	1 859	2 275	2 991	4 029	30 683	21.6	27 164	72.7	379	97.9	–	38 565
Clark	12 064	1 010	11 054	9 916	3 647	4 165	134 030	44.4	127 208	67.3	3 205	82.5	12.9	383 297
Columbia	172	4	168	188	4 090	4 672	2 018	-1.4	1 687	69.4	38	21.1	78.9	2 170
Cowlitz	5 438	335	5 103	3 526	5 869	4 294	38 624	16.0	35 850	67.6	514	67.9	29.6	55 807
Douglas	1 229	46	1 183	954	3 612	3 641	12 944	21.7	11 726	70.9	127	90.6	–	16 347
Ferry	102	2	100	151	1 406	2 399	3 775	16.5	2 823	73.0	46	67.4	32.6	4 093
Franklin	2 185	161	2 024	3 218	4 648	8 588	16 084	17.7	14 840	65.6	281	100.0	–	34 273
Garfield	89	8	81	85	3 776	3 781	1 288	6.5	987	74.0	1	100.0	–	100
Grant	3 588	235	3 353	2 983	5 120	5 740	29 081	27.5	25 204	66.7	222	84.7	–	27 035
Grays Harbor	3 488	144	3 344	3 589	5 089	5 636	32 489	8.5	26 808	69.0	220	84.5	10.9	26 083
Island	390	12	378	1 138	775	1 891	32 378	25.2	27 784	70.1	569	94.9	–	77 411
Jefferson	1 028	72	956	735	3 873	3 648	14 144	28.4	11 645	76.2	274	92.0	6.6	32 864
King	104 680	7 293	97 387	120 863	6 338	8 018	742 237	14.7	710 916	59.8	11 564	38.4	55.8	1 359 353
Kitsap	9 190	822	8 368	8 451	3 905	4 454	92 644	25.1	86 416	67.4	1 111	99.5	–	134 077
Kittitas	1 779	65	1 714	1 608	5 544	6 213	16 475	24.7	13 382	58.3	315	68.6	–	34 268
Klickitat	483	36	447	546	2 474	3 286	8 633	19.7	7 473	68.8	86	95.3	–	9 859
Lewis	3 146	204	2 942	2 721	4 562	4 584	29 585	16.1	26 306	71.4	184	98.9	–	19 181
Lincoln	184	8	176	224	1 961	2 527	5 298	15.0	4 151	76.8	33	100.0	–	2 788
Mason	2 850	163	2 687	1 908	5 741	4 976	25 515	14.5	18 912	79.0	404	90.1	5.9	29 642
Okanogan	1 040	95	945	1 461	3 227	4 381	19 085	14.8	15 027	68.6	219	88.1	11.0	19 868
Pacific	764	64	700	648	3 630	3 432	13 991	12.8	9 096	74.8	63	93.7	–	6 532
Pend Oreille	398	25	373	377	3 580	4 229	6 608	22.3	4 639	77.4	91	51.6	46.2	6 162
Pierce	42 714	4 380	38 334	40 916	6 395	7 054	277 060	21.1	260 800	63.5	4 688	80.1	7.6	514 133
San Juan	252	2	250	348	1 994	3 468	9 752	60.5	6 466	73.5	392	93.9	–	41 041
Skagit	6 365	165	6 200	2 611	6 332	3 551	42 681	27.1	38 852	69.7	677	83.3	12.6	88 192
Skamania	252	24	228	444	2 540	5 356	4 576	16.7	3 755	73.8	36	100.0	–	3 962
Snohomish	20 962	1 515	19 447	19 025	3 580	4 095	236 205	28.4	224 852	67.8	6 111	62.5	32.9	639 863
Spokane	24 633	1 899	22 734	22 104	6 013	6 352	175 005	16.6	163 611	65.5	2 094	63.4	31.9	209 244
Stevens	1 065	27	1 038	853	2 710	2 780	17 599	20.5	15 017	78.1	131	100.0	–	12 727
Thurston	7 712	561	7 151	6 783	3 769	4 268	86 652	30.4	81 625	66.6	1 299	87.7	8.8	165 904
Wahkiakum	75	3	72	112	1 922	3 366	1 792	19.8	1 553	79.7	12	100.0	–	1 080
Walla Walla	2 660	178	2 482	3 380	4 896	7 123	21 147	11.1	19 647	65.2	199	81.4	4.5	25 927
Whatcom	8 052	453	7 599	6 532	5 074	5 112	73 893	32.6	64 446	63.4	1 625	65.8	27.8	170 603
Whitman	930	48	882	1 352	2 472	3 661	16 676	14.2	15 257	47.9	247	25.5	72.9	15 407
Yakima	13 363	616	12 747	15 876	6 057	8 500	79 174	11.7	73 993	64.4	484	68.8	7.6	52 078
WEST VIRGINIA	37 289	4 831	32 458	44 890	2 451	2 503	844 623	8.1	736 481	75.2	3 763	87.6	9.5	359 560
Barbour	130	11	119	147	807	936	7 348	5.6	6 123	78.6	9	100.0	–	664
Berkeley	1 269	103	1 166	2 499	1 792	4 218	32 913	29.7	29 569	74.2	777	96.9	–	85 128
Boone	297	52	245	434	1 285	1 678	11 575	8.1	10 291	78.9	17	100.0	–	1 609
Braxton	211	40	171	114	1 604	877	7 374	29.2	5 771	78.2	–	–	–	–
Brooke	232	29	203	454	991	1 682	11 150	2.9	10 396	76.7	13	100.0	–	1 652
Cabell	873	33	840	5 636	17 558	5 821	45 615	4.6	41 180	64.6	50	100.0	–	6 162
Calhoun	55	8	47	66	694	837	3 848	11.7	3 071	78.9	X	X	X	X
Clay	124	39	85	113	1 180	1 132	4 836	10.9	4 020	79.2	25	100.0	–	1 314
Doddridge	82	25	57	62	1 088	886	3 661	12.6	2 845	81.2	X	X	X	X
Fayette	1 009	119	890	739	2 275	1 541	21 616	3.7	18 945	77.2	89	100.0	–	5 477
Gilmer	68	8	60	98	956	1 278	3 621	11.7	2 768	72.4	–	–	–	–
Grant	72	9	63	76	650	729	6 105	28.6	4 591	80.9	53	34.0	66.0	2 463
Greenbrier	384	57	327	348	1 088	1 003	17 644	5.3	14 571	76.6	105	92.4	7.6	8 262
Hampshire	292	45	247	290	1 537	1 758	11 185	26.9	7 955	81.1	111	100.0	–	12 527
Hancock	309	36	273	726	1 674	2 061	14 728	.2	13 678	77.1	21	100.0	–	2 810
Hardy	175	38	137	150	1 483	1 366	7 115	27.7	5 204	80.5	102	100.0	–	6 076
Harrison	1 378	153	1 225	1 504	2 006	2 168	31 112	3.7	27 867	74.8	166	71.7	28.3	14 338
Jackson	299	38	261	386	1 071	1 488	12 245	15.8	11 061	79.6	47	100.0	–	3 792
Jefferson	432	51	381	946	NA	2 633	17 623	20.7	16 165	75.8	483	89.9	10.1	52 418
Kanawha	10 324	1 155	9 169	9 314	5 121	4 486	93 788	1.1	86 226	70.3	96	88.5	6.3	15 008
Lewis	176	28	148	183	1 012	1 063	7 944	6.6	6 946	73.0	–	–	–	–
Lincoln	189	65	124	325	854	1 520	9 846	16.8	8 664	79.1	29	100.0	–	1 521
Logan	446	61	385	660	10 141	1 534	16 807	-.2	14 880	76.8	7	28.6	71.4	99
McDowell	372	78	294	285	1 261	809	13 582	-11.4	11 169	80.1	10	100.0	–	386

[1] Data on serious crimes have not been adjusted for underreporting; this may affect comparability over time or among geographic areas.   [2] Includes murder and nonnegligent manslaughter, forcible rape, robbery, and aggravated assault.   [3] Includes burglary, larceny-theft, and motor vehicle theft.   [4] Per 100,000 resident population provided by the U.S. Federal Bureau of Investigation.

Sources: Serious Crimes Known to Police—U.S. Federal Bureau of Investigation, Uniform Crime Reporting Program, unpublished data, annual (related Internet site <http://www.fbi.gov/ucr/ucr.htm>). Housing, 2000—U.S. Census Bureau, 2000 Census of Population and Housing, "Census 2000 Profiles of General Demographic Characteristics" data files, published May 2001 (related Internet site <http://www.census.gov/mp/www/pub/2000cen/mscen01.html>). Housing, 1990—U.S. Census Bureau, 1990 Census of Population and Housing, Summary Tape File (STF) 1C on CD-ROM (related Internet site <http://homer.ssd.census.gov/cdrom/lookup/>). Building Permits—U.S. Census Bureau, "New Residential Construction–Building Permits," e-mail from Manufacturing and Construction Division/Residential Construction Branch, subject: building permits by place 2000, 22 May 2001 (related Internet site <http://www.census.gov/const/www/permitsindex.html>).

[Includes U.S., states, and 3,142 counties or county equivalents defined as of January 1, 1992. For changes to these areas since January 1, 1992, see appendix B. Geographic Information]

County	Serious crimes known to police (as reported to the FBI)[1]						Housing, 2000				New private housing units authorized by building permits, 2000			
	Number				Rate[4]				Occupied units			Percent in structures with—		
	1999			1990	1999	1990	Total units	Percent change, 1990–2000	Number	Percent owner–occupied	Number	One unit	Five units or more	Valuation ($1,000)
	Total	Violent[2]	Property[3]											
WEST VIRGINIA—Con.														
Marion	881	81	800	1 299	1 598	2 269	26 660	4.6	23 652	74.8	21	100.0	–	1 410
Marshall	51	12	39	782	3 333	2 093	15 814	1.2	14 207	77.6	6	100.0	–	420
Mason	453	65	388	364	1 755	1 446	12 056	10.3	10 587	81.0	10	100.0	–	673
Mercer	2 202	314	1 888	1 913	3 490	2 944	30 143	6.0	26 509	76.8	33	78.8	–	2 499
Mineral	389	62	327	475	6 510	1 779	12 094	10.6	10 784	78.0	328	88.1	11.9	39 006
Mingo	321	66	255	504	1 047	1 494	12 898	-1.4	11 303	77.7	8	100.0	–	418
Monongalia	1 589	233	1 356	2 833	2 055	3 752	36 695	16.3	33 446	61.0	79	24.1	75.9	3 361
Monroe	95	26	69	103	721	830	7 267	21.2	5 447	84.5	1	100.0	–	27
Morgan	334	26	308	147	2 454	1 212	8 076	19.5	6 145	83.3	155	100.0	–	12 465
Nicholas	559	74	485	555	2 253	2 073	12 406	10.4	10 722	82.8	7	100.0	–	650
Ohio	963	123	840	1 263	2 119	2 483	22 166	-4.6	19 733	68.6	18	100.0	–	2 757
Pendleton	72	15	57	76	895	944	5 102	13.0	3 350	79.4	49	100.0	–	2 992
Pleasants	37	6	31	41	695	543	3 214	2.6	2 887	80.4	4	100.0	–	180
Pocahontas	140	20	120	48	1 514	533	7 594	36.1	3 835	80.3	–	–	–	–
Preston	282	36	246	406	964	1 398	13 444	10.8	11 544	83.0	5	100.0	–	325
Putnam	1 278	101	1 177	664	2 560	1 550	21 621	28.1	20 028	84.0	271	85.6	9.2	27 103
Raleigh	2 498	269	2 229	2 225	3 167	2 896	35 678	7.2	31 793	76.5	89	91.0	–	10 392
Randolph	744	123	621	420	2 602	1 511	13 478	7.4	11 072	75.7	29	51.7	48.3	1 566
Ritchie	82	29	53	91	2 649	889	5 513	11.7	4 184	81.7	4	100.0	–	203
Roane	355	70	285	210	2 319	1 389	7 360	11.3	6 161	79.6	–	–	–	–
Summers	175	39	136	68	1 334	479	7 331	8.3	5 530	79.1	24	100.0	–	2 053
Taylor	116	18	98	147	2 006	971	7 125	9.1	6 320	79.6	2	100.0	–	91
Tucker	76	11	65	107	998	1 385	4 634	18.8	3 052	82.6	9	100.0	–	583
Tyler	104	22	82	72	1 170	735	4 780	7.6	3 836	83.7	1	100.0	–	40
Upshur	378	31	347	421	1 610	1 841	10 751	13.1	8 972	76.7	101	50.5	49.5	6 246
Wayne	777	91	686	937	2 222	2 250	19 107	12.5	17 239	78.1	50	100.0	–	2 660
Webster	150	54	96	61	1 470	569	5 273	4.0	4 010	79.0	–	–	–	–
Wetzel	123	20	103	255	700	1 324	8 313	2.3	7 164	78.5	10	100.0	–	668
Wirt	79	15	64	90	1 397	1 733	3 266	16.9	2 284	83.1	–	–	–	–
Wood	2 394	451	1 943	2 344	2 766	2 697	39 785	5.8	36 275	73.4	237	69.6	8.4	18 871
Wyoming	394	47	347	414	1 442	1 428	11 698	-.5	10 454	83.3	2	100.0	–	195
WISCONSIN	171 155	12 796	158 359	5214 899	3 284	54 396	2 321 144	12.9	2 084 544	68.4	34 154	70.3	19.0	3 916 846
Adams	140	6	134	623	753	3 973	14 123	13.7	7 900	85.3	244	96.7	–	26 162
Ashland	448	14	434	492	2 705	3 017	8 883	6.1	6 718	70.7	49	83.7	16.3	4 015
Barron	702	47	655	976	1 669	2 395	20 969	8.3	17 851	75.8	337	75.1	–	30 193
Bayfield	273	21	252	330	1 793	2 356	11 640	6.6	6 207	82.6	146	98.6	–	12 260
Brown	6 879	427	6 452	7 800	3 178	4 008	90 199	20.7	87 295	65.4	1 559	72.5	15.8	197 642
Buffalo	163	8	155	162	1 134	1 193	6 098	9.2	5 511	76.5	81	85.2	–	7 739
Burnett	369	20	349	356	2 506	2 721	12 582	7.1	6 613	84.5	225	100.0	–	22 565
Calumet	569	34	535	857	1 475	2 499	15 758	26.4	14 910	80.4	388	83.5	4.1	50 582
Chippewa	1 318	48	1 270	1 469	2 403	2 806	22 821	8.5	21 356	75.7	442	90.0	–	48 470
Clark	479	17	462	489	1 438	1 545	13 531	4.9	12 047	81.2	134	79.1	6.0	12 912
Columbia	1 444	50	1 394	1 335	2 808	2 961	22 685	17.8	20 439	74.8	381	80.8	7.6	44 684
Crawford	434	16	418	457	2 605	2 867	8 480	15.9	6 677	76.8	56	89.3	–	4 974
Dane	13 326	1 109	12 217	19 440	3 122	5 296	180 398	22.0	173 484	57.6	3 986	50.0	34.0	465 508
Dodge	1 287	42	1 245	1 879	1 538	2 454	33 672	17.2	31 417	73.4	384	83.3	12.5	48 630
Door	576	5	571	665	2 120	2 589	19 587	8.6	11 828	79.4	458	71.4	11.6	45 236
Douglas	2 035	98	1 937	2 542	4 705	6 087	20 356	-1.2	17 808	71.3	251	89.2	4.4	21 337
Dunn	819	17	802	1 174	5 243	3 269	15 277	15.3	14 337	69.1	305	71.8	–	27 771
Eau Claire	3 005	150	2 855	3 702	3 403	4 346	37 444	14.5	35 822	65.0	731	60.3	18.5	80 941
Florence	123	6	117	105	2 354	2 288	4 239	12.3	2 133	85.7	–	–	–	–
Fond du Lac	2 353	51	2 302	3 328	2 472	3 694	39 271	13.7	36 931	72.9	415	83.6	9.6	56 667
Forest	359	5	354	327	3 703	3 726	8 322	15.5	4 043	78.9	96	100.0	–	7 341
Grant	869	72	797	956	1 911	1 941	19 940	8.1	18 465	72.3	159	89.9	–	16 571
Green	599	22	577	822	1 784	2 709	13 878	14.8	13 212	73.8	211	82.9	–	26 579
Green Lake	440	15	425	359	2 252	1 925	9 831	6.8	7 703	77.2	82	84.1	6.1	13 434
Iowa	370	35	335	285	1 642	1 414	9 579	16.5	8 764	75.9	198	67.7	26.3	18 212
Iron	211	13	198	185	3 306	3 007	5 706	8.8	3 083	80.7	73	100.0	–	7 908
Jackson	487	41	446	560	2 732	3 376	8 029	5.3	7 070	74.9	89	95.5	–	8 178
Jefferson	1 464	59	1 405	2 036	1 980	3 004	30 092	17.0	28 205	71.7	577	70.4	22.4	61 846
Juneau	594	48	546	663	2 481	3 062	12 370	8.3	9 696	77.0	187	76.5	21.4	16 362
Kenosha	4 565	530	4 035	6 236	3 146	4 865	59 989	17.0	56 057	69.1	1 014	61.7	34.7	105 536
Kewaunee	268	39	229	239	1 346	1 266	8 221	9.0	7 623	81.8	131	87.0	3.8	17 005
La Crosse	3 243	184	3 059	4 672	3 146	4 772	43 479	13.7	41 599	65.1	571	70.2	10.5	65 043

[1] Data on serious crimes have not been adjusted for underreporting; this may affect comparability over time or among geographic areas. [2] Includes murder and nonnegligent manslaughter, forcible rape, robbery, and aggravated assault. [3] Includes burglary, larceny-theft, and motor vehicle theft. [4] Per 100,000 resident population provided by the U.S. Federal Bureau of Investigation. [5] Includes data not distributed by county.

Sources: Serious Crimes Known to Police—U.S. Federal Bureau of Investigation, Uniform Crime Reporting Program, unpublished data, annual (related Internet site <http://www.fbi.gov/ucr/ucr.htm>). Housing, 2000—U.S. Census Bureau, 2000 Census of Population and Housing, "Census 2000 Profiles of General Demographic Characteristics" data files, published May 2001 (related Internet site <http://www.census.gov/mp/www/pub/2000cen/mscen01.html>). Housing, 1990—U.S. Census Bureau, 1990 Census of Population and Housing, Summary Tape File (STF) 1C on CD-ROM (related Internet site <http://homer.ssd.census.gov/cdrom/lookup>). Building Permits—U.S. Census Bureau, "New Residential Construction–Building Permits," e-mail from Manufacturing and Construction Division/Residential Construction Branch, subject: building permits by place 2000, 22 May 2001 (related Internet site <http://www.census.gov/const/www/permitsindex.html>).

Table B–6. Counties — Crime, Housing, and Building Permits–Con.

[Includes U.S., states, and 3,142 counties or county equivalents defined as of January 1, 1992. For changes to these areas since January 1, 1992, see appendix B. Geographic Information]

County	Serious crimes known to police (as reported to the FBI)[1] Number 1999 Total	Violent[2]	Property[3]	1990	Rate[4] 1999	1990	Housing, 2000 Total units	Percent change, 1990–2000	Occupied units Number	Percent owner–occupied	New private housing units authorized by building permits, 2000 Number	Percent in structures with— One unit	Five units or more	Valuation ($1,000)
WISCONSIN—Con.														
Lafayette	171	14	157	169	1 046	1 051	6 674	5.7	6 211	77.5	61	100.0	–	5 836
Langlade	714	28	686	656	3 471	3 363	11 187	3.3	8 452	79.0	153	100.0	–	12 590
Lincoln	876	53	823	690	2 932	2 556	14 681	10.7	11 721	78.2	219	96.3	–	22 853
Manitowoc	2 209	74	2 135	2 517	2 667	3 130	34 651	8.8	32 721	76.0	468	78.8	15.6	52 355
Marathon	2 721	149	2 572	3 843	2 197	3 330	50 360	15.0	47 702	75.7	803	81.2	13.0	88 640
Marinette	1 034	51	983	1 379	2 390	3 401	26 260	2.4	17 585	79.3	271	84.9	15.1	21 993
Marquette	287	12	275	303	1 891	2 757	8 664	7.8	5 986	82.3	128	90.6	–	12 640
Menominee	380	96	284	200	7 910	5 141	2 098	20.4	1 345	73.8	28	100.0	–	3 241
Milwaukee	59 043	6 574	52 469	74 483	6 446	7 765	400 093	2.4	377 729	52.6	1 750	42.1	54.2	160 776
Monroe	952	57	895	827	2 396	2 258	16 672	17.9	15 399	73.7	227	76.2	16.7	20 779
Oconto	696	42	654	409	2 036	1 353	19 812	5.2	13 979	83.0	461	97.0	2.6	44 092
Oneida	918	43	875	1 215	2 560	3 835	26 627	5.8	15 333	79.7	411	90.5	5.6	44 390
Outagamie	3 580	155	3 425	4 880	2 279	3 473	62 614	20.6	60 530	72.4	1 482	61.0	28.3	168 429
Ozaukee	1 020	30	990	1 354	1 252	1 859	32 034	21.0	30 857	76.3	502	71.7	9.6	95 126
Pepin	71	2	69	106	992	1 491	3 036	4.0	2 759	79.7	46	93.5	–	5 014
Pierce	800	26	774	771	2 235	2 353	13 493	17.0	13 015	73.1	309	90.3	–	38 229
Polk	535	33	502	597	1 408	1 717	21 129	13.8	16 254	80.2	431	89.3	1.9	44 492
Portage	1 618	84	1 534	2 326	2 486	3 788	26 589	16.1	25 040	70.9	468	63.9	13.7	48 226
Price	290	5	285	405	1 824	2 596	9 574	5.8	6 564	80.7	173	100.0	–	16 045
Racine	7 545	541	7 004	9 866	4 033	5 637	74 718	11.6	70 819	70.6	867	61.8	28.3	104 599
Richland	321	35	286	387	1 785	2 209	8 164	11.5	7 118	74.2	132	63.6	36.4	11 129
Rock	6 035	283	5 752	7 378	3 983	5 289	62 187	13.4	58 617	71.1	848	62.3	20.9	78 067
Rusk	429	61	368	365	2 798	2 421	7 609	–3.7	6 095	78.7	116	98.3	–	11 685
St. Croix	1 327	46	1 281	1 146	2 316	2 281	24 265	31.0	23 410	76.4	1 099	64.2	18.3	124 278
Sauk	1 695	45	1 650	1 394	3 160	2 968	24 297	18.9	21 644	73.3	575	69.7	19.8	58 830
Sawyer	267	5	262	451	1 898	3 180	13 722	5.4	6 640	77.1	274	96.4	2.2	24 538
Shawano	1 047	22	1 025	1 209	2 688	3 254	18 317	9.4	15 815	78.2	216	91.7	–	21 581
Sheboygan	3 010	120	2 890	4 239	2 718	4 081	45 947	12.9	43 545	71.4	675	53.5	30.8	78 949
Taylor	348	6	342	424	1 793	2 243	8 595	11.5	7 529	80.6	55	96.4	–	4 416
Trempealeau	364	32	332	264	1 368	1 113	11 482	13.7	10 747	74.1	153	92.8	–	15 429
Vernon	285	11	274	276	1 037	1 077	12 416	14.6	10 825	79.1	105	82.9	7.6	9 459
Vilas	543	32	511	676	2 748	3 818	22 397	10.7	9 066	81.8	360	85.8	11.1	31 868
Walworth	2 390	106	2 284	2 378	2 786	3 171	43 783	18.5	34 522	69.1	971	70.0	22.3	123 566
Washburn	471	9	462	359	3 039	2 607	10 814	10.0	6 604	80.8	241	97.5	–	18 565
Washington	2 745	83	2 662	2 943	2 398	3 087	45 808	33.2	43 842	76.0	931	68.4	15.5	122 470
Waukesha	6 349	289	6 060	8 096	1 789	2 657	140 309	27.0	135 229	76.4	2 448	75.5	15.2	419 523
Waupaca	1 235	27	1 208	1 316	2 431	2 854	22 508	11.8	19 863	77.0	272	75.0	8.8	29 287
Waushara	524	16	508	583	2 413	3 007	13 667	11.6	9 336	83.5	262	85.1	12.6	23 626
Winnebago	4 004	214	3 790	6 140	2 565	4 376	64 721	15.3	61 157	68.0	811	69.8	24.8	85 861
Wood	2 095	36	2 059	2 341	2 954	3 180	31 691	9.9	30 135	74.3	392	59.2	19.6	41 071
WYOMING	16 484	1 112	15 372	19 086	3 449	4 210	223 854	10.1	193 608	70.0	1 582	90.3	6.8	313 656
Albany	1 102	85	1 017	1 765	3 786	5 731	15 215	9.9	13 269	51.5	107	98.1	–	12 193
Big Horn	146	15	131	227	1 286	2 157	5 105	1.1	4 312	74.7	12	100.0	–	999
Campbell	1 363	102	1 261	1 273	4 210	4 334	13 288	15.2	12 207	73.6	61	100.0	–	7 769
Carbon	437	20	417	643	2 967	3 860	8 307	1.4	6 129	71.0	33	100.0	–	4 080
Converse	374	27	347	373	3 040	3 352	5 669	8.3	4 694	74.0	11	9.1	–	877
Crook	133	19	114	101	2 495	1 908	2 935	12.7	2 308	79.9	7	100.0	–	664
Fremont	1 247	73	1 174	1 311	3 469	3 895	15 541	7.6	13 545	72.9	43	86.0	–	2 573
Goshen	283	18	265	423	2 202	3 419	5 881	5.9	5 061	70.7	1	100.0	–	89
Hot Springs	159	3	156	249	3 373	5 178	2 536	4.4	2 108	68.4	4	100.0	–	352
Johnson	184	12	172	128	2 704	2 083	3 503	12.6	2 959	73.7	12	100.0	–	1 548
Laramie	2 953	169	2 784	3 369	3 735	4 606	34 213	12.1	31 927	69.1	245	100.0	–	33 834
Lincoln	223	28	195	301	1 672	2 384	6 831	26.3	5 266	81.3	145	100.0	–	19 480
Natrona	2 716	191	2 525	3 326	4 300	5 432	29 882	2.8	26 819	69.9	145	73.8	26.2	16 905
Niobrara	31	7	24	67	1 149	2 681	1 338	–8.1	1 011	72.9	–	–	–	–
Park	685	55	630	709	2 664	3 059	11 869	15.2	10 312	71.4	137	100.0	–	18 204
Platte	219	12	207	136	2 546	1 670	4 528	12.5	3 625	76.0	8	75.0	–	622
Sheridan	587	36	551	691	2 339	2 933	12 577	12.8	11 167	68.9	99	96.0	–	9 792
Sublette	170	20	150	147	2 971	3 035	3 552	22.0	2 371	73.3	54	100.0	–	7 052
Sweetwater	1 846	114	1 732	1 991	4 682	5 160	15 921	3.1	14 105	75.1	41	87.8	12.2	4 951
Teton	535	35	500	711	3 788	6 364	10 267	45.4	7 688	54.8	326	78.8	14.7	164 019
Uinta	775	41	734	772	3 797	4 127	8 011	10.6	6 823	75.3	72	100.0	–	6 590
Washakie	208	21	187	262	2 406	3 124	3 654	–2.1	3 278	73.1	8	12.5	87.5	595
Weston	108	9	99	111	1 673	1 703	3 231	4.6	2 624	77.9	11	9.1	90.9	468

[1] Data on serious crimes have not been adjusted for underreporting; this may affect comparability over time or among geographic areas. [2] Includes murder and nonnegligent manslaughter, forcible rape, robbery, and aggravated assault. [3] Includes burglary, larceny-theft, and motor vehicle theft. [4] Per 100,000 resident population provided by the U.S. Federal Bureau of Investigation.

Sources: Serious Crimes Known to Police—U.S. Federal Bureau of Investigation, Uniform Crime Reporting Program, unpublished data, annual (related Internet site <http://www.fbi.gov/ucr/ucr.htm>). Housing, 2000—U.S. Census Bureau, 2000 Census of Population and Housing, "Census 2000 Profiles of General Demographic Characteristics" data files, published May 2001 (related Internet site <http://www.census.gov/mp/www/pub/2000cen/mscen01.html>). Housing, 1990—U.S. Census Bureau, 1990 Census of Population and Housing, Summary Tape File (STF) 1C on CD-ROM (related Internet site <http://homer.ssd.census.gov/cdrom/lookup>). Building Permits—U.S. Census Bureau, "New Residential Construction–Building Permits," e-mail from Manufacturing and Construction Division/Residential Construction Branch, subject: building permits by place 2000, 22 May 2001 (related Internet site <http://www.census.gov/const/www/permitsindex.html>).

Table B–7. Counties — Labor Force and Private Business Establishments and Employment

[Includes U.S., states, and 3,142 counties/county equivalents defined as of January 1, 1992. For changes to these areas since January 1, 1992, see appendix B. Geographic Information]

County	Civilian labor force, 2000 Total	Percent change, 1999–2000	Unemployment Total	Rate[1]	Establishments 1998	Percent change, 1990–1998	1995	1990	Employment[2] 1998	Percent change, 1990–1998	1995	1990	Annual payroll per employee, 1998 Amount (dollars)	Percent of national average
UNITED STATES......	140 863 000	1.1	5 655 000	4.0	6 941 822	12.4	6 613 218	6 175 563	108 117 731	15.7	100 334 745	93 476 087	30 609	100.0
ALABAMA	2 154 273	.6	99 092	4.6	100 316	15.9	96 053	86 537	1 604 110	19.4	1 553 309	1 342 993	25 142	82.1
Autauga	22 598	.7	831	3.7	754	28.9	691	585	8 100	22.0	7 898	6 639	21 341	69.7
Baldwin..................	71 317	.6	2 243	3.1	3 760	57.7	3 238	2 384	39 662	69.7	34 395	23 368	19 825	64.8
Barbour..................	14 041	5.0	717	5.1	605	17.5	554	515	9 773	26.7	8 512	7 711	21 634	70.7
Bibb......................	7 277	1.2	487	6.7	340	28.8	327	264	3 636	9.6	4 001	3 318	20 225	66.1
Blount	24 163	.8	643	2.7	716	39.0	695	515	7 670	18.5	9 238	6 472	19 608	64.1
Bullock	4 569	2.5	454	9.9	147	2.8	150	143	2 414	23.5	2 416	1 954	18 578	60.7
Butler	9 325	–5.7	1 055	11.3	525	20.7	513	435	5 925	25.4	6 290	4 726	19 738	64.5
Calhoun	53 322	–1.9	2 778	5.2	2 549	10.9	2 540	2 299	39 928	19.4	38 500	33 433	20 645	67.4
Chambers	15 934	–3.2	747	4.7	653	23.0	597	531	11 930	1.0	11 706	11 815	22 537	73.6
Cherokee	10 269	.9	444	4.3	365	26.7	336	288	3 520	.6	3 567	3 500	17 197	56.2
Chilton	19 265	3.5	793	4.1	774	26.5	723	612	6 471	16.5	6 376	5 556	18 889	61.7
Choctaw	5 501	–5.2	473	8.6	315	–.6	321	317	3 984	–13.6	4 922	4 610	31 526	103.0
Clarke	13 667	.6	1 216	8.9	747	21.7	706	614	8 337	15.6	9 167	7 209	21 199	69.3
Clay.....................	6 729	1.6	530	7.9	231	4.5	231	221	4 461	33.5	4 556	3 342	19 269	63.0
Cleburne	7 232	Z	255	3.5	193	22.9	184	157	2 280	20.8	2 422	1 887	21 605	70.6
Coffee	21 665	–1.0	1 325	6.1	982	16.2	930	845	13 006	9.8	13 386	11 847	18 178	59.4
Colbert	25 531	.7	1 606	6.3	1 376	7.6	1 392	1 279	18 467	.3	19 760	18 407	23 694	77.4
Conecuh	5 935	.5	437	7.4	266	11.8	253	238	3 773	24.9	3 793	3 022	21 644	70.7
Coosa	5 234	–.7	309	5.9	134	6.3	140	126	1 773	31.7	1 782	1 346	20 746	67.8
Covington................	17 071	Z	1 579	9.2	912	9.1	914	836	12 157	2.6	12 525	11 854	19 757	64.5
Crenshaw	5 371	–.3	411	7.7	272	23.1	253	221	2 806	–6.1	3 557	2 989	17 200	56.2
Cullman	40 536	2.6	1 466	3.6	1 730	29.5	1 578	1 336	22 680	28.5	20 411	17 656	22 197	72.5
Dale	21 367	.4	1 150	5.4	876	22.3	842	716	10 421	–1.7	10 757	10 602	22 807	74.5
Dallas	19 690	.3	2 074	10.5	984	.2	973	982	15 011	10.2	14 430	13 627	21 305	69.6
DeKalb	33 419	2.9	1 177	3.5	1 228	18.3	1 196	1 038	20 861	27.0	22 172	16 422	20 024	65.4
Elmore	30 777	.9	1 023	3.3	1 065	43.3	957	743	9 782	28.0	8 961	7 641	18 613	60.8
Escambia	17 150	4.1	810	4.7	864	11.2	850	777	11 719	24.8	11 273	9 393	21 224	69.3
Etowah	49 821	.7	3 285	6.6	2 197	12.8	2 133	1 948	33 001	5.7	34 060	31 219	23 145	75.6
Fayette	7 626	–3.0	559	7.3	355	9.2	337	325	5 164	9.8	5 699	4 701	21 382	69.9
Franklin	16 823	.9	1 210	7.2	621	15.0	609	540	11 134	51.2	10 535	7 364	18 356	60.0
Geneva	10 513	–1.5	683	6.5	460	16.2	438	396	5 014	8.2	5 867	4 633	16 618	54.3
Greene	3 047	–1.5	313	10.3	136	–6.2	139	145	1 309	–7.5	1 604	1 415	17 747	58.0
Hale	7 244	3.2	547	7.6	229	16.2	221	197	3 140	28.5	2 613	2 444	17 702	57.8
Henry	6 540	1.7	390	6.0	331	7.5	313	308	4 046	1.6	4 037	3 984	20 159	65.9
Houston	45 576	1.0	2 169	4.8	2 822	17.4	2 639	2 403	46 545	24.2	42 019	37 490	24 011	78.4
Jackson	26 344	2.5	1 662	6.3	903	12.2	911	805	12 829	12.9	13 649	11 360	23 069	75.4
Jefferson	335 801	1.0	11 617	3.5	17 672	.6	17 834	17 565	354 243	6.5	361 636	332 538	29 839	97.5
Lamar	6 988	–2.9	670	9.6	289	–3.3	291	299	5 004	–5.9	4 951	5 316	25 026	81.8
Lauderdale...............	41 381	.7	2 258	5.5	2 089	16.4	2 045	1 794	30 630	26.9	29 266	24 141	19 456	63.6
Lawrence	16 703	.7	906	5.4	418	30.6	351	320	5 828	52.8	5 352	3 815	33 585	109.7
Lee	50 031	2.6	1 657	3.3	2 008	24.6	1 808	1 611	30 235	9.2	28 976	27 683	20 943	68.4
Limestone	29 524	1.8	971	3.3	1 087	31.8	940	825	16 425	16.9	14 881	14 048	30 731	100.4
Lowndes.................	4 253	2.3	501	11.8	152	18.8	144	128	1 602	4.4	1 676	1 535	30 917	101.0
Macon	7 936	3.5	487	6.1	255	2.4	257	249	6 429	13.5	5 966	5 663	22 181	72.5
Madison	145 450	1.7	4 101	2.8	6 996	22.8	6 584	5 695	119 763	19.3	116 332	100 398	28 428	92.9
Marengo.................	11 227	1.5	532	4.7	514	17.6	491	437	6 375	–4.1	6 585	6 646	25 429	83.1
Marion	14 973	–7.0	1 173	7.8	698	34.2	587	520	10 627	24.2	10 746	8 553	22 251	72.7
Marshall.................	39 111	–2.3	2 001	5.1	2 004	15.7	1 942	1 732	33 753	29.4	32 256	26 089	20 048	65.5
Mobile	200 525	.8	10 302	5.1	9 380	8.4	9 269	8 650	160 695	27.0	149 274	126 500	24 900	81.3
Monroe	9 666	.2	867	9.0	452	4.4	458	433	8 786	–1.9	8 366	8 954	25 083	81.9
Montgomery	111 083	.8	4 116	3.7	6 115	9.8	6 015	5 568	104 467	16.1	100 707	89 992	25 237	82.4
Morgan	57 195	1.1	2 338	4.1	2 808	15.1	2 735	2 439	45 996	24.5	41 850	36 955	25 084	81.9
Perry....................	4 570	–.3	536	11.7	157	–7.6	173	170	1 963	–11.6	2 253	2 220	17 439	57.0
Pickens..................	8 468	–1.4	898	10.6	356	3.8	359	343	3 320	–.7	3 766	3 345	18 942	61.9
Pike.....................	13 787	.8	896	6.5	678	8.7	638	624	9 389	11.5	9 395	8 420	20 120	65.7
Randolph	9 466	1.9	514	5.4	400	18.3	382	338	4 843	24.0	4 709	3 906	17 759	58.0
Russell	25 730	.5	1 142	4.4	882	14.0	859	774	10 868	20.5	10 253	9 021	23 735	77.5
St. Clair	31 609	.4	932	2.9	1 119	56.5	929	715	11 944	67.9	10 577	7 115	20 950	68.4
Shelby	83 378	.9	1 335	1.6	3 449	131.0	2 557	1 493	49 635	198.7	35 913	16 617	30 352	99.2
Sumter	5 375	–2.3	709	13.2	265	21.6	247	218	3 402	12.5	3 678	3 025	20 212	66.0
Talladega	33 793	–1.4	1 914	5.7	1 386	16.8	1 286	1 187	20 878	17.3	19 637	17 793	23 025	75.2
Tallapoosa	19 648	–1.1	1 012	5.2	843	20.1	783	702	22 801	38.8	23 605	16 432	22 549	73.7
Tuscaloosa	84 501	1.1	2 388	2.8	3 973	22.9	3 671	3 233	65 228	34.4	59 308	48 523	25 164	82.2
Walker	28 041	–2.2	2 070	7.4	1 451	7.6	1 494	1 348	16 159	6.1	15 261	15 223	21 450	70.1
Washington	5 828	–2.6	718	12.3	261	5.7	298	247	3 664	8.7	3 506	3 370	40 765	133.2
Wilcox	3 736	–2.0	439	11.8	227	–5.0	238	239	2 527	52.8	2 674	1 654	30 712	100.3
Winston	12 013	–3.2	1 243	10.3	481	–	523	481	10 381	30.4	10 769	7 958	22 537	73.6

[1] Civilian unemployed as a percent of total civilian labor force. [2] For pay period including March 12 of the year shown.

Sources: Civilian Labor Force—U.S. Bureau of Labor Statistics; Local Area Unemployment Statistics; 2000 data published 2 May 2001, 1999 data published 30 May 2001; <ftp://ftp.bls.gov/pub/time.series/la/> (related Internet site <http://www.bls.gov/lauhome.htm>). Private Business Establishments and Employment—U.S. Census Bureau; County Business Patterns on CD-ROM; annual (related Internet site <http://www.census.gov/epcd/cbp/view/cbpview.html>).

[Includes U.S., states, and 3,142 counties/county equivalents defined as of January 1, 1992. For changes to these areas since January 1, 1992, see appendix B. Geographic Information]

County	Civilian labor force, 2000 Total	Percent change, 1999–2000	Unemployment Total	Rate[1]	Establishments 1998	Percent change, 1990–1998	1995	1990	Employment[2] 1998	Percent change, 1990–1998	1995	1990	Annual payroll per employee, 1998 Amount (dollars)	Percent of national average
ALASKA	321 964	1.0	21 296	6.6	18 212	23.3	17 264	14 773	196 135	24.3	181 975	157 798	35 098	114.7
Aleutians East	1 537	−1.8	70	4.6	49	NA	55	(3)	1 995	NA	1 321	(3)	16 083	52.5
Aleutians West	2 027	−.6	175	8.6	112	NA	115	3127	4 375	NA	3 707	32 783	18 836	61.5
Anchorage	144 117	1.1	6 750	4.7	7 786	14.5	7 568	6 801	107 084	24.3	98 302	86 153	39 054	127.6
Bethel	6 276	−1.1	623	9.9	210	18.0	216	178	2 657	33.8	2 541	1 986	24 785	81.0
Bristol Bay	503	−.2	58	11.5	73	49.0	56	49	572	47.0	379	389	37 628	122.9
Denali	1 157	.4	112	9.7	70	NA	58	(4)	346	NA	497	(4)	61 032	199.4
Dillingham	1 787	−1.6	149	8.3	89	NA	111	5128	1 213	NA	1 015	51 184	31 751	103.7
Fairbanks North Star	43 443	−.6	2 673	6.2	2 173	18.5	2 091	1 834	21 009	22.6	19 460	17 136	31 213	102.0
Haines	1 225	−1.9	115	9.4	130	41.3	103	92	500	−1.6	392	508	26 272	85.8
Juneau	17 129	−.5	839	4.9	1 125	28.3	1 050	877	9 730	27.1	9 124	7 654	31 411	102.6
Kenai Peninsula	21 694	−1.6	2 204	10.2	1 703	34.8	1 599	1 263	11 104	31.3	10 166	8 455	30 276	98.9
Ketchikan Gateway	7 634	.1	580	7.6	582	18.1	570	493	4 982	−8.4	5 772	5 441	35 357	115.5
Kodiak Island	6 986	1.9	677	9.7	455	17.9	443	386	4 217	−.1	5 072	4 223	26 022	85.0
Lake and Peninsula	614	.3	62	10.1	56	NA	56	(5)	181	NA	164	(5)	45 453	148.5
Matanuska-Susitna	31 413	5.4	2 508	8.0	1 333	66.4	1 091	801	8 609	75.6	7 227	4 902	27 399	89.5
Nome	3 353	6.4	399	11.9	183	31.7	165	139	1 931	36.0	1 707	1 420	26 421	86.3
North Slope	3 357	7.6	313	9.3	137	69.1	124	81	1 698	78.5	1 595	951	48 403	158.1
Northwest Arctic	2 164	5.2	283	13.1	84	31.3	78	64	1 541	40.2	1 015	1 099	47 817	156.2
Prince of Wales-Outer Ketchikan	3 236	.6	454	14.0	175	62.0	142	108	1 349	5.3	1 327	1 281	29 307	95.7
Sitka	4 311	−.6	216	5.0	387	29.0	360	300	2 787	5.2	2 785	2 650	26 483	86.5
Skagway-Yakutat-Angoon	2 436	2.1	237	9.7	195	50.0	176	130	924	14.6	838	806	28 561	93.3
Southeast Fairbanks	2 606	1.0	304	11.7	142	19.3	141	119	572	24.6	539	459	22 080	72.1
Valdez-Cordova	5 049	−.9	444	8.8	464	44.1	420	322	2 249	19.1	2 027	1 888	31 907	104.2
Wade Hampton	2 230	1.4	397	17.8	64	12.3	65	57	698	63.8	515	426	11 216	36.6
Wrangell-Petersburg	3 556	.1	329	9.3	285	24.5	261	229	1 718	−2.2	1 568	1 756	27 222	88.9
Yukon-Koyukuk	2 128	1.0	327	15.4	133	NA	131	4149	522	NA	726	41 007	23 774	77.7
ARIZONA	2 346 997	−.5	91 223	3.9	110 245	27.5	99 583	86 489	1 763 508	42.6	1 507 132	1 236 401	27 815	90.9
Apache	19 702	−8.8	2 526	12.8	508	18.4	437	429	7 141	14.7	6 488	6 226	19 284	63.0
Cochise	39 327	−.8	1 777	4.5	2 169	22.0	2 003	1 778	21 008	36.6	18 849	15 382	21 168	69.2
Coconino	60 870	2.0	3 468	5.7	3 341	46.7	3 383	2 278	36 979	37.8	33 647	26 832	21 107	69.0
Gila	17 175	−1.3	989	5.8	1 110	33.1	1 004	834	13 714	49.8	12 470	9 152	25 405	83.0
Graham	10 295	−3.5	674	6.5	497	24.6	451	399	4 817	64.0	4 113	2 938	16 472	53.8
Greenlee	4 077	−2.6	228	5.6	104	4.0	102	100	3 643	NA	(6)	(7)	33 940	110.9
La Paz	7 048	2.2	507	7.2	357	19.4	310	299	3 695	52.6	2 705	2 421	17 006	55.6
Maricopa	1 503 466	−.5	39 573	2.6	68 955	29.3	61 372	53 343	1 246 448	47.0	1 035 214	847 908	29 692	97.0
Mohave	63 324	1.3	2 679	4.2	3 212	25.5	2 998	2 559	31 142	33.4	28 679	23 342	20 586	67.3
Navajo	31 120	−3.1	3 573	11.5	1 622	33.1	1 413	1 219	15 462	29.5	14 793	11 940	22 807	74.5
Pima	383 866	−.2	10 933	2.8	18 247	18.6	17 167	15 388	268 142	27.6	247 225	210 148	24 982	81.6
Pinal	59 426	−1.6	2 478	4.2	1 988	21.3	1 776	1 639	27 851	42.5	26 574	19 550	24 713	80.7
Santa Cruz	13 367	−1.4	1 840	13.8	1 070	11.8	1 051	957	10 403	5.9	9 808	9 825	20 555	67.2
Yavapai	68 231	1.1	1 885	2.8	4 603	40.7	3 743	3 271	41 861	67.5	32 441	24 992	20 366	66.5
Yuma	65 703	−1.5	18 092	27.5	2 443	24.3	2 358	1 965	30 497	33.3	30 257	22 884	19 515	63.8
ARKANSAS	1 238 151	.7	54 930	4.4	62 353	16.7	60 231	53 409	944 935	25.8	891 175	750 877	23 033	75.2
Arkansas	10 361	−2.4	543	5.2	587	−3.0	594	605	8 404	11.2	8 481	7 557	22 953	75.0
Ashley	10 585	−2.0	769	7.3	515	16.3	505	443	8 602	12.7	8 548	7 630	28 637	93.6
Baxter	14 497	2.1	561	3.9	1 034	25.0	981	827	11 273	25.2	10 908	9 001	21 728	71.0
Benton	69 136	2.7	1 370	2.0	3 393	62.4	3 063	2 089	57 907	50.8	53 135	38 405	27 305	89.2
Boone	14 878	2.1	694	4.7	908	22.2	857	743	13 275	25.2	13 641	10 606	21 932	71.7
Bradley	4 477	2.0	390	8.7	293	.7	326	291	3 015	3.1	3 043	2 923	16 484	53.9
Calhoun	2 227	−.8	167	7.5	103	21.2	99	85	974	46.7	762	664	20 633	67.4
Carroll	11 617	−.1	507	4.4	767	28.0	730	599	7 904	43.6	7 893	5 503	18 446	60.3
Chicot	6 281	.6	576	9.2	280	.4	290	279	3 116	31.5	2 895	2 369	16 117	52.7
Clark	12 004	2.7	392	3.3	588	15.7	583	508	8 204	42.7	7 702	5 748	18 633	60.9
Clay	7 805	−2.4	485	6.2	356	−1.4	386	361	5 276	27.4	4 626	4 140	17 272	56.4
Cleburne	9 580	.6	451	4.7	562	35.7	515	414	5 745	39.2	4 984	4 127	17 962	58.7
Cleveland	3 624	−2.8	202	5.6	111	29.1	96	86	718	18.3	760	607	15 826	51.7
Columbia	11 300	−.3	646	5.7	652	3.2	668	632	8 533	5.8	8 593	8 064	22 016	71.9
Conway	9 245	1.3	756	8.2	405	17.1	418	346	7 672	59.1	5 682	4 823	18 364	60.0
Craighead	43 005	1.4	1 603	3.7	2 289	26.6	2 126	1 808	32 834	26.5	30 689	25 948	22 999	75.1
Crawford	24 732	.7	874	3.5	916	24.6	880	735	13 681	44.4	11 395	9 473	21 241	69.4
Crittenden	22 646	.7	1 038	4.6	965	7.2	914	900	15 699	26.8	13 961	12 380	20 549	67.1
Cross	7 964	−.7	472	5.9	375	6.5	345	352	4 722	5.7	5 115	4 467	19 461	63.6
Dallas	3 558	.8	270	7.6	263	.8	287	261	2 996	3.7	2 650	2 889	21 025	68.7
Desha	6 972	−.6	791	11.3	409	5.4	375	388	5 005	28.8	4 569	3 886	21 530	70.3

[1] Civilian unemployed as a percent of total civilian labor force. [2] For pay period including March 12 of the year shown. [3] Aleutians East Borough included with Aleutians West Census Area; data not available separately. [4] Denali Borough included with Yukon-Koyukuk Census Area; data not available separately. [5] Lake and Peninsula Borough included with Dillingham Census Area; data not available separately. [6] 2,500–4,999 employees. [7] 1,000–2,499 employees.

Sources: Civilian Labor Force—U.S. Bureau of Labor Statistics; Local Area Unemployment Statistics; 2000 data published 2 May 2001, 1999 data published 30 May 2001; <ftp://ftp.bls.gov/pub/time.series/la/> (related Internet site <http://www.bls.gov/lauhome.htm>). Private Business Establishments and Employment—U.S. Census Bureau; County Business Patterns on CD-ROM; annual (related Internet site <http://www.census.gov/epcd/cbp/view/cbpview.html>).

[Includes U.S., states, and 3,142 counties/county equivalents defined as of January 1, 1992. For changes to these areas since January 1, 1992, see appendix B. Geographic Information]

County	Civilian labor force, 2000				Private nonfarm businesses								Annual payroll per employee, 1998	
		Percent change, 1999–2000	Unemployment		Establishments				Employment[2]				Amount (dollars)	Percent of national average
	Total		Total	Rate[1]	1998	Percent change, 1990–1998	1995	1990	1998	Percent change, 1990–1998	1995	1990		
ARKANSAS—Con.														
Drew	9 843	.4	665	6.8	462	31.6	416	351	6 923	44.0	6 392	4 806	19 037	62.2
Faulkner	42 681	.7	1 548	3.6	1 620	42.7	1 431	1 135	26 766	49.1	23 762	17 948	23 563	77.0
Franklin	7 572	.2	234	3.1	285	17.8	267	242	3 475	55.1	3 110	2 241	17 831	58.3
Fulton	4 139	.8	158	3.8	174	–7.9	166	189	1 368	3.4	1 364	1 323	16 417	53.6
Garland	35 729	.1	1 395	3.9	2 582	26.9	2 406	2 034	30 382	29.3	27 139	23 498	19 853	64.9
Grant	7 301	–	339	4.6	277	26.5	233	219	3 616	40.4	2 928	2 575	21 244	69.4
Greene	18 966	3.2	956	5.0	771	17.5	748	656	13 141	38.1	11 606	9 515	19 381	63.3
Hempstead	11 269	–.4	590	5.2	451	8.7	452	415	7 694	46.4	7 186	5 256	19 813	64.7
Hot Spring	12 188	1.1	582	4.8	556	22.5	528	454	5 805	24.5	5 292	4 663	20 567	67.2
Howard	6 835	.3	305	4.5	319	13.9	323	280	7 199	21.7	7 135	5 913	18 334	59.9
Independence	16 720	–1.1	902	5.4	815	13.8	796	716	13 925	18.9	13 669	11 708	20 870	68.2
Izard	4 334	1.2	209	4.8	246	20.6	236	204	2 238	27.9	1 959	1 750	17 505	57.2
Jackson	7 708	–1.8	739	9.6	444	–4.3	431	464	4 709	–3.1	4 821	4 862	21 026	68.7
Jefferson	36 154	–.1	2 581	7.1	1 640	–5.3	1 697	1 731	26 837	10.6	26 416	24 272	22 729	74.3
Johnson	10 628	.9	404	3.8	402	40.1	368	287	7 385	53.6	6 360	4 807	17 907	58.5
Lafayette	3 366	–1.1	249	7.4	154	–2.5	152	158	1 447	–2.7	1 423	1 487	19 105	62.4
Lawrence	7 236	–.5	465	6.4	380	11.4	369	341	4 180	13.6	3 903	3 679	17 674	57.7
Lee	4 740	5.1	372	7.8	157	6.1	159	148	1 285	3.9	1 360	1 237	18 076	59.1
Lincoln	5 272	.1	263	5.0	155	29.2	149	120	1 632	76.4	1 700	925	19 161	62.6
Little River	5 489	.5	316	5.8	244	14.6	263	213	3 565	14.2	3 741	3 121	32 082	104.8
Logan	9 326	–1.9	386	4.1	391	7.1	421	365	5 200	41.8	5 380	3 668	17 932	58.6
Lonoke	26 017	.6	751	2.9	868	36.3	792	637	8 228	36.9	7 468	6 011	18 317	59.8
Madison	6 748	2.0	181	2.7	182	19.0	177	153	1 641	9.8	1 721	1 494	20 347	66.5
Marion	6 215	1.6	168	2.7	236	38.8	221	170	3 194	44.0	3 287	2 218	16 435	53.7
Miller	16 998	–.3	678	4.0	719	5.1	759	684	10 320	–6.4	10 190	11 030	22 501	73.5
Mississippi	25 996	–1.8	2 613	10.1	1 002	3.2	949	971	18 275	25.3	16 700	14 583	23 920	78.1
Monroe	3 968	–.8	239	6.0	263	–.4	253	264	2 088	11.5	2 261	1 873	15 203	49.7
Montgomery	4 059	2.7	142	3.5	188	–6.0	187	200	1 121	–8.3	1 118	1 222	15 660	51.2
Nevada	4 871	–.7	261	5.4	151	–7.9	151	164	1 787	3.5	1 841	1 726	21 792	71.2
Newton	2 988	2.3	155	5.2	109	13.5	100	96	566	33.8	533	423	13 717	44.8
Ouachita	11 275	.1	902	8.0	637	–5.1	685	671	7 894	–23.2	8 908	10 282	23 756	77.6
Perry	3 655	2.6	262	7.2	114	72.7	103	66	595	9.8	569	542	16 176	52.8
Phillips	9 438	.1	787	8.3	553	–7.8	575	600	5 939	4.4	5 642	5 689	19 104	62.4
Pike	4 918	1.5	252	5.1	261	35.9	260	192	2 390	44.7	2 327	1 652	16 955	55.4
Poinsett	10 563	1.1	602	5.7	436	–1.1	431	441	4 600	–4.5	4 808	4 815	19 336	63.2
Polk	9 261	.6	363	3.9	488	53.5	453	318	5 334	46.2	5 152	3 649	18 577	60.7
Pope	27 090	.6	1 169	4.3	1 460	34.9	1 351	1 082	21 162	40.3	19 689	15 082	22 700	74.2
Prairie	4 071	4.0	195	4.8	194	4.9	187	185	1 205	–24.3	1 094	1 591	16 890	55.2
Pulaski	191 423	.4	6 893	3.6	11 744	6.9	11 748	10 983	216 792	18.8	207 814	182 557	26 848	87.7
Randolph	8 060	3.4	501	6.2	328	21.5	338	270	4 396	13.2	4 657	3 884	17 701	57.8
St. Francis	12 105	–.7	1 024	8.5	621	13.9	589	545	7 597	21.6	7 076	6 246	18 740	61.2
Saline	41 662	.5	1 193	2.9	1 325	52.3	1 151	870	14 865	70.8	12 328	8 704	20 977	68.5
Scott	4 794	–1.9	137	2.9	180	17.6	175	153	2 576	23.3	2 790	2 090	18 594	60.7
Searcy	2 953	.6	152	5.1	120	8.1	119	111	1 193	–19.7	1 483	1 486	11 965	39.1
Sebastian	55 596	.6	1 849	3.3	3 427	8.7	3 377	3 152	70 368	24.1	67 654	56 702	23 508	76.8
Sevier	6 892	1.4	266	3.9	297	3.5	295	287	4 748	22.0	4 690	3 892	16 706	54.6
Sharp	6 107	–1.1	355	5.8	369	44.1	341	256	3 057	67.5	2 832	1 825	15 753	51.5
Stone	5 131	.1	192	3.7	234	15.3	227	203	2 096	41.6	1 997	1 480	16 465	53.8
Union	20 965	1.4	1 087	5.2	1 267	–2.5	1 317	1 299	18 396	7.2	18 874	17 167	24 885	81.3
Van Buren	6 117	.6	356	5.8	315	20.7	312	261	2 780	10.4	2 500	2 518	15 893	51.9
Washington	79 061	2.7	1 797	2.3	4 039	35.3	3 711	2 986	65 847	45.8	59 189	45 164	23 022	75.2
White	32 011	2.1	1 508	4.7	1 388	23.2	1 322	1 127	20 657	44.9	19 089	14 258	21 269	69.5
Woodruff	3 849	–.4	308	8.0	160	5.3	163	152	1 981	25.4	2 025	1 580	17 758	58.0
Yell	9 311	.8	379	4.1	351	13.6	324	309	5 749	12.8	5 345	5 095	17 962	58.7
CALIFORNIA	17 090 815	3.0	845 192	4.9	773 925	3.8	740 583	745 686	12 026 989	6.3	10 959 318	11 318 516	33 797	110.4
Alameda	740 375	2.9	21 871	3.0	35 137	7.1	33 460	32 808	598 220	18.3	525 644	505 595	37 172	121.4
Alpine	488	–1.2	41	8.4	57	39.0	55	41	(3)	NA	1 122	1 048	D	D
Amador	14 201	4.2	624	4.4	819	4.7	789	782	7 377	23.3	6 723	5 985	20 620	67.4
Butte	87 933	2.0	6 127	7.0	4 494	–2.6	4 503	4 613	49 894	9.1	47 569	45 746	21 294	69.6
Calaveras	15 197	4.3	1 012	6.7	930	6.9	853	870	5 337	11.6	4 526	4 781	20 854	68.1
Colusa	8 834	.6	1 550	17.5	365	–3.2	369	377	3 273	12.8	3 434	2 902	25 690	83.9
Contra Costa	505 106	3.1	13 697	2.7	21 674	6.9	20 460	20 278	288 747	7.3	270 555	269 056	37 377	122.1
Del Norte	9 864	–.8	858	8.7	493	–15.0	508	580	4 159	–1.5	4 135	4 223	19 031	62.2
El Dorado	82 478	3.3	3 194	3.9	3 703	8.8	3 460	3 403	33 891	32.9	28 876	25 509	24 219	79.1

[1] Civilian unemployed as a percent of total civilian labor force.   [2] For pay period including March 12 of the year shown.   [3] 1,000–2,499 employees.

Sources: Civilian Labor Force—U.S. Bureau of Labor Statistics; Local Area Unemployment Statistics; 2000 data published 2 May 2001, 1999 data published 30 May 2001; <ftp://ftp.bls.gov/pub/time.series/la/> (related Internet site <http://www.bls.gov/lauhome.htm>).   Private Business Establishments and Employment—U.S. Census Bureau; County Business Patterns on CD-ROM; annual (related Internet site <http://www.census.gov/epcd/cbp/view/cbpview.html>).

[Includes U.S., states, and 3,142 counties/county equivalents defined as of January 1, 1992. For changes to these areas since January 1, 1992, see appendix B. Geographic Information]

County	Civilian labor force, 2000		Unemployment		Private nonfarm businesses								Annual payroll per employee, 1998	
					Establishments				Employment[2]					
	Total	Percent change, 1999–2000	Total	Rate[1]	1998	Percent change, 1990–1998	1995	1990	1998	Percent change, 1990–1998	1995	1990	Amount (dollars)	Percent of national average
CALIFORNIA—Con.														
Fresno	393 077	3.4	56 232	14.3	15 130	2.1	15 122	14 823	205 823	9.1	194 112	188 738	25 492	83.3
Glenn	10 537	.7	1 257	11.9	504	–.4	458	506	4 422	–6.5	4 147	4 727	25 852	84.5
Humboldt	60 370	.2	3 812	6.3	3 590	2.7	3 654	3 495	37 239	9.8	35 296	33 912	21 693	70.9
Imperial	58 475	5.4	15 383	26.3	2 230	.6	2 197	2 216	23 205	7.4	23 624	21 610	20 724	67.7
Inyo	7 165	–.3	400	5.6	609	–1.1	596	616	6 338	33.4	4 427	4 750	16 758	54.7
Kern	287 157	2.3	32 493	11.3	10 709	–.5	10 469	10 759	142 507	10.0	133 575	129 537	26 406	86.3
Kings	45 904	6.4	6 423	14.0	1 493	6.8	1 415	1 398	17 632	11.7	16 618	15 784	22 421	73.2
Lake	23 374	–1.5	1 870	8.0	1 069	–8.4	1 093	1 167	9 241	17.9	8 791	7 837	19 459	63.6
Lassen	11 044	–.9	761	6.9	533	–5.2	568	562	4 167	7.3	3 948	3 885	20 662	67.5
Los Angeles	4 761 357	2.1	255 253	5.4	219 933	.1	214 320	219 625	3 693 537	–4.0	3 494 193	3 847 918	33 513	109.5
Madera	54 615	2.7	6 469	11.8	1 811	10.8	1 718	1 634	22 178	43.0	17 665	15 509	20 349	66.5
Marin	139 759	3.4	2 329	1.7	10 031	6.1	9 646	9 453	97 596	9.3	91 503	89 295	36 542	119.4
Mariposa	6 656	–.6	520	7.8	359	–1.4	357	364	3 388	17.8	3 235	2 876	19 147	62.6
Mendocino	42 338	1.1	2 806	6.6	2 754	4.8	2 716	2 627	24 475	14.8	22 470	21 327	21 773	71.1
Merced	85 223	1.1	12 310	14.4	2 898	2.5	2 851	2 826	37 537	10.4	34 198	33 988	22 112	72.2
Modoc	3 994	–.7	333	8.3	195	–3.9	198	203	1 447	12.0	1 497	1 292	18 982	62.0
Mono	6 536	5.8	368	5.6	530	10.6	523	479	5 547	–4.3	5 704	5 795	16 251	53.1
Monterey	193 199	2.3	18 675	9.7	8 457	3.6	8 021	8 160	101 381	15.3	93 457	87 922	27 478	89.8
Napa	64 963	3.7	2 058	3.2	3 537	8.9	3 274	3 249	47 205	31.3	39 386	35 943	29 132	95.2
Nevada	45 880	4.6	1 656	3.6	2 800	8.3	2 600	2 586	23 644	25.1	21 261	18 897	22 945	75.0
Orange	1 512 941	2.8	38 369	2.5	75 154	5.5	70 783	71 255	1 274 074	7.0	1 151 819	1 191 075	33 955	110.9
Placer	124 781	3.3	3 975	3.2	6 562	18.5	5 760	5 537	81 772	53.0	61 887	53 443	29 233	95.5
Plumas	9 740	2.5	812	8.3	696	12.1	680	621	4 451	16.2	4 170	3 832	23 578	77.0
Riverside	731 422	5.0	40 006	5.5	24 817	10.7	22 752	22 423	341 885	17.1	297 865	292 031	24 807	81.0
Sacramento	605 760	3.3	25 658	4.2	25 062	1.6	24 450	24 675	388 764	15.0	372 814	337 951	30 229	98.8
San Benito	27 577	4.3	2 154	7.8	890	16.6	778	763	10 122	25.8	7 982	8 049	24 337	79.5
San Bernardino	791 536	4.9	37 626	4.8	26 132	4.6	24 702	24 987	425 068	13.7	371 796	373 719	25 475	83.2
San Diego	1 404 903	3.2	42 038	3.0	64 413	6.3	60 243	60 581	961 014	10.8	844 451	867 603	30 797	100.6
San Francisco	435 211	3.4	12 201	2.8	31 632	–1.6	30 668	32 149	531 023	2.1	484 846	520 059	44 509	145.4
San Joaquin	260 856	3.5	22 968	8.8	9 830	–.3	9 595	9 864	143 285	12.3	127 288	127 573	26 417	86.3
San Luis Obispo	115 736	3.3	3 440	3.0	6 557	7.7	6 077	6 089	69 698	14.5	60 590	60 893	23 085	75.4
San Mateo	411 280	3.3	6 555	1.6	20 014	7.0	19 602	18 699	333 418	12.1	298 393	297 544	43 812	143.1
Santa Barbara	204 463	2.7	7 484	3.7	10 535	1.3	10 157	10 396	129 260	.3	119 638	128 838	28 688	93.7
Santa Clara	1 003 926	4.0	19 943	2.0	44 204	12.4	40 442	39 340	946 363	17.0	800 990	808 990	50 287	164.3
Santa Cruz	141 915	1.5	8 005	5.6	6 737	.8	6 450	6 684	74 213	2.2	70 010	72 596	28 473	93.0
Shasta	75 035	3.2	5 170	6.9	4 380	–3.0	4 373	4 514	44 494	4.3	41 572	42 671	24 136	78.9
Sierra	1 643	.5	127	7.7	89	15.6	79	77	(3)	NA	613	447	D	D
Siskiyou	17 774	.4	1 685	9.5	1 261	–2.0	1 254	1 287	9 380	1.2	8 908	9 268	19 557	63.9
Solano	196 867	3.4	8 351	4.2	6 242	4.8	6 247	5 955	85 967	12.8	81 818	76 183	26 856	87.7
Sonoma	259 633	3.5	6 851	2.6	13 017	8.6	12 169	11 990	154 187	18.1	131 326	130 521	30 071	98.2
Stanislaus	207 261	1.8	21 488	10.4	8 027	3.8	7 693	7 732	113 536	10.0	103 226	103 228	25 876	84.5
Sutter	36 930	3.0	4 814	13.0	1 616	4.1	1 584	1 553	16 850	12.7	14 635	14 945	23 119	75.5
Tehama	25 391	4.3	1 757	6.9	1 014	7.2	938	946	11 518	22.7	10 339	9 384	22 462	73.4
Trinity	5 036	3.0	624	12.4	316	–1.3	298	320	1 811	.4	1 577	1 803	19 437	63.5
Tulare	170 116	2.6	26 234	15.4	5 812	–1	5 801	5 816	73 205	10.5	73 018	66 224	22 844	74.6
Tuolumne	20 647	3.4	1 245	6.0	1 405	–7.0	1 399	1 510	11 852	7.1	11 082	11 070	21 091	68.9
Ventura	411 353	3.5	18 663	4.5	16 463	8.1	15 346	15 223	217 737	6.1	201 758	205 176	29 133	95.2
Yolo	93 699	2.5	4 065	4.3	3 340	6.4	3 127	3 138	53 870	23.5	47 788	43 618	28 436	92.9
Yuba	21 282	3.2	2 504	11.8	807	–12.6	825	923	8 807	–.4	8 406	8 842	21 677	70.8
COLORADO	2 275 545	.5	62 501	2.7	130 354	34.6	118 192	96 828	1 757 628	40.8	1 558 141	1 248 022	30 604	100.0
Adams	183 875	.7	4 773	2.6	7 008	24.3	6 443	5 639	117 241	43.2	100 183	81 864	29 266	95.6
Alamosa	7 894	–1.9	398	5.0	525	29.6	469	405	4 920	55.4	4 414	3 167	18 426	60.2
Arapahoe	286 042	.7	5 769	2.0	16 039	34.8	14 664	11 894	271 272	69.4	225 174	160 153	37 822	123.6
Archuleta	4 795	4.2	170	3.5	410	105.0	335	200	2 400	118.2	1 855	1 100	17 157	56.1
Baca	2 163	–6.3	57	2.6	114		112	114	650	58.9	601	409	16 088	52.6
Bent	2 015	–5.5	73	3.6	75	2.7	82	73	1 076	10.8	1 014	971	30 714	100.3
Boulder	182 568	3.2	4 425	2.4	10 464	43.0	9 588	7 319	136 146	41.3	127 691	96 365	35 454	115.8
Chaffee	7 870	2.7	186	2.4	667	56.2	549	427	4 398	65.3	3 896	2 661	18 777	61.3
Cheyenne	1 162	–6.9	34	2.9	66	–2.9	66	68	478	21.6	357	393	22 983	75.1
Clear Creek	5 016	–3.4	151	3.0	318	74.7	232	182	2 646	14.6	2 193	2 308	24 101	78.7
Conejos	3 568	–2.2	243	6.8	113	27.0	112	89	940	46.2	745	643	16 205	52.9
Costilla	1 348	–	124	9.2	48	50.0	40	32	162	–31.6	239	237	13 994	45.7
Crowley	1 304	–2.5	57	4.4	46	39.4	43	33	255	30.8	247	195	19 455	63.6
Custer	1 851	5.1	53	2.9	124	103.3	97	61	515	201.2	410	171	19 130	62.5

[1] Civilian unemployed as a percent of total civilian labor force.   [2] For pay period including March 12 of the year shown.   [3] 500–999 employees.

Sources: Civilian Labor Force—U.S. Bureau of Labor Statistics; Local Area Unemployment Statistics; 2000 data published 2 May 2001, 1999 data published 30 May 2001; <ftp://ftp.bls.gov/pub/time.series/la/> (related Internet site <http://www.bls.gov/lauhome.htm>).   Private Business Establishments and Employment—U.S. Census Bureau; County Business Patterns on CD-ROM; annual (related Internet site <http://www.census.gov/epcd/cbp/view/cbpview.html>).

[Includes U.S., states, and 3,142 counties/county equivalents defined as of January 1, 1992. For changes to these areas since January 1, 1992, see appendix B. Geographic Information]

County	Civilian labor force, 2000		Unemployment		Private nonfarm businesses								Annual payroll per employee, 1998	
					Establishments				Employment[2]					
	Total	Percent change, 1999–2000	Total	Rate[1]	1998	Percent change, 1990–1998	1995	1990	1998	Percent change, 1990–1998	1995	1990	Amount (dollars)	Percent of national average
COLORADO—Con.														
Delta	10 628	−1.9	404	3.8	697	44.0	627	484	5 267	82.7	4 523	2 883	18 204	59.5
Denver	277 881	.7	8 468	3.0	21 317	9.6	20 793	19 455	384 052	15.4	361 212	332 733	35 102	114.7
Dolores	688	−1.3	64	9.3	44	41.9	38	31	192	20.0	187	160	22 276	72.8
Douglas	93 614	.8	1 282	1.4	3 572	165.6	2 603	1 345	29 453	227.0	20 571	9 006	25 236	82.4
Eagle	20 378	−1.9	441	2.2	2 564	85.4	1 995	1 383	26 617	74.8	21 825	15 230	24 388	79.7
Elbert	13 093	8.6	321	2.5	382	131.5	257	165	1 668	49.7	1 235	1 114	21 938	71.7
El Paso	258 399	−.2	8 312	3.2	13 057	36.4	11 826	9 575	194 751	54.4	165 390	126 113	27 969	91.4
Fremont	17 151	−1.1	538	3.1	853	31.4	733	649	7 920	34.4	6 792	5 893	18 813	61.5
Garfield	23 670	3.3	582	2.5	1 807	49.2	1 575	1 211	13 416	37.5	11 837	9 757	25 711	84.0
Gilpin	3 096	−5.0	63	2.0	90	60.7	87	56	3 352	2 364.7	4 025	136	25 606	83.7
Grand	5 860	−2.1	148	2.5	692	57.3	587	440	6 081	42.9	5 222	4 254	15 357	50.2
Gunnison	7 938	−1.0	360	4.5	785	52.7	724	514	6 785	63.5	6 309	4 150	15 971	52.2
Hinsdale	700	12.9	11	1.6	74	138.7	55	31	174	132.0	190	75	17 517	57.2
Huerfano	3 555	−2.6	182	5.1	206	38.3	174	149	1 425	104.2	971	698	17 831	58.3
Jackson	857	−3.8	28	3.3	57	18.8	55	48	213	−4.5	230	223	22 005	71.9
Jefferson	308 109	.6	6 174	2.0	15 132	40.9	13 565	10 736	167 896	26.1	151 938	133 154	30 317	99.0
Kiowa	766	−7.6	19	2.5	45	2.3	47	44	255	93.2	241	132	17 600	57.5
Kit Carson	3 404	−7.0	70	2.1	283	24.7	276	227	1 901	25.7	1 699	1 512	18 441	60.2
Lake	3 088	−1.9	143	4.6	210	23.5	194	170	1 480	18.4	1 292	1 250	18 576	60.7
La Plata	24 404	.8	917	3.8	1 886	51.5	1 678	1 245	16 444	56.9	14 542	10 479	21 813	71.3
Larimer	143 008	1.6	4 240	3.0	7 586	44.1	6 765	5 263	87 930	57.8	76 361	55 716	25 421	83.1
Las Animas	6 739	1.3	285	4.2	370	20.9	323	306	2 890	50.2	2 366	1 924	16 728	54.6
Lincoln	2 608	−.6	29	1.1	129	–	126	129	1 216	20.6	992	1 008	19 425	63.5
Logan	10 012	1.4	305	3.0	625	12.8	585	554	5 836	17.0	5 732	4 986	19 346	63.2
Mesa	58 532	−.2	2 176	3.7	3 528	40.0	3 113	2 520	39 408	44.9	34 086	27 205	23 768	77.7
Mineral	456	8.3	12	2.6	50	47.1	48	34	143	150.9	99	57	17 874	58.4
Moffat	5 987	−4.0	288	4.8	355	21.2	330	293	3 253	28.8	3 012	2 526	27 961	91.3
Montezuma	11 572	−1.1	615	5.3	754	47.0	682	513	6 302	60.8	6 339	3 918	21 242	69.4
Montrose	15 360	−.3	687	4.5	1 077	42.8	1 007	754	9 349	49.7	9 155	6 247	21 365	69.8
Morgan	12 164	−4.3	349	2.9	663	19.0	649	557	8 166	39.9	7 825	5 837	21 753	71.1
Otero	8 595	−2.0	451	5.2	536	4.7	534	512	5 133	20.4	4 705	4 262	18 318	59.8
Ouray	1 802	−.4	49	2.7	216	75.6	190	123	711	58.7	665	448	20 567	67.2
Park	8 470	5.6	204	2.4	354	195.0	258	120	1 215	217.2	836	383	20 383	66.6
Phillips	1 961	−3.7	38	1.9	150	17.2	139	128	977	40.6	891	695	19 042	62.2
Pitkin	8 757	−2.2	230	2.6	1 527	32.1	1 352	1 156	16 543	23.2	15 892	13 429	22 612	73.9
Prowers	6 667	−5.0	194	2.9	450	7.4	439	419	4 309	39.8	3 511	3 083	18 591	60.7
Pueblo	58 300	−3.1	2 513	4.3	3 178	17.7	2 954	2 701	45 760	34.2	40 168	34 095	22 116	72.3
Rio Blanco	3 071	.4	96	3.1	214	27.4	199	168	1 407	−23.5	1 955	1 840	25 777	84.2
Rio Grande	4 821	−3.2	340	7.1	372	15.2	348	323	2 859	20.6	2 495	2 370	19 337	63.2
Routt	11 049	−1.5	260	2.4	1 204	65.2	1 025	729	14 730	52.1	13 508	9 684	23 971	78.3
Saguache	2 647	−4.1	201	7.6	113	28.4	110	88	604	52.1	573	397	16 925	55.3
San Juan	272	−5.2	34	12.5	46	17.9	42	39	67	15.5	75	58	25 388	82.9
San Miguel	4 376	−5.0	158	3.6	485	79.0	415	271	4 307	183.9	3 435	1 517	18 809	61.5
Sedgwick	1 140	−4.4	29	2.5	91	−2.2	95	93	541	21.8	537	444	15 074	49.2
Summit	12 560	−1.7	257	2.0	1 683	72.4	1 419	976	18 787	37.3	16 400	13 682	18 085	59.1
Teller	13 549	.7	350	2.6	605	99.0	493	304	5 364	297.9	4 637	1 348	19 179	62.7
Washington	2 220	−6.2	48	2.2	119	10.2	112	108	759	16.2	709	653	18 810	61.5
Weld	85 810	Z	2 908	3.4	3 707	35.6	3 328	2 733	52 895	46.9	48 475	36 008	26 855	87.7
Yuma	4 290	−3.3	114	2.7	342	11.8	334	306	2 116	32.6	2 028	1 596	18 419	60.2
CONNECTICUT	1 746 489	2.2	39 345	2.3	92 362	−.5	91 189	92 816	1 493 964	.8	1 415 400	1 482 023	38 974	127.3
Fairfield	452 843	1.9	8 774	1.9	28 438	3.5	27 650	27 468	424 846	3.3	399 276	411 101	50 719	165.7
Hartford	424 766	2.3	10 710	2.5	23 275	−3.6	23 161	24 142	459 632	−3.9	440 154	478 285	37 770	123.4
Litchfield	100 914	1.0	1 862	1.8	5 146	.4	5 047	5 126	56 331	2.4	55 185	55 018	30 418	99.4
Middlesex	84 482	2.9	1 641	1.9	4 180	6.6	4 065	3 920	59 152	−2.9	56 104	60 888	32 498	106.2
New Haven	420 462	2.5	10 634	2.5	20 937	−3.5	20 851	21 701	334 737	1.5	314 290	329 737	32 808	107.2
New London	133 669	2.0	2 949	2.2	5 715	−2.3	5 811	5 848	103 413	9.2	98 665	94 678	31 058	101.5
Tolland	71 499	2.6	1 172	1.6	2 500	2.4	2 434	2 442	26 462	11.4	24 229	23 753	26 475	86.5
Windham	57 856	4.0	1 605	2.8	2 171	1.2	2 170	2 145	29 391	4.7	27 497	28 085	26 803	87.6
DELAWARE	409 058	5.0	16 247	4.0	22 871	21.9	20 991	18 761	354 643	14.0	324 498	311 017	33 361	109.0
Kent	71 339	4.4	3 024	4.2	2 966	14.6	2 729	2 588	42 453	19.5	38 068	35 537	22 716	74.2
New Castle	263 578	4.9	9 936	3.8	15 490	24.3	14 096	12 457	265 039	12.6	242 619	235 413	36 958	120.7
Sussex	74 141	5.9	3 287	4.4	4 415	19.3	4 166	3 701	47 151	18.1	43 811	39 937	22 721	74.2
DISTRICT OF COLUMBIA	278 875	−.7	16 112	5.8	19 571	−.1	19 451	19 587	402 070	−5.8	413 757	426 959	43 172	141.0
District of Columbia	278 875	−.7	16 112	5.8	19 571	−.1	19 451	19 587	402 070	−5.8	413 757	426 959	43 172	141.0

[1] Civilian unemployed as a percent of total civilian labor force.   [2] For pay period including March 12 of the year shown.

Sources: Civilian Labor Force—U.S. Bureau of Labor Statistics; Local Area Unemployment Statistics; 2000 data published 2 May 2001, 1999 data published 30 May 2001; <ftp://ftp.bls.gov/pub/time.series/la/> (related Internet site <http://www.bls.gov/lauhome.htm>).   Private Business Establishments and Employment—U.S. Census Bureau; County Business Patterns on CD-ROM; annual (related Internet site <http://www.census.gov/epcd/cbp/view/cbpview.html>).

Table B–7. Counties — Labor Force and Private Business Establishments and Employment–Con.

[Includes U.S., states, and 3,142 counties/county equivalents defined as of January 1, 1992. For changes to these areas since January 1, 1992, see appendix B. Geographic Information]

County	Civilian labor force, 2000		Unemployment		Private nonfarm businesses								Annual payroll per employee, 1998	
					Establishments				Employment[2]					
	Total	Percent change, 1999–2000	Total	Rate[1]	1998	Percent change, 1990–1998	1995	1990	1998	Percent change, 1990–1998	1995	1990	Amount (dollars)	Percent of national average
FLORIDA	7 490 307	1.8	268 808	3.6	420 638	16.4	398 232	361 330	5 756 353	24.9	5 208 285	4 607 247	26 047	85.1
Alachua	105 370	.2	1 991	1.9	5 124	9.1	5 071	4 698	75 584	23.9	71 759	61 018	23 426	76.5
Baker	8 989	2.8	261	2.9	277	19.4	264	232	3 589	104.2	3 604	1 758	20 419	66.7
Bay	64 938	−1.4	3 785	5.8	4 220	15.6	4 158	3 649	54 230	37.8	48 470	39 348	20 390	66.6
Bradford	9 348	−3.3	242	2.6	385	−2.8	399	396	4 042	4.6	3 549	3 866	17 002	55.5
Brevard	207 695	.9	7 009	3.4	11 330	16.3	10 739	9 744	154 136	12.8	145 351	136 686	27 059	88.4
Broward	779 445	1.7	29 107	3.7	49 026	22.8	46 105	39 915	585 668	27.0	526 178	461 330	27 382	89.5
Calhoun	4 574	−4.4	233	5.1	237	12.9	231	210	2 069	23.4	1 818	1 677	18 997	62.1
Charlotte	50 634	5.3	1 365	2.7	2 900	16.6	2 628	2 487	30 868	30.6	28 141	23 644	20 826	68.0
Citrus	37 698	4.1	1 763	4.7	2 271	15.7	2 136	1 963	22 282	17.9	22 522	18 903	22 014	71.9
Clay	70 268	2.0	1 913	2.6	2 770	25.1	2 400	2 221	29 361	27.0	26 781	23 115	20 236	66.1
Collier	100 050	5.5	3 502	3.5	7 959	34.6	6 939	5 913	82 383	35.5	71 444	60 794	24 938	81.5
Columbia	24 239	.2	1 037	4.3	1 149	15.4	1 095	996	15 306	20.0	13 732	12 750	22 143	72.3
Dade	1 053 924	.9	55 615	5.3	67 042	10.5	66 011	60 673	835 903	10.1	804 923	759 420	28 560	93.3
DeSoto	8 815	1.1	471	5.3	397	1.8	413	390	4 786	2.2	4 794	4 684	21 280	69.5
Dixie	3 480	−5.6	179	5.1	183	−3.7	200	190	1 341	−.1	1 555	1 343	17 242	56.3
Duval	392 748	3.0	12 913	3.3	20 774	10.9	19 860	18 733	381 829	25.6	348 695	304 076	28 085	91.8
Escambia	120 795	.8	4 799	4.0	6 728	7.4	6 544	6 266	107 234	24.2	100 900	86 313	23 211	75.8
Flagler	17 584	.1	486	2.8	955	63.2	744	585	9 356	54.6	7 522	6 050	19 620	64.1
Franklin	4 510	−1.7	122	2.7	287	22.6	302	234	1 910	29.9	2 437	1 470	16 112	52.6
Gadsden	20 014	1.5	728	3.6	594	−6.0	597	632	9 075	−12.5	9 055	10 371	24 915	81.4
Gilchrist	4 378	−2.4	152	3.5	179	20.9	152	148	1 057	7.9	994	980	16 433	53.7
Glades	3 713	−2.6	246	6.6	153	101.3	194	76	1 409	230.8	1 649	426	21 065	68.8
Gulf	4 861	−7.8	357	7.3	265	26.2	231	210	2 408	−2.6	2 843	2 473	23 402	76.5
Hamilton	3 310	−3.3	212	6.4	181	30.2	161	139	2 515	114.8	2 706	1 171	31 738	103.7
Hardee	9 616	4.2	802	8.3	357	−11.0	378	401	3 229	3.8	3 459	3 111	21 343	69.7
Hendry	15 125	−3.1	1 675	11.1	489	5.6	415	463	4 972	5.2	4 454	4 727	20 108	65.7
Hernando	49 074	2.9	1 612	3.3	2 258	16.9	2 118	1 932	23 665	38.4	21 273	17 098	20 154	65.8
Highlands	25 962	−.8	1 425	5.5	1 749	7.2	1 741	1 631	29 231	116.1	23 726	13 524	17 416	56.9
Hillsborough	564 858	2.9	14 629	2.6	26 125	12.4	24 734	23 242	493 710	31.8	431 933	374 452	28 379	92.7
Holmes	6 640	1.8	350	5.3	256	16.4	233	220	2 257	−2.0	2 387	2 302	14 957	48.9
Indian River	45 001	−1.0	2 884	6.4	3 474	19.5	3 209	2 908	37 569	29.8	30 373	28 953	21 787	71.2
Jackson	17 439	−2.2	798	4.6	802	5.9	765	757	8 776	13.6	8 842	7 726	16 879	55.1
Jefferson	4 540	−6.0	190	4.2	208	12.8	218	211	1 685	1.0	1 827	1 663	18 173	59.4
Lafayette	2 912	−.2	71	2.4	98	36.1	89	72	747	17.1	555	638	19 444	63.5
Lake	93 798	1.9	2 342	2.5	4 354	23.8	3 887	3 518	47 696	28.0	44 500	37 269	21 397	69.9
Lee	181 961	1.7	4 683	2.6	11 616	13.5	10 785	10 233	134 701	24.6	125 854	108 081	23 341	76.3
Leon	131 384	1.3	3 082	2.3	6 269	12.9	5 989	5 555	85 703	31.3	79 697	65 273	23 709	77.5
Levy	13 247	3.4	470	3.5	623	21.0	540	515	5 704	49.9	4 680	3 805	16 803	54.9
Liberty	2 206	−3.9	65	2.9	88	22.2	90	72	778	3.9	846	749	19 172	62.6
Madison	7 623	3.3	272	3.6	308	6.6	314	289	3 424	22.2	3 404	2 802	17 184	56.1
Manatee	123 345	2.7	2 787	2.3	5 441	25.8	5 149	4 325	106 633	65.3	88 504	64 508	21 652	70.7
Marion	99 349	1.2	3 688	3.7	5 383	15.6	5 015	4 658	69 245	34.7	61 146	51 403	21 345	69.7
Martin	49 480	2.4	2 178	4.4	4 181	18.7	3 821	3 522	44 730	20.7	38 309	37 056	24 801	81.0
Monroe	44 074	−3.8	897	2.0	3 762	31.1	3 507	2 869	32 132	22.0	28 998	26 341	19 697	64.4
Nassau	29 599	2.7	939	3.2	1 138	24.8	1 061	912	12 551	30.0	11 481	9 092	25 181	82.3
Okaloosa	82 486	2.5	2 710	3.3	4 779	26.8	4 446	3 768	55 450	30.7	50 977	42 423	20 799	68.0
Okeechobee	15 362	−2.9	1 014	6.6	685	11.2	687	616	6 403	19.6	6 270	5 354	18 821	61.5
Orange	496 692	1.7	12 644	2.5	25 218	21.8	23 539	20 705	528 249	36.3	436 522	387 529	27 228	89.0
Osceola	86 221	2.0	2 375	2.8	3 191	40.1	2 712	2 278	47 905	45.4	38 414	32 947	19 394	63.4
Palm Beach	517 893	2.4	22 798	4.4	35 287	25.5	32 701	28 111	414 845	24.9	379 154	332 174	29 237	95.5
Pasco	140 096	2.7	4 065	2.9	6 068	15.4	5 537	5 256	63 316	21.2	59 735	52 238	20 572	67.2
Pinellas	478 889	2.7	12 129	2.5	26 243	7.0	25 605	24 516	396 192	22.0	350 105	324 811	26 103	85.3
Polk	204 355	2.1	9 660	4.7	9 625	6.3	9 243	9 055	151 889	12.7	151 270	134 780	25 316	82.7
Putnam	27 189	−2.3	1 212	4.5	1 228	15.5	1 161	1 063	12 991	13.0	12 537	11 501	22 244	72.7
St. Johns	63 233	2.9	1 542	2.4	3 211	54.4	2 715	2 080	35 718	52.4	27 111	23 438	21 823	71.3
St. Lucie	78 757	1.5	6 026	7.7	3 752	14.0	3 490	3 290	40 612	15.2	36 472	35 265	21 977	71.8
Santa Rosa	53 318	Z	1 893	3.6	1 901	32.6	1 726	1 434	18 733	34.7	16 987	13 912	19 167	62.6
Sarasota	154 026	2.5	3 191	2.1	10 839	6.8	10 448	10 145	132 105	28.4	109 475	102 900	24 516	80.1
Seminole	220 706	1.8	5 555	2.5	10 272	30.6	9 408	7 863	122 055	38.8	110 883	87 934	26 423	86.3
Sumter	14 343	1.4	381	2.7	514	8.9	496	472	5 051	9.9	5 264	4 594	18 274	59.7
Suwannee	13 000	−2.2	469	3.6	614	23.3	522	498	7 098	30.4	6 519	5 445	18 238	59.6
Taylor	7 024	−3.6	469	6.7	404	−4.3	407	422	4 836	−5.8	4 793	5 135	25 258	82.5
Union	3 314	−3.4	107	3.2	117	2.6	129	114	1 480	−4.7	2 048	1 553	24 050	78.6
Volusia	174 212	.3	4 974	2.9	10 713	11.9	10 214	9 570	125 059	15.9	120 365	107 870	20 477	66.9
Wakulla	11 494	5.1	364	3.2	318	50.7	273	211	2 362	27.3	2 013	1 855	19 915	65.1
Walton	16 404	4.1	523	3.2	884	69.7	695	521	9 208	92.6	7 997	4 780	17 796	58.1
Washington	9 708	1.2	385	4.0	335	18.4	324	283	3 886	50.4	3 647	2 584	18 561	60.6

[1] Civilian unemployed as a percent of total civilian labor force.   [2] For pay period including March 12 of the year shown.

Sources: Civilian Labor Force—U.S. Bureau of Labor Statistics; Local Area Unemployment Statistics; 2000 data published 2 May 2001, 1999 data published 30 May 2001; <ftp://ftp.bls.gov/pub/time.series/la/> (related Internet site <http://www.bls.gov/lauhome.htm>).   Private Business Establishments and Employment—U.S. Census Bureau; County Business Patterns on CD-ROM; annual (related Internet site <http://www.census.gov/epcd/cbp/view/cbpview.html>).

[Includes U.S., states, and 3,142 counties/county equivalents defined as of January 1, 1992. For changes to these areas since January 1, 1992, see appendix B. Geographic Information]

County	Civilian labor force, 2000		Unemployment		Establishments				Employment[2]				Annual payroll per employee, 1998	
	Total	Percent change, 1999–2000	Total	Rate[1]	1998	Percent change, 1990–1998	1995	1990	1998	Percent change, 1990–1998	1995	1990	Amount (dollars)	Percent of national average
GEORGIA	4 173 274	2.3	154 398	3.7	194 213	23.2	179 006	157 667	3 198 950	28.0	2 920 361	2 498 877	29 599	96.7
Appling	8 146	−1.1	696	8.5	393	32.8	363	296	5 724	37.5	5 137	4 164	33 661	110.0
Atkinson	3 434	2.7	259	7.5	87	7.4	92	81	1 627	39.8	1 497	1 164	20 140	65.8
Bacon	4 386	2.9	267	6.1	198	3.7	195	191	2 870	−.3	3 025	2 880	21 158	69.1
Baker	1 621	.7	81	5.0	21	−8.7	23	23	232	−6.5	235	248	21 940	71.7
Baldwin.................	18 500	5.5	819	4.4	824	10.2	784	748	14 982	7.9	15 119	13 886	21 980	71.8
Banks	6 463	1.8	204	3.2	210	92.7	128	109	2 782	52.0	1 383	1 830	17 950	58.6
Barrow	21 706	3.2	681	3.1	770	45.8	658	528	8 958	26.6	7 725	7 076	23 148	75.6
Bartow	40 958	3.2	1 684	4.1	1 514	37.0	1 264	1 105	24 318	38.4	21 111	17 574	25 847	84.4
Ben Hill	9 457	−.2	582	6.2	380	1.1	385	376	6 927	43.5	6 669	4 826	22 478	73.4
Berrien	6 528	−4.2	368	5.6	280	19.1	284	235	4 003	−2.4	4 012	4 100	22 269	72.8
Bibb	73 073	.5	3 544	4.8	4 635	4.9	4 509	4 419	84 294	20.9	79 810	69 704	27 141	88.7
Bleckley	5 904	3.1	221	3.7	208	6.1	206	196	3 070	18.7	3 083	2 586	20 245	66.1
Brantley	6 388	7.7	368	5.8	170	33.9	134	127	1 166	50.3	926	776	20 065	65.6
Brooks	7 857	2.8	449	5.7	203	3.6	196	196	2 378	−8.5	2 954	2 599	19 026	62.2
Bryan	11 204	1.2	311	2.8	361	55.6	302	232	2 717	36.7	2 631	1 987	18 913	61.8
Bulloch	26 952	2.2	741	2.7	1 188	31.0	1 080	907	15 335	39.1	13 432	11 024	19 886	65.0
Burke	9 044	3.7	708	7.8	320	3.6	314	309	4 486	−7.1	4 647	4 827	29 066	95.0
Butts	9 101	5.5	476	5.2	321	26.4	295	254	3 915	27.4	3 889	3 072	21 525	70.3
Calhoun	2 497	4.0	202	8.1	101	−15.1	122	119	941	−21.4	1 186	1 197	13 953	45.6
Camden	17 064	2.2	601	3.5	677	44.3	579	469	7 849	32.7	6 704	5 913	20 993	68.6
Candler	3 907	−3.9	201	5.1	197	9.4	195	180	2 005	18.9	1 870	1 686	19 746	64.5
Carroll..................	45 486	2.5	1 861	4.1	1 739	19.6	1 615	1 454	26 389	4.0	27 371	25 365	24 631	80.5
Catoosa	27 199	2.0	683	2.5	739	31.7	682	561	10 393	27.8	11 386	8 133	21 780	71.2
Charlton	3 859	2.0	163	4.2	175	23.2	152	142	1 239	−1.9	1 277	1 263	19 967	65.2
Chatham	106 516	1.1	4 062	3.8	6 575	12.2	6 221	5 859	104 569	19.3	96 308	87 667	26 923	88.0
Chattahoochee........	2 457	2.2	193	7.9	60	140.0	47	25	1 404	NA	(3)	(3)	28 067	91.7
Chattooga	11 886	−.3	371	3.1	322	10.3	314	292	6 088	8.4	6 716	5 615	21 363	69.8
Cherokee	83 131	3.0	1 670	2.0	2 839	101.9	1 977	1 406	24 992	97.7	17 959	12 642	23 313	76.2
Clarke	46 256	1.0	1 231	2.7	2 529	5.7	2 642	2 392	40 179	5.7	44 446	38 015	23 042	75.3
Clay......................	1 587	.8	103	6.5	50	2.0	47	49	434	43.2	337	303	16 240	53.1
Clayton	126 858	3.1	4 540	3.6	4 344	15.3	4 104	3 768	83 840	56.2	76 304	53 662	26 577	86.8
Clinch	3 501	1.6	198	5.7	148	33.3	138	111	2 607	68.8	2 465	1 544	17 046	55.7
Cobb.....................	363 637	2.9	8 994	2.5	17 181	33.6	15 586	12 858	275 497	49.3	237 631	184 519	34 296	112.0
Coffee	20 990	1.3	1 120	5.3	828	22.5	776	676	14 798	52.7	12 780	9 693	21 801	71.2
Colquitt	19 672	1.1	1 156	5.9	908	16.0	885	783	11 501	20.5	11 036	9 543	20 017	65.9
Columbia	45 105	1.2	1 237	2.7	1 810	52.7	1 481	1 185	25 338	80.8	17 941	14 011	23 750	77.6
Cook.....................	8 380	6.9	431	5.1	329	25.1	311	263	4 126	10.7	3 910	3 727	21 918	71.6
Coweta..................	47 360	3.6	1 610	3.4	1 527	64.5	1 256	928	21 784	41.5	18 209	15 392	23 568	77.0
Crawford	6 134	6.2	254	4.1	78	9.9	63	71	531	24.6	504	426	16 831	55.0
Crisp	9 684	−2.1	593	6.1	556	6.1	523	524	7 417	20.0	7 494	6 179	20 001	65.3
Dade	7 520	1.5	194	2.6	212	49.3	195	142	2 404	26.5	1 866	1 901	19 173	62.6
Dawson	17 296	14.3	280	1.6	400	205.3	209	131	2 989	322.8	1 395	707	21 485	70.2
Decatur..................	11 857	.7	688	5.8	616	10.2	629	559	9 459	14.2	8 763	8 284	21 565	70.5
De Kalb	365 621	2.7	13 321	3.6	17 013	−.6	17 530	17 123	314 225	6.1	312 011	296 267	32 938	107.6
Dodge	9 918	2.1	458	4.6	374	−4.1	370	390	4 034	−7.7	4 760	4 369	17 697	57.8
Dooly	4 572	−2.4	296	6.5	191	4.4	198	183	2 753	43.3	1 787	1 921	19 413	63.4
Dougherty	44 424	−.7	3 051	6.9	2 632	1.3	2 688	2 599	45 671	19.4	39 697	38 264	25 108	82.0
Douglas	53 032	2.8	1 440	2.7	1 911	34.5	1 694	1 421	24 789	55.3	20 602	15 957	22 506	73.5
Early	4 768	2.5	362	7.6	247	4.7	249	236	2 969	−12.2	3 209	3 383	27 998	91.5
Echols...................	1 280	1.7	60	4.7	12	9.1	10	11	12	−64.7	(4)	34	26 417	86.3
Effingham..............	18 526	1.4	542	2.9	471	81.2	348	260	4 794	89.9	3 999	2 524	28 155	92.0
Elbert	9 063	3.5	707	7.8	536	1.5	548	528	5 848	−.5	6 133	5 875	20 030	65.4
Emanuel	8 803	1.5	835	9.5	424	1.9	422	416	5 401	−10.9	6 097	6 064	17 226	56.3
Evans	5 023	3.9	240	4.8	224	7.7	208	208	3 507	34.7	2 949	2 603	20 333	66.4
Fannin	9 329	6.8	286	3.1	417	26.0	372	331	3 844	42.4	3 567	2 699	18 068	59.0
Fayette..................	51 643	3.0	970	1.9	2 223	65.2	1 884	1 346	26 498	86.1	20 561	14 237	25 538	83.4
Floyd.....................	44 999	−.4	1 625	3.6	1 993	9.2	1 958	1 825	37 430	19.2	36 711	31 410	23 406	76.5
Forsyth..................	55 727	2.9	863	1.5	2 190	144.4	1 295	896	26 936	214.7	12 994	8 558	27 299	89.2
Franklin	10 562	3.2	368	3.5	443	17.5	417	377	6 313	49.0	5 535	4 238	19 574	63.9
Fulton...................	410 281	2.8	15 117	3.7	29 887	22.1	28 205	24 476	678 307	26.7	603 247	535 485	39 033	127.5
Gilmer	8 195	−1.3	271	3.3	426	40.1	366	304	5 758	48.2	5 200	3 886	19 824	64.8
Glascock	1 007	1.1	45	4.5	25	–	30	25	200	−36.5	318	315	14 940	48.8
Glynn	35 710	.4	1 262	3.5	2 392	16.3	2 242	2 056	29 800	19.5	29 749	24 927	21 948	71.7
Gordon	22 647	2.5	848	3.7	907	−5.9	859	964	19 580	−5.4	19 795	20 705	22 607	73.9
Grady	9 330	−.4	587	6.3	418	14.2	398	366	4 078	−3.5	4 503	4 228	19 334	63.2
Greene	5 812	−1.0	355	6.1	318	23.3	274	258	3 873	13.2	3 558	3 421	21 557	70.4

[1] Civilian unemployed as a percent of total civilian labor force.   [2] For pay period including March 12 of the year shown.   [3] 1,000–2,499 employees.   [4] 20–99 employees.

Sources: Civilian Labor Force—U.S. Bureau of Labor Statistics; Local Area Unemployment Statistics; 2000 data published 2 May 2001, 1999 data published 30 May 2001; <ftp://ftp.bls.gov/pub/time.series/la/> (related Internet site <http://www.bls.gov/lauhome.htm>).   Private Business Establishments and Employment—U.S. Census Bureau; County Business Patterns on CD-ROM; annual (related Internet site <http://www.census.gov/epcd/cbp/view/cbpview.html>).

[Includes U.S., states, and 3,142 counties/county equivalents defined as of January 1, 1992. For changes to these areas since January 1, 1992, see appendix B. Geographic Information]

County	Civilian labor force, 2000 Total	Percent change, 1999–2000	Unemployment Total	Rate[1]	Establishments 1998	Percent change, 1990–1998	1995	1990	Employment[2] 1998	Percent change, 1990–1998	1995	1990	Annual payroll per employee, 1998 Amount (dollars)	Percent of national average
GEORGIA—Con.														
Gwinnett	345 950	2.9	7 866	2.3	16 423	67.0	13 468	9 837	251 369	74.0	208 860	144 430	33 239	108.6
Habersham	15 864	.8	536	3.4	776	28.5	715	604	11 724	19.4	12 308	9 823	22 616	73.9
Hall	74 460	4.2	1 733	2.3	3 209	30.4	2 814	2 461	51 461	28.5	46 957	40 042	26 276	85.8
Hancock	4 017	.4	381	9.5	91	1.1	97	90	881	–9.6	1 125	975	14 991	49.0
Haralson	9 990	5.1	442	4.4	423	5.0	405	403	5 481	–10.8	5 353	6 143	20 113	65.7
Harris	12 168	1.4	356	2.9	413	71.4	274	241	3 996	60.0	3 350	2 497	18 311	59.8
Hart	9 985	6.6	438	4.4	375	28.0	326	293	5 446	–12.0	5 430	6 191	23 726	77.5
Heard	4 737	–1.0	262	5.5	106	35.9	95	78	1 136	–2.4	1 310	1 164	18 120	59.2
Henry	63 981	3.1	1 331	2.1	1 978	125.3	1 440	878	23 373	116.9	18 040	10 778	22 879	74.7
Houston	51 999	.2	1 733	3.3	1 903	18.8	1 834	1 052	24 990	38.7	23 204	18 018	21 200	69.5
Irwin	5 028	1.2	287	5.7	142	–6.0	137	151	2 065	29.6	1 864	1 593	16 669	54.5
Jackson	23 118	3.9	617	2.7	883	66.6	685	530	13 412	59.7	10 817	8 400	23 447	76.6
Jasper	4 863	1.9	191	3.9	158	45.0	116	109	1 592	12.8	1 545	1 411	24 242	79.2
Jeff Davis	5 254	–1.6	318	6.1	309	4.7	298	295	5 115	10.5	4 931	4 629	19 527	63.8
Jefferson	7 367	–2.9	678	9.2	351	17.4	342	299	4 974	3.6	5 633	4 799	23 595	77.1
Jenkins	4 664	3.7	278	6.0	148	4.2	143	142	2 459	36.3	1 839	1 804	17 917	58.5
Johnson	3 643	1.6	260	7.1	129	–10.4	140	144	1 411	–27.6	2 138	1 949	19 147	62.6
Jones	12 139	.8	502	4.1	245	66.7	190	147	1 845	55.6	1 766	1 186	21 149	69.1
Lamar	6 716	–1.9	431	6.4	225	13.6	198	198	3 303	13.3	3 289	2 915	18 429	60.2
Lanier	3 655	3.1	209	5.7	104	–	113	104	745	–14.3	975	869	19 342	63.2
Laurens	22 517	–.3	1 331	5.9	1 045	8.1	1 068	967	17 544	20.4	16 936	14 575	22 852	74.7
Lee	11 988	.4	485	4.0	195	119.1	158	89	1 768	108.7	1 036	847	19 010	62.1
Liberty	18 039	7.1	1 069	5.9	712	39.1	637	512	8 370	56.3	7 769	5 356	19 606	64.1
Lincoln	3 103	–10.8	292	9.4	151	34.8	145	112	1 514	117.8	1 502	695	16 617	54.3
Long	3 874	8.0	131	3.4	52	92.6	45	27	225	200.0	227	75	12 284	40.1
Lowndes	44 119	2.7	2 457	5.6	2 360	10.9	2 266	2 129	33 989	30.1	31 929	26 117	20 929	68.4
Lumpkin	11 225	4.9	200	1.8	353	75.6	296	201	3 658	57.2	3 075	2 327	21 352	69.8
McDuffie	9 699	.4	550	5.7	460	1.5	463	453	6 836	.1	6 780	6 831	21 490	70.2
McIntosh	4 581	–.1	233	5.1	240	72.7	184	139	1 966	22.6	1 106	1 604	15 087	49.3
Macon	5 763	8.6	555	9.6	232	.9	215	230	2 692	–17.7	3 027	3 270	26 585	86.9
Madison	13 605	.7	360	2.6	528	98.5	324	266	6 964	276.6	2 645	1 849	22 752	74.3
Marion	3 476	2.1	158	4.5	80	12.7	75	71	2 116	79.3	1 930	1 180	16 933	55.3
Meriwether	9 071	2.9	500	0.0	337	9.1	325	309	4 095	–2.0	4 848	5 027	21 819	71.3
Miller	3 167	–.3	172	5.4	142	34.0	128	106	1 009	29.7	1 028	778	15 916	52.0
Mitchell	12 205	3.1	750	6.1	416	5.9	437	393	3 631	–17.3	5 397	4 393	17 402	56.9
Monroe	8 690	10.0	441	5.1	367	40.6	332	261	3 293	–19.3	3 979	4 083	22 917	74.9
Montgomery	3 830	–.8	354	9.2	112	–14.5	113	131	1 214	–27.0	1 531	1 663	19 781	64.6
Morgan	7 447	4.6	307	4.1	376	35.3	320	278	5 579	48.7	5 012	3 751	23 027	75.2
Murray	20 107	5.0	753	3.7	479	161.7	462	183	8 836	64.5	10 316	5 373	23 304	76.1
Muscogee	86 436	.6	4 286	5.0	4 328	.6	4 352	4 301	84 737	19.2	75 920	71 067	25 221	82.4
Newton	30 873	2.9	1 013	3.3	1 101	49.0	920	739	13 521	33.3	13 092	10 145	23 993	78.4
Oconee	13 503	1.1	185	1.4	494	38.0	435	358	4 331	56.7	3 533	2 763	22 327	72.9
Oglethorpe	6 222	2.8	162	2.6	154	38.7	122	111	848	9.3	660	776	16 669	54.5
Paulding	43 595	3.1	962	2.2	869	86.5	676	466	7 989	101.7	5 662	3 961	21 034	68.7
Peach	11 261	.1	574	5.1	448	9.5	435	409	6 263	14.6	5 763	5 466	22 696	74.1
Pickens	11 274	3.1	305	2.7	442	52.4	341	290	4 692	32.4	3 905	3 543	22 656	74.0
Pierce	7 696	3.7	355	4.6	317	14.4	273	277	2 445	–11.8	2 074	2 773	18 907	61.8
Pike	6 599	1.9	287	4.3	171	50.0	145	114	1 149	45.8	804	788	21 199	69.3
Polk	17 251	7.0	738	4.3	595	11.8	569	532	7 674	–2.1	7 885	7 835	21 272	69.5
Pulaski	4 602	–.6	200	4.3	222	8.8	215	204	2 518	30.7	2 449	1 926	20 631	67.4
Putnam	9 576	1.1	306	3.2	314	42.1	262	221	4 375	48.0	3 529	2 957	25 657	83.8
Quitman	1 536	17.3	84	5.5	39	77.3	23	22	212	78.2	125	119	18 986	62.0
Rabun	7 388	1.6	135	1.8	466	23.9	421	376	4 921	24.2	4 688	3 963	20 322	66.4
Randolph	3 353	2.4	248	7.4	170	6.3	163	160	1 606	–6.6	1 884	1 720	18 465	60.3
Richmond	80 429	.9	4 668	5.8	4 513	.5	4 606	4 489	79 530	2.1	82 580	77 884	25 614	83.7
Rockdale	40 023	3.1	1 037	2.6	1 903	38.3	1 637	1 376	29 133	53.8	26 761	18 948	27 432	89.6
Schley	1 856	2.4	83	4.5	71	16.4	76	61	1 003	31.5	779	763	21 851	71.4
Screven	6 046	1.4	413	6.8	236	18.0	224	200	2 863	–14.2	3 044	3 335	21 324	69.7
Seminole	4 827	8.7	239	5.0	192	–6.3	213	205	1 424	–14.6	1 623	1 667	17 911	58.5
Spalding	30 043	3.8	1 485	4.9	1 187	9.1	1 153	1 088	18 880	15.9	18 264	16 286	22 291	72.8
Stephens	11 743	–3.5	428	3.6	570	–3.2	590	589	9 749	Z	10 615	9 751	20 284	66.3
Stewart	2 450	4.4	147	6.0	93	–5.1	91	98	913	2.9	948	887	20 501	67.0
Sumter	15 246	–.3	767	5.0	701	1.3	718	692	11 997	21.1	12 490	9 905	21 432	70.0
Talbot	3 037	4.0	196	6.5	67	–2.9	62	69	446	7.2	384	416	22 457	73.4
Taliaferro	844	4.7	44	5.2	25	4.2	19	24	96	–15.0	67	113	16 156	52.8
Tattnall	7 538	2.8	594	7.9	306	2.3	305	299	3 284	–6.5	3 859	3 513	15 927	52.0

[1] Civilian unemployed as a percent of total civilian labor force.   [2] For pay period including March 12 of the year shown.

Sources: Civilian Labor Force—U.S. Bureau of Labor Statistics; Local Area Unemployment Statistics; 2000 data published 2 May 2001, 1999 data published 30 May 2001; <ftp://ftp.bls.gov/pub/time.series/la/> (related Internet site <http://www.bls.gov/lauhome.htm>).   Private Business Establishments and Employment—U.S. Census Bureau; County Business Patterns on CD-ROM; annual (related Internet site <http://www.census.gov/epcd/cbp/view/cbpview.html>).

Table B–7. Counties — Labor Force and Private Business Establishments and Employment–Con.

[Includes U.S., states, and 3,142 counties/county equivalents defined as of January 1, 1992. For changes to these areas since January 1, 1992, see appendix B. Geographic Information]

County	Civilian labor force, 2000		Unemployment		Establishments				Employment²				Annual payroll per employee, 1998	
	Total	Percent change, 1999–2000	Total	Rate¹	1998	Percent change, 1990–1998	1995	1990	1998	Percent change, 1990–1998	1995	1990	Amount (dollars)	Percent of national average
GEORGIA—Con.														
Taylor	3 804	–2.8	212	5.6	143	10.0	142	130	1 112	–1.0	1 130	1 123	22 602	73.8
Telfair	5 030	1.2	514	10.2	239	2.6	225	233	3 935	–.3	3 697	3 947	16 890	55.2
Terrell	4 169	4.5	352	8.4	188	–3.1	188	194	2 013	–13.7	1 675	2 333	17 798	58.1
Thomas	21 696	–.4	1 052	4.8	1 107	5.5	1 108	1 049	18 085	35.6	16 348	13 335	21 068	68.8
Tift	20 741	.7	952	4.6	1 107	14.1	1 087	970	17 387	29.1	15 602	13 463	22 113	72.2
Toombs	12 750	.5	1 331	10.4	706	7.5	613	657	9 956	10.9	10 146	8 979	19 689	64.3
Towns	4 336	7.4	148	3.4	243	65.3	202	147	1 966	89.6	1 574	1 037	18 989	62.0
Treutlen	2 841	–3.4	277	9.8	99	11.2	98	89	812	–19.5	794	1 009	13 767	45.0
Troup	30 829	.7	1 262	4.1	1 400	7.3	1 360	1 305	28 425	7.7	27 021	26 405	26 448	86.4
Turner	4 230	–2.7	374	8.8	189	6.2	190	178	1 860	42.0	1 737	1 310	17 581	57.4
Twiggs	4 227	–.7	225	5.3	88	22.2	86	72	1 441	–7.3	1 607	1 554	38 187	124.8
Union	7 808	2.0	267	3.4	436	89.6	356	230	3 277	70.4	2 787	1 923	18 271	59.7
Upson	12 505	–3.2	796	6.4	530	5.2	492	504	9 406	5.3	9 038	8 932	20 438	66.8
Walker	31 864	2.1	1 101	3.5	865	4.0	840	832	14 831	10.8	13 727	13 380	22 338	73.0
Walton	30 419	2.7	924	3.0	1 070	103.8	799	525	9 326	36.1	9 001	6 852	23 497	76.8
Ware	16 110	2.2	867	5.4	976	2.6	970	951	12 660	17.7	12 424	10 758	20 447	66.8
Warren	2 673	–1.5	192	7.2	84	–1.2	80	85	1 418	5.6	1 385	1 343	22 434	73.3
Washington	9 827	.8	496	5.0	418	14.2	391	366	6 965	13.3	6 791	6 145	31 341	102.4
Wayne	11 771	2.2	708	6.0	509	14.4	484	445	7 735	27.1	7 155	6 084	19 488	63.7
Webster	1 142	–2.1	39	3.4	23	–17.9	25	28	267	11.3	278	240	24 573	80.3
Wheeler	2 083	1.2	196	9.4	75	27.1	73	59	544	5.2	654	517	22 096	72.2
White	9 237	–1.2	346	3.7	522	39.6	477	374	4 774	19.6	5 423	3 991	19 161	62.6
Whitfield	47 813	4.5	1 521	3.2	2 563	14.6	2 468	2 236	55 338	21.8	52 697	45 426	26 567	86.8
Wilcox	3 324	–2.9	168	5.1	103	–3.7	106	107	668	–31.0	1 060	968	17 786	58.1
Wilkes	5 486	–2.5	304	5.5	274	–1.1	289	277	3 585	5.9	3 933	3 384	22 052	72.0
Wilkinson	4 678	.1	243	5.2	160	–5.9	166	170	2 733	–9.1	3 209	3 006	30 393	99.3
Worth	9 418	–.4	580	6.2	291	18.3	278	246	2 518	7.9	2 215	2 333	18 522	60.5
HAWAII	595 432	.4	25 517	4.3	29 603	1.0	29 942	29 313	416 571	–3.7	423 822	432 663	27 107	88.6
Hawaii	70 107	1.0	4 666	6.7	3 552	5.2	3 649	3 376	38 917	1.3	37 217	38 421	23 727	77.5
Honolulu	423 493	.1	15 892	3.8	20 675	–2.4	21 004	21 176	309 487	–7.2	322 339	333 400	28 253	92.3
Kalawao	(³)	(³)	(³)	(³)	–	–	–	–	–	–	–	–	–	–
Kauai	29 414	1.8	1 901	6.5	1 630	7.6	1 649	1 515	19 400	5.9	(⁴)	18 325	22 275	72.8
Maui	³72 419	³1.4	³3 059	³4.2	3 746	15.7	3 639	3 239	48 767	14.9	46 141	42 427	24 454	79.9
IDAHO	657 712	1.0	31 914	4.9	35 961	35.6	32 972	26 513	423 615	41.1	379 161	300 163	25 012	81.7
Ada	170 914	3.0	5 070	3.0	9 377	43.3	8 389	6 544	140 801	53.4	126 168	91 764	30 396	99.3
Adams	1 626	.7	211	13.0	109	55.7	98	70	793	121.5	470	358	17 687	57.8
Bannock	39 502	.8	1 969	5.0	1 822	16.1	1 739	1 570	23 376	28.1	21 031	18 253	22 345	73.0
Bear Lake	2 831	–3.9	165	5.8	112	2.8	111	109	837	34.1	999	624	17 552	57.3
Benewah	4 444	.4	553	12.4	297	35.0	278	220	2 525	22.5	2 307	2 062	23 701	77.4
Bingham	21 908	.1	1 012	4.6	722	28.0	662	564	8 956	27.3	8 451	7 035	20 721	67.7
Blaine	11 328	2.3	373	3.3	1 252	32.3	1 163	946	9 714	29.4	9 021	7 505	23 779	77.7
Boise	2 343	–4.9	167	7.1	124	74.6	111	71	488	48.3	526	329	17 107	55.9
Bonner	17 396	–.1	1 560	9.0	1 233	43.7	1 185	858	10 236	36.7	8 772	7 489	20 521	67.0
Bonneville	46 479	.3	1 558	3.4	2 535	30.9	2 340	1 937	36 220	21.9	27 903	29 717	28 520	93.2
Boundary	4 466	Z	386	8.6	354	40.5	306	252	2 240	49.5	2 085	1 498	20 396	66.6
Butte	1 596	.3	59	3.7	63	16.7	62	54	336	76.8	362	190	17 759	58.0
Camas	406	–1.2	16	3.9	25	25.0	24	20	(⁵)	NA	107	99	D	D
Canyon	65 365	3.0	2 945	4.5	2 773	49.2	2 455	1 859	35 885	53.6	32 144	23 370	23 354	76.3
Caribou	3 083	–.5	186	6.0	193	12.9	188	171	2 112	21.5	1 845	1 738	33 932	110.9
Cassia	9 548	–1.1	595	6.2	586	7.9	571	543	5 732	1.7	5 985	5 638	19 770	64.6
Clark	577	4.5	28	4.9	16	45.5	17	11	99	200.0	70	33	13 273	43.4
Clearwater	3 936	–3.5	564	14.3	275	3.8	257	265	2 163	4.0	2 204	2 079	22 358	73.0
Custer	2 063	3.1	147	7.1	150	51.5	124	99	950	27.7	710	744	21 993	71.9
Elmore	9 163	–.6	556	6.1	400	19.8	370	334	3 769	24.2	3 394	3 035	18 239	59.6
Franklin	4 712	1.8	182	3.9	231	66.2	179	139	1 574	57.6	1 417	999	16 535	54.0
Fremont	4 694	–2.4	328	7.0	269	45.4	246	185	1 523	29.4	1 287	1 177	18 277	59.7
Gem	6 237	–.2	363	5.8	298	45.4	265	205	2 191	15.5	2 197	1 897	20 821	68.0
Gooding	6 584	–.2	254	3.9	325	22.2	301	266	3 907	146.5	2 143	1 585	15 513	50.7
Idaho	6 117	–2.3	626	10.2	445	24.0	406	359	2 605	–3.0	2 499	2 685	19 774	64.6
Jefferson	10 269	Z	396	3.9	334	47.8	261	226	2 685	26.9	2 609	2 116	18 061	59.0
Jerome	8 879	–.5	396	4.5	406	36.7	349	297	3 702	30.4	3 360	2 840	20 659	67.5

¹ Civilian unemployed as a percent of total civilian labor force. ² For pay period including March 12 of the year shown. ³ Kalawao County included with Maui County; data not available separately. ⁴ 10,000–24,999 employees. ⁵ 100–249 employees.

Sources: Civilian Labor Force—U.S. Bureau of Labor Statistics; Local Area Unemployment Statistics; 2000 data published 2 May 2001, 1999 data published 30 May 2001; <ftp://ftp.bls.gov/pub/time.series/la/> (related Internet site <http://www.bls.gov/lauhome.htm>). Private Business Establishments and Employment—U.S. Census Bureau; County Business Patterns on CD-ROM; annual (related Internet site <http://www.census.gov/epcd/cbp/view/cbpview.html>).

Table B–7. Counties — Labor Force and Private Business Establishments and Employment–Con.

[Includes U.S., states, and 3,142 counties/county equivalents defined as of January 1, 1992. For changes to these areas since January 1, 1992, see appendix B. Geographic Information]

County	Civilian labor force, 2000		Unemployment		Private nonfarm businesses								Annual payroll per employee, 1998	
					Establishments				Employment[2]					
	Total	Percent change, 1999–2000	Total	Rate[1]	1998	Percent change, 1990–1998	1995	1990	1998	Percent change, 1990–1998	1995	1990	Amount (dollars)	Percent of national average
IDAHO—Con.														
Kootenai	55 717	–.1	4 141	7.4	3 556	69.3	3 142	2 101	33 622	75.5	29 777	19 163	22 174	72.4
Latah	15 164	2.3	523	3.4	904	19.3	873	758	7 655	16.5	7 818	6 570	17 647	57.7
Lemhi	3 667	–4.7	330	9.0	284	27.9	280	222	1 633	39.7	1 735	1 169	19 641	64.2
Lewis	1 524	–.8	117	7.7	133	27.9	134	104	702	10.6	832	635	22 202	72.5
Lincoln	1 832	–1.8	89	4.9	69	60.5	52	43	488	13.8	476	429	18 840	61.6
Madison	11 021	5.9	272	2.5	503	20.6	484	417	9 644	42.0	8 269	6 792	14 924	48.8
Minidoka	9 722	–.9	703	7.2	374	18.0	347	317	5 043	19.7	4 791	4 212	21 182	69.2
Nez Perce	22 687	–2.7	947	4.2	1 224	12.9	1 238	1 084	16 063	21.1	16 209	13 265	25 836	84.4
Oneida	1 703	–1.5	62	3.6	70	20.7	60	58	523	45.7	490	359	16 444	53.7
Owyhee	4 251	–3.2	178	4.2	150	33.9	132	112	1 715	122.2	1 455	772	23 373	70.4
Payette	9 988	–1.8	690	6.9	427	47.8	390	289	3 869	14.0	4 012	3 395	19 076	62.3
Power	3 544	2.4	247	7.0	161	6.6	154	151	2 120	19.7	1 964	1 771	19 865	64.9
Shoshone	6 548	–.1	725	11.1	409	12.4	429	364	3 745	5.5	3 197	3 549	23 687	77.4
Teton	3 314	7.5	104	3.1	194	106.4	168	94	845	129.0	749	369	18 411	60.1
Twin Falls	31 891	–.9	1 414	4.4	2 076	22.6	1 969	1 694	25 929	49.1	23 014	17 394	20 502	67.0
Valley	4 107	1.6	320	7.8	467	48.3	439	315	2 332	44.9	2 155	1 609	16 344	53.4
Washington	4 575	–1.0	392	8.6	229	17.4	214	195	2 010	28.0	2 028	1 570	19 424	63.5
ILLINOIS	6 419 316	.6	279 433	4.4	304 533	11.7	293 694	272 738	5 221 782	12.4	4 950 462	4 647 094	33 648	109.9
Adams	36 718	–1.6	1 224	3.3	1 867	7.5	1 842	1 736	29 994	9.9	30 190	27 295	24 471	79.9
Alexander	4 333	1.6	355	8.2	173	–20.6	199	218	1 673	–14.8	1 805	1 963	20 919	68.3
Bond	8 326	.4	353	4.2	348	16.4	561	299	3 747	13.5	4 627	3 300	19 886	65.0
Boone	22 478	1.2	1 167	5.2	708	26.2	681	561	11 626	21.7	11 620	9 554	36 236	118.4
Brown	3 053	–2.0	83	2.7	121	–10.4	130	135	1 781	63.2	1 344	1 091	24 034	78.5
Bureau	19 023	–1.1	1 047	5.5	872	1.0	889	863	10 210	23.4	10 588	8 273	23 712	77.5
Calhoun	3 294	–2.4	156	4.7	120	8.1	110	111	723	11.2	623	650	16 620	54.3
Carroll	8 837	–3.1	562	6.4	447	10.6	453	404	3 702	25.7	3 684	2 945	22 955	75.0
Cass	7 307	–1.5	348	4.8	308	–	309	308	4 566	14.0	4 801	4 005	21 001	68.6
Champaign	99 387	1.8	2 420	2.4	4 065	8.1	4 010	3 759	67 242	17.8	64 027	57 093	23 114	75.5
Christian	19 194	–.6	1 038	5.4	807	10.2	804	732	10 430	29.0	10 690	8 088	20 859	68.1
Clark	10 661	1.7	455	4.3	379	1.1	388	375	4 542	40.7	4 018	3 229	20 909	68.3
Clay	7 365	–.4	523	7.1	396	10.9	384	357	5 190	44.4	5 111	3 594	20 994	68.6
Clinton	17 614	.8	721	4.1	810	9.3	751	741	7 681	10.6	8 875	6 943	19 548	63.9
Coles	27 753	–1.6	1 140	4.1	1 278	10.9	1 255	1 152	20 024	14.1	19 440	17 548	23 666	77.3
Cook	2 694 904	1.0	125 430	4.7	127 124	5.6	124 980	120 330	2 446 113	3.2	2 374 539	2 371 289	37 401	122.2
Crawford	9 876	–1.0	599	6.1	472	11.8	470	422	6 854	38.7	5 913	4 940	29 116	95.1
Cumberland	5 649	–1.1	294	5.2	186	12.0	164	166	1 391	13.8	1 283	1 222	16 572	54.1
DeKalb	48 420	.7	1 571	3.2	1 915	15.4	1 821	1 659	24 294	6.6	24 695	22 797	24 496	80.0
De Witt	8 003	–4.8	588	7.3	405	16.4	381	348	5 357	–6.3	5 523	5 716	32 970	107.7
Douglas	13 098	2.7	450	3.4	627	26.9	582	494	7 193	30.8	6 578	5 500	23 235	75.9
DuPage	530 868	.8	13 994	2.6	31 672	21.8	29 412	26 012	586 425	25.9	508 351	465 785	37 735	123.3
Edgar	10 403	–1.8	420	4.0	412	–3.3	430	426	4 710	19.4	4 380	3 946	20 607	67.3
Edwards	3 870	1.9	202	5.2	175	–17.5	168	212	2 998	8.6	2 872	2 760	21 200	69.3
Effingham	18 404	–2.3	806	4.4	1 110	17.6	1 094	944	19 080	24.0	18 541	15 384	22 257	72.7
Fayette	10 930	.7	766	7.0	477	4.4	462	457	5 063	22.8	4 717	4 123	19 271	63.0
Ford	6 794	.8	242	3.6	416	2.7	416	405	4 071	9.0	3 615	3 735	20 522	67.0
Franklin	17 107	.2	1 271	7.4	893	5.4	886	847	8 468	–1.4	8 980	8 589	21 461	70.1
Fulton	13 969	–3.6	1 012	7.2	722	–1.0	752	729	7 219	3.2	7 163	6 998	17 500	57.2
Gallatin	2 810	–1.3	190	6.8	142	–2.1	139	145	1 220	–15.9	1 077	1 450	25 477	83.2
Greene	7 580	–.2	379	5.0	309	8.4	301	285	1 990	.1	1 934	1 989	16 444	53.7
Grundy	19 320	.4	1 126	5.8	901	20.3	835	749	10 864	5.4	10 498	10 305	30 653	100.1
Hamilton	3 754	.1	211	5.6	189	.5	203	188	1 123	40.4	1 228	800	16 551	54.1
Hancock	12 528	–2.6	538	4.3	510	2.4	490	498	4 754	18.1	4 641	4 027	21 135	69.0
Hardin	1 864	–1.1	132	7.1	74	–12.9	84	85	795	–12.3	816	907	19 293	63.0
Henderson	5 096	–.7	205	4.0	126	–8.7	124	138	596	–12.0	634	677	15 230	49.8
Henry	27 622	.4	1 569	5.7	1 161	5.6	1 130	1 099	13 728	14.1	12 996	12 033	20 552	67.1
Iroquois	15 829	–3.1	724	4.6	731	5.6	716	692	7 467	8.7	7 861	6 872	19 878	64.9
Jackson	30 553	.1	1 060	3.5	1 411	10.6	1 392	1 276	17 365	16.4	17 316	14 923	19 965	65.2
Jasper	3 943	–2.4	307	7.8	271	14.3	226	237	3 182	25.3	3 015	2 539	24 816	81.1
Jefferson	19 243	1.9	1 147	6.0	1 074	11.6	1 016	962	15 673	22.0	14 810	12 848	23 808	77.8
Jersey	10 828	.9	561	5.2	424	22.9	382	345	4 591	37.3	3 844	3 344	16 283	53.2
Jo Daviess	13 201	–.6	584	4.4	746	38.9	719	537	7 757	55.4	7 411	4 992	20 368	66.5
Johnson	5 137	.7	315	6.1	192	11.0	176	173	983	19.2	953	825	18 128	59.2
Kane	222 285	1.1	8 765	3.9	9 916	19.4	9 317	8 305	162 347	19.4	152 648	135 956	30 739	100.4

[1] Civilian unemployed as a percent of total civilian labor force. [2] For pay period including March 12 of the year shown.

Sources: Civilian Labor Force—U.S. Bureau of Labor Statistics; Local Area Unemployment Statistics; 2000 data published 2 May 2001, 1999 data published 30 May 2001; <ftp://ftp.bls.gov/pub/time.series/la/> (related Internet site <http://www.bls.gov/lauhome.htm>). Private Business Establishments and Employment—U.S. Census Bureau; County Business Patterns on CD-ROM; annual (related Internet site <http://www.census.gov/epcd/cbp/view/cbpview.html>).

[Includes U.S., states, and 3,142 counties/county equivalents defined as of January 1, 1992. For changes to these areas since January 1, 1992, see appendix B. Geographic Information]

County	Civilian labor force, 2000		Unemployment		Private nonfarm businesses									
					Establishments				Employment[2]				Annual payroll per employee, 1998	
	Total	Percent change, 1999–2000	Total	Rate[1]	1998	Percent change, 1990–1998	1995	1990	1998	Percent change, 1990–1998	1995	1990	Amount (dollars)	Percent of national average
ILLINOIS—Con.														
Kankakee	52 664	.3	2 554	4.8	2 304	14.9	2 240	2 005	57 571	86.6	55 258	30 853	24 833	81.1
Kendall	30 395	.9	841	2.8	1 069	66.3	780	643	10 793	75.4	8 663	6 155	25 655	83.8
Knox	29 610	–.5	1 369	4.6	1 311	4.5	1 269	1 255	22 401	15.0	20 999	19 480	21 751	71.1
Lake	334 994	1.1	12 022	3.6	17 633	33.0	15 967	13 255	291 924	40.3	261 383	208 054	38 541	125.9
La Salle	56 396	–2.3	3 373	6.0	2 924	5.7	2 880	2 767	37 258	11.2	35 872	33 493	25 072	81.9
Lawrence	7 112	4.6	512	7.2	371	14.2	344	325	4 285	50.0	4 234	2 856	21 418	70.0
Lee	18 244	–.5	759	4.2	785	2.2	772	768	11 043	15.0	10 532	9 599	24 322	79.5
Livingston	20 534	–.9	690	3.4	947	4.6	910	905	12 167	9.8	12 928	11 082	27 790	90.8
Logan	14 167	–1.7	511	3.6	733	6.2	716	690	8 765	4.9	9 421	8 357	21 369	69.8
McDonough	19 143	–1.7	553	2.9	798	8.1	800	738	10 198	20.0	9 560	8 500	18 853	61.6
McHenry	139 396	.9	4 503	3.2	6 503	41.7	5 780	4 588	83 558	44.0	68 790	58 007	29 225	95.5
McLean	94 195	2.9	2 315	2.5	3 523	16.3	3 410	3 028	76 943	24.4	69 224	61 839	30 775	100.5
Macon	61 175	.4	3 063	5.0	2 802	1.3	2 835	2 765	54 225	7.8	52 973	50 292	29 116	95.1
Macoupin	23 423	.4	1 152	4.9	1 067	10.9	1 027	962	9 918	13.9	10 144	8 709	21 109	69.0
Madison	132 126	.9	6 230	4.7	5 914	10.5	5 771	5 354	82 009	6.7	80 855	76 853	26 350	86.1
Marion	21 093	Z	1 394	6.6	1 172	–.3	1 223	1 176	15 658	11.0	15 431	14 106	23 216	75.8
Marshall	6 515	–2.5	269	4.1	306	–1.3	299	310	2 835	10.7	2 992	2 562	22 631	73.9
Mason	8 659	2.3	528	6.1	357	–4.3	366	373	2 762	17.3	2 653	2 355	20 144	65.8
Massac	8 202	1.2	408	5.0	285	13.5	281	251	4 525	58.0	4 443	2 864	26 646	87.1
Menard	6 315	.5	229	3.6	274	13.2	266	242	1 409	9.1	1 473	1 292	21 539	70.4
Mercer	9 576	1.7	616	6.4	339	13.0	329	300	2 478	32.4	2 308	1 871	18 345	59.9
Monroe	14 604	.9	458	3.1	598	27.5	550	469	5 356	18.5	4 966	4 520	22 857	74.7
Montgomery	15 895	.7	930	5.9	778	6.0	762	734	8 639	9.2	8 049	7 910	21 033	68.7
Morgan	19 092	–.4	760	4.0	933	3.9	901	898	14 867	1.3	14 008	14 682	22 740	74.3
Moultrie	8 447	3.9	332	3.9	318	15.6	291	275	3 317	16.6	3 465	2 845	18 943	61.9
Ogle	28 401	.5	1 184	4.2	1 004	8.1	1 001	929	15 456	16.3	14 664	13 295	26 572	86.8
Peoria	95 579	.1	4 141	4.3	4 866	4.7	5 046	4 647	107 509	18.6	104 260	90 671	32 022	104.6
Perry	9 055	.1	877	9.7	458	–3.4	454	474	5 030	–16.3	4 859	6 009	19 088	62.4
Piatt	8 132	–3.1	282	3.5	359	6.5	372	337	2 553	–1.5	3 011	2 593	22 246	72.7
Pike	9 139	–1.0	501	5.5	398	–.5	414	400	3 310	18.9	3 200	2 783	17 860	58.3
Pope	1 797	–.7	150	8.3	67	21.8	65	55	(3)	NA	410	400	D	D
Pulaski	3 220	.5	274	8.5	132	10.0	128	120	1 363	30.9	1 034	1 041	27 408	89.5
Putnam	3 198	–1.5	171	5.3	134	12.6	132	119	1 738	20.3	1 617	1 445	37 262	121.7
Randolph	14 120	–1.2	766	5.4	770	4.2	763	739	10 720	14.3	11 135	9 382	22 720	74.2
Richland	8 749	–4.6	595	6.8	502	4.4	507	481	6 921	43.1	6 771	4 836	19 008	62.1
Rock Island	76 637	–.7	3 992	5.2	3 676	5.4	3 619	3 489	67 400	7.0	63 641	62 973	31 046	101.4
St. Clair	118 643	1.0	6 960	5.9	5 503	10.5	5 239	4 978	74 339	16.9	70 013	63 565	23 701	77.4
Saline	10 596	–.4	884	8.3	701	1.6	695	690	8 178	1.0	7 898	8 095	19 370	63.3
Sangamon	101 464	.5	3 636	3.6	5 357	16.0	5 248	4 618	80 769	17.4	78 235	68 820	25 707	84.0
Schuyler	4 264	–3.7	229	5.4	167	–1.8	183	170	1 326	15.2	1 336	1 151	20 333	66.4
Scott	2 951	–.6	152	5.2	108	–12.9	117	124	886	–15.6	993	1 050	48 843	159.6
Shelby	11 426	–2.5	586	5.1	498	19.1	482	418	4 793	16.5	4 882	4 114	20 859	68.1
Stark	2 876	–3.7	183	6.4	135	5.5	129	128	968	44.5	906	670	19 205	62.7
Stephenson	24 927	–2.9	1 558	6.3	1 122	6.1	1 132	1 057	21 597	13.4	20 651	19 048	28 679	93.7
Tazewell	71 215	–.4	2 622	3.7	2 783	13.1	2 663	2 460	41 640	12.1	39 518	37 158	29 085	95.0
Union	8 539	–.2	552	6.5	364	8.7	342	335	4 770	13.6	4 480	4 200	20 393	66.6
Vermilion	39 035	–.5	2 558	6.6	1 853	–1.3	1 857	1 878	29 209	.3	28 945	29 133	25 724	84.0
Wabash	4 999	–.1	402	8.0	325	–6.9	327	349	3 838	–30.5	4 801	5 521	20 399	66.6
Warren	10 184	–.4	435	4.3	378	–9.8	400	419	4 383	–14.3	4 807	5 113	18 396	60.1
Washington	8 814	–5.6	348	3.9	415	18.2	380	351	5 733	67.9	4 534	3 415	25 854	84.5
Wayne	8 257	–1.8	561	6.8	399	–1.7	412	406	3 719	11.7	3 799	3 329	21 222	69.3
White	7 275	–1.8	369	5.1	432	4.6	448	413	3 630	20.1	3 629	3 022	20 006	65.4
Whiteside	31 846	–1.5	1 267	4.0	1 442	12.8	1 390	1 278	21 890	16.6	20 683	18 780	24 627	80.5
Will	252 514	1.0	10 131	4.0	9 348	43.9	7 841	6 497	124 757	38.4	109 546	90 171	31 590	103.2
Williamson	29 386	1.3	1 933	6.6	1 531	22.7	1 434	1 248	20 365	40.9	16 970	14 449	20 314	66.4
Winnebago	151 515	.6	7 182	4.7	7 031	8.2	7 012	6 501	132 076	9.5	130 756	120 603	28 924	94.5
Woodford	19 371	–.2	537	2.8	718	29.1	632	556	8 309	45.3	7 083	5 720	23 546	76.9
INDIANA	3 084 135	.3	100 203	3.2	146 197	13.9	141 253	128 311	2 540 866	18.2	2 403 189	2 150 168	28 115	91.9
Adams	16 443	1.3	569	3.5	762	9.6	724	695	13 634	22.1	13 045	11 162	24 671	80.6
Allen	174 169	.1	5 307	3.0	8 813	9.1	8 557	8 077	178 109	6.3	166 194	167 485	28 822	94.2
Bartholomew	38 402	–1.7	905	2.4	2 019	18.3	1 925	1 707	36 972	14.1	36 088	32 416	27 032	88.3
Benton	5 200	–3.3	172	3.3	268	14.0	273	235	2 023	.8	2 010	2 007	19 679	64.3
Blackford	6 273	–1.8	370	5.9	293	3.2	284	284	3 816	1.6	4 002	3 756	22 589	73.8
Boone	25 159	2.3	425	1.7	1 214	24.6	1 136	974	11 516	27.9	11 078	9 004	22 890	74.8
Brown	8 577	–1.8	206	2.4	386	24.1	365	311	2 191	16.7	1 952	1 878	15 226	49.7
Carroll	11 957	–2.9	302	2.5	429	20.2	385	357	4 605	34.8	4 658	3 415	21 837	71.3
Cass	19 561	–1.4	650	3.3	870	–3.1	869	898	16 482	17.7	14 786	14 004	22 859	74.7

[1] Civilian unemployed as a percent of total civilian labor force.   [2] For pay period including March 12 of the year shown.   [3] 250–499 employees.

Sources: Civilian Labor Force—U.S. Bureau of Labor Statistics; Local Area Unemployment Statistics; 2000 data published 2 May 2001, 1999 data published 30 May 2001; <ftp://ftp.bls.gov/pub/time.series/la/> (related Internet site <http://www.bls.gov/lauhome.htm>).   Private Business Establishments and Employment—U.S. Census Bureau; County Business Patterns on CD-ROM; annual (related Internet site <http://www.census.gov/epcd/cbp/view/cbpview.html>).

Table B–7. Counties — Labor Force and Private Business Establishments and Employment–Con.

[Includes U.S., states, and 3,142 counties/county equivalents defined as of January 1, 1992. For changes to these areas since January 1, 1992, see appendix B. Geographic Information]

County	Civilian labor force, 2000				Private nonfarm businesses									
			Unemployment		Establishments				Employment²				Annual payroll per employee, 1998	
	Total	Percent change, 1999–2000	Total	Rate¹	1998	Percent change, 1990–1998	1995	1990	1998	Percent change, 1990–1998	1995	1990	Amount (dollars)	Percent of national average
INDIANA—Con.														
Clark	53 345	1.4	1 741	3.3	2 427	22.8	2 314	1 976	39 066	30.8	35 410	29 863	25 061	81.9
Clay	12 480	1.1	605	4.8	543	20.1	548	452	5 610	21.6	6 535	4 614	19 732	64.5
Clinton	15 713	−.3	426	2.7	717	3.3	727	694	10 910	31.1	10 617	8 324	23 083	75.4
Crawford	5 273	−.5	313	5.9	159	18.7	152	134	1 305	36.4	1 141	957	16 934	55.3
Daviess	13 503	−1.2	477	3.5	750	13.5	731	661	8 955	22.2	8 086	7 329	18 873	61.7
Dearborn	23 598	Z	730	3.1	982	37.7	952	713	12 648	46.3	10 581	8 646	24 659	80.6
Decatur	16 811	−.1	338	2.0	622	16.0	591	536	11 852	55.6	9 670	7 619	24 909	81.4
De Kalb	21 763	.3	751	3.5	986	26.1	882	782	21 324	55.4	17 384	13 719	30 581	99.9
Delaware	58 956	−2.4	1 952	3.3	2 762	6.4	2 753	2 597	49 162	11.1	49 968	44 235	24 430	79.8
Dubois	22 699	−1.3	514	2.3	1 226	15.8	1 163	1 059	27 299	29.7	25 321	21 054	27 454	89.7
Elkhart	98 037	1.5	2 777	2.8	5 030	8.5	4 993	4 637	109 830	16.3	110 515	94 406	27 618	90.2
Fayette	10 397	−4.6	627	6.0	554	11.7	541	496	10 103	−2.7	10 197	10 382	30 919	101.0
Floyd	39 298	1.5	1 161	3.0	1 747	31.7	1 605	1 326	25 635	53.8	22 233	16 672	22 464	73.4
Fountain	8 423	−2.3	293	3.5	383	1.9	385	376	4 886	21.1	4 369	4 034	22 852	74.7
Franklin	11 230	2.9	407	3.6	355	26.8	320	280	3 687	59.1	3 158	2 317	21 405	69.9
Fulton	9 807	−1.1	570	5.8	511	7.6	489	475	6 608	9.9	6 982	6 015	23 485	76.7
Gibson	17 597	5.6	673	3.8	756	4.1	732	726	10 281	21.0	8 868	8 495	24 057	78.6
Grant	31 929	−2.6	1 454	4.6	1 565	−.1	1 562	1 566	30 690	−.7	30 836	30 891	25 296	82.6
Greene	13 620	−4.8	956	7.0	640	9.0	701	587	5 899	9.8	6 304	5 371	18 058	59.0
Hamilton	99 980	2.5	1 377	1.4	5 000	58.5	4 275	3 155	72 679	84.4	56 343	39 408	35 183	114.9
Hancock	31 031	2.4	640	2.1	1 219	30.8	1 103	932	12 918	40.3	11 533	9 209	28 548	93.3
Harrison	19 046	1.1	546	2.9	649	21.1	617	536	7 731	49.5	7 062	5 171	20 149	65.8
Hendricks	55 289	2.4	915	1.7	2 061	59.6	1 732	1 291	22 967	86.3	17 517	12 331	23 316	76.2
Henry	23 676	−2.0	966	4.1	951	3.1	950	922	12 480	16.7	11 764	10 695	28 699	93.8
Howard	41 395	−.7	1 356	3.3	1 997	8.8	1 944	1 836	43 994	16.5	42 992	37 772	38 243	124.9
Huntington	20 369	.9	775	3.8	905	18.1	898	766	15 804	16.5	18 286	13 563	23 288	76.1
Jackson	21 640	.8	582	2.7	1 100	26.7	1 002	868	18 245	21.5	18 167	15 011	24 542	80.2
Jasper	14 297	Z	587	4.1	752	25.1	742	601	8 709	42.7	8 470	6 101	23 855	77.9
Jay	10 336	−3.7	407	3.9	449	7.4	460	418	7 372	15.7	6 900	6 374	19 897	65.0
Jefferson	13 235	−1.9	518	3.9	742	14.0	699	651	11 885	12.4	11 573	10 578	23 690	77.4
Jennings	14 325	−1.3	410	2.9	428	23.0	400	348	7 527	50.3	7 603	5 008	23 360	76.3
Johnson	63 956	2.4	1 200	1.9	2 684	30.0	2 524	2 065	37 074	43.7	32 446	25 800	22 362	73.1
Knox	18 815	−.9	768	4.1	1 052	2.5	1 039	1 026	14 476	28.0	14 453	11 312	21 217	69.3
Kosciusko	38 295	1.2	1 079	2.8	1 896	16.8	1 781	1 623	31 645	17.8	29 564	26 853	30 610	100.0
Lagrange	17 097	−1.4	476	2.8	685	28.0	650	535	10 000	25.6	10 445	7 964	25 661	83.8
Lake	219 092	−1.7	10 181	4.6	10 186	10.7	9 958	9 200	175 897	5.2	167 675	167 177	29 769	97.3
La Porte	52 908	.2	2 012	3.8	2 692	16.4	2 621	2 312	40 123	9.9	39 137	36 500	24 689	80.7
Lawrence	22 308	−1.3	1 078	4.8	890	14.7	886	776	13 990	26.1	13 960	11 093	24 860	81.2
Madison	65 885	2.4	2 171	3.3	2 780	7.8	2 712	2 579	43 904	.3	42 875	43 759	26 993	88.2
Marion	452 372	2.4	13 130	2.9	24 348	9.4	23 910	22 246	534 151	14.2	500 953	467 671	33 074	108.1
Marshall	24 205	−1.8	881	3.6	1 133	13.3	1 101	1 000	18 712	42.9	18 193	13 097	23 825	77.8
Martin	5 008	−1.5	199	4.0	227	9.1	227	208	2 244	−4.4	2 307	2 348	22 528	73.6
Miami	15 950	3.2	673	4.2	686	14.1	652	601	7 892	24.6	7 433	6 336	21 558	70.4
Monroe	60 420	−.7	1 226	2.0	2 874	12.8	2 815	2 549	45 630	18.4	41 990	38 545	23 285	76.1
Montgomery	17 566	−1.4	473	2.7	923	8.0	901	855	16 042	12.0	16 314	14 326	27 438	89.6
Morgan	36 210	2.2	860	2.4	1 293	29.9	1 197	995	12 549	16.1	12 080	10 812	22 836	74.6
Newton	6 302	−1.8	231	3.7	289	16.1	267	249	3 135	24.8	2 913	2 513	21 263	69.5
Noble	24 759	2.2	846	3.4	943	8.5	904	869	18 396	26.2	18 757	14 575	28 489	93.1
Ohio	2 663	.5	96	3.6	74	10.4	61	67	2 011	474.6	487	350	17 585	57.4
Orange	8 517	−2.8	525	6.2	387	10.9	394	349	6 966	18.4	6 787	5 884	21 162	69.1
Owen	10 787	−.5	350	3.2	313	28.8	289	243	3 282	45.9	2 732	2 250	19 400	63.4
Parke	7 602	−.8	289	3.8	293	5.0	294	279	2 295	10.0	2 272	2 087	17 839	58.3
Perry	8 837	−1.8	566	6.4	412	15.1	392	358	4 652	13.3	4 685	4 107	21 777	71.1
Pike	6 269	−.9	278	4.4	199	−2.5	194	204	2 058	20.1	2 086	1 714	28 332	92.6
Porter	74 214	−1.9	2 405	3.2	3 247	32.5	2 964	2 451	49 032	25.2	47 796	39 178	30 522	99.7
Posey	13 770	−.1	434	3.2	554	14.9	520	482	7 248	15.3	7 405	6 288	32 189	105.2
Pulaski	5 739	−6.6	393	6.8	341	20.1	321	284	3 700	18.9	3 692	3 113	25 584	83.6
Putnam	17 654	5.6	362	2.1	674	19.7	651	563	10 414	35.2	10 191	7 705	19 612	64.1
Randolph	10 881	−4.2	546	5.0	552	−3.2	587	570	6 184	−17.7	7 347	7 517	22 964	75.0
Ripley	13 795	2.1	379	2.7	727	25.6	678	579	10 596	16.3	10 242	9 109	30 864	100.8
Rush	9 263	−7.3	254	2.7	421	18.6	395	355	4 650	39.8	4 323	3 325	20 344	66.5
St. Joseph	134 598	.2	4 550	3.4	6 597	4.6	6 611	6 307	120 449	15.5	117 353	104 286	26 787	87.5
Scott	11 188	1.0	358	3.2	444	28.0	434	347	5 935	51.3	5 757	3 923	21 913	71.6
Shelby	23 748	2.0	649	2.7	938	15.2	909	814	15 042	23.7	14 709	12 158	26 858	87.7
Spencer	11 806	Z	496	4.2	428	13.5	396	377	5 710	17.8	5 584	4 849	26 906	87.9
Starke	10 600	−1.2	670	6.3	356	7.9	331	330	3 698	19.6	3 791	3 091	19 270	63.0
Steuben	17 256	−2.1	592	3.4	1 020	29.1	920	790	22 240	78.4	15 562	12 463	24 013	78.4
Sullivan	9 417	−.5	587	6.2	400	12.7	410	355	4 165	18.6	4 230	3 512	24 176	79.0
Switzerland	3 397	−7.5	335	9.9	111	19.4	112	93	1 235	8.5	1 273	1 138	17 936	58.6
Tippecanoe	73 858	−.3	1 695	2.3	3 100	13.5	2 992	2 732	61 322	26.2	55 580	48 580	27 864	91.0

¹ Civilian unemployed as a percent of total civilian labor force.   ² For pay period including March 12 of the year shown.

Sources: Civilian Labor Force—U.S. Bureau of Labor Statistics; Local Area Unemployment Statistics; 2000 data published 2 May 2001, 1999 data published 30 May 2001; <ftp://ftp.bls.gov/pub/time.series/la/> (related Internet site <http://www.bls.gov/lauhome.htm>).   Private Business Establishments and Employment—U.S. Census Bureau; County Business Patterns on CD-ROM; annual (related Internet site <http://www.census.gov/epcd/cbp/view/cbpview.html>).

[Includes U.S., states, and 3,142 counties/county equivalents defined as of January 1, 1992. For changes to these areas since January 1, 1992, see appendix B. Geographic Information]

County	Civilian labor force, 2000		Unemployment		Private nonfarm businesses								Annual payroll per employee, 1998	
					Establishments				Employment[2]					
	Total	Percent change, 1999–2000	Total	Rate[1]	1998	Percent change, 1990–1998	1995	1990	1998	Percent change, 1990–1998	1995	1990	Amount (dollars)	Percent of national average
INDIANA—Con.														
Tipton	8 603	–1.0	223	2.6	333	7.8	324	309	3 834	47.2	3 384	2 605	24 592	80.3
Union	3 733	–4.0	127	3.4	135	–4.3	139	141	929	35.4	855	686	18 916	61.8
Vanderburgh	90 206	–.2	2 973	3.3	5 347	6.5	5 196	5 019	105 914	14.2	102 461	92 710	26 857	87.7
Vermillion	7 761	1.0	459	5.9	288	4.7	283	275	4 563	48.2	4 099	3 079	32 765	107.0
Vigo	49 572	.7	2 364	4.8	2 678	8.3	2 682	2 473	45 531	7.4	46 777	42 410	23 544	76.9
Wabash	17 111	–1.4	567	3.3	833	6.4	874	783	12 851	1.0	13 203	12 721	23 422	76.5
Warren	3 863	–1.3	131	3.4	116	18.4	109	98	977	25.4		986	779	21 850	71.4
Warrick	29 150	.4	1 034	3.5	1 010	16.8	969	865	11 105	3.9	10 796	10 686	26 723	87.3
Washington	11 668	–	526	4.5	468	29.6	429	361	5 878	19.7	5 490	4 912	20 864	68.2
Wayne	36 242	–3.8	1 449	4.0	1 748	7.2	1 775	1 630	31 912	15.1	30 046	27 720	23 880	78.0
Wells	14 469	.3	377	2.6	638	11.1	628	574	10 510	31.7	9 257	7 980	23 665	77.3
White	13 344	–1.5	460	3.4	717	20.1	689	597	9 298	40.7	9 526	6 610	22 311	72.9
Whitley	16 576	.4	477	2.9	674	18.7	655	568	10 845	49.1	10 195	7 276	24 427	79.8
IOWA	1 563 063	–.6	40 922	2.6	80 838	10.5	78 464	73 130	1 213 285	20.4	1 138 402	1 007 900	25 064	81.9
Adair	4 511	2.4	110	2.4	212	–1.9	214	216	2 064	13.7	1 922	1 816	22 119	72.3
Adams	2 083	–8.0	92	4.4	128	2.4	126	125	945	22.6	1 082	771	19 044	62.2
Allamakee	7 325	–1.5	292	4.0	439	10.9	407	396	4 526	29.2	4 246	3 503	17 290	56.5
Appanoose	6 461	–3.7	278	4.3	346	5.5	328	328	3 571	19.1	3 344	2 998	18 944	61.9
Audubon	3 291	–4.8	99	3.0	230	15.6	217	199	1 432	10.7	1 503	1 294	16 794	54.9
Benton	11 607	.6	289	2.5	611	12.3	575	544	4 421	26.6	4 149	3 493	21 574	70.5
Black Hawk	66 958	–.7	2 050	3.1	3 210	6.6	3 134	3 011	58 478	24.1	54 088	47 126	25 485	83.3
Boone	14 154	.3	299	2.1	574	13.4	535	506	6 785	5.5	6 576	6 430	21 635	70.7
Bremer	12 332	–.8	266	2.2	631	8.0	631	584	7 938	5.3	7 142	7 538	22 858	74.7
Buchanan	10 712	–1.9	329	3.1	547	17.6	508	465	5 210	40.1	4 499	3 718	22 572	73.7
Buena Vista	10 639	–2.7	234	2.2	627	3.8	621	604	8 282	22.7	7 860	6 748	19 861	64.9
Butler	7 112	–6.9	270	3.8	389	5.7	377	368	2 270	13.8	2 442	1 995	17 253	56.4
Calhoun	4 687	–3.1	136	2.9	317	.3	339	316	2 444	7.3	2 496	2 278	15 992	52.2
Carroll	12 249	–2.1	288	2.4	842	12.7	829	747	10 289	36.2	8 744	7 552	20 172	65.9
Cass	7 183	–4.6	307	4.3	502	3.1	499	487	5 519	13.8	5 398	4 850	21 790	71.2
Cedar	9 266	–1.5	220	2.4	496	11.7	461	444	3 896	21.4	3 897	3 209	18 475	60.4
Cerro Gordo	25 492	–1.2	776	3.0	1 480	5.9	1 481	1 398	22 580	17.8	20 169	19 165	21 988	71.8
Cherokee	6 717	–2.0	145	2.2	391	2.6	376	381	4 283	3.8	4 307	4 128	22 227	72.6
Chickasaw	7 042	–7.6	564	8.0	399	8.4	390	368	4 156	11.9	4 073	3 715	22 298	72.8
Clarke	5 150	14.0	161	3.1	237	20.9	210	196	3 008	18.6	2 407	2 536	19 957	65.2
Clay	10 130	1.8	246	2.4	625	5.4	619	593	8 347	35.9	7 051	6 142	20 647	67.5
Clayton	9 981	–3.3	399	4.0	571	7.5	536	531	5 519	27.5	4 586	4 330	19 958	65.2
Clinton	25 991	–1.4	922	3.5	1 319	8.6	1 268	1 215	19 264	14.5	18 357	16 831	22 144	72.3
Crawford	8 654	–1.6	195	2.3	477	–.8	481	481	5 508	15.4	5 226	4 775	18 952	61.9
Dallas	20 700	.3	331	1.6	828	35.3	752	612	9 216	73.3	7 620	5 317	24 438	79.8
Davis	4 119	–1.0	116	2.8	179	2.9	177	174	1 654	39.1	1 604	1 189	18 629	60.9
Decatur	3 523	–2.9	163	4.6	174	3.0	169	169	2 402	12.5	2 347	2 135	13 954	45.6
Delaware	9 352	–.9	336	3.6	455	10.2	429	413	4 351	38.4	3 708	3 144	21 273	69.5
Des Moines	23 282	.2	770	3.3	1 231	3.8	1 225	1 186	20 967	9.8	20 376	19 101	24 272	79.3
Dickinson	9 787	1.4	235	2.4	728	19.7	689	608	7 040	36.3	7 068	5 164	21 996	71.9
Dubuque	48 515	–.1	1 612	3.3	2 599	10.3	2 567	2 357	47 588	12.8	47 808	42 195	24 888	81.3
Emmet	5 461	–.8	166	3.0	305	7.8	305	283	3 510	27.2	2 791	2 759	20 700	67.6
Fayette	10 803	–2.9	455	4.2	654	5.1	638	622	7 177	36.4	6 798	5 262	18 884	61.7
Floyd	7 569	–1.9	333	4.4	462	3.6	458	446	4 416	–8.3	4 491	4 815	19 598	64.0
Franklin	5 583	–5.4	153	2.7	342	12.5	334	304	3 034	21.2	2 614	2 503	22 194	72.5
Fremont	3 744	–2.1	86	2.3	187	–1.1	197	189	1 497	.9	1 336	1 483	19 971	65.2
Greene	4 792	–3.7	165	3.4	313	9.1	306	287	2 578	26.7	2 311	2 034	20 232	66.1
Grundy	6 038	–2.0	117	1.9	321	2.2	325	314	2 619	21.6	2 515	2 153	24 295	79.4
Guthrie	5 805	–2.9	148	2.5	291	15.9	277	251	1 841	12.5	1 883	1 637	16 714	54.6
Hamilton	8 350	–3.3	197	2.4	454	7.6	440	422	6 423	8.7	6 125	5 911	23 290	76.1
Hancock	9 504	–2.3	154	1.6	331	–3.8	351	344	3 033	5.1	3 870	2 887	21 195	69.2
Hardin	8 924	–4.3	265	3.0	656	.6	660	652	7 088	33.3	6 813	5 318	20 797	67.9
Harrison	7 816	.7	207	2.6	365	11.6	336	327	2 958	29.8	2 627	2 279	17 913	58.5
Henry	10 643	–2.4	295	2.8	539	11.4	518	484	11 127	23.0	10 343	9 045	22 909	74.8
Howard	5 426	–2.3	175	3.2	293	16.3	284	252	3 449	94.7	2 898	1 771	21 337	69.7
Humboldt	5 318	–3.4	125	2.4	315	1.3	313	311	3 944	62.3	2 967	2 430	19 655	64.2
Ida	3 869	–5.3	82	2.1	267	15.1	266	232	3 285	29.1	2 999	2 545	22 751	74.3
Iowa	9 305	.1	161	1.7	519	24.8	499	416	9 196	47.1	9 170	6 252	26 227	85.7
Jackson	10 209	–2.0	444	4.3	575	22.3	550	470	5 119	23.6	5 022	4 143	16 558	54.1
Jasper	19 493	1.8	410	2.1	852	12.4	820	758	13 041	29.6	11 647	10 064	24 818	81.1
Jefferson	9 370	–2.8	254	2.7	685	25.2	646	547	8 048	16.5	7 821	6 908	26 736	87.3
Johnson	68 494	1.6	1 420	2.1	2 607	25.6	2 413	2 076	45 266	20.9	42 798	37 436	23 694	77.4
Jones	9 475	–1.3	237	2.5	502	17.0	466	429	4 142	20.2	3 938	3 446	18 406	60.1
Keokuk	4 906	–3.4	200	4.1	272	–2.2	277	278	1 921	14.5	1 953	1 677	18 828	61.5

[1] Civilian unemployed as a percent of total civilian labor force. [2] For pay period including March 12 of the year shown.

Sources: Civilian Labor Force—U.S. Bureau of Labor Statistics; Local Area Unemployment Statistics; 2000 data published 2 May 2001, 1999 data published 30 May 2001; <ftp://ftp.bls.gov/pub/time.series/la/> (related Internet site <http://www.bls.gov/lauhome.htm>). Private Business Establishments and Employment—U.S. Census Bureau; County Business Patterns on CD-ROM; annual (related Internet site <http://www.census.gov/epcd/cbp/view/cbpview.html>).

[Includes U.S., states, and 3,142 counties/county equivalents defined as of January 1, 1992. For changes to these areas since January 1, 1992, see appendix B. Geographic Information]

| County | Civilian labor force, 2000 | | Unemployment | | Private nonfarm businesses | | | | | | | | Annual payroll per employee, 1998 | |
| | Total | Percent change, 1999-2000 | Total | Rate[1] | Establishments | | | | Employment[2] | | | | Amount (dollars) | Percent of national average |
					1998	Percent change, 1990-1998	1995	1990	1998	Percent change, 1990-1998	1995	1990		
IOWA—Con.														
Kossuth	8 245	−4.8	229	2.8	566	10.3	550	513	5 379	13.1	5 006	4 755	19 716	64.4
Lee	18 486	−2.6	865	4.7	1 062	4.7	1 052	1 014	16 666	14.3	15 949	14 580	24 474	80.0
Linn	114 258	1.2	2 098	1.8	5 297	18.2	5 081	4 482	110 504	27.0	98 757	87 000	31 095	101.6
Louisa	5 353	−1.9	181	3.4	222	−.4	229	223	2 586	−2.2	3 109	2 643	20 341	66.5
Lucas	3 939	−2.5	113	2.9	209	11.2	196	188	2 603	1.4	2 409	2 566	23 231	75.9
Lyon	5 306	−3.8	121	2.3	354	14.6	340	309	2 473	33.4	2 133	1 854	17 135	56.0
Madison	7 141	−5.6	258	3.6	337	16.2	335	290	2 705	38.4	2 381	1 955	18 450	60.3
Mahaska	10 969	−5.2	231	2.1	594	9.4	560	543	6 375	12.3	6 047	5 677	19 798	64.7
Marion	18 894	4.6	403	2.1	778	14.9	732	677	15 918	31.6	14 533	12 100	26 640	87.0
Marshall	19 971	−1.6	508	2.5	928	1.8	917	912	15 521	11.8	15 156	13 886	24 850	81.2
Mills	6 178	−1.7	112	1.8	241	4.8	245	230	2 707	−16.1	3 053	3 225	23 094	75.4
Mitchell	5 319	−2.3	142	2.7	348	8.1	350	322	3 212	34.4	2 963	2 390	19 201	62.7
Monona	4 784	−4.3	153	3.2	288	.3	284	287	2 736	18.3	2 871	2 312	17 262	56.4
Monroe	4 115	−.3	118	2.9	212	16.5	201	182	2 655	83.6	2 371	1 446	21 791	71.2
Montgomery	5 714	−2.3	193	3.4	349	6.1	339	329	4 664	15.5	4 087	4 037	19 672	64.3
Muscatine	21 475	.1	595	2.8	996	3.9	993	959	19 834	11.8	18 183	17 740	29 441	96.2
O'Brien	7 626	−2.1	161	2.1	559	8.8	532	514	5 264	11.3	4 975	4 728	17 905	58.5
Osceola	3 580	−8.4	83	2.3	213	4.4	212	204	1 825	20.7	1 680	1 512	19 127	62.5
Page	8 856	−.9	241	2.7	507	−1.6	525	515	6 714	14.0	6 581	5 890	22 514	73.6
Palo Alto	5 101	−5.2	104	2.0	333	7.8	337	309	2 687	33.7	2 637	2 010	15 978	52.2
Plymouth	13 101	1.1	356	2.7	682	9.6	617	622	8 024	31.9	7 487	6 082	24 791	81.0
Pocahontas	3 685	−9.8	105	2.8	278	−5.4	288	294	2 424	8.9	2 636	2 226	19 965	65.2
Polk	212 859	.5	4 316	2.0	11 307	12.3	11 008	10 068	229 586	17.6	221 914	195 268	30 211	98.7
Pottawattamie	48 530	2.3	1 094	2.3	1 896	6.4	1 810	1 782	28 219	27.8	23 776	22 089	22 056	72.1
Poweshiek	10 101	−.9	309	3.1	578	10.5	557	523	8 729	10.7	8 736	7 886	23 073	75.4
Ringgold	2 525	−3.0	73	2.9	135	−3.6	128	140	999	23.6	952	808	18 694	61.1
Sac	5 693	−3.2	153	2.7	387	2.4	369	378	2 651	14.0	2 546	2 326	16 484	53.9
Scott	85 191	.2	2 401	2.8	4 523	12.4	4 369	4 025	78 006	25.3	70 022	62 261	26 638	87.0
Shelby	6 670	−2.8	160	2.4	411	2.5	416	401	4 457	24.1	4 040	3 592	17 797	58.1
Sioux	17 433	−.7	405	2.3	1 095	24.7	1 057	878	15 280	28.9	13 307	11 855	18 938	61.9
Story	45 838	.2	944	2.1	1 842	10.4	1 842	1 669	26 903	17.7	26 099	22 857	22 714	74.2
Tama	8 496	−6.1	320	3.8	400	8.1	393	370	4 689	39.7	4 650	3 357	19 253	62.9
Taylor	3 256	−2.8	116	3.6	174	−2.2	183	178	961	−46.1	1 341	1 783	16 320	53.3
Union	6 285	−3.2	222	3.5	354	2.0	350	347	4 530	16.7	4 101	3 883	19 723	64.4
Van Buren	4 028	−2.0	130	3.2	179	7.2	187	167	1 590	50.6	1 383	1 050	20 795	67.9
Wapello	17 171	−.5	596	3.5	883	7.0	879	825	12 664	10.2	12 692	11 493	22 821	74.6
Warren	23 183	.5	433	1.9	765	22.4	690	625	6 911	29.6	6 030	5 334	18 004	58.8
Washington	11 035	−.9	223	2.0	686	18.7	644	578	5 971	33.7	5 635	4 467	20 988	68.6
Wayne	2 829	−4.4	83	2.9	197	1.0	195	195	1 508	10.2	1 678	1 368	16 768	54.8
Webster	19 689	−1.7	566	2.9	1 219	5.4	1 217	1 156	16 687	12.6	15 729	14 822	23 866	78.0
Winnebago	4 549	−3.7	117	2.6	354	8.9	337	325	7 342	54.5	7 147	4 753	24 499	80.0
Winneshiek	12 074	−5.0	383	3.2	597	7.0	579	558	8 975	20.5	8 106	7 450	19 547	63.9
Woodbury	52 932	−1.0	1 439	2.7	2 949	10.0	2 842	2 681	48 205	13.3	45 325	42 564	22 938	74.9
Worth	3 975	−1.1	133	3.3	191	12.4	192	170	1 579	13.2	1 391	1 395	18 900	61.7
Wright	6 735	.9	163	2.4	453	6.3	443	426	4 571	18.3	4 771	3 863	21 783	71.2
KANSAS	1 411 024	−1.6	52 323	3.7	74 019	12.4	70 894	65 858	1 081 941	21.0	982 066	893 830	26 570	86.8
Allen	7 393	.7	383	5.2	410	−.2	442	411	4 872	4.9	5 649	4 643	21 206	69.3
Anderson	3 984	−1.0	194	4.9	241	26.8	211	190	1 515	25.1	1 328	1 211	15 556	50.8
Atchison	8 940	−.1	400	4.5	392	8.6	399	361	5 485	16.1	5 573	4 724	23 277	76.0
Barber	2 421	−2.1	63	2.6	209	8.9	203	192	1 377	−4.2	1 373	1 437	21 126	69.0
Barton	14 158	−4.7	476	3.4	1 070	5.0	1 107	1 019	10 939	5.6	11 048	10 355	20 840	68.1
Bourbon	6 934	−.1	325	4.7	429	−32.3	456	634	6 522	23.6	6 034	5 276	20 551	67.1
Brown	5 944	.5	342	5.8	293	5.4	285	278	3 818	31.3	2 813	2 908	18 242	59.6
Butler	31 595	−1.9	1 263	4.0	1 219	24.3	1 113	981	11 075	22.7	10 100	9 024	22 028	72.0
Chase	1 433	−3.9	45	3.1	67	−5.6	73	71	406	−44.7	677	734	15 150	49.5
Chautauqua	1 630	−5.2	77	4.7	99	22.2	98	81	614	−11.0	645	690	12 993	42.4
Cherokee	10 172	−1.5	571	5.6	401	15.9	401	346	5 343	23.3	5 583	4 333	21 943	71.7
Cheyenne	1 507	−5.0	26	1.7	109	−4.4	112	114	572	−2.4	570	586	15 885	51.9
Clark	1 324	−1.4	29	2.2	82	−13.7	90	95	468	37.6	428	340	19 996	65.3
Clay	4 754	−3.1	143	3.0	304	22.1	286	249	2 501	37.0	2 433	1 825	17 485	57.1
Cloud	4 928	−1.9	179	3.6	356	9.9	338	324	3 057	2.2	2 984	2 992	18 170	59.4
Coffey	3 927	−6.3	192	4.9	266	19.8	247	222	2 935	137.3	2 701	1 237	31 856	104.1
Comanche	946	−8.4	12	1.3	79	−6.0	76	84	431	1.9	369	423	14 961	48.9
Cowley	17 033	−4.2	862	5.1	853	5.6	838	808	11 845	8.6	11 397	10 908	21 803	71.2
Crawford	18 531	−.6	826	4.5	1 006	15.6	924	870	13 684	26.5	12 667	10 819	20 301	66.3
Decatur	1 554	−7.0	32	2.1	122	−10.9	134	137	815	−9.0	865	896	14 811	48.4
Dickinson	10 073	−4.1	302	3.0	547	3.4	574	529	5 613	35.3	4 767	4 150	18 679	61.0

[1] Civilian unemployed as a percent of total civilian labor force. [2] For pay period including March 12 of the year shown.

Sources: Civilian Labor Force—U.S. Bureau of Labor Statistics; Local Area Unemployment Statistics; 2000 data published 2 May 2001, 1999 data published 30 May 2001; <ftp://ftp.bls.gov/pub/time.series/la/> (related Internet site <http://www.bls.gov/lauhome.htm>). Private Business Establishments and Employment—U.S. Census Bureau; County Business Patterns on CD-ROM; annual (related Internet site <http://www.census.gov/epcd/cbp/view/cbpview.html>).

[Includes U.S., states, and 3,142 counties/county equivalents defined as of January 1, 1992. For changes to these areas since January 1, 1992, see appendix B. Geographic Information]

| County | Civilian labor force, 2000 | | Unemployment | | Private nonfarm businesses | | | | | | | | Annual payroll per employee, 1998 | |
| | | | | | Establishments | | | | Employment[2] | | | | | |
	Total	Percent change, 1999–2000	Total	Rate[1]	1998	Percent change, 1990–1998	1995	1990	1998	Percent change, 1990–1998	1995	1990	Amount (dollars)	Percent of national average
KANSAS—Con.														
Doniphan	4 115	−4.0	239	5.8	165	15.4	155	143	2 191	35.2	1 878	1 620	25 079	81.9
Douglas	54 925	−1.9	2 190	4.0	2 590	38.2	2 334	1 874	35 809	39.8	30 088	25 615	20 407	66.7
Edwards	1 575	−7.6	32	2.0	102	−2.9	104	105	806	7.3	868	751	19 294	63.0
Elk	1 277	−5.3	65	5.1	63	−4.5	64	66	233	1.3	226	230	13 489	44.1
Ellis	16 130	−5.6	412	2.6	1 029	13.8	971	904	12 378	51.4	10 210	8 176	18 661	61.0
Ellsworth	2 799	−4.5	79	2.8	190	2.7	194	185	1 618	16.2	1 495	1 392	20 637	67.4
Finney	19 569	−2.1	569	2.9	1 002	9.6	972	914	15 887	20.9	15 035	13 140	22 343	73.0
Ford	15 396	−2.9	356	2.3	837	6.6	871	785	12 682	17.1	12 323	10 833	23 059	75.3
Franklin	12 921	−2.7	503	3.9	584	18.0	551	495	7 173	31.5	5 879	5 456	21 707	70.9
Geary	9 984	−1.1	641	6.4	576	−6.3	596	615	7 531	16.0	7 329	6 491	18 613	60.8
Gove	1 464	−3.9	23	1.6	134	19.6	109	112	793	28.9	677	615	17 723	57.9
Graham	1 462	−7.0	34	2.3	113	8.7	115	104	710	23.7	695	574	15 777	51.5
Grant	3 632	−6.2	124	3.4	253	16.6	249	217	2 414	37.5	2 363	1 756	24 500	80.0
Gray	3 238	−1.7	89	2.7	202	15.4	187	175	1 206	18.2	1 153	1 020	22 631	73.9
Greeley	781	−5.9	29	3.7	64	−4.5	63	67	340	−2.6	307	349	18 379	60.0
Greenwood	2 967	−7.6	187	6.3	255	2.4	234	249	1 600	9.7	1 460	1 458	16 914	55.3
Hamilton	1 224	−2.9	22	1.8	86	8.9	87	79	593	71.4	496	346	17 789	58.1
Harper	2 904	−4.2	118	4.1	231	4.1	228	222	1 622	14.7	1 403	1 414	17 803	58.2
Harvey	17 471	−2.0	642	3.7	826	9.0	791	758	12 256	15.2	11 254	10 636	22 491	73.5
Haskell	2 090	−3.5	43	2.1	119	19.0	105	100	758	40.9	638	538	21 001	68.6
Hodgeman	1 103	.6	39	3.5	46	21.1	39	38	292	111.6	250	138	18 911	61.8
Jackson	10 115	12.6	325	3.2	270	15.4	245	234	2 899	100.5	1 758	1 446	17 412	56.9
Jefferson	8 926	−8.7	379	4.2	345	21.9	297	283	2 019	37.1	1 779	1 473	19 364	63.3
Jewell	1 974	−4.9	32	1.6	121	7.1	117	113	567	30.3	516	435	13 457	44.0
Johnson	270 734	−.7	6 492	2.4	14 971	29.0	13 622	11 601	253 795	42.7	218 049	177 817	31 905	104.2
Kearny	2 071	−1.9	59	2.8	90	11.1	75	81	504	50.9	468	334	23 464	76.7
Kingman	4 225	−1.5	163	3.9	221	−.5	220	222	1 995	12.5	1 806	1 773	19 642	64.2
Kiowa	1 690	−.8	32	1.9	117	3.5	113	113	937	24.4	1 031	753	17 670	57.7
Labette	11 766	.1	650	5.5	528	−1.7	522	537	7 603	−5.2	7 579	8 023	21 907	71.6
Lane	1 076	−5.5	31	2.9	92	29.6	84	71	406	33.6	409	304	18 490	60.4
Leavenworth	29 351	−.4	1 179	4.0	1 089	18.2	1 003	921	14 079	18.9	13 589	11 837	23 095	75.5
Lincoln	1 771	−3.8	37	2.1	116	23.4	118	94	721	92.8	706	374	15 193	49.6
Linn	3 221	−2.7	249	7.7	199	5.3	164	189	1 287	−3.9	1 212	1 339	27 453	89.7
Logan	1 614	−1.7	58	3.6	136	3.8	140	131	748	24.7	849	600	17 733	57.9
Lyon	19 458	−3.1	700	3.6	917	11.2	894	825	15 129	22.1	14 709	12 395	21 644	70.7
McPherson	16 204	−.7	409	2.5	942	12.1	915	840	12 640	20.5	12 392	10 487	22 925	74.9
Marion	7 037	−2.1	163	2.3	348	−3.1	362	359	3 214	11.6	3 080	2 880	16 876	55.1
Marshall	5 808	−4.0	212	3.7	403	13.2	389	356	3 558	21.9	3 314	2 919	19 648	64.2
Meade	2 158	−4.7	44	2.0	155	14.8	140	135	857	55.8	819	550	19 092	62.4
Miami	14 376	−.8	460	3.2	610	28.2	536	476	6 146	26.4	5 402	4 863	21 425	70.0
Mitchell	3 848	.3	74	1.9	279	11.6	280	250	2 580	20.7	2 362	2 138	18 747	61.2
Montgomery	19 126	1.1	1 000	5.2	1 069	3.9	1 043	1 029	15 075	13.3	14 044	13 300	21 321	69.7
Morris	3 083	−2.7	103	3.3	167	18.4	150	141	1 238	35.9	1 131	911	16 752	54.7
Morton	1 742	−.7	48	2.8	127	35.1	116	94	929	72.0	883	540	23 384	76.4
Nemaha	5 546	−2.5	150	2.7	390	10.5	373	353	3 960	21.1	3 735	3 270	20 521	67.0
Neosho	8 546	−4.3	410	4.8	545	5.4	521	517	6 748	27.3	6 235	5 300	19 158	62.6
Ness	1 809	−3.2	37	2.0	153	6.3	151	144	1 005	43.6	901	700	17 442	57.0
Norton	3 080	−4.0	47	1.5	215	14.4	203	188	1 666	8.1	1 516	1 541	19 530	63.8
Osage	9 853	−1.5	424	4.3	336	8.4	322	310	3 657	71.3	2 282	2 135	13 680	44.7
Osborne	2 207	−4.7	43	1.9	175	6.1	170	165	1 267	11.3	1 433	1 138	15 509	50.7
Ottawa	3 161	−1.0	89	2.8	133	9.0	138	122	931	26.7	994	735	17 378	56.8
Pawnee	3 849	.1	68	1.8	196	−1.0	217	198	2 092	1.4	2 223	2 063	20 286	66.3
Phillips	3 175	−2.0	69	2.2	233	5.9	253	220	1 625	4.0	1 718	1 563	20 085	65.6
Pottawatomie	10 980	−.9	305	2.8	493	48.9	404	331	5 385	76.8	4 342	3 045	21 258	69.4
Pratt	4 660	−5.5	101	2.2	376	3.6	374	363	3 014	14.2	2 939	2 639	20 171	65.9
Rawlins	1 530	−2.0	40	2.6	110	12.2	115	98	569	17.6	672	484	17 297	56.5
Reno	32 113	−3.6	1 163	3.6	1 744	6.3	1 676	1 641	24 923	16.6	23 596	21 368	24 027	78.5
Republic	2 921	−5.7	55	1.9	219	11.2	206	197	1 888	9.8	1 974	1 720	16 572	54.1
Rice	4 541	−4.6	186	4.1	310	6.5	295	291	2 290	−9.1	2 312	2 519	19 257	62.9
Riley	30 525	−.8	1 099	3.6	1 402	10.2	1 418	1 272	17 523	14.2	16 676	15 342	18 556	60.6
Rooks	2 854	−5.7	82	2.9	213	−5.3	212	225	1 326	19.5	1 097	1 110	19 843	64.8
Rush	1 830	−3.2	49	2.7	101	−2.9	98	104	875	29.1	801	678	20 952	68.5
Russell	3 517	−1.0	134	3.8	294	−.3	286	295	2 166	−8.6	2 025	2 371	17 692	57.8
Saline	30 570	−1.1	863	2.8	1 706	12.2	1 645	1 521	26 327	19.7	25 855	21 989	23 937	78.2
Scott	2 722	−.1	54	2.0	215	18.1	207	182	1 389	7.0	1 295	1 298	19 258	62.9
Sedgwick	235 358	−2.1	10 080	4.3	11 776	10.6	11 453	10 646	232 884	15.3	203 765	202 027	30 127	98.4
Seward	10 988	−.8	313	2.8	702	7.3	666	654	9 117	19.1	8 662	7 658	23 825	77.8
Shawnee	90 077	−.5	3 441	3.8	4 609	3.3	4 529	4 460	81 210	14.3	75 290	71 049	26 758	87.4
Sheridan	1 387	−7.6	20	1.4	103	–	106	103	627	29.0	577	486	18 515	60.5

[1] Civilian unemployed as a percent of total civilian labor force. [2] For pay period including March 12 of the year shown.

Sources: Civilian Labor Force—U.S. Bureau of Labor Statistics; Local Area Unemployment Statistics; 2000 data published 2 May 2001, 1999 data published 30 May 2001; <ftp://ftp.bls.gov/pub/time.series/la/> (related Internet site <http://www.bls.gov/lauhome.htm>). Private Business Establishments and Employment—U.S. Census Bureau; County Business Patterns on CD-ROM; annual (related Internet site <http://www.census.gov/epcd/cbp/view/cbpview.html>).

[Includes U.S., states, and 3,142 counties/county equivalents defined as of January 1, 1992. For changes to these areas since January 1, 1992, see appendix B. Geographic Information]

| County | Civilian labor force, 2000 | | Unemployment | | Private nonfarm businesses | | | | | | | | | | |
| | | | | | Establishments | | | | Employment[2] | | | | Annual payroll per employee, 1998 | |
	Total	Percent change, 1999–2000	Total	Rate[1]	1998	Percent change, 1990–1998	1995	1990	1998	Percent change, 1990–1998	1995	1990	Amount (dollars)	Percent of national average
KANSAS—Con.														
Sherman	4 214	−1.1	90	2.1	269	3.5	275	260	2 150	24.4	2 034	1 728	16 881	55.2
Smith	2 300	−6.2	35	1.5	169	−1.7	166	172	1 092	1.4	1 205	1 077	14 850	48.5
Stafford	2 376	−2.7	66	2.8	143	−2.1	159	146	949	35.2	928	702	17 026	55.6
Stanton	1 106	−1.1	30	2.7	78	50.0	77	52	437	60.1	420	273	20 378	66.6
Stevens	2 778	−1.4	66	2.4	171	18.8	172	144	1 193	46.4	1 156	815	21 490	70.2
Sumner	13 850	−1.9	679	4.9	551	–	565	551	4 912	16.5	4 506	4 215	22 211	72.6
Thomas	4 602	−3.3	85	1.8	354	16.4	335	304	2 603	14.1	2 471	2 282	17 296	56.5
Trego	1 737	−8.3	32	1.8	127	10.4	133	115	737	12.0	776	658	15 753	51.5
Wabaunsee	3 581	−2.4	124	3.5	128	7.6	113	119	663	9.2	599	607	17 151	56.0
Wallace	840	−4.7	17	2.0	66	26.9	49	52	330	42.2	243	232	15 430	50.4
Washington	3 313	−4.2	108	3.3	236	1.7	250	232	1 461	12.1	1 584	1 303	13 686	44.7
Wichita	1 271	−4.4	37	2.9	98	19.5	86	82	493	56.5	430	315	17 414	56.9
Wilson	5 400	−3.2	189	3.5	266	12.2	237	237	3 043	20.8	3 488	2 519	21 200	69.3
Woodson	1 563	−2.4	84	5.4	108	–	97	108	555	10.6	484	502	16 787	54.8
Wyandotte	76 724	.2	5 289	6.9	3 115	−5.4	3 123	3 292	63 450	−9.1	63 518	69 787	30 765	100.5
KENTUCKY	1 981 868	.8	81 752	4.1	89 593	13.4	85 123	79 006	1 443 015	21.7	1 347 087	1 186 001	25 564	83.5
Adair	7 582	−.1	433	5.7	280	1.1	257	277	3 034	−3.0	3 934	3 128	18 576	60.7
Allen	8 620	−1.8	393	4.6	212	6.0	210	200	4 378	48.6	4 293	2 946	18 643	60.9
Anderson	10 110	.4	298	2.9	274	24.5	248	220	3 338	26.1	3 007	2 648	24 465	79.9
Ballard	4 331	1.4	310	7.2	156	−3.1	162	161	1 870	−16.3	1 881	2 234	32 527	106.3
Barren	18 715	−1.1	996	5.3	867	12.0	810	774	14 857	35.8	13 871	10 944	23 365	76.3
Bath	6 002	1.9	370	6.2	174	23.4	150	141	1 533	25.3	1 491	1 223	17 446	57.0
Bell	10 464	2.8	658	6.3	654	−5.2	637	690	8 202	6.3	7 655	7 715	19 627	64.1
Boone	46 973	1.4	1 330	2.8	2 240	41.2	1 897	1 586	52 131	62.7	39 931	32 033	26 203	85.6
Bourbon	10 215	1.1	234	2.3	404	5.5	387	383	5 138	20.6	5 046	4 260	25 588	83.6
Boyd	22 351	−1.1	1 191	5.3	1 570	4.5	1 526	1 502	25 638	−4.5	24 785	26 844	30 610	100.0
Boyle	15 283	4.8	480	3.1	760	11.6	698	681	15 119	38.6	13 877	10 907	23 021	75.2
Bracken	3 820	−4.0	131	3.4	125	15.7	117	108	1 125	71.8	930	655	16 429	53.7
Breathitt	4 270	.2	370	8.7	233	−4.9	241	245	2 451	−13.7	2 698	2 841	17 220	56.3
Breckinridge	7 873	.4	448	5.7	299	10.7	282	270	2 404	39.4	2 092	1 725	16 407	53.6
Bullitt	34 994	1.8	1 059	3.0	896	62.9	755	550	10 066	76.5	8 944	5 703	21 152	69.1
Butler	5 944	−.1	249	4.2	211	34.4	186	157	3 335	−13.9	3 004	3 874	17 285	56.5
Caldwell	6 528	−.3	271	4.2	292	1.4	300	288	3 074	11.8	3 074	2 755	19 802	64.0
Calloway	17 761	−.8	569	3.2	817	12.8	826	724	11 928	48.9	11 345	8 012	20 962	68.5
Campbell	46 405	1.2	1 513	3.3	1 611	11.0	1 576	1 451	23 449	26.5	20 206	18 544	25 237	82.5
Carlisle	2 786	−.6	154	5.5	80	5.3	81	76	677	26.3	590	536	16 300	53.3
Carroll	5 271	3.6	245	4.6	231	13.8	230	203	5 000	48.9	4 481	3 357	30 846	100.8
Carter	11 701	−3.5	1 068	9.1	446	20.2	439	371	4 215	3.7	4 006	4 064	14 564	47.6
Casey	6 732	−.2	309	4.6	203	1.5	209	200	2 463	4.2	2 730	2 364	16 144	52.7
Christian	28 994	3.4	1 214	4.2	1 347	10.7	1 299	1 217	21 380	25.3	19 575	17 059	21 915	71.6
Clark	16 941	1.0	515	3.0	751	21.3	655	619	11 522	34.5	9 287	8 567	23 117	75.5
Clay	7 344	−.5	451	6.1	295	12.2	280	263	2 899	23.4	3 026	2 349	17 949	58.6
Clinton	6 179	11.1	248	4.0	192	17.8	169	163	1 963	20.1	1 577	1 635	14 335	46.8
Crittenden	4 060	.7	357	8.8	171	1.2	184	169	1 755	−6.6	2 006	1 880	20 972	68.5
Cumberland	3 047	5.0	211	6.9	117	−4.9	123	123	1 042	−21.4	1 256	1 326	16 872	55.1
Daviess	50 364	Z	2 243	4.5	2 395	3.8	2 335	2 307	39 917	15.8	37 253	34 468	24 317	79.4
Edmonson	5 114	.5	245	4.8	99	5.3	103	94	651	4.7	682	622	16 195	52.9
Elliott	2 664	−4.9	312	11.7	57	26.7	46	45	413	82.7	276	226	15 298	50.0
Estill	5 679	−2.3	254	4.5	219	−2.2	216	224	2 072	22.5	1 880	1 691	14 908	48.7
Fayette	146 703	1.1	2 711	1.8	7 673	5.9	7 454	7 244	141 945	15.4	132 372	123 024	26 803	87.6
Fleming	6 425	2.4	323	5.0	263	21.2	244	217	2 485	20.2	2 725	2 068	18 478	60.4
Floyd	13 513	−2.2	1 000	7.4	877	−.2	829	879	9 880	9.0	9 040	9 063	25 184	82.3
Franklin	25 132	.6	676	2.7	1 145	13.5	1 083	1 009	15 986	17.7	14 703	13 580	22 316	72.9
Fulton	3 282	−3.4	185	5.6	206	−2.8	209	212	2 897	25.4	2 511	2 310	18 931	61.8
Gallatin	3 820	2.1	164	4.3	93	25.7	78	74	776	7.6	685	721	18 731	61.2
Garrard	7 915	4.8	207	2.6	236	24.9	179	189	2 049	28.9	1 735	1 590	17 902	58.5
Grant	10 442	1.9	475	4.5	428	34.2	389	319	3 839	25.6	3 887	3 056	20 009	65.4
Graves	17 553	−.7	828	4.7	682	13.7	649	600	10 097	16.9	10 027	8 640	23 067	75.4
Grayson	12 658	1.8	674	5.3	459	17.7	429	390	7 174	74.0	6 111	4 122	18 575	60.7
Green	4 124	−3.9	260	6.3	177	7.9	176	164	1 323	−21.1	1 788	1 676	17 709	57.9
Greenup	16 578	−.5	911	5.5	504	24.8	446	404	5 377	5.3	4 585	5 106	26 426	86.3
Hancock	4 150	−.9	273	6.6	128	9.4	124	117	2 677	44.1	2 643	1 858	38 019	124.2
Hardin	37 383	.7	1 934	5.2	1 943	17.4	1 812	1 655	30 894	31.2	28 265	23 549	21 692	70.9
Harlan	9 211	−.2	984	10.7	561	−11.8	588	636	5 778	−22.3	6 629	7 438	25 197	82.3
Harrison	7 384	−1.1	290	3.9	301	−.3	284	302	4 308	3.0	4 568	4 181	23 851	77.9
Hart	7 871	−1.8	362	4.6	265	12.3	281	236	2 459	2.3	2 627	2 404	17 017	55.6

[1] Civilian unemployed as a percent of total civilian labor force.   [2] For pay period including March 12 of the year shown.

Sources: Civilian Labor Force—U.S. Bureau of Labor Statistics; Local Area Unemployment Statistics; 2000 data published 2 May 2001, 1999 data published 30 May 2001; <ftp://ftp.bls.gov/pub/time.series/la/> (related Internet site <http://www.bls.gov/lauhome.htm>).   Private Business Establishments and Employment—U.S. Census Bureau; County Business Patterns on CD-ROM; annual (related Internet site <http://www.census.gov/epcd/cbp/view/cbpview.html>).

[Includes U.S., states, and 3,142 counties/county equivalents defined as of January 1, 1992. For changes to these areas since January 1, 1992, see appendix B. Geographic Information]

County	Civilian labor force, 2000		Unemployment		Establishments				Employment[2]				Annual payroll per employee, 1998	
	Total	Percent change, 1999–2000	Total	Rate[1]	1998	Percent change, 1990–1998	1995	1990	1998	Percent change, 1990–1998	1995	1990	Amount (dollars)	Percent of national average
KENTUCKY—Con.														
Henderson	24 229	.5	970	4.0	1 085	8.9	1 045	996	18 934	23.6	17 530	15 314	24 936	81.5
Henry	7 190	–4.9	196	2.7	239	10.1	200	217	2 354	12.3	2 066	2 096	21 593	70.5
Hickman	2 462	–2.1	93	3.8	95	–2.1	98	97	1 101	3.9	1 172	1 060	19 639	64.2
Hopkins	19 513	–1.0	1 313	6.7	1 104	5.6	1 078	1 045	15 133	–4.8	13 908	15 890	24 362	79.6
Jackson	7 570	9.6	319	4.2	140	32.1	116	106	1 826	67.2	1 865	1 092	17 548	57.3
Jefferson	386 243	1.7	13 856	3.6	19 803	11.7	19 102	17 724	396 681	18.6	377 188	334 590	29 384	96.0
Jessamine	21 451	1.3	350	1.6	827	31.5	719	629	11 372	52.9	8 791	7 438	21 483	70.2
Johnson	9 168	–1.5	558	6.1	501	4.2	514	481	4 656	–5.5	5 538	4 925	18 667	61.0
Kenton	81 298	1.4	2 728	3.4	3 240	21.9	3 073	2 657	57 159	25.6	55 238	45 502	29 269	95.6
Knott	5 829	–1.4	490	8.4	229	–9.8	218	254	2 408	23.9	2 321	1 944	26 692	87.2
Knox	11 360	.5	654	5.8	452	12.2	393	403	5 722	28.5	5 269	4 452	19 721	64.4
Larue	6 397	.8	285	4.5	231	11.1	215	208	1 805	11.2	1 649	1 623	17 062	55.7
Laurel	23 296	–.3	950	4.1	1 018	27.1	901	801	15 356	13.7	14 628	13 502	21 616	70.6
Lawrence	5 581	–.6	444	8.0	217	17.3	208	185	2 218	27.8	2 070	1 736	23 317	76.2
Lee	2 565	2.8	131	5.1	117	7.3	106	109	1 967	34.1	1 788	1 467	11 714	38.3
Leslie	4 349	–2.3	210	4.8	145	9.0	143	133	1 529	39.1	1 218	1 099	22 381	73.1
Letcher	8 119	2.2	861	10.6	437	–2.0	432	446	4 865	–6.5	4 503	5 203	24 647	80.5
Lewis	4 339	–9.1	685	15.8	138	14.0	130	121	1 728	.1	1 700	1 727	16 900	55.2
Lincoln	11 564	4.2	390	3.4	291	22.8	263	237	2 762	64.0	2 349	1 684	17 678	57.8
Livingston	5 036	1.5	322	6.4	153	1.3	150	151	1 748	40.4	1 739	1 245	24 660	80.6
Logan	13 220	–.2	458	3.5	525	18.8	496	442	8 634	26.6	8 924	6 821	23 774	77.7
Lyon	3 388	.3	167	4.9	190	29.3	173	147	1 398	29.4	1 373	1 080	11 907	38.9
McCracken	34 168	.8	1 466	4.3	2 148	18.9	1 993	1 807	35 552	26.7	32 404	28 057	24 447	79.9
McCreary	6 331	–.6	469	7.4	176	4.8	181	168	2 218	60.1	2 152	1 385	14 650	47.9
McLean	4 411	–3.1	266	6.0	180	33.3	177	135	1 224	36.9	1 138	894	18 371	60.0
Madison	37 204	1.3	1 003	2.7	1 369	22.1	1 199	1 121	20 775	36.7	17 911	15 197	21 812	71.3
Magoffin	5 113	–.6	715	14.0	207	39.9	200	148	1 893	48.8	1 737	1 272	18 839	61.5
Marion	11 150	.7	547	4.9	334	9.5	325	305	4 838	38.9	3 783	3 483	18 970	62.0
Marshall	14 832	.2	825	5.6	635	20.7	630	526	8 404	23.2	8 588	6 819	30 880	100.9
Martin	3 135	.7	252	8.0	178	–6.8	189	191	2 197	–6.0	2 522	2 338	31 640	103.4
Mason	8 310	–3.5	248	3.0	465	9.2	452	426	8 609	25.6	8 142	6 855	22 158	72.4
Meade	11 111	1.1	478	4.3	323	29.7	284	249	2 717	18.9	2 225	2 285	24 808	81.0
Menifee	2 976	1.3	182	6.1	75	50.0	64	50	637	86.3	415	342	15 008	49.0
Mercer	11 226	1.9	361	3.2	417	15.5	387	361	6 363	38.1	5 351	4 607	25 452	83.2
Metcalfe	4 815	–3.9	216	4.5	126	4.1	133	121	2 646	120.7	2 644	1 199	20 533	67.1
Monroe	5 109	–6.5	626	12.3	224	9.8	232	204	3 558	21.9	3 500	2 919	17 223	56.3
Montgomery	12 959	.8	517	4.0	509	11.4	469	457	7 634	37.4	4 924	5 558	19 537	63.8
Morgan	4 884	–2.0	333	6.8	173	18.5	163	146	1 916	35.6	1 601	1 413	20 888	68.2
Muhlenberg	12 556	–1.2	827	6.6	601	–4.0	622	626	6 907	–6.1	6 817	7 353	20 802	68.0
Nelson	19 432	2.1	1 078	5.5	878	34.9	767	651	12 060	39.1	10 849	8 672	22 395	73.2
Nicholas	2 750	–12.6	319	11.6	90	–7.2	90	97	1 248	–8.8	1 035	1 368	16 068	52.5
Ohio	9 711	–3.8	621	6.4	357	5.9	368	337	4 818	30.8	4 400	3 684	19 603	64.0
Oldham	25 951	2.2	570	2.2	950	57.0	742	605	8 623	41.9	7 704	6 075	23 174	75.7
Owen	4 394	1.1	147	3.3	119	–2.5	114	122	1 193	3.6	1 206	1 152	22 476	73.4
Owsley	1 735	–1.0	68	3.9	42	–14.3	42	49	269	–34.1	276	408	14 323	46.8
Pendleton	6 794	1.0	247	3.6	201	16.2	198	173	1 689	62.7	1 672	1 038	20 864	68.2
Perry	11 377	–3.2	703	6.2	750	26.5	670	593	9 581	30.3	8 404	7 352	24 420	79.8
Pike	26 725	–3.1	1 611	6.0	1 540	–1.1	1 605	1 557	18 713	6.4	18 969	17 585	24 992	81.6
Powell	6 319	–2.5	329	5.2	173	20.1	163	144	2 536	48.4	2 237	1 709	15 009	49.0
Pulaski	26 673	1.6	997	3.7	1 421	7.8	1 401	1 318	19 911	19.2	18 536	16 701	20 272	66.2
Robertson	1 018	–4.0	44	4.3	31	24.0	34	25	164	156.3	166	64	11 396	37.2
Rockcastle	6 211	–1.0	316	5.1	209	4.5	211	200	2 622	19.1	2 462	2 201	16 452	53.7
Rowan	9 837	3.7	353	3.6	451	18.7	418	380	6 090	26.1	5 112	4 828	17 433	57.0
Russell	5 812	–.2	476	8.2	343	47.2	309	233	3 860	–21.9	5 413	4 944	17 121	55.9
Scott	18 520	1.4	395	2.1	651	47.3	559	442	18 734	107.6	15 117	9 023	38 613	126.1
Shelby	18 504	2.4	447	2.4	707	33.4	607	530	10 802	32.5	9 814	8 155	25 297	82.6
Simpson	8 703	4.4	265	3.0	384	21.1	355	317	7 437	26.8	6 771	5 866	24 548	80.2
Spencer	5 762	8.4	173	3.0	160	72.0	117	93	804	50.0	797	536	17 419	56.9
Taylor	9 243	–5.5	627	6.8	666	24.5	616	535	8 250	–7.4	10 416	8 908	18 425	60.2
Todd	5 374	.3	230	4.3	218	27.5	202	171	2 401	14.3	2 543	2 100	18 390	60.1
Trigg	5 962	–.1	234	3.9	247	21.1	230	204	2 477	32.0	2 286	1 876	21 388	69.9
Trimble	3 201	.3	135	4.2	74	32.1	69	56	456	NA	820	(3)	24 967	81.6
Union	6 036	–3.3	329	5.5	311	1.3	317	307	5 929	6.4	6 063	5 571	30 607	100.0
Warren	50 695	1.2	1 626	3.2	2 495	26.1	2 365	1 979	40 955	39.3	37 550	29 406	24 273	79.3
Washington	6 140	6.1	212	3.5	212	6.5	205	199	2 435	23.2	2 459	1 977	18 994	62.1
Wayne	8 449	4.2	489	5.8	299	19.6	280	250	4 048	12.5	4 206	3 598	17 194	56.2
Webster	5 414	–1.9	386	7.1	260	–1.9	274	265	3 141	6.0	3 189	2 963	26 136	85.4
Whitley	14 358	–.9	670	4.7	811	1.8	834	797	13 185	12.2	12 663	11 751	19 222	62.8
Wolfe	3 300	–.8	294	8.9	80	–3.6	79	83	724	39.5	741	519	12 977	42.4
Woodford	13 758	1.2	221	1.6	496	9.0	480	455	8 136	26.3	7 348	6 442	26 656	87.1

[1] Civilian unemployed as a percent of total civilian labor force.   [2] For pay period including March 12 of the year shown.   [3] 500–999 employees.

Sources: Civilian Labor Force—U.S. Bureau of Labor Statistics; Local Area Unemployment Statistics; 2000 data published 2 May 2001, 1999 data published 30 May 2001; <ftp://ftp.bls.gov/pub/time.series/la/> (related Internet site <http://www.bls.gov/lauhome.htm>).   Private Business Establishments and Employment—U.S. Census Bureau; County Business Patterns on CD-ROM; annual (related Internet site <http://www.census.gov/epcd/cbp/view/cbpview.html>).

[Includes U.S., states, and 3,142 counties/county equivalents defined as of January 1, 1992. For changes to these areas since January 1, 1992, see appendix B. Geographic Information]

County	Civilian labor force, 2000		Unemployment		Private nonfarm businesses								Annual payroll per employee, 1998	
					Establishments				Employment[2]					
	Total	Percent change, 1999–2000	Total	Rate[1]	1998	Percent change, 1990–1998	1995	1990	1998	Percent change, 1990–1998	1995	1990	Amount (dollars)	Percent of national average
LOUISIANA	2 029 566	−1.1	112 475	5.5	100 667	14.0	96 063	88 290	1 577 220	24.1	1 452 355	1 271 219	25 870	84.5
Acadia	23 365	−2.5	1 611	6.9	979	15.3	916	849	12 220	31.4	11 324	9 301	19 517	63.8
Allen	9 582	−4.1	590	6.2	367	17.3	330	313	3 318	23.1	3 186	2 696	18 296	59.8
Ascension	36 735	1.7	2 155	5.9	1 462	42.1	1 242	1 029	23 839	44.3	20 651	16 518	30 288	98.9
Assumption	9 161	−.9	822	9.0	260	22.6	239	212	2 377	14.0	2 471	2 085	18 577	60.7
Avoyelles	16 684	1.2	1 194	7.2	729	26.1	671	578	8 195	54.4	8 046	5 307	16 044	52.4
Beauregard	12 159	−4.5	726	6.0	607	13.2	586	536	6 813	38.4	6 382	4 921	24 901	81.4
Bienville	5 560	−1.7	485	8.7	265	1.5	286	261	2 864	−17.3	3 608	3 464	21 832	71.3
Bossier	46 146	−1.9	2 241	4.9	1 883	22.4	1 697	1 539	29 730	65.5	21 926	17 966	20 334	66.4
Caddo	117 059	−1.5	6 071	5.2	6 345	2.2	6 292	6 207	106 029	12.8	105 946	94 019	25 694	83.9
Calcasieu	80 456	2.7	4 532	5.1	4 285	15.7	4 079	3 705	71 300	40.5	62 872	50 815	25 560	83.5
Caldwell	4 395	−.5	370	8.4	208	23.8	200	168	1 832	32.7	1 680	1 381	18 785	61.4
Cameron	3 894	−.6	233	6.0	182	3.4	174	176	2 050	−14.3	2 410	2 393	28 116	91.9
Catahoula	5 012	.2	618	12.3	198	16.5	197	170	1 910	63.8	1 653	1 166	14 881	48.6
Claiborne	5 622	−3.8	452	8.0	286	−4.0	285	298	2 922	5.0	2 814	2 784	18 889	61.7
Concordia	8 254	−4.3	957	11.6	354	4.7	340	338	3 521	12.6	3 329	3 126	18 430	60.2
De Soto	11 213	−2.7	815	7.3	375	8.7	408	345	4 358	20.8	4 035	3 609	24 792	81.0
East Baton Rouge	215 286	.9	9 046	4.2	11 459	18.2	10 869	9 694	204 953	30.0	189 080	157 670	27 222	88.9
East Carroll	3 228	2.8	482	14.9	148	7.2	150	138	946	−24.1	1 268	1 247	18 752	61.3
East Feliciana	7 411	−3.4	422	5.7	253	51.5	230	167	3 500	189.5	3 489	1 209	21 305	69.6
Evangeline	12 077	−2.2	697	5.8	555	11.2	550	499	6 114	21.4	5 381	5 036	19 421	63.4
Franklin	10 071	−.2	846	8.4	429	29.2	406	332	4 296	40.0	4 296	3 068	15 118	49.4
Grant	6 894	−3.3	614	8.9	200	35.1	191	148	1 639	6.4	1 688	1 541	19 361	63.3
Iberia	32 271	−3.1	2 258	7.0	1 636	11.8	1 549	1 463	28 258	43.2	23 091	19 730	26 005	85.0
Iberville	13 380	1.1	1 010	7.5	558	11.4	519	501	10 643	13.5	9 992	9 379	38 025	124.2
Jackson	5 942	2.4	377	6.3	261	3.6	272	252	2 958	7.0	3 207	2 764	26 679	87.2
Jefferson	229 800	−1.6	9 810	4.3	12 796	10.7	12 694	11 559	211 331	21.7	196 152	173 578	25 970	84.8
Jefferson Davis	11 472	−2.2	883	7.7	602	11.3	553	541	6 105	18.7	5 424	5 145	17 776	58.1
Lafayette	96 386	−1.8	3 913	4.1	6 575	27.4	5 963	5 160	99 052	39.8	84 937	70 868	26 693	87.2
Lafourche	42 787	.3	1 870	4.4	1 798	12.5	1 673	1 598	24 658	55.6	20 304	15 851	24 422	79.8
La Salle	5 258	−3.0	352	6.7	305	7.4	282	284	3 029	19.6	3 401	2 533	19 454	63.6
Lincoln	19 293	−2.3	589	3.1	907	17.2	825	774	13 884	16.3	12 584	11 940	21 095	68.9
Livingston	45 689	1.4	2 745	6.0	1 220	55.4	1 042	785	10 819	82.4	9 385	5 932	19 200	62.7
Madison	5 560	−.0	565	10.1	225	19.7	220	100	2 299	00.5	2 205	1 702	15 077	49.0
Morehouse	12 048	−2.1	1 386	11.5	543	12.2	524	484	6 455	8.0	6 503	5 976	24 014	78.5
Natchitoches	18 324	−.3	1 014	5.5	755	14.7	724	658	9 121	34.0	8 625	6 808	19 619	64.1
Orleans	194 237	−1.5	11 071	5.7	10 762	−2.0	10 862	10 983	211 827	3.8	209 110	204 031	28 661	93.6
Ouachita	71 975	.6	3 106	4.3	4 067	12.4	3 910	3 617	61 306	25.6	56 471	48 804	24 168	79.0
Plaquemines	10 591	−1.6	606	5.7	755	3.6	736	729	13 428	13.0	11 158	11 884	32 008	104.6
Pointe Coupee	9 622	−2.4	727	7.6	334	18.4	330	282	3 821	76.3	3 517	2 167	20 386	66.6
Rapides	60 838	−1.1	3 331	5.5	3 080	7.7	2 997	2 861	45 683	19.9	43 904	38 086	22 214	72.6
Red River	3 490	2.6	319	9.1	160	15.9	156	138	1 852	5.0	1 949	1 764	18 891	61.7
Richland	8 486	.4	856	10.1	418	5.6	426	396	4 547	23.7	4 911	3 675	18 717	61.1
Sabine	8 423	−3.6	445	5.3	481	24.3	471	387	4 760	25.3	4 561	3 800	18 478	60.4
St. Bernard	30 807	−.8	1 778	5.8	1 165	11.0	1 091	1 050	13 354	18.6	12 789	11 255	23 434	76.6
St. Charles	23 073	−.6	1 414	6.1	827	43.3	769	577	18 895	40.1	17 128	13 487	36 591	119.5
St. Helena	4 030	1.1	246	6.1	97	56.5	85	62	860	124.5	774	383	16 027	52.4
St. James	9 213	−1.1	1 024	11.1	311	5.8	305	294	6 222	20.0	6 718	5 184	36 497	119.2
St. John the Baptist	19 555	−.3	1 591	8.1	636	19.1	601	534	10 782	30.9	10 451	8 236	27 469	89.7
St. Landry	32 048	−1.2	2 536	7.9	1 540	8.3	1 473	1 422	16 440	16.5	16 036	14 115	20 111	65.7
St. Martin	21 325	−1.1	1 408	6.6	665	37.7	554	483	9 060	1.4	9 063	8 937	19 513	63.7
St. Mary	23 564	−3.8	2 378	10.1	1 485	8.5	1 387	1 369	25 701	29.5	20 696	19 851	27 507	89.9
St. Tammany	90 878	−1.5	3 375	3.7	4 433	49.9	3 812	2 958	48 247	65.7	40 490	29 120	21 273	69.5
Tangipahoa	45 664	1.6	3 691	8.1	1 901	24.5	1 766	1 527	23 496	39.9	22 617	16 795	19 212	62.8
Tensas	3 360	5.0	283	8.4	107	−4.5	114	112	716	−16.8	694	861	19 493	63.7
Terrebonne	48 916	−.3	2 130	4.4	2 680	19.1	2 467	2 251	43 874	47.1	34 234	29 830	28 379	92.7
Union	12 538	−2.4	649	5.2	331	14.5	336	289	4 749	61.8	3 260	2 936	19 192	62.7
Vermilion	21 849	−2.7	1 447	6.6	964	8.1	926	892	9 819	12.5	10 369	8 728	20 656	67.5
Vernon	16 888	−3.8	955	5.7	639	24.1	598	515	7 107	31.0	5 767	5 424	19 752	64.5
Washington	15 902	−4.7	1 163	7.3	734	6.7	720	688	8 584	26.9	8 492	6 765	21 109	69.0
Webster	19 052	−1.8	1 320	6.9	845	6.3	818	795	10 902	19.5	10 668	9 120	20 559	67.2
West Baton Rouge	10 298	1.3	542	5.3	413	32.4	382	312	8 346	32.0	8 088	6 321	30 480	99.6
West Carroll	5 636	2.6	767	13.6	191	18.6	178	161	1 775	18.5	1 630	1 498	19 412	63.4
West Feliciana	3 566	−5.8	179	5.0	162	31.7	126	123	2 784	4.7	2 851	2 660	39 902	130.4
Winn	6 256	−5.1	386	6.2	355	8.9	353	326	4 287	30.1	4 094	3 295	21 407	69.9

[1] Civilian unemployed as a percent of total civilian labor force.   [2] For pay period including March 12 of the year shown.

Sources: Civilian Labor Force—U.S. Bureau of Labor Statistics; Local Area Unemployment Statistics; 2000 data published 2 May 2001, 1999 data published 30 May 2001; <ftp://ftp.bls.gov/pub/time.series/la/> (related Internet site <http://www.bls.gov/lauhome.htm>).   Private Business Establishments and Employment—U.S. Census Bureau; County Business Patterns on CD-ROM; annual (related Internet site <http://www.census.gov/epcd/cbp/view/cbpview.html>).

[Includes U.S., states, and 3,142 counties/county equivalents defined as of January 1, 1992. For changes to these areas since January 1, 1992, see appendix B. Geographic Information]

County	Civilian labor force, 2000				Private nonfarm businesses									
			Unemployment		Establishments				Employment[2]				Annual payroll per employee, 1998	
	Total	Percent change, 1999–2000	Total	Rate[1]	1998	Percent change, 1990–1998	1995	1990	1998	Percent change, 1990–1998	1995	1990	Amount (dollars)	Percent of national average
MAINE	688 754	2.8	24 153	3.5	38 334	10.0	36 298	34 840	456 715	7.7	432 290	424 027	25 309	82.7
Androscoggin	61 976	3.7	2 139	3.5	2 763	–.3	2 659	2 770	39 769	3.5	39 431	38 438	23 549	76.9
Aroostook	38 415	2.0	1 678	4.4	2 273	–1.6	2 376	2 309	23 069	–.5	22 624	23 178	20 739	67.8
Cumberland	145 769	2.8	2 862	2.0	9 934	16.1	9 181	8 557	140 731	13.3	128 876	124 194	28 426	92.9
Franklin	14 759	–1.6	980	6.6	842	7.5	817	783	10 469	–9.8	10 939	11 608	21 934	71.7
Hancock	29 629	4.2	1 332	4.5	2 078	11.1	1 962	1 871	16 184	14.9	14 338	14 082	26 033	85.0
Kennebec	61 440	3.0	2 422	3.9	3 213	8.8	3 150	2 953	41 236	1.3	40 299	40 716	24 107	78.8
Knox	20 688	3.8	533	2.6	1 483	15.1	1 367	1 289	13 650	27.4	13 092	10 716	23 480	76.7
Lincoln	18 243	3.9	496	2.7	1 248	23.4	1 069	1 011	7 823	21.3	6 886	6 448	22 322	72.9
Oxford	26 709	1.0	1 454	5.4	1 372	12.1	1 293	1 224	15 002	13.1	14 383	13 266	22 740	74.3
Penobscot	79 369	2.6	2 984	3.8	4 061	5.5	3 958	3 848	53 154	2.0	52 579	52 094	24 137	78.9
Piscataquis	8 346	.2	545	6.5	464	3.8	459	447	4 943	16.7	4 641	4 236	22 335	73.0
Sagadahoc	16 772	3.0	432	2.6	756	8.6	692	696	13 318	–21.3	14 469	16 929	31 323	102.3
Somerset	26 139	1.4	1 606	6.1	1 195	5.1	1 176	1 137	15 110	8.2	14 414	13 969	27 265	89.1
Waldo	23 531	8.4	919	3.9	826	13.5	758	728	7 434	38.4	5 783	5 372	21 169	69.2
Washington	16 627	1.1	1 290	7.8	916	4.8	869	874	8 023	8.6	7 863	7 388	21 518	70.3
York	100 343	2.6	2 481	2.5	4 910	13.4	4 512	4 330	46 800	14.3	41 673	40 954	23 715	77.5
MARYLAND	2 804 827	1.1	108 284	3.9	126 577	10.2	122 350	114 874	1 938 727	7.1	1 820 731	1 810 796	30 854	100.8
Allegany	32 440	.6	2 541	7.8	1 843	–3.0	1 899	1 900	24 471	1.4	23 610	24 138	22 912	74.9
Anne Arundel	258 673	.4	7 476	2.9	11 894	15.7	11 420	10 282	165 599	13.6	155 704	145 770	30 089	98.3
Baltimore	398 590	.9	17 238	4.3	19 353	5.2	19 198	18 392	299 572	–.9	300 961	302 184	29 427	96.1
Calvert	38 571	1.3	1 013	2.6	1 440	36.9	1 269	1 052	13 644	41.5	12 682	9 645	26 626	87.0
Caroline	15 979	.5	651	4.1	579	2.8	549	563	5 887	–4.7	5 943	6 180	21 809	71.3
Carroll	83 421	.6	2 320	2.8	3 845	15.1	3 715	3 341	40 396	8.3	38 664	37 304	22 472	73.4
Cecil	42 078	1.2	2 337	5.6	1 601	13.0	1 507	1 417	18 482	11.0	17 072	16 657	27 040	88.3
Charles	62 972	1.3	1 616	2.6	2 411	20.3	2 334	2 004	28 147	25.1	26 833	22 495	21 957	71.7
Dorchester	14 804	–4.2	1 165	7.9	728	2.4	764	711	9 451	–7.9	9 531	10 266	23 132	75.6
Frederick	102 519	1.3	2 324	2.3	4 852	32.8	4 241	3 654	64 779	30.8	57 817	49 531	27 157	88.7
Garrett	13 453	–.4	1 146	8.5	869	19.5	806	727	8 323	9.3	8 207	7 615	19 546	63.9
Harford	115 486	.7	4 128	3.6	4 702	25.3	4 376	3 753	53 346	35.6	46 572	39 337	24 553	80.2
Howard	144 741	.5	2 753	1.9	6 962	29.3	6 374	5 384	125 515	39.0	97 851	90 310	38 012	124.2
Kent	10 044	Z	413	4.1	658	2.5	664	642	6 382	6.9	6 054	5 968	21 652	70.7
Montgomery	482 985	1.3	9 083	1.9	24 600	11.5	23 494	22 064	378 501	7.7	342 624	351 499	36 620	119.6
Prince George's	449 473	1.6	17 436	3.9	13 956	3.0	13 789	13 554	243 126	–2.9	233 595	250 372	30 455	99.5
Queen Anne's	21 541	.6	657	3.0	1 125	45.2	993	775	8 666	43.0	7 655	6 062	20 324	66.4
St. Mary's	52 784	6.2	1 637	3.1	1 646	16.2	1 503	1 417	20 782	29.7	16 688	16 028	26 763	87.4
Somerset	11 445	.4	868	7.6	403	6.9	373	377	2 921	–3.8	2 842	3 035	19 150	62.6
Talbot	18 862	–.1	582	3.1	1 425	15.6	1 335	1 233	16 275	7.4	14 964	15 152	23 969	78.3
Washington	68 329	.3	2 161	3.2	3 222	10.4	3 106	2 918	51 788	19.2	48 714	43 429	25 338	82.8
Wicomico	47 865	.8	2 379	5.0	2 451	9.1	2 369	2 246	35 020	11.5	33 067	31 396	24 306	79.4
Worcester	24 715	–.8	2 578	10.4	2 136	19.3	2 031	1 791	17 198	19.8	16 503	14 352	22 180	72.5
Independent City														
Baltimore city	293 059	1.2	23 782	8.1	13 855	–5.4	14 231	14 652	298 655	–4.0	295 031	311 161	31 871	104.1
MASSACHUSETTS	3 236 597	–1.4	85 610	2.6	167 929	6.1	160 350	158 329	2 924 913	5.5	2 735 963	2 772 444	36 196	118.3
Barnstable	106 356	–.7	3 838	3.6	7 938	10.5	7 410	7 181	66 257	9.4	59 987	60 557	26 843	87.7
Berkshire	62 681	–3.5	1 962	3.1	4 114	–.1	3 994	4 119	54 752	–4.5	52 756	57 345	27 842	91.0
Bristol	258 815	–2.0	10 028	3.9	12 399	4.2	12 001	11 902	195 504	7.3	183 206	182 282	26 326	86.0
Dukes	9 274	–.7	299	3.2	957	32.9	833	720	4 794	30.3	4 141	3 680	31 168	101.8
Essex	364 563	–1.3	9 964	2.7	17 706	6.9	16 763	16 563	268 252	4.8	251 278	255 967	31 871	104.1
Franklin	37 441	–1.4	961	2.6	1 625	–3.9	1 585	1 691	21 865	4.8	20 616	20 860	25 291	82.6
Hampden	205 182	–2.1	7 134	3.5	10 314	–4.9	10 207	10 851	180 610	–4.4	172 641	188 921	28 407	92.8
Hampshire	79 787	–1.9	1 595	2.0	3 316	3.5	3 215	3 204	44 100	2.0	43 492	43 239	24 073	78.6
Middlesex	813 747	–.8	15 792	1.9	41 848	8.9	39 745	38 442	787 896	6.2	734 997	741 652	41 122	134.3
Nantucket	6 309	–2.5	85	1.3	742	37.4	640	540	3 905	31.4	3 300	2 971	34 295	112.0
Norfolk	355 253	–1.0	7 173	2.0	18 905	7.5	18 041	17 594	326 590	10.1	292 097	296 612	36 301	118.6
Plymouth	242 366	–1.8	6 575	2.7	11 009	8.3	10 383	10 168	142 940	8.7	135 004	131 491	28 627	93.5
Suffolk	335 294	–1.2	9 904	3.0	19 870	5.1	19 136	18 913	539 259	5.7	511 455	510 072	45 718	149.4
Worcester	359 527	–2.5	10 298	2.9	17 171	4.6	16 387	16 409	287 961	4.2	270 856	276 265	30 671	100.2

[1] Civilian unemployed as a percent of total civilian labor force. [2] For pay period including March 12 of the year shown.

Sources: Civilian Labor Force—U.S. Bureau of Labor Statistics; Local Area Unemployment Statistics; 2000 data published 2 May 2001, 1999 data published 30 May 2001; <ftp://ftp.bls.gov/pub/time.series/la/> (related Internet site <http://www.bls.gov/lauhome.htm>). Private Business Establishments and Employment—U.S. Census Bureau; County Business Patterns on CD-ROM; annual (related Internet site <http://www.census.gov/epcd/cbp/view/cbpview.html>).

[Includes U.S., states, and 3,142 counties/county equivalents defined as of January 1, 1992. For changes to these areas since January 1, 1992, see appendix B. Geographic Information]

County	Civilian labor force, 2000		Unemployment		Private nonfarm businesses								Annual payroll per employee, 1998	
					Establishments				Employment[2]					
	Total	Percent change, 1999–2000	Total	Rate[1]	1998	Percent change, 1990–1998	1995	1990	1998	Percent change, 1990–1998	1995	1990	Amount (dollars)	Percent of national average
MICHIGAN	5 201 404	1.1	185 356	3.6	235 403	11.9	226 973	210 303	3 919 567	14.9	3 704 315	3 411 784	32 822	107.2
Alcona	4 952	−1.6	330	6.7	229	22.5	216	187	1 309	45.8	1 148	898	21 595	70.6
Alger	4 522	1.5	252	5.6	327	35.7	279	241	2 536	24.4	3 103	2 039	22 448	73.3
Allegan	59 084	2.3	1 753	3.0	2 069	29.4	1 821	1 599	36 293	43.2	33 311	25 348	29 755	97.2
Alpena	16 187	−.3	1 006	6.2	887	−.2	941	889	10 306	9.8	10 504	9 389	26 049	85.1
Antrim	10 870	1.8	584	5.4	632	30.0	548	486	5 378	43.1	4 426	3 757	19 614	64.1
Arenac	7 307	3.4	510	7.0	460	34.1	366	343	5 159	53.7	3 681	3 357	20 433	66.8
Baraga	4 467	1.1	321	7.2	232	11.0	212	209	2 136	17.1	2 018	1 824	22 512	73.5
Barry	34 021	3.0	1 040	3.1	1 005	40.0	827	718	11 151	33.5	9 698	8 354	23 966	78.3
Bay	55 956	−.3	2 338	4.2	2 635	11.7	2 577	2 359	35 189	15.1	32 941	30 577	27 138	88.7
Benzie	8 039	.9	424	5.3	443	31.8	300	336	2 901	42.4	2 782	2 079	19 155	62.6
Berrien	85 072	1.0	3 215	3.8	4 082	7.7	3 973	3 790	60 344	1.1	61 974	59 664	27 011	88.2
Branch	23 680	3.4	979	4.1	924	12.3	859	823	11 887	29.0	11 122	9 212	22 854	74.7
Calhoun	70 539	.4	3 046	4.3	3 058	5.0	3 068	2 911	60 436	16.3	58 742	51 983	28 650	93.6
Cass	26 971	−.4	910	3.4	821	9.2	834	752	8 765	5.9	9 398	8 278	24 822	81.1
Charlevoix	14 249	−1.3	726	5.1	1 019	49.2	840	683	9 922	41.0	8 501	7 037	26 289	85.9
Cheboygan	12 776	.4	1 307	10.2	922	−7.6	924	998	6 181	7.0	5 877	5 776	22 572	73.7
Chippewa	18 155	1.2	1 262	7.0	943	11.9	942	843	9 773	40.8	10 151	6 941	18 604	60.8
Clare	11 267	2.7	742	6.6	631	12.7	617	560	5 805	15.7	5 748	5 016	20 829	68.0
Clinton	35 070	1.2	754	2.1	1 165	25.7	1 089	927	12 621	35.1	11 948	9 342	26 894	87.9
Crawford	5 776	.4	332	5.7	307	5.1	316	292	2 994	−6.1	3 288	3 190	20 904	68.3
Delta	19 645	1.3	1 224	6.2	1 179	11.3	1 160	1 059	13 086	21.0	11 722	10 812	24 401	79.7
Dickinson	14 483	.8	635	4.4	952	15.5	883	824	12 997	14.3	11 722	11 371	26 728	87.3
Eaton	57 246	1.3	1 389	2.4	1 968	9.6	1 713	1 795	25 677	1.4	20 600	25 326	22 174	72.4
Emmet	18 456	.7	1 235	6.7	1 318	23.3	1 248	1 069	13 122	21.0	12 290	10 845	25 459	83.2
Genesee	192 251	−2.6	10 464	5.4	9 220	8.8	9 067	8 472	149 767	−.9	154 427	151 177	29 784	97.3
Gladwin	9 182	.2	607	6.6	475	43.1	435	332	4 253	39.6	4 110	3 047	22 578	73.8
Gogebic	8 157	1.1	515	6.3	490	−1.8	503	499	5 176	21.9	5 291	4 247	16 073	52.5
Grand Traverse	46 454	1.3	1 720	3.7	3 374	23.2	3 246	2 739	40 556	31.5	36 822	30 845	26 181	85.5
Gratiot	20 463	3.2	944	4.6	884	11.8	844	791	12 566	19.4	11 240	10 521	22 804	74.5
Hillsdale	24 841	.8	937	3.8	905	10.2	870	821	14 553	41.4	13 003	10 290	23 403	76.5
Houghton	17 497	−.1	850	4.9	946	14.9	912	823	9 577	17.2	8 638	8 170	18 473	60.4
Huron	18 663	3.3	908	4.9	1 047	11.3	1 056	941	11 013	28.9	10 789	8 546	25 312	82.7
Ingham	155 782	1.2	4 115	2.6	7 170	9.0	7 259	6 581	127 773	12.4	127 473	113 652	30 623	100.0
Ionia	28 051	.8	1 114	4.0	1 008	14.3	956	902	12 447	30.0	10 935	9 155	24 232	79.2
Iosco	11 653	−.9	868	7.4	682	−3.1	759	704	5 633	.5	5 967	5 607	21 180	69.2
Iron	5 533	−1.9	348	6.3	435	22.2	413	356	3 261	15.9	2 945	2 813	18 469	60.3
Isabella	33 676	1.8	979	2.9	1 315	15.5	1 307	1 139	18 049	25.9	16 370	14 337	20 243	66.1
Jackson	79 705	2.1	2 484	3.1	3 442	13.8	3 294	3 024	53 517	17.2	51 488	45 677	27 475	89.8
Kalamazoo	130 140	.2	3 698	2.8	5 960	11.0	5 865	5 367	109 688	13.3	109 215	96 837	30 959	101.1
Kalkaska	7 853	.8	459	5.8	383	40.8	334	272	4 122	42.3	3 998	2 897	26 383	86.2
Kent	336 728	2.2	10 416	3.1	15 198	14.6	14 618	13 256	324 049	23.2	303 241	263 085	31 188	101.9
Keweenaw	872	−1.2	67	7.7	61	19.6	60	51	310	10.3	207	281	17 261	56.4
Lake	3 682	5.4	255	6.9	180	30.4	165	138	1 125	24.4	1 102	904	16 306	53.3
Lapeer	46 145	1.6	1 921	4.2	1 709	33.6	1 504	1 279	19 962	49.9	16 219	13 313	22 916	74.9
Leelanau	11 332	.9	340	3.0	672	39.7	577	481	4 026	42.7	3 717	2 822	22 217	72.6
Lenawee	49 291	1.4	1 883	3.8	2 145	8.4	2 033	1 978	29 979	7.4	30 024	27 922	26 053	85.1
Livingston	83 617	1.0	1 648	2.0	3 629	56.8	2 938	2 314	42 785	53.7	34 814	27 840	28 443	92.9
Luce	2 611	−1.8	173	6.6	197	5.3	188	187	1 533	1.7	1 435	1 508	21 563	70.4
Mackinac	7 603	.9	637	8.4	533	24.2	512	429	2 714	24.6	2 507	2 179	25 337	82.8
Macomb	455 388	1.3	14 119	3.1	18 676	12.5	17 909	16 597	320 622	13.9	316 640	281 565	35 833	117.1
Manistee	11 398	3.2	691	6.1	643	6.3	612	605	5 737	5.2	5 643	5 455	23 060	75.3
Marquette	33 124	.6	1 614	4.9	1 718	7.6	1 720	1 596	20 557	10.0	20 785	18 683	25 351	82.8
Mason	15 070	4.6	828	5.5	803	13.1	763	710	8 969	31.4	8 112	6 827	24 584	80.3
Mecosta	18 110	−.1	733	4.0	920	22.3	831	752	9 753	43.7	8 265	6 786	19 439	63.5
Menominee	13 167	1.0	606	4.6	539	−.9	521	544	6 956	−4.2	7 255	7 261	22 843	74.6
Midland	43 913	.5	1 338	3.0	1 951	29.1	1 786	1 511	36 652	14.5	33 060	32 006	38 685	126.4
Missaukee	7 209	2.5	376	5.2	325	42.5	244	228	2 148	32.3	1 798	1 624	20 324	66.4
Monroe	76 609	1.5	2 428	3.2	2 476	14.9	2 327	2 154	36 779	20.5	34 405	30 524	32 116	104.9
Montcalm	26 122	2.0	1 324	5.1	1 062	6.5	1 071	997	14 910	11.6	15 571	13 356	23 816	77.8
Montmorency	3 579	−.9	375	10.5	251	14.1	265	220	1 700	−3.1	1 873	1 755	22 188	72.5
Muskegon	86 811	2.1	3 954	4.6	3 630	11.4	3 450	3 259	56 611	10.3	51 356	51 345	27 116	88.6
Newaygo	21 694	3.7	1 335	6.2	748	22.6	732	610	8 164	21.5	7 389	6 718	25 911	84.7
Oakland	697 142	1.1	15 419	2.2	41 626	10.8	40 440	37 572	746 998	26.0	665 004	592 646	39 462	128.9

[1] Civilian unemployed as a percent of total civilian labor force.   [2] For pay period including March 12 of the year shown.

Sources: Civilian Labor Force—U.S. Bureau of Labor Statistics; Local Area Unemployment Statistics; 2000 data published 2 May 2001, 1999 data published 30 May 2001; <ftp://ftp.bls.gov/pub/time.series/la/> (related Internet site <http://www.bls.gov/lauhome.htm>).   Private Business Establishments and Employment—U.S. Census Bureau; County Business Patterns on CD-ROM; annual (related Internet site <http://www.census.gov/epcd/cbp/view/cbpview.html>).

[Includes U.S., states, and 3,142 counties/county equivalents defined as of January 1, 1992. For changes to these areas since January 1, 1992, see appendix B. Geographic Information]

| County | Civilian labor force, 2000 | | Unemployment | | Private nonfarm businesses | | | | | | | | Annual payroll per employee, 1998 | |
| | | | | | Establishments | | | | Employment[2] | | | | | |
	Total	Percent change, 1999–2000	Total	Rate[1]	1998	Percent change, 1990–1998	1995	1990	1998	Percent change, 1990–1998	1995	1990	Amount (dollars)	Percent of national average
MICHIGAN—Con.														
Oceana.................	14 450	.2	998	6.9	574	–13.9	560	667	3 986	–11.8	3 834	4 521	21 399	69.9
Ogemaw...............	9 335	4.5	581	6.2	611	21.5	583	503	5 355	35.6	5 317	3 949	19 193	62.7
Ontonagon............	2 975	–2.7	245	8.2	232	.4	254	231	1 735	–40.0	2 899	2 894	23 465	76.7
Osceola...............	10 752	–.9	593	5.5	433	16.1	412	373	6 946	83.6	6 296	3 784	24 141	78.9
Oscoda................	3 657	–1.0	265	7.2	221	27.7	216	173	1 696	35.9	1 531	1 248	16 979	55.5
Otsego................	14 008	3.8	616	4.4	890	38.0	795	645	10 356	46.0	8 618	7 093	23 376	76.4
Ottawa................	144 969	2.1	3 645	2.5	5 614	27.3	5 309	4 410	98 821	39.0	90 179	71 073	28 677	93.7
Presque Isle	6 457	1.9	670	10.4	438	30.4	400	336	3 263	46.1	2 453	2 233	21 186	69.2
Roscommon	8 364	1.3	547	6.5	702	20.0	657	585	4 840	39.1	4 609	3 479	17 854	58.3
Saginaw...............	102 396	.1	4 262	4.2	5 035	6.6	4 982	4 724	86 367	8.7	83 741	79 490	31 446	102.7
St. Clair	83 648	1.3	3 533	4.2	3 577	23.5	3 427	2 897	47 265	31.2	42 996	36 027	26 548	86.7
St. Joseph.............	34 044	2.7	1 167	3.4	1 301	7.3	1 317	1 212	20 742	12.2	21 898	18 492	28 302	92.5
Sanilac	21 107	–	1 164	5.5	995	19.9	950	830	11 284	27.8	9 924	8 831	21 476	70.2
Schoolcraft............	4 386	.3	383	8.7	273	7.5	272	254	1 978	19.7	2 192	1 652	24 678	80.6
Shiawassee............	37 368	1.4	1 548	4.1	1 309	13.5	1 300	1 153	15 644	13.8	15 686	13 744	22 482	73.4
Tuscola................	27 699	–1.4	1 466	5.3	1 101	14.8	1 078	959	12 441	34.8	10 667	9 229	23 307	76.1
Van Buren	37 672	.3	1 661	4.4	1 451	12.2	1 387	1 293	16 113	22.3	15 220	13 176	25 745	84.1
Washtenaw.............	178 223	1.0	2 921	1.6	8 071	15.0	7 916	7 018	150 034	10.0	145 331	136 454	36 341	118.7
Wayne................	983 967	1.1	38 218	3.9	36 089	2.1	35 234	35 338	755 495	Z	727 006	755 297	36 410	119.0
Wexford	16 019	3.2	1 069	6.7	828	13.0	867	733	13 028	21.6	13 088	10 714	24 353	79.6
MINNESOTA...........	2 738 685	1.3	89 540	3.3	134 981	20.3	125 927	112 187	2 271 671	24.0	2 072 503	1 832 156	30 856	100.8
Aitkin.................	6 154	1.5	497	8.1	401	28.1	343	313	2 887	39.5	2 467	2 070	18 653	60.9
Anoka.................	181 664	1.3	4 813	2.6	6 278	40.0	5 456	4 483	92 836	36.1	80 651	68 234	31 379	102.5
Becker	14 834	5.3	947	6.4	953	42.2	777	670	14 405	108.1	8 623	6 922	19 068	62.3
Beltrami	20 319	2.3	1 156	5.7	989	14.9	968	861	11 744	28.5	11 470	9 142	21 129	69.0
Benton	21 094	2.2	774	3.7	672	23.1	512	546	10 806	45.4	8 195	7 430	24 407	79.7
Big Stone	2 703	1.5	128	4.7	204	3.0	198	198	1 604	28.6	1 399	1 247	16 107	52.6
Blue Earth	34 425	1.3	830	2.4	1 660	9.1	1 668	1 522	27 029	18.5	26 138	22 803	21 335	69.7
Brown.................	14 990	1.9	677	4.5	746	–2.4	755	764	12 389	12.6	12 610	11 001	21 916	71.6
Carlton	16 424	1.6	892	5.4	673	10.1	663	611	7 964	2.1	8 093	7 804	28 800	94.1
Carver.................	40 365	.9	854	2.1	1 646	58.7	1 314	1 037	25 950	58.6	24 195	16 360	29 669	96.9
Cass..................	12 748	2.7	833	6.5	770	29.0	749	597	4 873	48.3	4 822	3 285	17 131	56.0
Chippewa..............	6 654	–.9	434	6.5	393	2.9	405	382	4 485	37.3	4 367	3 266	20 252	66.2
Chisago	21 904	1.7	881	4.0	1 002	53.9	872	651	8 935	24.8	8 342	7 160	22 446	73.3
Clay..................	29 678	–.1	863	2.9	1 132	11.2	1 101	1 018	14 804	16.1	13 619	12 756	18 508	60.5
Clearwater	4 411	5.6	523	11.9	202	5.8	207	191	1 957	68.0	1 590	1 165	18 772	61.3
Cook	2 955	1.1	134	4.5	259	47.2	243	176	1 842	31.5	1 795	1 401	18 292	59.8
Cottonwood	5 769	3.9	336	5.8	389	.5	396	387	3 879	12.4	3 703	3 452	17 915	58.5
Crow Wing	28 318	2.2	1 300	4.6	1 817	33.2	1 665	1 364	19 398	46.2	17 516	13 265	23 165	75.7
Dakota................	215 912	1.3	4 783	2.2	8 099	39.0	7 106	5 826	140 687	50.6	117 207	93 410	32 626	106.6
Dodge.................	9 544	4.5	360	3.8	401	26.1	385	318	3 436	43.5	3 383	2 394	26 164	85.5
Douglas...............	16 793	1.5	625	3.7	1 198	30.2	1 014	920	13 232	46.8	11 655	9 014	21 554	70.4
Faribault	8 094	1.4	343	4.2	514	10.1	512	467	4 749	5.2	4 980	4 516	20 332	66.4
Fillmore	10 220	2.3	395	3.9	663	9.6	635	605	5 430	13.4	5 291	4 788	18 041	58.9
Freeborn	17 002	1.7	610	3.6	933	15.0	872	811	11 966	7.2	11 044	11 166	21 458	70.1
Goodhue	23 333	.6	841	3.6	1 245	15.0	1 199	1 083	19 286	30.7	17 692	14 758	23 457	76.6
Grant	2 893	3.4	195	6.7	231	11.6	227	207	1 723	46.9	1 790	1 173	16 746	54.7
Hennepin	655 599	1.3	16 967	2.6	38 350	15.5	36 725	33 207	820 439	16.4	765 277	704 799	36 803	120.2
Houston	11 322	1.6	450	4.0	418	9.7	405	381	4 212	38.3	3 869	3 046	18 806	61.4
Hubbard	8 577	2.7	506	5.9	564	28.5	486	439	4 672	67.0	3 485	2 797	20 138	65.8
Isanti.................	16 113	1.3	630	3.9	697	48.9	561	468	7 097	32.3	6 349	5 364	21 823	71.3
Itasca	19 928	.3	1 471	7.4	1 224	34.1	1 080	913	13 334	38.9	11 748	9 603	24 142	78.9
Jackson	6 044	–1.1	201	3.3	326	19.4	291	273	3 788	68.4	3 413	2 249	19 185	62.7
Kanabec...............	6 715	–.9	464	6.9	286	20.2	251	238	3 508	11.8	3 362	3 137	20 246	66.1
Kandiyohi..............	21 448	.2	797	3.7	1 255	18.8	1 211	1 056	18 294	36.7	15 650	13 380	22 044	72.0
Kittson	2 281	–.4	178	7.8	171	–5.0	165	180	1 146	19.5	1 184	959	17 390	56.8
Koochiching............	6 125	–2.7	402	6.6	459	5.5	454	435	4 949	14.2	4 627	4 334	23 944	78.2
Lac qui Parle	3 694	.3	139	3.8	261	20.3	228	217	2 371	46.5	1 905	1 618	19 023	62.1
Lake	5 394	–1.1	243	4.5	280	16.7	264	240	3 002	17.5	2 977	2 555	23 559	77.0
Lake of the Woods	2 402	–2.7	106	4.4	157	16.3	162	135	1 181	34.4	1 185	879	19 066	62.3
Le Sueur	15 149	1.8	571	3.8	672	27.8	544	526	8 280	54.5	6 391	5 358	24 031	78.5
Lincoln	2 939	–1.2	137	4.7	186	–	186	186	1 393	24.4	1 218	1 120	15 574	50.9
Lyon	14 784	–.9	458	3.1	775	12.2	758	691	13 476	44.8	13 077	9 305	24 689	80.7
McLeod	19 407	–4.1	761	3.9	912	10.8	908	823	18 060	41.2	16 373	12 787	27 133	88.6
Mahnomen.............	2 168	–.6	180	8.3	124	6.9	120	116	799	33.8	926	597	18 412	60.2
Marshall	4 726	4.7	534	11.3	344	32.3	280	260	2 120	41.6	1 684	1 497	19 928	65.1
Martin	10 709	–1.2	433	4.0	698	5.3	689	663	8 425	11.7	8 397	7 544	21 861	71.4
Meeker	9 806	3.4	627	6.4	587	20.0	500	489	5 763	8.7	5 532	5 301	22 331	73.0

[1] Civilian unemployed as a percent of total civilian labor force.   [2] For pay period including March 12 of the year shown.

Sources: Civilian Labor Force—U.S. Bureau of Labor Statistics; Local Area Unemployment Statistics; 2000 data published 2 May 2001, 1999 data published 30 May 2001; <ftp://ftp.bls.gov/pub/time.series/la/> (related Internet site <http://www.bls.gov/lauhome.htm>).   Private Business Establishments and Employment—U.S. Census Bureau; County Business Patterns on CD-ROM; annual (related Internet site <http://www.census.gov/epcd/cbp/view/cbpview.html>).

[Includes U.S., states, and 3,142 counties/county equivalents defined as of January 1, 1992. For changes to these areas since January 1, 1992, see appendix B. Geographic Information]

County	Civilian labor force, 2000				Private nonfarm businesses									
	Total	Percent change, 1999–2000	Unemployment		Establishments				Employment[2]				Annual payroll per employee, 1998	
			Total	Rate[1]	1998	Percent change, 1990–1998	1995	1990	1998	Percent change, 1990–1998	1995	1990	Amount (dollars)	Percent of national average
MINNESOTA—Con.														
Mille Lacs	9 884	4.4	621	6.3	605	16.6	599	519	8 583	42.8	7 936	6 010	19 568	63.9
Morrison	14 862	Z	973	6.5	781	18.3	742	660	8 435	27.5	7 263	6 617	19 834	64.8
Mower	19 518	3.3	512	2.6	918	9.5	909	838	12 340	12.1	12 302	11 012	25 955	84.8
Murray	4 409	3.1	214	4.9	288	18.5	266	243	2 101	14.8	2 085	1 830	18 171	59.4
Nicollet	18 957	1.6	418	2.2	619	17.9	562	525	11 487	8.3	11 095	10 611	24 119	78.8
Nobles	9 500	1.2	322	3.4	667	13.2	654	589	8 341	18.0	8 416	7 067	19 884	65.0
Norman	3 291	–	194	5.9	215	–.5	226	216	1 572	15.0	1 463	1 367	17 651	57.7
Olmsted	74 664	2.9	1 998	2.7	2 892	24.3	2 689	2 326	68 663	14.4	61 291	60 035	31 799	103.9
Otter Tail	27 232	.9	1 326	4.9	1 588	24.1	1 448	1 280	17 462	29.8	15 812	13 454	18 934	61.9
Pennington	8 013	–.1	552	6.9	363	–7.6	395	393	6 425	41.7	5 510	4 534	20 788	67.9
Pine	11 345	.8	815	7.2	602	40.7	486	428	4 820	47.8	3 864	3 261	17 098	55.9
Pipestone	4 991	2.1	201	4.0	330	11.1	343	297	3 705	44.4	3 129	2 565	17 211	56.2
Polk	16 811	.4	799	4.8	819	–.8	830	826	8 589	9.4	8 998	7 852	19 455	63.6
Pope	5 330	–.7	176	3.3	334	10.2	330	303	3 384	50.3	3 116	2 251	19 999	65.3
Ramsey	281 781	1.4	8 040	2.9	13 410	11.2	12 926	12 062	300 709	12.5	279 169	267 292	33 777	110.4
Red Lake	1 915	4.3	224	11.7	116	2.7	114	113	1 176	102.4	824	581	22 064	72.1
Redwood	8 880	1.2	301	3.4	604	20.3	576	502	5 447	32.8	6 892	4 101	20 364	66.5
Renville	8 244	2.3	424	5.1	604	22.5	525	493	6 074	50.8	5 427	4 029	20 300	66.3
Rice	28 047	Z	985	3.5	1 338	21.4	1 219	1 102	20 014	15.4	18 515	17 346	25 175	82.2
Rock	4 619	1.4	136	2.9	266	6.4	270	250	2 865	31.0	2 859	2 187	19 310	63.1
Roseau	8 629	–1.5	414	4.8	391	23.0	355	318	7 960	35.0	5 647	5 895	23 031	75.2
St. Louis	103 110	1.3	4 598	4.5	5 556	12.9	5 374	4 923	76 907	22.0	71 110	63 017	24 692	80.7
Scott	49 121	1.3	1 296	2.6	2 029	41.7	1 689	1 432	27 811	64.3	23 534	16 927	29 940	97.8
Sherburne	34 524	1.5	1 106	3.2	1 179	62.8	918	724	12 880	65.4	9 744	7 788	25 457	83.2
Sibley	6 519	1.4	301	4.6	355	17.9	339	301	3 304	14.3	3 163	2 890	21 596	70.6
Stearns	78 412	2.2	2 742	3.5	3 843	21.0	3 670	3 175	65 890	28.1	65 089	51 427	25 410	83.0
Steele	19 648	.9	612	3.1	898	23.4	808	728	20 163	47.1	16 673	13 704	27 572	90.1
Stevens	5 625	.8	179	3.2	354	25.1	331	283	3 575	39.1	3 214	2 570	20 954	68.5
Swift	5 435	–.9	219	4.0	333	8.5	338	307	3 522	66.4	3 032	2 116	19 022	62.1
Todd	9 402	2.1	537	5.7	546	14.7	480	476	4 666	13.9	4 456	4 097	20 887	68.2
Traverse	1 623	–3.3	96	5.9	132	–10.8	139	148	1 022	28.7	784	794	15 046	49.2
Wabasha	12 779	1.5	393	3.1	589	18.8	532	496	6 847	57.9	5 444	4 335	21 997	71.9
Wadena	7 383	3.5	416	5.6	299	–21.3	422	380	4 417	18.0	4 878	3 743	17 963	58.7
Waseca	9 567	1.0	329	3.4	481	16.7	464	412	6 982	14.7	6 796	6 089	23 843	77.9
Washington	118 021	1.3	2 600	2.2	4 197	54.5	3 531	2 716	52 281	53.8	43 196	33 982	30 603	100.0
Watonwan	5 673	.3	220	3.9	335	6.0	325	316	3 566	10.8	3 564	3 217	19 072	62.3
Wilkin	3 853	–2.7	103	2.7	173	–	180	173	1 936	30.6	2 030	1 482	17 985	58.8
Winona	28 333	1.4	895	3.2	1 267	12.1	1 244	1 130	24 355	31.6	20 374	18 501	22 585	73.8
Wright	48 897	1.5	1 696	3.5	2 078	42.1	1 806	1 462	22 644	63.9	18 654	13 817	24 003	78.4
Yellow Medicine	5 318	1.3	281	5.3	358	4.1	355	344	3 837	31.2	3 597	2 925	19 821	64.8
MISSISSIPPI	1 326 349	4.6	75 285	5.7	59 771	13.0	57 095	52 888	937 023	29.6	871 814	723 174	22 483	73.5
Adams	14 827	3.1	1 054	7.1	1 076	5.3	1 038	1 022	11 727	9.0	11 895	10 762	19 892	65.0
Alcorn	15 848	6.3	707	4.5	862	8.6	854	794	12 959	27.3	13 551	10 180	23 282	76.1
Amite	5 932	4.8	274	4.6	188	11.2	178	169	1 640	21.8	1 593	1 346	21 122	69.0
Attala	8 224	7.6	706	8.6	396	2.3	421	387	5 605	12.1	5 493	4 998	18 611	60.8
Benton	3 320	5.0	219	6.6	79	14.5	76	69	1 113	94.9	817	571	19 695	64.3
Bolivar	17 399	5.4	1 418	8.1	771	5.6	736	730	9 633	16.1	10 724	8 299	19 735	64.5
Calhoun	6 543	6.6	410	6.3	334	10.6	337	302	3 355	2.2	3 949	3 283	19 151	62.6
Carroll	4 620	5.3	330	7.1	115	30.7	105	88	778	72.1	665	452	16 532	54.0
Chickasaw	8 789	15.8	513	5.8	437	6.6	464	410	6 902	–8.6	8 158	7 552	18 746	61.2
Choctaw	3 605	18.0	370	10.3	157	14.6	130	137	1 502	–2.4	1 473	1 539	20 001	65.3
Claiborne	3 318	–1.4	400	12.1	145	9.0	138	133	2 278	2.8	2 510	2 217	36 518	119.3
Clarke	9 202	5.3	810	8.8	313	16.8	297	268	4 053	–2.5	4 644	4 158	19 969	65.2
Clay	9 277	5.1	713	7.7	433	6.9	391	405	7 804	.4	7 320	7 775	25 276	82.6
Coahoma	12 056	4.6	1 181	9.8	679	4.6	667	649	9 180	39.3	8 664	6 591	20 841	68.1
Copiah	11 334	3.3	871	7.7	463	15.2	421	402	5 946	17.9	5 976	5 045	17 369	56.7
Covington	8 726	6.6	486	5.6	308	22.2	303	252	4 298	46.7	4 140	2 930	17 377	56.8
DeSoto	57 466	6.0	1 626	2.8	1 749	47.0	1 470	1 190	28 534	55.9	23 966	18 304	22 848	74.6
Forrest	35 051	6.2	1 453	4.1	2 099	2.7	2 259	2 044	32 546	26.3	32 395	25 766	22 543	73.6
Franklin	3 282	–3.3	256	7.8	150	9.5	141	137	1 360	9.9	1 279	1 237	20 813	68.0
George	9 240	9.1	844	9.1	292	30.9	268	223	2 761	41.8	2 668	1 947	17 492	57.1
Greene	5 338	2.0	481	9.0	133	–	141	133	854	–3.3	867	883	14 568	47.6
Grenada	10 554	5.8	658	6.2	622	8.9	572	571	10 015	30.1	9 427	7 697	23 350	76.3
Hancock	18 794	3.0	743	4.0	718	49.3	630	481	8 672	37.9	8 304	6 289	23 993	78.4
Harrison	88 200	3.8	3 706	4.2	4 382	20.8	4 212	3 627	71 987	56.9	65 058	45 880	22 375	73.1
Hinds	131 690	5.6	6 222	4.7	6 768	–6.0	6 870	7 198	135 733	14.0	128 653	119 032	25 979	84.9
Holmes	7 211	4.2	1 520	21.1	289	–.3	289	290	3 899	64.6	3 355	2 369	16 249	53.1
Humphreys	5 112	7.6	600	11.7	190	–3.1	202	196	2 708	70.1	2 541	1 592	16 945	55.4
Issaquena	692	8.6	112	16.2	15	25.0	17	12	89	71.2	65	52	13 079	42.7

[1] Civilian unemployed as a percent of total civilian labor force. [2] For pay period including March 12 of the year shown.

Sources: Civilian Labor Force—U.S. Bureau of Labor Statistics; Local Area Unemployment Statistics; 2000 data published 2 May 2001, 1999 data published 30 May 2001; <ftp://ftp.bls.gov/pub/time.series/la/> (related Internet site <http://www.bls.gov/lauhome.htm>). Private Business Establishments and Employment—U.S. Census Bureau; County Business Patterns on CD-ROM; annual (related Internet site <http://www.census.gov/epcd/cbp/view/cbpview.html>).

Table B–7. Counties — Labor Force and Private Business Establishments and Employment–Con.

[Includes U.S., states, and 3,142 counties/county equivalents defined as of January 1, 1992. For changes to these areas since January 1, 1992, see appendix B. Geographic Information]

County	Civilian labor force, 2000				Private nonfarm businesses									
			Unemployment		Establishments				Employment[2]				Annual payroll per employee, 1998	
	Total	Percent change, 1999–2000	Total	Rate[1]	1998	Percent change, 1990–1998	1995	1990	1998	Percent change, 1990–1998	1995	1990	Amount (dollars)	Percent of national average
MISSISSIPPI—Con.														
Itawamba	11 862	6.3	592	5.0	334	13.6	328	294	4 662	2.2	4 719	4 562	21 185	69.2
Jackson	72 846	4.8	4 003	5.5	2 311	14.8	2 151	2 013	43 018	21.0	41 166	35 565	27 812	90.9
Jasper	8 503	4.8	432	5.1	287	24.8	287	230	3 948	107.7	3 222	1 901	18 849	61.6
Jefferson	2 760	4.5	534	19.3	79	17.9	77	67	745	17.0	642	637	18 250	59.6
Jefferson Davis	4 636	–2.0	731	15.8	194	5.4	195	184	2 471	59.4	2 006	1 550	14 005	45.8
Jones	32 213	4.4	1 051	3.3	1 442	7.5	1 387	1 341	21 443	32.5	19 690	16 179	22 222	72.6
Kemper	4 502	1.3	466	10.4	127	17.6	148	108	2 254	152.4	1 021	893	15 344	50.1
Lafayette	16 442	–5.7	364	2.2	897	35.5	783	662	12 302	67.1	9 430	7 360	18 258	59.6
Lamar	18 475	5.6	573	3.1	760	137.5	408	320	8 420	163.9	3 815	3 190	17 680	57.8
Lauderdale	35 532	3.7	2 088	5.9	2 109	10.1	2 007	1 916	33 674	21.4	30 578	27 728	23 203	75.8
Lawrence	5 595	7.5	622	11.1	234	19.4	222	196	2 675	23.2	2 846	2 171	24 775	80.9
Leake	9 558	2.5	641	6.7	347	8.8	339	319	5 605	49.5	4 196	3 750	16 000	52.3
Lee	42 325	5.6	1 665	3.9	2 284	13.2	2 203	2 017	46 890	29.2	45 317	36 298	25 056	81.9
Leflore	16 233	6.0	1 761	10.8	885	–4.6	937	928	13 262	15.2	12 523	11 510	20 726	67.7
Lincoln	14 875	7.6	781	5.3	787	18.9	706	662	10 022	25.9	9 176	7 961	21 616	70.6
Lowndes	27 089	1.9	1 632	6.0	1 673	13.0	1 584	1 480	25 209	20.5	24 436	20 918	21 991	71.8
Madison	38 831	5.5	1 398	3.6	1 795	67.9	1 463	1 069	24 706	84.5	18 838	13 391	22 975	75.1
Marion	11 034	4.8	685	6.2	563	9.5	544	514	6 289	16.2	5 974	5 414	18 843	61.6
Marshall	14 189	4.7	856	6.0	431	13.4	413	380	6 733	44.1	6 252	4 671	17 678	57.8
Monroe	15 616	3.9	1 605	10.3	762	5.1	772	725	10 338	–4.5	12 257	10 820	23 446	76.6
Montgomery	5 681	5.4	374	6.6	249	–	256	249	3 057	22.2	3 174	2 501	16 145	52.7
Neshoba	15 903	1.7	776	4.9	561	2.2	529	549	10 168	43.6	8 410	7 079	22 012	71.9
Newton	8 573	2.2	509	5.9	376	32.9	348	283	5 144	23.2	4 354	4 174	19 066	62.3
Noxubee	4 621	2.2	542	11.7	240	14.8	238	209	2 563	54.9	2 244	1 655	18 146	59.3
Oktibbeha	20 937	–2	598	2.9	793	11.5	740	711	9 543	29.8	9 269	7 352	17 729	57.9
Panola	13 268	7.3	1 274	9.6	651	24.5	644	523	9 490	20.4	9 389	7 882	19 636	64.1
Pearl River	20 604	4.2	935	4.5	778	38.2	682	563	7 603	46.7	6 163	5 182	17 345	56.7
Perry	4 341	6.8	337	7.8	152	22.6	148	124	2 044	27.2	1 957	1 607	27 403	89.5
Pike	17 519	6.5	1 121	6.4	993	16.7	944	851	12 879	28.3	12 063	10 035	19 480	63.6
Pontotoc	14 299	6.3	583	4.1	466	19.8	454	389	8 652	12.8	7 569	7 671	20 550	67.1
Prentiss	12 760	3.6	565	4.4	548	18.6	529	462	8 095	17.5	7 871	6 892	18 004	58.8
Quitman	3 477	6.7	354	10.2	146	–2.7	161	150	1 154	4.2	1 464	1 108	17 879	58.4
Rankin	63 134	5.3	1 581	2.5	2 408	42.6	2 119	1 689	38 772	57.1	33 900	24 674	24 256	79.2
Scott	12 758	5.1	526	4.1	517	3.4	507	500	9 538	19.7	10 695	7 965	17 878	58.4
Sharkey	2 548	2.2	364	14.3	143	6.7	145	134	1 009	–7.0	1 107	1 085	17 037	55.7
Simpson	10 557	8.5	492	4.7	439	–3.5	438	455	4 686	–16.6	5 946	5 616	16 219	53.0
Smith	6 089	6.5	294	4.8	205	15.2	191	178	3 458	19.3	3 054	2 899	23 534	76.9
Stone	5 315	6.0	373	7.0	273	11.4	270	245	2 759	31.4	2 706	2 099	19 881	65.0
Sunflower	11 554	6.7	1 269	11.0	498	–3.1	504	514	7 174	–25.4	8 714	9 621	19 727	64.4
Tallahatchie	5 599	6.2	656	11.7	191	–.5	190	192	1 494	–6.4	1 521	1 597	17 831	58.3
Tate	10 609	3.0	621	5.9	418	27.8	371	327	5 374	12.0	5 038	4 800	18 683	61.0
Tippah	10 381	5.7	594	5.7	411	10.5	414	372	6 810	42.7	6 644	4 771	21 257	69.4
Tishomingo	9 503	2.0	721	7.6	417	18.5	399	352	5 192	28.1	5 419	4 054	20 371	66.6
Tunica	4 250	–24.6	345	8.1	175	37.8	146	127	17 350	1 561.9	10 281	1 044	24 108	78.8
Union	13 116	5.4	488	3.7	459	17.7	437	390	9 121	13.9	7 695	8 010	21 772	71.1
Walthall	6 164	5.2	534	8.7	231	24.2	202	186	2 756	102.9	2 164	1 358	16 897	55.2
Warren	27 159	3.7	1 361	5.0	1 179	8.7	1 162	1 085	20 077	39.6	18 843	14 386	22 513	73.6
Washington	27 741	4.1	2 764	10.0	1 507	–.1	1 483	1 508	22 631	21.9	21 566	18 558	19 854	64.9
Wayne	8 945	6.8	659	7.4	379	12.5	361	337	5 257	47.8	4 886	3 558	19 671	64.3
Webster	4 436	2.2	211	4.8	195	10.2	199	177	3 047	48.0	2 374	2 059	15 938	52.1
Wilkinson	2 915	–1.6	346	11.9	170	–4.0	175	177	1 944	27.0	1 811	1 531	17 408	56.9
Winston	7 922	4.0	704	8.9	407	6.0	393	384	5 457	2.6	5 168	5 319	22 705	74.2
Yalobusha	4 960	7.3	342	6.9	238	2.6	242	232	3 035	2.7	3 153	2 954	19 531	63.8
Yazoo	9 959	7.5	913	9.2	452	5.4	439	429	5 579	25.3	5 238	4 451	22 590	73.8
MISSOURI	2 929 827	3.1	101 447	3.5	143 912	10.5	139 980	130 287	2 310 122	14.7	2 169 026	2 013 560	27 994	91.5
Adair	13 585	–.7	287	2.1	632	–.6	640	636	8 993	15.6	8 934	7 781	19 809	64.7
Andrew	8 354	1.8	254	3.0	241	20.5	231	200	2 228	52.1	1 620	1 465	17 365	56.7
Atchison	2 951	–4.1	66	2.2	223	–5.9	250	237	1 591	–15.7	1 459	1 888	16 336	53.4
Audrain	13 160	2.5	376	2.9	655	6.7	628	614	8 303	19.5	7 829	6 948	24 692	80.7
Barry	15 197	.4	508	3.3	783	29.0	719	607	12 292	30.5	11 678	9 420	21 026	68.7
Barton	7 061	–1.7	183	2.6	301	25.4	265	240	4 620	44.9	4 690	3 188	20 579	67.2
Bates	7 151	–2.6	334	4.7	389	17.5	378	331	2 871	23.6	2 814	2 322	16 729	54.7
Benton	5 924	–.6	405	6.8	407	19.7	400	340	2 402	29.8	2 256	1 851	15 315	50.0
Bollinger	5 458	2.0	265	4.9	212	19.8	173	177	1 411	–2.8	1 360	1 451	14 870	48.6
Boone	84 347	2.7	1 044	1.2	3 675	24.5	3 478	2 952	58 592	27.6	56 713	45 916	23 095	75.5
Buchanan	41 912	1.5	1 486	3.5	2 342	8.7	2 293	2 155	34 603	2.4	34 895	33 801	24 533	80.1
Butler	19 424	.3	980	5.0	1 067	6.8	1 033	999	14 393	25.6	13 066	11 459	20 242	66.1
Caldwell	3 093	–.6	146	4.7	185	36.0	170	136	1 011	4.4	1 292	968	17 012	55.6
Callaway	21 693	2.2	571	2.6	695	16.2	626	598	9 767	11.0	9 742	8 803	25 841	84.4

[1] Civilian unemployed as a percent of total civilian labor force.   [2] For pay period including March 12 of the year shown.

Sources: Civilian Labor Force—U.S. Bureau of Labor Statistics; Local Area Unemployment Statistics; 2000 data published 2 May 2001, 1999 data published 30 May 2001; <ftp://ftp.bls.gov/pub/time.series/la/> (related Internet site <http://www.bls.gov/lauhome.htm>).   Private Business Establishments and Employment—U.S. Census Bureau; County Business Patterns on CD-ROM; annual (related Internet site <http://www.census.gov/epcd/cbp/view/cbpview.html>).

Table B–7. Counties — Labor Force and Private Business Establishments and Employment–Con.

[Includes U.S., states, and 3,142 counties/county equivalents defined as of January 1, 1992. For changes to these areas since January 1, 1992, see appendix B. Geographic Information]

County	Civilian labor force, 2000 Total	Percent change, 1999–2000	Unemployment Total	Rate[1]	Establishments 1998	Percent change, 1990–1998	1995	1990	Employment[2] 1998	Percent change, 1990–1998	1995	1990	Annual payroll per employee, 1998 Amount (dollars)	Percent of national average
MISSOURI—Con.														
Camden	17 423	1.8	766	4.4	1 516	38.3	1 338	1 096	11 896	50.0	10 419	7 931	19 970	65.2
Cape Girardeau	37 781	1.4	1 122	3.0	2 282	9.5	2 214	2 084	34 596	20.4	34 093	28 725	22 636	74.0
Carroll	4 759	-.9	163	3.4	249	-.8	246	251	1 950	12.9	2 200	1 727	15 271	49.9
Carter	2 679	-1.7	145	5.4	137	20.2	132	114	818	1.2	892	808	14 329	46.8
Cass	46 784	5.1	1 204	2.6	1 631	32.5	1 489	1 231	13 180	46.6	12 448	8 991	20 189	66.0
Cedar	5 080	.5	175	3.4	301	12.3	296	268	2 615	22.7	2 435	2 131	16 831	55.0
Chariton	4 235	3.4	183	4.3	203	4.6	234	194	1 372	-12.1	1 453	1 561	17 046	55.7
Christian	29 398	5.6	720	2.4	1 103	63.2	962	676	9 918	75.2	8 353	5 661	18 395	60.1
Clark	3 658	.5	176	4.8	152	-1.9	153	155	888	6.7	898	832	15 670	51.2
Clay	109 830	4.7	2 396	2.2	4 504	16.4	4 406	3 868	78 899	31.2	72 541	60 131	30 310	99.0
Clinton	10 117	4.8	293	2.9	412	17.7	403	350	2 980	15.7	3 060	2 575	17 879	58.4
Cole	40 427	2.3	896	2.2	2 106	17.1	2 033	1 798	35 630	34.5	28 245	26 484	22 786	74.4
Cooper	8 305	.1	238	2.9	415	25.4	380	331	4 064	29.6	4 044	3 135	16 874	55.1
Crawford	9 996	4.1	581	5.8	487	21.4	461	401	4 917	2.8	5 428	4 782	19 032	62.2
Dade	3 420	2.3	136	4.0	150	12.8	147	133	1 171	6.6	1 201	1 099	17 377	56.8
Dallas	5 667	-12.1	358	6.3	263	20.6	262	218	2 869	23.2	2 716	2 328	12 036	39.3
Daviess	3 382	-2.6	121	3.6	183	22.0	179	150	1 352	21.1	1 175	1 116	14 780	48.3
DeKalb	4 570	-3.0	127	2.8	202	26.3	165	160	1 712	54.2	1 122	1 110	16 923	55.3
Dent	6 057	-4.6	378	6.2	337	9.1	328	309	3 742	20.0	3 911	3 118	21 142	69.1
Douglas	5 365	-2.2	316	5.9	201	16.2	189	173	1 719	-13.6	2 077	1 990	15 205	49.7
Dunklin	13 919	-.5	706	5.1	773	-1.0	769	781	7 863	11.9	7 597	7 027	17 915	58.5
Franklin	48 622	4.3	1 885	3.9	2 368	18.9	2 223	1 991	30 900	22.6	29 475	25 199	23 426	76.5
Gasconade	7 929	2.3	274	3.5	438	10.3	431	397	4 206	13.5	4 166	3 705	21 053	68.8
Gentry	3 620	1.4	106	2.9	206	-.5	210	207	1 770	13.4	1 578	1 561	16 732	54.7
Greene	130 508	5.7	3 069	2.4	7 533	16.7	7 269	6 453	129 375	26.4	119 485	102 354	23 582	77.0
Grundy	5 006	2.9	156	3.1	277	1.5	285	273	2 837	24.5	2 860	2 279	19 866	64.9
Harrison	4 155	-3.6	121	2.9	260	7.0	255	243	2 271	18.4	2 025	1 918	14 773	48.3
Henry	10 639	1.6	384	3.6	658	16.0	610	567	6 676	28.6	5 942	5 190	20 530	67.1
Hickory	2 653	-5.5	206	7.8	152	29.9	141	117	831	33.2	712	624	12 668	41.4
Holt	2 642	-1.8	82	3.1	130	-7.8	149	141	872	-5.2	954	920	18 975	62.0
Howard	4 402	-4.3	149	3.4	214	.5	210	213	1 901	8.6	1 763	1 751	17 510	57.2
Howell	17 183	-1.0	677	3.9	984	24.9	938	788	12 040	18.2	12 092	10 190	18 814	61.5
Iron	4 628	12.9	321	6.9	243	12.0	235	217	2 294	-7.2	2 121	2 473	24 268	79.3
Jackson	372 797	5.1	13 670	3.7	18 077	3.1	17 831	17 533	349 080	7.0	336 450	326 304	32 720	100.9
Jasper	54 803	.7	1 769	3.2	3 024	8.0	3 103	2 799	53 535	38.2	51 714	38 726	22 604	73.8
Jefferson	105 996	4.0	3 494	3.3	3 398	19.9	3 086	2 835	34 432	31.1	30 475	26 265	22 089	72.2
Johnson	23 149	1.9	675	2.9	832	18.3	776	703	9 110	19.8	8 841	7 602	19 153	62.6
Knox	1 950	-1.0	65	3.3	114	5.6	115	108	597	-18.7	535	734	15 923	52.0
Laclede	16 613	4.8	675	4.1	801	10.5	817	725	11 162	23.3	10 287	9 056	20 374	66.6
Lafayette	17 024	4.9	600	3.5	823	19.1	757	691	6 920	17.5	6 755	5 889	16 697	54.6
Lawrence	15 801	.6	535	3.4	627	11.2	565	564	7 043	21.6	5 997	5 793	20 503	67.0
Lewis	5 589	.9	165	3.0	232	11.0	235	209	2 127	31.3	1 970	1 620	17 638	57.6
Lincoln	19 040	4.2	658	3.5	730	30.4	660	560	6 654	58.5	5 691	4 198	20 772	67.9
Linn	6 361	-.5	458	7.2	354	-6.3	351	378	4 397	6.6	4 532	4 125	20 159	65.9
Livingston	7 286	1.3	176	2.4	463	6.9	476	433	5 172	10.5	4 996	4 679	19 720	64.4
McDonald	8 143	-2.5	324	4.0	336	20.4	316	279	4 856	34.3	3 884	3 616	18 340	59.9
Macon	7 416	-.6	388	5.2	360	6.8	360	337	3 824	33.8	3 494	2 858	16 238	53.0
Madison	4 479	4.2	297	6.6	272	3.8	263	262	2 588	-7.1	2 777	2 787	14 788	48.3
Maries	4 486	2.0	157	3.5	132	-3.6	155	137	1 054	11.2	1 053	948	19 603	64.0
Marion	15 498	.2	687	4.4	824	6.2	817	776	11 412	24.6	11 225	9 157	21 993	71.9
Mercer	1 497	-6.5	45	3.0	87	8.8	78	80	483	32.3	438	365	19 296	63.0
Miller	11 717	2.4	597	5.1	621	-1.9	719	633	6 099	.3	6 647	6 080	20 626	67.4
Mississippi	5 981	1.7	350	5.9	289	-3.0	288	298	2 832	-10.6	2 621	3 169	16 977	55.5
Moniteau	7 436	2.3	211	2.8	332	12.2	324	296	3 141	7.0	3 072	2 935	18 278	59.7
Monroe	4 327	-2.9	218	5.0	215	-11.9	227	244	2 204	-.1	2 090	2 206	21 496	70.2
Montgomery	5 544	-1.4	225	4.1	354	5.7	348	335	2 788	11.7	3 084	2 497	17 817	58.2
Morgan	8 469	1.4	367	4.3	505	10.5	471	457	3 161	17.4	2 926	2 693	16 622	54.3
New Madrid	8 588	1.2	463	5.4	375	10.6	373	339	6 006	21.4	4 581	4 949	24 394	79.7
Newton	27 697	.9	1 137	4.1	1 027	26.5	870	812	16 669	42.5	12 395	11 701	21 466	70.1
Nodaway	12 848	1.3	169	1.3	529	13.0	496	468	6 323	14.9	5 986	5 501	20 370	66.5
Oregon	4 305	-1.7	149	3.5	214	10.3	212	194	1 680	44.0	1 440	1 167	15 029	49.1
Osage	7 521	1.8	316	4.2	266	12.7	243	236	2 618	44.2	2 214	1 815	20 128	65.8
Ozark	4 044	.5	181	4.5	169	9.0	169	155	932	23.8	964	753	15 524	50.7
Pemiscot	8 157	-1.3	586	7.2	380	4.7	369	363	4 685	34.2	4 333	3 492	17 663	57.7
Perry	11 080	2.5	264	2.4	466	14.2	443	408	7 346	33.0	7 497	5 524	22 546	73.7
Pettis	21 701	1.2	748	3.4	1 034	4.6	1 030	989	16 743	36.5	15 456	12 266	21 678	70.8
Phelps	20 174	1.8	571	2.8	1 047	12.3	1 030	932	11 605	41.1	10 031	8 226	18 132	59.2
Pike	7 857	-1.6	310	3.9	409	2.8	409	398	3 556	1.3	3 435	3 511	22 150	72.4
Platte	45 463	5.0	898	2.0	1 762	33.4	1 585	1 321	33 722	43.6	28 113	23 477	25 244	82.5
Polk	11 940	-2.0	341	2.9	568	24.8	522	455	6 483	50.7	7 030	4 301	17 707	57.8

[1] Civilian unemployed as a percent of total civilian labor force. [2] For pay period including March 12 of the year shown.

Sources: Civilian Labor Force—U.S. Bureau of Labor Statistics; Local Area Unemployment Statistics; 2000 data published 2 May 2001, 1999 data published 30 May 2001; <ftp://ftp.bls.gov/pub/time.series/la/> (related Internet site <http://www.bls.gov/lauhome.htm>). Private Business Establishments and Employment—U.S. Census Bureau; County Business Patterns on CD-ROM; annual (related Internet site <http://www.census.gov/epcd/cbp/view/cbpview.html>).

[Includes U.S., states, and 3,142 counties/county equivalents defined as of January 1, 1992. For changes to these areas since January 1, 1992, see appendix B. Geographic Information]

County	Civilian labor force, 2000 Total	Percent change, 1999–2000	Unemployment Total	Rate[1]	Establishments 1998	Percent change, 1990–1998	1995	1990	Employment[2] 1998	Percent change, 1990–1998	1995	1990	Annual payroll per employee, 1998 Amount (dollars)	Percent of national average
MISSOURI—Con.														
Pulaski	12 590	3.9	756	6.0	676	9.2	638	619	5 598	–6.1	5 240	5 961	16 913	55.3
Putnam	1 895	–2.2	65	3.4	107	–15.7	119	127	598	5.3	692	568	14 890	48.6
Ralls	5 421	.1	238	4.4	175	13.6	165	154	2 067	31.8	1 934	1 568	22 078	72.1
Randolph	10 920	.5	473	4.3	556	7.8	576	516	7 284	.1	6 784	7 278	21 476	70.2
Ray	11 833	5.1	492	4.2	409	15.2	406	355	3 440	50.1	2 873	2 292	18 693	61.1
Reynolds	2 586	–18.2	239	9.2	168	7.7	156	156	1 766	20.5	1 838	1 466	24 175	79.0
Ripley	5 371	.5	299	5.6	234	16.4	252	201	1 886	36.0	1 806	1 387	16 095	52.6
St. Charles	163 089	4.0	3 563	2.2	6 001	31.3	5 306	4 571	85 552	46.7	68 426	58 309	25 599	83.6
St. Clair	3 954	3.6	164	4.1	190	4.4	187	182	1 473	40.8	1 253	1 046	13 834	45.2
Ste. Genevieve	8 871	1.3	314	3.5	368	15.0	362	320	4 869	11.1	4 874	4 383	23 186	75.7
St. Francois	24 217	–.5	1 593	6.6	1 283	23.4	1 130	1 040	16 284	26.8	15 221	12 839	19 158	62.6
St. Louis	563 492	3.9	15 552	2.8	30 262	2.3	29 630	29 574	582 360	4.1	528 032	559 457	32 543	106.3
Saline	11 916	.7	334	2.8	576	3.0	590	559	7 399	10.4	7 365	6 703	19 949	65.2
Schuyler	2 355	–.5	92	3.9	91	–	94	91	382	3.0	394	371	13 398	43.8
Scotland	2 147	–1.2	70	3.3	138	–7.4	151	149	771	2.9	909	749	15 131	49.4
Scott	20 510	1.6	945	4.6	1 143	.4	1 156	1 138	14 049	4.5	12 337	13 449	20 310	66.4
Shannon	3 916	–1.0	205	5.2	153	28.6	132	119	1 309	6.3	1 513	1 231	14 225	46.5
Shelby	3 417	–.1	216	6.3	198	5.9	194	187	1 691	51.3	1 513	1 118	21 378	69.8
Stoddard	13 237	1.3	647	4.9	740	4.5	721	708	7 572	–2.1	8 309	7 738	18 958	61.9
Stone	13 224	–2.9	1 059	8.0	648	33.3	640	486	4 173	35.2	3 930	3 086	22 295	72.8
Sullivan	3 785	–4.4	88	2.3	122	5.2	113	116	2 516	76.7	1 597	1 424	19 239	62.9
Taney	30 695	4.7	1 912	6.2	1 730	64.4	1 679	1 052	16 859	120.8	15 400	7 637	21 449	70.1
Texas	9 189	2.6	626	6.8	483	1.7	492	475	4 704	2.8	4 909	4 575	18 589	60.7
Vernon	8 829	–.8	260	2.9	501	18.4	476	423	5 925	24.6	5 790	4 757	19 862	64.9
Warren	12 993	3.8	425	3.3	536	31.7	497	407	5 864	40.3	5 863	4 181	21 672	70.8
Washington	9 418	–.9	711	7.5	335	28.4	293	261	2 755	57.0	1 874	1 755	19 003	62.1
Wayne	3 518	3.2	302	8.6	241	24.2	219	194	1 826	–26.0	1 663	2 467	14 004	45.8
Webster	15 032	5.8	464	3.1	593	27.3	541	466	4 902	42.0	4 725	3 451	18 928	61.8
Worth	756	–9.6	44	5.8	69	1.5	69	68	298	–4.2	329	311	12 993	42.4
Wright	7 000	–1.7	432	6.2	393	16.3	405	338	3 652	.7	3 712	3 626	17 960	58.7
Independent City														
St. Louis city	156 738	3.9	10 400	6.6	9 850	–.3	10 665	9 878	273 593	6.2	284 665	257 531	34 843	113.8
MONTANA	479 132	1.1	23 524	4.9	30 957	23.7	29 109	25 028	277 144	24.9	260 973	221 851	21 508	70.3
Beaverhead	4 877	–4.7	197	4.0	351	19.0	354	295	2 161	36.3	2 056	1 586	17 832	58.3
Big Horn	5 871	7.7	847	14.4	221	12.8	207	196	2 225	27.0	2 023	1 752	24 570	80.3
Blaine	2 937	–1.9	198	6.7	167	.6	178	166	1 035	4.5	1 024	990	21 008	68.6
Broadwater	2 157	.3	100	4.6	112	31.8	98	85	713	36.1	662	524	19 596	64.0
Carbon	4 883	–.1	251	5.1	313	33.8	271	234	1 866	42.0	1 662	1 314	15 501	50.6
Carter	1 098	1.1	23	2.1	28	–12.5	29	32	133	.8	133	132	14 496	47.4
Cascade	37 622	.1	1 895	5.0	2 522	8.2	2 460	2 331	26 152	9.0	25 574	23 984	20 407	66.7
Chouteau	2 960	.3	91	3.1	157	6.1	151	148	782	29.9	756	602	15 107	49.4
Custer	6 153	.6	266	4.3	398	9.6	378	363	3 839	21.2	3 520	3 167	19 036	62.2
Daniels	1 331	.5	40	3.0	82	9.3	87	75	572	49.0	608	384	19 773	64.6
Dawson	5 241	2.2	173	3.3	317	5.7	313	300	2 333	4.4	2 354	2 235	16 165	52.8
Deer Lodge	4 008	1.2	325	8.1	238	–4.4	224	249	2 401	11.2	2 769	2 159	19 507	63.7
Fallon	1 675	–3.8	60	3.6	116	11.5	111	104	750	41.8	622	529	20 431	66.7
Fergus	6 530	1.2	381	5.8	422	2.2	424	413	2 855	12.5	3 041	2 537	18 105	59.1
Flathead	38 645	1.7	2 374	6.1	3 051	37.6	2 829	2 218	24 981	37.7	23 259	18 139	22 573	73.7
Gallatin	43 810	2.7	1 184	2.7	3 104	56.7	2 677	1 981	25 362	60.5	22 544	15 800	20 078	65.6
Garfield	1 095	1.6	42	3.8	24	9.1	23	22	142	–4.1	160	148	12 683	41.4
Glacier	5 396	–2.2	710	13.2	279	–5.1	303	294	1 968	5.1	2 358	1 873	22 183	72.5
Golden Valley	599	2.7	34	5.7	15	–	13	15	47	6.8	40	44	10 702	35.0
Granite	1 260	1.7	95	7.5	84	15.1	90	73	469	13.6	344	413	17 139	56.0
Hill	9 032	–.2	455	5.0	524	6.1	522	494	4 692	18.3	4 446	3 965	17 616	57.6
Jefferson	5 260	2.2	267	5.1	196	45.2	183	135	1 349	70.3	1 280	792	26 585	86.9
Judith Basin	1 245	.5	54	4.3	55	17.0	44	47	144	–33.9	114	218	13 333	43.6
Lake	12 674	1.7	780	6.2	674	32.4	641	509	5 179	50.6	4 436	3 439	18 447	60.3
Lewis and Clark	28 464	1.3	1 213	4.3	1 911	22.5	1 834	1 560	20 267	23.5	19 042	16 410	21 715	70.9
Liberty	1 230	–.5	40	3.3	70	4.5	67	67	447	33.0	336	336	20 045	65.5
Lincoln	7 016	–1.4	821	11.7	577	11.4	538	518	3 797	–7.5	3 542	4 105	19 952	65.2
McCone	1 326	.8	42	3.2	46	–2.1	49	47	334	–8.0	369	363	19 374	63.3
Madison	4 051	.7	159	3.9	266	43.0	235	186	1 078	5.9	880	1 018	21 159	69.1
Meagher	1 126	3.8	81	7.2	61	–4.7	73	64	271	9.3	313	248	13 963	45.6
Mineral	1 682	–.1	151	9.0	108	27.1	108	85	700	3.2	770	678	15 071	49.2
Missoula	55 603	2.9	1 857	3.3	3 541	32.7	3 219	2 669	37 491	30.6	34 242	28 716	22 239	72.7
Musselshell	1 868	.8	139	7.4	142	23.5	150	115	649	4.3	732	622	14 707	48.0
Park	10 467	.5	559	5.3	692	41.8	661	488	4 165	22.0	4 745	3 415	18 281	59.7
Petroleum	382	2.1	21	5.5	9	12.5	11	8	18	38.5	21	13	6 722	22.0

[1] Civilian unemployed as a percent of total civilian labor force.   [2] For pay period including March 12 of the year shown.

Sources: Civilian Labor Force—U.S. Bureau of Labor Statistics; Local Area Unemployment Statistics; 2000 data published 2 May 2001, 1999 data published 30 May 2001; <ftp://ftp.bls.gov/pub/time.series/la/> (related Internet site <http://www.bls.gov/lauhome.htm>). Private Business Establishments and Employment—U.S. Census Bureau; County Business Patterns on CD-ROM; annual (related Internet site <http://www.census.gov/epcd/cbp/view/cbpview.html>).

Table B–7. Counties — Labor Force and Private Business Establishments and Employment–Con.

[Includes U.S., states, and 3,142 counties/county equivalents defined as of January 1, 1992. For changes to these areas since January 1, 1992, see appendix B. Geographic Information]

County	Civilian labor force, 2000		Unemployment		Establishments				Employment[2]				Annual payroll per employee, 1998	
	Total	Percent change, 1999–2000	Total	Rate[1]	1998	Percent change, 1990–1998	1995	1990	1998	Percent change, 1990–1998	1995	1990	Amount (dollars)	Percent of national average
MONTANA—Con.														
Phillips	2 388	−2.7	115	4.8	149	8.0	165	138	958	5.9	1 049	905	16 170	52.8
Pondera...................	3 494	.5	160	4.6	206	3.0	201	200	1 411	12.8	1 240	1 251	17 595	57.5
Powder River.............	1 319	.1	39	3.0	71	36.5	55	52	207	21.8	184	170	11 324	37.0
Powell....................	2 588	1.2	125	4.8	143	−4.0	143	149	1 014	1.9	994	995	19 536	63.8
Prairie...................	710	2.9	30	4.2	34	6.3	32	32	186	121.4	135	84	12 962	42.3
Ravalli...................	18 085	1.9	948	5.2	1 099	58.8	981	692	7 809	78.9	5 972	4 366	19 370	63.3
Richland..................	5 758	.1	359	6.2	396	9.4	387	362	3 134	17.2	3 023	2 674	19 325	63.1
Roosevelt.................	4 358	−.5	415	9.5	236	−2.9	237	243	1 761	−5.3	1 821	1 860	15 502	50.6
Rosebud...................	4 646	1.0	348	7.5	194	7.2	189	181	2 662	−9.0	2 874	2 925	30 260	98.9
Sanders...................	4 319	−.2	350	8.1	345	51.3	281	228	1 732	25.0	1 494	1 386	17 147	56.0
Sheridan..................	2 182	−.8	97	4.4	164	1.2	171	162	1 000	15.5	983	866	13 683	44.7
Silver Bow	16 866	−3.1	1 038	6.2	1 155	10.2	1 131	1 048	12 162	19.3	11 408	10 196	23 338	76.2
Stillwater	4 883	2.4	237	4.9	203	28.5	194	158	2 025	44.5	1 598	1 401	32 289	105.5
Sweet Grass	1 848	1.3	47	2.5	114	17.5	111	97	601	20.9	624	497	17 646	57.6
Teton	3 541	.6	146	4.1	190	18.8	181	160	1 083	40.1	978	773	18 073	59.0
Toole....................	2 961	−1.4	102	3.4	208	−2.3	212	213	1 314	25.9	1 334	1 044	19 687	64.3
Treasure..................	524	2.3	26	5.0	25	13.6	25	22	89	−14.4	97	104	15 258	49.8
Valley	4 296	−1.7	175	4.1	259	10.7	263	234	1 880	10.4	1 800	1 703	17 537	57.3
Wheatland	1 271	−1.1	58	4.6	63	6.8	61	59	335	26.4	321	265	12 081	39.5
Wibaux	607	1.8	25	4.1	25	13.6	23	22	154	69.2	181	91	12 890	42.1
Yellowstone...............	72 921	1.1	2 763	3.8	4 783	22.1	4 479	3 917	53 847	20.3	51 765	44 760	24 081	78.7
Yellowstone National Park	X	X	X	X	–	–	–	–	–	–	–	–	–	–
NEBRASKA.............	924 298	1.4	27 537	3.0	48 655	11.2	47 128	43 749	720 252	22.7	674 779	587 044	25 239	82.5
Adams	15 435	−1.5	360	2.3	962	9.6	940	878	13 812	14.7	13 540	12 047	21 152	69.1
Antelope..................	3 080	.9	115	3.7	243	.4	233	242	1 404	3.1	1 312	1 362	17 093	55.8
Arthur	202	3.1	7	3.5	12	–	11	12	(3)	NA	35	43	D	D
Banner	423	.7	12	2.8	7	75.0	9	4	20	25.0	23	16	18 400	60.1
Blaine	375	−.3	11	2.9	13	44.4	10	9	(3)	NA	24	33	D	D
Boone	2 804	−3.2	75	2.7	201	3.1	198	195	1 530	36.7	1 320	1 119	17 576	57.4
Box Butte	6 414	−.6	319	5.0	374	4.2	359	359	3 539	19.6	2 978	2 960	17 583	57.4
Boyd	1 080	−2.4	37	3.4	77	−1.3	87	78	424	39.0	420	305	14 042	45.9
Brown	1 735	−.3	59	3.4	148	9.6	144	135	791	17.2	721	675	14 794	48.3
Buffalo	25 031	1.9	792	3.2	1 269	12.9	1 215	1 124	19 485	34.1	17 265	14 530	21 670	70.8
Burt.....................	3 446	Z	166	4.8	221	−2.6	218	227	1 199	−2.8	1 156	1 234	18 055	59.0
Butler	4 357	3.7	138	3.2	183	2.2	167	179	1 674	38.9	1 552	1 205	19 389	63.3
Cass	13 147	2.2	362	2.8	495	28.9	447	384	3 593	38.4	3 253	2 596	21 131	69.0
Cedar	4 625	1.4	131	2.8	287	11.2	258	258	1 779	22.7	1 634	1 450	18 336	59.9
Chase	1 877	−1.9	46	2.5	135	−1.5	142	137	1 014	29.0	1 069	786	17 800	58.2
Cherry	3 400	.1	90	2.6	246	19.4	232	206	1 496	42.6	1 469	1 049	16 444	53.7
Cheyenne	6 246	17.0	134	2.1	328	5.8	328	310	3 778	42.7	3 546	2 647	21 628	70.7
Clay.....................	3 419	−1.3	91	2.7	203	12.2	197	181	1 237	39.9	1 172	884	18 520	60.5
Colfax	4 903	1.5	105	2.1	277	10.4	255	251	3 732	30.0	3 231	2 871	20 791	67.9
Cuming	5 298	.2	114	2.2	362	4.9	362	345	3 123	9.3	3 084	2 856	19 027	62.2
Custer....................	5 441	.4	128	2.4	374	4.2	386	359	2 533	2.6	2 561	2 468	17 188	56.2
Dakota	10 232	−.8	341	3.3	456	11.8	451	408	12 422	10.5	11 518	11 238	26 297	85.9
Dawes	4 614	–	215	4.7	293	2.1	284	287	2 282	34.3	2 039	1 699	13 911	45.4
Dawson	13 249	1.3	375	2.8	704	3.4	717	681	9 253	60.1	8 922	5 779	20 839	68.1
Deuel	865	1.2	33	3.8	82	18.8	78	69	451	22.9	356	367	16 534	54.0
Dixon	2 465	1.7	81	3.3	188	3.2	133	124	639	−52.2	693	1 336	14 504	47.4
Dodge....................	20 234	5.5	605	3.0	1 068	6.2	1 018	1 006	13 651	26.5	13 003	10 791	21 156	69.1
Douglas	260 391	2.2	8 056	3.1	13 789	10.8	13 377	12 450	293 617	22.2	275 647	240 223	30 066	98.2
Dundy	1 059	−1.2	18	1.7	73	2.8	77	71	469	37.1	436	342	17 437	57.0
Fillmore	3 208	3.0	79	2.5	238	3.0	238	231	1 640	11.5	1 604	1 471	20 279	66.3
Franklin	1 550	−2.8	33	2.1	104	10.6	102	94	539	31.8	509	409	15 434	50.4
Frontier..................	1 520	1.0	42	2.8	88	17.3	86	75	504	34.8	402	374	17 048	55.7
Furnas	2 448	−1.2	62	2.5	177	−3.8	182	184	1 335	38.2	1 211	966	19 103	62.4
Gage.....................	12 376	−.8	369	3.0	687	14.5	630	600	7 411	18.3	6 762	6 265	18 425	60.2
Garden	1 013	−7.0	25	2.5	61	−24.7	79	81	388	4.9	393	370	14 930	48.8
Garfield..................	968	−1.3	20	2.1	86	6.2	86	81	519	3.4	528	502	14 017	45.8
Gosper	1 328	1.7	25	1.9	54	8.0	54	50	176	13.5	151	155	15 523	50.7
Grant	354	1.1	7	2.0	24	9.1	25	22	99	59.7	99	62	21 202	69.3
Greeley	1 357	−2.0	45	3.3	85	18.1	80	72	428	17.3	410	365	15 696	51.3
Hall.....................	30 857	.2	887	2.9	1 845	15.2	1 831	1 601	26 442	19.7	26 424	22 092	22 627	73.9
Hamilton	5 422	.5	106	2.0	275	5.4	266	261	2 526	10.0	2 443	2 296	21 819	71.3
Harlan	1 707	−1.1	43	2.5	96	−2.0	101	98	556	−6.2	716	593	14 059	45.9
Hayes	465	−.4	18	3.9	21	5.0	19	20	63	−20.3	65	79	15 841	51.8
Hitchcock	1 551	−.8	34	2.2	62	−13.9	59	72	281	−19.3	308	348	19 480	63.6
Holt	6 340	−4.2	171	2.7	424	5.5	414	402	2 867	19.2	2 722	2 406	16 233	53.0

[1] Civilian unemployed as a percent of total civilian labor force.   [2] For pay period including March 12 of the year shown.   [3] 20–99 employees.

Sources: Civilian Labor Force—U.S. Bureau of Labor Statistics; Local Area Unemployment Statistics; 2000 data published 2 May 2001, 1999 data published 30 May 2001; <ftp://ftp.bls.gov/pub/time.series/la/> (related Internet site <http://www.bls.gov/lauhome.htm>).   Private Business Establishments and Employment—U.S. Census Bureau; County Business Patterns on CD-ROM; annual (related Internet site <http://www.census.gov/epcd/cbp/view/cbpview.html>).

[Includes U.S., states, and 3,142 counties/county equivalents defined as of January 1, 1992. For changes to these areas since January 1, 1992, see appendix B. Geographic Information]

County	Civilian labor force, 2000				Private nonfarm businesses									
			Unemployment		Establishments				Employment[2]				Annual payroll per employee, 1998	
	Total	Percent change, 1999–2000	Total	Rate[1]	1998	Percent change, 1990–1998	1995	1990	1998	Percent change, 1990–1998	1995	1990	Amount (dollars)	Percent of national average
NEBRASKA—Con.														
Hooker	444	5.0	14	3.2	35	66.7	35	21	179	50.4	192	119	17 916	58.5
Howard	3 494	Z	92	2.6	156	23.8	150	126	854	52.8	769	559	15 930	52.0
Jefferson	4 000	.2	128	3.2	251	–1.6	259	255	2 678	11.1	2 421	2 410	18 136	59.3
Johnson	2 075	–4.5	206	9.9	134	.8	131	133	778	–22.4	1 148	1 003	14 451	47.2
Kearney	3 790	1.8	82	2.2	192	4.9	178	183	1 623	12.5	1 499	1 443	17 097	55.9
Keith	4 619	1.7	135	2.9	375	9.0	351	344	2 989	9.7	2 810	2 724	16 859	55.1
Keya Paha	514	9.6	9	1.8	22	–4.3	19	23	(3)	NA	34	52	D	D
Kimball	1 979	2.5	46	2.3	161	–4.7	162	169	1 390	32.1	1 266	1 052	16 786	54.8
Knox	4 533	–4.0	191	4.2	285	7.5	280	265	1 481	9.8	1 331	1 349	13 274	43.4
Lancaster	144 894	1.6	3 797	2.6	6 696	19.1	6 403	5 624	117 339	25.4	108 537	93 607	24 955	81.5
Lincoln	16 792	–2.2	613	3.7	969	1.6	988	954	9 691	23.4	9 305	7 851	18 638	60.9
Logan	424	–2.8	9	2.1	15	–6.3	12	16	(3)	NA	40	45	D	D
Loup	367	–3.9	8	2.2	8	–20.0	8	10	(4)	NA	21	19	D	D
McPherson	286	–2.4	4	1.4	7	75.0	9	4	(4)	NA	11	22	D	D
Madison	19 797	.9	720	3.6	1 319	14.3	1 226	1 154	19 313	26.8	17 907	15 228	21 425	70.0
Merrick	4 562	.8	114	2.5	237	22.2	222	194	1 948	52.9	1 629	1 274	19 076	62.3
Morrill	2 687	–.6	101	3.8	117	–2.5	124	120	806	37.5	684	586	17 390	56.8
Nance	1 748	3.8	64	3.7	115	–8.7	105	126	490	–31.2	484	712	14 822	48.4
Nemaha	4 078	4.4	180	4.4	198	–2.0	194	202	1 687	17.2	1 648	1 439	18 231	59.6
Nuckolls	2 272	1.2	56	2.5	189	–7.4	207	204	1 270	–13.5	1 388	1 468	14 733	48.1
Otoe	7 733	1.9	266	3.4	445	21.9	420	365	4 583	18.7	4 540	3 862	19 303	63.1
Pawnee	1 640	3.1	52	3.2	81	14.1	75	71	456	32.2	406	345	15 175	49.6
Perkins	1 424	–2.9	32	2.2	110	4.8	115	105	771	50.3	771	513	18 567	60.7
Phelps	4 962	1.2	98	2.0	343	4.6	324	328	3 888	15.6	3 775	3 362	21 915	71.6
Pierce	4 034	1.4	114	2.8	212	–.5	216	213	1 440	22.1	1 318	1 179	17 354	56.7
Platte	17 330	2.3	556	3.2	992	19.2	959	832	15 781	25.2	14 160	12 602	22 883	74.8
Polk	2 281	–1.2	53	2.3	139	–7.3	147	150	944	1.6	923	929	17 479	57.1
Red Willow	5 888	–.8	148	2.5	430	–4.2	444	449	4 274	13.2	4 040	3 776	16 796	54.9
Richardson	4 260	–.5	266	6.2	305	5.9	304	288	2 176	4.9	2 275	2 074	16 518	54.0
Rock	817	–6.8	28	3.4	61	1.7	63	60	412	32.1	376	312	13 667	44.7
Saline	6 671	–4.9	171	2.6	311	3.7	315	300	5 227	19.7	5 015	4 366	21 654	70.7
Sarpy	62 230	2.0	1 374	2.2	2 010	40.7	1 819	1 429	26 503	19.5	22 680	22 170	24 654	80.5
Saunders	10 371	3.9	332	3.2	452	22.2	438	370	3 139	48.1	3 130	2 119	18 265	59.7
Scotts Bluff	18 340	.7	837	4.6	1 227	5.0	1 191	1 169	12 633	12.8	12 287	11 195	21 256	69.4
Seward	9 222	2.5	263	2.9	408	5.7	383	386	5 562	30.1	5 102	4 275	19 603	64.0
Sheridan	2 807	–1.1	96	3.4	198	7.6	201	184	1 179	20.9	1 350	975	13 585	44.4
Sherman	1 409	–3.2	49	3.5	80	–14.9	95	94	435	5.6	478	412	13 223	43.2
Sioux	750	–.4	9	1.2	16	–40.7	22	27	42	–77.9	68	190	9 762	31.9
Stanton	3 286	1.5	103	3.1	87	14.5	79	76	517	–46.3	378	962	14 273	46.6
Thayer	3 348	2.7	72	2.2	218	2.3	226	213	1 783	30.0	1 683	1 372	20 189	66.0
Thomas	419	–10.5	25	6.0	38	35.7	34	28	220	233.3	113	66	14 550	47.5
Thurston	2 802	–.7	276	9.9	135	13.4	120	119	1 457	30.1	1 399	1 120	20 478	66.9
Valley	2 440	–.9	63	2.6	175	–1.7	181	178	1 181	17.4	1 194	1 006	16 633	54.3
Washington	11 054	2.2	259	2.3	454	16.1	428	391	5 322	55.0	4 711	3 434	23 262	76.0
Wayne	6 368	–.2	230	3.6	256	18.5	236	216	3 686	107.7	3 679	1 775	17 875	58.4
Webster	1 732	–1.5	40	2.3	104	–9.6	108	115	644	16.2	709	554	15 388	50.3
Wheeler	376	–7.4	10	2.7	16	6.7	15	15	96	–32.9	60	143	8 760	28.6
York	8 651	–3.9	174	2.0	518	3.8	509	499	6 357	27.0	6 214	5 006	20 910	68.3
NEVADA	986 052	4.7	39 978	4.1	44 613	49.0	37 219	29 932	800 861	49.2	672 260	536 607	27 280	89.1
Churchill	9 215	–.5	754	8.2	511	23.1	456	415	4 687	38.8	4 369	3 376	22 083	72.1
Clark	688 494	5.9	28 524	4.1	26 691	63.7	21 289	16 305	549 060	64.3	449 215	334 100	27 315	89.2
Douglas	18 043	1.6	748	4.1	1 289	51.3	1 166	852	18 349	15.1	17 716	15 937	24 724	80.8
Elko	20 129	.2	899	4.5	1 012	40.0	873	723	17 108	49.3	14 536	11 458	26 243	85.7
Esmeralda	462	–24.3	46	10.0	15	–31.8	18	22	166	2.5	(5)	162	29 452	96.2
Eureka	848	–.9	22	2.6	39	30.0	32	30	2 767	NA	(6)	(7)	48 086	157.1
Humboldt	7 349	–5.4	378	5.1	409	31.5	357	311	6 615	71.4	5 273	3 859	30 029	98.1
Lander	2 313	–8.7	178	7.7	98	5.4	110	93	1 451	–14.8	1 591	1 704	28 802	94.1
Lincoln	1 010	–1.6	67	6.6	80	33.3	65	60	511	59.2	368	321	14 722	48.1
Lyon	13 301	1.0	919	6.9	546	42.6	427	383	6 001	66.5	4 093	3 604	22 947	75.0
Mineral	2 054	3.9	207	10.1	89	–16.0	97	106	1 551	–5.1	1 684	1 635	23 015	75.2
Nye	15 815	6.7	852	5.4	543	84.7	364	294	5 444	–37.8	3 943	8 748	24 706	80.7
Pershing	2 138	–1.8	87	4.1	95	14.5	93	83	1 470	66.5	985	883	33 929	110.8
Storey	1 547	1.3	45	2.9	82	57.7	68	52	321	52.9	(8)	210	15 623	51.0
Washoe	177 741	3.0	5 375	3.0	10 674	27.1	9 729	8 398	161 330	25.0	144 052	129 082	27 634	90.3
White Pine	2 855	–10.2	111	3.9	215	–.9	232	217	2 287	–12.2	2 021	2 606	28 835	94.2
Independent City														
Carson City city	22 739	1.6	765	3.4	2 209	41.5	1 817	1 561	21 677	38.8	19 085	15 618	25 973	84.9

[1] Civilian unemployed as a percent of total civilian labor force. [2] For pay period including March 12 of the year shown. [3] 20–99 employees. [4] 0–19 employees. [5] 100–249 employees. [6] 1,000–2,499 employees. [7] 2,500–4,999 employees. [8] 250–499 employees.

Sources: Civilian Labor Force—U.S. Bureau of Labor Statistics; Local Area Unemployment Statistics; 2000 data published 2 May 2001, 1999 data published 30 May 2001; <ftp://ftp.bls.gov/pub/time.series/la/> (related Internet site <http://www.bls.gov/lauhome.htm>). Private Business Establishments and Employment—U.S. Census Bureau; County Business Patterns on CD-ROM; annual (related Internet site <http://www.census.gov/epcd/cbp/view/cbpview.html>).

[Includes U.S., states, and 3,142 counties/county equivalents defined as of January 1, 1992. For changes to these areas since January 1, 1992, see appendix B. Geographic Information]

County	Civilian labor force, 2000		Unemployment		Establishments				Employment[2]				Annual payroll per employee, 1998	
	Total	Percent change, 1999– 2000	Total	Rate[1]	1998	Percent change, 1990– 1998	1995	1990	1998	Percent change, 1990– 1998	1995	1990	Amount (dollars)	Percent of national average
NEW HAMPSHIRE	685 511	2.6	19 191	2.8	36 842	10.8	34 647	33 249	518 526	17.9	464 122	439 636	28 666	93.7
Belknap	29 329	-2.5	755	2.6	1 865	1.8	1 834	1 832	20 889	12.4	19 336	18 589	24 936	81.5
Carroll	21 897	2.3	621	2.8	1 833	8.7	1 730	1 687	17 639	39.1	13 774	12 684	18 894	61.7
Cheshire	39 980	3.1	1 171	2.9	1 952	4.5	1 900	1 868	27 490	5.9	26 208	25 955	25 992	84.9
Coos	16 904	.9	802	4.7	975	-7.7	992	1 056	11 540	-5.7	11 291	12 244	23 050	75.3
Grafton	43 914	-.4	892	2.0	2 875	6.5	2 749	2 699	46 559	30.2	39 774	35 768	24 691	80.7
Hillsborough	213 388	3.3	5 635	2.6	10 779	9.4	10 050	9 853	176 318	12.5	155 400	156 662	31 198	101.9
Merrimack	77 198	3.0	1 776	2.3	3 991	12.7	3 747	3 542	51 764	16.1	48 823	44 602	28 201	92.1
Rockingham	161 484	3.5	5 480	3.4	9 078	21.4	8 343	7 476	114 513	28.5	103 207	89 112	31 027	101.4
Strafford	60 291	4.3	1 582	2.6	2 403	10.3	2 305	2 178	39 309	21.3	34 542	32 396	27 098	88.5
Sullivan	21 126	-1.6	478	2.3	1 091	5.0	997	1 039	12 505	10.9	11 767	11 273	24 048	78.6
NEW JERSEY	4 187 899	-.4	157 410	3.8	230 860	7.8	220 991	214 076	3 368 365	4.6	3 184 458	3 220 178	37 344	122.0
Atlantic	125 341	-2.0	7 119	5.7	6 310	4.2	6 055	6 054	121 092	1.8	115 881	118 916	27 030	88.3
Bergen	435 583	-1.2	13 420	3.1	32 941	4.7	32 034	31 468	446 352	1.6	424 051	439 302	40 025	130.8
Burlington	222 471	-1.0	6 431	2.9	10 086	11.3	9 497	9 065	158 802	12.9	137 050	140 683	32 225	105.3
Camden	253 052	-1.3	9 961	3.9	12 595	.3	12 447	12 556	178 439	-1.5	171 861	181 246	30 549	99.8
Cape May	44 663	-2.1	3 828	8.6	4 045	8.3	3 821	3 736	24 929	4.7	(3)	23 799	25 777	84.2
Cumberland	63 390	-2.5	4 565	7.2	3 058	-3.5	3 097	3 170	44 863	-10.8	47 555	50 314	27 873	91.1
Essex	365 941	-.6	17 210	4.7	19 880	-1.7	19 635	20 221	332 831	-6.1	333 646	354 333	37 376	122.1
Gloucester	129 514	-1.3	4 859	3.8	5 510	13.9	5 216	4 839	73 288	16.3	65 559	63 008	29 059	94.9
Hudson	280 974	-.5	15 975	5.7	13 254	8.5	13 143	12 211	210 152	2.9	215 395	204 302	37 126	121.3
Hunterdon	71 051	1.1	1 187	1.7	3 776	17.0	3 488	3 228	40 135	24.3	36 010	32 281	39 959	130.5
Mercer	174 296	1.5	5 313	3.0	9 317	6.3	9 067	8 762	156 991	-.7	163 644	158 026	36 265	118.5
Middlesex	411 155	.8	12 670	3.1	20 219	17.7	18 178	17 181	363 121	13.8	333 722	319 093	40 744	133.1
Monmouth	309 355	.3	10 041	3.2	18 278	14.1	17 362	16 015	200 524	9.1	187 447	183 832	33 491	109.4
Morris	263 176	Z	6 018	2.3	17 162	16.6	15 992	14 722	280 256	20.1	239 512	233 349	47 844	156.3
Ocean	213 290	.3	8 259	3.9	10 666	15.5	9 952	9 231	105 202	15.6	96 695	91 041	25 545	83.5
Passaic	227 774	-1.9	11 323	5.0	11 956	.4	11 800	11 909	164 987	-8.7	160 604	180 704	32 744	107.0
Salem	31 312	-.9	1 376	4.4	1 351	13.1	1 266	1 195	17 946	-4.1	18 378	18 710	35 307	115.3
Somerset	173 243	1.2	3 620	2.1	9 454	21.1	8 775	7 805	165 200	22.1	147 642	135 246	48 263	157.7
Sussex	76 560	-.1	2 189	2.9	3 470	10.9	3 306	3 129	27 181	9.8	25 894	24 750	26 845	87.7
Union	264 140	-.4	10 449	4.0	14 789	-1.5	14 164	15 017	225 532	-4.8	211 279	237 022	40 656	132.8
Warren	51 620	-.6	1 598	3.1	2 721	7.8	2 686	2 523	30 163	2.8	30 010	29 345	32 789	107.1
NEW MEXICO	832 835	2.9	40 400	4.9	42 608	19.4	40 631	35 700	540 186	29.2	506 634	417 986	24 313	79.4
Bernalillo	293 068	4.1	9 479	3.2	15 585	16.4	15 001	13 387	249 348	28.7	239 130	193 754	26 593	86.9
Catron	1 121	.7	91	8.1	59	22.9	58	48	238	38.4	204	172	12 966	42.4
Chaves	24 560	-1.7	1 536	6.3	1 525	9.9	1 485	1 387	16 056	1.5	15 525	15 822	20 092	65.6
Cibola	11 424	6.0	800	7.0	363	17.9	352	308	4 654	58.5	3 673	2 936	20 610	67.3
Colfax	6 705	2.1	338	5.0	500	23.2	445	406	3 963	32.6	4 020	2 988	17 343	56.7
Curry	19 128	.2	731	3.8	1 072	5.0	1 076	1 021	10 635	16.0	10 337	9 171	18 204	59.5
DeBaca	999	.3	45	4.5	62	-6.1	65	66	339	26.0	291	269	16 035	52.4
Dona Ana	70 923	3.9	4 645	6.5	3 183	23.7	3 071	2 574	34 739	33.0	32 071	26 119	19 389	63.3
Eddy	22 928	-1.2	1 516	6.6	1 283	11.9	1 281	1 147	15 947	18.3	14 502	13 478	24 115	78.8
Grant	12 546	.9	768	6.1	694	14.7	638	605	7 972	25.9	7 745	6 332	25 203	82.3
Guadalupe	1 824	-.7	150	8.2	113	10.8	101	102	1 077	33.5	895	807	14 257	46.6
Harding	431	-.1	15	3.5	20	17.6	19	17	54	-8.5	46	59	21 926	71.6
Hidalgo	1 974	-18.4	209	10.6	108	-4.4	128	113	1 451	9.8	l 517	1 321	23 881	78.0
Lea	24 634	3.8	1 173	4.8	1 487	.9	1 501	1 474	16 044	10.8	15 628	14 475	22 866	74.7
Lincoln	7 557	3.4	317	4.2	708	44.8	591	489	4 406	51.4	3 844	2 910	17 344	56.7
Los Alamos	10 425	3.8	202	1.9	446	7.7	433	414	5 830	5.1	6 222	5 547	29 738	97.2
Luna	11 240	2.3	2 575	22.9	414	19.7	381	346	3 408	30.9	2 912	2 604	16 621	54.3
McKinley	24 769	1.3	1 772	7.2	1 037	12.6	994	921	13 792	20.2	12 913	11 476	20 937	68.4
Mora	1 728	2.1	266	15.4	61	60.5	50	38	412	227.0	350	126	15 925	52.0
Otero	19 947	-.3	1 023	5.1	1 035	8.9	1 022	950	11 229	10.3	9 608	10 178	18 061	59.0
Quay	4 479	1.2	191	4.3	295	7.3	297	275	2 097	-3.5	2 080	2 174	15 338	50.1
Rio Arriba	19 865	3.6	1 377	6.9	637	32.4	591	481	6 248	60.1	6 240	3 903	19 082	62.3
Roosevelt	7 375	.1	250	3.4	342	-1.4	345	347	2 923	8.6	2 716	2 692	16 186	52.9
Sandoval	44 689	4.0	1 453	3.3	1 172	57.3	1 057	745	18 750	162.6	15 588	7 141	30 873	100.9
San Juan	49 009	1.1	3 522	7.2	2 416	26.2	2 253	1 914	31 938	32.8	30 045	24 053	27 180	88.8
San Miguel.............	12 061	3.2	748	6.2	536	32.3	504	405	5 063	18.2	4 991	4 285	19 817	64.7
Santa Fe	65 035	3.2	1 759	2.7	4 517	31.8	4 210	3 428	44 430	35.6	39 564	32 765	23 852	77.9
Sierra	4 017	.2	115	2.9	313	49.0	268	210	1 931	55.9	1 619	1 239	14 803	48.4
Socorro	6 515	3.8	357	5.5	271	3.0	267	263	2 410	5.6	2 371	2 282	16 983	55.5
Taos	12 638	-.2	1 327	10.5	1 109	36.4	1 019	813	8 242	26.9	8 011	6 496	16 733	54.7
Torrance	7 036	11.4	405	5.8	235	63.2	189	144	1 842	94.5	1 463	947	16 192	52.9
Union	2 000	1.7	54	2.7	119	-5.6	114	126	732	10.2	711	664	15 970	52.2
Valencia	30 187	4.3	1 193	4.0	833	32.6	759	628	8 267	58.7	7 106	5 209	18 163	59.3

[1] Civilian unemployed as a percent of total civilian labor force. [2] For pay period including March 12 of the year shown. [3] 10,000–24,999 employees.

Sources: Civilian Labor Force—U.S. Bureau of Labor Statistics; Local Area Unemployment Statistics; 2000 data published 2 May 2001, 1999 data published 30 May 2001; <ftp://ftp.bls.gov/pub/time.series/la/> (related Internet site <http://www.bls.gov/lauhome.htm>). Private Business Establishments and Employment—U.S. Census Bureau; County Business Patterns on CD-ROM; annual (related Internet site <http://www.census.gov/epcd/cbp/view/cbpview.html>).

[Includes U.S., states, and 3,142 counties/county equivalents defined as of January 1, 1992. For changes to these areas since January 1, 1992, see appendix B. Geographic Information]

County	Civilian labor force, 2000		Unemployment		Private nonfarm businesses								Annual payroll per employee, 1998	
					Establishments				Employment[2]					
	Total	Percent change, 1999–2000	Total	Rate[1]	1998	Percent change, 1990–1998	1995	1990	1998	Percent change, 1990–1998	1995	1990	Amount (dollars)	Percent of national average
NEW YORK	8 941 082	.7	407 769	4.6	481 962	3.3	467 262	466 762	6 993 814	-1.2	6 782 174	7 075 441	39 268	128.3
Albany	154 985	-.8	4 390	2.8	8 815	2.1	8 897	8 630	162 226	2.8	161 308	157 822	29 852	97.5
Allegany	22 823	-1.4	1 540	6.7	842	.6	798	837	12 131	3.1	12 328	11 768	20 352	66.5
Bronx	479 000	3.4	34 856	7.3	14 233	9.1	13 555	13 051	194 171	.4	196 713	193 458	29 763	97.2
Broome	97 109	-.5	3 248	3.3	4 280	-7.9	4 408	4 645	81 593	-7.4	82 685	88 087	27 261	89.1
Cattaraugus	39 740	-3.1	2 530	6.4	1 772	-2.0	1 810	1 809	24 039	1.4	24 837	23 713	22 837	74.6
Cayuga	37 313	-1.5	1 689	4.5	1 561	.6	1 571	1 552	19 050	2.0	19 075	18 672	22 944	75.0
Chautauqua	65 739	-.7	3 130	4.8	3 107	-6.1	3 115	3 309	46 937	-1.2	45 197	47 515	23 231	75.9
Chemung	43 061	-2.9	2 085	4.8	1 933	-4.4	1 972	2 023	36 456	4.5	34 491	34 898	24 550	80.2
Chenango	23 735	-1.3	1 139	4.8	1 027	-1.8	1 004	1 046	12 572	-7.3	12 587	13 566	24 278	79.3
Clinton	39 123	-1.3	2 030	5.2	1 888	1.3	1 940	1 864	23 507	3.0	23 918	22 814	22 917	74.9
Columbia	34 153	1.8	985	2.9	1 640	9.9	1 534	1 492	14 983	3.8	13 961	14 429	24 520	80.1
Cortland	22 134	-2.3	1 316	5.9	1 036	2.2	1 082	1 014	17 235	-3.4	17 902	17 840	20 252	66.2
Delaware	20 602	-.8	982	4.8	1 115	-14.8	1 145	1 308	12 610	-4.3	12 517	13 175	24 142	78.9
Dutchess	119 419	-.2	3 643	3.1	6 593	4.3	6 384	6 319	82 574	-15.6	80 182	97 812	28 045	91.6
Erie	451 115	-2.1	21 600	4.8	22 528	-1.6	23 014	22 890	399 282	.1	401 680	398 718	27 439	89.6
Essex	17 935	-1.5	1 187	6.6	1 168	2.6	1 142	1 138	9 786	5.9	8 927	9 237	22 519	73.6
Franklin	22 258	1.3	1 687	7.6	1 043	2.8	1 046	1 015	9 336	-2.1	9 789	9 541	20 691	67.6
Fulton	26 252	-1.5	1 532	5.8	1 080	-5.8	1 078	1 147	13 418	1.6	13 283	13 205	23 018	75.2
Genesee	31 405	-1.3	1 539	4.9	1 333	1.0	1 298	1 320	16 714	-2.6	16 256	17 154	23 662	77.3
Greene	21 088	-2.3	1 054	5.0	1 100	-5.3	1 083	1 162	8 915	-2.2	9 455	9 113	19 718	64.4
Hamilton	2 488	-3.3	204	8.2	203	-4.2	198	212	663	-6.1	690	706	20 661	67.5
Herkimer	30 817	-.4	1 532	5.0	1 178	-4.8	1 211	1 237	13 640	3.1	14 265	13 232	22 327	72.9
Jefferson	43 238	-1.7	3 553	8.2	2 304	-1.3	2 261	2 335	26 366	-4.0	25 506	27 472	23 541	76.9
Kings	995 580	3.1	67 313	6.8	36 980	9.6	34 154	33 752	409 117	2.1	403 635	400 652	28 362	92.7
Lewis	12 159	-.1	952	7.8	553	4.7	500	528	4 768	2.1	4 561	4 669	22 957	75.0
Livingston	34 024	-1.4	1 554	4.6	1 233	12.8	1 193	1 093	11 735	-5.9	11 727	12 473	20 956	68.5
Madison	35 160	-1.1	1 562	4.4	1 351	-1.7	1 398	1 374	18 837	28.6	16 141	14 649	21 256	69.4
Monroe	376 841	-1.1	14 145	3.8	16 463	-.2	16 415	16 504	361 798	-.3	365 112	363 015	32 665	106.7
Montgomery	23 064	-1.4	1 339	5.8	1 142	3.5	1 151	1 103	15 964	9.9	16 255	14 525	22 233	72.6
Nassau	685 677	-.5	18 745	2.7	46 238	-2.1	46 240	47 234	532 641	-6.8	522 215	571 682	33 859	110.6
New York	856 133	3.5	42 230	4.9	105 128	5.3	99 779	99 870	1 951 646	-3.2	1 819 293	2 015 135	62 774	205.1
Niagara	106 307	-2.0	6 244	5.9	4 590	-2.2	4 664	4 691	67 088	-5.4	66 480	70 908	26 061	85.1
Oneida	111 613	-.3	4 267	3.8	4 977	-8.7	5 189	5 453	86 713	2.1	89 639	84 953	23 093	75.4
Onondaga	230 285	-.9	8 003	3.5	11 571	-6.9	11 780	12 430	226 050	-2.6	223 633	232 120	29 221	95.5
Ontario	52 836	-1.4	1 942	3.7	2 518	8.4	2 382	2 323	36 166	17.5	32 841	30 771	26 358	86.1
Orange	156 730	-.9	4 914	3.1	7 867	7.8	7 250	7 295	87 960	4.9	82 009	83 870	26 333	86.0
Orleans	20 856	-.9	1 110	5.3	703	6.8	693	658	6 803	-1.5	7 024	6 904	20 615	67.4
Oswego	56 415	-.9	3 571	6.3	2 017	2.5	2 028	1 967	23 772	-2.6	25 046	24 396	27 441	89.6
Otsego	31 463	-.5	1 465	4.7	1 335	-4.8	1 373	1 402	17 455	8.9	16 682	16 028	22 537	73.6
Putnam	54 115	-.7	1 329	2.5	2 475	18.2	2 119	2 094	17 231	5.1	15 309	16 400	30 393	99.3
Queens	1 024 481	3.1	49 275	4.8	35 408	5.0	33 947	33 710	444 825	-2.2	421 561	454 973	31 116	101.7
Rensselaer	78 428	-.9	3 014	3.8	2 695	-3.0	2 696	2 778	41 552	.7	39 923	41 267	25 390	82.9
Richmond	205 730	3.3	9 887	4.8	7 073	8.1	6 766	6 540	79 611	11.3	77 792	71 525	27 454	89.7
Rockland	144 110	-1.5	4 329	3.0	8 297	8.0	7 853	7 682	92 559	5.5	92 059	87 775	32 356	105.7
St. Lawrence	50 540	-1.5	4 019	8.0	2 150	2.4	2 135	2 100	28 654	.5	28 895	28 509	23 823	77.8
Saratoga	104 001	-.8	3 375	3.2	3 955	8.1	3 778	3 660	50 296	26.1	44 091	39 892	26 370	86.2
Schenectady	71 092	-.9	2 455	3.5	2 995	-12.8	3 198	3 435	47 683	-9.2	49 035	52 513	30 883	100.9
Schoharie	14 899	-1.3	719	4.8	573	.4	539	571	5 747	19.0	5 299	4 831	20 639	67.4
Schuyler	8 913	-.9	489	5.5	344	7.8	308	319	3 065	-16.4	2 996	3 668	22 500	73.5
Seneca	15 378	-2.1	751	4.9	658	12.9	602	583	7 359	-6.7	7 676	7 888	25 169	82.2
Steuben	48 540	2.1	2 358	4.9	1 787	-6.1	1 787	1 903	29 921	-1.8	27 381	30 454	32 741	107.0
Suffolk	715 426	-.7	22 746	3.2	41 675	9.1	39 270	38 194	487 168	6.9	460 288	455 555	32 972	107.7
Sullivan	30 932	-.7	1 538	5.0	1 943	-5.4	2 168	2 054	17 387	-7.1	20 905	18 720	23 930	78.2
Tioga	26 242	-.2	865	3.3	786	.4	749	783	11 017	-3.3	10 140	11 397	33 264	108.7
Tompkins	50 830	-.9	1 354	2.7	2 122	-.7	2 090	2 138	39 804	-2.7	40 636	40 901	24 190	79.0
Ulster	82 114	-.2	2 748	3.3	4 253	1.6	4 080	4 185	46 526	6.9	42 704	43 540	22 794	74.5
Warren	30 970	-1.1	1 243	4.0	2 263	1.0	2 193	2 240	31 566	12.0	32 137	28 184	25 604	83.6
Washington	28 188	-.7	1 154	4.1	1 047	-2.3	974	1 072	9 778	-13.4	10 176	11 285	24 177	79.0
Wayne	49 130	-1.6	2 152	4.4	1 643	11.7	1 623	1 471	22 136	22.8	21 152	18 028	24 174	79.0
Westchester	442 296	-1.1	13 472	3.0	30 096	4.0	29 296	28 944	368 745	-6.4	376 884	393 824	40 962	133.8
Wyoming	20 548	-.1	1 189	5.8	763	3.1	844	740	8 586	9.9	10 211	7 812	21 599	70.6
Yates	13 509	.3	505	3.7	494	9.8	497	450	5 090	30.0	4 647	3 916	19 116	62.5

[1] Civilian unemployed as a percent of total civilian labor force.   [2] For pay period including March 12 of the year shown.

Sources: Civilian Labor Force—U.S. Bureau of Labor Statistics; Local Area Unemployment Statistics; 2000 data published 2 May 2001, 1999 data published 30 May 2001; <ftp://ftp.bls.gov/pub/time.series/la/> (related Internet site <http://www.bls.gov/lauhome.htm>).   Private Business Establishments and Employment—U.S. Census Bureau; County Business Patterns on CD-ROM; annual (related Internet site <http://www.census.gov/epcd/cbp/view/cbpview.html>).

[Includes U.S., states, and 3,142 counties/county equivalents defined as of January 1, 1992. For changes to these areas since January 1, 1992, see appendix B. Geographic Information]

County	Civilian labor force, 2000		Unemployment		Private nonfarm businesses								Annual payroll per employee, 1998	
					Establishments				Employment[2]					
	Total	Percent change, 1999–2000	Total	Rate[1]	1998	Percent change, 1990–1998	1995	1990	1998	Percent change, 1990–1998	1995	1990	Amount (dollars)	Percent of national average
NORTH CAROLINA......	3 958 354	2.3	144 079	3.6	198 690	20.4	181 972	165 076	3 223 178	20.3	2 992 175	2 678 669	26 924	88.0
Alamance................	66 468	2.0	1 893	2.8	3 275	7.4	3 112	3 048	57 559	13.7	56 258	50 631	23 621	77.2
Alexander...............	17 281	1.8	402	2.3	604	15.7	553	522	9 028	10.1	8 639	8 202	21 061	68.8
Alleghany...............	5 778	1.8	405	7.0	271	18.9	251	228	3 186	18.9	3 104	2 680	18 255	59.6
Anson	10 275	.4	681	6.6	456	–3.8	432	474	5 908	–20.2	7 104	7 404	23 193	75.8
Ashe	11 264	.2	699	6.2	522	18.6	479	440	5 873	4.6	6 036	5 617	19 913	65.1
Avery	7 713	–.7	266	3.4	574	11.5	509	515	5 791	19.7	4 725	4 836	18 948	61.9
Beaufort	19 623	–.4	1 496	7.6	1 146	12.8	1 056	1 016	15 433	13.0	15 438	13 659	22 123	72.3
Bertie	8 739	3.3	795	9.1	379	3.0	377	368	5 446	–.4	5 417	5 470	18 229	59.6
Bladen	19 544	.1	1 126	5.8	541	2.5	542	528	10 596	94.0	8 560	5 462	19 649	64.2
Brunswick	34 634	3.8	1 556	4.5	1 666	44.2	1 461	1 155	16 360	66.1	14 256	9 852	24 727	80.8
Buncombe	102 032	1.7	2 643	2.6	6 273	22.9	5 671	5 105	92 346	19.6	86 069	77 194	24 489	80.0
Burke	42 988	2.4	1 392	3.2	1 543	12.1	1 442	1 376	30 774	2.8	30 103	29 944	23 541	76.9
Cabarrus	69 371	4.7	1 784	2.6	2 906	22.5	2 612	2 373	45 564	29.5	40 105	35 191	26 752	87.4
Caldwell................	40 326	2.2	949	2.4	1 545	12.7	1 403	1 371	28 910	4.1	29 334	27 765	22 430	73.3
Camden	3 153	–.1	83	2.6	114	44.3	93	79	870	126.6	806	384	23 164	75.7
Carteret	29 075	1.0	1 274	4.4	1 879	25.2	1 733	1 501	17 308	32.2	14 907	13 094	17 766	58.0
Caswell.................	12 896	.5	339	2.6	232	11.0	219	209	1 580	9.0	1 511	1 449	16 685	54.5
Catawba	74 617	1.9	1 634	2.2	4 319	11.1	4 118	3 886	89 436	10.5	88 300	80 964	24 923	81.4
Chatham	26 954	3.1	499	1.9	961	28.8	860	746	13 343	30.3	12 658	10 242	21 822	71.3
Cherokee	11 454	.3	845	7.4	589	28.9	523	457	7 352	19.8	6 771	6 139	19 977	65.3
Chowan	6 459	.4	259	4.0	340	7.3	320	317	4 603	22.5	3 968	3 759	19 247	62.9
Clay	4 166	.9	171	4.1	201	46.7	186	137	1 326	15.8	1 292	1 145	18 700	61.1
Cleveland...............	44 440	3.0	2 659	6.0	2 128	6.2	2 055	2 003	35 351	2.4	34 513	34 514	24 129	78.8
Columbus...............	22 382	1.1	2 379	10.6	1 200	13.9	1 135	1 054	14 980	2.8	14 886	14 570	20 813	68.0
Craven	36 543	.5	1 534	4.2	2 138	21.8	1 948	1 756	26 162	23.8	22 645	21 135	23 427	76.5
Cumberland.............	119 619	1.9	5 023	4.2	5 312	11.6	5 247	4 760	86 766	29.7	77 585	66 882	21 926	71.6
Currituck...............	9 042	1.5	225	2.5	404	55.4	319	260	2 482	62.9	1 669	1 524	19 129	62.5
Dare	17 890	.9	917	5.1	1 626	26.4	1 460	1 286	11 401	26.2	9 813	9 034	20 492	66.9
Davidson	79 527	2.0	2 202	2.8	2 673	14.5	2 450	2 334	43 974	7.5	42 901	40 915	23 712	77.5
Davie	17 990	3.4	773	4.3	672	19.1	578	564	9 052	24.2	8 691	7 291	21 533	70.3
Duplin	21 371	–2.4	1 068	5.0	1 012	27.1	911	796	12 457	24.4	12 019	10 011	18 730	61.2
Durham	117 242	3.2	2 674	2.3	5 770	22.9	5 366	4 693	156 006	35.0	143 278	115 549	35 545	116.1
Edgecombe.............	23 770	–1.1	1 778	7.5	963	23.0	1 012	783	17 695	1.2	22 343	17 489	25 372	82.9
Forsyth	152 748	2.0	4 201	2.8	8 320	11.4	7 914	7 470	170 994	15.3	159 791	148 249	29 955	97.9
Franklin	23 781	3.1	629	2.6	730	27.0	637	575	7 891	9.9	0 790	7 101	23 050	75.3
Gaston	103 942	6.8	6 330	6.1	4 178	10.2	3 874	3 793	74 878	2.8	75 933	72 861	24 764	80.9
Gates	4 570	–.5	145	3.2	134	3.9	132	129	967	13.1	1 053	855	17 402	56.9
Graham	3 686	–.2	300	8.1	176	22.2	145	144	1 707	1.4	1 613	1 683	20 114	65.7
Granville...............	22 586	.5	934	4.1	795	22.1	713	651	13 930	40.5	12 339	9 918	24 185	79.0
Greene	9 001	.3	398	4.4	206	1.5	193	203	1 989	–8.0	1 838	2 162	17 808	58.2
Guilford.................	219 349	2.0	6 375	2.9	13 360	13.8	12 739	11 738	256 664	21.6	235 023	211 030	28 936	94.5
Halifax	21 934	–.4	1 649	7.5	1 133	–2.8	1 125	1 166	14 313	–5.5	15 324	15 144	21 723	71.0
Harnett	35 774	1.6	1 398	3.9	1 466	17.0	1 396	1 253	20 815	20.3	20 888	17 301	20 235	66.1
Haywood	23 280	–1.6	918	3.9	1 372	17.4	1 270	1 169	13 833	20.3	13 137	11 498	23 159	75.7
Henderson..............	38 300	2.7	816	2.1	2 102	11.3	1 952	1 889	29 114	28.0	26 197	22 750	24 940	81.5
Hertford................	10 500	2.3	578	5.5	574	.7	554	570	7 084	7.3	6 639	6 601	19 176	62.6
Hoke	12 105	3.1	966	8.0	284	22.9	271	231	5 217	–6.9	5 549	5 606	21 962	71.8
Hyde	3 014	–1.2	196	6.5	180	4.7	165	172	970	2.1	849	950	17 243	56.3
Iredell	64 528	3.7	2 153	3.3	3 119	33.2	2 632	2 342	46 931	22.6	42 020	38 291	25 339	82.8
Jackson	16 153	2.0	567	3.5	890	36.9	797	650	8 036	53.1	6 581	5 250	19 608	64.1
Johnston	61 228	3.2	1 317	2.2	2 489	27.6	2 186	1 950	28 497	30.2	25 392	21 881	22 486	73.5
Jones	4 382	.2	228	5.2	165	.6	187	164	1 298	12.1	1 683	1 158	20 343	66.5
Lee	26 423	2.1	1 081	4.1	1 391	8.8	1 346	1 279	24 645	29.7	24 196	19 007	24 236	79.2
Lenoir	29 124	–.4	1 602	5.5	1 531	3.3	1 511	1 482	27 563	6.6	28 003	25 864	23 268	76.0
Lincoln	32 996	5.5	1 357	4.1	1 275	16.4	1 135	1 095	18 081	21.0	16 933	14 949	23 677	77.4
McDowell	19 799	.2	911	4.6	763	12.7	711	677	14 898	10.2	14 408	13 513	20 912	68.3
Macon	13 816	1.3	484	3.5	1 026	31.7	920	779	8 352	44.4	7 686	5 782	20 840	68.1
Madison	9 043	1.9	298	3.3	305	24.5	266	245	2 991	34.5	2 072	2 223	20 126	65.8
Martin	11 154	.6	1 059	9.5	550	7.0	525	514	6 637	–7.2	7 484	7 150	18 440	60.2
Mecklenburg	378 054	4.6	9 519	2.5	23 466	27.5	20 929	18 404	456 674	24.7	414 113	366 224	34 743	113.5
Mitchell	7 015	–.1	355	5.1	358	13.7	344	315	4 306	.3	4 270	4 294	20 986	68.6
Montgomery	11 587	–1.2	469	4.0	536	6.1	492	505	8 976	–2.6	9 224	9 213	21 598	70.6
Moore	30 175	2.3	1 166	3.9	2 010	21.3	1 807	1 657	28 696	26.6	24 605	22 658	22 464	73.4
Nash	42 499	–.2	2 236	5.3	2 274	1.1	2 099	2 249	40 076	1.1	36 198	39 637	24 963	81.6
New Hanover	83 045	3.9	2 910	3.5	5 983	43.1	5 144	4 182	72 044	28.9	62 994	55 888	24 919	81.4
Northampton	8 098	–.8	529	6.5	319	–		314	319	2 912	7.9	2 849	2 698	20 417	66.7
Onslow	47 547	–.8	1 735	3.6	2 599	20.4	2 395	2 159	28 155	26.8	25 042	22 209	17 300	56.5

[1] Civilian unemployed as a percent of total civilian labor force. [2] For pay period including March 12 of the year shown.

Sources: Civilian Labor Force—U.S. Bureau of Labor Statistics; Local Area Unemployment Statistics; 2000 data published 2 May 2001, 1999 data published 30 May 2001; <ftp://ftp.bls.gov/pub/time.series/la/> (related Internet site <http://www.bls.gov/lauhome.htm>).   Private Business Establishments and Employment—U.S. Census Bureau; County Business Patterns on CD-ROM; annual (related Internet site <http://www.census.gov/epcd/cbp/view/cbpview.html>).

Table B–7. Counties — Labor Force and Private Business Establishments and Employment–Con.

[Includes U.S., states, and 3,142 counties/county equivalents defined as of January 1, 1992. For changes to these areas since January 1, 1992, see appendix B. Geographic Information]

| County | Civilian labor force, 2000 | | Unemployment | | Private nonfarm businesses | | | | | | | | | |
| | | | | | Establishments | | | | Employment[2] | | | | Annual payroll per employee, 1998 | |
	Total	Percent change, 1999–2000	Total	Rate[1]	1998	Percent change, 1990–1998	1995	1990	1998	Percent change, 1990–1998	1995	1990	Amount (dollars)	Percent of national average
NORTH CAROLINA–Con.														
Orange	64 448	3.1	850	1.3	2 783	31.3	2 484	2 119	33 867	23.2	31 041	27 496	25 240	82.5
Pamlico	5 418	.4	200	3.7	235	21.8	221	193	1 676	-.1	1 450	1 678	19 764	64.6
Pasquotank	14 899	Z	558	3.7	931	14.5	845	813	9 847	22.2	9 391	8 061	19 935	65.1
Pender	16 573	-.2	786	4.7	726	47.9	626	491	5 473	48.0	4 845	3 697	18 236	59.6
Perquimans	4 708	.6	173	3.7	180	6.5	176	169	1 215	-14.9	1 229	1 427	15 547	50.8
Person	17 166	1.6	799	4.7	760	29.9	656	585	11 189	26.8	10 133	8 826	22 793	74.5
Pitt	66 073	-1.2	3 114	4.7	3 051	26.3	2 818	2 416	50 143	43.6	45 669	34 918	23 425	76.5
Polk	7 782	-1.5	262	3.4	443	23.1	411	360	3 651	42.2	3 724	2 568	19 199	62.7
Randolph	71 289	2.0	2 188	3.1	2 754	29.1	2 433	2 134	46 166	27.5	41 784	36 200	23 700	77.4
Richmond	18 557	-1.0	1 234	6.6	978	2.2	939	957	13 514	-10.5	14 317	15 096	20 966	68.5
Robeson	53 200	.7	4 765	9.0	1 990	4.3	1 964	1 908	32 002	5.3	34 129	30 400	21 375	69.8
Rockingham	44 389	.5	2 376	5.4	1 789	9.3	1 725	1 637	30 153	-1.0	31 211	30 446	23 163	75.7
Rowan	68 035	6.1	3 279	4.8	2 460	14.0	2 164	2 157	43 574	20.8	41 645	36 084	25 392	83.0
Rutherford	28 250	-.6	2 133	7.6	1 303	7.1	1 231	1 217	21 816	-2.9	22 777	22 476	21 582	70.5
Sampson	22 861	-1.1	918	4.0	1 072	22.0	1 028	879	12 642	11.4	12 497	11 344	22 067	72.1
Scotland	17 235	.6	1 282	7.4	732	16.2	681	630	16 710	18.6	16 521	14 094	23 343	76.3
Stanly	26 980	1.2	1 135	4.2	1 390	13.1	1 283	1 229	19 078	5.4	18 298	18 094	22 439	73.3
Stokes	23 306	2.5	750	3.2	561	11.1	563	505	5 303	-15.0	5 166	6 242	21 691	70.9
Surry	34 156	.7	1 472	4.3	1 803	15.2	1 730	1 565	36 277	12.9	36 286	32 127	21 476	70.2
Swain	6 060	2.9	760	12.5	394	16.9	384	337	4 820	16.1	4 068	4 150	18 001	58.8
Transylvania	11 233	1.2	288	2.6	727	20.2	679	605	9 302	14.3	8 103	8 141	25 488	83.3
Tyrrell	1 850	2.0	179	9.7	74	2.8	73	72	329	-19.2	290	407	17 772	58.1
Union	63 203	4.4	1 450	2.3	2 675	32.4	2 266	2 021	37 152	23.8	32 931	30 003	25 385	82.9
Vance	19 734	2.8	1 756	8.9	940	10.2	910	853	15 073	-5.4	15 066	15 939	20 380	66.6
Wake	355 437	3.1	5 449	1.5	19 160	43.0	16 497	13 401	300 548	39.8	255 873	214 939	30 984	101.2
Warren	7 250	2.4	562	7.8	283	4.8	261	270	2 582	-3.0	2 932	2 662	17 723	57.9
Washington	6 093	.7	382	6.3	270	-.4	282	271	3 831	-16.2	4 335	4 573	33 664	110.0
Watauga	23 834	4.2	358	1.5	1 513	28.9	1 354	1 174	15 839	53.2	13 291	10 337	17 729	57.9
Wayne	48 467	.7	1 917	4.0	2 338	10.9	2 205	2 108	36 626	9.7	35 727	33 387	21 964	71.8
Wilkes	32 558	.9	1 069	3.3	1 285	7.5	1 217	1 195	22 541	9.1	21 727	20 659	22 635	73.9
Wilson	36 500	1.1	2 547	7.0	1 811	8.1	1 723	1 676	31 620	8.8	29 258	29 058	25 763	84.2
Yadkin	18 350	2.3	604	3.3	641	20.9	569	530	8 690	46.7	7 325	5 923	20 839	68.1
Yancey	6 608	2.0	261	3.9	321	10.7	302	290	3 643	6.6	3 563	3 417	21 640	70.7
NORTH DAKOTA	338 822	.6	10 106	3.0	20 288	6.9	20 269	18 979	249 476	26.8	230 090	196 675	22 182	72.5
Adams	1 380	1.0	35	2.5	104	-4.6	117	109	748	-4.8	810	786	20 266	66.2
Barnes	5 700	1.7	174	3.1	385	2.7	382	375	3 917	12.9	3 827	3 470	16 225	53.0
Benson	2 725	-1.1	214	7.9	117	-1.7	125	119	1 083	12.3	1 014	964	18 968	62.0
Billings	502	-2.1	19	3.8	27	17.4	26	23	148	60.9	73	92	30 358	99.2
Bottineau	3 280	-.7	131	4.0	269	-1.8	272	274	1 597	18.8	1 416	1 344	15 752	51.5
Bowman	1 812	1.5	31	1.7	165	3.1	146	160	953	5.8	923	901	16 044	52.4
Burke	966	-3.0	27	2.8	92	-20.7	100	116	389	-11.6	413	440	17 653	57.7
Burleigh	39 820	.9	891	2.2	2 252	15.0	2 178	1 959	32 964	27.5	29 796	25 856	23 193	75.8
Cass	72 697	1.5	1 174	1.6	4 059	17.5	4 056	3 454	71 056	34.1	64 576	52 984	25 228	82.4
Cavalier	2 480	.8	79	3.2	183	-14.5	194	214	1 282	24.1	1 165	1 033	17 466	57.1
Dickey	2 943	2.8	47	1.6	207	7.3	212	193	1 713	26.4	1 601	1 355	16 770	54.8
Divide	1 059	-3.7	23	2.2	83	-21.7	93	106	579	8.6	629	533	12 409	40.5
Dunn	2 021	5.4	70	3.5	90	4.7	129	86	659	60.0	984	412	18 390	60.1
Eddy	1 195	-7.3	60	5.0	86	19.4	75	72	525	-11.9	457	596	14 619	47.8
Emmons	2 032	1.1	89	4.4	146	4.3	153	140	1 106	63.1	954	678	20 115	65.7
Foster	2 242	-1.6	61	2.7	151	-10.7	149	169	1 548	53.4	1 232	1 009	18 811	61.5
Golden Valley	849	-6.2	30	3.5	77	2.7	73	75	438	1.2	467	433	16 137	52.7
Grand Forks	35 645	1.6	972	2.7	1 767	5.8	1 789	1 670	27 734	21.9	25 630	22 757	21 603	70.6
Grant	1 481	-2.8	41	2.8	86	-6.5	86	92	483	39.6	404	346	14 923	48.8
Griggs	1 554	.1	31	2.0	112	9.8	105	102	888	58.3	908	561	18 347	59.9
Hettinger	1 278	-3.1	33	2.6	99	-5.7	101	105	472	1.9	459	463	15 136	49.4
Kidder	1 426	-.7	68	4.8	64	-14.7	68	75	392	5.7	349	371	14 587	47.7
LaMoure	2 237	.1	57	2.5	157	5.4	149	149	897	31.1	780	684	15 349	50.1
Logan	1 137	2.1	20	1.8	75	-6.3	76	80	402	-10.3	407	448	12 254	40.0
McHenry	2 803	2.5	142	5.1	146	3.5	141	141	657	1.1	657	650	17 411	56.9
McIntosh	1 661	-1.8	40	2.4	121	-14.2	126	141	907	13.8	895	797	14 499	47.4
McKenzie	3 230	2.7	99	3.1	160	-4.8	157	168	1 127	1.2	1 139	1 114	17 936	58.6
McLean	4 274	-4.5	256	6.0	250	-4.2	256	261	2 040	21.9	1 911	1 673	26 032	85.0
Mercer	4 616	.9	259	5.6	259	12.6	257	230	3 592	57.6	3 448	2 279	34 177	111.7
Morton	13 554	.7	439	3.2	652	11.6	645	584	7 055	24.4	6 629	5 670	20 334	66.4
Mountrail	3 106	2.4	172	5.5	202	4.1	197	194	1 607	25.1	1 424	1 285	16 189	52.9
Nelson	1 507	-3.3	69	4.6	150	-2.0	156	153	928	11.9	873	829	15 880	51.9
Oliver	1 033	–	62	6.0	39	21.9	38	32	405	-7.1	476	436	50 642	165.4
Pembina	4 572	-6.5	314	6.9	329	-4.9	343	346	3 439	51.7	3 038	2 267	23 456	76.6
Pierce	2 750	8.6	70	2.5	160	1.3	161	158	1 443	14.9	1 526	1 256	17 701	57.8

[1] Civilian unemployed as a percent of total civilian labor force. [2] For pay period including March 12 of the year shown.

Sources: Civilian Labor Force—U.S. Bureau of Labor Statistics; Local Area Unemployment Statistics; 2000 data published 2 May 2001, 1999 data published 30 May 2001; <ftp://ftp.bls.gov/pub/time.series/la/> (related Internet site <http://www.bls.gov/lauhome.htm>).   Private Business Establishments and Employment—U.S. Census Bureau; County Business Patterns on CD-ROM; annual (related Internet site <http://www.census.gov/epcd/cbp/view/cbpview.html>).

[Includes U.S., states, and 3,142 counties/county equivalents defined as of January 1, 1992. For changes to these areas since January 1, 1992, see appendix B. Geographic Information]

| County | Civilian labor force, 2000 | | Unemployment | | Private nonfarm businesses | | | | | | | | Annual payroll per employee, 1998 | |
| | | | | | Establishments | | | | Employment[2] | | | | | |
	Total	Percent change, 1999–2000	Total	Rate[1]	1998	Percent change, 1990–1998	1995	1990	1998	Percent change, 1990–1998	1995	1990	Amount (dollars)	Percent of national average
NORTH DAKOTA—Con.														
Ramsey	6 145	-2.2	215	3.5	434	2.4	438	424	4 394	27.8	4 411	3 437	17 250	56.4
Ransom	2 805	3.9	61	2.2	208	15.6	190	180	1 494	30.0	1 305	1 149	17 206	56.2
Renville	1 368	2.0	29	2.1	90	-2.2	117	92	577	42.8	539	404	16 208	53.0
Richland	9 212	-1.3	241	2.6	566	19.2	541	475	6 582	32.7	6 213	4 961	21 551	70.4
Rolette	5 658	-.4	700	12.4	205	-10.9	219	230	3 409	53.1	2 826	2 226	18 715	61.1
Sargent	2 708	7.6	50	1.8	133	-1.5	131	135	1 999	30.5	1 759	1 532	35 012	114.4
Sheridan	693	-1.3	42	6.1	45	-4.3	50	47	187	10.7	180	169	18 802	61.4
Sioux	1 633	-1.1	102	6.2	35	12.9	36	31	735	165.3	640	277	21 297	69.6
Slope	390	-4.2	11	2.8	12	-20.0	11	15	81	50.0	23	54	20 025	65.4
Stark	12 121	-1.8	379	3.1	866	11.2	770	779	8 202	18.3	7 083	6 934	19 142	62.5
Steele	1 153	7.2	16	1.4	72	-7.7	74	78	364	33.3	333	273	20 170	65.9
Stutsman	11 355	-1.7	255	2.2	682	11.1	655	614	8 783	22.5	8 037	7 170	20 416	66.7
Towner	1 359	2.0	39	2.9	107	-11.6	114	121	778	-3.7	876	808	17 190	56.2
Traill	3 660	-2.3	111	3.0	309	-1.3	315	313	2 487	14.2	2 319	2 177	17 930	58.6
Walsh	6 196	-.7	259	4.2	445	-7.9	476	483	3 746	11.3	3 729	3 366	18 677	61.0
Ward	29 059	2.2	863	3.0	1 684	8.5	1 696	1 552	21 581	31.7	19 982	16 389	20 603	67.3
Wells	2 556	.7	94	3.7	212	8.2	195	196	1 380	17.9	1 166	1 170	15 280	49.9
Williams	9 185	-1.6	340	3.7	833	2.0	864	817	6 759	8.6	6 760	6 221	19 556	63.9
OHIO	5 782 649	.5	236 536	4.1	270 343	8.7	263 739	248 694	4 806 046	13.2	4 550 590	4 245 977	29 185	95.3
Adams	11 635	-.7	1 196	10.3	412	23.4	417	334	4 459	87.4	3 864	2 380	18 690	61.1
Allen	52 179	1.4	2 430	4.7	2 833	2.6	2 839	2 761	49 878	5.8	47 845	47 164	26 004	85.0
Ashland	25 899	-.7	1 075	4.2	1 069	11.1	1 086	962	17 971	18.3	17 000	15 193	24 443	79.9
Ashtabula	47 449	.3	2 604	5.5	2 269	14.9	2 158	1 975	29 842	16.5	27 840	25 624	23 012	75.2
Athens	27 283	2.2	1 295	4.7	1 174	14.5	1 135	1 025	12 428	15.7	11 742	10 740	18 711	61.1
Auglaize	25 020	.7	800	3.2	1 048	8.5	1 001	966	18 808	15.8	17 658	16 236	26 415	86.3
Belmont	32 206	-.5	1 632	5.1	1 654	13.8	1 561	1 454	19 491	19.6	17 062	16 299	19 493	64.2
Brown	20 288	1.4	1 227	6.0	572	16.5	525	491	6 344	4.3	6 037	6 085	22 326	72.9
Butler	189 277	1.7	5 664	3.0	6 197	16.8	5 833	5 306	102 274	21.0	94 630	84 530	29 091	95.0
Carroll	13 727	.5	601	4.4	475	12.6	415	422	5 274	14.9	4 570	4 591	21 925	71.6
Champaign	19 968	6.1	683	3.4	730	26.7	660	576	10 287	17.0	9 197	8 790	25 776	84.2
Clark	68 535	.2	3 142	4.6	2 808	1.5	2 871	2 766	49 917	7.8	49 295	46 323	25 832	84.4
Clermont	96 066	.6	3 476	3.6	3 221	32.1	2 647	2 439	45 663	47.2	37 699	31 019	29 196	95.4
Clinton	25 759	1.8	800	3.1	800	9.9	755	720	23 040	83.0	19 317	14 090	26 612	86.9
Columbiana	51 742	-1.9	2 642	5.1	2 440	6.4	2 410	2 294	30 406	12.0	29 343	27 144	22 985	75.1
Coshocton	17 468	-1.3	868	5.0	743	11.4	678	667	15 600	37.8	12 143	11 321	30 165	98.6
Crawford	21 513	-.8	1 122	5.2	1 016	4.0	1 008	977	15 362	-.5	16 321	15 445	25 093	82.0
Cuyahoga	680 600	.6	31 101	4.6	38 566	4.2	38 190	37 028	749 942	7.1	709 226	700 090	32 636	106.6
Darke	29 353	-.6	1 201	4.1	1 247	6.5	1 214	1 171	16 416	12.5	15 972	14 592	24 080	78.7
Defiance	21 190	-.2	850	4.0	883	6.4	844	830	17 186	13.5	15 434	15 137	30 393	99.3
Delaware	59 392	1.8	1 059	1.8	2 274	78.9	1 902	1 271	36 427	119.9	26 464	16 569	29 644	96.8
Erie	42 505	1.0	1 875	4.4	2 093	4.8	2 147	1 998	31 994	12.6	30 514	28 413	28 862	94.3
Fairfield	67 935	1.6	1 759	2.6	2 472	19.1	2 385	2 076	29 605	19.4	26 302	24 801	21 895	71.5
Fayette	15 086	-3.9	576	3.8	715	30.7	629	547	9 205	34.2	8 529	6 858	21 439	70.0
Franklin	604 308	1.8	14 714	2.4	27 644	11.0	26 702	24 896	589 962	18.4	539 282	498 255	31 039	101.4
Fulton	23 541	.3	948	4.0	1 081	8.1	1 091	1 000	18 876	30.6	19 168	14 454	26 513	86.6
Gallia	15 223	1.2	1 084	7.1	647	10.2	642	587	9 380	17.1	8 991	8 010	24 871	81.3
Geauga	48 156	.5	1 452	3.0	2 587	31.5	2 183	1 967	27 712	21.7	23 731	22 769	28 345	92.6
Greene	72 587	.2	2 466	3.4	2 893	19.7	2 791	2 416	43 882	39.8	39 767	31 380	24 200	79.1
Guernsey	19 009	Z	1 547	8.1	949	5.9	888	896	12 593	3.0	12 421	12 230	24 156	78.9
Hamilton	436 315	.7	15 507	3.6	24 944	1.5	25 577	24 571	531 128	2.7	522 152	517 092	32 995	107.8
Hancock	43 091	2.3	1 231	2.9	1 777	6.9	1 742	1 663	38 904	28.6	34 649	30 254	27 605	90.2
Hardin	15 424	-.8	607	3.9	526	–	525	526	8 132	11.5	7 645	7 295	22 938	74.9
Harrison	6 812	Z	370	5.4	341	2.7	326	332	3 121	27.4	2 835	2 450	21 630	70.7
Henry	15 819	-.6	783	4.9	626	2.3	653	612	8 936	4.0	8 873	8 591	27 387	89.5
Highland	18 600	-3.5	894	4.8	734	10.0	702	667	10 431	39.2	8 797	7 492	20 945	68.4
Hocking	11 785	-1.6	1 025	8.7	534	15.3	513	463	6 053	17.0	5 975	5 174	22 033	72.0
Holmes	19 109	1.5	512	2.7	923	48.2	776	623	11 878	40.3	10 710	8 468	21 999	71.9
Huron	29 773	-1.3	2 184	7.3	1 257	-.2	1 263	1 259	23 599	11.9	22 191	21 096	25 943	84.8
Jackson	14 479	Z	989	6.8	637	4.8	636	608	10 325	51.5	9 947	6 814	20 962	68.5
Jefferson	29 075	-2.5	1 526	5.2	1 642	.4	1 686	1 635	20 850	-5.7	21 939	22 104	23 605	77.1
Knox	26 014	-1.0	1 039	4.0	1 085	19.2	1 054	910	17 340	40.6	14 992	12 335	24 834	81.1
Lake	126 933	.3	4 586	3.6	6 442	14.4	6 246	5 632	94 736	13.8	87 700	83 223	27 930	91.2
Lawrence	27 005	.1	1 996	7.4	934	14.5	883	816	10 383	20.6	10 835	8 610	20 493	66.9
Licking	73 098	1.7	2 563	3.5	2 862	16.9	2 655	2 448	45 602	28.0	41 982	35 620	25 738	84.1
Logan	28 072	-1.3	901	3.2	930	2.5	941	907	18 710	57.8	16 374	11 857	28 576	93.4
Lorain	142 455	.9	7 259	5.1	5 708	11.8	5 484	5 106	91 049	10.9	91 279	82 123	27 824	90.9
Lucas	230 275	-.1	11 245	4.9	11 266	2.0	11 135	11 049	218 620	8.5	210 338	201 407	28 884	94.4
Madison	20 936	1.5	465	2.2	704	9.5	729	643	10 326	41.5	9 811	7 297	24 767	80.9
Mahoning	115 711	-1.1	6 444	5.6	6 506	1.5	6 598	6 408	96 202	4.1	95 450	92 452	24 219	79.1

[1] Civilian unemployed as a percent of total civilian labor force. [2] For pay period including March 12 of the year shown.

Sources: Civilian Labor Force—U.S. Bureau of Labor Statistics; Local Area Unemployment Statistics; 2000 data published 2 May 2001, 1999 data published 30 May 2001; <ftp://ftp.bls.gov/pub/time.series/la/> (related Internet site <http://www.bls.gov/lauhome.htm>). Private Business Establishments and Employment—U.S. Census Bureau; County Business Patterns on CD-ROM; annual (related Internet site <http://www.census.gov/epcd/cbp/view/cbpview.html>).

[Includes U.S., states, and 3,142 counties/county equivalents defined as of January 1, 1992. For changes to these areas since January 1, 1992, see appendix B. Geographic Information]

County	Civilian labor force, 2000		Unemployment		Private nonfarm businesses								Annual payroll per employee, 1998	
					Establishments				Employment[2]					
	Total	Percent change, 1999–2000	Total	Rate[1]	1998	Percent change, 1990–1998	1995	1990	1998	Percent change, 1990–1998	1995	1990	Amount (dollars)	Percent of national average
OHIO—Con.														
Marion	31 524	.1	1 267	4.0	1 411	7.3	1 377	1 315	24 668	15.1	24 808	21 429	25 134	82.1
Medina	80 063	.5	2 788	3.5	3 762	38.2	3 274	2 723	49 811	53.6	41 938	32 420	26 026	85.0
Meigs	8 365	–1.3	879	10.5	368	7.9	369	341	3 334	–6.6	3 362	3 571	28 912	94.5
Mercer	19 074	–4.2	1 072	5.6	972	9.8	957	885	13 854	10.5	13 325	12 541	22 205	72.5
Miami	50 461	–.5	1 691	3.4	2 244	11.6	2 185	2 011	37 906	14.9	37 083	32 995	27 061	88.4
Monroe	5 784	–1.8	541	9.4	283	3.3	292	274	3 876	–6.7	4 283	4 153	35 243	115.1
Montgomery	278 797	Z	10 464	3.8	13 428	–.7	13 650	13 522	282 914	5.3	282 871	268 727	30 177	98.6
Morgan	4 452	–5.7	553	12.4	202	9.8	201	184	2 319	–25.1	2 253	3 096	23 240	75.9
Morrow	14 217	–.1	596	4.2	401	2.6	376	391	4 502	–3.5	5 228	4 665	21 894	71.5
Muskingum	44 566	3.1	2 612	5.9	2 034	7.8	2 017	1 887	33 631	20.4	32 718	27 930	22 696	74.1
Noble	5 583	–.2	417	7.5	208	13.0	185	184	2 242	19.2	2 028	1 881	23 308	76.1
Ottawa	21 033	.5	1 226	5.8	1 146	6.7	1 088	1 074	11 942	–2.0	11 190	12 188	26 375	86.2
Paulding	9 918	–.3	409	4.1	338	3.0	342	328	4 205	9.4	4 084	3 845	22 292	72.8
Perry	14 196	–2.0	1 055	7.4	489	7.5	491	455	5 007	–5.8	5 015	5 313	21 900	71.5
Pickaway	25 121	1.7	780	3.1	839	18.5	859	708	12 124	19.1	11 678	10 182	27 370	89.4
Pike	11 797	1.2	920	7.8	455	20.7	410	377	9 775	49.6	7 925	6 532	27 958	91.3
Portage	83 576	.4	3 251	3.9	3 043	23.6	2 860	2 461	41 767	34.8	39 375	30 979	25 849	84.4
Preble	21 820	2.7	847	3.9	723	11.1	709	651	9 179	19.9	8 676	7 653	23 757	77.6
Putnam	20 742	.5	696	3.4	732	13.3	697	646	10 210	23.2	9 660	8 290	23 803	77.8
Richland	61 153	–1.2	3 449	5.6	3 061	6.9	3 075	2 864	53 050	4.3	53 453	50 882	24 936	81.5
Ross	35 294	2.0	1 814	5.1	1 364	11.9	1 315	1 219	22 006	27.1	20 706	17 308	27 476	89.8
Sandusky	30 883	–3.8	1 534	5.0	1 444	6.5	1 436	1 356	24 249	17.7	23 167	20 611	24 989	81.6
Scioto	32 837	–.3	2 898	8.8	1 496	4.1	1 466	1 437	18 044	11.8	17 382	16 138	19 527	63.8
Seneca	28 313	–.7	1 507	5.3	1 381	8.7	1 355	1 271	20 758	16.9	20 507	17 755	23 341	76.3
Shelby	28 633	1.5	1 201	4.2	1 030	14.8	966	897	23 816	26.6	23 480	18 818	32 289	105.5
Stark	190 089	1.2	7 816	4.1	9 362	6.7	9 508	8 776	161 496	10.8	155 526	145 769	26 044	85.1
Summit	282 109	.3	11 370	4.0	14 385	10.7	13 870	13 000	246 220	10.3	243 766	223 302	31 220	102.0
Trumbull	110 884	–1.3	5 697	5.1	4 776	7.5	4 516	4 443	87 887	1.0	85 271	87 029	29 479	96.3
Tuscarawas	44 404	.2	2 030	4.6	2 379	5.3	2 390	2 260	32 534	21.4	31 195	26 810	22 784	74.4
Union	18 355	2.3	513	2.8	788	30.7	656	603	19 557	15.9	16 429	16 881	44 096	144.1
Van Wert	16 928	1.3	774	4.6	643	5.8	588	608	11 157	13.3	10 504	9 847	24 519	80.1
Vinton	3 793	1.1	447	11.8	150	.7	161	149	1 715	–16.5	1 683	2 054	23 077	75.4
Warren	81 281	.7	2 367	2.9	2 806	34.6	2 422	2 084	52 958	83.2	39 436	28 910	27 920	91.2
Washington	32 658	.9	1 644	5.0	1 565	1.1	1 574	1 548	22 160	17.5	21 258	18 853	25 364	82.9
Wayne	57 155	–.4	1 879	3.3	2 570	17.9	2 414	2 179	43 616	25.9	40 459	34 639	26 946	88.0
Williams	21 081	–.1	783	3.7	921	8.2	900	851	17 476	14.1	16 919	15 315	25 314	82.7
Wood	67 690	.1	2 186	3.2	2 656	11.6	2 487	2 379	46 724	21.5	40 206	38 468	28 809	94.1
Wyandot	12 342	.1	549	4.4	568	9.2	546	520	9 276	28.3	8 379	7 231	22 586	73.8
OKLAHOMA	1 648 017	–.4	50 048	3.0	84 881	13.7	81 395	74 663	1 167 709	24.1	1 055 227	940 800	24 550	80.2
Adair	9 192	2.4	394	4.3	209	16.1	212	180	3 027	28.5	3 267	2 356	19 143	62.5
Alfalfa	2 585	2.1	48	1.9	145	1.4	146	143	860	13.5	883	758	15 312	50.0
Atoka	4 916	–.5	139	2.8	227	28.2	201	177	2 072	47.1	1 924	1 409	15 788	51.6
Beaver	2 567	–3.6	63	2.5	169	12.7	158	150	919	11.5	839	824	20 753	67.8
Beckham	10 142	3.0	300	3.0	625	17.5	592	532	5 558	35.2	4 593	4 111	16 840	55.0
Blaine	4 806	4.6	108	2.2	304	6.7	289	285	2 665	21.3	2 494	2 197	17 875	58.4
Bryan	16 822	.4	355	2.1	613	21.6	565	504	9 253	15.6	7 770	8 001	18 773	61.3
Caddo	12 429	–4.7	515	4.1	536	–2.7	524	551	4 409	5.8	4 326	4 169	19 835	64.8
Canadian	46 932	.4	918	2.0	1 586	29.8	1 388	1 222	17 871	70.9	12 113	10 459	20 577	67.2
Carter	20 234	–.3	890	4.4	1 363	9.5	1 299	1 245	16 627	28.9	15 082	12 897	21 905	71.6
Cherokee	18 483	–.1	557	3.0	671	23.8	627	542	6 403	34.5	5 712	4 761	16 596	54.2
Choctaw	5 448	–.9	331	6.1	274	6.6	284	257	2 946	22.4	2 476	2 406	14 624	47.8
Cimarron	1 707	–2.7	32	1.9	96	–6.8	93	103	500	35.5	487	369	15 466	50.5
Cleveland	113 413	.1	2 074	1.8	4 097	43.9	3 624	2 848	44 316	53.3	38 646	28 899	20 660	67.5
Coal	2 398	–4.7	127	5.3	63	–3.1	57	65	859	30.7	922	657	16 062	52.5
Comanche	40 851	–1.7	1 346	3.3	2 149	10.1	2 097	1 952	27 604	20.0	26 485	23 006	20 578	67.2
Cotton	2 155	–.6	70	3.2	95	–10.4	106	106	539	–24.2	848	711	11 408	37.3
Craig	6 668	–.6	234	3.5	381	21.3	353	314	5 200	34.2	4 491	3 874	20 448	66.8
Creek	33 584	–.3	1 129	3.4	1 240	19.1	1 194	1 041	15 256	44.8	13 645	10 533	21 907	71.6
Custer	11 630	–3.2	289	2.5	822	.1	822	821	7 922	4.5	8 609	7 581	18 378	60.0
Delaware	17 473	–.7	577	3.3	645	53.9	520	419	5 443	70.8	4 798	3 187	16 937	55.3
Dewey	1 884	–5.3	58	3.1	124	–17.9	133	151	766	–12.6	726	876	20 796	67.9
Ellis	1 575	–4.5	55	3.5	120	4.3	118	115	717	41.7	742	506	18 431	60.2
Garfield	26 360	–4.2	755	2.9	1 669	5.1	1 694	1 588	20 739	20.1	19 872	17 273	20 858	68.1
Garvin	10 958	–.1	456	4.2	635	1.4	627	626	6 366	31.0	5 737	4 860	19 510	63.7
Grady	19 468	.3	669	3.4	935	10.8	909	844	10 740	33.6	10 114	8 036	20 311	66.4
Grant	2 170	–3.1	52	2.4	142	–6.0	129	151	784	–19.2	688	970	23 953	78.3
Greer	2 417	–3.2	64	2.6	121	–8.3	114	132	871	28.5	835	678	16 746	54.7
Harmon	1 214	–3.8	35	2.9	82	10.8	87	74	513	–10.8	452	575	15 969	52.2
Harper	1 642	–6.1	35	2.1	117	.9	108	116	534	–6.2	585	569	16 809	54.9

[1] Civilian unemployed as a percent of total civilian labor force.   [2] For pay period including March 12 of the year shown.

Sources: Civilian Labor Force—U.S. Bureau of Labor Statistics; Local Area Unemployment Statistics; 2000 data published 2 May 2001, 1999 data published 30 May 2001; <ftp://ftp.bls.gov/pub/time.series/la/> (related Internet site <http://www.bls.gov/lauhome.htm>). Private Business Establishments and Employment—U.S. Census Bureau; County Business Patterns on CD-ROM; annual (related Internet site <http://www.census.gov/epcd/cbp/view/cbpview.html>).

[Includes U.S., states, and 3,142 counties/county equivalents defined as of January 1, 1992. For changes to these areas since January 1, 1992, see appendix B. Geographic Information]

County	Civilian labor force, 2000		Unemployment		Private nonfarm businesses								Annual payroll per employee, 1998	
					Establishments				Employment[2]					
	Total	Percent change, 1999–2000	Total	Rate[1]	1998	Percent change, 1990–1998	1995	1990	1998	Percent change, 1990–1998	1995	1990	Amount (dollars)	Percent of national average
OKLAHOMA—Con.														
Haskell	4 840	−1.4	260	5.4	210	17.3	184	179	2 073	58.1	1 765	1 311	15 845	51.8
Hughes	6 082	12.0	333	5.5	235	7.3	222	219	2 043	40.2	1 687	1 457	15 237	49.8
Jackson	12 816	−.2	348	2.7	570	−3.2	604	589	7 660	69.1	6 002	4 530	18 781	61.4
Jefferson	2 960	−5.8	86	2.9	142	−10.1	153	158	1 140	31.6	1 306	866	14 815	48.4
Johnston	4 845	−1.6	175	3.6	154	25.2	140	123	2 061	73.5	1 810	1 188	21 563	70.4
Kay	21 361	−3.1	1 200	5.6	1 286	2.5	1 334	1 255	18 153	−3.6	17 626	18 839	23 624	77.2
Kingfisher	6 385	−5.3	147	2.3	424	7.1	415	396	4 591	36.8	4 138	3 356	21 983	71.8
Kiowa	4 767	.3	130	2.7	238	−13.1	254	274	2 090	22.2	1 948	1 710	16 468	53.8
Latimer	4 592	−.8	251	5.5	168	3.1	173	163	1 713	30.0	1 494	1 318	17 792	58.1
Le Flore	18 963	−5.4	838	4.4	757	32.8	691	570	8 017	58.1	7 078	5 071	18 542	60.6
Lincoln	13 918	−2.5	450	3.2	540	26.8	522	426	5 195	39.2	4 792	3 732	18 063	59.0
Logan	14 625	.4	371	2.5	525	21.5	470	432	4 234	21.6	4 231	3 481	16 222	53.0
Love	3 813	1.0	152	4.0	143	21.2	133	118	1 464	12.8	1 548	1 298	18 402	60.1
McClain	13 408	.2	295	2.2	538	66.6	403	323	4 433	64.1	3 772	2 701	19 618	64.1
McCurtain	15 025	−3.0	895	6.0	610	20.6	611	506	8 315	20.6	8 131	6 894	20 872	68.2
McIntosh	7 734	−3.9	391	5.1	396	23.0	370	322	3 223	38.6	2 840	2 325	14 541	47.5
Major	3 729	−5.2	87	2.3	226	1.3	219	223	1 789	33.9	1 487	1 336	21 070	68.8
Marshall	5 391	−.3	189	3.5	287	25.3	265	229	3 395	66.2	3 112	2 043	18 897	61.7
Mayes	16 682	3.9	638	3.8	721	18.4	674	609	9 325	37.2	8 288	6 797	22 958	75.0
Murray	5 376	−1.0	232	4.3	263	15.9	263	227	2 369	5.9	2 357	2 238	17 583	57.4
Muskogee	30 972	−3.0	1 257	4.1	1 623	9.4	1 560	1 484	23 917	19.4	21 872	20 032	22 346	73.0
Noble	5 767	.6	115	2.0	245	6.1	243	231	3 606	22.5	3 615	2 944	23 910	78.1
Nowata	3 662	−2.3	165	4.5	177	4.1	175	170	1 418	12.4	1 357	1 262	16 970	55.4
Okfuskee	3 789	2.0	162	4.3	157	9.0	154	144	1 959	21.5	1 815	1 612	18 877	61.7
Oklahoma	334 201	.2	8 711	2.6	21 276	14.7	20 580	18 549	337 110	23.0	313 106	273 983	25 829	84.4
Okmulgee	14 421	.4	933	6.5	659	3.3	664	638	6 608	6.5	6 883	6 204	19 794	64.7
Osage	20 278	−.3	686	3.4	536	36.7	563	392	4 388	22.5	5 088	3 583	19 002	62.1
Ottawa	13 687	2.3	841	6.1	731	11.9	707	653	6 995	4.6	7 197	6 685	18 722	61.2
Pawnee	6 922	7.6	309	4.5	305	3.0	294	296	2 561	16.3	2 496	2 203	18 867	61.6
Payne	38 208	1.4	441	1.2	1 568	12.6	1 498	1 393	19 196	39.2	17 582	13 789	19 092	62.4
Pittsburg	17 681	−2.0	820	4.6	877	9.9	830	798	9 611	18.5	8 112	8 112	18 543	60.6
Pontotoc	17 443	1.2	542	3.1	878	1.7	870	863	11 208	17.0	10 006	9 579	18 506	60.5
Pottawatomie	29 004	Z	982	3.4	1 330	7.6	1 283	1 236	18 461	20.3	16 614	15 352	18 940	61.9
Pushmataha	4 992	Z	216	4.3	212	23.3	183	172	1 677	30.9	1 811	1 281	15 417	50.4
Roger Mills	1 965	−.7	47	2.4	83	–	86	83	502	44.7	469	347	16 540	54.0
Rogers	36 639	−.5	938	2.6	1 253	38.8	1 092	903	15 937	71.7	13 374	9 284	24 059	78.6
Seminole	10 302	2.5	532	5.2	528	1.3	537	521	6 127	23.2	5 811	4 973	16 790	54.9
Sequoyah	17 201	−1.1	766	4.5	609	22.8	579	496	5 936	38.7	5 593	4 279	15 340	50.1
Stephens	18 252	1.7	631	3.5	1 074	6.2	1 022	1 011	12 375	14.7	10 864	10 791	21 824	71.3
Texas	14 372	1.0	312	2.2	548	17.1	505	468	6 927	105.3	3 957	3 374	19 936	65.1
Tillman	3 441	−2.4	119	3.5	194	−8.9	220	213	1 635	−.7	2 187	1 647	18 521	60.5
Tulsa	299 966	−.5	8 501	2.8	18 112	10.2	17 508	16 437	314 790	22.5	273 399	256 884	29 595	96.7
Wagoner	28 979	−.2	734	2.5	733	69.7	639	432	6 841	38.5	5 785	4 938	19 358	63.2
Washington	18 743	−.2	656	3.5	1 179	3.7	1 164	1 137	16 607	−8.2	15 282	18 097	33 129	108.2
Washita	4 759	−3.6	123	2.6	258	11.7	245	231	1 721	16.1	1 630	1 482	15 433	50.4
Woods	4 427	−.1	67	1.5	284	.4	271	283	2 198	26.3	1 923	1 740	15 683	51.2
Woodward	8 511	−4.2	303	3.6	684	5.6	664	648	6 211	10.7	6 247	5 613	20 806	68.0
OREGON	1 802 889	2.4	87 486	4.9	99 183	22.3	93 468	81 077	1 310 750	28.9	1 185 415	1 017 239	28 780	94.0
Baker	7 378	1.0	536	7.3	568	27.4	565	446	3 781	13.3	3 740	3 337	19 105	62.4
Benton	39 887	1.2	968	2.4	1 968	13.4	2 264	1 736	29 170	40.3	28 560	20 793	31 611	103.3
Clackamas	199 025	2.7	6 426	3.2	9 332	33.1	8 409	7 011	106 042	24.0	106 947	85 490	28 801	94.1
Clatsop	17 481	1.0	804	4.6	1 351	20.7	1 290	1 119	11 729	23.2	10 842	9 522	19 233	62.8
Columbia	23 470	2.5	1 205	5.1	838	24.0	805	676	9 042	5.3	7 848	8 586	29 139	95.2
Coos	27 448	1.6	2 033	7.4	1 750	2.9	1 769	1 700	16 728	9.2	16 589	15 314	22 246	72.7
Crook	8 002	3.3	666	8.3	406	25.7	371	323	4 774	15.3	4 551	4 140	23 854	77.9
Curry	8 458	.2	528	6.2	692	15.7	662	598	4 700	14.0	4 559	4 122	19 786	64.6
Deschutes	61 461	6.0	3 234	5.3	4 137	45.7	3 621	2 839	39 781	43.2	35 046	27 785	23 603	77.1
Douglas	45 630	1.0	3 536	7.7	2 698	8.4	2 655	2 489	30 760	12.1	26 665	27 437	23 558	77.0
Gilliam	1 197	.8	56	4.7	57	50.0	59	38	556	69.5	533	328	24 000	78.4
Grant	3 987	−.1	444	11.1	294	22.5	295	240	1 604	−2.8	1 806	1 650	20 911	68.3
Harney	3 979	−1.4	380	9.6	211	3.4	209	204	1 463	−7.2	1 420	1 577	21 521	70.3
Hood River	11 189	2.1	868	7.8	744	36.0	672	547	7 241	16.0	7 323	6 240	19 333	63.2
Jackson	91 947	3.3	4 900	5.3	5 157	22.6	4 738	4 205	58 195	23.0	54 582	47 303	23 870	78.0
Jefferson	8 815	2.5	496	5.6	290	12.0	290	259	4 255	36.5	3 935	3 118	23 106	75.5
Josephine	29 631	1.8	2 062	7.0	1 817	12.9	1 799	1 610	16 368	7.6	16 076	15 217	21 381	69.9
Klamath	29 013	1.8	2 342	8.1	1 629	11.7	1 572	1 458	17 014	10.9	16 660	15 342	24 694	80.7
Lake	3 387	1.2	316	9.3	196	−1.0	212	198	1 311	13.4	1 546	1 156	19 516	63.8
Lane	166 885	2.2	8 534	5.1	9 726	17.9	9 170	8 247	114 500	19.8	106 351	95 541	25 171	82.2
Lincoln	21 077	.1	1 314	6.2	1 679	25.7	1 594	1 336	13 336	31.2	13 889	10 168	19 607	64.1

[1] Civilian unemployed as a percent of total civilian labor force.   [2] For pay period including March 12 of the year shown.

Sources: Civilian Labor Force—U.S. Bureau of Labor Statistics; Local Area Unemployment Statistics; 2000 data published 2 May 2001, 1999 data published 30 May 2001; <ftp://ftp.bls.gov/pub/time.series/la/> (related Internet site <http://www.bls.gov/lauhome.htm>).   Private Business Establishments and Employment—U.S. Census Bureau; County Business Patterns on CD-ROM; annual (related Internet site <http://www.census.gov/epcd/cbp/view/cbpview.html>).

[Includes U.S., states, and 3,142 counties/county equivalents defined as of January 1, 1992. For changes to these areas since January 1, 1992, see appendix B. Geographic Information]

County	Civilian labor force, 2000		Unemployment		Private nonfarm businesses								Annual payroll per employee, 1998	
					Establishments				Employment[2]					
	Total	Percent change, 1999–2000	Total	Rate[1]	1998	Percent change, 1990–1998	1995	1990	1998	Percent change, 1990–1998	1995	1990	Amount (dollars)	Percent of national average
OREGON—Con.														
Linn	52 008	-.8	3 669	7.1	2 514	14.0	2 182	2 206	34 977	32.5	28 820	26 395	26 274	85.8
Malheur	14 441	-.3	1 096	7.6	768	14.3	746	672	8 597	15.6	8 513	7 439	20 437	66.8
Marion	143 951	2.5	8 000	5.6	7 328	23.4	6 840	5 939	91 691	35.8	84 783	67 496	24 709	80.7
Morrow	4 163	2.0	497	11.9	158	12.9	147	140	1 899	22.3	1 657	1 553	25 604	83.6
Multnomah	373 536	2.6	16 159	4.3	23 396	17.0	22 627	19 993	399 456	21.2	367 961	329 650	31 894	104.2
Polk	31 640	2.7	1 513	4.8	1 149	20.4	1 071	954	12 653	54.5	9 354	8 192	21 566	70.5
Sherman	1 050	1.4	61	5.8	43	22.9	38	35	291	54.8	236	188	12 275	40.1
Tillamook	11 289	.2	500	4.4	718	18.5	659	606	6 181	36.6	5 658	4 525	20 655	67.5
Umatilla	37 103	1.7	2 366	6.4	1 586	14.0	1 541	1 391	18 721	26.8	16 642	14 766	21 833	71.3
Union	12 612	3.2	650	5.2	728	10.6	713	658	6 971	17.5	6 754	5 935	21 485	70.2
Wallowa	3 430	-1.7	298	8.7	322	37.0	288	235	1 500	10.4	1 375	1 359	19 847	64.8
Wasco	12 369	1.5	807	6.5	692	13.4	653	610	7 383	41.2	6 349	5 228	22 010	71.9
Washington	251 831	2.7	8 204	3.3	12 227	38.1	11 110	8 856	204 003	66.4	156 073	122 564	36 342	118.7
Wheeler	624	5.9	53	8.5	43	48.3	40	29	124	51.2	117	82	13 694	44.7
Yamhill	43 494	3.2	1 967	4.5	1 958	34.9	1 782	1 451	23 800	37.6	21 542	17 292	24 072	78.6
PENNSYLVANIA	5 971 913	-.1	249 922	4.2	292 659	4.7	283 998	279 595	4 906 190	6.7	4 702 892	4 598 441	29 670	96.9
Adams	43 384	3.1	1 408	3.2	1 788	14.3	1 760	1 564	26 680	21.1	26 346	22 033	22 478	73.4
Allegheny	645 352	-.3	23 733	3.7	34 987	1.2	34 506	34 564	672 404	3.8	654 009	647 782	32 068	104.8
Armstrong	31 482	.6	2 016	6.4	1 494	-2.9	1 547	1 538	15 767	-2.2	16 857	16 123	21 783	71.2
Beaver	85 038	-.7	3 617	4.3	3 485	6.8	3 316	3 263	50 231	18.5	47 150	42 372	25 606	83.7
Bedford	26 161	.7	1 591	6.1	1 068	5.4	1 065	1 013	12 861	26.5	11 619	10 170	21 113	69.0
Berks	184 173	.5	7 451	4.0	8 024	5.1	7 920	7 637	143 449	4.6	139 980	137 189	28 852	94.3
Blair	63 039	-.4	3 047	4.8	3 231	6.9	3 166	3 022	49 527	4.4	48 490	47 420	23 235	75.9
Bradford	27 964	1.3	1 063	3.8	1 306	9.0	1 262	1 198	18 449	4.7	18 025	17 625	24 790	81.0
Bucks	326 377	-.5	10 785	3.3	17 329	16.8	15 934	14 840	232 062	11.9	211 829	207 355	29 900	97.7
Butler	88 739	-.4	3 446	3.9	4 230	22.5	3 730	3 453	59 153	32.4	52 124	44 676	26 614	86.9
Cambria	65 569	.2	4 506	6.9	3 531	1.3	3 568	3 485	49 851	1.0	48 933	49 362	21 968	71.8
Cameron	2 867	2.4	237	8.3	146	2.1	138	143	2 026	18.0	1 974	1 717	23 733	77.5
Carbon	27 184	-.1	1 569	5.8	1 112	3.8	1 058	1 071	14 085	3.5	12 952	13 608	19 085	62.4
Centre	64 998	-.1	1 607	2.5	3 116	11.2	3 082	2 802	44 202	10.4	42 753	40 027	23 149	75.6
Chester	236 060	-.3	6 267	2.7	11 701	15.5	10 562	10 128	177 037	10.6	153 875	160 124	38 164	124.7
Clarion	19 069	Z	988	5.2	1 073	11.3	1 007	964	12 766	32.3	10 202	9 647	23 205	75.8
Clearfield	36 765	-1.8	2 521	6.9	1 937	-2.0	1 901	1 976	27 208	18.7	26 473	22 931	21 282	69.5
Clinton	18 151	1.9	975	5.4	761	9.2	724	697	9 737	11.0	9 113	8 774	20 814	68.0
Columbia	33 322	1.5	1 835	5.5	1 526	4.1	1 463	1 466	23 698	4.3	23 498	22 715	23 173	75.7
Crawford	41 662	-.3	2 291	5.5	2 114	10.2	2 042	1 919	27 645	8.6	26 022	25 455	23 755	77.6
Cumberland	120 550	-.5	2 874	2.4	5 358	11.8	5 131	4 792	111 899	14.1	104 829	98 062	27 318	89.2
Dauphin	137 279	-.9	4 094	3.0	6 535	7.9	6 421	6 055	138 356	17.2	125 490	118 086	28 976	94.7
Delaware	276 480	-.5	9 995	3.6	13 349	.4	13 225	13 302	211 561	6.2	204 898	199 294	35 600	116.3
Elk	17 445	-2.2	1 051	6.0	995	18.5	907	840	15 687	19.4	14 687	13 139	26 549	86.7
Erie	141 178	.5	6 957	4.9	6 859	8.4	6 508	6 325	116 678	8.5	112 125	107 548	26 022	85.0
Fayette	56 991	-.3	3 790	6.7	2 772	-4.5	3 045	2 903	32 766	-1.3	35 088	33 213	19 546	63.9
Forest	1 888	4.0	161	8.5	147	47.0	122	100	1 020	23.2	864	828	19 023	62.1
Franklin	63 761	-1.5	2 435	3.8	2 752	9.9	2 597	2 505	42 695	15.2	39 874	37 062	23 446	76.6
Fulton	6 527	-.9	262	4.0	292	15.4	258	253	5 135	54.7	3 889	3 319	23 869	78.0
Greene	15 951	-.7	1 049	6.6	668	6.5	643	627	8 270	18.5	8 152	6 977	29 662	96.9
Huntingdon	18 545	-1.5	1 356	7.3	836	4.6	790	799	9 584	.5	9 191	9 534	20 656	67.5
Indiana	35 577	-1.9	2 591	7.3	2 007	5.1	1 957	1 909	23 999	1.7	22 146	23 607	22 383	73.1
Jefferson	21 007	-1.8	1 287	6.1	1 215	10.7	1 145	1 098	13 635	9.4	13 026	12 467	22 581	73.8
Juniata	10 451	1.4	504	4.8	492	12.3	433	438	5 808	11.8	4 909	5 195	20 432	66.8
Lackawanna	103 805	.2	4 450	4.3	5 393	2.7	5 231	5 250	90 808	3.2	89 378	88 003	22 834	74.6
Lancaster	246 290	1.0	6 115	2.5	11 242	11.1	10 568	10 123	201 341	8.3	190 302	185 877	26 753	87.4
Lawrence	40 848	1.3	2 294	5.6	2 118	1.7	2 066	2 083	28 297	1.3	27 459	27 921	23 328	76.2
Lebanon	64 790	-.5	1 759	2.7	2 538	2.8	2 458	2 468	40 426	11.9	39 761	36 143	23 227	75.9
Lehigh	157 269	.3	5 347	3.4	8 187	4.4	8 206	7 841	158 672	12.0	151 950	141 625	32 184	105.1
Luzerne	155 373	.5	8 199	5.3	7 636	.1	7 539	7 631	122 507	3.3	120 902	118 650	23 853	77.9
Lycoming	56 345	-.3	2 632	4.7	2 883	-.4	2 921	2 895	47 148	2.0	44 913	46 207	22 705	74.2
McKean	21 050	-.4	1 122	5.3	1 151	5.1	1 117	1 095	15 364	11.8	14 885	13 740	22 449	73.3
Mercer	58 410	1.0	3 013	5.2	2 954	12.5	2 732	2 626	44 553	16.8	41 169	38 159	22 795	74.5
Mifflin	21 270	-2.4	959	4.5	937	3.3	909	907	14 430	5.2	14 347	13 716	23 816	77.8
Monroe	54 821	4.6	2 922	5.3	3 180	11.6	2 945	2 849	37 352	15.8	33 200	32 246	21 828	71.3
Montgomery	399 278	-.4	11 506	2.9	25 388	3.6	25 391	24 498	476 769	10.6	451 540	431 194	36 392	118.9
Montour	8 728	1.0	243	2.8	383	10.1	352	348	10 567	-.5	11 170	10 625	33 634	109.9
Northampton	131 496	.4	4 709	3.6	5 619	5.8	5 226	5 312	76 870	-1.6	75 018	78 082	26 463	86.5
Northumberland	43 620	.4	2 052	4.7	1 861	-4.3	1 864	1 945	25 010	-3.9	25 030	26 033	21 969	71.8
Perry	23 970	-.5	811	3.4	718	10.6	714	649	5 632	25.1	5 269	4 502	17 287	56.5
Philadelphia	628 687	-.3	38 573	6.1	26 181	-7.7	26 239	28 366	586 689	-4.2	594 043	612 419	34 420	112.5
Pike	18 757	-.1	627	3.3	688	8.3	650	635	5 328	-11.8	4 770	6 042	18 960	61.9
Potter	9 790	6.8	438	4.5	449	5.2	428	427	5 468	32.8	4 498	4 119	26 558	86.8

[1] Civilian unemployed as a percent of total civilian labor force.   [2] For pay period including March 12 of the year shown.

Sources: Civilian Labor Force—U.S. Bureau of Labor Statistics; Local Area Unemployment Statistics; 2000 data published 2 May 2001, 1999 data published 30 May 2001; <ftp://ftp.bls.gov/pub/time.series/la/> (related Internet site <http://www.bls.gov/lauhome.htm>). Private Business Establishments and Employment—U.S. Census Bureau; County Business Patterns on CD-ROM; annual (related Internet site <http://www.census.gov/epcd/cbp/view/cbpview.html>).

Table B–7. Counties — Labor Force and Private Business Establishments and Employment–Con.

[Includes U.S., states, and 3,142 counties/county equivalents defined as of January 1, 1992. For changes to these areas since January 1, 1992, see appendix B. Geographic Information]

County	Civilian labor force, 2000 Total	Percent change, 1999–2000	Unemployment Total	Rate[1]	Establishments 1998	Percent change, 1990–1998	1995	1990	Employment[2] 1998	Percent change, 1990–1998	1995	1990	Annual payroll per employee, 1998 Amount (dollars)	Percent of national average
PENNSYLVANIA—Con.														
Schuylkill	66 278	−1.6	4 467	6.7	3 175	.2	3 170	3 168	43 076	2.5	42 970	42 006	23 259	76.0
Snyder	18 919	−.4	582	3.1	808	4.0	793	777	12 746	1.0	12 905	12 618	20 018	65.4
Somerset	36 865	−.7	2 194	6.0	1 932	6.0	1 897	1 823	20 551	5.7	21 503	19 438	21 518	70.3
Sullivan	2 369	−6.1	130	5.5	179	7.8	163	166	1 368	15.2	1 325	1 187	18 262	59.7
Susquehanna	18 743	−.3	834	4.4	787	12.3	771	701	6 338	1.9	6 261	6 219	18 831	61.5
Tioga	20 045	3.2	903	4.5	859	5.3	818	816	10 443	13.0	9 954	9 243	19 653	64.2
Union	18 674	.3	485	2.6	827	4.9	800	788	14 600	4.8	12 333	13 932	21 910	71.6
Venango	26 298	.5	1 507	5.7	1 270	−.6	1 257	1 278	16 826	−4.7	15 865	17 657	23 829	77.9
Warren	19 841	−1.8	806	4.1	1 011	1.9	1 011	992	15 654	6.2	15 827	14 745	25 961	84.8
Washington	96 019	−.2	4 450	4.6	4 802	7.3	4 501	4 477	68 993	17.5	60 471	58 723	27 979	91.4
Wayne	19 765	1.2	1 067	5.4	1 430	3.5	1 350	1 381	12 669	8.0	11 561	11 732	19 804	64.7
Westmoreland	181 810	−.3	8 380	4.6	9 003	10.9	8 466	8 118	123 335	17.0	113 689	105 398	25 722	84.0
Wyoming	15 042	−.1	668	4.4	633	4.5	632	606	8 887	10.3	8 377	8 059	27 211	88.9
York	195 673	.4	6 322	3.2	8 160	4.7	7 760	7 791	149 419	5.0	146 495	142 256	27 886	91.1
RHODE ISLAND	504 800	.1	20 586	4.1	28 245	1.9	27 766	27 726	402 485	2.3	379 595	393 456	27 618	90.2
Bristol	25 415	.2	840	3.3	1 114	6.5	1 050	1 046	12 166	2.3	12 327	11 891	21 465	70.1
Kent	86 577	−.1	3 363	3.9	4 930	5.4	4 762	4 677	69 634	10.5	63 863	63 015	26 381	86.2
Newport	41 312	2.2	1 487	3.6	2 725	13.6	2 520	2 399	26 597	−.3	23 468	26 685	26 211	85.6
Providence	286 612	−.1	12 932	4.5	16 064	−3.4	16 276	16 622	261 016	.6	248 929	259 402	28 605	93.5
Washington	64 884	−.4	1 963	3.0	3 412	14.9	3 158	2 969	33 072	2.1	31 008	32 376	25 825	84.4
SOUTH CAROLINA	1 985 249	1.1	76 504	3.9	94 985	19.1	87 990	79 743	1 526 106	20.5	1 395 070	1 266 320	25 266	82.5
Abbeville	11 975	−2.8	502	4.2	329	7.9	314	305	6 408	27.9	6 233	5 009	24 268	79.3
Aiken	63 910	.3	2 779	4.3	2 593	15.8	2 479	2 239	49 345	4.5	54 793	47 237	33 725	110.2
Allendale	4 595	−5.5	218	4.7	165	−7.8	167	179	2 264	2.4	2 376	2 212	21 508	70.3
Anderson	86 021	1.6	2 243	2.6	3 640	14.4	3 299	3 182	55 329	13.6	52 726	48 703	24 135	78.8
Bamberg	7 791	−.1	401	5.1	297	2.8	296	289	3 499	5.6	3 298	3 312	20 155	65.8
Barnwell	11 173	−3.0	702	6.3	403	9.8	391	367	6 868	25.8	6 353	5 461	22 924	74.9
Beaufort	54 807	6.6	1 163	2.1	3 983	39.9	3 541	2 848	41 244	45.1	35 184	28 419	23 743	77.6
Berkeley	67 121	3.5	2 006	3.0	1 672	28.5	1 397	1 301	22 156	27.9	15 793	17 327	24 407	79.7
Calhoun	7 006	1.4	330	4.7	192	12.3	168	171	2 516	45.9	2 426	1 725	22 362	73.1
Charleston	167 178	3.9	5 071	3.0	10 218	16.3	9 414	8 700	102 111	31.1	140 536	123 699	24 647	80.5
Cherokee	26 551	2.7	1 302	4.9	1 054	22.4	901	861	20 287	15.0	17 109	17 646	23 617	77.2
Chester	15 683	−2.0	1 161	7.4	589	6.1	565	555	10 448	−1.4	10 002	10 595	24 809	81.1
Chesterfield	20 360	.2	1 127	5.5	729	11.3	701	655	13 120	−.4	12 514	13 177	22 747	74.3
Clarendon	13 471	3.3	924	6.9	533	14.6	503	465	5 968	6.9	5 393	5 581	18 023	58.9
Colleton	15 243	−.4	641	4.2	829	14.7	778	723	8 483	2.1	8 400	8 310	19 845	64.8
Darlington	30 387	−2.3	1 979	6.5	1 272	11.1	1 215	1 145	21 432	9.5	21 010	19 573	27 284	89.1
Dillon	13 793	−3.9	1 452	10.5	543	15.8	533	469	8 761	28.2	8 151	6 836	18 870	61.6
Dorchester	45 891	3.7	1 365	3.0	1 654	15.0	1 496	1 438	20 722	28.0	17 233	16 194	22 238	72.7
Edgefield	9 266	−1.4	308	3.3	364	24.2	322	293	4 400	21.8	4 427	3 613	20 390	66.6
Fairfield	10 349	−4.6	763	7.4	342	8.2	330	316	6 812	18.5	5 807	5 749	32 126	105.0
Florence	63 120	−.4	3 003	4.8	3 281	10.6	3 132	2 966	54 075	17.9	50 484	46 525	23 866	78.0
Georgetown	25 589	2.7	2 007	7.8	1 725	34.2	1 488	1 285	19 239	19.7	19 130	16 070	22 065	72.1
Greenville	196 671	1.7	3 865	2.0	11 405	28.6	10 748	8 869	244 949	22.1	221 686	200 545	29 615	96.8
Greenwood	32 443	−2.8	1 642	5.1	1 560	12.6	1 471	1 386	29 025	22.3	28 048	23 733	24 836	81.1
Hampton	8 577	−1.3	428	5.0	428	10.3	421	388	4 613	−1.9	4 374	4 700	21 843	71.4
Horry	106 955	2.6	3 857	3.6	6 991	32.5	6 271	5 278	80 708	46.7	68 314	55 009	20 007	65.4
Jasper	8 620	6.8	305	3.5	381	34.2	329	284	3 253	20.3	2 909	2 703	16 245	53.1
Kershaw	23 415	1.4	1 136	4.9	1 123	9.0	1 113	1 030	14 785	4.5	14 531	14 145	23 525	76.9
Lancaster	29 337	−.3	1 198	4.1	1 158	14.1	1 088	1 015	16 978	10.0	16 675	15 440	23 937	78.2
Laurens	27 935	.6	957	3.4	921	12.7	851	817	17 250	14.1	16 764	15 112	21 619	70.6
Lee	8 574	3.2	647	7.5	266	−5.7	287	282	2 350	−24.2	2 716	3 101	18 769	61.3
Lexington	121 035	−.2	2 456	2.0	4 878	32.9	4 352	3 670	63 898	44.9	54 281	44 107	23 806	77.8
McCormick	3 939	−5.4	310	7.9	129	−1.5	134	131	1 206	−19.2	1 203	1 492	18 805	61.4
Marion	16 127	−3.9	2 478	15.4	670	6.0	616	632	10 345	5.1	10 016	9 842	20 194	66.0
Marlboro	11 431	−3.2	1 200	10.5	426	4.4	417	408	6 323	.7	6 164	6 277	22 580	73.8
Newberry	18 010	−.4	848	4.7	720	14.3	718	630	11 652	23.2	11 686	9 461	20 400	66.6
Oconee	28 390	−1.4	1 073	3.8	1 432	26.5	1 282	1 132	20 842	32.8	19 605	15 690	24 727	80.8
Orangeburg	42 259	.2	3 374	8.0	1 901	9.1	1 847	1 743	28 575	9.6	26 157	26 078	22 401	73.2
Pickens	57 166	1.2	1 407	2.5	2 149	21.5	2 042	1 769	30 441	7.6	31 087	28 288	21 063	68.8
Richland	160 823	−.1	4 547	2.8	8 961	12.2	8 565	7 989	169 495	19.1	147 809	142 344	26 312	86.0
Saluda	9 001	−.1	385	4.3	266	−4.7	271	279	4 354	9.3	4 104	3 984	19 302	63.1
Spartanburg	134 734	1.2	4 623	3.4	6 170	13.8	5 645	5 420	115 285	9.9	109 827	104 895	26 979	88.1
Sumter	47 631	1.0	2 260	4.7	1 892	7.5	1 766	1 760	34 515	22.8	34 461	28 112	22 437	73.3
Union	14 428	−5.4	946	6.6	546	11.7	506	489	7 962	−6.1	9 588	8 483	20 345	66.5
Williamsburg	14 576	−2.2	1 804	12.4	535	4.9	541	510	8 565	1.1	8 288	8 473	19 721	64.4
York	91 897	2.8	3 314	3.6	3 651	23.4	3 262	2 958	50 990	25.3	44 827	40 703	26 454	86.4

[1] Civilian unemployed as a percent of total civilian labor force.　[2] For pay period including March 12 of the year shown.

Sources: Civilian Labor Force—U.S. Bureau of Labor Statistics; Local Area Unemployment Statistics; 2000 data published 2 May 2001, 1999 data published 30 May 2001; <ftp://ftp.bls.gov/pub/time.series/la/> (related Internet site <http://www.bls.gov/lauhome.htm>). Private Business Establishments and Employment—U.S. Census Bureau; County Business Patterns on CD-ROM; annual (related Internet site <http://www.census.gov/epcd/cbp/view/cbpview.html>).

[Includes U.S., states, and 3,142 counties/county equivalents defined as of January 1, 1992. For changes to these areas since January 1, 1992, see appendix B. Geographic Information]

County	Civilian labor force, 2000		Unemployment		Private nonfarm businesses								Annual payroll per employee, 1998	
					Establishments				Employment[2]					
	Total	Percent change, 1999–2000	Total	Rate[1]	1998	Percent change, 1990–1998	1995	1990	1998	Percent change, 1990–1998	1995	1990	Amount (dollars)	Percent of national average
SOUTH DAKOTA	401 151	.4	9 145	2.3	23 521	14.8	22 708	20 492	289 422	34.5	268 483	215 104	22 125	72.3
Aurora..................	1 231	−8.4	24	1.9	91	15.2	91	79	442	18.8	474	372	15 876	51.9
Beadle	8 558	−1.4	180	2.1	626	3.3	622	606	6 301	1.6	6 668	6 200	20 120	65.7
Bennett................	1 067	4.2	47	4.4	68	3.0	75	66	581	39.0	593	418	16 050	52.4
Bon Homme	3 045	−1.5	54	1.8	207	6.2	211	195	1 635	17.1	1 544	1 396	16 607	54.3
Brookings..............	17 030	3.3	196	1.2	729	23.8	643	589	10 480	49.8	9 581	6 994	20 412	66.7
Brown	20 744	Z	379	1.8	1 328	.8	1 332	1 317	16 515	27.4	16 159	12 962	20 113	65.7
Brule	2 499	−4.4	71	2.8	217	11.9	216	194	1 834	20.4	1 812	1 523	14 611	47.7
Buffalo	840	−.9	67	8.0	11	−21.4	10	14	(3)	NA	99	75	D	D
Butte	3 694	−.8	113	3.1	273	8.3	274	252	1 878	21.2	1 612	1 549	16 276	53.2
Campbell	855	−1.7	61	7.1	53	3.9	61	51	347	39.4	294	249	16 801	54.9
Charles Mix	4 435	−.8	109	2.5	285	13.5	302	251	2 487	52.8	2 688	1 628	16 038	52.4
Clark	1 838	−6.4	87	4.7	120	−4.0	115	125	694	13.0	629	614	16 117	52.7
Clay...................	7 586	.9	54	.7	306	8.1	302	283	2 619	6.6	2 277	2 456	13 541	44.2
Codington..............	14 822	2.1	398	2.7	997	26.2	912	790	12 851	37.3	12 111	9 360	21 040	68.7
Corson	1 462	−7.6	95	6.5	46	−28.1	65	64	268	7.6	295	249	10 347	33.8
Custer.................	3 453	.6	108	3.1	222	20.7	225	184	983	1.2	965	971	20 032	65.4
Davison	10 298	.7	198	1.9	748	19.1	685	628	8 995	18.8	8 371	7 572	21 144	69.1
Day	2 865	−3.8	130	4.5	200	−2.9	195	206	1 565	7.9	1 627	1 450	16 098	52.6
Deuel	2 372	−3.8	84	3.5	128	−5.2	125	135	837	11.0	765	754	18 388	60.1
Dewey	2 391	−.7	286	12.0	99	10.0	103	90	1 225	129.0	1 165	535	19 137	62.5
Douglas	1 539	−5.4	30	1.9	122	4.3	121	117	882	20.8	775	730	14 236	46.5
Edmunds	2 199	.1	33	1.5	114	.9	109	113	721	33.0	543	542	17 209	56.2
Fall River	3 249	.5	122	3.8	224	24.4	198	180	2 371	49.4	1 699	1 587	28 604	93.4
Faulk.................	1 075	−8.7	23	2.1	68	−2.9	75	70	413	29.9	313	318	14 971	48.9
Grant	4 224	.2	142	3.4	269	8.0	262	249	3 107	21.6	2 602	2 556	19 400	63.4
Gregory	2 400	−6.2	74	3.1	174	6.1	172	164	1 115	20.8	979	923	15 669	51.2
Haakon................	1 085	−2.3	22	2.0	95	17.3	103	81	623	16.0	626	537	17 226	56.3
Hamlin	2 620	2.5	70	2.7	148	19.4	145	124	728	32.1	682	551	16 522	54.0
Hand	1 957	−3.6	32	1.6	133	−2.2	128	136	936	1.5	899	922	15 907	52.0
Hanson	1 757	.3	28	1.6	50	−3.8	50	52	242	5.7	247	229	20 479	66.9
Harding................	744	−1.3	21	2.8	32	−27.3	39	44	183	−12.9	225	210	14 383	47.0
Hughes.................	9 594	−1.3	172	1.8	627	16.5	625	538	5 927	25.4	5 866	4 727	19 256	62.9
Hutchinson.............	3 733	−2.5	80	2.1	249	6.4	244	234	2 257	23.8	2 292	1 823	17 903	58.5
Hyde..................	872	−4.5	18	2.1	44	−6.4	52	47	562	57.9	459	356	16 423	53.7
Jackson	1 038	−6.6	57	5.5	64	12.3	62	57	294	37.4	302	214	14 741	48.2
Jerauld	1 479	14.6	24	1.6	77	30.5	69	59	493	15.5	466	427	16 195	52.9
Jones	748	−7.4	14	1.9	58	11.5	56	52	298	36.1	301	219	17 178	56.1
Kingsbury..............	2 414	−6.5	60	2.5	199	4.2	194	191	1 377	25.9	1 230	1 094	17 633	57.6
Lake	5 953	−1.7	144	2.4	351	13.6	323	309	3 446	22.4	3 294	2 815	19 802	64.7
Lawrence	10 547	1.2	269	2.6	821	17.3	815	700	8 606	21.3	8 903	7 093	19 306	63.1
Lincoln	13 246	2.3	151	1.1	518	50.1	378	345	4 510	61.5	2 967	2 793	22 559	73.7
Lyman	2 291	−6.5	95	4.1	72	1.4	79	71	589	43.0	330	412	15 547	50.8
McCook	2 406	−2.4	55	2.3	173	−1.7	176	176	1 140	5.9	1 195	1 076	15 824	51.7
McPherson	1 357	6.1	24	1.8	89	−9.2	93	98	492	−	512	492	13 018	42.5
Marshall	2 073	−8.1	85	4.1	141	10.2	149	128	1 270	53.0	1 354	830	20 694	67.6
Meade	13 174	.1	303	2.3	493	23.3	462	400	4 740	50.8	3 810	3 143	21 135	69.0
Mellette...............	660	−8.6	38	5.8	33	17.9	30	28	163	96.4	135	83	13 669	44.7
Miner.................	1 430	1.7	37	2.6	77	−23.8	78	101	395	−50.1	631	791	18 167	59.4
Minnehaha..............	91 615	2.5	1 405	1.5	5 009	19.5	4 862	4 190	92 181	36.7	84 431	67 421	24 685	80.6
Moody.................	3 486	−4.3	164	4.7	180	21.6	151	148	1 520	15.3	1 537	1 318	20 046	65.5
Pennington	48 248	2.4	955	2.0	3 178	19.7	3 056	2 654	38 208	29.5	37 007	29 504	22 266	72.7
Perkins................	1 880	−4.7	42	2.2	130	−7.1	138	140	1 027	6.1	916	968	13 449	43.9
Potter.................	1 391	−3.7	36	2.6	126	20.0	124	105	927	73.6	734	534	17 063	55.7
Roberts................	4 777	−.3	193	4.0	256	−1.9	259	261	1 888	12.7	1 960	1 675	14 461	47.2
Sanborn	1 426	−2.6	34	2.4	63	12.5	58	56	550	35.1	422	407	14 627	47.8
Shannon	3 137	−4.0	306	9.8	60	33.3	59	45	1 280	30.9	1 093	978	18 661	61.0
Spink..................	3 293	−4.6	95	2.9	186	−	179	186	1 227	8.2	1 192	1 134	17 007	55.6
Stanley	1 803	−1.4	35	1.9	88	31.3	80	67	658	52.0	675	433	22 833	74.6
Sully	823	−3.2	19	2.3	53	−1.9	51	54	244	9.9	253	222	16 258	53.1
Todd	2 983	2.2	172	5.8	58	5.5	63	55	948	32.8	955	714	23 687	77.4
Tripp	3 267	−7.1	84	2.6	236	12.9	223	209	1 722	25.6	1 483	1 371	17 506	57.2
Turner.................	4 031	−2.8	90	2.2	260	20.9	246	215	1 494	17.5	1 330	1 272	15 642	51.1
Union	7 046	−2.4	183	2.6	390	88.4	328	207	11 900	432.7	9 231	2 234	37 414	122.2
Walworth	3 049	−1.9	89	2.9	236	−1.3	247	239	1 884	21.8	1 889	1 547	15 497	50.6
Yankton	11 291	.1	200	1.8	723	12.6	714	642	11 038	33.1	9 770	8 291	19 387	63.3
Ziebach................	664	−3.9	81	12.2	17	−15.0	14	20	203	38.1	223	147	25 310	82.7

[1] Civilian unemployed as a percent of total civilian labor force.   [2] For pay period including March 12 of the year shown.   [3] 20–99 employees.

Sources: Civilian Labor Force—U.S. Bureau of Labor Statistics; Local Area Unemployment Statistics; 2000 data published 2 May 2001, 1999 data published 30 May 2001; <ftp://ftp.bls.gov/pub/time.series/la/> (related Internet site <http://www.bls.gov/lauhome.htm>). Private Business Establishments and Employment—U.S. Census Bureau; County Business Patterns on CD-ROM; annual (related Internet site <http://www.census.gov/epcd/cbp/view/cbpview.html>).

[Includes U.S., states, and 3,142 counties/county equivalents defined as of January 1, 1992. For changes to these areas since January 1, 1992, see appendix B. Geographic Information]

County	Civilian labor force, 2000		Unemployment		Private nonfarm businesses								Annual payroll per employee, 1998	
					Establishments				Employment[2]					
	Total	Percent change, 1999–2000	Total	Rate[1]	1998	Percent change, 1990–1998	1995	1990	1998	Percent change, 1990–1998	1995	1990	Amount (dollars)	Percent of national average
TENNESSEE	2 798 336	–.6	110 174	3.9	131 110	15.7	124 814	113 292	2 299 348	23.0	2 153 264	1 869 268	27 156	88.7
Anderson	35 461	–.1	1 292	3.6	1 726	11.7	1 678	1 545	38 946	18.8	36 541	32 787	34 579	113.0
Bedford.................	17 994	.7	1 033	5.7	726	16.2	677	625	11 816	11.4	11 954	10 604	23 267	76.0
Benton	7 679	2.0	677	8.8	347	12.3	346	309	3 643	13.9	3 628	3 198	19 235	62.8
Bledsoe	3 785	–3.4	152	4.0	142	14.5	131	124	1 557	15.8	1 303	1 344	19 545	63.9
Blount	51 166	–.8	1 579	3.1	2 132	23.7	1 947	1 723	32 936	44.3	27 858	22 828	27 370	89.4
Bradley	41 971	–2.7	1 442	3.4	1 904	16.1	1 833	1 640	37 841	20.4	34 633	31 431	25 234	82.4
Campbell	16 898	–.8	1 073	6.3	646	15.2	628	561	7 246	11.3	7 149	6 508	20 703	67.6
Cannon.................	5 148	2.5	214	4.2	157	9.0	162	144	1 488	3.7	1 594	1 435	17 638	57.6
Carroll.................	12 065	–4.3	1 478	12.3	544	2.3	552	532	8 071	5.7	8 969	7 636	18 161	59.3
Carter	25 265	–1.5	1 278	5.1	772	9.5	761	705	9 634	4.5	10 346	9 221	21 854	71.4
Cheatham	19 804	.2	445	2.2	485	70.2	401	285	6 219	69.0	5 305	3 680	23 405	76.5
Chester................	8 523	1.7	329	3.9	238	25.9	230	189	3 363	49.6	3 380	2 248	18 316	59.8
Claiborne	12 815	–3.3	646	5.0	470	20.2	434	391	7 493	4.9	7 789	7 142	19 206	62.7
Clay...................	2 661	–2.2	284	10.7	110	11.1	110	99	1 629	–26.9	2 243	2 229	18 958	61.9
Cocke..................	16 510	–.6	1 092	6.6	514	16.3	471	442	6 886	18.6	6 813	5 806	21 107	69.0
Coffee.................	22 378	–1.3	943	4.2	1 214	17.2	1 196	1 036	22 585	19.6	20 464	18 885	27 057	88.4
Crockett	7 082	–3.7	354	5.0	303	19.3	291	254	3 015	7.9	3 359	2 793	23 712	77.5
Cumberland.............	21 606	2.2	1 031	4.8	954	30.5	863	731	11 543	19.7	10 086	9 645	21 248	69.4
Davidson	305 847	.2	8 855	2.9	19 011	11.3	18 717	17 080	393 097	21.1	371 515	324 687	31 565	103.1
Decatur................	5 338	–3.0	335	6.3	256	11.3	252	230	3 483	26.9	3 586	2 745	21 101	68.9
DeKalb	8 124	.5	425	5.2	317	19.2	275	266	5 004	21.6	4 694	4 116	22 313	72.9
Dickson	22 082	.6	790	3.6	877	31.1	786	669	12 646	50.8	11 282	8 386	21 446	70.1
Dyer	18 161	–2.0	1 105	6.1	954	14.0	892	837	15 779	16.4	15 756	13 554	23 252	76.0
Fayette	14 577	.3	691	4.7	416	44.4	332	288	4 232	9.3	4 438	3 873	24 818	81.1
Fentress	6 365	–3.9	645	10.1	277	18.4	271	234	3 775	14.9	4 106	3 286	17 408	56.9
Franklin	17 972	–1.8	703	3.9	692	24.7	628	555	8 022	23.9	8 184	6 472	21 425	70.0
Gibson	21 123	–.9	1 444	6.8	1 080	2.4	1 102	1 055	16 783	4.0	18 037	16 130	22 178	72.5
Giles	16 276	–.2	708	4.3	571	15.4	535	495	9 290	33.0	8 629	6 985	24 425	79.8
Grainger	10 217	–.4	443	4.3	250	43.7	229	174	2 736	33.6	2 869	2 048	20 424	66.7
Greene	36 123	.7	2 166	6.0	1 187	11.8	1 134	1 062	20 966	2.5	20 754	20 463	22 172	72.4
Grundy	5 356	–2.5	289	5.4	190	–5.0	193	200	1 366	–24.9	1 295	1 818	14 284	46.7
Hamblen	29 980	–1.0	1 157	3.9	1 440	17.6	1 342	1 225	29 270	8.8	27 893	26 909	24 122	78.8
Hamilton...............	150 816	.1	4 291	2.8	9 059	8.7	8 741	8 335	166 300	10.3	152 420	138 585	26 356	86.1
Hancock...............	2 576	–6.8	134	5.2	63	–4.5	61	66	718	34.0	777	536	14 822	48.4
Hardeman	9 477	.1	596	6.3	432	9.6	442	394	5 748	–11.5	5 831	6 495	24 582	80.3
Hardin	11 970	–2.5	689	5.8	531	19.3	511	445	6 312	6.8	6 414	5 910	21 222	69.3
Hawkins	23 434	–2.3	1 057	4.5	615	16.7	571	527	11 152	18.5	10 686	9 400	26 641	87.0
Haywood	8 411	–.1	682	8.1	375	10.0	358	341	5 332	6.4	5 186	5 009	21 391	69.9
Henderson	14 461	Z	759	5.2	542	40.8	500	385	8 790	29.3	8 451	6 798	21 562	70.4
Henry	14 480	–.1	782	5.4	778	16.1	774	670	10 265	26.9	10 324	8 089	21 498	70.2
Hickman	7 677	–2.7	342	4.5	301	33.2	273	226	2 647	–5.3	2 806	2 795	21 791	71.2
Houston	2 729	Z	245	9.0	123	17.1	110	105	1 189	13.7	1 140	1 046	16 203	52.9
Humphreys	8 017	.4	510	6.4	323	9.1	301	296	4 756	8.8	4 417	4 370	29 421	96.1
Jackson	4 560	–1.7	363	8.0	109	–48.1	99	210	1 315	–38.9	1 497	2 153	20 902	68.3
Jefferson	24 099	–1.7	942	3.9	634	13.0	651	561	9 221	8.8	9 260	8 472	21 160	69.1
Johnson	6 541	–10.7	499	7.6	239	30.6	238	183	3 188	20.1	3 381	2 655	19 571	63.9
Knox	200 284	–.4	4 642	2.3	11 264	10.7	10 916	10 176	182 606	18.9	175 189	153 595	25 959	84.8
Lake	2 392	–6.4	135	5.6	100	–5.7	113	106	1 043	–26.8	1 251	1 424	15 621	51.0
Lauderdale..............	9 906	–1.5	640	6.5	379	4.7	382	362	7 173	2.2	6 464	7 022	19 705	64.4
Lawrence	19 774	–5.0	2 568	13.0	807	17.1	800	689	12 038	18.7	13 409	10 142	20 374	66.6
Lewis	4 027	–3.5	347	8.6	226	32.9	196	170	2 103	–18.1	2 865	2 567	18 610	60.8
Lincoln	14 277	.1	518	3.6	630	11.7	596	564	6 877	2.9	7 121	6 686	20 686	67.6
Loudon	20 678	–.3	576	2.8	748	41.1	675	530	9 582	27.1	8 473	7 540	23 780	77.7
McMinn................	20 985	–3.5	1 040	5.0	942	12.0	921	841	17 708	6.1	18 585	16 694	24 853	81.2
McNairy	10 330	–11.8	523	5.1	483	20.1	459	402	8 037	10.3	6 485	7 285	20 026	65.4
Macon.................	8 573	3.3	350	4.1	314	21.2	289	259	3 500	–3.4	3 923	3 625	18 195	59.4
Madison	60 053	1.8	2 084	3.5	2 662	18.4	2 525	2 249	49 684	36.6	45 461	36 361	24 912	81.4
Marion	12 698	.3	580	4.6	432	20.0	407	360	5 391	28.4	5 270	4 198	19 818	64.7
Marshall	12 425	1.3	496	4.0	503	16.4	465	432	11 455	23.9	11 155	9 247	24 466	79.9
Maury	36 794	–1.8	1 338	3.6	1 506	14.2	1 417	1 319	29 170	37.3	27 729	21 249	32 515	106.2
Meigs	4 439	–5.1	237	5.3	106	34.2	91	79	1 440	103.1	1 281	709	19 091	62.4
Monroe	18 723	–.9	1 014	5.4	654	16.6	645	561	10 029	38.8	9 511	7 225	22 752	74.3
Montgomery	59 205	1.0	1 841	3.1	2 319	28.1	2 180	1 810	30 945	48.4	27 712	20 855	21 191	69.2
Moore	2 852	–.7	77	2.7	53	1.9	60	52	784	21.4	707	646	23 844	77.9
Morgan	7 042	2.2	402	5.7	162	26.6	139	128	1 910	8.4	1 985	1 762	18 505	60.5
Obion	15 482	Z	686	4.4	765	5.1	762	728	14 187	11.5	13 515	12 727	26 182	85.5

[1] Civilian unemployed as a percent of total civilian labor force.　[2] For pay period including March 12 of the year shown.

Sources: Civilian Labor Force—U.S. Bureau of Labor Statistics; Local Area Unemployment Statistics; 2000 data published 2 May 2001, 1999 data published 30 May 2001; <ftp://ftp.bls.gov/pub/time.series/la/> (related Internet site <http://www.bls.gov/lauhome.htm>).　Private Business Establishments and Employment—U.S. Census Bureau; County Business Patterns on CD-ROM; annual (related Internet site <http://www.census.gov/epcd/cbp/view/cbpview.html>).

[Includes U.S., states, and 3,142 counties/county equivalents defined as of January 1, 1992. For changes to these areas since January 1, 1992, see appendix B. Geographic Information]

County	Civilian labor force, 2000		Unemployment		Private nonfarm businesses Establishments				Employment[2]				Annual payroll per employee, 1998	
	Total	Percent change, 1999–2000	Total	Rate[1]	1998	Percent change, 1990–1998	1995	1990	1998	Percent change, 1990–1998	1995	1990	Amount (dollars)	Percent of national average
TENNESSEE—Con.														
Overton	9 662	–.9	557	5.8	297	19.8	263	248	3 439	11.3	3 593	3 091	19 016	62.1
Perry	3 630	–4.9	201	5.5	121	11.0	116	109	2 556	55.8	2 074	1 641	20 824	68.0
Pickett	2 144	–2.6	103	4.8	80	23.1	80	65	1 188	25.8	1 033	944	17 767	58.0
Polk	6 668	–2.6	338	5.1	262	24.2	238	211	2 245	.2	2 890	2 240	18 275	59.7
Putnam	30 990	–1.1	1 377	4.4	1 677	26.9	1 601	1 321	26 478	25.1	26 324	21 751	21 751	71.1
Rhea	12 345	1.0	668	5.4	492	24.6	492	395	7 917	12.6	8 648	7 028	21 209	69.3
Roane	23 441	–5.3	996	4.2	712	7.1	690	665	8 900	22.9	8 491	7 244	18 753	61.3
Robertson	29 527	.4	1 039	3.5	942	53.9	868	612	12 631	36.2	11 934	9 272	22 715	74.2
Rutherford	98 188	.5	2 860	2.9	3 365	43.6	2 887	2 343	69 094	49.8	62 523	46 110	28 169	92.0
Scott	8 892	.2	505	5.7	344	16.2	302	296	6 239	33.1	6 036	4 688	17 544	57.3
Sequatchie	4 748	–3.0	181	3.8	171	13.2	179	151	2 301	26.4	2 480	1 821	16 801	54.9
Sevier	35 607	–.6	2 153	6.0	2 454	38.7	2 273	1 769	26 160	52.6	22 646	17 142	19 191	62.7
Shelby	442 764	–.6	17 470	3.9	21 376	6.2	20 766	20 120	453 920	23.0	406 899	368 959	30 082	98.3
Smith	9 622	–1.0	415	4.3	315	25.0	308	252	5 048	31.0	4 404	3 853	24 720	80.8
Stewart	3 481	1.3	248	7.1	155	42.2	142	109	1 098	–12.6	1 227	1 256	16 127	52.7
Sullivan	73 095	–2.1	2 567	3.5	3 655	12.3	3 621	3 256	65 273	7.9	67 742	60 519	28 957	94.6
Sumner	70 016	.5	2 130	3.0	2 523	23.1	2 356	2 049	32 828	31.8	33 313	24 901	24 236	79.2
Tipton	22 552	–.2	867	3.8	707	27.4	661	555	8 805	40.3	7 981	6 277	21 449	70.1
Trousdale	1 986	–5.1	103	5.2	120	11.1	121	108	1 617	2.8	1 634	1 573	21 004	68.6
Unicoi	8 012	.7	630	7.9	270	11.6	264	242	3 944	3.4	3 608	3 814	23 799	77.8
Union	7 845	–.4	257	3.3	184	50.8	172	122	2 144	67.6	2 016	1 279	20 063	65.5
Van Buren	2 338	–2.1	132	5.6	49	32.4	42	37	594	–38.7		712	969	27 626	90.3
Warren	19 109	–1.5	853	4.5	784	11.8	730	701	12 924	11.8	14 496	11 561	23 400	76.4
Washington	51 366	–1.4	1 927	3.8	2 773	16.9	2 583	2 372	51 322	32.8	45 412	38 634	21 462	70.1
Wayne	7 021	–7.0	703	10.0	237	21.5	235	195	2 941	–12.0	3 521	3 341	16 419	53.6
Weakley	16 183	–4.3	860	5.3	669	11.3	642	601	11 005	6.2	9 802	10 365	19 126	62.5
White	11 177	–1.5	520	4.7	405	17.1	396	346	6 428	13.3	6 457	5 672	22 034	72.0
Williamson	69 364	.1	1 284	1.9	4 020	64.3	3 209	2 446	63 258	98.4	47 441	31 883	33 697	110.1
Wilson	48 559	.5	1 483	3.1	1 846	43.1	1 491	1 290	22 262	37.7	20 013	16 168	25 714	84.0
TEXAS	10 324 527	1.0	437 488	4.2	462 875	17.3	438 262	394 482	7 570 820	29.1	6 786 893	5 864 637	30 272	98.9
Anderson	19 277	–5.6	901	4.7	929	7.6	907	863	11 463	35.2	10 645	8 479	21 833	71.3
Andrews	4 998	–5.4	291	5.8	301	–14.5	326	352	2 995	–21.3	3 088	3 806	22 142	72.3
Angelina	35 867	.5	1 824	5.1	1 822	10.6	1 727	1 648	28 986	15.6	26 880	25 064	24 793	81.0
Aransas	9 517	–1.7	576	6.1	471	31.6	413	358	3 499	39.8	3 270	2 503	18 512	60.5
Archer	3 981	–1.9	103	2.6	154	–8.3	148	168	751	1.9	746	737	17 537	57.3
Armstrong	1 150	11.7	19	1.7	42	35.5	34	31	316	32.8	297	238	21 608	70.6
Atascosa	18 406	3.1	710	3.9	540	21.9	530	443	5 182	31.1	4 396	3 953	19 623	64.1
Austin	12 858	–4.3	433	3.4	558	13.2	542	493	5 459	40.1	4 898	3 897	20 912	68.3
Bailey	3 461	–.2	177	5.1	180	–8.6	203	197	1 412	.3	1 327	1 408	18 198	59.5
Bandera	7 384	7.4	184	2.5	323	75.5	278	184	1 674	76.2	1 775	950	15 560	50.8
Bastrop	29 332	4.1	658	2.2	737	45.7	676	506	6 401	74.0	5 330	3 679	18 307	59.8
Baylor	1 633	–5.8	68	4.2	140	–7.3	139	151	1 178	36.5	890	863	12 067	39.4
Bee	10 385	–4.5	565	5.4	449	–8.2	468	489	4 427	2.1	4 596	4 334	18 041	58.9
Bell	94 332	.4	3 015	3.2	3 958	18.9	3 751	3 328	72 765	45.2	63 009	50 108	22 378	73.1
Bexar	676 590	1.2	23 903	3.5	29 487	16.8	28 091	25 241	529 247	32.3	479 745	399 919	25 732	84.1
Blanco	4 000	2.1	79	2.0	203	37.2	199	148	1 805	15.9	1 389	1 558	20 448	66.8
Borden	390	–.5	5	1.3	2	–33.3	3	3	(³)	NA	(³)	8	D	D
Bosque	6 715	–7.2	242	3.6	301	4.9	309	287	2 507	12.1	2 396	2 236	19 198	62.7
Bowie	38 586	–1.3	1 968	5.1	2 139	11.8	1 985	1 913	29 601	23.4	27 887	23 984	23 454	76.6
Brazoria	106 284	1.9	6 626	6.2	3 748	16.4	3 520	3 220	56 950	9.4	56 143	52 080	32 325	105.6
Brazos	76 482	1.3	1 161	1.5	3 167	30.6	2 945	2 425	42 899	43.7	38 078	29 845	21 772	71.1
Brewster	5 319	1.8	120	2.3	268	10.7	262	242	2 033	31.3	2 005	1 548	14 751	48.2
Briscoe	894	–1.8	25	2.8	49	–2.0	57	50	181	–10.4	253	202	17 901	58.5
Brooks	3 209	2.6	235	7.3	152	9.4	134	139	1 367	3.2	1 399	1 325	11 745	38.4
Brown	16 953	–1.0	647	3.8	884	5.6	897	837	11 944	22.1	11 315	9 780	21 095	68.9
Burleson	6 753	–.7	257	3.8	304	22.6	285	248	2 536	45.6	2 471	1 742	18 295	59.8
Burnet	14 377	2.7	373	2.6	826	37.2	765	602	5 931	31.3	5 384	4 516	19 383	63.3
Caldwell	16 890	4.2	548	3.2	508	15.5	478	440	4 053	1.1	3 606	4 009	16 923	55.3
Calhoun	10 044	4.4	465	4.6	420	2.2	419	411	7 888	25.1	7 840	6 303	37 725	123.2
Callahan	5 986	–2.3	223	3.7	194	–11.0	181	218	1 007	–9.3	926	1 110	16 822	55.0
Cameron	130 113	2.6	11 311	8.7	5 673	16.2	5 530	4 881	79 534	33.7	73 532	59 500	18 011	58.8
Camp	5 336	–.7	287	5.4	256	–6.2	249	273	2 861	12.9	2 711	2 535	25 036	81.8
Carson	3 122	–1.5	91	2.9	129	–11.6	138	146	795	–11.6	883	899	20 516	67.0
Cass	15 032	–2.4	872	5.8	617	22.4	609	504	5 422	23.3	5 234	4 396	19 214	62.8
Castro	3 690	–.7	143	3.9	199	–4.3	204	208	1 450	23.0	1 443	1 179	19 467	63.6

[1] Civilian unemployed as a percent of total civilian labor force. [2] For pay period including March 12 of the year shown. [3] 0–19 employees.

Sources: Civilian Labor Force—U.S. Bureau of Labor Statistics; Local Area Unemployment Statistics; 2000 data published 2 May 2001, 1999 data published 30 May 2001; <ftp://ftp.bls.gov/pub/time.series/la/> (related Internet site <http://www.bls.gov/lauhome.htm>). Private Business Establishments and Employment—U.S. Census Bureau; County Business Patterns on CD-ROM; annual (related Internet site <http://www.census.gov/epcd/cbp/view/cbpview.html>).

[Includes U.S., states, and 3,142 counties/county equivalents defined as of January 1, 1992. For changes to these areas since January 1, 1992, see appendix B. Geographic Information]

County	Civilian labor force, 2000					Private nonfarm businesses									
			Unemployment		Establishments				Employment[2]				Annual payroll per employee, 1998	
	Total	Percent change, 1999–2000	Total	Rate[1]	1998	Percent change, 1990–1998	1995	1990	1998	Percent change, 1990–1998	1995	1990	Amount (dollars)	Percent of national average
TEXAS—Con.														
Chambers	11 911	1.3	555	4.7	389	24.3	335	313	5 920	88.6	4 338	3 139	36 339	118.7
Cherokee	20 111	–3.1	814	4.0	827	13.3	794	730	11 527	14.6	11 996	10 059	19 809	64.7
Childress	2 887	–4.1	86	3.0	171	–7.1	185	184	1 253	17.0	1 281	1 071	17 116	55.9
Clay	5 717	2.9	158	2.8	121	–6.9	138	130	996	18.0	870	844	18 334	59.9
Cochran	1 361	2.6	106	7.8	66	–17.5	60	80	522	35.9	359	384	16 546	54.1
Coke	1 641	4.3	33	2.0	80	23.1	75	65	558	52.5	407	366	23 203	75.8
Coleman	3 167	–4.5	160	5.1	223	.5	229	222	1 527	2.2	1 851	1 494	15 445	50.5
Collin	287 350	2.7	5 768	2.0	9 598	88.8	6 875	5 085	154 811	96.8	104 583	78 648	39 701	129.7
Collingsworth	1 515	2.0	19	1.3	71	–17.4	83	86	513	7.5	608	477	16 938	55.3
Colorado	8 194	–1.5	272	3.3	538	4.7	517	514	5 209	18.7	4 769	4 387	20 364	66.5
Comal	39 947	.9	1 000	2.5	1 899	37.6	1 697	1 380	22 054	47.9	18 395	14 909	21 646	70.7
Comanche	6 615	–.1	168	2.5	318	12.4	306	283	2 737	40.2	2 473	1 952	18 362	60.0
Concho	1 534	–1.5	48	3.1	63	23.5	56	51	606	91.2	457	317	17 759	58.0
Cooke	17 061	–.1	543	3.2	846	21.4	797	697	10 521	34.6	8 896	7 817	20 646	67.5
Coryell	21 593	.8	861	4.0	710	19.3	689	595	7 488	61.0	5 549	4 652	16 169	52.8
Cottle	797	–4.6	34	4.3	47	–24.2	57	62	402	53.4	259	262	16 075	52.5
Crane	1 852	–8.0	101	5.5	88	–20.7	103	111	1 101	–7.6	1 076	1 191	23 916	78.1
Crockett	1 839	–9.8	66	3.6	133	14.7	115	116	1 017	44.3	825	705	17 857	58.3
Crosby	2 742	1.0	141	5.1	138	–6.8	137	148	912	–17.8	1 159	1 109	20 649	67.5
Culberson	1 083	–12.3	110	10.2	64	–15.8	66	76	572	22.2	661	468	13 941	45.5
Dallam	3 593	–1.6	102	2.8	250	11.1	287	225	1 642	30.3	1 815	1 260	19 406	63.4
Dallas	1 237 748	2.6	42 791	3.5	63 998	10.3	63 586	58 008	1 411 913	26.8	1 256 339	1 113 434	37 700	123.2
Dawson	6 413	5.4	314	4.9	362	–1.4	376	367	2 784	24.0	2 729	2 246	17 090	55.8
Deaf Smith	7 797	–.8	471	6.0	444	–7.7	477	481	4 507	–2.3	4 718	4 613	19 672	64.3
Delta	3 507	3.6	132	3.8	75	–5.1	88	79	583	–31.3	616	849	17 516	57.2
Denton	258 009	2.9	5 230	2.0	7 057	50.4	5 963	4 691	94 599	65.7	79 040	57 101	27 603	90.2
DeWitt	8 450	.5	299	3.5	375	2.7	337	365	3 713	24.8	2 961	2 975	18 204	59.5
Dickens	822	–5.4	35	4.3	60	7.1	54	56	328	9.3	401	300	21 070	68.8
Dimmit	3 605	–1.4	456	12.6	181	16.8	171	155	1 448	25.9	1 249	1 150	17 392	56.8
Donley	1 607	4.3	44	2.7	91	–7.1	102	98	403	–15.3	489	476	13 437	43.9
Duval	4 724	–6.0	438	9.3	160	6.0	144	151	1 834	32.8	1 261	1 381	19 184	62.7
Eastland	9 198	2.3	353	3.8	495	2.1	493	485	4 312	9.2	3 873	3 950	20 993	68.6
Ector	58 315	–4.3	3 752	6.4	3 154	–4.7	2 928	3 310	39 079	11.9	35 069	34 927	24 352	79.6
Edwards	770	–2.7	35	4.5	41	–4.7	46	43	145	–23.3	159	189	17 724	57.9
Ellis	57 325	2.8	1 831	3.2	1 943	30.1	1 712	1 493	26 556	45.4	22 772	18 262	24 594	80.3
El Paso	284 758	–1.1	23 440	8.2	12 409	11.9	11 963	11 092	198 571	24.9	185 943	158 999	21 947	71.7
Erath	16 548	.4	347	2.1	811	22.1	750	664	9 601	42.2	8 308	6 750	18 474	60.4
Falls	7 695	3.8	320	4.2	293	1.4	281	289	2 620	13.3	2 411	2 312	20 204	66.0
Fannin	12 674	–1.8	527	4.2	500	11.4	466	449	6 057	39.9	5 100	4 331	23 179	75.7
Fayette	10 744	–.5	261	2.4	705	15.4	651	611	6 047	33.1	5 384	4 544	18 821	61.5
Fisher	1 653	.4	54	3.3	86	–6.5	86	92	700	8.5	716	645	21 706	70.9
Floyd	3 148	–1.5	182	5.8	189	–6.9	199	203	1 207	7.2	1 375	1 126	18 012	58.8
Foard	866	1.6	22	2.5	43	–4.4	44	45	325	.6	469	323	12 142	39.7
Fort Bend	189 411	.7	5 478	2.9	5 325	100.0	4 036	2 663	72 243	104.8	57 448	35 277	31 938	104.3
Franklin	4 540	.1	156	3.4	181	40.3	148	129	4 834	6.2	4 069	4 552	10 241	33.5
Freestone	7 318	–1.8	363	5.0	330	11.5	301	296	3 303	9.2	3 007	3 025	26 602	86.9
Frio	5 854	–4.4	413	7.1	265	–5.4	281	280	2 016	5.1	2 017	1 918	18 333	59.9
Gaines	6 461	–3.8	286	4.4	324	9.8	312	295	2 526	38.9	2 154	1 819	20 379	66.6
Galveston	118 166	–3.3	7 002	5.9	4 769	12.0	4 541	4 257	68 024	5.7	65 343	64 349	25 838	84.4
Garza	2 193	10.5	88	4.0	129	–5.8	135	137	893	22.3	930	730	14 459	47.2
Gillespie	10 163	–.9	298	2.9	784	44.9	676	541	6 228	44.7	5 714	4 305	17 917	58.5
Glasscock	669	–3.9	20	3.0	20	17.6	18	17	123	112.1	97	58	21 114	69.0
Goliad	2 692	.4	95	3.5	104	–10.3	104	116	619	–4.3	683	647	19 670	64.3
Gonzales	7 580	1.2	231	3.0	388	–6.5	395	415	3 867	–13.0	4 113	4 443	20 222	66.1
Gray	9 104	–5.9	459	5.0	698	–2.8	729	718	6 964	1.3	6 946	6 874	23 856	77.9
Grayson	50 063	–.9	1 844	3.7	2 518	13.7	2 320	2 215	38 179	23.3	33 597	30 965	25 085	82.0
Gregg	58 230	–1.3	3 417	5.9	3 910	6.2	3 980	3 682	59 843	22.8	54 064	48 720	24 553	80.2
Grimes	8 557	–4.3	488	5.7	347	25.3	319	277	4 412	61.0	3 660	2 741	28 430	92.9
Guadalupe	43 472	.9	1 088	2.5	1 280	24.2	1 133	1 031	18 791	55.2	16 775	12 108	20 876	68.2
Hale	16 846	–.4	815	4.8	852	–1.5	874	865	11 567	21.2	11 148	9 547	20 570	67.2
Hall	1 711	6.8	81	4.7	93	–5.1	88	98	678	78.0	497	381	15 409	50.3
Hamilton	3 919	–2.0	94	2.4	227	4.1	224	218	1 830	18.8	1 779	1 541	18 858	61.6
Hansford	2 434	–.9	63	2.6	186	–6.1	180	198	1 258	36.3	1 187	923	21 063	68.8
Hardeman	1 844	–3.5	67	3.6	104	–28.3	125	145	915	.4	927	911	21 200	69.3
Hardin	23 245	–1.6	1 503	6.5	754	24.0	730	608	8 900	44.8	7 266	6 146	18 388	60.1
Harris	1 774 037	.6	76 083	4.3	83 308	13.7	80 034	73 250	1 592 279	19.7	1 475 299	1 330 126	35 765	116.8

[1] Civilian unemployed as a percent of total civilian labor force.   [2] For pay period including March 12 of the year shown.

Sources: Civilian Labor Force—U.S. Bureau of Labor Statistics; Local Area Unemployment Statistics; 2000 data published 2 May 2001, 1999 data published 30 May 2001; <ftp://ftp.bls.gov/pub/time.series/la/> (related Internet site <http://www.bls.gov/lauhome.htm>).   Private Business Establishments and Employment—U.S. Census Bureau; County Business Patterns on CD-ROM; annual (related Internet site <http://www.census.gov/epcd/cbp/view/cbpview.html>).

[Includes U.S., states, and 3,142 counties/county equivalents defined as of January 1, 1992. For changes to these areas since January 1, 1992, see appendix B. Geographic Information]

County	Civilian labor force, 2000 Total	Percent change, 1999–2000	Unemployment Total	Rate[1]	Establishments 1998	Percent change, 1990–1998	1995	1990	Employment[2] 1998	Percent change, 1990–1998	1995	1990	Annual payroll per employee, 1998 Amount (dollars)	Percent of national average
TEXAS—Con.														
Harrison	27 333	−1.0	1 555	5.7	1 226	25.4	1 028	978	15 294	24.7	12 581	12 260	22 464	73.4
Hartley	2 952	−1.6	41	1.4	73	87.2	44	39	733	149.3	274	294	18 995	62.1
Haskell	2 592	−4.4	93	3.6	169	−2.9	171	174	989	−1.0	1 018	999	16 522	54.0
Hays	55 058	4.1	1 294	2.4	2 015	80.6	1 613	1 116	22 634	99.3	18 171	11 358	20 600	67.3
Hemphill	1 706	−8.9	37	2.2	138	.7	151	137	1 008	20.4	860	837	22 299	72.8
Henderson	31 136	2.7	1 070	3.4	1 125	25.3	1 062	898	12 154	34.7	10 318	9 022	18 817	61.5
Hidalgo	203 863	4.8	27 676	13.6	7 990	28.5	7 231	6 216	101 510	34.4	90 975	75 510	18 568	60.7
Hill	16 242	Z	612	3.8	701	28.9	643	544	6 296	49.8	5 630	4 202	18 956	61.9
Hockley	10 804	−.4	427	4.0	512	−2.3	528	524	5 413	10.7	5 692	4 888	18 217	59.5
Hood	17 642	1.8	602	3.4	879	43.2	764	614	7 255	61.4	6 425	4 494	18 830	61.5
Hopkins	14 730	−6.4	560	3.8	752	15.7	723	650	9 758	36.5	8 596	7 151	20 758	67.8
Houston	9 323	2.0	354	3.8	406	2.0	389	398	3 969	17.5	4 038	3 379	17 727	57.9
Howard	13 543	−.8	623	4.6	797	−1.1	799	806	9 781	26.6	9 085	7 727	22 459	73.4
Hudspeth	1 487	2.4	52	3.5	44	18.9	44	37	240	20.0	219	200	17 079	55.8
Hunt	37 430	3.1	1 555	4.2	1 343	10.7	1 225	1 213	20 584	3.0	18 997	19 976	24 861	81.2
Hutchinson	8 939	−3.9	518	5.8	566	−3.7	583	588	7 338	7.2	7 448	6 842	28 958	94.6
Irion	672	−3.9	19	2.8	43	16.2	43	37	259	1.2	335	256	23 857	77.9
Jack	3 477	−.4	112	3.2	177	11.3	158	159	1 278	43.4	945	891	18 559	60.6
Jackson	8 253	−2.7	209	2.5	286	−1.7	284	291	5 478	158.9	2 761	2 116	24 236	79.2
Jasper	14 129	−3.4	1 387	9.8	749	17.2	721	639	8 710	29.6	9 628	6 723	22 427	73.3
Jeff Davis	1 371	−26.1	29	2.1	58	38.1	53	42	420	59.1	378	264	14 610	47.7
Jefferson	115 737	−.7	8 955	7.7	6 004	3.9	6 045	5 780	100 900	8.4	96 108	93 049	29 629	96.8
Jim Hogg	2 104	−7.0	161	7.7	106	−6.2	104	113	892	46.0	693	611	14 602	47.7
Jim Wells	16 466	−3.6	1 212	7.4	790	−1.3	736	800	10 114	22.4	8 474	8 260	18 942	61.9
Johnson	63 491	2.2	2 217	3.5	2 051	23.7	1 882	1 658	24 652	24.5	21 820	19 797	21 397	69.9
Jones	9 647	−1.9	308	3.2	335	1.5	334	330	3 344	7.2	3 199	3 118	17 863	58.4
Karnes	5 876	2.2	231	3.9	274	−7.1	279	295	2 116	3.9	2 053	2 036	17 457	57.0
Kaufman	34 392	2.9	1 426	4.1	1 421	40.1	1 262	1 014	18 713	97.1	14 024	9 494	22 231	72.6
Kendall	14 265	5.1	294	2.1	672	48.0	543	454	5 447	67.2	4 588	3 258	21 136	69.1
Kenedy	217	−4.4	3	1.4	4	−20.0	4	5	18	NA	(3)	(3)	14 000	45.7
Kent	432	−2.0	12	2.8	22	120.0	15	10	122	171.1	135	45	34 934	114.1
Kerr	17 543	.1	356	2.0	1 257	22.5	1 179	1 026	13 536	43.6	12 217	9 424	21 281	69.5
Kimble	2 320	−2.4	52	2.2	137	−1.4	139	139	1 148	29.4	1 008	887	16 908	55.2
King	129	4.9	4	3.1	3	−25.0	3	4	(3)	NA	4	15	D	D
Kinney	1 135	1.3	85	7.5	30	−14.3	33	35	219	−22.9	237	284	13 571	44.3
Kleberg	12 337	−4.0	658	5.3	545	−6.0	540	580	5 872	−1.9	5 851	5 985	17 214	56.2
Knox	1 875	−3.6	76	4.1	141	7.6	137	131	879	8.7	939	809	16 537	54.0
Lamar	21 645	−2.6	1 119	5.2	1 202	17.7	1 111	1 021	18 123	27.6	17 428	14 200	22 938	74.9
Lamb	6 242	−3.2	395	6.3	331	.3	339	330	2 737	9.9	2 688	2 490	21 810	71.3
Lampasas	8 605	7.2	248	2.9	356	26.2	326	282	2 912	19.5	2 746	2 436	17 989	58.8
La Salle	2 764	−4.0	200	7.2	89	−4.3	79	93	702	51.3	461	464	16 024	52.4
Lavaca	9 321	−1.7	146	1.6	501	−2.5	537	514	6 217	41.3	5 958	4 400	18 281	59.7
Lee	6 844	−4.7	209	3.1	401	17.6	381	341	3 635	22.8	3 726	2 961	21 290	69.6
Leon	6 566	3.8	339	5.2	316	29.0	289	245	3 243	36.0	2 915	2 385	27 885	91.1
Liberty	29 539	.3	1 980	6.7	1 056	14.4	1 017	923	10 794	11.2	10 385	9 709	22 541	73.6
Limestone	9 198	.4	376	4.1	408	16.2	376	351	4 437	26.8	3 881	3 500	17 792	58.1
Lipscomb	1 455	−3.7	36	2.5	107	11.5	89	96	459	12.2	347	409	19 841	64.8
Live Oak	4 330	−1.3	132	3.0	209	−5.0	193	220	1 701	14.5	1 520	1 486	22 277	72.8
Llano	5 450	−2.6	137	2.5	432	40.3	398	308	3 133	66.3	2 770	1 884	19 109	62.4
Loving	59	−22.4	7	11.9	1	—	2	1	(3)	NA	(3)	(3)	D	D
Lubbock	123 980	.4	3 251	2.6	6 480	10.9	6 351	5 841	90 311	16.5	84 865	77 550	22 089	72.2
Lynn	2 818	−1.9	108	3.8	105	−5.4	108	111	817	33.7	730	611	21 760	71.1
McCulloch	3 682	−.5	197	5.4	245	11.4	235	220	2 116	21.9	1 828	1 736	18 525	60.5
McLennan	101 514	−.2	3 288	3.2	4 742	6.7	4 760	4 444	82 466	16.2	82 519	70 978	23 196	75.8
McMullen	273	−2.8	10	3.7	18	−18.2	16	22	88	−7.4	85	95	31 614	103.3
Madison	4 225	−.8	119	2.8	217	10.7	212	196	1 921	36.4	2 282	1 408	18 252	59.6
Marion	3 614	−6.6	305	8.4	197	22.4	193	161	1 234	−9.8	1 250	1 368	16 812	54.9
Martin	1 829	3.0	79	4.3	90	−3.2	88	93	556	10.3	628	504	22 442	73.3
Mason	1 518	−2.3	24	1.6	109	7.9	101	101	631	−.3	540	633	13 236	43.2
Matagorda	14 773	−9.3	1 503	10.2	778	−2.0	759	794	9 612	19.1	8 675	8 071	34 479	112.6
Maverick	18 723	3.0	3 998	21.4	755	38.0	675	547	7 344	42.1	6 434	5 169	16 285	53.2
Medina	15 919	.2	569	3.6	572	22.7	533	466	4 854	28.5	4 345	3 776	18 994	62.1
Menard	992	−4.7	29	2.9	49	14.0	57	43	249	33.2	231	187	14 273	46.6
Midland	59 659	−2.3	2 818	4.7	4 147	18.2	4 229	3 508	48 297	31.0	45 370	36 874	26 674	87.1
Milam	9 589	1.4	326	3.4	408	−2.6	416	419	5 064	5.3	5 007	4 808	27 473	89.8
Mills	2 351	.5	44	1.9	131	22.4	112	107	878	14.5	719	767	18 562	60.6

[1] Civilian unemployed as a percent of total civilian labor force. [2] For pay period including March 12 of the year shown. [3] 0–19 employees.

Sources: Civilian Labor Force—U.S. Bureau of Labor Statistics; Local Area Unemployment Statistics; 2000 data published 2 May 2001, 1999 data published 30 May 2001; <ftp://ftp.bls.gov/pub/time.series/la/> (related Internet site <http://www.bls.gov/lauhome.htm>). Private Business Establishments and Employment—U.S. Census Bureau; County Business Patterns on CD-ROM; annual (related Internet site <http://www.census.gov/epcd/cbp/view/cbpview.html>).

[Includes U.S., states, and 3,142 counties/county equivalents defined as of January 1, 1992. For changes to these areas since January 1, 1992, see appendix B. Geographic Information]

County	Civilian labor force, 2000				Private nonfarm businesses									
			Unemployment		Establishments				Employment[2]				Annual payroll per employee, 1998	
	Total	Percent change, 1999–2000	Total	Rate[1]	1998	Percent change, 1990–1998	1995	1990	1998	Percent change, 1990–1998	1995	1990	Amount (dollars)	Percent of national average
TEXAS—Con.														
Mitchell	3 194	-4.7	128	4.0	147	-8.7	154	161	1 261	12.1	1 195	1 125	18 189	59.4
Montague	7 150	-2.6	388	5.4	450	13.1	421	398	3 314	14.6	3 339	2 893	18 143	59.3
Montgomery	144 944	.9	4 605	3.2	5 372	89.9	4 131	2 829	73 544	104.7	54 731	35 933	25 599	83.6
Moore	8 934	-3.5	262	2.9	447	14.6	428	390	6 584	30.1	6 175	5 062	22 750	74.3
Morris	6 073	-3.9	419	6.9	274	—	265	274	4 406	28.0	4 011	3 442	26 718	87.3
Motley	577	-2.0	10	1.7	47	9.3	41	43	180	-1.6	151	183	17 811	58.2
Nacogdoches	25 305	-.1	847	3.3	1 297	12.8	1 252	1 150	17 139	21.8	16 892	14 068	19 805	64.7
Navarro	21 797	.9	1 043	4.8	905	3.9	915	871	13 216	24.1	11 711	10 651	19 447	63.5
Newton	5 567	-4.1	607	10.9	162	-2.4	177	166	1 659	31.5	1 769	1 262	20 803	68.0
Nolan	6 905	-2.7	346	5.0	397	3.4	412	384	4 742	8.0	4 107	4 392	20 047	66.5
Nueces	144 369	-1.2	9 063	6.3	7 960	10.3	7 943	7 215	117 288	23.8	109 338	94 736	23 802	77.8
Ochiltree	4 838	-8.0	132	2.7	295	-8.7	323	323	2 495	-6.5	2 763	2 669	20 734	67.7
Oldham	1 267	3.1	28	2.2	49	40.0	48	35	481	206.4	511	157	18 214	59.5
Orange	41 000	-1.6	3 695	9.0	1 462	9.4	1 399	1 336	20 120	7.7	19 754	18 679	28 272	92.4
Palo Pinto	12 249	-.6	467	3.8	631	5.2	605	600	6 307	8.7	6 497	5 804	20 950	68.4
Panola	7 709	-4.2	599	7.8	476	17.2	464	406	5 031	9.4	4 929	4 599	20 379	66.6
Parker	43 692	2.4	1 316	3.0	1 503	50.5	1 362	999	14 326	65.9	12 091	8 633	21 235	69.4
Parmer	4 385	-1.4	120	2.7	203	2.0	214	199	3 234	14.3	2 962	2 830	21 585	70.5
Pecos	6 322	-5.7	341	5.4	335	-6.7	346	359	3 141	14.9	3 113	2 734	20 272	66.2
Polk	14 944	-.5	778	5.2	686	27.7	613	537	7 449	36.1	6 878	5 472	21 592	70.5
Potter	55 221	-.4	3 149	5.7	3 627	.7	3 517	3 602	58 880	19.3	54 633	49 367	26 087	85.2
Presidio	3 389	-2.5	935	27.6	101	-10.6	103	113	508	-11.2	581	572	15 390	50.3
Rains	3 691	-.3	114	3.1	125	33.0	118	94	840	36.4	1 021	616	16 544	54.0
Randall	57 639	-.3	825	1.4	1 925	31.6	1 920	1 463	20 804	31.7	20 749	15 801	20 962	68.5
Reagan	1 666	-11.5	58	3.5	98	-5.8	102	104	824	17.9	736	699	24 933	81.5
Real	1 301	-2.7	41	3.2	73	58.7	57	46	389	119.8	300	177	14 761	48.2
Red River	5 803	-2.6	275	4.7	220	-.5	210	221	2 702	26.7	2 617	2 132	16 719	54.6
Reeves	7 372	1.4	674	9.1	242	-15.1	267	285	2 775	3.1	2 388	2 691	19 199	62.7
Refugio	2 811	-2.6	127	4.5	168	-11.6	169	190	1 257	-5.8	1 258	1 335	21 816	71.3
Roberts	411	-4.9	7	1.7	15	7.1	13	14	78	-36.6	56	123	17 872	58.4
Robertson	6 386	1.4	296	4.6	233	-10.0	234	259	2 230	8.5	2 132	2 056	21 238	69.4
Rockwall	23 265	2.7	481	2.1	871	41.2	725	617	8 572	65.7	6 510	5 174	22 453	73.4
Runnels	4 926	-4.7	234	4.8	282	4.8	277	269	3 018	16.4	2 700	2 592	19 751	61.1
Rusk	21 342	1.7	990	4.6	764	2.8	748	743	8 878	5.2	8 606	8 436	25 316	82.7
Sabine	4 106	1.2	323	7.9	186	22.4	180	152	1 978	54.9	1 693	1 277	18 573	60.7
San Augustine	3 045	-3.3	159	5.2	161	8.8	153	148	1 425	42.4	1 304	1 001	16 912	55.3
San Jacinto	8 798	2.5	338	3.8	151	-3.8	149	157	1 181	-17.2	1 131	1 426	18 853	61.6
San Patricio	29 802	-.9	1 884	6.3	1 003	9.1	949	919	11 691	27.1	9 128	9 197	24 663	80.6
San Saba	2 500	-2.7	76	3.0	176	27.5	143	138	1 472	9.9	1 602	1 339	17 862	58.4
Schleicher	1 491	-.1	51	3.4	66	13.8	68	58	546	58.3	442	345	21 038	68.7
Scurry	6 924	-6.3	311	4.5	426	-14.3	451	497	5 066	18.6	4 978	4 273	20 841	68.1
Shackelford	1 267	-5.0	39	3.1	118	-1.7	112	120	585	-10.6	605	654	18 619	60.8
Shelby	8 983	-3.8	527	5.9	537	23.7	510	434	5 798	24.1	5 747	4 672	18 952	61.9
Sherman	1 792	18.8	29	1.6	69	-4.2	70	72	380	3.3	394	368	22 408	73.2
Smith	91 304	1.6	3 557	3.9	4 854	16.6	4 637	4 163	70 510	33.4	63 437	52 852	25 823	84.4
Somervell	2 066	.8	138	6.7	151	49.5	130	101	3 346	NA	2 289	(³)	31 288	102.2
Starr	21 239	-.2	4 743	22.3	414	3.2	446	401	4 626	56.8	4 124	2 950	12 750	41.7
Stephens	3 982	-3.8	155	3.9	300	-3.2	302	310	2 484	22.5	2 089	2 028	19 649	64.2
Sterling	675	.7	23	3.4	41	—	36	41	181	4.0	131	174	15 729	51.4
Stonewall	643	-7.2	27	4.2	62	8.8	69	57	436	24.9	411	349	20 278	66.2
Sutton	1 888	-7.5	75	4.0	147	13.1	141	130	1 127	43.6	1 086	785	21 011	68.6
Swisher	3 636	1.3	131	3.6	187	6.3	180	176	1 210	-4.3	1 202	1 265	17 772	58.1
Tarrant	791 873	2.1	24 813	3.1	32 593	17.0	30 368	27 853	591 128	32.2	514 017	447 271	28 688	93.7
Taylor	57 830	-3.1	2 063	3.6	3 558	7.3	3 528	3 316	48 503	19.3	44 958	40 649	20 074	65.6
Terrell	744	6.0	19	2.6	23	-14.8	20	27	65	-21.7	52	83	12 631	41.3
Terry	5 471	-2.6	294	5.4	252	-17.4	273	305	2 204	-17.8	2 929	2 680	19 626	64.1
Throckmorton	714	-3.5	19	2.7	67	-4.3	63	70	314	32.5	267	237	16 519	54.0
Titus	12 514	-.8	551	4.4	674	10.7	665	609	13 301	34.1	11 396	9 916	22 705	74.2
Tom Green	49 615	-1.2	1 574	3.2	2 565	8.6	2 562	2 362	34 098	15.7	31 846	29 467	21 690	70.9
Travis	482 165	4.2	10 004	2.1	22 483	38.1	20 537	16 277	386 568	56.1	336 854	247 618	34 622	113.1
Trinity	5 567	-3.8	250	4.5	239	16.0	240	206	1 797	24.4	1 723	1 444	16 661	54.4
Tyler	6 455	.5	504	7.8	310	15.7	279	268	3 134	56.4	2 560	2 004	18 196	59.4
Upshur	16 836	-.9	826	4.9	442	11.3	438	397	4 063	3.4	4 228	3 929	17 415	56.9
Upton	1 442	-8.1	80	5.5	72	-21.7	73	92	693	7.1	754	647	23 861	78.0
Uvalde	11 024	.4	785	7.1	579	12.0	547	517	5 657	21.6	5 187	4 651	17 926	58.6
Val Verde	18 022	-.3	1 251	6.9	795	16.4	734	683	8 383	43.8	7 318	5 830	15 906	52.0

[1] Civilian unemployed as a percent of total civilian labor force.   [2] For pay period including March 12 of the year shown.   [3] 1,000–2,499 employees.

Sources: Civilian Labor Force—U.S. Bureau of Labor Statistics; Local Area Unemployment Statistics; 2000 data published 2 May 2001, 1999 data published 30 May 2001; <ftp://ftp.bls.gov/pub/time.series/la/> (related Internet site <http://www.bls.gov/lauhome.htm>).   Private Business Establishments and Employment—U.S. Census Bureau; County Business Patterns on CD-ROM; annual (related Internet site <http://www.census.gov/epcd/cbp/view/cbpview.html>).

[Includes U.S., states, and 3,142 counties/county equivalents defined as of January 1, 1992. For changes to these areas since January 1, 1992, see appendix B. Geographic Information]

County	Civilian labor force, 2000		Unemployment		Private nonfarm businesses								Annual payroll per employee, 1998	
					Establishments				Employment[2]					
	Total	Percent change, 1999–2000	Total	Rate[1]	1998	Percent change, 1990–1998	1995	1990	1998	Percent change, 1990–1998	1995	1990	Amount (dollars)	Percent of national average
TEXAS—Con.														
Van Zandt	20 407	−.1	618	3.0	731	17.9	686	620	5 973	36.1	5 635	4 388	19 184	62.7
Victoria	43 165	Z	1 531	3.5	2 207	9.0	2 128	2 025	29 345	30.0	25 784	22 575	23 458	76.6
Walker	23 328	−.4	451	1.9	843	17.1	797	720	9 886	35.1	8 899	7 315	17 135	56.0
Waller	12 973	.8	652	5.0	489	46.0	373	335	6 257	59.8	4 226	3 916	26 081	85.2
Ward	4 013	−7.6	323	8.0	255	−24.6	282	338	2 569	−4.7	2 460	2 697	21 795	71.2
Washington	15 122	1.6	351	2.3	730	13.5	693	643	10 274	34.9	9 151	7 616	21 932	71.7
Webb	74 217	2.1	5 178	7.0	3 916	35.9	3 755	2 881	46 888	45.3	42 538	32 262	19 780	64.6
Wharton	19 040	−1.5	895	4.7	956	4.0	918	919	11 048	15.4	10 338	9 577	20 816	68.0
Wheeler	2 686	−2.1	93	3.5	185	6.9	171	173	1 135	15.6	1 294	982	15 405	50.3
Wichita	58 813	−1.9	2 428	4.1	3 378	.6	3 373	3 359	46 903	15.7	46 086	40 528	22 297	72.8
Wilbarger	7 268	−1.9	187	2.6	344	−10.9	335	386	4 622	43.2	4 564	3 228	21 024	68.7
Willacy	6 558	−4.8	1 019	15.5	207	−5.0	212	218	1 952	21.4	1 766	1 608	17 173	56.1
Williamson	154 337	4.2	2 168	1.4	4 286	81.0	3 286	2 368	60 075	163.9	38 119	22 763	38 972	127.3
Wilson	15 768	.8	402	2.5	381	34.2	353	284	2 805	63.2	2 404	1 719	16 017	52.3
Winkler	2 752	−9.6	192	7.0	172	−8.0	172	187	1 149	−30.8	1 168	1 661	21 701	70.9
Wise	24 190	3.5	666	2.8	842	46.4	693	575	8 875	54.7	6 848	5 736	24 083	78.7
Wood	13 977	.4	667	4.8	755	32.0	677	572	5 873	28.9	5 329	4 555	18 243	59.6
Yoakum	3 096	−13.0	223	7.2	200	−16.3	210	239	1 844	−19.0	1 768	2 277	23 026	75.2
Young	8 195	−.3	470	5.7	610	−.7	624	614	5 198	.6	5 445	5 166	22 350	73.0
Zapata	4 491	−1.2	399	8.9	137	25.7	129	109	1 337	96.6	1 149	680	18 430	60.2
Zavala	4 423	5.7	677	15.3	105	−6.3	116	112	1 648	19.7	1 342	1 377	11 445	37.4
UTAH	1 104 208	1.7	35 837	3.2	52 025	42.2	45 882	36 586	866 146	51.7	744 430	570 830	25 631	83.7
Beaver	2 414	1.2	87	3.6	141	34.3	125	105	1 275	70.5	975	748	15 268	49.9
Box Elder	17 226	−3.1	777	4.5	750	30.9	667	573	15 481	19.4	12 405	12 971	32 072	104.8
Cache	43 933	.5	1 110	2.5	2 174	65.8	1 771	1 311	31 339	64.1	28 483	19 097	18 872	61.7
Carbon	9 204	−4.1	538	5.8	511	15.1	476	444	6 647	40.6	5 625	4 728	24 625	80.4
Daggett	466	7.4	15	3.2	21	40.0	15	15	(3)	NA	115	94	D	D
Davis	122 671	1.6	3 621	3.0	4 270	62.4	3 504	2 629	56 666	66.0	44 817	34 143	22 409	73.2
Duchesne	5 641	−2.4	337	6.0	363	23.5	316	294	2 898	34.3	2 634	2 158	21 674	70.8
Emery	3 820	−2.2	247	6.5	185	14.9	162	161	2 651	−6.9	2 444	2 846	36 701	119.9
Garfield	2 713	−3.0	211	7.8	127	36.6	121	93	950	66.7	615	570	21 142	69.1
Grand	5 164	−4.5	337	6.5	360	67.4	306	215	2 780	96.5	2 288	1 415	15 188	49.6
Iron	14 905	1.8	455	3.1	799	38.5	722	577	8 636	63.0	7 430	5 299	17 661	57.7
Juab	3 445	−1.6	129	3.7	147	54.7	123	95	1 580	31.4	1 462	1 202	19 637	64.2
Kane	2 877	6.0	90	3.1	168	34.4	160	125	1 509	59.0	1 135	949	17 035	55.7
Millard	4 318	−4.0	172	4.0	239	19.5	236	200	2 573	17.0	2 451	2 200	23 763	77.6
Morgan	3 514	1.8	127	3.6	134	94.2	97	69	1 060	50.4	965	705	23 931	78.2
Piute	506	−3.3	24	4.7	18	50.0	16	12	83	15.3	83	72	12 627	41.3
Rich	961	−.1	36	3.7	62	148.0	39	25	322	198.1	229	108	17 978	58.7
Salt Lake	482 463	1.6	14 333	3.0	24 553	31.8	22 507	18 631	466 200	46.9	408 445	317 287	28 228	92.2
San Juan	4 593	−6.0	423	9.2	242	22.2	219	198	2 180	19.8	1 860	1 819	16 464	53.8
Sanpete	8 872	2.2	412	4.6	343	33.5	303	257	3 232	58.9	2 737	2 034	16 407	53.6
Sevier	8 240	.8	324	3.9	463	30.8	398	354	4 792	34.3	4 080	3 567	20 703	67.6
Summit	14 517	1.9	602	4.1	1 361	113.0	1 115	639	14 351	77.5	11 964	8 085	18 180	59.4
Tooele	12 187	2.5	642	5.3	438	50.0	362	292	6 168	83.2	4 462	3 366	28 822	94.2
Uintah	11 029	1.7	524	4.8	692	37.0	643	505	5 296	48.5	5 344	3 567	22 249	72.7
Utah	169 891	3.0	4 389	2.6	6 472	50.5	5 665	4 301	132 096	64.8	106 584	80 149	23 187	75.8
Wasatch	6 369	2.1	287	4.5	420	116.5	306	194	2 842	83.1	2 251	1 552	17 340	56.7
Washington	39 335	4.9	1 273	3.2	2 319	116.7	1 846	1 070	23 661	115.5	20 516	10 981	19 622	64.1
Wayne	1 552	7.6	71	4.6	79	119.4	60	36	(4)	NA	437	255	D	D
Weber	101 386	1.7	4 247	4.2	4 143	33.8	3 564	3 097	66 954	45.1	60 353	46 134	23 796	77.7
VERMONT	331 574	−1.3	9 657	2.9	21 261	7.2	20 542	19 839	239 034	11.1	224 327	215 222	24 716	80.7
Addison	20 096	−.4	531	2.6	1 028	5.5	983	974	10 441	3.8	9 842	10 058	23 622	77.2
Bennington	20 001	−2.0	650	3.2	1 552	7.6	1 495	1 442	16 270	11.7	15 352	14 565	22 466	73.4
Caledonia	15 015	−1.3	613	4.1	962	12.0	900	859	9 094	19.5	8 107	7 612	21 995	71.9
Chittenden	89 588	−.7	1 622	1.8	5 257	13.3	5 059	4 640	76 889	14.8	72 237	66 954	28 584	93.4
Essex	2 886	−.7	166	5.8	142	22.4	125	116	1 343	10.4	1 250	1 217	24 672	80.6
Franklin	23 919	.5	798	3.3	1 045	2.9	976	1 016	10 508	20.6	10 073	8 710	24 234	79.2
Grand Isle	3 497	.1	168	4.8	172	16.2	154	148	521	14.3	513	456	19 395	63.4
Lamoille	11 786	−1.4	506	4.3	970	8.5	924	894	8 932	17.6	8 384	7 594	17 985	58.8
Orange	15 553	−2.0	358	2.3	746	−10.1	807	830	6 423	−9.6	5 874	7 105	20 809	68.0
Orleans	12 526	.2	745	5.9	820	5.4	802	778	6 870	4.9	6 885	6 548	20 556	67.2
Rutland	30 979	−3.0	1 114	3.6	2 259	−.4	2 289	2 269	25 956	7.8	24 630	24 068	22 950	75.0
Washington	31 682	−.4	991	3.1	2 226	8.4	2 192	2 053	23 672	11.2	21 916	21 294	23 791	77.7
Windham	23 277	−1.4	689	3.0	1 827	1.3	1 791	1 803	22 321	9.0	21 946	20 479	23 945	78.2
Windsor	30 767	−3.4	705	2.3	2 255	12.3	2 045	2 008	19 794	7.3	17 318	18 444	23 809	77.8

[1] Civilian unemployed as a percent of total civilian labor force. [2] For pay period including March 12 of the year shown. [3] 100–249 employees. [4] 500–999 employees.

Sources: Civilian Labor Force—U.S. Bureau of Labor Statistics; Local Area Unemployment Statistics; 2000 data published 2 May 2001, 1999 data published 30 May 2001; <ftp://ftp.bls.gov/pub/time.series/la/> (related Internet site <http://www.bls.gov/lauhome.htm>). Private Business Establishments and Employment—U.S. Census Bureau; County Business Patterns on CD-ROM; annual (related Internet site <http://www.census.gov/epcd/cbp/view/cbpview.html>).

[Includes U.S., states, and 3,142 counties/county equivalents defined as of January 1, 1992. For changes to these areas since January 1, 1992, see appendix B. Geographic Information]

County	Civilian labor force, 2000				Private nonfarm businesses									
			Unemployment		Establishments				Employment[2]				Annual payroll per employee, 1998	
	Total	Percent change, 1999–2000	Total	Rate[1]	1998	Percent change, 1990–1998	1995	1990	1998	Percent change, 1990–1998	1995	1990	Amount (dollars)	Percent of national average
VIRGINIA	3 609 703	2.3	79 801	2.2	172 182	15.0	162 378	149 695	2 700 589	16.3	2 481 306	2 321 517	30 090	98.3
Accomack	14 820	.7	629	4.2	825	11.8	787	738	8 587	–3.0	8 726	8 857	16 954	55.4
Albemarle................	41 239	3.6	535	1.3	1 788	93.3	893	925	20 733	113.1	10 693	9 730	22 559	73.7
Alleghany	6 372	–1.2	198	3.1	162	55.8	96	104	2 703	94.0	1 758	1 393	23 646	77.3
Amelia	5 250	2.5	114	2.2	253	24.6	223	203	1 681	34.8	1 379	1 247	19 946	65.2
Amherst	14 915	1.9	242	1.6	578	17.5	561	492	8 613	11.0	6 426	7 758	22 069	72.1
Appomattox	5 332	–1.3	167	3.1	268	24.7	253	215	2 911	.1	2 996	2 909	18 411	60.1
Arlington	111 538	4.8	1 268	1.1	5 141	9.5	5 041	4 695	110 040	7.6	111 363	102 275	43 723	142.8
Augusta	31 806	.1	539	1.7	1 189	31.7	1 048	903	16 609	44.5	14 512	11 492	27 473	89.8
Bath	2 468	3.5	79	3.2	138	5.3	126	131	721	–52.1	1 213	1 504	27 178	88.8
Bedford..................	31 011	1.6	481	1.6	805	105.4	635	392	7 039	82.3	5 274	3 862	24 391	79.7
Bland	3 488	.6	206	5.9	106	29.3	103	82	1 479	57.8	1 217	937	25 513	83.3
Botetourt	16 818	1.2	199	1.2	585	49.6	506	391	6 395	98.4	5 254	3 223	26 286	85.9
Brunswick	7 734	1.1	238	3.1	337	12.3	312	300	3 730	21.9	3 446	3 060	18 539	60.6
Buchanan	7 847	–6.1	678	8.6	657	–8.6	662	719	7 055	–28.1	7 800	9 809	27 995	91.5
Buckingham	6 036	.9	187	3.1	229	1.3	209	226	1 887	–10.5	1 910	2 109	19 629	64.1
Campbell	26 956	2.1	589	2.2	1 025	46.2	886	701	14 341	28.2	13 155	11 183	22 190	72.5
Caroline	10 937	3.8	238	2.2	359	17.7	376	305	2 672	12.0	2 963	2 386	20 683	67.6
Carroll	13 819	–.7	804	5.8	477	33.2	416	358	5 631	55.1	4 617	3 631	18 093	59.1
Charles City..............	3 835	2.3	97	2.5	108	125.0	71	48	1 312	397.0	1 297	264	26 571	86.8
Charlotte	6 219	2.8	192	3.1	246	16.0	222	212	2 643	36.2	2 093	1 941	19 199	62.7
Chesterfield	143 783	2.2	2 184	1.5	5 516	24.7	5 052	4 424	74 635	16.5	68 875	64 086	27 523	89.9
Clarke	6 782	4.8	72	1.1	287	11.2	277	258	2 865	21.5	3 044	2 358	24 889	81.3
Craig	2 250	8.5	56	2.5	60	5.3	68	57	404	21.7	756	332	15 433	50.4
Culpeper	16 950	4.6	238	1.4	808	16.6	788	693	9 723	22.9	9 665	7 913	25 682	83.9
Cumberland	3 874	2.5	69	1.8	131	3.1	128	127	811	–41.7	790	1 391	18 617	60.8
Dickenson	5 321	–1.1	453	8.5	279	–2.4	311	286	2 091	–19.7	2 439	2 605	23 163	75.7
Dinwiddie	12 332	1.9	228	1.8	274	33.0	270	206	4 152	183.6	3 810	1 464	23 354	76.3
Essex	4 319	–.9	171	4.0	320	7.7	329	297	3 727	18.2	3 727	3 153	19 345	63.2
Fairfax	561 506	4.8	6 590	1.2	24 581	26.0	23 464	19 501	444 700	36.2	372 035	326 458	44 839	146.5
Fauquier.................	29 814	4.8	295	1.0	1 485	17.0	1 381	1 269	12 364	10.2	10 859	11 222	24 860	81.2
Floyd	6 934	2.5	319	4.6	240	27.0	232	189	1 788	15.8	1 694	1 544	16 623	54.3
Fluvanna	9 962	3.7	144	1.4	302	51.8	274	199	1 964	37.8	1 971	1 425	21 195	69.2
Franklin	25 019	–.2	907	3.6	935	29.9	837	720	10 780	16.6	10 057	9 249	21 984	71.8
Frederick	33 736	3.7	553	1.6	1 175	98.1	965	593	17 176	124.0	12 719	7 667	24 700	80.7
Giles	8 491	.9	419	4.9	320	4.2	298	307	5 000	–1.0	4 836	5 051	26 628	87.0
Gloucester	18 138	.8	309	1.7	766	21.2	738	632	6 199	23.5	5 931	5 020	16 876	55.1
Goochland	9 264	2.2	118	1.3	422	32.7	360	318	3 211	41.5	2 434	2 269	25 513	83.4
Grayson	8 395	1.8	594	7.1	183	15.8	191	158	1 793	–1.0	2 000	1 811	20 864	68.2
Greene	7 953	3.5	118	1.5	238	33.7	208	178	1 512	–22.6	1 530	1 953	20 443	66.8
Greensville...............	5 391	–.1	139	2.6	128	113.3	90	60	1 897	165.7	1 138	714	20 292	66.3
Halifax	18 397	.3	1 187	6.5	798	154.1	[3]338	[3]314	11 535	241.8	[3]4 780	[3]3 375	21 634	70.7
Hanover	48 446	2.3	585	1.2	2 590	31.6	2 295	1 968	30 817	26.7	28 234	24 324	25 847	84.4
Henrico..................	141 467	2.3	2 295	1.6	7 199	37.8	5 805	5 223	138 869	63.8	102 505	84 790	31 188	101.9
Henry	26 707	–2.9	1 980	7.4	916	14.9	816	797	15 315	–15.4	14 320	18 109	21 587	70.5
Highland.................	1 249	–.7	36	2.9	98	30.7	93	75	405	–14.6	(4)	474	15 684	51.2
Isle of Wight	15 237	.9	329	2.2	532	16.4	484	457	9 369	38.5	7 943	6 763	26 465	86.5
James City...............	25 271	1.0	369	1.5	1 017	197.4	990	342	10 880	69.2	12 346	6 429	23 183	75.7
King and Queen	2 920	.6	87	3.0	97	40.6	78	69	592	22.3	449	484	18 475	60.4
King George	9 035	4.8	134	1.5	349	30.2	336	268	3 984	27.7	3 151	3 121	30 278	98.9
King William	6 270	.3	123	2.0	293	24.2	278	236	3 118	2.9	3 028	3 031	32 426	105.9
Lancaster................	5 033	–2.1	392	7.8	479	–3.2	488	495	3 629	–.7	3 710	3 654	21 334	69.7
Lee	9 108	–4.5	452	5.0	366	3.1	369	355	3 867	6.0	3 583	3 649	19 690	64.3
Loudoun	94 734	5.1	872	.9	3 920	52.8	3 198	2 565	50 489	47.8	39 966	34 167	33 585	109.7
Louisa..................	9 866	2.6	301	3.1	488	34.8	434	362	3 950	16.7	3 938	3 384	31 034	101.4
Lunenburg	4 650	–2.4	224	4.8	209	–9.9	191	232	1 951	–29.4	1 971	2 764	18 500	60.4
Madison	8 794	.9	131	1.5	262	17.0	232	224	2 304	26.7	2 148	1 818	17 230	56.3
Mathews.................	4 675	1.0	81	1.7	198	1.0	186	196	1 097	13.4	966	967	16 874	55.1
Mecklenburg.............	15 060	.5	565	3.8	836	17.1	767	714	12 115	13.4	11 515	10 683	19 696	64.3
Middlesex...............	5 408	6.5	69	1.3	341	21.4	318	281	2 199	32.2	1 965	1 663	17 510	57.2
Montgomery	38 453	2.2	681	1.8	1 748	25.8	1 584	1 389	22 397	2.8	21 039	21 788	21 829	71.3
Nelson	6 836	–5.1	162	2.4	356	15.6	335	308	3 077	.5	2 855	3 061	16 149	52.8
New Kent	7 068	2.2	111	1.6	269	22.3	262	220	2 041	44.3	1 678	1 414	19 314	63.1
Northampton	5 328	1.3	153	2.9	329	5.4	288	312	2 994	–7.0	2 842	3 218	19 486	63.7
Northumberland	5 222	–1.4	336	6.4	316	24.9	287	253	2 021	9.7	1 685	1 842	18 571	60.7
Nottoway	6 668	–.8	170	2.5	366	15.5	333	317	3 997	22.8	3 365	3 256	17 860	58.3
Orange	11 066	.7	246	2.2	590	11.3	552	530	6 358	3.1	6 068	6 167	24 367	79.6
Page	11 884	–.3	296	2.5	448	–4.1	449	467	5 981	22.0	5 768	4 903	18 221	59.5
Patrick	8 552	–4.5	422	4.9	318	7.1	316	297	4 744	.5	4 613	4 722	19 398	63.4
Pittsylvania	31 200	–.4	1 347	4.3	1 008	48.5	899	679	11 703	39.7	11 783	8 375	20 840	68.1
Powhatan	11 352	2.3	142	1.3	461	65.8	337	278	3 529	140.7	1 758	1 466	19 890	65.0

[1] Civilian unemployed as a percent of total civilian labor force. [2] For pay period including March 12 of the year shown. [3] Excludes South Boston independent city which is included in the 1998 data; for more information, see appendix B. Geographic Information. [4] 250–499 employees.

Sources: Civilian Labor Force—U.S. Bureau of Labor Statistics; Local Area Unemployment Statistics; 2000 data published 2 May 2001, 1999 data published 30 May 2001; <ftp://ftp.bls.gov/pub/time.series/la/> (related Internet site <http://www.bls.gov/lauhome.htm>). Private Business Establishments and Employment—U.S. Census Bureau; County Business Patterns on CD-ROM; annual (related Internet site <http://www.census.gov/epcd/cbp/view/cbpview.html>).

[Includes U.S., states, and 3,142 counties/county equivalents defined as of January 1, 1992. For changes to these areas since January 1, 1992, see appendix B. Geographic Information]

County	Civilian labor force, 2000				Private nonfarm businesses									
			Unemployment		Establishments				Employment[2]				Annual payroll per employee, 1998	
	Total	Percent change, 1999–2000	Total	Rate[1]	1998	Percent change, 1990–1998	1995	1990	1998	Percent change, 1990–1998	1995	1990	Amount (dollars)	Percent of national average
VIRGINIA—Con.														
Prince Edward	8 292	1.8	231	2.8	536	18.1	512	454	7 282	16.1	7 567	6 273	18 247	59.6
Prince George	12 281	1.9	263	2.1	375	82.0	308	206	4 241	–3.0	5 520	4 370	21 878	71.5
Prince William	148 618	4.8	2 213	1.5	4 506	24.3	4 202	3 625	57 514	28.2	50 056	44 876	23 623	77.2
Pulaski	17 580	3.9	1 041	5.9	677	13.4	621	597	13 258	27.9	11 428	10 367	24 150	78.9
Rappahannock	3 965	–.3	52	1.3	203	37.2	183	148	1 173	26.9	928	924	21 258	69.5
Richmond	4 003	–.4	173	4.3	219	13.5	203	193	2 069	4.0	2 053	1 989	20 313	66.4
Roanoke	48 472	1.6	526	1.1	1 506	5.6	1 754	1 426	20 847	8.5	25 058	19 210	25 438	83.1
Rockbridge	10 412	2.0	182	1.7	308	1.0	218	305	4 500	.4	3 455	4 481	21 439	70.0
Rockingham	37 644	.9	349	.9	1 165	13.1	1 357	1 030	22 554	49.9	23 792	15 046	24 610	80.4
Russell	13 771	–2.2	846	6.1	579	26.1	512	459	6 817	7.0	5 820	6 369	22 032	72.0
Scott	9 048	–2.0	361	4.0	333	–	325	333	2 942	–14.7	3 304	3 451	18 348	59.9
Shenandoah	17 567	.3	234	1.3	859	10.1	840	780	12 326	12.7	12 036	10 937	21 774	71.1
Smyth	16 178	–2.0	932	5.8	662	5.8	651	626	12 124	10.2	11 818	10 999	20 461	66.8
Southampton	8 351	–1.9	212	2.5	292	32.7	260	220	4 495	19.0	4 627	3 778	35 758	116.8
Spotsylvania	46 564	4.9	596	1.3	1 386	230.0	492	420	16 194	326.9	5 581	3 793	22 651	74.0
Stafford	48 810	4.9	565	1.2	1 358	32.6	1 797	1 024	15 278	38.9	19 666	10 997	24 671	80.6
Surry	2 281	–5.0	128	5.6	76	13.4	73	67	1 427	–8.5	(3)	1 560	48 455	158.3
Sussex	6 149	–1.7	173	2.8	217	2.8	239	211	3 196	38.3	2 767	2 311	21 411	70.0
Tazewell	19 700	1.2	1 038	5.3	1 227	8.9	1 222	1 127	12 999	8.2	12 760	12 010	20 539	67.1
Warren	15 674	4.4	291	1.9	745	12.9	683	660	7 580	28.0	5 872	5 924	22 304	72.9
Washington	24 775	–.1	947	3.8	1 153	75.5	1 081	657	13 808	78.4	13 287	7 741	22 092	72.2
Westmoreland	7 514	2.7	349	4.6	371	13.5	350	327	2 549	12.2	2 378	2 271	15 630	51.1
Wise	14 751	–.2	865	5.9	938	5.4	923	890	9 188	–5.5	10 017	9 722	23 188	75.8
Wythe	14 605	2.6	857	5.9	728	23.2	662	591	8 698	14.8	9 272	7 576	19 605	64.0
York	28 968	1.0	453	1.6	1 165	59.4	974	731	13 577	109.6	10 924	6 479	18 435	60.2
Independent Cities														
Alexandria	77 542	4.5	1 193	1.5	4 571	12.6	4 296	4 061	75 301	5.3	69 906	71 518	37 169	121.4
Bedford	2 911	1.7	49	1.7	483	–23.2	552	629	5 998	–16.8	6 241	7 209	21 089	68.9
Bristol	7 630	–.1	213	2.8	688	–15.1	668	810	13 788	–11.5	14 783	15 582	23 076	75.4
Buena Vista	3 418	1.5	61	1.8	121	2.5	111	118	1 953	1.4	1 809	1 926	22 428	73.3
Charlottesville	18 769	3.6	370	2.0	2 209	–12.4	2 830	2 522	39 473	–2.7	42 836	40 550	29 447	96.2
Chesapeake	107 001	1.0	2 310	2.2	4 431	34.1	3 948	3 305	67 765	53.8	56 605	44 048	22 793	74.5
Clifton Forge	1 714	–.6	50	2.9	130	2.4	138	127	1 214	.2	956	1 211	15 962	52.1
Colonial Heights	8 582	2.4	197	2.3	656	29.4	592	507	9 414	40.0	6 986	6 725	17 464	57.1
Covington	3 252	–1.6	145	4.5	262	–10.6	314	293	4 667	–2.2	5 082	4 772	32 265	105.4
Danville	25 090	–.2	1 315	5.2	1 494	–4.7	1 456	1 567	25 915	–15.3	26 760	30 590	23 965	78.3
Emporia	2 464	–1.2	82	3.3	268	–20.0	308	335	4 021	–3.8	3 703	4 178	22 993	75.1
Fairfax	12 881	5.0	81	.6	2 108	11.8	1 401	1 886	32 986	3.4	28 287	31 910	40 893	133.6
Falls Church	6 100	5.1	69	1.1	836	2.0	624	820	13 598	5.9	12 904	12 845	35 893	117.3
Franklin	3 866	–2.3	126	3.3	223	–24.7	273	296	2 865	–16.5	3 154	3 430	19 033	62.2
Fredericksburg	9 944	4.6	229	2.3	1 484	–21.5	1 517	1 891	20 208	–11.0	18 057	22 704	23 249	76.0
Galax	3 237	.3	145	4.5	316	–.6	338	318	7 654	–10.0	8 508	8 508	19 850	64.8
Hampton	66 325	.3	1 897	2.9	2 503	1.9	2 390	2 457	46 772	15.9	41 620	40 364	21 907	71.6
Harrisonburg	18 758	1.0	202	1.1	1 435	11.2	1 117	1 290	23 203	8.0	17 685	21 478	21 543	70.4
Hopewell	10 785	1.4	324	3.0	474	–2.7	487	487	7 931	11.5	7 260	7 110	35 067	114.6
Lexington	3 062	2.0	34	1.1	435	–.5	486	437	5 573	24.2	4 926	4 486	15 975	52.2
Lynchburg	30 163	2.0	639	2.1	2 391	–2.7	2 469	2 458	51 457	.7	55 359	51 116	27 876	91.1
Manassas	19 651	4.8	237	1.2	1 568	29.2	1 290	1 214	20 894	13.7	17 961	18 371	34 482	112.7
Manassas Park	4 458	5.0	44	1.0	129	–12.2	190	147	1 983	32.6	2 439	1 496	30 073	98.2
Martinsville	6 701	–1.6	813	12.1	743	–1.6	794	755	18 055	–9.4	18 972	19 919	22 745	74.3
Newport News	84 294	.2	2 379	2.8	3 753	4.6	3 768	3 588	85 522	12.4	72 736	76 068	26 379	86.2
Norfolk	83 647	.4	3 518	4.2	5 454	–9.3	5 559	6 014	113 834	–1.2	112 562	115 187	27 211	88.9
Norton	1 458	1.0	78	5.3	287	9.1	275	263	4 763	20.2	4 940	3 961	25 832	84.4
Petersburg	15 717	.9	581	3.7	869	–17.1	976	1 048	13 287	–.8	13 104	13 396	24 714	80.7
Poquoson	6 154	1.0	106	1.7	174	7.4	175	162	1 226	9.8	1 268	1 117	16 935	55.3
Portsmouth	44 349	.6	1 858	4.2	1 736	–3.8	1 706	1 804	24 644	–5.3	26 832	26 035	23 771	77.7
Radford	6 766	2.3	193	2.9	348	–5.4	353	368	6 429	–3.1	6 525	6 638	25 091	82.0
Richmond	95 188	2.0	2 763	2.9	7 504	–12.2	8 470	8 550	159 003	–10.5	179 412	177 666	33 505	109.5
Roanoke	49 349	1.5	1 079	2.2	4 106	7.9	3 737	3 806	72 622	.6	72 317	72 174	24 614	80.4
Salem	13 573	1.5	169	1.2	963	6.9	927	901	22 047	4.8	20 199	21 039	27 163	88.7
South Boston	X	X	X	X	X	X	412	413	X	X	6 737	8 098	X	X
Staunton	11 482	.2	205	1.8	863	–2.6	829	886	10 863	12.6	10 763	9 650	20 441	66.8
Suffolk	30 817	.6	806	2.6	1 120	4.7	1 100	1 070	15 043	17.2	13 937	12 832	23 895	78.1
Virginia Beach	213 269	1.0	4 681	2.2	9 989	13.7	9 491	8 783	132 973	17.3	119 343	113 344	22 322	72.9
Waynesboro	9 270	.5	240	2.6	583	–6.3	591	622	11 160	–8.5	11 013	12 203	28 276	92.4
Williamsburg	6 120	.1	275	4.5	729	–39.3	654	1 200	15 520	–18.7	12 977	19 100	24 109	78.8
Winchester	13 376	3.4	242	1.8	1 217	–19.0	1 279	1 503	22 007	–8.0	21 785	23 921	26 537	86.7

[1] Civilian unemployed as a percent of total civilian labor force.   [2] For pay period including March 12 of the year shown.   [3] 1,000–2,499 employees.

Sources: Civilian Labor Force—U.S. Bureau of Labor Statistics; Local Area Unemployment Statistics; 2000 data published 2 May 2001, 1999 data published 30 May 2001; <ftp://ftp.bls.gov/pub/time.series/la/> (related Internet site <http://www.bls.gov/lauhome.htm>).   Private Business Establishments and Employment—U.S. Census Bureau; County Business Patterns on CD-ROM; annual (related Internet site <http://www.census.gov/epcd/cbp/view/cbpview.html>).

Table B–7. Counties — Labor Force and Private Business Establishments and Employment–Con.

[Includes U.S., states, and 3,142 counties/county equivalents defined as of January 1, 1992. For changes to these areas since January 1, 1992, see appendix B. Geographic Information]

County	Civilian labor force, 2000		Unemployment		Private nonfarm businesses								Annual payroll per employee, 1998	
					Establishments				Employment[2]					
	Total	Percent change, 1999–2000	Total	Rate[1]	1998	Percent change, 1990–1998	1995	1990	1998	Percent change, 1990–1998	1995	1990	Amount (dollars)	Percent of national average
WASHINGTON	3 045 244	−1.0	157 714	5.2	161 473	22.4	151 925	131 919	2 134 598	21.1	1 948 923	1 762 046	34 324	112.1
Adams	8 271	−3.0	849	10.3	403	8.6	412	371	4 039	29.3	3 770	3 124	20 704	67.6
Asotin	11 801	−3.8	537	4.6	452	31.0	397	345	3 909	29.6	3 526	3 016	21 549	70.4
Benton	71 821	.1	4 596	6.4	3 212	32.6	3 036	2 422	47 110	24.8	52 981	37 746	31 629	103.3
Chelan	34 334	−.5	3 045	8.9	2 292	21.4	2 213	1 888	24 925	22.9	23 628	20 278	24 324	79.5
Clallam	23 919	−5.9	1 894	7.9	2 060	14.3	1 941	1 802	15 482	16.4	14 130	13 304	21 683	70.8
Clark	177 960	−1.4	7 560	4.2	7 685	46.1	6 815	5 260	93 206	43.5	83 711	64 930	28 687	93.7
Columbia	1 451	−3.5	171	11.8	134	36.7	132	98	918	21.6	904	755	21 723	71.0
Cowlitz	41 084	−2.0	3 197	7.8	2 402	20.6	2 234	1 992	32 626	14.2	31 036	28 570	29 388	96.0
Douglas	19 211	−.1	1 432	7.5	547	26.6	534	432	3 892	21.7	4 031	3 197	20 520	67.0
Forry	2 570	1.4	351	13.7	140	22.1	162	122	1 075	−22.2	1 200	1 082	24 057	81.2
Franklin	22 661	−.7	2 161	9.5	1 086	15.5	998	940	13 522	15.4	11 854	11 717	23 602	77.1
Garfield	1 161	7.4	48	4.1	54	−3.6	60	56	350	41.1	345	248	20 071	65.6
Grant	37 149	−1.7	3 767	10.1	1 686	28.4	1 605	1 313	16 548	48.3	15 186	11 160	23 260	76.0
Grays Harbor	25 582	−2.2	2 532	9.9	1 980	7.0	1 948	1 850	17 697	−.9	17 622	17 862	24 714	80.7
Island	29 520	−.6	1 222	4.1	1 551	35.2	1 401	1 147	10 308	30.4	9 422	7 907	20 402	66.7
Jefferson	10 328	−5.6	587	5.7	998	41.2	905	707	5 781	42.4	5 273	4 059	21 471	70.1
King	1 023 199	−.5	36 666	3.6	58 839	15.1	56 521	51 125	955 805	13.7	862 946	840 297	43 538	142.2
Kitsap	94 048	−.7	5 297	5.6	5 071	32.2	4 698	3 835	45 673	26.9	43 735	35 999	21 859	71.4
Kittitas	14 891	.2	868	5.8	985	33.8	895	736	6 907	31.0	6 869	5 274	20 504	67.0
Klickitat	8 714	.3	917	10.5	509	29.8	467	392	3 537	22.7	3 408	2 883	28 707	93.8
Lewis	29 898	−.4	2 661	8.9	2 022	20.9	1 834	1 673	19 415	17.0	18 361	16 601	23 765	77.6
Lincoln	4 563	−2.9	233	5.1	300	13.2	291	265	1 996	72.2	1 677	1 159	20 808	68.0
Mason	19 655	1.1	1 402	7.1	1 051	26.5	1 004	831	8 552	32.4	7 407	6 461	22 297	72.8
Okanogan	20 859	−2.8	2 282	10.9	1 040	19.3	1 001	872	8 204	22.5	8 494	6 696	19 971	65.2
Pacific	7 726	−.8	647	8.4	671	21.1	669	554	4 218	5.3	4 380	4 006	18 235	59.6
Pend Oreille	4 175	−1.1	399	9.6	232	35.7	243	171	1 452	59.4	1 460	911	27 970	91.4
Pierce	331 374	−.8	17 574	5.3	15 257	23.8	14 316	12 322	190 567	23.7	178 569	153 998	27 078	88.5
San Juan	6 153	−5.6	230	3.7	804	47.0	690	547	3 526	32.2	2 836	2 668	24 917	81.4
Skagit	51 644	2.3	3 539	6.9	3 202	30.7	3 020	2 450	32 202	42.4	28 691	22 607	25 449	83.1
Skamania	4 028	−1.1	364	9.0	178	20.3	153	148	1 151	13.8	792	1 011	21 712	70.9
Snohomish	343 817	−.7	14 124	4.1	14 760	34.9	12 745	10 940	202 949	40.8	160 468	144 143	31 645	103.4
Spokane	208 495	−1.4	11 611	5.6	11 703	23.8	11 260	9 454	161 001	27.6	154 255	126 211	26 614	86.9
Stevens	16 604	1.4	1 680	0.5	703	24.0	785	605	6 000	20.7	7 001	5 907	23 200	75.8
Thurston	99 246	−2.9	5 008	5.0	4 960	29.7	4 673	3 823	49 668	24.1	44 585	40 015	24 565	80.3
Wahkiakum	1 800	−5.8	119	6.6	107	33.8	98	80	554	31.9	491	420	23 451	76.6
Walla Walla	25 734	−2.8	1 641	6.4	1 246	9.1	1 204	1 142	16 878	19.4	16 782	14 134	23 124	75.5
Whatcom	81 582	−.9	4 683	5.7	5 317	30.8	4 993	4 066	55 623	23.9	53 496	44 898	25 365	82.9
Whitman	19 473	2.8	425	2.2	887	12.1	847	791	7 027	29.1	6 447	5 442	19 312	63.1
Yakima	108 655	−2.5	11 498	10.6	4 830	12.8	4 710	4 281	58 832	16.7	56 692	50 420	24 518	80.1
WEST VIRGINIA	824 578	1.0	45 626	5.5	41 703	10.7	40 599	37 687	547 234	13.4	530 596	482 517	24 265	79.3
Barbour	6 308	1.6	652	10.3	269	8.0	254	249	2 739	11.5	2 711	2 457	16 490	53.9
Berkeley	36 537	2.3	1 075	2.9	1 432	25.7	1 325	1 139	19 735	29.0	18 006	15 301	24 633	80.5
Boone	7 986	−2.2	774	9.7	404	3.6	372	390	5 721	−4.2	6 454	5 972	36 300	118.6
Braxton	5 284	−1.4	524	9.9	331	14.9	311	288	3 158	26.8	2 585	2 490	18 729	61.2
Brooke	11 346	−1.8	431	3.8	455	18.5	418	384	7 529	−46.7	6 656	14 124	20 570	67.2
Cabell	43 807	.9	2 031	4.6	2 823	1.6	2 644	2 778	44 797	11.8	40 251	40 074	23 433	76.6
Calhoun	2 726	1.6	447	16.4	138	−19.8	150	172	1 064	−33.1	912	1 590	18 073	59.0
Clay	4 168	−3.1	407	9.8	136	54.5	130	88	1 312	150.9	927	523	26 251	85.8
Doddridge	3 354	.5	153	4.6	79	29.5	72	61	548	63.1	505	336	14 511	47.4
Fayette	17 603	−.5	1 471	8.4	960	3.1	956	931	10 150	11.1	10 324	9 135	21 224	69.3
Gilmer	2 640	−2.0	196	7.4	132	10.9	137	119	946	7.1	995	883	16 551	54.1
Grant	4 279	−4.9	299	7.0	280	3.3	292	271	3 380	−7.1	3 778	3 640	22 609	73.9
Greenbrier	16 010	1.6	1 120	7.0	1 029	16.5	1 011	883	10 041	19.4	9 447	8 410	20 946	68.4
Hampshire	9 218	4.1	384	4.2	338	23.4	322	274	2 883	38.5	2 555	2 081	16 425	53.7
Hancock	15 080	−1.7	605	4.0	706	9.0	714	648	14 430	68.2	16 452	8 578	29 167	95.3
Hardy	7 481	1.1	197	2.6	256	24.9	235	205	4 794	70.8	4 308	2 806	19 285	63.0
Harrison	35 262	.9	2 057	5.8	1 956	9.3	1 922	1 789	25 635	16.5	24 216	21 998	23 480	76.7
Jackson	12 905	−.1	889	6.9	530	28.3	489	413	7 391	34.3	7 516	5 505	26 347	86.1
Jefferson	22 336	2.6	536	2.4	811	18.6	762	684	9 756	25.1	7 866	7 797	19 852	64.9
Kanawha	109 477	1.9	4 674	4.3	5 972	9.0	5 847	5 478	93 918	11.3	88 894	84 383	27 192	88.8
Lewis	7 182	−.6	462	6.4	396	14.1	384	347	4 166	37.2	4 183	3 036	20 248	66.1
Lincoln	6 965	−1.8	678	9.7	244	15.6	265	211	1 548	13.2	1 610	1 367	19 438	63.5
Logan	12 846	−4.1	1 156	9.0	865	.2	883	863	10 404	15.8	10 182	8 988	25 342	82.8
McDowell	7 304	−3.8	812	11.1	441	−4.3	464	461	3 870	14.1	4 175	3 393	24 933	81.5

[1] Civilian unemployed as a percent of total civilian labor force.   [2] For pay period including March 12 of the year shown.

Sources: Civilian Labor Force—U.S. Bureau of Labor Statistics; Local Area Unemployment Statistics; 2000 data published 2 May 2001, 1999 data published 30 May 2001; <ftp://ftp.bls.gov/pub/time.series/la/> (related Internet site <http://www.bls.gov/lauhome.htm>).   Private Business Establishments and Employment—U.S. Census Bureau; County Business Patterns on CD-ROM; annual (related Internet site <http://www.census.gov/epcd/cbp/view/cbpview.html>).

[Includes U.S., states, and 3,142 counties/county equivalents defined as of January 1, 1992. For changes to these areas since January 1, 1992, see appendix B. Geographic Information]

County	Civilian labor force, 2000		Unemployment		Private nonfarm businesses								Annual payroll per employee, 1998	
					Establishments				Employment[2]					
	Total	Percent change, 1999–2000	Total	Rate[1]	1998	Percent change, 1990–1998	1995	1990	1998	Percent change, 1990–1998	1995	1990	Amount (dollars)	Percent of national average
WEST VIRGINIA—Con.														
Marion	24 724	1.3	1 514	6.1	1 305	4.2	1 283	1 252	15 176	4.1	15 777	14 578	24 833	81.1
Marshall	16 572	1.3	1 018	6.1	589	19.7	552	492	6 678	-4.0	7 471	6 959	24 696	80.7
Mason	9 249	.8	1 212	13.1	366	.3	361	365	5 113	-6.8	5 189	5 485	29 058	94.9
Mercer	28 475	-.6	1 288	4.5	1 461	5.1	1 435	1 390	20 307	19.1	18 915	17 047	22 463	73.4
Mineral	12 900	2.1	790	6.1	471	5.8	468	445	4 565	-6.5	4 544	4 880	20 310	66.4
Mingo	8 263	-4.4	784	9.5	674	-4.3	726	704	7 229	5.6	8 318	6 845	30 433	99.4
Monongalia	40 464	3.3	984	2.4	2 002	10.4	1 967	1 814	28 921	16.3	28 427	24 860	23 490	76.7
Monroe	5 559	2.8	233	4.2	207	21.1	203	171	1 197	11.1	1 166	1 077	19 785	64.6
Morgan	6 453	3.4	192	3.0	249	8.7	224	229	2 243	.3	2 011	2 236	19 920	65.1
Nicholas	11 299	2.0	899	8.0	687	13.6	677	605	6 520	7.9	6 940	6 040	19 964	65.2
Ohio	25 004	1.0	906	3.6	1 618	1.2	1 611	1 599	26 099	10.2	24 436	23 692	22 884	74.8
Pendleton	4 356	8.1	440	10.1	171	8.9	164	157	1 658	4.2	1 690	1 591	17 377	56.8
Pleasants	2 823	-1.7	227	8.0	132	7.3	125	123	1 686	-5.4	1 788	1 782	30 808	100.6
Pocahontas	4 302	-1.0	328	7.6	253	9.5	255	231	3 164	15.4	3 068	2 741	16 305	53.3
Preston	13 357	3.1	689	5.2	592	15.2	588	514	4 855	-.9	4 675	4 898	20 305	66.3
Putnam	28 381	2.1	1 250	4.4	1 091	45.1	931	752	12 325	54.9	11 894	7 955	25 241	82.5
Raleigh	35 184	-.4	2 150	6.1	2 035	16.8	1 950	1 742	23 791	15.9	22 213	20 531	24 021	78.5
Randolph	13 893	.7	863	6.2	772	15.7	738	667	8 206	12.5	8 473	7 293	18 963	62.0
Ritchie	4 413	.9	333	7.5	238	38.4	207	172	2 399	8.4	2 267	2 214	20 952	68.5
Roane	6 489	3.2	809	12.5	293	-6.7	306	314	2 733	37.8	2 747	1 984	18 160	59.3
Summers	4 418	.3	334	7.6	202	2.5	196	197	1 492	15.7	1 320	1 289	17 656	57.7
Taylor	7 113	-.4	393	5.5	227	15.2	222	197	1 949	23.9	1 889	1 573	19 613	64.1
Tucker	3 610	3.3	240	6.6	210	17.3	216	179	2 412	10.6	2 541	2 181	15 012	49.0
Tyler	4 362	1.3	241	5.5	157	12.9	141	139	1 846	22.4	1 722	1 508	33 810	110.5
Upshur	10 931	3.7	630	5.8	523	17.0	497	447	6 232	19.0	5 659	5 239	18 603	60.8
Wayne	17 235	.3	893	5.2	636	22.3	758	520	7 746	29.3	10 169	5 991	26 431	86.4
Webster	3 177	2.2	259	8.2	199	15.7	186	172	1 836	40.4	1 813	1 308	26 082	85.2
Wetzel	8 001	1.3	721	9.0	460	13.9	464	404	5 271	-2.2	5 646	5 388	32 191	105.2
Wirt	2 000	.1	240	12.0	80	33.3	77	60	351	31.5	336	267	13 972	45.6
Wood	45 428	2.4	2 032	4.5	2 350	12.8	2 301	2 083	37 199	14.2	36 237	32 561	25 404	83.0
Wyoming	8 041	-3.4	706	8.8	448	23.8	381	362	4 207	19.3	3 618	3 525	25 088	82.0
WISCONSIN	2 934 931	1.6	103 769	3.5	138 635	13.5	133 238	122 142	2 319 343	19.0	2 186 060	1 948 856	27 987	91.4
Adams	7 965	1.8	326	4.1	278	53.6	213	181	2 346	48.6	2 056	1 579	20 369	66.5
Ashland	7 775	1.5	576	7.4	580	5.1	571	552	6 787	5.3	6 876	6 444	22 031	72.0
Barron	23 786	2.2	1 133	4.8	1 274	12.4	1 257	1 133	16 788	33.2	15 521	12 608	20 773	67.9
Bayfield	7 367	2.4	479	6.5	411	17.1	384	351	2 171	20.8	2 263	1 797	16 383	53.5
Brown	135 539	2.1	3 603	2.7	6 050	20.4	5 671	5 025	121 799	29.8	107 195	93 869	29 087	95.0
Buffalo	8 016	2.4	271	3.4	344	16.2	351	296	3 300	9.6	3 678	3 012	28 531	93.2
Burnett	7 122	2.5	285	4.0	419	29.3	380	324	3 323	24.2	3 037	2 676	19 567	63.9
Calumet	25 284	2.4	639	2.5	791	28.2	763	617	12 298	15.1	12 791	10 684	25 097	82.0
Chippewa	30 493	1.0	1 347	4.4	1 207	4.5	1 254	1 155	17 406	16.9	15 849	14 893	23 391	76.4
Clark	15 759	1.7	899	5.7	802	2.2	802	785	7 948	16.5	7 751	6 821	19 857	64.9
Columbia	26 620	1.4	1 143	4.3	1 453	14.0	1 406	1 275	16 733	21.0	15 769	13 834	23 497	76.8
Crawford	10 043	2.7	372	3.7	376	2.2	387	368	5 912	37.3	5 270	4 307	19 653	64.2
Dane	262 802	1.6	4 375	1.7	12 058	21.1	11 413	9 953	214 837	29.5	198 563	165 858	28 018	91.5
Dodge	47 764	1.4	1 511	3.2	1 835	14.1	1 798	1 608	29 528	22.9	27 917	24 030	27 639	90.3
Door	15 390	1.1	704	4.6	1 320	25.4	1 167	1 053	10 311	17.1	9 257	8 804	21 191	69.2
Douglas	22 732	2.4	1 039	4.6	1 101	11.9	1 043	984	12 759	21.1	11 963	10 538	21 762	71.1
Dunn	21 753	.9	764	3.5	976	32.2	811	738	12 852	74.6	10 321	7 359	22 377	73.1
Eau Claire	51 780	1.0	1 756	3.4	2 585	16.1	2 479	2 226	41 277	26.9	38 105	32 528	22 674	74.1
Florence	1 580	-7.5	102	6.5	104	70.5	98	61	711	11.4	622	638	15 792	51.6
Fond du Lac	53 797	1.3	1 735	3.2	2 485	17.7	2 244	2 112	41 813	20.6	39 781	34 658	25 801	84.3
Forest	4 434	1.2	282	6.4	315	21.6	302	259	2 295	55.5	2 103	1 476	19 580	64.0
Grant	23 877	1.1	899	3.8	1 299	11.3	1 273	1 167	13 337	7.5	13 538	12 401	18 693	61.1
Green	18 552	3.3	685	3.7	950	15.6	875	822	12 857	24.2	12 096	10 350	23 189	75.8
Green Lake	10 387	1.0	432	4.2	622	15.6	628	538	6 738	16.8	6 425	5 769	22 910	74.8
Iowa	13 644	1.8	416	3.0	566	23.9	538	457	9 397	44.2	8 572	6 516	22 996	75.1
Iron	3 235	1.1	217	6.7	240	15.4	224	208	1 974	24.6	1 839	1 584	18 118	59.2
Jackson	11 955	-2.6	505	4.2	405	6.6	401	380	4 925	20.4	4 550	4 089	25 012	81.7
Jefferson	43 022	4.1	1 179	2.7	1 850	15.8	1 692	1 597	31 183	13.5	29 992	27 472	24 902	81.4
Juneau	10 382	-.1	734	7.1	618	19.3	560	518	7 881	28.7	7 236	6 124	21 151	69.1
Kenosha	81 749	1.7	3 086	3.8	3 053	20.3	2 877	2 537	46 908	30.7	43 625	35 882	27 612	90.2
Kewaunee	10 507	1.1	288	2.7	484	8.8	483	445	5 393	17.2	5 202	4 603	24 090	78.7
La Crosse	60 651	2.5	1 969	3.2	2 957	10.1	2 884	2 686	55 719	16.3	52 800	47 924	24 929	81.4

[1] Civilian unemployed as a percent of total civilian labor force.   [2] For pay period including March 12 of the year shown.

Sources: Civilian Labor Force—U.S. Bureau of Labor Statistics; Local Area Unemployment Statistics; 2000 data published 2 May 2001, 1999 data published 30 May 2001; <ftp://ftp.bls.gov/pub/time.series/la/> (related Internet site <http://www.bls.gov/lauhome.htm>). Private Business Establishments and Employment—U.S. Census Bureau; County Business Patterns on CD-ROM; annual (related Internet site <http://www.census.gov/epcd/cbp/view/cbpview.html>).

[Includes U.S., states, and 3,142 counties/county equivalents defined as of January 1, 1992. For changes to these areas since January 1, 1992, see appendix B. Geographic Information]

County	Civilian labor force, 2000		Unemployment		Private nonfarm businesses								Annual payroll per employee, 1998	
					Establishments				Employment[2]					
	Total	Percent change, 1999–2000	Total	Rate[1]	1998	Percent change, 1990–1998	1995	1990	1998	Percent change, 1990–1998	1995	1990	Amount (dollars)	Percent of national average
WISCONSIN—Con.														
Lafayette	7 266	-2.1	292	4.0	346	-1.7	323	352	2 842	19.7	2 747	2 375	20 412	66.7
Langlade	9 331	2.3	536	5.7	601	10.7	579	543	6 251	13.8	6 140	5 492	21 008	68.6
Lincoln	14 609	2.1	725	5.0	800	17.3	739	682	9 896	12.4	9 902	8 804	22 323	72.9
Manitowoc	44 455	1.7	1 558	3.5	1 857	5.7	1 859	1 757	33 320	15.8	31 529	28 779	26 768	87.5
Marathon	73 497	2.2	2 562	3.5	3 371	22.4	3 136	2 755	58 831	27.3	54 944	46 224	27 827	90.9
Marinette	21 121	1.7	1 038	4.9	1 070	7.9	1 107	992	15 939	15.8	15 289	13 769	25 350	82.8
Marquette	6 989	1.7	422	6.0	342	16.7	318	293	3 220	42.8	2 701	2 255	22 466	73.4
Menominee	2 371	-4.9	224	9.4	98	164.9	37	37	1 747	392.1	1 036	355	19 238	62.9
Milwaukee	474 330	1.1	22 287	4.7	21 384	-3.5	22 057	22 169	475 869	1.2	474 292	470 114	31 591	103.2
Monroe	19 758	2.6	889	4.5	868	9.2	831	795	13 017	18.3	12 466	11 001	23 135	75.6
Oconto	15 863	2.4	725	4.6	841	25.7	726	669	8 250	22.5	7 199	6 734	22 121	72.3
Oneida	20 183	.7	1 038	5.1	1 541	42.3	1 268	1 083	15 600	63.5	12 496	9 544	23 441	76.6
Outagamie	102 105	2.3	2 712	2.7	4 499	41.9	3 944	3 170	87 805	45.8	75 256	60 206	28 847	94.2
Ozaukee	48 217	.4	1 045	2.2	2 729	32.7	2 489	2 057	36 791	37.1	32 562	26 840	29 025	94.8
Pepin	3 171	-.1	151	4.8	195	5.4	192	185	1 622	6.7	1 564	1 520	21 790	71.2
Pierce	20 766	2.4	617	3.0	770	1.7	817	757	6 239	-15.1	7 370	7 345	19 987	65.3
Polk....................	22 305	3.2	831	3.7	1 063	21.6	984	874	11 625	36.8	9 899	8 495	21 154	69.1
Portage................	36 828	1.7	1 395	3.8	1 630	20.8	1 525	1 349	26 378	17.3	23 230	22 489	24 967	81.6
Price	6 819	-2.2	472	6.9	464	12.3	440	413	5 842	11.6	5 881	5 235	25 123	82.1
Racine	90 948	Z	4 310	4.7	4 210	3.1	4 141	4 083	76 877	6.7	73 331	72 070	29 413	96.1
Richland	8 329	1.6	337	4.0	348	-5.2	387	367	4 507	21.4	4 202	3 714	22 913	74.9
Rock	78 830	1.5	3 873	4.9	3 340	9.8	3 214	3 041	60 340	14.2	57 960	52 821	28 773	94.0
Rusk	7 079	1.1	478	6.8	360	11.1	364	324	4 164	6.0	3 790	3 927	22 720	74.2
St. Croix	33 683	2.1	848	2.5	1 579	34.6	1 362	1 173	20 449	60.6	17 101	12 735	24 392	79.7
Sauk	35 068	4.2	1 045	3.0	1 680	24.1	1 546	1 354	24 147	29.6	23 482	18 632	24 636	80.5
Sawyer	9 458	3.5	525	5.6	625	28.9	596	485	4 344	75.9	4 212	2 470	20 422	66.7
Shawano	19 900	.1	808	4.1	877	3.5	917	847	9 952	14.3	9 768	8 705	20 374	66.6
Sheboygan	62 622	2.9	1 446	2.3	2 584	13.2	2 505	2 282	53 132	19.8	51 026	44 351	27 948	91.3
Taylor	10 548	4.3	477	4.5	481	9.8	477	438	6 923	19.2	6 814	5 806	24 210	79.1
Trempealeau............	14 597	5.2	662	4.5	719	9.6	710	656	9 582	24.2	9 168	7 718	23 730	77.5
Vernon	13 813	3.0	577	4.2	659	12.1	642	588	5 951	20.2	5 743	4 950	18 249	59.6
Vilas	11 095	.7	564	5.1	810	-2.3	1 012	829	4 161	-20.5	6 326	5 236	18 849	61.6
Walworth	51 965	Z	1 407	2.7	2 573	20.8	2 449	2 130	35 171	41.2	31 943	24 910	23 346	76.3
Washburn	8 017	4.4	454	5.7	569	18.5	522	480	4 424	29.9	4 138	3 407	18 908	61.8
Washington	67 484	.6	1 812	2.7	3 053	38.0	2 712	2 213	46 100	43.0	40 593	32 234	26 229	85.7
Waukesha	212 569	.5	5 248	2.5	12 335	23.8	11 398	9 964	210 582	34.4	191 297	156 630	32 352	105.7
Waupaca	26 289	2.7	948	3.6	1 367	14.6	1 337	1 193	16 297	12.2	16 415	14 531	23 003	75.2
Waushara	10 935	7.6	498	4.6	525	23.0	464	427	4 009	32.1	3 507	3 034	18 953	61.9
Winnebago	96 034	2.5	2 430	2.5	3 749	-6.1	3 893	3 992	80 412	3.8	80 062	77 500	30 415	99.4
Wood	39 928	2.3	1 753	4.4	1 900	.2	1 977	1 897	36 761	8.4	35 801	33 922	29 673	96.9
WYOMING	266 945	1.9	10 377	3.9	17 888	22.3	17 133	14 630	163 791	24.0	157 472	132 061	24 300	79.4
Albany	18 601	1.9	298	1.6	996	23.4	947	807	9 255	31.4	8 547	7 045	18 930	61.8
Big Horn	6 031	4.3	335	5.6	287	20.1	283	239	2 428	45.7	1 991	1 666	23 607	77.1
Campbell	20 522	4.5	692	3.4	1 119	22.7	1 085	912	13 502	25.3	12 290	10 778	32 137	105.0
Carbon	8 367	-.3	339	4.1	566	14.8	528	493	2 809	4.6	4 461	3 976	22 534	73.6
Converse	6 919	4.0	305	4.4	377	19.3	364	316	2 809	24.7	2 830	2 253	23 746	77.6
Crook	3 214	5.0	131	4.1	190	13.8	179	167	1 412	22.1	1 302	1 156	25 360	82.9
Fremont	18 191	1.1	1 170	6.4	1 270	25.4	1 212	1 013	9 738	26.5	9 378	7 697	19 427	63.5
Goshen................	6 649	2.0	201	3.0	376	12.9	341	333	2 931	25.3	2 858	2 339	16 853	55.1
Hot Springs	2 454	.9	83	3.4	210	25.0	191	168	1 595	41.0	1 524	1 131	15 737	51.4
Johnson	4 060	3.9	114	2.8	298	29.6	273	230	1 583	28.2	1 476	1 235	18 888	61.7
Laramie	41 216	3.2	1 197	2.9	2 292	23.3	2 111	1 859	25 338	21.4	24 689	20 872	22 133	72.3
Lincoln	6 539	-1.1	344	5.3	478	29.5	451	369	3 804	22.1	3 753	3 115	24 907	81.4
Natrona	34 198	1.4	1 492	4.4	2 566	11.9	2 545	2 294	24 563	22.1	23 306	20 113	24 382	79.7
Niobrara	1 320	-.5	35	2.7	95	21.8	91	78	484	43.6	417	337	14 461	47.2
Park	15 466	.7	629	4.1	1 147	30.3	1 162	880	8 401	53.2	8 443	5 485	22 522	73.6
Platte	4 807	3.4	171	3.6	300	21.5	286	247	2 103	6.6	2 135	1 972	22 893	74.8
Sheridan...............	14 099	3.0	586	4.2	1 065	29.4	1 036	823	8 161	25.1	8 433	6 526	20 896	68.3
Sublette	3 243	3.2	81	2.5	311	48.1	300	210	1 258	18.3	1 183	1 063	22 568	73.7
Sweetwater	20 007	-3.0	977	4.9	1 124	11.5	1 131	1 008	14 765	12.4	14 899	13 134	33 022	107.9
Teton	12 281	5.6	212	1.7	1 595	45.8	1 452	1 094	13 291	67.7	11 678	7 924	23 318	76.2
Uinta	10 606	.9	582	5.5	587	27.9	522	459	5 680	16.3	5 317	4 885	24 964	81.6
Washakie	4 751	-2.7	250	5.3	379	19.2	364	318	3 057	30.4	2 995	2 345	20 286	66.3
Weston	3 406	1.3	152	4.5	218	-.5	220	219	1 553	-1.2	1 661	1 572	20 117	65.7

[1] Civilian unemployed as a percent of total civilian labor force.   [2] For pay period including March 12 of the year shown.

Sources: Civilian Labor Force—U.S. Bureau of Labor Statistics; Local Area Unemployment Statistics; 2000 data published 2 May 2001, 1999 data published 30 May 2001; <ftp://ftp.bls.gov/pub/time.series/la/> (related Internet site <http://www.bls.gov/lauhome.htm>). Private Business Establishments and Employment—U.S. Census Bureau; County Business Patterns on CD-ROM; annual (related Internet site <http://www.census.gov/epcd/cbp/view/cbpview.html>).

Table B–8. Counties — **Personal Income and Earnings**

[Includes U.S., states, and 3,142 counties/county equivalents defined as of January 1, 1992. For changes to these areas since January 1, 1992, see appendix B. Geographic Information]

County	Personal income, 1998													Manufacturing earnings		
		Per capita[1]				Earnings										
							Percent, by selected industry—									
							Goods-related		Service-related							
	Total (mil. dol.)	Percent change, 1990–1998	Amount (dollars)	Percent of national average	Transfer payments (mil. dol.)	Total[2] (mil. dol.)	Total[3]	Manufacturing	Total[4]	Retail trade	FIRE[5]	Services	Government	1998 ($1,000)	1997 ($1,000)	1996 ($1,000)
UNITED STATES	7 351 547.0	50.5	27 203	100.0	983 530.0	5 302 066.0	23.4	16.8	75.8	8.8	9.0	28.4	16.0	891 190 000	847 972 000	800 423 000
ALABAMA	95 955.6	49.7	22 054	81.1	15 961.2	66 930.1	27.7	20.5	70.8	9.4	5.6	23.1	20.0	13 753 680	13 376 333	12 886 639
Autauga	890.0	72.0	21 093	77.5	118.8	336.1	D	30.3	D	15.2	4.3	15.3	17.3	102 015	95 460	93 319
Baldwin	3 203.0	104.5	24 109	88.6	440.1	1 364.8	22.4	12.8	76.7	15.7	9.9	23.3	17.8	174 933	157 019	137 288
Barbour	521.5	52.7	19 360	71.2	111.2	330.7	41.9	37.5	53.1	7.9	3.2	13.5	17.7	124 117	106 705	103 672
Bibb	345.8	64.6	18 214	67.0	72.5	132.5	D	19.8	D	8.8	D	14.1	24.5	26 212	28 103	28 236
Blount	917.2	70.5	19 813	72.8	144.0	313.4	29.7	18.8	57.1	9.7	4.6	15.2	16.5	58 984	57 260	56 408
Bullock	179.3	57.8	15 833	58.2	50.4	99.4	D	D	D	7.4	3.0	13.0	22.6	D	21 538	18 329
Butler	363.3	47.4	16 776	61.7	97.7	203.3	33.7	28.0	61.8	12.5	2.9	19.9	15.7	56 897	57 090	60 719
Calhoun	2 378.6	37.7	20 315	74.7	445.5	1 695.0	D	19.0	D	9.9	2.7	16.3	36.8	321 613	313 407	293 056
Chambers	692.4	36.5	18 864	69.3	144.3	406.0	51.0	46.3	48.2	10.4	1.7	14.5	11.7	187 888	185 460	168 019
Cherokee	387.4	60.3	17 749	65.2	81.5	160.0	D	19.0	62.5	12.1	6.8	12.6	18.9	30 407	37 373	34 253
Chilton	716.3	69.9	19 398	71.3	131.5	253.2	D	17.5	D	17.3	3.4	14.1	18.0	44 406	45 133	44 750
Choctaw	281.4	39.8	17 780	65.4	68.2	217.3	D	61.9	D	4.9	1.3	9.1	8.5	134 450	131 151	134 451
Clarke	522.4	43.1	18 309	67.3	120.5	309.4	41.7	37.1	58.0	11.5	4.8	13.1	18.6	114 700	114 308	101 542
Clay	273.0	50.7	19 550	71.9	56.9	156.1	49.8	46.7	40.9	5.1	1.8	8.7	18.4	72 802	66 584	72 853
Cleburne	256.6	45.0	17 968	66.1	47.2	116.4	D	30.0	D	8.0	1.7	7.4	19.1	34 892	32 287	27 251
Coffee	911.6	43.7	21 590	79.4	159.5	456.9	30.6	26.5	59.6	12.7	4.0	17.8	15.8	120 926	117 042	115 269
Colbert	1 159.6	43.4	21 911	80.5	216.8	829.5	33.6	24.9	65.3	8.9	2.6	15.7	26.4	206 916	244 831	245 570
Conecuh	251.0	49.0	18 104	66.6	67.9	157.6	D	20.0	D	5.4	D	12.2	17.2	31 547	26 711	26 015
Coosa	203.6	50.6	17 499	64.3	43.7	74.2	57.4	52.7	D	5.0	D	10.5	18.2	39 121	37 478	37 549
Covington	698.5	45.7	18 646	68.5	167.4	418.6	D	23.5	D	10.9	3.1	18.6	15.5	98 502	101 725	95 005
Crenshaw	260.4	52.8	19 114	70.3	61.2	137.9	D	14.2	D	6.3	2.6	14.3	13.7	19 532	19 554	20 870
Cullman	1 506.5	56.0	20 101	73.9	271.9	887.2	29.5	23.2	59.9	15.4	3.0	19.2	12.3	205 400	195 233	185 357
Dale	944.9	27.4	19 318	71.0	173.3	888.6	D	23.2	D	4.2	1.5	9.1	53.4	205 775	187 579	176 428
Dallas	827.2	38.8	17 675	65.0	231.3	512.4	31.7	27.1	65.5	10.9	3.4	22.9	17.9	138 667	135 521	130 591
DeKalb	1 172.3	60.2	20 118	74.0	221.0	741.7	D	41.9	D	8.9	2.3	13.5	10.8	311 142	298 468	289 554
Elmore	1 294.8	78.7	20 889	76.8	221.2	414.8	D	21.2	D	11.9	3.5	16.8	24.7	87 788	80 418	66 864
Escambia	648.5	43.7	17 654	64.9	144.2	434.2	37.7	27.3	60.4	10.6	4.2	12.2	19.2	118 582	114 755	111 829
Etowah	2 112.6	44.4	20 328	74.7	440.1	1 255.1	D	28.9	D	11.3	3.6	25.7	13.4	363 323	359 887	356 301
Fayette	330.9	42.4	18 286	67.2	73.5	164.2	50.9	44.0	49.1	8.2	2.3	8.7	22.4	72 269	85 913	83 519
Franklin	580.4	57.2	19 553	71.9	129.7	339.6	D	39.0	D	9.6	2.7	17.0	16.7	132 526	122 179	119 759
Geneva	462.1	41.7	18 576	68.3	108.2	204.9	26.5	22.2	56.5	10.2	3.2	10.2	18.4	45 560	48 405	43 310
Greene	146.4	35.1	14 874	54.7	47.8	67.7	19.3	14.9	71.5	7.1	2.5	17.6	28.2	10 105	9 859	10 500
Hale	263.2	52.9	15 711	57.8	72.2	115.4	33.9	31.1	54.4	7.5	2.0	14.3	23.9	35 844	31 233	26 842
Henry	302.8	49.6	19 164	70.4	64.7	143.8	D	36.5	D	8.9	D	12.0	15.3	52 423	50 886	49 194
Houston	1 986.5	47.6	23 203	85.3	287.4	1 520.0	D	16.7	D	12.8	3.9	26.4	14.9	253 755	240 449	223 053
Jackson	1 024.3	45.3	19 952	73.3	180.9	578.3	D	40.4	D	8.7	2.6	10.4	20.4	233 659	224 138	212 088
Jefferson	18 000.8	43.6	27 272	100.3	2 625.7	16 071.2	17.6	10.0	82.4	8.4	10.0	30.7	14.5	1 614 625	1 565 185	1 522 114
Lamar	286.3	35.8	17 883	65.7	65.7	168.1	D	45.2	D	6.9	2.8	12.1	11.8	75 993	73 143	75 970
Lauderdale	1 727.5	35.2	20 515	75.4	321.2	946.7	D	21.9	D	13.0	5.3	22.7	21.1	206 864	224 279	223 234
Lawrence	639.7	58.1	19 127	70.3	105.3	327.3	D	D	D	6.4	1.6	8.7	13.7	D	143 517	136 071
Lee	1 892.1	51.8	18 831	69.2	254.1	1 247.9	D	20.3	D	11.6	4.0	16.8	32.9	253 786	271 166	266 801
Limestone	1 269.6	49.6	20 396	75.0	175.5	953.9	41.3	37.8	D	6.8	1.6	13.5	29.7	360 990	367 738	350 673
Lowndes	191.4	40.3	14 741	54.2	53.6	102.1	D	40.6	D	6.6	2.5	8.4	19.4	41 486	40 141	36 550
Macon	353.6	32.2	15 235	56.0	102.7	200.6	D	1.1	D	5.7	1.5	33.5	50.2	2 141	1 871	2 292
Madison	7 340.5	49.7	26 404	97.1	684.2	6 580.0	D	22.7	D	7.1	3.0	29.0	28.7	1 490 820	1 470 158	1 428 053
Marengo	443.2	46.7	18 959	69.7	99.3	268.7	38.3	32.3	58.0	8.8	3.2	11.4	18.7	86 731	77 091	78 118
Marion	585.1	62.8	18 961	69.7	123.3	401.2	D	49.4	D	6.6	2.8	13.6	11.6	198 126	190 843	184 994
Marshall	1 584.2	47.2	19 755	72.6	293.0	1 110.8	D	37.2	D	13.0	3.4	11.7	14.7	412 755	414 959	400 086
Mobile	7 996.8	44.0	20 048	73.7	1 476.1	6 163.8	26.1	16.3	73.5	10.1	5.0	27.3	16.5	1 007 142	1 009 106	973 235
Monroe	434.3	39.9	18 094	66.5	94.9	330.2	D	49.1	47.3	7.1	1.9	9.8	12.9	162 064	160 637	162 022
Montgomery	5 559.7	42.0	25 575	94.0	786.8	5 010.5	14.9	9.5	84.9	8.7	8.7	25.7	30.9	474 763	454 577	446 413
Morgan	2 608.4	47.8	23 882	87.8	401.3	1 731.2	45.6	36.5	53.5	9.5	4.2	16.7	13.1	631 902	589 079	550 015
Perry	180.0	40.4	14 190	52.2	64.3	82.9	D	30.0	D	6.9	3.6	20.5	22.7	24 867	22 806	22 200
Pickens	362.1	47.3	17 226	63.3	96.9	149.5	26.6	21.2	60.4	7.5	3.4	20.9	19.4	31 637	32 584	30 881
Pike	562.9	46.8	19 648	72.2	121.5	379.4	24.4	18.5	67.3	10.3	3.8	14.7	19.2	70 362	64 890	66 483
Randolph	362.8	41.4	18 119	66.6	86.6	175.1	37.4	34.0	55.6	10.2	2.5	10.8	22.2	59 523	57 199	57 404
Russell	944.7	49.4	18 756	68.9	182.5	451.5	45.8	36.6	52.9	10.4	3.2	15.6	16.3	165 118	158 997	153 205
St. Clair	1 221.6	80.8	19 698	72.4	182.1	431.2	D	20.6	D	12.1	3.5	18.2	16.9	88 989	81 746	78 157
Shelby	4 028.5	100.2	28 601	105.1	296.6	1 724.8	31.5	19.0	68.1	7.8	7.1	21.3	9.4	328 062	314 612	283 584
Sumter	237.6	35.3	15 071	55.4	68.3	144.5	26.1	23.1	65.4	8.3	1.6	15.3	27.0	33 393	31 200	35 672
Talladega	1 389.6	42.9	18 041	66.3	319.8	809.3	41.8	34.5	56.9	9.5	2.7	18.0	20.1	279 258	270 161	245 528
Tallapoosa	818.6	40.4	20 282	74.6	172.2	505.0	47.6	42.6	51.8	8.4	3.7	21.3	12.5	215 260	214 288	210 426
Tuscaloosa	3 546.8	48.6	22 063	81.1	625.1	2 650.6	35.3	21.9	64.4	10.2	3.8	17.5	24.9	580 977	497 354	460 276
Walker	1 407.9	38.8	19 828	72.9	328.4	658.3	24.7	6.9	72.1	15.3	4.4	23.5	16.1	45 342	46 731	46 304
Washington	316.4	46.8	17 912	65.8	68.7	236.1	D	59.2	D	3.3	1.5	5.5	11.4	139 849	117 417	115 714
Wilcox	184.7	36.0	13 728	50.5	68.2	134.6	49.4	45.8	45.9	5.8	1.8	10.6	19.1	61 603	59 329	61 533
Winston	461.9	65.2	19 141	70.4	103.3	347.2	D	51.1	D	6.5	2.1	11.0	9.5	177 318	172 387	183 018

[1] Based on resident population estimated as of July 1, 1998.   [2] Includes farm earnings; see table B-10 for these data.   [3] Includes mining and construction, not shown separately.   [4] Includes agricultural services, forestry, and fisheries; transportation and public utilities; and wholesale trade, not shown separately.   [5] Finance, insurance, and real estate.

Source: Personal Income and Earnings—U.S. Bureau of Economic Analysis, "Regional Economic Information System (REIS) 1969-1998" on CD-ROM (related Internet site <http://www.bea.doc.gov/bea/regional/data.htm>).

Table B–8. Counties — **Personal Income and Earnings**–Con.

[Includes U.S., states, and 3,142 counties/county equivalents defined as of January 1, 1992. For changes to these areas since January 1, 1992, see appendix B. Geographic Information]

| County | Personal income, 1998 | | | | | | | | | | | | | Manufacturing earnings | | |
	Total (mil. dol.)	Per capita[1] Percent change, 1990–1998	Per capita[1] Amount (dollars)	Per capita[1] Percent of national average	Transfer payments (mil. dol.)	Earnings Total[2] (mil. dol.)	Goods-related Total[3]	Goods-related Manufacturing	Service-related Total[4]	Retail trade	FIRE[5]	Services	Government	1998 ($1,000)	1997 ($1,000)	1996 ($1,000)
ALASKA	17 124.0	36.3	27 835	102.3	2 440.9	13 111.9	D	4.3	81.2	8.9	4.0	20.8	33.1	565 686	583 074	601 083
Aleutians East	53.5	18.6	24 069	88.5	6.1	50.8	D	D	D	2.7	1.6	D	16.5	D	31 964	36 155
Aleutians West	111.8	−44.5	28 356	104.2	11.7	137.7	45.8	44.3	54.1	6.3	2.8	14.2	16.7	61 062	57 037	74 174
Anchorage	8 348.1	39.8	32 659	120.1	989.2	6 486.2	15.4	1.5	84.6	9.4	5.3	23.9	30.4	99 173	89 395	87 479
Bethel	280.5	45.6	17 524	64.4	79.0	185.7	D	D	D	5.7	4.3	27.1	42.3	D	12 221	5 061
Bristol Bay	47.3	2.1	43 439	159.7	5.2	46.6	24.0	19.4	D	5.2	D	10.1	34.0	9 059	8 527	8 221
Denali	62.3	NA	32 152	118.2	12.5	75.0	D	–	D	3.0	D	37.4	29.5	–	–	
Dillingham	112.4	12.0	25 046	92.1	19.3	89.2	D	D	D	6.2	3.2	35.6	25.3	D	D	D
Fairbanks North Star	2 135.1	37.9	25 341	93.2	313.6	1 659.7	10.6	1.9	89.4	9.0	2.4	18.3	48.3	31 848	27 779	25 530
Haines	69.8	20.7	30 059	110.5	11.4	39.3	D	D	D	13.7	D	20.5	19.0	D	6 145	6 963
Juneau	1 010.3	39.9	33 516	123.2	110.4	731.9	D	2.1	D	8.6	4.7	15.3	49.4	15 426	14 971	14 208
Kenai Peninsula	1 213.8	37.5	25 120	92.3	205.1	744.4	29.2	11.1	70.7	10.9	1.9	16.7	25.7	82 804	88 433	97 397
Ketchikan Gateway	452.5	15.3	31 803	116.9	61.2	330.5	22.5	13.4	77.5	10.7	3.3	20.0	29.0	44 165	59 073	61 585
Kodiak Island	349.9	20.7	24 166	88.8	46.6	281.8	25.3	20.5	74.7	6.4	2.4	14.5	34.7	57 795	66 134	64 283
Lake and Peninsula	32.0	NA	18 419	67.7	7.6	21.5	D	23.9	D	5.4	.3	29.9	23.5	5 136	4 925	4 909
Matanuska-Susitna	1 046.3	59.6	18 752	68.9	199.5	484.2	D	1.2	D	13.8	3.2	24.8	26.8	6 007	5 879	5 458
Nome	184.7	45.9	20 508	75.4	47.2	125.5	D	1.1	93.6	7.7	5.6	29.9	42.1	1 400	1 577	2 336
North Slope	205.4	40.9	29 271	107.6	25.2	606.9	D	D	D	3.8	D	10.0	16.9	D	344	213
Northwest Arctic	140.0	47.9	20 700	76.1	37.2	128.9	D	.2	D	5.6	4.7	D	25.8	300	311	D
Prince of Wales- Outer Ketchikan	125.4	7.1	18 278	67.2	24.5	86.1	D	25.7	D	8.6	4.6	10.1	32.1	22 134	22 071	18 172
Sitka	236.5	20.6	28 480	104.7	33.6	170.3	D	5.0	D	9.6	2.1	26.1	33.8	8 495	9 034	12 311
Skagway-Yakutat-Angoon	109.6	17.2	51 438	189.1	19.1	70.7	27.0	19.9	D	11.7	D	14.7	31.5	14 075	24 943	21 964
Southeast Fairbanks	129.3	31.0	21 614	79.5	27.1	80.3	D	D	D	9.8	.5	11.9	61.7	D	659	689
Valdez-Cordova	289.8	21.0	28 256	103.9	37.1	243.3	19.9	7.0	80.1	5.6	2.3	12.6	23.6	17 000	21 452	22 112
Wade Hampton	87.1	45.7	12 684	46.6	38.8	46.0	D	1.1	D	7.6	3.5	9.7	63.9	492	D	663
Wrangell-Petersburg	177.0	4.8	25 983	95.5	31.4	115.7	23.3	17.8	D	8.5	3.0	7.6	33.9	20 614	18 695	19 286
Yukon-Koyukuk	113.6	−6.6	18 005	66.2	41.3	73.7	D	2.0	D	9.1	1.4	13.9	51.1	1 463	1 375	1 324
ARIZONA	112 973.9	78.4	24 206	89.0	15 261.1	79 155.1	21.8	13.5	77.2	10.4	9.5	28.6	15.9	10 709 917	9 634 054	8 774 355
Apache	811.7	53.7	11 809	43.4	304.9	525.4	D	1.7	D	5.6	D	35.9	41.8	9 166	9 567	13 584
Cochise	2 051.3	49.5	18 249	67.1	421.3	1 284.7	7.3	2.3	D	8.3	D	20.6	51.7	29 177	33 145	34 531
Coconino	2 204.0	67.5	20 020	73.0	313.9	1 553.5	14.3	7.5	85.5	13.3	4.3	27.6	32.9	116 029	107 999	109 043
Gila	887.8	63.5	18 178	66.8	253.8	459.1	D	17.3	70.9	11.1	4.7	26.3	21.0	79 432	81 187	82 935
Graham	447.6	63.9	14 115	51.9	119.6	228.4	D	2.9	D	14.4	2.1	20.5	42.3	6 632	6 107	5 520
Greenlee	180.0	70.9	19 305	71.0	29.8	185.9	D	.3	D	2.1	.4	2.0	9.1	517	424	584
La Paz	320.5	44.7	21 612	79.4	73.7	172.4	D	6.0	D	15.3	3.9	24.4	20.3	10 321	9 799	9 056
Maricopa	75 869.3	85.3	27 254	100.2	8 236.7	56 615.3	23.0	15.2	76.4	10.2	11.2	29.1	11.9	8 605 020	7 642 373	6 907 108
Mohave	2 487.4	72.9	19 039	70.0	584.8	1 102.4	19.8	8.9	79.8	16.6	5.9	28.1	18.2	98 031	86 409	81 049
Navajo	1 253.1	59.8	12 940	47.6	354.4	779.5	D	5.9	79.9	11.3	2.3	23.0	26.6	46 115	48 168	49 822
Pima	17 959.1	65.6	22 723	83.5	2 803.9	11 211.6	19.9	12.4	80.0	10.5	6.4	31.5	22.7	1 392 011	1 293 588	1 194 067
Pinal	2 340.8	64.3	15 930	58.6	628.6	1 430.5	27.1	7.6	64.8	9.7	2.4	18.9	27.4	109 052	112 410	110 100
Santa Cruz	600.0	65.5	15 725	57.8	100.4	401.6	D	7.7	D	12.3	2.9	15.4	28.0	30 756	29 409	27 519
Yavapai	3 070.7	84.6	20 643	75.9	610.6	1 433.3	22.5	7.7	76.9	13.6	6.7	29.3	18.4	110 773	115 619	97 506
Yuma	2 410.7	65.9	18 277	67.2	424.7	1 771.5	D	3.8	D	8.9	D	17.0	28.4	66 885	57 850	51 871
ARKANSAS	53 725.4	57.3	21 167	77.8	9 607.4	37 066.7	28.0	21.9	67.9	10.9	4.9	21.5	16.5	8 114 421	7 739 513	7 469 080
Arkansas	456.5	45.9	22 097	81.2	86.7	331.8	33.2	28.8	56.3	8.1	3.0	12.2	11.4	95 417	85 751	82 802
Ashley	492.7	49.4	20 245	74.4	100.9	380.7	D	38.8	D	6.3	2.1	D	9.2	185 643	178 997	181 670
Baxter	796.7	64.5	21 937	80.6	193.8	412.5	D	25.4	D	12.4	4.8	31.8	11.2	104 817	100 359	103 524
Benton	3 352.7	104.8	25 044	92.1	414.3	2 363.5	D	21.8	D	30.0	4.2	D	7.6	516 161	511 264	480 861
Boone	654.8	60.6	20 594	75.7	129.3	441.9	D	23.9	D	10.6	4.2	14.7	17.9	105 413	92 920	91 326
Bradley	236.3	39.9	20 716	76.2	62.8	133.5	D	40.6	D	7.1	2.7	16.1	15.4	54 277	51 593	47 359
Calhoun	89.6	32.5	15 764	57.9	21.8	112.4	D	69.6	D	2.0	D	3.2	13.4	78 301	73 287	63 860
Carroll	425.4	60.0	18 961	69.7	78.1	289.1	D	D	D	11.4	3.4	19.8	10.1	D	73 693	70 024
Chicot	240.0	45.7	15 975	58.7	69.1	131.8	D	D	D	7.5	3.8	12.7	25.1	D	19 798	18 661
Clark	416.1	52.9	19 277	70.9	93.1	273.3	34.0	32.0	62.7	10.3	3.7	19.6	20.7	87 538	85 534	82 334
Clay	305.1	44.0	17 820	65.5	78.6	171.6	39.6	35.5	D	7.5	D	8.7	14.3	60 999	56 398	49 463
Cleburne	440.7	69.2	19 252	70.8	100.3	207.8	33.3	24.7	60.1	12.3	3.5	20.0	12.1	51 266	46 400	40 208
Cleveland	155.9	67.2	18 510	68.0	29.8	44.5	D	13.1	D	4.9	D	9.8	21.4	5 844	5 964	6 175
Columbia	519.4	43.3	20 686	76.0	109.1	344.1	45.3	35.7	49.5	8.1	3.3	12.4	15.2	122 877	114 563	118 224
Conway	397.6	57.2	20 053	73.7	84.9	247.8	D	26.7	D	9.4	2.0	15.9	12.8	66 210	64 987	60 803
Craighead	1 603.5	63.4	20 771	76.4	252.7	1 205.0	D	22.2	69.0	10.8	4.4	27.2	14.9	267 693	243 518	226 486
Crawford	868.9	71.1	17 286	63.5	167.0	478.3	D	22.1	D	9.1	2.7	16.6	12.2	105 482	98 413	91 764
Crittenden	986.5	51.4	19 811	72.8	166.8	521.0	D	14.5	D	15.1	3.7	22.7	15.1	75 605	75 228	71 175
Cross	332.5	50.6	17 126	63.0	73.1	190.7	27.7	23.0	59.5	10.5	3.9	12.9	17.6	43 942	47 038	48 214
Dallas	179.5	35.9	19 835	72.9	46.9	114.6	47.0	41.5	51.5	9.6	2.2	18.0	11.3	47 564	45 935	40 511
Desha	258.4	39.5	17 142	63.0	65.0	186.4	D	24.8	D	8.5	3.1	12.2	18.1	46 257	43 772	42 332

[1] Based on resident population estimated as of July 1, 1998. [2] Includes farm earnings; see table B-10 for these data. [3] Includes mining and construction, not shown separately. [4] Includes agricultural services, forestry, and fisheries; transportation and public utilities; and wholesale trade, not shown separately. [5] Finance, insurance, and real estate.

Source: Personal Income and Earnings—U.S. Bureau of Economic Analysis, "Regional Economic Information System (REIS) 1969-1998" on CD-ROM (related Internet site <http://www.bea.doc.gov/bea/regional/data.htm>).

Table B–8. Counties — Personal Income and Earnings–Con.

[Includes U.S., states, and 3,142 counties/county equivalents defined as of January 1, 1992. For changes to these areas since January 1, 1992, see appendix B. Geographic Information]

County	Personal income, 1998 Total (mil. dol.)	Per capita Percent change, 1990–1998	Per capita Amount (dollars)	Per capita Percent of national average	Transfer payments (mil. dol.)	Earnings Total² (mil. dol.)	Goods-related Total³	Goods-related Manufacturing	Service-related Total⁴	Service-related Retail trade	Service-related FIRE⁵	Service-related Services	Service-related Government	Manufacturing earnings 1998 ($1,000)	Manufacturing earnings 1997 ($1,000)	Manufacturing earnings 1996 ($1,000)
ARKANSAS—Con.																
Drew	329.4	58.2	18 852	69.3	66.0	210.5	31.7	29.3	62.2	10.3	4.6	13.7	23.4	61 618	61 140	65 051
Faulkner	1 829.3	107.0	23 381	86.0	250.8	1 000.1	D	23.7	D	9.7	3.6	29.3	16.9	237 332	224 284	212 702
Franklin	301.4	64.7	17 917	65.9	65.4	165.4	D	17.2	57.5	6.9	3.9	11.7	24.8	28 498	29 547	30 396
Fulton	152.9	51.0	13 972	51.4	47.3	57.0	21.0	13.0	D	9.5	D	19.6	24.7	7 403	6 410	5 996
Garland	1 999.5	63.2	23 900	87.9	424.4	1 022.5	23.0	12.6	75.5	13.8	5.4	33.2	13.4	129 023	123 126	118 015
Grant	312.0	57.4	19 691	72.4	47.3	125.6	D	43.8	D	7.4	2.2	9.8	18.0	55 066	53 280	49 063
Greene	652.2	70.3	18 112	66.6	126.7	427.3	D	44.0	D	9.9	2.4	17.2	11.1	188 184	169 663	160 782
Hempstead	411.5	59.0	18 675	68.7	85.9	284.9	D	33.1	D	7.3	2.6	16.1	15.8	94 278	99 440	88 737
Hot Spring	488.0	49.3	16 900	62.1	116.1	233.0	40.6	32.1	57.6	9.7	3.6	13.1	20.5	74 779	71 110	70 952
Howard	292.1	49.3	21 348	78.5	56.0	260.3	49.0	46.7	35.0	5.9	1.6	9.5	9.1	121 449	118 179	115 749
Independence	662.8	52.3	20 142	74.0	129.7	498.3	38.3	33.5	58.3	8.7	2.4	20.8	11.0	167 000	156 603	153 793
Izard	210.7	44.5	16 070	59.1	63.8	93.9	D	20.3	D	11.6	4.9	17.0	24.3	19 060	17 376	12 902
Jackson	347.3	48.4	19 597	72.0	97.6	203.5	D	23.1	D	8.9	D	24.4	12.0	46 954	43 554	45 279
Jefferson	1 579.3	31.6	19 357	71.2	319.4	1 171.0	27.3	24.0	71.3	9.1	3.7	21.0	24.5	280 675	265 210	247 751
Johnson	376.3	74.6	17 537	64.5	79.9	232.8	D	36.3	D	15.4	3.0	15.3	12.7	84 452	81 225	76 432
Lafayette	145.4	37.6	16 261	59.8	37.8	74.1	28.8	20.3	46.6	6.4	3.9	9.0	17.3	15 011	14 862	13 253
Lawrence	291.7	50.2	16 950	62.3	79.4	158.4	28.2	21.8	59.3	10.6	2.6	11.9	20.3	34 543	37 144	34 877
Lee	175.9	39.7	13 620	50.1	54.1	84.1	D	8.8	D	8.5	2.5	15.0	29.8	7 422	6 250	8 487
Lincoln	198.5	64.3	13 858	50.9	43.9	118.5	D	14.1	D	4.5	1.7	8.7	32.8	16 715	16 600	16 917
Little River	271.6	31.3	20 648	75.9	50.2	208.4	D	50.4	D	4.8	1.8	5.3	10.8	104 968	102 818	102 862
Logan	394.8	53.4	18 714	68.8	98.5	209.8	D	33.1	D	9.0	2.8	12.7	17.5	69 477	69 124	66 917
Lonoke	1 046.3	86.1	20 925	76.9	148.9	330.0	27.3	18.0	D	12.5	4.3	16.4	17.6	59 280	52 390	56 397
Madison	243.4	68.3	18 380	67.6	44.2	118.4	27.9	21.2	40.2	6.3	2.3	10.8	14.0	25 086	22 954	23 802
Marion	240.3	62.7	16 172	59.4	63.5	104.9	D	39.7	D	8.7	4.3	14.6	15.5	41 608	39 020	37 158
Miller	724.2	45.6	18 321	67.3	143.3	453.7	36.2	27.6	60.7	11.1	3.4	17.7	12.9	125 322	127 854	136 234
Mississippi	954.7	24.1	18 899	69.5	196.5	734.1	D	45.6	D	7.7	3.0	13.8	11.6	334 806	339 030	322 183
Monroe	175.2	40.2	17 300	63.6	51.2	90.2	D	10.5	D	12.9	4.1	14.7	17.4	9 437	8 890	9 982
Montgomery	144.2	58.0	16 679	61.3	36.9	66.4	D	19.9	D	7.6	3.4	11.5	20.5	13 244	12 365	11 641
Nevada	173.4	50.3	17 369	63.8	44.4	83.6	D	D	D	7.1	1.9	12.1	17.2	D	25 842	22 722
Newton	109.3	55.4	13 388	49.2	32.8	32.0	D	13.1	D	8.6	D	16.1	41.7	4 190	3 564	3 458
Ouachita	520.9	25.7	18 752	68.9	129.3	257.4	31.3	25.7	67.5	11.6	3.7	20.5	18.6	66 186	71 386	74 558
Perry	148.5	53.0	15 422	56.7	35.9	51.1	D	7.6	D	8.3	D	15.7	24.1	3 879	5 241	6 090
Phillips	413.4	32.0	15 140	55.7	137.3	234.3	D	14.9	D	10.2	3.8	23.2	21.7	34 869	34 127	34 970
Pike	200.6	59.5	19 021	69.9	41.7	109.5	24.4	18.1	55.7	10.8	4.2	10.4	17.0	19 832	19 410	16 701
Poinsett	438.6	52.5	17 804	65.4	101.5	233.6	D	26.2	52.8	7.5	4.3	10.6	15.1	61 279	63 028	64 107
Polk	345.4	62.1	17 577	64.6	80.3	214.9	31.8	27.7	49.2	8.8	2.8	15.1	13.9	59 506	55 108	50 454
Pope	1 049.9	59.4	20 174	74.2	177.3	803.2	D	21.1	D	9.5	3.0	18.2	12.9	169 810	167 872	154 625
Prairie	160.1	49.4	17 137	63.0	39.1	70.9	14.3	9.9	55.6	8.1	2.0	12.5	16.9	7 003	6 349	6 582
Pulaski	9 922.0	48.7	28 445	104.6	1 231.3	9 346.2	13.9	9.0	86.1	8.4	8.6	27.1	22.4	839 269	805 032	792 110
Randolph	280.2	52.4	15 754	57.9	73.2	152.0	36.0	30.2	56.3	9.8	3.7	17.3	16.4	45 965	44 854	44 390
St. Francis	478.4	50.7	17 010	62.5	120.7	307.8	D	22.7	D	9.5	2.8	16.9	25.5	69 950	59 864	49 947
Saline	1 670.0	76.8	21 645	79.6	250.4	540.7	D	17.1	D	16.9	4.0	21.4	21.1	92 645	90 391	92 278
Scott	201.9	77.2	19 075	70.1	43.3	125.5	34.2	31.9	35.4	6.7	1.8	9.0	11.0	40 016	37 569	35 243
Searcy	123.3	54.7	15 935	58.6	38.3	52.8	D	15.7	D	10.7	D	16.3	25.9	8 319	8 361	8 738
Sebastian	2 611.8	55.2	24 664	90.7	379.6	2 422.2	37.4	31.0	62.0	8.7	3.9	29.7	18.8	750 157	706 815	689 548
Sevier	282.4	54.0	19 334	71.1	52.4	192.5	D	32.0	44.4	6.7	2.2	13.5	12.7	61 522	59 515	52 195
Sharp	278.0	63.1	16 448	60.5	90.3	111.4	D	8.0	D	14.7	5.6	20.5	19.0	8 889	8 693	8 467
Stone	185.5	69.9	16 721	61.5	52.0	92.3	25.5	20.7	57.3	13.2	2.7	17.0	18.0	19 059	16 588	17 914
Union	1 057.1	36.0	23 373	85.9	193.8	728.3	45.9	31.2	52.2	8.5	3.7	17.2	10.5	227 127	207 470	199 113
Van Buren	254.7	55.1	16 397	60.3	76.5	98.4	23.9	17.2	69.9	13.3	6.3	20.5	18.4	16 907	17 857	17 752
Washington	3 031.7	66.1	20 910	76.9	389.3	2 496.4	28.9	22.6	67.5	10.2	4.5	19.7	17.1	563 771	514 476	495 689
White	1 127.9	64.4	17 452	64.2	225.2	695.1	D	21.0	D	17.9	2.8	25.3	11.8	146 103	138 276	134 185
Woodruff	151.3	40.2	17 123	62.9	44.7	85.7	D	20.5	D	5.3	2.6	8.4	17.1	17 590	18 629	16 813
Yell	349.3	53.6	18 399	67.6	77.7	209.5	D	36.0	D	6.4	3.4	9.5	18.0	75 515	68 336	68 345
CALIFORNIA	920 452.2	40.4	28 163	103.5	109 387.7	677 217.3	20.8	15.2	78.0	8.8	8.9	31.6	15.6	102 939 260	95 856 549	87 524 160
Alameda	44 887.2	49.9	32 130	118.1	4 762.5	33 728.2	22.9	16.3	77.1	8.7	5.4	29.7	17.6	5 510 217	5 099 534	4 519 763
Alpine	27.0	27.8	22 688	83.4	6.0	23.9	D	D	D	2.9	D	61.8	19.9	D	(6)	D
Amador	692.4	39.0	20 721	76.2	134.2	362.5	16.9	10.1	82.5	14.1	3.8	27.0	26.2	36 581	38 642	42 942
Butte	4 049.8	40.3	20 838	76.6	888.3	2 299.1	14.4	8.1	84.2	13.0	6.1	32.3	21.7	185 297	186 141	165 605
Calaveras	799.7	42.4	20 172	74.2	173.5	300.3	D	5.1	D	11.5	7.5	26.5	25.3	15 409	14 351	13 411
Colusa	377.3	30.1	20 287	74.6	64.8	255.5	13.0	10.2	57.5	10.1	1.9	10.9	16.5	26 018	25 123	27 675
Contra Costa	33 052.4	51.8	36 006	132.4	2 966.8	17 491.3	21.0	12.1	78.9	9.7	12.4	31.4	11.7	2 108 653	1 870 941	1 802 972
Del Norte	442.5	33.4	16 385	60.2	119.4	266.1	10.8	6.3	84.1	10.4	2.2	21.7	39.3	16 643	17 310	15 005
El Dorado	4 282.0	63.8	27 046	99.4	493.0	1 688.2	19.6	6.1	80.4	12.3	6.3	35.6	18.2	103 313	105 824	98 006

[1] Based on resident population estimated as of July 1, 1998.   [2] Includes farm earnings; see table B-10 for these data.   [3] Includes mining and construction, not shown separately.   [4] Includes agricultural services, forestry, and fisheries; transportation and public utilities; and wholesale trade, not shown separately.   [5] Finance, insurance, and real estate.   [6] Less than $50,000.

Source: Personal Income and Earnings—U.S. Bureau of Economic Analysis, "Regional Economic Information System (REIS) 1969-1998" on CD-ROM (related Internet site <http://www.bea.doc.gov/bea/regional/data.htm>).

[Includes U.S., states, and 3,142 counties/county equivalents defined as of January 1, 1992. For changes to these areas since January 1, 1992, see appendix B. Geographic Information]

County	Personal income, 1998													Manufacturing earnings		
	Total (mil. dol.)	Per capita[1]			Transfer payments (mil. dol.)	Earnings								1998 ($1,000)	1997 ($1,000)	1996 ($1,000)
		Percent change, 1990–1998	Amount (dollars)	Percent of national average		Total[2] (mil. dol.)	Percent, by selected industry—									
							Goods-related		Service-related							
							Total[3]	Manu-facturing	Total[4]	Retail trade	FIRE[5]	Serv-ices	Gov-ern-ment			
CALIFORNIA—Con.																
Fresno	15 352.3	34.9	20 333	74.7	2 879.6	10 644.5	15.9	9.5	78.9	10.0	6.6	24.2	20.7	1 006 513	948 500	892 156
Glenn	441.9	21.7	16 882	62.1	101.1	266.1	28.1	17.3	67.2	8.2	2.1	13.1	26.4	45 924	51 429	44 562
Humboldt	2 695.6	37.1	22 066	81.1	528.3	1 728.3	D	14.8	D	12.4	5.1	25.2	22.1	255 024	251 973	252 678
Imperial	2 494.2	40.0	17 353	63.8	511.4	1 828.2	D	3.2	D	9.1	D	12.2	30.5	58 429	52 547	47 996
Inyo	424.1	26.3	23 468	86.3	81.0	247.3	12.9	3.6	88.4	15.5	2.5	25.8	34.9	8 837	9 056	8 440
Kern	12 406.9	36.3	19 643	72.2	2 146.4	9 041.1	19.4	5.3	76.4	8.8	4.0	20.1	25.7	477 781	438 769	424 695
Kings	1 838.4	35.5	15 492	56.9	342.8	1 330.6	D	9.5	D	9.1	D	14.3	43.3	126 619	135 085	115 939
Lake	1 194.9	38.6	21 696	79.8	319.8	445.6	D	4.0	D	13.8	4.9	30.0	24.1	17 718	15 745	16 534
Lassen	554.7	49.9	16 667	61.3	105.3	360.4	D	7.6	D	8.9	D	14.3	54.4	27 415	23 570	24 542
Los Angeles	246 949.2	26.2	26 773	98.4	32 720.7	200 847.0	18.8	15.0	81.1	8.2	9.6	36.5	12.9	30 184 599	28 724 644	26 973 576
Madera	1 993.0	49.9	17 403	64.0	409.4	1 184.1	D	11.7	D	9.7	D	22.5	22.5	138 579	133 711	125 607
Marin	12 497.0	51.5	52 869	194.3	736.6	6 186.5	D	4.6	D	10.8	14.8	44.0	9.8	287 101	248 429	236 697
Mariposa	335.2	34.7	21 231	78.0	72.4	170.7	D	3.7	D	8.5	2.7	38.5	39.4	6 297	6 210	6 365
Mendocino	1 903.5	40.2	22 728	83.5	370.9	1 105.0	D	16.5	D	14.4	3.6	25.4	18.4	182 128	193 839	174 534
Merced	3 497.8	28.3	17 732	65.2	755.6	2 178.5	22.1	17.6	63.4	10.5	3.7	16.4	19.2	383 958	353 335	336 715
Modoc	186.8	27.1	20 005	73.5	46.5	97.3	D	D	D	8.9	3.0	13.6	43.5	D	2 003	2 047
Mono	257.9	38.7	25 020	92.0	22.0	198.3	10.7	.9	90.0	16.9	6.6	35.4	27.8	1 716	1 647	1 717
Monterey	10 333.3	39.5	28 185	103.6	1 132.6	7 102.0	10.2	5.3	74.3	8.8	6.4	22.4	21.3	379 541	351 141	355 793
Napa	3 902.8	49.7	32 649	120.0	453.2	2 312.5	D	18.8	D	9.6	6.0	28.6	15.1	433 765	379 893	345 629
Nevada	2 282.5	54.2	25 051	92.1	346.2	1 037.3	24.7	11.8	75.5	14.2	7.2	29.7	17.2	122 058	120 963	110 828
Orange	88 634.5	43.1	32 541	119.6	7 140.4	65 281.6	24.0	18.0	75.7	9.3	12.1	30.0	9.6	11 767 476	10 692 324	9 816 785
Placer	7 408.1	86.5	32 319	118.8	723.4	4 037.2	27.3	15.5	72.7	13.6	8.6	26.1	12.4	625 465	564 322	502 440
Plumas	484.3	42.5	23 783	87.4	95.2	272.7	21.8	13.9	73.0	10.8	4.5	15.7	27.9	37 886	36 492	33 971
Riverside	33 243.5	46.9	22 451	82.5	4 920.3	16 333.5	22.7	12.0	74.4	12.0	5.8	26.5	20.0	1 960 286	1 710 708	1 567 435
Sacramento	30 634.5	42.3	26 257	96.5	4 552.1	24 433.2	13.6	7.7	86.1	8.0	9.3	26.2	33.6	1 871 534	1 659 587	1 518 514
San Benito	1 033.0	57.9	21 088	77.5	119.3	564.6	D	13.2	D	10.9	3.9	15.0	17.6	74 633	76 808	73 770
San Bernardino	33 141.7	33.3	20 258	74.5	5 153.9	19 531.7	19.8	12.4	78.8	11.7	5.3	24.2	22.9	2 414 003	2 233 815	2 111 220
San Diego	76 501.9	44.0	27 657	101.7	8 697.4	54 384.7	17.8	12.0	81.5	9.4	8.2	30.7	23.9	6 541 740	5 935 874	5 470 404
San Francisco	33 199.3	47.1	44 518	163.7	3 097.9	37 464.2	7.8	4.8	92.2	6.7	21.8	37.1	13.5	1 792 719	1 738 360	1 652 286
San Joaquin	11 440.4	39.1	20 813	76.5	2 154.0	7 166.4	20.5	13.6	74.9	10.6	6.6	21.7	19.4	975 178	958 525	916 663
San Luis Obispo	5 806.6	49.2	24 807	91.2	792.0	3 528.8	17.3	8.1	79.5	13.0	6.1	25.8	21.9	287 438	271 304	257 353
San Mateo	30 383.5	54.2	43 338	159.3	1 947.2	21 655.0	18.3	12.3	81.4	9.0	9.7	36.5	6.8	2 669 593	2 300 647	2 111 093
Santa Barbara	11 177.2	31.3	28 698	105.5	1 199.0	7 303.5	18.4	11.6	77.1	10.2	6.7	31.4	19.1	844 490	867 481	808 876
Santa Clara	67 033.6	70.9	40 828	150.1	4 382.5	62 529.7	40.4	35.9	59.4	5.9	4.0	32.3	7.3	22 462 045	20 948 318	17 993 441
Santa Cruz	7 612.6	50.4	31 302	115.1	722.1	4 199.7	21.4	14.5	73.2	11.6	5.1	30.5	15.4	607 220	639 553	650 086
Shasta	3 609.1	39.5	21 986	80.8	779.2	2 249.6	D	9.2	D	12.5	4.0	30.3	19.2	207 512	216 801	203 342
Sierra	78.2	41.7	23 175	85.2	13.9	41.3	D	D	D	5.6	D	10.3	51.6	D	9 813	D
Siskiyou	901.4	30.0	20 474	75.3	226.5	501.3	D	9.5	80.9	12.7	3.8	21.0	27.8	47 448	53 904	49 486
Solano	8 938.1	32.9	23 724	87.2	1 060.0	4 489.2	20.6	10.5	78.8	12.7	3.6	22.4	30.6	472 808	445 189	390 858
Sonoma	13 408.3	51.1	30 911	113.6	1 435.7	7 849.7	27.2	17.9	71.2	11.0	8.4	27.3	13.7	1 403 152	1 186 697	1 038 939
Stanislaus	9 022.2	42.4	21 136	77.7	1 545.6	5 715.9	D	19.2	D	10.9	4.2	23.0	16.6	1 099 685	1 037 840	962 387
Sutter	1 692.8	51.8	21 965	80.7	290.3	875.9	16.6	8.7	74.5	13.7	4.9	24.6	17.3	75 966	70 702	64 825
Tehama	950.7	42.6	17 600	64.7	237.2	488.5	23.9	18.6	73.2	17.1	4.4	20.2	21.8	90 999	90 966	81 462
Trinity	244.0	29.2	18 704	68.8	67.2	102.8	D	12.1	D	10.6	2.9	16.8	44.2	12 395	13 343	15 663
Tulare	6 698.2	43.7	18 893	69.5	1 331.5	4 439.9	14.3	9.3	71.1	10.8	4.0	15.8	20.5	414 307	388 343	363 907
Tuolumne	1 064.9	33.3	20 082	73.8	233.2	513.3	18.6	8.9	82.0	14.3	4.1	27.3	29.6	45 462	44 010	44 136
Ventura	21 020.3	39.0	28 711	105.5	2 006.8	12 342.1	20.2	13.3	76.2	9.9	6.6	30.3	17.9	1 643 841	1 546 338	1 309 024
Yolo	3 953.6	41.0	25 791	94.8	483.9	3 476.3	14.6	8.3	82.0	10.7	4.5	16.8	30.9	288 071	277 376	278 301
Yuba	983.5	25.2	16 405	60.3	289.8	717.0	12.9	6.6	84.2	6.6	2.1	16.3	50.4	47 123	40 717	45 499
COLORADO	119 043.7	82.9	29 994	110.3	11 098.4	90 240.5	20.3	11.0	78.9	9.0	9.0	28.6	16.0	9 915 018	9 169 829	8 532 923
Adams	7 611.3	77.8	23 533	86.5	915.8	5 131.8	28.0	15.8	71.6	11.5	3.9	16.3	14.4	810 659	733 554	641 671
Alamosa	288.8	51.3	19 858	73.0	55.8	210.8	D	1.1	D	13.0	4.4	27.3	29.0	2 310	2 197	2 130
Arapahoe	18 115.5	87.8	38 333	140.9	986.2	13 986.5	14.1	5.2	85.9	8.2	13.7	33.2	8.4	721 842	687 863	623 235
Archuleta	154.9	121.5	16 919	62.2	22.9	87.0	21.4	2.1	80.2	17.3	14.7	22.6	17.5	1 824	1 516	1 431
Baca	113.0	30.4	26 120	96.0	18.5	72.4	D	.8	D	6.9	1.5	5.8	23.0	603	607	529
Bent	98.0	34.1	16 894	62.1	23.2	62.3	D	D	D	4.3	2.8	D	60.9	D	169	D
Boulder	9 619.2	91.5	36 071	132.6	556.2	7 739.7	28.9	23.2	71.0	7.7	4.9	37.0	12.9	1 793 973	1 578 880	1 432 580
Chaffee	298.3	76.2	19 655	72.3	56.2	161.6	D	4.7	D	16.8	7.2	20.7	31.4	7 630	7 440	7 761
Cheyenne	58.1	25.2	25 031	92.0	8.6	40.4	D	D	D	4.6	D	5.5	21.0	D	233	244
Clear Creek	261.7	87.6	29 018	106.7	18.0	107.6	D	1.2	D	11.3	3.3	D	19.8	1 258	1 330	1 440
Conejos	110.8	51.7	13 880	51.0	36.4	49.3	D	4.2	D	8.8	2.5	23.1	32.9	2 056	2 322	2 471
Costilla	57.0	52.3	15 662	57.6	18.7	20.5	D	1.6	D	5.3	D	8.2	42.5	319	281	D
Crowley	72.1	51.7	16 713	61.4	17.2	51.0	D	–	D	4.2	D	9.3	35.8	–	–	–
Custer	63.0	117.0	18 336	67.4	10.2	23.6	33.0	2.8	D	12.6	6.1	17.9	25.1	673	743	759

[1] Based on resident population estimated as of July 1, 1998.   [2] Includes farm earnings; see table B-10 for these data.   [3] Includes mining and construction, not shown separately.   [4] Includes agricultural services, forestry, and fisheries; transportation and public utilities; and wholesale trade, not shown separately.   [5] Finance, insurance, and real estate.

Source: Personal Income and Earnings—U.S. Bureau of Economic Analysis, "Regional Economic Information System (REIS) 1969-1998" on CD-ROM (related Internet site <http://www.bea.doc.gov/bea/regional/data.htm>).

[Includes U.S., states, and 3,142 counties/county equivalents defined as of January 1, 1992. For changes to these areas since January 1, 1992, see appendix B. Geographic Information]

County	Personal income, 1998													Manufacturing earnings		
	Total (mil. dol.)	Per capita[1]			Transfer payments (mil. dol.)	Earnings								1998 ($1,000)	1997 ($1,000)	1996 ($1,000)
		Percent change, 1990–1998	Amount (dollars)	Percent of national average		Total[2] (mil. dol.)	Percent, by selected industry–									
							Goods-related		Service-related							
							Total[3]	Manufacturing	Total[4]	Retail trade	FIRE[5]	Services	Government			
COLORADO—Con.																
Delta	486.6	79.4	18 270	67.2	114.5	217.5	D	6.0	D	12.7	4.8	20.8	27.5	12 992	11 319	10 884
Denver	18 774.6	69.8	37 670	138.5	2 085.3	22 992.3	14.4	6.4	85.6	6.0	11.9	30.4	14.4	1 469 129	1 413 394	1 382 879
Dolores	33.4	56.5	18 363	67.5	7.2	16.5	D	D	D	7.0	D	5.4	23.8	D	264	200
Douglas	4 821.7	214.7	34 088	125.3	160.7	1 647.1	21.2	6.0	78.9	17.3	9.4	23.9	12.7	98 250	88 915	85 053
Eagle	1 247.2	151.5	37 000	136.0	34.8	1 056.0	D	2.9	D	14.9	17.8	32.1	7.9	30 828	26 042	28 808
Elbert	452.5	163.8	24 311	89.4	38.1	90.9	D	3.3	D	8.6	6.8	19.7	26.5	2 956	2 651	2 470
El Paso	12 873.3	82.0	26 270	96.6	1 256.1	9 748.2	18.6	11.6	81.5	8.4	6.1	27.9	28.5	1 129 899	1 035 346	977 693
Fremont	744.6	86.0	16 837	61.9	150.3	445.1	16.9	7.6	82.8	9.0	3.0	17.8	47.0	33 608	32 389	29 982
Garfield	945.5	84.2	24 011	88.3	88.3	647.1	26.1	2.7	73.7	14.8	7.4	25.3	17.1	17 263	15 735	16 212
Gilpin	123.7	146.9	29 565	108.7	7.1	143.4	D	D	D	1.8	.4	84.5	8.4	D	561	485
Grand	257.6	87.8	25 504	93.8	20.9	178.5	16.0	2.1	D	14.4	12.9	31.8	18.6	3 821	3 243	3 370
Gunnison	268.0	89.6	21 572	79.3	22.6	209.4	26.1	1.5	75.1	15.9	8.3	23.1	23.1	3 181	4 144	3 901
Hinsdale	16.1	92.0	21 807	80.2	1.7	8.1	D	D	D	19.2	11.9	25.3	21.2	D	225	244
Huerfano	127.2	86.0	18 739	68.9	38.3	61.8	D	6.2	D	12.3	4.9	36.9	20.9	3 852	3 789	3 266
Jackson	28.1	25.7	18 477	67.9	4.6	14.3	D	10.8	D	15.7	D	12.0	36.7	1 545	1 032	1 995
Jefferson	16 700.6	77.8	33 348	122.6	1 109.0	9 063.0	26.0	16.9	74.0	10.9	7.5	27.7	16.1	1 528 481	1 463 483	1 393 702
Kiowa	57.3	43.8	34 789	127.9	6.2	44.1	D	D	D	2.4	D	3.4	14.6	D	202	254
Kit Carson	194.1	37.7	26 550	97.6	25.0	126.2	D	4.1	53.4	8.9	3.1	10.5	15.5	5 186	4 623	4 276
Lake	151.8	69.4	23 898	87.9	16.0	62.8	D	1.7	D	11.8	4.0	24.0	31.9	1 092	870	748
La Plata	1 022.7	95.1	25 241	92.8	99.9	681.0	18.6	3.5	81.7	13.1	7.6	33.6	18.0	24 099	21 927	20 935
Larimer	6 380.0	92.7	27 607	101.5	558.9	4 338.8	35.2	25.4	64.3	10.8	5.5	22.1	19.6	1 103 588	976 273	885 152
Las Animas	255.5	51.9	17 561	64.6	80.2	142.0	14.5	2.7	88.5	11.4	5.0	20.5	32.7	3 835	3 557	3 096
Lincoln	98.9	31.2	17 395	63.9	17.2	62.1	3.9	.9	92.1	14.2	3.9	13.3	47.4	570	429	552
Logan	446.9	43.5	24 969	91.8	66.2	293.2	14.1	5.1	73.2	10.5	4.5	20.9	17.1	15 023	21 636	25 308
Mesa	2 539.2	75.4	22 491	82.7	409.6	1 599.3	19.9	8.3	79.4	13.5	6.0	28.2	18.7	133 218	132 800	107 637
Mineral	15.2	68.5	21 595	79.4	2.2	10.7	D	D	D	9.7	D	46.7	24.0	D	266	253
Moffat	266.1	45.2	21 179	77.9	33.9	177.5	26.3	1.3	74.3	11.5	2.2	16.1	23.6	2 219	2 878	2 542
Montezuma	457.7	72.3	20 464	75.2	76.1	281.5	D	4.3	D	12.7	4.1	25.5	20.0	12 103	11 078	12 023
Montrose	644.2	82.1	20 924	76.9	104.2	405.3	24.2	9.8	74.8	13.3	4.6	19.6	22.3	39 681	36 790	31 168
Morgan	544.4	49.6	21 699	79.8	82.5	383.9	29.3	22.0	58.1	7.1	4.5	15.7	16.5	84 459	80 125	72 251
Otero	407.7	45.2	19 729	72.5	114.4	223.3	13.1	9.5	82.0	10.3	4.1	23.4	24.7	21 263	19 892	19 256
Ouray	76.1	94.6	22 932	84.3	8.2	37.2	D	3.0	D	14.3	7.7	22.8	21.3	1 112	1 029	978
Park	309.4	146.4	23 081	84.8	23.3	71.4	25.4	1.6	75.5	8.5	5.8	21.9	29.8	1 174	1 020	1 034
Phillips	103.5	30.1	24 075	88.5	16.5	66.6	7.3	1.3	D	5.8	3.0	D	19.2	874	865	885
Pitkin	789.0	93.0	59 123	217.3	20.0	643.0	D	1.8	D	16.4	15.6	38.5	10.2	11 364	9 913	8 733
Prowers	313.2	51.1	22 853	84.0	54.7	216.2	17.8	12.6	57.1	9.9	3.5	11.4	21.5	27 214	24 118	19 403
Pueblo	2 884.5	63.1	21 379	78.6	721.9	1 722.8	20.6	12.0	79.5	13.7	7.0	26.0	22.5	206 460	198 189	191 715
Rio Blanco	139.3	48.2	22 236	81.7	17.1	114.0	54.3	.7	D	4.4	2.1	9.2	25.9	820	728	1 112
Rio Grande	234.6	40.0	20 450	75.2	46.4	144.8	11.8	6.7	72.6	7.6	4.6	13.1	20.7	9 688	10 159	8 658
Routt	556.1	84.6	31 795	116.9	26.7	428.4	31.3	1.6	69.7	12.5	8.9	26.7	11.8	6 785	6 014	5 768
Saguache	86.3	50.2	14 257	52.4	16.9	52.4	D	1.7	D	6.2	2.0	7.6	30.4	871	1 597	807
San Juan	11.6	−7.2	22 141	81.4	1.6	8.5	D	D	D	30.5	D	7.3	27.2	D	194	213
San Miguel	174.7	140.8	32 069	117.9	7.4	154.0	D	3.0	D	13.1	21.4	28.4	13.7	4 659	3 761	3 654
Sedgwick	65.1	37.5	25 505	93.8	13.2	37.7	D	D	D	8.3	2.7	8.6	21.0	D	1 251	836
Summit	685.7	131.7	36 508	134.2	20.7	578.3	D	1.3	D	17.7	13.9	36.8	10.0	7 483	5 844	4 586
Teller	501.8	131.2	24 415	89.8	39.7	206.7	D	4.2	D	8.6	7.8	41.0	16.6	8 762	6 881	5 239
Washington	109.1	15.5	23 977	88.1	17.2	66.0	D	3.3	D	7.0	2.5	5.6	19.9	2 209	2 004	1 738
Weld	3 477.6	67.9	21 803	80.1	439.3	2 433.4	31.1	20.3	61.2	8.3	7.1	18.7	14.9	493 408	460 210	434 130
Yuma	222.2	10.6	23 546	86.6	31.6	144.1	D	1.8	D	6.8	4.3	9.4	17.3	2 567	3 039	2 195
CONNECTICUT	122 190.7	39.0	37 338	137.3	14 121.6	86 121.4	25.1	20.1	74.7	7.5	13.7	29.5	11.9	17 311 162	16 436 269	15 337 069
Fairfield	43 436.8	51.4	51 866	190.7	3 529.0	30 193.5	D	20.8	D	7.0	18.5	29.8	6.8	6 278 232	5 966 222	5 563 619
Hartford	28 592.7	29.2	34 544	127.0	3 883.9	24 628.1	D	17.9	D	7.0	18.1	27.1	13.4	4 412 858	4 149 339	3 821 266
Litchfield	5 786.4	33.9	31 914	117.3	627.0	2 901.1	38.4	27.7	60.8	9.8	3.9	28.0	11.3	803 293	805 226	755 316
Middlesex	4 995.3	38.5	33 298	122.4	512.9	3 005.6	29.3	23.4	70.3	8.0	12.5	26.3	14.6	702 493	660 843	563 695
New Haven	25 601.8	35.4	32 290	118.7	3 777.4	16 683.3	D	19.6	D	8.4	6.1	33.0	13.0	3 264 587	3 117 781	2 934 381
New London	7 392.3	33.8	29 933	110.0	979.0	5 747.7	27.1	22.0	72.3	7.4	2.7	33.6	19.9	1 265 524	1 176 522	1 184 674
Tolland	3 729.7	33.6	28 393	104.4	375.9	1 583.8	20.4	12.1	78.3	9.2	3.9	23.9	35.3	191 029	178 595	159 353
Windham	2 655.8	34.7	25 328	93.1	436.6	1 378.4	34.9	28.5	64.2	10.8	3.4	23.8	18.3	393 146	381 741	354 765
DELAWARE	21 863.1	51.0	29 383	108.0	2 551.7	16 947.2	28.7	22.7	70.6	8.4	14.9	24.5	14.0	3 843 055	3 660 919	3 553 879
Kent	2 757.0	48.9	22 178	81.5	398.6	1 937.5	D	12.8	D	10.5	4.1	18.4	39.4	248 306	240 849	272 067
New Castle	15 982.9	49.9	33 121	121.8	1 540.0	13 151.1	D	24.5	D	7.1	17.4	25.8	10.4	3 224 842	3 066 677	2 932 593
Sussex	3 123.3	59.0	22 766	83.7	613.1	1 858.6	29.0	19.9	66.6	14.7	8.8	21.5	12.5	369 907	353 393	349 219
DISTRICT OF COLUMBIA	18 987.9	18.1	36 415	133.9	2 584.3	40 652.7	D	2.3	96.6	2.2	5.7	39.4	43.6	941 922	901 726	867 065
District of Columbia	18 987.9	18.1	36 415	133.9	2 584.3	40 652.7	D	2.3	96.6	2.2	5.7	39.4	43.6	941 922	901 726	867 065

[1] Based on resident population estimated as of July 1, 1998. [2] Includes farm earnings; see table B-10 for these data. [3] Includes mining and construction, not shown separately. [4] Includes agricultural services, forestry, and fisheries; transportation and public utilities; and wholesale trade, not shown separately. [5] Finance, insurance, and real estate.

Source: Personal Income and Earnings—U.S. Bureau of Economic Analysis, "Regional Economic Information System (REIS) 1969-1998" on CD-ROM (related Internet site <http://www.bea.doc.gov/bea/regional/data.htm>).

[Includes U.S., states, and 3,142 counties/county equivalents defined as of January 1, 1992. For changes to these areas since January 1, 1992, see appendix B. Geographic Information]

County	Personal income, 1998													Manufacturing earnings		
			Per capita[1]			Earnings										
							Percent, by selected industry–									
							Goods-related		Service-related							
	Total (mil. dol.)	Percent change, 1990–1998	Amount (dollars)	Percent of national average	Transfer payments (mil. dol.)	Total[2] (mil. dol.)	Total[3]	Manufacturing	Total[4]	Retail trade	FIRE[5]	Services	Government	1998 ($1,000)	1997 ($1,000)	1996 ($1,000)
FLORIDA	400 208.5	54.8	26 845	98.7	62 522.9	248 372.2	14.4	8.2	84.6	11.0	9.9	33.0	17.0	20 489 647	19 431 632	18 637 071
Alachua	4 887.3	56.1	24 656	90.6	692.6	3 700.7	D	5.2	D	9.3	6.5	30.4	38.0	193 603	191 129	182 164
Baker	382.9	55.7	18 191	66.9	69.7	166.4	10.8	5.6	83.2	9.4	2.8	11.6	51.4	9 391	8 657	8 155
Bay	3 252.0	60.6	22 163	81.5	547.5	2 213.7	16.2	6.9	83.8	12.7	5.7	26.9	28.3	153 159	130 029	105 007
Bradford	419.6	56.8	16 893	62.1	87.1	202.7	13.9	10.1	D	10.6	2.9	D	40.2	20 571	18 496	16 124
Brevard	11 043.3	47.5	23 758	87.3	1 936.6	6 790.3	D	19.9	D	9.6	4.1	35.9	17.9	1 347 983	1 293 864	1 242 827
Broward	43 040.5	45.0	28 546	104.9	5 934.7	24 224.9	13.6	7.3	86.3	12.8	10.9	33.2	14.9	1 758 256	1 714 971	1 741 913
Calhoun	190.9	55.4	15 380	56.5	52.2	103.0	17.3	8.0	79.5	9.9	2.2	25.9	29.9	8 261	8 712	8 177
Charlotte	3 200.9	56.4	23 752	87.3	791.1	1 109.6	D	2.7	D	16.9	6.7	38.4	16.7	30 399	29 675	27 892
Citrus	2 259.0	53.9	19 878	73.1	662.6	852.7	D	4.2	D	13.5	6.3	33.6	15.5	35 558	31 036	30 164
Clay	3 235.7	64.9	23 519	86.5	344.2	1 075.7	D	6.8	D	19.3	4.1	31.8	17.3	72 764	62 442	55 318
Collier	8 552.9	98.5	42 813	157.4	881.9	3 742.7	14.8	2.8	81.3	12.7	14.7	35.9	9.5	106 585	97 366	93 418
Columbia	1 005.6	72.9	19 004	69.9	217.0	598.0	18.6	11.2	80.7	13.9	2.9	20.4	31.9	66 700	65 518	59 276
Dade	51 447.9	42.3	23 919	87.9	8 987.2	39 463.0	10.4	6.7	89.2	9.7	10.4	32.2	16.3	2 658 549	2 539 348	2 509 753
DeSoto	532.7	50.6	21 560	79.3	123.6	313.9	D	2.7	D	7.5	1.9	12.5	30.0	8 327	8 505	8 289
Dixie	189.5	57.4	14 726	54.1	57.6	86.1	D	D	D	9.6	1.5	11.1	37.4	D	17 824	17 046
Duval	19 569.2	50.7	26 637	97.9	2 438.4	18 459.7	12.9	7.3	87.0	8.3	16.8	26.6	19.7	1 346 490	1 255 572	1 186 817
Escambia	6 159.7	43.3	21 682	79.7	1 046.2	4 808.9	D	8.7	D	10.1	4.2	27.0	33.1	418 228	413 250	404 006
Flagler	1 007.3	117.1	21 413	78.7	225.6	331.0	D	16.6	D	12.5	6.2	32.1	17.9	54 925	53 361	54 047
Franklin	191.8	61.7	18 988	69.8	50.0	86.1	D	5.3	D	15.4	6.5	21.1	24.3	4 598	4 485	3 918
Gadsden	782.0	52.6	17 771	65.3	182.1	433.4	D	12.2	D	7.4	1.9	10.1	40.7	53 003	48 179	38 795
Gilchrist	213.5	82.4	15 450	56.8	47.8	88.4	11.1	7.0	70.5	5.9	1.5	13.8	37.9	6 195	6 532	5 648
Glades	147.2	48.6	17 139	63.0	28.1	48.5	D	D	D	7.3	D	11.5	23.0	D	1 857	1 676
Gulf	226.0	52.7	16 754	61.6	63.9	121.4	30.9	25.6	69.1	7.0	3.0	17.4	29.4	31 108	46 017	42 370
Hamilton	177.1	36.7	13 967	51.3	47.5	150.1	D	D	D	3.8	.6	6.9	30.6	D	68 057	69 126
Hardee	422.5	41.5	20 081	73.8	87.6	258.1	D	3.4	65.0	6.8	3.1	14.8	22.8	8 736	8 283	6 977
Hendry	652.3	51.9	22 193	81.6	104.4	459.9	D	11.2	D	7.3	1.7	9.7	18.4	51 398	50 375	50 172
Hernando	2 732.7	68.1	21 587	79.4	774.0	850.7	14.9	5.6	84.2	15.5	6.0	31.6	21.1	47 615	47 277	45 097
Highlands	1 661.3	45.7	22 175	81.5	480.1	698.7	D	6.3	D	13.0	3.7	28.1	18.0	43 941	45 106	45 801
Hillsborough	24 389.3	62.1	26 355	96.9	3 259.6	21 492.3	12.2	6.7	86.9	9.8	10.6	35.6	14.7	1 442 112	1 329 906	1 259 119
Holmes	282.1	60.7	15 149	55.7	86.7	113.5	13.8	7.8	D	9.7	2.2	19.5	36.2	8 842	9 010	8 940
Indian River	3 617.7	54.5	36 501	134.2	578.3	1 419.6	D	7.4	D	14.2	9.9	32.8	13.2	104 365	89 187	79 797
Jackson	775.4	42.4	17 425	64.1	209.8	413.0	D	8.8	D	12.3	3.0	13.3	46.6	36 151	38 376	41 025
Jefferson	253.7	60.6	19 228	70.7	50.4	88.1	14.0	6.5	76.8	9.1	5.6	17.3	34.2	5 697	5 514	5 681
Lafayette	105.4	59.1	16 675	61.3	19.5	63.3	D	6.0	D	4.1	1.4	6.3	32.0	3 800	4 176	2 618
Lake	4 498.3	69.0	22 256	81.8	1 032.7	1 909.9	20.6	7.3	76.1	13.4	7.3	29.6	15.5	139 884	136 670	142 176
Lee	10 860.1	56.0	27 640	101.6	1 918.8	5 463.1	14.6	4.5	84.6	15.0	9.2	31.5	17.9	243 244	232 510	220 529
Leon	5 690.4	62.3	26 453	97.2	569.3	4 852.6	D	2.4	D	8.3	5.7	29.7	42.4	117 058	126 479	130 078
Levy	559.8	69.5	17 668	64.9	144.5	235.3	D	4.9	D	13.3	3.5	15.9	24.3	11 496	12 025	11 850
Liberty	101.9	49.0	15 139	55.7	21.1	53.7	D	14.8	D	4.6	D	11.3	45.8	7 930	8 057	7 695
Madison	283.1	48.1	15 959	58.7	78.0	148.5	23.1	21.7	70.0	8.8	1.7	19.2	32.1	32 160	31 968	31 884
Manatee	7 294.2	68.4	30 440	111.9	1 102.8	3 811.9	D	13.6	D	10.2	4.5	44.0	11.2	519 087	476 010	440 842
Marion	5 195.2	69.1	21 533	79.2	1 201.2	2 644.4	23.2	14.6	74.1	13.7	6.1	24.7	17.9	385 128	364 677	338 913
Martin	4 653.4	51.0	40 133	147.5	630.8	1 747.4	D	8.6	D	12.6	10.4	35.5	10.8	149 631	125 601	116 012
Monroe	2 627.8	45.9	32 501	119.5	266.7	1 320.2	D	1.4	D	17.4	6.4	36.0	23.4	18 507	16 317	15 337
Nassau	1 450.3	78.3	26 175	96.2	169.3	583.2	NA	18.6	72.8	11.1	5.0	21.7	25.0	108 414	105 891	96 277
Okaloosa	4 155.1	69.5	24 655	90.6	524.8	3 050.1	9.3	4.2	90.7	10.4	6.1	24.0	44.8	127 371	124 565	125 324
Okeechobee	598.7	48.9	18 725	68.8	153.5	323.2	6.8	1.9	73.5	12.5	2.6	26.5	20.0	6 115	6 754	6 628
Orange	21 066.2	62.9	26 186	96.3	2 510.8	21 762.7	14.3	8.5	85.3	10.0	8.6	41.0	11.1	1 848 324	1 660 116	1 550 877
Osceola	2 800.6	68.5	19 216	70.6	473.8	1 418.7	NA	5.4	85.9	17.7	6.8	35.2	18.3	76 647	80 498	72 783
Palm Beach	41 360.6	57.4	40 044	147.2	5 083.5	20 348.3	14.9	9.1	83.4	10.0	16.0	34.6	11.3	1 849 290	1 695 558	1 587 004
Pasco	7 377.5	66.3	22 691	83.4	1 788.8	2 260.8	13.5	5.1	85.3	11.5	5.4	37.1	18.6	115 489	121 931	112 965
Pinellas	26 873.6	46.8	30 633	112.6	4 358.9	15 358.6	D	11.7	D	11.0	10.9	37.5	11.7	1 798 886	1 713 629	1 645 588
Polk	10 234.1	57.1	22 609	83.1	1 862.4	6 398.5	23.0	14.0	75.0	14.5	5.8	26.1	14.0	897 916	855 885	832 886
Putnam	1 222.8	53.8	17 393	63.9	324.5	571.9	30.1	23.9	67.1	11.0	2.6	18.8	27.4	136 693	133 779	133 478
St. Johns	4 179.9	114.4	36 014	132.4	424.0	1 280.1	D	12.8	D	12.8	6.9	35.3	16.1	163 494	134 453	107 876
St. Lucie	3 831.5	59.5	21 362	78.5	915.9	1 636.6	11.7	4.8	85.9	12.6	5.7	28.7	21.3	79 369	76 911	78 290
Santa Rosa	2 566.3	97.2	21 808	80.2	332.4	934.8	22.0	8.6	77.2	9.8	4.3	25.9	29.3	80 223	77 441	79 641
Sarasota	11 263.3	43.4	37 131	136.5	1 767.7	4 691.0	14.8	6.7	84.9	14.5	11.9	39.6	10.5	313 724	294 166	286 922
Seminole	10 040.6	78.0	28 647	105.3	960.2	4 676.2	D	8.5	D	14.7	8.0	30.2	11.7	399 298	419 034	376 559
Sumter	687.2	79.0	16 549	60.8	196.5	285.9	16.0	8.7	80.0	10.2	2.3	12.9	39.6	24 860	25 548	21 902
Suwannee	616.5	59.8	18 972	69.7	153.3	328.8	D	D	D	12.1	3.4	17.4	17.4	D	39 432	38 109
Taylor	333.5	45.0	17 669	65.0	83.1	222.7	D	35.9	D	8.3	2.0	D	20.7	80 047	76 067	73 690
Union	153.0	53.4	12 194	44.8	29.1	127.9	D	7.7	D	3.4	.6	10.6	63.8	9 808	9 424	8 494
Volusia	9 221.3	48.3	21 920	80.6	1 985.6	4 252.5	D	9.1	D	14.5	6.4	35.5	17.5	388 370	437 801	423 100
Wakulla	449.9	117.9	24 169	88.8	61.4	147.6	37.5	26.1	60.8	7.8	3.9	15.2	27.3	38 509	24 665	21 573
Walton	623.6	87.1	16 664	61.3	138.3	306.1	D	8.6	D	14.4	5.5	26.8	24.0	26 341	24 226	23 992
Washington	331.5	65.1	16 381	60.2	93.7	182.2	D	12.5	D	9.3	1.8	12.7	42.3	22 831	21 452	20 644

[1] Based on resident population estimated as of July 1, 1998. [2] Includes farm earnings; see table B-10 for these data. [3] Includes mining and construction, not shown separately. [4] Includes agricultural services, forestry, and fisheries; transportation and public utilities; and wholesale trade, not shown separately. [5] Finance, insurance, and real estate.

Source: Personal Income and Earnings—U.S. Bureau of Economic Analysis, "Regional Economic Information System (REIS) 1969-1998" on CD-ROM (related Internet site <http://www.bea.doc.gov/bea/regional/data.htm>).

Table B–8. Counties — **Personal Income and Earnings**–Con.

[Includes U.S., states, and 3,142 counties/county equivalents defined as of January 1, 1992. For changes to these areas since January 1, 1992, see appendix B. Geographic Information]

County	Total (mil. dol.)	Per capita[1] Percent change, 1990–1998	Per capita Amount (dollars)	Per capita Percent of national average	Transfer payments (mil. dol.)	Earnings Total[2] (mil. dol.)	Goods-related Total[3]	Goods-related Manufacturing	Service-related Total[4]	Service-related Retail trade	Service-related FIRE[5]	Service-related Services	Government	Mfg. earnings 1998 ($1,000)	Mfg. earnings 1997 ($1,000)	Mfg. earnings 1996 ($1,000)
GEORGIA	197 318.7	71.0	25 839	95.0	22 733.9	151 756.3	21.5	15.6	77.3	8.8	7.8	26.0	16.2	23 644 729	22 168 568	21 008 774
Appling	285.4	51.4	17 250	63.4	62.7	238.7	22.5	17.2	70.9	6.6	2.5	7.6	14.2	41 151	41 894	37 560
Atkinson	138.3	76.4	19 326	71.0	27.1	87.2	D	34.9	D	4.3	2.0	4.6	11.5	30 440	26 833	29 235
Bacon	187.2	59.0	18 061	66.4	44.4	111.5	37.0	34.4	52.6	8.9	3.3	12.1	14.7	38 342	36 532	38 413
Baker	68.2	49.9	18 790	69.1	13.9	27.1	7.2	2.1	D	3.9	D	20.2	20.7	567	550	487
Baldwin	856.8	48.2	20 456	75.2	191.6	587.9	D	20.0	D	9.9	3.1	14.3	44.3	117 796	107 893	105 279
Banks	247.0	74.3	19 269	70.8	34.1	111.9	D	22.5	D	9.0	D	7.0	12.3	25 128	25 359	23 962
Barrow	807.6	86.5	19 971	73.4	114.3	397.9	D	31.6	D	12.0	3.2	14.5	15.2	125 756	110 117	96 602
Bartow	1 545.2	83.9	21 479	79.0	189.4	938.9	44.0	35.6	54.2	9.8	3.6	14.2	13.6	334 107	315 459	308 484
Ben Hill	360.5	63.9	20 634	75.9	73.5	279.7	49.6	45.7	44.7	7.5	3.0	10.3	15.3	127 851	104 674	104 150
Berrien	285.4	49.2	17 490	64.3	61.7	155.8	D	34.2	D	15.2	5.8	12.5	13.8	53 237	52 537	50 168
Bibb	3 933.2	48.7	25 222	92.7	662.7	3 250.9	D	20.0	D	9.8	9.3	31.7	12.3	650 063	656 475	610 932
Bleckley	235.2	59.8	21 078	77.5	43.7	113.6	D	D	D	7.9	2.5	11.2	24.1	D	41 133	36 795
Brantley	225.9	82.1	16 698	61.4	48.7	65.2	22.5	13.4	67.8	7.3	1.5	10.0	27.8	8 724	8 314	7 331
Brooks	268.0	54.5	16 839	61.9	64.5	104.5	25.1	21.4	54.6	6.1	3.1	12.5	20.0	22 389	22 185	23 841
Bryan	467.3	112.3	19 976	73.4	59.0	128.0	25.2	13.2	75.1	14.9	7.4	17.7	25.7	16 914	15 958	14 999
Bulloch	924.1	67.7	18 279	67.2	145.2	609.0	D	16.5	D	13.7	4.0	18.8	28.7	100 485	103 039	98 419
Burke	356.2	50.0	15 607	57.4	86.7	202.7	D	11.8	D	6.8	2.2	12.4	20.3	23 835	28 438	29 760
Butts	340.0	72.0	19 079	70.1	62.0	158.9	D	19.8	D	9.4	4.5	15.8	24.4	31 447	29 423	31 192
Calhoun	96.1	41.3	19 214	70.6	25.3	54.4	D	D	D	5.4	2.5	7.6	35.7	D	4 407	3 724
Camden	764.7	76.1	16 159	59.4	77.9	735.5	17.3	14.4	82.6	5.8	1.4	11.5	61.6	106 218	105 229	102 672
Candler	169.5	54.6	18 628	68.5	41.8	84.4	18.7	14.0	77.1	12.6	7.4	19.9	21.3	11 812	11 578	10 189
Carroll	1 676.4	63.6	20 221	74.3	259.8	1 061.1	D	32.3	D	9.4	4.3	19.5	15.4	342 380	321 698	322 584
Catoosa	959.5	69.4	18 922	69.6	139.2	441.8	D	26.2	D	13.6	4.2	24.7	12.6	115 939	106 364	109 618
Charlton	149.1	59.3	15 804	58.1	35.2	60.2	29.2	20.4	68.5	12.0	2.2	15.6	29.5	12 252	11 961	12 020
Chatham	5 944.2	48.1	26 384	97.0	855.5	4 677.9	D	18.4	D	9.7	4.7	30.1	18.3	859 965	740 835	731 552
Chattahoochee	373.9	35.3	22 790	83.8	13.0	574.4	D	D	D	1.8	D	1.9	95.1	D	609	598
Chattooga	429.2	50.1	18 866	69.4	91.7	240.8	D	50.6	D	9.9	2.1	10.8	18.1	121 912	117 939	112 402
Cherokee	3 485.3	123.3	25 941	95.4	236.4	1 121.4	D	10.9	D	12.0	8.2	24.0	14.0	122 633	108 154	99 983
Clarke	2 106.3	51.6	23 270	85.5	246.1	2 103.3	D	16.3	D	10.2	4.2	23.8	33.3	342 041	336 666	326 397
Clay	54.8	58.6	15 703	57.7	16.0	22.3	D	D	D	8.2	1.5	9.6	42.8	D	1 232	1 172
Clayton	4 571.2	51.3	21 872	80.4	497.2	4 666.8	D	6.0	D	9.8	2.6	17.0	10.4	281 672	247 311	237 481
Clinch	123.0	78.8	18 506	68.0	30.5	93.4	45.2	44.2	53.1	15.0	2.1	9.9	17.0	41 264	34 308	26 144
Cobb	19 459.7	90.7	34 377	126.4	1 101.2	13 731.2	17.8	10.4	82.2	11.1	9.2	29.6	9.6	1 422 513	1 308 659	1 218 872
Coffee	709.9	68.7	20 740	76.2	121.8	549.9	34.5	29.8	55.8	17.5	2.2	15.3	11.9	163 732	145 665	138 664
Colquitt	738.0	47.4	18 345	67.4	150.9	457.1	27.1	21.1	62.7	9.9	4.1	15.1	20.5	96 376	85 831	82 484
Columbia	2 043.1	70.7	22 488	82.7	186.3	623.8	D	22.4	D	11.3	5.9	24.7	15.3	139 698	144 412	117 308
Cook	258.5	65.5	17 246	63.4	58.6	150.3	37.8	32.7	52.9	10.0	3.1	14.7	14.3	49 165	47 773	43 739
Coweta	1 952.7	113.1	22 941	84.3	210.2	827.9	D	27.0	D	15.3	3.7	22.2	14.0	223 589	209 197	198 788
Crawford	179.9	57.7	16 880	62.1	28.4	37.2	D	9.0	D	5.3	D	14.2	31.3	3 332	2 878	2 877
Crisp	392.4	48.8	18 963	69.7	94.6	254.9	25.1	18.8	69.7	15.1	4.4	18.6	17.9	47 987	50 822	49 479
Dade	260.4	65.1	17 297	63.6	46.1	99.4	37.5	31.3	D	14.8	3.9	18.7	16.3	31 088	25 776	22 081
Dawson	338.3	137.8	22 709	83.5	34.9	121.5	29.6	11.2	61.1	17.0	5.3	18.0	14.4	13 647	12 309	11 474
Decatur	513.9	47.9	19 020	69.9	114.1	364.4	D	27.9	D	9.6	3.1	12.0	20.0	101 562	94 308	87 124
De Kalb	18 824.1	58.0	31 751	116.7	1 570.2	15 323.2	14.6	9.3	85.4	7.9	8.7	33.9	11.5	1 421 081	1 388 588	1 190 637
Dodge	317.9	51.3	17 543	64.5	73.8	158.9	22.2	16.7	75.0	10.7	3.4	16.9	35.2	26 510	23 486	23 189
Dooly	188.3	56.9	18 090	66.5	46.4	117.5	30.5	28.8	58.5	6.0	3.9	9.3	23.7	33 785	32 144	28 535
Dougherty	2 102.0	44.6	22 122	81.3	382.1	1 960.6	26.4	20.4	73.1	8.4	3.7	25.8	22.2	400 162	393 082	376 228
Douglas	2 084.7	81.3	23 319	85.7	205.4	870.6	D	9.2	D	17.4	4.0	25.0	15.5	80 458	74 544	65 888
Early	228.3	44.1	18 762	69.0	53.6	177.0	40.0	37.9	46.3	4.8	5.0	10.3	12.9	67 122	64 991	66 322
Echols	42.7	50.0	18 101	66.5	6.8	13.1	D	9.9	D	2.5	D	6.5	30.0	1 293	1 632	1 307
Effingham	758.5	100.5	20 743	76.3	85.9	229.8	47.4	35.5	52.3	10.6	2.7	9.7	21.1	81 644	71 601	65 635
Elbert	379.5	45.2	19 641	72.2	85.8	216.9	40.1	33.7	57.7	8.7	3.9	14.5	20.9	73 195	69 476	65 398
Emanuel	367.8	47.1	17 498	64.3	99.1	201.8	29.0	25.3	69.9	10.3	2.8	15.4	29.8	51 097	46 066	49 382
Evans	190.1	61.7	19 161	70.4	39.1	121.8	D	D	D	9.2	2.7	15.2	15.9	D	41 173	35 331
Fannin	326.9	67.9	17 598	64.7	86.0	145.2	24.3	16.8	D	19.8	D	21.3	16.8	24 328	22 783	23 168
Fayette	2 683.9	94.2	30 247	111.2	175.4	1 039.2	D	20.2	D	11.0	7.8	22.5	12.9	210 433	172 448	145 857
Floyd	1 957.0	48.6	22 987	84.5	335.4	1 346.9	D	27.2	D	9.3	4.0	28.5	15.0	366 932	369 569	354 098
Forsyth	2 565.2	206.2	29 687	109.1	145.8	1 124.6	D	21.8	D	8.1	4.0	18.5	8.5	244 665	201 926	185 954
Franklin	411.5	63.5	21 590	79.4	78.4	270.3	D	22.8	D	14.1	2.3	16.3	9.9	61 537	52 839	51 104
Fulton	30 465.5	77.8	41 325	151.9	2 337.5	39 118.6	11.4	8.5	88.6	5.9	13.1	33.7	12.0	3 324 458	2 938 209	2 902 967
Gilmer	361.7	83.6	19 294	70.9	76.9	216.2	D	33.8	D	10.3	3.9	D	12.3	73 103	67 279	63 514
Glascock	49.2	54.2	19 572	71.9	13.3	16.3	D	D	D	5.7	D	D	23.9	D	1 731	2 234
Glynn	1 755.5	56.2	26 129	96.1	269.1	1 162.5	22.0	14.7	78.0	12.1	6.2	27.8	24.2	170 640	162 641	159 340
Gordon	846.3	61.5	20 601	75.7	124.8	654.5	54.8	50.7	40.7	7.8	1.9	11.7	9.5	331 521	302 618	295 325
Grady	372.5	51.3	17 392	63.9	79.4	183.7	29.1	23.2	62.0	11.3	3.7	15.7	19.2	42 598	41 677	44 669
Greene	263.9	69.1	19 315	71.0	56.1	156.9	D	32.0	D	7.5	13.1	11.7	16.1	50 151	46 769	42 690

[1] Based on resident population estimated as of July 1, 1998. [2] Includes farm earnings; see table B-10 for these data. [3] Includes mining and construction, not shown separately. [4] Includes agricultural services, forestry, and fisheries; transportation and public utilities; and wholesale trade, not shown separately. [5] Finance, insurance, and real estate.

Source: Personal Income and Earnings—U.S. Bureau of Economic Analysis, "Regional Economic Information System (REIS) 1969-1998" on CD-ROM (related Internet site <http://www.bea.doc.gov/bea/regional/data.htm>).

Table B–8. Counties — **Personal Income and Earnings**–Con.

[Includes U.S., states, and 3,142 counties/county equivalents defined as of January 1, 1992. For changes to these areas since January 1, 1992, see appendix B. Geographic Information]

	Personal income, 1998													Manufacturing earnings		
			Per capita[1]			Earnings										
									Percent, by selected industry—							
								Goods-related		Service-related							
County	Total (mil. dol.)	Percent change, 1990–1998	Amount (dollars)	Percent of national average	Transfer payments (mil. dol.)	Total[2] (mil. dol.)	Total[3]	Manu-facturing	Total[4]	Retail trade	FIRE[5]	Serv-ices	Gov-ern-ment	1998 ($1,000)	1997 ($1,000)	1996 ($1,000)
GEORGIA—Con.																
Gwinnett	16 023.6	113.5	30 657	112.7	776.3	11 332.6	D	16.5	D	10.7	7.7	24.5	7.8	1 872 424	1 748 253	1 601 851
Habersham	712.3	70.8	22 445	82.5	110.0	479.0	D	30.8	D	9.5	4.7	14.0	16.6	147 499	136 238	137 132
Hall	2 862.9	78.6	23 991	88.2	337.2	2 075.6	35.9	28.8	62.0	9.2	6.1	23.2	12.0	597 475	547 652	505 609
Hancock	151.2	54.7	16 547	60.8	45.7	49.5	D	8.7	D	6.3	3.6	20.5	48.8	4 323	4 200	4 242
Haralson	461.0	55.6	18 747	68.9	89.2	210.0	38.7	28.2	58.5	10.3	2.5	16.8	18.3	59 309	58 059	55 278
Harris	550.1	87.2	24 672	90.7	61.4	145.4	31.5	22.0	67.4	10.9	3.7	28.7	18.5	31 980	25 243	20 630
Hart	434.9	53.3	19 955	73.4	82.5	246.6	D	43.7	D	7.2	D	14.0	13.0	107 871	92 435	82 084
Heard	169.2	69.6	18 772	61.7	32.4	95.6	D	39.8	D	2.3	1.1	4.8	15.3	38 028	32 380	29 362
Henry	2 289.4	128.0	21 819	80.2	221.7	890.8	D	11.7	D	13.4	5.9	20.5	22.9	104 037	106 208	99 679
Houston	2 315.0	51.5	21 914	80.6	257.8	1 898.5	12.0	8.5	87.7	7.5	2.5	14.5	59.5	160 784	151 316	134 866
Irwin	173.4	55.2	19 159	70.4	35.6	75.7	D	18.1	D	4.5	3.4	19.7	24.3	13 730	11 480	10 724
Jackson	853.6	95.4	22 634	83.2	121.0	543.0	D	27.9	D	9.8	4.4	8.5	11.5	151 774	144 607	126 573
Jasper	210.9	79.3	20 749	76.3	33.1	86.5	D	38.9	D	5.1	1.9	11.3	20.2	33 635	33 587	31 524
Jeff Davis	228.0	41.0	17 946	66.0	45.8	164.0	43.3	40.5	50.2	10.1	1.6	8.1	13.8	66 419	67 508	65 342
Jefferson	295.6	39.8	16 580	60.9	83.0	172.1	D	38.3	D	7.4	3.0	9.2	17.3	65 957	69 089	66 316
Jenkins	142.0	50.8	16 812	61.8	37.0	78.8	48.8	46.7	47.6	5.9	2.5	10.1	18.2	36 814	34 177	31 620
Johnson	147.8	56.1	17 822	65.5	39.1	64.5	22.5	17.4	68.8	4.8	1.6	12.7	32.4	11 192	13 404	13 672
Jones	482.1	46.7	20 964	77.1	54.4	100.4	D	7.6	D	7.1	3.5	19.0	23.2	7 581	7 478	7 417
Lamar	270.4	61.9	18 393	67.6	52.0	128.0	36.8	32.7	D	9.3	5.7	D	20.5	41 888	42 314	44 857
Lanier	114.4	64.5	16 365	60.2	25.3	36.4	21.0	8.6	D	10.1	D	22.1	27.7	3 139	2 806	2 026
Laurens	884.2	53.6	20 239	74.4	164.8	620.4	D	26.6	D	11.9	3.2	18.4	23.0	164 941	171 377	155 779
Lee	444.5	100.5	19 522	71.8	42.6	115.5	D	3.2	D	5.7	D	16.1	29.0	3 747	4 535	4 261
Liberty	944.4	71.7	15 985	58.8	110.1	1 082.3	D	3.7	D	3.9	1.7	4.7	81.9	39 954	37 926	35 774
Lincoln	147.8	49.2	17 970	66.1	30.4	52.3	38.0	30.6	D	8.6	2.1	12.5	22.8	15 979	16 517	16 698
Long	113.6	77.1	13 245	48.7	19.9	20.2	D	D	D	6.1	1.8	10.3	49.5	D	1 145	1 055
Lowndes	1 817.2	62.5	21 366	78.5	281.7	1 433.8	D	14.0	D	13.0	3.5	17.7	33.7	201 331	190 283	176 723
Lumpkin	409.3	99.7	21 539	79.2	52.2	210.4	D	15.9	D	10.4	5.3	18.2	26.2	33 532	30 493	31 077
McDuffie	418.6	44.9	19 293	70.9	79.2	234.6	D	27.1	D	15.4	3.4	16.6	18.9	63 468	59 424	59 659
McIntosh	155.9	63.5	15 557	57.2	40.2	58.3	9.3	4.7	90.7	19.0	6.1	15.9	29.7	2 726	2 937	2 837
Macon	247.4	51.1	18 734	68.9	56.4	164.4	37.4	34.1	41.1	5.4	1.3	11.8	16.8	56 049	52 444	54 729
Madison	518.2	74.7	21 217	78.0	78.0	156.4	D	13.2	D	6.1	2.2	13.8	16.6	20 671	19 053	20 811
Marion	103.7	68.7	15 476	56.9	21.0	63.8	D	D	D	4.7	1.7	8.6	17.7	D	29 450	24 870
Meriwether	415.6	62.6	18 007	66.2	86.1	220.1	33.8	27.2	64.7	9.0	7.9	15.3	23.3	59 764	58 879	58 299
Miller	126.9	50.4	19 952	73.3	26.4	51.7	6.2	1.7	72.2	9.5	6.8	13.3	26.2	888	858	865
Mitchell	415.4	61.1	19 596	72.0	84.5	253.6	29.4	25.8	52.5	6.4	2.9	9.9	22.1	65 362	55 610	49 086
Monroe	397.2	57.3	20 241	74.4	61.5	173.3	D	10.8	D	7.2	1.8	14.5	26.2	18 782	23 203	24 267
Montgomery	132.0	42.7	17 082	62.8	30.0	59.2	26.4	14.3	67.9	10.2	6.2	18.2	21.1	8 486	7 048	6 323
Morgan	341.9	72.7	22 658	83.3	49.6	204.9	35.7	30.2	55.8	13.1	3.7	10.6	12.4	61 910	58 968	56 127
Murray	579.4	73.0	17 710	65.1	82.9	377.2	D	60.0	D	5.2	1.8	9.7	10.8	226 153	195 961	216 062
Muscogee	4 222.0	45.8	23 145	85.1	667.5	3 442.5	D	17.2	D	9.6	11.6	25.9	23.2	591 786	581 185	558 110
Newton	1 140.0	86.4	19 702	72.4	172.2	595.8	D	32.6	D	9.1	3.2	17.6	13.5	194 205	195 347	180 420
Oconee	586.6	76.4	24 744	91.0	50.7	198.0	30.5	19.5	62.3	9.9	6.7	20.8	16.2	38 581	34 403	29 833
Oglethorpe	220.9	63.3	19 318	71.0	32.4	69.7	21.2	4.9	42.8	5.4	2.2	11.4	17.6	3 426	3 285	3 177
Paulding	1 226.1	105.6	16 593	61.0	126.7	363.8	D	11.7	D	14.3	3.9	13.6	23.4	42 548	33 285	24 398
Peach	471.0	35.5	19 245	70.7	88.0	264.1	D	38.1	D	9.2	3.4	9.2	26.2	100 725	96 231	125 574
Pickens	490.3	115.5	24 845	91.3	69.6	211.1	D	13.7	58.4	10.2	9.9	15.8	14.3	28 824	24 960	23 972
Pierce	298.1	76.1	18 913	69.5	60.5	110.0	22.6	13.6	66.4	10.9	5.1	15.3	17.8	14 944	14 228	14 414
Pike	248.1	69.1	19 587	72.0	36.5	71.4	D	19.9	D	4.7	3.8	15.4	22.3	14 233	13 948	12 656
Polk	675.7	50.3	18 625	68.5	148.5	303.6	D	28.3	D	10.5	3.5	16.4	18.7	85 910	87 423	86 757
Pulaski	186.7	62.3	22 197	81.6	36.1	102.7	D	14.3	D	8.6	3.3	30.2	23.0	14 646	14 804	14 904
Putnam	372.8	77.9	21 228	78.0	63.3	205.8	41.3	34.2	55.4	5.7	3.8	9.4	15.2	71 115	70 157	68 627
Quitman	42.9	63.2	17 261	63.5	12.5	8.7	D	21.3	D	13.4	D	9.2	37.9	1 844	1 697	1 414
Rabun	275.7	75.9	20 609	75.8	57.9	154.0	D	31.6	D	10.6	4.7	22.7	14.4	48 640	50 524	47 424
Randolph	133.9	43.4	16 838	61.9	36.3	75.5	30.8	26.3	61.4	7.2	2.3	12.9	26.8	19 860	23 402	22 480
Richmond	4 375.0	29.6	22 861	84.0	775.8	4 075.0	18.9	13.8	81.1	9.0	5.1	22.9	37.0	560 862	545 777	525 661
Rockdale	1 706.2	69.6	24 989	91.9	160.5	1 078.5	D	24.3	D	11.3	3.7	19.2	9.0	262 524	259 749	243 273
Schley	71.4	52.3	18 073	66.4	12.6	39.0	53.5	50.4	D	4.4	D	6.0	11.4	19 678	14 682	15 416
Screven	255.6	41.1	17 687	65.0	60.6	119.5	41.6	37.1	D	9.2	2.9	10.7	23.1	44 332	45 095	45 558
Seminole	170.3	52.7	17 444	64.1	43.3	79.3	D	8.4	76.5	11.2	5.0	21.1	18.6	6 684	6 161	5 780
Spalding	1 232.7	56.0	21 401	78.7	203.6	691.9	D	30.2	D	11.9	3.7	20.8	18.1	209 280	203 996	189 525
Stephens	528.0	57.7	20 824	76.6	108.3	346.4	D	37.9	D	9.8	4.6	17.2	14.2	131 127	134 904	124 596
Stewart	96.5	47.1	17 844	65.6	26.5	36.9	D	35.1	D	11.2	2.8	18.3	21.6	12 935	11 513	11 992
Sumter	652.1	56.6	20 841	76.6	127.0	466.2	D	25.1	D	8.8	2.4	19.2	18.6	117 171	114 436	116 283
Talbot	103.5	44.9	14 838	54.5	24.5	28.5	D	D	D	6.5	3.3	13.1	29.0	D	2 998	2 826
Taliaferro	31.5	32.9	16 455	60.5	9.4	7.0	D	D	D	8.9	D	9.9	35.4	D	1 000	932
Tattnall	363.0	56.4	19 068	70.1	75.4	228.6	11.7	8.2	60.6	5.8	2.6	8.6	33.8	18 770	18 805	17 860

[1] Based on resident population estimated as of July 1, 1998.   [2] Includes farm earnings; see table B-10 for these data.   [3] Includes mining and construction, not shown separately.   [4] Includes agricultural services, forestry, and fisheries; transportation and public utilities; and wholesale trade, not shown separately.   [5] Finance, insurance, and real estate.

Source: Personal Income and Earnings—U.S. Bureau of Economic Analysis, "Regional Economic Information System (REIS) 1969-1998" on CD-ROM (related Internet site <http://www.bea.doc.gov/bea/regional/data.htm>).

[Includes U.S., states, and 3,142 counties/county equivalents defined as of January 1, 1992. For changes to these areas since January 1, 1992, see appendix B. Geographic Information]

County	Personal income, 1998													Manufacturing earnings		
			Per capita[1]			Earnings										
									Percent, by selected industry–							
							Goods-related		Service-related							
	Total (mil. dol.)	Percent change, 1990–1998	Amount (dollars)	Percent of national average	Transfer payments (mil. dol.)	Total[2] (mil. dol.)	Total[3]	Manufacturing	Total[4]	Retail trade	FIRE[5]	Services	Government	1998 ($1,000)	1997 ($1,000)	1996 ($1,000)

County																
GEORGIA—Con.																
Taylor	146.5	50.2	17 805	65.5	36.0	74.9	D	5.7	70.9	9.1	3.7	11.5	20.3	4 264	3 868	4 507
Telfair	201.3	46.9	17 450	64.1	58.6	129.5	43.2	42.2	54.2	6.7	3.0	12.8	22.4	54 591	53 723	45 066
Terrell	171.6	40.5	15 405	56.6	45.9	79.5	20.3	18.3	68.9	8.6	4.8	14.5	24.2	14 521	13 838	12 855
Thomas	904.5	53.0	21 089	77.5	179.6	650.0	D	26.0	D	10.2	3.8	27.7	17.8	168 823	180 193	167 551
Tift	801.9	58.9	21 799	80.1	127.7	648.2	26.5	20.4	69.3	14.0	3.2	19.0	19.8	132 465	127 374	120 694
Toombs	473.1	45.2	18 321	67.3	107.6	288.8	24.5	18.0	70.0	12.6	3.5	21.9	14.3	52 006	52 444	54 800
Towns	175.5	94.0	20 708	76.1	44.7	74.0	D	1.6	D	12.0	7.7	36.5	12.7	1 184	1 131	2 813
Treutlen	95.7	48.6	16 043	59.0	24.9	35.5	26.4	17.2	65.3	9.5	3.6	13.3	30.1	6 100	6 153	5 847
Troup	1 317.8	51.3	22 499	82.7	210.5	1 058.0	D	40.2	D	8.7	3.5	14.7	15.2	425 220	407 414	378 311
Turner	154.5	47.3	16 814	61.8	37.0	77.1	21.3	17.2	62.8	10.5	4.9	9.7	20.7	13 272	12 876	12 833
Twiggs	160.9	54.6	15 908	58.5	36.1	90.6	62.4	3.1	D	2.9	1.1	8.0	14.0	2 779	2 013	1 828
Union	307.7	99.6	18 644	68.5	72.2	140.9	D	7.0	D	10.9	10.2	14.8	23.0	9 884	9 905	10 674
Upson	518.4	49.7	19 157	70.4	105.0	312.9	47.4	42.8	51.8	8.5	3.2	21.1	16.0	133 902	125 549	119 196
Walker	1 168.6	46.2	18 641	68.5	234.3	475.4	D	38.9	D	9.5	2.9	15.8	17.8	184 815	184 802	181 899
Walton	1 042.1	82.8	19 076	70.1	156.9	431.3	37.6	24.4	59.6	10.8	5.0	14.7	20.7	105 182	99 519	94 429
Ware	671.0	45.0	18 948	69.7	176.8	518.9	22.5	14.1	76.1	12.7	2.8	22.5	19.8	73 290	74 559	74 772
Warren	102.7	48.6	16 926	62.2	30.1	56.6	D	51.0	40.0	4.9	1.4	11.4	13.9	28 901	25 500	24 878
Washington	435.8	53.5	21 731	79.9	83.6	316.3	45.2	10.4	53.5	6.6	1.7	11.2	20.0	32 779	33 108	35 002
Wayne	463.9	51.8	18 294	67.2	98.1	294.0	39.5	32.0	59.1	11.0	1.7	11.3	27.7	93 934	86 234	79 888
Webster	42.0	55.8	19 110	70.2	7.9	16.3	27.1	26.7	D	3.8	D	D	21.6	4 347	5 833	4 683
Wheeler	86.6	49.1	17 671	65.0	23.1	33.6	15.9	13.8	D	4.2	D	16.3	25.5	4 657	4 168	3 655
White	378.4	84.4	21 642	79.6	62.3	196.8	28.5	18.4	60.2	14.8	4.3	17.9	14.8	36 194	39 692	37 545
Whitfield	2 037.5	62.6	24 834	91.3	234.4	1 972.7	D	51.3	D	7.3	2.4	13.3	8.4	1 012 770	958 429	882 555
Wilcox	137.4	65.3	18 670	68.6	35.3	55.9	D	5.2	D	5.6	3.1	11.0	32.8	2 906	2 759	4 817
Wilkes	216.3	37.6	20 397	75.0	47.3	131.0	D	37.2	D	7.1	3.2	13.0	18.4	48 707	46 886	40 204
Wilkinson	198.4	37.8	18 266	67.1	38.9	124.6	63.0	48.8	36.6	3.6	1.4	5.9	11.5	60 817	63 511	64 651
Worth	406.0	64.9	18 088	66.5	71.1	124.0	15.2	10.8	65.5	10.7	3.4	16.4	24.0	13 330	8 541	7 046
HAWAII	31 856.2	27.9	26 759	98.4	3 794.2	23 309.3	8.8	3.1	90.5	10.8	8.5	28.7	30.5	716 754	709 654	754 378
Hawaii	2 791.5	38.3	19 686	72.4	551.3	1 769.2	D	2.7	D	11.9	7.6	33.2	24.7	48 224	48 302	50 857
Honolulu	24 993.9	25.5	28 670	105.4	2 646.3	18 619.4	8.7	3.1	91.0	10.1	8.6	26.9	33.1	586 397	577 651	614 160
Kalawao	(6)	(6)	(6)	(6)	(6)	(6)	D	(6)	D	(6)	(6)	(6)	(6)	(6)	(6)	(6)
Kauai	1 255.7	30.1	22 340	82.1	206.9	867.9	D	1.7	D	14.2	7.0	38.9	20.7	15 012	13 159	17 534
Maui	6 2 815.1	6 40.1	6 23 325	6 85.7	6 389.7	6 2 052.7	D	6 3.3	D	6 15.1	6 9.5	6 37.5	6 16.1	6 67 121	6 70 542	6 71 827
IDAHO	27 177.4	69.3	22 079	81.2	3 552.1	18 941.1	D	17.1	D	10.1	5.2	22.3	18.2	3 241 927	3 093 699	2 937 750
Ada	8 332.1	101.6	30 230	111.1	695.4	6 659.3	32.1	21.9	67.4	9.4	7.3	22.3	14.4	1 459 405	1 368 050	1 308 265
Adams	68.0	51.0	17 955	66.0	13.7	32.1	D	22.8	D	8.9	2.4	7.1	37.9	7 321	8 438	8 480
Bannock	1 467.5	56.4	19 759	72.6	218.0	943.5	D	11.1	D	11.9	5.2	19.5	27.0	104 966	97 642	91 479
Bear Lake	100.1	50.9	15 378	56.5	20.7	41.9	9.2	5.2	D	16.0	3.9	D	34.9	2 199	1 977	2 599
Benewah	167.6	50.8	18 440	67.8	30.8	120.5	D	32.8	D	9.0	1.5	15.0	17.0	39 579	41 870	40 956
Bingham	704.2	32.0	16 837	61.9	115.3	408.7	D	18.3	D	8.3	D	13.6	24.2	74 915	74 634	68 187
Blaine	674.1	95.8	39 186	144.1	32.7	414.9	22.1	4.5	76.5	13.4	10.7	33.3	10.3	18 701	12 810	12 416
Boise	102.1	96.7	19 944	73.3	14.3	38.7	25.5	15.0	D	7.1	D	20.2	38.1	5 823	5 339	5 859
Bonner	644.3	80.0	18 232	67.0	112.9	362.8	27.2	18.2	72.2	17.9	5.6	20.0	17.8	65 996	63 703	62 989
Bonneville	1 743.8	39.3	21 608	79.4	221.3	1 237.7	D	4.9	D	11.3	3.9	39.2	15.0	60 345	53 503	47 100
Boundary	163.7	71.1	16 669	61.3	31.0	108.3	D	22.1	D	9.0	D	20.9	22.5	23 885	25 243	21 258
Butte	57.4	51.1	18 886	69.4	10.3	328.0	.6	.1	D	.9	.2	94.4	2.2	254	213	222
Camas	18.2	68.4	21 698	79.8	2.3	8.9	D	D	D	8.3	D	9.5	32.1	D	D	D
Canyon	2 146.9	72.4	17 833	65.6	371.3	1 395.6	35.9	27.1	57.7	9.8	3.3	18.9	13.1	378 548	361 583	339 526
Caribou	144.2	44.1	19 484	71.6	19.5	137.5	62.1	40.0	32.1	4.3	1.2	5.0	12.5	55 022	54 279	49 945
Cassia	424.8	31.1	19 923	73.2	62.1	289.8	D	12.5	D	11.0	3.6	14.5	15.6	36 203	37 654	33 588
Clark	17.0	−28.5	19 145	70.4	2.0	15.8	D	D	D	3.2	3.4	1.4	26.6	D	D	D
Clearwater	171.8	45.9	18 377	67.6	35.9	106.6	33.2	27.7	D	7.7	D	11.5	37.2	29 502	31 413	29 403
Custer	92.7	47.7	22 666	83.3	12.3	54.0	D	2.6	D	9.6	2.0	D	25.6	1 384	1 297	1 298
Elmore	524.4	42.0	20 679	76.0	49.6	386.4	5.1	2.5	87.1	6.1	1.6	6.6	68.9	9 720	8 622	8 472
Franklin	169.3	64.9	15 230	56.0	26.2	86.4	D	8.8	D	10.0	D	11.7	21.3	7 576	6 727	6 683
Fremont	178.7	26.2	14 979	55.1	31.1	93.0	D	2.9	D	8.8	D	11.1	33.0	2 710	2 693	2 354
Gem	260.1	61.0	17 516	64.4	50.7	100.3	D	23.4	D	9.2	D	15.2	23.5	23 459	23 668	24 846
Gooding	328.2	78.6	24 032	88.3	44.1	225.5	10.1	7.0	35.8	4.3	1.5	5.8	11.6	15 682	13 599	11 438
Idaho	258.5	32.1	17 226	63.3	55.6	136.9	D	16.2	D	9.9	3.9	14.3	34.7	22 216	21 799	24 441
Jefferson	323.6	52.8	16 564	60.9	44.3	140.3	D	12.1	D	7.7	D	7.7	20.9	17 041	15 940	15 093
Jerome	407.7	75.3	22 702	83.5	53.3	282.0	11.6	7.7	48.8	6.7	1.4	10.4	8.3	21 757	20 599	17 919

[1] Based on resident population estimated as of July 1, 1998. [2] Includes farm earnings; see table B-10 for these data. [3] Includes mining and construction, not shown separately. [4] Includes agricultural services, forestry, and fisheries; transportation and public utilities; and wholesale trade, not shown separately. [5] Finance, insurance, and real estate. [6] Kalawao County included with Maui County; data not available separately.

Source: Personal Income and Earnings—U.S. Bureau of Economic Analysis, "Regional Economic Information System (REIS) 1969-1998" on CD-ROM (related Internet site <http://www.bea.doc.gov/bea/regional/data.htm>).

[Includes U.S., states, and 3,142 counties/county equivalents defined as of January 1, 1992. For changes to these areas since January 1, 1992, see appendix B. Geographic Information]

County	Personal income, 1998														Manufacturing earnings		
	Total (mil. dol.)	Per capita[1]			Transfer payments (mil. dol.)	Earnings										
		Percent change, 1990–1998	Amount (dollars)	Percent of national average		Total[2] (mil. dol.)	Percent, by selected industry–							1998 ($1,000)	1997 ($1,000)	1996 ($1,000)
							Goods-related		Service-related							
							Total[3]	Manufacturing	Total[4]	Retail trade	FIRE[5]	Services	Government			
IDAHO—Con.																
Kootenai	2 232.6	98.0	22 038	81.0	317.4	1 275.0	26.1	14.3	73.9	14.0	6.0	23.5	18.2	182 382	177 788	162 942
Latah	681.0	50.7	20 846	76.6	86.1	405.3	D	6.6	D	11.2	2.7	18.9	47.8	26 820	25 599	24 811
Lemhi	150.1	64.7	18 671	68.6	31.4	81.6	D	6.6	D	13.0	2.4	D	35.2	5 356	5 190	5 500
Lewis	73.0	22.0	18 269	67.2	18.8	32.4	D	14.1	D	13.4	2.8	10.4	32.9	4 588	4 352	3 566
Lincoln	71.2	44.0	18 854	69.3	11.8	41.7	D	D	D	3.2	D	D	35.2	D	D	D
Madison	340.5	50.0	13 553	49.8	40.4	266.5	D	10.9	D	10.1	6.1	34.7	15.1	29 003	28 471	27 495
Minidoka	336.8	29.6	16 669	61.3	59.2	236.2	D	27.4	D	5.6	D	9.7	16.1	64 832	63 610	61 899
Nez Perce	873.4	51.2	23 707	87.1	148.0	696.8	D	25.6	D	11.2	7.2	23.9	14.0	178 303	177 872	164 758
Oneida	61.5	49.2	15 260	56.1	13.1	24.9	D	5.9	D	8.1	5.4	10.6	37.3	1 461	1 006	1 178
Owyhee	167.9	57.1	16 370	60.2	28.1	87.7	D	4.3	D	6.6	D	5.9	18.0	3 761	3 312	3 002
Payette	349.6	68.9	17 096	62.8	61.5	179.7	D	24.2	D	7.8	D	13.7	15.3	43 571	41 017	40 535
Power	146.6	14.9	17 427	64.1	19.6	149.2	52.6	49.7	34.5	D	1.3	3.7	11.6	74 170	73 481	71 985
Shoshone	267.5	34.4	19 296	70.9	67.1	159.8	38.6	5.4	61.4	14.7	2.5	15.6	23.3	8 672	8 462	7 544
Teton	81.4	95.0	14 826	54.5	11.4	40.2	14.9	1.9	72.0	14.6	4.7	15.2	26.7	761	604	655
Twin Falls	1 307.2	58.3	21 008	77.2	195.8	913.4	18.1	11.2	72.0	13.4	5.2	20.9	16.8	102 505	101 850	101 459
Valley	185.0	69.2	23 100	84.9	29.2	102.8	17.9	6.3	80.0	13.9	6.3	17.6	34.1	6 429	6 270	6 617
Washington	161.0	56.8	15 761	57.9	36.5	92.5	24.4	18.0	65.0	8.4	4.2	12.1	20.1	16 683	12 432	12 284
ILLINOIS	360 317.1	51.7	29 853	109.7	41 565.5	263 398.3	24.2	18.6	75.4	7.7	10.3	29.3	13.2	48 995 852	47 625 156	44 523 708
Adams	1 606.9	49.4	23 869	87.7	250.7	1 059.2	D	26.4	D	11.0	3.9	24.6	12.7	279 265	266 951	251 663
Alexander	159.6	33.6	15 868	58.3	53.1	75.6	D	16.7	D	7.0	2.1	17.8	27.2	12 625	13 092	12 218
Bond	348.6	60.8	20 168	74.1	59.0	155.9	19.3	15.7	68.9	6.7	3.3	18.5	25.3	24 503	22 708	21 311
Boone	1 063.5	87.3	27 446	100.9	99.6	631.6	64.1	53.2	34.0	6.9	2.2	10.4	7.7	336 319	314 423	325 092
Brown	117.5	79.2	17 070	62.8	18.9	86.0	D	D	D	4.2	2.8	8.5	21.0	D	889	1 201
Bureau	771.6	34.3	21 750	80.0	128.1	375.2	D	22.5	D	8.7	4.5	21.3	18.2	84 440	82 212	78 236
Calhoun	105.8	35.9	21 569	79.3	20.2	36.9	D	D	D	14.2	5.6	16.8	20.2	D	2 247	2 150
Carroll	402.1	55.0	23 795	87.5	64.7	219.4	21.8	15.7	60.5	6.5	3.2	10.0	21.1	34 534	32 036	30 790
Cass	297.6	46.5	22 430	82.5	52.4	185.5	D	6.5	D	6.5	2.8	13.0	12.3	D	59 750	55 408
Champaign	4 034.1	36.2	23 753	87.3	410.1	3 026.5	18.3	12.7	81.3	8.5	4.8	24.6	35.7	385 013	390 275	376 111
Christian	796.7	35.0	22 253	81.8	154.0	370.5	30.2	16.9	D	10.9	D	20.0	14.2	62 687	24 548	23 227
Clark	332.7	43.1	20 112	74.0	64.5	154.9	44.0	30.5	55.2	9.7	3.9	12.8	13.7	56 517	50 961	45 972
Clay	301.0	44.2	20 788	76.4	67.2	183.0	D	44.8	D	6.3	3.0	11.9	14.3	81 981	79 880	68 534
Clinton	805.6	48.2	22 582	83.0	120.9	354.1	21.6	10.3	69.6	12.6	3.3	18.7	21.8	36 460	33 051	33 560
Coles	1 150.8	47.2	22 148	81.4	180.9	909.1	31.8	27.1	67.6	8.4	2.7	25.6	20.7	246 570	235 153	206 944
Cook	165 150.2	45.8	31 806	116.9	20 183.1	138 378.4	20.8	16.5	79.2	6.6	13.4	32.0	11.8	22 890 484	22 941 465	21 257 069
Crawford	401.7	33.7	19 174	70.5	76.7	250.1	D	40.5	D	8.9	4.1	15.6	15.0	101 197	93 502	86 243
Cumberland	234.6	54.1	21 102	77.6	37.1	69.0	D	8.7	D	16.2	3.3	17.0	20.3	6 013	2 571	2 525
DeKalb	2 137.3	63.9	24 882	91.5	213.9	1 113.1	27.0	19.4	70.4	8.4	4.2	18.4	30.4	215 824	209 265	215 007
De Witt	389.6	53.2	23 276	85.6	64.6	317.3	NA	16.2	D	6.2	D	15.5	11.6	51 463	52 019	50 452
Douglas	433.9	42.4	21 820	80.2	66.9	264.4	D	39.1	D	13.3	3.4	9.6	9.8	103 370	94 782	87 959
DuPage	37 191.2	68.7	42 215	155.2	2 142.9	29 401.9	20.2	14.0	79.8	9.0	8.1	36.1	6.5	4 110 170	3 741 175	3 471 790
Edgar	437.0	50.8	22 094	81.2	78.3	240.3	D	15.3	D	6.6	3.9	15.2	17.1	36 790	37 201	35 216
Edwards	136.8	20.2	19 679	72.3	25.2	97.2	D	D	D	5.2	2.2	6.6	8.5	D	61 068	55 982
Effingham	802.8	51.2	23 939	88.0	106.4	624.3	38.7	31.6	59.5	11.7	3.3	22.4	10.2	196 968	177 497	174 417
Fayette	398.2	55.2	17 997	66.2	82.7	199.7	28.5	22.1	64.5	12.7	3.0	16.8	20.0	44 048	43 959	39 653
Ford	330.4	28.6	23 483	86.3	53.6	151.4	23.9	15.8	69.4	10.7	3.3	19.3	15.2	23 891	24 490	23 894
Franklin	697.1	28.6	17 232	63.3	196.1	314.9	D	16.0	70.4	13.4	2.4	22.2	22.4	50 256	45 192	42 314
Fulton	768.4	46.8	19 849	73.0	168.0	253.5	10.8	4.7	87.7	15.1	3.8	25.6	27.3	11 833	11 244	11 089
Gallatin	123.3	22.5	18 605	68.4	31.6	58.9	D	5.2	D	7.9	D	7.8	23.5	3 061	2 944	2 605
Greene	256.0	34.0	16 268	59.8	59.9	90.9	D	10.3	D	11.5	5.7	17.1	23.5	9 349	9 776	9 925
Grundy	1 039.1	65.6	28 277	103.9	112.3	596.6	25.1	17.5	D	7.7	2.2	D	11.0	104 473	102 640	100 627
Hamilton	148.2	32.8	17 206	63.3	38.6	49.9	10.3	4.6	80.3	12.1	3.4	15.4	35.2	2 316	2 104	2 241
Hancock	462.5	49.4	21 864	80.4	75.8	202.2	D	D	D	6.2	3.4	14.5	15.1	D	57 466	53 331
Hardin	80.9	20.9	16 407	60.3	24.8	35.3	D	D	D	5.7	D	21.4	26.4	D	3 319	3 381
Henderson	165.8	55.1	19 235	70.7	27.9	38.0	D	D	D	9.4	5.1	15.3	32.1	D	180	254
Henry	1 205.2	47.9	23 384	86.0	171.1	450.5	D	15.2	D	14.7	4.7	16.1	19.7	68 291	60 205	48 248
Iroquois	652.5	31.1	20 863	76.7	124.9	290.2	D	14.6	D	8.6	5.4	21.4	14.4	42 473	42 447	41 704
Jackson	1 174.1	44.7	19 294	70.9	199.9	870.3	D	10.3	D	10.1	3.2	23.8	45.4	37 731	33 241	33 153
Jasper	201.6	32.2	18 958	69.7	35.3	106.3	16.9	10.9	69.9	7.9	3.4	8.7	19.3	11 607	14 070	21 534
Jefferson	819.8	49.6	20 999	77.2	158.0	606.5	31.4	21.4	67.4	12.6	4.7	25.0	11.9	129 699	133 869	130 499
Jersey	452.3	51.4	21 021	77.3	72.4	135.6	8.2	2.2	92.6	16.1	3.7	32.0	26.8	2 963	3 590	3 900
Jo Daviess	590.1	61.6	27 442	100.9	72.5	288.5	D	24.7	D	10.7	3.4	21.8	11.3	71 357	62 207	60 894
Johnson	186.5	53.4	13 767	50.6	42.0	81.5	D	2.2	D	8.2	3.7	13.6	49.2	1 782	1 485	1 671
Kane	10 863.9	60.4	27 736	102.0	861.6	6 811.0	32.2	24.8	67.7	7.9	6.6	27.7	14.2	1 691 076	1 573 078	1 485 218

[1] Based on resident population estimated as of July 1, 1998.　[2] Includes farm earnings; see table B-10 for these data.　[3] Includes mining and construction, not shown separately.　[4] Includes agricultural services, forestry, and fisheries; transportation and public utilities; and wholesale trade, not shown separately.　[5] Finance, insurance, and real estate.

Source: Personal Income and Earnings—U.S. Bureau of Economic Analysis, "Regional Economic Information System (REIS) 1969-1998" on CD-ROM (related Internet site <http://www.bea.doc.gov/bea/regional/data.htm>).

[Includes U.S., states, and 3,142 counties/county equivalents defined as of January 1, 1992. For changes to these areas since January 1, 1992, see appendix B. Geographic Information]

County	Personal income, 1998 Total (mil. dol.)	Percent change, 1990–1998	Per capita¹ Amount (dollars)	Per capita¹ Percent of national average	Transfer payments (mil. dol.)	Earnings Total² (mil. dol.)	Total³	Manufacturing	Total⁴	Retail trade	FIRE⁵	Services	Government	Manufacturing earnings 1998 ($1,000)	1997 ($1,000)	1996 ($1,000)
ILLINOIS—Con.																
Kankakee	2 311.9	45.3	22 596	83.1	409.1	1 418.3	D	24.7	D	11.1	4.4	24.1	15.5	351 030	371 873	348 809
Kendall	1 451.6	85.4	28 026	103.0	97.9	637.1	D	48.3	D	8.6	3.5	9.7	10.7	307 841	299 487	270 101
Knox	1 269.5	47.4	22 830	83.9	249.8	850.3	NA	24.2	66.7	9.2	2.6	24.6	12.6	205 731	200 333	190 533
Lake	26 264.7	73.9	43 174	158.7	1 382.8	16 351.6	D	22.8	D	8.1	9.2	25.1	15.6	3 733 436	3 402 292	3 227 173
La Salle	2 510.4	48.2	22 782	83.7	409.4	1 537.3	27.7	20.1	71.7	11.2	4.5	19.9	13.4	309 315	292 946	283 598
Lawrence	347.9	40.7	22 699	83.4	77.3	158.6	D	3.8	D	7.1	9.6	17.6	16.5	5 958	6 461	8 896
Lee	758.4	40.3	21 083	77.5	124.5	429.6	34.7	29.6	65.0	8.1	3.8	23.0	20.4	127 328	132 096	120 296
Livingston	894.9	30.5	22 575	83.0	132.4	536.3	42.6	36.3	55.6	7.5	3.1	14.9	19.4	194 534	174 972	170 231
Logan	617.4	30.5	19 358	71.2	113.4	335.0	D	18.4	D	11.7	4.1	18.0	26.0	61 727	59 960	58 623
McDonough	677.0	53.6	19 080	70.1	105.5	482.9	19.5	15.3	77.5	19.7	3.0	12.3	36.0	73 681	74 779	68 102
McHenry	7 646.2	87.9	31 721	116.6	502.8	3 143.8	44.0	31.8	55.7	8.5	4.0	20.1	11.1	999 115	949 617	879 425
McLean	3 908.1	62.7	27 260	100.2	352.7	3 172.3	18.7	13.4	81.4	7.9	28.9	21.9	13.1	426 388	436 057	425 007
Macon	2 918.5	37.8	25 674	94.4	454.9	2 222.5	41.8	32.9	58.0	8.7	3.2	20.6	9.1	731 910	691 466	666 821
Macoupin	1 099.9	45.7	22 561	82.9	198.3	394.3	29.4	14.0	68.0	9.9	4.0	18.7	17.5	55 102	57 813	59 429
Madison	6 353.6	42.9	24 514	90.1	984.2	3 400.6	36.9	29.0	62.9	9.4	3.9	22.9	16.1	986 586	946 159	960 390
Marion	911.1	46.3	21 728	79.9	209.9	570.3	36.2	30.8	60.7	7.2	2.6	22.2	14.3	175 582	176 260	174 725
Marshall	294.4	40.3	22 828	83.9	49.7	116.9	D	33.2	D	8.5	4.3	18.6	9.7	38 779	36 960	35 117
Mason	357.9	56.8	21 261	78.2	71.0	144.6	D	12.9	67.6	10.0	3.0	14.0	22.4	18 612	17 302	15 806
Massac	302.6	50.4	19 486	71.6	70.4	174.6	D	22.8	D	7.9	3.1	25.3	14.8	39 727	36 528	25 119
Menard	314.9	64.5	25 142	92.4	38.0	84.8	D	2.0	D	10.6	5.5	16.6	23.1	1 710	1 795	1 587
Mercer	397.2	52.5	22 538	82.9	57.4	112.4	20.5	13.3	67.8	8.1	3.5	13.3	29.2	14 926	13 330	11 569
Monroe	705.3	75.7	26 474	97.3	79.4	215.5	20.4	4.1	73.7	14.0	4.7	22.2	17.3	8 878	8 658	8 654
Montgomery	629.2	41.1	20 014	73.6	128.3	342.7	23.6	16.3	72.2	9.3	4.1	22.6	19.0	55 942	60 839	56 061
Morgan	797.1	39.1	22 511	82.8	138.1	494.5	D	27.1	D	9.4	4.6	24.5	16.2	133 962	129 351	116 449
Moultrie	296.7	39.1	20 524	75.4	53.7	127.8	36.3	24.1	61.9	10.0	3.4	18.2	13.7	30 810	26 395	24 324
Ogle	1 181.0	55.1	23 377	85.9	144.2	645.3	36.7	31.4	61.0	6.3	3.1	14.8	13.0	202 425	197 384	189 220
Peoria	5 016.4	45.2	27 638	101.6	676.0	3 866.5	23.8	17.9	75.9	9.4	6.1	38.4	11.1	691 092	690 666	645 791
Perry	392.7	28.0	18 470	67.9	91.1	187.4	D	27.1	D	9.3	3.4	D	21.5	50 725	44 997	43 290
Piatt	405.5	40.5	24 681	90.7	53.4	139.5	D	11.5	D	10.1	4.7	29.3	18.2	16 066	15 558	15 996
Pike	328.3	48.0	19 002	69.9	71.1	156.0	D	5.4	D	12.4	4.2	17.3	17.7	8 401	8 612	8 787
Pope	71.5	42.4	14 966	55.0	17.7	32.1	D	3.8	D	5.4	1.0	D	42.8	1 219	952	1 068
Pulaski	122.8	37.2	16 860	62.0	37.3	63.7	26.1	4.7	71.6	4.6	1.5	15.8	38.8	3 021	2 785	10 494
Putnam	142.8	30.7	24 600	90.4	19.0	100.6	65.1	55.4	D	3.8	2.4	D	6.7	55 752	51 454	50 962
Randolph	632.4	25.5	18 781	69.0	124.7	400.2	D	21.9	66.1	9.4	3.5	13.5	27.4	87 592	80 851	77 630
Richland	371.1	51.6	22 115	81.3	66.9	238.6	D	22.6	66.4	12.4	4.6	15.5	21.5	53 822	61 094	54 521
Rock Island	3 952.3	41.5	26 719	98.2	525.9	3 451.8	31.1	25.1	68.7	7.2	5.2	21.2	20.9	868 085	882 343	750 569
St. Clair	5 897.4	38.5	22 527	82.8	1 042.5	3 452.6	15.6	9.4	84.1	10.1	5.3	26.5	30.2	324 702	305 447	290 302
Saline	501.3	28.4	19 145	70.4	137.2	297.4	31.1	3.7	67.3	9.8	3.4	21.7	20.7	10 934	8 157	7 143
Sangamon	5 237.3	46.4	27 351	100.5	646.4	4 131.9	9.3	4.0	90.2	7.3	8.9	32.4	30.7	164 540	151 926	144 229
Schuyler	144.0	46.7	19 019	69.9	26.2	65.4	25.1	4.2	66.0	10.1	2.7	17.7	21.7	2 713	2 874	2 430
Scott	100.0	35.8	17 804	65.4	20.2	74.3	50.0	2.2	D	3.4	2.3	D	12.3	1 655	1 575	1 744
Shelby	453.2	42.2	19 979	73.4	81.3	202.1	D	22.4	D	9.0	3.7	19.3	15.8	45 194	37 839	37 702
Stark	137.1	34.6	21 709	79.8	27.5	50.8	D	11.9	D	6.6	5.0	14.1	17.9	6 054	4 542	3 885
Stephenson	1 303.1	47.5	26 666	98.0	173.8	876.4	47.9	39.0	46.0	5.9	8.9	15.9	9.3	341 926	322 399	306 711
Tazewell	3 358.1	49.4	25 966	95.5	445.8	2 499.9	54.3	47.3	44.4	6.8	3.4	11.4	8.4	1 183 092	1 106 915	1 011 115
Union	348.4	44.3	19 353	71.1	84.4	170.2	D	12.3	D	9.4	2.6	19.8	37.6	20 849	18 819	17 783
Vermilion	1 726.2	28.1	20 436	75.1	348.0	1 127.4	32.0	26.6	67.9	9.6	4.5	19.0	20.5	300 246	293 645	281 845
Wabash	241.8	17.0	19 237	70.7	49.8	134.0	44.0	21.3	58.3	8.9	4.4	16.7	17.6	28 551	27 211	28 308
Warren	340.1	28.4	17 979	66.1	64.9	169.1	D	21.9	D	10.1	4.3	21.8	18.0	37 072	33 008	34 447
Washington	368.6	52.8	24 087	88.5	60.8	228.9	D	24.8	D	9.2	3.1	D	10.8	56 699	53 498	40 166
Wayne	338.0	44.0	19 932	73.3	69.9	171.4	34.5	24.6	59.1	9.5	4.8	16.2	14.6	42 240	40 399	37 848
White	335.4	36.7	21 496	79.0	75.7	172.6	27.0	5.0	68.0	12.3	4.0	17.8	19.6	8 648	8 009	7 534
Whiteside	1 421.6	45.3	23 761	87.3	231.2	836.4	D	37.6	D	8.8	4.1	16.1	14.3	314 110	302 839	286 601
Will	12 018.4	76.4	26 114	96.0	1 070.5	5 239.2	31.2	18.1	68.4	8.9	4.5	25.1	15.4	950 552	920 421	886 698
Williamson	1 298.4	50.9	21 165	77.8	248.2	748.6	19.7	11.3	80.2	15.7	6.6	20.2	25.7	84 939	80 973	75 248
Winnebago	7 013.6	47.6	26 203	96.3	894.8	5 473.6	42.1	36.7	57.7	7.8	5.7	23.4	9.5	2 007 487	1 933 065	1 808 147
Woodford	857.0	52.2	24 352	89.5	99.8	329.1	35.8	27.8	60.9	8.9	2.5	17.4	15.7	91 537	84 943	73 428
INDIANA	148 650.9	51.8	25 163	92.5	19 383.1	106 049.3	37.1	30.1	62.4	9.1	6.2	21.8	13.1	31 920 916	30 060 690	28 630 204
Adams	748.0	53.6	22 653	83.3	91.4	476.0	D	55.0	D	9.0	2.4	9.2	11.1	261 739	229 740	206 591
Allen	8 851.9	46.7	28 153	103.5	964.7	7 297.5	34.2	27.7	65.7	8.1	9.3	23.5	8.7	2 024 103	1 935 479	1 868 858
Bartholomew	1 947.3	61.9	28 046	103.1	209.8	1 746.3	55.5	50.4	44.4	6.8	6.3	13.7	10.0	879 272	808 111	768 648
Benton	206.7	35.3	21 189	77.9	31.6	73.9	D	21.6	D	9.4	5.6	17.7	24.5	15 942	14 745	14 168
Blackford	273.3	33.9	19 599	72.0	51.8	135.6	D	47.7	D	8.0	3.2	11.7	17.0	64 669	64 596	58 757
Boone	1 436.6	77.7	32 762	120.4	121.3	486.3	D	16.4	D	9.4	4.8	21.7	14.2	79 883	72 602	66 432
Brown	383.6	83.8	24 054	88.4	40.8	86.7	NA	9.1	D	15.9	4.2	28.7	23.8	7 902	6 975	6 637
Carroll	459.9	48.4	22 992	84.5	57.7	185.3	D	39.7	D	6.7	3.3	11.5	13.2	73 583	67 562	62 929
Cass	882.4	45.2	22 725	83.5	150.7	543.0	D	38.3	D	8.9	3.0	12.1	19.8	208 204	188 976	164 492

¹ Based on resident population estimated as of July 1, 1998.   ² Includes farm earnings; see table B-10 for these data.   ³ Includes mining and construction, not shown separately.   ⁴ Includes agricultural services, forestry, and fisheries; transportation and public utilities; and wholesale trade, not shown separately.   ⁵ Finance, insurance, and real estate.

Source: Personal Income and Earnings—U.S. Bureau of Economic Analysis, "Regional Economic Information System (REIS) 1969-1998" on CD-ROM (related Internet site <http://www.bea.doc.gov/bea/regional/data.htm>).

[Includes U.S., states, and 3,142 counties/county equivalents defined as of January 1, 1992. For changes to these areas since January 1, 1992, see appendix B. Geographic Information]

County	Personal income, 1998													Manufacturing earnings		
	Total (mil. dol.)	Per capita[1]			Transfer payments (mil. dol.)	Earnings								1998 ($1,000)	1997 ($1,000)	1996 ($1,000)
		Percent change, 1990–1998	Amount (dollars)	Percent of national average		Total[2] (mil. dol.)	Percent, by selected industry–									
							Goods-related		Service-related							
							Total[3]	Manu-facturing	Total[4]	Retail trade	FIRE[5]	Serv-ices	Gov-ern-ment			
INDIANA—Con.																
Clark	2 313.6	59.1	24 615	90.5	331.7	1 450.0	27.1	19.0	72.7	13.1	3.2	19.5	17.8	275 903	268 010	258 520
Clay	514.8	46.7	19 263	70.8	100.6	241.4	D	38.0	52.3	11.6	3.3	12.2	16.2	91 830	77 884	73 318
Clinton	730.6	48.6	22 011	80.9	110.2	383.3	NA	46.9	44.4	7.2	2.5	14.8	13.3	179 606	179 383	171 644
Crawford	182.4	59.1	17 226	63.3	41.2	56.1	D	D	D	12.8	4.0	D	25.4	D	6 320	5 703
Daviess	568.5	42.6	19 641	72.2	102.5	298.5	34.1	16.4	D	11.1	D	14.7	17.1	49 003	47 238	45 184
Dearborn	1 106.0	74.9	23 447	86.2	134.2	480.9	NA	21.6	68.2	10.2	4.1	26.4	15.4	103 673	98 142	96 818
Decatur	597.6	66.1	23 381	86.0	77.2	408.0	D	51.5	D	7.5	2.7	14.6	10.2	210 192	199 514	184 725
De Kalb	953.5	65.4	24 258	89.2	108.2	802.4	66.9	62.4	32.0	5.5	1.9	10.1	7.3	500 645	455 959	396 759
Delaware	2 739.1	37.9	23 545	86.6	433.7	1 886.6	D	26.2	D	9.8	4.3	25.6	17.8	494 094	556 150	523 774
Dubois	1 113.4	61.1	20 079	103.2	116.1	929.1	55.5	49.9	43.1	8.6	2.9	13.3	6.9	463 305	416 370	384 871
Elkhart	4 409.0	57.3	25 527	93.8	482.5	4 219.6	D	55.6	D	6.3	2.9	13.6	6.0	2 345 122	2 138 878	2 080 898
Fayette	552.2	36.6	21 218	78.0	107.7	418.5	D	57.7	D	7.0	1.8	15.4	11.5	241 351	249 429	241 554
Floyd	1 871.0	61.9	26 052	95.8	239.5	890.5	D	27.6	D	8.7	5.0	21.6	18.4	245 782	234 785	220 611
Fountain	362.2	43.1	19 763	72.7	65.8	184.0	D	49.8	D	8.7	3.2	11.0	14.4	91 578	76 464	64 978
Franklin	450.8	63.1	20 660	75.9	66.3	126.2	D	13.7	D	11.1	5.2	25.5	21.4	17 325	17 161	15 705
Fulton	421.5	50.2	20 398	75.0	68.0	248.1	D	40.8	D	9.9	4.2	11.9	14.2	101 226	103 118	93 520
Gibson	753.6	51.1	23 432	86.1	117.3	368.6	41.0	32.8	56.8	10.5	2.5	15.0	10.8	120 711	84 960	72 584
Grant	1 554.1	29.1	21 391	78.6	295.4	1 084.7	D	40.3	D	9.5	3.8	20.4	15.1	437 498	461 119	458 691
Greene	612.9	37.4	18 391	67.6	114.2	243.4	35.6	30.4	65.9	11.0	3.3	16.1	23.9	25 306	25 665	25 382
Hamilton	6 396.2	116.9	39 295	144.5	315.8	3 257.7	24.2	14.4	75.5	11.5	20.1	22.7	8.2	467 716	439 865	396 761
Hancock	1 544.2	77.3	28 337	104.2	143.7	616.4	D	33.3	D	8.8	4.1	15.4	16.3	205 321	181 339	151 995
Harrison	767.9	73.3	22 182	81.5	100.2	285.7	36.5	29.2	62.0	11.1	3.6	18.9	18.2	83 419	77 671	68 759
Hendricks	2 653.4	80.9	27 775	102.1	224.0	938.0	D	7.3	D	14.1	5.2	20.6	19.7	68 670	58 956	44 561
Henry	1 113.5	45.4	22 868	84.1	195.2	552.2	D	42.6	D	10.3	3.3	14.0	17.5	235 236	221 181	198 000
Howard	2 229.7	47.6	26 732	98.3	298.1	2 265.6	D	63.5	D	6.6	2.7	11.1	8.3	1 438 977	1 357 372	1 345 748
Huntington	884.7	49.3	23 725	87.2	115.8	510.4	D	45.7	D	9.5	3.5	13.6	12.8	233 190	235 903	229 597
Jackson	861.4	53.0	20 988	77.2	132.5	626.2	D	40.0	D	15.6	3.4	11.9	12.0	250 596	229 942	209 740
Jasper	578.4	54.3	19 896	73.1	87.1	344.1	27.3	16.3	68.7	11.0	2.6	13.7	14.4	56 234	52 400	44 516
Jay	401.7	38.1	18 499	68.0	76.7	237.9	D	45.8	D	8.9	3.0	13.6	15.1	109 006	109 785	105 219
Jefferson	614.0	45.8	19 521	71.8	117.7	404.1	D	30.6	64.1	11.5	2.8	24.6	16.1	123 775	135 514	137 911
Jennings	566.0	75.7	20 395	75.0	117.3	263.2	D	29.8	D	13.0	2.0	15.4	22.6	78 495	70 281	63 282
Johnson	2 992.6	75.6	27 357	100.6	284.9	1 229.1	30.8	20.8	69.0	16.6	5.7	24.8	14.4	255 479	248 374	222 913
Knox	852.1	41.6	21 704	79.8	173.2	525.6	17.5	11.5	79.4	10.9	5.7	19.4	29.8	60 283	58 982	52 935
Kosciusko	1 782.7	64.2	25 055	92.1	199.8	1 260.2	D	56.4	D	7.4	2.9	13.2	7.2	710 580	645 516	634 951
Lagrange	612.6	59.0	18 344	67.4	72.8	427.1	D	54.1	D	8.0	2.2	10.2	9.7	230 836	211 066	202 682
Lake	11 903.5	44.5	24 749	91.0	1 867.3	8 021.3	37.3	27.3	62.6	8.6	4.3	25.7	12.2	2 188 350	2 121 934	2 139 460
La Porte	2 535.6	44.4	23 084	84.9	374.7	1 572.1	35.8	29.3	63.2	10.4	2.9	22.3	15.3	461 020	458 856	443 329
Lawrence	962.1	48.4	21 056	77.4	165.1	561.7	49.4	43.1	50.5	10.5	2.6	16.7	14.4	241 875	243 224	230 917
Madison	3 047.3	43.2	23 220	85.4	507.2	1 780.5	D	39.3	D	9.8	4.0	22.6	12.9	698 974	721 255	761 561
Marion	23 446.4	41.9	28 851	106.1	2 808.3	25 347.9	26.6	21.3	73.3	8.8	9.6	26.7	12.0	5 387 573	4 847 116	4 457 689
Marshall	1 028.2	53.0	22 564	82.9	129.3	644.1	NA	45.4	48.0	8.2	4.0	15.0	10.5	292 282	284 064	273 304
Martin	207.8	37.9	19 845	73.0	34.4	365.0	D	6.1	D	2.0	.8	3.8	75.0	22 243	20 762	20 657
Miami	672.3	21.1	20 061	73.7	117.9	344.3	D	28.5	D	9.1	2.6	11.4	29.9	98 021	89 073	82 249
Monroe	2 638.7	54.9	22 636	83.2	291.9	1 995.6	25.9	19.6	74.1	9.7	5.0	21.2	30.5	391 637	369 428	343 892
Montgomery	830.2	44.8	22 767	83.7	124.1	633.3	D	51.1	D	7.9	2.5	16.5	9.2	323 592	321 620	313 769
Morgan	1 530.0	68.6	23 337	85.8	170.1	481.2	33.3	19.4	66.7	12.5	4.6	20.3	18.3	93 429	83 325	80 842
Newton	272.4	35.6	18 408	67.7	44.3	128.2	D	37.2	D	6.3	3.7	8.5	17.6	47 682	43 512	40 539
Noble	968.0	68.2	22 720	83.5	118.0	672.4	D	61.1	D	6.0	1.6	10.1	9.9	411 075	388 845	375 872
Ohio	120.2	69.6	22 065	81.1	16.1	66.3	D	D	D	3.6	1.4	D	12.6	D	1 332	1 212
Orange	364.3	51.0	18 593	68.3	73.2	212.4	48.4	33.0	49.8	9.0	2.8	14.2	16.1	70 133	68 575	63 154
Owen	350.3	55.7	17 146	63.0	62.2	127.9	D	34.1	D	8.8	4.5	13.2	18.5	43 679	39 583	36 073
Parke	328.2	46.0	19 473	71.6	59.0	100.3	D	19.9	D	10.3	3.5	20.9	30.3	19 986	17 113	17 985
Perry	377.7	48.5	19 563	71.9	64.4	183.8	D	34.3	D	9.3	4.2	13.7	25.1	63 082	52 093	43 346
Pike	265.6	36.0	20 588	75.7	50.7	122.6	33.4	5.6	65.0	5.2	2.4	9.5	14.5	6 817	6 308	6 128
Porter	4 059.8	61.2	27 758	102.0	396.9	2 206.5	D	34.4	D	8.7	3.6	19.4	12.6	759 288	720 441	724 301
Posey	670.8	55.9	25 357	93.2	81.2	410.7	D	50.6	D	4.6	1.5	11.1	10.1	207 790	201 595	184 133
Pulaski	289.7	41.5	21 566	79.3	45.1	171.5	D	33.8	D	6.8	3.5	10.6	17.5	57 991	55 878	53 340
Putnam	679.0	57.4	19 653	72.2	99.1	360.5	31.9	25.0	67.5	14.3	3.1	20.0	21.5	92 397	87 143	83 843
Randolph	576.0	40.8	20 945	77.0	99.0	260.2	D	39.4	D	7.7	2.5	11.5	17.6	102 458	106 045	113 619
Ripley	635.2	58.5	23 311	85.7	78.1	445.9	D	51.1	D	6.7	5.3	15.1	9.1	227 928	210 871	197 810
Rush	387.2	44.7	21 228	78.0	62.8	183.4	D	34.1	D	8.4	D	16.5	19.3	62 598	54 104	51 308
St. Joseph	6 656.6	51.2	25 782	94.8	884.3	4 699.3	D	21.7	D	9.2	6.1	32.3	10.1	1 018 654	988 766	960 171
Scott	441.2	58.7	19 139	70.4	81.7	209.5	D	40.3	D	11.5	2.7	15.3	18.3	84 371	79 547	76 024
Shelby	1 032.0	49.5	23 817	87.6	131.1	582.9	53.8	45.7	45.7	7.5	2.1	13.5	12.6	267 160	254 292	227 217
Spencer	431.0	50.7	20 509	75.4	61.9	268.0	32.0	25.2	67.0	5.4	3.7	16.8	11.0	67 485	48 363	43 220
Starke	388.3	45.5	16 222	59.6	80.8	148.8	D	23.7	D	11.7	2.7	19.5	19.3	35 343	34 635	32 717
Steuben	760.8	67.9	24 192	88.9	94.6	568.6	D	47.1	D	10.4	2.7	13.4	8.0	267 576	253 180	222 120
Sullivan	403.8	45.7	18 912	69.5	84.1	184.7	18.4	9.3	76.8	8.3	4.4	13.6	32.5	17 210	16 073	14 091
Switzerland	145.1	60.0	16 415	60.3	28.2	51.7	D	29.0	D	7.0	3.2	14.5	24.7	14 984	15 284	13 990
Tippecanoe	3 336.5	57.6	23 617	86.8	340.6	2 834.4	D	31.4	D	8.2	5.5	19.4	23.8	890 372	833 333	741 596

[1] Based on resident population estimated as of July 1, 1998. [2] Includes farm earnings; see table B–10 for these data. [3] Includes mining and construction, not shown separately. [4] Includes agricultural services, forestry, and fisheries; transportation and public utilities; and wholesale trade, not shown separately. [5] Finance, insurance, and real estate.

Source: Personal Income and Earnings—U.S. Bureau of Economic Analysis, "Regional Economic Information System (REIS) 1969-1998" on CD-ROM (related Internet site <http://www.bea.doc.gov/bea/regional/data.htm>).

Table B–8. Counties — **Personal Income and Earnings**–Con.

[Includes U.S., states, and 3,142 counties/county equivalents defined as of January 1, 1992. For changes to these areas since January 1, 1992, see appendix B. Geographic Information]

| County | Personal income, 1998 | | | | | | | | | | | | | Manufacturing earnings | | |
	Total (mil. dol.)	Per capita[1] Percent change, 1990–1998	Amount (dollars)	Percent of national average	Transfer payments (mil. dol.)	Earnings Total[2] (mil. dol.)	Percent, by selected industry — Goods-related Total[3]	Manufacturing	Service-related Total[4]	Retail trade	FIRE[5]	Services	Government	1998 ($1,000)	1997 ($1,000)	1996 ($1,000)
INDIANA—Con.																
Tipton	414.2	48.1	24 874	91.4	54.7	149.3	NA	23.4	65.4	10.4	2.6	14.1	23.1	34 971	32 455	29 680
Union	132.2	39.2	18 276	67.2	21.8	48.8	D	13.2	D	15.6	6.9	13.7	22.6	6 459	5 652	3 590
Vanderburgh	4 536.0	42.1	27 042	99.4	690.7	3 914.6	34.0	20.9	66.0	10.1	6.5	28.4	9.0	819 300	760 283	735 153
Vermillion	353.9	42.8	20 884	76.8	63.3	215.4	D	D	D	9.1	1.8	17.5	10.6	D	84 355	84 837
Vigo	2 275.5	36.8	21 679	79.7	417.2	1 687.0	27.6	20.5	72.4	14.1	4.0	25.8	18.2	346 180	335 140	324 261
Wabash	774.6	37.6	22 406	82.4	124.8	496.6	D	45.3	D	8.3	3.2	14.7	12.7	224 804	207 850	210 620
Warren	159.3	36.5	19 116	70.3	24.7	55.6	D	17.3	62.2	5.2	2.8	16.4	20.4	9 629	21 557	18 680
Warrick	1 308.7	61.7	25 385	93.3	138.7	534.8	52.1	38.7	48.2	6.5	3.9	16.2	11.5	207 237	183 676	174 579
Washington	530.6	66.8	19 087	70.2	86.4	210.1	D	39.4	D	10.0	3.1	12.0	19.5	82 766	80 324	71 758
Wayne	1 641.3	43.2	22 968	84.4	285.8	1 193.3	D	32.1	D	10.1	4.0	23.0	12.5	383 230	376 679	356 533
Wells	664.4	47.9	24 744	91.0	76.3	382.2	D	35.2	D	13.3	2.4	18.1	12.5	134 405	124 995	119 128
White	543.5	44.4	21 459	78.9	88.3	319.4	D	38.2	D	9.9	D	12.2	14.0	122 095	94 711	109 783
Whitley	727.0	55.9	23 948	88.0	88.5	401.3	NA	48.3	44.6	8.3	2.8	15.6	11.4	193 934	195 963	177 803
IOWA	70 797.1	46.5	24 745	91.0	9 742.0	49 141.5	27.5	21.1	69.0	9.2	7.7	22.3	15.8	10 356 843	9 803 023	9 189 590
Adair	173.3	32.3	21 382	78.6	30.2	86.7	D	22.4	D	8.3	3.9	D	16.4	19 415	18 043	17 963
Adams	90.5	30.2	20 639	75.9	19.1	49.1	D	19.2	D	7.2	3.6	26.2	15.5	9 431	8 984	8 679
Allamakee	287.2	41.3	20 441	75.1	48.9	172.8	D	21.5	D	10.1	3.7	13.3	14.8	37 090	36 258	33 616
Appanoose	259.1	42.0	19 096	70.2	60.8	144.0	D	32.2	D	10.7	3.2	17.9	17.0	46 400	41 001	35 321
Audubon	142.8	27.3	20 984	77.1	28.4	67.8	D	7.9	D	8.9	4.3	17.3	18.5	5 346	4 650	5 125
Benton	579.5	63.8	22 814	83.9	76.8	190.6	D	14.3	D	9.4	5.1	12.8	22.3	27 201	26 064	23 208
Black Hawk	2 960.6	43.8	24 484	90.0	467.3	2 345.1	D	30.5	D	9.1	5.0	23.5	15.9	714 331	726 612	659 917
Boone	641.2	46.3	24 554	90.3	119.7	300.0	D	9.7	80.1	14.3	2.9	16.2	22.7	29 096	29 007	27 022
Bremer	566.7	53.0	24 275	89.2	78.9	310.4	D	24.1	D	7.4	13.5	18.3	12.3	74 702	72 982	68 420
Buchanan	445.2	41.3	21 050	77.4	66.3	224.3	D	22.2	D	10.1	4.1	10.7	22.0	49 804	45 687	39 683
Buena Vista	450.1	40.1	23 184	85.2	72.9	303.2	30.4	25.6	57.4	10.0	4.3	17.4	13.7	77 610	69 770	67 073
Butler	323.5	34.0	20 699	76.1	57.0	132.6	D	14.2	58.6	7.5	3.7	14.2	14.8	18 778	16 184	14 480
Calhoun	227.5	31.8	20 002	73.5	49.0	98.3	D	7.2	D	8.3	5.4	25.7	24.0	7 072	6 630	6 487
Carroll	530.6	51.4	24 548	90.2	78.0	356.3	D	13.3	D	10.0	7.6	20.8	10.0	47 326	45 532	39 749
Cass	320.4	34.0	21 883	80.4	62.0	198.5	D	18.9	D	8.9	4.2	18.8	20.1	37 559	34 526	29 400
Cedar	439.2	45.8	24 460	89.9	54.5	166.9	D	15.3	D	9.8	4.1	16.8	17.6	25 455	25 966	24 387
Cerro Gordo	1 147.3	42.3	24 902	91.5	181.7	805.9	D	19.0	D	11.2	6.4	30.6	12.0	153 347	141 224	133 625
Cherokee	290.8	26.0	22 044	81.0	52.1	181.1	D	20.3	D	13.5	3.6	15.6	18.2	36 786	36 555	36 199
Chickasaw	299.6	48.6	22 320	82.0	46.3	186.5	D	33.6	D	6.8	3.2	13.8	10.4	62 765	56 391	50 117
Clarke	165.2	41.6	19 891	73.1	31.4	102.9	D	36.8	D	8.9	3.5	13.9	18.7	37 824	32 726	26 587
Clay	433.7	45.9	24 817	91.2	60.0	306.7	D	15.7	D	12.1	4.0	19.5	14.2	48 293	49 126	42 978
Clayton	407.8	41.6	21 796	80.1	69.3	233.2	D	16.7	D	7.9	D	17.4	16.5	39 004	37 678	35 456
Clinton	1 151.3	38.0	23 062	84.8	192.9	714.3	D	31.9	D	9.1	3.6	23.2	11.3	227 726	224 179	219 167
Crawford	334.9	33.6	20 342	74.8	60.6	218.8	D	29.9	D	9.0	3.1	15.2	15.8	65 484	59 249	57 445
Dallas	995.2	81.5	26 996	99.2	99.0	428.6	D	17.4	D	7.4	D	21.5	13.3	74 551	74 545	68 297
Davis	151.3	32.6	17 879	65.7	29.3	75.0	D	20.4	D	8.9	3.4	17.1	22.6	15 311	13 956	14 339
Decatur	129.0	25.8	15 654	57.5	33.0	64.4	D	11.6	D	7.3	D	30.5	26.1	7 483	7 006	4 212
Delaware	379.9	35.5	20 487	75.3	52.9	213.4	D	23.9	D	8.2	4.2	12.0	15.8	50 957	49 888	42 972
Des Moines	1 036.5	39.0	24 637	90.6	165.6	815.3	D	36.4	D	10.0	3.0	19.4	10.3	296 876	281 396	270 701
Dickinson	440.2	58.7	27 155	99.8	63.2	259.9	35.5	27.4	60.1	13.6	6.2	20.3	11.6	71 101	70 221	70 097
Dubuque	2 153.0	47.3	24 499	90.1	293.5	1 693.8	36.4	30.5	61.6	8.7	4.2	28.8	7.6	517 037	493 338	467 589
Emmet	252.6	41.9	23 283	85.6	48.4	156.2	D	19.0	D	8.1	3.1	18.8	16.0	29 643	25 717	20 946
Fayette	438.5	37.7	20 122	74.0	82.2	251.3	D	15.0	D	8.7	3.8	21.6	14.7	37 764	39 765	37 638
Floyd	360.5	27.9	22 025	81.0	71.4	177.9	27.6	19.5	61.2	10.1	4.3	18.7	17.1	34 660	37 389	39 150
Franklin	245.2	36.9	22 567	83.0	43.7	138.2	D	23.4	D	6.4	3.2	16.3	14.5	32 370	27 179	24 865
Fremont	158.5	32.8	20 392	75.0	32.9	96.8	D	42.0	D	6.4	3.9	14.6	13.3	40 682	34 039	30 831
Greene	211.7	35.8	21 010	77.2	40.9	105.2	D	17.7	D	8.4	4.9	14.1	23.0	18 578	15 640	13 929
Grundy	313.1	47.8	25 595	94.1	42.5	144.7	23.2	12.7	54.9	6.1	5.2	15.1	13.0	18 394	17 269	15 566
Guthrie	243.4	38.9	21 154	77.8	46.0	91.4	D	2.8	D	10.5	7.2	16.7	22.2	2 575	2 449	2 116
Hamilton	396.6	43.9	24 769	91.1	57.8	262.9	D	34.4	D	6.4	3.0	10.8	13.5	90 492	81 696	78 583
Hancock	261.6	31.0	21 716	79.8	41.7	228.5	D	60.0	D	4.0	2.0	6.3	9.0	137 105	121 296	117 958
Hardin	440.3	37.4	23 994	88.2	77.2	281.2	26.6	13.1	60.9	7.6	3.5	12.7	11.6	36 961	36 399	36 491
Harrison	302.9	47.2	19 748	72.6	61.4	118.9	D	7.5	D	13.8	3.6	19.9	21.3	8 926	8 427	8 698
Henry	443.4	40.0	22 130	81.4	63.0	335.0	D	32.1	D	19.7	2.3	16.3	16.6	107 417	98 819	92 945
Howard	222.1	50.7	22 942	84.3	36.1	138.7	40.5	36.5	46.8	8.1	3.4	9.8	14.4	50 566	43 059	36 893
Humboldt	243.4	40.6	23 572	86.7	42.2	136.9	D	23.9	D	6.6	D	11.1	14.7	32 789	32 425	29 824
Ida	180.4	36.7	22 784	83.8	28.9	126.0	38.6	30.1	D	6.6	3.6	12.7	10.3	37 872	37 524	36 245
Iowa	418.0	65.5	26 943	99.0	49.4	358.1	48.6	44.5	D	9.1	2.3	8.1	7.1	159 181	161 150	163 494
Jackson	395.3	35.8	19 630	72.2	75.0	175.3	30.0	20.9	66.3	12.0	4.6	17.9	20.6	36 602	34 249	31 544
Jasper	908.0	44.2	24 848	91.3	124.4	542.3	D	43.7	D	9.3	2.5	11.3	14.9	236 935	221 661	209 107
Jefferson	383.4	48.2	22 494	82.7	49.3	317.0	D	23.3	D	7.9	4.2	20.9	10.6	73 703	72 091	59 979
Johnson	2 849.6	60.3	27 785	102.1	209.0	2 256.4	D	8.8	D	8.4	4.3	19.6	45.7	197 899	177 350	169 584
Jones	376.9	35.1	18 715	68.8	61.5	188.7	D	19.8	D	10.4	3.7	14.0	22.2	37 278	37 515	34 617
Keokuk	221.0	23.3	19 268	70.8	46.2	87.1	D	16.9	69.5	8.6	5.0	14.4	18.1	14 718	14 738	8 489

[1] Based on resident population estimated as of July 1, 1998. [2] Includes farm earnings; see table B-10 for these data. [3] Includes mining and construction, not shown separately. [4] Includes agricultural services, forestry, and fisheries; transportation and public utilities; and wholesale trade, not shown separately. [5] Finance, insurance, and real estate.

Source: Personal Income and Earnings—U.S. Bureau of Economic Analysis, "Regional Economic Information System (REIS) 1969-1998" on CD-ROM (related Internet site <http://www.bea.doc.gov/bea/regional/data.htm>).

[Includes U.S., states, and 3,142 counties/county equivalents defined as of January 1, 1992. For changes to these areas since January 1, 1992, see appendix B. Geographic Information]

County	Personal income, 1998												Manufacturing earnings		
			Per capita[1]			Earnings									
									Percent, by selected industry–						
							Goods-related		Service-related						
	Total (mil. dol.)	Percent change, 1990–1998	Amount (dollars)	Percent of national average	Transfer payments (mil. dol.)	Total[2] (mil. dol.)	Total[3]	Man-ufac-turing	Total[4]	Retail trade	FIRE[5]	Serv-ices	Gov-ern-ment	1998 ($1,000)	1997 ($1,000)	1996 ($1,000)
IOWA—Con.															
Kossuth	385.0	31.4	21 726	79.9	64.4	221.9	D	17.9	D	9.6	6.3	16.6	13.8	39 830	37 304	35 146
Lee	873.7	41.0	22 701	83.5	148.0	659.5	D	38.0	D	8.1	2.4	19.7	12.1	250 673	234 009	227 917
Linn	5 420.6	60.2	29 656	109.0	550.9	4 488.2	32.6	25.9	67.1	8.5	7.8	25.9	9.1	1 161 140	1 061 625	983 483
Louisa	240.5	31.7	20 149	74.1	37.8	113.3	D	5.9	D	5.9	2.9	8.9	18.8	D	37 045	47 875
Lucas	180.3	29.3	19 817	72.8	37.5	94.4	14.2	9.1	D	39.5	4.9	D	20.8	8 638	7 247	7 077
Lyon	239.2	36.8	19 871	73.0	39.3	124.7	D	15.9	D	6.5	3.9	15.0	13.4	19 775	19 861	18 598
Madison	313.8	57.9	22 594	83.1	43.8	107.7	D	17.7	D	10.0	8.2	17.8	22.4	19 050	16 166	13 337
Mahaska	496.8	47.4	22 684	83.4	77.8	256.5	D	16.7	D	9.6	4.2	18.4	13.7	42 913	42 529	38 736
Marion	759.4	48.1	24 242	89.1	98.7	592.7	D	50.8	D	5.3	2.0	14.4	15.7	301 351	267 038	239 706
Marshall	936.6	35.6	24 177	88.9	155.3	640.6	D	35.7	D	8.4	3.2	18.0	15.4	228 537	219 761	205 581
Mills	374.1	52.5	25 837	95.0	97.7	119.8	D	2.9	D	8.8	5.2	19.8	42.7	3 451	2 476	2 223
Mitchell	259.2	32.0	23 495	86.4	40.2	138.1	D	20.7	D	7.4	3.9	15.5	13.6	28 643	28 871	27 151
Monona	199.6	40.3	19 829	72.9	47.9	99.3	13.0	5.6	81.0	11.5	4.5	32.5	17.9	5 590	5 360	4 525
Monroe	174.8	40.2	21 754	80.0	35.7	105.5	52.0	42.4	D	7.1	2.3	13.4	13.6	44 774	39 609	37 015
Montgomery	272.6	35.8	23 007	84.6	52.7	165.1	D	21.8	D	7.7	D	15.7	16.8	36 042	37 594	37 222
Muscatine	1 046.6	40.1	25 531	93.9	125.3	822.3	55.9	49.1	43.0	5.9	3.1	14.1	11.7	403 416	369 709	342 956
O'Brien	346.7	34.3	23 291	85.6	60.0	205.8	D	11.2	D	8.4	4.5	19.7	14.4	23 154	22 457	23 113
Osceola	151.9	36.7	21 841	80.3	23.1	87.5	D	19.4	D	5.6	D	11.6	11.5	16 996	14 998	14 189
Page	374.3	35.2	21 674	79.7	70.5	230.8	D	27.6	D	14.8	2.9	16.9	19.8	63 740	62 292	58 886
Palo Alto	218.7	32.8	21 743	79.9	41.0	125.2	D	15.0	D	8.1	4.1	15.9	21.6	18 776	15 817	14 608
Plymouth	559.3	47.0	22 728	83.5	72.7	324.9	D	D	D	8.2	4.9	12.5	11.5	D	68 740	64 481
Pocahontas	197.0	37.3	22 353	82.2	37.2	120.0	D	22.6	D	5.4	3.4	12.5	14.7	27 177	25 137	22 629
Polk	10 959.8	52.6	30 468	112.0	1 077.9	9 908.7	15.7	10.0	84.1	8.9	20.1	25.2	13.2	987 648	986 657	918 997
Pottawattamie	1 926.9	47.6	22 356	82.2	304.1	1 046.5	D	11.8	D	13.0	5.1	32.4	15.9	123 993	130 988	141 941
Poweshiek	456.5	40.2	24 333	89.4	64.1	330.8	D	21.0	D	7.1	9.4	26.5	8.2	69 577	63 574	57 149
Ringgold	98.8	38.8	18 447	67.8	23.4	46.0	D	7.9	D	10.2	D	18.4	28.6	3 627	3 338	3 223
Sac	235.9	27.8	19 832	72.9	44.3	112.4	16.0	8.2	71.2	9.1	5.0	19.4	18.0	9 215	6 743	5 852
Scott	4 146.2	45.8	26 186	96.3	475.2	3 025.1	30.5	22.8	69.0	10.9	4.5	29.3	9.9	689 192	661 020	624 767
Shelby	280.2	32.8	21 664	79.6	51.0	146.8	15.2	5.9	74.5	11.1	4.8	20.5	17.7	8 694	8 321	8 733
Sioux	706.3	51.8	22 476	82.6	88.2	502.2	D	27.3	D	7.9	3.6	15.1	10.0	137 058	126 411	117 076
Story	1 894.0	52.5	25 296	93.0	188.5	1 410.3	D	13.3	D	7.9	3.2	16.2	46.0	187 946	166 676	147 477
Tama	376.9	34.1	21 216	78.0	62.6	194.7	20.4	15.8	69.0	7.3	3.6	26.5	16.0	30 696	29 217	27 116
Taylor	126.4	42.2	17 676	65.0	28.1	58.9	D	D	D	7.4	3.2	12.4	20.5	D	8 327	7 196
Union	250.4	33.9	20 473	75.3	49.5	174.4	D	25.2	D	10.5	3.3	18.0	21.5	43 913	39 812	33 833
Van Buren	149.6	41.9	19 023	69.9	30.3	63.5	D	30.2	D	5.6	3.9	10.0	25.6	19 169	17 436	14 411
Wapello	749.1	34.8	21 168	77.8	159.0	470.6	31.3	25.0	68.3	11.5	2.7	24.9	17.8	117 655	112 111	122 793
Warren	941.9	59.3	23 426	86.1	104.9	259.9	D	7.4	D	13.4	5.0	26.9	21.1	19 229	16 944	15 989
Washington	484.5	44.9	23 140	85.1	74.6	234.5	D	18.5	D	9.6	3.6	16.9	15.2	43 440	40 898	37 454
Wayne	112.6	19.5	16 868	62.0	30.5	52.7	25.9	22.5	72.5	8.4	3.4	16.4	27.1	11 838	12 641	13 501
Webster	907.5	39.3	23 285	85.6	162.2	611.0	D	20.7	D	10.7	3.6	25.2	15.6	126 612	111 665	98 202
Winnebago	267.1	32.7	22 368	82.2	41.3	170.6	D	25.4	D	8.4	3.8	17.4	12.7	43 292	39 506	36 518
Winneshiek	461.8	41.6	22 032	81.0	61.6	315.4	32.6	19.4	59.2	8.7	3.1	22.2	15.9	61 263	53 474	44 390
Woodbury	2 524.7	48.5	24 863	91.4	343.5	1 727.0	D	16.2	D	10.2	4.8	31.8	13.3	279 502	252 402	242 320
Worth	167.4	26.7	21 624	79.5	27.3	78.8	D	24.0	D	4.7	3.6	10.8	13.7	18 884	16 057	13 795
Wright	326.6	42.3	23 265	85.5	60.9	195.8	D	25.6	D	10.9	D	11.7	14.4	50 123	49 940	50 600
KANSAS	67 383.4	49.4	25 537	93.9	8 466.9	47 411.8	25.3	18.3	72.2	9.6	6.1	23.4	17.2	8 676 091	8 164 979	7 515 145
Allen	283.6	41.5	19 513	71.7	57.0	182.3	36.5	29.6	65.3	17.0	4.4	15.7	19.8	53 980	52 752	48 337
Anderson	137.3	36.5	17 069	62.7	31.1	59.8	D	9.5	D	10.2	5.2	19.6	22.8	5 713	5 094	5 139
Atchison	326.8	36.7	19 386	71.3	59.7	205.4	33.9	28.2	63.2	9.4	2.8	20.5	17.0	57 858	52 547	49 489
Barber	105.2	16.9	19 714	72.5	26.0	54.5	D	D	D	9.4	5.8	13.9	28.3	D	6 643	6 753
Barton	634.3	29.9	21 922	80.6	107.7	403.0	26.8	12.4	D	11.6	D	25.5	14.5	49 990	44 894	40 780
Bourbon	311.3	41.8	20 535	75.5	65.5	187.6	D	21.8	D	14.5	10.3	22.0	15.9	40 935	38 452	34 644
Brown	232.9	42.4	21 092	77.5	45.9	145.3	D	15.2	D	7.0	3.1	34.7	15.8	22 135	21 920	20 577
Butler	1 417.7	64.5	22 909	84.2	167.8	515.1	28.5	16.3	71.6	12.1	4.3	21.2	23.3	83 768	75 987	74 820
Chase	69.7	59.1	23 693	87.1	12.3	35.2	D	1.6	D	8.1	4.8	11.6	18.3	565	626	513
Chautauqua	74.9	34.2	17 247	63.4	21.8	28.4	D	3.4	D	8.5	3.5	29.8	23.7	972	1 107	1 132
Cherokee	403.7	48.0	17 942	66.0	90.0	200.0	D	32.6	D	7.7	3.1	13.1	17.1	65 088	65 476	64 129
Cheyenne	69.3	11.8	21 943	80.7	14.3	39.8	D	D	D	8.2	4.3	15.7	15.9	D	418	394
Clark	58.0	8.3	24 641	90.6	9.9	28.4	10.7	1.9	D	8.5	6.7	8.7	31.6	533	454	497
Clay	200.6	29.1	22 083	81.2	34.4	102.6	21.1	12.4	62.7	10.4	4.1	13.7	19.1	12 692	12 521	11 433
Cloud	214.5	20.7	21 316	78.4	47.7	112.8	D	10.0	73.3	11.4	4.3	22.7	20.0	11 290	10 912	9 297
Coffey	182.3	45.1	21 007	77.2	32.7	149.6	D	6.4	D	5.7	2.7	6.6	18.4	9 588	5 510	4 726
Comanche	40.9	−10.1	20 418	75.1	9.8	18.1	D	7.7	D	8.8	7.5	20.0	33.4	1 391	1 307	1 258
Cowley	732.7	30.2	19 754	72.6	141.3	447.7	38.8	32.4	59.6	9.4	3.8	17.0	20.4	145 186	148 757	149 065
Crawford	752.8	42.5	20 703	76.1	156.5	465.6	24.6	20.3	74.5	11.4	3.5	21.9	24.7	94 394	91 417	86 034
Decatur	82.6	15.9	23 957	88.1	16.0	38.6	8.4	2.6	64.0	6.3	4.5	21.8	18.3	1 012	3 153	1 803
Dickinson	406.1	43.9	20 719	76.2	72.1	212.0	D	15.8	D	15.5	3.9	12.9	18.0	33 463	28 699	28 141

[1] Based on resident population estimated as of July 1, 1998. [2] Includes farm earnings; see table B-10 for these data. [3] Includes mining and construction, not shown separately. [4] Includes agricultural services, forestry, and fisheries; transportation and public utilities; and wholesale trade, not shown separately. [5] Finance, insurance, and real estate.

Source: Personal Income and Earnings—U.S. Bureau of Economic Analysis, "Regional Economic Information System (REIS) 1969-1998" on CD-ROM (related Internet site <http://www.bea.doc.gov/bea/regional/data.htm>).

[Includes U.S., states, and 3,142 counties/county equivalents defined as of January 1, 1992. For changes to these areas since January 1, 1992, see appendix B. Geographic Information]

County	Personal income, 1998													Manufacturing earnings		
			Per capita[1]			Earnings										
							Percent, by selected industry–									
							Goods-related		Service-related							
	Total (mil. dol.)	Percent change, 1990–1998	Amount (dollars)	Percent of national average	Transfer payments (mil. dol.)	Total[2] (mil. dol.)	Total[3]	Manu-facturing	Total[4]	Retail trade	FIRE[5]	Serv-ices	Gov-ern-ment	1998 ($1,000)	1997 ($1,000)	1996 ($1,000)
KANSAS—Con.																
Doniphan	162.6	38.1	20 650	75.9	31.0	107.8	D	34.7	D	4.7	3.2	8.2	16.7	37 437	33 627	30 514
Douglas	1 993.3	64.6	20 645	75.9	208.0	1 318.1	21.6	14.4	78.2	12.1	5.9	22.0	30.0	189 915	183 528	164 810
Edwards	87.5	25.6	26 611	97.8	16.2	52.2	D	13.5	D	4.8	1.8	12.6	13.3	7 023	6 581	5 714
Elk	57.8	28.3	17 060	62.7	17.3	19.3	D	D	D	9.2	3.6	10.4	48.5	D	165	204
Ellis	625.8	43.8	23 539	86.5	88.1	431.2	D	8.3	D	12.3	4.4	33.0	20.6	35 677	31 481	28 267
Ellsworth	129.4	33.8	20 617	75.8	28.5	73.4	D	14.1	D	6.3	4.6	17.7	27.5	10 353	9 760	8 074
Finney	772.2	49.2	21 087	77.5	77.3	629.2	33.8	23.1	60.6	9.9	3.7	19.9	13.6	145 525	145 669	137 792
Ford	657.1	43.6	22 305	82.0	83.4	505.6	D	29.5	D	11.7	3.7	18.3	13.9	149 360	137 267	130 009
Franklin	498.0	61.6	20 040	73.7	81.5	252.2	D	13.9	D	27.3	3.2	15.9	19.3	35 138	34 060	32 326
Geary	524.0	20.6	20 771	76.4	71.9	775.4	5.2	2.7	94.6	7.4	1.9	6.8	74.7	21 144	20 012	9 666
Gove	73.2	-7.4	24 041	88.4	13.1	46.3	D	5.9	D	9.8	3.1	13.4	20.7	2 727	2 412	1 936
Graham	72.6	27.3	22 779	83.7	14.9	43.3	D	D	D	7.5	4.0	13.7	22.9	D	328	363
Grant	170.7	45.5	21 344	78.5	19.2	138.5	30.1	5.7	57.8	6.4	3.3	15.7	14.2	7 831	6 463	5 829
Gray	151.6	52.7	27 196	100.0	15.1	113.4	11.1	2.1	46.9	3.3	4.4	7.3	15.3	2 337	2 244	2 044
Greeley	45.7	Z	26 995	99.2	5.9	34.2	D	.7	D	4.1	D	10.9	12.0	234	304	1 664
Greenwood	149.9	34.1	18 499	68.0	37.8	60.1	22.2	2.9	69.6	10.9	3.9	22.0	22.3	1 761	1 789	2 241
Hamilton	72.9	41.8	30 771	113.1	10.1	50.7	D	D	D	3.7	4.3	4.9	15.8	D	150	227
Harper	141.9	18.4	22 133	81.4	31.0	70.2	D	14.1	D	10.0	4.6	10.6	27.8	9 902	8 651	7 256
Harvey	826.5	54.5	24 204	89.0	117.1	484.9	40.1	32.0	57.1	8.8	2.8	25.1	10.2	155 139	133 653	130 943
Haskell	132.4	70.1	33 412	122.8	10.3	102.4	5.8	1.9	33.8	2.5	2.5	5.2	11.7	1 994	1 800	1 766
Hodgeman	49.8	17.1	22 465	82.6	7.9	29.0	D	D	D	6.0	3.0	6.4	24.3	D	–	–
Jackson	259.4	45.9	21 416	78.7	39.7	105.0	D	9.2	D	11.9	5.1	37.7	23.6	9 684	9 198	8 648
Jefferson	396.0	57.7	21 788	80.1	53.0	105.2	D	3.3	D	8.1	4.0	16.7	33.3	3 504	4 301	2 458
Jewell	86.9	15.5	22 450	82.5	16.7	44.6	D	D	D	5.7	5.7	7.5	24.0	D	224	299
Johnson	16 908.9	75.7	39 355	144.7	987.5	11 408.3	14.8	8.7	85.1	10.8	11.3	31.4	8.3	991 336	912 842	856 884
Kearny	97.3	.1	23 508	86.4	11.8	52.8	D	D	55.9	3.1	3.0	5.3	27.3	D	1 139	365
Kingman	176.3	37.8	20 598	75.7	34.7	79.6	32.5	13.7	63.9	9.1	6.4	20.2	18.4	10 885	5 989	5 358
Kiowa	77.0	20.7	22 513	82.8	16.0	38.0	D	.9	D	7.9	3.6	17.7	23.1	357	369	395
Labette	437.4	31.7	18 976	69.8	95.7	296.5	D	28.6	D	9.6	3.8	16.9	25.2	84 924	78 439	72 205
Lane	61.0	19.0	27 155	99.8	9.4	37.6	D	.4	D	4.8	D	5.4	17.6	165	151	192
Leavenworth	1 422.1	46.7	19 980	73.4	169.9	945.0	12.5	5.4	87.2	5.8	4.2	16.1	58.0	50 848	53 082	48 337
Lincoln	70.2	21.9	21 083	77.5	14.6	31.8	D	D	D	8.5	4.8	9.8	31.6	D	2 136	1 886
Linn	161.7	41.3	17 637	64.8	38.4	72.1	18.6	4.4	D	7.1	5.5	D	23.8	3 145	D	2 381
Logan	67.7	30.8	22 632	83.2	12.1	38.4	D	1.2	D	10.8	5.5	12.0	25.0	478	398	432
Lyon	722.7	43.3	21 390	78.6	107.7	515.5	38.0	34.0	61.3	9.3	2.6	15.9	21.8	175 395	160 440	146 510
McPherson	678.1	44.5	23 753	87.3	102.0	458.5	D	28.7	D	7.7	5.4	18.8	11.0	131 636	128 014	118 232
Marion	242.0	33.2	17 781	65.4	51.2	110.9	16.3	9.8	77.3	10.1	5.1	25.1	22.1	10 883	13 557	13 445
Marshall	268.7	37.6	24 445	89.9	53.7	159.3	D	18.8	D	8.2	5.9	14.5	12.1	29 957	28 317	26 543
Meade	115.2	53.3	25 993	95.6	16.5	70.3	D	1.0	D	4.1	2.7	8.1	16.7	715	725	516
Miami	597.5	60.5	22 586	83.0	85.4	242.8	24.7	10.3	75.2	10.5	5.7	17.6	22.7	24 955	24 940	21 992
Mitchell	164.9	31.0	23 724	87.2	28.4	117.9	17.0	13.6	69.1	8.6	2.9	18.3	18.3	16 038	16 469	12 416
Montgomery	735.5	28.8	19 854	73.0	161.4	483.4	40.5	35.6	58.2	9.5	3.1	20.7	14.4	172 312	166 818	154 196
Morris	117.5	35.3	19 097	70.2	25.5	53.4	D	11.7	D	11.2	D	14.7	23.2	6 261	6 145	5 772
Morton	75.5	44.0	22 017	80.9	12.0	55.2	D	D	D	6.0	3.7	D	29.2	D	955	798
Nemaha	246.9	40.7	24 192	88.9	39.1	141.7	22.6	18.3	60.7	7.8	3.9	17.7	13.8	25 965	29 183	27 899
Neosho	345.1	36.6	20 658	75.9	72.3	219.0	36.8	28.7	63.8	9.7	4.0	17.1	20.3	62 748	59 536	59 234
Ness	86.0	9.0	23 717	87.2	16.4	46.3	D	2.0	D	8.4	5.0	11.2	25.8	912	862	852
Norton	130.2	41.9	22 705	83.5	24.5	78.5	D	6.6	D	7.5	5.5	14.4	29.3	5 172	4 996	4 925
Osage	325.8	48.5	18 986	69.8	58.8	98.9	D	7.0	D	12.5	5.1	26.8	29.3	6 915	6 837	5 912
Osborne	96.9	13.5	20 711	76.1	21.8	48.6	D	10.3	D	10.8	6.5	16.8	18.2	5 005	4 946	4 631
Ottawa	120.0	40.3	20 407	75.0	21.5	43.5	D	4.9	D	6.5	6.9	22.8	24.4	2 127	2 503	3 691
Pawnee	162.9	18.7	22 487	82.7	26.9	103.8	D	1.5	D	5.9	4.3	12.6	46.8	1 592	1 533	1 379
Phillips	148.1	37.8	24 529	90.2	26.3	89.2	D	D	D	6.8	5.7	12.3	19.7	D	12 220	11 750
Pottawatomie	374.3	56.2	20 082	73.8	51.9	214.9	D	20.3	D	11.3	3.5	17.6	15.9	43 649	41 474	39 431
Pratt	220.7	36.6	22 790	83.8	39.2	135.3	12.4	3.1	81.2	10.7	4.2	25.1	20.3	4 201	3 833	3 544
Rawlins	67.7	20.4	21 629	79.5	13.1	35.1	D	1.4	D	4.7	5.5	17.1	24.8	492	385	996
Reno	1 430.7	38.7	22 622	83.2	235.2	952.5	30.3	22.7	68.0	15.7	3.8	24.1	14.8	216 217	203 094	186 332
Republic	124.7	17.0	20 455	75.2	26.5	65.7	D	12.7	D	8.5	7.1	16.4	22.7	8 320	8 659	8 035
Rice	207.8	21.1	19 933	73.3	41.7	111.4	D	10.6	D	6.9	3.8	14.4	21.0	11 839	10 200	9 133
Riley	1 325.3	31.3	20 728	76.2	123.6	712.4	D	3.2	D	11.2	7.9	24.2	41.1	22 516	21 560	17 375
Rooks	116.6	27.2	20 503	75.4	24.7	60.2	D	5.1	D	9.2	4.7	9.1	26.1	3 049	6 364	9 251
Rush	73.4	19.6	21 567	79.3	17.9	36.6	D	25.4	D	5.1	3.6	10.8	25.5	9 281	9 630	9 258
Russell	170.3	19.3	22 606	83.1	39.2	88.9	30.5	11.1	62.1	10.3	3.5	19.2	17.7	9 873	8 548	7 933
Saline	1 402.9	44.1	27 294	100.3	170.5	1 082.4	D	23.0	D	9.8	4.1	29.0	10.7	248 785	230 169	230 047
Scott	135.3	17.5	26 926	99.0	14.9	88.3	4.6	.5	57.4	6.2	3.8	10.2	13.9	459	389	427
Sedgwick	12 010.8	51.0	26 821	98.6	1 369.0	10 175.5	40.0	33.2	59.9	8.1	4.2	24.5	11.0	3 375 998	3 112 318	2 711 405
Seward	459.6	52.2	22 899	84.2	51.2	408.0	D	D	D	9.2	2.9	14.7	14.8	D	75 936	68 747
Shawnee	4 345.3	41.8	25 508	93.8	597.0	3 525.3	18.1	12.0	81.8	11.3	8.7	25.2	22.8	423 808	401 217	416 565
Sheridan	83.3	64.6	30 613	112.5	10.6	55.6	4.1	.7	49.9	9.8	4.6	8.0	13.4	399	418	580

[1] Based on resident population estimated as of July 1, 1998.   [2] Includes farm earnings; see table B-10 for these data.   [3] Includes mining and construction, not shown separately.   [4] Includes agricultural services, forestry, and fisheries; transportation and public utilities; and wholesale trade, not shown separately.   [5] Finance, insurance, and real estate.

Source: Personal Income and Earnings—U.S. Bureau of Economic Analysis, "Regional Economic Information System (REIS) 1969-1998" on CD-ROM (related Internet site <http://www.bea.doc.gov/bea/regional/data.htm>).

Table B–8. Counties — Personal Income and Earnings-Con.

[Includes U.S., states, and 3,142 counties/county equivalents defined as of January 1, 1992. For changes to these areas since January 1, 1992, see appendix B. Geographic Information]

County	Personal income, 1998													Manufacturing earnings		
	Total (mil. dol.)	Per capita[1]			Transfer payments (mil. dol.)	Earnings										
		Percent change, 1990–1998	Amount (dollars)	Percent of national average		Total[2] (mil. dol.)	Percent, by selected industry–							1998 ($1,000)	1997 ($1,000)	1996 ($1,000)
							Goods-related		Service-related							
							Total[3]	Manu-facturing	Total[4]	Retail trade	FIRE[5]	Serv-ices	Gov-ern-ment			
KANSAS—Con.																
Sherman	162.1	40.0	24 731	90.9	29.8	102.2	D	3.3	D	11.7	D	22.8	19.4	3 422	2 721	2 445
Smith	100.9	26.5	21 959	80.7	22.1	50.2	12.4	8.0	59.7	7.6	5.3	18.0	16.6	4 013	3 897	3 688
Stafford	117.2	31.8	23 208	85.3	25.8	64.9	10.2	2.8	56.9	5.8	5.0	12.6	21.1	1 796	D	D
Stanton	68.1	17.2	30 330	111.5	6.6	49.1	D	.6	D	2.7	D	4.9	14.8	316	306	279
Stevens	142.5	48.2	26 309	96.7	15.8	93.7	D	D	D	5.9	D	6.5	19.2	D	914	1 128
Sumner	636.2	49.8	23 393	86.0	93.1	239.4	D	22.6	D	10.2	4.9	17.3	20.9	54 063	49 664	39 983
Thomas	190.5	40.9	23 720	87.2	26.4	140.0	D	1.7	D	12.5	3.9	18.7	18.6	2 441	2 310	2 347
Trego	63.8	5.4	19 363	71.2	15.2	31.4	D	2.8	D	12.0	5.6	19.3	29.3	865	728	704
Wabaunsee	144.6	35.5	21 859	80.4	22.6	40.5	D	5.6	D	9.4	5.2	21.9	28.2	2 281	2 743	D
Wallace	39.7	39.1	21 887	80.5	7.2	23.2	D	D	D	6.5	2.3	9.9	17.1	D	178	191
Washington	130.3	23.7	20 003	73.5	29.3	63.7	D	3.0	D	7.6	5.2	11.2	26.6	1 934	1 636	1 396
Wichita	81.9	−11.7	30 952	113.8	9.0	60.4	D	D	D	3.4	D	5.1	10.6	D	1 268	1 207
Wilson	192.4	39.0	18 740	68.9	44.2	117.8	D	37.5	D	5.2	3.2	15.2	20.0	44 172	41 851	41 340
Woodson	67.3	18.9	17 061	62.7	18.3	26.2	D	4.2	D	10.8	4.0	11.3	23.2	1 102	252	345
Wyandotte	2 964.0	29.2	19 434	71.4	618.7	3 200.5	29.9	22.9	70.1	6.0	2.1	15.4	21.6	734 380	752 197	735 864
KENTUCKY	87 273.9	52.6	22 183	81.5	15 063.9	61 248.0	29.2	21.1	69.1	9.9	5.0	22.4	18.0	12 937 809	12 394 354	11 589 170
Adair	259.2	41.7	15 758	57.9	80.2	121.7	18.1	9.8	72.2	10.1	3.3	31.4	20.5	11 963	14 317	22 234
Allen	276.2	68.6	16 672	61.3	58.0	161.7	D	35.7	D	25.4	3.2	12.3	12.8	57 766	51 707	56 206
Anderson	404.1	76.9	21 841	80.3	48.1	139.3	D	43.1	D	9.6	4.0	12.6	16.2	60 016	56 174	50 677
Ballard	211.7	70.7	24 933	91.7	37.2	144.0	61.2	36.6	D	4.2	1.4	5.9	8.3	52 644	47 556	46 967
Barren	795.4	66.8	21 515	79.1	136.3	610.1	50.0	41.1	46.1	9.5	2.2	17.6	10.0	251 028	235 248	216 232
Bath	180.2	62.7	17 021	62.6	43.6	63.4	31.1	19.8	D	9.1	3.4	12.3	24.0	12 580	14 529	13 134
Bell	453.6	33.4	15 560	57.2	171.4	275.9	D	9.8	D	14.4	3.6	24.0	19.2	27 049	24 435	23 263
Boone	2 062.7	96.8	25 860	95.1	190.1	2 271.1	D	22.9	D	10.7	6.0	13.5	7.1	520 679	492 389	450 025
Bourbon	499.0	65.8	25 806	94.9	64.2	269.4	D	17.8	D	5.8	D	11.2	11.4	48 038	46 323	42 461
Boyd	1 167.1	29.6	23 571	86.6	236.8	1 033.3	D	23.9	D	9.5	3.4	29.8	11.5	246 870	259 368	258 109
Boyle	617.3	65.4	22 777	83.7	99.4	511.9	D	28.8	D	9.7	2.8	25.9	11.4	147 562	125 656	112 241
Bracken	146.3	52.3	17 375	63.9	28.5	50.9	D	D	D	6.4	3.2	16.6	20.5	D	9 041	9 327
Breathitt	222.0	35.2	14 116	51.9	90.5	96.7	D	2.8	D	16.0	4.1	25.7	33.6	2 700	2 900	2 715
Breckinridge	292.2	52.8	16 739	61.5	68.0	95.2	D	7.5	D	14.5	5.1	17.3	25.6	7 165	7 109	5 903
Bullitt	1 205.1	00.0	20 307	74.0	144.1	351.7	D	26.9	D	12.7	3.6	13.0	18.5	94 489	95 742	87 157
Butler	188.9	57.6	15 829	58.2	49.3	103.6	D	39.8	D	7.0	2.4	13.0	19.0	41 208	40 778	38 510
Caldwell	255.0	45.2	19 124	70.3	57.8	120.8	D	19.4	D	16.2	5.2	16.7	20.4	23 404	20 976	19 886
Calloway	730.3	63.0	21 850	80.3	125.1	493.8	25.4	18.0	71.5	14.3	2.4	13.9	25.8	88 984	89 179	84 702
Campbell	2 054.1	49.9	23 529	86.5	297.5	875.2	30.4	21.8	69.8	11.0	4.8	27.7	18.6	190 676	213 768	170 462
Carlisle	112.0	43.8	20 984	77.1	22.4	32.6	23.0	13.9	D	10.2	5.2	14.2	21.3	4 519	4 551	4 512
Carroll	196.6	49.9	20 424	75.1	38.1	208.9	61.9	55.6	D	7.6	.9	8.0	9.1	116 257	107 540	99 207
Carter	420.1	57.4	15 619	57.4	110.9	143.2	D	17.3	D	17.9	4.3	17.2	25.8	24 762	24 615	20 975
Casey	222.4	53.4	15 040	55.3	63.2	104.1	D	26.1	D	10.1	2.2	15.6	17.4	27 137	28 631	30 218
Christian	1 254.2	50.8	17 314	63.6	192.0	1 935.1	D	11.9	D	4.2	1.4	8.0	68.1	231 035	220 231	202 787
Clark	733.4	57.1	22 961	84.4	109.2	425.5	D	32.0	D	11.5	2.6	15.6	11.4	136 041	120 445	100 619
Clay	321.1	59.8	14 107	51.9	119.2	140.5	D	7.2	D	13.8	2.4	21.6	42.6	10 109	9 750	7 795
Clinton	139.2	63.8	14 888	54.7	55.9	63.7	D	19.5	D	12.3	2.8	19.9	22.4	12 397	10 743	9 475
Crittenden	151.9	37.3	15 846	58.3	41.4	68.0	38.1	27.2	61.9	9.7	3.5	23.2	17.3	18 515	20 132	18 199
Cumberland	97.9	45.7	14 296	52.6	40.2	42.9	18.5	14.8	D	11.5	5.7	29.5	24.5	6 353	5 154	4 274
Daviess	2 012.9	44.9	22 126	81.3	340.3	1 324.6	31.5	20.4	68.0	11.6	5.1	22.2	16.0	270 317	257 117	243 973
Edmonson	165.1	66.9	14 552	53.5	40.5	45.1	D	.8	D	8.2	3.8	22.6	47.2	371	D	510
Elliott	77.4	44.5	11 734	43.1	27.5	22.5	D	D	D	8.8	D	18.4	39.4	D	415	266
Estill	237.7	57.6	15 253	56.1	70.3	73.5	D	15.8	D	12.8	3.9	15.4	27.7	11 622	13 726	11 482
Fayette	7 234.7	51.8	29 933	110.0	705.4	6 342.8	21.4	13.3	77.0	9.9	6.1	28.9	19.5	846 346	771 064	738 308
Fleming	215.9	51.4	16 016	58.9	49.7	105.5	D	15.3	D	12.6	3.3	12.9	26.4	16 123	16 407	19 848
Floyd	699.5	38.0	16 145	59.4	232.6	395.3	24.7	3.7	D	9.3	D	27.5	19.3	14 707	14 698	13 378
Franklin	1 238.2	58.1	26 628	97.9	188.7	1 118.9	D	12.0	D	6.5	4.4	14.2	55.4	134 520	132 322	119 413
Fulton	152.5	34.0	20 198	74.2	40.8	99.1	D	31.9	D	10.8	3.6	13.5	18.4	31 578	34 591	31 669
Gallatin	121.0	87.4	16 853	62.0	21.1	69.8	D	48.6	D	6.3	1.6	8.3	13.1	33 941	32 647	26 627
Garrard	243.3	56.8	17 480	64.3	47.4	84.0	30.7	11.6	60.1	7.2	5.0	14.6	25.4	9 732	9 318	8 567
Grant	381.4	83.0	18 777	69.0	65.0	141.6	D	14.7	D	19.5	4.3	18.6	20.7	20 841	15 914	15 960
Graves	720.8	52.8	20 042	73.7	152.0	423.7	36.3	28.5	55.2	9.2	3.4	17.4	13.7	120 951	119 530	129 056
Grayson	388.7	62.0	16 377	60.2	96.8	217.5	39.8	30.6	D	9.9	3.0	11.5	18.5	66 527	62 197	57 158
Green	166.0	40.4	15 710	57.8	51.1	59.4	D	14.7	D	9.1	4.2	18.8	29.6	8 729	8 201	8 171
Greenup	708.5	33.3	19 165	70.5	164.7	323.1	D	31.6	D	7.8	2.6	13.7	14.3	102 135	117 488	118 137
Hancock	194.7	46.8	21 728	79.9	24.3	239.3	84.3	75.6	D	1.8	.8	D	5.0	180 793	171 070	156 668
Hardin	1 867.6	40.3	20 619	75.8	271.9	1 709.4	20.6	16.5	79.5	8.1	2.3	13.6	49.0	282 319	264 954	239 160
Harlan	496.7	23.8	14 265	52.4	196.4	261.8	D	3.2	D	9.6	3.6	22.4	23.5	8 320	7 455	6 098
Harrison	344.2	51.3	19 622	72.1	59.1	169.7	47.7	41.3	48.9	9.6	2.5	15.5	15.3	70 013	68 487	68 251
Hart	268.3	58.4	16 044	59.0	65.2	127.1	D	30.9	D	9.7	3.8	13.2	17.4	39 310	34 096	32 591

[1] Based on resident population estimated as of July 1, 1998.   [2] Includes farm earnings; see table B-10 for these data.   [3] Includes mining and construction, not shown separately.   [4] Includes agricultural services, forestry, and fisheries; transportation and public utilities; and wholesale trade, not shown separately.   [5] Finance, insurance, and real estate.

Source: Personal Income and Earnings—U.S. Bureau of Economic Analysis, "Regional Economic Information System (REIS) 1969-1998" on CD-ROM (related Internet site <http://www.bea.doc.gov/bea/regional/data.htm>).

Table B–8. Counties — **Personal Income and Earnings**–Con.

[Includes U.S., states, and 3,142 counties/county equivalents defined as of January 1, 1992. For changes to these areas since January 1, 1992, see appendix B. Geographic Information]

County	Personal income, 1998													Manufacturing earnings		
		Per capita[1]				Earnings										
								Percent, by selected industry–								
							Goods-related		Service-related							
	Total (mil. dol.)	Percent change, 1990–1998	Amount (dollars)	Percent of national average	Transfer payments (mil. dol.)	Total[2] (mil. dol.)	Total[3]	Manufacturing	Total[4]	Retail trade	FIRE[5]	Services	Government	1998 ($1,000)	1997 ($1,000)	1996 ($1,000)
KENTUCKY—Con.																
Henderson	1 053.3	54.6	23 680	87.0	169.5	720.4	47.6	39.2	50.0	7.8	3.1	18.7	11.0	282 329	266 707	230 782
Henry	293.6	59.6	19 875	73.1	52.0	109.7	D	21.6	D	9.3	4.1	17.7	19.0	23 720	27 910	27 725
Hickman	109.5	49.0	21 066	77.4	22.2	52.8	D	15.5	D	5.4	3.0	13.5	14.2	8 165	7 659	7 348
Hopkins	923.3	27.0	19 907	73.2	194.9	608.1	32.0	18.8	67.8	9.7	3.6	28.1	15.9	114 399	108 634	99 632
Jackson	179.5	72.6	13 879	51.0	59.3	78.0	D	30.3	D	7.3	1.9	12.2	24.6	23 649	20 782	17 212
Jefferson	19 794.2	47.6	29 473	108.3	2 677.0	16 828.4	25.2	19.4	74.8	9.5	8.0	28.1	10.8	3 266 247	3 154 887	3 087 517
Jessamine	806.4	76.0	22 048	81.0	94.1	442.0	D	21.2	D	11.3	2.4	14.9	12.4	93 524	85 251	77 336
Johnson	382.9	41.6	15 964	58.7	120.5	195.3	16.4	5.8	D	17.0	D	22.2	24.0	11 267	10 815	10 132
Kenton	4 006.3	59.2	27 303	100.4	465.9	2 018.2	NA	10.4	80.8	12.3	7.1	33.7	17.0	210 692	175 447	147 961
Knott	263.9	45.3	14 704	54.1	89.5	134.4	45.6	.6	54.5	6.2	1.8	13.1	21.1	749	623	690
Knox	441.3	51.0	13 839	50.9	149.6	218.5	21.2	15.0	78.5	15.1	3.6	20.6	25.3	32 847	32 673	35 304
Larue	263.7	43.0	20 183	74.2	50.0	75.0	27.6	17.1	66.1	8.8	4.8	19.2	22.8	12 817	11 294	10 617
Laurel	911.6	65.7	17 928	65.9	190.4	605.4	D	18.6	D	17.8	2.9	20.2	14.6	112 911	105 320	101 100
Lawrence	221.0	50.5	14 160	52.1	73.5	93.3	D	6.3	D	13.3	3.1	24.0	21.1	5 858	5 573	5 606
Lee	109.8	54.6	13 673	50.3	43.1	48.0	20.2	10.4	D	15.0	3.8	22.1	27.3	4 982	5 064	4 906
Leslie	213.1	60.4	15 684	57.7	77.5	150.0	D	D	D	3.9	1.3	13.0	13.5	D	10 139	8 352
Letcher	387.5	27.3	14 769	54.3	139.1	187.9	D	2.4	D	10.4	2.3	26.7	20.6	4 532	4 197	3 328
Lewis	182.4	49.9	13 495	49.6	56.9	70.2	32.3	25.1	D	9.0	4.3	14.4	23.5	17 587	18 674	19 583
Lincoln	378.3	69.3	16 886	62.1	88.5	136.6	30.3	22.2	D	9.9	4.9	13.5	23.0	30 331	28 802	20 782
Livingston	204.2	55.8	21 628	79.5	40.8	81.9	D	4.3	D	10.7	1.6	19.8	17.3	3 552	3 492	3 401
Logan	491.6	56.4	18 766	69.0	99.1	326.0	D	50.5	D	7.0	2.4	13.4	10.6	164 765	158 681	153 982
Lyon	125.1	64.5	15 623	57.4	32.4	55.6	23.1	8.9	D	13.9	3.4	14.9	39.1	4 952	5 288	4 795
McCracken	1 639.5	44.9	25 457	93.6	272.0	1 284.3	D	17.0	D	12.0	3.8	30.2	12.6	218 185	205 093	184 686
McCreary	210.4	69.3	12 647	46.5	91.2	85.5	D	25.1	D	11.7	3.1	15.0	32.8	21 433	20 258	18 818
McLean	188.2	51.1	19 124	70.3	39.3	78.2	D	6.2	D	9.2	2.7	D	17.5	4 838	5 666	5 509
Madison	1 346.8	73.1	20 266	74.5	212.6	812.5	D	27.9	D	11.7	2.5	20.2	26.2	226 788	205 308	188 783
Magoffin	177.9	53.2	12 849	47.2	71.6	75.6	28.7	10.9	D	8.2	D	D	25.4	8 281	8 407	7 376
Marion	320.5	57.1	18 809	69.1	68.6	166.7	39.5	32.0	D	8.7	2.7	21.9	14.9	53 255	41 924	36 514
Marshall	631.4	49.9	20 924	76.9	123.8	431.9	55.0	44.3	44.6	8.5	2.9	13.4	11.0	191 207	195 638	186 065
Martin	189.6	26.7	15 695	57.7	68.4	112.1	D	3.5	D	8.0	4.7	8.8	17.0	3 979	3 760	3 294
Mason	342.0	43.5	20 222	74.3	63.2	286.8	39.5	36.3	56.8	10.9	2.8	17.6	11.6	104 087	94 413	88 850
Meade	489.3	44.2	17 029	62.6	63.2	126.9	D	26.4	D	13.4	2.7	14.1	20.0	33 506	30 970	30 065
Menifee	82.5	71.1	14 284	52.5	24.7	30.8	D	15.3	D	7.1	2.0	19.6	34.6	4 693	4 309	4 539
Mercer	434.9	56.4	21 046	77.4	70.5	244.5	D	47.1	D	8.1	2.5	12.7	10.8	115 152	112 492	105 491
Metcalfe	155.6	57.3	16 255	59.8	40.7	80.4	D	38.1	D	6.6	3.2	7.9	16.8	30 663	30 711	30 619
Monroe	211.3	53.4	18 967	69.7	58.6	110.9	D	39.0	D	8.9	2.5	9.7	21.6	43 301	43 380	42 172
Montgomery	416.5	61.4	19 828	72.9	82.6	264.7	D	32.3	D	12.3	3.1	18.3	12.4	85 556	66 572	52 710
Morgan	170.7	60.3	12 574	46.2	54.4	92.8	D	11.6	D	12.4	3.7	19.0	34.7	10 751	9 675	8 313
Muhlenberg	559.1	36.3	17 438	64.1	134.6	328.5	27.7	13.2	66.8	8.7	2.4	16.5	26.6	43 270	40 218	38 412
Nelson	768.4	74.1	21 388	78.6	113.6	410.6	49.1	35.4	50.6	10.4	3.3	16.8	10.9	145 522	145 089	133 818
Nicholas	114.9	41.0	16 404	60.3	28.2	48.7	40.4	37.0	D	6.2	2.3	17.1	19.5	17 997	19 825	16 371
Ohio	375.3	51.4	17 051	62.7	96.1	183.2	35.3	26.8	D	9.0	2.3	13.1	20.5	49 023	44 660	37 207
Oldham	1 324.3	72.3	29 802	109.6	86.8	417.1	25.1	12.7	73.7	9.4	5.6	27.7	22.5	52 829	50 749	40 490
Owen	181.2	67.5	17 508	64.4	32.8	62.1	D	D	D	6.7	3.7	20.0	22.1	D	9 374	8 754
Owsley	68.8	65.8	12 754	46.9	36.0	20.0	D	D	D	9.1	D	22.6	43.1	D	278	179
Pendleton	246.1	65.1	17 921	65.9	40.9	88.1	D	15.0	D	7.0	3.5	D	21.3	13 218	12 080	10 597
Perry	530.5	40.2	17 115	62.9	171.6	376.4	D	4.9	D	12.3	3.2	28.2	19.3	18 321	17 483	14 543
Pike	1 291.4	32.6	17 931	65.9	356.0	836.2	34.2	2.7	65.8	11.9	3.5	23.9	14.0	22 798	14 662	12 225
Powell	184.2	55.3	14 262	52.4	48.5	86.3	D	29.6	D	10.8	2.7	12.2	24.9	25 574	24 974	24 949
Pulaski	1 028.9	62.4	18 270	67.2	253.6	674.3	D	19.6	D	12.6	4.2	23.6	16.4	132 124	131 838	120 216
Robertson	34.5	54.0	15 649	57.5	9.0	10.8	D	D	D	7.2	D	14.4	29.7	D	D	312
Rockcastle	238.8	59.9	14 998	55.1	68.1	91.1	D	17.4	D	9.6	D	28.8	24.2	15 855	15 990	16 514
Rowan	336.5	59.6	15 215	55.9	75.2	239.3	D	10.9	D	11.6	2.8	26.7	35.8	26 121	20 628	17 961
Russell	259.0	43.5	16 004	58.8	86.8	143.1	28.7	20.8	65.6	14.9	3.2	14.4	21.9	29 712	48 207	49 158
Scott	785.0	89.8	25 503	93.8	78.1	1 147.0	D	68.5	D	3.5	.8	8.2	4.3	785 287	701 132	564 167
Shelby	769.5	76.2	25 960	95.4	87.6	442.8	48.0	42.5	47.9	8.1	3.3	18.5	10.1	188 069	169 787	161 292
Simpson	308.6	49.8	18 741	68.9	53.8	240.8	D	55.9	D	11.6	2.3	10.0	10.7	134 625	125 757	113 050
Spencer	165.6	71.3	17 130	63.0	28.2	44.3	20.9	5.8	68.3	9.8	4.4	17.7	27.7	2 580	2 833	3 175
Taylor	391.1	38.0	17 017	62.6	107.8	246.5	D	28.0	D	12.7	4.8	17.7	18.2	69 087	116 949	120 942
Todd	212.2	57.2	18 844	69.3	41.1	114.5	D	33.8	D	5.7	2.1	8.7	12.5	38 643	36 290	35 436
Trigg	207.4	49.6	16 715	61.4	48.8	95.2	D	37.2	D	7.9	3.2	11.8	25.2	35 365	35 778	36 595
Trimble	122.0	64.4	15 877	58.4	25.5	34.8	D	5.4	D	6.1	4.4	13.4	25.1	1 894	1 712	1 890
Union	298.3	10.5	18 031	66.3	60.5	212.2	D	13.7	D	8.1	2.3	17.9	15.0	29 080	29 547	37 004
Warren	2 013.9	66.6	23 066	84.8	300.4	1 541.6	33.1	25.0	66.5	13.0	5.6	22.7	15.7	384 817	410 860	371 915
Washington	222.4	68.4	20 423	75.1	41.2	109.9	D	32.5	D	6.5	3.2	11.6	12.7	35 702	32 187	29 839
Wayne	287.1	69.8	15 065	55.4	89.4	152.7	D	29.0	D	10.1	3.1	13.8	18.7	44 315	41 212	37 721
Webster	249.4	19.4	18 422	67.7	53.3	155.1	51.3	14.6	46.7	6.6	3.1	8.4	13.0	22 612	20 252	19 824
Whitley	555.6	46.6	15 507	57.0	190.9	351.1	20.4	14.6	79.9	11.1	4.7	28.5	16.5	48 515	41 971	41 980
Wolfe	97.9	65.3	13 259	48.7	41.6	39.6	D	20.8	D	13.0	1.6	15.8	32.5	8 245	6 813	6 805
Woodford	692.3	58.5	30 458	112.0	57.7	476.0	D	33.3	D	4.3	2.5	11.7	5.7	158 700	147 097	140 371

[1] Based on resident population estimated as of July 1, 1998. [2] Includes farm earnings; see table B-10 for these data. [3] Includes mining and construction, not shown separately. [4] Includes agricultural services, forestry, and fisheries; transportation and public utilities; and wholesale trade, not shown separately. [5] Finance, insurance, and real estate.

Source: Personal Income and Earnings—U.S. Bureau of Economic Analysis, "Regional Economic Information System (REIS) 1969-1998" on CD-ROM (related Internet site <http://www.bea.doc.gov/bea/regional/data.htm>).

Table B–8. Counties — **Personal Income and Earnings**–Con.

[Includes U.S., states, and 3,142 counties/county equivalents defined as of January 1, 1992. For changes to these areas since January 1, 1992, see appendix B. Geographic Information]

County	Personal income, 1998													Manufacturing earnings		
	Total (mil. dol.)	Per capita[1]			Transfer payments (mil. dol.)	Earnings										
		Percent change, 1990–1998	Amount (dollars)	Percent of national average		Total[2] (mil. dol.)	Percent, by selected industry—							1998 ($1,000)	1997 ($1,000)	1996 ($1,000)
							Goods-related		Service-related							
							Total[3]	Manufacturing	Total[4]	Retail trade	FIRE[5]	Services	Government			
LOUISIANA	96 877.7	50.8	22 206	81.6	16 964.7	67 725.1	26.4	13.6	73.0	9.0	5.4	26.3	18.7	9 191 117	8 839 756	8 390 466
Acadia	1 003.2	54.5	17 352	63.8	245.9	437.9	25.8	11.9	70.0	10.5	3.7	22.9	18.8	52 247	54 330	46 237
Allen	383.2	79.8	15 833	58.2	94.1	233.7	D	8.8	D	7.0	D	39.6	32.6	20 555	20 114	19 859
Ascension	1 672.0	89.9	23 326	85.7	205.7	1 330.8	57.6	32.3	42.1	7.8	2.4	12.1	8.9	429 670	411 836	395 609
Assumption	434.0	60.2	18 852	69.3	88.8	189.6	53.8	47.9	42.1	6.3	2.6	12.0	15.7	90 886	99 789	72 507
Avoyelles	656.3	60.7	16 091	59.2	190.3	286.8	D	8.8	D	10.8	4.5	33.0	25.4	25 323	25 588	25 355
Beauregard	573.5	41.9	17 935	65.9	111.4	300.6	41.4	31.8	58.1	10.4	6.8	14.8	16.7	95 662	95 035	92 117
Bienville	270.2	43.7	17 102	62.9	79.6	115.4	39.8	30.2	57.9	8.3	4.2	14.4	19.1	34 855	35 486	45 528
Bossier	2 098.4	62.8	22 726	83.5	301.4	1 370.6	16.2	6.4	84.0	10.8	3.0	25.5	38.7	87 994	83 981	84 884
Caddo	5 729.8	36.0	23 630	86.9	990.5	4 330.9	25.1	15.5	75.0	8.5	4.7	28.2	19.4	672 336	648 264	648 110
Calcasieu	3 987.5	53.5	22 139	81.4	664.2	3 018.5	39.5	24.3	60.4	7.9	3.2	24.7	13.2	734 200	713 619	660 053
Caldwell	168.1	47.9	16 196	59.5	53.9	76.4	19.2	12.8	82.3	12.5	3.6	29.0	24.3	9 771	8 850	7 870
Cameron	195.3	65.1	21 615	79.5	26.3	168.2	26.7	11.9	72.3	3.3	.5	6.1	15.8	19 970	19 771	14 884
Catahoula	170.1	44.8	15 396	56.6	52.5	75.4	D	7.6	D	10.8	4.9	15.2	25.0	5 700	6 403	5 594
Claiborne	284.8	42.3	16 727	61.5	76.2	136.1	28.0	17.2	D	9.6	2.6	10.1	31.6	23 448	23 666	22 272
Concordia	334.7	40.4	16 130	59.3	91.5	144.7	D	12.4	D	13.2	4.9	20.8	28.9	17 904	18 439	16 930
De Soto	500.0	62.8	20 012	73.6	103.9	250.3	50.8	24.1	45.6	6.7	2.9	10.7	16.4	60 403	57 614	58 498
East Baton Rouge	10 074.5	45.8	25 592	94.1	1 276.3	8 283.1	23.0	10.2	77.0	9.0	8.3	28.0	19.9	843 256	816 920	802 182
East Carroll	131.9	46.3	14 872	54.7	51.6	65.2	13.9	9.9	71.0	5.5	2.5	11.5	32.8	6 478	5 667	5 296
East Feliciana	390.9	62.1	18 646	68.5	87.8	169.5	19.1	14.2	79.4	4.6	3.2	14.3	51.2	24 078	21 620	19 989
Evangeline	553.2	55.9	16 191	59.5	180.1	239.5	24.6	19.9	69.3	9.6	3.4	19.4	25.7	47 577	45 936	39 564
Franklin	333.9	45.5	15 112	55.6	112.3	148.2	D	8.9	D	16.4	4.9	19.4	25.7	13 220	15 439	16 623
Grant	305.3	58.9	16 109	59.2	75.6	90.0	D	29.4	D	6.6	2.4	12.5	32.6	26 417	25 993	25 330
Iberia	1 500.8	63.5	20 574	75.6	256.2	1 031.8	42.4	20.0	56.5	8.4	3.3	18.5	12.8	205 976	194 173	170 745
Iberville	632.9	51.6	20 118	74.0	129.9	659.3	D	49.0	D	3.9	1.4	9.8	15.0	323 048	302 629	294 684
Jackson	287.8	47.0	18 574	68.3	79.3	143.8	D	D	D	7.0	2.8	12.3	19.0	D	58 683	56 586
Jefferson	11 805.4	45.1	26 251	96.5	1 608.3	7 732.4	19.7	9.6	80.3	12.0	7.4	31.4	11.1	743 214	732 835	705 116
Jefferson Davis	510.0	47.2	16 155	59.4	127.5	217.1	19.1	10.6	73.6	14.4	4.4	19.3	21.2	23 022	19 042	16 238
Lafayette	4 821.8	71.1	25 903	95.2	545.3	4 297.8	33.4	7.4	66.6	9.8	4.0	27.7	10.3	316 801	290 414	252 282
Lafourche	1 889.4	68.3	21 226	78.0	308.5	1 017.3	23.8	14.6	75.6	8.2	2.8	18.1	20.6	148 410	137 147	111 003
La Salle	231.9	39.1	16 950	62.3	68.0	116.1	38.9	21.0	60.8	11.2	2.9	14.1	23.5	24 354	26 392	27 812
Lincoln	801.9	37.9	19 492	71.7	156.8	572.5	29.6	16.2	68.7	8.8	5.7	17.8	27.9	93 018	90 095	86 705
Livingston	1 782.6	93.0	20 194	74.2	247.5	481.5	32.0	14.7	67.7	12.7	4.7	17.0	21.5	70 976	67 395	68 871
Madison	187.3	59.4	14 480	53.2	59.9	93.8	9.0	6.6	84.3	9.9	2.7	30.7	31.0	6 176	5 772	5 196
Morehouse	527.8	38.9	16 772	61.7	160.8	267.5	D	23.7	D	10.9	3.1	20.9	16.4	63 427	64 759	65 283
Natchitoches	653.5	53.4	17 642	64.9	145.4	406.3	D	22.0	D	9.8	3.5	17.1	28.1	89 407	90 695	78 446
Orleans	11 818.6	34.1	25 439	93.5	2 257.1	11 725.1	14.8	5.3	85.2	6.5	7.4	37.8	21.0	620 950	605 782	584 947
Ouachita	3 117.2	50.3	21 230	78.0	547.7	2 283.6	22.4	16.7	77.3	10.5	8.2	25.6	16.1	380 293	375 892	380 749
Plaquemines	596.0	49.6	22 767	83.7	128.1	849.0	46.4	19.3	53.4	4.0	1.3	11.1	15.6	164 227	148 616	125 520
Pointe Coupee	436.6	56.7	18 559	68.2	97.3	169.3	24.7	14.3	D	12.3	3.6	14.6	22.9	24 234	21 976	21 631
Rapides	2 790.2	40.2	22 062	81.1	653.5	1 826.1	18.5	10.9	81.3	10.1	4.6	30.3	24.9	198 198	191 061	185 365
Red River	169.5	49.3	17 646	64.9	45.0	77.5	39.7	20.9	59.2	7.8	4.0	17.4	20.2	16 223	16 080	23 317
Richland	335.4	41.0	15 940	58.6	116.5	160.5	23.1	15.0	75.4	9.7	4.0	26.8	20.6	24 131	23 326	21 928
Sabine	404.2	54.3	16 979	62.4	102.1	207.0	39.3	34.9	51.6	10.4	3.9	12.8	16.2	72 214	72 838	70 130
St. Bernard	1 376.2	46.8	20 900	76.8	279.7	532.2	32.0	21.3	67.9	11.1	2.7	24.3	16.0	113 516	111 189	107 697
St. Charles	1 176.4	62.5	24 426	89.8	136.1	1 059.2	60.4	36.7	39.6	3.1	1.1	7.1	9.0	389 161	334 114	321 514
St. Helena	174.6	79.6	18 244	67.1	45.9	58.5	22.6	16.0	D	4.4	2.8	13.0	29.3	9 375	8 146	7 756
St. James	421.7	43.9	20 050	73.7	78.4	333.3	D	56.3	D	3.9	2.5	7.2	14.1	187 588	184 814	177 510
St. John the Baptist	864.1	49.6	20 480	75.3	126.4	448.0	45.8	32.4	53.8	8.1	2.8	17.6	12.6	145 056	137 778	130 248
St. Landry	1 447.3	51.5	17 275	63.5	391.4	638.5	25.8	17.8	73.9	12.0	4.7	23.2	23.9	113 478	114 514	121 475
St. Martin	789.5	67.2	16 640	61.2	160.6	306.7	39.5	24.2	57.2	10.3	4.4	14.9	20.8	74 117	89 151	92 301
St. Mary	1 133.5	54.2	19 805	72.8	213.9	1 108.7	44.9	17.3	54.5	5.8	2.0	15.0	10.9	191 755	177 212	142 737
St. Tammany	4 896.5	85.5	25 945	95.4	551.0	1 756.0	15.6	5.9	84.5	14.6	7.1	28.8	20.3	103 764	94 376	83 286
Tangipahoa	1 719.7	69.1	17 739	65.2	451.4	900.5	14.0	8.9	83.5	16.8	3.7	18.5	34.8	80 265	76 275	75 377
Tensas	116.3	47.3	17 622	64.8	38.4	56.7	D	D	D	4.6	D	16.7	23.0	D	3 572	3 054
Terrebonne	2 152.1	67.8	20 550	75.5	362.8	1 639.0	37.8	11.9	62.1	10.0	2.9	21.5	11.8	194 325	151 630	112 805
Union	406.4	58.5	18 442	67.8	95.7	174.0	D	34.6	D	7.4	2.2	13.3	15.9	60 155	55 850	47 143
Vermilion	965.1	56.9	18 540	68.2	201.0	517.4	36.2	9.8	59.4	10.0	3.4	12.9	17.0	50 548	58 401	55 588
Vernon	967.8	14.0	18 837	69.2	137.6	747.4	5.5	3.3	94.4	4.8	2.1	8.7	74.2	24 635	20 991	21 297
Washington	771.7	53.5	17 894	65.8	239.1	360.3	27.6	21.8	69.6	10.4	3.0	20.8	26.4	78 442	78 813	75 435
Webster	801.7	45.1	18 765	69.0	206.1	378.2	42.6	28.1	57.2	11.5	3.4	19.1	16.2	106 163	104 388	105 126
West Baton Rouge	483.8	67.8	23 467	86.3	75.3	413.2	D	30.9	D	4.4	2.2	10.1	10.1	127 655	121 911	114 760
West Carroll	185.1	61.3	15 235	56.0	65.1	75.1	21.6	14.1	D	8.5	2.4	15.4	29.1	10 583	9 816	8 892
West Feliciana	204.7	77.7	14 981	55.1	32.6	265.9	D	D	D	2.2	1.8	6.5	31.4	D	56 040	53 821
Winn	271.8	50.3	15 360	56.5	75.7	159.2	41.7	38.0	58.6	8.2	2.3	21.7	17.2	60 483	60 813	54 799

[1] Based on resident population estimated as of July 1, 1998.   [2] Includes farm earnings; see table B-10 for these data.   [3] Includes mining and construction, not shown separately.   [4] Includes agricultural services, forestry, and fisheries; transportation and public utilities; and wholesale trade, not shown separately.   [5] Finance, insurance, and real estate.

Source: Personal Income and Earnings—U.S. Bureau of Economic Analysis, "Regional Economic Information System (REIS) 1969-1998" on CD-ROM (related Internet site <http://www.bea.doc.gov/bea/regional/data.htm>).

[Includes U.S., states, and 3,142 counties/county equivalents defined as of January 1, 1992. For changes to these areas since January 1, 1992, see appendix B. Geographic Information]

County	Personal income, 1998													Manufacturing earnings		
			Per capita[1]			Earnings										
									Percent, by selected industry–							
							Goods-related		Service-related							
	Total (mil. dol.)	Percent change, 1990–1998	Amount (dollars)	Percent of national average	Transfer payments (mil. dol.)	Total[2] (mil. dol.)	Total[3]	Man-ufac-turing	Total[4]	Retail trade	FIRE[5]	Serv-ices	Gov-ern-ment	1998 ($1,000)	1997 ($1,000)	1996 ($1,000)
MAINE	29 315.8	36.2	23 499	86.4	4 964.7	19 645.5	24.2	17.7	75.3	11.6	6.6	27.0	18.3	3 481 402	3 411 038	3 256 430
Androscoggin	2 295.8	31.1	22 671	83.3	446.1	1 439.5	D	19.3	74.7	11.5	5.5	33.9	12.1	277 202	259 034	244 786
Aroostook	1 422.4	13.8	18 557	68.2	363.4	903.5	D	21.0	71.5	10.9	3.0	24.4	21.3	189 473	181 880	174 816
Cumberland..............	7 622.7	44.6	29 960	110.1	940.2	6 164.5	D	11.2	D	12.3	12.5	30.5	14.5	691 045	688 445	610 182
Franklin	575.3	33.1	19 940	73.3	119.9	388.5	D	37.8	D	11.2	4.2	D	14.9	146 760	150 755	143 450
Hancock	1 221.2	41.2	24 502	90.1	191.7	766.0	D	20.2	D	12.5	3.6	29.7	15.1	154 535	150 117	139 013
Kennebec................	2 705.5	29.0	23 502	86.4	474.3	1 940.2	D	9.2	D	9.5	3.2	26.9	31.1	179 087	194 225	188 376
Knox	929.7	44.8	24 475	90.0	151.2	557.1	D	12.0	D	12.3	8.0	29.1	14.6	66 662	66 530	71 630
Lincoln	804.2	36.8	25 321	93.1	126.5	337.7	19.6	10.1	79.8	16.5	4.4	29.3	14.9	34 256	31 485	28 977
Oxford	1 036.9	36.0	19 257	70.8	236.0	570.3	37.0	30.0	62.5	11.0	3.7	25.3	15.3	170 800	168 271	159 195
Penobscot	3 140.3	35.0	21 743	79.9	580.2	2 286.0	D	16.0	D	11.8	4.2	27.5	20.1	364 963	353 675	351 365
Piscataquis	322.7	28.6	17 742	65.2	80.0	184.6	D	D	D	10.5	D	16.1	18.6	D	66 973	60 150
Sagadahoc	828.4	31.4	23 236	85.4	108.5	622.0	D	D	D	5.6	1.7	14.7	14.1	D	305 165	324 325
Somerset	919.9	32.2	17 548	64.5	216.2	654.0	D	35.3	D	7.7	1.7	18.3	13.2	231 010	231 666	214 664
Waldo	696.6	50.6	19 070	70.1	138.6	309.9	NA	18.3	D	11.9	D	D	15.3	56 719	54 370	50 602
Washington	644.9	34.8	18 129	66.6	184.2	374.9	D	19.2	D	10.3	D	19.1	22.7	71 841	69 084	71 984
York	4 149.4	37.5	23 708	87.2	607.7	2 146.6	27.9	20.8	71.9	13.4	3.2	22.6	25.0	445 902	439 363	422 915
MARYLAND	156 759.3	41.9	30 557	112.3	16 347.9	101 409.6	15.2	8.5	84.5	9.0	8.1	31.9	23.7	8 617 296	8 180 182	7 785 154
Allegany	1 473.6	28.9	20 429	75.1	401.3	960.5	25.9	19.3	D	11.6	4.2	26.4	22.0	185 228	187 436	183 119
Anne Arundel	14 633.1	48.5	30 827	113.3	1 253.9	9 563.8	14.9	9.0	85.0	9.1	4.7	22.5	36.1	858 069	828 716	739 042
Baltimore	23 284.2	38.8	32 269	118.6	2 704.5	14 310.2	D	13.3	D	10.4	8.9	30.8	17.6	1 904 659	1 832 708	1 837 077
Calvert	1 941.9	71.9	27 063	99.5	166.9	640.8	17.9	3.4	D	11.1	4.2	D	17.6	21 890	20 654	18 057
Caroline	542.4	37.0	18 375	67.5	102.1	284.0	D	17.5	D	11.8	2.7	D	15.5	49 788	48 840	45 210
Carroll..................	4 099.9	52.3	27 389	100.7	411.7	1 497.0	30.5	15.6	68.3	11.3	5.4	22.3	15.9	233 240	211 214	202 779
Cecil	2 029.5	54.8	24 646	90.6	237.7	870.7	27.8	20.8	69.4	11.5	3.0	18.6	23.4	181 032	151 136	125 900
Charles	3 155.1	46.7	26 725	98.2	268.0	1 245.3	D	4.0	D	16.1	5.8	20.4	30.5	50 137	47 993	49 891
Dorchester	614.3	29.3	20 766	76.3	134.4	353.4	D	30.7	60.4	8.3	3.4	18.7	16.7	108 449	105 713	103 860
Frederick	5 602.5	80.6	30 021	110.4	429.8	2 704.1	22.7	11.0	76.2	10.0	9.9	26.8	19.2	298 187	270 075	255 656
Garrett	535.5	41.3	18 293	67.2	117.0	342.2	27.3	10.7	69.9	13.4	5.6	23.5	14.1	36 708	41 989	46 464
Harford	5 710.4	53.3	26 613	97.8	540.8	2 576.6	D	6.9	D	11.0	3.9	20.2	39.0	177 586	157 397	147 127
Howard..................	8 533.3	58.5	36 294	133.4	421.3	5 251.0	D	6.5	D	9.2	8.4	36.7	10.5	342 139	325 757	304 705
Kent	496.5	44.9	26 128	96.0	89.5	235.3	22.3	13.7	69.9	10.0	4.8	30.4	12.4	32 157	28 017	23 042
Montgomery	35 574.6	42.7	42 393	155.8	1 985.6	22 991.8	10.6	5.4	89.3	7.5	9.0	40.9	22.2	1 251 235	1 119 095	987 931
Prince George's	21 750.3	34.5	27 996	102.9	1 837.1	13 464.1	13.4	4.3	86.5	11.5	4.7	25.3	32.6	573 034	511 360	492 026
Queen Anne's	1 066.8	44.7	26 878	98.8	103.5	337.8	25.9	12.5	73.1	16.7	5.4	19.5	18.7	42 229	37 959	35 026
St. Mary's...............	2 397.4	77.1	27 354	100.6	203.5	1 660.5	D	1.2	D	6.1	2.2	28.4	49.7	19 576	21 654	18 350
Somerset	388.2	33.6	16 006	58.8	94.5	209.1	8.7	4.1	D	9.2	2.4	D	43.4	8 552	8 284	7 178
Talbot	1 085.9	42.4	32 754	120.4	138.8	613.9	D	13.5	D	12.7	6.2	36.9	13.6	83 096	82 529	74 357
Washington	2 967.9	48.2	23 282	85.6	452.7	2 022.5	D	19.5	D	10.9	3.4	29.5	15.7	393 791	355 686	330 192
Wicomico	1 821.5	43.2	22 929	84.3	295.5	1 334.2	D	19.2	D	10.1	4.9	28.0	15.2	256 091	248 773	227 621
Worcester	1 073.9	51.2	25 109	92.3	193.6	626.4	D	8.9	D	22.5	8.1	27.3	15.9	55 855	54 175	51 310
Independent City																
Baltimore city.............	15 980.4	19.6	24 750	91.0	3 764.6	17 314.7	11.6	8.4	88.4	5.2	14.0	36.8	20.3	1 454 568	1 483 022	1 479 234
MASSACHUSETTS......	205 813.6	47.2	33 496	123.1	26 554.9	154 005.8	20.9	16.0	79.0	8.3	10.6	35.6	12.3	24 677 689	23 543 236	22 254 146
Barnstable	6 798.9	55.0	32 612	119.9	1 127.0	3 260.7	D	5.2	D	17.7	6.8	33.4	17.8	170 709	126 110	116 810
Berkshire	3 683.7	31.9	27 731	101.9	693.7	2 355.0	26.9	20.6	73.0	12.0	4.5	34.7	12.3	486 115	500 403	470 630
Bristol	13 497.0	45.0	26 108	96.0	2 404.7	7 805.5	32.2	26.4	67.6	12.4	3.6	23.6	13.8	2 060 782	1 985 197	1 906 569
Dukes	465.4	68.7	33 599	123.5	52.3	272.4	15.6	1.3	84.2	21.5	7.6	27.9	15.9	3 460	3 266	3 318
Essex	22 930.1	49.4	32 740	120.4	3 004.8	12 864.4	32.0	26.8	67.8	9.9	5.1	29.2	12.2	3 445 561	3 331 560	3 216 465
Franklin	1 811.0	38.9	25 642	94.3	341.3	958.7	29.4	23.3	69.5	10.8	5.3	27.0	15.5	223 405	223 083	219 956
Hampden	11 616.5	30.7	26 441	97.2	2 522.7	7 575.3	24.6	19.5	75.3	9.5	8.6	28.6	18.2	1 480 910	1 465 174	1 398 156
Hampshire	3 792.4	41.0	25 225	92.7	447.3	2 154.3	16.9	10.8	82.3	10.4	3.1	32.5	27.6	232 703	227 690	215 790
Middlesex...............	56 695.3	50.4	39 857	146.5	5 115.8	44 843.7	24.4	19.4	75.5	7.1	5.3	42.1	8.5	8 692 442	8 002 934	7 394 687
Nantucket	349.3	82.4	44 267	162.7	25.0	251.9	16.3	1.2	83.7	23.7	10.3	26.2	12.2	3 103	3 007	3 058
Norfolk	25 332.6	48.9	39 453	145.0	2 314.7	15 356.6	18.9	13.0	81.1	10.8	13.2	32.3	9.0	2 003 453	1 967 297	1 905 700
Plymouth	13 680.4	52.2	29 292	107.7	1 766.9	7 141.2	17.0	9.9	82.5	13.7	5.5	27.0	17.7	705 745	693 526	661 336
Suffolk	24 270.4	47.4	37 844	139.1	3 752.6	35 881.9	D	5.4	D	4.1	23.8	41.0	13.1	1 934 009	1 867 965	1 727 933
Worcester	20 890.4	44.8	28 587	105.1	2 986.1	13 284.4	29.2	24.4	70.8	9.5	6.7	26.6	16.1	3 235 292	3 146 024	3 013 738

[1] Based on resident population estimated as of July 1, 1998. [2] Includes farm earnings; see table B-10 for these data. [3] Includes mining and construction, not shown separately. [4] Includes agricultural services, forestry, and fisheries; transportation and public utilities; and wholesale trade, not shown separately. [5] Finance, insurance, and real estate.

Source: Personal Income and Earnings—U.S. Bureau of Economic Analysis, "Regional Economic Information System (REIS) 1969-1998" on CD-ROM (related Internet site <http://www.bea.doc.gov/bea/regional/data.htm>).

Table B–8. Counties — **Personal Income and Earnings**–Con.

[Includes U.S., states, and 3,142 counties/county equivalents defined as of January 1, 1992. For changes to these areas since January 1, 1992, see appendix B. Geographic Information]

County	Personal income, 1998													Manufacturing earnings		
	Total (mil. dol.)	Per capita¹			Transfer payments (mil. dol.)	Earnings										
		Percent change, 1990–1998	Amount (dollars)	Percent of national average		Total² (mil. dol.)	Percent, by selected industry–							1998 ($1,000)	1997 ($1,000)	1996 ($1,000)
							Goods-related		Service-related							
							Total³	Manufacturing	Total⁴	Retail trade	FIRE⁵	Services	Government			
MICHIGAN	264 016.0	49.1	26 885	98.8	35 055.9	192 095.9	36.9	31.2	62.9	8.1	5.7	24.2	13.2	59 879 767	57 000 561	54 581 721
Alcona	205.7	47.3	18 593	68.3	61.2	61.7	NA	28.8	62.7	13.8	2.9	20.8	20.7	17 782	15 209	13 780
Alger	169.7	52.9	16 996	62.5	41.5	99.6	48.4	43.2	51.4	7.8	4.7	13.3	19.9	43 005	41 530	38 479
Allegan	2 476.5	69.7	24 356	89.5	274.5	1 448.8	62.4	56.1	35.7	6.9	2.1	9.6	10.6	813 439	741 676	674 189
Alpena	674.3	44.2	22 125	81.3	138.5	453.8	D	27.2	D	10.1	3.2	15.9	24.8	123 479	121 384	112 877
Antrim	474.0	74.4	22 073	81.1	88.4	190.0	D	28.2	D	9.4	3.7	21.0	19.6	53 625	41 895	37 193
Arenac	302.7	45.2	18 452	67.8	77.9	138.3	D	18.0	D	9.6	3.0	31.4	19.4	24 919	24 271	20 751
Baraga	152.1	55.1	17 678	65.0	36.3	98.9	D	29.8	D	6.5	2.8	23.6	25.8	29 475	26 867	23 224
Barry	1 342.6	68.0	24 650	90.6	158.5	438.0	D	31.7	D	8.1	6.1	19.6	16.3	139 044	128 933	120 010
Bay	2 689.9	41.4	24 458	89.9	435.9	1 573.2	34.5	29.2	65.1	10.5	5.0	24.2	15.6	459 209	452 374	431 530
Benzie	306.8	70.8	20 812	76.5	63.4	111.0	D	13.7	D	14.1	4.9	25.7	21.0	15 164	17 676	15 739
Berrien	3 873.5	45.9	24 235	89.1	636.5	2 594.6	42.3	37.0	57.0	8.5	3.5	22.9	11.5	960 518	957 414	899 406
Branch	843.7	40.4	19 306	71.0	147.4	466.5	D	30.6	D	8.7	3.0	14.2	28.4	142 787	134 603	121 254
Calhoun	3 285.4	42.0	23 333	85.8	542.8	2 629.0	41.7	37.1	58.3	9.3	4.8	17.8	18.2	974 398	976 605	914 227
Cass	1 048.6	44.4	20 982	77.1	169.8	375.9	44.2	37.9	56.0	7.3	4.1	15.8	19.7	142 419	128 499	132 945
Charlevoix	578.8	66.5	23 627	86.9	89.0	385.4	48.5	37.6	51.5	8.2	3.5	17.3	15.2	144 978	159 666	141 322
Cheboygan	498.4	67.0	20 928	76.9	112.7	230.1	NA	12.0	74.6	19.1	3.2	27.6	18.4	27 728	25 861	28 307
Chippewa	644.7	55.2	17 008	62.5	126.4	439.6	15.6	10.6	84.6	9.9	2.6	26.6	38.4	46 547	29 576	29 488
Clare	488.4	55.1	16 549	60.8	146.2	224.3	26.3	17.5	72.9	17.7	2.7	19.6	21.7	39 277	33 736	31 428
Clinton	1 541.4	60.7	24 310	89.4	154.3	498.2	35.0	23.8	63.1	10.8	2.5	19.7	20.3	118 664	113 172	111 563
Crawford	236.3	58.8	16 723	61.5	52.9	137.4	28.1	23.0	71.9	10.0	2.4	27.5	25.0	31 543	31 625	28 592
Delta	851.8	52.7	21 878	80.4	169.6	549.5	D	30.9	D	13.5	3.2	19.4	15.8	169 651	156 129	146 809
Dickinson	627.5	32.9	23 187	85.2	110.1	474.7	NA	25.4	61.3	9.0	2.1	16.3	22.1	120 386	117 033	114 319
Eaton	2 422.3	45.2	23 978	88.1	268.4	1 177.6	22.0	12.6	77.6	9.7	12.5	23.9	19.3	148 434	138 825	130 141
Emmet	750.8	56.1	26 222	96.4	101.2	541.0	D	12.5	D	13.5	5.5	36.6	11.4	67 751	64 261	59 122
Genesee	10 433.3	38.4	23 947	88.0	1 749.0	7 498.3	D	36.7	D	8.9	3.8	23.7	13.0	2 751 478	2 951 371	3 025 370
Gladwin	448.1	58.9	17 683	65.0	123.0	152.4	D	24.1	D	13.2	3.1	19.0	20.7	36 723	40 183	34 307
Gogebic	334.2	39.5	19 381	71.2	93.6	171.0	NA	14.7	81.1	11.5	3.8	31.2	28.5	25 111	23 955	25 956
Grand Traverse	1 969.5	67.7	26 535	97.5	244.1	1 600.2	26.7	14.5	73.2	13.1	6.7	31.8	12.9	231 830	220 109	196 920
Gratiot	784.6	39.4	19 545	71.8	147.9	449.8	30.5	26.6	68.8	8.2	3.4	28.4	16.9	119 850	135 724	120 999
Hillsdale	948.2	51.1	20 361	74.8	151.9	567.4	53.7	49.8	44.0	6.6	2.2	13.8	14.3	282 837	255 350	243 621
Houghton	667.2	42.5	18 732	68.9	147.9	398.8	D	8.4	D	9.6	5.1	22.0	39.4	33 359	28 778	29 431
Huron	852.9	53.9	24 179	88.9	157.1	493.4	D	32.7	D	9.0	2.9	18.4	13.7	161 447	147 789	131 335
Ingham	6 945.5	36.3	24 296	89.3	873.0	6 799.4	24.6	19.6	75.4	8.0	6.8	24.8	28.6	1 329 742	1 458 058	1 424 425
Ionia	1 122.9	48.2	16 832	61.9	157.2	560.6	D	9.4	D	9.4	4.0	14.3	30.6	154 293	156 100	156 729
Iosco	489.8	5.9	19 048	70.0	138.1	258.8	D	17.1	71.7	12.9	3.9	22.8	23.7	44 369	54 788	57 609
Iron	246.6	35.2	19 141	70.4	74.8	114.6	21.7	12.7	78.3	12.9	3.9	19.0	36.0	14 517	13 493	12 546
Isabella	1 150.1	47.7	19 696	72.4	186.7	789.7	22.5	11.4	77.1	11.3	3.0	28.5	27.0	90 151	85 975	84 399
Jackson	3 524.8	44.4	22 576	83.0	551.4	2 245.1	33.2	26.8	66.9	9.1	3.7	22.1	16.6	601 328	599 400	587 540
Kalamazoo	6 283.4	44.8	27 364	100.6	743.6	4 848.6	38.7	33.1	60.7	7.4	7.7	24.1	13.5	1 604 374	1 542 186	1 568 952
Kalkaska	266.3	57.9	17 122	62.9	57.4	170.4	45.3	16.9	54.3	8.1	1.9	12.2	13.2	28 763	31 724	28 977
Kent	15 700.6	61.2	28 820	105.9	1 593.9	13 742.3	36.9	30.2	62.8	9.5	6.4	23.3	8.2	4 156 926	3 967 409	3 640 396
Keweenaw	37.7	54.1	17 968	66.1	10.0	14.7	16.4	13.5	D	10.1	1.2	34.8	35.3	1 982	1 943	2 058
Lake	161.8	67.4	15 518	57.0	58.0	52.7	NA	17.6	D	14.4	3.3	20.2	29.1	9 262	9 243	8 322
Lapeer	2 005.1	56.7	22 727	83.5	224.6	719.9	39.6	29.1	60.0	12.1	3.2	14.6	23.0	209 480	203 188	192 217
Leelanau	506.3	71.4	26 448	97.2	67.8	181.0	D	5.5	D	11.9	5.4	36.5	14.6	10 033	10 387	10 619
Lenawee	2 307.4	46.8	23 400	86.0	324.3	1 253.4	D	38.9	D	10.3	4.0	17.1	16.8	487 984	463 807	446 037
Livingston	4 486.9	85.2	30 666	112.7	309.9	1 669.8	38.8	26.7	61.3	10.2	8.2	20.8	11.5	446 632	445 843	445 344
Luce	123.2	34.3	18 135	66.7	31.9	81.4	D	22.6	D	9.1	2.2	8.1	44.6	18 438	18 478	18 127
Mackinac	262.1	61.6	23 735	87.3	53.1	146.4	D	5.4	D	16.5	2.1	35.7	23.3	7 892	7 487	7 266
Macomb	22 254.7	45.4	28 283	104.0	2 663.4	15 779.3	51.9	45.3	48.0	7.7	3.1	18.8	10.5	7 152 468	7 007 654	6 631 787
Manistee	439.1	42.7	18 697	68.7	109.6	221.8	37.8	28.4	61.8	10.1	2.4	17.3	23.0	62 987	61 658	63 467
Marquette	1 307.7	22.0	20 894	76.8	239.5	873.0	D	3.6	D	8.9	4.1	D	25.8	31 015	23 007	23 141
Mason	573.3	52.1	20 551	75.5	115.9	353.4	D	35.4	D	9.5	2.5	18.9	17.9	125 124	117 837	105 600
Mecosta	689.9	55.8	17 181	63.2	134.4	382.2	D	18.2	D	10.4	2.2	16.5	37.8	69 539	64 245	57 177
Menominee	511.8	38.4	20 980	77.1	93.6	288.2	NA	36.5	58.4	8.3	2.5	17.2	16.2	105 168	100 040	93 966
Midland	2 438.5	46.7	29 897	109.9	244.3	1 757.3	D	51.2	D	4.9	2.5	21.9	8.1	900 359	868 518	853 919
Missaukee	236.9	54.4	17 058	62.7	48.3	95.8	33.2	23.5	55.1	10.0	2.9	11.3	19.0	22 487	21 689	19 957
Monroe	3 682.6	58.0	25 687	94.4	448.6	1 793.9	45.1	38.5	53.8	9.3	2.0	14.5	13.1	689 964	655 383	628 811
Montcalm	1 005.0	45.6	16 583	61.0	199.8	651.4	D	36.6	D	10.5	2.4	17.3	17.2	238 180	234 650	219 104
Montmorency	168.7	58.2	16 868	62.0	60.1	62.8	D	23.6	D	10.2	2.9	18.6	20.7	14 851	12 794	11 224
Muskegon	3 506.6	45.3	21 016	77.3	631.4	2 301.6	D	33.7	D	9.8	2.7	21.3	15.7	776 748	723 036	662 558
Newaygo	817.3	57.1	17 856	65.6	159.9	367.4	NA	23.5	67.1	9.2	4.4	20.1	24.5	86 237	80 030	80 945
Oakland	49 796.1	64.5	42 378	155.8	3 598.9	39 417.7	30.0	24.5	70.0	7.6	9.2	33.5	6.2	9 661 592	8 616 253	7 980 062

¹ Based on resident population estimated as of July 1, 1998.　² Includes farm earnings; see table B-10 for these data.　³ Includes mining and construction, not shown separately.　⁴ Includes agricultural services, forestry, and fisheries; transportation and public utilities; and wholesale trade, not shown separately.　⁵ Finance, insurance, and real estate.

Source: Personal Income and Earnings—U.S. Bureau of Economic Analysis, "Regional Economic Information System (REIS) 1969-1998" on CD-ROM (related Internet site <http://www.bea.doc.gov/bea/regional/data.htm>).

[Includes U.S., states, and 3,142 counties/county equivalents defined as of January 1, 1992. For changes to these areas since January 1, 1992, see appendix B. Geographic Information]

County	Personal income, 1998													Manufacturing earnings		
		Per capita[1]				Earnings										
							Percent, by selected industry–									
							Goods-related		Service-related							
	Total (mil. dol.)	Percent change, 1990–1998	Amount (dollars)	Percent of national average	Transfer payments (mil. dol.)	Total[2] (mil. dol.)	Total[3]	Manufacturing	Total[4]	Retail trade	FIRE[5]	Services	Government	1998 ($1,000)	1997 ($1,000)	1996 ($1,000)
MICHIGAN—Con.																
Oceana	468.5	51.7	18 934	69.6	97.3	213.3	31.0	21.6	61.4	9.7	2.6	19.4	20.4	46 157	47 428	41 919
Ogemaw	336.1	53.4	15 938	58.6	104.7	179.0	23.1	15.8	75.1	16.9	3.6	17.1	22.0	28 281	29 686	20 064
Ontonagon	148.9	20.6	18 985	69.8	42.3	83.5	D	30.5	D	9.7	2.7	11.9	27.8	25 488	26 194	26 274
Osceola	401.4	62.6	18 133	66.7	88.8	273.8	59.7	48.4	40.0	6.2	1.3	12.0	14.2	132 577	125 483	119 731
Oscoda	130.3	58.0	14 655	53.9	40.3	61.1	NA	34.7	59.0	13.1	2.7	15.7	22.2	21 192	19 773	19 455
Otsego	494.2	73.7	22 229	81.7	75.4	384.5	36.7	18.4	63.4	14.4	3.5	21.9	12.7	70 871	62 015	56 277
Ottawa	6 043.6	68.1	26 812	98.6	522.2	4 297.9	51.1	43.4	47.5	6.8	4.6	15.8	10.9	1 867 231	1 761 111	1 688 383
Presque Isle	246.4	31.9	16 951	62.3	69.6	107.1	D	8.4	D	14.2	3.3	D	21.6	9 046	8 455	7 051
Roscommon	435.7	53.7	18 656	68.6	145.7	183.7	D	7.3	D	21.4	3.8	20.0	26.2	13 475	14 250	15 067
Saginaw	4 915.2	40.0	23 402	86.0	839.0	3 945.6	42.8	37.7	57.1	9.0	4.0	23.1	11.0	1 488 612	1 468 567	1 408 970
St. Clair	3 823.4	48.6	23 976	88.1	529.0	1 841.3	32.9	25.1	67.3	10.2	4.4	21.7	14.9	462 183	471 587	450 062
St. Joseph	1 318.6	47.4	21 566	79.3	208.0	866.3	D	52.3	D	6.7	D	10.6	14.4	453 444	466 266	438 975
Sanilac	907.7	53.1	21 084	77.5	174.0	423.3	43.2	35.5	52.7	9.3	3.0	16.9	16.4	150 436	147 208	142 053
Schoolcraft	171.0	46.6	19 473	71.6	43.7	91.4	28.1	18.6	72.0	11.6	6.1	16.7	29.8	17 032	18 038	18 213
Shiawassee	1 453.8	33.7	20 056	73.7	244.5	593.0	29.6	22.5	71.0	11.8	5.5	22.7	20.2	133 560	133 956	125 862
Tuscola	1 129.5	37.8	19 487	71.6	208.8	471.7	30.1	22.9	67.5	9.3	4.3	14.7	28.2	107 830	106 041	104 148
Van Buren	1 460.8	44.7	19 313	71.0	269.1	750.3	D	27.5	D	9.6	D	13.5	22.4	206 123	188 020	172 985
Washtenaw	10 522.1	59.9	34 751	127.7	755.6	8 458.0	31.0	27.0	69.0	8.1	3.4	22.8	26.6	2 285 123	2 140 501	1 980 169
Wayne	53 051.1	35.2	25 065	92.1	9 263.9	43 742.7	36.8	33.3	63.2	6.7	5.8	23.1	13.2	14 553 438	13 473 701	13 289 363
Wexford	585.7	59.3	20 114	73.9	112.8	465.3	D	33.9	D	10.0	2.5	23.7	14.8	157 926	153 899	148 785
MINNESOTA	138 306.9	57.5	29 263	107.6	15 427.7	101 523.0	D	20.5	D	8.9	8.9	26.5	13.3	20 817 967	19 779 198	18 675 862
Aitkin	269.8	61.9	19 023	69.9	75.8	109.9	D	13.7	D	14.2	3.5	23.0	22.6	15 007	14 887	13 382
Anoka	7 703.9	72.7	26 354	96.9	622.1	4 058.4	42.5	33.3	57.5	10.4	2.6	20.6	12.7	1 350 420	1 274 743	1 162 375
Becker	590.3	50.3	20 012	73.6	117.0	342.5	D	14.5	D	11.0	D	25.1	20.2	49 602	43 904	39 982
Beltrami	759.0	61.1	19 630	72.2	151.7	495.2	16.1	6.1	83.7	11.9	3.3	29.2	27.5	30 316	28 089	29 521
Benton	742.0	64.7	21 751	80.0	86.8	424.2	D	27.4	D	12.2	2.1	15.5	10.0	116 329	112 048	107 420
Big Stone	116.6	21.7	20 627	75.8	27.4	53.1	D	2.6	D	10.8	5.5	17.5	28.8	1 398	1 278	1 180
Blue Earth	1 385.6	57.1	25 790	94.8	168.2	1 048.7	22.1	13.9	75.2	10.9	4.7	25.4	18.4	145 242	137 603	124 377
Brown	635.2	37.7	23 466	86.3	98.9	427.9	D	33.3	D	8.4	D	19.9	11.5	142 334	139 072	138 243
Carlton	655.7	55.2	20 948	77.0	120.6	431.4	39.7	26.9	60.7	7.7	3.0	18.0	22.0	116 076	114 668	106 747
Carver	2 059.7	96.8	31 775	116.8	127.2	1 104.4	D	39.6	D	6.2	4.1	20.4	12.6	437 607	450 250	436 049
Cass	503.2	67.7	19 126	70.3	120.8	253.3	12.6	3.2	87.5	13.7	4.7	33.8	27.2	7 987	7 037	6 274
Chippewa	313.2	37.4	23 998	88.2	48.4	194.7	D	21.7	D	9.2	3.7	13.9	15.0	42 237	42 332	35 002
Chisago	1 038.4	106.1	25 357	93.2	112.1	389.0	34.1	19.9	64.7	10.1	3.5	27.7	16.5	77 226	79 552	73 054
Clay	1 050.4	42.9	20 387	74.9	169.9	520.3	D	8.3	D	12.1	3.5	24.2	26.4	43 223	43 342	41 101
Clearwater	142.3	44.8	17 262	63.5	37.6	74.9	30.2	17.2	70.6	8.6	2.8	15.5	31.3	12 852	10 990	9 761
Cook	120.1	72.1	25 272	92.9	18.2	76.6	16.7	5.5	D	13.5	2.3	36.2	26.0	4 186	4 516	4 073
Cottonwood	271.9	33.2	22 596	83.1	52.8	154.9	D	18.7	D	8.0	4.5	17.3	16.5	29 004	24 913	22 971
Crow Wing	1 168.4	66.9	22 581	83.0	218.5	766.8	D	16.7	D	13.4	5.9	24.2	20.3	128 358	119 709	115 060
Dakota	10 849.1	75.4	31 717	116.6	689.9	5 537.1	29.0	21.2	70.8	10.5	7.5	22.4	12.2	1 171 453	1 090 339	1 010 492
Dodge	397.4	49.4	23 148	85.1	49.7	168.7	D	26.7	D	6.9	3.5	12.2	17.5	45 091	38 162	36 396
Douglas	710.4	63.2	22 860	84.0	118.7	449.3	32.2	20.7	67.1	13.2	4.0	19.4	17.9	93 153	88 967	85 358
Faribault	352.8	27.0	21 697	79.8	71.8	186.2	32.9	24.4	60.7	7.5	5.0	16.1	16.1	45 488	43 970	41 847
Fillmore	438.3	34.6	21 107	77.6	82.9	215.0	D	17.9	D	9.8	4.9	16.6	16.5	38 584	37 123	34 921
Freeborn	690.3	30.4	21 873	80.4	130.2	404.5	D	27.6	D	11.9	4.1	22.5	12.8	111 746	104 833	99 948
Goodhue	1 154.8	59.1	26 774	98.4	141.1	730.7	NA	25.8	65.5	7.3	3.6	24.3	12.4	188 846	185 540	170 165
Grant	131.5	30.9	21 529	79.1	27.9	71.3	D	10.7	D	6.8	4.8	23.7	15.7	7 599	7 392	7 551
Hennepin	42 491.0	57.1	40 126	147.5	3 764.5	41 517.1	20.7	16.4	79.3	8.4	13.6	29.8	9.5	6 798 755	6 464 862	6 097 361
Houston	464.3	49.9	24 100	88.6	65.3	168.5	D	13.8	D	7.0	4.1	23.1	17.3	23 331	21 147	17 783
Hubbard	334.7	67.5	19 791	72.8	74.1	169.7	D	23.9	D	11.6	4.6	24.3	17.7	40 498	36 646	33 697
Isanti	670.7	62.5	22 329	82.1	84.8	299.0	29.1	18.8	71.6	10.7	3.6	28.7	20.3	56 197	49 487	47 046
Itasca	882.8	49.5	20 100	73.9	182.2	525.2	D	18.2	D	10.1	3.5	D	20.7	95 448	95 336	84 057
Jackson	251.3	33.8	21 864	80.4	41.8	148.5	23.9	18.6	D	6.1	4.0	15.0	15.8	27 578	28 931	31 610
Kanabec	260.8	48.5	18 414	67.7	47.3	128.1	D	19.3	D	19.7	5.0	15.6	21.5	24 681	23 923	21 028
Kandiyohi	1 021.2	57.9	24 976	91.8	143.3	662.3	D	15.8	D	9.7	3.9	22.0	22.6	104 769	88 278	80 164
Kittson	115.6	4.5	21 808	80.2	23.8	54.0	D	4.4	78.1	8.4	4.3	20.9	23.3	2 373	2 373	2 285
Koochiching	328.8	34.5	21 823	80.2	64.8	212.7	D	34.4	D	9.6	2.2	21.9	18.2	73 256	72 317	70 549
Lac qui Parle	176.4	25.0	22 062	81.1	35.5	94.6	D	12.8	D	8.2	4.0	13.9	20.8	12 122	11 503	12 249
Lake	229.9	54.6	21 558	79.2	48.5	138.2	D	14.3	D	10.3	2.5	D	21.1	19 723	26 051	25 912
Lake of the Woods	90.2	40.4	19 763	72.7	16.9	44.0	D	26.0	D	10.2	2.1	26.9	23.6	11 440	9 965	9 340
Le Sueur	595.7	54.3	23 527	86.5	80.2	277.8	47.1	35.2	49.1	7.8	3.5	16.0	13.4	97 920	92 225	83 388
Lincoln	127.1	22.9	19 597	72.0	28.8	64.2	14.8	3.4	65.3	6.8	2.9	23.1	15.9	2 179	2 007	2 207
Lyon	621.9	50.2	25 488	93.7	85.5	463.5	D	29.3	D	8.0	5.8	14.1	18.6	135 958	122 508	120 842
McLeod	895.1	61.4	26 216	96.4	102.7	682.1	D	52.5	D	6.4	2.6	9.1	12.3	358 244	352 089	326 420
Mahnomen	83.0	30.2	16 434	60.4	23.9	53.5	D	D	D	8.4	8.6	47.0	19.8	D	994	1 163
Marshall	200.4	23.1	19 497	71.7	42.2	78.6	20.9	10.9	74.1	8.6	5.4	15.5	25.8	8 530	8 379	7 645
Martin	518.5	29.2	23 569	86.6	91.4	301.9	28.9	22.8	63.7	9.0	4.3	19.7	13.6	68 677	66 332	65 308
Meeker	457.9	37.1	21 064	77.4	72.4	201.0	D	25.2	D	9.4	D	14.7	18.2	50 636	53 294	44 103

[1] Based on resident population estimated as of July 1, 1998. [2] Includes farm earnings; see table B-10 for these data. [3] Includes mining and construction, not shown separately. [4] Includes agricultural services, forestry, and fisheries; transportation and public utilities; and wholesale trade, not shown separately. [5] Finance, insurance, and real estate.

Source: Personal Income and Earnings—U.S. Bureau of Economic Analysis, "Regional Economic Information System (REIS) 1969-1998" on CD-ROM (related Internet site <http://www.bea.doc.gov/bea/regional/data.htm>).

Table B–8. Counties — **Personal Income and Earnings**–Con.

[Includes U.S., states, and 3,142 counties/county equivalents defined as of January 1, 1992. For changes to these areas since January 1, 1992, see appendix B. Geographic Information]

County	Personal income, 1998 Total (mil. dol.)	Percent change, 1990–1998	Per capita Amount (dollars)	Per capita Percent of national average	Transfer payments (mil. dol.)	Earnings Total[2] (mil. dol.)	Goods-related Total[3]	Manufacturing	Service-related Total[4]	Retail trade	FIRE[5]	Services	Government	Manufacturing earnings 1998 ($1,000)	1997 ($1,000)	1996 ($1,000)
MINNESOTA—Con.																
Mille Lacs	410.6	53.7	19 490	71.6	92.9	252.1	D	18.1	D	9.1	4.8	33.3	17.0	45 678	47 650	43 941
Morrison	583.9	50.0	19 134	70.3	112.1	335.3	25.1	16.6	71.8	10.3	3.8	22.1	22.0	55 529	53 299	51 222
Mower	911.5	41.0	24 567	90.3	165.2	517.7	D	31.9	D	9.4	3.1	21.6	15.3	164 947	148 788	135 292
Murray	200.9	33.5	21 073	77.5	37.3	105.6	D	6.5	D	6.5	4.5	15.1	15.4	6 909	6 862	6 508
Nicollet	690.0	49.0	23 404	86.0	70.3	427.0	D	39.7	D	5.7	3.8	17.4	18.8	169 574	148 617	139 516
Nobles	449.5	26.9	23 319	85.7	75.4	307.7	D	22.8	D	10.9	3.8	14.6	17.3	70 299	75 203	77 542
Norman	159.5	13.9	21 159	77.8	35.2	76.4	D	D	D	9.9	5.6	20.3	20.7	D	2 102	2 334
Olmsted	3 610.9	58.4	30 880	113.5	333.5	3 184.5	D	22.3	71.6	7.1	3.6	45.6	9.0	708 865	634 147	534 604
Otter Tail	1 166.8	53.3	21 295	78.3	222.2	659.3	25.8	15.1	69.8	11.7	4.1	20.9	18.1	99 511	95 879	90 848
Pennington	308.3	46.2	22 765	83.7	50.4	232.9	D	23.6	D	9.1	2.9	20.0	17.7	54 856	55 541	52 058
Pine	443.4	63.7	18 403	67.7	95.2	218.8	D	5.9	D	12.6	3.0	31.7	27.7	12 961	11 832	10 673
Pipestone	216.2	37.0	21 499	79.0	40.6	135.1	D	17.4	D	11.2	D	17.1	18.2	23 572	20 693	20 129
Polk	684.5	32.6	22 024	81.0	128.2	371.5	20.8	15.2	70.3	8.9	3.4	21.1	22.7	56 525	51 710	49 803
Pope	226.9	49.6	20 792	76.4	47.3	110.0	D	15.2	72.1	10.5	3.8	16.8	20.7	16 661	15 425	14 596
Ramsey	15 961.7	46.6	32 863	120.8	1 900.2	14 041.3	29.7	24.9	70.3	6.8	8.8	27.2	16.7	3 497 897	3 422 467	3 418 720
Red Lake	77.6	33.6	18 303	67.3	17.9	40.6	D	8.1	D	10.8	3.4	15.8	20.6	3 302	3 243	3 442
Redwood	385.3	37.6	23 347	85.8	62.7	227.1	D	19.9	D	8.5	3.9	20.6	15.8	45 141	43 642	42 216
Renville	370.1	25.4	21 857	80.3	64.6	205.4	25.6	19.3	58.3	6.3	5.5	14.8	15.9	39 707	39 592	35 198
Rice	1 215.2	51.8	22 421	82.4	146.8	759.4	35.1	26.9	64.5	8.5	2.8	25.4	17.8	204 136	187 877	172 763
Rock	216.5	26.5	22 271	81.9	37.1	109.5	D	7.4	D	10.0	11.1	19.0	21.2	8 137	14 000	12 918
Roseau	348.9	36.8	21 690	79.7	45.2	268.0	63.3	61.5	37.4	5.6	2.3	13.3	11.1	164 783	162 963	166 469
St. Louis	4 958.4	47.2	25 630	94.2	854.9	3 372.9	22.6	9.4	77.4	10.1	3.6	28.4	19.8	316 013	295 214	277 702
Scott	2 298.2	103.4	29 049	106.8	142.7	1 166.9	40.0	23.4	59.8	8.3	3.3	25.0	11.7	273 033	217 715	202 842
Sherburne	1 342.4	97.2	22 248	81.8	115.3	603.2	D	18.5	D	11.7	3.8	15.5	19.1	111 439	102 517	93 926
Sibley	286.8	29.7	19 591	72.0	51.4	112.6	25.7	13.6	65.5	7.7	4.0	16.6	21.1	15 254	14 729	14 081
Stearns	2 928.4	55.9	22 747	83.6	361.9	2 473.5	24.0	17.6	73.9	17.0	4.6	23.3	16.4	435 277	400 785	377 504
Steele	868.3	54.9	27 371	100.6	95.6	672.2	D	39.6	D	7.6	D	13.7	9.0	266 266	257 820	245 925
Stevens	230.7	33.7	22 992	84.5	36.7	156.3	D	13.6	D	8.0	4.4	19.1	24.9	21 204	12 171	11 141
Swift	235.6	44.9	20 500	75.4	46.0	133.8	D	24.2	D	7.8	3.5	18.8	19.2	32 376	29 685	25 814
Todd	398.6	33.3	16 584	61.0	90.2	197.3	D	30.5	D	8.7	3.8	16.2	19.8	60 226	59 727	56 653
Traverse	94.5	17.9	22 240	81.8	21.2	44.5	D	13.6	D	8.1	6.4	12.4	24.9	6 074	5 365	4 995
Wabasha	505.1	49.7	24 176	88.9	71.3	245.8	36.0	29.0	55.5	8.6	3.2	14.9	14.3	71 188	60 215	52 720
Wadena	248.5	49.5	18 947	69.7	62.2	167.5	24.0	17.6	76.4	10.2	3.3	24.3	22.5	29 431	27 197	25 294
Waseca	415.8	39.6	22 433	82.5	57.2	272.9	D	41.5	D	5.3	3.2	14.1	17.5	113 270	113 519	106 411
Washington	5 978.7	82.4	30 399	111.7	364.3	2 330.8	35.9	29.1	63.5	12.0	9.2	19.1	14.0	678 343	635 762	553 577
Watonwan	254.5	37.9	22 093	81.2	45.4	156.9	D	27.2	D	6.1	3.8	16.0	13.9	42 690	41 474	40 472
Wilkin	148.7	29.4	20 172	74.2	26.9	71.5	D	3.7	D	7.0	5.5	26.0	18.2	2 629	2 418	1 978
Winona	1 128.3	44.0	23 495	86.4	149.9	776.1	D	32.3	D	8.1	2.4	19.2	15.5	250 906	236 349	227 858
Wright	2 052.7	77.2	24 143	88.8	201.1	875.7	D	18.1	D	11.7	4.5	19.1	16.4	158 193	135 664	123 914
Yellow Medicine	227.3	23.1	19 913	73.2	47.5	134.5	D	13.3	D	6.7	3.5	22.9	23.0	17 887	15 434	14 856
MISSISSIPPI	54 410.1	60.4	19 776	72.7	10 307.0	36 726.4	27.9	20.7	69.8	9.7	4.5	22.8	21.1	7 609 819	7 169 938	6 960 763
Adams	664.4	41.2	19 461	71.5	156.1	457.5	37.7	18.6	62.2	11.6	3.5	23.6	14.6	84 939	87 976	95 483
Alcorn	634.5	50.4	19 372	71.2	142.3	429.5	D	41.8	D	13.4	3.1	13.4	16.0	179 627	171 929	158 137
Amite	202.6	60.3	14 622	53.8	51.3	84.0	D	35.9	D	6.7	D	12.5	15.6	30 114	28 423	25 862
Attala	316.8	51.5	17 289	63.6	87.8	166.0	36.2	21.8	D	14.3	4.9	15.3	17.0	36 146	35 665	36 421
Benton	120.3	58.5	14 587	53.7	31.7	46.3	39.3	34.0	D	D	1.3	15.6	17.0	15 752	14 036	11 650
Bolivar	663.0	45.4	16 499	60.7	175.3	385.1	23.7	20.2	73.5	9.5	3.1	15.8	24.4	77 886	75 600	79 739
Calhoun	270.4	59.9	18 159	66.8	66.9	129.0	37.3	35.6	50.5	9.4	2.5	9.3	16.2	45 910	44 808	45 929
Carroll	170.1	69.3	17 029	62.6	35.6	40.6	D	17.7	D	9.2	D	19.6	21.1	7 209	6 391	5 707
Chickasaw	318.3	44.4	17 643	64.9	77.4	201.9	53.1	51.0	42.1	7.8	1.8	11.8	11.5	102 904	107 538	107 748
Choctaw	132.2	39.0	14 063	51.7	34.1	59.5	D	29.5	D	6.5	1.9	16.2	24.5	17 558	16 080	15 404
Claiborne	166.9	53.8	14 501	53.3	45.6	188.3	D	9.2	D	3.9	1.0	6.4	23.3	17 396	18 113	17 595
Clarke	292.1	42.9	16 013	58.9	70.2	133.8	48.9	43.4	48.3	5.7	2.4	14.2	14.7	58 112	58 144	56 088
Clay	383.5	44.2	17 735	65.2	82.9	277.6	D	52.2	D	6.8	2.0	16.4	10.0	144 948	129 477	127 451
Coahoma	523.2	39.3	16 727	61.5	154.6	308.0	D	14.2	D	10.2	5.1	34.3	19.0	43 801	45 063	48 174
Copiah	448.4	53.8	15 555	57.2	116.1	210.6	36.6	30.1	D	8.3	2.0	14.9	24.7	63 456	60 739	58 323
Covington	299.3	65.3	16 885	62.1	70.6	152.9	D	24.4	D	7.2	2.0	10.9	17.0	37 262	39 029	36 266
DeSoto	2 390.5	111.5	24 616	90.5	227.1	1 000.6	D	28.1	D	12.8	4.1	20.8	9.9	281 659	273 839	259 283
Forrest	1 438.5	55.4	19 313	71.0	286.3	1 144.8	18.5	11.8	80.9	10.2	5.6	22.9	31.7	135 132	135 737	123 885
Franklin	118.5	45.9	14 300	52.6	34.6	59.4	D	25.5	D	5.9	D	11.7	26.4	15 128	14 058	14 586
George	324.8	80.1	16 572	60.9	66.2	105.6	D	14.7	D	14.3	3.5	D	29.4	15 559	14 569	13 975
Greene	163.6	70.5	12 833	47.2	41.0	63.6	23.9	17.0	D	8.5	1.9	9.2	42.5	10 827	11 189	9 728
Grenada	428.1	54.3	19 103	70.2	101.0	342.7	46.2	41.4	53.4	11.2	3.1	15.3	16.1	141 773	128 385	124 449
Hancock	786.1	85.4	19 519	71.8	144.1	531.5	D	11.6	D	6.6	2.8	33.6	33.0	61 586	53 205	47 184
Harrison	4 046.8	71.5	22 838	84.0	655.6	3 239.2	12.5	6.5	87.6	9.5	4.0	28.5	35.1	211 338	189 452	160 839
Hinds	6 016.7	42.7	24 333	89.4	862.9	5 615.1	12.8	7.3	86.8	9.2	9.7	29.1	23.3	408 359	416 589	431 601
Holmes	289.8	44.5	13 472	49.5	112.8	138.4	D	28.8	D	10.1	2.6	21.8	22.5	39 834	38 198	36 141
Humphreys	194.7	37.1	17 204	63.2	54.5	115.4	23.7	21.6	48.3	7.0	2.7	14.2	15.2	24 881	23 376	21 428
Issaquena	21.0	4.6	12 859	47.3	5.6	6.2	D	4.6	D	D	D	14.5	38.4	283	284	250

[1] Based on resident population estimated as of July 1, 1998. [2] Includes farm earnings; see table B-10 for these data. [3] Includes mining and construction, not shown separately. [4] Includes agricultural services, forestry, and fisheries; transportation and public utilities; and wholesale trade, not shown separately. [5] Finance, insurance, and real estate.

Source: Personal Income and Earnings—U.S. Bureau of Economic Analysis, "Regional Economic Information System (REIS) 1969-1998" on CD-ROM (related Internet site <http://www.bea.doc.gov/bea/regional/data.htm>).

Table B–8. Counties — **Personal Income and Earnings**–Con.

[Includes U.S., states, and 3,142 counties/county equivalents defined as of January 1, 1992. For changes to these areas since January 1, 1992, see appendix B. Geographic Information]

County	Personal income, 1998 Total (mil. dol.)	Percent change, 1990–1998	Per capita¹ Amount (dollars)	Percent of national average	Transfer payments (mil. dol.)	Earnings Total² (mil. dol.)	Goods-related Total³	Manufacturing	Service-related Total⁴	Retail trade	FIRE⁵	Services	Government	Manufacturing earnings 1998 ($1,000)	1997 ($1,000)	1996 ($1,000)
MISSISSIPPI—Con.																
Itawamba	411.0	73.4	19 484	71.6	74.0	167.9	D	30.1	D	6.8	1.5	11.1	18.2	50 470	46 069	48 059
Jackson	2 769.0	68.2	21 170	77.8	402.6	2 110.7	D	40.0	D	6.6	2.1	16.0	19.7	843 670	668 690	714 013
Jasper	277.1	54.5	15 687	57.7	69.9	151.5	45.2	30.7	D	7.1	2.0	13.5	15.3	46 476	42 918	45 260
Jefferson	96.3	38.2	11 390	41.9	44.8	35.9	D	D	84.0	5.0	1.2	13.6	42.6	D	D	2 590
Jefferson Davis	206.4	47.5	14 944	54.9	55.4	79.9	D	16.3	D	11.4	2.3	14.5	22.7	13 027	12 475	12 493
Jones	1 310.3	61.0	20 598	75.7	290.8	894.3	40.4	25.3	53.9	8.7	2.3	14.5	18.9	226 132	214 087	204 180
Kemper	174.0	62.4	16 460	60.5	42.7	63.3	32.1	28.0	55.4	7.1	3.4	12.9	23.3	17 753	15 772	14 183
Lafayette	661.6	66.2	19 034	70.0	109.5	466.8	18.2	12.5	81.6	12.1	3.2	24.8	36.6	58 189	54 871	51 098
Lamar	694.9	70.4	18 761	69.0	98.4	364.4	17.6	9.5	79.8	21.7	3.3	34.3	9.8	34 617	34 079	30 921
Lauderdale	1 632.9	41.6	21 456	78.9	306.4	1 225.4	D	14.1	D	11.2	4.0	27.8	22.4	172 986	187 957	186 681
Lawrence	225.4	62.8	17 337	63.7	61.9	130.4	D	45.6	D	5.6	1.6	8.9	15.3	59 497	59 357	55 014
Leake	374.3	85.1	19 259	70.8	87.9	215.5	34.9	28.9	D	9.2	2.8	13.1	10.0	62 278	56 735	48 256
Lee	1 752.6	68.8	23 486	86.3	242.9	1 688.3	NA	34.6	61.7	9.6	4.4	27.0	8.8	584 400	559 758	532 505
Leflore	667.2	37.1	17 915	65.9	176.1	462.1	25.6	21.9	72.7	9.9	3.7	18.7	24.0	101 224	93 265	86 856
Lincoln	583.9	57.1	18 326	67.4	129.7	381.2	26.8	17.4	69.9	19.7	3.1	19.4	10.7	66 315	63 016	63 251
Lowndes	1 236.1	38.6	20 249	74.4	191.3	984.5	32.2	24.0	66.3	9.9	2.7	19.1	21.9	236 538	237 987	247 590
Madison	1 829.0	116.9	25 096	92.3	197.7	836.7	19.4	11.3	80.3	15.6	11.8	23.8	12.9	94 664	78 339	71 185
Marion	427.2	51.9	16 180	59.5	116.0	222.3	30.6	13.2	62.7	13.3	3.6	15.6	18.1	29 431	26 082	25 804
Marshall	575.1	70.7	17 878	65.7	118.4	227.8	D	27.4	D	9.1	4.2	23.0	15.7	62 465	58 728	50 012
Monroe	635.1	42.6	16 667	61.3	144.3	364.4	48.0	39.7	51.6	9.5	2.2	16.9	13.7	144 483	143 543	136 686
Montgomery	205.5	51.1	16 566	60.9	57.5	91.1	D	19.5	D	12.2	3.6	22.1	21.5	17 786	18 227	18 426
Neshoba	555.5	92.1	20 198	74.2	111.1	431.9	D	19.4	D	7.4	2.6	D	11.8	83 778	83 500	82 870
Newton	409.1	60.5	18 944	69.6	98.5	235.0	D	27.9	D	7.9	2.3	14.3	21.4	65 600	65 224	57 844
Noxubee	196.2	60.4	15 809	58.1	51.9	102.3	D	38.1	D	7.7	2.5	10.0	18.9	38 948	35 697	28 792
Oktibbeha	702.7	51.2	17 728	65.2	116.7	488.2	NA	15.3	81.8	9.9	3.7	12.7	52.7	74 526	71 286	70 006
Panola	512.2	47.7	15 368	56.5	129.6	315.4	36.2	28.4	63.9	12.2	2.4	16.9	19.2	89 432	84 748	82 371
Pearl River	763.6	71.1	16 304	59.9	180.8	278.1	D	11.3	D	18.3	3.6	21.7	22.6	31 426	29 769	27 351
Perry	163.3	55.7	13 774	50.6	44.7	94.3	D	51.3	D	6.4	2.2	6.6	17.4	48 340	49 179	48 428
Pike	671.1	60.8	17 737	65.2	167.5	454.3	D	23.9	D	13.1	3.1	17.0	22.4	108 507	96 150	92 833
Pontotoc	438.7	59.7	17 333	63.7	80.4	272.2	D	57.3	D	6.6	2.0	11.3	10.0	156 083	138 916	128 603
Prentiss	376.2	46.9	15 445	56.8	91.0	229.5	D	42.4	D	8.6	2.8	13.0	18.7	97 345	104 496	103 272
Quitman	137.8	27.4	13 980	51.4	49.4	52.2	D	15.6	79.5	11.5	11.8	23.9	21.8	7 876	7 500	D
Rankin	2 701.2	97.8	24 646	90.6	317.4	1 607.7	26.2	15.6	72.3	8.4	6.6	19.0	16.3	250 246	224 522	201 632
Scott	487.9	74.7	19 503	71.7	102.5	370.5	D	33.9	39.9	7.2	2.6	11.0	10.3	125 699	121 794	133 200
Sharkey	84.1	8.5	12 734	46.8	30.8	44.1	D	D	D	9.9	3.3	22.3	27.7	D	D	D
Simpson	467.7	65.2	18 489	68.0	118.1	228.1	D	10.8	D	10.9	2.6	20.4	19.2	24 529	36 629	33 966
Smith	300.9	83.7	19 709	72.5	60.8	189.7	D	32.5	D	3.3	.9	7.7	9.0	61 592	55 870	53 591
Stone	209.1	63.4	15 811	58.1	57.2	111.4	D	23.2	D	8.9	3.0	22.5	27.2	26 905	26 405	22 012
Sunflower	465.6	35.0	13 884	51.0	126.7	339.0	21.3	19.2	70.3	8.7	2.1	11.2	33.8	65 062	64 130	63 080
Tallahatchie	195.5	35.9	13 223	48.6	66.2	65.2	13.8	10.7	D	10.9	2.9	D	33.2	6 963	7 394	6 074
Tate	495.5	77.1	20 670	76.0	85.2	203.6	D	27.9	D	14.6	3.7	18.0	21.0	56 777	52 600	48 724
Tippah	361.5	55.8	17 202	63.2	90.0	222.9	D	50.2	D	8.5	3.4	9.6	12.3	111 984	99 452	92 565
Tishomingo	302.6	47.8	16 217	59.6	82.7	174.3	52.2	44.5	D	9.3	2.9	13.8	11.8	77 615	73 606	79 394
Tunica	151.6	88.3	18 857	69.3	33.9	461.6	5.1	2.4	94.9	1.8	.5	87.3	3.5	11 140	10 860	10 443
Union	457.3	60.0	19 166	70.5	86.5	259.6	45.9	42.3	53.2	15.8	2.6	15.0	11.1	109 852	107 289	105 408
Walthall	223.1	62.1	15 504	57.0	58.2	109.6	D	23.2	D	6.9	2.5	16.1	17.4	25 423	24 733	22 945
Warren	1 183.0	59.3	23 967	88.1	180.6	877.8	D	20.1	D	8.9	2.2	30.8	27.4	176 256	161 844	148 429
Washington	1 164.2	43.1	17 863	65.7	260.1	803.9	D	20.2	74.4	9.2	2.6	27.0	17.9	162 549	155 159	138 885
Wayne	345.7	59.9	17 032	62.6	72.8	209.0	35.0	19.3		11.5	3.0	12.0	15.1	40 027	37 624	37 112
Webster	174.7	50.5	16 502	60.7	48.6	87.3	48.0	42.1	51.5	8.7	2.3	17.6	13.5	36 761	35 614	33 176
Wilkinson	134.1	45.5	14 647	53.8	44.8	55.5	D	D	D	9.2	4.1	25.1	26.9	D	9 774	9 510
Winston	342.2	46.8	17 746	65.2	78.3	194.7	D	38.6	D	9.4	2.5	18.0	11.2	75 105	74 122	68 849
Yalobusha	211.4	35.7	17 026	62.6	59.9	102.9	D	40.9	D	10.4	3.7	9.0	19.4	42 136	41 919	41 914
Yazoo	455.1	44.5	17 847	65.6	116.1	257.4	D	27.9	63.0	7.9	7.2	15.4	23.1	71 710	65 595	63 683
MISSOURI	136 753.8	50.3	25 150	92.5	20 233.1	99 230.4	24.9	18.2	74.7	9.4	7.9	27.0	15.0	18 044 814	17 752 493	16 737 354
Adair	459.1	47.4	18 938	69.6	92.9	312.2	20.2	16.1	80.1	13.0	3.9	31.5	24.9	50 278	46 899	43 519
Andrew	329.7	54.1	21 202	77.9	46.3	79.2	D	3.3	D	15.1	D	19.0	22.5	2 642	2 601	2 469
Atchison	144.0	35.6	20 472	75.3	29.2	74.3	D	2.2	D	10.6	5.3	25.3	16.0	1 646	1 523	1 700
Audrain	536.2	51.7	22 765	83.7	104.2	345.7	D	39.8	D	9.3	3.5	11.6	21.2	137 549	112 076	95 671
Barry	604.3	73.7	18 215	67.0	130.3	440.3	D	41.1	D	8.6	2.5	16.0	11.2	181 106	178 964	167 649
Barton	231.0	54.8	19 138	70.4	46.3	146.3	50.1	44.0	48.6	9.5	3.4	11.3	14.5	64 420	58 419	53 788
Bates	284.8	47.9	17 995	66.2	69.8	110.7	D	8.0	D	12.5	4.7	15.9	24.6	8 830	8 242	8 581
Benton	267.8	66.3	15 792	58.1	89.9	97.7	D	9.5	D	18.0	6.2	18.4	26.7	9 243	10 147	10 393
Bollinger	168.2	47.3	14 556	53.5	44.3	52.8	D	12.8	D	10.8	D	18.3	23.0	6 780	6 602	6 896
Boone	3 302.2	70.5	25 606	94.1	348.9	2 514.5	14.3	8.5	85.6	9.6	9.1	22.2	36.9	214 380	209 664	196 669
Buchanan	1 854.3	41.2	22 669	83.3	345.3	1 356.2	D	23.5	D	9.8	5.4	25.7	15.1	318 817	302 026	285 917
Butler	825.1	67.6	20 407	75.0	214.2	549.1	D	16.6	D	11.7	2.9	27.4	19.6	91 380	78 278	67 959
Caldwell	150.4	47.7	17 067	62.7	34.7	50.1	D	2.0	D	13.8	5.1	14.2	28.3	1 010	3 491	5 708
Callaway	759.3	56.2	20 250	74.4	121.4	439.4	24.9	16.0	D	7.6	2.8	D	26.5	70 368	73 427	68 303

¹ Based on resident population estimated as of July 1, 1998.   ² Includes farm earnings; see table B-10 for these data.   ³ Includes mining and construction, not shown separately.   ⁴ Includes agricultural services, forestry, and fisheries; transportation and public utilities; and wholesale trade, not shown separately.   ⁵ Finance, insurance, and real estate.

Source: Personal Income and Earnings—U.S. Bureau of Economic Analysis, "Regional Economic Information System (REIS) 1969-1998" on CD-ROM (related Internet site <http://www.bea.doc.gov/bea/regional/data.htm>).

[Includes U.S., states, and 3,142 counties/county equivalents defined as of January 1, 1992. For changes to these areas since January 1, 1992, see appendix B. Geographic Information]

| County | Personal income, 1998 | | | | | | | | | | | | | Manufacturing earnings | | |
	Total (mil. dol.)	Percent change, 1990–1998	Per capita[1] Amount (dollars)	Percent of national average	Transfer payments (mil. dol.)	Earnings Total[2] (mil. dol.)	Goods-related Total[3]	Manu-facturing	Service-related Total[4]	Retail trade	FIRE[5]	Serv-ices	Gov-ern-ment	1998 ($1,000)	1997 ($1,000)	1996 ($1,000)
MISSOURI—Con.																
Camden	732.5	81.6	21 585	79.3	145.1	414.5	D	11.3	D	20.6	7.5	30.6	11.4	46 906	45 494	44 167
Cape Girardeau	1 561.2	58.6	23 573	86.7	227.2	1 190.3	25.7	18.1	74.4	11.6	4.5	28.9	13.9	215 122	204 352	193 926
Carroll	196.5	31.9	19 260	70.8	45.7	78.6	D	12.0	73.1	10.6	6.6	19.9	20.9	9 434	11 131	12 954
Carter	95.0	58.1	14 889	54.7	31.1	40.6	20.5	16.6	D	12.6	3.9	18.0	32.6	6 750	8 423	8 436
Cass	1 804.2	72.9	22 393	82.3	231.8	573.0	26.3	6.5	73.5	16.1	5.2	19.9	22.5	37 196	33 823	30 006
Cedar	222.1	53.8	16 833	61.9	66.6	93.5	D	16.4	D	14.9	4.3	17.4	25.9	15 373	16 006	16 653
Chariton	163.3	29.0	18 874	69.4	39.8	71.5	D	12.4	D	7.6	6.3	15.9	17.6	8 867	8 096	7 205
Christian	979.2	111.7	19 990	73.5	137.4	365.9	D	16.5	D	15.5	6.6	17.1	14.2	60 219	59 286	57 528
Clark	118.3	42.7	15 878	58.4	29.7	34.4	D	D	D	13.9	5.3	16.9	39.0	D	2 704	2 681
Clay	4 762.1	64.4	26 991	99.2	499.7	3 222.1	32.4	26.4	67.6	11.0	4.6	23.9	11.7	851 891	823 399	818 308
Clinton	416.4	67.5	21 860	80.4	59.5	130.0	D	4.6	D	14.9	11.8	30.0	19.2	6 037	5 745	5 115
Cole	1 827.5	62.9	26 399	97.0	213.9	1 680.0	D	7.0	D	7.3	5.8	21.3	41.0	116 931	117 760	107 394
Cooper	310.8	58.0	19 373	71.2	60.5	157.1	27.0	19.9	71.0	10.8	3.8	15.7	23.9	31 260	30 949	32 573
Crawford	398.8	65.0	17 888	65.8	93.0	169.0	D	29.2	D	17.4	3.6	19.6	13.8	49 343	51 657	49 458
Dade	142.7	54.9	18 208	66.9	34.5	56.1	D	10.0	D	8.0	3.5	14.2	25.3	5 604	5 840	5 595
Dallas	252.4	76.3	16 480	60.6	59.5	84.2	D	11.8	D	19.2	6.4	17.8	22.5	9 951	10 291	9 119
Daviess	143.6	46.9	18 180	66.8	30.1	59.7	30.4	17.5	D	8.9	4.5	9.6	24.8	10 481	10 436	8 637
DeKalb	164.2	60.7	14 651	53.9	35.7	93.1	D	2.4	D	10.5	3.4	11.2	45.7	2 224	2 403	2 325
Dent	261.9	55.3	18 531	68.1	70.2	138.2	D	13.4	D	12.4	4.3	13.9	19.2	18 482	16 413	15 124
Douglas	182.0	59.7	14 630	53.8	52.1	75.9	D	30.0	D	12.2	3.0	14.9	18.8	22 760	27 299	21 584
Dunklin	593.2	47.5	18 138	66.7	184.1	291.9	D	19.9	D	14.6	4.8	23.3	16.7	58 013	64 974	58 408
Franklin	2 103.4	65.0	22 900	84.2	285.7	1 052.8	44.1	34.5	55.7	11.7	3.7	17.7	11.7	362 804	342 093	315 263
Gasconade	309.1	54.0	20 853	76.7	60.8	159.3	D	38.7	D	11.2	3.0	13.7	15.2	61 616	51 518	50 647
Gentry	132.3	53.4	19 113	70.3	35.4	66.2	D	14.9	D	14.2	3.6	19.3	18.5	9 870	9 138	8 547
Greene	5 677.8	65.3	25 059	92.1	813.0	4 751.5	21.2	15.7	78.8	13.3	6.3	29.2	12.4	748 020	731 102	696 906
Grundy	203.6	40.9	19 980	73.4	47.2	103.8	D	22.9	D	11.4	4.3	21.9	23.3	23 749	25 764	24 918
Harrison	167.2	49.5	19 754	72.6	41.6	80.2	D	2.2	D	23.7	3.8	16.4	23.8	1 735	1 403	1 349
Henry	408.3	53.9	19 207	70.6	102.1	219.2	D	20.0	D	13.9	4.9	18.4	19.6	43 948	40 279	35 083
Hickory	124.3	58.8	14 446	53.1	51.1	34.3	D	8.2	D	16.0	5.3	21.0	26.3	2 805	2 600	2 618
Holt	112.9	33.6	20 386	74.9	25.5	51.9	D	6.2	63.0	10.1	4.5	12.2	18.6	3 202	3 237	3 163
Howard	188.3	46.0	19 352	71.1	40.1	77.7	D	22.3	D	8.4	4.0	23.3	17.2	17 300	14 788	14 316
Howell	628.5	70.5	17 582	64.6	167.8	387.3	28.4	23.2	71.8	14.6	3.7	24.9	16.0	89 971	85 424	81 801
Iron	176.1	46.0	16 144	59.3	57.3	110.3	D	20.0	D	7.1	2.4	18.4	14.0	22 071	26 323	24 708
Jackson	17 280.6	41.9	26 380	97.0	2 414.3	16 748.5	19.4	12.4	80.6	7.8	11.0	30.2	15.1	2 076 134	2 033 727	2 076 241
Jasper	2 205.6	63.5	22 140	81.4	406.3	1 857.0	28.6	23.6	70.9	11.0	3.3	24.2	9.9	438 753	425 598	391 579
Jefferson	4 074.3	61.9	20 843	76.6	521.7	1 262.8	28.8	15.7	71.4	13.1	4.8	22.7	18.6	198 147	183 493	174 865
Johnson	871.3	52.4	18 272	67.2	122.4	565.1	D	13.6	D	8.2	2.6	10.0	55.2	76 823	70 711	65 245
Knox	76.0	32.9	17 431	64.1	20.4	30.3	D	7.5	D	10.6	5.5	18.6	30.8	2 269	2 237	1 897
Laclede	577.6	67.5	18 649	68.6	112.7	380.8	D	39.8	D	16.4	2.8	16.5	10.7	151 604	141 839	129 350
Lafayette	698.2	45.3	21 371	78.6	141.6	264.3	20.3	12.1	75.1	13.3	5.2	20.2	23.3	31 943	29 542	27 850
Lawrence	574.3	55.0	17 338	63.7	129.9	248.8	D	15.1	D	16.2	4.1	14.9	19.2	37 524	41 161	41 950
Lewis	171.0	36.2	16 776	61.7	38.8	71.6	D	20.1	D	10.8	4.3	25.3	23.3	14 416	14 833	13 007
Lincoln	755.4	79.7	20 635	75.9	112.9	259.9	32.1	16.4	64.6	12.5	4.3	14.4	20.2	42 740	38 360	29 380
Linn	272.8	40.7	19 771	72.7	68.2	158.6	D	31.5	D	10.2	3.1	15.3	15.7	49 913	49 518	46 860
Livingston	323.4	43.0	22 872	84.1	61.8	193.2	25.6	17.1	72.2	12.3	6.5	21.6	17.8	33 024	33 350	29 056
McDonald	323.3	73.5	16 156	59.4	67.4	168.6	47.7	40.4	42.3	8.9	2.6	8.0	12.5	68 098	68 801	61 387
Macon	283.0	31.6	18 462	67.9	70.1	137.2	D	18.3	D	12.9	5.0	14.6	31.8	25 101	25 989	26 324
Madison	196.0	49.3	16 969	62.4	57.9	78.9	D	17.8	D	15.0	2.8	16.3	24.6	14 061	12 995	11 577
Maries	144.8	51.9	17 168	63.1	34.1	39.8	D	18.4	D	13.0	6.5	20.5	20.7	7 323	7 708	8 376
Marion	595.6	54.5	21 375	78.6	126.1	412.2	D	24.5	D	10.3	3.1	25.6	13.7	100 862	99 881	95 243
Mercer	32.5	-15.3	8 162	30.0	16.3	23.1	D	6.1	D	9.1	5.0	14.7	30.5	1 422	1 320	1 372
Miller	386.1	48.6	17 186	63.2	88.1	207.4	29.2	17.3	67.4	15.9	4.8	17.5	14.7	35 954	35 744	34 829
Mississippi	233.3	34.5	17 313	63.6	69.7	111.0	D	14.9	D	14.2	3.4	13.1	18.6	16 501	13 415	12 504
Moniteau	257.4	55.9	19 421	71.4	45.9	117.3	D	25.1	D	9.7	3.9	12.2	24.7	29 500	32 947	33 159
Monroe	170.2	28.2	18 826	69.2	37.5	89.8	D	40.7	D	7.7	2.9	10.2	21.7	36 528	36 010	34 381
Montgomery	235.5	47.0	19 518	71.7	51.9	105.5	35.1	24.0	67.9	10.4	5.5	16.8	16.6	25 358	23 109	22 216
Morgan	330.7	69.4	17 949	66.0	84.2	137.1	D	15.4	D	18.4	5.0	13.8	16.6	21 167	19 192	17 433
New Madrid	333.4	38.2	16 379	60.2	97.0	255.3	45.9	44.3	49.9	9.5	2.0	8.5	11.7	113 111	112 608	108 375
Newton	1 022.7	65.0	20 783	76.4	166.9	523.2	D	31.5	D	11.6	2.6	17.2	10.8	164 635	170 075	163 926
Nodaway	399.5	37.9	19 288	70.9	65.3	254.4	33.6	26.3	64.8	9.4	4.1	16.2	26.4	67 032	58 598	55 100
Oregon	142.2	48.2	13 975	51.4	51.1	62.9	D	18.0	D	15.5	5.6	17.1	20.2	11 298	9 688	8 189
Osage	273.1	57.1	21 907	80.5	39.3	100.5	D	30.9	D	11.6	3.8	14.1	17.4	31 011	31 252	30 327
Ozark	137.9	46.9	13 907	51.1	45.3	42.5	D	10.7	D	12.1	6.8	24.7	28.1	4 529	4 102	3 892
Pemiscot	347.6	39.4	16 207	59.6	116.7	172.7	D	14.6	D	10.7	3.3	17.5	30.9	25 225	24 788	19 961
Perry	360.8	55.0	20 618	75.8	62.3	237.4	D	42.1	D	9.0	3.4	13.2	11.2	99 966	86 133	75 548
Pettis	809.3	54.6	21 823	80.2	150.3	569.9	41.0	33.4	56.2	10.8	4.3	15.5	15.0	190 202	172 446	144 829
Phelps	770.3	57.5	19 980	73.4	146.6	476.2	13.6	8.0	87.2	13.0	3.3	21.4	41.4	38 311	31 162	29 313
Pike	304.6	46.6	18 581	68.3	71.4	158.1	D	20.5	D	10.7	3.8	15.7	27.5	32 474	31 943	30 746
Platte	2 155.9	76.7	30 801	113.2	159.9	1 258.6	14.7	9.0	84.5	6.9	6.0	23.5	8.3	113 315	97 924	83 880
Polk	439.1	65.6	17 181	63.2	103.2	204.0	D	9.3	D	13.4	4.5	28.9	21.7	18 995	20 691	21 924

[1] Based on resident population estimated as of July 1, 1998. [2] Includes farm earnings; see table B-10 for these data. [3] Includes mining and construction, not shown separately. [4] Includes agricultural services, forestry, and fisheries; transportation and public utilities; and wholesale trade, not shown separately. [5] Finance, insurance, and real estate.

Source: Personal Income and Earnings—U.S. Bureau of Economic Analysis, "Regional Economic Information System (REIS) 1969-1998" on CD-ROM (related Internet site <http://www.bea.doc.gov/bea/regional/data.htm>).

[Includes U.S., states, and 3,142 counties/county equivalents defined as of January 1, 1992. For changes to these areas since January 1, 1992, see appendix B. Geographic Information]

County	Personal income, 1998													Manufacturing earnings		
		Per capita[1]				Earnings										
							Percent, by selected industry–									
							Goods-related		Service-related							
	Total (mil. dol.)	Percent change, 1990–1998	Amount (dollars)	Percent of national average	Transfer payments (mil. dol.)	Total[2] (mil. dol.)	Total[3]	Manufacturing	Total[4]	Retail trade	FIRE[5]	Services	Government	1998 ($1,000)	1997 ($1,000)	1996 ($1,000)
MISSOURI—Con.																
Pulaski	801.1	34.6	20 369	74.9	104.3	622.4	D	2.2	D	6.5	1.7	8.7	74.4	13 879	13 419	12 866
Putnam	81.4	39.5	16 613	61.1	24.1	26.1	D	D	D	11.2	7.9	10.7	40.8	D	2 010	2 318
Ralls	186.6	54.8	21 026	77.3	33.7	85.3	43.3	37.6	D	6.5	3.7	11.3	14.1	32 044	28 445	27 199
Randolph	441.2	31.0	18 451	67.8	104.9	275.6	D	14.0	D	11.8	5.5	18.3	20.0	38 554	37 094	34 652
Ray	453.5	52.8	19 168	70.5	74.5	152.7	D	14.5	D	10.3	7.7	17.9	22.2	22 142	20 550	11 036
Reynolds	103.4	43.9	15 560	57.2	33.8	66.7	D	21.6	D	4.8	1.5	D	18.0	14 401	13 369	12 864
Ripley	190.3	59.8	13 545	49.8	72.4	70.8	D	18.1	D	15.8	3.6	18.4	27.7	12 797	11 282	10 205
St. Charles	7 229.6	81.8	26 570	97.7	615.2	3 157.7	34.4	21.9	65.4	13.1	4.1	24.7	12.2	691 538	663 731	675 279
St. Clair	147.7	48.8	16 283	59.9	45.1	55.2	D	2.4	D	15.3	4.8	24.5	33.1	1 335	1 292	1 364
Ste. Genevieve	350.7	57.4	20 204	74.3	60.4	177.7	D	33.6	D	8.6	4.0	11.8	15.0	59 792	56 462	55 161
St. Francois	897.5	49.3	16 214	59.6	248.7	549.8	26.0	18.7	73.9	13.2	4.0	24.9	22.8	102 785	85 875	81 851
St. Louis	36 702.4	41.0	36 800	135.3	3 466.4	28 210.8	27.2	20.9	72.8	8.4	9.6	31.3	7.4	5 885 918	5 985 597	5 418 444
Saline	499.7	44.8	22 044	81.0	128.0	294.1	D	25.7	D	8.5	3.4	18.0	21.5	75 480	70 137	67 176
Schuyler	63.1	27.7	14 174	52.1	19.8	20.1	D	6.5	D	18.5	4.8	13.7	37.3	1 300	1 183	1 185
Scotland	86.2	39.6	17 877	65.7	22.5	38.4	D	11.1	D	13.6	4.2	13.1	36.2	4 256	4 312	3 844
Scott	801.1	48.4	19 884	73.1	178.2	477.1	20.6	14.2	78.4	11.5	4.7	27.5	15.0	67 818	63 727	58 134
Shannon	114.4	56.5	13 782	50.7	35.6	53.2	D	32.9	D	9.4	3.0	16.1	25.5	17 524	16 191	14 297
Shelby	132.6	31.8	19 654	72.2	30.0	67.6	37.1	26.3	59.7	6.5	4.4	11.4	21.2	17 738	16 535	16 154
Stoddard	535.7	45.1	18 050	66.4	134.4	290.1	D	20.7	D	12.8	3.8	16.8	14.1	60 139	63 634	65 180
Stone	581.5	103.8	21 666	79.6	111.9	213.0	D	4.2	D	12.5	6.2	38.5	13.0	8 961	9 907	8 926
Sullivan	136.5	87.9	19 505	71.7	34.0	96.5	D	41.5	D	5.6	2.7	9.3	12.8	40 033	36 467	32 337
Taney	731.8	95.6	21 239	78.1	152.9	580.5	D	3.3	D	21.2	9.3	41.2	8.4	19 293	20 500	21 005
Texas	320.8	41.3	14 340	52.7	92.5	160.9	27.0	19.9	72.9	13.2	4.7	14.0	24.2	32 080	32 579	30 628
Vernon	355.4	35.1	18 238	67.0	102.6	207.2	D	25.1	D	11.8	5.7	19.8	24.3	51 981	51 124	50 306
Warren	511.9	74.4	20 885	76.8	81.8	189.8	43.7	33.0	55.9	11.2	5.5	14.1	13.3	62 644	62 353	60 039
Washington	362.1	67.6	15 714	57.8	94.1	138.9	D	8.7	D	12.2	3.7	21.1	36.2	12 093	11 316	9 046
Wayne	182.9	54.6	14 002	51.5	76.2	62.1	D	16.1	D	15.2	4.9	17.8	30.0	9 973	8 617	9 729
Webster	473.4	66.0	16 227	59.7	94.5	193.7	35.9	24.6	63.2	13.1	4.8	15.1	18.2	47 599	42 410	42 868
Worth	37.7	21.0	16 459	60.5	9.7	16.3	D	D	D	7.9	5.3	12.3	30.5	D	2 442	2 395
Wright	274.6	52.3	14 023	51.5	80.6	141.1	D	18.1	D	18.5	3.8	13.6	21.6	25 497	23 499	22 775
Independent City																
St. Louis city	8 925.1	26.7	26 332	96.8	1 901.9	11 871.6	D	17.1	D	5.7	9.8	29.8	16.9	2 034 421	2 021 035	1 934 263
MONTANA	18 671.5	50.4	21 229	78.0	3 063.2	12 009.4	17.9	7.9	80.1	11.8	5.9	26.6	21.8	949 555	853 721	817 339
Beaverhead	176.8	41.6	20 072	73.8	33.8	104.6	D	2.3	D	10.4	8.5	20.6	27.3	2 424	2 469	1 806
Big Horn	166.8	35.9	13 239	48.7	37.9	135.5	27.0	.8	67.4	5.9	2.8	20.8	32.7	1 048	1 047	1 069
Blaine	108.9	28.5	15 358	56.5	25.7	56.1	D	1.3	D	8.5	4.0	12.8	39.6	753	834	869
Broadwater	77.2	69.2	18 684	68.7	15.7	41.7	D	23.2	D	6.2	2.9	11.8	15.3	9 682	8 707	6 525
Carbon	185.6	53.7	19 745	72.6	33.0	68.0	15.1	4.2	82.4	15.2	7.4	28.4	21.7	2 882	2 972	2 522
Carter	19.9	5.2	13 139	48.3	4.7	6.2	D	10.1	D	9.5	6.8	D	42.7	625	531	515
Cascade	1 863.5	38.9	23 721	87.2	298.5	1 207.5	10.0	3.4	89.4	12.6	7.6	28.3	29.3	41 578	38 432	36 780
Chouteau	108.4	-3.7	20 905	76.8	20.7	44.7	5.1	1.9	67.1	8.8	5.5	11.5	28.6	862	948	917
Custer	246.8	31.4	20 487	75.3	48.1	140.0	D	2.7	D	14.7	5.9	26.3	30.8	3 847	4 271	4 184
Daniels	52.1	44.6	26 120	96.0	8.5	29.6	D	1.6	D	6.4	3.3	13.2	17.7	475	465	524
Dawson	181.6	37.8	20 612	75.8	34.6	113.6	D	1.3	D	10.2	3.4	18.9	21.0	1 521	1 509	1 636
Deer Lodge	174.2	34.3	17 490	64.3	47.6	85.9	D	3.9	D	11.3	3.1	33.5	35.3	3 379	3 247	3 786
Fallon	61.1	40.6	20 647	75.9	11.2	42.0	31.0	1.9	D	7.6	2.4	14.9	17.7	818	759	715
Fergus	241.0	30.4	19 630	72.2	50.5	128.2	15.5	4.7	78.8	12.1	4.8	26.3	24.1	6 030	6 650	5 940
Flathead	1 605.0	70.0	22 327	82.1	240.9	1 057.2	30.4	21.1	69.3	12.6	6.3	25.8	13.9	223 499	162 603	156 077
Gallatin	1 427.7	79.7	22 820	83.9	142.0	1 006.4	20.4	9.0	78.3	14.3	5.9	25.3	21.6	91 026	82 295	77 366
Garfield	22.3	3.9	15 761	57.9	4.2	10.7	9.0	4.8	D	8.2	D	D	29.9	513	480	529
Glacier	192.8	42.3	15 374	56.5	49.5	129.9	D	.8	D	10.0	3.0	26.8	34.9	991	965	1 094
Golden Valley	16.6	41.5	16 095	59.2	3.6	5.2	D	D	D	D	–	D	38.8	D	570	617
Granite	49.5	39.5	18 556	68.2	10.4	24.7	D	19.6	D	11.4	D	D	29.2	4 825	4 561	4 181
Hill	360.9	27.0	20 789	76.4	68.9	229.2	5.5	1.0	85.3	10.5	3.9	27.8	19.2	2 183	2 270	2 754
Jefferson	223.5	62.7	22 088	81.2	28.1	85.7	41.8	7.0	D	6.0	2.4	16.1	27.7	5 962	6 214	6 396
Judith Basin	41.0	12.6	17 882	65.7	7.6	14.6	D	1.9	D	6.5	6.5	7.2	34.8	280	D	D
Lake	423.6	51.7	16 574	60.9	94.6	224.5	22.0	13.1	78.7	13.1	4.5	36.5	17.2	29 516	25 542	23 868
Lewis and Clark	1 264.6	57.2	23 600	86.8	174.8	942.5	11.0	3.9	88.9	10.0	8.0	27.5	34.7	36 893	36 173	35 848
Liberty	45.9	-2.9	19 827	72.9	8.4	25.5	19.1	3.5	D	6.1	2.1	11.0	22.9	880	824	788
Lincoln	305.0	33.1	16 297	59.9	77.8	180.8	31.1	24.3	68.7	10.1	3.6	15.7	29.7	43 867	43 762	41 803
McCone	36.2	30.2	18 457	67.8	6.8	20.4	D	–	D	5.9	D	10.5	19.7	–	–	–
Madison	119.4	49.6	17 337	63.7	22.3	53.3	D	5.1	D	13.7	6.5	19.9	25.2	2 704	2 393	2 478
Meagher	35.6	28.6	19 870	73.0	7.5	18.6	D	5.4	D	8.8	D	25.2	22.0	999	916	787
Mineral	56.2	43.1	14 863	54.6	16.6	30.9	21.3	16.6	D	19.3	D	17.6	33.1	5 144	5 076	5 405
Missoula	2 065.7	64.2	23 234	85.4	273.3	1 521.4	16.5	8.9	83.8	12.5	6.5	29.9	19.3	135 654	130 816	127 778
Musselshell	65.6	29.1	14 351	52.8	19.5	27.0	19.6	5.1	D	11.6	4.1	20.3	25.2	1 387	1 157	1 080
Park	[6]295.5	[6]54.3	[6]18 708	[6]68.8	[6]54.2	[6]158.7	[6]20.0	[6]8.9	[6]76.8	[6]14.0	6.4	[6]32.2	[6]14.3	[6]14 183	[6]14 531	[6]13 378
Petroleum	7.2	17.9	14 151	52.0	1.7	3.4	D	–	D	D	2.6	D	35.9	–	–	D

[1] Based on resident population estimated as of July 1, 1998. [2] Includes farm earnings; see table B-10 for these data. [3] Includes mining and construction, not shown separately. [4] Includes agricultural services, forestry, and fisheries; transportation and public utilities; and wholesale trade, not shown separately. [5] Finance, insurance, and real estate. [6] Yellowstone National Park County included with Park County; data not available separately.

Source: Personal Income and Earnings—U.S. Bureau of Economic Analysis, "Regional Economic Information System (REIS) 1969-1998" on CD-ROM (related Internet site <http://www.bea.doc.gov/bea/regional/data.htm>).

[Includes U.S., states, and 3,142 counties/county equivalents defined as of January 1, 1992. For changes to these areas since January 1, 1992, see appendix B. Geographic Information]

County	Personal income, 1998													Manufacturing earnings		
	Total (mil. dol.)	Per capita[1]			Transfer payments (mil. dol.)	Earnings								1998 ($1,000)	1997 ($1,000)	1996 ($1,000)
		Percent change, 1990–1998	Amount (dollars)	Percent of national average		Total[2] (mil. dol.)	Percent, by selected industry–									
							Goods-related		Service-related							
							Total[3]	Manufacturing	Total[4]	Retail trade	FIRE[5]	Services	Government			
MONTANA—Con.																
Phillips	81.6	12.8	17 011	62.5	18.4	46.1	14.0	2.9	73.6	10.0	4.4	16.3	25.1	1 352	1 184	1 301
Pondera	126.1	22.5	19 866	73.0	26.2	62.9	D	3.1	D	10.0	4.8	16.9	20.6	1 927	1 672	1 751
Powder River	29.4	9.8	16 314	60.0	5.6	12.6	D	D	14.5	3.7	13.8	39.9	D	542	554
Powell	120.5	39.0	17 201	63.2	23.8	73.5	D	17.9	D	7.3	2.4	12.7	44.0	13 118	12 545	11 583
Prairie	25.1	26.3	18 533	68.1	5.9	11.6	D	D	D	6.0	D	5.9	29.5	D	396	464
Ravalli	622.8	81.9	17 737	65.2	121.7	300.2	D	12.9	D	12.1	7.5	22.7	19.9	38 843	34 125	32 003
Richland	196.1	33.2	19 298	70.9	36.0	121.8	D	9.8	D	11.3	3.3	21.0	16.4	11 936	11 149	9 948
Roosevelt	173.4	46.0	15 767	58.0	46.9	104.1	D	D	D	10.0	4.1	26.6	32.6	D	2 313	2 444
Rosebud	180.8	14.8	18 066	66.4	28.9	147.0	25.9	2.3	73.2	4.8	2.2	20.1	17.3	3 407	3 451	3 726
Sanders	155.7	46.4	15 284	56.2	41.7	72.7	D	12.7	D	9.9	3.6	24.6	28.1	9 229	8 695	9 065
Sheridan	93.1	39.9	21 947	80.7	18.4	46.5	D	2.3	D	9.7	3.8	19.5	24.1	1 093	1 111	1 167
Silver Bow	763.1	43.0	22 093	81.2	153.0	502.1	20.5	5.3	79.3	11.7	3.9	28.8	17.3	26 592	18 594	15 367
Stillwater	159.4	68.3	19 736	72.6	26.0	94.0	D	10.5	D	7.1	1.7	10.6	12.4	9 883	9 353	9 988
Sweet Grass	64.5	36.7	19 032	70.0	10.9	27.7	22.7	6.7	D	22.1	3.9	16.9	26.6	1 860	1 807	1 841
Teton	119.4	15.2	18 799	69.1	22.8	58.7	D	1.5	D	7.0	4.6	10.6	21.3	882	822	854
Toole	107.0	17.1	22 589	83.0	17.6	69.8	D	1.4	D	7.9	3.5	12.8	25.1	965	923	2 241
Treasure	13.8	.3	15 707	57.7	3.1	5.5	D	–	D	5.9	D	5.5	32.5	–	D	D
Valley	176.5	46.8	21 439	78.8	35.3	96.8	8.6	2.2	78.6	10.4	4.5	21.6	23.6	2 137	2 164	2 159
Wheatland	38.0	16.8	16 217	59.6	10.7	16.0	D	7.3	D	14.1	4.9	19.8	31.9	1 167	3 115	3 450
Wibaux	18.1	31.7	15 887	58.4	4.5	8.6	D	D	D	6.2	2.2	15.6	26.8	D	357	427
Yellowstone	3 083.3	54.9	24 425	89.8	422.8	2 156.8	16.2	6.7	83.4	12.4	6.6	31.0	14.5	143 956	145 131	136 753
Yellowstone National Park	(6)	(6)	(6)	(6)	(6)	(6)	(6)	(6)	(6)	(6)	(6)	(6)	(6)	(6)	(6)	(6)
NEBRASKA	43 053.2	50.6	25 924	95.3	5 494.6	31 163.1	19.9	13.7	75.4	8.6	7.3	25.2	17.0	4 260 189	4 091 261	3 852 984
Adams	714.2	35.1	24 280	89.3	108.0	462.9	26.5	19.7	68.5	10.0	3.2	25.7	16.5	91 223	91 317	85 640
Antelope	166.8	28.7	22 886	84.1	28.7	95.6	D	3.5	D	7.8	2.8	14.8	14.3	3 377	3 626	2 839
Arthur	3.0	-49.7	7 000	25.7	1.5	-1.6	NA	NA	D	D	NA	D	-45.1	(7)	(7)	(7)
Banner	13.2	3.2	15 122	55.6	2.2	6.7	D	1.7	D	3.0	24.8			112	112	100
Blaine	5.4	-48.5	9 358	34.4	1.5	1.3	D	D	D	30.7	D	35.1	179.7	D	120	109
Boone	130.1	18.2	20 399	75.0	24.3	66.2	D	3.0	D	9.4	3.9	12.5	23.9	2 008	530	549
Box Butte	295.3	29.3	23 134	85.0	41.4	229.5	NA	6.6	79.8	5.6	2.5	9.8	12.1	15 038	12 659	10 108
Boyd	44.1	8.4	17 195	63.2	12.2	20.7	D	D	D	8.7	5.4	16.7	28.9	D	663	653
Brown	66.3	10.1	18 763	69.0	14.5	30.8	D	D	D	10.5	6.4	16.9	33.9	D	470	430
Buffalo	910.1	60.8	22 564	82.9	116.7	669.5	24.8	19.0	71.4	14.0	3.4	25.8	15.9	127 122	118 274	113 153
Burt	169.5	41.1	21 396	78.7	35.7	82.1	NA	5.9	60.2	6.4	4.3	14.7	19.1	4 836	4 210	3 661
Butler	182.6	32.1	21 035	77.3	30.6	81.6	D	16.9	D	5.9	2.1	14.7	18.3	13 801	13 141	11 508
Cass	609.9	73.2	24 911	91.6	71.8	162.0	D	8.9	D	9.4	5.0	16.2	18.8	14 364	14 045	13 349
Cedar	203.9	35.7	21 173	77.8	31.8	109.9	D	8.5	D	5.6	D	14.1	17.9	9 358	9 564	8 292
Chase	110.9	34.6	26 008	95.6	17.4	69.2	NA	1.9	58.0	8.7	4.4	9.7	17.8	1 304	1 157	774
Cherry	113.5	19.7	18 046	66.3	21.1	52.7	D	1.4	D	18.4	6.5	22.9	26.5	713	675	670
Cheyenne	224.7	36.2	23 696	87.1	37.1	152.2	16.1	12.4	D	29.5	3.2	D	13.6	18 884	15 786	14 314
Clay	164.6	16.0	23 075	84.8	27.1	108.6	D	9.7	D	3.5	D	8.5	24.9	10 583	9 123	9 092
Colfax	205.4	28.4	19 274	70.9	37.9	144.3	D	D	D	5.2	2.8	12.5	10.9	D	55 205	50 653
Cuming	274.3	18.8	27 462	101.0	35.8	189.1	D	11.8	D	6.5	3.1	11.8	9.2	22 307	20 178	18 925
Custer	261.4	30.7	21 863	80.4	48.8	142.8	NA	9.5	60.7	8.2	5.1	17.1	16.8	13 523	13 034	12 480
Dakota	383.9	58.8	20 441	75.1	54.0	373.4	D	D	D	6.3	7.6	10.8	7.4	D	180 903	190 809
Dawes	153.4	36.8	17 293	63.6	32.7	82.2	D	1.0	D	17.6	3.8	24.4	40.9	794	891	4 653
Dawson	504.8	47.0	21 798	80.1	75.0	364.5	D	33.9	D	7.3	2.5	10.8	14.5	123 519	116 965	106 828
Deuel	47.0	20.2	23 239	85.4	9.2	20.5	D	D	D	11.2	7.0	13.9	25.2	D	476	143
Dixon	134.1	30.5	21 237	78.1	21.0	75.6	D	D	D	2.8	2.6	7.8	14.0	D	18 335	17 156
Dodge	835.4	52.7	23 662	87.0	137.6	476.8	D	22.1	D	12.6	4.0	19.3	16.8	105 333	100 214	93 248
Douglas	14 485.2	63.5	32 671	120.1	1 479.0	12 741.5	D	11.3	D	8.1	10.6	32.7	11.6	1 436 187	1 372 247	1 303 224
Dundy	67.2	25.9	29 441	108.2	10.6	35.6	D	D	D	3.6	D	10.9	16.9	D	161	180
Fillmore	185.4	23.7	26 716	98.2	24.6	106.2	NA	3.1	54.7	5.3	3.5	8.7	17.2	3 253	3 106	2 989
Franklin	75.9	22.6	20 425	75.1	16.9	31.9	D	1.3	D	7.0	6.0	12.8	22.9	419	285	230
Frontier	61.7	31.8	19 859	73.0	10.1	33.8	D	D	D	5.1	5.6	11.8	26.0	D	117	317
Furnas	114.8	14.0	21 135	77.7	26.4	55.4	D	2.2	D	7.8	4.6	22.7	24.0	1 208	1 034	839
Gage	549.7	40.5	24 120	88.7	131.3	294.4	D	21.0	D	10.2	3.1	19.1	22.2	61 924	63 689	51 568
Garden	46.4	15.4	21 802	80.1	10.3	20.1	D	D	D	15.7	7.1	8.5	36.1	D	116	134
Garfield	42.7	35.2	20 871	76.7	8.8	21.0	D	8.8	D	10.3	3.0	14.2	17.8	1 854	1 934	1 384
Gosper	46.5	22.7	19 988	73.5	8.9	16.5	NA	.8	D	6.3	8.5	8.4	25.3	130	D	D
Grant	8.7	-10.1	11 624	42.7	2.4	1.6	D	D	D	33.5	D	51.0	119.3	D	D	D
Greeley	51.0	.5	17 829	65.5	11.1	23.0	10.5	4.3	D	6.5	4.9	16.0	26.9	981	786	631
Hall	1 224.5	52.3	23 671	87.0	172.5	941.9	D	23.9	D	11.7	5.0	20.9	15.2	225 355	224 634	203 803
Hamilton	216.4	36.0	22 886	84.1	28.9	114.9	D	11.5	D	6.1	3.5	17.1	14.7	13 244	12 975	11 875
Harlan	76.4	6.0	20 656	75.9	16.2	38.4	D	D	D	8.5	3.6	12.2	19.0	D	521	261
Hayes	21.7	-24.0	20 486	75.3	3.1	10.9	D	D	D	3.2	3.4	D	19.5	D	1 171	593
Hitchcock	59.5	5.5	17 284	63.5	13.8	22.6	D	D	D	8.6	3.3	6.0	36.4	D	126	158
Holt	252.6	21.4	21 018	77.3	45.8	151.1	5.7	2.5	78.3	8.6	3.6	18.5	13.9	3 731	3 680	3 306

[1] Based on resident population estimated as of July 1, 1998. [2] Includes farm earnings; see table B-10 for these data. [3] Includes mining and construction, not shown separately. [4] Includes agricultural services, forestry, and fisheries; transportation and public utilities; and wholesale trade, not shown separately. [5] Finance, insurance, and real estate. [6] Yellowstone National Park County included with Park County; data not available separately. [7] Less than $50,000.

Source: Personal Income and Earnings—U.S. Bureau of Economic Analysis, "Regional Economic Information System (REIS) 1969-1998" on CD-ROM (related Internet site <http://www.bea.doc.gov/bea/regional/data.htm>).

[Includes U.S., states, and 3,142 counties/county equivalents defined as of January 1, 1992. For changes to these areas since January 1, 1992, see appendix B. Geographic Information]

County	Personal income, 1998 Total (mil. dol.)	Per capita Percent change, 1990–1998	Per capita Amount (dollars)	Per capita Percent of national average	Transfer payments (mil. dol.)	Earnings Total2 (mil. dol.)	Goods-related Total3	Manufacturing	Service-related Total4	Retail trade	FIRE5	Services	Government	Manufacturing earnings 1998 ($1,000)	1997 ($1,000)	1996 ($1,000)
NEBRASKA—Con.																
Hooker	9.9	-11.1	14 155	52.0	3.9	2.2	D	D	D	25.3	12.3	99.3	91.6	D	D	D
Howard	118.2	28.8	18 187	66.9	21.3	47.1	D	.8	D	11.4	3.9	11.2	23.7	398	303	315
Jefferson	183.9	24.8	22 029	81.0	35.2	99.5	D	19.4	D	10.0	3.0	14.4	14.5	19 288	14 938	14 017
Johnson	88.0	15.0	19 238	70.7	18.5	39.3	D	D	D	10.8	5.0	16.1	28.3	D	3 732	7 823
Kearney	172.9	32.2	25 244	92.8	26.7	94.6	NA	4.6	D	4.4	3.1	14.4	14.0	4 321	4 134	3 685
Keith	178.0	41.6	20 511	75.4	32.7	103.1	D	8.5	D	15.9	5.8	21.7	16.2	8 747	8 578	8 098
Keya Paha	10.5	-11.8	10 760	39.6	3.2	3.1	D	4.2	D	11.1	NA	D	43.6	129	164	192
Kimball	84.2	17.7	20 664	76.0	16.4	45.2	D	D	D	14.3	3.7	D	21.1	D	5 302	4 468
Knox	178.0	19.1	19 374	71.2	42.8	80.8	D	D	D	10.3	3.7	19.4	29.4	D	2 901	3 170
Lancaster	6 474.3	64.9	27 487	101.0	673.0	4 928.2	20.2	14.3	79.4	8.1	8.4	27.1	21.4	704 612	658 543	621 544
Lincoln	761.8	46.4	22 756	83.7	127.5	527.3	D	2.0	D	12.3	3.8	23.1	17.4	10 751	11 133	10 824
Logan	14.8	11.9	16 765	61.6	3.1	6.6	D	D	D	8.5	D	8.1	24.4	D	210	237
Loup	2.5	-62.1	3 674	13.5	2.1	-3.1	D	–	D	D	D	D	-36.9	–	–	–
McPherson	3.3	-56.1	5 926	21.8	1.6	-2.1	D	–	D	-12.5	–	D	-32.9	–	–	–
Madison	823.6	54.6	23 827	87.6	115.9	643.4	D	22.7	D	10.1	3.1	20.7	15.3	146 235	153 329	144 638
Merrick	165.6	21.4	20 538	75.5	28.2	83.3	D	3.7	D	6.1	4.9	12.1	18.3	3 064	2 976	2 787
Morrill	93.4	4.0	17 228	63.3	20.2	44.8	D	1.7	D	6.8	D	12.0	28.2	761	3 702	4 142
Nance	80.6	20.0	19 664	72.3	17.5	38.9	D	.9	D	5.0	4.9	13.9	23.0	364	438	562
Nemaha	199.6	53.7	26 008	95.6	31.4	147.6	NA	9.8	77.3	4.3	2.2	11.4	53.5	14 395	13 599	12 415
Nuckolls	108.2	15.0	20 783	76.4	25.4	51.5	D	.9	D	10.5	5.1	28.4	19.5	445	418	422
Otoe	318.0	43.3	21 605	79.4	56.5	172.3	D	23.6	D	11.1	4.1	17.7	19.9	40 659	40 850	37 895
Pawnee	68.7	19.7	21 968	80.8	14.8	29.2	D	10.1	D	6.8	3.3	15.2	22.7	2 942	2 052	1 772
Perkins	78.1	15.1	24 466	89.9	12.6	52.0	D	2.0	D	4.0	2.2	10.9	17.3	1 024	788	589
Phelps	268.6	33.1	27 140	99.8	39.6	190.3	NA	17.1	49.5	5.7	3.4	15.2	11.8	32 544	31 377	30 464
Pierce	162.4	30.7	20 392	75.0	25.5	76.3	NA	1.6	D	8.1	3.7	17.9	17.0	1 208	1 005	901
Platte	743.1	45.9	24 222	89.0	83.8	567.7	D	34.8	D	7.8	3.8	14.8	14.8	197 619	204 261	183 454
Polk	132.8	19.4	23 654	87.0	21.4	67.9	D	2.0	D	5.4	2.9	11.8	16.1	1 338	997	1 026
Red Willow	250.5	34.5	22 284	81.9	47.6	151.2	D	8.8	D	13.4	4.9	19.1	18.3	13 252	12 805	12 042
Richardson	208.4	31.4	22 087	81.2	44.7	110.1	D	7.2	D	8.9	3.7	18.7	14.9	7 933	8 269	8 113
Rock	35.9	-2.1	20 754	76.3	6.9	18.5	D	2.6	D	4.5	2.8	11.6	27.5	481	501	489
Saline	286.1	40.7	22 075	81.1	44.0	204.3	D	41.8	D	7.4	2.6	12.4	14.9	85 448	82 106	77 702
Sarpy	2 786.5	53.8	23 158	85.1	207.3	1 613.5	D	4.7	D	6.4	2.4	15.3	42.3	76 347	73 038	66 817
Saunders	410.0	48.4	21 321	78.4	60.9	170.0	D	7.3	D	8.7	4.2	15.1	19.3	12 494	11 418	10 353
Scotts Bluff	793.5	36.9	22 031	81.0	148.8	530.7	D	11.6	D	11.3	5.1	24.7	16.3	61 631	59 455	54 939
Seward	378.7	45.5	23 111	85.0	48.2	220.8	NA	16.5	61.2	6.4	3.4	20.1	14.2	36 340	37 573	34 166
Sheridan	113.3	21.1	17 572	64.6	26.2	46.2	D	1.0	D	16.5	7.6	18.7	37.3	458	1 356	1 395
Sherman	58.6	23.0	16 976	62.4	14.0	23.1	D	2.7	D	9.2	4.7	15.5	29.7	624	573	544
Sioux	15.8	-26.9	10 697	39.3	3.1	2.1	D	–	D	19.2	D	34.1	91.9	–	–	–
Stanton	123.4	25.4	19 788	72.7	14.3	80.5	D	D	D	1.6	1.7	7.1	9.4	D	38 165	35 381
Thayer	155.3	34.9	24 809	91.2	29.0	86.9	NA	17.5	52.9	6.2	4.9	10.2	17.8	15 198	14 078	11 650
Thomas	11.3	13.0	14 182	52.1	2.9	3.2	D	D	D	26.7	D	28.7	63.4	D	587	537
Thurston	120.5	36.1	16 807	61.8	29.8	83.5	D	10.0	D	4.3	3.6	32.0	25.1	8 356	8 637	10 046
Valley	96.6	5.9	20 848	76.6	20.5	49.7	D	2.0	78.6	9.2	5.3	14.4	32.1	973	1 151	862
Washington	502.9	65.1	26 933	99.0	50.6	243.5	D	15.1	D	8.6	2.6	21.6	27.3	36 709	30 049	26 082
Wayne	194.4	44.2	20 837	76.6	28.4	123.1	NA	15.6	57.8	6.4	5.3	12.8	26.2	19 214	16 788	14 968
Webster	82.0	.2	20 392	75.0	17.8	39.7	D	.8	D	8.6	4.4	12.1	19.2	309	288	272
Wheeler	21.0	-2.3	22 571	83.0	2.9	13.6	D	D	D	2.1	D	3.0	11.9	D	D	D
York	371.7	43.3	25 541	93.9	49.6	282.2	D	17.1	D	9.5	3.1	16.2	12.1	48 358	40 094	39 260
NEVADA	50 918.5	102.1	29 200	107.3	5 279.8	37 227.0	18.2	4.7	81.6	9.4	8.5	38.4	14.6	1 735 424	1 592 163	1 489 979
Churchill	510.2	80.3	22 041	81.0	69.4	353.0	15.2	6.2	82.3	9.4	2.9	25.2	38.7	21 964	17 528	12 549
Clark	33 541.7	121.2	28 884	106.2	3 573.6	25 278.1	16.2	3.2	83.7	9.7	9.6	41.2	13.1	800 528	746 102	688 217
Douglas	1 408.7	91.2	38 263	140.7	111.6	755.1	D	9.9	D	6.5	10.2	49.4	9.9	75 091	65 188	61 263
Elko	1 084.9	74.8	23 574	86.7	77.4	694.4	20.7	1.1	D	8.7	D	35.0	20.3	7 800	7 432	7 114
Esmeralda	19.8	9.0	17 235	63.4	3.5	11.9	D	1.9	D	3.2	–	D	26.2	222	221	189
Eureka	41.2	27.7	20 718	76.2	4.6	273.0	93.4	.1	D	.6	D	1.0	3.5	222	221	189
Humboldt	402.2	65.9	22 239	81.8	34.9	331.1	46.5	2.0	50.5	9.8	1.8	11.9	15.4	6 514	7 189	6 709
Lander	152.4	31.8	21 862	80.4	13.9	117.4	D	D	D	6.6	.6	8.3	19.1	D	D	D
Lincoln	85.1	23.6	20 375	74.9	15.0	58.9	D	D	D	6.9	1.3	D	38.5	D	924	659
Lyon	649.2	92.1	21 547	79.2	105.0	267.3	34.5	21.0	62.4	8.9	3.3	19.1	19.0	56 167	51 277	49 318
Mineral	130.3	24.3	24 443	89.9	23.9	81.3	23.5	.5	D	5.7	1.6	42.3	26.1	382	340	386
Nye	656.6	126.4	22 913	84.2	118.3	383.9	23.7	1.1	73.6	6.1	1.8	43.9	17.2	4 299	3 295	3 362
Pershing	114.0	65.9	23 585	86.7	14.3	88.9	52.9	1.4	D	7.2	D	3.5	27.4	1 243	998	802
Storey	78.1	72.1	26 462	97.3	7.1	37.0	D	D	D	10.7	D	14.2	18.7	D	D	D
Washoe	10 341.9	70.8	33 040	121.5	900.0	7 231.7	18.2	8.3	81.8	9.4	7.3	35.7	14.3	601 261	545 917	524 242
White Pine	202.3	29.1	20 068	73.8	31.5	144.7	32.0	.8	D	8.6	3.5	13.9	35.4	1 150	1 196	854
Independent City																
Carson City city	1 499.9	75.9	30 508	112.1	175.8	1 119.5	D	13.2	D	9.5	5.2	21.1	37.2	148 150	135 420	128 521

[1] Based on resident population estimated as of July 1, 1998. [2] Includes farm earnings; see table B-10 for these data. [3] Includes mining and construction, not shown separately. [4] Includes agricultural services, forestry, and fisheries; transportation and public utilities; and wholesale trade, not shown separately. [5] Finance, insurance, and real estate.

Source: Personal Income and Earnings—U.S. Bureau of Economic Analysis, "Regional Economic Information System (REIS) 1969-1998" on CD-ROM (related Internet site <http://www.bea.doc.gov/bea/regional/data.htm>).

Table B–8. Counties — **Personal Income and Earnings**–Con.

[Includes U.S., states, and 3,142 counties/county equivalents defined as of January 1, 1992. For changes to these areas since January 1, 1992, see appendix B. Geographic Information]

County	Personal income, 1998 Total (mil. dol.)	Percent change, 1990–1998	Per capita Amount (dollars)	Per capita Percent of national average	Transfer payments (mil. dol.)	Earnings Total[2] (mil. dol.)	Goods-related Total[3]	Manufacturing	Service-related Total[4]	Retail trade	FIRE[5]	Services	Government	Manufacturing earnings 1998 ($1,000)	1997 ($1,000)	1996 ($1,000)
NEW HAMPSHIRE	34 958.3	51.8	29 480	108.4	3 806.7	23 207.7	29.0	22.3	70.8	11.6	7.3	28.0	11.5	5 180 331	4 894 033	4 509 226
Belknap	1 472.8	52.0	27 824	102.3	205.6	870.1	31.1	20.8	68.9	16.9	3.2	27.0	12.3	180 800	171 827	150 264
Carroll	1 089.5	45.8	27 664	101.7	170.5	592.0	21.7	9.0	78.1	20.7	4.0	33.6	12.0	53 345	54 150	47 502
Cheshire	1 832.4	40.4	25 442	93.5	244.9	1 148.0	D	22.4	D	14.1	10.7	22.6	11.9	257 715	251 781	246 231
Coos	768.1	33.1	23 370	85.9	168.3	487.2	D	24.8	D	12.2	2.3	24.5	13.6	120 646	118 384	113 803
Grafton	2 255.3	52.0	28 826	106.0	285.8	1 835.1	24.8	20.0	75.0	10.8	3.6	41.9	11.1	366 537	352 401	310 054
Hillsborough	11 351.1	54.0	31 315	115.1	1 087.1	8 295.9	31.6	26.4	68.4	9.9	9.7	28.0	9.2	2 188 270	2 078 096	1 941 972
Merrimack	3 765.0	50.7	29 438	108.2	431.3	2 535.3	22.8	15.4	76.8	9.9	8.3	28.2	19.1	389 411	373 760	354 621
Rockingham	8 775.1	58.0	32 423	119.2	713.7	5 283.3	26.9	19.1	73.0	13.5	6.0	27.3	8.5	1 006 722	893 465	763 578
Strafford	2 684.3	45.1	24 615	90.1	343.8	1 640.3	32.8	27.3	67.1	10.2	5.5	20.2	10.0	450 633	438 855	422 104
Sullivan	964.9	43.2	24 199	89.0	155.7	511.5	D	32.5	D	11.6	3.4	19.2	15.3	166 252	161 314	159 017
NEW JERSEY	278 348.6	44.9	34 383	126.4	31 392.7	190 545.7	19.7	15.2	80.2	7.5	9.5	31.3	14.1	28 890 291	27 789 456	26 587 411
Atlantic	7 553.4	38.2	31 738	116.7	1 015.5	6 605.7	D	3.2	D	6.8	3.2	60.3	14.3	209 064	203 435	211 492
Bergen	40 244.5	48.3	47 101	173.1	3 078.2	27 377.6	19.3	16.1	80.7	7.3	8.0	34.7	7.3	4 395 077	4 175 363	4 059 641
Burlington	12 451.5	43.8	29 556	108.6	1 377.1	7 964.9	18.3	12.7	81.3	9.5	7.6	30.1	18.0	1 012 940	972 734	949 005
Camden	13 796.6	34.2	27 360	100.6	2 035.3	8 719.6	18.5	12.8	81.4	9.2	6.6	33.2	17.5	1 113 714	1 137 594	1 111 648
Cape May	2 773.1	37.7	28 297	104.0	529.9	1 306.7	D	2.5	D	17.8	6.6	D	27.0	32 585	32 838	30 831
Cumberland	3 194.6	32.3	22 756	83.7	642.9	2 225.4	29.0	22.7	68.9	8.3	4.7	20.7	22.8	505 744	485 400	470 552
Essex	24 771.2	29.5	33 102	121.7	3 722.4	19 669.4	13.0	9.9	87.0	5.2	14.7	31.1	18.7	1 954 206	1 922 803	1 927 017
Gloucester	6 447.0	47.5	25 995	95.6	815.9	3 304.5	28.6	19.9	70.5	11.6	3.2	21.9	17.5	659 006	635 775	597 975
Hudson	14 915.1	36.5	26 970	99.1	2 420.9	12 339.6	13.2	10.5	86.8	7.2	18.2	22.5	17.7	1 299 548	1 270 682	1 242 424
Hunterdon	5 198.0	66.0	42 471	156.1	300.2	2 551.6	32.1	24.9	67.7	8.9	7.5	28.4	12.7	635 339	574 190	492 917
Mercer	12 447.2	44.7	37 551	138.0	1 386.3	9 786.3	16.4	13.1	83.6	5.6	9.3	34.2	25.7	1 282 430	1 334 509	1 225 600
Middlesex	23 722.7	45.6	33 289	122.4	2 426.5	20 282.2	D	20.4	D	6.8	10.2	29.0	11.6	4 134 501	3 830 257	3 553 017
Monmouth	21 496.2	49.7	35 636	131.0	2 091.1	11 029.1	D	5.8	D	9.5	8.3	37.6	18.5	643 126	660 209	628 365
Morris	21 993.7	64.8	47 915	176.1	1 300.3	16 528.4	23.8	19.1	76.1	6.9	12.0	29.9	8.5	3 149 617	2 863 692	2 692 000
Ocean	13 142.3	44.8	26 815	98.6	2 509.7	4 928.3	15.3	5.8	84.5	14.9	5.3	32.8	21.3	287 043	284 858	271 703
Passaic	12 920.5	33.4	26 748	98.3	1 926.6	8 046.4	29.9	23.2	70.1	9.5	6.3	25.9	15.2	1 863 326	1 896 683	1 843 057
Salem	1 703.5	35.7	26 234	96.4	281.8	1 029.7	NA	25.8	D	7.0	2.7	D	15.5	265 789	258 783	261 752
Somerset	13 999.2	72.2	49 594	182.3	773.8	11 319.8	19.3	15.6	80.6	5.7	11.5	27.4	6.2	1 761 054	1 794 399	1 744 113
Sussex	4 176.8	43.2	29 180	107.3	371.2	1 446.6	18.3	9.1	81.7	10.2	8.6	31.8	20.6	131 018	123 602	114 786
Union	18 628.7	43.6	37 310	137.3	2 031.0	12 606.0	20.1	24.6	70.0	6.5	6.5	29.1	10.0	2 104 000	2 005 020	2 741 101
Warren	2 772.7	42.4	28 093	103.3	355.9	1 487.0	37.9	30.3	62.2	9.5	2.8	21.5	15.0	450 496	465 822	418 335
NEW MEXICO	36 688.2	61.3	21 164	77.8	5 593.0	25 319.8	17.0	7.3	80.6	10.6	5.2	27.2	27.2	1 851 778	1 820 127	1 680 938
Bernalillo	13 869.6	60.7	26 434	97.2	1 641.0	11 140.9	14.6	7.8	85.3	10.3	6.4	34.3	22.4	865 879	835 350	797 384
Catron	42.7	40.5	15 167	55.8	11.2	20.4	D	D	D	6.7	D	12.4	55.3	880	709	812
Chaves	1 188.4	44.4	18 979	69.8	226.0	766.0	22.7	12.8	60.7	9.7	3.5	17.4	20.4	97 974	83 002	71 922
Cibola	358.4	63.4	13 521	49.7	92.0	180.8	D	7.8	D	11.4	1.9	D	32.5	14 179	14 958	13 534
Colfax	257.6	49.0	18 960	69.7	56.2	150.8	D	5.4	D	13.6	5.2	D	28.9	8 090	7 740	7 000
Curry	906.5	47.3	20 201	74.3	156.4	621.4	D	1.9	D	9.9	3.0	13.6	42.7	11 985	11 461	11 907
DeBaca	38.6	35.9	16 324	60.0	10.4	20.1	NA	1.9	D	12.5	2.7	10.3	31.6	378	356	469
Dona Ana	2 804.7	62.2	16 599	61.0	494.9	1 777.4	D	4.8	D	10.4	4.0	21.4	37.8	84 493	79 623	75 971
Eddy	1 044.7	40.7	19 546	71.9	202.2	697.3	33.8	6.2	62.7	9.5	3.2	18.4	16.9	43 379	43 843	40 606
Grant	550.6	59.5	17 409	64.0	128.5	338.8	39.4	6.3	61.2	9.8	3.6	13.2	27.6	21 280	25 986	28 163
Guadalupe	57.1	35.9	14 120	51.9	18.2	34.6	D	D	D	21.4	D	17.5	30.8	D	225	323
Harding	15.0	22.7	16 645	61.2	3.4	7.4	D	D	D	5.7	D	D	35.2	D	211	311
Hidalgo	108.8	42.6	17 623	64.8	22.6	76.7	D	D	D	9.9	1.4	8.1	20.9		28 736	29 664
Lea	1 058.6	43.2	18 756	68.9	196.5	724.1	33.3	2.0	62.1	9.7	3.0	19.9	13.9	14 818	14 579	13 394
Lincoln	318.4	64.6	19 375	71.2	65.1	167.7	D	3.7	D	19.0	6.9	27.1	22.6	6 167	5 013	5 186
Los Alamos	700.8	33.7	38 350	141.0	33.8	923.9	2.0	.3	D	2.1	2.2	23.7	69.3	2 732	2 948	2 832
Luna	333.4	63.5	13 902	51.1	95.2	176.2	D	8.4	D	14.1	2.1	17.4	29.5	14 738	15 161	13 913
McKinley	907.8	55.9	13 482	49.6	228.9	598.0	D	3.7	D	16.3	3.1	18.4	37.6	21 860	19 685	20 481
Mora	61.2	60.0	12 667	46.6	22.4	20.7	NA	2.3	D	5.4	D	27.1	46.4	484	440	426
Otero	994.5	39.7	18 310	67.3	163.6	703.2	D	2.4	D	7.4	2.9	18.9	54.3	16 640	36 313	32 303
Quay	175.1	21.3	17 497	64.3	46.3	99.8	NA	2.0	D	12.1	4.5	20.0	29.9	2 033	1 479	1 520
Rio Arriba	542.6	62.8	14 340	52.7	142.5	250.6	11.2	4.9	88.8	11.6	3.3	33.1	33.1	12 374	11 900	11 343
Roosevelt	315.8	43.5	17 717	65.1	68.9	188.4	8.0	3.2	62.5	11.0	1.7	13.4	25.8	6 097	5 403	5 395
Sandoval	1 788.3	99.0	20 313	74.7	228.8	861.0	D	D	D	9.4	3.0	15.7	13.2		422 662	343 942
San Juan	1 928.2	67.2	18 161	66.8	307.6	1 472.6	29.3	3.2	66.8	11.3	2.9	19.3	17.6	47 806	43 212	41 102
San Miguel	439.1	61.0	15 291	56.2	130.8	222.3	D	2.2	D	11.7	3.5	22.2	49.9	4 805	4 569	8 184
Santa Fe	3 444.1	77.3	28 040	103.1	320.1	2 048.9	11.6	3.8	88.2	13.5	9.4	33.0	26.5	77 908	68 407	68 842
Sierra	213.2	69.8	19 406	71.3	70.8	88.4	D	1.0	D	13.2	7.3	22.9	30.8	876	906	1 081
Socorro	251.2	47.7	15 368	56.5	59.2	148.3	D	2.8	D	9.1	2.1	26.3	45.3	4 159	3 753	3 740
Taos	479.1	74.8	17 905	65.8	98.7	286.0	D	2.5	80.7	17.1	5.6	32.7	19.8	7 068	6 800	7 916
Torrance	252.0	112.2	15 726	57.8	46.5	85.8	NA	3.8	D	12.9	2.6	17.2	37.7	3 291	2 285	2 265
Union	93.9	42.5	23 568	86.6	17.1	63.1	D	1.1	D	6.3	4.9	11.2	16.7	675	985	934
Valencia	1 148.4	92.5	17 999	66.2	187.1	358.2	D	8.0	D	13.0	3.7	15.3	31.3	28 578	21 427	18 073

[1] Based on resident population estimated as of July 1, 1998.   [2] Includes farm earnings; see table B-10 for these data.   [3] Includes mining and construction, not shown separately.   [4] Includes agricultural services, forestry, and fisheries; transportation and public utilities; and wholesale trade, not shown separately.   [5] Finance, insurance, and real estate.

Source: Personal Income and Earnings—U.S. Bureau of Economic Analysis, "Regional Economic Information System (REIS) 1969-1998" on CD-ROM (related Internet site <http://www.bea.doc.gov/bea/regional/data.htm>).

[Includes U.S., states, and 3,142 counties/county equivalents defined as of January 1, 1992. For changes to these areas since January 1, 1992, see appendix B. Geographic Information]

County	Personal income, 1998													Manufacturing earnings		
			Per capita[1]			Earnings										
								Percent, by selected industry–								
								Goods-related		Service-related							
	Total (mil. dol.)	Percent change, 1990–1998	Amount (dollars)	Percent of national average	Transfer payments (mil. dol.)	Total[2] (mil. dol.)	Total[3]	Manufacturing	Total[4]	Retail trade	FIRE[5]	Services	Government	1998 ($1,000)	1997 ($1,000)	1996 ($1,000)
NEW YORK	583 061.2	38.9	32 108	118.0	93 972.1	432 571.5	15.3	11.6	84.6	6.4	20.7	31.0	14.5	50 071 702	47 925 703	46 366 814
Albany	8 959.4	34.5	30 576	112.4	1 413.4	9 299.5	D	6.4	D	7.6	9.2	28.5	32.0	593 028	576 950	547 129
Allegany	882.1	32.9	17 444	64.1	210.4	480.8	D	24.7	68.3	9.5	1.8	24.3	26.7	118 904	116 378	116 018
Bronx	23 637.0	29.1	19 841	72.9	7 611.0	8 744.9	D	4.8	D	7.1	7.9	47.2	14.1	419 420	407 582	423 422
Broome	4 817.8	22.5	24 514	90.1	902.5	3 549.4	D	24.6	D	8.8	4.4	27.6	18.4	873 196	820 793	807 570
Cattaraugus	1 600.7	32.0	18 845	69.3	358.7	1 011.9	28.6	25.0	70.7	9.7	2.9	20.8	23.6	252 606	252 318	236 091
Cayuga	1 699.7	32.9	20 687	76.0	314.2	849.8	24.1	18.9	73.1	8.7	2.7	24.1	24.6	160 952	169 428	154 934
Chautauqua	2 819.7	30.7	20 387	74.9	641.7	1 805.5	34.1	29.7	64.8	10.1	2.6	22.8	19.2	536 723	506 769	496 562
Chemung	2 076.9	33.5	22 524	82.8	423.1	1 371.4	32.6	26.4	67.2	9.9	3.7	24.1	18.5	361 812	341 664	322 689
Chenango	1 002.8	27.9	19 668	72.3	205.1	553.5	34.6	30.3	64.0	8.8	7.6	17.5	21.8	167 604	175 799	163 931
Clinton	1 648.6	25.3	20 664	76.0	307.5	1 132.7	D	18.1	D	10.8	2.6	20.1	28.7	205 114	188 792	183 208
Columbia	1 604.4	41.8	25 425	93.5	281.7	715.3	D	15.1	D	9.5	5.3	28.8	21.3	100 180	101 485	95 637
Cortland	943.5	30.3	19 570	71.9	184.0	604.5	D	26.6	D	11.3	3.2	25.8	20.6	160 942	165 157	152 815
Delaware	903.2	35.2	19 470	71.6	211.2	571.7	38.6	33.7	59.9	10.2	3.7	14.7	24.5	192 470	173 068	159 417
Dutchess	7 912.6	35.2	29 812	109.6	1 035.4	4 471.2	33.3	28.0	66.6	7.9	4.5	28.4	18.8	1 251 340	1 089 298	1 057 534
Erie	24 447.2	31.8	26 183	96.3	4 555.9	17 173.4	24.8	20.1	75.1	8.9	7.7	27.8	18.1	3 454 503	3 371 834	3 220 617
Essex	777.3	32.7	20 697	76.1	167.5	477.1	22.5	12.2	77.3	12.5	2.4	24.6	30.2	58 129	59 590	57 136
Franklin	873.9	38.9	17 956	66.0	204.8	538.5	D	6.2	D	9.6	3.1	28.0	41.3	33 253	34 683	34 226
Fulton	1 162.9	39.0	21 906	80.5	258.1	580.0	D	24.1	D	10.4	3.2	20.7	24.4	139 895	132 083	126 485
Genesee	1 335.6	28.2	22 007	80.9	235.4	727.7	27.3	21.6	68.6	9.4	2.5	20.3	24.6	157 065	156 352	153 123
Greene	1 046.0	43.2	21 726	79.9	206.7	422.4	D	10.0	D	10.6	3.9	21.1	35.4	42 100	38 064	35 579
Hamilton	114.4	33.6	22 051	81.1	26.4	48.9	18.4	5.8	81.6	13.9	3.2	21.0	39.0	2 836	3 203	2 866
Herkimer	1 271.1	31.6	19 854	73.0	289.5	542.2	D	26.4	D	11.3	3.1	18.9	25.1	143 281	145 988	148 365
Jefferson	2 312.6	31.8	20 832	76.6	394.9	1 740.5	D	9.6	D	8.9	2.9	16.9	49.1	166 756	158 163	155 858
Kings	54 561.0	32.8	24 076	88.5	14 297.1	17 530.0	D	7.7	D	7.7	14.5	38.8	10.4	1 355 533	1 345 642	1 377 806
Lewis	464.1	28.9	16 922	62.2	101.5	233.0	D	27.6	D	8.5	1.8	11.4	29.6	64 365	68 447	68 467
Livingston	1 367.1	31.4	20 827	76.6	219.1	601.1	20.3	14.1	78.4	12.6	2.7	15.5	40.2	84 907	81 033	80 146
Madison	1 554.9	34.9	21 926	80.6	245.2	707.0	19.9	14.0	78.1	11.3	4.8	29.9	20.7	98 670	97 895	90 487
Monroe	21 403.6	35.5	29 938	110.1	3 273.3	16 948.2	D	34.4	D	7.5	5.4	27.8	10.8	5 831 650	5 990 262	5 802 271
Montgomery	1 117.8	32.2	22 013	80.9	271.9	561.6	D	25.7	D	9.8	4.1	27.7	16.7	144 502	136 948	142 147
Nassau	55 120.0	35.2	42 368	155.7	5 910.3	28 864.6	12.1	7.3	87.9	10.8	12.4	36.6	13.7	2 105 925	2 091 066	1 964 035
New York	111 648.0	56.1	72 194	265.4	10 296.2	189 928.6	8.0	6.7	92.0	3.4	36.7	31.2	11.4	12 809 072	11 555 198	11 203 196
Niagara	5 093.5	32.5	23 387	86.0	1 007.6	2 892.2	D	35.5	D	9.8	2.8	18.9	17.8	1 025 693	1 047 492	1 035 359
Oneida	5 301.8	24.8	22 981	84.5	1 141.7	3 546.5	19.6	15.5	80.0	9.8	8.1	28.4	24.6	549 037	529 158	522 860
Onondaga	12 054.7	28.8	26 325	96.8	2 002.1	9 713.5	25.4	20.3	74.5	8.3	8.6	26.7	14.6	1 971 490	1 842 330	1 725 180
Ontario	2 504.1	35.7	25 160	92.5	365.5	1 480.5	30.6	21.6	68.5	12.9	3.6	21.3	20.2	319 792	292 767	271 233
Orange	8 242.4	36.6	24 992	91.9	1 237.6	4 309.8	15.2	10.2	84.4	11.3	5.4	24.6	28.1	441 703	432 060	424 739
Orleans	822.5	27.8	18 314	67.3	157.0	380.1	20.7	14.9	75.2	8.4	2.4	16.6	40.7	56 470	60 690	64 265
Oswego	2 487.2	28.8	20 088	73.8	451.8	1 288.6	D	21.8	D	9.4	2.1	16.8	28.4	280 767	283 568	283 803
Otsego	1 257.6	35.9	20 762	76.3	245.5	749.4	D	10.8	D	11.4	6.9	35.6	19.7	81 089	75 717	74 741
Putnam	3 122.8	46.8	33 453	123.0	292.5	934.7	D	12.0	D	8.3	9.0	30.6	19.8	111 846	101 632	97 151
Queens	56 656.2	32.7	28 425	104.5	12 515.5	20 362.7	19.4	9.4	80.6	7.9	6.4	31.4	8.9	1 921 968	1 876 762	1 752 584
Rensselaer	3 753.6	33.4	24 662	90.7	653.4	1 764.3	19.8	11.4	80.0	9.5	5.5	33.7	21.6	201 568	196 677	190 987
Richmond	12 690.1	46.0	31 187	114.6	2 636.4	3 604.2	NA	3.1	88.6	9.9	6.1	44.2	10.0	111 871	109 533	102 662
Rockland	10 298.6	48.7	36 654	134.7	1 155.5	5 096.0	D	13.3	D	8.5	6.4	30.3	16.7	675 693	650 920	620 157
St. Lawrence	2 052.6	37.6	18 141	66.7	479.1	1 333.9	27.2	21.0	71.5	9.9	2.4	21.0	30.3	279 539	265 921	260 032
Saratoga	5 217.0	45.0	26 424	97.1	623.4	2 275.7	D	16.0	D	12.0	7.8	26.0	21.2	364 624	356 729	340 819
Schenectady	4 196.9	34.5	28 922	106.3	696.2	2 686.3	29.2	23.3	70.8	9.0	4.3	35.3	14.0	625 735	623 423	611 086
Schoharie	639.0	36.0	19 922	73.2	123.2	288.2	D	9.6	D	14.7	5.7	15.7	35.9	27 757	24 418	22 051
Schuyler	340.0	35.0	17 715	65.1	79.1	140.1	25.4	19.4	74.3	12.3	2.1	25.0	26.2	27 105	31 543	33 111
Seneca	698.7	23.9	21 875	80.4	132.7	348.5	D	27.4	D	10.6	2.7	16.7	24.9	95 352	95 146	92 461
Steuben	2 219.6	33.3	22 657	83.3	430.2	1 584.4	D	43.5	D	7.5	4.7	17.3	17.8	689 129	656 778	692 823
Suffolk	44 745.1	41.0	32 648	120.0	5 525.7	24 387.5	20.0	13.6	79.9	8.9	7.8	29.5	19.7	3 319 832	3 127 007	3 072 583
Sullivan	1 660.2	31.7	23 925	87.9	375.1	851.8	7.7	2.7	92.1	8.8	8.0	30.5	26.0	22 971	21 842	23 361
Tioga	1 101.3	27.8	21 006	77.2	177.4	543.0	D	51.7	D	7.2	2.0	11.9	16.0	280 615	274 080	246 158
Tompkins	2 148.0	32.9	22 089	81.2	280.4	1 692.1	14.5	11.4	85.0	7.4	3.6	53.7	12.9	193 008	180 681	160 444
Ulster	3 973.2	27.2	23 817	87.6	727.8	1 953.9	18.5	13.4	81.0	11.1	5.6	28.5	25.4	261 649	239 500	224 915
Warren	1 558.7	41.9	25 445	93.5	254.0	1 148.1	D	16.6	D	12.3	7.9	33.3	13.1	191 046	200 298	194 004
Washington	1 125.9	34.0	18 712	68.8	237.3	585.8	33.6	27.1	63.6	7.8	1.8	15.3	32.1	158 719	151 043	152 377
Wayne	2 170.2	38.7	22 821	83.9	350.5	995.7	39.1	33.5	58.8	9.0	2.1	16.2	23.3	333 698	313 699	298 284
Westchester	42 581.3	44.3	47 267	173.8	4 320.9	22 204.4	20.2	14.6	79.8	7.1	11.7	32.4	14.1	3 238 198	3 193 559	3 090 876
Wyoming	801.7	35.3	18 157	66.7	146.8	451.8	24.4	19.7	67.4	8.9	3.6	11.7	33.9	88 870	90 176	84 235
Yates	461.1	40.8	19 004	69.9	96.8	191.0	D	15.8	D	11.5	3.5	26.2	20.4	30 215	28 622	21 706

[1] Based on resident population estimated as of July 1, 1998. [2] Includes farm earnings; see table B-10 for these data. [3] Includes mining and construction, not shown separately. [4] Includes agricultural services, forestry, and fisheries; transportation and public utilities; and wholesale trade, not shown separately. [5] Finance, insurance, and real estate.

Source: Personal Income and Earnings—U.S. Bureau of Economic Analysis, "Regional Economic Information System (REIS) 1969-1998" on CD-ROM (related Internet site <http://www.bea.doc.gov/bea/regional/data.htm>).

[Includes U.S., states, and 3,142 counties/county equivalents defined as of January 1, 1992. For changes to these areas since January 1, 1992, see appendix B. Geographic Information]

County	Personal income, 1998													Manufacturing earnings		
		Per capita[1]				Earnings										
							Percent, by selected industry–									
							Goods-related		Service-related							
	Total (mil. dol.)	Percent change, 1990–1998	Amount (dollars)	Percent of national average	Transfer payments (mil. dol.)	Total[2] (mil. dol.)	Total[3]	Manufacturing	Total[4]	Retail trade	FIRE[5]	Services	Government	1998 ($1,000)	1997 ($1,000)	1996 ($1,000)
NORTH CAROLINA......	190 008.5	64.4	25 181	92.6	26 130.9	138 538.5	29.3	22.5	69.1	9.2	7.0	22.6	17.7	31 119 905	30 152 031	28 669 590
Alamance.................	2 971.8	55.8	24 836	91.3	445.0	1 940.0	D	30.9	D	10.8	4.9	27.3	9.4	598 801	599 190	576 679
Alexander.................	666.4	53.8	21 298	78.3	94.8	328.1	56.0	50.5	38.6	7.5	1.7	12.7	11.5	165 693	156 782	144 341
Alleghany.................	232.3	73.7	23 687	87.1	44.8	134.5	D	7.2	D	3.3	15.9	11.8		37 754	33 972	30 416
Anson..................	499.9	49.8	20 496	75.3	111.9	278.4	37.6	31.8	52.2	6.6	1.5	10.7	23.1	88 499	93 928	89 499
Ashe	484.7	63.7	20 161	74.1	106.1	264.2	D	30.1	D	9.2	3.0	14.6	11.9	79 428	75 702	76 315
Avery	350.8	71.6	22 328	82.1	71.3	215.8	D	13.9	D	10.6	4.2	28.5	12.7	29 976	27 101	23 794
Beaufort.................	905.5	43.0	20 340	74.8	193.2	556.4	38.6	33.3	61.5	8.9	2.7	19.6	16.0	185 271	189 266	180 513
Bertie	377.4	45.7	18 497	68.0	100.8	212.9	37.5	35.2	44.3	4.6	1.8	11.7	16.8	75 025	71 132	69 159
Bladen..................	013.0	71.2	19 900	73.2	147.1	365.5	46.7	43.6	47.2	6.6	1.4	11.1	19.3	159 399	134 418	135 096
Brunswick...............	1 350.5	87.0	19 731	72.5	295.7	708.3	D	17.5	D	10.5	8.5	17.1	17.2	123 687	118 192	109 731
Buncombe................	5 055.5	60.7	25 998	95.6	775.3	3 498.3	25.3	18.5	74.0	11.3	4.8	30.5	15.9	646 330	647 864	625 103
Burke	1 700.1	42.1	20 644	75.9	297.6	1 175.3	D	42.8	D	7.6	1.8	16.8	21.1	503 558	486 984	478 869
Cabarrus.................	3 186.0	77.6	26 480	97.3	405.5	1 836.1	38.4	29.1	61.2	10.5	5.2	19.5	16.3	534 718	538 173	517 788
Caldwell.................	1 674.6	55.8	22 060	81.1	263.7	1 015.5	51.6	46.1	45.2	8.2	1.9	15.2	11.0	468 192	436 023	433 944
Camden..................	134.1	63.5	19 679	72.3	24.1	39.5	20.9	3.6	D	11.7	D	26.4	25.0	1 434	1 421	1 330
Carteret.................	1 401.9	74.8	23 442	86.2	225.2	594.3	D	7.6	D	17.8	6.7	21.4	23.5	45 429	37 130	34 728
Caswell.................	410.9	57.8	18 463	67.9	80.8	116.9	D	21.8	D	5.6	1.8	15.5	40.1	25 494	24 107	25 621
Catawba.................	3 595.6	61.1	27 157	99.8	433.2	3 141.8	D	43.1	D	10.1	2.8	16.2	8.9	1 352 904	1 300 294	1 221 940
Chatham.................	1 253.0	72.6	27 489	101.1	157.9	528.2	NA	38.4	D	7.7	2.4	16.7	11.6	202 851	197 567	190 652
Cherokee................	397.3	61.5	17 469	64.2	116.3	244.1	D	27.8	D	12.5	3.5	23.4	17.0	67 878	66 027	64 002
Chowan	301.7	50.7	21 238	78.1	67.3	168.1	D	22.2	D	9.2	3.4	21.7	15.6	37 359	34 492	32 955
Clay	161.6	74.4	18 861	69.3	39.9	55.0	D	6.3	D	13.0	6.1	24.2	21.3	3 461	2 446	3 342
Cleveland................	1 966.1	46.8	21 126	77.7	363.8	1 213.1	D	40.1	D	8.5	2.8	20.2	12.9	486 171	478 832	456 888
Columbus................	1 057.2	61.4	20 046	73.7	275.9	612.7	D	30.0	D	9.8	D	19.3	16.8	183 639	185 959	177 284
Craven	2 089.5	60.2	23 527	86.5	321.4	1 672.7	D	10.5	D	6.7	2.5	15.1	53.9	506 658	485 148	459 504
Cumberland..............	6 850.9	64.3	24 104	88.6	829.8	5 523.4	D	9.2	D	8.2	3.2	12.5	57.6	2 622	1 996	1 846
Currituck................	394.2	82.7	22 162	81.5	54.2	104.9	21.6	2.5	D	19.9	7.1	15.6	28.7	21 421	18 004	16 060
Dare	665.4	78.3	23 096	84.9	90.3	454.3	D	4.7	D	23.0	11.8	20.1	18.1	664 628	643 042	626 259
Davidson................	3 250.9	54.7	23 034	84.7	451.1	1 628.2	D	40.8	D	9.5	3.2	16.5	11.5	123 588	124 597	123 314
Davie	893.9	65.0	27 937	102.7	110.1	338.3	D	36.5	D	8.4	D	19.2	13.1			
Duplin	887.3	54.3	20 574	75.6	183.7	559.3	D	31.2	D	7.3	D	10.7	15.6	174 322	177 971	170 557
Durham	5 764.3	55.6	28 492	104.7	666.3	7 824.7	D	39.7	D	5.1	4.1	32.3	9.9	3 103 744	2 842 829	2 447 264
Edgecombe..............	1 004.4	09.1	19 040	71.1	255.2	783.0	D	20.0	D	6.9	D	15.4	20.0	163 506	164 155	178 055
Forsyth.................	9 005.7	52.1	31 304	115.1	1 001.4	7 106.5	D	24.0	D	9.5	9.9	30.0	8.2	1 703 500	1 689 552	1 599 941
Franklin.................	933.1	78.6	20 932	76.9	149.9	343.2	D	22.4	D	10.1	D	17.8	19.0	76 961	75 317	71 074
Gaston	4 267.4	46.6	23 210	85.3	674.4	2 743.3	D	40.5	D	9.3	3.4	19.7	10.6	1 110 892	1 095 761	1 083 030
Gates	180.4	42.6	17 775	65.3	40.1	56.3	D	10.1	68.3	5.9	2.3	13.9	32.9	5 669	5 621	5 231
Graham	128.2	70.5	16 877	62.0	37.8	69.7	D	D	D	8.4	1.9	10.5	21.1	D	14 537	13 464
Granville................	920.2	70.6	21 007	77.2	144.6	626.2	D	35.3	D	5.9	1.8	8.2	38.1	221 257	220 435	204 520
Greene	330.9	42.4	18 001	66.2	65.1	137.6	23.9	16.6	57.9	5.7	1.2	12.4	30.3	22 867	22 940	17 564
Guilford.................	11 330.0	52.6	29 229	107.4	1 310.1	10 323.8	30.6	24.4	69.1	9.3	7.9	23.7	10.4	2 514 940	2 403 576	2 317 438
Halifax.................	1 033.8	42.9	18 357	67.5	291.4	585.2	28.5	24.0	66.3	11.3	3.3	14.8	25.9	140 173	139 856	134 133
Harnett.................	1 576.5	73.1	19 129	70.3	264.6	722.4	D	23.9	D	10.8	3.0	19.8	19.3	172 317	173 331	169 283
Haywood................	1 106.8	54.8	21 494	79.0	237.7	557.8	D	24.8	D	14.6	3.2	20.7	19.1	138 547	165 795	163 035
Henderson..............	2 120.7	64.6	26 115	96.0	381.6	1 160.3	D	28.6	72.1	10.7	3.6	21.1	12.7	331 903	317 845	292 984
Hertford................	387.6	41.3	17 626	64.8	110.5	224.8	27.1	21.9	72.1	11.8	2.2	27.6	21.5	49 115	44 316	44 051
Hoke	412.2	57.1	13 582	49.9	91.0	220.3	46.3	38.3	48.2	4.6	1.4	10.7	27.1	84 387	83 808	80 816
Hyde	106.3	44.6	18 157	66.7	26.3	58.2	13.2	7.7	80.2	10.6	4.7	11.2	38.0	4 457	4 386	3 763
Iredell	2 767.9	75.7	24 382	89.6	380.6	1 817.4	40.5	32.6	57.1	11.7	2.5	21.5	11.3	591 721	566 864	540 814
Jackson	622.6	69.3	20 777	76.4	115.0	376.4	NA	8.4	81.3	10.6	3.3	32.4	29.7	31 587	31 641	32 181
Johnston	2 481.6	90.2	23 288	85.6	349.9	1 135.7	D	25.4	D	12.4	3.6	16.3	15.5	288 125	270 261	251 422
Jones	179.4	56.1	19 160	70.4	42.9	67.8	14.6	7.1	66.5	6.9	1.5	21.7	22.4	4 819	3 556	2 963
Lee	1 208.5	69.2	24 563	90.3	182.0	896.8	51.3	45.5	47.2	10.3	2.4	15.1	9.9	408 436	386 817	348 004
Lenoir	1 253.3	41.5	21 287	78.3	279.5	935.5	34.5	27.6	63.3	9.0	3.2	19.6	22.7	258 020	262 873	256 675
Lincoln	1 243.4	52.4	21 422	78.7	179.7	599.2	D	39.4	D	9.1	4.2	13.2	15.4	236 137	232 497	213 434
McDowell...............	782.0	61.4	19 522	71.8	145.4	563.7	D	53.3	D	7.4	1.4	11.5	12.5	300 673	282 967	268 346
Macon	599.3	75.5	21 191	77.9	132.1	305.2	D	12.0	D	15.6	5.8	28.7	14.8	36 751	36 099	31 400
Madison	349.2	61.4	18 599	68.4	78.3	124.0	30.8	23.5	D	6.9	2.2	22.7	21.3	29 090	28 113	25 356
Martin	488.0	41.3	18 657	68.6	116.2	340.3	48.6	43.4	46.3	7.5	1.6	10.4	17.8	147 705	166 642	162 837
Mecklenburg............	22 232.9	85.4	35 245	129.6	1 658.8	22 271.5	18.0	11.3	81.6	8.2	16.7	25.5	8.6	2 515 190	2 450 335	2 344 839
Mitchell.................	287.7	52.4	19 449	71.5	67.5	169.1	40.3	24.2	D	7.8	3.2	20.0	17.4	40 868	43 859	45 152
Montgomery.............	477.4	51.4	19 789	72.7	95.0	333.6	56.2	48.7	D	6.6	2.1	9.3	14.9	162 535	150 741	140 436
Moore	2 033.0	65.1	28 493	104.7	329.1	1 016.3	20.9	13.8	73.3	9.7	4.3	40.1	11.6	140 430	134 336	133 752
Nash	2 142.2	61.9	23 572	86.7	299.9	1 470.5	D	29.6	D	12.2	6.7	18.2	12.4	434 783	442 088	442 270
New Hanover............	3 947.7	83.3	26 346	96.8	564.4	2 871.6	25.1	15.9	74.7	13.1	7.0	26.0	17.6	457 234	467 087	436 455
Northampton............	393.6	52.7	18 452	67.8	108.6	191.6	D	17.2	D	5.0	D	12.2	23.4	33 039	32 299	31 809
Onslow	3 169.9	60.8	22 109	81.3	317.4	2 541.2	D	2.5	D	6.5	1.7	8.1	73.3	63 517	58 601	50 318

[1] Based on resident population estimated as of July 1, 1998. [2] Includes farm earnings; see table B-10 for these data. [3] Includes mining and construction, not shown separately. [4] Includes agricultural services, forestry, and fisheries; transportation and public utilities; and wholesale trade, not shown separately. [5] Finance, insurance, and real estate.

Source: Personal Income and Earnings—U.S. Bureau of Economic Analysis, "Regional Economic Information System (REIS) 1969-1998" on CD-ROM (related Internet site <http://www.bea.doc.gov/bea/regional/data.htm>).

[Includes U.S., states, and 3,142 counties/county equivalents defined as of January 1, 1992. For changes to these areas since January 1, 1992, see appendix B. Geographic Information]

County	Personal income, 1998													Manufacturing earnings		
		Per capita[1]				Earnings										
							Percent, by selected industry–									
							Goods-related		Service-related							
	Total (mil. dol.)	Percent change, 1990–1998	Amount (dollars)	Percent of national average	Transfer payments (mil. dol.)	Total[2] (mil. dol.)	Total[3]	Manufacturing	Total[4]	Retail trade	FIRE[5]	Services	Government	1998 ($1,000)	1997 ($1,000)	1996 ($1,000)
NORTH CAROLINA–Con.																
Orange	3 105.5	54.1	28 256	103.9	266.8	2 166.8	9.3	5.3	90.1	8.6	8.4	19.9	48.6	113 882	118 264	112 846
Pamlico	261.7	61.6	21 256	78.1	53.4	81.0	18.0	8.0	78.4	12.4	2.2	23.0	26.2	6 489	7 239	6 855
Pasquotank	696.9	50.7	19 581	72.0	139.6	455.8	11.0	5.7	88.0	12.1	4.5	17.3	44.0	25 810	26 230	30 515
Pender	729.7	78.6	18 535	68.1	146.9	263.7	D	13.1	D	9.3	D	16.4	25.4	34 600	33 381	32 638
Perquimans	197.1	51.9	17 609	64.7	50.5	61.0	D	D	D	9.4	D	16.7	29.7	D	2 572	2 406
Person	705.5	53.2	20 990	77.2	125.5	399.4	48.9	42.1	51.8	9.6	2.3	13.7	14.7	168 287	167 767	159 963
Pitt	2 883.6	61.0	22 772	83.7	419.9	2 002.7	D	18.0	D	10.6	4.1	19.5	31.1	360 316	366 984	365 302
Polk	478.7	58.4	28 614	105.2	81.4	136.7	30.3	22.0	D	9.5	4.3	30.4	17.3	30 138	29 196	27 608
Randolph	2 745.7	60.4	22 622	83.2	382.8	1 591.3	49.2	40.0	45.4	7.9	2.2	15.9	10.4	636 140	617 409	596 715
Richmond	866.6	42.7	18 845	69.3	224.7	508.0	31.4	25.9	62.1	10.7	2.7	18.6	17.9	131 754	141 145	141 531
Robeson	1 987.2	62.0	17 179	63.2	502.4	1 199.2	37.5	30.7	61.2	11.0	2.2	19.9	20.2	368 402	365 952	353 973
Rockingham	1 879.1	40.4	20 866	76.7	370.0	1 049.5	49.1	41.1	50.1	9.4	2.7	17.2	13.0	431 789	469 220	480 100
Rowan	2 700.5	52.2	21 594	79.4	437.7	1 636.0	41.7	34.2	57.0	10.4	2.3	17.6	17.3	558 716	511 381	486 724
Rutherford	1 229.5	50.6	20 183	74.2	240.9	784.8	D	44.9	D	9.0	2.6	15.8	12.7	352 537	342 392	338 662
Sampson	1 041.1	43.3	19 880	73.1	218.3	584.0	NA	22.9	54.5	8.5	2.2	13.0	19.2	133 701	131 008	124 816
Scotland	679.4	53.6	19 026	69.9	152.3	540.0	54.0	50.8	45.9	7.2	1.7	19.0	11.5	274 268	276 491	269 584
Stanly	1 211.0	48.0	21 689	79.7	204.9	686.9	47.2	38.8	49.7	10.2	2.4	17.2	13.5	266 676	248 589	237 985
Stokes	896.4	56.9	20 714	76.1	126.0	252.4	33.4	17.9	62.3	9.7	2.6	19.6	21.2	45 211	46 309	47 341
Surry	1 475.4	46.4	21 939	80.6	268.0	1 091.7	D	33.5	D	9.9	2.3	12.6	12.4	365 979	370 971	355 423
Swain	198.1	65.6	16 156	59.4	56.7	139.8	D	6.6	D	16.7	1.6	43.8	24.8	9 246	7 767	7 749
Transylvania	665.2	57.9	23 378	85.9	128.9	379.2	D	40.2	D	7.9	3.8	20.2	11.2	152 553	151 464	141 357
Tyrrell	62.0	18.6	15 475	56.9	17.2	24.0	12.6	9.5	87.6	12.1	3.0	14.4	44.2	2 281	2 273	1 898
Union	2 454.6	70.9	22 277	81.9	277.7	1 467.6	D	30.5	D	9.1	D	12.3	11.6	447 730	422 762	395 903
Vance	799.4	42.2	19 008	69.9	182.6	503.1	D	27.7	D	17.5	3.1	19.4	18.4	139 602	138 701	132 883
Wake	19 266.3	99.3	33 780	124.2	1 299.2	14 476.6	16.4	8.2	83.4	9.3	9.2	31.1	17.5	1 192 782	1 097 764	1 042 767
Warren	297.9	52.3	15 874	58.4	81.5	130.1	24.7	19.1	61.3	6.9	1.7	17.6	29.0	24 882	23 063	22 488
Washington	248.4	29.3	18 366	67.5	63.5	98.6	16.1	8.4	78.6	11.4	2.6	16.8	36.3	8 303	7 698	7 911
Watauga	858.8	61.5	20 996	77.2	118.9	585.3	D	7.1	D	15.4	5.2	27.5	27.1	41 372	39 791	35 444
Wayne	2 204.6	48.1	19 710	72.5	405.0	1 542.9	D	15.0	D	9.4	4.4	18.6	32.9	231 088	224 465	220 252
Wilkes	1 381.5	48.5	22 014	80.9	235.1	882.7	D	26.6	D	20.2	6.1	11.7	14.5	235 035	230 712	213 069
Wilson	1 625.8	50.1	23 823	87.6	288.8	1 250.7	D	28.6	D	8.7	7.5	17.4	14.8	358 274	325 834	306 205
Yadkin	762.7	57.1	21 860	80.4	121.3	328.2	46.0	34.4	48.2	10.5	1.8	14.3	13.5	112 889	116 004	100 625
Yancey	303.7	58.8	18 308	67.3	74.6	144.6	D	30.4	D	10.9	2.2	14.7	17.2	43 950	41 905	39 513
NORTH DAKOTA	14 600.4	44.3	22 892	84.2	2 292.5	10 196.3	16.6	8.0	77.9	9.5	5.6	25.0	20.8	818 283	754 696	686 991
Adams	50.2	14.6	18 543	68.2	13.3	25.7	D	1.9	D	14.7	3.7	45.3	16.6	499	556	487
Barnes	241.4	19.2	20 187	74.2	48.5	131.8	D	9.0	D	9.8	6.3	23.8	20.7	11 824	10 573	8 075
Benson	99.3	5.7	14 494	53.3	31.0	51.5	D	10.1	D	4.7	5.1	35.9	26.1	5 188	5 965	5 657
Billings	14.7	20.5	13 748	50.5	2.5	8.3	D	–	D	D	NA	D	40.0	–	–	–
Bottineau	152.1	18.7	20 837	76.6	32.0	73.9	D	2.5	D	11.8	4.9	20.6	20.2	1 875	1 612	1 577
Bowman	75.0	31.2	22 700	83.4	14.7	41.4	D	1.6	D	11.3	4.2	22.3	14.2	653	622	936
Burke	50.6	3.8	22 301	82.0	11.6	21.4	D	D	D	7.9	5.8	D	32.3	D	204	242
Burleigh	1 680.5	57.3	25 117	92.3	225.6	1 268.7	13.5	6.0	86.1	10.6	6.3	32.7	21.6	76 201	72 563	65 515
Cass	3 172.2	69.2	27 139	99.8	319.6	2 650.7	17.5	9.6	80.7	9.4	9.1	29.8	13.1	254 862	230 099	205 081
Cavalier	118.3	34.2	23 550	86.6	21.4	56.5	10.5	1.3	D	D	7.2	18.6	15.9	750	795	833
Dickey	116.8	26.7	20 654	75.9	26.3	66.1	13.0	9.5	63.2	8.5	2.8	22.8	11.4	6 267	4 969	3 940
Divide	55.4	37.9	23 380	85.9	11.3	25.6	D	D	D	7.6	4.7	23.3	18.0	D	318	290
Dunn	50.5	26.6	14 221	52.3	13.3	20.7	D	D	D	10.7	4.0	D	30.4	D	2 164	1 539
Eddy	51.7	8.5	18 140	66.7	14.3	24.6	D	D	D	8.7	5.5	22.1	19.7	D	1 084	D
Emmons	79.7	53.2	18 396	67.6	19.1	40.5	7.3	1.1	D	8.2	D	18.5	16.7	432	426	570
Foster	88.4	34.0	23 201	85.3	16.5	56.6	D	D	D	8.8	3.7	20.3	12.5	D	7 088	5 848
Golden Valley	30.0	1.3	16 234	59.7	7.6	12.6	D	D	D	11.3	7.4	31.8	30.0	D	239	500
Grand Forks	1 558.6	39.6	23 339	85.8	181.6	1 245.6	D	4.2	D	10.3	3.5	22.4	35.6	52 020	48 931	48 714
Grant	41.2	35.4	13 912	51.1	13.5	16.0	D	4.6	D	8.6	7.9	28.4	28.7	734	688	647
Griggs	65.8	18.3	23 128	85.0	13.2	38.5	9.8	8.1	60.9	6.9	3.8	13.8	13.1	3 102	3 196	2 755
Hettinger	61.0	41.1	20 997	77.2	14.1	31.1	D	2.8	D	4.4	3.9	13.0	18.1	863	877	692
Kidder	54.1	29.1	18 773	69.0	13.0	25.4	D	1.1	D	6.0	5.7	9.9	19.6	270	D	389
LaMoure	100.9	24.5	21 138	77.7	20.6	50.9	D	4.0	D	5.5	5.8	11.2	16.5	2 057	1 906	1 328
Logan	46.0	7.1	19 600	72.1	11.3	20.3	D	D	D	7.1	6.4	15.5	19.6	D	238	314
McHenry	105.1	21.2	17 310	63.6	27.9	40.7	D	D	D	6.6	3.5	12.1	26.2	D	2 933	2 644
McIntosh	72.2	34.6	20 892	76.8	21.1	33.3	10.2	6.1	74.3	9.1	6.1	30.7	14.5	2 046	1 777	1 578
McKenzie	106.7	31.9	18 781	69.0	21.3	69.5	D	1.3	D	4.2	3.7	32.0	19.5	936	845	758
McLean	206.3	30.0	21 246	78.1	44.0	114.4	D	1.1	D	5.3	3.6	13.1	18.5	1 263	1 255	1 261
Mercer	211.3	28.6	22 476	82.6	29.2	179.4	29.5	.6	72.3	4.8	1.6	10.2	9.1	1 063	1 076	1 287
Morton	505.3	56.0	20 533	75.5	96.4	265.0	D	13.2	D	11.6	4.2	21.9	15.5	34 854	32 284	31 610
Mountrail	137.8	39.5	20 907	76.9	30.8	76.1	D	D	D	7.1	6.6	15.2	20.1	D	3 420	2 388
Nelson	81.1	1.5	21 779	80.1	22.2	35.7	D	D	D	8.1	8.0	21.8	18.8	D	454	418
Oliver	39.6	47.7	17 962	66.0	6.1	30.5	D	.9	D	2.2	D	4.8	10.5	284	250	241
Pembina	250.6	48.6	29 538	108.6	33.8	188.8	D	22.3	D	6.1	D	9.4	12.0	42 095	38 105	35 872
Pierce	95.5	13.4	20 551	75.5	22.2	52.3	D	7.3	D	9.9	6.1	30.0	12.5	3 819	3 289	2 991

[1] Based on resident population estimated as of July 1, 1998.   [2] Includes farm earnings; see table B-10 for these data.   [3] Includes mining and construction, not shown separately.   [4] Includes agricultural services, forestry, and fisheries; transportation and public utilities; and wholesale trade, not shown separately.   [5] Finance, insurance, and real estate.

Source: Personal Income and Earnings–U.S. Bureau of Economic Analysis, "Regional Economic Information System (REIS) 1969-1998" on CD-ROM (related Internet site <http://www.bea.doc.gov/bea/regional/data.htm>).

Table B–8. Counties — **Personal Income and Earnings**–Con.

[Includes U.S., states, and 3,142 counties/county equivalents defined as of January 1, 1992. For changes to these areas since January 1, 1992, see appendix B. Geographic Information]

County	Personal income, 1998													Manufacturing earnings		
		Per capita[1]				Earnings										
								Percent, by selected industry–								
							Goods-related		Service-related							
	Total (mil. dol.)	Percent change, 1990–1998	Amount (dollars)	Percent of national average	Transfer payments (mil. dol.)	Total[2] (mil. dol.)	Total[3]	Man-ufac-turing	Total[4]	Retail trade	FIRE[5]	Serv-ices	Gov-ern-ment	1998 ($1,000)	1997 ($1,000)	1996 ($1,000)
NORTH DAKOTA—Con.																
Ramsey	272.8	32.3	22 525	82.8	53.3	160.7	D	3.7	D	15.6	6.6	25.4	23.7	5 881	5 923	5 506
Ransom	122.2	35.0	21 145	77.7	25.9	65.6	14.4	10.1	68.0	8.4	4.0	18.0	15.9	6 622	5 839	4 875
Renville	60.2	22.1	21 397	78.7	11.8	31.5	8.8	1.0	D	7.7	2.5	16.1	17.2	304	283	309
Richland	391.5	46.7	21 633	79.5	59.5	281.4	D	28.8	D	6.6	2.4	14.9	13.2	81 157	80 261	74 195
Rolette	207.3	57.9	14 654	53.9	67.0	127.5	D	7.5	D	8.9	4.7	33.3	37.6	9 533	10 662	10 150
Sargent	106.2	32.2	23 884	87.8	15.0	92.2	D	D	D	3.4	2.1	3.7	6.9	D	49 402	45 440
Sheridan	33.7	22.7	19 942	73.3	9.1	14.5	D	D	D	5.8	4.8	5.3	18.8	D	213	246
Sioux	42.9	43.0	10 341	38.0	16.2	34.5	D	D	D	3.7	D	60.8	37.8	D	–	–
Slope	12.3	59.7	13 927	51.2	2.4	5.8	D	D	D	D	–	D	11.1	D	D	D
Stark	475.0	47.8	20 921	76.9	84.0	306.2	25.0	9.2	D	12.7	D	25.0	16.5	28 260	24 518	20 232
Steele	51.0	20.9	22 907	84.2	8.2	26.9	12.0	6.8	D	5.0	5.0	D	13.7	1 839	1 784	1 546
Stutsman	495.5	33.2	23 614	86.8	88.5	326.2	D	15.6	D	10.2	4.8	21.9	18.0	50 819	42 586	35 007
Towner	64.9	30.8	21 537	79.2	13.9	32.7	D	16.4	D	8.6	5.2	22.2	14.5	5 375	5 132	4 660
Traill	193.1	37.7	22 619	83.1	33.6	117.3	D	D	D	6.7	4.3	13.8	15.0	D	11 460	11 065
Walsh	289.5	37.7	21 356	78.5	52.4	181.2	D	5.0	62.6	6.6	3.9	15.3	18.8	8 977	5 748	5 664
Ward	1 375.5	44.4	23 497	86.4	194.6	990.3	9.4	2.1	88.5	10.7	3.5	25.3	16.2	21 060	21 915	21 105
Wells	112.7	10.2	21 633	79.5	26.3	53.7	D	1.0	D	11.3	5.3	22.7	15.2	514	493	673
Williams	428.2	34.5	21 242	78.1	80.5	258.0	22.4	2.5	74.9	11.3	4.2	27.5	16.2	6 406	7 373	8 307
OHIO	292 999.2	43.5	26 073	95.8	42 197.2	208 359.9	31.4	25.5	68.1	9.2	6.8	24.8	14.6	53 090 841	51 501 318	49 364 389
Adams	449.5	58.6	15 735	57.8	123.7	215.9	D	15.8	D	12.3	3.0	14.1	21.9	34 186	32 163	30 243
Allen	2 391.1	31.0	22 295	82.0	402.2	1 873.2	36.0	29.5	64.1	9.9	3.0	24.4	14.2	552 004	536 939	536 728
Ashland	1 053.6	45.0	20 405	75.0	159.2	640.8	44.2	38.4	55.2	8.7	2.2	23.0	15.6	246 021	245 906	230 203
Ashtabula	2 190.9	45.6	21 221	78.0	450.5	1 122.9	42.1	35.0	57.7	9.9	2.7	19.3	15.6	392 727	378 224	367 720
Athens	1 075.7	47.5	17 459	64.2	200.3	653.4	8.0	3.9	92.1	11.2	3.2	17.8	54.1	25 189	24 501	23 422
Auglaize	1 129.6	44.0	24 012	88.3	154.9	721.1	56.4	49.2	41.1	7.7	2.4	12.7	13.0	354 761	336 844	328 577
Belmont	1 411.9	37.9	19 648	72.2	344.6	650.8	24.0	10.2	76.2	17.8	4.5	22.9	20.1	66 221	53 321	63 028
Brown	827.0	64.9	20 265	74.5	142.9	260.2	NA	21.7	66.5	9.6	2.6	20.5	25.3	56 522	52 878	48 024
Butler	8 395.4	57.7	25 372	93.3	1 008.6	4 481.8	33.8	25.4	66.3	10.4	7.1	19.6	15.2	1 138 257	1 071 298	1 039 818
Carroll	600.4	64.0	20 640	75.9	96.3	243.2	39.7	32.2	46.9	9.0	2.5	12.6	12.2	78 387	69 940	71 774
Champaign	902.8	46.8	23 543	86.5	127.3	397.2	48.0	42.4	47.0	8.5	3.4	13.7	15.2	168 382	175 505	142 084
Clark	3 467.5	38.2	23 870	87.7	614.8	2 064.3	D	35.1	D	10.3	3.5	21.5	14.1	723 623	650 192	613 060
Clermont	4 364.3	71.7	24 828	91.3	502.9	1 739.6	D	21.8	D	14.2	4.8	20.6	14.1	379 918	356 882	348 572
Clinton	1 008.0	78.8	25 114	92.3	135.8	870.6	D	21.6	D	6.0	3.4	10.9	11.6	187 649	174 606	159 234
Columbiana	2 282.4	42.1	20 487	75.3	454.9	1 139.1	36.8	27.8	61.7	9.7	3.3	20.4	15.6	316 391	305 570	293 593
Coshocton	740.3	44.6	20 491	75.3	140.5	461.8	44.5	38.5	53.0	7.1	2.4	18.6	11.6	177 583	176 411	169 216
Crawford	1 019.8	39.4	21 614	79.5	187.3	571.0	D	43.9	D	8.0	4.2	16.3	12.8	250 690	234 822	218 541
Cuyahoga	42 580.7	30.7	30 846	113.4	6 401.4	36 123.7	25.5	20.9	74.5	7.1	9.5	31.8	12.3	7 556 191	7 372 054	7 129 753
Darke	1 245.1	44.9	23 026	84.6	179.8	647.6	D	34.9	D	8.7	3.8	17.4	11.2	225 924	225 979	219 343
Defiance	953.9	39.1	23 944	88.0	126.5	759.4	NA	54.4	40.0	4.3	2.9	13.2	9.0	413 428	428 132	418 907
Delaware	3 301.2	122.1	33 614	123.6	227.0	1 136.2	29.2	19.6	69.9	11.4	7.1	25.4	15.3	222 903	197 312	181 042
Erie	2 106.0	49.4	26 922	99.0	300.4	1 433.9	41.8	36.2	57.6	9.2	3.0	24.8	13.1	519 508	515 654	502 119
Fairfield	3 145.4	69.3	25 376	93.3	362.7	1 083.3	28.7	21.1	71.4	12.6	6.2	21.4	22.6	229 080	221 765	216 942
Fayette	561.9	48.2	19 712	72.5	103.8	293.6	D	31.4	D	19.8	3.4	13.8	17.7	92 123	94 773	90 256
Franklin	30 060.3	51.8	29 425	108.2	3 236.0	27 567.8	17.2	12.1	82.8	11.9	12.6	27.3	17.2	3 326 498	3 196 022	2 995 974
Fulton	1 028.2	49.0	24 598	90.4	133.0	712.3	NA	48.5	D	6.8	2.4	12.1	11.4	345 270	332 537	294 387
Gallia	613.8	50.2	18 478	67.9	167.4	373.7	15.3	10.6	D	11.8	3.3	28.6	18.5	39 754	36 397	31 420
Geauga	2 902.7	57.4	32 765	120.4	241.4	1 178.6	43.6	33.3	56.4	8.0	3.7	22.1	10.6	392 007	371 295	348 058
Greene	3 798.2	51.9	25 674	94.4	414.6	2 691.1	11.5	7.9	88.0	8.7	2.7	19.1	52.5	211 617	193 431	178 394
Guernsey	727.6	38.0	17 781	65.4	174.9	439.2	31.5	23.3	68.9	11.0	3.5	22.0	21.2	102 405	101 845	99 880
Hamilton	26 863.3	36.8	31 708	116.6	3 331.7	25 043.3	28.0	23.0	72.0	7.5	9.1	28.7	10.8	5 752 435	5 402 259	5 155 010
Hancock	1 871.0	50.4	27 112	99.7	205.7	1 436.4	D	36.9	D	10.1	3.4	18.4	8.3	530 306	511 508	495 291
Hardin	615.8	44.0	19 431	71.4	106.3	324.2	D	35.2	D	7.9	2.5	21.0	15.1	114 054	98 952	92 449
Harrison	285.9	45.0	17 736	65.2	71.2	118.4	38.3	19.1	61.5	7.6	2.8	16.0	20.4	22 617	23 162	23 251
Henry	696.5	42.5	23 308	85.7	100.8	408.9	D	39.0	D	7.4	2.5	12.6	15.5	159 403	167 600	168 879
Highland	748.5	62.4	18 516	68.1	148.2	373.3	42.1	32.3	55.6	11.6	4.0	14.1	18.1	120 570	128 552	103 498
Hocking	545.2	56.0	18 848	69.3	104.6	232.4	D	34.2	D	8.8	3.1	13.6	24.6	79 428	81 361	74 400
Holmes	648.0	65.7	17 120	62.9	81.9	494.5	D	39.6	D	9.6	2.4	13.5	9.2	195 795	182 257	176 202
Huron	1 335.4	41.0	22 177	81.5	208.0	930.9	50.6	40.9	46.8	7.7	2.1	13.4	10.2	380 919	376 645	358 225
Jackson	573.0	49.4	17 591	64.7	129.9	334.3	D	36.2	D	12.4	3.6	12.3	14.6	120 992	113 539	102 458
Jefferson	1 442.3	17.6	19 335	71.1	384.7	846.7	29.8	23.3	70.0	10.3	3.1	26.1	15.3	197 190	121 035	193 285
Knox	1 102.4	54.2	20 644	75.9	209.9	635.9	41.2	30.0	55.6	8.2	2.7	23.2	15.0	190 959	197 576	185 667
Lake	6 427.5	43.7	28 337	104.2	803.1	3 672.6	D	35.8	D	9.8	4.1	19.5	12.3	1 313 497	1 280 686	1 210 888
Lawrence	1 097.8	37.7	17 035	62.6	301.5	390.4	D	18.6	D	13.4	2.9	18.0	29.0	72 563	70 971	72 010
Licking	3 480.9	59.2	25 791	94.8	445.2	1 817.9	32.5	24.3	65.4	12.9	7.5	20.4	14.5	441 775	437 824	420 391
Logan	1 122.1	59.9	24 205	89.0	159.9	759.4	48.5	42.1	48.5	7.3	2.8	17.0	9.7	319 442	302 141	277 428
Lorain	6 963.7	48.2	24 719	90.9	993.0	3 956.7	D	38.4	D	8.3	3.0	18.7	15.1	1 519 261	1 466 324	1 481 396
Lucas	11 814.8	33.7	26 335	96.8	1 940.8	9 248.3	30.1	23.2	69.6	9.0	5.1	28.9	14.1	2 142 548	2 277 305	2 123 302
Madison	872.5	56.1	21 235	78.1	119.4	433.2	D	27.4	D	8.4	2.6	15.8	27.3	118 881	112 455	101 106
Mahoning	5 918.5	31.5	23 183	85.2	1 249.8	3 624.4	21.1	13.4	78.6	12.8	5.7	29.8	15.9	485 719	494 715	453 289

[1] Based on resident population estimated as of July 1, 1998. [2] Includes farm earnings; see table B-10 for these data. [3] Includes mining and construction, not shown separately. [4] Includes agricultural services, forestry, and fisheries; transportation and public utilities; and wholesale trade, not shown separately. [5] Finance, insurance, and real estate.

Source: Personal Income and Earnings—U.S. Bureau of Economic Analysis, "Regional Economic Information System (REIS) 1969-1998" on CD-ROM (related Internet site <http://www.bea.doc.gov/bea/regional/data.htm>).

[Includes U.S., states, and 3,142 counties/county equivalents defined as of January 1, 1992. For changes to these areas since January 1, 1992, see appendix B. Geographic Information]

County	Personal income, 1998 Total (mil. dol.)	Percent change, 1990–1998	Per capita[1] Amount (dollars)	Per capita[1] Percent of national average	Transfer payments (mil. dol.)	Earnings Total[2] (mil. dol.)	Goods-related Total[3]	Goods-related Manufacturing	Service-related Total[4]	Service-related Retail trade	Service-related FIRE[5]	Service-related Services	Government	Manufacturing earnings 1998 ($1,000)	Manufacturing earnings 1997 ($1,000)	Manufacturing earnings 1996 ($1,000)
OHIO—Con.																
Marion	1 448.0	45.7	21 583	79.3	253.6	945.6	33.7	28.8	65.5	9.4	2.9	17.7	21.7	272 596	267 186	270 759
Medina	3 981.2	66.4	27 675	101.7	416.4	1 811.5	33.7	25.1	65.6	10.8	7.2	23.2	12.4	454 007	406 069	379 846
Meigs	382.1	39.7	15 951	58.6	100.5	196.3	D	2.9	D	11.4	2.5	D	17.3	5 785	5 683	5 976
Mercer	961.9	41.8	23 406	86.0	131.7	574.7	D	28.3	D	8.2	4.3	11.3	13.8	162 627	157 963	145 643
Miami	2 630.8	54.7	26 788	98.5	321.1	1 557.8	D	40.0	D	10.3	3.7	20.4	11.1	622 356	622 676	597 316
Monroe	265.3	29.7	17 251	63.4	61.6	193.9	D	56.4	D	4.9	2.0	D	14.1	109 322	105 111	111 110
Montgomery	15 509.7	36.3	27 203	100.0	2 163.7	12 358.2	33.3	28.5	66.7	7.4	5.0	28.1	14.1	3 515 918	3 541 489	3 382 142
Morgan	260.8	28.3	17 952	66.0	60.6	145.4	D	22.5	D	5.6	2.2	8.1	14.7	32 738	33 909	31 821
Morrow	543.6	47.6	17 286	63.5	88.8	189.6	34.3	24.9	60.2	9.1	2.7	16.8	23.1	47 205	46 944	47 613
Muskingum	1 790.5	43.2	21 155	77.8	333.6	1 153.8	32.8	25.0	67.3	12.2	3.2	24.8	14.1	288 351	268 417	270 961
Noble	199.9	46.1	13 564	49.9	43.8	106.3	D	28.8	D	8.5	3.1	12.9	35.0	D	24 309	22 009
Ottawa	1 076.2	41.6	26 242	96.5	174.7	529.0	31.9	24.6	67.2	11.2	3.5	16.5	15.6	130 362	119 647	114 881
Paulding	395.7	31.8	19 703	72.4	62.3	165.3	D	34.8	D	8.5	2.3	11.2	22.1	57 596	57 062	54 472
Perry	541.4	37.3	15 821	58.2	129.0	221.5	40.9	26.1	57.5	7.6	2.6	14.9	21.8	57 732	55 874	50 617
Pickaway	1 053.7	52.2	19 777	72.7	149.1	615.4	D	39.4	D	7.9	2.6	9.9	26.7	242 432	234 370	233 555
Pike	494.6	65.7	17 836	65.6	123.6	405.1	D	57.6	D	7.5	1.2	11.3	13.5	233 343	228 271	220 583
Portage	3 521.9	50.6	23 350	85.8	457.1	1 917.8	36.8	29.8	62.6	8.8	2.5	15.2	26.1	571 026	536 887	477 760
Preble	934.8	48.5	21 681	79.7	138.7	385.7	D	37.1	D	9.1	2.8	14.4	16.4	143 110	132 369	159 353
Putnam	839.5	46.3	23 820	87.6	104.7	392.2	D	40.6	D	8.4	D	10.9	14.0	159 393	150 963	149 890
Richland	2 833.3	33.6	21 846	80.3	485.6	2 082.7	D	34.5	D	9.8	3.7	19.7	14.7	719 424	710 998	676 307
Ross	1 474.8	51.3	19 557	71.9	252.5	982.8	D	28.8	D	10.9	2.3	17.3	26.9	282 599	263 824	246 364
Sandusky	1 403.9	34.1	22 615	83.1	222.5	928.5	NA	43.7	D	8.5	2.8	18.2	12.7	406 197	383 570	382 294
Scioto	1 468.3	42.7	18 178	66.8	418.3	764.3	20.8	14.0	79.2	12.9	3.6	27.8	25.1	107 145	92 005	86 660
Seneca	1 261.7	29.6	21 036	77.3	243.2	741.7	D	38.3	D	8.8	3.1	18.7	14.3	283 914	275 598	267 189
Shelby	1 198.6	51.9	25 209	92.7	143.9	1 085.8	65.1	59.3	33.4	4.2	1.4	11.5	8.4	644 129	614 117	569 854
Stark	9 287.4	40.8	24 898	91.5	1 472.9	6 097.0	39.6	32.2	60.1	10.6	4.6	22.9	11.4	1 966 008	1 868 741	1 789 948
Summit	15 008.1	47.7	27 940	102.7	2 158.6	10 202.9	31.6	25.9	68.4	9.7	5.4	25.7	12.7	2 640 857	2 512 451	2 510 563
Trumbull	5 492.4	34.3	24 264	89.2	970.8	3 800.0	54.1	50.3	45.8	8.9	3.0	15.9	10.3	1 913 251	2 053 220	2 002 447
Tuscarawas	1 845.7	43.7	20 845	76.6	316.3	1 140.6	39.6	31.2	58.3	11.9	3.4	18.2	13.6	355 594	345 704	353 315
Union	924.9	52.8	23 191	85.3	97.1	1 193.7	D	68.6	D	3.5	D	7.7	8.1	818 614	774 864	674 288
Van Wert	662.5	34.4	22 025	81.0	96.6	400.4	D	46.4	D	8.0	6.1	15.5	11.0	185 737	182 040	169 230
Vinton	193.6	46.0	15 916	58.5	47.2	71.1	D	D	D	7.9	5.6	12.9	30.1	D	19 867	18 848
Warren	3 956.9	87.0	27 097	99.6	397.2	1 828.9	34.9	27.3	65.0	13.6	7.1	19.6	14.1	499 550	448 611	406 810
Washington	1 366.7	44.4	21 586	79.4	244.6	862.6	38.4	28.4	61.0	9.7	3.7	23.3	13.3	245 224	234 633	226 368
Wayne	2 542.3	49.2	23 079	84.8	350.1	1 732.5	46.6	38.2	49.6	8.7	4.1	14.0	14.0	661 343	652 596	612 629
Williams	924.8	45.1	24 428	89.8	129.2	642.5	D	51.3	D	6.4	3.1	15.0	10.6	329 922	303 874	286 136
Wood	3 064.0	45.6	25 624	94.2	345.7	1 991.5	38.8	32.3	59.9	7.7	3.2	15.6	20.7	644 162	626 117	567 411
Wyandot	497.9	43.1	21 817	80.2	79.3	315.7	53.7	42.2	44.0	7.0	2.6	9.8	12.2	133 305	133 224	132 684
OKLAHOMA	73 349.9	43.7	21 964	80.7	11 445.4	51 096.2	25.9	16.0	72.8	9.4	5.3	24.0	20.5	8 151 721	7 724 507	7 314 517
Adair	319.9	54.7	15 678	57.6	75.4	155.3	D	32.4	D	7.4	1.9	11.9	21.2	50 353	47 605	42 953
Alfalfa	107.9	3.8	17 904	65.8	23.9	57.7	7.3	2.4	D	7.8	3.8	10.7	23.8	1 406	1 291	1 366
Atoka	190.8	60.4	14 343	52.7	50.1	104.0	D	15.9	D	13.1	2.4	10.9	35.0	16 495	13 221	12 250
Beaver	117.5	19.7	19 431	71.4	18.7	58.4	25.5	5.0	D	4.8	2.7	7.3	23.9	2 931	2 542	1 854
Beckham	322.9	35.1	16 184	59.5	70.8	185.3	23.8	4.3	74.7	16.5	4.5	28.6	15.3	7 913	4 693	3 021
Blaine	205.3	30.8	19 706	72.4	44.0	106.7	26.9	19.7	57.0	7.7	3.8	13.9	24.2	21 002	20 408	19 669
Bryan	619.6	57.8	17 848	65.6	144.1	323.1	D	11.8	D	11.3	3.5	34.2	21.9	38 187	32 259	29 585
Caddo	500.7	28.7	16 215	59.6	111.9	267.8	D	2.9	D	7.6	3.9	20.2	26.2	7 699	7 310	7 668
Canadian	1 872.2	54.4	21 917	80.6	215.5	776.0	41.5	30.8	57.5	9.7	3.1	15.3	22.2	239 387	236 351	214 859
Carter	946.8	40.9	21 344	78.5	183.1	697.0	41.6	19.2	58.9	11.9	3.3	21.5	11.8	133 591	128 279	132 550
Cherokee	643.0	36.0	16 480	60.6	146.7	345.5	D	1.0	D	11.2	2.9	26.5	36.1	3 592	3 396	3 477
Choctaw	230.1	32.2	15 237	56.0	74.5	103.8	D	1.9	84.1	14.1	3.0	22.3	27.7	1 978	2 740	4 486
Cimarron	63.1	-3.5	21 098	77.6	10.6	36.2	D	1.6	D	9.3	3.3	7.5	25.9	573	553	675
Cleveland	4 261.2	52.8	21 203	77.9	439.8	1 718.1	16.6	8.1	83.6	13.2	4.8	23.3	35.6	139 764	123 995	116 656
Coal	80.7	39.1	13 386	49.2	26.0	32.2	D	D	D	10.6	D	25.1	31.4	D	9 190	8 527
Comanche	2 298.8	35.4	21 257	78.1	323.2	1 747.2	D	10.0	D	7.3	2.8	13.2	57.6	174 225	164 397	154 311
Cotton	119.0	18.1	17 924	65.9	25.3	40.3	D	2.5	D	7.9	3.8	15.3	27.7	1 014	940	907
Craig	260.5	48.0	18 008	66.2	67.6	179.1	D	18.0	D	9.4	3.5	16.2	33.1	32 263	29 713	24 556
Creek	1 165.0	40.3	17 358	63.8	218.4	562.8	41.4	29.7	59.4	8.4	3.6	17.8	15.3	167 389	165 320	166 421
Custer	489.4	24.6	19 140	70.4	89.1	308.8	22.0	13.5	74.7	11.8	4.3	19.9	26.2	41 691	44 135	50 168
Delaware	609.0	70.2	17 753	65.3	131.8	222.4	21.3	12.6	64.0	12.8	4.9	24.6	18.0	28 012	17 770	17 192
Dewey	95.0	8.2	19 306	71.0	19.8	47.2	D	5.5	D	6.8	4.5	13.3	29.6	2 608	2 418	2 275
Ellis	82.1	15.4	19 335	71.1	16.9	37.0	D	2.1	D	11.5	D	13.0	35.6	772	755	753
Garfield	1 293.7	32.4	22 720	83.5	254.3	830.7	19.6	8.2	77.9	10.0	4.0	23.6	23.9	68 511	65 313	54 188
Garvin	525.2	40.1	19 590	72.0	163.5	261.2	33.3	12.5	67.7	11.4	3.8	12.3	25.8	32 576	31 774	29 238
Grady	781.6	44.3	17 078	62.8	137.7	390.1	35.0	25.9	61.8	9.6	3.3	18.6	19.6	100 880	93 791	88 549
Grant	118.5	10.1	22 204	81.6	22.9	59.6	11.4	1.7	D	3.5	4.8	D	17.4	990	765	776
Greer	125.3	31.7	19 704	72.4	30.0	59.2	4.8	3.2	D	5.5	2.8	12.3	43.4	1 888	1 626	1 601
Harmon	61.7	14.2	17 736	65.2	17.3	31.1	D	6.9	D	8.3	5.2	7.9	30.4	2 137	2 142	1 764
Harper	85.2	12.3	23 708	87.2	14.8	42.7	15.6	1.6	D	6.7	4.3	12.2	26.8	667	587	706

[1] Based on resident population estimated as of July 1, 1998.   [2] Includes farm earnings; see table B-10 for these data.   [3] Includes mining and construction, not shown separately.   [4] Includes agricultural services, forestry, and fisheries; transportation and public utilities; and wholesale trade, not shown separately.   [5] Finance, insurance, and real estate.

Source: Personal Income and Earnings—U.S. Bureau of Economic Analysis, "Regional Economic Information System (REIS) 1969-1998" on CD-ROM (related Internet site <http://www.bea.doc.gov/bea/regional/data.htm>).

[Includes U.S., states, and 3,142 counties/county equivalents defined as of January 1, 1992. For changes to these areas since January 1, 1992, see appendix B. Geographic Information]

County	Personal income, 1998 Total (mil. dol.)	Per capita Percent change, 1990–1998	Per capita Amount (dollars)	Per capita Percent of national average	Transfer payments (mil. dol.)	Earnings Total[2] (mil. dol.)	Goods-related Total[3]	Goods-related Manufacturing	Service-related Total[4]	Service-related Retail trade	Service-related FIRE[5]	Service-related Services	Service-related Government	Manufacturing earnings 1998 ($1,000)	Manufacturing earnings 1997 ($1,000)	Manufacturing earnings 1996 ($1,000)
OKLAHOMA—Con.																
Haskell	181.8	46.0	16 009	58.9	52.0	78.9	18.3	4.0	76.5	12.8	2.3	21.8	28.3	3 136	2 369	2 107
Hughes	204.5	38.1	14 499	53.3	63.5	79.7	10.0	1.5	79.8	12.9	3.2	18.7	33.4	1 170	873	786
Jackson	562.2	32.5	19 700	72.4	94.7	423.9	D	6.6	D	8.2	3.0	12.1	56.8	27 933	23 583	18 566
Jefferson	116.0	31.1	17 630	64.8	31.8	56.1	D	19.3	65.8	13.9	4.5	13.4	23.6	10 856	11 028	10 432
Johnston	144.7	48.6	14 046	51.6	42.9	79.4	D	D	D	6.9	.9	12.8	29.0	D	19 101	16 837
Kay	1 037.3	21.8	22 273	81.9	175.0	724.9	D	27.1	D	10.2	2.7	D	11.8	196 198	188 609	180 770
Kingfisher	292.7	43.6	21 715	79.8	45.7	190.2	25.1	7.5	66.6	8.2	3.5	14.8	12.2	14 289	13 436	12 993
Kiowa	189.8	18.3	17 789	65.4	51.0	94.0	D	D	8.4	4.0	17.2	27.0		D	9 748	8 362
Latimer	181.8	52.3	17 093	05.0	49.2	108.2	30.2	7.9	05.8	5.4	1.7	12.0	09.0	0 590	0 490	7 007
Le Flore	789.5	52.1	16 919	62.2	190.0	368.6	D	16.6	D	10.3	4.2	14.5	25.7	61 269	56 132	49 450
Lincoln	563.0	49.5	17 976	66.1	98.8	189.2	20.9	9.2	82.0	11.0	11.6	18.3	20.4	17 402	18 420	23 101
Logan	617.1	48.5	20 509	75.4	96.7	199.2	19.9	5.2	78.2	10.6	4.6	24.9	27.6	10 268	9 530	10 209
Love	134.9	28.2	15 774	58.0	31.2	49.8	D	29.4	D	13.8	2.6	16.8	23.2	14 674	13 470	11 358
McClain	492.9	50.1	18 809	69.1	76.7	180.3	31.2	11.3	67.4	16.1	4.6	14.2	23.3	20 398	18 088	18 019
McCurtain	598.6	57.7	17 210	63.3	141.0	411.1	D	33.6	D	7.8	2.1	16.0	17.4	138 241	124 560	115 346
McIntosh	292.4	51.8	15 386	56.6	92.3	105.6	13.8	8.0	88.9	19.0	4.8	29.7	24.8	8 425	9 846	9 613
Major	147.3	27.6	18 874	69.4	26.2	83.8	D	7.0	D	8.3	3.7	13.8	15.6	5 880	5 382	4 951
Marshall	204.6	50.2	16 697	61.4	57.2	103.7	D	32.2	D	12.0	3.6	15.4	19.6	33 351	32 262	31 597
Mayes	685.2	53.2	18 205	66.9	140.1	358.9	D	38.2	D	9.5	2.7	13.6	20.5	137 123	127 901	120 173
Murray	206.1	43.2	16 720	61.5	52.8	105.4	D	7.5	D	13.2	3.1	17.6	34.6	7 900	7 479	6 540
Muskogee	1 299.3	44.8	18 538	68.1	292.1	924.9	29.3	20.3	71.0	10.0	3.0	18.7	26.6	187 396	177 600	165 303
Noble	221.6	38.5	19 503	71.7	40.2	143.8	D	D	D	7.9	3.2	11.3	17.0	D	57 379	50 275
Nowata	161.6	27.9	16 188	59.5	40.3	56.2	D	17.9	D	7.3	5.1	22.5	25.1	10 048	9 278	8 602
Okfuskee	168.2	42.3	14 767	54.3	51.6	76.1	28.6	6.9	70.7	8.8	3.4	20.8	32.1	5 254	5 047	5 041
Oklahoma	15 841.3	41.7	25 031	92.0	2 036.6	14 977.2	20.2	11.1	79.8	9.4	6.6	27.5	23.0	1 669 707	1 589 335	1 494 050
Okmulgee	603.1	34.8	15 599	57.3	170.0	281.2	30.2	23.1	71.1	11.6	4.1	22.1	25.5	65 030	55 176	50 508
Osage	755.7	42.2	17 618	64.8	122.5	247.5	48.8	14.7	52.8	6.0	2.7	15.1	24.2	36 322	28 768	32 780
Ottawa	572.6	37.5	18 537	68.1	145.8	288.6	D	18.2	D	11.2	3.2	22.7	19.4	52 421	53 147	52 839
Pawnee	298.0	38.7	18 181	66.8	58.6	97.7	D	4.5	D	11.8	4.8	28.2	29.5	4 414	4 054	4 854
Payne	1 266.6	45.9	19 405	71.3	188.9	863.6	D	10.7	D	9.9	3.4	20.2	43.5	92 313	95 036	92 308
Pittsburg	739.3	43.0	17 184	63.2	172.9	438.7	20.6	13.6	80.3	11.2	3.4	18.7	37.0	59 596	63 025	51 402
Pontotoc	653.4	39.3	18 868	69.4	148.2	400.4	20.4	13.5	80.3	11.2	6.1	33.0	21.0	53 967	52 188	46 126
Pottawatomie	1 135.2	39.3	18 224	07.0	210.7	594.5	30.8	23.1	00.8	10.4	3.3	20.0	15.8	137 043	129 747	120 554
Pushmataha	155.0	48.5	13 512	49.7	56.6	68.7	13.5	7.3	94.0	13.9	3.3	31.3	37.3	4 983	4 459	4 319
Roger Mills	66.1	22.2	18 457	67.8	12.7	29.6	14.9	1.9	D	7.6	3.8	13.3	38.7	550	491	606
Rogers	1 404.9	65.1	20 657	75.9	186.7	710.5	42.8	33.6	57.7	7.6	3.3	15.3	15.8	238 863	210 236	186 689
Seminole	385.1	25.2	15 555	57.2	118.8	189.3	33.9	19.7	D	11.5	3.0	20.1	24.3	37 347	38 704	36 567
Sequoyah	636.9	67.4	16 964	62.4	145.1	248.7	14.9	9.1	85.5	14.4	4.3	32.3	25.3	22 668	22 639	21 600
Stephens	845.4	40.1	19 422	71.4	174.6	499.5	39.5	24.6	60.3	11.6	4.6	25.0	12.9	122 740	116 818	101 796
Texas	496.0	95.3	26 751	98.3	48.9	380.3	D	D	D	6.4	2.0	9.7	11.8	D	63 390	41 833
Tillman	154.8	10.2	16 259	59.8	40.4	81.8	D	18.7	58.9	5.8	3.2	11.4	24.9	15 306	14 147	12 980
Tulsa	16 297.0	50.8	29 990	110.2	1 740.0	14 363.2	30.5	20.8	69.5	8.2	6.3	27.3	7.8	2 981 500	2 847 596	2 758 704
Wagoner	985.0	45.3	17 836	65.6	140.7	225.9	30.3	16.8	69.1	10.9	3.5	28.0	19.1	37 857	37 639	34 500
Washington	1 248.5	21.4	26 271	96.6	183.9	695.2	D	10.6	D	9.7	4.1	D	10.0	73 494	73 440	69 224
Washita	180.7	13.7	15 261	56.1	45.9	75.4	D	6.3	D	7.3	3.3	18.3	28.7	4 740	5 172	4 945
Woods	187.9	32.9	22 640	83.2	36.5	102.9	9.6	4.7	71.2	12.0	6.8	12.5	28.9	4 879	4 914	5 534
Woodward	356.7	35.9	19 151	70.4	59.4	257.4	27.2	4.2	68.5	11.7	6.8	13.0	21.9	10 687	9 492	8 530
OREGON	85 043.5	63.0	25 912	95.3	11 139.7	60 103.3	26.1	18.6	72.7	10.4	7.1	25.2	15.7	11 151 563	10 617 275	9 686 341
Baker	312.6	40.9	19 049	70.0	71.1	158.7	D	12.8	83.1	12.6	4.2	23.5	30.3	20 373	18 598	17 309
Benton	2 125.1	73.3	27 307	100.4	186.8	1 452.3	D	32.6	D	6.6	2.9	22.3	24.2	473 578	470 769	428 043
Clackamas	10 280.6	73.3	30 709	112.9	865.4	5 152.2	25.5	15.9	72.6	12.3	8.2	22.9	12.1	816 632	714 727	662 326
Clatsop	801.4	37.9	22 662	83.3	134.3	499.5	NA	23.1	69.2	15.1	2.9	23.1	20.5	115 631	115 742	116 257
Columbia	1 024.0	64.8	23 004	84.6	137.0	380.9	34.4	25.6	62.8	10.5	3.6	13.0	18.6	97 605	95 662	93 477
Coos	1 325.9	40.9	21 332	78.4	305.4	708.9	D	14.4	D	13.0	3.9	21.3	26.8	101 936	101 537	98 358
Crook	344.3	66.8	19 905	73.2	66.5	205.7	D	27.4	D	7.7	2.8	13.6	21.6	56 336	55 279	55 945
Curry	463.4	48.5	21 993	80.8	115.6	185.3	D	15.8	D	18.5	4.7	20.8	22.3	29 323	29 093	26 693
Deschutes	2 620.5	83.2	24 784	91.1	354.5	1 626.4	24.8	11.7	75.4	13.2	9.7	28.0	15.0	191 026	174 011	172 446
Douglas	2 092.1	44.4	20 543	75.5	435.7	1 249.2	32.6	27.0	67.3	9.9	3.4	20.9	21.8	337 782	336 794	313 002
Gilliam	29.0	18.3	14 353	52.8	6.5	17.7	5.4	2.1	D	11.9	2.4	9.6	34.9	370	D	D
Grant	160.4	35.6	19 963	73.4	33.5	87.0	NA	15.6	80.3	8.8	3.5	12.7	44.2	13 577	15 180	16 042
Harney	147.9	46.2	20 534	75.5	28.8	90.1	26.1	20.0	72.3	11.2	1.7	16.5	35.1	18 009	13 954	11 254
Hood River	416.6	50.5	21 262	78.2	57.2	280.3	20.2	12.6	72.6	11.8	2.2	23.4	16.7	35 282	36 925	37 168
Jackson	4 021.7	63.0	23 214	85.3	659.7	2 412.8	23.1	15.3	76.5	16.4	5.7	26.8	16.1	368 829	363 554	349 730
Jefferson	306.9	60.9	18 328	67.4	59.6	198.0	35.5	32.4	61.4	8.3	2.0	17.8	22.9	64 171	60 518	60 672
Josephine	1 473.1	57.3	19 862	73.0	373.8	697.0	23.7	15.0	75.9	16.1	5.5	26.0	18.9	104 871	97 964	87 313
Klamath	1 250.6	48.0	19 800	72.8	259.0	764.1	D	18.1	D	10.7	4.7	23.9	22.3	138 436	142 483	145 052
Lake	143.1	27.4	19 996	73.5	31.4	78.4	D	D	D	10.5	2.6	12.6	43.3	D	9 363	10 916
Lane	7 567.7	58.1	24 151	88.8	1 138.5	4 854.9	27.2	19.2	72.2	12.0	5.6	26.3	17.7	930 630	881 637	798 100
Lincoln	992.3	56.5	21 913	80.6	205.8	521.1	D	10.3	D	17.6	4.7	27.1	24.9	53 517	50 339	53 803

[1] Based on resident population estimated as of July 1, 1998.   [2] Includes farm earnings; see table B–10 for these data.   [3] Includes mining and construction, not shown separately.   [4] Includes agricultural services, forestry, and fisheries; transportation and public utilities; and wholesale trade, not shown separately.   [5] Finance, insurance, and real estate.

Source: Personal Income and Earnings—U.S. Bureau of Economic Analysis, "Regional Economic Information System (REIS) 1969-1998" on CD-ROM (related Internet site <http://www.bea.doc.gov/bea/regional/data.htm>).

Table B–8. Counties — **Personal Income and Earnings**–Con.

[Includes U.S., states, and 3,142 counties/county equivalents defined as of January 1, 1992. For changes to these areas since January 1, 1992, see appendix B. Geographic Information]

County	Personal income, 1998 Total (mil. dol.)	Percent change, 1990–1998	Per capita¹ Amount (dollars)	Per capita¹ Percent of national average	Transfer payments (mil. dol.)	Earnings Total² (mil. dol.)	Goods-related Total³	Goods-related Manufacturing	Service-related Total⁴	Service-related Retail trade	Service-related FIRE⁵	Service-related Services	Service-related Government	Manufacturing earnings 1998 ($1,000)	Manufacturing earnings 1997 ($1,000)	Manufacturing earnings 1996 ($1,000)
OREGON—Con.																
Linn	2 216.5	57.3	21 218	78.0	389.2	1 495.4	42.3	34.4	54.4	9.2	4.0	16.0	13.5	514 572	529 015	481 565
Malheur	557.9	46.0	19 542	71.8	105.6	394.2	D	11.3	74.0	11.7	3.0	19.4	25.3	44 448	42 133	39 582
Marion	6 249.6	59.3	23 240	85.4	957.1	4 339.4	D	11.5	D	10.3	5.8	24.1	28.3	498 199	495 700	485 566
Morrow	182.7	49.3	18 353	67.5	25.9	130.9	30.2	26.7	52.5	4.4	1.6	8.4	19.8	34 967	31 747	25 817
Multnomah	19 334.3	56.5	30 662	112.7	2 223.9	19 148.7	19.2	12.8	80.7	8.8	10.4	29.3	14.4	2 445 663	2 402 857	2 203 350
Polk	1 371.4	76.5	22 334	82.1	184.4	528.2	30.0	20.8	62.9	7.7	2.7	26.7	17.1	109 641	100 815	92 708
Sherman	29.2	–10.6	16 247	59.7	7.6	16.1	D	D	D	29.1	1.4	18.6	64.4	D	D	D
Tillamook	500.6	56.3	20 613	75.8	106.0	262.6	NA	17.5	67.6	12.0	3.4	20.7	22.6	45 850	44 993	42 718
Umatilla	1 378.6	58.7	21 018	77.3	235.7	891.7	D	15.0	D	12.5	2.8	19.3	22.6	133 322	125 702	122 089
Union	504.3	42.2	20 272	74.5	97.3	306.4	D	19.0	D	12.3	3.0	18.6	25.1	58 264	56 000	54 717
Wallowa	144.0	34.2	19 636	72.2	30.1	72.9	24.9	17.2	82.7	16.1	6.0	16.5	32.1	12 571	13 911	12 401
Wasco	528.5	46.8	22 876	84.1	89.6	311.1	D	16.7	D	14.0	3.2	23.5	23.5	51 999	50 574	46 970
Washington	12 270.1	83.9	30 621	112.6	913.3	9 596.5	38.8	31.1	60.5	9.2	5.8	23.2	6.2	2 985 342	2 700 200	2 296 432
Wheeler	24.4	35.9	15 555	57.2	6.4	7.1	D	D	D	17.5	4.7	11.3	63.8	D	560	1 049
Yamhill	1 852.4	74.1	22 586	83.0	241.2	981.5	33.6	24.5	58.3	10.2	4.7	20.2	15.3	240 413	238 397	226 610
PENNSYLVANIA	329 687.1	39.8	27 469	101.0	53 391.1	226 718.2	26.9	20.6	72.8	8.7	8.0	29.9	13.3	46 774 842	45 013 390	43 118 436
Adams	2 000.4	44.6	23 083	84.9	265.8	961.8	35.7	26.4	62.2	10.0	2.7	22.2	16.8	253 693	241 429	239 170
Allegheny	40 149.8	34.3	31 665	116.4	6 429.3	31 897.5	22.2	16.2	77.8	7.8	9.4	35.2	10.9	5 182 275	5 103 599	5 016 001
Armstrong	1 593.0	41.0	21 728	79.9	342.2	694.2	30.7	15.3	67.1	12.4	2.7	22.0	16.3	106 037	102 983	96 557
Beaver	4 250.8	43.3	23 066	84.8	873.6	2 120.1	D	22.9	D	9.3	3.3	25.1	13.9	486 142	475 789	448 622
Bedford	921.7	50.9	18 657	68.6	191.2	529.9	D	27.6	D	15.3	2.4	14.9	14.8	146 396	132 885	118 740
Berks	9 787.4	44.3	27 511	101.1	1 407.9	6 703.2	35.5	29.4	63.7	9.2	6.4	25.8	10.7	1 972 768	1 990 244	1 833 824
Blair	2 900.3	45.6	22 216	81.7	610.4	2 042.4	D	17.5	D	13.1	3.2	26.4	14.9	357 422	341 187	324 849
Bradford	1 231.9	35.2	19 746	72.6	232.3	793.6	D	33.7	D	9.3	2.8	25.4	13.2	267 560	256 214	249 238
Bucks	19 189.5	51.6	32 643	120.0	1 938.3	9 795.1	30.0	20.8	69.8	11.6	6.4	28.6	10.0	2 040 713	2 010 115	1 912 607
Butler	4 112.4	54.2	24 078	88.5	627.0	2 454.2	38.0	29.4	61.9	9.3	3.2	19.1	14.3	722 578	662 683	634 212
Cambria	3 276.4	31.2	21 058	77.4	911.4	1 911.8	21.2	13.2	78.6	10.6	6.3	31.4	18.5	252 733	238 692	235 799
Cameron	132.8	38.4	23 672	87.0	28.1	84.4	D	59.9	D	6.5	D	8.1	15.7	50 583	48 990	44 351
Carbon	1 294.6	39.5	22 059	81.1	274.4	500.7	D	25.3	D	11.0	5.7	24.5	18.4	126 792	131 951	122 509
Centre	3 071.8	45.8	23 272	85.5	358.0	2 399.2	18.7	13.8	80.8	7.7	3.6	21.7	38.9	330 816	328 387	312 119
Chester	17 581.6	68.7	41 675	153.2	1 375.6	10 836.6	26.5	21.0	72.6	8.0	13.1	30.3	7.5	2 272 314	2 115 551	2 023 989
Clarion	852.6	41.2	20 435	75.1	178.1	540.4	30.1	19.7	69.2	12.6	2.6	16.2	22.8	106 688	100 615	88 689
Clearfield	1 645.9	40.7	20 390	75.0	361.9	1 048.6	27.7	17.9	72.1	17.5	3.1	22.4	15.8	187 427	176 802	165 933
Clinton	731.7	38.2	19 810	72.8	161.2	406.4	38.3	34.1	60.9	11.8	2.9	15.3	22.6	138 412	133 026	125 488
Columbia	1 352.6	39.5	21 165	77.8	254.5	853.7	D	30.5	D	10.4	2.7	19.6	18.0	260 041	257 417	242 672
Crawford	1 836.7	41.8	20 576	75.6	378.4	1 160.5	43.3	37.2	55.8	9.5	2.3	22.9	13.8	431 174	409 015	377 982
Cumberland	6 124.4	45.8	29 218	107.4	668.3	5 161.2	15.8	11.1	83.9	10.2	11.4	24.8	17.5	572 352	544 217	523 597
Dauphin	7 211.5	42.3	29 380	108.0	934.0	6 765.8	21.7	16.5	78.2	6.4	7.3	25.0	25.4	1 115 514	1 043 925	1 006 849
Delaware	17 519.3	35.1	32 288	118.7	2 313.5	10 264.8	24.1	18.5	75.9	9.9	9.7	34.8	9.8	1 903 609	1 837 076	1 874 276
Elk	844.1	43.7	24 385	89.6	147.8	594.5	63.4	58.9	36.7	5.7	1.8	14.7	8.1	349 916	341 958	326 981
Erie	6 569.7	41.1	23 622	86.8	1 099.0	4 621.2	38.3	32.5	61.3	9.6	5.4	23.8	13.3	1 502 231	1 458 350	1 398 981
Fayette	2 886.7	39.4	19 996	73.5	802.9	1 203.6	22.9	15.1	77.1	14.6	2.9	27.1	17.4	181 797	174 706	187 548
Forest	88.8	44.1	17 947	66.0	26.9	45.7	D	14.9	D	9.6	1.0	30.2	30.9	6 797	6 749	6 063
Franklin	2 986.0	42.7	23 282	85.6	486.3	1 785.0	D	29.4	D	10.8	3.3	19.8	19.5	525 673	509 016	494 852
Fulton	288.1	52.3	19 830	72.9	46.3	197.5	D	50.2	D	6.9	D	10.5	12.5	99 162	88 225	88 327
Greene	734.1	39.5	17 385	63.9	190.7	466.5	45.2	4.7	55.4	7.7	2.0	14.2	20.9	21 898	20 878	19 188
Huntingdon	782.8	38.2	17 491	64.3	160.3	430.9	D	20.9	D	9.5	4.3	19.9	25.6	89 965	88 176	78 200
Indiana	1 839.3	31.3	20 809	76.5	365.3	1 198.7	33.4	12.1	65.7	9.8	4.9	16.9	21.7	145 150	141 940	145 100
Jefferson	968.9	34.9	20 979	77.1	209.6	561.8	43.6	32.6	55.7	9.1	2.4	19.5	12.0	182 870	171 056	159 409
Juniata	423.3	33.7	19 140	70.4	76.8	192.1	43.9	34.5	52.2	10.5	3.8	12.4	11.2	66 278	66 555	59 220
Lackawanna	5 120.5	32.8	24 572	90.3	1 119.6	3 341.8	27.6	22.6	72.4	10.3	7.2	30.0	13.2	755 095	747 599	737 821
Lancaster	12 012.2	45.0	26 303	96.7	1 405.2	8 378.8	40.2	30.4	58.7	10.1	5.8	21.7	8.7	2 547 631	2 433 885	2 335 994
Lawrence	2 014.2	35.1	21 223	78.0	481.0	1 140.1	30.6	21.4	69.1	11.3	6.7	24.2	15.2	243 564	239 863	236 012
Lebanon	2 858.8	40.9	24 303	89.3	427.8	1 453.2	D	24.9	D	12.2	3.1	22.5	19.0	362 404	324 856	317 268
Lehigh	8 861.1	43.2	29 657	109.0	1 227.9	7 140.7	D	26.8	D	8.0	6.6	29.7	8.5	1 911 304	1 827 048	1 698 024
Luzerne	7 559.7	32.6	24 029	88.3	1 690.2	4 877.1	25.5	19.4	74.4	9.8	6.4	25.5	15.5	948 378	930 808	870 523
Lycoming	2 558.4	33.7	21 791	80.1	468.6	1 773.3	31.7	26.0	67.8	10.4	5.0	25.2	14.3	460 510	435 973	425 105
McKean	1 021.1	43.5	22 045	81.0	203.3	645.4	45.3	36.5	54.4	8.5	2.1	18.4	16.8	235 720	239 216	234 661
Mercer	2 585.0	36.7	21 231	78.0	556.9	1 613.9	35.5	29.9	63.9	11.3	3.9	26.3	12.1	482 939	448 147	441 907
Mifflin	881.1	36.4	18 761	69.0	192.3	562.9	42.2	36.5	55.8	10.5	2.9	19.4	11.0	205 549	200 006	198 729
Monroe	2 808.6	58.1	22 396	82.3	413.7	1 539.3	D	14.5	D	11.9	4.6	25.8	26.2	223 183	198 895	187 004
Montgomery	30 531.9	43.8	42 431	156.0	2 780.1	24 495.8	30.2	23.8	69.7	6.8	13.7	30.4	6.4	5 836 679	5 543 172	5 087 037
Montour	552.2	53.6	31 402	115.4	126.5	525.2	D	6.3	D	3.2	2.3	68.0	9.8	33 324	29 267	32 509
Northampton	6 846.6	43.8	26 479	97.3	1 023.7	3 292.5	30.3	22.8	69.6	9.9	6.1	27.4	14.4	749 070	759 679	775 850
Northumberland	1 981.3	31.3	21 089	77.5	438.0	1 025.9	39.0	32.8	60.4	13.2	2.9	16.8	14.7	336 171	316 743	314 642
Perry	937.0	44.2	21 163	77.8	129.9	261.0	D	10.1	D	13.7	3.2	17.3	23.3	26 251	24 143	22 003
Philadelphia	35 542.2	22.6	24 769	91.1	8 929.6	32 161.9	D	9.7	D	5.8	10.4	48.2	18.3	3 103 874	2 963 199	2 880 481
Pike	856.4	67.5	21 332	78.4	131.8	256.8	D	6.3	D	14.2	7.3	29.8	25.1	16 207	15 587	15 861
Potter	370.8	56.8	21 644	79.6	72.1	244.0	20.6	15.2	76.7	7.4	1.5	19.1	13.9	37 024	36 010	34 253

¹ Based on resident population estimated as of July 1, 1998.   ² Includes farm earnings; see table B-10 for these data.   ³ Includes mining and construction, not shown separately.   ⁴ Includes agricultural services, forestry, and fisheries; transportation and public utilities; and wholesale trade, not shown separately.   ⁵ Finance, insurance, and real estate.

Source: Personal Income and Earnings—U.S. Bureau of Economic Analysis, "Regional Economic Information System (REIS) 1969-1998" on CD-ROM (related Internet site <http://www.bea.doc.gov/bea/regional/data.htm>).

[Includes U.S., states, and 3,142 counties/county equivalents defined as of January 1, 1992. For changes to these areas since January 1, 1992, see appendix B. Geographic Information]

County	Personal income, 1998													Manufacturing earnings		
		Per capita[1]				Earnings										
								Percent, by selected industry–								
							Goods-related		Service-related							
	Total (mil. dol.)	Percent change, 1990–1998	Amount (dollars)	Percent of national average	Transfer payments (mil. dol.)	Total[2] (mil. dol.)	Total[3]	Manufacturing	Total[4]	Retail trade	FIRE[5]	Services	Government	1998 ($1,000)	1997 ($1,000)	1996 ($1,000)
PENNSYLVANIA—Con.																
Schuylkill	3 268.0	32.2	21 777	80.1	714.5	1 702.3	39.0	30.6	60.5	10.0	3.1	20.3	15.5	521 058	496 021	500 790
Snyder	958.1	50.4	25 237	92.8	288.4	514.3	D	32.1	D	13.0	2.7	14.3	18.5	165 083	157 713	146 985
Somerset	1 611.1	32.2	20 091	73.9	375.2	916.4	34.5	19.4	63.3	11.4	3.2	20.1	16.6	177 381	169 121	158 311
Sullivan	122.6	34.4	20 179	74.2	30.4	58.8	D	D	D	10.9	3.7	26.5	20.9	D	12 062	11 209
Susquehanna	858.9	36.9	20 409	75.0	155.3	325.8	29.4	13.3	65.7	11.9	3.6	19.1	19.6	43 444	43 396	46 077
Tioga	780.6	39.2	18 799	69.1	160.1	439.9	30.3	25.6	66.2	10.7	5.7	17.4	23.3	112 634	105 783	89 920
Union	866.4	42.5	21 516	79.1	183.9	627.5	D	18.9	D	7.1	2.2	29.7	27.8	118 344	104 377	99 375
Venango	1 420.8	39.8	24 583	90.4	470.1	744.6	35.3	30.3	64.9	10.1	3.2	21.1	19.3	225 422	213 107	189 769
Warren	993.4	26.7	22 685	83.4	219.5	592.4	38.6	32.1	61.0	17.2	3.2	16.2	16.4	190 057	189 277	176 169
Washington	5 377.9	48.5	26 190	96.3	1 046.3	2 709.8	33.3	20.6	66.8	11.2	3.2	26.1	13.6	558 029	527 584	530 657
Wayne	940.5	42.0	20 701	76.1	198.4	448.3	22.3	8.5	76.0	12.4	5.8	26.6	20.1	38 319	35 889	34 989
Westmoreland	9 235.0	43.1	24 799	91.2	1 767.7	4 884.7	32.3	24.2	67.6	11.3	3.8	24.5	12.7	1 181 717	1 114 537	1 021 461
Wyoming	608.7	33.7	20 838	76.6	103.1	407.2	D	D	D	7.6	2.3	13.4	10.0	D	152 193	146 180
York	9 565.0	40.6	25 596	94.1	1 132.9	6 393.0	43.7	36.1	56.1	10.1	4.0	20.5	10.5	2 304 857	2 227 833	2 138 918
RHODE ISLAND	27 914.2	37.6	28 262	103.9	4 691.5	17 890.2	22.6	17.6	77.2	8.8	8.0	31.2	17.9	3 154 097	3 088 475	2 986 736
Bristol	1 615.2	41.3	32 832	120.7	195.8	489.4	30.6	22.4	69.2	9.3	4.0	29.7	16.7	109 695	102 564	94 082
Kent	4 672.4	38.9	28 946	106.4	722.8	2 586.1	D	19.3	D	12.6	9.9	28.8	13.8	500 302	526 468	508 491
Newport	2 564.6	34.2	31 054	114.2	322.5	1 647.8	D	8.8	D	8.9	2.7	29.0	41.4	145 527	133 954	128 931
Providence	15 463.1	34.0	26 953	99.1	3 024.0	11 510.1	22.8	18.0	77.1	7.5	9.1	33.1	14.8	2 072 088	2 049 056	1 992 161
Washington	3 599.0	54.7	29 792	109.5	426.4	1 656.8	25.8	19.7	73.6	11.9	3.8	24.1	22.9	326 485	276 433	263 071
SOUTH CAROLINA	85 897.9	53.0	22 372	82.2	13 265.7	60 400.1	30.1	22.9	69.4	10.6	6.2	22.1	19.5	13 813 387	13 425 772	12 907 490
Abbeville	468.7	56.4	19 019	69.9	87.9	269.4	58.1	53.1	41.0	4.8	1.8	11.7	15.0	143 185	138 023	126 566
Aiken	3 166.2	42.3	23 627	86.9	464.1	2 395.5	55.0	44.7	44.2	7.0	4.3	16.5	11.6	1 070 170	1 072 518	1 072 885
Allendale	185.8	57.9	16 293	59.9	50.1	138.1	37.3	30.0	61.2	9.1	1.4	11.2	30.7	48 278	42 694	38 314
Anderson	3 556.6	56.4	22 130	81.4	548.2	2 055.2	41.4	33.5	57.9	12.3	4.5	17.0	16.0	688 154	688 722	679 080
Bamberg	281.7	49.7	17 130	63.0	74.3	130.5	D	26.2	D	10.7	3.4	17.2	27.2	34 163	33 174	33 492
Barnwell	503.8	75.3	23 086	84.9	96.6	423.0	26.1	22.4	D	4.9	1.3	D	10.5	94 854	84 358	82 128
Beaufort	3 386.9	85.4	30 765	113.1	370.8	2 110.9	11.7	2.5	88.1	12.2	12.3	23.8	32.8	52 265	42 957	35 940
Berkeley	2 236.9	20.9	16 258	59.8	307.4	1 091.5	D	31.9	D	8.0	2.1	13.2	21.7	348 166	310 963	278 821
Calhoun	276.2	54.0	19 625	72.1	43.4	152.3	59.2	54.0	D	3.9	D	8.5	15.4	82 231	80 466	90 135
Charleston	7 611.3	44.6	24 040	88.4	1 010.2	6 593.4	D	5.8	D	11.1	7.1	29.8	28.9	384 750	370 931	365 313
Cherokee	930.0	53.0	18 894	69.5	167.4	645.2	D	45.7	D	9.8	1.8	11.8	10.3	294 677	279 628	255 674
Chester	601.9	49.4	17 521	64.4	126.7	380.1	47.5	42.2	52.0	7.9	1.5	8.5	19.0	160 571	156 139	150 742
Chesterfield	737.8	48.0	17 965	66.0	157.3	475.5	57.4	52.7	39.5	7.5	2.5	10.9	12.5	250 683	246 992	252 296
Clarendon	492.8	58.4	16 016	58.9	133.0	212.2	27.0	19.2	70.8	13.1	4.0	18.0	27.2	40 692	38 451	34 137
Colleton	644.0	45.8	17 243	63.4	160.2	329.5	30.5	22.5	68.5	11.4	4.3	19.3	18.6	74 090	76 694	73 908
Darlington	1 303.6	49.8	19 652	72.2	278.3	849.2	50.4	39.7	48.9	8.0	2.2	16.8	10.6	337 441	323 578	313 766
Dillon	498.7	52.4	16 788	61.7	138.6	279.1	36.9	35.1	61.9	14.8	2.6	20.9	16.1	97 905	86 864	83 960
Dorchester	1 825.4	35.1	20 735	76.2	312.8	787.9	34.9	26.3	64.6	11.7	3.1	18.6	18.5	207 352	199 740	180 375
Edgefield	376.3	52.7	18 809	69.1	70.5	169.5	40.8	36.2	57.2	7.6	1.7	11.9	28.6	61 435	57 680	52 368
Fairfield	442.3	54.6	19 730	72.5	97.2	301.0	D	38.5	D	3.8	1.2	9.4	15.2	115 966	103 995	90 265
Florence	2 757.3	55.0	22 114	81.3	531.7	2 096.5	D	20.0	D	10.3	8.5	24.9	18.6	420 066	406 827	388 234
Georgetown	1 138.7	63.4	21 207	78.0	230.9	648.9	D	21.9	D	13.9	8.4	21.3	19.1	141 943	145 288	146 177
Greenville	9 604.0	59.1	27 131	99.7	1 096.8	8 494.6	32.1	24.1	67.9	10.7	6.9	25.0	10.1	2 049 784	2 000 490	1 930 156
Greenwood	1 434.8	53.9	22 562	82.9	224.7	1 112.6	45.8	39.3	53.6	10.7	3.8	15.8	17.6	436 715	453 398	410 796
Hampton	361.9	60.3	18 900	69.5	86.2	202.6	30.7	26.9	68.8	10.8	2.8	18.6	26.0	54 491	55 857	53 071
Horry	4 030.1	77.4	23 088	84.9	629.5	2 766.0	17.1	8.6	82.8	20.4	10.2	32.5	12.4	238 539	216 626	204 705
Jasper	310.8	62.3	18 225	67.0	60.2	126.4	22.5	7.2	D	10.3	1.6	26.7	25.0	9 144	7 526	5 255
Kershaw	995.8	41.3	20 484	75.3	170.2	596.8	46.4	36.1	51.6	8.7	4.5	13.3	16.4	215 269	204 376	198 798
Lancaster	1 151.4	46.8	19 557	71.9	201.1	621.7	45.7	39.1	52.4	12.9	5.1	16.8	13.1	242 907	241 675	240 330
Laurens	1 311.2	51.1	20 762	76.3	357.4	654.5	D	34.4	D	16.0	2.6	15.4	18.7	224 986	221 639	229 448
Lee	271.8	45.0	13 390	49.2	75.2	115.0	D	24.9	D	10.3	3.2	17.7	23.4	28 602	28 529	29 462
Lexington	5 161.7	63.3	25 174	92.5	527.5	2 700.2	29.5	19.8	69.4	11.4	5.2	20.7	13.8	535 180	530 227	486 671
McCormick	148.6	61.5	15 591	57.3	37.1	70.0	D	22.0	D	4.7	D	14.2	43.6	15 414	15 889	15 430
Marion	583.6	44.9	16 892	62.1	158.3	338.8	D	41.7	D	9.5	3.6	14.3	21.7	141 407	138 025	125 182
Marlboro	441.6	38.3	14 921	54.9	126.9	248.6	D	39.8	D	7.5	1.4	14.8	22.3	98 960	101 238	92 072
Newberry	677.3	48.1	19 671	72.3	128.6	382.9	46.8	40.7	50.0	7.7	2.1	14.9	16.8	155 966	158 046	149 921
Oconee	1 456.1	52.9	22 702	83.5	232.5	894.8	45.9	38.0	D	7.1	2.2	D	13.1	339 709	336 440	315 721
Orangeburg	1 646.9	45.2	18 777	69.0	367.7	1 036.2	35.2	30.0	63.7	11.6	3.5	18.4	22.3	310 728	300 726	277 956
Pickens	2 190.1	56.4	20 460	75.2	296.2	1 170.6	D	24.5	D	11.7	6.2	19.0	23.4	286 814	289 366	292 041
Richland	8 094.1	51.5	26 547	97.6	1 074.4	7 723.2	11.3	6.6	88.7	8.6	11.5	26.0	32.5	512 810	489 432	482 888
Saluda	337.0	48.6	19 783	72.7	63.3	138.5	43.0	37.7	46.7	6.8	4.7	9.5	17.6	52 227	48 956	42 667
Spartanburg	5 506.2	48.5	22 274	81.9	806.4	4 376.6	43.6	36.6	56.3	11.0	3.3	17.8	12.2	1 602 431	1 525 441	1 456 638
Sumter	1 942.6	45.6	17 294	63.6	362.5	1 425.3	D	25.2	D	8.4	3.2	17.0	31.8	358 808	330 127	312 978
Union	548.4	42.8	17 967	66.0	124.0	298.6	D	48.6	D	7.9	2.7	10.1	23.2	145 199	154 219	144 936
Williamsburg	558.8	39.7	15 111	55.5	159.4	275.1	37.0	31.4	60.7	8.6	3.5	13.6	22.6	86 468	83 198	91 762
York	3 710.3	60.5	24 051	88.4	442.0	2 096.2	D	24.9	D	10.4	3.5	23.9	13.2	521 792	507 644	494 030

[1] Based on resident population estimated as of July 1, 1998.   [2] Includes farm earnings; see table B-10 for these data.   [3] Includes mining and construction, not shown separately.   [4] Includes agricultural services, forestry, and fisheries; transportation and public utilities; and wholesale trade, not shown separately.   [5] Finance, insurance, and real estate.

Source: Personal Income and Earnings—U.S. Bureau of Economic Analysis, "Regional Economic Information System (REIS) 1969-1998" on CD-ROM (related Internet site <http://www.bea.doc.gov/bea/regional/data.htm>).

[Includes U.S., states, and 3,142 counties/county equivalents defined as of January 1, 1992. For changes to these areas since January 1, 1992, see appendix B. Geographic Information]

County	Personal income, 1998													Manufacturing earnings		
	Total (mil. dol.)	Per capita[1]			Transfer payments (mil. dol.)	Earnings								1998 ($1,000)	1997 ($1,000)	1996 ($1,000)
		Percent change, 1990–1998	Amount (dollars)	Percent of national average		Total[2] (mil. dol.)	Goods-related		Service-related							
							Total[3]	Manufacturing	Total[4]	Retail trade	FIRE[5]	Services	Government			
SOUTH DAKOTA	17 331.0	53.2	23 715	87.2	2 430.2	11 909.9	20.9	14.2	71.2	10.0	7.0	23.8	17.0	1 694 918	1 542 794	1 419 254
Aurora	57.9	28.7	19 194	70.6	11.5	29.4	4.9	2.3	D	7.9	4.7	D	29.2	687	657	808
Beadle	410.3	33.8	23 944	88.0	70.3	254.6	D	11.8	D	8.7	4.5	24.2	19.0	30 006	42 071	47 195
Bennett	48.8	19.3	14 403	52.9	13.6	24.5	D	D	D	14.1	2.0	6.8	40.2	D	696	913
Bon Homme	140.5	45.8	19 356	71.2	26.7	76.8	17.3	11.5	D	9.4	6.0	16.4	19.3	8 801	8 408	7 993
Brookings	589.9	62.7	22 729	83.6	66.5	423.0	D	28.1	D	8.2	3.4	11.1	28.0	118 983	107 632	95 129
Brown	919.0	47.3	25 960	95.4	124.9	629.5	NA	12.5	75.8	11.1	6.0	29.8	14.9	78 743	75 373	72 795
Brule	115.5	40.3	20 883	76.8	19.7	64.2	D	2.5	D	15.0	4.5	28.0	15.6	1 631	1 502	1 235
Buffalo	21.0	29.0	11 952	43.9	8.6	15.7	D	D	D	D	D	35.5	44.6	D	64	76
Butte	147.4	48.8	16 522	60.7	29.9	72.6	D	3.0	D	15.0	5.0	21.1	21.6	2 180	1 998	2 191
Campbell	38.7	53.1	20 639	75.9	7.9	21.7	D	D	D	5.1	D	4.7	11.9	D	2 738	2 919
Charles Mix	190.4	49.6	20 467	75.2	39.0	121.9	NA	3.5	70.0	9.1	3.6	23.1	18.2	4 277	4 103	3 390
Clark	88.2	20.4	20 331	74.7	15.6	49.2	D	D	D	5.7	2.3	8.0	12.2	D	D	D
Clay	269.5	58.3	20 427	75.1	38.0	160.1	D	2.4	D	8.5	2.6	16.4	45.5	3 858	3 725	3 707
Codington	620.4	66.2	24 393	89.7	75.0	457.7	34.3	27.7	61.0	12.7	4.9	19.4	11.4	126 924	120 379	106 625
Corson	52.8	45.9	12 636	46.5	18.4	22.6	D	D	D	4.1	1.4	19.1	44.6	D	377	475
Custer	124.0	31.8	17 856	65.6	23.9	57.5	D	3.3	D	14.7	3.1	24.6	39.9	1 909	1 799	1 606
Davison	449.0	57.2	25 320	93.1	68.3	309.2	D	18.0	D	15.8	4.3	29.8	11.2	55 557	50 746	46 110
Day	123.9	18.0	19 372	71.2	27.5	65.3	D	13.7	D	7.6	5.4	15.0	16.3	8 933	9 257	7 982
Deuel	98.9	57.1	21 975	80.8	15.9	58.1	19.2	13.6	48.1	5.8	4.7	9.5	10.3	7 915	6 957	5 703
Dewey	80.1	49.9	13 650	50.2	20.3	51.3	6.4	1.8	D	6.3	4.1	D	41.8	928	768	768
Douglas	74.1	47.6	21 071	77.5	13.4	44.3	D	5.6	D	6.1	2.7	17.2	10.3	2 498	2 347	2 065
Edmunds	103.8	41.3	24 611	90.5	17.2	51.8	7.1	1.1	49.0	7.2	3.1	8.6	16.1	570	537	626
Fall River	142.6	39.0	20 765	76.3	34.8	82.8	D	2.1	D	12.0	2.4	13.8	47.3	1 738	1 758	1 844
Faulk	61.8	32.4	24 537	90.2	11.6	33.1	D	D	D	9.4	D	8.6	12.4	D	459	520
Grant	187.8	34.2	23 321	85.7	28.5	127.5	D	12.5	D	7.6	7.4	14.7	8.9	15 908	16 273	16 159
Gregory	103.5	30.2	20 895	76.8	21.4	54.0	D	2.8	D	12.9	5.5	20.0	14.2	1 528	1 520	1 402
Haakon	56.0	19.3	23 735	87.3	7.0	36.4	D	10.8	D	8.8	4.7	20.4	11.7	3 922	3 602	3 163
Hamlin	105.5	38.7	19 821	72.9	18.9	51.2	D	7.6	D	7.0	3.5	9.3	21.3	3 870	3 605	3 621
Hand	89.5	19.3	21 515	79.1	14.6	47.0	D	3.3	D	7.1	4.4	16.2	13.0	1 562	1 458	1 381
Hanson	57.5	65.2	19 458	71.5	7.6	28.2	D	8.0	D	4.5	4.3	4.3	12.1	2 247	2 250	2 368
Harding	16.4	-17.5	11 002	40.4	3.4	5.6	D	D	D	16.3	D	48.2	58.9	D	(6)	(6)
Hughes	412.2	59.2	26 857	98.7	45.6	301.6	D	1.3	D	10.3	6.5	24.3	43.3	3 829	5 036	5 127
Hutchinson	183.2	48.0	22 760	83.7	33.9	100.0	12.5	8.6	52.5	7.5	4.8	17.6	11.4	8 561	8 155	7 799
Hyde	36.0	29.5	22 232	81.7	6.4	19.3	7.3	2.2	62.6	12.2	2.5	12.0	12.3	415	384	487
Jackson	38.6	22.1	13 271	48.8	10.6	18.2	D	2.9	D	15.2	D	15.0	37.0	533	485	614
Jerauld	52.6	16.8	23 822	87.6	10.0	31.5	D	D	D	6.7	3.7	29.0	13.7	D	D	D
Jones	29.5	10.8	24 046	88.4	3.7	19.0	D	D	D	22.8	3.3	13.3	13.5	D	361	464
Kingsbury	138.5	53.1	24 041	88.4	25.2	77.1	NA	12.1	46.3	6.2	5.2	11.6	10.4	9 344	8 827	7 909
Lake	251.3	47.8	23 529	86.5	37.7	157.7	D	17.7	D	10.1	3.9	16.9	15.7	27 882	26 241	23 432
Lawrence	447.8	37.1	20 437	75.1	70.9	297.0	29.6	7.7	70.5	11.3	3.1	34.0	17.6	22 974	22 500	21 014
Lincoln	499.3	90.7	24 417	89.8	44.3	202.4	NA	13.0	56.0	9.4	2.8	19.2	9.7	26 294	23 957	21 918
Lyman	78.2	39.4	20 720	76.2	14.1	45.1	D	D	D	9.3	3.6	23.9	16.1	D	441	561
McCook	122.8	43.2	21 886	80.5	20.7	64.4	13.4	10.9	47.4	7.5	3.0	12.1	11.9	7 009	6 740	6 020
McPherson	54.8	15.7	20 046	73.7	11.4	27.1	12.7	6.8	D	5.9	5.5	15.9	14.5	1 845	1 618	1 456
Marshall	103.1	16.8	22 633	83.2	17.3	60.3	D	20.2	D	4.3	4.8	9.1	13.6	12 178	11 803	12 018
Meade	501.1	46.3	23 182	85.2	60.2	225.6	D	5.2	D	9.5	4.1	16.2	36.8	11 660	9 819	9 644
Mellette	27.0	6.2	13 233	48.6	8.9	10.1	D	D	D	8.8	D	3.7	35.1	D	(6)	(6)
Miner	62.2	20.1	22 142	81.4	11.8	32.8	D	D	D	7.6	2.9	23.9	13.3	D	496	614
Minnehaha	4 186.2	71.8	29 817	109.6	393.1	3 448.3	D	13.9	D	9.8	12.4	29.3	9.7	478 605	425 194	394 196
Moody	155.3	39.8	23 904	87.9	19.1	93.1	D	D	D	4.0	2.5	18.9	16.1	D	5 922	5 803
Pennington	2 083.4	50.7	23 858	87.7	275.2	1 530.4	16.8	8.6	82.9	13.0	6.2	28.2	23.7	132 131	126 360	122 108
Perkins	73.3	9.8	20 983	77.1	15.0	37.9	D	D	D	9.7	5.2	19.1	18.9	D	4 314	4 164
Potter	81.4	53.4	28 398	104.4	12.2	43.8	D	5.0	D	5.1	4.1	13.5	12.5	2 204	2 460	2 195
Roberts	172.0	35.5	17 438	64.1	37.1	96.0	D	4.5	D	8.8	4.4	22.2	19.5	4 321	4 587	4 245
Sanborn	65.0	42.0	23 908	87.9	10.3	28.9	D	D	D	6.3	2.0	9.1	13.3	D	3 897	3 453
Shannon	132.8	98.4	10 885	40.0	51.1	91.9	3.6	–	D	3.6	D	43.9	38.7	–	–	–
Spink	178.5	12.4	23 648	86.9	46.9	96.7	4.6	1.4	64.2	7.3	3.9	12.0	27.0	1 348	1 904	1 644
Stanley	61.9	77.2	21 186	77.9	7.1	29.2	41.2	1.0	D	9.2	D	7.7	13.8	294	300	263
Sully	51.4	21.7	34 804	127.9	4.4	33.7	D	D	D	6.8	2.7	2.4	9.3	D	D	D
Todd	97.7	62.5	10 507	38.6	36.6	62.7	D	D	D	5.2	D	38.6	43.7	D	100	86
Tripp	132.5	20.4	19 702	72.4	25.0	77.1	D	1.6	D	11.2	4.7	24.5	14.2	1 272	1 036	1 008
Turner	200.6	46.0	23 267	85.5	30.1	93.9	11.8	5.4	49.0	6.1	5.7	12.5	11.9	5 066	4 453	3 893
Union	398.5	130.4	32 505	119.5	35.4	489.2	D	69.2	D	3.4	3.9	8.0	3.5	338 652	277 756	239 887
Walworth	125.1	30.7	22 361	82.2	23.8	69.3	D	2.1	D	14.0	4.1	29.5	15.9	1 436	1 430	1 360
Yankton	490.6	59.9	23 375	85.9	68.1	362.7	D	23.6	D	11.0	6.4	23.5	15.0	85 630	78 462	70 648
Ziebach	22.0	12.8	10 206	37.5	7.1	9.4	D	D	D	9.1	D		27.4	D	161	201

[1] Based on resident population estimated as of July 1, 1998. [2] Includes farm earnings; see table B-10 for these data. [3] Includes mining and construction, not shown separately. [4] Includes agricultural services, forestry, and fisheries; transportation and public utilities; and wholesale trade, not shown separately. [5] Finance, insurance, and real estate.

Source: Personal Income and Earnings—U.S. Bureau of Economic Analysis, "Regional Economic Information System (REIS) 1969-1998" on CD-ROM (related Internet site <http://www.bea.doc.gov/bea/regional/data.htm>).

[Includes U.S., states, and 3,142 counties/county equivalents defined as of January 1, 1992. For changes to these areas since January 1, 1992, see appendix B. Geographic Information]

County	Personal income, 1998													Manufacturing earnings		
		Per capita[1]				Earnings										
							Percent, by selected industry–									
							Goods-related		Service-related							
	Total (mil. dol.)	Percent change, 1990–1998	Amount (dollars)	Percent of national average	Transfer payments (mil. dol.)	Total[2] (mil. dol.)	Total[3]	Manufacturing	Total[4]	Retail trade	FIRE[5]	Services	Government	1998 ($1,000)	1997 ($1,000)	1996 ($1,000)
TENNESSEE	132 756.5	61.4	24 437	89.8	20 540.0	98 605.3	27.0	20.4	72.8	10.4	6.8	27.7	13.5	20 152 760	19 683 235	18 911 753
Anderson	1 725.3	44.5	24 337	89.5	304.4	1 494.5	39.2	33.4	D	D	2.3	31.5	14.5	498 836	484 616	480 635
Bedford	732.6	57.9	21 219	78.0	119.8	479.2	50.8	43.0	48.1	8.6	3.9	13.6	11.3	206 170	188 146	168 219
Benton	303.5	46.4	18 633	68.5	77.8	137.3	D	24.9	D	12.7	2.9	15.7	16.8	34 221	36 385	32 336
Bledsoe	186.1	75.2	17 293	63.6	42.1	100.0	25.4	20.2	D	5.3	2.5	D	27.3	20 227	16 005	14 264
Blount	2 249.6	58.6	22 227	81.7	359.5	1 280.2	40.4	32.3	59.8	12.4	5.4	18.5	13.2	413 188	385 522	345 424
Bradley	1 935.4	62.2	23 214	85.3	287.0	1 380.6	D	34.9	D	8.9	4.5	26.4	11.3	482 308	490 704	440 270
Campbell	620.1	56.8	16 249	59.7	211.1	289.6	29.8	19.5	70.5	14.2	7.6	16.5	22.1	56 489	57 228	46 733
Cannon	232.5	62.6	10 130	70.4	52.0	56.4	D	10.2	D	13.7	4.1	20.2	21.0	9 143	8 194	8 863
Carroll	574.7	56.5	19 691	72.4	143.8	267.9	40.5	34.7	60.5	10.9	4.2	21.1	15.4	93 091	92 051	90 704
Carter	916.0	42.9	17 179	63.2	223.2	332.8	D	19.9	D	14.2	5.4	23.6	18.9	66 124	68 001	77 816
Cheatham	747.4	91.2	21 197	77.9	90.1	263.7	D	D	D	7.5	3.4	17.4	15.1	D	82 559	81 528
Chester	254.7	82.8	17 356	63.8	53.4	109.0	D	22.9	D	13.3	D	20.5	18.2	24 971	24 264	24 593
Claiborne	501.9	63.9	17 010	62.5	146.7	240.5	D	33.3	D	11.6	3.8	15.2	18.6	80 070	82 555	77 362
Clay	119.0	36.5	16 368	60.2	37.6	54.7	D	38.7	D	9.2	1.8	18.8	20.1	21 164	19 658	28 687
Cocke	542.4	60.4	16 975	62.4	147.3	258.5	D	34.7	D	16.3	2.6	18.8	15.5	89 789	81 001	80 805
Coffee	1 008.2	49.8	22 005	80.9	189.2	822.1	D	21.5	D	10.7	3.0	40.2	13.6	177 166	170 932	152 396
Crockett	285.4	51.2	20 359	74.8	63.7	134.2	47.6	38.0	52.0	6.1	3.5	16.2	13.0	51 036	47 312	47 542
Cumberland	861.3	86.3	19 512	71.7	214.9	476.6	D	20.2	D	14.6	9.1	25.3	10.4	96 440	88 085	84 301
Davidson	17 505.5	64.8	32 827	120.7	1 948.4	18 267.0	16.4	10.2	83.5	10.4	9.0	39.0	10.5	1 863 993	1 825 387	1 757 360
Decatur	209.8	65.6	19 501	71.7	61.3	112.5	D	26.1	D	8.8	3.4	21.7	15.6	29 368	34 751	29 857
DeKalb	319.6	54.2	19 964	73.4	72.5	171.5	D	27.2	D	8.0	3.0	30.9	11.2	46 577	49 481	46 736
Dickson	919.2	74.6	21 740	79.9	143.3	540.2	D	35.3	D	13.2	4.0	20.2	12.0	190 927	171 464	151 817
Dyer	776.7	43.8	21 235	78.1	150.9	588.2	44.4	37.2	55.4	10.3	4.5	18.9	12.1	218 650	209 250	197 239
Fayette	633.3	94.8	20 828	76.6	99.3	222.7	44.1	31.7	55.0	7.6	9.3	11.9	18.0	70 513	69 960	67 974
Fentress	275.1	70.3	17 030	62.6	91.8	136.6	D	17.7	D	14.3	4.0	24.0	14.9	24 189	23 959	25 317
Franklin	759.3	58.7	20 192	74.2	154.9	341.4	D	22.2	D	12.3	3.2	30.6	13.0	75 682	70 385	59 152
Gibson	1 006.6	50.0	20 964	77.1	234.1	610.6	49.3	42.7	50.3	11.1	3.3	15.0	12.2	260 495	271 605	252 178
Giles	615.6	64.3	21 299	78.3	109.7	362.9	D	49.3	D	10.3	3.6	14.4	10.5	178 792	160 911	151 225
Grainger	323.3	67.7	16 328	60.0	81.4	131.9	D	39.9	D	6.9	1.8	15.4	14.7	52 602	45 113	42 362
Greene	1 256.1	55.5	20 846	76.6	319.7	782.8	41.4	37.1	58.6	11.0	2.8	20.1	13.1	290 704	261 183	263 663
Grundy	235.2	63.8	16 744	61.6	74.1	70.9	D	12.9	D	10.8	D	15.5	20.2	9 884	8 735	8 498
Hamblen	1 236.4	60.6	22 913	84.2	219.1	1 086.3	D	48.0	D	9.2	3.4	15.0	8.9	521 587	492 797	459 908
Hamilton	8 161.1	46.1	27 712	101.9	1 221.3	6 908.8	D	18.5	D	10.9	9.3	24.8	16.2	1 277 150	1 217 300	1 164 546
Hancock	87.2	45.3	12 813	47.1	33.8	32.5	D	25.0	D	12.1	D	17.4	27.0	8 116	7 002	6 847
Hardeman	397.1	38.3	16 352	60.1	117.2	209.8	42.4	35.0	58.7	9.4	3.7	13.8	25.0	73 400	71 871	70 694
Hardin	480.3	72.9	19 284	70.9	120.1	283.1	D	38.6	D	11.0	3.2	9.8	15.3	109 238	107 191	98 577
Hawkins	926.3	48.0	18 703	68.8	195.1	432.5	D	55.0	D	7.8	1.6	10.2	15.8	238 000	244 830	243 745
Haywood	361.1	49.1	18 487	68.0	85.0	205.2	40.0	35.2	55.5	8.7	6.9	12.2	15.9	72 132	71 113	69 284
Henderson	486.3	70.0	19 914	73.2	102.3	297.7	54.3	46.9	46.9	9.7	3.2	15.0	10.7	144 454	143 665	121 386
Henry	627.0	57.6	20 921	76.9	142.1	393.6	D	32.1	D	13.0	3.5	16.2	15.9	126 257	120 570	117 614
Hickman	366.1	75.4	17 719	65.1	73.5	130.9	41.5	31.3	D	11.0	D	15.3	26.5	40 939	36 572	33 117
Houston	124.7	51.5	15 902	58.5	39.8	45.8	19.9	11.7	D	11.5	D	43.0	21.8	5 364	6 923	15 499
Humphreys	323.7	49.5	19 011	69.9	72.4	226.4	D	41.3	D	8.3	1.8	11.7	21.0	93 602	85 839	84 066
Jackson	185.8	71.0	19 326	71.0	49.2	65.3	37.0	27.5	D	8.2	5.6	D	16.1	17 945	17 838	18 384
Jefferson	779.2	68.9	17 868	65.7	168.3	372.1	D	26.3	61.3	10.2	2.5	17.6	14.0	97 891	95 904	91 870
Johnson	233.5	62.3	13 973	51.4	77.3	107.5	D	30.2	D	13.3	3.1	14.5	15.2	32 490	32 026	30 500
Knox	9 911.0	55.2	26 451	97.2	1 313.8	7 739.8	18.9	11.7	81.1	12.8	6.7	30.5	16.2	908 648	856 277	817 300
Lake	94.3	25.4	11 495	42.3	37.1	38.7	D	D	D	15.0	2.4	19.3	48.1	D	6 724	7 460
Lauderdale	426.0	52.1	17 624	64.8	108.5	286.2	D	44.5	D	8.3	2.9	11.9	16.5	127 336	119 399	102 074
Lawrence	750.3	52.9	19 082	70.1	165.7	420.2	D	37.0	D	13.6	3.3	15.0	13.0	155 575	167 442	170 931
Lewis	173.0	65.1	15 901	58.5	49.3	77.6	D	31.1	D	15.1	3.1	17.8	16.8	24 122	23 949	26 987
Lincoln	585.1	43.8	19 713	72.5	114.2	266.2	D	30.6	D	12.2	3.5	13.3	20.4	81 402	73 921	73 243
Loudon	883.8	79.5	22 648	83.3	161.6	364.2	D	30.9	D	10.3	3.8	16.5	15.6	112 378	109 169	105 711
McMinn	882.2	44.6	19 092	70.2	188.9	626.7	D	50.1	D	9.2	3.6	12.5	11.0	313 738	301 426	280 663
McNairy	453.0	56.8	18 883	69.4	118.7	249.9	D	34.7	59.6	8.4	2.4	24.8	13.5	86 754	81 426	77 375
Macon	309.2	55.1	17 115	62.9	74.2	123.8	D	25.1	D	12.9	5.3	16.9	17.3	31 086	28 960	34 762
Madison	2 129.7	63.1	24 814	91.2	332.3	1 890.1	D	25.7	D	9.3	3.6	23.6	18.1	485 964	464 875	422 636
Marion	521.2	56.1	19 536	71.8	122.1	197.8	D	29.3	D	16.9	4.0	15.9	15.3	57 860	54 110	47 066
Marshall	567.4	65.2	21 607	79.4	89.6	401.8	D	58.7	D	7.5	3.0	9.5	9.3	236 018	225 125	217 916
Maury	1 458.6	72.7	20 960	77.1	240.2	1 486.1	D	48.0	D	6.3	4.6	17.2	11.5	713 605	756 103	821 077
Meigs	161.0	58.7	16 147	59.4	43.0	57.5	D	31.7	D	9.6	D	13.4	18.2	18 234	17 098	13 718
Monroe	619.4	68.1	17 775	65.3	148.5	363.8	D	51.0	D	11.4	3.8	12.9	10.8	185 613	166 681	145 160
Montgomery	2 828.6	87.2	22 245	81.8	329.3	1 177.3	D	19.8	D	15.5	5.3	23.0	18.6	233 232	221 417	213 628
Moore	99.7	49.5	19 343	71.1	16.8	46.8	D	15.1	D	3.5	D	7.6	39.1	7 057	7 424	7 724
Morgan	270.2	54.5	14 468	53.2	80.1	110.7	33.7	26.4	67.0	6.8	1.9	11.5	36.6	29 174	30 899	26 723
Obion	714.9	39.8	22 227	81.7	128.9	547.3	54.1	49.0	45.0	9.8	2.3	14.3	8.7	268 338	255 054	242 153

[1] Based on resident population estimated as of July 1, 1998.   [2] Includes farm earnings; see table B-10 for these data.   [3] Includes mining and construction, not shown separately.   [4] Includes agricultural services, forestry, and fisheries; transportation and public utilities; and wholesale trade, not shown separately.   [5] Finance, insurance, and real estate.

Source: Personal Income and Earnings—U.S. Bureau of Economic Analysis, "Regional Economic Information System (REIS) 1969-1998" on CD-ROM (related Internet site <http://www.bea.doc.gov/bea/regional/data.htm>).

Table B–8. Counties — **Personal Income and Earnings**–Con.

[Includes U.S., states, and 3,142 counties/county equivalents defined as of January 1, 1992. For changes to these areas since January 1, 1992, see appendix B. Geographic Information]

County	Personal income, 1998														Manufacturing earnings		
			Per capita[1]			Earnings											
									Percent, by selected industry–								
							Goods-related		Service-related								
	Total (mil. dol.)	Percent change, 1990–1998	Amount (dollars)	Percent of national average	Transfer payments (mil. dol.)	Total[2] (mil. dol.)	Total[3]	Manufacturing	Total[4]	Retail trade	FIRE[5]	Services	Government	1998 ($1,000)	1997 ($1,000)	1996 ($1,000)
TENNESSEE—Con.																
Overton	324.7	63.3	16 635	61.2	90.6	148.6	D	29.4	D	11.5	4.2	19.3	18.3	43 722	38 815	34 632
Perry	141.2	81.2	18 756	68.9	37.4	89.3	D	56.3	D	5.2	2.9	19.9	10.7	50 250	54 592	42 388
Pickett	82.1	54.9	17 658	64.9	24.3	35.4	31.7	23.1	D	16.0	4.1	14.7	19.8	8 167	8 357	7 613
Polk	270.2	63.1	18 097	66.5	72.5	86.1	D	23.3	D	9.3	5.5	20.9	23.0	20 100	20 985	21 176
Putnam	1 321.0	66.5	22 371	82.2	233.2	1 024.6	D	29.0	D	11.3	4.3	17.7	19.1	297 082	287 244	269 270
Rhea	468.8	44.4	16 847	61.9	122.3	361.8	42.1	36.7	57.8	7.2	2.1	9.6	35.2	132 746	126 012	118 213
Roane	1 032.5	41.1	20 673	76.0	233.4	883.6	D	27.7	D	43.7	1.4	14.6	14.6	244 980	253 340	291 758
Robertson	1 193.1	91.4	22 429	82.5	166.8	486.2	D	33.4	D	11.6	2.7	15.3	16.0	162 377	146 392	133 637
Rutherford	4 187.3	105.1	25 212	92.7	385.2	3 128.7	D	30.7	D	8.0	6.0	25.4	12.9	960 207	985 354	889 110
Scott	304.2	47.8	15 155	55.7	104.1	166.0	D	33.6	D	10.9	2.4	17.6	19.0	55 871	47 254	46 215
Sequatchie	182.0	65.2	17 375	63.9	41.7	78.4	D	31.0	D	10.0	5.4	14.3	16.2	24 293	22 935	24 842
Sevier	1 410.5	78.0	21 913	80.6	223.3	898.5	D	9.0	D	27.5	6.1	34.4	12.2	80 425	78 194	73 671
Shelby	25 152.3	57.1	28 984	106.5	3 101.0	21 985.9	D	10.7	D	9.1	8.8	29.1	13.2	2 352 501	2 284 166	2 180 090
Smith	329.6	61.5	20 154	74.1	68.1	184.2	D	33.6	53.2	12.0	3.6	18.7	11.8	61 947	55 172	53 177
Stewart	189.3	61.7	16 427	60.4	49.4	85.8	12.8	5.4	D	10.7	4.2	10.5	56.2	4 604	3 877	5 326
Sullivan	3 513.3	41.4	23 368	85.9	629.4	2 706.3	43.4	36.0	56.7	9.5	3.4	25.0	8.7	975 405	1 075 344	1 147 684
Sumner	2 970.8	67.5	23 969	88.1	370.2	1 386.4	39.8	30.1	60.2	9.2	4.6	22.6	13.2	416 978	421 463	396 589
Tipton	890.7	67.5	18 832	69.2	153.7	388.6	D	32.5	D	10.2	4.0	17.2	15.4	126 195	107 751	103 303
Trousdale	110.3	56.3	16 078	59.1	29.9	51.5	D	32.9	D	10.5	5.7	16.5	21.5	16 932	16 202	15 080
Unicoi	347.6	43.8	20 198	74.2	86.4	169.0	D	43.2	D	5.2	2.2	11.2	16.1	72 965	69 601	63 451
Union	239.6	68.1	14 796	54.4	59.4	79.4	D	36.6	D	7.3	D	12.3	19.9	29 021	22 127	21 889
Van Buren	79.6	63.1	15 828	58.2	20.1	33.8	D	D	D	3.2	2.0	8.0	18.6	D	14 663	15 594
Warren	761.5	65.4	21 074	77.5	162.9	569.0	D	48.1	D	8.2	D	12.5	8.7	273 623	271 124	253 665
Washington	2 333.1	54.0	22 830	83.9	400.6	1 792.3	D	19.5	D	12.1	3.6	30.1	20.1	349 300	330 418	313 782
Wayne	245.0	54.7	14 904	54.8	66.6	104.8	D	27.9	D	9.7	3.4	22.0	22.0	29 238	30 420	31 274
Weakley	640.7	46.2	19 471	71.6	132.1	370.0	31.9	25.4	66.8	8.6	3.2	15.5	24.3	94 126	95 482	96 774
White	402.7	59.1	17 733	65.2	99.2	236.6	D	44.6	D	14.4	3.3	13.3	10.9	105 506	95 212	90 460
Williamson	4 296.5	114.0	36 508	134.2	237.9	2 309.2	17.9	8.5	82.1	11.7	16.4	35.8	7.8	195 550	182 630	172 906
Wilson	2 090.5	81.4	24 914	91.6	253.8	972.5	33.7	21.0	66.5	16.2	4.5	25.2	9.6	204 122	193 787	181 984
TEXAS	500 086.8	68.1	25 369	93.3	59 395.9	388 313.5	25.3	14.1	74.0	8.9	7.4	26.5	14.8	54 748 360	49 906 807	46 321 126
Anderson	897.4	55.9	17 218	63.3	191.7	612.4	14.7	5.6	86.0	16.7	3.4	22.1	29.4	34 026	29 537	30 068
Andrews	243.7	19.5	17 351	63.8	46.9	152.5	41.4	8.7	D	6.8	D	12.6	23.9	13 273	12 125	11 709
Angelina	1 602.6	53.3	20 735	76.2	316.7	1 133.5	32.1	26.5	67.7	11.9	4.1	24.2	16.1	300 566	304 122	298 447
Aransas	489.8	88.1	21 464	78.9	94.6	166.1	26.8	7.9	73.3	15.9	4.3	19.9	17.3	13 176	13 001	9 164
Archer	179.2	41.9	21 638	79.5	26.1	68.2	D	.6	D	5.2	2.8	11.2	20.7	432	359	357
Armstrong	39.9	26.0	18 489	68.0	9.0	12.2	D	D	D	7.3	10.0	22.6	32.4	D	157	135
Atascosa	622.4	70.8	17 105	62.9	121.5	262.0	17.4	4.2	80.2	10.7	3.2	27.0	21.5	10 963	11 459	9 693
Austin	527.2	63.3	22 531	82.8	83.4	289.4	37.5	23.0	63.1	7.8	5.0	19.2	14.4	66 703	63 775	60 822
Bailey	146.0	28.0	21 331	78.4	27.9	89.3	NA	5.0	56.5	7.0	4.8	6.9	18.1	4 506	3 495	2 676
Bandera	354.6	112.4	22 422	82.4	52.5	72.6	D	3.3	D	11.8	5.2	26.1	24.6	2 374	2 253	2 467
Bastrop	1 012.0	94.5	20 065	73.8	139.9	314.2	D	7.0	D	13.9	4.2	18.7	33.8	22 073	27 824	29 878
Baylor	80.5	17.1	19 366	71.2	23.9	37.7	10.6	1.7	83.1	9.4	3.3	27.7	23.0	622	534	898
Bee	432.0	39.7	15 574	57.3	104.0	254.1	15.3	4.0	84.5	8.6	4.0	22.6	42.8	10 262	8 347	7 249
Bell	5 121.4	70.3	22 949	84.4	601.9	4 518.2	11.2	7.2	88.8	7.1	2.6	15.8	56.9	326 999	320 340	340 168
Bexar	32 316.2	65.6	23 852	87.7	4 300.6	26 012.4	14.0	6.0	85.8	9.8	8.7	25.2	25.4	1 557 112	1 429 423	1 377 794
Blanco	172.1	70.3	20 642	75.9	46.2	77.7	D	2.0	D	9.4	9.9	D	16.6	1 564	1 439	1 350
Borden	8.5	–42.3	11 140	41.0	1.9	1.5	D	–	D	D	D	41.4	183.0	–	–	–
Bosque	319.2	45.4	19 292	70.9	74.0	118.9	24.5	14.5	68.6	9.3	4.1	21.0	21.1	17 190	17 093	16 006
Bowie	1 810.7	39.3	21 747	79.9	338.6	1 257.7	D	9.0	D	12.8	4.1	28.6	27.6	112 720	114 471	103 755
Brazoria	5 228.0	57.1	22 844	84.0	595.6	3 083.1	51.8	34.4	47.9	7.8	2.5	14.8	14.1	1 060 471	1 102 864	1 040 389
Brazos	2 674.5	65.6	20 121	74.0	282.3	2 077.6	15.2	7.0	84.8	11.0	5.4	23.0	39.4	144 967	126 199	109 470
Brewster	165.4	45.2	18 729	68.8	30.9	101.0	D	1.5	D	12.3	2.9	22.7	43.6	1 507	1 076	1 236
Briscoe	35.8	7.8	18 990	69.8	8.9	17.9	D	6.6	D	7.5	5.7	D	19.1	1 177	423	410
Brooks	115.0	43.4	13 644	50.2	41.6	50.1	D	1.6	D	13.8	3.5	23.4	43.9	815	472	316
Brown	693.1	51.3	18 816	69.2	175.8	448.9	34.6	28.9	65.1	10.8	3.0	24.7	17.9	129 934	123 002	117 878
Burleson	271.4	54.5	17 441	64.1	63.4	102.8	31.1	5.5	71.4	11.7	4.6	14.8	23.4	5 670	8 290	7 426
Burnet	642.5	77.6	19 910	73.2	119.9	298.9	26.0	11.4	75.3	15.6	6.7	22.8	18.8	33 988	33 239	31 472
Caldwell	559.5	75.9	17 471	64.2	107.1	181.4	D	6.3	D	11.4	3.6	31.2	25.4	11 387	11 852	12 104
Calhoun	402.2	47.6	19 535	71.8	71.4	497.0	72.5	51.0	27.5	4.4	2.0	7.5	8.5	253 579	239 916	235 677
Callahan	236.7	51.2	18 500	68.0	51.6	62.0	24.8	4.3	75.9	10.8	5.4	16.5	31.1	2 671	2 482	1 956
Cameron	4 460.7	71.4	13 766	50.6	1 134.2	2 857.4	D	11.3	D	11.3	5.6	27.6	26.4	322 195	327 282	301 725
Camp	265.5	69.9	24 280	89.3	50.8	145.6	17.9	9.5	52.1	9.3	4.6	12.3	9.8	13 834	13 189	12 732
Carson	173.5	59.9	25 863	95.1	21.7	245.5	D	D	D	1.5	2.1	3.8	11.6	D	167 264	165 837
Cass	618.1	56.9	20 105	73.9	145.3	329.5	38.5	29.6	55.8	9.7	2.9	13.7	17.9	97 463	96 242	89 526
Castro	239.3	38.4	28 778	105.8	28.7	189.6	NA	6.0	34.6	4.5	2.2	4.8	10.4	11 355	9 855	8 952

[1] Based on resident population estimated as of July 1, 1998.   [2] Includes farm earnings; see table B-10 for these data.   [3] Includes mining and construction, not shown separately.   [4] Includes agricultural services, forestry, and fisheries; transportation and public utilities; and wholesale trade, not shown separately.   [5] Finance, insurance, and real estate.

Source: Personal Income and Earnings—U.S. Bureau of Economic Analysis, "Regional Economic Information System (REIS) 1969-1998" on CD-ROM (related Internet site <http://www.bea.doc.gov/bea/regional/data.htm>).

Table B–8. Counties — **Personal Income and Earnings**–Con.

[Includes U.S., states, and 3,142 counties/county equivalents defined as of January 1, 1992. For changes to these areas since January 1, 1992, see appendix B. Geographic Information]

County	Personal income, 1998													Manufacturing earnings		
		Per capita[1]				Earnings										
								Percent, by selected industry–								
							Goods-related		Service-related							
	Total (mil. dol.)	Percent change, 1990–1998	Amount (dollars)	Percent of national average	Transfer payments (mil. dol.)	Total[2] (mil. dol.)	Total[3]	Manufacturing	Total[4]	Retail trade	FIRE[5]	Services	Government	1998 ($1,000)	1997 ($1,000)	1996 ($1,000)
TEXAS—Con.																
Chambers	564.4	82.1	23 722	87.2	69.3	279.2	52.1	38.3	43.7	5.3	1.6	8.8	16.0	106 928	91 778	91 168
Cherokee	941.0	66.9	21 728	79.9	190.0	578.8	20.1	16.3	58.8	12.4	3.5	14.5	20.5	94 505	90 350	83 399
Childress	116.1	33.6	15 310	56.3	28.5	66.8	D	2.7	D	14.3	3.0	14.3	50.1	1 816	1 331	1 223
Clay	209.6	40.0	19 902	73.2	35.7	77.8	D	12.3	D	10.1	D	24.8	18.7	9 567	8 716	8 043
Cochran	68.0	–2.1	17 349	63.8	16.2	38.8	D	1.2	D	5.7	2.7	10.6	31.1	473	397	474
Coke	62.8	36.5	18 607	68.4	16.5	25.8	D	3.4	D	15.9	6.0	22.6	37.3	887	749	763
Coleman	176.5	43.0	18 550	68.2	59.4	73.1	D	3.4	D	15.7	4.1	22.0	28.6	2 491	6 721	5 575
Collin	16 542.0	156.3	38 618	142.0	617.0	7 304.0	D	22.2	D	9.4	7.8	35.1	9.1	1 638 359	1 320 117	1 263 024
Collingsworth	59.0	3.8	18 065	66.4	17.3	28.1	4.3	1.4	81.0	8.8	5.8	15.0	31.1	398	474	423
Colorado	427.1	52.6	22 589	83.0	89.4	206.6	25.6	13.1	66.9	11.7	7.0	19.6	14.3	27 012	26 327	22 835
Comal	2 026.2	114.8	27 560	101.3	240.6	857.6	33.4	17.9	66.8	16.9	4.5	22.7	13.4	153 733	136 734	120 064
Comanche	266.5	32.8	19 701	72.4	68.6	119.3	13.0	7.0	74.7	10.6	3.3	16.6	20.2	8 370	8 201	8 207
Concho	46.2	18.0	14 913	54.8	13.5	23.4	D	D	D	7.5	4.5	37.0	30.2	D	246	322
Cooke	727.5	59.2	22 099	81.2	125.8	379.7	36.1	25.3	64.0	12.5	3.8	14.6	19.7	96 014	88 099	75 307
Coryell	1 168.1	54.7	15 824	58.2	125.1	364.2	D	4.4	D	9.6	4.3	15.3	50.4	16 122	15 109	13 771
Cottle	36.7	9.1	19 119	70.3	10.6	16.0	D	7.8	D	9.4	3.6	20.6	29.2	1 251	1 219	722
Crane	74.4	17.9	16 735	61.5	13.1	57.1	D	D	D	5.1	1.9	9.6	19.8	D	899	898
Crockett	64.6	11.9	14 340	52.7	12.6	38.2	41.3	.6	D	14.5	D	15.2	27.8	223	149	162
Crosby	127.7	24.6	17 670	65.0	37.5	59.6	D	D	D	5.6	3.9	12.9	24.8	D	2 057	1 583
Culberson	40.5	27.8	13 482	49.6	9.8	33.7	D	D	D	13.4	D	9.5	32.7	158	1 589	1 506
Dallam	183.1	56.9	27 935	102.7	24.9	163.8	5.8	1.9	59.6	5.4	3.1	9.7	14.2	3 158	2 385	2 120
Dallas	68 758.0	62.7	33 617	123.6	5 385.9	78 324.4	20.8	13.3	79.2	7.6	11.9	31.2	7.4	10 380 371	9 517 142	8 750 027
Dawson	259.0	19.2	17 705	65.1	67.4	144.9	14.7	4.5	79.8	10.0	4.4	13.1	26.5	6 521	6 487	6 770
Deaf Smith	427.9	30.7	22 436	82.5	65.7	300.6	13.2	9.7	44.4	4.4	2.7	8.3	12.9	29 017	30 651	29 467
Delta	102.5	53.6	20 714	76.1	24.0	36.0	D	D	D	5.5	4.9	24.2	24.9	D	6 069	4 174
Denton	10 685.2	104.5	27 872	102.5	624.9	3 982.7	29.1	19.6	70.9	12.3	5.0	21.9	17.5	781 180	688 341	662 615
DeWitt	370.0	41.3	18 903	69.5	93.6	187.8	D	17.5	D	10.0	6.0	20.3	32.8	32 900	31 120	27 899
Dickens	44.0	24.1	19 698	72.4	16.1	20.4	D	D	D	9.9	4.5	16.2	24.5	D	96	102
Dimmit	125.0	43.8	12 005	44.1	46.3	68.5	D	D	D	10.0	3.5	14.0	44.7	D	2 085	1 994
Donley	65.5	10.4	17 091	62.8	18.8	27.9	D	1.7	D	13.3	5.0	16.0	37.7	465	399	467
Duval	176.3	45.4	12 042	47.6	67.0	94.7	D	D	D	4.2	D	18.7	36.9	D	304	174
Eastland	333.9	43.8	18 943	69.6	99.4	178.9	41.3	20.6	D	10.0	D	14.6	21.0	36 905	33 436	29 390
Ector	2 473.9	45.9	19 824	72.9	411.5	1 756.2	34.8	12.1	65.4	11.1	3.0	20.2	16.7	211 669	197 154	178 902
Edwards	30.7	18.5	8 401	30.9	10.1	10.6	D	D	D	11.3	5.8	13.7	49.4	D	89	106
Ellis	2 398.3	78.3	23 119	85.0	319.4	1 100.7	47.3	38.2	52.9	7.8	3.3	17.2	12.7	420 187	393 923	356 085
El Paso	11 363.1	53.9	16 359	60.1	2 071.1	8 513.3	19.7	14.6	80.1	9.8	6.2	22.6	27.7	1 245 791	1 144 958	1 100 288
Erath	660.5	53.4	21 059	77.4	116.2	433.3	24.3	18.9	57.8	9.2	3.2	18.6	17.5	81 913	72 695	67 369
Falls	286.7	38.2	16 385	60.2	78.4	126.4	D	7.9	D	7.7	1.9	16.8	47.3	9 933	10 590	9 592
Fannin	546.4	58.1	19 263	70.8	129.0	273.9	28.1	21.9	71.9	13.2	5.5	12.5	30.9	60 067	52 538	48 058
Fayette	471.7	47.9	22 170	81.5	103.6	245.6	22.7	11.4	77.2	11.0	6.0	20.7	21.5	27 948	27 370	25 125
Fisher	73.3	1.6	17 143	63.0	21.9	21.7	D	D	D	8.6	8.3	17.0	46.9	D	4 119	4 075
Floyd	181.5	15.9	22 126	81.3	34.1	118.5	NA	2.7	52.4	4.1	3.8	7.4	15.6	3 204	2 784	2 521
Foard	33.2	5.5	19 804	72.8	9.8	12.8	D	D	D	5.6	D	17.0	26.9	D	1 554	2 936
Fort Bend	8 861.5	96.3	26 309	96.7	512.4	3 858.3	36.5	17.2	62.2	7.8	8.6	21.1	14.2	661 772	604 172	569 321
Franklin	191.1	70.2	19 623	72.1	35.5	85.7	D	7.8	D	21.8	5.2	23.1	12.2	6 705	5 442	3 557
Freestone	287.9	38.4	16 315	60.0	67.6	141.9	28.3	5.6	78.1	13.8	2.9	15.5	24.5	8 011	9 539	7 923
Frio	214.4	49.8	13 536	49.8	56.1	123.2	11.0	1.9	71.9	8.8	2.6	17.7	29.6	2 396	2 339	2 267
Gaines	270.5	34.4	18 191	66.9	44.5	191.0	17.6	.9	51.6	5.4	2.4	6.4	16.9	1 808	1 611	2 361
Galveston	5 954.1	51.7	24 303	89.3	812.3	3 244.7	24.4	16.1	75.6	9.3	7.0	18.4	31.2	523 633	485 275	476 002
Garza	83.7	33.0	18 198	66.9	21.7	44.0	35.8	1.8	67.9	9.1	7.8	19.0	21.8	784	742	646
Gillespie	463.9	67.7	23 200	85.3	87.7	206.6	D	10.0	D	17.5	5.6	31.0	14.6	20 756	22 001	20 154
Glasscock	18.4	–27.5	13 325	49.0	2.1	10.2	D	–	D	D	D	7.2	39.6	–	–	–
Goliad	108.0	36.3	15 451	56.8	27.4	37.7	D	.4	D	10.4	2.9	14.8	32.7	155	165	190
Gonzales	372.6	61.5	21 311	78.3	78.7	232.2	D	7.3	D	5.9	3.5	13.7	15.0	17 005	21 251	22 594
Gray	566.7	32.9	24 021	88.3	110.7	355.8	41.6	25.2	54.7	9.0	2.9	18.1	13.2	89 779	83 730	75 454
Grayson	2 287.0	50.2	22 417	82.4	427.5	1 472.0	39.3	32.0	60.5	11.1	6.4	23.0	11.9	471 501	447 044	447 160
Gregg	2 821.7	52.5	24 983	91.8	468.4	2 143.8	32.7	18.0	67.4	12.7	4.2	25.4	10.0	385 055	362 524	346 537
Grimes	366.0	52.9	15 686	57.7	70.4	243.1	43.6	34.5	55.3	6.0	2.1	16.0	24.3	83 991	77 095	69 325
Guadalupe	1 712.2	81.5	21 282	78.2	237.0	710.8	42.7	34.0	56.6	10.8	3.7	16.1	18.4	241 930	216 062	201 874
Hale	738.0	39.3	20 107	73.9	140.3	512.4	18.6	14.5	64.6	17.6	2.8	15.2	14.8	74 267	70 104	64 842
Hall	55.6	–1.8	15 325	56.3	20.8	25.6	13.3	9.7	D	11.4	5.2	D	36.6	2 499	2 182	1 577
Hamilton	171.5	52.7	22 415	82.4	43.0	81.8	D	8.1	D	13.9	2.6	17.5	19.1	6 600	6 887	6 127
Hansford	178.5	20.3	33 376	122.7	18.0	136.4	12.4	1.1	D	3.5	2.6	D	10.8	1 509	1 583	1 826
Hardeman	93.6	18.6	20 496	75.3	23.8	46.6	D	26.4	D	8.4	3.7	12.1	25.9	12 313	12 085	11 688
Hardin	1 000.7	74.8	20 361	74.8	183.4	322.5	34.6	13.7	65.6	13.1	3.0	18.3	19.6	44 267	41 451	38 530
Harris	102 632.7	71.1	32 052	117.8	8 190.5	96 481.4	29.8	12.5	70.2	7.5	7.0	28.7	8.7	12 031 996	11 299 709	10 183 073

[1] Based on resident population estimated as of July 1, 1998. [2] Includes farm earnings; see table B-10 for these data. [3] Includes mining and construction, not shown separately. [4] Includes agricultural services, forestry, and fisheries; transportation and public utilities; and wholesale trade, not shown separately. [5] Finance, insurance, and real estate.

Source: Personal Income and Earnings—U.S. Bureau of Economic Analysis, "Regional Economic Information System (REIS) 1969-1998" on CD-ROM (related Internet site <http://www.bea.doc.gov/bea/regional/data.htm>).

[Includes U.S., states, and 3,142 counties/county equivalents defined as of January 1, 1992. For changes to these areas since January 1, 1992, see appendix B. Geographic Information]

County	Personal income, 1998													Manufacturing earnings		
			Per capita[1]			Earnings										
									Percent, by selected industry–							
							Goods-related		Service-related							
	Total (mil. dol.)	Percent change, 1990–1998	Amount (dollars)	Percent of national average	Transfer payments (mil. dol.)	Total[2] (mil. dol.)	Total[3]	Manu-facturing	Total[4]	Retail trade	FIRE[5]	Serv-ices	Gov-ern-ment	1998 ($1,000)	1997 ($1,000)	1996 ($1,000)

TEXAS—Con.

County																
Harrison	1 148.5	44.0	19 211	70.6	216.5	793.2	48.2	35.6	51.3	7.0	4.3	18.4	11.4	282 385	290 995	310 842
Hartley	143.5	51.7	27 901	102.6	7.8	90.8	D	D	D	2.5	D	5.6	12.9	D	D	D
Haskell	110.7	7.0	18 071	66.4	34.1	46.2	7.0	1.3	91.1	16.4	6.5	20.9	29.3	619	518	499
Hays	1 910.6	109.3	21 394	78.6	204.0	919.1	25.9	16.3	74.6	16.0	4.6	21.6	25.3	150 002	136 104	116 220
Hemphill	100.9	46.7	28 621	105.2	11.1	69.0	D	1.8	76.1	5.3	6.2	7.1	15.8	1 239	979	869
Henderson	1 383.9	75.2	20 060	73.7	292.7	489.6	23.5	11.9	76.1	15.5	10.0	24.0	16.0	58 356	49 841	43 420
Hidalgo	6 630.5	83.6	12 759	46.9	1 705.8	4 223.7	15.0	7.5	82.9	14.0	4.4	24.6	27.8	315 920	312 529	297 366
Hill	568.7	61.8	18 609	68.4	138.2	238.3	D	17.4	D	18.7	4.8	17.4	22.3	41 405	39 075	34 393
Hockley	438.9	34.5	18 516	68.1	90.7	265.7	D	2.6	D	6.9	3.5	15.3	19.0	6 853	6 540	5 409
Hood	972.7	86.1	26 106	96.0	158.5	262.5	14.9	4.2	82.6	18.4	9.3	23.4	17.6	11 058	9 147	8 195
Hopkins	658.9	55.9	21 711	79.8	123.0	436.6	D	23.5	D	11.5	3.4	12.3	13.5	102 689	58 113	50 132
Houston	442.7	50.9	20 091	73.9	110.3	251.5	24.5	17.0	74.5	8.4	5.3	19.6	24.5	42 816	42 422	38 011
Howard	648.7	32.4	20 224	74.3	140.8	407.3	D	12.8	D	9.8	4.3	18.3	31.6	52 344	47 419	46 606
Hudspeth	38.7	45.5	12 131	44.6	9.4	24.1	D	D	D	6.0	D	7.4	53.6	D	D	D
Hunt	1 434.1	46.5	20 418	75.1	269.4	847.0	D	37.1	D	9.9	2.8	15.0	21.1	314 402	305 350	287 400
Hutchinson	519.5	16.5	21 609	79.4	90.4	369.6	60.0	31.4	39.2	7.1	1.8	9.8	13.5	116 195	112 575	111 872
Irion	30.9	23.6	17 911	65.8	5.4	13.2	D	D	D	9.9	D	14.8	25.1	D	205	170
Jack	140.3	49.9	18 862	69.3	30.3	64.5	33.3	2.8	70.7	7.3	5.4	22.7	23.7	1 797	1 320	634
Jackson	288.3	47.1	21 086	77.5	59.1	162.8	53.8	35.3	47.7	7.6	2.3	10.2	16.8	57 445	60 827	59 152
Jasper	697.8	68.9	20 867	76.7	162.4	389.0	41.0	32.7	59.4	11.1	3.2	18.9	16.0	127 316	126 959	118 634
Jeff Davis	32.9	30.1	13 932	51.2	6.8	18.4	D	D	D	10.5	6.1	38.1	40.0	D	D	D
Jefferson	5 741.6	39.9	23 802	87.5	1 104.3	4 751.2	33.0	21.6	66.9	9.2	3.7	28.7	14.2	1 027 595	971 885	913 004
Jim Hogg	82.1	39.7	16 391	60.3	22.8	39.3	19.5	2.1	D	13.2	D	9.3	40.6	842	775	580
Jim Wells	663.4	50.6	16 563	60.9	180.4	378.8	28.4	1.9	71.3	11.0	4.0	28.8	17.4	7 325	6 535	6 375
Johnson	2 404.1	64.3	20 339	74.8	364.7	1 013.1	33.6	22.9	65.6	12.6	3.3	20.5	14.8	232 354	222 166	187 884
Jones	287.3	28.3	15 428	56.7	77.9	154.4	13.4	6.3	88.9	6.4	4.7	17.5	48.3	9 713	10 786	12 785
Karnes	219.0	50.0	14 417	53.0	59.7	112.9	18.8	8.3	85.5	7.9	3.6	20.5	43.1	9 403	9 697	8 797
Kaufman	1 411.2	77.7	21 534	79.2	241.5	627.4	31.3	22.1	68.8	13.4	4.2	20.4	20.7	138 560	129 940	120 734
Kendall	583.6	98.9	27 542	101.2	71.8	224.8	26.4	8.8	75.4	16.0	10.9	24.5	15.6	19 769	15 433	11 610
Kenedy	9.1	11.8	20 226	74.4	1.1	7.0	D	–	D	D	.9	14.9	22.1	–	–	–
Kent	17.3	47.2	19 662	72.3	4.7	7.3	D	–	D	8.6	D	8.4	59.0	–	–	–
Kerr	1 085.8	62.8	25 448	93.5	200.4	507.0	18.6	7.9	81.8	12.1	5.3	32.6	23.2	40 065	37 291	31 951
Kimble	72.4	35.8	17 496	64.3	18.4	41.1	31.1	19.6	D	15.1	4.6	26.6	22.9	8 060	7 664	7 453
King	4.9	2.0	13 783	50.7	.7	3.7	D	1.4	D	D	–	D	51.4	51	50	(6)
Kinney	45.2	56.4	13 006	47.8	15.1	15.1	5.6	1.1	D	4.3	D	15.3	69.9	170	111	129
Kleberg	536.5	44.0	17 822	65.5	122.0	342.6	12.4	1.9	86.3	10.8	2.9	18.9	48.1	6 665	7 416	6 189
Knox	82.9	20.4	19 630	72.2	23.6	45.3	16.1	1.0	64.7	5.3	3.6	14.2	27.9	473	489	280
Lamar	993.2	50.8	21 648	79.6	200.6	704.8	36.3	30.2	64.6	9.6	3.1	23.4	12.9	212 834	207 235	193 211
Lamb	315.6	24.7	21 378	78.6	70.9	207.3	12.1	9.7	50.2	5.6	2.2	8.0	14.3	20 026	19 380	18 766
Lampasas	284.7	61.1	16 052	59.0	70.7	103.7	30.0	11.4	73.6	13.8	4.2	22.4	25.3	11 837	11 351	10 025
La Salle	76.7	54.2	12 704	46.7	23.7	39.6	13.4	–	77.0	6.4	2.5	16.6	42.1	–	–	–
Lavaca	394.1	42.7	20 918	76.9	97.0	161.5	37.3	29.2	64.7	12.9	3.8	20.6	15.3	47 089	42 212	41 786
Lee	266.6	52.7	17 909	65.8	50.9	154.0	36.0	9.5	66.1	8.7	3.9	14.7	22.3	14 694	14 178	12 650
Leon	270.3	54.9	18 665	68.6	71.6	159.3	58.0	22.8	46.1	7.6	3.7	10.2	13.1	36 296	35 038	34 324
Liberty	1 191.1	62.7	18 281	67.2	252.2	520.0	29.2	17.6	70.4	12.1	3.8	19.8	21.9	91 541	85 944	79 693
Limestone	392.9	38.7	18 939	69.6	104.7	208.0	16.4	8.5	84.9	10.0	2.6	18.2	35.4	17 695	16 239	14 071
Lipscomb	77.0	25.7	25 999	95.6	10.9	43.4	D	D	D	3.7	3.7	6.1	20.3	D	3 380	3 032
Live Oak	187.8	63.1	18 500	68.0	39.1	96.7	D	D	D	10.7	3.3	13.5	39.5	D	18 366	16 673
Llano	315.0	65.7	23 422	86.1	82.7	117.8	D	2.3	D	11.4	8.6	28.3	23.4	2 668	2 430	2 143
Loving	3.8	63.1	32 853	120.8	.3	2.3	D	–	D	NA	D	D	14.6	–	–	–
Lubbock	5 352.0	46.7	23 451	86.2	836.3	3 860.1	15.4	8.7	83.8	13.2	6.5	28.3	20.1	334 130	284 955	270 213
Lynn	119.1	12.7	17 743	65.2	27.4	61.4	3.3	1.5	75.7	3.4	5.2	7.7	22.4	896	664	544
McCulloch	158.6	40.4	18 204	66.9	44.0	77.6	D	8.6	D	13.4	5.8	22.1	24.2	6 655	7 165	6 726
McLennan	4 435.3	56.9	21 826	80.2	701.8	3 210.8	26.6	20.2	73.2	9.5	11.2	24.3	16.9	647 575	616 217	582 277
McMullen	19.3	42.0	24 335	89.5	2.6	9.2	D	–	D	3.3	D	D	33.7	–	–	–
Madison	220.7	52.0	18 623	68.5	45.8	133.7	5.2	1.1	67.0	9.4	5.4	19.9	25.7	1 472	1 192	1 086
Marion	167.8	41.0	15 403	56.6	50.5	63.6	D	25.3	D	12.5	2.9	19.9	20.6	16 113	15 868	18 058
Martin	69.4	–7.4	13 833	50.9	17.2	37.3	13.4	2.8	96.8	13.5	5.2	14.1	31.3	1 036	1 193	1 019
Mason	59.2	20.3	16 105	59.2	16.5	21.3	D	D	D	13.4	6.3	20.8	31.6	D	424	355
Matagorda	735.6	34.8	19 364	71.2	140.2	501.1	17.0	6.5	78.6	8.7	2.3	18.7	15.6	32 438	33 638	36 870
Maverick	488.9	88.8	10 258	37.7	169.6	282.4	10.9	7.3	88.6	12.0	3.5	16.6	41.0	20 670	19 277	17 809
Medina	662.1	90.1	17 939	65.9	122.1	229.4	16.5	6.4	81.8	13.5	4.4	17.9	32.2	14 774	15 445	16 863
Menard	34.7	31.8	14 958	55.0	11.6	11.4	D	D	D	20.0	6.2	12.6	49.6	D	91	126
Midland	3 555.2	48.8	29 846	109.7	341.5	2 744.0	47.7	3.5	52.4	7.3	4.4	18.0	10.2	96 340	92 572	81 332
Milam	441.2	42.6	18 234	67.0	102.1	251.1	50.1	37.3	49.9	8.4	4.1	13.6	14.1	93 679	90 790	85 457
Mills	92.4	41.1	19 460	71.5	26.5	40.1	NA	6.9	D	14.3	D	26.2	23.4	2 763	3 090	3 143

[1] Based on resident population estimated as of July 1, 1998. [2] Includes farm earnings; see table B-10 for these data. [3] Includes mining and construction, not shown separately. [4] Includes agricultural services, forestry, and fisheries; transportation and public utilities; and wholesale trade, not shown separately. [5] Finance, insurance, and real estate. [6] Less than $50,000.

Source: Personal Income and Earnings—U.S. Bureau of Economic Analysis, "Regional Economic Information System (REIS) 1969-1998" on CD-ROM (related Internet site <http://www.bea.doc.gov/bea/regional/data.htm>).

[Includes U.S., states, and 3,142 counties/county equivalents defined as of January 1, 1992. For changes to these areas since January 1, 1992, see appendix B. Geographic Information]

County	Personal income, 1998													Manufacturing earnings		
			Per capita[1]			Earnings										
									Percent, by selected industry–							
							Goods-related		Service-related							
	Total (mil. dol.)	Percent change, 1990–1998	Amount (dollars)	Percent of national average	Transfer payments (mil. dol.)	Total[2] (mil. dol.)	Total[3]	Man-ufac-turing	Total[4]	Retail trade	FIRE[5]	Serv-ices	Gov-ern-ment	1998 ($1,000)	1997 ($1,000)	1996 ($1,000)
TEXAS—Con.																
Mitchell	137.7	25.4	15 588	57.3	39.8	67.1	13.2	2.2	98.3	9.8	2.8	13.7	56.5	1 443	1 224	1 189
Montague	350.5	46.5	18 873	69.4	91.6	146.9	D	12.2	D	11.6	4.9	20.1	24.7	17 854	17 059	16 575
Montgomery	7 146.0	119.2	26 291	96.6	703.0	2 724.2	26.6	11.1	73.0	11.5	6.2	28.3	13.1	301 203	270 539	235 725
Moore	416.7	46.4	21 278	78.2	51.4	338.8	38.7	30.4	45.0	6.1	1.8	10.0	12.1	102 871	101 679	90 258
Morris	258.3	50.3	19 334	71.1	67.2	199.1	53.9	50.4	42.9	4.3	2.5	12.2	10.8	100 355	120 914	103 382
Motley	19.9	-13.5	14 962	55.0	7.2	7.2	D	18.4	D	14.3	5.6	20.5	40.6	1 331	1 442	1 607
Nacogdoches	1 097.9	50.7	19 520	71.8	209.7	674.1	D	20.1	D	11.8	3.5	21.7	23.0	135 751	135 179	133 545
Navarro	844.2	52.6	20 294	74.6	179.3	477.2	24.2	16.7	76.6	15.6	3.7	26.9	17.6	79 466	78 001	73 683
Newton	219.0	59.2	15 357	56.5	57.4	69.3	D	32.8	D	6.5	D	18.2	27.2	22 730	22 211	22 911
Nolan	299.0	31.8	18 198	66.9	75.1	183.2	27.2	17.8	73.1	9.1	4.0	18.3	26.1	32 688	31 389	29 277
Nueces	7 032.6	54.0	22 275	81.9	1 111.6	5 439.3	21.7	10.0	78.0	10.2	5.1	28.1	21.4	544 741	522 644	511 946
Ochiltree	232.8	29.8	26 480	97.3	24.7	177.0	35.3	2.0	D	6.6	D	9.4	11.0	3 517	3 455	3 701
Oldham	50.5	10.1	23 385	86.0	6.2	36.2	D	D	D	3.9	D	D	22.7	D	101	88
Orange	1 828.9	56.5	21 575	79.3	352.5	972.4	51.6	42.2	48.4	8.4	2.6	16.8	13.9	410 602	390 901	366 597
Palo Pinto	509.6	47.2	19 682	72.4	107.5	240.6	D	19.4	D	13.3	4.5	19.4	22.1	46 643	39 860	37 384
Panola	420.4	45.2	18 242	67.1	91.7	218.6	34.9	14.0	57.7	7.3	3.3	15.7	19.7	30 576	25 673	22 353
Parker	1 978.5	88.4	24 050	88.4	224.0	614.7	32.3	15.0	67.1	13.1	5.5	19.5	18.9	92 205	88 879	83 617
Parmer	226.3	15.8	21 971	80.8	30.8	201.8	D	D	D	2.1	1.4	5.8	11.1	D	D	D
Pecos	213.5	41.2	13 271	48.8	47.2	146.8	21.2	2.3	77.8	9.3	2.5	15.7	37.2	3 446	3 335	3 306
Polk	862.3	98.1	17 184	63.2	264.7	321.0	30.2	21.9	70.1	12.8	3.7	17.5	23.2	70 273	69 597	68 159
Potter	2 448.8	58.9	22 613	83.1	498.4	2 673.9	19.7	8.3	80.4	11.3	6.9	30.3	15.8	221 781	208 919	213 385
Presidio	88.1	44.8	10 296	37.8	26.8	44.6	D	1.2	D	7.2	3.0	14.0	60.7	529	478	401
Rains	140.7	62.0	16 378	60.2	34.5	45.8	D	6.7	D	13.4	3.6	19.3	21.1	3 064	2 740	4 327
Randall	2 416.2	49.1	24 461	89.9	164.1	743.2	22.4	9.4	73.7	11.0	5.8	22.1	18.1	70 189	66 662	66 777
Reagan	53.6	-.2	12 672	46.6	10.2	35.3	D	2.1	D	5.7	3.6	11.8	28.8	752	794	604
Real	46.5	63.6	17 206	63.3	16.0	14.6	D	D	D	10.2	3.7	27.9	34.6	D	430	402
Red River	238.2	32.6	17 339	63.7	74.1	95.7	D	30.7	D	10.4	2.3	18.3	23.7	29 340	30 363	30 394
Reeves	195.0	19.0	13 626	50.1	50.5	112.7	D	D	D	10.8	2.8	13.3	30.6	D	9 156	8 019
Refugio	187.7	50.9	23 766	87.4	35.5	77.5	36.0	.6	61.7	11.2	4.1	9.2	23.8	463	452	330
Roberts	16.6	-6.5	17 777	65.3	2.8	7.3	D	D	D	5.3	D	D	32.1	D	161	149
Robertson	248.3	36.5	15 904	58.5	72.0	107.0	31.8	19.2	74.3	9.3	5.0	13.7	25.3	20 400	21 030	21 615
Rockwall	1 174.8	110.9	31 580	116.1	85.7	426.2	22.9	9.9	77.1	11.8	6.3	29.9	10.8	42 119	38 526	37 031
Runnels	208.7	34.7	18 118	66.6	52.4	114.0	35.8	28.2	59.4	8.7	5.9	14.7	20.8	32 143	30 527	27 465
Rusk	898.0	40.2	19 632	72.2	167.5	501.7	38.6	12.2	58.1	7.0	3.0	20.4	13.3	61 408	56 474	50 958
Sabine	210.8	62.2	20 055	73.7	69.6	85.6	D	D	D	8.0	2.8	18.2	19.3	D	21 068	20 506
San Augustine	150.9	57.3	18 626	68.5	50.9	62.2	D	9.6	D	9.7	2.8	21.1	20.4	5 996	5 481	4 855
San Jacinto	381.8	87.1	17 493	64.3	81.7	66.8	D	8.8	D	7.9	3.4	22.7	30.8	5 858	5 320	4 556
San Patricio	1 209.0	70.1	17 091	62.8	232.2	658.7	30.4	22.5	68.0	6.8	1.9	13.5	41.0	147 878	136 033	131 240
San Saba	105.1	38.5	18 061	66.4	27.9	52.6	D	2.4	D	17.6	D	19.3	34.6	1 237	1 555	1 652
Schleicher	44.8	28.3	15 075	55.4	10.9	23.6	D	.4	D	5.3	3.7	16.4	31.3	87	D	D
Scurry	337.4	30.2	18 742	68.9	67.0	208.0	42.7	4.4	61.1	7.5	3.2	10.5	24.1	9 222	7 114	6 046
Shackelford	70.9	19.1	21 550	79.2	14.7	34.2	57.2	1.5	48.0	6.1	4.8	14.6	17.8	517	492	696
Shelby	488.9	65.1	21 368	78.6	117.2	287.0	D	22.5	D	7.9	3.2	15.6	12.6	64 447	60 178	57 715
Sherman	111.1	22.4	38 754	142.5	8.3	90.8	2.5	.5	D	2.7	D	4.4	8.1	455	318	312
Smith	4 233.6	61.0	25 190	92.6	632.9	3 042.1	27.5	16.6	71.5	12.1	5.9	30.0	12.8	506 428	475 661	486 593
Somervell	173.7	106.3	27 205	100.0	21.1	156.8	D	2.9	D	3.0	1.8	17.6	11.1	4 472	3 531	3 165
Starr	456.0	103.3	8 225	30.2	177.5	244.2	D	.5	D	12.6	1.7	20.2	46.8	1 300	1 198	1 164
Stephens	192.1	54.3	19 743	72.6	43.7	106.1	D	17.8	D	8.9	3.5	15.5	20.8	18 929	15 605	16 189
Sterling	20.7	48.4	14 928	54.9	4.2	13.6	D	D	D	9.7	D	14.6	28.1	D	D	D
Stonewall	36.4	8.7	20 273	74.5	9.4	19.3	D	D	D	4.5	D	11.5	26.4	D	(6)	D
Sutton	75.2	31.3	16 830	61.9	13.6	53.7	54.5	.9	D	8.3	4.1	14.2	22.4	490	361	217
Swisher	204.8	12.6	24 730	90.9	32.9	136.5	D	2.9	41.9	4.2	2.2	6.6	15.7	3 902	3 827	4 343
Tarrant	37 287.7	61.9	27 538	101.2	3 427.9	28 043.2	26.1	17.7	73.8	10.7	6.4	24.9	11.7	4 962 175	4 585 936	4 262 938
Taylor	2 808.3	45.7	23 012	84.6	447.9	2 040.9	20.5	11.7	79.0	10.5	4.8	27.4	26.2	239 519	241 094	234 257
Terrell	21.4	-.7	18 266	67.1	5.2	8.5	D	D	D	6.3	3.8	16.5	44.3	D	D	D
Terry	253.4	36.0	19 657	72.3	58.4	144.6	17.3	1.1	62.2	10.3	3.3	9.6	23.1	1 594	1 723	1 525
Throckmorton	41.2	-5.4	24 190	88.9	8.6	18.3	D	D	D	3.9	2.5	7.7	26.7	D	280	298
Titus	534.9	47.1	21 042	77.4	96.4	459.1	D	33.2	D	9.7	2.4	12.9	17.5	152 455	142 626	127 632
Tom Green	2 273.5	46.0	22 140	81.4	367.4	1 539.8	20.7	11.4	79.4	10.0	4.9	24.4	25.9	175 358	166 245	168 954
Travis	22 798.9	100.7	32 148	118.2	1 586.0	22 597.8	26.4	20.4	73.6	7.5	7.3	29.1	17.2	4 601 963	3 164 749	2 852 078
Trinity	226.2	55.9	17 938	65.9	69.6	74.2	D	13.3	D	11.7	3.7	20.8	24.8	9 846	8 183	8 026
Tyler	343.5	57.8	16 862	62.0	94.0	115.8	D	13.8	D	10.6	5.0	15.3	36.0	15 980	15 520	17 438
Upshur	645.1	57.2	18 010	66.2	143.8	204.5	24.7	10.2	73.2	14.6	5.6	18.0	21.3	20 935	20 384	17 666
Upton	63.9	5.3	16 952	62.3	13.2	41.6	D	.7	D	4.7	3.0	6.9	31.0	306	303	335
Uvalde	432.5	52.4	16 997	62.5	104.2	248.8	14.7	6.4	83.0	11.6	3.5	20.0	29.8	15 999	14 499	12 914
Val Verde	660.5	52.2	15 137	55.6	139.2	451.6	D	2.7	D	9.9	2.7	15.2	55.5	12 200	10 966	10 868

[1] Based on resident population estimated as of July 1, 1998. [2] Includes farm earnings; see table B-10 for these data. [3] Includes mining and construction, not shown separately. [4] Includes agricultural services, forestry, and fisheries; transportation and public utilities; and wholesale trade, not shown separately. [5] Finance, insurance, and real estate. [6] Less than $50,000.

Source: Personal Income and Earnings—U.S. Bureau of Economic Analysis, "Regional Economic Information System (REIS) 1969-1998" on CD-ROM (related Internet site <http://www.bea.doc.gov/bea/regional/data.htm>).

[Includes U.S., states, and 3,142 counties/county equivalents defined as of January 1, 1992. For changes to these areas since January 1, 1992, see appendix B. Geographic Information]

County	Personal income, 1998 Total (mil. dol.)	Percent change, 1990–1998	Per capita Amount (dollars)	Per capita Percent of national average	Transfer payments (mil. dol.)	Earnings Total[2] (mil. dol.)	Goods-related Total[3]	Manufacturing	Service-related Total[4]	Retail trade	FIRE[5]	Services	Government	Manufacturing earnings 1998 ($1,000)	1997 ($1,000)	1996 ($1,000)
TEXAS—Con.																
Van Zandt	868.0	68.6	19 745	72.6	194.5	270.5	23.2	2.9	72.0	14.2	3.2	21.6	20.0	7 967	7 935	8 741
Victoria	1 970.8	49.5	24 131	88.7	283.0	1 232.3	28.0	12.3	72.8	14.0	5.4	26.3	15.7	151 806	147 303	137 190
Walker	918.3	52.3	16 757	61.6	151.8	646.9	D	7.3	D	9.3	2.9	13.4	59.3	46 905	48 345	47 166
Waller	555.8	67.8	20 398	75.0	97.8	277.2	33.0	23.2	68.6	13.2	3.3	12.1	31.5	64 387	64 577	57 939
Ward	208.1	15.0	17 639	64.8	43.0	121.0	D	D	D	8.0	3.1	12.2	27.5	D	2 078	5 085
Washington	747.4	64.6	25 667	94.4	120.4	403.3	D	22.9	D	10.9	9.3	16.2	19.2	92 384	89 689	86 337
Webb	2 590.9	104.1	13 870	51.0	526.1	1 958.1	13.7	2.2	86.3	12.0	6.0	19.7	25.3	43 452	35 842	31 878
Wharton	854.5	39.1	21 298	78.3	156.4	467.1	22.0	11.9	67.0	9.4	3.8	21.5	18.6	55 741	54 245	51 353
Wheeler	137.8	35.2	26 061	95.8	29.9	79.9	D	1.8	D	8.0	2.3	15.5	18.1	1 426	1 290	1 210
Wichita	2 946.3	41.1	22 929	84.3	455.2	2 166.3	26.3	14.6	73.4	9.1	3.8	20.3	30.6	316 889	306 550	281 864
Wilbarger	291.6	24.4	20 717	76.2	66.8	182.5	19.1	14.3	76.8	9.4	4.2	13.3	39.0	26 176	22 222	20 684
Willacy	234.5	74.4	11 965	44.0	83.2	105.0	D	D	D	10.3	3.1	20.2	35.0	D	1 934	1 693
Williamson	5 848.7	156.5	26 149	96.1	406.4	3 037.2	21.4	11.8	78.8	7.7	4.5	18.5	11.1	359 325	342 540	297 851
Wilson	600.6	100.7	19 185	70.5	89.5	135.2	23.3	5.8	78.1	11.7	4.1	19.8	33.6	7 837	7 517	7 112
Winkler	136.3	27.3	17 103	62.9	30.9	77.2	39.4	.5	D	7.7	2.5	12.8	23.2	380	381	518
Wise	945.9	90.2	21 339	78.4	122.1	398.0	35.5	17.3	65.1	12.8	3.9	15.7	15.9	69 029	61 037	55 176
Wood	646.4	54.6	18 837	69.2	173.0	284.5	19.1	8.9	69.8	11.2	4.5	23.7	17.7	25 355	26 466	25 901
Yoakum	143.8	16.2	18 046	66.3	24.9	112.1	43.8	1.8	53.0	5.2	1.5	9.0	19.5	1 973	907	752
Young	410.5	35.2	23 384	86.0	87.0	236.3	D	18.4	D	8.6	4.6	14.8	16.2	43 503	37 019	33 987
Zapata	138.8	84.6	12 126	44.6	41.4	71.9	36.6	.8	D	7.0	3.3	14.3	32.0	600	373	398
Zavala	121.4	45.9	10 215	37.6	48.7	61.9	D	D	D	6.4	1.9	18.7	34.6	D	5 784	6 626
UTAH	46 717.0	80.1	22 240	81.8	4 857.4	35 540.3	23.0	13.9	76.5	10.3	7.9	26.7	18.2	4 955 043	4 798 736	4 487 879
Beaver	98.6	65.5	16 705	61.4	19.7	68.4	D	4.8	D	10.6	2.1	13.0	24.1	3 294	D	1 890
Box Elder	895.6	60.9	21 359	78.5	97.3	793.9	D	56.8	D	10.1	1.8	8.3	9.3	450 560	433 058	407 365
Cache	1 560.2	67.2	17 887	65.8	172.8	1 079.7	D	26.9	D	8.6	3.1	21.7	24.5	290 100	294 786	270 595
Carbon	418.9	43.2	19 930	73.3	85.7	286.8	31.9	5.4	69.2	9.5	2.1	21.5	21.5	15 358	13 273	11 852
Daggett	12.8	38.8	17 734	65.2	2.2	11.8	D	D	D	3.7	.5	19.8	64.0	D	D	D
Davis	5 046.5	78.2	21 603	79.4	405.2	2 936.6	21.2	12.5	78.5	11.4	4.5	18.6	36.5	368 235	353 380	341 641
Duchesne	236.6	53.7	16 301	59.9	47.0	147.0	26.8	5.3	D	9.1	D	12.8	30.5	7 852	8 010	8 583
Emery	179.3	41.2	16 276	59.8	31.2	153.5	40.5	.7	D	3.6	.7	D	17.3	1 101	949	1 031
Garfield	75.5	53.4	17 589	64.7	14.2	51.7	D	8.4	D	6.8	1.8	32.9	32.3	4 365	4 170	4 552
Grand	157.4	89.5	19 505	71.7	25.2	105.1	D	D	D	20.8	D	31.1	24.3	D	1 258	1 220
Iron	491.8	97.2	17 090	62.8	76.2	342.6	D	14.4	D	12.1	5.6	21.1	28.8	49 380	43 195	35 790
Juab	113.1	66.7	14 883	54.7	22.9	63.8	D	19.4	D	14.0	1.6	29.6	23.3	12 355	11 655	9 492
Kane	128.1	86.5	20 600	75.7	20.9	67.5	D	D	D	13.7	2.7	26.6	26.1	D	6 229	1 411
Millard	193.2	26.6	15 734	57.8	34.1	136.1	D	4.5	D	9.6	D	15.5	22.0	6 124	6 631	6 684
Morgan	134.1	76.7	19 066	70.1	11.7	57.5	38.1	18.6	D	7.2	2.4	D	17.4	10 711	11 647	9 807
Piute	20.3	47.8	14 428	53.0	5.1	9.3	D	D	D	2.9	D	D	37.5	D	263	334
Rich	28.8	34.7	15 526	57.1	4.8	14.3	D	D	D	6.1	D	20.8	36.6	D	241	D
Salt Lake	22 078.7	81.6	26 100	95.9	1 973.7	19 138.7	19.9	11.6	80.1	10.2	10.6	26.9	14.8	2 221 102	2 155 206	2 003 633
San Juan	173.0	55.3	12 685	46.6	41.4	120.1	25.0	5.7	D	8.2	D	19.4	37.6	6 898	7 919	8 647
Sanpete	302.0	62.5	13 989	51.4	58.0	170.2	D	13.0	D	8.3	2.4	15.4	33.7	22 157	20 594	18 216
Sevier	303.7	58.0	16 474	60.6	61.2	199.1	D	7.4	D	11.2	2.4	17.9	23.2	14 795	14 556	13 056
Summit	1 062.4	189.1	39 645	145.7	37.1	524.9	17.9	6.0	81.1	14.5	16.7	33.5	11.1	31 725	31 322	32 885
Tooele	610.7	53.8	18 244	67.1	64.7	425.1	23.2	14.0	76.4	5.7	3.8	13.3	37.8	59 456	57 471	50 868
Uintah	378.1	51.2	14 749	54.2	71.5	267.3	27.7	1.8	D	10.3	D	22.9	22.6	4 743	4 883	4 822
Utah	6 103.2	91.5	17 956	66.0	679.1	4 512.2	D	15.2	D	9.0	4.9	39.7	13.4	687 756	662 513	647 621
Wasatch	281.4	108.1	21 199	77.9	28.7	119.1	D	7.8	D	12.5	4.2	25.2	22.4	9 345	7 451	5 551
Washington	1 516.2	145.2	18 428	67.7	262.1	929.5	23.5	7.2	76.6	15.8	6.4	27.8	16.2	66 458	63 283	60 083
Wayne	40.6	72.1	17 231	63.3	7.2	27.6	NA	2.6	D	10.3	D	29.3	32.3	709	704	644
Weber	4 076.2	59.1	22 178	81.5	496.4	2 781.0	29.2	21.6	70.6	10.4	4.8	25.4	22.9	600 056	581 194	529 271
VERMONT	14 529.4	42.5	24 602	90.4	2 046.8	9 988.8	27.4	20.2	71.1	10.0	5.6	28.5	16.0	2 018 648	1 906 589	1 829 927
Addison	776.1	44.2	22 081	81.2	95.6	459.4	26.6	19.1	68.2	11.8	3.0	33.8	12.2	87 819	79 739	77 464
Bennington	919.9	35.4	25 599	94.1	138.0	581.5	D	26.7	D	14.1	4.6	30.6	11.3	155 434	133 930	121 811
Caledonia	582.5	38.3	20 394	75.0	105.1	357.6	31.8	23.0	65.0	11.0	3.6	24.9	15.7	82 301	80 826	75 126
Chittenden	4 119.2	48.8	28 909	106.3	402.1	3 555.9	30.6	23.7	69.1	8.5	6.2	29.1	14.1	842 944	793 812	768 845
Essex	104.1	32.2	15 805	58.1	23.2	67.1	62.1	58.3	D	3.5	.7	7.5	16.2	39 129	37 410	33 461
Franklin	888.1	42.3	20 197	74.2	132.4	487.2	26.8	21.3	65.8	11.8	3.4	19.5	21.8	104 007	102 230	98 035
Grand Isle	154.2	56.0	24 761	91.0	18.5	32.7	D	4.0	D	10.0	4.1	24.1	22.9	1 300	1 282	1 234
Lamoille	502.5	47.8	23 221	85.4	71.8	303.1	22.3	12.8	75.6	13.6	3.5	37.1	15.4	38 656	38 103	35 229
Orange	569.5	42.2	20 438	75.1	84.1	252.8	24.0	12.5	72.3	8.8	3.4	28.1	20.6	31 678	33 698	34 543
Orleans	482.2	40.1	19 010	69.9	107.9	288.2	27.1	19.8	65.7	10.6	3.8	23.8	17.5	56 968	55 824	53 802
Rutland	1 477.1	38.7	23 617	86.8	298.5	951.8	26.8	19.6	72.6	11.5	3.6	29.2	15.4	187 009	183 073	174 993
Washington	1 392.5	37.1	24 787	91.1	218.7	1 019.6	17.6	11.6	82.1	9.6	11.8	27.0	24.1	118 131	111 575	113 492
Windham	1 083.2	39.8	25 368	93.3	156.5	827.1	D	15.9	D	9.5	5.7	29.2	10.0	131 549	124 974	117 353
Windsor	1 478.3	41.7	26 700	98.2	194.4	804.8	26.1	17.6	73.4	10.1	4.0	28.8	21.8	141 723	130 113	124 539

[1] Based on resident population estimated as of July 1, 1998. [2] Includes farm earnings; see table B-10 for these data. [3] Includes mining and construction, not shown separately. [4] Includes agricultural services, forestry, and fisheries; transportation and public utilities; and wholesale trade, not shown separately. [5] Finance, insurance, and real estate.

Source: Personal Income and Earnings—U.S. Bureau of Economic Analysis, "Regional Economic Information System (REIS) 1969-1998" on CD-ROM (related Internet site <http://www.bea.doc.gov/bea/regional/data.htm>).

Table B–8. Counties — **Personal Income and Earnings**–Con.

[Includes U.S., states, and 3,142 counties/county equivalents defined as of January 1, 1992. For changes to these areas since January 1, 1992, see appendix B. Geographic Information]

County	Personal income, 1998														Manufacturing earnings		
			Per capita[1]			Earnings											
							Percent, by selected industry–										
							Goods-related		Service-related								
	Total (mil. dol.)	Percent change, 1990–1998	Amount (dollars)	Percent of national average	Transfer payments (mil. dol.)	Total[2] (mil. dol.)	Total[3]	Manufacturing	Total[4]	Retail trade	FIRE[5]	Services	Government	1998 ($1,000)	1997 ($1,000)	1996 ($1,000)
VIRGINIA	190 528.1	49.3	28 063	103.2	18 822.9	138 258.4	18.2	11.9	81.6	8.1	7.2	29.6	24.3	16 445 718	15 868 028	15 224 623
Accomack	613.8	35.1	19 032	70.0	132.0	369.7	D	20.5	D	8.3	3.0	18.6	29.3	75 776	71 486	72 605
Albemarle	[6]3 602.4	[6]54.1	[6]30 947	[6]113.8	[6]329.2	[6]2 872.9	[6]19.4	[6]10.5	[6]80.4	[6]8.9	[6]7.7	[6]22.9	[6]34.3	[6]300 667	[6]280 098	[6]281 152
Alleghany	[7]512.7	[7]38.4	[7]21 940	[7]80.7	[7]105.6	[7]392.3	D	D	D	[7]7.5	[7]1.5	[7]15.4	[7]12.4	D	[7]155 177	[7]149 594
Amelia	204.7	52.7	19 687	72.4	32.5	84.5	D	12.6	D	6.7	D	14.2	19.1	10 671	10 342	10 018
Amherst	535.6	37.3	17 866	65.7	90.2	293.1	35.7	26.5	D	9.5	D	15.2	29.0	77 802	70 274	56 652
Appomattox	251.0	40.8	19 093	70.2	42.7	119.9	D	D	D	9.4	4.4	11.0	19.4	D	40 002	35 604
Arlington	8 150.2	50.1	46 677	171.6	353.8	11 107.1	D	2.1	D	4.0	5.4	35.2	39.8	233 967	250 472	222 723
Augusta	[8]2 342.3	[8]39.3	[8]22 526	[8]82.8	[8]343.0	[8]1 578.2	D	[8]30.2	D	[8]10.4	[8]3.5	[8]17.4	[8]16.8	[8]476 823	[8]464 796	[8]435 835
Bath	108.1	38.0	22 020	80.9	20.1	70.7	D	D	D	3.4	2.3	48.0	15.9	D	5 966	6 175
Bedford	[9]1 537.3	[9]71.0	[9]24 279	[9]89.3	[9]190.1	[9]493.7	D	[9]29.0	D	[9]7.5	D	[9]23.5	[9]14.4	[9]143 091	[9]139 043	[9]128 409
Bland	111.3	37.1	16 357	60.1	24.5	61.2	35.3	31.4	D	4.6	1.0	D	29.1	19 245	17 743	16 471
Botetourt	683.7	73.8	23 859	87.7	83.5	241.6	41.0	22.7	58.7	8.6	2.8	13.1	15.5	54 761	51 813	49 386
Brunswick	268.4	41.8	15 439	56.8	68.2	136.5	D	19.0	D	5.6	2.3	20.2	28.3	25 884	23 999	22 659
Buchanan	500.7	15.6	17 274	63.5	161.9	310.4	44.2	4.1	55.7	7.4	4.4	15.2	16.3	12 792	12 729	14 385
Buckingham	229.7	45.3	15 698	57.7	49.8	103.7	D	15.3	D	6.0	D	18.4	32.2	15 836	16 156	15 476
Campbell	[10]2 551.2	[10]27.8	[10]22 308	[10]82.0	[10]463.2	[10]2 416.6	D	[10]35.8	D	[10]9.1	[10]7.8	[10]22.6	[10]9.8	[10]865 009	[10]828 479	[10]820 640
Caroline	435.9	50.6	19 825	72.9	66.5	144.6	D	14.3	D	11.6	5.4	13.5	32.1	20 694	21 597	19 464
Carroll	[11]633.3	[11]42.7	[11]18 395	[11]67.6	[11]154.5	[11]401.6	D	[11]37.8	D	[11]10.7	[11]2.2	[11]19.3	[11]15.5	[11]151 685	[11]148 075	[11]143 063
Charles City	133.1	41.9	18 604	68.4	20.4	45.6	D	20.3	D	4.5	2.2	12.8	22.6	9 251	4 990	7 814
Charlotte	212.0	47.0	17 206	63.3	52.7	108.4	44.8	38.4	51.9	5.5	2.8	10.9	19.0	41 585	36 269	30 524
Chesterfield	7 576.9	62.5	30 288	111.3	477.1	3 816.7	D	18.2	D	11.0	7.1	21.0	18.0	696 408	660 385	663 944
Clarke	351.1	54.4	27 607	101.5	30.6	130.5	D	34.1	D	6.2	4.6	21.1	14.7	44 462	42 507	39 853
Craig	96.1	62.7	19 697	72.4	14.6	19.4	D	D	D	6.4	4.6	11.6	33.5	D	2 766	2 936
Culpeper	847.2	63.6	25 589	94.1	91.4	431.2	22.2	14.0	77.1	9.0	5.5	24.9	19.1	60 439	59 125	54 193
Cumberland	144.1	32.0	18 363	67.5	30.0	40.4	23.5	7.8	69.4	12.3	2.0	17.1	24.6	3 140	2 880	2 026
Dickenson	254.8	23.1	15 107	55.5	95.9	107.0	32.3	1.5	67.4	8.8	1.5	18.8	23.0	1 650	2 988	2 931
Dinwiddie	[12]1 837.0	[12]40.0	[12]23 931	[12]88.0	[12]375.1	[12]947.3	D	[12]12.8	D	[12]17.0	[12]4.5	[12]18.9	[12]29.0	[12]121 179	[12]110 293	[12]105 282
Essex	185.1	40.5	20 388	74.9	37.7	102.5	31.0	25.7	70.0	18.4	5.0	26.6	13.7	26 368	26 480	25 954
Fairfax	[13]42 461.8	[13]59.7	[13]44 303	[13]162.9	[13]1 575.9	[13]30 866.9	[13]8.4	[13]3.7	[13]91.6	[13]6.5	[13]8.9	[13]46.2	[13]15.0	[13]1 127 413	[13]1 012 711	[13]989 456
Fauquier	1 893.5	53.7	35 104	129.0	115.4	577.3	D	6.8	D	10.1	7.0	31.8	16.5	39 136	34 443	31 626
Floyd	218.3	38.8	16 709	61.4	42.9	75.6	30.1	19.7	65.4	10.2	4.1	17.4	19.5	14 929	14 271	14 550
Fluvanna	389.7	94.1	20 610	75.8	55.1	107.2	23.0	9.2	76.0	5.6	2.8	23.7	27.0	9 903	9 839	9 983
Franklin	882.6	53.6	19 787	72.7	135.4	387.3	46.7	35.9	51.2	9.1	3.2	16.3	13.4	138 989	123 295	118 482
Frederick	[14]1 901.8	[14]59.2	[14]24 362	[14]89.6	[14]204.5	[14]1 507.0	[14]34.6	[14]27.6	[14]65.0	[14]11.4	[14]3.9	[14]28.0	[14]10.6	[14]415 681	[14]405 500	[14]380 262
Giles	311.5	30.0	19 176	70.5	67.3	201.0	54.9	49.7	D	7.5	D	14.3	11.1	99 924	105 129	109 308
Gloucester	742.9	45.6	21 261	78.2	89.7	231.2	D	4.3	D	15.3	4.7	24.0	29.1	9 827	10 068	10 397
Goochland	561.6	69.8	32 265	118.6	43.3	221.1	D	1.7	D	19.4	8.4	22.7	16.8	3 774	3 247	2 828
Grayson	274.5	37.0	16 738	61.5	61.4	89.8	42.0	36.3	54.2	6.8	3.2	15.5	20.8	32 608	33 849	31 013
Greene	266.5	74.1	18 978	69.8	32.5	103.5	D	30.0	D	8.0	D	17.2	19.5	31 079	16 209	14 818
Greensville	[15]293.4	[15]49.3	[15]17 615	[15]64.8	[15]63.0	[15]238.1	D	[15]35.4	D	[15]7.8	D	[15]17.7	[15]23.3	[15]84 312	[15]78 205	[15]72 346
Halifax	660.8	36.2	17 989	66.1	146.0	409.3	D	32.4	D	11.5	2.0	18.8	14.7	132 576	129 445	135 641
Hanover	2 222.7	69.5	27 007	99.3	204.8	1 265.6	D	14.0	D	9.1	4.8	20.5	10.3	177 300	175 944	167 883
Henrico	7 436.9	40.9	30 761	113.1	651.1	6 025.5	18.1	12.6	81.8	12.8	20.5	25.6	7.8	758 714	797 003	697 902
Henry	[16]1 456.9	[16]18.7	[16]20 483	[16]75.3	[16]272.6	[16]1 082.0	D	[16]48.3	D	[16]9.1	[16]3.6	[16]15.9	[16]11.1	[16]522 445	[16]529 600	[16]505 170
Highland	55.0	40.4	22 141	81.4	9.9	19.8	D	23.8	D	4.5	4.4	16.8	18.1	4 703	4 543	4 570
Isle of Wight	718.9	67.2	24 637	90.6	90.1	489.5	D	60.6	D	3.7	D	6.8	8.0	296 707	282 420	257 715
James City	[17]1 790.8	[17]80.5	[17]31 499	[17]115.8	[17]175.1	[17]1 128.2	[17]17.2	[17]11.0	[17]82.8	[17]13.6	[17]9.5	[17]32.5	[17]23.6	[17]124 064	[17]123 795	[17]120 298
King and Queen	130.2	36.6	20 034	73.6	21.7	34.8	35.3	21.2	D	4.1	D	10.5	43.4	7 385	6 498	6 016
King George	432.5	59.5	25 166	92.5	32.5	516.9	4.6	1.9	95.5	1.8	.9	21.8	68.4	10 025	8 738	9 533
King William	300.4	48.4	23 437	86.2	36.2	135.5	54.6	45.1	46.4	7.6	5.4	12.7	13.7	61 158	72 526	68 388
Lancaster	307.7	33.8	27 133	99.7	62.7	124.8	13.3	4.2	87.0	12.4	10.7	41.9	11.8	5 274	4 896	4 448
Lee	378.3	38.5	15 853	58.3	129.1	157.4	28.5	10.9	69.2	8.8	3.8	24.7	23.7	17 227	16 928	14 894
Loudoun	4 985.0	123.4	34 495	126.8	195.4	2 931.3	17.6	7.1	82.3	8.2	4.0	28.5	19.2	206 906	169 403	150 564
Louisa	534.4	69.5	21 778	80.1	75.7	252.4	D	20.2	D	4.9	3.8	D	12.8	50 905	45 983	41 688
Lunenburg	193.3	33.0	16 121	59.3	45.7	81.3	33.7	20.9	60.1	7.4	3.0	12.1	31.0	17 013	16 331	16 553
Madison	240.3	52.8	19 014	69.9	37.9	89.3	30.9	21.7	68.0	13.1	1.5	26.9	17.9	19 393	16 777	15 551
Mathews	232.2	42.8	25 507	93.8	37.9	45.8	27.4	11.6	70.1	14.7	3.8	17.7	23.6	5 322	5 590	5 733
Mecklenburg	603.8	44.1	19 449	71.5	126.9	384.8	D	27.8	D	13.1	D	17.6	17.3	106 915	112 545	104 939
Middlesex	224.0	46.6	23 255	85.5	43.0	76.3	21.1	10.8	78.1	12.6	5.8	20.2	29.4	8 273	8 666	8 271
Montgomery	[18]1 710.8	[18]41.2	[18]18 506	[18]68.0	[18]217.4	[18]1 334.0	D	[18]22.0	D	[18]10.3	[18]4.5	[18]18.6	[18]35.3	[18]293 293	[18]282 645	[18]270 247
Nelson	273.3	52.1	19 659	72.3	54.2	96.7	D	7.6	D	5.8	3.3	34.2	17.8	7 345	7 384	7 133
New Kent	305.1	59.7	23 705	87.1	31.1	76.9	D	4.7	D	11.4	3.7	33.5	22.1	3 639	3 144	3 524
Northampton	241.6	31.8	18 992	69.8	61.7	130.4	11.3	7.1	77.1	10.4	2.0	31.3	24.3	9 248	8 381	7 539
Northumberland	253.6	44.7	22 105	81.3	55.6	83.1	D	30.6	D	7.7	5.9	20.1	15.7	25 421	28 241	27 539
Nottoway	280.9	34.6	18 522	68.1	67.8	170.2	D	16.0	D	9.5	2.9	12.0	37.9	27 151	21 661	25 532
Orange	532.6	51.0	20 988	77.2	92.0	227.3	D	24.2	D	12.0	4.9	13.6	21.4	55 089	52 079	52 286
Page	421.6	45.3	18 285	67.2	77.7	198.7	44.7	35.8	52.2	8.1	2.5	17.2	17.6	71 192	69 305	68 806
Patrick	331.0	38.0	17 945	66.0	66.4	152.8	50.4	45.8	48.4	7.2	2.1	15.7	13.0	69 947	70 899	66 330
Pittsylvania	[19]2 136.6	[19]33.3	[19]19 738	[19]72.6	[19]407.7	[19]1 368.4	D	[19]37.5	D	[19]10.5	[19]3.3	[19]20.5	[19]13.8	[19]513 127	[19]504 901	[19]487 029
Powhatan	450.1	81.5	20 942	77.0	42.9	166.2	D	2.9	D	7.3	5.6	12.9	40.0	4 802	4 372	4 102

[1] Based on resident population estimated as of July 1, 1998. [2] Includes farm earnings; see table B-10 for these data. [3] Includes mining and construction, not shown separately. [4] Includes agricultural services, forestry, and fisheries; transportation and public utilities; and wholesale trade, not shown separately. [5] Finance, insurance, and real estate. [6] Albemarle County includes Charlottesville city. [7] Alleghany County includes Clifton Forge and Covington cities. [8] Augusta County includes Staunton and Waynesboro cities. [9] Bedford County includes Bedford city. [10] Campbell County includes Lynchburg city [11] Carroll County includes Galax city. [12] Dinwiddie County includes Colonial Heights and Petersburg cities. [13] Fairfax County includes Fairfax and Falls Church cities. [14] Frederick County includes Winchester city. [15] Greensville County includes Emporia city. [16] Henry County includes Martinsville city. [17] James City County includes Williamsburg city. [18] Montgomery County includes Radford city. [19] Pittsylvania County includes Danville city.

Source: Personal Income and Earnings—U.S. Bureau of Economic Analysis, "Regional Economic Information System (REIS) 1969-1998" on CD-ROM (related Internet site <http://www.bea.doc.gov/bea/regional/data.htm>).

[Includes U.S., states, and 3,142 counties/county equivalents defined as of January 1, 1992. For changes to these areas since January 1, 1992, see appendix B. Geographic Information]

County	Personal income, 1998													Manufacturing earnings		
	Per capita[1]				Transfer payments (mil. dol.)	Earnings										
							Percent, by selected industry–									
							Goods-related		Service-related							
	Total (mil. dol.)	Percent change, 1990–1998	Amount (dollars)	Percent of national average		Total[2] (mil. dol.)	Total[3]	Manufacturing	Total[4]	Retail trade	FIRE[5]	Services	Government	1998 ($1,000)	1997 ($1,000)	1996 ($1,000)
VIRGINIA—Con.																
Prince Edward	293.1	36.1	15 237	56.0	64.4	226.5	D	8.6	D	18.5	3.2	31.1	24.5	19 571	19 054	23 460
Prince George	[6]1 120.6	[6]38.0	[6]21 846	[6]80.3	[6]144.6	[6]1 037.3	[6]25.2	[6]18.3	[6]74.9	[6]5.4	[6]1.2	[6]10.8	[6]53.3	[6]190 111	[6]187 410	[6]185 822
Prince William	[7]8 405.5	756.7	[7]27 759	[7]102.0	[7]427.3	[7]3 833.2	D	[7]10.2	D	[7]13.8	D	[7]21.4	726.9	[7]392 523	[7]371 239	[7]309 443
Pulaski	662.1	40.3	19 244	70.7	134.4	504.6	D	46.9	D	6.6	1.9	13.5	12.2	236 501	214 187	181 471
Rappahannock	184.5	53.5	25 170	92.5	21.1	56.3	25.5	3.9	73.4	18.5	3.1	25.4	16.9	2 203	2 365	2 073
Richmond	141.1	30.6	16 258	59.8	30.6	84.3	D	D	D	7.8	3.2	15.4	32.7	D	11 919	11 019
Roanoke	[8]3 341.3	[8]51.7	[8]31 675	[8]116.4	[8]307.1	[8]2 073.9	D	[8]21.9	D	[8]9.1	[8]9.3	[8]26.5	[8]15.7	[8]453 231	[8]450 166	[8]420 632
Rockbridge	[9]654.9	[9]41.9	[9]19 701	[9]72.4	[9]112.8	[9]399.0	D	[9]26.2	D	[9]11.4	[9]9.3	[9]23.6	[9]21.3	[9]104 545	[9]97 100	[9]91 881
Rockingham	[10]2 144.6	[10]51.2	[10]22 072	[10]81.1	[10]250.7	[10]1 726.6	D	[10]29.4	D	[10]10.0	[10]3.8	[10]19.9	[10]14.7	[10]507 552	[10]483 458	[10]444 669
Russell	486.9	41.8	16 855	62.0	143.2	253.9	37.4	20.0	61.6	9.0	2.4	16.1	18.9	50 704	50 025	44 459
Scott	365.0	29.1	16 119	59.3	104.8	115.2	D	15.5	D	15.3	4.4	20.2	27.0	17 807	20 362	25 228
Shenandoah	725.5	44.0	20 896	76.8	109.4	429.0	D	37.9	D	8.9	3.2	15.4	11.7	162 775	151 623	148 638
Smyth	602.0	35.2	18 360	67.5	128.0	428.5	D	43.9	D	7.2	1.7	16.0	18.1	188 009	174 083	160 198
Southampton	[11]566.1	[11]41.9	[11]21 776	[11]80.0	[11]104.6	[11]249.7	D	[11]13.4	D	[11]9.6	D	[11]22.3	[11]29.9	[11]133 352	[11]131 383	[11]129 956
Spotsylvania	[12]2 731.8	[12]83.9	[12]26 555	[12]97.6	[12]236.2	[12]1 327.5	D	[12]9.7	D	[12]16.0	[12]6.9	[12]29.7	[12]16.7	[12]128 919	[12]122 303	[12]115 008
Stafford	2 065.2	74.2	23 031	84.7	119.4	769.6	14.5	3.5	85.6	7.3	15.2	18.0	29.8	26 777	21 121	20 820
Surry	114.9	21.5	17 682	65.0	20.7	102.8	9.8	3.2	D	1.5	D	6.9	13.4	3 279	3 044	3 589
Sussex	211.4	38.3	21 030	77.3	45.7	100.7	23.8	15.7	73.9	11.6	2.8	13.9	30.7	15 858	15 028	13 615
Tazewell	828.9	30.6	17 766	65.3	223.3	457.2	D	11.0	D	16.0	3.3	26.6	19.6	50 176	53 336	50 048
Warren	717.7	67.0	23 857	87.7	80.7	279.1	31.9	19.7	67.9	13.7	4.4	25.9	15.8	55 041	46 882	42 114
Washington	[13]1 389.6	[13]48.1	[13]20 877	[13]76.7	[13]257.8	[13]973.4	D	[13]28.0	D	[13]13.0	[13]6.3	[13]18.4	[13]15.1	[13]272 612	[13]268 765	[13]265 559
Westmoreland	331.5	44.4	20 313	74.7	64.8	90.1	D	20.0	D	13.9	5.0	18.6	23.4	18 011	16 982	14 825
Wise	[14]789.2	[14]27.1	[14]18 277	[14]67.2	[14]239.5	[14]556.8	[14]28.6	[14]3.8	D	[14]11.0	D	[14]22.7	[14]19.9	[14]20 970	[14]21 927	[14]21 371
Wythe	512.9	42.2	19 523	71.8	105.5	305.6	29.5	23.6	70.0	14.0	2.7	21.2	19.9	72 051	73 250	72 235
York	[15]1 726.7	[15]51.0	[15]25 030	[15]92.0	[15]138.0	[15]584.8	NA	[15]5.9	D	[15]10.0	[15]3.3	[15]19.7	[15]40.6	[15]34 334	[15]31 757	[15]28 974
Independent Cities																
Alexandria	5 322.4	50.5	46 290	170.2	313.8	4 591.5	6.1	2.7	93.9	6.9	6.6	46.4	24.9	123 015	121 801	126 433
Bedford	(16)	(16)	(16)	(16)	(16)	(16)	D	(16)	D	(16)	D	(16)	(16)	(16)	(16)	(16)
Bristol	(13)	(13)	(13)	(13)	(13)	(13)	D	(13)	D	(13)	(13)	(13)	(13)	(13)	(13)	(13)
Buena Vista	(9)	(9)	(9)	(9)	(9)	(9)	D	(9)	D	(9)	(9)	(9)	(9)	(9)	(9)	(9)
Charlottesville	(17)	(17)	(17)	(17)	(17)	(17)	(17)	(17)	(17)	(17)	(17)	(17)	(17)	(17)	(17)	(17)
Chesapeake	4 707.2	65.5	23 606	86.8	441.5	2 400.9	22.9	9.8	76.9	12.9	4.9	22.3	22.4	234 153	219 468	183 944
Clifton Forge	(18)	(18)	(18)	(18)	(18)	(18)	D	(18)	D	(18)	(18)	(18)	(18)	(18)	(18)	(18)
Colonial Heights	(19)	(19)	(19)	(19)	(19)	(19)	D	(19)	D	(19)	(19)	(19)	(19)	(19)	(19)	(19)
Covington	(18)	(18)	(18)	(18)	(18)	(18)	D	(18)	D	(18)	(18)	(18)	(18)	(18)	(18)	(18)
Danville	(20)	(20)	(20)	(20)	(20)	(20)	D	(20)	D	(20)	(20)	(20)	(20)	(20)	(20)	(20)
Emporia	(21)	(21)	(21)	(21)	(21)	(21)	D	(21)	D	(21)	D	(21)	(21)	(21)	(21)	(21)
Fairfax	(22)	(22)	(22)	(22)	(22)	(22)	(22)	(22)	(22)	(22)	(22)	(22)	(22)	(22)	(22)	(22)
Falls Church	(22)	(22)	(22)	(22)	(22)	(22)	(22)	(22)	(22)	(22)	(22)	(22)	(22)	(22)	(22)	(22)
Franklin	(11)	(11)	(11)	(11)	(11)	(11)	D	(11)	D	(11)	(11)	(11)	(11)	(11)	(11)	(11)
Fredericksburg	(12)	(12)	(12)	(12)	(12)	(12)	D	(12)	D	(12)	(12)	(12)	(12)	(12)	(12)	(12)
Galax	(23)	(23)	(23)	(23)	(23)	(23)	D	(23)	D	(23)	(23)	(23)	(23)	(23)	(23)	(23)
Hampton	2 959.2	32.7	21 646	79.6	401.7	2 708.9	12.3	8.5	87.7	8.4	2.5	21.4	49.4	230 868	168 721	132 432
Harrisonburg	(10)	(10)	(10)	(10)	(10)	(10)	(10)	(10)	(10)	(10)	(10)	(10)	(10)	(10)	(10)	(10)
Hopewell	(6)	(6)	(6)	(6)	(6)	(6)	(6)	(6)	(6)	(6)	(6)	(6)	(6)	(6)	(6)	(6)
Lexington	(9)	(9)	(9)	(9)	(9)	(9)	D	(9)	D	(9)	(9)	(9)	(9)	(9)	(9)	(9)
Lynchburg	(24)	(24)	(24)	(24)	(24)	(24)	D	(24)	D	(24)	(24)	(24)	(24)	(24)	(24)	(24)
Manassas	(7)	(7)	(7)	(7)	(7)	(7)	D	(7)	D	(7)	D	(7)	(7)	(7)	(7)	(7)
Manassas Park	(7)	(7)	(7)	(7)	(7)	(7)	D	(7)	D	(7)	(7)	(7)	(7)	(7)	(7)	(7)
Martinsville	(25)	(25)	(25)	(25)	(25)	(25)	D	(25)	D	(25)	(25)	(25)	(25)	(25)	(25)	(25)
Newport News	3 811.9	31.3	21 415	78.7	504.9	3 613.2	NA	29.8	66.1	6.5	3.6	22.8	26.7	1 075 651	1 051 247	1 076 183
Norfolk	4 761.7	12.7	20 967	77.1	764.6	8 257.3	D	7.0	D	4.5	5.2	17.8	51.4	576 932	565 900	584 028
Norton	(14)	(14)	(14)	(14)	(14)	(14)	(14)	(14)	(14)	(14)	D	(14)	(14)	(14)	(14)	(14)
Petersburg	(19)	(19)	(19)	(19)	(19)	(19)	(19)	(19)	(19)	(19)	(19)	(19)	(19)	(19)	(19)	(19)
Poquoson	(15)	(15)	(15)	(15)	(15)	(15)	NA	(15)	D	(15)	(15)	(15)	(15)	(15)	(15)	(15)
Portsmouth	2 030.7	26.6	20 502	75.4	382.8	1 859.1	D	5.2	D	4.2	1.6	18.5	58.8	96 786	97 420	92 474
Radford	(26)	(26)	(26)	(26)	(26)	(26)	D	(26)	D	(26)	(26)	(26)	(26)	(26)	(26)	(26)
Richmond	5 622.8	20.1	29 439	108.2	901.9	7 806.5	19.0	15.2	81.0	4.1	13.4	24.3	25.4	1 182 954	1 207 812	1 200 838
Roanoke	2 271.6	28.6	24 218	89.0	443.7	2 671.5	D	10.4	D	12.4	8.6	30.0	11.7	277 161	268 167	289 568
Salem	(8)	(8)	(8)	(8)	(8)	(8)	D	(8)	D	(8)	(8)	(8)	(8)	(8)	(8)	(8)
South Boston	X	X	X	X	X	X	X	X	X	X	X	X	X	X	X	X
Staunton	(27)	(27)	(27)	(27)	(27)	(27)	D	(27)	D	(27)	(27)	(27)	(27)	(27)	(27)	(27)
Suffolk	1 365.4	59.3	21 786	80.1	202.0	611.3	22.4	15.0	77.1	9.7	3.4	23.8	22.1	91 708	88 643	90 993
Virginia Beach	11 613.3	40.5	26 967	99.1	858.9	5 963.3	D	3.0	D	10.8	8.1	29.3	30.6	177 244	155 741	143 962
Waynesboro	(27)	(27)	(27)	(27)	(27)	(27)	(27)	(27)	(27)	(27)	(27)	(27)	(27)	(27)	(27)	(27)
Williamsburg	(28)	(28)	(28)	(28)	(28)	(28)	(28)	(28)	(28)	(28)	(28)	(28)	(28)	(28)	(28)	(28)
Winchester	(29)	(29)	(29)	(29)	(29)	(29)	(29)	(29)	(29)	(29)	(29)	(29)	(29)	(29)	(29)	(29)

[1] Based on resident population estimated as of July 1, 1998.   [2] Includes farm earnings; see table B-10 for these data.   [3] Includes mining and construction, not shown separately.   [4] Includes agricultural services, forestry, and fisheries; transportation and public utilities; and wholesale trade, not shown separately.   [5] Finance, insurance, and real estate.   [6] Prince George County includes Hopewell city.   [7] Prince William County includes Manassas and Manassas Park cities.   [8] Roanoke County includes Salem city.   [9] Rockbridge County includes Buena Vista and Lexington cities.   [10] Rockingham County includes Harrisonburg city.   [11] Southampton County includes Franklin city.   [12] Spotsylvania County includes Fredericksburg city.   [13] Washington County includes Bristol city.   [14] Wise County includes Norton city.   [15] York County includes Poquoson city.   [16] Bedford County includes Bedford city.   [17] Albemarle County includes Charlottesville city.   [18] Alleghany County includes Clifton Forge and Covington cities.   [19] Dinwiddie County includes Colonial Heights and Petersburg cities.   [20] Pittsylvania County includes Danville city.   [21] Greenville County includes Emporia city.   [22] Fairfax County includes Fairfax and Falls Church cities.   [23] Carroll County includes Galax city.   [24] Campbell County includes Lynchburg city.   [25] Henry County includes Martinsville city.   [26] Montgomery County includes Radford city.   [27] Augusta County includes Staunton and Waynesboro cities.   [28] James City County includes Williamsburg city.   [29] Frederick County includes Winchester city.

Source: Personal Income and Earnings—U.S. Bureau of Economic Analysis, "Regional Economic Information System (REIS) 1969-1998" on CD-ROM (related Internet site <http://www.bea.doc.gov/bea/regional/data.htm>).

[Includes U.S., states, and 3,142 counties/county equivalents defined as of January 1, 1992. For changes to these areas since January 1, 1992, see appendix B. Geographic Information]

County	Personal income, 1998													Manufacturing earnings		
	Total (mil. dol.)	Per capita[1]		Transfer payments (mil. dol.)	Earnings								1998 ($1,000)	1997 ($1,000)	1996 ($1,000)
		Percent change, 1990–1998	Amount (dollars)	Percent of national average		Total[2] (mil. dol.)	Percent, by selected industry–									
							Goods-related		Service-related							
							Total[3]	Manufacturing	Total[4]	Retail trade	FIRE[5]	Services	Government			
WASHINGTON	163 347.9	66.4	28 719	105.6	19 389.8	118 132.7	22.5	15.9	76.3	8.9	6.5	29.0	17.8	18 811 380	17 770 966	15 998 788
Adams	316.1	32.7	20 605	75.7	64.9	188.8	18.9	15.8	65.1	8.1	2.3	10.3	21.5	29 916	28 706	29 060
Asotin	443.4	68.0	20 829	76.6	92.8	152.0	D	7.4	D	15.7	3.2	29.8	21.5	11 193	9 234	8 327
Benton	3 310.0	62.6	24 315	89.4	419.7	2 437.8	D	7.8	D	7.8	2.6	31.7	18.1	191 318	190 305	178 652
Chelan	1 483.4	62.5	24 654	90.6	237.3	1 129.1	D	9.0	D	11.7	4.5	23.4	20.8	101 565	96 208	94 024
Clallam	1 464.5	45.2	22 786	83.8	310.0	706.6	D	11.9	D	12.7	4.8	21.4	29.6	84 374	91 334	87 918
Clark	8 801.6	95.6	26 882	98.8	960.5	4 554.5	32.8	20.7	66.9	9.7	6.1	21.9	16.4	944 602	893 985	845 872
Columbia	84.0	27.8	20 211	74.3	17.9	48.8	D	D	D	6.1	2.2	D	32.4	D	10 509	10 153
Cowlitz	1 997.4	42.6	21 851	80.3	380.4	1 381.1	44.1	33.9	55.4	10.1	3.3	18.0	14.3	468 514	456 289	453 416
Douglas	640.0	03.4	19 072	70.1	108.4	225.4	12.2	3.8	79.2	13.8	3.3	15.7	29.0	8 635	9 081	5 185
Ferry	114.8	44.2	16 031	58.9	29.1	64.2	D	D	D	8.2	2.1	D	34.7	D	8 582	8 375
Franklin	859.5	59.3	18 479	67.9	166.2	678.4	14.7	8.3	68.2	8.3	1.7	18.3	20.6	56 023	50 547	45 777
Garfield	44.7	11.8	19 293	70.9	9.2	22.9	D	D	D	5.3	3.0	7.8	56.0	D	112	D
Grant	1 434.6	83.4	20 301	74.6	256.2	980.6	D	16.6	D	9.0	D	11.0	21.4	162 950	149 515	130 226
Grays Harbor	1 361.8	34.5	20 186	74.2	327.1	802.1	D	24.3	D	12.5	D	19.9	21.0	195 130	199 006	186 772
Island	1 703.5	58.9	23 743	87.3	209.9	865.7	D	3.1	D	7.2	4.5	12.0	61.9	27 194	22 729	20 748
Jefferson	621.6	67.2	23 658	87.0	120.1	239.1	D	14.7	D	11.5	3.7	21.5	26.2	35 063	33 720	34 363
King	67 670.7	73.4	40 905	150.4	5 410.3	60 095.9	20.0	14.6	79.9	7.8	8.0	36.7	10.6	8 795 157	8 262 859	7 409 457
Kitsap	5 347.5	45.9	22 957	84.4	660.8	3 422.4	7.6	2.2	92.4	8.4	3.5	19.0	57.3	76 193	66 761	64 493
Kittitas	635.6	56.3	20 241	74.4	106.6	371.3	14.1	8.4	82.1	13.4	2.7	15.2	35.9	31 025	32 400	29 702
Klickitat	378.2	51.1	19 535	71.8	76.3	216.8	35.0	27.4	60.7	5.5	3.3	9.1	24.2	59 308	57 556	69 578
Lewis	1 359.8	49.2	19 969	73.4	300.3	851.3	D	17.4	D	15.6	D	17.5	19.3	148 344	159 296	153 773
Lincoln	207.7	30.9	21 269	78.2	42.0	89.9	6.1	2.1	89.2	8.4	3.7	17.3	39.5	1 904	1 778	1 698
Mason	957.7	66.7	19 220	70.7	211.3	428.7	D	19.7	D	10.5	4.0	16.3	28.0	84 580	81 664	77 660
Okanogan	751.4	54.7	19 626	72.1	174.6	465.5	13.5	7.8	75.9	10.8	2.3	20.1	30.9	36 288	39 764	39 969
Pacific	420.0	49.4	20 139	74.0	112.5	199.7	25.5	21.0	68.0	10.6	3.7	18.1	27.6	41 973	40 767	40 449
Pend Oreille	205.3	76.2	17 813	65.5	53.9	97.4	D	31.3	D	8.6	2.5	11.9	32.6	30 462	28 742	26 412
Pierce	16 561.2	57.1	24 500	90.1	2 316.2	9 538.6	18.8	11.8	80.8	10.2	6.5	23.0	30.6	1 126 577	1 080 303	963 830
San Juan	446.3	82.6	35 573	130.8	46.4	163.4	D	5.0	D	14.4	7.0	26.9	17.9	8 244	7 467	9 268
Skagit	2 393.1	65.6	24 079	88.5	393.0	1 422.5	D	14.2	D	13.0	D	20.3	19.6	202 511	190 150	180 195
Skamania	204.5	55.2	20 915	76.9	29.1	67.5	D	18.3	D	5.4	2.0	17.4	41.2	12 322	11 242	9 087
Snohomish	15 816.7	73.5	27 015	99.3	1 617.9	9 489.5	46.7	38.9	53.1	8.9	5.1	15.6	15.8	3 694 852	3 397 196	2 821 784
Spokane	9 572.8	50.5	23 450	86.2	1 573.3	6 773.7	20.7	13.5	79.1	10.7	7.4	27.1	20.0	913 713	878 769	829 016
Stevens	674.1	67.0	17 028	62.6	153.5	348.4	33.9	26.9	64.5	9.0	2.4	21.6	23.1	93 617	87 531	80 949
Thurston	5 035.4	66.2	24 895	91.5	683.2	3 052.2	12.0	6.0	87.1	10.1	4.4	23.1	42.6	183 411	175 795	173 243
Wahkiakum	78.1	44.6	20 216	74.3	15.1	29.9	39.2	35.2	NA	6.8	2.7	11.9	24.9	10 522	10 259	D
Walla Walla	1 118.8	51.5	20 845	76.6	202.7	769.0	D	18.7	D	9.0	3.7	23.6	24.2	143 422	144 118	139 287
Whatcom	3 574.5	59.6	22 732	83.6	518.4	2 384.6	28.2	16.9	67.9	11.7	5.7	22.5	14.7	404 011	397 973	394 148
Whitman	723.6	38.0	18 696	68.7	110.9	489.9	D	3.6	91.3	6.7	2.8	11.3	59.1	17 537	15 052	13 074
Yakima	4 533.2	52.8	20 718	76.2	871.9	2 887.5	18.0	12.5	68.2	10.0	3.5	22.5	17.5	360 835	353 662	325 578
WEST VIRGINIA	36 569.4	39.9	20 185	74.2	8 561.0	22 682.7	27.3	15.0	72.7	9.5	4.1	25.0	21.3	3 393 792	3 296 656	3 313 567
Barbour	238.2	40.2	14 789	54.4	75.6	89.1	D	7.1	D	9.7	3.7	26.1	27.4	6 371	5 663	5 355
Berkeley	1 579.1	68.0	22 234	81.7	232.0	868.3	D	13.7	D	9.3	4.0	D	32.8	118 651	107 337	103 598
Boone	502.2	40.5	19 193	70.6	128.3	360.0	D	D	D	6.0	D	9.4	12.9	D	3 181	2 761
Braxton	209.9	41.3	15 880	58.4	62.7	110.2	D	15.8	D	17.0	2.4	21.3	22.2	17 364	15 745	13 237
Brooke	518.0	29.3	19 910	73.2	113.0	301.5	D	42.0	D	7.8	1.9	16.8	11.1	126 750	120 439	139 131
Cabell	2 166.9	34.6	23 024	84.6	493.5	1 657.0	21.4	14.8	78.6	10.7	4.5	32.7	17.3	245 507	245 318	238 795
Calhoun	106.9	33.4	13 454	49.5	37.0	45.0	38.0	4.6	D	8.7	D	16.9	26.0	2 064	2 334	3 428
Clay	142.7	55.2	13 561	49.9	45.5	65.8	45.1	5.0	D	6.0	1.9	12.9	26.5	3 258	3 176	2 866
Doddridge	118.3	56.2	15 764	57.9	24.5	28.9	29.2	9.0	D	7.6	6.6	15.8	34.1	2 613	2 918	2 695
Fayette	815.6	43.7	17 318	63.7	278.1	386.0	23.7	11.4	76.3	10.6	3.0	25.4	27.2	43 981	40 830	38 194
Gilmer	121.3	36.9	16 898	62.1	34.7	56.5	40.8	10.7	D	6.7	1.8	11.3	36.1	6 033	5 223	4 224
Grant	198.1	29.9	17 823	65.5	47.5	139.0	35.0	18.0	64.5	5.8	3.0	11.5	21.9	25 072	22 582	20 171
Greenbrier	662.1	35.1	18 731	68.9	176.6	378.5	19.2	10.1	80.3	12.2	3.1	36.8	18.6	38 198	36 827	35 433
Hampshire	298.6	51.7	15 593	57.3	69.4	113.2	D	9.3	D	9.6	4.5	23.2	29.3	10 529	10 831	10 270
Hancock	762.3	25.0	22 413	82.4	169.9	564.7	D	56.8	D	5.3	1.9	20.0	8.4	320 592	337 422	375 541
Hardy	220.0	54.4	18 555	68.2	39.5	140.1	D	53.3	D	7.8	2.7	9.3	13.7	74 607	70 582	67 464
Harrison	1 593.4	50.0	22 504	82.7	342.2	1 099.9	20.5	8.6	79.7	9.5	2.8	21.8	29.5	94 497	94 014	94 203
Jackson	507.2	53.7	18 128	66.6	115.7	314.3	D	37.5	D	11.8	2.4	14.4	14.0	117 722	117 459	120 359
Jefferson	1 050.8	74.2	25 353	93.2	129.0	379.9	D	22.2	D	12.3	3.6	23.8	26.2	84 469	70 905	65 813
Kanawha	5 323.3	37.4	26 421	97.1	1 051.9	4 184.6	20.9	12.2	79.1	8.5	7.0	30.5	17.9	508 946	496 285	502 593
Lewis	283.8	33.7	16 116	59.2	76.2	160.2	26.3	11.6	74.1	12.0	1.9	21.8	26.7	18 557	17 194	17 049
Lincoln	307.0	46.8	13 836	50.9	93.8	88.1	28.6	4.8	D	8.3	D	16.8	34.2	4 255	3 847	4 052
Logan	709.8	31.0	17 303	63.6	244.6	438.2	32.3	5.3	67.6	11.1	2.4	27.0	15.6	23 250	22 060	21 963
McDowell	413.5	13.2	13 786	50.7	191.3	167.5	26.9	1.3	73.1	9.5	4.6	14.7	34.5	2 205	2 241	3 353

[1] Based on resident population estimated as of July 1, 1998. [2] Includes farm earnings; see table B-10 for these data. [3] Includes mining and construction, not shown separately. [4] Includes agricultural services, forestry, and fisheries; transportation and public utilities; and wholesale trade, not shown separately. [5] Finance, insurance, and real estate.

Source: Personal Income and Earnings—U.S. Bureau of Economic Analysis, "Regional Economic Information System (REIS) 1969-1998" on CD-ROM (related Internet site <http://www.bea.doc.gov/bea/regional/data.htm>).

[Includes U.S., states, and 3,142 counties/county equivalents defined as of January 1, 1992. For changes to these areas since January 1, 1992, see appendix B. Geographic Information]

County	Personal income, 1998													Manufacturing earnings		
			Per capita[1]			Earnings										
									Percent, by selected industry–							
							Goods-related		Service-related							
	Total (mil. dol.)	Percent change, 1990–1998	Amount (dollars)	Percent of national average	Transfer payments (mil. dol.)	Total[2] (mil. dol.)	Total[3]	Manufacturing	Total[4]	Retail trade	FIRE[5]	Services	Government	1998 ($1,000)	1997 ($1,000)	1996 ($1,000)
WEST VIRGINIA—Con.																
Marion	1 094.0	26.5	19 374	71.2	275.0	638.9	28.9	9.8	71.2	9.5	4.0	23.7	20.7	62 503	62 218	70 585
Marshall	665.5	27.2	18 888	69.4	151.5	429.3	52.6	35.3	D	7.4	1.5	D	14.6	151 372	148 355	150 925
Mason	436.8	36.1	16 844	61.9	117.7	240.0	D	23.7	D	6.0	2.1	17.6	19.3	56 985	58 616	59 891
Mercer	1 311.6	34.8	20 384	74.9	378.9	716.4	14.4	7.8	85.8	12.4	4.2	30.5	22.6	56 220	57 223	55 547
Mineral	487.7	40.0	18 035	66.3	122.1	187.7	D	22.7	D	12.1	2.7	18.8	25.0	42 543	46 621	48 930
Mingo	535.9	26.1	16 792	61.7	171.9	383.5	48.5	3.3	51.5	4.7	2.4	13.3	13.7	12 591	10 998	10 787
Monongalia	1 762.6	48.5	22 758	83.7	309.3	1 312.2	15.5	8.9	84.7	8.3	3.2	25.4	40.7	116 274	99 933	95 186
Monroe	196.8	29.0	14 917	54.8	55.2	69.9	26.8	18.8	D	5.9	D	13.1	39.5	13 155	14 057	12 680
Morgan	264.3	59.7	19 281	70.9	61.8	91.3	D	14.2	D	10.0	4.0	20.4	24.0	12 939	11 438	11 636
Nicholas	433.0	29.1	15 713	57.8	128.4	250.6	34.1	12.1	66.1	12.8	2.7	16.5	22.5	30 392	28 186	24 381
Ohio	1 238.4	28.8	25 677	94.4	255.3	881.9	D	8.0	D	8.8	6.3	44.5	14.3	70 831	68 458	68 110
Pendleton	149.7	50.1	18 563	68.2	32.6	71.7	D	15.6	D	6.2	2.5	16.1	38.2	11 206	11 974	11 106
Pleasants	151.0	38.3	20 136	74.0	40.6	116.0	50.3	31.3	49.8	4.5	1.7	7.7	14.9	36 360	33 693	33 218
Pocahontas	173.5	57.4	19 082	70.1	52.2	104.2	D	15.9	D	7.9	2.3	31.2	21.4	16 600	15 722	14 228
Preston	452.5	24.8	15 183	55.8	123.8	193.9	27.2	13.8	72.8	10.2	3.1	15.9	25.3	26 734	23 356	22 277
Putnam	1 181.8	79.1	23 084	84.9	168.2	611.7	26.0	10.8	74.0	11.7	3.5	20.7	12.5	65 897	51 310	46 875
Raleigh	1 586.8	45.4	20 027	73.6	421.6	975.0	20.1	3.7	80.0	12.8	4.3	29.9	21.2	35 662	33 582	30 908
Randolph	517.1	45.2	18 035	66.3	146.2	305.6	19.8	12.0	79.7	11.0	3.3	30.0	22.3	36 637	35 748	33 286
Ritchie	162.7	42.2	15 672	57.6	44.9	80.0	D	41.0	D	8.1	3.1	10.5	19.3	32 780	29 949	25 626
Roane	240.9	53.2	15 720	57.8	67.0	117.3	D	23.1	D	8.8	4.2	18.3	18.1	27 060	22 497	20 754
Summers	198.7	40.1	14 274	52.5	78.0	67.3	D	2.5	D	11.8	4.7	22.3	30.3	1 698	1 471	954
Taylor	229.0	41.4	14 908	54.8	68.3	95.8	D	28.5	D	7.8	1.4	11.1	33.2	27 279	26 940	25 883
Tucker	124.1	26.5	16 351	60.1	36.9	69.7	34.6	14.6	65.6	7.6	4.6	22.2	23.9	10 179	10 516	10 942
Tyler	153.6	29.8	15 691	57.7	37.6	94.0	D	54.5	D	4.6	1.7	8.6	17.0	51 220	48 564	48 640
Upshur	369.4	31.1	15 688	57.7	92.6	220.9	36.0	17.8	65.0	12.1	2.3	24.7	18.0	39 309	37 290	36 111
Wayne	656.4	30.4	15 638	57.5	156.4	324.2	26.3	12.3	D	7.6	D	13.0	36.6	39 798	39 691	38 732
Webster	130.3	34.0	12 723	46.8	50.4	73.0	43.4	8.7	D	5.2	D	12.1	26.2	6 366	6 699	5 188
Wetzel	350.8	28.2	19 161	70.4	89.8	129.8	19.0	5.4	81.3	16.9	3.6	16.5	28.7	6 974	8 276	8 839
Wirt	84.9	60.2	14 872	54.7	20.4	20.3	D	D	D	8.7	4.5	20.5	41.8	D	2 238	3 036
Wood	1 979.2	36.7	22 829	83.9	393.4	1 471.1	34.7	26.3	65.3	10.5	4.8	24.6	16.2	386 499	387 417	387 766
Wyoming	401.6	25.9	14 690	54.0	140.3	203.2	45.7	4.2	D	8.1	D	11.4	20.6	8 540	9 207	7 992
WISCONSIN	137 256.4	54.2	26 284	96.6	17 160.5	96 051.0	33.6	27.2	65.6	8.7	6.9	23.2	14.4	26 116 131	25 050 743	23 492 974
Adams	324.9	72.5	17 629	64.8	75.9	138.5	D	D	D	8.1	1.6	16.7	31.0	D	20 629	19 968
Ashland	328.0	48.7	19 948	73.3	69.8	254.6	D	22.3	D	2.6	29.4	18.6	56 741	61 998	58 417
Barron	904.9	54.0	20 640	75.9	160.6	621.5	D	32.2	D	10.1	2.7	19.2	16.3	200 155	181 728	172 870
Bayfield	288.0	50.6	18 963	69.7	58.0	108.4	17.8	7.0	82.1	11.9	3.7	27.7	27.3	7 642	6 611	8 470
Brown	6 042.8	62.9	28 114	103.3	570.5	5 032.9	32.7	25.8	66.7	9.1	7.6	23.1	10.1	1 297 233	1 267 300	1 109 324
Buffalo	307.0	47.5	21 558	79.2	48.7	179.1	13.8	9.3	D	5.5	2.4	D	18.3	16 617	15 794	13 961
Burnett	265.3	64.3	18 124	66.6	63.9	127.2	D	30.2	D	11.7	2.7	21.9	16.8	38 425	36 278	33 472
Calumet	940.0	65.5	24 435	89.8	88.3	424.4	D	48.6	D	6.6	2.5	10.1	10.2	206 189	211 765	200 190
Chippewa	1 237.0	55.0	22 670	83.3	196.2	745.7	46.4	36.7	51.9	9.6	1.7	15.2	16.4	273 748	253 798	237 501
Clark	617.3	47.0	18 627	68.5	116.1	320.1	D	28.0	D	7.2	2.5	13.5	18.8	89 713	82 278	77 862
Columbia	1 190.4	56.3	23 273	85.6	171.8	638.3	D	27.0	D	10.2	5.3	19.0	17.6	172 218	158 649	157 983
Crawford	313.4	49.4	18 883	69.4	59.0	193.0	D	35.0	D	15.4	2.7	22.4	14.2	67 611	65 483	61 899
Dane	12 830.8	64.2	30 214	111.1	1 016.2	10 033.3	19.2	12.4	80.4	8.5	10.0	24.3	26.8	1 242 667	1 164 031	1 101 666
Dodge	1 801.4	59.3	21 702	79.8	240.5	1 206.6	D	41.7	D	6.2	2.5	15.2	12.6	502 666	462 509	444 458
Door	685.0	49.1	25 326	93.1	106.4	372.5	D	16.5	D	15.5	6.9	26.5	14.0	61 509	56 466	42 969
Douglas	879.7	43.4	20 396	75.0	177.9	536.2	20.1	11.0	80.0	10.0	2.6	17.6	20.1	58 989	55 747	57 802
Dunn	777.2	60.3	19 910	73.2	107.2	484.8	25.6	18.7	71.8	15.8	2.3	15.5	27.2	90 704	94 420	93 640
Eau Claire	2 132.4	55.8	23 896	87.8	283.0	1 623.2	17.5	11.7	81.9	20.0	5.0	27.1	17.3	190 123	163 812	138 553
Florence	100.6	62.0	19 428	71.4	18.9	27.4	31.5	24.1	70.0	10.7	2.3	13.9	33.2	6 608	5 611	4 923
Fond du Lac	2 540.5	54.3	26 867	98.8	305.3	1 704.5	45.8	36.0	52.6	8.0	3.5	16.5	11.3	613 781	605 713	573 595
Forest	171.8	67.7	17 757	65.3	41.7	88.6	D	18.4	D	9.1	2.6	26.4	24.9	16 327	15 438	14 414
Grant	988.9	38.3	20 062	73.7	170.6	532.5	D	20.2	D	10.2	4.1	18.1	26.4	107 773	97 367	88 852
Green	758.9	38.9	22 676	83.4	103.4	439.2	31.1	24.1	65.9	16.8	3.1	22.2	13.6	105 996	109 002	100 617
Green Lake	458.5	46.4	23 503	86.4	73.7	242.2	37.0	24.2	58.5	9.2	3.3	23.0	13.0	58 694	60 679	56 042
Iowa	467.2	61.2	20 919	76.9	59.1	316.8	D	7.2	D	2.2	13.5	13.5	22 695	21 814	20 647	
Iron	130.5	56.9	20 572	75.6	32.0	67.1	D	17.1	D	12.9	2.0	28.2	17.2	11 485	11 176	8 648
Jackson	362.0	58.9	20 412	75.0	61.7	200.7	D	12.8	D	10.1	3.5	D	19.1	25 655	22 599	19 093
Jefferson	1 758.2	53.4	23 888	87.8	240.9	1 118.3	D	41.6	D	9.7	2.4	15.4	12.2	465 338	447 665	424 681
Juneau	456.1	51.8	19 165	70.5	94.8	279.4	NA	36.7	D	9.2	D	14.6	19.2	102 563	102 756	99 491
Kenosha	3 729.9	64.3	25 833	95.0	441.6	1 865.8	D	32.3	D	9.0	3.9	20.2	15.9	603 014	542 662	514 687
Kewaunee	419.0	46.8	21 080	77.5	61.3	223.2	D	34.2	D	6.8	3.1	12.0	14.7	76 411	68 784	65 446
La Crosse	2 546.5	44.5	24 862	91.4	318.0	2 106.9	D	20.2	D	10.6	5.2	28.3	14.1	424 808	398 972	381 492

[1] Based on resident population estimated as of July 1, 1998.   [2] Includes farm earnings; see table B-10 for these data.   [3] Includes mining and construction, not shown separately.   [4] Includes agricultural services, forestry, and fisheries; transportation and public utilities; and wholesale trade, not shown separately.   [5] Finance, insurance, and real estate.

Source: Personal Income and Earnings—U.S. Bureau of Economic Analysis, "Regional Economic Information System (REIS) 1969-1998" on CD-ROM (related Internet site <http://www.bea.doc.gov/bea/regional/data.htm>).

[Includes U.S., states, and 3,142 counties/county equivalents defined as of January 1, 1992. For changes to these areas since January 1, 1992, see appendix B. Geographic Information]

County	Personal income, 1998													Manufacturing earnings		
	Total (mil. dol.)	Per capita[1]			Transfer payments (mil. dol.)	Earnings										
							Percent, by selected industry–									
							Goods-related		Service-related							
		Percent change, 1990–1998	Amount (dollars)	Percent of national average		Total[2] (mil. dol.)	Total[3]	Man-ufac-turing	Total[4]	Retail trade	FIRE[5]	Serv-ices	Gov-ern-ment	1998 ($1,000)	1997 ($1,000)	1996 ($1,000)
WISCONSIN—Con.																
Lafayette	293.2	23.2	18 123	66.6	48.2	124.7	19.3	13.3	71.2	7.1	5.7	11.0	28.1	16 537	14 452	14 521
Langlade	399.5	50.4	19 503	71.7	82.8	236.0	D	22.1	D	12.3	D	19.7	16.3	52 160	50 000	45 313
Lincoln	610.9	58.2	20 535	75.5	110.2	385.6	D	38.8	D	8.5	6.3	11.4	16.3	149 496	143 274	140 141
Manitowoc	2 001.7	52.2	24 276	89.2	288.5	1 293.2	47.6	40.8	49.4	6.6	2.3	17.7	11.6	528 158	494 956	473 392
Marathon	3 050.1	57.1	24 781	91.1	356.6	2 220.0	38.0	31.7	60.1	8.1	9.7	16.8	11.8	703 053	681 593	600 909
Marinette	886.5	46.6	20 611	75.8	172.9	613.2	D	44.3	D	8.4	2.3	16.4	12.8	271 657	269 075	250 710
Marquette	266.1	50.4	17 594	64.7	62.0	113.1	42.4	32.0	56.3	9.1	3.7	14.5	18.4	36 160	32 970	31 783
Menominee	66.5	64.4	13 362	49.1	16.6	54.3	D	D	D	1.5	D	51.0	20.0	D	9 230	7 441
Milwaukee	25 165.2	35.3	27 607	101.5	3 944.5	21 510.5	25.3	22.2	74.7	7.6	10.7	31.3	12.9	4 773 508	4 744 525	4 521 626
Monroe	776.6	51.2	19 655	72.3	123.1	534.3	D	17.8	D	7.7	2.7	13.5	33.8	95 244	97 894	96 416
Oconto	626.3	52.4	18 488	68.0	111.9	284.5	D	28.1	D	10.1	2.5	15.3	19.2	80 072	71 415	65 675
Oneida	850.9	62.0	23 803	87.5	156.6	540.7	D	18.5	D	12.4	4.1	27.3	18.0	99 765	98 040	96 569
Outagamie	4 266.6	65.1	27 281	100.3	386.1	3 263.4	D	25.6	D	9.4	9.0	20.4	9.5	836 215	894 227	855 162
Ozaukee	3 239.9	71.5	39 934	146.8	215.7	1 468.7	D	37.4	D	7.9	7.4	22.5	9.4	549 157	521 699	483 516
Pepin	138.9	37.2	19 442	71.5	25.8	72.1	17.0	6.8	D	10.3	3.2	16.9	22.4	4 872	4 378	3 988
Pierce	851.9	62.3	23 978	88.1	88.8	294.7	D	14.7	D	8.9	4.0	17.4	34.5	43 350	35 595	35 309
Polk	824.8	64.5	21 265	78.2	129.4	425.4	D	31.1	D	9.9	3.7	17.8	16.9	132 413	118 904	107 230
Portage	1 455.3	53.5	22 452	82.5	180.0	1 048.3	D	20.8	D	8.9	14.6	16.4	16.8	218 307	217 888	205 648
Price	341.6	48.6	21 737	79.9	65.4	214.6	D	50.2	D	6.6	2.4	13.0	15.0	107 781	107 743	96 521
Racine	5 141.5	50.5	27 712	101.9	604.2	3 117.3	48.6	42.8	51.0	7.2	2.8	20.3	12.0	1 333 140	1 337 462	1 205 842
Richland	333.0	49.6	18 646	68.5	58.5	171.9	D	33.1	D	10.9	3.0	16.3	19.3	56 975	55 556	49 737
Rock	3 671.0	49.2	24 356	89.5	476.8	2 537.4	46.6	39.9	52.9	9.2	2.7	18.0	12.4	1 011 510	1 006 405	955 055
Rusk	270.0	48.4	17 772	65.3	60.5	170.6	D	36.9	D	9.3	2.1	11.9	21.3	62 910	50 507	50 098
St. Croix	1 692.7	76.2	28 731	105.6	136.9	748.1	D	31.8	D	11.3	3.6	21.2	13.7	237 717	232 296	217 369
Sauk	1 259.7	60.2	23 602	86.8	175.5	935.2	D	24.6	D	11.7	3.8	23.7	10.5	230 369	212 908	203 424
Sawyer	304.6	72.4	18 940	69.6	66.6	175.8	25.9	16.7	73.1	13.6	4.9	28.2	18.5	29 351	29 619	28 234
Shawano	772.7	56.5	19 906	73.2	135.4	384.5	D	21.6	D	12.0	4.1	20.1	16.0	83 193	80 370	64 496
Sheboygan	2 876.0	51.7	26 149	96.1	337.0	2 097.3	52.9	46.8	46.1	7.4	4.4	16.8	10.4	981 719	912 863	863 693
Taylor	375.3	47.5	19 497	71.7	61.9	263.3	D	40.6	D	7.9	3.1	14.9	11.4	106 907	95 586	94 404
Trempealeau	543.4	45.9	20 510	75.4	99.9	347.6	D	40.0	D	6.5	2.6	13.9	11.0	139 043	126 821	121 042
Vernon	474.8	41.0	17 352	63.8	96.4	213.1	D	12.1	D	11.3	6.5	21.1	23.2	25 741	25 127	23 560
Vilas	450.7	71.0	21 200	77.9	96.9	220.1	D	9.0	D	17.2	5.1	29.8	14.8	19 779	18 667	18 134
Walworth	2 061.1	60.1	24 112	88.6	256.2	1 231.4	D	29.5	D	9.4	3.4	19.3	17.3	362 953	336 682	334 944
Washburn	294.0	63.5	19 058	70.1	71.7	158.4	24.5	18.1	74.2	12.9	4.7	20.0	25.7	28 597	24 675	24 021
Washington	3 383.7	73.8	29 708	109.2	287.3	1 682.4	44.5	36.4	55.1	7.9	5.2	16.6	13.1	612 005	572 585	536 061
Waukesha	12 848.2	73.8	36 394	133.8	920.1	8 783.1	37.8	29.2	62.1	7.2	7.4	22.3	7.4	2 564 011	2 352 595	2 182 209
Waupaca	1 185.7	62.5	23 473	86.3	210.2	665.6	D	36.7	D	9.3	3.3	17.2	15.8	244 343	227 687	202 041
Waushara	406.1	46.2	18 761	69.0	84.8	161.1	20.3	12.8	70.4	12.1	4.1	16.3	19.9	20 634	17 521	16 021
Winnebago	3 987.1	52.9	26 581	97.7	453.8	3 334.1	D	46.6	D	6.0	3.7	18.5	11.5	1 553 558	1 403 588	1 324 004
Wood	2 058.4	53.5	27 054	99.5	271.8	1 702.2	32.9	27.5	D	8.3	D	33.4	9.8	468 790	453 831	443 082
WYOMING	11 670.9	43.0	24 312	89.4	1 474.7	7 804.1	28.6	5.7	70.6	9.7	4.9	18.6	24.3	444 781	417 095	409 989
Albany	655.9	46.2	22 423	82.4	84.3	419.6	15.0	8.7	D	10.3	3.9	22.5	42.5	36 704	33 777	36 799
Big Horn	201.2	35.0	17 759	65.3	39.7	135.7	34.8	6.8	D	6.7	D	7.5	25.7	9 224	9 507	8 863
Campbell	800.9	48.7	24 729	90.9	61.7	701.0	53.1	2.9	47.5	6.7	1.9	12.0	13.5	19 996	16 197	15 028
Carbon	328.2	14.6	21 117	77.6	48.1	210.9	28.1	10.5	70.3	10.1	2.8	14.4	26.8	22 070	22 823	22 592
Converse	245.3	40.1	19 977	73.4	32.3	163.2	37.4	1.8	D	7.3	2.0	D	19.6	2 913	2 823	3 097
Crook	118.8	23.4	20 553	75.6	15.9	54.6	36.1	12.5	D	8.9	2.7	9.9	31.9	6 834	6 923	6 956
Fremont	690.5	49.3	19 113	70.3	144.2	404.2	20.0	4.1	79.2	14.5	2.9	25.3	26.5	16 599	17 319	17 986
Goshen	247.4	25.4	19 322	71.0	47.3	133.1	D	6.7	D	7.9	3.4	17.4	26.8	8 861	9 035	9 014
Hot Springs	99.8	28.1	21 488	79.0	23.7	51.1	D	D	D	8.7	4.3	27.1	27.4	D	1 491	1 255
Johnson	145.0	39.7	21 339	78.4	22.9	70.2	D	4.3	D	13.5	7.3	20.0	30.4	3 049	3 174	2 408
Laramie	2 012.7	44.3	25 613	94.2	241.9	1 378.2	11.4	5.1	87.5	9.9	8.0	16.6	40.2	69 756	63 719	59 067
Lincoln	261.2	42.0	18 918	69.5	37.1	160.2	35.6	9.4	63.8	9.4	2.8	9.5	23.1	14 994	15 499	14 632
Natrona	1 784.5	36.5	28 217	103.7	217.1	1 182.4	34.7	4.4	65.2	9.1	4.7	22.1	14.6	51 593	49 622	51 078
Niobrara	49.3	17.8	18 265	67.1	9.9	22.1	D	D	D	11.1	3.3	10.7	44.2	D	573	595
Park	598.2	50.8	23 231	85.4	84.1	364.5	22.8	4.3	74.6	10.9	5.0	22.0	27.4	15 739	15 651	16 189
Platte	172.4	28.0	19 999	73.5	31.3	112.8	D	1.6	D	10.3	D	D	22.9	1 824	1 934	1 619
Sheridan	648.1	39.0	25 767	94.7	91.7	333.4	11.9	3.9	87.7	11.4	7.6	24.1	30.1	13 131	13 411	12 068
Sublette	126.1	37.5	21 940	80.7	14.9	69.8	33.0	1.3	63.2	10.3	3.7	16.3	25.6	938	889	885
Sweetwater	1 006.8	43.7	25 345	93.2	95.9	858.5	53.7	11.2	46.4	7.4	2.9	9.3	14.3	95 885	83 936	82 136
Teton	748.3	93.1	52 723	193.8	31.0	510.4	18.3	2.8	81.7	14.6	10.8	38.0	12.9	14 312	13 607	13 176
Uinta	397.4	44.6	19 485	71.6	50.0	262.2	32.9	3.9	67.5	9.7	2.9	19.9	21.5	10 120	8 609	8 297
Washakie	185.4	40.7	21 347	78.5	27.3	119.3	31.6	16.6	65.3	8.2	3.1	17.6	21.4	19 821	18 443	18 675
Weston	147.4	30.9	22 673	83.3	22.1	86.5	31.8	9.9	D	8.8	3.1	18.7	21.1	8 545	8 133	7 574

[1] Based on resident population estimated as of July 1, 1998. [2] Includes farm earnings; see table B-10 for these data. [3] Includes mining and construction, not shown separately. [4] Includes agricultural services, forestry, and fisheries; transportation and public utilities; and wholesale trade, not shown separately. [5] Finance, insurance, and real estate.

Source: Personal Income and Earnings—U.S. Bureau of Economic Analysis, "Regional Economic Information System (REIS) 1969-1998" on CD-ROM (related Internet site <http://www.bea.doc.gov/bea/regional/data.htm>).

Table B–9. Counties — Manufacturing and Water Use

[Includes U.S., states, and 3,142 counties/county equivalents defined as of January 1, 1992. For changes to these areas since January 1, 1992, see appendix B. Geographic Information]

County	Manufacturing (NAICS 31-33), 1997								Water use per day,[3] 1995					
	Establishments		All employees		Production workers		Value added by manufacture (mil. dol.)	Value of shipments (mil. dol.)	Withdrawals					Consumptive use (mil. gal.)
	Total	Percent with 20 or more employees	Number[1]	Annual payroll (mil. dol.)	Number[2]	Wages (mil. dol.)			Total (mil. gal.)	Percent ground water	By selected major use– (mil. gal.)			
											Irrigation	Public supply	Industrial	
UNITED STATES	363 753	33.1	16 888 016	572 101.1	12 124 001	339 723.0	1 826 590.0	3 842 061.4	398 514	19.4	133 626	39 779	22 367	101 052
ALABAMA	5 444	38.4	352 618	10 187.8	275 637	6 928.4	29 221.5	67 970.1	7 097	6.3	139	813	733	532
Autauga	38	36.8	2 130	69.2	1 582	45.1	152.5	366.4	40	18.9	Z	5	34	9
Baldwin	138	21.7	5 150	127.1	4 130	80.0	366.4	809.5	42	88.4	25	12	Z	31
Barbour	41	53.7	3 680	93.0	2 783	58.8	276.3	689.7	15	44.3	8	5	1	11
Bibb	27	63.0	1 218	23.9	975	19.4	130.5	244.3	3	75.3	–	2	–	1
Blount	60	21.7	2 742	49.5	2 451	42.0	272.5	403.5	51	7.1	Z	49	–	2
Bullock	6	33.3	(4)	D	D	D	D	D	5	40.1	2	2	–	3
Butler	27	55.6	2 044	41.9	1 799	33.6	142.7	305.5	4	75.1	–	2	Z	2
Calhoun	149	43.6	10 841	257.8	8 573	178.4	718.0	1 504.5	26	86.6	2	22	1	5
Chambers	40	57.5	5 612	147.2	4 947	121.7	266.4	765.8	13	2.9	Z	6	6	2
Cherokee	21	28.6	1 194	25.4	1 048	20.7	41.1	121.2	6	12.4	4	2	–	5
Chilton	54	37.0	1 488	30.3	1 181	21.4	66.0	162.1	6	62.4	Z	3	Z	2
Choctaw	12	50.0	(5)	D	D	D	D	D	52	5.7	–	1	48	4
Clarke	32	46.9	2 888	82.7	2 391	59.0	198.5	540.1	26	6.9	–	3	22	6
Clay	15	40.0	2 789	49.6	2 365	33.4	96.4	212.4	3	27.5	–	1	–	1
Cleburne	10	50.0	1 108	19.9	850	15.3	48.1	175.1	3	68.2	–	1	1	1
Coffee	39	35.9	4 725	89.8	3 828	63.6	279.0	679.8	16	44.2	8	5	1	11
Colbert	118	28.0	5 581	205.8	4 236	141.0	195.0	1 491.6	91	5.6	6	8	57	9
Conecuh	21	47.6	821	17.0	642	10.1	39.6	98.8	2	91.9	–	2	–	1
Coosa	11	54.5	978	22.3	824	18.4	54.0	123.1	1	29.0	–	Z	–	1
Covington	30	50.0	3 872	83.5	3 504	71.2	162.2	388.0	12	43.9	1	4	1	4
Crenshaw	15	46.7	830	9.6	684	6.6	16.8	26.1	3	84.1	Z	2	–	1
Cullman	123	31.7	5 994	147.4	4 778	99.8	338.4	964.1	20	7.8	–	14	3	6
Dale	26	30.8	1 254	23.0	891	14.2	32.0	70.0	14	84.4	2	5	–	6
Dallas	53	50.9	5 336	137.6	4 240	92.5	457.4	1 064.8	57	19.2	Z	8	38	14
DeKalb	216	46.3	11 774	237.3	10 267	177.3	537.9	1 286.0	10	36.5	Z	6	1	4
Elmore	51	27.5	2 340	57.1	1 765	31.1	131.4	280.3	6	51.4	1	4	–	2
Escambia	53	32.1	3 145	79.5	2 666	59.6	362.4	689.5	49	23.6	4	5	37	14
Etowah	136	34.6	8 775	277.0	6 778	184.5	679.0	1 577.0	265	1.8	9	21	93	26
Fayette	33	42.4	2 617	55.9	2 246	44.9	126.8	372.0	3	28.8	Z	2	–	1
Franklin	64	35.9	5 348	97.0	4 532	73.2	174.7	645.8	5	38.8	Z	3	–	2
Geneva	26	30.8	2 123	34.1	1 933	28.9	79.2	171.1	4	72.1	Z	2	–	2
Greene	NA	NA	NA	NA	NA	NA	NA	NA	320	.6	–	1	–	11
Hale	16	56.3	1 443	28.5	1 246	19.8	82.1	210.0	39	15.3	Z	2	–	37
Henry	18	44.4	1 410	33.9	1 196	24.5	142.6	382.5	9	30.8	7	1	Z	8
Houston	125	37.6	9 233	231.9	7 254	156.3	667.7	1 457.7	120	25.8	14	18	–	18
Jackson	83	31.3	6 557	182.4	5 319	136.1	479.9	1 253.5	1 302	.1	1	8	4	6
Jefferson	817	35.5	35 972	1 168.7	25 373	723.6	3 194.7	7 475.6	92	19.6	1	56	Z	35
Lamar	22	54.5	2 589	61.3	2 100	46.1	142.1	313.4	4	85.0	–	2	1	2
Lauderdale	115	33.9	7 545	169.9	6 301	124.1	412.5	885.1	16	14.7	Z	14	–	4
Lawrence	29	31.0	(5)	D	D	D	D	D	62	1.8	1	2	56	9
Lee	88	44.3	7 016	194.9	5 906	146.8	665.6	1 232.9	19	16.4	1	13	2	6
Limestone	69	43.5	6 780	309.0	5 999	270.2	858.7	1 321.0	792	.7	9	4	–	14
Lowndes	10	40.0	(4)	D	D	D	D	D	9	19.7	6	1	–	8
Macon	NA	NA	NA	NA	NA	NA	NA	NA	7	14.9	2	3	–	4
Madison	335	33.7	28 280	1 079.1	17 934	608.7	2 813.0	6 991.7	54	53.7	1	48	1	10
Marengo	18	61.1	1 701	54.1	1 366	38.6	201.4	404.8	32	14.4	–	2	27	6
Marion	53	58.5	6 423	154.8	5 103	104.9	458.7	964.2	7	16.1	–	5	–	2
Marshall	152	48.7	15 773	338.5	13 341	244.6	1 002.5	2 616.7	22	24.7	Z	19	1	5
Mobile	445	33.5	22 130	835.3	15 383	523.1	2 549.6	5 494.8	1 106	2.7	5	154	4	39
Monroe	28	53.6	4 748	165.0	3 718	115.0	514.7	1 094.0	64	9.9	1	5	57	8
Montgomery	214	38.3	11 343	299.4	8 019	183.1	1 041.2	2 024.6	60	58.0	1	55	1	10
Morgan	214	38.8	(6)	D	D	D	D	D	140	6.5	Z	29	108	8
Perry	8	62.5	926	21.7	775	16.2	46.2	96.9	8	41.7	–	1	–	7
Pickens	21	52.4	1 051	18.3	958	15.1	46.1	113.7	6	61.6	2	3	Z	4
Pike	32	50.0	2 302	47.1	1 991	36.6	126.4	356.1	12	59.5	6	4	–	8
Randolph	28	35.7	2 322	39.0	1 998	32.6	97.5	218.5	2	67.7	–	Z	–	2
Russell	49	38.8	3 295	107.8	2 757	80.7	540.6	1 000.4	34	4.8	1	8	25	4
St. Clair	85	37.6	3 180	85.1	2 536	56.1	190.8	480.2	9	91.5	Z	7	–	3
Shelby	158	41.1	6 076	174.8	4 670	116.8	436.6	876.6	720	2.2	2	14	–	11
Sumter	15	53.3	832	17.4	618	12.6	38.5	89.4	10	7.2	–	2	–	7
Talladega	100	44.0	7 160	201.1	5 984	150.1	582.1	1 420.6	77	11.3	1	12	61	8
Tallapoosa	53	64.2	5 868	112.8	5 278	91.0	343.8	1 074.8	13	5.7	1	11	–	4
Tuscaloosa	160	35.6	10 738	378.9	8 500	266.2	926.4	2 557.9	37	14.8	1	25	3	10
Walker	72	25.0	1 709	32.8	1 376	21.8	126.8	381.3	907	.2	Z	52	–	11
Washington	12	41.7	(5)	D	D	D	D	D	86	10.9	Z	1	17	6
Wilcox	12	41.7	(5)	D	D	D	D	D	43	4.3	1	21	20	6
Winston	87	48.3	6 573	135.8	5 465	95.4	301.3	838.7	3	58.1	–	1	–	1

[1] Average number of production workers plus the number of other (nonproduction) employees for the pay period including March 12. [2] Average number of production workers for the pay periods including the 12th of March, May, August, and November. [3] In millions of gallons per day. [4] 500 to 999 employees. [5] 1,000 to 2,499 employees. [6] 10,000 to 24,999 employees.

Sources: Manufacturing—U.S. Census Bureau, 1997 Economic Census – Manufacturing, generated by Statistical Compendia Branch, using American Factfinder at <http://www.census.gov/>, (June 2000) [related Internet site <http://www.census.gov/epcd/www/97EC31.HTM>]. Water Use—U.S. Geological Survey, "Water Use in the United States," individual state/county and US by state files from <http://water.usgs.gov/watuse/spread95.html>, (accessed: September 1999).

Table B–9. Counties — **Manufacturing and Water Use**–Con.

[Includes U.S., states, and 3,142 counties/county equivalents defined as of January 1, 1992. For changes to these areas since January 1, 1992, see appendix B. Geographic Information]

County	Manufacturing (NAICS 31-33), 1997								Water use per day,[3] 1995					
	Establishments		All employees		Production workers		Value added by manu-facture (mil. dol.)	Value of ship-ments (mil. dol.)	Withdrawals					Consump-tive use (mil. gal.)
	Total	Percent with 20 or more employ-ees	Number[1]	Annual payroll (mil. dol.)	Number[2]	Wages (mil. dol.)			Total (mil. gal.)	Percent ground water	By selected major use– (mil. gal.)			
											Irrigation	Public supply	Industrial	
ALASKA	488	20.9	10 770	331.2	8 805	238.2	1 159.3	3 305.0	329	40.3	1	81	57	35
Aleutians East	2	100.0	(4)	D	D	D	D	D	3	NA	–	1	3	1
Aleutians West	8	75.0	(5)	D	D	D	D	D	3	NA	–	3	–	Z
Anchorage	187	13.9	2 022	62.9	1 459	38.8	157.8	322.3	45	39.0	–	36	Z	5
Bethel	NA	NA	NA	NA	NA	NA	NA	NA	Z	NA	–	Z	–	Z
Bristol Bay	NA	NA	NA	NA	NA	NA	NA	NA	Z	100.0	–	Z	Z	Z
Denali	NA	NA	NA	NA	NA	NA	NA	NA	17	NA	–	Z	–	2
Dillingham	NA	NA	NA	NA	NA	NA	NA	NA	Z	NA	–	Z	–	Z
Fairbanks North Star	NA	NA	NA	NA	NA	NA	NA	NA	32	40.5	Z	7	Z	3
Haines	NA	NA	NA	NA	NA	NA	NA	NA	1	3.9	–	Z	–	Z
Juneau	NA	NA	NA	NA	NA	NA	NA	NA	5	98.7	–	4	Z	1
Kenai Peninsula	56	21.4	1 246	56.7	977	41.8	283.0	1 027.0	9	88.6	Z	4	3	2
Ketchikan Gateway	18	38.9	762	31.1	579	21.5	27.5	131.3	54	–	–	4	50	8
Kodiak Island	25	52.0	1 576	35.4	1 405	28.6	82.5	204.3	5	4.8	–	5	Z	1
Lake and Peninsula	NA	NA	NA	NA	NA	NA	NA	NA	Z	NA	–	Z	–	Z
Matanuska-Susitna	NA	NA	NA	NA	NA	NA	NA	NA	6	70.1	1	1	Z	1
Nome	NA	NA	NA	NA	NA	NA	NA	NA	1	57.6	–	1	–	Z
North Slope	NA	NA	NA	NA	NA	NA	NA	NA	116	64.0	–	Z	–	9
Northwest Arctic	NA	NA	NA	NA	NA	NA	NA	NA	6	8.5	–	Z	–	1
Prince of Wales-Outer Ketchikan	NA	NA	NA	NA	NA	NA	NA	NA	1	.7	–	1	–	Z
Sitka	NA	NA	NA	NA	NA	NA	NA	NA	5	–	–	5	Z	1
Skagway-Yakutat-Angoon	NA	NA	NA	NA	NA	NA	NA	NA	1	86.2	–	1	–	Z
Southeast Fairbanks	NA	NA	NA	NA	NA	NA	NA	NA	3	12.8	–	Z	–	Z
Valdez-Cordova	NA	NA	NA	NA	NA	NA	NA	NA	5	51.1	–	4	Z	Z
Wade Hampton	NA	NA	NA	NA	NA	NA	NA	NA	Z	66.7	–	Z	–	Z
Wrangell-Petersburg	NA	NA	NA	NA	NA	NA	NA	NA	2	2.1	–	2	–	Z
Yukon-Koyukuk	NA	NA	NA	NA	NA	NA	NA	NA	8	NA	–	Z	–	Z
ARIZONA	4 917	27.9	193 616	6 753.6	121 994	3 000.1	26 898.9	43 030.3	6 830	41.7	5 672	807	39	3 843
Apache	NA	NA	NA	NA	NA	NA	NA	NA	39	63.2	16	5	–	28
Cochise	53	30.2	921	20.9	641	12.4	62.6	153.8	234	97.3	211	12	1	125
Coconino	95	13.7	(5)	D	D	D	D	D	47	45.5	8	17	–	34
Gila	34	17.0	(5)	D	D	D	D	D	43	56.8	15	5	–	27
Graham	NA	NA	NA	NA	NA	NA	NA	NA	176	44.1	173	3	–	89
Greenlee	NA	NA	NA	NA	NA	NA	NA	NA	44	50.8	19	1	–	29
La Paz	NA	NA	NA	NA	NA	NA	NA	NA	629	3.4	627	1	–	341
Maricopa	3 364	29.6	143 683	5 045.0	88 996	2 213.6	22 363.5	32 782.1	2 392	43.1	1 764	588	6	1 356
Mohave	156	21.2	3 807	85.2	3 166	60.8	344.0	760.4	140	98.5	104	15	–	100
Navajo	45	17.8	1 346	44.2	1 130	34.7	100.9	275.9	64	98.4	24	5	16	46
Pima	764	26.2	26 746	1 064.7	15 013	356.9	2 350.1	4 455.2	264	86.2	94	103	16	160
Pinal	74	40.5	4 594	154.8	3 466	101.2	723.9	2 530.6	1 262	39.6	1 205	15	1	645
Santa Cruz	35	25.7	(4)	D	D	D	D	D	15	98.4	11	3	–	9
Yavapai	189	19.0	3 511	91.3	2 625	62.7	262.4	445.8	82	71.6	39	14	–	52
Yuma	66	25.8	3 041	54.6	2 701	42.9	158.0	389.5	1 399	28.0	1 364	22	–	801
ARKANSAS	3 316	37.6	230 153	5 778.4	187 493	4 192.7	19 346.8	45 186.0	8 767	62.2	5 936	381	187	4 761
Arkansas	28	46.4	2 768	66.4	2 160	48.4	140.9	916.2	821	58.4	733	5	–	560
Ashley	24	70.8	3 792	141.7	3 247	114.4	371.5	921.4	135	69.4	77	3	40	69
Baxter	56	23.2	3 185	74.1	2 408	47.7	209.3	350.8	6	30.7	–	4	–	1
Benton	194	37.6	14 220	346.5	11 438	257.9	1 179.6	2 491.8	336	1.6	Z	10	–	9
Boone	67	26.9	2 808	70.4	2 361	53.0	221.4	495.0	5	29.1	Z	3	–	3
Bradley	9	33.3	594	12.5	519	10.3	38.1	90.0	1	94.5	–	1	–	1
Calhoun	NA	NA	NA	NA	NA	NA	NA	NA	1	93.6	–	1	–	Z
Carroll	41	14.6	3 408	62.8	2 548	53.7	283.9	426.5	7	22.1	Z	5	–	2
Chicot	11	45.5	1 019	12.8	968	10.8	21.2	67.1	233	66.7	198	2	–	166
Clark	31	51.6	2 960	64.2	2 659	52.7	153.8	401.1	5	22.7	1	3	1	2
Clay	23	52.2	2 475	42.0	2 256	33.5	97.8	188.6	176	97.8	173	2	–	129
Cleburne	34	29.4	1 687	39.1	1 225	22.1	242.7	367.0	7	17.8	Z	4	–	3
Cleveland	NA	NA	NA	NA	NA	NA	NA	NA	1	87.7	–	1	–	Z
Columbia	39	46.2	2 957	96.6	2 210	65.5	291.3	602.3	6	97.1	–	4	2	1
Conway	23	39.1	2 108	49.4	1 763	37.6	164.3	334.8	29	5.2	5	2	21	7
Craighead	122	36.9	6 886	184.9	5 474	125.9	507.6	1 257.6	350	90.9	337	12	–	252
Crawford	62	38.7	(6)	D	D	D	D	D	16	3.7	Z	14	Z	4
Crittenden	45	51.1	2 323	56.2	1 824	36.6	224.5	620.6	112	99.7	103	10	Z	77
Cross	17	35.3	1 698	37.8	1 500	29.5	78.6	286.0	299	95.2	295	3	–	220
Dallas	15	46.7	786	21.9	710	18.6	51.5	131.3	1	95.8	–	1	–	Z
Desha	16	56.3	1 611	45.1	1 317	32.6	128.8	319.2	330	71.9	281	2	19	226

[1] Average number of production workers plus the number of other (nonproduction) employees for the pay period including March 12. [2] Average number of production workers for the pay periods including the 12th of March, May, August, and November. [3] In millions of gallons per day. [4] 500 to 999 employees. [5] 1,000 to 2,499 employees. [6] 2,500 to 4,999 employees.

Sources: Manufacturing—U.S. Census Bureau, 1997 Economic Census – Manufacturing, generated by Statistical Compendia Branch, using American Factfinder at <http://www.census.gov/>, (June 2000) [related Internet site <http://www.census.gov/epcd/www/97EC31.HTM>]. Water Use—U.S. Geological Survey, "Water Use in the United States," individual state/county and US by state files from <http://water.usgs.gov/watuse/spread95.html>, (accessed: September 1999).

[Includes U.S., states, and 3,142 counties/county equivalents defined as of January 1, 1992. For changes to these areas since January 1, 1992, see appendix B. Geographic Information]

County	Maunfacturing (NAICS 31-33), 1997								Water use per day,[3] 1995					
	Establishments		All employees		Production workers		Value added by manufacture (mil. dol.)	Value of shipments (mil. dol.)	Withdrawals					Consumptive use (mil. gal.)
	Total	Percent with 20 or more employees	Number[1]	Annual payroll (mil. dol.)	Number[2]	Wages (mil. dol.)			Total (mil. gal.)	Percent ground water	By selected major use— (mil. gal.)			
											Irrigation	Public supply	Industrial	
ARKANSAS—Con.														
Drew	33	48.5	2 429	51.2	2 098	38.7	102.4	222.0	71	81.5	64	2	–	49
Faulkner	93	34.4	7 556	189.0	5 902	133.2	582.6	1 230.5	12	32.8	1	8	–	5
Franklin	16	56.3	1 284	24.2	1 132	18.7	105.9	216.0	13	7.6	Z	3	–	2
Fulton	NA	NA	NA	NA	NA	NA	NA	NA	74	1.7	Z	Z	–	10
Garland	108	23.1	3 827	100.0	2 823	65.7	258.1	795.5	266	.6	Z	15	2	3
Grant	25	36.0	1 481	42.0	1 229	30.8	142.2	314.6	2	94.7	–	2	Z	1
Greene	47	40.4	5 223	126.6	4 440	95.0	467.9	961.3	154	98.9	149	3	Z	112
Hempstead	32	46.9	3 565	75.9	2 849	51.2	203.6	558.9	9	33.8	–	3	–	3
Hot Spring	47	36.2	1 764	45.3	1 457	34.7	136.1	315.2	8	7.0	4	3	1	4
Howard	26	57.7	5 067	94.5	4 723	82.8	452.6	1 120.2	6	13.2	–	4	1	1
Independence	54	37.0	5 168	123.3	4 318	88.3	468.1	1 013.3	37	51.6	20	7	Z	24
Izard	NA	NA	NA	NA	NA	NA	NA	NA	3	81.9	–	2	–	1
Jackson	23	39.1	1 129	31.5	930	22.2	75.2	199.9	298	95.2	288	2	–	218
Jefferson	84	44.0	7 774	218.8	6 471	167.1	741.1	1 741.5	455	84.4	332	17	76	277
Johnson	39	46.2	3 318	65.1	2 899	53.0	237.6	409.4	4	21.0	Z	3	–	2
Lafayette	NA	NA	NA	NA	NA	NA	NA	NA	33	75.6	28	1	–	24
Lawrence	37	32.4	1 615	31.2	1 412	23.1	127.2	215.5	281	92.1	278	2	–	207
Lee	NA	NA	NA	NA	NA	NA	NA	NA	167	98.4	160	2	–	122
Lincoln	8	25.0	(4)	D	D	D	D	D	151	87.7	147	1	–	111
Little River	16	25.0	(5)	D	D	D	D	D	5	37.3	3	1	–	3
Logan	36	30.6	2 569	44.8	2 084	32.6	162.4	393.0	5	31.1	Z	3	–	3
Lonoke	39	25.6	1 739	45.4	1 376	31.9	143.2	269.8	373	82.2	296	3	1	261
Madison	19	26.3	738	12.8	608	8.7	38.8	170.7	4	44.4	–	2	–	2
Marion	23	30.4	1 847	29.5	1 394	18.7	68.6	133.7	2	19.0	–	1	–	1
Miller	25	32.0	2 274	99.7	1 648	68.0	263.4	495.6	100	10.0	94	5	–	71
Mississippi	62	56.5	7 644	252.7	6 425	201.2	1 123.9	2 801.7	153	97.4	136	9	8	103
Monroe	NA	NA	NA	NA	NA	NA	NA	NA	194	92.6	192	2	–	143
Montgomery	NA	NA	NA	NA	NA	NA	NA	NA	2	41.0	Z	1	Z	1
Nevada	8	25.0	(4)	D	D	D	D	D	2	38.7	–	1	–	1
Newton	NA	NA	NA	NA	NA	NA	NA	NA	1	76.7	Z	Z	–	1
Ouachita	33	51.5	2 961	96.0	2 358	70.4	418.3	854.3	36	4.6	–	4	9	2
Perry	NA	NA	NA	NA	NA	NA	NA	NA	4	13.0	3	1	–	3
Phillips	19	57.9	983	24.1	647	14.3	95.5	411.8	314	44.1	133	5	Z	100
Pike	13	38.5	596	12.0	529	10.2	47.4	121.5	2	46.0	–	1	–	1
Poinsett	27	44.4	1 895	42.5	1 586	32.2	125.4	367.1	501	89.2	479	3	–	365
Polk	29	37.9	1 933	38.2	1 632	30.5	138.8	322.2	5	21.4	Z	3	–	2
Pope	82	37.8	4 940	118.4	4 059	84.4	507.9	1 222.1	980	.3	1	9	–	30
Prairie	NA	NA	NA	NA	NA	NA	NA	NA	297	75.7	256	1	–	212
Pulaski	431	36.0	20 557	572.8	15 210	354.1	1 971.2	4 342.4	86	21.5	23	61	–	26
Randolph	32	28.1	1 688	37.6	1 356	26.9	93.3	190.5	80	74.7	78	1	–	59
St. Francis	27	44.4	1 606	41.1	1 227	26.5	119.4	628.2	201	94.1	193	4	–	146
Saline	72	27.8	1 827	56.8	1 459	40.6	140.2	352.7	10	40.9	Z	6	1	4
Scott	19	31.6	1 367	27.1	1 158	21.2	55.2	220.7	3	35.8	–	1	–	2
Searcy	NA	NA	NA	NA	NA	NA	NA	NA	2	35.2	–	1	–	1
Sebastian	233	43.3	22 891	582.0	18 649	421.6	1 974.2	4 319.3	32	1.3	Z	32	–	7
Sevier	15	40.0	1 985	37.3	1 848	32.1	127.7	402.0	4	30.2	–	3	–	2
Sharp	NA	NA	NA	NA	NA	NA	NA	NA	2	50.0	–	1	–	1
Stone	26	15.4	602	10.4	485	7.2	18.0	39.8	2	27.8	–	1	–	1
Union	63	46.0	5 443	158.1	4 314	110.2	868.8	2 082.2	16	98.9	–	9	6	3
Van Buren	15	20.0	638	12.5	573	10.2	24.5	111.5	3	28.2	–	1	–	1
Washington	193	39.9	14 795	357.1	12 125	261.5	1 071.6	2 388.9	27	14.8	Z	22	–	8
White	75	42.7	4 149	103.3	3 326	72.1	300.4	646.5	114	51.9	102	7	–	81
Woodruff	9	55.6	796	14.0	712	11.9	39.6	78.4	275	92.7	270	1	Z	202
Yell	22	27.3	2 880	52.4	2 609	44.4	99.8	337.7	10	23.6	2	4	–	4
CALIFORNIA	49 418	30.9	1 809 667	65 762.8	1 181 865	31 140.0	195 872.8	379 612.4	45 937	31.9	28 894	5 622	575	25 558
Alameda	2 507	34.4	93 809	3 803.0	60 299	1 914.3	10 363.3	22 337.8	237	18.7	13	215	7	67
Alpine	NA	NA	NA	NA	NA	NA	NA	NA	24	23.2	24	Z	–	24
Amador	51	19.6	732	19.5	552	13.6	67.8	136.8	27	46.2	16	10	–	17
Butte	232	22.8	4 944	128.4	3 939	89.7	377.3	771.6	958	31.8	853	45	–	772
Calaveras	NA	NA	NA	NA	NA	NA	NA	NA	15	26.2	6	5	1	6
Colusa	20	40.0	651	20.8	520	13.7	75.4	265.8	1 049	31.4	1 045	3	Z	839
Contra Costa	723	21.9	19 366	889.0	12 384	499.5	3 831.5	11 644.8	885	15.7	89	135	107	147
Del Norte	NA	NA	NA	NA	NA	NA	NA	NA	20	51.5	16	3	Z	16
El Dorado	144	19.4	1 775	56.4	1 342	36.5	134.0	287.9	74	17.0	19	52	Z	29

[1] Average number of production workers plus the number of other (nonproduction) employees for the pay period including March 12.   [2] Average number of production workers for the pay periods including the 12th of March, May, August, and November.   [3] In millions of gallons per day.   [4] 500 to 999 employees.   [5] 1,000 to 2,499 employees.

Sources: Manufacturing—U.S. Census Bureau, 1997 Economic Census – Manufacturing, generated by Statistical Compendia Branch, using American Factfinder at <http://www.census.gov/>, (June 2000) [related Internet site <http://www.census.gov/epcd/www/97EC31.HTM>].   Water Use—U.S. Geological Survey, "Water Use in the United States," individual state/county and US by state files from <http://water.usgs.gov/watuse/spread95.html>, (accessed: September 1999).

[Includes U.S., states, and 3,142 counties/county equivalents defined as of January 1, 1992. For changes to these areas since January 1, 1992, see appendix B. Geographic Information]

| County | Maunfacturing (NAICS 31-33), 1997 | | | | | | | | Water use per day,[3] 1995 | | | | | |
| | Establishments | | All employees | | Production workers | | Value added by manu-facture (mil. dol.) | Value of ship-ments (mil. dol.) | Withdrawals | | By selected major use— (mil. gal.) | | | Consump-tive use (mil. gal.) |
	Total	Percent with 20 or more employ-ees	Number[1]	Annual payroll (mil. dol.)	Number[2]	Wages (mil. dol.)			Total (mil. gal.)	Percent ground water	Irrigation	Public supply	Industrial	
CALIFORNIA—Con.														
Fresno	696	32.9	27 552	704.3	19 949	428.5	2 347.6	5 667.6	3 554	49.4	3 329	169	5	2 654
Glenn	29	31.0	946	29.2	790	23.6	68.0	290.6	848	34.1	840	4	1	687
Humboldt	178	23.6	5 540	161.4	4 628	125.9	454.6	1 041.9	200	43.1	45	37	32	66
Imperial	61	29.5	1 481	40.6	1 202	26.7	94.7	241.6	2 609	3.6	2 570	23	Z	2 308
Inyo	NA	NA	NA	NA	NA	NA	NA	NA	149	48.1	50	3	Z	105
Kern	390	22.6	14 306	379.2	11 322	251.0	1 608.5	2 824.6	2 515	55.9	2 288	146	3	1 805
Kings	65	35.4	2 796	90.6	2 312	68.0	249.6	748.7	1 413	53.7	1 369	26	Z	1 074
Lake	NA	NA	NA	NA	NA	NA	NA	NA	64	81.1	50	6	Z	56
Lassen	NA	NA	NA	NA	NA	NA	NA	NA	301	40.7	294	5	Z	260
Los Angeles	17 915	32.6	622 302	20 311.3	430 159	10 295.1	53 692.0	106 706.4	1 147	18.2	36	1 473	167	400
Madera	94	36.2	3 913	120.8	2 978	84.3	450.6	952.3	981	32.0	949	17	4	773
Marin	341	14.1	4 605	160.0	2 953	78.2	333.1	656.2	41	5.1	1	37	–	12
Mariposa	NA	NA	NA	NA	NA	NA	NA	NA	8	43.9	5	2	Z	5
Mendocino	160	22.5	4 287	124.1	3 182	85.2	374.9	769.3	53	51.4	36	9	3	41
Merced	123	41.5	8 381	198.2	6 660	146.7	665.3	2 431.5	1 688	33.6	1 586	34	5	1 323
Modoc	NA	NA	NA	NA	NA	NA	NA	NA	429	33.6	426	1	–	333
Mono	NA	NA	NA	NA	NA	NA	NA	NA	221	40.7	209	3	–	202
Monterey	302	22.2	7 070	223.7	5 110	132.5	698.4	1 329.4	1 295	43.8	585	41	27	456
Napa	277	30.7	8 466	320.7	4 576	129.0	1 198.8	2 139.7	67	24.6	46	16	1	51
Nevada	174	14.4	2 311	74.1	1 457	37.7	211.2	372.9	41	22.4	26	12	–	28
Orange	5 767	31.7	215 936	7 643.6	142 728	3 654.1	21 157.8	39 134.1	669	62.9	44	440	31	155
Placer	260	20.4	9 244	403.4	4 310	120.5	1 671.3	3 808.4	200	24.6	156	38	2	138
Plumas	23	17.4	643	21.9	559	19.0	54.3	176.7	130	19.0	120	4	4	112
Riverside	1 420	29.8	46 134	1 329.1	34 135	797.6	3 977.1	7 736.0	1 432	26.9	1 028	354	1	1 004
Sacramento	910	25.2	30 493	1 017.0	19 650	483.5	5 233.1	8 939.6	876	39.6	450	330	24	478
San Benito	75	29.3	2 160	64.2	1 662	43.0	162.8	365.3	88	89.1	80	5	Z	62
San Bernardino	1 992	34.3	63 448	1 830.4	49 119	1 179.5	5 517.3	11 618.7	618	68.2	186	313	31	316
San Diego	3 407	28.0	118 868	4 223.5	73 111	1 868.8	10 999.2	22 233.6	3 169	1.9	355	405	12	422
San Francisco	1 247	24.8	25 037	642.4	19 500	392.8	1 998.4	3 978.9	563	1.2	–	95	7	22
San Joaquin	553	38.0	24 646	749.6	19 276	527.2	2 900.8	5 879.1	1 817	44.4	1 674	87	14	1 476
San Luis Obispo	323	21.4	6 322	182.3	4 157	94.4	619.7	1 156.3	2 703	5.7	144	38	–	121
San Mateo	1 019	27.5	34 438	1 649.6	19 609	626.1	4 364.7	6 690.1	111	44.1	10	92	5	36
Santa Barbara	502	26.9	14 985	584.2	8 254	205.1	1 463.9	2 770.4	326	79.8	243	77	Z	209
Santa Clara	3 464	34.6	249 947	13 094.0	116 800	4 149.5	44 011.3	72 528.3	350	68.0	10	248	47	112
Santa Cruz	387	23.0	10 011	315.2	6 213	152.9	1 140.0	2 135.0	72	80.8	42	26	1	38
Shasta	177	18.1	3 526	118.7	2 549	79.5	261.7	635.0	311	38.1	165	49	5	157
Sierra	NA	NA	NA	NA	NA	NA	NA	NA	41	15.7	39	1	Z	37
Siskiyou	41	24.4	1 016	30.1	889	22.3	78.1	207.3	475	24.5	422	9	1	276
Solano	277	30.0	9 175	331.0	6 822	206.5	1 224.0	3 496.4	527	23.8	458	64	2	387
Sonoma	793	27.5	24 209	968.8	15 754	464.9	2 883.7	5 119.8	141	41.3	57	45	2	89
Stanislaus	435	37.5	25 056	823.1	18 871	524.3	3 081.1	6 886.6	1 438	37.8	1 295	65	7	1 130
Sutter	70	22.9	1 589	49.3	1 245	33.0	161.1	354.0	1 054	27.9	1 037	13	1	848
Tehama	48	31.3	2 228	62.9	1 965	53.5	180.7	455.2	400	49.3	330	12	Z	298
Trinity	NA	NA	NA	NA	NA	NA	NA	NA	26	10.4	3	1	Z	3
Tulare	282	35.8	11 439	314.5	8 825	214.6	1 109.6	3 167.3	2 209	55.0	2 082	83	4	1 648
Tuolumne	65	16.9	880	22.5	665	15.3	75.6	155.2	38	9.6	11	6	Z	12
Ventura	1 008	31.8	33 562	1 136.3	22 137	555.5	3 352.4	6 163.4	799	23.4	204	147	6	202
Yolo	175	30.3	6 178	212.0	4 214	116.4	632.0	1 514.9	1 090	32.5	1 045	39	5	820
Yuba	44	34.1	1 203	26.8	981	19.3	78.0	248.2	355	26.1	344	9	–	309
COLORADO	5 480	23.1	173 069	6 176.8	115 308	3 177.7	20 673.0	40 012.8	13 840	16.4	12 735	705	123	5 235
Adams	436	28.2	13 151	428.4	8 926	244.3	1 098.9	3 045.1	132	41.2	76	48	5	58
Alamosa	NA	NA	NA	NA	NA	NA	NA	NA	414	29.0	411	2	Z	171
Arapahoe	549	18.0	18 852	798.0	14 246	514.8	2 992.9	5 017.3	87	29.0	5	73	4	25
Archuleta	NA	NA	NA	NA	NA	NA	NA	NA	48	2.2	46	2	–	17
Baca	NA	NA	NA	NA	NA	NA	NA	NA	106	100.0	104	1	–	50
Bent	NA	NA	NA	NA	NA	NA	NA	NA	426	2.0	425	1	Z	180
Boulder	686	25.7	26 225	1 052.1	15 182	402.0	3 184.3	5 196.3	174	8.1	117	42	4	67
Chaffee	NA	NA	NA	NA	NA	NA	NA	NA	57	3.6	52	4	Z	23
Cheyenne	NA	NA	NA	NA	NA	NA	NA	NA	26	84.3	25	Z	–	22
Clear Creek	NA	NA	NA	NA	NA	NA	NA	NA	7	7.7	–	1	–	1
Conejos	NA	NA	NA	NA	NA	NA	NA	NA	732	3.9	727	3	–	264
Costilla	NA	NA	NA	NA	NA	NA	NA	NA	197	10.7	196	Z	–	66
Crowley	NA	NA	NA	NA	NA	NA	NA	NA	65	7.5	63	1	–	31
Custer	NA	NA	NA	NA	NA	NA	NA	NA	42	1.7	41	Z	–	19

[1] Average number of production workers plus the number of other (nonproduction) employees for the pay period including March 12. [2] Average number of production workers for the pay periods including the 12th of March, May, August, and November. [3] In millions of gallons per day.

Sources: Manufacturing—U.S. Census Bureau, 1997 Economic Census – Manufacturing, generated by Statistical Compendia Branch, using American Factfinder at <http://www.census.gov/>, (June 2000) [related Internet site <http://www.census.gov/epcd/www/97EC31.HTM>]. Water Use—U.S. Geological Survey, "Water Use in the United States," individual state/county and US by state files from <http://water.usgs.gov/watuse/spread95.html>, (accessed: September 1999).

Table B–9. Counties — **Manufacturing and Water Use**–Con.

[Includes U.S., states, and 3,142 counties/county equivalents defined as of January 1, 1992. For changes to these areas since January 1, 1992, see appendix B. Geographic Information]

County	Establishments — Total	Establishments — Percent with 20 or more employees	All employees — Number[1]	All employees — Annual payroll (mil. dol.)	Production workers — Number[2]	Production workers — Wages (mil. dol.)	Value added by manufacture (mil. dol.)	Value of shipments (mil. dol.)	Withdrawals — Total (mil. gal.)	Withdrawals — Percent ground water	By selected major use (mil. gal.) — Irrigation	By selected major use (mil. gal.) — Public supply	By selected major use (mil. gal.) — Industrial	Consumptive use (mil. gal.)
COLORADO—Con.														
Delta	NA	NA	NA	NA	NA	NA	NA	NA	704	.9	695	7	Z	179
Denver	976	29.6	26 320	816.2	18 087	456.2	2 525.0	4 867.8	123	9.1	–	90	12	35
Dolores	NA	NA	NA	NA	NA	NA	NA	NA	28	5.5	28	Z	–	12
Douglas	119	23.5	1 941	58.8	1 403	35.7	170.7	289.7	29	43.7	12	13	Z	11
Eagle	43	11.6	502	14.9	383	10.5	37.7	85.3	138	3.7	128	9	Z	27
Elbert	NA	NA	NA	NA	NA	NA	NA	NA	34	75.4	31	1	Z	20
El Paso	499	24.0	21 593	700.6	15 148	358.9	2 966.2	5 698.9	135	17.2	28	101	2	38
Fremont	47	17.0	950	26.8	651	14.2	98.2	146.9	159	2.3	113	9	1	50
Garfield	NA	NA	NA	NA	NA	NA	NA	NA	563	1.7	549	9	Z	112
Gilpin	NA	NA	NA	NA	NA	NA	NA	NA	1	44.2	–	Z	–	Z
Grand	NA	NA	NA	NA	NA	NA	NA	NA	204	.6	201	2	Z	42
Gunnison	NA	NA	NA	NA	NA	NA	NA	NA	286	1.7	283	2	Z	70
Hinsdale	NA	NA	NA	NA	NA	NA	NA	NA	13	.6	13	Z	–	5
Huerfano	NA	NA	NA	NA	NA	NA	NA	NA	91	.3	89	1	–	42
Jackson	NA	NA	NA	NA	NA	NA	NA	NA	401	.2	400	Z	–	139
Jefferson	559	17.4	17 871	803.0	10 584	353.9	2 448.1	3 711.2	97	10.3	8	71	14	28
Kiowa	NA	NA	NA	NA	NA	NA	NA	NA	15	99.3	14	Z	–	9
Kit Carson	NA	NA	NA	NA	NA	NA	NA	NA	166	99.8	163	1	Z	147
Lake	NA	NA	NA	NA	NA	NA	NA	NA	26	9.3	7	3	–	7
La Plata	66	16.7	752	19.3	509	12.1	29.4	51.8	378	1.0	366	6	Z	136
Larimer	384	22.9	15 840	645.0	8 321	256.2	1 995.8	3 890.7	271	17.3	218	41	2	123
Las Animas	NA	NA	NA	NA	NA	NA	NA	NA	121	2.1	112	7	Z	55
Lincoln	NA	NA	NA	NA	NA	NA	NA	NA	18	98.9	16	1	–	11
Logan	19	21.1	736	15.2	634	12.4	33.3	163.2	336	29.5	326	5	1	168
Mesa	167	20.4	3 605	99.2	2 614	60.7	262.6	484.2	973	.7	943	21	1	181
Mineral	NA	NA	NA	NA	NA	NA	NA	NA	2	2.4	2	Z	–	1
Moffat	NA	NA	NA	NA	NA	NA	NA	NA	207	1.1	192	2	Z	59
Montezuma	NA	NA	NA	NA	NA	NA	NA	NA	314	.5	308	6	Z	119
Montrose	64	20.3	1 540	31.5	1 226	22.5	91.0	156.0	644	.8	635	6	Z	173
Morgan	25	24.0	(4)	D	D	D	D	D	336	55.6	320	6	1	188
Otero	17	35.3	534	10.7	436	6.9	19.8	36.2	425	4.7	418	5	Z	181
Ouray	NA	NA	NA	NA	NA	NA	NA	NA	58	.2	57	1	–	12
Park	NA	NA	NA	NA	NA	NA	NA	NA	9	9.8	7	1	–	4
Phillips	NA	NA	NA	NA	NA	NA	NA	NA	86	99.1	84	2	–	77
Pitkin	NA	NA	NA	NA	NA	NA	NA	NA	47	1.9	39	6	Z	8
Prowers	20	30.0	(5)	D	D	D	D	D	695	22.4	678	3	Z	308
Pueblo	107	29.9	4 688	147.0	3 392	98.7	500.3	1 021.3	246	8.6	131	35	67	86
Rio Blanco	NA	NA	NA	NA	NA	NA	NA	NA	135	9.9	120	2	–	29
Rio Grande	NA	NA	NA	NA	NA	NA	NA	NA	405	26.4	400	4	Z	167
Routt	NA	NA	NA	NA	NA	NA	NA	NA	307	1.7	294	4	–	72
Saguache	NA	NA	NA	NA	NA	NA	NA	NA	426	34.1	423	2	–	174
San Juan	NA	NA	NA	NA	NA	NA	NA	NA	Z	6.9	–	Z	–	Z
San Miguel	NA	NA	NA	NA	NA	NA	NA	NA	63	.3	62	1	–	24
Sedgwick	NA	NA	NA	NA	NA	NA	NA	NA	95	55.7	94	Z	Z	58
Summit	NA	NA	NA	NA	NA	NA	NA	NA	29	9.2	23	5	Z	6
Teller	NA	NA	NA	NA	NA	NA	NA	NA	9	13.2	1	3	–	2
Washington	NA	NA	NA	NA	NA	NA	NA	NA	48	94.2	44	1	Z	38
Weld	208	32.2	10 773	345.4	7 751	197.5	1 788.9	4 338.5	1 162	23.1	1 106	32	8	558
Yuma	NA	NA	NA	NA	NA	NA	NA	NA	273	98.4	267	2	–	252
CONNECTICUT	5 844	33.0	252 330	10 452.1	153 045	4 895.3	27 295.2	46 938.2	4 453	3.7	28	393	10	171
Fairfield	1 316	30.9	57 560	2 495.9	32 808	1 106.7	7 220.2	12 115.5	330	10.8	4	103	3	20
Hartford	1 592	35.2	71 982	3 113.1	43 849	1 477.2	6 478.6	11 319.8	94	42.9	14	65	1	30
Litchfield	448	34.8	17 288	589.8	12 311	379.7	1 922.9	3 246.8	93	18.3	1	80	1	5
Middlesex	309	34.0	13 132	513.5	9 515	323.3	1 479.6	2 999.3	626	1.5	1	6	1	9
New Haven	1 592	33.4	59 380	2 285.0	37 796	1 124.6	7 084.5	12 073.9	764	3.8	5	96	2	94
New London	237	24.9	19 888	1 035.1	7 433	255.7	1 834.6	2 962.8	2 515	.5	1	30	1	6
Tolland	152	23.0	4 487	145.8	2 746	71.8	456.4	739.2	17	50.9	1	8	Z	4
Windham	198	37.4	8 613	273.8	6 587	156.3	818.4	1 480.9	15	87.8	1	3	1	3
DELAWARE	675	34.4	41 084	1 474.3	28 959	899.8	5 389.5	13 397.3	1 495	7.4	48	89	64	74
Kent	82	34.1	7 985	209.8	5 343	144.4	1 086.0	1 965.5	34	84.6	17	9	2	19
New Castle	458	33.2	22 610	1 000.1	15 063	587.0	3 047.6	8 735.0	1 080	2.9	2	69	19	12
Sussex	135	38.5	10 489	264.4	8 553	168.5	1 255.8	2 696.8	382	13.2	29	12	43	43
DISTRICT OF COLUMBIA	200	17.5	2 858	101.1	1 926	60.9	170.8	320.2	10	4.9	–	–	1	15
District of Columbia	200	17.5	2 858	101.1	1 926	60.9	170.8	320.2	10	4.9	–	–	1	15

[1] Average number of production workers plus the number of other (nonproduction) employees for the pay period including March 12. [2] Average number of production workers for the pay periods including the 12th of March, May, August, and November. [3] In millions of gallons per day. [4] 2,500 to 4,999 employees. [5] 500 to 999 employees.

Sources: Manufacturing—U.S. Census Bureau, 1997 Economic Census – Manufacturing, generated by Statistical Compendia Branch, using American Factfinder at <http://www.census.gov/>, (June 2000) [related Internet site <http://www.census.gov/epcd/www/97EC31.HTM>]. Water Use—U.S. Geological Survey, "Water Use in the United States," individual state/county and US by state files from <http://water.usgs.gov/watuse/spread95.html>, (accessed: September 1999).

CO(Delta)–DC(District of Columbia)   U.S. Census Bureau, County and City Data Book: 2000

[Includes U.S., states, and 3,142 counties/county equivalents defined as of January 1, 1992. For changes to these areas since January 1, 1992, see appendix B. Geographic Information]

County	Manufacturing (NAICS 31-33), 1997								Water use per day,[3] 1995					
	Establishments		All employees		Production workers		Value added by manu-facture (mil. dol.)	Value of ship-ments (mil. dol.)	Withdrawals					
											By selected major use– (mil. gal.)			
	Total	Percent with 20 or more employ-ees	Number[1]	Annual payroll (mil. dol.)	Number[2]	Wages (mil. dol.)			Total (mil. gal.)	Percent ground water	Irrigation	Public supply	Industrial	Consump-tive use (mil. gal.)
FLORIDA	15 992	22.7	433 149	13 185.1	291 452	6 826.0	40 213.4	77 477.5	18 183	23.9	3 469	2 065	353	2 782
Alachua	151	27.8	5 251	157.1	4 196	112.6	458.3	1 010.3	48	98.4	12	24	1	18
Baker	NA	NA	NA	NA	NA	NA	NA	NA	5	88.3	2	1	Z	2
Bay	136	20.6	3 492	108.7	2 588	71.3	330.5	719.0	319	4.5	2	49	Z	14
Bradford	15	40.0	698	10.7	584	7.7	22.0	44.1	8	99.3	1	1	Z	2
Brevard	494	22.9	20 832	753.9	10 572	260.8	1 855.7	3 450.7	1 333	8.5	101	27	Z	67
Broward	1 967	18.9	37 134	1 115.4	24 291	551.4	3 288.9	5 788.3	1 516	17.7	62	222	Z	63
Calhoun	NA	NA	NA	NA	NA	NA	NA	NA	4	80.7	2	1	–	1
Charlotte	74	8.1	587	13.8	362	7.4	39.0	77.7	50	72.5	29	8	Z	26
Citrus	58	17.2	1 025	18.2	856	13.3	43.8	92.4	1 685	1.7	5	10	Z	9
Clay	74	21.6	1 579	43.7	1 062	21.3	120.9	247.2	22	98.9	1	12	7	4
Collier	205	12.7	2 305	62.4	1 732	39.7	141.7	259.0	208	89.8	160	39	–	54
Columbia	35	28.6	1 798	46.3	1 454	30.8	106.6	244.5	17	96.5	9	3	–	4
Dade	3 031	21.9	66 391	1 663.8	48 587	954.5	4 856.0	8 523.9	652	85.1	124	387	5	130
DeSoto	NA	NA	NA	NA	NA	NA	NA	NA	71	82.6	52	12	Z	44
Dixie	NA	NA	NA	NA	NA	NA	NA	NA	3	100.0	1	1	Z	1
Duval	754	31.2	28 237	944.1	19 977	559.7	3 893.9	7 231.0	720	20.1	3	100	20	30
Escambia	236	20.3	7 526	294.6	5 502	199.2	977.6	2 214.1	270	32.2	7	38	56	19
Flagler	42	31.0	1 560	45.9	1 248	28.6	109.7	260.7	14	94.0	8	5	–	6
Franklin	NA	NA	NA	NA	NA	NA	NA	NA	3	100.0	1	2	–	1
Gadsden	32	31.3	1 399	32.3	1 144	20.9	78.8	187.8	16	47.1	7	4	Z	7
Gilchrist	NA	NA	NA	NA	NA	NA	NA	NA	9	98.9	6	Z	–	6
Glades	NA	NA	NA	NA	NA	NA	NA	NA	100	21.0	83	Z	–	55
Gulf	12	58.3	(4)	D	D	D	D	D	37	8.4	1	1	34	4
Hamilton	4	50.0	(4)	D	D	D	D	D	46	100.0	5	1	–	6
Hardee	NA	NA	NA	NA	NA	NA	NA	NA	51	99.0	43	2	Z	36
Hendry	22	22.7	724	26.8	512	18.1	141.9	437.7	557	28.1	550	4	Z	366
Hernando	72	18.1	1 192	29.4	861	15.7	150.6	235.2	42	95.1	7	17	Z	10
Highlands	54	18.5	1 199	27.0	953	19.0	71.4	191.6	119	94.4	100	8	Z	88
Hillsborough	960	27.9	30 861	859.3	21 533	497.6	2 707.2	6 019.8	2 628	6.4	67	130	24	71
Holmes	NA	NA	NA	NA	NA	NA	NA	NA	7	90.2	1	1	–	4
Indian River	116	15.5	1 825	55.4	1 177	29.7	103.7	219.8	266	28.7	195	11	Z	134
Jackson	26	34.6	1 344	27.3	1 172	22.0	61.3	182.1	81	34.8	21	2	–	18
Jefferson	NA	NA	NA	NA	NA	NA	NA	NA	12	95.5	9	1	–	7
Lafayette	NA	NA	NA	NA	NA	NA	NA	NA	7	95.4	4	Z	–	5
Lake	164	25.6	3 730	90.2	2 783	57.2	234.6	578.5	83	90.8	43	26	2	25
Lee	357	17.9	5 363	141.1	3 904	85.6	388.9	741.8	499	22.5	76	41	–	62
Leon	127	17.3	2 676	68.0	1 842	36.4	253.0	557.6	39	98.1	3	29	–	11
Levy	NA	NA	NA	NA	NA	NA	NA	NA	23	89.4	12	2	Z	13
Liberty	NA	NA	NA	NA	NA	NA	NA	NA	2	95.7	Z	Z	Z	1
Madison	11	45.5	1 114	25.8	907	17.8	73.4	270.3	9	94.1	6	2	Z	5
Manatee	284	25.0	11 156	348.4	7 477	188.7	685.7	2 115.7	123	73.9	75	42	Z	55
Marion	215	32.1	9 620	238.0	6 841	146.4	640.4	1 287.8	52	98.0	9	20	Z	16
Martin	172	15.1	3 274	101.7	2 188	69.2	295.6	555.2	170	29.3	127	14	1	114
Monroe	NA	NA	NA	NA	NA	NA	NA	NA	2	100.0	1	–	–	3
Nassau	34	23.5	1 790	77.3	1 437	58.4	298.5	630.6	47	95.0	1	5	37	4
Okaloosa	133	20.3	3 448	81.5	2 301	42.1	167.7	296.5	30	99.2	2	21	Z	7
Okeechobee	NA	NA	NA	NA	NA	NA	NA	NA	41	86.7	33	2	–	21
Orange	889	27.1	32 437	1 213.4	18 156	468.2	3 402.7	5 786.6	260	88.1	62	165	3	70
Osceola	77	24.7	1 295	37.1	998	25.0	190.7	379.9	81	83.8	54	19	–	41
Palm Beach	1 051	17.5	26 262	1 138.1	13 889	372.9	4 116.1	6 344.5	1 433	15.3	733	187	23	480
Pasco	213	18.3	4 091	100.7	2 851	57.5	264.4	713.3	1 169	11.1	16	94	9	23
Pinellas	1 335	24.1	40 954	1 256.8	25 346	575.3	3 195.1	5 732.8	530	8.1	4	35	Z	25
Polk	480	38.8	20 627	633.5	15 251	382.2	2 587.4	5 999.9	392	62.0	110	58	38	113
Putnam	48	33.3	2 556	88.9	2 100	67.1	283.5	730.2	88	43.1	15	4	40	40
St. Johns	88	13.6	2 277	53.8	1 731	33.8	163.7	299.6	46	98.6	33	10	–	22
St. Lucie	124	27.4	2 230	60.1	1 722	39.7	228.4	542.7	1 485	5.4	280	15	Z	208
Santa Rosa	59	23.7	1 895	41.6	1 585	30.3	229.2	427.7	23	99.1	4	12	6	6
Sarasota	379	17.7	7 809	222.9	5 461	112.6	473.8	872.6	48	81.2	8	26	Z	15
Seminole	434	20.3	9 624	287.1	5 931	120.8	851.8	1 582.2	70	98.7	10	51	Z	18
Sumter	30	30.0	907	19.6	725	13.9	51.8	200.9	66	19.0	9	2	Z	10
Suwannee	19	10.5	(5)	D	D	D	D	D	142	20.4	22	1	1	18
Taylor	20	55.0	1 594	58.0	1 243	40.8	270.8	496.1	53	96.3	Z	2	47	2
Union	NA	NA	NA	NA	NA	NA	NA	NA	3	95.2	1	Z	Z	1
Volusia	392	20.2	10 216	263.2	7 297	156.4	683.2	1 212.6	157	51.8	33	49	Z	33
Wakulla	NA	NA	NA	NA	NA	NA	NA	NA	73	5.0	1	1	1	1
Walton	35	17.1	937	12.5	601	7.0	47.4	108.7	12	90.0	5	4	1	6
Washington	14	14.3	754	15.7	668	13.1	40.3	85.8	5	94.1	1	1	–	2

[1] Average number of production workers plus the number of other (nonproduction) employees for the pay period including March 12. [2] Average number of production workers for the pay periods including the 12th of March, May, August, and November. [3] In millions of gallons per day. [4] 500 to 999 employees. [5] 2,500 to 4,999 employees.

Sources: Manufacturing—U.S. Census Bureau, 1997 Economic Census – Manufacturing, generated by Statistical Compendia Branch, using American Factfinder at <http://www.census.gov/>, (June 2000) [related Internet site <http://www.census.gov/epcd/www/97EC31.HTM>]. Water Use—U.S. Geological Survey, "Water Use in the United States," individual state/county and US by state files from <http://water.usgs.gov/watuse/spread95.html>, (accessed: September 1999).

[Includes U.S., states, and 3,142 counties/county equivalents defined as of January 1, 1992. For changes to these areas since January 1, 1992, see appendix B. Geographic Information]

| County | Manufacturing (NAICS 31-33), 1997 | | | | | | | | Water use per day,[3] 1995 | | | | | |
| | Establishments | | All employees | | Production workers | | Value added by manufacture (mil. dol.) | Value of shipments (mil. dol.) | Withdrawals | | By selected major use– (mil. gal.) | | | Consumptive use (mil. gal.) |
	Total	Percent with 20 or more employees	Number[1]	Annual payroll (mil. dol.)	Number[2]	Wages (mil. dol.)			Total (mil. gal.)	Percent ground water	Irrigation	Public supply	Industrial	
GEORGIA	9 083	36.3	533 830	15 534.1	410 713	10 173.4	55 550.1	124 526.8	5 818	20.5	722	1 153	664	1 173
Appling	25	56.0	1 160	28.7	857	17.9	103.2	432.9	63	4.0	2	1	–	32
Atkinson	13	30.8	1 081	24.1	967	19.0	44.8	123.8	3	57.9	2	Z	–	3
Bacon	14	50.0	1 373	27.8	1 109	21.9	64.5	210.9	3	89.0	1	1	Z	2
Baker	NA	NA	NA	NA	NA	NA	NA	NA	24	78.7	23	Z	–	24
Baldwin	20	40.0	3 454	91.2	3 098	78.2	172.9	624.9	7	.7	Z	5	1	1
Banks	14	28.6	(4)	D	D	D	D	D	2	35.5	Z	Z	–	1
Barrow	64	17.2	2 217	64.0	1 801	45.2	185.5	509.9	6	22.4	1	3	–	2
Bartow	126	46.8	10 115	303.1	8 231	226.1	1 387.6	2 918.4	58	13.9	Z	13	5	22
Ben Hill	34	61.8	3 621	93.6	3 195	73.0	260.3	641.5	17	73.5	13	4	–	14
Berrien	17	47.1	1 987	45.0	1 740	37.7	93.1	231.6	13	57.6	11	1	Z	12
Bibb	179	34.1	(5)	D	D	D	D	D	107	3.3	Z	32	16	7
Bleckley	6	33.3	(6)	D	D	D	D	D	9	31.6	8	Z	–	9
Brantley	NA	NA	NA	NA	NA	NA	NA	NA	2	91.1	Z	Z	–	1
Brooks	12	75.0	1 077	17.4	942	11.3	47.8	106.3	6	84.5	4	1	–	5
Bryan	NA	NA	NA	NA	NA	NA	NA	NA	2	96.0	Z	1	–	1
Bulloch	41	36.6	3 210	84.3	2 683	59.1	276.8	493.4	17	81.0	9	5	1	11
Burke	16	50.0	1 035	21.3	587	11.7	49.2	84.4	75	13.2	9	2	–	73
Butts	18	55.6	1 127	22.3	964	16.7	105.2	181.4	6	9.1	Z	5	–	1
Calhoun	3	66.7	(4)	D	D	D	D	D	19	70.7	18	1	–	18
Camden	21	33.3	1 364	52.7	1 039	36.3	237.5	528.8	48	85.4	3	3	38	7
Candler	NA	NA	NA	NA	NA	NA	NA	NA	3	61.1	2	1	–	2
Carroll	121	44.6	9 590	229.6	7 860	175.0	663.8	2 156.7	14	20.5	1	10	–	3
Catoosa	64	34.4	2 291	56.2	1 813	40.5	182.3	458.5	11	85.8	1	8	–	3
Charlton	NA	NA	NA	NA	NA	NA	NA	NA	2	92.0	Z	1	–	Z
Chatham	207	28.0	(5)	D	D	D	D	D	606	13.4	5	77	75	25
Chattahoochee	NA	NA	NA	NA	NA	NA	NA	NA	14	3.8	Z	7	–	2
Chattooga	23	65.2	3 996	91.0	3 568	75.9	464.7	873.6	5	41.4	Z	4	–	1
Cherokee	152	23.0	3 886	100.5	2 971	60.3	247.4	656.7	14	10.9	Z	12	1	3
Clarke	90	37.8	9 388	234.9	7 520	168.5	577.4	1 368.5	18	7.3	Z	17	–	3
Clay	NA	NA	NA	NA	NA	NA	NA	NA	6	24.3	5	Z	–	5
Clayton	167	35.3	5 901	184.1	4 216	109.8	789.3	1 641.6	26	5.9	1	24	–	4
Clinch	11	45.5	918	18.8	834	15.5	49.7	148.9	1	84.5	1	Z	–	1
Cobb	604	26.5	24 499	980.2	14 336	437.7	2 146.6	4 134.7	440	.4	2	80	2	14
Coffee	45	48.9	5 377	116.1	4 667	86.6	294.8	773.8	13	62.2	6	5	–	8
Colquitt	55	32.7	3 503	67.1	2 577	42.5	151.0	452.2	40	49.7	33	3	1	35
Columbia	77	31.2	5 323	154.3	3 690	84.3	683.3	1 356.1	12	20.3	Z	10	Z	2
Cook	35	42.9	1 582	34.1	1 313	23.6	100.3	227.4	12	75.9	9	2	–	10
Coweta	76	39.5	5 589	147.8	4 120	94.7	389.8	1 093.2	353	1.3	Z	5	–	7
Crawford	NA	NA	NA	NA	NA	NA	NA	NA	6	57.7	3	Z	–	5
Crisp	27	51.9	2 067	53.1	1 714	35.1	185.6	340.5	19	96.2	13	1	–	14
Dade	22	40.9	907	19.9	819	16.1	47.2	98.5	2	5.2	Z	2	–	Z
Dawson	NA	NA	NA	NA	NA	NA	NA	NA	1	39.2	–	1	–	1
Decatur	35	34.3	3 538	84.2	2 833	57.3	292.3	632.8	65	91.4	58	3	2	59
De Kalb	697	29.3	24 358	942.8	17 939	627.9	2 718.4	8 018.5	86	3.0	2	81	–	13
Dodge	16	25.0	867	17.5	773	13.8	49.5	155.0	7	62.2	5	1	–	6
Dooly	12	66.7	1 521	30.4	1 320	24.4	104.1	186.8	13	93.8	10	2	–	11
Dougherty	90	47.8	8 627	312.0	7 065	229.8	1 905.0	4 275.5	134	29.0	12	20	8	16
Douglas	95	22.1	2 211	54.5	1 747	36.0	165.5	371.2	8	3.2	Z	7	–	1
Early	12	33.3	1 071	45.0	857	21.3	166.0	475.2	142	16.6	32	Z	109	40
Echols	NA	NA	NA	NA	NA	NA	NA	NA	3	76.8	3	Z	–	3
Effingham	11	45.5	(6)	D	D	D	D	D	146	4.8	Z	2	10	2
Elbert	112	28.6	2 954	64.6	2 383	47.7	206.6	441.7	3	30.4	Z	2	–	1
Emanuel	36	44.4	2 191	38.4	1 764	28.1	125.6	253.5	6	92.7	2	2	2	2
Evans	14	50.0	1 677	34.2	1 449	25.9	60.6	184.9	3	73.8	1	1	2	2
Fannin	28	25.0	922	15.7	820	13.8	67.9	146.6	2	34.5	Z	1	–	1
Fayette	85	28.2	5 595	170.2	3 959	95.4	617.3	1 345.1	14	43.8	3	9	–	5
Floyd	120	46.7	9 583	280.0	8 115	205.2	765.5	1 892.4	452	.3	1	14	34	6
Forsyth	129	27.9	4 337	127.7	3 489	88.1	329.3	701.3	14	22.6	Z	10	–	3
Franklin	46	39.1	1 852	43.2	1 488	28.2	134.6	281.1	4	41.2	Z	2	–	2
Fulton	897	35.0	37 948	1 283.6	26 734	777.6	6 945.1	14 240.9	226	.9	–	224	Z	34
Gilmer	34	29.4	3 404	52.3	3 127	39.6	99.3	303.0	3	22.8	Z	2	–	1
Glascock	NA	NA	NA	NA	NA	NA	NA	NA	Z	74.4	Z	Z	–	Z
Glynn	71	31.0	3 784	124.9	2 651	76.0	382.7	993.6	124	54.0	Z	12	74	11
Gordon	102	55.9	10 527	255.4	7 798	158.8	801.5	2 419.0	18	21.9	Z	13	3	3
Grady	19	31.6	1 402	29.6	1 231	23.3	78.7	153.7	12	61.7	8	3	–	9
Greene	19	57.9	1 533	33.1	1 339	24.2	98.6	448.4	5	11.7	3	1	Z	4

[1] Average number of production workers plus the number of other (nonproduction) employees for the pay period including March 12. [2] Average number of production workers for the pay periods including the 12th of March, May, August, and November. [3] In millions of gallons per day. [4] 500 to 999 employees. [5] 10,000 to 24,999 employees. [6] 1,000 to 2,499 employees.

Sources: Manufacturing—U.S. Census Bureau, 1997 Economic Census – Manufacturing, generated by Statistical Compendia Branch, using American Factfinder at <http://www.census.gov/>, (June 2000) [related Internet site <http://www.census.gov/epcd/www/97EC31.HTM>]. Water Use—U.S. Geological Survey, "Water Use in the United States," individual state/county and US by state files from <http://water.usgs.gov/watuse/spread95.html>, (accessed: September 1999).

Table B–9. Counties — **Manufacturing and Water Use**–Con.

[Includes U.S., states, and 3,142 counties/county equivalents defined as of January 1, 1992. For changes to these areas since January 1, 1992, see appendix B. Geographic Information]

County	Establishments Total	Establishments Percent with 20 or more employees	All employees Number[1]	All employees Annual payroll (mil. dol.)	Production workers Number[2]	Production workers Wages (mil. dol.)	Value added by manufacture (mil. dol.)	Value of shipments (mil. dol.)	Withdrawals Total (mil. gal.)	Withdrawals Percent ground water	By selected major use (mil. gal.) Irrigation	By selected major use (mil. gal.) Public supply	By selected major use (mil. gal.) Industrial	Consumptive use (mil. gal.)
GEORGIA—Con.														
Gwinnett	737	32.2	29 121	1 071.3	19 123	535.5	3 402.7	6 241.7	72	1.1	Z	71	–	11
Habersham	69	36.2	4 354	111.8	3 530	76.6	402.1	681.2	10	18.4	Z	6	Z	2
Hall	226	42.0	16 519	443.1	13 361	306.3	1 835.8	4 293.7	20	19.9	1	14	1	5
Hancock	NA	NA	NA	NA	NA	NA	NA	NA	1	48.6	Z	1	–	Z
Haralson	35	51.4	2 552	59.4	2 083	42.6	147.1	340.0	2	1.4	–	2	–	1
Harris	19	26.3	(4)	D	D	D	D	D	10	11.5	Z	1	8	2
Hart	36	41.7	2 540	61.1	2 144	47.4	271.8	465.6	4	36.0	1	1	–	2
Heard	9	33.3	550	12.8	459	9.0	32.5	77.6	1	56.4	Z	Z	–	Z
Henry	68	36.8	3 392	106.1	2 471	64.4	401.3	854.8	7	10.0	Z	7	–	1
Houston	66	25.8	(5)	D	D	D	D	D	29	97.2	9	15	Z	13
Irwin	7	57.1	746	13.7	664	10.5	23.4	38.5	10	70.5	9	1	Z	9
Jackson	65	43.1	5 896	135.8	4 768	96.9	415.2	1 204.5	6	50.5	Z	3	1	2
Jasper	19	52.6	737	21.4	640	17.7	50.4	176.7	2	33.3	–	1	1	Z
Jeff Davis	23	34.8	2 493	49.0	1 989	40.9	154.6	304.4	5	71.8	3	1	Z	4
Jefferson	28	39.3	1 999	51.9	1 647	37.8	62.8	294.2	15	52.3	6	2	7	7
Jenkins	4	75.0	1 294	25.0	1 202	19.1	86.5	154.3	5	69.6	4	1	Z	5
Johnson	8	87.5	762	8.8	642	6.9	20.2	34.9	3	70.7	2	Z	–	3
Jones	NA	NA	NA	NA	NA	NA	NA	NA	2	87.1	Z	1	Z	1
Lamar	13	46.2	1 605	35.1	1 351	25.4	72.2	190.9	5	26.4	1	2	–	2
Lanier	NA	NA	NA	NA	NA	NA	NA	NA	3	71.4	2	1	–	3
Laurens	43	58.1	5 703	134.2	4 509	91.3	383.5	888.6	33	21.5	7	5	20	10
Lee	NA	NA	NA	NA	NA	NA	NA	NA	26	93.1	24	1	–	25
Liberty	14	64.3	1 020	33.9	782	24.1	110.7	319.0	17	99.9	–	6	8	2
Lincoln	7	42.9	688	10.9	629	9.4	17.6	55.8	1	71.6	Z	1	–	Z
Long	NA	NA	NA	NA	NA	NA	NA	NA	1	76.3	Z	Z	–	Z
Lowndes	98	37.8	5 492	146.7	4 234	98.0	460.9	1 468.9	28	94.1	3	9	12	6
Lumpkin	17	35.3	879	21.0	760	16.9	41.7	85.9	3	34.1	Z	Z	–	1
McDuffie	26	50.0	1 677	41.7	1 414	32.7	83.6	297.8	4	37.4	1	1	–	2
McIntosh	NA	NA	NA	NA	NA	NA	NA	NA	1	99.3	–	1	–	Z
Macon	14	35.7	1 624	46.7	1 348	33.8	103.5	369.0	24	42.1	10	1	12	12
Madison	31	19.4	826	18.9	704	14.9	32.1	69.0	3	61.5	Z	Z	–	2
Marion	5	40.0	(4)	D	D	D	D	D	3	64.3	1	2	–	1
Meriwether	22	59.1	2 105	46.1	1 640	30.0	127.3	273.7	6	49.2	1	2	Z	3
Miller	NA	NA	NA	NA	NA	NA	NA	NA	29	91.9	28	Z	–	28
Mitchell	17	47.1	1 016	15.4	913	12.3	30.3	72.2	32	92.1	29	3	–	30
Monroe	21	28.6	515	10.7	434	7.9	27.9	57.1	35	9.9	Z	1	–	33
Montgomery	NA	NA	NA	NA	NA	NA	NA	NA	4	63.0	4	Z	–	4
Morgan	20	40.0	1 512	39.8	1 266	29.6	112.7	262.1	3	30.6	1	1	–	1
Murray	100	32.0	5 321	121.8	4 602	95.3	336.7	1 201.9	4	46.1	1	2	–	1
Muscogee	158	47.5	(6)	D	D	D	D	D	39	.3	Z	39	Z	6
Newton	62	37.1	3 976	146.4	2 527	70.6	757.0	1 348.8	4	57.2	Z	3	Z	1
Oconee	30	40.0	746	20.8	579	13.6	78.4	208.8	3	61.4	1	1	–	1
Oglethorpe	NA	NA	NA	NA	NA	NA	NA	NA	2	55.7	Z	Z	–	1
Paulding	38	28.9	1 161	26.0	914	20.7	75.2	137.3	4	18.2	Z	3	–	1
Peach	32	40.6	(5)	D	D	D	D	D	7	97.2	4	2	–	4
Pickens	35	34.3	1 155	26.7	913	18.7	74.2	135.8	3	42.5	Z	1	–	1
Pierce	17	41.2	521	9.1	468	7.1	22.1	77.2	6	67.2	4	Z	–	5
Pike	NA	NA	NA	NA	NA	NA	NA	NA	3	55.7	2	1	–	2
Polk	35	42.9	2 273	62.1	1 844	46.0	218.2	423.1	11	59.5	Z	8	2	2
Pulaski	11	18.2	(7)	D	D	D	D	D	12	84.8	11	1	–	11
Putnam	24	58.3	2 030	56.8	1 733	45.0	144.8	424.8	1 010	.1	Z	1	Z	1
Quitman	NA	NA	NA	NA	NA	NA	NA	NA	2	12.7	2	Z	–	2
Rabun	27	29.6	1 870	44.1	1 711	37.7	135.3	316.0	4	24.0	–	1	2	1
Randolph	NA	NA	NA	NA	NA	NA	NA	NA	11	54.4	9	1	Z	9
Richmond	134	45.5	12 084	423.4	8 547	258.7	2 266.6	4 092.6	127	18.4	7	38	80	19
Rockdale	116	37.9	6 730	200.0	4 659	121.3	743.4	1 625.1	2	11.9	Z	2	–	1
Schley	9	77.8	589	14.6	498	10.6	49.4	115.4	2	36.4	1	Z	–	2
Screven	13	30.8	1 289	33.9	1 125	26.8	76.3	127.8	8	81.3	5	1	2	5
Seminole	NA	NA	NA	NA	NA	NA	NA	NA	24	94.6	22	1	–	23
Spalding	70	44.3	6 328	150.7	5 250	113.1	512.3	1 118.8	10	13.3	Z	8	–	2
Stephens	64	43.8	3 970	88.4	3 190	63.1	262.7	634.8	3	13.8	Z	2	–	1
Stewart	NA	NA	NA	NA	NA	NA	NA	NA	4	38.6	2	1	–	2
Sumter	38	42.1	3 163	71.3	2 582	52.4	185.0	475.4	28	64.1	24	4	–	25
Talbot	NA	NA	NA	NA	NA	NA	NA	NA	3	58.2	Z	Z	–	Z
Taliaferro	NA	NA	NA	NA	NA	NA	NA	NA	Z	75.0	–	Z	–	Z
Tattnall	12	25.0	762	8.4	622	7.5	39.0	62.9	18	52.2	15	1	–	16

[1] Average number of production workers plus the number of other (nonproduction) employees for the pay period including March 12. [2] Average number of production workers for the pay periods including the 12th of March, May, August, and November. [3] In millions of gallons per day. [4] 1,000 to 2,499 employees. [5] 2,500 to 4,999 employees. [6] 10,000 to 24,999 employees. [7] 500 to 999 employees.

Sources: Manufacturing—U.S. Census Bureau, 1997 Economic Census – Manufacturing, generated by Statistical Compendia Branch, using American Factfinder at <http://www.census.gov/>, (June 2000) [related Internet site <http://www.census.gov/epcd/www/97EC31.HTM>]. Water Use—U.S. Geological Survey, "Water Use in the United States," individual state/county and US by state files from <http://water.usgs.gov/watuse/spread95.html>, (accessed: September 1999).

[Includes U.S., states, and 3,142 counties/county equivalents defined as of January 1, 1992. For changes to these areas since January 1, 1992, see appendix B. Geographic Information]

County	Establishments Total	Establishments Percent with 20 or more employees	All employees Number[1]	All employees Annual payroll (mil. dol.)	Production workers Number[2]	Production workers Wages (mil. dol.)	Value added by manufacture (mil. dol.)	Value of shipments (mil. dol.)	Withdrawals Total (mil. gal.)	Withdrawals Percent ground water	Irrigation	Public supply	Industrial	Consumptive use (mil. gal.)
GEORGIA—Con.														
Taylor	NA	NA	NA	NA	NA	NA	NA	NA	2	76.2	1	1	–	1
Telfair	14	42.9	1 946	37.0	1 770	31.6	158.8	566.3	10	74.1	8	2	Z	9
Terrell	13	46.2	786	15.1	693	12.0	37.4	141.6	21	49.5	19	1	–	19
Thomas	72	41.7	4 926	108.6	3 748	68.9	421.3	933.7	13	90.0	5	6	1	7
Tift	51	47.1	4 449	103.7	3 878	81.5	204.0	613.3	35	54.4	27	6	–	29
Toombs	38	44.7	2 516	41.6	2 093	30.4	79.9	169.3	7	57.3	4	2	–	5
Towns	NA	NA	NA	NA	NA	NA	NA	NA	2	14.3	Z	2	–	1
Treutlen	NA	NA	NA	NA	NA	NA	NA	NA	2	88.0	1	1	–	1
Troup	101	56.4	9 369	284.2	7 131	177.2	712.1	1 807.7	13	9.2	Z	11	1	2
Turner	10	60.0	686	11.8	611	8.9	31.2	66.1	19	47.0	16	2	1	16
Twiggs	NA	NA	NA	NA	NA	NA	NA	NA	23	99.3	1	Z	21	4
Union	NA	NA	NA	NA	NA	NA	NA	NA	1	52.6	Z	1	–	Z
Upson	26	53.8	4 241	82.9	3 476	63.2	251.2	555.1	11	25.9	Z	3	3	5
Walker	77	32.5	6 555	159.9	5 820	122.9	575.9	1 207.7	11	81.2	Z	8	2	2
Walton	55	41.8	2 611	70.4	2 122	50.6	190.0	441.5	6	29.8	1	4	–	2
Ware	42	33.3	2 121	55.8	1 779	37.0	126.5	287.4	6	90.7	1	3	Z	2
Warren	6	83.3	798	20.0	706	13.8	62.3	131.0	5	33.1	3	1	1	3
Washington	18	33.3	917	22.3	802	15.7	93.4	131.7	24	94.8	4	2	17	7
Wayne	23	34.8	1 816	56.0	1 441	41.6	238.9	460.6	66	99.1	1	2	62	9
Webster	NA	NA	NA	NA	NA	NA	NA	NA	5	12.5	5	Z	–	5
Wheeler	NA	NA	NA	NA	NA	NA	NA	NA	3	85.4	3	Z	–	3
White	28	17.9	952	27.0	808	15.7	88.2	172.8	6	26.4	Z	3	–	1
Whitfield	379	43.3	27 373	687.5	21 626	505.8	2 444.7	6 166.5	39	.4	Z	38	–	5
Wilcox	NA	NA	NA	NA	NA	NA	NA	NA	15	67.8	14	1	–	15
Wilkes	23	52.2	1 584	36.8	1 359	28.7	131.0	315.4	4	19.7	1	2	–	2
Wilkinson	14	28.6	1 307	49.7	763	24.0	279.5	391.2	23	99.9	–	2	17	3
Worth	NA	NA	NA	NA	NA	NA	NA	NA	29	30.7	11	1	–	12
HAWAII	921	17.3	15 109	405.0	9 899	231.6	1 262.4	3 192.5	1 934	27.5	652	214	20	551
Hawaii	106	12.3	1 588	37.5	1 076	21.1	81.2	192.5	132	82.6	13	26	–	33
Honolulu	685	19.4	11 161	300.9	7 034	164.8	1 042.8	2 692.2	1 111	23.0	83	142	13	143
Kalawao	–	–	–	–	–	–	–	–	–	–	–	–	–	–
Kauai	NA	NA	NA	NA	NA	NA	NA	NA	261	16.4	223	14	5	147
Maui	100	9.0	1 919	51.3	1 509	36.3	123.3	259.6	430	28.8	333	33	2	228
IDAHO	1 647	25.4	66 184	2 099.8	50 362	1 277.2	6 393.1	16 952.9	15 141	18.7	13 048	189	47	4 342
Ada	395	24.6	20 850	862.6	13 866	416.0	2 242.4	6 318.4	1 098	7.7	1 033	42	9	339
Adams	NA	NA	NA	NA	NA	NA	NA	NA	64	1.9	62	Z	–	20
Bannock	62	32.3	3 482	119.2	2 420	60.7	406.0	775.1	314	20.2	263	20	2	91
Bear Lake	NA	NA	NA	NA	NA	NA	NA	NA	117	1.9	115	1	–	38
Benewah	8	37.5	586	20.2	532	17.4	43.7	141.8	8	56.8	6	1	Z	2
Bingham	44	20.5	2 413	64.2	1 995	42.0	187.7	366.1	1 094	34.1	1 079	4	4	352
Blaine	NA	NA	NA	NA	NA	NA	NA	NA	160	25.0	147	3	1	48
Boise	NA	NA	NA	NA	NA	NA	NA	NA	15	7.7	14	1	–	5
Bonner	86	23.3	1 898	56.8	1 563	41.8	126.8	382.1	35	22.9	12	5	–	4
Bonneville	115	22.6	2 550	55.8	1 917	36.5	136.0	267.9	645	15.9	618	22	1	202
Boundary	NA	NA	NA	NA	NA	NA	NA	NA	2	71.4	1	1	–	Z
Butte	NA	NA	NA	NA	NA	NA	NA	NA	168	49.5	164	Z	–	54
Camas	NA	NA	NA	NA	NA	NA	NA	NA	27	84.8	27	Z	–	9
Canyon	176	33.0	9 817	268.2	7 863	181.2	1 144.9	3 581.7	639	5.6	594	12	3	195
Caribou	7	57.1	(4)	D	D	D	D	D	225	14.0	190	1	6	66
Cassia	24	20.8	(5)	D	D	D	D	D	585	61.5	576	3	3	188
Clark	NA	NA	NA	NA	NA	NA	NA	NA	106	33.2	105	Z	–	34
Clearwater	NA	NA	NA	NA	NA	NA	NA	NA	36	5.7	–	2	–	Z
Custer	NA	NA	NA	NA	NA	NA	NA	NA	142	13.2	113	Z	–	37
Elmore	NA	NA	NA	NA	NA	NA	NA	NA	327	35.0	320	2	–	105
Franklin	NA	NA	NA	NA	NA	NA	NA	NA	178	23.3	175	2	–	57
Fremont	NA	NA	NA	NA	NA	NA	NA	NA	338	10.2	333	2	–	108
Gem	NA	NA	NA	NA	NA	NA	NA	NA	136	15.2	133	1	–	43
Gooding	NA	NA	NA	NA	NA	NA	NA	NA	1 289	10.0	621	1	1	274
Idaho	NA	NA	NA	NA	NA	NA	NA	NA	30	9.2	11	1	–	4
Jefferson	17	17.6	664	11.9	567	8.0	57.1	94.4	1 544	18.2	1 540	1	1	501
Jerome	19	36.8	803	15.9	672	12.9	75.8	176.3	1 109	8.1	1 005	2	1	327

[1] Average number of production workers plus the number of other (nonproduction) employees for the pay period including March 12. [2] Average number of production workers for the pay periods including the 12th of March, May, August, and November. [3] In millions of gallons per day. [4] 500 to 999 employees. [5] 1,000 to 2,499 employees.

Sources: Manufacturing—U.S. Census Bureau, 1997 Economic Census – Manufacturing, generated by Statistical Compendia Branch, using American Factfinder at <http://www.census.gov/>, (June 2000) [related Internet site <http://www.census.gov/epcd/www/97EC31.HTM>]. Water Use—U.S. Geological Survey, "Water Use in the United States," individual state/county and US by state files from <http://water.usgs.gov/watuse/spread95.html>, (accessed: September 1999).

Table B-9. Counties — **Manufacturing and Water Use**–Con.

[Includes U.S., states, and 3,142 counties/county equivalents defined as of January 1, 1992. For changes to these areas since January 1, 1992, see appendix B. Geographic Information]

County	Manufacturing (NAICS 31-33), 1997								Water use per day,[3] 1995					
	Establishments		All employees		Production workers		Value added by manu-facture (mil. dol.)	Value of ship-ments (mil. dol.)	Withdrawals					Consump-tive use (mil. gal.)
											By selected major use— (mil. gal.)			
	Total	Percent with 20 or more employ-ees	Number[1]	Annual payroll (mil. dol.)	Number[2]	Wages (mil. dol.)			Total (mil. gal.)	Percent ground water	Irrigation	Public supply	Industrial	
IDAHO—Con.														
Kootenai	195	25.6	4 472	116.9	3 459	83.6	275.5	592.1	47	44.5	26	18	–	9
Latah	NA	NA	NA	NA	NA	NA	NA	NA	12	40.7	7	3	–	2
Lemhi	NA	NA	NA	NA	NA	NA	NA	NA	124	3.7	121	1	–	40
Lewis	NA	NA	NA	NA	NA	NA	NA	NA	1	92.7	–	1	–	Z
Lincoln	NA	NA	NA	NA	NA	NA	NA	NA	421	11.8	418	Z	1	136
Madison	21	38.1	1 326	25.5	963	17.1	85.4	141.4	295	33.9	290	3	2	94
Minidoka	18	44.4	1 638	44.3	1 432	35.2	170.4	425.7	527	36.0	521	2	2	170
Nez Perce	55	21.8	3 263	128.0	2 656	95.6	395.3	769.1	19	28.6	9	4	5	4
Oneida	NA	NA	NA	NA	NA	NA	NA	NA	103	19.8	102	Z	–	33
Owyhee	5	40.0	613	12.2	563	9.5	56.9	225.2	474	11.3	472	7	–	154
Payette	24	37.5	(4)	D	D	D	62.9	155.3	254	7.6	249	2	Z	81
Power	8	75.0	889	21.3	744	16.9	62.9	155.3	306	60.9	262	1	1	85
Shoshone	NA	NA	NA	NA	NA	NA	NA	NA	10	21.5	–	3	–	1
Teton	NA	NA	NA	NA	NA	NA	NA	NA	116	27.6	115	Z	–	38
Twin Falls	95	24.2	3 588	82.9	3 031	57.8	286.4	723.3	1 891	4.4	1 108	19	2	362
Valley	NA	NA	NA	NA	NA	NA	NA	NA	28	4.8	13	1	Z	4
Washington	NA	NA	NA	NA	NA	NA	NA	NA	83	78.7	80	2	–	26
ILLINOIS	17 953	36.6	887 350	31 837.9	629 423	18 713.8	95 287.3	200 020.0	19 922	4.8	180	1 823	452	882
Adams	85	35.3	5 707	190.4	3 647	93.6	634.2	1 868.3	24	68.7	1	9	13	4
Alexander	NA	NA	NA	NA	NA	NA	NA	NA	2	57.6	1	1	Z	1
Bond	16	31.3	695	19.2	517	13.1	79.0	166.0	2	52.9	Z	1	–	Z
Boone	63	36.5	5 846	283.9	5 175	240.3	500.4	2 300.0	6	100.0	1	4	Z	2
Brown	NA	NA	NA	NA	NA	NA	NA	NA	Z	100.0	Z	Z	–	Z
Bureau	41	53.7	2 499	72.0	1 818	43.1	239.9	413.7	8	81.0	2	2	Z	4
Calhoun	NA	NA	NA	NA	NA	NA	NA	NA	8	19.9	Z	Z	–	1
Carroll	33	36.4	1 015	27.0	802	18.3	134.6	235.2	9	99.8	3	1	2	4
Cass	13	46.2	(4)	D	D	D	D	D	10	99.8	5	1	2	6
Champaign	152	36.2	10 857	292.4	8 396	204.8	1 165.9	2 689.5	36	85.1	5	23	2	9
Christian	30	26.7	1 388	53.2	847	24.0	142.9	479.3	776	.6	Z	3	–	13
Clark	24	41.7	1 682	44.6	1 314	26.9	188.9	435.5	4	100.0	2	2	–	2
Clay	23	43.5	2 453	62.8	1 932	42.5	220.4	480.1	2	62.8	Z	1	–	1
Clinton	39	30.8	963	22.4	709	15.0	108.1	175.9	8	57.0	1	2	–	3
Coles	57	36.8	5 754	182.9	4 844	142.4	766.5	1 455.6	8	15.0	Z	7	–	1
Cook	7 966	37.0	362 364	13 032.0	250 025	7 309.3	38 114.9	74 563.3	1 691	1.4	3	1 134	111	92
Crawford	20	50.0	2 547	90.4	2 132	68.4	343.3	2 175.4	61	14.7	1	2	5	7
Cumberland	NA	NA	NA	NA	NA	NA	NA	NA	2	62.0	Z	1	–	Z
DeKalb	137	40.9	6 957	207.7	4 859	110.2	875.8	1 511.7	12	87.3	1	7	1	3
De Witt	15	53.3	1 300	39.6	1 037	26.2	139.2	267.1	712	.3	Z	1	–	26
Douglas	65	29.2	2 711	79.2	2 111	49.5	240.9	481.7	6	37.5	Z	1	3	1
DuPage	2 033	36.4	71 351	2 503.0	50 090	1 411.8	6 631.9	11 938.5	18	83.3	1	12	Z	11
Edgar	27	40.7	1 539	36.9	1 229	24.9	100.6	248.7	3	52.1	Z	2	–	1
Edwards	8	50.0	(4)	D	D	D	D	D	2	92.8	Z	1	–	1
Effingham	59	45.8	5 660	148.7	4 827	111.3	379.3	978.7	6	59.0	Z	3	–	1
Fayette	22	36.4	1 529	37.8	1 384	32.3	148.2	277.9	7	44.7	Z	1	–	2
Ford	22	40.9	951	23.7	756	16.8	89.7	322.4	4	90.9	1	2	Z	1
Franklin	43	27.9	1 632	36.6	1 329	24.9	85.7	233.7	16	4.2	Z	13	–	1
Fulton	NA	NA	NA	NA	NA	NA	NA	NA	273	1.2	Z	3	–	7
Gallatin	NA	NA	NA	NA	NA	NA	NA	NA	10	99.2	5	4	–	6
Greene	NA	NA	NA	NA	NA	NA	NA	NA	3	89.2	1	1	–	2
Grundy	33	42.4	2 015	87.8	1 469	59.8	384.5	875.4	2 560	.4	Z	1	7	75
Hamilton	NA	NA	NA	NA	NA	NA	NA	NA	1	97.0	Z	–	–	1
Hancock	28	21.4	1 862	42.5	1 287	23.2	120.4	193.2	3	71.0	1	1	–	1
Hardin	NA	NA	NA	NA	NA	NA	NA	NA	3	96.4	Z	Z	–	1
Henderson	NA	NA	NA	NA	NA	NA	NA	NA	15	100.0	8	6	–	9
Henry	53	32.1	4 019	124.3	3 222	95.3	210.0	1 288.0	9	100.0	2	4	Z	4
Iroquois	30	46.7	1 723	43.0	1 333	27.1	108.1	296.9	4	100.0	2	1	Z	1
Jackson	35	22.9	1 062	29.0	846	20.8	61.6	151.8	191	1.9	Z	7	–	5
Jasper	15	40.0	874	15.2	731	10.7	28.9	66.4	532	.5	Z	1	–	10
Jefferson	44	25.0	2 922	104.5	2 334	77.2	371.1	743.1	4	58.4	Z	1	–	2
Jersey	NA	NA	NA	NA	NA	NA	NA	NA	7	34.9	Z	1	–	1
Jo Daviess	33	39.4	1 590	46.2	1 304	32.5	158.7	312.6	9	99.3	Z	3	3	2
Johnson	NA	NA	NA	NA	NA	NA	NA	NA	2	58.2	Z	1	–	Z
Kane	877	42.5	40 200	1 443.8	28 591	837.6	4 360.1	8 226.1	53	56.4	2	48	2	18

[1] Average number of production workers plus the number of other (nonproduction) employees for the pay period including March 12. [2] Average number of production workers for the pay periods including the 12th of March, May, August, and November. [3] In millions of gallons per day. [4] 1,000 to 2,499 employees.

Sources: Manufacturing—U.S. Census Bureau, 1997 Economic Census – Manufacturing, generated by Statistical Compendia Branch, using American Factfinder at <http://www.census.gov/>, (June 2000) [related Internet site <http://www.census.gov/epcd/www/97EC31.HTM>].   Water Use—U.S. Geological Survey, "Water Use in the United States," individual state/county and US by state files from <http://water.usgs.gov/watuse/spread95.html>, (accessed: September 1999).

Table B–9. Counties — **Manufacturing and Water Use**–Con.

[Includes U.S., states, and 3,142 counties/county equivalents defined as of January 1, 1992. For changes to these areas since January 1, 1992, see appendix B. Geographic Information]

| County | Manufacturing (NAICS 31-33), 1997 | | | | | | | | Water use per day,[3] 1995 | | | | | |
| | Establishments | | All employees | | Production workers | | Value added by manufacture (mil. dol.) | Value of shipments (mil. dol.) | Withdrawals | | By selected major use— (mil. gal.) | | | Consumptive use (mil. gal.) |
	Total	Percent with 20 or more employees	Number[1]	Annual payroll (mil. dol.)	Number[2]	Wages (mil. dol.)			Total (mil. gal.)	Percent ground water	Irrigation	Public supply	Industrial	
ILLINOIS—Con.														
Kankakee	116	44.0	6 937	263.8	4 879	159.6	914.9	2 253.2	29	59.8	12	14	Z	14
Kendall	66	24.2	2 303	69.5	1 800	39.2	229.0	369.6	6	100.0	Z	2	Z	1
Knox	56	44.6	5 528	165.0	4 477	119.8	370.7	1 058.8	9	100.0	Z	6	–	2
Lake	969	32.0	62 535	2 660.2	37 779	1 163.1	7 361.4	13 686.2	2 449	.6	2	60	16	80
La Salle	152	42.8	6 752	232.1	5 272	163.6	789.9	1 732.6	888	2.4	1	15	3	34
Lawrence	NA	NA	NA	NA	NA	NA	NA	NA	14	100.0	5	1	Z	12
Lee	35	60.0	3 798	115.3	2 798	71.8	404.9	739.4	16	99.7	7	4	2	8
Livingston	51	43.1	4 573	170.5	3 580	121.1	537.1	1 055.8	7	55.6	Z	5	Z	1
Logan	24	25.0	1 401	44.9	1 164	33.8	170.6	318.2	5	100.0	1	3	–	1
McDonough	30	46.7	1 956	61.2	1 615	48.0	140.2	255.9	5	39.5	Z	3	Z	1
McHenry	583	36.4	22 949	760.4	16 601	458.7	1 966.5	3 930.4	40	89.9	9	15	4	13
McLean	112	33.9	8 388	357.7	6 751	276.3	975.0	3 870.3	17	70.9	Z	11	–	2
Macon	134	33.6	11 616	479.4	8 240	319.7	2 182.9	6 114.2	47	9.6	Z	40	5	2
Macoupin	35	22.9	697	18.9	515	12.3	65.4	156.5	10	32.3	Z	5	–	2
Madison	224	31.7	19 074	743.8	14 679	521.0	2 799.8	7 676.5	308	17.4	1	53	81	15
Marion	65	44.6	5 220	152.6	4 267	113.5	440.0	768.3	6	19.3	Z	5	–	1
Marshall	18	61.1	921	28.3	763	19.9	95.5	179.6	4	100.0	1	2	1	2
Mason	NA	NA	NA	NA	NA	NA	NA	NA	119	41.6	36	1	–	45
Massac	12	33.3	732	31.2	553	21.2	133.0	191.5	592	1.7	2	1	4	11
Menard	NA	NA	NA	NA	NA	NA	NA	NA	2	100.0	1	1	–	1
Mercer	NA	NA	NA	NA	NA	NA	NA	NA	5	100.0	2	1	–	3
Monroe	NA	NA	NA	NA	NA	NA	NA	NA	3	77.8	Z	1	–	1
Montgomery	37	40.5	1 752	48.3	1 422	35.1	117.7	300.7	334	.6	Z	3	Z	6
Morgan	36	38.9	3 566	110.6	2 670	73.0	664.6	1 213.4	159	7.4	1	6	5	4
Moultrie	20	25.0	796	19.8	676	14.8	81.4	210.8	3	68.8	Z	1	–	Z
Ogle	70	38.6	5 859	166.2	4 762	118.4	424.2	1 020.5	31	38.3	2	5	Z	5
Peoria	177	43.5	14 351	610.6	9 859	383.8	2 038.7	4 392.7	110	32.0	2	25	81	13
Perry	22	36.4	1 481	35.3	1 189	24.7	119.9	262.3	11	9.1	Z	1	Z	3
Piatt	NA	NA	NA	NA	NA	NA	NA	NA	3	100.0	Z	1	1	Z
Pike	NA	NA	NA	NA	NA	NA	NA	NA	23	15.2	1	2	–	2
Pope	NA	NA	NA	NA	NA	NA	NA	NA	1	86.8	–	Z	–	Z
Pulaski	NA	NA	NA	NA	NA	NA	NA	NA	1	100.0	Z	1	–	Z
Putnam	9	33.3	(4)	D	D	D	D	D	167	1.0	Z	Z	4	3
Randolph	32	46.9	2 353	51.8	2 146	42.3	165.2	398.6	1 179	.2	Z	4	–	19
Richland	34	29.4	1 814	37.0	1 499	25.0	101.0	218.3	3	50.5	Z	2	Z	1
Rock Island	197	34.0	10 675	493.8	7 994	354.4	1 913.4	3 508.8	925	1.1	3	17	6	37
St. Clair	198	30.8	7 123	249.3	5 300	159.7	602.9	1 763.5	47	61.4	Z	19	22	7
Saline	NA	NA	NA	NA	NA	NA	NA	NA	1	64.0	Z	–	–	1
Sangamon	134	30.6	(5)	D	D	D	D	D	337	2.1	Z	24	–	8
Schuyler	NA	NA	NA	NA	NA	NA	NA	NA	2	98.6	Z	1	–	Z
Scott	NA	NA	NA	NA	NA	NA	NA	NA	6	99.7	2	4	Z	2
Shelby	14	28.6	1 191	32.4	1 029	26.5	103.6	205.7	4	73.2	Z	2	–	1
Stark	NA	NA	NA	NA	NA	NA	NA	NA	1	100.0	1	Z	–	1
Stephenson	62	37.1	8 386	300.3	5 988	194.9	646.8	1 239.2	11	100.0	Z	5	2	3
Tazewell	118	39.8	7 015	311.1	4 985	195.5	1 160.7	2 512.9	798	5.6	12	15	36	29
Union	11	54.5	616	17.0	481	11.1	59.1	132.2	4	97.1	Z	1	–	1
Vermilion	104	42.3	7 055	228.9	5 467	161.4	657.4	1 696.1	16	39.1	Z	11	3	2
Wabash	15	26.7	611	20.5	466	13.4	40.6	55.8	8	82.1	Z	6	–	2
Warren	19	26.3	(6)	D	D	D	D	D	4	100.0	Z	2	–	1
Washington	16	31.3	1 397	44.5	1 036	25.8	104.2	222.4	3	72.6	Z	1	Z	1
Wayne	20	10.0	(6)	D	D	D	D	D	5	75.6	Z	1	–	3
White	NA	NA	NA	NA	NA	NA	NA	NA	6	100.0	2	1	–	5
Whiteside	102	39.2	7 374	245.0	6 187	179.6	547.5	1 381.8	33	99.0	18	6	5	20
Will	527	35.7	24 090	988.2	16 559	557.2	3 209.3	7 594.7	3 908	1.6	3	37	15	98
Williamson	51	23.5	2 551	69.2	1 720	43.8	161.7	425.1	14	14.3	Z	3	–	2
Winnebago	779	37.9	39 740	1 483.6	27 007	844.5	3 791.4	6 608.4	47	99.2	1	36	4	6
Woodford	55	34.5	2 272	74.7	1 847	49.0	406.3	644.9	11	39.2	Z	9	Z	1
INDIANA	9 303	42.4	625 692	22 121.4	478 248	14 956.5	67 210.9	142 270.7	9 139	7.8	116	669	2 275	505
Adams	67	55.2	6 536	189.6	5 323	133.7	485.4	1 428.9	7	66.1	–	3	2	1
Allen	576	38.7	36 585	1 362.0	26 869	891.3	3 762.1	9 182.2	55	20.2	Z	38	8	6
Bartholomew	145	46.9	13 311	412.1	10 184	282.5	1 321.9	3 096.7	22	87.3	2	12	2	4
Benton	16	43.8	562	12.6	404	8.2	29.8	58.8	2	89.2	Z	1	–	Z
Blackford	28	67.9	2 081	58.6	1 711	40.5	143.2	299.2	2	90.0	–	1	1	Z
Boone	73	28.8	1 769	48.5	1 365	31.1	108.1	190.9	5	70.8	Z	2	1	1
Brown	NA	NA	NA	NA	NA	NA	NA	NA	1	51.8	–	Z	–	Z
Carroll	33	27.3	2 191	50.3	1 935	39.1	120.4	500.8	5	82.7	Z	1	1	2
Cass	60	58.3	6 129	157.9	5 258	121.9	362.1	994.3	29	12.4	Z	4	Z	2

[1] Average number of production workers plus the number of other (nonproduction) employees for the pay period including March 12.   [2] Average number of production workers for the pay periods including the 12th of March, May, August, and November.   [3] In millions of gallons per day.   [4] 500 to 999 employees.   [5] 2,500 to 4,999 employees.   [6] 1,000 to 2,499 employees.

Sources: Manufacturing—U.S. Census Bureau, 1997 Economic Census – Manufacturing, generated by Statistical Compendia Branch, using American Factfinder at <http://www.census.gov/>, (June 2000) [related Internet site <http://www.census.gov/epcd/www/97EC31.HTM>].   Water Use—U.S. Geological Survey, "Water Use in the United States," individual state/county and US by state files from <http://water.usgs.gov/watuse/spread95.html>, (accessed: September 1999).

[Includes U.S., states, and 3,142 counties/county equivalents defined as of January 1, 1992. For changes to these areas since January 1, 1992, see appendix B. Geographic Information]

County	Establishments Total	Establishments Percent with 20 or more employees	All employees Number[1]	All employees Annual payroll (mil. dol.)	Production workers Number[2]	Production workers Wages (mil. dol.)	Value added by manufacture (mil. dol.)	Value of shipments (mil. dol.)	Withdrawals Total (mil. gal.)	Withdrawals Percent ground water	By selected major use Irrigation	By selected major use Public supply	By selected major use Industrial	Consumptive use (mil. gal.)
INDIANA—Con.														
Clark	163	36.2	(4)	D	D	D	D	D	31	44.5	–	13	4	3
Clay	34	38.2	(5)	D	D	D	D	D	2	81.0	–	1	Z	1
Clinton	49	51.0	4 959	148.1	4 263	103.6	672.7	1 565.1	7	98.2	Z	4	–	1
Crawford	NA	NA	NA	NA	NA	NA	NA	NA	6	43.7	–	2	3	1
Daviess	51	31.4	1 947	37.4	1 560	26.8	118.7	350.0	9	65.1	1	3	Z	3
Dearborn	39	35.9	(5)	D	D	D	D	D	622	1.7	–	4	6	13
Decatur	52	34.6	4 926	155.6	4 141	123.6	448.7	847.9	4	54.5	–	2	–	1
De Kalb	119	59.7	11 000	364.3	8 336	247.8	982.9	2 040.2	8	84.9	Z	4	2	1
Delaware	176	43.8	9 972	402.6	7 525	264.1	882.9	1 764.5	19	31.4	Z	12	4	2
Dubois	114	57.9	12 450	327.9	10 442	251.3	815.2	1 637.0	10	22.2	–	7	–	2
Elkhart	894	51.9	56 087	1 610.8	44 247	1 093.8	3 861.8	8 999.9	43	90.0	7	14	14	10
Fayette	36	47.2	4 809	217.0	3 860	164.3	688.0	1 254.3	4	96.4	–	3	–	1
Floyd	135	44.4	7 499	204.1	5 970	140.8	668.2	1 243.2	272	.4	–	6	Z	6
Fountain	22	50.0	2 616	67.8	2 193	50.6	155.7	282.8	4	94.6	Z	1	2	1
Franklin	19	31.6	812	23.3	566	13.6	68.3	134.5	3	81.5	Z	1	Z	1
Fulton	52	50.0	3 004	79.1	2 435	57.9	191.2	424.4	8	87.8	5	1	Z	5
Gibson	42	42.9	2 142	54.3	1 744	41.0	135.1	336.1	49	15.4	Z	2	–	2
Grant	80	48.8	9 375	395.2	7 924	313.5	736.8	1 784.4	14	67.1	–	7	3	2
Greene	26	30.8	1 136	18.5	973	13.9	37.4	171.7	24	18.9	13	3	1	13
Hamilton	191	29.3	5 687	185.8	4 065	104.2	491.5	836.3	76	20.6	Z	17	12	6
Hancock	66	24.2	2 564	88.4	1 901	54.3	273.5	712.9	5	95.6	Z	3	Z	1
Harrison	38	39.5	(6)	D	D	D	D	D	3	83.3	–	2	–	1
Hendricks	80	27.5	1 537	48.5	1 090	28.1	108.3	248.4	10	88.4	–	4	Z	2
Henry	57	29.8	3 516	164.8	2 818	131.3	297.3	688.7	12	74.4	Z	4	5	2
Howard	80	38.8	20 018	1 077.9	13 762	728.0	2 341.4	4 732.2	23	35.3	Z	13	Z	3
Huntington	78	53.8	7 451	207.8	5 618	121.9	652.8	1 245.5	5	95.3	–	3	Z	1
Jackson	90	43.3	5 848	179.4	4 560	116.3	544.7	1 182.7	10	44.3	1	4	2	2
Jasper	33	39.4	1 479	35.2	1 239	24.7	134.3	279.4	31	27.1	14	1	1	14
Jay	39	59.0	3 751	86.6	3 250	69.0	236.4	539.1	4	81.0	Z	2	1	1
Jefferson	51	39.2	3 655	97.3	2 787	64.8	257.5	548.9	1 318	.4	–	4	–	27
Jennings	42	52.4	2 410	55.7	2 002	41.6	145.4	263.2	4	16.9	–	1	–	1
Johnson	126	38.1	6 486	204.6	4 977	124.5	531.0	1 305.5	13	98.2	Z	11	Z	2
Knox	44	36.4	1 715	46.2	1 370	33.3	122.5	289.1	61	16.9	4	5	1	6
Kosciusko	186	45.7	14 949	514.1	11 122	311.2	1 716.5	2 969.2	23	78.9	8	4	3	10
Lagrange	77	42.9	4 765	154.3	3 832	114.5	371.7	887.4	12	68.1	6	1	–	7
Lake	423	39.0	37 109	1 748.3	28 136	1 262.2	5 978.4	14 297.9	2 174	.7	12	84	1 284	115
La Porte	189	50.3	10 835	351.2	7 863	213.3	1 065.6	2 007.9	86	18.6	10	11	1	12
Lawrence	75	40.0	5 322	195.0	4 457	154.1	448.7	1 063.0	9	14.4	–	6	2	1
Madison	133	37.6	12 144	534.3	10 033	428.7	925.4	2 256.8	22	80.9	Z	13	3	3
Marion	1 194	36.6	66 571	2 898.6	46 673	1 800.7	11 970.6	19 561.3	318	14.4	Z	132	12	21
Marshall	143	58.0	8 588	230.2	6 756	159.8	718.5	1 516.0	7	89.2	1	3	1	2
Martin	9	44.4	575	17.7	502	13.8	57.9	133.4	3	58.8	–	1	1	1
Miami	50	42.0	2 491	64.0	1 793	42.9	228.5	385.9	7	58.2	Z	2	Z	1
Monroe	122	32.0	8 817	302.6	7 410	221.8	1 094.0	2 444.2	15	3.2	–	14	Z	2
Montgomery	67	43.3	7 634	264.1	5 828	181.8	890.6	1 878.7	7	91.4	Z	3	1	1
Morgan	65	30.8	2 869	78.7	2 109	46.6	252.1	472.3	151	6.5	–	5	2	4
Newton	29	37.9	1 474	34.4	1 235	24.5	88.9	176.5	4	80.6	3	1	–	3
Noble	143	55.9	10 818	309.2	8 831	221.3	874.3	1 821.7	10	87.7	1	3	2	3
Ohio	NA	NA	NA	NA	NA	NA	NA	NA	1	89.7	–	1	–	Z
Orange	34	47.1	2 478	55.3	2 114	43.0	137.8	296.4	3	34.8	–	1	Z	1
Owen	24	25.0	1 242	31.5	870	18.1	52.9	109.2	2	90.9	–	1	–	Z
Parke	17	41.2	641	13.7	525	9.4	41.7	92.1	2	88.9	Z	1	–	Z
Perry	27	40.7	1 211	33.6	1 069	28.0	77.5	141.1	2	89.3	–	2	Z	Z
Pike	NA	NA	NA	NA	NA	NA	NA	NA	473	.7	–	1	–	10
Porter	146	35.6	12 353	624.5	9 171	462.3	1 713.9	4 353.6	679	2.0	4	16	395	35
Posey	31	48.4	(6)	D	D	D	D	D	20	13.7	1	2	10	2
Pulaski	20	55.0	1 353	41.1	1 079	25.9	79.0	218.1	10	56.7	5	1	1	5
Putnam	25	44.0	2 482	64.8	2 017	45.8	187.4	421.7	8	78.0	–	4	1	1
Randolph	54	42.6	3 080	86.5	2 264	62.8	194.8	361.0	4	72.6	–	2	1	1
Ripley	35	28.6	3 168	109.9	2 071	59.4	567.5	755.2	4	27.3	–	3	–	1
Rush	32	37.5	1 081	32.4	786	19.9	188.9	289.1	3	76.3	Z	1	1	1
St. Joseph	457	39.2	20 435	698.9	14 401	410.9	1 998.9	4 149.7	94	66.6	5	31	16	15
Scott	34	52.9	(6)	D	D	D	D	D	4	3.3	–	3	Z	1
Shelby	86	48.8	6 656	218.5	5 151	149.5	509.7	1 188.8	8	78.4	1	3	1	2
Spencer	19	47.4	1 369	36.3	1 106	26.9	73.0	134.0	32	10.0	Z	2	–	1
Starke	19	57.9	1 357	29.7	1 082	19.3	72.3	143.3	7	56.1	5	1	Z	5
Steuben	110	58.2	6 774	189.0	5 457	138.2	517.6	1 056.5	4	85.9	Z	1	Z	1
Sullivan	18	38.9	579	14.3	473	9.6	31.8	73.0	450	1.4	2	2	1	11
Switzerland	6	50.0	619	10.7	567	9.4	29.0	58.7	4	96.5	–	1	–	Z
Tippecanoe	113	46.0	16 695	692.2	12 922	443.9	2 585.8	7 519.0	45	95.8	Z	14	21	5

[1] Average number of production workers plus the number of other (nonproduction) employees for the pay period including March 12.   [2] Average number of production workers for the pay periods including the 12th of March, May, August, and November.   [3] In millions of gallons per day.   [4] 5,000 to 9,999 employees.   [5] 1,000 to 2,499 employees.   [6] 2,500 to 4,999 employees.

Sources: Manufacturing—U.S. Census Bureau, 1997 Economic Census – Manufacturing, generated by Statistical Compendia Branch, using American Factfinder at <http://www.census.gov/>, (June 2000) [related Internet site <http://www.census.gov/epcd/www/97EC31.HTM>].   Water Use—U.S. Geological Survey, "Water Use in the United States," individual state/county and US by state files from <http://water.usgs.gov/watuse/spread95.html>, (accessed: September 1999).

Table B–9. Counties — **Manufacturing and Water Use**–Con.

[Includes U.S., states, and 3,142 counties/county equivalents defined as of January 1, 1992. For changes to these areas since January 1, 1992, see appendix B. Geographic Information]

County	Manufacturing (NAICS 31-33), 1997								Water use per day,[3] 1995					
	Establishments		All employees		Production workers		Value added by manu-facture (mil. dol.)	Value of ship-ments (mil. dol.)	Withdrawals					Consump-tive use (mil. gal.)
	Total	Percent with 20 or more employ-ees	Number[1]	Annual payroll (mil. dol.)	Number[2]	Wages (mil. dol.)			Total (mil. gal.)	Percent ground water	By selected major use– (mil. gal.)			
											Irrigation	Public supply	Industrial	
INDIANA—Con.														
Tipton	22	31.8	954	30.5	753	21.0	85.0	199.3	2	97.3	–	1	Z	1
Union	NA	NA	NA	NA	NA	NA	NA	NA	1	86.4	–	Z	–	Z
Vanderburgh	271	38.4	17 536	607.7	11 415	330.5	2 317.4	3 824.6	30	4.4	Z	28	Z	4
Vermillion	10	40.0	(4)	D	D	D	D	D	470	2.4	–	1	9	10
Vigo	137	40.1	7 464	255.2	5 627	172.2	989.3	1 891.8	328	7.1	Z	12	8	9
Wabash	77	50.6	5 300	156.3	4 254	106.4	354.0	812.8	10	84.1	Z	6	2	5
Warren	NA	NA	NA	NA	NA	NA	NA	NA	6	98.6	Z	1	5	1
Warrick	53	20.8	(5)	D	D	D	D	D	709	1.1	–	2	412	32
Washington	40	35.0	2 824	66.9	2 450	53.8	164.7	298.7	4	26.6	–	2	–	1
Wayne	132	56.1	8 940	270.0	7 107	185.0	715.3	1 598.7	16	39.8	Z	8	3	2
Wells	49	57.1	3 615	106.2	2 475	62.3	245.1	490.2	4	84.5	–	2	1	1
White	56	37.5	3 402	90.6	2 817	66.9	229.2	638.0	6	90.5	1	2	Z	2
Whitley	66	47.0	4 327	117.3	3 642	86.4	317.5	908.8	4	89.9	Z	1	Z	1
IOWA	3 749	37.7	235 880	7 573.3	175 933	4 936.1	28 673.3	62 413.7	3 035	17.4	39	373	258	290
Adair	8	37.5	527	15.1	469	12.0	33.3	101.9	2	62.0	–	1	–	1
Adams	NA	NA	NA	NA	NA	NA	NA	NA	2	39.5	–	Z	–	1
Allamakee	26	30.8	1 505	27.4	1 313	22.3	82.5	209.7	212	1.8	–	1	1	2
Appanoose	15	26.7	1 070	30.1	890	21.2	84.1	156.5	5	12.2	Z	1	–	1
Audubon	NA	NA	NA	NA	NA	NA	NA	NA	2	80.8	–	1	–	1
Benton	NA	NA	NA	NA	NA	NA	NA	NA	3	87.3	–	1	–	2
Black Hawk	165	42.4	13 542	555.7	9 967	382.1	2 258.4	5 133.1	57	66.3	Z	20	19	10
Boone	26	46.2	914	22.5	733	16.0	67.8	131.9	3	93.8	Z	2	–	1
Bremer	39	43.6	1 993	58.6	1 485	40.4	126.8	446.3	5	66.2	Z	2	–	2
Buchanan	35	37.1	1 230	31.7	1 068	24.3	78.1	277.7	4	81.1	Z	1	Z	2
Buena Vista	28	28.6	2 546	55.2	2 185	46.0	112.3	688.6	5	93.7	Z	4	–	2
Butler	23	30.4	601	16.3	504	12.1	36.4	70.7	8	30.2	Z	1	–	2
Calhoun	NA	NA	NA	NA	NA	NA	NA	NA	2	91.5	Z	1	–	1
Carroll	39	33.3	1 588	41.7	1 375	33.5	205.8	423.8	5	82.3	Z	2	Z	3
Cass	25	40.0	1 112	29.8	844	20.2	71.2	150.7	4	74.9	–	2	–	1
Cedar	25	32.0	810	19.4	588	11.4	53.4	122.3	3	86.3	–	1	Z	2
Cerro Gordo	61	41.0	3 703	98.9	2 789	67.5	275.6	719.8	9	82.7	Z	7	–	2
Cherokee	15	40.0	904	24.6	758	19.2	42.5	188.5	5	92.1	Z	3	Z	2
Chickasaw	25	32.0	1 674	42.2	1 367	28.6	158.0	414.4	3	87.5	Z	1	–	2
Clarke	19	47.4	1 152	21.4	1 009	16.9	89.6	209.4	2	47.4	–	1	–	1
Clay	28	39.3	1 180	34.9	989	26.5	97.9	202.3	3	94.3	Z	2	Z	1
Clayton	31	38.7	1 538	28.6	1 289	19.6	73.8	184.6	5	84.6	–	1	Z	4
Clinton	59	47.5	5 148	175.6	4 072	123.8	1 097.5	2 106.9	279	5.8	Z	5	138	21
Crawford	22	45.5	1 879	49.5	1 648	38.1	131.5	908.9	4	88.8	Z	Z	1	2
Dallas	41	46.3	2 489	59.7	2 095	46.0	132.8	451.2	6	91.5	Z	3	1	2
Davis	NA	NA	NA	NA	NA	NA	NA	NA	1	57.8	–	Z	–	1
Decatur	NA	NA	NA	NA	NA	NA	NA	NA	2	69.1	–	1	–	1
Delaware	34	26.5	1 144	33.7	906	24.3	171.0	327.5	6	76.1	–	1	Z	4
Des Moines	66	48.5	6 772	228.9	5 119	155.4	553.6	1 320.8	115	1.9	Z	6	Z	2
Dickinson	31	25.8	2 386	60.3	1 892	39.8	117.0	353.4	3	29.8	Z	2	–	1
Dubuque	133	48.9	10 687	386.9	7 698	248.1	1 391.5	3 074.9	82	28.1	Z	10	21	10
Emmet	15	46.7	752	18.2	567	12.4	39.6	115.8	2	71.2	Z	1	Z	1
Fayette	24	58.3	1 539	38.9	1 271	29.5	94.0	262.4	5	80.4	Z	2	Z	3
Floyd	17	29.4	591	16.6	470	11.1	30.5	94.5	4	87.5	Z	2	1	2
Franklin	22	27.3	790	21.6	663	16.4	40.3	83.9	3	68.4	Z	1	–	1
Fremont	NA	NA	NA	NA	NA	NA	NA	NA	6	41.5	Z	1	Z	1
Greene	17	29.4	525	14.4	393	8.8	36.3	83.4	2	82.7	Z	1	–	1
Grundy	NA	NA	NA	NA	NA	NA	NA	NA	2	88.8	–	1	–	1
Guthrie	NA	NA	NA	NA	NA	NA	NA	NA	2	76.0	Z	1	–	1
Hamilton	30	46.7	2 861	75.8	2 377	55.6	161.3	472.0	3	91.5	Z	2	–	1
Hancock	27	33.3	1 126	29.7	797	17.9	55.0	221.2	4	78.1	Z	1	1	2
Hardin	39	41.0	1 580	34.8	1 309	26.2	91.0	375.8	5	72.3	Z	2	Z	2
Harrison	NA	NA	NA	NA	NA	NA	NA	NA	12	87.2	8	1	–	9
Henry	34	35.3	2 839	85.2	2 130	57.8	357.0	717.4	3	49.0	–	2	–	1
Howard	20	25.0	1 405	29.2	1 169	25.7	91.5	177.7	2	80.5	Z	1	–	1
Humboldt	28	50.0	1 257	31.8	902	19.9	80.6	159.7	4	42.1	Z	1	–	1
Ida	9	44.4	1 112	32.5	887	18.1	75.7	165.0	2	86.6	Z	1	–	1
Iowa	31	32.3	4 698	144.7	3 813	101.2	283.7	678.8	3	89.7	Z	1	1	2
Jackson	34	50.0	1 208	25.7	1 019	18.2	80.6	194.5	9	41.6	Z	1	–	3
Jasper	46	28.3	3 702	132.4	3 067	99.9	494.9	740.0	8	91.9	Z	2	–	3
Jefferson	37	35.1	1 751	56.4	1 508	43.8	150.0	256.6	3	94.0	–	5	–	1
Johnson	89	15.7	3 639	121.1	2 940	89.5	1 857.6	2 510.4	63	11.3	Z	9	Z	5
Jones	23	34.8	889	23.5	716	16.9	79.0	170.1	4	86.1	Z	2	–	2
Keokuk	NA	NA	NA	NA	NA	NA	NA	NA	3	70.0	–	1	–	2

[1] Average number of production workers plus the number of other (nonproduction) employees for the pay period including March 12. [2] Average number of production workers for the pay periods including the 12th of March, May, August, and November. [3] In millions of gallons per day. [4] 1,000 to 2,499 employees. [5] 2,500 to 4,999 employees.

Sources: Manufacturing—U.S. Census Bureau, 1997 Economic Census – Manufacturing, generated by Statistical Compendia Branch, using American Factfinder at <http://www.census.gov/>, (June 2000) [related Internet site <http://www.census.gov/epcd/www/97EC31.HTM>]. Water Use—U.S. Geological Survey, "Water Use in the United States," individual state/county and US by state files from <http://water.usgs.gov/watuse/spread95.html>, (accessed: September 1999).

Table B–9. Counties — Manufacturing and Water Use–Con.

[Includes U.S., states, and 3,142 counties/county equivalents defined as of January 1, 1992. For changes to these areas since January 1, 1992, see appendix B. Geographic Information]

County	Establishments Total	Establishments Percent with 20 or more employees	All employees Number[1]	All employees Annual payroll (mil. dol.)	Production workers Number[2]	Production workers Wages (mil. dol.)	Value added by manufacture (mil. dol.)	Value of shipments (mil. dol.)	Withdrawals Total (mil. gal.)	Withdrawals Percent ground water	Irrigation	Public supply	Industrial	Consumptive use (mil. gal.)
IOWA—Con.														
Kossuth	30	33.3	1 126	33.7	918	25.1	92.9	207.3	3	89.5	Z	1	—	2
Lee	70	51.4	6 397	209.0	4 910	144.8	762.0	1 671.5	19	32.5	Z	11	5	4
Linn	239	39.7	22 877	935.0	11 730	388.4	3 617.0	6 376.1	260	21.2	Z	42	10	13
Louisa	11	36.4	[4]	D	D	D	D	D	10	98.6	3	1	2	4
Lucas	NA	NA	NA	NA	NA	NA	NA	NA	1	45.7	—	1	—	1
Lyon	NA	NA	NA	NA	NA	NA	NA	NA	4	87.9	Z	2	—	3
Madison	NA	NA	NA	NA	NA	NA	NA	NA	2	85.2	—	1	—	1
Mahaska	26	42.3	1 020	26.3	805	18.1	112.0	230.6	4	91.4	Z	2	—	2
Marion	44	31.8	6 687	229.8	5 426	167.4	690.7	1 388.5	6	73.9	Z	3	—	2
Marshall	44	38.6	5 363	174.0	3 719	102.4	516.7	1 413.2	11	79.3	Z	6	1	3
Mills	NA	NA	NA	NA	NA	NA	NA	NA	3	93.7	1	1	—	2
Mitchell	16	56.3	1 021	27.4	842	17.0	104.4	186.3	2	77.3	Z	Z	—	2
Monona	NA	NA	NA	NA	NA	NA	NA	NA	12	98.1	10	1	—	11
Monroe	18	50.0	863	32.8	542	20.0	163.7	593.2	1	85.7	—	Z	Z	1
Montgomery	11	45.5	1 365	32.4	1 222	26.6	92.7	185.0	2	92.6	—	1	—	1
Muscatine	70	47.1	6 523	252.7	4 937	176.2	1 506.7	2 631.1	270	15.2	3	27	27	12
O'Brien	NA	NA	NA	NA	NA	NA	NA	NA	4	88.8	Z	2	—	2
Osceola	NA	NA	NA	NA	NA	NA	NA	NA	3	83.4	Z	1	—	1
Page	27	33.3	2 271	78.0	1 937	62.0	296.5	477.3	3	56.5	Z	2	—	1
Palo Alto	NA	NA	NA	NA	NA	NA	NA	NA	3	83.7	1	1	—	2
Plymouth	26	30.8	[4]	D	D	D	D	D	6	88.5	Z	3	—	4
Pocahontas	19	31.6	821	20.3	630	12.9	53.8	91.8	2	89.7	Z	1	—	1
Polk	410	32.0	19 790	688.6	13 985	427.6	2 106.9	5 054.9	57	19.7	Z	50	—	11
Pottawattamie	59	44.1	4 109	113.2	3 285	84.6	429.4	888.7	469	1.0	1	14	Z	6
Poweshiek	32	46.9	1 533	42.7	1 249	30.1	108.9	226.6	3	81.8	—	2	—	2
Ringgold	NA	NA	NA	NA	NA	NA	NA	NA	1	62.2	—	Z	—	1
Sac	NA	NA	NA	NA	NA	NA	NA	NA	3	81.3	Z	1	Z	2
Scott	210	37.1	11 845	478.3	8 748	323.8	2 189.8	4 614.8	101	4.4	Z	19	1	6
Shelby	NA	NA	NA	NA	NA	NA	NA	NA	3	87.5	Z	1	—	2
Sioux	67	41.8	4 610	104.6	3 387	74.8	305.7	822.0	16	77.0	3	6	Z	8
Story	75	37.3	3 577	108.4	2 449	58.2	652.1	988.6	13	97.8	Z	9	—	4
Tama	14	42.9	911	22.5	757	16.1	59.8	236.1	5	93.3	—	2	2	2
Taylor	NA	NA	NA	NA	NA	NA	NA	NA	1	62.2	—	Z	—	1
Union	19	42.1	1 031	24.6	774	16.6	53.1	113.2	3	25.7	—	2	—	1
Van Buren	14	35.7	653	14.8	559	11.0	30.2	54.4	1	64.1		Z		1
Wapello	22	40.9	2 701	92.5	2 139	64.7	290.7	741.8	20	3.7	—	6	7	8
Warren	NA	NA	NA	NA	NA	NA	NA	NA	8	49.7	Z	2	—	2
Washington	32	40.6	1 441	41.2	1 160	26.6	96.7	196.2	4	84.5	Z	1	—	2
Wayne	13	53.8	[5]	D	D	D	D	D	1	61.5	—	7	—	1
Webster	60	33.3	2 554	81.7	1 625	48.2	748.3	1 110.9	9	76.0	Z	4	1	2
Winnebago	13	38.5	4 006	105.5	3 292	70.2	262.8	640.5	2	94.3	Z	1	—	1
Winneshiek	29	31.0	1 453	38.0	1 233	27.9	99.7	215.0	5	87.3	Z	2	Z	3
Woodbury	113	52.2	[6]	D	D	D	D	D	672	5.8	Z	15	15	9
Worth	12	25.0	596	12.5	458	8.3	26.2	49.2	5	18.2	Z	Z	—	1
Wright	25	40.0	1 318	39.2	1 021	27.1	131.0	546.5	3	96.7	Z	1	1	1
KANSAS	3 309	34.8	193 742	6 532.5	141 169	4 052.5	17 650.6	46 296.4	5 235	67.1	3 383	370	53	3 620
Allen	28	42.9	1 722	45.7	1 296	29.3	165.1	277.3	3	6.9	Z	2	Z	2
Anderson	NA	NA	NA	NA	NA	NA	NA	NA	2	18.6	Z	Z	—	1
Atchison	24	41.7	1 753	53.7	1 415	37.7	119.3	360.1	6	14.9	Z	5	—	3
Barber	NA	NA	NA	NA	NA	NA	NA	NA	5	99.6	2	1	—	4
Barton	45	22.2	1 608	34.0	1 102	21.6	112.5	308.1	38	100.0	31	3	1	35
Bourbon	29	55.2	1 295	29.4	999	19.0	80.2	149.0	3	9.3	Z	2	—	2
Brown	18	33.3	820	18.0	699	12.8	37.8	75.8	2	71.8	Z	1	—	1
Butler	52	26.9	1 704	58.8	1 237	35.8	243.7	1 132.7	13	25.0	1	9	Z	9
Chase	NA	NA	NA	NA	NA	NA	NA	NA	1	64.4	Z	Z	—	1
Chautauqua	NA	NA	NA	NA	NA	NA	NA	NA	1	61.3	Z	Z	—	1
Cherokee	44	36.4	2 291	59.6	1 613	34.5	120.9	343.5	92	3.9	Z	3	Z	4
Cheyenne	NA	NA	NA	NA	NA	NA	NA	NA	38	99.8	36	1	—	37
Clark	NA	NA	NA	NA	NA	NA	NA	NA	5	96.0	4	Z	—	5
Clay	NA	NA	NA	NA	NA	NA	NA	NA	15	94.6	12	2	—	13
Cloud	NA	NA	NA	NA	NA	NA	NA	NA	15	94.9	12	1	Z	13
Coffey	NA	NA	NA	NA	NA	NA	NA	NA	24	1.9	Z	Z	—	14
Comanche	NA	NA	NA	NA	NA	NA	NA	NA	8	99.2	7	Z	—	7
Cowley	47	40.4	3 793	107.3	3 123	78.5	367.2	1 176.7	10	70.0	1	5	1	5
Crawford	74	40.5	3 206	77.2	2 557	55.3	238.8	519.3	7	76.2	1	5	—	4
Decatur	NA	NA	NA	NA	NA	NA	NA	NA	13	100.0	11	2	—	13
Dickinson	25	28.0	1 161	24.6	945	15.7	87.5	160.9	5	79.4	2	2	—	4

[1] Average number of production workers plus the number of other (nonproduction) employees for the pay period including March 12. [2] Average number of production workers for the pay periods including the 12th of March, May, August, and November. [3] In millions of gallons per day. [4] 1,000 to 2,499 employees. [5] 500 to 999 employees. [6] 5,000 to 9,999 employees.

Sources: Manufacturing—U.S. Census Bureau, 1997 Economic Census – Manufacturing, generated by Statistical Compendia Branch, using American Factfinder at <http://www.census.gov/>, (June 2000) [related Internet site <http://www.census.gov/epcd/www/97EC31.HTM>]. Water Use—U.S. Geological Survey, "Water Use in the United States," individual state/county and US by state files from <http://water.usgs.gov/watuse/spread95.html>, (accessed: September 1999).

Table B–9. Counties — **Manufacturing and Water Use**–Con.

[Includes U.S., states, and 3,142 counties/county equivalents defined as of January 1, 1992. For changes to these areas since January 1, 1992, see appendix B. Geographic Information]

County	Manufacturing (NAICS 31-33), 1997 Establishments Total	Percent with 20 or more employees	All employees Number[1]	Annual payroll (mil. dol.)	Production workers Number[2]	Wages (mil. dol.)	Value added by manufacture (mil. dol.)	Value of shipments (mil. dol.)	Water use per day,[3] 1995 Withdrawals Total (mil. gal.)	Percent ground water	By selected major use Irrigation (mil. gal.)	Public supply	Industrial	Consumptive use (mil. gal.)
KANSAS—Con.														
Doniphan	8	50.0	(4)	D	D	D	D	D	1	97.6	Z	Z	–	1
Douglas	76	32.9	4 240	120.0	3 213	76.9	393.4	728.8	22	29.2	1	12	3	12
Edwards	NA	NA	NA	NA	NA	NA	NA	NA	95	100.0	94	Z	–	94
Elk	NA	NA	NA	NA	NA	NA	NA	NA	1	3.5	–	Z	–	1
Ellis	28	28.6	1 061	20.6	916	12.9	47.1	95.1	5	96.3	1	2	Z	3
Ellsworth	NA	NA	NA	NA	NA	NA	NA	NA	3	73.4	Z	1	Z	2
Finney	38	26.3	5 416	123.4	4 675	102.4	272.5	2 420.2	295	100.0	276	6	6	282
Ford	29	37.9	(5)	D	D	D	D	D	104	99.9	90	5	4	99
Franklin	25	32.0	806	22.0	596	14.2	60.2	151.0	3	25.3	Z	2	–	2
Geary	NA	NA	NA	NA	NA	NA	NA	NA	9	93.4	2	6	–	4
Gove	NA	NA	NA	NA	NA	NA	NA	NA	20	100.0	18	Z	–	20
Graham	NA	NA	NA	NA	NA	NA	NA	NA	11	99.8	10	Z	Z	10
Grant	NA	NA	NA	NA	NA	NA	NA	NA	173	100.0	167	1	1	169
Gray	NA	NA	NA	NA	NA	NA	NA	NA	226	99.1	222	1	–	221
Greeley	NA	NA	NA	NA	NA	NA	NA	NA	26	100.0	25	Z	Z	26
Greenwood	NA	NA	NA	NA	NA	NA	NA	NA	2	20.2	Z	1	–	2
Hamilton	NA	NA	NA	NA	NA	NA	NA	NA	47	85.2	45	1	–	45
Harper	NA	NA	NA	NA	NA	NA	NA	NA	3	90.2	1	1	–	2
Harvey	55	41.8	2 855	87.9	2 235	60.4	195.5	446.6	42	99.4	22	19	Z	24
Haskell	NA	NA	NA	NA	NA	NA	NA	NA	291	99.9	287	1	–	284
Hodgeman	NA	NA	NA	NA	NA	NA	NA	NA	33	98.6	31	Z	Z	32
Jackson	NA	NA	NA	NA	NA	NA	NA	NA	2	84.7	–	1	–	2
Jefferson	NA	NA	NA	NA	NA	NA	NA	NA	3	88.3	1	2	–	2
Jewell	NA	NA	NA	NA	NA	NA	NA	NA	78	3.0	77	1	–	9
Johnson	551	34.1	20 590	662.8	13 670	355.2	1 813.4	3 659.3	12	50.5	2	9	Z	26
Kearny	NA	NA	NA	NA	NA	NA	NA	NA	192	61.3	189	1	–	167
Kingman	NA	NA	NA	NA	NA	NA	NA	NA	16	96.0	13	1	Z	15
Kiowa	NA	NA	NA	NA	NA	NA	NA	NA	51	100.0	50	Z	–	50
Labette	40	42.5	2 298	64.4	1 616	35.8	142.2	254.5	5	6.5	Z	Z	Z	3
Lane	NA	NA	NA	NA	NA	NA	NA	NA	20	100.0	19	Z	–	20
Leavenworth	36	25.0	645	16.2	474	10.0	35.4	62.3	10	71.3	Z	8	Z	6
Lincoln	NA	NA	NA	NA	NA	NA	NA	NA	1	84.0	Z	Z	Z	1
Linn	NA	NA	NA	NA	NA	NA	NA	NA	727	Z	Z	1	–	8
Logan	NA	NA	NA	NA	NA	NA	NA	NA	8	100.0	7	1	–	8
Lyon	40	42.5	6 478	167.1	4 210	100.1	443.6	2 054.1	9	4.3	Z	7	–	5
McPherson	68	42.6	3 845	131.2	2 709	82.1	632.4	1 633.5	30	95.1	21	4	3	26
Marion	NA	NA	NA	NA	NA	NA	NA	NA	3	59.9	1	1	Z	3
Marshall	21	33.3	880	23.0	685	16.6	46.6	106.8	3	74.8	1	1	Z	2
Meade	NA	NA	NA	NA	NA	NA	NA	NA	157	100.0	156	1	–	153
Miami	31	19.4	682	19.1	519	12.4	36.0	58.2	4	5.7	Z	3	–	2
Mitchell	NA	NA	NA	NA	NA	NA	NA	NA	12	9.9	10	1	Z	9
Montgomery	61	49.2	4 590	121.6	3 435	80.9	434.8	1 482.9	9	2.9	Z	6	1	4
Morris	NA	NA	NA	NA	NA	NA	NA	NA	2	59.4	Z	Z	Z	2
Morton	NA	NA	NA	NA	NA	NA	NA	NA	56	100.0	54	1	Z	54
Nemaha	19	42.1	1 047	30.3	771	14.7	68.1	209.5	3	92.4	Z	1	Z	2
Neosho	40	55.0	2 281	53.7	1 796	36.3	137.1	289.0	3	2.2	Z	2	Z	2
Ness	NA	NA	NA	NA	NA	NA	NA	NA	6	91.7	4	Z	–	5
Norton	NA	NA	NA	NA	NA	NA	NA	NA	12	84.1	11	1	–	11
Osage	NA	NA	NA	NA	NA	NA	NA	NA	2	18.5	Z	1	–	2
Osborne	NA	NA	NA	NA	NA	NA	NA	NA	5	66.9	3	1	–	6
Ottawa	NA	NA	NA	NA	NA	NA	NA	NA	3	91.1	2	Z	–	3
Pawnee	NA	NA	NA	NA	NA	NA	NA	NA	68	99.3	65	1	–	66
Phillips	NA	NA	NA	NA	NA	NA	NA	NA	32	27.4	30	1	–	11
Pottawatomie	22	36.4	720	25.8	501	16.9	74.3	134.2	40	40.0	6	5	–	33
Pratt	NA	NA	NA	NA	NA	NA	NA	NA	77	99.8	73	2	–	75
Rawlins	NA	NA	NA	NA	NA	NA	NA	NA	16	99.7	15	Z	–	16
Reno	97	42.3	5 141	161.3	3 869	111.4	438.3	849.7	58	96.6	26	8	17	48
Republic	8	25.0	(4)	D	D	D	D	D	29	83.9	26	1	–	52
Rice	NA	NA	NA	NA	NA	NA	NA	NA	20	98.6	16	1	2	19
Riley	28	17.9	533	14.4	422	10.6	45.8	75.8	6	91.7	2	2	Z	7
Rooks	NA	NA	NA	NA	NA	NA	NA	NA	17	14.7	15	1	–	3
Rush	NA	NA	NA	NA	NA	NA	NA	NA	10	99.6	9	1	–	9
Russell	NA	NA	NA	NA	NA	NA	NA	NA	1	45.5	–	1	–	1
Saline	87	34.5	6 434	193.2	5 294	145.5	386.7	1 212.2	10	68.1	3	6	–	6
Scott	NA	NA	NA	NA	NA	NA	NA	NA	64	100.0	59	1	–	62
Sedgwick	595	37.6	61 675	2 569.7	40 767	1 400.1	5 282.8	10 638.7	89	70.9	27	44	4	60
Seward	10	40.0	(5)	D	D	D	D	D	160	100.0	150	4	2	152
Shawnee	140	35.0	7 722	265.4	6 334	196.6	949.4	1 805.6	43	31.3	7	28	5	22
Sheridan	NA	NA	NA	NA	NA	NA	NA	NA	78	99.9	77	Z	–	77

[1] Average number of production workers plus the number of other (nonproduction) employees for the pay period including March 12. [2] Average number of production workers for the pay periods including the 12th of March, May, August, and November. [3] In millions of gallons per day. [4] 500 to 999 employees. [5] 2,500 to 4,999 employees.

Sources: Manufacturing—U.S. Census Bureau, 1997 Economic Census – Manufacturing, generated by Statistical Compendia Branch, using American Factfinder at <http://www.census.gov/>, (June 2000) [related Internet site <http://www.census.gov/epcd/www/97EC31.HTM>]. Water Use—U.S. Geological Survey, "Water Use in the United States," individual state/county and US by state files from <http://water.usgs.gov/watuse/spread95.html>, (accessed: September 1999).

Table B–9. Counties — **Manufacturing and Water Use**–Con.

[Includes U.S., states, and 3,142 counties/county equivalents defined as of January 1, 1992. For changes to these areas since January 1, 1992, see appendix B. Geographic Information]

| County | Maunfacturing (NAICS 31-33), 1997 | | | | | | | | Water use per day[3] 1995 | | | | | |
| | Establishments | | All employees | | Production workers | | Value added by manufacture (mil. dol.) | Value of shipments (mil. dol.) | Withdrawals | | By selected major use– (mil. gal.) | | | Consumptive use (mil. gal.) |
	Total	Percent with 20 or more employees	Number[1]	Annual payroll (mil. dol.)	Number[2]	Wages (mil. dol.)			Total (mil. gal.)	Percent ground water	Irrigation	Public supply	Industrial	
KANSAS—Con.														
Sherman	NA	NA	NA	NA	NA	NA	NA	NA	90	100.0	87	1	Z	88
Smith	NA	NA	NA	NA	NA	NA	NA	NA	5	83.6	3	1	–	11
Stafford	NA	NA	NA	NA	NA	NA	NA	NA	76	100.0	73	Z	–	74
Stanton	NA	NA	NA	NA	NA	NA	NA	NA	164	100.0	162	1	Z	160
Stevens	NA	NA	NA	NA	NA	NA	NA	NA	189	100.0	186	1	–	186
Sumner	44	18.2	1 262	45.1	998	32.4	95.6	194.6	7	88.7	3	3	Z	6
Thomas	NA	NA	NA	NA	NA	NA	NA	NA	91	100.0	88	2	–	89
Trego	NA	NA	NA	NA	NA	NA	NA	NA	5	99.4	3	Z	–	4
Wabaunsee	NA	NA	NA	NA	NA	NA	NA	NA	4	78.9	2	Z	–	3
Wallace	NA	NA	NA	NA	NA	NA	NA	NA	62	100.0	61	Z	–	61
Washington	NA	NA	NA	NA	NA	NA	NA	NA	6	72.6	3	1	–	5
Wichita	NA	NA	NA	NA	NA	NA	NA	NA	76	100.0	73	Z	Z	73
Wilson	29	34.5	1 256	35.0	984	22.6	82.0	261.5	3	4.0	Z	1	Z	2
Woodson	NA	NA	NA	NA	NA	NA	NA	NA	1	2.1	Z	Z	–	1
Wyandotte	262	43.9	15 083	638.9	11 778	466.8	2 872.9	7 678.2	479	.9	Z	84	1	13
KENTUCKY	4 218	40.6	288 405	9 198.1	223 868	6 251.6	38 337.6	86 636.1	4 420	5.1	12	496	347	318
Adair	20	20.0	533	8.3	437	6.4	18.8	30.8	2	5.5	Z	1	–	1
Allen	12	66.7	1 858	41.6	1 648	34.1	110.6	285.1	2	3.8	Z	1	–	1
Anderson	20	50.0	(4)	D	D	D	D	D	3	2.4	Z	2	1	1
Ballard	12	41.7	(5)	D	D	D	D	D	23	7.6	Z	Z	22	2
Barren	55	56.4	5 672	154.5	4 635	120.1	325.7	796.0	8	4.7	Z	6	–	2
Bath	NA	NA	NA	NA	NA	NA	NA	NA	5	.9	Z	Z	–	1
Bell	22	36.4	858	18.6	681	12.3	50.6	125.8	8	13.1	–	3	Z	Z
Boone	134	46.3	9 050	305.7	6 878	190.3	880.4	1 857.4	8	11.0	Z	Z	–	1
Bourbon	19	47.4	(4)	D	D	D	D	D	3	8.1	Z	2	–	1
Boyd	42	40.5	4 395	203.4	3 491	158.6	668.2	2 930.8	80	1.8	Z	10	70	3
Boyle	33	60.6	4 604	130.5	3 537	89.8	370.5	778.3	5	1.9	Z	4	–	1
Bracken	NA	NA	NA	NA	NA	NA	NA	NA	2	73.0	Z	1	Z	1
Breathitt	NA	NA	NA	NA	NA	NA	NA	NA	1	36.2	–	1	–	Z
Breckinridge	NA	NA	NA	NA	NA	NA	NA	NA	2	18.6	Z	1	–	1
Bullitt	49	24.5	2 959	85.6	2 438	63.7	172.0	344.8	4	27.1	Z	–	2	1
Butler	15	60.0	1 886	37.6	1 664	29.2	228.7	355.1	2	3.3	Z	1	–	Z
Caldwell	19	21.1	659	18.7	537	12.9	49.4	121.6	1	3.9	–	1	–	Z
Calloway	28	28.6	2 983	69.1	2 639	52.7	519.8	817.4	5	88.5	Z	3	1	1
Campbell	83	38.6	3 043	105.0	2 062	71.2	400.2	726.1	32	.1	Z	30	1	2
Carlisle	NA	NA	NA	NA	NA	NA	NA	NA	3	90.6	Z	Z	2	Z
Carroll	18	61.1	2 378	94.8	1 658	58.7	634.9	1 408.7	43	37.7	Z	1	16	23
Carter	18	44.4	612	8.9	559	7.5	29.4	40.0	3	6.8	Z	3	–	Z
Casey	27	33.3	946	16.0	742	12.4	34.5	80.3	2	26.6	Z	1	–	1
Christian	56	42.9	4 469	115.4	3 632	79.9	332.2	780.8	10	6.1	Z	9	–	2
Clark	46	60.9	3 635	87.0	3 032	65.9	252.4	661.1	109	.1	Z	5	Z	2
Clay	NA	NA	NA	NA	NA	NA	NA	NA	3	20.1	Z	2	–	Z
Clinton	15	40.0	671	9.9	572	7.8	24.2	45.7	1	2.3	Z	1	–	Z
Crittenden	NA	NA	NA	NA	NA	NA	NA	NA	1	22.3	–	Z	–	Z
Cumberland	NA	NA	NA	NA	NA	NA	NA	NA	1	3.7	Z	1	–	Z
Daviess	114	45.6	8 011	276.8	6 002	187.3	1 106.8	2 938.2	220	10.4	Z	15	8	2
Edmonson	NA	NA	NA	NA	NA	NA	NA	NA	1	3.3	Z	1	–	1
Elliott	NA	NA	NA	NA	NA	NA	NA	NA	Z	75.0	Z	Z	–	Z
Estill	NA	NA	NA	NA	NA	NA	NA	NA	2	4.5	Z	1	–	Z
Fayette	283	32.5	17 403	654.0	10 380	275.0	2 147.7	4 313.9	43	1.5	1	41	–	4
Fleming	19	31.6	650	14.6	560	11.6	22.3	54.8	2	4.3	Z	1	–	1
Floyd	NA	NA	NA	NA	NA	NA	NA	NA	4	11.9	–	3	Z	Z
Franklin	40	45.0	3 435	97.8	2 804	70.6	302.0	592.4	9	1.4	Z	7	Z	1
Fulton	14	64.3	1 087	23.4	895	17.9	80.5	194.1	2	97.0	–	2	Z	Z
Gallatin	NA	NA	NA	NA	NA	NA	NA	NA	1	43.2	Z	Z	Z	Z
Garrard	NA	NA	NA	NA	NA	NA	NA	NA	2	3.6	Z	1	–	1
Grant	16	37.5	(5)	D	D	D	D	D	2	3.9	Z	2	–	1
Graves	50	34.0	3 053	101.4	2 282	72.2	208.8	537.6	15	94.1	Z	3	11	2
Grayson	31	41.9	2 462	47.8	2 223	41.0	107.9	382.5	3	2.7	Z	2	–	1
Green	NA	NA	NA	NA	NA	NA	NA	NA	2	3.0	Z	1	–	1
Greenup	13	53.8	600	23.4	479	17.3	48.5	108.6	16	10.0	Z	3	13	1
Hancock	13	53.8	1 862	80.9	1 330	54.0	222.8	1 049.0	251	10.2	Z	1	25	1
Hardin	68	44.1	7 162	216.8	5 575	155.8	734.4	1 633.9	13	60.2	Z	12	1	2
Harlan	NA	NA	NA	NA	NA	NA	NA	NA	5	19.4	Z	3	–	1
Harrison	19	36.8	1 730	54.9	1 372	37.9	196.4	353.3	3	2.4	1	2	–	1
Hart	10	40.0	(5)	D	D	D	D	D	4	2.5	Z	3	–	1

[1] Average number of production workers plus the number of other (nonproduction) employees for the pay period including March 12. [2] Average number of production workers for the pay periods including the 12th of March, May, August, and November. [3] In millions of gallons per day. [4] 1,000 to 2,499 employees. [5] 500 to 999 employees.

Sources: Manufacturing—U.S. Census Bureau, 1997 Economic Census – Manufacturing, generated by Statistical Compendia Branch, using American Factfinder at <http://www.census.gov/>, (June 2000) [related Internet site <http://www.census.gov/epcd/www/97EC31.HTM>]. Water Use—U.S. Geological Survey, "Water Use in the United States," individual state/county and US by state files from <http://water.usgs.gov/watuse/spread95.html>, (accessed: September 1999).

Table B–9. Counties — **Manufacturing and Water Use**–Con.

[Includes U.S., states, and 3,142 counties/county equivalents defined as of January 1, 1992. For changes to these areas since January 1, 1992, see appendix B. Geographic Information]

County	Manufacturing (NAICS 31-33), 1997 Establishments Total	Establishments Percent with 20 or more employees	All employees Number[1]	All employees Annual payroll (mil. dol.)	Production workers Number[2]	Production workers Wages (mil. dol.)	Value added by manufacture (mil. dol.)	Value of shipments (mil. dol.)	Water use per day,[3] 1995 Withdrawals Total (mil. gal.)	Withdrawals Percent ground water	By selected major use (mil. gal.) Irrigation	By selected major use Public supply	By selected major use Industrial	Consumptive use (mil. gal.)
KENTUCKY—Con.														
Henderson	78	56.4	6 862	208.0	5 465	148.5	912.2	1 722.9	118	2.6	–	7	1	36
Henry	8	50.0	555	17.1	490	13.9	73.0	213.9	3	68.9	Z	2	–	1
Hickman	NA	NA	NA	NA	NA	NA	NA	NA	1	38.2	Z	Z	–	1
Hopkins	55	38.2	2 606	89.7	1 939	60.5	245.2	572.8	18	33.8	Z	7	5	1
Jackson	13	38.5	1 940	28.4	1 603	18.7	5.4	173.3	1	6.7	Z	1	–	Z
Jefferson	873	41.9	56 948	2 201.4	43 631	1 551.9	15 278.7	30 261.6	928	2.3	Z	140	72	25
Jessamine	67	37.3	2 379	67.9	1 834	45.4	327.0	675.4	4	2.8	Z	3	–	1
Johnson	NA	NA	NA	NA	NA	NA	NA	NA	2	19.2	–	2	–	Z
Kenton	161	39.8	6 810	233.4	4 874	133.1	860.5	1 482.8	8	6.0	Z	8	–	1
Knott	NA	NA	NA	NA	NA	NA	NA	NA	1	69.1	–	Z	–	Z
Knox	17	35.3	877	20.6	725	16.7	67.9	160.6	1	49.5	Z	Z	–	Z
Larue	12	33.3	641	10.1	548	7.3	11.4	25.3	1	12.8	Z	Z	–	1
Laurel	44	40.9	2 595	57.4	1 849	35.0	130.6	319.1	10	1.3	Z	9	–	1
Lawrence	NA	NA	NA	NA	NA	NA	NA	NA	16	2.4	Z	1	8	7
Lee	NA	NA	NA	NA	NA	NA	NA	NA	1	10.0	–	1	–	Z
Leslie	NA	NA	NA	NA	NA	NA	NA	NA	3	12.7	–	1	–	Z
Letcher	NA	NA	NA	NA	NA	NA	NA	NA	2	55.0	–	1	–	Z
Lewis	15	46.7	804	15.7	773	14.8	67.0	89.9	1	72.5	Z	1	–	1
Lincoln	18	33.3	737	18.9	504	8.4	20.2	54.7	2	15.1	Z	1	–	1
Livingston	NA	NA	NA	NA	NA	NA	NA	NA	24	11.8	Z	1	22	1
Logan	41	48.8	4 650	126.0	3 966	92.1	394.5	781.7	5	2.4	Z	2	1	1
Lyon	NA	NA	NA	NA	NA	NA	NA	NA	2	21.2	Z	2	–	Z
McCracken	58	48.3	4 081	155.2	2 559	81.0	543.2	978.9	1 006	.1	Z	8	16	1
McCreary	16	37.5	(4)	D	D	D	D	D	1	4.4	–	1	–	Z
McLean	NA	NA	NA	NA	NA	NA	NA	NA	1	14.5	–	1	–	Z
Madison	68	52.9	5 460	160.3	3 916	106.1	543.5	1 576.1	12	1.7	Z	11	–	2
Magoffin	NA	NA	NA	NA	NA	NA	NA	NA	1	40.4	–	1	–	Z
Marion	22	63.6	1 554	34.4	1 327	24.9	87.2	175.1	3	1.7	Z	2	Z	1
Marshall	35	51.4	2 881	141.0	2 022	93.1	747.1	1 715.5	22	20.2	Z	3	18	1
Martin	NA	NA	NA	NA	NA	NA	NA	NA	6	8.1	–	3	Z	Z
Mason	19	73.7	3 167	85.6	2 478	55.9	200.4	545.5	45	87.2	Z	3	3	8
Meade	NA	NA	NA	NA	NA	NA	NA	NA	25	45.2	Z	2	22	2
Menifee	NA	NA	NA	NA	NA	NA	NA	NA	Z	57.1	Z	–	–	Z
Mercer	16	50.0	3 053	94.9	2 357	62.5	272.4	888.7	20	.4	Z	2	–	14
Metcalfe	13	53.8	1 829	37.0	1 695	31.8	107.9	231.4	1	26.4	Z	–	–	1
Monroe	32	43.8	1 966	35.8	1 696	28.1	80.5	160.9	2	7.7	Z	1	–	1
Montgomery	32	53.1	2 124	45.4	1 770	31.4	99.5	281.4	2	2.8	Z	2	–	1
Morgan	NA	NA	NA	NA	NA	NA	NA	NA	1	31.2	Z	1	–	Z
Muhlenberg	36	36.1	1 399	26.8	1 245	20.4	78.5	130.1	488	.1	Z	3	41	41
Nelson	56	28.6	3 616	99.0	2 716	70.2	528.6	960.2	8	3.3	Z	4	3	2
Nicholas	5	40.0	(4)	D	D	D	D	D	2	1.6	Z	2	–	Z
Ohio	27	37.0	2 010	37.4	1 755	29.9	107.3	177.1	8	1.9	Z	2	–	5
Oldham	41	24.4	1 004	37.5	779	24.6	101.4	252.5	5	86.8	Z	4	–	1
Owen	NA	NA	NA	NA	NA	NA	NA	NA	2	3.9	Z	1	–	1
Owsley	NA	NA	NA	NA	NA	NA	NA	NA	Z	16.7	–	Z	–	Z
Pendleton	12	58.3	(4)	D	D	D	D	D	2	5.2	–	1	–	1
Perry	9	44.4	614	16.5	500	12.4	43.3	91.4	6	8.4	–	3	–	1
Pike	26	11.5	587	10.7	515	8.8	27.9	74.3	8	29.0	–	4	–	1
Powell	16	43.8	1 185	19.2	1 060	15.4	138.2	175.3	Z	7.7	Z	Z	–	1
Pulaski	84	31.0	4 564	107.1	3 696	76.6	322.6	672.1	390	Z	Z	6	Z	8
Robertson	NA	NA	NA	NA	NA	NA	NA	NA	Z	31.8	Z	2	–	Z
Rockcastle	11	18.2	(4)	D	D	D	D	D	1	2.7	Z	1	–	Z
Rowan	13	53.8	647	10.5	555	7.6	86.2	111.6	3	1.4	–	3	–	Z
Russell	24	25.0	2 098	40.5	1 971	36.5	220.3	348.9	3	16.1	Z	2	–	1
Scott	45	46.7	(5)	D	D	D	D	D	3	16.0	1	2	Z	1
Shelby	42	61.9	4 095	126.2	3 180	87.9	392.3	942.2	5	2.8	Z	3	Z	2
Simpson	34	38.2	3 390	107.2	2 954	88.4	235.7	549.4	2	2.9	Z	2	–	2
Spencer	NA	NA	NA	NA	NA	NA	NA	NA	1	6.9	Z	1	–	1
Taylor	38	28.9	4 088	96.6	3 602	80.4	293.3	599.8	6	1.8	Z	5	–	1
Todd	19	36.8	1 299	25.7	1 171	21.4	51.8	147.3	2	26.7	Z	1	–	1
Trigg	19	36.8	1 083	26.5	931	20.5	73.1	158.0	2	1.8	Z	2	–	Z
Trimble	NA	NA	NA	NA	NA	NA	NA	NA	1	72.1	Z	2	–	Z
Union	18	38.9	1 214	29.3	934	20.8	102.6	167.0	7	1.0	–	2	–	1
Warren	104	41.3	(5)	D	D	D	D	D	17	1.5	Z	14	–	2
Washington	13	61.5	1 049	25.1	804	13.9	56.4	179.6	2	7.6	Z	1	–	1
Wayne	33	39.4	1 877	33.4	1 666	27.4	78.2	190.0	2	15.4	Z	1	–	1
Webster	19	42.1	798	16.4	671	11.6	48.0	82.5	152	.5	Z	2	–	48
Whitley	33	33.3	1 927	43.5	1 331	24.4	106.0	201.1	2	4.0	Z	1	–	Z
Wolfe	NA	NA	NA	NA	NA	NA	NA	NA	1	33.3	Z	1	–	Z
Woodford	22	40.9	(6)	D	D	D	D	D	17	.6	Z	3	–	1

[1] Average number of production workers plus the number of other (nonproduction) employees for the pay period including March 12.   [2] Average number of production workers for the pay periods including the 12th of March, May, August, and November.   [3] In millions of gallons per day.   [4] 500 to 999 employees.   [5] 5,000 to 9,999 employees.   [6] 2,500 to 4,999 employees.

Sources: Manufacturing—U.S. Census Bureau, 1997 Economic Census – Manufacturing, generated by Statistical Compendia Branch, using American Factfinder at <http://www.census.gov/>, (June 2000) [related Internet site <http://www.census.gov/epcd/www/97EC31.HTM>].   Water Use—U.S. Geological Survey, "Water Use in the United States," individual state/county and US by state files from <http://water.usgs.gov/watuse/spread95.html>, (accessed: September 1999).

[Includes U.S., states, and 3,142 counties/county equivalents defined as of January 1, 1992. For changes to these areas since January 1, 1992, see appendix B. Geographic Information]

County	Manufacturing (NAICS 31-33), 1997 — Establishments Total	Percent with 20 or more employees	All employees Number[1]	Annual payroll (mil. dol.)	Production workers Number[2]	Wages (mil. dol.)	Value added by manufacture (mil. dol.)	Value of shipments (mil. dol.)	Water use per day,[3] 1995 — Withdrawals Total (mil. gal.)	Percent ground water	By selected major use (mil. gal.) Irrigation	Public supply	Industrial	Consumptive use (mil. gal.)
LOUISIANA	3 545	33.0	165 777	6 054.5	123 566	3 967.7	29 066.9	80 424.0	9 848	13.7	769	638	2 582	1 925
Acadia	47	36.2	2 247	38.5	1 940	27.7	91.7	283.9	110	91.9	93	5	Z	79
Allen	11	54.5	658	16.7	577	13.7	29.3	97.5	24	93.0	20	3	Z	17
Ascension	86	34.9	5 577	300.0	3 528	173.5	4 095.6	7 012.9	227	6.1	–	4	218	29
Assumption	NA	NA	NA	NA	NA	NA	NA	NA	29	37.2	–	3	24	16
Avoyelles	20	40.0	622	11.4	560	9.4	45.7	92.8	17	85.2	10	4	Z	16
Beauregard	26	26.9	1 413	63.0	1 036	43.0	250.7	627.1	30	99.5	4	4	21	11
Bienville	14	57.1	1 052	33.0	698	25.0	67.3	226.3	2	96.1	–	1	Z	2
Bossier	76	36.8	2 578	65.4	2 087	45.6	140.3	376.5	12	28.5	Z	10	Z	11
Caddo	216	36.6	11 997	445.7	9 108	315.1	1 606.9	4 515.6	87	4.3	1	33	Z	28
Calcasieu	134	37.3	11 274	542.4	8 113	344.4	3 018.4	10 153.5	312	36.6	24	22	239	86
Caldwell	NA	NA	NA	NA	NA	NA	NA	NA	3	56.5	2	1	–	3
Cameron	NA	NA	NA	NA	NA	NA	NA	NA	28	10.5	17	2	1	26
Catahoula	NA	NA	NA	NA	NA	NA	NA	NA	17	80.2	9	1	–	15
Claiborne	10	50.0	507	11.5	434	9.6	34.8	109.5	3	100.0	–	2	Z	2
Concordia	NA	NA	NA	NA	NA	NA	NA	NA	32	94.5	21	3	–	24
De Soto	16	31.3	1 166	43.9	952	33.0	285.0	493.3	14	13.2	Z	3	9	5
East Baton Rouge	354	27.7	12 159	570.1	7 833	299.8	2 707.7	9 831.6	152	86.9	Z	55	89	98
East Carroll	NA	NA	NA	NA	NA	NA	NA	NA	38	89.2	36	1	–	27
East Feliciana	NA	NA	NA	NA	NA	NA	NA	NA	3	94.6	Z	2	–	3
Evangeline	18	22.2	944	36.0	736	25.4	75.4	191.0	188	36.4	49	4	2	63
Franklin	13	38.5	506	6.9	374	3.6	11.5	36.1	27	81.7	8	3	1	24
Grant	NA	NA	NA	NA	NA	NA	NA	NA	4	49.3	–	2	2	4
Iberia	100	36.0	4 962	141.8	4 234	104.3	575.5	911.0	31	42.8	2	7	7	21
Iberville	39	56.4	4 360	270.0	2 822	158.0	891.1	4 176.1	1 218	1.9	–	4	510	31
Jackson	5	40.0	(4)	D	D	D	D	D	21	99.3	–	2	19	2
Jefferson	444	26.4	16 356	508.6	11 560	335.9	1 346.4	2 893.2	1 140	.8	Z	79	21	84
Jefferson Davis	21	23.8	598	13.9	516	10.2	46.9	110.2	152	71.0	142	3	–	116
Lafayette	215	26.0	5 419	150.1	3 698	83.5	437.1	868.5	33	96.0	8	19	Z	22
Lafourche	66	30.3	2 464	72.9	1 927	53.6	147.3	424.2	30	5.2	–	11	7	22
La Salle	8	50.0	(4)	D	D	D	D	D	2	75.1	Z	1	Z	2
Lincoln	35	40.0	1 788	53.0	1 465	38.8	185.2	346.0	8	95.4	Z	7	1	5
Livingston	54	25.9	1 342	39.6	1 002	28.2	106.0	227.4	16	99.9	Z	7	Z	15
Madison	NA	NA	NA	NA	NA	NA	NA	NA	19	95.9	16	2	–	13
Morehouse	14	21.4	(5)	D	D	D	D	D	73	45.4	34	4	34	30
Natchitoches	18	27.8	1 664	42.5	1 461	33.6	205.8	537.9	24	18.7	3	6	9	12
Orleans	261	29.5	10 453	362.2	7 022	226.5	1 064.6	2 305.0	636	2.0	Z	125	2	65
Ouachita	152	40.8	8 235	287.6	6 176	198.2	861.2	1 983.4	112	19.0	2	22	33	75
Plaquemines	44	43.2	2 231	102.1	1 544	58.7	451.2	2 779.2	116	Z	–	7	108	5
Pointe Coupee	11	45.5	539	12.9	468	9.9	76.6	146.1	290	3.6	1	3	4	154
Rapides	73	32.9	3 179	103.0	2 201	59.9	722.2	1 165.9	498	6.6	9	31	Z	28
Red River	NA	NA	NA	NA	NA	NA	NA	NA	2	89.5	Z	1	–	1
Richland	14	28.6	600	16.6	475	11.6	38.4	132.1	25	81.6	21	2	–	18
Sabine	19	36.8	1 121	28.8	1 017	25.3	65.7	253.1	4	62.8	–	2	Z	3
St. Bernard	54	18.5	1 769	83.1	1 269	54.6	325.2	2 603.6	306	Z	–	11	295	44
St. Charles	37	40.5	5 068	302.2	3 383	193.3	3 734.4	8 501.5	1 953	.3	–	9	460	17
St. Helena	NA	NA	NA	NA	NA	NA	NA	NA	6	99.7	–	Z	5	2
St. James	26	73.1	2 858	149.5	1 919	92.1	745.6	3 842.3	247	23.5	–	3	236	14
St. John the Baptist	29	44.8	2 304	104.2	1 604	66.9	630.7	3 057.5	731	1.3	–	5	90	46
St. Landry	57	31.6	1 919	50.8	1 537	36.7	154.5	904.7	48	85.1	14	10	4	38
St. Martin	44	29.5	3 501	69.7	3 243	62.3	807.2	1 259.8	45	80.5	5	5	Z	42
St. Mary	67	49.3	5 098	163.6	4 201	120.0	500.4	944.4	219	.6	–	11	60	16
St. Tammany	127	26.8	2 699	61.3	2 173	41.5	154.1	373.7	24	96.7	1	15	Z	20
Tangipahoa	74	37.8	2 933	59.5	2 488	42.5	184.9	420.4	18	97.1	Z	9	1	16
Tensas	NA	NA	NA	NA	NA	NA	NA	NA	12	79.2	10	1	–	9
Terrebonne	119	26.9	3 990	129.3	3 217	92.0	289.6	539.5	33	.3	–	13	2	28
Union	NA	NA	NA	NA	NA	NA	NA	NA	5	82.9	–	3	Z	3
Vermilion	27	29.6	1 348	28.6	1 208	23.7	86.5	203.9	262	18.1	182	4	3	248
Vernon	NA	NA	NA	NA	NA	NA	NA	NA	9	98.4	–	3	–	8
Washington	28	42.9	1 536	54.7	1 266	38.8	171.2	466.3	32	62.3	–	6	24	19
Webster	45	40.0	2 336	67.2	1 926	47.0	201.7	504.6	8	84.2	–	5	2	5
West Baton Rouge	39	56.4	2 452	84.0	1 942	63.5	432.8	1 376.7	10	94.6	–	4	4	6
West Carroll	NA	NA	NA	NA	NA	NA	NA	NA	25	74.4	23	2	Z	13
West Feliciana	6	16.7	(4)	D	D	D	D	D	47	10.6	–	2	30	17
Winn	24	45.8	1 252	37.8	1 083	28.2	74.3	300.0	3	92.6	–	2	1	2

[1] Average number of production workers plus the number of other (nonproduction) employees for the pay period including March 12. [2] Average number of production workers for the pay periods including the 12th of March, May, August, and November. [3] In millions of gallons per day. [4] 500 to 999 employees. [5] 1,000 to 2,499 employees.

Sources: Manufacturing—U.S. Census Bureau, 1997 Economic Census – Manufacturing, generated by Statistical Compendia Branch, using American Factfinder at <http://www.census.gov/>, (June 2000) [related Internet site <http://www.census.gov/epcd/www/97EC31.HTM>]. Water Use—U.S. Geological Survey, "Water Use in the United States," individual state/county and US by state files from <http://water.usgs.gov/watuse/spread95.html>, (accessed: September 1999).

[Includes U.S., states, and 3,142 counties/county equivalents defined as of January 1, 1992. For changes to these areas since January 1, 1992, see appendix B. Geographic Information]

County	Maunfacturing (NAICS 31-33), 1997								Water use per day,[3] 1995					
	Establishments		All employees		Production workers		Value added by manu-facture (mil. dol.)	Value of ship-ments (mil. dol.)	Withdrawals					
	Total	Percent with 20 or more employ-ees	Number[1]	Annual payroll (mil. dol.)	Number[2]	Wages (mil. dol.)			Total (mil. gal.)	Percent ground water	By selected major use– (mil. gal.)			Consump-tive use (mil. gal.)
											Irrigation	Public supply	Industrial	
MAINE	1 812	28.3	82 288	2 591.1	62 647	1 746.0	6 530.6	14 097.6	326	24.6	27	100	11	50
Androscoggin	183	36.6	8 233	226.6	5 966	145.8	705.6	1 218.6	14	29.2	1	10	Z	3
Aroostook	89	32.6	3 906	125.4	3 260	98.3	355.5	895.0	25	31.2	14	6	1	14
Cumberland	382	24.6	14 304	477.2	10 291	289.8	1 174.2	2 232.7	87	14.0	2	25	Z	7
Franklin	53	39.6	3 457	110.3	2 920	86.2	353.8	867.8	5	51.7	Z	2	1	1
Hancock	94	16.0	2 397	103.8	1 944	75.9	268.8	551.0	61	5.1	Z	2	1	1
Kennebec	129	27.1	5 488	165.8	4 338	112.1	345.7	753.4	30	28.4	1	11	1	3
Knox	92	22.8	1 602	44.3	1 127	24.2	146.2	267.7	5	32.8	Z	3	Z	1
Lincoln	68	11.8	(4)	D	D	D	D	D	3	67.4	Z	1	Z	1
Oxford	84	35.7	4 038	118.7	3 118	83.0	383.0	758.5	10	49.2	2	3	1	4
Penobscot	155	32.3	8 897	285.9	6 871	203.7	870.9	1 658.6	21	42.8	2	12	2	5
Piscataquis	26	38.5	1 905	36.1	1 192	26.3	71.6	114.7	3	46.7	Z	1	Z	1
Sagadahoc	29	24.1	(5)	D	D	D	D	D	5	40.3	Z	3	Z	1
Somerset	76	26.3	4 441	143.7	3 543	99.0	522.6	1 239.9	8	55.3	Z	3	1	2
Waldo	53	22.6	1 180	24.8	1 001	17.3	57.9	117.8	4	78.3	Z	1	Z	1
Washington	41	39.0	1 676	52.6	1 284	38.8	102.8	364.8	5	55.6	2	1	Z	2
York	258	30.2	11 649	360.2	8 594	220.3	632.3	2 093.5	38	26.0	2	15	Z	5
MARYLAND	3 996	30.4	163 992	5 840.5	109 564	3 249.2	18 721.6	36 505.9	7 729	3.2	62	834	326	229
Allegany	67	31.3	4 169	139.2	3 206	95.6	396.4	785.9	45	3.9	Z	1	43	8
Anne Arundel	339	19.5	14 878	618.4	8 189	284.8	1 641.7	2 703.8	735	6.5	1	32	2	7
Baltimore	575	30.4	31 065	1 235.1	20 081	712.4	3 918.7	6 883.3	906	.9	2	273	256	42
Calvert	NA	NA	NA	NA	NA	NA	NA	NA	3 228	.2	1	2	Z	17
Caroline	31	45.2	1 533	36.6	1 247	26.9	81.7	167.7	20	53.8	16	1	Z	17
Carroll	144	27.1	4 330	131.1	3 084	78.0	337.5	716.9	15	66.8	1	6	Z	3
Cecil	55	40.0	2 766	100.9	1 618	48.4	385.2	678.3	9	67.0	Z	4	Z	2
Charles	58	32.8	1 100	38.5	745	22.5	74.0	170.3	1 103	1.2	Z	7	Z	12
Dorchester	48	39.6	3 580	86.9	2 598	51.0	323.3	867.2	25	66.4	13	3	1	14
Frederick	162	36.4	7 795	268.5	5 451	152.2	832.1	1 509.1	39	36.0	Z	14	3	5
Garrett	49	28.6	1 135	22.8	868	16.7	46.5	103.5	9	35.6	Z	3	Z	1
Harford	152	28.3	5 301	178.8	4 067	115.4	672.0	1 274.6	18	59.1	Z	8	1	3
Howard	245	27.8	6 927	257.2	4 391	128.9	562.0	1 177.3	4	85.7	Z	–	Z	3
Kent	27	33.3	1 031	25.4	713	13.0	62.1	189.4	6	79.4	4	1	Z	4
Montgomery	527	19.7	15 190	680.5	7 196	230.1	1 861.8	3 111.9	729	.6	1	395	Z	14
Prince George's	372	32.5	11 179	408.5	7 185	211.8	1 010.4	2 008.1	620	1.0	1	48	Z	27
Queen Anne's	34	29.4	877	21.8	743	15.7	48.4	106.7	14	61.8	9	1	Z	10
St. Mary's	NA	NA	NA	NA	NA	NA	NA	NA	11	86.4	Z	3	Z	1
Somerset	NA	NA	NA	NA	NA	NA	NA	NA	7	87.4	2	2	Z	3
Talbot	54	27.8	3 035	69.1	2 445	47.4	431.9	836.1	7	92.3	2	2	1	2
Washington	147	37.4	9 173	294.2	7 154	217.9	940.9	1 924.5	60	16.7	1	13	2	4
Wicomico	95	42.1	5 690	158.1	4 300	103.1	461.2	1 041.6	20	94.2	6	6	2	9
Worcester	38	28.9	1 754	30.9	1 435	21.5	97.7	275.4	15	93.9	2	8	2	4
Independent City														
Baltimore city	688	39.7	30 216	1 006.2	21 898	636.2	4 452.9	9 822.2	86	5.6	Z	–	13	16
MASSACHUSETTS	9 554	34.7	417 135	16 379.0	257 050	7 734.8	44 337.8	77 876.6	5 511	6.4	82	725	85	186
Barnstable	226	10.2	2 561	82.4	1 540	35.5	229.5	349.4	422	7.4	8	28	Z	11
Berkshire	207	30.4	9 176	344.7	5 359	156.5	795.2	1 423.0	24	21.7	1	18	3	3
Bristol	915	39.7	49 363	1 654.2	35 735	910.6	3 890.6	7 651.4	1 482	4.7	4	60	8	12
Dukes	NA	NA	NA	NA	NA	NA	NA	NA	3	96.1	Z	2	Z	Z
Essex	1 200	34.9	57 660	2 362.4	36 217	1 185.6	7 537.5	13 728.1	600	1.7	1	102	10	12
Franklin	119	43.7	5 700	182.2	3 763	108.7	414.5	756.0	9	67.2	Z	4	1	3
Hampden	802	36.3	33 350	1 204.0	22 875	659.2	3 213.8	5 953.5	232	9.3	1	60	8	8
Hampshire	180	32.2	5 760	192.3	3 985	108.1	493.7	1 048.3	26	51.8	1	12	3	8
Middlesex	2 437	34.9	118 002	5 216.5	61 016	1 998.8	13 888.8	22 587.1	840	6.6	2	78	20	24
Nantucket	NA	NA	NA	NA	NA	NA	NA	NA	2	98.1	Z	1	Z	Z
Norfolk	863	36.7	36 648	1 515.2	22 383	747.2	3 662.6	6 528.4	57	76.8	1	40	12	12
Plymouth	613	29.0	16 063	534.4	10 774	289.8	1 246.5	2 210.8	1 014	5.1	61	36	3	73
Suffolk	624	30.8	21 366	745.4	14 111	391.6	2 606.9	4 317.9	495	Z	Z	–	4	5
Worcester	1 336	37.9	61 344	2 340.9	39 194	1 140.1	6 347.5	11 303.4	306	12.8	2	283	11	14

[1] Average number of production workers plus the number of other (nonproduction) employees for the pay period including March 12.   [2] Average number of production workers for the pay periods including the 12th of March, May, August, and November.   [3] In millions of gallons per day.   [4] 500 to 999 employees.   [5] 5,000 to 9,999 employees.

Sources: Manufacturing—U.S. Census Bureau, 1997 Economic Census – Manufacturing, generated by Statistical Compendia Branch, using American Factfinder at <http://www.census.gov/>, (June 2000) [related Internet site <http://www.census.gov/epcd/www/97EC31.HTM>].   Water Use—U.S. Geological Survey, "Water Use in the United States," individual state/county and US by state files from <http://water.usgs.gov/watuse/spread95.html>, (accessed: September 1999).

Table B–9. Counties — **Manufacturing and Water Use**-Con.

[Includes U.S., states, and 3,142 counties/county equivalents defined as of January 1, 1992. For changes to these areas since January 1, 1992, see appendix B. Geographic Information]

County	Manufacturing (NAICS 31-33), 1997								Water use per day,[3] 1995					
	Establishments		All employees		Production workers		Value added by manu- facture (mil. dol.)	Value of ship- ments (mil. dol.)	Withdrawals					Consump- tive use (mil. gal.)
	Total	Percent with 20 or more employ- ees	Number[1]	Annual payroll (mil. dol.)	Number[2]	Wages (mil. dol.)			Total (mil. gal.)	Percent ground water	By selected major use— (mil. gal.)			
											Irrigation	Public supply	Industrial	
MICHIGAN	16 045	35.9	833 429	34 418.9	630 390	23 486.0	93 809.5	214 900.7	12 064	7.1	227	1 300	1 854	668
Alcona	NA	NA	NA	NA	NA	NA	NA	NA	2	86.9	–	1	Z	Z
Alger	13	38.5	873	29.7	693	22.2	82.4	195.8	4	43.7	Z	1	2	Z
Allegan	203	41.4	15 984	585.9	11 317	321.1	1 742.8	3 108.9	51	33.3	9	6	28	13
Alpena	58	36.2	2 445	90.8	1 823	52.5	257.6	480.1	409	.4	Z	3	305	25
Antrim	56	25.0	1 323	38.7	1 025	26.2	90.0	164.9	8	73.3	5	2	Z	5
Arenac	37	32.4	732	18.9	571	11.5	47.8	91.8	53	2.4	2	50	Z	2
Baraga	26	30.8	715	21.6	566	16.2	49.5	115.2	2	22.6	–	1	1	Z
Barry	71	25.4	3 145	102.1	2 351	67.2	274.9	525.2	9	74.9	1	3	2	2
Bay	152	34.2	7 459	347.0	5 607	225.4	1 067.0	1 928.6	628	.6	4	19	11	9
Benzie	23	34.8	657	12.3	537	9.1	35.0	70.1	4	71.7	1	1	1	I
Berrien	397	40.3	16 996	539.1	12 678	335.9	1 266.2	2 394.2	2 196	.7	5	21	21	46
Branch	90	42.2	3 572	102.4	2 749	68.6	269.6	516.5	21	61.2	12	4	3	12
Calhoun	222	40.5	16 973	613.8	13 210	437.7	2 376.3	4 514.8	61	93.5	2	14	37	9
Cass	87	32.2	3 384	95.9	2 678	62.9	204.4	570.8	18	50.6	7	3	3	8
Charlevoix	69	40.6	3 624	116.9	2 743	75.5	392.6	724.1	117	2.7	Z	3	12	2
Cheboygan	37	24.3	711	17.9	587	12.4	48.7	76.6	4	67.2	Z	1	1	1
Chippewa	31	41.9	818	15.0	694	11.0	32.9	63.2	10	20.3	–	3	5	1
Clare	28	42.9	924	23.9	769	16.7	53.0	120.9	4	82.3	Z	2	1	1
Clinton	62	25.8	2 586	100.3	2 019	68.4	202.9	450.3	12	68.4	2	4	2	4
Crawford	17	47.1	503	15.8	396	10.1	32.8	104.3	3	92.6	–	1	1	1
Delta	59	33.9	2 834	124.3	2 099	80.3	355.4	702.4	76	3.7	Z	3	48	4
Dickinson	50	38.0	2 478	100.6	1 912	70.9	338.1	655.3	11	37.8	Z	3	7	1
Eaton	94	37.2	(4)	D	D	D	D	D	18	80.5	1	10	2	3
Emmet	57	22.8	1 377	39.1	973	22.0	81.6	168.2	6	80.8	Z	3	1	1
Genesee	355	32.4	34 414	1 744.6	28 473	1 388.8	3 592.6	11 240.3	55	47.3	1	12	33	10
Gladwin	46	34.8	1 406	42.1	1 123	30.0	113.9	206.8	3	77.2	1	1	1	1
Gogebic	27	37.0	709	14.8	617	11.7	28.0	62.5	4	75.6	–	3	1	Z
Grand Traverse	190	31.1	5 867	177.1	4 542	118.0	487.6	875.9	18	45.5	2	4	5	3
Gratiot	51	37.3	2 282	77.0	1 827	40.5	141.9	265.7	9	64.9	1	4	2	2
Hillsdale	104	44.2	6 510	176.1	5 276	128.1	493.5	1 134.5	62	14.4	1	3	53	6
Houghton	43	20.9	698	16.3	540	10.4	36.6	72.1	6	85.4	Z	5	1	1
Huron	67	50.7	4 216	126.9	3 417	94.8	326.2	612.8	53	8.1	2	3	3	4
Ingham	272	34.2	(5)	D	D	D	D	D	163	41.5	1	62	3	10
Ionia	80	42.5	4 308	138.0	3 333	89.5	375.4	852.8	13	77.6	2	0	2	3
Iosco	34	32.4	1 299	31.5	962	21.8	83.1	164.7	6	64.5	Z	4	Z	1
Iron	NA	NA	NA	NA	NA	NA	NA	NA	5	88.2	Z	4	Z	Z
Isabella	58	22.4	2 221	61.2	1 650	38.4	165.2	402.5	10	85.7	1	6	1	2
Jackson	351	39.9	12 248	422.0	8 735	246.1	1 082.9	2 271.8	37	66.6	4	17	10	7
Kalamazoo	399	38.3	22 007	820.9	15 620	520.9	1 744.2	4 108.6	112	69.9	11	30	63	19
Kalkaska	19	47.4	1 187	34.5	946	32.6	83.3	178.2	4	59.4	2	1	1	2
Kent	1 205	42.2	80 020	3 189.9	57 080	1 912.2	8 338.4	14 765.5	184	17.7	6	80	84	18
Keweenaw	NA	NA	NA	NA	NA	NA	NA	NA	Z	74.1	–	Z	Z	Z
Lake	NA	NA	NA	NA	NA	NA	NA	NA	1	87.9	–	Z	Z	Z
Lapeer	139	31.7	6 118	155.6	4 380	96.2	392.2	837.2	14	57.8	1	2	5	3
Leelanau	NA	NA	NA	NA	NA	NA	NA	NA	7	45.4	4	1	Z	5
Lenawee	163	39.9	8 940	359.3	6 671	229.3	774.4	1 736.1	24	44.8	1	9	11	3
Livingston	264	39.8	10 560	374.1	7 592	218.5	1 075.2	2 782.8	25	53.7	1	5	9	4
Luce	NA	NA	NA	NA	NA	NA	NA	NA	1	99.1	Z	1	Z	Z
Mackinac	NA	NA	NA	NA	NA	NA	NA	NA	15	4.9	Z	1	11	1
Macomb	2 116	35.2	93 551	4 321.9	73 377	3 128.1	9 148.9	23 988.0	80	13.4	2	18	52	18
Manistee	31	38.7	1 300	48.4	993	35.1	140.6	244.6	37	21.4	2	2	31	6
Marquette	39	20.5	730	16.0	484	10.2	39.0	81.0	257	5.1	–	13	Z	2
Mason	40	45.0	2 682	84.2	2 092	55.5	289.4	435.8	28	74.7	2	1	21	5
Mecosta	41	31.7	1 837	50.7	1 544	33.6	178.9	363.2	16	30.1	10	3	1	10
Menominee	56	48.2	2 901	78.0	2 319	56.4	233.1	425.2	8	21.7	Z	1	5	1
Midland	71	16.9	5 613	285.4	3 247	142.7	783.1	1 690.8	89	4.4	1	Z	85	5
Missaukee	23	30.4	548	17.5	436	11.7	37.7	73.0	5	65.1	2	1	Z	2
Monroe	138	40.6	9 278	425.6	7 346	316.9	1 310.3	2 560.1	1 764	.4	2	9	17	38
Montcalm	77	31.2	5 456	172.0	4 561	131.0	464.3	923.8	27	81.9	17	4	2	17
Montmorency	NA	NA	NA	NA	NA	NA	NA	NA	3	41.3	Z	Z	1	Z
Muskegon	335	41.2	16 398	562.1	11 708	355.4	1 521.9	2 903.3	322	3.6	14	25	30	20
Newaygo	46	23.9	1 727	51.7	1 325	34.6	277.7	484.7	17	45.6	9	2	2	10
Oakland	2 366	33.8	90 481	3 747.5	64 198	2 271.6	12 724.1	27 172.7	111	38.6	1	21	65	30

[1] Average number of production workers plus the number of other (nonproduction) employees for the pay period including March 12. [2] Average number of production workers for the pay periods including the 12th of March, May, August, and November. [3] In millions of gallons per day. [4] 2,500 to 4,999 employees. [5] 10,000 to 24,999 employees.

Sources: Manufacturing—U.S. Census Bureau, 1997 Economic Census – Manufacturing, generated by Statistical Compendia Branch, using American Factfinder at <http://www.census.gov/>, (June 2000) [related Internet site <http://www.census.gov/epcd/www/97EC31.HTM>]. Water Use—U.S. Geological Survey, "Water Use in the United States," individual state/county and US by state files from <http://water.usgs.gov/watuse/spread95.html>, (accessed: September 1999).

Table B–9. Counties — Manufacturing and Water Use–Con.

[Includes U.S., states, and 3,142 counties/county equivalents defined as of January 1, 1992. For changes to these areas since January 1, 1992, see appendix B. Geographic Information]

County	Manufacturing (NAICS 31-33), 1997								Water use per day,[3] 1995					
	Establishments		All employees		Production workers		Value added by manufacture (mil. dol.)	Value of shipments (mil. dol.)	Withdrawals					Consumptive use (mil. gal.)
	Total	Percent with 20 or more employees	Number[1]	Annual payroll (mil. dol.)	Number[2]	Wages (mil. dol.)			Total (mil. gal.)	Percent ground water	By selected major use– (mil. gal.)			
											Irrigation	Public supply	Industrial	
MICHIGAN—Con.														
Oceana	51	23.5	1 385	31.2	1 141	23.1	103.9	214.5	8	61.8	3	2	2	3
Ogemaw	29	34.5	872	23.3	660	15.9	52.6	85.9	4	65.1	Z	1	1	1
Ontonagon	NA	NA	NA	NA	NA	NA	NA	NA	31	10.8	–	1	15	2
Osceola	36	36.1	3 582	99.2	3 051	73.3	350.3	661.3	7	56.4	Z	1	3	1
Oscoda	NA	NA	NA	NA	NA	NA	NA	NA	1	47.9	–	Z	1	Z
Otsego	39	38.5	1 870	53.8	1 545	34.6	125.7	255.5	4	54.6	–	1	1	Z
Ottawa	591	36.7	38 244	1 310.8	27 338	797.7	3 645.7	7 688.1	640	3.9	9	14	32	18
Presque Isle	NA	NA	NA	NA	NA	NA	NA	NA	6	34.4	Z	1	Z	1
Roscommon	NA	NA	NA	NA	NA	NA	NA	NA	4	69.8	–	1	Z	1
Saginaw	239	34.7	20 681	1 148.6	16 429	901.9	2 456.5	5 172.2	32	20.4	1	1	26	7
St. Clair	294	38.4	14 162	431.5	10 456	276.4	1 110.8	2 667.6	1 563	1.0	Z	19	23	18
St. Joseph	163	48.5	10 651	371.4	8 359	263.4	1 390.5	2 402.7	58	47.8	38	6	12	37
Sanilac	88	45.5	5 244	123.6	4 166	82.3	359.3	726.3	17	48.2	4	4	4	8
Schoolcraft	NA	NA	NA	NA	NA	NA	NA	NA	12	16.9	–	1	8	1
Shiawassee	86	43.0	4 139	99.6	3 037	63.0	207.5	453.8	12	61.0	1	4	4	2
Tuscola	65	30.8	2 818	96.9	2 017	61.4	197.0	486.4	13	68.4	4	4	1	5
Van Buren	127	34.6	4 879	152.1	3 772	100.1	563.2	1 007.8	102	14.5	10	6	6	32
Washtenaw	412	36.4	29 254	1 395.5	23 147	1 036.9	3 167.6	7 350.2	55	33.2	3	23	20	8
Wayne	2 390	33.1	133 703	6 514.3	104 295	4 787.5	21 498.0	54 375.0	2 165	.8	Z	677	586	99
Wexford	57	42.1	4 331	126.7	3 179	72.4	353.9	719.1	9	96.0	Z	3	4	1
MINNESOTA	8 091	33.7	382 530	13 126.1	260 158	7 250.1	36 629.9	76 244.9	3 392	21.0	157	485	140	417
Aitkin	NA	NA	NA	NA	NA	NA	NA	NA	5	26.2	4	Z	–	4
Anoka	614	30.0	24 754	908.7	16 979	525.3	2 186.2	3 860.7	142	21.8	1	131	Z	10
Becker	42	26.2	1 320	35.7	907	22.5	96.1	193.0	5	99.4	2	1	–	3
Beltrami	43	23.3	1 112	32.0	882	23.6	67.8	175.9	8	50.5	4	2	Z	5
Benton	53	47.2	2 797	71.4	1 921	38.7	184.0	300.2	18	48.7	5	2	9	8
Big Stone	NA	NA	NA	NA	NA	NA	NA	NA	1	89.0	Z	Z	Z	1
Blue Earth	78	46.2	4 144	126.7	2 823	75.8	350.9	1 160.8	32	36.3	Z	3	4	3
Brown	41	43.9	4 292	113.0	3 419	79.6	849.9	1 580.8	4	94.7	1	1	Z	3
Carlton	30	16.7	2 131	89.8	1 764	71.1	260.7	425.0	22	63.9	Z	13	8	3
Carver	143	48.3	10 470	391.7	6 484	193.6	972.7	1 920.0	8	99.4	Z	5	1	3
Cass	NA	NA	NA	NA	NA	NA	NA	NA	4	97.7	1	Z	Z	3
Chippewa	24	37.5	1 498	34.5	1 164	22.0	65.7	116.3	9	17.9	Z	1	–	1
Chisago	101	32.7	2 462	70.3	1 916	42.9	138.2	282.1	4	93.5	Z	1	–	2
Clay	38	28.9	1 225	35.7	999	27.5	57.5	229.4	8	86.0	1	5	Z	2
Clearwater	NA	NA	NA	NA	NA	NA	NA	NA	13	8.1	12	Z	Z	11
Cook	NA	NA	NA	NA	NA	NA	NA	NA	126	.2	Z	Z	–	4
Cottonwood	16	25.0	930	20.5	762	15.1	176.6	486.9	3	93.7	Z	1	Z	1
Crow Wing	95	29.5	2 957	91.2	2 184	63.6	248.2	458.3	9	65.6	1	2	3	4
Dakota	439	37.8	17 957	636.3	11 717	345.9	2 282.5	5 922.4	224	22.9	12	28	8	22
Dodge	29	34.5	1 322	37.5	1 034	27.7	119.1	398.6	2	98.5	Z	1	–	1
Douglas	72	30.6	2 806	76.0	2 199	51.1	276.2	448.4	6	91.8	1	2	Z	3
Faribault	28	64.3	1 578	36.5	1 222	24.1	87.8	260.6	3	100.0	Z	1	1	1
Fillmore	42	28.6	1 122	27.9	917	18.7	124.2	224.8	15	22.6	Z	1	Z	2
Freeborn	66	36.4	3 062	86.7	2 380	61.2	221.1	564.5	7	99.8	Z	4	1	2
Goodhue	81	44.4	5 522	166.6	4 094	105.5	403.8	972.8	600	1.4	1	3	2	25
Grant	NA	NA	NA	NA	NA	NA	NA	NA	2	100.0	1	2	–	1
Hennepin	2 404	34.7	106 772	4 090.1	65 257	1 954.5	9 754.7	17 291.6	253	36.2	2	76	2	20
Houston	NA	NA	NA	NA	NA	NA	NA	NA	3	100.0	Z	1	–	2
Hubbard	32	31.3	940	19.6	770	13.2	73.7	166.1	7	99.7	4	Z	1	5
Isanti	59	28.8	1 330	35.6	953	22.2	81.3	153.5	3	100.0	Z	1	Z	2
Itasca	58	22.4	2 432	92.0	1 958	70.4	249.3	534.3	175	2.4	Z	2	17	13
Jackson	18	22.2	(4)	D	D	D	D	D	2	98.3	Z	Z	–	1
Kanabec	17	29.4	803	19.4	637	7.7	49.9	96.7	2	99.4	Z	Z	–	1
Kandiyohi	66	33.3	3 265	84.0	2 666	60.0	243.7	605.5	9	83.5	2	4	Z	4
Kittson	NA	NA	NA	NA	NA	NA	NA	NA	1	82.4	Z	Z	Z	Z
Koochiching	11	36.4	(5)	D	D	D	D	D	43	1.4	Z	1	41	6
Lac qui Parle	NA	NA	NA	NA	NA	NA	NA	NA	4	97.2	1	Z	2	2
Lake	12	41.7	507	18.6	396	12.4	45.4	84.4	133	.3	–	1	–	1
Lake of the Woods	NA	NA	NA	NA	NA	NA	NA	NA	1	41.1	1	Z	–	1
Le Sueur	51	39.2	2 751	79.5	2 229	53.7	382.7	728.9	4	100.0	Z	1	Z	2
Lincoln	NA	NA	NA	NA	NA	NA	NA	NA	1	99.2	Z	Z	–	1
Lyon	28	39.3	1 833	40.5	1 487	31.5	133.3	456.0	6	97.0	Z	4	Z	2
McLeod	67	46.3	9 080	291.0	7 268	206.5	1 005.4	1 670.5	7	94.6	Z	3	3	2
Mahnomen	NA	NA	NA	NA	NA	NA	NA	NA	1	100.0	–	Z	Z	Z
Marshall	NA	NA	NA	NA	NA	NA	NA	NA	1	96.0	Z	Z	–	1
Martin	44	29.5	2 111	61.6	1 422	33.6	167.9	294.1	45	7.8	Z	2	Z	3
Meeker	58	44.8	1 740	41.1	1 286	23.8	119.7	356.8	4	97.2	1	1	Z	3

[1] Average number of production workers plus the number of other (nonproduction) employees for the pay period including March 12.   [2] Average number of production workers for the pay periods including the 12th of March, May, August, and November.   [3] In millions of gallons per day.   [4] 500 to 999 employees.   [5] 1,000 to 2,499 employees.

Sources: Manufacturing—U.S. Census Bureau, 1997 Economic Census – Manufacturing, generated by Statistical Compendia Branch, using American Factfinder at <http://www.census.gov/>, (June 2000) [related Internet site <http://www.census.gov/epcd/www/97EC31.HTM>].   Water Use—U.S. Geological Survey, "Water Use in the United States," individual state/county and US by state files from <http://water.usgs.gov/watuse/spread95.html>, (accessed: September 1999).

[Includes U.S., states, and 3,142 counties/county equivalents defined as of January 1, 1992. For changes to these areas since January 1, 1992, see appendix B. Geographic Information]

County	Manufacturing (NAICS 31-33), 1997								Water use per day,[3] 1995					
	Establishments		All employees		Production workers		Value added by manu-facture (mil. dol.)	Value of ship-ments (mil. dol.)	Withdrawals					Consump-tive use (mil. gal.)
	Total	Percent with 20 or more employ-ees	Number[1]	Annual payroll (mil. dol.)	Number[2]	Wages (mil. dol.)			Total (mil. gal.)	Percent ground water	By selected major use– (mil. gal.)			
											Irrigation	Public supply	Industrial	
MINNESOTA—Con.														
Mille Lacs	38	21.1	1 029	24.4	883	18.4	61.2	158.0	3	91.4	Z	1	Z	2
Morrison	44	27.3	1 883	47.3	1 595	34.7	104.1	256.3	10	98.5	5	1	–	8
Mower	37	29.7	(4)	D	D	D	D	D	7	100.0	Z	3	3	3
Murray	NA	NA	NA	NA	NA	NA	NA	NA	2	96.1	Z	1	–	1
Nicollet	34	52.9	3 748	79.9	2 555	46.9	265.2	868.2	6	100.0	Z	4	Z	2
Nobles	24	33.3	2 690	62.9	2 157	44.4	236.5	823.8	5	96.4	Z	3	Z	2
Norman	NA	NA	NA	NA	NA	NA	NA	NA	1	100.0	Z	Z	–	1
Olmsted	77	39.0	10 477	482.1	4 949	126.9	1 040.9	3 085.4	41	65.1	Z	12	–	6
Otter Tail	91	33.0	3 732	82.1	2 875	55.3	260.7	661.7	77	49.5	21	4	Z	33
Pennington	16	50.0	2 047	50.9	1 366	25.3	270.1	594.7	3	19.4	1	1	–	2
Pine	NA	NA	NA	NA	NA	NA	NA	NA	3	98.5	Z	1	–	2
Pipestone	15	20.0	652	16.6	534	13.0	45.1	96.9	3	96.3	Z	2	Z	1
Polk	40	30.0	1 350	36.3	1 107	26.6	130.0	300.3	18	10.9	7	9	Z	8
Pope	29	24.1	529	13.3	429	9.2	34.9	84.6	12	98.3	1	Z	Z	11
Ramsey	765	38.4	41 550	1 581.6	25 442	784.6	5 009.5	9 294.6	143	33.8	1	23	12	11
Red Lake	NA	NA	NA	NA	NA	NA	NA	NA	1	98.3	Z	Z	–	Z
Redwood	21	33.3	1 250	34.9	926	20.1	75.2	165.9	3	97.9	Z	1	Z	2
Renville	34	32.4	884	21.5	648	13.3	64.4	155.7	3	98.0	Z	1	1	2
Rice	86	34.9	4 838	161.3	3 518	112.0	450.1	954.9	7	98.1	Z	3	Z	3
Rock	NA	NA	NA	NA	NA	NA	NA	NA	3	97.2	Z	2	Z	1
Roseau	18	27.8	(5)	D	D	D	D	D	2	100.0	–	1	–	1
St. Louis	228	25.0	5 446	155.8	3 851	96.0	462.2	879.4	204	1.2	Z	32	4	7
Scott	148	23.0	5 039	180.8	3 626	116.6	442.6	989.5	10	99.6	Z	6	2	3
Sherburne	96	32.3	3 278	103.2	2 574	67.6	272.2	463.2	87	25.6	17	2	Z	37
Sibley	25	40.0	1 054	28.7	834	16.7	129.2	352.1	3	97.0	Z	1	Z	2
Stearns	219	30.1	12 609	369.1	10 193	266.8	919.2	2 216.6	28	98.4	9	10	1	16
Steele	67	44.8	6 292	191.7	4 612	122.3	517.4	1 006.9	4	89.2	Z	2	–	2
Stevens	NA	NA	NA	NA	NA	NA	NA	NA	4	97.1	2	1	–	3
Swift	13	38.5	829	19.3	667	15.2	21.8	56.5	8	99.5	7	1	–	7
Todd	47	23.4	1 519	46.4	1 221	35.1	104.5	278.2	7	95.6	4	1	Z	6
Traverse	NA	NA	NA	NA	NA	NA	NA	NA	1	100.0	–	Z	–	Z
Wabasha	39	33.3	1 934	51.3	1 474	39.6	161.1	368.5	4	98.7	Z	1	Z	2
Wadena	21	38.1	784	19.8	623	12.9	43.0	74.4	8	83.7	6	1	–	6
Waseca	29	41.4	3 298	108.6	2 455	61.5	265.9	467.1	3	100.0	Z	2	–	1
Washington	210	25.2	9 456	436.0	6 653	271.4	1 062.7	2 795.0	321	18.1	1	36	12	11
Watonwan	21	33.3	1 102	22.7	823	15.2	62.2	139.3	3	99.7	Z	2	–	1
Wilkin	NA	NA	NA	NA	NA	NA	NA	NA	1	79.0	Z	Z	–	1
Winona	116	44.0	7 115	196.1	4 942	111.6	489.4	1 071.9	12	75.3	Z	4	1	3
Wright	179	29.6	4 315	127.4	3 051	69.6	301.1	583.6	348	2.4	1	3	Z	5
Yellow Medicine	NA	NA	NA	NA	NA	NA	NA	NA	2	98.0	Z	1	–	1
MISSISSIPPI	3 008	42.6	227 800	5 599.4	182 630	3 905.8	17 088.5	39 658.3	3 200	80.8	1 742	344	290	1 572
Adams	38	28.9	2 299	76.0	1 910	58.3	275.2	550.0	51	99.9	–	5	46	9
Alcorn	58	37.9	4 918	150.8	4 179	115.4	371.6	955.6	3	84.5	Z	2	–	1
Amite	10	50.0	691	17.2	609	14.7	33.0	97.3	2	82.8	Z	1	–	1
Attala	22	50.0	1 267	21.8	926	12.1	46.8	119.9	4	96.7	Z	4	Z	1
Benton	NA	NA	NA	NA	NA	NA	NA	NA	1	91.8	Z	Z	–	Z
Bolivar	22	54.5	2 724	67.0	2 061	44.2	237.1	417.8	472	95.1	443	5	1	289
Calhoun	34	38.2	1 874	35.4	1 745	29.6	88.5	296.2	46	97.5	1	1	43	9
Carroll	NA	NA	NA	NA	NA	NA	NA	NA	6	94.7	4	1	–	4
Chickasaw	80	41.3	4 896	93.4	4 326	75.2	162.4	420.8	2	84.7	Z	2	–	1
Choctaw	10	50.0	598	13.9	495	11.8	45.0	105.0	2	91.6	–	2	–	1
Claiborne	10	60.0	629	13.9	523	10.3	33.9	88.6	34	98.6	Z	1	–	20
Clarke	18	61.1	2 084	51.4	1 825	38.8	147.7	304.1	3	92.2	Z	2	Z	1
Clay	25	44.0	3 640	113.6	2 805	74.9	406.2	926.0	7	96.8	–	5	1	2
Coahoma	28	46.4	1 353	35.6	1 144	24.9	85.2	236.6	146	95.4	134	5	Z	91
Copiah	32	56.3	2 735	52.6	2 122	35.2	142.0	407.7	5	90.4	Z	3	Z	1
Covington	17	35.3	1 950	32.2	1 735	26.4	67.9	194.2	7	95.8	Z	2	4	2
DeSoto	131	48.1	7 232	213.4	5 374	137.7	565.1	1 369.6	17	96.9	8	7	1	7
Forrest	84	34.5	5 170	116.3	3 783	73.1	420.0	1 037.1	42	34.0	Z	10	3	4
Franklin	NA	NA	NA	NA	NA	NA	NA	NA	1	90.5	Z	1	–	Z
George	NA	NA	NA	NA	NA	NA	NA	NA	2	74.7	Z	Z	–	1
Greene	NA	NA	NA	NA	NA	NA	NA	NA	1	70.6	Z	1	–	1
Grenada	24	58.3	4 194	109.5	3 364	81.4	233.6	571.8	21	76.2	8	2	10	8
Hancock	NA	NA	NA	NA	NA	NA	NA	NA	6	98.4	Z	3	1	1
Harrison	139	27.3	4 498	133.6	3 525	89.2	566.8	1 079.7	266	13.8	Z	27	3	15
Hinds	208	33.2	11 540	314.8	9 002	217.1	1 001.5	2 484.4	48	29.4	–	43	10	10
Holmes	14	57.1	1 674	31.4	1 544	26.0	82.1	214.5	48	95.9	37	3	1	31
Humphreys	4	75.0	(6)	D	D	D	D	D	158	98.3	54	1	1	112
Issaquena	NA	NA	NA	NA	NA	NA	NA	NA	34	95.9	28	Z	–	22

[1] Average number of production workers plus the number of other (nonproduction) employees for the pay period including March 12. [2] Average number of production workers for the pay periods including the 12th of March, May, August, and November. [3] In millions of gallons per day. [4] 2,500 to 4,999 employees. [5] 5,000 to 9,999 employees. [6] 500 to 999 employees.

Sources: Manufacturing—U.S. Census Bureau, 1997 Economic Census – Manufacturing, generated by Statistical Compendia Branch, using American Factfinder at <http://www.census.gov/>, (June 2000) [related Internet site <http://www.census.gov/epcd/www/97EC31.HTM>]. Water Use—U.S. Geological Survey, "Water Use in the United States," individual state/county and US by state files from <http://water.usgs.gov/watuse/spread95.html>, (accessed: September 1999).

[Includes U.S., states, and 3,142 counties/county equivalents defined as of January 1, 1992. For changes to these areas since January 1, 1992, see appendix B. Geographic Information]

	Maunfacturing (NAICS 31-33), 1997								Water use per day,[3] 1995					
	Establishments		All employees		Production workers				Withdrawals					
County							Value added by manu- facture (mil. dol.)	Value of ship- ments (mil. dol.)			By selected major use– (mil. gal.)			
	Total	Percent with 20 or more employ- ees	Number[1]	Annual payroll (mil. dol.)	Number[2]	Wages (mil. dol.)			Total (mil. gal.)	Percent ground water	Irrigation	Public supply	Industrial	Consump- tive use (mil. gal.)
MISSISSIPPI—Con.														
Itawamba	40	40.0	1 366	30.1	1 158	22.6	129.4	371.6	2	89.2	Z	2	–	1
Jackson	98	34.7	16 340	534.5	9 998	308.9	1 735.8	4 447.7	68	26.7	1	10	56	13
Jasper	15	66.7	1 720	30.0	1 447	21.6	70.3	151.3	3	91.4	Z	2	Z	1
Jefferson	NA	NA	NA	NA	NA	NA	NA	NA	2	94.7	–	1	–	Z
Jefferson Davis	9	55.6	769	8.9	738	7.5	30.0	56.0	2	86.2	Z	1	–	1
Jones	68	32.4	6 820	162.7	5 786	117.5	464.5	991.3	17	95.3	Z	10	3	5
Kemper	NA	NA	NA	NA	NA	NA	NA	NA	2	78.5	Z	1	–	1
Lafayette	29	31.0	2 017	43.2	1 661	31.1	117.0	304.5	5	97.3	Z	3	Z	1
Lamar	22	27.3	770	16.4	646	12.2	36.5	116.8	9	97.5	Z	4	1	3
Lauderdale	83	39.8	6 076	164.2	4 441	111.4	471.5	916.6	15	98.8	Z	11	2	3
Lawrence	9	44.4	(4)	D	D	D	D	D	34	7.5	Z	1	32	6
Leake	18	55.6	2 481	29.8	2 403	27.9	179.2	242.0	4	76.2	–	3	–	2
Lee	191	48.2	17 717	472.9	14 552	335.5	1 192.2	2 708.4	13	29.0	Z	11	Z	2
Leflore	40	47.5	3 572	76.6	2 867	47.2	219.1	510.9	193	96.4	137	5	Z	127
Lincoln	28	39.3	1 383	35.1	1 187	23.6	129.7	301.4	13	97.6	Z	3	9	3
Lowndes	71	39.4	7 611	223.2	5 582	140.9	617.3	1 313.9	15	97.3	Z	8	4	3
Madison	57	40.4	2 414	57.2	1 891	33.9	174.5	396.6	12	90.7	1	10	Z	3
Marion	26	19.2	1 000	15.7	861	12.5	52.5	103.9	4	81.9	Z	3	Z	1
Marshall	29	48.3	1 777	41.2	1 533	31.1	102.6	201.3	3	91.3	Z	2	–	1
Monroe	71	46.5	4 889	124.8	4 078	88.7	430.1	1 121.2	19	95.1	1	4	12	4
Montgomery	21	52.4	1 165	21.8	948	17.4	39.9	116.6	2	83.3	Z	1	–	1
Neshoba	32	40.6	2 572	57.1	2 157	49.5	132.3	347.8	4	90.6	Z	3	Z	1
Newton	20	40.0	2 256	49.5	1 968	42.9	89.6	165.7	4	87.0	–	2	Z	1
Noxubee	20	65.0	1 201	22.8	1 011	16.1	68.2	210.8	4	43.9	2	1	–	3
Oktibbeha	35	48.6	2 132	49.8	1 566	28.2	164.7	372.3	8	97.8	Z	6	1	2
Panola	44	45.5	2 943	68.5	2 447	51.0	289.7	575.0	15	95.4	11	3	Z	8
Pearl River	47	27.7	905	20.3	703	13.5	91.0	190.3	6	95.3	Z	3	1	1
Perry	7	57.1	(5)	D	D	D	D	D	20	5.9	Z	1	19	4
Pike	36	50.0	3 924	64.7	3 456	49.8	195.8	580.3	7	91.0	Z	5	1	2
Pontotoc	92	50.0	5 549	116.5	4 671	91.4	366.6	720.2	3	92.8	Z	2	–	1
Prentiss	46	58.7	4 507	86.1	3 752	63.6	371.6	702.2	2	95.6	Z	2	–	1
Quitman	NA	NA	NA	NA	NA	NA	NA	NA	112	95.1	109	1	Z	70
Rankin	127	37.8	5 763	150.3	4 555	101.2	558.8	1 088.2	13	95.4	Z	10	1	3
Scott	28	53.6	5 487	95.9	4 880	80.2	225.8	607.4	10	85.6	Z	8	–	3
Sharkey	NA	NA	NA	NA	NA	NA	NA	NA	64	96.3	47	Z	–	43
Simpson	15	40.0	1 182	22.2	947	14.8	334.2	360.4	4	86.5	Z	3	Z	2
Smith	17	58.8	1 801	41.2	1 520	31.9	138.8	392.8	6	64.3	2	3	–	3
Stone	15	46.7	682	15.3	583	12.2	34.5	124.6	2	84.2	Z	1	–	1
Sunflower	22	63.6	2 654	48.3	2 237	35.6	204.9	508.3	353	96.2	268	5	1	228
Tallahatchie	7	71.4	500	5.6	423	3.9	27.2	41.2	107	95.2	103	1	–	72
Tate	16	37.5	2 047	45.3	1 728	33.2	98.0	199.9	6	93.5	3	1	–	3
Tippah	42	45.2	3 247	71.2	2 639	46.4	160.9	344.1	2	95.6	Z	2	Z	1
Tishomingo	46	45.7	3 361	70.8	2 564	46.0	126.8	321.6	4	98.9	–	4	–	1
Tunica	NA	NA	NA	NA	NA	NA	NA	NA	140	95.5	127	1	–	87
Union	39	41.0	4 204	97.2	3 387	60.7	228.8	445.8	3	95.6	Z	2	Z	1
Walthall	24	50.0	940	15.8	785	10.6	37.8	68.9	2	83.7	–	1	Z	1
Warren	43	60.5	4 698	131.7	3 800	98.0	349.7	1 181.8	82	16.6	Z	10	21	7
Washington	65	44.6	5 067	121.8	4 320	94.4	492.2	1 030.3	303	87.2	209	10	1	177
Wayne	16	56.3	1 323	28.7	1 040	22.7	100.4	294.9	2	84.3	Z	1	–	1
Webster	17	52.9	1 567	25.2	1 424	21.3	92.1	149.8	1	91.3	Z	1	–	Z
Wilkinson	NA	NA	NA	NA	NA	NA	NA	NA	2	91.9	Z	2	–	1
Winston	26	38.5	1 850	53.5	1 385	33.8	133.8	318.3	3	92.4	Z	3	–	1
Yalobusha	17	41.2	1 576	33.4	1 371	24.8	109.2	224.2	3	97.1	–	2	–	1
Yazoo	21	47.6	1 987	52.1	1 560	27.4	101.4	236.1	30	98.0	1	4	10	14
MISSOURI	7 497	33.3	371 448	11 647.1	270 297	7 197.3	43 186.1	93 115.5	7 029	12.7	567	699	39	692
Adair	10	50.0	1 619	39.8	1 392	31.9	221.7	412.4	4	27.1	1	3	–	2
Andrew	NA	NA	NA	NA	NA	NA	NA	NA	3	71.7	2	1	–	2
Atchison	NA	NA	NA	NA	NA	NA	NA	NA	19	86.8	18	1	–	16
Audrain	38	60.5	2 721	79.7	2 258	61.5	208.2	531.3	10	38.2	7	2	Z	7
Barry	61	50.8	7 537	154.3	5 259	98.9	486.4	1 096.2	7	81.7	Z	4	1	3
Barton	19	21.1	2 080	52.0	1 829	43.2	129.5	269.6	5	65.4	2	2	–	3
Bates	NA	NA	NA	NA	NA	NA	NA	NA	3	13.9	Z	1	–	2
Benton	NA	NA	NA	NA	NA	NA	NA	NA	2	73.0	Z	1	–	1
Bollinger	NA	NA	NA	NA	NA	NA	NA	NA	10	96.7	8	Z	–	8
Boone	87	31.0	5 703	165.3	4 450	107.9	855.1	1 595.0	18	88.4	2	15	–	5
Buchanan	96	51.0	7 365	235.1	5 688	159.1	860.2	2 293.8	58	2.3	Z	17	–	3
Butler	53	24.5	3 010	66.7	2 673	53.5	266.4	494.5	156	97.9	151	4	–	110
Caldwell	NA	NA	NA	NA	NA	NA	NA	NA	1	47.4	Z	Z	–	1
Callaway	37	40.5	1 896	59.6	1 489	41.9	145.8	320.6	27	17.6	1	3	–	14

[1] Average number of production workers plus the number of other (nonproduction) employees for the pay period including March 12. [2] Average number of production workers for the pay periods including the 12th of March, May, August, and November. [3] In millions of gallons per day. [4] 1,000 to 2,499 employees. [5] 500 to 999 employees.

Sources: Manufacturing—U.S. Census Bureau, 1997 Economic Census – Manufacturing, generated by Statistical Compendia Branch, using American Factfinder at <http://www.census.gov/>, (June 2000) [related Internet site <http://www.census.gov/epcd/www/97EC31.HTM>]. Water Use—U.S. Geological Survey, "Water Use in the United States," individual state/county and US by state files from <http://water.usgs.gov/watuse/spread95.html>, (accessed: September 1999).

Table B–9. Counties — **Manufacturing and Water Use**–Con.

[Includes U.S., states, and 3,142 counties/county equivalents defined as of January 1, 1992. For changes to these areas since January 1, 1992, see appendix B. Geographic Information]

County	Manufacturing (NAICS 31-33), 1997								Water use per day,[3] 1995					
	Establishments		All employees		Production workers		Value added by manufacture (mil. dol.)	Value of shipments (mil. dol.)	Withdrawals					Consumptive use (mil. gal.)
	Total	Percent with 20 or more employees	Number[1]	Annual payroll (mil. dol.)	Number[2]	Wages (mil. dol.)			Total (mil. gal.)	Percent ground water	By selected major use– (mil. gal.)			
											Irrigation	Public supply	Industrial	
MISSOURI—Con.														
Camden	53	22.6	1 269	32.6	1 010	20.8	69.4	132.0	4	84.4	Z	2	–	1
Cape Girardeau	93	34.4	5 912	163.3	4 486	113.3	878.1	1 569.7	12	58.9	4	7	Z	5
Carroll	NA	NA	NA	NA	NA	NA	NA	NA	3	82.6	1	1	–	2
Carter	NA	NA	NA	NA	NA	NA	NA	NA	1	86.2	Z	Z	–	Z
Cass	71	19.7	1 057	24.6	790	16.2	47.7	116.6	6	27.6	2	3	–	3
Cedar	15	33.3	505	9.9	417	7.5	37.5	76.5	2	76.1	Z	1	Z	1
Chariton	NA	NA	NA	NA	NA	NA	NA	NA	2	63.3	Z	Z	–	1
Christian	101	18.8	(4)	D	D	D	D	D	5	83.7	Z	2	Z	2
Clark	NA	NA	NA	NA	NA	NA	NA	NA	2	82.2	1	Z	–	1
Clay	214	45.8	14 743	569.6	11 547	427.1	4 117.9	9 891.7	26	95.0	Z	12	6	5
Clinton	NA	NA	NA	NA	NA	NA	NA	NA	2	11.7	Z	1	–	1
Cole	53	24.5	(4)	D	D	D	D	D	9	57.3	Z	7	–	2
Cooper	16	43.8	865	19.2	670	13.2	80.8	138.6	3	30.3	Z	2	–	1
Crawford	52	30.8	1 639	33.8	1 214	20.2	74.7	142.9	2	76.0	Z	1	–	1
Dade	NA	NA	NA	NA	NA	NA	NA	NA	4	67.7	2	Z	–	3
Dallas	11	27.3	530	8.7	489	7.8	18.0	40.2	2	67.3	Z	Z	–	1
Daviess	NA	NA	NA	NA	NA	NA	NA	NA	2	41.7	Z	1	–	1
DeKalb	NA	NA	NA	NA	NA	NA	NA	NA	1	58.1	Z	Z	–	1
Dent	27	29.6	951	17.3	841	13.1	22.9	84.3	2	72.7	Z	1	–	1
Douglas	NA	NA	NA	NA	NA	NA	NA	NA	3	57.4	Z	1	–	2
Dunklin	26	30.8	1 281	28.5	1 084	21.5	135.6	259.7	45	98.9	41	4	–	32
Franklin	210	40.0	10 640	284.4	8 557	201.3	952.8	1 836.3	967	1.1	Z	6	–	5
Gasconade	38	44.7	1 643	41.9	1 300	22.3	75.6	161.8	3	81.2	Z	1	–	1
Gentry	NA	NA	NA	NA	NA	NA	NA	NA	1	41.3	–	1	–	1
Greene	371	31.0	19 475	513.1	14 253	321.4	1 722.1	3 788.6	176	6.8	Z	28	2	10
Grundy	11	36.4	798	20.7	669	16.0	173.6	242.4	3	29.9	1	2	–	1
Harrison	NA	NA	NA	NA	NA	NA	NA	NA	2	22.0	1	1	–	1
Henry	32	31.3	1 780	33.0	1 430	23.0	103.8	390.1	358	.3	Z	2	–	5
Hickory	NA	NA	NA	NA	NA	NA	NA	NA	1	64.5	Z	Z	–	1
Holt	NA	NA	NA	NA	NA	NA	NA	NA	2	93.1	2	Z	–	2
Howard	NA	NA	NA	NA	NA	NA	NA	NA	2	24.4	Z	1	–	1
Howell	70	35.7	3 690	72.5	2 888	52.6	238.1	485.6	5	81.3	Z	3	–	2
Iron	NA	NA	NA	NA	NA	NA	NA	NA	6	94.2	Z	1	4	1
Jackson	907	31.6	38 785	1 301.5	24 744	695.3	5 394.9	8 984.7	547	6.2	Z	86	6	24
Jasper	198	39.4	11 904	289.8	9 293	207.0	003.1	2 154.0	20	30.0	Z	16	4	7
Jefferson	182	24.7	5 304	168.2	4 018	112.2	558.3	1 199.3	835	1.4	Z	9	3	4
Johnson	31	25.8	1 856	46.7	1 431	25.2	105.1	183.3	5	77.3	Z	4	–	2
Knox	NA	NA	NA	NA	NA	NA	NA	NA	1	21.3	Z	Z	–	1
Laclede	57	38.6	5 177	130.4	4 142	85.6	352.9	809.7	5	83.5	Z	3	Z	2
Lafayette	42	31.0	1 166	22.9	960	16.0	44.6	130.4	4	28.6	1	2	–	2
Lawrence	54	44.4	1 614	34.8	1 247	25.7	112.3	259.0	5	67.1	1	2	–	3
Lewis	NA	NA	NA	NA	NA	NA	NA	NA	2	67.1	Z	1	–	1
Lincoln	43	23.3	1 078	29.0	848	19.4	100.2	176.8	3	79.9	Z	1	–	1
Linn	24	41.7	1 739	45.0	1 240	25.2	92.5	137.8	2	25.9	Z	1	–	1
Livingston	28	42.9	903	23.6	762	18.2	70.9	117.1	3	80.2	Z	2	–	1
McDonald	34	32.4	3 052	52.5	2 674	40.7	182.5	469.8	5	71.0	Z	2	1	2
Macon	15	26.7	(5)	D	D	D	D	D	3	11.7	Z	2	–	1
Madison	16	25.0	553	8.3	459	6.0	18.6	28.7	1	48.1	Z	1	–	1
Maries	NA	NA	NA	NA	NA	NA	NA	NA	3	84.8	Z	Z	Z	1
Marion	46	41.3	3 179	87.5	2 343	55.4	1 382.3	1 707.1	8	38.7	1	4	2	3
Mercer	NA	NA	NA	NA	NA	NA	NA	NA	2	37.9	Z	Z	–	2
Miller	29	34.5	1 500	31.8	1 218	22.8	66.4	128.5	3	65.5	Z	1	–	2
Mississippi	14	42.9	571	10.7	473	7.6	34.0	66.4	19	99.7	17	2	–	15
Moniteau	22	27.3	1 095	19.5	932	14.7	114.7	173.8	3	77.0	Z	2	–	1
Monroe	7	42.9	1 047	27.9	811	25.6	45.5	74.8	3	30.5	1	2	–	2
Montgomery	32	37.5	811	16.6	601	10.3	37.2	82.1	2	61.0	1	1	–	1
Morgan	29	17.2	649	12.0	574	9.1	65.4	115.0	2	73.8	Z	1	–	1
New Madrid	17	35.3	2 504	83.4	2 074	61.9	267.2	529.8	849	9.6	78	2	1	67
Newton	63	27.0	4 315	109.8	3 696	91.7	288.9	692.9	7	50.8	Z	4	–	3
Nodaway	23	39.1	1 677	48.2	1 328	34.4	366.7	647.2	4	28.6	Z	2	–	2
Oregon	NA	NA	NA	NA	NA	NA	NA	NA	4	85.5	Z	3	–	1
Osage	24	25.0	914	20.3	786	12.7	58.3	169.8	35	4.5	Z	1	–	2
Ozark	NA	NA	NA	NA	NA	NA	NA	NA	5	84.5	Z	4	–	1
Pemiscot	12	41.7	893	19.8	825	14.4	48.0	131.1	28	99.5	25	4	–	19
Perry	31	51.6	2 855	61.9	2 298	41.6	288.4	609.3	3	54.7	Z	2	–	1
Pettis	69	34.8	5 324	130.2	4 650	102.0	438.4	958.9	6	52.2	Z	4	Z	2
Phelps	55	16.4	1 132	29.6	833	17.6	106.5	218.2	4	92.3	Z	2	–	1
Pike	27	25.9	771	25.7	544	16.7	127.6	277.4	10	10.7	Z	1	5	2
Platte	47	44.7	1 599	52.4	1 093	28.4	104.8	344.7	365	1.7	Z	3	–	2
Polk	34	26.5	859	13.9	636	8.2	47.7	81.1	4	70.7	Z	2	–	2

[1] Average number of production workers plus the number of other (nonproduction) employees for the pay period including March 12. [2] Average number of production workers for the pay periods including the 12th of March, May, August, and November. [3] In millions of gallons per day. [4] 2,500 to 4,999 employees. [5] 1,000 to 2,499 employees.

Sources: Manufacturing—U.S. Census Bureau, 1997 Economic Census – Manufacturing, generated by Statistical Compendia Branch, using American Factfinder at <http://www.census.gov/>, (June 2000) [related Internet site <http://www.census.gov/epcd/www/97EC31.HTM>]. Water Use—U.S. Geological Survey, "Water Use in the United States," individual state/county and US by state files from <http://water.usgs.gov/watuse/spread95.html>, (accessed: September 1999).

[Includes U.S., states, and 3,142 counties/county equivalents defined as of January 1, 1992. For changes to these areas since January 1, 1992, see appendix B. Geographic Information]

County	Establishments Total	Establishments Percent with 20 or more employees	All employees Number[1]	All employees Annual payroll (mil. dol.)	Production workers Number[2]	Production workers Wages (mil. dol.)	Value added by manufacture (mil. dol.)	Value of shipments (mil. dol.)	Withdrawals Total (mil. gal.)	Withdrawals Percent ground water	Irrigation	Public supply	Industrial	Consumptive use (mil. gal.)
MISSOURI—Con.														
Pulaski	18	16.7	682	9.4	582	7.0	17.6	36.4	7	47.5	Z	6	–	1
Putnam	NA	NA	NA	NA	NA	NA	NA	NA	2	25.0	Z	Z	–	2
Ralls	10	60.0	913	21.6	762	17.0	161.6	253.9	2	20.5	Z	1	Z	1
Randolph	37	29.7	1 381	30.5	1 170	21.6	82.5	182.6	877	Z	Z	2	–	12
Ray	21	19.0	654	16.5	511	9.7	39.2	63.9	4	85.7	Z	3	–	1
Reynolds	33	24.2	634	10.9	541	8.5	23.4	52.7	4	96.8	Z	Z	Z	1
Ripley	42	11.9	629	10.0	545	8.2	24.1	42.8	19	75.4	18	1	–	13
St. Charles	279	30.1	12 160	431.9	9 801	317.5	2 094.5	4 432.9	446	4.6	1	16	1	5
St. Clair	NA	NA	NA	NA	NA	NA	NA	NA	2	49.7	Z	Z	–	1
Ste. Genevieve	32	34.4	1 752	47.8	1 438	35.3	130.2	208.2	2	80.4	–	1	–	1
St. Francois	66	33.3	3 797	80.3	2 963	53.6	224.6	394.6	307	1.8	Z	4	–	2
St. Louis	1 272	34.1	78 218	3 359.8	46 676	1 712.9	8 581.8	25 347.9	176	3.0	Z	164	Z	29
Saline	24	37.5	2 530	55.4	2 266	46.1	223.1	647.5	5	83.8	Z	4	–	2
Schuyler	NA	NA	NA	NA	NA	NA	NA	NA	1	28.8	Z	Z	–	Z
Scotland	NA	NA	NA	NA	NA	NA	NA	NA	1	22.8	Z	Z	–	1
Scott	77	32.5	3 008	66.1	2 556	51.1	234.6	532.6	20	99.3	13	5	–	11
Shannon	22	31.8	710	8.1	592	6.3	20.3	40.9	1	79.4	Z	Z	–	Z
Shelby	5	60.0	(4)	D	D	D	D	D	3	57.3	1	Z	–	2
Stoddard	40	45.0	2 372	42.4	2 051	34.2	149.1	264.0	153	99.5	149	3	–	108
Stone	NA	NA	NA	NA	NA	NA	NA	NA	4	88.8	Z	2	–	1
Sullivan	5	40.0	(5)	D	D	D	D	D	3	26.1	Z	1	Z	2
Taney	59	13.6	798	15.8	622	10.6	49.3	87.8	10	49.4	Z	9	Z	1
Texas	53	18.9	1 399	26.2	1 200	21.3	78.9	169.6	5	54.0	1	1	1	3
Vernon	21	52.4	1 561	44.0	1 286	31.9	280.1	425.8	5	64.0	1	2	–	3
Warren	37	43.2	2 042	50.1	1 590	36.2	117.1	242.7	4	64.2	1	1	Z	2
Washington	NA	NA	NA	NA	NA	NA	NA	NA	9	74.7	Z	1	–	1
Wayne	28	21.4	510	8.3	454	5.5	24.2	44.0	2	67.2	Z	1	–	Z
Webster	44	29.5	(5)	D	D	D	D	D	4	59.4	1	1	–	2
Worth	NA	NA	NA	NA	NA	NA	NA	NA	Z	29.2	Z	Z	–	Z
Wright	18	33.3	730	14.2	678	12.7	59.5	102.0	4	54.4	1	1	–	2
Independent City														
St. Louis city	802	39.0	33 836	1 243.6	23 100	723.4	5 088.6	8 605.5	148	–	–	148	–	23
MONTANA	1 160	15.4	19 611	560.1	14 988	394.0	1 732.2	4 866.3	8 860	2.5	8 546	143	60	1 957
Beaverhead	NA	NA	NA	NA	NA	NA	NA	NA	571	.5	565	2	Z	111
Big Horn	NA	NA	NA	NA	NA	NA	NA	NA	316	2.7	311	1	Z	71
Blaine	NA	NA	NA	NA	NA	NA	NA	NA	274	2.2	272	Z	–	70
Broadwater	NA	NA	NA	NA	NA	NA	NA	NA	241	1.0	239	1	Z	49
Carbon	NA	NA	NA	NA	NA	NA	NA	NA	454	1.5	446	2	Z	73
Carter	NA	NA	NA	NA	NA	NA	NA	NA	4	9.3	3	Z	–	3
Cascade	80	16.3	925	23.9	691	15.4	58.1	228.5	153	1.1	136	15	1	41
Chouteau	NA	NA	NA	NA	NA	NA	NA	NA	36	3.8	34	1	Z	10
Custer	NA	NA	NA	NA	NA	NA	NA	NA	75	1.5	72	2	Z	26
Daniels	NA	NA	NA	NA	NA	NA	NA	NA	5	48.2	4	Z	–	3
Dawson	NA	NA	NA	NA	NA	NA	NA	NA	72	1.3	69	2	Z	21
Deer Lodge	NA	NA	NA	NA	NA	NA	NA	NA	48	9.5	43	4	–	11
Fallon	NA	NA	NA	NA	NA	NA	NA	NA	11	53.8	5	Z	Z	4
Fergus	NA	NA	NA	NA	NA	NA	NA	NA	75	5.3	70	2	Z	19
Flathead	124	16.9	3 887	121.5	2 820	86.4	353.1	790.5	65	26.8	51	6	6	33
Gallatin	148	18.9	1 992	48.3	1 498	30.7	133.4	273.8	489	2.2	479	8	Z	109
Garfield	NA	NA	NA	NA	NA	NA	NA	NA	12	10.2	11	Z	–	7
Glacier	NA	NA	NA	NA	NA	NA	NA	NA	87	3.3	84	2	Z	17
Golden Valley	NA	NA	NA	NA	NA	NA	NA	NA	85	.6	85	Z	–	15
Granite	NA	NA	NA	NA	NA	NA	NA	NA	104	.9	102	Z	Z	25
Hill	NA	NA	NA	NA	NA	NA	NA	NA	18	14.5	16	2	Z	6
Jefferson	NA	NA	NA	NA	NA	NA	NA	NA	148	2.0	145	2	Z	32
Judith Basin	NA	NA	NA	NA	NA	NA	NA	NA	65	1.6	64	Z	–	11
Lake	30	23.3	840	19.5	688	14.0	56.7	115.3	309	1.1	305	1	Z	81
Lewis and Clark	46	15.2	(4)	D	D	D	D	D	183	5.4	173	8	1	46
Liberty	NA	NA	NA	NA	NA	NA	NA	NA	22	1.0	22	Z	–	5
Lincoln	33	12.1	657	21.3	599	19.1	48.2	125.4	37	6.8	20	1	14	10
McCone	NA	NA	NA	NA	NA	NA	NA	NA	15	4.6	14	Z	–	8
Madison	NA	NA	NA	NA	NA	NA	NA	NA	540	.2	538	Z	–	91
Meagher	NA	NA	NA	NA	NA	NA	NA	NA	350	.2	348	Z	Z	53
Mineral	NA	NA	NA	NA	NA	NA	NA	NA	8	37.5	4	Z	3	3
Missoula	136	15.4	2 690	89.4	2 226	70.6	218.6	562.3	114	31.5	65	25	22	32
Musselshell	NA	NA	NA	NA	NA	NA	NA	NA	83	3.6	80	1	Z	15
Park	36	8.3	535	13.3	438	9.8	24.3	63.3	333	1.7	329	3	Z	57
Petroleum	NA	NA	NA	NA	NA	NA	NA	NA	57	1.2	56	Z	–	15

[1] Average number of production workers plus the number of other (nonproduction) employees for the pay period including March 12. [2] Average number of production workers for the pay periods including the 12th of March, May, August, and November. [3] In millions of gallons per day. [4] 500 to 999 employees. [5] 1,000 to 2,499 employees.

Sources: Manufacturing—U.S. Census Bureau, 1997 Economic Census – Manufacturing, generated by Statistical Compendia Branch, using American Factfinder at <http://www.census.gov/>, (June 2000) [related Internet site <http://www.census.gov/epcd/www/97EC31.HTM>]. Water Use—U.S. Geological Survey, "Water Use in the United States," individual state/county and US by state files from <http://water.usgs.gov/watuse/spread95.html>, (accessed: September 1999).

Table B–9. Counties — **Manufacturing and Water Use**–Con.

[Includes U.S., states, and 3,142 counties/county equivalents defined as of January 1, 1992. For changes to these areas since January 1, 1992, see appendix B. Geographic Information]

County	Establishments Total	Establishments Percent with 20 or more employees	All employees Number[1]	All employees Annual payroll (mil. dol.)	Production workers Number[2]	Production workers Wages (mil. dol.)	Value added by manufacture (mil. dol.)	Value of shipments (mil. dol.)	Withdrawals Total (mil. gal.)	Withdrawals Percent ground water	Withdrawals Irrigation	Withdrawals Public supply	Withdrawals Industrial	Consumptive use (mil. gal.)
MONTANA—Con.														
Phillips	NA	NA	NA	NA	NA	NA	NA	NA	210	1.6	208	Z	—	49
Pondera	NA	NA	NA	NA	NA	NA	NA	NA	212	1.5	211	1	—	58
Powder River	NA	NA	NA	NA	NA	NA	NA	NA	16	18.5	13	Z	—	8
Powell	NA	NA	NA	NA	NA	NA	NA	NA	211	.8	209	1	—	46
Prairie	NA	NA	NA	NA	NA	NA	NA	NA	74	3.4	74	—	—	21
Ravalli	66	18.2	870	21.3	674	14.7	42.1	95.2	167	3.0	161	3	Z	48
Richland	NA	NA	NA	NA	NA	NA	NA	NA	317	.9	313	1	1	55
Roosevelt	NA	NA	NA	NA	NA	NA	NA	NA	45	6.1	42	1	Z	12
Rosebud	NA	NA	NA	NA	NA	NA	NA	NA	165	1.6	145	2	Z	53
Sanders	NA	NA	NA	NA	NA	NA	NA	NA	76	4.1	74	1	Z	19
Sheridan	NA	NA	NA	NA	NA	NA	NA	NA	5	82.7	4	Z	—	4
Silver Bow	NA	NA	NA	NA	NA	NA	NA	NA	39	5.0	25	13	2	10
Stillwater	NA	NA	NA	NA	NA	NA	NA	NA	114	4.5	112	1	—	24
Sweet Grass	NA	NA	NA	NA	NA	NA	NA	NA	324	.4	322	Z	—	49
Teton	NA	NA	NA	NA	NA	NA	NA	NA	519	.4	517	1	—	104
Toole	NA	NA	NA	NA	NA	NA	NA	NA	9	15.7	7	1	Z	3
Treasure	NA	NA	NA	NA	NA	NA	NA	NA	117	1.1	116	Z	—	28
Valley	NA	NA	NA	NA	NA	NA	NA	NA	153	3.3	150	2	Z	44
Wheatland	NA	NA	NA	NA	NA	NA	NA	NA	185	1.4	184	Z	—	29
Wibaux	NA	NA	NA	NA	NA	NA	NA	NA	3	9.6	2	Z	—	1
Yellowstone	182	15.4	3 223	110.1	2 177	68.5	561.0	1 797.9	440	1.4	399	23	10	110
Yellowstone National Park	–	–	–	–	–	–	–	–	Z	100.0	–	Z	—	—
NEBRASKA	1 960	31.2	106 690	3 040.5	84 085	2 132.7	10 822.7	27 859.2	10 548	58.8	7 550	286	30	7 021
Adams	63	38.1	3 526	88.9	2 606	62.4	238.5	593.0	189	96.5	177	7	1	174
Antelope	NA	NA	NA	NA	NA	NA	NA	NA	130	96.3	125	1	—	127
Arthur	NA	NA	NA	NA	NA	NA	NA	NA	18	99.7	18	—	—	18
Banner	NA	NA	NA	NA	NA	NA	NA	NA	27	85.3	25	Z	—	25
Blaine	NA	NA	NA	NA	NA	NA	NA	NA	30	28.3	29	Z	—	9
Boone	NA	NA	NA	NA	NA	NA	NA	NA	88	96.6	85	1	—	85
Box Butte	NA	NA	NA	NA	NA	NA	NA	NA	171	97.5	167	3	—	166
Boyd	NA	NA	NA	NA	NA	NA	NA	NA	4	59.3	3	7	—	4
Brown	NA	NA	NA	NA	NA	NA	NA	NA	19	84.0	18	Z	Z	46
Buffalo	47	34.0	4 392	122.1	3 371	87.3	354.1	817.1	207	85.6	192	7	1	170
Burt	NA	NA	NA	NA	NA	NA	NA	NA	46	92.2	44	1	—	44
Butler	NA	NA	NA	NA	NA	NA	NA	NA	101	96.9	98	1	—	95
Cass	NA	NA	NA	NA	NA	NA	NA	NA	16	37.6	2	3	1	5
Cedar	NA	NA	NA	NA	NA	NA	NA	NA	53	94.6	48	1	Z	51
Chase	NA	NA	NA	NA	NA	NA	NA	NA	180	98.8	177	1	—	177
Cherry	NA	NA	NA	NA	NA	NA	NA	NA	99	35.9	95	1	—	37
Cheyenne	NA	NA	NA	NA	NA	NA	NA	NA	66	95.3	62	2	Z	63
Clay	NA	NA	NA	NA	NA	NA	NA	NA	198	95.2	192	1	—	187
Colfax	4	25.0	[4]	D	D	D	D	D	60	93.5	53	1	2	53
Cuming	30	16.7	803	18.0	641	13.0	427.7	522.2	44	74.7	28	2	1	33
Custer	NA	NA	NA	NA	NA	NA	NA	NA	241	76.3	233	2	Z	206
Dakota	23	60.9	[5]	D	D	D	D	D	21	98.5	14	3	3	16
Dawes	NA	NA	NA	NA	NA	NA	NA	NA	43	31.1	35	2	—	22
Dawson	26	46.2	3 899	88.8	3 339	72.1	185.8	1 300.0	333	70.2	319	8	Z	282
Deuel	NA	NA	NA	NA	NA	NA	NA	NA	43	48.0	40	1	—	22
Dixon	NA	NA	NA	NA	NA	NA	NA	NA	43	82.5	12	1	Z	41
Dodge	67	46.3	3 437	87.5	2 703	59.9	317.3	1 009.7	101	93.4	90	4	1	91
Douglas	555	31.9	27 335	897.4	20 962	603.3	3 274.2	7 140.4	364	6.5	11	54	1	44
Dundy	NA	NA	NA	NA	NA	NA	NA	NA	103	94.9	101	Z	—	104
Fillmore	NA	NA	NA	NA	NA	NA	NA	NA	163	96.5	161	1	—	158
Franklin	NA	NA	NA	NA	NA	NA	NA	NA	100	86.0	95	1	—	98
Frontier	NA	NA	NA	NA	NA	NA	NA	NA	76	96.3	75	Z	—	72
Furnas	NA	NA	NA	NA	NA	NA	NA	NA	74	52.8	71	1	—	60
Gage	34	50.0	1 700	43.9	1 314	31.3	134.9	305.5	42	77.1	32	5	Z	35
Garden	NA	NA	NA	NA	NA	NA	NA	NA	58	66.2	54	Z	—	53
Garfield	NA	NA	NA	NA	NA	NA	NA	NA	103	8.5	102	Z	—	12
Gosper	NA	NA	NA	NA	NA	NA	NA	NA	165	44.0	164	Z	—	86
Grant	NA	NA	NA	NA	NA	NA	NA	NA	4	97.9	3	Z	—	4
Greeley	NA	NA	NA	NA	NA	NA	NA	NA	45	96.9	43	Z	—	47
Hall	81	30.9	5 791	156.3	4 873	122.2	475.6	1 823.3	170	95.9	147	11	2	146
Hamilton	21	28.6	691	19.9	508	14.0	160.6	332.7	225	99.1	223	1	Z	215
Harlan	NA	NA	NA	NA	NA	NA	NA	NA	122	66.0	119	1	Z	89
Hayes	NA	NA	NA	NA	NA	NA	NA	NA	61	67.0	61	Z	—	41
Hitchcock	NA	NA	NA	NA	NA	NA	NA	NA	51	31.8	47	1	—	25
Holt	NA	NA	NA	NA	NA	NA	NA	NA	168	93.7	157	2	—	160

[1] Average number of production workers plus the number of other (nonproduction) employees for the pay period including March 12. [2] Average number of production workers for the pay periods including the 12th of March, May, August, and November. [3] In millions of gallons per day. [4] 1,000 to 2,499 employees. [5] 5,000 to 9,999 employees.

Sources: Manufacturing—U.S. Census Bureau, 1997 Economic Census – Manufacturing, generated by Statistical Compendia Branch, using American Factfinder at <http://www.census.gov/>, (June 2000) [related Internet site <http://www.census.gov/epcd/www/97EC31.HTM>]. Water Use—U.S. Geological Survey, "Water Use in the United States," individual state/county and US by state files from <http://water.usgs.gov/watuse/spread95.html>, (accessed: September 1999).

[Includes U.S., states, and 3,142 counties/county equivalents defined as of January 1, 1992. For changes to these areas since January 1, 1992, see appendix B. Geographic Information]

County	Establishments Total	Establishments Percent with 20 or more employees	All employees Number[1]	All employees Annual payroll (mil. dol.)	Production workers Number[2]	Production workers Wages (mil. dol.)	Value added by manufacture (mil. dol.)	Value of shipments (mil. dol.)	Withdrawals Total (mil. gal.)	Withdrawals Percent ground water	Irrigation	Public supply	Industrial	Consumptive use (mil. gal.)
NEBRASKA—Con.														
Hooker	NA	NA	NA	NA	NA	NA	NA	NA	6	92.9	6	Z	–	6
Howard	NA	NA	NA	NA	NA	NA	NA	NA	42	83.4	39	1	–	74
Jefferson	11	54.5	649	11.8	572	8.9	38.0	67.5	41	83.7	37	1	Z	38
Johnson	NA	NA	NA	NA	NA	NA	NA	NA	8	86.8	6	2	–	7
Kearney	NA	NA	NA	NA	NA	NA	NA	NA	168	98.3	165	1	–	188
Keith	NA	NA	NA	NA	NA	NA	NA	NA	123	78.7	110	2	–	111
Keya Paha	NA	NA	NA	NA	NA	NA	NA	NA	9	83.3	8	Z	–	9
Kimball	NA	NA	NA	NA	NA	NA	NA	NA	39	90.9	36	1	–	36
Knox	NA	NA	NA	NA	NA	NA	NA	NA	51	74.6	43	2	Z	46
Lancaster	267	34.5	15 322	502.3	11 577	323.9	1 962.9	3 855.1	21	90.7	14	2	Z	27
Lincoln	NA	NA	NA	NA	NA	NA	NA	NA	1 086	18.5	371	7	Z	257
Logan	NA	NA	NA	NA	NA	NA	NA	NA	20	99.0	19	Z	–	20
Loup	NA	NA	NA	NA	NA	NA	NA	NA	36	21.7	35	–	–	12
McPherson	NA	NA	NA	NA	NA	NA	NA	NA	9	97.6	8	–	–	9
Madison	52	36.5	4 908	154.3	3 959	116.4	486.3	1 402.4	69	86.4	52	6	3	54
Merrick	NA	NA	NA	NA	NA	NA	NA	NA	125	98.3	121	1	–	118
Morrill	NA	NA	NA	NA	NA	NA	NA	NA	116	38.9	110	1	2	174
Nance	NA	NA	NA	NA	NA	NA	NA	NA	39	75.6	38	Z	–	41
Nemaha	NA	NA	NA	NA	NA	NA	NA	NA	637	.4	2	1	–	3
Nuckolls	NA	NA	NA	NA	NA	NA	NA	NA	54	86.4	52	1	–	56
Otoe	17	29.4	1 354	35.0	1 149	28.3	97.3	212.3	308	1.5	1	3	–	4
Pawnee	NA	NA	NA	NA	NA	NA	NA	NA	2	29.6	2	Z	–	2
Perkins	NA	NA	NA	NA	NA	NA	NA	NA	141	99.6	140	1	–	140
Phelps	8	37.5	(4)	D	D	D	D	D	338	60.1	331	2	–	276
Pierce	NA	NA	NA	NA	NA	NA	NA	NA	78	95.7	75	1	–	77
Platte	74	36.5	6 120	164.1	4 613	113.3	551.1	1 217.2	117	93.2	97	5	4	100
Polk	NA	NA	NA	NA	NA	NA	NA	NA	116	98.9	113	1	–	110
Red Willow	NA	NA	NA	NA	NA	NA	NA	NA	64	65.7	55	3	Z	61
Richardson	NA	NA	NA	NA	NA	NA	NA	NA	3	78.4	1	1	–	2
Rock	NA	NA	NA	NA	NA	NA	NA	NA	26	93.3	24	Z	–	26
Saline	19	36.8	2 512	64.7	2 262	48.9	238.5	659.9	66	90.8	62	2	2	61
Sarpy	55	30.9	(5)	D	D	D	D	D	65	91.7	6	46	2	15
Saunders	NA	NA	NA	NA	NA	NA	NA	NA	123	88.2	75	36	Z	75
Scotts Bluff	54	25.9	1 732	46.2	1 397	31.6	134.8	357.5	371	14.2	354	7	3	274
Seward	18	16.7	1 039	30.1	892	23.3	27.0	111.7	99	88.0	96	2	Z	94
Sheridan	NA	NA	NA	NA	NA	NA	NA	NA	81	92.2	79	1	–	86
Sherman	NA	NA	NA	NA	NA	NA	NA	NA	115	31.2	114	Z	–	47
Sioux	NA	NA	NA	NA	NA	NA	NA	NA	30	41.6	29	Z	–	59
Stanton	NA	NA	NA	NA	NA	NA	NA	NA	22	85.4	19	Z	–	20
Thayer	NA	NA	NA	NA	NA	NA	NA	NA	111	91.5	104	1	Z	102
Thomas	NA	NA	NA	NA	NA	NA	NA	NA	8	58.0	4	Z	–	5
Thurston	NA	NA	NA	NA	NA	NA	NA	NA	8	87.4	6	1	–	7
Valley	NA	NA	NA	NA	NA	NA	NA	NA	46	63.9	43	1	–	62
Washington	21	28.6	861	25.1	559	13.7	94.1	372.1	445	3.1	16	4	Z	18
Wayne	15	33.3	1 473	28.6	1 284	22.4	83.0	221.3	21	94.4	19	1	–	20
Webster	NA	NA	NA	NA	NA	NA	NA	NA	117	32.6	113	Z	–	48
Wheeler	NA	NA	NA	NA	NA	NA	NA	NA	30	98.6	28	Z	–	30
York	33	33.3	1 207	32.8	962	22.4	78.2	214.6	232	98.7	228	2	1	220
NEVADA	1 615	25.3	37 849	1 178.0	26 247	677.2	3 298.1	6 361.8	2 301	39.0	1 644	468	15	1 364
Churchill	NA	NA	NA	NA	NA	NA	NA	NA	161	24.5	134	3	Z	101
Clark	814	23.2	(6)	D	D	D	D	D	413	19.5	32	339	7	170
Douglas	65	16.9	1 897	66.3	905	21.5	143.1	241.8	131	18.8	118	10	Z	87
Elko	NA	NA	NA	NA	NA	NA	NA	NA	359	15.4	335	12	–	229
Esmeralda	NA	NA	NA	NA	NA	NA	NA	NA	46	88.5	35	Z	–	35
Eureka	NA	NA	NA	NA	NA	NA	NA	NA	103	85.0	81	Z	–	71
Humboldt	NA	NA	NA	NA	NA	NA	NA	NA	281	78.1	259	4	1	200
Lander	NA	NA	NA	NA	NA	NA	NA	NA	95	68.8	87	1	–	55
Lincoln	NA	NA	NA	NA	NA	NA	NA	NA	54	65.3	52	2	–	32
Lyon	50	46.0	1 561	47.9	1 201	30.0	135.6	280.4	194	20.7	178	5	4	115
Mineral	NA	NA	NA	NA	NA	NA	NA	NA	23	36.6	19	1	–	19
Nye	NA	NA	NA	NA	NA	NA	NA	NA	73	82.6	59	5	–	37
Pershing	NA	NA	NA	NA	NA	NA	NA	NA	86	34.3	83	2	–	56
Storey	NA	NA	NA	NA	NA	NA	NA	NA	3	19.9	1	Z	–	3
Washoe	418	29.4	11 522	361.9	7 519	184.0	922.3	1 931.3	159	27.9	73	71	2	76
White Pine	NA	NA	NA	NA	NA	NA	NA	NA	105	55.6	91	3	–	71
Independent City														
Carson City city	186	25.3	4 157	120.8	3 011	70.5	297.3	514.5	15	41.2	6	8	Z	7

[1] Average number of production workers plus the number of other (nonproduction) employees for the pay period including March 12.   [2] Average number of production workers for the pay periods including the 12th of March, May, August, and November.   [3] In millions of gallons per day.   [4] 500 to 999 employees.   [5] 1,000 to 2,499 employees.   [6] 10,000 to 24,999 employees.

Sources: Manufacturing—U.S. Census Bureau, 1997 Economic Census – Manufacturing, generated by Statistical Compendia Branch, using American Factfinder at <http://www.census.gov/>, (June 2000) [related Internet site <http://www.census.gov/epcd/www/97EC31.HTM>].   Water Use—U.S. Geological Survey, "Water Use in the United States," individual state/county and US by state files from <http://water.usgs.gov/watuse/spread95.html>, (accessed: September 1999).

Table B–9. Counties — **Manufacturing and Water Use**–Con.

[Includes U.S., states, and 3,142 counties/county equivalents defined as of January 1, 1992. For changes to these areas since January 1, 1992, see appendix B. Geographic Information]

County	Establishments Total	Establishments Percent with 20 or more employees	All employees Number[1]	All employees Annual payroll (mil. dol.)	Production workers Number[2]	Production workers Wages (mil. dol.)	Value added by manufacture (mil. dol.)	Value of shipments (mil. dol.)	Withdrawals Total (mil. gal.)	Withdrawals Percent ground water	Irrigation	Public supply	Industrial	Consumptive use (mil. gal.)
NEW HAMPSHIRE	2 328	32.5	98 934	3 361.4	68 942	1 935.5	11 320.1	19 813.1	1 323	6.2	6	98	43	35
Belknap	133	32.3	4 658	133.4	3 373	84.4	306.3	497.4	7	41.7	Z	3	Z	1
Carroll	93	28.0	1 634	45.9	1 095	23.3	93.3	180.7	8	52.5	1	3	Z	1
Cheshire	168	29.2	6 212	196.4	4 036	110.8	480.4	787.3	9	65.9	Z	5	Z	2
Coos	50	36.0	3 051	94.0	2 394	69.5	255.2	494.3	46	6.8	Z	5	34	5
Grafton	148	30.4	6 886	205.6	5 069	125.3	509.0	881.5	19	35.6	1	8	1	3
Hillsborough	737	32.6	36 656	1 397.9	25 257	782.1	3 527.2	6 260.7	59	35.3	2	40	4	9
Merrimack	224	38.8	9 674	304.9	7 282	186.0	677.3	1 314.4	245	3.4	1	10	1	7
Rockingham	500	29.8	16 582	573.3	10 704	312.9	3 730.2	6 596.5	902	2.2	1	10	1	5
Strafford	159	35.2	9 080	281.5	6 019	146.0	1 306.4	2 106.2	22	33.8	Z	12	1	2
Sullivan	116	37.9	4 501	128.6	3 713	95.2	434.7	694.2	6	43.6	Z	3	1	1
NEW JERSEY..........	11 812	32.4	409 788	15 430.2	275 840	8 152.1	50 101.7	97 060.8	6 113	9.5	125	1 037	396	257
Atlantic	160	25.6	4 927	143.0	3 801	91.8	338.3	600.3	46	94.5	9	29	1	11
Bergen	1 806	32.9	59 877	2 223.7	39 181	1 087.6	5 527.7	10 419.7	122	27.1	2	102	15	16
Burlington	464	37.5	18 766	740.7	12 947	445.7	2 082.7	3 945.9	234	22.7	81	37	4	18
Camden	677	30.3	21 055	729.5	14 193	392.3	1 916.7	3 617.6	73	95.5	1	65	Z	10
Cape May	82	12.2	813	19.1	665	13.7	52.6	110.4	300	6.1	1	12	Z	7
Cumberland.............	210	42.9	12 985	398.3	10 077	277.2	979.5	1 896.1	87	38.2	10	15	4	16
Essex	1 206	33.6	35 578	1 359.9	23 210	655.0	5 014.0	8 416.4	46	55.0	Z	30	16	16
Gloucester	290	37.6	11 013	416.5	7 301	231.4	2 187.4	6 882.8	73	48.8	6	22	39	16
Hudson	979	28.9	26 470	787.8	18 236	420.5	2 063.4	4 220.8	444	Z	–	–	3	8
Hunterdon	175	28.0	5 064	194.8	3 434	110.4	562.8	1 104.4	73	18.7	Z	4	46	6
Mercer	352	30.4	13 537	579.7	8 353	291.7	1 315.2	2 413.6	506	2.5	Z	41	1	8
Middlesex..............	977	39.3	49 983	1 950.6	34 434	1 123.6	6 290.5	13 688.0	94	48.3	1	40	4	13
Monmouth	587	21.8	12 820	402.7	8 814	218.8	1 136.8	2 318.3	79	29.8	4	69	1	11
Morris	749	29.0	24 461	979.6	15 757	490.3	4 780.5	7 531.5	102	43.9	1	79	4	7
Ocean...................	309	22.7	7 174	201.1	5 384	119.8	510.9	939.8	1 441	3.5	1	44	1	7
Passaic..................	1 059	34.8	34 589	1 237.6	24 529	668.9	3 764.9	6 464.2	300	2.8	Z	297	Z	12
Salem	48	29.2	4 188	207.5	2 475	108.2	604.3	1 156.2	1 551	.8	4	4	20	29
Somerset	376	35.6	16 289	856.7	8 173	285.5	3 139.3	5 148.4	127	7.8	Z	121	Z	3
Sussex	146	19.9	2 854	87.2	1 956	45.6	194.7	320.8	20	63.1	Z	5	Z	2
Union	996	35.4	40 157	1 619.7	28 056	888.9	6 438.3	13 883.3	326	4.2	Z	15	188	32
Warren	164	37.8	7 188	294.4	4 864	185.0	1 201.1	1 982.3	69	30.1	1	5	50	11
NEW MEXICO	1 593	18.4	39 664	1 135.8	29 334	721.4	13 440.2	17 906.1	3 505	48.6	2 993	311	8	1 980
Bernalillo	703	21.8	(4)	D	D	D	D	D	190	69.3	62	121	1	79
Catron..................	NA	NA	NA	NA	NA	NA	NA	NA	17	5.0	17	7	–	3
Chaves..................	51	23.5	(5)	D	D	D	D	D	290	90.7	262	17	1	195
Cibola...................	NA	NA	NA	NA	NA	NA	NA	NA	9	68.2	5	3	Z	4
Colfax...................	NA	NA	NA	NA	NA	NA	NA	NA	48	4.8	43	2	–	20
Curry....................	NA	NA	NA	NA	NA	NA	NA	NA	230	100.0	219	8	–	184
DeBaca..................	NA	NA	NA	NA	NA	NA	NA	NA	53	24.0	52	Z	–	26
Dona Ana...............	111	21.6	2 290	46.9	1 849	31.9	153.5	395.5	441	24.2	399	31	Z	223
Eddy	41	19.5	1 057	43.9	709	26.2	342.7	641.4	238	53.1	212	14	1	148
Grant	NA	NA	NA	NA	NA	NA	NA	NA	61	53.4	33	4	Z	28
Guadalupe..............	NA	NA	NA	NA	NA	NA	NA	NA	19	14.1	18	1	–	8
Harding..................	NA	NA	NA	NA	NA	NA	NA	NA	4	97.6	3	Z	–	4
Hidalgo..................	2	50.0	(6)	D	D	D	D	D	41	85.5	34	1	Z	25
Lea	45	13.3	524	14.8	315	8.2	98.5	379.7	158	100.0	117	14	1	116
Lincoln..................	NA	NA	NA	NA	NA	NA	NA	NA	35	36.0	30	3	Z	16
Los Alamos.............	16	25.0	776	10.7	564	7.8	23.2	49.5	5	100.0	–	5	–	5
McKinley	NA	NA	NA	NA	NA	NA	NA	NA	18	76.1	4	4	1	12
Mora	NA	NA	NA	NA	NA	NA	NA	NA	33	1.9	33	Z	–	16
Otero	26	19.2	593	10.5	547	9.0	46.9	93.8	47	68.6	33	11	Z	32
Quay....................	NA	NA	NA	NA	NA	NA	NA	NA	134	20.5	132	2	–	56
Rio Arriba...............	NA	NA	NA	NA	NA	NA	NA	NA	85	5.6	80	2	Z	32
Roosevelt...............	NA	NA	NA	NA	NA	NA	NA	NA	144	100.0	136	5	Z	119
Sandoval	57	29.8	(7)	D	D	D	D	D	68	27.6	50	14	1	27
San Juan	71	16.9	1 147	30.3	883	19.2	90.3	257.8	345	.9	278	16	Z	224
San Miguel..............	NA	NA	NA	NA	NA	NA	NA	NA	31	4.9	26	3	–	12
Santa Fe	162	8.6	1 436	31.7	1 038	19.7	72.8	124.8	46	52.4	29	14	Z	25
Sierra	NA	NA	NA	NA	NA	NA	NA	NA	42	39.4	39	2	Z	23
Socorro..................	NA	NA	NA	NA	NA	NA	NA	NA	147	25.6	143	2	Z	54
Taos	NA	NA	NA	NA	NA	NA	NA	NA	98	6.6	93	2	Z	38
Torrance.................	NA	NA	NA	NA	NA	NA	NA	NA	42	100.0	40	1	Z	31
Union	NA	NA	NA	NA	NA	NA	NA	NA	76	95.4	75	Z	–	64
Valencia.................	40	12.5	967	22.3	779	15.4	55.5	110.3	180	9.3	171	4	Z	55

[1] Average number of production workers plus the number of other (nonproduction) employees for the pay period including March 12. [2] Average number of production workers for the pay periods including the 12th of March, May, August, and November. [3] In millions of gallons per day. [4] 10,000 to 24,999 employees. [5] 2,500 to 4,999 employees. [6] 500 to 999 employees. [7] 5,000 to 9,999 employees.

Sources: Manufacturing—U.S. Census Bureau, 1997 Economic Census – Manufacturing, generated by Statistical Compendia Branch, using American Factfinder at <http://www.census.gov/>, (June 2000) [related Internet site <http://www.census.gov/epcd/www/97EC31.HTM>]. Water Use—U.S. Geological Survey, "Water Use in the United States," individual state/county and US by state files from <http://water.usgs.gov/watuse/spread95.html>, (accessed: September 1999).

Table B–9. Counties — **Manufacturing and Water Use**–Con.

[Includes U.S., states, and 3,142 counties/county equivalents defined as of January 1, 1992. For changes to these areas since January 1, 1992, see appendix B. Geographic Information]

County	Manufacturing (NAICS 31-33), 1997 — Establishments Total	Establishments Percent with 20 or more employees	All employees Number[1]	All employees Annual payroll (mil. dol.)	Production workers Number[2]	Production workers Wages (mil. dol.)	Value added by manufacture (mil. dol.)	Value of shipments (mil. dol.)	Water use per day,[3] 1995 — Withdrawals Total (mil. gal.)	Withdrawals Percent ground water	By selected major use (mil. gal.) Irrigation	By selected major use (mil. gal.) Public supply	By selected major use (mil. gal.) Industrial	Consumptive use (mil. gal.)
NEW YORK	23 908	28.0	785 891	26 515.8	538 186	14 695.8	76 999.8	146 720.2	16 782	6.0	30	3 000	259	603
Albany	272	30.9	9 065	335.9	6 082	189.5	1 086.5	2 182.4	567	1.4	1	49	4	17
Allegany	57	28.1	2 919	102.4	1 899	54.0	242.6	542.8	10	74.8	Z	5	2	2
Bronx	527	30.7	12 941	319.6	9 928	202.1	725.5	1 252.3	197	3.8	–	–	8	8
Broome	242	44.6	20 429	787.8	12 357	314.0	1 631.9	3 147.6	133	17.1	Z	33	4	7
Cattaraugus	95	43.2	5 341	162.9	4 110	115.7	529.7	930.5	16	77.7	Z	8	2	3
Cayuga	100	33.0	3 859	110.4	2 824	71.0	312.0	618.6	17	22.7	Z	12	1	3
Chautauqua	222	41.4	13 084	409.1	9 651	267.2	1 459.6	2 973.6	1 204	1.1	1	14	5	28
Chemung	94	46.8	9 098	278.1	6 214	170.4	765.6	1 357.3	18	61.0	Z	13	2	2
Chenango	86	38.4	3 829	120.3	2 643	62.3	497.9	790.4	9	69.7	Z	3	2	2
Clinton	82	34.1	4 188	131.8	3 422	98.3	359.5	777.9	16	28.0	Z	8	2	3
Columbia	86	30.2	2 531	62.2	1 882	38.6	156.2	331.1	9	68.6	1	3	1	2
Cortland	70	41.4	4 521	123.5	3 190	76.7	400.6	736.1	11	95.3	Z	7	1	2
Delaware	60	46.7	4 386	147.9	3 169	92.7	418.0	783.7	490	1.3	Z	485	1	2
Dutchess	210	28.1	11 848	521.3	5 675	153.8	937.5	3 032.9	40	41.6	Z	27	2	5
Erie	1 251	36.8	63 234	2 422.1	45 098	1 541.8	7 064.6	14 054.5	1 095	.7	1	215	26	42
Essex	40	12.5	1 474	50.4	1 132	35.3	130.0	285.2	12	14.0	Z	7	Z	2
Franklin	26	30.8	1 165	24.9	971	18.2	71.6	144.4	11	44.4	Z	6	1	2
Fulton	116	37.1	3 548	86.6	2 845	58.8	220.6	443.6	8	45.4	Z	3	2	1
Genesee	107	37.4	3 979	127.0	2 834	75.5	335.2	778.1	11	65.4	Z	5	2	2
Greene	37	16.2	740	22.4	472	11.9	57.8	118.4	11	37.6	1	3	Z	2
Hamilton	NA	NA	NA	NA	NA	NA	NA	NA	1	41.0	–	1	Z	Z
Herkimer	71	42.3	4 971	135.8	3 982	96.5	411.9	662.4	16	19.7	1	11	1	3
Jefferson	84	36.9	3 896	132.0	2 791	85.2	357.6	812.6	31	23.5	Z	16	6	4
Kings	2 672	23.2	48 589	1 139.9	37 284	718.3	3 014.6	5 725.5	51	48.8	–	–	12	6
Lewis	24	41.7	1 560	53.1	1 207	35.4	130.3	505.3	8	48.9	Z	2	2	2
Livingston	48	37.5	2 196	59.5	1 725	39.1	327.0	500.5	13	31.2	Z	6	1	2
Madison	69	30.4	2 526	69.3	2 040	45.7	159.9	506.7	12	36.4	–	6	1	2
Monroe	1 007	37.5	82 459	3 521.8	52 189	1 861.6	12 355.0	21 774.7	344	3.4	1	128	25	21
Montgomery	84	42.9	4 790	123.6	3 686	75.9	345.4	637.7	15	18.9	1	9	2	3
Nassau	1 653	22.3	42 717	1 550.8	26 522	704.5	4 093.7	7 117.3	546	39.6	Z	187	13	27
New York	5 165	23.2	93 784	2 551.8	63 917	1 336.4	6 420.9	14 028.9	340	24.0	–	–	29	28
Niagara	310	39.4	18 164	836.5	13 605	578.6	2 530.6	4 403.5	434	.5	Z	52	9	14
Oneida	280	36.4	15 079	447.1	10 928	283.0	1 170.6	2 485.3	39	14.8	1	26	5	5
Onondaga	510	37.5	33 289	1 296.3	21 138	682.3	3 649.8	6 614.4	170	9.0	Z	143	11	17
Ontario	161	41.0	7 196	226.4	4 896	119.9	561.9	999.1	18	31.1	Z	11	3	3
Orange	346	30.9	(4)	D	D	D	D	D	1 369	1.5	1	29	4	32
Orleans	48	50.0	2 269	71.2	1 631	42.9	230.6	496.0	5	53.7	Z	2	1	1
Oswego	108	29.6	5 082	204.9	3 929	140.2	534.5	2 210.7	1 172	1.1	2	14	3	66
Otsego	68	25.0	1 481	38.0	1 151	24.7	131.0	225.0	10	40.9	Z	5	Z	2
Putnam	74	18.9	1 595	60.3	967	27.8	163.1	258.9	131	3.7	Z	126	Z	1
Queens	2 043	26.5	50 505	1 433.2	36 736	806.8	3 566.3	6 412.8	2 216	2.0	–	24	8	48
Rensselaer	110	39.1	5 023	169.1	3 030	84.8	301.7	767.2	38	27.9	Z	27	4	4
Richmond	162	12.3	2 156	59.6	1 404	37.8	148.8	316.2	493	.6	–	–	Z	11
Rockland	309	23.3	10 739	413.3	6 958	215.6	2 642.4	3 649.8	1 218	3.0	Z	34	8	27
St. Lawrence	85	36.5	5 311	201.4	3 994	137.7	606.3	1 602.2	22	31.7	Z	8	2	4
Saratoga	139	28.8	6 400	263.2	4 662	166.3	720.5	1 513.9	21	50.5	Z	12	2	3
Schenectady	119	33.6	5 134	212.2	3 759	142.9	756.4	1 687.8	31	98.9	Z	27	2	3
Schoharie	28	21.4	1 024	24.0	817	17.3	128.9	180.8	132	3.5	1	123	Z	2
Schuyler	17	35.3	574	18.3	395	12.7	49.9	88.8	5	42.1	Z	1	Z	1
Seneca	31	25.8	2 037	71.2	1 362	43.4	221.0	457.2	5	44.9	Z	3	Z	1
Steuben	74	37.8	8 070	264.2	6 029	169.0	803.8	1 338.5	65	21.9	1	11	5	5
Suffolk	2 535	26.5	70 317	2 433.5	44 634	1 179.1	7 090.4	12 009.2	1 011	17.1	9	127	14	42
Sullivan	54	13.0	(5)	D	D	D	D	D	151	4.0	Z	146	Z	1
Tioga	48	29.2	5 055	239.8	1 694	42.4	1 200.3	1 569.6	9	91.1	Z	4	1	2
Tompkins	94	26.6	3 613	123.6	2 619	76.2	303.1	667.1	261	1.2	Z	12	Z	7
Ulster	215	26.0	6 449	183.7	4 355	105.1	450.5	785.0	482	2.1	2	470	1	4
Warren	84	22.6	4 014	144.0	2 634	72.8	423.6	820.7	14	9.8	Z	10	1	2
Washington	99	37.4	3 852	122.7	2 912	78.6	347.2	642.0	11	47.8	1	4	1	3
Wayne	145	37.2	8 041	221.8	5 883	141.5	752.9	1 435.2	484	1.3	Z	11	2	12
Westchester	869	23.7	18 797	626.3	13 047	342.3	1 431.7	3 012.0	1 380	1.8	Z	260	16	40
Wyoming	55	50.9	3 011	79.1	2 400	54.7	195.7	371.9	11	48.7	Z	4	Z	3
Yates	27	22.2	522	15.6	351	9.5	91.2	225.2	113	1.6	Z	1	Z	3

[1] Average number of production workers plus the number of other (nonproduction) employees for the pay period including March 12. [2] Average number of production workers for the pay periods including the 12th of March, May, August, and November. [3] In millions of gallons per day. [4] 10,000 to 24,999 employees. [5] 500 to 999 employees.

Sources: Manufacturing—U.S. Census Bureau, 1997 Economic Census – Manufacturing, generated by Statistical Compendia Branch, using American Factfinder at <http://www.census.gov/>, (June 2000) [related Internet site <http://www.census.gov/epcd/www/97EC31.HTM>]. Water Use—U.S. Geological Survey, "Water Use in the United States," individual state/county and US by state files from <http://water.usgs.gov/watuse/spread95.html>, (accessed: September 1999).

[Includes U.S., states, and 3,142 counties/county equivalents defined as of January 1, 1992. For changes to these areas since January 1, 1992, see appendix B. Geographic Information]

| County | Manufacturing (NAICS 31-33), 1997 | | | | | | | | Water use per day,[3] 1995 | | | | | |
| | Establishments | | All employees | | Production workers | | Value added by manufacture (mil. dol.) | Value of shipments (mil. dol.) | Withdrawals | | By selected major use– (mil. gal.) | | | Consumptive use (mil. gal.) |
	Total	Percent with 20 or more employees	Number[1]	Annual payroll (mil. dol.)	Number[2]	Wages (mil. dol.)			Total (mil. gal.)	Percent ground water	Irrigation	Public supply	Industrial	
NORTH CAROLINA	11 306	40.9	773 548	21 297.9	601 190	14 061.0	78 638.0	161 900.5	9 286	5.8	239	769	369	730
Alamance	282	54.3	21 490	588.2	17 603	406.5	1 415.5	3 324.8	28	16.0	4	14	5	10
Alexander	99	50.5	5 512	129.2	4 741	101.3	295.5	635.0	5	36.3	Z	2	Z	3
Alleghany	22	45.5	1 422	27.2	1 124	19.6	80.0	245.3	3	47.4	1	Z	Z	2
Anson	37	59.5	3 426	74.3	2 867	53.4	174.0	364.8	13	32.9	Z	6	5	5
Ashe	37	32.4	2 093	42.2	1 823	33.2	99.2	242.1	4	56.0	1	Z	–	2
Avery	11	45.5	802	14.6	749	13.1	49.0	85.4	9	22.9	4	1	1	4
Beaufort	65	41.5	5 772	139.8	4 606	95.5	328.0	927.8	17	91.0	1	2	Z	12
Bertie	16	50.0	(4)	D	D	D	D	D	8	57.6	3	1	Z	7
Bladen	36	58.3	6 559	127.4	5 846	103.4	-192.5	1 040.9	9	77.0	1	2	2	5
Brunswick	57	31.6	2 340	86.9	1 785	58.4	458.3	1 013.3	1 565	.3	8	2	1	28
Buncombe	332	38.3	(5)	D	D	D	D	D	38	18.4	2	24	3	10
Burke	171	48.5	17 279	416.7	14 305	297.2	1 026.7	2 126.9	29	16.7	3	16	7	9
Cabarrus	166	33.7	13 099	409.7	10 652	295.3	6 096.7	7 991.8	31	21.2	2	9	17	8
Caldwell	167	52.7	15 254	344.4	13 275	269.4	831.9	1 633.1	13	21.1	3	6	2	6
Camden	NA	NA	NA	NA	NA	NA	NA	NA	1	97.7	Z	Z	–	1
Carteret	69	17.4	1 576	29.4	1 369	21.6	72.5	173.1	8	94.5	2	4	Z	4
Caswell	NA	NA	NA	NA	NA	NA	NA	NA	4	84.8	2	1	–	2
Catawba	575	51.3	40 469	1 035.2	33 729	741.3	2 527.8	5 512.8	806	1.1	4	17	6	10
Chatham	76	47.4	7 109	158.2	6 261	122.7	431.5	1 014.3	396	1.5	Z	4	Z	15
Cherokee	27	44.4	2 776	56.3	2 375	44.8	136.5	315.0	8	15.3	Z	2	–	1
Chowan	18	44.4	1 061	23.8	890	17.1	53.5	114.2	3	57.1	1	2	Z	2
Clay	NA	NA	NA	NA	NA	NA	NA	NA	5	18.6	Z	Z	–	1
Cleveland	173	47.4	14 655	399.9	11 767	293.3	1 321.2	2 497.0	39	10.7	2	13	2	7
Columbus	46	54.3	4 767	129.9	3 707	83.1	379.4	895.5	7	74.5	1	2	1	3
Craven	86	26.7	4 344	118.5	3 477	87.8	237.6	796.4	14	95.4	3	10	Z	6
Cumberland	121	43.0	12 282	384.6	9 912	281.9	1 419.4	2 766.9	36	23.8	5	25	2	13
Currituck	NA	NA	NA	NA	NA	NA	NA	NA	2	74.1	1	Z	–	2
Dare	NA	NA	NA	NA	NA	NA	NA	NA	6	90.3	2	4	–	3
Davidson	326	40.5	21 576	521.7	17 683	384.5	1 229.8	2 249.4	22	6.2	2	15	5	7
Davie	45	40.0	2 886	76.4	2 423	52.6	178.1	406.9	6	31.4	2	2	Z	3
Duplin	48	43.8	4 688	95.2	3 763	68.7	190.3	675.9	29	86.7	4	11	1	17
Durham	181	33.1	31 489	1 027.2	10 092	252.1	2 961.1	11 223.8	31	14.6	3	21	4	9
Edgecombe	50	56.0	7 720	234.0	5 995	136.7	539.1	1 606.6	12	42.6	3	4	1	6
Forsyth	399	36.8	26 545	908.6	20 891	642.1	5 769.3	9 676.3	62	7.9	6	43	9	19
Franklin	55	47.3	2 259	67.3	1 859	43.9	259.1	444.6	0	36.0	4	2	Z	6
Gaston	492	39.6	31 175	863.2	25 139	617.1	2 758.2	5 772.7	399	1.7	2	33	45	19
Gates	NA	NA	NA	NA	NA	NA	NA	NA	2	79.7	1	1	–	2
Graham	3	66.7	(6)	D	D	D	D	D	42	1.0	Z	Z	–	Z
Granville	57	52.6	6 990	185.2	5 353	121.5	945.0	1 534.2	7	33.4	2	2	1	4
Greene	NA	NA	NA	NA	NA	NA	NA	NA	5	87.1	1	2	–	3
Guilford	862	42.5	47 158	1 431.2	34 628	875.9	6 136.4	10 546.4	95	13.9	11	42	34	29
Halifax	59	47.5	4 136	113.7	3 442	84.2	211.4	567.7	13	23.3	3	6	2	6
Harnett	82	40.2	5 959	149.3	5 020	104.1	309.1	633.7	97	7.1	3	7	84	23
Haywood	49	26.5	3 321	130.2	2 645	97.6	178.7	726.3	85	2.2	1	6	26	8
Henderson	132	28.0	8 361	260.1	6 845	190.0	848.5	1 745.8	14	22.6	4	6	2	6
Hertford	30	56.7	1 695	37.2	1 364	25.8	105.8	459.2	5	80.0	2	1	–	3
Hoke	11	45.5	3 151	72.8	2 903	62.5	238.4	414.8	5	79.7	1	2	Z	2
Hyde	NA	NA	NA	NA	NA	NA	NA	NA	1	97.4	–	1	Z	Z
Iredell	263	46.0	16 978	476.5	12 941	304.6	1 289.0	3 172.6	24	28.8	2	9	7	8
Jackson	36	25.0	699	15.9	530	11.2	36.3	76.3	5	42.1	1	1	Z	1
Johnston	114	39.5	6 588	192.1	4 713	111.2	682.4	1 622.3	14	49.6	5	5	Z	8
Jones	NA	NA	NA	NA	NA	NA	NA	NA	5	52.1	1	1	3	2
Lee	108	50.0	12 130	319.4	9 340	193.0	1 180.2	2 167.9	9	20.4	2	5	–	4
Lenoir	82	43.9	7 120	201.4	5 411	127.3	650.9	1 596.1	12	83.7	1	7	Z	5
Lincoln	112	47.3	8 047	196.4	6 834	150.1	470.9	990.9	11	31.8	1	6	1	3
McDowell	63	49.2	6 084	140.9	5 186	109.9	382.5	866.3	11	40.1	1	2	2	2
Macon	34	29.4	1 358	32.5	1 134	23.6	98.0	174.7	17	8.7	1	1	Z	2
Madison	NA	NA	NA	NA	NA	NA	NA	NA	4	33.7	1	Z	Z	1
Martin	22	36.4	1 902	40.6	1 673	30.3	96.4	307.9	6	81.6	1	3	–	3
Mecklenburg	1 001	33.8	42 494	1 429.8	27 420	767.9	4 383.6	8 831.4	2 749	.5	12	73	5	31
Mitchell	32	28.1	1 868	37.1	1 706	30.6	64.5	151.4	7	13.4	Z	1	–	1
Montgomery	78	56.4	5 292	112.1	4 493	83.8	303.4	666.7	7	30.6	1	3	Z	4
Moore	105	39.0	5 943	129.9	4 945	93.4	366.9	903.7	27	44.0	14	5	Z	21
Nash	104	50.0	9 879	267.8	7 876	190.6	860.4	1 721.8	24	17.1	6	13	2	11
New Hanover	203	26.6	8 378	338.8	5 922	211.4	1 615.2	2 698.2	67	14.4	4	20	Z	13
Northampton	13	61.5	749	20.5	601	14.5	84.3	233.0	5	79.4	1	1	Z	3
Onslow	37	32.4	1 829	37.7	1 554	29.2	169.4	346.4	15	97.1	2	8	–	6

[1] Average number of production workers plus the number of other (nonproduction) employees for the pay period including March 12. [2] Average number of production workers for the pay periods including the 12th of March, May, August, and November. [3] In millions of gallons per day. [4] 2,500 to 4,999 employees. [5] 10,000 to 24,999 employees. [6] 500 to 999 employees.

Sources: Manufacturing—U.S. Census Bureau, 1997 Economic Census – Manufacturing, generated by Statistical Compendia Branch, using American Factfinder at <http://www.census.gov/>, (June 2000) [related Internet site <http://www.census.gov/epcd/www/97EC31.HTM>]. Water Use—U.S. Geological Survey, "Water Use in the United States," individual state/county and US by state files from <http://water.usgs.gov/watuse/spread95.html>, (accessed: September 1999).

[Includes U.S., states, and 3,142 counties/county equivalents defined as of January 1, 1992. For changes to these areas since January 1, 1992, see appendix B. Geographic Information]

| | Manufacturing (NAICS 31-33), 1997 | | | | | | | | Water use per day,[3] 1995 | | | | | |
| County | Establishments | | All employees | | Production workers | | Value added by manu-facture (mil. dol.) | Value of ship-ments (mil. dol.) | Withdrawals | | By selected major use– (mil. gal.) | | | Consump-tive use (mil. gal.) |
	Total	Percent with 20 or more employ-ees	Number[1]	Annual payroll (mil. dol.)	Number[2]	Wages (mil. dol.)			Total (mil. gal.)	Percent ground water	Irrigation	Public supply	Industrial	
NORTH CAROLINA–Con.														
Orange	78	19.2	1 209	34.0	913	21.5	69.7	142.1	16	19.4	3	11	–	6
Pamlico	NA	NA	NA	NA	NA	NA	NA	NA	3	100.0	2	1	–	2
Pasquotank	31	35.5	884	18.5	698	12.6	75.2	148.6	5	90.2	1	4	Z	2
Pender	39	30.8	1 123	24.3	902	17.3	41.3	135.8	4	59.9	2	1	–	3
Perquimans	NA	NA	NA	NA	NA	NA	NA	NA	2	95.8	Z	1	–	1
Person	39	48.7	5 138	135.5	4 048	95.6	471.6	1 084.8	678	.3	2	4	1	34
Pitt	119	42.0	9 305	280.8	6 985	174.5	1 707.3	2 741.9	26	58.3	3	14	6	9
Polk	25	40.0	904	19.9	771	15.0	72.2	150.9	3	41.4	1	1	Z	1
Randolph	411	43.3	24 954	559.8	20 933	410.7	1 853.7	3 612.7	24	48.6	2	7	3	12
Richmond	58	43.1	4 814	114.5	4 033	89.0	384.4	719.7	12	32.2	2	5	2	6
Robeson	96	52.1	11 890	264.0	10 112	194.3	1 305.3	2 407.9	38	46.9	3	17	6	13
Rockingham	124	51.6	13 958	387.0	11 643	297.2	1 169.0	3 214.4	69	3.4	5	22	1	9
Rowan	201	51.7	14 324	413.8	11 907	316.3	1 506.1	3 677.9	72	9.9	2	12	2	7
Rutherford	97	49.5	11 480	278.6	9 409	198.5	524.1	1 514.2	33	9.0	2	10	11	14
Sampson	61	47.5	4 202	102.4	3 176	59.9	207.6	768.5	21	77.3	6	3	Z	16
Scotland	59	59.3	8 534	234.0	7 422	174.9	716.1	1 533.3	9	59.0	1	3	3	3
Stanly	124	48.4	8 086	210.3	6 544	152.1	547.1	1 167.5	13	27.3	2	8	1	4
Stokes	33	33.3	1 218	37.0	958	21.9	75.1	167.7	898	.2	1	2	–	2
Surry	149	43.6	14 915	300.1	13 186	238.5	762.3	1 697.3	26	29.1	2	7	10	8
Swain	NA	NA	NA	NA	NA	NA	NA	NA	23	3.7	Z	Z	–	1
Transylvania	28	35.7	3 071	119.3	2 337	79.7	435.5	715.1	30	7.0	2	2	Z	3
Tyrrell	NA	NA	NA	NA	NA	NA	NA	NA	1	100.0	1	Z	–	Z
Union	228	39.5	13 113	356.9	10 261	223.6	1 256.3	2 543.5	27	37.4	1	10	5	13
Vance	53	60.4	5 085	119.2	4 217	80.9	464.6	1 218.0	22	59.8	1	5	14	5
Wake	639	27.1	23 789	784.7	15 855	388.3	6 075.3	10 420.0	79	23.1	10	43	8	28
Warren	13	69.2	813	15.3	757	13.6	36.6	95.5	3	43.0	1	Z	Z	2
Washington	15	46.7	(4)	D	D	D	D	D	6	91.8	1	3	–	3
Watauga	56	16.1	1 223	24.8	1 014	18.3	54.5	97.4	6	19.8	1	4	–	2
Wayne	101	43.6	9 495	231.1	7 597	159.2	646.7	1 417.5	32	29.9	3	9	6	12
Wilkes	108	37.0	8 082	168.1	7 025	129.4	403.7	1 081.2	18	35.0	1	7	–	11
Wilson	96	40.6	8 954	288.1	7 218	195.8	2 605.9	4 980.3	17	30.1	3	8	3	7
Yadkin	43	39.5	3 616	94.5	3 068	68.2	231.7	787.3	6	74.0	1	2	–	3
Yancey	21	61.9	1 645	39.3	1 369	28.2	92.4	373.4	2	57.6	1	Z	–	1
NORTH DAKOTA	704	26.7	21 956	604.8	16 364	386.9	1 802.4	5 115.9	1 122	10.9	117	73	11	181
Adams	NA	NA	NA	NA	NA	NA	NA	NA	1	62.2	Z	Z	–	1
Barnes	NA	NA	NA	NA	NA	NA	NA	NA	2	44.0	Z	1	Z	1
Benson	NA	NA	NA	NA	NA	NA	NA	NA	3	93.7	1	1	–	1
Billings	NA	NA	NA	NA	NA	NA	NA	NA	1	56.3	Z	Z	Z	1
Bottineau	NA	NA	NA	NA	NA	NA	NA	NA	2	64.7	Z	1	Z	1
Bowman	NA	NA	NA	NA	NA	NA	NA	NA	3	27.2	1	Z	–	2
Burke	NA	NA	NA	NA	NA	NA	NA	NA	1	50.0	Z	Z	–	1
Burleigh	54	22.2	1 310	47.3	927	30.5	–	99.7	12	20.1	2	9	Z	5
Cass	183	37.2	6 757	173.5	4 947	106.5	625.8	1 512.2	19	31.5	3	14	1	6
Cavalier	NA	NA	NA	NA	NA	NA	NA	NA	1	28.7	Z	1	–	Z
Dickey	NA	NA	NA	NA	NA	NA	NA	NA	7	87.7	5	1	–	6
Divide	NA	NA	NA	NA	NA	NA	NA	NA	2	90.2	2	Z	Z	2
Dunn	NA	NA	NA	NA	NA	NA	NA	NA	3	50.1	2	Z	Z	1
Eddy	NA	NA	NA	NA	NA	NA	NA	NA	2	72.0	1	Z	–	1
Emmons	NA	NA	NA	NA	NA	NA	NA	NA	6	23.4	5	Z	–	6
Foster	NA	NA	NA	NA	NA	NA	NA	NA	2	94.1	1	Z	Z	2
Golden Valley	NA	NA	NA	NA	NA	NA	NA	NA	3	14.0	2	Z	Z	3
Grand Forks	52	25.0	1 737	39.0	1 387	28.3	145.3	251.5	16	36.2	5	10	–	7
Grant	NA	NA	NA	NA	NA	NA	NA	NA	8	11.0	7	Z	–	7
Griggs	NA	NA	NA	NA	NA	NA	NA	NA	2	94.9	1	Z	Z	Z
Hettinger	NA	NA	NA	NA	NA	NA	NA	NA	1	63.2	Z	Z	–	Z
Kidder	NA	NA	NA	NA	NA	NA	NA	NA	6	91.0	5	Z	–	6
LaMoure	NA	NA	NA	NA	NA	NA	NA	NA	5	93.0	4	Z	–	4
Logan	NA	NA	NA	NA	NA	NA	NA	NA	2	84.5	1	Z	–	2
McHenry	NA	NA	NA	NA	NA	NA	NA	NA	19	33.7	17	1	Z	16
McIntosh	NA	NA	NA	NA	NA	NA	NA	NA	1	76.9	–	Z	Z	1
McKenzie	NA	NA	NA	NA	NA	NA	NA	NA	13	14.2	11	Z	Z	11
McLean	NA	NA	NA	NA	NA	NA	NA	NA	161	2.5	3	1	Z	14
Mercer	NA	NA	NA	NA	NA	NA	NA	NA	278	.6	1	5	6	19
Morton	27	37.0	883	27.2	641	17.7	109.8	573.4	38	4.6	1	3	2	4
Mountrail	NA	NA	NA	NA	NA	NA	NA	NA	2	52.9	1	Z	–	1
Nelson	NA	NA	NA	NA	NA	NA	NA	NA	1	91.2	Z	Z	–	1
Oliver	NA	NA	NA	NA	NA	NA	NA	NA	435	.2	3	Z	Z	4
Pembina	16	6.3	(5)	D	D	D	D	D	2	57.7	Z	1	Z	1
Pierce	NA	NA	NA	NA	NA	NA	NA	NA	2	84.5	1	1	–	1

[1] Average number of production workers plus the number of other (nonproduction) employees for the pay period including March 12.   [2] Average number of production workers for the pay periods including the 12th of March, May, August, and November.   [3] In millions of gallons per day.   [4] 1,000 to 2,499 employees.   [5] 500 to 999 employees.

Sources: Manufacturing—U.S. Census Bureau, 1997 Economic Census – Manufacturing, generated by Statistical Compendia Branch, using American Factfinder at <http://www.census.gov/>, (June 2000) [related Internet site <http://www.census.gov/epcd/www/97EC31.HTM>].   Water Use—U.S. Geological Survey, "Water Use in the United States," individual state/county and US by state files from <http://water.usgs.gov/watuse/spread95.html>, (accessed: September 1999).

Table B–9. Counties — **Manufacturing and Water Use**–Con.

[Includes U.S., states, and 3,142 counties/county equivalents defined as of January 1, 1992. For changes to these areas since January 1, 1992, see appendix B. Geographic Information]

County	Manufacturing (NAICS 31-33), 1997								Water use per day,[3] 1995					
	Establishments		All employees		Production workers		Value added by manu-facture (mil. dol.)	Value of ship-ments (mil. dol.)	Withdrawals		By selected major use– (mil. gal.)			Consump-tive use (mil. gal.)
	Total	Percent with 20 or more employ-ees	Number[1]	Annual payroll (mil. dol.)	Number[2]	Wages (mil. dol.)			Total (mil. gal.)	Percent ground water	Irrigation	Public supply	Industrial	
NORTH DAKOTA—Con.														
Ramsey	NA	NA	NA	NA	NA	NA	NA	NA	1	66.7	Z	Z	–	Z
Ransom	NA	NA	NA	NA	NA	NA	NA	NA	13	90.1	12	1	Z	11
Renville	NA	NA	NA	NA	NA	NA	NA	NA	Z	80.8	Z	Z	Z	Z
Richland	34	38.2	2 261	69.2	1 758	50.0	120.5	373.0	4	94.8	Z	2	Z	1
Rolette	NA	NA	NA	NA	NA	NA	NA	NA	2	94.0	Z	1	–	1
Sargent	5	60.0	(4)	D	D	D	D	D	6	97.6	6	Z	–	6
Sheridan	NA	NA	NA	NA	NA	NA	NA	NA	1	73.6	Z	Z	–	Z
Sioux	NA	NA	NA	NA	NA	NA	NA	NA	1	64.4	Z	Z	–	1
Slope	NA	NA	NA	NA	NA	NA	NA	NA	1	30.6	1	Z	–	1
Stark	30	20.0	718	17.6	508	10.2	36.6	75.8	2	41.8	1	Z	Z	3
Steele	NA	NA	NA	NA	NA	NA	NA	NA	1	95.7	1	Z	–	1
Stutsman	28	35.7	1 446	41.0	1 001	20.8	110.1	250.3	6	93.2	1	2	2	4
Towner	NA	NA	NA	NA	NA	NA	NA	NA	1	55.6	Z	Z	Z	Z
Traill	NA	NA	NA	NA	NA	NA	NA	NA	1	62.4	Z	1	–	Z
Walsh	NA	NA	NA	NA	NA	NA	NA	NA	2	46.4	Z	1	–	1
Ward	58	19.0	770	18.0	499	10.4	91.6	281.6	9	91.7	1	7	Z	3
Wells	NA	NA	NA	NA	NA	NA	NA	NA	1	84.7	Z	Z	–	Z
Williams	NA	NA	NA	NA	NA	NA	NA	NA	11	47.7	7	3	Z	7
OHIO	17 974	38.4	984 201	35 950.5	730 170	23 561.0	112 491.4	241 902.9	10 523	8.6	27	1 420	557	791
Adams	31	19.4	(5)	D	D	D	D	D	735	.6	Z	2	–	6
Allen	132	37.9	9 529	407.8	7 458	299.7	2 753.8	6 631.7	40	23.5	Z	31	5	8
Ashland	98	44.9	7 135	215.7	5 681	145.3	580.0	1 157.5	6	93.7	Z	4	Z	1
Ashtabula	175	41.7	9 984	302.6	7 607	206.4	921.2	1 794.3	211	1.0	Z	9	12	15
Athens	43	16.3	1 351	32.5	983	22.3	123.1	222.1	7	68.8	Z	6	–	1
Auglaize	93	40.9	8 236	288.7	6 053	187.8	829.7	1 737.6	15	66.1	Z	5	Z	4
Belmont	55	23.6	1 523	36.9	1 190	26.4	111.4	272.5	240	3.4	Z	9	1	2
Brown	25	28.0	1 110	33.4	872	24.8	85.9	280.8	4	78.8	Z	3	–	1
Butler	396	39.1	20 391	819.2	14 957	562.3	4 325.4	6 567.8	74	83.3	1	37	33	29
Carroll	40	37.5	1 782	56.7	1 267	43.0	138.8	302.3	4	87.3	Z	1	1	1
Champaign	55	40.0	3 452	101.3	2 853	71.9	493.4	946.8	5	92.7	Z	2	–	1
Clark	230	39.6	13 231	520.0	10 009	369.1	1 575.2	4 071.5	25	88.8	1	19	Z	5
Clermont	167	33.5	7 092	305.5	5 123	170.6	807.1	1 544.3	547	3.1	Z	14	–	24
Clinton	50	52.0	4 969	135.5	3 897	86.6	352.4	809.6	2	55.4	–	1	–	1
Columbiana	209	39.2	8 616	246.3	7 016	169.8	583.2	1 109.3	14	48.6	Z	10	Z	3
Coshocton	55	50.9	4 814	162.9	3 508	105.0	513.4	1 191.3	238	7.7	Z	9	6	13
Crawford	90	51.1	6 575	211.6	5 213	156.6	674.5	1 194.7	6	29.5	Z	4	–	2
Cuyahoga	2 712	36.0	116 680	4 640.6	79 865	2 783.6	11 552.7	23 382.3	429	.1	Z	282	99	38
Darke	92	31.5	5 811	172.4	4 299	107.1	545.2	1 147.4	8	61.2	Z	3	–	3
Defiance	48	50.0	7 150	329.2	6 119	272.2	645.8	1 338.9	6	25.9	Z	5	–	1
Delaware	117	34.2	5 131	187.6	3 234	97.7	725.1	1 285.7	17	26.7	1	8	Z	5
Erie	117	51.3	9 176	409.2	7 192	304.1	1 006.3	2 251.5	22	8.0	Z	14	7	9
Fairfield	154	26.6	6 251	188.2	4 762	125.4	464.3	833.7	13	97.0	Z	9	–	3
Fayette	45	48.9	2 959	83.5	2 426	66.2	241.0	572.8	4	46.6	Z	2	–	1
Franklin	1 061	35.4	48 265	1 754.6	34 268	1 059.5	6 256.9	11 837.7	162	19.2	2	150	1	29
Fulton	110	53.6	9 108	276.5	7 288	165.5	807.8	1 673.4	6	29.9	Z	4	–	1
Gallia	18	27.8	948	26.9	759	19.2	72.7	117.6	1 285	.4	–	3	–	178
Geauga	233	35.2	9 851	306.2	7 117	180.7	692.6	1 380.2	8	88.0	Z	1	–	2
Greene	141	34.0	4 952	166.2	3 542	103.0	430.5	738.0	18	86.0	Z	9	1	6
Guernsey	59	44.1	3 773	113.7	3 048	86.3	399.8	899.9	7	27.7	Z	5	–	1
Hamilton	1 450	37.9	76 053	3 027.9	48 484	1 593.5	10 255.8	20 077.9	311	21.3	1	155	15	70
Hancock	97	44.3	11 964	422.5	9 302	293.0	1 330.2	2 792.4	18	24.1	Z	14	1	5
Hardin	38	50.0	2 412	84.6	1 975	63.0	213.0	484.3	4	93.2	Z	2	–	1
Harrison	24	37.5	678	14.2	535	8.9	40.7	105.8	2	45.4	–	1	–	Z
Henry	54	44.4	3 947	148.6	3 239	114.7	1 145.5	1 721.1	9	17.0	Z	2	6	2
Highland	41	39.0	3 851	94.4	3 297	68.3	280.7	653.8	4	31.5	–	2	–	1
Hocking	26	50.0	2 102	60.4	1 804	47.3	174.5	341.3	5	97.1	Z	3	–	1
Holmes	164	31.7	4 621	100.2	3 889	76.3	329.0	710.1	5	79.2	–	1	Z	2
Huron	110	50.9	11 114	326.0	9 239	239.8	988.3	2 152.7	11	23.3	1	7	Z	2
Jackson	37	37.8	3 631	83.4	3 174	65.1	422.8	780.5	2	68.9	–	2	–	Z
Jefferson	45	26.7	2 244	78.7	1 579	49.6	187.6	463.3	2 147	.6	Z	5	149	32
Knox	72	41.7	4 924	174.4	3 550	104.6	399.3	972.3	7	74.7	Z	4	–	1
Lake	769	34.1	25 423	893.2	18 166	518.8	2 746.8	4 661.0	804	.2	4	29	1	47
Lawrence	44	27.3	1 969	65.0	1 462	46.8	530.9	998.1	9	72.4	–	5	3	1
Licking	150	36.7	9 489	321.1	7 635	239.6	1 315.7	2 455.1	18	52.5	Z	11	1	3
Logan	58	43.1	6 295	238.9	5 088	186.3	1 334.7	3 766.0	6	90.4	Z	3	Z	1
Lorain	437	37.8	27 252	1 054.4	21 092	730.1	4 578.7	11 225.5	544	.3	1	37	2	7
Lucas	652	36.0	33 116	1 404.8	26 522	1 050.6	3 742.1	12 071.0	754	.9	1	82	34	17
Madison	51	45.1	3 401	102.8	2 744	72.1	287.0	606.5	4	92.2	Z	2	–	1
Mahoning	405	36.3	13 001	398.6	9 883	259.2	953.7	2 110.0	8	19.7	Z	6	Z	2

[1] Average number of production workers plus the number of other (nonproduction) employees for the pay period including March 12.   [2] Average number of production workers for the pay periods including the 12th of March, May, August, and November.   [3] In millions of gallons per day.   [4] 1,000 to 2,499 employees.   [5] 500 to 999 employees.

Sources: Manufacturing—U.S. Census Bureau, 1997 Economic Census – Manufacturing, generated by Statistical Compendia Branch, using American Factfinder at <http://www.census.gov/>, (June 2000) [related Internet site <http://www.census.gov/epcd/www/97EC31.HTM>].   Water Use—U.S. Geological Survey, "Water Use in the United States," individual state/county and US by state files from <http://water.usgs.gov/watuse/spread95.html>, (accessed: September 1999).

Table B–9. Counties — Manufacturing and Water Use–Con.

[Includes U.S., states, and 3,142 counties/county equivalents defined as of January 1, 1992. For changes to these areas since January 1, 1992, see appendix B. Geographic Information]

County	Establishments Total	Establishments Percent with 20 or more employees	All employees Number[1]	All employees Annual payroll (mil. dol.)	Production workers Number[2]	Production workers Wages (mil. dol.)	Value added by manufacture (mil. dol.)	Value of shipments (mil. dol.)	Withdrawals Total (mil. gal.)	Withdrawals Percent ground water	Irrigation	Public supply	Industrial	Consumptive use (mil. gal.)
OHIO—Con.														
Marion	86	45.3	6 842	229.8	5 270	160.0	837.5	1 924.7	9	48.1	Z	6	1	3
Medina	306	40.5	10 672	346.7	7 492	195.6	890.0	1 744.7	17	59.4	Z	7	–	4
Meigs	NA	NA	NA	NA	NA	NA	NA	NA	9	76.9	–	2	–	3
Mercer	62	41.9	4 473	130.8	3 720	93.6	413.2	775.7	7	71.5	Z	2	Z	3
Miami	265	35.8	13 848	454.9	9 839	265.4	1 338.5	2 611.8	42	30.0	1	11	Z	3
Monroe	21	14.3	(4)	D	D	D	D	D	4	54.5	Z	2	–	2
Montgomery	927	38.4	56 299	2 337.3	41 924	1 592.6	7 143.4	15 734.7	179	74.3	2	99	16	33
Morgan	10	30.0	921	27.5	736	18.6	72.3	135.5	4	88.5	Z	1	1	1
Morrow	27	37.0	1 778	57.5	1 169	28.2	147.5	366.2	3	90.7	Z	1	–	1
Muskingum	113	34.5	10 096	248.8	8 869	199.2	765.7	1 214.6	19	79.0	Z	10	5	7
Noble	12	41.7	(5)	D	D	D	D	D	1	31.2	–	1	–	Z
Ottawa	56	42.9	2 886	100.8	2 308	74.5	319.6	634.2	51	15.1	Z	3	6	12
Paulding	39	43.6	1 628	46.4	1 263	32.8	109.0	256.5	3	64.6	–	1	1	1
Perry	35	42.9	1 763	50.8	1 515	38.4	148.5	238.9	4	40.9	–	1	–	1
Pickaway	44	43.2	4 726	188.6	3 369	116.0	609.7	1 134.4	37	42.9	1	4	9	6
Pike	28	35.7	4 953	190.2	3 161	103.1	762.1	1 202.3	4	90.0	Z	2	–	1
Portage	298	41.6	12 984	417.8	9 633	265.1	1 109.2	2 154.2	17	76.6	Z	10	Z	5
Preble	61	37.7	3 274	109.2	2 451	68.7	352.4	698.0	4	91.5	–	2	–	1
Putnam	42	52.4	4 005	129.9	3 433	98.8	345.5	1 237.1	5	61.6	Z	3	–	1
Richland	220	42.3	15 212	567.1	11 809	412.8	1 199.6	2 444.7	16	47.2	Z	13	–	3
Ross	48	29.2	(6)	D	D	D	D	D	42	91.9	Z	7	32	8
Sandusky	124	40.3	10 156	307.1	8 377	226.9	1 243.5	2 533.6	20	17.7	Z	6	8	5
Scioto	63	25.4	1 942	55.0	1 426	34.7	112.5	290.8	12	27.3	Z	11	–	2
Seneca	101	44.6	6 882	231.2	5 485	167.1	662.2	1 124.6	5	48.0	Z	2	1	2
Shelby	136	52.9	13 278	470.5	10 060	304.3	1 464.3	5 129.2	13	80.4	Z	4	1	8
Stark	629	39.7	39 352	1 324.1	30 632	910.4	4 062.7	8 222.5	45	88.9	1	31	4	8
Summit	1 091	37.3	42 312	1 506.1	29 183	905.5	3 596.2	6 846.7	83	28.9	1	57	15	14
Trumbull	282	41.1	34 101	1 622.1	27 999	1 261.5	3 663.6	11 235.6	231	1.7	Z	16	62	33
Tuscarawas	226	40.3	9 823	304.1	7 495	198.9	896.1	2 054.6	40	92.9	1	25	11	8
Union	40	45.0	8 462	370.7	6 799	288.6	2 696.9	7 467.2	6	71.6	Z	2	1	2
Van Wert	50	46.0	4 553	140.8	3 853	112.8	420.5	942.1	5	60.2	Z	3	–	1
Vinton	17	58.8	624	15.4	460	10.0	34.3	91.2	1	65.9	–	Z	Z	1
Warren	198	46.5	12 145	407.3	8 177	225.4	875.1	2 186.4	22	89.6	Z	18	Z	4
Washington	104	41.3	5 242	187.8	3 591	113.6	932.5	1 900.9	690	1.4	Z	8	1	6
Wayne	252	40.9	16 172	521.5	11 720	333.2	1 607.8	3 105.0	19	79.8	Z	9	1	4
Williams	131	51.1	9 132	267.1	6 835	170.3	849.7	1 831.5	5	94.4	Z	3	Z	1
Wood	192	51.0	13 357	512.7	10 085	358.0	1 182.6	2 602.3	12	51.6	Z	5	Z	4
Wyandot	53	47.2	4 188	112.1	3 488	83.9	281.7	573.1	7	89.1	Z	2	Z	5
OKLAHOMA	4 087	29.1	164 060	4 963.2	122 705	3 229.5	17 233.7	37 453.2	2 040	59.7	864	567	21	716
Adair	14	42.9	1 626	33.9	1 216	21.0	102.6	312.6	10	5.5	2	5	–	5
Alfalfa	NA	NA	NA	NA	NA	NA	NA	NA	4	88.6	Z	Z	–	2
Atoka	NA	NA	NA	NA	NA	NA	NA	NA	55	1.2	Z	53	–	2
Beaver	NA	NA	NA	NA	NA	NA	NA	NA	36	98.8	31	Z	Z	24
Beckham	NA	NA	NA	NA	NA	NA	NA	NA	8	82.4	3	3	Z	5
Blaine	15	20.0	622	17.1	532	13.1	55.0	98.0	6	71.6	2	1	–	4
Bryan	31	35.5	949	19.3	783	14.0	40.2	122.5	19	22.8	3	4	–	7
Caddo	NA	NA	NA	NA	NA	NA	NA	NA	52	70.2	31	10	–	37
Canadian	64	26.6	3 003	82.3	2 121	52.3	610.7	1 024.4	11	78.9	2	3	Z	8
Carter	45	20.0	2 801	105.4	2 455	90.7	228.6	1 012.6	61	94.5	2	1	–	4
Cherokee	NA	NA	NA	NA	NA	NA	NA	NA	23	3.8	3	18	–	4
Choctaw	NA	NA	NA	NA	NA	NA	NA	NA	13	10.1	Z	6	–	6
Cimarron	NA	NA	NA	NA	NA	NA	NA	NA	217	98.8	212	Z	–	52
Cleveland	151	23.2	4 287	116.4	3 161	69.0	426.6	902.3	26	33.8	1	19	–	7
Coal	NA	NA	NA	NA	NA	NA	NA	NA	7	10.1	1	4	–	3
Comanche	51	25.5	3 325	119.8	2 914	102.5	509.6	900.8	21	14.4	1	17	–	10
Cotton	NA	NA	NA	NA	NA	NA	NA	NA	4	60.4	Z	1	–	2
Craig	18	33.3	978	21.7	828	14.1	73.7	128.1	3	22.3	–	Z	–	3
Creek	96	32.3	4 032	116.4	3 123	85.2	465.9	703.3	37	85.3	Z	5	Z	3
Custer	23	26.1	(4)	D	D	D	D	D	13	43.1	3	8	Z	6
Delaware	30	16.7	673	12.1	567	9.5	16.7	45.2	6	46.8	2	1	–	4
Dewey	NA	NA	NA	NA	NA	NA	NA	NA	7	85.1	3	Z	–	4
Ellis	NA	NA	NA	NA	NA	NA	NA	NA	47	99.8	42	1	Z	25
Garfield	66	21.2	2 389	62.7	2 090	42.0	232.6	506.2	8	77.3	1	2	Z	4
Garvin	26	42.3	1 153	29.4	799	19.0	128.8	615.4	12	72.9	1	2	–	4
Grady	64	23.4	2 792	70.0	2 402	55.8	412.3	747.1	20	64.5	9	4	–	11
Grant	NA	NA	NA	NA	NA	NA	NA	NA	4	65.7	Z	1	–	2
Greer	NA	NA	NA	NA	NA	NA	NA	NA	5	76.4	2	1	–	3
Harmon	NA	NA	NA	NA	NA	NA	NA	NA	16	96.0	15	Z	–	16
Harper	NA	NA	NA	NA	NA	NA	NA	NA	27	74.9	11	1	–	12

[1] Average number of production workers plus the number of other (nonproduction) employees for the pay period including March 12. [2] Average number of production workers for the pay periods including the 12th of March, May, August, and November. [3] In millions of gallons per day. [4] 1,000 to 2,499 employees. [5] 500 to 999 employees. [6] 2,500 to 4,999 employees.

Sources: Manufacturing—U.S. Census Bureau, 1997 Economic Census – Manufacturing, generated by Statistical Compendia Branch, using American Factfinder at <http://www.census.gov/>, (June 2000) [related Internet site <http://www.census.gov/epcd/www/97EC31.HTM>]. Water Use—U.S. Geological Survey, "Water Use in the United States," individual state/county and US by state files from <http://water.usgs.gov/watuse/spread95.html>, (accessed: September 1999).

[Includes U.S., states, and 3,142 counties/county equivalents defined as of January 1, 1992. For changes to these areas since January 1, 1992, see appendix B. Geographic Information]

County	Manufacturing (NAICS 31-33), 1997								Water use per day,[3] 1995					
	Establishments		All employees		Production workers		Value added by manu-facture (mil. dol.)	Value of ship-ments (mil. dol.)	Withdrawals					Consump-tive use (mil. gal.)
	Total	Percent with 20 or more employ-ees	Number[1]	Annual payroll (mil. dol.)	Number[2]	Wages (mil. dol.)			Total (mil. gal.)	Percent ground water	Irrigation	Public supply	Industrial	
OKLAHOMA—Con.														
Haskell	NA	NA	NA	NA	NA	NA	NA	NA	4	17.4	Z	1	–	3
Hughes	NA	NA	NA	NA	NA	NA	NA	NA	18	18.9	13	1	–	8
Jackson	12	25.0	896	16.3	799	13.1	83.2	205.1	46	18.1	44	Z	Z	43
Jefferson	NA	NA	NA	NA	NA	NA	NA	NA	9	74.6	Z	6	–	2
Johnston	10	40.0	678	17.1	562	10.8	32.5	98.4	6	31.9	2	1	Z	3
Kay	74	39.2	4 019	126.5	3 136	87.4	517.7	2 001.2	29	57.0	4	17	3	3
Kingfisher	NA	NA	NA	NA	NA	NA	NA	NA	10	75.3	4	1	Z	8
Kiowa	NA	NA	NA	NA	NA	NA	NA	NA	12	31.9	3	7	–	5
Latimer	NA	NA	NA	NA	NA	NA	NA	NA	2	11.0	Z	1	–	1
Le Flore	32	21.9	1 104	24.4	889	16.5	50.0	137.0	14	16.2	1	9	–	5
Lincoln	21	23.8	737	14.1	648	11.3	67.2	132.0	12	72.6	3	2	–	3
Logan	NA	NA	NA	NA	NA	NA	NA	NA	9	61.9	Z	2	–	3
Love	NA	NA	NA	NA	NA	NA	NA	NA	3	59.6	1	Z	–	2
McClain	19	31.6	(4)	D	D	D	D	D	6	52.5	1	2	–	3
McCurtain	25	52.0	2 758	79.6	2 539	67.4	299.6	794.7	11	13.0	Z	7	–	4
McIntosh	NA	NA	NA	NA	NA	NA	NA	NA	5	11.7	–	3	–	2
Major	NA	NA	NA	NA	NA	NA	NA	NA	12	99.2	4	5	–	6
Marshall	20	35.0	1 196	24.3	1 084	20.7	56.5	130.5	3	30.8	Z	1	–	2
Mayes	68	39.7	3 357	102.4	2 653	77.7	361.6	731.5	84	.7	–	71	–	13
Murray	NA	NA	NA	NA	NA	NA	NA	NA	16	21.6	1	12	–	3
Muskogee	87	31.0	4 780	155.3	3 927	119.7	581.0	990.3	86	7.6	5	15	16	23
Noble	13	23.1	(5)	D	D	D	D	D	6	52.3	Z	1	–	2
Nowata	NA	NA	NA	NA	NA	NA	NA	NA	7	79.2	Z	Z	–	1
Okfuskee	NA	NA	NA	NA	NA	NA	NA	NA	4	52.0	Z	Z	–	2
Oklahoma	851	30.0	39 462	1 281.5	28 036	809.3	4 630.1	9 922.1	83	31.8	3	57	Z	25
Okmulgee	35	28.6	1 120	38.5	901	27.4	202.3	295.4	10	23.3	Z	7	–	2
Osage	21	19.0	939	31.2	561	12.7	52.8	137.1	20	15.3	Z	15	Z	4
Ottawa	67	23.9	1 819	41.4	1 415	24.8	103.7	276.4	5	59.7	–	2	–	3
Pawnee	NA	NA	NA	NA	NA	NA	NA	NA	28	13.6	Z	3	–	9
Payne	60	26.7	2 584	76.5	1 928	50.0	456.1	846.8	18	77.0	1	3	–	4
Pittsburg	27	22.2	875	20.7	751	16.0	102.3	217.1	10	9.2	Z	6	1	5
Pontotoc	47	25.5	1 743	36.6	1 425	25.5	81.2	209.7	23	80.0	1	2	–	5
Pottawatomie	72	25.0	3 673	119.7	2 818	83.9	328.6	654.9	23	65.4	2	6	Z	6
Pushmataha	NA	NA	NA	NA	NA	NA	NA	NA	7	16.6	Z	1	–	2
Roger Mills	NA	NA	NA	NA	NA	NA	NA	NA	7	68.3	4	i	–	6
Rogers	122	34.4	4 562	147.4	3 316	87.9	428.3	822.9	79	1.1	Z	65	–	13
Seminole	30	23.3	1 689	33.4	1 371	24.5	84.0	252.3	33	54.4	Z	2	–	6
Sequoyah	NA	NA	NA	NA	NA	NA	NA	NA	14	3.1	Z	10	–	4
Stephens	58	20.7	1 941	49.8	1 556	37.5	306.2	470.4	25	76.4	Z	4	–	4
Texas	13	38.5	(5)	D	D	D	D	D	382	100.0	360	3	1	136
Tillman	NA	NA	NA	NA	NA	NA	NA	NA	7	64.4	5	1	–	6
Tulsa	1 136	33.1	39 402	1 310.7	26 754	750.4	3 586.7	7 858.1	19	65.2	2	9	–	22
Wagoner	66	27.3	1 924	50.8	1 457	33.0	266.2	432.7	21	6.1	Z	18	–	3
Washington	48	16.7	1 327	50.0	880	20.7	106.2	183.8	6	40.1	Z	3	–	3
Washita	NA	NA	NA	NA	NA	NA	NA	NA	7	63.5	4	1	–	6
Woods	NA	NA	NA	NA	NA	NA	NA	NA	8	99.1	2	2	–	4
Woodward	30	16.7	591	21.5	384	12.8	122.0	260.5	16	95.0	5	7	–	9
OREGON	5 768	29.0	213 111	7 095.3	158 506	4 545.8	25 077.2	47 666.0	7 906	13.2	6 168	504	378	3 206
Baker	NA	NA	NA	NA	NA	NA	NA	NA	463	3.8	457	3	Z	223
Benton	106	28.3	8 547	494.5	6 417	359.5	736.2	1 391.9	81	24.6	47	9	Z	30
Clackamas	589	25.5	18 655	632.2	12 495	333.6	1 723.5	3 667.4	228	22.2	78	38	40	58
Clatsop	49	24.5	858	21.2	707	14.5	50.9	142.4	127	.4	5	10	80	8
Columbia	57	31.6	3 079	128.4	2 563	98.6	523.3	1 008.5	100	3.8	28	2	55	22
Coos	104	16.3	1 937	57.6	1 627	44.8	114.1	391.2	37	11.1	24	6	2	16
Crook	21	38.1	1 506	39.4	1 324	31.2	76.1	225.3	226	6.2	223	1	–	113
Curry	32	12.5	727	26.2	618	21.1	39.9	116.2	20	8.4	4	3	–	3
Deschutes	202	21.3	4 884	129.5	3 868	84.1	328.6	698.6	181	7.2	152	11	–	72
Douglas	157	32.5	7 141	226.4	6 043	177.9	533.9	1 494.7	190	2.3	112	11	44	69
Gilliam	NA	NA	NA	NA	NA	NA	NA	NA	31	26.8	30	Z	–	16
Grant	NA	NA	NA	NA	NA	NA	NA	NA	223	1.3	221	1	–	102
Harney	NA	NA	NA	NA	NA	NA	NA	NA	549	15.3	546	1	Z	251
Hood River	58	25.9	1 128	27.2	886	18.6	67.7	157.5	117	.3	61	3	Z	37
Jackson	301	23.3	7 428	201.7	5 740	141.1	512.5	1 424.0	364	2.8	224	30	–	126
Jefferson	21	38.1	1 793	52.2	1 530	41.4	77.2	351.3	164	3.7	125	3	–	58
Josephine	117	24.8	2 812	76.8	2 163	52.0	192.1	439.6	60	13.9	52	2	–	29
Klamath	72	36.1	3 013	86.1	2 500	60.7	218.3	562.6	695	16.1	670	8	2	299
Lake	NA	NA	NA	NA	NA	NA	NA	NA	686	21.1	683	1	–	300
Lane	624	27.6	19 262	589.8	14 171	383.1	1 674.9	3 881.8	350	14.6	101	47	33	70
Lincoln	59	10.2	1 060	34.4	843	17.8	73.0	255.2	42	2.3	4	7	11	4

[1] Average number of production workers plus the number of other (nonproduction) employees for the pay period including March 12. [2] Average number of production workers for the pay periods including the 12th of March, May, August, and November. [3] In millions of gallons per day. [4] 500 to 999 employees. [5] 1,000 to 2,499 employees.

Sources: Manufacturing—U.S. Census Bureau, 1997 Economic Census – Manufacturing, generated by Statistical Compendia Branch, using American Factfinder at <http://www.census.gov/>, (June 2000) [related Internet site <http://www.census.gov/epcd/www/97EC31.HTM>]. Water Use—U.S. Geological Survey, "Water Use in the United States," individual state/county and US by state files from <http://water.usgs.gov/watuse/spread95.html>, (accessed: September 1999).

Table B–9. Counties — Manufacturing and Water Use–Con.

[Includes U.S., states, and 3,142 counties/county equivalents defined as of January 1, 1992. For changes to these areas since January 1, 1992, see appendix B. Geographic Information]

County	Manufacturing (NAICS 31-33), 1997 Establishments Total	Establishments Percent with 20 or more employees	All employees Number[1]	All employees Annual payroll (mil. dol.)	Production workers Number[2]	Production workers Wages (mil. dol.)	Value added by manufacture (mil. dol.)	Value of shipments (mil. dol.)	Water use per day,[3] 1995 Withdrawals Total (mil. gal.)	Withdrawals Percent ground water	By selected major use (mil. gal.) Irrigation	By selected major use (mil. gal.) Public supply	By selected major use (mil. gal.) Industrial	Consumptive use (mil. gal.)
OREGON—Con.														
Linn	184	39.1	9 794	347.8	7 366	235.5	933.7	1 918.8	184	24.3	98	12	57	64
Malheur	28	14.3	(4)	D	D	D	D	D	610	3.8	602	2	2	344
Marion	402	30.8	12 651	354.4	9 815	219.2	942.6	2 232.8	266	50.1	188	53	—	116
Morrow	10	40.0	741	20.9	662	17.2	85.3	183.4	348	25.5	306	2	—	145
Multnomah	1 309	30.5	47 763	1 600.4	35 901	1 085.3	4 195.5	8 715.4	198	8.3	16	178	3	25
Polk	63	33.3	2 358	63.4	1 995	49.6	146.9	357.4	68	22.1	64	4	—	37
Sherman	NA	NA	NA	NA	NA	NA	NA	NA	22	37.0	21	Z	—	15
Tillamook	31	32.3	1 227	32.5	1 052	23.9	100.2	317.8	85	2.6	6	3	Z	5
Umatilla	75	32.0	4 623	107.2	4 047	83.7	369.0	790.6	378	18.5	362	12	—	199
Union	28	28.6	1 250	37.2	1 107	29.4	86.2	273.9	203	8.4	185	4	—	84
Wallowa	NA	NA	NA	NA	NA	NA	NA	NA	168	3.5	149	1	—	71
Wasco	26	23.1	751	28.1	600	20.5	103.8	374.7	130	15.0	76	6	15	46
Washington	828	33.7	38 997	1 413.2	25 297	722.1	10 277.6	14 360.2	107	16.1	85	19	—	63
Wheeler	NA	NA	NA	NA	NA	NA	NA	NA	51	.6	51	Z	—	28
Yamhill	159	30.2	6 092	194.9	4 494	122.6	540.4	1 268.3	156	18.2	112	10	31	59
PENNSYLVANIA	17 128	37.1	826 521	27 641.3	597 544	17 045.1	86 212.1	172 193.2	9 685	8.9	16	1 546	1 682	565
Adams	127	43.3	8 209	214.1	6 599	152.2	727.7	1 401.3	27	64.6	2	10	1	7
Allegheny	1 500	30.5	55 620	2 130.8	36 517	1 178.6	5 105.8	10 576.1	904	4.7	Z	210	430	33
Armstrong	92	41.3	3 617	94.9	2 855	65.2	228.1	409.2	145	10.5	Z	5	Z	15
Beaver	221	36.7	10 311	383.1	7 825	260.1	1 413.6	3 161.9	696	2.8	Z	22	432	57
Bedford	61	23.0	3 231	76.6	2 639	54.4	203.5	472.8	12	35.2	Z	8	Z	1
Berks	587	41.1	41 614	1 510.7	30 925	954.0	3 865.1	7 729.4	85	56.3	1	34	6	8
Blair	157	38.9	8 966	251.7	6 960	165.5	865.1	1 592.4	36	30.3	Z	15	16	5
Bradford	73	34.2	6 405	191.5	5 278	143.1	629.5	1 273.7	14	93.2	Z	4	5	3
Bucks	1 236	34.6	41 592	1 518.9	26 985	816.9	3 414.8	7 593.0	95	31.3	1	46	28	7
Butler	276	38.4	14 891	533.0	10 912	340.4	1 358.1	2 990.0	31	36.2	Z	11	10	10
Cambria	153	36.6	7 403	186.3	4 970	113.4	515.0	1 349.5	23	27.0	Z	16	Z	4
Cameron	20	45.0	1 259	34.6	999	22.9	87.9	151.4	1	19.0	—	1	Z	Z
Carbon	63	50.8	3 646	76.2	3 036	58.4	177.5	311.9	37	13.1	Z	34	Z	2
Centre	159	36.5	8 546	255.4	5 941	148.7	790.1	1 409.3	34	91.8	Z	17	Z	5
Chester	629	33.1	20 791	771.1	13 708	425.6	2 343.6	4 332.2	274	10.8	1	37	6	7
Clarion	49	49.0	2 711	76.4	2 281	58.9	217.1	441.7	5	54.5	Z	2	Z	1
Clearfield	107	43.0	4 864	120.2	3 789	84.1	302.7	791.0	320	.9	Z	6	Z	3
Clinton	54	37.0	3 212	89.2	2 659	64.9	330.5	677.1	36	4.7	Z	5	29	1
Columbia	100	43.0	(5)	D	D	D	D	D	9	65.5	Z	6	1	1
Crawford	301	34.6	8 714	289.4	6 350	178.9	760.3	1 263.4	17	96.0	Z	8	4	2
Cumberland	221	37.6	13 804	444.8	9 986	288.0	1 574.0	3 307.3	55	72.4	Z	18	3	5
Dauphin	222	37.8	14 871	522.4	11 743	378.1	1 670.9	3 590.9	123	16.1	Z	35	47	34
Delaware	522	26.1	19 341	867.0	12 311	447.4	3 117.8	7 315.2	828	.3	Z	24	107	17
Elk	130	43.1	8 338	288.0	6 616	208.8	668.4	1 393.3	18	6.9	Z	6	11	2
Erie	570	44.4	32 813	1 142.3	24 172	739.3	3 128.3	5 779.3	97	10.3	Z	49	42	13
Fayette	128	31.3	3 842	106.0	2 987	69.7	318.9	656.7	43	8.7	Z	39	Z	2
Forest	NA	NA	NA	NA	NA	NA	NA	NA	1	96.0	—	Z	Z	Z
Franklin	191	38.7	12 763	379.5	9 223	226.9	975.3	2 212.0	21	58.1	1	10	1	4
Fulton	22	27.3	(6)	D	D	D	D	D	2	74.6	Z	Z	—	1
Greene	27	25.9	630	15.1	521	10.6	39.9	81.5	44	27.7	Z	Z	Z	16
Huntingdon	44	38.6	2 300	59.5	1 932	45.2	308.4	493.0	9	42.6	Z	3	Z	1
Indiana	88	30.7	3 175	98.9	2 158	61.9	152.9	344.1	240	8.0	Z	4	Z	29
Jefferson	88	47.7	4 634	132.0	3 774	94.5	368.6	680.9	7	41.9	Z	2	2	1
Juniata	57	31.6	2 443	61.1	2 150	44.6	205.0	290.6	4	81.7	Z	1	1	2
Lackawanna	306	42.2	16 052	463.0	12 611	318.7	1 266.3	2 562.7	52	7.1	Z	45	4	2
Lancaster	918	40.3	52 908	1 752.0	40 403	1 178.5	5 658.5	10 585.4	166	30.1	2	71	4	16
Lawrence	169	34.9	5 092	156.4	3 740	96.4	455.5	1 076.6	154	5.9	Z	9	5	3
Lebanon	199	45.2	9 376	254.3	7 154	173.3	681.3	1 710.3	24	93.8	Z	2	2	4
Lehigh	504	36.7	23 277	877.2	15 685	485.2	5 212.2	7 690.1	49	67.7	Z	36	8	3
Luzerne	408	41.9	24 362	700.8	18 860	487.2	2 350.2	4 501.1	105	12.0	Z	26	1	32
Lycoming	208	45.7	12 982	370.2	9 691	229.9	1 189.4	2 460.4	16	44.5	1	11	Z	2
McKean	67	46.3	5 346	158.7	4 266	116.9	455.9	875.7	15	72.4	—	7	7	1
Mercer	198	38.9	10 457	326.8	7 788	220.9	990.4	2 440.8	85	7.1	Z	13	67	19
Mifflin	72	34.7	5 373	163.1	4 406	124.3	491.0	922.7	15	17.0	Z	4	9	2
Monroe	113	28.3	4 744	171.1	2 994	74.1	547.9	812.9	15	76.5	Z	8	Z	1
Montgomery	1 398	35.9	67 234	2 649.5	43 314	1 434.6	11 564.6	20 666.6	142	45.4	Z	69	10	41
Montour	22	36.4	1 530	65.8	1 168	42.2	517.8	820.4	21	7.1	Z	2	Z	11
Northampton	353	43.3	18 244	546.1	13 613	355.4	1 496.7	2 638.4	472	8.8	Z	10	193	12
Northumberland	115	53.9	7 812	217.3	5 854	155.0	826.9	1 526.7	31	34.9	Z	11	9	3
Perry	32	25.0	845	19.1	689	12.4	39.9	82.7	4	92.1	Z	1	Z	1
Philadelphia	1 342	32.0	47 908	1 582.4	33 884	926.0	3 997.5	11 098.1	575	Z	—	359	33	16
Pike	NA	NA	NA	NA	NA	NA	NA	NA	4	97.1	—	2	—	Z
Potter	29	51.7	1 166	28.8	982	21.1	62.3	117.6	4	92.2	Z	1	Z	Z

[1] Average number of production workers plus the number of other (nonproduction) employees for the pay period including March 12. [2] Average number of production workers for the pay periods including the 12th of March, May, August, and November. [3] In millions of gallons per day. [4] 1,000 to 2,499 employees. [5] 5,000 to 9,999 employees. [6] 2,500 to 4,999 employees.

Sources: Manufacturing—U.S. Census Bureau, 1997 Economic Census – Manufacturing, generated by Statistical Compendia Branch, using American Factfinder at <http://www.census.gov/>, (June 2000) [related Internet site <http://www.census.gov/epcd/www/97EC31.HTM>]. Water Use—U.S. Geological Survey, "Water Use in the United States," individual state/county and US by state files from <http://water.usgs.gov/watuse/spread95.html>, (accessed: September 1999).

[Includes U.S., states, and 3,142 counties/county equivalents defined as of January 1, 1992. For changes to these areas since January 1, 1992, see appendix B. Geographic Information]

County	Maunfacturing (NAICS 31-33), 1997								Water use per day,[3] 1995					
	Establishments		All employees		Production workers		Value added by manu- facture (mil. dol.)	Value of ship- ments (mil. dol.)	Withdrawals					
											By selected major use– (mil. gal.)			
	Total	Percent with 20 or more employ- ees	Number[1]	Annual payroll (mil. dol.)	Number[2]	Wages (mil. dol.)			Total (mil. gal.)	Percent ground water	Irrigation	Public supply	Industrial	Consump- tive use (mil. gal.)
PENNSYLVANIA—Con.														
Schuylkill	226	50.4	14 370	393.7	11 600	272.8	1 341.3	2 625.1	55	51.8	Z	29	1	9
Snyder	65	52.3	4 413	111.3	3 575	79.5	181.6	414.3	299	1.4	Z	2	Z	3
Somerset	118	38.1	4 828	117.1	3 764	79.4	301.6	644.1	40	23.0	Z	33	Z	2
Sullivan	NA	NA	NA	NA	NA	NA	NA	NA	3	18.5	Z	3	–	1
Susquehanna	51	25.5	1 160	22.1	939	14.4	54.2	132.6	6	63.5	Z	2	Z	1
Tioga	46	39.1	2 930	69.4	2 501	56.0	216.3	415.9	6	62.0	Z	2	1	1
Union	36	44.4	3 394	86.0	2 673	60.6	228.4	434.5	7	40.3	Z	4	1	1
Venango	89	37.1	3 950	137.8	2 767	83.4	383.7	1 084.6	13	62.3	Z	6	3	3
Warren	81	42.0	4 670	147.8	3 256	88.8	395.7	1 116.3	72	18.9	Z	5	7	3
Washington	278	38.8	11 725	402.3	7 983	245.4	1 137.6	2 788.4	452	2.6	Z	8	11	8
Wayne	68	16.2	1 039	24.5	821	16.9	71.0	182.3	5	80.7	Z	2	Z	1
Westmoreland	597	33.7	24 404	800.2	16 883	493.5	1 786.6	4 000.2	120	5.8	Z	41	71	32
Wyoming	35	34.3	(4)	D	D	D	D	D	18	14.6	Z	1	12	2
York	661	47.5	45 754	1 557.5	33 469	975.5	4 627.8	8 156.9	2 350	.7	1	32	35	32
RHODE ISLAND	2 535	27.8	75 599	2 288.6	52 889	1 279.8	5 484.2	10 482.0	411	6.7	2	114	1	24
Bristol	100	34.0	2 634	73.0	1 966	47.2	157.0	267.0	5	24.6	Z	5	Z	1
Kent	411	25.8	12 933	417.1	8 912	228.0	1 060.9	2 115.3	7	48.7	Z	2	Z	3
Newport	98	15.3	2 304	100.0	988	25.7	174.9	296.1	11	11.5	Z	9	Z	2
Providence	1 774	28.5	49 910	1 440.9	35 529	831.8	3 413.8	6 435.0	366	2.3	Z	89	Z	14
Washington	152	28.3	7 818	257.6	5 494	147.1	677.6	1 368.6	21	60.6	1	9	Z	5
SOUTH CAROLINA	4 450	42.1	346 142	10 369.4	267 548	6 856.0	33 657.8	70 797.0	6 203	5.2	52	543	700	321
Abbeville	36	72.2	3 978	101.4	3 437	78.0	237.3	607.5	4	25.0	–	2	Z	1
Aiken	99	40.4	19 999	896.7	10 215	409.7	3 405.4	4 256.3	303	6.9	Z	18	119	25
Allendale	14	64.3	1 440	33.6	1 199	24.1	135.1	310.3	11	86.2	6	1	4	6
Anderson	240	42.9	20 589	611.4	16 627	431.7	1 739.5	4 180.1	82	.8	Z	21	1	5
Bamberg	24	45.8	1 175	28.5	879	16.6	100.4	180.4	3	96.6	1	1	–	1
Barnwell	22	63.6	3 376	75.9	2 858	51.0	203.7	450.3	4	91.2	Z	2	–	1
Beaufort	94	13.8	1 087	28.7	781	16.5	75.8	137.5	30	70.7	5	23	1	9
Berkeley	75	44.0	6 396	210.6	4 561	132.6	1 232.6	2 811.2	491	1.5	Z	10	9	13
Calhoun	18	33.3	809	22.9	637	15.4	20.5	97.6	125	4.7	18	1	106	34
Charleston	261	26.7	10 530	366.3	7 467	200.7	1 400.1	3 039.4	148	7.5	1	106	37	25
Cherokee	76	67.1	8 195	231.4	6 800	174.9	911.4	1 767.1	9	8.0	Z	5	3	2
Chester	54	55.6	5 260	145.8	4 503	111.5	441.2	964.1	4	33.9	–	2	Z	1
Chesterfield	58	62.1	7 450	196.4	5 702	134.8	614.1	1 408.2	10	31.7	Z	5	Z	2
Clarendon	24	58.3	1 396	26.1	1 245	20.3	74.5	122.4	4	94.1	1	1	–	2
Colleton	26	57.7	1 779	46.9	1 470	33.5	86.9	196.0	8	50.3	Z	2	–	1
Darlington	63	54.0	6 002	185.9	5 088	146.4	749.2	2 054.6	38	35.3	Z	7	21	5
Dillon	25	64.0	3 613	62.9	3 308	49.9	155.4	394.3	5	99.8	Z	4	Z	1
Dorchester	79	41.8	3 669	110.6	2 881	73.1	388.2	738.3	7	91.5	–	1	3	1
Edgefield	28	39.3	2 041	44.6	1 676	32.0	123.0	333.3	3	.6	Z	3	–	1
Fairfield	20	55.0	2 239	79.8	1 966	63.0	453.3	1 001.9	861	.1	–	2	–	7
Florence	139	44.6	11 011	328.2	7 889	200.3	973.0	2 114.2	50	36.9	Z	12	33	8
Georgetown	78	39.7	4 974	146.6	4 094	108.6	431.7	1 057.6	46	15.7	1	6	32	7
Greenville	672	40.5	45 372	1 431.8	34 483	916.5	4 595.2	9 507.5	177	1.9	Z	50	123	27
Greenwood	93	44.1	11 612	339.6	9 767	250.4	944.9	1 875.1	13	11.1	Z	11	Z	2
Hampton	20	40.0	1 307	44.2	1 055	30.4	97.5	196.7	4	99.8	–	2	1	1
Horry	160	19.4	6 687	173.4	4 559	98.9	565.2	927.8	94	13.3	7	30	Z	13
Jasper	NA	NA	NA	NA	NA	NA	NA	NA	2	100.0	Z	1	–	1
Kershaw	62	46.8	4 916	151.8	3 894	113.0	979.9	1 637.9	19	15.3	Z	10	9	4
Lancaster	54	48.1	5 341	145.5	4 627	112.8	510.4	1 561.6	19	5.1	–	8	10	3
Laurens	72	44.4	6 447	171.7	5 483	128.0	405.3	834.1	7	20.9	–	5	Z	1
Lee	9	77.8	641	18.3	503	15.2	60.5	172.4	3	99.7	–	1	2	1
Lexington	225	30.2	9 964	324.2	7 032	186.7	1 035.4	2 080.7	189	8.3	1	12	39	12
McCormick	NA	NA	NA	NA	NA	NA	NA	NA	3	22.4	Z	2	–	2
Marion	32	59.4	5 007	112.5	4 046	83.1	389.0	727.0	12	99.8	Z	5	–	1
Marlboro	22	63.6	2 935	82.1	2 362	58.9	318.9	755.2	10	36.3	Z	3	6	2
Newberry	49	59.2	5 553	130.5	4 983	106.5	304.0	735.4	6	18.4	–	5	Z	1
Oconee	80	46.3	7 487	202.8	5 877	137.7	637.5	1 136.0	2 534	Z	Z	9	Z	22
Orangeburg	90	48.9	9 370	222.9	7 235	141.6	644.2	1 700.3	25	52.4	7	9	6	10
Pickens	134	41.0	11 790	305.7	9 973	226.9	616.8	1 916.3	18	13.7	Z	11	1	3
Richland	235	40.0	13 558	460.8	9 617	275.7	1 464.1	3 220.7	495	1.1	Z	46	29	21
Saluda	14	71.4	2 565	46.9	2 287	35.7	144.8	375.2	4	82.4	–	Z	2	1
Spartanburg	481	43.0	35 102	1 108.6	27 391	746.0	3 172.2	7 534.6	66	6.8	–	58	3	10
Sumter	84	59.5	12 655	303.0	10 941	227.7	976.8	2 050.4	32	99.4	1	16	12	6
Union	43	60.5	5 355	129.2	4 341	91.3	341.6	679.6	7	2.6	–	5	2	1
Williamsburg	34	55.9	3 392	86.8	2 828	63.2	246.6	533.4	5	99.6	–	1	2	1
York	222	40.5	11 731	391.8	8 688	250.3	1 163.0	2 325.7	216	19.8	Z	7	83	16

[1] Average number of production workers plus the number of other (nonproduction) employees for the pay period including March 12.   [2] Average number of production workers for the pay periods including the 12th of March, May, August, and November.   [3] In millions of gallons per day.   [4] 2,500 to 4,999 employees.

Sources: Manufacturing—U.S. Census Bureau, 1997 Economic Census – Manufacturing, generated by Statistical Compendia Branch, using American Factfinder at <http://www.census.gov/>, (June 2000) [related Internet site <http://www.census.gov/epcd/www/97EC31.HTM>]. Water Use—U.S. Geological Survey, "Water Use in the United States," individual state/county and US by state files from <http://water.usgs.gov/watuse/spread95.html>, (accessed: September 1999).

Table B–9. Counties — Manufacturing and Water Use–Con.

[Includes U.S., states, and 3,142 counties/county equivalents defined as of January 1, 1992. For changes to these areas since January 1, 1992, see appendix B. Geographic Information]

County	Manufacturing (NAICS 31-33), 1997								Water use per day,[3] 1995					
	Establishments		All employees		Production workers		Value added by manu-facture (mil. dol.)	Value of ship-ments (mil. dol.)	Withdrawals					Consump-tive use (mil. gal.)
	Total	Percent with 20 or more employ-ees	Number[1]	Annual payroll (mil. dol.)	Number[2]	Wages (mil. dol.)			Total (mil. gal.)	Percent ground water	By selected major use– (mil. gal.)			
											Irrigation	Public supply	Industrial	
SOUTH DAKOTA........	888	32.9	46 539	1 162.6	33 230	707.4	3 880.9	12 305.5	460	40.7	269	88	5	249
Aurora...................	NA	NA	NA	NA	NA	NA	NA	NA	1	44.9	Z	Z	–	1
Beadle	21	33.3	1 134	25.7	921	19.6	66.3	263.5	9	56.3	4	3	1	5
Bennett.................	NA	NA	NA	NA	NA	NA	NA	NA	7	95.6	6	Z	–	6
Bon Homme	NA	NA	NA	NA	NA	NA	NA	NA	4	45.1	3	1	–	3
Brookings...............	31	48.4	3 449	92.4	2 459	64.2	469.7	902.0	7	91.7	2	4	Z	3
Brown	38	39.5	2 492	61.0	1 905	42.8	230.6	397.5	8	52.6	2	3	–	4
Brule	NA	NA	NA	NA	NA	NA	NA	NA	4	37.6	1	1	–	2
Buffalo	NA	NA	NA	NA	NA	NA	NA	NA	3	27.1	3	–	–	3
Butte...................	NA	NA	NA	NA	NA	NA	NA	NA	89	3.3	86	1	Z	36
Campbell	NA	NA	NA	NA	NA	NA	NA	NA	3	50.7	2	Z	–	2
Charles Mix	NA	NA	NA	NA	NA	NA	NA	NA	11	25.3	7	2	–	7
Clark	NA	NA	NA	NA	NA	NA	NA	NA	3	81.1	1	1	Z	2
Clay....................	NA	NA	NA	NA	NA	NA	NA	NA	5	89.4	3	2	Z	3
Codington	63	42.9	4 115	102.6	3 138	66.4	201.2	395.8	11	62.8	1	3	1	4
Corson.................	NA	NA	NA	NA	NA	NA	NA	NA	2	35.0	1	Z	–	2
Custer..................	NA	NA	NA	NA	NA	NA	NA	NA	4	27.1	2	Z	Z	2
Davison	36	36.1	1 719	47.2	1 329	31.1	196.2	365.9	4	30.3	2	3	Z	1
Day	NA	NA	NA	NA	NA	NA	NA	NA	1	68.3	Z	Z	–	1
Deuel	NA	NA	NA	NA	NA	NA	NA	NA	1	68.1	Z	Z	–	1
Dewey	NA	NA	NA	NA	NA	NA	NA	NA	2	30.7	Z	1	–	1
Douglas	NA	NA	NA	NA	NA	NA	NA	NA	2	77.0	1	Z	–	2
Edmunds	NA	NA	NA	NA	NA	NA	NA	NA	2	72.4	Z	Z	Z	1
Fall River	NA	NA	NA	NA	NA	NA	NA	NA	38	3.9	35	1	–	24
Faulk...................	NA	NA	NA	NA	NA	NA	NA	NA	1	41.7	Z	Z	–	1
Grant	6	66.7	(4)	D	D	D	D	D	6	53.8	1	1	–	2
Gregory	NA	NA	NA	NA	NA	NA	NA	NA	2	37.9	1	Z	–	2
Haakon	NA	NA	NA	NA	NA	NA	NA	NA	2	51.4	2	Z	–	1
Hamlin	NA	NA	NA	NA	NA	NA	NA	NA	3	90.7	2	Z	–	2
Hand	NA	NA	NA	NA	NA	NA	NA	NA	2	60.2	Z	Z	–	1
Hanson.................	NA	NA	NA	NA	NA	NA	NA	NA	1	27.3	Z	–	–	1
Harding.................	NA	NA	NA	NA	NA	NA	NA	NA	1	39.0	Z	Z	Z	1
Hughes.................	NA	NA	NA	NA	NA	NA	NA	NA	22	23.9	18	3	–	16
Hutchinson.............	NA	NA	NA	NA	NA	NA	NA	NA	3	68.4	1	Z	–	2
Hyde	NA	NA	NA	NA	NA	NA	NA	NA	1	50.0	Z	Z	–	1
Jackson	NA	NA	NA	NA	NA	NA	NA	NA	2	26.3	1	Z	–	2
Jerauld	NA	NA	NA	NA	NA	NA	NA	NA	1	61.7	Z	Z	–	1
Jones	NA	NA	NA	NA	NA	NA	NA	NA	1	21.2	Z	Z	–	1
Kingsbury..............	NA	NA	NA	NA	NA	NA	NA	NA	3	87.0	Z	2	–	1
Lake	23	52.2	950	19.7	767	12.9	74.4	167.2	3	40.1	Z	1	–	2
Lawrence	30	16.7	502	13.1	424	10.1	31.9	88.2	15	29.7	1	4	Z	4
Lincoln	30	26.7	(4)	D	D	D	D	D	3	81.4	1	2	–	1
Lyman..................	NA	NA	NA	NA	NA	NA	NA	NA	5	12.3	4	Z	–	4
McCook	NA	NA	NA	NA	NA	NA	NA	NA	2	68.7	Z	1	–	1
McPherson	NA	NA	NA	NA	NA	NA	NA	NA	2	38.1	Z	Z	–	1
Marshall	NA	NA	NA	NA	NA	NA	NA	NA	2	65.6	2	1	–	1
Meade	NA	NA	NA	NA	NA	NA	NA	NA	5	54.6	2	1	Z	3
Mellette................	NA	NA	NA	NA	NA	NA	NA	NA	1	35.8	Z	Z	–	1
Miner..................	NA	NA	NA	NA	NA	NA	NA	NA	1	50.7	Z	Z	–	1
Minnehaha.............	168	34.5	(5)	D	D	D	D	D	25	60.2	1	20	1	6
Moody..................	NA	NA	NA	NA	NA	NA	NA	NA	2	71.3	Z	1	–	1
Pennington	134	28.4	4 263	100.8	3 214	62.4	318.5	867.3	30	56.1	4	12	1	9
Perkins	NA	NA	NA	NA	NA	NA	NA	NA	2	45.3	Z	Z	–	1
Potter	NA	NA	NA	NA	NA	NA	NA	NA	4	33.2	3	Z	–	3
Roberts	NA	NA	NA	NA	NA	NA	NA	NA	2	74.1	Z	1	Z	1
Sanborn	NA	NA	NA	NA	NA	NA	NA	NA	1	54.4	Z	Z	–	1
Shannon................	NA	NA	NA	NA	NA	NA	NA	NA	1	82.6	Z	Z	–	1
Spink	NA	NA	NA	NA	NA	NA	NA	NA	8	90.5	7	Z	–	7
Stanley	NA	NA	NA	NA	NA	NA	NA	NA	3	24.8	Z	Z	–	1
Sully	NA	NA	NA	NA	NA	NA	NA	NA	13	19.8	12	Z	–	10
Todd	NA	NA	NA	NA	NA	NA	NA	NA	8	93.3	7	Z	–	6
Tripp	NA	NA	NA	NA	NA	NA	NA	NA	5	55.1	2	1	–	3
Turner..................	NA	NA	NA	NA	NA	NA	NA	NA	15	94.6	13	1	–	12
Union	26	57.7	(6)	D	D	D	D	D	16	94.8	14	1	Z	12
Walworth	NA	NA	NA	NA	NA	NA	NA	NA	6	9.4	2	4	–	2
Yankton	30	46.7	2 517	62.3	1 961	42.9	166.9	452.2	11	40.9	5	5	Z	5
Ziebach	NA	NA	NA	NA	NA	NA	NA	NA	1	43.2	Z	–	–	1

[1] Average number of production workers plus the number of other (nonproduction) employees for the pay period including March 12.   [2] Average number of production workers for the pay periods including the 12th of March, May, August, and November.   [3] In millions of gallons per day.   [4] 500 to 999 employees.   [5] 10,000 to 24,999 employees.   [6] 5,000 to 9,999 employees.

Sources: Manufacturing—U.S. Census Bureau, 1997 Economic Census – Manufacturing, generated by Statistical Compendia Branch, using American Factfinder at <http://www.census.gov/>, (June 2000) [related Internet site <http://www.census.gov/epcd/www/97EC31.HTM>].   Water Use—U.S. Geological Survey, "Water Use in the United States," individual state/county and US by state files from <http://water.usgs.gov/watuse/spread95.html>, (accessed: September 1999).

[Includes U.S., states, and 3,142 counties/county equivalents defined as of January 1, 1992. For changes to these areas since January 1, 1992, see appendix B. Geographic Information]

County	Manufacturing (NAICS 31-33), 1997								Water use per day,[3] 1995					
	Establishments		All employees		Production workers		Value added by manu-facture (mil. dol.)	Value of ship-ments (mil. dol.)	Withdrawals					
	Total	Percent with 20 or more employ-ees	Number[1]	Annual payroll (mil. dol.)	Number[2]	Wages (mil. dol.)			Total (mil. gal.)	Percent ground water	By selected major use– (mil. gal.)			Consump-tive use (mil. gal.)
											Irrigation	Public supply	Industrial	
TENNESSEE	7 407	39.2	483 823	14 351.9	375 121	9 468.8	44 355.2	98 503.1	10 076	4.3	24	777	863	233
Anderson	107	39.3	8 559	328.0	4 679	135.2	994.5	1 336.2	508	.3	Z	17	2	2
Bedford	64	31.3	5 582	146.6	4 694	112.0	518.1	1 302.7	7	18.5	Z	6	–	1
Benton	17	58.8	1 150	23.7	988	17.9	51.7	97.5	4	43.1	Z	1	–	2
Bledsoe	NA	NA	NA	NA	NA	NA	NA	NA	2	45.5	Z	1	–	1
Blount	126	29.4	7 027	251.9	5 466	175.4	1 306.8	2 806.9	14	14.3	Z	12	–	2
Bradley	142	40.1	12 974	363.8	10 883	258.9	1 616.6	2 931.7	19	21.8	Z	12	5	2
Campbell	53	35.8	1 945	49.1	1 529	31.2	112.1	243.7	4	30.8	Z	4	–	Z
Cannon	NA	NA	NA	NA	NA	NA	NA	NA	1	39.5	Z	1	–	Z
Carroll	50	38.0	3 103	64.1	2 585	47.9	181.0	456.7	5	99.4	Z	3	1	1
Carter	48	33.3	1 960	50.7	1 556	35.1	138.9	273.4	20	75.5	Z	7	12	2
Cheatham	42	23.8	3 060	81.9	2 757	62.2	300.7	579.7	2	16.5	Z	2	Z	Z
Chester	24	37.5	853	18.7	716	12.6	29.0	76.0	2	98.7	Z	1	–	Z
Claiborne	34	55.9	3 584	67.1	3 010	44.9	160.4	317.1	3	37.9	Z	2	–	Z
Clay	8	62.5	771	13.7	641	8.7	46.9	85.7	2	32.1	Z	1	–	1
Cocke	40	40.0	2 627	64.6	2 058	45.8	161.7	382.8	7	15.3	Z	4	Z	3
Coffee	67	59.7	5 595	178.4	4 376	115.5	476.4	1 082.9	6	11.5	Z	5	Z	1
Crockett	16	43.8	1 241	26.6	1 036	13.1	61.2	160.8	3	100.0	Z	2	1	Z
Cumberland	47	40.4	2 437	58.9	1 994	41.2	228.4	442.9	8	4.3	1	6	–	2
Davidson	752	34.7	31 716	1 100.0	23 000	688.6	3 419.6	6 721.8	148	1.9	1	107	38	15
Decatur	35	28.6	1 113	21.8	922	16.0	66.8	137.0	7	49.1	–	1	–	6
DeKalb	28	53.6	2 740	65.7	2 062	38.8	140.1	333.9	2	17.6	Z	1	–	Z
Dickson	51	41.2	3 574	102.5	3 130	79.0	348.9	710.3	4	21.8	Z	4	–	Z
Dyer	42	42.9	6 404	183.5	5 059	120.3	494.7	1 121.4	7	100.0	Z	6	1	1
Fayette	39	38.5	1 193	33.3	918	23.4	166.4	271.6	6	99.2	Z	1	3	1
Fentress	31	38.7	1 471	22.5	1 299	18.3	62.1	141.4	20	4.2	–	1	–	2
Franklin	43	32.6	1 872	53.1	1 539	37.8	164.8	438.2	5	45.4	Z	4	–	1
Gibson	90	42.2	7 607	200.7	5 856	138.7	530.0	1 085.6	8	98.3	1	6	–	2
Giles	48	43.8	3 515	104.6	3 001	75.1	370.5	679.7	5	14.9	Z	4	Z	1
Grainger	35	45.7	1 321	30.6	1 099	21.1	71.2	180.9	2	87.3	Z	Z	–	1
Greene	107	45.8	7 990	198.0	6 430	128.2	465.7	1 296.7	10	8.4	Z	8	1	2
Grundy	NA	NA	NA	NA	NA	NA	NA	NA	2	24.7	Z	1	–	Z
Hamblen	129	53.5	14 586	369.6	12 020	265.8	956.0	2 039.2	8	11.2	Z	8	–	1
Hamilton	515	40.4	32 559	991.4	23 344	590.1	2 198.2	6 403.2	1 533	.8	1	51	13	7
Hancock	NA	NA	NA	NA	NA	NA	NA	NA	1	86.2	Z	Z	–	Z
Hardeman	37	37.8	1 957	51.4	1 637	37.8	98.7	274.7	3	99.0	Z	2	–	1
Hardin	52	42.3	2 628	70.0	2 185	53.5	201.7	530.2	29	8.6	1	2	25	4
Hawkins	50	48.0	6 534	219.4	5 342	158.6	557.0	1 040.9	553	.5	Z	4	1	1
Haywood	23	52.2	2 477	64.1	2 111	49.1	159.4	425.5	3	99.7	Z	2	Z	Z
Henderson	47	34.0	4 302	101.6	3 485	77.7	253.7	710.9	3	17.5	Z	3	Z	Z
Henry	66	31.8	3 483	79.7	2 775	52.2	202.3	506.1	4	95.3	Z	3	–	1
Hickman	31	29.0	1 017	22.2	800	17.9	74.0	139.5	3	42.3	Z	2	–	1
Houston	NA	NA	NA	NA	NA	NA	NA	NA	1	46.6	–	1	–	Z
Humphreys	29	48.3	1 976	75.4	1 440	51.0	500.3	854.1	1 221	.1	Z	2	67	8
Jackson	8	62.5	681	11.8	585	8.0	68.3	104.9	1	27.3	–	Z	Z	Z
Jefferson	56	44.6	2 880	59.7	2 352	41.0	205.2	434.0	7	85.2	Z	3	1	2
Johnson	19	47.4	1 392	29.2	1 261	26.0	95.1	206.4	3	46.0	Z	2	–	1
Knox	493	31.2	20 782	550.3	15 926	347.0	1 486.5	3 245.5	63	7.2	1	58	Z	7
Lake	NA	NA	NA	NA	NA	NA	NA	NA	2	100.0	1	1	–	1
Lauderdale	22	63.6	3 525	74.4	3 226	60.0	194.6	353.8	5	98.6	Z	4	Z	1
Lawrence	56	39.3	5 501	145.8	4 943	122.9	405.1	1 063.8	6	53.5	Z	4	–	2
Lewis	22	13.6	600	16.4	486	12.5	47.0	101.1	2	97.5	–	1	Z	Z
Lincoln	43	34.9	2 381	62.9	1 834	42.1	200.6	455.0	5	38.3	Z	4	–	1
Loudon	45	48.9	3 150	93.0	2 575	68.8	458.5	806.7	17	25.2	Z	9	7	3
McMinn	74	51.4	8 791	279.4	6 641	197.4	763.6	1 572.2	85	3.0	Z	5	79	10
McNairy	48	43.8	2 632	58.2	1 990	37.9	195.7	328.1	4	95.1	Z	3	–	1
Macon	38	31.6	1 403	25.9	1 203	19.5	30.6	80.1	2	86.4	Z	1	–	Z
Madison	138	47.8	12 429	382.5	9 959	260.5	1 512.6	3 473.4	19	99.7	1	12	4	3
Marion	29	44.8	1 726	38.5	1 594	31.4	92.0	212.8	3	46.2	Z	2	–	Z
Marshall	45	57.8	7 552	169.4	6 365	124.9	633.0	1 349.1	3	19.6	Z	3	–	1
Maury	75	41.3	11 361	532.6	9 315	417.1	1 995.3	4 431.7	19	32.7	Z	11	6	3
Meigs	13	46.2	764	14.2	702	12.4	31.7	125.1	1	72.1	Z	1	–	Z
Monroe	84	41.7	5 488	144.8	4 402	97.8	373.6	834.9	5	26.7	Z	4	–	1
Montgomery	83	38.6	6 519	182.7	5 474	133.9	715.7	1 271.6	25	.9	Z	22	3	2
Moore	NA	NA	NA	NA	NA	NA	NA	NA	1	75.6	–	Z	Z	Z
Morgan	24	25.0	925	20.1	804	13.2	45.2	98.8	1	34.1	–	1	–	Z
Obion	46	52.2	5 656	195.5	4 804	157.4	665.7	1 140.0	6	100.0	Z	5	Z	1

[1] Average number of production workers plus the number of other (nonproduction) employees for the pay period including March 12.   [2] Average number of production workers for the pay periods including the 12th of March, May, August, and November.   [3] In millions of gallons per day.

Sources: Manufacturing—U.S. Census Bureau, 1997 Economic Census – Manufacturing, generated by Statistical Compendia Branch, using American Factfinder at <http://www.census.gov/>, (June 2000) [related Internet site <http://www.census.gov/epcd/www/97EC31.HTM>]. Water Use—U.S. Geological Survey, "Water Use in the United States," individual state/county and US by state files from <http://water.usgs.gov/watuse/spread95.html>, (accessed: September 1999).

[Includes U.S., states, and 3,142 counties/county equivalents defined as of January 1, 1992. For changes to these areas since January 1, 1992, see appendix B. Geographic Information]

County	Establishments Total	Establishments Percent with 20 or more employees	All employees Number[1]	All employees Annual payroll (mil. dol.)	Production workers Number[2]	Production workers Wages (mil. dol.)	Value added by manufacture (mil. dol.)	Value of shipments (mil. dol.)	Withdrawals Total (mil. gal.)	Withdrawals Percent ground water	Irrigation	Public supply	Industrial	Consumptive use (mil. gal.)
TENNESSEE—Con.														
Overton	29	41.4	1 249	23.7	1 065	17.7	48.6	126.4	1	5.0	Z	1	–	Z
Perry	15	33.3	1 689	34.9	1 518	27.8	58.4	169.8	1	33.0	–	1	–	Z
Pickett	NA	NA	NA	NA	NA	NA	NA	NA	1	13.3	–	1	–	Z
Polk	22	50.0	1 061	18.3	875	13.0	34.5	72.1	33	3.5	Z	1	32	4
Putnam	141	41.1	9 927	232.3	7 927	156.4	736.4	1 757.7	11	4.9	Z	10	Z	1
Rhea	40	35.0	4 674	105.6	4 082	85.8	233.8	434.7	4	32.0	Z	3	–	1
Roane	42	40.5	2 075	47.1	1 628	30.4	143.4	256.0	1 254	.2	–	6	1	1
Robertson	74	50.0	5 019	127.2	3 948	84.6	296.3	730.9	6	23.3	Z	4	–	1
Rutherford	191	38.7	19 096	754.7	14 819	516.2	2 481.1	8 851.9	25	7.8	1	22	–	3
Scott	40	27.5	2 915	56.5	2 483	39.1	143.1	330.0	2	9.8	–	2	–	Z
Sequatchie	11	36.4	948	18.3	858	14.6	77.8	223.8	1	32.4	Z	1	–	Z
Sevier	103	22.3	2 611	64.5	2 046	43.3	141.6	272.4	10	27.6	Z	7	Z	1
Shelby	902	39.4	44 145	1 476.9	29 794	815.7	4 800.5	11 758.7	638	32.6	3	163	39	23
Smith	23	47.8	1 710	44.9	1 361	33.3	149.3	396.6	3	18.6	Z	2	–	Z
Stewart	NA	NA	NA	NA	NA	NA	NA	NA	2 197	Z	–	1	–	Z
Sullivan	182	32.4	18 602	816.7	12 238	430.1	2 364.7	4 245.2	544	.2	Z	24	519	59
Sumner	205	37.6	11 852	333.8	9 157	218.5	803.8	1 932.0	792	Z	Z	19	–	2
Tipton	39	53.8	3 327	88.6	2 651	62.6	326.2	604.8	6	99.5	Z	4	Z	1
Trousdale	12	50.0	693	14.4	552	10.0	32.3	63.8	1	7.6	Z	1	–	Z
Unicoi	22	45.5	1 518	36.3	1 330	27.3	129.7	202.5	2	99.6	–	2	–	Z
Union	20	55.0	1 099	23.6	870	17.3	42.2	141.1	3	93.8	–	1	–	Z
Van Buren	NA	NA	NA	NA	NA	NA	NA	NA	1	6.3	Z	Z	–	Z
Warren	73	47.9	6 610	192.5	5 542	150.6	523.3	1 133.3	6	3.8	Z	5	–	1
Washington	151	45.7	10 370	257.6	8 085	174.8	546.1	1 300.9	22	29.1	1	19	–	3
Wayne	28	39.3	1 487	23.0	1 224	17.8	50.7	99.6	5	52.3	Z	1	–	3
Weakley	45	53.3	3 287	74.9	2 781	54.6	213.7	574.0	4	100.0	Z	3	–	1
White	49	38.8	3 442	81.0	2 963	63.3	254.5	457.3	3	5.9	–	3	–	Z
Williamson	115	32.2	4 723	130.7	3 581	73.9	373.7	846.6	5	57.6	2	Z	–	3
Wilson	114	35.1	5 533	161.1	3 989	104.7	360.6	1 122.9	10	12.4	Z	9	–	1
TEXAS	21 808	31.1	959 665	32 760.8	663 929	18 163.1	129 390.0	297 657.0	29 608	29.7	9 451	3 294	2 296	11 124
Anderson	41	24.4	1 419	36.1	1 138	24.6	123.8	287.4	13	63.6	Z	8	–	6
Andrews	NA	NA	NA	NA	NA	NA	NA	NA	49	99.9	17	3	–	23
Angelina	88	34.1	7 536	212.8	6 405	168.3	511.3	1 363.6	41	57.5	Z	10	31	11
Aransas	NA	NA	NA	NA	NA	NA	NA	NA	1	98.1	–	Z	Z	1
Archer	NA	NA	NA	NA	NA	NA	NA	NA	24	8.8	–	12	–	10
Armstrong	NA	NA	NA	NA	NA	NA	NA	NA	11	98.7	9	Z	–	10
Atascosa	NA	NA	NA	NA	NA	NA	NA	NA	56	96.9	40	4	–	51
Austin	32	46.9	947	26.8	728	18.1	68.4	153.6	13	88.0	8	2	Z	9
Bailey	NA	NA	NA	NA	NA	NA	NA	NA	173	99.8	170	1	Z	172
Bandera	NA	NA	NA	NA	NA	NA	NA	NA	2	91.1	Z	1	Z	2
Bastrop	52	23.1	801	18.5	570	11.8	38.6	78.3	12	64.0	1	6	Z	7
Baylor	NA	NA	NA	NA	NA	NA	NA	NA	4	43.9	Z	2	–	2
Bee	NA	NA	NA	NA	NA	NA	NA	NA	4	71.9	1	1	–	4
Bell	135	34.1	7 365	224.5	5 778	158.2	696.9	1 351.3	48	3.9	1	45	1	12
Bexar	1 101	26.0	35 919	986.5	25 245	539.7	2 716.4	5 565.5	838	30.7	21	209	16	122
Blanco	NA	NA	NA	NA	NA	NA	NA	NA	2	76.9	Z	Z	–	2
Borden	NA	NA	NA	NA	NA	NA	NA	NA	6	91.9	1	–	Z	2
Bosque	18	44.4	548	13.4	406	7.8	34.5	74.9	6	59.8	2	2	1	4
Bowie	75	33.3	4 056	128.0	3 017	84.7	359.1	975.5	58	5.0	5	48	1	12
Brazoria	199	30.2	14 149	682.9	10 011	425.1	2 579.3	10 761.0	1 095	2.7	82	20	983	713
Brazos	101	24.8	3 126	79.6	2 203	44.3	175.6	382.2	38	91.0	8	24	Z	18
Brewster	NA	NA	NA	NA	NA	NA	NA	NA	4	88.2	Z	1	–	3
Briscoe	NA	NA	NA	NA	NA	NA	NA	NA	27	94.5	25	2	–	25
Brooks	NA	NA	NA	NA	NA	NA	NA	NA	2	81.1	Z	1	–	2
Brown	39	33.3	3 055	98.7	2 393	73.3	489.4	848.5	19	10.5	10	6	Z	14
Burleson	NA	NA	NA	NA	NA	NA	NA	NA	17	94.1	8	2	Z	10
Burnet	42	11.9	714	16.7	599	11.9	41.8	72.5	134	1.5	Z	3	Z	4
Caldwell	18	38.9	556	9.7	375	6.2	19.6	39.2	7	56.9	1	3	–	3
Calhoun	20	35.0	3 815	208.8	2 274	132.7	520.8	2 689.3	241	1.2	48	2	43	35
Callahan	NA	NA	NA	NA	NA	NA	NA	NA	4	48.1	1	1	–	3
Cameron	235	28.5	12 694	242.4	10 505	169.6	775.2	1 732.8	457	.3	406	46	–	275
Camp	NA	NA	NA	NA	NA	NA	NA	NA	3	68.0	Z	2	–	2
Carson	NA	NA	NA	NA	NA	NA	NA	NA	72	99.5	62	2	5	65
Cass	26	26.9	546	11.4	451	8.0	35.1	63.9	80	4.7	Z	1	76	30
Castro	NA	NA	NA	NA	NA	NA	NA	NA	401	99.6	388	3	2	398

[1] Average number of production workers plus the number of other (nonproduction) employees for the pay period including March 12. [2] Average number of production workers for the pay periods including the 12th of March, May, August, and November. [3] In millions of gallons per day.

Sources: Manufacturing—U.S. Census Bureau, 1997 Economic Census – Manufacturing, generated by Statistical Compendia Branch, using American Factfinder at <http://www.census.gov/>, (June 2000) [related Internet site <http://www.census.gov/epcd/www/97EC31.HTM>]. Water Use—U.S. Geological Survey, "Water Use in the United States," individual state/county and US by state files from <http://water.usgs.gov/watuse/spread95.html>, (accessed: September 1999).

Table B–9. Counties — **Manufacturing and Water Use**–Con.

[Includes U.S., states, and 3,142 counties/county equivalents defined as of January 1, 1992. For changes to these areas since January 1, 1992, see appendix B. Geographic Information]

County	Manufacturing (NAICS 31-33), 1997								Water use per day,[3] 1995					
	Establishments		All employees		Production workers		Value added by manu-facture (mil. dol.)	Value of ship-ments (mil. dol.)	Withdrawals					Consump-tive use (mil. gal.)
	Total	Percent with 20 or more employ-ees	Number[1]	Annual payroll (mil. dol.)	Number[2]	Wages (mil. dol.)			Total (mil. gal.)	Percent ground water	By selected major use– (mil. gal.)			
											Irrigation	Public supply	Industrial	
TEXAS—Con.														
Chambers	15	46.7	1 499	83.5	751	32.2	910.1	1 989.7	1 228	.7	103	2	4	62
Cherokee	91	41.8	3 178	67.0	2 681	49.4	167.0	327.4	347	2.0	Z	6	–	8
Childress	NA	NA	NA	NA	NA	NA	NA	NA	7	94.3	6	–	–	7
Clay	NA	NA	NA	NA	NA	NA	NA	NA	17	15.7	1	13	–	3
Cochran	NA	NA	NA	NA	NA	NA	NA	NA	59	99.8	52	1	–	54
Coke	NA	NA	NA	NA	NA	NA	NA	NA	33	4.8	1	30	–	2
Coleman	NA	NA	NA	NA	NA	NA	NA	NA	4	11.4	1	2	–	2
Collin	318	30.2	21 326	972.3	11 033	343.1	3 447.7	6 235.9	339	.8	Z	133	1	24
Collingsworth	NA	NA	NA	NA	NA	NA	NA	NA	28	97.6	27	1	–	28
Colorado	29	20.7	825	17.4	694	13.3	41.4	76.0	231	11.5	198	2	Z	100
Comal	84	33.3	4 016	101.2	3 036	62.6	344.5	558.6	28	69.5	Z	11	8	14
Comanche	NA	NA	NA	NA	NA	NA	NA	NA	46	55.9	40	2	–	42
Concho	NA	NA	NA	NA	NA	NA	NA	NA	8	67.4	4	2	–	5
Cooke	68	41.2	3 318	88.2	2 713	64.7	209.6	437.7	10	85.6	Z	4	–	5
Coryell	25	24.0	556	12.0	393	7.8	19.7	52.3	2	47.4	Z	Z	–	5
Cottle	NA	NA	NA	NA	NA	NA	NA	NA	3	85.9	2	Z	–	3
Crane	NA	NA	NA	NA	NA	NA	NA	NA	15	91.7	Z	1	–	3
Crockett	NA	NA	NA	NA	NA	NA	NA	NA	8	94.1	Z	2	Z	3
Crosby	NA	NA	NA	NA	NA	NA	NA	NA	92	97.7	88	2	–	90
Culberson	NA	NA	NA	NA	NA	NA	NA	NA	8	99.9	5	1	–	7
Dallam	NA	NA	NA	NA	NA	NA	NA	NA	329	99.8	324	2	–	328
Dallas	3 383	34.4	151 686	5 499.4	97 974	2 612.1	17 555.1	29 962.5	729	.7	1	83	1	147
Dawson	NA	NA	NA	NA	NA	NA	NA	NA	50	99.9	44	Z	Z	46
Deaf Smith	32	28.1	1 128	28.9	857	19.6	125.0	376.7	279	98.9	258	3	1	276
Delta	NA	NA	NA	NA	NA	NA	NA	NA	1	13.2	–	Z	–	Z
Denton	305	26.2	13 556	459.8	9 544	247.4	1 393.8	2 741.8	166	5.0	1	163	Z	18
DeWitt	24	33.3	721	16.4	563	11.2	39.1	87.9	5	69.5	Z	2	–	4
Dickens	NA	NA	NA	NA	NA	NA	NA	NA	6	92.9	4	Z	–	5
Dimmit	NA	NA	NA	NA	NA	NA	NA	NA	14	60.4	10	2	–	12
Donley	NA	NA	NA	NA	NA	NA	NA	NA	15	76.5	11	4	–	12
Duval	NA	NA	NA	NA	NA	NA	NA	NA	23	96.1	6	2	–	16
Eastland	25	36.0	713	17.4	566	11.3	41.8	98.3	16	60.0	12	2	Z	13
Ector	203	27.6	3 526	115.6	2 536	71.4	489.5	1 286.2	40	98.3	6	1	2	25
Edwards	NA	NA	NA	NA	NA	NA	NA	NA	1	90.4	Z	Z	–	1
Ellis	174	39.1	9 635	285.0	7 726	205.4	1 109.8	2 397.9	16	39.0	Z	11	3	7
El Paso	652	33.1	36 723	773.9	29 598	528.7	3 300.0	7 966.5	393	22.7	256	123	8	189
Erath	37	24.3	2 186	53.3	1 534	33.0	119.0	387.7	25	72.2	13	2	Z	24
Falls	NA	NA	NA	NA	NA	NA	NA	NA	9	44.4	4	2	–	7
Fannin	40	35.0	1 784	43.6	1 510	30.7	139.4	340.6	477	1.0	3	3	–	9
Fayette	39	35.9	1 056	23.2	821	14.9	57.6	148.6	24	41.4	1	2	Z	16
Fisher	NA	NA	NA	NA	NA	NA	NA	NA	4	77.8	2	–	Z	3
Floyd	NA	NA	NA	NA	NA	NA	NA	NA	226	99.9	224	Z	Z	226
Foard	NA	NA	NA	NA	NA	NA	NA	NA	5	94.6	4	Z	–	5
Fort Bend	270	33.0	11 923	452.7	7 187	202.3	1 493.4	2 704.9	217	32.4	73	45	64	81
Franklin	NA	NA	NA	NA	NA	NA	NA	NA	5	49.8	Z	2	–	3
Freestone	NA	NA	NA	NA	NA	NA	NA	NA	868	.4	Z	2	Z	15
Frio	NA	NA	NA	NA	NA	NA	NA	NA	102	98.4	96	2	–	98
Gaines	NA	NA	NA	NA	NA	NA	NA	NA	579	99.9	543	2	1	548
Galveston	160	21.9	7 279	392.5	4 817	244.5	1 761.8	9 182.6	587	.8	3	3	130	56
Garza	NA	NA	NA	NA	NA	NA	NA	NA	10	95.6	4	–	–	5
Gillespie	45	13.3	721	13.1	554	9.7	27.0	70.7	7	78.7	3	2	Z	6
Glasscock	NA	NA	NA	NA	NA	NA	NA	NA	56	99.9	52	Z	–	52
Goliad	NA	NA	NA	NA	NA	NA	NA	NA	8	15.3	Z	Z	–	8
Gonzales	19	36.8	747	16.8	586	10.9	44.5	173.6	10	33.1	1	4	Z	7
Gray	20	30.0	1 082	53.2	704	30.2	190.1	419.9	27	91.6	15	3	3	20
Grayson	140	33.6	10 223	365.4	7 871	224.9	2 188.0	3 557.3	29	55.8	1	18	6	8
Gregg	205	40.5	13 008	447.6	9 627	279.6	1 391.9	3 408.6	42	45.0	Z	19	3	8
Grimes	21	42.9	1 910	63.3	1 666	47.0	203.2	386.9	10	46.0	Z	2	Z	8
Guadalupe	90	38.9	5 592	150.4	4 115	93.9	616.7	1 320.3	10	32.9	Z	5	2	7
Hale	32	40.6	(4)	D	D	D	D	D	355	99.8	346	4	2	351
Hall	NA	NA	NA	NA	NA	NA	NA	NA	12	97.8	11	Z	–	12
Hamilton	NA	NA	NA	NA	NA	NA	NA	NA	3	39.5	1	Z	–	3
Hansford	NA	NA	NA	NA	NA	NA	NA	NA	167	98.2	160	1	–	166
Hardeman	NA	NA	NA	NA	NA	NA	NA	NA	13	65.8	6	Z	–	11
Hardin	37	35.1	1 016	30.0	808	21.1	62.7	173.1	186	8.4	164	11	Z	13
Harris	4 374	31.7	158 572	5 991.3	108 800	3 390.2	29 799.7	73 227.7	895	40.1	19	370	170	275

[1] Average number of production workers plus the number of other (nonproduction) employees for the pay period including March 12.   [2] Average number of production workers for the pay periods including the 12th of March, May, August, and November.   [3] In millions of gallons per day.   [4] 2,500 to 4,999 employees.

Sources: Manufacturing—U.S. Census Bureau, 1997 Economic Census – Manufacturing, generated by Statistical Compendia Branch, using American Factfinder at <http://www.census.gov/>, (June 2000) [related Internet site <http://www.census.gov/epcd/www/97EC31.HTM>].   Water Use—U.S. Geological Survey, "Water Use in the United States," individual state/county and US by state files from <http://water.usgs.gov/watuse/spread95.html>, (accessed: September 1999).

[Includes U.S., states, and 3,142 counties/county equivalents defined as of January 1, 1992. For changes to these areas since January 1, 1992, see appendix B. Geographic Information]

County	Manufacturing (NAICS 31-33), 1997								Water use per day,[3] 1995					
	Establishments		All employees		Production workers		Value added by manu-facture (mil. dol.)	Value of ship-ments (mil. dol.)	Withdrawals					Consump-tive use (mil. gal.)
	Total	Percent with 20 or more employ-ees	Number[1]	Annual payroll (mil. dol.)	Number[2]	Wages (mil. dol.)			Total (mil. gal.)	Percent ground water	By selected major use– (mil. gal.)			
											Irrigation	Public supply	Industrial	
TEXAS—Con.														
Harrison	90	42.2	3 128	83.2	2 368	55.3	301.4	600.4	82	4.4	Z	7	63	41
Hartley	NA	NA	NA	NA	NA	NA	NA	NA	212	98.9	206	Z	–	212
Haskell	NA	NA	NA	NA	NA	NA	NA	NA	98	32.3	31	2	–	32
Hays	108	26.9	3 389	96.2	2 388	50.7	249.9	477.0	17	85.6	Z	13	Z	7
Hemphill	NA	NA	NA	NA	NA	NA	NA	NA	4	74.3	1	Z	–	4
Henderson	49	28.6	1 880	38.3	1 490	26.2	127.2	214.3	126	5.0	Z	122	–	5
Hidalgo	261	25.7	10 284	178.3	8 159	123.1	671.9	1 428.2	932	2.3	853	71	1	554
Hill	37	27.0	1 237	30.7	1 055	23.7	78.6	174.4	6	42.1	Z	4	–	3
Hockley	NA	NA	NA	NA	NA	NA	NA	NA	176	99.7	151	1	–	156
Hood	NA	NA	NA	NA	NA	NA	NA	NA	3 333	.1	4	5	Z	9
Hopkins	43	37.2	1 463	41.4	1 103	27.7	229.4	526.1	13	39.8	Z	5	–	9
Houston	24	37.5	618	13.3	530	9.8	50.9	131.8	6	52.2	Z	3	–	4
Howard	27	48.1	1 124	34.6	851	23.5	157.9	726.2	14	71.7	1	1	1	7
Hudspeth	NA	NA	NA	NA	NA	NA	NA	NA	158	100.0	157	Z	–	213
Hunt	58	44.8	7 223	256.0	5 621	180.6	669.4	1 478.9	97	1.5	Z	95	–	5
Hutchinson	30	33.3	1 718	89.1	1 346	55.0	373.7	1 949.1	147	55.6	56	66	23	61
Irion	NA	NA	NA	NA	NA	NA	NA	NA	6	66.6	3	Z	–	3
Jack	NA	NA	NA	NA	NA	NA	NA	NA	3	48.0	–	Z	–	2
Jackson	11	27.3	(4)	D	D	D	D	D	88	72.8	65	1	19	43
Jasper	29	31.0	1 911	76.6	1 524	58.9	234.3	543.2	57	84.6	Z	3	52	4
Jeff Davis	NA	NA	NA	NA	NA	NA	NA	NA	1	88.1	Z	Z	–	1
Jefferson	230	34.3	14 471	727.0	10 170	469.7	4 398.7	15 920.2	172	2.2	42	20	107	104
Jim Hogg	NA	NA	NA	NA	NA	NA	NA	NA	2	68.7	Z	1	–	1
Jim Wells	NA	NA	NA	NA	NA	NA	NA	NA	5	70.5	1	1	–	5
Johnson	170	28.8	5 942	161.3	4 521	106.1	523.9	981.4	13	65.1	–	9	1	8
Jones	NA	NA	NA	NA	NA	NA	NA	NA	287	1.5	5	1	1	9
Karnes	NA	NA	NA	NA	NA	NA	NA	NA	5	74.8	1	2	Z	3
Kaufman	109	31.2	4 274	120.4	3 132	68.1	267.2	521.3	7	5.3	2	3	–	5
Kendall	NA	NA	NA	NA	NA	NA	NA	NA	4	66.4	1	2	Z	3
Kenedy	NA	NA	NA	NA	NA	NA	NA	NA	1	46.2	Z	Z	–	1
Kent	NA	NA	NA	NA	NA	NA	NA	NA	10	95.9	1	Z	–	2
Kerr	49	10.2	960	24.9	652	14.2	53.5	92.9	8	51.0	1	5	Z	4
Kimble	NA	NA	NA	NA	NA	NA	NA	NA	3	27.1	1	1	1	2
King	NA	NA	NA	NA	NA	NA	NA	NA	4	90.0	Z	Z	–	1
Kinney	NA	NA	NA	NA	NA	NA	NA	NA	9	98.8	7	1	–	8
Kleberg	NA	NA	NA	NA	NA	NA	NA	NA	8	80.6	Z	4	–	5
Knox	NA	NA	NA	NA	NA	NA	NA	NA	27	97.0	25	Z	–	26
Lamar	60	36.7	4 809	161.0	4 036	125.7	1 336.7	2 056.3	22	3.7	4	11	5	13
Lamb	14	21.4	678	16.7	567	13.3	53.6	123.6	294	99.8	269	3	–	285
Lampasas	NA	NA	NA	NA	NA	NA	NA	NA	2	60.2	Z	Z	–	3
La Salle	NA	NA	NA	NA	NA	NA	NA	NA	7	91.4	5	1	–	6
Lavaca	46	47.8	2 127	37.2	1 568	20.9	92.8	192.5	17	89.6	12	1	–	12
Lee	NA	NA	NA	NA	NA	NA	NA	NA	10	88.6	1	2	–	4
Leon	NA	NA	NA	NA	NA	NA	NA	NA	9	57.8	–	1	2	4
Liberty	41	29.3	1 220	36.1	986	26.7	84.9	209.8	613	4.1	95	385	121	43
Limestone	17	35.3	790	15.4	686	11.2	40.6	80.1	24	15.8	–	2	Z	22
Lipscomb	NA	NA	NA	NA	NA	NA	NA	NA	18	96.7	16	1	–	17
Live Oak	NA	NA	NA	NA	NA	NA	NA	NA	10	70.2	1	2	1	8
Llano	NA	NA	NA	NA	NA	NA	NA	NA	5	45.3	1	3	Z	3
Loving	NA	NA	NA	NA	NA	NA	NA	NA	2	69.0	1	–	–	1
Lubbock	258	27.5	7 286	203.8	5 026	100.0	881.4	1 566.4	219	95.4	198	13	2	216
Lynn	NA	NA	NA	NA	NA	NA	NA	NA	51	91.9	50	Z	–	50
McCulloch	NA	NA	NA	NA	NA	NA	NA	NA	6	96.5	2	3	Z	5
McLennan	261	38.7	16 474	481.7	11 828	291.2	2 100.4	3 855.6	57	22.1	2	35	5	30
McMullen	NA	NA	NA	NA	NA	NA	NA	NA	2	77.9	–	Z	–	1
Madison	NA	NA	NA	NA	NA	NA	NA	NA	3	81.1	Z	2	Z	2
Marion	NA	NA	NA	NA	NA	NA	NA	NA	5	21.8	Z	2	–	4
Martin	NA	NA	NA	NA	NA	NA	NA	NA	14	99.2	6	1	Z	8
Mason	NA	NA	NA	NA	NA	NA	NA	NA	13	96.7	11	1	–	12
Matagorda	29	17.2	(5)	D	D	D	D	D	124	18.9	88	4	9	126
Maverick	19	36.8	1 091	13.2	1 001	10.5	20.3	78.0	135	1.3	126	5	–	75
Medina	23	17.4	556	13.8	418	9.9	33.2	50.5	50	62.4	43	5	–	41
Menard	NA	NA	NA	NA	NA	NA	NA	NA	6	16.1	5	Z	–	5
Midland	135	23.0	2 435	76.5	1 558	35.6	168.3	326.1	60	82.8	38	9	Z	50
Milam	9	55.6	1 559	65.3	1 251	44.5	129.8	456.0	50	61.3	1	4	38	11
Mills	NA	NA	NA	NA	NA	NA	NA	NA	4	22.6	2	Z	–	3

[1] Average number of production workers plus the number of other (nonproduction) employees for the pay period including March 12. [2] Average number of production workers for the pay periods including the 12th of March, May, August, and November. [3] In millions of gallons per day. [4] 1,000 to 2,499 employees. [5] 500 to 999 employees.

Sources: Manufacturing—U.S. Census Bureau, 1997 Economic Census – Manufacturing, generated by Statistical Compendia Branch, using American Factfinder at <http://www.census.gov/>, (June 2000) [related Internet site <http://www.census.gov/epcd/www/97EC31.HTM>]. Water Use—U.S. Geological Survey, "Water Use in the United States," individual state/county and US by state files from <http://water.usgs.gov/watuse/spread95.html>, (accessed: September 1999).

Table B-9. Counties — **Manufacturing and Water Use**-Con.

[Includes U.S., states, and 3,142 counties/county equivalents defined as of January 1, 1992. For changes to these areas since January 1, 1992, see appendix B. Geographic Information]

County	Manufacturing (NAICS 31-33), 1997								Water use per day,[3] 1995					
	Establishments		All employees		Production workers		Value added by manu-facture (mil. dol.)	Value of ship-ments (mil. dol.)	Withdrawals					
	Total	Percent with 20 or more employ-ees	Number[1]	Annual payroll (mil. dol.)	Number[2]	Wages (mil. dol.)			Total (mil. gal.)	Percent ground water	By selected major use— (mil. gal.)			Consump-tive use (mil. gal.)
											Irrigation	Public supply	Industrial	
TEXAS—Con.														
Mitchell	NA	NA	NA	NA	NA	NA	NA	NA	7	58.4	1	Z	–	5
Montague	21	28.6	505	8.9	374	5.4	22.2	44.1	6	43.7	Z	2	–	3
Montgomery	285	26.0	6 706	219.1	4 837	134.8	722.5	1 540.9	39	91.2	–	26	2	20
Moore	19	21.1	2 865	72.5	2 411	56.1	534.0	2 663.2	312	99.7	296	5	6	307
Morris	16	56.3	2 224	95.7	1 601	65.5	247.4	688.0	86	1.0	Z	Z	83	12
Motley	NA	NA	NA	NA	NA	NA	NA	NA	6	93.7	5	Z	–	6
Nacogdoches	60	41.7	3 475	99.3	2 817	72.9	265.9	771.3	14	68.0	1	10	1	6
Navarro	49	40.8	2 191	58.5	1 628	38.8	183.9	336.0	9	7.2	–	7	Z	4
Newton	10	30.0	620	15.8	525	13.2	34.1	133.2	5	84.6	2	1	Z	3
Nolan	17	52.9	1 043	27.7	758	18.4	125.9	170.7	8	78.8	2	1	Z	5
Nueces	223	27.4	8 925	373.8	5 951	226.1	2 452.5	9 988.5	926	.2	–	113	46	27
Ochiltree	NA	NA	NA	NA	NA	NA	NA	NA	86	98.2	81	2	–	84
Oldham	NA	NA	NA	NA	NA	NA	NA	NA	7	79.9	4	1	–	6
Orange	82	30.5	6 137	302.4	4 477	203.7	1 190.2	2 893.4	1 191	1.5	5	18	46	29
Palo Pinto	37	37.8	1 183	32.6	803	14.8	76.4	134.2	462	.1	Z	4	–	5
Panola	12	16.7	1 092	19.7	961	15.7	98.8	125.0	12	44.1	–	3	3	7
Parker	101	28.7	2 538	63.5	1 940	39.8	164.0	310.8	19	29.6	Z	5	Z	7
Parmer	6	50.0	(4)	D	D	D	D	D	342	99.4	329	1	1	340
Pecos	NA	NA	NA	NA	NA	NA	NA	NA	86	97.8	65	3	Z	67
Polk	25	32.0	1 693	54.6	1 498	45.0	101.9	295.8	9	45.8	Z	7	1	3
Potter	145	26.9	(5)	D	D	D	D	D	29	65.2	17	Z	5	35
Presidio	NA	NA	NA	NA	NA	NA	NA	NA	22	16.0	20	1	–	15
Rains	NA	NA	NA	NA	NA	NA	NA	NA	1	18.7	Z	1	–	1
Randall	58	24.1	(4)	D	D	D	D	D	55	93.6	27	22	–	39
Reagan	NA	NA	NA	NA	NA	NA	NA	NA	34	99.9	28	1	–	30
Real	NA	NA	NA	NA	NA	NA	NA	NA	1	60.6	Z	Z	–	1
Red River	18	44.4	1 171	24.4	1 048	16.5	59.7	127.0	5	35.9	2	1	–	4
Reeves	4	25.0	(6)	D	D	D	D	D	98	98.0	92	1	1	95
Refugio	NA	NA	NA	NA	NA	NA	NA	NA	6	92.5	–	1	–	1
Roberts	NA	NA	NA	NA	NA	NA	NA	NA	6	94.4	5	Z	–	6
Robertson	NA	NA	NA	NA	NA	NA	NA	NA	24	86.7	16	3	Z	21
Rockwall	56	19.6	927	24.0	686	14.8	59.1	114.8	Z	44.4	–	–	–	2
Runnels	15	50.0	1 453	20.1	979	13.9	81.2	151.1	7	34.8	3	2	–	5
Rusk	51	31.4	1 302	29.4	1 006	20.7	85.8	170.3	28	36.3	Z	4	1	21
Sabine	NA	NA	NA	NA	NA	NA	NA	NA	2	57.7	Z	1	Z	1
San Augustine	NA	NA	NA	NA	NA	NA	NA	NA	2	54.9	Z	1	–	1
San Jacinto	NA	NA	NA	NA	NA	NA	NA	NA	2	86.4	–	1	Z	2
San Patricio	45	26.7	2 510	103.2	1 896	71.0	459.5	1 235.3	12	22.9	Z	1	9	9
San Saba	NA	NA	NA	NA	NA	NA	NA	NA	5	46.4	3	1	Z	4
Schleicher	NA	NA	NA	NA	NA	NA	NA	NA	3	96.4	2	Z	–	3
Scurry	NA	NA	NA	NA	NA	NA	NA	NA	26	44.4	1	14	–	6
Shackelford	NA	NA	NA	NA	NA	NA	NA	NA	2	72.6	Z	–	–	2
Shelby	29	34.5	1 989	39.3	1 419	31.5	199.3	303.2	6	39.1	Z	4	Z	4
Sherman	NA	NA	NA	NA	NA	NA	NA	NA	244	99.7	240	1	–	244
Smith	213	31.0	10 969	381.1	8 450	262.6	1 113.0	2 299.1	39	50.4	Z	32	3	14
Somervell	NA	NA	NA	NA	NA	NA	NA	NA	6	22.1	Z	Z	–	6
Starr	NA	NA	NA	NA	NA	NA	NA	NA	50	3.3	40	7	–	34
Stephens	18	27.8	562	13.0	479	8.8	57.8	94.3	10	40.8	Z	5	–	2
Sterling	NA	NA	NA	NA	NA	NA	NA	NA	3	97.5	1	Z	–	2
Stonewall	NA	NA	NA	NA	NA	NA	NA	NA	4	84.4	1	–	–	2
Sutton	NA	NA	NA	NA	NA	NA	NA	NA	3	86.2	2	1	–	3
Swisher	NA	NA	NA	NA	NA	NA	NA	NA	181	99.4	175	Z	–	181
Tarrant	2 009	33.5	95 970	3 583.2	60 428	1 701.5	9 393.8	18 621.6	176	7.3	Z	138	32	90
Taylor	118	23.7	3 062	79.9	2 121	44.6	531.2	1 010.7	26	7.2	Z	21	1	10
Terrell	NA	NA	NA	NA	NA	NA	NA	NA	1	99.1	Z	Z	–	1
Terry	NA	NA	NA	NA	NA	NA	NA	NA	155	99.8	149	1	Z	151
Throckmorton	NA	NA	NA	NA	NA	NA	NA	NA	2	57.5	–	Z	–	1
Titus	42	45.2	4 792	102.4	4 411	89.8	188.8	845.3	1 421	.2	–	6	2	25
Tom Green	100	28.0	4 452	105.1	3 579	74.7	367.3	827.6	258	23.5	98	18	Z	98
Travis	774	26.2	52 353	1 986.2	26 364	764.7	11 400.7	14 692.9	590	1.6	1	117	9	50
Trinity	NA	NA	NA	NA	NA	NA	NA	NA	2	53.4	–	1	–	1
Tyler	13	23.1	565	8.9	372	6.4	18.8	42.1	3	94.8	Z	2	–	1
Upshur	31	22.6	603	13.2	383	7.2	25.3	81.1	7	62.6	Z	4	–	4
Upton	NA	NA	NA	NA	NA	NA	NA	NA	29	99.9	16	1	–	20
Uvalde	17	23.5	710	9.4	611	6.7	29.7	50.7	61	97.5	53	4	Z	57
Val Verde	24	29.2	522	10.2	314	3.8	37.3	125.4	12	53.6	1	10	–	6

[1] Average number of production workers plus the number of other (nonproduction) employees for the pay period including March 12. [2] Average number of production workers for the pay periods including the 12th of March, May, August, and November. [3] In millions of gallons per day. [4] 1,000 to 2,499 employees. [5] 5,000 to 9,999 employees. [6] 500 to 999 employees.

Sources: Manufacturing—U.S. Census Bureau, 1997 Economic Census – Manufacturing, generated by Statistical Compendia Branch, using American Factfinder at <http://www.census.gov/>, (June 2000) [related Internet site <http://www.census.gov/epcd/www/97EC31.HTM>]. Water Use—U.S. Geological Survey, "Water Use in the United States," individual state/county and US by state files from <http://water.usgs.gov/watuse/spread95.html>, (accessed: September 1999).

Table B–9. Counties — **Manufacturing and Water Use**–Con.

[Includes U.S., states, and 3,142 counties/county equivalents defined as of January 1, 1992. For changes to these areas since January 1, 1992, see appendix B. Geographic Information]

County	Manufacturing (NAICS 31-33), 1997								Water use per day,[3] 1995					
	Establishments		All employees		Production workers		Value added by manu-facture (mil. dol.)	Value of ship-ments (mil. dol.)	Withdrawals					Consump-tive use (mil. gal.)
	Total	Percent with 20 or more employ-ees	Number[1]	Annual payroll (mil. dol.)	Number[2]	Wages (mil. dol.)			Total (mil. gal.)	Percent ground water	By selected major use– (mil. gal.)			
											Irrigation	Public supply	Industrial	
TEXAS—Con.														
Van Zandt	38	13.2	622	16.2	490	11.6	38.4	68.2	10	64.8	Z	3	Z	6
Victoria	71	23.9	3 064	119.5	2 265	82.4	592.5	1 245.3	48	61.3	13	9	17	36
Walker	38	28.9	677	14.7	557	10.1	40.5	90.8	5	93.1	Z	4	Z	4
Waller	43	37.2	1 283	43.3	836	22.6	127.9	245.6	24	97.5	19	3	Z	16
Ward	NA	NA	NA	NA	NA	NA	NA	NA	40	56.4	18	10	Z	18
Washington	41	58.5	2 982	81.9	2 277	56.2	280.6	529.2	7	45.7	Z	3	Z	4
Webb	87	17.2	1 402	28.1	969	15.5	136.8	258.6	43	2.5	7	32	Z	20
Wharton	46	32.6	2 152	51.9	1 874	39.2	160.2	372.3	273	50.1	264	4	Z	145
Wheeler	NA	NA	NA	NA	NA	NA	NA	NA	6	74.7	3	1	–	5
Wichita	153	28.1	7 927	254.9	6 263	183.3	769.8	1 435.9	31	17.0	21	2	2	22
Wilbarger	9	33.3	681	19.8	552	14.9	99.9	236.7	29	93.6	24	3	–	26
Willacy	NA	NA	NA	NA	NA	NA	NA	NA	1	85.1	–	–	–	37
Williamson	240	32.5	11 727	418.8	7 137	164.6	3 673.8	9 637.4	26	64.6	–	20	1	14
Wilson	NA	NA	NA	NA	NA	NA	NA	NA	17	80.8	11	3	–	14
Winkler	NA	NA	NA	NA	NA	NA	NA	NA	7	99.9	–	2	–	3
Wise	54	29.6	1 340	37.8	1 004	25.4	107.0	180.3	22	20.3	Z	3	2	20
Wood	45	15.6	649	13.5	562	9.9	37.3	143.4	16	88.3	Z	4	–	6
Yoakum	NA	NA	NA	NA	NA	NA	NA	NA	127	98.2	96	2	–	104
Young	28	35.7	1 043	28.3	787	14.9	142.4	248.4	9	22.5	–	4	–	5
Zapata	NA	NA	NA	NA	NA	NA	NA	NA	6	1.5	3	2	–	3
Zavala	NA	NA	NA	NA	NA	NA	NA	NA	71	73.9	66	2	1	67
UTAH	2 860	30.1	119 140	3 726.1	84 129	2 218.7	11 343.5	24 014.4	4 459	17.7	3 533	497	86	2 333
Beaver	NA	NA	NA	NA	NA	NA	NA	NA	136	34.3	121	2	–	66
Box Elder	51	23.5	5 725	270.7	4 340	189.5	661.5	1 271.6	371	21.3	341	25	2	205
Cache	149	32.2	8 355	195.0	6 089	132.9	534.2	1 785.6	293	12.1	243	22	2	151
Carbon	NA	NA	NA	NA	NA	NA	NA	NA	72	6.5	63	5	Z	52
Daggett	NA	NA	NA	NA	NA	NA	NA	NA	15	1.7	15	Z	–	12
Davis	227	28.6	7 170	202.8	5 664	136.4	634.8	1 592.1	159	13.2	113	43	2	85
Duchesne	NA	NA	NA	NA	NA	NA	NA	NA	172	.6	169	1	Z	128
Emery	NA	NA	NA	NA	NA	NA	NA	NA	153	1.1	123	3	1	114
Garfield	NA	NA	NA	NA	NA	NA	NA	NA	71	3.6	69	1	–	23
Grand	NA	NA	NA	NA	NA	NA	NA	NA	10	27.6	7	3	Z	6
Iron	50	24.0	1 520	37.9	1 208	23.7	103.5	206.4	154	70.6	146	7	–	106
Juab	NA	NA	NA	NA	NA	NA	NA	NA	111	20.9	106	4	Z	42
Kane	NA	NA	NA	NA	NA	NA	NA	NA	10	16.9	8	2	–	8
Millard	NA	NA	NA	NA	NA	NA	NA	NA	285	27.1	245	4	17	223
Morgan	NA	NA	NA	NA	NA	NA	NA	NA	107	1.6	105	1	Z	22
Piute	NA	NA	NA	NA	NA	NA	NA	NA	72	2.5	60	Z	–	28
Rich	NA	NA	NA	NA	NA	NA	NA	NA	153	3.7	151	1	–	57
Salt Lake	1 441	30.7	53 424	1 706.4	35 180	879.9	4 968.6	10 012.2	386	22.4	174	190	12	129
San Juan	NA	NA	NA	NA	NA	NA	NA	NA	42	13.0	36	2	Z	30
Sanpete	18	27.8	908	16.9	808	13.6	53.2	116.7	149	14.5	142	5	–	86
Sevier	NA	NA	NA	NA	NA	NA	NA	NA	209	3.4	193	2	Z	61
Summit	40	17.5	861	21.4	505	15.4	38.9	86.2	91	8.0	83	7	–	48
Tooele	27	33.3	1 737	56.8	1 382	39.5	169.4	342.8	211	32.7	61	8	30	155
Uintah	NA	NA	NA	NA	NA	NA	NA	NA	195	5.3	183	5	Z	146
Utah	390	32.3	15 949	461.0	11 682	299.9	1 191.9	2 667.3	299	33.0	214	73	8	124
Wasatch	NA	NA	NA	NA	NA	NA	NA	NA	97	7.6	93	3	–	33
Washington	92	31.5	1 949	48.4	1 501	33.8	133.8	243.4	84	31.6	60	24	Z	33
Wayne	NA	NA	NA	NA	NA	NA	NA	NA	58	7.6	26	Z	–	26
Weber	210	32.4	18 446	635.0	13 353	402.9	2 606.3	5 242.4	295	10.2	184	54	10	136
VERMONT	1 226	27.7	42 533	1 459.6	29 318	758.0	4 044.6	7 803.0	565	8.8	4	47	9	24
Addison	61	27.9	1 871	59.4	1 227	33.5	184.7	321.9	7	66.7	Z	3	Z	2
Bennington	88	30.7	3 090	94.1	2 305	62.2	250.0	504.8	8	46.4	Z	4	Z	1
Caledonia	55	29.1	1 950	54.0	1 505	36.7	115.5	198.0	7	42.1	Z	2	1	1
Chittenden	234	26.9	14 302	624.0	7 867	196.1	2 056.8	3 942.1	20	22.9	1	15	Z	3
Essex	11	36.4	883	25.7	732	21.0	32.0	86.0	2	27.8	Z	Z	2	Z
Franklin	68	41.2	2 603	78.8	1 980	53.0	209.0	546.6	8	47.5	Z	3	1	2
Grand Isle	NA	NA	NA	NA	NA	NA	NA	NA	7	3.8	Z	Z	–	Z
Lamoille	51	17.6	697	18.0	516	10.2	46.9	85.2	4	65.9	Z	1	Z	1
Orange	58	25.9	1 220	29.3	921	19.2	64.4	128.5	3	80.2	Z	1	Z	1
Orleans	45	20.0	1 565	37.2	1 336	29.5	78.5	138.1	5	69.5	Z	2	Z	1
Rutland	123	34.1	4 635	150.5	3 856	116.4	311.0	542.2	16	36.2	Z	5	4	2
Washington	152	21.1	2 901	84.7	1 937	47.8	218.4	446.2	8	43.6	Z	4	Z	1
Windham	120	30.8	3 473	99.5	2 771	69.1	240.1	442.8	460	.6	Z	2	2	5
Windsor	155	25.8	3 300	103.2	2 330	62.5	235.6	417.1	11	86.5	Z	4	Z	2

[1] Average number of production workers plus the number of other (nonproduction) employees for the pay period including March 12.   [2] Average number of production workers for the pay periods including the 12th of March, May, August, and November.   [3] In millions of gallons per day.

Sources: Manufacturing—U.S. Census Bureau, 1997 Economic Census – Manufacturing, generated by Statistical Compendia Branch, using American Factfinder at <http://www.census.gov/>, (June 2000) [related Internet site <http://www.census.gov/epcd/www/97EC31.HTM>].   Water Use—U.S. Geological Survey, "Water Use in the United States," individual state/county and US by state files from <http://water.usgs.gov/watuse/spread95.html>, (accessed: September 1999).

[Includes U.S., states, and 3,142 counties/county equivalents defined as of January 1, 1992. For changes to these areas since January 1, 1992, see appendix B. Geographic Information]

County	Manufacturing (NAICS 31-33), 1997								Water use per day,[3] 1995					
	Establishments		All employees		Production workers		Value added by manufacture (mil. dol.)	Value of shipments (mil. dol.)	Withdrawals		By selected major use– (mil. gal.)			Consumptive use (mil. gal.)
	Total	Percent with 20 or more employees	Number[1]	Annual payroll (mil. dol.)	Number[2]	Wages (mil. dol.)			Total (mil. gal.)	Percent ground water	Irrigation	Public supply	Industrial	
VIRGINIA	5 986	34.1	370 595	11 557.8	279 682	7 412.2	43 563.0	83 814.0	8 262	4.3	30	786	583	226
Accomack	32	21.9	3 209	52.6	2 533	44.2	105.5	244.5	9	91.6	2	1	3	3
Albemarle	54	27.8	(4)	D	D	D	D	D	16	21.8	Z	12	Z	2
Alleghany	NA	NA	NA	NA	NA	NA	NA	NA	57	6.3	–	2	55	7
Amelia	NA	NA	NA	NA	NA	NA	NA	NA	2	47.2	1	Z	Z	1
Amherst	44	31.8	1 678	53.8	1 272	39.9	209.6	395.1	18	6.3	Z	13	4	1
Appomattox	18	22.2	1 216	28.5	1 027	24.3	65.5	112.7	2	63.2	Z	Z	–	1
Arlington	57	14.0	509	16.3	373	11.2	36.3	59.5	Z	35.7	–	–	Z	2
Augusta	66	43.9	5 372	175.1	4 406	129.2	709.8	1 312.4	17	76.4	1	9	2	4
Bath	3	33.3	(5)	D	D	D	D	D	2	90.5	–	Z	–	Z
Bedford	45	37.0	1 489	49.7	984	22.7	95.9	262.0	17	26.8	Z	3	9	3
Bland	7	71.4	656	15.8	493	10.0	41.6	85.5	1	59.1	–	Z	–	Z
Botetourt	23	60.9	1 422	39.3	1 007	24.2	110.7	210.4	18	19.7	–	16	Z	1
Brunswick	19	52.6	937	18.7	795	13.7	44.5	84.3	4	29.5	1	1	–	1
Buchanan	NA	NA	NA	NA	NA	NA	NA	NA	2	36.4	–	Z	Z	1
Buckingham	NA	NA	NA	NA	NA	NA	NA	NA	4	23.5	Z	4	5	2
Campbell	62	33.9	5 098	123.5	4 272	88.5	890.6	1 383.7	11	23.5	Z	4	5	2
Caroline	NA	NA	NA	NA	NA	NA	NA	NA	3	67.1	Z	1	Z	1
Carroll	35	37.1	2 430	45.3	2 199	39.1	112.8	286.3	4	65.4	Z	1	Z	1
Charles City	10	40.0	680	16.0	522	11.4	36.4	62.2	2	39.2	1	Z	Z	1
Charlotte	15	60.0	1 178	25.4	1 055	21.4	46.4	143.6	2	50.3	Z	Z	Z	1
Chesterfield	164	30.5	10 166	412.6	7 324	255.7	1 361.2	2 671.2	1 008	.2	Z	32	60	10
Clarke	13	23.1	1 167	33.7	920	23.4	129.3	190.3	2	56.9	Z	1	Z	1
Craig	NA	NA	NA	NA	NA	NA	NA	NA	1	100.0	–	Z	–	Z
Culpeper	28	35.7	1 484	45.3	1 107	28.7	127.6	278.9	4	40.8	–	2	Z	1
Cumberland	NA	NA	NA	NA	NA	NA	NA	NA	1	70.3	–	Z	–	Z
Dickenson	NA	NA	NA	NA	NA	NA	NA	NA	3	26.7	–	3	–	Z
Dinwiddie	NA	NA	NA	NA	NA	NA	NA	NA	4	34.7	1	Z	–	1
Essex	18	44.4	1 140	24.8	996	18.6	45.6	119.4	1	86.9	Z	Z	–	Z
Fairfax	478	22.4	13 181	551.9	7 658	262.2	1 437.1	2 594.5	77	5.8	Z	72	Z	10
Fauquier	36	25.0	867	25.7	627	15.4	50.9	107.8	7	68.0	Z	2	Z	2
Floyd	22	22.7	547	11.2	455	8.6	22.7	48.0	2	64.2	–	Z	–	1
Fluvanna	NA	NA	NA	NA	NA	NA	NA	NA	118	1.2	–	1	Z	Z
Franklin	66	33.3	4 677	113.0	3 717	75.8	255.1	519.6	6	54.8	1	1	–	2
Frederick	69	53.6	3 416	97.0	2 299	61.1	362.2	741.1	6	48.6	Z	3	Z	1
Giles	15	66.7	2 701	90.5	2 109	63.6	304.2	538.6	309	2.2	–	1	66	8
Gloucester	NA	NA	NA	NA	NA	NA	NA	NA	3	65.7	–	1	–	Z
Goochland	NA	NA	NA	NA	NA	NA	NA	NA	3	52.6	–	Z	–	Z
Grayson	18	61.1	1 085	25.8	787	16.7	74.4	123.4	2	70.0	–	Z	Z	1
Greene	NA	NA	NA	NA	NA	NA	NA	NA	2	65.0	–	Z	–	Z
Greensville	5	60.0	733	15.0	678	13.2	36.4	120.3	3	29.5	Z	Z	1	1
Halifax	42	47.6	4 707	113.8	4 122	92.2	251.8	652.9	7	31.4	1	Z	Z	4
Hanover	150	28.7	3 803	111.8	3 009	72.2	257.5	579.7	26	20.3	1	7	–	3
Henrico	216	38.4	10 857	379.0	7 656	253.9	1 502.1	2 432.3	8	85.1	–	4	1	4
Henry	70	48.6	7 970	189.1	7 068	145.6	447.9	858.4	42	12.6	Z	8	30	4
Highland	NA	NA	NA	NA	NA	NA	NA	NA	6	99.8	–	Z	5	1
Isle of Wight	17	35.3	4 698	106.6	3 798	77.4	793.9	1 546.8	56	68.8	Z	15	40	6
James City	26	38.5	(4)	D	D	D	D	D	33	12.1	Z	31	Z	1
King and Queen	NA	NA	NA	NA	NA	NA	NA	NA	1	86.4	Z	Z	Z	Z
King George	NA	NA	NA	NA	NA	NA	NA	NA	4	57.4	Z	1	Z	1
King William	13	38.5	1 114	56.5	833	38.9	164.3	357.2	22	97.8	Z	Z	21	3
Lancaster	NA	NA	NA	NA	NA	NA	NA	NA	2	92.3	–	1	Z	Z
Lee	17	41.2	784	10.8	686	9.1	43.0	70.8	4	63.5	–	1	–	1
Loudoun	128	30.5	3 459	132.8	2 379	76.3	265.7	480.8	18	23.9	Z	15	Z	2
Louisa	29	27.6	633	16.4	489	10.1	51.1	89.3	2 078	.1	–	Z	Z	1
Lunenburg	16	50.0	900	16.2	758	12.5	32.2	76.3	2	35.6	1	Z	–	1
Madison	NA	NA	NA	NA	NA	NA	NA	NA	2	59.6	–	Z	Z	1
Mathews	NA	NA	NA	NA	NA	NA	NA	NA	1	98.7	–	Z	–	Z
Mecklenburg	41	56.1	4 589	102.7	3 845	75.6	340.2	859.1	11	21.9	1	2	4	2
Middlesex	NA	NA	NA	NA	NA	NA	NA	NA	1	91.4	Z	Z	Z	Z
Montgomery	68	32.4	4 836	153.9	3 796	109.9	481.8	699.1	25	7.8	1	9	13	3
Nelson	14	21.4	621	8.7	563	7.1	21.2	41.2	3	42.0	1	Z	Z	1
New Kent	NA	NA	NA	NA	NA	NA	NA	NA	40	2.6	Z	39	–	1
Northampton	NA	NA	NA	NA	NA	NA	NA	NA	6	79.2	4	Z	Z	3
Northumberland	19	36.8	575	12.9	316	6.5	35.6	59.6	1	97.5	Z	Z	Z	1
Nottoway	18	50.0	681	11.3	604	9.3	40.4	139.9	3	25.2	Z	2	Z	1
Orange	35	37.1	2 529	68.8	1 975	46.1	205.0	445.6	3	26.1	Z	2	Z	1
Page	16	56.3	2 883	47.5	2 352	33.5	197.9	461.8	5	87.8	Z	2	1	1
Patrick	38	47.4	2 610	55.7	2 342	43.8	109.3	249.7	2	68.9	Z	2	1	1
Pittsylvania	59	39.0	(6)	D	D	D	D	D	11	37.1	Z	1	3	3
Powhatan	NA	NA	NA	NA	NA	NA	NA	NA	2	88.5	–	Z	–	Z

[1] Average number of production workers plus the number of other (nonproduction) employees for the pay period including March 12. [2] Average number of production workers for the pay periods including the 12th of March, May, August, and November. [3] In millions of gallons per day. [4] 1,000 to 2,499 employees. [5] 500 to 999 employees. [6] 2,500 to 4,999 employees.

Sources: Manufacturing—U.S. Census Bureau, 1997 Economic Census – Manufacturing, generated by Statistical Compendia Branch, using American Factfinder at <http://www.census.gov/>, (June 2000) [related Internet site <http://www.census.gov/epcd/www/97EC31.HTM>]. Water Use—U.S. Geological Survey, "Water Use in the United States," individual state/county and US by state files from <http://water.usgs.gov/watuse/spread95.html>, (accessed: September 1999).

Table B–9. Counties — **Manufacturing and Water Use**–Con.

[Includes U.S., states, and 3,142 counties/county equivalents defined as of January 1, 1992. For changes to these areas since January 1, 1992, see appendix B. Geographic Information]

County	Establishments Total	Percent with 20 or more employees	All employees Number[1]	Annual payroll (mil. dol.)	Production workers Number[2]	Wages (mil. dol.)	Value added by manufacture (mil. dol.)	Value of shipments (mil. dol.)	Total (mil. gal.)	Percent ground water	Irrigation	Public supply	Industrial	Consumptive use (mil. gal.)
VIRGINIA—Con.														
Prince Edward	18	27.8	(4)	D	D	D	D	D	3	41.1	Z	1	–	1
Prince George	NA	NA	NA	D	NA	NA	NA	NA	22	14.0	Z	Z	13	3
Prince William	109	28.4	2 974	115.9	2 030	67.9	187.2	378.1	330	3.9	Z	61	Z	4
Pulaski	41	61.0	6 509	169.6	5 444	131.5	349.2	1 655.8	9	12.0	1	6	Z	1
Rappahannock	NA	NA	NA	NA	NA	NA	NA	NA	1	71.0	–	Z	–	Z
Richmond	NA	NA	NA	NA	NA	NA	NA	NA	2	34.6	1	Z	Z	1
Roanoke	64	31.3	3 450	107.6	2 389	67.8	287.5	598.7	8	75.7	Z	6	1	1
Rockbridge	24	50.0	2 090	50.0	1 755	40.6	108.7	335.4	7	75.9	Z	3	2	1
Rockingham	74	39.2	9 272	269.7	7 474	184.4	2 021.4	4 112.5	29	61.6	1	12	9	6
Russell	26	30.8	1 614	28.8	1 379	22.6	64.8	129.2	16	14.0	–	1	Z	10
Scott	NA	NA	NA	NA	NA	NA	NA	NA	3	42.4	–	1	Z	1
Shenandoah	47	51.1	5 436	139.4	4 375	105.2	329.7	840.5	7	57.2	Z	2	2	2
Smyth	53	47.2	4 913	109.2	4 158	81.8	335.6	692.6	6	85.7	Z	4	–	1
Southampton	16	50.0	2 874	131.1	2 082	92.5	393.8	710.0	25	29.6	Z	18	6	1
Spotsylvania	40	42.5	1 698	60.4	1 325	41.7	127.2	304.9	8	37.2	1	4	1	1
Stafford	47	17.0	711	17.2	568	13.3	48.8	99.2	11	26.2	Z	6	Z	1
Surry	NA	NA	NA	NA	NA	NA	NA	NA	1 758	.1	–	Z	Z	Z
Sussex	9	77.8	1 138	26.5	987	21.4	99.1	283.5	2	93.3	–	1	Z	Z
Tazewell	58	32.8	1 517	30.6	1 122	19.9	57.6	161.2	7	29.6	–	4	Z	1
Warren	27	25.9	1 540	37.7	1 366	29.1	227.4	511.0	8	19.6	–	7	Z	1
Washington	65	30.8	2 031	53.2	1 503	32.0	176.0	315.8	13	27.0	Z	10	1	2
Westmoreland	16	43.8	694	13.5	612	9.0	34.7	124.6	3	62.4	1	1	Z	1
Wise	24	8.3	556	10.1	466	8.1	30.4	64.2	8	22.8	–	5	–	1
Wythe	45	37.8	2 129	51.6	1 766	37.9	159.9	276.9	5	54.0	–	3	–	1
York	28	10.7	(4)	D	D	D	D	D	515	.3	–	24	62	8
Independent Cities														
Alexandria	114	20.2	1 907	59.4	1 230	33.8	194.8	328.1	282	Z	–	–	Z	2
Bedford	30	40.0	2 278	62.2	1 788	41.9	122.4	254.3	–	–	–	–	–	Z
Bristol	41	53.7	6 954	184.4	5 554	132.8	474.9	1 222.9	–	–	–	–	–	Z
Buena Vista	10	90.0	(4)	D	D	D	D	D	Z	25.0	–	–	Z	Z
Charlottesville	67	28.4	(5)	D	D	D	D	D	–	–	–	–	–	1
Chesapeake	132	34.1	4 558	147.0	2 967	80.9	336.7	1 085.0	556	.8	–	10	Z	2
Clifton Forge	NA	NA	NA	NA	NA	NA	NA	NA	–	–	–	–	–	Z
Colonial Heights	14	35.7	838	20.4	711	14.9	146.5	215.4	–	–	–	–	–	Z
Covington	11	54.5	2 615	113.4	1 842	74.0	510.9	1 004.9	3	–	–	2	1	Z
Danville	47	48.9	(6)	D	D	D	D	D	19	–	–	9	10	2
Emporia	13	76.9	1 055	29.0	868	22.3	72.4	158.7	1	–	–	1	–	Z
Fairfax	NA	NA	NA	NA	NA	NA	NA	NA	Z	–	–	–	–	Z
Falls Church	NA	NA	NA	NA	NA	NA	NA	NA	–	–	–	–	–	Z
Franklin	NA	NA	NA	NA	NA	NA	NA	NA	1	100.0	–	1	–	Z
Fredericksburg	41	26.8	1 059	28.6	830	19.5	88.5	240.7	4	–	–	4	–	Z
Galax	24	54.2	4 460	86.8	4 042	71.8	172.7	380.2	3	–	–	3	–	Z
Hampton	80	28.8	4 636	123.4	3 636	81.3	422.7	971.0	2	3.7	Z	1	–	2
Harrisonburg	38	47.4	3 687	102.6	2 985	73.9	254.3	725.8	–	–	–	–	–	1
Hopewell	19	42.1	2 907	147.4	2 191	96.1	743.9	1 328.1	156	–	–	23	133	18
Lexington	NA	NA	NA	NA	NA	NA	NA	NA	–	–	–	–	–	Z
Lynchburg	117	44.4	12 535	481.1	8 365	257.1	1 602.6	3 096.4	1	3.0	–	Z	1	1
Manassas	34	32.4	2 822	188.5	582	20.2	594.7	791.6	Z	100.0	–	Z	Z	Z
Manassas Park	NA	NA	NA	NA	NA	NA	NA	NA	Z	100.0	–	Z	–	Z
Martinsville	39	61.5	8 726	203.0	7 241	146.2	345.4	724.1	Z	77.8	–	–	–	1
Newport News	131	33.6	24 707	898.4	19 157	574.7	1 653.6	3 300.5	37	1.0	Z	32	5	3
Norfolk	199	34.2	10 996	402.2	8 838	303.4	2 789.7	5 737.3	14	2.0	–	13	Z	4
Norton	NA	NA	NA	NA	NA	NA	NA	NA	1	–	–	1	–	Z
Petersburg	43	46.5	2 553	72.4	1 771	39.1	145.4	409.6	Z	100.0	–	–	–	Z
Poquoson	NA	NA	NA	NA	NA	NA	NA	NA	–	–	–	–	–	Z
Portsmouth	71	21.1	1 812	52.0	1 341	33.6	143.6	368.7	2	98.8	–	–	2	2
Radford	21	52.4	2 838	84.6	2 111	57.3	185.4	393.4	3	–	–	3	–	Z
Richmond	325	36.6	21 879	941.2	14 775	539.5	8 229.6	11 748.3	70	Z	–	70	Z	4
Roanoke	152	38.2	8 489	242.9	5 819	144.1	1 213.4	2 156.3	9	78.6	–	4	Z	2
Salem	73	38.4	6 478	202.3	4 367	115.3	555.1	1 035.6	3	3.6	–	3	Z	1
South Boston	X	X	X	X	X	X	X	X	2	–	–	2	–	Z
Staunton	NA	NA	NA	NA	NA	NA	NA	NA	–	–	–	–	–	Z
Suffolk	52	44.2	2 257	63.8	1 920	48.6	539.6	1 103.5	89	9.9	Z	87	Z	1
Virginia Beach	236	20.3	5 806	139.3	3 913	82.1	380.4	967.2	8	42.7	–	4	Z	4
Waynesboro	31	51.6	4 558	160.2	2 589	81.6	452.5	802.5	12	60.9	–	4	8	1
Williamsburg	14	14.3	(7)	D	D	D	D	D	2	96.2	–	–	–	1
Winchester	43	58.1	6 047	196.1	4 647	130.9	791.1	1 431.3	Z	79.2	–	–	Z	1

[1] Average number of production workers plus the number of other (nonproduction) employees for the pay period including March 12. [2] Average number of production workers for the pay periods including the 12th of March, May, August, and November. [3] In millions of gallons per day. [4] 500 to 999 employees. [5] 2,500 to 4,999 employees. [6] 10,000 to 24,999 employees. [7] 1,000 to 2,499 employees.

Sources: Manufacturing—U.S. Census Bureau, 1997 Economic Census – Manufacturing, generated by Statistical Compendia Branch, using American Factfinder at <http://www.census.gov/>, (June 2000) [related Internet site <http://www.census.gov/epcd/www/97EC31.HTM>]. Water Use—U.S. Geological Survey, "Water Use in the United States," individual state/county and US by state files from <http://water.usgs.gov/watuse/spread95.html>, (accessed: September 1999).

Table B-9. Counties — **Manufacturing and Water Use**-Con.

[Includes U.S., states, and 3,142 counties/county equivalents defined as of January 1, 1992. For changes to these areas since January 1, 1992, see appendix B. Geographic Information]

County	Establishments Total	Establishments Percent with 20 or more employees	All employees Number[1]	All employees Annual payroll (mil. dol.)	Production workers Number[2]	Production workers Wages (mil. dol.)	Value added by manufacture (mil. dol.)	Value of shipments (mil. dol.)	Water use Total (mil. gal.)	Water use Percent ground water	By selected major use (mil. gal.) Irrigation	By selected major use (mil. gal.) Public supply	By selected major use (mil. gal.) Industrial	Consumptive use (mil. gal.)
WASHINGTON	7 801	27.7	328 511	13 004.1	213 330	7 046.4	30 434.8	78 852.5	8 860	19.9	6 469	1 179	649	3 081
Adams	13	15.4	1 088	25.9	967	20.5	127.6	274.7	346	37.2	340	2	2	168
Asotin	NA	NA	NA	NA	NA	NA	NA	NA	6	78.2	1	4	–	1
Benton	121	19.8	3 672	139.5	2 634	78.9	425.2	885.5	1 078	4.9	566	25	125	271
Chelan	88	26.1	2 535	76.2	2 066	55.0	195.1	552.2	128	9.9	100	11	16	46
Clallam	75	20.0	1 481	49.0	1 184	37.8	151.0	359.2	102	57.3	34	65	Z	20
Clark	421	31.1	19 537	715.2	15 316	489.4	1 985.4	3 854.3	195	65.5	30	38	114	35
Columbia	NA	NA	NA	NA	NA	NA	NA	NA	17	8.6	16	1	Z	7
Cowlitz	125	36.8	8 309	364.4	6 330	263.4	1 051.5	2 496.5	208	3.0	10	13	183	24
Douglas	NA	NA	NA	NA	NA	NA	NA	NA	63	18.5	54	5	3	24
Ferry	NA	NA	NA	NA	NA	NA	NA	NA	13	18.6	12	Z	Z	6
Franklin	47	14.9	3 092	69.1	2 668	55.4	221.5	1 160.5	844	12.6	825	15	Z	358
Garfield	NA	NA	NA	NA	NA	NA	NA	NA	2	33.7	1	Z	Z	1
Grant	56	39.3	4 090	111.3	3 276	78.2	438.3	806.9	1 795	12.8	1 777	11	2	768
Grays Harbor	97	27.8	3 792	125.7	3 164	96.7	337.8	822.9	104	43.0	10	79	12	15
Island	49	10.2	625	17.0	494	12.1	32.7	62.5	14	70.9	3	10	Z	3
Jefferson	56	16.1	(4)	D	D	D	D	D	32	35.0	4	21	7	5
King	2 993	27.6	134 028	5 682.6	75 310	2 515.5	10 459.9	26 480.3	292	33.8	4	267	6	37
Kitsap	143	11.2	1 441	36.8	1 016	20.9	81.3	142.7	40	80.5	1	30	Z	5
Kittitas	32	15.6	662	15.6	577	12.0	59.7	102.4	453	1.8	443	6	1	179
Klickitat	25	16.0	(5)	D	D	D	D	D	99	41.9	89	2	6	48
Lewis	115	35.7	3 630	97.1	3 036	75.0	262.2	648.0	54	34.7	30	7	3	18
Lincoln	NA	NA	NA	NA	NA	NA	NA	NA	72	69.0	69	2	Z	41
Mason	52	21.2	1 664	51.7	1 452	39.7	128.0	343.9	19	53.8	1	6	8	3
Okanogan	28	14.3	794	20.9	697	17.4	36.0	123.6	140	19.9	127	4	5	57
Pacific	36	27.8	848	19.0	756	16.1	46.4	112.8	10	29.4	3	5	1	2
Pend Oreille	NA	NA	NA	NA	NA	NA	NA	NA	5	54.6	1	2	1	1
Pierce	680	30.6	22 283	705.2	16 834	479.5	1 882.2	4 275.9	219	62.2	12	147	35	32
San Juan	NA	NA	NA	NA	NA	NA	NA	NA	3	51.6	Z	2	Z	1
Skagit	185	29.7	5 026	148.9	3 737	92.1	691.5	2 917.7	46	39.7	13	26	Z	13
Skamania	NA	NA	NA	NA	NA	NA	NA	NA	13	8.5	1	1	11	2
Snohomish	837	28.0	58 170	2 918.1	33 010	1 534.6	7 380.4	19 903.2	173	21.6	7	115	36	22
Spokane	572	30.8	20 892	681.4	14 631	406.8	1 811.2	3 994.6	189	83.9	44	93	36	52
Stevens	40	30.0	1 540	53.0	1 293	41.2	120.0	303.0	29	20.0	17	4	Z	0
Thurston	156	23.7	3 218	100.7	2 503	69.9	304.4	761.0	50	87.4	15	19	5	14
Wahkiakum	NA	NA	NA	NA	NA	NA	NA	NA	3	23.7	2	1	Z	1
Walla Walla	66	22.7	2 400	89.4	1 907	64.8	245.5	544.7	354	17.4	321	15	15	147
Whatcom	314	26.8	9 184	281.4	6 856	183.1	841.8	3 947.0	161	53.9	53	92	7	45
Whitman	NA	NA	NA	NA	NA	NA	NA	NA	15	62.3	6	8	–	4
Yakima	239	37.2	10 163	264.6	8 183	186.9	762.0	2 090.5	1 475	6.4	1 427	25	6	595
WEST VIRGINIA	1 505	34.4	72 813	2 460.7	55 643	1 658.9	9 311.0	18 293.3	4 619	3.2	Z	176	1 316	353
Barbour	NA	NA	NA	NA	NA	NA	NA	NA	2	29.9	–	1	Z	Z
Berkeley	38	52.6	3 093	85.1	2 582	62.3	267.3	470.4	21	28.2	–	7	10	3
Boone	NA	NA	NA	NA	NA	NA	NA	NA	4	44.9	–	1	Z	1
Braxton	NA	NA	NA	NA	NA	NA	NA	NA	6	14.1	–	1	4	1
Brooke	22	59.1	1 275	49.6	897	32.4	138.4	637.6	83	3.4	–	5	45	7
Cabell	112	40.2	5 766	199.9	4 435	145.5	690.3	1 199.5	83	3.4	–	14	66	11
Calhoun	NA	NA	NA	NA	NA	NA	NA	NA	2	33.3	–	Z	1	Z
Clay	NA	NA	NA	NA	NA	NA	NA	NA	1	54.3	–	Z	Z	Z
Doddridge	NA	NA	NA	NA	NA	NA	NA	NA	1	64.4	–	Z	Z	Z
Fayette	34	20.6	807	27.5	618	19.1	76.2	169.4	33	12.0	–	4	10	19
Gilmer	NA	NA	NA	NA	NA	NA	NA	NA	1	43.1	–	Z	Z	Z
Grant	18	38.9	929	15.6	806	12.8	37.5	106.2	1 006	.5	–	1	4	12
Greenbrier	38	26.3	923	26.2	615	14.9	47.9	99.7	11	50.6	–	3	3	2
Hampshire	NA	NA	NA	NA	NA	NA	NA	NA	3	54.1	–	1	Z	Z
Hancock	37	59.5	8 011	330.3	6 113	242.6	893.1	2 105.3	176	2.3	–	2	173	27
Hardy	20	50.0	2 940	57.7	2 685	43.2	142.7	435.6	14	9.5	–	2	11	2
Harrison	68	19.1	2 022	72.7	1 524	49.2	185.4	394.0	60	2.9	–	8	29	19
Jackson	16	37.5	(6)	D	D	D	D	D	51	5.3	–	1	47	8
Jefferson	26	50.0	2 172	60.1	1 839	38.8	194.5	444.1	14	39.5	Z	2	6	2
Kanawha	141	29.8	6 590	273.3	4 697	182.0	1 945.8	3 071.3	638	1.4	–	32	275	45
Lewis	18	22.2	538	13.5	473	11.1	33.3	52.6	6	16.1	–	1	3	1
Lincoln	NA	NA	NA	NA	NA	NA	NA	NA	2	67.5	–	1	Z	Z
Logan	39	23.1	853	20.2	592	11.2	42.2	82.6	6	39.3	–	3	Z	1
McDowell	NA	NA	NA	NA	NA	NA	NA	NA	7	92.3	–	5	Z	1

[1] Average number of production workers plus the number of other (nonproduction) employees for the pay period including March 12. [2] Average number of production workers for the pay periods including the 12th of March, May, August, and November. [3] In millions of gallons per day. [4] 500 to 999 employees. [5] 1,000 to 2,499 employees. [6] 2,500 to 4,999 employees.

Sources: Manufacturing—U.S. Census Bureau, 1997 Economic Census – Manufacturing, generated by Statistical Compendia Branch, using American Factfinder at <http://www.census.gov/>, (June 2000) [related Internet site <http://www.census.gov/epcd/www/97EC31.HTM>]. Water Use—U.S. Geological Survey, "Water Use in the United States," individual state/county and US by state files from <http://water.usgs.gov/watuse/spread95.html>, (accessed: September 1999).

Table B–9. Counties — Manufacturing and Water Use–Con.

[Includes U.S., states, and 3,142 counties/county equivalents defined as of January 1, 1992. For changes to these areas since January 1, 1992, see appendix B. Geographic Information]

County	Manufacturing (NAICS 31-33), 1997								Water use per day,[3] 1995					
	Establishments		All employees		Production workers		Value added by manu-facture (mil. dol.)	Value of ship-ments (mil. dol.)	Withdrawals		By selected major use– (mil. gal.)			Consump-tive use (mil. gal.)
	Total	Percent with 20 or more employ-ees	Number[1]	Annual payroll (mil. dol.)	Number[2]	Wages (mil. dol.)			Total (mil. gal.)	Percent ground water	Irrigation	Public supply	Industrial	
WEST VIRGINIA—Con.														
Marion	62	35.5	1 501	42.0	1 175	30.1	151.7	347.0	56	1.9	–	8	13	3
Marshall	NA	NA	NA	NA	NA	NA	NA	NA	751	.7	–	3	96	29
Mason	16	37.5	1 173	47.1	829	30.1	110.4	466.3	662	.5	–	2	42	28
Mercer	56	44.6	1 908	61.8	1 300	29.7	147.8	298.5	22	26.2	–	5	10	2
Mineral	16	50.0	1 138	40.4	828	24.7	101.8	136.3	5	23.0	–	1	2	1
Mingo	NA	NA	NA	NA	NA	NA	NA	NA	7	42.0	–	2	1	1
Mcnongalia	58	27.6	2 055	77.8	1 395	39.3	287.4	598.0	132	2.4	–	8	37	12
Monroe	NA	NA	NA	NA	NA	NA	NA	NA	3	56.4	–	Z	1	1
Morgan	NA	NA	NA	NA	NA	NA	NA	NA	3	80.3	–	1	Z	Z
Nicholas	27	37.0	768	18.2	620	12.2	67.4	123.1	5	24.3	–	2	1	1
Ohio	58	36.2	(4)	D	D	D	D	D	44	1.7	–	9	35	6
Pendleton	7	28.6	595	10.4	545	9.1	20.2	47.3	5	74.8	–	1	Z	1
Pleasants	6	50.0	(5)	D	D	D	D	D	123	.9	–	1	26	15
Pocahontas	NA	NA	NA	NA	NA	NA	NA	NA	5	71.5	–	1	1	Z
Preston	28	28.6	664	14.1	590	11.5	32.2	69.0	147	1.6	–	1	13	2
Putnam	35	25.7	1 091	38.5	737	22.4	95.8	234.0	70	2.5	–	2	24	33
Raleigh	56	19.6	999	32.6	701	19.8	57.2	164.9	15	36.9	–	7	2	1
Randolph	29	48.3	1 397	27.3	1 257	23.2	60.8	169.4	15	31.6	–	2	5	2
Ritchie	21	38.1	1 035	27.2	751	14.8	67.0	116.6	4	16.8	–	Z	3	1
Roane	18	22.2	790	12.9	737	10.9	83.2	170.4	3	25.9	–	1	2	Z
Summers	NA	NA	NA	NA	NA	NA	NA	NA	2	51.0	–	Z	Z	Z
Taylor	NA	NA	NA	NA	NA	NA	NA	NA	7	5.2	–	2	5	1
Tucker	NA	NA	NA	NA	NA	NA	NA	NA	17	4.4	–	1	15	2
Tyler	12	66.7	(5)	D	D	D	D	D	25	3.2	–	Z	24	4
Upshur	26	46.2	947	22.5	792	15.8	73.1	152.5	4	21.5	–	2	1	1
Wayne	33	42.4	1 770	47.3	1 183	25.5	152.6	325.0	21	7.2	–	2	17	3
Webster	NA	NA	NA	NA	NA	NA	NA	NA	2	37.1	–	Z	Z	Z
Wetzel	18	22.2	(4)	D	D	D	D	D	92	4.2	–	2	89	14
Wirt	NA	NA	NA	NA	NA	NA	NA	NA	3	19.9	–	Z	2	Z
Wood	78	34.6	7 010	293.3	5 137	195.4	1 485.9	2 301.9	169	7.5	–	10	156	25
Wyoming	NA	NA	NA	NA	NA	NA	NA	NA	6	35.9	–	2	3	1
WISCONSIN	9 936	39.3	562 479	18 766.4	416 254	11 952.6	54 947.1	117 383.0	7 252	10.5	169	600	441	443
Adams	NA	NA	NA	NA	NA	NA	NA	NA	38	100.0	37	Z	Z	33
Ashland	28	53.6	1 661	44.8	1 341	32.2	73.7	150.7	35	2.2	–	2	–	1
Barron	96	33.3	5 430	133.9	4 488	94.2	403.4	891.5	16	91.6	7	4	3	9
Bayfield	NA	NA	NA	NA	NA	NA	NA	NA	5	96.9	Z	Z	Z	1
Brown	396	42.4	25 825	1 015.7	18 473	602.6	2 588.4	6 457.4	497	3.5	Z	30	65	20
Buffalo	NA	NA	NA	NA	NA	NA	NA	NA	178	3.4	2	1	–	5
Burnett	32	37.5	1 106	30.3	882	23.1	100.2	176.7	2	99.1	1	Z	Z	1
Calumet	64	48.4	6 078	190.9	4 730	131.5	487.9	1 018.9	6	97.6	Z	3	Z	2
Chippewa	112	34.8	6 442	203.7	4 731	140.6	440.2	989.8	11	97.9	2	5	1	4
Clark	87	41.4	2 863	70.7	2 371	50.1	199.8	799.6	5	95.7	Z	2	Z	2
Columbia	108	40.7	5 311	159.1	4 059	104.3	509.0	1 262.4	17	48.9	Z	4	2	2
Crawford	20	55.0	2 252	50.8	1 802	35.7	366.9	509.1	3	97.5	Z	1	Z	1
Dane	564	33.2	26 568	864.4	18 841	507.8	2 484.9	4 840.5	113	49.1	Z	47	2	12
Dodge	164	49.4	12 667	413.8	9 898	293.8	1 111.7	3 159.9	14	97.5	Z	7	2	4
Door	63	27.0	2 222	59.7	1 803	40.8	136.1	267.5	5	99.0	Z	2	Z	1
Douglas	56	25.0	1 543	45.4	1 216	31.9	128.1	500.2	7	13.1	Z	4	1	1
Dunn	60	23.3	2 910	92.0	2 356	62.5	518.0	875.4	15	99.1	9	3	1	10
Eau Claire	107	34.6	4 182	110.9	3 311	75.7	369.9	651.3	18	81.8	1	9	6	4
Florence	NA	NA	NA	NA	NA	NA	NA	NA	1	98.2	Z	Z	–	Z
Fond du Lac	158	37.3	11 150	393.2	8 065	249.1	1 135.1	2 115.7	17	98.8	Z	12	1	3
Forest	NA	NA	NA	NA	NA	NA	NA	NA	1	96.0	Z	Z	–	Z
Grant	57	36.8	2 996	68.5	2 499	52.2	405.9	718.1	252	3.4	Z	3	1	6
Green	77	37.7	3 667	93.5	2 936	64.8	380.2	840.2	6	96.7	1	3	Z	2
Green Lake	61	39.3	2 383	55.8	1 884	38.1	153.2	262.0	5	96.8	Z	2	1	2
Iowa	34	20.6	815	18.4	647	12.9	53.6	156.7	3	95.8	Z	1	–	1
Iron	12	50.0	534	10.5	462	7.3	28.2	64.2	1	100.0	–	1	Z	Z
Jackson	20	40.0	810	17.8	608	12.8	72.5	134.2	9	99.1	Z	1	Z	2
Jefferson	165	49.7	12 201	371.8	8 988	234.1	912.4	2 431.5	23	98.9	1	9	4	5
Juneau	47	44.7	3 503	103.0	2 431	62.0	247.8	522.7	8	99.5	6	1	Z	6
Kenosha	204	40.2	9 526	396.2	7 325	281.5	881.6	2 031.0	35	7.2	Z	15	4	3
Kewaunee	45	40.0	2 359	67.1	1 803	40.2	148.5	314.0	726	.4	Z	1	Z	8
La Crosse	161	34.8	10 171	313.7	7 230	182.7	499.7	1 382.7	69	40.2	Z	17	4	5

[1] Average number of production workers plus the number of other (nonproduction) employees for the pay period including March 12. [2] Average number of production workers for the pay periods including the 12th of March, May, August, and November. [3] In millions of gallons per day. [4] 1,000 to 2,499 employees. [5] 500 to 999 employees.

Sources: Manufacturing—U.S. Census Bureau, 1997 Economic Census – Manufacturing, generated by Statistical Compendia Branch, using American Factfinder at <http://www.census.gov/>, (June 2000) [related Internet site <http://www.census.gov/epcd/www/97EC31.HTM>]. Water Use—U.S. Geological Survey, "Water Use in the United States," individual state/county and US by state files from <http://water.usgs.gov/watuse/spread95.html>, (accessed: September 1999).

[Includes U.S., states, and 3,142 counties/county equivalents defined as of January 1, 1992. For changes to these areas since January 1, 1992, see appendix B. Geographic Information]

County	Manufacturing (NAICS 31-33), 1997								Water use per day,[3] 1995					
	Establishments		All employees		Production workers		Value added by manu-facture (mil. dol.)	Value of ship-ments (mil. dol.)	Withdrawals					
											By selected major use– (mil. gal.)			
	Total	Percent with 20 or more employ-ees	Number[1]	Annual payroll (mil. dol.)	Number[2]	Wages (mil. dol.)			Total (mil. gal.)	Percent ground water	Irrigation	Public supply	Industrial	Consump-tive use (mil. gal.)
WISCONSIN—Con.														
Lafayette	21	47.6	661	14.5	603	11.8	54.1	134.5	3	94.9	Z	1	–	2
Langlade	39	41.0	1 493	35.9	1 232	25.0	89.5	184.0	13	83.3	4	1	Z	5
Lincoln	63	36.5	3 637	101.2	2 922	71.9	261.9	532.4	11	32.0	Z	2	7	2
Manitowoc	180	50.6	13 474	407.2	10 278	269.1	1 111.2	2 134.1	1 261	.5	Z	11	2	16
Marathon	232	42.2	16 839	502.6	13 422	354.8	1 295.2	3 181.9	183	13.1	1	15	29	13
Marinette	82	37.8	6 766	217.9	5 215	152.6	489.6	1 139.1	22	45.2	2	4	12	6
Marquette	24	50.0	996	27.3	815	16.1	69.4	135.8	2	96.9	Z	Z	Z	Z
Menominee	6	66.7	705	16.6	463	9.1	23.6	51.0	Z	92.9	Z	Z	–	Z
Milwaukee	1 463	38.0	86 933	3 213.2	60 161	1 920.8	8 383.2	16 535.5	1 974	.4	Z	171	12	42
Monroe	58	34.5	3 397	79.9	2 601	54.3	291.9	745.0	6	98.0	Z	3	Z	2
Oconto	61	42.6	2 445	56.6	2 048	36.8	135.5	297.7	6	79.1	2	1	1	3
Oneida	68	22.1	2 526	78.3	2 163	62.5	182.8	395.3	33	13.4	Z	3	28	6
Outagamie	303	41.9	21 410	750.7	15 718	490.8	2 319.3	5 315.4	68	30.3	Z	16	46	11
Ozaukee	242	41.3	13 420	485.8	9 040	267.2	1 463.8	2 763.1	224	3.4	Z	6	Z	4
Pepin	NA	NA	NA	NA	NA	NA	NA	NA	1	97.9	1	Z	–	1
Pierce	40	30.0	942	24.7	715	16.4	92.5	216.7	4	97.2	Z	2	Z	2
Polk	95	42.1	3 912	90.7	3 010	59.2	270.5	628.1	5	97.3	Z	2	Z	2
Portage	83	36.1	5 534	178.3	4 609	133.5	683.6	1 265.8	85	91.0	58	8	16	57
Price	46	39.1	2 957	91.7	2 168	59.5	232.8	449.6	9	22.3	Z	1	7	2
Racine	379	37.2	18 869	664.1	13 445	393.0	3 236.9	5 229.5	38	29.5	1	28	3	7
Richland	26	34.6	1 851	52.7	1 464	32.8	140.1	373.3	3	97.1	Z	1	Z	1
Rock	234	34.6	19 547	785.3	15 128	553.5	3 905.9	10 105.6	152	19.2	3	21	2	9
Rusk	30	43.3	1 722	41.0	1 392	30.9	84.2	203.1	4	68.5	1	1	1	2
St. Croix	150	34.0	5 867	174.3	4 387	106.8	399.7	827.0	8	98.6	Z	3	2	2
Sauk	114	43.9	6 570	180.8	5 245	130.0	511.3	1 121.2	13	98.9	Z	6	4	3
Sawyer	39	28.2	859	22.4	695	16.2	60.7	137.3	2	99.3	Z	Z	Z	Z
Shawano	67	34.3	1 985	51.0	1 539	33.8	131.1	330.3	6	96.0	Z	3	Z	2
Sheboygan	239	49.0	20 047	628.3	14 618	383.8	2 035.0	4 252.7	465	2.0	Z	19	1	9
Taylor	43	37.2	2 987	83.8	2 383	59.4	178.3	592.7	2	96.8	Z	1	–	1
Trempealeau	62	38.7	4 678	121.8	3 782	76.0	258.3	799.9	6	96.1	Z	2	Z	2
Vernon	37	32.4	970	20.7	823	15.4	86.7	168.1	201	2.9	Z	1	–	4
Vilas	NA	NA	NA	NA	NA	NA	NA	NA	1	100.0	Z	Z	Z	Z
Walworth	218	41.7	10 377	311.7	7 685	185.5	771.0	1 496.2	15	99.2	Z	7	1	3
Washburn	36	20.0	793	17.1	676	11.8	39.7	91.7	2	98.4	1	1	–	1
Washington	321	39.3	15 660	499.2	11 444	307.9	1 234.3	2 360.2	13	99.5	Z	9	Z	3
Waukesha	1 148	40.4	49 130	1 760.3	34 599	1 051.1	4 944.8	9 434.6	43	80.6	2	25	10	9
Waupaca	105	38.1	5 995	176.0	4 999	130.8	586.7	1 235.3	10	98.6	1	6	Z	3
Waushara	32	28.1	746	14.9	658	11.1	38.8	79.2	26	99.9	24	Z	–	22
Winnebago	316	52.5	27 191	976.5	19 575	642.6	2 873.8	6 026.6	69	19.2	Z	20	45	9
Wood	117	38.5	9 421	363.3	7 764	268.2	996.7	2 535.6	122	9.1	1	7	111	18
WYOMING	503	17.9	8 448	256.4	6 426	174.8	1 031.1	2 955.1	7 059	4.8	6 595	90	3	2 809
Albany	33	18.2	531	13.5	412	9.4	46.6	89.1	180	2.4	172	6	Z	105
Big Horn	NA	NA	NA	NA	NA	NA	NA	NA	741	.9	735	2	Z	239
Campbell	NA	NA	NA	NA	NA	NA	NA	NA	61	78.8	–	4	Z	25
Carbon	NA	NA	NA	NA	NA	NA	NA	NA	787	.9	777	3	Z	182
Converse	NA	NA	NA	NA	NA	NA	NA	NA	226	4.2	41	2	Z	27
Crook	NA	NA	NA	NA	NA	NA	NA	NA	46	17.5	38	Z	Z	16
Fremont	41	7.3	(4)	D	D	D	D	D	594	.8	586	4	Z	422
Goshen	NA	NA	NA	NA	NA	NA	NA	NA	166	26.8	158	3	Z	86
Hot Springs	NA	NA	NA	NA	NA	NA	NA	NA	205	3.8	202	1	Z	50
Johnson	NA	NA	NA	NA	NA	NA	NA	NA	300	.7	296	1	Z	64
Laramie	48	35.4	1 349	45.2	985	28.4	173.8	606.3	113	61.9	90	20	–	82
Lincoln	20	35.0	579	17.4	424	12.1	139.3	200.8	499	2.5	483	3	Z	202
Natrona	91	17.6	1 440	40.7	1 165	28.7	92.2	328.3	193	10.7	163	11	1	61
Niobrara	NA	NA	NA	NA	NA	NA	NA	NA	28	99.0	27	1	Z	21
Park	41	17.1	524	13.9	388	7.6	37.9	66.1	869	.8	857	4	Z	402
Platte	NA	NA	NA	NA	NA	NA	NA	NA	130	17.0	110	2	Z	87
Sheridan	NA	NA	NA	NA	NA	NA	NA	NA	857	.4	847	5	Z	166
Sublette	NA	NA	NA	NA	NA	NA	NA	NA	449	.3	446	1	Z	319
Sweetwater	29	20.7	696	36.1	471	23.9	290.3	458.2	74	7.5	40	8	–	42
Teton	NA	NA	NA	NA	NA	NA	NA	NA	89	3.8	85	3	Z	27
Uinta	NA	NA	NA	NA	NA	NA	NA	NA	180	1.2	176	2	Z	107
Washakie	NA	NA	NA	NA	NA	NA	NA	NA	259	4.0	256	2	Z	73
Weston	NA	NA	NA	NA	NA	NA	NA	NA	14	44.6	8	2	Z	4

[1] Average number of production workers plus the number of other (nonproduction) employees for the pay period including March 12. [2] Average number of production workers for the pay periods including the 12th of March, May, August, and November. [3] In millions of gallons per day. [4] 500 to 999 employees.

Sources: Manufacturing—U.S. Census Bureau, 1997 Economic Census – Manufacturing, generated by Statistical Compendia Branch, using American Factfinder at <http://www.census.gov/>, (June 2000) [related Internet site <http://www.census.gov/epcd/www/97EC31.HTM>]. Water Use—U.S. Geological Survey, "Water Use in the United States," individual state/county and US by state files from <http://water.usgs.gov/watuse/spread95.html>, (accessed: September 1999).

Table B–10. Counties — Farm Population, Farm Earnings, and Agriculture

[Includes U.S., states, and 3,142 counties/county equivalents defined as of January 1, 1992. For changes to these areas since January 1, 1992, see appendix B. Geographic Information]

County	Farm population, 1990 Number	Farm population, 1990 Percent of total[1]	Farm earnings 1998 Total ($1,000)	Farm earnings 1998 Percent of total[2]	Farm earnings 1997 ($1,000)	Farms Number	Farms Percent Less than 50 acres	Farms Percent 500 acres or more	Land in farms Total acreage (1,000)	Land in farms Net change, 1992–1997[3] (1,000)	Land in farms Average size of farm	Land in farms Total cropland (1,000)	Value of farm products sold Total ($1,000)	Value of farm products sold Average per farm (dollars)	Value of farm products sold Percent from Crops[4]	Value of farm products sold Percent from Livestock and poultry[5]
UNITED STATES......	3 871 583	1.6	43 016 000	.8	45 698 000	1 911 859	29.5	18.4	931 795	−13 736	487	431 145	196 864 649	102 970	49.8	50.2
ALABAMA	59 349	1.5	1 045 235	1.6	932 599	41 384	33.8	9.2	8 704	254	210	4 198	3 098 989	74 884	20.4	79.6
Autauga	614	1.8	7 629	2.3	10 252	348	26.1	12.4	105	−2	301	46	11 174	32 109	62.0	38.0
Baldwin.................	1 675	1.7	12 345	.9	20 949	977	45.8	8.4	166	−2	169	117	62 291	63 757	76.7	23.3
Barbour	614	2.4	16 294	4.9	12 528	417	14.9	20.1	154	−23	369	63	24 261	58 180	51.8	48.2
Bibb....................	145	.9	3 284	2.5	3 217	177	21.5	15.8	47	−1	265	16	2 150	12 147	11.5	88.5
Blount	1 831	4.7	41 208	13.1	37 456	1 191	39.0	2.7	139	1	116	73	137 982	115 854	3.7	96.3
Bullock	289	2.6	16 200	16.3	13 907	277	12.6	33.2	169	24	609	59	24 691	89 137	65.4	34.6
Butler	774	3.5	9 129	4.5	6 333	440	22.5	7.5	97	1	221	36	30 773	69 939	10.7	89.3
Calhoun.................	768	.7	13 343	.8	15 987	629	39.1	3.8	77	4	123	39	53 885	85 668	12.5	87.5
Chambers	434	1.2	3 246	.8	2 632	324	22.2	15.7	94	−15	291	28	4 269	13 176	27.8	72.2
Cherokee	759	3.9	21 944	13.7	19 036	494	24.7	10.7	123	2	249	69	49 324	99 846	47.9	52.1
Chilton	981	3.0	11 410	4.5	13 544	663	34.5	5.0	99	−1	149	44	9 449	14 252	62.2	37.8
Choctaw	541	3.4	5 083	2.3	4 378	225	29.8	14.2	65	−3	289	16	6 669	29 640	8.5	91.5
Clarke	472	1.7	956	.3	1 003	248	25.4	11.3	61	Z	248	17	1 998	8 056	32.4	67.6
Clay....................	561	4.2	14 571	9.3	13 056	397	20.9	6.3	75	7	190	32	24 729	62 290	1.7	98.3
Cleburne	601	4.7	16 740	14.4	14 017	340	27.9	3.8	51	4	149	21	45 854	134 865	3.6	96.4
Coffee..................	1 405	3.5	44 741	9.8	31 098	788	26.5	10.7	187	12	237	95	136 282	172 947	13.2	86.8
Colbert	718	1.4	8 875	1.1	10 282	557	37.3	8.4	116	−23	207	70	32 590	58 510	36.1	63.9
Conecuh.................	361	2.6	6 047	3.8	5 494	366	22.1	8.5	88	6	241	33	5 709	15 598	35.3	64.7
Coosa..................	474	4.3	2 776	3.7	2 508	213	16.9	8.0	42	1	196	15	1 323	6 211	19.6	80.4
Covington.............	1 442	4.0	25 409	6.1	21 396	899	26.1	7.3	180	14	200	81	65 735	73 120	29.7	70.3
Crenshaw.............	897	6.6	27 577	20.0	14 705	488	19.5	12.9	129	18	265	51	54 066	110 791	9.3	90.7
Cullman.................	2 855	4.2	94 830	10.7	77 320	2 151	47.8	1.8	203	6	94	115	334 148	155 345	2.6	97.4
Dale	729	1.5	10 401	1.2	6 304	422	22.5	15.4	131	−4	310	63	34 339	81 372	33.2	66.8
Dallas	368	.8	14 208	2.8	14 389	435	25.5	29.4	249	15	572	98	29 813	68 536	51.8	48.2
DeKalb	2 843	5.2	70 118	9.5	63 487	2 080	42.9	2.9	224	13	108	130	234 276	112 633	4.7	95.3
Elmore	966	2.0	2 998	.7	8 187	560	28.2	10.4	124	20	222	62	19 419	34 677	68.9	31.1
Escambia	531	1.5	8 202	1.9	10 537	380	35.0	11.6	87	1	229	52	18 348	48 284	80.3	19.7
Etowah.................	912	.9	19 788	1.6	19 580	904	47.3	3.1	95	9	105	47	54 944	60 779	6.2	93.8
Fayette	299	1.7	−59	X	1 642	305	21.6	8.5	63	−2	206	26	8 149	26 718	23.8	76.2
Franklin.................	1 142	4.1	18 988	5.6	23 268	833	26.2	5.0	128	−2	154	61	90 361	108 477	1.2	98.8
Geneva.................	1 376	5.8	34 780	17.0	30 787	872	26.5	11.2	207	11	237	120	108 157	124 033	25.9	74.1
Greene.................	475	4.7	6 254	9.2	5 925	261	13.8	30.3	123	−5	472	47	11 520	44 138	13.1	86.9
Hale	710	4.6	13 585	11.8	10 626	411	16.3	18.0	158	−10	384	54	32 222	78 399	6.3	93.7
Henry	594	3.9	9 311	6.5	5 588	334	19.8	28.1	154	−13	460	90	27 199	81 434	85.4	14.6
Houston.................	1 192	1.5	11 587	.8	11 364	690	31.9	16.2	198	6	287	137	56 290	81 580	67.9	32.1
Jackson.................	1 221	2.6	18 557	3.2	17 330	1 296	37.8	7.5	221	17	171	131	64 157	49 504	20.6	79.4
Jefferson.................	718	.1	3 325	Z	4 125	426	52.3	3.1	41	6	97	19	16 049	37 674	19.4	80.6
Lamar.................	507	3.2	3 113	1.9	1 969	387	31.0	8.5	71	15	184	27	5 389	13 925	20.0	80.0
Lauderdale.................	1 627	2.0	7 658	.8	5 513	1 355	40.5	6.0	212	10	156	134	29 079	21 461	48.6	51.4
Lawrence	1 492	4.7	38 783	11.8	22 535	1 287	40.0	4.7	205	32	159	139	79 910	62 090	18.6	81.4
Lee	962	1.1	7 715	.6	7 091	347	32.9	10.7	76	8	218	22	19 857	57 225	86.4	13.6
Limestone	1 281	2.4	21 412	2.2	10 099	1 127	39.5	10.3	254	47	225	181	53 026	47 051	43.6	56.4
Lowndes.................	583	4.6	10 265	10.1	10 819	330	20.3	30.0	173	−27	524	63	31 024	94 012	17.1	82.9
Macon.................	691	2.8	4 784	2.4	6 608	300	16.7	22.7	127	−11	424	43	9 577	31 923	70.0	30.0
Madison	1 552	.6	6 062	.1	478	973	40.8	9.5	210	−14	216	158	29 160	29 969	59.6	40.4
Marengo.................	428	1.9	9 968	3.7	8 236	464	19.4	21.1	198	−1	428	68	14 868	32 043	13.5	86.5
Marion	678	2.3	9 446	2.4	7 229	677	26.7	3.5	98	9	145	44	26 143	38 616	6.8	93.2
Marshall.................	1 592	2.2	47 035	4.2	44 488	1 583	51.0	1.8	146	3	92	85	200 632	126 742	2.4	97.6
Mobile.................	1 430	.4	23 276	.4	26 978	755	55.2	7.8	121	17	161	61	62 661	82 995	84.5	15.5
Monroe.................	898	3.7	4 098	1.2	8 858	422	27.3	14.0	135	24	319	57	22 891	54 244	77.8	22.2
Montgomery.............	847	.4	12 003	.2	12 032	654	25.2	20.9	241	10	368	102	33 114	50 633	29.1	70.9
Morgan	1 420	1.4	16 872	1.0	17 265	1 214	41.8	4.1	159	3	131	95	78 185	64 403	7.4	92.6
Perry.................	492	3.9	6 680	8.1	6 215	340	19.1	19.4	145	Z	425	58	10 214	30 041	23.8	76.2
Pickens.................	498	2.4	19 435	13.0	13 209	454	21.6	12.6	123	17	271	45	60 574	133 423	4.6	95.4
Pike....................	840	3.0	31 239	8.2	25 340	580	19.5	19.1	174	−6	299	80	60 737	104 719	21.7	78.3
Randolph.................	719	3.6	12 260	7.0	16 608	599	22.5	7.2	108	12	181	43	54 311	90 669	1.2	98.8
Russell.................	575	1.2	5 814	1.3	5 914	246	27.2	21.5	96	−17	391	33	7 577	30 801	74.1	25.9
St. Clair.................	821	1.6	12 946	3.0	16 236	594	37.5	3.2	77	−1	129	37	51 728	87 084	12.1	87.9
Shelby.................	803	.8	7 993	.5	7 011	435	38.2	7.1	68	−3	157	39	11 216	25 784	66.6	33.4
Sumter.................	511	3.2	12 298	8.5	9 970	369	19.0	26.6	175	7	474	59	11 237	30 453	7.9	92.1
Talladega	674	.9	11 281	1.4	10 368	523	29.3	9.2	110	5	209	60	40 341	77 134	14.9	85.1
Tallapoosa	510	1.3	3 250	.6	2 635	344	23.5	7.8	78	−1	227	27	7 434	21 610	17.2	82.7
Tuscaloosa	794	.5	6 225	.2	3 659	510	30.8	10.0	100	4	196	43	20 529	40 253	30.1	69.9
Walker.................	789	1.2	21 257	3.2	12 735	470	44.3	4.3	55	5	117	27	54 765	116 521	1.5	98.5
Washington	570	3.4	327	.1	6 586	397	27.2	9.3	87	2	220	26	21 886	55 128	10.1	89.9
Wilcox.................	666	4.9	6 404	4.8	6 196	248	19.0	32.7	154	13	621	39	7 218	29 105	34.5	65.5
Winston.................	812	3.7	19 656	5.7	15 482	582	38.7	1.7	59	2	102	29	59 110	101 564	.5	99.5

[1] For 1990 corrected population, see table B-1. Percent is based on 1990 uncorrected population because only total population is corrected. [2] For total earnings, see table B-8. [3] Most data are comparable between 1992 and 1997; however, it should be noted that farms with all acreage in Conservation or Wetlands Reserve Programs (excluded in 1992) are included in 1997, as are short rotation woody crops which includes Christmas trees and maple sap gathering (in Forestry in 1992). [4] Includes nursery and greenhouse crops. [5] Includes related products.

Sources: Farm Population—U.S. Census Bureau, 1990 Census of Population and Housing, Summary Tape File (STF) 3C on CD-ROM (related Internet site <http://homer.ssd.census.gov/cdrom/lookup>). Farm Earnings—U.S. Bureau of Economic Analysis, "Regional Economic Information System (REIS) 1969-1998" on CD-ROM (related Internet site <http://www.bea.doc.gov/bea/regional/reis/ca45/>). Agriculture—U.S. Department of Agriculture, National Agricultural Statistics Service, 1997 Census of Agriculture, Volume 1, Geographic Area Series, 1A, 1B, 1C CD-ROM Set (related Internet site <http://www.nass.usda.gov/census/>).

[Includes U.S., states, and 3,142 counties/county equivalents defined as of January 1, 1992. For changes to these areas since January 1, 1992, see appendix B. Geographic Information]

County	Farm population, 1990 Number	Percent of total[1]	Farm earnings 1998 Total ($1,000)	1998 Percent of total[2]	1997 ($1,000)	Farms Number	Percent Less than 50 acres	Percent 500 acres or more	Land in farms Total acreage (1,000)	Net change, 1992–1997[3] (1,000)	Average size of farm	Total cropland (1,000)	Value Total ($1,000)	Average per farm (dollars)	Percent from Crops[4]	Percent from Livestock and poultry[5]
ALASKA	1 160	.2	18 649	.1	21 672	548	35.4	16.4	881	–42	1 608	95	24 650	44 982	64.8	35.2
Aleutians East	–	–	–	–	–	(6)	(6)	(6)	(6)	(6)	(6)	(6)	(6)	(6)	(6)	(6)
Aleutians West	–	–	144	.1	-783	[6]636	[6]19.4	[6]30.6	[6]665	[6]-19	[6]18 470	D	[6]1 352	[6]37 556	D	D
Anchorage	18	Z	–	–	–	[7]222	[7]44.6	77.7	740	[7]-7	[7]182	[7]18	[7]15 851	[7]71 401	[7]66.5	[7]33.5
Bethel	–	–	–	–	–	(6)	(6)	(6)	(6)	(6)	(6)	(6)	(6)	(6)	(6)	(6)
Bristol Bay	–	–	–	–	–	(9)	(9)	(9)	(9)	(9)	(9)	(9)	(9)	(9)	(9)	(9)
Denali	(8)	(8)	–	–	–	(6)	(6)	(6)	(6)	(6)	(6)	(6)	(6)	(6)	(6)	(6)
Dillingham	–	–	–	–	–	(6)	(6)	(6)	(6)	(6)	(6)	(6)	(6)	(6)	(6)	(6)
Fairbanks North Star	99	.1	158	Z	1 312	[9]179	[9]19.0	[9]28.5	[9]119	[9]-23	[9]664	[9]69	[9]5 822	[9]32 525	[9]72.7	[9]27.3
Haines	–	–	–	–	–	(10)	(10)	(10)	(10)	(10)	(10)	(10)	(10)	(10)	(10)	(10)
Juneau	–	–	607	.1	163	[10]22	[10]90.9	[10]–	[10]1	Z	[10]24	D	[10]366	[10]16 636	D	D
Kenai Peninsula	151	.4	520	.1	937	89	38.2	12.4	56	6	635	8	1 259	14 146	71.8	28.2
Ketchikan Gateway	–	–	–	–	–	(10)	(10)	(10)	(10)	(10)	(10)	(10)	(10)	(10)	(10)	(10)
Kodiak Island	39	.3	–	–	–	(6)	(6)	(6)	(6)	(6)	(6)	(6)	(6)	(6)	(6)	(6)
Lake and Peninsula	7	.4	–	–	–	(6)	(6)	(6)	(6)	(6)	(6)	(6)	(6)	(6)	(6)	(6)
Matanuska-Susitna	521	1.3	17 220	3.6	20 043	(7)	(7)	(7)	(7)	(7)	(7)	(7)	(7)	(7)	(7)	(7)
Nome	–	–	–	–	–	(6)	(6)	(6)	(6)	(6)	(6)	(6)	(6)	(6)	(6)	(6)
North Slope	–	–	–	–	–	(6)	(6)	(6)	(6)	(6)	(6)	(6)	(6)	(6)	(6)	(6)
Northwest Arctic	–	–	–	–	–	(6)	(6)	(6)	(6)	(6)	(6)	(6)	(6)	(6)	(6)	(6)
Prince of Wales-Outer Ketchikan	71	1.1	–	–	–	(10)	(10)	(10)	(10)	(10)	(10)	(10)	(10)	(10)	(10)	(10)
Sitka	–	–	–	–	–	(10)	(10)	(10)	(10)	(10)	(10)	(10)	(10)	(10)	(10)	(10)
Skagway-Yakutat-Angoon	40	.9	–	–	–	(10)	(10)	(10)	(10)	(10)	(10)	(10)	(10)	(10)	(10)	(10)
Southeast Fairbanks	100	1.7	–	–	–	(9)	(9)	(9)	(9)	(9)	(9)	(9)	(9)	(9)	(9)	(9)
Valdez-Cordova	77	.8	–	–	–	(7)	(7)	(7)	(7)	(7)	(7)	(7)	(7)	(7)	(7)	(7)
Wade Hampton	–	–	–	–	–	(6)	(6)	(6)	(6)	(6)	(6)	(6)	(6)	(6)	(6)	(6)
Wrangell-Petersburg	–	–	–	–	–	(10)	(10)	(10)	(10)	(10)	(10)	(10)	(10)	(10)	(10)	(10)
Yukon-Koyukuk	[8]37	[8].4	–	–	–	(9)	(9)	(9)	(9)	(9)	(9)	(9)	(9)	(9)	(9)	(9)
ARIZONA	6 967	.2	800 723	1.0	648 200	6 135	44.8	27.1	26 867	–8 171	4 379	1 277	1 903 408	310 254	64.2	35.8
Apache	419	.7	-1 358	X	-2 679	288	30.9	34.7	D	D	D	17	6 732	23 375	3.9	96.1
Cochise	925	.9	35 658	2.8	24 989	824	23.7	38.3	1 260	-632	1 529	116	60 154	73 002	68.2	31.8
Coconino	01	.1	3 074	.2	2 059	199	37.2	33.2	6 209	219	31 203	D	10 687	53 704	3.8	96.2
Gila	179	.4	-422	X	-1 507	148	45.9	18.2	D	D	D	8	2 927	19 777	2.6	97.4
Graham	351	1.3	12 619	5.5	10 529	281	41.3	28.1	1 245	-602	4 430	D	56 005	199 306	90.0	10.0
Greenlee	103	1.3	4 968	2.7	4 189	99	37.4	14.1	29	-108	297	8	4 744	47 919	30.5	69.5
La Paz	162	1.2	22 307	12.9	23 956	97	24.7	44.3	279	33	2 875	D	94 665	975 928	99.2	.8
Maricopa	2 124	.1	318 588	.6	259 627	1 643	67.4	12.5	700	-21	431	341	664 057	404 170	57.0	42.4
Mohave	108	.1	3 931	.4	2 361	212	34.4	41.5	997	-985	4 704	19	14 983	70 675	54.5	45.5
Navajo	166	.2	1 400	.2	14 376	310	37.7	32.3	3 903	-3 327	12 589	19	25 697	82 894	4.1	95.9
Pima	451	.1	14 997	.1	15 525	419	60.1	22.0	2 914	-559	6 954	D	46 861	111 840	80.6	19.4
Pinal	881	.8	116 473	8.1	114 059	541	26.1	44.7	1 303	-599	2 409	D	363 479	671 865	52.3	47.7
Santa Cruz	171	.6	384	.1	-252	156	19.2	34.0	265	-69	1 701	11	3 706	23 756	D	D
Yavapai	302	.3	8 742	.6	5 010	453	47.5	26.3	772	-1 337	1 703	24	26 648	58 826	8.5	91.5
Yuma	544	.5	258 762	14.6	175 958	465	44.7	25.6	238	8	511	215	522 063	1 122 716	D	D
ARKANSAS	63 589	2.7	1 515 409	4.1	1 700 883	45 142	24.1	16.4	14 365	237	318	10 062	5 479 692	121 388	39.9	60.1
Arkansas	1 020	4.7	34 886	10.5	43 783	518	7.9	58.5	426	15	823	376	142 405	274 913	99.4	.6
Ashley	414	1.7	13 647	3.6	20 123	299	23.7	31.8	166	15	555	138	59 378	198 589	86.4	13.6
Baxter	540	1.7	6 895	1.7	6 240	492	22.8	9.8	105	13	214	40	21 046	42 776	1.2	98.8
Benton	3 568	3.7	97 684	4.1	96 627	2 323	44.2	3.9	297	3	128	168	337 522	145 296	1.4	98.6
Boone	1 618	5.7	18 108	4.1	17 760	1 259	25.3	8.7	258	7	205	116	59 906	47 582	1.2	98.8
Bradley	228	1.9	8 692	6.5	7 517	249	29.3	2.8	29	-1	116	15	14 410	57 871	23.5	76.5
Calhoun	127	2.2	319	.3	410	112	23.2	3.6	18	-1	157	10	1 714	15 304	11.0	89.1
Carroll	1 464	7.8	41 940	14.5	44 350	1 032	20.7	10.7	242	-4	235	105	146 376	141 837	.5	99.5
Chicot	701	4.5	21 645	16.4	30 141	361	8.3	47.4	288	19	798	254	101 250	280 471	74.8	25.2
Clark	512	2.4	8 952	3.3	7 088	376	19.1	14.1	96	-3	256	51	18 725	49 801	15.4	84.6
Clay	1 241	6.9	18 992	11.1	31 385	611	16.9	36.7	324	10	530	296	88 096	144 183	98.0	2.0
Cleburne	899	4.6	13 576	6.5	13 173	710	24.4	4.9	117	9	165	55	46 486	65 473	1.4	98.6
Cleveland	322	4.1	13 551	30.4	14 055	222	31.5	4.1	33	-1	148	14	50 722	228 477	.3	99.7
Columbia	568	2.2	17 860	5.2	16 767	313	24.0	7.0	58	Z	184	26	40 862	130 550	8.0	92.0
Conway	952	5.0	25 923	10.5	28 932	729	19.6	8.0	163	-5	223	96	83 395	114 396	6.6	93.4
Craighead	1 260	1.8	31 659	2.6	44 934	754	21.6	33.8	363	13	482	335	122 723	162 763	98.3	1.7
Crawford	897	2.1	19 279	4.0	19 893	806	35.7	7.6	139	-7	172	78	60 016	74 462	17.5	82.5
Crittenden	546	1.1	16 122	3.1	23 373	259	11.2	62.5	320	-7	1 235	304	82 402	318 154	99.7	.3
Cross	762	4.0	24 531	12.9	29 230	382	15.2	50.3	344	19	900	317	102 850	269 241	98.5	1.5
Dallas	102	1.1	1 761	1.5	1 516	121	15.7	9.9	23	3	192	9	1 950	16 116	33.2	66.8
Desha	568	3.4	24 676	13.2	31 039	302	12.6	55.0	276	14	914	257	100 873	334 017	92.9	7.1

[1] For 1990 corrected population, see table B-1. Percent is based on 1990 uncorrected population because only total population is corrected. [2] For total earnings, see table B-8. [3] Most data are comparable between 1992 and 1997; however, it should be noted that farms with all acreage in Conservation or Wetlands Reserve Programs (excluded in 1992) are included in 1997, as are short rotation woody crops which includes Christmas trees and maple sap gathering (in Forestry in 1992). [4] Includes nursery and greenhouse crops. [5] Includes related products. [6] Aleutians East, Bethel, Bristol Bay, Dillingham, Kodiak Island, Lake and Peninsula, Nome, North Slope, Northwest Arctic, and Wade Hampton included with Aleutians West; data not available separately. [7] Matanuska-Susitna and Valdez-Cordova included with Anchorage; data not available separately. [8] Denali Borough included with Yukon-Koyukuk Census Area; data not available separately. [9] Denali, Southeast Fairbanks, and Yukon-Koyukuk included with Fairbanks Northstar; data not available separately. [10] Haines, Ketchikan Gateway, Prince of Wales-Outer Ketchikan, Sitka, Skagway-Yakutat-Angoon, and Wrangell-Petersburg included with Juneau; data not available separately.

Sources: Farm Population—U.S. Census Bureau, 1990 Census of Population and Housing, Summary Tape File (STF) 3C on CD-ROM (related Internet site <http://homer.ssd.census.gov/cdrom/lookup>).   Farm Earnings—U.S. Bureau of Economic Analysis, "Regional Economic Information System (REIS) 1969-1998" on CD-ROM (related Internet site <http://www.bea.doc.gov/bea/regional/reis/ca45/>).   Agriculture—U.S. Department of Agriculture, National Agricultural Statistics Service, 1997 Census of Agriculture, Volume 1, Geographic Area Series, 1A, 1B, 1C CD-ROM Set (related Internet site <http://www.nass.usda.gov/census/>).

[Includes U.S., states, and 3,142 counties/county equivalents defined as of January 1, 1992. For changes to these areas since January 1, 1992, see appendix B. Geographic Information]

County	Farm population, 1990 Number	Farm population, 1990 Percent of total[1]	Farm earnings 1998 Total ($1,000)	Farm earnings 1998 Percent of total[2]	Farm earnings 1997 ($1,000)	Farms Number	Farms Percent Less than 50 acres	Farms Percent 500 acres or more	Land in farms (acres) Total acreage (1,000)	Land in farms Net change, 1992–1997[3] (1,000)	Land in farms Average size of farm	Land in farms Total cropland (1,000)	Value of farm products sold Total ($1,000)	Value of farm products sold Average per farm (dollars)	Value Percent from Crops[4]	Value Percent from Live-stock and poultry[5]
ARKANSAS—Con.																
Drew	488	2.8	12 801	6.1	12 926	342	23.1	20.2	123	12	358	94	35 809	104 705	78.4	21.6
Faulkner	1 300	2.2	7 400	.7	6 109	1 111	29.3	8.8	211	1	190	120	21 059	18 955	27.2	72.8
Franklin	898	6.0	26 926	16.3	26 627	783	22.1	9.6	171	3	219	86	99 719	127 355	1.7	98.3
Fulton	993	9.9	5 015	8.8	5 078	737	12.2	17.0	228	4	309	92	15 186	20 605	4.2	95.8
Garland	524	.7	15 307	1.5	14 808	360	36.1	3.1	43	1	121	21	25 478	70 772	6.3	93.7
Grant	240	1.7	1 927	1.5	1 672	215	38.6	2.8	33	−5	151	16	4 704	21 879	3.0	97.0
Greene	1 224	3.8	21 956	5.1	28 174	733	22.6	23.2	263	11	359	230	63 989	87 297	93.6	6.4
Hempstead	676	3.1	41 004	14.4	40 071	752	24.2	14.6	189	21	252	90	142 070	188 923	1.1	98.9
Hot Spring	558	2.1	4 142	1.8	3 609	447	25.1	5.4	75	−3	168	37	10 135	22 673	9.8	90.2
Howard	1 107	8.2	41 498	15.9	45 429	656	30.5	6.7	108	2	165	54	128 526	195 924	.4	99.6
Independence	1 173	3.8	16 908	3.4	16 323	1 044	21.6	13.8	283	20	271	154	72 510	69 454	18.0	82.0
Izard	714	6.3	7 342	7.8	5 744	703	16.6	13.7	188	4	267	80	27 980	39 801	1.5	98.5
Jackson	719	3.8	27 354	13.4	21 662	461	11.3	38.8	335	−33	727	295	80 192	173 952	97.3	2.7
Jefferson	615	.7	15 494	1.3	27 093	362	25.7	37.0	289	7	797	258	95 248	263 116	85.0	15.0
Johnson	811	4.5	21 982	9.4	23 122	606	23.8	6.6	115	6	189	66	82 274	135 766	3.7	96.3
Lafayette	373	3.9	18 270	24.7	19 495	261	24.1	19.2	98	−10	374	67	71 925	275 575	13.3	86.7
Lawrence	767	4.4	19 957	12.6	23 603	661	12.7	30.4	294	12	444	238	74 889	113 297	85.3	14.7
Lee	554	4.2	19 998	23.8	23 325	273	13.2	47.3	280	−19	1 024	263	80 407	294 531	98.0	2.0
Lincoln	471	3.4	28 640	24.2	28 834	292	12.3	34.6	184	−2	631	156	109 772	375 932	47.6	52.4
Little River	691	4.9	14 582	7.0	15 888	381	19.4	16.0	146	3	384	83	37 130	97 454	17.5	82.5
Logan	1 144	5.6	29 208	13.9	31 422	953	23.0	8.6	199	12	209	107	92 617	97 185	3.3	96.7
Lonoke	1 471	3.7	35 400	10.7	42 063	869	22.8	28.2	391	8	450	327	125 997	144 991	78.9	21.1
Madison	1 587	13.7	37 722	31.8	37 314	1 203	16.0	11.0	282	14	235	125	104 648	86 989	.8	99.2
Marion	801	6.7	6 160	5.9	6 293	495	16.2	14.5	140	−3	282	53	21 653	43 743	1.6	98.4
Miller	621	1.6	14 086	3.1	15 547	502	25.7	14.1	154	−20	307	105	46 594	92 817	24.3	75.7
Mississippi	955	1.7	22 275	3.0	46 806	462	14.5	57.8	489	4	1 059	480	166 810	361 061	99.4	.6
Monroe	477	4.2	15 246	16.9	19 337	245	12.7	58.0	236	16	962	211	63 191	257 922	96.9	3.1
Montgomery	609	7.8	15 474	23.3	17 133	417	20.1	6.2	74	−6	178	36	43 159	103 499	1.0	99.0
Nevada	496	4.9	13 101	15.7	12 362	372	23.1	7.8	73	3	196	37	33 254	89 392	1.3	98.7
Newton	600	7.8	324	1.0	1 755	521	15.2	7.9	109	6	209	37	9 929	19 058	2.2	97.8
Ouachita	269	.9	2 986	1.2	2 720	177	35.0	8.5	29	−3	166	13	6 692	37 808	5.8	94.2
Perry	416	5.2	10 995	21.5	11 371	391	24.0	7.2	73	6	186	45	36 785	94 079	14.0	86.0
Phillips	937	3.2	9 267	4.0	23 100	323	13.6	50.5	361	4	1 118	346	113 700	352 012	99.4	.6
Pike	694	6.9	21 877	20.0	24 740	406	26.1	7.4	73	2	180	33	57 070	140 567	1.0	99.0
Poinsett	816	3.3	39 665	17.0	50 505	570	9.6	54.2	401	−3	704	375	139 716	245 116	98.6	1.4
Polk	1 252	7.2	40 917	19.0	41 003	850	34.2	6.2	133	10	157	61	99 264	116 781	.3	99.7
Pope	956	2.1	27 999	3.5	36 322	917	31.0	5.6	152	−4	166	85	110 368	120 358	2.5	97.5
Prairie	875	9.2	21 325	30.1	27 335	420	11.2	48.1	302	−11	719	257	90 082	214 481	93.2	6.8
Pulaski	374	.1	5 363	.1	6 584	421	40.1	12.6	111	−1	263	77	24 761	58 815	55.1	44.9
Randolph	528	3.2	11 622	7.6	15 046	694	13.3	21.9	266	12	383	163	44 112	63 562	64.1	35.9
St. Francis	725	2.5	14 353	4.7	20 627	328	12.5	45.7	290	−16	884	244	68 925	210 137	96.0	4.0
Saline	475	.7	1 600	.3	1 515	329	38.0	5.8	50	5	153	26	4 049	12 307	40.1	59.9
Scott	975	9.6	38 194	30.4	33 222	655	24.4	6.3	116	1	177	56	88 942	135 789	.4	99.6
Searcy	632	8.1	2 458	4.7	2 835	614	15.3	16.1	188	−7	307	69	10 248	16 691	3.1	96.9
Sebastian	902	.9	14 035	.6	12 389	724	33.8	6.9	115	Z	159	64	36 854	50 903	4.8	95.2
Sevier	613	4.5	39 379	20.5	40 650	588	27.9	8.2	133	2	227	63	128 522	218 575	.4	99.6
Sharp	624	4.4	12 796	11.5	12 186	618	13.4	12.5	174	15	281	69	33 090	53 544	2.6	97.4
Stone	891	9.1	15 898	17.2	15 478	601	19.5	12.3	142	6	237	56	37 335	62 121	2.0	98.0
Union	402	.9	13 714	1.9	11 812	281	43.4	3.9	34	3	122	14	49 711	176 907	.5	99.5
Van Buren	777	5.5	6 080	6.2	4 780	578	15.2	10.7	132	12	229	62	19 863	34 365	2.8	97.2
Washington	4 461	3.9	88 467	3.5	90 689	2 476	38.1	4.8	335	−18	135	175	359 423	145 163	1.1	98.9
White	1 716	3.1	16 765	2.4	18 243	1 667	26.3	11.0	394	35	237	268	62 828	37 689	49.8	50.2
Woodruff	222	2.3	14 481	16.9	19 524	239	12.1	61.9	285	10	1 191	255	74 080	309 958	98.3	1.7
Yell	1 091	6.1	26 976	12.9	30 247	826	22.3	10.0	188	−2	228	107	113 307	137 176	3.5	96.5
CALIFORNIA	150 535	.5	8 002 197	1.2	8 407 862	74 126	60.6	11.7	27 699	−1 280	374	10 804	23 032 259	310 718	74.0	26.0
Alameda	458	Z	12 003	Z	22 926	458	49.6	16.8	258	−28	563	42	41 905	91 496	70.4	29.6
Alpine	–	–	–	–	–	12	58.3	25.0	4	−1	329	3	307	25 583	D	D
Amador	422	1.4	2 340	.6	4 307	360	41.1	14.2	204	−32	568	25	21 137	58 714	44.3	55.7
Butte	2 818	1.5	31 154	1.4	56 062	1 942	58.7	9.4	404	−48	208	247	286 227	147 388	96.9	3.1
Calaveras	429	1.3	−4 300	X	−3 676	457	45.1	23.0	245	−1	536	21	9 841	21 534	17.9	82.1
Colusa	1 259	7.7	75 513	29.5	105 961	810	25.7	27.5	431	−19	532	317	276 538	341 405	97.8	2.2
Contra Costa	607	.1	21 423	.1	28 194	587	64.6	11.6	148	−15	252	44	67 068	114 256	78.1	21.9
Del Norte	154	.7	13 653	5.1	10 246	66	45.5	7.6	13	1	202	8	20 797	315 106	51.9	48.1
El Dorado	1 083	.9	344	Z	3 006	763	74.2	2.8	103	1	135	13	13 479	17 666	74.9	25.1

[1] For 1990 corrected population, see table B-1. Percent is based on 1990 uncorrected population because only total population is corrected. [2] For total earnings, see table B-8. [3] Most data are comparable between 1992 and 1997; however, it should be noted that farms with all acreage in Conservation or Wetlands Reserve Programs (excluded in 1992) are included in 1997, as are short rotation woody crops which includes Christmas trees and maple sap gathering (in Forestry in 1992). [4] Includes nursery and greenhouse crops. [5] Includes related products.

Sources: Farm Population—U.S. Census Bureau, 1990 Census of Population and Housing, Summary Tape File (STF) 3C on CD-ROM (related Internet site <http://homer.ssd.census.gov/cdrom/lookup>). Farm Earnings—U.S. Bureau of Economic Analysis, "Regional Economic Information System (REIS) 1969-1998" on CD-ROM (related Internet site <http://www.bea.doc.gov/bea/regional/reis/ca45/>). Agriculture—U.S. Department of Agriculture, National Agricultural Statistics Service, 1997 Census of Agriculture, Volume 1, Geographic Area Series, 1A, 1B, 1C CD-ROM Set (related Internet site <http://www.nass.usda.gov/census/>).

[Includes U.S., states, and 3,142 counties/county equivalents defined as of January 1, 1992. For changes to these areas since January 1, 1992, see appendix B. Geographic Information]

County	Farm population, 1990 Number	Farm population, 1990 Percent of total[1]	Farm earnings 1998 Total ($1,000)	Farm earnings 1998 Percent of total[2]	Farm earnings 1997 ($1,000)	Farms Number	Farms Percent— Less than 50 acres	Farms Percent— 500 acres or more	Land in farms Total acreage (1,000)	Land in farms Net change, 1992–1997[3] (1,000)	Land in farms Average size of farm	Land in farms Total cropland (1,000)	Value of farm products sold Total ($1,000)	Value of farm products sold Average per farm (dollars)	Percent from— Crops[4]	Percent from— Livestock and poultry[5]
CALIFORNIA—Con.																
Fresno	18 440	2.8	554 061	5.2	744 202	6 592	58.6	11.2	1 881	107	285	1 251	2 772 785	420 629	76.3	23.7
Glenn	2 499	10.1	12 426	4.7	55 607	1 189	44.6	16.0	483	9	406	256	228 221	191 944	78.7	21.3
Humboldt	897	.8	28 007	1.6	22 055	792	40.9	20.2	585	–13	738	51	75 475	95 297	32.9	67.1
Imperial	1 030	.9	411 772	22.5	350 129	557	24.6	37.7	490	–43	879	459	850 351	1 526 662	69.4	30.6
Inyo	139	.8	–3 110	X	–2 468	82	37.8	34.1	199	–49	2 423	D	5 038	61 439	20.1	79.9
Kern	3 307	.6	386 059	4.3	530 002	1 997	35.1	30.3	2 851	12	1 428	1 054	1 968 513	985 735	90.8	9.2
Kings	2 679	2.6	97 808	7.4	154 491	1 079	50.6	18.9	657	–119	609	526	693 677	642 889	53.2	46.8
Lake	799	1.6	9 451	2.1	13 487	776	66.2	5.4	138	–26	178	33	40 366	52 018	95.1	4.9
Lassen	958	3.5	1 270	.4	5 031	365	32.1	33.4	454	–34	1 243	118	26 399	72 326	55.8	44.2
Los Angeles	1 154	Z	214 416	.1	189 942	1 226	84.7	4.7	131	–53	107	49	237 665	193 854	94.3	5.7
Madera	3 839	4.4	96 073	8.1	149 214	1 673	44.6	13.8	642	–108	383	333	627 210	374 901	81.0	19.0
Marin	635	.3	11 132	.2	10 350	276	34.1	34.1	150	–19	542	28	53 879	195 214	6.6	93.4
Mariposa	251	1.8	–4 540	X	–4 240	252	38.9	27.8	198	–8	787	9	5 615	22 282	6.6	93.4
Mendocino	2 123	2.6	29 386	2.7	39 750	1 092	45.1	19.3	639	–87	585	66	116 859	107 014	87.7	12.3
Merced	8 893	5.0	317 439	14.6	356 971	2 831	52.5	10.8	882	–97	311	532	1 273 475	449 832	45.4	54.6
Modoc	689	7.1	12 478	12.8	13 890	440	16.1	41.8	663	–24	1 507	183	63 797	144 993	63.8	36.2
Mono	82	.8	–1 325	X	–1 241	63	27.0	39.7	69	–34	1 092	D	6 502	103 206	49.8	50.2
Monterey	3 414	1.0	1 098 336	15.5	1 029 277	1 209	40.7	29.9	1 544	171	1 277	389	1 749 747	1 447 268	98.0	2.0
Napa	2 018	1.8	60 253	2.6	84 902	1 318	68.2	6.6	212	–23	161	75	238 696	181 105	98.0	2.0
Nevada	522	.7	–1 719	X	–1 137	412	70.1	8.0	63	–10	152	15	3 974	9 646	45.9	54.1
Orange	46	Z	199 428	.3	176 139	349	74.8	3.2	58	–3	167	17	228 881	655 819	98.6	1.4
Placer	1 696	1.0	717	Z	5 028	997	71.8	6.9	140	2	140	62	36 985	37 096	68.4	31.6
Plumas	103	.5	14 300	5.2	15 233	117	32.5	29.9	109	–11	931	43	23 125	197 650	70.8	29.2
Riverside	4 464	.4	468 951	2.9	348 575	3 048	79.3	4.8	509	85	167	280	1 047 525	343 676	55.0	45.0
Sacramento	2 696	.3	81 683	.3	55 554	1 288	63.0	11.3	308	–71	239	159	218 023	169 273	62.3	37.7
San Benito	1 693	4.6	73 681	13.0	79 207	562	48.0	24.9	512	–89	910	73	156 707	278 838	84.8	15.2
San Bernardino	2 049	.1	278 375	1.4	211 497	1 455	78.9	3.2	924	–363	635	58	617 833	424 627	12.0	88.0
San Diego	8 200	.3	348 399	.6	315 624	5 925	90.2	2.0	475	–43	80	113	632 731	106 790	86.6	13.4
San Francisco	–	–	–	–	–	9	100.0	–	Z	Z	2	D	880	97 778	100.0	–
San Joaquin	10 337	2.2	327 146	4.6	417 942	3 862	62.6	8.3	809	25	209	559	1 179 706	305 465	73.4	26.6
San Luis Obispo	2 806	1.3	111 326	3.2	131 658	1 916	49.3	19.7	1 302	–23	679	281	312 950	163 335	89.5	10.5
San Mateo	212	Z	73 071	.3	91 880	240	60.8	8.3	45	–13	186	15	138 669	577 788	99.1	.9
Santa Barbara	2 362	.8	334 813	4.6	337 101	1 451	59.0	16.1	817	–20	563	157	659 741	454 680	94.3	5.7
Santa Clara	2 064	.1	139 396	.2	125 646	985	74.5	7.8	319	–24	324	32	188 485	191 355	89.6	10.4
Santa Cruz	899	.4	225 319	5.4	259 552	722	75.8	3.5	71	18	98	28	247 815	343 234	94.9	5.1
Shasta	1 299	.9	10 667	.5	13 642	850	61.3	14.0	317	–71	373	59	31 349	36 881	58.6	41.4
Sierra	51	1.5	–1 927	X	–1 863	47	14.9	31.9	46	–9	986	15	1 304	27 745	23.9	76.1
Siskiyou	1 599	3.7	19 482	3.9	21 871	733	32.5	27.3	629	–19	858	182	74 244	101 288	70.3	29.7
Solano	2 015	.6	27 503	.6	43 656	795	57.7	15.5	362	22	455	210	161 418	203 042	83.8	16.2
Sonoma	6 567	1.7	120 878	1.5	152 534	2 745	66.3	7.3	571	54	208	145	463 616	168 895	69.1	30.9
Stanislaus	12 388	3.3	351 101	6.1	340 647	4 009	65.5	6.5	733	–27	183	382	1 208 524	301 453	45.5	54.5
Sutter	2 922	4.5	78 215	8.9	84 963	1 314	45.7	12.8	348	30	265	297	279 653	212 826	97.5	2.5
Tehama	2 480	5.0	14 077	2.9	21 775	1 362	57.3	13.1	885	–131	650	127	107 102	78 636	62.4	37.6
Trinity	91	.7	271	.3	–65	116	41.4	19.8	118	2	1 019	7	1 797	15 491	D	D
Tulare	11 069	3.8	651 038	14.7	567 251	5 446	59.7	8.2	1 310	–45	240	703	1 921 381	352 806	58.4	41.6
Tuolumne	116	.2	–3 309	X	–3 212	264	43.2	23.5	152	15	577	13	19 177	72 640	6.3	93.7
Ventura	4 111	.6	436 056	3.5	435 705	2 214	73.3	5.6	346	26	156	132	845 613	381 939	98.0	2.0
Yolo	2 709	1.9	119 170	3.4	162 927	923	45.6	21.1	537	18	581	381	344 894	373 666	96.9	3.1
Yuba	1 263	2.2	20 567	2.9	30 155	706	49.3	11.2	208	–26	295	97	106 587	150 973	86.8	13.2
COLORADO	45 118	1.4	719 814	.8	599 652	28 268	28.4	34.2	32 634	–1 349	1 154	10 509	4 534 213	160 401	29.3	70.7
Adams	953	.4	19 659	.4	20 925	696	36.1	29.2	674	–12	968	530	87 739	126 062	78.1	21.9
Alamosa	589	4.3	13 723	6.5	7 382	306	14.7	35.3	190	–17	621	103	57 195	186 912	90.4	9.6
Arapahoe	583	.1	4 250	Z	5 514	258	34.5	30.2	333	10	1 290	169	23 612	91 519	61.7	38.3
Archuleta	202	3.8	–1 419	X	–965	206	26.2	21.4	113	–43	547	18	6 149	29 850	6.4	93.6
Baca	504	11.1	33 656	46.5	17 454	608	3.0	67.6	1 142	–115	1 879	633	77 369	127 252	36.1	63.9
Bent	693	13.7	3 664	5.9	6 505	270	13.7	49.3	784	–13	2 905	D	50 975	188 796	24.6	75.4
Boulder	1 863	.8	10 268	.1	10 812	657	60.4	6.7	128	–29	195	59	43 671	66 470	63.9	36.1
Chaffee	127	1.0	–875	X	–318	189	21.7	19.6	86	1	453	24	5 161	27 307	40.3	59.7
Cheyenne	429	17.9	12 830	31.8	7 917	333	3.0	73.0	796	–118	2 390	434	33 645	101 036	57.0	43.0
Clear Creek	22	.3	–	–	–	12	58.3	25.0	5	–2	426	D	30	2 500	–	100.0
Conejos	493	6.6	1 862	3.8	3 921	429	16.3	30.5	285	–20	664	135	25 488	59 413	54.6	45.4
Costilla	253	7.9	4 229	20.6	3 133	171	20.5	29.8	363	32	2 124	D	15 978	93 439	83.7	16.3
Crowley	394	10.0	22 752	44.6	18 792	203	14.8	42.9	390	–34	1 920	54	73 487	362 005	6.4	93.6
Custer	145	7.5	–1 961	X	–825	152	15.1	36.8	144	–13	949	24	4 816	31 684	40.6	59.4

[1] For 1990 corrected population, see table B–1. Percent is based on 1990 uncorrected population because only total population is corrected. [2] For total earnings, see table B–8. [3] Most data are comparable between 1992 and 1997; however, it should be noted that farms with all acreage in Conservation or Wetlands Reserve Programs (excluded in 1992) are included in 1997, as are short rotation woody crops which includes Christmas trees and maple sap gathering (in Forestry in 1992). [4] Includes nursery and greenhouse crops. [5] Includes related products.

Sources: Farm Population—U.S. Census Bureau, 1990 Census of Population and Housing, Summary Tape File (STF) 3C on CD-ROM (related Internet site <http://homer.ssd.census.gov/cdrom/lookup>). Farm Earnings—U.S. Bureau of Economic Analysis, "Regional Economic Information System (REIS) 1969-1998" on CD-ROM (related Internet site <http://www.bea.doc.gov/bea/regional/reis/ca45/>). Agriculture—U.S. Department of Agriculture, National Agricultural Statistics Service, 1997 Census of Agriculture, Volume 1, Geographic Area Series, 1A, 1B, 1C CD-ROM Set (related Internet site <http://www.nass.usda.gov/census/>).

[Includes U.S., states, and 3,142 counties/county equivalents defined as of January 1, 1992. For changes to these areas since January 1, 1992, see appendix B. Geographic Information]

County	Farm population, 1990 Number	Percent of total[1]	Farm earnings 1998 Total ($1,000)	Percent of total[2]	1997 ($1,000)	Farms Number	Percent Less than 50 acres	Percent 500 acres or more	Total acreage (1,000)	Net change, 1992–1997[3] (1,000)	Average size of farm	Total cropland (1,000)	Value of farm products sold Total ($1,000)	Average per farm (dollars)	Percent from Crops[4]	Percent from Live-stock and poultry[5]
COLORADO—Con.																
Delta	1 562	7.4	9 857	4.5	6 084	1 041	51.7	9.3	282	21	271	75	39 083	37 544	38.8	61.2
Denver	20	Z	643	Z	553	16	100.0	—	Z	D	5	D	2 174	135 875	99.6	.4
Dolores	146	9.7	2 605	15.8	3 481	160	8.8	49.4	156	−11	973	68	8 601	53 756	57.1	42.9
Douglas	768	1.3	−1 470	X	−1 683	574	42.9	16.4	204	−27	356	40	17 119	29 824	56.5	43.5
Eagle	193	.9	−772	X	159	124	27.4	33.9	185	−28	1 492	19	7 413	59 782	9.6	90.4
Elbert	925	9.6	−4 627	X	−1 542	822	23.5	38.4	1 095	−10	1 332	179	31 249	38 016	14.1	85.9
El Paso	868	.2	−1 748	X	−430	851	32.2	32.0	867	10	1 019	78	30 330	35 640	41.5	58.5
Fremont	634	2.0	1 361	.3	1 265	561	62.9	16.0	283	−48	505	19	12 126	21 615	28.7	71.3
Garfield	654	2.2	718	.1	2 353	475	36.2	27.6	427	−13	899	63	22 817	48 036	40.1	59.9
Gilpin	6	.2	—	—	—	11	27.3	27.3	9	−5	797	D	D	D	D	D
Grand	108	1.4	−873	X	69	161	20.5	50.9	251	−48	1 560	38	8 833	54 863	18.5	81.5
Gunnison	302	2.9	−2 546	X	−1 557	187	19.3	37.4	195	18	1 043	38	8 436	45 112	10.9	89.1
Hinsdale	13	2.8	−305	X	−244	14	—	57.1	9	Z	631	2	377	26 929	D	D
Huerfano	336	5.6	−1 831	X	−1 032	273	14.3	52.7	641	−1	2 348	28	9 681	35 462	9.0	91.0
Jackson	215	13.4	−1 275	X	393	126	15.1	70.6	477	5	3 786	86	15 593	123 754	17.4	82.6
Jefferson	353	.1	6 272	.1	5 643	377	67.1	11.1	98	−6	259	15	19 474	51 655	89.3	10.7
Kiowa	211	12.5	28 877	65.5	19 593	339	.9	72.0	914	35	2 696	494	61 724	182 077	27.8	72.2
Kit Carson	889	12.5	49 096	38.9	28 703	718	7.8	66.6	1 346	4	1 874	839	177 051	246 589	39.6	60.4
Lake	14	.2	—	—	—	20	30.0	45.0	17	3	859	D	513	25 650	4.1	95.9
La Plata	1 188	3.7	−2 132	X	(6)	781	33.5	16.6	580	−7	743	91	15 797	20 227	31.3	68.7
Larimer	2 172	1.2	22 258	.5	20 731	1 298	50.5	13.0	542	2	418	127	100 483	77 414	38.1	61.9
Las Animas	664	4.8	−4 304	X	−2 320	485	10.5	60.4	2 215	−72	4 567	77	20 336	41 930	10.1	89.9
Lincoln	849	18.7	2 494	4.0	588	467	6.9	75.4	1 648	−12	3 530	D	44 773	95 874	33.4	66.6
Logan	1 811	10.3	37 119	12.7	30 434	879	9.0	53.2	1 129	62	1 284	524	292 740	333 038	16.8	83.2
Mesa	1 676	1.8	10 530	.7	9 216	1 489	64.1	8.3	417	−4	280	92	50 450	33 882	39.9	60.1
Mineral	—	—	−108	X	−87	10	20.0	30.0	D	D	D	Z	146	14 600	D	D
Moffat	520	4.6	−1 048	X	2 634	389	18.0	44.0	1 031	−129	2 651	104	18 938	48 684	15.4	84.6
Montezuma	828	4.4	1 955	.7	5 025	718	34.8	18.1	935	101	1 303	103	21 874	30 465	59.0	41.0
Montrose	1 553	6.4	3 837	.9	3 664	866	38.8	14.9	372	−76	429	89	88 274	101 933	22.3	77.7
Morgan	1 584	7.2	48 427	12.6	39 188	759	12.1	38.3	741	−11	976	342	405 945	534 842	18.9	81.1
Otero	831	4.1	10 946	4.9	10 665	512	33.2	23.2	580	−54	1 132	65	100 214	195 730	21.2	78.8
Ouray	112	4.9	−447	X	(6)	79	19.0	43.0	117	−2	1 480	15	3 237	40 975	17.9	82.1
Park	150	2.1	−611	X	−311	183	16.9	44.3	311	−78	1 700	25	3 622	19 792	20.9	79.1
Phillips	278	6.6	25 817	38.7	25 829	344	7.6	61.6	463	4	1 347	389	117 064	340 302	45.8	54.2
Pitkin	98	.8	−1 076	X	−979	70	20.0	20.0	25	−7	360	10	1 527	21 814	39.5	60.5
Prowers	1 034	7.7	54 202	25.1	37 983	522	12.6	53.3	863	−141	1 653	445	150 677	288 653	28.2	71.8
Pueblo	917	.7	−1 758	X	−706	664	31.3	34.2	823	−74	1 239	90	33 642	50 666	42.3	57.7
Rio Blanco	341	5.7	−3 851	X	−915	255	22.0	43.1	466	−80	1 829	56	14 086	55 239	8.7	91.3
Rio Grande	749	7.0	22 610	15.6	12 206	348	14.9	37.9	232	12	666	134	72 818	209 247	92.7	7.3
Routt	747	5.3	−4 328	X	−2 308	494	25.9	35.8	521	−56	1 054	102	22 858	46 271	15.4	84.6
Saguache	535	11.6	12 397	23.7	8 578	248	9.7	56.9	482	19	1 942	140	50 305	202 843	81.3	18.7
San Juan	—	—	−733	X	—	4	50.0	50.0	D	D	D	D	D	D	D	D
San Miguel	123	3.4	−733	X	(6)	83	24.1	39.8	162	−39	1 951	28	2 897	34 904	16.4	83.6
Sedgwick	255	9.5	16 359	43.4	10 172	215	4.2	58.6	294	−16	1 368	197	54 751	254 656	45.2	54.8
Summit	27	.2	−634	X	−358	35	17.1	40.0	35	−4	987	7	1 511	43 171	52.5	47.5
Teller	57	.5	−449	X	−272	84	35.7	34.5	83	−21	993	5	1 277	15 202	21.6	78.4
Washington	1 199	24.9	21 746	32.9	21 393	792	7.7	62.1	1 394	61	1 760	853	97 898	123 609	52.2	47.8
Weld	7 468	5.7	186 562	7.7	153 820	2 959	28.6	24.6	1 914	−173	647	882	1 286 636	434 821	16.3	83.7
Yuma	1 885	21.1	57 414	39.8	53 749	896	8.5	60.3	1 365	−68	1 524	633	481 374	537 248	24.8	75.2
CONNECTICUT	5 250	.2	188 342	.2	161 504	3 687	54.7	2.8	359	1	97	181	421 648	114 361	62.6	37.4
Fairfield	266	Z	10 327	Z	9 594	255	71.8	—	12	2	47	6	16 837	66 027	64.7	35.3
Hartford	623	.1	54 729	.2	50 880	627	58.4	1.9	53	−4	84	33	112 189	178 930	91.3	8.7
Litchfield	1 179	.7	22 285	.8	17 752	689	48.5	4.6	91	4	131	45	27 461	39 856	38.2	61.8
Middlesex	623	.4	12 481	.4	11 033	288	64.2	1.4	19	−1	65	8	33 944	117 861	92.6	7.4
New Haven	410	.1	19 905	.1	16 275	423	68.8	1.2	25	−1	58	13	43 284	102 326	85.1	14.9
New London	725	.3	34 657	.6	34 194	610	45.4	3.1	68	2	111	30	125 805	206 238	43.8	56.2
Tolland	469	.4	20 574	1.3	12 752	355	51.8	3.7	36	−2	102	17	27 268	76 811	39.2	60.8
Windham	955	.9	13 384	1.0	9 024	440	44.8	4.5	57	1	128	29	34 861	79 230	16.9	83.1
DELAWARE	6 486	1.0	118 522	.7	86 564	2 460	47.6	11.9	580	−10	236	487	690 794	280 811	25.3	74.7
Kent	2 520	2.3	26 181	1.4	17 702	767	40.3	12.0	195	−3	254	168	153 691	200 379	40.7	59.3
New Castle	899	.2	10 381	.1	9 432	327	46.8	13.1	77	−10	236	67	36 943	112 976	71.3	28.7
Sussex	3 067	2.7	81 960	4.4	59 430	1 366	51.9	11.5	308	3	225	253	500 160	366 149	17.2	82.8
DISTRICT OF COLUMBIA	—	—	—	—	—	X	X	X	X	X	X	X	X	X	X	X
District of Columbia	—	—	—	—	—	X	X	X	X	X	X	X	X	X	X	X

[1] For 1990 corrected population, see table B-1. Percent is based on 1990 uncorrected population because only total population is corrected. [2] For total earnings, see table B-8. [3] Most data are comparable between 1992 and 1997; however, it should be noted that farms with all acreage in Conservation or Wetlands Reserve Programs (excluded in 1992) are included in 1997, as are short rotation woody crops which includes Christmas trees and maple sap gathering (in Forestry in 1992). [4] Includes nursery and greenhouse crops. [5] Includes related products. [6] Less than $50,000.

Sources: Farm Population—U.S. Census Bureau, 1990 Census of Population and Housing, Summary Tape File (STF) 3C on CD-ROM (related Internet site <http://homer.ssd.census.gov/cdrom/lookup>). Farm Earnings—U.S. Bureau of Economic Analysis, "Regional Economic Information System (REIS) 1969-1998" on CD-ROM (related Internet site <http://www.bea.doc.gov/bea/regional/reis/ca45/>). Agriculture—U.S. Department of Agriculture, National Agricultural Statistics Service, 1997 Census of Agriculture, Volume 1, Geographic Area Series, 1A, 1B, 1C CD-ROM Set (related Internet site <http://www.nass.usda.gov/census/>).

Table B–10. Counties — **Farm Population, Farm Earnings, and Agriculture**–Con.

[Includes U.S., states, and 3,142 counties/county equivalents defined as of January 1, 1992. For changes to these areas since January 1, 1992, see appendix B. Geographic Information]

County	Farm population, 1990 Number	Farm population, 1990 Percent of total[1]	Farm earnings 1998 Total ($1,000)	Farm earnings 1998 Percent of total[2]	Farm earnings 1997 ($1,000)	Farms Number	Farms Percent– Less than 50 acres	Farms Percent– 500 acres or more	Land in farms (acres) Total acreage (1,000)	Land in farms (acres) Net change, 1992–1997[3] (1,000)	Land in farms (acres) Average size of farm	Land in farms (acres) Total cropland (1,000)	Value of farm products sold Total ($1,000)	Value of farm products sold Average per farm (dollars)	Value of farm products sold Percent from– Crops[4]	Value of farm products sold Percent from– Livestock and poultry[5]
FLORIDA	47 436	.4	2 492 670	1.0	2 169 340	34 799	57.9	8.7	10 454	–312	300	3 640	6 004 554	172 550	80.2	19.8
Alachua	2 295	1.3	19 470	.5	18 941	1 086	57.9	6.2	198	7	182	75	50 256	46 276	61.9	38.1
Baker	335	1.8	9 983	6.0	9 238	157	66.2	3.8	13	–11	83	5	25 204	160 535	38.6	61.4
Bay	168	.1	1 574	.1	1 564	70	60.0	4.3	7	–2	96	3	2 672	38 171	91.8	8.2
Bradford	667	3.0	5 175	2.6	4 765	274	55.8	4.0	44	7	159	10	17 402	63 511	6.7	93.3
Brevard	226	.1	12 213	.2	10 576	470	74.9	8.7	277	77	588	27	37 956	80 757	85.6	14.4
Broward	186	Z	24 364	.1	22 341	347	86.2	2.3	31	7	89	7	49 024	141 280	85.8	14.2
Calhoun	233	2.1	3 372	3.3	4 801	130	33.1	16.2	44	Z	337	27	16 197	124 592	89.5	10.5
Charlotte	196	.2	12 573	1.1	10 527	209	47.8	22.0	290	63	1 389	45	50 162	240 010	89.4	10.6
Citrus	797	.9	1 398	.2	1 558	294	64.0	8.5	49	–21	167	21	6 172	20 993	59.8	40.2
Clay......................	585	.6	9 276	.9	7 521	211	64.0	6.6	71	–15	336	8	30 118	142 739	10.9	89.1
Collier	311	.2	145 812	3.9	123 525	235	53.6	23.0	277	–25	1 180	69	276 924	1 178 400	96.7	3.3
Columbia	803	1.9	3 749	.6	4 787	600	48.3	6.8	97	Z	162	46	22 060	36 767	46.4	53.6
Dade	1 635	.1	166 897	.4	148 070	1 576	87.2	2.9	85	1	54	68	416 502	264 278	98.2	1.8
DeSoto	676	2.8	67 261	21.4	55 052	715	53.1	11.9	322	–12	451	127	180 983	253 123	87.6	12.4
Dixie	142	1.3	1 716	2.0	1 589	155	51.0	10.3	34	2	216	6	4 626	29 845	34.2	65.8
Duval	116	Z	12 804	.1	12 530	320	70.3	6.6	36	–5	111	11	26 463	82 697	36.9	63.1
Escambia	648	.2	3 640	.1	6 162	466	59.0	4.5	55	–3	117	35	16 183	34 727	58.3	41.7
Flagler	228	.8	9 124	2.8	9 161	91	39.6	28.6	88	35	964	13	27 837	305 901	95.6	4.4
Franklin	7	.1	–	–	–	19	57.9	10.5	5	D	270	D	D	D	D	D
Gadsden	1 408	3.4	46 584	10.7	45 277	290	37.9	10.3	58	Z	200	24	92 632	319 421	92.2	7.8
Gilchrist	519	5.4	16 244	18.4	14 800	365	40.0	10.1	78	7	214	44	52 043	142 584	15.0	85.0
Glades	84	1.1	13 205	27.2	10 279	188	39.4	28.7	380	10	2 023	41	58 589	311 644	64.7	35.3
Gulf	116	1.0	–	–	–	33	54.5	9.1	4	–10	116	1	359	10 879	13.1	86.9
Hamilton	310	2.8	3 351	2.2	5 354	256	26.2	12.1	66	–3	259	25	13 080	51 094	52.6	47.4
Hardee	1 202	6.2	62 359	24.2	52 407	1 045	51.8	9.8	346	18	331	106	154 837	148 169	75.9	24.1
Hendry	202	.8	132 823	28.9	105 605	403	40.0	24.8	605	75	1 500	205	323 438	802 576	95.4	4.6
Hernando	620	.6	7 985	.9	7 430	432	62.7	6.5	53	–8	123	21	23 011	53 266	27.6	72.4
Highlands...............	787	1.2	71 967	10.3	58 124	779	53.8	13.7	490	6	628	122	202 863	260 415	82.4	17.6
Hillsborough	3 452	.4	194 123	.9	173 198	2 639	75.8	3.3	248	–18	94	103	332 736	126 084	79.3	20.7
Holmes	835	5.3	13 923	12.3	13 807	578	28.2	4.5	88	1	152	41	31 534	54 557	16.5	83.5
Indian River	267	.3	34 367	2.4	27 589	437	58.6	10.8	168	–6	385	86	95 144	217 721	94.7	5.3
Jackson	1 449	3.5	8 025	1.9	14 686	844	25.5	14.6	245	Z	290	136	51 455	60 966	74.6	25.4
Jefferson	468	4.1	8 107	9.2	8 850	342	35.7	13.7	127	8	370	33	18 050	52 778	77.4	22.6
Lafayette	686	12.3	20 473	32.3	18 792	221	27.1	14.0	93	–2	423	22	54 322	245 801	10.8	89.2
Lake	1 582	1.0	63 847	3.3	59 479	1 389	68.5	6.2	185	–14	133	80	168 137	121 049	85.7	14.3
Lee	372	.1	44 288	.8	41 467	509	70.9	10.0	129	22	253	34	116 397	228 678	98.0	2.0
Leon	577	.3	2 386	Z	2 504	243	51.9	6.2	68	–33	278	16	3 463	14 251	38.8	61.2
Levy	473	1.8	32 819	13.9	30 037	549	43.4	13.5	157	–33	287	68	51 822	94 393	32.0	68.0
Liberty	56	1.0	395	.7	367	47	46.8	4.3	7	–5	154	1	551	11 723	7.6	92.6
Madison	716	4.3	10 271	6.9	12 859	486	20.0	11.1	132	–1	271	54	31 992	65 827	36.5	63.5
Manatee	966	.5	135 230	3.5	118 653	697	54.1	13.5	268	–32	384	106	239 624	343 793	91.6	8.4
Marion	2 062	1.1	71 009	2.7	62 381	1 669	62.1	5.0	266	–31	159	100	101 530	60 833	22.6	77.4
Martin	367	.4	50 104	2.9	39 300	305	59.0	19.0	184	–7	602	75	145 023	475 485	80.5	19.5
Monroe..................	23	Z	–	–	–	13	61.5	–	1	1	95	D	D	D	D	D
Nassau	421	1.0	15 595	2.7	14 715	238	55.5	5.0	35	–10	148	6	27 572	115 849	2.0	98.0
Okaloosa	402	.3	988	Z	2 313	342	37.1	6.4	51	–6	149	21	8 711	25 471	60.9	39.1
Okeechobee	945	3.2	63 730	19.7	55 773	459	35.9	23.1	392	40	854	73	138 006	300 667	24.1	75.9
Orange	1 066	.2	104 239	.5	97 388	862	77.0	7.0	175	37	203	44	247 759	287 423	98.6	1.4
Osceola	798	.7	28 286	2.0	23 047	485	55.9	15.3	611	–106	1 259	51	88 784	183 060	68.1	31.9
Palm Beach	1 009	.1	336 284	1.7	246 026	855	76.0	10.4	605	–33	707	529	872 877	1 020 909	99.5	.5
Pasco	1 602	.6	28 929	1.3	25 824	951	65.0	6.6	162	–59	170	58	84 301	88 645	35.8	64.2
Pinellas.................	25	Z	4 569	Z	4 589	129	91.5	–	2	–2	15	1	11 867	91 992	98.7	1.3
Polk	2 366	.6	125 029	2.0	106 807	2 464	62.3	8.6	621	10	252	187	253 459	102 865	80.5	19.5
Putnam	694	1.1	15 880	2.8	15 173	391	57.0	8.7	86	–20	219	17	34 023	87 015	89.8	10.2
St. Johns	330	.4	12 616	1.0	12 550	149	55.0	21.5	50	1	333	25	46 047	309 040	95.6	4.4
St. Lucie	257	.2	38 713	2.4	26 163	500	50.8	13.8	227	–73	455	136	173 137	346 274	94.2	5.8
Santa Rosa	916	1.1	7 186	.8	10 265	438	43.6	11.6	88	9	201	59	29 971	68 427	93.1	6.9
Sarasota	443	.2	13 460	.3	12 642	315	70.5	9.2	129	–23	408	19	24 147	76 657	70.6	29.4
Seminole	477	.2	9 959	.2	9 597	344	83.1	2.6	37	–22	108	7	19 966	58 041	91.3	8.7
Sumter	732	2.3	11 222	3.9	11 175	718	49.7	7.9	183	–70	255	55	34 442	47 969	27.5	72.5
Suwannee	1 596	6.0	48 453	14.7	46 325	840	37.5	8.1	158	–4	189	87	121 153	144 230	33.4	66.6
Taylor	353	2.1	2 068	.9	1 843	126	38.1	12.7	57	D	451	6	4 312	34 222	19.6	80.4
Union	316	3.1	2 771	2.2	2 765	213	45.1	8.5	63	14	293	16	11 009	51 685	34.2	65.8
Volusia	1 258	.3	58 033	1.4	56 753	910	73.0	4.0	112	–27	123	30	120 358	132 262	94.7	5.3
Wakulla	168	1.2	2 422	1.6	2 309	88	58.0	8.0	11	3	130	4	3 062	34 795	16.3	83.7
Walton	697	2.5	6 048	2.0	6 736	476	30.7	5.7	79	–18	166	35	19 768	41 529	24.0	76.0
Washington	712	4.2	1 904	1.0	2 609	322	28.0	6.8	55	10	172	26	9 352	29 043	38.8	61.2

[1] For 1990 corrected population, see table B-1. Percent is based on 1990 uncorrected population because only total population is corrected.   [2] For total earnings, see table B-8.   [3] Most data are comparable between 1992 and 1997; however, it should be noted that farms with all acreage in Conservation or Wetlands Reserve Programs (excluded in 1992) are included in 1997, as are short rotation woody crops which includes Christmas trees and maple sap gathering (in Forestry in 1992).   [4] Includes nursery and greenhouse crops.   [5] Includes related products.

Sources: Farm Population—U.S. Census Bureau, 1990 Census of Population and Housing, Summary Tape File (STF) 3C on CD-ROM (related Internet site <http://homer.ssd.census.gov/cdrom/lookup/>).   Farm Earnings—U.S. Bureau of Economic Analysis, "Regional Economic Information System (REIS) 1969-1998" on CD-ROM (related Internet site <http://www.bea.doc.gov/bea/regional/reis/ca45/>).   Agriculture—U.S. Department of Agriculture, National Agricultural Statistics Service, 1997 Census of Agriculture, Volume 1, Geographic Area Series, 1A, 1B, 1C CD-ROM Set (related Internet site <http://www.nass.usda.gov/census/>).

Table B–10. Counties — Farm Population, Farm Earnings, and Agriculture–Con.

[Includes U.S., states, and 3,142 counties/county equivalents defined as of January 1, 1992. For changes to these areas since January 1, 1992, see appendix B. Geographic Information]

County	Farm population, 1990 Number	Percent of total[1]	Farm earnings 1998 Total ($1,000)	Percent of total[2]	1997 ($1,000)	Farms Number	Percent– Less than 50 acres	500 acres or more	Land in farms (acres) Total acreage (1,000)	Net change, 1992–1997[3] (1,000)	Average size of farm	Total cropland (1,000)	Value of farm products sold Total ($1,000)	Average per farm (dollars)	Percent from– Crops[4]	Livestock and poultry[5]
GEORGIA	80 083	1.2	1 774 258	1.2	1 802 887	40 334	31.4	12.6	10 671	646	265	5 371	4 992 918	123 789	38.5	61.5
Appling	1 094	6.9	15 826	6.6	17 036	494	32.8	10.5	108	2	218	52	46 374	93 874	45.4	54.6
Atkinson	522	8.4	31 036	35.6	27 824	196	20.9	20.4	63	−15	320	31	58 586	298 908	27.1	72.9
Bacon	661	6.9	11 669	10.5	11 653	324	29.3	8.3	70	−8	217	25	34 904	107 728	31.9	68.1
Baker	422	11.7	10 542	39.0	12 290	131	21.4	40.5	119	10	910	63	38 766	295 924	69.8	30.2
Baldwin	470	1.2	1 349	.2	1 182	137	24.8	14.6	30	−3	221	12	3 253	23 745	7.8	92.2
Banks	767	7.4	39 669	35.5	34 171	446	40.8	2.5	47	−2	106	21	103 426	231 897	2.6	97.4
Barrow	916	3.1	20 991	5.3	17 432	361	46.0	3.0	41	5	114	20	52 349	145 011	1.1	98.9
Bartow	762	1.4	17 149	1.8	14 017	400	35.3	7.8	84	−1	211	36	44 429	111 073	11.5	88.5
Ben Hill	404	2.5	15 892	5.7	16 419	159	28.9	16.4	53	6	335	34	16 381	103 025	76.3	23.7
Berrien	793	5.6	10 189	6.5	12 996	399	19.3	19.0	131	2	328	66	39 358	98 642	78.2	21.8
Bibb	211	.1	1 684	.1	996	149	34.9	4.7	22	5	148	9	5 459	36 638	18.4	81.6
Bleckley	434	4.2	3 294	2.9	3 243	221	23.5	18.1	71	8	321	45	11 578	52 389	89.8	10.2
Brantley	331	3.0	6 345	9.7	6 196	207	31.4	4.3	28	Z	134	10	13 445	64 952	17.8	82.2
Brooks	810	5.3	21 155	20.2	30 673	430	20.0	22.6	189	21	440	96	59 058	137 344	73.0	27.0
Bryan	90	.6	−367	X	(6)	61	44.3	16.4	25	10	418	6	1 782	29 213	92.1	7.9
Bulloch	1 623	3.8	10 975	1.8	28 124	524	26.1	21.2	200	−14	382	132	72 520	138 397	84.1	15.9
Burke	887	4.3	−1 552	X	6 290	346	17.9	30.9	210	43	606	119	42 194	121 948	75.6	24.4
Butts	252	1.6	2 229	1.4	2 189	148	31.1	6.8	27	−2	186	11	3 072	20 757	20.6	79.4
Calhoun	329	6.6	13 490	24.8	13 635	122	13.1	50.0	129	15	1 054	65	40 189	329 418	71.0	29.0
Camden	37	.1	702	.1	626	46	43.5	17.4	19	1	412	1	653	14 196	88.5	11.5
Candler	449	5.8	3 559	4.2	8 446	264	15.5	16.7	78	21	297	34	18 662	70 689	68.6	31.4
Carroll	1 031	1.4	33 260	3.1	26 811	702	34.0	3.1	78	−5	111	41	90 272	128 593	3.5	96.5
Catoosa	116	.3	11 357	2.6	9 412	215	42.8	2.3	22	−8	102	13	24 769	115 205	7.7	92.3
Charlton	205	2.4	1 390	2.3	1 160	75	36.0	9.3	20	−1	271	4	2 939	39 187	25.3	74.7
Chatham	124	.1	686	Z	636	42	45.2	11.9	9	Z	207	2	2 935	69 881	94.3	5.7
Chattahoochee	17	.1	(6)	Z	(6)	13	23.1	15.4	4	−2	313	1	79	6 077	D	D
Chattooga	584	2.6	1 374	.6	1 186	278	24.8	8.3	55	3	199	23	4 882	17 561	16.4	83.6
Cherokee	970	1.1	19 934	1.8	16 407	493	64.9	.6	32	−1	65	13	54 634	110 819	10.7	89.3
Clarke	165	.2	5 016	.2	4 030	80	43.8	7.5	13	1	158	5	11 429	142 863	27.6	72.4
Clay	218	6.5	3 169	14.2	4 120	56	10.7	44.6	44	2	791	24	10 070	179 821	84.2	15.8
Clayton	152	.1	419	Z	460	54	50.0	–	5	Z	91	3	773	14 315	44.2	55.8
Clinch	91	1.5	1 614	1.7	2 569	93	52.7	8.6	16	3	174	4	4 385	47 151	48.8	51.2
Cobb	42	Z	1 178	Z	981	128	63.3	3.1	10	Z	77	4	4 986	38 953	64.7	35.3
Coffee	1 558	5.3	53 167	9.7	49 780	656	22.1	13.9	204	25	311	104	141 424	215 585	39.5	60.5
Colquitt	1 180	3.2	46 840	10.2	54 607	634	23.2	20.0	229	31	362	136	122 000	192 429	76.3	23.7
Columbia	450	.7	3 611	.6	3 594	169	42.6	7.7	29	2	172	9	3 352	19 834	35.4	64.6
Cook	661	4.9	13 926	9.3	14 496	226	31.0	16.8	84	11	371	53	47 371	209 606	95.4	4.6
Coweta	768	1.4	2 080	.3	1 512	316	40.2	4.1	43	1	135	19	6 737	21 320	65.0	35.0
Crawford	307	3.4	3 450	9.3	5 637	123	28.5	13.0	37	−1	304	18	14 894	121 089	62.7	37.3
Crisp	341	1.7	13 202	5.2	15 965	213	20.7	31.9	115	5	542	75	43 152	202 592	75.3	24.7
Dade	109	.8	3 265	3.3	2 536	175	37.1	5.7	26	Z	147	11	9 035	51 629	.9	99.1
Dawson	371	3.9	11 370	9.4	9 508	160	53.8	7.5	19	Z	120	9	29 640	185 250	2.2	97.8
Decatur	644	2.5	25 598	7.0	32 034	335	20.0	22.4	164	−4	491	102	76 139	227 281	86.8	13.2
De Kalb	150	Z	1 141	Z	1 138	46	78.3	2.2	6	3	134	1	1 905	41 413	50.5	49.6
Dodge	663	3.8	4 515	2.8	5 746	491	17.3	12.2	156	58	317	64	18 211	37 090	82.8	17.2
Dooly	624	6.3	12 944	11.0	15 611	259	18.9	34.4	165	8	636	122	54 570	210 695	79.9	20.1
Dougherty	377	.4	10 572	.5	14 032	139	43.9	25.9	83	12	599	44	26 626	191 554	91.8	8.2
Douglas	120	.2	−288	X	−341	107	57.9	1.9	10	2	91	3	1 269	11 860	44.1	55.9
Early	500	4.2	24 138	13.6	26 214	279	16.1	31.5	173	−11	619	107	45 430	162 832	94.0	6.0
Echols	162	6.9	3 614	27.6	3 912	67	34.3	9.0	18	2	267	4	5 059	75 507	93.9	6.1
Effingham	616	2.4	742	.3	3 362	203	30.0	12.8	52	9	259	25	8 220	40 493	70.4	29.6
Elbert	436	2.3	4 896	2.3	3 901	320	20.3	6.3	57	3	178	28	14 397	44 991	16.7	83.3
Emanuel	1 122	5.5	2 242	1.1	10 352	441	16.3	19.7	153	30	347	61	22 525	51 077	77.5	22.6
Evans	261	3.0	4 861	4.0	5 504	183	28.4	14.2	43	3	237	22	21 237	116 049	39.6	60.4
Fannin	307	1.9	3 880	2.7	3 536	151	37.1	.7	15	−1	100	6	10 022	66 371	13.9	86.1
Fayette	384	.6	2 771	.3	2 686	184	44.6	2.7	18	−4	100	9	4 029	21 897	62.9	37.1
Floyd	483	.6	8 611	.6	8 067	437	29.1	5.7	83	10	191	36	31 009	70 959	9.6	90.4
Forsyth	988	2.2	23 477	2.4	23 477	434	60.1	1.6	31	−5	71	13	62 238	143 406	9.0	91.0
Franklin	801	4.8	56 539	20.9	45 999	699	36.3	2.3	77	3	111	40	147 703	211 306	.9	99.1
Fulton	365	.1	1 661	Z	1 448	257	56.0	3.9	27	5	106	10	4 096	15 938	71.2	28.8
Gilmer	538	4.0	30 745	14.2	26 125	267	51.3	1.1	23	−2	86	9	77 159	288 985	1.6	98.4
Glascock	74	3.1	−615	X	−550	76	15.8	18.4	20	−8	266	8	930	12 237	48.8	51.2
Glynn	135	.2	53	Z	71	36	55.6	16.7	8	−2	215	1	375	10 417	30.1	69.6
Gordon	905	2.6	29 529	4.5	24 937	535	43.7	4.5	69	−5	129	41	88 329	165 101	4.9	95.1
Grady	1 119	5.5	16 403	8.9	20 611	462	28.6	13.9	127	−10	276	72	70 172	151 887	77.1	22.9
Greene	349	3.0	9 324	5.9	7 138	198	27.8	14.6	52	6	265	22	29 257	147 763	D	D

[1] For 1990 corrected population, see table B–1. Percent is based on 1990 uncorrected population because only total population is corrected. [2] For total earnings, see table B–8. [3] Most data are comparable between 1992 and 1997; however, it should be noted that farms with all acreage in Conservation or Wetlands Reserve Programs (excluded in 1992) are included in 1997, as are short rotation woody crops which includes Christmas trees and maple sap gathering (in Forestry in 1992). [4] Includes nursery and greenhouse crops. [5] Includes related products. [6] Less than $50,000.

Sources: Farm Population—U.S. Census Bureau, 1990 Census of Population and Housing, Summary Tape File (STF) 3C on CD-ROM (related Internet site <http://homer.ssd.census.gov/cdrom/lookup/>). Farm Earnings—U.S. Bureau of Economic Analysis, "Regional Economic Information System (REIS) 1969-1998" on CD-ROM (related Internet site <http://www.bea.doc.gov/bea/regional/reis/ca45/>). Agriculture—U.S. Department of Agriculture, National Agricultural Statistics Service, 1997 Census of Agriculture, Volume 1, Geographic Area Series, 1A, 1B, 1C CD-ROM Set (related Internet site <http://www.nass.usda.gov/census/>).

[Includes U.S., states, and 3,142 counties/county equivalents defined as of January 1, 1992. For changes to these areas since January 1, 1992, see appendix B. Geographic Information]

County	Farm population, 1990 Number	Percent of total[1]	Farm earnings 1998 Total ($1,000)	1998 Percent of total[2]	1997 ($1,000)	Farms Number	Percent Less than 50 acres	Percent 500 acres or more	Land in farms Total acreage (1,000)	Net change, 1992–1997[3]	Average size of farm	Total cropland (1,000)	Value Total ($1,000)	Average per farm (dollars)	Percent Crops[4]	Percent Livestock and poultry[5]
GEORGIA—Con.																
Gwinnett	519	.1	2 862	Z	2 354	303	57.4	2.3	31	7	103	9	10 611	35 020	51.6	48.4
Habersham	829	3.0	44 900	9.4	36 551	407	55.5	1.0	31	−5	77	15	113 883	279 811	.8	99.2
Hall	1 732	1.8	44 113	2.1	34 648	666	53.5	1.4	51	−3	77	25	137 873	207 017	.9	99.1
Hancock	622	7.0	2 545	5.1	2 896	103	11.7	14.6	34	−2	327	7	3 273	31 777	4.6	95.4
Haralson	430	2.0	5 864	2.8	4 673	260	36.9	3.5	31	−1	118	14	16 635	63 981	2.7	97.3
Harris	588	3.3	1 631	1.1	1 709	207	33.8	10.6	47	16	227	13	3 020	14 589	50.4	49.6
Hart	888	4.5	16 147	6.5	13 661	460	33.9	4.8	58	−1	126	36	55 925	121 576	3.8	96.2
Heard	204	2.4	8 926	9.3	6 980	160	21.3	5.6	28	3	173	12	21 061	131 631	.6	99.4
Henry	630	1.1	1 520	.2	1 407	327	45.6	5.5	45	−1	137	20	6 650	20 336	72.1	27.9
Houston	337	.4	4 667	.2	7 711	249	39.4	16.1	87	14	350	49	27 835	111 787	57.8	42.2
Irwin	862	10.0	7 324	9.7	12 221	288	14.9	26.7	132	−4	457	82	40 940	142 153	87.6	12.4
Jackson	1 525	5.1	103 663	19.1	91 212	719	47.8	3.2	77	−6	108	38	190 865	265 459	1.3	98.7
Jasper	278	3.3	6 499	7.5	5 694	185	15.7	11.9	52	−9	281	20	14 091	76 168	3.4	96.6
Jeff Davis	331	2.8	10 703	6.5	8 927	220	25.0	16.8	71	−1	324	36	23 324	106 018	70.7	29.3
Jefferson	757	4.3	2 960	1.7	9 553	356	14.6	19.1	142	6	399	84	24 395	68 525	75.9	24.1
Jenkins	531	6.4	2 821	3.6	6 590	248	12.9	21.4	93	16	375	44	20 150	81 250	52.4	47.6
Johnson	484	5.8	5 586	8.7	6 291	288	15.6	13.9	96	25	334	40	6 483	22 510	72.8	27.2
Jones	384	1.9	3 293	3.3	2 573	157	27.4	8.3	31	Z	197	11	7 408	47 185	7.6	92.4
Lamar	408	3.1	6 495	5.1	5 577	188	30.9	8.0	38	−2	202	20	14 783	78 633	13.7	86.3
Lanier	289	5.2	2 283	6.3	2 589	92	25.0	22.8	43	2	466	15	7 291	79 250	90.2	9.8
Laurens	1 109	2.8	8 151	1.3	9 784	688	23.0	12.8	198	30	288	85	23 757	34 531	79.7	20.3
Lee	272	1.7	14 364	12.4	16 721	157	29.9	38.9	138	33	879	76	37 849	241 076	79.5	20.5
Liberty	111	.2	132	Z	64	43	25.6	25.6	21	5	488	2	913	21 233	78.5	21.5
Lincoln	389	5.2	1 149	2.2	1 000	163	27.0	9.2	31	−1	191	12	1 818	11 153	4.5	95.5
Long	157	2.5	1 816	9.0	1 907	64	26.6	18.8	19	7	295	4	6 064	94 750	13.7	86.3
Lowndes	662	.9	8 931	.6	11 921	373	40.5	10.2	72	−1	193	38	22 919	61 445	88.9	11.1
Lumpkin	302	2.1	17 621	8.4	13 507	198	35.4	5.1	25	2	127	10	64 445	325 480	1.8	98.2
McDuffie	437	2.2	6 690	2.9	5 985	217	33.2	10.6	41	7	190	18	16 296	75 097	D	D
McIntosh	240	2.8	(6)	Z	(6)	24	33.3	8.3	4	−4	175	1	159	6 625	46.5	53.5
Macon	585	4.5	35 383	21.5	30 821	282	19.9	23.4	119	−2	421	69	99 108	351 447	24.8	75.2
Madison	979	4.7	40 305	25.8	32 758	622	38.3	2.4	70	8	112	34	107 419	172 699	1.7	98.3
Marion	382	6.0	7 024	11.5	5 820	147	12.2	19.0	52	6	351	18	33 642	228 857	10.3	89.7
Meriwether	652	2.9	3 247	1.5	2 906	257	24.9	13.6	69	Z	268	22	6 386	24 848	32.7	67.3
Miller	644	10.3	11 121	21.5	13 480	251	16.3	27.9	116	−6	462	79	38 183	152 124	82.1	17.9
Mitchell	910	4.5	45 911	18.1	45 063	464	22.4	25.4	221	16	477	135	141 351	304 636	49.0	51.0
Monroe	298	1.7	7 512	4.3	5 373	179	25.7	19.0	57	12	317	15	28 346	158 358	1.7	98.3
Montgomery	360	5.0	3 372	5.7	3 716	252	20.6	19.8	75	10	298	22	9 260	36 746	64.4	35.6
Morgan	487	3.8	17 304	8.4	14 102	390	27.2	13.1	88	−5	225	43	42 595	109 218	5.5	94.5
Murray	542	2.1	11 968	3.2	9 454	238	42.9	5.0	35	2	146	21	43 704	183 630	3.1	96.9
Muscogee	45	Z	−698	X	−645	39	43.6	10.3	8	4	218	2	188	4 821	68.6	31.4
Newton	570	1.4	1 058	.2	589	260	40.4	7.7	46	Z	175	17	9 730	37 423	9.7	90.3
Oconee	620	3.5	14 214	7.2	11 811	305	35.1	8.5	51	−1	168	21	44 026	144 348	14.5	85.5
Oglethorpe	860	8.8	25 143	36.1	24 295	319	27.0	8.8	63	7	196	27	56 802	178 063	2.4	97.6
Paulding	611	1.5	427	.1	−175	218	50.9	.5	18	Z	84	8	11 171	51 243	5.9	94.1
Peach	281	1.3	11 328	4.3	17 538	157	35.0	15.9	51	6	325	35	30 528	194 446	83.1	16.9
Pickens	409	2.8	19 906	9.4	16 160	194	49.5	.5	16	−2	82	7	54 012	278 412	.3	99.7
Pierce	651	4.9	12 111	11.0	13 592	379	27.2	13.2	100	20	265	41	29 642	78 211	69.2	30.8
Pike	376	3.7	8 797	12.3	7 617	252	30.2	9.5	48	3	190	24	19 187	76 139	11.5	88.5
Polk	1 061	3.1	6 754	2.2	5 808	344	38.4	4.4	50	4	147	23	18 673	54 282	8.8	91.2
Pulaski	229	2.8	6 017	5.9	8 573	161	23.6	30.4	92	12	574	64	27 627	171 596	83.2	16.8
Putnam	292	2.1	6 777	3.3	3 937	152	27.0	8.6	31	−3	206	14	21 459	141 178	1.5	98.5
Quitman	103	4.7	55	.6	(6)	17	11.8	47.1	11	Z	668	6	1 461	85 941	91.2	8.8
Rabun	144	1.2	4 544	3.0	3 793	122	51.6	2.5	11	−2	89	5	12 995	106 516	18.0	82.0
Randolph	241	3.0	5 909	7.8	7 636	119	10.9	47.9	94	−2	792	64	20 419	171 588	86.0	14.0
Richmond	262	.1	1 221	Z	1 494	106	49.1	3.8	15	−1	139	10	4 107	38 745	59.6	40.5
Rockdale	183	.3	−74	X	−61	102	64.7	6.9	12	−1	118	4	1 206	11 824	47.4	52.6
Schley	134	3.7	4 213	10.8	5 205	91	19.8	22.0	41	3	449	16	12 024	132 132	24.8	75.2
Screven	669	4.8	2 337	2.0	11 379	325	14.2	27.4	165	26	507	90	29 841	91 818	86.9	13.1
Seminole	400	4.4	9 775	12.3	14 572	183	24.6	28.4	107	−2	587	68	39 861	217 820	92.3	7.7
Spalding	350	.6	763	.1	288	193	40.4	5.2	27	3	138	13	5 042	26 124	21.9	78.1
Stephens	423	1.8	14 469	4.2	11 627	188	38.8	2.7	20	4	104	10	41 286	219 606	1.2	98.8
Stewart	96	1.7	1 520	4.1	1 806	77	13.0	33.8	56	7	730	17	6 252	81 195	60.0	40.0
Sumter	961	3.2	38 096	8.2	45 732	314	16.9	31.5	186	17	594	122	91 581	291 659	80.8	19.2
Talbot	329	5.0	799	2.8	657	111	16.2	20.7	36	−2	329	11	1 828	16 468	10.0	90.0
Taliaferro	161	8.4	1 168	16.6	721	55	12.7	18.2	16	−3	297	5	3 103	56 418	2.3	97.7
Tattnall	830	4.7	63 345	27.7	69 896	589	31.2	10.5	137	17	232	66	144 237	244 885	42.5	57.5

[1] For 1990 corrected population, see table B-1. Percent is based on 1990 uncorrected population because only total population is corrected.   [2] For total earnings, see table B-8.   [3] Most data are comparable between 1992 and 1997; however, it should be noted that farms with all acreage in Conservation or Wetlands Reserve Programs (excluded in 1992) are included in 1997, as are short rotation woody crops which includes Christmas trees and maple sap gathering (in Forestry in 1992).   [4] Includes nursery and greenhouse crops.   [5] Includes related products.   [6] Less than $50,000.

Sources: Farm Population—U.S. Census Bureau, 1990 Census of Population and Housing, Summary Tape File (STF) 3C on CD-ROM (related Internet site <http://homer.ssd.census.gov/cdrom/lookup>).   Farm Earnings—U.S. Bureau of Economic Analysis, "Regional Economic Information System (REIS) 1969-1998" on CD-ROM (related Internet site <http://www.bea.doc.gov/bea/regional/reis/ca45/>).   Agriculture—U.S. Department of Agriculture, National Agricultural Statistics Service, 1997 Census of Agriculture, Volume 1, Geographic Area Series, 1A, 1B, 1C CD-ROM Set (related Internet site <http://www.nass.usda.gov/census/>).

Table B–10. Counties — Farm Population, Farm Earnings, and Agriculture–Con.

[Includes U.S., states, and 3,142 counties/county equivalents defined as of January 1, 1992. For changes to these areas since January 1, 1992, see appendix B. Geographic Information]

County	Farm population, 1990 Number	Farm population, 1990 Percent of total[1]	Farm earnings 1998 Total ($1,000)	Farm earnings 1998 Percent of total[2]	Farm earnings 1997 ($1,000)	Farms Number	Farms Percent Less than 50 acres	Farms Percent 500 acres or more	Land in farms Total acreage (1,000)	Land in farms Net change, 1992–1997[3] (1,000)	Land in farms Average size of farm	Land in farms Total cropland (1,000)	Value Total ($1,000)	Value Average per farm (dollars)	Value Percent from Crops[4]	Value Percent from Live-stock and poultry[5]
GEORGIA—Con.																
Taylor	294	3.8	12 019	16.0	11 398	196	11.2	20.9	70	15	355	27	29 113	148 536	24.7	75.3
Telfair	332	3.0	3 355	2.6	5 409	271	13.7	16.2	86	15	318	32	10 393	38 351	79.5	20.5
Terrell	499	4.7	8 629	10.9	10 720	174	17.2	43.1	139	−4	797	88	27 812	159 839	97.1	2.9
Thomas	582	1.5	10 136	1.6	18 252	421	31.8	20.9	180	6	427	79	37 646	89 420	87.0	13.0
Tift	836	2.4	26 978	4.2	28 805	359	30.9	16.7	106	−8	296	67	53 813	149 897	93.8	6.2
Toombs	470	2.0	16 010	5.5	18 303	401	21.4	13.2	100	11	249	42	29 371	73 244	87.5	12.5
Towns	163	2.4	−126	X	−138	121	45.5	−	9	−1	72	5	1 008	8 331	15.2	84.7
Treutlen	169	2.8	2 924	8.2	2 802	157	17.8	11.5	42	9	268	12	2 900	18 471	88.8	11.2
Troup	430	.8	1 127	.1	610	221	24.4	9.0	43	2	195	20	4 326	19 575	24.3	75.7
Turner	531	6.1	12 237	15.9	11 229	230	12.2	26.5	98	−1	427	63	34 534	150 148	80.3	19.7
Twiggs	191	1.9	5 274	5.8	4 498	98	28.6	14.3	26	−5	267	11	3 686	37 612	76.9	23.1
Union	474	4.0	7 701	5.5	6 794	256	53.5	2.3	22	Z	87	11	16 961	66 254	D	D
Upson	556	2.1	2 488	.8	1 867	185	22.7	8.6	38	5	203	15	9 891	53 465	9.4	90.6
Walker	529	.9	8 785	1.8	7 196	478	34.3	6.3	86	−3	179	39	28 171	58 935	4.4	95.6
Walton	756	2.0	12 018	2.8	10 489	493	42.6	4.3	60	4	121	31	29 226	59 282	26.1	73.9
Ware	591	1.7	6 960	1.3	8 054	274	34.3	11.3	64	10	235	20	17 953	65 522	57.1	42.9
Warren	322	5.3	2 594	4.6	2 582	134	17.2	17.9	44	−3	332	15	4 394	32 791	10.3	89.7
Washington	857	4.5	4 128	1.3	4 840	327	17.1	19.3	111	−1	339	56	11 607	35 495	72.2	27.8
Wayne	513	2.3	4 003	1.4	7 008	276	30.8	10.9	65	11	236	33	17 036	61 725	80.9	19.1
Webster	243	10.7	4 171	25.6	4 848	76	10.5	34.2	58	4	758	29	8 985	118 224	94.1	5.9
Wheeler	177	3.6	5 603	16.7	6 538	176	9.1	22.2	71	23	405	20	8 853	50 301	91.5	8.5
White	382	2.9	22 196	11.3	22 268	284	51.8	2.1	26	2	93	12	53 189	187 285	1.7	98.3
Whitfield	583	.8	14 001	7.1	11 099	325	42.2	4.3	39	Z	119	20	46 046	141 680	2.4	97.6
Wilcox	798	11.4	16 890	30.2	16 567	273	16.1	25.3	123	8	451	73	51 948	190 286	47.4	52.6
Wilkes	366	3.5	5 145	3.9	7 238	298	15.8	14.4	95	2	319	32	22 033	73 936	4.2	95.8
Wilkinson	156	1.5	551	.4	617	88	11.4	18.2	28	−4	313	8	1 272	14 455	45.0	55.0
Worth	999	5.1	23 899	19.3	25 140	406	24.6	30.0	191	−9	470	122	64 652	159 241	87.2	12.8
HAWAII	6 277	.6	164 304	.7	159 179	5 473	89.0	2.6	1 439	−150	263	292	496 935	90 798	80.8	19.2
Hawaii	2 991	2.5	42 504	2.4	41 543	3 319	89.0	2.6	870	−57	262	103	168 111	50 651	76.7	23.3
Honolulu	1 164	.1	55 062	.3	53 143	880	93.2	1.7	80	−12	91	29	142 965	162 460	72.4	27.6
Kalawao	–	–	(6)	(6)	(6)	–	–	–	–	–	–	–	–	–	–	–
Kauai	794	1.6	17 426	2.0	17 948	468	84.8	3.0	197	−17	421	D	57 474	122 808	91.9	8.1
Maui	1 328	1.3	6,49 312	6,2.4	6,46 545	806	87.0	3.5	292	−64	362	D	128 385	159 287	90.4	9.6
IDAHO	44 869	4.5	867 410	4.6	648 342	22 314	39.0	22.6	11 830	−1 639	530	6 309	3 345 864	149 945	53.0	47.0
Ada	2 037	1.0	33 201	.5	21 255	1 221	70.7	5.7	231	−2	189	90	93 719	76 756	38.8	61.2
Adams	411	12.6	−102	X	−98	279	40.9	27.6	200	−21	719	48	8 339	29 889	13.4	86.6
Bannock	877	1.3	4 173	.4	3 063	664	44.0	20.6	309	−16	466	167	25 032	37 699	62.3	37.7
Bear Lake	332	5.5	3 872	9.2	2 607	410	20.2	28.5	222	−48	541	121	14 876	36 283	23.1	76.9
Benewah	374	4.7	863	.7	709	226	26.1	31.4	126	14	557	77	11 434	50 593	91.9	8.1
Bingham	2 665	7.1	43 060	10.5	42 736	1 168	44.6	22.9	796	−576	682	378	225 493	193 059	75.0	25.0
Blaine	428	3.2	5 933	1.4	5 359	195	31.3	31.3	215	−51	1 102	70	23 584	120 944	53.8	46.2
Boise	32	.9	219	.6	121	78	25.6	24.4	45	−35	583	7	2 253	28 885	52.6	47.4
Bonner	686	2.6	1 964	.5	646	501	43.3	8.8	99	−51	197	37	7 269	14 509	55.4	44.6
Bonneville	1 959	2.7	16 960	1.4	16 909	787	44.0	23.8	449	−4	571	312	90 589	115 107	79.7	20.3
Boundary	481	5.8	7 338	6.8	5 105	312	37.2	11.9	73	Z	233	51	13 541	43 401	86.5	13.5
Butte	473	16.2	4 044	1.2	3 492	207	21.3	31.9	130	−30	626	70	21 514	103 932	69.3	30.7
Camas	66	9.1	2 248	25.1	1 778	98	10.2	55.1	128	−2	1 301	80	8 815	89 949	77.3	22.7
Canyon	4 878	5.4	88 876	6.4	67 598	1 898	56.4	7.5	355	−36	187	235	311 397	164 066	50.2	49.8
Caribou	486	7.0	7 991	5.8	10 738	427	15.2	46.6	469	−118	1 099	265	42 918	100 511	68.6	31.4
Cassia	1 877	9.6	67 642	23.3	48 634	729	30.6	35.9	657	−10	901	378	332 819	456 542	42.8	57.2
Clark	113	14.8	3 413	21.6	3 238	83	8.4	59.0	215	−71	2 594	D	32 029	385 892	74.9	25.1
Clearwater	359	4.2	(7)	Z	−107	210	24.3	20.5	73	−30	348	42	4 849	23 090	79.8	20.2
Custer	327	7.9	3 077	5.7	3 055	268	26.5	32.8	148	7	552	68	17 557	65 511	20.6	79.4
Elmore	328	1.5	30 258	7.8	21 760	301	34.6	32.6	356	2	1 181	127	220 121	731 299	D	D
Franklin	1 079	11.7	24 224	28.0	14 721	655	31.1	22.0	246	16	376	148	57 212	87 347	19.3	80.7
Fremont	855	7.8	14 036	15.1	14 277	493	32.3	30.6	334	−47	678	193	81 004	164 308	85.9	14.1
Gem	1 022	8.6	4 323	4.3	1 482	552	50.5	10.7	183	−14	331	48	29 606	53 634	38.2	61.8
Gooding	1 413	12.1	122 221	54.2	78 938	675	44.7	13.0	220	−7	326	D	249 436	369 535	20.7	79.3
Idaho	1 452	10.5	−1 375	X	−3 119	661	20.9	42.4	650	−94	983	226	32 553	49 248	58.2	41.8
Jefferson	1 815	11.0	24 195	17.2	18 978	773	41.9	19.9	333	21	430	234	136 132	176 109	61.8	38.2
Jerome	1 639	10.8	111 708	39.6	72 819	683	41.7	15.4	194	−14	284	160	250 374	366 580	33.3	66.7

[1] For 1990 corrected population, see table B-1. Percent is based on 1990 uncorrected population because only total population is corrected. [2] For total earnings, see table B-8. [3] Most data are comparable between 1992 and 1997; however, it should be noted that farms with all acreage in Conservation or Wetlands Reserve Programs (excluded in 1992) are included in 1997, as are short rotation woody crops which includes Christmas trees and maple sap gathering (in Forestry in 1992). [4] Includes nursery and greenhouse crops. [5] Includes related products. [6] Kalawao County included with Maui County; data not available separately. [7] Less than $50,000.

Sources: Farm Population—U.S. Census Bureau, 1990 Census of Population and Housing, Summary Tape File (STF) 3C on CD-ROM (related Internet site <http://homer.ssd.census.gov/cdrom/lookup>). Farm Earnings—U.S. Bureau of Economic Analysis, "Regional Economic Information System (REIS) 1969-1998" on CD-ROM (related Internet site <http://www.bea.doc.gov/bea/regional/reis/ca45/>). Agriculture—U.S. Department of Agriculture, National Agricultural Statistics Service, 1997 Census of Agriculture, Volume 1, Geographic Area Series, 1A, 1B, 1C CD-ROM Set (related Internet site <http://www.nass.usda.gov/census/>).

Table B–10. Counties — Farm Population, Farm Earnings, and Agriculture–Con.

[Includes U.S., states, and 3,142 counties/county equivalents defined as of January 1, 1992. For changes to these areas since January 1, 1992, see appendix B. Geographic Information]

County	Farm population, 1990 Number	Farm population, 1990 Percent of total[1]	Farm earnings 1998 Total ($1,000)	Farm earnings 1998 Percent of total[2]	Farm earnings 1997 ($1,000)	Farms Number	Farms Percent Less than 50 acres	Farms Percent 500 acres or more	Land in farms Total acreage (1,000)	Land in farms Net change, 1992–1997[3] (1,000)	Land in farms Average size of farm	Land in farms Total cropland (1,000)	Value of farm products sold Total ($1,000)	Value of farm products sold Average per farm (dollars)	Percent from Crops[4]	Percent from Livestock and poultry[5]
IDAHO—Con.																
Kootenai	1 089	1.6	–717	X	–1 669	598	48.0	13.0	131	Z	219	77	13 581	22 711	80.9	19.1
Latah	1 210	4.0	2 500	.6	–569	659	26.6	29.1	325	–22	494	238	37 541	56 967	91.5	8.5
Lemhi	559	8.1	385	.5	664	308	33.8	33.4	197	3	638	84	18 782	60 981	8.6	91.4
Lewis	262	7.5	–1 058	X	–2 455	182	12.6	52.7	194	–17	1 064	140	20 157	110 753	93.5	6.5
Lincoln	707	21.4	11 071	26.5	8 406	281	18.5	24.9	131	–1	468	D	43 896	156 214	61.1	38.9
Madison	922	3.9	15 763	5.9	14 309	470	40.2	23.4	223	–2	474	174	80 475	171 223	90.9	9.1
Minidoka	2 176	11.2	32 720	13.9	25 215	674	42.4	18.2	207	–1	307	D	152 214	225 837	75.4	24.6
Nez Perce	538	1.6	2 278	.3	–78	383	27.2	43.9	339	–138	886	208	37 756	98 580	87.7	12.3
Oneida	598	17.1	2 585	10.4	2 368	387	19.4	39.3	271	Z	701	188	15 164	39 183	60.1	39.9
Owyhee	1 212	14.4	28 946	33.0	23 907	570	29.5	28.6	683	–69	1 198	158	102 974	180 656	45.6	54.4
Payette	1 188	7.2	22 357	12.4	16 538	564	55.0	7.3	148	Z	263	D	48 801	86 527	55.6	44.4
Power	221	3.1	19 112	12.8	20 904	323	17.3	55.7	424	–11	1 313	354	120 975	374 536	72.0	28.0
Shoshone	29	.2	–99	X	–52	44	50.0	2.3	4	Z	93	2	388	8 818	D	D
Teton	388	11.3	5 278	13.1	4 265	270	22.2	28.9	133	–2	491	102	22 864	84 681	74.1	25.9
Twin Falls	4 379	8.2	90 059	9.9	69 465	1 439	38.3	15.6	456	–34	317	308	239 410	166 372	56.3	43.7
Valley	145	2.4	2 098	2.0	1 974	119	36.1	32.8	64	–15	540	23	7 608	63 933	17.1	82.9
Washington	782	9.1	9 817	10.6	8 456	489	36.8	29.4	443	–113	906	107	38 816	79 378	60.8	39.2
ILLINOIS	207 016	1.8	1 115 205	.4	1 729 734	73 051	23.1	25.1	27 205	–46	372	23 921	8 556 486	117 130	76.8	23.2
Adams	3 675	5.6	21 007	2.0	27 119	1 415	20.8	20.4	442	–23	312	340	120 787	85 362	61.6	38.4
Alexander	434	4.1	199	.3	2 705	166	16.9	22.9	71	2	429	58	13 213	79 596	95.8	4.2
Bond	1 663	11.1	18 399	11.8	13 009	616	27.8	19.8	180	–3	292	156	45 785	74 326	73.5	26.5
Boone	1 418	4.6	12 028	1.9	9 658	490	35.1	19.6	141	6	289	130	53 693	109 578	75.2	24.8
Brown	796	13.6	10 483	12.2	7 584	377	19.1	24.4	152	8	404	101	30 356	80 520	69.6	30.4
Bureau	3 682	10.3	8 734	2.3	36 079	1 155	15.3	31.6	484	2	419	441	198 887	172 197	82.2	17.8
Calhoun	1 044	19.6	5 365	14.5	8 970	433	22.4	10.6	99	Z	230	59	18 517	42 764	70.6	29.4
Carroll	2 179	13.0	38 813	17.7	16 780	625	18.6	24.8	243	4	389	214	123 059	196 894	49.7	50.3
Cass	1 162	8.6	21 862	11.8	20 519	417	21.8	32.6	192	–17	461	160	74 171	177 868	56.1	43.9
Champaign	3 073	1.8	12 498	.4	45 643	1 371	17.4	31.1	568	–4	414	549	190 040	138 614	96.2	3.8
Christian	2 022	5.9	18 348	5.0	39 783	820	23.3	34.9	390	Z	476	366	123 058	150 071	93.7	6.3
Clark	2 280	14.3	1 183	.8	11 168	603	25.2	31.3	269	9	446	225	63 239	104 874	87.2	12.8
Clay	1 992	13.8	5 684	3.1	9 932	627	21.2	26.6	239	15	381	207	49 244	78 539	87.2	12.8
Clinton	2 784	8.2	31 191	8.8	22 660	860	23.1	14.2	234	5	272	211	106 672	124 037	38.5	61.5
Coles	1 894	3.7	5 560	.6	17 144	681	26.6	28.3	257	–6	377	237	72 881	107 021	93.5	6.5
Cook	196	Z	1 448	Z	8 039	237	53.6	11.0	39	–2	166	30	21 387	90 241	97.2	2.8
Crawford	1 804	9.3	–2 854	X	3 855	473	24.5	30.4	209	–15	442	183	52 005	109 947	81.6	18.4
Cumberland	1 694	15.9	9 182	13.3	11 149	547	23.9	21.4	170	–6	310	148	53 864	98 472	67.1	32.9
DeKalb	2 768	3.6	29 067	2.6	32 480	828	19.4	30.6	368	–9	445	355	183 396	221 493	61.7	38.3
De Witt	1 479	9.0	–528	X	12 670	463	23.3	33.3	205	–1	443	197	68 830	148 661	93.8	6.2
Douglas	1 737	8.9	4 791	1.8	15 673	630	27.0	29.8	250	–10	396	239	80 387	127 598	89.2	10.8
DuPage	83	Z	–4 869	X	4 612	93	59.1	10.8	17	–1	184	14	17 637	189 645	96.7	3.3
Edgar	2 155	11.0	58 314	24.3	35 750	766	17.2	33.7	352	–2	460	322	165 386	215 909	54.5	45.5
Edwards	994	13.4	2 241	2.3	12 972	329	24.3	23.1	113	–3	343	95	27 708	84 219	67.4	32.6
Effingham	3 121	9.8	11 463	1.8	12 927	1 035	25.1	13.9	257	–1	248	222	79 036	76 363	57.1	42.9
Fayette	2 747	13.1	13 936	7.0	16 053	1 119	26.1	18.4	333	–4	298	276	71 974	64 320	85.1	14.9
Ford	1 477	10.3	10 278	6.8	22 576	550	11.1	43.8	315	15	572	300	100 000	181 982	89.7	10.3
Franklin	1 559	3.9	858	.3	6 163	658	33.6	13.8	180	19	273	152	31 638	48 082	78.4	21.6
Fulton	2 986	7.8	3 699	1.5	12 588	1 101	20.8	26.2	425	–6	386	319	98 853	89 785	80.9	19.1
Gallatin	349	5.1	2 574	4.4	9 872	238	20.2	39.9	191	19	803	165	45 212	189 966	94.1	5.9
Greene	1 840	12.0	13 795	15.2	13 977	720	20.6	28.6	328	24	455	261	105 750	146 875	62.3	37.7
Grundy	1 741	6.4	–4 134	X	7 682	463	17.5	30.9	201	–24	435	190	59 233	127 933	93.7	6.3
Hamilton	1 304	15.3	4 656	9.3	11 931	563	22.6	20.2	215	13	381	181	38 810	68 934	93.5	6.5
Hancock	3 213	15.0	25 955	12.8	30 235	1 137	17.2	28.2	438	5	386	354	125 938	110 763	74.3	25.7
Hardin	255	4.9	1 339	3.8	591	172	16.9	7.0	39	1	228	24	3 160	18 372	34.4	65.6
Henderson	1 351	16.7	5 607	14.8	11 287	414	16.7	36.7	202	–2	488	169	60 210	145 435	81.1	18.9
Henry	4 694	9.2	17 137	3.8	24 938	1 344	21.6	24.0	457	3	340	413	179 062	133 231	57.8	42.2
Iroquois	4 190	13.6	31 730	10.9	48 212	1 393	14.0	37.6	667	5	479	634	240 042	172 320	81.1	18.9
Jackson	1 718	2.8	9 960	1.1	8 684	680	24.0	14.3	203	16	298	161	37 015	54 434	74.7	25.3
Jasper	2 795	26.3	14 023	13.2	30 776	729	22.2	27.8	252	–6	346	225	85 983	117 947	61.3	38.7
Jefferson	2 423	6.5	7 290	1.2	2 462	962	28.4	11.5	230	12	239	184	35 217	36 608	80.0	20.0
Jersey	1 584	7.7	–1 136	X	5 015	481	24.7	22.7	164	–17	341	131	40 316	83 817	80.1	19.9
Jo Daviess	2 694	12.3	19 466	6.7	1 394	941	18.5	15.0	276	–15	293	189	72 580	77 131	37.9	62.1
Johnson	578	5.1	3 016	3.7	2 161	515	21.2	8.2	104	10	203	70	10 720	20 816	56.9	43.1
Kane	2 094	.7	10 467	.2	30 629	650	36.3	21.5	210	6	323	197	122 734	188 822	84.7	15.3

[1] For 1990 corrected population, see table B-1. Percent is based on 1990 uncorrected population because only total population is corrected. [2] For total earnings, see table B-8. [3] Most data are comparable between 1992 and 1997; however, it should be noted that farms with all acreage in Conservation or Wetlands Reserve Programs (excluded in 1992) are included in 1997, as are short rotation woody crops which includes Christmas trees and maple sap gathering (in Forestry in 1992). [4] Includes nursery and greenhouse crops. [5] Includes related products.

Sources: Farm Population—U.S. Census Bureau, 1990 Census of Population and Housing, Summary Tape File (STF) 3C on CD-ROM (related Internet site <http://homer.ssd.census.gov/cdrom/lookup>). Farm Earnings—U.S. Bureau of Economic Analysis, "Regional Economic Information System (REIS) 1969-1998" on CD-ROM (related Internet site <http://www.bea.doc.gov/bea/regional/reis/ca45/>). Agriculture—U.S. Department of Agriculture, National Agricultural Statistics Service, 1997 Census of Agriculture, Volume 1, Geographic Area Series, 1A, 1B, 1C CD-ROM Set (related Internet site <http://www.nass.usda.gov/census/>).

Table B–10. Counties — Farm Population, Farm Earnings, and Agriculture–Con.

[Includes U.S., states, and 3,142 counties/county equivalents defined as of January 1, 1992. For changes to these areas since January 1, 1992, see appendix B. Geographic Information]

County	Farm population, 1990 Number	Farm population, 1990 Percent of total[1]	Farm earnings 1998 Total ($1,000)	Farm earnings 1998 Percent of total[2]	Farm earnings 1997 ($1,000)	Farms Number	Farms Percent Less than 50 acres	Farms Percent 500 acres or more	Land in farms Total acreage (1,000)	Land Net change, 1992–1997[3] (1,000)	Land Average size of farm	Land Total cropland (1,000)	Value Total ($1,000)	Value Average per farm (dollars)	Percent from Crops[4]	Percent from Livestock and poultry[5]
ILLINOIS—Con.																
Kankakee	3 214	3.3	17 368	1.2	24 397	831	21.8	31.0	352	−7	423	338	132 882	159 906	89.0	11.0
Kendall	1 554	3.9	2 172	.3	7 859	441	23.4	25.9	167	−11	380	158	58 758	133 238	85.6	14.4
Knox	2 430	4.3	31 142	3.7	29 272	928	22.2	27.4	390	4	420	318	130 303	140 413	69.6	30.4
Lake	586	.1	1 116	Z	7 944	335	65.4	6.6	51	−22	152	42	32 246	96 257	87.1	12.9
La Salle	4 806	4.5	9 214	.6	33 351	1 581	17.0	26.2	588	−24	372	552	183 148	115 843	90.1	9.9
Lawrence	1 154	7.2	6 556	4.1	10 074	376	25.5	31.1	183	13	485	162	55 206	146 824	66.1	33.9
Lee	2 970	8.6	1 644	.4	19 751	904	16.2	30.3	393	−21	435	369	136 216	150 681	81.9	18.1
Livingston	4 007	10.2	9 307	1.7	52 409	1 380	12.3	36.9	614	−24	445	589	213 643	154 814	77.5	22.5
Logan	1 943	6.3	−2 678	X	21 270	739	15.3	40.5	381	11	515	361	133 249	180 310	84.1	15.9
McDonough	1 932	5.5	14 479	3.0	26 338	824	22.5	28.4	340	−5	413	292	96 818	117 498	84.1	15.9
McHenry	2 611	1.4	9 136	.3	15 937	921	42.6	14.8	242	−7	263	220	109 147	118 509	71.4	28.6
McLean	4 002	3.1	−2 630	X	44 049	1 475	18.0	35.5	697	−13	472	666	238 243	161 521	89.0	11.0
Macon	1 753	1.5	4 891	.2	24 811	665	24.7	36.7	323	12	486	303	105 734	158 998	96.0	4.0
Macoupin	3 622	7.6	10 280	2.6	20 302	1 206	24.3	22.3	396	−7	328	336	120 711	100 092	71.2	28.8
Madison	3 310	1.3	6 853	.2	11 467	1 195	34.9	14.6	284	−16	237	248	86 104	72 054	79.0	21.0
Marion	2 068	5.0	17 440	3.1	11 764	882	24.5	17.6	249	−5	283	203	55 599	63 037	65.3	34.7
Marshall	1 205	9.4	8 739	7.5	12 513	494	12.3	30.6	228	24	461	197	67 644	136 931	88.7	11.3
Mason	1 361	8.4	22 910	15.8	13 309	486	15.4	45.5	292	9	600	264	84 384	173 630	90.9	9.1
Massac	829	5.6	2 948	1.7	3 091	400	27.5	13.0	104	5	259	84	19 919	49 798	69.5	30.5
Menard	1 233	11.0	10 343	12.2	15 292	352	21.3	34.1	170	6	484	153	52 380	148 807	81.4	18.6
Mercer	2 181	12.6	13 118	11.7	18 076	754	21.9	28.5	310	−3	411	261	92 148	122 212	76.2	23.8
Monroe	2 123	9.5	12 580	5.8	7 744	556	29.0	21.0	187	Z	336	154	49 384	88 820	65.3	34.7
Montgomery	2 704	8.8	14 540	4.2	23 598	980	19.6	27.3	361	−11	368	324	109 153	111 381	78.2	21.8
Morgan	1 973	5.4	4 514	.9	18 310	780	21.5	27.7	306	−6	392	267	96 148	123 267	78.0	21.9
Moultrie	1 346	9.7	2 323	1.8	11 339	464	29.1	25.6	173	−12	372	165	55 951	120 584	86.9	13.1
Ogle	3 451	7.5	14 812	2.3	24 370	1 099	24.1	23.1	379	−13	345	343	148 907	135 493	65.9	34.1
Peoria	2 238	1.2	11 697	.3	17 632	924	28.8	19.2	267	6	289	224	77 189	83 538	86.3	13.7
Perry	1 363	6.4	4 127	2.2	4 325	551	25.2	21.1	172	4	312	145	28 517	51 755	81.0	19.0
Piatt	956	6.1	3 686	2.6	18 614	448	14.1	44.9	253	2	565	245	83 439	186 248	93.7	6.3
Pike	2 721	15.5	31 660	20.3	22 006	1 028	16.4	26.4	461	18	449	342	123 842	120 469	65.2	34.8
Pope	325	7.4	551	1.7	179	282	13.1	12.1	72	4	256	43	4 720	16 738	60.7	39.3
Pulaski	557	7.4	1 476	2.3	2 542	239	18.4	19.2	83	1	348	71	15 328	64 134	83.7	16.3
Putnam	324	5.7	1 196	1.2	9 769	190	18.9	29.5	77	−1	405	65	41 977	220 932	89.8	10.2
Randolph	2 363	6.8	9 880	2.5	9 014	843	23.5	18.4	262	−8	311	208	50 239	59 595	70.5	29.5
Richland	1 858	11.2	9 804	4.1	12 602	495	24.8	26.7	197	8	398	175	59 412	120 024	65.5	34.5
Rock Island	1 927	1.3	5 777	.2	11 654	618	32.7	18.3	170	−6	275	135	49 789	80 565	72.9	27.1
St. Clair	2 950	1.1	11 284	.3	16 456	844	29.1	18.5	265	Z	313	239	78 193	92 646	81.5	18.5
Saline	691	2.6	4 485	1.5	8 751	441	32.9	16.8	131	−11	296	115	33 115	75 091	62.8	37.2
Sangamon	2 636	1.5	20 399	.5	44 519	993	31.4	31.1	467	20	470	436	162 564	163 710	88.6	11.4
Schuyler	1 505	20.1	5 861	9.0	7 876	477	13.2	28.9	209	2	438	144	39 747	83 327	79.0	21.0
Scott	752	13.3	3 662	4.9	5 619	327	24.5	30.3	146	17	445	117	34 929	106 817	84.3	15.7
Shelby	2 938	13.2	16 236	8.0	25 126	1 250	23.9	21.0	419	16	335	376	112 466	89 973	78.1	21.9
Stark	1 164	17.8	11 057	21.8	15 926	354	17.8	39.0	180	10	508	165	65 450	184 887	84.8	15.2
Stephenson	3 717	7.7	53 398	6.1	25 491	1 081	24.4	15.1	309	−6	285	277	142 015	131 374	41.6	58.4
Tazewell	2 352	1.9	32 382	1.3	35 084	909	26.2	27.0	328	−8	361	305	123 163	135 493	76.0	24.0
Union	1 456	8.3	3 480	2.0	3 207	591	23.0	11.7	136	17	230	95	20 720	35 059	77.8	22.2
Vermilion	2 757	3.1	1 057	.1	23 464	984	22.1	36.1	485	−3	493	458	140 159	142 438	95.7	4.3
Wabash	1 005	7.7	−3 137	X	2 406	212	28.3	40.6	122	6	574	112	30 784	145 208	91.9	8.1
Warren	2 109	11.0	13 817	8.2	24 999	710	16.5	34.2	315	−2	444	278	105 083	148 004	80.0	20.0
Washington	2 335	15.6	24 398	10.7	19 844	777	16.6	25.6	309	12	397	279	87 954	113 197	62.7	37.3
Wayne	2 898	16.8	11 031	6.4	13 364	972	22.4	20.0	321	−12	330	274	70 920	72 963	70.0	30.0
White	1 183	7.2	8 634	5.0	18 915	432	22.5	29.4	256	21	594	224	61 272	141 833	86.9	13.1
Whiteside	3 073	5.1	18 839	2.3	28 311	1 039	22.7	24.4	385	−15	370	353	156 992	151 099	64.4	35.6
Will	2 999	.8	20 648	.4	22 817	910	32.7	20.7	294	−32	323	275	107 129	117 724	92.0	8.0
Williamson	1 132	2.0	195	Z	781	585	33.3	6.0	92	3	158	67	11 422	19 525	70.0	30.0
Winnebago	1 987	.8	13 650	.2	12 814	687	35.1	18.0	196	−8	285	178	68 904	100 297	73.1	26.9
Woodford	2 656	8.1	10 743	3.3	20 884	923	22.5	22.2	300	4	325	275	107 254	116 202	78.6	21.4
INDIANA	188 133	3.4	507 141	.5	922 905	57 916	31.4	15.1	15 111	−508	261	12 849	5 229 977	90 303	62.1	37.9
Adams	4 322	13.9	5 076	1.1	16 023	1 093	41.6	10.4	209	11	191	191	95 237	87 134	48.0	52.0
Allen	4 946	1.6	8 101	.1	22 066	1 440	36.4	9.5	276	−9	192	247	89 877	62 415	69.3	30.7
Bartholomew	2 450	3.8	1 571	.1	6 368	577	32.3	19.1	167	2	289	146	46 702	80 939	82.0	18.0
Benton	1 141	12.1	−2 342	X	13 327	433	10.2	42.0	257	−14	593	248	79 373	183 309	95.7	4.3
Blackford	1 149	8.2	−237	X	5 758	303	36.3	14.5	86	−1	284	77	25 295	83 482	72.4	27.6
Boone	2 258	5.9	12 491	2.6	20 901	611	33.6	25.4	228	5	374	212	81 519	133 419	74.0	26.0
Brown	349	2.5	306	.4	(6)	173	34.7	1.7	22	−1	125	10	2 203	12 734	52.0	48.0
Carroll	2 006	10.7	14 112	7.6	24 969	563	28.8	24.9	218	−2	388	198	116 937	207 703	52.1	47.9
Cass	2 227	5.8	10 502	1.9	19 646	700	34.6	17.7	205	−22	293	179	77 559	110 799	69.0	31.0

[1] For 1990 corrected population, see table B-1. Percent is based on 1990 uncorrected population because only total population is corrected. [2] For total earnings, see table B-8. [3] Most data are comparable between 1992 and 1997; however, it should be noted that farms with all acreage in Conservation or Wetlands Reserve Programs (excluded in 1992) are included in 1997, as are short rotation woody crops which includes Christmas trees and maple sap gathering (in Forestry in 1992). [4] Includes nursery and greenhouse crops. [5] Includes related products. [6] Less than $50,000.

Sources: Farm Population—U.S. Census Bureau, 1990 Census of Population and Housing, Summary Tape File (STF) 3C on CD-ROM (related Internet site <http://homer.ssd.census.gov/cdrom/lookup>). Farm Earnings—U.S. Bureau of Economic Analysis, "Regional Economic Information System (REIS) 1969-1998" on CD-ROM (related Internet site <http://www.bea.doc.gov/bea/regional/reis/ca45/>). Agriculture—U.S. Department of Agriculture, National Agricultural Statistics Service, 1997 Census of Agriculture, Volume 1, Geographic Area Series, 1A, 1B, 1C CD-ROM Set (related Internet site <http://www.nass.usda.gov/census/>).

[Includes U.S., states, and 3,142 counties/county equivalents defined as of January 1, 1992. For changes to these areas since January 1, 1992, see appendix B. Geographic Information]

County	Farm population, 1990 Number	Farm population, 1990 Percent of total[1]	Farm earnings 1998 Total ($1,000)	Farm earnings 1998 Percent of total[2]	Farm earnings 1997 ($1,000)	Farms Number	Farms Percent Less than 50 acres	Farms Percent 500 acres or more	Land in farms Total acreage (1,000)	Land in farms Net change, 1992–1997[3] (1,000)	Land in farms Average size of farm	Land in farms Total cropland (1,000)	Value of farm products sold Total ($1,000)	Value of farm products sold Average per farm (dollars)	Percent from Crops[4]	Percent from Livestock and poultry[5]
INDIANA—Con.																
Clark	1 310	1.5	3 087	.2	2 080	647	33.1	7.3	109	3	168	76	21 878	33 815	71.2	28.8
Clay	1 811	7.3	1 392	.6	8 564	520	26.9	20.8	159	−3	307	135	42 549	81 825	71.6	28.4
Clinton	2 019	6.5	10 180	2.7	24 759	585	25.6	26.8	236	Z	404	223	106 004	181 203	60.5	39.5
Crawford	522	5.3	166	.3	1 767	410	19.8	3.9	61	2	150	30	3 502	8 541	31.1	68.9
Daviess	3 639	13.2	9 463	3.2	13 648	1 101	41.9	10.9	217	−5	197	189	117 889	107 074	34.0	66.0
Dearborn	1 662	4.3	1 690	.4	685	679	24.0	2.2	81	−5	120	45	8 965	13 203	58.3	41.7
Decatur	2 499	10.6	1 863	.5	12 879	654	24.0	19.9	199	−4	304	171	82 874	126 719	52.8	47.2
De Kalb	2 508	7.1	9 496	1.2	10 138	785	27.3	9.8	163	10	208	135	38 669	49 260	65.9	34.1
Delaware	2 246	1.9	13 154	.7	14 812	635	38.0	13.7	173	4	273	160	52 625	82 874	84.3	15.7
Dubois	2 149	5.9	12 881	1.4	15 890	812	22.2	11.3	191	−2	235	138	144 151	177 526	15.5	84.5
Elkhart	5 856	3.7	12 167	.3	16 636	1 335	45.9	6.2	183	−10	137	160	124 038	92 912	28.0	72.0
Fayette	1 338	5.1	585	.1	1 227	420	29.8	15.0	107	−5	254	85	26 419	62 902	64.9	35.1
Floyd	670	1.0	594	.1	471	310	47.1	3.2	29	−1	93	18	3 716	11 987	71.7	28.3
Fountain	1 707	9.6	−4 387	X	−4 008	550	23.8	26.5	205	−25	372	177	49 371	89 765	85.9	14.1
Franklin	2 546	13.0	−2 001	X	382	776	23.3	7.2	139	−10	179	92	31 237	40 254	48.1	51.9
Fulton	2 396	12.7	7 716	3.1	10 102	622	29.4	17.7	171	−24	274	151	55 452	89 151	70.8	29.2
Gibson	2 247	7.0	7 970	2.2	9 385	579	27.8	25.4	233	−8	402	212	69 056	119 268	81.3	18.7
Grant	2 613	3.5	2 436	.2	14 554	575	28.9	23.5	192	−4	334	178	62 549	108 781	83.2	16.8
Greene	1 937	6.4	−3 481	X	5 884	878	25.1	11.3	206	−2	234	147	77 483	88 249	30.3	69.7
Hamilton	2 350	2.2	8 749	.3	14 660	591	47.9	14.6	141	−22	238	127	59 491	100 662	87.2	12.8
Hancock	2 266	5.0	2 259	.4	13 674	549	39.5	17.1	164	Z	298	155	55 797	101 634	79.8	20.2
Harrison	2 189	7.3	4 397	1.5	409	1 108	32.5	4.9	161	Z	146	110	46 049	41 560	30.0	70.0
Hendricks	2 700	3.6	2 191	.2	6 641	631	38.0	13.5	167	−20	265	150	49 154	77 899	81.7	18.3
Henry	2 687	5.6	4 968	.9	9 560	770	39.6	13.8	178	−13	231	161	52 177	67 762	81.0	19.0
Howard	2 089	2.6	9 334	.4	18 366	486	28.4	19.5	148	−1	304	138	62 587	128 780	69.2	30.8
Huntington	2 349	6.6	7 581	1.5	19 371	651	29.5	18.7	184	−4	283	169	69 752	107 146	63.6	36.4
Jackson	2 009	5.3	5 384	.9	13 400	809	30.7	15.9	201	−2	248	157	92 711	114 600	35.5	64.5
Jasper	2 394	9.6	13 697	4.0	20 093	618	24.4	34.3	283	−19	458	258	111 015	179 636	66.9	33.1
Jay	2 930	13.6	9 209	3.9	13 076	839	32.9	10.8	180	−3	214	157	83 241	99 215	42.4	57.6
Jefferson	2 176	7.3	3 544	.9	4 483	796	33.3	5.0	126	−4	159	81	23 445	29 454	76.9	23.1
Jennings	1 979	8.4	1 941	.7	3 360	605	33.7	10.4	130	6	215	91	45 214	74 734	43.6	56.4
Johnson	1 907	2.2	2 268	.2	6 869	526	41.4	17.7	136	−4	258	121	46 342	88 103	80.7	19.3
Knox	1 920	4.8	16 518	3.1	25 413	584	22.3	27.6	281	−25	481	256	101 195	173 279	70.7	29.3
Kosciusko	3 875	5.9	21 003	1.7	26 170	1 130	35.0	12.0	247	−5	219	210	146 062	129 258	33.4	66.6
Lagrange	5 639	19.1	17 018	4.0	20 761	1 392	38.2	5.3	190	2	136	156	103 278	74 194	36.2	63.8
Lake	1 135	.2	10 833	.1	12 163	442	32.6	20.1	149	5	337	139	47 827	108 206	89.4	10.6
La Porte	2 527	2.4	15 887	1.0	21 489	749	30.4	21.8	248	−20	331	227	95 814	127 923	71.0	29.0
Lawrence	1 328	3.1	816	.1	817	875	26.1	8.3	171	12	195	100	22 317	25 505	46.7	53.3
Madison	2 597	2.0	8 790	.5	16 513	738	37.1	19.9	224	Z	303	209	77 512	105 030	88.0	12.0
Marion	−	−	15 895	.1	15 899	225	62.2	8.0	29	−10	129	24	32 681	145 249	59.5	40.5
Marshall	3 211	7.6	13 750	2.1	15 836	865	31.9	11.9	202	−18	233	177	62 187	71 892	69.6	30.4
Martin	695	6.7	2 876	.8	3 353	335	28.7	9.6	70	−1	209	46	23 997	71 633	26.6	73.4
Miami	2 407	6.5	5 406	1.6	13 758	678	27.4	18.0	197	8	291	175	74 763	110 270	58.4	41.6
Monroe	1 224	1.1	1 866	.1	1 474	473	33.4	5.5	62	3	131	36	8 406	17 772	58.5	41.5
Montgomery	2 269	6.6	12 878	2.0	18 350	681	28.5	27.5	273	−10	401	244	85 081	124 935	73.1	26.9
Morgan	1 916	3.4	157	Z	4 535	601	41.9	12.5	134	−6	223	111	34 315	57 097	82.1	17.9
Newton	1 061	7.8	4 060	3.2	8 127	381	20.5	36.7	207	Z	544	193	84 301	221 262	68.4	31.6
Noble	3 298	8.7	9 643	1.4	10 245	942	31.7	10.1	182	−2	193	147	58 841	62 464	51.8	48.2
Ohio	668	12.6	1 214	1.8	−135	252	27.0	1.6	30	−2	119	16	3 764	14 937	71.8	28.2
Orange	1 236	6.7	3 897	1.8	2 202	531	21.3	12.6	123	7	232	78	22 143	41 701	44.2	55.8
Owen	1 018	5.9	−1 376	X	1 335	569	27.8	8.8	107	−6	189	70	16 417	28 852	62.2	37.8
Parke	1 165	7.6	(6)	Z	3 022	471	26.3	23.1	189	7	401	146	43 384	92 110	79.8	20.2
Perry	887	4.6	−278	X	719	484	19.8	5.4	84	4	174	44	13 184	27 240	28.0	72.0
Pike	913	7.3	1 956	1.6	1 708	288	26.0	18.1	84	−1	292	70	20 050	69 618	68.8	31.2
Porter	1 386	1.1	9 053	.4	11 310	476	31.5	19.7	135	−8	283	123	42 227	88 712	86.3	13.7
Posey	1 352	5.2	−1 571	X	4 794	437	25.9	27.5	195	−26	447	180	59 770	136 773	84.3	15.7
Pulaski	1 462	11.6	19 427	11.3	26 558	531	21.5	29.2	236	−6	445	216	98 057	184 665	62.4	37.6
Putnam	2 072	6.8	2 219	.6	3 878	794	34.0	14.4	195	−9	246	153	48 773	61 427	70.0	30.0
Randolph	3 618	13.3	5 960	2.3	12 617	851	29.8	16.2	224	−13	263	202	67 766	79 631	70.2	29.8
Ripley	2 762	11.2	−990	X	1 476	821	28.7	8.4	159	−5	194	124	56 909	69 317	46.9	53.1
Rush	2 797	15.4	755	.4	14 464	663	22.5	24.6	228	−5	344	207	85 928	129 605	65.4	34.6
St. Joseph	2 691	1.1	13 485	.3	14 244	666	41.3	13.7	154	−18	231	140	55 178	82 850	72.6	27.4
Scott	980	4.7	−339	X	−87	348	40.2	6.9	57	−6	165	41	9 183	26 388	83.8	16.2
Shelby	2 433	6.0	2 831	.5	14 134	641	34.9	20.7	201	−17	313	186	66 936	104 424	78.8	21.2
Spencer	2 254	11.6	2 827	1.1	7 152	638	27.3	13.0	173	−2	271	142	51 896	81 342	56.5	43.5
Starke	1 508	6.6	11 247	7.6	12 875	410	30.5	19.5	136	1	331	116	33 138	80 824	96.2	3.8
Steuben	1 596	5.8	4 852	.9	5 748	581	24.3	9.1	124	2	213	99	25 641	44 133	65.4	34.6
Sullivan	1 353	7.1	8 854	4.8	9 051	473	28.5	21.6	177	−4	374	154	43 806	92 613	87.2	12.8
Switzerland	1 700	22.0	2 085	4.0	2 450	541	34.9	2.6	68	−11	125	34	13 331	24 641	70.2	29.8
Tippecanoe	2 218	1.7	3 253	.1	12 877	665	35.8	23.9	242	−16	363	221	79 502	119 552	77.1	22.9

[1] For 1990 corrected population, see table B-1. Percent is based on 1990 uncorrected population because only total population is corrected. [2] For total earnings, see table B-8. [3] Most data are comparable between 1992 and 1997; however, it should be noted that farms with all acreage in Conservation or Wetlands Reserve Programs (excluded in 1992) are included in 1997, as are short rotation woody crops which includes Christmas trees and maple sap gathering (in Forestry in 1992). [4] Includes nursery and greenhouse crops. [5] Includes related products. [6] Less than $50,000.

Sources: Farm Population—U.S. Census Bureau, 1990 Census of Population and Housing, Summary Tape File (STF) 3C on CD-ROM (related Internet site <http://homer.ssd.census.gov/cdrom/lookup>). Farm Earnings—U.S. Bureau of Economic Analysis, "Regional Economic Information System (REIS) 1969-1998" on CD-ROM (related Internet site <http://www.bea.doc.gov/bea/regional/reis/ca45/>). Agriculture—U.S. Department of Agriculture, National Agricultural Statistics Service, 1997 Census of Agriculture, Volume 1, Geographic Area Series, 1A, 1B, 1C CD-ROM Set (related Internet site <http://www.nass.usda.gov/census/>).

[Includes U.S., states, and 3,142 counties/county equivalents defined as of January 1, 1992. For changes to these areas since January 1, 1992, see appendix B. Geographic Information]

County	Farm population, 1990 Number	Farm population, 1990 Percent of total[1]	Farm earnings 1998 Total ($1,000)	Farm earnings 1998 Percent of total[2]	Farm earnings 1997 ($1,000)	Farms Number	Farms Percent Less than 50 acres	Farms Percent 500 acres or more	Land in farms (acres) Total acreage (1,000)	Land in farms Net change, 1992–1997[3] (1,000)	Land in farms Average size of farm	Land in farms Total cropland (1,000)	Value of farm products sold Total ($1,000)	Value of farm products sold Average per farm (dollars)	Percent from Crops[4]	Percent from Livestock and poultry[5]
INDIANA—Con.																
Tipton	1 483	9.2	6 869	4.6	18 961	415	28.4	25.1	158	−2	382	148	65 838	158 646	79.7	20.3
Union	1 014	14.5	564	1.2	4 251	268	17.9	23.1	83	2	308	69	25 709	95 929	68.9	31.1
Vanderburgh	1 003	.6	−1 995	X	−320	271	36.5	14.0	72	−9	266	67	20 875	77 030	88.9	11.1
Vermillion	748	4.5	−459	X	1 680	249	18.9	29.3	118	−1	474	101	30 490	122 450	73.6	26.4
Vigo	1 436	1.4	−937	X	1 218	455	40.2	14.9	115	−30	253	99	26 017	57 180	87.1	12.9
Wabash	2 610	7.4	7 111	1.4	18 359	762	27.0	14.3	188	−10	247	163	97 747	128 277	42.7	57.3
Warren	1 360	16.6	7 846	14.1	8 638	378	22.2	31.7	185	−17	489	162	57 996	153 429	70.8	29.2
Warrick	1 150	2.6	−1 995	X	2 154	356	28.7	16.0	99	2	277	81	23 671	66 492	80.9	19.1
Washington	2 119	8.9	5 433	2.6	2 835	914	25.3	9.4	181	−8	198	125	40 119	43 894	41.2	58.8
Wayne	2 337	3.2	−2 025	X	4 050	814	29.2	12.2	173	−17	212	142	51 021	62 679	63.7	36.3
Wells	2 913	11.2	13 263	3.5	20 870	660	28.9	19.5	196	−3	297	182	74 294	112 567	67.3	32.7
White	1 940	8.3	11 834	3.7	18 876	620	26.5	31.6	272	−13	439	253	118 603	191 295	62.0	38.0
Whitley	2 301	8.3	4 842	1.2	11 124	787	32.9	9.5	165	3	210	139	51 930	65 985	59.0	41.0
IOWA	256 562	9.2	1 693 638	3.4	3 030 950	90 792	18.3	22.8	31 167	−180	343	26 822	11 947 894	131 596	51.8	48.2
Adair	2 344	27.9	8 810	10.2	13 934	792	13.0	29.0	336	7	424	284	82 545	104 223	51.9	48.1
Adams	1 424	29.3	4 758	9.7	11 610	573	14.0	27.6	235	−4	411	185	49 642	86 635	51.8	48.2
Allamakee	2 635	19.0	23 831	13.8	21 616	958	15.0	18.6	296	−26	309	180	80 826	84 370	26.7	73.3
Appanoose	1 454	10.6	1 632	1.1	6 323	797	17.4	19.4	241	2	303	176	28 757	36 082	53.8	46.2
Audubon	2 047	27.9	11 129	16.4	29 308	649	15.9	28.5	272	4	420	248	114 110	175 824	46.0	54.0
Benton	3 430	15.3	15 923	8.4	34 780	1 210	20.0	24.0	418	−9	346	376	157 977	130 560	65.1	34.9
Black Hawk	2 834	2.3	29 874	1.3	39 060	1 002	25.1	18.2	286	−14	285	263	127 892	127 637	60.4	39.6
Boone	2 589	10.3	12 936	4.3	27 780	863	22.4	27.0	329	−1	381	297	119 995	139 044	71.4	28.6
Bremer	2 788	12.2	28 989	9.3	35 171	982	24.5	13.2	239	2	243	211	101 575	103 437	55.1	44.9
Buchanan	3 643	17.5	22 297	9.9	36 908	1 136	21.3	19.1	337	4	297	304	137 169	120 747	57.7	42.3
Buena Vista	2 624	13.1	36 842	12.2	64 687	867	15.3	31.3	357	15	411	326	210 089	242 317	43.4	56.6
Butler	3 077	19.6	28 247	21.3	39 759	1 085	21.4	16.8	324	9	299	295	131 473	121 173	56.2	43.8
Calhoun	2 439	21.2	10 414	10.6	32 807	793	16.0	33.5	337	−9	424	317	140 244	176 852	63.7	36.3
Carroll	3 486	16.3	22 065	6.2	53 198	1 102	17.1	20.4	353	−7	320	324	221 458	200 960	35.1	64.9
Cass	2 628	17.4	11 753	5.9	17 896	804	16.4	32.7	331	−16	412	288	94 100	117 040	56.4	43.6
Cedar	3 239	18.6	22 010	13.2	32 722	965	19.4	24.8	326	−13	338	292	128 566	133 229	61.9	38.1
Cerro Gordo	2 114	4.5	25 567	3.2	38 221	822	22.7	26.5	301	−8	366	282	120 620	146 740	67.5	32.5
Cherokee	2 330	16.5	21 129	11.7	36 035	890	14.8	26.5	330	−6	371	287	145 854	163 881	48.9	51.1
Chickasaw	2 647	19.9	25 799	13.8	36 007	926	19.3	18.6	272	−3	294	243	122 131	131 891	46.6	53.4
Clarke	1 311	15.8	6 581	6.4	9 010	678	14.6	18.6	222	−15	327	151	38 534	56 835	33.8	66.2
Clay	2 167	12.3	25 354	8.3	33 217	668	15.9	32.8	286	−29	428	263	120 624	180 575	56.5	43.5
Clayton	4 756	25.0	35 726	15.3	39 276	1 638	14.2	14.7	452	−5	276	337	171 442	104 665	31.4	68.6
Clinton	3 866	7.6	25 026	3.5	38 275	1 268	20.0	19.7	368	Z	290	325	148 387	117 024	57.9	42.1
Crawford	3 322	19.8	11 829	5.4	28 295	1 107	18.8	26.4	432	17	390	375	143 011	129 188	56.4	43.6
Dallas	2 779	9.3	28 509	6.7	37 335	918	28.0	24.2	324	11	353	288	117 622	128 129	65.8	34.2
Davis	2 251	27.1	3 301	4.4	10 240	884	16.1	17.3	267	−9	301	189	55 850	63 179	33.1	66.9
Decatur	1 272	15.3	−108	X	9 371	730	17.1	22.5	262	Z	359	171	54 349	74 451	26.5	73.5
Delaware	3 900	21.6	35 223	16.5	51 248	1 278	14.7	11.0	326	−10	255	287	195 918	153 300	26.3	73.7
Des Moines	1 571	3.7	6 804	.8	18 816	650	22.3	18.8	192	Z	296	156	69 769	107 337	62.2	37.8
Dickinson	1 325	8.9	11 459	4.4	12 510	512	16.8	29.1	201	−1	393	181	72 854	142 293	57.1	42.9
Dubuque	5 161	6.0	33 802	2.0	39 664	1 579	17.9	7.3	336	−7	213	258	171 651	108 709	18.0	82.0
Emmet	1 378	11.9	19 309	12.4	26 478	519	15.2	36.2	220	−5	424	205	91 349	176 010	59.0	41.0
Fayette	4 701	21.5	43 184	17.2	54 002	1 295	18.0	18.5	404	3	312	344	181 137	139 874	42.4	57.6
Floyd	2 405	14.1	19 921	11.2	25 080	850	19.5	24.7	300	13	353	274	113 534	133 569	67.8	32.2
Franklin	2 822	24.8	21 383	15.8	33 209	856	16.1	30.8	344	1	402	316	180 192	210 505	48.0	52.0
Fremont	1 660	20.2	6 879	7.1	18 593	568	10.9	38.7	318	16	560	268	88 185	155 255	74.3	25.7
Greene	2 041	20.3	11 887	11.3	29 793	763	14.7	35.1	343	−24	450	317	122 235	160 203	71.3	28.7
Grundy	2 229	18.5	31 692	21.9	48 005	754	18.0	27.9	321	4	426	299	149 118	197 769	61.5	38.5
Guthrie	2 053	18.8	7 635	8.4	15 054	847	17.7	24.0	304	−25	359	242	95 779	113 080	46.3	53.7
Hamilton	2 311	14.4	34 011	12.9	56 269	790	16.8	32.2	349	16	441	330	227 219	287 619	42.2	57.8
Hancock	2 709	21.4	18 996	8.3	36 770	849	14.7	29.6	334	5	393	315	140 661	165 678	61.2	38.8
Hardin	2 577	13.5	34 970	12.4	60 453	857	20.8	29.6	340	8	397	314	201 877	235 562	43.0	57.0
Harrison	2 268	15.4	6 630	5.6	28 761	876	17.0	30.8	393	−6	448	342	112 981	128 974	72.3	27.7
Henry	2 152	11.2	3 183	1.0	14 533	835	18.4	17.2	245	19	293	201	77 086	92 319	60.1	39.9
Howard	2 327	23.7	17 537	12.6	24 223	862	16.1	17.3	270	9	313	241	95 130	110 360	57.8	42.2
Humboldt	1 823	16.9	13 527	9.9	30 984	600	12.3	33.3	257	−23	429	245	100 520	167 533	72.2	27.8
Ida	2 256	27.0	16 283	12.9	24 894	637	17.3	27.5	253	−20	398	231	95 685	150 212	57.8	42.2
Iowa	2 774	19.0	15 651	4.4	28 317	976	17.2	18.8	332	11	340	272	104 865	107 444	51.0	49.0
Jackson	3 409	17.1	6 655	3.8	12 343	1 280	17.0	13.4	335	−12	262	234	96 659	75 515	27.7	72.3
Jasper	3 949	11.3	29 185	5.4	49 919	1 204	21.3	25.4	421	−11	349	366	153 843	127 777	58.0	42.0
Jefferson	1 895	11.6	8 428	2.7	19 276	765	16.3	17.1	228	1	298	178	57 520	75 190	60.9	39.1
Johnson	4 049	4.2	10 067	.4	24 066	1 261	24.0	13.3	288	4	229	249	100 391	79 612	50.6	49.4
Jones	3 659	18.8	16 933	9.0	28 529	1 029	18.8	20.9	322	Z	313	267	136 937	133 078	44.3	55.7
Keokuk	2 489	21.4	1 640	1.9	23 451	968	15.4	22.4	323	1	334	263	96 734	99 932	52.9	47.1

[1] For 1990 corrected population, see table B-1. Percent is based on 1990 uncorrected population because only total population is corrected. [2] For total earnings, see table B-8. [3] Most data are comparable between 1992 and 1997; however, it should be noted that farms with all acreage in Conservation or Wetlands Reserve Programs (excluded in 1992) are included in 1997, as are short rotation woody crops which includes Christmas trees and maple sap gathering (in Forestry in 1992). [4] Includes nursery and greenhouse crops. [5] Includes related products.

Sources: Farm Population—U.S. Census Bureau, 1990 Census of Population and Housing, Summary Tape File (STF) 3C on CD-ROM (related Internet site <http://homer.ssd.census.gov/cdrom/lookup>). Farm Earnings—U.S. Bureau of Economic Analysis, "Regional Economic Information System (REIS) 1969-1998" on CD-ROM (related Internet site <http://www.bea.doc.gov/bea/regional/reis/ca45/>). Agriculture—U.S. Department of Agriculture, National Agricultural Statistics Service, 1997 Census of Agriculture, Volume 1, Geographic Area Series, 1A, 1B, 1C CD-ROM Set (related Internet site <http://www.nass.usda.gov/census/>).

Table B–10. Counties — **Farm Population, Farm Earnings, and Agriculture**–Con.

[Includes U.S., states, and 3,142 counties/county equivalents defined as of January 1, 1992. For changes to these areas since January 1, 1992, see appendix B. Geographic Information]

County	Farm population, 1990 Number	Farm population, 1990 Per-cent of total[1]	Farm earnings 1998 Total ($1,000)	Farm earnings 1998 Per-cent of total[2]	Farm earnings 1997 ($1,000)	Farms Number	Farms Percent Less than 50 acres	Farms Percent 500 acres or more	Land in farms Total acreage (1,000)	Land in farms Net change, 1992–1997[3] (1,000)	Land in farms Average size of farm	Land in farms Total cropland (1,000)	Value of farm products sold Total ($1,000)	Value of farm products sold Average per farm (dollars)	Value Percent from Crops[4]	Value Percent from Live-stock and poultry[5]
IOWA—Con.																
Kossuth	4 241	22.8	32 762	14.8	59 965	1 404	11.8	29.6	581	−34	414	548	242 775	172 917	62.9	37.1
Lee	2 513	6.5	4 103	.6	19 265	861	19.0	20.6	257	−9	298	190	77 358	89 847	54.1	45.9
Linn	3 511	2.1	13 543	.3	25 204	1 480	28.9	11.6	339	−10	229	292	113 460	76 662	66.2	33.8
Louisa	1 815	15.7	12 753	11.3	23 803	593	16.9	23.3	201	10	340	168	81 296	137 093	52.1	47.9
Lucas	1 368	15.1	−1 645	X	3 665	706	16.6	18.3	227	8	322	157	29 371	41 602	46.1	53.9
Lyon	3 291	27.5	27 400	22.0	45 815	1 149	20.5	18.9	348	1	303	315	198 795	173 016	35.5	64.5
Madison	2 055	16.5	−645	X	5 336	986	18.6	19.3	317	11	321	229	73 550	74 594	48.8	51.2
Mahaska	3 351	15.6	17 708	6.9	42 499	1 022	15.2	21.4	329	14	322	274	156 722	153 348	38.3	61.7
Marion	2 533	8.4	3 107	.5	16 826	971	20.2	18.3	286	17	294	219	73 114	75 298	60.9	39.1
Marshall	2 459	6.4	21 538	3.4	33 149	912	21.3	24.7	319	7	350	290	117 640	128 991	67.6	32.4
Mills	1 355	10.3	3 680	3.1	13 995	496	15.3	34.5	232	−6	468	205	59 190	119 335	84.5	15.5
Mitchell	2 598	23.8	29 005	21.0	45 355	824	21.7	22.8	265	2	322	243	160 571	194 868	38.3	61.7
Monona	1 883	18.8	5 959	6.0	20 930	697	11.5	36.3	368	−25	527	317	100 554	144 267	67.1	32.9
Monroe	1 429	17.6	2 067	2.0	5 969	691	12.4	19.0	217	−6	314	151	39 323	56 907	37.0	63.0
Montgomery	1 568	13.0	10 863	6.6	19 711	577	13.0	31.2	243	3	421	209	82 602	143 158	56.9	43.1
Muscatine	2 369	5.9	8 994	1.1	16 460	783	25.4	17.9	219	−1	280	190	73 835	94 298	63.8	36.2
O'Brien	3 000	19.4	35 286	17.1	53 905	977	13.8	26.4	358	−4	367	330	180 036	184 274	49.7	50.3
Osceola	1 847	25.4	25 581	29.2	35 064	649	14.6	26.7	241	−20	371	222	139 942	215 627	39.9	60.1
Page	2 095	12.4	5 549	2.4	21 918	845	16.1	26.7	309	−10	366	260	79 419	93 987	65.7	34.3
Palo Alto	2 234	20.9	24 555	19.6	46 832	787	13.6	32.7	328	−11	416	306	155 767	197 925	52.5	47.5
Plymouth	4 714	20.2	47 003	14.5	69 582	1 490	18.5	22.6	512	−6	344	456	238 391	159 994	41.4	58.6
Pocahontas	2 418	25.4	25 398	21.2	42 036	778	9.8	37.1	357	−2	459	339	138 598	178 147	71.9	28.1
Polk	2 088	.6	13 889	.1	23 728	800	36.9	18.0	226	−4	282	201	71 221	89 026	86.2	13.8
Pottawattamie	3 510	4.2	9 208	.9	31 703	1 325	21.2	30.6	537	−6	405	483	190 001	143 397	65.1	34.9
Poweshiek	2 557	13.4	18 739	5.7	32 204	934	15.8	25.5	335	−6	359	293	107 375	114 963	59.0	41.0
Ringgold	1 540	28.4	3 234	7.0	12 474	671	13.3	24.6	264	−30	393	210	48 665	72 526	38.2	61.8
Sac	2 683	21.8	14 338	12.8	48 729	813	15.0	28.3	345	−19	424	312	190 949	234 870	43.1	56.9
Scott	1 943	1.3	13 416	.4	21 266	799	24.8	18.4	225	−8	282	206	95 104	119 029	64.9	35.1
Shelby	3 156	23.9	15 160	10.3	34 909	921	14.0	26.6	342	−11	372	315	132 843	144 238	57.5	42.5
Sioux	5 522	18.5	74 367	14.8	118 222	1 752	24.2	16.8	494	−2	282	453	507 960	289 932	21.7	78.3
Story	2 333	3.1	21 391	1.5	36 913	946	23.4	25.4	341	10	360	317	130 832	138 300	71.7	28.3
Tama	3 392	19.5	20 512	10.5	35 856	1 152	18.1	22.3	396	−6	344	348	127 816	110 951	67.5	32.5
Taylor	1 807	25.4	10 948	18.6	19 775	746	11.1	23.1	291	13	391	229	62 200	83 378	49.0	51.0
Union	1 624	12.0	2 883	1.7	6 430	671	10.0	21.0	225	−11	330	109	39 032	58 170	51.1	48.9
Van Buren	1 694	22.1	1 791	2.8	11 068	807	13.8	19.2	257	16	319	172	43 027	53 317	57.5	42.5
Wapello	1 860	5.2	1 764	.4	9 806	781	20.2	16.4	208	13	267	160	44 604	57 111	65.0	35.0
Warren	2 823	7.8	2 511	1.0	11 975	1 214	27.5	13.3	300	−3	247	220	59 615	49 106	64.3	35.7
Washington	2 897	14.8	22 815	9.7	50 888	1 061	19.4	19.0	318	8	299	274	174 186	164 172	33.7	66.3
Wayne	1 560	22.1	850	1.6	10 219	729	12.2	27.2	286	4	393	219	36 564	50 156	59.3	40.7
Webster	2 307	5.7	8 367	1.4	40 975	937	15.3	30.5	413	4	440	386	166 258	177 436	68.0	32.0
Winnebago	1 702	14.0	17 455	10.2	20 375	607	20.8	28.2	242	10	398	227	78 356	129 087	81.7	18.3
Winneshiek	4 674	22.4	25 960	8.2	28 810	1 450	18.3	12.6	361	3	249	287	131 310	90 559	32.7	67.3
Woodbury	2 930	3.0	12 518	.7	28 006	1 306	20.8	24.2	497	55	381	428	151 324	115 868	59.3	40.7
Worth	1 897	23.7	21 751	27.6	31 279	608	20.1	30.1	228	3	375	209	76 626	126 030	75.0	25.0
Wright	2 127	14.9	21 660	11.1	49 966	717	14.6	39.2	350	−4	488	330	175 045	244 135	54.7	45.3
KANSAS	108 083	4.4	1 201 726	2.5	1 325 029	61 593	14.9	37.9	46 089	−583	748	30 021	9 207 130	149 483	35.0	65.0
Allen	1 254	8.6	−3 208	X	4 885	604	17.1	25.3	271	−12	449	182	33 031	54 687	65.7	34.3
Anderson	1 593	20.4	3 284	5.5	16 136	688	15.4	33.3	367	−11	533	242	53 256	77 407	57.1	42.9
Atchison	1 551	9.2	5 985	2.9	7 131	632	16.6	21.8	242	−3	383	178	35 657	56 419	66.5	33.5
Barber	776	13.2	−1 916	X	2 427	433	8.5	54.7	595	−44	1 374	194	48 183	111 277	34.9	65.1
Barton	917	3.1	15 208	3.8	15 651	742	10.9	44.9	613	32	826	488	185 656	250 210	28.5	71.5
Bourbon	1 298	8.7	−91	X	2 998	805	14.8	24.1	329	−8	409	158	29 604	36 775	42.0	58.0
Brown	1 742	15.7	17 697	12.2	16 250	599	15.5	33.6	333	−6	556	267	70 253	117 284	67.0	33.0
Butler	2 638	5.2	−688	X	3 606	1 256	20.9	26.7	759	−7	604	314	133 456	106 255	21.7	78.3
Chase	576	19.1	11 654	33.1	7 191	285	11.6	48.8	409	57	1 436	88	64 779	227 295	11.7	88.3
Chautauqua	529	12.0	883	3.1	656	376	12.2	43.1	391	4	1 041	61	29 016	77 170	23.5	76.5
Cherokee	1 396	6.5	10 882	5.4	15 758	725	26.3	19.0	269	−2	371	208	52 187	71 982	57.0	43.0
Cheyenne	493	15.2	10 965	27.6	3 620	398	4.8	61.1	562	−30	1 413	368	53 543	134 530	54.3	45.7
Clark	270	11.2	7 136	25.2	7 557	260	7.3	56.5	546	−20	2 098	196	105 342	405 162	12.0	88.0
Clay	1 627	17.8	16 661	16.2	24 645	546	11.5	44.0	369	−12	675	258	64 130	117 454	51.8	48.2
Cloud	862	7.8	10 639	9.4	10 856	545	14.3	44.0	393	−14	722	280	45 832	84 095	73.3	26.7
Coffey	1 207	14.4	1 652	1.1	9 994	555	11.0	32.1	307	−47	553	201	39 308	70 825	59.4	40.6
Comanche	281	12.1	767	4.2	943	256	5.5	65.6	504	17	1 969	168	29 110	113 711	40.0	60.0
Cowley	1 868	5.1	7 361	1.6	9 694	962	16.5	27.3	643	15	668	276	67 530	70 198	34.5	65.5
Crawford	1 935	5.4	4 377	.9	11 344	787	21.9	21.0	291	−12	369	189	35 206	44 734	66.0	34.0
Decatur	806	20.0	10 654	27.6	6 717	396	10.1	60.1	515	−11	1 301	322	67 589	170 679	37.8	62.2
Dickinson	1 593	8.4	18 783	8.9	22 591	893	13.0	38.1	514	Z	576	381	91 842	102 847	47.3	52.7

[1] For 1990 corrected population, see table B-1. Percent is based on 1990 uncorrected population because only total population is corrected. [2] For total earnings, see table B-8. [3] Most data are comparable between 1992 and 1997; however, it should be noted that farms with all acreage in Conservation or Wetlands Reserve Programs (excluded in 1992) are included in 1997, as are short rotation woody crops which includes Christmas trees and maple sap gathering (in Forestry in 1992). [4] Includes nursery and greenhouse crops. [5] Includes related products.

Sources: Farm Population—U.S. Census Bureau, 1990 Census of Population and Housing, Summary Tape File (STF) 3C on CD-ROM (related Internet site <http://homer.ssd.census.gov/cdrom/lookup>). Farm Earnings—U.S. Bureau of Economic Analysis, "Regional Economic Information System (REIS) 1969-1998" on CD-ROM (related Internet site <http://www.bea.doc.gov/bea/regional/reis/ca45/>). Agriculture—U.S. Department of Agriculture, National Agricultural Statistics Service, 1997 Census of Agriculture, Volume 1, Geographic Area Series, 1A, 1B, 1C CD-ROM Set (related Internet site <http://www.nass.usda.gov/census/>).

[Includes U.S., states, and 3,142 counties/county equivalents defined as of January 1, 1992. For changes to these areas since January 1, 1992, see appendix B. Geographic Information]

County	Farm population, 1990 Number	Farm population, 1990 Percent of total[1]	Farm earnings 1998 Total ($1,000)	Farm earnings 1998 Percent of total[2]	Farm earnings 1997 ($1,000)	Farms Number	Farms Percent Less than 50 acres	Farms Percent 500 acres or more	Land in farms (acres) Total acreage (1,000)	Land in farms Net change, 1992–1997[3] (1,000)	Land in farms Average size of farm	Land in farms Total cropland (1,000)	Value of farm products sold Total ($1,000)	Value of farm products sold Average per farm (dollars)	Value Percent from Crops[4]	Value Percent from Livestock and poultry[5]
KANSAS—Con.																
Doniphan	1 100	13.5	13 820	12.8	12 290	507	17.6	29.4	222	20	438	174	47 107	92 913	84.6	15.4
Douglas	1 716	2.1	2 568	.2	6 798	839	30.3	13.8	219	-4	260	147	38 885	46 347	55.6	44.4
Edwards	310	8.2	19 148	36.7	12 148	302	3.0	59.9	357	-47	1 181	283	81 908	271 219	50.2	49.8
Elk	553	16.6	413	2.1	1 505	383	12.0	41.0	331	7	864	78	20 518	53 572	20.4	79.6
Ellis	847	3.3	6 765	1.6	8 689	674	8.2	42.4	507	-40	753	313	50 199	74 479	30.9	69.1
Ellsworth	778	11.8	7 576	10.3	5 367	424	6.6	50.9	376	-67	886	234	29 181	68 823	62.4	37.6
Finney	876	2.6	34 921	5.5	29 099	520	9.4	62.3	761	16	1 464	631	479 824	922 738	21.7	78.3
Ford	822	3.0	24 266	4.8	23 586	692	11.1	49.3	669	-2	967	524	308 296	445 514	15.8	84.2
Franklin	2 067	9.4	2 847	1.1	7 770	956	22.7	16.9	303	-13	317	193	47 289	49 465	51.0	49.0
Geary	558	1.8	1 859	.2	5 208	223	17.5	41.7	154	-10	690	74	19 012	85 256	36.9	63.1
Gove	518	16.0	13 140	28.4	4 831	439	5.9	62.0	649	-23	1 478	389	121 705	277 232	24.2	75.8
Graham	391	11.0	11 654	26.9	3 759	382	6.5	56.0	486	-27	1 271	304	41 736	109 257	45.2	54.8
Grant	269	3.8	16 753	12.1	24 541	257	6.2	62.6	333	-9	1 294	277	291 279	1 133 381	14.8	85.2
Gray	767	14.2	47 582	42.0	29 880	461	5.4	66.4	556	38	1 206	469	373 688	810 603	20.8	79.2
Greeley	140	7.9	18 656	54.6	9 245	273	2.9	62.3	442	18	1 618	399	122 580	449 011	21.0	79.0
Greenwood	1 138	14.5	4 975	8.3	2 954	593	11.1	39.0	634	30	1 069	153	57 960	97 740	14.8	85.2
Hamilton	211	8.8	27 830	54.9	18 270	267	4.1	70.0	528	-5	1 976	397	175 865	658 670	12.5	87.5
Harper	700	9.8	7 192	10.2	13 711	529	9.6	46.3	461	-38	871	319	55 184	104 318	56.9	43.1
Harvey	1 739	5.6	13 629	2.8	25 428	779	23.2	27.5	321	1	412	282	71 397	91 652	58.4	41.6
Haskell	190	4.9	61 885	60.5	50 538	241	3.3	70.5	369	2	1 530	327	432 446	1 794 382	17.4	82.6
Hodgeman	339	15.6	11 491	39.6	12 220	359	4.5	67.7	485	5	1 351	344	96 423	268 588	20.2	79.8
Jackson	1 972	17.1	-3 212	X	-1 731	1 050	18.1	17.1	321	-19	306	190	28 913	27 536	47.9	52.1
Jefferson	1 985	12.5	4 030	3.8	3 747	1 018	22.1	13.6	269	-3	264	176	34 740	34 126	55.4	44.6
Jewell	1 088	25.6	17 946	40.2	15 534	579	7.4	47.5	459	-26	793	315	51 224	88 470	62.6	37.4
Johnson	963	.3	12 380	.1	7 930	604	41.6	11.9	136	-6	225	88	37 332	61 808	39.7	60.3
Kearny	479	11.9	21 337	40.4	21 752	271	2.6	66.8	526	8	1 940	381	184 714	681 601	24.5	75.5
Kingman	1 186	14.3	2 849	3.6	14 546	759	11.7	40.8	521	-23	686	351	56 075	73 880	61.4	38.6
Kiowa	356	9.7	6 500	17.1	5 111	318	3.8	58.2	442	42	1 390	268	47 386	149 013	57.5	42.5
Labette	1 772	7.5	3 993	1.3	8 158	901	17.8	22.3	331	-15	368	212	58 555	64 989	35.4	64.6
Lane	243	10.2	15 834	42.1	6 628	287	5.9	65.5	435	16	1 517	321	134 362	468 160	16.2	83.8
Leavenworth	2 182	3.4	2 624	.3	5 808	1 046	33.0	8.3	202	-5	193	126	42 483	40 615	66.2	33.8
Lincoln	629	17.2	7 161	22.5	5 605	454	8.1	51.8	428	-55	942	248	34 411	75 795	67.8	32.2
Linn	1 219	14.8	1 437	2.0	7 207	757	16.0	21.4	278	4	367	157	30 012	39 646	46.9	53.1
Logan	341	11.1	7 254	18.9	2 088	326	5.5	66.6	628	25	1 926	362	36 271	111 261	62.9	37.1
Lyon	2 022	5.8	3 694	.7	11 289	855	15.3	29.2	496	10	580	257	77 424	90 554	30.8	69.2
McPherson	2 191	8.0	20 379	4.4	39 351	1 163	16.2	30.8	523	-15	449	412	113 040	97 197	53.4	46.6
Marion	2 020	11.9	7 055	6.4	16 082	968	16.2	36.3	563	-25	582	368	81 302	83 990	45.6	54.4
Marshall	2 398	20.5	20 258	12.7	23 091	922	13.8	40.3	514	-59	558	358	70 264	76 208	63.1	36.9
Meade	306	7.2	32 857	46.7	15 183	416	6.5	62.0	555	-42	1 333	349	112 668	270 837	45.9	54.1
Miami	2 060	8.8	137	.1	-331	1 245	33.5	10.5	280	-7	225	175	39 902	32 050	45.2	54.8
Mitchell	650	9.0	16 322	13.8	16 187	487	11.5	54.2	455	-25	933	357	86 545	177 710	49.3	50.7
Montgomery	1 387	3.6	6 677	1.4	12 604	964	19.7	16.2	328	5	341	184	45 525	47 225	37.3	62.7
Morris	969	15.6	5 119	9.6	5 891	489	13.3	41.3	396	-14	810	186	47 229	96 583	37.1	62.9
Morton	157	4.5	4 062	7.4	8 951	233	3.4	59.2	422	-5	1 813	268	57 746	247 837	35.4	64.6
Nemaha	2 717	26.0	23 620	16.7	32 974	1 007	12.3	28.6	418	-24	415	305	90 606	89 976	37.0	63.0
Neosho	1 296	7.6	-1 200	X	5 121	722	18.8	26.0	345	18	478	221	37 946	52 557	52.3	47.7
Ness	592	14.7	3 831	8.3	4 312	516	3.1	62.6	623	-45	1 208	414	34 357	66 583	56.2	43.8
Norton	592	10.0	11 435	14.6	7 468	399	10.5	56.6	479	13	1 200	289	41 674	104 446	50.0	50.0
Osage	1 915	12.6	2 259	2.3	6 281	890	18.4	22.2	360	11	404	221	40 717	45 749	58.9	41.1
Osborne	660	13.6	8 032	16.5	9 799	465	6.0	55.5	505	-42	1 087	306	40 964	88 095	61.4	38.6
Ottawa	613	10.9	6 654	15.3	9 414	498	12.9	45.0	400	20	803	238	61 877	124 251	44.4	55.6
Pawnee	668	8.8	13 306	12.8	16 115	425	6.8	51.3	480	31	1 129	388	117 557	276 605	36.1	63.9
Phillips	848	12.9	14 005	15.7	11 428	501	10.6	54.1	555	-27	1 107	322	44 760	89 341	51.9	48.1
Pottawatomie	1 464	9.1	4 334	2.0	7 151	787	15.1	32.8	443	-8	563	199	51 811	65 834	33.4	66.6
Pratt	553	5.7	8 680	6.4	11 594	434	6.5	52.3	437	5	1 008	365	147 530	339 931	32.1	67.9
Rawlins	924	27.1	8 641	24.6	2 603	431	3.9	70.8	647	6	1 500	407	38 079	88 350	68.8	31.2
Reno	2 243	3.6	15 592	1.6	24 984	1 363	18.6	29.9	662	-39	486	500	133 987	98 303	44.0	56.0
Republic	1 500	23.1	7 583	11.5	11 210	684	9.1	42.0	428	-15	626	321	92 892	135 807	48.8	51.2
Rice	562	5.3	16 035	14.4	22 148	519	12.1	47.8	458	25	882	346	96 849	186 607	46.8	53.2
Riley	986	1.5	501	.1	1 423	468	20.9	31.2	238	10	508	122	30 199	64 528	45.9	54.1
Rooks	641	10.6	6 816	11.3	2 406	435	9.4	53.6	570	-9	1 309	330	41 103	94 490	47.8	52.2
Rush	477	12.4	1 789	4.9	3 572	486	4.7	47.3	412	-15	848	329	29 523	60 747	72.5	27.5
Russell	430	5.5	6 630	7.5	3 661	494	7.1	45.3	429	-34	869	261	27 357	55 379	59.8	40.2
Saline	708	1.4	8 473	.8	12 684	720	15.3	33.1	414	10	575	284	45 312	62 933	67.7	32.3
Scott	223	4.2	33 546	38.0	32 500	335	10.1	63.0	476	-8	1 422	394	451 264	1 347 057	9.5	90.5
Sedgwick	2 734	.7	9 164	.1	27 065	1 395	30.9	21.9	540	29	387	413	81 798	58 637	70.0	30.0
Seward	412	2.2	27 645	6.8	39 466	251	10.4	59.4	328	Z	1 306	237	256 618	1 022 382	13.4	86.6
Shawnee	1 543	1.0	5 483	.2	7 305	823	30.6	14.2	224	-3	272	148	29 103	35 362	73.7	26.3
Sheridan	490	16.1	25 550	45.9	14 405	442	5.2	63.1	507	-28	1 148	364	79 802	180 548	55.9	44.1

[1] For 1990 corrected population, see table B-1. Percent is based on 1990 uncorrected population because only total population is corrected. [2] For total earnings, see table B-8. [3] Most data are comparable between 1992 and 1997; however, it should be noted that farms with all acreage in Conservation or Wetlands Reserve Programs (excluded in 1992) are included in 1997, as are short rotation woody crops which includes Christmas trees and maple sap gathering (in Forestry in 1992). [4] Includes nursery and greenhouse crops. [5] Includes related products.

Sources: Farm Population—U.S. Census Bureau, 1990 Census of Population and Housing, Summary Tape File (STF) 3C on CD-ROM (related Internet site <http://homer.ssd.census.gov/cdrom/lookup>). Farm Earnings—U.S. Bureau of Economic Analysis, "Regional Economic Information System (REIS) 1969-1998" on CD-ROM (related Internet site <http://www.bea.doc.gov/bea/regional/reis/ca45/>). Agriculture—U.S. Department of Agriculture, National Agricultural Statistics Service, 1997 Census of Agriculture, Volume 1, Geographic Area Series, 1A, 1B, 1C CD-ROM Set (related Internet site <http://www.nass.usda.gov/census/>).

Table B-10. Counties — **Farm Population, Farm Earnings, and Agriculture**–Con.

[Includes U.S., states, and 3,142 counties/county equivalents defined as of January 1, 1992. For changes to these areas since January 1, 1992, see appendix B. Geographic Information]

County	Farm population, 1990 Number	Farm population, 1990 Percent of total[1]	Farm earnings 1998 Total ($1,000)	Farm earnings 1998 Percent of total[2]	Farm earnings 1997 ($1,000)	Farms Number	Farms Percent Less than 50 acres	Farms Percent 500 acres or more	Land in farms Total acreage (1,000)	Land in farms Net change, 1992–1997[3] (1,000)	Land in farms Average size of farm	Land in farms Total cropland (1,000)	Value of farm products sold Total ($1,000)	Value Average per farm (dollars)	Value Percent from Crops[4]	Value Percent from Livestock and poultry[5]
KANSAS—Con.																
Sherman	514	7.4	20 132	19.7	10 860	478	4.8	63.0	653	33	1 365	527	82 964	173 565	64.5	35.5
Smith	1 038	20.4	13 978	27.9	11 326	557	11.7	54.9	492	−45	883	344	51 974	93 311	55.9	44.1
Stafford	552	10.3	21 351	32.9	18 781	475	7.2	52.4	435	−2	915	351	100 008	210 543	46.3	53.7
Stanton	299	12.8	27 894	56.8	35 405	253	4.3	68.0	400	−12	1 582	344	118 707	469 198	38.6	61.4
Stevens	331	6.6	29 862	31.9	23 739	304	6.3	62.5	512	61	1 684	408	154 227	507 326	44.4	55.6
Sumner	2 556	9.9	10 268	4.3	31 625	1 064	15.1	39.1	667	−20	627	555	89 103	83 743	80.1	19.9
Thomas	792	9.6	29 355	21.0	18 687	553	6.1	61.5	679	−23	1 229	584	117 634	212 720	53.4	46.6
Trego	598	16.2	517	1.6	−210	399	4.8	63.7	462	−22	1 159	302	41 008	102 777	33.5	66.5
Wabaunsee	1 199	18.2	1 545	3.8	3 050	597	12.7	36.2	478	55	801	155	41 235	69 070	30.4	69.6
Wallace	354	19.4	8 896	38.4	4 688	277	6.5	57.4	480	8	1 733	266	36 042	130 116	60.7	39.3
Washington	1 699	24.0	16 610	26.1	22 448	780	14.6	41.0	536	15	688	348	84 751	108 655	42.6	57.4
Wichita	418	15.2	37 043	61.4	44 246	310	7.1	67.4	450	6	1 450	363	273 853	883 397	13.5	86.5
Wilson	1 277	12.4	−1 771	X	7 520	541	12.6	33.6	301	−11	557	176	35 259	65 174	65.9	34.1
Woodson	698	17.0	2 547	9.7	6 391	371	14.6	38.8	254	−11	686	122	26 907	72 526	45.8	54.2
Wyandotte	151	.1	747	Z	216	189	57.7	3.7	22	Z	118	17	4 658	24 646	68.2	31.9
KENTUCKY	174 204	4.7	1 065 729	1.7	1 065 618	82 273	33.9	5.9	13 334	−332	162	8 549	3 064 460	37 247	51.5	48.5
Adair	3 086	20.1	11 840	9.7	9 869	1 350	34.6	2.4	160	−17	119	98	29 640	21 956	37.3	62.7
Allen	1 962	13.4	2 162	1.3	8 460	1 097	30.5	4.3	159	3	145	96	35 124	32 018	22.7	77.3
Anderson	1 284	8.8	774	.6	897	691	32.9	2.0	84	−6	121	53	11 397	16 493	54.2	45.8
Ballard	793	10.0	6 621	4.6	10 967	482	29.7	12.4	119	7	246	96	34 703	71 998	62.8	37.2
Barren	4 918	14.5	23 947	3.9	18 412	2 000	36.4	4.0	250	1	125	185	59 789	29 895	42.6	57.4
Bath	1 565	16.1	7 614	12.0	6 290	799	30.0	6.4	129	−4	161	82	22 751	28 474	66.5	33.5
Bell	90	.3	−160	X	−132	54	44.4	–	4	−2	68	2	127	2 352	24.4	75.6
Boone	1 350	2.3	2 617	.1	2 551	691	49.1	3.5	80	−1	116	48	15 856	22 946	75.2	24.8
Bourbon	2 059	10.7	72 944	27.1	61 265	910	33.8	10.3	197	−10	216	141	89 869	98 757	31.8	68.2
Boyd	202	.4	294	Z	385	207	35.7	2.9	26	−2	126	11	2 271	10 971	20.3	79.7
Boyle	1 539	6.0	7 057	1.4	9 778	673	40.1	4.9	95	−13	141	66	27 040	40 178	38.9	61.1
Bracken	1 426	18.4	7 226	14.2	6 034	656	26.4	3.0	92	−7	140	54	17 639	26 889	80.0	20.0
Breathitt	541	3.4	−380	X	(6)	193	33.2	9.3	47	4	242	6	1 419	7 352	83.9	16.1
Breckinridge	2 908	17.8	6 348	6.7	9 429	1 379	28.1	7.0	268	1	194	147	31 955	23 173	62.0	38.0
Bullitt	541	1.1	−2 340	X	−1 570	564	49.8	2.5	57	−4	100	32	7 583	13 445	50.6	49.4
Butler	961	8.6	217	.2	9 700	700	20.0	9.7	151	11	216	79	21 536	30 766	39.9	60.1
Caldwell	951	7.2	4 860	4.0	8 859	608	19.2	12.5	148	19	243	99	22 631	37 222	70.2	29.7
Calloway	1 867	6.1	14 939	3.0	18 823	749	39.3	9.9	146	9	195	117	49 112	65 570	69.1	30.9
Campbell	967	1.2	−1 384	X	−919	503	36.4	.6	45	2	90	25	5 441	10 817	59.1	40.9
Carlisle	677	12.9	4 961	15.2	7 951	323	26.6	9.9	90	11	279	74	24 949	77 241	65.7	34.3
Carroll	879	9.5	2 813	1.3	3 459	324	25.9	6.5	60	−1	185	29	8 693	26 830	77.8	22.2
Carter	1 804	7.4	2 210	1.5	1 183	872	31.0	2.5	109	−4	125	42	9 373	10 749	67.8	32.2
Casey	2 685	18.9	11 593	11.1	10 910	1 332	32.0	4.5	191	−2	143	95	28 805	21 625	51.2	48.8
Christian	2 281	3.3	10 684	.6	23 888	1 158	25.0	12.3	310	10	267	230	82 557	71 293	76.5	23.5
Clark	1 608	5.5	13 583	3.2	14 590	847	41.3	7.9	147	2	173	102	35 471	41 878	45.2	54.8
Clay	1 200	5.5	989	.7	1 203	402	33.3	6.0	57	−11	142	16	5 297	13 177	84.3	15.7
Clinton	1 218	13.3	4 563	7.2	4 067	639	38.0	2.8	78	3	122	44	10 978	17 180	43.1	56.9
Crittenden	881	9.6	(6)	Z	1 399	599	18.2	9.2	142	16	236	85	9 884	16 501	50.3	49.7
Cumberland	899	13.3	2 569	6.0	2 383	524	28.6	9.7	108	Z	207	40	7 611	14 525	62.1	37.9
Daviess	3 243	3.7	7 249	.5	19 609	1 042	43.2	11.8	251	1	241	207	71 279	68 406	82.1	17.9
Edmonson	1 243	12.0	2 004	4.4	2 766	706	35.0	3.4	90	−3	127	53	10 713	15 174	40.9	59.1
Elliott	900	13.9	1 951	8.7	1 592	439	28.0	3.0	58	−3	131	21	4 041	9 205	81.5	18.5
Estill	807	5.5	−124	X	210	432	27.8	4.4	62	−7	144	28	4 520	10 463	72.0	28.1
Fayette	1 118	.5	103 943	1.6	70 316	745	42.7	8.6	136	−11	182	91	139 292	186 969	16.2	83.8
Fleming	2 395	19.5	11 425	10.8	8 919	1 132	27.7	6.4	189	−5	167	125	37 044	32 724	47.2	52.8
Floyd	95	.2	−200	X	−120	59	44.1	3.4	7	−4	124	2	508	8 610	84.1	16.1
Franklin	1 627	3.7	5 846	.5	4 445	675	35.0	2.8	83	−3	122	51	15 871	23 513	71.1	28.9
Fulton	389	4.7	4 263	4.3	8 529	162	22.8	32.1	94	−3	578	83	23 260	143 580	94.2	5.8
Gallatin	399	7.4	1 950	2.8	2 472	253	28.9	4.3	36	−5	144	21	6 746	26 664	78.3	21.7
Garrard	1 802	15.6	7 756	9.2	9 371	880	32.6	5.0	125	−13	142	86	29 852	33 923	49.7	50.3
Grant	2 277	14.5	1 247	.9	1 743	936	30.7	2.6	115	−12	123	71	15 554	16 618	76.2	23.8
Graves	2 633	7.8	36 089	8.5	32 431	1 371	35.8	8.2	237	27	173	186	114 700	83 662	37.6	62.4
Grayson	3 121	14.8	8 128	3.7	8 924	1 412	27.8	3.9	209	3	148	130	32 844	23 261	36.7	63.3
Green	2 504	24.1	7 554	12.7	5 987	1 059	31.2	2.6	129	−6	122	85	23 858	22 529	53.9	46.1
Greenup	1 369	3.7	5 039	1.6	4 105	733	33.8	3.4	98	−3	134	37	8 303	11 327	64.4	35.6
Hancock	786	10.0	1 738	.7	4 809	449	30.5	3.8	65	−5	145	37	12 088	26 922	69.7	30.3
Hardin	3 536	4.0	−196	X	6 737	1 637	41.7	4.9	223	−3	136	158	38 948	23 792	58.8	41.2
Harlan	131	.4	(6)	Z	(6)	27	48.1	–	2	−3	86	1	184	6 815	35.9	64.1
Harrison	2 270	14.0	5 739	3.4	5 772	1 079	27.7	5.6	169	−9	157	113	28 984	26 862	72.1	27.9
Hart	2 971	20.0	16 100	12.7	12 254	1 352	26.8	2.7	186	−14	138	113	35 089	25 953	56.3	43.7

[1] For 1990 corrected population, see table B-1. Percent is based on 1990 uncorrected population because only total population is corrected. [2] For total earnings, see table B-8. [3] Most data are comparable between 1992 and 1997; however, it should be noted that farms with all acreage in Conservation or Wetlands Reserve Programs (excluded in 1992) are included in 1997, as are short rotation woody crops which includes Christmas trees and maple sap gathering (in Forestry in 1992). [4] Includes nursery and greenhouse crops. [5] Includes related products. [6] Less than $50,000.

Sources: Farm Population—U.S. Census Bureau, 1990 Census of Population and Housing, Summary Tape File (STF) 3C on CD-ROM (related Internet site <http://homer.ssd.census.gov/cdrom/lookup>). Farm Earnings—U.S. Bureau of Economic Analysis, "Regional Economic Information System (REIS) 1969-1998" on CD-ROM (related Internet site <http://www.bea.doc.gov/bea/regional/reis/ca45/>). Agriculture—U.S. Department of Agriculture, National Agricultural Statistics Service, 1997 Census of Agriculture, Volume 1, Geographic Area Series, 1A, 1B, 1C CD-ROM Set (related Internet site <http://www.nass.usda.gov/census/>).

[Includes U.S., states, and 3,142 counties/county equivalents defined as of January 1, 1992. For changes to these areas since January 1, 1992, see appendix B. Geographic Information]

County	Farm population, 1990 Number	Farm population, 1990 Percent of total[1]	Farm earnings 1998 Total ($1,000)	Farm earnings 1998 Percent of total[2]	Farm earnings 1997 ($1,000)	Farms Number	Farms Percent Less than 50 acres	Farms Percent 500 acres or more	Land in farms Total acreage (1,000)	Land in farms Net change, 1992–1997[3] (1,000)	Land in farms Average size of farm	Land in farms Total cropland (1,000)	Value Total ($1,000)	Value Average per farm (dollars)	Value Percent Crops[4]	Value Percent Livestock and poultry[5]
KENTUCKY—Con.																
Henderson	1 246	2.9	17 262	2.4	7 975	526	37.3	18.3	196	−2	373	163	50 142	95 327	78.4	21.6
Henry	2 043	15.9	15 420	14.1	12 293	955	28.8	5.2	149	−11	156	101	36 835	38 571	69.9	30.1
Hickman	823	14.8	16 462	31.2	8 688	294	28.2	21.1	115	16	390	101	43 958	149 517	58.4	41.6
Hopkins	996	2.2	1 729	.3	6 259	538	26.2	11.2	141	−4	263	105	27 411	50 950	62.9	37.1
Jackson	1 359	11.4	1 267	1.6	1 929	689	38.8	2.2	74	−7	107	34	9 326	13 536	62.3	37.7
Jefferson	432	.1	3 159	Z	4 513	475	61.5	1.7	34	−11	72	20	12 295	25 884	78.6	21.4
Jessamine	1 502	4.9	49 836	11.3	34 929	754	47.9	4.5	89	−10	117	61	66 452	88 133	22.0	78.0
Johnson	340	1.5	−338	X	−81	182	36.3	1.1	20	−3	112	5	1 259	6 918	81.1	18.9
Kenton	688	.5	−753	X	−832	442	45.9	1.1	38	−6	85	23	5 094	11 525	61.7	38.3
Knott	185	1.0	−200	X	−166	21	23.8	9.5	4	Z	177	1	64	3 048	18.8	81.3
Knox	571	1.9	842	.4	698	322	33.2	5.3	46	Z	144	19	3 173	9 854	64.8	35.2
Larue	1 999	17.1	4 739	6.3	5 654	806	35.2	5.1	117	−4	145	84	24 766	30 727	51.4	48.6
Laurel	2 134	4.9	2 590	.4	3 198	1 083	48.3	1.6	96	−4	88	55	14 402	13 298	61.7	38.3
Lawrence	401	2.9	−628	X	−558	297	25.6	4.0	49	Z	165	12	2 009	6 764	75.3	24.6
Lee	371	5.0	387	.8	433	161	32.3	5.0	24	3	149	9	1 779	11 050	67.1	32.9
Leslie	168	1.2	86	.1	96	17	41.2	5.9	3	1	157	D	114	6 706	89.5	10.5
Letcher	123	.5	−98	X	−76	31	29.0	–	3	−1	87	Z	59	1 903	11.9	88.1
Lewis	1 611	12.4	7 662	10.9	6 574	774	26.1	7.1	143	−17	185	47	14 264	18 429	73.9	26.1
Lincoln	3 417	17.0	14 807	10.8	15 119	1 258	40.5	5.3	170	−4	135	110	38 573	30 662	44.0	56.0
Livingston	659	7.3	1 834	2.2	2 634	405	15.1	14.1	117	−2	290	74	9 938	24 538	39.7	60.3
Logan	3 087	12.6	7 273	2.2	18 232	1 203	26.2	10.4	273	−5	227	206	63 634	52 896	75.3	24.7
Lyon	429	6.5	539	1.0	1 607	249	22.1	7.6	48	−1	194	33	6 114	24 554	66.3	33.7
McCracken	1 169	1.9	2 743	.2	3 799	457	48.1	5.3	67	4	146	55	16 468	36 035	69.7	30.3
McCreary	116	.7	−673	X	−647	108	38.9	.9	11	−3	101	5	515	4 769	25.4	74.6
McLean	1 068	11.1	20 903	26.7	15 678	422	32.2	17.5	134	−1	318	113	53 771	127 419	49.4	50.6
Madison	2 666	4.6	8 249	1.0	13 026	1 444	40.4	6.0	222	−26	153	140	44 288	30 670	48.2	51.8
Magoffin	602	4.6	689	.9	903	373	42.1	2.1	41	−4	109	10	2 682	7 190	89.7	10.3
Marion	2 641	16.0	13 441	8.1	14 212	983	27.4	5.3	166	−9	169	101	33 590	34 171	43.4	56.6
Marshall	1 294	4.8	1 926	.4	1 563	673	37.6	4.0	89	13	133	62	17 746	26 368	44.1	55.9
Martin	42	.3	−74	X	−51	9	11.1	–	2	−3	248	D	50	5 556	14.0	86.0
Mason	1 971	11.8	10 786	3.8	7 870	751	28.6	6.4	131	−13	175	92	30 991	41 266	61.7	38.3
Meade	1 862	7.7	1 688	1.3	3 292	841	41.3	5.4	121	1	143	80	17 578	20 901	51.0	49.0
Menifee	1 025	20.1	1 392	4.5	1 517	346	34.1	2.6	38	−5	110	16	3 802	10 988	74.0	26.0
Mercer	2 079	10.9	6 279	2.6	5 824	976	38.2	3.2	126	−7	129	92	30 601	31 353	48.9	51.1
Metcalfe	2 090	23.3	12 093	15.0	11 684	950	28.2	3.5	134	−3	141	71	24 993	26 308	43.2	56.8
Monroe	1 587	13.9	9 900	8.9	7 952	973	31.1	7.0	167	1	172	91	25 602	26 312	36.4	63.6
Montgomery	1 347	6.9	6 089	2.3	6 668	734	36.4	6.0	112	−2	152	79	22 680	30 899	63.3	36.7
Morgan	1 797	15.4	2 096	2.3	2 487	698	30.1	5.9	111	6	159	41	9 768	13 994	76.5	23.5
Muhlenberg	937	3.0	18 055	5.5	14 342	559	25.9	8.9	115	−3	205	72	32 419	57 995	29.2	70.8
Nelson	2 507	8.4	1 469	.4	8 218	1 249	37.2	5.0	176	−15	141	118	38 646	30 942	37.0	63.0
Nicholas	1 219	18.1	4 666	9.6	4 185	567	26.6	8.8	106	−6	187	67	16 024	28 261	69.3	30.7
Ohio	1 593	7.5	18 915	10.3	15 408	943	28.5	5.5	162	2	172	94	36 980	39 215	36.0	64.0
Oldham	827	2.5	5 287	1.3	4 947	392	42.1	9.7	71	−14	180	46	16 085	41 033	46.3	53.7
Owen	2 166	24.0	5 757	9.3	5 346	803	20.3	7.8	150	−26	187	85	22 337	27 817	74.0	26.0
Owsley	720	14.3	1 282	6.4	1 280	246	38.2	3.7	32	−4	129	9	2 914	11 846	92.5	7.5
Pendleton	1 647	13.7	3 909	4.4	4 180	816	24.9	4.3	117	−11	143	67	14 793	18 129	72.8	27.2
Perry	222	.7	60	Z	107	29	41.4	20.7	7	2	234	3	457	15 759	51.4	48.6
Pike	488	.7	−235	X	−192	37	10.8	8.1	6	Z	158	1	176	4 757	31.3	68.8
Powell	503	4.3	1 040	1.2	1 370	231	35.1	4.3	28	−5	123	12	2 558	11 074	70.6	29.4
Pulaski	3 912	7.9	12 727	1.9	11 786	1 958	39.1	2.2	215	−3	110	138	35 952	18 362	45.1	54.9
Robertson	762	35.9	2 043	18.9	2 126	272	18.8	5.5	48	−5	176	26	6 677	24 548	75.8	24.2
Rockcastle	1 342	9.1	2 115	2.3	2 113	771	39.4	3.9	94	1	121	45	10 417	13 511	58.6	41.4
Rowan	761	3.7	1 892	.8	1 871	413	44.3	2.2	42	−7	103	21	4 430	10 726	75.6	24.4
Russell	2 036	13.8	8 099	5.7	10 266	943	46.7	2.3	95	3	101	64	27 945	29 634	32.9	67.1
Scott	2 000	8.4	61 739	5.4	53 215	851	35.5	8.2	146	−8	171	100	65 483	76 948	40.5	59.5
Shelby	3 505	14.1	17 930	4.0	18 554	1 399	38.7	4.6	199	−31	142	140	56 164	40 146	59.2	40.8
Simpson	944	6.2	876	.4	8 304	582	35.2	8.2	115	−3	198	98	32 107	55 167	77.1	22.9
Spencer	1 203	17.7	4 779	10.8	4 935	592	36.0	3.9	81	−13	137	56	19 997	33 779	60.2	39.8
Taylor	2 045	9.7	3 408	1.4	4 730	971	39.8	2.6	112	−16	116	73	24 457	25 187	47.7	52.3
Todd	1 744	15.9	22 972	20.1	26 906	679	21.2	15.3	190	25	280	144	69 686	102 630	59.5	40.5
Trigg	779	7.5	1 193	1.3	6 321	411	28.2	13.4	117	5	285	81	26 535	64 562	67.4	32.6
Trimble	1 121	18.4	3 285	9.4	3 294	526	33.7	2.3	64	−7	122	34	10 812	20 555	83.5	16.5
Union	1 041	6.3	4 170	2.0	14 040	352	23.3	31.3	212	15	601	185	58 623	166 543	81.9	18.1
Warren	3 736	4.9	7 079	.5	19 968	1 819	41.9	5.5	255	2	140	171	65 241	35 866	37.8	62.2
Washington	2 142	20.5	13 740	12.5	11 654	1 050	26.2	3.4	157	−8	150	107	32 584	31 032	52.1	47.9
Wayne	1 526	8.7	24 110	15.8	19 014	803	36.6	6.7	131	−4	164	60	49 995	62 260	18.5	81.5
Webster	1 025	7.3	3 146	2.0	6 447	455	25.3	14.9	136	−4	300	110	31 584	69 415	72.7	27.3
Whitley	233	.7	−1 021	X	−851	368	31.5	2.2	44	−1	118	24	3 141	8 535	35.5	64.5
Wolfe	939	14.4	1 793	4.5	1 657	382	31.7	6.8	57	−4	148	14	3 876	10 147	84.5	15.5
Woodford	1 891	9.5	121 381	25.5	100 095	678	36.9	8.8	123	−1	181	79	115 401	170 208	18.6	81.4

[1] For 1990 corrected population, see table B-1. Percent is based on 1990 uncorrected population because only total population is corrected. [2] For total earnings, see table B-8. [3] Most data are comparable between 1992 and 1997; however, it should be noted that farms with all acreage in Conservation or Wetlands Reserve Programs (excluded in 1992) are included in 1997, as are short rotation woody crops which includes Christmas trees and maple sap gathering (in Forestry in 1992). [4] Includes nursery and greenhouse crops. [5] Includes related products.

Sources: Farm Population—U.S. Census Bureau, 1990 Census of Population and Housing, Summary Tape File (STF) 3C on CD-ROM (related Internet site <http://homer.ssd.census.gov/cdrom/lookup>). Farm Earnings—U.S. Bureau of Economic Analysis, "Regional Economic Information System (REIS) 1969-1998" on CD-ROM (related Internet site <http://www.bea.doc.gov/bea/regional/reis/ca45/>). Agriculture—U.S. Department of Agriculture, National Agricultural Statistics Service, 1997 Census of Agriculture, Volume 1, Geographic Area Series, 1A, 1B, 1C CD-ROM Set (related Internet site <http://www.nass.usda.gov/census/>).

[Includes U.S., states, and 3,142 counties/county equivalents defined as of January 1, 1992. For changes to these areas since January 1, 1992, see appendix B. Geographic Information]

County	Farm population, 1990 Number	Per-cent of total[1]	Farm earnings 1998 Total ($1,000)	Per-cent of total[2]	1997 ($1,000)	Farms Number	Percent– Less than 50 acres	Percent– 500 acres or more	Land in farms (acres) Total acreage (1,000)	Net change, 1992–1997[3] (1,000)	Aver-age size of farm	Total cropland (1,000)	Value of farm products sold Total ($1,000)	Average per farm (dollars)	Percent from– Crops[4]	Percent from– Live-stock and poultry[5]
LOUISIANA	40 103	1.0	380 617	.6	573 615	23 823	34.1	17.3	7 877	39	331	5 331	2 031 277	85 265	69.5	30.5
Acadia	1 291	2.3	18 202	4.2	24 992	638	34.5	29.0	273	5	428	240	66 593	104 378	96.0	4.0
Allen	527	2.5	5 335	2.3	3 984	343	36.2	17.5	116	–2	337	58	11 474	33 452	84.5	15.5
Ascension	586	1.0	3 466	.3	2 979	279	53.8	8.6	55	–8	198	32	15 277	54 756	90.1	9.9
Assumption	319	1.4	7 835	4.1	6 620	102	36.3	44.1	64	–4	628	53	32 066	314 373	93.4	6.6
Avoyelles	1 590	4.1	(6)	Z	18 477	827	31.9	17.9	259	3	314	211	61 085	73 863	93.2	6.8
Beauregard	793	2.6	1 632	.5	3 110	676	32.8	10.7	165	29	244	62	10 947	16 194	37.1	62.9
Bienville	498	3.1	2 655	2.3	2 943	221	25.3	7.2	47	–5	212	16	5 875	26 584	9.5	90.5
Bossier	481	.6	–2 558	X	–936	372	35.2	18.8	111	1	300	56	8 909	23 949	42.9	57.1
Caddo	565	.2	–539	X	5 094	473	33.8	17.3	173	2	365	94	27 441	58 015	69.3	30.7
Calcasieu	739	.4	2 728	.1	3 191	749	36.5	17.5	312	–16	416	140	20 453	27 307	68.6	31.4
Caldwell	478	4.9	–1 174	X	3 843	217	28.6	14.7	70	4	324	49	11 306	52 101	88.3	11.7
Cameron	258	2.8	1 557	.9	262	384	23.4	22.9	245	–13	638	75	11 058	28 797	64.3	35.7
Catahoula	595	5.4	9 228	12.2	12 693	381	22.0	31.0	229	–22	600	171	42 950	112 730	90.8	9.2
Claiborne	356	2.0	11 864	8.7	13 279	261	23.0	10.3	58	–5	224	22	36 465	139 713	2.5	97.5
Concordia	412	2.0	3 359	2.3	17 627	292	17.5	50.7	253	26	867	221	60 844	208 370	88.2	11.8
De Soto	554	2.2	9 009	3.6	8 171	516	26.0	15.7	157	9	304	50	19 430	37 655	7.3	92.7
East Baton Rouge	516	.1	–2 322	X	–2 541	441	44.4	7.5	66	–13	150	32	8 266	18 744	37.9	62.1
East Carroll	417	4.3	9 845	15.1	17 986	244	15.6	50.8	210	16	862	186	62 163	254 766	98.3	1.7
East Feliciana	410	2.1	2 529	1.5	2 441	386	29.5	14.2	115	–22	298	40	7 540	19 534	16.2	83.9
Evangeline.............	740	2.2	14 775	6.2	22 481	588	35.5	11.7	181	4	308	147	44 482	75 650	85.1	14.9
Franklin	1 939	8.7	13 370	9.0	29 051	732	24.7	21.7	269	4	367	220	88 027	120 255	77.1	22.9
Grant	239	1.4	–1 409	X	2 152	186	32.8	13.4	49	4	261	28	6 037	32 457	85.9	14.1
Iberia.................	783	1.1	11 659	1.1	10 302	298	47.0	22.1	103	–8	344	90	49 797	167 104	98.1	1.9
Iberville	575	1.9	6 432	1.0	7 326	161	21.1	35.4	96	15	599	71	37 183	230 950	94.1	5.9
Jackson	306	1.9	7 637	5.3	8 651	183	43.7	1.6	16	–1	86	6	25 452	139 082	1.1	98.9
Jefferson..............	47	Z	1 687	Z	2 106	62	54.8	–	5	1	78	2	2 353	37 952	16.4	83.5
Jefferson Davis	928	3.0	16 015	7.4	16 979	576	26.2	34.9	304	12	527	252	52 360	90 903	93.1	6.9
Lafayette	801	.5	3 130	.1	6 341	577	62.4	7.3	88	Z	152	74	24 007	41 607	88.7	11.3
Lafourche	667	.8	6 470	.6	6 033	398	33.7	17.6	135	2	339	69	32 207	80 922	83.1	16.9
La Salle	112	.8	290	.2	111	160	41.9	5.0	27	Z	170	11	1 146	7 163	40.3	59.6
Lincoln	478	1.1	9 823	1.7	10 909	287	27.9	3.8	41	–17	144	20	35 276	122 913	4.2	95.8
Livingston.............	626	.9	1 762	.4	1 759	345	58.3	2.3	40	4	117	19	8 594	24 910	19.2	80.8
Madison	571	4.6	6 361	6.8	13 586	279	11.5	53.4	266	20	955	237	63 455	227 437	99.2	.8
Morehouse.............	386	1.2	8 104	3.0	25 515	402	18.2	40.3	258	16	642	224	78 408	195 045	97.1	2.9
Natchitoches	753	2.1	11 402	2.8	19 818	530	23.2	17.5	189	6	356	109	50 068	94 468	35.1	64.9
Orleans................	27	Z	–	–	–	10	100.0	–	Z	Z	4	Z	21	2 100	D	D
Ouachita...............	595	.4	7 022	.3	10 512	377	37.9	11.9	89	14	236	60	25 729	68 247	64.5	35.5
Plaquemines	247	1.0	2 287	.3	1 032	127	64.6	9.4	37	–9	289	5	4 653	36 638	71.9	28.1
Pointe Coupee	579	2.6	914	.5	12 815	402	30.6	25.9	201	8	500	160	53 662	133 488	90.3	9.7
Rapides	1 490	1.1	3 649	.2	8 308	817	39.4	11.9	194	–16	238	122	55 175	67 534	88.5	11.5
Red River..............	217	2.3	836	1.1	4 135	218	23.9	20.2	113	16	519	51	10 925	50 115	68.3	31.7
Richland	1 467	7.1	2 365	1.5	16 215	483	19.0	35.0	237	–10	490	197	57 475	118 996	94.3	5.7
Sabine	655	2.9	18 757	9.1	20 214	373	30.6	5.4	57	–1	152	24	53 434	143 255	.6	99.4
St. Bernard	19	Z	309	.1	300	27	59.3	7.4	3	–3	126	2	425	15 741	D	D
St. Charles............	18	Z	–68	X	–188	71	32.4	11.3	21	–2	301	9	5 065	71 338	87.5	12.5
St. Helena	518	5.2	11 089	18.9	11 752	333	30.6	4.5	66	15	197	24	30 224	90 763	1.6	98.4
St. James	269	1.3	7 530	2.3	6 333	65	38.5	46.2	45	2	698	40	26 691	410 631	99.8	.2
St. John the Baptist	15	Z	1 470	.3	1 349	27	40.7	22.2	10	–8	353	6	3 546	131 333	98.4	1.7
St. Landry	1 639	2.0	1 800	.3	14 534	966	44.5	15.7	265	–18	274	224	63 850	66 097	86.6	13.4
St. Martin	737	1.7	10 080	3.3	9 714	243	42.0	20.2	78	7	321	66	30 648	126 123	90.7	9.3
St. Mary	288	.5	7 049	.6	6 165	103	20.4	49.5	83	1	807	65	39 430	382 816	99.2	.8
St. Tammany	816	.6	–2 256	X	–2 287	451	64.7	2.9	42	2	93	17	12 404	27 503	66.6	33.4
Tangipahoa	1 886	2.2	22 579	2.5	20 211	923	41.4	3.5	120	–7	130	73	59 280	64 225	16.5	83.5
Tensas	500	7.0	11 395	20.1	14 537	202	7.9	54.5	241	–5	1 193	197	70 700	350 000	99.6	.4
Terrebonne	247	.3	2 908	.2	2 490	137	38.0	21.2	53	9	386	31	14 180	103 504	85.6	14.4
Union	573	2.8	19 969	11.5	32 052	436	30.3	3.2	63	1	145	27	86 387	198 135	.5	99.5
Vermilion	1 516	3.0	22 863	4.4	21 959	995	34.0	20.7	329	12	330	256	70 111	70 463	90.8	9.2
Vernon	781	1.3	356	Z	328	387	40.1	3.1	44	–8	113	19	8 271	21 372	4.2	95.8
Washington	1 138	2.6	10 177	2.8	7 899	814	37.7	3.1	100	–16	123	60	45 118	55 428	26.1	73.9
Webster	592	1.4	936	.2	817	341	35.5	5.0	50	–8	147	23	5 642	16 545	9.1	90.9
West Baton Rouge	164	.8	10 461	2.5	12 231	95	49.5	22.1	29	–10	304	22	29 414	309 621	D	D
West Carroll	1 430	11.8	5 553	7.4	12 306	539	21.5	19.5	167	40	310	134	43 339	80 406	94.4	5.6
West Feliciana	106	.8	885	.3	818	148	21.6	27.7	76	–11	515	24	3 406	23 014	51.9	48.1
Winn	238	1.5	–461	X	–271	147	37.4	3.4	18	–5	122	8	3 076	20 925	6.2	93.8

[1] For 1990 corrected population, see table B-1. Percent is based on 1990 uncorrected population because only total population is corrected. [2] For total earnings, see table B-8. [3] Most data are comparable between 1992 and 1997; however, it should be noted that farms with all acreage in Conservation or Wetlands Reserve Programs (excluded in 1992) are included in 1997, as are short rotation woody crops which includes Christmas trees and maple sap gathering (in Forestry in 1992). [4] Includes nursery and greenhouse crops. [5] Includes related products. [6] Less than $50,000.

Sources: Farm Population—U.S. Census Bureau, 1990 Census of Population and Housing, Summary Tape File (STF) 3C on CD-ROM (related Internet site <http://homer.ssd.census.gov/cdrom/lookup>). Farm Earnings—U.S. Bureau of Economic Analysis, "Regional Economic Information System (REIS) 1969-1998" on CD-ROM (related Internet site <http://www.bea.doc.gov/bea/regional/reis/ca45/>). Agriculture—U.S. Department of Agriculture, National Agricultural Statistics Service, 1997 Census of Agriculture, Volume 1, Geographic Area Series, 1A, 1B, 1C CD-ROM Set (related Internet site <http://www.nass.usda.gov/census/>).

Table B–10. Counties — **Farm Population, Farm Earnings, and Agriculture**–Con.

[Includes U.S., states, and 3,142 counties/county equivalents defined as of January 1, 1992. For changes to these areas since January 1, 1992, see appendix B. Geographic Information]

County	Farm population, 1990 Number	Percent of total[1]	Farm earnings 1998 Total ($1,000)	Percent of total[2]	1997 ($1,000)	Farms Number	Less than 50 acres Percent	500 acres or more Percent	Land in farms Total acreage (1,000)	Net change, 1992–1997[3] (1,000)	Average size of farm	Total cropland (1,000)	Value of farm products sold Total ($1,000)	Average per farm (dollars)	Crops[4] Percent	Livestock and poultry[5] Percent
MAINE	11 008	.9	100 487	.5	79 231	5 810	29.6	9.3	1 212	−47	209	540	438 673	75 503	48.4	51.6
Androscoggin	605	.6	6 303	.4	9 840	288	27.4	9.7	56	−6	194	23	62 377	216 587	12.7	87.3
Aroostook	1 236	1.4	26 190	2.9	17 529	889	12.8	21.0	325	−9	365	188	109 619	123 306	95.5	4.5
Cumberland................	831	.3	2 796	Z	1 490	455	47.3	3.5	50	−4	110	26	17 318	38 062	64.5	35.5
Franklin	530	1.8	265	.1	−383	223	22.0	5.8	40	1	180	15	5 570	24 978	D	D
Hancock	451	1.0	9 886	1.3	7 850	310	41.9	4.2	43	−7	137	11	30 448	98 219	D	D
Kennebec................	1 370	1.2	11 732	.6	11 051	455	27.7	7.7	88	−7	194	45	45 181	99 299	13.7	86.3
Knox	327	.9	−51	X	128	194	35.6	1.5	25	−2	130	10	5 603	28 881	60.4	39.6
Lincoln	460	1.5	1 936	.6	1 479	210	37.6	4.3	26	2	123	11	6 329	30 138	35.9	64.1
Oxford	569	1.1	2 801	.5	2 730	358	32.1	7.5	64	Z	179	21	19 549	54 606	53.2	46.8
Penobscot	1 196	.8	5 954	.3	2 380	525	31.0	11.4	117	−2	222	49	29 978	57 101	37.2	62.8
Piscataquis	325	1.7	1 349	.7	508	141	22.0	13.5	34	−2	242	10	5 561	39 440	30.8	69.2
Sagadahoc	277	.8	356	.1	(6)	118	34.7	5.9	18	−1	151	7	3 067	25 992	46.0	54.0
Somerset	820	1.6	6 241	1.0	3 008	431	18.3	11.8	101	−6	235	36	24 727	57 371	19.8	80.2
Waldo	787	2.4	2 534	.8	805	315	23.8	9.5	69	−3	218	28	14 768	46 883	17.2	82.8
Washington	390	1.1	17 417	4.6	16 558	399	37.8	7.5	98	4	246	36	43 074	107 955	61.1	38.9
York	834	.5	4 778	.2	4 298	499	40.3	2.8	58	−3	117	24	15 503	31 068	66.2	33.8
MARYLAND	32 596	.7	300 133	.3	226 722	12 084	43.3	8.2	2 155	−69	178	1 613	1 312 086	108 580	35.0	65.0
Allegany	273	.4	121	Z	−563	239	21.8	8.4	42	4	175	20	3 322	13 900	34.6	65.4
Anne Arundel	1 301	.3	6 842	.1	6 257	412	60.0	3.4	35	−9	84	23	12 621	30 633	79.5	20.5
Baltimore	1 734	.3	40 436	.3	30 642	7 781	760.2	72.9	776	7–7	797	754	751 179	765 530	768.3	731.7
Calvert	1 153	2.2	309	Z	1 309	349	52.7	3.7	33	−4	96	18	7 704	22 074	89.1	10.9
Caroline	2 062	7.6	3 207	1.1	1 910	525	38.5	11.2	111	−16	212	95	95 120	181 181	30.2	69.8
Carroll................	2 935	2.4	17 917	1.2	9 755	1 041	48.9	5.8	160	3	154	125	71 272	68 465	36.2	63.8
Cecil	1 497	2.1	24 066	2.8	18 298	464	43.5	9.1	86	5	185	63	59 052	127 267	38.8	61.2
Charles................	1 369	1.4	−327	X	1 445	410	43.4	5.4	56	−3	136	33	10 816	26 380	86.6	13.4
Dorchester	842	2.8	11 438	3.2	12 101	297	26.6	27.9	123	−1	414	99	82 391	277 411	41.9	58.1
Frederick	2 950	2.0	30 750	1.1	14 783	1 304	35.9	5.6	216	−7	166	171	101 660	77 960	17.2	82.8
Garrett	1 522	5.4	9 826	2.9	5 279	649	19.7	4.6	108	−3	166	54	20 997	32 353	11.5	88.5
Harford	1 102	.6	25 010	1.0	18 460	651	48.2	5.7	94	−3	145	72	38 807	59 611	42.0	58.0
Howard	886	.5	16 102	.3	13 125	318	58.2	6.3	40	−5	125	31	19 610	61 667	61.6	38.4
Kent	1 207	6.8	18 326	7.8	10 612	314	21.0	20.4	118	−14	374	98	60 957	194 131	55.8	44.2
Montgomery	1 110	.1	15 826	.1	11 672	526	56.5	6.5	77	−5	147	61	28 563	54 302	69.4	30.6
Prince George's	719	.1	14 063	.1	12 063	473	59.2	3.0	48	−7	101	28	18 708	39 552	89.4	10.6
Queen Anne's	1 191	3.5	3 573	1.1	2 504	419	28.2	27.4	168	3	401	146	68 736	164 048	63.4	36.6
St. Mary's................	2 454	3.2	−194	X	5 960	621	43.6	3.7	72	−6	116	43	21 056	33 907	83.3	16.7
Somerset	896	3.8	2 724	1.3	−1 113	288	43.4	8.7	55	−1	190	40	96 532	335 181	13.5	86.5
Talbot	1 164	3.8	3 200	.5	3 548	240	25.4	24.2	110	Z	457	93	48 530	202 208	50.0	50.0
Washington	1 617	1.3	7 163	.4	3 249	768	34.1	4.7	126	2	164	95	60 604	78 911	21.1	78.9
Wicomico	1 789	2.4	29 595	2.2	26 777	580	56.2	9.1	91	−1	156	71	186 294	321 197	16.0	84.0
Worcester	823	2.3	20 560	3.3	18 649	415	50.8	16.4	112	4	269	83	147 553	355 549	16.6	83.4
Independent City																
Baltimore city.............	–	–	–	–	–	(7)	(7)	(7)	(7)	(7)	(7)	(7)	(7)	(7)	(7)	(7)
MASSACHUSETTS......	9 342	.2	165 502	.1	195 405	5 574	56.0	2.7	518	−8	93	224	454 404	81 522	78.6	21.4
Barnstable	172	.1	6 805	.2	8 902	221	89.6	–	5	−1	21	2	18 225	82 466	94.5	5.5
Berkshire	490	.4	3 156	.1	3 740	387	39.5	8.8	63	2	162	31	20 725	53 553	40.0	60.0
Bristol	879	.2	20 716	.3	21 070	555	58.7	1.3	37	3	67	18	34 102	61 445	73.6	26.4
Dukes	71	.6	610	.2	688	64	76.6	3.1	5	−1	77	1	1 250	19 531	78.9	21.1
Essex	672	.1	13 056	.1	13 477	396	64.6	1.0	26	Z	65	12	25 091	63 361	79.2	20.8
Franklin	1 114	1.6	10 702	1.1	14 818	543	35.0	4.4	75	1	138	32	40 704	74 961	61.6	38.4
Hampden	343	.1	7 062	.1	10 739	418	51.9	2.2	37	Z	90	16	29 107	69 634	85.8	14.2
Hampshire	1 185	.8	17 907	.8	24 246	539	53.2	3.0	52	−1	97	27	35 514	65 889	70.8	29.2
Middlesex	812	.1	35 393	.1	38 076	531	67.4	1.3	31	−1	58	15	57 572	108 422	86.5	13.5
Nantucket	–	–	–	–	–	14	85.7	7.1	1	D	75	D	2 951	210 786	100.0	–
Norfolk	252	Z	4 859	Z	4 907	185	73.0	.5	10	Z	53	4	8 266	44 681	88.8	11.2
Plymouth	1 277	.3	35 696	.5	41 963	732	66.5	3.0	73	1	100	21	122 687	167 605	96.7	3.3
Suffolk	–	–	–	–	–	5	100.0	–	Z	D	1	D	263	52 600	100.0	–
Worcester	2 075	.3	9 540	.1	12 779	984	45.3	2.4	103	−11	105	44	57 949	58 891	54.9	45.1

[1] For 1990 corrected population, see table B-1. Percent is based on 1990 uncorrected population because only total population is corrected. [2] For total earnings, see table B-8. [3] Most data are comparable between 1992 and 1997; however, it should be noted that farms with all acreage in Conservation or Wetlands Reserve Programs (excluded in 1992) are included in 1997, as are short rotation woody crops which includes Christmas trees and maple sap gathering (in Forestry in 1992). [4] Includes nursery and greenhouse crops. [5] Includes related products. [6] Less than $50,000. [7] Independent city of Baltimore included with Baltimore County; data not available separately.

Sources: Farm Population—U.S. Census Bureau, 1990 Census of Population and Housing, Summary Tape File (STF) 3C on CD-ROM (related Internet site <http://homer.ssd.census.gov/cdrom/lookup>). Farm Earnings—U.S. Bureau of Economic Analysis, "Regional Economic Information System (REIS) 1969-1998" on CD-ROM (related Internet site <http://www.bea.doc.gov/bea/regional/reis/ca45/>). Agriculture—U.S. Department of Agriculture, National Agricultural Statistics Service, 1997 Census of Agriculture, Volume 1, Geographic Area Series, 1A, 1B, 1C CD-ROM Set (related Internet site <http://www.nass.usda.gov/census/>).

Table B–10. Counties — **Farm Population, Farm Earnings, and Agriculture**–Con.

[Includes U.S., states, and 3,142 counties/county equivalents defined as of January 1, 1992. For changes to these areas since January 1, 1992, see appendix B. Geographic Information]

County	Farm population, 1990 Number	Farm population, 1990 Percent of total[1]	Farm earnings 1998 Total ($1,000)	Farm earnings 1998 Percent of total[2]	Farm earnings 1997 ($1,000)	Farms Number	Farms Percent Less than 50 acres	Farms Percent 500 acres or more	Land in farms Total acreage (1,000)	Land in farms Net change, 1992–1997[3] (1,000)	Land in farms Average size of farm	Land in farms Total cropland (1,000)	Value of farm products sold Total ($1,000)	Value of farm products sold Average per farm (dollars)	Value Percent from Crops[4]	Value Percent from Livestock and poultry[5]
MICHIGAN............	120 496	1.3	468 037	.2	513 620	46 027	31.9	10.7	9 873	–215	215	7 892	3 567 825	77 516	61.7	38.3
Alcona	304	3.0	–347	X	–920	207	17.9	8.2	43	1	210	30	5 592	27 014	39.1	60.9
Alger	126	1.4	223	.2	–106	60	18.3	13.3	16	Z	267	9	2 028	33 800	28.8	71.2
Allegan	3 936	4.3	27 026	1.9	30 815	1 337	40.6	8.3	237	–9	177	198	186 757	139 684	39.5	60.5
Alpena	836	2.7	–2 615	X	–3 821	412	24.0	8.3	78	1	189	56	11 156	27 078	39.4	60.6
Antrim	433	2.4	5 673	3.0	5 005	261	26.4	8.4	55	4	211	33	17 206	65 923	72.9	27.1
Arenac	609	4.1	6 017	4.4	5 595	325	17.8	12.9	86	4	265	69	23 118	71 132	71.1	28.9
Baraga	109	1.4	(6)	Z	–241	54	16.7	25.9	15	1	278	9	1 134	21 000	36.7	63.3
Barry	2 094	4.2	2 506	.6	449	881	27.1	8.3	165	–1	187	126	47 801	54 258	30.2	69.8
Bay	2 134	1.9	5 846	.4	9 798	730	28.2	14.2	176	–5	241	162	61 423	84 141	93.1	6.9
Benzie	247	2.0	1 631	1.5	2 285	140	30.7	7.1	23	3	161	12	6 636	47 400	71.2	28.8
Berrien	3 398	2.1	17 832	.7	21 758	1 182	49.1	5.8	174	7	147	146	81 376	68 846	88.5	11.5
Branch	2 645	6.4	2 351	.5	13 587	980	26.2	11.9	234	6	239	185	77 249	78 826	57.7	42.3
Calhoun	2 827	2.1	1 633	.1	3 068	1 085	24.4	11.0	243	–2	224	188	60 985	56 207	57.3	42.7
Cass	2 427	4.9	–714	X	12 495	700	29.0	14.3	177	–10	253	141	67 491	96 416	47.0	53.0
Charlevoix	341	1.6	(6)	Z	–425	188	24.5	8.0	31	–10	165	18	4 151	22 080	39.3	60.7
Cheboygan	239	1.1	571	.2	–288	210	21.0	11.9	51	10	241	28	5 848	27 848	20.7	79.3
Chippewa	506	1.5	–730	X	–1 658	319	11.3	20.4	99	6	310	68	7 351	23 044	39.3	60.7
Clare	495	2.0	1 914	.9	451	350	24.0	9.4	63	–1	180	41	12 950	37 000	13.4	86.6
Clinton	4 685	8.1	9 178	1.8	11 780	1 123	29.4	9.7	244	–12	217	210	91 515	81 492	44.8	55.2
Crawford	–	–	–	–	–	27	48.1	3.7	3	1	95	1	117	4 333	34.2	65.8
Delta	489	1.3	963	.2	474	253	14.6	15.8	70	–3	278	41	8 162	32 261	45.5	54.5
Dickinson	126	.5	62	Z	–275	116	26.7	11.2	28	Z	244	14	3 941	33 974	46.5	53.5
Eaton	3 650	3.9	4 267	.4	2 816	1 062	33.9	9.4	232	–2	218	190	54 948	51 740	71.8	28.2
Emmet	232	.9	83	Z	–603	207	23.2	8.2	40	Z	194	25	5 449	26 324	35.9	64.1
Genesee	1 850	.4	–3 043	X	–3 210	796	49.5	6.4	118	–19	148	99	27 995	35 170	73.2	26.8
Gladwin	699	3.2	490	.3	732	424	21.5	5.4	68	7	160	49	9 557	22 540	41.9	58.1
Gogebic	90	.5	–218	X	–238	48	25.0	.	4	–2	87	2	232	4 833	77.6	22.4
Grand Traverse	723	1.1	483	Z	713	413	39.7	5.8	62	–5	150	42	17 155	41 538	79.9	20.1
Gratiot	3 610	9.3	3 304	.7	16 237	873	26.0	18.1	277	–1	317	245	102 439	117 341	63.9	36.1
Hillsdale	3 356	7.7	12 682	2.2	15 772	1 236	29.6	9.9	257	26	208	210	71 729	58 033	58.3	41.7
Houghton	245	.7	–285	X	–804	128	21.1	4.7	23	–6	181	12	2 206	17 234	30.6	69.4
Huron	3 607	10.3	34 358	7.0	26 242	1 184	20.5	21.4	424	–15	358	384	211 414	178 559	47.5	52.5
Ingham	2 173	.8	4 862	.1	3 380	827	42.1	10.5	190	–3	230	159	53 394	64 563	60.8	39.2
Ionia	3 726	6.5	3 292	.6	7 413	1 004	28.1	11.8	237	–18	236	197	87 194	86 847	40.2	59.8
Iosco	329	1.1	1 073	.4	118	238	30.7	8.4	43	–5	179	29	6 769	28 441	23.8	76.2
Iron	144	1.1	–76	X	–326	86	17.4	14.0	24	–6	277	12	1 593	18 523	65.1	34.9
Isabella	1 679	3.1	3 166	.4	3 531	911	23.4	12.8	217	17	238	176	56 825	62 377	47.3	52.7
Jackson	2 812	1.9	–823	X	–1 153	987	34.7	8.0	181	–29	184	138	44 311	44 895	53.7	46.3
Kalamazoo	1 916	.9	30 483	.6	27 174	696	44.0	12.8	147	–8	211	120	105 494	151 572	64.2	35.8
Kalkaska	120	.9	788	.5	665	139	30.9	4.3	21	5	154	13	5 060	36 403	78.0	22.0
Kent	3 018	.6	30 597	.2	34 044	1 136	42.3	7.0	186	–4	164	150	121 041	106 550	76.0	24.0
Keweenaw	–	–	–	–	–	5	60.0	.	D	D	D	Z	5	1 000	.	100.0
Lake	162	1.9	(6)	Z	–224	126	24.6	6.3	23	5	182	14	2 073	16 452	48.3	51.7
Lapeer	3 317	4.4	2 951	.4	1 159	1 020	37.8	7.9	178	–16	175	144	54 255	53 191	59.5	40.5
Leelanau	763	4.6	6 101	3.4	7 457	369	26.3	4.9	62	–3	168	38	28 725	77 846	82.9	17.1
Lenawee	3 975	4.3	18 382	1.5	16 990	1 317	30.1	14.7	336	Z	255	302	102 849	78 093	76.2	23.8
Livingston..............	1 565	1.4	–609	X	–1 098	637	51.8	6.9	98	–20	154	75	28 455	44 670	65.1	34.9
Luce	23	.4	1 309	1.6	1 027	31	29.0	22.6	D	D	D	7	2 326	75 032	81.5	18.5
Mackinac	192	1.8	–266	X	–742	72	15.3	15.3	22	–1	299	14	2 547	35 375	13.5	86.5
Macomb	1 066	.1	9 439	.1	9 061	523	49.5	5.5	69	–1	132	59	44 734	85 533	92.3	7.7
Manistee	347	1.6	947	.4	1 148	284	23.2	6.7	48	–1	167	28	9 096	32 028	89.2	10.8
Marquette	119	.2	–102	X	–519	108	33.3	11.1	27	3	247	12	2 946	27 278	38.2	61.8
Mason.................	736	2.9	3 754	1.1	2 938	413	30.0	8.7	77	4	187	56	23 621	57 194	67.8	32.2
Mecosta	1 099	2.9	5 016	1.3	2 572	597	17.9	8.0	112	–9	188	82	24 866	41 652	40.4	59.6
Menominee	629	2.5	3 035	1.1	–395	348	14.1	19.3	110	Z	315	63	18 302	52 592	13.3	86.7
Midland...............	1 266	1.7	–3 481	X	–1 378	418	33.7	9.6	80	–10	191	62	17 254	41 278	76.1	23.9
Missaukee	590	4.9	11 288	11.8	4 744	335	17.9	18.2	90	2	269	66	34 697	103 573	13.5	86.5
Monroe	3 440	2.6	19 595	1.1	18 311	1 058	44.0	11.2	210	–7	198	196	94 138	88 977	89.8	10.2
Montcalm	1 678	3.2	15 071	2.3	19 014	954	25.3	12.8	238	14	249	186	87 860	92 096	71.9	28.1
Montmorency	217	2.4	–120	X	–310	103	15.5	13.6	21	–1	204	14	3 271	31 757	36.7	63.3
Muskegon	823	.5	9 202	.4	7 338	410	44.6	7.1	73	–1	178	53	44 435	108 378	54.0	46.0
Newaygo	1 177	3.1	10 750	2.9	5 879	670	27.6	8.7	122	7	183	90	48 541	72 449	41.5	58.5
Oakland	943	.1	8 985	Z	8 199	544	66.9	2.2	45	–3	83	33	32 452	59 654	91.6	8.4

[1] For 1990 corrected population, see table B-1. Percent is based on 1990 uncorrected population because only total population is corrected. [2] For total earnings, see table B-8. [3] Most data are comparable between 1992 and 1997; however, it should be noted that farms with all acreage in Conservation or Wetlands Reserve Programs (excluded in 1992) are included in 1997, as are short rotation woody crops which includes Christmas trees and maple sap gathering (in Forestry in 1992). [4] Includes nursery and greenhouse crops. [5] Includes related products. [6] Less than $50,000.

Sources: Farm Population—U.S. Census Bureau, 1990 Census of Population and Housing, Summary Tape File (STF) 3C on CD-ROM (related Internet site <http://homer.ssd.census.gov/cdrom/lookup>). Farm Earnings—U.S. Bureau of Economic Analysis, "Regional Economic Information System (REIS) 1969-1998" on CD-ROM (related Internet site <http://www.bea.doc.gov/bea/regional/reis/ca45/>). Agriculture—U.S. Department of Agriculture, National Agricultural Statistics Service, 1997 Census of Agriculture, Volume 1, Geographic Area Series, 1A, 1B, 1C CD-ROM Set (related Internet site <http://www.nass.usda.gov/census/>).Sources: Farm Population—U.S. Census Bureau, 1990 Census of Population and Housing, Summary Tape File (STF) 3C on CD-ROM (related Internet site <http://homer.ssd.census.gov/cdrom/lookup>). Farm Earnings—U.S. Bureau of Economic Analysis, "Regional Economic Information System (REIS) 1969-1998" on CD-ROM (related Internet site <http://www.bea.doc.gov/bea/regional/reis/ca45/>). Agriculture—U.S. Department of Agriculture, National Agricultural Statistics Service, 1997 Census of Agriculture, Volume 1, Geographic Area Series, 1A, 1B, 1C CD-ROM Set (related Internet site <http://www.nass.usda.gov/census/>).

Table B–10. Counties — Farm Population, Farm Earnings, and Agriculture–Con.

[Includes U.S., states, and 3,142 counties/county equivalents defined as of January 1, 1992. For changes to these areas since January 1, 1992, see appendix B. Geographic Information]

County	Farm population, 1990 Number	Percent of total[1]	Farm earnings 1998 Total ($1,000)	Percent of total[2]	1997 ($1,000)	Farms Number	Percent— Less than 50 acres	500 acres or more	Total acreage (1,000)	Net change, 1992-1997[3] (1,000)	Average size of farm	Total cropland (1,000)	Value of farm products sold Total ($1,000)	Average per farm (dollars)	Percent from— Crops[4]	Livestock and poultry[5]
MICHIGAN—Con.																
Oceana	1 000	4.5	16 256	7.6	15 275	573	28.1	11.0	128	−1	223	86	49 792	86 897	74.7	25.3
Ogemaw	328	1.8	3 129	1.7	1 130	261	15.3	13.8	73	−2	281	51	22 144	84 843	13.6	86.4
Ontonagon	153	1.7	−109	X	−446	92	5.4	20.7	33	Z	353	17	2 205	23 967	24.9	75.1
Osceola	907	4.5	868	.3	−2 161	496	16.5	8.5	108	Z	218	72	19 284	38 879	17.7	82.3
Oscoda	188	2.4	247	.4	(6)	80	21.3	5.0	14	Z	174	8	1 880	23 500	19.1	80.9
Otsego	224	1.2	−345	X	−709	139	17.3	13.7	34	−2	248	19	3 810	27 410	65.7	34.3
Ottawa	3 273	1.7	61 178	1.4	70 962	1 292	48.4	5.4	171	−6	132	141	299 985	232 187	53.4	46.6
Presque Isle	478	3.5	2 703	2.5	2 165	296	12.2	12.8	82	3	279	54	13 085	44 206	59.7	40.3
Roscommon	23	.1	(6)	Z	(6)	36	44.4	2.8	4	Z	115	3	513	14 250	73.1	26.9
Saginaw	4 583	2.2	2 391	.1	10 750	1 163	30.0	13.8	298	−20	256	268	84 034	72 256	89.0	11.0
St. Clair	2 131	1.5	−2 180	X	−1 679	940	35.0	6.7	163	−19	173	141	36 076	38 379	76.7	23.3
St. Joseph	2 542	4.3	6 336	.7	17 709	791	28.2	15.8	217	−17	275	185	81 103	102 532	77.1	22.9
Sanilac	3 162	7.9	17 411	4.1	12 754	1 448	21.5	16.2	430	−15	297	381	132 513	91 515	56.6	43.4
Schoolcraft	63	.8	−109	X	−140	45	22.2	22.2	16	2	350	9	1 230	27 333	47.6	52.4
Shiawassee	3 671	5.3	−3 587	X	1 387	915	30.1	12.9	214	−23	234	184	45 200	49 399	72.2	27.8
Tuscola	3 914	7.1	11 718	2.5	13 764	1 140	25.4	16.8	333	9	292	292	105 723	92 739	80.7	19.3
Van Buren	2 756	3.9	20 000	2.7	24 430	1 059	37.5	6.1	177	−29	167	136	100 641	95 034	86.6	13.4
Washtenaw	3 299	1.2	801	Z	1 390	1 030	39.9	8.8	180	−9	175	153	56 521	54 875	61.1	38.9
Wayne	396	Z	4 600	Z	3 117	303	65.3	5.9	39	17	129	30	27 159	89 634	96.2	3.8
Wexford	293	1.1	1 034	.2	457	251	21.9	5.6	43	12	173	29	8 690	34 622	63.8	36.2
MINNESOTA	207 956	4.8	965 470	1.0	734 669	73 367	18.0	20.8	25 995	328	354	21 492	8 290 264	112 997	50.7	49.3
Aitkin	828	6.7	−1 387	X	−1 534	587	13.3	14.8	164	−5	279	81	14 419	24 564	36.2	63.8
Anoka	694	.3	847	Z	−1 742	473	49.0	4.4	57	−5	121	40	23 794	50 304	70.5	29.5
Becker	2 427	8.7	15 464	4.5	13 632	1 084	11.4	16.4	389	11	359	269	99 870	92 131	33.4	66.6
Beltrami	1 145	3.3	804	.2	−683	656	8.5	21.0	225	Z	343	121	17 231	26 267	30.4	69.6
Benton	2 595	8.6	10 909	2.6	6 563	834	21.9	7.8	176	−7	211	131	89 610	107 446	21.8	78.2
Big Stone	1 127	17.9	4 590	8.6	4 642	420	13.1	45.7	254	−8	605	227	54 617	130 040	70.1	29.9
Blue Earth	3 674	6.8	28 413	2.7	40 144	1 037	19.1	29.4	403	20	389	370	221 470	213 568	44.8	55.2
Brown	3 585	13.3	12 462	2.9	21 974	1 054	13.1	20.2	350	3	332	321	181 843	172 527	42.8	57.2
Carlton	817	2.8	−1 680	X	−3 026	527	12.9	5.9	107	−6	203	56	8 451	16 036	19.6	80.4
Carver	3 056	6.4	12 230	1.1	2 464	779	28.5	5.6	153	−13	197	126	62 056	79 661	36.8	63.2
Cass	1 093	5.0	−430	X	−644	598	13.9	17.6	192	−8	321	95	20 639	34 513	12.2	87.8
Chippewa	2 352	17.8	16 230	8.3	8 698	618	14.7	33.7	318	−8	515	298	101 231	163 804	82.6	17.4
Chisago	2 233	7.3	4 684	1.2	1 866	762	30.8	5.8	122	−17	159	84	30 249	39 697	62.2	37.8
Clay	2 286	4.5	8 506	1.6	2 184	887	14.0	39.8	581	14	655	529	137 664	155 202	81.7	18.3
Clearwater	1 207	14.5	−615	X	−2 361	570	6.3	19.6	212	1	372	115	20 421	35 826	45.3	54.7
Cook	4	.1	–	–	–	11	9.1	9.1	D	D	D	1	101	9 182	77.2	22.8
Cottonwood	2 493	19.6	23 812	15.4	22 000	784	11.5	29.6	368	−7	470	333	160 266	204 421	49.8	50.2
Crow Wing	774	1.7	−3 289	X	−4 339	593	20.9	10.6	135	5	228	69	14 219	23 978	27.1	72.9
Dakota	2 200	.8	11 615	.2	10 273	890	36.3	14.4	221	Z	249	196	102 979	115 707	62.5	37.5
Dodge	2 253	14.3	17 218	10.2	13 230	674	24.6	22.0	247	6	366	224	104 794	155 481	55.8	44.2
Douglas	2 381	8.3	2 875	.6	−1 491	1 042	14.8	11.0	268	8	257	201	58 881	56 508	36.2	63.8
Faribault	2 932	17.3	11 934	6.4	21 155	878	13.4	35.0	413	−1	471	389	171 051	194 819	66.3	33.7
Fillmore	4 796	23.1	26 349	12.3	22 246	1 546	19.2	16.2	435	−9	281	327	148 261	95 900	41.3	58.7
Freeborn	3 804	11.5	12 844	3.2	22 873	1 151	25.0	24.0	380	13	330	351	163 067	141 674	61.6	38.4
Goodhue	4 806	11.8	31 466	4.3	20 612	1 489	25.5	14.4	385	5	258	315	160 642	107 886	40.3	59.7
Grant	1 241	19.9	9 862	13.8	7 613	468	13.5	36.1	278	9	595	251	60 726	129 756	81.7	18.3
Hennepin	1 094	.1	5 252	Z	5 599	574	56.3	5.1	69	−10	120	54	43 748	76 216	77.3	22.7
Houston	2 822	15.3	10 564	6.3	7 027	954	11.4	17.7	298	26	313	187	77 659	81 404	38.1	61.9
Hubbard	757	5.1	1 210	.7	−104	431	10.4	14.2	131	18	303	71	23 359	54 197	77.8	22.2
Isanti	1 953	7.5	−2 196	X	−3 302	746	34.7	8.4	139	8	187	99	24 923	33 409	65.8	34.2
Itasca	763	1.9	−1 969	X	−2 053	415	14.9	11.1	104	−4	250	55	4 962	11 957	34.0	66.0
Jackson	2 960	25.3	23 208	15.6	23 146	963	13.7	28.6	384	−17	398	355	150 391	156 169	59.1	40.9
Kanabec	1 552	12.1	−2 440	X	−4 224	626	17.7	8.8	139	−7	222	68	16 633	26 570	26.4	73.6
Kandiyohi	3 717	9.6	15 481	2.3	3 000	1 131	22.3	20.3	379	18	335	327	223 670	197 763	32.5	67.5
Kittson	903	15.7	7 309	13.5	−548	558	5.4	52.9	501	18	899	431	55 591	99 625	90.7	9.3
Koochiching	385	2.4	−786	X	−953	213	4.2	25.8	77	8	360	42	3 519	16 521	29.9	70.1
Lac qui Parle	2 734	30.6	22 563	23.9	20 522	790	10.1	37.5	398	−8	503	362	113 080	143 139	62.4	37.6
Lake	59	.6	−146	X	−141	37	29.7	2.7	4	−1	107	2	124	3 351	46.0	54.0
Lake of the Woods	314	7.7	−1 779	X	−1 881	196	11.2	34.2	118	14	600	78	7 818	39 888	81.5	18.5
Le Sueur	2 726	11.7	10 571	3.8	9 751	877	24.9	12.4	215	10	245	184	84 524	96 379	48.9	51.1
Lincoln	2 209	32.1	12 739	19.8	5 613	724	13.0	25.4	270	14	372	234	68 956	95 243	44.7	55.3
Lyon	3 016	12.2	26 120	5.6	22 301	931	15.5	33.1	403	8	433	366	147 152	158 058	49.7	50.3
McLeod	3 851	12.0	14 858	2.2	6 495	1 008	22.9	12.5	250	Z	248	223	82 787	82 130	55.4	44.6
Mahnomen	1 042	20.7	−3 849	X	−2 970	341	8.5	36.4	190	3	557	153	24 657	72 308	73.6	26.4
Marshall	2 125	19.3	3 921	5.0	4 146	1 144	6.6	41.1	774	30	677	691	91 090	79 624	89.7	10.3
Martin	3 178	13.9	22 292	7.4	39 019	987	16.6	32.3	421	8	426	398	253 722	257 064	43.2	56.8
Meeker	3 245	15.6	2 611	1.3	−210	1 016	21.8	15.8	293	−8	289	249	139 385	137 190	34.2	65.8

[1] For 1990 corrected population, see table B-1. Percent is based on 1990 uncorrected population because only total population is corrected. [2] For total earnings, see table B-8. [3] Most data are comparable between 1992 and 1997; however, it should be noted that farms with all acreage in Conservation or Wetlands Reserve Programs (excluded in 1992) are included in 1997, as are short rotation woody crops which includes Christmas trees and maple sap gathering (in Forestry in 1992). [4] Includes nursery and greenhouse crops. [5] Includes related products. [6] Less than $50,000.

Sources: Farm Population—U.S. Census Bureau, 1990 Census of Population and Housing, Summary Tape File (STF) 3C on CD-ROM (related Internet site <http://homer.ssd.census.gov/cdrom/lookup>). Farm Earnings—U.S. Bureau of Economic Analysis, "Regional Economic Information System (REIS) 1969-1998" on CD-ROM (related Internet site <http://www.bea.doc.gov/bea/regional/reis/ca45/>). Agriculture—U.S. Department of Agriculture, National Agricultural Statistics Service, 1997 Census of Agriculture, Volume 1, Geographic Area Series, 1A, 1B, 1C CD-ROM Set (related Internet site <http://www.nass.usda.gov/census/>).

Table B–10. Counties — Farm Population, Farm Earnings, and Agriculture–Con.

[Includes U.S., states, and 3,142 counties/county equivalents defined as of January 1, 1992. For changes to these areas since January 1, 1992, see appendix B. Geographic Information]

County	Farm population, 1990 Number	Farm population, 1990 Percent of total[1]	Farm earnings 1998 Total ($1,000)	Farm earnings 1998 Percent of total[2]	Farm earnings 1997 ($1,000)	Farms Number	Farms Percent Less than 50 acres	Farms Percent 500 acres or more	Land in farms (acres) Total acreage (1,000)	Land in farms (acres) Net change, 1992–1997[3] (1,000)	Land in farms Average size of farm	Land in farms Total cropland (1,000)	Value of farm products sold Total ($1,000)	Value Average per farm (dollars)	Percent from Crops[4]	Percent from Livestock and poultry[5]
MINNESOTA—Con.																
Mille Lacs	1 767	9.5	5 247	2.1	2 295	711	21.9	7.3	135	−8	189	84	26 221	36 879	25.5	74.5
Morrison	5 364	18.1	10 451	3.1	−1 930	1 808	12.3	8.3	430	8	238	250	156 769	86 709	16.2	83.8
Mower	3 562	9.5	24 509	4.7	29 967	1 123	20.8	23.1	404	12	360	375	162 784	144 955	62.0	38.0
Murray	3 031	31.4	26 404	25.0	16 814	836	13.8	35.8	384	8	459	355	126 415	151 214	54.6	45.4
Nicollet	2 577	9.2	10 465	2.5	15 314	723	16.3	22.0	249	7	345	233	172 307	238 322	35.2	64.8
Nobles	3 744	18.6	22 210	7.2	17 380	1 021	14.1	24.2	390	−26	382	366	158 548	155 287	48.5	51.5
Norman	1 173	14.7	11 099	14.5	−2 823	670	10.6	45.4	483	25	721	435	75 243	112 303	91.2	8.8
Olmsted	3 532	3.3	22 986	.7	15 013	1 317	28.3	10.9	304	−2	231	245	106 320	80 729	48.4	51.6
Otter Tail	6 626	13.1	28 947	4.4	15 180	2 647	11.6	16.7	840	19	317	595	201 431	76 098	40.1	59.9
Pennington	1 231	9.3	−050	X	−6 020	528	7.0	32.4	313	33	592	264	23 895	45 256	81.2	18.8
Pine	1 850	8.7	2 174	1.0	−1 628	950	12.4	11.6	247	−16	260	129	37 856	39 848	26.0	74.0
Pipestone	2 201	21.0	10 956	8.1	11 940	690	18.7	23.3	244	−9	353	213	118 444	171 658	29.6	70.4
Polk	2 183	6.7	32 998	8.9	−3 459	1 366	8.6	45.0	1 052	9	770	937	193 650	141 764	91.8	8.2
Pope	2 366	22.0	7 552	6.9	5 795	825	12.8	22.3	325	15	394	268	80 204	97 217	60.7	39.3
Ramsey	–	–	1 724	Z	1 590	59	74.6	1.7	D	D	D	3	6 235	105 678	98.6	1.4
Red Lake	844	18.7	5 628	13.9	586	376	7.4	33.8	205	22	545	172	21 104	56 128	67.8	32.2
Redwood	4 087	23.7	20 163	8.9	27 800	1 168	11.8	34.5	508	16	435	473	209 724	179 558	55.8	44.2
Renville	4 237	24.0	33 018	16.1	34 286	1 114	12.4	35.8	601	1	540	567	300 612	269 849	56.1	43.9
Rice	3 480	7.1	2 948	.4	9 617	1 191	24.9	9.8	251	24	211	209	127 410	106 977	36.2	63.8
Rock	2 467	25.2	17 078	15.6	17 887	704	19.7	25.1	281	10	399	260	134 842	191 537	40.7	59.3
Roseau	2 159	14.4	−1 843	X	−9 795	1 051	9.2	31.6	577	41	549	467	53 348	50 759	64.5	35.5
St. Louis	902	.5	181	Z	−364	713	19.5	8.4	155	2	218	87	9 679	13 575	51.0	49.0
Scott	2 456	4.2	2 577	.2	1 906	805	46.5	6.0	118	−14	146	100	46 150	57 329	46.8	53.2
Sherburne	1 265	3.0	5 980	1.0	4 811	512	36.5	9.4	105	−13	205	77	42 760	83 516	64.1	35.9
Sibley	3 310	23.0	9 951	8.8	3 022	958	20.6	18.1	310	−2	323	283	144 034	150 349	47.7	52.3
Stearns	9 855	8.3	51 907	2.1	29 573	2 982	16.8	6.5	646	2	217	492	302 244	101 356	18.1	81.9
Steele	2 822	9.2	16 461	2.4	12 539	774	23.5	15.9	227	−5	293	210	96 432	124 589	58.2	41.8
Stevens	1 663	15.6	14 352	9.2	16 795	497	16.5	44.1	299	13	602	284	106 646	214 579	55.8	44.2
Swift	1 959	18.3	8 439	6.3	7 185	739	10.8	37.9	388	−2	525	352	119 209	161 311	64.0	36.0
Todd	4 116	17.6	5 584	2.8	−2 866	1 741	13.7	8.0	387	−8	223	248	112 540	64 641	22.7	77.3
Traverse	835	18.7	4 191	9.4	5 804	385	7.3	56.9	315	5	818	300	68 215	177 182	88.4	11.6
Wabasha	2 981	15.1	20 665	8.4	9 821	963	16.0	12.0	253	8	263	184	93 514	97 107	33.3	66.7
Wadena	1 304	9.9	−768	X	−1 494	625	13.3	13.4	175	3	280	100	52 948	84 717	22.9	77.1
Waseca	2 270	12.0	12 075	4.4	13 005	709	19.2	22.7	235	−2	332	213	118 269	166 811	51.2	48.8
Washington	1 084	.7	12 633	.5	12 214	653	49.0	6.3	90	−11	138	69	57 258	87 685	87.3	12.7
Watonwan	1 879	16.1	19 710	12.6	27 168	576	12.5	31.1	256	6	444	237	120 131	208 561	54.3	45.7
Wilkin	1 031	13.7	6 477	9.1	6 129	441	8.8	54.9	458	37	1 038	435	100 540	227 982	94.4	5.6
Winona	3 801	7.9	32 758	4.2	17 832	1 044	14.7	14.6	290	−1	277	191	122 064	116 920	21.3	78.7
Wright	4 710	6.9	9 545	1.1	1 440	1 422	31.6	7.5	252	−21	177	201	92 839	65 288	47.1	52.9
Yellow Medicine	3 016	25.8	17 641	13.1	18 364	876	11.9	38.5	415	7	474	380	125 126	142 838	66.0	34.0
MISSISSIPPI	56 225	2.2	839 778	2.3	828 297	31 318	22.3	14.5	10 125	−64	323	5 947	3 127 383	99 859	41.3	58.7
Adams	316	.9	474	.1	1 508	132	26.5	21.2	65	−15	489	29	5 787	43 841	79.4	20.6
Alcorn	510	1.6	745	.2	966	449	28.5	8.0	81	2	180	43	7 577	16 875	67.1	32.9
Amite	781	5.9	11 730	14.0	9 102	471	15.1	9.6	118	5	251	43	28 071	59 599	1.8	98.2
Attala	378	2.0	1 473	.9	2 879	385	12.7	14.3	129	21	334	43	13 153	34 164	61.5	38.5
Benton	357	4.4	409	.9	1 125	213	15.5	17.4	81	−10	382	43	8 181	38 408	86.8	13.2
Bolivar	935	2.2	10 587	2.7	35 778	394	11.7	57.4	455	28	1 154	416	156 531	397 287	92.3	7.7
Calhoun	820	5.5	15 704	12.2	13 497	427	11.5	18.5	142	14	332	83	24 705	57 857	88.0	12.0
Carroll	735	8.0	1 342	3.3	2 141	423	12.8	19.6	143	−9	338	64	15 467	36 565	70.1	29.9
Chickasaw	752	4.2	9 550	4.7	9 965	447	17.4	15.0	138	−11	309	81	30 171	67 497	26.3	73.7
Choctaw	395	4.4	2 654	4.5	2 547	217	11.1	7.4	58	15	267	16	8 554	39 419	9.9	90.1
Claiborne	252	2.2	2 699	1.4	2 284	170	13.5	25.3	81	−7	478	29	6 204	36 494	42.5	57.5
Clarke	636	3.7	3 664	2.7	2 881	269	29.0	8.9	52	−17	193	19	4 787	17 796	6.2	93.8
Clay	842	4.0	880	.3	1 060	367	16.6	14.4	132	5	359	61	11 325	30 858	38.6	61.4
Coahoma	598	1.9	5 899	1.9	20 483	181	10.5	59.1	273	−22	1 507	252	96 217	531 586	95.7	4.3
Copiah	816	3.0	12 487	5.9	8 378	510	18.2	11.6	121	−6	237	45	45 263	88 751	5.3	94.7
Covington	810	4.9	13 994	9.2	10 082	475	22.3	7.4	86	6	180	33	43 452	91 478	8.8	91.2
DeSoto	910	1.3	−2 789	X	1 845	467	41.8	12.4	149	10	320	103	26 937	57 681	87.5	12.5
Forrest	490	.7	6 365	.6	4 558	291	36.8	5.2	46	9	158	16	11 952	41 072	23.2	76.8
Franklin	123	1.5	685	1.2	284	158	17.7	12.0	42	−4	269	13	3 658	23 152	19.9	80.1
George	509	3.1	2 804	2.7	3 515	419	47.0	3.1	42	−2	100	19	9 105	21 730	67.8	32.2
Greene	466	4.6	5 610	8.8	4 275	334	23.4	7.2	59	10	176	17	11 830	35 419	7.8	92.2
Grenada	401	1.9	1 278	.4	1 755	211	13.3	19.9	91	−9	431	45	9 703	45 986	73.6	26.4
Hancock	239	.8	−973	X	−899	239	33.1	5.0	36	6	152	17	2 139	8 950	23.0	77.0
Harrison	582	.4	−1 153	X	−905	275	60.0	.7	18	1	65	8	2 572	9 353	59.1	40.9
Hinds	1 098	.4	18 252	.3	15 325	723	23.5	13.8	196	−34	272	89	51 506	71 239	21.7	78.3
Holmes	1 106	5.1	6 815	4.9	5 792	352	11.1	25.0	190	−34	539	119	37 086	105 358	93.9	6.1
Humphreys	798	6.6	32 370	28.0	27 320	240	15.8	45.4	198	18	826	145	123 981	516 588	40.0	60.0
Issaquena	196	10.3	(6)	NA	2 657	82	7.3	54.9	113	−1	1 375	96	29 964	365 415	90.8	9.2

[1] For 1990 corrected population, see table B-1. Percent is based on 1990 uncorrected population because only total population is corrected. [2] For total earnings, see table B-8. [3] Most data are comparable between 1992 and 1997; however, it should be noted that farms with all acreage in Conservation or Wetlands Reserve Programs (excluded in 1992) are included in 1997, as are short rotation woody crops which includes Christmas trees and maple sap gathering (in Forestry in 1992). [4] Includes nursery and greenhouse crops. [5] Includes related products. [6] Less than $50,000.

Sources: Farm Population—U.S. Census Bureau, 1990 Census of Population and Housing, Summary Tape File (STF) 3C on CD-ROM (related Internet site <http://homer.ssd.census.gov/cdrom/lookup/>). Farm Earnings—U.S. Bureau of Economic Analysis, "Regional Economic Information System (REIS) 1969-1998" on CD-ROM (related Internet site <http://www.bea.doc.gov/bea/regional/reis/ca45/>). Agriculture—U.S. Department of Agriculture, National Agricultural Statistics Service, 1997 Census of Agriculture, Volume 1, Geographic Area Series, 1A, 1B, 1C CD-ROM Set (related Internet site <http://www.nass.usda.gov/census/>).

[Includes U.S., states, and 3,142 counties/county equivalents defined as of January 1, 1992. For changes to these areas since January 1, 1992, see appendix B. Geographic Information]

County	Farm population, 1990		Farm earnings			Agriculture (NAICS 111-112), 1997										
			1998			Farms			Land in farms (acres)				Value of farm products sold			
							Percent—								Percent from—	
	Number	Percent of total[1]	Total ($1,000)	Percent of total[2]	1997 ($1,000)	Number	Less than 50 acres	500 acres or more	Total acreage (1,000)	Net change, 1992–1997[3] (1,000)	Average size of farm	Total cropland (1,000)	Total ($1,000)	Average per farm (dollars)	Crops[4]	Livestock and poultry[5]
MISSISSIPPI—Con.																
Itawamba	732	3.7	7 944	4.7	6 137	387	19.4	9.8	82	5	211	37	14 480	37 416	19.9	80.1
Jackson	385	.3	−729	X	−993	321	53.9	4.0	33	8	102	15	4 792	14 928	54.9	45.1
Jasper	1 037	6.1	14 652	9.7	11 337	367	15.5	7.6	75	−14	204	25	28 471	77 578	.6	99.4
Jefferson	166	1.9	2 067	5.8	2 100	158	12.7	23.4	64	−3	402	25	7 731	48 930	53.8	46.2
Jefferson Davis	599	4.3	7 575	9.5	5 871	389	16.7	7.5	79	−2	202	34	15 337	39 427	7.3	92.7
Jones	1 123	1.8	51 173	5.7	39 724	773	37.9	2.6	91	−6	118	39	99 339	128 511	1.5	98.5
Kemper	677	6.5	7 952	12.6	6 922	382	17.5	13.6	97	3	253	33	8 370	21 911	3.6	96.4
Lafayette	681	2.1	912	.2	758	372	12.6	11.3	102	3	275	44	6 125	16 465	69.9	30.1
Lamar	500	1.6	9 701	2.7	8 453	401	31.4	6.5	74	21	185	25	33 705	84 052	6.0	94.0
Lauderdale	719	1.0	2 171	.2	1 941	356	25.6	9.6	75	−6	210	22	4 733	13 295	44.6	55.4
Lawrence	451	3.6	12 956	9.9	10 079	308	16.9	7.5	55	−8	179	24	23 819	77 334	5.7	94.3
Leake	632	3.4	48 851	22.7	37 879	583	22.5	6.2	104	8	178	40	97 366	167 009	1.7	98.3
Lee	1 159	1.8	2 555	.2	2 030	488	27.7	11.9	135	−5	277	93	20 823	42 670	60.0	40.0
Leflore	821	2.2	7 825	1.7	17 140	246	8.9	56.5	267	5	1 087	230	114 960	467 317	73.3	26.7
Lincoln	672	2.2	12 485	3.3	9 562	499	18.6	6.4	99	Z	198	44	31 483	63 092	4.6	95.4
Lowndes	907	1.5	14 878	1.5	22 139	378	22.8	21.4	145	19	384	71	45 309	119 865	21.2	78.8
Madison	786	1.5	3 072	.4	5 087	465	22.2	20.4	182	−17	392	90	24 186	52 013	77.1	22.9
Marion	706	2.8	14 753	6.6	11 436	485	23.1	9.3	97	8	201	36	28 576	58 920	1.7	98.3
Marshall	1 409	4.6	−1 421	X	987	469	21.7	16.6	181	−1	387	88	14 102	30 068	68.2	31.8
Monroe	880	2.4	1 358	.4	1 092	504	19.2	18.7	162	−13	322	100	16 888	33 508	61.0	39.0
Montgomery	317	2.6	2 334	2.6	3 484	286	15.7	18.5	92	12	323	38	9 990	34 930	67.0	33.0
Neshoba	675	2.7	34 478	8.0	25 403	608	20.1	5.1	141	3	231	51	87 249	143 502	1.0	99.0
Newton	727	3.6	39 945	17.0	29 184	543	21.0	5.9	100	4	185	44	88 505	162 993	1.2	98.8
Noxubee	879	7.0	9 493	9.3	11 392	454	16.7	23.3	194	−8	426	100	43 558	95 943	33.8	66.2
Oktibbeha	599	1.6	2 304	.5	1 886	329	21.0	14.0	85	5	259	42	8 788	26 711	17.4	82.6
Panola	1 161	3.9	−480	X	4 461	573	14.7	20.1	238	20	416	151	31 022	54 140	88.1	11.9
Pearl River	777	2.0	−1 559	X	−1 413	609	36.8	6.6	103	10	169	44	8 838	14 512	26.7	73.3
Perry	398	3.7	4 318	4.6	3 528	246	32.5	4.9	32	Z	130	11	9 167	37 264	6.4	93.6
Pike	808	2.2	14 086	3.1	9 304	437	23.3	4.1	71	−10	161	35	49 577	113 449	1.4	98.6
Pontotoc	843	3.8	3 770	1.4	2 039	552	25.0	9.8	115	−10	208	65	8 620	15 616	61.9	38.1
Prentiss	853	3.7	−513	X	61	412	20.9	8.3	88	2	214	51	7 577	18 391	70.0	30.0
Quitman	766	7.3	683	1.3	7 034	179	10.6	50.8	170	−17	947	156	46 178	257 978	98.0	2.0
Rankin	1 594	1.8	24 196	1.5	18 015	558	26.9	10.6	117	−1	210	50	51 306	91 946	8.0	92.0
Scott	1 146	4.7	84 138	22.7	65 701	674	29.1	5.0	107	−3	159	46	174 534	258 953	.7	99.3
Sharkey	284	4.0	3 784	8.6	5 896	110	9.1	65.5	166	−16	1 505	153	59 095	537 227	81.9	18.1
Simpson	803	3.4	45 396	19.9	37 437	550	25.5	5.3	94	−3	170	39	103 126	187 502	1.2	98.8
Smith	876	5.9	66 196	34.9	54 781	635	26.8	4.9	95	Z	149	36	129 243	203 532	.9	99.1
Stone	339	3.2	427	.4	414	212	33.5	5.7	42	9	196	13	4 152	19 585	43.2	56.9
Sunflower	865	2.6	28 325	8.4	36 701	350	8.9	52.6	348	−13	995	296	164 335	469 529	61.7	38.3
Tallahatchie	913	6.0	746	1.1	16 616	355	12.4	38.0	297	24	836	250	82 675	232 887	96.9	3.1
Tate	803	3.7	5 753	2.8	7 144	508	24.0	13.2	135	−7	265	77	24 406	48 043	47.4	52.6
Tippah	577	3.0	3 219	1.4	3 542	501	18.4	7.8	114	6	227	47	9 480	18 922	65.1	34.9
Tishomingo	378	2.1	369	.2	(6)	258	21.7	6.2	45	4	174	17	2 778	10 767	32.1	67.8
Tunica	445	5.5	(6)	Z	8 965	95	1.1	74.7	202	−28	2 130	185	64 267	676 495	89.9	10.1
Union	743	3.4	2 103	.8	696	549	23.3	6.4	102	2	186	50	9 866	17 971	46.0	54.0
Walthall	929	6.5	18 941	17.3	14 168	538	21.4	6.7	110	2	205	50	50 771	94 370	2.4	97.6
Warren	782	1.6	88	Z	1 926	159	17.0	32.7	98	−16	615	51	12 298	77 346	92.5	7.5
Washington	759	1.1	22 547	2.8	34 534	283	8.8	60.4	343	1	1 211	308	146 480	517 597	78.6	21.4
Wayne	678	3.5	24 736	11.8	18 061	458	31.2	6.1	76	3	165	28	62 626	136 738	2.1	97.9
Webster	424	4.1	442	.5	2 029	289	19.4	11.4	79	3	272	35	12 512	43 294	56.7	43.3
Wilkinson	319	3.3	298	.5	147	196	19.9	26.5	109	19	557	38	5 296	27 020	28.8	71.2
Winston	664	3.4	3 684	1.9	3 059	458	19.9	7.2	88	5	192	36	8 282	18 083	14.4	85.6
Yalobusha	507	4.2	(6)	Z	−219	278	14.4	13.7	86	7	308	41	9 494	34 151	80.0	20.0
Yazoo	703	2.8	11 222	4.4	12 466	424	9.7	39.9	312	−49	737	209	74 823	176 469	78.5	21.5
MISSOURI	180 097	3.5	424 624	.4	995 172	98 860	20.1	15.5	28 826	279	292	19 229	5 367 813	54 297	43.0	57.0
Adair	1 466	6.0	−1 058	X	3 349	861	14.4	18.2	268	1	311	171	21 804	25 324	47.7	52.3
Andrew	1 666	11.4	3 812	4.8	10 682	820	18.4	15.5	227	Z	276	178	40 440	49 317	70.0	30.0
Atchison	1 019	13.7	10 146	13.7	18 019	471	11.9	46.5	294	−10	625	256	62 548	132 798	89.1	10.9
Audrain	2 421	10.3	2 832	.8	15 972	1 005	15.1	23.5	382	5	381	316	81 984	81 576	63.0	37.0
Barry	2 277	8.3	31 953	7.3	20 339	1 598	27.8	6.4	285	−7	178	163	151 993	95 115	2.7	97.3
Barton	1 683	14.9	1 919	1.3	13 608	896	15.3	24.2	335	24	374	252	64 242	71 699	52.3	47.7
Bates	2 212	14.7	6 876	6.2	17 343	1 250	17.3	18.9	445	14	356	297	65 806	52 645	49.1	50.9
Benton	1 357	9.8	1 382	1.4	2 440	804	14.1	15.0	232	−7	289	124	30 667	38 143	20.6	79.4
Bollinger	1 435	13.5	577	1.1	2 651	832	13.5	12.5	209	12	251	117	19 060	22 909	42.7	57.3
Boone	2 058	1.8	1 576	.1	2 323	1 227	28.8	10.8	250	−22	204	172	40 103	32 684	42.0	58.0
Buchanan	1 464	1.8	5 052	.4	6 848	776	28.5	12.5	182	Z	234	145	32 194	41 487	79.4	20.6
Butler	1 741	4.5	18 304	3.3	24 285	678	22.3	25.1	255	Z	376	218	59 893	88 338	91.5	8.5
Caldwell	1 437	17.1	3 760	7.5	5 235	845	17.0	13.6	227	−5	269	164	25 546	30 232	52.6	47.4
Callaway	2 298	7.0	10 137	2.3	8 993	1 338	19.7	10.3	330	−9	247	210	54 401	40 658	40.1	59.9

[1] For 1990 corrected population, see table B-1. Percent is based on 1990 uncorrected population because only total population is corrected. [2] For total earnings, see table B-8. [3] Most data are comparable between 1992 and 1997; however, it should be noted that farms with all acreage in Conservation or Wetlands Reserve Programs (excluded in 1992) are included in 1997, as are short rotation woody crops which includes Christmas trees and maple sap gathering (in Forestry in 1992). [4] Includes nursery and greenhouse crops. [5] Includes related products. [6] Less than $50,000.

Sources: Farm Population—U.S. Census Bureau, 1990 Census of Population and Housing, Summary Tape File (STF) 3C on CD-ROM (related Internet site <http://homer.ssd.census.gov/cdrom/lookup>). Farm Earnings—U.S. Bureau of Economic Analysis, "Regional Economic Information System (REIS) 1969-1998" on CD-ROM (related Internet site <http://www.bea.doc.gov/bea/regional/reis/ca45/>). Agriculture—U.S. Department of Agriculture, National Agricultural Statistics Service, 1997 Census of Agriculture, Volume 1, Geographic Area Series, 1A, 1B, 1C CD-ROM Set (related Internet site <http://www.nass.usda.gov/census/>).

[Includes U.S., states, and 3,142 counties/county equivalents defined as of January 1, 1992. For changes to these areas since January 1, 1992, see appendix B. Geographic Information]

County	Farm population, 1990 Number	Percent of total[1]	Farm earnings 1998 Total ($1,000)	Percent of total[2]	1997 ($1,000)	Farms Number	Percent Less than 50 acres	Percent 500 acres or more	Land in farms Total acreage (1,000)	Net change, 1992–1997[3] (1,000)	Average size of farm	Total cropland (1,000)	Value of farm products sold Total ($1,000)	Average per farm (dollars)	Percent from Crops[4]	Percent from Livestock and poultry[5]
MISSOURI—Con.																
Camden	984	3.6	–201	X	1 517	584	14.0	15.6	172	9	295	71	15 614	26 736	3.2	96.8
Cape Girardeau	2 299	3.7	–1 574	X	4 454	1 161	21.7	9.7	261	8	225	197	46 225	39 815	50.0	50.0
Carroll	1 772	16.5	6 931	8.8	17 001	952	15.7	25.8	396	19	416	324	58 965	61 938	75.5	24.5
Carter	212	3.8	–656	X	497	202	15.3	15.3	63	8	311	20	3 069	15 193	7.5	92.5
Cass	2 919	4.6	759	.1	9 149	1 519	31.4	8.7	310	–15	204	229	55 600	36 603	61.2	38.8
Cedar	1 358	11.2	1 996	2.1	1 971	865	18.3	11.2	204	16	235	111	20 870	24 127	12.4	87.6
Chariton	2 316	25.2	11 268	15.8	20 505	1 071	14.5	23.4	414	11	387	332	85 215	79 566	56.0	44.0
Christian	2 078	6.4	–962	X	766	1 209	34.7	5.0	203	–8	168	115	25 739	21 289	7.9	92.1
Clark	1 600	21.2	–4 836	X	11 610	634	9.5	24.3	248	4	392	184	35 554	56 079	81.8	18.2
Clay	696	.5	1 092	Z	1 604	634	34.7	9.8	134	4	212	93	26 319	41 513	43.6	56.4
Clinton	1 373	8.3	–1 636	X	3 440	768	25.0	14.6	216	9	282	156	34 565	45 007	51.8	48.2
Cole	1 816	2.9	4 079	.2	3 198	1 045	20.0	5.4	179	–8	171	98	26 464	25 324	18.8	81.2
Cooper	1 727	11.6	3 067	2.0	8 772	879	15.1	20.7	302	3	343	224	52 827	60 099	45.3	54.7
Crawford	891	4.6	–3 151	X	–2 417	691	15.8	12.7	182	–20	264	82	8 727	12 630	17.1	82.9
Dade	1 414	19.0	2 361	4.2	4 325	808	17.3	17.3	249	–4	308	159	30 609	37 882	32.0	68.0
Dallas	2 021	16.0	–412	X	–1 040	1 130	23.3	8.2	222	–6	196	127	28 355	25 093	4.7	95.3
Daviess	1 754	22.3	5 907	9.9	19 010	886	15.8	20.2	302	23	341	209	57 180	64 537	42.2	57.8
DeKalb	1 392	14.0	6 012	6.5	10 313	769	17.7	16.8	215	4	280	162	29 270	38 062	51.4	48.6
Dent	909	6.6	253	.2	546	727	11.8	17.3	222	3	305	96	9 871	13 578	7.7	92.3
Douglas	1 936	16.3	4 549	6.0	3 795	1 206	16.7	12.1	302	1	250	135	29 531	24 487	4.5	95.5
Dunklin	1 224	3.7	3 266	1.1	29 010	473	16.5	43.3	313	24	662	303	110 022	232 605	98.7	1.3
Franklin	2 554	3.2	2 048	.2	6 187	1 592	25.4	7.4	290	–7	182	180	46 634	29 293	31.7	68.3
Gasconade	917	6.5	–971	X	1 317	762	11.7	10.0	188	–9	247	96	15 186	19 929	26.6	73.4
Gentry	1 261	18.4	10 073	15.2	28 809	667	13.5	22.0	249	3	373	191	54 100	81 109	33.4	66.6
Greene	2 695	1.3	2 299	Z	1 970	1 997	40.7	5.0	277	–8	139	183	33 414	16 732	16.0	84.0
Grundy	1 400	13.3	274	.3	7 111	667	15.0	18.4	222	–4	333	170	28 852	43 256	72.9	27.1
Harrison	1 625	19.2	9 636	12.0	9 351	901	13.2	25.7	387	–12	430	255	44 394	49 272	56.2	43.8
Henry	1 802	9.0	2 974	1.4	5 642	938	17.9	19.0	315	–6	336	235	42 642	45 461	40.8	59.2
Hickory	987	13.5	279	.8	383	521	10.4	19.0	172	–3	330	85	14 580	27 985	8.5	91.5
Holt	1 115	18.5	13 367	25.7	17 621	465	12.0	34.2	231	–2	497	204	53 269	114 557	83.8	16.2
Howard	1 287	13.4	2 142	2.8	5 637	709	13.3	18.2	242	3	342	159	31 428	44 327	64.2	35.8
Howell	3 058	9.7	–688	X	1 714	1 637	22.0	9.2	387	15	236	162	50 152	30 637	3.3	96.7
Iron	301	2.8	230	.2	562	274	14.6	11.3	63	–6	228	29	6 378	23 277	D	D
Jackson	1 277	.2	–476	X	3 323	765	45.0	7.2	151	16	197	114	27 586	36 060	80.7	19.3
Jasper	2 169	2.4	9 196	.5	13 481	1 355	30.0	8.5	271	–10	200	180	76 421	56 399	36.7	63.3
Jefferson	862	.5	–2 487	X	–1 275	659	31.1	5.8	109	–10	166	57	8 966	13 605	41.6	58.4
Johnson	2 981	7.0	–3 400	X	1 208	1 626	21.9	12.1	400	29	246	279	53 791	33 082	38.4	61.6
Knox	1 262	28.2	1 445	4.8	8 656	602	10.6	29.7	281	12	466	207	36 610	60 814	59.5	40.5
Laclede	1 683	6.2	220	.1	–183	1 300	18.1	12.5	317	12	244	166	32 154	24 734	6.1	93.9
Lafayette	3 036	9.8	11 941	4.5	30 852	1 215	25.3	16.8	349	–7	287	286	107 890	88 798	53.4	46.6
Lawrence	3 151	10.4	11 474	4.6	10 859	1 733	28.7	8.3	338	5	195	223	121 838	70 305	7.8	92.2
Lewis	1 132	11.1	–2 706	X	9 666	719	15.2	20.6	269	20	374	190	40 639	56 522	70.6	29.4
Lincoln	2 741	9.5	8 658	3.3	13 983	989	25.8	14.6	262	9	265	188	52 365	52 947	53.5	46.5
Linn	1 621	11.7	5 230	3.3	11 776	933	14.1	22.5	346	8	371	251	48 596	52 086	33.9	66.1
Livingston	1 745	12.0	4 368	2.3	11 404	738	15.4	20.5	273	2	370	213	37 179	50 378	78.7	21.3
McDonald	1 845	10.9	16 774	9.9	16 985	1 078	23.1	7.6	232	32	215	97	155 015	143 799	1.0	99.0
Macon	2 192	14.3	–5 238	X	2 892	1 155	13.7	17.3	381	–1	329	249	34 916	30 230	55.0	45.0
Madison	387	3.5	–228	X	–102	386	10.9	15.5	110	–1	285	48	6 565	17 008	7.7	92.3
Maries	1 252	15.7	–3 726	X	–1 076	817	12.9	16.5	229	–4	280	105	19 246	23 557	8.4	91.6
Marion	1 574	5.7	2 931	.7	10 822	695	15.7	18.7	221	1	318	164	39 955	57 489	62.2	37.8
Mercer	761	20.4	–295	X	30 309	539	12.1	24.9	230	19	426	159	122 780	227 792	D	D
Miller	1 680	8.1	7 128	3.4	10 953	1 067	12.7	9.5	255	13	239	118	75 961	71 191	3.2	96.8
Mississippi	483	3.3	12 094	10.9	23 095	267	10.5	57.3	264	–2	987	255	79 847	299 052	99.1	.9
Moniteau	2 194	17.8	5 154	4.4	7 386	1 024	17.5	9.7	223	6	218	147	52 868	51 629	17.7	82.3
Monroe	1 946	21.4	2 018	2.2	16 708	886	12.4	21.0	328	22	370	240	55 533	62 678	52.9	47.1
Montgomery	1 315	11.6	–3 169	X	2 997	765	17.1	20.3	248	23	324	171	36 604	47 848	62.2	37.8
Morgan	1 684	10.8	16 140	11.8	15 278	869	19.4	10.8	202	1	233	112	91 101	104 834	6.1	93.9
New Madrid	830	4.0	10 755	4.2	19 785	429	7.7	55.5	386	17	899	375	109 408	255 030	97.0	3.0
Newton	3 127	7.0	19 395	3.7	13 272	1 622	31.3	6.0	256	Z	158	168	123 381	76 067	4.8	95.2
Nodaway	3 244	14.9	4 007	1.6	19 249	1 257	14.3	26.1	492	–16	391	396	83 850	66 706	63.5	36.5
Oregon	1 199	12.7	–2 621	X	–733	798	17.3	14.8	248	–4	311	100	20 325	25 470	5.9	94.1
Osage	2 124	17.7	1 824	1.8	4 228	1 147	13.3	11.5	305	–12	266	140	51 424	44 833	10.2	89.8
Ozark	1 464	17.0	–999	X	–937	781	12.5	14.7	253	2	324	85	21 034	26 932	2.9	97.1
Pemiscot	921	4.2	3 002	1.7	24 314	306	12.7	58.2	296	4	966	291	85 856	280 575	99.3	.7
Perry	1 629	9.8	–2 689	X	4 098	857	20.0	10.6	201	–8	235	131	32 213	37 588	48.9	51.1
Pettis	2 977	8.4	15 873	2.8	18 014	1 249	20.7	16.1	366	7	293	263	104 015	83 279	28.1	71.9
Phelps	970	2.8	–4 002	X	–3 160	758	21.0	12.9	196	–5	259	84	9 254	12 208	13.7	86.3
Pike	2 182	13.7	1 612	1.0	10 731	944	17.1	18.8	317	–7	336	218	54 572	57 809	63.5	36.5
Platte	1 249	2.2	10 312	.8	11 368	714	31.4	13.6	180	–8	253	139	35 776	50 106	84.2	15.8
Polk	2 749	12.6	740	.4	1 231	1 575	23.5	9.7	348	2	221	209	49 516	31 439	9.6	90.4

[1] For 1990 corrected population, see table B-1. Percent is based on 1990 uncorrected population because only total population is corrected. [2] For total earnings, see table B-8. [3] Most data are comparable between 1992 and 1997; however, it should be noted that farms with all acreage in Conservation or Wetlands Reserve Programs (excluded in 1992) are included in 1997, as are short rotation woody crops which includes Christmas trees and maple sap gathering (in Forestry in 1992). [4] Includes nursery and greenhouse crops. [5] Includes related products.

Sources: Farm Population—U.S. Census Bureau, 1990 Census of Population and Housing, Summary Tape File (STF) 3C on CD-ROM (related Internet site <http://homer.ssd.census.gov/cdrom/lookup>). Farm Earnings—U.S. Bureau of Economic Analysis, "Regional Economic Information System (REIS) 1969-1998" on CD-ROM (related Internet site <http://www.bea.doc.gov/bea/regional/reis/ca45/>). Agriculture—U.S. Department of Agriculture, National Agricultural Statistics Service, 1997 Census of Agriculture, Volume 1, Geographic Area Series, 1A, 1B, 1C CD-ROM Set (related Internet site <http://www.nass.usda.gov/census/>).

[Includes U.S., states, and 3,142 counties/county equivalents defined as of January 1, 1992. For changes to these areas since January 1, 1992, see appendix B. Geographic Information]

County	Farm population, 1990 Number	Farm population, 1990 Percent of total[1]	Farm earnings 1998 Total ($1,000)	Farm earnings 1998 Percent of total[2]	Farm earnings 1997 ($1,000)	Farms Number	Farms Percent Less than 50 acres	Farms Percent 500 acres or more	Land in farms Total acreage (1,000)	Land in farms Net change, 1992–1997[3] (1,000)	Land in farms Average size of farm	Land in farms Total cropland (1,000)	Value of farm products sold Total ($1,000)	Value of farm products sold Average per farm (dollars)	Value Percent from Crops[4]	Value Percent from Livestock and poultry[5]
MISSOURI—Con.																
Pulaski	719	1.7	2 624	.4	−396	539	16.7	15.8	140	1	259	65	11 952	22 174	6.7	93.3
Putnam	1 130	22.2	−897	X	2 602	615	12.7	24.7	261	7	425	154	26 900	43 740	27.8	72.2
Ralls	1 452	17.1	5 150	6.0	11 510	550	13.8	26.2	232	3	421	172	38 747	70 449	66.7	33.3
Randolph	1 151	4.7	2 829	1.0	4 123	801	16.0	14.2	230	9	287	143	26 725	33 365	40.7	59.3
Ray	2 207	10.0	2 840	1.9	7 010	1 075	23.7	12.3	274	−3	255	202	39 060	36 335	63.6	36.4
Reynolds	309	4.6	−692	X	−545	302	10.9	19.9	113	24	375	34	3 105	10 281	8.6	91.4
Ripley	661	5.4	2 284	3.2	3 478	472	13.8	18.2	152	−1	322	70	10 729	22 731	50.5	49.5
St. Charles	1 486	.7	7 516	.2	8 804	680	29.4	16.0	187	−17	275	148	42 456	62 435	79.9	20.1
St. Clair	1 555	18.4	−1 826	X	678	778	16.1	22.1	263	6	338	162	24 614	31 638	36.2	63.8
Ste. Genevieve	1 052	6.6	636	.4	3 253	631	17.7	11.6	168	Z	266	86	17 905	28 376	38.9	61.1
St. Francois	794	1.6	1 029	.2	1 362	649	25.6	6.3	113	−4	174	61	13 299	20 492	46.3	53.7
St. Louis	283	Z	6 079	Z	6 769	[6]291	[6]45.7	[6]9.6	[6]45	[6]−9	[6]155	[6]31	[6]21 334	[6]73 313	[6]84.3	[6]15.7
Saline	2 233	9.5	15 804	5.4	31 425	936	14.4	28.8	430	15	459	347	102 633	109 651	66.6	33.4
Schuyler	781	18.4	−1 727	X	908	493	13.8	18.1	160	−6	324	111	14 345	29 097	43.0	57.0
Scotland	1 221	25.3	1 129	2.9	9 866	600	12.3	22.2	225	8	374	165	34 078	56 797	60.6	39.4
Scott	1 320	3.4	4 751	1.0	19 619	541	21.8	26.1	241	22	445	223	76 630	141 645	77.7	22.3
Shannon	746	9.8	−677	X	497	470	16.8	15.7	133	13	284	51	5 500	11 702	5.8	94.2
Shelby	1 445	20.8	2 188	3.2	18 262	644	12.3	27.3	272	−1	423	210	58 535	90 893	50.8	49.2
Stoddard	1 984	6.9	23 029	7.9	48 876	941	22.6	27.1	449	10	477	415	153 640	163 273	76.3	23.7
Stone	1 211	6.3	1 538	.7	917	684	23.4	9.4	136	−2	199	62	15 888	23 228	4.8	95.2
Sullivan	1 227	19.4	17 539	18.2	16 967	791	9.2	25.7	326	−4	412	212	185 404	234 392	4.9	95.1
Taney	595	2.3	665	.1	1 045	459	17.0	17.4	158	−2	345	40	9 937	21 649	5.3	94.7
Texas	2 818	13.1	213	.1	1 468	1 478	16.6	13.3	430	−30	291	206	36 547	24 727	6.0	94.0
Vernon	1 841	9.7	−5 099	X	16 783	1 265	21.1	17.2	389	−14	307	274	87 731	69 353	31.5	68.5
Warren	1 171	6.0	912	.5	5 025	555	26.8	13.3	133	6	239	85	22 492	40 526	55.0	45.0
Washington	770	3.8	−1 967	X	6 131	499	14.6	11.6	127	15	254	53	24 682	49 463	1.8	98.2
Wayne	478	4.1	−234	X	673	380	10.3	12.4	98	5	257	38	4 205	11 066	27.5	72.5
Webster	2 802	11.8	1 681	.9	1 327	1 691	31.3	6.9	297	7	176	166	46 348	27 409	5.0	95.0
Worth	532	21.8	1 517	9.3	3 618	356	12.4	26.1	150	16	422	105	13 045	36 643	53.1	46.9
Wright	2 258	13.5	8 492	6.0	5 243	1 331	19.8	12.1	312	−4	235	163	41 994	31 551	3.8	96.2
Independent City																
St. Louis city	–	–	–	–	–	(6)	(6)	(6)	(6)	(6)	(6)	(6)	(6)	(6)	(6)	(6)
MONTANA	45 718	5.7	244 124	2.0	172 663	24 279	18.4	53.0	58 608	−1 035	2 414	17 629	1 870 732	77 051	48.3	51.7
Beaverhead	902	10.7	7 246	6.9	6 912	360	19.2	57.2	1 152	−190	3 200	203	55 374	153 817	18.4	81.6
Big Horn	846	7.5	7 529	5.6	3 254	530	13.4	60.0	2 770	−232	5 227	408	61 126	115 332	45.0	55.0
Blaine	1 205	17.9	10 748	19.2	4 484	541	6.3	68.8	2 258	−81	4 173	660	47 937	88 608	53.3	46.7
Broadwater	378	11.4	4 720	11.3	5 338	219	13.2	51.1	453	3	2 067	131	20 177	92 132	66.8	33.2
Carbon	1 392	17.2	1 729	2.5	2 342	623	15.4	35.6	736	137	1 181	172	43 770	70 257	35.5	64.5
Carter	765	50.9	−1 683	X	−1 808	305	3.3	88.5	1 589	−30	5 211	245	26 991	88 495	13.9	86.1
Cascade	1 819	2.3	7 044	.6	9 144	903	20.3	44.3	1 441	17	1 596	508	66 731	73 899	48.0	52.0
Chouteau	1 657	30.4	12 423	27.8	12 540	750	2.8	84.0	2 212	−66	2 949	1 346	92 706	123 608	83.9	16.1
Custer	995	8.5	−1 420	X	−2 667	405	18.8	53.3	1 898	−188	4 685	170	32 586	80 459	21.8	78.2
Daniels	498	22.0	6 419	21.7	4 520	363	3.3	80.4	765	3	2 106	529	25 644	70 645	79.4	20.6
Dawson	873	9.2	6 689	5.9	2 687	502	8.2	72.5	1 417	83	2 823	466	34 748	69 219	59.3	40.7
Deer Lodge	148	1.4	175	.2	(7)	83	24.1	44.6	102	−33	1 225	22	4 217	50 807	20.3	79.7
Fallon	629	20.3	1 506	3.6	909	309	7.1	73.1	953	8	3 084	232	20 407	66 042	27.3	72.7
Fergus	1 592	13.2	7 389	5.8	8 521	816	11.0	67.2	2 249	16	2 756	676	71 841	88 040	44.7	55.3
Flathead	1 718	2.9	3 190	.3	1 861	898	49.0	12.6	216	−61	241	106	26 664	29 693	67.0	33.0
Gallatin	1 770	3.5	13 087	1.3	9 765	835	31.3	30.4	760	61	910	253	58 905	70 545	52.5	47.5
Garfield	751	47.3	2 534	23.6	917	244	3.3	90.2	2 163	163	8 866	302	32 030	131 270	30.5	69.5
Glacier	650	5.4	10 338	8.0	10 058	425	9.4	68.5	1 623	−108	3 818	497	45 418	106 866	62.6	37.4
Golden Valley	200	21.9	1 075	20.8	820	118	7.6	72.9	638	2	5 407	117	12 942	109 678	35.0	65.0
Granite	337	13.2	1 134	4.6	1 106	117	8.5	67.5	268	−82	2 294	45	9 642	82 410	15.0	85.0
Hill	1 060	6.0	21 123	9.2	12 577	692	4.2	73.4	1 643	−1	2 374	1 080	67 060	96 908	82.6	17.4
Jefferson	236	3.0	(7)	Z	−327	266	28.2	36.5	364	−3	1 369	76	8 565	32 199	22.9	77.1
Judith Basin	779	34.1	3 966	27.1	3 956	329	8.5	72.9	835	−33	2 537	289	37 595	114 271	38.5	61.5
Lake	2 210	10.5	−1 639	X	−1 971	1 011	40.2	14.5	597	−35	590	150	37 543	37 135	42.8	57.2
Lewis and Clark	746	1.6	1 522	.2	1 389	502	43.6	25.5	822	−61	1 638	97	18 997	37 843	35.4	64.6
Liberty	411	17.9	7 477	29.3	6 025	280	1.1	88.6	915	−36	3 269	631	38 479	137 425	76.1	23.9
Lincoln	319	1.8	264	.1	(7)	252	35.3	6.7	46	−4	183	17	3 675	14 583	38.8	61.2
McCone	749	32.9	5 403	26.4	2 136	430	2.8	83.7	1 313	23	3 053	555	28 698	66 740	62.2	37.8
Madison	751	12.5	−1 093	X	−535	460	16.7	47.0	1 080	−192	2 347	154	35 456	77 078	27.9	72.1
Meagher	190	10.4	3 359	18.0	3 423	142	9.9	65.5	940	28	6 620	114	22 898	161 254	18.2	81.8
Mineral	84	2.5	130	.4	(7)	71	36.6	14.1	16	−3	230	6	1 183	16 662	25.1	74.9
Missoula	744	.9	−3 696	X	−4 431	482	53.1	13.9	262	14	544	47	8 022	16 643	27.4	72.6
Musselshell	405	9.9	1 652	6.1	1 442	232	9.1	63.8	953	−79	4 106	134	17 441	75 177	32.3	67.7
Park	803	5.5	[8]4 988	[8]3.1	[8]3 677	420	20.0	50.0	749	−29	1 784	132	20 457	48 707	30.2	69.8
Petroleum	175	33.7	1 289	37.7	809	88	2.3	81.8	541	−128	6 152	64	9 371	106 489	23.8	76.2

[1] For 1990 corrected population, see table B-1. Percent is based on 1990 uncorrected population because only total population is corrected. [2] For total earnings, see table B-8. [3] Most data are comparable between 1992 and 1997; however, it should be noted that farms with all acreage in Conservation or Wetlands Reserve Programs (excluded in 1992) are included in 1997, as are short rotation woody crops which includes Christmas trees and maple sap gathering (in Forestry in 1992). [4] Includes nursery and greenhouse crops. [5] Includes related products. [6] Independent city of St. Louis included with St. Louis County; data not available separately. [7] Less than $50,000. [8] Yellowstone National Park County included with Park County; data not available separately.

Sources: Farm Population—U.S. Census Bureau, 1990 Census of Population and Housing, Summary Tape File (STF) 3C on CD-ROM (related Internet site <http://homer.ssd.census.gov/cdrom/lookup/>). Farm Earnings—U.S. Bureau of Economic Analysis, "Regional Economic Information System (REIS) 1969-1998" on CD-ROM (related Internet site <http://www.bea.doc.gov/bea/regional/reis/ca45/>). Agriculture—U.S. Department of Agriculture, National Agricultural Statistics Service, 1997 Census of Agriculture, Volume 1, Geographic Area Series, 1A, 1B, 1C CD-ROM Set (related Internet site <http://www.nass.usda.gov/census/>).

Table B–10. Counties — Farm Population, Farm Earnings, and Agriculture–Con.

[Includes U.S., states, and 3,142 counties/county equivalents defined as of January 1, 1992. For changes to these areas since January 1, 1992, see appendix B. Geographic Information]

County	Farm population, 1990 Number	Farm population, 1990 Percent of total[1]	Farm earnings 1998 Total ($1,000)	Farm earnings 1998 Percent of total[2]	Farm earnings 1997 ($1,000)	Farms Number	Farms Percent Less than 50 acres	Farms Percent 500 acres or more	Land in farms Total acreage (1,000)	Land in farms Net change, 1992–1997[3] (1,000)	Land in farms Average size of farm	Land in farms Total cropland (1,000)	Value of farm products sold Total ($1,000)	Value of farm products sold Average per farm (dollars)	Value of farm products sold Percent from Crops[4]	Value of farm products sold Percent from Livestock and poultry[5]
MONTANA—Con.																
Phillips	1 024	19.8	5 736	12.4	728	489	8.2	71.0	1 978	9	4 045	634	40 865	83 569	39.8	60.2
Pondera	694	10.8	11 311	18.0	10 002	474	8.9	69.0	878	−15	1 853	564	57 683	121 694	75.2	24.8
Powder River	711	34.0	−209	X	−690	297	4.7	81.5	1 559	−70	5 250	166	27 293	91 896	11.5	88.5
Powell	384	5.8	2 430	3.3	3 159	230	13.9	57.4	649	−26	2 824	75	17 807	77 422	12.7	87.3
Prairie	436	31.5	4 275	36.9	1 512	158	5.7	75.3	613	−70	3 879	123	20 292	128 430	30.9	69.1
Ravalli	1 436	5.7	−151	X	−810	1 080	56.8	6.8	184	−58	170	83	23 949	22 175	25.3	74.7
Richland	1 162	10.8	9 297	7.6	3 629	571	10.3	62.7	1 215	18	2 127	507	54 075	94 702	65.0	35.0
Roosevelt	908	8.3	10 474	10.1	8 252	609	4.9	71.8	1 430	16	2 348	784	38 812	63 731	77.4	22.6
Rosebud	727	6.9	1 364	.9	−53	362	7.5	68.8	2 681	95	7 406	207	37 666	104 050	23.1	76.9
Sanders	707	8.2	−2 724	X	−3 445	412	18.9	25.5	410	29	995	62	11 534	27 995	36.7	63.3
Sheridan	611	12.9	10 575	22.7	4 911	581	2.6	77.5	1 001	39	1 723	677	35 949	61 874	80.6	19.4
Silver Bow	195	.6	626	.1	592	116	17.2	32.8	100	Z	864	15	3 238	27 914	7.0	93.0
Stillwater	998	15.3	1 196	1.3	1 067	473	18.6	53.1	897	7	1 896	250	29 001	61 313	28.1	71.9
Sweet Grass	584	18.5	−1 212	X	−757	301	12.3	57.1	839	1	2 789	101	21 345	70 914	9.4	90.6
Teton	1 709	27.3	11 358	19.3	12 970	557	10.2	58.2	1 117	−62	2 005	581	71 962	129 196	63.9	36.1
Toole	446	8.8	6 997	10.0	7 297	382	2.6	80.9	1 091	28	2 856	680	39 178	102 560	79.2	20.8
Treasure	185	21.2	1 107	20.0	509	110	5.5	64.5	606	7	5 505	47	17 567	159 700	35.5	64.5
Valley	1 418	17.2	12 476	12.9	7 883	655	5.6	69.2	1 787	99	2 728	740	47 785	72 954	54.0	46.0
Wheatland	376	16.7	1 568	9.8	1 989	144	3.5	80.6	834	−17	5 790	182	22 834	158 569	28.2	71.8
Wibaux	240	20.2	2 445	28.5	771	178	5.6	69.1	475	−16	2 671	139	10 562	59 337	40.0	60.0
Yellowstone	1 980	1.7	8 521	.4	4 335	1 097	32.5	32.0	1 526	71	1 391	381	96 044	87 552	31.4	68.6
Yellowstone National Park	–	–	(6)	(6)	(6)	–	–	–	–	–	–	–	–	–	–	–
NEBRASKA	117 658	7.5	1 481 636	4.8	1 610 749	51 454	14.2	42.2	45 525	1 132	885	22 093	9 831 519	191 074	38.6	61.4
Adams	1 147	3.9	23 212	5.0	23 818	623	15.2	44.6	344	9	553	288	159 384	255 833	49.3	50.7
Antelope	2 010	25.2	34 312	35.9	36 005	803	12.0	41.2	492	3	613	378	156 180	194 496	49.2	50.8
Arthur	254	55.0	−3 655	X	−4 504	83	4.8	88.0	465	5	5 606	59	13 487	162 494	14.8	85.2
Banner	395	46.4	3 254	48.9	4 521	220	3.6	77.3	446	39	2 029	210	48 750	221 591	29.4	70.6
Blaine	259	38.4	−3 163	X	−2 801	118	10.2	72.0	452	−8	3 831	44	16 287	138 025	11.0	89.0
Boone	1 680	25.2	16 923	25.6	25 101	767	9.8	38.1	448	10	584	317	163 955	213 761	33.7	66.3
Box Butte	900	6.9	22 236	9.7	25 854	508	6.5	61.0	697	47	1 371	389	150 821	296 892	40.8	59.2
Boyd	692	24.4	−209	X	936	361	9.7	54.3	297	Z	822	113	30 723	85 105	33.5	66.5
Brown	472	12.9	−676	X	1 765	349	14.3	56.7	701	51	2 008	133	87 369	250 341	18.1	81.9
Buffalo	1 830	4.9	25 354	3.8	26 750	1 081	16.1	39.0	621	34	575	380	158 551	146 671	51.7	48.3
Burt	1 384	17.6	23 783	29.0	27 057	580	14.7	35.5	292	22	504	264	112 520	194 000	53.7	46.3
Butler	2 268	26.4	22 456	27.5	24 416	804	13.4	32.6	354	18	440	307	102 471	127 451	65.8	34.2
Cass	2 348	11.0	17 155	10.6	18 368	694	22.6	28.2	301	5	433	255	67 160	96 772	83.8	16.2
Cedar	3 199	31.6	31 926	29.1	39 623	971	12.5	33.5	445	17	459	359	153 567	158 153	31.9	68.1
Chase	504	11.5	25 489	36.9	22 873	374	7.2	68.4	557	35	1 488	317	104 194	278 594	68.6	31.4
Cherry	1 652	26.2	−889	X	1 212	672	9.2	75.7	3 882	−6	5 777	395	100 280	149 226	7.7	92.3
Cheyenne	1 060	11.2	8 398	5.5	8 616	645	4.7	62.8	779	7	1 208	559	111 325	172 597	34.1	65.9
Clay	1 158	16.3	27 240	25.1	26 912	538	14.9	46.5	365	8	678	288	170 597	317 095	43.8	56.2
Colfax	1 708	18.7	24 638	17.1	29 890	604	20.4	28.3	230	1	381	203	178 632	295 748	25.1	74.9
Cuming	2 885	28.5	74 978	39.6	86 723	995	19.8	23.7	360	14	361	313	506 954	509 502	11.8	88.2
Custer	2 664	21.7	37 266	26.1	43 114	1 307	13.4	57.3	1 552	127	1 188	486	288 541	220 766	26.4	73.6
Dakota	739	4.4	7 755	2.1	8 373	289	13.8	27.7	142	4	492	120	28 954	100 187	80.9	19.1
Dawes	985	10.9	−7 100	X	−7 659	471	10.0	59.2	822	−20	1 745	198	28 195	59 862	27.0	73.0
Dawson	1 470	7.4	52 181	14.3	54 816	858	16.2	45.1	650	−9	757	354	399 475	465 589	22.4	77.6
Deuel	359	16.0	3 050	14.9	1 887	251	5.6	62.9	282	16	1 122	231	21 073	83 956	73.9	26.1
Dixon	1 361	22.2	25 547	33.8	32 092	583	14.9	27.8	243	Z	416	194	117 176	200 988	24.0	76.0
Dodge	2 014	5.8	28 689	6.0	32 844	798	19.7	29.1	323	24	405	295	141 098	176 815	51.0	49.0
Douglas	1 186	.3	10 308	.1	11 366	368	37.0	19.3	113	17	306	92	44 144	119 957	56.4	43.6
Dundy	582	22.5	15 444	43.4	14 672	323	6.8	68.7	591	62	1 830	217	86 632	268 211	46.3	53.7
Fillmore	1 553	21.9	37 973	35.7	36 505	584	9.8	50.5	357	16	611	326	141 652	242 555	62.0	38.0
Franklin	753	19.1	10 510	33.0	8 694	430	10.5	48.8	351	28	816	192	55 688	129 495	66.9	33.1
Frontier	852	27.5	9 509	28.2	9 015	362	8.3	68.8	531	5	1 467	226	75 638	208 945	36.2	63.8
Furnas	798	14.4	9 384	16.9	10 384	432	10.6	55.3	450	19	1 042	279	76 853	177 900	50.1	49.9
Gage	2 767	12.1	33 974	11.5	28 353	1 144	16.3	34.4	519	10	454	410	114 773	100 326	55.1	44.9
Garden	558	22.7	2 303	11.5	2 712	308	7.1	61.0	1 078	8	3 499	197	57 551	186 854	24.4	75.6
Garfield	494	23.1	3 477	16.5	3 992	206	11.2	51.0	308	−30	1 495	67	28 865	140 121	14.4	85.6
Gosper	541	28.1	5 325	32.3	5 784	252	6.7	58.3	234	4	929	127	51 653	204 972	51.1	48.9
Grant	110	14.3	−3 179	X	−3 968	88	14.8	76.1	477	−69	5 419	41	11 183	127 080	5.6	94.4
Greeley	814	27.1	4 092	17.8	6 259	387	8.8	49.1	291	−13	752	124	46 419	119 946	40.4	59.6
Hall	1 346	2.8	18 827	2.0	17 838	702	20.8	32.3	342	26	488	258	146 375	208 511	47.1	52.9
Hamilton	1 631	18.4	32 895	28.6	31 638	661	11.3	43.9	344	23	520	310	149 283	225 844	64.4	35.6
Harlan	761	20.0	11 696	30.5	9 825	371	11.9	52.3	325	20	877	219	82 735	223 005	41.9	58.1
Hayes	469	38.4	5 470	50.1	5 256	257	5.8	63.8	426	24	1 659	173	68 171	265 257	26.9	73.1
Hitchcock	695	18.5	3 198	14.2	2 841	339	8.6	65.2	406	3	1 198	239	33 700	99 410	66.8	33.2
Holt	2 463	19.5	24 292	16.1	37 667	1 291	12.3	54.0	1 464	76	1 134	618	246 073	190 607	35.1	64.9

[1] For 1990 corrected population, see table B-1. Percent is based on 1990 uncorrected population because only total population is corrected. [2] For total earnings, see table B-8. [3] Most data are comparable between 1992 and 1997; however, it should be noted that farms with all acreage in Conservation or Wetlands Reserve Programs (excluded in 1992) are included in 1997, as are short rotation woody crops which includes Christmas trees and maple sap gathering (in Forestry in 1992). [4] Includes nursery and greenhouse crops. [5] Includes related products. [6] Yellowstone National Park County included with Park County; data not available separately.

Sources: Farm Population—U.S. Census Bureau, 1990 Census of Population and Housing, Summary Tape File (STF) 3C on CD-ROM (related Internet site <http://homer.ssd.census.gov/cdrom/lookup>). Farm Earnings—U.S. Bureau of Economic Analysis, "Regional Economic Information System (REIS) 1969-1998" on CD-ROM (related Internet site <http://www.bea.doc.gov/bea/regional/reis/ca45/>). Agriculture—U.S. Department of Agriculture, National Agricultural Statistics Service, 1997 Census of Agriculture, Volume 1, Geographic Area Series, 1A, 1B, 1C CD-ROM Set (related Internet site <http://www.nass.usda.gov/census/>).

[Includes U.S., states, and 3,142 counties/county equivalents defined as of January 1, 1992. For changes to these areas since January 1, 1992, see appendix B. Geographic Information]

County	Farm population, 1990		Farm earnings			Agriculture (NAICS 111-112), 1997										
			1998			Farms			Land in farms (acres)				Value of farm products sold			
							Percent–									Percent from–
	Number	Per-cent of total[1]	Total ($1,000)	Per-cent of total[2]	1997 ($1,000)	Number	Less than 50 acres	500 acres or more	Total acreage (1,000)	Net change, 1992–1997[3] (1,000)	Aver-age size of farm	Total cropland (1,000)	Total ($1,000)	Average per farm (dollars)	Crops[4]	Live-stock and poultry[5]
NEBRASKA—Con.																
Hooker	63	7.9	−4 425	X	−4 289	88	4.5	76.1	371	−4	4 221	20	8 541	97 057	1.6	98.4
Howard	1 492	24.6	15 360	32.6	17 749	646	12.4	34.2	330	5	511	210	115 694	179 093	32.7	67.3
Jefferson	1 560	17.8	18 156	18.2	15 386	626	11.2	37.2	315	−12	503	238	76 996	122 997	54.5	45.5
Johnson	1 161	24.8	4 334	11.0	3 781	491	9.8	29.7	197	10	401	146	29 602	60 289	59.4	40.6
Kearney	627	9.5	35 270	37.3	39 270	492	10.4	52.4	320	10	650	267	196 557	399 506	43.2	56.8
Keith	381	4.4	11 878	11.5	10 581	375	10.1	51.7	607	−62	1 618	254	102 788	274 101	32.0	68.0
Keya Paha	438	42.6	−112	X	472	225	3.1	79.6	500	54	2 221	104	27 142	120 631	16.1	83.9
Kimball	441	10.7	1 254	2.8	1 159	326	4.9	71.8	565	60	1 734	339	22 884	70 196	60.8	39.2
Knox	2 692	28.2	10 183	12.6	20 237	1 053	12.2	40.2	596	−17	566	327	164 667	156 379	17.1	82.9
Lancaster	3 081	1.4	20 658	.4	18 128	1 457	32.3	19.1	421	6	289	344	82 386	56 545	72.4	27.6
Lincoln	1 873	5.8	6 588	1.2	10 044	1 019	15.8	52.4	1 420	−30	1 394	434	192 318	188 732	36.6	63.4
Logan	328	37.4	2 338	35.3	2 572	124	8.9	58.1	323	−13	2 605	58	19 107	154 089	33.9	66.1
Loup	373	54.6	−5 303	X	−4 940	143	7.0	60.1	339	9	2 372	39	14 933	104 427	17.2	82.8
McPherson	359	65.8	−3 471	X	−3 135	112	7.1	80.4	443	−21	3 958	36	13 951	124 563	7.2	92.8
Madison	2 170	6.6	21 630	3.4	24 195	782	19.8	30.7	329	7	421	275	115 769	148 042	44.9	55.1
Merrick	1 505	18.7	25 688	30.8	28 595	553	13.6	37.4	274	−17	495	220	163 159	295 043	36.0	64.0
Morrill	927	17.1	10 489	23.4	13 960	474	12.0	53.2	861	136	1 816	232	147 631	311 458	24.6	75.4
Nance	952	22.3	14 455	37.1	16 484	419	13.6	41.5	244	7	583	165	66 566	158 869	46.5	53.5
Nemaha	945	11.8	12 211	8.3	16 894	483	9.7	36.9	239	13	495	202	56 089	116 126	64.2	35.8
Nuckolls	1 189	20.5	7 047	13.7	3 732	496	9.9	51.0	327	−6	660	228	54 141	109 155	70.5	29.5
Otoe	2 237	15.7	10 745	6.2	13 657	821	19.2	29.2	354	29	432	276	71 162	86 677	67.7	32.3
Pawnee	905	27.3	9 289	31.8	7 395	444	8.3	33.6	230	6	517	145	28 031	63 133	50.9	49.1
Perkins	611	18.1	20 437	39.3	14 788	490	4.3	59.4	553	20	1 128	446	64 853	132 353	83.1	16.9
Phelps	1 070	11.0	54 720	28.8	51 808	552	11.8	50.5	379	3	686	302	336 390	609 402	25.5	74.5
Pierce	2 147	27.4	17 650	23.1	21 409	717	14.6	31.9	309	11	431	258	108 138	150 820	42.2	57.8
Platte	3 353	11.2	41 661	7.3	53 213	1 024	18.8	30.1	420	10	410	356	224 770	219 502	36.1	63.9
Polk	1 374	24.2	29 929	44.1	31 206	601	16.6	34.1	259	8	430	220	165 623	275 579	38.1	61.9
Red Willow	616	5.3	16 303	10.8	14 985	438	17.6	53.4	436	−3	996	262	92 436	211 041	41.0	59.0
Richardson	1 315	13.2	24 177	22.0	24 405	717	12.1	29.4	319	17	444	242	69 242	96 572	60.7	39.3
Rock	417	20.7	4 355	23.5	5 691	316	8.2	64.6	631	−27	1 997	169	55 629	176 041	26.7	73.3
Saline	1 966	15.5	23 635	11.6	20 437	727	14.7	31.9	318	5	437	265	76 552	105 298	67.9	32.1
Sarpy	926	.9	6 597	.4	7 982	367	30.8	19.9	102	−3	277	90	57 209	155 883	38.5	61.5
Saunders	3 175	17.4	38 821	22.8	42 079	1 176	18.8	25.9	436	−1	371	382	143 667	122 166	57.3	42.7
Scotts Bluff	1 932	5.4	39 050	7.4	39 807	789	14.6	26.5	443	25	561	227	231 796	293 785	24.6	75.4
Seward	2 111	13.7	37 822	17.1	38 584	833	22.2	30.1	321	6	385	279	146 802	176 233	46.8	53.2
Sheridan	1 359	20.1	−4 205	X	−2 614	656	10.8	60.4	1 487	5	2 267	335	66 111	100 779	29.1	70.9
Sherman	1 149	30.9	4 540	19.6	4 689	483	9.1	41.8	324	26	671	178	43 128	89 292	54.5	45.5
Sioux	618	39.9	−2 052	X	−1 448	343	8.2	65.0	1 115	109	3 250	97	70 652	205 983	13.0	87.0
Stanton	1 441	23.1	16 969	21.1	22 477	609	13.8	27.4	226	9	372	183	103 785	170 419	26.8	73.2
Thayer	1 405	21.2	22 866	26.3	19 695	569	8.6	45.2	368	21	648	288	107 464	188 865	59.0	41.0
Thomas	180	21.2	−3 242	X	−2 992	87	8.0	75.9	369	8	4 236	14	8 363	96 126	9.5	90.5
Thurston	992	14.3	9 811	11.8	11 638	379	13.2	33.8	189	−5	499	170	59 553	157 132	50.6	49.4
Valley	962	18.6	7 556	15.2	8 685	445	11.9	48.3	333	−7	747	154	90 249	202 807	29.7	70.3
Washington	2 366	14.2	16 142	6.6	17 632	692	25.6	20.8	219	−9	317	196	92 545	133 736	48.7	51.3
Wayne	1 475	15.8	24 229	19.7	26 979	612	17.0	30.7	257	9	420	233	92 485	151 119	41.4	58.6
Webster	856	20.0	11 928	30.0	12 063	433	12.0	46.2	314	6	725	183	113 702	262 591	23.2	76.8
Wheeler	386	40.7	9 557	70.3	13 833	186	10.8	61.3	293	29	1 574	122	126 843	681 952	10.6	89.4
York	1 987	13.8	32 470	11.5	34 357	712	14.5	40.9	353	7	496	320	178 311	250 437	56.5	43.5
NEVADA	4 831	.4	61 446	.2	47 573	2 829	39.6	26.1	6 409	−2 854	2 266	847	356 565	126 039	42.5	57.5
Churchill	1 184	6.6	8 872	2.5	4 712	511	50.1	9.8	129	−139	253	54	38 058	74 477	29.7	70.3
Clark	71	Z	6 703	Z	6 135	209	70.3	3.8	71	−11	338	9	18 926	90 555	33.4	66.6
Douglas	278	1.0	−256	X	−376	156	53.2	14.1	90	11	579	26	8 796	56 385	24.4	75.6
Elko	722	2.2	6 531	.9	5 805	402	25.1	49.5	2 855	−294	7 103	237	49 228	122 458	8.6	91.4
Esmeralda	77	5.7	352	3.0	349	20	10.0	35.0	27	−1 922	1 373	12	4 016	200 800	83.8	16.2
Eureka	212	13.7	2 619	1.0	2 214	84	4.8	45.2	215	−21	2 559	41	13 133	156 345	52.8	47.2
Humboldt	606	4.7	10 041	3.0	6 622	218	20.2	49.1	733	−5	3 364	172	57 315	262 913	67.8	32.2
Lander	108	1.7	2 341	2.0	1 856	76	21.1	46.1	486	−8	6 395	32	12 794	168 342	42.1	57.9
Lincoln	60	1.6	855	1.5	405	121	30.6	19.8	49	Z	404	17	7 317	60 471	54.4	45.6
Lyon	594	3.0	8 487	3.2	7 923	305	42.6	22.0	174	−15	572	79	53 656	175 921	54.9	45.1
Mineral	73	1.1	−495	X	−651	37	54.1	21.6	D	D	D	11	1 809	48 892	40.5	59.5
Nye	207	1.2	10 380	2.7	7 730	144	42.4	23.6	86	−55	594	28	27 792	193 000	26.6	73.4
Pershing	213	4.9	2 759	3.1	2 931	120	15.8	35.0	119	−505	995	50	32 679	272 325	44.5	55.5
Storey	37	1.5	–	–	–	8	62.5	–	D	D	D	Z	93	11 625	D	D
Washoe	201	.1	1 844	Z	1 843	285	56.1	17.5	772	61	2 709	42	22 518	79 011	67.4	32.6
White Pine	188	2.0	672	.5	352	115	24.3	35.7	247	16	2 152	34	8 236	71 617	21.9	78.1
Independent City																
Carson City city	–	–	−259	X	−277	18	33.3	27.8	7	2	401	1	198	11 000	D	D

[1] For 1990 corrected population, see table B-1. Percent is based on 1990 uncorrected population because only total population is corrected. [2] For total earnings, see table B-8. [3] Most data are comparable between 1992 and 1997; however, it should be noted that farms with all acreage in Conservation or Wetlands Reserve Programs (excluded in 1992) are included in 1997, as are short rotation woody crops which includes Christmas trees and maple sap gathering (in Forestry in 1992). [4] Includes nursery and greenhouse crops. [5] Includes related products.

Sources: Farm Population—U.S. Census Bureau, 1990 Census of Population and Housing, Summary Tape File (STF) 3C on CD-ROM (related Internet site <http://homer.ssd.census.gov/cdrom/lookup>). Farm Earnings—U.S. Bureau of Economic Analysis, "Regional Economic Information System (REIS) 1969-1998" on CD-ROM (related Internet site <http://www.bea.doc.gov/bea/regional/reis/ca45/>). Agriculture—U.S. Department of Agriculture, National Agricultural Statistics Service, 1997 Census of Agriculture, Volume 1, Geographic Area Series, 1A, 1B, 1C CD-ROM Set (related Internet site <http://www.nass.usda.gov/census/>).

[Includes U.S., states, and 3,142 counties/county equivalents defined as of January 1, 1992. For changes to these areas since January 1, 1992, see appendix B. Geographic Information]

County	Farm population, 1990 Number	Percent of total[1]	Farm earnings 1998 Total ($1,000)	Percent of total[2]	1997 ($1,000)	Agriculture (NAICS 111-112), 1997 — Farms Number	Percent Less than 50 acres	500 acres or more	Land in farms (acres) Total acreage (1,000)	Net change, 1992–1997[3] (1,000)	Average size of farm	Total cropland (1,000)	Value of farm products sold Total ($1,000)	Average per farm (dollars)	Percent from Crops[4]	Livestock and poultry[5]
NEW HAMPSHIRE	5 576	.5	35 293	.2	36 105	2 937	41.2	5.2	415	29	141	133	149 467	50 891	49.3	50.7
Belknap	391	.8	105	Z	127	184	41.8	3.8	21	Z	112	5	3 666	19 924	65.2	34.8
Carroll	499	1.4	1 205	.2	1 055	177	36.7	4.5	24	-1	136	6	3 556	20 090	63.7	36.3
Cheshire	370	.5	6 508	.6	7 180	293	40.6	5.8	42	8	142	12	27 534	93 973	11.5	88.5
Coos	230	.7	2 289	.5	1 321	185	24.3	10.3	43	-3	232	14	7 791	42 114	20.3	79.7
Grafton	659	.9	2 580	.1	2 246	406	27.8	8.4	76	Z	187	27	17 380	42 808	17.4	82.6
Hillsborough	804	.2	3 220	Z	4 110	391	51.2	1.8	38	-2	96	15	16 260	41 586	72.1	27.9
Merrimack	928	.8	10 008	.4	8 984	413	41.4	6.5	63	17	154	17	29 239	70 797	70.8	29.2
Rockingham	959	.4	3 577	.1	4 534	407	55.0	1.5	35	1	87	14	16 770	41 204	74.0	26.0
Strafford	425	.4	1 848	.1	2 079	235	45.5	3.0	26	1	111	9	9 133	38 864	64.0	36.0
Sullivan	311	.8	3 953	.8	4 469	246	35.8	8.1	47	9	192	13	18 140	73 740	58.7	41.3
NEW JERSEY	17 283	.2	249 918	.1	228 337	9 101	66.5	3.8	833	-15	91	595	697 380	76 627	85.0	15.0
Atlantic	661	.3	28 334	.4	27 187	421	69.8	1.9	31	1	73	19	63 469	149 691	99.0	1.0
Bergen	16	Z	9 291	Z	8 782	121	92.6	.8	3	Z	22	1	9 008	74 446	96.0	4.0
Burlington	1 430	.4	31 726	.4	30 892	857	64.8	6.0	104	6	121	70	87 535	102 141	86.6	13.4
Camden	99	Z	10 537	.1	9 248	211	79.6	1.4	9	1	43	7	17 473	82 810	98.5	1.5
Cape May	428	.5	2 464	.2	2 248	149	70.5	2.0	10	-2	65	6	6 807	45 685	95.9	4.1
Cumberland	943	.7	47 719	2.1	41 177	573	61.8	4.7	66	-2	116	51	94 152	164 314	96.0	4.0
Essex	–	–	2 923	Z	2 872	21	90.5	–	D	D	D	Z	1 223	58 238	99.3	.7
Gloucester	1 501	.7	30 111	.9	27 795	652	66.3	3.2	58	-3	90	46	66 972	102 718	91.5	8.5
Hudson	–	–	–	–	–	–	–	–	–	–	–	–	–	–	–	–
Hunterdon	2 886	2.7	5 312	.2	4 790	1 313	65.0	3.0	105	-1	80	78	36 057	27 462	78.1	21.9
Mercer	575	.2	2 360	Z	3 014	285	64.9	4.6	28	-7	100	23	13 255	46 509	92.5	7.5
Middlesex	422	.1	12 918	.1	12 708	275	73.5	5.5	28	3	102	22	34 355	124 927	96.7	3.3
Monmouth	1 355	.2	22 335	.2	19 869	874	80.0	1.5	59	1	68	46	67 973	77 772	92.2	7.8
Morris	814	.2	15 910	.1	14 320	383	73.6	1.8	22	-2	58	14	29 956	78 214	96.0	4.0
Ocean	706	.2	6 361	.1	5 669	235	83.4	2.1	11	1	48	6	8 170	34 766	68.1	31.9
Passaic	–	–	3 351	Z	3 095	55	80.0	–	2	Z	41	Z	3 863	70 236	93.9	6.1
Salem	1 479	2.3	13 013	1.3	12 052	660	50.8	6.5	92	-6	139	75	67 908	102 891	64.2	35.8
Somerset	799	.3	1 992	Z	1 167	437	66.4	4.8	46	2	106	31	14 026	32 096	71.0	29.0
Sussex	1 769	1.4	402	Z	-958	827	62.2	3.4	73	-3	88	41	19 187	23 201	58.7	41.3
Union	–	–	3 562	Z	3 317	19	94.7	–	D	D	D	Z	9 986	525 579	99.8	.2
Warren	1 400	1.5	-703	X	-907	730	54.4	4.7	83	-5	114	58	46 005	63 021	42.8	57.2
NEW MEXICO	15 090	1.0	600 214	2.4	522 883	14 094	37.0	35.5	45 787	-1 062	3 249	2 179	1 617 708	114 780	28.6	71.4
Bernalillo	208	Z	14 859	.1	12 273	468	76.9	7.3	465	50	993	18	31 028	66 299	17.9	82.1
Catron	149	5.8	-1 048	X	-75	217	9.7	59.9	1 795	242	8 274	12	14 494	66 793	.5	99.5
Chaves	803	1.4	127 184	16.6	66 892	562	29.9	44.1	2 944	-168	5 239	D	220 127	391 685	15.4	84.6
Cibola	96	.4	1 261	.7	2 261	166	24.7	59.0	1 699	-381	10 237	21	5 692	34 289	3.7	96.3
Colfax	415	3.2	3 061	2.0	3 647	322	14.3	51.9	2 227	142	6 917	46	40 236	124 957	3.5	96.5
Curry	880	2.1	55 472	8.9	54 034	655	13.4	51.0	948	23	1 447	444	195 438	298 379	24.4	75.6
DeBaca	323	14.3	3 728	18.6	4 205	191	24.1	52.9	1 442	98	7 548	18	25 173	131 796	18.1	81.9
Dona Ana	1 361	1.0	129 948	7.3	105 781	1 290	75.7	7.8	581	55	451	91	235 484	182 546	54.5	45.5
Eddy	807	1.7	24 357	3.5	27 758	467	34.3	34.5	1 276	137	2 731	65	84 586	181 126	29.7	70.3
Grant	240	.9	-1 968	X	-523	286	19.6	52.4	1 174	-36	4 103	13	7 319	25 591	3.0	97.0
Guadalupe	183	4.4	-1 779	X	(6)	236	15.7	64.8	1 419	-114	6 013	7	12 424	52 644	2.1	97.9
Harding	219	22.2	1 474	19.9	3 205	172	3.5	78.5	1 255	-35	7 296	20	13 733	79 843	.2	99.8
Hidalgo	231	3.9	8 970	11.7	9 360	146	10.3	65.1	1 105	261	7 567	23	18 311	125 418	69.2	30.8
Lea	491	.9	32 955	4.6	14 954	528	19.1	47.0	2 002	-148	3 792	104	60 392	114 379	25.6	74.4
Lincoln	292	2.4	-972	X	1 957	337	21.4	57.0	1 975	93	5 861	9	14 026	41 620	.8	99.2
Los Alamos	–	–	–	–	–	4	100.0	–	D	D	D	D	D	D	D	D
Luna	272	1.5	17 911	10.2	26 601	192	17.7	48.4	603	-194	3 143	D	49 067	255 557	78.3	21.7
McKinley	568	.9	94	Z	2 802	224	21.4	47.8	3 157	-67	14 094	D	9 330	41 652	.8	99.2
Mora	646	15.2	-2 198	X	-797	398	19.1	34.9	975	70	2 449	41	11 059	27 786	3.9	96.1
Otero	500	1.0	2 967	.4	2 923	417	48.9	21.3	1 081	-85	2 592	D	9 694	23 247	35.7	64.3
Quay	594	5.5	5 678	5.7	11 089	583	9.4	60.4	1 856	87	3 183	245	40 630	69 691	32.9	67.1
Rio Arriba	302	.9	(6)	Z	1 593	940	56.6	16.5	1 463	-89	1 557	65	10 435	11 101	19.7	80.3
Roosevelt	1 254	7.5	55 501	29.5	45 848	738	15.2	49.1	1 419	-227	1 923	349	128 293	173 839	30.3	69.7
Sandoval	172	.3	1 480	.2	4 663	353	48.4	22.4	780	10	2 209	32	9 987	28 292	21.4	78.6
San Juan	875	1.0	57 711	3.9	62 568	666	64.3	7.5	D	D	D	84	D	D	D	D
San Miguel	294	1.1	216	.1	2 774	643	18.5	46.3	2 557	-23	3 976	50	20 654	32 121	5.3	94.7
Santa Fe	231	.2	3 139	.2	2 694	336	53.9	23.2	652	134	1 940	23	12 507	37 223	52.6	47.4
Sierra	326	3.3	5 962	6.7	5 509	180	24.4	49.4	1 287	53	7 149	D	15 766	87 589	27.7	72.3
Socorro	691	4.7	8 991	6.1	5 503	395	41.5	32.4	1 651	-217	4 180	20	25 229	63 871	18.6	81.4
Taos	195	.8	807	.3	1 172	422	53.1	11.1	310	-14	735	27	3 748	8 882	35.1	64.9
Torrance	332	3.2	5 635	6.6	5 713	473	15.2	51.2	1 477	-320	3 123	65	30 847	65 216	38.2	61.8
Union	773	18.7	29 232	46.4	29 195	448	7.8	70.8	2 227	-137	4 972	90	130 494	291 281	10.3	89.7
Valencia	367	.8	9 547	2.7	7 305	639	80.8	4.2	384	34	600	17	26 599	41 626	23.6	76.4

[1] For 1990 corrected population, see table B-1. Percent is based on 1990 uncorrected population because only total population is corrected. [2] For total earnings, see table B-8. [3] Most data are comparable between 1992 and 1997; however, it should be noted that farms with all acreage in Conservation or Wetlands Reserve Programs (excluded in 1992) are included in 1997, as are short rotation woody crops which includes Christmas trees and maple sap gathering (in Forestry in 1992). [4] Includes nursery and greenhouse crops. [5] Includes related products. [6] Less than $50,000.

Sources: Farm Population—U.S. Census Bureau, 1990 Census of Population and Housing, Summary Tape File (STF) 3C on CD-ROM (related Internet site <http://homer.ssd.census.gov/cdrom/lookup>). Farm Earnings—U.S. Bureau of Economic Analysis, "Regional Economic Information System (REIS) 1969-1998" on CD-ROM (related Internet site <http://www.bea.doc.gov/bea/regional/reis/ca45/>). Agriculture—U.S. Department of Agriculture, National Agricultural Statistics Service, 1997 Census of Agriculture, Volume 1, Geographic Area Series, 1A, 1B, 1C CD-ROM Set (related Internet site <http://www.nass.usda.gov/census/>).

[Includes U.S., states, and 3,142 counties/county equivalents defined as of January 1, 1992. For changes to these areas since January 1, 1992, see appendix B. Geographic Information]

County	Farm population, 1990		Farm earnings			Agriculture (NAICS 111-112), 1997										
			1998			Farms			Land in farms (acres)				Value of farm products sold			
							Percent–								Percent from–	
	Number	Percent of total[1]	Total ($1,000)	Percent of total[2]	1997 ($1,000)	Number	Less than 50 acres	500 acres or more	Total acreage (1,000)	Net change, 1992–1997[3] (1,000)	Average size of farm	Total cropland (1,000)	Total ($1,000)	Average per farm (dollars)	Crops[4]	Live-stock and poultry[5]
NEW YORK	82 256	.5	551 355	.1	346 757	31 757	24.3	10.7	7 254	−204	228	4 722	2 834 512	89 256	35.3	64.7
Albany	540	.2	1 237	Z	883	396	35.6	3.8	57	−1	143	36	15 770	39 823	42.7	57.3
Allegany	1 701	3.4	4 775	1.0	1 927	724	14.0	8.6	158	−4	218	90	34 852	48 138	11.8	88.2
Bronx	–	–	–	–	–	–	–	–	–	–	–	–	–	–	–	–
Broome	869	.4	3 109	.1	1 036	511	26.6	4.9	86	−12	168	47	24 016	46 998	19.4	80.6
Cattaraugus	2 539	3.0	7 558	.7	2 263	946	17.0	7.2	192	−12	203	105	53 473	56 525	19.5	80.5
Cayuga	2 902	3.5	23 566	2.8	13 272	846	17.3	15.7	252	−2	298	193	115 438	136 452	32.6	67.4
Chautauqua	4 277	3.0	19 245	1.1	11 641	1 557	33.2	5.3	245	−15	157	145	88 673	56 951	32.9	67.1
Chemung	471	.5	2 415	.2	670	313	23.3	8.0	59	Z	189	36	12 898	41 208	31.1	68.9
Chenango	1 801	3.5	7 705	1.4	−701	801	18.6	10.2	183	−5	229	104	53 154	66 360	7.3	92.7
Clinton	1 289	1.5	13 934	1.2	10 778	488	15.6	16.0	149	−10	305	77	69 328	142 066	23.0	77.0
Columbia	1 658	2.6	20 310	2.8	20 740	464	31.0	13.4	115	3	248	79	72 675	156 627	26.0	74.0
Cortland	1 201	2.5	5 886	1.0	1 875	452	15.3	14.4	121	−18	267	67	37 447	82 847	8.2	91.8
Delaware	1 841	3.9	8 129	1.4	2 556	717	15.9	12.3	184	−8	256	95	43 498	60 667	11.1	88.9
Dutchess	1 188	.5	4 748	.1	4 639	539	33.0	9.8	107	−3	198	63	33 964	63 013	48.5	51.5
Erie	2 245	.2	11 638	.1	6 559	973	37.2	5.4	143	−2	147	103	77 830	79 990	39.9	60.1
Essex	338	.9	885	.2	149	197	22.8	14.2	48	−7	245	25	8 006	40 640	31.6	68.4
Franklin	1 171	2.5	9 730	1.8	2 471	476	9.9	14.3	163	25	342	78	44 285	93 036	12.6	87.4
Fulton	386	.7	1 703	.3	−65	176	18.8	5.1	34	−1	195	22	9 625	54 688	13.2	86.8
Genesee	1 557	2.6	29 325	4.0	24 000	516	28.7	15.5	171	−1	331	143	109 614	212 430	43.9	56.1
Greene	457	1.0	1 136	.3	698	244	24.2	10.7	49	3	200	25	8 781	35 988	36.4	63.6
Hamilton	20	.4	–	–	–	13	61.5	–	1	D	61	D	79	6 077	89.9	10.1
Herkimer	1 371	2.1	9 392	1.7	3 168	583	15.6	11.8	142	−21	243	90	45 824	78 600	7.9	92.1
Jefferson	2 261	2.0	15 617	.9	3 618	916	12.9	17.4	291	−9	318	194	77 076	84 144	9.2	90.8
Kings	–	–	–	–	–	8	100.0	–	Z	Z	1	Z	374	46 750	100.0	–
Lewis	1 865	7.0	9 279	4.0	−430	623	9.5	12.8	180	10	288	102	61 686	99 014	5.1	94.9
Livingston	1 949	3.1	7 901	1.3	5 359	625	21.8	17.9	197	−8	316	154	72 936	116 698	36.9	63.1
Madison	1 956	2.8	13 706	1.9	5 655	692	16.8	14.2	186	−10	269	121	65 690	94 928	13.4	86.6
Monroe	1 180	.2	10 398	.1	8 283	480	46.7	12.3	103	−7	215	90	47 954	99 904	79.8	20.2
Montgomery	1 488	2.9	7 106	1.3	2 611	542	18.1	11.8	135	−4	249	105	48 723	89 895	16.0	84.0
Nassau	–	–	552	Z	1 229	55	83.6	–	1	−1	25	1	3 119	56 709	91.7	8.3
New York	–	–	–	–	–	2	100.0	–	D	D	D	D	D	D	D	D
Niagara	1 865	.8	11 388	.4	10 165	687	39.9	7.7	127	−8	185	112	57 726	84 026	66.1	33.9
Oneida	2 775	1.1	16 229	.5	8 321	928	18.8	11.2	216	−27	233	139	74 056	79 802	21.5	78.5
Onondaga	1 726	.4	12 040	.1	6 463	602	33.1	12.6	147	2	244	112	70 951	117 859	29.4	70.6
Ontario	1 850	1.9	12 368	.8	7 099	692	28.6	16.2	186	4	269	154	77 983	112 692	48.4	51.6
Orange	1 910	.6	18 784	.4	10 643	624	38.5	5.0	95	−8	152	66	69 847	111 934	63.6	36.4
Orleans	1 487	3.6	15 680	4.1	13 974	456	29.6	15.4	143	10	314	122	62 128	136 246	85.5	14.5
Oswego	1 469	1.2	7 928	.6	4 751	605	25.1	4.8	103	−10	169	59	31 454	51 990	56.6	43.4
Otsego	2 148	3.5	6 522	.9	1 958	865	13.9	11.8	207	−11	239	116	51 612	59 667	8.6	91.4
Putnam	33	Z	934	.1	905	48	54.2	–	3	Z	72	2	2 928	61 000	96.9	3.1
Queens	–	–	–	–	–	2	100.0	–	D	D	D	D	D	D	D	D
Rensselaer	1 416	.9	3 173	.2	398	459	26.8	9.8	99	6	216	59	28 700	62 527	33.5	66.5
Richmond	–	–	–	–	–	7	100.0	–	Z	D	4	D	472	67 429	D	D
Rockland	–	–	934	Z	905	21	81.0	–	1	Z	27	Z	2 361	112 429	D	D
St. Lawrence	2 952	2.6	17 244	1.3	730	1 363	10.3	14.9	396	Z	291	220	89 078	65 354	7.5	92.5
Saratoga	1 447	.8	3 977	.2	1 292	472	36.9	6.6	73	3	155	46	29 855	63 252	29.6	70.4
Schenectady	293	.2	155	Z	−248	151	33.1	1.3	18	−1	120	11	6 108	40 450	71.8	28.2
Schoharie	1 093	3.4	3 591	1.2	1 712	518	21.2	9.5	111	−7	214	70	26 973	52 071	21.7	78.3
Schuyler	552	3.0	473	.3	−205	318	19.5	6.3	65	Z	205	37	14 034	44 132	24.8	75.2
Seneca	1 208	3.6	4 578	1.3	5 991	413	24.0	16.0	117	2	284	97	41 069	99 441	49.4	50.6
Steuben	3 153	3.2	12 915	.8	8 212	1 295	14.1	13.7	349	−14	269	217	78 665	60 745	30.2	69.8
Suffolk	406	Z	43 653	.2	43 809	606	71.6	2.3	36	1	59	30	167 858	276 993	92.8	7.2
Sullivan	723	1.0	1 604	.2	326	311	24.8	8.4	58	2	187	35	23 364	75 125	9.1	90.9
Tioga	1 262	2.4	5 239	1.0	2 336	497	18.7	9.7	109	−6	220	63	27 536	55 404	11.7	88.3
Tompkins	1 141	1.2	8 344	.5	6 389	447	30.0	11.4	95	4	214	64	47 548	106 371	16.2	83.8
Ulster	1 411	.9	9 343	.5	12 007	409	38.4	5.1	69	−1	169	38	42 278	103 369	87.5	12.5
Warren	114	.2	196	Z	243	58	37.9	5.2	9	3	158	2	2 180	37 586	61.1	38.9
Washington	2 133	3.6	16 204	2.8	7 579	738	18.0	14.8	195	−11	264	123	77 544	105 073	13.1	86.9
Wayne	2 829	3.2	21 137	2.1	32 317	840	31.2	8.8	167	−7	199	125	107 566	128 055	66.0	34.0
Westchester	128	Z	2 946	Z	3 351	91	60.4	3.3	8	2	83	3	10 568	116 132	69.6	30.4
Wyoming	2 538	6.0	37 150	8.2	17 547	702	19.8	13.4	195	−15	278	136	134 654	191 815	10.0	90.0
Yates	1 673	7.3	5 641	3.0	2 903	657	19.8	4.3	105	3	159	77	40 259	61 277	48.1	51.9

[1] For 1990 corrected population, see table B-1. Percent is based on 1990 uncorrected population because only total population is corrected. [2] For total earnings, see table B-8. [3] Most data are comparable between 1992 and 1997; however, it should be noted that farms with all acreage in Conservation or Wetlands Reserve Programs (excluded in 1992) are included in 1997, as are short rotation woody crops which includes Christmas trees and maple sap gathering (in Forestry in 1992). [4] Includes nursery and greenhouse crops. [5] Includes related products.

Sources: Farm Population—U.S. Census Bureau, 1990 Census of Population and Housing, Summary Tape File (STF) 3C on CD-ROM (related Internet site <http://homer.ssd.census.gov/cdrom/lookup>). Farm Earnings—U.S. Bureau of Economic Analysis, "Regional Economic Information System (REIS) 1969-1998" on CD-ROM (related Internet site <http://www.bea.doc.gov/bea/regional/reis/ca45/>). Agriculture—U.S. Department of Agriculture, National Agricultural Statistics Service, 1997 Census of Agriculture, Volume 1, Geographic Area Series, 1A, 1B, 1C CD-ROM Set (related Internet site <http://www.nass.usda.gov/census/>).

Table B–10. Counties — Farm Population, Farm Earnings, and Agriculture–Con.

[Includes U.S., states, and 3,142 counties/county equivalents defined as of January 1, 1992. For changes to these areas since January 1, 1992, see appendix B. Geographic Information]

County	Farm population, 1990 Number	Farm population, 1990 Percent of total[1]	Farm earnings 1998 Total ($1,000)	Farm earnings 1998 Percent of total[2]	Farm earnings 1997 ($1,000)	Farms Number	Farms Percent Less than 50 acres	Farms Percent 500 acres or more	Land in farms Total acreage (1,000)	Land in farms Net change, 1992-1997[3] (1,000)	Land in farms Average size of farm	Land in farms Total cropland (1,000)	Value of farm products sold Total ($1,000)	Value of farm products sold Average per farm (dollars)	Value percent from Crops[4]	Value percent from Livestock and poultry[5]
NORTH CAROLINA	116 801	1.8	2 174 674	1.6	2 984 233	49 406	39.6	8.2	9 122	186	185	5 608	7 676 523	155 376	33.8	66.2
Alamance	1 485	1.4	8 249	.4	8 722	731	34.3	4.5	108	7	147	59	34 603	47 337	37.7	62.3
Alexander	693	2.5	17 645	5.4	15 568	565	41.9	2.8	60	7	106	35	46 791	82 816	9.9	90.1
Alleghany	576	6.0	23 354	17.4	20 679	545	38.3	7.2	86	13	158	42	25 340	46 495	43.8	56.2
Anson	785	3.3	28 415	10.2	31 399	442	26.0	8.4	82	11	185	35	98 554	222 973	5.2	94.8
Ashe	1 614	7.3	37 414	14.2	35 805	1 043	48.7	3.0	105	Z	101	47	22 160	21 246	74.9	25.1
Avery	605	4.1	30 763	14.3	28 955	429	59.0	.7	27	7	63	14	16 907	39 410	98.1	1.9
Beaufort	1 323	3.1	–716	X	13 411	385	27.3	23.4	155	11	404	136	81 695	212 195	68.2	31.8
Bertie	1 116	5.5	38 690	18.2	37 622	371	25.9	19.9	154	–16	416	97	110 924	298 987	59.8	40.2
Bladen	1 427	5.0	22 221	6.1	84 961	553	34.7	13.4	128	Z	232	75	238 728	431 696	15.2	84.8
Brunswick	695	1.4	2 147	.3	7 362	213	44.6	7.0	37	–3	173	24	30 306	142 282	41.9	58.1
Buncombe	2 198	1.3	25 128	.7	24 868	1 009	59.3	2.3	87	–6	87	36	34 413	34 106	73.0	27.0
Burke	517	.7	25 745	2.2	24 549	354	55.6	1.7	29	–2	83	14	28 242	79 780	34.1	65.9
Cabarrus	631	.6	7 770	.4	8 869	481	34.1	4.4	63	Z	131	40	20 860	43 368	24.8	75.2
Caldwell	538	.8	31 818	3.1	30 728	331	42.9	3.6	37	6	112	18	23 712	71 637	58.1	41.9
Camden	171	2.9	–233	X	2 772	76	27.6	39.5	52	9	680	48	19 747	259 829	93.7	6.3
Carteret	402	.8	1 668	.3	3 292	101	47.5	7.9	60	–4	593	46	18 958	187 703	96.0	4.0
Caswell	1 617	7.8	5 622	4.8	9 633	564	24.6	13.8	138	12	244	54	28 385	50 328	77.1	22.9
Catawba	786	.7	12 386	.4	11 236	596	40.6	3.7	72	9	121	48	24 396	40 933	27.1	72.9
Chatham	1 561	4.0	31 281	5.9	29 135	956	39.0	2.5	113	5	118	54	120 705	126 260	3.8	96.2
Cherokee	264	1.3	4 389	1.8	3 955	243	50.6	3.7	25	1	101	10	12 611	51 897	11.3	88.7
Chowan	535	4.0	20 468	12.2	20 476	151	26.5	27.2	51	–3	340	38	34 002	225 179	76.7	23.3
Clay	259	3.6	1 448	2.6	1 036	166	41.0	4.8	18	2	110	9	4 678	28 181	14.4	85.6
Cleveland	1 636	1.9	15 033	1.2	13 557	864	33.9	3.1	104	10	120	62	33 687	38 990	27.0	73.0
Columbus	2 927	5.9	60 795	9.9	89 880	884	35.9	11.2	170	7	192	116	139 913	158 273	48.0	52.0
Craven	1 088	1.3	–472	X	11 225	277	34.3	18.4	84	–5	303	62	66 933	241 635	52.9	47.1
Cumberland	1 173	.4	10 002	.2	19 157	433	37.9	12.9	103	5	238	57	67 684	156 314	32.8	67.2
Currituck	374	2.7	–208	X	874	86	40.7	29.1	40	–2	460	34	14 964	174 000	93.1	6.9
Dare	48	.2	–		–	9	55.6	33.3	5	–2	551	4	836	92 889	D	D
Davidson	1 883	1.5	7 282	.4	7 659	929	40.7	3.3	99	7	107	56	23 645	25 452	44.9	55.1
Davie	1 019	3.7	1 077	.3	467	557	35.7	3.8	71	2	127	42	15 651	28 099	38.1	61.9
Duplin	3 554	8.9	101 609	18.2	264 862	1 224	40.1	10.0	238	–10	195	157	746 449	609 844	9.5	90.5
Durham	325	.2	4 877	.1	5 660	159	40.3	8.2	22	3	140	11	7 247	45 579	85.6	14.4
Edgecombe	1 358	2.4	43 515	5.6	64 516	315	29.2	33.0	172	–9	545	116	148 778	472 311	43.5	56.5
Forsyth	1 184	.4	6 021	.1	7 555	621	56.2	2.3	51	3	82	30	16 262	26 187	83.8	16.2
Franklin	1 687	4.6	32 125	9.4	37 788	524	23.1	13.9	137	19	261	72	60 792	116 015	66.0	34.0
Gaston	638	.4	9 768	.4	8 650	333	41.7	1.8	35	Z	105	20	9 947	29 871	33.4	66.6
Gates	864	9.3	9 880	17.6	12 109	147	21.1	26.5	62	–3	422	49	44 943	305 735	38.3	61.7
Graham	255	3.5	2 464	3.5	2 279	110	60.9	.9	7	–2	65	3	1 094	9 945	21.7	78.3
Granville	1 660	4.3	5 853	.9	11 119	637	22.8	11.5	162	6	254	59	37 011	58 102	85.9	14.1
Greene	1 100	7.2	25 000	18.2	68 148	313	26.2	20.8	103	–9	330	80	180 964	578 160	29.1	70.9
Guilford	1 915	.6	34 348	.3	37 870	920	43.9	4.6	112	–2	122	60	48 872	53 122	68.2	31.8
Halifax	1 083	2.0	30 213	5.2	33 330	339	26.0	28.0	185	–19	547	128	97 223	286 794	54.7	45.3
Harnett	2 182	3.2	23 887	3.3	34 292	626	40.9	9.6	116	–12	185	73	94 083	150 292	47.1	52.9
Haywood	1 451	3.1	12 626	2.3	11 000	776	56.6	2.2	65	–5	84	28	14 646	18 874	37.3	62.7
Henderson	1 224	1.8	71 763	6.2	64 963	488	56.8	2.9	45	–8	91	28	46 743	95 785	85.9	14.1
Hertford	514	2.3	1 697	.8	4 789	169	16.0	26.0	76	1	452	53	60 556	358 320	44.4	55.6
Hoke	581	2.5	12 118	5.5	18 723	162	37.0	20.4	67	10	413	42	66 083	407 920	27.5	72.5
Hyde	418	7.7	3 818	6.6	10 031	100	17.0	53.0	95	2	953	83	32 996	329 960	91.1	8.9
Iredell	1 660	1.8	42 371	2.3	37 730	1 189	39.4	5.1	157	9	132	98	99 614	83 780	9.6	90.4
Jackson	175	.7	10 787	2.9	9 675	217	56.7	2.8	19	6	87	6	6 236	28 737	89.3	10.7
Johnston	3 946	4.9	67 638	6.0	94 820	1 216	40.1	8.0	211	–19	174	138	179 430	147 558	53.9	46.1
Jones	510	5.4	12 833	18.9	34 672	154	24.7	26.6	72	3	466	50	107 629	698 890	24.2	75.8
Lee	890	2.2	13 427	1.5	15 847	311	43.1	4.5	45	8	145	22	26 078	83 852	59.2	40.8
Lenoir	1 624	2.8	20 260	2.2	49 805	447	30.9	20.4	150	8	335	110	199 573	446 472	36.5	63.5
Lincoln	897	1.8	14 171	2.4	13 273	497	39.0	3.8	63	5	127	39	19 214	38 660	16.3	83.7
McDowell	312	.9	19 174	3.4	18 228	223	43.9	3.1	21	–1	93	9	13 473	60 417	61.7	38.3
Macon	516	2.2	4 610	1.5	4 091	309	50.8	–	23	1	74	11	3 447	11 155	46.4	53.6
Madison	2 273	13.4	7 560	6.1	7 701	907	49.4	1.5	80	–13	88	27	10 120	11 158	77.6	22.4
Martin	1 418	5.7	17 321	5.1	19 256	389	25.7	19.0	115	–17	296	81	62 958	161 846	85.6	14.4
Mecklenburg	557	.1	96 903	.4	91 279	295	47.8	2.4	29	1	98	16	43 002	145 769	79.4	20.6
Mitchell	496	3.4	5 651	3.3	5 484	306	58.8	2.0	25	2	82	11	3 792	12 392	80.0	20.0
Montgomery	459	2.0	19 533	5.9	19 210	256	35.2	6.3	42	5	163	15	46 160	180 313	7.8	92.2
Moore	961	1.6	58 848	5.8	61 197	683	41.6	6.0	101	14	147	37	113 221	165 770	18.2	81.8
Nash	1 836	2.4	60 277	4.1	73 599	472	32.8	16.1	175	–4	371	110	167 761	355 426	50.8	49.2
New Hanover	–		6 752	.2	6 848	62	67.7	4.8	5	2	88	4	4 325	69 758	D	D
Northampton	1 023	4.9	46 530	24.3	48 223	342	24.6	31.3	160	5	469	104	92 228	269 673	45.1	54.9
Onslow	1 161	.8	17 956	.7	32 573	369	40.7	8.4	63	–1	172	42	101 549	275 201	21.6	78.4

[1] For 1990 corrected population, see table B-1. Percent is based on 1990 uncorrected population because only total population is corrected. [2] For total earnings, see table B-8. [3] Most data are comparable between 1992 and 1997; however, it should be noted that farms with all acreage in Conservation or Wetlands Reserve Programs (excluded in 1992) are included in 1997, as are short rotation woody crops which includes Christmas trees and maple sap gathering (in Forestry in 1992). [4] Includes nursery and greenhouse crops. [5] Includes related products.

Sources: Farm Population—U.S. Census Bureau, 1990 Census of Population and Housing, Summary Tape File (STF) 3C on CD-ROM (related Internet site <http://homer.ssd.census.gov/cdrom/lookup>). Farm Earnings—U.S. Bureau of Economic Analysis, "Regional Economic Information System (REIS) 1969-1998" on CD-ROM (related Internet site <http://www.bea.doc.gov/bea/regional/reis/ca45/>). Agriculture—U.S. Department of Agriculture, National Agricultural Statistics Service, 1997 Census of Agriculture, Volume 1, Geographic Area Series, 1A, 1B, 1C CD-ROM Set (related Internet site <http://www.nass.usda.gov/census/>).

Table B–10. Counties — Farm Population, Farm Earnings, and Agriculture–Con.

[Includes U.S., states, and 3,142 counties/county equivalents defined as of January 1, 1992. For changes to these areas since January 1, 1992, see appendix B. Geographic Information]

County	Farm population, 1990 Number	Farm population, 1990 Percent of total[1]	Farm earnings 1998 Total ($1,000)	Farm earnings 1998 Percent of total[2]	Farm earnings 1997 ($1,000)	Farms Number	Farms Percent Less than 50 acres	Farms Percent 500 acres or more	Land in farms Total acreage (1,000)	Land in farms Net change, 1992–1997[3] (1,000)	Land in farms Average size of farm	Land in farms Total cropland (1,000)	Value of farm products sold Total ($1,000)	Value of farm products sold Average per farm (dollars)	Value Percent from Crops[4]	Value Percent from Livestock and poultry[5]
NORTH CAROLINA–Con.																
Orange	1 079	1.1	13 144	.6	13 605	485	32.6	6.0	73	5	150	41	25 835	53 268	46.6	53.4
Pamlico	178	1.6	2 975	3.7	4 331	67	25.4	38.8	50	6	750	43	22 871	341 358	90.5	9.5
Pasquotank	723	2.3	4 734	1.0	9 538	174	25.9	29.9	86	3	496	79	33 107	190 270	96.7	3.3
Pender	803	2.8	20 583	7.8	38 196	283	31.4	13.4	69	4	243	42	109 576	387 194	20.7	79.3
Perquimans	751	7.2	7 719	12.7	11 040	202	21.8	25.7	77	8	382	70	38 044	188 337	58.4	41.6
Person	1 670	5.5	-2 884	X	5 245	401	27.9	15.2	120	5	300	56	29 042	72 424	85.9	14.1
Pitt	2 089	1.9	15 401	.8	47 218	474	26.8	23.0	193	-1	408	144	196 139	413 795	49.8	50.2
Polk	310	2.2	3 412	2.5	2 950	188	38.3	4.3	31	8	163	10	3 315	17 633	50.6	49.4
Randolph	2 148	2.0	86 655	5.4	83 981	1 366	39.5	2.7	148	3	109	78	147 329	107 854	10.3	89.7
Richmond	538	1.2	33 231	6.5	35 569	251	29.5	9.2	54	3	217	26	66 100	263 347	16.6	83.4
Robeson	3 276	3.1	16 400	1.4	53 088	1 004	35.8	14.8	285	-7	284	214	221 444	220 562	45.8	54.2
Rockingham	1 666	1.9	8 189	.8	13 542	780	32.2	6.8	134	3	172	55	37 172	47 656	81.1	18.9
Rowan	1 222	1.1	21 553	1.3	19 505	779	35.4	4.7	108	3	138	71	31 828	40 858	41.2	58.8
Rutherford	801	1.4	313	Z	-663	505	32.5	3.4	61	6	121	30	5 438	10 768	23.7	76.3
Sampson	2 981	6.3	100 644	17.2	224 518	1 186	36.6	9.9	271	5	228	183	732 859	617 925	13.7	86.3
Scotland	301	.9	729	.1	6 539	123	28.5	24.4	54	Z	435	36	55 056	447 610	23.0	77.0
Stanly	936	1.8	21 469	3.1	21 625	558	34.8	5.7	95	6	170	67	67 689	121 306	20.4	79.6
Stokes	2 384	6.4	10 855	4.3	15 508	926	38.0	3.0	110	5	119	50	33 786	36 486	68.9	31.1
Surry	2 162	3.5	54 918	5.0	61 129	1 194	42.3	2.8	130	8	109	70	98 364	82 382	32.4	67.6
Swain	115	1.0	857	.6	806	77	46.8	3.9	7	1	86	2	2 322	30 156	31.8	68.2
Transylvania	200	.8	9 290	2.4	8 570	174	60.9	1.7	13	Z	73	6	10 314	59 276	33.3	66.7
Tyrrell	228	5.9	-59	X	7 183	83	25.3	28.9	55	-13	661	51	35 687	429 964	54.6	45.4
Union	2 432	2.9	57 416	3.9	57 502	1 142	48.9	5.7	178	11	156	131	283 564	248 305	10.9	89.1
Vance	694	1.8	6 636	1.3	10 325	232	17.2	16.8	67	-1	287	27	19 567	84 341	97.4	2.6
Wake	3 015	.7	35 963	.2	44 171	772	43.0	5.8	113	-7	147	60	70 808	91 720	80.3	19.7
Warren	788	4.6	18 276	14.0	22 437	282	19.1	14.9	80	-7	284	35	37 607	133 358	35.8	64.2
Washington	604	4.3	5 210	5.3	12 529	203	35.5	27.1	107	4	528	92	67 555	332 783	62.2	37.8
Watauga	1 269	3.4	14 011	2.4	13 624	674	57.7	2.1	57	10	84	24	11 641	17 272	58.9	41.1
Wayne	2 356	2.3	42 146	2.7	72 083	827	39.5	13.1	229	50	277	147	337 089	407 605	21.4	78.6
Wilkes	1 461	2.5	65 087	7.4	58 740	1 170	45.6	2.3	127	12	109	59	214 889	183 666	4.1	95.9
Wilson	2 258	3.4	23 859	1.9	36 268	385	33.8	22.6	128	-14	333	91	120 443	312 839	70.1	29.9
Yadkin	1 601	5.3	18 973	5.8	20 981	884	42.2	3.8	102	-2	115	67	50 160	56 742	44.7	55.3
Yancey	1 109	7.2	13 604	9.4	13 503	604	63.9	1.3	40	2	66	14	5 347	8 853	80.0	20.0
NORTH DAKOTA	60 288	9.4	563 763	5.5	-41 978	30 504	6.4	63.9	39 359	-79	1 290	27 025	2 869 322	94 064	76.5	23.5
Adams	733	23.1	-1 742	X	-3 767	367	4.4	72.8	630	35	1 716	375	27 845	75 872	53.9	46.1
Barnes	2 084	16.6	6 829	5.2	-12 622	772	7.5	60.0	870	12	1 127	767	79 968	103 585	87.7	12.3
Benson	1 341	18.6	2 834	5.5	-7 176	604	4.6	64.2	758	-19	1 255	610	49 972	82 735	78.5	21.5
Billings	564	50.9	430	5.2	-2 623	237	5.5	67.5	794	-25	3 350	124	12 190	51 435	30.0	70.0
Bottineau	1 091	13.6	11 815	16.0	-3 790	808	4.8	61.5	960	10	1 188	811	60 921	75 397	90.5	9.5
Bowman	598	16.6	5 602	13.5	-871	358	6.1	65.1	715	37	1 998	335	26 207	73 204	49.1	50.9
Burke	664	22.1	2 178	10.2	-6 688	479	2.3	71.2	615	56	1 285	455	28 788	60 100	86.6	13.4
Burleigh	1 112	1.8	5 895	.5	-5 198	867	12.8	50.4	896	18	1 033	480	36 039	41 567	52.3	47.7
Cass	2 672	2.6	46 736	1.8	37 144	919	10.8	61.8	1 068	-3	1 162	1 013	169 041	183 940	91.7	8.3
Cavalier	709	11.7	7 669	13.6	-2 454	682	2.9	74.6	875	20	1 284	812	72 240	105 924	97.6	2.4
Dickey	1 219	20.0	15 734	23.8	7 082	517	7.0	58.6	580	-48	1 122	454	63 602	123 021	68.3	31.7
Divide	605	20.9	7 098	27.7	-4 256	535	4.3	76.1	733	7	1 371	555	35 014	65 447	84.9	15.1
Dunn	1 599	39.9	-3 061	X	-9 905	618	8.1	72.3	1 336	-17	2 161	429	39 412	63 773	29.9	70.1
Eddy	664	22.5	1 415	5.8	-394	288	3.8	74.0	344	-25	1 195	258	22 522	78 201	66.1	33.9
Emmons	1 493	30.9	8 411	20.8	-6 791	744	3.2	65.1	824	-10	1 107	509	51 263	68 902	50.1	49.9
Foster	684	17.2	10 174	18.0	-570	282	5.7	65.6	370	4	1 313	312	35 956	127 504	69.3	30.7
Golden Valley	317	15.0	-3 861	X	-6 236	244	4.9	71.3	579	73	2 372	221	18 266	74 861	56.5	43.5
Grand Forks	1 373	1.9	45 423	3.6	12 272	768	8.1	55.1	775	6	1 009	719	129 611	168 764	91.5	8.5
Grant	1 176	33.1	-1 368	X	-10 011	596	6.5	71.1	970	-50	1 627	448	34 897	58 552	37.6	62.4
Griggs	875	26.5	11 291	29.4	-693	357	7.0	58.5	390	-6	1 092	318	28 120	78 768	83.7	16.3
Hettinger	947	27.5	11 371	36.5	3 345	436	3.9	71.3	707	19	1 622	578	44 440	101 927	81.1	18.9
Kidder	1 174	35.2	8 309	32.8	-2 095	513	3.7	71.5	725	1	1 413	416	33 940	66 160	46.8	53.2
LaMoure	1 132	21.0	17 197	33.8	1 236	616	5.8	62.8	671	2	1 089	570	72 829	118 229	74.1	25.9
Logan	997	35.0	5 320	26.2	-3 369	401	3.5	73.3	531	-68	1 325	287	32 325	80 611	35.2	64.8
McHenry	1 797	27.5	7 165	17.6	-5 196	905	5.2	61.7	1 067	18	1 179	683	56 541	62 476	63.4	36.6
McIntosh	836	20.8	5 185	15.6	-3 359	505	4.8	60.4	508	-37	1 006	348	35 286	69 873	43.8	56.2
McKenzie	1 513	23.7	5 288	7.6	-9 172	668	6.0	67.2	1 170	4	1 751	522	46 500	69 611	54.9	45.1
McLean	2 016	19.3	16 336	14.3	-1 768	969	5.1	63.1	1 143	14	1 179	866	74 274	76 650	82.8	17.2
Mercer	960	9.8	-3 237	X	-5 735	473	7.0	53.9	551	20	1 165	284	23 039	48 708	53.5	46.5
Morton	2 107	8.9	4 074	1.5	-12 355	907	9.0	62.1	1 229	-5	1 355	565	60 312	66 496	30.3	69.7
Mountrail	1 163	16.6	17 711	23.3	-1 232	755	2.8	70.3	997	-4	1 321	650	49 173	65 130	78.0	22.0
Nelson	616	14.0	5 616	15.7	-3 875	471	3.8	62.6	535	-18	1 136	441	36 662	77 839	84.6	15.4
Oliver	654	27.5	-285	X	-4 859	327	6.1	59.0	400	16	1 224	186	19 086	58 367	38.8	61.2
Pembina	601	6.5	49 429	26.2	13 351	615	7.3	57.9	633	32	1 030	587	127 506	207 327	96.7	3.3
Pierce	1 248	24.7	2 684	5.1	-5 908	491	5.1	69.2	567	-19	1 155	444	36 083	73 489	75.4	24.6

[1] For 1990 corrected population, see table B-1. Percent is based on 1990 uncorrected population because only total population is corrected. [2] For total earnings, see table B-8. [3] Most data are comparable between 1992 and 1997; however, it should be noted that farms with all acreage in Conservation or Wetlands Reserve Programs (excluded in 1992) are included in 1997, as are short rotation woody crops which includes Christmas trees and maple sap gathering (in Forestry in 1992). [4] Includes nursery and greenhouse crops. [5] Includes related products.

Sources: Farm Population—U.S. Census Bureau, 1990 Census of Population and Housing, Summary Tape File (STF) 3C on CD-ROM (related Internet site <http://homer.ssd.census.gov/cdrom/lookup>). Farm Earnings—U.S. Bureau of Economic Analysis, "Regional Economic Information System (REIS) 1969-1998" on CD-ROM (related Internet site <http://www.bea.doc.gov/bea/regional/reis/ca45/>). Agriculture—U.S. Department of Agriculture, National Agricultural Statistics Service, 1997 Census of Agriculture, Volume 1, Geographic Area Series, 1A, 1B, 1C CD-ROM Set (related Internet site <http://www.nass.usda.gov/census/>).

Table B–10. Counties — Farm Population, Farm Earnings, and Agriculture–Con.

[Includes U.S., states, and 3,142 counties/county equivalents defined as of January 1, 1992. For changes to these areas since January 1, 1992, see appendix B. Geographic Information]

County	Farm population, 1990 Number	Farm population, 1990 Percent of total[1]	Farm earnings 1998 Total ($1,000)	Farm earnings 1998 Percent of total[2]	Farm earnings 1997 ($1,000)	Farms Number	Farms Less than 50 acres	Farms 500 acres or more	Land in farms Total acreage (1,000)	Land in farms Net change, 1992–1997[3] (1,000)	Land in farms Average size of farm	Land in farms Total cropland (1,000)	Value of farm products sold Total ($1,000)	Value of farm products sold Average per farm (dollars)	Value of farm products sold Percent from Crops[4]	Value of farm products sold Percent from Livestock and poultry[5]
NORTH DAKOTA—Con.																
Ramsey	1 199	9.5	3 825	2.4	−12 267	525	7.0	66.3	658	18	1 254	597	44 935	85 590	93.9	6.1
Ransom	1 405	23.7	11 521	17.6	9 730	485	10.3	52.6	515	30	1 062	360	61 387	126 571	76.7	23.3
Renville	664	21.0	10 246	32.5	−292	390	1.8	74.1	516	12	1 322	456	37 791	96 900	92.1	7.9
Richland	1 801	9.9	40 611	14.4	45 128	874	10.2	55.6	809	10	926	748	165 985	189 914	82.1	17.9
Rolette	1 062	8.3	−3 319	X	−5 938	511	7.6	58.5	493	−29	965	356	29 604	57 933	73.4	26.6
Sargent	1 353	29.7	11 457	12.4	12 446	449	8.0	60.8	477	−19	1 062	403	64 534	143 728	74.2	25.8
Sheridan	768	35.8	4 498	31.1	−2 684	380	3.2	71.3	492	−29	1 295	340	27 388	72 074	63.8	36.2
Sioux	589	15.7	−4 583	X	−4 137	193	3.6	76.7	705	−41	3 652	D	14 528	75 275	22.8	77.2
Slope	613	67.6	3 587	61.5	−1 955	263	4.2	72.6	757	−29	2 879	D	21 432	81 490	57.3	42.7
Stark	1 339	5.9	2 635	.9	−7 460	802	12.8	56.1	806	−36	1 005	536	45 785	57 089	47.6	52.4
Steele	905	37.4	11 395	42.3	3 995	290	5.5	75.2	413	−27	1 423	377	46 718	161 097	95.9	4.1
Stutsman	1 964	8.8	16 225	5.0	−14 882	979	6.8	64.9	1 265	−5	1 292	985	92 543	94 528	72.6	27.4
Towner	511	14.1	3 517	10.7	−6 894	428	6.5	72.0	570	−21	1 332	499	42 394	99 051	93.1	6.9
Traill	1 120	12.8	35 245	30.0	16 635	471	8.5	67.1	494	−7	1 050	480	84 519	179 446	97.3	2.7
Walsh	1 279	9.2	51 332	28.3	12 175	755	5.7	57.9	718	−20	950	642	122 394	162 111	96.0	4.0
Ward	1 967	3.4	21 400	2.2	−7 084	1 172	8.1	57.8	1 208	47	1 030	949	82 909	70 741	82.8	17.2
Wells	1 163	19.8	5 526	10.3	−473	593	4.9	65.3	744	−6	1 255	617	61 586	103 855	83.8	16.2
Williams	1 252	5.9	6 980	2.7	−9 483	850	6.0	67.3	1 205	23	1 418	829	53 022	62 379	80.5	19.5
OHIO	198 914	1.8	1 009 065	.5	1 453 217	68 591	30.7	10.0	14 103	−145	206	11 341	4 684 277	68 293	60.4	39.6
Adams	2 638	10.4	10 922	5.1	6 884	1 315	30.5	4.9	195	−2	148	110	27 278	20 744	58.6	41.4
Allen	3 139	2.9	−1 043	X	16 029	918	27.7	12.0	190	−4	207	173	59 375	64 679	76.6	23.4
Ashland	3 299	6.9	4 053	.6	9 957	929	26.9	7.8	164	−7	176	128	48 933	52 673	38.4	61.6
Ashtabula	2 486	2.5	2 545	.2	9 993	993	28.9	4.4	149	−7	150	103	34 907	35 153	43.7	56.3
Athens	928	1.6	−791	X	94	481	18.5	4.4	83	2	172	39	6 208	12 906	33.9	66.1
Auglaize	3 661	8.2	18 627	2.6	24 079	1 001	27.3	10.8	213	8	213	195	85 557	85 472	55.3	44.7
Belmont	1 099	1.5	−1 588	X	−2 298	622	16.7	9.5	148	22	238	65	12 308	19 788	18.7	81.3
Brown	3 479	9.9	11 311	4.3	13 099	1 378	36.3	5.2	196	−7	142	144	37 773	27 411	81.8	18.2
Butler	2 387	.8	−2 253	X	3 557	849	40.8	6.6	135	−4	158	108	35 032	41 263	61.4	38.6
Carroll	1 469	5.5	32 636	13.4	8 164	683	21.5	4.2	113	−9	166	68	21 278	31 154	45.2	54.8
Champaign	2 393	6.6	19 777	5.0	25 528	836	35.8	16.6	222	6	265	196	71 281	85 264	76.0	24.0
Clark	2 254	1.5	13 936	.7	27 884	671	42.0	14.8	172	−7	256	154	73 418	109 416	86.7	13.3
Clermont	2 076	1.4	−2 860	X	3 116	744	50.0	5.1	88	−11	119	66	16 665	22 399	84.2	15.8
Clinton	2 752	7.8	8 765	1.0	24 851	761	28.3	19.6	223	−4	293	201	65 828	86 502	84.4	15.6
Columbiana	2 159	2.0	17 434	1.5	14 213	980	36.2	4.4	138	−6	141	99	46 923	47 881	36.1	63.9
Coshocton	2 187	6.2	11 267	2.4	12 573	864	20.1	8.0	170	8	197	104	37 124	42 968	39.6	60.4
Crawford	2 410	5.0	9 915	1.7	28 212	712	25.3	17.6	227	3	318	207	75 204	105 624	71.1	28.9
Cuyahoga	16	Z	14 922	Z	10 452	118	78.8	—	4	Z	36	3	17 147	145 314	97.0	3.0
Darke	6 640	12.4	26 731	4.1	58 512	1 726	33.8	6.0	329	−6	191	302	247 071	143 147	30.1	69.9
Defiance	2 913	7.4	5 784	.8	15 075	861	25.7	10.6	186	−10	216	166	45 248	52 553	74.2	25.8
Delaware	2 291	3.4	10 475	.9	20 879	627	41.8	14.2	161	−8	256	145	53 806	85 815	85.8	14.2
Erie	1 117	1.5	9 668	.7	12 324	380	36.1	15.0	90	1	237	81	35 462	93 321	83.1	16.9
Fairfield	3 058	3.0	(6)	Z	10 957	1 024	37.5	9.2	197	−1	192	162	51 306	50 104	74.0	26.0
Fayette	1 744	6.3	4 014	1.4	17 705	520	26.5	32.5	243	7	466	224	72 179	138 806	89.5	10.5
Franklin	1 155	.1	9 902	Z	21 443	407	46.4	11.5	80	−17	196	69	41 165	101 143	92.3	7.7
Fulton	3 577	9.3	24 454	3.4	38 812	794	30.4	14.0	197	−8	249	185	87 848	110 640	64.5	35.5
Gallia	1 245	4.0	3 015	.8	(6)	776	24.7	3.4	117	7	151	53	15 155	19 530	41.2	58.8
Geauga	1 820	2.2	787	.1	6 326	661	44.9	2.1	59	−6	90	38	18 282	27 658	49.0	51.0
Greene	2 516	1.8	11 577	.4	20 434	764	40.8	13.5	178	−6	233	155	58 595	76 695	82.8	17.2
Guernsey	1 405	3.6	−1 421	X	328	802	20.6	5.0	138	10	172	70	10 754	13 409	22.4	77.6
Hamilton	362	Z	7 161	Z	9 989	302	59.9	3.6	29	Z	97	21	17 301	57 288	83.2	16.8
Hancock	3 651	5.6	12 963	.9	28 397	979	25.4	18.1	277	2	283	259	81 864	83 620	82.3	17.7
Hardin	3 454	11.1	24 908	7.7	37 700	837	23.2	17.9	247	−2	295	225	114 970	137 360	47.4	52.6
Harrison	734	4.6	239	.2	1 591	423	15.6	11.6	110	−4	259	53	10 010	23 664	23.6	76.4
Henry	3 128	10.7	10 971	2.7	28 862	872	22.7	16.6	244	−1	280	230	75 092	86 115	89.5	10.5
Highland	3 381	9.5	8 479	2.3	11 120	1 239	28.2	10.0	242	11	196	190	46 179	37 271	73.8	26.2
Hocking	667	2.6	−3 174	X	−1 593	353	24.4	1.4	48	Z	136	23	3 432	9 722	68.5	31.5
Holmes	5 661	17.2	20 003	4.0	20 820	1 404	24.6	2.5	172	−5	122	113	87 815	62 546	8.9	91.1
Huron	2 708	4.8	24 207	2.6	33 165	782	24.9	16.0	232	13	296	203	77 539	99 155	82.3	17.7
Jackson	507	1.7	8 647	2.6	10 143	408	17.4	6.4	74	Z	181	43	17 515	42 929	75.1	24.9
Jefferson	739	.9	1 377	.2	1 782	410	16.8	6.6	71	3	174	40	6 703	16 349	29.1	70.9
Knox	2 801	5.9	20 388	3.2	27 345	1 103	28.6	8.4	206	−4	187	159	61 891	56 112	45.5	54.5
Lake	274	.1	63 824	1.7	49 929	274	68.6	2.2	19	2	70	13	73 572	268 511	99.3	.7
Lawrence	820	1.3	−179	X	390	490	28.6	2.4	59	−3	121	23	3 954	8 069	56.3	43.7
Licking	2 847	2.2	37 853	2.1	30 892	1 218	35.0	8.3	237	10	195	184	128 880	105 813	32.7	67.3
Logan	2 466	5.8	22 988	3.0	27 512	895	30.5	12.7	219	16	245	188	89 077	99 527	45.9	54.1
Lorain	1 775	.7	26 408	.7	32 456	778	43.7	6.8	131	−12	168	110	82 972	106 648	83.1	16.9
Lucas	1 417	.3	24 915	.3	26 978	385	53.0	14.3	80	6	207	75	60 875	158 117	75.1	24.9
Madison	2 200	5.9	7 913	1.8	20 861	667	28.5	24.7	262	1	393	238	80 277	120 355	83.9	16.1
Mahoning	1 374	.5	11 443	.3	10 824	542	39.5	3.7	73	Z	135	56	31 997	59 035	56.1	43.9

[1] For 1990 corrected population, see table B-1. Percent is based on 1990 uncorrected population because only total population is corrected. [2] For total earnings, see table B-8. [3] Most data are comparable between 1992 and 1997; however, it should be noted that farms with all acreage in Conservation or Wetlands Reserve Programs (excluded in 1992) are included in 1997, as are short rotation woody crops which includes Christmas trees and maple sap gathering (in Forestry in 1992). [4] Includes nursery and greenhouse crops. [5] Includes related products. [6] Less than $50,000.

Sources: Farm Population—U.S. Census Bureau, 1990 Census of Population and Housing, Summary Tape File (STF) 3C on CD-ROM (related Internet site <http://homer.ssd.census.gov/cdrom/lookup>). Farm Earnings—U.S. Bureau of Economic Analysis, "Regional Economic Information System (REIS) 1969-1998" on CD-ROM (related Internet site <http://www.bea.doc.gov/bea/regional/reis/ca45/>). Agriculture—U.S. Department of Agriculture, National Agricultural Statistics Service, 1997 Census of Agriculture, Volume 1, Geographic Area Series, 1A, 1B, 1C CD-ROM Set (related Internet site <http://www.nass.usda.gov/census/>).

Table B–10. Counties — Farm Population, Farm Earnings, and Agriculture–Con.

[Includes U.S., states, and 3,142 counties/county equivalents defined as of January 1, 1992. For changes to these areas since January 1, 1992, see appendix B. Geographic Information]

County	Farm population, 1990 Number	Farm population, 1990 Percent of total[1]	Farm earnings 1998 Total ($1,000)	Farm earnings 1998 Percent of total[2]	Farm earnings 1997 ($1,000)	Farms Number	Farms Percent Less than 50 acres	Farms Percent 500 acres or more	Land in farms Total acreage (1,000)	Land in farms Net change, 1992–1997[3] (1,000)	Land in farms Average size of farm	Land in farms Total cropland (1,000)	Value of farm products sold Total ($1,000)	Value of farm products sold Average per farm (dollars)	Percent from Crops[4]	Percent from Livestock and poultry[5]
OHIO—Con.																
Marion	1 730	2.7	7 611	.8	19 088	543	28.2	22.7	221	3	406	207	64 262	118 346	81.3	18.7
Medina	2 368	1.9	11 614	.6	7 477	851	47.9	4.6	104	Z	122	81	34 080	40 047	52.7	47.3
Meigs	866	3.8	14 847	7.6	7 927	491	17.7	4.7	85	-2	173	39	12 982	26 440	69.8	30.2
Mercer	5 282	13.4	80 197	14.0	83 342	1 255	26.6	10.4	261	-8	208	237	287 662	229 213	19.1	80.9
Miami	4 283	4.6	10 443	.7	24 784	983	42.6	11.5	192	-8	196	174	64 097	65 205	77.8	22.2
Monroe	1 103	7.1	-1 544	X	-2 446	589	12.4	4.9	110	Z	186	48	7 398	12 560	13.7	86.3
Montgomery	2 072	.4	11 041	.1	11 670	760	50.7	6.4	106	-1	139	93	36 178	47 603	81.8	18.2
Morgan	780	5.5	2 234	1.5	1 933	500	12.2	6.8	98	-16	197	42	8 402	16 804	19.8	80.2
Morrow	2 438	8.8	10 505	5.5	17 369	759	31.2	9.4	161	-3	212	132	41 635	54 855	66.7	33.3
Muskingum	1 662	2.0	-1 057	X	3 348	1 018	22.7	7.1	180	-8	177	103	25 776	25 320	38.6	61.4
Noble	797	7.0	-2 399	X	-2 049	519	15.0	4.6	99	-5	191	51	3 823	7 366	16.9	83.1
Ottawa	1 605	4.0	4 699	.9	7 976	474	31.4	12.4	106	-1	223	97	28 643	60 428	93.1	6.9
Paulding	1 761	8.6	2 972	1.8	18 306	542	21.2	26.6	210	-9	387	196	54 144	99 897	82.8	17.2
Perry	1 206	3.8	3 555	1.6	2 762	606	25.1	5.0	97	1	159	63	15 351	25 332	62.0	37.9
Pickaway	2 527	5.2	6 137	1.0	22 835	703	31.4	21.5	267	8	380	241	79 338	112 856	83.1	16.9
Pike	707	2.9	-1 603	X	-674	435	19.8	6.2	78	-10	180	44	7 517	17 280	52.1	47.9
Portage	1 641	1.2	10 141	.5	11 080	719	45.9	4.0	87	-9	122	62	23 778	33 071	55.7	44.3
Preble	3 446	8.6	12 132	3.1	9 101	977	35.9	10.4	197	-7	202	172	67 931	69 530	64.5	35.5
Putnam	4 709	13.9	16 039	4.1	36 101	1 352	23.1	10.3	292	6	216	275	102 883	76 097	68.0	32.0
Richland	2 979	2.4	12 720	.6	15 087	908	28.6	7.0	156	-5	171	120	47 145	51 922	49.0	51.0
Ross	1 621	2.3	3 554	.4	9 432	885	25.2	13.1	252	-2	284	184	45 806	51 758	80.4	19.6
Sandusky	2 914	4.7	12 138	1.3	26 715	795	30.3	14.1	199	-3	251	186	66 000	83 019	85.7	14.3
Scioto	874	1.1	111	Z	1 213	630	28.4	5.6	103	7	163	59	13 937	22 122	61.9	38.1
Seneca	3 927	6.6	-443	X	22 742	1 210	24.0	13.7	293	-4	242	261	83 691	69 166	73.2	26.8
Shelby	3 463	7.7	16 657	1.5	18 340	991	27.7	10.3	202	-2	204	181	71 798	72 450	57.4	42.6
Stark	2 719	.7	15 280	.3	18 316	1 086	45.5	4.7	137	Z	126	107	72 998	67 217	39.0	61.0
Summit	245	Z	526	Z	3 695	251	64.5	1.2	17	-2	69	11	8 932	35 586	84.7	15.3
Trumbull	2 288	1.0	576	Z	4 210	788	33.0	4.2	112	-8	143	82	25 467	32 319	53.7	46.3
Tuscarawas	2 131	2.5	24 134	2.1	15 758	920	28.2	5.3	141	-7	154	90	56 229	61 118	20.5	79.5
Union	2 545	8.0	9 483	.8	17 840	811	31.8	14.5	205	-18	252	185	69 625	85 851	61.7	38.3
Van Wert	2 664	8.7	5 171	1.3	22 047	707	21.9	23.9	237	-5	336	225	72 552	102 620	86.7	13.3
Vinton	320	2.9	-559	X	-234	202	19.3	4.5	37	-5	184	20	1 704	8 436	40.2	59.8
Warren	2 022	1.8	475	Z	9 744	741	49.7	6.7	118	-11	160	94	33 781	45 588	84.0	16.0
Washington	1 656	2.7	4 758	.6	4 560	900	19.6	4.0	147	7	163	72	20 428	22 698	36.8	63.2
Wayne	5 848	5.8	65 566	3.8	46 881	1 601	35.5	5.8	241	-6	150	195	155 757	97 287	22.1	77.9
Williams	2 756	7.5	4 934	.8	14 375	908	25.7	10.9	203	16	224	175	51 383	56 589	69.0	31.0
Wood	3 374	3.0	25 258	1.3	36 710	1 015	27.1	19.8	304	2	299	288	96 452	95 027	90.8	9.2
Wyandot	2 306	10.4	7 294	2.3	17 475	608	24.2	22.0	209	-7	344	191	63 690	104 753	71.9	28.1
OKLAHOMA	82 929	2.6	658 277	1.3	711 656	74 214	20.5	21.6	33 219	1 076	448	14 844	4 146 351	55 870	21.9	78.1
Adair	1 983	10.8	25 757	16.6	19 946	1 090	26.0	8.4	225	18	207	100	74 320	68 183	1.6	98.4
Alfalfa	1 034	16.1	18 352	31.8	21 899	709	8.9	43.4	502	14	708	376	89 885	126 777	35.3	64.7
Atoka	1 220	9.5	1 157	1.1	927	1 087	16.7	15.5	421	45	387	128	20 444	18 808	7.7	92.3
Beaver	796	13.2	9 745	16.7	9 008	738	3.9	56.9	1 048	61	1 420	397	88 602	120 057	16.0	84.0
Beckham	624	3.3	2 709	1.5	3 314	825	14.4	34.8	499	6	605	222	24 755	30 006	33.2	66.8
Blaine	898	7.8	17 137	16.1	11 159	841	8.2	39.4	547	33	650	304	77 367	91 994	22.7	77.3
Bryan	1 807	5.6	-1 405	X	321	1 516	20.0	14.2	420	7	277	192	32 547	21 469	27.6	72.4
Caddo	1 710	5.8	27 892	10.4	28 647	1 496	11.8	29.4	727	Z	486	403	91 135	60 919	47.9	52.1
Canadian	1 505	2.0	8 002	1.0	5 269	1 165	25.2	26.0	467	-33	401	280	66 587	57 156	29.1	70.9
Carter	501	1.2	-3 962	X	-2 218	1 165	22.1	15.0	382	9	328	118	21 961	18 851	9.5	90.5
Cherokee	1 505	4.4	40 878	11.8	36 085	1 154	27.5	7.5	238	19	206	91	65 681	56 916	58.9	41.1
Choctaw	1 059	6.9	1 860	1.8	3 591	991	17.7	18.9	338	37	341	132	24 209	24 429	12.9	87.1
Cimarron	535	16.2	13 803	38.1	12 199	481	3.1	66.3	1 077	42	2 239	454	180 548	375 360	16.8	83.2
Cleveland	960	.6	-3 304	X	-1 583	1 017	42.4	7.4	162	5	160	84	12 173	11 970	32.3	67.7
Coal	933	16.1	-2 819	X	-1 280	586	13.0	26.8	273	8	466	90	17 859	30 476	4.2	95.8
Comanche	1 178	1.1	6 410	.4	5 068	1 030	18.2	25.2	435	29	422	194	32 321	31 380	35.0	65.0
Cotton	805	12.1	10 068	25.0	10 178	512	8.8	36.5	350	-8	684	194	36 399	71 092	29.5	70.5
Craig	1 383	9.8	-2 172	X	-1 246	1 120	18.3	17.3	418	-29	374	166	61 663	55 056	10.1	89.9
Creek	998	1.6	-4 363	X	-3 561	1 475	32.7	10.4	351	15	238	122	14 592	9 893	14.6	85.4
Custer	1 054	3.9	10 005	3.2	7 608	788	10.3	41.9	625	-9	793	312	64 735	82 151	31.5	68.5
Delaware	1 862	6.6	32 704	14.7	28 208	1 303	24.2	8.6	265	23	203	129	94 390	72 441	3.1	96.9
Dewey	781	14.1	6 407	13.6	4 975	713	6.2	43.3	619	36	869	227	34 260	48 050	31.5	68.5
Ellis	616	13.7	8 624	23.3	5 481	622	5.1	50.0	670	-30	1 077	194	35 306	56 762	24.5	75.5
Garfield	1 800	3.2	20 937	2.5	23 111	1 069	13.5	35.3	615	-47	575	459	82 977	77 621	46.5	53.5
Garvin	1 803	6.8	-2 549	X	2 000	1 380	19.9	18.3	449	29	325	196	34 245	24 815	25.4	74.6
Grady	2 184	5.2	12 680	3.3	11 528	1 625	20.6	19.5	609	43	375	278	89 271	54 936	15.5	84.5
Grant	699	12.3	16 969	28.5	19 242	688	4.5	50.9	585	-15	850	431	61 155	88 888	64.1	35.9
Greer	317	4.8	9 963	16.8	8 865	478	7.3	38.3	314	-24	658	173	17 260	36 109	52.7	47.3
Harmon	318	8.4	7 432	23.9	6 824	338	5.6	48.5	304	18	900	161	21 738	64 314	56.1	43.9
Harper	414	10.2	11 881	27.8	16 914	443	5.6	56.7	580	-28	1 308	201	100 021	225 781	8.7	91.3

[1] For 1990 corrected population, see table B-1. Percent is based on 1990 uncorrected population because only total population is corrected. [2] For total earnings, see table B-8. [3] Most data are comparable between 1992 and 1997; however, it should be noted that farms with all acreage in Conservation or Wetlands Reserve Programs (excluded in 1992) are included in 1997, as are short rotation woody crops which includes Christmas trees and maple sap gathering (in Forestry in 1992). [4] Includes nursery and greenhouse crops. [5] Includes related products.

Sources: Farm Population—U.S. Census Bureau, 1990 Census of Population and Housing, Summary Tape File (STF) 3C on CD-ROM (related Internet site <http://homer.ssd.census.gov/cdrom/lookup>). Farm Earnings—U.S. Bureau of Economic Analysis, "Regional Economic Information System (REIS) 1969-1998" on CD-ROM (related Internet site <http://www.bea.doc.gov/bea/regional/reis/ca45/>). Agriculture—U.S. Department of Agriculture, National Agricultural Statistics Service, 1997 Census of Agriculture, Volume 1, Geographic Area Series, 1A, 1B, 1C CD-ROM Set (related Internet site <http://www.nass.usda.gov/census/>).

[Includes U.S., states, and 3,142 counties/county equivalents defined as of January 1, 1992. For changes to these areas since January 1, 1992, see appendix B. Geographic Information]

County	Farm population, 1990 Number	Farm population, 1990 Percent of total[1]	Farm earnings 1998 Total ($1,000)	Farm earnings 1998 Percent of total[2]	Farm earnings 1997 ($1,000)	Farms Number	Farms Percent Less than 50 acres	Farms Percent 500 acres or more	Land in farms Total acreage (1,000)	Land in farms Net change, 1992–1997[3] (1,000)	Land in farms Average size of farm	Land in farms Total cropland (1,000)	Value of farm products sold Total ($1,000)	Value of farm products sold Average per farm (dollars)	Value Percent from Crops[4]	Value Percent from Livestock and poultry[5]
OKLAHOMA—Con.																
Haskell	741	6.8	4 063	5.1	4 169	872	17.3	15.7	268	Z	307	116	33 304	38 193	3.3	96.7
Hughes	764	5.9	8 141	10.2	15 117	897	11.5	17.9	355	9	396	116	40 524	45 177	10.2	89.8
Jackson	701	2.4	22 186	5.2	19 149	723	16.0	34.3	477	7	659	333	68 685	95 000	61.2	38.8
Jefferson	704	10.0	4 585	8.2	9 366	499	11.4	36.9	441	36	884	135	50 810	101 824	8.9	91.1
Johnston	693	6.9	2 888	3.6	4 031	624	20.0	21.3	334	11	535	92	27 559	44 165	6.9	93.1
Kay	1 448	3.0	9 559	1.3	18 995	929	18.5	32.2	469	–8	505	331	56 486	60 803	65.8	34.2
Kingfisher	1 240	9.4	15 802	8.3	18 264	998	12.0	34.7	555	33	556	367	99 470	99 669	21.5	78.5
Kiowa	662	5.8	17 480	18.6	10 101	702	9.5	46.4	595	37	848	362	51 826	73 826	36.8	63.2
Latimer	648	6.3	–2 159	X	–1 887	643	20.2	14.5	202	8	314	63	10 712	16 659	5.7	94.3
Le Flore	1 691	3.9	38 433	10.4	31 597	1 744	29.0	9.9	407	27	234	189	118 708	68 067	6.5	93.5
Lincoln	2 379	8.1	–5 435	X	–2 876	1 916	19.0	9.9	431	33	225	181	23 511	12 271	12.8	87.2
Logan	1 159	4.0	3 910	2.0	6 096	983	20.7	20.8	381	36	387	183	39 403	40 084	27.3	72.7
Love	813	10.0	–3 618	X	–1 864	629	16.2	18.6	266	11	423	87	15 551	24 723	22.1	77.9
McClain	1 017	4.5	2 607	1.4	6 009	1 046	30.1	13.5	268	14	256	121	31 467	30 083	21.5	78.5
McCurtain	1 689	5.1	47 029	11.4	35 297	1 573	28.0	8.0	328	13	208	135	137 081	87 146	3.0	97.0
McIntosh	938	5.6	–2 951	X	–1 485	906	20.2	10.9	254	17	280	105	15 887	17 535	16.5	83.5
Major	1 156	14.4	8 873	10.6	12 652	877	11.1	35.5	491	–3	560	244	54 803	62 489	27.0	73.0
Marshall	505	4.7	–3 432	X	–2 892	414	18.6	17.9	164	1	395	42	6 076	14 676	19.5	80.5
Mayes	1 932	5.8	2 596	.7	3 873	1 406	29.9	8.6	284	6	202	147	33 422	23 771	13.5	86.5
Murray	454	3.8	1 140	1.1	1 359	454	18.5	19.6	203	–27	448	49	20 459	45 064	3.0	97.0
Muskogee	1 947	2.9	–2 968	X	3 299	1 468	28.3	8.7	333	–15	227	183	31 658	21 565	39.6	60.4
Noble	823	7.5	5 179	3.6	8 489	739	11.1	31.9	413	22	559	222	39 677	53 690	45.3	54.7
Nowata	995	10.0	194	.3	1 677	764	18.5	17.9	309	27	405	99	28 516	37 325	6.6	93.4
Okfuskee	783	6.8	512	.7	2 029	784	14.5	17.5	282	25	360	101	17 549	22 384	11.9	88.1
Oklahoma	619	.1	2 156	Z	2 942	996	46.0	7.0	160	4	161	78	14 943	15 003	56.7	43.3
Okmulgee	921	2.5	–3 536	X	173	1 107	23.6	11.5	302	22	273	123	18 819	17 000	22.3	77.7
Osage	1 092	2.6	–4 008	X	963	1 196	20.7	29.3	1 207	91	1 010	158	102 882	86 022	5.5	94.5
Ottawa	1 536	5.0	24 131	X	25 864	972	31.4	9.1	215	8	221	130	52 773	54 293	53.4	46.6
Pawnee	771	5.0	–3 307	X	258	671	18.0	23.0	263	–19	393	93	17 876	26 641	19.9	80.1
Payne	1 465	2.4	–2 987	X	–2 022	1 281	26.9	14.0	339	10	265	142	22 375	17 467	17.4	82.6
Pittsburg	1 736	4.3	–3 958	X	–2 247	1 586	21.7	14.6	491	10	310	148	24 631	15 530	13.0	87.0
Pontotoc	1 143	3.4	–2 578	X	–431	1 133	22.9	13.9	335	–18	296	130	23 345	20 605	8.0	92.0
Pottawatomie	1 018	1.7	2 271	.4	6 715	1 448	22.5	10.4	336	37	232	155	32 999	22 789	13.7	86.3
Pushmataha	756	6.9	–5 149	X	–3 894	776	19.2	14.4	256	16	330	71	7 704	9 928	4.7	95.3
Roger Mills	734	17.7	3 210	10.8	3 493	680	3.5	52.1	691	30	1 016	162	27 511	40 457	16.6	83.4
Rogers	1 290	2.3	–3 793	X	–188	1 408	38.2	9.3	313	3	222	125	27 129	19 268	21.9	78.1
Seminole	827	3.3	–2 844	X	–1 299	1 018	20.2	11.3	278	27	273	109	14 427	14 172	16.2	83.8
Sequoyah	1 014	3.0	–958	X	–603	1 125	30.0	7.7	293	78	261	95	39 105	34 760	12.1	87.9
Stephens	1 259	3.0	1 010	.2	1 981	1 165	20.5	17.4	427	6	366	171	24 287	20 847	13.0	87.0
Texas	1 030	6.3	117 855	31.0	117 937	785	6.5	58.2	1 087	35	1 384	632	668 024	850 986	7.8	92.2
Tillman	732	7.0	15 626	19.1	10 691	638	7.5	42.0	466	–15	730	322	41 124	64 458	59.2	40.8
Tulsa	792	.2	7 305	.1	8 576	954	50.3	6.6	143	9	150	72	19 725	20 676	65.8	34.2
Wagoner	1 281	2.7	1 288	.6	8 099	973	32.2	10.1	241	24	247	139	28 856	29 657	64.5	35.5
Washington	830	1.7	2 571	.4	3 455	768	32.8	10.8	238	21	309	74	16 421	21 382	26.2	73.8
Washita	1 202	10.5	7 646	10.1	8 210	994	9.7	38.7	586	8	589	399	68 746	69 161	36.3	63.7
Woods	717	7.9	19 803	19.2	16 348	705	7.2	51.9	805	61	1 141	290	81 400	115 461	27.3	72.7
Woodward	1 000	5.3	11 111	4.3	13 591	800	12.1	39.0	722	35	902	214	49 697	62 121	17.7	82.3
OREGON	68 729	2.4	747 932	1.2	790 214	34 030	56.3	12.9	17 449	–160	513	5 286	2 969 194	87 252	71.2	28.8
Baker	1 189	7.8	–5 010	X	5 669	704	27.0	35.9	1 008	189	1 431	161	53 876	76 528	25.3	74.7
Benton	1 852	2.6	28 037	1.9	24 882	726	65.4	7.4	131	12	180	92	70 202	96 697	87.3	12.7
Clackamas	7 517	2.7	96 752	1.9	90 229	3 745	78.9	1.0	180	31	48	107	276 251	73 765	78.4	21.6
Clatsop	567	1.7	1 486	.3	2 187	229	49.8	3.1	23	–2	99	13	5 325	23 253	13.4	86.6
Columbia	1 364	3.6	10 646	2.8	11 670	686	63.4	2.3	66	–6	96	23	24 851	36 226	81.4	18.6
Coos	1 297	2.2	13 326	1.9	21 569	675	42.1	9.6	163	–12	242	43	30 527	45 225	46.7	53.3
Crook	782	5.5	–830	X	246	521	46.1	26.9	916	22	1 759	77	31 436	60 338	42.5	57.5
Curry	314	1.6	–1 771	X	1 085	168	33.9	26.8	85	10	505	17	13 061	77 744	67.1	32.9
Deschutes	1 998	2.7	–2 756	X	–2 296	1 235	74.7	3.5	124	–15	101	44	21 495	17 405	45.9	54.1
Douglas	2 425	2.6	1 032	.1	9 269	1 908	49.5	9.1	402	Z	211	118	35 338	18 521	27.8	72.2
Gilliam	430	25.0	–6 841	X	–1 968	166	2.4	81.3	743	–24	4 474	298	24 526	147 747	81.0	19.0
Grant	746	9.5	–1 430	X	3 598	407	23.8	49.6	1 081	–74	2 655	87	17 093	41 998	14.5	85.5
Harney	669	9.5	1 419	1.6	5 210	504	17.9	52.6	1 359	–98	2 696	215	38 883	77 149	19.3	80.7
Hood River	1 300	7.7	20 344	7.3	28 076	537	67.2	.7	28	1	53	21	63 306	117 888	98.6	1.4
Jackson	2 349	1.6	9 113	.4	14 703	1 623	66.7	4.7	246	–16	152	70	50 957	31 397	74.5	25.5
Jefferson	931	6.8	6 114	3.1	2 798	399	30.8	26.3	783	253	1 964	100	43 152	108 150	81.2	18.8
Josephine	653	1.0	3 048	.4	774	616	74.0	1.1	35	3	56	17	16 204	26 305	54.0	46.0
Klamath	1 776	3.1	9 127	1.2	18 679	1 066	35.2	22.6	714	–7	669	235	100 622	94 392	51.0	49.0
Lake	748	10.4	–635	X	8 589	418	17.0	39.7	737	–96	1 762	187	42 759	102 294	47.3	52.7
Lane	4 514	1.6	29 131	.6	24 603	2 104	65.3	4.2	224	–18	106	120	87 170	41 431	62.2	37.8
Lincoln	609	1.6	–1 103	X	–187	306	54.9	3.9	32	–2	104	10	4 127	13 487	61.8	38.2

[1] For 1990 corrected population, see table B-1. Percent is based on 1990 uncorrected population because only total population is corrected. [2] For total earnings, see table B-8. [3] Most data are comparable between 1992 and 1997; however, it should be noted that farms with all acreage in Conservation or Wetlands Reserve Programs (excluded in 1992) are included in 1997, as are short rotation woody crops which includes Christmas trees and maple sap gathering in Forestry in 1992). [4] Includes nursery and greenhouse crops. [5] Includes related products.

Sources: Farm Population—U.S. Census Bureau, 1990 Census of Population and Housing, Summary Tape File (STF) 3C on CD-ROM (related Internet site <http://homer.ssd.census.gov/cdrom/lookup>). Farm Earnings—U.S. Bureau of Economic Analysis, "Regional Economic Information System (REIS) 1969-1998" on CD-ROM (related Internet site <http://www.bea.doc.gov/bea/regional/reis/ca45/>). Agriculture—U.S. Department of Agriculture, National Agricultural Statistics Service, 1997 Census of Agriculture, Volume 1, Geographic Area Series, 1A, 1B, 1C CD-ROM Set (related Internet site <http://www.nass.usda.gov/census/>).

Table B–10. Counties — **Farm Population, Farm Earnings, and Agriculture**–Con.

[Includes U.S., states, and 3,142 counties/county equivalents defined as of January 1, 1992. For changes to these areas since January 1, 1992, see appendix B. Geographic Information]

County	Farm population, 1990 Number	Percent of total[1]	Farm earnings 1998 Total ($1,000)	Percent of total[2]	1997 ($1,000)	Farms Number	Percent Less than 50 acres	500 acres or more	Total acreage (1,000)	Net change, 1992–1997[3] (1,000)	Average size of farm	Total cropland (1,000)	Value Total ($1,000)	Average per farm (dollars)	Percent from Crops[4]	Live-stock and poultry[5]
OREGON—Con.																
Linn	4 571	5.0	49 830	3.3	56 277	2 009	57.4	9.2	393	13	196	305	174 215	86 717	78.5	21.5
Malheur	3 184	12.2	40 288	10.2	39 713	1 207	28.7	22.5	1 257	–61	1 042	279	208 218	172 509	58.7	41.3
Marion	7 079	3.1	162 395	3.7	141 307	2 546	65.0	5.8	306	4	120	251	438 369	172 179	83.6	16.4
Morrow	629	8.2	22 649	17.3	16 514	420	24.8	52.6	1 118	–1	2 662	486	141 531	336 979	77.0	23.0
Multnomah	1 115	.2	19 182	.1	14 905	577	82.1	1.6	34	3	60	19	41 326	71 622	96.2	3.8
Polk	2 690	5.4	37 818	7.2	32 429	1 147	60.0	6.8	171	4	149	128	91 094	79 419	77.3	22.7
Sherman	427	22.3	–6 104	X	–5 058	168	9.5	76.8	425	–62	2 530	278	23 937	142 482	82.8	17.2
Tillamook	980	4.5	18 395	7.0	16 634	313	37.4	2.6	36	–4	114	20	62 504	199 693	.6	99.4
Umatilla	2 656	4.5	34 989	3.9	47 692	1 488	48.6	27.8	1 345	–121	904	707	249 201	167 474	76.2	23.8
Union	1 326	5.6	1 750	.6	10 131	832	39.7	25.1	532	59	639	176	47 731	57 369	70.7	29.3
Wallowa	989	14.3	–5 569	X	2 216	459	29.0	38.6	621	–73	1 353	109	27 436	59 773	35.5	64.5
Wasco	1 079	5.0	17 514	5.6	17 564	470	32.3	36.2	1 135	–18	2 415	214	56 987	121 249	82.8	17.2
Washington	4 141	1.3	67 253	.7	57 970	1 681	72.5	3.3	131	–9	78	100	186 045	110 675	90.6	9.4
Wheeler	231	16.5	–1 252	X	–161	157	7.6	54.8	680	–48	4 331	35	6 602	42 051	9.5	90.5
Yamhill	3 602	5.5	79 595	8.1	72 696	1 813	67.1	4.9	186	7	103	128	162 837	89 816	79.2	20.8
PENNSYLVANIA	117 119	1.0	696 848	.3	582 340	45 457	29.2	5.4	7 168	–22	158	5 032	3 997 565	87 942	32.1	67.9
Adams	2 799	3.6	20 661	2.1	28 700	984	36.8	7.7	179	6	182	138	150 040	152 480	40.1	59.9
Allegheny	586	Z	1 630	Z	1 315	334	52.1	1.2	27	–6	81	18	9 037	27 057	76.3	23.7
Armstrong	1 230	1.7	14 988	2.2	13 599	654	18.8	6.4	120	Z	183	80	40 773	62 344	69.8	30.2
Beaver	954	.5	332	Z	–1 026	499	35.1	1.6	54	–4	108	34	12 418	24 886	40.5	59.5
Bedford	2 042	4.3	7 433	1.4	5 899	943	17.4	8.4	199	Z	211	125	58 065	61 575	16.9	83.1
Berks	4 627	1.4	56 753	.8	54 837	1 586	39.0	5.0	222	Z	140	188	247 789	156 235	47.7	52.3
Blair	1 224	.9	9 250	.5	7 604	422	20.6	10.2	84	7	199	60	51 001	120 855	13.9	86.1
Bradford	2 641	4.3	13 649	1.7	12 619	1 279	15.1	11.1	307	–4	240	192	96 969	75 816	9.6	90.4
Bucks	1 811	.3	16 221	.2	13 778	739	58.9	5.4	84	7	113	71	69 717	94 340	79.1	20.9
Butler	2 553	1.7	2 622	.1	2 752	972	30.7	2.8	119	–11	122	83	27 671	28 468	46.5	53.5
Cambria	1 119	.7	3 822	.2	2 645	525	26.1	7.6	88	11	167	59	22 008	41 920	53.8	46.2
Cameron	5	.1	(6)	Z	(6)	26	30.8	3.8	4	D	159	2	228	8 769	D	D
Carbon	360	.6	1 089	.2	817	167	40.1	3.6	20	1	119	14	7 639	45 743	83.7	16.3
Centre	2 071	1.7	12 960	.5	8 247	788	26.8	6.1	136	–4	173	93	50 518	64 109	26.3	73.7
Chester	4 597	1.2	98 580	.9	103 603	1 424	45.6	4.8	175	–1	123	139	342 868	240 778	77.5	22.5
Clarion	1 053	2.5	3 760	.7	1 782	457	15.8	9.4	94	–1	206	63	16 527	36 164	25.3	74.7
Clearfield	625	.8	1 784	.2	702	339	25.1	4.4	53	–2	155	35	8 644	25 499	38.1	61.9
Clinton	737	2.0	3 337	.8	1 169	266	24.1	6.0	41	2	155	30	20 746	77 992	32.4	67.6
Columbia	1 850	2.9	–471	X	–1 042	702	24.5	4.8	110	9	157	83	38 239	54 472	58.8	41.2
Crawford	3 047	3.5	9 699	.8	8 814	1 069	19.5	6.9	207	–4	194	135	58 428	54 657	17.2	82.8
Cumberland	2 711	1.4	14 890	.3	11 878	970	31.6	4.9	143	1	148	122	84 519	87 133	24.1	75.9
Dauphin	1 888	.8	7 478	.1	5 060	625	34.2	4.2	87	–4	138	70	53 592	85 747	22.7	77.3
Delaware	74	Z	1 835	Z	1 662	63	68.3	3.2	5	Z	77	3	7 048	111 873	90.5	9.5
Elk	181	.5	–801	X	–1 168	145	25.5	1.4	17	1	118	11	2 062	14 221	30.1	69.9
Erie	2 923	1.1	19 278	.4	14 678	1 123	31.7	4.2	168	Z	149	114	68 914	61 366	63.4	36.6
Fayette	1 247	.9	134	Z	–2 108	747	28.8	4.7	109	2	145	70	20 005	26 780	42.5	57.5
Forest	34	.7	(6)	NA	–143	34	17.6	5.9	5	1	158	3	1 011	29 735	18.5	81.5
Franklin	4 235	3.5	28 531	1.6	26 766	1 304	27.7	6.1	238	3	182	191	194 983	149 527	10.9	89.1
Fulton	768	5.6	1 792	.9	499	449	12.0	6.7	94	5	210	51	21 185	47 183	16.4	83.6
Greene	894	2.3	–2 795	X	–4 020	666	17.4	7.8	131	5	197	67	7 095	10 653	24.5	75.5
Huntingdon	1 239	2.8	13 685	3.2	7 286	586	15.7	7.5	125	–5	213	76	41 128	70 184	12.5	87.5
Indiana	1 792	2.0	11 255	.9	7 616	767	22.0	6.4	139	–5	181	90	46 070	60 065	56.0	44.0
Jefferson	931	2.0	4 063	.7	2 449	436	19.3	4.8	80	1	183	52	15 820	36 284	43.6	56.4
Juniata	1 210	5.9	7 352	3.8	6 581	611	27.7	2.6	87	2	142	58	63 814	104 442	10.1	89.9
Lackawanna	481	.2	1 632	Z	656	238	30.3	2.5	30	–7	124	20	11 123	46 735	50.1	49.9
Lancaster	18 182	4.3	90 756	1.1	81 282	4 556	39.6	1.3	392	3	86	331	766 743	168 293	13.3	86.7
Lawrence	1 610	1.7	2 758	.2	–162	621	26.4	3.5	87	1	140	63	25 396	40 895	25.5	74.5
Lebanon	2 588	2.3	12 752	.9	13 407	885	36.4	2.5	111	6	125	96	171 137	193 375	10.8	89.2
Lehigh	1 138	.4	6 766	.1	6 518	425	42.6	10.6	92	9	216	81	56 719	133 456	69.4	30.6
Luzerne	915	.3	3 505	.1	2 303	451	35.3	3.5	57	7	127	37	18 317	40 614	66.9	33.1
Lycoming	1 739	1.5	9 160	.5	6 693	841	19.9	4.8	136	3	161	87	43 191	51 357	36.9	63.1
McKean	260	.6	1 808	.3	1 166	209	17.7	7.2	39	–1	187	18	4 281	20 483	24.7	75.3
Mercer	2 572	2.1	9 841	.6	4 289	1 030	20.4	4.7	167	6	162	113	46 096	44 753	39.0	61.0
Mifflin	1 770	3.8	11 651	2.1	10 367	619	25.5	1.8	79	–2	128	53	51 842	83 751	9.3	90.7
Monroe	406	.4	340	Z	360	176	34.7	5.1	26	5	149	14	5 301	30 119	56.3	43.7
Montgomery	929	.1	2 514	Z	1 550	462	55.4	2.2	42	–3	90	34	29 395	63 626	56.9	43.1
Montour	662	3.7	7 282	1.4	6 525	259	23.2	5.8	40	–1	154	30	26 389	101 888	68.2	31.8
Northampton	1 104	.4	3 294	.1	836	396	44.4	11.1	78	–3	198	69	28 593	72 205	68.0	32.0
Northumberland	1 636	1.7	6 820	.7	5 575	596	30.4	7.6	115	5	193	91	59 370	99 614	36.8	63.2
Perry	1 696	4.1	13 527	5.2	11 489	618	21.8	6.1	115	11	186	79	58 647	94 898	15.6	84.4
Philadelphia	–	–	135	Z	113	9	66.7	–	Z	D	32	D	773	85 889	D	D
Pike	46	.2	158	.1	85	40	45.0	7.5	6	–1	139	D	1 385	34 625	83.6	16.4
Potter	613	3.7	6 565	2.7	4 713	292	14.4	13.7	83	–7	286	44	19 780	67 740	24.7	75.3

[1] For 1990 corrected population, see table B-1.   Percent is based on 1990 uncorrected population because only total population is corrected.   [2] For total earnings, see table B-8.   [3] Most data are comparable between 1992 and 1997; however, it should be noted that farms with all acreage in Conservation or Wetlands Reserve Programs (excluded in 1992) are included in 1997, as are short rotation woody crops which includes Christmas trees and maple sap gathering (in Forestry in 1992).   [4] Includes nursery and greenhouse crops.   [5] Includes related products.   [6] Less than $50,000.

Sources: Farm Population—U.S. Census Bureau, 1990 Census of Population and Housing, Summary Tape File (STF) 3C on CD-ROM (related Internet site <http://homer.ssd.census.gov/cdrom/lookup/>).   Farm Earnings—U.S. Bureau of Economic Analysis, "Regional Economic Information System (REIS) 1969-1998" on CD-ROM (related Internet site <http://www.bea.doc.gov/bea/regional/reis/ca45/>).   Agriculture—U.S. Department of Agriculture, National Agricultural Statistics Service, 1997 Census of Agriculture, Volume 1, Geographic Area Series, 1A, 1B, 1C CD-ROM Set (related Internet site <http://www.nass.usda.gov/census/>).

Table B–10. Counties — **Farm Population, Farm Earnings, and Agriculture**–Con.

[Includes U.S., states, and 3,142 counties/county equivalents defined as of January 1, 1992. For changes to these areas since January 1, 1992, see appendix B. Geographic Information]

County	Farm population, 1990 Number	Farm population, 1990 Percent of total[1]	Farm earnings 1998 Total ($1,000)	Farm earnings 1998 Percent of total[2]	Farm earnings 1997 ($1,000)	Farms Number	Farms Percent Less than 50 acres	Farms Percent 500 acres or more	Land in farms Total acreage (1,000)	Land in farms Net change, 1992–1997[3] (1,000)	Land in farms Average size of farm	Land in farms Total cropland (1,000)	Value of farm products sold Total ($1,000)	Value Average per farm (dollars)	Value Percent from Crops[4]	Value Percent from Livestock and poultry[5]
PENNSYLVANIA—Con.																
Schuylkill	1 444	.9	9 459	.6	8 679	605	32.9	6.8	90	1	149	70	66 919	110 610	31.0	69.0
Snyder	2 146	5.9	15 755	3.1	17 497	671	27.6	3.3	93	5	138	68	74 867	111 575	12.5	87.5
Somerset	2 308	3.0	19 263	2.1	11 199	958	15.9	8.2	206	−14	215	128	59 914	62 541	12.7	87.3
Sullivan	170	2.8	832	1.4	−361	123	10.6	8.1	27	−3	222	17	7 063	57 423	5.8	94.2
Susquehanna	1 135	2.8	15 799	4.8	9 647	703	13.2	10.1	169	−9	240	95	43 016	61 189	7.3	92.7
Tioga	2 266	5.5	15 629	3.6	9 611	823	13.7	11.2	202	−10	246	124	47 317	57 493	12.7	87.3
Union	1 634	4.5	12 978	2.1	11 287	498	28.9	2.6	63	Z	127	54	49 406	99 209	16.8	83.2
Venango	588	1.0	−845	X	−1 882	351	21.9	1.4	46	−7	132	28	6 515	18 561	27.0	73.0
Warren	696	1.5	2 206	.4	156	390	21.0	4.1	64	−3	165	32	14 631	37 515	14.3	85.7
Washington	2 130	1.0	−2 604	X	−5 610	1 307	23.1	3.1	186	−17	142	115	26 606	20 357	38.5	61.5
Wayne	1 050	2.6	7 661	1.7	3 614	564	14.7	6.0	110	−12	194	60	25 143	44 580	11.1	88.9
Westmoreland	1 618	.4	3 552	.1	106	1 035	27.6	4.6	148	−6	143	101	36 458	35 225	45.0	55.0
Wyoming	727	2.6	7 806	1.9	5 848	307	16.6	7.5	61	−2	199	37	30 042	97 857	13.3	86.7
York	4 802	1.4	13 252	.2	10 919	1 698	43.9	6.8	261	9	154	217	128 620	75 748	39.9	60.1
RHODE ISLAND	1 124	.1	27 214	.2	23 131	735	59.6	2.0	55	6	75	26	48 200	65 578	81.8	18.2
Bristol	18	Z	941	.2	798	37	62.2	–	2	Z	46	1	2 790	75 405	92.9	7.1
Kent	110	.1	1 302	.1	1 003	74	64.9	2.7	6	1	87	2	2 685	36 284	85.3	14.7
Newport	352	.4	9 438	.6	8 461	139	56.1	2.2	10	1	75	7	14 512	104 403	81.0	19.0
Providence	240	Z	4 488	Z	3 173	255	63.1	.4	15	2	58	6	9 672	37 929	64.7	35.2
Washington	404	.4	11 045	.7	9 696	230	55.7	3.9	22	2	95	10	18 542	80 617	89.1	10.9
SOUTH CAROLINA	48 565	1.4	306 125	.5	445 975	20 189	34.4	10.6	4 593	121	228	2 463	1 588 173	78 665	49.8	50.2
Abbeville	631	2.6	2 630	1.0	3 541	471	25.7	6.2	81	−9	172	36	8 289	17 599	17.4	82.6
Aiken	1 528	1.3	17 761	.7	15 758	729	37.6	7.4	134	−2	184	62	58 754	80 595	24.5	75.5
Allendale	159	1.4	2 138	1.5	4 184	131	21.4	31.3	92	11	701	55	13 824	105 527	92.3	7.7
Anderson	1 971	1.4	14 470	.7	12 906	1 271	38.9	4.4	166	5	131	90	34 538	27 174	41.7	58.3
Bamberg	598	3.5	1 415	1.1	7 497	254	21.3	25.6	101	14	397	53	20 715	81 555	67.1	32.9
Barnwell	415	2.0	2 330	.6	5 054	325	28.3	15.4	97	22	299	48	14 615	44 969	78.1	21.9
Beaufort	458	.5	3 453	.2	3 205	99	56.6	18.2	39	−6	395	11	8 353	84 374	90.6	9.4
Berkeley	1 137	.9	9 484	.9	9 591	292	47.9	7.2	51	Z	176	18	22 123	75 764	92.5	7.5
Calhoun	777	6.1	1 031	2.6	7 000	290	21.5	21.2	102	11	349	62	26 322	89 836	83.8	16.2
Charleston	1 124	.4	15 233	.2	13 219	266	53.4	8.6	44	12	166	17	26 859	100 974	85.3	14.7
Cherokee	530	1.2	1 760	.3	4 817	412	32.3	4.9	65	−1	157	31	13 193	32 022	23.0	77.0
Chester	695	2.2	2 077	.5	2 696	340	21.8	11.2	81	−14	237	33	11 675	34 338	11.4	88.6
Chesterfield	887	2.3	14 409	3.0	17 818	537	23.1	10.2	124	15	231	55	71 856	133 810	12.3	87.7
Clarendon	1 482	5.2	4 726	2.2	20 780	304	30.3	27.0	142	6	468	112	76 646	252 125	56.7	43.3
Colleton	1 164	3.4	3 144	1.0	5 285	416	33.4	4.4	155	28	372	50	15 191	36 517	75.7	24.3
Darlington	1 937	3.1	5 908	.7	15 323	346	32.4	23.7	158	1	457	115	61 257	177 043	77.2	22.8
Dillon	939	3.2	3 241	1.2	19 787	199	21.6	26.6	91	−18	458	69	65 919	331 251	52.0	48.0
Dorchester	763	.9	3 600	.5	8 547	314	41.7	9.6	65	3	208	38	21 506	68 490	48.7	51.3
Edgefield	579	3.2	3 316	2.0	4 060	271	29.5	13.3	71	3	264	28	15 240	56 236	65.6	34.4
Fairfield	671	3.0	4 133	1.4	3 325	172	27.9	16.3	47	−9	271	15	13 504	78 512	2.3	97.7
Florence	3 071	2.7	6 746	.3	18 313	615	33.5	15.4	169	−26	274	114	69 106	112 367	89.4	10.6
Georgetown	719	1.6	4 890	.8	6 112	206	41.7	15.0	53	16	258	15	14 889	72 277	87.4	12.6
Greenville	1 162	.4	6 716	.1	5 661	761	50.3	2.5	70	4	92	38	17 512	23 012	75.4	24.6
Greenwood	1 055	1.8	7 024	.6	7 020	377	37.9	8.2	68	−2	181	28	12 291	32 602	D	D
Hampton	709	3.9	957	.5	2 316	207	25.1	24.2	117	20	567	58	15 774	76 203	91.7	8.3
Horry	2 701	1.9	3 504	.1	26 342	896	31.1	9.8	184	−12	205	117	82 788	92 397	86.8	13.2
Jasper	426	2.8	1 954	1.5	2 152	123	35.8	13.8	68	−4	554	16	4 713	38 317	93.9	6.2
Kershaw	687	1.6	12 145	2.0	8 790	324	35.2	9.6	73	20	224	24	59 748	184 407	4.3	95.7
Lancaster	883	1.6	11 781	1.9	8 037	500	32.6	5.6	75	17	150	31	40 680	81 360	4.7	95.3
Laurens	1 446	2.5	6 527	1.0	4 556	686	30.2	9.2	127	−1	185	62	18 565	27 063	40.5	59.5
Lee	1 153	6.3	6 858	6.0	14 445	222	18.5	30.6	120	−16	539	89	45 383	204 428	61.6	38.4
Lexington	1 667	1.0	29 116	1.1	23 318	799	44.1	3.8	93	11	117	49	108 429	135 706	20.9	79.1
McCormick	209	2.4	2 539	3.6	2 491	92	28.3	12.0	20	1	221	7	6 963	75 685	D	D
Marion	1 076	3.2	−1 142	X	6 336	200	25.0	23.0	80	2	401	53	32 719	163 595	94.8	5.2
Marlboro	452	1.5	3 540	1.4	12 400	180	22.8	33.9	117	12	647	84	36 469	202 606	79.1	20.9
Newberry	851	2.6	11 992	3.1	10 697	499	24.2	8.2	95	1	190	49	42 734	85 639	7.5	92.5
Oconee	891	1.5	8 277	.9	11 082	611	40.4	3.1	66	−3	109	31	44 308	72 517	8.7	91.3
Orangeburg	2 274	2.7	10 961	1.1	21 599	965	25.9	14.9	272	10	282	164	87 899	91 087	55.7	44.3
Pickens	370	.4	1 966	.2	1 777	532	53.2	1.9	47	3	88	25	5 908	11 105	61.3	38.7
Richland	887	.3	4 285	.1	3 391	350	42.6	6.6	57	−10	162	28	10 830	30 943	43.4	56.6
Saluda	857	5.2	14 252	10.3	14 248	556	26.3	8.8	111	1	200	54	55 937	100 606	10.4	89.6
Spartanburg	1 293	.6	8 036	.2	5 987	1 067	48.0	2.7	107	Z	100	64	23 114	21 663	57.6	42.4
Sumter	1 733	1.7	7 046	.5	14 034	396	35.9	16.7	139	1	352	95	60 173	151 952	52.0	48.0
Union	346	1.1	1 255	.4	984	255	23.5	7.5	53	−3	208	22	1 817	7 125	21.1	78.9
Williamsburg	2 237	6.1	6 380	2.3	13 963	602	28.1	19.8	189	16	315	93	47 872	79 522	87.0	13.0
York	965	.7	9 261	.4	15 138	726	31.8	6.3	115	−5	159	56	41 172	56 711	37.3	62.7

[1] For 1990 corrected population, see table B-1. Percent is based on 1990 uncorrected population because only total population is corrected. [2] For total earnings, see table B-8. [3] Most data are comparable between 1992 and 1997; however, it should be noted that farms with all acreage in Conservation or Wetlands Reserve Programs (excluded in 1992) are included in 1997, as are short rotation woody crops which includes Christmas trees and maple sap gathering (in Forestry in 1992). [4] Includes nursery and greenhouse crops. [5] Includes related products.

Sources: Farm Population—U.S. Census Bureau, 1990 Census of Population and Housing, Summary Tape File (STF) 3C on CD-ROM (related Internet site <http://homer.ssd.census.gov/cdrom/lookup>). Farm Earnings—U.S. Bureau of Economic Analysis, "Regional Economic Information System (REIS) 1969-1998" on CD-ROM (related Internet site <http://www.bea.doc.gov/bea/regional/reis/ca45/>). Agriculture—U.S. Department of Agriculture, National Agricultural Statistics Service, 1997 Census of Agriculture, Volume 1, Geographic Area Series, 1A, 1B, 1C CD-ROM Set (related Internet site <http://www.nass.usda.gov/census/>).

Table B–10. Counties — Farm Population, Farm Earnings, and Agriculture–Con.

[Includes U.S., states, and 3,142 counties/county equivalents defined as of January 1, 1992. For changes to these areas since January 1, 1992, see appendix B. Geographic Information]

County	Farm population, 1990 Number	Farm population, 1990 Percent of total[1]	Farm earnings 1998 Total ($1,000)	Farm earnings 1998 Percent of total[2]	Farm earnings 1997 ($1,000)	Farms Number	Farms Percent Less than 50 acres	Farms Percent 500 acres or more	Land in farms Total acreage (1,000)	Land in farms Net change, 1992–1997[3] (1,000)	Land in farms Average size of farm	Land in farms Total cropland (1,000)	Value of farm products sold Total ($1,000)	Value of farm products sold Average per farm (dollars)	Percent from Crops[4]	Percent from Livestock and poultry[5]
SOUTH DAKOTA........	76 170	10.9	941 499	7.9	804 134	31 284	11.5	52.2	44 355	−473	1 418	19 355	3 569 951	114 114	46.3	53.7
Aurora..............	1 026	32.7	5 952	20.3	8 037	421	11.4	54.4	343	−37	814	226	54 960	130 546	34.1	65.9
Beadle..............	1 979	10.8	19 188	7.5	22 928	731	13.1	52.9	707	−17	968	493	96 202	131 603	45.4	54.6
Bennett.............	400	12.5	3 334	13.6	2 253	258	5.8	69.8	797	9	3 090	234	28 772	111 519	34.7	65.3
Bon Homme..........	1 599	22.6	17 154	22.3	13 792	672	10.4	34.4	311	−12	462	247	65 507	97 481	42.1	57.9
Brookings...........	2 467	9.8	26 455	6.3	19 485	886	19.4	31.5	408	−37	460	331	87 628	98 903	44.0	56.0
Brown...............	2 012	5.7	36 941	5.9	36 890	1 006	15.7	52.0	1 070	43	1 063	818	146 001	145 130	63.2	36.8
Brule...............	1 269	23.1	9 007	14.0	4 913	382	7.6	65.4	461	−36	1 206	272	45 785	119 856	39.3	60.7
Buffalo.............	279	15.9	1 336	8.5	2 898	77	3.9	79.2	302	23	3 923	85	21 647	281 130	37.2	62.8
Butte...............	837	10.6	−1 548	X	91	547	14.1	45.7	1 166	−77	2 132	162	41 119	75 172	13.8	86.2
Campbell............	574	29.2	8 583	39.6	5 080	286	4.5	69.9	396	−22	1 383	212	30 515	106 696	39.2	60.8
Charles Mix.........	1 821	19.9	27 138	22.3	31 995	735	10.2	57.7	680	−8	925	496	111 347	151 493	44.6	55.4
Clark...............	1 472	33.4	22 954	46.7	24 466	563	8.2	54.5	514	−21	913	359	72 689	129 110	43.0	57.0
Clay................	1 164	8.8	16 888	10.5	17 068	397	9.8	43.1	226	−11	569	208	46 140	116 222	81.3	18.7
Codington...........	1 391	6.1	21 809	4.8	17 973	619	19.4	38.8	385	−8	621	286	64 636	104 420	42.1	57.9
Corson..............	868	20.7	3 294	14.6	2 004	425	6.1	74.1	1 605	−97	3 775	336	30 558	71 901	32.1	67.9
Custer..............	445	7.2	−4 503	X	−6 020	326	12.9	46.9	476	14	1 462	71	11 404	34 982	10.4	89.6
Davison.............	866	4.9	14 160	4.6	13 695	429	21.4	37.8	274	4	640	215	39 238	91 464	60.5	39.5
Day.................	1 612	23.1	13 151	20.1	11 190	693	8.2	49.1	536	−25	774	385	49 180	70 967	61.1	38.9
Deuel...............	1 306	28.9	18 998	32.7	12 332	564	9.8	38.5	311	−31	551	216	47 430	84 096	41.9	58.1
Dewey...............	589	10.7	−1 760	X	−1 391	375	6.1	72.5	1 851	−8	4 935	240	26 356	70 283	22.9	77.1
Douglas.............	1 397	37.3	14 771	33.4	16 886	392	11.5	49.2	247	−5	630	197	54 808	139 816	35.6	64.4
Edmunds.............	890	20.4	22 716	43.9	15 853	449	7.3	69.0	635	−7	1 415	431	61 619	137 236	44.3	55.7
Fall River..........	508	6.9	−4 396	X	−4 464	309	7.4	69.6	978	3	3 165	119	60 382	195 411	4.2	95.8
Faulk...............	846	30.8	17 081	51.6	11 014	316	7.9	71.8	571	11	1 808	344	53 289	168 636	53.0	47.0
Grant...............	1 772	21.2	28 868	22.6	30 384	534	10.1	42.9	359	−15	672	271	77 839	145 766	46.6	53.4
Gregory.............	1 371	25.6	10 740	19.9	10 279	570	11.1	56.8	566	−36	992	264	43 104	75 621	39.4	60.6
Haakon..............	657	25.0	10 325	28.3	2 936	309	4.9	79.6	1 325	121	4 288	428	40 786	131 994	34.4	65.6
Hamlin..............	1 412	28.4	17 692	34.6	9 077	413	15.0	44.8	279	2	675	232	48 593	117 659	56.1	43.9
Hand................	1 511	35.4	17 507	37.3	8 889	488	6.6	69.3	811	−50	1 662	472	65 978	135 201	44.4	55.6
Hanson..............	916	30.6	13 804	48.9	7 050	326	10.7	47.5	231	−14	710	183	43 346	132 963	49.3	50.7
Harding.............	625	37.4	−5 032	X	−3 577	275	7.3	82.9	1 702	45	6 190	193	27 931	101 567	11.0	89.0
Hughes..............	423	2.9	12 040	4.0	6 090	287	11.8	55.1	391	1	1 364	237	36 908	128 599	56.8	43.2
Hutchinson..........	2 294	27.8	35 049	35.1	28 776	804	9.5	45.9	479	−23	596	404	102 970	128 072	47.4	52.6
Hyde................	603	35.6	5 813	30.1	1 736	229	9.2	68.6	532	−13	2 324	214	30 352	132 541	40.8	59.2
Jackson.............	611	21.7	1 854	10.2	4 257	295	4.7	80.0	1 354	−7	4 591	267	28 273	95 841	31.7	68.3
Jerauld.............	598	24.7	5 792	18.4	6 384	276	9.8	56.2	346	12	1 255	184	37 186	134 732	30.9	69.1
Jones...............	299	22.6	5 046	26.5	2 262	203	4.4	70.9	589	4	2 900	214	18 584	91 547	28.8	71.2
Kingsbury...........	1 361	23.0	28 434	36.9	22 493	580	12.1	49.5	481	20	828	386	73 110	126 052	59.0	41.0
Lake................	1 424	13.5	21 489	13.6	17 649	500	15.6	45.4	307	9	614	260	67 886	135 772	55.8	44.2
Lawrence............	385	1.9	−148	X	−198	270	19.3	31.1	171	−24	635	48	9 487	35 137	12.6	87.4
Lincoln.............	2 329	15.1	39 687	19.6	37 324	806	17.4	28.5	319	−4	395	291	100 154	124 261	61.1	38.9
Lyman...............	637	17.5	13 974	31.0	6 870	414	5.6	74.2	944	97	2 279	418	40 437	97 674	48.8	51.2
McCook..............	1 425	25.1	25 287	39.3	21 264	544	13.1	43.4	312	−14	574	254	63 627	116 961	60.3	39.7
McPherson...........	812	25.2	9 202	33.9	4 472	397	3.8	70.5	569	−92	1 433	311	56 423	142 123	18.2	81.8
Marshall............	1 128	23.3	20 319	33.7	22 911	490	8.4	57.8	505	19	1 030	325	79 596	162 441	37.4	62.6
Meade...............	1 727	7.9	4 333	1.9	1 732	829	11.0	62.2	2 074	−2	2 502	432	52 063	62 802	19.4	80.6
Mellette............	398	18.6	2 622	26.0	2 081	217	3.2	82.5	655	−47	3 017	161	17 739	81 747	19.9	80.1
Miner...............	1 270	38.8	12 042	36.7	11 777	369	9.2	46.9	280	−33	760	199	40 045	108 523	48.9	51.1
Minnehaha...........	3 242	2.6	35 361	1.0	31 740	1 125	26.3	24.6	406	−19	361	352	103 938	92 389	59.6	40.4
Moody...............	1 727	26.5	28 960	31.1	24 606	549	12.6	35.7	284	−1	517	237	67 768	123 439	56.9	43.1
Pennington..........	1 036	1.3	4 795	.3	2 317	637	16.2	46.8	1 044	−22	1 639	288	39 678	62 289	29.2	70.7
Perkins.............	1 073	27.3	4 107	10.8	1 582	520	6.2	76.3	1 705	−21	3 279	454	42 287	81 321	22.5	77.5
Potter..............	536	16.8	19 216	43.8	9 036	285	8.4	67.0	530	23	1 860	352	44 689	156 804	57.2	42.8
Roberts.............	2 039	20.6	24 413	25.4	30 349	803	10.8	46.8	571	−33	711	441	86 630	107 883	63.3	36.7
Sanborn.............	1 001	35.3	10 422	36.1	9 386	382	11.0	51.6	347	24	907	220	41 350	108 246	35.7	64.3
Shannon.............	368	3.7	3 457	3.8	2 231	175	8.0	62.9	1 474	57	8 423	102	12 690	72 514	25.6	74.4
Spink...............	2 069	25.9	30 134	31.2	35 539	647	7.0	66.3	849	−41	1 313	686	116 647	180 289	63.9	36.1
Stanley.............	381	15.5	3 541	12.1	−273	194	6.7	78.4	896	−8	4 617	243	22 941	118 253	46.1	53.9
Sully...............	266	16.7	22 922	67.9	10 672	261	4.6	72.8	599	−16	2 295	470	52 729	202 027	76.8	23.2
Todd................	691	8.3	−987	X	−841	210	2.9	78.1	1 084	5	5 164	173	25 130	119 667	29.4	70.6
Tripp...............	1 455	21.0	14 804	19.2	12 301	654	7.0	62.5	930	−76	1 423	454	65 717	100 485	30.8	69.2
Turner..............	2 213	25.8	36 789	39.2	32 642	832	15.3	31.9	352	−15	424	312	97 247	116 883	53.0	47.0
Union...............	1 523	14.9	25 865	5.3	31 812	494	15.0	38.3	254	−5	514	236	86 335	174 767	58.6	41.4
Walworth............	772	12.7	8 420	12.1	3 781	338	10.9	61.8	437	−12	1 294	246	31 214	92 349	46.9	53.1
Yankton.............	1 643	8.5	21 336	5.9	22 579	636	16.7	32.4	261	−10	410	219	60 401	94 970	57.6	42.4
Ziebach.............	530	23.9	2 502	26.5	2 789	259	4.6	81.9	1 499	93	5 788	240	22 926	88 517	41.9	58.1

[1] For 1990 corrected population, see table B-1. Percent is based on 1990 uncorrected population because only total population is corrected. [2] For total earnings, see table B-8. [3] Most data are comparable between 1992 and 1997; however, it should be noted that farms with all acreage in Conservation or Wetlands Reserve Programs (excluded in 1992) are included in 1997, as are short rotation woody crops which includes Christmas trees and maple sap gathering (in Forestry in 1992). [4] Includes nursery and greenhouse crops. [5] Includes related products.

Sources: Farm Population—U.S. Census Bureau, 1990 Census of Population and Housing, Summary Tape File (STF) 3C on CD-ROM (related Internet site <http://homer.ssd.census.gov/cdrom/lookup>). Farm Earnings—U.S. Bureau of Economic Analysis, "Regional Economic Information System (REIS) 1969-1998" on CD-ROM (related Internet site <http://www.bea.doc.gov/bea/regional/reis/ca45/>). Agriculture—U.S. Department of Agriculture, National Agricultural Statistics Service, 1997 Census of Agriculture, Volume 1, Geographic Area Series, 1A, 1B, 1C CD-ROM Set (related Internet site <http://www.nass.usda.gov/census/>).

[Includes U.S., states, and 3,142 counties/county equivalents defined as of January 1, 1992. For changes to these areas since January 1, 1992, see appendix B. Geographic Information]

County	Farm population, 1990 Number	Farm population, 1990 Percent of total[1]	Farm earnings 1998 Total ($1,000)	Farm earnings 1998 Percent of total[2]	Farm earnings 1997 ($1,000)	Farms Number	Farms Percent— Less than 50 acres	Farms Percent— 500 acres or more	Land in farms (acres) Total acreage (1,000)	Land in farms (acres) Net change, 1992–1997[3] (1,000)	Land in farms (acres) Average size of farm	Total cropland (1,000)	Value of farm products sold Total ($1,000)	Value of farm products sold Average per farm (dollars)	Value of farm products sold Percent from— Crops[4]	Value of farm products sold Percent from— Livestock and poultry[5]
TENNESSEE	111 680	2.3	110 619	.1	268 145	76 818	39.5	5.0	11 122	−47	145	7 069	2 178 389	28 358	52.5	47.5
Anderson	391	.6	−1 585	X	−1 206	462	47.8	1.9	41	−1	89	21	5 474	11 848	49.7	50.3
Bedford	1 892	6.2	5 558	1.2	3 751	1 408	33.3	5.3	207	−6	147	125	69 049	49 040	7.4	92.6
Benton	627	4.3	−1 387	X	−1 023	433	27.9	4.8	69	6	159	36	4 364	10 079	41.1	58.9
Bledsoe	709	7.3	17 800	17.8	12 549	525	24.4	6.7	96	3	183	57	41 498	79 044	10.6	89.4
Blount	1 544	1.8	−1 605	X	−616	1 053	52.9	2.6	93	−3	89	64	18 568	17 633	45.2	54.8
Bradley	849	1.2	3 601	.3	3 295	781	44.6	4.1	90	−2	115	51	54 891	70 283	4.7	95.3
Campbell	758	2.2	−840	X	−890	398	45.2	1.3	31	Z	77	19	2 740	6 884	48.7	51.3
Cannon	873	8.3	−3 326	X	−2 155	754	33.7	2.9	103	6	136	53	12 117	16 070	36.0	63.9
Carroll	1 388	5.0	−2 616	X	640	851	25.5	8.0	172	6	202	108	22 233	26 126	78.4	21.6
Carter	594	1.2	−775	X	−74	622	64.6	.8	39	2	63	22	7 296	11 730	42.6	57.4
Cheatham	598	2.2	233	.1	1 892	556	35.3	3.8	68	10	123	38	8 851	15 919	70.5	29.4
Chester	577	4.5	−1 706	X	147	410	24.6	7.3	73	2	178	42	5 864	14 302	69.8	30.1
Claiborne	2 192	8.4	3 671	1.5	2 849	1 397	43.7	2.1	144	1	103	73	20 200	14 460	40.6	59.4
Clay	972	13.4	−689	X	385	503	30.4	3.8	72	1	142	34	6 292	12 509	56.4	43.6
Cocke	1 431	4.9	2 456	1.0	3 049	886	45.5	1.0	75	−9	85	41	14 137	15 956	46.4	53.6
Coffee	1 423	3.5	1 295	.2	1 723	968	41.5	5.6	136	3	140	89	29 859	30 846	38.0	62.0
Crockett	1 501	11.2	558	.4	9 972	380	34.2	22.6	151	6	396	135	48 056	126 463	97.1	2.9
Cumberland	791	2.3	15 030	3.2	12 335	726	40.8	5.8	100	3	138	57	37 229	51 280	21.4	78.6
Davidson	81	Z	498	Z	843	533	47.1	2.4	52	5	98	27	10 646	19 974	76.0	24.0
Decatur	488	4.7	−2 384	X	−1 447	437	19.7	8.7	88	2	202	42	4 271	9 773	30.6	69.4
DeKalb	1 109	7.7	1 849	1.1	4 246	806	40.0	3.5	99	3	123	56	26 091	32 371	80.7	19.3
Dickson	1 868	5.3	−6 653	X	−4 638	1 106	32.8	3.8	149	4	134	77	12 068	10 911	41.5	58.5
Dyer	1 028	2.9	854	.1	13 997	526	30.2	25.5	234	3	445	217	55 625	105 751	94.3	5.7
Fayette	1 276	5.0	2 112	.9	11 861	716	28.4	15.6	271	12	378	180	51 388	71 771	70.8	29.2
Fentress	781	5.3	2 190	1.6	3 592	504	35.9	4.8	70	Z	139	34	21 824	43 302	13.9	86.1
Franklin	1 658	4.8	15 877	4.7	11 492	985	45.1	6.1	132	−3	134	94	62 540	63 492	27.8	72.2
Gibson	2 685	5.8	2 425	.4	14 261	874	36.5	17.4	278	6	318	249	68 474	78 346	87.0	13.0
Giles	2 111	8.2	−295	X	−2 327	1 570	26.0	5.2	249	−7	159	139	30 281	19 287	16.6	83.4
Grainger	1 591	9.3	3 794	2.9	3 027	1 095	45.5	1.3	97	−8	88	52	16 253	14 843	62.3	37.7
Greene	4 362	7.8	63	Z	2 320	3 086	56.3	1.1	226	−11	73	153	51 213	16 595	36.8	63.2
Grundy	590	4.4	6 873	8.9	6 376	337	49.6	3.9	36	−6	108	18	30 792	91 371	17.2	82.8
Hamblen	1 209	2.4	−333	X	−126	667	57.9	1.9	52	−5	78	37	13 724	20 576	41.3	58.7
Hamilton	569	.2	333	Z	258	604	49.2	2.5	57	−6	94	30	8 282	13 712	21.8	78.3
Hancock	1 134	16.8	197	.6	674	633	39.5	1.7	68	−13	107	32	7 562	11 946	44.8	55.2
Hardeman	663	2.8	−2 241	X	1 730	559	22.4	15.2	166	6	297	91	18 721	33 490	72.7	27.3
Hardin	490	2.2	−240	X	590	594	28.1	7.6	116	5	195	65	9 648	16 242	65.3	34.7
Hawkins	2 700	6.1	−4 177	X	−3 129	1 813	48.5	.7	147	−9	81	76	15 977	8 812	54.4	45.6
Haywood	888	4.6	9 185	4.5	16 219	360	24.2	31.1	212	−12	589	186	63 051	175 142	97.4	2.6
Henderson	1 448	6.6	−3 383	X	−2 898	858	21.4	7.1	152	5	177	89	18 155	21 160	33.6	66.4
Henry	1 810	6.5	1 567	.4	7 736	831	25.5	8.7	185	−6	223	118	37 755	45 433	58.0	42.0
Hickman	1 378	8.2	−3 473	X	−2 431	678	21.7	7.2	128	−2	189	64	8 647	12 754	22.8	77.2
Houston	224	3.2	−1 249	X	−1 034	289	23.9	5.2	49	4	169	24	4 022	13 917	22.0	78.0
Humphreys	826	5.2	−3 824	X	−2 757	577	24.6	9.9	122	3	211	56	8 166	14 153	44.0	56.0
Jackson	965	10.4	−1 222	X	−439	605	31.7	3.8	83	−4	138	34	5 083	8 402	50.2	49.8
Jefferson	1 812	5.5	−671	X	−383	1 147	50.2	1.0	98	−1	85	68	20 019	17 453	30.2	69.8
Johnson	1 748	12.7	−453	X	976	679	58.2	1.2	49	−5	73	26	7 608	11 205	56.6	43.4
Knox	1 233	.4	−1 268	X	−516	1 193	58.1	1.3	88	−6	74	53	15 483	12 978	57.6	42.4
Lake	201	2.8	−1 599	X	3 316	80	15.0	51.3	90	−2	1 120	86	23 404	292 550	99.5	.5
Lauderdale	845	3.6	2 981	1.0	13 454	505	28.3	18.8	192	9	380	161	47 293	93 650	94.0	6.0
Lawrence	1 933	5.5	−4 526	X	−2 823	1 617	33.0	3.8	214	17	132	134	26 942	16 662	29.2	70.8
Lewis	193	2.1	−1 204	X	−983	222	23.0	3.6	37	Z	166	16	2 392	10 775	37.7	62.3
Lincoln	2 455	8.7	2 642	1.0	1 915	1 661	31.7	6.6	276	1	166	158	49 394	29 738	32.1	67.9
Loudon	887	2.8	21 392	5.9	21 362	763	51.6	2.4	74	Z	97	48	45 067	59 066	D	D
McMinn	960	2.3	1 534	.2	228	1 074	39.9	4.0	127	4	119	79	34 171	31 817	10.5	89.5
McNairy	847	3.8	−2 221	X	163	720	22.1	7.1	130	8	181	70	11 116	15 439	60.4	39.6
Macon	2 211	13.9	518	.4	5 994	1 238	40.0	1.9	135	−4	109	74	20 117	16 250	71.0	29.0
Madison	863	1.1	3 084	.2	5 953	571	30.8	11.2	146	4	255	104	28 896	50 606	79.4	20.6
Marion	280	1.1	−677	X	−909	294	37.1	6.5	51	Z	174	30	10 685	36 344	15.3	84.7
Marshall	1 283	6.0	−1 310	X	−816	1 097	32.1	4.7	167	5	152	96	21 622	19 710	15.7	84.3
Maury	2 198	4.0	−3 027	X	−1 201	1 532	31.1	5.5	243	−3	158	145	27 442	17 913	29.6	70.4
Meigs	429	5.3	−462	X	−188	339	32.2	3.8	49	−7	144	27	4 783	14 109	15.9	84.1
Monroe	1 019	3.3	152	Z	−110	855	39.8	2.8	97	−3	113	66	18 881	22 083	17.2	82.8
Montgomery	1 439	1.4	3 788	.3	7 691	988	35.1	8.4	165	−10	167	109	30 810	31 184	73.4	26.6
Moore	557	11.8	290	.6	64	371	30.2	3.2	52	4	140	29	9 309	25 092	9.8	90.2
Morgan	319	1.8	−827	X	−1 115	328	29.6	3.0	46	3	140	22	5 247	15 997	13.3	86.7
Obion	1 390	4.4	4 816	.9	17 099	705	26.1	18.2	242	−15	344	209	63 751	90 427	78.5	21.5

[1] For 1990 corrected population, see table B-1.   Percent is based on 1990 uncorrected population because only total population is corrected.   [2] For total earnings, see table B-8.   [3] Most data are comparable between 1992 and 1997; however, it should be noted that farms with all acreage in Conservation or Wetlands Reserve Programs (excluded in 1992) are included in 1997, as are short rotation woody crops which includes Christmas trees and maple sap gathering (in Forestry in 1992).   [4] Includes nursery and greenhouse crops.   [5] Includes related products.

Sources: Farm Population—U.S. Census Bureau, 1990 Census of Population and Housing, Summary Tape File (STF) 3C on CD-ROM (related Internet site <http://homer.ssd.census.gov/cdrom/lookup>). Farm Earnings—U.S. Bureau of Economic Analysis, "Regional Economic Information System (REIS) 1969-1998" on CD-ROM (related Internet site <http://www.bea.doc.gov/bea/regional/reis/ca45/>). Agriculture—U.S. Department of Agriculture, National Agricultural Statistics Service, 1997 Census of Agriculture, Volume 1, Geographic Area Series, 1A, 1B, 1C CD-ROM Set (related Internet site <http://www.nass.usda.gov/census/>).

Table B–10. Counties — Farm Population, Farm Earnings, and Agriculture–Con.

[Includes U.S., states, and 3,142 counties/county equivalents defined as of January 1, 1992. For changes to these areas since January 1, 1992, see appendix B. Geographic Information]

County	Farm population, 1990 Number	Farm population, 1990 Percent of total[1]	Farm earnings 1998 Total ($1,000)	Farm earnings 1998 Percent of total[2]	Farm earnings 1997 ($1,000)	Farms Number	Farms Percent Less than 50 acres	Farms Percent 500 acres or more	Land in farms Total acreage (1,000)	Land in farms Net change, 1992–1997[3] (1,000)	Land in farms Average size of farm	Land in farms Total cropland (1,000)	Value of farm products sold Total ($1,000)	Value of farm products sold Average per farm (dollars)	Value Percent from Crops[4]	Value Percent from Livestock and poultry[5]
TENNESSEE—Con.																
Overton	1 090	6.2	525	.4	621	889	36.4	4.0	109	4	123	63	11 704	13 165	30.1	69.9
Perry	215	3.3	-1 290	X	-699	235	21.3	9.4	54	1	231	21	3 723	15 843	41.7	58.3
Pickett	502	11.0	1 683	4.8	1 216	374	43.3	1.6	37	Z	100	21	4 699	12 564	55.9	44.1
Polk	529	3.9	4 083	4.7	3 420	255	47.1	3.9	32	1	126	20	22 149	86 859	9.5	90.5
Putnam	1 275	2.5	-3 053	X	-1 736	1 120	42.9	2.6	112	-5	100	59	11 911	10 635	32.9	67.1
Rhea	291	1.2	552	.2	570	404	34.4	3.7	56	4	139	35	7 575	18 750	51.3	48.7
Roane	687	1.5	-3 002	X	-2 549	539	39.5	1.3	53	1	99	28	5 771	10 707	36.2	63.8
Robertson	2 915	7.0	11 705	2.4	19 046	1 474	40.3	6.2	236	3	160	183	71 904	48 782	69.3	30.7
Rutherford	2 198	1.9	-2 456	X	-2 703	1 591	39.8	3.6	195	-5	123	115	19 841	12 471	23.3	76.7
Scott	135	.7	123	.1	-382	228	34.2	2.6	30	-3	130	13	4 874	21 377	D	D
Sequatchie	203	2.3	-184	X	-180	169	34.9	6.5	26	1	151	14	4 864	28 781	15.2	84.8
Sevier	800	1.6	-4 033	X	-3 159	801	46.1	1.2	72	-2	89	41	9 456	11 805	25.0	75.0
Shelby	747	.1	-997	Z	4 770	683	53.1	8.8	128	-17	188	98	29 103	42 611	91.6	8.4
Smith	1 656	11.7	-1 041	X	-400	1 045	25.8	3.6	138	-12	132	73	12 840	12 287	47.8	52.2
Stewart	723	7.6	221	.3	1 289	350	25.4	4.6	57	3	161	26	5 298	15 137	70.1	29.9
Sullivan	1 478	1.0	-2 685	X	-329	1 315	62.4	1.5	86	-6	66	55	18 253	13 881	39.1	60.9
Sumner	2 608	2.5	159	Z	2 441	1 703	47.7	2.6	182	4	107	120	34 343	20 166	61.3	38.7
Tipton	1 143	3.0	4 629	1.2	8 805	592	43.6	13.5	170	-13	287	149	38 561	65 137	95.2	4.8
Trousdale	752	12.7	-638	X	451	405	35.6	4.2	52	-3	128	31	6 941	17 138	68.1	31.9
Unicoi	520	3.1	(6)	Z	140	155	60.6	.6	8	-4	48	4	1 002	6 465	57.3	42.6
Union	763	5.6	169	.2	-90	544	44.9	1.8	51	2	94	27	3 842	7 063	43.9	56.2
Van Buren	221	4.6	(6)	(6)	(6)	228	34.2	6.1	32	-1	139	18	2 847	12 487	21.8	78.2
Warren	1 774	5.4	23 753	4.2	26 201	1 347	45.1	3.5	162	-3	120	112	83 004	61 621	84.7	15.3
Washington	2 641	2.9	8 065	.4	9 901	1 807	62.3	1.2	120	2	66	88	44 742	24 760	55.1	44.9
Wayne	542	3.9	-1 824	X	-839	700	21.7	5.9	130	5	186	60	8 207	11 724	25.6	74.4
Weakley	2 024	6.3	4 893	1.3	14 033	1 010	29.4	10.7	223	18	220	178	54 638	54 097	63.4	36.6
White	1 194	5.9	-3 482	X	-2 650	1 034	43.3	3.6	119	-5	115	74	16 887	16 332	20.1	79.9
Williamson	1 463	1.8	-1 695	X	442	1 410	40.6	4.8	198	-6	140	110	28 689	20 347	31.8	68.2
Wilson	2 447	3.6	-2 531	X	-3 283	1 676	33.5	2.9	211	-4	126	118	17 310	10 328	17.6	82.4
TEXAS	192 392	1.1	2 511 051	.6	2 579 353	194 301	27.6	21.4	131 308	422	676	37 662	13 766 527	70 852	31.2	68.8
Anderson	1 204	2.5	-3 759	X	-2 031	1 542	30.2	8.9	354	1	230	138	24 258	15 732	14.1	85.9
Andrews	51	.4	-1 750	X	1 571	142	28.9	43.7	829	-134	5 837	70	9 278	65 338	59.6	40.4
Angelina	575	.8	2 508	.2	1 264	790	41.1	4.8	118	15	149	48	15 913	20 143	4.2	95.8
Aransas	158	.9	-73	X	-308	54	37.0	18.5	19	Z	347	4	304	5 630	13.2	86.5
Archer	487	6.1	16 667	24.4	11 182	496	11.5	40.1	611	-2	1 232	123	63 394	127 810	7.8	92.2
Armstrong	203	10.0	-632	X	614	235	3.4	59.1	560	60	2 385	D	27 901	118 728	19.9	80.1
Atascosa	1 318	4.3	6 333	2.4	5 640	1 322	21.9	23.2	708	-57	536	215	46 170	34 924	48.9	51.1
Austin	1 968	9.9	-1 742	X	2 166	1 820	33.0	8.3	367	30	202	161	24 550	13 489	29.3	70.7
Bailey	609	8.6	29 566	33.1	27 828	441	12.0	49.0	409	-24	927	275	171 675	389 286	21.3	78.7
Bandera	654	6.2	-1 348	X	-1 700	650	22.2	27.5	364	-32	560	48	4 713	7 251	16.9	83.1
Bastrop	2 089	5.5	736	.2	4 980	1 765	33.1	9.3	392	-3	222	141	27 946	15 833	26.0	74.0
Baylor	280	6.4	2 357	6.3	-862	270	13.3	46.3	378	20	1 400	156	38 007	140 767	22.2	77.8
Bee	684	2.7	505	.2	5 707	686	18.1	26.8	421	-21	614	128	27 688	40 362	36.7	63.3
Bell	2 240	1.2	2 206	Z	8 951	1 741	36.2	10.9	407	-10	234	214	51 485	29 572	35.7	64.3
Bexar	2 172	.2	51 308	.2	45 761	1 964	46.1	7.8	448	39	228	177	68 282	34 767	67.4	32.6
Blanco	554	9.3	5 905	7.6	5 198	617	18.3	30.5	381	10	618	56	13 007	21 081	D	D
Borden	243	30.4	-2 967	X	1 371	107	4.7	72.9	515	-115	4 810	70	12 436	116 224	49.9	50.1
Bosque	909	6.0	8 249	6.9	5 795	1 077	16.2	21.7	548	1	509	138	41 354	38 397	22.1	77.9
Bowie	1 039	1.3	14 217	1.1	14 724	1 138	31.7	10.5	281	18	247	135	40 158	35 288	19.7	80.3
Brazoria	1 318	.7	10 646	.3	5 122	1 783	45.4	13.8	567	3	318	203	42 621	23 904	58.9	41.1
Brazos	888	.7	-830	X	4 628	1 084	35.4	11.5	265	-30	245	104	41 184	37 993	18.9	81.1
Brewster	112	1.3	-5 611	X	-5 618	129	13.2	73.6	2 397	-8	18 581	6	9 009	69 837	D	D
Briscoe	171	8.7	3 316	18.5	3 778	232	8.6	50.0	533	124	2 298	154	22 613	97 470	74.4	25.6
Brooks	101	1.2	-1 332	X	-1 147	283	13.4	23.7	458	-108	1 620	64	8 662	30 608	13.1	86.9
Brown	932	2.7	1 581	.4	547	1 228	19.5	23.1	516	3	420	141	32 860	26 759	12.3	87.7
Burleson	1 474	10.8	-2 608	X	-757	1 337	27.3	11.0	322	4	241	144	27 388	20 485	45.7	54.3
Burnet	1 119	4.9	-3 788	X	-1 777	1 110	25.4	24.1	537	-11	484	95	10 369	9 341	7.7	92.3
Caldwell	964	3.7	-675	X	238	1 068	26.1	11.8	265	1	248	105	32 384	30 322	14.5	85.5
Calhoun	411	2.2	(6)	Z	5 943	257	23.0	36.6	213	5	830	76	20 502	79 774	75.4	24.6
Callahan	512	4.3	-441	X	-668	849	23.4	22.3	489	-2	576	133	20 970	24 700	13.6	86.4
Cameron	1 941	.7	65 614	2.3	39 660	902	55.0	16.9	369	39	409	230	79 414	88 042	87.7	12.3
Camp	373	3.8	43 774	30.1	33 184	427	32.6	5.4	63	-5	148	34	150 735	353 009	.8	99.2
Carson	292	4.4	22 454	9.1	11 941	348	10.6	60.6	468	-155	1 344	272	72 471	208 250	31.1	68.9
Cass	777	2.6	18 967	5.8	15 563	852	25.1	7.7	171	4	200	72	22 716	26 662	10.0	90.0
Castro	567	6.3	109 674	57.9	107 149	489	5.1	59.3	559	40	1 142	409	668 439	1 366 951	13.4	86.6

[1] For 1990 corrected population, see table B-1. Percent is based on 1990 uncorrected population because only total population is corrected. [2] For total earnings, see table B-8. [3] Most data are comparable between 1992 and 1997; however, it should be noted that farms with all acreage in Conservation or Wetlands Reserve Programs (excluded in 1992) are included in 1997, as are short rotation woody crops which includes Christmas trees and maple sap gathering (in Forestry in 1992). [4] Includes nursery and greenhouse crops. [5] Includes related products. [6] Less than $50,000.

Sources: Farm Population—U.S. Census Bureau, 1990 Census of Population and Housing, Summary Tape File (STF) 3C on CD-ROM (related Internet site <http://homer.ssd.census.gov/cdrom/lookup>).   Farm Earnings—U.S. Bureau of Economic Analysis, "Regional Economic Information System (REIS) 1969-1998" on CD-ROM (related Internet site <http://www.bea.doc.gov/bea/regional/reis/ca45/>).   Agriculture—U.S. Department of Agriculture, National Agricultural Statistics Service, 1997 Census of Agriculture, Volume 1, Geographic Area Series, 1A, 1B, 1C CD-ROM Set (related Internet site <http://www.nass.usda.gov/census/>).

Table B–10. Counties — **Farm Population, Farm Earnings, and Agriculture**–Con.

[Includes U.S., states, and 3,142 counties/county equivalents defined as of January 1, 1992. For changes to these areas since January 1, 1992, see appendix B. Geographic Information]

County	Farm population, 1990		Farm earnings			Agriculture (NAICS 111-112), 1997										
			1998		1997	Farms			Land in farms (acres)				Value of farm products sold			
							Percent–								Percent from–	
	Number	Per-cent of total[1]	Total ($1,000)	Per-cent of total[2]	($1,000)	Number	Less than 50 acres	500 acres or more	Total acreage (1,000)	Net change, 1992–1997[3] (1,000)	Aver-age size of farm	Total cropland (1,000)	Total ($1,000)	Average per farm (dollars)	Crops[4]	Live-stock and poultry[5]
TEXAS—Con.																
Chambers	189	.9	11 517	4.1	7 232	421	33.5	25.4	242	–9	575	118	15 702	37 297	73.9	26.1
Cherokee	1 293	3.1	121 601	21.0	106 954	1 429	28.7	7.2	283	14	198	140	103 024	72 095	58.3	41.7
Childress	231	3.9	2 014	3.0	5 615	284	7.7	43.3	393	–57	1 384	D	19 256	67 803	71.2	28.8
Clay	756	7.5	5 396	6.9	1 824	818	16.4	28.7	604	–67	738	160	37 592	45 956	13.1	86.9
Cochran	417	9.5	6 716	17.3	22 511	276	4.0	63.8	402	31	1 457	283	51 283	185 808	72.2	27.8
Coke	140	4.1	–5 057	X	–4 286	336	6.5	54.5	482	–41	1 436	55	7 990	23 780	8.3	91.7
Coleman	480	4.9	–1 693	X	–995	837	10.5	41.3	737	56	880	199	20 781	24 828	18.4	81.6
Collin	1 424	.5	6 874	.1	6 046	1 407	49.0	8.3	270	–5	192	190	33 996	24 162	66.0	34.0
Collingsworth	250	7.0	4 128	14.7	5 200	547	21.0	32.5	488	26	893	177	30 582	55 909	65.1	34.9
Colorado	989	5.4	15 571	7.5	12 675	1 562	21.3	15.4	521	–29	333	222	53 274	34 106	63.7	36.3
Comal	487	.9	–1 888	X	–1 433	657	31.1	16.4	183	–24	279	42	5 166	7 863	32.4	67.6
Comanche	1 538	11.5	14 684	12.3	9 586	1 438	19.8	18.4	535	–8	372	225	94 223	65 524	18.7	81.3
Concho	492	16.2	–115	X	2 806	380	4.5	56.1	636	64	1 673	129	19 766	52 016	36.7	63.3
Cooke	1 981	6.4	–271	X	–874	1 487	29.5	14.2	479	48	322	188	37 287	25 075	16.7	83.3
Coryell	1 097	1.7	–2 270	X	–2 625	1 075	17.3	26.2	646	41	601	156	28 029	26 073	15.9	84.1
Cottle	257	11.4	1 207	7.6	2 065	225	3.1	57.8	507	35	2 253	127	14 753	65 569	32.0	68.0
Crane	–	–	–1 758	X	–1 587	53	26.4	66.0	491	96	9 266	28	2 059	38 849	–	100.0
Crockett	211	5.2	–5 924	X	–4 769	170	6.5	83.5	1 935	–66	11 383	D	15 195	89 382	.5	99.5
Crosby	368	5.0	12 044	20.2	25 697	385	5.5	57.9	563	111	1 462	368	74 257	192 875	95.6	4.4
Culberson	55	1.6	88	.3	–434	92	6.5	76.1	1 569	–15	17 057	27	6 026	65 500	38.2	61.8
Dallam	458	8.4	56 612	34.6	78 331	414	7.2	69.6	932	151	2 250	D	356 988	862 290	29.6	70.4
Dallas	200	Z	19 741	Z	18 680	768	54.6	8.7	149	25	194	75	22 279	29 009	73.1	26.9
Dawson	545	3.8	8 033	5.5	29 315	583	7.7	59.3	605	52	1 038	504	89 602	153 691	96.9	3.1
Deaf Smith	930	4.9	127 436	42.4	123 786	647	11.7	62.8	880	23	1 360	572	656 636	1 014 893	8.2	91.8
Delta	466	9.6	1 934	5.4	4 460	419	26.3	13.4	120	13	287	82	11 584	27 647	53.4	46.6
Denton	2 066	.8	–550	X	3 545	1 782	52.6	8.6	363	–3	204	198	53 547	30 049	24.1	75.9
DeWitt	1 336	7.1	–3 359	X	–714	1 502	18.7	16.6	560	–9	373	150	23 240	15 473	9.5	90.5
Dickens	203	7.9	2 890	14.1	3 135	366	6.6	39.9	533	–29	1 456	140	14 144	38 645	46.4	53.6
Dimmit	89	.9	2 027	3.0	705	218	13.8	48.6	518	–160	2 375	44	19 902	91 294	13.1	86.9
Donley	216	5.8	3 398	12.2	8 586	393	6.1	40.2	643	44	1 637	93	91 967	234 013	7.6	92.4
Duval	515	4.0	–4 724	X	–4 272	880	6.7	32.7	844	43	959	131	12 939	14 703	35.4	64.6
Eastland	740	4.0	–1 929	X	–1 170	1 137	12.8	20.9	497	4	437	172	25 882	22 763	29.1	70.9
Ector	189	.2	–4 110	X	–5 336	208	63.9	19.7	462	–56	2 223	D	3 400	16 346	5.3	94.7
Edwards	128	5.6	–2 481	X	–2 651	283	6.4	68.6	1 142	25	4 035	17	9 085	32 102	2.0	98.0
Ellis	2 026	2.4	–2 384	X	8 508	1 713	38.1	10.9	426	Z	249	255	40 430	23 602	61.1	38.9
El Paso	530	.1	21 510	.3	13 191	415	67.7	11.6	244	D	587	47	76 673	184 754	48.0	52.0
Erath	2 361	8.4	77 373	17.9	55 983	1 787	21.8	18.1	613	32	343	218	232 917	130 340	3.6	96.4
Falls	1 441	8.1	–3 969	X	4 611	1 027	19.9	17.8	362	–16	353	223	52 345	50 969	37.4	62.6
Fannin	1 354	5.5	82	Z	6 086	1 604	25.7	13.2	445	32	277	264	39 220	24 451	43.5	56.5
Fayette	2 759	13.7	207	.1	228	2 659	27.0	7.7	515	18	194	222	59 679	22 444	9.1	90.9
Fisher	591	12.2	–7 374	X	7 822	603	9.1	40.5	575	29	954	222	30 848	51 158	59.0	41.0
Floyd	596	7.0	49 409	41.7	48 882	517	4.6	57.3	556	–73	1 075	409	130 709	252 822	53.6	46.4
Foard	189	10.5	2 221	17.3	1 668	238	7.1	42.9	308	–14	1 293	128	11 108	46 672	46.1	53.9
Fort Bend	1 425	.6	48 954	1.3	51 300	1 295	40.1	15.1	432	9	333	193	76 397	58 994	84.1	15.9
Franklin	543	7.0	13 837	16.1	10 824	510	24.5	12.7	135	6	265	55	49 185	96 441	2.5	97.5
Freestone	1 019	6.4	–9 045	X	–6 268	1 205	26.1	14.8	423	52	351	133	19 648	16 305	7.3	92.7
Frio	795	5.9	21 053	17.1	15 874	485	9.7	43.5	662	–87	1 365	149	68 083	140 377	58.3	41.7
Gaines	427	3.0	58 948	30.9	56 412	712	7.3	59.8	772	86	1 085	591	218 298	306 598	D	D
Galveston	216	.1	–134	X	–932	519	59.3	8.3	105	3	202	30	6 805	13 112	31.4	68.6
Garza	336	6.5	–1 619	X	1 572	259	9.3	56.4	514	–59	1 986	D	14 820	57 220	67.7	32.3
Gillespie	1 643	9.6	(6)	Z	522	1 462	21.3	26.4	694	6	475	118	29 261	20 014	16.4	83.6
Glasscock	363	25.1	1 064	10.4	8 342	200	3.0	76.0	437	–41	2 183	132	23 740	118 700	87.9	12.1
Goliad	464	7.8	–1 831	X	1 538	786	17.9	20.5	434	–32	552	76	12 352	15 715	15.7	84.3
Gonzales	1 668	9.7	87 246	37.6	73 507	1 629	20.5	19.8	710	44	436	178	294 402	180 726	4.7	95.3
Gray	185	.8	13 059	3.7	5 511	341	10.6	50.7	561	–15	1 645	D	85 164	249 748	11.2	88.8
Grayson	1 916	2.0	2 562	.2	395	2 080	39.6	8.7	417	8	201	245	35 476	17 056	44.2	55.8
Gregg	276	.3	–2 150	X	–2 089	363	42.4	4.4	51	4	142	26	2 761	7 606	17.5	82.5
Grimes	1 170	6.2	2 589	1.1	1 816	1 423	30.7	12.2	370	17	260	132	23 345	16 405	13.2	86.8
Guadalupe	1 898	2.9	5 281	.7	7 421	1 841	37.9	7.3	348	Z	189	165	31 361	17 035	44.4	55.6
Hale	925	2.7	85 914	16.8	92 899	840	7.7	50.0	587	26	698	512	239 579	285 213	48.7	51.3
Hall	191	4.9	–520	X	5 529	311	2.3	52.7	448	5	1 440	172	23 597	75 875	76.2	23.8
Hamilton	1 211	15.7	8 942	10.9	9 034	966	11.5	26.4	466	5	482	134	52 410	54 255	5.6	94.4
Hansford	33	.6	74 590	54.7	57 092	279	5.4	76.3	582	6	2 086	314	346 244	1 241 018	11.4	88.6
Hardeman	195	3.7	1 986	4.3	4 615	342	6.1	44.4	323	9	944	167	15 887	46 453	44.1	55.9
Hardin	144	.3	–636	X	–939	354	61.0	5.4	65	33	185	18	2 873	8 116	33.3	66.7
Harris	1 356	Z	34 488	Z	28 664	1 727	55.8	7.7	311	3	180	119	43 301	25 073	69.9	30.1

[1] For 1990 corrected population, see table B-1. Percent is based on 1990 uncorrected population because only total population is corrected.   [2] For total earnings, see table B-8.   [3] Most data are comparable between 1992 and 1997; however, it should be noted that farms with all acreage in Conservation or Wetlands Reserve Programs (excluded in 1992) are included in 1997, as are short rotation woody crops which includes Christmas trees and maple sap gathering (in Forestry in 1992).   [4] Includes nursery and greenhouse crops.   [5] Includes related products.   [6] Less than $50,000.

Sources: Farm Population—U.S. Census Bureau, 1990 Census of Population and Housing, Summary Tape File (STF) 3C on CD-ROM (related Internet site <http://homer.ssd.census.gov/cdrom/lookup>).   Farm Earnings—U.S. Bureau of Economic Analysis, "Regional Economic Information System (REIS) 1969-1998" on CD-ROM (related Internet site <http://www.bea.doc.gov/bea/regional/reis/ca45/>).   Agriculture—U.S. Department of Agriculture, National Agricultural Statistics Service, 1997 Census of Agriculture, Volume 1, Geographic Area Series, 1A, 1B, 1C CD-ROM Set (related Internet site <http://www.nass.usda.gov/census/>).

Table B–10. Counties — **Farm Population, Farm Earnings, and Agriculture**–Con.

[Includes U.S., states, and 3,142 counties/county equivalents defined as of January 1, 1992. For changes to these areas since January 1, 1992, see appendix B. Geographic Information]

County	Farm population, 1990 Number	Farm population, 1990 Percent of total[1]	Farm earnings 1998 Total ($1,000)	Farm earnings 1998 Percent of total[2]	Farm earnings 1997 ($1,000)	Farms Number	Farms Percent Less than 50 acres	Farms Percent 500 acres or more	Land in farms Total acreage (1,000)	Land in farms Net change, 1992–1997[3] (1,000)	Land in farms Average size of farm	Land in farms Total cropland (1,000)	Value Total ($1,000)	Value Average per farm (dollars)	Value Percent Crops[4]	Value Percent Livestock and poultry[5]
TEXAS—Con.																
Harrison	1 101	1.9	4 320	.5	3 551	1 107	36.3	10.1	214	13	194	96	12 084	10 916	14.5	85.5
Hartley	305	8.4	57 193	63.0	45 620	245	5.7	69.4	823	136	3 359	D	349 970	1 428 449	15.0	85.0
Haskell	522	7.7	884	1.9	9 314	611	11.0	40.6	469	−25	767	292	39 735	65 033	71.7	28.3
Hays	947	1.4	−4 212	X	−2 947	816	33.6	16.1	298	−165	366	74	10 759	13 185	41.2	58.8
Hemphill	206	5.5	17 712	25.7	16 360	230	8.3	62.2	624	78	2 711	D	103 109	448 300	1.5	98.5
Henderson	1 582	2.7	2 049	.4	3 990	1 630	34.8	8.4	367	11	225	155	29 496	18 096	34.3	65.7
Hidalgo	3 642	.9	89 896	2.1	42 817	1 373	49.5	18.9	636	−25	463	439	197 235	143 653	91.8	8.2
Hill	1 858	6.8	177	.1	10 684	1 563	25.6	14.3	464	−6	297	292	57 711	36 923	59.7	40.3
Hockley	913	3.8	26 727	10.1	30 641	675	15.6	47.7	572	81	847	430	89 315	132 319	75.7	24.3
Hood	581	2.0	6 516	2.5	6 137	799	41.2	12.4	225	Z	282	78	18 252	22 844	47.7	52.3
Hopkins	2 454	8.5	40 053	9.2	33 547	1 758	25.3	9.8	386	Z	220	222	127 100	72 298	3.0	97.0
Houston	1 246	5.8	2 662	1.1	5 247	1 369	21.4	15.6	440	23	322	168	27 388	20 006	14.5	85.5
Howard	390	1.2	−4 823	X	11 601	436	20.0	45.0	544	54	1 247	202	31 487	72 218	69.4	30.6
Hudspeth	28	1.0	1 857	7.7	−918	147	7.5	61.9	2 503	269	17 026	40	24 993	170 020	66.2	33.8
Hunt	1 591	2.5	−608	X	−276	2 049	38.8	6.4	353	8	172	215	24 085	11 755	44.3	55.7
Hutchinson	248	1.0	2 824	.8	4 203	190	13.7	53.7	400	−3	2 106	126	42 969	226 153	31.9	68.1
Irion	164	10.1	−2 793	X	−2 580	146	21.9	54.8	652	−5	4 464	D	5 980	40 959	8.8	91.2
Jack	453	6.5	−2 590	X	−2 896	730	9.7	31.8	532	13	728	71	16 919	23 177	6.0	94.0
Jackson	638	4.9	−2 349	X	3 345	790	20.5	30.4	463	1	586	240	47 257	59 819	79.6	20.4
Jasper	543	1.7	−1 819	X	−1 715	639	55.6	2.0	87	17	136	26	3 480	5 446	28.5	71.5
Jeff Davis	69	3.5	−3 381	X	−3 480	83	7.2	77.1	1 482	−43	17 851	D	9 344	112 578	.7	99.3
Jefferson	438	.2	7 313	.2	5 694	562	39.1	25.6	434	111	772	181	25 957	46 187	70.8	29.2
Jim Hogg	137	2.7	−361	X	−1 453	188	7.4	61.2	768	32	4 086	25	6 500	34 574	.1	99.9
Jim Wells	1 038	2.8	1 287	.3	5 164	738	22.6	24.4	496	−21	673	199	35 618	48 263	50.1	49.9
Johnson	2 368	2.4	7 274	.7	5 065	2 062	48.6	6.1	333	3	161	175	48 119	23 336	13.5	86.5
Jones	682	4.1	−3 468	X	10 118	867	17.2	27.5	459	−54	530	300	39 133	45 136	56.2	43.8
Karnes	874	7.0	−4 960	X	−993	1 051	12.7	20.3	417	34	397	162	15 890	15 119	23.7	76.3
Kaufman	1 759	3.4	−665	X	1 052	1 883	44.6	7.7	389	2	206	181	29 022	15 413	18.1	81.9
Kendall	706	4.8	−4 136	X	−3 203	730	25.5	22.2	325	−30	446	49	6 488	8 888	14.2	85.8
Kenedy	56	12.2	−481	X	−1 251	31	3.2	71.0	563	10	18 159	D	6 832	220 387	D	D
Kent	178	17.6	−91	X	−692	171	5.8	51.5	561	−34	3 280	51	7 279	42 567	16.0	84.0
Kerr	694	1.9	−2 278	X	−3 065	778	23.3	26.9	548	17	704	51	7 192	9 244	14.6	85.4
Kimble	402	9.8	−3 765	X	−3 778	485	12.2	52.6	773	−2	1 594	33	7 223	14 893	11.6	88.4
King	5	1.4	489	13.1	1 355	43	2.3	62.8	D	D	D	22	6 598	153 442	9.0	91.0
Kinney	161	5.2	−2 195	X	−2 784	128	6.3	76.6	629	−70	4 913	20	6 093	47 602	D	D
Kleberg	224	.7	4 662	1.4	4 833	272	41.5	16.9	D	D	D	116	44 258	162 713	D	D
Knox	284	5.9	8 704	19.2	4 692	296	8.1	52.0	658	81	2 224	220	49 037	165 666	31.5	68.5
Lamar	1 194	2.7	−6 517	X	2 041	1 539	24.9	14.4	431	6	280	248	35 385	22 992	31.8	68.2
Lamb	734	4.9	78 266	37.8	59 782	865	7.4	42.1	539	21	624	439	253 464	293 022	39.8	60.2
Lampasas	875	6.5	−3 706	X	−2 551	746	21.0	26.7	435	2	583	71	12 952	17 362	13.8	86.2
La Salle	150	2.9	3 808	9.6	2 320	280	5.7	53.2	527	−239	1 882	72	18 689	66 746	22.1	77.9
Lavaca	2 352	12.6	−3 127	X	−1 780	2 558	26.5	7.7	526	−2	206	220	42 657	16 676	9.8	90.2
Lee	1 300	10.1	−3 308	X	−384	1 685	26.2	8.5	344	26	204	130	22 533	13 373	23.9	76.1
Leon	1 164	9.2	−6 552	X	−3 283	1 633	24.9	15.5	515	33	315	183	27 062	16 572	12.3	87.7
Liberty	1 026	1.9	2 496	.5	4 346	1 138	44.6	11.5	307	−35	270	160	23 723	20 846	69.6	30.4
Limestone	860	4.1	−2 696	X	−765	1 212	19.7	16.8	443	15	365	174	25 809	21 295	11.8	88.2
Lipscomb	266	8.5	8 680	20.0	9 004	302	7.0	61.3	529	−60	1 751	146	45 321	150 070	25.0	75.0
Live Oak	556	5.8	−7 144	X	−4 089	732	15.7	33.2	520	−38	711	128	11 768	16 077	36.7	63.3
Llano	529	4.5	−1 826	X	−1 861	565	17.0	40.9	532	25	942	44	9 810	17 363	5.2	94.8
Loving	–	–	147	6.3	180	14	7.1	92.9	352	5	25 148	–	880	62 857	–	100.0
Lubbock	1 372	.6	32 743	.8	41 453	1 068	29.1	32.1	541	59	506	456	133 755	125 239	70.6	29.4
Lynn	682	10.1	12 930	21.1	35 468	490	7.3	60.6	563	72	1 149	421	71 417	145 749	97.2	2.8
McCulloch	595	6.8	1 406	1.8	1 417	545	7.9	43.7	641	−35	1 175	135	18 034	33 090	29.0	71.0
McLennan	2 467	1.3	7 929	.2	15 304	2 006	38.8	11.1	493	20	246	299	92 952	46 337	36.7	63.3
McMullen	177	21.7	534	5.8	50	210	2.4	74.8	521	5	2 481	26	5 552	26 438	6.6	93.4
Madison	747	6.8	37 151	27.8	32 655	816	24.4	12.5	224	−20	274	79	42 710	52 341	D	D
Marion	260	2.6	369	.6	449	207	19.3	16.4	62	12	299	27	2 048	9 894	24.0	76.0
Martin	346	7.0	−3 826	X	13 058	353	8.5	57.2	539	27	1 527	272	39 930	113 116	91.4	8.6
Mason	352	10.3	−971	X	−817	565	11.5	48.5	595	48	1 054	65	19 575	34 646	21.0	79.0
Matagorda	532	1.4	21 826	4.4	19 494	768	24.1	31.3	551	−12	717	240	58 020	75 547	73.1	26.9
Maverick	232	.6	1 153	.4	1 158	169	24.3	33.1	470	−208	2 783	29	19 576	115 834	29.7	70.3
Medina	1 868	6.8	3 770	1.6	3 556	1 570	26.2	22.7	750	91	477	226	59 937	38 176	43.7	56.3
Menard	291	12.9	−4 087	X	−2 445	291	12.4	53.3	496	8	1 704	25	12 856	44 179	6.0	94.0
Midland	313	.3	−2 620	X	268	411	44.5	24.1	863	138	2 100	69	18 742	45 601	44.8	55.2
Milam	1 529	6.7	(6)	Z	8 216	1 655	24.4	14.4	545	−6	329	248	62 585	37 816	29.7	70.3
Mills	545	12.0	104	.3	1 691	731	12.7	32.7	425	−3	582	91	22 902	31 330	20.0	80.0

[1] For 1990 corrected population, see table B-1. Percent is based on 1990 uncorrected population because only total population is corrected. [2] For total earnings, see table B-8. [3] Most data are comparable between 1992 and 1997; however, it should be noted that farms with all acreage in Conservation or Wetlands Reserve Programs (excluded in 1992) are included in 1997, as are short rotation woody crops which includes Christmas trees and maple sap gathering (in Forestry in 1992). [4] Includes nursery and greenhouse crops. [5] Includes related products. [6] Less than $50,000.

Sources: Farm Population—U.S. Census Bureau, 1990 Census of Population and Housing, Summary Tape File (STF) 3C on CD-ROM (related Internet site <http://homer.ssd.census.gov/cdrom/lookup/>). Farm Earnings—U.S. Bureau of Economic Analysis, "Regional Economic Information System (REIS) 1969-1998" on CD-ROM (related Internet site <http://www.bea.doc.gov/bea/regional/reis/ca45/>). Agriculture—U.S. Department of Agriculture, National Agricultural Statistics Service, 1997 Census of Agriculture, Volume 1, Geographic Area Series, 1A, 1B, 1C CD-ROM Set (related Internet site <http://www.nass.usda.gov/census/>).

Table B–10. Counties — Farm Population, Farm Earnings, and Agriculture–Con.

[Includes U.S., states, and 3,142 counties/county equivalents defined as of January 1, 1992. For changes to these areas since January 1, 1992, see appendix B. Geographic Information]

County	Farm population, 1990 Number	Farm population, 1990 Percent of total[1]	Farm earnings 1998 Total ($1,000)	Farm earnings 1998 Percent of total[2]	Farm earnings 1997 ($1,000)	Farms Number	Farms Percent Less than 50 acres	Farms Percent 500 acres or more	Land in farms (acres) Total acreage (1,000)	Land in farms Net change, 1992–1997[3] (1,000)	Land in farms Average size of farm	Land in farms Total cropland (1,000)	Value of farm products sold Total ($1,000)	Value of farm products sold Average per farm (dollars)	Value Percent from Crops[4]	Value Percent from Livestock and poultry[5]
TEXAS—Con.																
Mitchell	424	5.3	-7 726	X	2 644	378	12.4	42.9	541	-46	1 432	162	20 321	53 759	63.4	36.6
Montague	834	4.8	-964	X	-1 362	1 234	18.4	18.4	494	-2	400	163	29 559	23 954	11.8	88.2
Montgomery	1 499	.8	8 657	.3	7 479	1 163	56.1	6.0	193	-1	166	48	15 676	13 479	59.3	40.7
Moore	45	.3	55 234	16.3	52 485	263	8.0	69.6	555	-32	2 112	258	294 150	1 118 441	15.2	84.8
Morris	393	3.0	6 426	3.2	5 510	372	29.6	9.1	66	-7	179	36	14 628	39 323	3.0	97.0
Motley	168	11.0	-1 603	X	2 159	214	4.7	62.1	590	110	2 757	D	18 641	87 107	49.5	50.5
Nacogdoches	1 849	3.4	42 839	6.4	26 188	1 200	27.3	7.3	372	152	310	102	166 892	139 077	.7	99.3
Navarro	1 126	2.8	-3 743	X	1 174	1 513	22.5	15.5	516	-9	341	237	33 574	22 190	37.3	62.7
Newton	248	1.8	-978	X	-787	294	49.7	3.1	62	32	211	10	1 445	4 915	25.9	74.2
Nolan	424	2.6	-479	X	9 911	445	10.3	42.7	520	-16	1 169	153	32 422	72 858	37.8	62.2
Nueces	585	.2	14 514	.3	16 411	569	30.4	32.9	438	-5	770	351	66 254	116 439	95.3	4.7
Ochiltree	321	3.5	40 025	22.6	16 112	361	5.3	68.7	564	-30	1 563	348	104 000	288 089	25.2	74.8
Oldham	205	9.0	14 827	41.0	12 748	140	1.4	76.4	842	-6	6 014	D	88 490	632 071	4.7	95.3
Orange	223	.3	-469	X	-450	334	65.3	8.7	88	31	263	26	3 318	9 934	42.8	57.2
Palo Pinto	543	2.2	-1 380	X	-1 769	830	25.8	24.0	524	7	632	83	14 972	18 039	10.9	89.1
Panola	972	4.4	16 321	7.5	13 066	866	23.7	12.1	202	7	234	84	45 898	53 000	1.8	98.2
Parker	3 299	5.1	3 712	.6	2 706	2 301	50.8	8.2	480	64	209	170	43 837	19 051	24.6	75.4
Parmer	926	9.4	80 285	39.8	80 078	599	7.2	57.9	547	21	913	434	550 904	919 706	18.2	81.8
Pecos	285	1.9	1 590	1.1	2 892	284	14.1	70.8	2 943	52	10 363	D	40 231	141 658	41.8	58.2
Polk	447	1.5	-956	X	-887	551	35.4	9.3	136	-5	247	42	4 461	8 096	10.0	90.0
Potter	175	.2	-1 813	X	-2 662	214	28.0	33.6	450	48	2 102	D	18 620	87 009	14.4	85.6
Presidio	25	.4	1 296	2.9	-151	138	11.6	73.2	1 690	-5	12 247	D	13 580	98 406	36.4	63.6
Rains	479	7.1	4 418	9.6	5 109	493	36.5	8.5	94	-4	192	46	15 844	32 138	25.7	74.3
Randall	830	.9	29 034	3.9	31 950	583	22.3	39.5	460	-37	789	277	202 949	348 111	9.4	90.6
Reagan	272	6.0	-4 438	X	-1 639	123	3.3	79.7	624	6	5 072	57	12 499	101 618	65.9	34.1
Real	267	11.1	-1 618	X	-2 318	207	8.7	60.4	378	15	1 826	10	2 483	11 995	5.9	94.1
Red River	790	5.5	328	.3	2 666	1 088	19.4	17.9	445	19	409	173	39 391	36 205	16.6	83.4
Reeves	98	.6	6 278	5.6	8 478	176	12.5	59.7	1 014	-542	5 760	D	42 076	239 068	31.1	68.9
Refugio	350	4.4	1 742	2.2	222	230	17.0	33.5	550	-117	2 392	111	23 833	103 622	68.5	31.5
Roberts	72	7.0	1 742	23.7	553	96	1.0	85.4	566	56	5 896	51	14 064	146 500	13.1	86.9
Robertson	1 153	7.4	-6 524	X	-1 009	1 289	23.0	15.4	425	33	329	177	31 479	24 421	35.6	64.4
Rockwall	402	1.6	97	Z	-395	265	47.9	5.3	46	-1	174	32	3 735	14 094	53.8	46.2
Runnels	1 006	8.9	5 484	4.8	4 032	896	12.4	34.8	581	9	649	293	27 400	30 580	56.7	43.3
Rusk	1 461	3.3	17 025	3.4	15 601	1 296	24.2	9.0	267	-1	206	131	29 051	22 416	29.0	71.0
Sabine	157	1.6	3 144	3.7	2 473	194	36.1	4.6	25	-8	129	13	10 941	56 397	2.1	97.9
San Augustine	225	2.8	7 580	12.2	6 103	291	26.8	10.3	65	11	224	26	25 127	86 347	4.0	96.0
San Jacinto	375	2.3	599	.9	636	398	43.5	7.0	85	2	213	28	4 613	11 590	22.8	77.2
San Patricio	1 066	1.8	10 471	1.6	9 902	496	30.2	36.9	406	47	818	265	74 334	149 867	77.0	23.0
San Saba	538	10.0	1 743	3.3	1 281	653	11.2	42.4	733	-11	1 122	139	25 133	38 489	18.6	81.4
Schleicher	285	9.5	-3 809	X	-1 858	284	7.4	69.0	739	-26	2 601	45	11 683	41 137	15.1	84.9
Scurry	823	4.4	-7 850	X	4 146	606	15.0	35.6	479	-40	790	210	24 355	40 190	57.7	42.3
Shackelford	248	7.5	-1 774	X	-2 709	250	7.6	48.8	516	-49	2 063	54	11 271	45 084	17.3	82.7
Shelby	1 339	6.1	58 428	20.4	43 445	1 047	24.6	7.0	201	14	192	86	181 243	173 107	1.2	98.8
Sherman	73	2.6	66 342	73.0	53 517	293	5.8	70.3	607	100	2 072	355	295 013	1 006 870	17.4	82.6
Smith	2 073	1.4	28 385	.9	26 146	1 844	43.0	4.6	251	3	136	127	38 352	20 798	52.0	48.0
Somervell	310	5.8	-613	X	-422	245	32.7	17.1	72	9	293	20	2 194	8 955	17.1	82.9
Starr	426	1.1	16 679	6.8	11 375	609	8.5	33.2	636	3	1 044	127	50 558	83 018	41.8	58.2
Stephens	165	1.8	-3 048	X	-2 638	454	7.5	42.3	465	-72	1 024	60	7 984	17 586	7.3	92.7
Sterling	184	12.8	-1 939	X	-3 998	67	9.0	73.1	706	-130	10 532	14	8 531	127 328	2.0	98.0
Stonewall	164	8.1	1 225	6.4	-968	305	4.9	49.8	484	-29	1 585	109	10 641	34 889	30.4	69.6
Sutton	69	1.7	-6 580	X	-6 059	211	5.2	80.6	925	-1	4 383	9	9 184	43 526	2.1	97.9
Swisher	430	5.3	73 404	53.8	65 233	529	7.2	53.9	516	11	975	355	364 094	688 268	12.8	87.2
Tarrant	280	Z	8 132	Z	7 388	1 048	60.6	6.5	184	17	176	70	20 870	19 914	50.5	49.5
Taylor	983	.8	10 327	.5	9 399	1 048	27.5	23.8	492	-17	469	207	52 867	50 446	17.9	82.1
Terrell	91	6.5	-1 820	X	-1 953	85	4.7	88.2	1 291	-106	15 186	D	4 600	54 118	D	D
Terry	769	5.8	29 551	20.4	40 453	562	13.0	52.5	468	9	833	378	92 288	164 214	95.0	5.0
Throckmorton	144	7.7	2 108	11.5	1 355	249	4.0	57.0	562	-19	2 257	115	20 469	82 205	28.9	71.1
Titus	713	3.0	6 342	1.4	5 324	722	30.3	8.4	174	-6	242	73	41 393	57 331	2.0	98.0
Tom Green	1 211	1.2	-1 491	X	8 389	880	34.9	33.2	959	-62	1 089	217	85 876	97 586	31.4	68.6
Travis	1 294	.2	996	Z	3 568	1 038	39.4	12.8	396	63	382	113	16 433	15 831	58.7	41.3
Trinity	321	2.8	3 121	4.2	1 674	518	26.8	6.8	99	-11	191	49	6 083	11 743	6.8	93.2
Tyler	284	1.7	-1 306	X	-1 060	463	50.3	3.9	53	-5	115	25	3 115	6 728	20.8	79.2
Upshur	1 095	3.5	4 198	2.1	3 461	1 110	35.9	5.0	175	-19	158	72	30 913	27 850	3.6	96.4
Upton	119	2.7	-2 689	X	-2 520	96	10.4	69.8	746	51	7 774	D	7 653	79 719	53.5	46.5
Uvalde	593	2.5	5 838	2.3	5 201	593	17.5	44.7	943	25	1 590	159	68 485	115 489	40.9	59.1
Val Verde	187	.5	-7 953	X	-9 138	238	24.8	63.4	1 748	-59	7 345	11	19 450	81 723	1.2	98.8

[1] For 1990 corrected population, see table B-1. Percent is based on 1990 uncorrected population because only total population is corrected. [2] For total earnings, see table B-8. [3] Most data are comparable between 1992 and 1997; however, it should be noted that farms with all acreage in Conservation or Wetlands Reserve Programs (excluded in 1992) are included in 1997, as are short rotation woody crops which includes Christmas trees and maple sap gathering (in Forestry in 1992). [4] Includes nursery and greenhouse crops. [5] Includes related products.

Sources: Farm Population—U.S. Census Bureau, 1990 Census of Population and Housing, Summary Tape File (STF) 3C on CD-ROM (related Internet site <http://homer.ssd.census.gov/cdrom/lookup>). Farm Earnings—U.S. Bureau of Economic Analysis, "Regional Economic Information System (REIS) 1969-1998" on CD-ROM (related Internet site <http://www.bea.doc.gov/bea/regional/reis/ca45/>). Agriculture—U.S. Department of Agriculture, National Agricultural Statistics Service, 1997 Census of Agriculture, Volume 1, Geographic Area Series, 1A, 1B, 1C CD-ROM Set (related Internet site <http://www.nass.usda.gov/census/>).

Table B–10. Counties — **Farm Population, Farm Earnings, and Agriculture**–Con.

[Includes U.S., states, and 3,142 counties/county equivalents defined as of January 1, 1992. For changes to these areas since January 1, 1992, see appendix B. Geographic Information]

County	Farm population, 1990 Number	Percent of total[1]	Farm earnings 1998 Total ($1,000)	Percent of total[2]	1997 ($1,000)	Farms Number	Percent Less than 50 acres	500 acres or more	Land in farms (acres) Total acreage (1,000)	Net change, 1992–1997[3] (1,000)	Average size of farm	Total cropland (1,000)	Value of farm products sold Total ($1,000)	Average per farm (dollars)	Percent from Crops[4]	Livestock and poultry[5]
TEXAS—Con.																
Van Zandt	2 598	6.8	13 107	4.8	14 398	2 423	39.7	5.3	361	−17	149	201	55 941	23 087	36.7	63.3
Victoria	916	1.2	−10 311	X	−2 883	1 084	32.4	16.6	458	27	423	155	28 638	26 419	59.8	40.2
Walker	457	.9	−1 427	X	−947	826	38.3	8.7	184	−30	223	60	10 892	13 186	25.3	74.7
Waller	711	3.0	−4 510	X	−2 433	1 066	43.6	9.3	238	−5	223	116	29 126	27 323	51.5	48.5
Ward	16	.1	−3 888	X	−4 135	85	23.5	51.8	363	−93	4 271	D	1 800	21 176	48.1	51.9
Washington	2 198	8.4	−170	X	4 388	1 986	32.2	5.8	336	8	169	162	26 086	13 135	20.3	79.7
Webb	394	.3	59	Z	952	453	6.0	61.1	2 176	464	4 804	52	28 198	62 247	9.9	90.1
Wharton	1 587	4.0	51 386	11.0	44 048	1 347	24.3	28.1	679	35	504	443	133 550	99 146	79.7	20.3
Wheeler	428	7.3	28 034	35.1	25 924	505	9.7	45.0	514	13	1 018	155	80 652	159 707	4.7	95.3
Wichita	581	.5	7 263	.3	2 899	560	38.4	20.4	339	31	605	143	21 861	39 038	33.7	66.3
Wilbarger	464	3.1	7 593	4.2	2 751	476	13.9	38.2	884	20	1 857	260	33 237	69 826	57.0	43.0
Willacy	536	3.0	8 419	8.0	8 710	243	21.0	49.4	286	25	1 178	234	49 496	203 687	91.2	8.8
Williamson	2 879	2.1	−6 357	X	3 228	2 034	36.8	12.7	538	−8	265	296	48 071	23 634	65.8	34.2
Wilson	2 057	9.1	−2 007	X	489	1 794	27.5	9.9	446	−31	248	217	46 047	25 667	30.2	69.8
Winkler	20	.2	−426	X	−520	39	28.2	59.0	488	55	12 506	D	1 841	47 205	D	D
Wise	2 192	6.3	−2 433	X	2 316	2 075	41.1	8.4	412	−49	198	177	34 276	16 519	12.7	87.3
Wood	1 029	3.5	31 475	11.1	28 566	1 331	35.8	5.9	215	11	161	107	74 572	56 027	17.9	82.1
Yoakum	291	3.3	3 628	3.2	20 183	278	9.4	58.6	343	−2	1 234	247	52 195	187 752	93.7	6.3
Young	340	1.9	3 797	1.6	−272	709	12.0	32.4	553	−10	781	155	23 193	32 712	22.6	77.4
Zapata	40	.4	−804	X	−503	323	2.8	57.6	403	−82	1 249	33	7 282	22 545	D	D
Zavala	256	2.1	8 660	14.0	8 506	232	4.3	62.5	591	−132	2 546	78	45 385	195 625	40.0	60.0
UTAH	11 685	.7	192 929	.5	171 817	14 181	46.3	16.4	12 025	2 400	848	2 070	877 295	61 864	28.2	71.8
Beaver	87	1.8	12 723	18.6	11 225	219	31.1	21.5	131	−61	598	39	58 525	267 237	11.2	88.8
Box Elder	1 328	3.6	30 511	3.8	28 089	1 077	36.9	26.7	1 358	−92	1 261	344	102 173	94 868	35.6	64.4
Cache	1 429	2.0	27 139	2.5	21 955	1 232	42.1	9.5	266	−2	216	177	104 809	85 072	13.4	86.6
Carbon	183	.9	−3 077	X	−2 777	199	48.2	18.1	202	−90	1 013	17	3 622	18 201	11.2	88.8
Daggett	119	17.2	−151	X	−97	36	8.3	36.1	26	5	736	13	1 440	40 000	29.7	70.3
Davis	154	.1	9 713	.3	8 763	559	74.4	3.0	68	18	121	27	33 385	59 723	82.2	17.8
Duchesne	1 239	9.8	2 609	1.8	2 930	811	29.6	17.8	1 328	929	1 638	125	27 568	33 993	16.9	83.1
Emery	414	4.0	1 817	1.2	1 850	450	33.8	19.1	159	−82	353	53	10 970	24 378	18.3	81.7
Garfield	142	3.6	−485	X	−322	285	30.2	18.9	121	−16	426	36	7 583	26 607	17.7	82.3
Grand	102	1.5	(6)	Z	82	85	52.9	15.3	76	13	892	6	2 289	26 929	37.1	62.9
Iron	176	.8	10 193	3.0	11 254	375	32.0	34.4	405	−30	1 079	71	42 126	112 336	66.9	33.1
Juab	193	3.3	−187	X	295	228	22.8	32.5	276	−57	1 209	66	8 353	36 636	34.5	65.5
Kane	62	1.2	585	.9	702	143	21.0	43.4	175	−34	1 226	15	3 230	22 587	7.6	92.4
Millard	598	5.3	15 326	11.3	13 784	650	23.1	30.3	458	−26	704	163	71 047	109 303	39.7	60.3
Morgan	214	3.9	5 847	10.2	5 106	243	55.1	18.5	179	−55	738	22	13 213	54 374	9.1	90.9
Piute	84	6.6	2 873	31.0	2 414	106	12.3	24.5	45	−14	420	21	7 216	68 075	9.1	90.8
Rich	87	5.0	2 176	15.2	2 640	162	20.4	53.1	524	31	3 233	87	15 538	95 914	7.1	92.9
Salt Lake	73	Z	3 528	Z	2 911	593	78.9	3.9	114	6	192	40	22 983	38 757	55.0	45.0
San Juan	45	.4	1 178	1.0	1 457	231	12.6	55.0	1 673	1 348	7 243	150	9 097	39 381	38.5	61.5
Sanpete	380	2.3	16 975	10.0	13 093	776	34.9	18.6	360	−88	464	113	82 785	106 682	9.3	90.7
Sevier	225	1.5	12 809	6.4	11 668	478	44.4	9.2	147	−11	308	50	39 668	82 987	16.3	83.7
Summit	440	2.8	5 390	1.0	4 602	476	46.6	20.0	590	216	1 239	40	17 057	35 834	5.7	94.3
Tooele	254	1.0	1 927	.5	1 985	332	40.7	23.2	292	−145	879	42	17 381	52 352	13.5	86.5
Uintah	893	4.0	1 399	.5	2 229	795	41.5	15.6	2 268	973	2 853	91	21 466	27 001	26.2	73.8
Utah	1 539	.6	22 673	.5	19 744	1 790	68.2	6.5	375	−75	209	150	97 009	54 195	40.4	59.6
Wasatch	183	1.8	2 539	2.1	2 226	294	60.9	5.8	106	−33	361	17	7 747	26 350	14.4	85.6
Washington	89	.2	−736	X	−582	429	46.9	20.0	163	−4	380	35	9 342	21 776	34.3	65.7
Wayne	146	6.7	3 385	12.3	2 791	191	28.8	9.9	60	−46	312	18	11 200	58 639	8.9	91.1
Weber	807	.5	4 220	.2	1 800	936	73.8	2.1	81	−175	87	40	28 474	30 421	25.0	75.0
VERMONT	11 810	2.1	147 264	1.5	112 250	5 828	25.0	10.0	1 262	−16	217	617	476 343	81 734	12.5	87.5
Addison	1 851	5.6	23 865	5.2	16 884	683	20.8	18.7	205	−5	300	135	112 718	165 034	8.6	91.4
Bennington	323	.9	2 758	.5	2 306	171	38.0	6.4	32	−1	189	12	8 084	47 275	29.0	71.0
Caledonia	938	3.4	11 716	3.3	8 895	452	21.5	9.5	94	−2	209	43	29 357	64 949	10.6	89.4
Chittenden	806	.6	9 610	.3	8 162	456	35.7	7.2	83	1	183	42	25 544	56 018	28.9	71.1
Essex	249	3.9	2 013	3.0	1 434	79	15.2	17.7	25	8	323	9	6 769	85 684	19.2	80.8
Franklin	1 809	4.5	35 684	7.3	25 582	740	18.5	12.8	190	−13	257	99	99 610	134 608	4.3	95.7
Grand Isle	293	5.5	3 035	9.3	2 305	107	29.0	13.1	21	−4	197	16	9 605	89 766	11.2	88.8
Lamoille	468	2.4	6 446	2.1	5 086	297	31.0	6.1	49	8	165	20	15 470	52 088	14.1	85.9
Orange	1 049	4.0	9 282	3.7	7 269	537	20.9	6.9	98	5	183	42	26 079	48 564	16.9	83.1
Orleans	1 360	5.7	20 744	7.2	14 816	569	18.5	11.8	144	−5	253	74	59 522	104 608	6.4	93.6
Rutland	769	1.2	6 441	.7	4 547	530	23.4	12.8	126	−7	237	53	28 357	53 504	11.3	88.7
Washington	738	1.3	3 562	.3	2 913	344	28.8	3.5	56	−3	164	23	15 041	43 724	21.4	78.6
Windham	383	.9	7 787	.9	8 093	305	34.8	4.6	47	3	154	19	20 366	66 774	44.8	55.2
Windsor	774	1.4	4 321	.5	3 958	558	30.8	5.4	90	Z	161	30	19 820	35 520	22.6	77.4

[1] For 1990 corrected population, see table B-1. Percent is based on 1990 uncorrected population because only total population is corrected. [2] For total earnings, see table B-8. [3] Most data are comparable between 1992 and 1997; however, it should be noted that farms with all acreage in Conservation or Wetlands Reserve Programs (excluded in 1992) are included in 1997, as are short rotation woody crops which includes Christmas trees and maple sap gathering (in Forestry in 1992). [4] Includes nursery and greenhouse crops. [5] Includes related products. [6] Less than $50,000.

Sources: Farm Population—U.S. Census Bureau, 1990 Census of Population and Housing, Summary Tape File (STF) 3C on CD-ROM (related Internet site <http://homer.ssd.census.gov/cdrom/lookup>). Farm Earnings—U.S. Bureau of Economic Analysis, "Regional Economic Information System (REIS) 1969-1998" on CD-ROM (related Internet site <http://www.bea.doc.gov/bea/regional/reis/ca45/>). Agriculture—U.S. Department of Agriculture, National Agricultural Statistics Service, 1997 Census of Agriculture, Volume 1, Geographic Area Series, 1A, 1B, 1C CD-ROM Set (related Internet site <http://www.nass.usda.gov/census/>).

Table B-10. Counties — **Farm Population, Farm Earnings, and Agriculture**–Con.

[Includes U.S., states, and 3,142 counties/county equivalents defined as of January 1, 1992. For changes to these areas since January 1, 1992, see appendix B. Geographic Information]

County	Farm population, 1990		Farm earnings			Agriculture (NAICS 111-112), 1997										
			1998			Farms			Land in farms (acres)				Value of farm products sold			
							Percent–								Percent from–	
	Number	Percent of total[1]	Total ($1,000)	Percent of total[2]	1997 ($1,000)	Number	Less than 50 acres	500 acres or more	Total acreage (1,000)	Net change, 1992–1997[3] (1,000)	Average size of farm	Total cropland (1,000)	Total ($1,000)	Average per farm (dollars)	Crops[4]	Livestock and poultry[5]
VIRGINIA	80 560	1.3	373 498	.3	379 798	41 095	32.0	9.0	8 228	–69	200	4 322	2 343 518	57 027	33.3	66.7
Accomack	1 079	3.4	14 157	3.8	14 014	268	38.1	21.3	92	1	345	75	84 849	316 601	41.4	58.6
Albemarle	1 494	2.2	[6]7 634	[6].3	[6]6 661	[6]747	[6]30.4	[6]10.4	[6]172	[6]–16	[6]231	[6]75	[6]21 450	[6]28 715	[6]21.6	[6]78.4
Alleghany	253	1.9	[7]554	[7].1	[7]526	[7]160	[7]22.5	[7]5.6	[7]31	[7]5	[7]194	[7]13	[7]2 132	[7]13 325	[7]10.6	[7]89.4
Amelia	724	8.2	11 174	13.2	8 857	336	24.1	11.6	78	8	234	37	57 543	171 259	7.1	92.9
Amherst	469	1.6	1 228	.4	825	406	21.4	9.9	93	2	228	34	5 105	12 574	29.4	70.6
Appomattox	604	4.9	383	.3	([8])	353	16.1	8.8	77	–2	217	39	6 764	19 161	27.9	72.1
Arlington	–	–	–	–	–	1	100.0	–	D	D	D	D	D	D	D	D
Augusta	3 265	6.0	[9]25 559	[9]1.6	[9]19 036	[9]1 499	[9]36.6	[9]9.1	[9]282	[9]–5	[9]188	[9]147	[9]138 673	[9]92 510	[9]9.9	[9]90.1
Bath	194	4.0	410	.6	260	129	14.7	28.7	58	11	452	21	2 011	15 589	13.7	86.2
Bedford	1 654	3.6	[10]1 320	[10].3	([8])	[10]1 198	[10]27.4	[10]6.1	[10]195	[10]–6	[10]163	[10]102	[10]19 755	[10]16 490	[10]12.6	[10]87.4
Bland	408	6.3	857	1.4	675	346	21.7	11.6	83	2	241	28	7 088	20 486	6.8	93.2
Botetourt	689	2.8	682	.3	–437	505	26.9	7.9	91	–6	179	41	10 733	21 253	16.5	83.5
Brunswick	832	5.2	1 613	1.2	5 824	294	20.1	13.9	79	–6	269	33	18 063	61 439	67.9	32.1
Buchanan	479	1.5	104	Z	([8])	70	42.9	1.4	6	–2	90	2	341	4 871	58.7	41.3
Buckingham	513	4.0	3 647	3.5	4 090	370	20.8	8.4	76	10	205	38	18 084	48 876	4.8	95.2
Campbell	1 142	2.4	[11]1 882	[11].1	[11]1 373	[11]621	[11]18.4	[11]10.8	[11]141	[11]6	[11]227	[11]63	[11]14 613	[11]23 531	[11]40.9	[11]59.1
Caroline	467	2.4	–523	X	3 288	179	31.3	18.4	55	4	310	39	11 599	64 799	86.4	13.6
Carroll	892	3.4	[12]3 811	[12].9	[12]3 260	913	33.8	3.0	110	–3	121	63	18 358	20 107	24.7	75.3
Charles City	112	1.8	311	.7	1 045	59	30.5	37.3	D	D	D	D	6 643	112 593	89.9	10.1
Charlotte	733	6.3	3 521	3.2	3 548	493	20.5	12.4	132	19	267	54	16 518	33 505	57.4	42.6
Chesterfield	457	.2	2 202	.1	2 350	[13]159	[13]47.8	[13]7.5	[13]20	[13]3	[13]127	[13]10	[13]8 543	[13]53 730	[13]60.1	[13]39.9
Clarke	769	6.4	947	.7	595	325	31.1	10.5	71	3	220	48	13 056	40 172	33.6	66.4
Craig	178	4.1	893	4.6	664	176	17.6	11.9	46	Z	260	20	2 635	14 972	10.1	89.9
Culpeper	924	3.3	3 020	.7	2 346	521	32.4	10.6	115	Z	221	72	21 582	41 424	35.3	64.7
Cumberland	597	7.6	2 881	7.1	3 077	248	20.6	12.5	61	–1	246	29	24 971	100 690	7.7	92.3
Dickenson	430	2.4	381	.4	328	102	39.2	2.0	9	D	89	5	489	4 794	33.5	66.5
Dinwiddie	1 131	5.4	[14]1 297	[14].1	[14]3 875	[15]351	[15]25.9	[15]11.7	[15]89	[15]3	[15]254	[15]44	[15]18 143	[15]51 689	[15]76.3	[15]23.7
Essex	368	4.2	–1 041	X	1 074	114	21.1	36.0	62	5	540	43	10 287	90 237	95.1	4.9
Fairfax	196	Z	[16]1 323	Z	[16]1 509	[17]121	[17]60.3	[17]4.1	[17]12	[17]–3	[17]102	[17]4	[17]5 233	[17]43 248	[17]68.5	[17]31.5
Fauquier	2 267	4.7	8 152	1.4	8 051	957	35.2	10.3	239	4	250	122	47 474	49 607	28.4	71.6
Floyd	985	8.2	3 362	4.4	3 810	731	25.4	5.6	123	6	168	61	30 063	41 126	38.7	61.3
Fluvanna	426	3.4	1 057	1.0	561	256	19.5	9.0	59	1	230	26	6 281	24 535	12.5	87.5
Franklin	1 713	4.3	8 374	2.2	5 722	890	23.5	7.8	159	–8	178	82	40 924	45 982	18.4	81.6
Frederick	999	2.2	[10]5 730	[10].4	[10]4 336	[10]568	[10]31.0	[10]7.9	[18]100	[18]2	[18]176	[18]60	[18]20 530	[18]36 144	[18]69.6	[18]30.4
Giles	518	3.2	–222	X	–209	341	20.8	8.2	67	–6	197	28	4 122	12 088	13.0	87.0
Gloucester	406	1.3	–135	X	365	108	45.4	12.0	23	–1	215	17	5 068	46 926	95.5	4.5
Goochland	623	4.4	581	.3	1 084	229	35.8	10.5	47	–5	204	26	6 857	29 943	29.3	70.6
Grayson	844	5.2	3 440	3.8	2 526	[19]054	[19]05.0	[19]7.1	[19]130	Z	[19]100	[19]05	[10]19 314	[10]22 616	[10]21.1	[10]78.9
Greene	371	3.6	578	.6	492	198	22.2	6.6	34	–3	170	18	4 450	22 475	9.2	90.8
Greensville	472	5.3	[20]4 995	[20]2.1	[20]5 061	[20]134	[20]20.1	[20]23.9	[20]58	[20]7	[20]435	[20]40	[20]14 465	[20]107 948	[20]88.9	[20]11.1
Halifax	2 176	7.5	10 301	2.5	13 065	940	21.7	11.1	228	–5	242	92	40 179	42 744	81.7	18.3
Hanover	1 164	1.8	5 388	.4	7 337	501	39.1	8.6	98	2	196	61	28 727	57 339	75.6	24.4
Henrico	308	.1	4 770	.1	5 600	[21]154	[21]49.4	[21]6.5	[21]26	[21]2	[21]171	[21]14	[21]9 835	[21]63 864	[21]64.3	[21]35.7
Henry	842	1.5	[22]3 960	[22].4	[22]3 916	[22]288	[22]27.4	[22]6.3	[22]48	[22]–1	[22]168	[22]24	[22]8 016	[22]27 833	[22]39.2	[22]60.8
Highland	436	16.5	1 968	10.0	1 778	283	11.0	17.0	91	–6	323	35	12 256	43 307	2.2	97.8
Isle of Wight	933	3.7	5 434	1.1	6 541	190	24.7	32.6	88	2	463	61	41 025	215 921	51.9	48.1
James City	167	.5	[23]431	Z	[23]534	[23]58	[23]48.3	[23]10.3	[23]9	[23]–1	[23]153	[23]6	[23]1 892	[23]32 621	[23]79.5	[23]20.5
King and Queen	420	6.7	–2 316	X	1 445	127	15.7	18.1	51	–2	400	34	10 171	80 087	80.9	19.1
King George	398	2.9	–863	X	555	139	29.5	11.5	34	–4	246	20	4 687	33 719	89.4	10.6
King William	339	3.1	–1 256	X	1 618	123	17.9	26.0	56	–3	457	38	11 658	94 780	78.4	21.6
Lancaster	221	2.0	–371	X	468	70	25.7	14.3	17	–2	246	14	3 291	47 014	97.5	2.5
Lee	1 816	7.4	3 647	2.3	1 549	1 106	37.9	2.9	127	–2	115	63	13 100	11 844	50.8	49.2
Loudoun	2 103	2.4	1 532	.1	1 601	1 032	53.3	7.4	185	–10	179	117	25 978	25 172	42.5	57.5
Louisa	955	4.7	525	.2	712	385	26.0	10.9	79	–2	205	41	9 542	24 784	25.8	74.2
Lunenburg	827	7.2	5 021	6.2	5 258	339	20.1	10.0	78	–8	229	31	16 473	48 593	57.4	42.6
Madison	874	7.3	1 017	1.1	750	422	30.6	12.1	100	–1	237	55	16 784	39 773	17.6	82.4
Mathews	103	1.2	1 126	2.5	1 160	58	50.0	8.6	8	2	145	6	3 565	61 466	95.0	5.0
Mecklenburg	1 247	4.3	9 587	2.5	9 957	604	20.7	14.4	167	–1	276	83	41 948	69 450	78.1	21.9
Middlesex	295	3.4	561	.7	1 410	67	29.9	19.4	18	–3	273	15	5 189	77 448	96.7	3.3
Montgomery	784	1.1	[24]3 225	[24].2	[24]2 095	[24]517	[24]32.9	[24]7.4	[24]93	[24]–6	[24]180	[24]44	[24]14 792	[24]28 611	[24]14.9	[24]85.1
Nelson	543	4.2	2 132	2.2	1 409	357	23.5	8.1	73	1	205	35	6 844	19 171	58.4	41.6
New Kent	313	3.0	–329	X	374	64	29.7	14.1	16	–2	256	12	2 941	45 953	94.8	5.2
Northampton	593	4.5	15 129	11.6	16 720	152	30.3	24.3	56	4	371	50	38 597	253 928	70.3	29.7
Northumberland	503	4.8	–633	X	2 337	122	26.2	15.6	38	–3	313	31	9 645	79 057	98.4	1.6
Nottoway	729	4.9	3 266	1.9	2 956	317	15.1	10.1	69	5	218	36	22 057	69 580	15.4	84.6
Orange	724	3.4	5 233	2.3	5 151	437	28.4	11.2	101	–6	232	56	25 872	59 204	39.2	60.8
Page	720	3.3	6 223	3.1	7 863	541	43.8	4.3	68	3	125	39	115 209	212 956	2.0	98.0
Patrick	817	4.7	1 888	1.2	1 229	536	32.6	3.4	74	–5	138	36	13 312	24 836	51.8	48.2
Pittsylvania	3 606	6.5	[25]16 770	[25]1.2	[25]18 827	[25]1 235	[25]20.4	[25]10.3	[25]267	[25]–30	[25]216	[25]124	[25]58 864	[25]47 663	[25]75.0	[25]25.0
Powhatan	341	2.2	1 428	.9	904	208	33.7	8.7	43	Z	207	19	6 867	33 014	21.2	78.8

[1] For 1990 corrected population, see table B-1. Percent is based on 1990 uncorrected population because only total population is corrected. [2] For total earnings, see table B-8. [3] Most data are comparable between 1992 and 1997; however, it should be noted that farms with all acreage in Conservation or Wetlands Reserve Programs (excluded in 1992) are included in 1997, as are short rotation woody crops which includes Christmas trees and maple sap gathering (in Forestry in 1992). [4] Includes nursery and greenhouse crops. [5] Includes related products. [6] Albemarle County includes Charlottesville city. [7] Alleghany County includes Clifton Forge and Covington cities. [8] Less than $50,000. [9] Augusta County includes Staunton and Waynesboro cities. [10] Bedford County includes Bedford city. [11] Campbell County includes Lynchburg city. [12] Carroll County includes Galax city. [13] Chesterfield County includes Colonial Heights city. [14] Dinwiddie County includes Colonial Heights and Petersburg cities. [15] Dinwiddie County includes Petersburg city. [16] Fairfax County includes Fairfax and Falls Church cities. [17] Fairfax County includes Alexandria, Fairfax, and Falls Church cities. [18] Frederick County includes Winchester city. [19] Grayson County includes Galax city. [20] Greensville County includes Emporia city. [21] Henrico County includes Richmond city. [22] Henry County includes Martinsville city. [23] James City County includes Williamsburg city. [24] Montgomery County includes Radford city. [25] Pittsylvania County includes Danville city.

Sources: Farm Population—U.S. Census Bureau, 1990 Census of Population and Housing, Summary Tape File (STF) 3C on CD-ROM (related Internet site <http://homer.ssd.census.gov/cdrom/lookup>). Farm Earnings—U.S. Bureau of Economic Analysis, "Regional Economic Information System (REIS) 1969-1998" on CD-ROM (related Internet site <http://www.bea.doc.gov/bea/regional/reis/ca45/>). Agriculture—U.S. Department of Agriculture, National Agricultural Statistics Service, 1997 Census of Agriculture, Volume 1, Geographic Area Series, 1A, 1B, 1C CD-ROM Set (related Internet site <http://www.nass.usda.gov/census/>).

Table B-10. Counties — **Farm Population, Farm Earnings, and Agriculture**–Con.

[Includes U.S., states, and 3,142 counties/county equivalents defined as of January 1, 1992. For changes to these areas since January 1, 1992, see appendix B. Geographic Information]

County	Farm population, 1990		Farm earnings			Agriculture (NAICS 111-112), 1997										
			1998			Farms			Land in farms (acres)				Value of farm products sold			
							Percent–								Percent from–	
	Number	Percent of total[1]	Total ($1,000)	Percent of total[2]	1997 ($1,000)	Number	Less than 50 acres	500 acres or more	Total acreage (1,000)	Net change, 1992–1997[3] (1,000)	Average size of farm	Total cropland (1,000)	Total ($1,000)	Average per farm (dollars)	Crops[4]	Livestock and poultry[5]
VIRGINIA—Con.																
Prince Edward	565	3.3	3 106	1.4	2 971	312	17.6	10.9	73	4	234	35	13 521	43 337	13.7	86.3
Prince George	336	1.2	[6]–1 020	X	[6]383	[6]133	[6]28.6	[6]16.5	[6]45	[6]–4	[6]338	[6]21	[6]5 829	[6]43 827	[6]88.0	[6]12.0
Prince William	653	.3	[7]1 681	Z	[7]1 968	[7]261	[7]47.9	[7]4.6	[7]36	[7]3	[7]138	[7]26	[7]9 733	[7]37 291	[7]50.2	[7]49.8
Pulaski	667	1.9	1 670	.3	841	370	31.6	8.9	80	9	217	40	12 973	35 062	7.5	92.5
Rappahannock	427	6.4	592	1.1	280	335	34.6	11.9	72	–7	215	36	5 539	16 534	35.4	64.6
Richmond	537	7.4	–1 408	X	1 644	139	27.3	18.7	36	–3	262	26	8 885	63 921	94.5	5.5
Roanoke	339	.4	[8]–116	X	[8]–93	[9]273	[9]48.7	[9]1.8	[9]27	[9]2	[9]98	[9]12	[9]5 042	[9]18 469	[9]51.2	[9]48.8
Rockbridge	940	5.1	[10]2 584	[10].6	[10]1 648	[10]631	[10]24.1	[10]8.9	[10]140	[10]–2	[10]222	[10]64	[10]15 446	[10]24 479	[10]10.8	[10]89.2
Rockingham	4 032	7.0	[11]71 329	[11]4.1	[11]47 433	[11]1 834	[11]38.5	[11]3.8	[11]230	[11]–6	[11]126	[11]145	[11]438 103	[11]238 878	[11]2.7	[11]97.3
Russell	1 287	4.5	2 374	.9	1 645	1 026	37.0	5.1	153	–8	149	62	18 600	18 129	31.0	69.0
Scott	2 280	9.8	1 386	1.2	551	1 400	39.5	1.7	138	3	98	54	14 205	10 146	58.3	41.7
Shenandoah	1 270	4.0	18 353	4.3	14 824	841	35.3	5.5	127	1	151	73	73 044	86 854	10.2	89.8
Smyth	1 439	4.4	2 187	.5	373	774	41.7	7.0	125	5	162	57	19 579	25 296	18.1	81.9
Southampton	901	5.1	[12]10 740	[12]4.3	[12]15 692	[12]277	[12]13.4	[12]41.2	[12]185	[12]7	[12]670	[12]103	[12]55 090	[12]198 881	[12]76.3	[12]23.7
Spotsylvania	840	1.5	[13]–207	X	(14)	[13]253	[13]34.4	[13]8.7	[13]48	[13]–5	[13]190	[13]24	[13]6 069	[13]23 988	[13]36.7	[13]63.3
Stafford	255	.4	–174	X	(14)	158	44.3	4.4	20	Z	126	11	2 043	12 930	60.1	39.9
Surry	491	8.0	–177	X	3 046	115	27.0	28.7	45	–8	390	32	19 536	169 878	44.5	55.5
Sussex	685	6.7	2 255	2.2	7 608	134	19.4	35.8	82	–1	608	45	D	D	D	D
Tazewell	383	.8	3 539	.8	3 145	488	30.7	13.3	134	–5	274	50	13 037	26 715	6.1	93.9
Warren	239	.9	494	.2	198	259	35.5	9.3	45	6	173	23	5 539	21 386	10.8	89.2
Washington	2 847	6.2	[15]8 376	[15].9	[15]8 606	[15]1 744	[15]51.3	[15]3.6	[15]178	[15]–12	[15]102	[15]91	[15]50 809	[15]29 134	[15]25.5	[15]74.5
Westmoreland	531	3.4	2 123	2.4	4 351	160	24.4	23.8	63	6	392	42	19 743	123 394	93.9	6.1
Wise	263	.7	[16]–565	X	[16]–566	[16]137	[16]53.3	[16]5.8	[16]16	[16]3	[16]118	[16]7	[16]1 264	[16]9 226	[16]30.5	[16]69.5
Wythe	818	3.2	1 503	.5	658	734	27.9	9.3	140	8	190	78	24 415	33 263	7.1	92.9
York	52	.1	[17]511	[17].1	[17]624	[18]39	[18]64.1	[18]2.6	[18]2	Z	[18]51	[18]1	[18]2 294	[18]58 821	D	D
Independent Cities																
Alexandria	–	–	–	–	–	(19)	(19)	(19)	(19)	(19)	(19)	(19)	(19)	(19)	(19)	(19)
Bedford	–	–	(20)	(20)	(14)	(20)	(20)	(20)	(20)	(20)	(20)	(20)	(20)	(20)	(20)	(20)
Bristol	–	–	(15)	(15)	(15)	(15)	(15)	(15)	(15)	(15)	(15)	(15)	(15)	(15)	(15)	(15)
Buena Vista	–	–	(10)	(10)	(10)	(10)	(10)	(10)	(10)	(10)	(10)	(10)	(10)	(10)	(10)	(10)
Charlottesville	–	–	(21)	(21)	(21)	(21)	(21)	(21)	(21)	(21)	(21)	(21)	(21)	(21)	(21)	(21)
Chesapeake	339	.2	4 946	.2	7 399	[22]201	[22]53.7	[22]15.4	[22]61	[22]6	[22]302	[22]51	[22]36 314	[22]180 667	[22]90.3	[22]9.7
Clifton Forge	–	–	(23)	(23)	(23)	(23)	(23)	(23)	(23)	(23)	(23)	(23)	(23)	(23)	(23)	(23)
Colonial Heights	–	–	(24)	(24)	(24)	(25)	(25)	(25)	(25)	(25)	(25)	(25)	(25)	(25)	(25)	(25)
Covington	–	–	(23)	(23)	(23)	(23)	(23)	(23)	(23)	(23)	(23)	(23)	(23)	(23)	(23)	(23)
Danville	–	–	(26)	(26)	(26)	(26)	(26)	(26)	(26)	(26)	(26)	(26)	(26)	(26)	(26)	(26)
Emporia	–	–	(27)	(27)	(27)	(27)	(27)	(27)	(27)	(27)	(27)	(27)	(27)	(27)	(27)	(27)
Fairfax	–	–	(28)	(28)	(28)	(19)	(19)	(19)	(19)	(19)	(19)	(19)	(19)	(19)	(19)	(19)
Falls Church	–	–	(28)	(28)	(28)	(19)	(19)	(19)	(19)	(19)	(19)	(19)	(19)	(19)	(19)	(19)
Franklin	–	–	(12)	(12)	(12)	(12)	(12)	(12)	(12)	(12)	(12)	(12)	(12)	(12)	(12)	(12)
Fredericksburg	–	–	(13)	(13)	(14)	(13)	(13)	(13)	(13)	(13)	(13)	(13)	(13)	(13)	(13)	(13)
Galax	–	–	(29)	(29)	(29)	(30)	(30)	(30)	(30)	(30)	(30)	(30)	(30)	(30)	(30)	(30)
Hampton	–	–	–	–	–	(18)	(18)	(18)	(18)	(18)	(18)	(18)	(18)	(18)	(18)	(18)
Harrisonburg	–	–	(11)	(11)	(11)	(11)	(11)	(11)	(11)	(11)	(11)	(11)	(11)	(11)	(11)	(11)
Hopewell	–	–	(6)	(6)	(6)	(6)	(6)	(6)	(6)	(6)	(6)	(6)	(6)	(6)	(6)	(6)
Lexington	–	–	(10)	(10)	(10)	(10)	(10)	(10)	(10)	(10)	(10)	(10)	(10)	(10)	(10)	(10)
Lynchburg	–	–	(31)	(31)	(31)	(31)	(31)	(31)	(31)	(31)	(31)	(31)	(31)	(31)	(31)	(31)
Manassas	–	–	(7)	(7)	(7)	(7)	(7)	(7)	(7)	(7)	(7)	(7)	(7)	(7)	(7)	(7)
Manassas Park	–	–	(7)	(7)	(7)	(7)	(7)	(7)	(7)	(7)	(7)	(7)	(7)	(7)	(7)	(7)
Martinsville	–	–	(32)	(32)	(32)	(32)	(32)	(32)	(32)	(32)	(32)	(32)	(32)	(32)	(32)	(32)
Newport News	–	–	–	–	–	(18)	(18)	(18)	(18)	(18)	(18)	(18)	(18)	(18)	(18)	(18)
Norfolk	–	–	–	–	–	(22)	(22)	(22)	(22)	(22)	(22)	(22)	(22)	(22)	(22)	(22)
Norton	–	–	(16)	(16)	(16)	(16)	(16)	(16)	(16)	(16)	(16)	(16)	(16)	(16)	(16)	(16)
Petersburg	–	–	(24)	(24)	(24)	(33)	(33)	(33)	(33)	(33)	(33)	(33)	(33)	(33)	(33)	(33)
Poquoson	–	–	(17)	(17)	(17)	(18)	(18)	(18)	(18)	(18)	(18)	(18)	(18)	(18)	(18)	(18)
Portsmouth	–	–	–	–	–	(22)	(22)	(22)	(22)	(22)	(22)	(22)	(22)	(22)	(22)	(22)
Radford	–	–	(34)	(34)	(34)	(34)	(34)	(34)	(34)	(34)	(34)	(34)	(34)	(34)	(34)	(34)
Richmond	–	–	–	–	–	(35)	(35)	(35)	(35)	(35)	(35)	(35)	(35)	(35)	(35)	(35)
Roanoke	–	–	–	–	–	(9)	(9)	(9)	(9)	(9)	(9)	(9)	(9)	(9)	(9)	(9)
Salem	–	–	(8)	(8)	(8)	(9)	(9)	(9)	(9)	(9)	(9)	(9)	(9)	(9)	(9)	(9)
South Boston	–	–	X	X	X	X	X	X	X	X	X	X	X	X	X	X
Staunton	44	.2	(36)	(36)	(36)	(36)	(36)	(36)	(36)	(36)	(36)	(36)	(36)	(36)	(36)	(36)
Suffolk	896	1.7	2 826	.5	3 854	218	34.4	20.2	76	–7	350	57	38 672	177 394	84.1	15.9
Virginia Beach	230	.1	3 648	.1	5 124	147	61.9	8.8	30	–13	204	25	13 638	92 776	76.8	23.2
Waynesboro	–	–	(36)	(36)	(36)	(36)	(36)	(36)	(36)	(36)	(36)	(36)	(36)	(36)	(36)	(36)
Williamsburg	–	–	(37)	(37)	(37)	(37)	(37)	(37)	(37)	(37)	(37)	(37)	(37)	(37)	(37)	(37)
Winchester	–	–	(38)	(38)	(38)	(38)	(38)	(38)	(38)	(38)	(38)	(38)	(38)	(38)	(38)	(38)

[1] For 1990 corrected population, see table B-1. Percent is based on 1990 uncorrected population because only total population is corrected. [2] For total earnings, see table B-8. [3] Most data are comparable between 1992 and 1997; however, it should be noted that farms with all acreage in Conservation or Wetlands Reserve Programs (excluded in 1992) are included in 1997, as are short rotation woody crops which includes Christmas trees and maple sap gathering (in Forestry in 1992). [4] Includes nursery and greenhouse crops. [5] Includes related products. [6] Prince George County includes Hopewell city. [7] Prince William County includes Manassas and Manassas Park cities. [8] Roanoke County includes Salem city. [9] Roanoke County includes Roanoke and Salem cities. [10] Rockbridge County includes Buena Vista and Lexington cities. [11] Rockingham County includes Harrisonburg city. [12] Southhampton County includes Franklin city. [13] Spotsylvania County includes Fredericksburg city. [14] Less than $50,000. [15] Washington County includes Bristol city. [16] Wise County includes Norton city. [17] York County includes Poquoson city. [18] York County includes Hampton, Newport News, and Poquoson cities. [19] Fairfax County includes Alexandria, Fairfax, and Falls Church cities. [20] Bedford County includes Bedford city. [21] Albemarle County includes Charlottesville city. [22] Chesapeake City includes Norfolk and Portsmouth cities. [23] Alleghany County includes Clifton Forge and Covington cities. [24] Dinwiddie County includes Colonial Heights and Petersburg cities. [25] Chesterfield County includes Colonial Heights city. [26] Pittsylvania County includes Danville city. [27] Greensville County includes Emporia city. [28] Fairfax County includes Fairfax and Falls Church cities. [29] Carroll County includes Galax city. [30] Grayson County includes Galax city. [31] Campbell County includes Lynchburg city. [32] Henry County includes Martinsville city. [33] Dinwiddie County includes Petersburg city. [34] Montgomery County includes Radford city. [35] Henrico County includes Richmond city. [36] Augusta County includes Staunton and Waynesboro cities. [37] James City County includes Williamsburg city. [38] Frederick County includes Winchester city.

Sources: Farm Population—U.S. Census Bureau, 1990 Census of Population and Housing, Summary Tape File (STF) 3C on CD-ROM (related Internet site <http://homer.ssd.census.gov/cdrom/lookup>). Farm Earnings—U.S. Bureau of Economic Analysis, "Regional Economic Information System (REIS) 1969-1998" on CD-ROM (related Internet site <http://www.bea.doc.gov/bea/regional/reis/ca45/>). Agriculture—U.S. Department of Agriculture, National Agricultural Statistics Service, 1997 Census of Agriculture, Volume 1, Geographic Area Series, 1A, 1B, 1C CD-ROM Set (related Internet site <http://www.nass.usda.gov/census/>).

Table B–10. Counties — Farm Population, Farm Earnings, and Agriculture–Con.

[Includes U.S., states, and 3,142 counties/county equivalents defined as of January 1, 1992. For changes to these areas since January 1, 1992, see appendix B. Geographic Information]

County	Farm population, 1990 Number	Farm population, 1990 Percent of total[1]	Farm earnings 1998 Total ($1,000)	Farm earnings 1998 Percent of total[2]	Farm earnings 1997 ($1,000)	Farms Number	Farms Percent– Less than 50 acres	Farms Percent– 500 acres or more	Land in farms (acres) Total acreage (1,000)	Land in farms (acres) Net change, 1992–1997[3] (1,000)	Land in farms (acres) Average size of farm	Land in farms (acres) Total cropland (1,000)	Value of farm products sold Total ($1,000)	Value of farm products sold Average per farm (dollars)	Value of farm products sold Percent from– Crops[4]	Value of farm products sold Percent from– Livestock and poultry[5]
WASHINGTON	60 243	1.2	1 503 168	1.3	1 291 353	29 011	51.4	16.2	15 180	−546	523	7 914	4 767 727	164 342	68.2	31.8
Adams	823	6.1	30 161	16.0	29 005	628	10.5	56.7	1 096	100	1 746	809	201 873	321 454	92.0	8.0
Asotin	292	1.7	−2 830	X	−689	140	22.1	62.1	304	30	2 175	87	9 743	69 593	65.5	34.5
Benton	1 613	1.4	105 759	4.3	93 324	1 078	67.3	10.4	612	−28	568	440	300 530	278 785	97.1	2.9
Chelan	3 029	5.8	90 514	8.0	84 636	1 113	71.1	3.3	124	12	111	41	146 403	131 539	99.5	.5
Clallam	543	1.0	2 385	.3	1 702	292	66.8	2.1	21	−3	72	12	6 011	20 586	45.4	54.6
Clark	2 274	1.0	12 457	.3	9 091	1 175	71.5	1.6	73	−10	62	43	43 083	36 666	39.6	60.4
Columbia	263	6.5	5 987	12.3	4 556	198	20.7	51.5	310	5	1 567	178	24 477	123 621	92.0	8.0
Cowlitz	713	.9	7 064	.5	5 991	349	59.3	2.6	31	−5	89	15	15 919	45 613	45.6	54.4
Douglas	1 533	5.9	19 452	8.6	15 427	853	51.3	27.8	906	−12	1 063	533	117 623	137 893	95.5	4.5
Ferry	325	5.2	2 355	3.7	2 456	179	18.4	31.3	810	62	4 524	22	5 013	28 006	26.5	73.5
Franklin	2 040	5.4	116 120	17.1	104 964	848	30.8	26.5	564	−106	665	D	332 935	392 612	86.5	13.5
Garfield	428	19.0	312	1.4	430	182	11.0	65.9	325	Z	1 787	192	24 685	135 632	88.9	11.1
Grant	3 779	6.9	211 825	21.6	174 337	1 699	28.5	28.0	1 095	9	645	786	804 252	473 368	68.9	31.1
Grays Harbor	831	1.3	9 897	1.2	7 914	389	50.9	5.4	42	−2	109	24	15 029	38 635	32.6	67.4
Island	343	.6	3 830	.4	2 448	261	67.8	.8	16	−4	61	11	10 538	40 375	14.8	85.2
Jefferson	266	1.3	2 248	.9	1 780	144	54.9	2.1	13	3	91	8	4 321	30 007	12.9	87.1
King	1 954	.1	39 454	.1	28 851	1 091	83.9	1.0	42	−1	38	24	93 791	85 968	41.1	58.9
Kitsap	822	.4	1 759	.1	1 030	359	84.7	.6	19	9	53	6	12 233	34 075	32.6	67.4
Kittitas	1 150	4.3	14 274	3.8	15 488	757	50.3	12.2	178	−178	235	87	79 634	105 197	60.4	39.6
Klickitat	693	4.2	9 278	4.3	8 686	530	36.0	30.0	589	−101	1 111	186	33 231	62 700	71.4	28.6
Lewis	1 687	2.8	27 529	3.2	21 279	1 117	51.7	1.8	118	5	105	62	82 778	74 107	28.3	71.7
Lincoln	1 278	14.4	4 252	4.7	14 111	707	7.1	73.8	1 376	−90	1 946	876	107 808	152 487	91.9	8.1
Mason	335	.9	822	.2	−509	211	75.4	1.9	20	9	95	7	13 365	63 341	D	D
Okanogan	2 404	7.2	49 645	10.7	44 788	1 270	47.5	18.0	1 179	−112	928	142	133 521	105 135	87.1	12.9
Pacific	232	1.2	12 931	6.5	10 906	253	48.6	7.1	40	8	159	15	16 964	67 051	48.5	51.5
Pend Oreille	185	2.1	1 514	1.6	1 462	225	30.7	14.7	63	8	281	27	2 879	12 796	40.0	60.0
Pierce	1 528	.3	31 289	.3	24 314	989	75.4	.9	51	−8	51	24	69 835	70 612	39.7	60.3
San Juan	188	1.9	−486	X	−642	174	56.3	2.9	17	−4	97	12	2 653	15 247	14.1	85.9
Skagit	1 843	2.3	87 225	6.1	71 094	714	53.8	5.5	93	1	131	73	171 690	240 462	52.6	47.4
Skamania	140	1.7	−541	X	−553	63	52.4	–	4	Z	67	2	1 532	24 317	86.7	13.3
Snohomish	3 157	.7	24 876	.3	14 777	1 139	75.9	1.8	61	−14	53	40	112 881	99 105	30.8	69.2
Spokane	3 210	.9	11 400	.2	10 052	1 643	44.1	17.3	590	−36	359	398	78 704	47 903	74.2	25.8
Stevens	1 831	5.9	5 484	1.6	5 877	989	27.8	16.8	525	−21	531	123	22 815	23 069	39.5	60.5
Thurston	1 865	1.2	27 776	.9	19 302	832	72.7	2.4	56	−4	68	27	120 712	145 087	29.9	70.1
Wahkiakum	288	8.7	240	.8	−97	108	33.3	5.6	13	1	124	9	2 715	25 139	3.3	96.7
Walla Walla	1 065	2.2	45 007	5.9	43 386	716	36.9	36.3	715	4	998	598	256 930	358 841	D	D
Whatcom	3 596	2.8	92 157	3.9	64 349	1 228	57.1	2.4	104	−15	84	81	241 643	196 778	16.5	83.5
Whitman	2 457	6.3	3 603	.7	11 520	1 003	12.4	68.3	1 301	−103	1 297	1 067	173 483	172 964	93.5	6.5
Yakima	9 237	4.9	396 084	13.7	344 510	3 365	63.0	6.6	1 683	43	500	D	873 495	259 582	66.5	33.5
WEST VIRGINIA	23 753	1.3	−4 845	X	−6 461	17 772	21.1	7.5	3 456	188	194	1 337	447 428	25 176	14.5	85.5
Barbour	438	2.8	−552	X	−465	437	14.4	7.8	87	10	198	39	3 927	8 986	11.7	88.3
Berkeley	879	1.5	2 758	.3	3 632	509	36.5	3.9	73	−1	143	47	18 171	35 699	64.3	35.7
Boone	169	.7	(6)	Z	(6)	23	39.1	–	2	Z	102	Z	45	1 957	71.1	28.9
Braxton	301	2.3	−639	X	−977	280	11.8	11.1	67	−6	240	24	1 731	6 182	9.9	90.1
Brooke	112	.4	82	Z	87	95	25.3	4.2	14	1	143	7	1 100	11 579	30.9	69.2
Cabell	417	.4	−207	X	−293	305	28.9	1.3	32	−4	105	10	2 263	7 420	81.0	19.0
Calhoun	105	1.3	−238	X	−254	171	8.2	7.6	38	4	225	12	686	4 012	8.9	91.3
Clay	301	3.0	74	.1	(6)	100	7.0	3.0	17	2	173	5	540	5 400	24.6	75.2
Doddridge	161	2.3	−1 036	X	−1 050	302	10.3	10.3	71	11	234	27	1 046	3 464	18.1	81.9
Fayette	289	.6	157	Z	(6)	205	25.9	2.0	23	3	113	10	1 573	7 673	27.9	72.1
Gilmer	330	4.3	−1 039	X	−920	214	5.1	17.3	63	11	296	25	1 949	9 107	8.7	91.3
Grant	474	4.5	650	.5	781	375	17.9	22.1	122	16	325	34	34 412	91 765	1.2	98.8
Greenbrier	986	2.8	1 855	.5	1 546	727	23.0	12.1	184	5	254	62	40 278	55 403	2.7	97.3
Hampshire	882	5.3	1 919	1.7	1 144	547	21.8	12.4	140	5	257	50	15 709	28 718	18.5	81.5
Hancock	161	.5	−82	X	−70	64	37.5	1.6	7	−1	112	3	578	9 031	74.2	25.8
Hardy	707	6.4	3 122	2.2	3 406	467	22.9	15.8	143	1	306	43	109 461	234 392	1.5	98.5
Harrison	750	1.1	−2 288	X	−2 430	601	23.5	6.0	103	15	172	48	4 756	7 913	14.3	85.7
Jackson	587	2.3	−3 264	X	−3 253	730	18.9	4.0	117	15	160	48	4 362	5 975	30.0	70.0
Jefferson	886	2.5	2 833	.7	3 911	357	40.9	10.4	73	−1	204	56	19 412	54 375	42.7	57.3
Kanawha	181	.1	−87	X	−76	154	35.1	1.9	19	−1	126	6	1 419	9 214	74.0	25.9
Lewis	475	2.8	−623	X	−179	364	16.5	10.2	79	−2	218	33	2 996	8 231	15.6	84.4
Lincoln	467	2.2	496	.6	278	214	30.4	3.3	27	−3	128	9	1 187	5 547	85.5	14.5
Logan	179	.4	106	Z	128	10	40.0	–	D	D	D	D	D	D	D	D
McDowell	221	.6	–		–	7	42.9	–	Z	−1	70	Z	D	D	D	D

[1] For 1990 corrected population, see table B-1. Percent is based on 1990 uncorrected population because only total population is corrected. [2] For total earnings, see table B-8. [3] Most data are comparable between 1992 and 1997; however, it should be noted that farms with all acreage in Conservation or Wetlands Reserve Programs (excluded in 1992) are included in 1997, as are short rotation woody crops which includes Christmas trees and maple sap gathering (in Forestry in 1992). [4] Includes nursery and greenhouse crops. [5] Includes related products. [6] Less than $50,000.

Sources: Farm Population—U.S. Census Bureau, 1990 Census of Population and Housing, Summary Tape File (STF) 3C on CD-ROM (related Internet site <http://homer.ssd.census.gov/cdrom/lookup>). Farm Earnings—U.S. Bureau of Economic Analysis, "Regional Economic Information System (REIS) 1969-1998" on CD-ROM (related Internet site <http://www.bea.doc.gov/bea/regional/reis/ca45/>). Agriculture—U.S. Department of Agriculture, National Agricultural Statistics Service, 1997 Census of Agriculture, Volume 1, Geographic Area Series, 1A, 1B, 1C CD-ROM Set (related Internet site <http://www.nass.usda.gov/census/>).

[Includes U.S., states, and 3,142 counties/county equivalents defined as of January 1, 1992. For changes to these areas since January 1, 1992, see appendix B. Geographic Information]

County	Farm population, 1990		Farm earnings			Agriculture (NAICS 111-112), 1997										
			1998			Farms			Land in farms (acres)				Value of farm products sold			
							Percent–								Percent from–	
	Number	Percent of total[1]	Total ($1,000)	Percent of total[2]	1997 ($1,000)	Number	Less than 50 acres	500 acres or more	Total acreage (1,000)	Net change, 1992–1997[3]	Average size of farm	Total cropland (1,000)	Total ($1,000)	Average per farm (dollars)	Crops[4]	Livestock and poultry[5]
WEST VIRGINIA—Con.																
Marion	470	.8	-833	X	-832	317	19.6	1.6	39	-1	124	19	1 629	5 139	43.8	56.3
Marshall	484	1.3	-1 085	X	-1 219	536	16.2	1.5	78	14	146	32	2 923	5 453	19.0	81.0
Mason	939	3.7	-420	X	-815	742	22.6	5.1	121	3	162	49	15 092	20 340	49.3	50.7
Mercer	364	.6	-925	X	-933	409	29.3	3.4	53	-3	131	18	2 539	6 208	28.0	72.0
Mineral	431	1.6	1 443	.8	590	343	22.2	11.1	80	5	232	27	8 372	24 408	8.5	91.5
Mingo	60	.2	–	–	–	5	80.0	–	D	D	D	D	6	1 200	–	100.0
Monongalia	693	.9	-2 491	X	-2 623	430	24.9	2.8	58	3	135	28	2 890	6 721	18.5	81.5
Monroe	828	6.7	-419	X	-311	617	18.0	9.9	139	-10	225	48	19 321	31 314	9.9	90.1
Morgan	191	1.6	-238	X	-235	161	21.7	5.0	28	6	175	11	1 308	8 124	63.1	36.9
Nicholas	380	1.4	-590	X	-340	304	28.9	3.0	40	7	130	17	2 542	8 362	12.7	87.3
Ohio	164	.3	-69	X	-251	136	14.7	3.7	21	Z	155	13	1 790	13 162	12.7	87.3
Pendleton	910	11.3	2 744	3.8	2 755	590	19.5	17.3	175	-3	297	45	67 654	114 668	1.1	98.9
Pleasants	171	2.3	-175	X	-84	132	15.9	6.1	21	6	162	6	766	5 803	22.2	77.8
Pocahontas	454	5.0	(6)	Z	-211	357	14.0	18.5	129	13	361	38	5 141	14 401	11.5	88.5
Preston	1 030	3.5	(6)	Z	-240	866	20.3	4.5	152	13	175	74	10 597	12 237	22.1	77.9
Putnam	569	1.3	310	.1	85	454	24.7	.9	57	1	126	21	4 372	9 630	77.9	22.1
Raleigh	257	.3	-513	X	-424	260	33.8	4.2	35	3	136	14	2 013	7 742	38.6	61.4
Randolph	459	1.7	1 449	.5	1 350	396	18.9	16.4	104	Z	263	36	5 646	14 258	13.7	86.3
Ritchie	366	3.6	-1 760	X	-1 699	352	8.8	11.1	87	16	247	35	2 244	6 375	17.4	82.7
Roane	453	3.0	-1 618	X	-1 613	454	12.1	6.6	93	11	204	41	2 626	5 784	11.5	88.5
Summers	358	2.5	-1 856	X	-1 859	316	19.0	5.7	57	-1	181	20	3 642	11 525	20.5	79.6
Taylor	540	3.6	1 351	1.4	735	278	29.5	6.5	44	2	157	17	3 675	13 219	42.2	57.7
Tucker	322	4.2	-147	X	-160	191	19.9	5.8	35	3	184	11	1 138	5 958	19.0	80.9
Tyler	126	1.3	505	.5	338	234	13.7	6.8	48	1	205	20	1 115	4 765	16.4	83.6
Upshur	469	2.1	-2 151	X	-1 896	399	23.8	4.5	64	6	161	28	2 532	6 346	16.5	83.5
Wayne	276	.7	55	Z	(6)	151	17.9	7.9	29	–	190	8	1 447	9 583	45.7	54.3
Webster	90	.8	(6)	Z	-57	74	28.4	–	8	-1	109	3	194	2 622	23.7	76.3
Wetzel	308	1.6	-396	X	-396	260	11.2	4.6	48	11	184	13	735	2 827	25.9	74.1
Wirt	266	5.1	-180	X	-276	199	15.1	6.0	37	1	186	15	2 633	13 231	54.2	45.8
Wood	471	.5	-760	X	-740	520	21.5	1.5	67	7	128	29	2 836	5 454	35.3	64.7
Wyoming	396	1.4	(6)	Z	(6)	31	38.7	6.5	4	-2	128	1	180	5 806	58.3	41.7
WISCONSIN	195 550	4.0	839 302	.9	456 193	65 602	19.5	9.2	14 900	-563	227	10 353	5 579 861	85 056	29.4	70.6
Adams	730	4.7	12 273	8.9	13 350	360	15.3	14.7	122	2	338	84	58 306	161 961	90.4	9.6
Ashland	413	2.5	-1 091	X	-1 746	186	10.8	9.7	47	-5	250	24	4 921	26 457	11.0	89.0
Barron	4 303	10.6	27 402	4.4	17 360	1 384	13.5	7.9	325	-26	235	218	164 557	118 900	14.1	85.9
Bayfield	711	5.1	159	.1	-1 148	325	13.8	12.0	84	-13	259	48	9 839	30 274	19.6	80.4
Brown	3 495	1.8	31 215	.6	14 729	1 059	31.4	6.2	196	-9	185	168	128 466	121 309	13.9	86.1
Buffalo	2 759	20.3	7 020	3.9	-1 649	1 000	11.2	17.7	309	-15	309	171	102 160	102 160	15.1	84.9
Burnett	938	7.2	-113	X	-182	351	12.5	10.3	83	-1	236	45	14 187	40 419	39.0	61.0
Calumet	2 570	7.5	14 734	3.5	5 984	703	23.0	6.5	144	-19	204	122	75 984	108 085	17.1	82.9
Chippewa	4 907	9.4	12 691	1.7	1 753	1 471	10.7	10.5	373	-14	253	238	118 689	80 686	15.8	84.2
Clark	6 553	20.7	29 938	9.4	8 895	1 883	11.3	6.5	414	-13	220	289	159 135	84 511	9.7	90.3
Columbia	4 148	9.2	2 369	.4	2 868	1 359	21.5	12.2	326	-1	240	253	106 871	78 639	43.2	56.8
Crawford	2 522	15.8	-654	X	-3 231	958	12.8	9.3	233	-15	244	114	39 983	41 736	21.5	78.5
Dane	7 307	2.0	43 194	.4	25 465	2 595	30.1	8.1	513	-26	198	414	284 637	109 687	31.1	68.9
Dodge	7 100	9.3	35 523	2.9	27 133	1 807	20.0	8.7	392	-22	217	331	193 585	107 131	26.4	73.6
Door	1 680	6.5	10 742	2.9	5 748	702	23.4	4.1	122	-8	174	93	38 296	54 553	31.2	68.8
Douglas	374	.9	-464	X	-736	267	15.0	11.6	71	Z	265	34	5 689	21 307	21.2	78.8
Dunn	4 017	11.2	12 896	2.7	8 167	1 397	14.3	11.3	369	2	264	235	114 375	81 872	25.6	74.4
Eau Claire	2 659	3.1	9 781	.6	5 627	927	17.0	5.7	191	1	206	133	57 778	62 328	30.0	70.0
Florence	152	3.3	-411	X	-1 016	86	10.5	9.3	19	-2	225	11	1 850	21 512	26.2	73.8
Fond du Lac	4 803	5.3	27 348	1.6	13 331	1 488	17.6	8.2	325	-27	218	273	151 140	101 573	25.5	74.5
Forest	128	1.5	-189	X	-515	111	17.1	8.1	26	Z	236	12	3 698	33 315	11.4	88.6
Grant	7 343	14.9	19 344	3.6	8 826	2 238	13.7	12.0	600	-21	268	376	204 300	91 287	17.9	82.1
Green	4 138	13.6	13 381	3.0	4 146	1 295	17.4	9.8	305	12	235	249	125 372	96 812	23.3	76.7
Green Lake	1 658	8.9	11 084	4.6	8 941	584	17.5	8.7	134	-29	230	106	45 256	77 493	36.8	63.2
Iowa	3 787	18.8	4 910	1.6	-2 257	1 394	14.1	11.6	367	5	263	232	110 905	79 559	20.6	79.4
Iron	35	.6	-220	X	-255	38	7.9	10.5	10	-1	254	5	819	21 553	38.0	62.0
Jackson	2 181	13.1	22 493	11.2	17 810	774	13.2	13.4	244	26	315	133	77 915	100 665	53.2	46.8
Jefferson	3 935	5.8	16 901	1.5	14 081	1 240	25.8	7.0	242	10	195	200	131 266	105 860	45.2	54.8
Juneau	1 984	9.2	11 120	4.0	7 534	654	16.5	10.1	169	-26	259	110	52 541	80 338	54.3	45.7
Kenosha	1 191	.9	1 955	.1	2 602	388	40.5	12.4	85	-8	218	74	33 251	85 698	63.9	36.1
Kewaunee	2 722	14.4	15 713	7.0	5 162	795	16.4	6.4	161	-9	203	132	80 730	101 547	18.6	81.4
La Crosse	2 103	2.1	6 903	.3	4 133	759	14.9	9.2	170	-13	223	89	45 758	60 287	19.7	80.3

[1] For 1990 corrected population, see table B-1. Percent is based on 1990 uncorrected population because only total population is corrected. [2] For total earnings, see table B-8. [3] Most data are comparable between 1992 and 1997; however, it should be noted that farms with all acreage in Conservation or Wetlands Reserve Programs (excluded in 1992) are included in 1997, as are short rotation woody crops which includes Christmas trees and maple sap gathering (in Forestry in 1992). [4] Includes nursery and greenhouse crops. [5] Includes related products. [6] Less than $50,000.

Sources: Farm Population—U.S. Census Bureau, 1990 Census of Population and Housing, Summary Tape File (STF) 3C on CD-ROM (related Internet site <http://homer.ssd.census.gov/cdrom/lookup>). Farm Earnings—U.S. Bureau of Economic Analysis, "Regional Economic Information System (REIS) 1969-1998" on CD-ROM (related Internet site <http://www.bea.doc.gov/bea/regional/reis/ca45/>). Agriculture—U.S. Department of Agriculture, National Agricultural Statistics Service, 1997 Census of Agriculture, Volume 1, Geographic Area Series, 1A, 1B, 1C CD-ROM Set (related Internet site <http://www.nass.usda.gov/census/>).

Table B–10. Counties — Farm Population, Farm Earnings, and Agriculture–Con.

[Includes U.S., states, and 3,142 counties/county equivalents defined as of January 1, 1992. For changes to these areas since January 1, 1992, see appendix B. Geographic Information]

County	Farm population, 1990 Number	Farm population, 1990 Per-cent of total[1]	Farm earnings 1998 Total ($1,000)	Farm earnings 1998 Per-cent of total[2]	Farm earnings 1997 ($1,000)	Farms Number	Farms Percent Less than 50 acres	Farms Percent 500 acres or more	Land in farms Total acreage (1,000)	Land in farms Net change, 1992–1997[3] (1,000)	Land in farms Aver-age size of farm	Land in farms Total cropland (1,000)	Value Total ($1,000)	Value Average per farm (dollars)	Value Percent from Crops[4]	Value Percent from Live-stock and poultry[5]
WISCONSIN—Con.																
Lafayette	3 977	24.7	11 920	9.6	6 076	1 127	16.0	14.2	338	−18	300	263	136 208	120 859	28.6	71.4
Langlade	1 009	5.2	8 532	3.6	7 823	453	19.4	13.0	124	4	273	82	50 915	112 395	57.3	42.7
Lincoln	1 204	4.5	1 759	.5	227	425	15.1	6.4	84	−2	197	44	20 290	47 741	33.4	66.6
Manitowoc	4 488	5.6	38 805	3.0	21 383	1 227	23.3	8.1	245	−4	200	206	138 456	112 841	13.6	86.4
Marathon	8 047	7.0	41 901	1.9	16 898	2 703	23.3	6.2	516	−14	191	337	204 288	75 578	24.7	75.3
Marinette	1 284	3.2	9 689	1.6	5 522	551	15.6	11.1	132	−14	239	83	39 586	71 844	18.4	81.6
Marquette	1 029	8.4	1 484	1.3	2 752	443	17.8	14.4	125	−11	282	86	32 281	72 869	53.5	46.5
Menominee	15	.4	–	–	–	5	60.0	–	Z	D	77	D	13	2 600	D	D
Milwaukee	–	–	1 019	Z	1 095	83	67.5	2.4	6	−2	76	D	6 820	82 169	D	D
Monroe	4 742	12.9	22 781	4.3	11 100	1 567	14.3	7.0	330	−17	210	178	101 789	64 958	33.5	66.5
Oconto	2 533	8.4	11 235	3.9	4 727	940	15.1	8.1	204	−5	217	144	66 618	70 870	19.4	80.6
Oneida	85	.3	3 844	.7	3 304	117	25.6	14.5	39	7	334	16	13 290	113 590	85.5	14.5
Outagamie	4 414	3.1	31 685	1.0	18 868	1 286	26.4	7.6	252	−11	196	212	142 184	110 563	23.7	76.3
Ozaukee	1 074	1.5	3 909	.3	1 017	427	34.7	6.1	70	−9	164	59	32 047	75 052	34.5	65.5
Pepin	1 339	18.8	3 997	5.5	1 547	425	15.8	10.4	104	−10	245	66	29 421	69 226	27.0	73.0
Pierce	3 449	10.5	4 391	1.5	1 448	1 265	20.5	7.9	268	−5	212	184	76 374	60 375	30.2	69.8
Polk	3 147	9.1	8 729	2.1	2 179	1 301	17.6	8.2	268	−15	206	171	67 944	52 224	23.5	76.5
Portage	2 860	4.7	21 760	2.1	18 975	913	14.8	12.2	263	−3	288	189	115 093	126 060	67.6	32.4
Price	846	5.4	2 563	1.2	710	370	10.0	10.5	93	−2	250	40	15 155	40 959	27.6	72.4
Racine	1 435	.8	12 877	.4	12 846	554	41.0	9.4	123	−10	222	110	78 438	141 585	53.7	46.3
Richland	3 059	17.5	6 063	3.5	2 605	1 032	13.2	8.5	238	−33	231	128	61 143	59 247	14.9	85.1
Rock	3 863	2.8	12 858	.5	11 416	1 324	32.6	12.9	351	8	265	308	129 628	97 906	56.9	43.1
Rusk	1 902	12.6	5 125	3.0	891	578	9.3	10.7	159	−9	275	83	32 479	56 192	6.9	93.1
St. Croix	4 259	8.5	6 109	.8	−117	1 520	23.9	7.4	312	4	205	237	91 606	60 267	28.2	71.8
Sauk	4 398	9.4	10 176	1.1	7 431	1 452	16.9	10.6	333	−3	229	213	121 224	83 488	18.2	81.8
Sawyer	384	2.7	1 686	1.0	1 018	184	16.8	13.6	48	1	263	27	10 220	55 543	33.6	66.4
Shawano	4 261	11.5	28 601	7.4	14 308	1 337	15.3	6.4	270	−28	202	184	126 533	94 639	10.0	90.0
Sheboygan	3 003	2.9	20 688	1.0	10 308	968	32.2	8.5	182	−25	188	153	92 206	95 254	19.1	80.9
Taylor	3 171	16.8	2 555	1.0	−5 311	887	13.0	10.5	224	−8	252	122	61 754	69 621	9.0	91.0
Trempealeau	3 803	15.1	13 309	3.8	5 061	1 408	11.4	9.4	341	−8	242	211	124 348	88 315	16.2	83.8
Vernon	5 958	23.3	4 495	2.1	−2 637	1 893	17.9	5.7	344	−21	182	203	86 491	45 690	16.1	83.9
Vilas	48	.3	3 753	1.7	3 365	44	31.8	4.5	8	D	172	D	6 190	140 682	97.9	2.1
Walworth	2 890	3.9	9 288	.8	9 203	853	32.6	15.1	220	−6	258	187	93 389	109 483	48.3	51.7
Washburn	666	4.8	2 025	1.3	1 244	354	12.4	13.0	98	12	276	46	15 933	45 008	37.8	62.2
Washington	1 989	2.1	6 895	.4	2 776	787	30.9	5.6	127	−20	162	105	61 445	78 075	33.1	66.9
Waukesha	1 034	.3	3 433	Z	3 866	630	46.8	7.8	106	−9	168	88	42 099	66 824	64.2	35.8
Waupaca	3 359	7.3	14 228	2.1	6 219	1 129	19.8	7.2	227	−15	201	162	86 182	76 335	26.2	73.8
Waushara	1 702	8.8	14 954	9.3	14 002	634	22.7	12.0	175	7	275	127	75 001	118 298	75.3	24.7
Winnebago	2 354	1.7	3 843	.1	285	860	24.0	9.0	167	−2	195	136	61 689	71 731	31.7	68.3
Wood	3 124	4.2	28 391	1.7	20 193	968	16.9	8.6	219	−2	227	138	90 831	93 834	47.5	52.5
WYOMING	15 919	3.5	58 011	.7	167 912	9 232	16.9	50.5	34 089	1 213	3 692	2 968	898 527	97 327	19.3	80.7
Albany	390	1.3	1 601	.4	6 032	315	10.5	65.1	1 922	54	6 103	133	34 209	108 600	4.9	95.1
Big Horn	957	9.1	6 206	4.6	10 056	495	17.6	32.7	443	2	896	131	43 416	87 709	57.9	42.1
Campbell	844	2.9	−4 631	X	1 020	531	11.9	72.3	2 944	239	5 544	157	34 924	65 770	5.8	94.2
Carbon	630	3.8	3 338	1.6	10 174	310	12.9	66.8	2 282	−439	7 360	158	43 444	140 142	5.8	94.2
Converse	703	6.3	932	.6	2 061	348	8.6	69.0	2 515	152	7 228	79	26 785	76 968	6.1	93.9
Crook	746	14.1	−1 749	X	6 033	498	6.2	73.3	1 690	147	3 393	181	31 546	63 345	7.1	92.9
Fremont	1 862	5.5	2 983	.7	11 824	983	25.8	29.1	2 619	203	2 664	D	61 497	62 561	27.8	72.2
Goshen	1 478	11.9	17 937	13.5	23 569	688	12.9	51.0	1 266	31	1 840	289	130 856	190 198	20.2	79.8
Hot Springs	337	7.0	(6)	Z	2 162	147	21.1	35.4	944	36	6 423	36	9 560	65 034	10.3	89.7
Johnson	398	6.5	−3 904	X	1 557	315	10.5	71.7	2 132	76	6 767	61	27 819	88 314	4.9	95.1
Laramie	862	1.2	15 163	1.1	24 355	615	10.4	55.9	1 728	28	2 810	D	95 959	156 031	20.8	79.2
Lincoln	508	4.0	960	.6	5 202	504	27.8	25.4	408	−151	810	115	22 969	45 573	13.2	86.8
Natrona	500	.8	1 289	.1	2 560	311	20.6	48.9	2 807	298	9 025	52	26 788	86 135	11.7	88.3
Niobrara	506	20.2	−1 248	X	4 612	278	3.6	84.9	1 608	264	5 785	91	27 766	99 878	4.3	95.7
Park	1 195	5.2	9 435	2.6	13 365	588	24.3	29.3	1 011	214	1 720	121	65 553	111 485	47.8	52.2
Platte	966	11.9	1 657	1.5	10 355	461	15.2	56.0	1 285	−80	2 787	170	68 242	148 030	16.5	83.5
Sheridan	1 116	4.7	1 354	.4	6 321	568	23.2	45.6	1 608	399	2 831	129	38 387	67 583	9.8	90.2
Sublette	361	7.5	2 638	3.8	7 647	275	18.9	54.2	592	−1	2 152	169	27 208	98 938	4.7	95.3
Sweetwater	378	1.0	−364	X	1 682	160	13.8	39.4	1 421	−300	8 881	42	6 963	43 519	18.7	81.3
Teton	108	1.0	−119	X	1 180	104	27.9	25.0	52	−10	504	21	4 654	44 750	29.8	70.2
Uinta	385	2.1	−974	X	4 534	300	23.0	40.3	940	60	3 133	108	22 325	74 417	2.5	97.5
Washakie	284	3.4	3 726	3.1	6 641	205	28.3	45.9	450	52	2 195	58	28 741	140 200	45.5	54.5
Weston	405	6.2	1 768	2.0	4 970	233	7.7	77.7	1 421	−64	6 097	96	18 918	81 193	4.3	95.7

[1] For 1990 corrected population, see table B–1. Percent is based on 1990 uncorrected population because only total population is corrected. [2] For total earnings, see table B–8. [3] Most data are comparable between 1992 and 1997; however, it should be noted that farms with all acreage in Conservation or Wetlands Reserve Programs (excluded in 1992) are included in 1997, as are short rotation woody crops which includes Christmas trees and maple sap gathering (in Forestry in 1992). [4] Includes nursery and greenhouse crops. [5] Includes related products. [6] Less than $50,000.

Sources: Farm Population—U.S. Census Bureau, 1990 Census of Population and Housing, Summary Tape File (STF) 3C on CD-ROM (related Internet site <http://homer.ssd.census.gov/cdrom/lookup/>). Farm Earnings—U.S. Bureau of Economic Analysis, "Regional Economic Information System (REIS) 1969-1998" on CD-ROM (related Internet site <http://www.bea.doc.gov/bea/regional/reis/ca45/>). Agriculture—U.S. Department of Agriculture, National Agricultural Statistics Service, 1997 Census of Agriculture, Volume 1, Geographic Area Series, 1A, 1B, 1C CD-ROM Set (related Internet site <http://www.nass.usda.gov/census/>).

Table B–11. Counties — Wholesale Trade and Retail Trade

[Includes U.S., states, and 3,142 counties/county equivalents defined as of January 1, 1992. For changes to these areas since January 1, 1992, see appendix B. Geographic Information]

County	Wholesale trade[1] (NAICS 42), 1997						Retail trade[1] (NAICS 44-45), 1997							
	Sales							Sales					Annual payroll	
									Per capita[3]		Percent from general merchandise stores			
	Establishments	Total (mil. dol.)	Merchant wholesalers (mil. dol.)	Paid employees[2]	Annual payroll (mil. dol.)	Operating expenses (mil. dol.)	Establishments	Total (mil. dol.)	Amount (dollars)	Percent of national average		Paid employees[2]	Total (mil. dol.)	Per paid employee (dollars)
UNITED STATES	453 470	4 059 657.8	2 333 131.2	5 796 557	214 915.4	443 572.9	1 118 447	2 460 886.0	9 190	100.0	13.4	13 991 103	237 195.5	16 953
ALABAMA	6 315	40 986.3	26 045.8	79 229	2 394.7	4 844.9	20 163	36 623.3	8 477	92.2	15.5	231 665	3 381.7	14 598
Autauga	29	39.7	D	81	2.1	4.6	161	367.3	8 895	96.8	D	2 200	32.1	14 575
Baldwin	151	493.5	357.6	1 248	42.9	83.0	801	1 215.3	9 438	102.7	14.9	7 850	114.8	14 622
Barbour	32	79.6	D	228	4.2	9.7	129	163.2	6 102	66.4	17.1	1 076	15.0	13 895
Bibb	15	53.2	D	82	1.9	4.1	60	77.2	4 141	45.1	14.5	527	6.7	12 643
Blount	51	D	D	(4)	D	D	143	202.0	4 499	49.0	D	1 328	17.8	13 373
Bullock	10	D	D	(5)	D	D	38	40.3	3 564	38.8	D	289	3.8	13 007
Butler	23	58.1	D	148	3.6	8.6	122	144.2	6 624	72.1	15.9	1 023	13.9	13 540
Calhoun	130	890.9	798.5	1 688	47.0	111.4	578	982.0	8 384	91.2	19.3	6 747	92.5	13 715
Chambers	23	89.3	89.3	158	3.9	9.0	131	216.0	5 895	64.1	D	1 502	19.7	13 143
Cherokee	22	65.2	65.2	161	4.0	10.3	88	123.1	5 701	62.0	12.5	678	9.0	13 235
Chilton	29	64.2	54.9	193	3.8	8.6	180	246.6	6 793	73.9	D	1 510	21.8	14 407
Choctaw	19	108.0	D	191	5.7	12.6	76	69.1	4 352	47.4	4.3	386	6.1	15 816
Clarke	23	34.3	D	125	2.4	5.5	188	233.2	8 151	88.7	22.2	1 669	21.4	12 842
Clay	4	D	D	(5)	D	D	49	45.7	3 301	35.9	D	376	4.6	12 106
Cleburne	13	D	D	(5)	D	D	47	54.0	3 829	41.7	D	262	3.6	13 760
Coffee	47	141.0	131.6	259	5.8	16.9	223	411.0	9 775	106.4	D	2 405	34.6	14 384
Colbert	109	404.3	D	1 173	30.4	63.2	273	527.5	9 935	108.1	16.9	2 915	45.0	15 436
Conecuh	14	57.4	D	102	2.3	5.4	49	39.1	2 785	30.3	D	275	3.8	13 691
Coosa	6	D	D	(5)	D	D	28	15.3	1 317	14.3	D	130	1.8	14 062
Covington	49	223.1	D	585	12.2	25.4	239	287.9	7 692	83.7	11.8	1 974	27.8	14 086
Crenshaw	15	D	D	(4)	D	D	54	56.6	4 132	45.0	D	444	5.3	12 025
Cullman	95	256.1	216.0	637	16.2	34.6	360	650.9	8 786	95.6	13.1	3 334	52.1	15 632
Dale	37	118.6	D	537	8.1	20.8	182	201.8	4 110	44.7	16.4	1 402	18.1	12 911
Dallas	52	213.2	146.6	517	12.0	24.9	232	339.0	7 195	78.3	18.9	2 430	31.9	13 115
DeKalb	62	309.6	224.6	602	12.4	31.6	269	343.0	5 950	64.7	21.0	2 576	31.3	12 158
Elmore	47	116.6	D	309	7.1	18.5	199	296.8	4 919	53.5	D	1 780	23.7	13 342
Escambia	53	117.8	D	532	11.6	24.5	210	295.1	8 058	87.7	14.3	2 097	28.0	13 349
Etowah	135	D	D	(6)	D	D	452	737.8	7 110	77.4	18.8	4 935	65.9	13 362
Fayette	11	D	D	(5)	D	D	82	111.1	6 134	66.7	14.2	709	9.4	13 262
Franklin	27	99.8	60.1	287	6.0	11.8	144	184.5	6 230	67.8	11.4	1 167	15.5	13 260
Geneva	28	D	D	(4)	D	D	124	108.5	4 366	47.5	D	813	10.5	12 918
Greene	10	D	D	(5)	D	D	34	31.3	3 156	34.3	D	232	2.7	11 547
Hale	5	D	D	(5)	D	D	45	52.8	3 212	35.0	5.2	322	4.1	12 780
Henry	15	68.0	68.0	323	6.4	14.9	81	84.6	5 388	58.6	3.3	524	7.9	15 095
Houston	206	705.0	D	2 149	54.8	111.1	656	1 288.2	15 131	164.6	17.9	7 801	124.6	15 966
Jackson	47	203.2	D	630	12.8	24.7	218	299.8	5 912	64.3	14.9	1 849	25.7	13 918
Jefferson	1 480	14 471.2	7 459.1	23 438	824.1	1 546.3	3 020	7 636.8	11 567	125.9	13.1	44 165	705.6	15 977
Lamar	10	D	D	(5)	D	D	69	65.0	4 076	44.4	5.6	445	5.4	12 049
Lauderdale	100	368.9	D	1 959	45.4	91.6	462	780.8	9 306	101.3	24.2	5 546	74.9	13 512
Lawrence	19	D	D	(5)	D	D	100	116.6	3 503	38.1	13.8	721	9.6	13 361
Lee	86	308.0	288.2	727	18.6	38.9	425	774.4	7 867	85.6	15.4	5 437	73.7	13 555
Limestone	49	D	D	(4)	D	D	255	404.6	6 618	72.0	D	2 539	37.8	14 887
Lowndes	8	26.6	26.6	82	1.7	4.0	29	34.7	2 695	29.3	D	215	3.7	17 419
Macon	8	D	D	(5)	D	D	66	64.1	2 777	30.2	D	437	6.0	13 703
Madison	471	D	D	(7)	D	D	1 224	2 610.7	9 585	104.3	D	17 275	253.6	14 678
Marengo	25	91.8	78.8	229	5.0	11.1	140	143.5	6 104	66.4	13.0	1 060	13.6	12 819
Marion	44	243.7	D	387	10.8	28.4	138	167.6	5 422	59.0	17.9	1 063	14.2	13 404
Marshall	115	858.8	809.9	1 424	39.0	135.3	560	1 008.2	12 610	137.2	13.0	5 254	73.6	14 004
Mobile	699	3 332.9	2 520.6	8 647	252.1	498.1	1 681	3 404.5	8 549	93.0	17.4	22 860	338.1	14 789
Monroe	25	85.0	D	267	7.1	15.5	120	170.4	7 058	76.8	11.7	1 086	15.2	14 007
Montgomery	392	2 938.8	2 072.5	5 460	157.0	314.3	1 144	2 482.8	11 404	124.1	14.7	15 998	237.8	14 865
Morgan	180	D	D	(6)	D	D	583	1 136.5	10 487	114.1	12.0	6 426	95.5	14 867
Perry	4	D	D	(5)	D	D	41	31.7	2 517	27.4	8.3	249	3.7	15 032
Pickens	16	33.8	D	67	1.5	4.3	96	130.6	6 235	67.8	4.0	654	9.0	13 830
Pike	44	177.5	D	472	9.6	30.6	145	223.2	7 819	85.1	12.5	1 559	19.9	12 781
Randolph	14	30.6	D	74	.9	2.7	89	89.4	4 476	48.7	16.2	722	9.3	12 884
Russell	23	D	D	(4)	D	D	168	229.6	4 525	49.2	28.0	1 797	23.1	12 853
St. Clair	68	D	D	(8)	D	D	205	270.6	4 462	48.6	D	1 724	21.5	12 443
Shelby	372	3 529.0	2 077.4	5 413	186.1	349.3	476	891.3	6 563	71.4	12.3	5 173	85.2	16 462
Sumter	15	47.0	D	162	2.9	6.5	66	69.3	4 358	47.4	13.9	511	6.0	11 748
Talladega	57	183.0	D	618	17.0	33.9	348	474.7	6 194	67.4	18.0	3 236	43.5	13 455
Tallapoosa	37	D	73.4	(6)	D	D	196	239.0	5 933	64.6	D	1 800	24.1	13 363
Tuscaloosa	185	858.1	705.6	1 981	61.1	106.9	790	1 543.2	9 652	105.0	D	10 852	151.0	13 910
Walker	69	210.8	D	677	12.4	26.8	359	679.0	9 607	104.5	16.3	3 923	54.7	13 946
Washington	11	D	D	(5)	D	D	53	52.1	2 961	32.2	D	319	4.2	13 273
Wilcox	8	18.3	18.3	36	.7	1.8	62	53.0	3 940	42.9	D	331	5.0	14 964
Winston	37	127.2	D	560	11.6	21.5	108	103.8	4 329	47.1	D	751	10.8	14 445

[1] Includes only establishments with payroll.   [2] For pay period including March 12.   [3] Based on resident population estimated as of July 1, 1997.   [4] 250 to 499 employees.   [5] 20 to 99 employees.   [6] 1,000 to 2,499 employees.   [7] 5,000 to 9,999 employees.   [8] 500 to 999 employees.

Sources: Wholesale Trade—U.S. Census Bureau, 1997 Economic Census, ECON97 Report Series CD-ROM, CD-EC97-1, Disc 1E, issued February 2001 (related Internet site <http://www.census.gov/epcd/www/97EC42.HTM>).   Retail Trade—U.S. Census Bureau, 1997 Economic Census, ECON97 Report Series CD-ROM, CD-EC97-1, Disc 1E, issued February 2001 (related Internet site <http://www.census.gov/epcd/www/97EC44.HTM>).

Table B–11. Counties — Wholesale Trade and Retail Trade–Con.

[Includes U.S., states, and 3,142 counties/county equivalents defined as of January 1, 1992. For changes to these areas since January 1, 1992, see appendix B. Geographic Information]

County	Wholesale trade[1] (NAICS 42), 1997						Retail trade[1] (NAICS 44-45), 1997							
	Sales						Sales					Annual payroll		
									Per capita[3]		Percent from general merchandise stores			
	Establishments	Total (mil. dol.)	Merchant wholesalers (mil. dol.)	Paid employees[2]	Annual payroll (mil. dol.)	Operating expenses (mil. dol.)	Establishments	Total (mil. dol.)	Amount (dollars)	Percent of national average		Paid employees[2]	Total (mil. dol.)	Per paid employee (dollars)
ALASKA	784	2 989.8	2 148.8	6 860	256.8	507.9	2 866	6 251.4	10 268	111.7	20.0	32 502	670.5	20 628
Aleutians East	2	D	D	(4)	D	D	6	7.2	3 130	34.1	D	56	1.0	18 518
Aleutians West	14	61.4	61.4	110	3.2	7.4	20	41.2	10 044	109.3	5.9	197	4.2	21 457
Anchorage	434	1 989.1	1 393.4	4 748	181.4	351.8	1 001	3 114.9	12 392	134.8	22.5	15 115	319.3	21 124
Bethel	3	1.1	1.1	9	.2	.5	59	77.2	4 896	53.3	25.5	829	8.5	10 298
Bristol Bay	2	D	D	(4)	D	D	13	12.8	11 712	127.4	D	91	2.1	22 692
Denali	2	D	D	(4)	D	D	7	D	D	D	D	(5)	D	D
Dillingham	4	4.7	4.7	10	.5	1.3	16	33.1	7 435	80.9	5.3	220	3.6	16 359
Fairbanks North Star	75	266.0	D	737	27.7	50.3	359	927.9	11 144	121.3	24.9	4 431	99.5	22 455
Haines	3	D	D	(4)	D	D	26	13.1	5 653	61.5	D	98	2.0	20 827
Juneau	33	206.3	87.8	196	8.2	17.0	173	312.7	10 323	112.3	33.2	1 807	37.2	20 582
Kenai Peninsula	70	242.0	D	337	12.6	25.4	292	426.5	8 922	97.1	D	2 219	45.1	20 308
Ketchikan Gateway	31	78.8	D	190	4.7	13.3	119	205.1	14 009	152.4	3.3	1 164	28.6	24 578
Kodiak Island	35	50.8	D	87	4.4	8.1	67	102.9	6 990	76.1	D	590	11.9	20 088
Lake and Peninsula	NA	NA	NA	NA	NA	NA	10	D	D	D	D	(5)	D	D
Matanuska-Susitna	22	D	D	(6)	D	D	201	477.3	8 851	96.3	12.4	2 149	46.6	21 661
Nome	1	D	D	(4)	D	D	41	57.0	6 377	69.4	D	442	5.8	13 100
North Slope	4	42.5	D	26	2.0	3.4	22	45.0	6 234	67.8	24.4	293	7.4	25 137
Northwest Arctic	NA	NA	NA	NA	NA	NA	30	40.8	6 129	66.7	38.3	286	5.4	18 853
Prince of Wales-Outer Ketchikan	6	21.6	21.6	32	1.0	3.5	40	26.0	3 716	40.4	5.5	158	2.7	16 930
Sitka	9	D	D	(5)	D	D	75	78.2	9 211	100.2	D	534	10.3	19 358
Skagway-Yakutat-Angoon	3	D	D	NA	D	D	51	30.6	6 592	71.7	D	238	4.0	16 895
Southeast Fairbanks	3	D	D	(4)	D	D	30	28.4	4 829	52.5	2.5	193	2.9	14 943
Valdez-Cordova	20	D	D	(5)	D	D	78	81.7	7 904	86.0	D	417	8.2	19 746
Wade Hampton	1	D	D	(4)	D	D	29	27.3	4 018	43.7	24.9	353	3.1	8 666
Wrangell-Petersburg	7	D	D	(5)	D	D	61	54.1	7 840	85.3	D	406	8.2	20 244
Yukon-Koyukuk	NA	NA	NA	NA	NA	NA	40	22.3	3 543	38.6	16.9	147	2.1	14 531
ARIZONA	6 689	45 899.1	26 412.6	80 155	2 748.9	5 311.0	16 283	43 960.9	9 657	105.1	13.0	232 050	4 223.9	18 202
Apache	9	D	D	(5)	D	D	126	170.0	2 448	26.6	5.6	1 242	17.0	13 716
Cochise	68	132.3	D	468	11.4	25.7	421	712.1	6 378	69.4	17.2	4 557	68.1	14 946
Coconino	112	D	D	(7)	D	D	653	1 081.2	9 507	103.4	D	7 217	112.1	15 529
Gila	42	60.7	D	220	6.4	13.4	170	329.6	8 835	74.4	D	2 040	32.9	16 107
Graham	25	59.1	D	193	3.9	9.0	110	205.4	6 573	71.5	D	1 377	19.4	14 089
Greenlee	7	D	D	(5)	D	D	22	20.8	2 208	24.0	D	146	1.8	12 027
La Paz	14	56.4	D	183	3.9	8.6	79	177.5	12 027	130.9	–	830	10.8	12 963
Maricopa	4 752	39 518.5	D	61 594	2 265.9	4 344.3	9 214	29 331.0	10 870	118.3	11.9	144 912	2 792.4	19 269
Mohave	106	D	D	(8)	D	D	578	1 236.9	9 638	104.9	D	6 944	111.1	15 996
Navajo	50	98.7	D	266	7.3	15.4	296	602.7	6 364	69.2	13.7	3 667	55.2	15 062
Pima	929	2 759.8	1 724.1	9 257	266.0	507.4	2 785	6 853.8	8 802	95.8	14.9	39 285	693.4	17 650
Pinal	88	206.4	D	690	18.1	40.0	404	680.8	4 763	51.8	9.2	4 355	63.9	14 664
Santa Cruz	205	1 124.9	673.4	1 859	49.9	105.3	207	320.3	8 604	93.6	18.8	2 169	30.7	14 163
Yavapai	150	480.6	447.7	1 134	29.1	60.6	757	1 203.1	8 335	90.7	15.1	7 325	120.8	16 491
Yuma	132	512.9	D	2 376	41.3	78.6	455	1 035.7	8 024	87.3	D	5 984	94.5	15 787
ARKANSAS	3 619	27 515.4	14 409.6	41 385	1 136.6	2 271.9	12 600	21 643.7	8 575	93.3	18.4	132 335	1 904.4	14 391
Arkansas	39	233.0	D	485	15.1	30.1	143	201.1	9 690	105.4	D	1 190	17.7	14 852
Ashley	28	D	D	(9)	D	D	117	133.8	5 502	59.9	16.7	961	12.3	12 827
Baxter	27	22.9	20.2	130	2.8	6.7	227	298.2	8 241	89.7	D	1 713	27.1	15 802
Benton	167	2 480.5	D	1 886	52.6	101.9	548	1 015.6	7 797	84.8	D	6 217	93.2	14 997
Boone	45	D	D	(7)	D	D	194	368.9	11 633	126.6	D	2 205	30.4	13 785
Bradley	11	25.6	25.6	37	1.0	2.3	62	65.1	5 672	61.7	6.2	385	4.9	12 714
Calhoun	2	D	D	(5)	D	D	22	13.3	2 328	25.3	D	91	1.1	12 549
Carroll	26	25.6	D	126	3.0	6.1	202	174.9	7 812	85.0	D	1 204	17.3	14 330
Chicot	23	87.6	D	216	5.7	11.9	80	87.1	5 726	62.3	6.3	627	7.1	11 333
Clark	25	39.1	D	128	3.4	10.9	116	171.3	7 723	84.0	D	1 100	14.8	13 464
Clay	23	98.8	98.8	350	7.4	15.6	86	106.2	6 112	66.5	9.9	632	8.1	12 767
Cleburne	33	63.9	D	255	5.3	13.7	111	135.7	6 019	65.5	D	982	12.4	12 626
Cleveland	6	D	D	(5)	D	D	19	9.2	1 107	12.0	D	94	.8	9 032
Columbia	30	47.1	D	177	3.7	7.7	136	157.8	6 250	68.0	D	1 205	14.9	12 405
Conway	23	D	D	(6)	D	D	91	157.1	7 874	85.7	D	948	12.3	12 987
Craighead	140	509.7	433.3	1 548	35.6	70.9	480	854.3	11 204	121.9	21.7	5 589	80.8	14 452
Crawford	58	170.1	D	373	9.3	19.6	171	268.5	5 428	59.1	D	1 599	22.8	14 262
Crittenden	64	D	D	(8)	D	D	206	496.9	10 034	109.2	D	2 722	33.1	12 172
Cross	22	102.7	102.7	344	7.1	15.4	80	129.8	6 695	72.9	15.3	720	10.5	14 583
Dallas	13	D	D	(5)	D	D	63	63.3	6 919	75.3	D	480	6.1	12 652
Desha	23	D	D	(6)	D	D	99	159.4	10 472	113.9	D	859	12.2	14 248

[1] Includes only establishments with payroll. [2] For pay period including March 12. [3] Based on resident population estimated as of July 1, 1997. [4] 0 to 19 employees. [5] 20 to 99 employees. [6] 100 to 249 employees. [7] 1,000 to 2,499 employees. [8] 500 to 999 employees. [9] 250 to 499 employees.

Sources: Wholesale Trade—U.S. Census Bureau, 1997 Economic Census, ECON97 Report Series CD-ROM, CD-EC97-1, Disc 1E, issued February 2001 (related Internet site <http://www.census.gov/epcd/www/97EC42.HTM>). Retail Trade—U.S. Census Bureau, 1997 Economic Census, ECON97 Report Series CD-ROM, CD-EC97-1, Disc 1E, issued February 2001 (related Internet site <http://www.census.gov/epcd/www/97EC44.HTM>).

[Includes U.S., states, and 3,142 counties/county equivalents defined as of January 1, 1992. For changes to these areas since January 1, 1992, see appendix B. Geographic Information]

County	Wholesale trade[1] (NAICS 42), 1997						Retail trade[1] (NAICS 44-45), 1997							
	Sales			Paid employees[2]	Annual payroll (mil. dol.)	Operating expenses (mil. dol.)	Estab-lishments	Sales			Percent from general merchandise stores	Paid employees[2]	Annual payroll	
	Estab-lishments	Total (mil. dol.)	Merchant whole-salers (mil. dol.)					Total (mil. dol.)	Per capita[3]				Total (mil. dol.)	Per paid employee (dollars)
									Amount (dollars)	Percent of national average				
ARKANSAS—Con.														
Drew	21	78.4	D	170	4.8	11.2	102	153.7	8 731	95.0	D	952	12.3	12 944
Faulkner	76	242.0	D	826	17.0	34.1	309	571.2	7 465	81.2	D	3 423	51.5	15 044
Franklin	8	D	D	(4)	D	D	63	71.2	4 301	46.8	D	461	5.9	12 870
Fulton	8	D	D	(4)	D	D	40	21.8	2 012	21.9	D	184	1.9	10 500
Garland	110	966.5	D	898	25.5	53.5	498	875.8	10 579	115.1	18.2	5 023	74.8	14 886
Grant	14	28.7	28.7	113	2.2	5.0	54	58.5	3 744	40.7	D	450	6.0	13 222
Greene	55	115.5	D	571	9.9	23.3	183	263.2	7 425	80.8	D	1 649	22.0	13 347
Hempstead	17	D	D	(5)	D	D	111	134.4	6 115	66.5	D	925	12.0	12 996
Hot Spring	28	54.0	36.9	170	4.1	7.1	99	144.6	5 052	55.0	D	787	11.1	14 161
Howard	14	12.7	12.7	44	.7	1.7	73	88.2	6 424	69.9	24.1	634	8.0	12 587
Independence	50	172.5	D	624	12.6	31.0	195	284.2	8 689	94.5	D	1 741	23.2	13 324
Izard	9	D	D	(4)	D	D	57	71.0	5 453	59.3	3.2	374	4.8	12 861
Jackson	29	D	D	(5)	D	D	108	152.4	8 524	92.8	D	862	12.0	13 937
Jefferson	77	309.8	D	780	18.9	43.3	393	726.6	8 848	96.3	15.5	4 785	71.8	14 995
Johnson	9	D	D	(4)	D	D	104	155.5	7 338	79.8	D	988	13.4	13 535
Lafayette	2	D	D	(6)	D	D	40	22.1	2 444	26.6	10.2	216	2.1	9 690
Lawrence	21	85.2	85.2	173	3.7	7.6	88	122.0	6 997	76.1	D	710	9.5	13 323
Lee	10	63.7	63.7	95	2.3	4.5	39	40.8	3 207	34.9	9.0	273	3.6	13 286
Lincoln	7	D	D	(4)	D	D	28	30.6	2 140	23.3	6.8	228	2.9	12 851
Little River	16	22.5	D	76	2.2	4.0	57	77.4	5 852	63.7	D	396	5.2	13 237
Logan	17	D	D	(5)	D	D	94	119.5	5 640	61.4	D	707	9.5	13 491
Lonoke	37	144.4	D	321	7.3	14.4	178	269.1	5 474	59.6	D	1 622	23.3	14 345
Madison	2	D	D	(6)	D	D	41	47.7	3 649	39.7	D	282	4.0	14 007
Marion	8	D	D	(4)	D	D	39	46.2	3 195	34.8	D	360	4.5	12 394
Miller	49	D	176.1	(7)	D	D	167	254.1	6 425	69.9	D	1 512	21.0	13 870
Mississippi	60	237.9	D	457	13.1	25.2	261	361.8	7 181	78.1	14.6	2 117	29.1	13 757
Monroe	13	33.6	D	65	1.7	3.6	72	89.8	8 702	94.7	D	488	7.2	14 775
Montgomery	12	16.6	16.6	34	.6	4.6	36	20.9	2 453	26.7	D	174	2.4	13 851
Nevada	5	18.2	18.2	21	.9	1.8	40	37.0	3 683	40.1	7.1	261	3.1	11 812
Newton	7	D	D	(4)	D	D	16	15.1	1 846	20.1	D	121	1.5	12 289
Ouachita	31	121.0	D	264	6.8	17.5	148	198.2	7 082	77.1	14.8	1 380	19.3	14 009
Perry	3	D	D	(4)	D	D	27	19.0	2 011	21.9	D	154	1.7	11 201
Phillips	30	D	D	(8)	D	D	151	187.6	6 792	73.9	21.5	1 310	16.9	12 921
Pike	13	45.5	D	107	1.6	3.7	60	72.7	6 939	75.5	4.8	441	5.2	11 857
Poinsett	24	179.0	179.0	267	7.7	15.5	111	118.1	4 809	52.3	11.8	760	10.0	13 218
Polk	18	10.1	D	65	.8	2.2	99	121.3	6 224	67.7	D	828	10.2	12 362
Pope	81	193.9	D	543	16.6	29.5	302	502.4	9 801	106.6	15.9	3 168	45.4	14 345
Prairie	8	18.5	D	53	1.3	3.0	54	36.6	3 943	42.9	7.8	246	3.1	12 419
Pulaski	882	9 759.8	4 597.7	14 654	455.7	864.6	1 847	4 584.4	13 140	143.0	D	26 898	415.1	15 434
Randolph	16	28.5	28.5	95	2.2	4.0	73	96.1	5 436	59.2	D	705	9.1	12 949
St. Francis	36	303.7	D	392	9.1	21.6	144	259.3	9 138	99.4	D	1 485	21.3	14 329
Saline	78	204.2	137.7	514	14.1	28.9	250	793.4	10 454	113.8	D	2 860	51.9	18 155
Scott	8	39.4	D	84	1.2	5.7	40	42.2	3 890	42.3	D	343	4.1	11 936
Searcy	7	D	D	(6)	D	D	40	31.4	4 046	44.0	D	253	2.6	10 182
Sebastian	245	708.5	638.9	2 101	56.8	121.8	659	1 360.6	12 844	139.8	22.2	8 721	128.1	14 686
Sevier	12	39.7	39.7	88	3.1	4.7	70	86.4	5 947	64.7	D	710	8.1	11 373
Sharp	11	D	D	(4)	D	D	91	112.6	6 764	73.6	D	778	8.6	11 012
Stone	11	D	D	(4)	D	D	63	66.3	6 047	65.8	D	470	6.4	13 611
Union	78	119.7	111.4	511	12.3	26.2	263	408.6	9 032	98.3	D	2 603	36.5	14 016
Van Buren	9	4.2	D	17	.2	.4	78	71.7	4 609	50.2	D	536	6.5	12 203
Washington	278	6 815.1	D	3 203	101.4	205.6	762	1 444.9	10 060	109.5	D	9 555	141.6	14 817
White	85	243.0	216.0	624	14.2	30.9	312	509.0	8 064	87.7	D	2 997	42.5	14 176
Woodruff	17	112.0	112.0	163	5.3	11.9	48	34.1	3 807	41.4	10.5	268	3.2	12 052
Yell	19	17.0	17.0	68	1.3	3.2	70	93.2	4 889	53.2	15.1	638	7.3	11 433
CALIFORNIA	57 841	548 864.5	342 227.7	757 294	29 875.0	64 165.6	106 357	263 118.3	8 167	88.9	13.1	1 354 797	26 362.7	19 459
Alameda	3 232	47 790.8	24 563.8	51 312	2 155.3	4 289.8	4 363	12 404.9	9 040	98.4	10.8	59 289	1 227.8	20 709
Alpine	NA	NA	NA	NA	NA	NA	7	2.3	1 900	20.7	D	28	.2	8 143
Amador	28	D	D	(5)	D	D	158	475.0	14 213	154.7	D	1 570	25.7	16 358
Butte	179	637.9	583.2	1 792	56.9	117.5	777	1 502.6	7 783	84.7	16.9	9 004	154.0	17 107
Calaveras	27	D	D	(5)	D	D	136	135.5	3 461	37.7	D	862	14.0	16 226
Colusa	25	152.3	D	318	8.3	17.7	67	121.7	6 606	71.9	D	545	10.8	19 894
Contra Costa	1 159	14 968.0	5 950.9	11 092	518.5	1 080.9	2 705	7 376.8	8 201	89.2	15.7	37 550	752.8	20 049
Del Norte	15	D	D	(5)	D	D	88	123.1	4 527	49.3	D	982	12.5	12 741
El Dorado	108	249.7	170.1	684	19.3	41.9	546	926.8	5 987	65.1	D	4 894	91.1	18 624

[1] Includes only establishments with payroll. [2] For pay period including March 12. [3] Based on resident population estimated as of July 1, 1997. [4] 20 to 99 employees. [5] 100 to 249 employees. [6] 0 to 19 employees. [7] 500 to 999 employees. [8] 250 to 499 employees.

Sources: Wholesale Trade—U.S. Census Bureau, 1997 Economic Census, ECON97 Report Series CD-ROM, CD-EC97-1, Disc 1E, issued February 2001 (related Internet site <http://www.census.gov/epcd/www/97EC42.HTM>). Retail Trade—U.S. Census Bureau, 1997 Economic Census, ECON97 Report Series CD-ROM, CD-EC97-1, Disc 1E, issued February 2001 (related Internet site <http://www.census.gov/epcd/www/97EC44.HTM>).

[Includes U.S., states, and 3,142 counties/county equivalents defined as of January 1, 1992. For changes to these areas since January 1, 1992, see appendix B. Geographic Information]

County	Wholesale trade[1] (NAICS 42), 1997						Retail trade[1] (NAICS 44-45), 1997							
		Sales						Sales				Annual payroll	
									Per capita[3]		Percent from general mer-chandise stores			
	Estab-lishments	Total (mil. dol.)	Merchant whole-salers (mil. dol.)	Paid em-ployees[2]	Annual payroll (mil. dol.)	Operating expenses (mil. dol.)	Estab-lishments	Total (mil. dol.)	Amount (dollars)	Percent of national average		Paid em-ployees[2]	Total (mil. dol.)	Per paid em-ployee (dollars)
CALIFORNIA—Con.														
Fresno	971	5 845.2	4 188.6	13 004	415.5	842.5	2 492	5 574.6	7 427	80.8	D	30 231	548.9	18 158
Glenn	36	125.8	D	298	8.6	25.0	79	98.9	3 773	41.1	D	720	10.5	14 522
Humboldt	128	493.6	389.1	1 306	37.1	92.0	668	1 024.0	8 350	90.9	D	6 816	108.7	15 942
Imperial	189	673.7	557.2	1 951	41.0	87.6	521	989.4	6 960	75.7	20.5	5 991	98.8	16 488
Inyo	24	D	D	(4)	D	D	145	171.1	9 365	101.9	8.9	1 092	17.8	16 267
Kern	612	4 313.9	3 446.4	7 930	256.4	512.4	1 918	4 224.4	6 764	73.6	14.2	22 792	412.1	18 080
Kings	60	411.6	D	623	15.8	40.3	316	629.3	5 504	59.9	16.0	3 690	60.0	16 254
Lake	39	D	D	(5)	D	D	197	309.3	5 639	61.4	14.6	1 954	30.7	15 695
Lassen	11	D	D	(6)	D	D	106	159.2	4 761	51.8	D	1 032	15.5	15 043
Los Angeles	21 474	177 244.9	127 905.3	259 217	9 450.4	21 599.1	27 577	69 534.2	7 619	82.9	12.2	343 656	6 769.0	19 697
Madera	87	265.8	198.9	623	18.8	41.4	313	527.3	4 690	51.0	D	3 173	53.0	16 708
Marin	570	2 414.8	1 660.8	4 167	170.4	354.1	1 291	2 775.7	11 836	128.8	11.8	14 793	322.0	21 767
Mariposa	7	D	D	(6)	D	D	78	57.4	3 687	40.1	D	397	6.3	15 950
Mendocino	108	308.7	271.6	1 095	27.0	57.9	490	711.4	8 543	93.0	D	4 572	76.8	16 797
Merced	117	699.9	663.7	1 333	36.4	75.8	551	1 102.1	5 684	61.8	D	6 122	108.0	17 634
Modoc	11	D	D	(4)	D	D	46	34.3	3 570	38.8	–	256	3.5	13 695
Mono	2	D	D	(7)	D	D	79	84.0	8 069	87.8	D	683	10.2	14 880
Monterey	473	4 747.4	3 024.0	7 530	267.9	554.5	1 558	3 035.9	8 459	92.0	12.9	16 413	327.9	19 977
Napa	153	533.0	422.7	1 296	46.4	90.3	525	952.6	8 077	87.9	D	5 292	102.8	19 427
Nevada	90	118.7	82.5	453	13.1	25.7	430	654.8	7 277	79.2	D	3 914	73.7	18 839
Orange	7 029	94 403.4	51 630.8	103 113	3 999.6	9 312.6	9 084	26 172.8	9 819	106.8	12.9	126 575	2 572.0	20 320
Placer	283	1 792.6	1 125.6	3 888	147.7	269.9	875	2 666.6	12 095	131.6	D	11 769	254.7	21 645
Plumas	12	D	D	(4)	D	D	119	127.5	6 242	67.9	D	829	16.1	19 452
Riverside	1 200	6 715.6	4 705.4	12 649	416.6	903.9	4 030	10 609.0	7 369	80.2	14.0	54 433	1 028.9	18 902
Sacramento	1 287	8 555.8	5 442.2	18 090	626.7	1 247.3	3 587	9 502.3	8 245	89.7	15.4	51 962	990.0	19 053
San Benito	43	211.1	171.8	752	21.6	39.6	117	276.8	5 936	64.6	D	1 731	30.9	17 847
San Bernardino	1 747	14 254.1	9 369.8	24 756	805.8	1 753.6	4 372	11 342.8	7 049	76.7	15.9	60 940	1 100.5	18 058
San Diego	4 159	26 543.9	16 589.5	53 589	2 273.7	4 302.5	9 109	22 215.3	8 161	88.8	13.9	119 022	2 241.1	18 829
San Francisco	1 900	12 219.1	8 973.1	17 677	779.8	1 501.5	3 841	6 795.0	9 170	99.8	9.6	39 693	830.6	20 926
San Joaquin	560	7 651.7	5 938.9	9 751	319.3	692.0	1 594	3 679.6	6 814	74.1	14.9	19 957	364.7	18 273
San Luis Obispo	244	561.5	469.9	1 904	46.8	104.2	1 132	1 780.7	7 694	83.7	9.8	10 917	182.4	16 708
San Mateo	1 687	14 662.6	9 144.6	21 640	1 088.3	2 316.1	2 285	7 335.4	10 544	114.7	13.9	33 757	735.4	21 786
Santa Barbara	469	1 636.0	1 166.6	4 282	137.5	314.2	1 653	3 183.5	8 231	89.6	11.8	19 187	354.0	18 451
Santa Clara	3 468	68 095.4	33 562.5	66 542	3 891.8	7 811.0	5 278	16 673.6	10 282	111.9	12.9	79 921	1 696.7	21 230
Santa Cruz	342	1 541.8	D	4 472	140.3	261.0	986	1 970.2	8 248	89.7	D	11 794	215.5	18 274
Shasta	217	566.6	487.3	1 786	51.9	106.2	713	1 354.5	8 330	90.6	17.9	8 113	140.3	17 293
Sierra	NA	NA	NA	NA	NA	NA	13	8.8	2 620	28.5	–	64	.9	14 266
Siskiyou	35	D	D	(5)	D	D	233	256.1	5 785	62.9	D	1 770	25.4	14 370
Solano	262	2 170.1	930.8	3 909	145.7	296.6	1 116	2 789.4	7 517	81.8	D	15 046	281.0	18 674
Sonoma	619	3 069.7	2 531.6	7 430	259.4	536.2	1 808	4 146.2	9 723	105.8	12.3	22 190	443.7	19 995
Stanislaus	417	2 264.4	D	5 118	159.1	322.9	1 368	3 282.2	7 825	85.1	16.7	17 706	319.2	18 027
Sutter	90	D	247.4	(8)	D	D	291	606.7	7 936	86.4	26.7	3 604	61.1	16 962
Tehama	40	D	D	(4)	D	D	176	360.6	6 700	72.9	D	1 953	33.0	16 909
Trinity	6	D	D	(7)	D	D	54	38.9	2 957	32.2	D	334	4.6	13 647
Tulare	343	2 527.7	1 912.3	5 120	135.1	319.5	1 107	2 135.7	6 099	66.4	18.1	12 742	211.8	16 625
Tuolumne	37	96.2	D	280	8.8	27.5	228	341.4	6 524	71.0	D	2 343	38.0	16 239
Ventura	1 088	10 402.7	D	13 811	522.6	1 107.3	2 348	6 476.6	8 968	97.6	12.6	30 831	608.7	19 743
Yolo	282	5 000.2	4 438.8	7 829	257.8	510.1	458	1 026.7	6 777	73.7	7.9	5 776	110.6	19 153
Yuba	40	D	D	(4)	D	D	155	244.6	4 066	44.2	D	1 525	25.6	16 782
COLORADO	7 383	60 310.4	27 610.4	88 364	3 282.0	6 213.5	18 299	40 536.0	10 417	113.4	12.8	225 647	4 163.3	18 451
Adams	732	7 044.5	5 061.3	12 884	443.5	851.5	952	2 859.1	9 052	98.5	D	14 489	308.8	21 316
Alamosa	30	68.8	59.7	225	5.3	10.6	97	167.2	11 562	125.8	D	1 090	17.2	15 737
Arapahoe	1 156	22 395.3	6 336.0	15 912	813.5	1 471.4	2 003	6 353.6	13 726	149.4	13.2	30 860	603.5	19 557
Archuleta	9	10.2	D	13	.6	1.0	67	54.6	6 407	69.7	D	370	5.9	16 016
Baca	11	24.1	24.1	51	1.0	2.7	27	18.6	4 240	46.1	3.2	127	1.7	13 134
Bent	2	D	D	(7)	D	D	16	11.6	2 144	23.3	D	94	1.1	12 106
Boulder	539	3 906.0	1 943.8	5 558	234.9	438.7	1 275	2 915.0	11 150	121.3	10.6	17 269	309.9	17 948
Chaffee	25	37.4	31.8	130	2.1	4.2	112	124.4	8 301	90.3	D	928	14.0	15 091
Cheyenne	5	39.7	D	43	1.1	2.4	13	11.4	5 044	54.9	D	68	.9	12 529
Clear Creek	17	30.7	D	97	2.7	5.8	50	39.3	4 421	48.1	–	299	3.9	13 060
Conejos	6	11.4	11.4	57	.9	2.3	22	22.5	2 866	31.2	D	139	2.0	14 719
Costilla	NA	NA	NA	NA	NA	NA	11	3.6	1 012	11.0	D	24	.3	14 250
Crowley	NA	NA	NA	NA	NA	NA	10	12.6	2 932	31.9	–	87	1.3	15 414
Custer	4	1.6	D	8	.1	.3	21	13.9	4 213	45.8	D	100	1.4	13 940

[1] Includes only establishments with payroll. [2] For pay period including March 12. [3] Based on resident population estimated as of July 1, 1997. [4] 100 to 249 employees. [5] 250 to 499 employees. [6] 20 to 99 employees. [7] 0 to 19 employees. [8] 500 to 999 employees.

Sources: Wholesale Trade—U.S. Census Bureau, 1997 Economic Census, ECON[97] Report Series CD-ROM, CD-EC97-1, Disc 1E, issued February 2001 (related Internet site <http://www.census.gov/epcd/www/97EC42.HTM>). Retail Trade—U.S. Census Bureau, 1997 Economic Census, ECON[97] Report Series CD-ROM, CD-EC97-1, Disc 1E, issued February 2001 (related Internet site <http://www.census.gov/epcd/www/97EC44.HTM>).

Table B–11. Counties — Wholesale Trade and Retail Trade—Con.

[Includes U.S., states, and 3,142 counties/county equivalents defined as of January 1, 1992. For changes to these areas since January 1, 1992, see appendix B. Geographic Information]

County	Wholesale trade[1] (NAICS 42), 1997						Retail trade[1] (NAICS 44-45), 1997							
	Sales						Sales					Annual payroll	
									Per capita[3]		Percent from general merchandise stores			
	Establishments	Total (mil. dol.)	Merchant wholesalers (mil. dol.)	Paid employees[2]	Annual payroll (mil. dol.)	Operating expenses (mil. dol.)	Establishments	Total (mil. dol.)	Amount (dollars)	Percent of national average		Paid employees[2]	Total (mil. dol.)	Per paid employee (dollars)
COLORADO—Con.														
Delta	26	40.8	D	272	4.9	9.5	129	156.8	6 054	65.9	4.2	957	15.0	15 700
Denver	1 681	16 177.1	7 593.4	26 604	972.8	1 846.9	2 410	5 600.9	11 217	122.1	8.7	30 080	628.0	20 879
Dolores	6	23.7	23.7	45	.9	1.6	6	4.5	2 650	28.8	–	34	.4	12 676
Douglas	198	943.9	D	967	34.5	79.4	500	1 212.0	9 550	103.9	D	8 052	123.5	15 337
Eagle	62	189.0	D	242	8.5	19.1	367	497.2	15 556	169.3	5.1	3 313	67.3	20 329
Elbert	18	39.3	D	60	2.8	4.1	40	34.9	1 999	21.8	–	188	2.8	15 101
El Paso	498	1 417.9	1 079.7	6 513	213.3	384.3	1 901	5 015.1	10 449	113.7	D	27 806	503.6	18 111
Fremont	28	42.8	25.3	120	3.0	6.2	143	203.8	4 726	51.4	16.8	1 311	21.6	16 457
Garfield	52	112.8	D	379	8.7	18.2	277	552.5	14 642	159.3	10.0	2 635	55.7	21 149
Gilpin	1	D	D	(4)	D	D	7	2.8	697	7.6	–	27	.4	15 222
Grand	10	12.9	D	52	1.0	2.3	116	95.6	9 749	106.1	–	706	10.5	14 868
Gunnison	9	9.1	9.1	40	.7	1.7	139	135.6	11 054	120.3	D	969	13.6	14 075
Hinsdale	1	D	D	(4)	D	D	14	5.1	7 257	79.0	D	15	.5	33 333
Huerfano	7	2.9	2.9	26	.6	1.1	39	33.0	4 903	53.4	D	211	3.3	15 649
Jackson	3	3.6	D	25	.6	1.4	6	6.2	4 068	44.3	–	50	.6	12 720
Jefferson	771	2 805.6	D	4 994	178.2	342.5	1 986	5 114.8	10 309	112.2	17.3	28 098	509.2	18 122
Kiowa	6	8.0	8.0	16	.3	.8	8	4.4	2 660	28.9	–	52	.5	9 481
Kit Carson	28	122.5	D	241	4.8	10.6	64	100.1	13 934	151.6	D	462	7.6	16 478
Lake	4	D	D	(5)	D	D	33	25.9	4 094	44.5	–	202	2.7	13 569
La Plata	71	119.4	98.3	511	15.4	32.1	317	440.6	10 994	119.6	6.6	2 848	49.5	17 371
Larimer	311	805.6	528.0	2 630	75.9	142.8	1 201	2 440.5	10 823	117.8	14.2	13 810	234.2	16 957
Las Animas	17	33.8	28.5	117	3.3	6.7	54	84.8	5 872	63.9	D	576	8.0	13 868
Lincoln	9	20.6	D	61	.9	2.4	36	58.3	10 324	112.3	D	320	5.1	15 900
Logan	32	97.4	72.6	338	6.4	11.9	115	199.5	11 023	119.9	D	1 149	16.5	14 367
Mesa	198	531.1	429.1	1 461	42.8	80.9	600	1 152.7	10 411	113.3	19.2	6 409	115.0	17 942
Mineral	NA	NA	NA	NA	NA	NA	10	3.7	5 558	60.5	D	34	.5	14 941
Moffat	28	35.6	D	123	3.3	7.9	77	117.4	9 523	103.6	D	706	12.1	17 173
Montezuma	23	18.4	18.4	112	2.0	4.3	136	228.6	10 268	111.7	D	1 302	22.4	17 239
Montrose	44	88.7	70.0	377	6.7	14.6	171	304.1	10 069	109.6	13.9	1 710	31.3	18 287
Morgan	41	416.9	107.7	403	9.0	26.1	119	157.6	6 290	68.4	D	996	15.0	15 092
Otero	34	118.9	D	286	6.1	12.8	101	141.2	6 775	73.7	23.5	932	13.6	14 628
Ouray	2	D	D	(4)	D	D	41	11.9	3 720	40.5	D	99	1.4	14 242
Park	15	D	D	(5)	D	D	35	28.2	2 232	24.3	D	175	3.1	17 497
Phillips	15	142.3	142.3	170	4.7	13.6	23	28.4	6 593	71.7	–	165	2.4	14 273
Pitkin	26	79.0	D	204	9.3	22.6	265	288.9	21 304	231.8	–	2 264	41.0	18 128
Prowers	25	82.0	D	403	7.4	15.7	93	112.9	8 261	89.9	14.7	826	11.4	13 771
Pueblo	113	390.3	279.0	1 101	27.5	53.6	600	1 180.7	8 915	97.0	20.3	7 040	121.7	17 280
Rio Blanco	6	6.6	6.6	23	.5	1.4	36	21.5	3 408	37.1	D	201	2.2	11 045
Rio Grande	31	98.1	D	564	9.1	19.9	77	96.8	8 508	92.6	D	476	8.6	18 130
Routt	31	51.4	D	185	5.3	11.2	184	190.3	10 998	119.7	9.6	1 484	22.5	15 185
Saguache	8	8.7	8.7	92	1.1	2.7	24	30.1	5 084	55.3	D	118	2.4	20 314
San Juan	NA	NA	NA	NA	NA	NA	18	5.1	9 423	102.5	–	39	.8	19 538
San Miguel	5	2.2	2.2	28	.6	1.2	76	44.6	8 398	91.4	–	524	6.5	12 334
Sedgwick	10	36.9	36.9	71	1.7	4.6	24	25.6	9 850	107.2	D	129	2.0	15 659
Summit	41	58.5	D	191	4.5	10.2	339	387.9	21 009	228.6	D	2 801	45.8	16 346
Teller	15	19.5	D	57	2.3	3.6	72	77.6	3 913	42.6	–	516	8.6	16 678
Washington	10	53.1	53.1	147	3.4	7.4	21	23.0	5 009	54.5	D	162	2.8	17 099
Weld	247	1 334.6	1 185.3	2 829	84.9	167.3	505	1 155.5	7 429	80.8	13.9	6 195	109.2	17 624
Yuma	30	112.4	D	239	4.8	10.9	68	89.4	9 543	103.8	D	529	8.6	16 338
CONNECTICUT	5 283	76 167.9	54 110.8	77 716	3 595.3	7 560.0	14 574	34 938.9	10 690	116.3	9.5	186 935	3 634.3	19 442
Fairfield	1 768	48 325.4	36 875.9	28 573	1 559.1	3 507.3	4 008	11 563.9	13 868	150.9	7.7	54 012	1 218.0	22 550
Hartford	1 369	16 831.0	9 077.6	25 741	1 108.2	2 245.5	3 683	8 829.0	10 669	116.1	10.4	51 121	943.6	18 457
Litchfield	240	779.0	536.5	2 203	90.7	174.0	816	1 611.0	8 928	97.1	6.2	8 193	158.0	19 288
Middlesex	218	823.0	520.3	2 045	74.2	145.7	742	1 345.0	9 038	98.3	D	8 050	143.1	17 780
New Haven	1 316	8 028.3	6 130.3	15 458	633.3	1 222.0	3 335	7 725.2	9 752	106.1	11.9	41 942	775.9	18 500
New London	201	801.6	517.9	2 279	81.9	169.3	1 182	2 405.0	9 608	104.5	12.9	13 923	240.3	17 263
Tolland	89	246.5	147.8	602	23.2	42.9	428	763.9	5 846	63.6	D	5 028	81.8	16 262
Windham	82	333.1	304.6	815	24.7	53.2	380	695.8	6 641	72.3	10.9	4 666	73.6	15 776
DELAWARE	906	12 585.5	2 943.2	13 509	619.5	1 262.7	3 736	8 237.0	11 206	121.9	13.5	47 116	798.7	16 952
Kent	110	D	D	(6)	D	D	594	1 325.4	10 806	117.6	20.2	7 864	128.3	16 311
New Castle	637	D	D	(7)	D	D	2 079	5 367.0	11 217	122.1	12.9	30 375	523.1	17 220
Sussex	159	481.2	D	1 435	35.9	81.0	1 063	1 544.5	11 536	125.5	9.4	8 877	147.4	16 602
DISTRICT OF COLUMBIA	348	3 918.6	1 091.0	5 008	223.0	411.3	2 075	2 788.8	5 274	57.4	6.3	19 608	351.5	17 925
District of Columbia	348	3 918.6	1 091.0	5 008	223.0	411.3	2 075	2 788.8	5 274	57.4	6.3	19 608	351.5	17 925

[1] Includes only establishments with payroll. [2] For pay period including March 12. [3] Based on resident population estimated as of July 1, 1997. [4] 0 to 19 employees. [5] 20 to 99 employees.
[6] 1,000 to 2,499 employees. [7] 10,000 to 24,999 employees.

Sources: Wholesale Trade—U.S. Census Bureau, 1997 Economic Census, ECON97 Report Series CD-ROM, CD-EC97-1, Disc 1E, issued February 2001 (related Internet site <http://www.census.gov/epcd/www/97EC42.HTM>). Retail Trade—U.S. Census Bureau, 1997 Economic Census, ECON97 Report Series CD-ROM, CD-EC97-1, Disc 1E, issued February 2001 (related Internet site <http://www.census.gov/epcd/www/97EC44.HTM>).

Table B–11. Counties — **Wholesale Trade and Retail Trade**–Con.

[Includes U.S., states, and 3,142 counties/county equivalents defined as of January 1, 1992. For changes to these areas since January 1, 1992, see appendix B. Geographic Information]

County	Wholesale trade[1] (NAICS 42), 1997 Sales Establishments	Total (mil. dol.)	Merchant wholesalers (mil. dol.)	Paid employees[2]	Annual payroll (mil. dol.)	Operating expenses (mil. dol.)	Retail trade[1] (NAICS 44-45), 1997 Sales Establishments	Total (mil. dol.)	Per capita[3] Amount (dollars)	Percent of national average	Percent from general merchandise stores	Annual payroll Paid employees[2]	Total (mil. dol.)	Per paid employee (dollars)
FLORIDA	31 214	187 079.9	121 260.1	296 139	9 678.2	20 378.7	66 643	151 191.2	10 297	112.0	13.0	841 814	14 169.5	16 832
Alachua	224	738.0	508.5	1 824	54.5	114.8	923	1 934.5	9 791	106.5	16.2	12 726	186.2	14 629
Baker	7	D	D	(4)	D	D	61	95.7	4 597	50.0	D	630	7.3	11 619
Bay	173	422.1	279.4	1 406	34.2	72.1	832	1 496.8	10 228	111.3	21.2	9 558	148.1	15 496
Bradford	20	31.1	D	78	1.7	3.8	94	151.7	6 165	67.1	D	930	12.7	13 649
Brevard	577	1 362.4	1 019.1	4 389	136.2	261.5	1 856	3 900.5	8 495	92.4	16.0	23 867	370.3	15 514
Broward	4 359	26 122.2	16 434.4	38 614	1 414.7	3 086.7	6 804	17 979.8	12 174	132.5	10.8	89 290	1 639.9	18 366
Calhoun	13	D	D	(4)	D	D	49	81.0	6 545	71.2	2.9	478	6.4	13 295
Charlotte	103	117.2	D	446	11.2	24.1	515	1 063.3	8 035	87.4	22.6	6 840	100.4	14 679
Citrus	88	90.4	74.2	383	7.1	15.8	429	800.6	7 191	78.2	14.0	5 049	71.8	14 212
Clay	104	220.6	D	503	12.7	30.7	516	1 100.5	8 231	89.6	18.2	6 956	106.0	15 235
Collier	350	813.8	644.4	2 076	63.0	131.7	1 343	2 627.1	13 624	148.2	11.4	15 366	274.1	17 836
Columbia	87	286.7	231.0	859	21.6	41.2	239	556.0	10 764	117.1	D	3 132	49.0	15 636
Dade	8 935	43 604.4	35 347.4	70 050	2 235.9	4 972.9	9 814	20 720.6	9 718	105.7	12.7	110 292	1 995.8	18 096
DeSoto	19	D	D	(5)	D	D	81	197.0	7 961	86.6	9.7	937	14.9	15 876
Dixie	4	D	D	(4)	D	D	42	39.2	3 090	33.6	D	271	3.6	13 244
Duval	1 394	16 590.0	9 552.0	21 860	760.3	1 565.2	3 134	8 034.1	11 003	119.7	12.7	44 276	761.4	17 197
Escambia	388	1 616.0	1 165.8	4 769	128.3	237.1	1 301	2 874.7	10 265	111.7	D	16 602	261.4	15 744
Flagler	39	94.6	D	272	7.9	17.4	119	244.1	5 435	59.1	D	1 608	22.2	13 820
Franklin	26	64.1	64.1	309	4.4	10.9	69	57.0	5 643	61.4	D	389	5.6	14 411
Gadsden	21	D	D	(6)	D	D	157	179.8	4 076	44.4	D	1 228	16.2	13 207
Gilchrist	11	D	D	(4)	D	D	34	29.9	2 236	24.3	3.9	206	2.8	13 374
Glades	4	D	D	(7)	D	D	27	35.2	4 164	45.3	D	211	2.7	12 730
Gulf	8	28.2	D	24	.6	3.2	60	48.9	3 623	39.4	D	404	4.7	11 733
Hamilton	5	D	D	(7)	D	D	55	53.6	4 293	46.7	D	393	4.3	10 936
Hardee	21	92.4	74.4	164	5.1	10.9	79	116.8	5 544	60.3	D	721	10.6	14 713
Hendry	23	D	D	(5)	D	D	104	202.6	6 925	75.4	15.0	1 030	16.8	16 285
Hernando	98	142.3	D	513	13.8	25.8	371	821.5	6 626	72.1	15.8	5 270	74.3	14 097
Highlands	85	184.1	D	618	13.1	28.6	349	618.2	8 239	89.7	13.5	4 035	57.1	14 151
Hillsborough	2 233	23 668.5	12 171.9	33 851	1 151.4	2 353.9	3 821	10 931.6	12 018	130.8	10.9	57 038	1 001.4	17 557
Holmes	11	D	D	(4)	D	D	55	46.3	2 517	27.4	D	327	3.9	12 043
Indian River	147	D	D	(8)	D	D	667	1 143.9	11 683	127.1	15.7	7 793	121.5	15 594
Jackson	42	86.0	D	301	7.1	16.1	221	376.9	8 460	92.1	12.8	2 289	31.6	13 810
Jefferson	10	D	D	(4)	D	D	55	51.5	3 942	42.9	D	426	4.3	10 188
Lafayette	9	D	D	(4)	D	D	17	10.0	1 604	17.5	D	93	1.2	12 559
Lake	229	680.2	540.1	2 137	48.2	104.5	760	1 514.3	7 781	84.7	15.5	9 663	148.2	15 335
Lee	586	1 450.3	1 081.5	4 593	135.3	263.9	1 924	4 367.0	11 320	123.2	14.2	25 417	430.5	16 936
Leon	260	D	D	(9)	D	D	1 038	2 244.4	10 476	114.0	D	15 478	229.7	14 838
Levy	21	37.7	D	141	2.2	4.9	132	234.5	7 541	82.1	D	1 455	19.2	13 203
Liberty	1	D	D	(7)	D	D	17	11.9	1 766	19.2	–	83	1.2	14 651
Madison	15	60.9	D	128	2.3	4.7	72	64.1	3 653	39.7	3.0	567	6.6	11 668
Manatee	270	1 087.6	734.0	2 348	76.5	150.7	938	2 141.0	9 110	99.1	15.5	12 165	194.4	15 984
Marion	309	999.6	691.8	3 219	80.0	168.9	1 014	2 221.4	9 423	102.5	15.4	13 159	202.1	15 361
Martin	174	423.8	204.3	695	23.7	47.4	712	1 454.0	12 779	139.1	D	8 425	147.5	17 504
Monroe	131	217.5	D	870	19.5	40.5	707	914.2	11 300	123.0	8.3	6 246	99.5	15 931
Nassau	40	158.4	D	238	8.9	19.2	215	332.2	6 156	67.0	11.0	2 172	28.6	13 145
Okaloosa	139	248.3	D	959	23.9	55.1	931	1 754.9	10 468	113.9	18.2	11 322	165.7	14 631
Okeechobee	31	D	D	(5)	D	D	149	270.1	8 741	95.1	D	1 657	23.6	14 243
Orange	1 931	24 089.1	9 826.6	25 730	868.5	1 637.1	3 911	10 450.9	13 312	144.9	11.4	53 854	913.6	16 964
Osceola	108	1 070.1	1 058.2	1 499	41.3	82.7	612	1 349.7	9 579	104.2	16.9	8 289	124.8	15 052
Palm Beach	2 187	11 544.5	7 574.6	17 864	707.0	1 593.6	4 967	11 731.2	11 561	125.8	12.0	61 563	1 126.1	18 292
Pasco	243	351.6	D	1 378	34.1	71.1	1 055	2 247.1	7 057	76.8	17.2	14 200	212.5	14 962
Pinellas	1 730	11 558.7	8 803.3	17 616	609.3	1 194.9	3 895	10 183.9	11 665	126.9	10.7	51 843	911.4	17 581
Polk	639	4 176.2	2 753.1	8 329	212.7	450.4	1 816	3 844.3	8 606	93.6	16.0	22 751	360.9	15 861
Putnam	56	D	D	(6)	D	D	250	397.7	5 679	61.8	14.3	2 395	36.1	15 071
St. Johns	179	428.0	314.0	1 050	31.1	65.6	549	862.5	7 731	84.1	9.4	5 640	81.0	14 364
St. Lucie	198	581.5	381.6	2 262	53.8	112.0	610	1 387.2	7 818	85.1	D	7 644	125.1	16 361
Santa Rosa	82	103.1	70.4	296	7.1	15.3	319	561.1	4 932	53.7	D	3 615	44.2	12 227
Sarasota	527	1 035.9	761.5	3 122	86.2	180.3	1 669	3 606.6	12 011	130.7	10.7	20 311	343.8	16 926
Seminole	881	3 669.7	1 899.0	7 301	242.9	484.8	1 512	3 550.1	10 333	112.4	15.8	21 219	352.1	16 593
Sumter	18	84.4	D	236	4.5	9.1	111	185.3	4 578	49.8	8.3	1 192	14.8	12 438
Suwannee	35	D	D	(6)	D	D	137	205.0	6 438	70.1	9.2	1 333	19.2	14 440
Taylor	16	D	D	(5)	D	D	97	144.2	7 724	84.0	D	945	12.6	13 348
Union	3	D	D	(4)	D	D	28	27.2	2 185	23.8	D	180	2.8	15 328
Volusia	488	1 629.7	D	4 314	105.4	234.9	1 865	3 887.6	9 349	101.7	20.0	23 251	360.5	15 505
Wakulla	15	D	D	(4)	D	D	53	57.6	3 127	34.0	4.6	418	5.0	11 873
Walton	29	98.2	D	283	6.6	16.1	215	262.6	7 177	78.1	D	1 959	27.0	13 777
Washington	5	D	D	(7)	D	D	70	104.4	5 158	56.1	D	742	9.1	12 311

[1] Includes only establishments with payroll. [2] For pay period including March 12. [3] Based on resident population estimated as of July 1, 1997. [4] 20 to 99 employees. [5] 100 to 249 employees. [6] 250 to 499 employees. [7] 0 to 19 employees. [8] 1,000 to 2,499 employees. [9] 2,500 to 4,999 employees.

Sources: Wholesale Trade—U.S. Census Bureau, 1997 Economic Census, ECON97 Report Series CD-ROM, CD-EC97-1, Disc 1E, issued February 2001 (related Internet site <http://www.census.gov/epcd/www/97EC42.HTM>). Retail Trade—U.S. Census Bureau, 1997 Economic Census, ECON97 Report Series CD-ROM, CD-EC97-1, Disc 1E, issued February 2001 (related Internet site <http://www.census.gov/epcd/www/97EC44.HTM>).

Wholesale Trade and Retail Trade–Con.

[Includes U.S., states, and 3,142 counties/county equivalents defined as of January 1, 1992. For changes to these areas since January 1, 1992, see appendix B. Geographic Information]

County	Wholesale trade[1] (NAICS 42), 1997						Retail trade[1] (NAICS 44-45), 1997							
		Sales						Sales				Annual payroll		
									Per capita[3]		Percent from general merchandise stores			
	Establishments	Total (mil. dol.)	Merchant wholesalers (mil. dol.)	Paid employees[2]	Annual payroll (mil. dol.)	Operating expenses (mil. dol.)	Establishments	Total (mil. dol.)	Amount (dollars)	Percent of national average		Paid employees[2]	Total (mil. dol.)	Per paid employee (dollars)
GEORGIA	13 978	163 782.6	69 922.1	191 087	7 519.7	15 252.1	33 073	72 212.5	9 646	105.0	12.9	420 676	6 943.6	16 506
Appling	14	41.0	D	92	2.8	5.7	88	116.9	7 131	77.6	2.5	616	9.7	15 672
Atkinson	9	11.9	11.9	67	.9	2.1	30	20.9	2 923	31.8	D	154	1.9	12 104
Bacon	10	40.4	D	141	2.4	7.4	37	47.1	4 569	49.7	D	291	4.1	14 058
Baker	1	D	D	(4)	D	D	5	4.4	1 174	12.8	–	45	.4	9 800
Baldwin	23	57.6	D	169	3.8	8.4	218	372.0	8 877	96.6	22.9	2 407	34.3	14 234
Banks	12	44.6	44.6	331	8.5	13.9	69	75.7	6 064	66.0	D	560	7.1	12 620
Barrow	30	73.8	D	223	5.6	10.9	145	344.8	8 863	96.4	D	1 798	30.8	17 144
Bartow	92	258.2	208.7	814	23.1	58.2	246	580.0	8 380	91.2	17.5	3 219	53.3	16 543
Ben Hill	20	D	D	(5)	D	D	93	144.0	8 290	90.2	D	884	12.3	13 922
Berrien	24	40.5	D	110	2.4	5.2	62	79.3	4 976	54.1	D	471	8.1	17 176
Bibb	272	1 511.7	1 009.5	3 545	110.7	207.5	912	1 977.3	12 668	137.8	15.5	12 885	194.2	15 069
Bleckley	4	D	D	(4)	D	D	53	59.0	5 327	58.0	4.9	392	4.8	12 291
Brantley	7	6.5	6.5	44	1.2	2.4	32	26.4	1 986	21.6	D	180	2.1	11 622
Brooks	9	5.8	D	36	.5	1.1	57	63.5	4 016	43.7	3.8	349	5.3	15 315
Bryan	14	D	D	(6)	D	D	61	85.3	3 692	40.2	D	537	7.4	13 762
Bulloch	54	333.4	310.9	582	13.9	34.4	259	471.9	9 462	103.0	20.6	3 386	44.0	12 994
Burke	19	128.0	128.0	208	6.1	14.9	81	118.6	5 280	57.5	4.0	700	10.6	15 074
Butts	12	143.4	143.4	169	6.7	11.9	71	111.9	6 493	70.7	D	613	8.3	13 618
Calhoun	6	18.8	D	44	1.1	3.3	25	29.0	5 720	62.2	D	212	2.6	12 491
Camden	9	12.5	12.5	63	1.0	2.0	143	275.7	6 050	65.8	15.7	1 687	21.7	12 842
Candler	16	54.3	D	146	3.2	8.1	50	74.6	8 409	91.5	2.5	388	5.5	14 121
Carroll	84	1 286.3	D	1 232	48.2	121.0	348	574.5	7 082	77.1	15.5	3 505	53.2	15 184
Catoosa	39	747.7	D	638	15.7	33.1	172	406.2	8 224	89.5	25.7	2 524	35.4	14 017
Charlton	8	85.0	D	37	.9	2.1	49	31.8	3 432	37.3	8.1	201	3.1	15 214
Chatham	348	2 445.1	1 671.3	4 347	142.9	292.6	1 261	2 466.9	10 940	119.0	16.1	15 625	244.0	15 619
Chattahoochee	1	D	D	(4)	D	D	6	4.2	258	2.8	–	26	.4	14 154
Chattooga	12	12.4	D	54	1.0	1.7	82	122.5	5 351	58.2	D	922	11.9	12 858
Cherokee	201	490.8	264.7	1 103	34.7	65.6	351	968.9	7 622	82.9	D	5 202	86.7	16 665
Clarke	81	D	225.7	(7)	D	D	540	1 118.8	12 336	134.2	D	7 760	110.3	14 218
Clay	5	3.8	D	16	.3	.6	17	10.5	3 040	33.1	D	123	1.2	9 805
Clayton	316	3 345.2	2 042.3	6 142	217.5	394.0	832	2 731.7	13 338	145.1	16.1	16 204	285.3	17 609
Clinch	8	11.7	D	60	1.2	2.4	32	25.1	3 805	41.4	10.4	220	2.5	11 455
Cobb	1 632	23 231.5	7 766.9	24 859	1 270.8	2 335.9	2 234	6 971.6	12 646	137.6	12.4	37 323	663.6	17 779
Coffee	55	183.3	D	469	11.2	22.3	210	389.9	11 535	125.5	D	2 120	33.0	15 562
Colquitt	53	156.4	118.7	436	9.8	18.7	214	326.0	8 233	89.6	12.3	2 026	29.4	14 535
Columbia	91	D	314.5	(8)	D	D	247	613.0	6 911	75.2	D	3 731	60.0	16 077
Cook	20	86.0	D	231	3.9	8.5	89	121.1	8 280	90.1	1.9	824	10.7	13 038
Coweta	79	513.5	D	735	16.8	41.5	259	550.0	6 812	74.1	D	3 728	52.7	14 138
Crawford	2	D	D	(6)	D	D	14	11.2	1 043	11.3	D	84	1.2	14 000
Crisp	29	266.8	D	483	12.5	28.1	158	234.5	11 419	124.3	D	1 859	23.7	12 732
Dade	8	D	D	(6)	D	D	54	92.3	6 318	68.7	2.6	476	5.9	12 466
Dawson	19	71.0	46.4	56	2.1	5.1	106	119.4	8 558	93.1	–	704	12.2	17 293
Decatur	35	341.1	D	452	11.0	25.9	172	243.6	9 132	99.4	7.8	1 656	21.7	13 079
De Kalb	1 518	19 215.9	6 425.6	23 560	964.4	1 845.2	2 407	6 229.3	10 550	114.8	10.6	34 901	635.7	18 214
Dodge	20	D	D	(5)	D	D	84	102.4	5 661	61.6	20.3	799	9.0	11 263
Dooly	15	56.7	D	120	3.2	7.0	51	65.7	6 267	68.2	D	336	4.8	14 193
Dougherty	184	D	D	(7)	D	D	574	1 154.7	12 085	131.5	18.5	7 707	113.9	14 774
Douglas	105	1 100.1	947.4	1 492	43.7	108.0	312	974.7	11 251	122.4	D	4 781	82.6	17 275
Early	19	133.3	D	277	5.7	11.1	68	69.9	5 758	62.7	5.3	519	6.4	12 293
Echols	1	D	D	(4)	D	D	3	D	D	D	D	(4)	D	D
Effingham	12	D	D	(6)	D	D	91	165.8	4 729	51.5	D	1 193	15.7	13 171
Elbert	50	68.2	68.2	294	6.6	16.7	85	130.7	6 813	74.1	D	726	10.5	14 459
Emanuel	25	126.3	61.7	239	4.0	9.8	102	139.6	6 649	72.4	13.6	902	12.0	13 271
Evans	10	35.0	D	74	1.3	3.3	60	85.8	8 837	96.2	D	444	7.1	16 032
Fannin	16	21.1	D	56	1.4	3.4	103	126.7	6 978	75.9	D	779	10.7	13 715
Fayette	135	545.5	276.1	1 236	42.3	92.1	298	677.6	7 967	86.7	21.9	4 697	69.9	14 871
Floyd	112	523.3	424.6	1 163	35.8	69.7	442	808.1	9 536	103.8	21.9	4 991	75.0	15 035
Forsyth	228	1 140.8	D	3 138	110.0	215.2	255	653.9	8 566	93.2	D	3 503	63.5	18 140
Franklin	32	56.5	D	208	3.9	8.1	92	202.3	10 909	118.7	2.6	937	15.2	16 247
Fulton	2 462	55 915.1	16 692.3	40 435	1 823.9	3 610.7	3 569	9 248.2	12 779	139.1	11.4	51 556	990.1	19 205
Gilmer	17	44.4	D	170	2.9	8.6	89	136.1	7 565	82.3	D	778	11.9	15 343
Glascock	NA	NA	NA	NA	NA	NA	7	2.9	1 153	12.5	–	30	.3	9 800
Glynn	118	461.5	411.2	903	30.7	63.2	504	716.1	10 766	117.1	15.1	4 847	69.6	14 359
Gordon	57	150.6	D	675	16.5	35.8	241	360.1	8 945	97.3	D	2 260	33.9	15 000
Grady	24	125.3	D	272	5.7	11.9	111	130.1	6 054	65.9	D	824	12.2	14 829
Greene	16	102.0	25.0	90	2.2	5.2	56	66.8	4 997	54.4	D	465	6.2	13 340

[1] Includes only establishments with payroll. [2] For pay period including March 12. [3] Based on resident population estimated as of July 1, 1997. [4] 0 to 19 employees. [5] 100 to 249 employees. [6] 20 to 99 employees. [7] 1,000 to 2,499 employees. [8] 500 to 999 employees.

Sources: Wholesale Trade—U.S. Census Bureau, 1997 Economic Census, ECON[97] Report Series CD-ROM, CD-EC97-1, Disc 1E, issued February 2001 (related Internet site <http://www.census.gov/epcd/www/97EC42.HTM>).   Retail Trade—U.S. Census Bureau, 1997 Economic Census, ECON[97] Report Series CD-ROM, CD-EC97-1, Disc 1E, issued February 2001 (related Internet site <http://www.census.gov/epcd/www/97EC44.HTM>).

[Includes U.S., states, and 3,142 counties/county equivalents defined as of January 1, 1992. For changes to these areas since January 1, 1992, see appendix B. Geographic Information]

County	Wholesale trade[1] (NAICS 42), 1997 — Sales — Establishments	Total (mil. dol.)	Merchant whole-salers (mil. dol.)	Paid em-ployees[2]	Annual payroll (mil. dol.)	Operating expenses (mil. dol.)	Retail trade[1] (NAICS 44-45), 1997 — Sales — Estab-lishments	Total (mil. dol.)	Per capita[3] Amount (dollars)	Percent of national average	Percent from general mer-chandise stores	Paid em-ployees[2]	Annual payroll Total (mil. dol.)	Per paid em-ployee (dollars)
GEORGIA—Con.														
Gwinnett	1 959	29 114.6	16 191.9	31 305	1 365.0	3 130.6	2 013	6 829.0	13 640	148.4	10.0	33 639	632.5	18 802
Habersham	34	35.1	D	203	4.8	8.8	153	256.3	8 207	89.3	21.4	1 677	24.1	14 358
Hall	238	1 777.8	1 368.0	3 407	100.6	190.5	548	1 240.8	10 713	116.6	17.5	6 357	114.6	18 022
Hancock	3	D	D	(4)	D	D	24	17.0	1 888	20.5	D	149	2.0	13 597
Haralson	16	50.8	D	121	4.3	7.4	98	145.7	6 025	65.6	D	845	11.3	13 350
Harris	9	D	D	(4)	D	D	59	31.3	1 409	15.3	D	259	3.2	12 525
Hart	25	35.6	D	113	2.6	5.7	78	96.9	4 503	49.0	D	778	9.6	12 302
Heard	2	D	D	(4)	D	D	21	17.2	1 718	18.7	D	117	1.7	14 299
Henry	84	377.1	D	1 136	29.1	69.8	300	660.7	6 760	73.6	D	3 580	58.9	16 457
Houston	54	236.5	80.1	454	14.7	30.9	403	941.2	9 069	98.7	12.5	5 818	86.6	14 879
Irwin	10	13.3	D	54	1.1	2.2	31	28.3	3 160	34.4	D	226	3.1	13 588
Jackson	48	502.2	425.0	867	25.4	59.7	218	288.4	7 917	86.1	7.7	1 673	25.5	15 266
Jasper	3	D	D	(5)	D	D	21	19.9	2 018	22.0	D	148	2.0	13 547
Jeff Davis	23	177.9	D	228	6.1	15.8	79	127.9	10 089	109.8	D	660	9.2	14 012
Jefferson	19	59.8	D	188	3.1	6.7	83	94.3	5 298	57.6	4.5	681	10.2	15 023
Jenkins	8	10.9	10.9	44	.7	1.7	34	38.0	4 501	49.0	4.7	235	3.2	13 557
Johnson	13	25.4	25.4	56	.9	2.1	29	27.3	3 271	35.6	D	250	2.9	11 660
Jones	15	D	D	(5)	D	D	36	37.7	1 666	18.1	D	249	3.6	14 506
Lamar	6	10.0	10.0	63	1.2	2.2	51	74.1	5 130	55.8	3.4	440	6.8	15 545
Lanier	3	D	D	(4)	D	D	29	24.0	3 550	38.6	D	167	2.3	13 922
Laurens	64	125.3	D	390	9.5	19.8	265	417.5	9 645	105.0	16.2	2 872	38.4	13 379
Lee	7	D	D	(5)	D	D	39	54.0	2 467	26.8	–	362	4.4	12 144
Liberty	14	D	D	(5)	D	D	165	255.0	4 248	46.2	18.3	1 762	22.2	12 593
Lincoln	6	4.1	4.1	33	.6	1.1	21	15.9	1 962	21.3	D	118	1.4	12 108
Long	1	D	D	(4)	D	D	9	7.1	857	9.3	D	37	.4	12 108
Lowndes	135	452.9	382.2	1 155	31.5	61.7	533	1 008.5	11 914	129.6	15.3	6 187	91.3	14 754
Lumpkin	10	8.1	D	42	.7	1.7	64	120.1	6 626	72.1	D	740	11.8	15 959
McDuffie	12	D	D	(5)	D	D	112	312.3	14 470	157.5	D	1 382	25.0	18 063
McIntosh	7	D	D	(4)	D	D	106	104.9	10 588	115.2	D	732	9.1	12 428
Macon	15	63.6	D	129	2.6	5.8	52	57.7	4 349	47.3	5.1	409	5.5	13 411
Madison	47	514.3	D	1 146	39.3	64.8	74	76.4	3 161	34.4	D	453	5.9	12 956
Marion	4	1.2	D	11	.1	.3	23	30.1	4 611	50.2	D	181	2.7	14 923
Meriwether	8	3.1	3.1	21	.3	.8	85	99.4	4 339	47.2	4.5	556	9.4	16 973
Miller	7	D	D	(6)	D	D	43	39.2	6 189	67.3	D	286	3.4	11 976
Mitchell	39	148.5	D	408	8.2	18.8	107	122.3	5 800	63.1	10.9	897	12.1	13 474
Monroe	13	26.4	D	59	1.0	2.1	75	70.3	3 625	39.4	D	503	6.7	13 340
Montgomery	5	36.5	36.5	106	2.7	7.1	29	20.2	2 603	28.3	D	138	1.9	14 065
Morgan	17	66.7	66.7	186	4.2	9.8	71	166.3	11 461	124.7	D	886	15.6	17 570
Murray	33	537.2	D	320	10.5	39.5	108	166.9	5 234	57.0	3.9	743	13.6	18 238
Muscogee	208	1 316.5	D	2 884	91.3	211.3	845	1 950.9	10 675	116.2	D	11 718	186.6	15 920
Newton	52	D	D	(7)	D	D	173	319.8	5 792	63.0	D	2 023	32.4	16 036
Oconee	22	D	D	(6)	D	D	55	166.6	7 186	78.2	D	799	14.7	18 342
Oglethorpe	10	6.3	D	84	1.2	2.5	25	27.9	2 487	27.1	–	140	1.9	13 921
Paulding	45	98.6	D	260	7.4	15.8	124	390.8	5 678	61.8	D	2 137	31.4	14 686
Peach	18	D	D	(5)	D	D	110	146.7	6 147	66.9	D	862	11.5	13 379
Pickens	23	D	D	(6)	D	D	74	238.5	12 820	139.5	D	694	12.9	18 588
Pierce	15	D	D	(7)	D	D	69	68.6	4 428	48.2	D	417	6.5	15 528
Pike	13	14.4	D	44	1.4	2.9	23	15.9	1 300	14.1	D	109	1.4	13 284
Polk	20	121.5	D	318	9.5	22.8	146	183.9	5 126	55.8	15.3	1 377	18.3	13 286
Pulaski	16	162.7	D	215	5.5	12.8	53	48.8	5 875	63.9	D	319	4.6	14 476
Putnam	8	63.7	63.7	88	2.6	5.7	56	83.7	4 960	54.0	3.1	490	8.3	16 984
Quitman	2	D	D	(4)	D	D	6	4.1	1 668	18.2	–	30	.4	11 900
Rabun	8	D	D	(4)	D	D	91	97.6	7 370	80.2	1.8	561	8.7	15 594
Randolph	10	33.5	33.5	54	1.2	3.1	40	27.5	3 457	37.6	7.6	261	3.3	12 558
Richmond	245	756.9	649.2	2 262	68.8	136.6	912	1 909.9	9 964	108.4	D	12 332	189.3	15 352
Rockdale	124	1 230.4	324.9	1 267	47.3	86.8	281	766.0	11 440	124.5	D	4 411	71.4	16 184
Schley	9	21.5	D	57	1.5	3.2	14	9.9	2 568	27.9	D	96	1.1	11 135
Screven	8	9.8	D	41	.7	1.3	56	82.1	5 705	62.1	3.1	483	7.0	14 482
Seminole	14	83.0	D	182	2.0	5.1	61	71.5	7 434	80.9	3.7	413	5.4	13 123
Spalding	49	338.5	D	611	18.4	39.1	248	521.5	9 080	98.8	14.9	3 119	52.1	16 693
Stephens	28	50.8	48.5	222	5.1	10.3	121	203.9	8 082	87.9	D	1 247	17.8	14 290
Stewart	5	9.7	D	39	1.2	1.8	26	14.5	2 670	29.1	D	133	1.3	10 143
Sumter	42	168.9	D	430	11.0	21.3	162	283.9	9 012	98.1	D	1 984	28.1	14 142
Talbot	2	D	D	(4)	D	D	13	7.1	1 033	11.2	D	68	.7	9 691
Taliaferro	2	D	D	(4)	D	D	4	D	D	D	D	(5)	D	D
Tattnall	19	58.4	D	389	7.3	17.0	78	76.2	4 001	43.5	D	581	6.7	11 540

[1] Includes only establishments with payroll.   [2] For pay period including March 12.   [3] Based on resident population estimated as of July 1, 1997.   [4] 0 to 19 employees.   [5] 20 to 99 employees.   [6] 100 to 249 employees.   [7] 250 to 499 employees.

Sources: Wholesale Trade—U.S. Census Bureau, 1997 Economic Census, ECON97 Report Series CD-ROM, CD-EC97-1, Disc 1E, issued February 2001 (related Internet site <http://www.census.gov/epcd/www/97EC42.HTM>).   Retail Trade—U.S. Census Bureau, 1997 Economic Census, ECON97 Report Series CD-ROM, CD-EC97-1, Disc 1E, issued February 2001 (related Internet site <http://www.census.gov/epcd/www/97EC44.HTM>).

Table B–11. Counties — Wholesale Trade and Retail Trade–Con.

[Includes U.S., states, and 3,142 counties/county equivalents defined as of January 1, 1992. For changes to these areas since January 1, 1992, see appendix B. Geographic Information]

County	Wholesale trade[1] (NAICS 42), 1997 Sales — Establishments	Total (mil. dol.)	Merchant wholesalers (mil. dol.)	Paid employees[2]	Annual payroll (mil. dol.)	Operating expenses (mil. dol.)	Retail trade[1] (NAICS 44-45), 1997 Sales — Establishments	Total (mil. dol.)	Per capita[3] Amount (dollars)	Per capita[3] Percent of national average	Percent from general merchandise stores	Paid employees[2]	Annual payroll Total (mil. dol.)	Annual payroll Per paid employee (dollars)
GEORGIA—Con.														
Taylor	7	D	D	(4)	D	D	36	36.5	4 463	48.6	D	227	2.8	12 278
Telfair	14	53.6	D	237	4.5	11.0	60	49.5	4 327	47.1	5.3	407	4.9	11 921
Terrell	17	125.8	125.8	198	4.3	10.4	57	55.3	4 987	54.3	3.5	321	4.2	12 941
Thomas	64	293.0	D	701	21.0	38.5	256	395.8	9 298	101.2	16.3	2 661	39.0	14 656
Tift	88	459.4	356.7	1 117	26.6	55.7	260	440.4	12 028	130.9	11.9	2 500	36.1	14 433
Toombs	39	203.6	D	333	8.4	28.7	152	253.7	9 884	107.6	17.5	1 706	23.1	13 549
Towns	7	D	D	(5)	D	D	52	42.4	5 170	56.3	D	289	3.9	13 574
Treutlen	2	D	D	(5)	D	D	23	14.2	2 387	26.0	D	111	1.3	12 126
Troup	69	270.8	250.7	681	22.6	47.6	293	526.0	9 016	98.1	11.3	3 500	52.7	15 062
Turner	16	203.8	D	230	5.8	13.1	54	58.3	6 396	69.6	3.7	316	4.4	13 940
Twiggs	3	D	D	(5)	D	D	14	17.2	1 760	19.2	D	116	1.6	13 431
Union	15	37.3	D	92	2.1	3.5	75	101.8	6 463	70.3	5.3	592	8.2	13 895
Upson	17	17.0	D	112	1.4	2.6	121	174.5	6 430	70.0	D	1 119	14.5	12 980
Walker	58	D	D	(6)	D	D	180	240.1	3 861	42.0	7.4	1 515	22.4	14 752
Walton	45	239.9	D	322	10.4	31.7	162	247.6	4 813	52.4	D	1 567	25.0	15 977
Ware	62	169.4	D	493	10.4	24.6	226	390.1	10 949	119.1	21.9	2 628	35.8	13 604
Warren	3	.8	.8	6	.1	.2	22	12.5	2 077	22.6	D	128	1.9	15 133
Washington	24	37.8	D	157	4.0	8.1	108	139.3	6 958	75.7	D	925	13.2	14 307
Wayne	17	50.7	D	159	3.9	11.6	125	172.5	6 905	75.1	8.7	1 145	16.6	14 528
Webster	2	D	D	(5)	D	D	8	7.6	3 374	36.7	36.3	80	.8	9 375
Wheeler	3	D	D	(5)	D	D	13	11.1	2 218	24.1	–	64	.7	11 594
White	12	23.6	D	110	1.8	4.1	139	230.4	13 682	148.9	D	1 028	18.3	17 787
Whitfield	340	3 475.7	D	4 254	122.9	241.1	508	1 068.1	13 158	143.2	13.4	5 908	103.7	17 551
Wilcox	5	D	D	(5)	D	D	30	20.1	2 745	29.9	D	138	1.8	13 043
Wilkes	18	61.5	D	138	3.1	6.3	65	56.3	5 293	57.6	5.9	414	5.2	12 655
Wilkinson	7	24.8	24.8	125	3.3	6.0	29	29.5	2 740	29.8	D	190	2.3	12 068
Worth	32	118.7	98.3	308	7.9	19.5	62	101.5	4 554	49.6	3.0	461	8.1	17 616
HAWAII	1 872	7 147.5	5 088.7	18 532	576.0	1 213.5	5 088	11 317.8	9 516	103.5	20.1	64 218	1 161.8	18 092
Hawaii	179	457.3	367.2	1 362	35.9	79.7	688	1 183.1	8 401	91.4	20.6	7 587	128.5	16 941
Honolulu	1 463	6 079.9	4 215.7	15 423	487.0	1 017.7	3 269	8 264.7	9 466	103.0	21.0	44 960	823.6	18 317
Kalawao	NA	NA	D	NA	NA	NA	(7)	(7)	(7)	(7)	(7)	(7)	(7)	(7)
Kauai	64	176.7	D	423	11.9	29.0	326	510.7	9 078	98.8	17.5	3 427	59.0	17 217
Maui	166	433.6	D	1 324	41.2	87.1	7805	71 359.3	711 410	7124.2	714.8	78 244	7150.7	718 283
IDAHO	1 980	10 127.8	6 081.3	22 828	628.0	1 303.0	5 848	11 649.6	9 623	104.7	13.1	63 732	1 079.7	16 941
Ada	578	5 362.7	2 009.8	7 610	273.5	534.3	1 264	3 163.2	11 847	128.9	16.0	16 663	300.9	18 060
Adams	1	D	NA	(5)	D	D	16	13.4	3 527	38.4	–	81	.9	11 457
Bannock	104	282.6	253.1	935	25.2	49.8	343	705.7	9 544	103.9	14.6	4 177	65.1	15 590
Bear Lake	3	20.2	20.2	88	1.5	2.6	34	40.2	6 161	67.0	5.8	271	3.3	12 295
Benewah	8	17.6	17.6	52	1.2	3.7	41	50.2	5 587	60.8	–	313	4.9	15 649
Bingham	54	189.4	171.3	974	18.0	42.2	125	243.8	5 880	64.0	D	1 363	22.0	16 106
Blaine	41	172.3	D	301	12.3	38.6	189	226.9	13 213	143.8	D	1 372	26.3	19 160
Boise	NA	NA	NA	NA	NA	NA	18	6.6	1 311	14.3	–	65	.5	8 138
Bonner	37	69.8	66.1	256	6.2	13.6	200	573.8	16 521	179.8	6.5	2 325	41.5	17 870
Bonneville	181	808.0	689.7	2 484	63.2	123.1	480	933.4	11 664	126.9	21.5	5 615	90.1	16 045
Boundary	12	16.7	16.7	89	2.9	5.1	54	61.6	6 259	68.1	1.6	373	6.1	16 383
Butte	3	D	D	(5)	D	D	15	10.6	3 425	37.3	–	81	.9	10 765
Camas	1	D	D	(5)	D	D	4	3.0	3 539	38.5	–	11	.1	12 091
Canyon	157	555.2	451.3	1 512	38.4	86.9	429	1 014.1	8 701	94.7	9.3	4 724	88.9	18 827
Caribou	15	25.3	25.3	64	1.6	3.5	42	57.8	7 931	86.3	D	301	4.5	14 797
Cassia	40	218.6	168.7	271	6.3	15.3	116	193.0	9 002	98.0	D	1 144	19.2	16 753
Clark	1	D	D	(4)	D	D	4	4.5	5 368	58.4	D	40	.3	8 700
Clearwater	5	D	D	(5)	D	D	45	56.8	6 039	65.7	D	331	5.0	14 994
Custer	3	D	D	(4)	D	D	25	14.7	3 467	37.7	–	106	1.2	11 585
Elmore	11	20.1	D	64	1.6	3.4	84	231.0	9 361	101.9	D	894	17.3	19 334
Franklin	19	30.1	30.1	122	2.9	5.4	45	55.1	5 093	55.4	D	383	4.8	12 452
Fremont	17	83.0	68.8	235	4.2	9.1	50	53.0	4 508	49.1	D	285	4.2	14 744
Gem	18	35.7	D	155	3.0	6.1	42	49.5	3 423	37.2	D	326	5.4	16 623
Gooding	13	58.5	D	197	3.3	8.2	54	66.8	4 919	53.5	D	480	6.5	13 577
Idaho	15	38.6	D	168	2.8	5.3	81	75.2	5 001	54.4	1.5	540	8.0	14 794
Jefferson	30	101.2	D	511	8.0	18.5	48	59.9	3 130	34.1	D	438	5.7	13 071
Jerome	37	251.9	186.2	312	6.1	12.1	57	107.6	6 139	66.8	D	624	10.3	16 460

[1] Includes only establishments with payroll. [2] For pay period including March 12. [3] Based on resident population estimated as of July 1, 1997. [4] 20 to 99 employees. [5] 0 to 19 employees. [6] 500 to 999 employees. [7] Kalawao County included with Maui County; data not available separately.

Sources: Wholesale Trade—U.S. Census Bureau, 1997 Economic Census, ECON97 Report Series CD-ROM, CD-EC97-1, Disc 1E, issued February 2001 (related Internet site <http://www.census.gov/epcd/www/97EC42.HTM>).   Retail Trade—U.S. Census Bureau, 1997 Economic Census, ECON97 Report Series CD-ROM, CD-EC97-1, Disc 1E, issued February 2001 (related Internet site <http://www.census.gov/epcd/www/97EC44.HTM>).

[Includes U.S., states, and 3,142 counties/county equivalents defined as of January 1, 1992. For changes to these areas since January 1, 1992, see appendix B. Geographic Information]

County	Wholesale trade[1] (NAICS 42), 1997						Retail trade[1] (NAICS 44-45), 1997							
	Sales							Sales					Annual payroll	
									Per capita[3]		Percent from general mer-chandise stores			
	Estab-lishments	Total (mil. dol.)	Merchant whole-salers (mil. dol.)	Paid em-ployees[2]	Annual payroll (mil. dol.)	Operating expenses (mil. dol.)	Estab-lishments	Total (mil. dol.)	Amount (dollars)	Percent of national average		Paid em-ployees[2]	Total (mil. dol.)	Per paid em-ployee (dollars)
IDAHO—Con.														
Kootenai	121	402.9	361.6	1 171	35.7	82.6	545	1 022.7	10 351	112.6	11.3	5 590	100.5	17 978
Latah	44	111.6	D	255	6.0	13.5	176	253.8	7 654	83.3	16.5	1 982	26.7	13 474
Lemhi	10	8.0	8.0	28	.6	1.3	54	54.5	6 752	73.5	D	384	5.1	13 362
Lewis	8	27.2	27.2	87	1.8	3.7	27	21.0	5 212	56.7	–	137	2.5	18 044
Lincoln	1	D	NA	(4)	D	D	12	11.2	2 957	32.2	D	57	.7	12 667
Madison	40	94.3	77.7	605	8.4	18.5	93	211.9	8 520	92.7	D	1 286	18.9	14 706
Minidoka	42	158.4	D	776	16.8	31.0	76	130.4	6 361	69.2	D	775	12.1	15 575
Nez Perce	66	214.1	D	725	16.9	32.0	231	464.3	12 607	137.2	D	2 832	48.7	17 200
Oneida	1	D	D	(5)	D	D	11	10.3	2 588	28.2	D	78	.9	11 090
Owyhee	13	40.6	D	161	4.0	7.7	33	31.6	3 126	34.0	D	202	2.9	14 114
Payette	25	58.0	D	308	5.0	10.5	66	89.5	4 433	48.2	–	490	8.8	18 014
Power	11	72.9	D	143	3.2	7.9	23	35.9	4 367	47.5	D	191	3.1	16 073
Shoshone	13	33.1	33.1	95	2.6	6.5	76	243.5	17 454	189.9	D	687	12.8	18 702
Teton	4	.5	.5	6	.1	.2	37	34.7	6 568	71.5	D	217	3.0	13 977
Twin Falls	159	450.7	382.9	1 600	37.9	85.4	378	837.9	13 623	148.2	21.8	4 721	76.8	16 261
Valley	9	3.8	3.8	21	.9	2.1	65	66.2	8 200	89.2	D	436	6.7	15 433
Washington	9	46.7	D	322	4.2	9.2	40	58.7	5 841	63.6	D	341	5.5	16 073
ILLINOIS	21 951	275 968.4	142 923.4	325 752	13 324.5	27 788.1	44 568	108 002.2	8 992	97.8	13.0	610 790	10 596.0	17 348
Adams	127	686.7	606.9	1 650	45.7	92.3	341	669.5	9 913	107.9	19.6	4 752	68.2	14 347
Alexander	10	D	D	(4)	D	D	35	29.1	2 903	31.6	D	237	2.9	12 105
Bond	19	143.4	D	264	6.5	14.6	60	97.7	5 704	62.1	D	496	7.1	14 230
Boone	43	D	D	(6)	D	D	91	198.7	5 239	57.0	D	1 156	19.4	16 796
Brown	11	D	D	(7)	D	D	21	16.5	2 438	26.5	D	138	1.5	10 986
Bureau	58	D	D	(7)	D	D	145	229.5	6 423	69.9	D	1 379	20.7	15 019
Calhoun	4	D	D	(4)	D	D	24	26.8	5 365	58.4	D	134	2.0	14 843
Carroll	26	111.6	D	190	5.0	9.1	72	81.4	4 814	52.4	8.1	560	7.1	12 625
Cass	20	240.0	240.0	193	5.4	12.1	59	68.3	5 151	56.1	D	520	6.3	12 173
Champaign	199	2 419.0	1 759.1	3 737	111.5	224.0	675	1 556.7	9 131	99.4	20.9	10 645	151.9	14 268
Christian	51	363.6	D	482	15.0	30.7	156	283.1	7 899	86.0	D	1 644	24.7	15 021
Clark	22	104.8	104.8	199	4.6	9.4	77	106.7	6 508	70.8	11.6	627	8.5	13 624
Clay	31	84.2	D	316	6.1	12.8	66	92.1	6 395	69.6	D	662	7.4	11 224
Clinton	54	D	D	(7)	D	D	136	243.8	6 904	75.1	D	1 373	30.9	22 517
Coles	67	327.2	D	663	15.4	34.7	233	526.5	10 099	109.9	26.2	3 210	46.2	14 391
Cook	9 574	120 551.8	61 229.4	149 994	6 467.2	13 145.6	17 318	42 547.2	8 199	89.2	12.0	240 539	4 369.9	18 167
Crawford	24	246.8	D	151	3.4	7.3	93	136.4	6 495	70.7	D	907	12.5	13 792
Cumberland	16	48.7	D	87	1.9	5.1	42	37.2	3 342	36.4	D	253	3.3	13 154
DeKalb	75	871.8	D	835	32.2	64.5	309	642.3	7 565	82.3	D	4 008	63.1	15 735
De Witt	22	138.0	138.0	127	5.5	11.0	70	142.0	8 475	92.2	D	756	12.4	16 376
Douglas	33	203.4	200.0	370	8.6	22.0	165	185.8	9 349	101.7	D	1 299	16.7	12 831
DuPage	3 351	74 318.8	29 301.2	64 415	2 918.5	6 137.8	3 625	12 825.3	14 742	160.4	11.1	64 962	1 231.1	18 951
Edgar	31	163.8	D	260	5.4	15.8	68	108.3	5 451	59.3	D	721	9.8	13 614
Edwards	15	105.7	105.7	188	6.1	9.5	34	28.4	4 038	43.9	D	235	2.4	10 272
Effingham	58	265.9	241.8	879	29.6	54.1	236	561.3	16 814	183.0	D	3 205	50.2	15 678
Fayette	27	186.3	D	372	8.8	21.7	103	153.3	6 938	75.5	D	933	12.7	13 610
Ford	33	298.9	298.9	335	11.4	24.0	93	120.2	8 502	92.5	7.1	716	9.6	13 466
Franklin	47	72.6	D	258	6.1	12.1	192	276.9	6 826	74.3	12.6	1 707	27.1	15 864
Fulton	36	95.4	86.3	235	5.0	10.4	156	248.4	6 398	69.6	15.7	1 718	24.8	14 416
Gallatin	8	D	D	(8)	D	D	29	23.4	3 522	38.3	D	144	2.0	13 764
Greene	22	70.1	64.1	108	2.4	5.9	70	71.1	4 527	49.3	D	480	6.6	13 660
Grundy	40	387.3	D	347	12.3	23.9	137	288.0	7 949	86.5	D	1 604	27.2	16 979
Hamilton	13	54.3	54.3	68	1.4	2.9	37	37.7	4 385	47.7	6.4	207	2.7	13 000
Hancock	32	211.9	211.9	220	5.1	11.7	101	101.5	4 800	52.2	.9	601	8.8	14 646
Hardin	NA	NA	NA	NA	NA	NA	15	8.6	1 732	18.8	–	60	.8	13 783
Henderson	10	21.6	21.6	40	.7	1.9	23	21.0	2 426	26.4	–	125	1.7	13 416
Henry	81	521.6	D	775	19.9	41.6	217	371.9	7 222	78.6	D	2 583	37.1	14 348
Iroquois	65	405.3	D	524	12.8	32.1	118	176.1	5 606	61.0	D	1 139	17.2	15 067
Jackson	45	78.4	65.2	289	7.6	17.2	287	551.9	9 029	98.2	25.2	3 992	60.7	15 217
Jasper	22	120.1	D	206	5.1	11.5	45	78.5	7 395	80.5	D	366	5.9	16 063
Jefferson	64	362.9	D	667	18.5	58.4	216	385.2	9 862	107.3	18.4	2 678	36.8	13 754
Jersey	28	D	D	(8)	D	D	82	171.0	8 037	87.5	D	1 031	14.2	13 794
Jo Daviess	31	130.4	113.5	176	5.5	12.3	144	150.2	6 931	75.4	D	897	12.4	13 807
Johnson	12	38.5	D	90	1.7	4.4	34	42.8	3 251	35.4	D	235	4.1	17 340
Kane	787	8 557.1	4 086.7	9 948	392.4	778.2	1 353	3 116.6	8 163	88.8	16.0	19 688	331.1	16 817

[1] Includes only establishments with payroll. [2] For pay period including March 12. [3] Based on resident population estimated as of July 1, 1997. [4] 20 to 99 employees. [5] 0 to 19 employees. [6] 250 to 499 employees. [7] 500 to 999 employees. [8] 100 to 249 employees.

Sources: Wholesale Trade—U.S. Census Bureau, 1997 Economic Census, ECON97 Report Series CD-ROM, CD-EC97-1, Disc 1E, issued February 2001 (related Internet site <http://www.census.gov/epcd/www/97EC42.HTM>). Retail Trade—U.S. Census Bureau, 1997 Economic Census, ECON97 Report Series CD-ROM, CD-EC97-1, Disc 1E, issued February 2001 (related Internet site <http://www.census.gov/epcd/www/97EC44.HTM>).

Table B–11. Counties — Wholesale Trade and Retail Trade–Con.

[Includes U.S., states, and 3,142 counties/county equivalents defined as of January 1, 1992. For changes to these areas since January 1, 1992, see appendix B. Geographic Information]

County	Wholesale trade[1] (NAICS 42), 1997						Retail trade[1] (NAICS 44-45), 1997							
	Sales			Paid employees[2]	Annual payroll (mil. dol.)	Operating expenses (mil. dol.)	Sales					Paid employees[2]	Annual payroll	
	Establishments	Total (mil. dol.)	Merchant wholesalers (mil. dol.)				Establishments	Total (mil. dol.)	Per capita[3]		Percent from general merchandise stores		Total (mil. dol.)	Per paid employee (dollars)
									Amount (dollars)	Percent of national average				
ILLINOIS—Con.														
Kankakee	126	809.3	D	1 628	47.2	102.1	388	907.0	8 878	96.6	22.0	5 594	88.5	15 812
Kendall	61	348.0	D	585	18.6	35.1	118	371.0	7 441	81.0	D	1 755	36.6	20 876
Knox	75	381.7	330.2	933	25.2	54.1	252	489.9	8 804	95.8	20.2	3 785	52.5	13 863
Lake	1 411	19 079.1	10 299.3	20 149	932.4	2 342.4	2 391	8 562.3	14 316	155.8	7.9	38 002	785.9	20 679
La Salle	168	1 292.6	1 240.7	1 729	55.8	109.0	502	1 047.7	9 529	103.7	17.3	6 352	96.8	15 236
Lawrence	16	64.0	64.0	248	6.7	10.9	63	71.8	4 624	50.3	D	535	6.9	12 929
Lee	55	248.5	D	525	14.7	30.2	138	234.8	6 525	71.0	D	1 379	23.6	17 100
Livingston	48	255.6	D	431	11.1	25.0	186	336.3	8 451	92.0	10.2	1 909	28.7	15 028
Logan	45	252.3	D	433	12.2	28.0	140	238.0	7 574	82.4	13.1	1 283	20.3	15 784
McDonough	37	164.8	D	233	5.6	13.5	167	246.6	6 966	75.8	D	1 870	24.8	13 288
McHenry	497	2 874.1	1 732.8	5 381	210.7	407.8	813	2 034.6	8 620	93.8	D	10 457	188.3	18 010
McLean	212	1 348.4	D	2 268	87.1	168.2	632	1 474.6	10 406	113.2	13.5	9 242	142.3	15 399
Macon	158	3 249.3	3 114.5	1 815	57.4	115.9	506	1 129.6	9 895	107.7	17.4	6 967	110.4	15 845
Macoupin	76	238.9	230.0	749	19.6	37.7	188	309.4	6 331	68.9	7.3	1 695	26.0	15 323
Madison	259	2 264.4	1 168.4	2 860	91.6	190.1	969	2 057.0	7 945	86.5	D	11 722	181.4	15 478
Marion	53	166.7	D	474	11.8	25.5	226	309.4	7 352	80.0	18.7	2 119	30.2	14 239
Marshall	16	232.5	D	127	3.9	7.4	49	68.7	5 350	58.2	D	395	6.4	16 258
Mason	32	305.2	299.1	225	5.6	13.4	59	98.4	5 838	63.5	D	601	9.5	15 812
Massac	6	D	D	(4)	D	D	55	79.7	5 143	56.0	D	414	6.4	15 575
Menard	15	74.7	D	104	2.7	5.5	41	58.3	4 681	50.9	D	320	4.6	14 503
Mercer	21	102.2	D	103	3.1	7.7	57	88.5	5 036	54.8	D	586	8.6	14 594
Monroe	29	D	D	(5)	D	D	85	175.2	6 771	73.7	D	858	15.4	17 955
Montgomery	46	215.1	198.6	351	9.0	19.4	142	236.6	7 532	82.0	D	1 344	19.3	14 311
Morgan	45	D	D	(5)	D	D	192	344.7	9 628	104.8	16.3	2 207	31.9	14 448
Moultrie	28	103.2	D	211	5.1	11.1	46	42.5	2 940	32.0	D	303	3.9	12 861
Ogle	54	D	D	(6)	D	D	150	268.3	5 344	58.2	D	1 491	24.0	16 099
Peoria	299	5 876.5	D	4 755	171.6	345.7	801	1 847.4	10 138	110.3	18.0	11 817	182.6	15 451
Perry	14	D	D	(4)	D	D	98	113.8	5 329	58.0	D	789	14.3	18 142
Piatt	29	332.4	D	335	7.6	16.3	55	99.4	6 031	65.6	D	432	7.8	18 153
Pike	37	175.1	D	319	8.0	19.5	85	119.9	6 938	75.5	D	725	10.6	14 567
Pope	2	D	D	(7)	D	D	12	7.5	1 585	17.2	–	36	.5	13 167
Pulaski	9	D	D	(4)	D	D	27	15.5	2 150	23.4	D	127	1.4	10 717
Putnam	7	D	D	(4)	D	D	22	23.4	4 032	43.9	–	126	1.9	15 024
Randolph	32	D	D	(5)	D	D	140	261.7	7 743	84.3	D	1 601	27.3	17 066
Richland	38	266.2	D	641	14.0	44.2	94	149.0	8 834	96.1	D	940	13.8	14 688
Rock Island	239	2 042.8	D	4 530	148.4	285.7	623	1 427.4	9 640	104.9	D	8 593	142.2	16 547
St. Clair	214	1 615.1	1 349.3	2 169	64.2	131.2	965	2 048.5	7 768	84.5	21.5	12 887	197.7	15 339
Saline	26	D	D	(5)	D	D	154	232.5	8 868	96.5	D	1 404	32.3	23 021
Sangamon	259	1 513.4	D	3 517	119.7	222.2	836	1 991.9	10 404	113.2	D	12 054	187.0	15 514
Schuyler	8	62.5	62.5	93	2.3	5.8	37	45.5	5 937	64.6	D	303	4.3	14 343
Scott	13	152.5	D	123	3.4	8.3	13	20.5	3 652	39.7	D	113	1.5	13 602
Shelby	37	153.1	146.8	237	5.6	14.2	86	123.9	5 465	59.5	2.5	554	7.7	13 935
Stark	12	52.0	52.0	73	1.6	4.0	23	27.4	4 326	47.1	–	124	2.4	19 460
Stephenson	54	129.6	127.2	429	10.0	21.9	191	414.6	8 451	92.0	15.5	2 522	40.3	15 992
Tazewell	140	D	D	(8)	D	D	473	1 275.2	9 896	107.7	D	6 813	112.1	16 457
Union	14	25.0	D	93	2.6	7.3	66	96.8	5 354	58.3	D	641	9.4	14 705
Vermilion	102	1 257.5	1 209.4	2 221	68.5	130.3	351	639.2	7 540	82.0	20.7	4 505	64.4	14 291
Wabash	21	52.3	D	116	2.8	8.0	49	75.6	5 965	64.9	D	508	6.7	13 234
Warren	23	164.4	D	274	7.3	21.0	67	97.7	5 162	56.2	D	632	9.1	14 394
Washington	27	128.9	128.9	245	6.9	17.0	83	157.1	10 237	111.4	3.3	662	13.0	19 573
Wayne	32	113.3	D	176	4.2	8.8	80	103.6	6 086	66.2	D	703	9.9	14 151
White	33	104.7	D	152	3.7	9.2	84	109.7	6 993	76.1	D	644	9.3	14 483
Whiteside	75	481.9	D	522	15.3	32.1	241	515.4	8 575	93.3	17.6	3 303	54.1	16 386
Will	577	3 946.2	2 518.9	6 563	230.2	486.6	1 157	3 286.2	7 388	80.4	11.4	17 267	301.3	17 447
Williamson	80	189.3	170.2	629	15.0	34.3	306	576.2	9 414	102.4	D	3 405	51.1	15 003
Winnebago	510	2 530.0	1 740.1	6 308	216.5	433.2	1 090	2 754.5	10 316	112.3	D	17 044	270.3	15 861
Woodford	55	D	D	(9)	D	D	101	229.4	6 585	71.7	D	1 009	16.8	16 654
INDIANA	8 896	66 350.1	38 354.0	112 705	3 737.8	7 412.2	24 954	57 241.7	9 748	106.1	15.4	337 867	5 273.8	15 609
Adams	43	151.3	151.3	314	7.5	17.7	172	344.6	10 528	114.6	10.0	1 824	27.9	15 315
Allen	686	6 586.2	4 806.2	10 861	357.8	682.0	1 320	3 534.6	11 335	123.3	19.7	21 917	351.1	16 021
Bartholomew	114	714.3	589.9	910	29.8	61.2	397	680.6	9 888	107.6	16.4	4 658	66.1	14 190
Benton	27	109.0	109.0	181	4.3	10.1	59	70.0	7 243	78.8	D	413	7.0	16 884
Blackford	15	20.8	20.8	110	2.9	6.9	56	82.9	5 924	64.5	D	515	6.8	13 217
Boone	94	500.9	202.0	629	18.8	35.3	173	261.0	6 068	66.0	D	1 632	25.3	15 473
Brown	9	D	D	(4)	D	D	102	42.1	2 709	29.5	D	432	5.3	12 227
Carroll	33	145.8	D	224	6.4	14.6	61	90.9	4 567	49.7	D	574	8.8	15 392
Cass	49	220.0	187.6	453	13.7	25.8	169	339.1	8 755	95.3	D	2 046	31.5	15 404

[1] Includes only establishments with payroll. [2] For pay period including March 12. [3] Based on resident population estimated as of July 1, 1997. [4] 20 to 99 employees. [5] 250 to 499 employees. [6] 1,000 to 2,499 employees. [7] 0 to 19 employees. [8] 2,500 to 4,999 employees. [9] 500 to 999 employees.

Sources: Wholesale Trade—U.S. Census Bureau, 1997 Economic Census, ECON97 Report Series CD-ROM, CD-EC97-1, Disc 1E, issued February 2001 (related Internet site <http://www.census.gov/epcd/www/97EC42.HTM>). Retail Trade—U.S. Census Bureau, 1997 Economic Census, ECON97 Report Series CD-ROM, CD-EC97-1, Disc 1E, issued February 2001 (related Internet site <http://www.census.gov/epcd/www/97EC44.HTM>).

[Includes U.S., states, and 3,142 counties/county equivalents defined as of January 1, 1992. For changes to these areas since January 1, 1992, see appendix B. Geographic Information]

County	Wholesale trade[1] (NAICS 42), 1997 — Sales						Retail trade[1] (NAICS 44-45), 1997 — Sales		Per capita[3]		Percent from general merchandise stores	Annual payroll		
	Establishments	Total (mil. dol.)	Merchant wholesalers (mil. dol.)	Paid employees[2]	Annual payroll (mil. dol.)	Operating expenses (mil. dol.)	Establishments	Total (mil. dol.)	Amount (dollars)	Percent of national average		Paid employees[2]	Total (mil. dol.)	Per paid employee (dollars)
INDIANA—Con.														
Clark	128	686.5	D	1 486	37.8	84.0	471	1 261.0	13 530	147.2	16.8	7 887	114.9	14 568
Clay	18	D	D	(4)	D	D	105	190.1	7 172	78.0	D	1 076	16.1	14 962
Clinton	47	D	D	(5)	D	D	126	193.5	5 835	63.5	D	1 200	18.8	15 698
Crawford	4	D	D	(6)	D	D	36	36.3	3 483	37.9	D	322	4.0	12 292
Daviess	22	76.6	D	233	6.0	13.4	145	260.5	9 033	98.3	D	1 490	21.4	14 339
Dearborn	37	D	D	(4)	D	D	158	344.3	7 424	80.8	D	1 896	29.0	15 273
Decatur	36	231.2	D	423	10.4	20.8	128	230.9	9 099	99.0	D	1 414	20.2	14 278
De Kalb	49	254.5	224.7	413	15.6	34.3	152	291.8	7 492	81.5	D	1 667	25.1	15 034
Delaware	119	653.4	330.7	1 501	45.8	91.3	548	1 118.7	9 504	103.4	20.6	7 340	105.4	14 355
Dubois	72	781.8	D	1 417	52.1	181.6	231	551.7	14 133	153.8	11.1	2 951	50.7	17 174
Elkhart	382	2 246.1	1 885.5	5 031	160.0	303.0	751	1 973.6	11 555	125.7	14.8	10 866	179.6	16 531
Fayette	19	69.5	D	227	6.2	10.5	94	193.4	7 403	80.6	D	1 202	16.8	13 951
Floyd	97	298.0	D	1 076	30.1	57.5	231	331.0	4 631	50.4	1.9	2 366	36.8	15 543
Fountain	22	D	D	(4)	D	D	75	120.4	6 616	72.0	D	675	8.9	13 142
Franklin	14	28.1	D	81	2.1	4.3	63	66.5	3 097	33.7	D	443	6.5	14 603
Fulton	35	70.0	59.7	175	4.0	7.8	91	143.8	7 051	76.7	D	936	11.6	12 444
Gibson	38	D	D	(4)	D	D	148	252.0	7 859	85.5	15.6	1 694	21.9	12 936
Grant	72	200.2	168.4	770	20.4	47.1	318	629.5	8 641	94.0	D	3 864	54.8	14 177
Greene	30	89.2	D	145	3.1	7.4	135	178.5	5 398	58.7	D	1 252	16.7	13 369
Hamilton	508	5 171.0	1 643.5	5 552	223.2	410.3	574	1 786.5	11 525	125.4	15.5	9 896	176.8	17 870
Hancock	62	258.7	D	665	17.9	33.6	149	341.4	6 419	69.8	8.8	1 639	25.4	15 520
Harrison	27	70.9	D	264	6.0	11.0	133	234.9	6 894	75.0	D	1 540	20.6	13 400
Hendricks	100	263.9	236.8	725	23.2	42.6	289	756.5	8 208	89.3	D	4 363	65.5	15 017
Henry	46	197.3	D	498	13.8	29.4	189	426.6	8 727	95.0	9.8	2 107	33.4	15 844
Howard	110	D	D	(7)	D	D	409	959.6	11 455	124.6	23.3	6 078	89.1	14 666
Huntington	54	265.1	184.6	485	12.9	30.7	169	312.8	8 417	91.6	13.3	1 943	28.1	14 441
Jackson	46	206.0	D	553	14.7	27.6	242	389.5	9 513	103.5	17.9	2 444	36.6	14 970
Jasper	43	283.7	D	299	8.6	18.9	149	278.5	9 737	106.0	8.6	1 718	24.7	14 349
Jay	21	122.7	98.5	231	5.2	14.3	82	115.0	5 308	57.8	D	707	17.0	23 992
Jefferson	27	40.3	34.6	226	4.8	7.5	167	281.2	8 963	97.5	23.3	1 766	24.5	13 895
Jennings	16	39.9	D	115	2.7	5.9	72	136.0	5 012	54.5	D	764	12.1	15 895
Johnson	113	659.9	D	788	26.6	54.0	490	1 171.2	10 957	119.2	30.1	7 338	109.2	14 877
Knox	68	373.7	303.4	842	19.3	35.5	234	399.9	10 099	109.9	18.4	2 668	36.7	13 759
Kosciusko	105	372.3	254.5	737	22.4	47.8	333	551.9	7 832	85.2	11.8	3 460	55.3	15 984
Lagrange	91	132.4	D	479	9.8	18.7	145	203.9	6 200	67.5	3.3	1 184	17.6	14 880
Lake	547	3 876.3	2 117.6	7 094	249.7	472.4	1 736	4 380.6	9 100	99.0	13.5	25 503	398.6	15 631
La Porte	135	658.5	551.9	1 525	44.6	94.2	552	1 041.7	9 501	103.4	15.9	6 312	95.7	15 156
Lawrence	26	54.7	D	228	5.3	15.3	207	372.1	8 183	89.0	16.1	2 108	31.6	15 001
Madison	105	428.6	326.2	1 157	31.3	61.7	521	1 123.4	8 510	92.6	17.8	6 790	101.3	14 924
Marion	1 953	21 284.8	10 532.7	32 619	1 245.4	2 381.2	3 654	10 757.4	13 203	143.7	12.5	59 830	1 038.3	17 355
Marshall	71	265.5	220.7	696	18.4	36.3	202	367.9	8 115	88.3	12.8	2 103	31.2	14 857
Martin	6	D	D	(4)	D	D	52	58.6	5 562	60.5	2.5	385	4.7	12 177
Miami	41	270.9	D	564	16.4	32.5	121	205.0	6 171	67.1	D	1 068	17.9	16 785
Monroe	102	D	D	(8)	D	D	514	1 073.7	9 262	100.8	19.5	6 846	97.5	14 236
Montgomery	56	176.4	D	271	8.9	23.0	167	293.8	8 096	88.1	16.2	1 947	27.2	13 971
Morgan	56	150.5	D	303	8.8	23.1	207	432.9	6 688	72.8	D	2 372	35.7	15 037
Newton	24	82.4	D	131	4.1	10.0	53	70.6	4 804	52.3	D	418	5.7	13 531
Noble	39	208.3	181.9	392	13.0	24.3	157	258.3	6 159	67.0	12.9	1 642	23.5	14 289
Ohio	NA	NA	NA	NA	NA	NA	12	13.7	2 520	27.4	D	108	1.4	12 593
Orange	19	33.4	D	109	2.0	4.8	89	103.2	5 325	57.9	D	574	9.0	15 716
Owen	15	13.0	D	60	1.4	2.6	59	71.3	3 519	38.3	D	510	6.1	11 949
Parke	12	21.0	21.0	67	1.1	2.6	50	48.8	2 944	32.0	D	367	4.8	13 005
Perry	15	77.3	D	178	5.8	16.0	85	131.2	6 797	74.0	D	974	11.7	12 016
Pike	12	37.1	D	113	3.2	7.0	38	41.1	3 209	34.9	D	266	3.1	11 805
Porter	174	941.7	605.2	1 823	56.1	122.1	436	1 040.3	7 215	78.5	17.5	6 231	98.6	15 819
Posey	30	D	D	(7)	D	D	95	151.5	5 726	62.3	D	906	13.9	15 360
Pulaski	36	167.3	D	356	9.7	17.8	58	73.9	5 539	60.3	D	419	6.9	16 368
Putnam	24	39.2	D	110	2.7	5.5	126	186.0	5 485	59.7	D	1 278	18.4	14 423
Randolph	21	76.5	D	120	3.1	6.3	111	152.2	5 532	60.2	D	978	13.7	14 056
Ripley	34	108.0	D	532	25.5	34.0	130	197.4	7 269	79.1	4.4	1 124	18.4	16 394
Rush	30	119.0	D	189	3.9	8.5	75	114.8	6 257	68.1	12.7	678	10.3	15 134
St. Joseph	472	3 389.0	2 666.7	7 080	230.7	447.7	1 069	2 782.9	10 780	117.3	19.4	16 822	249.0	14 802
Scott	15	13.9	D	83	1.8	3.5	105	168.2	7 366	80.2	D	1 134	15.9	14 003
Shelby	49	215.6	190.4	530	18.4	41.3	146	310.8	7 199	78.3	D	1 577	26.3	16 706
Spencer	24	217.5	209.7	308	8.4	18.2	80	94.6	4 556	49.6	D	661	9.7	14 604
Starke	20	75.8	D	127	3.2	8.1	95	110.3	4 657	50.7	9.9	812	11.2	13 743
Steuben	39	98.7	60.1	252	5.9	13.3	238	397.5	12 813	139.4	D	2 280	35.5	15 561
Sullivan	23	113.6	D	155	3.7	8.6	68	95.3	4 445	48.4	D	648	8.6	13 247
Switzerland	3	D	D	(6)	D	D	20	17.1	1 971	21.4	D	125	1.4	11 344
Tippecanoe	117	D	D	(8)	D	D	564	1 479.8	10 682	116.2	D	9 688	137.8	14 221

[1] Includes only establishments with payroll. [2] For pay period including March 12. [3] Based on resident population estimated as of July 1, 1997. [4] 100 to 249 employees. [5] 250 to 499 employees. [6] 0 to 19 employees. [7] 500 to 999 employees. [8] 1,000 to 2,499 employees.

Sources: Wholesale Trade—U.S. Census Bureau, 1997 Economic Census, ECON[97] Report Series CD-ROM, CD-EC97-1, Disc 1E, issued February 2001 (related Internet site <http://www.census.gov/epcd/www/97EC42.HTM>). Retail Trade—U.S. Census Bureau, 1997 Economic Census, ECON[97] Report Series CD-ROM, CD-EC97-1, Disc 1E, issued February 2001 (related Internet site <http://www.census.gov/epcd/www/97EC44.HTM>).

Table B–11. Counties — Wholesale Trade and Retail Trade–Con.

[Includes U.S., states, and 3,142 counties/county equivalents defined as of January 1, 1992. For changes to these areas since January 1, 1992, see appendix B. Geographic Information]

County	Wholesale trade[1] (NAICS 42), 1997 — Sales — Establishments	Total (mil. dol.)	Merchant wholesalers (mil. dol.)	Paid employees[2]	Annual payroll (mil. dol.)	Operating expenses (mil. dol.)	Retail trade[1] (NAICS 44-45), 1997 — Sales — Establishments	Total (mil. dol.)	Per capita[3] Amount (dollars)	Percent of national average	Percent from general merchandise stores	Paid employees[2]	Annual payroll Total (mil. dol.)	Per paid employee (dollars)
INDIANA—Con.														
Tipton	20	D	D	(4)	D	D	52	118.1	7 189	78.2	2.8	478	7.3	15 201
Union	10	44.9	D	94	1.7	4.3	31	28.9	3 965	43.1	–	221	3.5	15 674
Vanderburgh	352	D	1 273.8	(5)	D	D	932	2 282.8	13 565	147.6	19.1	14 807	229.6	15 506
Vermillion	15	D	D	(6)	D	D	61	123.8	7 293	79.4	D	726	9.4	12 963
Vigo	143	682.4	402.9	1 646	43.0	96.7	509	2 321.3	21 958	238.9	D	9 685	158.4	16 360
Wabash	38	86.4	77.1	233	6.0	13.6	169	289.8	8 336	90.7	11.1	1 853	27.5	14 847
Warren	12	74.8	D	129	3.5	6.6	16	19.8	2 398	26.1	–	101	1.4	13 644
Warrick	48	D	D	(4)	D	D	170	219.1	4 303	46.8	D	1 438	20.2	14 072
Washington	16	D	D	(6)	D	D	88	176.1	6 495	70.7	D	731	11.8	16 105
Wayne	96	1 256.3	639.6	1 657	53.8	103.3	338	690.6	9 612	104.6	17.5	4 233	64.3	15 182
Wells	38	455.3	D	1 735	37.9	80.6	116	164.0	6 132	66.7	D	1 113	16.1	14 423
White	46	196.7	D	358	8.5	19.2	131	209.7	8 370	91.1	8.8	1 173	19.6	16 673
Whitley	29	168.0	D	240	6.1	12.8	108	221.0	7 371	80.2	D	1 657	22.8	13 760
IOWA	5 399	35 453.7	25 728.6	63 596	1 820.1	3 746.2	14 695	26 723.8	9 362	101.9	13.0	175 694	2 633.4	14 989
Adair	16	83.1	D	142	3.7	9.3	49	46.2	5 671	61.7	D	320	3.7	11 656
Adams	9	18.5	18.5	52	.9	3.4	22	16.0	3 621	39.4	D	131	1.5	11 389
Allamakee	34	158.2	D	512	9.8	18.6	95	101.2	7 224	78.6	4.2	652	8.1	12 465
Appanoose	12	25.7	D	65	1.0	2.2	73	92.4	6 843	74.5	D	702	9.4	13 356
Audubon	24	76.2	76.2	169	3.5	8.0	34	51.9	7 607	82.8	D	254	4.0	15 890
Benton	40	186.3	155.7	506	12.5	26.5	101	144.1	5 768	62.8	4.8	789	12.2	15 436
Black Hawk	169	952.7	888.2	2 690	77.0	147.4	598	1 344.8	11 082	120.6	15.7	9 386	139.3	14 845
Boone	25	155.2	D	216	5.2	13.7	98	173.2	6 618	72.0	D	1 134	15.5	13 705
Bremer	42	151.8	D	293	6.0	13.5	115	144.7	6 211	67.6	D	1 037	13.7	13 230
Buchanan	38	222.7	D	311	8.4	19.8	106	154.9	7 322	79.7	D	911	13.8	15 167
Buena Vista	42	287.3	284.7	392	11.3	27.0	122	192.1	9 784	106.5	D	1 450	20.1	13 854
Butler	42	158.5	D	257	6.1	14.2	86	67.6	4 300	46.8	D	428	5.5	12 738
Calhoun	15	184.9	D	222	6.3	13.8	71	81.3	7 103	77.3	D	484	6.1	12 655
Carroll	53	354.5	D	868	21.4	45.6	176	226.0	10 454	113.8	14.3	1 706	22.9	13 437
Cass	41	D	D	(7)	D	D	99	122.3	8 292	90.2	9.3	927	11.9	12 796
Cedar	39	137.8	113.0	370	8.3	17.6	85	100.8	5 604	61.0	D	689	8.6	12 459
Cerro Gordo	85	489.6	439.2	875	24.5	48.7	292	609.9	13 168	143.3	D	3 995	54.9	13 744
Cherokee	22	59.1	59.1	184	3.9	9.6	83	107.7	8 058	87.7	9.3	787	10.3	13 050
Chickasaw	32	179.2	D	362	9.6	21.7	62	73.4	5 470	59.5	6.7	480	6.4	13 263
Clarke	8	D	D	(6)	D	D	39	51.3	6 239	67.9	D	402	5.3	13 256
Clay	58	246.8	224.5	612	14.8	33.9	141	215.0	12 221	133.0	14.8	1 529	25.7	16 793
Clayton	52	269.9	251.0	335	7.1	16.3	120	133.4	7 099	77.2	.9	670	10.4	15 451
Clinton	68	217.7	205.1	492	12.1	26.6	227	418.3	8 350	90.9	12.5	2 523	43.3	17 163
Crawford	27	191.4	D	309	6.0	12.8	97	111.7	6 785	73.8	D	919	9.9	10 818
Dallas	53	D	D	(8)	D	D	134	220.7	6 167	67.1	D	1 371	21.1	15 402
Davis	15	62.6	D	136	2.4	5.8	42	43.4	5 129	55.8	D	294	4.2	14 412
Decatur	11	68.3	D	129	2.0	4.3	35	24.8	3 047	33.2	D	205	2.4	11 810
Delaware	39	250.5	D	444	10.0	23.3	80	110.8	6 005	65.3	14.8	726	10.7	14 698
Des Moines	67	375.8	346.1	618	14.5	30.9	238	499.9	11 875	129.2	22.6	3 724	51.7	13 881
Dickinson	26	176.1	167.4	738	17.6	29.7	143	172.2	10 728	116.7	D	1 087	17.0	15 626
Dubuque	157	926.5	779.1	1 845	50.8	108.6	525	935.5	10 608	115.4	15.4	6 583	100.2	15 227
Emmet	14	56.8	56.8	260	4.5	8.7	61	79.2	7 225	78.6	5.9	550	7.7	13 967
Fayette	41	D	D	(8)	D	D	133	174.3	7 955	86.6	D	1 089	16.6	15 200
Floyd	31	112.2	D	258	5.3	11.3	95	119.3	7 233	78.7	13.3	839	10.5	12 511
Franklin	24	144.8	144.8	241	5.2	11.5	65	61.1	5 600	60.9	D	459	5.8	12 630
Fremont	15	97.4	D	108	3.6	8.2	32	26.8	3 434	37.4	–	212	2.5	11 745
Greene	19	116.8	D	207	4.7	11.5	47	53.1	5 266	57.3	7.9	381	4.8	12 714
Grundy	20	171.9	D	231	8.2	20.0	49	61.4	4 991	54.3	–	377	5.3	14 072
Guthrie	14	70.6	D	121	2.1	6.3	53	57.9	5 046	54.9	D	359	5.0	13 861
Hamilton	36	D	D	(7)	D	D	82	90.8	5 659	61.6	8.3	747	9.0	12 092
Hancock	30	179.8	164.9	285	6.7	18.0	55	55.4	4 616	50.2	D	425	4.4	10 348
Hardin	63	554.5	D	1 095	31.5	62.0	114	151.0	8 167	88.9	12.6	1 097	13.6	12 401
Harrison	26	106.5	D	228	5.1	13.0	78	166.9	10 919	118.8	D	647	11.5	17 723
Henry	34	93.6	D	246	5.4	12.6	88	161.8	8 161	88.8	D	970	13.5	13 908
Howard	22	102.6	102.6	159	3.9	10.2	54	54.4	5 609	61.0	3.8	361	4.0	11 100
Humboldt	37	199.0	D	285	7.7	19.4	56	71.3	6 883	74.9	7.7	496	7.3	14 619
Ida	23	211.1	D	166	5.0	14.5	44	52.8	6 591	71.7	D	389	4.6	11 949
Iowa	28	112.4	D	217	4.8	12.4	164	153.6	9 940	108.2	D	1 250	14.7	11 798
Jackson	35	73.7	D	197	4.3	10.0	110	165.5	8 244	89.7	D	889	12.0	13 543
Jasper	47	465.2	441.9	465	11.3	24.1	175	232.3	6 492	70.6	10.0	1 703	25.2	14 820
Jefferson	50	78.3	72.1	275	6.6	16.8	107	279.2	16 363	178.1	D	1 165	38.5	33 089
Johnson	89	D	D	(9)	D	D	467	990.9	9 722	105.8	D	6 924	104.7	15 125
Jones	34	101.6	D	236	5.6	11.7	90	124.4	6 113	66.5	11.9	771	11.4	14 825
Keokuk	21	90.8	90.8	178	3.9	8.6	55	94.3	8 202	89.2	D	449	6.6	14 628

[1] Includes only establishments with payroll. [2] For pay period including March 12. [3] Based on resident population estimated as of July 1, 1997. [4] 100 to 249 employees. [5] 2,500 to 4,999 employees. [6] 20 to 99 employees. [7] 500 to 999 employees. [8] 250 to 499 employees. [9] 1,000 to 2,499 employees.

Sources: Wholesale Trade—U.S. Census Bureau, 1997 Economic Census, ECON97 Report Series CD-ROM, CD-EC97-1, Disc 1E, issued February 2001 (related Internet site <http://www.census.gov/epcd/www/97EC42.HTM>). Retail Trade—U.S. Census Bureau, 1997 Economic Census, ECON97 Report Series CD-ROM, CD-EC97-1, Disc 1E, issued February 2001 (related Internet site <http://www.census.gov/epcd/www/97EC44.HTM>).

Table B–11. Counties — Wholesale Trade and Retail Trade–Con.

[Includes U.S., states, and 3,142 counties/county equivalents defined as of January 1, 1992. For changes to these areas since January 1, 1992, see appendix B. Geographic Information]

County	Wholesale trade[1] (NAICS 42), 1997						Retail trade[1] (NAICS 44-45), 1997							
	Sales						Sales					Annual payroll		
									Per capita[3]		Percent from general merchandise stores			
	Establishments	Total (mil. dol.)	Merchant wholesalers (mil. dol.)	Paid employees[2]	Annual payroll (mil. dol.)	Operating expenses (mil. dol.)	Establishments	Total (mil. dol.)	Amount (dollars)	Percent of national average		Paid employees[2]	Total (mil. dol.)	Per paid employee (dollars)
IOWA—Con.														
Kossuth	32	176.3	D	279	6.7	14.0	118	152.2	8 501	92.5	D	1 091	13.6	12 478
Lee	50	178.8	D	486	11.9	26.0	194	344.2	8 902	96.9	14.3	2 166	34.0	15 688
Linn	375	2 324.1	1 780.2	5 653	166.0	304.2	874	2 040.9	11 242	122.3	14.7	13 337	213.9	16 039
Louisa	14	70.9	D	185	5.1	8.9	39	45.7	3 844	41.8	D	256	3.6	14 004
Lucas	14	35.0	D	134	2.8	6.5	45	50.2	5 514	60.0	11.8	399	4.8	12 120
Lyon	24	133.7	D	243	5.7	12.8	62	63.8	5 332	58.0	D	476	5.5	11 571
Madison	15	62.8	D	89	2.3	5.3	61	82.8	6 025	65.6	6.8	522	7.1	13 557
Mahaska	43	192.8	D	374	10.3	24.0	114	190.8	8 746	95.2	D	1 246	17.1	13 761
Marion	42	98.6	D	510	7.2	16.5	156	243.1	7 813	85.0	8.1	1 519	22.4	14 770
Marshall	58	227.6	153.1	488	16.6	32.0	182	319.9	9 249	89.8	10.1	2 457	33.9	13 787
Mills	15	51.1	51.1	110	2.8	5.8	41	52.8	3 684	40.1	D	322	4.4	13 547
Mitchell	24	D	D	(4)	D	D	91	71.0	6 403	69.7	D	541	6.0	11 096
Monona	22	88.1	D	159	4.3	11.2	61	95.4	9 406	102.4	7.2	576	8.4	14 566
Monroe	11	20.9	20.9	73	1.4	2.8	43	51.7	6 400	69.6	D	363	4.7	12 923
Montgomery	30	151.3	135.7	214	5.1	11.5	68	82.8	6 990	76.1	10.4	581	7.4	12 752
Muscatine	63	264.1	254.2	381	10.1	22.4	177	337.6	8 254	89.8	D	2 390	34.5	14 428
O'Brien	41	201.1	D	367	8.9	22.5	111	169.5	11 314	123.1	4.4	976	14.0	14 314
Osceola	13	65.8	65.8	128	4.8	10.4	36	32.0	4 537	49.4	D	211	2.6	12 133
Page	26	87.4	D	223	5.0	10.8	108	148.5	8 573	93.3	17.1	1 185	14.3	12 048
Palo Alto	22	164.6	D	172	4.2	12.4	60	75.4	7 480	81.4	D	479	6.5	13 503
Plymouth	39	401.8	D	938	27.2	52.0	118	194.9	7 895	85.9	D	1 052	16.2	15 371
Pocahontas	18	197.4	D	277	6.8	16.7	46	43.4	4 918	53.5	D	301	3.4	11 302
Polk	901	D	D	(5)	D	D	1 680	4 454.0	12 503	136.1	13.4	28 123	461.4	16 408
Pottawattamie	101	D	D	(6)	D	D	382	978.5	11 469	124.8	D	5 742	87.1	15 170
Poweshiek	36	124.9	D	298	8.0	18.5	103	190.6	10 065	109.5	8.9	1 122	15.4	13 682
Ringgold	8	19.6	19.6	35	.9	2.7	28	38.2	7 117	77.4	D	214	2.7	12 612
Sac	37	144.5	144.5	230	6.6	14.8	76	83.7	7 022	76.4	–	491	6.2	12 656
Scott	389	3 366.3	1 562.6	4 535	151.6	351.6	747	1 831.5	11 610	126.3	15.8	11 397	187.3	16 433
Shelby	27	D	D	(7)	D	D	80	117.4	8 984	97.8	5.4	645	9.6	14 868
Sioux	92	470.8	401.4	1 144	27.7	61.4	182	285.2	9 113	99.2	5.9	1 557	21.4	13 766
Story	95	321.2	267.2	772	21.7	44.4	359	631.3	8 426	91.7	D	4 729	65.8	13 918
Tama	31	215.9	D	221	4.9	12.0	90	90.8	5 133	55.9	5.5	646	8.1	12 475
Taylor	15	26.2	D	72	1.4	3.4	34	24.8	3 477	37.8	D	193	2.3	12 031
Union	24	108.9	D	318	5.6	11.9	72	114.6	9 167	99.7	D	800	11.5	14 349
Van Buren	8	35.2	D	60	.5	1.0	34	19.0	2 529	27.5	–	154	1.9	12 513
Wapello	38	140.6	D	321	9.1	18.1	185	330.9	9 325	101.5	20.4	2 538	32.7	12 899
Warren	54	D	D	(7)	D	D	113	244.8	6 154	67.0	D	1 314	20.8	15 811
Washington	40	134.2	D	298	6.5	15.3	128	155.6	7 451	81.1	9.7	1 036	16.2	15 608
Wayne	17	53.5	D	130	2.2	5.2	38	31.6	4 663	50.7	D	252	3.5	13 782
Webster	71	710.2	D	885	31.4	62.3	252	438.7	11 338	123.4	21.0	3 142	44.9	14 290
Winnebago	17	D	D	(4)	D	D	74	81.6	6 767	73.6	D	573	6.2	10 869
Winneshiek	39	131.4	D	449	10.5	20.9	124	180.1	8 645	94.1	D	1 113	15.0	13 437
Woodbury	209	1 222.1	D	2 476	70.5	141.5	523	1 143.5	11 226	122.2	D	7 771	116.0	14 928
Worth	17	85.6	D	97	2.6	6.4	41	28.8	3 701	40.3	–	213	2.3	10 995
Wright	28	D	D	(7)	D	D	83	73.9	5 228	56.9	6.7	639	7.8	12 150
KANSAS	5 085	42 209.9	23 579.8	59 954	1 946.8	3 921.6	12 271	22 571.9	8 627	93.9	15.3	140 412	2 191.1	15 604
Allen	18	35.5	D	186	3.2	5.8	83	85.3	5 893	64.1	D	590	8.1	13 810
Anderson	12	48.4	D	77	1.4	3.8	38	43.0	5 340	58.1	D	207	2.9	14 116
Atchison	17	270.8	D	449	9.9	18.8	68	86.1	5 118	55.7	D	659	7.9	11 920
Barber	12	35.7	35.7	97	2.0	4.0	39	35.1	6 514	70.9	D	271	3.9	14 354
Barton	92	206.2	164.2	737	18.2	37.0	185	282.8	9 719	105.8	D	1 803	28.7	15 911
Bourbon	24	233.2	D	475	9.8	21.9	69	95.2	6 253	68.0	D	606	8.8	14 541
Brown	27	73.6	D	152	3.7	7.6	51	67.1	6 071	66.1	D	407	5.4	13 307
Butler	67	136.2	D	368	8.8	28.3	194	350.3	5 764	62.7	D	1 875	29.3	15 623
Chase	2	D	D	(8)	D	D	14	8.3	2 838	30.9	D	103	.8	8 184
Chautauqua	7	9.3	D	39	.8	1.4	19	10.9	2 492	27.1	D	98	.9	8 694
Cherokee	18	210.5	210.5	134	3.4	7.7	91	93.2	4 128	44.9	D	621	7.8	12 585
Cheyenne	11	57.8	D	118	2.7	6.0	30	17.7	5 522	60.1	D	125	1.4	11 544
Clark	5	D	D	(9)	D	D	19	7.6	3 154	34.3	–	62	.8	12 887
Clay	18	55.4	55.4	140	3.2	6.5	61	63.4	6 909	75.2	11.4	487	6.3	12 864
Cloud	22	110.5	D	238	5.5	12.2	71	83.2	8 159	88.8	D	608	7.7	12 635
Coffey	9	38.5	D	76	2.1	4.4	50	58.8	6 718	73.1	D	418	5.2	12 433
Comanche	4	D	D	(9)	D	D	14	8.4	4 148	45.1	D	71	.8	11 239
Cowley	38	118.9	D	343	8.9	22.6	173	255.5	6 829	74.3	D	1 682	24.2	14 401
Crawford	53	173.3	D	624	17.0	33.6	180	296.5	8 120	88.4	D	2 132	27.7	12 999
Decatur	15	74.3	D	144	2.9	6.1	23	10.2	2 907	31.6	–	108	1.1	10 352
Dickinson	25	220.6	D	365	8.8	18.0	110	125.0	6 324	68.8	D	900	11.4	12 704

[1] Includes only establishments with payroll. [2] For pay period including March 12. [3] Based on resident population estimated as of July 1, 1997. [4] 100 to 249 employees. [5] 10,000 to 24,999 employees. [6] 1,000 to 2,499 employees. [7] 250 to 499 employees. [8] 0 to 19 employees. [9] 20 to 99 employees.

Sources: Wholesale Trade—U.S. Census Bureau, 1997 Economic Census, ECON97 Report Series CD-ROM, CD-EC97-1, Disc 1E, issued February 2001 (related Internet site <http://www.census.gov/epcd/www/97EC42.HTM>). Retail Trade—U.S. Census Bureau, 1997 Economic Census, ECON97 Report Series CD-ROM, CD-EC97-1, Disc 1E, issued February 2001 (related Internet site <http://www.census.gov/epcd/www/97EC44.HTM>).

Table B–11. Counties — Wholesale Trade and Retail Trade–Con.

[Includes U.S., states, and 3,142 counties/county equivalents defined as of January 1, 1992. For changes to these areas since January 1, 1992, see appendix B. Geographic Information]

County	Wholesale trade[1] (NAICS 42), 1997 Sales — Establishments	Total (mil. dol.)	Merchant wholesalers (mil. dol.)	Paid employees[2]	Annual payroll (mil. dol.)	Operating expenses (mil. dol.)	Retail trade[1] (NAICS 44-45), 1997 Sales — Establishments	Total (mil. dol.)	Per capita[3] Amount (dollars)	Percent of national average	Percent from general merchandise stores	Annual payroll — Paid employees[2]	Total (mil. dol.)	Per paid employee (dollars)
KANSAS—Con.														
Doniphan	11	D	D	(4)	D	D	27	43.2	5 519	60.1	–	322	4.0	12 407
Douglas	88	248.8	187.5	777	21.0	38.7	453	758.5	7 994	87.0	14.8	5 664	80.3	14 185
Edwards	8	57.6	57.6	87	2.6	8.1	15	7.6	2 232	24.3	D	64	.7	11 328
Elk	6	10.9	10.9	18	.4	.9	8	3.7	1 086	11.8	–	30	.2	6 100
Ellis	46	93.1	D	411	8.3	17.4	216	326.7	12 271	133.5	D	2 207	32.3	14 630
Ellsworth	12	D	D	(5)	D	D	41	30.3	4 788	52.1	D	242	2.5	10 488
Finney	84	495.5	D	791	26.2	53.1	186	405.0	11 264	122.6	17.3	2 502	38.3	15 326
Ford	55	347.8	220.9	607	17.3	38.1	169	367.4	12 616	137.3	15.9	2 016	31.9	15 822
Franklin	29	298.4	D	487	11.4	20.8	89	167.2	6 815	74.2	D	1 114	15.3	13 719
Geary	18	60.1	D	153	2.7	6.1	99	181.1	7 212	78.5	18.8	1 174	17.9	15 282
Gove	11	31.8	D	74	1.7	4.0	22	19.3	6 247	68.0	–	122	1.4	11 828
Graham	9	16.9	D	39	1.0	2.3	21	25.3	7 817	85.1	D	133	2.1	15 827
Grant	20	97.8	D	165	4.9	10.6	39	60.1	7 652	83.3	D	371	6.1	16 321
Gray	23	126.5	126.5	189	6.0	13.6	28	33.2	6 036	65.7	–	163	2.7	16 613
Greeley	3	D	D	(5)	D	D	11	9.2	5 301	57.7	–	59	.9	14 576
Greenwood	14	6.2	6.2	70	.7	1.5	41	36.6	4 555	49.6	D	215	2.9	13 572
Hamilton	11	53.8	53.8	136	3.0	7.1	16	14.3	6 260	68.1	D	81	1.0	12 222
Harper	18	76.8	76.8	168	3.8	7.4	39	38.7	5 961	64.9	D	266	2.9	10 846
Harvey	35	181.2	D	280	7.7	18.3	156	185.8	5 473	59.6	D	1 608	19.1	11 886
Haskell	13	92.3	92.3	146	4.7	10.2	15	10.6	2 645	28.8	–	84	.9	11 012
Hodgeman	4	D	D	(5)	D	D	9	11.3	5 064	55.1	–	55	.6	11 382
Jackson	12	25.0	D	45	.8	1.7	50	73.9	6 148	66.9	D	489	6.4	13 182
Jefferson	10	9.6	D	30	.5	1.3	60	51.4	2 866	31.2	D	353	4.2	11 878
Jewell	8	50.2	D	76	1.2	3.3	27	9.3	2 357	25.6	D	89	.9	10 022
Johnson	1 502	21 107.6	7 491.9	19 597	789.6	1 516.4	1 903	5 418.8	12 934	140.7	14.8	30 545	543.2	17 785
Kearny	7	24.1	24.1	35	1.0	2.2	14	5.8	1 387	15.1	D	69	.6	8 638
Kingman	15	51.6	D	129	3.7	8.1	41	36.2	4 235	46.1	10.2	290	3.6	12 483
Kiowa	7	30.2	30.2	50	1.4	3.5	21	20.2	5 852	63.7	D	176	1.9	10 813
Labette	29	81.7	D	214	4.6	8.5	120	147.5	6 374	69.4	D	1 021	14.1	13 787
Lane	9	36.0	36.0	69	1.6	4.5	17	8.9	4 061	44.2	–	62	.8	12 226
Leavenworth	24	D	D	(5)	D	D	178	359.2	5 091	55.4	D	2 081	31.6	15 164
Lincoln	15	37.5	D	93	1.4	3.2	22	14.6	4 330	47.1	D	104	1.2	11 962
Linn	6	8.6	D	24	.4	.9	34	30.1	3 328	36.2	D	241	2.7	11 133
Logan	8	30.6	30.6	72	1.5	3.7	28	43.9	14 487	157.6	D	249	3.1	12 297
Lyon	41	197.3	189.3	571	14.0	26.3	172	285.5	8 399	91.4	D	1 982	29.3	14 786
McPherson	52	165.6	161.1	337	9.4	19.0	155	213.7	7 494	81.5	10.7	1 378	19.4	14 065
Marion	17	79.0	79.0	215	4.6	9.5	80	97.3	7 095	77.2	D	482	7.8	16 098
Marshall	24	115.2	D	206	5.6	11.4	74	76.5	6 879	74.9	D	490	6.0	12 190
Meade	10	66.8	66.8	87	2.4	6.0	32	21.3	4 857	52.9	D	171	2.0	11 912
Miami	21	D	D	(6)	D	D	91	170.6	6 505	70.8	D	1 163	16.3	13 982
Mitchell	25	133.5	133.5	247	6.1	16.3	61	79.7	11 382	123.9	D	448	6.7	15 063
Montgomery	52	124.4	97.7	472	10.9	21.9	223	264.2	7 108	77.3	18.2	2 013	25.4	12 629
Morris	6	8.0	8.0	24	.5	1.0	39	40.1	6 435	70.0	D	239	2.9	12 113
Morton	13	78.8	78.8	146	3.7	8.7	19	10.8	3 160	34.4	D	84	1.2	14 202
Nemaha	21	58.5	D	135	3.0	7.4	82	88.1	8 624	93.8	D	490	6.5	13 186
Neosho	37	125.2	D	297	8.2	19.7	107	149.1	8 853	96.3	D	925	12.7	13 729
Ness	18	39.4	D	118	2.9	5.5	25	13.3	3 711	40.4	D	103	1.2	11 738
Norton	15	66.1	D	92	1.5	4.0	37	32.7	5 636	61.3	D	263	2.8	10 631
Osage	9	45.7	D	90	1.6	3.7	65	67.7	3 975	43.3	D	444	5.7	12 827
Osborne	13	65.9	D	156	2.8	6.7	45	34.2	7 271	79.1	D	244	2.8	11 516
Ottawa	12	72.1	72.1	92	2.6	5.3	24	16.8	2 878	31.3	1.8	132	1.7	12 788
Pawnee	11	43.1	D	92	2.3	4.8	42	40.8	5 592	60.8	8.3	298	4.2	14 020
Phillips	16	58.8	58.8	138	2.9	7.1	39	34.7	5 697	62.0	14.2	281	3.0	10 708
Pottawatomie	22	113.9	D	266	5.0	9.7	94	119.6	6 545	71.2	.6	854	12.1	14 197
Pratt	30	258.0	D	357	8.7	18.5	62	88.0	9 110	99.1	D	632	9.5	14 995
Rawlins	12	47.0	D	77	2.0	3.7	23	13.8	4 308	46.9	D	114	1.2	10 421
Reno	94	474.6	329.5	1 239	36.3	72.6	327	667.0	10 587	115.2	15.8	3 961	65.7	16 557
Republic	24	85.8	85.8	153	2.3	6.1	51	34.5	5 605	61.0	4.3	255	3.6	14 110
Rice	19	47.7	47.7	116	3.1	6.4	50	40.1	3 831	41.7	D	337	4.1	12 187
Riley	42	140.7	126.1	493	12.1	22.4	305	442.9	6 852	74.6	19.7	3 331	43.6	13 083
Rooks	17	53.8	D	114	2.6	7.3	43	37.3	6 528	71.0	2.1	258	3.0	11 438
Rush	16	58.8	D	160	4.2	6.3	18	13.5	3 943	42.9	D	93	1.2	13 258
Russell	17	108.7	D	138	3.2	6.3	53	42.0	5 490	59.7	10.3	310	4.2	13 465
Saline	103	841.2	728.2	1 261	36.0	72.3	313	679.3	13 155	143.1	20.7	4 340	63.8	14 694
Scott	22	67.4	D	149	3.7	9.2	40	48.9	9 783	106.5	D	297	3.9	13 199
Sedgwick	798	5 875.1	D	9 903	336.3	663.3	1 804	4 265.4	9 711	105.7	17.2	25 223	423.1	16 776
Seward	48	133.3	120.4	299	9.2	18.3	135	249.1	12 450	135.5	D	1 394	21.5	15 403
Shawnee	204	947.1	790.1	2 298	65.9	130.1	768	1 619.6	9 560	104.0	20.2	10 625	166.7	15 689
Sheridan	9	56.6	D	109	3.1	5.9	22	15.9	5 802	63.1	D	110	1.4	12 873

[1] Includes only establishments with payroll. [2] For pay period including March 12. [3] Based on resident population estimated as of July 1, 1997. [4] 250 to 499 employees. [5] 20 to 99 employees. [6] 100 to 249 employees.

Sources: Wholesale Trade—U.S. Census Bureau, 1997 Economic Census, ECON[97] Report Series CD-ROM, CD-EC97-1, Disc 1E, issued February 2001 (related Internet site <http://www.census.gov/epcd/www/97EC42.HTM>). Retail Trade—U.S. Census Bureau, 1997 Economic Census, ECON[97] Report Series CD-ROM, CD-EC97-1, Disc 1E, issued February 2001 (related Internet site <http://www.census.gov/epcd/www/97EC44.HTM>).

Table B–11. Counties — **Wholesale Trade and Retail Trade**–Con.

[Includes U.S., states, and 3,142 counties/county equivalents defined as of January 1, 1992. For changes to these areas since January 1, 1992, see appendix B. Geographic Information]

County	Wholesale trade[1] (NAICS 42), 1997						Retail trade[1] (NAICS 44-45), 1997							
	Sales			Paid employees[2]	Annual payroll (mil. dol.)	Operating expenses (mil. dol.)	Sales		Per capita[3]		Percent from general merchandise stores	Annual payroll		
	Establishments	Total (mil. dol.)	Merchant wholesalers (mil. dol.)				Establishments	Total (mil. dol.)	Amount (dollars)	Percent of national average		Paid employees[2]	Total (mil. dol.)	Per paid employee (dollars)
KANSAS—Con.														
Sherman	21	126.6	D	203	5.7	13.5	62	88.7	13 480	146.7	19.0	453	7.4	16 347
Smith	15	61.4	D	133	2.4	5.6	39	25.7	5 566	60.6	6.2	230	2.5	11 004
Stafford	15	57.1	57.1	157	3.4	8.6	21	12.0	2 359	25.7	D	108	1.1	10 352
Stanton	16	65.5	65.5	132	3.7	7.3	12	13.1	5 703	62.1	D	61	1.2	19 164
Stevens	19	113.9	113.9	181	4.9	12.0	23	26.4	4 936	53.7	D	138	2.1	15 254
Sumner	33	143.2	143.2	212	6.1	14.3	93	114.5	4 253	46.3	D	733	9.4	12 834
Thomas	28	207.8	197.2	255	6.5	14.7	70	81.5	9 986	108.7	D	606	8.0	13 175
Trego	11	38.6	38.6	52	1.1	3.2	29	21.4	6 407	69.7	D	177	2.0	11 412
Wabaunsee	5	6.7	6.7	21	.2	.5	30	18.4	2 762	30.1	D	139	1.9	13 410
Wallace	6	D	D	(4)	D	D	12	7.7	4 251	46.3	D	68	.7	11 000
Washington	21	83.8	D	226	4.7	11.0	42	19.6	2 966	32.3	D	211	1.8	8 564
Wichita	8	31.7	D	43	1.2	3.9	22	19.1	7 041	76.6	D	104	1.7	16 048
Wilson	11	D	D	(4)	D	D	38	26.8	2 603	28.3	D	253	2.6	10 138
Woodson	9	D	D	(4)	D	D	25	11.7	2 933	31.9	D	101	1.2	12 267
Wyandotte	311	4 013.4	3 456.4	6 891	224.7	476.4	436	932.9	6 106	66.4	11.2	5 172	91.8	17 743
KENTUCKY	5 051	37 242.9	23 683.8	69 309	2 071.2	4 190.9	17 369	33 332.7	8 530	92.8	16.1	212 189	3 128.1	14 742
Adair	16	29.4	D	131	3.6	8.7	65	83.0	5 042	54.9	D	525	6.3	11 945
Allen	11	15.3	15.3	102	1.8	3.0	70	78.6	4 856	52.8	D	469	5.9	12 569
Anderson	10	D	D	(4)	D	D	54	92.7	5 131	55.8	D	528	8.0	15 064
Ballard	5	28.7	28.7	50	1.1	2.7	37	49.0	5 834	63.5	D	264	3.6	13 784
Barren	35	97.6	D	328	8.1	17.4	208	355.5	9 694	105.5	21.4	2 171	31.2	14 388
Bath	1	D	D	(5)	D	D	42	38.5	3 716	40.4	D	238	2.9	12 092
Bell	26	88.9	D	328	7.6	17.4	163	299.2	10 049	109.3	28.2	1 955	36.2	18 512
Boone	122	1 005.0	485.5	1 683	59.6	111.1	435	1 666.2	21 890	238.2	20.7	8 561	132.5	15 481
Bourbon	18	D	D	(6)	D	D	75	127.9	6 616	72.0	D	781	10.1	12 954
Boyd	94	515.3	D	1 435	38.7	96.4	345	641.6	12 894	140.3	19.4	4 313	60.8	14 094
Boyle	33	197.0	D	285	4.8	11.1	149	301.8	11 200	121.9	D	2 152	29.0	13 454
Bracken	4	18.2	18.2	47	1.0	1.8	27	19.7	2 361	25.7	D	127	1.5	12 165
Breathitt	5	40.1	40.1	75	1.7	4.8	52	102.8	6 564	71.4	D	715	8.7	12 189
Breckinridge	10	D	D	(4)	D	D	69	95.1	5 492	59.8	D	525	7.4	14 154
Bullitt	31	92.8	D	288	7.1	15.7	151	243.3	4 203	45.7	D	1 547	22.5	14 546
Butler	8	13.9	13.9	31	.5	1.6	41	35.7	3 030	33.0	D	270	3.1	11 663
Caldwell	11	27.2	D	61	1.3	2.7	64	126.3	9 466	103.0	D	752	11.8	15 727
Calloway	53	D	D	(7)	D	D	192	336.5	10 141	110.3	D	2 020	28.4	14 056
Campbell	78	230.1	164.6	649	26.0	55.4	266	644.1	7 360	80.1	11.0	3 874	57.6	14 870
Carlisle	8	22.0	22.0	28	.6	2.2	19	20.3	3 784	41.2	D	134	3.0	22 731
Carroll	13	03.4	D	234	3.8	9.2	59	121.8	12 694	138.1	2.4	549	8.7	15 821
Carter	12	D	D	(4)	D	D	130	179.2	6 753	73.5	10.5	1 071	14.8	13 843
Casey	17	18.2	D	87	1.4	4.5	53	44.2	3 043	33.1	4.3	310	4.2	13 652
Christian	79	682.5	D	1 281	39.9	74.6	301	464.9	6 344	69.0	D	2 836	43.7	15 398
Clark	34	D	D	(6)	D	D	147	348.2	11 003	119.7	14.4	1 922	30.3	15 781
Clay	14	13.4	D	70	1.1	3.1	78	110.2	4 886	53.2	D	812	9.4	11 612
Clinton	8	12.8	D	55	1.0	2.4	55	47.2	5 092	55.4	3.5	374	4.5	12 152
Crittenden	7	D	D	(4)	D	D	29	28.9	3 071	33.4	8.8	261	3.2	12 284
Cumberland	2	D	D	(4)	D	D	34	35.1	5 115	55.7	5.7	231	3.1	13 225
Daviess	141	872.9	797.6	1 678	43.7	122.5	470	853.8	9 397	102.3	20.3	6 011	84.5	14 055
Edmonson	2	D	D	(5)	D	D	22	18.9	1 688	18.4	5.9	140	1.5	10 650
Elliott	NA	NA	NA	NA	NA	NA	20	11.5	1 755	19.1	D	87	.9	9 977
Estill	11	D	D	(8)	D	D	61	58.9	3 818	41.5	4.5	375	4.5	12 112
Fayette	492	4 181.5	2 659.7	6 529	203.8	390.1	1 251	3 133.1	13 078	142.3	D	20 363	308.7	15 162
Fleming	20	58.2	D	126	2.1	4.6	68	108.2	8 194	89.2	2.4	526	9.5	17 975
Floyd	55	312.6	D	771	19.7	39.8	185	259.4	5 984	65.1	D	1 568	22.9	14 603
Franklin	33	D	D	(8)	D	D	202	443.4	9 588	104.3	16.7	3 096	39.2	12 651
Fulton	12	D	D	(8)	D	D	61	70.5	9 249	100.6	D	498	7.0	14 082
Gallatin	6	D	D	(6)	D	D	19	21.6	3 178	34.6	6.6	179	2.0	11 011
Garrard	5	D	D	(8)	D	D	44	33.8	2 488	27.1	D	238	3.0	12 487
Grant	18	D	D	(8)	D	D	100	181.3	9 159	99.7	D	1 098	16.5	15 048
Graves	37	201.8	D	571	14.3	26.9	141	286.2	8 031	87.4	D	1 580	24.4	15 451
Grayson	17	D	D	(6)	D	D	103	131.4	5 646	61.4	D	942	12.0	12 742
Green	7	6.7	6.7	31	.3	.9	41	33.4	3 162	34.4	5.1	230	3.1	13 496
Greenup	18	D	D	(8)	D	D	111	119.7	3 225	35.1	4.1	788	11.2	14 201
Hancock	1	D	D	(5)	D	D	22	29.3	3 308	36.0	D	168	2.3	13 542
Hardin	68	134.7	D	596	13.1	27.9	422	897.0	9 982	108.6	D	5 431	82.9	15 273
Harlan	31	108.9	D	242	6.3	12.6	132	168.8	4 786	52.1	21.3	1 261	17.1	13 600
Harrison	11	D	D	(8)	D	D	64	106.6	6 181	67.3	D	695	9.0	12 895
Hart	10	D	D	(4)	D	D	90	76.7	4 642	50.5	4.0	589	7.3	12 362

[1] Includes only establishments with payroll. [2] For pay period including March 12. [3] Based on resident population estimated as of July 1, 1997. [4] 20 to 99 employees. [5] 0 to 19 employees. [6] 250 to 499 employees. [7] 500 to 999 employees. [8] 100 to 249 employees.

Sources: Wholesale Trade—U.S. Census Bureau, 1997 Economic Census, ECON97 Report Series CD-ROM, CD-EC97-1, Disc 1E, issued February 2001 (related Internet site <http://www.census.gov/epcd/www/97EC42.HTM>). Retail Trade—U.S. Census Bureau, 1997 Economic Census, ECON97 Report Series CD-ROM, CD-EC97-1, Disc 1E, issued February 2001 (related Internet site <http://www.census.gov/epcd/www/97EC44.HTM>).

[Includes U.S., states, and 3,142 counties/county equivalents defined as of January 1, 1992. For changes to these areas since January 1, 1992, see appendix B. Geographic Information]

County	Wholesale trade[1] (NAICS 42), 1997						Retail trade[1] (NAICS 44-45), 1997							
		Sales						Sales					Annual payroll	
									Per capita[3]		Percent from general merchandise stores			
	Establishments	Total (mil. dol.)	Merchant wholesalers (mil. dol.)	Paid employees[2]	Annual payroll (mil. dol.)	Operating expenses (mil. dol.)	Establishments	Total (mil. dol.)	Amount (dollars)	Percent of national average		Paid employees[2]	Total (mil. dol.)	Per paid employee (dollars)
KENTUCKY—Con.														
Henderson	71	728.4	D	798	23.9	56.3	208	422.2	9 495	103.3	D	2 252	36.8	16 330
Henry	18	114.4	D	247	5.7	13.9	53	90.5	6 159	67.0	D	470	7.0	14 930
Hickman	6	40.4	40.4	97	2.3	4.8	19	13.5	2 581	28.1	–	93	1.4	14 570
Hopkins	57	190.0	D	435	10.5	21.1	246	409.0	8 850	96.3	16.8	2 805	39.9	14 230
Jackson	2	D	D	(4)	D	D	30	31.2	2 432	26.5	12.5	179	2.3	12 799
Jefferson	1 509	15 932.9	7 870.0	24 651	852.5	1 584.0	2 950	7 200.8	10 726	116.7	16.2	47 517	761.6	16 029
Jessamine	46	513.7	D	1 010	27.9	68.0	132	394.0	10 922	118.8	D	2 078	32.7	15 757
Johnson	24	60.1	41.3	187	5.4	10.8	127	229.2	9 537	103.8	21.7	1 606	20.7	12 890
Kenton	198	1 370.3	1 056.5	3 123	109.3	197.9	452	829.4	5 675	61.8	9.7	5 904	86.6	14 671
Knott	6	3.6	3.6	59	.7	1.5	48	35.4	1 964	21.4	D	242	3.4	14 025
Knox	14	52.4	52.4	140	3.4	10.1	123	254.4	8 081	87.9	15.0	1 556	20.6	13 226
Larue	7	3.4	3.4	19	.2	.4	41	42.5	3 296	35.9	D	294	4.3	14 714
Laurel	67	520.2	431.5	1 239	28.3	62.6	230	499.8	9 976	108.6	D	2 827	40.6	14 344
Lawrence	9	D	D	(5)	D	D	51	63.7	4 125	44.9	11.7	440	5.5	12 532
Lee	6	16.3	16.3	50	2.0	4.2	27	25.8	3 232	35.2	D	179	2.8	15 408
Leslie	2	D	D	(6)	D	D	42	30.2	2 241	24.4	7.4	215	2.8	13 228
Letcher	14	111.3	111.3	374	5.1	15.7	92	110.2	4 158	45.2	D	837	10.8	12 883
Lewis	5	5.6	5.6	13	.2	.5	34	22.6	1 669	18.2	D	241	2.0	8 336
Lincoln	13	12.1	12.1	68	.8	2.0	64	70.9	3 214	35.0	D	471	6.6	13 975
Livingston	4	4.4	D	39	.4	.9	33	22.7	2 418	26.3	–	188	2.7	14 261
Logan	27	79.8	64.2	203	3.5	8.4	106	147.8	5 662	61.6	D	975	13.8	14 104
Lyon	4	42.7	D	27	.7	1.4	68	52.4	6 565	71.4	D	461	5.2	11 204
McCracken	136	1 557.0	1 498.8	2 700	72.3	144.8	515	1 012.0	15 636	170.1	25.7	6 266	91.1	14 546
McCreary	4	1.0	1.0	18	.2	.3	50	52.4	3 161	34.4	5.0	318	4.2	13 097
McLean	11	52.5	52.5	134	2.4	6.5	30	40.8	4 179	45.5	D	209	3.4	16 105
Madison	49	285.7	88.5	720	24.8	56.1	288	565.0	8 629	93.9	D	3 824	51.4	13 435
Magoffin	6	45.2	45.2	36	.9	2.1	47	46.9	3 370	36.7	D	314	3.5	11 232
Marion	14	40.3	12.7	143	1.9	4.7	79	84.8	4 986	54.3	19.3	642	7.1	11 131
Marshall	38	124.2	D	292	7.6	17.6	128	179.2	5 999	65.3	11.9	1 054	16.4	15 554
Martin	8	73.9	D	48	2.1	3.9	51	58.0	4 741	51.6	5.0	344	5.3	15 294
Mason	31	93.7	D	394	7.4	29.4	109	246.3	14 529	158.1	20.7	1 467	20.2	13 738
Meade	12	59.0	D	51	1.5	5.3	85	122.8	4 354	47.4	D	570	9.4	16 502
Menifee	NA	NA	NA	NA	NA	NA	16	11.8	2 089	22.7	D	81	.8	9 914
Mercer	18	23.7	D	67	1.2	2.9	84	125.6	6 151	66.9	D	637	10.1	15 788
Metcalfe	3	11.8	D	44	1.2	1.7	40	39.8	4 186	45.5	1.7	272	3.5	12 904
Monroe	12	D	D	(5)	D	D	64	63.7	5 641	61.4	D	405	5.3	12 963
Montgomery	31	126.7	D	243	5.2	11.8	117	225.2	10 854	118.1	D	1 479	18.1	12 205
Morgan	4	D	D	(4)	D	D	52	65.7	4 869	53.0	8.7	388	5.6	14 384
Muhlenberg	16	D	D	(7)	D	D	130	198.7	6 218	67.7	26.3	1 405	20.0	14 216
Nelson	41	133.3	D	448	12.8	39.5	178	218.8	6 222	67.7	D	1 445	19.5	13 474
Nicholas	1	D	D	(6)	D	D	14	18.5	2 631	28.6	D	114	1.6	13 868
Ohio	8	45.4	D	198	3.0	9.4	75	89.8	4 089	44.5	D	614	8.2	13 305
Oldham	58	272.6	D	451	15.0	32.6	113	192.1	4 442	48.3	D	1 209	19.1	15 767
Owen	6	3.0	D	17	.2	.4	23	50.4	4 997	54.4	D	220	2.9	13 145
Owsley	NA	NA	NA	NA	NA	NA	16	25.9	4 844	52.7	D	99	1.0	10 414
Pendleton	10	D	D	(4)	D	D	40	35.5	2 561	27.9	D	287	2.9	10 223
Perry	50	233.7	213.7	467	14.4	31.0	183	294.6	9 462	103.0	18.7	1 917	25.7	13 431
Pike	78	318.4	270.2	711	21.3	47.9	347	664.7	9 170	99.8	16.3	4 618	61.2	13 251
Powell	8	23.2	D	115	2.2	4.3	39	38.1	3 004	32.7	5.3	297	3.0	10 148
Pulaski	76	318.4	271.0	1 068	21.1	45.3	336	543.3	9 739	106.0	17.0	3 508	48.7	13 885
Robertson	NA	NA	NA	NA	NA	NA	7	2.4	1 102	12.0	D	25	.2	6 880
Rockcastle	9	11.4	11.4	62	.9	1.7	54	44.3	2 820	30.7	7.0	365	4.3	11 773
Rowan	28	61.2	59.9	230	4.2	9.3	131	180.7	8 243	89.7	D	1 319	15.6	11 799
Russell	10	83.2	D	356	7.2	10.2	88	104.9	6 426	69.9	15.5	797	14.0	17 518
Scott	25	319.5	D	816	26.3	46.9	115	230.7	7 829	85.2	D	1 396	17.5	12 534
Shelby	46	140.4	103.0	375	11.2	25.1	111	253.0	8 779	95.5	D	1 338	19.6	14 675
Simpson	18	130.6	114.3	411	4.6	10.6	77	205.7	12 761	138.9	D	914	13.9	15 252
Spencer	7	D	D	(4)	D	D	23	16.9	1 843	20.1	D	147	2.5	17 259
Taylor	33	37.1	24.3	175	3.1	6.9	152	252.8	11 057	120.3	D	1 555	22.5	14 437
Todd	16	54.1	D	227	2.8	6.3	48	45.7	4 078	44.4	2.8	274	3.3	12 047
Trigg	10	18.3	D	66	1.8	3.5	52	51.8	4 263	46.4	6.1	324	4.1	12 660
Trimble	1	D	NA	(6)	D	D	14	11.1	1 526	16.6	–	96	1.1	11 125
Union	21	66.8	D	226	4.4	9.0	77	91.4	5 555	60.1	D	623	7.7	12 409
Warren	155	1 367.4	684.7	2 029	57.4	137.0	525	1 108.8	12 815	139.4	D	7 144	102.5	14 346
Washington	10	D	38.6	(5)	D	D	41	44.6	4 125	44.9	D	301	3.9	12 944
Wayne	10	15.2	7.8	113	1.3	2.0	65	99.0	5 271	57.4	D	663	13.0	19 567
Webster	3	D	D	(6)	D	D	59	73.3	5 414	58.9	D	431	6.5	15 012
Whitley	28	D	D	(7)	D	D	164	275.6	7 743	84.3	D	1 609	23.5	14 606
Wolfe	3	3.9	D	15	.1	.3	27	25.7	3 534	38.5	11.6	161	1.7	10 752
Woodford	20	D	60.5	(7)	D	D	75	124.9	5 596	60.9	D	724	9.7	13 431

[1] Includes only establishments with payroll.   [2] For pay period including March 12.   [3] Based on resident population estimated as of July 1, 1997.   [4] 20 to 99 employees.   [5] 100 to 249 employees.   [6] 0 to 19 employees.   [7] 250 to 499 employees.

Sources: Wholesale Trade—U.S. Census Bureau, 1997 Economic Census, ECON[97] Report Series CD-ROM, CD-EC97-1, Disc 1E, issued February 2001 (related Internet site <http://www.census.gov/epcd/www/97EC42.HTM>).   Retail Trade—U.S. Census Bureau, 1997 Economic Census, ECON[97] Report Series CD-ROM, CD-EC97-1, Disc 1E, issued February 2001 (related Internet site <http://www.census.gov/epcd/www/97EC44.HTM>).

Table B–11. Counties — Wholesale Trade and Retail Trade–Con.

[Includes U.S., states, and 3,142 counties/county equivalents defined as of January 1, 1992. For changes to these areas since January 1, 1992, see appendix B. Geographic Information]

County	Wholesale trade[1] (NAICS 42), 1997						Retail trade[1] (NAICS 44-45), 1997							
		Sales						Sales				Annual payroll		
									Per capita[3]		Percent from general mer-chandise stores			
	Estab-lishments	Total (mil. dol.)	Merchant whole-salers (mil. dol.)	Paid em-ployees[2]	Annual payroll (mil. dol.)	Operating expenses (mil. dol.)	Estab-lishments	Total (mil. dol.)	Amount (dollars)	Percent of national average		Paid em-ployees[2]	Total (mil. dol.)	Per paid em-ployee (dollars)
LOUISIANA	6 390	46 972.3	34 931.9	76 350	2 375.2	4 827.7	17 863	35 807.9	8 229	89.5	16.2	224 412	3 307.9	14 740
Acadia	61	280.7	235.5	598	12.9	29.8	199	278.0	4 828	52.5	D	2 093	27.9	13 333
Allen	16	37.7	D	113	2.0	4.9	93	99.1	4 162	45.3	D	672	7.8	11 655
Ascension	94	314.1	305.0	950	26.8	55.9	304	578.0	8 261	89.9	D	3 777	48.9	12 942
Assumption	15	32.5	D	114	2.7	5.3	59	75.1	3 290	35.8	12.9	599	7.5	12 454
Avoyelles	26	83.3	D	236	3.3	10.4	169	212.0	5 213	56.7	16.4	1 606	18.2	11 308
Beauregard	21	43.4	43.4	130	2.2	7.9	115	222.4	6 986	76.0	D	1 293	18.9	14 596
Bienville	10	188.8	D	76	2.2	5.8	65	57.3	3 616	39.3	D	414	5.0	12 162
Bossier	121	D	D	[4]	D	D	363	834.1	8 923	97.1	D	4 838	72.9	15 073
Caddo	451	2 586.1	1 965.0	5 864	176.2	339.7	1 053	2 338.2	9 594	104.4	14.1	13 945	221.5	15 883
Calcasieu	244	1 732.7	814.2	3 136	90.8	221.3	775	1 606.2	8 962	97.5	19.9	10 400	147.1	14 148
Caldwell	12	D	D	[5]	D	D	34	48.4	4 679	50.9	D	274	3.7	13 536
Cameron	19	416.8	D	115	4.7	13.3	34	29.1	3 256	35.4	D	240	2.4	9 867
Catahoula	15	111.8	111.8	193	3.0	7.4	52	62.2	5 634	61.3	D	407	4.9	12 034
Claiborne	20	121.7	D	173	4.2	11.7	63	63.7	3 746	40.8	D	486	6.3	13 041
Concordia	17	113.6	D	224	4.7	11.9	94	126.0	6 099	66.4	11.1	853	10.8	12 607
De Soto	17	D	D	[6]	D	D	83	116.3	4 644	50.5	D	748	9.6	12 832
East Baton Rouge	764	4 006.6	2 630.1	9 966	345.9	691.5	1 822	4 468.8	11 337	123.4	D	27 428	423.7	15 447
East Carroll	9	97.5	97.5	147	4.4	10.2	36	41.3	4 613	50.2	D	245	3.5	14 143
East Feliciana	11	D	D	[6]	D	D	45	45.0	2 162	23.5	D	373	4.3	11 568
Evangeline	17	30.4	30.4	122	2.3	5.1	129	144.5	4 239	46.1	D	1 012	13.4	13 252
Franklin	29	D	D	[6]	D	D	90	168.1	7 608	82.8	D	1 119	13.7	12 241
Grant	4	D	D	[7]	D	D	31	49.3	2 649	28.8	D	168	3.3	19 601
Iberia	118	359.2	312.2	1 447	44.4	82.8	282	613.9	8 503	92.5	11.3	3 354	54.1	16 122
Iberville	27	89.7	D	251	5.7	12.3	100	159.1	5 110	55.6	11.1	1 036	14.3	13 831
Jackson	8	28.0	D	36	1.1	2.3	53	59.8	3 833	41.7	D	521	5.6	10 825
Jefferson	1 168	10 041.1	6 673.7	15 313	500.0	1 004.8	2 038	5 787.0	12 826	139.6	15.9	32 403	535.8	16 535
Jefferson Davis	36	270.7	D	359	9.7	19.8	131	232.9	7 358	80.1	D	1 406	18.7	13 326
Lafayette	484	2 620.5	2 084.1	6 260	223.5	413.0	990	2 465.4	13 385	145.6	D	14 462	231.6	16 016
Lafourche	88	328.5	D	722	18.8	41.7	323	570.0	6 459	70.3	D	3 869	50.4	13 016
La Salle	8	8.8	8.8	43	.8	1.6	64	68.4	4 976	54.1	D	515	6.0	11 695
Lincoln	34	105.8	D	376	9.1	18.3	163	328.0	7 886	85.8	D	2 233	28.8	12 907
Livingston	55	140.1	D	502	12.8	22.0	213	368.9	4 313	46.9	D	2 403	32.4	13 481
Madison	14	D	D	[0]	D	D	53	83.8	6 428	69.9	D	512	6.5	12 664
Morehouse	15	45.8	45.8	143	4.0	7.9	126	216.2	6 821	74.2	14.5	1 263	16.3	12 896
Natchitoches	33	91.0	91.0	247	4.6	9.7	141	230.4	6 205	67.5	D	1 612	19.7	12 221
Orleans	484	2 450.5	1 718.5	6 086	210.2	405.8	1 871	2 771.3	5 908	64.3	9.5	20 405	315.6	15 465
Ouachita	248	1 257.2	1 117.2	2 912	82.4	169.7	753	1 483.5	10 094	109.8	23.7	9 649	134.0	13 884
Plaquemines	87	837.8	D	1 168	36.4	79.1	76	85.8	3 311	36.0	D	674	8.4	12 479
Pointe Coupee	13	D	D	[6]	D	D	84	159.0	6 742	73.4	11.4	807	11.6	14 320
Rapides	173	581.1	475.9	1 789	45.6	93.9	586	1 188.3	9 404	102.3	21.5	7 397	108.5	14 666
Red River	6	13.8	13.8	53	.9	1.8	39	53.6	5 557	60.5	D	265	3.7	14 015
Richland	28	160.4	D	259	5.6	16.3	85	188.0	8 983	97.7	19.0	840	11.2	13 325
Sabine	13	D	D	[5]	D	D	93	120.2	5 056	55.0	D			
St. Bernard	62	D	D	[8]	D	D	214	362.7	5 470	59.5	24.9	2 887	33.6	11 628
St. Charles	84	2 627.1	2 454.3	1 485	50.7	100.4	119	210.8	4 430	48.2	D	1 316	17.5	13 292
St. Helena	1	D	D	[5]	D	D	17	11.1	1 145	12.5	D	101	1.1	10 743
St. James	15	277.7	D	282	10.5	19.5	55	72.4	3 461	37.7	2.8	609	7.4	12 212
St. John the Baptist	30	D	D	[9]	D	D	119	231.5	5 524	60.1	D	1 643	19.9	12 122
St. Landry	85	415.1	D	948	21.5	44.9	327	515.8	6 192	67.4	D	3 552	43.9	12 456
St. Martin	36	116.5	D	332	8.2	17.9	121	192.4	4 111	44.7	D	1 260	17.2	13 620
St. Mary	124	705.3	D	1 384	46.9	95.4	256	396.1	6 957	75.7	D	2 829	38.3	13 532
St. Tammany	252	6 604.0	D	2 070	75.3	148.6	749	1 511.5	8 199	89.2	16.5	9 479	135.3	14 274
Tangipahoa	106	725.4	694.2	1 482	38.0	90.6	415	894.8	9 384	102.1	D	5 442	74.6	13 700
Tensas	8	50.5	50.5	103	3.3	5.7	22	27.5	4 110	44.7	D	114	1.5	13 088
Terrebonne	212	790.5	D	2 467	69.5	133.5	482	1 064.1	10 320	112.3	D	6 237	93.3	14 966
Union	11	9.0	9.0	75	1.3	2.9	73	92.3	4 231	46.0	D	578	7.8	13 512
Vermilion	66	361.9	334.9	738	19.6	46.1	198	277.5	5 374	58.5	12.7	1 836	23.7	12 908
Vernon	30	53.6	D	221	4.8	9.1	143	216.1	4 177	45.5	D	1 392	19.3	13 833
Washington	28	57.0	57.0	178	3.7	9.1	184	241.2	5 587	60.8	13.5	1 627	20.0	12 322
Webster	36	D	D	[8]	D	D	197	293.5	6 886	74.9	D	1 844	24.5	13 294
West Baton Rouge	38	444.2	D	575	19.1	42.9	63	124.3	6 094	66.3	D	843	11.9	14 173
West Carroll	9	8.9	8.9	19	.4	1.1	37	54.0	4 432	48.2	D	426	4.6	10 704
West Feliciana	7	11.7	11.7	30	.8	1.5	35	40.7	3 066	33.4	D	275	3.5	12 702
Winn	17	56.7	56.7	159	4.9	11.3	65	81.1	4 565	49.7	19.7	692	7.9	11 434

[1] Includes only establishments with payroll. [2] For pay period including March 12. [3] Based on resident population estimated as of July 1, 1997. [4] 1,000 to 2,499 employees. [5] 20 to 99 employees. [6] 100 to 249 employees. [7] 0 to 19 employees. [8] 250 to 499 employees. [9] 500 to 999 employees.

Sources: Wholesale Trade—U.S. Census Bureau, 1997 Economic Census, ECON97 Report Series CD-ROM, CD-EC97-1, Disc 1E, issued February 2001 (related Internet site <http://www.census.gov/epcd/www/97EC42.HTM>). Retail Trade—U.S. Census Bureau, 1997 Economic Census, ECON97 Report Series CD-ROM, CD-EC97-1, Disc 1E, issued February 2001 (related Internet site <http://www.census.gov/epcd/www/97EC44.HTM>).

[Includes U.S., states, and 3,142 counties/county equivalents defined as of January 1, 1992. For changes to these areas since January 1, 1992, see appendix B. Geographic Information]

County	Wholesale trade[1] (NAICS 42), 1997						Retail trade[1] (NAICS 44-45), 1997							
	Sales						Sales						Annual payroll	
									Per capita[3]		Percent from general merchandise stores			
	Establishments	Total (mil. dol.)	Merchant wholesalers (mil. dol.)	Paid employees[2]	Annual payroll (mil. dol.)	Operating expenses (mil. dol.)	Establishments	Total (mil. dol.)	Amount (dollars)	Percent of national average		Paid employees[2]	Total (mil. dol.)	Per paid employee (dollars)
MAINE	1 726	7 305.6	6 051.1	19 932	616.2	1 231.5	7 074	12 737.1	10 229	111.3	10.9	72 897	1 164.2	15 970
Androscoggin	126	277.8	270.2	1 244	35.7	71.8	533	1 247.1	12 357	134.5	11.6	6 362	96.4	15 150
Aroostook	101	211.1	197.9	766	19.8	40.0	471	591.9	7 604	82.7	14.0	4 285	57.9	13 503
Cumberland	574	3 673.3	2 801.9	8 884	296.8	582.0	1 570	3 825.9	15 175	165.1	10.2	20 735	346.5	16 710
Franklin	16	26.8	D	91	2.7	5.6	179	245.5	8 462	92.1	12.4	1 537	22.4	14 605
Hancock	73	138.6	138.6	354	8.4	19.3	388	490.0	9 880	107.5	10.2	2 895	49.3	17 045
Kennebec	133	821.9	795.3	2 135	67.6	132.7	589	1 289.7	11 155	121.4	13.6	7 166	120.5	16 811
Knox	79	171.7	D	550	13.8	29.4	278	394.0	10 411	113.3	9.2	2 309	35.8	15 513
Lincoln	52	66.5	D	259	5.5	10.8	236	299.7	9 466	103.0	3.4	1 545	25.2	16 337
Oxford	36	122.2	114.3	366	9.8	24.2	280	320.4	5 961	64.9	10.8	2 104	30.6	14 567
Penobscot	196	938.0	805.8	2 786	85.6	175.0	796	1 654.6	11 408	124.1	14.2	9 433	148.0	15 692
Piscataquis	11	D	D	(4)	D	D	100	120.6	6 569	71.5	13.4	871	12.3	14 163
Sagadahoc	21	78.7	D	111	1.9	5.1	124	183.5	5 176	56.3	2.8	1 044	17.1	16 346
Somerset	30	120.9	D	473	18.9	36.6	260	356.5	6 808	74.1	12.5	2 234	35.1	15 718
Waldo	29	149.2	149.2	165	4.2	10.2	165	192.5	5 334	58.0	9.0	1 226	18.2	14 875
Washington	50	438.6	D	(5)	D	D	204	260.2	7 241	78.8	10.8	1 712	23.5	13 748
York	199	438.6	382.3	1 479	41.1	77.8	901	1 265.1	7 286	79.3	7.4	7 439	125.1	16 823
MARYLAND	6 283	54 906.7	31 714.9	92 458	3 656.3	7 019.8	19 798	46 428.2	9 116	99.2	12.5	274 260	4 914.0	17 917
Allegany	71	D	D	(6)	D	D	385	663.5	9 133	99.4	19.4	4 719	63.5	13 457
Anne Arundel	653	8 829.7	5 974.0	9 148	366.4	751.1	1 863	4 757.6	10 127	110.2	16.5	27 922	487.0	17 443
Baltimore	1 003	6 707.2	3 143.5	12 047	491.6	943.7	3 138	8 243.4	11 448	124.6	13.4	49 690	902.7	18 166
Calvert	29	61.7	D	202	4.8	9.7	190	404.0	5 830	63.4	D	2 566	42.7	16 655
Caroline	26	163.2	D	325	9.1	19.7	104	191.3	6 490	70.6	D	901	13.7	15 175
Carroll	146	292.9	220.0	966	27.8	52.7	604	1 160.6	7 899	86.0	14.4	7 366	116.5	15 818
Cecil	53	D	D	(6)	D	D	284	613.4	7 599	82.7	11.6	3 526	58.2	16 518
Charles	75	234.9	D	1 088	27.6	50.9	490	1 243.6	10 793	117.4	D	7 750	128.0	16 520
Dorchester	51	121.6	D	402	10.7	24.2	132	285.9	9 567	104.1	D	1 476	27.7	18 788
Frederick	212	847.7	686.1	2 783	94.0	163.9	741	1 839.3	10 048	109.3	13.6	10 644	186.8	17 547
Garrett	40	121.7	D	303	5.7	13.8	157	222.9	7 576	82.4	2.8	1 367	20.6	15 055
Harford	198	1 024.7	667.0	1 502	47.1	108.2	741	1 755.4	8 265	89.9	14.1	10 518	174.6	16 599
Howard	631	9 392.3	4 999.3	13 185	528.3	1 040.3	766	2 010.8	8 783	95.6	D	11 823	216.2	18 283
Kent	25	49.8	D	162	3.5	6.3	125	132.3	6 969	75.8	D	908	13.9	15 316
Montgomery	971	8 795.9	D	14 752	778.9	1 319.5	3 000	8 914.4	10 758	117.1	9.8	46 311	957.8	20 681
Prince George's	759	9 053.7	4 910.6	13 904	542.9	1 122.8	2 425	6 390.5	8 301	90.3	11.9	38 214	675.8	17 685
Queen Anne's	71	209.0	149.3	526	14.3	29.9	217	321.5	8 252	89.8	D	1 833	28.7	15 672
St. Mary's	27	D	D	(5)	D	D	278	553.2	6 476	70.5	D	3 615	55.4	15 311
Somerset	19	D	D	(5)	D	D	73	68.0	2 784	30.3	D	485	6.1	12 480
Talbot	69	243.4	D	527	15.5	32.6	262	457.5	13 977	152.1	D	2 621	47.0	17 916
Washington	156	922.7	D	2 184	62.9	123.3	598	1 220.5	9 589	104.3	15.5	7 450	117.3	15 751
Wicomico	130	502.1	384.8	1 410	41.7	81.8	464	994.1	12 567	136.7	20.8	6 111	100.0	16 369
Worcester	76	476.0	D	1 181	39.1	70.8	505	546.0	12 958	141.0	10.2	3 285	59.1	17 979
Independent City														
Baltimore city	792	6 171.2	4 215.8	14 152	499.2	957.4	2 256	3 438.4	5 229	56.9	D	23 159	414.7	17 907
MASSACHUSETTS	9 993	112 792.4	61 530.3	146 827	6 484.8	12 686.7	26 209	58 578.0	9 579	104.2	10.1	335 736	5 894.8	17 558
Barnstable	259	462.8	350.6	1 361	45.5	89.6	1 592	2 518.8	12 275	133.6	6.3	13 675	256.5	18 754
Berkshire	136	D	D	(7)	D	D	832	1 280.7	9 564	104.1	11.5	8 513	137.7	16 179
Bristol	709	11 586.3	5 929.8	12 089	471.3	953.5	2 365	5 158.7	10 026	109.1	16.8	32 400	511.1	15 773
Dukes	22	D	D	(4)	D	D	222	207.6	15 272	166.2	D	931	24.3	26 100
Essex	1 071	9 270.7	6 727.0	14 836	671.4	1 329.2	2 703	6 156.2	8 867	96.5	9.5	34 590	585.5	16 926
Franklin	87	349.0	261.3	782	29.3	68.2	295	410.8	5 800	63.1	D	2 880	46.2	16 026
Hampden	573	4 481.2	3 152.1	7 696	285.4	535.9	1 862	3 919.9	8 902	96.9	13.5	24 675	384.7	15 591
Hampshire	109	D	D	(7)	D	D	604	964.6	6 415	69.8	5.9	6 976	107.5	15 417
Middlesex	2 914	33 893.5	17 452.6	49 166	2 386.3	4 448.3	5 701	14 462.1	10 205	111.0	9.2	78 812	1 491.7	18 927
Nantucket	13	D	D	(4)	D	D	178	195.7	26 126	284.3	D	799	23.0	28 826
Norfolk	1 451	21 949.4	9 793.9	23 872	1 128.8	2 193.2	2 599	7 332.9	11 461	124.7	10.5	38 832	715.5	18 425
Plymouth	700	5 772.6	3 078.4	9 214	361.1	783.7	1 917	4 895.9	10 611	115.5	8.3	27 147	472.3	17 396
Suffolk	923	10 935.6	7 837.8	11 910	523.8	1 091.3	2 543	4 842.5	7 539	82.0	6.2	30 091	532.2	17 687
Worcester	1 026	12 038.3	5 001.9	12 865	493.9	985.7	2 796	6 231.7	8 604	93.6	11.3	35 415	606.7	17 132

[1] Includes only establishments with payroll. [2] For pay period including March 12. [3] Based on resident population estimated as of July 1, 1997. [4] 20 to 99 employees. [5] 100 to 249 employees. [6] 500 to 999 employees. [7] 1,000 to 2,499 employees.

Sources: Wholesale Trade—U.S. Census Bureau, 1997 Economic Census, ECON97 Report Series CD-ROM, CD-EC97-1, Disc 1E, issued February 2001 (related Internet site <http://www.census.gov/epcd/www/97EC42.HTM>). Retail Trade—U.S. Census Bureau, 1997 Economic Census, ECON97 Report Series CD-ROM, CD-EC97-1, Disc 1E, issued February 2001 (related Internet site <http://www.census.gov/epcd/www/97EC44.HTM>).

Table B-11. Counties — Wholesale Trade and Retail Trade-Con.

[Includes U.S., states, and 3,142 counties/county equivalents defined as of January 1, 1992. For changes to these areas since January 1, 1992, see appendix B. Geographic Information]

County	Wholesale trade[1] (NAICS 42), 1997						Retail trade[1] (NAICS 44-45), 1997							
	Sales						Sales					Annual payroll		
									Per capita[3]		Percent from general merchandise stores			
	Establishments	Total (mil. dol.)	Merchant wholesalers (mil. dol.)	Paid employees[2]	Annual payroll (mil. dol.)	Operating expenses (mil. dol.)	Establishments	Total (mil. dol.)	Amount (dollars)	Percent of national average		Paid employees[2]	Total (mil. dol.)	Per paid employee (dollars)
MICHIGAN	13 936	159 432.3	70 982.0	189 057	7 629.6	15 704.7	39 564	93 706.1	9 576	104.2	16.1	529 441	8 922.3	16 852
Alcona	1	D	NA	(4)	D	D	40	49.7	4 561	49.6	D	290	3.9	13 600
Alger	7	D	D	(5)	D	D	55	37.1	3 712	40.4	D	294	3.3	11 139
Allegan	100	369.4	245.2	1 003	29.9	59.4	365	642.0	6 389	69.5	7.2	3 757	59.5	15 836
Alpena	45	143.3	D	396	10.3	22.7	162	288.5	9 429	102.6	20.0	1 719	25.0	14 568
Antrim	24	32.5	30.8	96	3.0	6.6	96	106.5	5 079	55.3	D	628	11.6	18 451
Arenac	27	74.6	D	227	5.3	11.3	79	127.8	7 815	85.0	6.1	758	10.6	13 992
Baraga	6	27.0	D	67	1.8	5.3	43	48.8	5 774	62.8	D	337	4.2	12 537
Barry	50	87.0	D	317	8.4	17.1	180	262.3	4 832	52.6	D	1 697	24.0	14 162
Bay	123	600.0	311.5	1 393	41.7	84.5	541	1 101.7	9 980	108.6	19.2	6 661	104.8	15 739
Benzie	9	4.6	4.6	48	.7	1.8	78	104.8	7 007	79.5	2.1	502	10.0	10 070
Berrien	193	938.3	442.8	1 887	60.0	130.3	674	1 302.5	8 121	88.4	17.8	8 078	125.6	15 554
Branch	49	411.8	D	639	19.0	37.2	174	321.3	7 342	79.9	14.6	2 002	30.4	15 162
Calhoun	145	1 392.4	D	1 646	60.8	150.3	567	1 239.0	8 884	96.7	D	7 779	114.7	14 741
Cass	54	252.5	165.7	351	11.1	23.1	143	159.0	3 191	34.7	D	985	14.6	14 866
Charlevoix	14	33.9	21.3	113	3.4	6.4	172	202.8	8 414	91.6	7.7	1 288	19.3	14 984
Cheboygan	21	48.9	D	85	3.0	5.9	195	254.0	10 834	117.9	15.2	1 475	24.0	16 291
Chippewa	21	24.9	D	140	3.2	7.6	187	289.6	7 673	83.5	D	1 839	25.5	13 858
Clare	15	47.2	D	90	2.8	6.5	140	217.8	7 517	81.8	D	1 319	21.4	16 226
Clinton	56	522.2	D	685	23.2	47.2	207	426.2	6 779	73.8	10.1	2 378	40.1	16 863
Crawford	11	D	D	(6)	D	D	65	116.0	8 340	90.8	8.9	629	9.3	14 769
Delta	59	95.5	D	452	10.9	21.4	232	380.0	9 766	106.3	D	2 552	35.7	13 985
Dickinson	54	119.1	D	505	14.1	31.1	177	316.6	11 663	126.9	D	2 222	31.4	14 138
Eaton	86	673.9	D	774	25.1	51.1	342	898.7	8 954	97.4	24.0	5 587	82.4	14 750
Emmet	32	75.4	55.7	228	6.7	12.7	298	404.7	14 277	155.4	D	2 509	41.9	16 703
Genesee	422	1 899.4	1 134.3	5 884	217.2	427.6	1 809	4 521.3	10 386	113.0	18.3	25 369	409.3	16 132
Gladwin	15	11.2	D	40	1.1	2.2	90	152.8	6 139	66.8	8.2	895	14.2	15 850
Gogebic	16	35.4	D	115	2.6	6.4	102	135.0	7 704	83.8	D	920	11.4	12 418
Grand Traverse	167	729.9	458.8	1 580	51.9	99.2	634	1 232.7	16 916	184.1	22.1	7 300	117.5	16 089
Gratiot	37	196.0	D	493	14.1	29.5	200	295.8	7 399	80.5	17.7	1 891	26.9	14 237
Hillsdale	48	215.6	D	416	12.7	28.7	163	255.8	5 513	60.0	D	1 556	23.2	14 936
Houghton	27	33.7	33.7	179	5.3	9.3	181	262.3	7 337	79.8	18.1	2 052	25.4	12 401
Huron	51	194.5	D	536	14.0	31.0	211	262.6	7 441	81.0	16.0	1 800	23.3	12 958
Ingham	365	3 313.4	2 243.2	5 830	213.5	412.9	1 207	2 992.6	10 424	113.4	19.7	18 762	301.9	16 092
Ionia	42	143.5	D	325	11.1	22.7	184	331.2	5 014	54.6	10.7	2 109	32.1	14 072
Iosco	11	7.9	7.9	79	1.4	3.1	160	224.3	8 772	95.5	D	1 475	21.7	14 698
Iron	17	18.4	D	86	2.1	3.7	77	92.9	7 141	77.7	5.8	632	9.2	14 597
Isabella	69	327.9	D	817	23.7	49.8	220	458.6	7 946	86.5	34.0	3 187	44.0	13 803
Jackson	196	1 047.2	659.6	2 339	83.7	159.0	564	1 289.4	8 292	90.2	28.1	8 108	126.9	15 651
Kalamazoo	337	1 870.1	1 010.7	6 278	233.2	539.7	978	2 388.2	10 407	113.2	25.6	15 421	230.2	14 926
Kalkaska	27	76.2	72.9	225	8.2	14.6	70	144.3	9 353	101.8	D	660	11.6	17 579
Kent	1 314	15 882.2	11 414.4	28 386	1 043.6	1 942.8	2 194	6 491.8	11 996	130.5	16.9	38 200	658.0	17 226
Keweenaw	3	.7	.7	7	.2	.3	10	2.7	1 293	14.1	–	19	.3	13 368
Lake	7	4.0	4.0	27	.5	1.1	36	36.8	3 626	39.5	D	244	3.7	15 012
Lapeer	68	136.0	111.1	373	13.2	27.2	278	705.7	8 124	88.4	18.7	3 706	58.2	15 714
Leelanau	18	20.0	8.0	90	1.7	3.2	143	92.0	4 887	53.2		661	10.5	15 924
Lenawee	92	429.5	278.5	685	22.6	51.6	375	826.3	8 441	91.8	19.3	4 859	75.8	15 594
Livingston	246	1 064.1	432.5	1 859	73.2	126.8	476	1 308.4	9 223	100.4	15.5	6 435	121.7	18 911
Luce	10	10.8	D	61	1.2	3.0	36	64.7	9 792	106.6	D	333	4.6	13 817
Mackinac	12	29.6	29.6	92	1.6	3.9	133	83.7	7 549	82.1	D	448	8.2	18 225
Macomb	1 040	6 608.7	3 536.5	12 592	521.7	966.2	2 901	9 010.8	11 508	125.2	16.3	47 125	859.9	18 248
Manistee	26	D	D	(7)	D	D	116	189.8	8 156	88.7	D	947	16.3	17 183
Marquette	68	159.1	D	545	15.4	29.6	331	522.7	8 400	91.4	17.1	3 822	51.1	13 363
Mason	25	41.0	D	118	3.2	6.8	159	223.0	8 027	87.3	19.5	1 470	21.0	14 286
Mecosta	31	43.0	D	187	4.9	10.7	175	301.1	7 643	83.2	18.4	1 925	25.6	13 307
Menominee	24	192.4	192.4	337	10.5	24.8	85	162.0	6 626	72.1	D	967	12.5	12 898
Midland	73	311.0	254.6	758	29.0	59.7	353	722.1	8 893	96.8	20.5	4 449	72.2	16 218
Missaukee	11	17.6	D	57	1.3	2.8	57	103.1	7 566	82.3	3.8	506	7.8	15 344
Monroe	96	731.5	403.2	1 213	46.2	94.9	448	1 035.0	7 283	79.2	17.9	5 489	91.1	16 602
Montcalm	48	158.7	D	287	7.1	16.6	217	403.7	6 763	73.6	D	2 613	36.5	13 971
Montmorency	3	D	D	(4)	D	D	48	49.9	5 000	54.4	5.0	312	4.1	13 189
Muskegon	162	891.4	536.5	1 852	57.6	113.9	591	1 365.4	8 230	89.6	25.6	8 672	132.3	15 256
Newaygo	27	56.0	56.0	323	9.4	20.5	156	244.2	5 423	59.0	D	1 394	22.8	16 383
Oakland	3 526	69 194.0	19 649.1	45 311	2 332.1	5 035.7	5 530	16 585.0	14 175	154.2	13.4	83 826	1 623.9	19 373

[1] Includes only establishments with payroll.   [2] For pay period including March 12.   [3] Based on resident population estimated as of July 1, 1997.   [4] 0 to 19 employees.   [5] 20 to 99 employees.   [6] 100 to 249 employees.   [7] 250 to 499 employees.

Sources: Wholesale Trade—U.S. Census Bureau, 1997 Economic Census, ECON97 Report Series CD-ROM, CD-EC97-1, Disc 1E, issued February 2001 (related Internet site <http://www.census.gov/epcd/www/97EC42.HTM>).   Retail Trade—U.S. Census Bureau, 1997 Economic Census, ECON97 Report Series CD-ROM, CD-EC97-1, Disc 1E, issued February 2001 (related Internet site <http://www.census.gov/epcd/www/97EC44.HTM>).

Table B–11. Counties — Wholesale Trade and Retail Trade–Con.

[Includes U.S., states, and 3,142 counties/county equivalents defined as of January 1, 1992. For changes to these areas since January 1, 1992, see appendix B. Geographic Information]

County	Wholesale trade[1] (NAICS 42), 1997						Retail trade[1] (NAICS 44-45), 1997							
	Sales							Sales				Annual payroll		
									Per capita[3]		Percent from general merchandise stores			
	Estab-lishments	Total (mil. dol.)	Merchant whole-salers (mil. dol.)	Paid em-ployees[2]	Annual payroll (mil. dol.)	Operating expenses (mil. dol.)	Estab-lishments	Total (mil. dol.)	Amount (dollars)	Percent of national average		Paid em-ployees[2]	Total (mil. dol.)	Per paid em-ployee (dollars)

County	Estab	Total	Merch	Paid emp	Ann payroll	Op exp	Estab	Total	Per cap Amt	Per cap %	% gen mer	Paid emp	Total payroll	Per emp
MICHIGAN—Con.														
Oceana	11	14.6	D	72	2.3	4.2	110	124.3	5 043	54.9	3.1	786	10.7	13 660
Ogemaw	18	69.9	D	207	6.0	11.7	148	230.8	11 018	119.9	D	1 351	20.1	14 857
Ontonagon	2	D	D	(4)	D	D	51	60.4	7 455	81.1	D	388	5.2	13 309
Osceola	11	51.2	D	129	3.0	6.3	88	105.5	4 788	52.1	D	694	9.8	14 097
Oscoda	3	D	D	(5)	D	D	44	44.7	5 059	55.0	D	318	4.2	13 343
Otsego	38	207.8	D	387	11.3	22.9	163	334.8	15 382	167.4	16.3	1 903	29.9	15 700
Ottawa	326	2 213.3	1 154.5	3 471	110.2	399.5	828	1 920.7	8 709	94.8	22.1	12 375	193.1	15 603
Presque Isle	15	41.7	D	181	3.6	7.0	93	122.5	8 528	92.8	2.3	768	11.0	14 303
Roscommon	22	10.5	D	72	1.3	2.9	149	267.0	11 503	125.2	D	1 553	25.5	16 446
Saginaw	269	1 614.3	1 318.0	3 643	120.1	236.2	1 101	2 477.0	11 753	127.9	17.6	14 917	228.2	15 299
St. Clair	131	596.4	216.3	1 415	50.6	92.3	629	1 315.1	8 350	90.9	18.4	7 801	124.8	15 997
St. Joseph	59	252.1	D	680	27.8	49.7	230	399.3	6 535	71.1	15.4	2 627	37.4	14 239
Sanilac	37	99.5	79.1	238	5.2	10.8	183	287.6	6 733	73.3	D	1 707	25.7	15 037
Schoolcraft	12	D	D	(5)	D	D	56	78.6	9 042	98.4	D	410	6.2	15 115
Shiawassee	67	182.6	104.1	476	11.5	24.3	234	571.4	7 902	86.0	19.0	3 080	46.6	15 137
Tuscola	54	202.4	198.7	408	9.8	20.7	212	412.6	7 119	77.5	D	2 048	33.1	16 146
Van Buren	61	160.5	D	405	11.7	26.4	267	503.8	6 686	72.8	D	2 694	44.2	16 416
Washtenaw	435	3 338.4	1 961.3	4 778	182.3	337.9	1 204	3 371.9	11 267	122.6	14.6	18 464	329.6	17 849
Wayne	2 357	37 963.4	17 972.3	40 193	1 614.4	3 278.7	6 690	15 852.1	7 449	81.1	13.3	85 476	1 483.7	17 358
Wexford	29	83.5	65.5	334	9.0	17.2	174	359.1	12 330	134.2	16.8	2 127	33.1	15 562
MINNESOTA	9 348	99 444.5	56 577.7	131 787	5 024.0	10 030.4	20 888	48 098.0	10 260	111.6	12.9	282 413	4 528.5	16 035
Aitkin	16	D	D	(6)	D	D	60	77.7	5 611	61.1	9.3	490	6.5	13 267
Anoka	351	1 824.1	1 240.4	4 520	161.2	322.7	826	2 232.6	7 789	84.8	17.7	13 478	206.0	15 283
Becker	42	78.6	D	263	7.4	15.1	182	258.6	8 822	96.0	12.5	1 609	22.7	14 114
Beltrami	44	101.2	D	414	10.0	25.0	200	365.8	9 454	102.9	17.1	2 453	34.5	14 069
Benton	45	535.4	D	1 083	28.4	53.1	102	186.8	5 543	60.3	D	1 356	20.6	15 192
Big Stone	15	D	D	(6)	D	D	42	26.9	4 745	51.6	D	254	2.6	10 327
Blue Earth	108	558.0	D	1 520	39.0	72.8	325	744.4	13 868	150.9	D	5 166	70.4	13 621
Brown	41	417.7	D	438	9.8	22.8	152	234.7	8 618	93.8	10.5	1 850	22.2	12 006
Carlton	25	193.2	D	417	11.5	23.6	129	226.6	7 344	79.9	D	1 364	19.5	14 317
Carver	122	570.1	D	2 205	59.8	119.0	177	413.8	6 554	71.3	D	2 389	40.0	16 741
Cass	18	D	D	(6)	D	D	163	164.8	6 368	69.3	D	959	15.9	16 602
Chippewa	27	191.4	D	240	6.9	14.4	75	125.9	9 629	104.8	D	844	10.8	12 799
Chisago	33	D	D	(7)	D	D	148	221.9	5 609	61.0	.3	1 421	20.0	14 056
Clay	67	410.6	D	765	17.8	34.1	193	458.0	8 867	96.5	D	2 828	37.8	13 373
Clearwater	10	17.7	17.7	75	1.4	2.8	40	34.5	4 170	45.4	D	260	3.0	11 388
Cook	2	D	D	(4)	D	D	48	44.0	9 302	101.2	D	271	4.5	16 428
Cottonwood	28	169.6	D	206	4.5	12.7	72	103.2	8 501	92.5	D	665	8.7	13 032
Crow Wing	79	178.7	151.2	713	16.4	36.5	376	708.3	13 861	150.8	19.6	3 749	61.9	16 521
Dakota	686	5 578.3	3 504.6	9 650	359.6	714.1	1 140	4 010.9	11 981	130.4	D	22 202	374.2	16 856
Dodge	22	156.1	D	321	10.1	26.3	68	70.5	4 133	45.0	D	448	6.5	14 522
Douglas	56	174.6	D	488	13.1	23.2	233	368.7	12 005	130.6	D	2 472	33.3	13 491
Faribault	40	D	D	(7)	D	D	84	80.5	4 903	53.4	D	634	7.7	12 162
Fillmore	35	240.8	D	319	8.4	18.5	135	149.2	7 210	78.5	D	810	12.7	15 632
Freeborn	68	522.1	D	646	19.1	42.0	183	310.8	9 838	107.1	16.6	1 965	29.5	15 037
Goodhue	63	680.4	D	1 051	31.3	89.9	244	337.0	7 888	85.8	D	2 390	32.7	13 677
Grant	18	209.1	D	168	3.8	7.8	44	53.4	8 665	94.3	D	287	4.1	14 111
Hennepin	3 723	59 929.0	28 192.0	61 454	2 700.6	5 112.2	4 644	14 615.8	13 856	150.8	11.4	78 226	1 409.6	18 019
Houston	31	70.0	D	536	10.1	20.4	70	76.3	3 970	43.2	D	500	6.0	11 962
Hubbard	22	29.0	25.3	111	2.2	4.4	107	125.2	7 512	81.7	D	846	11.4	13 455
Isanti	19	D	D	(5)	D	D	103	193.6	6 562	71.4	D	1 195	15.7	13 146
Itasca	43	467.5	D	395	9.7	20.0	256	361.0	8 285	90.2	D	2 376	34.0	14 303
Jackson	23	131.3	D	254	6.9	15.6	55	57.6	4 941	53.8	D	478	5.6	11 697
Kanabec	9	D	D	(5)	D	D	75	114.0	8 156	88.7	D	665	9.5	14 253
Kandiyohi	73	548.8	D	1 071	31.5	83.1	267	447.6	10 924	118.9	17.9	3 022	44.2	14 634
Kittson	20	89.3	89.3	171	3.3	8.6	36	38.0	7 096	77.2	–	220	2.7	12 164
Koochiching	10	D	D	(5)	D	D	104	124.6	8 204	89.3	D	787	11.9	15 150
Lac qui Parle	21	124.6	D	207	5.2	10.9	56	50.1	6 170	67.1	1.3	355	3.8	10 727
Lake	9	D	D	(5)	D	D	53	121.4	11 379	123.8	4.6	407	9.3	22 951
Lake of the Woods	8	15.8	D	43	.8	1.6	29	26.2	5 798	63.1	D	202	2.5	12 441
Le Sueur	30	154.0	D	415	11.6	23.4	117	150.1	5 993	65.2	.7	955	13.1	13 723
Lincoln	15	40.2	40.2	99	1.9	4.5	34	35.9	5 438	59.2	–	228	4.2	18 338
Lyon	54	915.8	D	889	31.7	62.4	155	290.5	11 884	129.3	14.2	2 013	27.6	13 720
McLeod	43	239.0	D	413	13.6	24.3	188	286.6	8 502	92.5	16.6	2 079	27.7	13 312
Mahnomen	8	29.7	29.7	48	1.2	3.5	28	28.8	5 640	61.4	–	147	2.7	18 252
Marshall	32	D	D	(7)	D	D	45	72.0	6 860	74.6	–	293	5.6	18 959
Martin	53	419.4	D	377	12.6	25.5	131	250.4	11 289	122.8	11.0	1 552	21.3	13 743
Meeker	26	100.8	100.8	203	5.3	13.9	103	128.2	5 957	64.8	D	787	11.9	15 074

[1] Includes only establishments with payroll. [2] For pay period including March 12. [3] Based on resident population estimated as of July 1, 1997. [4] 0 to 19 employees. [5] 20 to 99 employees. [6] 100 to 249 employees. [7] 250 to 499 employees.

Sources: Wholesale Trade—U.S. Census Bureau, 1997 Economic Census, ECON97 Report Series CD-ROM, CD-EC97-1, Disc 1E, issued February 2001 (related Internet site <http://www.census.gov/epcd/www/97EC42.HTM>). Retail Trade—U.S. Census Bureau, 1997 Economic Census, ECON97 Report Series CD-ROM, CD-EC97-1, Disc 1E, issued February 2001 (related Internet site <http://www.census.gov/epcd/www/97EC44.HTM>).

Table B–11. Counties — Wholesale Trade and Retail Trade–Con.

[Includes U.S., states, and 3,142 counties/county equivalents defined as of January 1, 1992. For changes to these areas since January 1, 1992, see appendix B. Geographic Information]

County	Wholesale trade[1] (NAICS 42), 1997						Retail trade[1] (NAICS 44-45), 1997							
	Sales						Sales					Annual payroll		
									Per capita[3]		Percent from general merchandise stores			
	Establishments	Total (mil. dol.)	Merchant wholesalers (mil. dol.)	Paid employees[2]	Annual payroll (mil. dol.)	Operating expenses (mil. dol.)	Establishments	Total (mil. dol.)	Amount (dollars)	Percent of national average		Paid employees[2]	Total (mil. dol.)	Per paid employee (dollars)
MINNESOTA—Con.														
Mille Lacs	27	87.1	87.1	219	5.1	10.5	118	133.1	6 429	70.0	5.8	997	12.2	12 206
Morrison	31	161.5	D	282	5.3	8.9	141	247.8	8 134	88.5	D	1 468	20.1	13 694
Mower	44	443.3	D	279	9.8	55.9	191	269.0	7 255	78.9	13.7	1 957	26.0	13 270
Murray	15	78.6	78.6	124	3.0	6.9	53	54.0	5 652	61.5	D	335	4.3	12 815
Nicollet	41	207.3	D	492	21.1	44.7	80	121.7	4 078	44.4	D	756	10.3	13 642
Nobles	43	D	D	(4)	D	D	155	206.6	10 497	114.2	D	1 376	19.0	13 830
Norman	15	57.6	D	141	3.3	7.3	43	80.5	10 534	114.6	D	357	5.7	15 919
Olmsted	125	605.4	584.4	1 176	37.5	65.5	586	1 432.7	12 508	136.1	D	9 277	136.9	14 760
Otter Tail	73	233.4	D	602	10.2	21.3	317	474.8	8 736	95.1	12.9	2 922	43.3	14 817
Pennington	19	302.9	302.9	939	21.0	50.3	85	149.5	10 966	119.3	13.2	1 000	15.3	15 303
Pine	14	25.4	D	101	2.0	3.7	116	153.2	6 477	70.5	D	875	12.3	14 097
Pipestone	31	256.1	D	457	9.1	18.3	67	94.3	9 329	101.5	D	557	6.6	11 903
Polk	57	206.2	D	415	10.0	21.2	152	211.7	6 626	72.1	D	1 377	19.7	14 317
Pope	22	192.2	D	290	8.0	22.9	54	58.7	5 360	58.3	D	379	5.1	13 420
Ramsey	927	9 328.6	6 210.4	15 680	633.3	1 379.1	1 879	5 504.5	11 355	123.6	13.5	32 615	567.0	17 384
Red Lake	10	35.0	35.0	70	1.8	3.9	30	32.5	7 501	81.6	–	150	2.6	17 253
Redwood	51	400.0	D	478	16.1	37.6	87	126.9	7 632	83.0	D	927	11.7	12 586
Renville	31	364.7	D	478	13.3	26.1	104	111.7	6 555	71.3	D	681	9.8	14 357
Rice	63	543.5	528.8	1 009	32.2	66.8	242	416.8	7 779	84.6	10.8	2 788	40.5	14 533
Rock	22	108.5	D	126	3.2	8.1	50	85.6	8 667	94.3	D	517	7.2	13 905
Roseau	20	69.7	D	145	4.0	9.4	89	119.7	7 354	80.0	D	769	10.3	13 432
St. Louis	280	D	D	(5)	D	D	1 088	1 892.4	9 720	105.8	D	12 389	186.4	15 045
Scott	153	1 917.8	1 187.9	1 613	64.5	145.9	229	419.3	5 493	59.8	D	2 318	37.0	15 961
Sherburne	51	78.5	D	351	7.1	14.3	154	502.9	8 672	94.4	D	2 120	34.4	16 208
Sibley	13	146.7	146.7	110	3.6	12.6	62	63.1	4 313	46.9	D	497	5.3	10 718
Stearns	193	1 068.9	D	3 688	117.1	205.7	661	1 664.3	12 990	141.3	D	9 866	149.4	15 141
Steele	55	225.7	210.9	415	13.1	32.8	174	272.4	8 665	94.3	D	2 042	27.5	13 491
Stevens	22	151.6	D	379	11.0	22.2	64	119.4	11 839	128.8	D	569	8.5	14 917
Swift	21	180.6	D	266	6.5	17.3	65	68.5	6 328	68.9	D	486	6.7	13 765
Todd	32	49.3	D	217	4.1	7.8	112	124.1	5 168	56.2	D	780	10.1	12 923
Traverse	8	96.4	96.4	72	2.9	10.6	31	31.6	7 402	80.5	D	213	2.7	12 737
Wabasha	25	49.0	49.0	199	4.3	9.1	107	124.7	6 031	65.6	1.2	882	13.1	14 859
Wadena	17	D	D	(6)	D	D	66	104.8	8 078	87.9	D	589	9.0	15 205
Waseca	26	62.6	55.1	156	3.3	6.7	70	106.3	5 748	62.5	D	742	10.0	13 532
Washington	205	2 029.3	333.1	1 471	69.8	142.6	601	1 674.4	8 725	94.9	D	9 304	142.6	15 324
Watonwan	24	211.8	211.8	219	6.0	14.7	59	55.3	4 758	51.8	D	427	5.0	11 691
Wilkin	20	149.7	D	260	6.8	14.9	36	38.1	5 166	56.2	–	272	3.8	13 926
Winona	80	418.3	402.0	682	17.8	37.1	224	384.8	7 969	86.7	D	2 506	36.5	14 565
Wright	85	221.2	168.7	669	18.2	40.0	283	682.9	8 222	89.5	10.5	3 870	59.7	15 427
Yellow Medicine	24	91.7	91.7	124	2.7	6.8	66	79.7	6 872	74.8	D	514	6.5	12 607
MISSISSIPPI	3 173	18 445.2	13 925.7	36 520	1 012.1	2 143.3	12 791	20 774.5	7 605	82.8	17.3	138 372	1 935.3	13 986
Adams	57	80.4	57.4	369	9.2	19.8	225	328.9	9 528	103.7	30.8	2 356	33.3	14 138
Alcorn	49	264.3	D	692	16.9	32.4	200	315.1	9 607	104.5	25.4	2 152	29.4	13 679
Amite	7	D	9.3	(7)	D	D	44	34.6	2 530	27.5	D	228	3.1	13 395
Attala	18	46.2	30.0	210	3.9	8.8	93	146.7	7 956	86.6	D	1 022	13.9	13 574
Benton	1	D	D	(8)	D	D	24	23.6	2 935	31.9	D	178	1.8	10 230
Bolivar	41	355.4	D	685	18.8	67.8	187	296.3	7 305	79.5	11.6	1 775	24.1	13 576
Calhoun	12	27.3	27.3	130	2.7	4.7	86	63.2	4 215	45.9	6.8	525	6.6	12 583
Carroll	9	17.3	D	32	.9	3.3	24	15.5	1 544	16.8	D	161	1.9	11 789
Chickasaw	29	66.6	D	244	3.3	7.5	94	102.0	5 594	60.9	D	741	9.1	12 217
Choctaw	5	D	D	(7)	D	D	29	26.5	2 848	31.0	D	183	2.3	12 661
Claiborne	1	D	D	(8)	D	D	34	46.8	4 029	43.8	5.2	229	4.3	18 638
Clarke	14	33.1	33.1	142	2.3	4.5	63	38.3	2 125	23.1	11.8	325	3.7	11 422
Clay	18	561.8	D	217	14.1	36.7	94	109.5	5 079	55.3	14.3	771	9.4	12 197
Coahoma	37	203.2	D	529	14.3	33.0	160	250.4	7 957	86.6	12.5	1 613	22.2	13 760
Copiah	20	66.4	D	187	3.6	8.2	107	100.1	3 468	37.7	18.4	815	9.4	11 588
Covington	15	426.1	D	150	2.6	6.9	63	92.4	5 274	57.4	4.6	479	7.2	15 054
DeSoto	78	D	D	(9)	D	D	278	663.2	7 186	78.2	D	4 248	58.5	13 772
Forrest	113	1 282.5	D	1 602	37.6	94.2	427	852.4	11 577	126.0	25.9	5 509	77.9	14 143
Franklin	5	D	D	(8)	D	D	37	25.4	3 062	33.3	5.0	198	2.2	11 187
George	12	D	D	(6)	D	D	70	92.4	4 866	52.9	D	706	8.0	11 299
Greene	5	18.6	18.6	92	1.9	4.9	36	28.2	2 283	24.8	10.5	203	2.1	10 507
Grenada	34	123.2	D	252	5.6	15.1	139	249.5	11 131	121.1	23.4	1 506	20.9	13 906
Hancock	30	68.8	D	251	7.6	14.3	128	214.2	5 447	59.3	17.9	1 583	19.9	12 545
Harrison	195	650.9	D	2 082	51.9	107.9	883	1 613.9	11 154	99.6	20.0	10 553	153.3	14 527
Hinds	454	2 600.7	1 979.3	6 671	206.0	396.0	1 092	2 760.8	11 154	121.4	13.3	17 356	280.3	16 152
Holmes	10	22.5	D	73	.6	1.8	95	95.0	4 428	48.2	5.5	673	8.6	12 796
Humphreys	14	D	D	(6)	D	D	44	70.4	6 216	67.6	4.9	334	5.0	15 042
Issaquena	2	D	D	(8)	D	D	2	D	D	D	D	(8)	D	D

[1] Includes only establishments with payroll. [2] For pay period including March 12. [3] Based on resident population estimated as of July 1, 1997. [4] 500 to 999 employees. [5] 2,500 to 4,999 employees. [6] 100 to 249 employees. [7] 20 to 99 employees. [8] 0 to 19 employees. [9] 1,000 to 2,499 employees.

Sources: Wholesale Trade—U.S. Census Bureau, 1997 Economic Census, ECON97 Report Series CD-ROM, CD-EC97-1, Disc 1E, issued February 2001 (related Internet site <http://www.census.gov/epcd/www/97EC42.HTM>). Retail Trade—U.S. Census Bureau, 1997 Economic Census, ECON97 Report Series CD-ROM, CD-EC97-1, Disc 1E, issued February 2001 (related Internet site <http://www.census.gov/epcd/www/97EC44.HTM>).

Table B-11. Counties — Wholesale Trade and Retail Trade-Con.

[Includes U.S., states, and 3,142 counties/county equivalents defined as of January 1, 1992. For changes to these areas since January 1, 1992, see appendix B. Geographic Information]

County	Wholesale trade[1] (NAICS 42), 1997 Estab-lishments	Sales Total (mil. dol.)	Sales Merchant whole-salers (mil. dol.)	Paid em-ployees[2]	Annual payroll (mil. dol.)	Operating expenses (mil. dol.)	Retail trade[1] (NAICS 44-45), 1997 Estab-lishments	Sales Total (mil. dol.)	Per capita[3] Amount (dollars)	Per capita[3] Percent of national average	Percent from general mer-chandise stores	Annual payroll Paid em-ployees[2]	Annual payroll Total (mil. dol.)	Annual payroll Per paid em-ployee (dollars)
MISSISSIPPI—Con.														
Itawamba	13	43.2	43.2	188	3.9	7.7	65	85.1	4 042	44.0	D	555	6.8	12 205
Jackson	70	272.6	D	576	16.7	31.9	512	948.6	7 354	80.0	16.6	6 119	82.3	13 447
Jasper	9	11.1	11.1	61	1.5	3.1	63	76.1	4 330	47.1	3.9	480	7.2	15 046
Jefferson	4	D	D	(4)	D	D	22	D	D	D	D	(5)	D	D
Jefferson Davis	4	2.0	2.0	17	.2	1.1	51	45.5	3 275	35.6	11.3	357	4.6	12 969
Jones	102	211.8	169.8	764	20.8	47.9	303	467.1	7 363	80.1	18.0	3 059	43.3	14 162
Kemper	4	D	D	(4)	D	D	37	27.7	2 654	28.9	D	176	2.5	14 153
Lafayette	22	46.8	D	89	2.0	14.1	174	254.2	7 378	80.3	D	2 099	26.4	12 558
Lamar	29	D	D	(5)	D	D	170	283.4	7 908	86.1	18.0	2 250	28.0	12 466
Lauderdale	106	973.6	818.1	1 869	50.4	99.4	496	793.7	10 359	112.7	16.8	5 305	76.2	14 367
Lawrence	9	8.5	8.5	43	.6	1.2	62	40.1	3 102	33.8	5.8	350	4.0	11 463
Leake	17	17.7	D	105	1.5	2.9	99	125.2	6 465	70.3	D	769	10.9	14 192
Lee	201	831.0	644.4	2 121	56.7	123.6	541	975.8	13 239	144.1	22.4	6 341	92.3	14 557
Leflore	56	905.1	854.3	803	23.4	45.2	222	277.8	7 407	80.6	12.8	2 033	26.4	12 999
Lincoln	37	415.6	403.4	762	17.9	38.6	164	315.2	9 962	108.4	D	1 809	24.7	13 637
Lowndes	93	333.5	316.9	1 098	30.0	60.0	367	601.2	9 815	106.8	16.4	3 856	54.3	14 069
Madison	118	1 180.0	929.6	1 565	45.4	97.4	377	679.8	9 590	104.4	24.8	4 987	69.6	13 964
Marion	29	D	D	(5)	D	D	130	167.4	6 362	69.2	16.9	1 154	15.0	13 041
Marshall	14	46.1	46.1	99	2.1	5.2	115	102.0	3 173	34.5	D	892	10.8	12 163
Monroe	33	104.5	D	200	5.4	11.8	169	228.1	5 992	65.2	D	1 525	21.3	13 957
Montgomery	10	20.7	D	57	1.0	2.7	68	63.1	5 068	55.1	22.2	507	5.5	10 919
Neshoba	32	85.3	85.3	297	5.9	10.8	117	226.0	8 312	90.4	D	1 384	18.4	13 302
Newton	8	D	D	(6)	D	D	91	116.0	5 402	58.8	12.4	829	10.6	12 830
Noxubee	9	21.2	D	57	.9	3.1	62	50.9	4 111	44.7	5.7	378	4.3	11 397
Oktibbeha	11	25.3	D	63	1.5	3.6	172	241.4	6 080	66.2	19.3	2 029	23.5	11 582
Panola	37	248.0	216.5	465	14.6	28.8	186	239.7	7 300	79.4	11.6	1 525	20.8	13 656
Pearl River	34	58.0	D	276	3.8	8.9	178	336.3	7 367	80.2	21.5	2 086	30.2	14 462
Perry	3	D	D	(4)	D	D	36	29.4	2 478	27.0	12.4	253	2.7	10 775
Pike	64	164.0	130.2	527	11.9	25.9	252	343.0	9 040	98.4	14.6	2 339	33.2	14 204
Pontotoc	24	73.1	D	204	4.6	12.2	103	120.2	4 852	52.8	D	808	9.7	12 045
Prentiss	29	85.3	69.5	223	4.7	9.6	129	138.4	5 706	62.1	14.4	891	11.5	12 895
Quitman	4	D	D	(4)	D	D	35	44.4	4 522	49.2	D	249	3.9	15 771
Rankin	200	1 609.8	1 079.8	3 150	112.2	200.0	350	808.9	7 565	82.3	11.1	5 001	72.9	14 586
Scott	34	103.6	D	208	3.6	6.9	144	156.2	6 227	67.8	D	1 216	14.6	12 025
Sharkey	10	18.3	D	91	1.8	3.7	33	25.4	3 840	41.8	10.3	204	2.8	13 814
Simpson	13	31.3	31.3	76	1.6	4.9	103	147.9	5 874	63.9	16.7	1 039	13.3	12 837
Smith	7	D	22.3	(6)	D	D	49	35.5	2 342	25.5	6.6	279	3.4	12 258
Stone	17	17.0	17.0	76	1.3	3.3	59	63.6	4 958	53.9	5.0	425	6.7	15 809
Sunflower	31	D	D	(7)	D	D	144	212.3	6 181	67.3	D	1 250	16.8	13 414
Tallahatchie	10	24.2	24.2	59	1.5	3.1	45	35.3	2 365	25.7	D	276	3.3	11 783
Tate	15	34.2	D	151	2.1	4.9	93	220.4	9 350	101.7	D	1 182	17.0	14 420
Tippah	20	59.9	59.9	181	2.8	8.2	105	106.7	5 095	55.4	D	831	10.2	12 237
Tishomingo	31	82.7	D	288	6.3	11.5	98	91.1	4 907	53.4	14.5	635	8.7	13 765
Tunica	11	110.6	D	109	2.9	10.6	40	61.8	7 659	83.3	D	304	4.8	15 888
Union	21	334.5	D	217	9.2	34.1	107	138.3	5 868	63.9	D	1 084	12.8	11 792
Walthall	14	53.3	D	181	1.9	5.3	54	56.2	3 929	42.8	7.8	378	5.3	14 103
Warren	46	151.6	D	359	10.6	21.9	281	454.7	9 241	100.6	15.7	3 316	43.7	13 177
Washington	78	393.8	372.7	795	24.5	46.1	324	507.2	7 741	84.2	20.0	3 441	48.2	14 017
Wayne	25	174.4	D	159	7.6	17.9	99	124.1	6 162	67.1	22.9	868	12.7	14 590
Webster	6	D	D	(6)	D	D	45	42.4	4 052	44.1	7.4	329	3.9	11 778
Wilkinson	12	27.3	27.3	88	1.5	3.1	31	31.1	3 380	36.8	D	228	2.7	11 886
Winston	13	98.0	D	242	8.6	15.1	90	103.9	5 360	58.3	D	741	10.2	13 825
Yalobusha	11	48.9	D	36	1.1	3.3	50	41.0	3 336	36.3	10.5	372	4.2	11 242
Yazoo	28	93.5	D	224	6.1	10.1	121	196.5	7 742	84.2	9.9	1 043	16.0	15 299
MISSOURI	9 522	91 411.9	47 744.0	125 929	4 639.8	9 354.1	24 181	51 269.9	9 482	103.2	15.2	297 556	4 945.0	16 619
Adair	30	87.6	66.2	376	6.8	12.7	143	225.2	9 255	100.7	D	1 595	21.7	13 617
Andrew	9	D	D	(6)	D	D	47	86.8	5 648	61.5	D	513	7.1	13 864
Atchison	13	D	D	(6)	D	D	45	59.5	8 389	91.3	D	376	4.8	12 872
Audrain	46	125.1	D	356	7.4	14.2	122	166.5	7 096	77.2	D	1 108	16.8	15 129
Barry	39	98.1	71.0	252	5.3	11.1	160	255.3	7 801	84.9	D	1 383	19.8	14 281
Barton	17	D	D	(5)	D	D	58	78.4	6 577	71.6	D	546	6.7	12 335
Bates	23	72.0	D	183	3.7	8.4	82	81.4	5 172	56.3	D	636	7.8	12 263
Benton	13	29.6	29.6	131	1.9	4.7	82	99.3	5 987	65.1	D	587	8.2	13 894
Bollinger	16	56.6	D	135	3.4	7.4	41	40.5	3 536	38.5	4.4	274	3.8	14 011
Boone	138	684.7	D	1 651	49.9	105.1	602	1 469.7	11 495	125.1	D	8 880	135.3	15 232
Buchanan	153	D	1 032.6	(8)	D	D	399	797.9	9 756	106.2	D	4 841	73.4	15 156
Butler	66	170.0	D	523	12.2	26.3	248	425.7	10 544	114.7	D	2 419	35.9	14 823
Caldwell	14	22.9	22.9	57	.9	2.0	31	25.4	2 912	31.7	D	175	2.2	12 423
Callaway	35	130.0	D	238	5.0	9.4	119	208.2	5 639	61.4	D	1 109	16.3	14 666

[1] Includes only establishments with payroll. [2] For pay period including March 12. [3] Based on resident population estimated as of July 1, 1997. [4] 0 to 19 employees. [5] 100 to 249 employees. [6] 20 to 99 employees. [7] 500 to 999 employees. [8] 1,000 to 2,499 employees.

Sources: Wholesale Trade—U.S. Census Bureau, 1997 Economic Census, ECON97 Report Series CD-ROM, CD-EC97-1, Disc 1E, issued February 2001 (related Internet site <http://www.census.gov/epcd/www/97EC42.HTM>). Retail Trade—U.S. Census Bureau, 1997 Economic Census, ECON97 Report Series CD-ROM, CD-EC97-1, Disc 1E, issued February 2001 (related Internet site <http://www.census.gov/epcd/www/97EC44.HTM>).

Table B–11. Counties — Wholesale Trade and Retail Trade-Con.

[Includes U.S., states, and 3,142 counties/county equivalents defined as of January 1, 1992. For changes to these areas since January 1, 1992, see appendix B. Geographic Information]

County	Wholesale trade[1] (NAICS 42), 1997 — Sales — Estab-lishments	Total (mil. dol.)	Merchant whole-salers (mil. dol.)	Paid em-ployees[2]	Annual payroll (mil. dol.)	Operating expenses (mil. dol.)	Retail trade[1] (NAICS 44-45), 1997 — Sales — Estab-lishments	Total (mil. dol.)	Per capita[3] Amount (dollars)	Per capita[3] Percent of national average	Percent from general mer-chandise stores	Annual payroll — Paid em-ployees[2]	Total (mil. dol.)	Per paid em-ployee (dollars)
MISSOURI—Con.														
Camden	58	88.4	46.0	244	5.0	11.1	328	437.0	13 150	143.1	D	2 639	42.1	15 971
Cape Girardeau	144	647.2	577.3	1 585	42.0	82.6	473	959.5	14 537	158.2	23.3	5 997	88.0	14 675
Carroll	24	78.8	78.8	105	2.1	5.3	52	36.3	3 556	38.7	D	286	3.2	11 259
Carter	5	4.7	4.7	20	.4	.7	29	17.9	2 829	30.8	D	149	1.3	8 852
Cass	58	D	D	(4)	D	D	218	492.9	6 315	68.7	D	2 833	44.4	15 679
Cedar	12	11.4	D	40	.6	1.3	67	70.0	5 357	58.3	5.8	416	5.5	13 269
Chariton	20	121.4	D	190	4.2	10.1	49	47.9	5 437	59.2	D	260	3.6	13 938
Christian	58	134.3	D	403	8.6	18.4	176	247.7	5 268	57.3	D	1 298	20.7	15 941
Clark	17	69.1	D	155	3.5	7.1	38	44.2	5 892	64.1	D	327	3.8	11 596
Clay	334	5 773.2	D	4 707	165.4	315.8	721	2 476.5	14 230	154.8	16.4	11 919	211.4	17 732
Clinton	14	D	D	(5)	D	D	72	129.3	6 927	75.4	D	787	11.5	14 633
Cole	100	897.5	833.4	3 286	65.9	129.3	349	764.1	11 108	120.9	22.6	4 884	72.0	14 737
Cooper	26	63.2	63.2	125	2.8	7.1	71	96.5	6 010	65.4	D	640	8.6	13 406
Crawford	19	46.3	D	117	3.8	6.6	83	224.5	10 222	111.2	4.7	1 014	14.2	13 959
Dade	8	104.6	104.6	328	8.0	14.5	27	20.9	2 648	28.8	D	156	1.7	11 096
Dallas	17	23.8	D	75	1.2	2.8	59	80.9	5 371	58.4	D	423	6.8	15 981
Daviess	13	41.6	D	119	2.1	4.9	45	24.8	3 178	34.6	D	203	2.3	11 266
DeKalb	12	29.6	D	77	2.2	4.0	28	44.9	4 063	44.2	D	232	3.1	13 284
Dent	11	D	D	(6)	D	D	77	105.5	7 485	81.4	D	675	9.1	13 536
Douglas	8	27.1	27.1	56	.8	1.5	40	46.6	3 790	41.2	D	324	4.3	13 142
Dunklin	53	134.3	129.9	384	9.0	16.5	186	256.6	7 811	85.0	D	1 690	25.2	14 918
Franklin	104	185.3	181.7	753	19.5	39.7	398	803.1	8 846	96.3	D	4 495	74.5	16 565
Gasconade	26	D	D	(7)	D	D	84	91.2	6 120	66.6	14.5	605	9.8	16 255
Gentry	12	D	D	(5)	D	D	48	40.9	5 938	64.6	D	304	4.1	13 408
Greene	576	5 101.7	3 732.9	8 856	263.9	489.8	1 302	3 271.8	14 503	157.8	D	17 819	294.0	16 499
Grundy	13	59.1	59.1	136	2.6	6.2	54	65.7	6 430	70.0	10.2	451	6.5	14 426
Harrison	19	74.6	74.6	225	4.6	15.5	56	92.7	10 991	119.6	D	605	8.7	14 456
Henry	48	218.6	D	534	14.2	25.9	136	177.1	8 393	91.3	D	1 126	15.0	13 348
Hickory	4	2.0	2.0	3	.2	.4	28	22.5	2 618	28.5	–	141	1.7	12 050
Holt	6	45.7	45.7	34	1.2	2.6	28	39.4	6 990	76.1	–	191	2.9	15 393
Howard	13	48.4	48.4	129	3.1	6.9	41	24.8	2 544	27.7	D	199	2.1	10 347
Howell	55	273.4	141.8	418	10.5	30.7	213	351.7	9 894	107.7	D	2 123	30.1	14 163
Iron	5	D	D	(5)	D	D	53	56.1	5 109	55.6	4.5	317	4.3	13 562
Jackson	1 197	11 305.8	5 889.8	19 252	712.5	1 524.9	2 670	7 239.1	11 066	120.4	12.6	30 108	704.0	17 980
Jasper	190	897.0	D	2 164	54.3	106.1	597	1 153.1	11 656	126.8	D	7 658	108.8	14 214
Jefferson	158	352.6	273.1	1 115	35.7	65.3	549	1 110.0	5 757	62.6	D	6 265	99.9	15 953
Johnson	37	93.8	53.4	373	8.0	15.2	154	243.8	5 169	56.2	D	1 551	22.1	14 256
Knox	7	D	D	(5)	D	D	31	20.4	4 693	51.1	6.5	115	1.3	11 078
Laclede	44	126.4	D	337	7.3	16.1	191	318.9	10 468	113.9	D	1 964	28.1	14 331
Lafayette	48	220.3	D	362	9.1	19.4	185	201.4	6 200	67.5	6.7	1 516	19.3	12 703
Lawrence	26	205.6	D	108	2.2	6.1	120	270.8	8 260	89.9	D	1 202	21.4	17 844
Lewis	13	D	D	(5)	D	D	49	47.2	4 652	50.6	D	261	4.0	15 456
Lincoln	47	144.2	139.1	254	6.5	18.5	110	234.1	6 647	72.3	D	1 249	18.9	15 158
Linn	23	34.0	D	123	2.8	5.1	71	80.4	5 766	62.7	18.5	531	7.0	13 256
Livingston	36	196.3	106.1	591	12.6	28.8	83	150.4	10 562	114.9	D	987	14.8	15 009
McDonald	16	D	D	(4)	D	D	79	82.6	4 191	45.6	2.2	478	6.4	13 324
Macon	23	82.9	D	227	3.7	7.8	73	85.6	5 599	60.9	D	642	7.7	12 048
Madison	11	19.0	D	64	.6	1.7	53	62.9	5 481	59.6	D	475	7.0	14 653
Maries	8	87.0	D	142	.7	1.6	30	31.5	3 778	41.1	4.0	199	2.3	11 799
Marion	37	138.6	D	437	8.4	16.5	178	298.6	10 744	116.9	18.0	1 889	25.4	13 444
Mercer	4	11.8	11.8	33	.6	1.0	16	17.5	4 365	47.5	–	78	1.1	14 244
Miller	22	62.8	D	182	2.9	6.9	130	208.1	9 233	100.5	D	1 004	17.8	17 717
Mississippi	22	313.2	D	236	6.2	12.8	67	94.7	7 021	76.4	D	588	7.6	12 986
Moniteau	19	D	D	(7)	D	D	59	108.9	8 208	89.3	D	447	7.2	16 022
Monroe	13	17.0	17.0	40	.9	1.6	42	47.1	5 238	57.0	D	267	3.8	14 199
Montgomery	21	93.7	D	180	4.0	11.4	67	74.4	6 303	68.6	4.6	438	6.3	14 363
Morgan	23	31.1	D	129	2.0	3.8	112	146.0	8 081	87.9	D	921	12.8	13 909
New Madrid	31	310.5	D	482	11.2	28.3	95	145.0	7 072	77.0	4.4	741	10.4	14 004
Newton	52	195.1	D	411	10.0	18.9	193	291.2	6 016	65.5	D	1 644	24.8	15 107
Nodaway	29	240.0	D	266	5.0	12.3	100	128.1	6 119	66.6	D	1 029	12.5	12 159
Oregon	14	29.0	D	113	2.0	5.1	46	57.1	5 715	62.2	18.7	378	4.9	13 085
Osage	15	24.4	D	34	.9	1.9	52	91.9	7 367	80.2	D	387	7.1	18 233
Ozark	8	D	3.9	(5)	D	D	37	39.6	4 105	44.7	1.7	249	3.2	12 815
Pemiscot	25	213.8	184.1	239	5.7	14.5	91	129.8	6 025	65.6	10.0	667	10.4	15 612
Perry	17	39.1	D	122	3.9	6.9	83	170.2	9 722	105.8	D	880	14.7	16 676
Pettis	67	211.6	131.3	765	18.3	36.6	204	355.7	9 646	105.0	D	2 230	33.5	15 020
Phelps	44	99.0	68.4	428	9.6	20.0	209	375.8	9 823	106.9	D	2 352	33.7	14 347
Pike	28	D	D	(7)	D	D	95	86.1	5 354	58.3	12.9	636	9.0	14 208
Platte	119	3 334.6	D	1 943	92.4	193.0	204	581.5	8 451	92.0	D	2 471	40.4	16 360
Polk	26	120.2	D	788	7.0	16.2	110	167.2	6 586	71.7	19.1	919	14.6	15 842

[1] Includes only establishments with payroll. [2] For pay period including March 12. [3] Based on resident population estimated as of July 1, 1997. [4] 250 to 499 employees. [5] 20 to 99 employees. [6] 500 to 999 employees. [7] 100 to 249 employees.

Sources: Wholesale Trade—U.S. Census Bureau, 1997 Economic Census, ECON97 Report Series CD-ROM, CD-EC97-1, Disc 1E, issued February 2001 (related Internet site <http://www.census.gov/epcd/www/97EC42.HTM>). Retail Trade—U.S. Census Bureau, 1997 Economic Census, ECON97 Report Series CD-ROM, CD-EC97-1, Disc 1E, issued February 2001 (related Internet site <http://www.census.gov/epcd/www/97EC44.HTM>).

[Includes U.S., states, and 3,142 counties/county equivalents defined as of January 1, 1992. For changes to these areas since January 1, 1992, see appendix B. Geographic Information]

County	Wholesale trade[1] (NAICS 42), 1997						Retail trade[1] (NAICS 44-45), 1997							
		Sales						Sales					Annual payroll	
									Per capita[3]		Percent from general merchandise stores			
	Establishments	Total (mil. dol.)	Merchant wholesalers (mil. dol.)	Paid employees[2]	Annual payroll (mil. dol.)	Operating expenses (mil. dol.)	Establishments	Total (mil. dol.)	Amount (dollars)	Percent of national average		Paid employees[2]	Total (mil. dol.)	Per paid employee (dollars)
MISSOURI—Con.														
Pulaski	15	D	D	(4)	D	D	143	178.8	4 723	51.4	D	1 041	15.6	14 951
Putnam	10	D	D	(4)	D	D	18	17.7	3 572	38.9	–	116	1.4	12 181
Ralls	12	61.3	D	86	2.6	5.8	31	23.2	2 646	28.8	–	172	2.3	13 453
Randolph	26	76.9	D	188	4.7	10.6	110	211.7	8 839	96.2	D	1 384	19.1	13 779
Ray	19	D	D	(5)	D	D	72	109.9	4 714	51.3	D	608	8.9	14 706
Reynolds	7	8.3	D	59	.7	1.5	27	19.1	2 864	31.2	D	123	1.5	12 431
Ripley	7	11.0	D	32	.5	1.4	54	68.4	4 929	53.6	D	371	5.1	13 685
St. Charles	345	1 831.7	1 336.4	2 729	91.9	194.4	934	2 343.7	8 879	96.6	D	13 688	220.7	16 123
St. Clair	8	34.4	D	38	.5	1.1	48	42.5	4 663	50.7	3.8	314	3.5	11 303
Ste. Genevieve	24	36.0	D	137	3.2	6.5	64	82.5	4 810	52.3	D	469	6.7	14 348
St. Francois	51	145.1	110.9	556	14.4	28.6	260	440.1	8 053	87.6	D	2 792	39.9	14 284
St. Louis	2 639	39 755.5	17 530.1	38 765	1 890.0	3 695.5	4 287	12 385.5	12 364	134.5	14.1	72 497	1 347.8	18 591
Saline	41	226.2	221.6	459	12.0	26.2	122	140.9	6 174	67.2	D	1 025	12.9	12 600
Schuyler	3	D	D	(6)	D	D	22	22.6	5 147	56.0	–	138	1.6	11 674
Scotland	9	25.3	D	56	.7	2.2	33	24.2	4 981	54.2	D	170	2.1	12 412
Scott	80	629.5	D	1 142	30.8	61.3	243	355.1	8 801	95.8	13.8	2 248	34.3	15 264
Shannon	10	22.3	D	61	1.5	4.9	29	19.1	2 341	25.5	D	128	1.5	11 391
Shelby	20	32.3	D	98	1.9	4.8	45	28.0	4 123	44.9	D	233	2.8	11 880
Stoddard	52	177.2	D	355	8.1	16.8	152	245.1	8 296	90.3	9.0	1 292	18.7	14 449
Stone	17	28.0	14.2	51	1.2	3.0	131	134.0	5 066	55.1	D	828	13.1	15 857
Sullivan	2	D	D	(4)	D	D	31	34.4	5 103	55.5	D	191	2.7	13 916
Taney	40	73.0	62.5	302	6.9	13.8	391	442.6	13 015	141.6	13.3	2 976	47.3	15 895
Texas	26	66.7	D	184	3.0	8.9	105	136.7	6 114	66.5	8.5	916	11.9	12 998
Vernon	29	56.3	D	164	3.3	7.8	89	143.7	7 454	81.1	D	1 003	14.5	14 466
Warren	26	53.7	36.9	145	4.3	7.6	114	188.8	7 973	86.8	D	1 027	15.3	14 855
Washington	15	11.3	D	65	1.0	2.1	67	101.7	4 481	48.8	D	633	11.6	18 308
Wayne	5	3.6	3.6	18	.2	.6	53	57.5	4 472	48.7	D	457	5.2	11 422
Webster	23	25.8	D	120	2.2	5.7	114	146.3	5 139	55.9	D	876	11.9	13 632
Worth	7	D	D	(4)	D	D	14	6.1	2 623	28.5	D	58	.6	10 603
Wright	20	94.8	D	147	2.4	4.7	94	130.4	6 713	73.0	D	795	10.7	13 443
Independent City														
St. Louis city	902	10 582.9	5 698.4	16 599	646.4	1 321.6	1 241	2 361.7	6 856	74.6	D	14 511	282.4	19 463
MONTANA	1 574	7 596.8	6 045.5	14 356	371.6	765.3	5 042	7 779.1	8 853	96.3	14.7	48 337	746.5	15 443
Beaverhead	11	16.3	D	95	1.6	3.3	60	69.5	7 765	84.5	D	474	7.2	15 162
Big Horn	10	D	D	(4)	D	D	50	56.5	4 483	48.8	D	415	5.7	13 781
Blaine	13	58.2	58.2	81	1.2	3.3	36	30.5	4 273	46.5	–	204	2.7	13 426
Broadwater	8	37.1	37.1	61	1.8	3.0	17	12.7	3 097	33.7	D	103	1.1	10 816
Carbon	13	9.9	9.9	55	1.0	3.0	45	32.8	3 469	37.7	–	267	3.2	11 940
Carter	1	D	D	(6)	D	D	4	2.6	1 717	18.7	–	18	.2	10 056
Cascade	141	1 114.8	991.4	1 231	32.6	64.4	427	803.0	10 168	110.6	D	5 049	81.8	16 194
Chouteau	14	108.7	108.7	89	2.1	4.5	34	33.5	6 393	69.6	D	169	2.4	13 959
Custer	20	94.3	D	147	2.6	5.9	72	113.5	9 371	102.0	D	770	10.7	13 918
Daniels	7	23.7	D	29	.7	1.6	17	30.9	15 013	163.4	–	125	2.7	21 280
Dawson	22	39.7	33.7	117	2.6	5.6	61	69.6	7 736	84.2	D	522	6.9	13 169
Deer Lodge	2	D	D	(6)	D	D	42	49.5	4 952	53.9	D	259	3.8	14 846
Fallon	7	15.1	D	52	.5	1.4	20	22.5	7 497	81.6	D	120	1.6	13 225
Fergus	27	187.8	175.9	199	4.4	10.0	80	89.6	7 186	78.2	D	581	7.2	12 411
Flathead	102	347.1	220.2	784	19.7	40.7	475	696.4	9 706	105.6	19.6	4 285	70.0	16 342
Gallatin	129	476.1	340.4	1 126	31.9	69.1	472	710.3	11 603	126.3	10.4	4 594	73.6	16 019
Garfield	1	D	D	(6)	D	D	5	4.4	3 074	33.4	–	35	.4	11 829
Glacier	15	72.2	D	77	1.5	4.4	54	71.1	5 635	61.3	3.5	426	6.8	15 939
Golden Valley	2	D	D	(6)	D	D	2	D	D	D	D	(6)	D	D
Granite	3	3.6	3.6	12	.3	1.3	11	13.2	4 985	54.2	–	73	.9	12 630
Hill	28	145.2	D	218	4.9	11.7	90	140.7	8 043	87.5	D	907	13.0	14 325
Jefferson	10	6.9	D	18	.5	1.0	25	17.8	1 815	19.7	D	148	1.9	12 655
Judith Basin	6	D	D	(6)	D	D	8	4.4	1 889	20.6	–	26	.2	8 346
Lake	23	34.1	D	129	2.2	5.0	125	157.5	6 197	67.4	D	1 056	15.8	14 932
Lewis and Clark	76	217.0	144.4	772	18.2	36.1	304	529.4	9 934	108.1	15.4	3 196	49.7	15 540
Liberty	5	43.9	43.9	40	.9	1.8	14	11.1	4 730	51.5	–	72	.9	12 208
Lincoln	10	4.9	4.9	30	.7	1.4	94	91.5	4 886	53.2	8.5	602	8.7	14 444
McCone	5	25.1	25.1	55	1.3	2.4	8	8.0	3 942	42.9	–	58	.7	11 810
Madison	6	5.7	D	17	.4	.9	40	24.6	3 571	38.9	–	165	2.3	14 055
Meagher	1	D	D	(6)	D	D	12	8.2	4 550	49.5	D	43	.6	13 302
Mineral	NA	NA	NA	NA	NA	NA	19	20.3	5 432	59.1	–	164	2.5	15 067
Missoula	183	775.9	558.5	1 991	50.0	101.9	540	1 069.0	12 032	130.9	20.0	6 800	105.7	15 548
Musselshell	7	7.8	D	28	.6	1.6	22	15.6	3 391	36.9	D	134	1.6	12 239
Park	23	33.9	33.9	138	3.3	7.7	111	102.7	6 384	69.5	D	588	8.5	14 452
Petroleum	1	D	D	(6)	D	D	2	D	D	D	D	(6)	D	D

[1] Includes only establishments with payroll. [2] For pay period including March 12. [3] Based on resident population estimated as of July 1, 1997. [4] 20 099 employees. [5] 100 to 249 employees. [6] 0 to 19 employees.

Sources: Wholesale Trade—U.S. Census Bureau, 1997 Economic Census, ECON97 Report Series CD-ROM, CD-EC97-1, Disc 1E, issued February 2001 (related Internet site <http://www.census.gov/epcd/www/97EC42.HTM>). Retail Trade—U.S. Census Bureau, 1997 Economic Census, ECON97 Report Series CD-ROM, CD-EC97-1, Disc 1E, issued February 2001 (related Internet site <http://www.census.gov/epcd/www/97EC44.HTM>).

[Includes U.S., states, and 3,142 counties/county equivalents defined as of January 1, 1992. For changes to these areas since January 1, 1992, see appendix B. Geographic Information]

County	Wholesale trade[1] (NAICS 42), 1997						Retail trade[1] (NAICS 44-45), 1997						Annual payroll	
	Sales						Sales							
									Per capita[3]		Percent from general merchandise stores			
	Establishments	Total (mil. dol.)	Merchant wholesalers (mil. dol.)	Paid employees[2]	Annual payroll (mil. dol.)	Operating expenses (mil. dol.)	Establishments	Total (mil. dol.)	Amount (dollars)	Percent of national average		Paid employees[2]	Total (mil. dol.)	Per paid employee (dollars)
MONTANA—Con.														
Phillips	5	15.7	15.7	37	.8	2.0	29	31.1	6 323	68.8	D	209	2.8	13 158
Pondera	21	55.3	55.3	132	2.4	6.7	32	51.8	8 047	87.6	–	260	4.2	15 996
Powder River	NA	NA	NA	NA	NA	NA	14	9.0	4 750	51.7	–	78	.9	12 051
Powell	6	D	D	(4)	D	D	24	15.8	2 247	24.5	D	131	1.9	14 344
Prairie	3	D	D	(5)	D	D	5	5.2	3 917	42.6	–	37	.4	11 405
Ravalli	44	166.4	145.9	283	8.7	16.8	154	179.8	5 207	56.7	D	1 197	16.8	14 025
Richland	26	188.7	130.8	228	4.2	10.4	66	83.6	8 198	89.2	D	506	7.5	14 874
Roosevelt	10	57.5	57.5	42	1.1	2.6	53	53.0	4 767	51.9	D	367	5.2	14 237
Rosebud	NA	NA	NA	NA	NA	NA	39	42.4	4 166	45.3	D	392	4.6	11 666
Sanders	12	65.0	D	51	1.2	2.4	51	33.2	3 244	35.3	D	239	3.2	13 527
Sheridan	13	44.1	D	67	1.1	3.0	41	26.2	6 105	66.4	D	176	2.3	12 938
Silver Bow	55	192.0	D	534	10.7	21.7	220	333.1	9 691	105.5	D	2 147	32.0	14 924
Stillwater	6	6.1	D	14	.3	.6	37	47.7	6 067	66.0	D	339	4.0	11 829
Sweet Grass	2	D	D	(4)	D	D	26	36.4	10 762	117.1	D	177	2.9	16 232
Teton	10	31.2	31.2	66	1.6	3.6	33	50.1	7 928	86.3	–	247	3.6	14 425
Toole	18	71.5	D	99	2.8	7.2	30	24.2	5 018	54.6	D	181	2.5	13 851
Treasure	3	8.8	D	22	.6	1.3	5	2.2	2 616	28.5	–	25	.2	7 320
Valley	15	71.2	D	126	2.5	6.2	52	53.1	6 383	69.5	5.7	342	4.8	14 178
Wheatland	3	3.8	3.8	17	.3	.6	14	10.6	4 527	49.3	–	89	.8	8 775
Wibaux	1	D	D	(5)	D	D	2	D	D	D	D	(5)	D	D
Yellowstone	389	2 648.9	2 062.5	4 915	143.4	280.7	717	1 575.6	12 509	136.1	17.9	8 736	144.9	16 585
Yellowstone National Park	–	D	–	–	–	–	–	–	–	–	–	–	–	–
NEBRASKA	3 157	38 015.4	17 741.8	41 002	1 170.2	2 461.1	8 295	16 529.3	9 981	108.6	13.3	102 684	1 554.6	15 140
Adams	60	D	D	(6)	D	D	180	289.5	9 779	106.4	18.1	2 204	30.4	13 782
Antelope	21	88.4	D	162	3.1	8.4	51	52.1	7 085	77.1	D	314	3.7	11 869
Arthur	NA	NA	NA	NA	NA	NA	3	.3	778	8.5	–	5	Z	5 200
Banner	1	D	D	(5)	D	D	4	.9	1 498	16.3	D	7	.1	8 571
Blaine	3	D	D	(5)	D	D	–	–	–	–	–	–	–	–
Boone	21	164.8	D	200	4.2	9.0	49	60.5	9 404	102.3	D	334	5.2	15 677
Box Butte	24	84.0	84.0	250	6.1	12.4	72	107.3	8 269	90.0	12.0	698	9.7	13 890
Boyd	6	D	D	(4)	D	D	15	7.9	2 983	32.5	–	62	.6	10 290
Brown	9	D	D	(4)	D	D	30	28.8	8 010	87.2	D	191	2.5	12 869
Buffalo	68	589.2	494.4	915	22.5	48.5	239	455.3	11 343	123.4	22.0	3 234	48.7	15 048
Burt	18	52.2	52.2	129	3.8	8.1	51	49.2	6 212	67.6	D	241	3.7	15 332
Butler	13	D	D	(7)	D	D	25	23.3	2 705	29.4	D	210	2.4	11 376
Cass	28	D	D	(7)	D	D	77	113.5	4 743	51.6	8.2	740	8.8	11 916
Cedar	24	79.8	79.8	154	3.2	8.6	51	62.9	6 421	69.9	D	308	4.3	14 107
Chase	19	118.5	D	222	5.4	12.2	35	44.8	10 525	114.5	D	240	3.7	15 550
Cherry	13	37.2	37.2	51	1.2	2.9	49	60.7	9 446	102.8	11.7	399	5.8	14 464
Cheyenne	18	D	D	(4)	D	D	61	649.8	68 085	740.9	D	964	22.2	23 053
Clay	19	100.2	100.2	185	4.1	11.0	40	43.9	6 157	67.0	–	202	2.9	14 124
Colfax	23	81.4	D	207	4.5	10.6	51	76.3	7 242	78.8	2.3	383	5.9	15 292
Cuming	24	D	D	(7)	D	D	60	97.8	9 763	106.2	4.1	466	6.7	14 326
Custer	19	74.3	D	142	2.7	5.7	83	81.2	6 707	73.0	6.9	534	6.7	12 481
Dakota	30	D	D	(6)	D	D	80	105.0	5 638	61.3	D	878	11.5	13 090
Dawes	16	D	D	(7)	D	D	61	81.4	9 112	99.2	19.0	663	6.7	10 094
Dawson	46	306.3	D	504	11.4	24.8	149	185.4	8 004	87.1	12.2	1 401	18.9	13 510
Deuel	5	D	D	(4)	D	D	15	24.6	12 138	132.1	D	136	1.6	11 787
Dixon	9	47.1	47.1	80	1.7	3.5	16	23.5	3 711	40.4	–	97	1.4	13 969
Dodge	71	587.7	453.6	748	21.1	50.4	185	479.8	13 656	148.6	13.5	2 313	37.8	16 325
Douglas	1 039	11 542.8	D	17 083	574.0	1 169.0	1 931	5 634.5	12 773	139.0	11.4	34 920	591.7	16 945
Dundy	5	D	D	(4)	D	D	17	15.7	6 829	74.3	–	84	1.4	16 071
Fillmore	21	83.0	83.0	170	4.5	9.5	38	30.5	4 417	48.1	5.6	229	2.5	10 913
Franklin	7	20.9	20.9	43	.9	2.2	23	13.0	3 418	37.2	D	97	1.2	12 392
Frontier	7	D	D	(4)	D	D	17	6.3	1 985	21.6	–	78	.6	8 000
Furnas	11	D	17.5	(4)	D	D	41	55.2	10 155	110.5	.7	285	4.0	14 028
Gage	46	148.3	D	277	6.6	17.6	153	190.1	8 321	90.5	11.8	1 310	15.8	12 077
Garden	4	D	D	(5)	D	D	15	9.6	4 369	47.5	–	80	.9	11 613
Garfield	3	D	D	(4)	D	D	26	33.0	15 972	173.8	D	135	1.8	13 496
Gosper	4	D	D	(5)	D	D	5	2.0	870	9.5	–	17	.1	6 588
Grant	2	D	D	(5)	D	D	6	2.9	3 934	42.8	–	41	.4	8 829
Greeley	7	D	D	(4)	D	D	19	32.8	11 307	123.0	D	111	1.9	17 378
Hall	116	690.4	D	1 534	41.5	90.5	347	722.1	14 033	152.7	27.5	4 646	69.2	14 904
Hamilton	26	208.8	D	376	8.1	21.5	35	39.9	4 222	45.9	D	302	4.2	13 980
Harlan	7	D	D	(7)	D	D	20	17.0	4 509	49.1	D	103	1.3	12 223
Hayes	2	D	D	(4)	D	D	1	D	D	D	–	(5)	D	D
Hitchcock	7	D	D	(4)	D	D	14	18.2	5 329	58.0	–	93	1.3	14 215
Holt	40	166.2	D	341	4.7	11.1	95	99.6	8 202	89.2	10.0	610	7.5	12 361

[1] Includes only establishments with payroll. [2] For pay period including March 12. [3] Based on resident population estimated as of July 1, 1997. [4] 20 to 99 employees. [5] 0 to 19 employees. [6] 500 to 999 employees. [7] 100 to 249 employees.

Sources: Wholesale Trade—U.S. Census Bureau, 1997 Economic Census, ECON97 Report Series CD-ROM, CD-EC97-1, Disc 1E, issued February 2001 (related Internet site <http://www.census.gov/epcd/www/97EC42.HTM>). Retail Trade—U.S. Census Bureau, 1997 Economic Census, ECON97 Report Series CD-ROM, CD-EC97-1, Disc 1E, issued February 2001 (related Internet site <http://www.census.gov/epcd/www/97EC44.HTM>).

[Includes U.S., states, and 3,142 counties/county equivalents defined as of January 1, 1992. For changes to these areas since January 1, 1992, see appendix B. Geographic Information]

County	Wholesale trade[1] (NAICS 42), 1997						Retail trade[1] (NAICS 44-45), 1997							
	Sales				Annual payroll (mil. dol.)	Operating expenses (mil. dol.)	Sales					Annual payroll		
									Per capita[3]		Percent from general merchandise stores			
	Establishments	Total (mil. dol.)	Merchant wholesalers (mil. dol.)	Paid employees[2]			Establishments	Total (mil. dol.)	Amount (dollars)	Percent of national average		Paid employees[2]	Total (mil. dol.)	Per paid employee (dollars)
NEBRASKA—Con.														
Hooker	1	D	D	(4)	D	D	8	4.1	5 812	63.2	D	43	.5	11 674
Howard	7	30.7	D	54	1.7	3.2	38	25.1	3 894	42.4	3.9	210	2.8	13 500
Jefferson	22	144.3	D	246	5.7	15.0	51	60.6	7 202	78.4	D	448	6.1	13 712
Johnson	7	29.0	D	71	1.1	3.9	34	29.1	6 330	68.9	D	196	2.6	13 173
Kearney	11	135.3	135.3	131	3.8	10.1	28	24.2	3 606	39.2	D	166	2.1	12 584
Keith	24	190.6	D	213	4.8	8.5	75	97.8	11 338	123.4	10.5	669	9.6	14 336
Keya Paha	3	D	D	(4)	D	D	6	2.1	2 122	23.1	—	12	.2	15 417
Kimball	10	D	D	(5)	D	D	30	21.1	5 244	57.1	7.2	183	2.1	11 514
Knox	17	D	D	(6)	D	D	73	61.3	6 560	71.4	2.7	373	4.5	12 043
Lancaster	304	D	D	(7)	D	D	996	2 270.4	9 730	105.9	15.8	15 734	232.0	14 745
Lincoln	56	259.7	208.1	461	11.9	26.7	198	314.5	9 390	102.2	20.5	2 107	28.9	13 727
Logan	NA	NA	NA	NA	NA	NA	2	D	D	D	D	(4)	D	D
Loup	NA	NA	NA	NA	NA	NA	3	D	D	D	D	(4)	D	D
McPherson	2	D	D	(4)	D	D	2	D	D	D	D	(4)	D	D
Madison	81	D	D	(8)	D	D	226	479.6	13 783	150.0	21.9	3 048	41.6	13 635
Merrick	20	109.4	109.4	137	3.7	7.8	39	31.5	3 852	41.9	4.2	250	3.2	12 872
Morrill	11	30.7	30.7	119	2.7	6.5	23	23.9	4 427	48.2	10.1	162	2.0	12 426
Nance	10	D	D	(5)	D	D	21	14.8	3 520	38.3	D	111	1.2	10 937
Nemaha	12	D	D	(5)	D	D	45	51.5	6 590	71.7	D	323	3.7	11 563
Nuckolls	13	44.9	44.9	109	1.7	3.9	40	43.2	8 099	88.1	D	284	3.7	13 169
Otoe	21	131.3	131.3	159	3.6	8.1	98	110.6	7 617	82.9	D	694	9.5	13 644
Pawnee	6	D	D	(4)	D	D	12	7.1	2 250	24.5	—	53	.6	11 321
Perkins	20	136.7	136.7	125	2.8	7.6	18	12.4	3 820	41.6	—	92	1.2	13 152
Phelps	25	D	D	(9)	D	D	70	81.8	8 220	89.4	D	533	7.4	13 795
Pierce	18	40.0	D	97	1.9	4.9	51	45.1	5 702	62.0	D	312	3.6	11 407
Platte	55	324.8	221.2	680	14.8	27.6	176	293.7	9 586	104.3	D	1 984	27.9	14 039
Polk	11	117.1	D	141	4.0	8.6	24	23.8	4 238	46.1	—	126	1.7	13 516
Red Willow	20	D	D	(9)	D	D	109	176.3	15 516	168.8	D	1 124	15.7	13 946
Richardson	25	74.0	D	119	2.6	5.8	66	59.4	6 283	68.4	D	387	4.6	11 997
Rock	7	D	D	(5)	D	D	10	6.4	3 619	39.4	D	57	.6	11 333
Saline	15	72.7	72.7	109	2.8	7.1	62	95.6	7 345	79.9	D	584	8.9	15 154
Sarpy	84	D	D	(8)	D	D	291	695.6	5 866	63.8	24.3	4 663	63.7	13 654
Saunders	21	72.1	D	150	2.7	6.7	79	92.8	4 842	52.7	4.6	602	7.5	12 482
Scotts Bluff	79	225.8	D	826	19.0	35.5	239	391.9	10 790	117.4	D	2 624	38.8	14 798
Seward	25	94.2	94.2	235	5.9	12.4	63	80.7	4 978	54.2	17.2	564	6.8	11 975
Sheridan	17	117.2	D	245	3.6	7.3	58	56.9	8 625	93.9	9.0	397	4.4	11 121
Sherman	4	D	D	(5)	D	D	18	17.8	5 035	54.8	D	84	1.2	14 357
Sioux	2	D	D	(4)	D	D	5	2.2	1 430	15.6	D	17	.2	10 706
Stanton	5	D	D	(5)	D	D	13	8.2	1 335	14.5	—	59	.8	13 576
Thayer	16	96.0	D	112	2.1	5.1	45	44.2	7 046	76.7	—	285	3.5	12 389
Thomas	1	D	D	(4)	D	D	6	4.2	5 163	56.2	—	27	.3	10 963
Thurston	9	31.4	31.4	54	1.2	2.7	29	42.4	5 887	64.1	—	239	3.1	12 954
Valley	13	101.4	101.4	151	3.1	8.5	38	27.3	5 749	62.6	15.4	226	2.9	12 876
Washington	22	D	D	(5)	D	D	72	233.9	12 740	138.6	D	675	14.3	21 228
Wayne	11	D	D	(5)	D	D	46	47.0	4 978	54.2	D	386	4.5	11 663
Webster	13	48.4	48.4	103	2.0	4.0	22	21.3	5 308	57.8	—	143	2.0	14 133
Wheeler	1	D	NA	(5)	D	D	4	1.7	1 805	19.6	—	16	.1	7 875
York	38	207.4	D	363	10.2	18.5	98	160.2	10 948	119.1	12.7	1 027	13.9	13 548
NEVADA	2 253	12 806.9	8 185.7	27 251	918.5	1 865.4	6 222	18 220.8	10 874	118.3	13.5	89 452	1 798.2	20 103
Churchill	17	29.3	D	123	2.3	4.2	87	177.6	7 789	84.8	D	1 023	16.9	16 519
Clark	1 298	6 366.0	4 550.3	15 824	526.9	1 047.6	3 803	12 321.5	11 151	121.3	D	58 477	1 201.7	20 549
Douglas	46	67.6	D	205	6.8	15.0	141	203.3	5 637	61.3	—	1 143	23.5	20 563
Elko	61	268.9	D	636	24.2	44.4	171	426.8	9 369	101.9	12.3	2 226	39.1	17 560
Esmeralda	1	D	D	(4)	D	D	2	D	D	D	D	(4)	D	D
Eureka	3	3.4	3.4	4	.1	.2	7	D	D	D	D	(5)	D	D
Humboldt	29	64.2	D	161	4.4	9.4	79	193.7	11 085	120.6	D	967	15.7	16 231
Lander	7	19.8	19.8	46	1.0	3.2	20	36.6	5 060	55.1	—	311	4.0	12 855
Lincoln	1	D	D	(4)	D	D	15	12.5	3 034	33.0	D	141	1.5	10 546
Lyon	26	46.0	46.0	145	4.5	9.4	81	140.6	4 876	53.1	D	723	13.9	19 165
Mineral	2	D	D	(5)	D	D	23	32.1	5 672	61.7	—	172	2.7	15 715
Nye	19	D	D	(5)	D	D	107	140.4	5 207	56.7	D	777	13.0	16 730
Pershing	2	D	D	(4)	D	D	21	36.4	7 589	82.6	D	177	2.4	13 746
Storey	2	D	D	(4)	D	D	24	7.5	2 602	28.3	—	82	1.4	16 805
Washoe	639	5 663.6	2 951.6	9 339	324.9	682.1	1 328	3 751.1	12 247	133.3	16.2	19 418	389.5	20 059
White Pine	12	17.6	17.6	64	1.6	4.3	51	55.5	5 440	59.2	D	376	6.1	16 239
Independent City														
Carson City city	88	222.4	D	557	18.7	39.0	262	678.4	13 942	151.7	D	3 383	66.1	19 533

[1] Includes only establishments with payroll. [2] For pay period including March 12. [3] Based on resident population estimated as of July 1, 1997. [4] 0 to 19 employees. [5] 20 to 99 employees. [6] 100 to 249 employees. [7] 5,000 to 9,999 employees. [8] 1,000 to 2,499 employees. [9] 250 to 499 employees.

Sources: Wholesale Trade—U.S. Census Bureau, 1997 Economic Census, ECON97 Report Series CD-ROM, CD-EC97-1, Disc 1E, issued February 2001 (related Internet site <http://www.census.gov/epcd/www/97EC42.HTM>). Retail Trade—U.S. Census Bureau, 1997 Economic Census, ECON97 Report Series CD-ROM, CD-EC97-1, Disc 1E, issued February 2001 (related Internet site <http://www.census.gov/epcd/www/97EC44.HTM>).

Table B–11. Counties — **Wholesale Trade and Retail Trade**–Con.

[Includes U.S., states, and 3,142 counties/county equivalents defined as of January 1, 1992. For changes to these areas since January 1, 1992, see appendix B. Geographic Information]

County	Wholesale trade[1] (NAICS 42), 1997						Retail trade[1] (NAICS 44-45), 1997							
	Sales						Sales						Annual payroll	
									Per capita[3]		Percent from general merchandise stores			
	Establishments	Total (mil. dol.)	Merchant wholesalers (mil. dol.)	Paid employees[2]	Annual payroll (mil. dol.)	Operating expenses (mil. dol.)	Establishments	Total (mil. dol.)	Amount (dollars)	Percent of national average		Paid employees[2]	Total (mil. dol.)	Per paid employee (dollars)
NEW HAMPSHIRE	2 033	11 371.1	7 618.2	22 631	875.0	1 731.7	6 645	15 812.0	13 477	146.6	13.1	84 170	1 422.0	16 894
Belknap	74	181.7	132.0	628	25.9	53.6	414	713.8	13 676	148.8	14.6	4 073	69.2	16 990
Carroll	61	80.8	D	371	10.6	19.7	428	551.1	14 227	154.8	5.0	3 267	55.4	16 965
Cheshire	92	403.5	348.4	1 187	37.6	76.8	402	1 077.3	14 995	163.2	9.4	5 097	85.8	16 829
Coos	27	81.0	D	308	6.6	14.3	229	423.8	12 777	139.0	3.4	1 959	32.8	16 738
Grafton	112	333.4	234.1	944	31.6	72.3	589	1 031.6	13 234	144.0	8.7	6 164	110.2	17 872
Hillsborough	721	4 792.9	2 661.2	8 588	366.4	667.6	1 692	4 927.0	13 777	149.9	13.9	25 208	455.6	18 074
Merrimack	189	799.5	665.4	2 328	78.0	167.1	628	1 500.7	11 856	129.0	11.6	7 629	127.7	16 734
Rockingham	605	4 328.9	3 209.4	6 504	271.2	563.4	1 617	4 218.8	15 824	172.2	16.8	22 905	356.8	15 578
Strafford	109	281.0	D	1 508	39.9	79.6	436	1 020.0	9 378	102.0	10.8	5 807	92.8	15 975
Sullivan	43	88.4	D	265	7.4	17.3	210	347.8	8 746	95.2	13.6	2 061	35.8	17 367
NEW JERSEY	17 812	227 309.0	129 415.1	266 944	11 886.1	26 750.7	34 837	79 914.9	9 922	108.0	10.2	420 724	7 926.0	18 839
Atlantic	234	831.5	D	2 312	81.0	161.8	1 258	2 513.2	10 639	115.8	14.4	14 308	253.8	17 737
Bergen	3 876	62 435.3	37 790.9	55 657	2 713.6	6 592.5	4 284	10 766.1	12 646	137.6	9.5	52 065	1 052.8	20 220
Burlington	769	16 206.9	5 487.8	13 262	547.1	1 353.4	1 570	4 410.8	10 510	114.4	11.4	22 857	426.6	18 664
Camden	922	6 139.0	3 552.8	10 789	400.0	835.8	2 052	4 612.4	9 139	99.4	9.9	26 577	481.0	18 097
Cape May	74	201.0	D	907	21.6	40.5	784	961.1	9 814	106.8	5.6	4 990	102.7	20 577
Cumberland	189	989.4	D	2 230	69.4	150.0	578	1 226.5	8 702	94.7	10.7	7 157	130.1	18 177
Essex	1 478	17 599.5	10 483.6	23 082	1 025.5	2 531.0	2 819	4 518.1	6 018	65.5	7.8	27 068	512.9	18 949
Gloucester	381	6 023.1	3 338.3	6 268	218.8	475.3	989	2 441.7	9 929	108.0	D	14 030	231.3	16 483
Hudson	1 065	11 271.5	9 154.5	21 629	864.6	1 940.9	2 327	3 842.9	6 941	75.5	8.6	22 670	384.9	16 980
Hunterdon	208	1 201.5	430.2	1 595	74.9	134.1	600	1 454.5	12 064	131.3	4.1	6 415	143.7	22 394
Mercer	472	4 403.0	D	8 480	291.5	720.0	1 442	3 183.1	9 650	105.0	10.4	18 217	326.1	17 900
Middlesex	1 866	24 256.4	15 820.8	36 168	1 554.4	3 362.9	2 785	7 364.0	10 407	113.2	D	39 421	720.8	18 286
Monmouth	1 197	6 298.1	4 216.1	9 577	410.3	930.9	2 870	6 400.5	10 725	116.7	11.5	34 839	627.7	18 017
Morris	1 397	20 939.4	11 834.7	20 533	1 027.2	2 316.4	2 241	6 499.9	14 305	155.7	8.1	30 767	635.5	20 655
Ocean	429	937.2	782.8	2 903	95.4	193.6	1 923	4 728.3	9 802	106.7	10.4	23 431	431.5	18 414
Passaic	1 006	9 085.0	4 990.9	13 154	601.8	1 168.1	1 843	4 659.9	9 665	105.2	14.5	25 468	469.0	18 416
Salem	45	440.3	426.2	517	19.3	54.4	226	401.3	6 151	66.9	D	2 682	41.5	15 460
Somerset	672	18 285.3	9 178.1	12 018	643.4	1 464.1	1 178	3 305.8	11 959	130.1	D	15 351	306.7	19 978
Sussex	181	D	D	(4)	D	D	502	953.6	6 722	73.1	D	4 689	92.7	19 762
Union	1 222	15 712.5	7 236.1	22 744	1 085.7	2 079.2	2 100	4 809.2	9 662	105.1	4.6	22 616	464.9	20 558
Warren	129	D	D	(4)	D	D	466	862.2	8 789	95.6	D	5 106	90.1	17 637
NEW MEXICO	2 182	7 397.6	5 400.6	21 344	601.1	1 201.7	7 421	14 984.5	8 697	94.6	14.2	86 300	1 455.5	16 865
Bernalillo	1 037	4 594.3	3 175.6	12 824	388.2	748.0	2 307	6 497.7	12 372	134.6	13.9	34 361	623.6	18 149
Catron	NA	NA	NA	NA	NA	NA	12	3.1	1 128	12.3	52.9	37	.3	9 162
Chaves	74	231.3	D	599	13.8	29.5	269	411.0	6 569	71.5	18.8	2 702	40.5	14 981
Cibola	17	21.8	21.8	82	1.4	3.0	77	149.3	5 704	62.1	4.6	809	11.3	13 972
Colfax	13	D	D	(5)	D	D	95	104.6	7 613	82.8	8.4	606	9.1	15 074
Curry	44	120.5	107.2	342	7.3	16.2	235	342.6	7 355	80.0	19.4	2 455	34.6	14 078
DeBaca	1	D	D	(6)	D	D	13	8.7	3 707	40.3	-	59	.8	12 864
Dona Ana	122	283.6	229.7	978	25.0	54.7	511	1 059.1	6 364	69.2	15.1	6 266	98.1	15 661
Eddy	69	274.7	D	384	10.3	21.7	232	372.7	7 014	76.3	15.0	2 312	38.9	16 814
Grant	32	56.6	D	198	4.1	9.4	125	190.4	6 060	65.9	D	1 165	17.9	15 399
Guadalupe	5	9.8	9.8	7	.2	.6	27	32.0	7 820	85.1	-	333	3.5	10 429
Harding	NA	NA	NA	NA	NA	NA	3	8.1	9 072	98.7	D	13	.5	36 538
Hidalgo	3	D	D	(5)	D	D	36	49.3	7 890	85.9	D	238	3.7	15 429
Lea	121	308.7	248.5	964	27.2	62.2	248	405.3	7 229	78.7	14.9	2 375	42.6	17 928
Lincoln	16	7.7	D	35	.6	2.2	148	149.1	9 307	101.3	D	1 079	15.1	14 016
Los Alamos	9	41.4	D	75	4.1	8.1	59	74.1	4 065	44.2	D	555	8.0	14 395
Luna	22	49.3	D	233	3.1	7.3	95	177.5	7 539	82.0	D	950	12.3	12 934
McKinley	74	191.9	D	761	13.5	29.9	269	585.5	8 710	94.8	14.7	3 670	59.6	16 246
Mora	NA	NA	NA	NA	NA	NA	12	7.3	1 528	16.6	-	57	.7	12 614
Otero	22	29.7	13.6	121	2.5	5.2	215	326.5	5 897	64.2	14.6	2 281	32.3	14 161
Quay	10	4.5	4.5	33	.4	1.2	71	99.6	9 875	107.5	D	594	8.5	14 391
Rio Arriba	19	40.2	D	84	1.6	4.4	104	189.0	5 029	54.7	2.8	1 149	18.2	15 806
Roosevelt	17	33.7	D	103	2.0	4.3	71	121.2	6 680	72.7	6.4	626	10.6	16 968
Sandoval	48	248.3	D	456	11.2	20.0	155	274.0	3 191	34.7	D	1 902	31.0	16 290
San Juan	158	381.9	292.7	1 278	35.7	75.7	494	990.8	9 579	104.2	20.1	5 896	96.7	16 407
San Miguel	16	19.4	11.9	62	1.3	2.5	114	168.4	5 844	63.6	D	1 087	15.1	13 931
Santa Fe	167	340.2	D	1 260	39.3	78.6	846	1 422.9	11 708	127.4	D	7 868	149.4	18 992
Sierra	7	7.5	7.5	21	.8	1.4	60	62.6	5 733	62.4	7.3	379	5.2	13 718
Socorro	6	12.3	D	102	1.4	2.9	57	70.6	4 339	47.2	3.2	385	6.3	16 356
Taos	16	11.8	D	59	1.0	2.0	259	206.8	7 794	84.8	D	1 554	23.7	15 237
Torrance	10	10.4	10.4	57	1.2	2.3	44	73.2	4 960	54.0	D	441	5.6	12 587
Union	2	D	D	(6)	D	D	27	15.3	3 778	41.1	5.3	103	1.3	13 010
Valencia	25	38.1	D	104	1.7	3.5	131	336.2	5 411	58.9	D	1 993	30.4	15 244

[1] Includes only establishments with payroll. [2] For pay period including March 12. [3] Based on resident population estimated as of July 1, 1997. [4] 1,000 to 2,499 employees. [5] 20 to 99 employees. [6] 0 to 19 employees.

Sources: Wholesale Trade—U.S. Census Bureau, 1997 Economic Census, ECON97 Report Series CD-ROM, CD-EC97-1, Disc 1E, issued February 2001 (related Internet site <http://www.census.gov/epcd/www/97EC42.HTM>). Retail Trade—U.S. Census Bureau, 1997 Economic Census, ECON97 Report Series CD-ROM, CD-EC97-1, Disc 1E, issued February 2001 (related Internet site <http://www.census.gov/epcd/www/97EC44.HTM>).

Table B–11. Counties — **Wholesale Trade and Retail Trade**–Con.

[Includes U.S., states, and 3,142 counties/county equivalents defined as of January 1, 1992. For changes to these areas since January 1, 1992, see appendix B. Geographic Information]

County	Wholesale trade[1] (NAICS 42), 1997						Retail trade[1] (NAICS 44-45), 1997							
	Sales			Paid employees[2]	Annual payroll (mil. dol.)	Operating expenses (mil. dol.)	Establishments	Sales				Paid employees[2]	Annual payroll	
	Establishments	Total (mil. dol.)	Merchant wholesalers (mil. dol.)					Total (mil. dol.)	Per capita[3]		Percent from general merchandise stores		Total (mil. dol.)	Per paid employee (dollars)
									Amount (dollars)	Percent of national average				
NEW YORK	37 499	319 697.6	217 216.8	414 249	17 185.8	37 754.1	75 241	139 303.9	7 678	83.5	11.4	805 208	14 329.8	17 796
Albany	581	4 335.8	2 686.3	8 866	322.3	608.6	1 483	3 567.2	12 112	131.8	13.8	21 444	348.1	16 233
Allegany	26	54.8	D	235	3.9	7.9	181	210.6	4 143	45.1	D	1 646	20.4	12 413
Bronx	755	5 373.6	D	10 728	389.9	791.4	3 110	3 434.9	2 884	31.4	D	21 641	352.5	16 291
Broome	261	D	D	(4)	D	D	829	1 763.3	8 902	96.9	16.5	11 881	164.2	13 825
Cattaraugus	86	409.1	358.0	979	28.0	56.5	380	570.7	6 704	72.9	18.0	4 190	56.1	13 390
Cayuga	78	201.3	D	746	20.7	39.1	265	516.8	6 271	68.2	D	3 250	50.5	15 526
Chautauqua	159	748.6	D	2 171	57.6	114.4	591	1 011.1	7 254	78.9	16.8	7 096	96.6	13 615
Chemung	107	447.2	D	1 667	49.2	90.7	412	875.9	9 464	103.0	D	5 963	82.9	13 911
Chenango	30	64.3	D	332	6.7	15.3	204	293.8	5 692	61.9	D	1 793	27.3	15 200
Clinton	115	407.0	D	1 515	29.6	86.4	445	756.6	9 450	102.8	18.2	4 967	70.8	14 263
Columbia	81	250.6	D	686	20.2	40.7	260	424.1	6 701	72.9	D	2 647	42.0	15 878
Cortland	35	195.7	D	401	11.8	27.7	200	423.9	8 806	95.8	11.1	2 658	38.5	14 490
Delaware	40	150.8	D	278	7.4	16.3	243	307.8	6 625	72.1	7.7	1 810	29.2	16 113
Dutchess	274	D	D	(4)	D	D	1 097	2 259.5	8 571	93.3	14.5	13 506	225.7	16 712
Erie	1 680	14 962.5	D	25 712	884.6	1 725.2	3 628	8 036.3	8 524	92.8	12.1	55 286	797.2	14 420
Essex	22	49.7	D	178	5.2	13.2	251	283.8	7 531	81.9	5.3	1 611	25.9	16 096
Franklin	37	126.7	D	310	6.8	15.2	215	283.9	5 784	62.9	7.9	1 834	26.0	14 184
Fulton	78	336.1	D	763	22.7	46.8	195	331.8	6 210	67.6	D	2 019	30.1	14 924
Genesee	99	385.6	303.7	1 140	31.5	63.1	231	366.4	6 007	65.4	15.1	2 649	35.6	13 441
Greene	39	222.6	D	516	14.8	32.7	230	278.3	5 841	63.6	D	1 673	27.1	16 219
Hamilton	2	D	D	(5)	D	D	35	23.7	4 577	49.8	15.8	140	2.6	18 771
Herkimer	33	D	D	(6)	D	D	254	313.4	4 821	52.5	7.0	2 183	29.7	13 587
Jefferson	93	280.7	256.9	958	26.0	52.9	514	1 016.3	9 042	98.4	14.0	5 679	90.8	15 985
Kings	2 953	11 371.6	10 591.2	25 838	742.8	1 583.3	6 994	7 983.6	3 523	38.3	8.2	45 941	821.8	17 888
Lewis	25	68.8	D	186	3.7	8.5	99	134.0	4 859	52.9	D	743	11.1	14 898
Livingston	68	212.6	D	633	18.7	38.7	245	411.3	6 260	68.1	D	2 676	38.4	14 334
Madison	63	159.8	D	473	13.4	26.9	260	463.3	6 538	71.1	D	2 935	43.2	14 732
Monroe	1 113	9 311.1	3 803.7	15 298	634.8	1 151.1	2 546	6 513.2	9 076	98.8	11.1	43 294	634.1	14 647
Montgomery	54	148.6	D	561	14.7	27.5	222	378.4	7 385	80.4	D	2 381	34.0	14 299
Nassau	4 124	23 793.6	16 613.4	36 401	1 597.9	3 381.8	6 751	16 483.6	12 686	138.0	10.5	81 902	1 615.9	19 730
New York	11 629	151 792.8	102 916.5	119 913	6 473.4	15 323.3	11 222	19 502.4	12 652	137.7	11.4	102 965	2 447.2	23 767
Niagara	237	656.6	D	2 573	64.4	136.1	886	1 607.6	7 324	79.7	13.9	11 500	159.9	13 908
Oneida	245	D	D	(4)	D	D	971	1 846.1	7 941	86.4	16.8	12 664	180.5	14 253
Onondaga	992	11 159.8	6 070.5	13 949	526.1	1 004.1	1 974	4 372.3	9 491	103.3	13.0	30 203	443.4	14 680
Ontario	152	471.6	D	1 092	36.4	71.6	520	1 118.6	11 225	122.1	20.1	7 791	106.3	13 644
Orange	448	D	D	(7)	D	D	1 438	3 047.7	9 332	101.5	D	17 131	290.4	16 955
Orleans	26	36.3	D	205	3.9	8.5	139	191.5	4 273	46.5	D	1 371	18.1	13 215
Oswego	73	140.0	102.9	443	11.0	22.0	396	747.1	5 992	65.2	D	4 609	69.5	15 074
Otsego	50	99.4	D	427	9.8	20.3	298	539.3	8 887	96.7	14.4	3 064	47.4	15 454
Putnam	126	278.2	230.1	729	27.0	65.2	320	497.6	5 397	58.7	5.4	2 707	49.9	18 426
Queens	2 787	12 942.0	9 764.4	27 165	952.6	2 026.1	5 933	8 756.0	4 416	48.1	8.3	48 425	890.1	18 382
Rensselaer	131	780.5	411.8	1 066	33.5	70.9	440	854.3	5 587	60.8	10.4	5 814	86.0	14 794
Richmond	358	627.1	D	1 763	55.5	137.0	1 197	2 235.3	5 562	60.5	D	13 522	219.4	16 228
Rockland	662	5 826.0	2 599.1	5 606	221.0	500.5	1 114	2 229.9	8 012	87.2	12.7	11 601	228.2	19 667
St. Lawrence	74	316.4	D	665	18.3	37.1	483	791.8	6 966	75.8	15.3	5 161	73.6	14 266
Saratoga	195	1 539.6	971.3	2 324	74.8	169.0	721	1 509.8	7 716	84.0	11.0	9 063	139.0	15 342
Schenectady	121	618.3	548.5	1 733	60.0	104.8	582	1 174.0	8 028	87.4	D	7 606	119.1	15 657
Schoharie	12	24.4	D	89	1.9	4.3	134	190.1	5 893	64.1	D	1 364	18.4	13 458
Schuyler	14	D	D	(8)	D	D	72	119.5	6 268	68.2	D	713	11.7	16 403
Seneca	28	53.9	38.3	311	6.0	11.7	174	250.3	7 781	84.7	D	1 560	22.6	14 464
Steuben	46	89.9	79.4	366	8.1	17.8	403	663.4	6 745	73.4	10.3	4 526	63.8	14 104
Suffolk	3 400	21 953.6	18 261.5	42 107	1 616.1	3 400.9	6 393	13 509.7	9 933	108.1	11.0	68 059	1 352.7	19 876
Sullivan	82	235.8	D	688	16.7	32.3	344	485.9	6 984	76.0	4.9	2 842	49.0	17 252
Tioga	31	D	D	(6)	D	D	145	218.1	4 165	45.3	2.3	1 205	20.0	16 617
Tompkins	71	239.6	D	432	13.8	35.4	373	616.3	6 335	68.9	10.5	4 367	65.7	15 043
Ulster	183	522.0	441.3	2 163	59.5	120.5	771	1 278.3	7 658	83.3	D	8 107	132.1	16 294
Warren	93	D	D	(9)	D	D	466	850.6	13 883	151.1	12.5	5 236	83.9	16 031
Washington	44	D	D	(6)	D	D	209	265.2	4 394	47.8	7.6	1 693	25.9	15 307
Wayne	78	327.1	D	745	26.0	54.0	296	576.4	6 091	66.3	8.3	3 569	54.2	15 188
Westchester	1 947	23 918.0	13 523.2	31 486	1 313.0	3 014.8	4 191	9 189.0	10 248	111.5	11.1	46 984	958.6	20 404
Wyoming	32	107.4	97.9	202	4.7	9.2	159	247.0	5 572	60.6	8.8	1 609	23.8	14 772
Yates	21	D	D	(10)	D	D	107	105.4	4 360	47.4	D	739	10.6	14 398

[1] Includes only establishments with payroll. [2] For pay period including March 12. [3] Based on resident population estimated as of July 1, 1997. [4] 2,500 to 4,999 employees. [5] 0 to 19 employees. [6] 250 to 499 employees. [7] 5,000 to 9,999 employees. [8] 20 to 99 employees. [9] 500 to 999 employees. [10] 100 to 249 employees.

Sources: Wholesale Trade—U.S. Census Bureau, 1997 Economic Census, ECON[97] Report Series CD-ROM, CD-EC97-1, Disc 1E, issued February 2001 (related Internet site <http://www.census.gov/epcd/www/97EC42.HTM>). Retail Trade—U.S. Census Bureau, 1997 Economic Census, ECON[97] Report Series CD-ROM, CD-EC97-1, Disc 1E, issued February 2001 (related Internet site <http://www.census.gov/epcd/www/97EC44.HTM>).

Wholesale Trade and Retail Trade–Con.

[Includes U.S., states, and 3,142 counties/county equivalents defined as of January 1, 1992. For changes to these areas since January 1, 1992, see appendix B. Geographic Information]

County	Wholesale trade[1] (NAICS 42), 1997						Retail trade[1] (NAICS 44-45), 1997							
	Sales							Sales					Annual payroll	
										Per capita[3]		Percent from general merchandise stores		
	Establishments	Total (mil. dol.)	Merchant wholesalers (mil. dol.)	Paid employees[2]	Annual payroll (mil. dol.)	Operating expenses (mil. dol.)	Establishments	Total (mil. dol.)	Amount (dollars)	Percent of national average		Paid employees[2]	Total (mil. dol.)	Per paid employee (dollars)
NORTH CAROLINA	12 284	98 080.1	48 386.9	157 774	5 574.1	11 039.1	35 563	72 356.8	9 740	106.0	11.9	416 287	6 697.4	16 088
Alamance	172	550.7	411.6	1 756	53.7	105.7	643	1 245.1	10 545	114.7	10.3	7 630	117.8	15 433
Alexander	24	23.1	D	91	1.9	4.2	100	142.5	4 649	50.6	10.9	900	11.6	12 874
Alleghany	3	D	D	(4)	D	D	53	59.0	6 056	65.9	3.2	317	4.7	14 694
Anson	17	86.2	D	208	6.5	17.0	96	105.4	4 338	47.2	13.1	771	9.8	12 672
Ashe	24	44.2	39.9	69	1.3	3.3	103	163.0	6 825	74.3	D	830	13.2	15 849
Avery	19	35.1	D	98	2.6	5.6	108	130.9	8 366	91.0	D	822	11.9	14 456
Beaufort	77	245.4	D	683	16.6	36.3	234	386.0	8 731	95.0	11.0	2 398	33.1	13 818
Bertie	21	158.6	116.6	268	4.8	12.0	69	70.8	3 456	37.6	2.4	458	6.5	14 262
Bladen	29	144.7	D	298	7.5	17.4	111	129.4	4 225	46.0	D	895	11.9	13 332
Brunswick	57	77.0	D	367	8.6	17.4	276	441.9	6 712	73.0	11.2	2 490	38.1	15 284
Buncombe	340	D	D	(5)	D	D	1 136	2 193.4	11 393	124.0	15.1	13 179	210.4	15 966
Burke	78	248.4	D	583	16.0	32.4	315	557.8	6 828	74.3	9.9	3 079	46.2	15 016
Cabarrus	157	953.9	D	1 480	45.4	86.2	468	1 131.8	9 736	105.9	14.8	6 467	103.6	16 018
Caldwell	77	791.3	D	842	31.6	53.9	330	515.1	6 823	74.2	12.0	3 329	45.8	13 750
Camden	5	D	D	(4)	D	D	24	14.9	2 218	24.1	D	128	1.6	12 586
Carteret	61	141.3	134.7	623	13.5	31.2	406	598.7	10 089	109.8	17.5	3 510	53.4	15 218
Caswell	5	4.5	4.5	75	1.1	2.2	49	44.0	1 990	21.7	4.7	267	3.9	14 442
Catawba	308	2 543.2	2 120.7	5 844	177.7	322.1	779	1 719.8	13 197	143.6	14.5	10 011	161.1	16 090
Chatham	58	262.9	D	523	12.8	28.0	177	226.1	5 036	54.8	D	1 451	21.3	14 701
Cherokee	24	51.1	51.1	186	3.1	6.4	139	217.0	9 744	106.0	D	1 266	18.3	14 421
Chowan	14	72.1	D	207	5.7	12.2	67	109.6	7 738	84.2	D	730	9.8	13 403
Clay	1	D	NA	(6)	D	D	38	52.2	6 269	68.2	2.3	324	3.8	11 818
Cleveland	126	1 355.9	1 243.7	1 434	39.1	73.6	431	707.4	7 690	83.7	12.9	4 707	68.9	14 639
Columbus	62	241.3	182.6	463	10.6	23.7	296	387.7	7 400	80.5	13.6	2 565	37.4	14 580
Craven	76	307.6	277.4	746	23.2	47.4	443	772.6	8 780	95.5	11.5	4 560	71.3	15 631
Cumberland	205	845.3	600.3	2 454	66.5	128.7	1 061	2 563.3	8 975	97.7	16.3	14 929	239.3	16 027
Currituck	20	D	D	(4)	D	D	81	98.6	5 729	62.3	D	541	10.2	18 860
Dare	41	103.9	95.3	374	7.1	15.3	389	442.4	15 854	172.5	13.5	2 494	43.4	17 388
Davidson	193	791.9	600.3	1 972	67.8	123.3	494	892.0	6 412	69.8	9.5	5 131	88.7	17 294
Davie	33	109.2	91.3	406	8.3	19.2	107	166.2	5 335	58.1	D	902	14.4	15 950
Duplin	44	D	D	(7)	D	D	226	280.4	6 547	71.2	D	1 879	25.2	13 398
Durham	249	2 306.3	1 527.9	4 343	158.4	293.7	1 010	2 032.6	10 169	110.7	D	13 322	213.2	16 006
Edgecombe	47	454.3	431.2	602	19.9	55.4	196	214.2	3 850	41.9	D	1 631	21.5	13 166
Forsyth	478	3 625.1	2 027.3	6 706	219.9	435.2	1 489	3 731.2	13 048	142.0	12.0	20 888	344.9	16 510
Franklin	34	166.1	118.3	481	13.8	30.3	127	176.2	4 043	44.0	D	1 057	15.0	14 198
Gaston	269	958.5	562.8	2 047	67.6	132.6	767	1 587.9	8 678	94.4	13.8	9 662	146.5	15 162
Gates	6	16.7	16.7	51	1.1	2.2	29	41.8	4 196	45.7	D	248	3.1	12 363
Graham	2	D	D	(6)	D	D	36	44.6	5 838	63.5	3.3	278	3.5	12 507
Granville	32	219.0	111.1	222	8.2	15.4	151	217.1	5 156	56.1	9.7	1 334	19.9	14 903
Greene	13	34.8	D	122	2.7	5.0	38	47.7	2 648	28.8	D	302	4.2	13 954
Guilford	1 347	13 448.1	5 986.2	21 568	882.9	1 906.7	2 059	5 179.3	13 546	147.4	10.7	29 817	530.8	17 804
Halifax	36	101.7	82.3	424	11.1	20.4	306	462.0	8 172	88.9	13.3	3 255	43.7	13 418
Harnett	62	257.7	246.4	756	18.5	40.0	284	443.2	5 494	59.8	13.2	2 713	37.0	13 650
Haywood	49	127.3	D	349	9.4	19.4	266	569.8	11 171	121.6	11.1	2 847	46.5	16 342
Henderson	91	228.0	D	613	15.8	36.9	386	901.3	11 280	122.7	7.9	4 192	75.2	17 933
Hertford	27	126.0	D	264	5.7	13.8	134	176.9	7 991	87.0	D	1 313	17.7	13 457
Hoke	7	30.3	D	102	2.8	7.1	74	67.5	2 302	25.0	7.2	486	5.9	12 160
Hyde	9	21.8	21.8	61	1.3	3.1	36	26.8	4 913	53.5	D	164	2.5	15 482
Iredell	196	1 373.6	D	2 443	76.5	161.8	510	1 065.8	9 758	106.2	12.2	5 993	93.2	15 546
Jackson	16	18.2	D	66	1.6	2.9	178	220.6	7 440	81.0	D	1 472	20.1	13 638
Johnston	117	836.8	400.2	1 269	26.3	59.7	486	857.9	8 404	91.4	8.9	4 580	71.5	15 620
Jones	7	12.9	12.9	60	1.2	3.8	30	33.7	3 572	38.9	D	142	2.2	15 345
Lee	75	517.1	497.0	1 159	32.2	62.8	292	591.9	12 287	133.7	9.5	3 109	51.0	16 415
Lenoir	80	486.7	283.4	1 382	28.2	54.9	352	565.6	9 594	104.4	10.9	3 597	51.2	14 240
Lincoln	73	629.9	D	1 035	29.4	57.2	212	406.2	7 103	77.3	13.2	2 346	36.6	15 598
McDowell	30	59.0	D	293	6.1	13.6	167	273.4	6 931	75.4	14.1	1 557	22.0	14 101
Macon	30	16.5	D	101	1.7	3.6	241	308.1	11 110	120.9	14.4	1 750	27.5	15 687
Madison	9	D	D	(4)	D	D	51	49.0	2 660	28.9	5.2	327	4.0	12 306
Martin	32	76.1	52.4	220	5.3	10.5	117	195.1	7 409	80.6	12.4	1 263	17.1	13 534
Mecklenburg	2 638	35 019.8	11 330.8	38 333	1 574.3	3 019.6	2 971	8 517.2	13 867	150.9	10.7	44 557	815.7	18 308
Mitchell	11	D	D	(4)	D	D	81	97.3	6 595	71.8	2.5	486	7.3	14 955
Montgomery	22	58.6	D	110	3.0	7.2	100	137.0	5 732	62.4	2.2	825	11.7	14 200
Moore	92	297.6	127.4	579	16.5	55.7	360	616.7	8 806	95.8	13.7	4 003	60.5	15 105
Nash	125	1 038.8	971.8	2 204	67.9	130.0	524	1 035.5	11 550	125.7	11.9	5 885	93.0	15 803
New Hanover	324	1 216.9	D	3 528	95.4	191.4	1 026	2 461.1	16 751	182.3	11.9	12 352	210.9	17 075
Northampton	22	214.8	D	243	6.1	12.8	66	85.4	4 004	43.6	D	532	8.9	16 688
Onslow	69	D	D	(8)	D	D	564	1 090.1	7 707	83.9	15.7	6 542	96.7	14 777

[1] Includes only establishments with payroll.   [2] For pay period including March 12.   [3] Based on resident population estimated as of July 1, 1997.   [4] 20 to 99 employees.   [5] 2,500 to 4,999 employees.   [6] 0 to 19 employees.   [7] 500 to 999 employees.   [8] 250 to 499 employees.

Sources: Wholesale Trade—U.S. Census Bureau, 1997 Economic Census, ECON97 Report Series CD-ROM, CD-EC97-1, Disc 1E, issued February 2001 (related Internet site <http://www.census.gov/epcd/www/97EC42.HTM>).   Retail Trade—U.S. Census Bureau, 1997 Economic Census, ECON97 Report Series CD-ROM, CD-EC97-1, Disc 1E, issued February 2001 (related Internet site <http://www.census.gov/epcd/www/97EC44.HTM>).

[Includes U.S., states, and 3,142 counties/county equivalents defined as of January 1, 1992. For changes to these areas since January 1, 1992, see appendix B. Geographic Information]

County	Wholesale trade[1] (NAICS 42), 1997						Retail trade[1] (NAICS 44-45), 1997							
	Sales			Paid employees[2]	Annual payroll (mil. dol.)	Operating expenses (mil. dol.)	Sales					Paid employees[2]	Annual payroll	
	Establishments	Total (mil. dol.)	Merchant wholesalers (mil. dol.)				Establishments	Total (mil. dol.)	Per capita[3]		Percent from general merchandise stores		Total (mil. dol.)	Per paid employee (dollars)
									Amount (dollars)	Percent of national average				
NORTH CAROLINA–Con.														
Orange	78	312.3	D	428	12.0	27.9	387	837.2	7 719	84.0	D	5 549	95.0	17 125
Pamlico	12	19.0	19.0	144	2.4	5.6	49	53.8	4 429	48.2	3.9	364	5.0	13 687
Pasquotank	46	150.7	126.2	606	12.8	25.2	201	405.0	11 498	125.1	14.5	2 548	37.6	14 773
Pender	33	99.1	D	326	8.0	16.9	131	153.9	4 060	44.2	2.6	906	13.5	14 860
Perquimans	9	32.6	D	87	1.7	3.7	38	31.7	2 862	31.1	5.3	274	3.0	10 956
Person	30	81.1	67.9	273	6.4	15.6	160	250.2	7 546	82.1	11.8	1 556	22.7	14 580
Pitt	181	1 246.8	1 024.5	2 153	66.4	133.7	643	1 384.8	11 130	121.1	10.5	7 956	124.8	15 681
Polk	14	19.7	4.8	39	.8	1.7	61	63.3	3 794	41.3	D	417	5.9	14 252
Randolph	174	582.0	476.1	1 637	44.5	95.7	457	845.0	7 077	77.0	13.1	4 821	77.1	15 987
Richmond	38	96.9	D	368	8.9	18.0	229	368.2	8 024	87.3	10.5	2 165	32.8	15 153
Robeson	82	349.6	285.0	843	22.0	48.2	450	1 011.7	8 844	96.2	9.6	4 844	79.8	16 473
Rockingham	59	177.6	D	394	10.0	22.9	421	619.8	6 907	75.2	12.3	3 974	55.4	13 945
Rowan	117	548.3	354.1	1 392	39.7	78.3	450	799.2	6 461	70.3	8.8	4 820	74.3	15 419
Rutherford	66	334.9	309.7	525	15.0	32.8	286	443.5	7 361	80.1	13.8	2 861	41.1	14 364
Sampson	52	231.1	193.9	587	17.6	33.7	246	373.8	7 231	78.7	9.5	2 125	31.1	14 630
Scotland	29	75.0	70.4	212	6.1	12.2	178	255.3	7 185	78.2	18.1	1 856	26.1	14 038
Stanly	61	228.3	151.7	474	15.8	27.0	265	472.3	8 509	92.6	11.5	2 722	44.5	16 342
Stokes	18	D	D	(4)	D	D	118	135.5	3 179	34.6	D	774	11.7	15 061
Surry	90	646.3	412.2	1 147	24.8	71.0	381	780.0	11 753	127.9	16.4	5 594	75.6	13 510
Swain	9	27.3	D	109	2.7	6.5	118	62.1	5 103	55.5	4.0	472	6.3	13 271
Transylvania	16	20.9	20.1	68	1.8	4.5	110	158.2	5 675	61.8	21.7	1 127	14.9	13 256
Tyrrell	4	16.0	D	14	.3	1.2	19	18.1	4 828	52.5	D	107	1.4	13 505
Union	241	813.4	D	2 214	75.6	157.6	383	753.0	7 106	77.3	10.6	4 245	69.2	16 305
Vance	33	274.0	239.0	489	13.2	25.9	251	454.0	10 911	118.7	12.6	2 763	42.1	15 222
Wake	1 249	13 259.1	5 708.5	18 833	826.0	1 488.3	2 719	7 391.9	13 396	145.8	11.7	38 755	664.3	17 141
Warren	9	5.6	D	22	.6	1.1	55	44.1	2 435	26.5	6.4	369	5.3	14 385
Washington	15	36.4	D	91	2.5	5.6	65	71.0	5 178	56.3	4.1	446	6.4	14 247
Watauga	47	166.1	124.1	422	12.0	22.4	342	519.8	12 766	138.9	12.7	3 207	44.3	13 801
Wayne	151	891.1	D	2 217	59.4	116.3	523	1 033.0	9 227	100.4	16.8	6 169	88.1	14 278
Wilkes	66	431.1	267.1	818	22.8	47.6	259	458.6	7 361	80.1	15.6	2 906	41.3	14 195
Wilson	121	471.1	289.7	1 264	33.6	73.4	393	735.4	10 845	118.0	11.2	4 416	66.2	14 995
Yadkin	32	D	D	(5)	D	D	144	167.9	4 868	53.0	2.0	851	13.6	16 009
Yancey	5	1.5	1.5	15	.2	.5	66	112.6	6 834	74.4	D	541	8.8	16 327
NORTH DAKOTA	1 604	8 618.4	7 464.2	16 992	454.4	934.3	3 569	6 702.1	10 457	113.8	13.9	40 685	616.1	15 144
Adams	10	51.0	51.0	67	1.4	3.6	21	34.3	12 397	134.9	D	169	2.7	16 000
Barnes	35	150.2	D	281	6.3	13.6	76	81.1	6 728	73.2	D	602	7.4	12 329
Benson	10	31.8	31.8	36	1.3	2.9	18	14.7	2 152	23.4	D	76	.7	9 066
Billings	1	D	D	(6)	D	D	6	1.4	1 244	13.5	–	10	.2	16 900
Bottineau	13	84.2	84.2	71	2.4	5.7	54	57.3	7 725	84.1	D	325	4.7	14 529
Bowman	5	56.1	56.1	97	2.2	5.3	27	43.5	13 123	142.8	D	196	2.8	14 286
Burke	7	33.4	D	41	.7	2.3	16	14.5	6 209	67.6	D	89	.9	10 596
Burleigh	143	619.8	D	1 574	43.5	86.2	366	814.6	12 279	133.6	D	5 114	82.5	16 129
Cass	366	2 755.5	D	5 945	182.6	341.4	572	1 669.2	14 516	158.0	D	9 697	161.3	16 635
Cavalier	20	93.6	D	113	3.2	7.6	33	48.7	9 549	103.9	D	241	3.4	14 145
Dickey	22	93.2	D	153	3.5	10.8	41	46.9	8 321	90.5	3.5	297	4.3	14 407
Divide	8	59.8	59.8	45	1.2	2.7	15	9.0	3 720	40.5	–	70	1.0	14 814
Dunn	9	9.5	D	35	.8	1.4	19	29.3	8 085	88.0	–	110	1.6	14 918
Eddy	7	23.1	23.1	42	.9	2.4	11	9.9	3 463	37.7	–	59	.7	11 508
Emmons	9	34.3	D	64	.8	2.3	34	35.1	8 005	87.1	D	174	2.4	13 644
Foster	17	68.0	D	109	2.7	6.1	30	38.7	10 287	111.9	D	222	3.2	14 401
Golden Valley	4	32.8	32.8	58	1.3	2.6	17	17.7	9 281	101.0	D	88	1.2	13 295
Grand Forks	130	552.4	D	1 511	41.3	86.5	351	934.7	13 453	146.4	D	5 596	81.4	14 541
Grant	10	19.4	D	51	.9	2.4	15	14.0	4 617	50.2	–	77	1.1	13 870
Griggs	15	36.7	36.7	83	2.1	4.4	22	22.6	7 914	86.1	D	133	1.9	14 233
Hettinger	9	27.3	D	54	1.2	2.5	13	16.9	5 701	62.0	–	79	1.1	14 215
Kidder	5	9.8	9.8	23	.4	.9	11	13.9	4 744	51.6	–	62	.6	10 161
LaMoure	17	88.6	D	155	2.9	6.7	22	18.7	3 831	41.7	–	105	1.6	15 486
Logan	8	96.9	D	111	1.2	2.7	12	11.8	4 913	53.5	–	52	.8	14 519
McHenry	19	64.7	D	92	2.3	5.1	23	14.3	2 314	25.2	–	109	1.1	10 523
McIntosh	8	22.2	22.2	43	.9	2.2	27	29.0	8 118	88.3	D	146	2.1	14 521
McKenzie	11	18.3	D	62	1.6	3.3	27	23.8	4 142	45.1	–	179	2.2	12 011
McLean	22	114.3	114.3	124	3.2	7.7	46	47.0	4 820	52.4	D	343	3.9	11 446
Mercer	12	22.8	D	58	1.1	2.3	46	56.2	5 920	64.4	D	440	5.2	11 882
Morton	49	193.4	D	409	9.2	19.2	101	196.0	8 032	87.4	D	944	18.4	19 517
Mountrail	13	D	D	(4)	D	D	46	47.0	7 057	76.8	D	299	3.7	12 365
Nelson	20	92.1	92.1	188	3.4	6.9	22	15.5	4 018	43.7	–	114	1.2	10 509
Oliver	2	D	D	(6)	D	D	3	4.0	1 797	19.6	–	23	.2	8 478
Pembina	28	113.7	113.7	211	4.4	11.8	77	103.0	11 943	130.0	D	620	8.4	13 474
Pierce	13	90.1	D	183	3.5	8.4	30	42.5	9 165	99.7	D	252	3.0	11 913

[1] Includes only establishments with payroll. [2] For pay period including March 12. [3] Based on resident population estimated as of July 1, 1997. [4] 20 to 99 employees. [5] 100 to 249 employees. [6] 0 to 19 employees.

Sources: Wholesale Trade—U.S. Census Bureau, 1997 Economic Census, ECON97 Report Series CD-ROM, CD-EC97-1, Disc 1E, issued February 2001 (related Internet site <http://www.census.gov/epcd/www/97EC42.HTM>). Retail Trade—U.S. Census Bureau, 1997 Economic Census, ECON97 Report Series CD-ROM, CD-EC97-1, Disc 1E, issued February 2001 (related Internet site <http://www.census.gov/epcd/www/97EC44.HTM>).

Table B–11. Counties — Wholesale Trade and Retail Trade–Con.

[Includes U.S., states, and 3,142 counties/county equivalents defined as of January 1, 1992. For changes to these areas since January 1, 1992, see appendix B. Geographic Information]

County	Wholesale trade[1] (NAICS 42), 1997 — Sales — Establishments	Total (mil. dol.)	Merchant wholesalers (mil. dol.)	Paid employees[2]	Annual payroll (mil. dol.)	Operating expenses (mil. dol.)	Retail trade[1] (NAICS 44-45), 1997 — Sales — Establishments	Total (mil. dol.)	Per capita[3] Amount (dollars)	Per capita[3] Percent of national average	Percent from general merchandise stores	Paid employees[2]	Annual payroll Total (mil. dol.)	Annual payroll Per paid employee (dollars)
NORTH DAKOTA—Con.														
Ramsey	35	170.5	D	374	9.3	20.0	92	141.2	11 449	124.6	19.8	1 014	14.0	13 812
Ransom	9	130.2	130.2	154	4.6	9.2	39	39.4	6 776	73.7	D	275	3.3	12 156
Renville	15	57.8	D	56	1.4	2.9	14	27.7	9 752	106.1	–	105	1.9	17 857
Richland	54	208.3	D	479	8.7	19.5	91	137.9	7 526	81.9	D	797	11.9	14 886
Rolette	10	79.4	79.4	71	1.5	3.9	49	79.7	5 649	61.5	D	486	6.5	13 302
Sargent	11	48.5	48.5	80	1.6	4.2	28	25.5	5 761	62.7	–	161	2.0	12 727
Sheridan	5	7.5	7.5	25	.4	1.0	8	6.1	3 442	37.5	–	33	.5	14 576
Sioux	2	D	D	(4)	D	D	11	14.0	3 412	37.1	–	60	.7	11 283
Slope	NA	NA	NA	NA	NA	NA	–	–	–	–	–	–	–	–
Stark	57	276.6	168.2	434	9.8	22.0	100	255.9	11 289	122.8	D	1 591	23.5	14 799
Steele	7	47.1	47.1	42	1.4	3.2	8	12.3	5 463	59.4	–	51	.7	14 275
Stutsman	37	235.0	D	300	8.0	17.9	137	207.8	9 863	107.3	D	1 419	19.4	13 677
Towner	11	D	D	(5)	D	D	19	10.4	3 389	36.9	–	87	.8	9 471
Traill	30	184.0	D	293	6.6	15.4	47	49.2	5 719	62.2	D	314	4.4	13 933
Walsh	42	151.7	D	383	8.2	18.8	91	116.1	8 474	92.2	6.2	706	10.2	14 402
Ward	95	701.6	D	1 203	32.9	70.0	339	753.7	12 764	138.9	D	4 819	74.3	15 411
Wells	18	91.2	91.2	148	3.7	9.0	42	41.4	7 930	86.3	D	238	3.4	14 298
Williams	89	331.0	272.9	693	17.4	36.5	138	207.5	10 231	111.3	D	1 417	19.7	13 915
OHIO	17 322	160 415.6	76 172.9	254 226	9 192.2	18 406.0	44 521	102 938.8	9 181	99.9	14.6	630 098	9 924.5	15 751
Adams	9	32.1	32.1	50	1.2	2.8	105	134.5	4 749	51.7	15.7	913	12.0	13 149
Allen	190	D	D	(6)	D	D	542	1 291.4	11 964	130.2	23.4	7 908	116.0	14 671
Ashland	47	121.3	68.2	282	7.3	16.5	183	311.1	6 076	66.1	D	2 242	33.0	14 736
Ashtabula	86	152.0	D	572	12.9	25.3	429	711.1	6 903	75.1	13.1	4 962	68.9	13 876
Athens	37	72.5	D	298	7.7	14.3	232	345.7	5 634	61.3	10.6	2 609	36.3	13 930
Auglaize	46	D	D	(7)	D	D	192	341.5	7 281	79.2	10.8	2 114	30.1	14 245
Belmont	58	D	D	(7)	D	D	383	737.6	10 272	111.8	23.5	5 359	68.3	12 737
Brown	15	73.7	D	239	5.6	11.1	114	141.7	3 531	38.4	7.2	922	12.4	13 491
Butler	454	D	2 445.6	(8)	D	D	922	2 188.6	6 679	72.7	D	13 529	208.5	15 409
Carroll	25	83.6	D	180	5.2	9.2	79	129.6	4 491	48.9	D	819	11.3	13 796
Champaign	31	160.8	D	427	11.4	25.4	124	204.1	5 358	58.3	D	1 254	18.3	14 569
Clark	124	1 035.2	985.2	1 704	49.6	108.0	528	1 102.9	7 561	82.3	D	7 439	107.9	14 498
Clermont	186	1 935.9	D	2 602	96.5	196.4	540	1 656.2	9 583	104.3	21.5	8 901	141.0	15 839
Clinton	39	192.2	183.5	360	11.1	25.7	154	404.7	11 013	119.8	D	2 101	33.4	15 886
Columbiana	111	278.0	234.2	866	24.5	51.5	468	823.4	7 395	80.5	10.6	4 934	68.7	13 934
Coshocton	31	70.5	D	203	4.7	9.9	146	209.8	5 803	63.1	14.8	1 538	20.1	13 058
Crawford	52	175.4	113.0	520	13.3	28.0	173	251.8	5 333	58.0	5.7	1 726	23.6	13 691
Cuyahoga	3 292	31 169.4	14 989.7	52 577	2 131.0	4 264.5	5 700	12 662.9	9 116	99.2	11.2	78 658	1 310.3	16 659
Darke	65	491.2	D	985	30.1	63.7	206	385.4	7 103	77.3	13.0	2 398	37.4	15 617
Defiance	46	306.7	198.4	568	16.4	40.0	195	424.8	10 617	115.5	D	2 580	39.7	15 386
Delaware	173	828.4	D	1 596	62.2	108.3	258	792.9	8 578	93.3	8.6	4 080	70.2	17 199
Erie	94	397.0	348.4	1 123	31.0	64.6	382	732.0	9 313	101.3	23.7	4 784	71.4	14 925
Fairfield	104	209.1	D	649	18.6	37.1	405	841.7	6 927	75.4	16.1	5 430	81.9	15 079
Fayette	44	749.2	D	329	10.8	28.8	246	329.8	11 559	125.8	D	2 154	30.6	14 228
Franklin	1 843	22 320.0	9 745.0	36 442	1 411.7	2 906.1	4 276	13 622.2	13 387	145.7	14.6	76 175	1 355.4	17 793
Fulton	68	365.4	310.3	603	16.9	34.8	179	294.2	7 104	77.3	D	1 715	26.3	15 329
Gallia	27	45.2	D	187	2.6	6.2	172	281.5	8 497	92.5	12.2	1 665	24.0	14 432
Geauga	194	691.5	D	1 425	53.9	95.9	317	565.0	6 456	70.3	D	3 311	55.6	16 785
Greene	110	1 540.4	D	1 316	47.0	99.5	564	1 321.9	9 055	98.5	22.2	8 922	125.0	14 005
Guernsey	42	97.3	84.1	390	10.8	20.7	167	294.0	7 236	78.7	14.3	1 722	24.9	14 470
Hamilton	2 047	32 788.6	8 728.5	37 207	1 413.1	2 673.4	3 774	9 310.4	10 932	119.0	13.0	59 154	938.2	15 861
Hancock	103	507.6	451.0	1 053	30.5	60.2	323	767.9	11 196	121.8	D	4 557	67.6	14 842
Hardin	19	D	D	(9)	D	D	111	160.7	5 072	55.2	11.5	1 089	14.5	13 310
Harrison	18	63.1	D	185	6.0	11.1	60	55.2	3 421	37.2	D	379	5.0	13 259
Henry	43	216.7	211.8	283	7.8	18.5	106	191.5	6 408	69.7	D	1 060	16.3	15 360
Highland	45	218.2	D	424	7.8	16.3	160	258.5	6 512	70.9	18.2	1 698	22.9	13 499
Hocking	14	D	D	(9)	D	D	92	145.1	5 059	55.0	D	880	14.3	16 218
Holmes	38	92.5	D	418	9.4	17.7	159	242.0	6 488	70.6	8.8	1 495	24.0	16 074
Huron	54	204.4	171.5	573	16.0	31.1	234	445.0	7 422	80.8	9.6	2 616	38.1	14 580
Jackson	27	72.5	D	304	7.2	14.9	162	234.8	7 241	78.8	18.5	1 542	21.5	13 929
Jefferson	69	D	D	(10)	D	D	335	531.4	6 991	76.1	17.4	3 969	52.9	13 324
Knox	58	168.3	128.8	362	9.0	17.5	183	313.4	5 951	64.8	15.6	2 076	28.8	13 894
Lake	425	1 590.9	1 073.5	4 392	148.8	270.6	975	2 831.2	12 517	136.2	14.6	15 509	260.7	16 808
Lawrence	37	D	D	(7)	D	D	206	360.7	5 604	61.0	31.4	2 503	31.7	12 672
Licking	144	623.1	551.6	1 600	45.1	89.4	502	1 105.2	8 484	92.3	16.5	6 392	104.2	16 305
Logan	45	844.2	D	1 671	47.2	97.4	187	309.0	6 739	73.3	12.6	1 919	26.9	13 998
Lorain	245	997.6	702.3	2 627	74.8	154.4	929	2 379.8	8 441	91.8	12.5	13 595	210.1	15 455
Lucas	751	6 302.2	3 960.6	10 580	377.3	777.8	1 860	4 842.2	10 746	116.9	19.8	29 585	473.7	16 011
Madison	38	355.4	315.3	904	26.2	42.1	122	276.8	6 791	73.9	6.8	1 423	22.5	15 796
Mahoning	407	2 132.4	1 503.7	5 559	177.3	353.8	1 187	2 547.9	9 901	107.7	14.0	16 420	235.5	14 345

[1] Includes only establishments with payroll. [2] For pay period including March 12. [3] Based on resident population estimated as of July 1, 1997. [4] 0 to 19 employees. [5] 20 to 99 employees. [6] 2,500 to 4,999 employees. [7] 250 to 499 employees. [8] 5,000 to 9,999 employees. [9] 100 to 249 employees. [10] 500 to 999 employees.

Sources: Wholesale Trade—U.S. Census Bureau, 1997 Economic Census, ECON97 Report Series CD-ROM, CD-EC97-1, Disc 1E, issued February 2001 (related Internet site <http://www.census.gov/epcd/www/97EC42.HTM>). Retail Trade—U.S. Census Bureau, 1997 Economic Census, ECON97 Report Series CD-ROM, CD-EC97-1, Disc 1E, issued February 2001 (related Internet site <http://www.census.gov/epcd/www/97EC44.HTM>).

[Includes U.S., states, and 3,142 counties/county equivalents defined as of January 1, 1992. For changes to these areas since January 1, 1992, see appendix B. Geographic Information]

County	Wholesale trade[1] (NAICS 42), 1997						Retail trade[1] (NAICS 44-45), 1997							
		Sales						Sales				Annual payroll		
									Per capita[3]		Percent from general merchandise stores			
	Establishments	Total (mil. dol.)	Merchant wholesalers (mil. dol.)	Paid employees[2]	Annual payroll (mil. dol.)	Operating expenses (mil. dol.)	Establishments	Total (mil. dol.)	Amount (dollars)	Percent of national average		Paid employees[2]	Total (mil. dol.)	Per paid employee (dollars)
OHIO—Con.														
Marion	61	219.3	192.9	559	17.5	37.9	237	548.9	8 150	88.7	27.0	3 549	53.8	15 155
Medina	295	1 155.8	775.5	2 724	93.5	185.4	524	1 346.0	9 508	103.5	D	7 764	123.4	15 889
Meigs	12	21.7	D	70	1.5	3.1	98	113.9	4 747	51.7	8.3	798	11.0	13 779
Mercer	57	384.7	384.3	952	24.1	43.9	192	330.0	8 057	87.7	D	2 151	32.3	15 033
Miami	110	3 072.8	D	1 832	56.2	217.7	371	845.4	8 651	94.1	D	5 018	72.4	14 428
Monroe	8	D	D	(4)	D	D	58	50.5	3 301	35.9	D	445	5.3	11 883
Montgomery	888	7 638.5	3 170.1	12 913	508.0	987.9	2 143	5 603.5	9 797	106.6	18.8	35 936	549.9	15 301
Morgan	10	D	D	(5)	D	D	35	45.4	3 123	34.0	7.7	345	3.8	11 084
Morrow	8	D	D	(5)	D	D	65	113.5	3 659	39.8	5.5	670	8.6	12 870
Muskingum	79	415.6	332.8	1 114	30.0	58.8	428	787.9	9 334	101.6	13.0	4 690	68.1	14 513
Noble	8	28.2	D	109	2.1	4.4	47	54.0	3 740	40.7	D	393	4.9	12 387
Ottawa	42	85.8	D	184	5.1	11.3	171	353.3	8 670	94.3	D	1 648	29.3	17 801
Paulding	19	69.8	69.8	155	4.0	8.7	62	102.4	5 063	55.1	D	638	8.9	13 940
Perry	15	D	D	(6)	D	D	83	105.2	3 075	33.5	D	648	8.9	13 762
Pickaway	38	141.8	D	326	9.1	20.3	147	284.0	5 392	58.7	15.3	1 630	23.8	14 586
Pike	16	26.1	D	103	2.8	5.1	98	153.5	5 578	60.7	20.8	1 105	12.9	11 690
Portage	183	1 180.5	837.2	2 648	96.5	217.2	465	1 117.9	7 435	80.9	8.7	5 828	92.8	15 931
Preble	32	249.6	D	586	20.2	42.5	112	218.3	5 082	55.3	D	1 334	18.7	14 026
Putnam	51	162.0	157.0	330	7.7	16.4	115	181.2	5 172	56.3	D	1 344	17.2	12 780
Richland	157	633.2	454.1	1 902	53.8	112.4	590	1 297.7	9 994	108.7	24.8	8 848	127.7	14 434
Ross	63	147.5	125.1	531	12.8	27.6	279	581.9	7 771	84.6	D	3 882	52.7	13 585
Sandusky	64	213.7	195.8	880	24.2	40.9	241	470.3	7 541	82.1	16.9	2 945	43.2	14 670
Scioto	68	219.3	D	550	12.3	24.3	321	543.0	6 687	72.8	18.2	3 629	53.4	14 704
Seneca	63	359.2	D	756	20.7	44.9	231	407.9	6 778	73.8	8.5	2 447	38.9	15 909
Shelby	51	276.3	D	666	18.6	32.6	167	309.4	6 545	71.2	D	2 126	28.4	13 348
Stark	517	4 151.7	D	8 242	275.8	528.8	1 618	3 671.2	9 821	106.9	D	23 170	357.2	15 415
Summit	1 070	8 443.7	4 514.9	13 375	501.6	986.6	2 172	2 515.7	10 280	111.9	12.3	32 463	546.7	16 840
Trumbull	231	1 212.0	922.5	2 867	80.4	154.4	913	1 943.2	8 551	93.0	14.8	12 617	192.9	15 290
Tuscarawas	109	300.2	261.9	1 096	26.4	52.2	439	758.8	8 615	93.7	16.4	5 240	75.6	14 420
Union	38	165.6	D	280	11.5	25.7	103	279.1	7 186	78.2	11.3	1 291	22.0	17 009
Van Wert	40	D	D	(7)	D	D	110	207.6	6 838	74.4	14.0	1 279	17.9	13 969
Vinton	4	D	D	(5)	D	D	28	27.1	2 260	24.6	D	201	2.3	11 667
Warren	181	6 034.5	D	2 324	91.2	197.6	455	1 111.7	7 941	86.4	15.8	6 709	106.3	15 851
Washington	74	166.6	152.5	826	19.3	40.2	279	501.0	7 879	85.7	13.2	3 063	45.8	14 957
Wayne	144	654.1	547.3	1 489	41.5	85.2	393	801.4	7 321	79.7	9.8	5 250	79.5	15 151
Williams	49	344.7	301.5	557	17.4	50.7	153	227.7	6 001	65.3	D	1 573	21.4	13 580
Wood	169	1 496.8	1 096.6	2 731	82.5	156.3	436	947.2	8 000	87.1	D	5 864	83.4	14 222
Wyandot	28	129.6	D	296	7.4	14.6	94	109.4	4 833	52.6	5.1	842	11.2	13 357
OKLAHOMA	5 191	32 132.3	20 292.5	59 641	1 756.1	3 612.6	14 352	27 065.6	8 166	88.9	16.7	161 613	2 406.9	14 893
Adair	4	5.6	5.6	31	.4	.9	54	67.0	3 328	36.2	D	482	5.1	10 548
Alfalfa	19	52.0	D	129	2.1	5.1	25	18.4	3 038	33.1	D	136	1.5	10 779
Atoka	19	48.8	D	124	2.2	4.0	49	71.9	5 377	58.5	D	530	6.2	11 781
Beaver	10	10.3	10.3	30	.7	1.9	25	14.4	2 434	26.5	D	116	1.1	9 655
Beckham	31	58.0	30.5	163	3.5	6.8	130	204.1	10 554	114.8	17.0	1 036	13.6	13 121
Blaine	17	D	D	(6)	D	D	69	42.6	4 008	43.6	9.1	357	3.7	10 322
Bryan	44	287.4	D	597	12.3	32.0	127	206.8	6 032	65.6	D	1 243	17.6	14 143
Caddo	26	111.4	111.4	284	5.8	13.9	142	128.7	4 170	45.4	D	998	11.7	11 732
Canadian	87	819.0	D	670	17.5	39.3	212	620.1	7 350	80.0	D	2 957	46.6	15 764
Carter	78	244.7	D	835	23.7	51.1	275	413.3	9 327	101.5	20.9	2 594	35.5	13 699
Cherokee	21	44.5	D	201	2.7	5.1	144	235.0	6 112	66.5	D	1 843	20.2	10 980
Choctaw	14	D	D	(5)	D	D	71	75.4	4 968	54.1	D	551	5.9	10 704
Cimarron	7	13.7	13.7	36	.6	1.5	19	24.4	7 940	86.4	—	116	1.5	13 069
Cleveland	159	528.6	D	1 462	37.2	74.4	616	1 318.6	6 659	72.5	D	7 679	115.2	15 006
Coal	2	D	D	(8)	D	D	18	17.1	2 801	30.5	D	150	1.4	9 007
Comanche	84	200.6	D	766	16.4	31.0	436	691.8	6 364	69.2	29.2	5 216	67.8	12 993
Cotton	7	10.7	10.7	40	.6	1.5	20	21.7	3 233	35.2	D	114	1.3	11 825
Craig	24	74.9	D	208	3.7	8.5	67	99.2	6 869	74.7	D	571	8.6	15 070
Creek	77	255.9	204.3	914	25.4	50.5	186	284.4	4 294	46.7	D	1 854	23.7	12 778
Custer	45	211.8	D	367	9.9	19.7	172	235.0	9 197	100.1	18.0	1 472	18.9	12 863
Delaware	15	27.1	D	82	1.1	2.4	132	148.9	4 408	48.0	D	1 067	13.8	12 887
Dewey	7	D	D	(5)	D	D	32	20.8	4 177	45.5	D	174	1.8	10 218
Ellis	7	14.9	14.9	34	.8	1.8	28	20.1	4 770	51.9	D	143	1.7	11 853
Garfield	122	570.1	D	1 967	48.9	99.4	302	501.7	8 833	96.1	20.2	3 423	47.8	13 960
Garvin	26	67.8	D	287	5.3	9.0	127	172.0	6 416	69.8	D	1 097	13.4	12 244
Grady	63	173.4	D	576	14.7	33.0	162	241.3	5 312	57.8	D	1 512	19.7	13 005
Grant	18	D	D	(5)	D	D	18	12.8	2 352	25.6	D	92	.9	10 304
Greer	5	13.4	13.4	49	.4	.9	26	15.4	2 396	26.1	D	129	1.5	11 519
Harmon	3	D	D	(5)	D	D	25	20.2	5 746	62.5	D	154	1.9	12 110
Harper	9	13.4	13.4	42	.9	2.1	17	10.8	2 992	32.6	D	90	.9	10 500

[1] Includes only establishments with payroll. [2] For pay period including March 12. [3] Based on resident population estimated as of July 1, 1997. [4] 1,000 to 2,499 employees. [5] 20 to 99 employees. [6] 100 to 249 employees. [7] 250 to 499 employees. [8] 0 to 19 employees.

Sources: Wholesale Trade—U.S. Census Bureau, 1997 Economic Census, ECON97 Report Series CD-ROM, CD-EC97-1, Disc 1E, issued February 2001 (related Internet site <http://www.census.gov/epcd/www/97EC42.HTM>). Retail Trade—U.S. Census Bureau, 1997 Economic Census, ECON97 Report Series CD-ROM, CD-EC97-1, Disc 1E, issued February 2001 (related Internet site <http://www.census.gov/epcd/www/97EC44.HTM>).

[Includes U.S., states, and 3,142 counties/county equivalents defined as of January 1, 1992. For changes to these areas since January 1, 1992, see appendix B. Geographic Information]

County	Wholesale trade[1] (NAICS 42), 1997 — Sales — Estab-lishments	Total (mil. dol.)	Merchant whole-salers (mil. dol.)	Paid em-ployees[2]	Annual payroll (mil. dol.)	Operating expenses (mil. dol.)	Retail trade[1] (NAICS 44-45), 1997 — Sales — Estab-lishments	Total (mil. dol.)	Per capita[3] Amount (dollars)	Percent of national average	Percent from general mer-chandise stores	Paid em-ployees[2]	Annual payroll Total (mil. dol.)	Per paid em-ployee (dollars)
OKLAHOMA—Con.														
Haskell	7	41.5	D	90	1.2	2.0	42	57.9	5 095	55.4	21.3	395	5.2	13 081
Hughes	14	35.7	D	222	2.8	5.3	64	58.6	4 168	45.4	D	431	4.8	11 037
Jackson	34	66.7	D	161	3.9	10.2	125	241.2	8 502	92.5	D	1 420	19.8	13 954
Jefferson	5	D	D	(4)	D	D	30	25.5	3 831	41.7	D	164	1.8	11 146
Johnston	7	14.4	14.4	54	1.1	3.3	37	22.1	2 139	23.3	D	167	1.9	11 515
Kay	61	210.2	D	444	12.0	32.2	263	397.6	8 505	92.5	22.1	2 718	36.5	13 437
Kingfisher	33	159.3	D	234	7.3	13.7	60	90.0	6 683	72.7	D	576	7.3	12 689
Kiowa	18	44.7	D	123	2.4	5.6	56	37.5	3 457	37.6	D	353	3.3	9 482
Latimer	6	D	D	(4)	D	D	31	26.1	2 544	27.7	D	237	2.9	12 405
Le Flore	27	42.4	D	120	2.3	5.1	162	247.2	5 325	57.9	25.1	1 578	20.0	12 698
Lincoln	21	D	D	(5)	D	D	154	136.3	4 388	47.7	D	1 011	12.6	12 436
Logan	18	D	D	(4)	D	D	96	133.3	4 455	48.5	D	816	10.5	12 904
Love	6	28.7	D	79	1.9	3.3	35	51.7	6 030	65.6	D	290	3.5	12 210
McClain	19	D	D	(5)	D	D	96	192.0	7 442	81.0	D	940	14.6	15 561
McCurtain	30	69.8	D	239	4.8	11.1	138	167.2	4 835	52.6	D	1 119	15.1	13 489
McIntosh	10	6.7	6.7	17	.3	.7	94	140.1	7 457	81.1	D	650	9.2	14 192
Major	17	69.4	D	151	2.3	5.1	48	59.6	7 671	83.5	D	323	4.1	12 607
Marshall	12	48.7	D	124	3.5	5.6	56	56.6	4 694	51.1	D	416	5.3	12 659
Mayes	36	71.5	56.1	216	5.2	10.8	135	191.8	5 175	56.3	D	1 313	16.5	12 554
Murray	10	25.5	D	73	1.1	2.6	49	93.1	7 522	81.8	D	492	7.3	14 793
Muskogee	91	313.2	268.0	1 185	30.4	63.5	349	561.7	8 048	87.6	17.2	3 613	52.8	14 625
Noble	9	17.2	D	50	.9	2.3	57	72.3	6 406	69.7	D	478	6.4	13 387
Nowata	9	28.4	D	107	1.6	2.8	33	27.3	2 765	30.1	13.3	180	2.1	11 656
Okfuskee	2	D	D	(6)	D	D	33	37.5	3 301	35.9	D	235	2.7	11 340
Oklahoma	1 517	15 144.3	6 586.9	21 108	638.9	1 358.3	3 098	7 479.8	11 857	129.0	D	41 034	681.3	16 603
Okmulgee	30	42.7	D	150	3.2	5.9	142	207.3	5 383	58.6	D	1 324	17.8	13 464
Osage	23	29.5	D	147	3.2	7.2	112	95.8	2 257	24.6	D	748	8.8	11 770
Ottawa	30	D	D	(7)	D	D	138	180.8	5 891	64.1	D	1 136	15.2	13 342
Pawnee	9	D	D	(4)	D	D	55	69.9	4 313	46.9	D	484	6.2	12 874
Payne	62	211.2	173.3	664	13.1	40.3	299	466.1	7 174	78.1	D	3 336	43.4	13 003
Pittsburg	51	114.2	D	333	8.2	16.8	185	326.3	7 592	82.6	D	2 059	26.7	12 983
Pontotoc	53	257.6	D	492	10.4	22.0	180	266.9	7 708	83.9	D	1 859	23.5	12 630
Pottawatomie	44	D	D	(7)	D	D	276	397.8	6 496	70.7	D	2 847	37.0	12 996
Pushmataha	10	11.1	11.1	130	1.4	3.7	56	42.0	3 640	39.6	D	294	3.3	11 150
Roger Mills	3	4.6	4.6	6	1	.4	22	14.8	4 132	45.0	D	110	1.4	12 682
Rogers	65	357.8	D	518	16.7	40.7	192	353.2	5 383	58.6	D	1 994	28.6	14 346
Seminole	28	53.8	D	169	4.6	13.6	104	116.1	4 648	50.6	D	813	10.6	13 012
Sequoyah	15	47.6	D	110	1.4	2.9	159	218.9	5 920	64.4	D	1 387	17.0	12 287
Stephens	53	90.6	D	441	10.0	19.6	221	314.1	7 250	78.9	15.0	2 074	27.7	13 378
Texas	40	D	D	(7)	D	D	99	130.2	7 219	78.6	15.7	936	11.6	12 364
Tillman	13	33.4	33.4	155	3.0	6.8	43	31.4	3 268	35.6	9.2	346	2.6	7 442
Tulsa	1 438	9 427.0	7 662.0	18 675	658.2	1 258.8	2 440	6 410.4	11 952	130.1	D	35 520	590.8	16 632
Wagoner	34	98.3	D	209	4.3	8.1	109	149.2	2 756	30.0	D	971	12.0	12 344
Washington	34	52.0	D	284	7.1	18.1	216	425.8	8 970	97.6	26.8	2 613	38.7	14 817
Washita	16	33.2	D	118	2.0	4.8	51	46.2	3 975	43.3	D	310	3.8	12 177
Woods	21	48.0	D	170	3.2	6.8	58	65.4	7 869	85.6	D	533	6.8	12 715
Woodward	50	68.9	58.4	342	6.7	14.5	128	179.2	9 624	104.7	D	1 074	15.3	14 265
OREGON	5 943	53 679.1	38 230.9	74 790	2 578.7	5 192.5	14 467	33 396.8	10 297	112.0	16.8	178 349	3 308.8	18 552
Baker	19	13.2	13.2	90	2.0	3.6	93	121.3	7 409	80.6	D	805	11.7	14 507
Benton	63	112.6	D	681	15.9	34.8	294	473.9	6 112	66.5	11.8	3 175	53.2	16 766
Clackamas	685	6 383.3	4 210.2	8 723	314.7	638.5	1 092	3 448.3	10 438	113.6	D	16 098	312.3	19 401
Clatsop	39	88.4	76.4	383	7.0	14.4	274	332.4	9 382	102.1	D	2 173	36.8	16 928
Columbia	26	61.5	61.5	161	4.4	10.3	137	199.8	4 590	49.9	D	1 360	22.1	16 243
Coos	60	233.2	D	496	14.6	36.2	289	505.2	8 081	87.9	18.1	3 040	52.1	17 147
Crook	16	21.5	D	72	1.5	3.6	57	89.3	5 274	57.4	—	494	8.4	16 964
Curry	20	14.2	D	62	1.1	2.9	121	148.4	7 045	76.7	D	1 041	16.8	16 097
Deschutes	191	571.0	512.3	1 303	39.7	76.3	687	1 297.1	12 759	138.8	21.2	7 130	128.7	18 045
Douglas	84	404.1	389.7	1 152	27.0	52.0	457	669.0	6 584	71.6	18.5	4 416	71.2	16 122
Gilliam	3	D	D	(6)	D	D	13	8.7	4 431	48.2	—	72	1.1	15 139
Grant	4	5.9	5.9	28	.8	1.4	45	42.4	5 297	57.6	D	316	4.4	14 044
Harney	6	9.7	9.7	31	.7	1.7	41	51.5	7 341	79.9	—	299	5.4	18 114
Hood River	27	92.2	D	181	9.9	29.7	129	170.3	8 845	96.2	D	1 286	19.8	15 362
Jackson	284	1 022.7	953.5	2 678	69.8	147.3	835	2 075.3	12 167	132.4	17.1	9 564	172.2	18 007
Jefferson	18	78.0	78.0	221	5.3	13.7	57	109.9	6 643	72.3	1.9	647	11.4	17 569
Josephine	59	175.6	D	441	9.2	20.4	326	590.3	8 065	87.8	17.6	3 322	57.9	17 427
Klamath	66	293.1	267.5	954	22.1	54.2	290	544.8	8 678	94.4	19.5	3 116	55.5	17 805
Lake	7	D	D	(4)	D	D	48	39.4	5 429	59.1	D	266	4.3	16 241
Lane	535	2 498.6	1 883.1	6 144	179.6	360.3	1 462	3 322.6	10 680	116.2	16.0	18 145	328.3	18 096
Lincoln	39	72.5	D	296	7.0	15.4	372	415.2	9 139	99.4	15.8	2 794	43.8	15 660

[1] Includes only establishments with payroll. [2] For pay period including March 12. [3] Based on resident population estimated as of July 1, 1997. [4] 20 to 99 employees. [5] 100 to 249 employees. [6] 0 to 19 employees. [7] 250 to 499 employees.

Sources: Wholesale Trade—U.S. Census Bureau, 1997 Economic Census, ECON97 Report Series CD-ROM, CD-EC97-1, Disc 1E, issued February 2001 (related Internet site <http://www.census.gov/epcd/www/97EC42.HTM>). Retail Trade—U.S. Census Bureau, 1997 Economic Census, ECON97 Report Series CD-ROM, CD-EC97-1, Disc 1E, issued February 2001 (related Internet site <http://www.census.gov/epcd/www/97EC44.HTM>).

[Includes U.S., states, and 3,142 counties/county equivalents defined as of January 1, 1992. For changes to these areas since January 1, 1992, see appendix B. Geographic Information]

County	Wholesale trade[1] (NAICS 42), 1997						Retail trade[1] (NAICS 44-45), 1997							
	Sales						Sales					Annual payroll		
									Per capita[3]		Percent from general merchandise stores			
	Establishments	Total (mil. dol.)	Merchant wholesalers (mil. dol.)	Paid employees[2]	Annual payroll (mil. dol.)	Operating expenses (mil. dol.)	Establishments	Total (mil. dol.)	Amount (dollars)	Percent of national average		Paid employees[2]	Total (mil. dol.)	Per paid employee (dollars)
OREGON—Con.														
Linn	131	766.0	721.6	1 534	44.5	100.7	391	800.9	7 731	84.1	D	4 662	78.7	16 871
Malheur	50	171.0	D	951	18.0	36.9	163	302.9	10 678	116.2	21.7	1 903	30.7	16 138
Marion	326	1 184.0	899.7	3 247	91.9	189.7	1 081	2 672.5	10 089	109.8	D	14 637	266.3	18 190
Morrow	12	103.1	D	73	2.1	5.9	30	38.8	4 060	44.2	–	217	3.2	14 581
Multnomah	1 850	25 188.5	19 894.5	28 384	1 017.7	2 042.3	3 025	7 334.5	11 680	127.1	14.7	39 841	791.4	19 864
Polk	41	87.3	62.2	425	8.7	15.3	143	232.4	3 881	42.2	D	1 592	24.3	15 239
Sherman	2	D	D	(4)	D	D	13	12.9	7 145	77.7	D	91	1.3	14 209
Tillamook	22	18.8	D	114	2.0	5.2	123	144.1	5 924	64.5	D	1 044	15.0	14 414
Umatilla	75	331.6	244.5	954	22.8	48.1	290	567.2	8 808	95.8	D	3 188	53.7	16 854
Union	34	96.2	68.7	301	7.4	15.1	129	227.7	9 097	99.0	16.2	1 355	23.5	17 328
Wallowa	4	5.1	5.1	11	.2	.6	52	61.8	8 264	89.9	D	336	6.2	18 518
Wasco	36	115.7	92.5	550	11.3	26.0	134	256.9	11 120	121.0	18.9	1 468	26.1	17 800
Washington	1 035	13 153.8	6 578.7	13 622	603.2	1 154.9	1 499	5 453.5	13 937	151.7	18.6	25 124	512.3	20 389
Wheeler	1	D	NA	(4)	D	D	6	8.5	5 310	57.8	–	19	.5	28 526
Yamhill	73	259.1	234.4	485	14.8	30.7	269	627.2	7 855	85.5	D	3 313	58.4	17 614
PENNSYLVANIA	17 138	159 354.2	80 673.7	237 567	8 588.2	17 081.0	50 208	109 948.5	9 150	99.6	11.5	650 144	10 561.9	16 245
Adams	88	909.7	604.5	1 211	33.2	91.3	330	472.7	5 520	60.1	10.8	3 072	45.6	14 858
Allegheny	2 490	28 256.0	11 089.4	33 034	1 269.4	2 480.9	5 353	12 929.7	10 099	109.9	11.8	78 841	1 218.0	15 449
Armstrong	48	65.1	56.6	285	5.9	13.8	310	487.1	6 639	72.2	10.2	3 255	43.3	13 301
Beaver	148	570.5	D	1 515	46.5	102.6	668	1 180.5	6 362	69.2	18.0	8 513	113.7	13 361
Bedford	44	207.7	D	451	11.7	30.6	216	438.9	8 911	97.0	D	2 298	35.6	15 481
Berks	439	3 121.7	2 553.4	7 051	253.0	456.7	1 468	3 330.7	9 412	102.4	12.3	19 302	326.2	16 901
Blair	160	1 641.3	1 469.7	2 836	82.3	222.0	639	1 331.2	10 165	110.6	18.9	8 310	117.7	14 166
Bradford	55	175.1	166.5	512	10.7	23.8	296	521.2	8 361	91.0	13.6	3 315	46.4	14 007
Bucks	1 433	8 415.9	4 419.0	16 257	684.2	1 334.3	2 549	7 217.4	12 391	134.8	9.9	36 195	701.3	19 375
Butler	272	4 540.8	D	4 732	140.5	259.1	709	1 480.2	8 761	95.3	14.5	9 317	137.0	14 701
Cambria	144	580.7	D	2 115	57.5	114.4	693	1 244.8	7 910	86.1	14.5	8 555	111.5	13 028
Cameron	2	D	D	(4)	D	D	27	31.0	5 456	59.4	D	287	3.8	13 146
Carbon	34	91.4	D	240	7.0	15.8	219	316.7	5 387	58.6	D	2 102	30.9	14 720
Centre	100	D	D	(5)	D	D	617	1 153.9	8 710	94.8	15.1	7 861	108.7	13 822
Chester	1 013	15 420.9	3 761.8	10 955	459.6	953.9	1 517	5 879.6	14 144	153.9	3.8	22 625	490.8	21 691
Clarion	47	568.5	D	470	13.8	27.3	226	330.5	7 906	86.0	10.0	2 100	32.3	15 404
Clearfield	80	280.5	D	713	17.7	39.4	397	768.4	9 500	103.4	17.7	4 935	68.8	13 948
Clinton	28	D	D	(6)	D	D	176	296.2	8 006	87.1	9.0	1 877	24.6	13 092
Columbia	50	D	D	(6)	D	D	317	533.9	8 323	90.6	D	3 462	45.1	13 024
Crawford	81	175.5	108.4	652	14.6	32.5	360	628.8	7 039	76.6	12.2	3 970	58.6	14 770
Cumberland	260	2 439.6	1 204.9	3 589	122.7	254.0	955	2 759.5	13 289	144.6	11.3	15 697	268.2	17 088
Dauphin	341	8 700.1	7 370.4	9 844	320.2	651.8	1 125	2 532.8	10 310	112.2	12.9	15 204	246.1	16 185
Delaware	807	9 506.8	6 231.7	9 947	438.9	903.8	2 080	5 003.6	9 202	100.1	10.0	28 710	516.4	17 985
Elk	40	89.7	D	335	8.7	20.9	163	219.9	6 316	68.7	D	1 668	20.4	12 214
Erie	334	1 277.8	999.7	4 069	131.9	258.0	1 225	2 562.1	9 166	99.7	13.6	16 323	239.0	14 645
Fayette	123	406.8	D	1 566	29.3	70.0	599	1 110.2	7 652	83.3	21.1	7 056	96.3	13 647
Forest	4	D	D	(7)	D	D	35	28.6	5 759	62.7	1.3	162	2.3	14 037
Franklin	102	610.3	D	1 862	49.0	89.4	566	1 035.7	8 122	88.4	12.8	6 249	94.4	15 105
Fulton	7	6.6	6.6	32	.5	1.2	55	70.7	4 870	53.0	2.7	402	5.3	13 286
Greene	34	78.9	42.9	364	6.9	15.7	136	259.2	6 145	66.9	3.8	1 240	18.4	14 874
Huntingdon	24	D	D	(6)	D	D	169	252.8	5 650	61.5	D	1 495	22.5	15 048
Indiana	80	418.8	D	870	19.6	43.7	391	723.6	8 116	88.3	17.3	4 986	64.3	12 904
Jefferson	62	121.4	D	515	12.0	23.8	209	299.2	6 437	70.0	D	1 828	24.6	13 432
Juniata	24	D	D	(8)	D	D	71	123.6	5 642	61.4	1.8	649	9.0	13 884
Lackawanna	286	1 126.0	881.9	3 636	95.7	187.1	1 039	1 966.3	9 350	101.7	14.2	13 167	189.8	14 411
Lancaster	663	10 936.6	3 414.0	11 020	341.6	669.5	2 012	4 671.7	10 298	112.1	9.5	29 237	480.8	16 445
Lawrence	90	430.2	365.5	1 070	29.0	71.4	370	627.1	6 583	71.6	13.6	4 286	61.4	14 335
Lebanon	118	D	D	(9)	D	D	490	1 209.1	10 327	112.4	11.2	6 480	106.8	16 476
Lehigh	560	4 668.7	2 551.4	7 469	255.6	514.6	1 376	3 509.2	11 768	128.1	12.2	18 976	333.2	17 561
Luzerne	388	2 149.6	1 672.5	5 697	152.3	302.9	1 406	2 856.4	8 998	97.9	15.2	18 945	269.2	14 209
Lycoming	137	481.9	D	2 195	51.4	113.4	605	1 149.3	9 732	105.9	15.4	7 600	108.4	14 265
McKean	44	229.2	D	426	12.7	32.1	200	280.5	6 009	65.4	D	1 969	26.8	13 607
Mercer	124	656.3	D	1 692	41.9	91.1	618	1 285.0	10 525	114.5	D	7 852	112.8	14 369
Mifflin	53	111.7	D	552	12.4	24.3	195	368.4	7 849	85.4	D	2 427	34.8	14 336
Monroe	93	345.3	267.2	1 012	28.5	59.7	658	1 160.6	9 460	102.9	D	7 621	111.7	14 642
Montgomery	2 004	22 878.2	8 916.6	29 378	1 395.6	2 744.3	3 689	9 607.4	13 462	146.5	11.7	54 728	1 025.8	18 744
Montour	15	65.8	D	209	5.2	10.8	76	131.3	7 378	80.3	D	797	10.0	12 514
Northampton	312	2 066.2	D	4 465	167.7	312.5	832	1 831.8	7 114	77.4	D	10 051	168.1	16 724
Northumberland	72	582.6	D	1 016	26.5	57.0	367	658.7	6 927	75.4	D	3 689	58.9	15 953
Perry	17	D	D	(8)	D	D	141	205.3	4 652	50.6	.8	1 280	17.5	13 655
Philadelphia	1 403	12 004.0	7 486.7	22 298	848.4	1 629.6	4 782	8 118.2	5 592	60.8	9.3	51 398	887.1	17 260
Pike	23	D	D	(8)	D	D	107	182.6	4 659	50.7	D	1 203	16.9	14 034
Potter	13	17.4	17.4	58	1.0	3.4	77	88.3	5 158	56.1	3.5	611	8.3	13 563

[1] Includes only establishments with payroll.   [2] For pay period including March 12.   [3] Based on resident population estimated as of July 1, 1997.   [4] 0 to 19 employees.   [5] 500 to 999 employees.   [6] 250 to 499 employees.   [7] 20 to 99 employees.   [8] 100 to 249 employees.   [9] 1,000 to 2,499 employees.

Sources: Wholesale Trade—U.S. Census Bureau, 1997 Economic Census, ECON97 Report Series CD-ROM, CD-EC97-1, Disc 1E, issued February 2001 (related Internet site <http://www.census.gov/epcd/www/97EC42.HTM>). Retail Trade—U.S. Census Bureau, 1997 Economic Census, ECON97 Report Series CD-ROM, CD-EC97-1, Disc 1E, issued February 2001 (related Internet site <http://www.census.gov/epcd/www/97EC44.HTM>).

[Includes U.S., states, and 3,142 counties/county equivalents defined as of January 1, 1992. For changes to these areas since January 1, 1992, see appendix B. Geographic Information]

County	Wholesale trade[1] (NAICS 42), 1997						Retail trade[1] (NAICS 44-45), 1997							
	Sales							Sales					Annual payroll	
									Per capita[3]		Percent from general merchandise stores			
	Establishments	Total (mil. dol.)	Merchant wholesalers (mil. dol.)	Paid employees[2]	Annual payroll (mil. dol.)	Operating expenses (mil. dol.)	Establishments	Total (mil. dol.)	Amount (dollars)	Percent of national average		Paid employees[2]	Total (mil. dol.)	Per paid employee (dollars)
PENNSYLVANIA—Con.														
Schuylkill	134	632.2	467.4	1 798	42.0	90.8	659	1 062.5	7 028	76.5	9.2	7 129	106.3	14 913
Snyder	29	160.4	D	444	11.8	21.3	190	365.6	9 565	104.1	27.4	2 558	33.5	13 077
Somerset	87	274.5	D	840	21.8	42.1	367	543.1	6 744	73.4	7.1	3 361	46.2	13 756
Sullivan	5	D	D	(4)	D	D	29	24.7	4 048	44.0	4.8	186	2.3	12 108
Susquehanna	34	D	D	(5)	D	D	161	217.8	5 179	56.4	D	1 221	17.3	14 169
Tioga	28	93.3	D	293	6.8	18.9	170	287.9	6 942	75.5	13.4	1 924	26.3	13 677
Union	33	89.9	82.9	313	10.0	18.0	140	225.3	5 516	60.0	D	1 492	19.6	13 117
Venango	53	128.3	94.2	530	12.1	24.8	247	417.4	7 180	78.1	13.8	2 792	37.8	13 549
Warren	36	67.1	60.5	285	8.4	16.6	185	718.6	16 287	177.2	D	2 742	52.9	19 278
Washington	305	1 481.0	064.0	3 003	132.5	263.8	778	1 531.6	7 443	81.0	9.7	9 187	152.6	16 612
Wayne	35	67.5	D	262	5.9	13.0	246	397.0	8 785	95.6	9.9	2 444	38.4	15 730
Westmoreland	473	3 967.1	3 273.9	6 482	221.0	429.4	1 557	3 230.2	8 644	94.1	13.8	19 333	280.5	14 508
Wyoming	23	D	D	(6)	D	D	126	214.3	7 323	79.7	D	1 241	17.4	14 010
York	450	3 428.1	1 768.5	9 498	275.9	539.9	1 447	3 250.6	8 765	95.4	14.7	20 356	315.4	15 492
RHODE ISLAND	1 590	7 602.7	5 058.1	18 762	635.2	1 276.1	4 169	7 505.8	7 605	82.8	10.2	45 747	752.2	16 442
Bristol	55	108.4	D	324	9.4	17.0	168	211.6	4 316	47.0	D	1 311	20.6	15 682
Kent	312	1 778.6	996.3	3 491	128.9	271.0	804	1 985.9	12 309	133.9	18.8	11 839	187.9	15 874
Newport	102	242.3	D	561	18.6	39.2	485	626.2	7 543	82.1	D	3 844	66.1	17 198
Providence	1 003	5 094.4	3 554.5	13 417	450.9	892.3	2 163	3 663.7	6 378	69.4	7.7	22 850	374.6	16 393
Washington	118	378.9	249.3	969	27.2	56.7	549	1 018.3	8 545	93.0	7.9	5 903	103.0	17 444
SOUTH CAROLINA	5 035	34 179.8	19 994.2	58 910	1 866.8	3 763.1	18 481	33 634.3	8 874	96.6	13.0	209 256	3 107.2	14 849
Abbeville	10	12.1	D	36	.9	1.5	65	58.6	2 398	26.1	3.0	469	5.2	11 179
Aiken	97	D	D	(7)	D	D	533	936.6	7 028	76.5	D	6 455	87.1	13 500
Allendale	11	17.9	17.9	44	.9	2.9	46	53.6	4 653	50.6	D	311	3.8	12 122
Anderson	186	873.0	527.9	1 704	46.4	105.2	743	1 349.1	8 506	92.6	14.1	8 860	124.7	14 076
Bamberg	10	D	D	(4)	D	D	78	68.4	4 125	44.9	4.7	524	6.4	12 300
Barnwell	8	D	D	(4)	D	D	107	116.2	5 337	58.1	23.6	1 020	11.6	11 380
Beaufort	118	169.4	129.6	548	15.2	30.5	751	1 340.9	12 508	136.1	11.0	7 444	129.2	17 353
Berkeley	75	577.6	D	926	25.7	54.1	292	537.5	4 010	43.6	7.9	3 347	47.1	14 070
Calhoun	10	24.1	24.1	114	2.9	5.9	37	31.1	2 255	24.5	D	267	2.9	10 944
Charleston	472	3 727.1	D	5 290	175.5	341.0	1 850	3 483.7	11 113	120.9	14.5	22 298	347.7	15 594
Cherokee	42	D	D	(7)	D	D	232	366.7	7 549	82.1	9.7	2 137	30.3	14 167
Chester	27	331.5	D	905	24.2	45.2	129	186.1	5 508	59.9	9.4	1 142	14.4	12 605
Chesterfield	33	91.8	D	330	8.6	16.4	182	240.9	5 924	64.5	D	1 632	21.4	13 125
Clarendon	22	56.2	D	187	4.2	7.2	130	165.6	5 394	58.7	D	1 120	14.9	13 283
Colleton	44	212.5	D	487	11.9	28.2	188	259.4	6 995	76.1	13.8	1 890	23.5	12 410
Darlington	81	728.0	D	858	19.1	37.6	310	423.4	6 441	70.1	8.7	2 715	36.3	13 354
Dillon	29	177.3	D	292	9.4	21.3	151	196.0	6 632	72.2	12.1	1 612	19.6	12 182
Dorchester	59	97.3	D	422	7.9	16.8	282	516.9	5 976	65.0	16.5	3 450	46.3	13 419
Edgefield	10	D	14.4	(4)	D	D	79	78.8	3 994	43.5	D	455	6.5	14 376
Fairfield	8	29.5	29.5	94	2.6	4.6	70	82.8	3 706	40.3	D	764	7.1	9 346
Florence	206	1 017.6	811.6	2 847	81.0	150.5	759	1 467.3	11 799	128.4	14.5	8 935	138.4	15 485
Georgetown	56	119.6	89.6	363	9.6	22.5	346	481.9	9 197	100.1	15.4	3 178	47.6	14 969
Greenville	930	10 685.9	D	12 025	451.4	869.3	1 852	4 496.4	12 873	140.1	11.9	24 775	380.2	15 347
Greenwood	52	148.1	D	760	13.6	30.0	339	606.1	9 588	104.3	15.3	4 601	60.7	13 190
Hampton	11	D	D	(6)	D	D	131	114.1	5 978	65.0	4.0	952	10.8	11 377
Horry	230	481.5	437.0	1 824	49.5	94.5	1 522	2 505.2	14 790	160.9	13.6	14 457	230.7	15 960
Jasper	12	65.5	D	177	4.7	9.1	79	76.9	4 528	49.3	D	531	6.8	12 714
Kershaw	24	36.9	D	113	3.1	7.3	221	296.5	6 198	67.4	14.8	2 150	27.2	12 663
Lancaster	48	136.3	116.5	353	9.2	16.8	264	401.3	6 947	75.6	14.2	2 608	36.3	13 934
Laurens	40	86.5	72.6	351	9.5	19.5	200	296.2	4 749	51.7	13.5	1 743	24.4	13 987
Lee	15	38.5	D	124	2.7	5.4	74	72.4	3 583	39.0	2.4	576	6.6	11 523
Lexington	301	2 282.6	1 696.5	4 749	152.0	302.5	803	1 803.7	8 997	97.9	D	10 332	156.6	15 154
McCormick	5	D	D	(4)	D	D	41	23.5	2 465	26.8	D	204	2.0	9 755
Marion	31	91.6	D	235	5.3	11.3	178	215.7	6 191	67.4	11.3	1 609	20.9	13 001
Marlboro	16	54.3	D	133	3.8	7.4	115	122.3	4 119	44.8	3.9	796	10.6	13 339
Newberry	22	D	D	(7)	D	D	152	198.1	5 786	63.0	15.1	1 388	19.4	13 973
Oconee	57	D	D	(5)	D	D	276	403.9	6 372	69.3	15.8	2 738	35.1	12 824
Orangeburg	103	380.9	268.4	933	25.4	51.3	461	704.3	8 040	87.5	12.6	4 793	65.2	13 612
Pickens	86	D	162.4	(7)	D	D	372	655.2	6 248	68.0	11.2	4 237	58.1	13 708
Richland	540	2 989.4	2 025.7	7 346	251.7	546.9	1 558	3 475.6	11 523	125.4	17.8	22 311	350.7	15 718
Saluda	11	38.7	D	102	1.7	5.0	67	76.4	4 512	49.1	3.3	415	5.4	12 930
Spartanburg	484	3 965.3	3 296.3	6 234	214.8	446.6	1 117	2 311.6	9 432	102.6	12.7	13 785	213.5	15 490
Sumter	84	208.6	D	671	18.1	37.0	425	782.0	7 019	76.4	11.6	4 841	72.8	15 029
Union	13	14.2	D	38	1.1	2.8	113	155.2	5 077	55.2	15.8	1 228	15.0	12 178
Williamsburg	39	98.0	74.7	367	7.0	15.8	146	155.6	4 190	45.6	5.7	1 006	13.3	13 267
York	267	3 001.9	1 202.1	3 598	124.2	246.1	615	1 244.4	8 275	90.0	9.3	7 155	112.7	15 755

[1] Includes only establishments with payroll. [2] For pay period including March 12. [3] Based on resident population estimated as of July 1, 1997. [4] 20 to 99 employees. [5] 250 to 499 employees. [6] 100 to 249 employees. [7] 500 to 999 employees.

Sources: Wholesale Trade—U.S. Census Bureau, 1997 Economic Census, ECON97 Report Series CD-ROM, CD-EC97-1, Disc 1E, issued February 2001 (related Internet site <http://www.census.gov/epcd/www/97EC42.HTM>). Retail Trade—U.S. Census Bureau, 1997 Economic Census, ECON97 Report Series CD-ROM, CD-EC97-1, Disc 1E, issued February 2001 (related Internet site <http://www.census.gov/epcd/www/97EC44.HTM>).

[Includes U.S., states, and 3,142 counties/county equivalents defined as of January 1, 1992. For changes to these areas since January 1, 1992, see appendix B. Geographic Information]

County	Wholesale trade[1] (NAICS 42), 1997						Retail trade[1] (NAICS 44-45), 1997							
		Sales						Sales				Annual payroll		
									Per capita[3]		Percent from general mer-			
	Estab-lishments	Total (mil. dol.)	Merchant whole-salers (mil. dol.)	Paid em-ployees[2]	Annual payroll (mil. dol.)	Operating expenses (mil. dol.)	Estab-lishments	Total (mil. dol.)	Amount (dollars)	Percent of national average	chandise stores	Paid em-ployees[2]	Total (mil. dol.)	Per paid em-ployee (dollars)
SOUTH DAKOTA	1 402	7 874.2	6 181.7	15 509	389.8	794.3	4 311	11 707.1	16 018	174.3	8.2	45 867	689.6	15 034
Aurora	4	13.4	13.4	38	1.1	2.0	18	D	D	D	D	(4)	D	D
Beadle	27	183.9	107.3	279	5.8	12.7	120	152.9	8 530	92.8	D	1 082	15.5	14 319
Bennett	4	44.9	D	59	.5	1.7	21	D	D	D	D	(5)	D	D
Bon Homme	17	51.4	D	129	1.8	4.1	43	D	D	D	D	(5)	D	D
Brookings	29	265.8	D	505	8.3	20.0	139	169.2	6 476	70.5	18.2	1 513	17.5	11 589
Brown	83	637.3	539.9	897	21.5	44.7	237	497.4	13 943	151.7	D	3 128	47.9	15 308
Brule	9	36.5	18.3	94	1.7	3.5	51	D	D	D	D	(6)	D	D
Buffalo	NA	NA	NA	NA	NA	NA	2	D	D	D	D	(7)	D	D
Butte	19	83.1	D	139	2.4	5.2	59	66.7	7 471	81.3	D	402	6.5	16 269
Campbell	6	D	D	(4)	D	D	10	D	D	D	D	(4)	D	D
Charles Mix	16	63.6	63.6	120	2.3	5.7	73	63.9	6 775	73.7	D	497	5.7	11 370
Clark	7	80.6	D	76	1.4	4.5	16	D	D	D	D	(5)	D	D
Clay	9	18.3	18.3	44	1.2	3.0	52	75.4	5 703	62.1	D	493	6.8	13 840
Codington	74	320.7	251.4	560	15.8	32.9	191	347.2	13 640	148.4	D	2 382	32.8	13 770
Corson	5	D	D	(4)	D	D	14	D	D	D	D	(4)	D	D
Custer	2	D	D	(7)	D	D	32	D	D	D	D	(5)	D	D
Davison	36	216.7	D	504	12.6	23.5	153	230.7	12 964	141.1	16.1	1 747	21.8	12 469
Day	7	53.2	53.2	85	1.8	4.0	42	D	D	D	D	(6)	D	D
Deuel	6	7.6	7.6	19	.2	.9	26	D	D	D	D	(5)	D	D
Dewey	6	12.6	12.6	33	.7	1.9	27	D	D	D	D	(5)	D	D
Douglas	9	17.4	17.4	60	1.2	1.9	18	D	D	D	D	(5)	D	D
Edmunds	11	101.5	D	147	3.3	7.0	21	D	D	D	D	(5)	D	D
Fall River	6	5.5	D	31	.5	.9	45	D	D	D	D	(6)	D	D
Faulk	6	10.6	10.6	25	.4	.8	11	D	D	D	D	(4)	D	D
Grant	18	106.2	106.2	413	7.4	15.6	55	68.1	8 431	91.7	D	451	5.3	11 670
Gregory	14	39.2	D	88	1.3	3.0	44	D	D	D	D	(5)	D	D
Haakon	10	62.4	D	124	1.6	3.5	20	D	D	D	D	(5)	D	D
Hamlin	10	38.3	38.3	60	1.4	3.4	29	D	D	D	D	(5)	D	D
Hand	12	58.5	58.5	156	3.0	5.8	22	D	D	D	D	(5)	D	D
Hanson	9	34.3	34.3	30	.5	1.5	10	D	D	D	D	(4)	D	D
Harding	2	D	D	(7)	D	D	6	4.9	3 285	35.7	–	28	.5	18 929
Hughes	22	85.8	D	159	4.2	9.9	121	194.7	12 673	137.9	16.1	1 221	17.4	14 265
Hutchinson	23	147.3	147.3	245	5.3	10.9	53	D	D	D	D	(6)	D	D
Hyde	3	D	D	(4)	D	D	11	D	D	D	D	(4)	D	D
Jackson	2	D	D	(7)	D	D	17	D	D	D	D	(5)	D	D
Jerauld	6	D	D	(4)	D	D	16	D	D	D	D	(5)	D	D
Jones	3	7.5	7.5	9	.3	.6	13	D	D	D	D	(5)	D	D
Kingsbury	10	69.3	69.3	94	2.4	5.7	40	D	D	D	D	(5)	D	D
Lake	12	81.0	D	125	3.5	7.6	67	115.0	10 747	116.9	D	581	10.4	17 849
Lawrence	21	12.1	D	59	.9	2.1	147	226.1	10 187	110.8	14.9	1 334	18.6	13 909
Lincoln	39	200.4	146.7	305	8.0	16.7	72	150.5	7 726	84.1	D	625	11.1	17 760
Lyman	5	D	D	(4)	D	D	18	D	D	D	D	(5)	D	D
McCook	13	33.5	33.5	53	1.0	2.5	31	D	D	D	D	(5)	D	D
McPherson	2	D	D	(7)	D	D	16	D	D	D	D	(5)	D	D
Marshall	10	43.0	D	82	1.2	2.8	23	D	D	D	D	(5)	D	D
Meade	22	94.8	D	134	2.4	6.2	81	115.9	5 308	57.8	D	630	9.8	15 494
Mellette	NA	NA	NA	NA	NA	NA	9	5.1	2 532	27.6	–	58	.5	8 069
Miner	8	19.9	19.9	39	.7	2.2	15	D	D	D	D	(4)	D	D
Minnehaha	356	2 145.1	1 674.4	5 412	163.3	307.9	770	1 999.4	14 417	156.9	D	12 238	191.7	15 662
Moody	6	13.1	13.1	32	.8	1.7	23	D	D	D	D	(5)	D	D
Pennington	173	675.7	645.8	2 027	57.8	110.4	581	1 132.0	13 013	141.6	18.0	6 870	112.2	16 336
Perkins	8	49.4	D	62	.8	2.6	26	15.8	4 452	48.4	D	159	1.8	11 132
Potter	11	57.3	D	98	2.3	5.3	28	D	D	D	D	(5)	D	D
Roberts	19	202.6	D	144	2.6	6.5	49	D	D	D	D	(6)	D	D
Sanborn	9	15.6	D	39	.7	1.5	8	D	D	D	D	(4)	D	D
Shannon	NA	NA	NA	NA	NA	NA	15	D	D	D	D	(5)	D	D
Spink	16	133.0	D	146	3.8	8.1	39	51.7	6 777	73.7	D	261	4.0	15 421
Stanley	5	D	D	(4)	D	D	19	D	D	D	D	(5)	D	D
Sully	4	D	D	(4)	D	D	14	D	D	D	D	(4)	D	D
Todd	1	D	D	(7)	D	D	17	D	D	D	D	(5)	D	D
Tripp	17	82.4	D	175	3.1	6.3	52	52.1	7 620	82.9	D	364	4.5	12 486
Turner	14	99.5	99.5	76	1.8	5.1	42	D	D	D	D	(5)	D	D
Union	26	225.0	220.9	210	6.1	17.1	45	D	D	D	D	(8)	D	D
Walworth	11	34.2	D	69	1.5	3.8	61	54.3	9 594	104.4	11.2	398	4.9	12 279
Yankton	50	290.1	168.4	428	8.6	17.7	162	229.6	11 016	119.9	19.2	1 988	25.2	12 687
Ziebach	2	D	D	(7)	D	D	3	D	D	D	D	(7)	D	D

[1] Includes only establishments with payroll. [2] For pay period including March 12. [3] Based on resident population estimated as of July 1, 1997. [4] 20 to 99 employees. [5] 100 to 249 employees. [6] 250 to 499 employees. [7] 0 to 19 employees. [8] 500 to 999 employees.

Sources: Wholesale Trade—U.S. Census Bureau, 1997 Economic Census, ECON97 Report Series CD-ROM, CD-EC97-1, Disc 1E, issued February 2001 (related Internet site <http://www.census.gov/epcd/www/97EC42.HTM>). Retail Trade—U.S. Census Bureau, 1997 Economic Census, ECON97 Report Series CD-ROM, CD-EC97-1, Disc 1E, issued February 2001 (related Internet site <http://www.census.gov/epcd/www/97EC44.HTM>).

Table B–11. Counties — **Wholesale Trade and Retail Trade**–Con.

[Includes U.S., states, and 3,142 counties/county equivalents defined as of January 1, 1992. For changes to these areas since January 1, 1992, see appendix B. Geographic Information]

County	Wholesale trade[1] (NAICS 42), 1997						Retail trade[1] (NAICS 44-45), 1997							
		Sales							Sales				Annual payroll	
										Per capita[3]		Percent from general mer-		
	Estab-lishments	Total (mil. dol.)	Merchant whole-salers (mil. dol.)	Paid em-ployees[2]	Annual payroll (mil. dol.)	Operating expenses (mil. dol.)	Estab-lishments	Total (mil. dol.)	Amount (dollars)	Percent of national average	chandise stores	Paid em-ployees[2]	Total (mil. dol.)	Per paid em-ployee (dollars)
TENNESSEE	8 234	82 626.4	47 023.5	120 228	3 975.4	8 044.6	24 808	50 813.2	9 448	102.8	15.3	304 452	4 810.3	15 800
Anderson	51	105.9	D	342	9.9	20.2	331	700.9	9 821	106.9	D	3 923	60.8	15 507
Bedford	43	72.3	D	284	7.7	14.8	145	207.4	6 068	66.0	D	1 298	18.1	13 924
Benton	14	35.2	35.2	99	2.5	5.6	78	92.5	5 698	62.0	D	746	9.4	12 625
Bledsoe	2	D		(4)	D	D	31	23.6	2 234	24.3	D	162	1.8	10 932
Blount	97	655.2	551.1	1 347	38.2	83.7	385	1 189.1	11 925	129.8	D	5 590	99.3	17 760
Bradley	93	1 651.3	D	2 328	51.0	110.0	392	745.7	9 066	98.7	16.7	4 103	66.1	16 120
Campbell	26	117.6	D	477	15.0	31.0	159	228.9	6 047	65.8	13.4	1 551	21.3	13 732
Cannon	8	D	D	(5)	D	D	30	33.3	2 771	30.2	D	213	2.9	13 770
Carroll	26	48.2	D	210	4.6	9.2	121	127.4	4 417	48.1	D	950	11.6	12 246
Carter	28	D	D	(6)	D	D	156	265.1	4 992	54.3	18.1	1 602	23.2	14 458
Cheatham	20	29.3	D	119	3.1	6.6	75	130.0	3 781	41.1	D	729	10.5	14 385
Chester	10	34.4	34.4	62	1.3	2.0	65	99.8	6 903	75.1	3.8	481	7.8	16 239
Claiborne	17	D	D	(6)	D	D	97	111.5	3 855	41.9	D	736	10.2	13 844
Clay	2	D	D	(5)	D	D	23	19.0	2 598	28.3	D	127	1.7	13 079
Cocke	19	68.9	D	167	5.3	9.1	126	191.3	6 044	65.8	D	1 361	16.3	11 940
Coffee	50	127.4	120.1	482	10.7	22.2	283	490.6	10 818	117.7	18.4	3 127	43.8	14 020
Crockett	15	D	D	(6)	D	D	58	58.4	4 218	45.9	20.8	339	4.4	12 956
Cumberland	35	130.5	D	276	7.7	17.1	222	368.6	8 540	92.9	20.8	2 171	32.4	14 941
Davidson	1 445	17 005.2	9 431.5	26 012	962.7	1 914.1	3 017	7 737.6	14 440	157.1	13.2	44 452	782.7	17 608
Decatur	7	3.3	3.3	36	.5	.8	50	65.1	6 036	65.7	8.4	371	5.2	14 008
DeKalb	8	96.3	D	271	6.6	13.6	65	67.3	4 269	46.5	5.0	419	5.7	13 704
Dickson	27	274.7	224.9	471	11.5	26.4	185	412.9	10 083	109.7	D	2 158	35.2	16 293
Dyer	47	221.2	D	572	15.7	28.8	220	362.4	9 954	108.3	19.5	2 237	30.4	13 587
Fayette	21	102.8	63.3	163	5.1	11.2	69	77.4	2 635	28.7	D	459	7.0	15 166
Fentress	8	4.3	D	20	.4	1.0	64	77.2	4 856	52.8	18.5	570	7.1	12 470
Franklin	23	46.9	D	145	3.4	7.3	164	231.0	6 186	67.3	20.4	1 555	21.9	14 076
Gibson	51	333.2	314.4	520	14.4	23.8	248	358.4	7 461	81.2	14.8	2 221	33.0	14 872
Giles	34	93.1	82.8	302	9.5	20.9	137	201.7	7 069	76.9	D	1 218	16.9	13 911
Grainger	9	18.6	D	46	1.0	1.9	59	57.2	2 937	32.0	D	385	4.5	11 813
Greene	44	283.5	D	679	12.4	26.8	253	440.2	7 427	80.8	14.0	2 871	39.9	13 898
Grundy	4	2.1	D	20	.4	.7	57	51.5	3 684	40.1	6.0	414	5.4	13 152
Hamblen	70	460.2	375.0	1 199	35.1	84.5	323	645.9	12 034	130.9	14.3	3 595	54.7	15 214
Hamilton	094	D	2 722.3	(7)	D	D	1 531	3 269.6	11 084	120.6	D	20 122	325.8	16 193
Hancock	4	3.2	3.2	25	.2	.5	20	13.4	1 970	21.4	D	100	1.4	13 990
Hardeman	22	D	D	(6)	D	D	103	120.7	5 006	54.5	15.9	860	11.2	13 026
Hardin	18	35.9	D	92	3.0	6.2	131	183.3	7 387	80.4	16.1	1 079	15.4	14 317
Hawkins	11	D	D	(5)	D	D	138	194.9	3 997	43.5	8.5	1 230	16.0	13 020
Haywood	12	114.6	D	135	3.4	7.9	100	146.4	7 421	80.8	10.6	830	12.0	14 489
Henderson	20	44.1	D	150	3.1	5.9	124	177.7	7 405	80.6	D	1 090	16.0	14 703
Henry	41	198.0	168.3	625	16.1	30.1	167	244.6	8 204	89.3	D	1 608	21.9	13 640
Hickman	8	9.2	9.2	35	.5	1.3	66	48.8	2 441	26.6	D	360	4.5	12 381
Houston	4	D	D	(4)	D	D	29	23.7	3 052	33.2	D	164	2.0	12 165
Humphreys	11	52.0	52.0	142	3.0	6.0	77	110.8	6 581	71.6	D	657	9.5	14 458
Jackson	1	D	D	(4)	D	D	27	20.5	2 144	23.3	D	145	1.4	9 421
Jefferson	42	73.8	55.7	246	6.2	12.0	120	249.5	5 910	64.3	D	1 415	21.1	14 912
Johnson	3	D	D	(5)	D	D	57	67.5	4 067	44.3	4.4	417	6.3	15 074
Knox	950	7 507.7	5 111.0	12 580	449.4	830.2	1 946	5 029.7	13 470	146.6	13.1	28 344	478.9	16 897
Lake	9	D	D	(5)	D	D	26	20.1	2 427	26.4	D	172	2.0	11 756
Lauderdale	26	364.9	D	548	18.4	38.6	100	123.9	5 151	56.1	D	867	11.4	13 187
Lawrence	42	174.6	D	296	8.7	21.8	200	315.2	8 066	87.8	D	1 822	27.1	14 889
Lewis	8	11.6	11.6	67	1.3	2.9	59	66.3	6 143	66.8	D	367	5.4	14 583
Lincoln	29	102.6	D	211	3.9	8.3	138	205.6	7 015	76.3	D	1 360	18.0	13 260
Loudon	41	93.1	45.0	232	6.0	12.8	137	271.7	7 109	77.4	D	1 407	21.0	14 923
McMinn	32	D	D	(8)	D	D	209	361.7	7 868	85.6	17.4	2 119	30.3	14 311
McNairy	21	D	D	(6)	D	D	100	117.2	4 952	53.9	D	728	9.9	13 657
Macon	12	19.2	19.2	84	1.2	2.8	81	89.3	5 010	54.5	D	582	7.8	13 364
Madison	161	756.4	566.5	2 186	60.5	117.6	582	1 196.5	14 113	153.6	19.9	8 169	114.9	14 064
Marion	15	D	D	(6)	D	D	111	186.5	7 041	76.6	D	1 232	15.2	12 351
Marshall	17	21.4	21.4	104	2.4	4.7	122	180.9	7 050	76.7	D	1 153	16.7	14 462
Maury	54	251.3	D	631	17.9	38.4	306	572.9	8 396	91.4	13.6	3 451	55.7	16 136
Meigs	3	D	D	(4)	D	D	21	24.2	2 493	27.1	D	163	2.3	13 877
Monroe	22	48.3	D	171	2.8	5.6	165	234.5	6 908	75.2	14.4	1 505	19.9	13 215
Montgomery	93	281.8	D	716	19.0	42.2	523	1 175.8	9 455	102.9	D	6 895	108.1	15 682
Moore	1	D	D	(4)	D	D	12	5.6	1 077	11.7	–	51	.5	9 647
Morgan	9	D	D	(4)	D	D	41	31.2	1 690	18.4	D	209	2.8	13 244
Obion	43	243.7	223.2	768	19.1	37.2	183	296.5	9 250	100.7	D	1 834	26.8	14 628

[1] Includes only establishments with payroll. [2] For pay period including March 12. [3] Based on resident population estimated as of July 1, 1997. [4] 0 to 19 employees. [5] 20 to 99 employees. [6] 100 to 249 employees. [7] 5,000 to 9,999 employees. [8] 250 to 499 employees.

Sources: Wholesale Trade—U.S. Census Bureau, 1997 Economic Census, ECON[97] Report Series CD-ROM, CD-EC97-1, Disc 1E, issued February 2001 (related Internet site <http://www.census.gov/epcd/www/97EC42.HTM>). Retail Trade—U.S. Census Bureau, 1997 Economic Census, ECON[97] Report Series CD-ROM, CD-EC97-1, Disc 1E, issued February 2001 (related Internet site <http://www.census.gov/epcd/www/97EC44.HTM>).

[Includes U.S., states, and 3,142 counties/county equivalents defined as of January 1, 1992. For changes to these areas since January 1, 1992, see appendix B. Geographic Information]

County	Wholesale trade[1] (NAICS 42), 1997						Retail trade[1] (NAICS 44-45), 1997							
	Sales			Paid employees[2]	Annual payroll (mil. dol.)	Operating expenses (mil. dol.)	Estab-lishments	Sales				Paid employees[2]	Annual payroll	
	Estab-lishments	Total (mil. dol.)	Merchant whole-salers (mil. dol.)					Total (mil. dol.)	Per capita[3]		Percent from general mer-chandise stores		Total (mil. dol.)	Per paid em-ployee (dollars)
									Amount (dollars)	Percent of national average				
TENNESSEE—Con.														
Overton	10	D	D	(4)	D	D	64	77.1	4 024	43.8	7.8	439	5.9	13 483
Perry	2	D	D	(4)	D	D	27	21.5	2 890	31.4	D	145	1.7	11 862
Pickett	2	D	D	(5)	D	D	20	17.0	3 682	40.1	D	109	1.3	12 165
Polk	9	D	D	(6)	D	D	53	47.0	3 198	34.8	D	366	4.4	11 921
Putnam	88	425.9	225.3	1 188	31.6	63.4	379	648.6	11 114	120.9	18.2	3 925	60.2	15 327
Rhea	15	26.8	D	98	2.7	7.7	100	137.8	4 981	54.2	D	903	12.3	13 616
Roane	22	139.8	D	345	10.2	28.0	176	308.9	6 194	67.4	12.5	1 832	25.9	14 164
Robertson	68	233.0	D	785	19.0	41.5	178	331.4	6 432	70.0	12.4	1 823	29.1	15 968
Rutherford	189	2 177.0	1 859.8	3 908	129.4	275.9	594	1 515.6	9 486	103.2	D	8 766	144.4	16 470
Scott	20	50.1	50.1	158	2.9	7.4	74	88.0	4 437	48.3	D	555	7.3	13 119
Sequatchie	10	D	D	(6)	D	D	42	56.1	5 539	60.3	D	288	4.2	14 531
Sevier	50	D	D	(7)	D	D	683	857.5	13 658	148.6	D	5 554	86.3	15 546
Shelby	1 851	35 419.2	16 570.7	34 481	1 214.8	2 437.4	3 574	8 959.2	10 359	112.7	15.2	56 612	891.3	15 744
Smith	15	55.7	D	105	2.4	4.3	62	100.8	6 286	68.4	D	642	8.9	13 787
Stewart	NA	NA	NA	NA	NA	NA	35	43.5	3 877	42.2	D	260	3.4	13 012
Sullivan	236	1 268.6	727.2	2 971	78.9	164.8	754	1 515.6	10 091	109.8	20.5	8 945	141.2	15 787
Sumner	141	500.2	431.1	1 369	37.9	91.1	403	665.2	5 458	59.4	D	4 252	64.4	15 148
Tipton	36	101.7	87.2	229	4.2	8.5	169	279.7	6 085	66.2	D	1 571	23.0	14 630
Trousdale	8	38.6	D	224	3.3	10.7	28	23.4	3 475	37.8	D	190	2.3	11 916
Unicoi	9	70.3	D	121	5.0	12.0	50	59.1	3 437	37.4	D	342	4.9	14 251
Union	9	D	D	(4)	D	D	36	28.2	1 770	19.3	D	204	2.3	11 451
Van Buren	2	D	D	(5)	D	D	10	7.4	1 464	15.9	–	30	.4	14 500
Warren	45	101.5	D	339	8.6	18.7	177	267.0	7 468	81.3	D	1 803	26.2	14 556
Washington	162	1 192.8	1 053.8	2 131	55.5	115.0	540	1 123.1	11 071	120.5	D	6 873	103.1	14 999
Wayne	8	D	D	(4)	D	D	67	45.8	2 777	30.2	9.4	370	4.2	11 389
Weakley	49	320.2	D	680	19.9	57.3	153	171.8	5 237	57.0	D	1 211	16.1	13 264
White	22	62.8	D	190	4.3	8.4	90	183.5	8 265	89.9	D	856	13.2	15 471
Williamson	228	2 559.9	531.8	1 749	95.7	185.1	540	1 421.4	12 758	138.8	D	7 729	142.1	18 381
Wilson	95	605.8	220.8	1 075	29.4	75.5	290	566.5	6 956	75.7	D	3 216	49.6	15 423
TEXAS	33 346	323 111.7	170 652.6	425 750	15 504.9	31 787.8	74 105	182 516.1	9 430	102.6	14.2	950 848	16 197.1	17 034
Anderson	46	166.1	163.2	338	9.7	25.8	194	316.1	6 066	66.0	D	1 877	27.2	14 490
Andrews	20	24.6	D	103	2.3	4.7	52	59.7	4 281	46.6	7.3	356	5.7	15 921
Angelina	81	288.2	242.0	1 237	31.1	63.7	343	688.8	9 024	98.2	18.1	4 238	62.7	14 786
Aransas	16	24.8	D	63	1.7	3.5	90	124.8	5 551	60.4	D	771	11.8	15 363
Archer	18	41.5	D	142	2.3	4.9	27	23.4	2 853	31.0	D	111	2.0	18 207
Armstrong	2	D	D	(5)	D	D	6	2.9	1 345	14.6	–	19	.2	8 000
Atascosa	30	89.6	D	227	6.6	12.9	108	177.2	5 015	54.6	D	1 246	16.3	13 104
Austin	22	212.8	177.2	390	11.3	28.0	123	211.4	9 211	100.2	9.4	1 114	16.7	14 994
Bailey	20	112.1	D	203	4.3	8.4	36	33.9	5 009	54.5	D	271	3.1	11 546
Bandera	5	.9	.9	7	.1	.2	54	50.9	3 406	37.1	D	275	3.9	14 273
Bastrop	28	69.0	D	205	3.4	7.4	135	397.0	8 129	88.5	D	1 450	20.8	14 343
Baylor	14	D	D	(4)	D	D	21	21.4	5 152	56.1	D	126	1.5	11 619
Bee	18	92.3	D	128	3.2	9.1	92	141.8	5 079	55.3	D	1 008	15.5	15 405
Bell	150	D	D	(8)	D	D	829	1 733.5	7 821	85.1	D	10 409	163.4	15 701
Bexar	1 829	12 639.2	8 177.0	25 191	810.7	1 601.5	4 505	11 657.5	8 725	94.9	D	64 928	1 111.1	17 112
Blanco	7	D	D	(4)	D	D	46	35.2	4 285	46.6	D	231	3.4	14 706
Borden	1	D	NA	(5)	D	D	1	D	D	D	D	(5)	D	D
Bosque	11	63.3	D	105	1.6	2.9	73	73.2	4 387	47.7	3.4	443	6.0	13 578
Bowie	134	D	921.6	(9)	D	D	445	940.7	11 251	122.4	D	5 222	83.0	15 894
Brazoria	220	840.2	525.2	2 524	102.1	292.1	629	1 534.4	6 871	74.8	21.2	8 945	136.0	15 203
Brazos	130	426.5	351.7	1 655	41.9	85.1	569	1 336.2	10 106	110.0	19.7	7 994	122.2	15 288
Brewster	12	18.3	18.3	62	1.1	3.3	56	58.1	6 563	71.4	7.9	460	6.1	13 183
Briscoe	6	D	D	(4)	D	D	9	4.3	2 253	24.5	–	29	.3	11 345
Brooks	5	3.8	3.8	14	.2	.7	32	38.4	4 574	49.8	D	287	3.8	13 366
Brown	42	95.7	70.5	337	8.5	17.7	194	302.0	8 216	89.4	D	1 843	24.6	13 323
Burleson	26	133.1	95.7	136	4.3	10.4	66	81.4	5 302	57.7	15.0	477	6.5	13 669
Burnet	27	34.9	D	163	4.2	9.4	159	281.0	9 108	99.1	D	1 534	24.6	16 049
Caldwell	25	63.1	D	166	2.9	7.1	92	128.4	4 104	44.7	D	806	10.1	12 510
Calhoun	29	51.9	D	135	3.7	8.9	77	111.1	5 387	58.6	D	725	10.3	14 171
Callahan	8	7.2	7.2	38	.8	1.9	36	65.4	5 130	55.8	D	266	4.3	16 218
Cameron	387	1 218.9	955.5	3 772	81.6	170.4	1 117	1 904.0	5 993	65.2	22.1	13 089	179.3	13 700
Camp	11	13.2	9.8	80	.9	3.7	58	109.6	9 996	108.8	D	532	9.1	17 102
Carson	6	20.4	20.4	37	.8	2.2	29	25.2	3 782	41.2	D	233	2.3	9 721
Cass	30	106.8	106.8	222	6.1	19.1	137	161.5	5 268	57.3	D	1 261	16.8	13 353
Castro	20	D	D	(7)	D	D	41	47.7	5 757	62.6	D	208	3.2	15 284

[1] Includes only establishments with payroll.   [2] For pay period including March 12.   [3] Based on resident population estimated as of July 1, 1997.   [4] 20 to 99 employees.   [5] 0 to 19 employees.   [6] 100 to 249 employees.   [7] 250 to 499 employees.   [8] 2,500 to 4,999 employees.   [9] 1,000 to 2,499 employees.

Sources: Wholesale Trade—U.S. Census Bureau, 1997 Economic Census, ECON97 Report Series CD-ROM, CD-EC97-1, Disc 1E, issued February 2001 (related Internet site <http://www.census.gov/epcd/www/97EC42.HTM>).   Retail Trade—U.S. Census Bureau, 1997 Economic Census, ECON97 Report Series CD-ROM, CD-EC97-1, Disc 1E, issued February 2001 (related Internet site <http://www.census.gov/epcd/www/97EC44.HTM>).

Table B–11. Counties — Wholesale Trade and Retail Trade–Con.

[Includes U.S., states, and 3,142 counties/county equivalents defined as of January 1, 1992. For changes to these areas since January 1, 1992, see appendix B. Geographic Information]

County	Wholesale trade[1] (NAICS 42), 1997						Retail trade[1] (NAICS 44-45), 1997							
	Sales							Sales					Annual payroll	
									Per capita[3]		Percent from general merchandise stores			
	Establishments	Total (mil. dol.)	Merchant wholesalers (mil. dol.)	Paid employees[2]	Annual payroll (mil. dol.)	Operating expenses (mil. dol.)	Establishments	Total (mil. dol.)	Amount (dollars)	Percent of national average		Paid employees[2]	Total (mil. dol.)	Per paid employee (dollars)
TEXAS—Con.														
Chambers	22	D	D	(4)	D	D	83	133.8	5 750	62.6	D	648	9.4	14 539
Cherokee	39	75.5	69.4	250	8.4	15.3	146	262.6	6 135	66.8	D	1 542	21.5	13 947
Childress	14	51.7	D	101	2.3	5.0	38	43.7	5 678	61.8	D	309	3.8	12 159
Clay	7	17.3	17.3	51	1.2	2.9	34	53.3	5 099	55.5	D	267	4.1	15 202
Cochran	7	7.9	7.9	26	.5	1.2	15	15.6	3 982	43.3	D	87	1.5	17 437
Coke	3	D	D	(5)	D	D	21	24.2	7 124	77.5	–	98	1.3	13 367
Coleman	18	29.9	D	102	1.2	2.8	53	57.1	5 891	64.1	4.3	324	4.2	12 910
Collin	737	7 169.8	2 679.2	7 373	326.9	674.4	1 301	4 220.4	10 536	114.6	14.3	20 311	407.2	20 048
Collingsworth	5	7.4	D	18	.4	.7	17	17.4	5 249	57.1	D	113	2.1	18 752
Colorado	40	84.9	D	235	4.3	11.0	113	160.0	8 052	94.1	9.3	879	13.3	15 148
Comal	99	320.1	186.1	653	20.0	46.7	317	633.3	8 990	97.8	D	3 242	55.7	17 183
Comanche	29	124.5	70.4	370	8.5	16.1	77	79.6	5 875	63.9	2.7	456	6.4	13 978
Concho	4	2.7	2.7	20	.4	1.0	14	14.1	4 563	49.7	–	82	1.2	14 195
Cooke	45	102.5	D	354	6.6	15.2	240	355.6	10 833	117.9	D	2 013	28.9	14 346
Coryell	17	D	D	(6)	D	D	144	268.7	3 652	39.7	D	1 781	22.0	12 361
Cottle	1	D	D	(5)	D	D	10	10.3	5 291	57.6	–	40	.6	15 750
Crane	6	D	D	(5)	D	D	17	21.7	4 868	53.0	D	129	1.8	13 837
Crockett	6	6.7	6.7	15	.4	.9	31	26.6	5 914	64.4	D	263	3.2	12 061
Crosby	12	65.4	65.4	171	4.8	9.2	33	41.8	5 698	62.0	D	226	3.2	14 323
Culberson	1	D	D	(5)	D	D	25	28.2	9 084	98.8	–	162	1.7	10 660
Dallam	22	191.7	D	275	10.0	22.0	43	65.3	10 233	111.3	9.4	250	4.3	17 376
Dallas	6 054	100 787.3	34 969.2	108 131	4 621.7	9 301.4	7 878	24 538.2	12 166	132.4	11.2	117 812	2 400.4	20 375
Dawson	25	91.4	D	122	2.8	8.2	68	95.8	6 511	70.8	D	553	8.6	15 609
Deaf Smith	46	120.8	102.7	368	10.0	24.3	88	113.9	5 935	64.6	D	595	8.9	14 960
Delta	2	D	D	(6)	D	D	19	16.2	3 271	35.6	–	94	1.2	12 500
Denton	423	2 762.2	1 740.4	3 935	141.4	300.6	1 143	3 180.1	8 738	95.1	D	16 966	284.9	16 794
DeWitt	22	86.4	45.3	155	2.6	6.3	81	93.0	4 727	51.4	D	663	9.1	13 688
Dickens	1	D	D	(5)	D	D	12	7.4	3 268	35.6	D	54	.5	9 204
Dimmit	7	6.2	6.2	17	.4	1.1	34	50.3	4 819	52.4	D	328	4.5	13 851
Donley	2	D	D	(5)	D	D	20	23.6	6 200	67.5	D	114	1.7	15 114
Duval	6	D	D	(5)	D	D	36	35.2	2 593	28.2	D	203	2.6	12 901
Eastland	29	255.7	D	368	9.1	15.4	113	116.5	6 569	71.5	12.5	682	8.8	12 937
Ector	355	1 047.6	863.8	3 518	117.9	226.7	638	1 100.9	9 205	101.0	20.3	6 060	104.4	17 227
Edwards	2	D	D	(5)	D	D	9	5.8	1 609	17.5	D	47	.4	8 404
Ellis	94	375.7	D	751	19.6	42.7	310	572.7	5 696	62.0	D	3 054	47.5	15 539
El Paso	1 000	6 089.3	4 702.2	11 129	309.6	700.1	2 134	4 698.9	6 856	74.6	19.7	28 986	430.5	14 851
Erath	43	118.9	82.6	378	6.8	17.5	157	274.1	8 745	95.2	D	1 674	24.6	14 693
Falls	14	D	D	(4)	D	D	68	65.4	3 701	40.3	17.8	435	5.4	12 347
Fannin	26	187.8	D	321	7.7	18.1	101	193.8	6 955	75.7	D	929	14.8	15 931
Fayette	39	318.6	223.4	411	10.6	21.8	141	185.9	8 840	96.2	9.3	1 063	15.2	14 340
Fisher	3	D	D	(5)	D	D	17	12.4	2 859	31.1	D	96	1.3	13 073
Floyd	19	58.0	D	181	2.7	6.8	32	47.7	5 831	63.4	D	206	3.2	15 646
Foard	2	D	D	(5)	D	D	6	4.3	2 546	27.7	–	22	.3	14 000
Fort Bend	405	2 972.1	2 367.5	3 793	143.0	284.3	825	2 229.9	6 965	75.8	18.4	11 992	196.4	16 381
Franklin	5	2.6	2.6	19	.4	.7	32	37.2	3 893	42.4	7.3	220	3.3	15 205
Freestone	15	26.4	D	61	1.2	3.2	63	105.9	6 042	65.7	2.2	481	7.7	15 963
Frio	23	D	D	(4)	D	D	52	82.1	5 196	56.5	D	461	6.2	13 388
Gaines	22	135.6	D	182	5.2	9.5	62	88.9	6 041	65.7	13.6	470	7.4	15 643
Galveston	198	561.3	470.2	1 522	46.6	92.3	921	1 786.9	7 375	80.3	15.1	10 591	165.8	15 653
Garza	8	18.7	18.7	32	.8	1.9	29	18.3	3 909	42.5	D	123	1.5	11 797
Gillespie	36	89.8	D	334	5.8	12.4	153	172.9	8 745	95.2	10.6	1 361	18.6	13 655
Glasscock	1	D	D	(5)	D	D	5	D	D	D	D	(5)	D	D
Goliad	4	2.8	D	12	.2	.4	20	17.4	2 549	27.7	D	100	1.3	12 610
Gonzales	38	153.3	D	353	6.0	15.1	82	99.2	5 664	61.6	16.0	728	8.4	11 518
Gray	42	178.7	174.2	309	9.6	20.3	130	169.1	7 150	77.8	16.0	1 068	16.0	14 938
Grayson	132	406.1	291.8	958	25.1	56.5	474	1 092.0	10 847	118.0	25.3	6 213	98.5	15 857
Gregg	342	1 863.5	D	3 564	114.0	245.3	734	1 549.7	13 783	150.0	D	8 825	145.1	16 442
Grimes	19	137.0	D	187	4.1	8.8	73	120.5	5 271	57.4	D	663	9.9	14 986
Guadalupe	82	366.1	196.6	681	20.6	43.2	215	498.1	6 420	69.9	D	2 665	41.7	15 649
Hale	74	294.5	D	540	13.3	38.2	164	264.7	7 253	78.9	17.9	1 566	23.6	15 093
Hall	6	10.1	D	25	.5	1.4	22	43.1	11 741	127.8	D	137	2.1	15 270
Hamilton	10	42.1	D	118	2.2	4.9	57	45.4	5 946	64.7	D	301	4.0	13 213
Hansford	23	116.1	116.1	139	4.3	11.1	38	39.0	7 286	79.3	D	233	3.6	15 536
Hardeman	9	12.2	12.2	41	.6	1.7	21	16.3	3 494	38.0	D	115	1.5	12 861
Hardin	28	33.4	D	150	3.3	7.8	152	350.6	7 207	78.4	D	1 630	24.5	15 054
Harris	7 564	110 399.7	62 116.8	101 357	4 129.7	8 563.0	11 596	31 045.1	9 857	107.3	13.1	168 038	2 921.9	17 388

[1] Includes only establishments with payroll. [2] For pay period including March 12. [3] Based on resident population estimated as of July 1, 1997. [4] 100 to 249 employees. [5] 0 to 19 employees. [6] 20 to 99 employees.

Sources: Wholesale Trade—U.S. Census Bureau, 1997 Economic Census, ECON97 Report Series CD-ROM, CD-EC97-1, Disc 1E, issued February 2001 (related Internet site <http://www.census.gov/epcd/www/97EC42.HTM>). Retail Trade—U.S. Census Bureau, 1997 Economic Census, ECON97 Report Series CD-ROM, CD-EC97-1, Disc 1E, issued February 2001 (related Internet site <http://www.census.gov/epcd/www/97EC44.HTM>).

Wholesale Trade and Retail Trade-Con.

[Includes U.S., states, and 3,142 counties/county equivalents defined as of January 1, 1992. For changes to these areas since January 1, 1992, see appendix B. Geographic Information]

County	Wholesale trade[1] (NAICS 42), 1997						Retail trade[1] (NAICS 44-45), 1997							
	Sales						Sales					Annual payroll		
									Per capita[3]		Percent from general merchandise stores			
	Establishments	Total (mil. dol.)	Merchant wholesalers (mil. dol.)	Paid employees[2]	Annual payroll (mil. dol.)	Operating expenses (mil. dol.)	Establishments	Total (mil. dol.)	Amount (dollars)	Percent of national average		Paid employees[2]	Total (mil. dol.)	Per paid employee (dollars)
TEXAS—Con.														
Harrison	65	321.2	D	747	20.8	43.0	220	378.6	6 375	69.4	D	2 270	33.2	14 605
Hartley	5	D	D	(4)	D	D	10	14.4	2 797	30.4	–	84	1.2	14 845
Haskell	8	23.3	D	40	.6	1.2	41	58.9	9 618	104.7	D	238	3.3	14 029
Hays	75	174.1	125.0	559	15.9	29.2	382	698.0	8 156	88.7	D	4 056	61.0	15 042
Hemphill	7	10.5	10.5	33	.8	1.8	22	19.7	5 472	59.5	D	132	2.0	15 379
Henderson	42	98.3	D	215	4.6	11.1	221	381.1	5 666	61.7	D	2 586	34.3	13 263
Hidalgo	600	1 981.7	1 592.1	6 395	124.6	261.1	1 582	3 337.6	6 621	72.0	20.0	20 862	313.1	15 006
Hill	26	46.8	D	119	2.5	5.6	229	331.1	11 011	119.8	6.3	1 800	26.4	14 646
Hockley	40	81.5	D	255	6.3	12.2	86	150.6	6 319	68.8	12.0	725	11.3	15 548
Hood	29	32.5	D	83	2.0	4.3	159	346.6	9 625	104.7	D	1 702	30.3	17 796
Hopkins	48	607.1	D	1 088	27.0	49.0	174	357.2	11 851	129.0	D	1 753	27.8	15 863
Houston	16	49.4	D	136	2.4	5.4	91	122.4	5 605	61.0	D	772	10.6	13 724
Howard	50	215.5	D	559	22.0	45.2	149	248.6	7 746	84.3	D	1 509	21.1	13 999
Hudspeth	4	1.9	1.9	7	.1	.2	9	6.1	1 913	20.8	–	52	.5	8 673
Hunt	54	263.6	245.6	447	10.1	23.3	258	479.9	6 982	76.0	D	3 013	41.7	13 848
Hutchinson	31	163.9	D	192	5.5	11.0	104	151.0	6 308	68.6	D	1 028	13.8	13 422
Irion	3	5.1	D	19	.4	.8	4	1.5	911	9.9	–	19	.1	7 789
Jack	7	13.0	13.0	64	1.8	4.4	35	21.3	2 907	31.6	D	181	2.3	12 829
Jackson	22	58.4	D	177	3.3	6.7	63	90.6	6 617	72.0	D	479	7.6	15 772
Jasper	49	103.4	100.2	247	6.5	13.9	190	301.0	9 046	98.4	D	1 658	23.7	14 321
Jeff Davis	NA	NA	NA	NA	NA	NA	8	3.7	1 667	18.1	–	37	.5	12 595
Jefferson	368	2 081.2	D	4 827	163.7	327.0	1 084	2 570.9	10 650	115.9	D	14 964	230.1	15 374
Jim Hogg	5	25.3	D	40	.8	1.6	34	31.4	6 410	69.7	6.4	207	2.5	12 309
Jim Wells	56	139.8	115.3	522	14.1	29.3	160	258.1	6 490	70.6	D	1 531	23.4	15 255
Johnson	87	261.8	D	762	18.2	38.1	358	706.8	6 208	67.6	D	3 995	62.2	15 570
Jones	24	145.1	D	140	3.4	9.7	58	163.1	8 727	95.0	8.6	498	8.0	16 036
Karnes	14	45.8	D	168	2.4	5.4	54	59.8	3 924	42.7	D	434	5.1	11 838
Kaufman	77	189.3	D	665	16.8	34.2	286	573.3	8 999	97.9	D	2 693	43.0	15 959
Kendall	31	141.1	132.5	378	8.5	16.3	93	305.8	15 012	163.4	D	1 012	20.1	19 821
Kenedy	NA	NA	NA	NA	NA	NA	–	–	–	–	–	–	–	–
Kent	1	D	D	(4)	D	D	4	D	D	D	D	(4)	D	D
Kerr	48	65.6	D	271	6.4	15.8	210	436.1	10 391	113.1	15.9	2 467	38.4	15 584
Kimble	5	D	D	(5)	D	D	33	31.4	7 565	82.3	D	201	2.8	13 701
King	NA	NA	NA	NA	NA	NA	–	–	–	–	–	–	–	–
Kinney	2	D	D	(4)	D	D	9	4.2	1 243	13.5	–	41	.4	9 561
Kleberg	10	8.2	8.2	42	.9	2.0	113	214.3	7 098	77.2	D	1 414	20.0	14 126
Knox	13	29.8	29.8	79	1.7	4.2	31	24.7	5 735	62.4	D	163	2.0	12 270
Lamar	68	152.4	D	519	12.7	27.1	242	482.5	10 582	115.1	20.2	2 591	40.0	15 419
Lamb	25	72.6	72.6	146	3.1	8.0	63	75.4	5 088	55.4	6.1	450	5.9	13 024
Lampasas	16	36.3	D	79	.7	1.6	65	94.4	5 406	58.8	D	562	7.8	13 831
La Salle	3	D	D	(4)	D	D	27	20.0	3 350	36.5	D	142	1.8	12 415
Lavaca	30	202.6	D	818	14.6	39.2	108	118.1	6 308	68.6	11.2	797	10.7	13 415
Lee	35	322.4	D	324	7.1	16.5	59	79.9	5 426	59.0	D	665	9.0	13 562
Leon	15	56.2	D	149	3.2	6.8	72	77.4	5 372	58.5	D	494	6.0	12 192
Liberty	53	D	100.2	(6)	D	D	204	441.7	6 869	74.7	D	2 472	36.5	14 778
Limestone	15	D	D	(7)	D	D	91	137.6	6 649	72.4	D	831	11.3	13 539
Lipscomb	11	12.5	12.5	32	.6	2.1	17	10.6	3 528	38.4	–	82	.8	10 195
Live Oak	9	25.4	D	77	.9	2.2	45	75.0	7 414	80.7	2.6	397	5.1	12 851
Llano	15	85.5	58.1	222	5.4	11.0	77	69.1	5 245	57.1	D	380	5.3	14 061
Loving	1	D	D	(4)	D	D	–	–	–	–	–	–	–	–
Lubbock	505	3 867.8	2 985.1	6 628	181.3	388.9	1 084	2 673.0	11 618	126.4	16.5	14 538	238.0	16 371
Lynn	7	D	D	(5)	D	D	24	30.6	4 646	50.6	D	122	2.1	17 082
McCulloch	14	14.9	D	91	1.4	2.4	55	75.5	8 651	94.1	D	473	5.9	12 533
McLennan	315	1 716.3	1 394.5	3 755	102.1	209.9	862	1 797.8	8 883	96.7	18.1	10 227	162.7	15 908
McMullen	NA	NA	NA	NA	NA	NA	5	1.9	2 398	26.1	–	13	.2	12 923
Madison	5	12.1	12.1	23	.8	1.9	46	137.0	11 648	126.7	D	462	7.5	16 199
Marion	9	19.1	D	31	1.0	5.2	41	37.4	3 534	38.5	D	246	2.8	11 280
Martin	10	22.2	22.2	53	1.4	2.7	17	27.9	5 580	60.7	–	116	2.1	18 198
Mason	9	38.3	D	56	1.1	2.8	20	10.9	2 973	32.4	D	107	1.0	9 804
Matagorda	33	D	D	(6)	D	D	152	224.7	5 936	64.6	D	1 443	21.7	15 064
Maverick	35	85.3	85.3	165	3.7	8.9	184	233.3	4 995	54.4	D	1 716	21.1	12 304
Medina	28	75.7	D	241	4.4	11.9	117	215.2	5 990	65.2	D	955	18.0	18 819
Menard	4	13.9	D	34	1.0	1.8	11	10.2	4 326	47.1	D	60	.7	10 867
Midland	297	1 938.6	1 358.6	2 708	93.9	180.1	549	1 226.3	10 434	113.5	17.0	6 649	108.5	16 317
Milam	22	119.8	44.3	177	3.2	8.3	82	106.8	4 434	48.2	16.0	701	9.8	13 924
Mills	7	28.2	D	75	.4	.9	36	32.3	6 845	74.5	D	159	2.4	14 868

[1] Includes only establishments with payroll. [2] For pay period including March 12. [3] Based on resident population estimated as of July 1, 1997. [4] 0 to 19 employees. [5] 20 to 99 employees. [6] 250 to 499 employees. [7] 100 to 249 employees.

Sources: Wholesale Trade—U.S. Census Bureau, 1997 Economic Census, ECON97 Report Series CD-ROM, CD-EC97-1, Disc 1E, issued February 2001 (related Internet site <http://www.census.gov/epcd/www/97EC42.HTM>). Retail Trade—U.S. Census Bureau, 1997 Economic Census, ECON97 Report Series CD-ROM, CD-EC97-1, Disc 1E, issued February 2001 (related Internet site <http://www.census.gov/epcd/www/97EC44.HTM>).

Table B–11. Counties — Wholesale Trade and Retail Trade–Con.

[Includes U.S., states, and 3,142 counties/county equivalents defined as of January 1, 1992. For changes to these areas since January 1, 1992, see appendix B. Geographic Information]

| County | Wholesale trade[1] (NAICS 42), 1997 | | | | | | Retail trade[1] (NAICS 44-45), 1997 | | | | | | | |
	Estab-lishments	Sales Total (mil. dol.)	Sales Merchant whole-salers (mil. dol.)	Paid em-ployees[2]	Annual payroll (mil. dol.)	Operating expenses (mil. dol.)	Estab-lishments	Total (mil. dol.)	Per capita[3] Amount (dollars)	Per capita[3] Percent of national average	Percent from general mer-chandise stores	Paid em-ployees[2]	Annual payroll Total (mil. dol.)	Annual payroll Per paid em-ployee (dollars)
TEXAS—Con.														
Mitchell	9	5.2	D	93	.8	1.4	38	35.8	4 111	44.7	D	226	3.5	15 398
Montague	30	53.7	D	118	1.9	4.3	86	97.9	5 322	57.9	D	640	8.0	12 434
Montgomery	337	2 129.7	1 124.1	3 271	118.8	245.1	835	2 224.8	8 625	93.9	D	11 926	187.4	15 718
Moore	26	137.7	137.7	187	6.0	14.0	83	127.5	6 624	72.1	17.1	724	11.0	15 149
Morris	15	100.2	100.2	230	6.9	14.8	53	38.9	2 922	31.8	D	342	4.2	12 386
Motley	3	2.4	2.4	24	.4	.6	11	6.1	4 685	51.0	–	37	.5	13 000
Nacogdoches	57	161.6	135.9	593	14.1	32.1	279	501.2	8 852	96.3	D	3 036	45.0	14 835
Navarro	45	227.5	209.9	409	10.7	20.3	196	347.9	8 467	92.1	15.4	2 007	29.4	14 649
Newton	3	9.4	9.4	22	.5	2.5	36	26.8	1 860	20.2	D	185	2.1	11 427
Nolan	24	48.7	D	171	4.5	9.7	83	121.1	7 381	80.3	D	786	10.2	12 996
Nueces	493	1 803.1	D	5 029	154.0	298.4	1 286	2 783.5	8 824	96.0	17.8	17 018	265.9	15 622
Ochiltree	33	78.3	74.4	175	4.3	10.8	44	63.3	7 188	78.2	10.5	377	5.5	14 602
Oldham	5	5.2	5.2	27	.5	1.1	11	8.0	3 604	39.2	–	60	.8	13 667
Orange	49	61.6	D	316	7.4	15.5	290	546.1	6 459	70.3	D	3 310	44.8	13 549
Palo Pinto	30	62.4	D	223	4.7	11.2	132	171.9	6 731	73.2	D	1 072	14.5	13 568
Panola	25	135.3	29.5	161	3.9	7.6	90	97.1	4 214	45.9	D	696	8.1	11 616
Parker	75	231.6	D	579	15.6	27.7	236	602.3	7 646	83.2	D	2 657	49.3	18 563
Parmer	28	122.0	122.0	186	4.1	11.1	42	48.3	4 666	50.8	D	279	3.8	13 573
Pecos	15	28.2	28.2	101	2.8	6.2	75	84.1	5 185	56.4	D	576	8.3	14 398
Polk	26	114.6	87.1	214	3.7	8.5	132	272.1	5 725	62.3	D	1 701	24.8	14 571
Potter	247	1 209.8	D	3 204	105.5	203.8	641	1 531.3	14 122	153.7	D	7 939	137.3	17 297
Presidio	6	4.1	4.1	14	.2	.4	27	21.4	2 588	28.2	D	152	1.6	10 257
Rains	5	D	D	(4)	D	D	33	22.3	2 720	29.6	–	186	2.4	13 022
Randall	110	1 180.9	D	1 620	47.5	87.3	346	838.3	8 582	93.4	D	4 299	72.4	16 847
Reagan	4	D	D	(4)	D	D	16	19.5	4 632	50.4	D	84	1.3	14 988
Real	3	D	D	(5)	D	D	19	6.3	2 376	25.9	–	57	.6	10 947
Red River	4	D	D	(4)	D	D	59	61.2	4 442	48.3	D	482	4.8	10 017
Reeves	13	12.0	12.0	138	1.7	3.7	43	64.2	4 404	47.9	21.4	383	5.7	14 950
Refugio	12	19.3	D	60	1.3	2.9	38	49.6	6 283	68.4	D	258	4.0	15 450
Roberts	2	D	D	(5)	D	D	4	1.7	1 765	19.2	–	20	.2	10 400
Robertson	11	84.2	D	49	.7	2.4	55	52.0	3 371	36.7	6.4	364	4.5	12 467
Rockwall	58	133.2	D	343	7.8	16.6	112	266.9	7 500	81.6	D	1 488	24.1	16 165
Runnels	17	64.8	D	614	12.6	22.6	57	69.5	6 080	66.2	D	413	5.5	13 223
Rusk	41	137.0	D	516	11.9	24.2	144	188.0	4 136	45.0	D	1 305	17.0	13 019
Sabine	5	4.0	4.0	18	.4	.7	47	40.6	3 843	41.8	4.8	284	4.0	14 155
San Augustine	11	13.3	D	67	1.1	2.5	42	45.0	5 533	60.2	4.2	312	3.6	11 606
San Jacinto	6	4.8	4.8	31	.5	1.9	33	29.7	1 425	15.5	D	235	2.9	12 549
San Patricio	42	105.9	D	262	6.8	14.4	200	348.7	5 038	54.8	9.6	1 988	29.6	14 902
San Saba	15	48.2	D	105	1.2	2.6	38	51.1	8 639	94.0	D	254	3.6	14 146
Schleicher	2	D	D	(5)	D	D	11	7.7	2 548	27.7	D	45	.7	15 133
Scurry	27	50.0	45.3	215	5.9	10.2	80	135.3	7 468	81.3	D	762	10.9	14 318
Shackelford	6	2.7	2.7	13	.3	.6	22	14.8	4 480	48.7	D	86	1.0	11 047
Shelby	27	99.7	D	168	4.3	8.8	103	155.0	6 866	74.7	D	984	12.4	12 637
Sherman	9	35.1	D	40	.9	4.5	12	8.1	2 799	30.5	D	47	.8	17 404
Smith	297	1 237.7	702.2	3 103	93.9	191.0	805	1 868.6	11 278	122.7	17.4	9 773	170.2	17 418
Somervell	4	D	D	(5)	D	D	29	29.1	4 694	51.1	D	220	2.5	11 386
Starr	21	37.2	37.2	105	2.3	5.2	131	201.2	3 700	40.3	D	1 379	16.3	11 830
Stephens	16	10.9	D	45	1.2	2.5	47	56.1	5 641	61.4	D	421	5.8	13 701
Sterling	3	1.5	1.5	8	.2	.4	5	5.8	4 246	46.2	–	38	.4	10 711
Stonewall	2	D	D	(5)	D	D	10	5.7	3 149	34.3	D	39	.5	13 103
Sutton	14	18.9	D	63	1.7	3.9	31	56.3	12 729	138.5	D	206	4.0	19 573
Swisher	15	42.2	42.2	94	2.1	4.6	39	41.2	4 941	53.8	D	255	3.2	12 463
Tarrant	2 399	22 102.4	11 605.6	33 372	1 219.5	2 589.2	5 015	14 097.9	10 636	115.7	D	71 758	1 326.3	18 483
Taylor	219	933.9	832.9	1 996	54.1	114.7	635	1 297.7	10 673	116.1	20.6	7 211	116.7	16 189
Terrell	1	D	D	(5)	D	D	7	2.7	2 309	25.1	–	26	.3	12 115
Terry	22	108.6	108.6	216	5.2	10.0	46	81.3	6 262	68.1	14.3	458	7.3	15 910
Throckmorton	5	2.1	2.1	8	.2	.5	11	4.9	2 845	31.0	–	37	.4	11 541
Titus	48	203.3	145.8	539	14.2	29.3	147	271.1	10 805	117.6	19.6	1 483	23.7	15 991
Tom Green	159	D	320.9	(6)	D	D	471	890.7	8 708	94.8	19.6	5 404	84.3	15 606
Travis	1 268	8 991.9	4 533.4	18 345	717.9	1 300.3	2 925	16 072.8	23 228	252.8	D	45 335	916.0	20 205
Trinity	5	D	D	(4)	D	D	60	56.1	4 502	49.0	D	365	4.5	12 384
Tyler	5	D	D	(4)	D	D	72	85.2	4 218	45.9	D	612	7.5	12 248
Upshur	17	104.5	D	49	2.3	6.0	101	145.1	4 090	44.5	D	895	11.7	13 107
Upton	8	24.7	24.7	41	.9	2.4	16	14.7	3 875	42.2	D	94	1.1	11 404
Uvalde	40	165.3	D	318	6.2	14.1	124	178.0	6 985	76.0	D	1 054	15.5	14 750
Val Verde	30	54.5	45.4	291	5.1	11.5	173	278.1	6 488	70.6	19.4	1 798	25.3	14 092

[1] Includes only establishments with payroll. [2] For pay period including March 12. [3] Based on resident population estimated as of July 1, 1997. [4] 20 to 99 employees. [5] 0 to 19 employees. [6] 1,000 to 2,499 employees.

Sources: Wholesale Trade—U.S. Census Bureau, 1997 Economic Census, ECON97 Report Series CD-ROM, CD-EC97-1, Disc 1E, issued February 2001 (related Internet site <http://www.census.gov/epcd/www/97EC42.HTM>). Retail Trade—U.S. Census Bureau, 1997 Economic Census, ECON97 Report Series CD-ROM, CD-EC97-1, Disc 1E, issued February 2001 (related Internet site <http://www.census.gov/epcd/www/97EC44.HTM>).

[Includes U.S., states, and 3,142 counties/county equivalents defined as of January 1, 1992. For changes to these areas since January 1, 1992, see appendix B. Geographic Information]

County	Wholesale trade[1] (NAICS 42), 1997						Retail trade[1] (NAICS 44-45), 1997							
	Sales			Paid employees[2]	Annual payroll (mil. dol.)	Operating expenses (mil. dol.)	Estab-lishments	Sales					Annual payroll	
	Estab-lishments	Total (mil. dol.)	Merchant whole-salers (mil. dol.)					Total (mil. dol.)	Per capita[3]		Percent from general mer-chandise stores	Paid employees[2]	Total (mil. dol.)	Per paid em-ployee (dollars)
									Amount (dollars)	Percent of national average				
TEXAS—Con.														
Van Zandt	31	70.8	51.4	179	4.1	9.6	145	245.2	5 695	62.0	D	1 339	20.2	15 106
Victoria	141	422.1	D	1 665	46.0	85.6	398	868.7	10 771	117.2	21.3	5 052	80.1	15 858
Walker	36	89.5	D	247	4.4	9.3	174	386.7	7 107	77.3	D	2 245	32.0	14 247
Waller	38	D	D	(4)	D	D	80	480.4	17 970	195.5	D	1 280	25.6	20 000
Ward	15	74.4	D	103	2.9	5.8	49	54.0	4 590	49.9	D	381	5.5	14 402
Washington	36	289.2	269.9	543	14.6	28.4	143	270.3	9 396	102.2	D	1 565	22.8	14 592
Webb	339	1 105.4	D	2 453	51.1	125.2	730	1 524.6	8 453	92.0	19.8	9 051	138.8	15 334
Wharton	69	326.6	221.8	1 005	23.7	47.8	217	301.0	7 525	81.9	8.5	1 799	27.4	15 223
Wheeler	11	30.8	30.8	80	1.6	5.3	45	33.1	6 207	67.5	D	226	2.7	12 004
Wichita	211	434.6	D	1 906	44.8	89.1	598	1 198.7	9 315	101.4	D	7 268	107.3	14 762
Wilbarger	21	30.6	D	81	1.9	4.6	76	111.5	7 845	85.4	D	737	8.9	12 080
Willacy	10	16.9	16.9	68	1.6	3.1	43	61.8	3 167	34.5	D	386	4.6	11 930
Williamson	217	750.3	625.2	1 723	57.6	114.2	623	1 582.1	7 523	81.9	D	8 402	152.9	18 200
Wilson	16	36.7	36.7	82	1.6	3.4	68	109.5	3 626	39.5	D	625	8.9	14 160
Winkler	6	7.6	D	26	.9	1.6	32	43.6	5 527	60.1	8.6	225	3.3	14 596
Wise	38	197.2	D	343	6.8	16.5	122	689.2	16 239	176.7	D	1 692	31.3	18 490
Wood	47	189.5	161.6	364	10.0	22.0	146	211.1	6 214	67.6	D	1 173	17.3	14 711
Yoakum	22	73.4	29.4	119	2.9	6.1	42	34.0	4 251	46.3	D	246	3.2	13 004
Young	39	83.9	D	194	3.3	7.3	100	113.5	6 451	70.2	17.7	737	10.1	13 746
Zapata	3	D	D	(5)	D	D	37	26.8	2 399	26.1	D	221	2.3	10 561
Zavala	3	6.8	6.8	42	.7	1.6	20	22.5	1 905	20.7	D	178	2.3	12 781
UTAH	3 277	21 271.9	13 618.2	44 312	1 420.4	2 763.4	7 656	19 964.6	9 666	105.2	12.8	114 474	1 856.9	16 221
Beaver	3	4.0	4.0	19	.3	.5	30	29.4	5 013	54.5	D	205	2.1	10 088
Box Elder	28	73.4	73.4	245	6.1	16.9	126	250.1	6 089	66.3	8.0	1 452	19.5	13 428
Cache	85	146.4	112.8	696	12.4	25.4	349	682.7	7 957	86.6	D	5 242	70.7	13 491
Carbon	46	175.3	151.6	348	9.4	20.6	94	174.9	8 365	91.0	24.2	1 310	17.6	13 441
Daggett	NA	NA	NA	NA	NA	NA	6	1.6	2 162	23.5	–	16	.3	15 750
Davis	241	1 184.9	597.9	2 868	70.7	149.5	582	1 809.7	7 970	86.7	12.5	9 488	157.6	16 607
Duchesne	20	31.1	30.3	103	1.9	4.4	62	96.3	6 754	73.5	3.4	541	8.4	15 529
Emery	7	5.8	2.3	15	.3	.9	37	48.4	4 443	48.3	–	359	3.7	10 295
Garfield	3	D	D	(5)	D	D	23	16.9	4 021	43.8	–	122	1.4	11 410
Grand	11	8.8	7.1	46	1.2	2.6	74	77.0	9 506	103.4	3.0	528	8.4	15 864
Iron	32	113.6	109.2	266	6.1	14.7	135	286.9	10 330	112.4	14.7	1 663	24.2	14 544
Juab	8	10.7	10.7	52	.7	1.5	29	40.3	5 556	60.5	D	267	3.0	11 270
Kane	5	D	D	(5)	D	D	42	35.0	5 760	62.7	D	308	4.0	13 078
Millard	16	28.8	28.8	82	1.4	3.0	58	82.2	6 698	72.9	D	495	6.4	12 925
Morgan	7	D	D	(6)	D	D	20	24.7	3 575	38.9	–	151	1.9	12 285
Piute	1	D	D	(5)	D	D	7	2.0	1 461	15.9	–	25	.2	6 040
Rich	1	D	D	(5)	D	D	13	6.0	3 310	36.0	–	43	.6	13 442
Salt Lake	2 013	15 365.4	8 951.4	29 521	1 018.0	1 892.3	3 230	10 139.4	12 046	131.1	11.8	53 236	937.0	17 600
San Juan	11	12.6	12.6	105	1.2	2.9	41	33.7	2 491	27.1	D	304	3.4	11 332
Sanpete	8	15.1	14.5	36	.6	1.3	73	90.1	4 321	47.0	D	688	7.3	10 606
Sevier	19	78.1	34.4	238	3.9	7.9	102	167.5	9 288	101.1	D	1 067	14.1	13 224
Summit	47	116.9	27.0	147	6.0	16.4	242	307.9	12 003	130.6	D	2 520	32.0	12 692
Tooele	9	10.3	4.9	120	1.4	2.6	74	182.8	5 802	63.1	D	1 170	16.7	14 274
Uintah	49	77.6	49.3	291	7.4	14.9	104	180.4	7 094	77.2	D	1 190	16.9	14 169
Utah	320	2 763.6	2 504.5	6 272	190.4	416.3	978	2 486.4	7 549	82.1	15.6	15 868	245.1	15 444
Wasatch	14	14.3	11.0	65	2.5	3.3	56	69.1	5 417	58.9	D	454	6.3	13 769
Washington	85	238.5	223.3	641	18.0	39.4	406	879.4	11 074	120.5	10.7	4 829	77.3	16 007
Wayne	1	D	D	(5)	D	D	16	9.9	4 124	44.9	D	86	.8	9 547
Weber	187	640.6	503.0	2 025	57.3	112.1	647	1 753.5	9 620	104.7	18.0	10 847	170.3	15 698
VERMONT	941	4 731.4	4 109.5	10 987	330.6	740.3	4 093	5 898.6	10 020	109.0	7.5	36 306	603.3	16 618
Addison	41	90.2	60.1	296	7.7	17.5	186	316.1	9 075	98.7	3.7	1 523	30.3	19 916
Bennington	49	87.0	66.7	250	6.2	14.7	359	553.4	15 346	167.0	6.1	3 160	53.0	16 766
Caledonia	34	179.4	168.7	431	10.2	27.9	199	232.8	8 148	88.7	D	1 644	24.3	14 808
Chittenden	303	1 834.9	1 373.1	4 167	140.4	303.4	958	1 863.7	13 160	143.2	12.0	11 254	189.6	16 847
Essex	3	D	D	(5)	D	D	18	D	D	D	D	(6)	D	D
Franklin	49	381.6	D	582	15.8	39.3	237	324.4	7 451	81.1	4.6	1 734	28.6	16 470
Grand Isle	7	D	D	(5)	D	D	33	D	D	D	D	(7)	D	D
Lamoille	30	57.7	38.9	270	8.3	14.8	183	169.6	7 920	86.2	6.1	1 380	19.8	14 341
Orange	33	D	D	(4)	D	D	109	145.8	5 251	57.1	2.3	798	15.6	19 486
Orleans	36	D	D	(7)	D	D	174	220.4	8 711	94.8	D	1 161	19.9	17 137
Rutland	97	218.3	206.9	934	22.0	48.7	502	646.3	10 335	112.5	9.9	4 344	66.6	15 330
Washington	99	D	D	(8)	D	D	421	542.4	9 640	104.9	D	3 614	58.9	16 296
Windham	73	1 244.0	D	1 920	62.5	155.1	342	444.8	10 355	112.7	D	2 950	50.0	16 962
Windsor	87	242.9	227.5	704	19.1	45.0	372	415.5	7 533	82.0	D	2 559	44.7	17 480

[1] Includes only establishments with payroll.　[2] For pay period including March 12.　[3] Based on resident population estimated as of July 1, 1997.　[4] 250 to 499 employees.　[5] 0 to 19 employees.　[6] 20 to 99 employees.　[7] 100 to 249 employees.　[8] 500 to 999 employees.

Sources: Wholesale Trade—U.S. Census Bureau, 1997 Economic Census, ECON97 Report Series CD-ROM, CD-EC97-1, Disc 1E, issued February 2001 (related Internet site <http://www.census.gov/epcd/www/97EC42.HTM>). Retail Trade—U.S. Census Bureau, 1997 Economic Census, ECON97 Report Series CD-ROM, CD-EC97-1, Disc 1E, issued February 2001 (related Internet site <http://www.census.gov/epcd/www/97EC44.HTM>).

Table B–11. Counties — Wholesale Trade and Retail Trade–Con.

[Includes U.S., states, and 3,142 counties/county equivalents defined as of January 1, 1992. For changes to these areas since January 1, 1992, see appendix B. Geographic Information]

County	Wholesale trade[1] (NAICS 42), 1997						Retail trade[1] (NAICS 44-45), 1997							
	Sales							Sales					Annual payroll	
									Per capita[3]		Percent from general merchandise stores			
	Establishments	Total (mil. dol.)	Merchant wholesalers (mil. dol.)	Paid employees[2]	Annual payroll (mil. dol.)	Operating expenses (mil. dol.)	Establishments	Total (mil. dol.)	Amount (dollars)	Percent of national average		Paid employees[2]	Total (mil. dol.)	Per paid employee (dollars)
VIRGINIA	7 868	61 046.7	34 446.6	106 365	3 784.4	7 276.7	29 032	62 569.9	9 293	101.1	13.8	379 039	6 202.6	16 364
Accomack	36	47.1	37.1	250	5.5	10.7	208	180.5	5 622	61.2	D	1 335	18.6	13 966
Albemarle	64	181.6	D	547	20.5	31.8	314	718.0	9 251	100.7	20.1	4 270	67.4	15 775
Alleghany	8	2.8	2.8	31	.7	1.2	38	65.3	5 345	58.2	D	430	6.1	14 119
Amelia	9	41.1	41.1	167	4.8	11.2	36	41.0	4 018	43.7	3.7	226	4.0	17 584
Amherst	18	D	D	(4)	D	D	104	190.2	6 356	69.2	18.0	1 082	18.0	16 628
Appomattox	9	5.7	D	50	.9	2.0	60	75.5	5 817	63.3	4.6	536	8.3	15 550
Arlington	110	819.8	440.9	1 208	57.2	93.6	665	1 819.4	10 448	113.7	D	10 098	188.7	18 685
Augusta	54	153.8	130.3	622	16.8	32.0	214	310.8	5 205	56.6	D	1 925	29.4	15 249
Bath	2	D	D	(5)	D	D	25	10.8	2 218	24.1	D	105	1.2	11 400
Bedford	34	281.9	D	170	4.8	10.3	92	83.0	1 511	10.4	D	604	10.0	16 483
Bland	6	D	D	(4)	D	D	18	19.8	2 909	31.7	–	145	1.4	9 986
Botetourt	34	213.9	185.8	464	12.5	23.0	81	130.2	4 612	50.2	D	796	11.0	13 827
Brunswick	7	27.6	D	54	1.3	2.5	60	49.6	2 980	32.4	3.1	455	5.3	11 657
Buchanan	34	140.3	D	296	8.7	20.7	130	135.2	4 607	50.1	D	1 018	13.7	13 504
Buckingham	5	6.6	6.6	16	.3	.8	42	34.4	2 359	25.7	10.8	254	3.7	14 720
Campbell	53	D	D	(6)	D	D	209	338.0	6 756	73.5	D	2 169	31.3	14 413
Caroline	16	27.8	27.8	74	2.0	6.0	69	118.4	5 460	59.4	1.9	608	8.5	13 929
Carroll	25	42.9	D	164	3.2	7.5	114	162.6	5 839	63.5	3.6	957	13.8	14 370
Charles City	1	D	NA	(5)	D	D	6	3.3	482	5.2	–	24	.3	11 667
Charlotte	10	18.4	18.4	108	2.4	4.8	46	42.2	3 467	37.7	3.2	286	3.7	12 776
Chesterfield	372	1 447.5	803.2	3 154	116.3	214.0	938	2 412.6	9 762	106.2	18.5	15 275	230.7	15 104
Clarke	13	D	D	(7)	D	D	44	44.8	3 519	38.3	D	297	3.7	12 579
Craig	3	.5	.5	5	.1	.2	8	3.7	754	8.2	–	25	.3	11 880
Culpeper	24	122.5	D	287	7.6	13.4	153	307.0	9 459	102.9	D	1 812	28.4	15 655
Cumberland	6	2.1	2.1	22	.3	.6	29	31.4	4 034	43.9	D	230	3.6	15 622
Dickenson	6	4.7	4.7	30	1.2	1.4	71	64.2	3 739	40.7	3.8	447	6.1	13 747
Dinwiddie	9	D	D	(4)	D	D	44	64.5	2 580	28.1	D	514	6.0	11 761
Essex	7	21.4	D	46	1.2	2.7	68	126.0	13 704	149.1	D	787	12.1	15 362
Fairfax	1 142	15 659.4	6 916.4	18 462	944.7	1 754.3	3 025	9 261.0	10 094	109.8	12.4	48 037	980.6	20 414
Fauquier	45	171.6	D	434	13.8	26.6	223	353.1	6 677	72.7	D	2 052	36.6	17 812
Floyd	6	10.7	10.7	18	.4	1.0	45	55.3	4 254	46.3	3.5	364	4.3	11 712
Fluvanna	10	D	4.8	(7)	D	D	33	24.5	1 377	15.0	D	196	2.6	13 372
Franklin	33	85.4	D	186	5.2	8.8	180	257.7	5 861	63.8	D	1 707	23.4	13 681
Frederick	82	302.0	D	1 246	33.2	55.1	211	464.7	8 522	92.7	13.1	2 574	46.1	17 901
Giles	6	D	2.2	(7)	D	D	71	91.2	5 045	61.4	0.4	563	8.2	14 531
Gloucester	30	42.5	40.7	360	5.6	11.7	134	228.1	6 636	72.2	D	1 505	20.7	13 779
Goochland	25	72.8	D	168	4.9	9.4	50	72.5	4 253	46.3	D	391	6.7	17 161
Grayson	3	.9	.9	5	.1	.4	38	33.4	2 037	22.2	4.5	176	2.3	12 790
Greene	5	D	D	(7)	D	D	37	33.8	2 527	27.5	D	254	4.1	16 087
Greensville	10	18.4	D	45	.9	2.0	26	23.0	2 087	22.7	D	179	1.9	10 352
Halifax	24	76.9	63.1	262	5.3	12.9	164	215.9	5 863	63.8	16.3	1 570	20.6	13 112
Hanover	240	3 044.5	2 306.2	4 199	150.2	291.4	309	830.0	10 473	114.0	D	4 693	80.6	17 176
Henrico	474	5 902.5	2 796.5	7 602	310.0	586.3	1 148	2 974.4	12 329	134.2	18.1	19 119	302.4	15 819
Henry	45	136.4	94.0	408	9.8	20.3	240	346.3	6 169	67.1	D	2 263	30.7	13 556
Highland	5	D	D	(5)	D	D	18	4.1	1 606	17.5	–	36	.3	9 417
Isle of Wight	28	D	D	(4)	D	D	97	141.9	4 965	54.0	2.8	1 049	12.4	11 837
James City	27	27.0	13.1	71	2.2	4.2	190	303.8	7 024	76.4	D	2 064	31.0	15 000
King and Queen	1	D	D	(7)	D	D	9	5.2	805	8.8	–	40	.5	11 650
King George	7	7.3	D	46	.9	1.9	48	53.2	3 151	34.3	D	306	4.8	15 624
King William	7	D	D	(4)	D	D	58	88.8	7 125	77.5	D	485	8.9	18 353
Lancaster	26	38.4	D	171	3.4	8.4	89	98.5	8 726	95.0	3.2	687	10.9	15 821
Lee	18	47.0	33.4	171	1.5	3.3	90	86.4	3 589	39.1	3.1	578	7.7	13 306
Loudoun	177	1 301.3	D	1 773	70.8	137.2	478	1 282.0	9 555	104.0	D	6 933	129.0	18 601
Louisa	14	29.1	D	105	2.9	5.6	73	77.7	3 257	35.4	4.7	530	7.4	13 879
Lunenburg	11	25.9	D	55	1.3	3.5	56	39.7	3 268	35.6	4.9	368	4.9	13 277
Madison	9	7.6	D	30	.6	1.2	48	86.9	6 949	75.6	D	418	7.4	17 699
Mathews	9	D	D	(7)	D	D	42	33.5	3 677	40.0	D	287	3.6	12 582
Mecklenburg	38	71.1	D	230	4.9	10.3	200	272.5	8 796	95.7	12.2	2 109	26.3	12 461
Middlesex	17	26.2	D	121	2.7	5.5	53	48.4	5 051	55.0	D	358	5.4	15 142
Montgomery	39	169.8	D	581	16.6	48.5	355	749.7	9 922	108.0	D	4 976	74.4	14 942
Nelson	7	6.1	D	13	.3	.7	51	27.6	2 004	21.8	D	225	2.6	11 604
New Kent	9	D	D	(7)	D	D	39	53.7	4 289	46.7	–	412	4.9	11 927
Northampton	22	D	D	(8)	D	D	79	73.0	5 716	62.2	18.7	594	7.5	12 603
Northumberland	13	D	D	(8)	D	D	54	42.4	3 722	40.5	D	338	5.0	14 831
Nottoway	14	D	D	(8)	D	D	80	86.3	5 732	62.4	3.3	676	8.8	13 009
Orange	23	68.4	55.4	163	4.1	7.8	104	160.1	6 426	69.9	3.1	946	15.8	16 655
Page	13	4.5	D	49	.7	1.5	83	97.2	4 256	46.3	D	645	8.9	13 730
Patrick	11	24.5	24.5	194	3.7	5.6	59	66.1	3 618	39.4	3.9	432	6.1	14 086
Pittsylvania	46	D	D	(4)	D	D	213	300.5	5 334	58.0	D	2 170	27.9	12 865
Powhatan	21	D	11.3	(7)	D	D	55	78.8	3 826	41.6	D	391	7.3	18 645

[1] Includes only establishments with payroll. [2] For pay period including March 12. [3] Based on resident population estimated as of July 1, 1997. [4] 250 to 499 employees. [5] 0 to 19 employees. [6] 500 to 999 employees. [7] 20 to 99 employees. [8] 100 to 249 employees.

Sources: Wholesale Trade—U.S. Census Bureau, 1997 Economic Census, ECON97 Report Series CD-ROM, CD-EC97-1, Disc 1E, issued February 2001 (related Internet site <http://www.census.gov/epcd/www/97EC42.HTM>). Retail Trade—U.S. Census Bureau, 1997 Economic Census, ECON97 Report Series CD-ROM, CD-EC97-1, Disc 1E, issued February 2001 (related Internet site <http://www.census.gov/epcd/www/97EC44.HTM>).

Table B–11. Counties — Wholesale Trade and Retail Trade-Con.

[Includes U.S., states, and 3,142 counties/county equivalents defined as of January 1, 1992. For changes to these areas since January 1, 1992, see appendix B. Geographic Information]

County	Wholesale trade[1] (NAICS 42), 1997						Retail trade[1] (NAICS 44-45), 1997							
	Sales							Sales					Annual payroll	
									Per capita[3]					
	Establishments	Total (mil. dol.)	Merchant wholesalers (mil. dol.)	Paid employees[2]	Annual payroll (mil. dol.)	Operating expenses (mil. dol.)	Establishments	Total (mil. dol.)	Amount (dollars)	Percent of national average	Percent from general merchandise stores	Paid employees[2]	Total (mil. dol.)	Per paid employee (dollars)
VIRGINIA—Con.														
Prince Edward	20	30.9	25.2	143	3.4	6.5	125	267.4	14 163	154.1	24.6	1 703	24.4	14 356
Prince George	16	62.4	62.4	189	5.8	10.4	66	91.8	3 250	35.4	D	632	8.4	13 285
Prince William	150	1 191.2	684.7	1 736	61.7	117.9	915	2 563.1	10 021	109.0	12.0	13 936	240.5	17 257
Pulaski	21	152.0	53.7	299	7.9	19.6	133	250.9	7 296	79.4	13.5	1 541	21.6	14 038
Rappahannock	6	D	D	(4)	D	D	33	49.0	6 799	74.0	D	244	4.3	17 455
Richmond	17	18.7	D	89	2.2	4.6	49	62.6	7 266	79.1	13.0	460	5.8	12 635
Roanoke	95	399.4	226.4	796	24.5	46.4	202	461.8	5 688	61.9	4.3	2 559	41.7	16 293
Rockbridge	10	D	D	(4)	D	D	79	165.3	8 621	93.8	7.6	961	13.9	14 492
Rockingham	57	539.7	D	1 140	30.6	48.5	242	356.2	5 616	61.1	.8	2 075	35.4	17 048
Russell	15	93.9	93.9	98	2.6	5.5	102	154.2	5 318	57.9	3.7	910	14.5	15 934
Scott	11	D	D	(5)	D	D	91	143.0	6 293	68.5	3.0	788	11.0	13 952
Shenandoah	24	85.9	D	241	4.9	9.6	158	279.3	8 180	89.0	2.0	1 574	23.6	14 980
Smyth	25	65.7	D	237	6.8	13.8	170	232.1	7 057	76.8	14.4	1 560	20.8	13 314
Southampton	17	D	D	(5)	D	D	56	41.3	2 338	25.4	5.9	378	4.6	12 063
Spotsylvania	67	686.0	D	821	19.5	34.7	261	737.6	9 161	99.7	25.2	4 038	66.6	16 497
Stafford	47	D	D	(6)	D	D	202	413.5	4 820	52.4	D	2 336	39.7	17 001
Surry	3	8.6	D	52	.8	1.4	17	8.9	1 386	15.1	-	84	1.0	12 274
Sussex	14	30.7	30.7	106	2.1	4.9	47	71.5	7 108	77.3	2.6	358	5.6	15 774
Tazewell	81	215.1	207.1	781	15.8	33.0	267	565.5	12 079	131.4	20.5	3 193	47.2	14 775
Warren	18	D	D	(4)	D	D	142	199.7	6 670	72.6	10.7	1 354	19.6	14 450
Washington	51	847.5	625.8	1 125	29.3	47.1	253	408.9	8 323	90.6	10.7	2 609	40.8	15 652
Westmoreland	17	35.9	D	64	1.6	3.6	71	83.4	5 127	55.8	D	546	8.0	14 626
Wise	46	177.5	D	354	9.7	19.6	183	310.9	7 925	86.2	11.5	1 961	28.3	14 411
Wythe	21	73.0	D	184	4.9	9.2	204	346.1	13 149	143.1	5.7	1 933	27.2	14 054
York	45	137.9	D	415	10.5	20.6	255	326.9	5 767	62.8	D	2 681	32.6	12 146
Independent Cities														
Alexandria	137	899.6	395.0	1 830	75.1	146.6	593	1 507.6	13 261	144.3	D	7 746	160.0	20 651
Bedford	19	D	D	(5)	D	D	81	136.3	21 704	236.2	D	975	13.5	13 840
Bristol	40	D	D	(7)	D	D	155	331.7	19 296	210.0	34.0	2 266	29.2	12 888
Buena Vista	2	D	D	(4)	D	D	32	33.2	5 076	55.2	-	257	3.5	13 790
Charlottesville	81	265.9	D	954	29.7	63.2	360	730.3	19 304	210.1	D	4 345	73.2	16 850
Chesapeake	246	1 768.2	1 069.1	3 833	115.7	233.6	779	1 993.3	10 171	110.7	21.4	12 554	184.5	14 695
Clifton Forge	2	D	D	(4)	D	D	34	47.4	10 913	118.7	D	321	4.6	14 287
Colonial Heights	12	D	D	(4)	D	D	205	496.4	30 410	330.9	D	3 776	46.5	12 326
Covington	9	15.3	15.3	44	1.1	2.0	61	90.4	12 805	139.3	4.6	539	7.9	14 588
Danville	55	211.8	D	964	22.6	42.7	334	585.5	11 159	121.4	17.7	3 787	56.9	15 026
Emporia	8	D	D	(5)	D	D	81	97.3	16 519	179.7	D	714	9.7	13 543
Fairfax	48	515.2	114.2	519	22.3	42.7	305	1 288.0	62 760	682.9	6.2	5 870	115.5	19 680
Falls Church	22	D	D	(5)	D	D	120	355.6	37 317	406.1	D	1 536	34.7	22 570
Franklin	7	48.9	D	121	2.3	4.5	57	95.0	10 792	117.4	D	635	9.3	14 720
Fredericksburg	53	427.3	327.8	723	23.3	47.3	317	567.3	27 071	294.6	D	3 701	60.7	16 403
Galax	6	6.0	D	42	1.0	2.0	71	134.6	20 153	219.3	D	906	12.6	13 891
Hampton	94	370.7	D	1 073	31.3	57.2	514	1 638.9	11 804	128.4	18.5	9 930	150.5	15 161
Harrisonburg	62	749.2	D	971	25.5	88.8	308	690.8	20 570	223.8	21.0	4 161	64.0	15 381
Hopewell	18	92.7	D	268	9.5	19.5	83	100.9	4 489	48.8	D	754	10.6	14 024
Lexington	5	16.9	D	27	1.4	3.4	68	108.9	14 952	162.7	D	686	9.6	14 042
Lynchburg	100	504.6	298.1	1 292	43.8	86.3	446	1 228.5	18 869	205.3	15.3	7 209	115.8	16 061
Manassas	59	626.3	524.7	1 008	41.0	66.8	230	647.5	20 115	218.9	16.2	3 355	64.9	19 349
Manassas Park	13	36.7	D	180	6.4	13.5	16	28.7	3 852	41.9	D	142	2.9	20 683
Martinsville	23	143.7	D	202	6.9	13.3	142	248.8	16 020	174.3	31.9	1 927	25.3	13 109
Newport News	132	604.2	482.9	1 634	50.3	99.3	681	1 488.6	8 516	92.7	13.1	9 284	143.6	15 465
Norfolk	324	2 914.6	2 003.5	5 845	183.9	361.9	918	1 900.4	8 069	87.8	15.0	12 628	207.3	16 416
Norton	15	174.9	D	292	9.9	20.1	66	127.8	31 407	341.8	D	921	11.9	12 934
Petersburg	35	139.2	D	538	16.8	32.0	189	290.0	8 229	89.5	D	1 764	29.5	16 735
Poquoson	11	D	D	(4)	D	D	28	29.8	2 627	28.6	-	247	3.0	12 121
Portsmouth	63	167.3	141.1	712	23.6	44.5	295	468.4	4 712	51.3	3.5	3 291	51.2	15 562
Radford	8	51.7	D	296	3.3	7.0	58	79.2	5 054	55.0	D	561	8.6	15 415
Richmond	464	5 979.5	3 318.3	7 572	283.5	539.0	1 013	1 738.1	9 112	99.2	D	11 579	193.5	16 708
Roanoke	299	1 292.7	796.5	3 768	121.0	229.9	792	1 843.7	19 422	211.3	D	12 425	191.3	15 393
Salem	86	635.8	280.6	1 809	58.6	93.0	174	452.5	18 761	204.1	D	3 089	51.8	16 768
South Boston	X	X	X	X	X	X	X	X	X	X	X	X	X	X
Staunton	33	132.0	D	327	7.4	17.4	168	330.5	13 492	146.8	27.0	2 213	32.0	14 467
Suffolk	61	822.5	344.6	1 305	43.7	87.2	212	380.0	6 214	67.6	D	2 697	38.0	14 074
Virginia Beach	479	1 922.8	1 506.5	5 642	159.4	300.6	1 621	3 342.7	7 754	84.4	13.6	21 987	337.2	15 337
Waynesboro	21	D	D	(5)	D	D	115	216.6	11 261	122.5	11.6	1 512	22.2	14 655
Williamsburg	16	D	D	(4)	D	D	163	330.2	27 130	295.2	D	2 262	33.7	14 890
Winchester	39	301.1	D	569	16.4	45.9	283	571.3	25 519	277.7	D	3 667	58.7	16 007

[1] Includes only establishments with payroll. [2] For pay period including March 12. [3] Based on resident population estimated as of July 1, 1997. [4] 20 to 99 employees. [5] 100 to 249 employees. [6] 1,000 to 2,499 employees. [7] 500 to 999 employees.

Sources: Wholesale Trade—U.S. Census Bureau, 1997 Economic Census, ECON97 Report Series CD-ROM, CD-EC97-1, Disc 1E, issued February 2001 (related Internet site <http://www.census.gov/epcd/www/97EC42.HTM>). Retail Trade—U.S. Census Bureau, 1997 Economic Census, ECON97 Report Series CD-ROM, CD-EC97-1, Disc 1E, issued February 2001 (related Internet site <http://www.census.gov/epcd/www/97EC44.HTM>).

Table B–11. Counties — Wholesale Trade and Retail Trade–Con.

[Includes U.S., states, and 3,142 counties/county equivalents defined as of January 1, 1992. For changes to these areas since January 1, 1992, see appendix B. Geographic Information]

County	Wholesale trade[1] (NAICS 42), 1997 — Sales — Establishments	Total (mil. dol.)	Merchant wholesalers (mil. dol.)	Paid employees[2]	Annual payroll (mil. dol.)	Operating expenses (mil. dol.)	Retail trade[1] (NAICS 44-45), 1997 — Sales — Establishments	Total (mil. dol.)	Per capita[3] Amount (dollars)	Per capita[3] Percent of national average	Percent from general merchandise stores	Paid employees[2]	Annual payroll Total (mil. dol.)	Annual payroll Per paid employee (dollars)
WASHINGTON	10 039	75 397.8	47 863.7	118 810	4 376.0	8 684.1	22 841	52 472.9	9 363	101.9	14.2	283 653	5 385.9	18 988
Adams	36	158.5	D	408	11.2	23.7	71	100.2	6 544	71.2	D	526	9.7	18 511
Asotin	15	D	264.1	(4)	D	D	66	160.1	7 631	83.0	D	714	13.7	19 188
Benton	106	305.3	264.1	1 050	22.7	47.4	574	1 208.8	8 940	97.3	14.1	7 091	115.6	16 302
Chelan	115	782.5	552.2	1 760	53.1	107.0	415	697.7	11 727	127.6	18.5	4 030	73.3	18 185
Clallam	51	299.8	D	358	11.0	22.2	292	453.6	7 129	77.6		2 990	50.3	16 818
Clark	458	2 138.8	1 410.3	3 751	137.3	314.6	868	2 214.7	6 971	75.9		12 284	230.9	18 796
Columbia	14	D	D	(5)	D	D	29	23.2	5 512	60.0	D	147	2.5	17 224
Cowlitz	81	D	D	(6)	D	D	414	811.5	8 956	97.5	18.4	4 744	82.1	17 315
Douglas	31	81.8	81.8	188	5.6	10.3	91	184.9	5 615	61.1	D	1 109	17.4	15 712
Ferry	2	D	D	(7)	D	D	32	33.9	4 679	50.9		212	2.0	10 566
Franklin	93	550.7	436.1	1 111	33.0	69.5	196	487.4	10 678	116.2	D	2 205	45.9	20 828
Garfield	5	D	D	(4)	D	D	12	10.9	4 738	51.6	—	75	1.2	16 107
Grant	109	365.5	289.0	1 089	28.5	60.4	326	576.4	8 349	90.8	9.2	3 291	58.0	17 619
Grays Harbor	68	139.0	136.7	566	15.9	32.8	324	473.4	6 960	75.7	14.5	3 005	52.0	17 294
Island	33	40.9	D	126	3.2	6.8	231	311.9	4 375	47.6	3.1	2 000	33.5	16 763
Jefferson	23	D	D	(5)	D	D	149	146.0	5 677	61.8	D	974	14.3	14 718
King	4 937	50 226.1	D	63 696	2 641.6	5 204.6	7 031	19 399.8	11 871	129.2	20.1	99 542	2 025.3	20 346
Kitsap	135	330.9	213.9	925	29.9	60.4	773	1 722.1	7 393	80.4		10 338	179.5	17 365
Kittitas	36	129.9	D	350	9.2	15.5	178	230.8	7 367	80.2	D	1 427	23.0	16 085
Klickitat	22	33.9	D	120	2.2	5.2	69	47.4	2 501	27.2	D	346	5.4	15 494
Lewis	90	D	D	(6)	D	D	388	597.7	8 851	96.3	D	3 699	63.5	17 158
Lincoln	37	131.4	D	272	7.3	15.0	54	57.2	5 905	64.3	—	305	4.9	16 030
Mason	35	105.1	D	271	8.8	17.2	148	233.5	4 713	51.3	13.9	1 530	21.9	14 327
Okanogan	44	368.7	D	1 472	20.5	37.8	204	263.2	6 885	74.9	D	1 657	25.9	15 605
Pacific	14	D	D	(4)	D	D	115	87.1	4 149	45.1	8.6	680	11.0	16 115
Pend Oreille	5	D	D	(7)	D	D	44	35.8	3 185	34.7	D	247	3.3	13 219
Pierce	781	4 618.9	3 741.5	9 324	327.0	637.2	2 289	5 468.2	8 248	89.7	14.3	28 956	550.1	18 998
San Juan	17	D	D	(5)	D	D	115	81.7	6 709	73.0	1.6	561	10.1	18 007
Skagit	122	344.4	D	1 018	30.2	62.9	614	1 070.7	11 024	120.0	D	6 096	107.0	17 552
Skamania	2	D	D	(7)	D	D	15	14.2	1 464	15.9	—	137	1.7	12 109
Snohomish	755	3 561.6	D	6 808	232.3	475.5	2 027	5 303.0	9 359	101.8	15.5	26 302	524.2	19 931
Spokane	788	4 878.5	3 457.7	11 268	360.9	671.3	1 730	4 122.6	10 165	110.6	17.6	22 246	433.9	19 503
Stevens	28	39.8	D	133	3.2	6.7	141	184.0	4 684	51.0	19.0	1 230	18.6	14 990
Thurston	201	580.3	433.2	1 805	57.5	104.5	730	1 616.8	8 096	88.1		9 008	166.3	18 463
Wahkiakum	NA	NA	NA	NA	NA	NA	14	7.3	1 896	20.6	D	62	.9	13 758
Walla Walla	78	318.1	D	726	16.4	38.1	222	376.4	7 200	76.4	16.2	2 426	41.9	17 268
Whatcom	308	1 042.7	899.0	2 451	76.0	170.0	840	1 673.3	10 803	117.6		9 758	165.7	16 976
Whitman	73	D	D	(6)	D	D	156	243.9	6 342	69.0	D	1 520	24.0	15 759
Yakima	291	1 853.8	1 460.9	4 871	141.9	272.9	854	1 741.6	8 057	87.7	18.5	10 174	174.9	17 186
WEST VIRGINIA	1 956	10 290.4	6 503.4	23 805	681.1	1 396.6	8 082	14 057.9	7 743	84.3	16.2	90 087	1 309.3	14 534
Barbour	9	12.7	12.7	75	1.2	2.8	57	69.3	4 318	47.0	D	509	6.7	13 218
Berkeley	52	D	D	(8)	D	D	335	546.7	7 917	86.1	D	4 000	52.2	13 062
Boone	19	52.9	D	121	3.5	7.3	110	146.3	5 544	60.3	D	984	14.4	14 676
Braxton	17	38.8	D	119	3.5	8.6	87	111.1	8 402	91.4	3.1	678	10.2	14 987
Brooke	10	D	D	(4)	D	D	86	91.3	3 488	38.0	6.5	684	8.7	12 693
Cabell	169	D	760.9	(8)	D	D	553	1 120.1	11 771	128.1	D	7 592	113.1	14 895
Calhoun	1	D	D	(7)	D	D	29	20.7	2 617	28.5	12.0	168	1.9	11 417
Clay	1	D	D	(7)	D	D	33	37.9	3 604	39.2	D	208	2.6	12 611
Doddridge	2	D	D	(7)	D	D	15	7.0	946	10.3	D	47	.6	12 979
Fayette	29	84.6	66.2	402	11.4	22.4	206	328.6	6 882	74.9	17.7	2 103	31.3	14 893
Gilmer	5	5.7	5.7	16	.3	.8	25	23.4	3 292	35.8	9.2	164	2.3	14 317
Grant	8	D	D	(5)	D	D	54	53.0	4 770	51.9	3.8	349	4.9	14 097
Greenbrier	32	47.0	38.4	211	5.0	9.8	217	329.0	9 277	100.9	19.8	2 176	31.1	14 285
Hampshire	14	11.5	11.5	67	1.2	2.8	59	67.8	3 584	39.0	3.5	440	5.9	13 343
Hancock	21	42.6	D	133	3.5	7.4	135	206.0	6 001	65.3	21.4	1 682	20.2	11 998
Hardy	5	D	D	(5)	D	D	50	53.2	4 537	49.4	D	426	6.0	14 077
Harrison	91	452.2	178.5	1 434	43.2	88.5	391	766.7	10 784	117.3	18.0	4 956	70.2	14 173
Jackson	28	145.5	137.7	394	8.9	19.6	115	293.5	10 622	115.6	14.7	1 442	23.2	16 066
Jefferson	19	D	D	(4)	D	D	142	197.7	4 840	52.7	D	1 291	21.0	16 283
Kanawha	388	2 162.1	D	4 807	146.8	288.3	976	2 428.6	11 952	130.1	15.9	14 450	217.7	15 067
Lewis	15	26.8	D	125	2.9	6.7	89	143.6	8 206	89.3	D	946	12.7	13 438
Lincoln	5	D	D	(5)	D	D	51	52.3	2 358	25.7	D	358	4.7	13 196
Logan	46	158.7	D	398	11.4	26.3	204	335.7	8 133	88.5	13.0	1 996	31.0	15 506
McDowell	14	157.6	D	102	3.0	5.5	97	108.3	3 542	38.5	D	860	11.9	13 856

[1] Includes only establishments with payroll. [2] For pay period including March 12. [3] Based on resident population estimated as of July 1, 1997. [4] 100 to 249 employees. [5] 20 to 99 employees. [6] 500 to 999 employees. [7] 0 to 19 employees. [8] 1,000 to 2,499 employees.

Sources: Wholesale Trade—U.S. Census Bureau, 1997 Economic Census, ECON97 Report Series CD-ROM, CD-EC97-1, Disc 1E, issued February 2001 (related Internet site <http://www.census.gov/epcd/www/97EC42.HTM>). Retail Trade—U.S. Census Bureau, 1997 Economic Census, ECON97 Report Series CD-ROM, CD-EC97-1, Disc 1E, issued February 2001 (related Internet site <http://www.census.gov/epcd/www/97EC44.HTM>).

Table B–11. Counties — Wholesale Trade and Retail Trade—Con.

[Includes U.S., states, and 3,142 counties/county equivalents defined as of January 1, 1992. For changes to these areas since January 1, 1992, see appendix B. Geographic Information]

County	Wholesale trade[1] (NAICS 42), 1997						Retail trade[1] (NAICS 44-45), 1997							
	Sales							Sales					Annual payroll	
									Per capita[3]		Percent from general merchandise stores			
	Estab-lishments	Total (mil. dol.)	Merchant whole-salers (mil. dol.)	Paid em-ployees[2]	Annual payroll (mil. dol.)	Operating expenses (mil. dol.)	Estab-lishments	Total (mil. dol.)	Amount (dollars)	Percent of national average		Paid em-ployees[2]	Total (mil. dol.)	Per paid employee (dollars)
WEST VIRGINIA—Con.														
Marion	67	154.8	112.8	695	18.3	38.1	236	421.5	7 409	80.6	D	2 567	35.7	13 911
Marshall	21	D	D	(4)	D	D	114	204.3	5 756	62.6	D	1 523	18.3	12 011
Mason	6	47.9	47.9	75	1.9	10.8	80	79.5	3 064	33.3	3.8	557	7.2	12 883
Mercer	72	354.4	143.9	1 265	31.1	54.6	321	588.2	9 099	99.0	16.1	3 683	53.0	14 394
Mineral	18	D	D	(4)	D	D	103	142.7	5 284	57.5	32.2	982	12.6	12 821
Mingo	30	54.0	D	234	5.7	13.6	122	176.1	5 420	59.0	3.6	1 006	15.9	15 764
Monongalia	81	439.0	D	688	19.7	38.3	373	677.2	8 708	94.8	19.0	4 750	70.5	14 849
Monroe	10	14.1	D	56	.9	2.0	37	27.7	2 112	23.0	D	192	2.1	11 078
Morgan	7	D	D	(5)	D	D	53	59.7	4 404	47.9	D	355	6.2	17 454
Nicholas	31	64.1	D	255	5.9	13.4	139	213.7	7 752	84.4	15.8	1 333	18.6	13 984
Ohio	110	D	D	(6)	D	D	247	387.0	7 953	86.5	D	2 706	43.2	15 973
Pendleton	5	2.9	2.9	24	.3	.6	33	29.4	3 657	39.8	6.4	210	2.8	13 305
Pleasants	3	D	D	(7)	D	D	28	41.8	5 585	60.8	D	248	3.5	14 282
Pocahontas	4	8.7	D	25	.4	1.0	55	46.4	5 134	55.9	2.7	373	4.5	12 040
Preston	26	97.3	56.0	199	4.7	12.4	87	147.0	4 939	53.7	D	828	11.6	14 052
Putnam	60	423.2	D	1 255	43.4	79.2	201	365.0	7 250	78.9	10.4	2 119	30.1	14 185
Raleigh	131	378.1	302.2	1 146	32.8	76.0	390	826.8	10 460	113.8	20.4	4 889	75.9	15 519
Randolph	37	152.5	D	355	8.6	18.5	149	201.1	7 009	76.3	23.6	1 343	18.4	13 674
Ritchie	8	11.2	D	52	1.2	2.1	48	42.0	4 109	44.7	7.2	282	3.7	13 227
Roane	10	D	D	(5)	D	D	58	75.1	4 894	53.3	3.0	475	7.1	14 998
Summers	10	29.5	29.5	121	2.4	4.6	45	36.0	2 611	28.4	15.0	247	3.9	15 652
Taylor	5	D	9.8	(5)	D	D	47	55.7	3 636	39.6	D	318	4.5	14 233
Tucker	3	D	D	(7)	D	D	38	40.9	5 302	57.7	2.8	266	3.8	14 132
Tyler	2	D	D	(5)	D	D	32	25.6	2 563	27.9	D	191	2.1	11 058
Upshur	20	75.7	42.3	310	3.6	7.6	101	155.2	6 542	71.2	D	837	14.0	16 755
Wayne	31	D	D	(8)	D	D	111	168.5	4 004	43.6	D	1 127	15.4	13 687
Webster	7	D	D	(5)	D	D	32	31.2	3 027	32.9	D	212	2.8	13 297
Wetzel	14	32.7	32.7	69	1.4	4.1	112	145.5	7 875	85.7	D	1 070	14.1	13 131
Wirt	2	D	D	(7)	D	D	14	10.6	1 873	20.4	D	72	.7	10 125
Wood	116	489.8	D	1 357	34.0	71.8	462	990.2	11 364	123.7	24.0	6 058	91.0	15 029
Wyoming	9	47.9	D	53	1.7	3.7	98	108.4	3 918	42.6	11.9	759	11.3	14 928
WISCONSIN	8 025	57 192.9	35 760.6	110 309	3 764.9	7 173.4	21 717	50 520.5	9 715	105.7	13.4	305 255	4 826.2	15 810
Adams	11	28.0	D	146	2.8	5.3	37	64.7	3 560	38.7	D	327	5.5	16 768
Ashland	18	40.5	D	130	3.3	6.9	113	149.7	9 060	98.6	D	1 041	13.4	12 915
Barron	66	153.8	D	763	17.6	35.8	254	451.6	10 359	112.7	21.6	2 812	41.9	14 903
Bayfield	7	5.6	5.6	36	.8	1.5	66	51.0	3 359	36.6	D	328	4.2	12 771
Brown	461	2 848.1	1 810.7	6 480	212.1	411.4	950	2 569.1	12 000	130.6	19.9	14 976	239.7	16 008
Buffalo	17	47.6	D	180	4.2	7.5	46	45.7	3 208	34.9	D	305	3.8	12 351
Burnett	9	10.2	D	20	.5	1.5	71	77.1	5 311	57.8	5.1	530	7.6	14 323
Calumet	45	98.6	73.9	474	12.1	20.6	106	232.7	6 124	66.6	D	1 615	20.1	12 471
Chippewa	49	237.4	D	654	21.7	50.9	205	481.3	8 865	96.5	D	2 475	39.9	16 120
Clark	51	71.3	66.3	278	6.6	15.0	137	198.0	5 993	65.2	D	1 071	16.1	15 036
Columbia	64	352.5	206.3	735	18.5	39.7	228	407.4	8 083	88.0	D	2 434	37.7	15 477
Crawford	19	220.9	D	118	3.9	10.4	88	133.6	8 086	88.0	D	915	12.3	13 479
Dane	675	4 350.1	3 306.8	10 048	342.7	643.5	1 845	4 860.9	11 515	125.3	11.6	30 150	507.2	16 824
Dodge	86	528.9	437.8	1 087	33.7	68.3	277	544.2	6 609	71.9	16.8	3 220	49.6	15 404
Door	34	38.9	D	159	3.3	7.9	281	258.9	9 623	104.7	D	1 581	24.8	15 681
Douglas	59	D	D	(9)	D	D	161	334.1	7 754	84.4	D	2 075	31.1	14 974
Dunn	43	98.2	D	433	9.5	18.7	156	324.0	8 370	91.1	16.4	2 060	30.0	14 568
Eau Claire	135	613.5	D	1 463	42.2	77.4	459	1 036.0	11 621	126.5	D	7 405	100.7	13 600
Florence	5	D	D	(7)	D	D	12	15.1	2 882	31.4	–	78	.8	10 218
Fond du Lac	116	528.2	D	1 204	36.0	74.0	413	891.2	9 442	102.7	16.8	5 744	86.6	15 079
Forest	11	13.5	13.5	76	1.9	4.0	42	50.9	5 332	58.0	D	345	4.9	14 252
Grant	66	174.5	129.8	613	11.2	23.0	243	357.6	7 254	78.9	13.3	2 310	32.3	13 966
Green	66	208.8	D	588	14.1	33.1	181	572.9	17 305	188.3	8.6	3 025	66.3	21 917
Green Lake	19	32.6	26.3	149	3.8	5.8	113	161.4	8 332	90.7	D	1 297	15.7	12 069
Iowa	39	109.9	D	331	10.7	19.0	105	1 211.4	54 744	595.7	D	4 409	107.7	24 435
Iron	8	11.9	11.9	48	1.1	2.2	38	49.4	7 675	83.5	D	337	4.5	13 359
Jackson	10	8.7	8.7	74	1.1	2.0	83	124.7	7 075	77.0	D	919	11.6	12 674
Jefferson	92	466.5	288.1	1 483	42.2	84.6	253	568.2	7 750	84.3	12.3	3 519	53.1	15 076
Juneau	22	77.5	D	200	4.5	10.3	102	170.5	7 133	77.6	D	1 056	15.1	14 268
Kenosha	135	1 385.3	1 162.1	2 515	91.5	158.5	546	1 072.4	7 502	81.6	12.3	6 442	95.7	14 861
Kewaunee	20	35.5	35.5	139	3.4	6.5	72	113.6	5 776	62.9	D	655	10.3	15 675
La Crosse	154	1 921.6	D	3 217	102.5	178.4	509	1 452.6	14 230	154.8	D	9 005	135.6	15 063

[1] Includes only establishments with payroll. [2] For pay period including March 12. [3] Based on resident population estimated as of July 1, 1997. [4] 100 to 249 employees. [5] 20 to 99 employees. [6] 1,000 to 2,499 employees. [7] 0 to 19 employees. [8] 250 to 499 employees. [9] 500 to 999 employees.

Sources: Wholesale Trade—U.S. Census Bureau, 1997 Economic Census, ECON97 Report Series CD-ROM, CD-EC97-1, Disc 1E, issued February 2001 (related Internet site <http://www.census.gov/epcd/www/97EC42.HTM>). Retail Trade—U.S. Census Bureau, 1997 Economic Census, ECON97 Report Series CD-ROM, CD-EC97-1, Disc 1E, issued February 2001 (related Internet site <http://www.census.gov/epcd/www/97EC44.HTM>).

Table B–11. Counties — **Wholesale Trade and Retail Trade**–Con.

[Includes U.S., states, and 3,142 counties/county equivalents defined as of January 1, 1992. For changes to these areas since January 1, 1992, see appendix B. Geographic Information]

County	Wholesale trade[1] (NAICS 42), 1997						Retail trade[1] (NAICS 44-45), 1997							
	Sales			Paid employees[2]	Annual payroll (mil. dol.)	Operating expenses (mil. dol.)	Sales					Paid employees[2]	Annual payroll	
	Estab-lishments	Total (mil. dol.)	Merchant whole-salers (mil. dol.)				Estab-lishments	Total (mil. dol.)	Per capita[3]		Percent from general mer-chandise stores		Total (mil. dol.)	Per paid em-ployee (dollars)
									Amount (dollars)	Percent of national average				
WISCONSIN—Con.														
Lafayette	23	62.2	D	170	4.0	8.8	62	94.8	5 806	63.2	—	526	8.8	16 681
Langlade	39	217.8	211.5	348	11.0	22.9	114	255.7	12 440	135.4	D	1 270	20.5	16 154
Lincoln	25	D	D	(4)	D	D	142	220.1	7 452	81.1	D	1 504	20.6	13 714
Manitowoc	67	257.1	190.6	611	22.0	48.7	295	561.0	6 831	74.3	17.8	3 856	55.1	14 296
Marathon	221	1 002.0	725.1	3 395	102.5	181.1	565	1 421.6	11 630	126.6	16.7	9 236	142.6	15 438
Marinette	33	93.2	D	485	14.8	29.8	187	285.9	6 661	72.5	D	2 008	27.4	13 650
Marquette	10	D	D	(5)	D	D	47	56.6	3 789	41.2	D	444	5.6	12 532
Menominee	2	D	D	(6)	D	D	13	15.2	3 061	33.3	—	113	1.2	10 398
Milwaukee	1 393	13 007.5	7 363.2	22 559	845.3	1 610.3	3 224	8 065.2	8 786	95.6	D	52 471	839.2	15 994
Monroe	46	241.6	D	465	12.2	26.1	139	201.8	8 680	72.7	D	1 618	22.8	14 112
Oconto	28	45.1	38.1	121	3.8	7.5	118	178.6	5 353	58.2	D	1 017	14.2	13 962
Oneida	45	119.9	D	441	12.8	24.0	294	471.5	13 234	144.0	14.5	3 030	45.3	14 959
Outagamie	291	1 694.0	1 290.5	4 066	147.5	266.2	712	1 936.3	12 549	136.6	D	11 218	182.2	16 238
Ozaukee	204	627.1	340.9	1 314	49.6	93.7	352	940.1	11 651	126.8	7.1	4 453	75.3	16 921
Pepin	11	27.4	27.4	90	2.1	4.1	38	88.7	12 383	134.7	D	434	8.6	19 749
Pierce	29	D	D	(4)	D	D	112	151.6	4 316	47.0	D	1 047	13.6	13 000
Polk	38	112.5	D	432	11.0	26.4	183	221.6	5 792	63.0	D	1 552	19.7	12 699
Portage	93	380.9	295.6	1 307	39.8	90.2	262	603.2	9 332	101.5	D	3 916	56.8	14 493
Price	19	41.5	D	211	3.3	6.9	97	106.9	6 784	73.8	7.8	726	9.9	13 617
Racine	234	3 816.9	D	4 560	142.4	306.8	664	1 564.1	8 452	92.0	14.5	9 693	142.0	14 651
Richland	16	32.2	D	122	1.6	3.5	76	128.5	7 179	78.1	D	821	11.4	13 856
Rock	152	1 706.4	1 614.5	2 823	95.8	219.0	584	1 599.7	10 654	115.9	15.2	8 484	148.4	17 492
Rusk	9	4.8	4.8	35	.6	1.0	62	78.7	5 144	56.0	D	486	6.7	13 844
St. Croix	80	210.3	D	484	14.9	28.0	224	590.3	10 283	111.9	D	3 053	52.2	17 094
Sauk	68	426.4	415.3	1 090	33.6	67.1	295	582.6	10 987	119.6	12.5	4 083	62.2	15 243
Sawyer	8	23.8	23.8	79	3.4	5.8	100	133.6	8 333	90.7	D	778	12.0	15 434
Shawano	40	191.8	D	450	12.3	23.6	153	267.5	6 943	75.5	15.9	1 747	26.2	15 017
Sheboygan	119	1 185.0	889.3	2 041	65.4	113.7	398	911.0	8 298	90.3	D	5 831	88.0	15 099
Taylor	19	80.8	D	467	9.1	17.0	88	141.8	7 358	80.1	D	896	11.4	12 735
Trempealeau	39	125.6	D	215	5.2	11.8	126	169.4	6 417	69.8	D	1 017	13.5	13 294
Vernon	37	75.6	D	217	4.5	8.9	108	161.1	5 908	64.3	D	1 139	16.9	14 812
Vilas	20	17.0	12.4	69	1.5	3.6	150	122.8	5 827	63.4	D	764	12.8	16 712
Walworth	128	883.1	588.5	1 554	46.8	100.7	371	627.2	7 439	80.9	13.5	3 880	59.2	15 266
Washburn	16	21.9	21.9	90	2.1	3.6	90	173.0	11 408	124.1	D	975	15.4	15 779
Washington	181	1 107.9	1 004.9	2 658	97.0	181.2	390	1 201.5	10 679	116.2	D	5 184	86.0	16 595
Waukesha	1 272	11 523.8	5 074.4	16 570	672.1	1 181.6	1 385	4 094.2	11 751	127.9	14.7	24 345	392.4	16 117
Waupaca	58	116.3	D	406	9.5	17.4	242	416.3	8 316	90.5	13.2	2 473	36.8	14 868
Waushara	21	54.5	54.5	156	3.6	6.4	91	148.3	6 916	75.3	D	817	12.9	15 838
Winnebago	194	1 088.8	598.9	3 387	111.9	224.3	611	1 489.6	9 950	108.3	D	8 712	141.4	16 234
Wood	85	636.9	D	1 421	44.1	85.9	355	950.5	12 535	136.4	D	5 177	83.0	16 033
WYOMING	800	2 547.1	1 995.0	5 761	161.9	323.7	2 939	4 530.5	9 438	102.7	14.7	26 934	426.7	15 841
Albany	24	84.9	84.9	132	2.7	6.3	168	339.7	11 450	124.6	D	1 663	27.5	16 509
Big Horn	15	14.9	D	64	1.2	2.1	59	50.7	4 570	49.7	3.7	340	5.0	14 626
Campbell	78	235.4	209.1	658	22.9	39.9	179	280.3	8 739	95.1	D	1 733	28.0	16 140
Carbon	18	25.5	D	70	1.3	3.2	103	141.2	8 982	97.7	D	847	11.7	13 786
Converse	15	42.0	D	128	2.2	4.0	59	64.2	5 208	56.7	D	430	5.6	12 970
Crook	2	D	D	(7)	D	D	27	25.7	4 428	48.2	—	180	2.4	13 294
Fremont	43	85.2	D	260	3.9	8.9	204	296.8	8 229	89.5	13.5	1 735	27.8	16 043
Goshen	21	210.9	D	240	4.1	8.9	65	69.3	5 352	58.2	10.4	509	7.7	15 051
Hot Springs	3	D	D	(6)	D	D	32	20.4	4 339	47.2	D	229	2.2	9 546
Johnson	12	6.9	6.9	53	.9	1.9	56	38.5	5 701	62.0	D	287	3.9	13 697
Laramie	81	267.5	245.2	665	18.6	34.8	358	855.5	10 881	118.4	17.2	4 851	77.8	16 041
Lincoln	10	9.8	9.8	23	.5	1.2	80	86.4	6 250	68.0	3.4	623	7.3	11 690
Natrona	206	984.1	851.5	1 853	59.2	115.7	399	645.6	10 135	110.3	D	3 985	65.2	16 370
Niobrara	3	D	D	(7)	D	D	14	11.9	4 517	49.2	D	84	1.0	11 571
Park	44	51.8	D	178	4.1	9.8	219	271.3	10 573	115.0	15.9	1 528	24.5	16 024
Platte	8	D	D	(6)	D	D	46	68.5	8 010	87.2	D	374	4.8	12 869
Sheridan	40	146.1	110.8	246	6.4	14.4	179	240.8	9 576	104.2	D	1 561	23.9	15 294
Sublette	7	10.8	D	26	.6	1.4	33	26.4	4 672	50.8	D	189	2.7	14 397
Sweetwater	82	188.5	134.6	469	15.0	32.2	212	402.8	10 128	110.2	12.8	2 399	38.6	16 079
Teton	35	49.3	D	201	5.7	13.2	242	300.9	21 642	235.5	D	1 619	33.7	20 820
Uinta	32	73.2	71.1	226	7.3	15.4	96	174.5	8 608	93.7	D	1 027	15.0	14 618
Washakie	15	31.8	15.6	156	2.4	5.1	70	80.7	9 365	101.9	D	474	7.2	15 213
Weston	6	4.2	4.2	26	.9	1.6	39	38.4	5 892	64.1	D	267	3.3	12 382

[1] Includes only establishments with payroll. [2] For pay period including March 12. [3] Based on resident population estimated as of July 1, 1997. [4] 250 to 499 employees. [5] 100 to 249 employees. [6] 20 to 99 employees. [7] 0 to 19 employees.

Sources: Wholesale Trade—U.S. Census Bureau, 1997 Economic Census, ECON97 Report Series CD-ROM, CD-EC97-1, Disc 1E, issued February 2001 (related Internet site <http://www.census.gov/epcd/www/97EC42.HTM>). Retail Trade—U.S. Census Bureau, 1997 Economic Census, ECON97 Report Series CD-ROM, CD-EC97-1, Disc 1E, issued February 2001 (related Internet site <http://www.census.gov/epcd/www/97EC44.HTM>).

Table B–12. Counties — Accommodation and Foodservices, Banking, and Federal Funds

[Includes U.S., states, and 3,142 counties/county equivalents defined as of January 1, 1992. For changes to these areas since January 1, 1992, see appendix B. Geographic Information]

| County | Accommodation and foodservices[1] (NAICS 72), 1997 | | | | | Banking,[4] 1999 | | Federal funds and grants, 1999 | | | | | | |
| | Sales | | | Paid employ-ees[3] | Annual payroll ($1,000) | Offices | Deposits (mil. dol.) | Total expenditures or obligations (mil. dol.) | Percent change, 1990–1999 | Per capita[5] (dollars) | | | | |
	Estab-lishments	Total ($1,000)	Percent from food-services[2]							Total	Direct payments for individuals	Procure-ment contract awards	Salaries and wages	Grant awards
UNITED STATES	545 068	350 399 194	71.9	9 451 226	97 007 396	83 684	3 749 761.0	1 516 775.0	51.6	5 562	2 946	760	646	1 058
ALABAMA	6 955	3 881 782	84.0	134 719	1 059 642	1 419	52 700.3	26 775.6	54.3	6 127	3 449	846	640	1 060
Autauga	50	27 950	D	1 036	8 685	14	308.5	154.7	79.1	3 586	2 840	30	120	515
Baldwin	303	224 330	66.2	6 337	61 034	58	1 540.3	563.3	120.7	4 147	3 332	64	105	344
Barbour	42	17 254	75.4	600	4 283	14	304.4	130.2	61.2	4 873	3 316	41	147	1 195
Bibb	12	D	D	(6)	D	10	141.6	81.9	92.8	4 176	3 116	44	177	830
Blount	42	13 710	D	461	3 341	11	375.0	138.6	85.6	2 923	2 293	26	94	492
Bullock	12	D	D	(7)	D	3	114.3	61.1	76.0	5 383	3 248	33	171	1 842
Butler	31	17 190	84.1	595	4 843	9	211.1	121.7	105.8	5 656	3 581	30	121	1 852
Calhoun	185	114 365	88.6	4 262	31 272	32	1 132.0	865.7	22.0	7 429	4 205	1 356	1 253	588
Chambers	44	18 255	92.7	671	4 616	13	228.9	157.7	57.0	4 336	3 447	63	96	693
Cherokee	26	6 853	83.9	251	1 785	8	184.8	92.4	53.2	4 219	3 049	314	120	602
Chilton	50	18 371	87.0	744	4 972	12	319.7	142.4	80.6	3 787	2 912	25	96	719
Choctaw	15	5 594	83.2	233	1 457	6	176.5	78.9	43.7	5 087	3 293	266	127	1 385
Clarke	41	17 150	85.6	665	4 231	18	360.5	144.7	109.6	5 033	3 138	82	177	1 623
Clay	11	3 233	100.0	171	828	5	133.7	64.3	90.2	4 587	3 429	32	214	840
Cleburne	11	D	D	(7)	D	4	119.7	58.0	84.1	4 015	2 816	41	227	919
Coffee	63	26 863	89.5	1 092	7 234	14	409.9	405.2	32.9	9 618	3 852	4 655	302	610
Colbert	103	46 270	85.1	1 766	12 266	27	598.0	367.6	50.7	6 995	3 944	660	1 498	773
Conecuh	17	6 051	75.9	279	1 360	5	106.7	76.7	46.5	5 590	3 892	42	159	1 367
Coosa	3	D	D	(8)	D	2	22.9	46.9	74.6	4 001	3 081	94	141	673
Covington	58	20 067	86.7	830	4 955	9	493.9	196.5	62.8	5 227	3 826	58	198	1 014
Crenshaw	11	3 767	D	138	645	5	144.9	77.6	81.9	5 698	3 630	242	216	1 447
Cullman	94	52 758	93.2	1 980	14 377	27	810.2	306.0	89.3	4 045	3 226	32	152	611
Dale	82	26 900	85.1	1 204	6 980	15	253.6	455.5	17.0	9 271	4 030	364	4 197	585
Dallas	63	25 999	85.6	887	6 290	10	381.9	314.8	70.6	6 745	3 919	1 006	183	1 524
DeKalb	100	40 842	78.4	1 419	10 676	24	586.8	236.5	82.3	4 012	2 857	31	136	940
Elmore	62	33 091	D	1 117	9 077	19	415.0	236.5	89.8	3 725	3 035	30	131	478
Escambia	56	23 992	89.8	905	6 022	16	413.2	175.1	80.1	4 776	3 332	24	117	1 002
Etowah	169	85 035	91.5	3 223	23 603	26	886.7	481.9	58.8	4 658	3 664	66	155	740
Fayette	18	D	D	(6)	D	7	214.1	74.4	43.1	4 107	3 017	34	162	840
Franklin	44	12 710	93.7	529	3 262	18	461.5	148.4	78.7	4 995	3 542	30	142	1 231
Geneva	31	6 069	D	343	1 739	7	276.7	136.9	90.6	5 484	3 909	41	185	942
Greene	5	1 346	100.0	105	459	2	40.9	68.6	57.2	7 029	3 396	41	196	3 232
Hale	12	D	D	(7)	D	6	148.5	86.6	96.3	5 133	3 486	60	176	1 317
Henry	12	D	D	(7)	D	7	188.1	92.1	95.8	5 835	3 512	199	163	1 001
Houston	198	121 559	86.0	3 945	31 367	35	1 197.9	386.3	80.7	4 486	3 099	382	179	709
Jackson	70	25 936	88.9	848	6 851	22	502.2	348.7	118.0	6 767	3 226	1 913	652	890
Jefferson	1 197	796 095	82.0	25 250	225 209	191	14 689.1	3 775.1	66.9	5 742	3 579	406	706	992
Lamar	17	3 488	D	106	888	11	219.9	74.7	74.5	4 382	3 382	133	209	878
Lauderdale	146	67 231	95.5	2 558	19 479	38	1 236.9	364.1	74.8	4 318	3 400	45	190	599
Lawrence	33	13 489	87.1	524	3 589	11	183.0	123.9	83.8	3 666	2 302	31	144	912
Lee	199	110 294	80.5	4 165	29 560	31	977.6	329.9	58.2	3 229	2 118	85	206	794
Limestone	71	45 859	D	1 759	12 835	13	488.9	212.9	91.0	3 377	2 409	88	113	561
Lowndes	4	D	D	(8)	D	5	79.4	71.1	114.6	5 457	2 722	131	156	2 308
Macon	21	9 919	D	393	2 313	3	105.6	196.8	47.8	8 560	3 789	142	1 996	2 503
Madison	513	345 904	D	11 052	94 634	78	2 937.3	3 958.8	11.0	14 119	2 935	7 901	2 587	628
Marengo	34	12 649	84.5	465	3 199	12	321.8	114.1	79.3	4 925	3 040	220	181	1 374
Marion	41	D	D	(9)	D	18	463.0	155.1	74.4	5 092	3 178	78	147	1 595
Marshall	157	70 739	89.0	2 732	17 862	37	1 082.2	358.2	80.5	4 448	3 402	171	198	635
Mobile	649	370 123	83.0	12 767	102 236	103	3 793.8	1 900.4	48.5	4 755	3 161	335	369	763
Monroe	34	15 215	87.6	591	3 452	11	253.6	108.0	82.0	4 531	3 031	26	126	1 086
Montgomery	422	279 507	82.9	10 064	77 068	69	3 526.3	2 514.5	71.4	11 651	3 757	1 251	2 018	4 568
Morgan	185	101 119	87.6	3 752	28 967	38	1 282.0	489.1	13.8	4 460	2 942	81	836	566
Perry	11	2 970	D	178	816	3	105.0	70.8	59.8	5 613	3 499	38	184	1 675
Pickens	14	D	D	(7)	D	11	225.3	109.5	69.3	5 207	3 550	30	155	1 389
Pike	58	25 780	85.3	1 135	7 211	12	399.4	162.5	83.6	5 709	3 584	498	197	1 264
Randolph	27	7 955	100.0	335	2 228	10	235.3	101.4	32.7	5 005	3 555	370	122	940
Russell	71	32 154	92.7	938	8 344	17	364.3	230.9	77.2	4 612	3 575	28	106	849
St. Clair	78	31 337	D	1 170	8 392	20	463.0	185.8	92.3	2 910	2 428	30	96	347
Shelby	188	120 146	90.0	3 762	32 471	34	790.2	270.5	43.5	1 848	1 512	30	110	185
Sumter	21	6 961	89.7	327	1 959	4	108.6	81.0	22.2	5 189	3 110	69	168	1 773
Talladega	94	37 939	91.4	1 504	9 982	19	607.2	394.1	77.5	5 084	3 508	309	361	858
Tallapoosa	51	21 370	80.6	788	5 692	13	434.0	178.7	80.5	4 431	3 380	62	125	821
Tuscaloosa	317	202 525	82.5	7 396	55 562	43	1 753.8	697.6	61.9	4 321	2 770	218	403	900
Walker	93	43 519	94.5	1 650	10 786	24	815.1	404.3	93.9	5 670	4 000	35	151	1 462
Washington	13	D	D	(10)	D	5	114.5	78.7	43.4	4 435	3 012	30	120	1 233
Wilcox	17	4 483	D	178	1 120	3	115.5	81.9	65.2	6 105	3 586	55	287	2 072
Winston	33	11 139	100.0	426	2 687	12	323.8	107.9	91.3	4 412	3 457	62	210	651

[1] Includes only establishments with payroll.   [2] Includes full-service restaurants, limited-service eating places, special food services, and drinking places (alcoholic beverages).   [3] For pay period including March 12.   [4] As of June 30. Covers all FDIC-insured commercial banks and savings institutions.   [5] Based on resident population estimated as of July 1, 1999.   [6] 250 to 499 employees.   [7] 100 to 249 employees.   [8] 0 to 19 employees.   [9] 500 to 999 employees.   [10] 20 to 99 employees.

Sources: Accommodation and Foodservices—U.S. Census Bureau, 1997 Economic Census, ECON97 Report Series CD-ROM, CD-EC97-1, Disc 1E, issued February 2001 (related Internet site <http://www.census.gov/epcd/www/97EC72.HTM>). Banking—U.S. Federal Deposit Insurance Corporation and Office of Thrift Supervision, "1999 Bank and Thrift Branch Office Data Book: Summary of Deposits," national and 6 regional data books (related Internet site <http://www2.fdic.gov/sod/>). Federal Funds and Grants—U.S. Census Bureau, County Aggregate files for each state, <http://www.census.gov/govs/www/cffr99.html>, (accessed: August 2000).

Table B–12. Counties — **Accommodation and Foodservices, Banking, and Federal Funds**–Con.

[Includes U.S., states, and 3,142 counties/county equivalents defined as of January 1, 1992. For changes to these areas since January 1, 1992, see appendix B. Geographic Information]

| County | Accommodation and foodservices[1] (NAICS 72), 1997 | | | | | Banking,[4] 1999 | | Federal funds and grants, 1999 | | | | | | |
	Estab-lishments	Sales Total ($1,000)	Sales Percent from food-services[2]	Paid employ-ees[3]	Annual payroll ($1,000)	Offices	Deposits (mil. dol.)	Total expenditures or obligations (mil. dol.)	Percent change, 1990–1999	Per capita[5] (dollars) Total	Direct payments for individuals	Procure-ment contract awards	Salaries and wages	Grant awards
ALASKA	1 763	1 065 459	68.5	20 587	301 523	137	4 542.6	5 278.7	60.9	8 521	1 912	1 365	2 053	3 114
Aleutians East	8	D	D	(6)	D	–	–	19.4	1 040.2	8 911	2 073	3 137	542	3 146
Aleutians West	11	7 637	D	165	3 414	1	18.4	68.6	–53.3	17 533	561	15 259	581	1 125
Anchorage	640	573 955	71.1	11 364	165 792	45	2 029.6	1 961.4	53.4	7 608	1 727	1 391	2 747	1 677
Bethel	12	3 191	34.9	44	620	2	38.8	185.2	145.6	11 423	1 111	259	511	9 087
Bristol Bay	12	4 505	34.3	71	1 334	1	14.9	22.0	26.3	20 756	3 886	3 614	2 531	10 708
Denali	18	8 669	30.7	80	2 641	–	–	23.3	–	12 352	469	8 613	3 115	148
Dillingham	18	8 944	D	73	2 188	2	32.7	50.5	90.0	11 070	1 706	1 365	601	7 331
Fairbanks North Star	184	112 087	70.6	2 488	29 449	16	568.0	760.0	23.4	9 009	1 603	1 663	3 825	1 903
Haines	19	5 349	54.9	84	1 399	1	19.0	21.1	310.6	9 241	2 396	555	251	6 036
Juneau	94	57 721	69.8	1 117	16 123	12	455.2	440.5	56.9	14 590	1 907	225	1 714	10 545
Kenai Peninsula	213	65 224	66.8	1 251	16 240	10	339.4	196.4	138.1	4 009	1 867	138	427	1 537
Ketchikan Gateway	57	25 243	61.3	476	7 108	9	230.5	101.1	114.8	7 170	1 768	1 282	1 378	2 736
Kodiak Island	41	18 440	58.4	378	5 279	4	112.4	136.4	304.7	9 505	710	3 853	2 883	2 034
Lake and Peninsula	16	D	D	(6)	D	–	–	11.2	S	6 399	2 074	137	852	3 312
Matanuska-Susitna	126	43 903	86.2	928	10 243	9	184.9	188.0	122.3	3 245	1 566	271	123	1 282
Nome	20	6 567	69.1	215	2 071	1	30.2	89.9	40.8	10 092	1 330	1 538	597	6 078
North Slope	31	32 395	82.1	313	11 986	1	45.3	48.5	194.5	6 846	932	1 167	211	4 056
Northwest Arctic	13	11 086	77.1	159	4 228	1	15.6	65.7	158.7	9 770	1 209	555	600	7 378
Prince of Wales- Outer Ketchikan	25	8 235	56.0	135	2 398	3	42.6	37.2	71.8	5 559	946	1 155	581	2 687
Sitka	32	15 527	66.2	331	4 354	4	112.4	79.4	159.9	9 689	2 171	706	1 831	4 898
Skagway-Yakutat-Angoon	45	12 211	D	195	3 553	3	36.6	25.6	36.7	6 009	1 232	1 566	1 350	1 845
Southeast Fairbanks	28	6 619	54.7	140	1 806	2	20.0	63.1	51.6	10 790	1 958	2 146	2 710	3 966
Valdez-Cordova	58	19 792	50.0	315	4 873	5	99.4	84.5	138.2	8 258	1 313	2 908	778	3 245
Wade Hampton	2	D	D	(7)	D	–	–	56.5	206.5	8 118	1 452	120	291	6 245
Wrangell-Petersburg	23	6 320	D	120	1 707	5	96.6	43.2	111.1	6 358	2 191	1 867	1 147	1 148
Yukon-Koyukuk	17	4 424	66.3	38	671	–	–	121.1	18.0	19 575	1 945	7 040	981	9 580
ARIZONA	9 094	6 634 744	66.5	184 382	1 823 706	947	40 171.6	26 959.3	77.9	5 642	2 869	1 001	557	950
Apache	65	37 655	37.8	1 310	9 984	6	92.6	538.5	80.0	7 855	1 987	485	1 108	4 128
Cochise	270	94 239	77.0	3 310	23 909	23	588.3	1 086.7	57.7	9 638	3 847	1 898	2 761	1 056
Coconino	477	407 661	40.2	9 409	105 750	26	389.8	552.4	75.4	4 824	2 122	323	972	1 386
Gila	148	56 184	72.2	1 675	14 642	10	042.0	275.8	41.0	5 622	4 089	108	391	1 017
Graham	59	18 971	D	734	4 849	5	134.8	142.4	74.2	4 451	2 453	212	516	1 163
Greenlee	15	3 867	D	180	1 063	2	33.1	26.5	52.8	2 934	2 064	30	172	636
La Paz	76	23 172	72.0	795	6 501	5	74.3	118.0	28.3	7 935	3 123	3 428	404	572
Maricopa	4 903	4 196 807	68.4	112 091	1 170 527	546	27 274.7	12 976.7	60.9	4 535	2 474	896	399	739
Mohave	324	144 587	65.9	4 516	39 306	32	1 012.7	665.4	124.5	4 957	4 197	63	170	516
Navajo	222	118 479	52.0	2 890	26 242	21	329.3	447.6	90.1	4 553	2 247	102	608	1 511
Pima	1 525	1 042 213	70.2	32 316	292 317	157	6 510.6	5 700.9	80.1	7 094	3 129	2 178	717	1 058
Pinal	233	139 639	50.3	3 995	36 842	26	599.0	717.0	108.9	4 708	2 972	186	235	1 101
Santa Cruz	87	40 349	71.1	1 374	11 698	9	588.7	165.6	121.7	4 229	1 877	78	1 103	1 150
Yavapai	444	180 446	74.1	5 614	48 649	53	1 520.2	732.7	98.8	4 790	3 874	79	330	503
Yuma	246	130 475	69.2	4 173	31 427	23	680.8	775.0	76.2	5 715	2 946	419	1 399	854
ARKANSAS	4 663	2 179 696	81.9	73 397	589 917	1 198	31 798.8	13 630.8	62.8	5 343	3 421	183	437	1 025
Arkansas	43	10 513	90.5	340	2 774	12	441.3	148.0	50.9	7 144	3 453	624	370	979
Ashley	24	9 899	D	280	2 250	13	228.4	129.7	81.0	5 342	3 290	32	159	1 309
Baxter	106	32 315	68.4	1 060	9 074	15	654.0	213.7	62.4	5 828	5 104	84	212	418
Benton	230	98 940	90.2	3 585	26 932	57	1 964.9	448.5	70.8	3 240	2 772	107	141	206
Boone	65	26 656	86.6	1 015	6 998	17	529.3	147.9	48.2	4 645	3 627	125	310	477
Bradley	16	5 019	100.0	193	1 322	8	192.1	70.4	61.2	6 171	4 158	34	190	1 752
Calhoun	4	416	100.0	13	54	2	42.0	29.7	–35.2	5 246	2 675	1 240	116	1 180
Carroll	157	41 343	56.1	1 117	10 904	19	374.0	86.8	62.3	3 853	3 136	73	283	331
Chicot	23	3 975	80.3	124	955	7	156.3	103.3	54.8	6 956	3 487	25	100	2 034
Clark	45	23 259	85.9	862	6 590	13	348.0	99.3	38.7	4 638	3 508	38	230	773
Clay	17	D	D	(8)	D	10	222.5	118.6	57.2	6 968	3 892	44	200	1 198
Cleburne	49	21 016	72.2	735	6 215	17	305.9	114.2	82.0	4 901	4 115	47	200	504
Cleveland	2	D	D	(7)	D	5	42.3	31.9	62.8	3 731	2 867	28	100	713
Columbia	50	19 484	84.4	755	4 759	15	531.0	123.4	56.2	5 000	3 645	230	124	985
Conway	29	10 390	79.7	342	2 568	9	205.3	98.3	76.0	4 953	3 751	44	173	857
Craighead	133	80 216	89.1	2 720	21 556	48	1 160.6	301.2	64.0	3 877	2 561	60	291	632
Crawford	65	32 457	88.9	961	7 861	21	455.5	177.2	84.9	3 446	2 738	59	100	519
Crittenden	84	51 090	72.2	1 561	13 264	19	374.5	234.3	85.0	4 673	2 586	28	113	1 534
Cross	21	8 269	91.2	412	2 297	10	314.2	116.6	36.1	6 043	2 844	658	147	1 122
Dallas	10	D	D	(6)	D	6	132.9	45.6	47.5	5 116	3 831	37	235	986
Desha	35	7 966	78.8	263	1 711	10	187.5	130.3	101.9	8 774	3 426	2 105	356	1 512

[1] Includes only establishments with payroll. [2] Includes full-service restaurants, limited-service eating places, special food services, and drinking places (alcoholic beverages). [3] For pay period including March 12. [4] As of June 30. Covers all FDIC-insured commercial banks and savings institutions. [5] Based on resident population estimated as of July 1, 1999. [6] 20 to 99 employees. [7] 0 to 19 employees. [8] 100 to 249 employees.

Sources: Accommodation and Foodservices—U.S. Census Bureau, 1997 Economic Census, ECON97 Report Series CD-ROM, CD-EC97-1, Disc 1E, issued February 2001 (related Internet site <http://www.census.gov/epcd/www/97EC72.HTM>). Banking—U.S. Federal Deposit Insurance Corporation and Office of Thrift Supervision, "1999 Bank and Thrift Branch Office Data Book: Summary of Deposits," national and 6 regional data books (related Internet site <http://www2.fdic.gov/sod/>). Federal Funds and Grants—U.S. Census Bureau, County Aggregate files for each state, <http://www.census.gov/govs/www/cffr99.html>, (accessed: August 2000).

Table B–12. Counties — Accommodation and Foodservices, Banking, and Federal Funds-Con.

[Includes U.S., states, and 3,142 counties/county equivalents defined as of January 1, 1992. For changes to these areas since January 1, 1992, see appendix B. Geographic Information]

| County | Accommodation and foodservices[1] (NAICS 72), 1997 | | | | | Banking,[4] 1999 | | Federal funds and grants, 1999 | | | | | | |
| | Estab-lishments | Total ($1,000) | Percent from food-services[2] | Paid employ-ees[3] | Annual payroll ($1,000) | Offices | Deposits (mil. dol.) | Total expenditures or obligations (mil. dol.) | Percent change, 1990–1999 | Per capita[5] (dollars) | | | | |
										Total	Direct payments for individuals	Procure-ment contract awards	Salaries and wages	Grant awards
ARKANSAS—Con.														
Drew	31	15 306	D	507	3 740	11	251.1	92.0	81.4	5 274	2 999	129	229	1 531
Faulkner	112	69 287	88.0	2 389	18 975	30	778.7	256.7	98.0	3 208	2 242	103	126	699
Franklin	27	5 880	D	211	1 473	9	190.8	85.6	47.2	5 093	3 386	498	675	483
Fulton	17	3 351	72.1	106	972	4	111.5	51.6	76.0	4 683	3 811	37	139	656
Garland	222	120 203	66.2	4 005	36 757	36	938.7	490.6	63.5	5 808	4 886	122	327	458
Grant	11	D	D	(6)	D	5	125.0	53.6	82.0	3 353	2 528	31	133	651
Greene	54	20 837	93.1	768	5 897	14	427.6	149.9	71.3	4 118	2 777	63	134	620
Hempstead	34	14 946	79.8	519	3 798	11	303.2	94.6	63.7	4 283	3 168	33	212	801
Hot Spring	33	13 542	92.4	454	3 643	12	318.4	134.7	90.8	4 619	3 324	56	151	1 050
Howard	18	6 694	D	224	1 823	9	211.1	61.1	63.0	4 469	3 451	41	226	689
Independence	48	22 649	88.3	812	5 822	19	438.5	162.6	79.3	4 916	3 167	294	317	988
Izard	20	2 099	84.4	88	564	8	138.1	75.6	86.5	5 767	4 274	96	130	1 217
Jackson	28	8 581	D	284	2 283	11	215.1	132.0	59.2	7 538	4 326	56	169	1 323
Jefferson	131	57 867	85.6	2 049	15 014	23	732.8	536.5	40.1	6 640	3 410	772	805	1 354
Johnson	36	13 742	79.6	456	3 439	11	263.6	97.9	71.9	4 584	3 137	58	232	1 132
Lafayette	9	1 573	100.0	61	353	4	114.7	56.8	71.0	6 421	3 591	48	190	2 003
Lawrence	28	7 707	D	284	2 139	11	214.6	124.6	75.6	7 183	3 839	48	214	1 981
Lee	8	D	D	(7)	D	3	72.2	89.9	61.7	7 079	2 986	54	216	2 181
Lincoln	7	1 919	100.0	63	416	6	64.1	63.7	74.6	4 432	2 263	85	66	983
Little River	23	D	D	(6)	D	8	142.0	62.4	68.2	4 778	3 511	72	147	803
Logan	33	8 661	97.0	335	2 204	12	259.1	98.6	61.9	4 668	3 615	59	288	659
Lonoke	53	21 285	93.7	728	5 300	22	444.5	197.6	78.6	3 841	2 690	89	104	447
Madison	9	2 075	100.0	79	639	6	137.9	48.0	54.5	3 604	2 770	94	177	499
Marion	30	6 096	76.0	191	1 637	7	153.5	65.3	64.0	4 384	3 799	39	96	416
Miller	79	45 789	80.7	1 363	11 635	12	476.1	196.9	77.8	4 999	3 154	90	67	1 484
Mississippi	74	36 207	79.0	1 254	8 572	24	511.6	272.3	10.1	5 454	3 063	214	137	1 213
Monroe	24	11 959	79.6	430	2 880	6	157.6	90.5	75.8	9 059	3 691	61	184	3 413
Montgomery	14	9 365	20.0	148	2 008	3	73.3	41.0	63.2	4 689	3 716	106	280	565
Nevada	9	3 758	D	113	1 196	2	83.2	47.4	35.0	4 729	3 525	59	208	877
Newton	10	1 912	D	69	479	2	55.2	37.5	72.7	4 564	3 019	37	281	1 144
Ouachita	40	18 025	75.3	626	4 355	16	342.7	172.6	34.5	6 279	4 037	923	272	994
Perry	8	1 036	D	31	242	3	70.0	51.3	109.1	5 299	3 431	110	220	1 445
Phillips	39	9 406	88.3	369	2 488	13	275.6	195.1	67.9	7 213	3 525	97	146	2 496
Pike	26	4 847	70.1	205	1 269	8	178.4	45.3	44.4	4 330	3 370	49	284	583
Poinsett	34	9 486	83.4	249	1 960	16	309.2	153.3	57.8	6 233	3 297	99	146	1 277
Polk	34	14 461	87.4	435	3 616	12	240.0	91.7	66.2	4 676	3 725	71	229	606
Pope	106	50 484	85.2	2 025	13 834	27	675.7	198.0	62.7	3 765	2 669	134	262	656
Prairie	17	3 483	D	132	771	5	73.8	70.7	81.0	7 617	3 359	117	248	1 288
Pulaski	801	507 968	79.9	16 728	144 694	157	5 197.9	2 595.2	56.6	7 431	3 424	298	1 622	2 040
Randolph	27	D	D	(8)	D	5	201.6	82.0	72.8	4 580	3 310	29	99	761
St. Francis	54	24 162	68.6	822	6 371	13	231.3	183.6	80.9	6 612	3 169	255	731	1 837
Saline	83	46 257	91.6	1 368	12 159	23	483.9	175.1	82.1	2 234	1 882	22	65	259
Scott	17	D	D	(6)	D	5	122.3	49.4	58.2	4 639	3 291	85	307	919
Searcy	10	2 086	75.8	88	684	4	74.1	49.8	89.8	6 393	4 108	55	289	1 843
Sebastian	257	138 872	89.2	4 669	38 118	47	1 666.7	448.5	50.2	4 221	3 103	142	514	443
Sevier	22	D	D	(8)	D	8	209.5	56.6	54.6	3 859	3 015	48	270	477
Sharp	41	10 142	89.5	379	2 579	11	241.3	96.0	64.3	5 617	4 735	47	187	631
Stone	21	7 588	D	278	1 930	4	122.6	58.0	92.7	5 168	3 821	29	201	1 060
Union	68	28 132	82.8	1 007	6 604	24	722.7	208.6	45.1	4 640	3 667	44	204	715
Van Buren	27	8 856	78.0	336	2 389	10	140.1	78.8	58.8	5 028	4 313	33	154	498
Washington	372	183 358	79.4	6 181	50 853	68	1 806.7	501.1	62.7	3 418	2 276	195	381	551
White	95	48 070	94.6	1 323	11 029	30	783.1	252.0	71.9	3 872	2 992	49	141	535
Woodruff	6	888	100.0	34	186	6	102.6	89.0	103.5	10 221	4 048	89	232	3 322
Yell	18	D	D	(6)	D	9	261.0	104.1	82.6	5 520	3 652	622	348	796
CALIFORNIA	62 629	42 312 641	73.8	1 054 106	11 455 306	6 103	427 750.1	166 049.7	41.2	5 010	2 532	778	535	1 097
Alameda	2 775	1 573 988	81.5	38 391	418 219	267	17 884.4	8 052.8	32.4	5 689	2 353	1 513	531	1 257
Alpine	16	5 952	20.4	148	1 422	–	–	9.1	268.6	7 842	4 033	1 397	266	2 110
Amador	106	29 956	78.9	918	8 139	14	402.1	149.5	89.5	4 377	3 634	34	128	576
Butte	380	156 249	91.3	5 920	43 277	43	1 808.3	935.2	68.7	4 790	3 475	109	138	895
Calaveras	95	21 397	74.7	753	5 670	14	256.8	185.7	113.1	4 636	3 688	192	140	608
Colusa	43	17 086	83.3	508	4 877	7	182.5	120.2	91.7	6 380	2 507	205	152	1 151
Contra Costa	1 517	903 631	86.1	23 407	239 007	205	17 747.0	3 329.3	44.9	3 568	2 423	204	354	573
Del Norte	82	24 077	69.9	710	5 820	5	149.9	120.2	73.3	4 538	3 048	76	247	1 162
El Dorado	410	208 973	55.3	5 539	55 345	37	1 172.6	522.5	84.0	3 238	2 557	95	189	390

[1] Includes only establishments with payroll. [2] Includes full-service restaurants, limited-service eating places, special food services, and drinking places (alcoholic beverages). [3] For pay period including March 12. [4] As of June 30. Covers all FDIC-insured commercial banks and savings institutions. [5] Based on resident population estimated as of July 1, 1999. [6] 100 to 249 employees. [7] 20 to 99 employees. [8] 250 to 499 employees.

Sources: Accommodation and Foodservices—U.S. Census Bureau, 1997 Economic Census, ECON97 Report Series CD-ROM, CD-EC97-1, Disc 1E, issued February 2001 (related Internet site <http://www.census.gov/epcd/www/97EC72.HTM>). Banking—U.S. Federal Deposit Insurance Corporation and Office of Thrift Supervision, "1999 Bank and Thrift Branch Office Data Book: Summary of Deposits," national and 6 regional data books (related Internet site <http://www2.fdic.gov/sod/>). Federal Funds and Grants—U.S. Census Bureau, County Aggregate files for each state, <http://www.census.gov/govs/www/cffr99.html>, (accessed: August 2000).

[Includes U.S., states, and 3,142 counties/county equivalents defined as of January 1, 1992. For changes to these areas since January 1, 1992, see appendix B. Geographic Information]

County	Accommodation and foodservices[1] (NAICS 72), 1997					Banking,[4] 1999		Federal funds and grants, 1999						
		Sales								Per capita[5] (dollars)				
												By selected type—		
	Estab-lishments	Total ($1,000)	Percent from food-services[2]	Paid employ-ees[3]	Annual payroll ($1,000)	Offices	Deposits (mil. dol.)	Total expenditures or obligations (mil. dol.)	Percent change, 1990–1999	Total	Direct payments for individuals	Procure-ment contract awards	Salaries and wages	Grant awards
CALIFORNIA—Con.														
Fresno	1 258	632 164	88.3	19 900	169 742	138	5 479.4	3 028.3	80.9	3 969	2 145	126	519	1 060
Glenn	50	17 785	88.6	549	4 261	8	207.4	154.7	83.2	5 875	2 690	321	434	1 006
Humboldt	371	134 191	73.1	4 312	36 392	29	1 004.8	591.9	59.2	4 877	3 159	200	368	1 130
Imperial	238	89 264	79.9	2 723	22 990	18	948.6	585.1	92.1	4 027	2 115	189	602	1 040
Inyo	100	54 352	56.4	1 248	13 492	5	234.4	259.8	46.7	14 465	3 866	7 726	687	2 180
Kern	1 013	493 178	84.8	14 724	129 106	91	3 267.7	3 150.3	45.5	4 903	2 373	515	1 013	897
Kings	156	65 128	94.1	2 037	16 249	20	659.2	631.7	90.5	5 125	1 802	544	1 666	864
Lake	132	29 147	81.2	978	6 862	18	519.1	332.5	60.5	6 001	4 663	88	131	1 108
Lassen	68	25 784	81.7	733	7 036	6	129.9	145.6	32.9	4 409	2 404	440	910	630
Los Angeles	15 737	11 084 321	80.3	267 406	2 994 342	1 499	131 995.8	43 465.6	28.6	4 659	2 147	1 081	317	1 008
Madera	162	73 007	75.4	2 136	18 676	22	613.1	417.7	111.1	3 578	2 297	94	106	916
Marin	687	417 478	80.4	10 256	120 797	76	4 713.5	859.1	61.8	3 628	2 789	171	247	394
Mariposa	56	80 873	12.5	1 112	14 823	2	68.3	118.8	108.4	7 615	3 757	1 564	1 309	980
Mendocino	322	124 889	60.2	3 636	33 501	26	957.5	465.2	104.0	5 533	3 064	628	174	1 648
Merced	270	108 738	88.2	3 272	27 331	28	1 070.6	734.8	27.7	3 661	2 263	134	109	1 021
Modoc	27	4 925	67.2	178	1 141	3	85.3	58.4	54.2	6 344	3 355	338	1 094	1 229
Mono	134	114 283	27.9	3 210	35 338	4	70.6	36.1	69.2	3 434	1 384	587	1 109	350
Monterey	908	837 250	45.3	16 903	226 541	71	3 849.7	1 670.5	17.9	4 493	2 508	249	1 012	711
Napa	347	287 127	55.4	6 250	80 293	43	1 575.9	518.0	57.3	4 282	3 390	50	130	705
Nevada	231	118 160	55.9	3 993	33 731	29	1 054.6	450.0	86.0	4 890	3 190	608	191	895
Orange	5 405	4 248 476	72.7	105 484	1 135 774	557	36 457.2	9 292.5	17.3	3 366	2 017	612	257	474
Placer	546	334 114	74.4	10 083	93 987	70	2 188.6	836.2	88.4	3 491	2 723	127	169	440
Plumas	116	23 467	59.4	512	5 597	10	204.7	110.9	53.7	5 445	3 728	316	637	748
Riverside	2 161	1 620 059	63.1	41 960	448 083	223	10 949.2	5 154.1	79.0	3 367	2 528	104	224	503
Sacramento	2 189	1 197 664	83.6	36 472	321 040	186	10 491.8	12 388.6	59.6	10 458	3 110	828	577	5 881
San Benito	80	29 989	90.5	962	7 895	12	459.4	142.5	95.8	2 778	1 515	600	125	506
San Bernardino	2 323	1 279 705	86.7	37 291	334 980	204	9 632.1	5 898.9	37.3	3 532	2 101	273	494	655
San Diego	5 441	4 246 590	66.2	105 287	1 160 544	491	26 517.3	17 857.4	44.4	6 330	2 656	1 095	1 701	869
San Francisco	3 264	3 283 495	50.7	60 178	956 602	255	48 149.3	5 673.6	46.1	7 597	3 078	671	1 372	2 390
San Joaquin	826	376 916	89.4	11 413	96 497	99	6 273.1	2 126.5	68.7	3 776	2 321	154	271	952
San Luis Obispo	675	383 166	62.8	10 553	101 966	62	2 602.2	882.9	69.1	3 726	2 803	65	160	662
San Mateo	1 497	1 379 760	69.2	28 013	386 246	156	12 040.3	2 612.7	47.7	3 721	2 355	355	413	586
Santa Barbara	954	634 492	68.6	17 242	177 652	92	5 114.4	2 097.6	29.1	5 364	2 607	1 236	708	797
Santa Clara	3 499	2 591 903	77.8	60 369	678 075	317	30 098.2	8 637.6	18.4	5 243	1 892	2 163	374	817
Santa Cruz	592	306 824	81.6	8 250	81 253	47	2 441.9	808.1	58.8	3 296	2 186	149	118	832
Shasta	402	161 680	71.9	5 070	41 725	38	1 371.4	845.6	86.0	5 139	3 518	163	356	1 094
Sierra	22	5 393	46.2	86	1 191	2	16.5	22.7	17.3	6 805	3 702	205	796	2 089
Siskiyou	160	46 895	64.5	1 396	12 363	24	429.8	275.3	66.8	6 320	3 934	193	629	1 471
Solano	569	291 986	90.4	8 798	74 332	55	2 087.2	1 885.2	8.7	4 887	2 661	564	1 090	551
Sonoma	1 012	492 828	84.7	14 082	133 147	109	5 896.0	1 630.5	69.0	3 706	2 712	107	264	610
Stanislaus	678	313 809	89.7	9 918	80 622	89	3 690.8	1 539.1	82.6	3 524	2 317	172	138	842
Sutter	102	44 924	96.8	1 443	12 760	15	697.1	333.5	94.2	4 253	2 772	60	118	725
Tehama	102	36 692	83.0	1 128	9 187	10	396.8	243.0	76.1	4 499	3 167	90	199	911
Trinity	57	11 055	54.5	296	2 490	4	73.4	79.2	48.0	6 128	3 864	181	556	1 519
Tulare	510	232 318	82.4	7 020	56 835	61	2 162.4	1 317.8	77.9	3 676	2 052	94	141	1 191
Tuolumne	168	58 447	72.0	1 747	15 233	22	610.9	246.1	57.1	4 578	3 609	137	322	506
Ventura	1 201	775 634	84.4	21 884	209 465	129	7 147.6	3 190.8	49.0	4 283	2 203	587	928	553
Yolo	302	140 051	85.8	4 379	36 209	29	1 158.9	798.0	104.2	5 130	2 163	315	901	1 580
Yuba	85	30 956	78.3	940	9 136	7	282.7	457.2	64.1	7 671	3 223	191	2 560	1 425
COLORADO	10 073	6 710 540	68.7	195 262	1 939 282	1 202	45 923.9	21 755.4	47.0	5 364	2 409	1 095	863	850
Adams	512	288 779	84.2	8 990	79 285	54	1 815.7	1 126.3	45.8	3 402	2 055	363	501	442
Alamosa	49	20 651	69.8	938	5 832	5	231.5	63.1	63.3	4 326	2 062	183	468	1 500
Arapahoe	915	684 015	82.3	19 374	188 812	127	5 759.1	1 978.7	124.3	4 104	1 975	1 293	363	460
Archuleta	56	15 063	60.0	530	4 366	7	117.1	28.0	92.8	2 917	2 282	51	235	340
Baca	7	1 271	79.8	41	294	3	77.3	47.5	43.2	10 991	3 602	83	346	831
Bent	8	2 225	D	83	587	2	60.8	50.7	9.8	8 747	3 742	317	2 698	1 504
Boulder	709	453 926	82.8	13 844	131 438	84	3 373.0	1 348.3	69.3	4 937	1 827	1 247	653	1 199
Chaffee	100	30 860	53.6	969	8 603	7	217.5	61.7	54.1	3 956	3 079	73	275	520
Cheyenne	4	D	D	(6)	D	3	74.3	25.9	59.5	11 635	3 175	103	325	627
Clear Creek	48	18 823	79.8	539	5 168	4	37.8	18.2	84.4	1 982	1 262	28	173	516
Conejos	14	1 921	D	44	461	2	29.9	43.0	91.9	5 325	2 613	213	207	2 182
Costilla	7	D	D	(6)	D	1	6.6	25.2	95.6	7 039	3 990	29	215	2 592
Crowley	5	D	D	(6)	D	1	23.6	19.8	67.9	4 461	2 659	48	171	1 237
Custer	14	4 205	24.2	103	978	1	21.3	12.7	49.3	3 520	2 834	51	170	457

[1] Includes only establishments with payroll. [2] Includes full-service restaurants, limited-service eating places, special food services, and drinking places (alcoholic beverages). [3] For pay period including March 12. [4] As of June 30. Covers all FDIC-insured commercial banks and savings institutions. [5] Based on resident population estimated as of July 1, 1999. [6] 20 to 99 employees.

Sources: Accommodation and Foodservices—U.S. Census Bureau, 1997 Economic Census, ECON97 Report Series CD-ROM, CD-EC97-1, Disc 1E, issued February 2001 (related Internet site <http://www.census.gov/epcd/www/97EC72.HTM>). Banking—U.S. Federal Deposit Insurance Corporation and Office of Thrift Supervision, "1999 Bank and Thrift Branch Office Data Book: Summary of Deposits," national and 6 regional data books (related Internet site <http://www2.fdic.gov/sod/>). Federal Funds and Grants—U.S. Census Bureau, County Aggregate files for each state, <http://www.census.gov/govs/www/cffr99.html>, (accessed: August 2000).

Table B–12. Counties — Accommodation and Foodservices, Banking, and Federal Funds–Con.

[Includes U.S., states, and 3,142 counties/county equivalents defined as of January 1, 1992. For changes to these areas since January 1, 1992, see appendix B. Geographic Information]

County	Accommodation and foodservices[1] (NAICS 72), 1997 — Sales — Estab-lishments	Total ($1,000)	Percent from food-services[2]	Paid employ-ees[3]	Annual payroll ($1,000)	Banking,[4] 1999 Offices	Deposits (mil. dol.)	Federal funds and grants, 1999 Total expenditures or obligations (mil. dol.)	Percent change, 1990–1999	Per capita[5] (dollars) Total	Direct payments for individuals	Procure-ment contract awards	Salaries and wages	Grant awards
COLORADO—Con.														
Delta	68	15 232	80.7	559	4 234	11	279.8	124.1	54.1	4 561	3 540	54	315	620
Denver	1 564	1 335 200	69.7	33 749	385 979	131	11 605.3	5 019.2	-2.1	10 043	3 342	2 412	1 627	2 580
Dolores	7	D	D	(6)	D	1	17.0	9.4	-40.4	5 037	2 991	61	241	672
Douglas	178	109 055	91.5	3 593	32 064	34	708.6	141.2	158.4	900	752	54	55	35
Eagle	223	288 121	41.6	7 181	100 331	32	610.9	51.9	131.7	1 484	661	72	213	532
Elbert	11	2 387	D	73	701	6	52.7	55.0	232.2	2 786	1 310	37	73	1 217
El Paso	999	772 632	64.7	21 494	217 183	101	3 115.8	3 753.9	58.8	7 508	2 816	1 937	2 389	357
Fremont	82	29 805	79.3	1 008	7 627	13	364.8	218.4	108.0	4 886	2 892	46	1 352	592
Garfield	155	72 559	62.0	1 906	21 266	23	488.8	103.1	-2.1	2 535	1 863	73	338	246
Gilpin	9	61 137	2.1	647	11 430	–	–	5.0	56.4	1 117	760	34	79	241
Grand	127	51 931	41.0	1 531	15 524	6	121.6	28.5	95.4	2 717	1 917	102	410	283
Gunnison	114	84 331	34.5	2 765	22 637	10	206.7	75.3	296.5	5 988	1 374	3 569	427	612
Hinsdale	18	3 686	20.5	71	780	1	16.2	2.3	158.2	3 105	2 082	66	224	726
Huerfano	28	5 851	73.3	201	1 672	3	73.5	42.5	87.3	6 250	4 544	33	138	1 508
Jackson	7	938	D	48	276	1	8.6	5.6	68.6	3 653	2 415	206	766	247
Jefferson	969	586 497	90.6	18 993	172 760	158	5 140.4	2 491.2	110.7	4 892	1 763	1 918	963	244
Kiowa	5	D	D	(6)	D	1	15.9	26.1	57.8	15 961	3 357	95	419	1 581
Kit Carson	20	9 788	D	360	2 618	7	177.7	72.5	107.5	9 779	2 969	80	259	909
Lake	44	8 375	67.0	342	2 086	3	57.8	17.2	23.6	2 694	1 898	51	332	410
La Plata	169	143 236	36.2	4 281	44 064	14	504.8	129.1	56.8	3 138	2 023	134	411	543
Larimer	648	344 242	76.1	10 797	95 196	67	2 380.6	751.9	76.6	3 175	1 968	117	433	634
Las Animas	42	13 590	D	462	3 410	5	210.6	95.0	61.2	6 460	3 906	168	228	2 084
Lincoln	25	8 045	73.6	238	2 157	4	100.7	34.7	50.6	6 114	2 679	52	228	984
Logan	51	20 427	76.8	769	5 818	9	262.6	88.4	34.8	4 932	3 007	154	202	593
Mesa	247	124 668	81.4	4 555	36 298	38	1 081.1	539.4	65.3	4 684	2 969	729	465	510
Mineral	11	2 017	D	19	597	2	9.7	2.0	49.4	2 748	2 257	59	320	105
Moffat	27	12 043	66.0	372	3 398	3	97.1	44.2	67.0	3 475	2 247	131	468	461
Montezuma	82	27 782	61.8	987	7 831	10	286.5	100.1	30.0	4 415	2 661	153	511	1 034
Montrose	76	29 286	77.1	825	7 345	13	395.1	127.6	61.1	4 058	2 914	157	432	527
Morgan	63	19 612	85.7	789	5 355	12	376.3	106.8	82.6	4 207	2 432	201	235	592
Otero	63	15 909	76.2	618	3 843	14	267.0	121.3	68.3	5 886	3 745	61	257	1 536
Ouray	45	10 882	44.0	223	2 800	1	37.6	9.2	105.3	2 634	1 950	49	131	497
Park	38	9 914	57.7	270	2 753	1	12.3	25.8	139.2	1 818	1 500	57	151	106
Phillips	10	D	D	(6)	D	4	72.7	40.0	90.0	9 476	3 740	74	283	1 181
Pitkin	191	229 874	40.7	5 765	82 443	10	491.2	23.7	82.3	1 779	953	90	328	400
Prowers	40	12 325	69.9	470	3 542	8	236.5	67.6	64.9	4 905	2 599	33	160	896
Pueblo	321	142 381	86.3	4 969	38 107	30	1 110.6	695.5	53.4	5 077	3 536	155	262	1 099
Rio Blanco	25	7 468	45.4	182	2 331	2	66.3	24.5	98.1	3 952	2 199	99	463	1 143
Rio Grande	41	10 888	60.4	353	2 955	10	176.5	52.7	62.2	4 581	2 653	121	408	1 184
Routt	108	98 089	43.2	3 225	28 082	7	295.1	-18.1	-177.8	-1 008	1 182	-2 800	327	210
Saguache	10	D	D	(6)	D	1	5.9	24.9	51.9	4 027	2 132	113	287	1 122
San Juan	15	1 991	75.9	6	493	1	3.1	1.6	66.4	3 130	2 105	186	218	615
San Miguel	59	25 087	63.6	848	8 839	7	139.3	10.6	89.4	1 943	827	146	270	652
Sedgwick	11	D	D	(6)	D	3	54.4	27.0	84.4	10 427	4 538	97	333	1 118
Summit	204	226 554	37.1	7 781	67 560	13	344.1	25.8	171.6	1 313	914	92	147	157
Teller	68	94 755	11.4	1 848	26 000	6	157.9	46.3	-19.4	2 180	1 918	46	101	113
Washington	11	D	D	(6)	D	5	90.5	56.2	109.6	12 898	3 444	91	507	2 323
Weld	271	106 785	93.1	4 047	29 403	48	1 558.4	486.7	76.3	2 935	1 899	68	186	612
Yuma	25	4 737	91.0	217	1 316	8	191.7	73.8	18.8	7 828	2 607	64	232	593
CONNECTICUT	6 903	3 746 560	83.5	96 556	1 062 812	1 202	58 734.2	19 240.5	30.2	5 862	3 098	1 108	411	1 172
Fairfield	1 772	1 113 311	80.1	24 643	311 260	320	16 355.9	4 108.8	6.2	4 884	2 728	1 084	271	764
Hartford	1 778	995 364	85.7	28 579	289 124	290	19 669.5	5 087.3	26.9	6 132	3 141	619	448	1 826
Litchfield	369	150 619	80.7	3 709	43 196	81	2 972.6	642.8	67.8	3 524	2 734	171	146	459
Middlesex	355	171 999	80.4	4 231	49 310	70	2 063.3	526.1	19.5	3 473	2 597	114	147	602
New Haven	1 644	804 654	89.2	21 581	221 393	273	12 224.3	4 007.1	60.9	5 052	3 154	187	384	1 278
New London	590	332 965	74.2	8 652	95 682	89	2 988.1	3 278.2	46.0	13 323	3 126	8 041	1 475	668
Tolland	208	101 433	94.2	3 148	32 613	44	1 443.3	384.5	93.6	2 898	1 998	196	133	559
Windham	187	76 215	80.7	2 013	20 234	35	1 017.2	438.9	75.3	4 170	2 881	88	152	1 028
DELAWARE	1 605	1 008 954	85.3	26 969	280 815	254	52 948.8	3 765.7	71.3	4 997	3 002	294	539	1 095
Kent	234	118 385	84.8	3 796	31 929	33	1 051.6	902.6	76.8	7 161	2 880	545	1 611	2 042
New Castle	929	656 109	86.1	17 837	187 374	169	40 839.4	2 002.3	58.7	4 110	2 500	295	366	916
Sussex	442	234 460	83.3	5 336	61 512	52	11 057.8	702.8	104.8	5 009	3 993	62	176	719
DISTRICT OF COLUMBIA	1 700	2 263 498	52.2	42 650	701 354	206	10 903.4	27 033.7	52.8	52 088	5 100	12 338	23 074	10 198
District of Columbia	1 700	2 263 498	52.2	42 650	701 354	206	10 903.4	27 033.7	52.8	52 088	5 100	12 338	23 074	10 198

[1] Includes only establishments with payroll. [2] Includes full-service restaurants, limited-service eating places, special food services, and drinking places (alcoholic beverages). [3] For pay period including March 12. [4] As of June 30. Covers all FDIC-insured commercial banks and savings institutions. [5] Based on resident population estimated as of July 1, 1999. [6] 20 to 99 employees.

Sources: Accommodation and Foodservices—U.S. Census Bureau, 1997 Economic Census, ECON97 Report Series CD-ROM, CD-EC97-1, Disc 1E, issued February 2001 (related Internet site <http://www.census.gov/epcd/www/97EC72.HTM>). Banking—U.S. Federal Deposit Insurance Corporation and Office of Thrift Supervision, "1999 Bank and Thrift Branch Office Data Book: Summary of Deposits," national and 6 regional data books (related Internet site <http://www2.fdic.gov/sod/>). Federal Funds and Grants—U.S. Census Bureau, County Aggregate files for each state, <http://www.census.gov/govs/www/cffr99.html>, (accessed: August 2000).

Table B–12. Counties — Accommodation and Foodservices, Banking, and Federal Funds–Con.

[Includes U.S., states, and 3,142 counties/county equivalents defined as of January 1, 1992. For changes to these areas since January 1, 1992, see appendix B. Geographic Information]

County	Accommodation and foodservices[1] (NAICS 72), 1997					Banking,[4] 1999		Federal funds and grants, 1999						
		Sales								Per capita[5] (dollars)				
												By selected type—		
	Estab-lishments	Total ($1,000)	Percent from food-services[2]	Paid employ-ees[3]	Annual payroll ($1,000)	Offices	Deposits (mil. dol.)	Total expenditures or obligations (mil. dol.)	Percent change, 1990–1999	Total	Direct payments for individuals	Procure-ment contract awards	Salaries and wages	Grant awards
FLORIDA	28 999	24 165 336	63.5	608 834	6 239 469	4 509	200 783.4	87 214.9	69.1	5 772	3 872	572	518	741
Alachua	431	263 040	82.3	8 981	67 776	56	1 567.1	1 038.6	81.6	5 233	2 797	281	723	1 398
Baker	18	9 780	D	380	2 449	4	118.0	73.4	119.8	3 467	2 594	27	117	710
Bay	483	336 289	60.3	9 268	84 781	46	1 330.5	1 211.3	89.8	8 187	4 740	1 054	1 876	451
Bradford	28	17 261	83.5	698	4 827	5	119.7	96.3	77.9	3 871	2 911	30	283	614
Brevard	860	495 297	80.4	16 207	136 263	124	4 182.3	4 132.0	25.1	8 785	4 355	3 436	708	273
Broward	3 206	2 474 496	69.9	61 243	615 469	404	22 770.6	6 375.8	57.2	4 152	3 451	125	252	310
Calhoun	13	4 118	95.7	120	1 106	4	90.6	56.5	89.0	4 540	2 984	28	89	1 308
Charlotte	218	123 457	83.0	3 935	31 928	47	1 884.6	776.7	88.5	5 670	5 363	40	99	160
Citrus	166	66 323	77.8	2 393	18 957	39	1 524.0	635.8	84.3	5 476	5 153	26	90	200
Clay	195	114 573	96.9	3 990	32 748	26	500.4	467.3	90.4	3 306	2 962	57	128	155
Collier	518	536 740	50.5	11 599	140 916	98	4 102.8	893.2	102.0	4 315	3 750	44	147	369
Columbia	99	54 117	75.2	2 118	14 845	14	376.0	272.4	108.3	5 069	3 384	121	771	757
Dade	3 835	3 199 453	66.3	75 597	878 468	535	39 633.1	10 358.7	69.1	4 761	2 905	145	468	1 216
DeSoto	33	12 413	80.5	412	2 978	6	207.5	118.1	86.1	4 796	3 918	26	121	708
Dixie	22	3 543	D	152	910	4	58.4	67.1	144.1	5 192	4 445	15	74	594
Duval	1 420	917 173	83.7	28 354	244 243	168	8 417.9	4 901.5	51.7	6 637	3 142	889	1 917	655
Escambia	493	350 884	86.7	11 101	92 309	79	2 493.0	2 190.0	52.8	7 754	4 020	607	2 319	745
Flagler	88	42 350	69.3	1 465	12 839	13	569.6	246.4	179.7	5 017	4 592	116	110	185
Franklin	43	14 942	55.7	393	3 402	9	110.3	51.0	73.7	5 109	4 003	34	122	803
Gadsden	39	10 731	86.4	321	2 567	9	186.5	215.2	51.8	4 882	3 017	71	136	1 633
Gilchrist	16	D	D	(6)	D	4	84.4	45.7	112.4	3 251	2 674	22	82	366
Glades	20	4 698	57.4	129	983	2	17.1	28.0	111.8	3 221	2 649	110	53	371
Gulf	21	4 631	D	155	1 198	5	101.4	75.0	139.1	5 527	4 126	15	56	1 306
Hamilton	13	3 708	55.6	161	853	5	41.6	52.4	87.1	4 101	2 742	32	118	1 097
Hardee	17	7 351	91.4	225	1 631	5	249.7	84.9	79.7	4 040	2 991	30	130	855
Hendry	48	18 414	87.7	644	4 997	13	282.7	105.7	120.1	3 589	2 534	53	142	832
Hernando	184	74 047	92.2	2 772	19 891	37	1 737.4	845.3	132.0	6 579	6 053	38	121	357
Highlands	118	52 337	90.1	1 817	13 783	27	1 036.5	505.0	88.2	6 751	6 023	66	174	466
Hillsborough	1 552	1 248 260	76.3	34 618	330 422	227	9 995.8	4 436.3	70.8	4 717	2 964	328	728	670
Holmes	13	4 530	70.9	160	1 158	3	112.4	104.8	105.2	5 585	3 690	86	154	1 514
Indian River	204	112 351	85.2	3 527	31 602	60	2 126.3	645.9	78.3	6 443	5 772	129	183	347
Jackson	58	25 991	86.4	931	7 612	16	346.0	264.5	61.7	5 938	3 430	56	626	1 599
Jefferson	13	3 351	84.7	121	930	2	84.6	00.2	149.7	0 124	2 962	36	114	2 895
Lafayette	13	3 120	D	94	701	2	40.1	22.1	106.0	3 416	2 021	407	110	746
Lake	291	154 595	74.6	5 161	42 408	82	2 563.1	1 145.8	120.1	5 461	4 958	66	122	307
Lee	824	699 097	59.6	17 424	175 213	146	5 628.2	2 031.6	79.7	5 072	4 459	73	240	283
Leon	456	296 768	83.3	9 884	77 068	70	2 473.8	2 974.3	122.5	13 775	2 659	218	421	10 286
Levy	57	19 497	87.2	809	5 112	15	280.1	148.3	105.4	4 578	3 732	33	128	567
Liberty	3	D	D	(6)	D	1	43.0	30.5	136.5	4 550	2 395	91	237	1 819
Madison	29	9 941	68.3	433	2 433	6	122.9	97.3	101.5	5 428	3 165	29	122	2 016
Manatee	390	241 506	81.9	7 480	64 498	92	2 962.1	1 143.7	71.6	4 697	4 069	105	234	273
Marion	363	200 914	85.8	6 558	54 103	71	2 542.1	1 325.7	105.5	5 389	4 519	198	138	519
Martin	258	167 804	75.0	4 676	46 449	63	2 002.1	658.3	80.6	5 574	5 043	160	123	239
Monroe	567	569 086	41.0	10 939	151 297	48	1 286.0	480.6	60.1	6 012	3 088	857	1 160	381
Nassau	100	143 312	27.8	3 102	37 399	14	374.8	244.4	97.5	4 302	2 854	148	930	363
Okaloosa	401	261 745	80.9	8 450	72 995	68	1 803.3	1 764.4	41.6	10 376	4 464	2 690	2 825	356
Okeechobee	60	34 804	86.8	988	8 853	8	289.4	162.0	108.6	5 002	4 246	73	115	544
Orange	1 720	4 058 657	34.7	73 124	962 746	197	9 098.4	4 791.7	47.1	5 863	2 724	2 154	460	512
Osceola	423	762 955	35.0	12 152	152 219	40	1 106.8	480.5	122.7	3 191	2 661	69	95	357
Palm Beach	2 087	1 659 834	73.6	41 031	440 949	426	20 527.8	6 887.8	84.9	6 563	4 304	1 541	277	424
Pasco	437	246 305	76.0	7 654	62 638	95	3 976.7	1 695.5	59.4	5 127	4 602	35	112	358
Pinellas	1 965	1 383 434	66.1	36 685	367 626	315	13 415.5	5 493.9	36.8	6 254	4 798	727	369	335
Polk	711	419 264	80.7	13 383	113 216	111	3 932.0	1 983.0	91.5	4 336	3 491	81	159	585
Putnam	88	37 485	86.5	1 318	9 777	15	479.7	347.0	96.4	4 941	3 796	27	100	986
St. Johns	332	263 564	48.0	6 999	71 143	36	1 040.9	559.0	97.9	4 671	3 392	594	189	487
St. Lucie	245	147 643	75.6	3 959	36 555	53	1 784.7	945.1	122.0	5 197	4 573	77	145	389
Santa Rosa	119	53 759	89.7	1 970	14 597	30	686.5	560.8	98.1	4 636	3 141	353	484	593
Sarasota	687	481 774	71.5	13 051	132 072	148	6 673.6	1 986.0	63.4	6 479	5 985	65	152	265
Seminole	579	423 115	87.6	12 966	117 300	85	2 883.0	1 087.3	117.1	3 042	2 378	110	225	318
Sumter	48	23 597	78.3	661	5 728	10	154.2	242.3	111.9	5 668	3 942	231	976	456
Suwannee	32	15 512	92.0	512	3 748	7	288.7	163.7	93.9	4 966	3 936	40	193	714
Taylor	36	11 881	82.0	364	3 006	4	112.2	107.9	118.8	5 665	3 396	1 242	98	895
Union	5	D	D	(6)	D	1	30.0	33.0	70.4	2 592	1 805	41	75	614
Volusia	1 051	635 582	69.2	19 758	167 040	132	5 216.0	2 169.6	60.3	5 098	4 306	150	163	466
Wakulla	28	9 751	78.3	293	2 333	6	115.1	64.9	107.5	3 385	2 553	66	166	474
Walton	87	107 172	36.0	2 446	29 444	15	286.5	396.5	360.7	10 399	3 206	43	6 610	445
Washington	22	8 771	94.7	317	2 554	4	96.6	114.3	84.7	5 546	3 720	23	116	1 612

[1] Includes only establishments with payroll.   [2] Includes full-service restaurants, limited-service eating places, special food services, and drinking places (alcoholic beverages).   [3] For pay period including March 12.   [4] As of June 30. Covers all FDIC-insured commercial banks and savings institutions.   [5] Based on resident population estimated as of July 1, 1999.   [6] 20 to 99 employees.

Sources: Accommodation and Foodservices—U.S. Census Bureau, 1997 Economic Census, ECON97 Report Series CD-ROM, CD-EC97-1, Disc 1E, issued February 2001 (related Internet site <http://www.census.gov/epcd/www/97EC72.HTM>). Banking—U.S. Federal Deposit Insurance Corporation and Office of Thrift Supervision, "1999 Bank and Thrift Branch Office Data Book: Summary of Deposits," national and 6 regional data books (related Internet site <http://www2.fdic.gov/sod/>). Federal Funds and Grants—U.S. Census Bureau, County Aggregate files for each state, <http://www.census.gov/govs/www/cffr99.html>, (accessed: August 2000).

[Includes U.S., states, and 3,142 counties/county equivalents defined as of January 1, 1992. For changes to these areas since January 1, 1992, see appendix B. Geographic Information]

County	Accommodation and foodservices[1] (NAICS 72), 1997					Banking,[4] 1999		Federal funds and grants, 1999					
		Sales								Per capita[5] (dollars)			
											By selected type—		
	Estab-lishments	Total ($1,000)	Percent from food-services[2]	Paid employ-ees[3]	Annual payroll ($1,000)	Offices	Deposits (mil. dol.)	Total expenditures or obligations (mil. dol.)	Percent change, 1990–1999	Total	Direct payments for individuals	Procure-ment contract awards	Salaries and wages	Grant awards
GEORGIA	13 829	9 689 927	76.7	274 322	2 695 138	2 252	89 625.3	39 215.0	84.3	5 035	2 597	661	808	867
Appling	29	10 539	92.0	350	2 901	4	163.0	72.5	56.6	4 346	2 761	49	147	1 091
Atkinson	7	1 714	100.0	69	451	3	48.2	40.3	126.5	5 530	2 854	34	118	2 161
Bacon	17	D	D	(6)	D	4	160.0	58.5	133.6	5 640	2 891	40	126	2 289
Baker	3	157	100.0	7	32	1	12.6	17.6	102.1	4 860	2 414	24	95	1 213
Baldwin	66	37 798	90.2	1 507	9 829	11	438.8	157.1	87.3	3 723	2 699	109	106	791
Banks	22	16 726	85.8	372	4 566	3	63.2	33.5	111.7	2 547	1 853	16	63	600
Barrow	47	24 076	96.1	642	5 672	14	408.1	123.2	77.6	2 941	2 211	72	209	429
Bartow	123	65 261	87.6	1 827	17 732	18	663.0	200.3	112.0	2 684	2 071	75	112	403
Ben Hill	26	D	D	(7)	D	7	194.2	77.6	53.2	4 443	3 165	28	99	1 017
Berrien	15	5 530	95.6	169	1 251	7	187.0	70.8	82.7	4 283	3 085	27	98	647
Bibb....................	340	229 762	83.4	7 265	62 101	57	2 063.6	915.5	77.1	5 889	3 757	201	565	1 317
Bleckley	15	5 423	92.7	176	1 472	2	141.3	60.8	85.8	5 378	4 083	25	99	807
Brantley	10	2 093	100.0	59	541	2	43.5	48.5	124.1	3 491	2 822	26	97	520
Brooks	13	D	D	(6)	D	7	159.9	72.8	71.4	4 513	2 695	24	91	1 035
Bryan	29	D	D	(8)	D	3	127.7	619.0	609.7	25 375	2 288	2 960	19 549	561
Bulloch	99	52 479	87.4	1 894	13 543	17	516.8	160.1	76.7	3 154	2 171	36	162	607
Burke	21	7 369	D	283	1 941	9	190.1	99.4	80.9	4 280	2 563	46	126	1 132
Butts	28	10 546	D	272	2 758	4	173.1	70.0	87.3	3 808	2 864	28	141	765
Calhoun	8	D	D	(9)	D	4	63.1	35.6	74.9	7 208	4 287	87	179	1 780
Camden	68	35 268	80.3	1 220	9 882	11	187.6	450.4	126.1	9 577	1 591	1 224	5 723	1 036
Candler	17	7 694	84.8	262	1 998	7	124.2	40.9	85.0	4 565	2 996	31	117	1 065
Carroll	124	63 063	94.8	2 196	16 812	29	945.6	273.2	84.0	3 223	2 546	47	129	488
Catoosa	57	34 322	90.4	920	8 324	13	566.8	117.1	91.2	2 247	1 843	60	66	272
Charlton	11	3 799	92.4	104	1 112	2	76.7	41.6	109.9	4 399	3 021	59	211	1 064
Chatham	581	427 646	72.4	12 599	116 370	72	2 479.9	1 389.8	70.3	6 159	3 274	921	1 100	762
Chattahoochee	2	D	D	(10)	D	8	54.4	128.6	102.6	7 719	552	6 901	23	243
Chattooga	31	10 071	94.8	378	2 643	6	182.3	99.0	84.7	4 329	3 299	24	86	887
Cherokee	139	75 201	97.3	2 314	20 995	39	1 156.4	243.0	149.9	1 715	1 279	30	94	308
Clarke	240	125 546	89.9	4 371	33 769	33	1 160.1	431.3	49.8	4 758	2 262	230	803	1 412
Clay	2	D	D	(10)	D	1	15.8	24.1	51.4	6 850	2 993	407	555	2 484
Clayton	376	422 948	81.4	10 412	123 160	38	1 196.0	571.1	75.2	2 672	2 034	108	301	225
Clinch	8	D	D	(9)	D	1	49.1	35.5	37.5	5 318	3 335	659	144	1 132
Cobb...................	1 098	847 338	80.3	23 334	236 296	141	4 403.3	3 973.5	185.5	6 809	1 650	4 674	286	191
Coffee	47	26 133	85.5	810	6 479	12	366.6	135.5	105.7	3 877	2 472	48	145	984
Colquitt	52	23 295	88.4	754	6 447	8	351.8	181.1	76.8	4 446	2 910	28	117	1 058
Columbia	100	63 342	95.3	1 813	16 210	19	551.6	550.9	204.3	5 904	1 672	899	3 171	159
Cook	30	9 658	80.1	278	2 740	6	144.0	63.0	89.0	4 144	2 832	28	100	878
Coweta	103	58 512	89.7	1 880	15 163	23	616.1	227.0	111.2	2 540	2 040	50	110	323
Crawford	2	D	D	(10)	D	2	47.8	26.0	87.2	2 494	1 853	15	53	517
Crisp	51	26 241	57.2	913	7 991	9	250.2	103.2	79.7	5 003	3 198	34	138	1 281
Dade	22	10 453	97.6	319	2 468	5	95.9	48.4	105.1	3 151	2 521	62	76	486
Dawson	16	D	D	(6)	D	7	198.0	38.3	53.7	2 401	1 828	31	100	434
Decatur	30	14 043	D	455	3 241	8	226.1	115.9	61.5	4 272	2 732	68	115	1 044
De Kalb	1 232	809 662	77.7	21 365	215 439	127	6 092.9	1 992.5	37.0	3 338	1 808	77	1 039	401
Dodge	22	8 431	81.0	324	2 325	7	190.4	90.6	72.7	4 995	3 406	27	123	1 119
Dooly	16	3 248	57.5	89	791	6	160.4	85.0	64.8	6 481	3 212	38	186	1 680
Dougherty	192	118 067	D	3 736	31 590	25	782.9	661.9	67.4	7 036	3 369	978	1 555	1 063
Douglas	127	96 818	88.4	3 049	25 478	25	636.2	201.6	83.3	2 211	1 862	30	104	210
Early	17	D	D	(6)	D	3	120.8	63.8	81.9	5 261	2 960	149	160	1 345
Echols	–	–	–	–	–	–	–	6.3	50.5	2 469	1 511	11	40	781
Effingham..............	31	D	D	(7)	D	8	190.1	90.7	135.8	2 364	1 748	21	85	478
Elbert	34	11 602	88.4	396	2 652	8	237.6	97.6	69.0	5 039	3 549	118	371	938
Emanuel	26	9 501	92.9	310	2 457	8	223.7	116.5	73.8	5 536	3 321	50	233	1 660
Evans	19	6 416	D	174	1 811	8	127.3	45.6	93.1	4 519	3 011	34	229	1 112
Fannin	35	11 311	76.9	431	3 294	7	225.2	93.7	86.4	4 946	3 990	27	130	779
Fayette	118	102 342	68.1	2 750	27 627	26	888.1	203.0	138.3	2 197	1 939	47	126	82
Floyd..................	151	87 756	94.3	2 572	22 852	25	974.5	332.2	65.1	3 884	3 054	58	132	604
Forsyth	89	54 532	95.1	1 523	15 006	21	656.4	126.1	137.6	1 304	1 057	21	79	144
Franklin	35	16 794	88.9	621	4 314	12	281.2	85.8	92.8	4 442	3 443	37	135	770
Fulton	2 292	2 364 425	65.8	57 973	682 112	259	22 790.8	6 801.8	90.3	9 132	3 017	1 235	1 630	3 141
Gilmer.................	30	11 115	96.9	428	2 850	6	295.2	80.9	141.5	4 091	3 300	32	164	580
Glascock	2	D	D	(10)	D	1	10.6	13.1	72.3	5 139	3 648	61	218	1 037
Glynn	214	251 537	45.5	7 051	84 275	29	850.7	412.2	90.2	6 066	3 475	699	1 212	657
Gordon	76	40 843	88.5	1 201	11 290	9	399.9	132.5	119.3	3 157	2 397	52	134	543
Grady	26	8 152	89.7	300	1 996	9	207.9	86.6	65.6	4 011	2 725	22	80	843
Greene	19	6 302	77.8	208	1 614	5	205.4	61.7	88.7	4 379	3 146	35	174	965

[1] Includes only establishments with payroll.   [2] Includes full-service restaurants, limited-service eating places, special food services, and drinking places (alcoholic beverages).   [3] For pay period including March 12.   [4] As of June 30. Covers all FDIC-insured commercial banks and savings institutions.   [5] Based on resident population estimated as of July 1, 1999.   [6] 100 to 249 employees.   [7] 250 to 499 employees.   [8] 500 to 999 employees.   [9] 20 to 99 employees.   [10] 0 to 19 employees.

Sources: Accommodation and Foodservices—U.S. Census Bureau, 1997 Economic Census, ECON[97] Report Series CD-ROM, CD-EC97-1, Disc 1E, issued February 2001 (related Internet site <http://www.census.gov/epcd/www/97EC72.HTM>).   Banking—U.S. Federal Deposit Insurance Corporation and Office of Thrift Supervision, "1999 Bank and Thrift Branch Office Data Book: Summary of Deposits," national and 6 regional data books (related Internet site <http://www2.fdic.gov/sod/>).   Federal Funds and Grants—U.S. Census Bureau, County Aggregate files for each state, <http://www.census.gov/govs/www/cffr99.html>, (accessed: August 2000).

[Includes U.S., states, and 3,142 counties/county equivalents defined as of January 1, 1992. For changes to these areas since January 1, 1992, see appendix B. Geographic Information]

County	Accommodation and foodservices[1] (NAICS 72), 1997					Banking,[4] 1999		Federal funds and grants, 1999							
		Sales								Per capita[5] (dollars)					
												By selected type—			
	Estab-lishments	Total ($1,000)	Percent from food-services[2]	Paid employ-ees[3]	Annual payroll ($1,000)	Offices	Deposits (mil. dol.)	Total expenditures or obligations (mil. dol.)	Percent change, 1990–1999	Total	Direct payments for individuals	Procure-ment contract awards	Salaries and wages	Grant awards
GEORGIA—Con.														
Gwinnett	896	720 365	79.0	19 623	199 844	146	5 144.6	926.6	86.7	1 698	972	274	307	134
Habersham	64	26 005	87.0	879	7 337	19	629.8	117.6	74.5	3 614	2 920	36	172	476
Hall	202	148 511	74.6	4 192	41 607	37	1 654.3	372.8	48.7	3 024	2 257	147	178	431
Hancock	5	1 207	100.0	46	321	2	65.4	52.7	86.7	5 831	3 902	24	84	1 777
Haralson	31	D	D	(6)	D	11	269.9	99.5	102.3	3 971	2 808	31	110	1 004
Harris	35	D	D	(7)	D	5	68.3	73.0	84.3	3 224	2 439	27	111	639
Hart	22	9 043	D	268	2 359	8	225.1	90.9	95.9	4 107	2 665	275	193	922
Heard	5	D	D	(8)	D	3	54.4	30.3	80.3	2 890	2 151	24	76	622
Henry	139	74 463	87.6	2 485	20 011	28	845.9	311.5	111.5	2 746	1 910	45	564	218
Houston	183	102 469	83.4	3 753	28 385	22	639.5	1 214.2	39.4	11 229	3 334	1 933	5 606	362
Irwin	9	2 013	D	70	454	3	63.7	41.9	88.4	4 569	2 574	29	182	1 010
Jackson	53	65 327	D	1 318	16 657	16	320.4	131.3	108.6	3 361	2 421	181	139	599
Jasper	7	2 239	D	78	634	2	107.7	35.7	80.5	3 369	2 430	27	106	768
Jeff Davis	20	D	D	(6)	D	5	121.8	49.7	87.4	3 911	2 791	29	103	748
Jefferson	17	6 365	D	207	1 516	13	175.1	95.7	57.0	5 361	3 329	29	124	1 537
Jenkins	12	D	D	(9)	D	2	57.2	44.6	79.6	5 313	3 123	38	117	1 444
Johnson	7	D	D	(8)	D	1	49.5	42.7	90.6	5 145	3 496	34	104	1 261
Jones	8	D	D	(9)	D	4	158.7	61.5	76.3	2 639	1 956	22	66	586
Lamar	18	6 575	D	217	1 629	4	156.1	61.5	97.8	4 094	3 224	31	156	613
Lanier	5	D	D	(8)	D	1	107.8	27.9	70.5	4 006	2 777	34	101	920
Laurens	76	40 850	89.3	1 448	10 031	17	597.7	230.9	65.5	5 257	3 134	153	821	999
Lee	9	2 427	D	94	768	5	50.9	46.8	104.3	2 007	1 409	17	64	286
Liberty	65	35 827	89.9	1 209	9 041	10	215.4	231.0	7.6	3 870	1 856	36	1 087	888
Lincoln	12	D	D	(9)	D	2	54.1	38.9	104.3	4 664	3 294	493	112	729
Long	6	1 134	100.0	39	303	1	12.2	29.6	204.2	3 403	1 733	16	58	1 572
Lowndes	194	109 330	85.3	3 700	30 801	26	950.6	532.8	92.6	6 238	2 802	884	1 841	667
Lumpkin	34	16 492	81.6	465	4 004	8	247.9	58.5	84.0	2 957	1 914	32	506	495
McDuffie	34	17 783	86.1	572	4 824	10	254.1	89.4	85.9	4 096	2 960	23	172	918
McIntosh	23	8 951	73.2	332	2 670	3	67.5	59.6	42.6	5 897	3 283	31	122	2 457
Macon	15	D	D	(9)	D	3	56.7	68.9	79.7	5 251	2 998	24	123	1 542
Madison	50	33 379	70.3	1 032	9 823	7	122.6	83.0	103.8	3 293	2 547	35	118	561
Marion	5	D	D	(10)	D	1	25.3	27.7	87.1	4 086	2 144	19	187	582
Meriwether	29	8 994	93.3	269	2 487	8	158.7	89.7	72.1	3 895	2 747	34	99	983
Miller	7	2 738	D	121	719	4	93.7	33.1	91.7	5 247	3 004	29	149	1 056
Mitchell	30	11 604	58.9	292	4 028	7	201.6	101.8	62.1	4 796	2 788	34	149	1 255
Monroe	33	21 606	D	616	4 740	4	117.4	57.9	80.2	2 891	2 253	38	123	458
Montgomery	7	1 995	D	90	506	4	130.9	34.0	56.5	4 328	2 929	36	139	1 088
Morgan	37	16 752	69.9	574	4 386	6	154.6	52.8	81.9	3 420	2 583	32	120	604
Murray	39	19 981	69.8	493	5 144	8	211.6	77.7	85.2	2 290	1 814	39	127	302
Muscogee	365	D	D	(11)	D	51	2 436.1	1 586.7	54.4	8 715	3 598	58	4 278	750
Newton	58	30 864	91.4	1 074	8 190	12	487.8	178.7	107.3	2 950	2 252	53	117	515
Oconee	13	3 546	100.0	134	821	9	214.1	57.8	119.0	2 355	1 890	43	175	213
Oglethorpe	8	1 392	100.0	59	409	2	67.5	31.8	57.5	2 747	1 799	144	79	672
Paulding	51	D	D	(7)	D	16	422.4	120.1	104.0	1 509	1 129	18	63	293
Peach	44	D	D	(7)	D	5	183.3	138.4	105.5	5 537	3 964	127	197	1 151
Pickens	25	11 283	100.0	331	3 002	6	335.0	90.6	158.0	4 312	2 732	146	123	1 303
Pierce	21	5 620	D	229	1 834	5	158.5	64.6	84.2	4 090	2 990	54	126	654
Pike	10	2 136	100.0	77	654	5	113.1	47.3	101.6	3 613	2 458	36	425	644
Polk	43	D	D	(7)	D	10	320.2	169.5	79.9	4 628	3 367	298	108	819
Pulaski	16	5 575	D	326	1 885	3	98.0	50.8	71.7	6 076	3 971	29	125	1 161
Putnam	22	6 122	93.0	191	1 322	4	166.3	67.4	101.7	3 705	2 914	35	149	548
Quitman	1	D	D	(8)	D	1	3.8	17.4	-73.0	7 116	4 353	80	206	2 382
Rabun	47	19 008	51.4	573	5 285	7	315.2	64.9	90.6	4 742	3 691	47	186	783
Randolph	14	2 597	D	88	566	3	63.8	45.7	74.9	5 699	3 234	36	112	1 935
Richmond	400	255 627	79.1	8 301	70 404	59	2 053.7	1 142.2	32.0	6 002	3 779	172	1 040	973
Rockdale	122	86 634	88.6	2 657	23 487	18	609.7	147.1	91.8	2 133	1 810	27	95	195
Schley	4	266	100.0	6	53	1	44.1	14.5	48.4	3 681	2 266	25	100	1 111
Screven	18	3 952	84.5	89	911	6	140.7	70.1	79.5	4 850	3 091	35	133	1 248
Seminole	10	2 937	D	82	627	6	127.9	48.0	84.1	4 892	3 309	28	103	1 015
Spalding	92	46 724	94.0	1 524	12 611	13	572.2	228.5	90.2	3 951	3 042	52	118	730
Stephens	44	21 344	90.0	844	5 730	7	267.4	111.4	74.2	4 399	3 549	40	155	610
Stewart	6	1 654	D	30	366	2	30.5	34.1	79.2	6 342	3 595	40	141	2 357
Sumter	51	23 509	82.4	770	6 248	10	322.2	142.0	77.3	4 528	2 882	47	204	1 121
Talbot	6	D	D	(8)	D	2	41.8	32.8	100.0	4 708	3 264	42	116	1 228
Taliaferro	1	D	D	(10)	D	1	14.4	19.4	191.2	10 068	4 147	59	210	5 538
Tattnall	19	6 641	77.0	241	1 641	10	214.6	89.5	76.6	4 666	3 276	29	107	1 099

[1] Includes only establishments with payroll. [2] Includes full-service restaurants, limited-service eating places, special food services, and drinking places (alcoholic beverages). [3] For pay period including March 12. [4] As of June 30. Covers all FDIC-insured commercial banks and savings institutions. [5] Based on resident population estimated as of July 1, 1999. [6] 250 to 499 employees. [7] 500 to 999 employees. [8] 20 to 99 employees. [9] 100 to 249 employees. [10] 0 to 19 employees. [11] 5,000 to 9,999 employees.

Sources: Accommodation and Foodservices—U.S. Census Bureau, 1997 Economic Census, ECON97 Report Series CD-ROM, CD-EC97-1, Disc 1E, issued February 2001 (related Internet site <http://www.census.gov/epcd/www/97EC72.HTM>). Banking—U.S. Federal Deposit Insurance Corporation and Office of Thrift Supervision, "1999 Bank and Thrift Branch Office Data Book: Summary of Deposits," national and 6 regional data books (related Internet site <http://www2.fdic.gov/sod/>). Federal Funds and Grants—U.S. Census Bureau, County Aggregate files for each state, <http://www.census.gov/govs/www/cffr99.html>, (accessed: August 2000).

[Includes U.S., states, and 3,142 counties/county equivalents defined as of January 1, 1992. For changes to these areas since January 1, 1992, see appendix B. Geographic Information]

County	Accommodation and foodservices[1] (NAICS 72), 1997 Sales Establishments	Sales Total ($1,000)	Percent from food-services[2]	Paid employees[3]	Annual payroll ($1,000)	Banking,[4] 1999 Offices	Deposits (mil. dol.)	Federal funds and grants, 1999 Total expenditures or obligations (mil. dol.)	Percent change, 1990–1999	Per capita[5] (dollars) Total	By selected type— Direct payments for individuals	Procure-ment contract awards	Salaries and wages	Grant awards
GEORGIA—Con.														
Taylor	6	1 313	100.0	48	344	2	52.2	46.4	81.1	5 603	3 598	36	128	1 669
Telfair	19	4 923	D	175	1 077	6	133.3	71.2	88.6	6 244	4 307	44	136	1 526
Terrell	9	D	D	(6)	D	4	135.4	61.3	–5.0	5 472	2 904	427	288	1 402
Thomas	64	36 879	76.9	1 100	9 615	15	643.1	200.9	75.0	4 683	3 251	33	211	984
Tift	80	44 283	78.3	1 434	12 791	15	444.7	143.6	72.8	3 884	2 647	34	265	780
Toombs	60	22 761	88.8	814	5 724	12	442.8	108.4	74.0	4 172	2 887	31	141	1 010
Towns	24	14 776	D	381	4 787	7	197.5	48.6	138.0	5 526	4 500	–9	143	882
Treutlen	8	2 257	100.0	131	686	1	36.4	28.5	47.3	4 796	2 911	29	116	1 597
Troup	111	50 601	83.7	1 757	12 798	23	841.0	230.5	–34.8	3 920	2 893	86	117	799
Turner	16	6 027	42.4	194	948	4	188.5	48.3	89.8	5 226	3 095	32	138	1 257
Twiggs	4	D	D	(7)	D	1	16.7	38.9	97.6	3 810	2 612	20	54	1 038
Union	27	8 443	86.6	272	2 309	4	328.6	80.1	135.2	4 647	3 654	46	173	764
Upson	46	14 559	94.0	502	3 750	7	281.8	110.4	66.7	3 140	3 140	51	103	759
Walker	51	19 972	95.9	658	5 077	12	393.8	240.3	65.3	3 817	3 194	24	100	484
Walton	45	D	D	(8)	D	11	443.3	157.2	105.6	2 687	2 164	29	116	350
Ware	63	34 399	D	1 180	9 919	10	383.0	193.5	70.3	5 493	4 034	50	219	1 130
Warren	1	D	D	(9)	D	1	39.2	34.0	60.6	5 592	3 557	101	158	1 651
Washington	20	D	D	(10)	D	7	243.0	91.7	85.8	4 539	3 041	44	131	1 180
Wayne	34	15 678	88.0	555	4 107	8	165.9	138.6	134.5	5 412	2 982	722	780	802
Webster	–	–	–	–	–	1	4.2	9.8	56.1	4 460	2 677	52	210	877
Wheeler	3	387	100.0	8	47	2	22.0	26.4	62.5	5 425	3 353	38	126	1 655
White	73	25 320	70.9	666	6 617	7	297.8	64.2	128.5	3 527	2 890	42	114	463
Whitfield	143	91 981	87.1	2 565	25 365	23	1 126.0	242.9	77.7	2 919	2 256	79	109	469
Wilcox	1	D	D	(9)	D	7	88.0	45.1	81.4	6 081	3 809	36	137	1 295
Wilkes	13	D	D	(6)	D	5	173.3	53.8	80.0	5 099	3 698	32	164	1 084
Wilkinson	8	D	D	(7)	D	3	84.4	47.1	87.4	4 315	3 166	28	97	990
Worth	18	D	D	(6)	D	3	144.0	80.7	77.1	3 588	2 202	20	81	755
HAWAII	3 081	5 007 899	39.6	88 083	1 507 538	306	17 844.3	8 568.2	52.1	7 228	2 981	963	2 055	1 126
Hawaii	326	546 576	26.5	10 441	188 103	38	1 287.1	597.0	73.6	4 193	2 875	104	293	913
Honolulu	2 125	3 036 837	48.0	53 916	852 782	209	14 620.5	6 944.7	45.7	8 033	2 906	1 203	2 713	1 191
Kalawao	(11)	(11)	(11)	(11)	(11)	–	–	–	–	–	–	–	–	–
Kauai	210	293 784	33.7	5 775	102 273	22	594.2	253.7	69.5	4 488	2 555	741	438	747
Maui	11 420	11 1 130 702	11 24.6	11 117 951	11 364 380	37	1 342.5	393.1	91.0	3 224	2 109	368	197	528
IDAHO	2 980	1 233 215	72.5	42 087	345 955	435	10 141.7	6 164.7	61.2	4 925	2 521	695	554	940
Ada	649	370 525	74.8	12 115	104 022	95	2 659.7	1 304.4	82.9	4 603	2 115	350	797	1 316
Adams	14	3 377	D	134	1 701	2	20.4	28.9	156.1	7 640	3 244	216	856	3 278
Bannock	188	75 270	D	2 792	20 510	22	398.4	272.1	71.1	3 634	2 344	170	307	726
Bear Lake	13	2 799	63.0	90	659	5	67.5	30.9	24.8	4 708	2 760	88	261	1 164
Benewah	26	4 219	92.3	181	1 263	5	71.3	46.4	64.2	5 117	3 140	84	294	1 142
Bingham	51	12 575	D	583	3 730	10	199.8	151.9	80.9	3 606	1 925	173	243	834
Blaine	131	115 305	38.2	3 365	34 332	10	228.5	40.1	71.1	2 312	1 455	72	226	485
Boise	23	3 083	92.1	110	734	1	24.4	28.6	17.3	5 378	2 397	639	735	1 585
Bonner	115	33 566	61.0	1 385	11 135	10	292.7	131.1	82.7	3 633	2 715	81	260	571
Bonneville	181	90 586	83.7	3 391	26 022	27	700.8	808.4	–12.7	9 915	2 126	6 646	516	463
Boundary	24	13 287	D	276	2 494	4	82.5	45.7	116.1	4 577	2 614	182	462	1 141
Butte	9	1 506	70.7	50	335	2	25.9	26.1	114.9	8 680	2 840	52	2 275	2 675
Camas	5	D	D	(7)	D	1	4.6	5.4	61.7	6 286	2 572	223	771	1 341
Canyon	188	71 422	92.8	2 619	19 112	30	817.2	433.4	93.5	3 483	2 207	305	134	771
Caribou	16	2 698	74.6	129	656	3	50.4	33.9	70.7	4 656	2 267	96	224	866
Cassia	48	17 886	68.0	653	4 837	9	254.2	85.3	82.3	3 956	2 089	57	317	620
Clark	3	D	D	(9)	D	1	4.5	13.8	131.9	15 152	2 039	204	1 507	9 266
Clearwater	31	4 688	80.3	186	1 274	5	71.6	52.3	77.2	5 586	3 096	438	1 029	917
Custer	26	5 758	23.7	131	1 686	2	31.2	20.4	73.8	4 989	2 912	256	863	892
Elmore	53	13 531	83.1	479	3 851	7	99.8	288.0	89.7	11 239	2 488	1 409	6 306	896
Franklin	14	3 327	80.1	171	894	3	68.1	33.8	64.3	2 977	2 079	47	200	310
Fremont	32	8 599	50.6	172	2 002	6	60.3	50.5	82.7	4 243	2 347	115	435	672
Gem	22	5 362	D	189	1 159	4	121.0	57.2	74.7	3 779	2 827	46	253	549
Gooding	28	4 957	92.8	254	1 525	6	112.5	53.9	72.6	3 924	2 710	49	185	701
Idaho	56	9 731	71.2	323	2 481	9	135.4	91.0	83.6	6 055	3 004	391	1 004	1 190
Jefferson	18	D	D	(6)	D	5	90.1	55.8	110.6	2 795	1 751	72	120	441
Jerome	30	6 949	82.4	210	1 704	7	122.7	61.1	71.1	3 374	2 172	47	141	669

[1] Includes only establishments with payroll. [2] Includes full-service restaurants, limited-service eating places, special food services, and drinking places (alcoholic beverages). [3] For pay period including March 12. [4] As of June 30. Covers all FDIC-insured commercial banks and savings institutions. [5] Based on resident population estimated as of July 1, 1999. [6] 100 to 249 employees. [7] 20 to 99 employees. [8] 500 to 999 employees. [9] 0 to 19 employees. [10] 250 to 499 employees. [11] Kalawao County included with Maui County; data not available separately.

Sources: Accommodation and Foodservices—U.S. Census Bureau, 1997 Economic Census, ECON97 Report Series CD-ROM, CD-EC97-1, Disc 1E, issued February 2001 (related Internet site <http://www.census.gov/epcd/www/97EC72.HTM>). Banking—U.S. Federal Deposit Insurance Corporation and Office of Thrift Supervision, "1999 Bank and Thrift Branch Office Data Book: Summary of Deposits," national and 6 regional data books (related Internet site <http://www2.fdic.gov/sod/>). Federal Funds and Grants—U.S. Census Bureau, County Aggregate files for each state, <http://www.census.gov/govs/www/cffr99.html>, (accessed: August 2000).

Table B–12. Counties — Accommodation and Foodservices, Banking, and Federal Funds–Con.

[Includes U.S., states, and 3,142 counties/county equivalents defined as of January 1, 1992. For changes to these areas since January 1, 1992, see appendix B. Geographic Information]

| County | Accommodation and foodservices[1] (NAICS 72), 1997 | | | | | Banking,[4] 1999 | | Federal funds and grants, 1999 | | | | | | |
	Estab-lishments	Sales — Total ($1,000)	Sales — Percent from food-services[2]	Paid employ-ees[3]	Annual payroll ($1,000)	Offices	Deposits (mil. dol.)	Total expenditures or obligations (mil. dol.)	Percent change, 1990–1999	Per capita[5] — Total	Direct payments for individuals	Procure-ment contract awards	Salaries and wages	Grant awards
IDAHO—Con.														
Kootenai	298	137 688	64.4	4 086	37 946	35	848.7	376.4	99.1	3 591	2 628	163	293	478
Latah	91	33 527	68.4	1 348	8 606	13	291.6	140.4	62.8	4 318	2 112	248	343	1 212
Lemhi	36	6 521	60.5	209	1 990	3	71.1	45.5	72.5	3 551		307	1 169	651
Lewis	18	4 156	D	109	1 162	3	42.0	37.2	107.8	9 431	4 974	125	351	2 205
Lincoln	7	1 543	100.0	63	432	2	24.8	16.2	54.3	4 228	2 375	94	822	376
Madison	40	D	D	(6)	D	6	149.5	49.8	84.3	2 007	1 327	27	102	276
Minidoka	25	5 710	D	274	1 888	5	130.5	72.7	77.2	3 583	2 467	67	158	420
Nez Perce	103	43 015	81.3	1 439	12 542	16	374.8	210.1	91.0	5 692	3 356	435	263	1 344
Oneida	7	D	D	(7)	D	2	38.1	20.7	29.4	5 099	2 722	57	214	650
Owyhee	18	2 435	100.0	107	708	3	34.4	32.9	68.0	3 158	1 799	184	209	646
Payette	25	4 689	100.0	208	1 060	5	137.5	98.3	124.4	4 714	2 520	207	79	1 783
Power	16	2 331	91.4	76	563	4	46.7	36.3	35.7	4 321	1 697	42	136	438
Shoshone	49	8 129	77.0	326	2 266	8	131.7	101.4	120.8	7 426	4 125	2 284	264	747
Teton	19	4 145	53.7	104	1 081	2	35.4	18.8	61.6	3 286	1 657	67	201	790
Twin Falls	148	62 688	86.5	2 303	18 122	29	786.9	253.8	80.8	4 031	2 574	208	419	651
Valley	65	13 935	76.1	484	3 908	4	76.3	53.9	138.5	6 860	3 803	777	1 190	1 076
Washington	21	D	D	(8)	D	4	106.1	49.8	46.2	4 837	3 137	38	209	1 222
ILLINOIS	23 984	14 826 805	79.4	397 300	4 018 697	3 881	220 296.8	55 836.0	50.3	4 604	2 769	287	495	873
Adams	139	65 890	84.8	2 204	18 205	37	1 139.8	290.3	44.6	4 336	3 061	110	239	722
Alexander	23	4 342	D	130	1 022	3	66.5	68.6	59.6	6 916	3 891	39	196	2 502
Bond	36	11 042	86.1	407	3 062	9	203.7	85.4	106.7	4 980	2 742	87	1 079	553
Boone	53	18 556	94.4	556	4 749	12	385.7	95.6	63.7	2 417	1 900	28	100	185
Brown	12	1 754	D	77	495	6	87.1	26.3	61.4	3 799	2 116	57	234	645
Bureau	86	20 711	92.7	766	5 390	25	667.3	150.8	50.1	4 266	3 093	43	218	237
Calhoun	18	3 615	100.0	96	836	5	87.0	27.0	-9.7	5 545	3 501	465	268	626
Carroll	55	8 950	94.2	317	2 126	12	332.3	107.7	49.9	6 451	3 582	985	694	480
Cass	36	7 672	D	237	1 778	9	240.0	63.0	58.1	4 752	3 199	81	311	391
Champaign	449	248 630	80.4	8 944	70 646	67	2 351.2	772.7	26.2	4 538	1 999	304	421	1 624
Christian	76	21 567	92.9	763	5 372	23	521.3	162.9	53.0	4 550	3 341	43	130	426
Clark	40	12 418	89.2	530	3 214	10	244.9	83.3	69.7	5 035	3 312	54	162	731
Clay	30	5 819	84.2	216	1 592	9	213.9	70.2	68.9	4 906	3 391	50	192	704
Clinton	92	D	D	(6)	D	20	682.7	125.0	70.0	3 529	2 075	176	130	260
Coles	136	59 840	86.3	2 058	15 413	28	654.7	185.2	60.8	3 574	2 586	38	148	526
Cook	9 912	7 770 045	74.7	177 351	2 092 358	1 146	120 547.5	24 312.3	42.9	4 682	2 723	334	496	1 045
Crawford	34	D	D	(9)	D	14	351.1	92.3	67.9	4 424	3 088	61	148	416
Cumberland	14	D	D	(8)	D	4	130.3	46.5	76.6	4 186	2 696	40	152	632
DeKalb	190	73 198	88.8	2 664	17 759	30	1 268.2	226.5	71.6	2 604	1 925	33	133	253
De Witt	42	11 148	84.2	384	2 850	10	225.1	78.8	79.5	4 726	3 158	45	175	598
Douglas	47	17 269	89.0	692	4 834	17	303.2	76.7	67.6	3 858	2 401	394	160	287
DuPage	1 698	1 495 412	75.3	37 452	405 678	300	17 294.2	2 301.6	72.3	2 579	1 887	199	344	122
Edgar	31	6 059	92.5	264	1 575	12	352.7	98.5	69.3	5 044	3 289	65	192	586
Edwards	7	D	D	(8)	D	3	122.5	29.1	52.7	4 231	3 024	52	184	445
Effingham	90	59 206	68.2	2 061	15 797	16	684.0	130.2	60.7	3 855	2 609	72	258	644
Fayette	39	12 458	84.4	477	3 524	9	238.0	90.2	69.9	4 096	2 778	46	154	532
Ford	32	7 532	D	290	2 039	13	324.4	72.6	65.1	5 167	3 434	51	190	481
Franklin	82	26 697	82.5	983	7 496	18	481.5	246.7	76.8	6 111	3 966	719	250	993
Fulton	81	20 407	97.2	837	5 847	21	504.2	174.9	24.4	4 521	3 479	149	172	357
Gallatin	8	1 320	100.0	45	257	4	77.6	41.5	75.2	6 298	3 772	-282	209	974
Greene	31	D	D	(8)	D	7	209.5	81.3	77.0	5 166	3 224	49	187	999
Grundy	72	32 797	81.6	999	8 358	24	572.4	124.6	72.3	3 351	2 485	38	163	310
Hamilton	7	2 070	100.0	88	514	4	150.9	47.4	59.2	5 519	3 448	51	202	744
Hancock	44	7 822	95.8	321	2 012	17	330.9	96.0	47.6	4 580	3 081	112	208	376
Hardin	6	D	D	(7)	D	3	44.8	25.9	44.8	5 277	3 763	38	178	1 125
Henderson	12	1 964	100.0	83	329	5	130.2	38.3	40.0	4 457	2 639	95	213	495
Henry	113	32 892	94.5	1 309	9 140	30	829.5	195.5	50.3	3 769	2 837	41	168	237
Iroquois	67	14 469	91.3	435	3 347	26	584.1	154.5	63.7	4 951	3 201	50	188	558
Jackson	156	65 356	90.9	2 379	17 750	22	574.1	223.6	47.0	3 686	2 411	129	280	755
Jasper	18	2 283	100.0	87	527	6	182.7	47.5	78.8	4 498	2 561	91	195	645
Jefferson	72	41 883	84.0	1 270	11 278	19	506.3	171.2	57.0	4 368	3 149	54	231	724
Jersey	50	15 975	70.9	612	4 597	9	246.4	69.8	69.7	3 237	2 413	29	109	372
Jo Daviess	101	61 778	33.4	1 755	16 042	17	490.4	96.0	68.9	4 453	3 120	128	194	565
Johnson	15	3 642	D	111	1 051	4	129.3	52.0	75.8	3 822	2 722	49	272	582
Kane	633	367 015	95.3	11 078	106 306	114	4 829.8	1 290.3	56.3	3 205	1 795	818	308	246

[1] Includes only establishments with payroll. [2] Includes full-service restaurants, limited-service eating places, special food services, and drinking places (alcoholic beverages). [3] For pay period including March 12. [4] As of June 30. Covers all FDIC-insured commercial banks and savings institutions. [5] Based on resident population estimated as of July 1, 1999. [6] 500 to 999 employees. [7] 20 to 99 employees. [8] 100 to 249 employees. [9] 250 to 499 employees.

Sources: Accommodation and Foodservices—U.S. Census Bureau, 1997 Economic Census, ECON97 Report Series CD-ROM, CD-EC97-1, Disc 1E, issued February 2001 (related Internet site <http://www.census.gov/epcd/www/97EC72.HTM>). Banking—U.S. Federal Deposit Insurance Corporation and Office of Thrift Supervision, "1999 Bank and Thrift Branch Office Data Book: Summary of Deposits," national and 6 regional data books (related Internet site <http://www2.fdic.gov/sod/>). Federal Funds and Grants—U.S. Census Bureau, County Aggregate files for each state, <http://www.census.gov/govs/www/cffr99.html>, (accessed: August 2000).

Table B–12. Counties — Accommodation and Foodservices, Banking, and Federal Funds–Con.

[Includes U.S., states, and 3,142 counties/county equivalents defined as of January 1, 1992. For changes to these areas since January 1, 1992, see appendix B. Geographic Information]

County	Accommodation and foodservices[1] (NAICS 72), 1997 Sales Establishments	Total ($1,000)	Percent from food-services[2]	Paid employ-ees[3]	Annual payroll ($1,000)	Banking,[4] 1999 Offices	Deposits (mil. dol.)	Federal funds and grants, 1999 Total expenditures or obligations (mil. dol.)	Percent change, 1990–1999	Per capita[5] (dollars) Total	Direct payments for individuals	Procure-ment contract awards	Salaries and wages	Grant awards
ILLINOIS–Con.														
Kankakee	229	100 367	92.1	3 563	27 356	37	1 209.8	420.4	49.5	4 093	2 978	61	209	646
Kendall	76	28 202	90.5	869	6 605	18	577.1	96.2	75.7	1 793	1 281	30	233	70
Knox	132	54 489	86.1	1 863	14 802	20	686.7	251.0	48.8	4 532	3 456	49	200	525
Lake	1 245	775 839	83.4	20 090	210 277	172	10 377.9	2 776.5	80.5	4 493	1 847	389	2 032	215
La Salle	332	109 747	82.6	3 830	30 798	63	2 018.9	432.4	44.6	3 922	3 022	46	173	375
Lawrence	24	5 644	D	199	1 465	10	240.8	84.3	65.2	5 562	3 752	36	178	706
Lee	68	20 126	84.7	638	4 960	17	483.0	139.0	63.7	3 891	2 754	43	154	297
Livingston	86	26 500	94.0	1 001	7 246	26	743.8	156.1	56.3	3 939	2 613	38	153	264
Logan	77	23 959	88.1	864	6 355	21	425.1	134.7	68.8	4 244	2 803	41	189	534
McDonough	78	29 771	93.2	1 303	8 123	17	437.5	118.0	50.7	3 350	2 313	63	163	385
McHenry	409	175 759	91.7	5 347	46 390	84	3 186.0	506.8	86.0	2 053	1 645	59	119	185
McLean	336	200 528	80.3	7 104	58 320	58	1 677.1	457.0	71.8	3 141	1 898	64	278	441
Macon	233	123 573	87.1	4 105	35 653	40	1 468.4	508.4	64.3	4 490	3 120	265	185	730
Macoupin	90	24 691	93.8	783	5 738	32	681.6	221.5	57.5	4 518	3 507	50	151	415
Madison	537	253 806	89.5	8 326	68 086	85	3 211.0	1 101.7	32.1	4 246	3 171	283	150	581
Marion	95	31 385	93.3	1 056	8 490	22	440.8	222.3	65.7	5 316	4 055	74	267	681
Marshall	31	7 657	94.9	422	2 147	9	238.3	56.3	4.5	4 342	3 019	58	165	245
Mason	48	8 300	94.7	294	2 052	9	241.0	83.5	63.0	4 971	3 470	51	179	476
Massac	38	10 272	81.7	343	2 604	4	213.0	119.2	149.6	7 736	3 523	2 785	137	1 021
Menard	24	D	D	(6)	D	8	170.9	46.8	54.4	3 675	2 505	22	89	374
Mercer	34	5 564	100.0	215	1 484	10	213.5	69.2	18.8	3 925	2 708	51	177	241
Monroe	51	D	D	(7)	D	19	457.8	85.0	90.6	3 115	2 420	113	116	213
Montgomery	77	25 672	84.5	924	6 461	24	514.7	146.4	55.6	4 674	3 170	48	200	702
Morgan	78	34 032	87.5	1 165	9 463	20	538.3	165.5	77.6	4 707	3 116	58	163	960
Moultrie	27	6 230	D	283	1 893	10	218.6	65.5	63.5	4 493	3 287	32	141	255
Ogle	93	27 595	77.8	999	7 162	27	657.2	160.8	67.1	3 155	2 207	189	156	186
Peoria	494	246 341	83.3	8 204	70 717	73	2 097.9	902.8	58.9	4 984	3 071	394	703	713
Perry	34	10 379	D	428	2 913	9	269.5	93.8	65.2	4 398	3 476	34	127	493
Piatt	28	D	D	(8)	D	11	321.5	67.8	61.0	4 080	2 902	40	148	191
Pike	39	9 310	83.0	389	2 435	16	379.7	96.7	71.0	5 616	3 347	281	211	830
Pope	8	1 800	100.0	36	396	1	24.0	26.4	87.1	5 482	3 023	157	620	1 329
Pulaski	10	1 645	D	64	364	4	43.4	53.8	74.3	7 371	3 914	379	394	2 246
Putnam	11	D	D	(9)	D	3	97.7	23.5	60.7	4 017	2 947	36	136	140
Randolph	75	20 354	93.7	749	5 265	20	584.7	138.1	67.1	4 111	3 122	135	179	447
Richland	34	12 887	89.2	439	3 403	10	264.5	73.3	57.5	4 400	3 102	46	188	621
Rock Island	373	161 423	90.6	5 780	43 925	51	2 264.2	891.6	16.5	6 044	3 238	554	1 715	458
St. Clair	477	245 005	95.0	8 481	66 694	81	2 969.2	1 653.4	44.6	6 358	3 420	470	1 379	992
Saline	58	19 688	96.0	709	5 124	17	492.5	163.5	67.2	6 276	4 012	764	237	1 010
Sangamon	497	D	D	(10)	D	75	3 089.9	2 412.4	80.1	12 610	3 448	112	576	8 258
Schuyler	15	D	D	(6)	D	4	115.7	38.1	83.8	5 081	2 864	59	186	1 094
Scott	9	1 239	100.0	90	316	4	104.5	28.6	77.7	5 095	2 834	148	162	744
Shelby	40	15 429	61.7	473	4 154	18	312.8	104.7	68.8	4 652	3 190	90	200	350
Stark	6	D	D	(9)	D	5	145.0	36.5	66.7	5 805	3 467	104	199	477
Stephenson	103	37 054	91.2	1 259	8 704	21	858.3	192.8	55.8	3 953	2 882	50	161	527
Tazewell	265	115 831	87.2	4 329	33 683	47	1 409.7	452.4	71.5	3 486	2 634	37	214	452
Union	26	D	D	(8)	D	9	223.4	87.3	69.8	4 846	3 226	38	156	1 207
Vermilion	185	68 520	90.2	2 570	20 049	38	963.6	476.2	45.4	5 681	3 494	616	682	596
Wabash	24	7 883	D	367	2 399	7	242.1	53.6	65.4	4 286	3 172	39	137	503
Warren	37	9 775	95.9	334	2 675	12	324.1	87.8	40.2	4 637	2 955	139	195	537
Washington	43	10 878	85.4	380	2 612	13	255.6	70.4	71.7	4 632	3 261	49	196	297
Wayne	20	D	D	(8)	D	7	256.9	82.2	70.5	4 844	3 275	47	191	630
White	28	10 720	D	404	3 326	11	283.6	108.7	88.8	6 983	4 000	982	189	1 061
Whiteside	112	42 900	89.3	1 567	10 855	21	1 021.6	239.2	65.9	4 013	3 065	89	157	391
Will	646	291 636	92.1	9 054	75 194	117	4 420.4	980.4	58.4	2 049	1 648	54	98	216
Williamson	135	68 107	86.2	2 155	18 102	28	763.6	380.1	56.2	6 175	3 268	1 369	883	584
Winnebago	556	306 279	86.9	9 693	84 054	71	3 396.2	943.0	53.7	3 517	2 506	272	217	452
Woodford	63	18 782	94.6	789	4 749	16	378.6	109.1	80.5	3 068	2 162	54	103	197
INDIANA	11 705	6 646 318	84.1	215 710	1 865 305	2 239	70 354.5	26 828.1	57.5	4 514	2 773	374	332	792
Adams	61	27 440	94.5	1 103	7 929	13	479.7	111.3	72.5	3 356	2 285	27	100	680
Allen	626	414 040	88.2	13 472	122 249	86	3 369.2	1 284.4	41.9	4 059	2 351	854	376	434
Bartholomew	135	102 393	81.6	3 114	28 369	24	1 188.5	264.3	22.2	3 791	2 453	270	263	682
Benton	19	D	D	(6)	D	7	168.3	51.4	76.1	5 254	2 841	42	166	829
Blackford	21	D	D	(6)	D	9	122.4	51.9	36.0	3 729	2 993	39	117	440
Boone	85	37 489	89.6	1 303	11 026	17	539.0	122.9	70.9	2 741	2 204	38	114	172
Brown	46	18 422	43.4	623	6 051	4	71.8	27.9	62.4	1 746	1 415	16	58	238
Carroll	26	9 783	D	339	2 984	8	205.4	64.5	71.6	3 225	2 144	33	160	339
Cass	88	30 708	89.8	1 125	9 034	14	482.1	156.0	42.9	4 004	3 095	136	153	383

[1] Includes only establishments with payroll. [2] Includes full-service restaurants, limited-service eating places, special food services, and drinking places (alcoholic beverages). [3] For pay period including March 12. [4] As of June 30. Covers all FDIC-insured commercial banks and savings institutions. [5] Based on resident population estimated as of July 1, 1999. [6] 100 to 249 employees. [7] 500 to 999 employees. [8] 250 to 499 employees. [9] 20 to 99 employees. [10] 5,000 to 9,999 employees.

Sources: Accommodation and Foodservices—U.S. Census Bureau, 1997 Economic Census, ECON97 Report Series CD-ROM, CD-EC97-1, Disc 1E, issued February 2001 (related Internet site <http://www.census.gov/epcd/www/97EC72.HTM>). Banking—U.S. Federal Deposit Insurance Corporation and Office of Thrift Supervision, "1999 Bank and Thrift Branch Office Data Book: Summary of Deposits," national and 6 regional data books (related Internet site <http://www2.fdic.gov/sod/>). Federal Funds and Grants—U.S. Census Bureau, County Aggregate files for each state, <http://www.census.gov/govs/www/cffr99.html>, (accessed: August 2000).

Table B–12. Counties — Accommodation and Foodservices, Banking, and Federal Funds–Con.

[Includes U.S., states, and 3,142 counties/county equivalents defined as of January 1, 1992. For changes to these areas since January 1, 1992, see appendix B. Geographic Information]

County	Accommodation and foodservices[1] (NAICS 72), 1997					Banking,[4] 1999		Federal funds and grants, 1999							
	Sales									Per capita[5] (dollars)				
												By selected type—		
	Estab-lishments	Total ($1,000)	Percent from food-services[2]	Paid employ-ees[3]	Annual payroll ($1,000)	Offices	Deposits (mil. dol.)	Total expenditures or obligations (mil. dol.)	Percent change, 1990–1999	Total	Direct payments for individuals	Procure-ment contract awards	Salaries and wages	Grant awards
INDIANA—Con.														
Clark	192	121 706	84.1	3 876	34 789	46	993.1	441.2	24.9	4 638	2 989	96	963	551
Clay	50	13 665	84.2	516	3 765	13	291.4	114.2	61.4	4 244	3 243	40	167	576
Clinton	63	19 380	D	753	5 181	14	374.1	122.4	61.3	3 714	2 804	32	126	407
Crawford	18	D	D	(6)	D	6	92.1	46.0	58.1	4 280	3 088	52	169	909
Daviess	59	20 384	91.3	899	5 583	17	342.6	117.0	45.4	4 024	3 007	30	147	530
Dearborn	79	31 655	D	1 068	8 576	21	582.0	132.2	64.7	2 754	2 201	24	83	427
Decatur	47	19 572	87.8	765	5 656	12	287.2	89.7	58.5	3 490	2 493	30	117	463
De Kalb	78	33 996	89.0	1 008	8 769	13	389.4	112.7	-16.1	2 839	2 127	396	108	11
Delaware	228	126 656	94.0	4 981	35 561	44	1 348.4	445.9	51.2	3 862	2 839	53	189	699
Dubois	91	39 431	84.4	1 480	11 512	31	909.1	153.0	108.4	3 815	2 266	572	155	624
Elkhart	354	189 394	90.2	6 202	51 749	62	1 620.7	462.3	43.8	2 647	2 094	83	89	344
Fayette	49	22 018	D	759	5 948	13	303.9	105.4	39.9	4 075	3 128	26	107	663
Floyd	107	54 941	D	1 830	15 838	30	801.4	256.5	76.0	3 551	2 683	70	130	635
Fountain	48	16 380	92.8	546	5 106	15	236.2	91.3	77.2	4 969	3 274	43	162	942
Franklin	38	12 625	D	554	3 465	8	289.9	60.3	74.6	2 728	1 911	25	100	517
Fulton	46	14 220	D	551	3 851	9	234.3	76.3	66.6	3 650	2 719	33	127	363
Gibson	62	20 965	92.7	894	6 291	18	374.4	137.2	69.0	4 256	3 075	109	128	521
Grant	140	74 253	87.8	2 579	20 187	29	669.4	361.0	68.2	5 008	3 351	71	549	911
Greene	49	D	D	(7)	D	17	385.1	152.3	65.4	4 594	3 228	563	143	496
Hamilton	252	165 558	88.5	5 154	49 175	69	1 367.2	298.5	73.9	1 734	1 409	43	114	130
Hancock	79	41 490	91.3	1 470	11 004	16	375.6	148.9	94.5	2 677	2 200	32	107	225
Harrison	44	21 409	D	690	5 542	17	415.3	109.7	91.6	3 100	2 369	35	154	456
Hendricks	127	72 157	94.8	2 581	20 888	39	892.0	246.2	135.2	2 491	1 843	65	95	423
Henry	68	30 426	91.2	1 082	8 329	21	608.0	199.1	47.3	4 116	3 137	31	113	689
Howard	182	115 066	94.8	3 913	31 714	32	778.8	327.1	61.4	3 906	2 979	51	206	564
Huntington	85	32 348	93.0	1 260	9 047	17	444.2	136.6	66.9	3 655	2 604	54	129	683
Jackson	72	35 311	86.9	1 042	10 098	21	572.2	143.7	51.4	3 477	2 631	46	138	465
Jasper	57	24 086	92.6	810	6 554	13	381.3	101.6	77.1	3 449	2 480	38	147	296
Jay	41	14 359	95.4	528	3 798	11	218.8	88.1	56.2	4 064	2 911	31	111	573
Jefferson	77	29 594	89.0	1 068	8 706	15	322.2	132.0	45.9	4 148	2 904	215	163	767
Jennings	31	10 039	D	392	2 704	11	222.2	86.3	74.3	3 070	2 249	25	108	539
Johnson	214	121 570	94.8	4 190	34 932	47	1 013.8	309.2	75.9	2 743	2 162	163	139	231
Knox	80	36 063	85.4	1 375	10 338	18	620.6	199.0	58.7	5 097	3 520	65	214	855
Kosciusko	152	58 679	86.9	2 116	16 613	41	740.4	193.4	61.2	2 711	2 173	41	142	209
Lagrange	60	23 998	81.2	702	6 885	13	330.5	70.2	70.2	2 065	1 619	25	97	199
Lake	931	463 083	90.6	15 407	126 006	154	5 912.6	2 086.1	55.3	4 341	3 029	107	230	935
La Porte	234	106 115	89.6	3 394	28 984	33	1 074.0	385.6	59.1	3 507	2 782	54	120	456
Lawrence	74	38 002	94.6	1 321	10 504	14	418.4	197.4	71.4	4 314	3 088	104	167	878
Madison	244	139 848	91.8	4 794	38 384	57	1 203.2	566.8	63.0	4 327	3 349	75	132	685
Marion	1 893	1 523 692	77.8	43 946	432 381	242	13 203.7	5 623.1	53.8	6 934	3 068	1 314	838	1 695
Marshall	97	37 086	91.9	1 418	10 005	15	509.5	138.8	79.7	3 009	2 183	50	114	477
Martin	21	D	D	(8)	D	5	116.8	295.8	56.2	28 497	3 722	4 281	19 373	976
Miami	58	18 239	96.7	706	5 095	14	302.3	171.2	5.2	5 096	3 083	40	1 266	461
Monroe	302	176 573	81.7	6 312	48 773	45	1 124.7	457.9	65.6	3 916	2 114	117	187	1 481
Montgomery	88	33 659	78.8	1 054	8 630	21	525.7	140.9	64.9	3 852	2 725	64	166	533
Morgan	80	45 102	96.7	1 411	13 277	24	559.8	188.1	80.6	2 807	2 188	72	101	366
Newton	28	D	D	(8)	D	9	167.3	50.0	60.1	3 371	2 179	40	151	302
Noble	69	29 761	93.6	961	7 707	17	367.2	114.8	66.2	2 654	2 110	31	103	283
Ohio	9	D	D	(9)	D	3	40.5	16.9	58.3	3 093	2 395	42	148	456
Orange	35	9 975	76.2	610	3 148	7	216.7	77.5	68.1	3 908	2 877	33	85	759
Owen	20	D	D	(8)	D	6	164.6	60.1	71.4	2 913	2 259	50	114	387
Parke	34	D	D	(6)	D	9	139.5	69.5	48.2	4 109	2 712	47	171	723
Perry	44	14 060	D	465	3 592	11	315.9	75.7	62.1	3 964	2 724	108	191	880
Pike	12	D	D	(10)	D	7	146.5	53.8	-57.2	4 131	3 154	36	139	540
Porter	259	126 495	90.0	4 385	35 881	58	1 403.8	387.7	83.9	2 624	2 114	56	143	270
Posey	35	D	D	(8)	D	12	311.6	88.4	72.2	3 364	2 404	44	140	361
Pulaski	22	D	D	(6)	D	8	243.0	55.0	65.5	4 066	2 780	37	148	297
Putnam	75	27 797	71.0	1 022	7 533	14	378.6	105.0	56.3	3 019	2 339	27	116	323
Randolph	44	11 942	97.4	438	3 090	15	302.9	112.2	59.3	4 094	2 943	52	158	609
Ripley	58	19 774	78.9	787	5 182	15	465.3	100.2	44.7	3 621	2 707	109	151	467
Rush	30	D	D	(8)	D	9	207.6	78.0	77.7	4 283	2 765	46	154	703
St. Joseph	537	305 241	87.0	10 620	86 871	76	3 019.9	1 363.3	34.2	5 273	2 792	1 518	238	688
Scott	38	19 609	D	716	5 884	9	191.6	96.5	72.0	4 119	2 874	104	133	924
Shelby	57	31 151	90.2	1 059	9 305	17	399.0	142.1	66.7	3 257	2 396	67	222	365
Spencer	28	D	D	(8)	D	12	181.0	72.3	73.7	3 414	2 384	37	162	538
Starke	37	D	D	(8)	D	9	185.3	83.2	56.8	3 526	2 536	31	116	596
Steuben	88	41 643	81.2	1 300	11 848	14	321.7	101.6	75.8	3 201	2 482	49	145	346
Sullivan	28	D	D	(8)	D	12	221.9	97.3	57.1	4 517	3 229	67	171	613
Switzerland	9	D	D	(6)	D	3	64.1	31.0	65.2	3 457	2 470	38	149	692
Tippecanoe	312	194 298	D	6 722	55 993	44	1 552.6	497.4	48.1	3 491	1 964	77	199	1 174

[1] Includes only establishments with payroll. [2] Includes full-service restaurants, limited-service eating places, special food services, and drinking places (alcoholic beverages). [3] For pay period including March 12. [4] As of June 30. Covers all FDIC-insured commercial banks and savings institutions. [5] Based on resident population estimated as of July 1, 1999. [6] 100 to 249 employees. [7] 500 to 999 employees. [8] 250 to 499 employees. [9] 1,000 to 2,499 employees. [10] 20 to 99 employees.

Sources: Accommodation and Foodservices—U.S. Census Bureau, 1997 Economic Census, ECON[97] Report Series CD-ROM, CD-EC97-1, Disc 1E, issued February 2001 (related Internet site <http://www.census.gov/epcd/www/97EC72.HTM>). Banking—U.S. Federal Deposit Insurance Corporation and Office of Thrift Supervision, "1999 Bank and Thrift Branch Office Data Book: Summary of Deposits," national and 6 regional data books (related Internet site <http://www2.fdic.gov/sod/>). Federal Funds and Grants—U.S. Census Bureau, County Aggregate files for each state, <http://www.census.gov/govs/www/cffr99.html>, (accessed: August 2000).

[Includes U.S., states, and 3,142 counties/county equivalents defined as of January 1, 1992. For changes to these areas since January 1, 1992, see appendix B. Geographic Information]

County	Accommodation and foodservices[1] (NAICS 72), 1997					Banking,[4] 1999		Federal funds and grants, 1999						
		Sales								Per capita[5] (dollars)				
											By selected type—			
	Establishments	Total ($1,000)	Percent from food-services[2]	Paid employees[3]	Annual payroll ($1,000)	Offices	Deposits (mil. dol.)	Total expenditures or obligations (mil. dol.)	Percent change, 1990–1999	Total	Direct payments for individuals	Procurement contract awards	Salaries and wages	Grant awards
INDIANA—Con.														
Tipton	25	9 248	88.5	319	2 548	6	160.3	62.6	66.5	3 762	2 715	178	128	302
Union	10	D	D	(6)	D	4	113.9	27.8	88.8	3 816	2 517	33	118	566
Vanderburgh	426	267 277	88.5	8 841	78 503	57	3 114.1	798.7	51.4	4 756	3 269	386	301	750
Vermillion	35	13 714	95.9	463	3 414	9	167.5	72.1	18.2	4 254	3 093	169	161	624
Vigo	268	148 890	89.1	5 027	42 679	31	1 456.5	527.1	55.5	5 051	3 186	223	706	854
Wabash	71	D	D	(7)	D	15	321.8	160.2	58.9	4 639	2 764	50	125	1 449
Warren	7	D	D	(8)	D	4	53.1	32.8	65.5	3 926	2 206	32	131	390
Warrick	68	D	D	(7)	D	13	440.8	133.4	68.2	2 538	2 013	28	117	303
Washington	31	D	D	(9)	D	11	224.1	90.4	73.2	3 202	2 322	53	117	537
Wayne	145	83 708	87.9	2 808	24 190	33	966.1	334.8	66.4	4 706	3 202	75	129	1 175
Wells	36	15 288	D	597	4 378	11	279.0	81.7	73.9	3 046	2 262	29	122	294
White	66	17 164	92.4	459	4 583	11	320.0	114.4	83.6	4 483	3 021	39	146	726
Whitley	61	23 319	D	871	6 593	13	318.1	94.8	53.8	3 077	2 438	145	120	174
IOWA	6 830	2 762 766	80.3	99 148	769 461	1 499	41 705.2	15 601.5	54.2	5 437	2 889	313	338	904
Adair	19	5 386	89.8	246	1 396	7	143.3	42.8	43.6	5 310	2 908	39	170	982
Adams	9	1 236	D	55	278	5	58.7	25.7	32.3	5 843	3 370	71	313	519
Allamakee	42	6 111	84.6	293	1 493	8	297.6	59.2	15.1	4 205	2 695	96	213	528
Appanoose	35	7 352	91.9	284	1 785	6	140.8	75.5	41.6	5 618	3 613	56	288	1 336
Audubon	16	D	D	(10)	D	5	114.8	42.8	46.0	6 297	3 332	52	228	1 154
Benton	43	6 128	D	249	1 646	19	343.9	104.4	77.6	4 048	2 411	277	135	350
Black Hawk	293	135 821	89.4	5 544	39 167	39	1 274.6	511.8	12.5	4 267	2 971	90	268	804
Boone	48	15 118	86.6	574	4 400	12	312.1	106.0	40.2	4 030	2 794	41	286	390
Bremer	47	13 594	D	578	3 989	14	374.1	95.8	51.0	4 086	2 788	48	121	586
Buchanan	38	D	D	(9)	D	11	267.1	86.0	48.1	4 062	2 613	39	153	454
Buena Vista	47	14 981	92.9	604	4 010	17	421.3	94.3	43.8	4 861	3 141	180	297	425
Butler	29	D	D	(6)	D	12	188.7	77.0	36.5	4 970	3 231	39	154	561
Calhoun	17	D	D	(6)	D	10	185.3	64.7	44.9	5 713	3 561	52	194	435
Carroll	64	19 275	82.7	785	4 853	19	440.0	96.7	59.3	4 493	2 922	63	237	574
Cass	43	10 215	88.5	443	2 786	11	234.4	75.2	29.3	5 182	3 599	51	256	486
Cedar	37	8 100	D	375	1 917	13	262.1	72.0	43.6	3 986	2 448	38	256	302
Cerro Gordo	139	60 971	82.3	2 286	16 676	29	769.1	220.6	46.3	4 830	3 190	106	203	970
Cherokee	35	8 280	86.1	350	2 164	10	254.4	66.6	52.4	5 103	3 295	51	203	481
Chickasaw	33	D	D	(9)	D	11	321.9	118.8	144.0	8 849	2 764	4 535	187	413
Clarke	26	12 214	62.0	399	2 791	6	147.8	37.1	37.8	4 490	2 894	52	184	613
Clay	53	17 176	77.6	682	4 753	13	378.2	89.9	57.6	5 211	2 874	48	239	555
Clayton	51	7 160	80.2	266	1 462	15	310.7	87.4	39.1	4 701	2 894	57	238	598
Clinton	132	39 282	81.3	1 516	10 902	26	654.8	203.3	41.8	4 098	3 096	36	144	434
Crawford	49	11 415	90.6	477	2 878	13	278.4	86.2	50.1	5 245	2 890	438	284	706
Dallas	55	13 061	82.3	596	3 877	18	437.4	127.7	59.1	3 342	2 208	37	136	640
Davis	13	2 551	100.0	126	653	3	74.6	40.1	45.9	4 713	2 716	45	194	1 015
Decatur	16	2 243	76.3	110	588	6	85.7	43.8	16.9	5 267	3 073	56	225	1 209
Delaware	34	5 637	D	269	1 307	11	296.1	69.9	53.5	3 784	2 148	43	154	457
Des Moines	109	47 774	88.2	1 841	13 441	23	639.0	202.3	24.4	4 822	3 166	626	232	602
Dickinson	98	29 054	68.1	857	8 277	13	271.1	77.6	70.2	4 767	3 276	38	145	771
Dubuque	233	94 697	85.2	3 838	27 399	36	1 222.1	322.2	31.3	3 656	2 705	63	194	547
Emmet	25	5 517	D	218	1 414	9	168.5	61.7	25.9	5 805	3 541	351	228	674
Fayette	50	10 825	D	504	3 019	18	345.8	103.5	44.4	4 798	3 128	54	220	533
Floyd	37	8 878	94.8	368	1 976	7	290.4	120.0	98.2	7 383	3 544	95	173	2 754
Franklin	19	3 129	93.0	164	896	12	166.3	59.6	24.4	5 525	2 905	47	192	850
Fremont	18	2 612	68.5	83	627	9	137.0	48.5	46.5	6 290	3 638	124	211	819
Greene	22	D	D	(6)	D	7	217.3	58.6	52.5	5 844	3 426	57	233	657
Grundy	23	D	D	(6)	D	8	240.2	60.6	56.4	4 932	2 960	39	149	559
Guthrie	30	5 798	92.9	158	1 435	10	225.9	57.7	44.1	4 975	3 219	66	228	509
Hamilton	35	8 431	85.1	311	2 224	9	282.5	76.5	47.2	4 808	3 150	44	169	471
Hancock	22	3 900	D	199	912	11	208.0	56.9	50.3	4 730	2 900	47	198	263
Hardin	43	9 389	97.1	371	2 435	15	397.1	103.8	56.4	5 715	3 658	441	232	523
Harrison	30	8 589	95.1	318	2 472	11	172.0	79.7	48.8	5 240	3 288	55	266	747
Henry	44	16 744	91.9	612	4 477	13	220.4	90.8	76.0	4 508	2 653	43	174	1 106
Howard	29	D	D	(6)	D	6	180.3	48.3	23.5	5 048	2 963	89	173	631
Humboldt	21	4 462	92.6	210	1 282	9	174.1	55.6	51.3	5 435	3 420	57	265	466
Ida	22	D	D	(6)	D	8	215.3	41.7	46.2	5 255	3 147	50	217	431
Iowa	54	30 445	73.9	999	8 486	8	174.1	65.4	57.9	4 173	2 629	50	208	380
Jackson	58	11 387	95.5	515	2 598	13	302.6	95.4	56.0	4 730	2 971	38	177	949
Jasper	74	25 899	78.5	961	7 289	19	478.1	140.7	53.3	3 838	2 761	54	147	414
Jefferson	41	10 742	66.0	365	2 656	9	229.8	60.5	47.6	3 606	2 254	49	272	502
Johnson	271	144 291	79.8	5 496	40 789	32	1 356.2	532.8	82.8	5 133	1 582	1 096	614	1 709
Jones	37	7 733	97.8	366	1 938	12	315.7	75.6	45.8	3 763	2 435	53	136	410
Keokuk	20	1 680	D	86	465	10	195.1	69.2	57.0	6 104	3 484	68	262	834

[1] Includes only establishments with payroll. [2] Includes full-service restaurants, limited-service eating places, special food services, and drinking places (alcoholic beverages). [3] For pay period including March 12. [4] As of June 30. Covers all FDIC-insured commercial banks and savings institutions. [5] Based on resident population estimated as of July 1, 1999. [6] 100 to 249 employees. [7] 500 to 999 employees. [8] 0 to 19 employees. [9] 250 to 499 employees. [10] 20 to 99 employees.

Sources: Accommodation and Foodservices—U.S. Census Bureau, 1997 Economic Census, ECON97 Report Series CD-ROM, CD-EC97-1, Disc 1E, issued February 2001 (related Internet site <http://www.census.gov/epcd/www/97EC72.HTM>). Banking—U.S. Federal Deposit Insurance Corporation and Office of Thrift Supervision, "1999 Bank and Thrift Branch Office Data Book: Summary of Deposits," national and 6 regional data books (related Internet site <http://www2.fdic.gov/sod/>). Federal Funds and Grants—U.S. Census Bureau, County Aggregate files for each state, <http://www.census.gov/govs/www/cffr99.html>, (accessed: August 2000).

Table B–12. Counties — Accommodation and Foodservices, Banking, and Federal Funds–Con.

[Includes U.S., states, and 3,142 counties/county equivalents defined as of January 1, 1992. For changes to these areas since January 1, 1992, see appendix B. Geographic Information]

County	Accommodation and foodservices[1] (NAICS 72), 1997 Estab-lishments	Sales Total ($1,000)	Sales Percent from food-services[2]	Paid employ-ees[3]	Annual payroll ($1,000)	Banking,[4] 1999 Offices	Deposits (mil. dol.)	Total expenditures or obligations (mil. dol.)	Percent change, 1990–1999	Per capita[5] (dollars) Total	Direct payments for individuals	Procure-ment contract awards	Salaries and wages	Grant awards
IOWA—Con.														
Kossuth	42	9 244	90.2	417	2 226	17	335.0	95.5	49.7	5 416	3 048	69	235	474
Lee	108	32 962	87.3	1 257	8 775	24	589.9	157.2	47.8	4 104	3 038	48	171	628
Linn	439	240 106	82.2	7 853	68 191	68	2 244.6	962.9	51.5	5 208	2 386	1 875	298	563
Louisa	27	3 960	D	191	969	7	130.4	51.3	55.9	4 296	2 405	391	206	485
Lucas	18	3 456	90.8	148	841	6	122.0	47.6	35.7	5 214	3 427	51	228	893
Lyon	26	D	D	(6)	D	10	208.3	51.3	55.0	4 266	2 591	46	144	358
Madison	21	4 776	D	154	1 291	8	169.7	52.2	38.0	3 703	2 582	38	153	433
Mahaska	43	15 624	90.8	656	4 300	11	337.1	95.7	50.0	4 360	2 754	45	172	741
Marion	59	20 513	88.2	900	5 434	17	403.5	155.4	38.9	4 929	3 050	107	976	518
Marshall	86	29 741	86.0	1 070	8 411	10	070.7	190.5	68.0	4 912	3 029	555	171	761
Mills	23	5 708	93.3	221	1 616	9	151.2	67.1	67.2	4 561	2 831	47	190	887
Mitchell	21	D	D	(6)	D	8	305.9	55.7	56.1	5 018	3 310	47	179	362
Monona	36	6 403	89.4	267	1 620	10	182.5	66.1	55.4	6 555	3 886	56	244	915
Monroe	18	D	D	(6)	D	5	116.0	43.1	40.2	5 381	3 707	41	193	893
Montgomery	32	7 029	D	291	1 796	10	192.8	60.6	40.4	5 180	3 573	52	252	559
Muscatine	85	29 318	90.7	1 057	7 950	16	601.9	147.3	48.4	3 576	2 438	244	149	505
O'Brien	44	8 065	93.0	392	1 857	16	307.5	78.9	55.2	5 394	3 412	52	230	657
Osceola	14	2 342	D	117	538	6	131.6	35.5	21.4	5 140	2 966	49	203	367
Page	41	10 052	95.1	466	3 055	11	280.7	82.5	39.2	4 813	3 325	52	210	684
Palo Alto	30	D	D	(6)	D	8	170.0	63.9	51.5	6 440	3 522	52	213	1 138
Plymouth	57	D	D	(7)	D	14	476.9	97.8	53.3	3 941	2 480	65	196	421
Pocahontas	25	3 017	D	179	790	10	164.2	56.0	54.7	6 381	3 678	58	252	494
Polk	897	534 440	77.5	17 068	156 145	124	5 575.7	3 064.3	79.1	8 403	2 491	270	825	2 015
Pottawattamie	197	186 136	D	3 782	48 397	29	778.1	791.2	107.4	9 155	2 947	30	137	738
Poweshiek	43	13 187	89.0	677	4 073	11	320.3	78.7	8.5	4 210	2 925	39	144	337
Ringgold	9	1 271	100.0	64	313	6	59.6	32.0	39.5	5 970	3 329	72	292	789
Sac	25	3 851	100.0	207	1 074	14	219.6	61.9	50.9	5 260	3 394	56	197	375
Scott	378	234 224	81.0	8 050	70 038	49	2 029.5	610.1	50.0	3 826	2 677	174	347	544
Shelby	34	7 438	91.9	343	2 112	11	269.8	72.6	63.7	5 680	3 506	49	205	806
Sioux	71	19 822	94.4	1 098	5 021	24	618.7	117.4	56.1	3 744	2 298	88	148	493
Story	202	89 081	77.3	3 598	24 520	36	1 006.5	359.5	49.8	4 769	2 135	518	576	1 339
Tama	33	7 789	85.8	311	1 828	13	233.1	86.6	49.1	4 868	2 961	51	226	584
Taylor	11	1 412	100.0	77	316	5	63.8	41.2	33.2	5 861	3 272	67	269	902
Union	28	10 028	D	379	2 728	8	201.1	63.7	28.5	5 052	3 289	60	319	871
Van Buren	10	2 003	D	83	255	0	102.4	38.8	42.2	4 925	3 280	61	258	540
Wapello	85	29 820	84.0	1 076	7 813	13	392.4	182.3	41.6	5 142	3 639	85	199	1 025
Warren	58	18 279	92.6	809	5 073	15	306.3	109.5	51.9	2 696	2 027	30	132	289
Washington	42	10 784	92.0	506	3 071	15	355.4	88.4	54.3	4 179	2 859	36	171	390
Wayne	17	1 679	D	99	445	7	79.0	45.2	32.7	6 865	3 926	70	307	1 203
Webster	93	37 072	83.6	1 322	10 489	17	552.7	199.8	41.4	5 145	3 434	153	411	656
Winnebago	28	6 162	D	259	1 396	9	226.7	57.1	40.5	4 771	3 042	52	193	504
Winneshiek	51	14 535	82.9	573	3 953	11	346.2	82.5	48.8	3 945	2 406	41	197	608
Woodbury	246	109 240	D	3 812	29 861	40	1 420.1	443.9	41.4	4 376	2 743	211	443	793
Worth	9	D	D	(8)	D	7	104.7	38.8	34.0	5 065	3 056	59	223	426
Wright	40	7 320	97.7	292	1 802	12	258.7	81.6	54.3	5 876	3 669	66	293	622
KANSAS	5 677	2 685 732	83.9	91 173	757 095	1 374	38 835.0	14 447.0	50.4	5 443	2 868	476	660	822
Allen	38	13 658	D	534	4 128	11	215.7	68.8	53.6	4 767	3 234	35	236	888
Anderson	22	4 896	74.7	206	1 058	9	135.3	37.9	49.2	4 667	3 439	54	225	323
Atchison	32	8 189	D	340	2 158	10	276.8	74.2	37.1	4 402	3 090	165	161	643
Barber	16	2 405	75.6	121	668	9	130.4	35.4	48.5	6 750	4 144	68	267	406
Barton	71	26 784	87.2	959	7 235	20	511.1	126.8	23.1	4 425	3 187	72	167	344
Bourbon	60	D	D	(9)	D	8	201.8	78.1	53.5	5 214	3 692	72	303	866
Brown	20	5 416	D	248	1 403	10	194.2	65.1	37.5	5 960	3 357	65	339	1 127
Butler	96	37 587	92.7	1 400	10 578	30	587.5	178.7	68.4	2 846	2 194	37	114	294
Chase	8	D	D	(8)	D	3	36.4	17.4	69.7	6 094	3 462	69	393	1 470
Chautauqua	10	987	D	58	220	3	43.4	24.6	51.2	5 757	4 153	63	235	966
Cherokee	29	7 330	100.0	285	2 038	11	205.6	102.7	51.3	4 584	3 173	68	135	949
Cheyenne	9	1 174	D	51	251	3	65.7	33.6	95.1	10 410	4 016	48	207	459
Clark	6	D	D	(8)	D	3	75.1	17.0	31.4	7 272	4 075	42	195	269
Clay	21	4 614	D	256	1 316	7	147.5	49.2	38.9	5 489	3 643	46	199	522
Cloud	28	7 889	83.0	314	2 023	11	170.0	66.5	40.6	6 644	4 265	55	238	957
Coffey	21	4 627	81.2	172	1 230	11	165.1	42.7	59.3	4 882	3 191	216	240	591
Comanche	10	982	100.0	32	188	4	53.0	16.1	8.3	8 226	4 521	44	180	460
Cowley	74	25 636	89.4	1 002	6 498	21	481.9	161.3	53.3	4 366	3 065	220	134	643
Crawford	96	50 730	94.3	1 623	14 025	21	570.1	175.3	44.0	4 823	3 444	64	191	961
Decatur	7	D	D	(8)	D	6	81.1	30.6	53.0	9 074	4 255	80	297	446
Dickinson	49	12 642	81.7	494	3 593	14	274.4	101.3	16.4	5 158	3 633	106	250	503

[1] Includes only establishments with payroll.   [2] Includes full-service restaurants, limited-service eating places, special food services, and drinking places (alcoholic beverages).   [3] For pay period including March 12.   [4] As of June 30.   Covers all FDIC-insured commercial banks and savings institutions.   [5] Based on resident population estimated as of July 1, 1999.   [6] 100 to 249 employees.   [7] 500 to 999 employees.   [8] 20 to 99 employees.   [9] 1,000 to 2,499 employees.

Sources: Accommodation and Foodservices—U.S. Census Bureau, 1997 Economic Census, ECON97 Report Series CD-ROM, CD-EC97-1, Disc 1E, issued February 2001 (related Internet site <http://www.census.gov/epcd/www/97EC72.HTM>).   Banking—U.S. Federal Deposit Insurance Corporation and Office of Thrift Supervision, "1999 Bank and Thrift Branch Office Data Book: Summary of Deposits," national and 6 regional data books (related Internet site <http://www2.fdic.gov/sod/>).   Federal Funds and Grants—U.S. Census Bureau, County Aggregate files for each state, <http://www.census.gov/govs/www/cffr99.html>, (accessed: August 2000).

Table B–12. Counties — Accommodation and Foodservices, Banking, and Federal Funds–Con.

[Includes U.S., states, and 3,142 counties/county equivalents defined as of January 1, 1992. For changes to these areas since January 1, 1992, see appendix B. Geographic Information]

County	Accommodation and foodservices[1] (NAICS 72), 1997 — Sales — Establishments	Total ($1,000)	Percent from foodservices[2]	Paid employees[3]	Annual payroll ($1,000)	Banking,[4] 1999 — Offices	Deposits (mil. dol.)	Federal funds and grants, 1999 — Total expenditures or obligations (mil. dol.)	Percent change, 1990–1999	Per capita[5] (dollars) — Total	Direct payments for individuals	Procurement contract awards	Salaries and wages	Grant awards
KANSAS—Con.														
Doniphan	10	1 309	D	51	355	10	138.3	41.6	47.1	5 234	3 079	109	227	820
Douglas	240	120 735	81.0	4 627	34 206	42	1 083.2	290.5	34.8	2 953	1 680	120	268	838
Edwards	11	D	D	(6)	D	4	73.4	35.0	63.0	10 682	4 192	270	335	793
Elk	8	D	D	(6)	D	4	28.1	19.8	40.6	5 853	4 160	76	312	818
Ellis	89	43 564	78.5	1 717	11 786	15	413.5	105.6	55.9	4 009	2 835	50	318	457
Ellsworth	16	3 467	D	122	883	8	110.0	36.0	35.8	5 792	3 813	59	179	369
Finney	68	40 206	67.5	1 310	11 135	15	425.2	110.9	66.0	2 965	1 609	23	192	454
Ford	69	35 406	81.8	1 102	9 552	18	385.3	114.6	41.9	3 872	2 253	44	360	463
Franklin	43	17 109	89.3	603	4 650	11	335.3	94.5	61.9	3 759	2 782	42	182	571
Geary	77	28 669	88.2	1 128	9 480	9	211.2	566.8	8.3	22 754	3 429	2 954	15 315	951
Gove	7	D	D	(6)	D	4	68.0	29.5	109.6	9 744	3 682	75	283	376
Graham	10	1 373	D	108	334	5	74.3	26.8	38.7	8 605	3 957	112	270	589
Grant	23	7 028	82.0	243	1 609	3	101.2	31.5	60.2	3 998	1 808	29	121	230
Gray	9	1 008	100.0	44	250	4	77.4	43.6	96.8	7 821	2 243	41	160	340
Greeley	5	475	D	30	118	1	25.9	23.8	84.8	14 471	2 900	43	198	638
Greenwood	27	D	D	(7)	D	9	108.5	43.8	35.7	5 496	4 200	97	288	700
Hamilton	7	1 193	D	59	255	3	75.4	24.7	46.6	10 413	3 784	42	202	305
Harper	22	4 410	91.0	172	1 055	7	124.9	46.4	41.0	7 352	4 177	70	276	421
Harvey	65	25 515	89.0	942	7 477	19	408.4	150.1	80.5	4 381	2 942	32	109	902
Haskell	8	1 201	D	51	275	2	73.2	36.2	128.2	8 959	2 002	28	185	337
Hodgeman	4	D	D	(8)	D	2	30.6	19.8	28.8	8 846	3 202	70	290	287
Jackson	20	5 754	D	271	1 635	9	193.2	49.5	62.5	4 068	2 724	55	249	632
Jefferson	33	4 173	87.1	148	680	8	128.8	61.2	53.6	3 374	2 638	48	177	245
Jewell	11	1 188	D	75	419	7	71.0	34.5	52.1	9 121	3 941	98	448	1 053
Johnson	827	636 252	80.7	19 029	188 473	179	7 675.3	1 491.7	84.0	3 389	2 000	296	453	226
Kearny	6	1 104	D	47	226	2	80.3	30.3	101.0	7 336	2 239	24	111	631
Kingman	18	4 401	92.8	197	1 171	5	116.9	51.5	46.2	5 956	3 380	57	242	304
Kiowa	11	1 794	D	89	566	5	58.8	27.9	52.7	8 337	4 023	76	297	638
Labette	45	13 348	93.0	548	3 720	15	292.7	113.6	5.8	4 951	3 426	96	198	931
Lane	4	D	D	(6)	D	2	63.2	24.2	93.5	11 139	3 921	39	177	1 074
Leavenworth	85	37 420	D	1 409	10 840	28	694.0	558.3	31.6	7 779	2 819	1 294	3 260	368
Lincoln	7	1 031	D	62	231	5	67.5	26.0	21.3	7 783	3 979	77	414	657
Linn	12	1 836	D	54	392	7	90.5	48.1	73.6	5 170	3 638	84	194	759
Logan	11	2 051	52.4	77	506	3	67.6	26.5	78.5	9 017	3 885	44	208	609
Lyon	104	37 265	84.6	1 633	10 017	19	468.3	112.3	41.7	3 323	2 494	48	220	364
McPherson	64	22 914	86.2	992	6 321	20	395.5	121.7	55.4	4 225	2 972	105	155	286
Marion	34	5 359	D	264	1 525	14	197.3	67.6	60.4	4 991	3 359	76	226	377
Marshall	36	6 083	80.2	257	1 547	13	290.1	73.4	52.9	6 732	3 739	60	314	1 163
Meade	8	1 441	D	62	314	4	86.5	32.7	28.7	7 411	3 331	22	128	379
Miami	36	11 230	D	456	3 321	13	370.6	87.5	69.8	3 231	2 501	37	133	462
Mitchell	24	5 122	93.2	274	1 483	9	134.6	47.7	21.6	6 859	3 665	63	250	817
Montgomery	87	30 271	86.6	1 164	8 521	20	477.5	182.9	40.0	4 973	3 647	84	213	905
Morris	10	D	D	(7)	D	6	100.4	34.3	46.7	5 556	3 838	142	261	471
Morton	10	2 374	D	90	559	4	69.2	25.2	−27.6	7 229	2 759	41	197	349
Nemaha	31	4 980	D	256	1 407	16	275.2	59.8	42.7	5 871	3 289	68	295	944
Neosho	41	11 050	80.3	497	2 953	15	265.3	77.6	41.1	4 665	3 470	81	179	587
Ness	14	D	D	(6)	D	4	73.5	36.3	74.0	10 175	4 259	88	378	2 194
Norton	14	3 985	D	157	867	6	133.0	43.2	50.4	7 674	3 596	50	262	1 832
Osage	32	5 198	95.9	189	1 104	12	200.7	73.4	66.5	4 265	3 011	57	222	631
Osborne	11	1 354	D	83	486	5	117.4	37.5	27.0	8 175	4 135	199	305	705
Ottawa	14	1 380	D	50	282	5	131.2	31.5	21.7	5 356	3 051	54	185	515
Pawnee	18	8 616	D	195	1 310	4	133.8	48.5	48.4	6 723	3 366	58	285	558
Phillips	18	3 129	81.3	150	761	9	170.0	39.1	38.4	6 560	3 826	88	352	632
Pottawatomie	32	7 295	74.6	320	1 893	8	261.0	61.5	52.5	3 244	2 446	46	152	340
Pratt	34	10 297	83.6	478	2 972	6	214.0	62.4	48.3	6 551	3 700	48	193	384
Rawlins	7	D	D	(8)	D	6	62.6	31.7	56.4	10 495	3 824	71	274	842
Reno	141	67 469	84.7	2 382	17 616	27	724.8	268.4	51.2	4 213	3 106	42	205	503
Republic	12	3 099	D	172	798	7	132.3	45.6	43.5	7 637	3 891	67	292	1 041
Rice	28	6 221	D	317	1 731	12	151.9	59.9	36.9	5 856	3 464	57	222	410
Riley	156	74 576	D	2 998	21 035	21	826.1	209.0	57.1	3 280	1 806	262	303	839
Rooks	19	1 553	90.5	79	386	7	106.4	37.7	45.6	6 697	4 095	58	229	572
Rush	8	D	D	(6)	D	5	79.2	31.7	32.0	9 432	4 918	180	372	712
Russell	21	6 214	82.4	288	1 633	7	143.4	49.0	34.5	6 560	4 287	68	273	468
Saline	136	68 923	81.7	2 464	21 008	22	1 149.5	252.5	75.3	4 914	2 944	130	356	1 269
Scott	12	3 348	D	148	835	3	134.7	32.0	74.4	6 484	1 974	49	187	357
Sedgwick	969	585 552	82.8	17 828	166 705	143	5 929.5	2 446.9	33.3	5 417	2 488	1 528	745	592
Seward	56	24 228	75.9	820	6 201	9	252.6	122.8	49.4	6 103	1 895	2 757	225	463
Shawnee	374	199 223	88.2	6 745	54 344	76	2 777.8	1 462.9	89.7	8 566	3 296	197	935	3 219
Sheridan	4	D	D	(6)	D	3	94.2	30.8	105.8	11 520	3 210	86	201	508

[1] Includes only establishments with payroll.   [2] Includes full-service restaurants, limited-service eating places, special food services, and drinking places (alcoholic beverages).   [3] For pay period including March 12.   [4] As of June 30. Covers all FDIC-insured commercial banks and savings institutions.   [5] Based on resident population estimated as of July 1, 1999.   [6] 20 to 99 employees.   [7] 100 to 249 employees.   [8] 0 to 19 employees.

Sources: Accommodation and Foodservices—U.S. Census Bureau, 1997 Economic Census, ECON97 Report Series CD-ROM, CD-EC97-1, Disc 1E, issued February 2001 (related Internet site <http://www.census.gov/epcd/www/97EC72.HTM>).   Banking—U.S. Federal Deposit Insurance Corporation and Office of Thrift Supervision, "1999 Bank and Thrift Branch Office Data Book: Summary of Deposits," national and 6 regional data books (related Internet site <http://www2.fdic.gov/sod/>).   Federal Funds and Grants—U.S. Census Bureau, County Aggregate files for each state, <http://www.census.gov/govs/www/cffr99.html>, (accessed: August 2000).

Table B–12. Counties — **Accommodation and Foodservices, Banking, and Federal Funds**–Con.

[Includes U.S., states, and 3,142 counties/county equivalents defined as of January 1, 1992. For changes to these areas since January 1, 1992, see appendix B. Geographic Information]

County	Accommodation and foodservices[1] (NAICS 72), 1997 — Estab-lishments	Sales Total ($1,000)	Sales Percent from food-services[2]	Paid employ-ees[3]	Annual payroll ($1,000)	Banking,[4] 1999 Offices	Deposits (mil. dol.)	Federal funds and grants, 1999 Total expenditures or obligations (mil. dol.)	Percent change, 1990–1999	Per capita[5] (dollars) Total	Direct payments for individuals	Procure-ment contract awards	Salaries and wages	Grant awards
KANSAS—Con.														
Sherman	20	6 594	D	246	1 715	3	161.8	54.8	86.5	8 399	3 577	44	437	624
Smith	14	2 287	D	81	560	6	101.3	36.3	48.5	7 944	4 259	81	401	443
Stafford	14	D	D	(6)	D	6	110.6	39.3	25.2	7 868	3 606	68	336	349
Stanton	6	D	D	(6)	D	2	36.4	25.8	70.4	11 600	2 368	32	129	572
Stevens	13	3 044	D	94	625	3	91.5	37.9	86.7	7 010	2 492	44	180	301
Sumner	36	10 732	81.6	444	3 200	15	354.3	128.6	60.7	4 734	3 076	59	162	433
Thomas	34	13 459	74.4	487	3 929	8	156.4	59.1	39.3	7 422	2 925	68	306	485
Trego	13	D	D	(7)	D	3	67.7	24.8	43.7	7 594	4 031	57	230	633
Wabaunsee	8	1 375	100.0	21	206	7	72.8	78.8	240.0	11 975	7 553	50	208	3 607
Wallace	2	D	D	(8)	D	1	21.0	22.6	93.3	12 540	3 550	159	259	504
Washington	17	2 781	D	159	722	9	123.5	56.8	61.2	8 769	3 900	99	405	2 260
Wichita	1	D	D	(8)	D	2	52.4	60.5	302.6	23 467	2 635	12 934	209	543
Wilson	13	D	D	(7)	D	6	160.4	53.0	50.2	5 127	3 400	50	200	933
Woodson	10	1 264	D	55	358	4	35.7	22.9	39.4	5 860	3 994	111	271	621
Wyandotte	230	109 268	91.7	3 191	30 324	44	1 565.6	897.2	62.3	5 927	3 218	282	908	1 453
KENTUCKY	6 546	4 056 107	83.3	129 442	1 140 617	1 591	48 237.3	22 198.1	61.9	5 604	3 126	574	660	1 110
Adair	19	7 269	93.0	221	2 006	7	176.4	93.9	114.7	5 701	3 265	734	133	1 469
Allen	20	6 333	93.3	232	1 658	4	163.6	67.2	85.6	3 985	2 730	43	107	1 017
Anderson	19	6 509	100.0	283	2 231	5	193.6	49.0	88.9	2 606	2 033	29	90	433
Ballard	6	D	D	(6)	D	6	116.1	45.6	76.3	5 357	3 984	50	193	633
Barren	85	44 616	85.3	1 338	11 850	16	426.5	141.5	77.0	3 788	2 670	46	177	815
Bath	11	2 720	D	105	655	6	138.9	47.6	71.7	4 429	2 864	29	137	1 312
Bell	50	25 995	96.9	766	6 545	13	346.6	506.7	−25.4	17 455	4 274	11 129	257	1 758
Boone	171	156 022	81.6	4 381	43 193	40	857.7	247.9	60.6	2 974	1 834	469	468	193
Bourbon	27	9 895	100.0	308	2 635	8	193.6	84.5	−54.0	4 366	2 741	34	111	1 340
Boyd	109	68 673	87.3	2 172	18 142	29	789.0	287.7	72.5	5 891	4 186	195	636	854
Boyle	54	32 500	92.7	1 088	8 822	19	407.3	108.4	66.4	3 962	2 916	56	153	802
Bracken	11	D	D	(6)	D	5	88.5	33.8	76.0	3 981	2 810	44	159	909
Breathitt	19	9 965	D	329	2 694	4	150.3	101.0	90.4	6 406	3 734	25	228	2 402
Breckinridge	22	4 684	100.0	188	1 523	9	171.2	81.0	72.8	4 570	3 174	34	172	916
Bullitt	56	35 994	81.2	1 169	10 417	10	356.7	199.3	50.6	3 270	1 670	1 301	47	245
Butler	12	3 039	100.0	134	895	7	124.6	49.6	69.9	4 129	2 785	34	138	992
Caldwell	24	7 209	D	283	1 993	6	201.1	63.5	53.0	4 752	3 111	38	101	811
Calloway	63	26 475	88.4	995	7 229	11	511.2	130.8	71.6	3 929	3 008	22	145	555
Campbell	169	D	D	(9)	D	33	987.0	308.9	53.3	3 542	2 768	92	158	512
Carlisle	7	D	D	(6)	D	5	91.7	27.2	68.0	5 058	3 584	42	180	624
Carroll	27	12 676	69.5	430	3 323	4	84.6	40.7	69.0	4 166	2 857	172	164	914
Carter	33	14 156	D	445	3 991	9	226.0	136.6	103.1	5 038	3 034	601	139	1 243
Casey	16	D	D	(7)	D	7	119.5	65.2	85.7	4 375	2 827	29	107	1 332
Christian	101	55 527	88.0	2 208	18 218	20	568.2	1 175.5	87.5	16 340	2 285	2 154	11 012	684
Clark	58	31 143	D	1 105	8 538	12	446.4	119.8	66.8	3 690	2 831	88	171	549
Clay	20	9 602	D	281	2 448	6	157.9	105.0	44.6	4 609	2 985	−1 419	885	2 146
Clinton	16	6 490	45.0	155	1 782	3	101.3	59.2	99.3	6 255	3 812	30	146	2 213
Crittenden	12	D	D	(7)	D	5	95.2	44.9	66.1	4 698	3 445	66	173	767
Cumberland	12	4 267	41.3	123	1 231	3	82.3	42.2	99.5	6 131	3 895	33	126	1 953
Daviess	150	100 566	79.3	3 331	26 599	40	1 115.1	360.4	73.8	3 953	2 924	125	172	649
Edmonson	11	6 092	D	179	1 920	2	131.6	50.8	90.5	4 383	2 403	76	643	1 181
Elliott	4	D	D	(8)	D	3	29.6	25.7	79.1	3 931	2 351	20	69	1 446
Estill	17	D	D	(7)	D	5	128.3	81.9	95.3	5 280	3 908	23	110	1 199
Fayette	610	508 106	72.2	15 216	146 858	88	3 204.7	1 247.1	85.8	5 115	2 443	802	775	1 057
Fleming	9	3 614	D	143	970	8	190.6	59.4	86.5	4 368	2 606	43	171	1 406
Floyd	43	19 329	80.9	608	5 443	15	402.7	244.3	62.7	5 647	3 973	217	172	1 265
Franklin	89	47 157	82.9	1 518	13 156	20	652.3	954.2	74.3	20 482	4 612	74	540	15 232
Fulton	15	D	D	(10)	D	5	166.3	55.4	55.8	7 434	4 654	317	283	1 514
Gallatin	9	4 689	100.0	103	684	2	32.3	24.5	84.7	3 299	2 321	63	166	720
Garrard	13	2 709	100.0	112	670	6	132.5	46.5	74.7	3 242	2 444	30	110	596
Grant	37	D	D	(11)	D	13	200.1	69.2	107.5	3 324	2 447	54	131	662
Graves	49	15 652	96.2	592	4 167	12	447.6	176.4	71.7	4 866	3 424	68	232	826
Grayson	36	12 886	93.1	370	2 982	12	232.3	106.8	84.5	4 484	3 116	48	130	1 089
Green	11	3 173	100.0	115	842	5	150.7	47.4	77.7	4 476	3 379	30	107	889
Greenup	33	20 259	D	789	5 624	18	285.5	155.5	77.7	4 234	3 517	56	87	563
Hancock	8	D	D	(6)	D	3	84.1	26.4	48.2	2 936	2 127	32	118	534
Hardin	141	85 665	86.1	2 975	24 281	36	955.9	862.6	51.5	9 420	3 409	44	5 529	397
Harlan	32	14 956	96.2	457	3 944	11	288.5	295.0	−58.6	8 607	6 743	331	170	1 348
Harrison	18	D	D	(10)	D	11	207.8	69.7	63.7	3 946	2 632	46	164	1 031
Hart	17	5 520	D	189	1 533	7	174.4	68.9	88.4	4 089	2 794	26	98	1 072

[1] Includes only establishments with payroll. [2] Includes full-service restaurants, limited-service eating places, special food services, and drinking places (alcoholic beverages). [3] For pay period including March 12. [4] As of June 30. Covers all FDIC-insured commercial banks and savings institutions. [5] Based on resident population estimated as of July 1, 1999. [6] 20 to 99 employees. [7] 100 to 249 employees. [8] 0 to 19 employees. [9] 2,500 to 4,999 employees. [10] 250 to 499 employees. [11] 500 to 999 employees.

Sources: Accommodation and Foodservices—U.S. Census Bureau, 1997 Economic Census, ECON97 Report Series CD-ROM, CD-EC97-1, Disc 1E, issued February 2001 (related Internet site <http://www.census.gov/epcd/www/97EC72.HTM>). Banking—U.S. Federal Deposit Insurance Corporation and Office of Thrift Supervision, "1999 Bank and Thrift Branch Office Data Book: Summary of Deposits," national and 6 regional data books (related Internet site <http://www2.fdic.gov/sod/>). Federal Funds and Grants—U.S. Census Bureau, County Aggregate files for each state, <http://www.census.gov/govs/www/cffr99.html>, (accessed: August 2000).

Table B–12. Counties — **Accommodation and Foodservices, Banking, and Federal Funds**–Con.

[Includes U.S., states, and 3,142 counties/county equivalents defined as of January 1, 1992. For changes to these areas since January 1, 1992, see appendix B. Geographic Information]

County	Accommodation and foodservices[1] (NAICS 72), 1997					Banking,[4] 1999		Federal funds and grants, 1999						
		Sales								Per capita[5] (dollars)				
												By selected type—		
	Establishments	Total ($1,000)	Percent from foodservices[2]	Paid employees[3]	Annual payroll ($1,000)	Offices	Deposits (mil. dol.)	Total expenditures or obligations (mil. dol.)	Percent change, 1990–1999	Total	Direct payments for individuals	Procurement contract awards	Salaries and wages	Grant awards
KENTUCKY—Con.														
Henderson	81	41 323	88.7	1 403	11 841	14	446.9	170.9	80.6	3 849	2 932	113	135	474
Henry	7	3 123	100.0	99	848	9	225.1	53.3	102.0	3 546	2 557	42	178	693
Hickman	3	D	D	(6)	D	2	72.2	27.8	47.9	5 406	2 834	36	181	1 126
Hopkins	74	30 426	88.6	982	8 334	25	519.1	246.3	91.0	5 336	3 386	825	425	601
Jackson	8	D	D	(6)	D	4	76.5	67.1	77.3	5 142	3 107	28	114	1 842
Jefferson	1 394	1 081 920	82.6	34 303	314 768	257	12 545.0	3 831.2	81.9	5 694	3 110	1 204	545	783
Jessamine	44	23 588	D	799	6 184	16	270.0	109.1	137.2	2 924	2 008	204	100	595
Johnson	28	15 318	89.6	470	4 276	10	280.7	126.6	58.9	5 275	3 573	31	136	1 514
Kenton	294	236 874	78.1	6 542	65 482	61	1 856.3	608.9	42.4	4 136	2 536	94	905	584
Knott	10	D	D	(6)	D	3	90.7	87.8	77.1	4 896	3 136	38	138	1 574
Knox	33	15 852	D	561	4 266	14	281.9	153.7	56.2	4 807	2 806	23	241	1 727
Larue	10	D	D	(7)	D	9	176.3	54.6	73.1	4 154	3 136	35	155	679
Laurel	64	50 876	86.9	1 698	14 386	20	480.1	214.9	76.6	4 131	2 545	250	307	1 010
Lawrence	18	8 291	D	280	2 187	4	90.8	78.7	83.9	4 980	3 286	117	139	1 420
Lee	8	D	D	(6)	D	2	76.3	46.2	78.6	5 778	3 612	32	125	1 972
Leslie	6	D	D	(6)	D	3	76.5	78.7	104.3	5 801	3 716	69	140	1 871
Letcher	19	9 498	D	314	2 673	10	234.2	149.4	47.7	5 731	3 886	43	148	1 645
Lewis	14	D	D	(6)	D	8	124.9	59.7	81.6	4 431	2 860	20	77	1 423
Lincoln	15	4 694	100.0	176	1 263	8	184.2	97.1	96.3	4 307	2 876	29	124	1 220
Livingston	11	8 692	D	249	3 086	5	76.8	59.4	118.8	6 268	3 636	1 452	354	602
Logan	29	11 595	91.8	479	2 634	13	328.8	117.7	92.5	4 478	2 999	59	126	871
Lyon	21	7 162	66.6	216	1 800	4	53.3	33.1	70.1	4 110	3 273	30	186	478
McCracken	184	125 093	81.8	4 116	35 262	21	1 017.7	641.9	58.6	9 966	3 462	5 191	603	619
McCreary	10	3 009	70.1	117	926	5	99.1	235.4	344.7	14 050	3 610	8 672	235	1 522
McLean	10	1 578	100.0	58	372	7	123.3	52.3	99.7	5 280	3 294	39	167	1 347
Madison	126	75 539	84.7	2 664	21 206	30	573.4	255.3	70.5	3 772	2 467	129	393	749
Magoffin	11	4 849	D	161	1 351	4	78.2	70.5	75.9	5 024	3 022	29	88	1 861
Marion	28	8 254	97.0	296	2 499	9	213.8	74.1	78.6	4 329	2 792	39	179	1 193
Marshall	72	23 956	64.8	774	6 324	9	406.4	121.1	74.1	4 005	3 347	44	151	391
Martin	15	7 615	D	235	2 100	3	84.8	67.2	96.1	5 646	3 886	97	82	1 570
Mason	42	20 153	89.8	526	4 851	13	286.1	84.1	97.5	4 998	2 830	33	190	1 853
Meade	24	9 386	85.9	284	2 682	6	131.4	69.4	93.2	2 377	1 901	18	73	306
Menifee	4	D	D	(6)	D	1	19.2	40.8	80.8	6 949	3 246	113	1 453	2 107
Mercer	36	13 985	73.1	403	3 684	8	223.5	72.8	68.1	3 500	2 691	30	121	604
Metcalfe	9	1 998	100.0	83	446	5	95.6	42.1	86.8	4 391	2 835	37	150	1 279
Monroe	21	D	D	(7)	D	8	135.2	69.8	103.3	6 254	3 770	40	200	2 105
Montgomery	38	20 487	86.9	785	5 498	13	348.4	94.5	105.9	4 370	2 813	28	158	1 303
Morgan	9	D	D	(7)	D	4	114.4	62.3	81.9	4 564	2 723	42	115	1 659
Muhlenberg	41	13 217	88.9	502	3 802	8	321.5	226.7	79.9	7 093	3 575	1 861	920	676
Nelson	55	27 228	82.2	863	7 517	14	379.8	108.5	80.2	2 934	2 183	58	136	496
Nicholas	4	827	100.0	59	242	3	66.8	30.5	81.7	4 274	2 993	30	178	975
Ohio	24	10 287	100.0	363	2 383	15	220.6	92.9	70.4	4 198	3 193	47	177	656
Oldham	51	29 151	90.9	957	8 414	11	281.4	67.3	98.9	1 470	1 122	24	84	211
Owen	6	1 838	100.0	75	512	5	91.5	29.5	62.1	2 836	2 151	29	107	508
Owsley	2	D	D	(8)	D	1	30.1	38.4	84.0	7 147	4 012	48	169	2 891
Pendleton	12	D	D	(7)	D	7	143.5	46.5	100.1	3 331	2 265	31	108	881
Perry	51	34 569	91.2	1 008	8 733	13	364.1	182.0	73.9	5 909	4 085	205	257	1 347
Pike	84	44 891	89.3	1 425	10 866	29	891.2	422.7	98.3	5 909	3 718	159	199	1 826
Powell	15	D	D	(7)	D	4	91.2	43.1	79.0	3 247	1 991	25	124	1 079
Pulaski	82	45 410	90.9	1 548	13 167	26	682.5	260.0	107.8	4 552	3 168	50	172	1 128
Robertson	3	122	100.0	12	27	1	15.4	8.9	70.7	3 919	2 759	25	106	892
Rockcastle	17	8 635	77.6	270	2 323	4	172.6	96.2	107.4	6 023	2 766	26	97	3 103
Rowan	43	24 016	88.2	899	6 814	7	175.8	82.2	56.0	3 708	2 431	34	188	1 026
Russell	29	9 807	91.6	324	2 662	8	173.3	86.3	81.1	5 332	3 421	61	159	1 644
Scott	51	43 241	88.3	1 209	12 217	15	314.1	87.8	32.2	2 722	1 899	25	94	654
Shelby	43	21 384	85.3	685	5 831	14	416.0	91.3	81.2	2 988	2 071	189	139	513
Simpson	37	23 669	89.4	697	6 308	10	236.9	61.6	58.9	3 712	2 549	27	101	689
Spencer	7	D	D	(6)	D	3	68.0	27.6	112.5	2 646	1 954	71	127	413
Taylor	45	18 808	94.5	685	4 969	11	253.5	99.3	87.2	4 328	3 269	67	194	705
Todd	10	2 002	100.0	75	498	8	144.2	53.1	81.3	4 705	2 912	45	146	1 008
Trigg	18	6 077	69.6	224	1 817	6	138.8	65.0	101.2	5 161	3 698	96	485	618
Trimble	7	569	100.0	30	155	3	99.2	24.5	99.9	3 095	2 456	29	103	456
Union	23	D	D	(9)	D	8	176.3	-89.6	-203.2	-5 433	2 905	-9 482	155	532
Warren	192	135 964	82.0	4 375	40 041	31	840.4	349.4	91.8	3 984	2 636	115	436	716
Washington	13	4 101	D	131	985	7	170.9	41.5	79.9	3 756	2 590	35	165	878
Wayne	20	D	D	(9)	D	6	197.2	93.9	103.4	4 894	2 945	20	103	1 775
Webster	15	3 116	100.0	138	899	9	270.8	87.1	69.4	6 471	3 276	2 051	150	597
Whitley	68	35 084	81.2	1 128	9 366	14	380.6	232.1	102.4	6 423	4 388	257	204	1 553
Wolfe	6	D	D	(6)	D	1	29.1	44.5	86.5	5 926	3 326	74	201	2 278
Woodford	41	14 901	D	529	4 344	8	296.7	59.0	83.9	2 592	2 065	45	93	322

[1] Includes only establishments with payroll.　[2] Includes full-service restaurants, limited-service eating places, special food services, and drinking places (alcoholic beverages).　[3] For pay period including March 12.　[4] As of June 30. Covers all FDIC-insured commercial banks and savings institutions.　[5] Based on resident population estimated as of July 1, 1999.　[6] 20 to 99 employees.　[7] 100 to 249 employees.　[8] 0 to 19 employees.　[9] 250 to 499 employees.

Sources: Accommodation and Foodservices—U.S. Census Bureau, 1997 Economic Census, ECON97 Report Series CD-ROM, CD-EC97-1, Disc 1E, issued February 2001 (related Internet site <http://www.census.gov/epcd/www/97EC72.HTM>). Banking—U.S. Federal Deposit Insurance Corporation and Office of Thrift Supervision, "1999 Bank and Thrift Branch Office Data Book: Summary of Deposits," national and 6 regional data books (related Internet site <http://www2.fdic.gov/sod/>). Federal Funds and Grants—U.S. Census Bureau, County Aggregate files for each state, <http://www.census.gov/govs/www/cffr99.html>, (accessed: August 2000).

Table B–12. Counties — Accommodation and Foodservices, Banking, and Federal Funds-Con.

[Includes U.S., states, and 3,142 counties/county equivalents defined as of January 1, 1992. For changes to these areas since January 1, 1992, see appendix B. Geographic Information]

County	Accommodation and foodservices[1] (NAICS 72), 1997					Banking,[4] 1999		Federal funds and grants, 1999						
	Sales			Paid employees[3]	Annual payroll ($1,000)	Offices	Deposits (mil. dol.)	Total expenditures or obligations (mil. dol.)	Percent change, 1990–1999	Per capita[5] (dollars)				
	Establishments	Total ($1,000)	Percent from foodservices[2]							Total	Direct payments for individuals	Procurement contract awards	Salaries and wages	Grant awards
LOUISIANA	7 151	5 259 921	69.4	147 016	1 408 910	1 462	44 762.9	24 384.3	59.1	5 577	3 121	610	495	1 196
Acadia	58	D	D	(6)	D	20	548.2	271.5	63.1	4 685	2 745	251	105	1 158
Allen	26	10 873	53.2	288	2 278	10	136.9	144.9	60.6	5 984	2 863	138	1 594	1 099
Ascension	103	58 750	87.9	1 729	15 874	19	492.1	205.7	105.3	2 777	2 016	72	93	583
Assumption	13	3 276	D	116	907	8	118.1	90.7	89.1	3 903	2 719	20	107	1 045
Avoyelles	37	131 212	D	1 931	34 574	20	355.6	216.9	82.8	5 329	3 124	143	134	1 609
Beauregard	32	15 696	D	449	3 210	11	253.6	132.6	62.6	4 109	3 027	32	194	771
Bienville	16	D	D	(7)	D	6	119.7	88.8	68.5	5 640	3 778	82	161	1 586
Bossier	173	300 760	29.3	5 610	69 807	20	577.1	681.8	16.5	7 302	3 465	482	2 624	625
Caddo	408	236 946	86.9	7 743	66 000	71	2 252.1	1 166.0	31.8	4 828	3 114	188	471	1 011
Calcasieu	294	306 387	52.9	8 019	75 424	59	1 599.3	700.6	28.5	3 879	2 784	164	182	694
Caldwell	8	D	D	(8)	D	4	117.4	58.3	80.4	5 566	3 614	28	138	1 216
Cameron	11	2 010	D	54	447	6	87.6	33.8	92.4	3 771	2 084	278	168	742
Catahoula	11	2 698	100.0	100	666	6	99.4	84.5	117.0	7 753	3 345	704	221	1 845
Claiborne	18	D	D	(7)	D	8	110.6	79.5	62.3	4 723	3 122	50	141	1 360
Concordia	27	D	D	(9)	D	5	288.7	123.6	82.1	6 009	3 169	289	166	1 626
De Soto	15	D	D	(7)	D	13	185.7	119.5	76.7	4 751	3 170	29	129	1 321
East Baton Rouge	754	504 675	85.3	16 452	138 339	142	5 190.8	2 415.6	77.0	6 142	2 694	191	350	2 891
East Carroll	6	D	D	(8)	D	2	64.5	73.3	76.7	8 409	3 660	41	131	2 902
East Feliciana	17	3 433	D	150	929	6	121.7	84.9	84.7	4 018	2 676	28	159	1 127
Evangeline	34	D	D	(7)	D	13	378.9	205.4	70.6	5 983	3 344	26	89	2 110
Franklin	18	D	D	(7)	D	8	202.0	134.8	83.1	6 127	3 171	28	158	1 722
Grant	3	D	D	(10)	D	5	58.6	87.7	13.0	4 563	3 108	107	222	998
Iberia	83	33 875	D	1 302	8 973	30	822.7	267.9	77.9	3 648	2 534	46	104	949
Iberville	31	13 000	D	478	3 522	14	300.7	158.7	74.5	5 060	3 146	188	345	1 354
Jackson	18	D	D	(7)	D	5	130.0	82.0	84.0	5 310	3 875	60	226	1 127
Jefferson	948	681 211	83.0	18 676	185 739	125	4 733.1	1 815.7	57.4	4 055	2 745	467	205	573
Jefferson Davis	44	20 386	D	684	5 360	17	326.4	144.9	66.7	4 611	2 799	86	121	951
Lafayette	382	270 121	86.7	9 058	78 805	77	2 278.0	622.9	91.4	3 324	2 138	206	278	666
Lafourche	129	48 637	85.3	1 554	10 886	42	1 051.5	510.8	52.7	5 710	2 498	2 440	93	653
La Salle	13	4 602	D	150	1 170	9	145.9	68.2	62.1	4 977	3 515	38	156	1 230
Lincoln	66	34 505	80.7	1 206	8 415	17	418.4	155.4	66.8	3 778	2 600	33	149	979
Livingston	84	37 096	95.7	1 282	9 455	17	381.0	237.9	110.6	2 609	1 982	18	74	512
Madison	15	D	D	(7)	D	4	108.8	93.0	75.0	7 157	3 478	130	164	2 249
Morehouse	28	D	D	(8)	D	8	214.9	203.5	86.1	6 513	3 613	32	121	1 843
Natchitoches	65	40 867	65.4	1 370	11 168	15	272.9	200.6	66.6	5 394	3 085	90	242	1 693
Orleans	1 105	1 371 830	49.4	32 081	377 486	105	7 977.5	4 811.7	40.5	10 439	3 797	3 122	1 531	1 809
Ouachita	265	170 104	86.7	5 360	42 565	56	1 608.8	572.4	68.6	3 903	2 769	87	180	810
Plaquemines	51	55 492	D	1 600	20 439	8	205.1	204.0	66.3	7 817	2 446	3 503	1 122	696
Pointe Coupee	26	D	D	(9)	D	13	209.9	100.2	62.9	4 273	2 429	30	133	1 342
Rapides	224	119 801	82.0	3 985	31 736	47	1 184.9	689.1	22.4	5 435	3 366	292	730	946
Red River	6	D	D	(8)	D	2	92.0	57.0	70.4	6 005	3 346	107	171	1 836
Richland	27	8 662	81.6	296	2 135	9	211.9	136.8	94.8	6 491	3 266	32	231	1 781
Sabine	24	7 611	D	217	2 171	15	184.1	120.1	78.0	5 044	3 418	33	104	1 456
St. Bernard	107	43 031	D	1 431	11 587	19	690.8	286.4	79.8	4 379	3 519	341	98	379
St. Charles	47	18 973	86.5	701	5 227	15	314.5	158.0	60.3	3 248	2 041	585	157	448
St. Helena	5	D	D	(8)	D	3	46.0	38.2	97.5	3 981	2 308	16	71	1 541
St. James	14	6 599	D	203	1 763	10	238.6	113.9	131.8	5 374	2 797	1 452	152	931
St. John the Baptist	36	21 793	D	783	5 701	8	265.5	156.6	153.9	3 685	2 230	795	107	522
St. Landry	76	32 165	92.1	1 034	8 585	39	750.4	444.2	73.1	5 273	3 190	30	117	1 766
St. Martin	52	D	D	(6)	D	17	330.1	170.6	93.1	3 582	2 223	157	88	1 072
St. Mary	91	41 331	83.4	1 385	10 348	27	667.1	236.1	60.3	4 158	2 659	279	154	1 041
St. Tammany	345	170 691	90.8	5 415	44 825	57	1 441.4	566.1	104.7	2 934	2 337	86	153	327
Tangipahoa	159	79 678	90.1	2 898	21 865	31	708.9	424.1	84.5	4 315	2 968	41	152	1 132
Tensas	8	1 612	D	25	179	6	78.6	61.0	8.2	9 336	3 589	31	127	2 668
Terrebonne	173	105 933	90.7	3 133	31 081	39	944.3	365.0	94.4	3 472	2 565	95	146	625
Union	19	D	D	(7)	D	8	182.9	100.9	86.1	4 553	3 247	63	188	1 024
Vermilion	64	22 632	D	775	5 542	27	644.8	215.8	67.1	4 129	2 717	32	135	761
Vernon	58	22 979	85.3	782	5 878	13	150.6	612.0	33.2	11 867	2 720	2 218	6 321	587
Washington	49	18 326	D	626	4 403	18	328.5	248.8	87.5	5 764	4 172	73	145	1 331
Webster	56	18 091	91.4	637	4 157	13	373.1	211.3	40.8	4 938	3 705	29	136	1 040
West Baton Rouge	31	18 052	67.6	591	4 487	5	120.0	113.9	113.7	5 576	2 621	2 044	141	742
West Carroll	7	D	D	(8)	D	5	102.4	73.1	78.6	6 005	3 360	31	163	1 565
West Feliciana	18	7 120	D	176	1 797	2	61.2	37.9	35.3	2 740	1 423	608	63	617
Winn	20	6 211	D	209	1 498	3	106.1	79.1	66.5	4 521	3 025	44	183	1 233

[1] Includes only establishments with payroll. [2] Includes full-service restaurants, limited-service eating places, special food services, and drinking places (alcoholic beverages). [3] For pay period including March 12. [4] As of June 30. Covers all FDIC-insured commercial banks and savings institutions. [5] Based on resident population estimated as of July 1, 1999. [6] 500 to 999 employees. [7] 100 to 249 employees. [8] 20 to 99 employees. [9] 250 to 499 employees. [10] 0 to 19 employees.

Sources: Accommodation and Foodservices—U.S. Census Bureau, 1997 Economic Census, ECON[97] Report Series CD-ROM, CD-EC97-1, Disc 1E, issued February 2001 (related Internet site <http://www.census.gov/epcd/www/97EC72.HTM>). Banking—U.S. Federal Deposit Insurance Corporation and Office of Thrift Supervision, "1999 Bank and Thrift Branch Office Data Book: Summary of Deposits," national and 6 regional data books (related Internet site <http://www2.fdic.gov/sod/>). Federal Funds and Grants—U.S. Census Bureau, County Aggregate files for each state, <http://www.census.gov/govs/www/cffr99.html>, (accessed: August 2000).

[Includes U.S., states, and 3,142 counties/county equivalents defined as of January 1, 1992. For changes to these areas since January 1, 1992, see appendix B. Geographic Information]

County	Accommodation and foodservices[1] (NAICS 72), 1997					Banking,[4] 1999		Federal funds and grants, 1999						
	Sales			Paid employees[3]	Annual payroll ($1,000)	Offices	Deposits (mil. dol.)	Total expenditures or obligations (mil. dol.)	Percent change, 1990–1999	Per capita[5] (dollars)				
												By selected type—		
	Estab-lishments	Total ($1,000)	Percent from food-services[2]							Total	Direct payments for individuals	Procure-ment contract awards	Salaries and wages	Grant awards
MAINE	3 716	1 510 182	70.5	39 657	429 143	509	13 472.1	7 281.5	46.9	5 811	3 143	641	634	1 328
Androscoggin	180	77 432	85.9	2 438	23 332	36	951.0	443.3	55.6	4 374	3 055	60	197	1 042
Aroostook	162	49 993	81.3	1 807	14 845	35	680.7	463.3	24.5	6 109	3 432	381	415	1 804
Cumberland	793	430 482	74.1	11 767	121 464	94	3 820.9	1 277.1	56.0	4 980	2 757	428	971	794
Franklin	94	33 612	71.8	1 328	11 021	19	300.0	120.3	78.5	4 176	2 946	49	155	1 009
Hancock	315	104 992	56.2	1 741	28 366	28	661.5	268.1	54.8	5 397	3 093	249	583	1 453
Kennebec	257	109 078	77.8	3 282	32 000	45	1 120.8	898.5	71.6	7 798	3 212	103	657	3 798
Knox	131	58 008	55.8	1 306	17 494	20	640.8	175.2	53.6	4 586	3 170	50	183	1 178
Lincoln	158	49 070	52.9	870	14 445	18	460.7	145.8	64.7	4 565	3 379	79	177	921
Oxford	140	44 207	55.5	1 203	12 199	21	494.8	231.7	59.8	4 268	3 115	45	154	937
Penobscot	344	151 277	79.0	4 778	45 826	54	1 251.0	735.0	65.5	5 089	2 953	189	568	1 351
Piscataquis	50	10 841	70.2	351	2 802	7	129.3	87.5	57.0	4 842	3 498	35	147	1 142
Sagadahoc	64	25 629	77.8	743	7 674	12	220.1	652.8	−25.8	17 999	2 539	13 924	746	784
Somerset	105	25 964	77.8	778	6 829	22	429.6	217.0	65.5	4 124	2 754	42	169	1 139
Waldo	86	23 188	71.7	546	6 249	10	227.2	186.5	108.6	5 046	2 638	1 142	156	1 093
Washington	113	21 952	77.9	707	6 345	21	369.6	225.3	57.7	6 374	3 526	298	502	1 948
York	724	294 457	63.5	6 012	78 252	67	1 714.1	873.2	98.0	4 917	2 929	211	1 241	527
MARYLAND	9 049	5 972 467	81.2	161 273	1 644 729	1 671	60 524.0	41 990.2	53.9	8 119	3 057	2 046	1 614	1 111
Allegany	165	75 460	D	2 434	19 799	28	695.2	475.1	70.1	6 677	4 383	203	461	1 608
Anne Arundel	852	637 267	81.0	17 645	175 602	150	4 122.0	3 390.4	62.3	7 056	2 965	1 714	1 660	703
Baltimore	1 359	842 416	88.0	24 414	233 515	277	9 820.3	3 715.9	49.9	5 133	3 090	483	1 111	445
Calvert	94	56 886	85.3	1 859	15 521	19	477.6	220.7	72.1	2 993	2 497	72	105	310
Caroline	27	7 864	91.7	255	1 898	14	248.3	123.9	85.6	4 170	2 848	43	147	974
Carroll	214	110 321	94.2	3 906	31 390	58	1 739.7	475.5	7.0	3 119	2 479	236	111	270
Cecil	131	75 176	79.5	2 011	20 051	20	564.4	335.1	56.9	3 978	2 522	325	710	386
Charles	186	125 329	91.9	3 895	33 496	34	1 016.7	587.2	82.6	4 855	2 603	457	1 315	466
Dorchester	60	21 335	93.8	765	5 990	15	379.1	182.6	83.5	6 146	3 612	567	259	1 533
Frederick	304	193 177	87.4	6 028	54 474	78	1 936.9	741.6	80.4	3 885	2 132	451	868	396
Garrett	73	26 716	65.0	961	8 010	13	359.2	125.6	89.2	4 273	2 858	148	156	1 094
Harford	293	185 882	90.9	5 777	51 550	74	1 548.3	1 314.2	41.7	6 031	2 462	1 376	1 858	323
Howard	366	242 517	84.2	7 078	68 549	58	1 941.4	780.0	44.9	3 208	1 607	1 071	185	334
Kent	66	20 095	85.8	585	5 689	16	330.4	113.5	55.3	5 947	4 215	187	203	1 014
Montgomery	1 407	1 062 058	82.0	25 248	297 974	279	13 349.4	9 210.8	57.4	10 809	2 729	4 041	3 225	789
Prince George's	1 027	718 399	84.3	20 122	193 791	171	5 331.1	6 874.6	56.0	8 794	2 649	3 247	2 204	678
Queen Anne's	80	54 887	84.1	1 482	15 681	16	399.6	128.3	74.3	3 153	2 310	163	107	384
St. Mary's	111	62 559	92.1	2 017	17 530	19	582.2	2 143.6	221.5	24 151	2 685	14 437	6 389	622
Somerset	28	10 457	D	335	2 980	8	151.2	121.3	80.9	5 005	2 905	284	155	1 582
Talbot	96	69 755	64.3	1 639	20 000	20	586.6	199.8	100.7	5 957	3 861	749	416	728
Washington	230	127 582	78.8	4 135	36 436	60	1 339.3	510.8	36.4	3 997	2 906	151	220	690
Wicomico	159	86 796	84.9	2 964	25 035	49	963.4	326.8	80.3	4 108	2 696	268	225	885
Worcester	393	309 679	55.3	5 697	77 802	42	735.3	287.3	87.2	6 580	4 033	1 318	198	944
Independent City														
Baltimore city	1 328	849 854	72.1	20 021	231 966	153	11 906.5	7 444.8	40.6	11 767	4 206	1 896	1 132	4 402
MASSACHUSETTS	14 827	9 282 541	78.4	227 898	2 579 922	1 987	131 158.7	37 803.0	24.9	6 122	3 209	932	473	1 431
Barnstable	1 144	624 340	66.0	11 852	177 312	111	3 859.4	1 419.8	81.6	6 681	4 696	479	559	934
Berkshire	485	247 325	56.1	7 060	75 553	58	2 082.3	869.0	.6	6 572	3 658	1 721	290	890
Bristol	1 113	557 475	93.1	16 990	152 727	158	5 923.8	2 560.5	13.0	4 922	2 980	725	161	1 033
Dukes	139	87 860	56.8	888	25 290	14	369.7	54.3	63.8	3 866	3 025	131	222	464
Essex	1 575	872 605	86.8	22 567	238 827	236	10 541.1	3 821.7	5.8	5 425	2 981	1 400	288	741
Franklin	150	49 828	90.2	1 715	14 325	19	765.4	276.7	49.2	3 907	2 862	96	173	753
Hampden	935	433 459	89.2	13 582	120 923	130	5 507.8	2 338.0	46.8	5 335	3 290	249	671	1 091
Hampshire	334	149 026	89.9	4 845	43 099	52	1 838.1	595.6	36.9	3 947	2 378	371	425	761
Middlesex	3 053	2 058 172	77.9	48 948	559 296	453	24 389.6	9 077.0	3.7	6 363	2 766	1 866	469	1 241
Nantucket	106	69 071	70.1	899	20 139	4	294.7	29.4	58.6	3 588	2 480	80	410	602
Norfolk	1 303	804 120	88.4	21 164	222 348	219	11 075.2	2 791.6	67.5	4 338	2 643	934	107	646
Plymouth	889	483 191	90.8	14 440	135 427	142	4 383.4	1 709.8	61.3	3 615	2 571	136	316	575
Suffolk	2 076	2 129 480	66.9	41 660	598 585	198	52 908.0	7 600.3	47.7	11 844	3 912	663	1 600	5 531
Worcester	1 525	716 589	85.6	21 288	196 071	193	7 220.3	3 066.2	52.0	4 151	2 861	180	250	842

[1] Includes only establishments with payroll.   [2] Includes full-service restaurants, limited-service eating places, special food services, and drinking places (alcoholic beverages).   [3] For pay period including March 12.   [4] As of June 30. Covers all FDIC-insured commercial banks and savings institutions.   [5] Based on resident population estimated as of July 1, 1999.

Sources: Accommodation and Foodservices—U.S. Census Bureau, 1997 Economic Census, ECON97 Report Series CD-ROM, CD-EC97-1, Disc 1E, issued February 2001 (related Internet site <http://www.census.gov/epcd/www/97EC72.HTM>).   Banking—U.S. Federal Deposit Insurance Corporation and Office of Thrift Supervision, "1999 Bank and Thrift Branch Office Data Book: Summary of Deposits," national and 6 regional data books (related Internet site <http://www2.fdic.gov/sod/>).   Federal Funds and Grants—U.S. Census Bureau, County Aggregate files for each state, <http://www.census.gov/govs/www/cffr99.html>, (accessed: August 2000).

Table B–12. Counties — Accommodation and Foodservices, Banking, and Federal Funds–Con.

[Includes U.S., states, and 3,142 counties/county equivalents defined as of January 1, 1992. For changes to these areas since January 1, 1992, see appendix B. Geographic Information]

County	Accommodation and foodservices[1] (NAICS 72), 1997 Estab-lishments	Sales Total ($1,000)	Sales Percent from food-services[2]	Paid employ-ees[3]	Annual payroll ($1,000)	Banking,[4] 1999 Offices	Deposits (mil. dol.)	Federal funds and grants, 1999 Total expenditures or obligations (mil. dol.)	Percent change, 1990–1999	Per capita[5] (dollars) Total	By selected type— Direct payments for individuals	Procure-ment contract awards	Salaries and wages	Grant awards
MICHIGAN..............	18 958	10 158 693	84.8	320 014	2 835 825	2 983	111 363.8	43 871.6	49.1	4 448	2 880	209	297	990
Alcona	38	5 458	D	194	1 274	2	24.8	72.0	63.1	6 460	4 755	57	185	1 421
Alger...................	57	12 648	70.2	392	3 064	8	94.0	49.2	55.7	4 878	3 548	62	335	898
Allegan	174	65 601	85.5	2 136	18 071	33	585.9	256.6	62.2	2 482	1 833	54	86	420
Alpena	74	27 218	78.1	1 130	7 420	12	303.8	169.1	67.8	5 524	3 733	402	184	1 163
Antrim	71	49 330	D	930	15 600	11	194.7	93.1	72.9	4 239	3 072	372	135	610
Arenac	51	14 741	88.5	499	3 822	7	138.5	86.0	58.5	5 198	3 799	85	147	974
Baraga	21	4 575	D	211	1 254	4	90.0	119.8	274.3	13 819	3 226	397	168	10 004
Barry	84	28 016	94.7	1 095	7 913	11	310.1	141.5	54.9	2 589	1 992	49	98	364
Bay	241	106 454	90.4	3 922	29 599	41	954.7	446.7	48.3	4 079	3 027	44	130	809
Benzie	60	28 674	39.1	819	8 044	7	172.2	61.5	58.7	4 028	3 115	50	172	679
Berrien	383	163 476	87.9	5 328	44 007	70	1 844.2	712.0	49.2	4 458	3 123	68	142	1 079
Branch	78	30 017	84.7	1 026	7 422	23	424.2	152.7	61.6	3 483	2 525	30	113	573
Calhoun	307	147 476	91.2	5 010	42 501	45	994.9	740.3	39.1	5 236	3 126	262	863	912
Cass	76	19 989	95.8	708	5 177	15	267.2	165.5	60.0	3 302	2 329	65	94	664
Charlevoix	84	45 006	58.2	1 384	16 414	15	278.4	90.4	55.4	3 610	2 808	129	194	462
Cheboygan	128	33 593	65.3	715	8 628	12	247.1	111.5	73.4	4 618	3 321	82	237	958
Chippewa	147	48 997	63.6	1 475	12 261	14	311.7	186.2	56.0	4 913	2 700	323	491	1 295
Clare	80	25 224	75.8	895	6 723	12	233.7	151.1	73.8	5 044	3 985	32	103	871
Clinton	83	32 424	D	1 213	9 208	15	333.6	168.5	14.5	2 630	1 599	34	370	465
Crawford	47	14 719	73.5	409	3 913	5	113.9	57.0	47.2	3 996	2 855	101	564	465
Delta	132	39 976	81.3	1 529	10 458	17	403.4	180.7	59.3	4 651	3 427	79	257	834
Dickinson	92	26 671	76.7	1 124	7 702	14	355.7	139.2	15.7	5 166	3 346	214	973	594
Eaton	156	88 389	D	3 008	25 358	37	904.8	595.7	58.7	5 863	1 731	20	208	3 833
Emmet	143	88 527	47.7	1 970	24 732	20	439.4	112.0	69.3	3 861	2 900	123	181	640
Genesee	794	403 858	92.8	13 618	111 154	100	3 402.5	1 820.0	65.7	4 161	2 914	75	178	960
Gladwin	42	11 657	84.1	475	3 431	7	141.4	116.3	71.2	4 525	3 707	29	105	612
Gogebic	70	39 975	29.6	1 175	10 508	8	189.2	110.2	45.3	6 467	4 606	109	430	1 306
Grand Traverse	233	134 161	71.8	3 895	37 286	29	909.9	295.5	78.8	3 922	2 768	149	394	592
Gratiot	67	29 796	98.0	1 009	7 602	20	397.5	174.3	74.7	4 355	2 826	46	149	988
Hillsdale	75	23 559	87.7	815	6 283	15	366.0	160.8	57.3	3 417	2 399	47	124	616
Houghton	118	30 296	76.7	1 272	8 250	24	474.0	168.9	39.2	4 765	3 119	175	276	1 176
Huron	103	23 199	92.1	719	6 125	27	566.6	179.9	55.9	5 099	3 457	45	154	872
Ingham	597	368 882	86.2	13 137	104 754	91	3 110.9	2 524.3	105.0	8 853	3 155	179	383	5 061
Ionia	85	26 001	94.5	893	6 501	21	402.4	173.8	63.5	2 589	1 800	76	90	603
Iosco	88	25 838	73.3	795	6 631	13	257.8	151.8	-13.7	5 855	4 773	158	197	673
Iron	49	11 478	66.7	577	3 933	9	148.2	78.6	47.2	6 134	4 605	72	221	1 191
Isabella	103	68 513	76.9	2 498	19 525	22	463.0	159.2	49.3	2 693	1 882	28	123	527
Jackson	267	136 985	91.9	4 467	37 735	54	1 387.7	575.6	54.5	3 660	2 703	104	162	642
Kalamazoo	452	260 623	89.1	9 317	78 222	75	2 062.8	857.8	61.7	3 732	2 410	145	401	739
Kalkaska	29	8 999	77.9	296	2 398	4	91.8	51.3	73.6	3 245	2 428	35	99	664
Kent	954	617 519	83.4	20 741	181 578	192	7 183.8	1 841.8	50.2	3 346	2 165	226	302	636
Keweenaw	21	D	D	(6)	D	1	7.3	11.8	4.0	5 506	4 250	27	186	1 039
Lake	36	7 863	79.1	201	1 919	3	57.2	61.2	69.7	5 756	4 076	39	224	1 377
Lapeer	119	52 068	90.4	2 045	14 129	26	517.7	215.8	65.3	2 415	1 752	26	95	471
Leelanau	78	32 464	68.3	884	10 124	7	133.4	60.2	49.1	3 108	2 519	56	263	249
Lenawee	182	73 461	93.0	2 485	19 613	46	1 023.4	346.6	61.2	3 474	2 582	33	117	572
Livingston	193	116 055	92.1	3 494	29 882	44	1 324.1	288.2	93.1	1 902	1 433	46	90	307
Luce	33	7 326	62.7	275	1 986	3	59.3	34.3	51.8	5 077	3 471	34	141	1 401
Mackinac	129	50 388	40.4	723	13 316	11	148.1	52.3	30.8	4 715	3 472	101	356	762
Macomb	1 342	796 531	93.5	24 413	216 427	207	10 789.1	3 479.3	44.8	4 393	2 781	832	421	351
Manistee	73	18 508	79.2	671	5 221	14	227.0	108.1	57.6	4 569	3 590	106	218	620
Marquette	175	64 669	80.0	2 642	20 079	32	519.2	270.6	-1.6	4 312	3 173	113	248	759
Mason	80	29 468	79.7	1 010	8 381	10	266.7	114.9	49.2	4 109	3 121	113	180	642
Mecosta	87	41 228	73.4	1 587	11 408	14	265.0	136.2	63.9	3 346	2 517	32	132	559
Menominee	51	D	D	(7)	D	12	189.4	101.1	54.4	4 133	2 977	163	164	670
Midland	132	78 129	77.7	2 688	22 935	26	739.8	244.7	71.3	2 985	2 238	64	116	528
Missaukee	25	4 631	D	179	1 171	4	88.3	48.0	72.8	3 395	2 523	42	119	519
Monroe	219	98 028	91.1	3 339	26 199	42	1 464.0	426.5	54.7	2 943	2 373	38	90	379
Montcalm	89	27 716	94.1	1 027	7 527	25	443.0	217.2	59.9	3 537	2 609	32	128	626
Montmorency	38	7 095	D	275	1 732	3	78.4	61.6	56.0	6 154	5 218	24	86	795
Muskegon	321	153 779	87.5	5 256	42 230	43	1 155.7	744.5	59.3	4 430	2 810	611	130	861
Newaygo	62	19 927	86.9	686	5 398	13	255.9	149.0	61.6	3 213	2 416	55	101	577
Oakland	2 453	1 667 951	87.3	48 174	478 594	345	20 325.9	3 931.6	58.0	3 332	2 495	139	242	435

[1] Includes only establishments with payroll. [2] Includes full-service restaurants, limited-service eating places, special food services, and drinking places (alcoholic beverages). [3] For pay period including March 12. [4] As of June 30. Covers all FDIC-insured commercial banks and savings institutions. [5] Based on resident population estimated as of July 1, 1999. [6] 100 to 249 employees. [7] 500 to 999 employees.

Sources: Accommodation and Foodservices—U.S. Census Bureau, 1997 Economic Census, ECON97 Report Series CD-ROM, CD-EC97-1, Disc 1E, issued February 2001 (related Internet site <http://www.census.gov/epcd/www/97EC72.HTM>). Banking—U.S. Federal Deposit Insurance Corporation and Office of Thrift Supervision, "1999 Bank and Thrift Branch Office Data Book: Summary of Deposits," national and 6 regional data books (related Internet site <http://www2.fdic.gov/sod/>). Federal Funds and Grants—U.S. Census Bureau, County Aggregate files for each state, <http://www.census.gov/govs/www/cffr99.html>, (accessed: August 2000).

Table B–12. Counties — **Accommodation and Foodservices, Banking, and Federal Funds**–Con.

[Includes U.S., states, and 3,142 counties/county equivalents defined as of January 1, 1992. For changes to these areas since January 1, 1992, see appendix B. Geographic Information]

County	Accommodation and foodservices[1] (NAICS 72), 1997 Sales — Establishments	Total ($1,000)	Percent from foodservices[2]	Paid employees[3]	Annual payroll ($1,000)	Banking,[4] 1999 Offices	Deposits (mil. dol.)	Federal funds and grants, 1999 Total expenditures or obligations (mil. dol.)	Percent change, 1990–1999	Per capita[5] (dollars) Total	Direct payments for individuals	Procurement contract awards	Salaries and wages	Grant awards
MICHIGAN—Con.														
Oceana	66	16 862	60.7	410	5 219	9	180.4	103.9	75.5	4 173	2 999	353	130	631
Ogemaw	69	20 776	85.4	654	5 721	9	210.3	96.5	66.0	4 550	3 592	29	139	687
Ontonagon	40	6 467	73.2	303	1 825	6	80.6	59.6	72.8	7 776	4 472	1 001	322	1 918
Osceola	43	10 605	98.6	334	2 564	7	167.4	100.1	51.0	4 505	3 204	66	141	953
Oscoda	24	5 592	D	210	1 721	3	64.3	36.5	67.6	4 101	3 383	33	204	471
Otsego	69	56 935	46.2	1 686	18 340	10	278.8	95.2	106.5	4 189	2 647	102	481	921
Ottawa	328	173 154	85.5	6 073	50 366	87	2 577.1	655.1	99.9	2 845	1 856	567	120	272
Presque Isle	57	9 053	90.2	295	2 492	5	115.4	72.6	55.4	4 973	3 918	70	157	731
Roscommon	79	26 466	86.7	994	7 500	9	199.7	143.7	76.5	6 097	5 287	22	83	702
Saginaw	408	270 546	87.3	9 236	78 917	73	1 796.3	937.2	57.2	4 479	2 969	137	342	953
St. Clair	290	138 296	85.9	4 520	38 368	44	1 421.2	510.0	47.8	3 153	2 236	112	158	608
St. Joseph	128	45 485	87.4	1 436	11 362	35	575.3	214.6	50.5	3 492	2 590	89	116	553
Sanilac	75	21 283	87.7	736	6 099	23	451.2	183.8	63.7	4 230	2 964	91	136	646
Schoolcraft	43	7 489	72.5	221	1 886	6	130.5	54.8	83.7	6 231	3 899	815	291	1 188
Shiawassee	110	41 051	96.4	1 467	10 954	21	587.4	246.1	64.3	3 402	2 640	26	109	525
Tuscola	84	28 996	91.0	1 101	8 202	25	482.6	213.2	68.9	3 663	2 658	40	130	626
Van Buren	146	51 587	90.7	1 677	15 145	25	536.1	294.8	63.4	3 883	2 608	143	110	960
Washtenaw	627	430 165	84.0	13 266	119 497	93	3 460.2	1 446.0	66.2	4 724	1 950	464	548	1 732
Wayne	3 313	2 023 660	84.5	58 336	542 489	387	26 097.0	10 602.9	44.6	5 033	3 145	129	434	1 298
Wexford	88	39 747	72.8	1 487	11 576	14	297.9	138.9	53.5	4 698	2 920	629	245	877
MINNESOTA	9 982	5 934 155	74.4	179 487	1 688 779	1 557	66 928.2	21 665.8	44.9	4 537	2 425	378	372	942
Aitkin	59	16 505	66.8	469	4 437	5	127.0	83.9	73.2	5 870	3 928	51	161	1 677
Anoka	351	215 438	94.4	7 744	62 349	44	1 449.9	1 148.2	176.4	3 841	1 158	27	41	271
Becker	104	33 299	53.9	973	8 407	10	263.4	150.7	67.9	5 065	2 793	213	323	1 322
Beltrami	100	40 850	75.0	1 339	11 371	14	443.0	183.6	68.2	4 683	2 464	138	381	1 634
Benton	53	26 841	89.0	962	7 539	9	160.2	103.8	45.3	2 980	2 225	13	100	481
Big Stone	21	3 312	88.5	155	789	5	124.9	37.8	46.3	6 783	3 648	64	337	885
Blue Earth	137	72 637	90.4	2 657	19 489	27	803.6	215.9	51.9	4 007	2 429	101	391	710
Brown	62	23 512	81.9	1 044	6 458	15	483.5	112.1	52.3	4 169	2 740	89	155	405
Carlton	74	23 402	88.2	808	6 420	8	153.1	144.0	72.7	4 572	2 851	46	414	1 199
Carver	109	43 602	87.7	1 566	12 818	24	618.4	139.9	109.7	2 087	1 214	362	186	213
Cass	121	26 792	56.1	669	6 033	16	275.3	146.9	60.6	5 431	3 271	50	370	1 711
Chippewa	30	7 585	95.5	329	2 034	7	284.7	61.9	54.6	4 748	2 591	41	220	700
Chisago	67	18 507	92.1	772	5 197	14	290.3	105.4	70.8	2 491	1 990	37	133	260
Clay	107	40 684	85.4	1 615	11 365	21	455.7	187.6	52.2	3 627	2 339	32	131	676
Clearwater	20	D	D	(6)	D	4	94.5	44.2	52.6	5 431	2 979	47	189	2 026
Cook	71	36 086	21.6	748	9 837	3	49.2	26.4	94.1	5 524	2 845	202	781	1 684
Cottonwood	24	6 007	100.0	258	1 577	6	194.0	68.9	56.2	5 783	3 244	62	241	701
Crow Wing	211	121 295	45.7	2 480	33 182	38	650.0	228.6	63.2	4 346	3 259	72	169	828
Dakota	488	344 933	88.3	11 244	100 755	76	2 304.7	709.2	68.6	2 031	1 287	258	299	156
Dodge	24	D	D	(7)	D	9	152.7	61.9	71.8	3 561	1 974	31	118	671
Douglas	106	42 175	69.4	1 258	11 104	13	478.4	131.5	67.0	4 205	2 920	51	201	779
Faribault	31	D	D	(7)	D	15	346.7	90.0	49.5	5 538	3 277	48	179	647
Fillmore	60	D	D	(7)	D	18	376.1	100.1	48.3	4 838	3 032	52	196	759
Freeborn	79	26 534	82.5	978	7 013	21	427.0	157.0	62.4	4 983	3 188	445	159	620
Goodhue	104	39 429	73.9	1 623	12 023	16	613.3	153.1	18.3	3 531	2 447	52	150	503
Grant	11	D	D	(8)	D	8	100.4	44.0	81.0	7 237	3 530	63	234	1 320
Hennepin	2 196	2 078 397	72.3	54 567	616 362	228	25 533.8	5 584.8	36.5	5 247	2 468	1 033	651	1 059
Houston	33	6 851	88.4	260	1 345	10	189.6	68.9	54.3	3 535	2 473	56	172	477
Hubbard	70	16 881	69.3	429	3 801	5	205.3	77.8	72.0	4 571	3 303	35	132	1 035
Isanti	43	14 461	92.1	570	4 083	5	224.2	76.3	72.6	2 469	1 802	43	116	390
Itasca	116	41 856	69.5	1 365	10 919	18	501.5	191.9	35.3	4 346	3 034	77	190	1 037
Jackson	16	D	D	(7)	D	9	184.9	58.9	51.8	5 173	2 558	44	172	511
Kanabec	23	D	D	(7)	D	4	159.0	52.3	74.1	3 628	2 303	36	164	1 019
Kandiyohi	88	41 503	74.7	1 551	10 959	19	578.0	177.0	76.7	4 336	2 530	438	251	669
Kittson	11	D	D	(8)	D	7	89.8	45.2	67.1	8 739	3 471	72	521	1 009
Koochiching	52	18 058	59.5	599	5 125	6	150.9	68.6	44.0	4 609	3 207	71	407	894
Lac qui Parle	17	D	D	(6)	D	7	122.7	49.0	49.7	6 272	3 269	68	246	723
Lake	49	15 624	56.4	481	3 928	5	77.6	51.7	88.8	4 807	3 743	151	133	775
Lake of the Woods	35	11 324	18.4	304	2 568	3	55.6	20.2	61.4	4 375	2 792	40	251	909
Le Sueur	47	D	D	(9)	D	11	339.4	92.1	63.0	3 616	2 401	33	120	592
Lincoln	15	2 284	100.0	83	379	4	51.6	40.8	52.8	6 352	3 324	51	211	756
Lyon	52	22 042	80.2	879	6 393	16	433.4	106.5	54.8	4 392	2 553	179	271	680
McLeod	67	26 939	87.7	1 040	7 142	19	552.8	111.9	52.0	3 238	2 129	57	130	588
Mahnomen	14	D	D	(6)	D	2	52.4	31.0	69.8	6 086	2 816	172	155	1 698
Marshall	27	D	D	(6)	D	10	150.4	84.6	78.4	8 377	3 058	106	340	987
Martin	52	18 121	78.5	775	5 204	14	419.7	113.4	59.2	5 206	3 108	47	166	746
Meeker	36	D	D	(7)	D	9	220.0	80.4	51.7	3 694	2 369	35	193	465

[1] Includes only establishments with payroll. [2] Includes full-service restaurants, limited-service eating places, special food services, and drinking places (alcoholic beverages). [3] For pay period including March 12. [4] As of June 30. Covers all FDIC-insured commercial banks and savings institutions. [5] Based on resident population estimated as of July 1, 1999. [6] 100 to 249 employees. [7] 250 to 499 employees. [8] 20 to 99 employees. [9] 500 to 999 employees.

Sources: Accommodation and Foodservices—U.S. Census Bureau, 1997 Economic Census, ECON97 Report Series CD-ROM, CD-EC97-1, Disc 1E, issued February 2001 (related Internet site <http://www.census.gov/epcd/www/97EC72.HTM>). Banking—U.S. Federal Deposit Insurance Corporation and Office of Thrift Supervision, "1999 Bank and Thrift Branch Office Data Book: Summary of Deposits," national and 6 regional data books (related Internet site <http://www2.fdic.gov/sod/>). Federal Funds and Grants—U.S. Census Bureau, County Aggregate files for each state, <http://www.census.gov/govs/www/cffr99.html>, (accessed: August 2000).

Table B–12. Counties — **Accommodation and Foodservices, Banking, and Federal Funds**–Con.

[Includes U.S., states, and 3,142 counties/county equivalents defined as of January 1, 1992. For changes to these areas since January 1, 1992, see appendix B. Geographic Information]

County	Estab-lishments	Sales Total ($1,000)	Percent from food-services[2]	Paid employ-ees[3]	Annual payroll ($1,000)	Offices	Deposits (mil. dol.)	Total expenditures or obligations (mil. dol.)	Percent change, 1990–1999	Per capita[5] Total	Direct payments for individuals	Procure-ment contract awards	Salaries and wages	Grant awards
MINNESOTA—Con.														
Mille Lacs	65	D	D	(6)	D	9	216.6	101.8	63.4	4 769	3 375	47	151	1 081
Morrison	91	22 409	82.5	804	5 648	12	362.2	141.0	37.7	4 620	2 689	98	618	943
Mower	87	31 466	82.8	1 211	8 453	18	467.4	185.6	46.5	4 996	3 445	122	210	618
Murray	22	D	D	(7)	D	7	167.3	53.2	61.6	5 588	2 870	58	226	495
Nicollet	44	22 920	81.2	826	6 129	10	289.3	68.6	67.7	2 342	1 495	17	93	294
Nobles	44	17 604	80.6	737	5 524	15	345.6	93.4	51.7	4 885	2 851	47	249	851
Norman	26	D	D	D	D	8	121.1	57.8	79.5	7 689	3 215	76	272	811
Olmsted	274	204 252	59.9	5 924	58 527	36	1 109.4	443.8	74.9	3 727	1 937	118	426	1 132
Otter Tail	138	37 863	84.6	1 354	9 708	26	656.5	242.6	53.2	4 365	2 935	103	200	759
Pennington	32	22 043	45.9	839	6 960	5	190.8	70.2	53.8	5 182	2 651	59	325	1 242
Pine	68	27 676	86.2	911	7 893	12	187.1	119.0	75.4	4 835	2 851	66	726	1 092
Pipestone	28	D	D	(8)	D	7	205.7	52.6	44.1	5 261	3 000	52	279	862
Polk	80	25 021	D	1 127	6 670	15	409.8	190.1	60.6	6 173	2 942	74	210	1 435
Pope	36	D	D	(8)	D	8	155.7	55.5	57.0	5 102	3 307	52	163	607
Ramsey	1 011	654 925	90.1	20 952	196 577	100	8 508.2	3 385.4	37.3	6 962	3 034	647	619	2 574
Red Lake	9	D	D	(9)	D	3	50.9	35.0	91.4	8 340	2 828	2 104	267	1 211
Redwood	41	10 517	83.7	397	2 935	14	364.3	93.9	61.0	5 715	2 912	75	210	894
Renville	33	39 861	D	1 068	12 548	14	256.5	93.4	71.7	5 555	2 851	61	213	663
Rice	110	54 970	90.8	1 825	15 540	19	593.1	161.5	55.3	2 937	1 981	98	139	545
Rock	20	D	D	(8)	D	8	183.7	47.9	51.7	4 982	2 964	41	177	596
Roseau	44	14 596	55.3	718	5 242	7	228.1	64.9	65.9	4 033	1 973	36	193	697
St. Louis	591	289 755	63.8	8 610	73 255	67	1 894.1	1 003.9	50.9	5 190	3 289	184	601	1 092
Scott	122	56 976	93.1	2 049	16 097	24	602.0	122.4	66.9	1 474	1 055	51	161	133
Sherburne	74	33 357	84.3	1 095	9 668	14	375.5	108.0	110.5	1 705	1 177	29	155	276
Sibley	18	4 189	100.0	180	826	11	158.2	61.9	66.4	4 189	2 426	38	158	516
Stearns	309	150 448	82.9	5 558	39 992	47	1 947.7	441.9	71.3	3 397	1 957	191	508	573
Steele	65	26 392	87.4	1 004	7 032	15	376.5	107.5	60.4	3 351	2 227	206	129	367
Stevens	24	D	D	(8)	D	8	135.3	61.1	79.3	6 128	2 835	66	403	1 168
Swift	28	6 588	86.4	219	1 481	9	178.6	63.4	58.2	5 584	2 954	198	252	736
Todd	49	D	D	(8)	D	11	231.9	102.4	53.9	4 225	2 503	38	169	1 177
Traverse	10	D	D	(9)	D	5	82.8	33.3	92.8	8 000	3 671	72	264	742
Wabasha	51	D	D	(8)	D	11	319.8	92.8	14.9	4 388	2 635	661	154	463
Wadena	22	D	D	(8)	D	6	184.6	66.7	52.3	5 036	3 341	51	201	1 259
Waseca	32	D	D	(8)	D	8	254.5	86.3	89.5	4 649	2 279	296	802	457
Washington	296	165 189	95.0	5 543	50 987	39	1 174.0	260.9	78.3	1 288	1 001	37	77	160
Watonwan	20	D	D	(8)	D	10	201.3	59.4	55.1	5 145	2 924	515	220	297
Wilkin	19	D	D	(7)	D	5	105.6	40.3	76.8	5 526	2 559	59	194	658
Winona	115	45 692	86.0	1 725	11 932	16	704.8	156.8	45.6	3 281	2 316	116	153	470
Wright	130	54 343	86.4	2 159	15 082	31	698.1	187.1	75.0	2 130	1 602	31	117	274
Yellow Medicine	21	D	D	(7)	D	10	221.0	71.9	62.7	6 353	3 251	153	221	1 008
MISSISSIPPI	4 050	3 064 753	55.7	84 834	814 454	1 101	27 913.6	16 487.9	61.6	5 955	3 237	700	613	1 223
Adams	88	37 670	69.1	1 189	10 331	12	327.5	175.0	64.6	5 199	3 493	279	182	1 142
Alcorn	66	26 910	86.4	913	6 782	15	396.1	148.7	65.2	4 494	3 327	62	142	823
Amite	4	D	D	(9)	D	3	61.0	58.3	71.8	4 192	2 957	58	185	903
Attala	28	10 834	87.0	373	2 305	8	242.1	100.0	49.9	5 452	3 810	64	165	1 293
Benton	1	D	D	(10)	D	3	32.9	38.5	63.8	4 764	3 051	65	135	1 320
Bolivar	49	17 896	90.6	626	4 340	19	332.7	239.3	71.4	6 008	3 017	30	123	2 063
Calhoun	16	D	D	(7)	D	8	192.2	74.5	57.7	5 005	3 358	74	182	1 022
Carroll	2	D	D	(10)	D	3	39.0	43.7	90.3	4 382	2 550	103	113	1 230
Chickasaw	27	D	D	(7)	D	7	183.9	88.5	70.2	4 886	3 381	41	163	1 067
Choctaw	5	D	D	(9)	D	4	65.8	36.5	70.6	3 901	2 526	66	216	1 020
Claiborne	6	1 460	D	46	357	2	98.4	48.7	67.6	4 198	2 773	76	96	1 136
Clarke	12	3 354	D	94	884	10	156.6	72.2	62.9	3 914	2 938	26	104	833
Clay	32	11 454	91.5	408	3 065	10	184.0	94.7	31.8	4 371	2 777	303	213	951
Coahoma	37	17 192	85.5	540	4 297	16	329.9	188.6	53.8	6 064	3 385	38	153	1 747
Copiah	30	12 615	91.1	425	3 003	12	200.7	150.7	64.2	5 216	3 377	695	140	969
Covington	15	D	D	(8)	D	7	143.2	84.9	73.3	4 747	3 268	27	168	1 252
DeSoto	114	72 652	82.9	2 639	18 632	39	848.7	246.6	120.0	2 414	1 964	32	72	298
Forrest	163	D	D	(6)	D	33	986.6	376.7	67.8	5 027	3 267	250	573	906
Franklin	4	D	D	(10)	D	5	89.7	48.6	95.2	5 955	3 295	76	259	2 282
George	25	D	D	(8)	D	6	178.6	73.7	87.1	3 649	3 005	27	117	430
Greene	9	1 783	100.0	78	521	4	54.8	37.4	71.5	2 963	2 214	29	68	630
Grenada	46	24 377	85.7	806	5 918	11	265.8	113.6	69.9	5 062	3 499	113	463	830
Hancock	72	24 679	85.7	784	6 194	14	370.9	473.8	59.9	11 413	3 109	4 971	2 894	414
Harrison	377	323 431	55.3	9 573	87 828	61	1 798.2	1 578.1	55.4	8 838	3 681	1 319	3 213	502
Hinds	449	322 431	81.3	10 351	92 626	87	3 598.0	1 913.9	63.4	7 788	3 078	233	919	3 523
Holmes	18	3 093	D	113	795	10	191.6	151.2	78.2	7 010	3 859	374	142	2 186
Humphreys	9	D	D	(9)	D	4	157.2	76.4	75.5	6 816	3 353	223	131	1 990
Issaquena	–	–	–	–	–	1	3.7	14.2	110.6	8 700	2 193	738	185	1 801

[1] Includes only establishments with payroll.   [2] Includes full-service restaurants, limited-service eating places, special food services, and drinking places (alcoholic beverages).   [3] For pay period including March 12.   [4] As of June 30. Covers all FDIC-insured commercial banks and savings institutions.   [5] Based on resident population estimated as of July 1, 1999.   [6] 2,500 to 4,999 employees.   [7] 100 to 249 employees.   [8] 250 to 499 employees.   [9] 20 to 99 employees.   [10] 0 to 19 employees.

Sources: Accommodation and Foodservices—U.S. Census Bureau, 1997 Economic Census, ECON[97] Report Series CD-ROM, CD-EC97-1, Disc 1E, issued February 2001 (related Internet site <http://www.census.gov/epcd/www/97EC72.HTM>). Banking—U.S. Federal Deposit Insurance Corporation and Office of Thrift Supervision, "1999 Bank and Thrift Branch Office Data Book: Summary of Deposits," national and 6 regional data books (related Internet site <http://www2.fdic.gov/sod/>). Federal Funds and Grants—U.S. Census Bureau, County Aggregate files for each state, <http://www.census.gov/govs/www/cffr99.html>, (accessed: August 2000).

Table B–12. Counties — **Accommodation and Foodservices, Banking, and Federal Funds**–Con.

[Includes U.S., states, and 3,142 counties/county equivalents defined as of January 1, 1992. For changes to these areas since January 1, 1992, see appendix B. Geographic Information]

County	Accommodation and foodservices[1] (NAICS 72), 1997					Banking,[4] 1999		Federal funds and grants, 1999							
	Estab-lishments	Sales		Paid employ-ees[3]	Annual payroll ($1,000)	Offices	Deposits (mil. dol.)	Total expenditures or obligations (mil. dol.)	Percent change, 1990–1999	Per capita[5] (dollars)				
		Total ($1,000)	Percent from food-services[2]							Total	Direct payments for individuals	Procure-ment contract awards	Salaries and wages	Grant awards
MISSISSIPPI—Con.														
Itawamba	29	6 925	D	341	1 503	6	182.9	72.9	55.2	3 456	2 502	59	120	716
Jackson	191	97 369	83.0	3 469	25 452	34	935.1	1 439.5	20.7	10 814	2 803	6 505	765	517
Jasper	12	D	D	(6)	D	8	128.9	77.8	41.2	4 297	3 025	28	167	1 060
Jefferson	5	2 261	D	131	546	2	19.8	58.8	46.4	7 011	3 858	41	150	2 802
Jefferson Davis	16	D	D	(6)	D	3	114.1	61.2	52.9	4 442	2 877	21	96	1 399
Jones	84	37 272	86.1	1 309	10 012	28	712.8	275.8	46.9	4 374	3 380	40	183	745
Kemper	4	637	100.0	30	191	4	69.5	48.7	40.0	4 645	2 992	34	174	1 391
Lafayette	109	43 221	81.1	1 665	11 506	17	368.6	126.8	35.0	3 631	1 917	214	434	1 010
Lamar	48	D	D	(7)	D	10	322.0	89.3	57.0	2 342	1 851	16	68	375
Lauderdale	147	87 383	80.5	2 855	23 911	40	776.2	435.1	43.7	5 726	3 436	210	1 250	791
Lawrence	15	2 889	100.0	126	706	3	80.7	69.2	72.3	5 296	4 069	44	265	855
Leake	20	D	D	(6)	D	11	207.6	98.9	86.0	5 047	3 613	33	200	1 151
Lee	158	84 683	84.5	3 037	23 207	41	1 107.0	281.5	66.8	3 743	2 668	86	381	552
Leflore	51	28 023	74.3	841	7 314	15	368.9	212.3	58.1	5 767	3 297	142	262	1 457
Lincoln	42	21 224	92.1	715	5 167	11	312.5	124.6	67.9	3 881	2 856	32	170	790
Lowndes	105	59 453	88.4	2 071	14 949	29	591.7	345.7	42.1	5 711	2 679	1 015	1 220	721
Madison	113	78 832	86.5	2 402	20 805	33	693.1	428.3	125.4	5 744	2 340	2 441	128	748
Marion	32	10 543	D	434	2 802	8	324.3	131.0	57.5	4 938	3 369	287	126	1 108
Marshall	19	7 740	81.0	322	1 881	11	240.8	152.8	76.7	4 728	2 824	50	139	1 611
Monroe	46	13 439	85.8	503	3 075	21	459.0	171.2	97.2	4 477	2 924	53	144	1 228
Montgomery	20	5 399	83.2	196	1 324	8	179.0	76.9	51.4	6 207	3 673	56	318	2 017
Neshoba	37	17 102	84.0	725	3 816	16	332.4	120.8	59.0	4 372	2 721	22	187	1 419
Newton	26	D	D	(8)	D	9	211.0	113.5	67.6	5 220	3 970	33	212	943
Noxubee	8	3 006	45.7	105	1 041	5	112.5	65.9	61.1	5 277	2 830	146	151	1 747
Oktibbeha	85	40 222	77.9	1 546	10 181	13	418.9	203.0	64.8	5 106	2 370	233	407	2 056
Panola	46	23 009	84.2	829	5 559	12	272.4	152.0	66.5	4 482	2 813	86	169	1 098
Pearl River	66	23 245	94.5	877	5 746	16	334.3	200.8	54.7	4 186	3 176	470	110	404
Perry	6	1 484	100.0	68	434	4	79.9	42.3	32.6	3 510	2 578	29	118	741
Pike	61	25 955	89.8	923	6 455	19	449.4	184.4	59.7	4 863	3 574	54	196	989
Pontotoc	25	8 041	92.6	340	1 902	6	258.2	85.1	66.4	3 315	2 422	34	118	608
Prentiss	34	10 912	D	425	2 824	11	245.9	101.2	65.1	4 131	3 123	20	112	784
Quitman	5	D	D	(9)	D	6	65.9	67.7	68.7	6 926	3 582	35	141	2 064
Rankin	127	78 113	92.4	2 286	20 663	39	784.3	291.4	81.2	2 593	1 983	27	258	311
Scott	36	13 006	83.3	448	3 373	9	327.1	124.1	87.5	4 983	3 293	32	320	1 302
Sharkey	3	D	D	(9)	D	4	49.7	42.8	71.3	6 546	3 088	73	236	1 507
Simpson	21	D	D	(8)	D	9	228.9	112.9	90.6	4 450	3 019	27	113	1 271
Smith	8	1 564	100.0	53	379	6	125.0	62.3	63.3	4 040	2 778	31	178	1 031
Stone	18	D	D	(6)	D	4	143.3	70.2	106.1	5 203	3 962	66	277	871
Sunflower	27	9 810	88.0	299	2 548	13	279.4	152.7	61.6	4 593	2 483	24	121	1 256
Tallahatchie	11	1 137	100.0	56	250	5	79.7	95.1	72.8	6 520	3 104	348	179	1 839
Tate	25	10 381	89.9	357	2 426	9	250.8	91.9	66.4	3 766	2 588	47	152	804
Tippah	21	D	D	(6)	D	10	283.6	97.2	84.6	4 613	3 382	65	155	939
Tishomingo	21	D	D	(6)	D	13	253.2	115.6	100.7	6 170	3 812	1 385	181	747
Tunica	26	826 930	.4	11 575	226 071	2	84.4	48.0	52.2	6 053	2 816	27	119	1 834
Union	38	D	D	(7)	D	8	299.9	91.0	71.4	3 772	2 798	123	132	622
Walthall	17	4 269	D	149	1 158	3	128.0	63.4	66.7	4 465	3 024	21	100	1 185
Warren	97	160 787	24.8	3 294	38 037	21	469.2	383.2	44.1	7 796	3 359	1 786	1 916	641
Washington	95	47 513	78.7	1 486	12 344	25	543.1	331.1	49.2	5 151	2 978	131	333	1 285
Wayne	20	D	D	(6)	D	11	248.4	71.5	51.1	3 466	2 471	32	94	845
Webster	5	D	D	(9)	D	4	105.2	59.6	93.4	5 604	3 276	32	175	1 888
Wilkinson	9	2 159	79.5	79	615	5	96.8	45.3	54.5	5 008	3 282	16	56	1 608
Winston	22	8 921	68.3	326	2 415	10	235.2	88.2	58.8	4 582	3 156	31	135	1 212
Yalobusha	10	D	D	(6)	D	6	140.0	76.2	72.0	6 035	4 289	86	299	1 202
Yazoo	24	9 880	D	340	2 499	11	252.9	183.9	114.7	7 296	3 476	172	710	2 286
MISSOURI	11 150	6 780 812	74.7	203 849	1 933 340	2 066	74 262.9	33 231.0	36.1	6 077	3 123	1 043	606	1 002
Adair	59	28 958	87.1	1 364	8 702	7	400.2	93.0	47.2	3 841	2 525	79	182	908
Andrew	14	3 500	D	149	997	5	109.0	51.6	61.9	3 312	2 063	31	197	716
Atchison	21	D	D	(6)	D	5	119.4	47.0	59.0	6 697	3 144	116	276	1 735
Audrain	46	17 095	96.0	626	4 177	11	370.6	117.3	61.4	5 004	3 634	45	176	629
Barry	66	17 891	91.1	667	4 626	22	398.8	137.4	68.0	4 139	3 216	74	188	645
Barton	25	7 222	D	324	1 972	8	205.7	51.4	49.8	4 239	2 902	47	177	466
Bates	23	7 095	89.5	282	1 832	12	208.5	76.8	61.6	4 784	3 301	49	180	662
Benton	43	9 621	80.1	427	2 533	7	186.3	93.6	88.0	5 396	4 469	63	246	537
Bollinger	10	1 533	D	61	308	4	49.6	49.6	81.8	4 197	2 641	34	137	1 210
Boone	312	180 132	83.6	5 983	48 437	46	1 463.7	537.9	62.7	4 132	2 154	174	711	1 052
Buchanan	196	96 209	D	3 208	26 746	31	1 167.1	380.5	50.0	4 661	3 471	50	292	791
Butler	76	36 360	85.5	1 210	9 329	19	513.2	255.2	63.8	6 320	3 698	125	522	1 534
Caldwell	9	1 001	D	58	355	7	77.0	40.6	56.3	4 546	3 236	56	215	472
Callaway	48	22 562	91.1	739	5 920	15	328.2	141.2	19.0	3 724	2 487	82	580	419

[1] Includes only establishments with payroll. [2] Includes full-service restaurants, limited-service eating places, special food services, and drinking places (alcoholic beverages). [3] For pay period including March 12. [4] As of June 30. Covers all FDIC-insured commercial banks and savings institutions. [5] Based on resident population estimated as of July 1, 1999. [6] 100 to 249 employees. [7] 500 to 999 employees. [8] 250 to 499 employees. [9] 20 to 99 employees.

Sources: Accommodation and Foodservices—U.S. Census Bureau, 1997 Economic Census, ECON97 Report Series CD-ROM, CD-EC97-1, Disc 1E, issued February 2001 (related Internet site <http://www.census.gov/epcd/www/97EC72.HTM>). Banking—U.S. Federal Deposit Insurance Corporation and Office of Thrift Supervision, "1999 Bank and Thrift Branch Office Data Book: Summary of Deposits," national and 6 regional data books (related Internet site <http://www2.fdic.gov/sod/>). Federal Funds and Grants—U.S. Census Bureau, County Aggregate files for each state, <http://www.census.gov/govs/www/cffr99.html>, (accessed: August 2000).

Table B–12. Counties — Accommodation and Foodservices, Banking, and Federal Funds–Con.

[Includes U.S., states, and 3,142 counties/county equivalents defined as of January 1, 1992. For changes to these areas since January 1, 1992, see appendix B. Geographic Information]

| County | Accommodation and foodservices[1] (NAICS 72), 1997 | | | | | Banking,[4] 1999 | | Federal funds and grants, 1999 | | | | | | | |
	Estab-lishments	Sales Total ($1,000)	Sales Percent from food-services[2]	Paid employ-ees[3]	Annual payroll ($1,000)	Offices	Deposits (mil. dol.)	Total expenditures or obligations (mil. dol.)	Percent change, 1990–1999	Per capita[5] (dollars) Total	Direct payments for individuals	Procure-ment contract awards	Salaries and wages	Grant awards
MISSOURI—Con.														
Camden	200	103 944	52.9	2 412	31 408	20	595.3	152.2	94.4	4 399	3 417	27	96	853
Cape Girardeau	137	89 379	83.4	3 017	24 891	28	1 029.2	254.3	73.0	3 784	2 567	116	333	678
Carroll	13	D	D	(6)	D	10	218.6	62.7	55.5	6 203	3 626	75	276	760
Carter	18	1 951	76.4	63	487	5	60.3	38.7	103.2	6 150	3 756	32	384	1 971
Cass	104	50 407	D	1 647	12 762	25	579.8	300.8	115.0	3 620	2 413	85	470	470
Cedar	33	6 426	90.7	291	1 713	9	237.4	69.9	63.4	5 218	4 026	104	183	836
Chariton	11	1 050	D	39	189	8	162.3	54.8	66.0	6 407	3 476	215	266	1 005
Christian	62	20 322	94.4	841	5 941	25	410.4	137.4	151.3	2 676	2 144	28	118	376
Clark	4	804	100.0	31	252	7	112.1	36.3	66.3	4 923	2 851	54	217	768
Clay	320	527 207	32.3	12 228	145 207	60	2 011.3	450.2	45.1	2 500	1 884	98	228	230
Clinton	22	D	D	(6)	D	10	168.9	69.9	64.1	3 579	2 682	45	155	482
Cole	134	84 530	74.6	2 751	24 602	28	1 426.6	1 103.5	93.6	15 875	3 547	139	239	11 793
Cooper	32	10 180	84.7	391	2 806	14	246.3	72.0	64.3	4 459	2 975	40	179	795
Crawford	47	11 606	70.3	447	3 086	8	170.2	94.5	91.4	4 213	2 959	83	84	1 073
Dade	11	D	D	(7)	D	6	93.7	39.2	60.4	4 940	3 462	54	206	855
Dallas	27	6 715	89.1	298	1 903	7	169.0	59.5	81.1	3 823	2 823	31	118	832
Daviess	10	2 152	100.0	79	500	7	111.4	43.7	41.8	5 424	3 098	197	272	959
DeKalb	27	10 278	84.0	415	2 922	12	197.0	35.2	33.3	3 118	2 025	36	138	460
Dent	22	8 342	72.8	300	2 242	6	174.6	81.6	81.1	5 720	3 558	683	246	1 226
Douglas	8	3 578	D	148	955	5	117.0	53.8	94.6	4 334	2 867	33	160	1 249
Dunklin	51	14 627	93.4	563	3 654	19	420.6	220.1	88.7	6 768	3 671	55	163	2 121
Franklin	160	70 948	90.9	2 514	20 181	35	1 188.3	291.1	74.0	3 125	2 587	34	134	338
Gasconade	36	7 425	90.1	357	2 029	10	213.6	62.7	65.1	4 190	3 489	36	142	445
Gentry	12	1 269	D	62	329	5	99.3	45.2	62.8	6 576	4 087	107	346	977
Greene	595	350 262	82.5	11 812	100 041	92	3 333.4	983.0	73.1	4 330	2 889	140	567	584
Grundy	17	4 999	76.5	238	1 505	7	151.1	57.8	50.4	5 706	3 779	68	279	928
Harrison	17	8 796	70.4	320	2 209	9	187.8	53.9	50.0	6 411	3 956	94	309	887
Henry	53	16 230	79.5	568	4 136	17	334.1	117.6	80.9	5 522	3 951	66	203	1 055
Hickory	20	3 540	78.5	121	817	4	59.8	49.5	83.4	5 666	4 579	151	209	683
Holt	12	2 725	85.1	99	693	7	77.4	37.4	64.4	6 723	3 709	68	305	893
Howard	12	2 914	D	152	807	6	153.6	50.8	45.8	5 258	3 349	136	190	1 096
Howell	76	29 296	86.5	1 093	7 967	19	439.6	189.1	37.8	5 243	3 414	241	153	1 417
Iron	18	3 791	D	151	967	8	111.5	57.4	59.5	5 244	3 849	33	115	1 239
Jackson	1 393	1 005 294	76.7	28 200	292 523	185	10 343.7	4 249.3	30.9	6 493	3 231	1 202	1 232	805
Jasper	222	109 542	96.4	4 100	31 712	48	1 281.7	580.4	117.8	5 789	3 336	1 472	187	743
Jefferson	214	113 813	94.3	3 981	31 757	39	1 116.5	470.7	84.5	2 376	1 960	37	89	285
Johnson	83	31 543	80.9	1 144	8 150	17	385.7	303.8	50.6	6 322	2 243	550	3 057	334
Knox	4	748	D	24	171	2	56.8	30.2	52.3	6 994	3 888	110	432	785
Laclede	62	27 923	74.0	827	6 901	13	428.3	129.9	92.8	4 134	3 109	31	140	832
Lafayette	70	D	D	(8)	D	18	543.0	145.8	66.3	4 445	3 090	111	203	718
Lawrence	54	17 565	93.1	690	4 840	15	314.0	126.5	66.5	3 776	2 872	32	196	619
Lewis	18	2 101	D	66	404	8	135.6	49.4	13.2	4 830	2 978	114	269	718
Lincoln	48	19 447	D	700	5 112	12	367.8	108.0	84.7	2 861	2 149	36	130	355
Linn	26	6 571	D	241	1 658	12	221.8	80.0	50.8	5 769	4 073	125	225	774
Livingston	28	11 714	89.1	405	3 092	10	333.6	82.9	91.7	5 909	3 443	73	375	1 301
McDonald	34	7 167	84.7	218	2 024	8	133.5	82.0	103.0	4 069	2 477	41	232	1 304
Macon	26	9 763	88.7	355	2 959	9	319.3	81.6	58.2	5 285	3 585	150	289	770
Madison	23	5 698	87.9	278	1 593	7	138.8	63.9	88.7	5 486	3 666	31	116	1 503
Maries	9	D	D	(7)	D	7	125.2	29.7	76.7	3 531	2 749	24	84	638
Marion	69	28 863	86.3	1 053	8 241	20	426.7	133.2	64.2	4 804	3 425	64	100	995
Mercer	8	826	D	49	306	3	55.1	25.3	41.8	6 402	3 322	50	237	1 632
Miller	63	39 963	42.4	1 090	12 472	11	285.9	96.2	77.9	4 253	3 477	34	130	591
Mississippi	16	D	D	(6)	D	7	159.7	93.3	93.0	6 994	3 423	39	155	2 502
Moniteau	21	5 463	D	210	1 433	10	194.9	49.5	63.9	3 721	2 808	39	174	487
Monroe	22	3 366	85.7	160	926	7	139.2	51.0	69.9	5 578	3 391	132	332	891
Montgomery	17	4 731	D	240	1 208	9	173.8	60.8	77.0	5 024	3 319	58	216	882
Morgan	51	11 386	89.6	330	3 214	10	199.1	88.4	92.9	4 673	3 789	34	123	681
New Madrid	26	7 935	86.2	298	2 152	12	179.1	140.7	97.3	7 060	2 897	40	171	2 387
Newton	87	49 958	70.4	1 664	14 314	16	346.4	149.2	44.6	3 001	2 147	76	177	567
Nodaway	41	18 360	90.8	764	4 702	13	401.8	85.7	42.6	4 173	2 496	62	272	772
Oregon	18	4 162	D	139	1 108	5	79.7	54.5	73.1	5 295	3 556	54	163	1 503
Osage	21	D	D	(6)	D	8	145.6	41.3	53.1	3 301	2 493	67	147	474
Ozark	14	2 331	27.9	63	485	5	90.7	49.3	87.2	4 947	3 476	61	137	1 254
Pemiscot	36	10 550	83.2	404	2 978	8	231.3	157.6	81.6	7 454	3 418	64	168	2 847
Perry	39	12 470	D	469	3 473	12	307.1	65.2	55.0	3 743	2 632	304	163	424
Pettis	76	36 152	89.7	1 313	10 813	20	605.7	169.3	62.0	4 562	3 287	83	204	726
Phelps	103	45 059	74.9	1 346	12 063	17	505.3	206.6	59.7	5 304	3 326	147	838	981
Pike	25	8 745	74.6	304	2 344	9	251.3	91.1	95.4	5 553	3 224	704	226	951
Platte	157	139 204	D	3 218	38 340	23	493.6	205.3	81.4	2 864	1 789	90	640	287
Polk	40	12 042	92.9	462	3 266	13	331.8	109.1	82.9	4 238	3 217	38	150	804

[1] Includes only establishments with payroll.   [2] Includes full-service restaurants, limited-service eating places, special food services, and drinking places (alcoholic beverages).   [3] For pay period including March 12.   [4] As of June 30. Covers all FDIC-insured commercial banks and savings institutions.   [5] Based on resident population estimated as of July 1, 1999.   [6] 100 to 249 employees.   [7] 20 to 99 employees.   [8] 500 to 999 employees.

Sources: Accommodation and Foodservices—U.S. Census Bureau, 1997 Economic Census, ECON97 Report Series CD-ROM, CD-EC97-1, Disc 1E, issued February 2001 (related Internet site <http://www.census.gov/epcd/www/97EC72.HTM>).   Banking—U.S. Federal Deposit Insurance Corporation and Office of Thrift Supervision, "1999 Bank and Thrift Branch Office Data Book: Summary of Deposits," national and 6 regional data books (related Internet site <http://www2.fdic.gov/sod/>).   Federal Funds and Grants—U.S. Census Bureau, County Aggregate files for each state, <http://www.census.gov/govs/www/cffr99.html>, (accessed: August 2000).

Table B–12. Counties — **Accommodation and Foodservices, Banking, and Federal Funds**-Con.

[Includes U.S., states, and 3,142 counties/county equivalents defined as of January 1, 1992. For changes to these areas since January 1, 1992, see appendix B. Geographic Information]

County	Accommodation and foodservices[1] (NAICS 72), 1997 Estab-lishments	Sales Total ($1,000)	Percent from food-services[2]	Paid employ-ees[3]	Annual payroll ($1,000)	Banking,[4] 1999 Offices	Deposits (mil. dol.)	Federal funds and grants, 1999 Total expenditures or obligations (mil. dol.)	Percent change, 1990–1999	Per capita[5] (dollars) Total	Direct payments for individuals	Procure-ment contract awards	Salaries and wages	Grant awards
MISSOURI—Con.														
Pulaski	77	29 516	78.7	914	10 738	14	292.7	676.8	52.9	17 704	3 169	2 350	11 114	1 064
Putnam	5	D	D	(6)	D	3	96.2	29.3	59.6	6 011	3 945	69	260	922
Ralls	17	6 108	D	239	2 124	3	79.4	36.5	30.9	3 986	2 197	114	448	564
Randolph	45	16 118	91.4	656	4 163	12	314.3	112.1	52.7	4 699	3 414	49	169	836
Ray	26	7 094	100.0	244	1 834	8	217.3	75.3	63.1	3 168	2 350	31	129	364
Reynolds	14	3 021	30.7	70	1 008	6	50.1	34.8	75.7	5 244	3 520	152	192	1 365
Ripley	16	4 071	80.3	156	1 043	6	121.1	77.3	80.9	5 456	3 566	33	164	1 593
St. Charles	418	245 195	91.7	8 656	71 326	63	2 168.7	697.8	68.0	2 488	1 823	359	107	171
St. Clair	14	D	D	(7)	D	7	123.7	58.2	104.6	6 272	3 768	44	167	1 942
Ste. Genevieve	32	9 495	84.2	399	2 622	6	230.4	62.6	90.3	3 583	2 622	365	96	365
St. Francois	100	45 131	88.7	1 602	13 062	22	606.5	247.7	78.1	4 439	3 356	44	127	903
St. Louis	2 030	1 579 700	79.1	46 507	465 687	263	14 982.2	3 898.3	59.6	3 913	2 996	168	337	406
Saline	50	15 315	92.0	603	3 954	13	309.4	116.2	53.3	5 100	3 354	51	206	872
Schuyler	8	807	100.0	51	242	3	43.0	25.6	44.6	5 794	3 819	87	448	832
Scotland	10	2 267	D	66	539	4	100.8	29.2	46.6	5 941	3 383	58	239	649
Scott	78	35 100	83.1	1 102	9 811	15	509.2	190.7	79.3	4 702	3 073	127	142	1 104
Shannon	16	2 145	66.2	44	514	6	67.2	38.3	90.8	4 617	2 868	30	258	1 454
Shelby	11	1 517	D	94	396	7	115.2	39.2	64.2	5 879	3 891	88	343	677
Stoddard	47	14 551	95.1	504	4 067	19	351.6	176.4	89.6	5 954	3 346	65	277	1 262
Stone	86	19 240	72.6	530	5 796	13	223.7	109.7	105.0	3 988	3 289	27	72	594
Sullivan	7	D	D	(8)	D	6	85.2	40.7	51.1	5 925	3 419	66	362	1 267
Taney	328	245 412	38.7	4 947	68 586	25	464.4	152.2	84.6	4 289	3 552	151	143	440
Texas	32	4 715	87.1	212	1 291	10	251.3	107.9	78.5	4 804	3 627	41	181	931
Vernon	41	13 765	86.3	520	3 629	10	260.8	89.9	53.5	4 613	3 267	47	254	647
Warren	34	14 341	D	503	4 140	6	217.5	76.7	99.2	3 017	2 414	44	127	296
Washington	17	D	D	(7)	D	7	153.1	83.7	96.9	3 586	2 475	30	118	958
Wayne	20	3 532	87.2	144	873	7	93.1	84.1	92.9	6 447	4 580	255	231	1 346
Webster	38	11 731	93.3	420	3 144	13	316.8	104.1	86.6	3 472	2 599	41	136	677
Worth	6	369	100.0	13	76	2	31.2	15.2	44.6	6 604	3 549	331	481	856
Wright	40	8 300	89.8	303	2 042	9	220.2	90.6	77.8	4 544	3 097	38	146	1 212
Independent City														
St. Louis city	954	686 612	73.4	18 843	195 758	93	8 646.3	7 490.4	-7.8	22 429	4 396	12 315	2 188	3 385
MONTANA	3 280	1 199 251	71.8	38 551	325 510	336	9 013.6	6 225.0	81.9	7 052	3 034	589	755	1 585
Beaverhead	47	11 083	60.4	337	2 428	3	101.7	52.9	71.2	6 015	3 132	192	869	1 672
Big Horn	35	8 098	72.9	241	1 975	4	78.8	94.6	35.9	7 528	1 953	259	1 333	3 187
Blaine	18	2 470	73.0	101	655	3	48.4	64.0	77.1	9 043	2 412	467	1 097	2 781
Broadwater	17	3 298	90.0	128	844	2	32.0	21.8	73.8	5 232	3 121	77	331	778
Carbon	52	14 255	72.8	417	4 354	4	71.3	38.4	59.1	4 028	2 953	55	288	441
Carter	5	364	100.0	17	64	1	16.1	14.2	50.3	9 792	2 305	201	525	2 470
Cascade	267	109 667	80.8	3 592	29 350	21	713.8	1 076.0	88.5	13 746	3 532	936	2 316	1 056
Chouteau	22	1 678	91.7	71	417	4	84.7	67.9	111.3	13 409	3 279	214	286	836
Custer	43	17 158	83.8	629	4 919	5	216.3	74.2	48.4	6 270	3 289	85	1 012	1 538
Daniels	10	D	D	(8)	D	1	26.6	24.0	27.6	12 208	4 025	1 250	528	398
Dawson	29	9 373	62.2	415	2 579	4	112.8	47.9	53.0	5 524	3 197	70	294	624
Deer Lodge	39	12 209	D	420	3 345	3	89.4	51.4	21.1	5 289	3 853	44	339	998
Fallon	12	2 928	82.5	88	521	2	43.9	16.1	72.5	5 588	2 827	72	149	477
Fergus	49	16 531	80.7	652	4 241	5	163.7	73.9	72.7	6 068	3 344	154	508	843
Flathead	319	132 137	64.1	3 940	35 862	23	683.3	306.8	77.5	4 216	2 821	153	432	773
Gallatin	286	154 147	51.5	4 703	44 090	26	652.7	224.2	82.2	3 510	1 795	227	402	1 003
Garfield	5	D	D	(6)	D	1	19.1	13.4	14.1	9 457	2 392	112	504	441
Glacier	52	18 501	39.1	403	4 445	4	78.2	98.5	82.0	7 817	2 289	402	1 130	2 704
Golden Valley	4	456	100.0	13	80	1	1.6	7.3	36.7	6 969	3 166	81	289	54
Granite	15	1 792	87.2	85	414	1	25.0	18.1	115.1	6 801	2 884	56	511	3 323
Hill	53	18 632	91.2	679	4 896	6	194.9	132.8	79.9	7 791	3 051	130	354	2 150
Jefferson	27	5 057	84.0	205	1 156	3	31.3	39.9	77.6	3 847	2 305	204	775	511
Judith Basin	13	D	D	(8)	D	1	33.8	16.2	77.4	7 082	2 835	106	560	404
Lake	86	20 537	71.9	594	5 261	13	200.4	131.5	59.4	5 082	2 842	354	217	1 594
Lewis and Clark	183	67 905	81.3	2 352	18 184	18	517.4	756.9	147.6	13 998	3 311	2 782	1 099	6 766
Liberty	4	543	100.0	16	119	2	22.3	29.3	142.7	12 986	4 045	101	520	291
Lincoln	68	16 688	72.4	439	3 800	5	99.4	108.8	91.7	5 784	3 416	447	903	1 014
McCone	5	D	D	(6)	D	1	12.5	31.4	63.8	16 301	2 849	67	355	5 184
Madison	44	7 676	52.7	117	1 884	3	66.9	38.7	102.2	5 594	2 724	87	381	2 205
Meagher	16	2 640	46.7	57	596	1	17.9	11.9	70.2	6 693	3 378	488	555	1 488
Mineral	24	4 752	74.2	178	1 501	3	20.1	21.5	95.7	5 547	3 645	168	480	1 237
Missoula	329	145 646	77.0	4 782	40 350	29	945.1	385.9	67.3	4 320	2 414	235	695	963
Musselshell	20	D	D	(7)	D	2	47.1	27.9	92.0	6 124	3 450	44	172	1 793
Park	111	33 953	45.5	1 043	9 652	8	192.7	74.2	77.5	4 645	3 095	42	235	1 173
Petroleum	3	D	D	(6)	D	–	–	3.2	76.6	6 393	2 427	85	393	808

[1] Includes only establishments with payroll. [2] Includes full-service restaurants, limited-service eating places, special food services, and drinking places (alcoholic beverages). [3] For pay period including March 12. [4] As of June 30. Covers all FDIC-insured commercial banks and savings institutions. [5] Based on resident population estimated as of July 1, 1999. [6] 0 to 19 employees. [7] 100 to 249 employees. [8] 20 to 99 employees.

Sources: Accommodation and Foodservices—U.S. Census Bureau, 1997 Economic Census, ECON97 Report Series CD-ROM, CD-EC97-1, Disc 1E, issued February 2001 (related Internet site <http://www.census.gov/epcd/www/97EC72.HTM>). Banking—U.S. Federal Deposit Insurance Corporation and Office of Thrift Supervision, "1999 Bank and Thrift Branch Office Data Book: Summary of Deposits," national and 6 regional data books (related Internet site <http://www2.fdic.gov/sod/>). Federal Funds and Grants—U.S. Census Bureau, County Aggregate files for each state, <http://www.census.gov/govs/www/cffr99.html>, (accessed: August 2000).

Table B–12. Counties — Accommodation and Foodservices, Banking, and Federal Funds–Con.

[Includes U.S., states, and 3,142 counties/county equivalents defined as of January 1, 1992. For changes to these areas since January 1, 1992, see appendix B. Geographic Information]

| County | Accommodation and foodservices[1] (NAICS 72), 1997 | | | | | Banking,[4] 1999 | | Federal funds and grants, 1999 | | Per capita[5] (dollars) | | | | |
| | Sales | | | | | | | | | | By selected type— | | | |
	Establishments	Total ($1,000)	Percent from foodservices[2]	Paid employees[3]	Annual payroll ($1,000)	Offices	Deposits (mil. dol.)	Total expenditures or obligations (mil. dol.)	Percent change, 1990–1999	Total	Direct payments for individuals	Procurement contract awards	Salaries and wages	Grant awards
MONTANA—Con.														
Phillips	23	3 966	84.0	140	887	3	88.8	38.7	48.4	8 253	3 141	87	499	1 609
Pondera	18	D	D	(6)	D	5	83.0	81.5	249.5	13 053	3 323	4 258	341	1 893
Powder River	7	D	D	(7)	D	1	18.7	15.4	183.2	8 687	2 324	255	445	2 580
Powell	25	D	D	(6)	D	3	70.8	26.8	47.0	3 858	2 750	73	433	535
Prairie	5	D	D	(8)	D	1	32.1	10.0	23.4	7 365	3 418	103	267	468
Ravalli	92	21 099	91.9	793	5 962	15	357.1	151.0	75.6	4 217	3 110	149	500	443
Richland	40	10 325	78.9	401	2 701	6	137.4	87.5	175.1	8 709	2 847	3 634	340	669
Roosevelt	29	5 869	72.1	210	1 492	5	101.0	160.2	147.7	14 677	2 613	6 115	818	3 701
Rosebud	29	7 470	76.0	301	1 840	4	70.1	61.0	66.9	6 184	1 978	186	642	2 597
Sanders	27	4 862	87.6	189	1 194	4	95.2	51.2	60.3	5 006	3 516	58	440	963
Sheridan	26	D	D	(6)	D	3	109.2	44.8	60.3	10 916	3 891	119	736	2 762
Silver Bow	130	47 814	79.9	1 354	12 286	10	378.3	205.2	39.8	6 042	3 611	946	400	1 045
Stillwater	24	D	D	(6)	D	4	73.1	33.4	75.0	4 012	2 510	126	191	415
Sweet Grass	15	6 211	39.5	170	1 675	3	60.1	16.5	74.2	4 597	2 574	70	367	1 390
Teton	26	3 346	72.3	122	816	3	87.8	46.4	101.0	7 215	2 987	71	339	528
Toole	27	4 773	87.4	135	1 044	4	83.1	42.0	69.8	9 060	2 828	295	683	742
Treasure	4	D	D	(8)	D	1	7.8	4.4	163.2	5 083	2 956	111	335	246
Valley	33	7 612	68.1	261	1 782	5	122.2	68.6	26.8	8 432	3 601	412	835	1 071
Wheatland	14	1 812	D	77	378	1	24.9	16.5	80.4	7 256	3 911	77	638	1 362
Wibaux	9	D	D	(7)	D	1	8.6	9.1	33.0	8 102	2 639	79	222	1 287
Yellowstone	365	205 329	79.3	6 691	58 688	41	1 343.0	560.6	58.6	4 405	2 691	182	729	645
Yellowstone National Park	–	–	–	–	–	–	–	Z	-35.1	436	436	–	–	–
NEBRASKA	4 070	1 726 647	83.5	61 048	488 208	930	27 225.8	8 793.3	44.5	5 278	2 755	282	596	991
Adams	82	29 087	89.8	1 230	8 356	14	508.4	136.6	55.2	4 665	2 942	132	210	759
Antelope	17	2 811	D	146	743	7	130.8	57.8	76.4	7 986	2 932	141	241	2 131
Arthur	–	–	–	–	–	1	1.4	1.9	21.3	4 718	3 143	68	245	141
Banner	–	D	–	–	–	1	18.0	7.1	42.2	8 581	1 433	34	173	112
Blaine	1	D	D	(8)	D	1	19.9	2.9	15.9	4 981	2 247	148	527	1 290
Boone	14	1 803	D	60	353	7	146.9	41.0	49.4	6 445	2 940	56	243	567
Box Butte	35	10 254	81.5	441	3 082	6	172.7	53.4	56.1	4 216	2 564	68	239	402
Boyd	6	484	100.0	17	64	4	39.5	17.2	63.6	6 838	4 013	90	362	1 589
Brown	16	2 316	D	95	640	4	98.2	21.8	53.1	6 240	3 268	57	240	1 210
Buffalo	118	65 828	77.8	2 322	18 733	19	744.9	144.8	66.4	3 598	2 224	167	198	569
Burt	17	3 144	100.0	141	686	5	119.3	47.5	50.0	6 010	3 555	54	215	704
Butler	18	D	D	(7)	D	8	166.0	48.6	50.2	5 644	2 745	77	281	613
Cass	45	10 348	87.9	340	2 608	16	241.8	97.3	75.3	3 919	2 622	65	147	659
Cedar	21	D	D	(6)	D	10	157.9	50.3	14.1	5 228	2 539	62	368	765
Chase	12	1 771	D	75	511	5	118.8	35.0	79.6	8 238	3 221	43	213	639
Cherry	27	5 870	58.0	179	1 477	6	140.6	26.4	11.7	4 181	2 781	107	319	675
Cheyenne	37	12 544	74.6	456	3 384	9	189.0	60.7	65.4	6 437	3 427	81	301	770
Clay	21	D	D	(7)	D	7	113.3	58.8	55.6	8 287	3 100	306	1 180	996
Colfax	31	D	D	(6)	D	7	176.1	55.5	88.9	5 194	3 022	478	271	498
Cuming	33	6 238	92.1	265	1 470	11	269.9	48.4	70.1	4 847	2 735	41	231	844
Custer	32	5 047	87.5	206	959	11	233.3	68.9	53.1	5 828	3 197	54	236	680
Dakota	41	21 154	D	656	6 105	9	197.1	91.5	107.0	4 780	2 176	1 473	184	680
Dawes	37	9 369	80.3	398	2 496	6	127.4	44.4	46.5	5 024	2 980	156	631	767
Dawson	63	19 361	79.4	759	4 792	17	383.5	96.7	67.9	4 153	2 398	91	201	527
Deuel	10	1 128	D	50	370	2	41.0	21.5	101.5	10 831	4 096	43	230	1 943
Dixon	9	1 370	100.0	39	238	4	62.7	32.7	.6	5 139	2 761	215	240	495
Dodge	99	41 265	91.0	1 490	10 174	19	661.1	149.4	56.1	4 243	3 135	63	193	482
Douglas	1 033	618 847	84.1	19 822	184 379	152	7 818.0	2 093.4	45.9	4 691	2 730	235	678	1 016
Dundy	8	D	D	(7)	D	2	40.4	21.4	56.0	9 817	3 926	78	299	761
Fillmore	23	3 746	100.0	121	725	9	171.8	45.5	54.3	6 576	3 036	66	249	536
Franklin	10	1 338	100.0	44	206	5	71.3	26.1	.3	7 107	3 732	85	326	446
Frontier	4	D	D	(7)	D	3	64.0	21.6	41.1	6 856	2 525	93	283	652
Furnas	17	D	D	(7)	D	8	129.8	48.7	60.6	8 992	4 277	79	318	1 451
Gage	50	15 564	87.6	583	4 124	19	407.2	115.3	54.3	5 075	3 112	58	233	776
Garden	10	1 070	D	42	155	3	48.1	26.7	134.6	12 881	4 638	4 059	336	747
Garfield	8	870	D	61	244	1	24.5	10.7	23.0	5 299	3 750	49	228	594
Gosper	5	648	D	16	127	2	24.7	18.2	80.0	8 046	3 268	38	158	63
Grant	3	D	D	(8)	D	2	15.6	5.1	108.0	7 078	2 926	99	353	3 686
Greeley	6	945	100.0	25	107	4	54.2	21.0	65.1	7 460	3 102	95	332	1 262
Hall	155	71 465	82.4	2 833	20 993	25	942.1	237.2	54.4	4 582	2 733	143	559	747
Hamilton	12	2 890	D	129	930	9	173.1	54.2	59.6	5 669	2 415	45	166	918
Harlan	15	D	D	(6)	D	5	95.1	28.9	60.0	7 861	3 649	66	369	477
Hayes	1	D	D	(8)	D	1	10.4	11.0	75.0	10 350	2 087	26	169	345
Hitchcock	4	D	D	(8)	D	4	44.3	26.6	68.2	7 907	3 509	55	239	1 208
Holt	30	7 294	85.5	313	1 587	8	232.0	67.3	54.7	5 660	2 928	46	214	962

[1] Includes only establishments with payroll. [2] Includes full-service restaurants, limited-service eating places, special food services, and drinking places (alcoholic beverages). [3] For pay period including March 12. [4] As of June 30. Covers all FDIC-insured commercial banks and savings institutions. [5] Based on resident population estimated as of July 1, 1999. [6] 100 to 249 employees. [7] 20 to 99 employees. [8] 0 to 19 employees.

Sources: Accommodation and Foodservices—U.S. Census Bureau, 1997 Economic Census, ECON97 Report Series CD-ROM, CD-EC97-1, Disc 1E, issued February 2001 (related Internet site <http://www.census.gov/epcd/www/97EC72.HTM>). Banking—U.S. Federal Deposit Insurance Corporation and Office of Thrift Supervision, "1999 Bank and Thrift Branch Office Data Book: Summary of Deposits," national and 6 regional data books (related Internet site <http://www2.fdic.gov/sod/>). Federal Funds and Grants—U.S. Census Bureau, County Aggregate files for each state, <http://www.census.gov/govs/www/cffr99.html>, (accessed: August 2000).

[Includes U.S., states, and 3,142 counties/county equivalents defined as of January 1, 1992. For changes to these areas since January 1, 1992, see appendix B. Geographic Information]

County	Accommodation and foodservices[1] (NAICS 72), 1997					Banking,[4] 1999		Federal funds and grants, 1999						
	Sales									Per capita[5] (dollars)				
											By selected type—			
	Estab-lishments	Total ($1,000)	Percent from food-services[2]	Paid employ-ees[3]	Annual payroll ($1,000)	Offices	Deposits (mil. dol.)	Total expenditures or obligations (mil. dol.)	Percent change, 1990–1999	Total	Direct payments for individuals	Procure-ment contract awards	Salaries and wages	Grant awards
NEBRASKA—Con.														
Hooker	4	515	D	19	84	1	12.2	4.2	46.7	6 067	4 242	41	369	1 347
Howard	17	1 910	88.6	107	488	8	89.3	33.0	49.5	5 039	2 815	52	209	607
Jefferson	19	D	D	(6)	D	9	181.2	54.3	58.5	6 551	3 406	54	223	1 247
Johnson	10	1 407	D	73	351	7	98.0	27.4	44.4	6 026	3 210	73	380	872
Kearney	15	D	D	(6)	D	4	149.5	45.5	78.1	6 628	2 815	95	191	301
Keith	57	19 971	55.0	584	4 688	6	203.7	46.6	53.7	5 245	2 856	91	199	810
Keya Paha	2	D	D	(7)	D	1	10.5	4.6	13.2	4 811	2 503	60	212	783
Kimball	18	6 302	D	205	1 705	3	90.4	37.6	101.2	9 333	3 450	83	162	3 161
Knox	30	3 440	D	122	581	9	185.8	60.4	58.9	6 676	3 488	218	274	1 599
Lancaster	545	318 475	84.0	11 230	91 802	102	3 144.7	1 250.5	69.1	5 262	2 320	223	593	2 037
Lincoln	96	44 766	69.0	1 645	13 059	22	544.2	166.1	64.9	4 903	3 072	187	355	699
Logan	2	D	D	(7)	D	1	9.9	7.4	115.2	8 229	2 773	31	113	3 622
Loup	1	D	D	(7)	D	1	18.5	3.0	78.5	4 572	2 625	21	76	810
McPherson	1	D	D	(7)	D	—		3.6	90.4	6 590	3 272	51	185	2 280
Madison	101	40 243	87.1	1 541	11 292	21	708.4	133.9	57.5	3 917	2 578	79	355	563
Merrick	17	3 416	D	168	873	6	97.6	42.6	46.8	5 294	2 927	66	205	559
Morrill	16	2 325	D	109	650	3	68.3	27.1	29.3	5 116	2 966	48	196	515
Nance	4	391	100.0	12	72	3	89.0	24.7	52.9	6 096	2 966	42	178	1 026
Nemaha	21	4 837	D	221	1 351	7	148.8	38.2	40.9	5 021	3 097	105	233	561
Nuckolls	14	D	D	(8)	D	6	130.4	35.8	48.6	6 988	3 896	64	273	790
Otoe	47	17 400	62.2	658	4 726	11	239.2	66.9	42.5	4 519	2 941	98	193	501
Pawnee	8	875	D	36	153	7	49.1	23.5	40.2	7 604	4 125	87	337	805
Perkins	9	D	D	(8)	D	5	62.5	37.0	76.9	11 533	3 248	58	241	123
Phelps	20	5 729	88.9	221	1 543	8	253.2	55.9	56.9	5 682	2 948	45	184	427
Pierce	14	1 650	100.0	58	333	4	109.0	40.1	67.5	5 041	2 524	41	173	574
Platte	75	29 722	85.2	1 130	8 307	18	616.9	132.4	91.8	4 358	2 213	856	219	342
Polk	12	1 524	100.0	56	284	5	98.9	32.8	38.3	5 945	3 092	53	178	291
Red Willow	39	12 728	77.1	536	3 454	10	312.1	60.8	58.5	5 382	3 327	67	321	534
Richardson	26	4 728	85.7	214	1 334	11	196.7	57.0	46.3	6 112	3 813	73	240	869
Rock	9	658	D	33	158	1	25.9	10.0	16.5	5 893	3 012	42	203	544
Saline	39	9 964	D	442	2 651	11	268.3	65.9	-15.5	5 023	2 864	463	248	471
Sarpy	155	72 207	89.9	2 462	20 544	30	669.1	710.7	6.9	5 802	1 633	1 242	2 555	342
Saunders	39	D	D	(9)	D	17	272.2	88.1	72.3	4 572	2 682	222	278	601
Scotts Bluff	100	33 126	88.9	1 207	9 163	20	652.1	177.3	46.4	4 916	3 172	102	257	1 122
Seward	37	12 603	D	589	3 152	10	271.0	62.0	55.3	3 775	2 319	49	161	344
Sheridan	24	D	D	(6)	D	6	170.2	35.6	38.8	5 536	3 357	112	164	769
Sherman	9	D	D	(8)	D	3	44.3	24.2	52.6	6 983	3 154	61	244	1 605
Sioux	2	D	D	(7)	D	1	16.3	5.6	3.7	3 912	1 362	39	275	926
Stanton	6	D	D	(8)	D	3	57.4	19.8	46.7	3 249	1 452	23	162	334
Thayer	14	2 375	100.0	124	468	10	188.7	41.5	41.6	6 720	3 565	93	266	597
Thomas	4	982	D	43	263	1	7.1	4.1	51.0	5 121	2 878	163	1 800	136
Thurston	8	3 031	D	95	1 299	2	68.2	72.1	88.4	10 216	2 690	1 496	848	4 203
Valley	20	D	D	(6)	D	5	115.7	30.5	32.2	6 744	3 651	70	313	1 270
Washington	45	11 821	D	489	3 013	6	237.9	64.2	92.3	3 409	2 097	120	129	612
Wayne	26	7 605	D	411	2 049	9	185.0	35.1	46.6	3 820	2 205	37	218	361
Webster	9	1 281	D	40	291	3	69.6	28.6	49.4	7 269	3 862	72	310	736
Wheeler	5	D	D	(7)	D	1	16.8	6.4	18.2	6 895	2 300	92	328	201
York	43	22 146	84.0	804	6 254	14	325.9	68.5	47.2	4 762	2 872	41	196	299
NEVADA	3 633	15 323 751	12.8	241 682	4 665 524	403	16 689.3	7 941.9	89.9	4 390	2 719	443	499	690
Churchill	53	26 036	48.6	706	7 976	6	156.6	193.2	102.8	8 253	3 024	2 342	2 280	585
Clark	2 164	12 412 281	11.8	185 322	3 771 036	241	11 398.4	4 842.7	80.9	3 979	2 550	504	498	408
Douglas	92	523 877	5.7	8 414	151 107	13	361.1	119.8	160.9	3 185	2 572	145	118	344
Elko	134	301 016	12.1	6 268	78 645	15	243.2	108.2	113.0	2 380	1 111	73	340	824
Esmeralda	5	510	100.0	12	120	—	–	12.5	178.9	11 126	9 690	88	372	963
Eureka	6	1 977	D	55	407	1	9.8	9.4	246.6	5 067	1 878	23	97	2 996
Humboldt	53	46 433	D	1 125	15 195	4	113.3	42.3	105.2	2 365	1 489	53	335	426
Lander	19	5 810	81.1	160	1 276	2	21.0	18.6	103.1	2 778	1 380	158	518	709
Lincoln	18	2 514	84.6	100	665	4	26.3	19.4	70.0	4 586	3 740	104	340	389
Lyon	43	15 841	63.0	465	4 373	6	103.8	114.8	72.2	3 649	3 034	142	107	358
Mineral	12	9 718	D	258	3 178	1	8.4	71.4	18.2	13 790	4 702	7 282	781	1 020
Nye	54	40 492	30.6	1 035	12 807	6	156.1	131.1	179.4	4 414	3 602	62	281	463
Pershing	21	7 646	83.3	289	2 215	2	23.8	14.8	74.6	3 079	1 919	40	111	909
Storey	10	2 390	D	49	705	1	5.5	4.8	72.7	1 601	1 004	14	51	525
Washoe	779	1 816 785	17.0	34 527	583 270	81	3 406.4	1 204.5	77.9	3 766	2 347	187	511	709
White Pine	37	17 374	25.4	493	4 823	3	75.5	40.0	56.2	4 066	2 440	236	664	712
Independent City														
Carson City city	133	93 051	51.0	2 404	27 726	17	680.3	530.8	166.6	10 606	3 487	300	509	6 303

[1] Includes only establishments with payroll. [2] Includes full-service restaurants, limited-service eating places, special food services, and drinking places (alcoholic beverages). [3] For pay period including March 12. [4] As of June 30. Covers all FDIC-insured commercial banks and savings institutions. [5] Based on resident population estimated as of July 1, 1999. [6] 100 to 249 employees. [7] 0 to 19 employees. [8] 20 to 99 employees. [9] 250 to 499 employees.

Sources: Accommodation and Foodservices—U.S. Census Bureau, 1997 Economic Census, ECON97 Report Series CD-ROM, CD-EC97-1, Disc 1E, issued February 2001 (related Internet site <http://www.census.gov/epcd/www/97EC72.HTM>). Banking—U.S. Federal Deposit Insurance Corporation and Office of Thrift Supervision, "1999 Bank and Thrift Branch Office Data Book: Summary of Deposits," national and 6 regional data books (related Internet site <http://www2.fdic.gov/sod/>). Federal Funds and Grants—U.S. Census Bureau, County Aggregate files for each state, <http://www.census.gov/govs/www/cffr99.html>, (accessed: August 2000).

Accommodation and Foodservices, Banking, and Federal Funds–Con.

[Includes U.S., states, and 3,142 counties/county equivalents defined as of January 1, 1992. For changes to these areas since January 1, 1992, see appendix B. Geographic Information]

County	Accommodation and foodservices[1] (NAICS 72), 1997					Banking,[4] 1999		Federal funds and grants, 1999						
		Sales								Per capita[5] (dollars)				
												By selected type—		
	Estab-lishments	Total ($1,000)	Percent from food-services[2]	Paid employ-ees[3]	Annual payroll ($1,000)	Offices	Deposits (mil. dol.)	Total expenditures or obligations (mil. dol.)	Percent change, 1990–1999	Total	Direct payments for individuals	Procure-ment contract awards	Salaries and wages	Grant awards
NEW HAMPSHIRE	3 033	1 544 942	76.4	43 996	450 258	408	19 430.6	5 301.4	47.0	4 414	2 646	401	377	932
Belknap	213	89 079	73.0	2 237	26 095	22	6 118.7	251.3	88.7	4 681	3 312	158	218	982
Carroll....................	271	143 671	47.2	3 821	42 558	22	645.1	175.5	80.6	4 368	3 511	48	189	611
Cheshire..................	133	68 941	87.2	2 178	21 207	23	864.1	265.7	68.2	3 670	2 671	71	138	775
Coos	121	56 244	34.1	1 572	18 210	15	428.6	406.4	62.9	5 358	3 792	51	233	1 269
Grafton...................	325	156 275	61.4	4 761	47 271	50	1 176.4	608.1	65.9	5 173	2 797	514	371	1 472
Hillsborough	704	413 613	84.7	12 063	120 963	103	4 276.4	1 608.1	49.3	4 379	2 322	844	580	603
Merrimack	261	126 064	88.6	3 807	36 240	50	1 630.1	693.6	78.2	5 339	2 648	112	345	2 197
Rockingham	727	384 161	81.2	9 947	109 345	78	2 813.2	942.1	2.6	3 420	2 246	319	377	468
Strafford.................	209	84 256	94.2	2 830	22 064	27	975.8	450.7	82.6	4 072	2 647	81	180	1 146
Sullivan	69	22 638	86.7	780	6 305	18	502.1	162.3	56.8	4 032	3 020	66	139	791
NEW JERSEY...........	16 975	13 416 088	53.6	252 031	3 610 740	2 967	141 283.2	40 397.6	41.9	4 961	3 052	517	442	892
Atlantic	766	5 015 195	5.9	55 638	1 328 253	82	2 513.8	1 249.3	72.3	5 214	3 114	541	714	801
Bergen	1 910	1 116 936	78.4	24 315	303 971	437	23 616.8	3 661.8	45.8	4 273	2 984	686	202	387
Burlington................	711	391 449	85.7	11 085	109 318	139	4 369.8	2 664.1	31.1	6 276	2 777	2 092	986	412
Camden	881	440 391	91.2	11 826	120 162	143	5 690.8	2 331.0	49.2	4 633	3 026	455	334	782
Cape May	961	368 063	57.2	4 642	95 042	65	1 678.4	552.9	36.9	5 641	4 261	166	439	746
Cumberland	218	78 778	89.1	2 554	21 063	45	1 493.5	670.5	59.6	4 786	3 166	199	290	1 088
Essex	1 320	853 827	78.8	16 915	234 183	236	12 321.2	4 518.1	29.9	6 046	3 029	293	572	2 054
Gloucester	386	201 646	94.6	6 419	53 560	87	2 455.5	862.2	33.8	3 442	2 498	405	113	419
Hudson	1 127	466 491	80.3	10 056	119 647	164	14 246.9	2 726.6	52.0	4 932	2 515	286	772	1 279
Hunterdon	237	102 452	88.7	2 439	28 870	54	1 777.5	289.9	66.7	2 327	1 864	83	151	215
Mercer	703	393 956	83.9	9 870	109 917	125	6 692.6	2 960.9	43.5	8 869	3 375	805	457	4 164
Middlesex................	1 319	770 473	78.5	18 100	203 481	217	14 275.8	2 711.4	54.0	3 777	2 480	389	287	602
Monmouth	1 377	689 798	88.3	18 131	194 477	221	8 784.3	3 080.6	44.4	5 038	2 791	962	832	429
Morris....................	1 080	665 781	78.5	14 790	183 980	196	8 087.3	1 576.0	12.7	3 400	2 240	421	497	233
Ocean....................	946	420 236	88.5	10 569	108 736	190	8 263.0	2 579.2	74.8	5 184	4 228	250	390	307
Passaic...................	764	338 917	92.3	8 212	91 015	149	7 030.9	1 939.9	26.7	3 999	2 523	429	201	821
Salem	109	45 131	86.3	1 246	12 460	27	746.0	264.9	-20.3	4 104	3 143	97	189	634
Somerset	618	356 552	87.0	8 092	102 157	100	4 134.2	837.8	42.7	2 908	2 077	181	343	294
Sussex	254	106 194	75.7	3 006	31 363	57	1 416.0	373.3	63.5	2 580	1 998	179	136	260
Union	1 064	513 246	82.3	11 982	138 312	189	10 230.2	2 024.4	35.8	4 059	2 964	142	294	625
Warren	224	80 576	81.1	2 144	20 773	44	1 458.8	364.9	58.3	3 638	2 862	202	154	394
NEW MEXICO	3 827	2 146 558	73.1	67 203	599 757	501	14 092.2	13 580.2	56.2	7 805	2 893	2 259	946	1 581
Bernalillo	1 203	879 397	76.0	26 792	248 636	137	4 537.0	4 929.3	42.5	9 417	3 003	3 826	1 468	1 099
Catron....................	11	1 651	45.9	45	363	1	10.0	19.1	51.5	6 671	4 041	749	1 191	660
Chaves...................	115	54 822	80.4	1 970	14 732	23	546.0	263.1	50.9	4 216	2 876	133	294	848
Cibola	46	21 354	77.7	642	5 274	6	85.0	94.4	127.4	5 573	3 325	156	213	1 817
Colfax....................	79	34 571	D	1 205	12 686	10	197.5	76.2	61.5	7 740	2 945	366	2 888	882
Curry.....................	83	45 924	85.9	1 631	13 098	17	436.3	337.3	27.2	5 133	3 746	54	242	883
DeBaca	8	1 185	D	44	295	1	20.4	12.1	-18.5	5 434	2 457	1 005	905	1 041
Dona Ana................	253	121 657	84.7	4 278	32 591	44	1 495.5	925.7	28.0	6 476	3 012	2 094	472	856
Eddy.....................	103	52 931	70.3	1 782	14 519	16	558.5	344.0	61.8	4 478	3 123	57	329	962
Grant	72	25 144	78.1	823	6 246	8	220.9	140.3	96.1	6 932	3 378	77	287	3 160
Guadalupe	33	10 051	D	317	2 411	2	23.5	27.9	84.3	6 281	3 916	133	582	701
Harding...................	3	132	D	10	22	1	7.1	5.4	37.5	3 006	2 715	43	457	935
Hidalgo	24	7 913	72.1	301	2 617	3	41.2	28.2	93.9	3 649	2 715	25	103	694
Lea	109	42 047	89.4	1 510	11 298	16	401.5	200.9	74.9	3 425	2 715	103	278	739
Lincoln	99	30 063	74.6	866	7 606	15	231.2	76.7	80.1	4 572	1 780	103	588	1 103
Los Alamos	42	20 452	77.2	696	6 273	7	465.3	1 476.1	39.4	80 742	1 780	77 266	588	1 103
Luna	51	16 014	73.8	595	4 419	7	172.5	112.1	75.8	4 601	3 159	62	375	908
McKinley	133	69 291	72.2	2 061	17 533	10	294.7	405.5	70.2	6 059	2 029	266	1 376	2 380
Mora	4	228	100.0	12	73	2	20.1	30.7	37.2	6 212	2 907	63	355	2 870
Otero	99	36 956	73.4	1 324	9 931	20	426.6	492.7	36.5	9 093	3 379	1 393	3 517	749
Quay.....................	46	16 173	D	526	3 878	5	132.5	62.7	54.0	6 355	3 820	102	315	1 050
Rio Arriba	89	33 878	72.7	1 059	9 477	8	270.7	201.6	85.4	5 280	2 443	248	350	2 209
Roosevelt................	30	12 433	93.2	581	3 312	6	143.0	91.5	49.2	5 251	3 008	57	159	1 033
Sandoval	92	45 981	87.1	1 501	12 115	14	297.9	261.2	102.1	2 895	2 010	88	139	644
San Juan	173	100 040	82.0	3 478	27 260	24	807.1	417.4	88.0	3 798	2 047	102	659	947
San Miguel...............	69	23 990	70.8	796	5 781	11	179.1	171.1	109.2	6 004	2 717	45	255	2 957
Santa Fe	361	304 791	57.9	7 498	89 148	38	1 146.7	894.3	119.7	7 199	2 370	310	466	4 005
Sierra....................	47	12 968	67.2	437	3 174	5	110.0	97.6	80.0	8 868	5 860	287	439	2 225
Socorro...................	51	18 709	78.0	658	5 193	6	97.1	86.7	71.3	5 255	2 414	505	502	1 828
Taos	167	63 731	47.8	2 232	19 081	12	219.0	131.5	104.7	4 850	2 550	130	415	1 725
Torrance..................	32	8 925	78.6	361	2 475	6	71.6	62.5	2.9	3 807	2 035	829	145	719
Union	20	4 837	74.1	226	1 203	3	77.1	36.8	33.0	9 420	3 500	91	555	4 203
Valencia	80	28 319	85.3	946	7 037	17	349.3	230.4	105.1	3 540	2 584	21	89	833

[1] Includes only establishments with payroll. [2] Includes full-service restaurants, limited-service eating places, special food services, and drinking places (alcoholic beverages). [3] For pay period including March 12. [4] As of June 30. Covers all FDIC-insured commercial banks and savings institutions. [5] Based on resident population estimated as of July 1, 1999.

Sources: Accommodation and Foodservices—U.S. Census Bureau, 1997 Economic Census, ECON97 Report Series CD-ROM, CD-EC97-1, Disc 1E, issued February 2001 (related Internet site <http://www.census.gov/epcd/www/97EC72.HTM>). Banking—U.S. Federal Deposit Insurance Corporation and Office of Thrift Supervision, "1999 Bank and Thrift Branch Office Data Book: Summary of Deposits," national and 6 regional data books (related Internet site <http://www2.fdic.gov/sod/>). Federal Funds and Grants—U.S. Census Bureau, County Aggregate files for each state, <http://www.census.gov/govs/www/cffr99.html>, (accessed: August 2000).

Table B–12. Counties — Accommodation and Foodservices, Banking, and Federal Funds–Con.

[Includes U.S., states, and 3,142 counties/county equivalents defined as of January 1, 1992. For changes to these areas since January 1, 1992, see appendix B. Geographic Information]

County	Accommodation and foodservices[1] (NAICS 72), 1997					Banking,[4] 1999		Federal funds and grants, 1999						
	Sales							Total expenditures or obligations (mil. dol.)	Percent change, 1990–1999	Per capita[5] (dollars)				
											By selected type—			
	Estab-lishments	Total ($1,000)	Percent from food-services[2]	Paid employ-ees[3]	Annual payroll ($1,000)	Offices	Deposits (mil. dol.)			Total	Direct payments for individuals	Procure-ment contract awards	Salaries and wages	Grant awards
NEW YORK	38 051	21 680 529	74.5	473 481	6 104 432	4 548	418 861.5	101 808.6	45.6	5 595	3 134	372	413	1 587
Albany	841	449 212	74.4	12 586	125 018	116	6 061.7	4 981.3	53.2	17 059	4 053	345	1 080	11 421
Allegany	87	29 108	94.2	961	7 844	21	317.6	201.6	64.5	3 989	2 748	135	140	935
Bronx	1 067	371 580	95.2	8 264	95 747	111	8 688.6	(6)	(6)	(6)	(6)	(6)	(6)	(6)
Broome	476	204 243	D	6 940	58 109	56	2 635.3	953.6	35.2	4 884	3 293	460	223	890
Cattaraugus	227	79 500	77.7	3 309	23 404	28	675.1	394.4	79.1	4 669	2 911	438	182	1 097
Cayuga	172	52 527	89.1	1 688	14 246	21	717.4	317.9	59.7	3 892	2 693	92	128	908
Chautauqua	368	124 873	73.0	4 323	35 359	50	1 112.9	631.6	49.5	4 596	3 114	227	168	1 057
Chemung	213	86 223	91.5	2 965	24 435	24	961.7	424.8	44.3	4 630	3 207	85	278	1 037
Chenango	97	23 980	81.6	848	5 959	15	455.7	202.0	53.2	3 985	2 791	79	129	946
Clinton	189	64 698	78.9	2 243	19 981	26	856.5	321.5	6.2	4 033	2 592	128	335	916
Columbia	142	41 873	75.0	1 130	11 067	21	771.2	272.6	62.1	4 327	2 964	144	154	1 022
Cortland	126	53 099	89.3	1 849	13 767	16	514.5	172.7	59.9	3 598	2 427	138	136	864
Delaware	124	31 051	72.9	740	7 335	19	602.2	308.0	134.9	6 644	3 610	337	214	2 453
Dutchess	558	252 143	75.5	6 243	64 378	82	2 870.4	993.5	59.7	3 704	2 630	74	233	757
Erie	2 143	935 441	85.3	31 916	271 630	232	14 009.7	4 836.7	51.9	5 223	3 308	264	472	1 143
Essex	219	86 895	43.8	1 942	28 098	15	292.1	194.8	58.4	5 193	3 339	151	581	1 109
Franklin	127	30 607	67.2	899	7 943	19	426.7	216.5	60.0	4 463	2 675	171	182	1 317
Fulton	112	28 153	86.6	957	7 283	16	542.5	205.7	45.3	3 891	2 889	58	106	816
Genesee	131	51 654	85.8	1 770	14 495	17	1 093.8	247.7	61.3	4 097	2 843	196	389	597
Greene	207	62 566	41.2	1 508	16 352	20	588.2	189.7	56.7	3 923	2 988	64	134	718
Hamilton	59	10 379	47.8	140	2 796	4	44.3	29.1	75.6	5 606	3 946	63	225	1 364
Herkimer	153	40 647	84.1	1 225	10 570	20	526.2	264.4	22.1	4 173	3 114	93	122	810
Jefferson	295	102 469	83.2	2 835	28 065	39	946.9	874.4	61.4	7 955	2 520	527	3 840	1 025
Kings	2 221	734 498	97.0	15 748	188 129	241	24 744.5	[6]44 212.6	[6]56.4	[6]5 952	[6]2 957	[6]342	[6]433	[6]2 129
Lewis	67	10 932	D	314	2 410	9	201.4	99.8	44.3	3 658	2 386	115	129	965
Livingston	138	39 279	93.0	1 399	10 311	20	519.4	202.2	51.5	3 071	2 276	67	131	500
Madison	171	59 913	89.1	1 948	17 473	20	587.1	225.1	63.0	3 165	2 373	40	124	589
Monroe	1 439	760 564	84.0	22 914	219 357	185	9 647.6	3 233.0	59.0	4 538	2 931	214	250	1 119
Montgomery	115	36 891	87.5	910	8 513	23	719.5	246.2	43.2	4 888	3 790	140	130	765
Nassau	2 882	1 544 948	89.4	35 716	431 396	429	33 953.2	6 254.5	-7.3	4 793	3 354	627	296	505
New York	7 219	8 318 219	59.5	127 621	2 423 407	464	179 972.3	(6)	(6)	(6)	(6)	(6)	(6)	(6)
Niagara	593	207 768	78.5	6 877	58 272	49	2 273.5	1 015.0	60.7	4 695	3 249	173	358	869
Oneida	528	180 099	86.1	5 931	50 789	76	2 695.7	1 307.3	14.9	5 691	3 620	383	525	1 130
Onondaga	1 063	509 905	80.1	16 012	151 555	124	5 429.5	2 261.2	24.1	4 956	2 850	674	498	898
Ontario	262	110 676	82.2	3 516	31 500	28	946.5	401.4	58.5	4 023	2 740	116	461	644
Orange	687	256 534	86.2	6 763	66 990	118	3 633.0	1 545.1	94.1	4 623	2 394	430	1 143	631
Orleans	66	15 212	96.5	598	4 142	10	304.9	156.6	64.8	3 477	2 353	154	108	741
Oswego	262	87 032	89.0	3 128	25 372	33	909.4	420.8	66.0	3 397	2 445	67	120	751
Otsego	165	62 798	72.4	1 675	16 671	28	744.1	253.9	55.9	4 188	2 902	101	156	995
Putnam	144	45 699	90.5	1 207	12 032	24	6 894.2	235.7	80.8	2 485	2 036	41	121	282
Queens	2 668	1 344 780	88.4	25 458	360 360	322	28 283.9	(6)	(6)	(6)	(6)	(6)	(6)	(6)
Rensselaer	269	92 036	91.2	3 092	25 752	46	1 550.7	810.7	92.5	5 353	2 906	72	202	2 132
Richmond	553	239 599	97.8	5 427	55 318	71	5 779.3	(6)	(6)	(6)	(6)	(6)	(6)	(6)
Rockland	558	246 568	82.2	5 553	64 357	95	5 256.6	1 026.7	74.0	3 615	2 568	73	133	830
St. Lawrence	259	74 868	85.6	2 497	20 314	40	973.8	484.2	62.5	4 291	2 726	67	230	1 211
Saratoga	380	197 272	79.6	5 431	58 388	65	1 737.4	600.6	70.0	3 007	2 233	44	343	375
Schenectady	313	106 618	93.4	3 126	29 777	50	2 043.0	1 019.2	-2.7	7 084	3 483	2 290	342	931
Schoharie	51	14 377	74.4	547	4 100	12	295.3	123.0	76.8	3 838	2 702	41	149	911
Schuyler	49	11 400	D	281	3 083	6	110.1	74.5	56.3	3 873	2 595	55	158	1 046
Seneca	72	23 319	D	646	7 003	12	280.3	129.6	3.2	4 061	3 026	45	262	641
Steuben	211	74 665	74.3	2 332	21 420	36	679.5	454.4	45.6	4 651	3 128	171	409	899
Suffolk	2 795	1 266 920	88.2	29 208	336 294	391	24 347.6	6 150.5	53.7	4 445	2 681	600	468	687
Sullivan	246	148 122	23.9	3 607	43 351	34	795.6	369.5	56.1	5 330	3 446	136	181	1 550
Tioga	84	24 247	D	749	6 748	15	319.4	463.4	-7.6	8 876	2 271	5 963	155	466
Tompkins	312	113 177	76.7	3 477	31 665	31	957.0	444.9	27.2	4 556	1 926	147	195	2 261
Ulster	468	215 653	58.1	5 662	63 109	55	1 692.4	654.5	56.4	3 912	2 783	90	167	853
Warren	407	179 524	D	4 078	51 631	28	912.2	253.1	58.9	4 120	3 012	97	257	746
Washington	100	19 832	D	584	4 823	19	493.6	214.7	57.5	3 569	2 648	67	134	677
Wayne	140	46 151	96.4	1 473	12 419	22	622.3	339.1	61.7	3 550	2 567	55	121	717
Westchester	1 833	1 018 091	81.4	19 829	285 073	307	21 167.8	4 059.9	49.4	4 483	3 006	375	322	761
Wyoming	73	16 449	90.5	544	4 110	16	457.3	141.1	76.0	3 193	2 294	219	130	451
Yates	55	12 973	86.5	322	3 137	6	219.4	96.4	51.9	3 926	3 046	41	198	568

[1] Includes only establishments with payroll. [2] Includes full-service restaurants, limited-service eating places, special food services, and drinking places (alcoholic beverages). [3] For pay period including March 12. [4] As of June 30. Covers all FDIC-insured commercial banks and savings institutions. [5] Based on resident population estimated as of July 1, 1999. [6] Bronx, New York, Queens, and Richmond Counties included with Kings County; data not available separately.

Sources: Accommodation and Foodservices—U.S. Census Bureau, 1997 Economic Census, ECON97 Report Series CD-ROM, CD-EC97-1, Disc 1E, issued February 2001 (related Internet site <http://www.census.gov/epcd/www/97EC72.HTM>). Banking—U.S. Federal Deposit Insurance Corporation and Office of Thrift Supervision, "1999 Bank and Thrift Branch Office Data Book: Summary of Deposits," national and 6 regional data books (related Internet site <http://www2.fdic.gov/sod/>). Federal Funds and Grants—U.S. Census Bureau, County Aggregate files for each state, <http://www.census.gov/govs/www/cffr99.html>, (accessed: August 2000).

Table B–12. Counties — Accommodation and Foodservices, Banking, and Federal Funds–Con.

[Includes U.S., states, and 3,142 counties/county equivalents defined as of January 1, 1992. For changes to these areas since January 1, 1992, see appendix B. Geographic Information]

County	Accommodation and foodservices[1] (NAICS 72), 1997					Banking,[4] 1999		Federal funds and grants, 1999						
		Sales								Per capita[5] (dollars)				
												By selected type—		
	Establishments	Total ($1,000)	Percent from foodservices[2]	Paid employees[3]	Annual payroll ($1,000)	Offices	Deposits (mil. dol.)	Total expenditures or obligations (mil. dol.)	Percent change, 1990–1999	Total	Direct payments for individuals	Procurement contract awards	Salaries and wages	Grant awards
NORTH CAROLINA	14 579	8 624 993	80.2	262 848	2 393 158	2 458	101 651.7	37 227.6	81.0	4 866	2 834	268	689	994
Alamance	246	145 090	89.8	5 028	39 944	44	1 600.2	438.7	18.7	3 623	2 912	56	111	524
Alexander	38	15 506	D	575	4 518	11	285.0	86.7	75.1	2 712	2 182	35	85	386
Alleghany	25	6 156	88.8	246	1 823	5	154.7	52.7	85.9	5 351	3 732	143	219	1 196
Anson	30	12 121	92.9	406	3 349	8	204.0	126.3	94.9	5 209	3 128	732	119	1 156
Ashe	43	12 543	D	464	3 782	10	2 270.7	109.2	95.0	4 499	3 049	34	168	1 214
Avery	47	22 057	52.2	468	5 634	5	133.8	75.3	97.3	4 750	3 504	34	146	1 057
Beaufort	68	29 144	84.6	924	7 162	18	434.8	217.5	97.8	4 817	3 187	64	139	977
Bertie	15	4 357	D	162	1 138	7	125.8	120.7	95.8	5 920	3 420	117	204	1 901
Bladen	50	17 885	75.0	544	4 668	9	185.4	157.8	85.0	5 104	3 112	252	184	1 394
Brunswick	155	67 361	84.3	1 843	16 745	26	704.7	318.0	104.4	4 466	3 448	232	201	552
Buncombe	506	334 308	D	9 130	98 878	60	2 446.7	963.0	61.4	4 907	3 285	309	606	674
Burke	118	63 148	92.2	2 451	16 660	17	600.6	291.1	66.1	3 502	2 549	146	82	713
Cabarrus	155	123 695	93.2	3 317	31 695	35	1 247.1	409.2	88.3	3 278	2 697	31	121	415
Caldwell	102	40 853	D	1 332	10 778	17	655.3	238.2	77.9	3 117	2 496	46	91	473
Camden	3	D	D	(6)	D	1	8.5	32.1	84.3	4 671	3 357	27	225	718
Carteret	202	106 021	65.5	3 010	28 652	23	613.8	294.8	88.9	4 910	3 657	366	346	485
Caswell	14	2 715	100.0	88	694	2	46.1	81.2	90.6	3 619	2 338	37	102	1 102
Catawba	315	179 690	89.6	6 274	52 024	52	1 692.2	445.6	85.2	3 318	2 465	88	224	520
Chatham	51	D	D	(7)	D	15	383.7	157.0	102.5	3 377	2 357	294	132	574
Cherokee	47	15 423	D	525	3 979	11	288.9	119.7	89.1	5 166	3 730	52	270	1 092
Chowan	27	10 083	84.2	364	2 479	6	127.5	72.4	77.2	5 060	3 589	50	145	1 028
Clay	13	D	D	(6)	D	3	83.8	43.2	94.7	4 942	3 740	41	152	991
Cleveland	131	60 547	91.8	2 422	17 606	31	902.7	444.3	132.8	4 725	2 798	1 002	107	786
Columbus	75	26 711	D	1 058	6 699	18	484.4	284.3	104.5	5 370	3 543	30	129	1 494
Craven	159	87 133	81.3	3 004	24 840	26	713.7	924.5	55.6	10 343	3 570	935	4 990	771
Cumberland	495	318 413	86.2	10 654	91 208	59	1 527.8	3 103.1	90.9	10 940	3 054	1 152	5 919	782
Currituck	45	13 671	85.2	339	4 022	4	57.8	75.6	108.6	4 128	3 044	475	116	395
Dare	274	139 959	65.6	2 854	37 574	20	494.3	125.0	89.5	4 218	2 886	249	401	630
Davidson	177	87 377	95.4	2 802	24 800	39	1 394.5	401.6	73.6	2 811	2 200	151	69	377
Davie	41	D	D	(7)	D	8	315.3	109.1	94.2	3 337	2 595	172	93	456
Duplin	65	28 583	95.7	976	7 594	15	323.0	208.8	86.4	4 814	2 981	189	155	1 259
Durham	468	378 507	66.8	9 414	105 661	76	2 408.9	1 533.5	81.2	7 514	2 395	1 635	1 118	2 325
Edgecombe	52	22 133	D	747	6 184	11	262.2	269.1	87.9	4 924	2 805	128	489	1 306
Forsyth	632	407 986	87.1	12 945	116 178	104	8 599.2	1 159.9	71.8	4 016	2 762	90	221	917
Franklin	37	D	D	(7)	D	7	234.8	149.6	110.1	3 280	2 263	35	93	840
Gaston	297	158 728	93.8	5 315	42 310	57	1 615.3	622.7	70.9	3 363	2 694	44	109	506
Gates	4	1 231	100.0	53	364	4	76.8	47.7	90.9	4 690	3 164	35	128	1 045
Graham	17	7 686	30.3	160	2 445	3	79.9	37.8	49.5	4 973	3 437	46	234	1 249
Granville	52	23 314	88.6	680	5 855	11	360.9	219.1	149.6	4 919	2 458	757	921	734
Greene	10	2 935	100.0	117	800	3	76.8	66.6	109.6	3 592	2 123	22	111	1 001
Guilford	924	637 543	79.6	19 991	185 375	128	5 221.8	1 728.5	26.3	4 416	2 613	495	583	693
Halifax	76	51 742	76.8	1 531	13 436	19	485.0	327.6	96.3	5 867	3 697	77	118	1 811
Harnett	88	37 070	94.6	1 289	9 964	24	606.2	281.4	91.4	3 330	2 249	159	76	736
Haywood	151	65 903	65.0	2 038	17 458	12	509.8	256.4	90.5	4 930	3 582	321	139	870
Henderson	167	97 233	70.9	3 146	28 613	27	987.5	393.3	69.7	4 781	4 055	77	132	490
Hertford	39	16 786	88.9	632	4 615	8	255.6	118.3	84.1	5 394	3 315	28	163	1 728
Hoke	19	5 409	D	189	1 304	4	93.8	92.5	116.0	2 953	1 860	76	94	853
Hyde	33	10 168	67.2	158	2 369	4	45.7	38.3	100.6	6 571	3 057	900	260	1 406
Iredell	195	117 486	82.1	3 470	31 875	38	1 251.5	366.9	91.5	3 122	2 513	47	106	425
Jackson	102	32 903	79.0	942	8 599	14	258.5	113.3	82.8	3 744	2 747	21	106	863
Johnston	151	90 860	85.2	2 548	23 680	37	854.8	367.2	99.6	3 313	2 291	39	93	804
Jones	6	1 338	100.0	41	316	3	53.7	55.6	88.5	5 963	3 868	57	124	1 364
Lee	83	40 450	87.1	1 390	11 401	17	552.0	204.8	93.9	4 140	3 174	81	148	705
Lenoir	95	51 489	90.9	1 678	14 589	20	537.4	321.9	91.0	5 470	3 601	102	326	1 276
Lincoln	73	26 793	92.9	962	7 073	22	544.7	171.8	106.5	2 917	2 341	64	97	390
McDowell	64	26 676	82.8	861	6 992	7	254.3	144.3	65.8	3 558	2 695	23	97	739
Macon	92	30 676	74.7	943	8 190	15	405.5	147.4	79.7	5 100	3 890	153	287	762
Madison	24	6 062	D	230	1 876	5	123.4	129.1	182.6	6 828	2 875	299	137	3 430
Martin	43	17 477	85.3	659	4 811	10	264.4	128.7	92.4	4 924	3 216	26	145	1 289
Mecklenburg	1 553	1 194 234	74.2	33 351	330 168	228	26 742.6	2 011.7	85.3	3 103	1 934	189	430	527
Mitchell	25	8 932	D	324	2 569	6	164.0	77.8	79.4	5 271	3 405	32	156	1 642
Montgomery	28	D	D	(8)	D	14	233.3	102.7	68.2	4 223	2 900	337	105	847
Moore	154	132 972	40.7	3 202	34 598	40	1 041.0	358.3	94.5	4 916	4 208	33	114	521
Nash	168	111 649	D	3 481	30 221	40	1 209.4	334.6	65.0	3 623	2 642	64	39	806
New Hanover	455	281 368	79.6	8 834	76 717	60	1 890.1	674.4	88.9	4 469	3 052	259	324	749
Northampton	12	D	D	(6)	D	6	87.7	130.9	101.6	6 166	3 623	36	121	2 001
Onslow	249	127 923	88.9	4 420	34 525	25	530.7	1 538.9	46.2	10 801	2 455	978	6 809	533

[1] Includes only establishments with payroll. [2] Includes full-service restaurants, limited-service eating places, special food services, and drinking places (alcoholic beverages). [3] For pay period including March 12. [4] As of June 30. Covers all FDIC-insured commercial banks and savings institutions. [5] Based on resident population estimated as of July 1, 1999. [6] 20 to 99 employees. [7] 500 to 999 employees. [8] 250 to 499 employees.

Sources: Accommodation and Foodservices—U.S. Census Bureau, 1997 Economic Census, ECON97 Report Series CD-ROM, CD-EC97-1, Disc 1E, issued February 2001 (related Internet site <http://www.census.gov/epcd/www/97EC72.HTM>). Banking—U.S. Federal Deposit Insurance Corporation and Office of Thrift Supervision, "1999 Bank and Thrift Branch Office Data Book: Summary of Deposits," national and 6 regional data books (related Internet site <http://www2.fdic.gov/sod/>). Federal Funds and Grants—U.S. Census Bureau, County Aggregate files for each state, <http://www.census.gov/govs/www/cffr99.html>, (accessed: August 2000).

[Includes U.S., states, and 3,142 counties/county equivalents defined as of January 1, 1992. For changes to these areas since January 1, 1992, see appendix B. Geographic Information]

County	Accommodation and foodservices[1] (NAICS 72), 1997					Banking,[4] 1999		Federal funds and grants, 1999						
	Sales									Per capita[5] (dollars)				
											By selected type—			
	Estab-lishments	Total ($1,000)	Percent from food-services[2]	Paid employ-ees[3]	Annual payroll ($1,000)	Offices	Deposits (mil. dol.)	Total expenditures or obligations (mil. dol.)	Percent change, 1990–1999	Total	Direct payments for individuals	Procure-ment contract awards	Salaries and wages	Grant awards
NORTH CAROLINA–Con.														
Orange	283	154 075	73.4	4 443	44 340	39	1 150.9	547.0	88.9	4 905	1 961	222	177	2 522
Pamlico	18	13 571	D	293	4 396	4	87.6	62.8	102.5	5 098	3 687	49	150	956
Pasquotank	74	31 710	D	1 183	9 301	13	473.2	221.0	74.5	6 203	3 248	287	1 311	1 214
Pender	48	15 216	D	499	4 480	8	177.3	156.6	115.7	3 886	2 786	74	95	848
Perquimans	11	D	D	(6)	D	2	68.4	65.0	108.3	5 753	3 929	162	126	1 105
Person	45	20 770	90.4	716	5 368	8	341.4	125.9	87.7	3 717	2 620	22	95	934
Pitt	237	153 479	88.5	5 342	41 804	40	1 058.1	467.4	95.9	3 652	2 280	56	159	1 055
Polk	36	10 898	78.4	431	3 276	8	251.5	84.0	75.6	4 975	4 031	38	137	750
Randolph	150	75 898	92.5	2 433	20 973	41	1 173.2	326.4	91.5	2 645	2 117	52	85	376
Richmond	69	28 559	91.6	1 140	7 113	15	343.5	213.3	75.7	4 665	3 434	44	129	1 022
Robeson	171	85 261	81.5	2 685	22 379	35	721.4	554.0	116.7	4 751	2 806	60	240	1 495
Rockingham	124	60 167	85.5	1 913	16 508	31	980.3	355.9	66.3	3 942	3 008	83	99	738
Rowan	158	82 409	87.3	2 891	22 443	32	1 032.0	484.1	77.3	3 824	2 654	45	501	570
Rutherford	93	37 359	91.0	1 280	10 203	18	586.5	236.8	80.0	3 850	2 851	33	105	847
Sampson	66	26 558	91.5	903	7 272	19	346.5	235.9	96.6	4 467	2 798	70	131	1 155
Scotland	52	28 906	87.0	1 134	6 950	10	238.1	156.0	101.3	4 347	2 661	27	93	1 464
Stanly	92	34 133	96.2	1 338	9 128	21	660.6	194.7	79.5	3 442	2 783	31	161	425
Stokes	39	D	D	(7)	D	10	206.8	111.7	107.5	2 546	1 944	28	87	475
Surry	149	56 577	90.5	1 899	15 356	26	932.5	285.7	101.5	4 206	3 026	29	120	1 004
Swain	79	38 121	44.2	796	10 352	5	126.1	92.5	48.1	7 495	3 430	414	992	2 573
Transylvania	72	34 026	57.2	798	10 696	10	320.5	133.9	86.5	4 641	3 854	88	228	453
Tyrrell	8	D	D	(8)	D	2	31.5	36.9	185.3	9 353	2 981	37	131	5 247
Union	151	73 045	91.9	2 618	18 557	28	843.2	249.8	76.5	2 169	1 632	88	87	313
Vance	66	38 570	D	1 532	10 670	10	340.7	192.3	103.4	4 525	2 957	214	112	1 223
Wake	1 229	896 627	82.8	24 776	251 020	197	6 588.7	3 073.8	86.4	5 237	1 935	186	441	2 645
Warren	13	D	D	(6)	D	5	103.9	91.8	90.6	4 872	2 965	27	108	1 702
Washington	22	9 587	D	334	2 530	6	109.4	69.2	80.1	5 147	3 321	87	161	1 250
Watauga	165	91 269	67.0	2 847	24 994	14	434.1	124.6	95.3	3 009	2 083	46	124	740
Wayne	158	84 388	85.5	2 953	23 124	32	856.7	719.0	87.9	6 436	3 053	487	1 718	1 000
Wilkes	97	42 921	88.0	1 436	10 751	17	583.3	228.7	91.7	3 593	2 530	35	143	869
Wilson	138	85 352	89.0	2 771	23 084	24	591.4	304.9	91.2	4 432	2 936	104	124	1 161
Yadkin	70	26 216	76.9	922	7 698	10	324.8	126.7	90.9	3 595	2 502	32	102	906
Yancey	26	7 368	87.4	268	2 231	5	141.6	78.5	93.3	4 654	3 169	41	138	1 257
NORTH DAKOTA	1 827	684 930	77.7	26 330	188 982	401	9 793.1	4 535.2	54.0	7 157	2 844	402	975	1 593
Adams	9	1 239	D	54	352	5	46.5	19.7	39.7	7 437	3 439	65	312	852
Barnes	36	8 084	80.3	318	2 148	7	215.1	85.8	61.6	7 235	3 268	272	403	1 033
Benson	12	D	D	(8)	D	5	46.3	79.4	49.4	11 713	2 826	736	730	4 850
Billings	8	6 680	D	92	1 879	1	2.7	5.1	−5.5	4 793	1 221	123	1 028	740
Bottineau	30	4 775	78.3	151	1 308	9	150.4	58.1	59.1	8 020	3 590	77	416	689
Bowman	18	3 225	83.3	128	719	5	80.2	26.0	84.6	7 955	3 616	57	242	1 956
Burke	18	D	D	(8)	D	4	42.9	26.6	41.9	12 148	4 611	118	1 058	1 843
Burleigh	156	96 754	78.0	3 485	27 819	23	845.7	573.2	89.5	8 509	2 687	106	748	4 744
Cass	294	195 010	73.8	7 184	55 195	54	2 066.3	495.6	39.3	4 186	2 027	209	844	766
Cavalier	23	D	D	(6)	D	5	148.3	63.8	137.8	13 236	3 468	65	341	627
Dickey	20	3 227	D	177	768	4	82.2	46.3	73.1	8 177	3 361	83	280	1 633
Divide	8	1 399	D	52	214	4	67.9	23.4	17.4	10 221	4 126	88	475	1 052
Dunn	10	D	D	(8)	D	3	36.6	22.5	46.7	6 494	2 457	724	298	1 265
Eddy	13	1 865	D	55	430	2	18.7	21.3	26.2	7 603	3 744	151	359	813
Emmons	15	D	D	(8)	D	4	97.3	31.0	15.7	7 208	3 442	56	257	947
Foster	14	D	D	(6)	D	5	97.1	47.5	196.3	12 547	3 340	1 137	383	4 804
Golden Valley	7	1 268	100.0	57	348	2	44.2	14.9	47.0	8 371	3 884	56	256	990
Grand Forks	180	93 822	D	4 126	27 065	26	731.6	424.3	35.2	6 560	2 023	1 028	2 108	920
Grant	8	1 032	100.0	37	192	3	46.6	24.6	24.3	8 626	3 813	65	369	1 379
Griggs	12	1 716	61.6	71	496	4	58.7	26.5	64.1	9 543	3 603	82	379	608
Hettinger	9	938	100.0	34	184	3	46.6	32.7	53.6	11 527	4 004	55	382	1 497
Kidder	5	1 269	D	49	392	2	40.6	23.2	22.9	8 286	3 426	81	381	1 305
LaMoure	16	D	D	(8)	D	6	69.2	45.6	91.9	9 696	3 470	157	393	1 629
Logan	8	931	100.0	33	153	3	48.1	19.5	21.3	8 612	3 413	69	285	923
McHenry	14	D	D	(8)	D	9	68.1	50.7	39.1	8 511	3 967	98	451	1 389
McIntosh	16	1 466	D	67	300	4	74.1	28.8	29.4	8 484	4 883	67	339	812
McKenzie	21	2 259	87.0	75	473	4	84.4	32.0	55.2	5 776	2 422	521	397	993
McLean	35	4 185	D	155	850	10	146.3	77.5	37.3	8 066	3 600	599	493	1 202
Mercer	32	6 342	87.4	276	1 867	7	107.0	32.8	43.2	3 556	2 304	129	207	429
Morton	49	15 729	78.5	580	4 128	9	265.7	104.3	36.8	4 246	2 685	120	211	788
Mountrail	30	4 075	81.8	158	950	6	112.3	58.5	39.2	8 983	3 326	70	679	3 017
Nelson	17	2 028	D	68	472	6	111.4	43.4	72.4	11 858	4 771	97	371	1 349
Oliver	5	D	D	(9)	D	1	16.3	12.0	60.4	5 568	1 739	13	87	2 176
Pembina	29	5 507	80.4	244	1 278	10	196.7	73.4	50.5	8 791	3 299	244	805	975
Pierce	17	3 196	77.1	104	850	3	83.5	34.1	38.3	7 431	3 285	66	291	1 108

[1] Includes only establishments with payroll. [2] Includes full-service restaurants, limited-service eating places, special food services, and drinking places (alcoholic beverages). [3] For pay period including March 12. [4] As of June 30. Covers all FDIC-insured commercial banks and savings institutions. [5] Based on resident population estimated as of July 1, 1999. [6] 100 to 249 employees. [7] 250 to 499 employees. [8] 20 to 99 employees. [9] 0 to 19 employees.

Sources: Accommodation and Foodservices—U.S. Census Bureau, 1997 Economic Census, ECON97 Report Series CD-ROM, CD-EC97-1, Disc 1E, issued February 2001 (related Internet site <http://www.census.gov/epcd/www/97EC72.HTM>). Banking—U.S. Federal Deposit Insurance Corporation and Office of Thrift Supervision, "1999 Bank and Thrift Branch Office Data Book: Summary of Deposits," national and 6 regional data books (related Internet site <http://www2.fdic.gov/sod/>). Federal Funds and Grants—U.S. Census Bureau, County Aggregate files for each state, <http://www.census.gov/govs/www/cffr99.html>, (accessed: August 2000).

[Includes U.S., states, and 3,142 counties/county equivalents defined as of January 1, 1992. For changes to these areas since January 1, 1992, see appendix B. Geographic Information]

County	Accommodation and foodservices[1] (NAICS 72), 1997 Estab-lishments	Sales Total ($1,000)	Sales Percent from food-services[2]	Paid employ-ees[3]	Annual payroll ($1,000)	Banking,[4] 1999 Offices	Deposits (mil. dol.)	Federal funds and grants, 1999 Total expenditures or obligations (mil. dol.)	Percent change, 1990–1999	Per capita[5] (dollars) Total	Direct payments for individuals	Procure-ment contract awards	Salaries and wages	Grant awards
NORTH DAKOTA—Con.														
Ramsey	43	15 197	76.3	551	4 219	12	302.3	109.6	103.0	9 179	3 523	1 061	807	1 642
Ransom	25	4 161	87.6	176	892	7	133.7	41.7	67.1	7 272	3 363	105	309	701
Renville	12	D	D	(6)	D	4	37.8	23.6	60.5	8 414	3 640	76	337	556
Richland	44	11 339	87.6	384	2 615	11	278.6	89.5	49.3	4 992	2 482	55	207	596
Rolette	21	3 646	86.2	109	739	5	98.9	147.7	56.3	10 380	2 308	2 315	1 595	3 404
Sargent	17	D	D	(7)	D	4	69.1	34.0	85.1	7 939	2 882	106	430	925
Sheridan	5	1 584	D	46	272	2	30.3	20.2	25.3	12 142	4 055	167	288	2 496
Sioux	3	870	100.0	23	180	–	–	40.3	36.4	9 703	1 835	613	1 663	4 187
Slope	2	D	D	(6)	D	–	–	7.0	47.9	7 847	1 515	32	114	605
Stark	64	26 615	75.8	1 059	7 233	14	338.1	99.3	35.6	4 414	2 722	35	297	873
Steele	8	794	100.0	21	113	3	48.8	26.0	92.2	11 932	3 478	157	384	922
Stutsman	61	22 188	83.5	850	6 337	10	335.9	139.9	41.1	6 636	3 066	119	443	1 414
Towner	9	1 509	100.0	40	316	5	68.8	33.7	77.1	11 396	3 569	58	342	1 489
Traill	36	6 942	93.8	363	1 816	9	152.6	60.4	87.8	7 058	3 154	122	244	873
Walsh	41	7 385	90.9	271	1 727	15	269.8	92.0	73.1	6 891	3 073	67	240	1 244
Ward	158	72 091	80.4	2 896	20 902	24	776.7	469.4	58.4	8 043	2 733	1 008	3 222	670
Wells	21	2 885	93.3	164	713	7	121.5	46.4	30.3	9 117	3 973	78	293	1 187
Williams	63	20 768	72.5	819	5 987	11	334.2	99.1	28.9	5 015	3 129	206	244	740
OHIO	22 631	12 410 978	86.6	401 206	3 444 193	3 863	156 316.7	53 262.2	38.9	4 732	2 947	400	386	911
Adams	37	13 869	93.8	508	3 681	11	227.8	152.3	72.8	5 305	2 933	38	134	2 081
Allen	231	127 461	90.1	4 260	33 143	43	1 373.9	561.7	-34.2	5 254	4 010	225	229	696
Ashland	102	40 673	85.6	1 440	11 421	21	505.6	147.7	51.4	2 841	2 255	54	110	352
Ashtabula	235	83 834	83.2	2 759	21 703	33	907.3	425.7	59.2	4 119	3 083	292	134	562
Athens	141	57 442	87.2	2 364	16 242	28	416.4	260.9	72.9	4 235	2 329	111	316	1 459
Auglaize	102	37 908	82.2	1 533	10 415	24	586.4	148.0	42.5	3 139	2 420	93	106	292
Belmont	152	67 587	89.8	2 281	18 025	44	1 036.6	353.3	52.6	4 958	3 786	59	142	954
Brown	60	15 634	94.1	531	3 841	16	343.7	137.3	74.0	3 302	2 313	35	106	690
Butler	519	286 267	D	9 919	79 648	92	2 580.7	972.4	73.6	2 916	2 146	150	94	503
Carroll	45	10 478	96.1	459	2 703	10	187.4	78.0	64.3	2 665	1 929	27	87	584
Champaign	64	20 021	96.1	776	5 223	17	540.2	132.9	47.1	3 444	2 397	211	110	481
Clark	248	132 788	90.8	4 662	36 609	35	1 284.0	669.9	47.9	4 621	3 377	84	266	825
Clermont	224	133 850	93.0	4 370	37 703	57	1 238.2	377.9	56.3	2 114	1 595	32	92	380
Clinton	74	36 291	94.4	1 268	10 120	16	468.8	163.6	60.0	3 773	2 658	44	190	609
Columbiana	210	70 052	95.7	2 526	19 157	50	1 127.5	465.2	58.1	4 179	3 138	65	229	719
Coshocton	52	19 159	92.1	719	5 664	12	381.7	134.2	62.2	3 708	2 640	94	146	729
Crawford	94	30 549	94.3	1 160	7 801	21	653.1	186.4	53.2	3 964	3 092	31	88	535
Cuyahoga	3 031	1 846 316	82.8	55 025	493 420	442	36 973.7	7 902.0	34.5	5 761	3 501	450	621	1 141
Darke	91	32 376	89.9	1 143	8 464	26	829.0	188.3	71.6	3 483	2 490	51	113	557
Defiance	72	33 369	92.2	1 281	8 942	15	635.1	137.7	64.4	3 473	2 470	115	126	502
Delaware	160	79 264	94.6	2 623	23 883	29	636.3	266.5	141.4	2 571	1 787	118	114	465
Erie	248	167 886	63.2	4 622	46 628	24	807.3	328.2	68.0	4 214	3 066	143	151	788
Fairfield	185	106 810	94.1	3 478	30 427	32	1 050.2	338.9	61.3	2 675	2 041	74	103	388
Fayette	56	32 373	D	1 002	9 170	8	291.3	108.6	60.1	3 824	2 600	37	91	739
Franklin	2 330	1 669 929	82.8	49 486	483 195	294	17 254.9	6 051.1	68.1	5 887	2 423	462	575	2 391
Fulton	78	27 844	93.3	1 002	7 306	22	658.4	144.0	61.7	3 411	2 482	67	156	423
Gallia	59	30 868	88.0	970	7 896	12	387.2	147.9	74.8	4 450	2 909	89	119	1 294
Geauga	146	58 581	89.5	1 977	16 752	32	981.0	170.0	82.8	1 897	1 640	26	77	140
Greene	248	157 349	86.0	5 129	44 311	42	1 082.6	1 755.5	20.8	11 770	2 377	3 762	5 165	425
Guernsey	91	49 294	71.9	1 459	14 065	13	445.6	184.3	38.8	4 501	3 094	40	140	1 174
Hamilton	1 967	1 365 873	83.3	40 513	387 363	334	18 349.6	5 353.7	7.4	6 370	3 128	1 532	646	1 013
Hancock	172	87 524	87.7	3 184	25 786	25	736.5	196.1	27.7	2 826	2 038	30	130	430
Hardin	58	17 150	97.8	647	5 046	14	320.0	100.6	64.9	3 180	2 006	132	184	512
Harrison	37	5 726	D	225	1 443	7	132.2	73.1	43.3	4 549	3 530	53	204	729
Henry	60	D	D	(8)	D	18	371.9	107.1	83.0	3 584	2 434	43	164	491
Highland	58	22 862	95.2	743	5 784	19	565.6	163.7	71.8	3 983	2 766	40	132	811
Hocking	51	20 428	81.3	619	5 514	7	223.4	98.0	72.1	3 358	2 470	32	91	738
Holmes	58	26 002	72.6	845	7 544	16	458.3	59.8	61.6	1 562	1 082	32	97	296
Huron	110	43 606	96.5	1 696	12 465	25	634.2	210.8	46.7	3 484	2 763	36	126	414
Jackson	49	21 688	94.2	694	5 566	13	334.0	145.5	62.3	4 456	2 775	40	113	1 496
Jefferson	166	48 588	D	1 724	13 620	37	905.0	430.6	24.6	5 846	4 357	136	189	1 136
Knox	96	36 874	91.6	1 418	10 506	13	507.0	187.2	64.9	3 473	2 580	31	105	651
Lake	482	257 225	87.1	9 435	68 558	79	3 011.1	724.5	60.8	3 189	2 675	80	114	314
Lawrence	73	32 103	91.6	1 078	8 291	20	477.0	304.1	5.5	4 727	3 316	43	106	1 248
Licking	266	124 391	89.1	4 206	35 838	43	1 326.2	562.6	59.0	4 122	2 555	732	183	569
Logan	101	36 979	82.5	1 502	10 497	21	547.8	173.6	58.8	3 708	2 695	89	228	475
Lorain	489	215 891	92.1	7 639	56 237	87	2 485.0	983.3	52.3	3 486	2 567	48	291	549
Lucas	1 034	601 988	89.2	18 683	161 571	143	5 103.2	1 965.7	43.4	4 403	3 050	122	268	930
Madison	61	39 577	D	1 219	11 030	12	305.1	148.5	96.4	3 592	2 235	29	108	957
Mahoning	536	255 768	93.6	8 653	69 301	99	3 078.6	1 341.3	50.4	5 310	3 725	93	338	1 121

[1] Includes only establishments with payroll. [2] Includes full-service restaurants, limited-service eating places, special food services, and drinking places (alcoholic beverages). [3] For pay period including March 12. [4] As of June 30. Covers all FDIC-insured commercial banks and savings institutions. [5] Based on resident population estimated as of July 1, 1999. [6] 0 to 19 employees. [7] 20 to 99 employees. [8] 500 to 999 employees.

Sources: Accommodation and Foodservices—U.S. Census Bureau, 1997 Economic Census, ECON97 Report Series CD-ROM, CD-EC97-1, Disc 1E, issued February 2001 (related Internet site <http://www.census.gov/epcd/www/97EC72.HTM/>). Banking—U.S. Federal Deposit Insurance Corporation and Office of Thrift Supervision, "1999 Bank and Thrift Branch Office Data Book: Summary of Deposits," national and 6 regional data books (related Internet site <http://www2.fdic.gov/sod/>). Federal Funds and Grants—U.S. Census Bureau, County Aggregate files for each state, <http://www.census.gov/govs/www/cffr99.html>, (accessed: August 2000).

[Includes U.S., states, and 3,142 counties/county equivalents defined as of January 1, 1992. For changes to these areas since January 1, 1992, see appendix B. Geographic Information]

County	Accommodation and foodservices[1] (NAICS 72), 1997					Banking,[4] 1999		Federal funds and grants, 1999						
		Sales						Total expenditures or obligations (mil. dol.)	Percent change, 1990– 1999	Per capita[5] (dollars)				
												By selected type—		
	Estab- lishments	Total ($1,000)	Percent from food- services[2]	Paid employ- ees[3]	Annual payroll ($1,000)	Offices	Deposits (mil. dol.)			Total	Direct payments for individuals	Procure- ment contract awards	Salaries and wages	Grant awards
OHIO—Con.														
Marion	116	57 708	94.1	1 947	15 357	26	685.8	261.3	68.7	3 907	2 826	60	132	686
Medina	229	117 627	93.5	4 400	33 625	48	1 390.7	349.7	84.0	2 374	2 007	64	110	175
Meigs	26	10 103	D	313	2 340	10	189.7	104.1	58.4	4 333	2 873	44	144	1 208
Mercer	79	27 489	94.5	1 027	7 387	22	641.2	84.5	73.7	2 061	1 222	34	128	319
Miami	178	91 434	92.9	3 231	26 203	42	1 063.7	350.5	56.9	3 550	2 598	395	119	353
Monroe	18	D	D	(6)	D	5	100.6	68.9	74.9	4 461	2 934	207	194	1 108
Montgomery	1 129	717 508	88.6	23 022	202 654	164	6 292.3	3 096.6	25.4	5 472	3 298	778	490	870
Morgan	15	4 198	100.0	178	1 237	7	117.9	59.6	73.9	4 103	2 717	82	255	990
Morrow	39	10 202	88.0	370	2 531	6	145.9	76.2	56.9	2 372	1 703	24	89	374
Muskingum	189	91 585	89.5	3 177	25 225	28	969.4	359.0	67.3	4 233	2 936	53	200	999
Noble	18	6 143	D	204	1 699	3	120.0	39.9	51.1	2 697	1 795	66	95	717
Ottawa	168	62 600	81.9	1 346	15 730	21	542.6	166.5	32.6	4 034	3 247	69	274	344
Paulding	32	10 147	100.0	332	2 552	9	225.6	61.8	53.5	3 080	1 809	35	126	518
Perry	38	8 268	100.0	294	1 978	10	231.1	131.6	65.9	3 842	2 858	36	100	797
Pickaway	72	31 678	D	1 069	9 192	13	426.6	157.5	68.7	2 947	2 023	31	90	570
Pike	51	21 151	90.4	643	5 560	5	178.1	311.2	–51.2	11 117	2 598	6 253	124	2 075
Portage	267	124 587	86.2	4 761	35 050	43	1 077.4	420.8	56.5	2 776	2 117	83	108	451
Preble	67	22 103	83.5	689	5 993	19	347.0	136.4	81.1	3 138	2 367	29	113	420
Putnam	54	D	D	(7)	D	20	526.6	86.2	73.1	2 449	1 567	89	115	305
Richland	272	140 136	90.7	4 613	38 648	42	1 371.3	491.1	52.9	3 789	2 749	97	330	560
Ross	119	61 264	89.3	2 225	16 796	20	595.2	337.2	54.4	4 453	2 622	81	768	856
Sandusky	110	50 001	86.8	1 699	12 876	27	652.5	201.7	44.0	3 263	2 505	41	100	465
Scioto	151	65 444	89.5	2 199	17 891	22	620.7	428.3	54.9	5 330	3 580	34	124	1 545
Seneca	128	33 905	92.2	1 325	9 720	23	785.4	233.7	55.8	3 910	3 021	30	124	507
Shelby	95	48 629	79.0	1 554	12 350	26	595.9	140.2	60.4	2 923	2 083	29	96	533
Stark	761	389 778	91.9	14 302	107 550	114	4 104.9	1 486.6	48.9	3 984	3 041	123	200	596
Summit	1 156	612 199	90.6	20 197	173 066	170	6 581.1	2 365.8	37.5	4 399	2 910	513	277	663
Trumbull	449	203 506	90.3	7 323	55 728	75	2 479.2	908.1	61.8	4 030	3 263	54	120	566
Tuscarawas	212	90 633	90.2	3 365	25 676	37	1 031.7	312.0	55.1	3 514	2 722	48	128	588
Union	57	23 073	D	766	6 781	12	306.4	93.9	4.5	2 302	1 545	35	92	383
Van Wert	58	21 949	94.7	878	5 558	9	353.9	92.3	61.8	3 068	2 129	50	116	354
Vinton	15	D	D	(8)	D	3	131.6	46.1	66.5	3 726	2 436	54	114	1 102
Warren	243	154 654	80.4	4 694	44 565	58	1 200.9	347.1	75.8	2 265	1 698	81	97	356
Washington	122	65 386	87.9	2 023	18 560	33	823.8	262.3	53.4	4 162	3 000	58	180	897
Wayne	178	78 957	93.8	3 206	23 904	49	1 325.0	321.7	59.8	2 897	2 223	44	125	443
Williams	84	30 283	83.5	1 197	9 135	24	608.0	132.5	68.2	3 510	2 596	46	122	460
Wood	270	134 399	82.0	4 905	36 992	51	1 336.1	347.0	70.0	2 885	2 011	53	114	550
Wyandot	57	16 277	D	656	4 490	14	376.6	86.5	72.9	3 774	2 612	90	135	452
OKLAHOMA	6 534	3 151 332	86.7	105 934	856 753	1 118	36 602.8	19 188.7	60.4	5 714	3 215	497	822	962
Adair	15	D	D	(6)	D	6	113.6	113.5	75.1	5 524	2 820	576	111	1 994
Alfalfa	6	D	D	(9)	D	7	95.3	47.5	66.6	8 072	3 822	111	383	1 379
Atoka	15	D	D	(6)	D	3	102.0	67.8	28.8	5 065	3 065	44	227	1 531
Beaver	8	D	D	(8)	D	4	84.3	38.4	42.9	6 389	2 467	64	239	1 426
Beckham	56	19 725	81.7	721	5 056	11	359.5	83.6	45.1	4 224	2 909	32	131	708
Blaine	24	5 034	93.9	236	1 494	8	162.8	71.7	84.5	6 975	3 601	71	323	1 849
Bryan	50	23 459	79.5	733	5 833	9	431.6	204.3	62.2	5 847	3 566	363	186	1 568
Caddo	48	8 045	85.2	277	1 985	17	315.5	180.6	54.4	5 890	3 437	76	557	1 175
Canadian	122	49 398	93.3	1 704	12 699	24	594.4	280.1	33.3	3 238	2 088	119	635	258
Carter	97	44 305	82.2	1 466	12 509	23	548.5	202.5	62.0	4 546	3 506	33	162	812
Cherokee	78	26 579	90.8	930	7 038	10	252.3	227.0	62.3	5 746	2 938	167	514	2 026
Choctaw	25	D	D	(6)	D	4	129.6	120.8	83.2	8 039	4 090	92	194	2 808
Cimarron	11	1 774	D	91	414	2	51.0	29.3	14.8	10 029	3 408	67	286	509
Cleveland	330	188 129	83.4	6 474	51 575	40	1 122.1	683.3	42.6	3 358	2 335	253	228	518
Coal	3	D	D	(9)	D	1	33.4	34.7	58.8	5 660	3 573	44	207	1 605
Comanche	203	96 899	90.6	3 660	28 929	26	698.6	1 153.6	38.9	10 820	3 511	1 335	5 271	610
Cotton	7	D	D	(8)	D	2	59.0	42.3	69.1	6 398	3 728	49	240	997
Craig	39	14 109	85.9	409	3 926	6	238.1	75.0	66.3	5 186	3 572	47	203	1 209
Creek	86	31 218	94.0	991	7 761	21	505.7	212.0	81.4	3 110	2 479	27	103	483
Custer	65	27 709	76.2	1 110	7 797	16	438.6	100.2	–57.9	3 919	2 324	50	315	668
Delaware	67	24 117	80.4	808	6 652	13	276.5	140.4	63.4	4 015	3 061	25	97	816
Dewey	5	D	D	(8)	D	6	123.2	32.4	49.2	6 676	3 966	88	347	485
Ellis	7	D	D	(8)	D	3	52.8	29.9	61.4	7 124	3 815	61	248	1 406
Garfield	123	51 876	89.7	1 896	14 659	24	753.5	369.1	52.0	6 481	3 430	1 210	1 032	463
Garvin	44	13 318	94.8	458	3 526	13	301.4	173.3	102.2	6 485	4 233	1 030	175	897
Grady	63	24 480	89.7	983	6 493	14	433.6	164.2	66.3	3 563	2 644	28	116	615
Grant	7	810	D	30	197	7	138.7	50.1	90.4	9 562	3 965	199	345	755
Greer	8	1 356	D	55	416	6	73.3	44.2	45.2	6 922	4 413	49	211	1 079
Harmon	3	D	D	(9)	D	1	32.2	27.4	39.7	8 218	4 308	55	277	1 305
Harper	8	749	D	34	180	2	58.0	24.6	36.1	6 883	3 780	68	296	386

[1] Includes only establishments with payroll. [2] Includes full-service restaurants, limited-service eating places, special food services, and drinking places (alcoholic beverages). [3] For pay period including March 12. [4] As of June 30. Covers all FDIC-insured commercial banks and savings institutions. [5] Based on resident population estimated as of July 1, 1999. [6] 100 to 249 employees. [7] 500 to 999 employees. [8] 20 to 99 employees. [9] 0 to 19 employees.

Sources: Accommodation and Foodservices—U.S. Census Bureau, 1997 Economic Census, ECON97 Report Series CD-ROM, CD-EC97-1, Disc 1E, issued February 2001 (related Internet site <http://www.census.gov/epcd/www/97EC72.HTM>). Banking—U.S. Federal Deposit Insurance Corporation and Office of Thrift Supervision, "1999 Bank and Thrift Branch Office Data Book: Summary of Deposits," national and 6 regional data books (related Internet site <http://www2.fdic.gov/sod/>). Federal Funds and Grants—U.S. Census Bureau, County Aggregate files for each state, <http://www.census.gov/govs/www/cffr99.html>, (accessed: August 2000).

Table B–12. Counties — Accommodation and Foodservices, Banking, and Federal Funds–Con.

[Includes U.S., states, and 3,142 counties/county equivalents defined as of January 1, 1992. For changes to these areas since January 1, 1992, see appendix B. Geographic Information]

County	Accommodation and foodservices[1] (NAICS 72), 1997 — Sales — Establishments	Total ($1,000)	Percent from food-services[2]	Paid employ-ees[3]	Annual payroll ($1,000)	Banking,[4] 1999 — Offices	Deposits (mil. dol.)	Federal funds and grants, 1999 — Total expenditures or obligations (mil. dol.)	Percent change, 1990–1999	Per capita[5] (dollars) — Total	Direct payments for individuals	Procure-ment contract awards	Salaries and wages	Grant awards
OKLAHOMA—Con.														
Haskell	16	D	D	(6)	D	3	73.0	70.7	76.6	6 192	4 148	56	246	1 546
Hughes	21	D	D	(6)	D	4	110.8	84.9	56.9	6 035	4 043	39	315	1 417
Jackson	56	24 232	88.8	841	6 259	13	310.9	291.5	51.3	10 265	3 639	1 095	3 818	1 078
Jefferson	13	D	D	(6)	D	5	93.9	45.3	64.3	6 945	4 396	70	262	1 523
Johnston	12	2 830	100.0	142	938	3	62.8	59.2	73.0	5 739	3 375	427	245	1 527
Kay	102	40 344	91.0	1 446	10 758	25	585.9	276.6	100.5	5 955	3 408	1 421	202	523
Kingfisher	27	D	D	(6)	D	11	256.0	65.5	17.1	4 856	2 981	347	227	394
Kiowa	15	D	D	(7)	D	8	156.6	82.6	52.2	7 871	4 381	60	280	1 611
Latimer	14	2 847	D	107	835	5	85.8	49.0	69.6	4 798	3 480	40	117	1 110
Le Flore	55	18 200	86.6	616	4 689	12	336.7	254.0	70.7	5 431	3 523	80	195	1 527
Lincoln	46	12 373	D	570	3 314	14	299.8	118.7	73.7	3 732	2 882	31	155	594
Logan	43	D	D	(8)	D	10	197.5	122.4	60.7	4 021	2 619	395	127	714
Love	17	5 272	82.4	157	1 298	4	59.6	38.2	79.0	4 455	3 183	28	110	926
McClain	38	D	D	(8)	D	11	257.5	97.5	106.5	3 649	2 662	31	124	711
McCurtain	51	14 948	77.8	537	3 745	12	299.2	200.1	78.4	5 752	3 468	43	180	1 921
McIntosh	46	12 589	68.7	439	3 406	8	229.3	113.7	66.5	5 901	4 471	46	116	1 203
Major	16	D	D	(6)	D	5	108.5	37.9	44.7	4 945	3 024	59	228	496
Marshall	27	7 339	82.8	222	1 805	5	122.0	63.6	57.0	5 136	4 183	22	106	735
Mayes	72	19 654	96.5	755	5 006	12	339.2	147.3	78.6	3 848	2 868	25	96	833
Murray	24	8 414	85.6	266	2 304	7	132.1	64.8	55.1	5 193	3 695	30	278	1 097
Muskogee	135	58 820	89.3	2 097	15 174	20	658.8	407.0	51.4	5 807	3 650	108	832	1 161
Noble	20	7 234	81.7	316	2 028	4	205.1	55.2	60.5	4 871	2 886	92	211	909
Nowata	12	3 081	D	139	868	5	111.8	47.5	62.7	4 710	3 488	214	159	754
Okfuskee	12	2 893	D	96	741	5	77.8	89.3	124.2	7 944	3 975	1 713	167	1 962
Oklahoma	1 493	918 611	85.8	29 780	255 930	198	8 669.3	5 233.2	70.5	8 221	3 199	1 462	2 015	1 527
Okmulgee	59	20 718	89.5	664	5 506	11	294.5	212.5	42.7	5 478	3 584	42	164	1 622
Osage	42	9 490	94.8	389	2 463	13	212.3	136.3	49.7	5 173	1 888	54	651	511
Ottawa	59	18 104	88.9	676	5 127	14	278.4	198.1	77.6	6 415	4 331	742	212	976
Pawnee	28	5 667	82.8	199	1 350	7	113.7	73.1	65.7	4 419	3 088	61	278	881
Payne	149	66 534	89.6	2 867	18 304	16	825.0	290.0	58.6	4 433	2 457	337	302	1 288
Pittsburg	75	37 284	78.5	1 275	10 233	13	615.6	272.8	52.3	6 276	3 818	409	986	981
Pontotoc	59	29 283	91.6	1 151	8 158	15	461.4	196.8	50.7	5 674	3 624	166	387	1 408
Pottawatomie	135	76 262	94.2	2 726	21 078	17	555.9	281.4	61.1	4 491	3 329	52	157	900
Pushmataha	17	3 280	66.8	96	837	4	82.3	76.2	79.7	6 604	4 102	42	149	2 145
Roger Mills	9	1 319	31.6	57	314	2	71.7	23.0	55.8	6 389	3 268	100	462	967
Rogers	89	38 004	91.9	1 324	10 009	14	490.9	202.6	111.6	2 872	2 000	34	299	510
Seminole	33	11 726	D	413	2 925	10	214.3	151.7	73.7	6 182	3 922	54	244	1 882
Sequoyah	74	24 025	80.8	900	6 285	9	258.7	178.7	94.4	4 718	3 103	67	202	1 322
Stephens	85	30 873	78.7	1 159	8 349	19	566.8	212.8	68.4	4 940	3 679	156	129	885
Texas	55	16 744	80.3	617	4 380	7	272.4	96.0	72.1	5 236	2 283	107	176	709
Tillman	14	D	D	(6)	D	6	111.1	71.5	42.7	7 589	3 803	150	213	1 324
Tulsa	1 316	771 286	85.7	23 663	207 654	155	7 357.2	2 158.7	55.6	3 937	2 806	224	379	503
Wagoner	60	23 080	96.1	786	5 136	9	197.8	126.6	65.9	2 255	1 724	12	63	401
Washington	92	51 637	91.2	1 595	13 997	13	517.9	190.8	53.6	4 003	3 511	33	38	398
Washita	9	892	D	37	143	10	155.3	70.8	74.8	6 056	3 513	524	195	496
Woods	23	6 328	89.3	317	1 808	6	218.3	55.4	52.1	6 782	4 110	251	254	659
Woodward	46	18 314	86.8	613	4 621	10	312.0	72.7	54.1	3 910	2 768	108	274	384
OREGON	8 371	4 388 304	77.3	124 506	1 237 426	953	28 345.5	15 592.3	58.2	4 702	2 866	231	454	1 061
Baker	62	19 049	D	540	4 740	7	167.9	103.7	63.6	6 378	3 564	186	748	1 772
Benton	206	85 974	84.3	2 815	24 026	18	509.2	308.9	56.1	4 002	2 102	169	434	1 283
Clackamas	571	331 094	84.1	10 002	94 577	84	2 021.5	985.6	51.5	2 914	2 117	109	267	413
Clatsop	201	89 736	65.4	2 260	25 618	13	294.8	171.1	29.3	4 845	3 191	399	549	696
Columbia	75	24 279	88.1	782	7 198	10	197.8	137.4	73.2	3 028	2 347	127	101	450
Coos	186	61 364	76.0	2 004	16 959	23	555.1	345.7	76.0	5 606	3 841	297	415	1 037
Crook	34	12 689	81.8	383	3 358	5	108.6	81.1	90.6	4 587	3 064	208	747	529
Curry	112	30 482	57.3	785	8 098	8	201.0	128.9	65.9	6 087	5 040	137	283	622
Deschutes	306	194 578	58.7	4 730	55 720	42	1 009.0	378.3	77.1	3 414	2 634	82	305	386
Douglas	274	138 119	56.7	3 635	37 918	29	687.9	504.3	63.0	4 954	3 511	140	618	675
Gilliam	8	1 691	D	67	438	3	17.9	19.8	29.9	9 555	3 019	34	159	2 268
Grant	32	5 752	65.1	179	1 409	4	62.4	46.6	54.4	5 929	3 308	330	1 395	880
Harney	25	5 186	86.6	170	1 457	3	70.5	43.0	53.7	5 895	2 991	222	1 160	1 307
Hood River	76	36 150	58.6	1 107	10 816	6	161.6	71.7	-19.4	3 599	2 258	297	299	729
Jackson	474	205 345	78.9	6 253	60 307	63	1 515.0	763.4	70.1	4 342	3 095	127	445	657
Jefferson	31	11 886	D	371	3 236	4	84.3	77.4	99.3	4 593	2 818	58	389	1 133
Josephine	168	66 897	81.4	1 928	17 960	22	717.2	378.0	45.6	5 046	3 884	84	197	872
Klamath	156	73 109	59.9	1 899	17 185	15	675.2	304.4	69.6	4 798	3 184	173	679	711
Lake	26	6 091	82.0	196	1 507	3	51.6	54.1	85.1	7 547	3 695	1 371	1 481	886
Lane	810	388 432	81.9	12 040	110 684	82	2 350.9	1 306.4	72.0	4 149	2 758	109	306	961
Lincoln	275	134 856	53.4	3 647	37 857	21	484.9	228.0	60.6	5 067	3 807	250	297	679

[1] Includes only establishments with payroll. [2] Includes full-service restaurants, limited-service eating places, special food services, and drinking places (alcoholic beverages). [3] For pay period including March 12. [4] As of June 30. Covers all FDIC-insured commercial banks and savings institutions. [5] Based on resident population estimated as of July 1, 1999. [6] 100 to 249 employees. [7] 20 to 99 employees. [8] 500 to 999 employees.

Sources: Accommodation and Foodservices—U.S. Census Bureau, 1997 Economic Census, ECON97 Report Series CD-ROM, CD-EC97-1, Disc 1E, issued February 2001 (related Internet site <http://www.census.gov/epcd/www/97EC72.HTM>). Banking—U.S. Federal Deposit Insurance Corporation and Office of Thrift Supervision, "1999 Bank and Thrift Branch Office Data Book: Summary of Deposits," national and 6 regional data books (related Internet site <http://www2.fdic.gov/sod/>). Federal Funds and Grants—U.S. Census Bureau, County Aggregate files for each state, <http://www.census.gov/govs/www/cffr99.html>, (accessed: August 2000).

[Includes U.S., states, and 3,142 counties/county equivalents defined as of January 1, 1992. For changes to these areas since January 1, 1992, see appendix B. Geographic Information]

County	Accommodation and foodservices[1] (NAICS 72), 1997 — Establishments	Sales Total ($1,000)	Percent from foodservices[2]	Paid employees[3]	Annual payroll ($1,000)	Banking,[4] 1999 Offices	Deposits (mil. dol.)	Federal funds and grants, 1999 Total expenditures or obligations (mil. dol.)	Percent change, 1990–1999	Per capita[5] (dollars) Total	Direct payments for individuals	Procurement contract awards	Salaries and wages	Grant awards
OREGON—Con.														
Linn	183	73 130	90.2	2 400	20 324	29	660.4	408.6	63.9	3 879	2 771	78	199	816
Malheur	73	33 304	78.8	947	9 082	12	509.4	121.2	66.1	4 263	2 668	64	309	926
Marion	529	281 581	90.3	8 872	78 133	80	2 175.8	1 543.9	46.5	5 660	2 871	79	294	2 403
Morrow	18	4 204	66.1	123	906	6	57.2	55.7	89.8	5 299	2 270	312	227	1 103
Multnomah	1 939	1 315 906	77.1	33 972	373 886	160	7 910.3	3 783.4	55.4	5 975	2 857	585	1 026	1 471
Polk	77	30 682	94.8	997	7 813	11	295.9	280.2	64.9	4 490	1 805	31	107	2 397
Sherman	9	D	D	(6)	D	1	7.7	31.2	96.1	17 444	4 079	1 560	1 929	3 374
Tillamook	128	35 486	62.9	1 086	10 080	8	203.4	125.4	69.8	5 135	3 781	99	272	865
Umatilla	160	66 675	77.2	1 961	17 285	25	507.8	369.7	98.3	5 534	2 675	914	508	981
Union	77	23 557	80.4	773	6 274	9	209.4	112.4	57.0	4 532	3 068	69	371	768
Wallowa	47	5 815	61.0	198	1 433	5	101.3	49.0	65.8	6 748	3 498	300	606	1 894
Wasco	73	34 340	64.1	925	11 813	9	238.7	134.1	82.8	5 745	3 149	511	627	1 142
Washington	798	495 779	83.8	14 299	140 625	104	2 928.7	833.8	63.1	2 037	1 497	101	105	324
Wheeler	6	D	D	(7)	D	1	9.9	7.2	51.6	4 643	4 041	37	235	135
Yamhill	146	58 314	94.5	1 997	16 960	28	585.5	273.5	54.4	3 278	2 312	96	375	440
PENNSYLVANIA	24 465	12 227 177	80.9	365 158	3 364 117	4 509	175 347.4	69 448.0	52.3	5 790	3 640	495	452	1 096
Adams	190	89 338	68.5	2 789	25 537	34	883.5	306.8	79.1	3 499	2 560	138	243	521
Allegheny	2 912	1 711 395	82.2	52 581	477 501	489	32 406.7	9 270.3	53.1	7 376	4 154	1 314	635	1 224
Armstrong	135	32 806	91.2	1 133	8 237	33	1 005.7	386.5	69.2	5 295	4 033	55	171	1 015
Beaver	307	108 332	94.9	3 796	28 143	65	1 851.5	834.5	52.9	4 568	3 736	79	113	617
Bedford	108	49 502	75.1	1 674	14 387	24	531.6	215.3	76.5	4 332	3 164	184	146	792
Berks	706	330 380	87.7	10 091	90 949	129	4 632.6	1 343.0	59.5	3 749	2 876	168	179	503
Blair	254	108 842	91.4	4 003	29 614	59	1 461.7	673.8	52.7	5 186	3 649	105	349	1 057
Bradford	117	35 298	82.7	1 185	9 714	33	680.5	286.8	73.3	4 615	2 955	365	185	1 064
Bucks	1 047	569 330	88.0	15 741	147 782	210	7 394.5	1 943.0	58.4	3 271	2 581	251	131	300
Butler	317	156 605	80.3	5 439	42 754	67	1 941.9	772.3	94.3	4 476	3 017	536	346	565
Cambria	314	111 354	87.8	4 143	30 627	82	2 107.0	992.0	59.9	6 451	4 185	814	486	924
Cameron	14	2 578	D	106	699	2	61.0	37.0	87.5	6 635	4 402	51	181	1 991
Carbon	97	41 767	78.2	1 200	11 325	25	735.9	268.3	43.6	4 566	3 835	58	115	544
Centre	287	154 826	73.7	5 241	41 236	62	1 389.4	678.4	76.2	5 132	2 192	555	219	2 148
Chester	642	365 448	88.9	10 790	102 672	175	5 147.0	1 500.0	68.3	3 488	2 236	476	378	380
Clarion	108	38 697	81.4	1 331	9 918	21	525.4	187.8	63.8	4 509	3 399	63	145	847
Clearfield	153	56 099	82.5	1 840	14 469	36	967.9	365.8	60.2	4 531	3 462	71	189	789
Clinton	79	28 563	87.7	932	6 872	12	257.9	171.0	60.2	4 650	3 334	404	222	652
Columbia	154	59 282	87.1	2 218	15 881	33	784.7	257.6	-60.3	4 046	3 123	200	140	538
Crawford	180	67 340	82.3	2 357	18 969	30	865.1	382.6	65.4	4 293	3 263	72	144	771
Cumberland	415	235 235	82.3	7 623	65 573	94	2 786.4	1 187.1	37.5	5 635	3 278	284	1 694	359
Dauphin	611	394 373	64.2	10 456	107 288	97	3 170.6	3 331.4	80.8	13 566	3 930	574	702	8 273
Delaware	1 025	514 134	85.2	13 991	134 089	157	6 514.6	2 495.7	53.0	4 609	3 478	336	239	531
Elk	82	18 462	86.3	617	4 437	18	497.3	140.9	54.6	4 104	3 355	46	162	522
Erie	614	265 234	85.9	9 599	73 349	89	2 722.6	1 194.3	54.3	4 312	2 994	150	289	845
Fayette	278	157 328	54.0	4 886	47 676	43	1 646.5	913.4	58.5	6 353	4 623	59	179	1 457
Forest	20	4 871	54.8	142	1 158	2	29.7	32.4	78.3	6 564	5 026	214	436	872
Franklin	217	105 819	87.2	3 274	28 139	57	1 409.9	614.8	29.9	4 773	3 205	417	615	501
Fulton	24	10 047	93.8	278	2 666	8	185.5	57.9	83.5	3 963	2 823	149	109	804
Greene	56	19 369	90.4	620	4 724	12	447.6	200.0	43.7	4 753	3 673	-348	193	1 223
Huntingdon	84	22 940	75.1	778	6 279	24	398.0	190.5	73.4	4 257	3 011	65	146	977
Indiana	167	64 845	91.4	2 707	17 478	36	1 207.4	415.7	64.4	4 732	3 399	72	176	1 054
Jefferson	89	23 871	79.7	928	6 350	18	642.6	217.8	46.7	4 727	3 678	38	168	816
Juniata	33	8 499	90.8	312	2 013	11	289.7	75.8	60.4	3 415	2 661	39	166	487
Lackawanna	520	219 292	85.8	7 421	59 388	88	3 180.7	1 235.6	47.0	5 983	4 223	660	286	784
Lancaster	877	506 427	76.9	15 724	145 587	185	5 311.6	1 510.9	68.7	3 284	2 480	193	196	398
Lawrence	196	67 333	93.2	2 488	17 238	33	1 316.1	524.0	55.1	5 544	4 261	196	269	767
Lebanon	209	76 007	89.9	2 687	22 296	43	1 207.5	539.9	18.4	4 581	3 147	137	815	464
Lehigh	648	412 687	86.4	11 892	114 678	108	3 688.5	1 207.7	59.9	4 028	2 798	364	243	600
Luzerne	694	292 707	83.8	9 780	79 830	129	4 322.8	1 830.4	38.5	5 867	4 309	237	489	805
Lycoming	283	106 140	85.2	3 571	28 520	46	1 150.2	525.9	37.9	4 506	3 199	190	310	773
McKean	118	29 963	83.1	1 057	7 779	20	522.3	230.0	53.1	5 002	3 435	99	595	853
Mercer	270	113 272	91.7	3 953	32 577	48	1 546.1	586.7	67.4	4 830	3 883	36	141	730
Mifflin	83	26 006	93.5	989	6 975	21	510.3	206.6	68.3	4 416	3 163	48	139	1 031
Monroe	345	241 754	44.5	6 179	67 691	50	1 269.9	546.2	53.5	4 249	2 779	440	747	272
Montgomery	1 504	915 384	82.2	23 896	253 994	338	12 336.3	3 241.4	40.7	4 477	3 176	586	332	372
Montour	39	15 802	72.8	586	4 526	7	192.9	79.1	21.4	4 504	3 358	40	119	935
Northampton	513	195 017	91.4	5 497	50 008	111	3 522.5	1 159.9	75.3	4 466	3 424	108	288	608
Northumberland	180	43 673	93.7	1 641	11 712	35	1 029.5	439.6	44.5	4 718	3 776	49	135	709
Perry	61	14 811	85.5	467	3 382	18	417.6	159.6	92.8	3 603	2 640	57	112	745
Philadelphia	2 989	1 691 565	75.2	38 521	461 137	316	27 327.0	12 566.5	38.8	8 865	4 231	868	1 182	2 482
Pike	91	48 968	40.1	1 221	15 224	15	287.0	119.0	105.7	2 878	2 479	31	237	127
Potter	49	9 089	67.7	270	1 842	8	178.7	79.0	67.9	4 613	3 206	54	166	1 141

[1] Includes only establishments with payroll.   [2] Includes full-service restaurants, limited-service eating places, special food services, and drinking places (alcoholic beverages).   [3] For pay period including March 12.   [4] As of June 30. Covers all FDIC-insured commercial banks and savings institutions.   [5] Based on resident population estimated as of July 1, 1999.   [6] 100 to 249 employees.   [7] 0 to 19 employees.

Sources: Accommodation and Foodservices—U.S. Census Bureau, 1997 Economic Census, ECON97 Report Series CD-ROM, CD-EC97-1, Disc 1E, issued February 2001 (related Internet site <http://www.census.gov/epcd/www/97EC72.HTM>).   Banking—U.S. Federal Deposit Insurance Corporation and Office of Thrift Supervision, "1999 Bank and Thrift Branch Office Data Book: Summary of Deposits," national and 6 regional data books (related Internet site <http://www2.fdic.gov/sod/>).   Federal Funds and Grants—U.S. Census Bureau, County Aggregate files for each state, <http://www.census.gov/govs/www/cffr99.html>, (accessed: August 2000).

[Includes U.S., states, and 3,142 counties/county equivalents defined as of January 1, 1992. For changes to these areas since January 1, 1992, see appendix B. Geographic Information]

County	Accommodation and foodservices[1] (NAICS 72), 1997					Banking,[4] 1999		Federal funds and grants, 1999						
	Sales									Per capita[5] (dollars)				
												By selected type—		
	Establishments	Total ($1,000)	Percent from foodservices[2]	Paid employees[3]	Annual payroll ($1,000)	Offices	Deposits (mil. dol.)	Total expenditures or obligations (mil. dol.)	Percent change, 1990–1999	Total	Direct payments for individuals	Procurement contract awards	Salaries and wages	Grant awards
PENNSYLVANIA—Con.														
Schuylkill	297	85 184	92.1	2 931	22 802	77	1 819.1	751.9	44.8	5 053	4 068	101	275	580
Snyder	78	36 896	88.6	1 218	10 288	18	448.0	119.5	63.3	3 154	2 558	30	118	411
Somerset	168	54 356	81.7	1 902	15 383	34	927.6	374.1	64.5	4 674	3 551	101	148	840
Sullivan	24	3 923	D	105	928	4	84.5	31.6	59.6	5 233	3 979	119	251	835
Susquehanna	79	22 154	88.6	693	5 341	18	434.3	159.6	55.6	3 783	2 955	48	168	583
Tioga	89	31 833	75.7	1 091	7 926	16	414.7	213.8	95.6	5 131	3 070	50	211	1 756
Union	90	46 318	83.1	1 501	12 148	16	443.4	229.7	143.3	5 665	2 390	279	2 103	851
Venango	99	31 465	92.8	1 143	9 239	20	560.6	273.6	55.8	4 753	3 599	44	133	955
Warren	112	27 890	83.8	984	6 704	16	486.8	180.2	50.0	4 143	3 246	132	216	530
Washington	351	133 031	90.5	4 812	38 765	64	2 550.2	1 063.0	55.3	5 188	4 025	65	160	922
Wayne	172	106 736	29.7	2 459	32 217	25	796.8	336.6	180.9	7 305	4 027	2 571	159	534
Westmoreland	710	320 914	90.2	12 235	93 453	141	4 635.3	1 747.4	61.3	4 714	3 797	63	162	676
Wyoming	56	19 037	96.5	722	4 941	15	268.7	100.7	53.0	3 437	2 752	36	134	491
York	635	318 734	88.5	10 721	91 093	139	4 580.2	1 742.3	96.0	4 627	2 500	1 425	269	411
RHODE ISLAND	2 617	1 220 865	85.0	34 162	340 552	217	12 771.8	6 036.1	39.2	6 092	3 439	425	729	1 424
Bristol	104	38 932	D	1 386	10 727	14	521.0	194.4	53.3	3 958	3 159	56	168	567
Kent	409	221 358	86.0	6 904	61 540	33	1 913.3	715.6	54.7	4 414	3 405	75	259	669
Newport	328	207 082	64.4	4 643	59 835	19	800.9	1 013.0	-.7	12 201	3 423	3 560	4 487	678
Providence	1 338	581 361	92.8	17 307	162 595	121	8 136.1	3 308.6	52.9	5 763	3 251	158	441	1 874
Washington	438	172 132	D	3 922	45 855	30	1 400.4	482.6	43.1	3 941	2 676	162	382	709
SOUTH CAROLINA	7 775	4 835 839	75.0	150 621	1 313 837	1 214	35 959.9	20 833.2	50.6	5 361	3 008	654	628	998
Abbeville	26	8 279	85.9	368	2 470	9	195.4	92.7	81.0	3 757	2 601	22	106	1 005
Aiken	212	99 420	91.6	3 618	26 343	38	1 026.5	1 969.8	-7.5	14 548	2 892	10 543	398	691
Allendale	6	1 718	D	50	387	7	69.5	60.5	74.4	5 343	2 876	33	118	2 008
Anderson	283	144 565	92.1	4 919	37 134	58	1 612.8	570.4	70.5	3 504	2 757	37	136	558
Bamberg	24	6 492	95.8	310	1 741	7	144.1	93.1	75.1	5 716	3 100	351	139	1 932
Barnwell	33	10 647	D	327	2 644	10	204.4	118.6	96.8	5 445	3 294	323	114	1 469
Beaufort	353	337 616	56.6	7 838	93 239	48	1 529.5	765.3	86.8	6 774	3 277	829	2 209	453
Berkeley	135	63 792	88.7	2 304	17 414	14	303.9	404.4	83.5	2 842	2 068	74	150	534
Calhoun	7	D	D	(6)	D	3	66.3	52.7	67.6	3 704	2 107	21	111	1 125
Charleston	847	710 650	64.2	19 759	197 975	105	3 160.5	2 677.1	7.9	8 368	3 284	1 637	2 385	1 037
Cherokee	85	40 587	86.8	1 771	10 823	13	417.9	174.8	106.2	3 492	2 487	24	96	867
Chester	46	19 190	90.9	660	5 046	7	186.0	130.4	75.3	3 733	2 790	27	97	793
Chesterfield	65	23 300	91.5	882	6 371	13	300.1	178.1	85.7	4 289	2 624	35	114	1 470
Clarendon	50	16 158	D	617	4 328	6	176.4	159.1	95.5	5 148	3 049	24	108	1 737
Colleton	57	26 234	67.9	856	7 561	11	283.0	185.5	97.9	4 926	3 370	211	142	1 143
Darlington	91	31 378	92.4	964	8 282	20	410.3	259.1	82.1	3 896	2 629	29	98	1 046
Dillon	54	25 995	70.5	929	7 108	10	221.4	147.1	105.3	4 949	3 047	22	130	1 535
Dorchester	115	61 758	82.6	2 188	17 424	26	526.5	342.4	100.5	3 780	3 036	43	108	566
Edgefield	23	6 012	95.8	289	1 695	8	122.3	91.3	113.3	4 566	2 265	121	1 195	943
Fairfield	21	7 799	89.0	297	1 803	7	137.0	96.2	83.7	4 262	2 885	46	116	1 192
Florence	245	147 063	70.1	4 857	40 469	45	1 185.2	564.7	96.5	4 509	2 844	88	293	1 200
Georgetown	151	86 946	90.9	2 804	25 794	18	512.5	290.6	59.7	5 289	4 058	229	112	863
Greenville	818	506 621	83.2	17 006	141 758	139	5 361.0	1 346.1	90.8	3 750	2 566	329	265	574
Greenwood	122	64 489	93.1	2 320	17 456	26	659.8	250.4	71.3	3 930	2 957	31	166	768
Hampton	30	10 421	76.9	393	2 876	9	204.7	121.0	113.3	6 332	3 460	169	1 038	1 478
Horry	1 044	881 722	57.6	20 246	228 524	89	2 682.7	729.8	38.7	4 087	3 060	97	131	739
Jasper	35	21 747	D	769	5 820	4	155.1	70.3	28.8	4 080	2 512	24	108	1 411
Kershaw	80	31 024	82.8	1 197	7 991	14	390.2	193.8	84.8	3 932	3 059	26	126	702
Lancaster	76	33 202	95.4	1 112	8 160	8	271.9	200.4	85.5	3 364	2 592	53	94	614
Laurens	68	31 320	89.8	1 218	8 568	16	457.8	215.1	80.7	3 394	2 630	20	97	608
Lee	14	D	D	(7)	D	4	91.9	87.6	79.8	4 311	2 501	34	99	1 355
Lexington	338	203 297	87.4	7 502	55 385	47	1 307.9	612.1	110.6	2 929	2 214	54	141	500
McCormick	8	2 217	D	127	601	3	50.3	52.5	104.6	5 463	3 431	431	381	1 306
Marion	45	14 241	89.2	610	3 613	12	247.2	218.9	40.2	6 350	3 274	1 255	143	1 547
Marlboro	36	10 524	88.9	403	2 592	8	156.7	154.8	56.6	5 250	3 016	26	145	1 876
Newberry	43	16 709	91.4	697	4 249	14	397.2	155.2	77.8	4 514	3 187	43	215	1 016
Oconee	101	42 156	94.2	1 845	10 999	19	671.1	244.4	99.0	3 756	3 071	33	126	504
Orangeburg	149	72 094	73.6	2 583	18 634	24	694.3	438.7	88.3	5 013	3 175	38	135	1 541
Pickens	193	97 900	89.4	3 985	27 260	30	861.6	364.3	94.3	3 369	2 402	62	130	770
Richland	695	418 633	81.4	13 674	117 031	100	3 934.1	2 621.1	41.9	8 530	3 137	456	2 276	2 625
Saluda	18	D	D	(7)	D	5	129.7	59.6	73.8	3 509	2 311	133	154	829
Spartanburg	465	244 223	91.7	9 520	68 714	78	2 250.5	865.2	75.2	3 466	2 600	60	120	663
Sumter	133	70 008	89.1	2 311	19 075	19	624.9	673.0	53.5	5 987	2 823	295	1 741	1 074
Union	36	13 524	93.3	646	3 580	9	258.5	122.5	74.1	4 034	3 120	29	156	713
Williamsburg	35	10 055	D	334	3 089	12	213.2	173.8	89.7	4 717	2 708	28	123	1 629
York	264	152 857	83.3	5 073	39 049	42	1 096.2	458.7	97.6	2 900	2 247	44	118	476

[1] Includes only establishments with payroll. [2] Includes full-service restaurants, limited-service eating places, special food services, and drinking places (alcoholic beverages). [3] For pay period including March 12. [4] As of June 30. Covers all FDIC-insured commercial banks and savings institutions. [5] Based on resident population estimated as of July 1, 1999. [6] 20 to 99 employees. [7] 100 to 249 employees.

Sources: Accommodation and Foodservices—U.S. Census Bureau, 1997 Economic Census, ECON97 Report Series CD-ROM, CD-EC97-1, Disc 1E, issued February 2001 (related Internet site <http://www.census.gov/epcd/www/97EC72.HTM>). Banking—U.S. Federal Deposit Insurance Corporation and Office of Thrift Supervision, "1999 Bank and Thrift Branch Office Data Book: Summary of Deposits," national and 6 regional data books (related Internet site <http://www2.fdic.gov/sod/>). Federal Funds and Grants—U.S. Census Bureau, County Aggregate files for each state, <http://www.census.gov/govs/www/cffr99.html>, (accessed: August 2000).

[Includes U.S., states, and 3,142 counties/county equivalents defined as of January 1, 1992. For changes to these areas since January 1, 1992, see appendix B. Geographic Information]

| County | Accommodation and foodservices[1] (NAICS 72), 1997 | | | | | Banking,[4] 1999 | | Federal funds and grants, 1999 | | | | | | |
	Estab-lishments	Sales Total ($1,000)	Sales Percent from food-services[2]	Paid employ-ees[3]	Annual payroll ($1,000)	Offices	Deposits (mil. dol.)	Total expenditures or obligations (mil. dol.)	Percent change, 1990–1999	Per capita[5] (dollars) Total	Direct payments for individuals	Procure-ment contract awards	Salaries and wages	Grant awards
SOUTH DAKOTA	2 259	888 148	69.6	30 136	234 413	417	12 271.1	4 909.0	71.6	6 696	2 942	714	762	1 440
Aurora	15	1 337	D	49	288	3	67.3	19.0	60.1	6 328	3 034	52	242	882
Beadle	66	17 155	74.2	671	4 787	8	248.0	123.3	78.5	7 414	3 574	147	1 188	1 399
Bennett	6	1 325	D	47	211	1	21.2	247.7	1 937.9	74 802	2 555	68 648	273	1 799
Bon Homme	22	D	D	(6)	D	5	82.9	37.7	63.7	5 253	3 229	51	199	568
Brookings	62	26 869	82.7	1 236	7 167	12	529.2	100.5	37.5	3 875	2 167	56	259	846
Brown	105	47 368	76.8	1 616	13 292	19	594.7	210.6	59.5	5 977	3 269	108	752	980
Brule	30	10 169	D	276	2 774	5	114.1	35.5	78.3	6 449	2 972	178	339	1 776
Buffalo	–	–	–	–	–	–	–	21.4	86.6	12 046	1 845	1 143	2 783	5 252
Butte	23	D	D	(6)	D	4	124.6	37.1	22.9	4 229	3 007	50	233	634
Campbell	8	735	D	20	103	2	30.8	18.5	83.9	10 034	4 482	77	309	1 548
Charles Mix	27	38 757	D	592	6 768	6	161.0	72.3	74.1	7 861	3 046	247	838	2 127
Clark	11	1 376	D	56	274	5	66.0	33.9	75.4	7 900	3 141	353	283	764
Clay	46	15 491	86.8	812	3 817	7	112.4	57.6	63.2	4 394	2 152	43	218	1 283
Codington	78	33 096	79.0	1 185	9 102	13	369.3	101.7	48.8	4 010	2 425	260	399	535
Corson	3	235	100.0	5	29	3	24.7	37.5	77.1	9 129	3 552	475	922	2 581
Custer	46	14 797	45.2	243	3 873	2	37.7	45.4	94.8	6 460	3 524	255	941	1 659
Davison	79	33 237	71.7	1 190	9 401	10	272.2	91.9	46.8	5 146	3 123	668	304	676
Day	20	2 713	88.2	125	744	7	89.4	54.8	59.5	8 874	3 805	187	452	1 658
Deuel	12	1 628	D	65	319	4	63.5	30.3	52.6	6 801	3 005	194	329	641
Dewey	7	1 666	D	64	464	3	32.1	53.1	31.6	8 840	2 137	766	2 090	2 841
Douglas	9	577	D	28	85	3	43.8	23.0	90.4	6 567	3 140	154	346	1 107
Edmunds	10	1 390	100.0	61	267	4	75.4	27.8	62.8	6 637	3 239	100	206	485
Fall River	35	12 383	79.9	278	1 748	4	68.1	73.3	56.3	10 749	5 575	941	2 861	1 131
Faulk	6	542	D	14	124	2	28.2	20.3	57.5	8 116	3 851	174	332	466
Grant	22	5 715	76.8	221	1 534	5	112.8	40.8	45.4	5 132	2 986	60	276	567
Gregory	19	2 303	85.5	91	516	4	104.2	33.3	21.9	6 784	3 787	686	360	1 192
Haakon	9	1 270	D	44	269	2	80.8	16.5	13.5	7 127	2 745	37	311	185
Hamlin	13	D	D	(7)	D	7	76.1	29.7	76.3	5 489	2 693	65	242	437
Hand	9	1 237	D	46	221	2	85.8	38.1	108.9	9 208	2 674	31	180	3 613
Hanson	4	536	100.0	25	114	3	45.7	13.8	45.5	4 574	2 082	57	201	285
Harding	7	1 004	D	77	201	1	16.4	9.6	49.9	6 617	2 238	117	608	389
Hughes	55	25 695	58.7	894	7 680	10	289.2	238.7	63.9	15 445	2 999	378	709	10 816
Hutchinson	16	D	D	(7)	D	8	244.7	50.2	70.6	6 224	3 426	58	273	793
Hyde	4	D	D	(7)	D	2	27.7	11.9	44.7	7 502	3 165	39	129	1 339
Jackson	17	3 794	61.2	66	765	1	14.3	16.1	45.9	5 444	1 988	495	827	911
Jerauld	7	814	D	38	182	2	38.2	15.2	61.7	7 124	4 165	73	303	449
Jones	12	2 421	D	41	734	3	29.8	10.5	44.4	8 753	2 778	132	275	1 503
Kingsbury	22	3 336	80.8	98	530	7	113.7	41.4	60.3	7 216	3 935	85	357	491
Lake	34	8 127	D	353	2 226	8	171.0	53.8	56.2	5 032	3 091	105	260	655
Lawrence	111	59 240	34.1	1 728	15 736	10	234.9	87.4	70.9	4 089	2 912	113	367	686
Lincoln	33	7 828	98.3	344	1 998	10	138.3	92.5	158.3	4 272	3 212	26	91	334
Lyman	15	3 150	D	96	715	3	30.6	41.9	46.8	11 085	2 517	1 340	732	3 510
McCook	23	2 682	82.5	132	556	5	76.7	39.4	89.6	7 099	3 058	78	318	1 906
McPherson	10	D	D	(7)	D	2	35.0	16.9	14.7	6 288	2 889	53	224	799
Marshall	18	1 931	83.6	71	477	5	53.9	35.5	93.2	7 858	3 359	60	258	1 632
Meade	54	15 669	75.1	517	4 061	5	170.2	137.4	48.1	6 420	2 825	1 445	1 239	631
Mellette	4	623	D	14	94	1	8.2	12.9	60.8	6 296	2 334	42	205	2 687
Miner	8	1 010	D	43	217	3	31.0	20.2	66.0	7 535	3 781	69	301	968
Minnehaha	386	223 384	79.8	8 074	63 980	81	4 230.9	611.4	66.7	4 281	2 335	443	749	613
Moody	17	D	D	(7)	D	3	62.0	42.4	64.2	6 599	2 661	401	851	1 114
Pennington	326	163 660	64.5	5 125	44 264	22	944.8	559.1	39.1	6 345	3 058	396	1 908	911
Perkins	15	1 558	D	91	385	3	84.1	26.3	48.9	7 594	3 692	74	360	974
Potter	12	3 162	75.8	79	622	3	92.6	26.7	71.7	9 403	3 938	78	387	1 236
Roberts	29	4 643	90.9	187	1 092	7	137.9	71.1	61.2	7 256	2 880	253	594	1 931
Sanborn	6	D	D	(7)	D	3	27.9	24.4	121.5	9 119	3 347	79	299	2 765
Shannon	6	1 183	100.0	39	375	–	142.6	160.2	11 438	2 115	517	1 694	6 923
Spink	18	4 229	D	191	1 014	9	129.5	62.5	85.8	8 403	3 540	77	348	1 221
Stanley	8	1 460	D	55	379	1	9.0	15.4	45.1	5 314	2 117	15	87	484
Sully	6	1 853	37.4	87	330	2	27.8	21.2	96.9	14 269	2 514	38	180	2 772
Todd	5	1 161	D	40	262	1	13.7	72.9	56.2	7 674	1 866	61	1 192	4 435
Tripp	19	4 937	80.7	184	1 449	4	112.5	35.5	35.6	5 368	2 915	59	290	669
Turner	17	2 153	100.0	92	406	8	117.3	45.6	65.9	5 271	2 995	65	219	707
Union	37	15 719	82.1	473	3 814	11	149.6	130.2	276.8	10 440	2 666	5 784	170	851
Walworth	31	6 391	67.2	218	1 549	4	137.3	29.8	34.6	5 305	2 762	81	297	863
Yankton	67	23 614	87.9	989	6 181	12	443.9	89.6	63.6	4 228	2 622	164	472	573
Ziebach	2	D	D	(8)	D	1	64.3	12.1	40.0	5 585	1 783	192	89	1 536

[1] Includes only establishments with payroll. [2] Includes full-service restaurants, limited-service eating places, special food services, and drinking places (alcoholic beverages). [3] For pay period including March 12. [4] As of June 30. Covers all FDIC-insured commercial banks and savings institutions. [5] Based on resident population estimated as of July 1, 1999. [6] 100 to 249 employees. [7] 20 to 99 employees. [8] 0 to 19 employees.

Sources: Accommodation and Foodservices—U.S. Census Bureau, 1997 Economic Census, ECON97 Report Series CD-ROM, CD-EC97-1, Disc 1E, issued February 2001 (related Internet site <http://www.census.gov/epcd/www/97EC72.HTM>). Banking—U.S. Federal Deposit Insurance Corporation and Office of Thrift Supervision, "1999 Bank and Thrift Branch Office Data Book: Summary of Deposits," national and 6 regional data books (related Internet site <http://www2.fdic.gov/sod/>). Federal Funds and Grants—U.S. Census Bureau, County Aggregate files for each state, <http://www.census.gov/govs/www/cffr99.html>, (accessed: August 2000).

[Includes U.S., states, and 3,142 counties/county equivalents defined as of January 1, 1992. For changes to these areas since January 1, 1992, see appendix B. Geographic Information]

County	Accommodation and foodservices[1] (NAICS 72), 1997 — Sales — Establishments	Total ($1,000)	Percent from food-services[2]	Paid employees[3]	Annual payroll ($1,000)	Banking,[4] 1999 — Offices	Deposits (mil. dol.)	Federal funds and grants, 1999 — Total expenditures or obligations (mil. dol.)	Percent change, 1990-1999	Per capita[5] (dollars) — Total	By selected type — Direct payments for individuals	Procurement contract awards	Salaries and wages	Grant awards
TENNESSEE	9 604	6 790 159	74.7	197 881	1 880 279	1 981	68 584.7	30 866.8	73.3	5 629	3 140	824	496	1 076
Anderson	129	71 576	87.5	2 384	19 935	22	714.0	2 209.7	34.1	31 121	3 777	25 420	1 018	889
Bedford	49	19 801	88.9	727	4 878	10	366.8	121.2	79.1	3 473	2 641	29	127	600
Benton	39	10 679	D	339	2 111	8	229.1	82.4	23.3	4 994	3 944	43	157	792
Bledsoe	8	1 807	100.0	82	508	2	70.1	42.5	84.7	3 886	2 610	33	79	1 096
Blount	167	97 341	77.5	3 223	26 455	36	1 105.1	673.1	224.0	6 548	3 019	2 775	142	601
Bradley	138	81 837	86.7	2 533	21 832	33	884.6	280.3	88.8	3 332	2 614	46	153	504
Campbell	60	26 596	81.7	910	6 707	15	384.0	223.8	69.9	5 817	4 088	417	123	1 140
Cannon	10	2 857	100.0	119	753	5	115.2	51.5	77.2	4 206	3 338	33	107	673
Carroll	45	12 048	94.4	532	2 942	17	343.6	155.0	−19.5	5 263	3 698	160	156	1 093
Carter	47	21 862	92.7	846	5 843	13	480.5	214.3	68.0	4 021	2 904	56	98	944
Cheatham	29	10 969	92.1	348	2 751	8	218.2	81.0	89.7	2 241	1 785	50	115	282
Chester	19	6 592	D	306	2 133	8	151.1	57.6	82.7	3 879	2 536	22	114	1 143
Claiborne	22	12 055	D	412	3 202	11	336.0	166.7	−15.4	5 603	3 519	33	112	1 910
Clay	20	3 425	D	73	790	3	66.8	38.9	47.4	5 358	3 011	99	256	1 939
Cocke	52	30 471	80.5	978	8 285	11	307.8	155.7	155.2	4 823	3 237	31	114	1 401
Coffee	106	56 506	86.2	1 949	15 733	17	432.1	538.9	7.5	11 625	3 526	6 880	522	652
Crockett	16	4 814	D	82	675	12	198.5	74.1	77.9	5 265	3 222	98	179	1 149
Cumberland	75	39 577	88.0	1 300	11 423	18	452.1	214.3	130.3	4 727	3 864	150	102	579
Davidson	1 407	1 511 748	62.8	37 523	426 301	166	9 898.4	3 562.8	128.5	6 722	2 993	312	830	2 527
Decatur	21	3 917	80.3	175	874	8	147.8	61.7	125.5	5 722	4 064	45	196	1 343
DeKalb	22	6 637	D	317	1 714	10	216.2	82.2	98.2	5 079	3 433	108	132	1 360
Dickson	70	37 670	88.3	1 116	10 598	16	453.3	145.7	90.4	3 386	2 723	30	126	495
Dyer	67	30 162	92.5	998	7 569	21	491.5	173.5	56.4	4 723	3 120	76	170	1 059
Fayette	18	5 049	D	196	1 473	13	276.8	117.6	93.7	3 742	1 995	23	95	1 344
Fentress	18	5 955	91.3	225	1 485	7	152.9	91.9	84.6	5 618	3 902	58	137	1 478
Franklin	50	16 884	93.9	592	4 399	10	328.0	166.2	85.5	4 395	3 302	184	210	614
Gibson	62	22 094	96.3	815	5 870	32	661.9	268.8	82.2	5 595	3 649	59	194	1 268
Giles	38	14 664	91.6	615	3 744	14	437.7	123.4	67.3	4 250	3 055	44	145	933
Grainger	10	D	D	(6)	D	5	103.9	105.8	146.6	5 235	2 991	31	148	2 045
Greene	102	42 071	90.1	1 622	11 897	24	719.1	303.3	72.6	4 980	3 094	805	159	865
Grundy	8	1 923	D	60	462	5	78.8	67.5	88.6	4 808	3 639	27	103	1 007
Hamblen	100	58 316	D	2 269	15 611	19	687.8	225.2	87.1	4 156	3 025	36	173	865
Hamilton	711	453 239	82.2	13 376	128 162	108	3 500.6	2 155.8	69.2	7 315	3 557	1 448	1 374	895
Hancock	2	D	D	(7)	D	2	39.2	41.1	93.3	6 068	3 289	30	82	2 600
Hardeman	30	8 227	D	291	1 797	12	319.2	153.1	66.8	6 261	3 434	874	132	1 686
Hardin	49	17 153	80.1	576	4 409	12	272.5	141.8	128.9	5 618	3 299	43	212	1 983
Hawkins	45	18 007	D	788	4 856	20	449.0	304.7	64.6	6 080	2 885	1 990	272	910
Haywood	26	11 394	86.5	350	2 908	7	400.5	107.6	86.5	5 543	2 978	27	157	1 877
Henderson	36	13 548	90.8	568	3 714	15	340.1	129.8	129.1	5 241	3 235	286	119	1 490
Henry	61	22 126	87.0	890	5 971	16	410.3	171.6	73.9	5 702	3 864	121	257	1 276
Hickman	23	D	D	(6)	D	4	153.9	73.3	91.7	3 443	2 618	31	151	612
Houston	12	1 894	D	59	448	3	47.7	39.8	52.4	5 040	3 791	43	163	1 015
Humphreys	35	13 354	74.8	358	3 202	6	179.5	177.3	172.6	10 313	3 320	4 354	1 268	1 316
Jackson	7	1 393	100.0	41	311	4	104.4	47.1	101.6	4 889	3 225	42	137	1 450
Jefferson	51	24 605	85.8	790	6 426	12	319.1	183.8	124.9	4 074	3 101	35	131	786
Johnson	16	5 251	D	197	1 501	5	167.2	82.2	97.9	4 914	3 514	37	123	1 197
Knox	769	550 896	85.3	17 252	157 553	127	4 563.0	1 821.9	74.1	4 845	2 979	393	572	856
Lake	15	3 940	D	140	1 168	4	43.6	47.5	54.7	5 840	3 069	443	147	1 604
Lauderdale	22	7 474	D	283	1 767	15	280.4	131.3	79.8	5 418	3 277	61	135	1 498
Lawrence	45	21 641	88.7	740	5 825	17	473.0	170.7	87.2	4 307	3 211	59	155	799
Lewis	19	D	D	(6)	D	4	85.9	44.2	99.6	3 973	2 954	22	127	847
Lincoln	44	D	D	(8)	D	13	355.3	131.0	73.7	4 401	3 149	33	142	981
Loudon	56	26 336	87.0	825	7 281	17	460.7	176.4	76.2	4 421	3 531	42	214	607
McMinn	84	41 649	74.8	1 303	10 211	21	569.1	198.9	97.2	4 288	3 180	103	128	839
McNairy	28	6 835	93.7	360	1 715	14	281.3	162.6	120.9	6 690	3 685	41	185	2 670
Macon	19	6 206	95.2	253	1 490	8	237.6	71.8	96.6	3 873	2 669	25	110	957
Madison	183	137 702	D	4 110	37 100	37	998.9	378.9	69.2	4 368	2 919	69	334	927
Marion	41	20 400	89.0	673	5 444	14	205.5	123.4	75.0	4 587	3 446	36	147	933
Marshall	34	12 870	88.5	446	3 237	13	340.7	92.0	67.3	3 481	2 636	76	126	599
Maury	96	58 341	92.1	2 152	16 520	25	850.5	252.9	75.3	3 590	2 633	89	158	682
Meigs	7	1 910	100.0	83	566	5	74.3	43.4	125.6	4 284	3 152	28	163	914
Monroe	55	27 720	88.3	770	7 025	23	355.2	154.0	98.0	4 328	3 020	40	124	1 115
Montgomery	237	132 321	89.7	4 699	37 287	41	1 054.4	496.2	145.6	3 834	2 702	78	558	461
Moore	5	D	D	(7)	D	1	64.7	15.0	121.6	2 921	2 224	21	69	578
Morgan	8	3 763	D	289	1 092	5	101.0	73.2	82.3	3 914	2 668	24	214	989
Obion	51	19 861	87.5	927	5 272	20	500.5	158.9	56.0	4 930	3 378	30	194	957

[1] Includes only establishments with payroll. [2] Includes full-service restaurants, limited-service eating places, special food services, and drinking places (alcoholic beverages). [3] For pay period including March 12. [4] As of June 30. Covers all FDIC-insured commercial banks and savings institutions. [5] Based on resident population estimated as of July 1, 1999. [6] 100 to 249 employees. [7] 20 to 99 employees. [8] 250 to 499 employees.

Sources: Accommodation and Foodservices—U.S. Census Bureau, 1997 Economic Census, ECON97 Report Series CD-ROM, CD-EC97-1, Disc 1E, issued February 2001 (related Internet site <http://www.census.gov/epcd/www/97EC72.HTM>). Banking—U.S. Federal Deposit Insurance Corporation and Office of Thrift Supervision, "1999 Bank and Thrift Branch Office Data Book: Summary of Deposits," national and 6 regional data books (related Internet site <http://www2.fdic.gov/sod/>). Federal Funds and Grants—U.S. Census Bureau, County Aggregate files for each state, <http://www.census.gov/govs/www/cffr99.html>, (accessed: August 2000).

[Includes U.S., states, and 3,142 counties/county equivalents defined as of January 1, 1992. For changes to these areas since January 1, 1992, see appendix B. Geographic Information]

County	Accommodation and foodservices[1] (NAICS 72), 1997					Banking,[4] 1999		Federal funds and grants, 1999						
		Sales						Total expenditures or obligations (mil. dol.)	Percent change, 1990–1999	Per capita[5] (dollars)				
												By selected type—		
	Estab-lishments	Total ($1,000)	Percent from food-services[2]	Paid employ-ees[3]	Annual payroll ($1,000)	Offices	Deposits (mil. dol.)			Total	Direct payments for individuals	Procure-ment contract awards	Salaries and wages	Grant awards
TENNESSEE—Con.														
Overton	21	7 583	91.8	263	1 928	6	219.8	92.5	102.1	4 706	3 290	31	140	1 201
Perry	6	665	D	19	132	3	86.6	37.3	86.5	4 935	3 709	30	151	987
Pickett	7	D	D	(6)	D	2	75.7	24.0	86.5	5 096	3 326	40	86	1 498
Polk	18	4 830	D	160	1 203	11	208.7	86.4	95.5	5 725	3 930	46	261	1 433
Putnam	119	82 234	86.1	2 960	22 578	28	805.0	271.0	102.5	4 537	3 247	100	217	947
Rhea	46	17 310	83.8	531	4 339	7	238.6	186.5	–13.1	6 633	3 358	273	2 129	841
Roane	60	27 196	87.3	1 083	7 641	14	381.9	306.7	120.3	6 133	3 900	528	540	1 141
Robertson	54	28 350	91.7	1 213	7 400	14	442.4	169.4	104.4	3 087	2 344	32	93	508
Rutherford	244	191 451	88.1	6 157	56 044	48	1 450.2	492.8	93.5	2 875	1 838	151	507	362
Scott	22	9 331	91.2	292	2 692	7	178.1	132.5	25.2	6 548	3 458	1 278	186	1 616
Sequatchie	16	D	D	(7)	D	5	76.7	47.2	171.3	4 355	2 614	978	83	665
Sevier	453	384 086	47.0	8 176	105 491	40	1 061.2	219.1	99.1	3 330	2 639	39	219	428
Shelby	1 429	1 362 627	66.1	35 241	371 525	239	14 166.5	4 822.2	49.7	5 524	2 708	865	848	1 057
Smith	19	D	D	(8)	D	9	289.6	77.6	61.0	4 629	3 278	66	282	922
Stewart	12	3 228	D	97	730	5	117.4	107.7	248.5	9 158	4 001	2 145	2 192	788
Sullivan	266	169 467	86.8	5 599	48 681	44	1 555.2	661.6	75.1	4 404	3 442	61	169	716
Sumner	144	67 078	87.0	2 207	18 573	41	1 079.0	394.2	116.2	3 129	2 314	265	176	352
Tipton	44	18 170	D	581	4 642	19	379.5	189.1	113.5	3 911	2 718	134	121	784
Trousdale	10	2 166	D	115	551	3	100.8	31.4	136.7	4 510	3 037	350	309	724
Unicoi	19	7 072	D	337	1 803	5	143.7	98.5	–10.4	5 690	4 051	494	241	893
Union	10	2 981	100.0	101	772	6	89.2	50.7	120.9	3 059	2 178	19	69	778
Van Buren	2	D	D	(9)	D	1	23.1	22.9	157.4	4 567	2 498	25	50	1 980
Warren	56	23 996	92.8	880	6 620	17	502.4	162.6	91.4	4 466	3 463	42	166	750
Washington	190	140 570	89.0	4 858	41 078	41	1 289.8	539.3	60.1	5 246	3 440	325	793	650
Wayne	19	D	D	(7)	D	10	209.1	72.4	124.4	4 409	2 684	28	99	1 564
Weakley	55	18 744	95.7	797	4 682	16	422.6	146.0	77.3	4 432	3 027	80	221	865
White	17	D	D	(8)	D	6	282.0	106.9	97.8	4 676	3 300	113	136	1 103
Williamson	189	160 552	78.3	4 711	44 922	53	1 667.4	247.4	100.9	1 998	1 603	55	124	203
Wilson	111	68 664	92.0	2 225	19 835	32	934.3	240.7	104.2	2 783	2 235	24	118	391
TEXAS	34 160	22 698 848	80.1	638 333	6 175 414	4 620	207 774.7	97 987.6	68.3	4 889	2 507	724	589	916
Anderson	58	29 711	87.9	1 031	8 087	11	327.1	214.1	75.0	4 101	2 872	259	137	788
Andrews	20	D	D	(7)	D	3	81.5	44.0	69.5	3 203	2 422	16	76	397
Angelina	119	60 739	85.8	1 908	17 385	22	747.4	322.6	82.0	4 157	3 041	59	249	778
Aransas	72	24 901	74.9	823	6 794	5	162.3	87.7	92.0	3 794	3 315	17	59	375
Archer	5	1 046	D	31	223	4	50.4	59.0	108.0	7 147	3 776	22	2 487	392
Armstrong	4	444	100.0	21	120	1	17.5	15.1	57.1	6 873	3 065	32	160	596
Atascosa	44	13 405	92.7	450	3 646	8	205.0	134.3	96.2	3 588	2 286	21	75	1 137
Austin	46	15 402	90.2	425	3 788	9	452.5	427.1	743.6	17 911	2 786	14 141	200	632
Bailey	17	D	D	(7)	D	2	94.6	49.0	70.4	7 298	2 830	38	185	811
Bandera	36	9 959	59.1	288	3 016	5	107.3	64.1	114.2	3 857	3 354	24	230	236
Bastrop	68	25 716	93.6	889	7 305	13	353.8	185.5	94.0	3 529	2 348	30	377	728
Baylor	9	1 889	D	74	423	3	72.6	30.6	43.2	7 486	4 821	53	179	1 205
Bee	47	14 115	90.9	503	3 735	4	165.7	129.1	18.0	4 426	2 886	31	95	1 132
Bell	376	202 925	85.0	6 673	53 464	55	1 664.0	2 622.6	81.4	11 777	3 021	1 095	7 152	467
Bexar	2 558	2 027 776	75.8	56 118	563 127	200	14 725.9	9 212.5	62.7	6 710	3 084	1 050	1 688	858
Blanco	22	6 224	92.0	239	1 925	5	111.4	58.5	150.7	6 878	6 232	23	358	241
Borden	–	–	–	–	–	–	–	3.7	1.1	4 778	1 195	18	65	129
Bosque	19	2 808	71.7	99	660	9	166.9	78.1	56.8	4 677	3 777	41	187	582
Bowie	142	82 869	87.4	2 456	19 967	24	751.9	587.7	18.3	7 038	3 961	551	1 199	1 245
Brazoria	295	148 369	86.9	4 787	41 761	44	1 354.1	584.2	59.7	2 493	1 892	104	123	284
Brazos	275	170 723	81.8	5 668	48 179	29	1 233.5	506.2	77.3	3 772	1 711	255	371	1 405
Brewster	45	15 127	48.5	579	3 993	3	67.0	40.4	60.6	4 600	2 945	48	823	732
Briscoe	2	D	D	(9)	D	2	39.0	19.1	38.1	10 493	4 049	62	270	1 394
Brooks	21	7 242	67.8	201	1 954	3	80.0	59.3	113.6	7 041	2 944	460	493	2 909
Brown	77	31 653	91.7	1 048	8 308	14	331.9	176.2	63.2	4 782	3 607	152	157	805
Burleson	25	6 215	89.8	234	1 649	7	247.6	82.7	74.8	5 297	3 169	67	153	1 615
Burnet	63	33 935	62.4	878	10 536	13	366.7	121.1	59.9	3 549	3 013	25	99	391
Caldwell	36	14 140	97.8	370	3 745	7	233.4	117.1	88.5	3 567	2 455	26	87	895
Calhoun	53	15 209	83.1	524	4 157	8	290.4	82.9	89.2	4 060	2 464	39	149	944
Callahan	15	2 898	100.0	130	814	4	100.9	54.1	47.3	4 191	3 275	54	113	556
Cameron	513	278 174	75.1	8 349	71 674	56	2 362.3	1 281.6	103.3	3 894	2 003	68	311	1 426
Camp	17	3 480	D	96	870	6	147.7	60.1	87.7	5 494	3 970	54	137	1 237
Carson	10	D	D	(6)	D	4	62.3	38.4	–33.7	5 678	2 765	103	127	752
Cass	47	14 680	94.0	548	4 049	9	265.5	174.8	101.7	5 708	3 794	33	125	1 728
Castro	14	D	D	(6)	D	4	78.5	58.8	60.1	7 117	2 085	24	103	685

[1] Includes only establishments with payroll.   [2] Includes full-service restaurants, limited-service eating places, special food services, and drinking places (alcoholic beverages).   [3] For pay period including March 12.   [4] As of June 30. Covers all FDIC-insured commercial banks and savings institutions.   [5] Based on resident population estimated as of July 1, 1999.   [6] 20 to 99 employees.   [7] 100 to 249 employees.   [8] 250 to 499 employees.   [9] 0 to 19 employees.

Sources: Accommodation and Foodservices—U.S. Census Bureau, 1997 Economic Census, ECON97 Report Series CD-ROM, CD-EC97-1, Disc 1E, issued February 2001 (related Internet site <http://www.census.gov/epcd/www/97EC72.HTM>). Banking—U.S. Federal Deposit Insurance Corporation and Office of Thrift Supervision, "1999 Bank and Thrift Branch Office Data Book: Summary of Deposits," national and 6 regional data books (related Internet site <http://www2.fdic.gov/sod/>). Federal Funds and Grants—U.S. Census Bureau, County Aggregate files for each state, <http://www.census.gov/govs/www/cffr99.html>, (accessed: August 2000).

[Includes U.S., states, and 3,142 counties/county equivalents defined as of January 1, 1992. For changes to these areas since January 1, 1992, see appendix B. Geographic Information]

County	Accommodation and foodservices[1] (NAICS 72), 1997					Banking,[4] 1999		Federal funds and grants, 1999						
		Sales								Per capita[5] (dollars)				
												By selected type—		
	Establishments	Total ($1,000)	Percent from food-services[2]	Paid employees[3]	Annual payroll ($1,000)	Offices	Deposits (mil. dol.)	Total expenditures or obligations (mil. dol.)	Percent change, 1990–1999	Total	Direct payments for individuals	Procurement contract awards	Salaries and wages	Grant awards
TEXAS—Con.														
Chambers	31	14 929	82.8	577	3 928	6	143.2	69.8	15.1	2 911	1 872	158	98	333
Cherokee	47	20 264	97.2	632	4 917	11	442.1	172.4	50.4	3 949	2 931	28	98	815
Childress	24	7 181	65.6	256	1 769	4	109.9	44.6	63.8	5 908	2 926	45	198	1 823
Clay	11	1 454	100.0	61	390	4	71.9	39.8	64.8	3 789	2 715	34	127	569
Cochran	5	466	100.0	16	136	2	50.5	34.3	59.9	9 059	2 876	38	177	762
Coke	7	D	D	(6)	D	2	58.9	16.4	35.0	4 903	3 782	51	203	506
Coleman	21	4 172	78.3	173	1 221	5	128.5	66.1	71.0	6 999	4 770	87	247	1 502
Collin	563	430 946	90.8	11 830	119 604	89	2 701.9	905.2	171.3	1 983	1 039	667	102	150
Collingsworth	7	995	D	43	218	2	42.8	26.7	45.0	8 415	4 091	88	384	1 144
Colorado	48	15 314	81.8	569	3 733	12	355.7	103.6	57.9	5 437	3 317	35	146	1 149
Comal	172	80 444	81.6	2 468	22 817	15	507.3	317.5	69.5	4 136	3 156	148	216	316
Comanche	22	4 788	D	165	1 335	9	212.7	73.0	50.4	5 375	3 865	61	166	905
Concho	9	2 770	D	81	622	2	35.5	20.9	34.8	6 960	3 410	52	261	938
Cooke	64	28 982	88.9	965	7 588	10	379.8	124.5	57.2	3 729	3 005	31	117	445
Coryell	60	30 391	93.8	1 201	9 855	10	309.3	209.1	85.9	2 840	2 136	110	145	412
Cottle	5	D	D	(6)	D	1	36.5	17.8	33.9	9 436	4 188	52	307	1 173
Crane	7	1 932	100.0	83	509	2	37.5	11.6	76.8	2 710	2 357	17	59	245
Crockett	24	6 350	70.1	218	1 654	2	74.1	18.1	23.9	4 115	2 042	13	62	1 802
Crosby	5	1 100	100.0	34	279	5	76.1	55.2	85.8	7 816	3 474	30	121	909
Culberson	21	6 011	D	224	1 458	1	16.5	12.2	72.5	4 039	2 176	81	764	604
Dallam	27	8 652	66.4	264	1 936	6	168.2	57.6	81.3	8 696	3 267	107	158	1 709
Dallas	4 194	4 045 939	68.6	98 652	1 102 651	485	33 064.6	8 971.8	55.6	4 351	1 995	1 056	687	593
Dawson	30	9 800	96.2	283	2 739	3	247.3	101.6	98.3	7 032	3 350	32	182	1 080
Deaf Smith	29	D	D	(7)	D	3	138.7	90.2	44.3	4 795	2 334	59	107	690
Delta	2	D	D	(8)	D	4	49.7	33.5	−6.2	6 733	3 888	302	202	1 742
Denton	488	324 968	89.3	9 742	90 429	82	2 118.7	671.1	−13.0	1 661	1 123	243	138	140
DeWitt	37	8 932	86.5	290	2 610	13	305.7	103.4	86.3	5 364	3 171	31	146	1 806
Dickens	7	1 466	100.0	38	305	1	23.6	21.8	31.1	10 017	5 936	59	254	1 288
Dimmit	12	3 992	89.1	125	967	2	44.3	70.4	132.9	6 805	2 501	20	534	3 686
Donley	14	2 205	D	79	475	4	75.3	22.8	47.6	5 945	3 963	34	170	649
Duval	16	2 848	72.4	88	660	3	66.6	81.4	82.7	5 965	3 167	16	210	2 303
Eastland	43	9 250	81.7	382	2 590	8	100.6	105.1	50.5	6 010	4 474	49	178	1 109
Ector	234	119 917	88.4	3 806	32 853	23	959.9	379.2	83.6	3 065	2 385	27	91	556
Edwards	3	D	D	(8)	D	1	27.3	13.1	4.7	3 577	2 529	25	241	597
Ellis	113	52 510	92.7	1 652	14 724	28	704.5	318.7	−2.4	2 963	2 140	30	95	572
El Paso	1 094	703 263	74.5	19 292	194 004	69	3 219.3	3 073.8	59.0	4 379	2 255	355	904	849
Erath	68	30 247	91.5	1 029	7 919	12	351.2	113.7	64.9	3 614	2 872	30	126	479
Falls	20	3 722	D	92	906	8	185.4	113.0	54.3	6 543	3 417	53	634	1 833
Fannin	33	9 878	D	281	2 708	12	266.8	169.6	57.7	5 913	3 539	51	698	1 137
Fayette	55	20 938	89.6	780	6 029	14	417.8	109.8	63.5	5 132	3 705	93	173	1 006
Fisher	6	D	D	(6)	D	2	47.9	38.7	65.5	9 234	3 976	58	259	1 001
Floyd	16	2 019	100.0	75	574	4	104.4	66.4	57.5	8 180	2 875	49	177	970
Foard	3	222	100.0	8	53	1	21.1	18.9	80.6	11 595	4 303	35	180	3 197
Fort Bend	319	205 432	90.7	5 880	56 181	62	2 125.0	527.2	108.4	1 491	933	38	82	319
Franklin	18	5 106	D	198	1 275	5	94.3	34.7	106.7	3 486	2 690	24	76	536
Freestone	24	9 164	D	297	2 598	9	136.9	69.6	44.5	3 942	2 810	39	105	850
Frio	23	5 677	D	168	1 487	4	167.4	62.5	68.0	3 927	2 056	39	64	1 577
Gaines	21	D	D	(9)	D	3	131.0	81.7	83.5	5 535	1 968	16	76	446
Galveston	485	301 528	79.2	9 156	82 424	63	2 108.4	1 044.3	70.7	4 203	2 569	538	223	760
Garza	13	2 691	90.4	115	704	2	52.4	25.0	53.9	5 541	3 397	38	146	781
Gillespie	67	25 873	74.8	815	7 593	10	404.1	95.0	63.3	4 659	4 040	72	188	305
Glasscock	1	D	D	(8)	D	1	6.6	16.0	164.5	11 114	1 103	19	70	1 525
Goliad	13	2 648	D	114	660	2	39.5	30.1	80.4	4 221	2 870	28	122	947
Gonzales	26	7 083	87.6	242	1 891	7	191.8	97.6	17.9	5 559	3 293	36	442	1 463
Gray	55	18 969	84.8	658	4 971	7	282.0	108.3	34.5	4 648	3 702	85	142	440
Grayson	200	104 782	86.5	3 312	30 745	31	1 146.6	469.8	64.4	4 529	3 351	90	151	838
Gregg	274	146 329	89.1	4 575	41 484	40	1 502.2	460.3	65.5	4 068	3 205	36	154	667
Grimes	25	D	D	(9)	D	7	227.1	83.1	74.5	3 459	2 369	30	94	913
Guadalupe	127	D	D	(10)	D	14	470.6	358.6	118.1	4 330	2 839	31	135	553
Hale	67	25 924	97.5	923	6 935	11	404.3	184.4	58.5	5 053	2 704	59	153	856
Hall	10	D	D	(9)	D	4	63.6	35.7	61.8	9 935	4 131	63	294	1 950
Hamilton	13	2 591	D	103	706	5	108.5	42.8	46.0	5 631	4 436	73	200	732
Hansford	11	D	D	(6)	D	4	147.1	37.2	45.8	6 896	2 648	29	137	362
Hardeman	10	D	D	(9)	D	4	80.6	32.4	31.3	7 393	4 310	49	196	1 073
Hardin	50	16 430	D	538	4 477	10	314.4	164.3	66.0	3 306	2 692	21	84	495
Harris	5 470	4 379 041	80.3	111 869	1 160 739	705	43 500.1	13 997.9	88.8	4 307	1 792	1 365	422	698

[1] Includes only establishments with payroll. [2] Includes full-service restaurants, limited-service eating places, special food services, and drinking places (alcoholic beverages). [3] For pay period including March 12. [4] As of June 30. Covers all FDIC-insured commercial banks and savings institutions. [5] Based on resident population estimated as of July 1, 1999. [6] 20 to 99 employees. [7] 250 to 499 employees. [8] 0 to 19 employees. [9] 100 to 249 employees. [10] 1,000 to 2,499 employees.

Sources: Accommodation and Foodservices—U.S. Census Bureau, 1997 Economic Census, ECON97 Report Series CD-ROM, CD-EC97-1, Disc 1E, issued February 2001 (related Internet site <http://www.census.gov/epcd/www/97EC72.HTM>). Banking—U.S. Federal Deposit Insurance Corporation and Office of Thrift Supervision, "1999 Bank and Thrift Branch Office Data Book: Summary of Deposits," national and 6 regional data books (related Internet site <http://www2.fdic.gov/sod/>). Federal Funds and Grants—U.S. Census Bureau, County Aggregate files for each state, <http://www.census.gov/govs/www/cffr99.html>, (accessed: August 2000).

[Includes U.S., states, and 3,142 counties/county equivalents defined as of January 1, 1992. For changes to these areas since January 1, 1992, see appendix B. Geographic Information]

County	Accommodation and foodservices[1] (NAICS 72), 1997					Banking,[4] 1999		Federal funds and grants, 1999						
		Sales								Per capita[5] (dollars)				
												By selected type—		
	Estab-lishments	Total ($1,000)	Percent from food-services[2]	Paid employ-ees[3]	Annual payroll ($1,000)	Offices	Deposits (mil. dol.)	Total expenditures or obligations (mil. dol.)	Percent change, 1990–1999	Total	Direct payments for individuals	Procure-ment contract awards	Salaries and wages	Grant awards
TEXAS—Con.														
Harrison	75	35 132	92.2	1 017	9 257	14	517.9	234.1	19.9	3 916	2 678	38	117	1 070
Hartley	4	256	100.0	15	76	–		19.4	57.9	3 683	520	11	57	71
Haskell	8	2 276	D	97	661	5	119.8	54.9	72.2	9 200	4 308	57	259	1 513
Hays	177	88 449	87.7	2 890	25 423	21	442.8	280.0	100.1	3 019	1 787	491	91	597
Hemphill	12	1 402	D	69	325	3	72.2	11.7	12.9	3 377	2 441	29	141	255
Henderson	95	40 692	92.6	1 389	10 293	20	541.5	236.8	93.7	3 351	2 658	22	73	573
Hidalgo	626	352 082	86.0	10 871	90 083	87	4 246.3	1 810.5	97.4	3 385	1 811	192	238	1 083
Hill	67	25 303	83.5	785	6 447	12	271.0	185.7	93.9	5 979	3 539	99	156	1 769
Hockley	38	13 293	D	544	3 511	8	268.4	117.4	89.5	5 022	2 518	28	103	1 198
Hood	74	28 146	D	966	7 553	14	415.2	158.4	126.5	4 089	3 725	34	120	190
Hopkins	56	25 538	87.9	747	7 443	9	381.1	140.7	95.4	4 596	3 040	38	155	1 103
Houston	27	7 221	77.4	231	2 043	8	241.1	122.6	74.0	5 517	3 675	71	164	1 382
Howard	73	24 175	91.9	981	6 719	6	402.8	231.3	89.5	7 299	3 785	1 050	1 136	792
Hudspeth	5	1 426	D	35	163	1	12.7	14.0	89.6	4 313	1 844	145	1 194	660
Hunt	117	50 940	90.5	1 729	15 050	20	575.1	598.7	68.4	8 348	2 988	4 047	231	993
Hutchinson	48	15 103	D	578	3 992	5	172.4	93.4	48.1	3 938	3 089	27	151	344
Irion	5	D	D	(6)	D	1	39.1	6.4	21.6	3 759	2 775	42	149	487
Jack	11	D	D	(7)	D	4	123.3	27.5	42.1	3 678	2 973	40	151	389
Jackson	18	7 006	D	205	1 500	7	162.0	75.5	75.1	5 530	3 092	26	111	745
Jasper	49	21 557	D	714	5 648	9	322.2	161.1	60.6	4 809	3 493	45	117	1 138
Jeff Davis	12	4 455	28.1	138	1 347	1	20.3	13.3	108.5	5 494	2 565	29	404	2 313
Jefferson	426	261 863	86.9	8 206	69 938	50	2 639.4	1 350.9	54.4	5 598	3 352	797	583	786
Jim Hogg	14	2 976	D	106	864	3	86.3	30.8	92.0	6 198	3 171	113	523	2 264
Jim Wells	68	25 612	97.3	823	6 578	8	305.7	194.6	97.1	4 840	2 863	24	153	1 591
Johnson	134	60 179	D	1 885	16 602	28	764.8	350.3	86.9	2 858	2 418	26	93	284
Jones	24	3 727	90.2	119	1 014	6	141.2	91.7	51.0	4 867	2 921	31	138	688
Karnes	23	5 100	D	192	1 342	5	143.8	74.8	58.3	4 949	2 847	33	119	1 715
Kaufman	91	39 873	91.8	1 342	10 749	17	592.5	287.4	93.1	4 222	3 519	37	140	475
Kendall	50	27 658	56.8	858	8 530	8	266.8	104.1	124.3	4 762	4 069	338	123	221
Kenedy	1	D	D	(6)	D	–		1.4	71.3	3 252	1 702	99	860	489
Kent	1	D	D	(6)	D	1	10.3	10.1	88.6	11 802	3 891	67	440	4 018
Kerr	100	54 332	53.7	1 417	15 284	11	585.0	246.6	66.6	5 703	4 758	52	560	323
Kimble	27	6 738	62.0	212	1 891	2	52.5	18.2	16.3	4 294	3 428	3	156	597
King	1	D	D	(6)	D	–		2.5	–11.7	7 984	1 679	135	638	594
Kinney	3	417	100.0	18	130	1	12.1	22.7	56.0	6 549	4 379	53	1 062	855
Kleberg	74	31 573	85.3	1 048	8 465	5	189.9	253.0	–7.8	8 524	2 826	2 933	1 511	1 110
Knox	13	D	D	(7)	D	1	28.1	36.9	54.3	8 999	4 172	132	364	1 745
Lamar	96	45 894	88.8	1 466	13 049	14	669.4	243.3	76.0	5 283	3 300	54	179	1 504
Lamb	27	D	D	(8)	D	14	205.3	94.9	48.4	6 425	3 195	30	123	896
Lampasas	28	D	D	(9)	D	7	155.4	86.5	83.4	4 886	4 252	31	119	458
La Salle	8	3 448	D	93	895	1	27.8	34.5	52.6	5 750	2 513	36	351	2 484
Lavaca	32	9 169	92.6	375	2 598	10	427.6	112.8	74.2	5 963	4 220	40	152	1 374
Lee	24	8 183	86.9	252	2 090	7	203.3	45.8	75.3	3 079	2 311	32	94	556
Leon	24	9 289	78.2	385	2 645	7	151.0	94.6	99.9	6 365	4 293	52	178	1 651
Liberty	65	32 883	90.4	984	8 455	13	436.1	266.1	88.1	3 963	2 779	49	91	825
Limestone	33	9 722	92.0	290	2 386	9	220.0	111.0	71.3	5 384	3 476	96	155	1 409
Lipscomb	4	D	D	(6)	D	3	58.5	15.5	20.1	5 132	3 089	70	296	306
Live Oak	29	9 504	78.9	278	2 171	4	115.4	71.6	5.8	7 089	2 594	1 774	1 721	612
Llano	47	10 501	82.6	298	2 840	12	235.4	87.8	70.1	6 343	5 782	53	141	340
Loving	–	–	–	–	–	–		.9	170.5	7 540	1 903	381	1 336	2 894
Lubbock	522	332 126	89.2	11 154	87 593	69	2 764.3	951.1	49.0	4 174	2 817	166	301	752
Lynn	7	1 028	100.0	48	266	4	101.8	54.9	86.9	8 240	2 922	38	158	967
McCulloch	23	7 091	86.3	181	1 611	3	129.6	47.1	47.6	5 346	3 718	42	198	1 049
McLennan	400	220 665	88.6	6 900	59 809	42	2 204.4	1 023.7	44.6	5 012	3 021	598	504	830
McMullen	2	D	D	(6)	D	1	21.9	6.7	171.9	8 358	2 466	71	322	4 926
Madison	19	7 888	88.7	213	2 090	5	191.1	42.5	66.0	3 578	2 459	32	92	927
Marion	35	4 978	70.9	185	1 306	2	72.0	55.2	67.0	5 022	3 157	82	212	1 555
Martin	4	594	100.0	28	165	2	55.3	37.8	62.9	7 569	2 371	46	166	1 000
Mason	8	1 302	68.4	46	333	3	65.5	18.9	37.8	5 190	3 902	31	248	825
Matagorda	77	26 636	82.6	804	6 973	9	350.4	178.6	86.6	4 722	2 549	331	134	996
Maverick	46	23 676	83.7	670	6 126	6	324.8	183.7	112.5	3 776	1 927	46	406	1 374
Medina	46	12 946	83.8	413	3 205	12	295.4	141.1	83.8	3 742	2 545	24	329	691
Menard	9	1 877	90.8	42	368	2	29.0	13.2	28.7	5 849	4 144	45	202	1 073
Midland	231	123 908	90.7	3 814	34 197	29	1 458.0	332.9	69.1	2 810	2 128	61	232	342
Milam	43	10 747	88.7	342	2 916	10	246.1	128.0	88.3	5 268	3 029	44	123	1 655
Mills	6	1 406	D	55	391	2	94.4	26.5	41.6	5 601	4 131	51	207	1 015

[1] Includes only establishments with payroll. [2] Includes full-service restaurants, limited-service eating places, special food services, and drinking places (alcoholic beverages). [3] For pay period including March 12. [4] As of June 30. Covers all FDIC-insured commercial banks and savings institutions. [5] Based on resident population estimated as of July 1, 1999. [6] 0 to 19 employees. [7] 20 to 99 employees. [8] 100 to 249 employees. [9] 250 to 499 employees.

Sources: Accommodation and Foodservices—U.S. Census Bureau, 1997 Economic Census, ECON97 Report Series CD-ROM, CD-EC97-1, Disc 1E, issued February 2001 (related Internet site <http://www.census.gov/epcd/www/97EC72.HTM>). Banking—U.S. Federal Deposit Insurance Corporation and Office of Thrift Supervision, "1999 Bank and Thrift Branch Office Data Book: Summary of Deposits," national and 6 regional data books (related Internet site <http://www2.fdic.gov/sod/>). Federal Funds and Grants—U.S. Census Bureau, County Aggregate files for each state, <http://www.census.gov/govs/www/cffr99.html>, (accessed: August 2000).

[Includes U.S., states, and 3,142 counties/county equivalents defined as of January 1, 1992. For changes to these areas since January 1, 1992, see appendix B. Geographic Information]

County	Accommodation and foodservices[1] (NAICS 72), 1997					Banking,[4] 1999		Federal funds and grants, 1999						
	Sales			Paid employees[3]	Annual payroll ($1,000)	Offices	Deposits (mil. dol.)	Total expenditures or obligations (mil. dol.)	Percent change, 1990–1999	Per capita[5] (dollars)				
												By selected type—		
	Establishments	Total ($1,000)	Percent from foodservices[2]							Total	Direct payments for individuals	Procurement contract awards	Salaries and wages	Grant awards
TEXAS—Con.														
Mitchell	17	3 892	D	146	851	3	91.9	50.9	68.4	5 796	3 238	36	137	1 285
Montague	38	10 397	D	360	2 219	7	246.3	93.9	66.9	5 009	4 036	44	160	602
Montgomery	284	230 238	77.2	6 044	62 622	61	1 752.8	657.5	119.5	2 286	1 849	38	99	217
Moore	46	20 278	73.5	630	5 245	6	157.2	61.9	37.7	3 136	1 819	17	188	172
Morris	21	D	D	(6)	D	9	155.7	71.8	68.3	5 468	4 177	34	122	1 064
Motley	3	294	100.0	15	52	1	8.7	14.3	65.6	10 860	4 561	65	309	2 273
Nacogdoches	87	57 082	85.3	1 897	15 604	18	598.1	234.6	80.3	4 179	2 914	47	173	1 004
Navarro	54	25 489	93.8	878	6 684	15	506.2	194.3	69.7	4 640	3 114	36	138	1 161
Newton	15	3 045	D	87	796	2	42.2	59.3	85.2	4 133	2 864	29	102	1 096
Nolan	35	11 736	84.5	426	2 014	4	105.1	82.8	65.8	5 097	3 475	34	140	798
Nueces	730	418 558	84.9	12 846	111 588	75	2 351.6	1 715.7	66.1	5 439	2 699	890	925	824
Ochiltree	20	7 049	78.3	254	1 802	3	167.2	36.3	30.8	4 182	2 093	29	132	139
Oldham	3	1 175	D	60	418	1	13.9	11.1	6.1	5 037	2 576	45	181	312
Orange	115	58 555	D	2 096	16 164	16	636.9	324.7	72.0	3 810	3 015	131	92	545
Palo Pinto	66	21 256	86.4	657	5 634	14	298.6	113.2	58.5	4 327	3 385	61	117	724
Panola	26	10 891	83.6	342	3 157	5	300.6	96.4	81.8	4 193	2 954	32	148	977
Parker	93	41 489	90.2	1 316	10 796	14	550.8	227.7	98.1	2 665	2 309	33	96	210
Parmer	15	D	D	(6)	D	5	166.3	67.5	39.8	6 520	2 059	32	234	392
Pecos	32	12 706	D	392	3 109	4	105.3	47.8	76.2	2 973	1 913	27	129	724
Polk	55	21 514	86.5	732	6 237	10	403.3	262.5	157.4	4 998	4 242	46	70	606
Potter	337	190 998	81.6	5 864	51 333	33	1 731.9	928.9	55.3	8 513	4 062	2 398	835	959
Presidio	15	3 316	41.2	130	1 034	3	52.2	39.8	51.4	4 444	1 968	81	1 031	1 314
Rains	14	2 877	60.2	87	729	5	70.6	31.3	116.3	3 492	2 709	27	96	464
Randall	143	71 585	96.8	2 428	19 596	17	409.5	102.4	44.3	1 028	786	5	24	104
Reagan	9	D	D	(7)	D	2	29.9	13.9	86.9	3 587	1 737	22	104	216
Real	6	2 133	D	42	509	2	39.5	19.9	112.9	7 314	4 740	67	148	2 229
Red River	15	D	D	(6)	D	6	112.7	99.5	66.6	7 269	4 215	61	160	2 388
Reeves	28	8 369	72.2	285	2 315	2	105.8	58.3	78.0	4 161	2 254	75	185	1 310
Refugio	23	6 074	95.8	215	1 729	3	85.2	41.7	65.8	5 394	3 511	42	198	845
Roberts	1	D	D	(8)	D	1	11.9	4.6	14.5	4 936	2 613	62	279	246
Robertson	18	5 926	84.3	211	2 128	5	180.9	89.7	75.8	5 693	3 356	37	149	1 706
Rockwall	44	26 741	98.6	831	8 117	15	371.7	89.1	165.5	2 256	1 676	328	100	119
Runnels	21	3 236	D	110	729	9	159.2	64.3	49.8	5 674	3 464	45	197	898
Rusk	45	15 280	D	518	4 332	12	480.2	171.4	63.6	3 741	2 645	29	113	913
Sabine	19	4 274	54.8	166	1 232	4	134.6	73.0	85.2	6 919	5 600	38	202	1 054
San Augustine	8	1 919	100.0	57	435	5	91.8	51.6	33.5	6 388	4 280	38	137	1 861
San Jacinto	9	4 551	D	126	1 106	4	58.5	74.3	93.2	3 293	2 555	17	65	626
San Patricio	109	31 759	87.0	1 037	8 343	16	324.3	422.4	179.9	5 896	2 427	894	1 471	818
San Saba	12	D	D	(7)	D	2	57.6	38.1	61.8	6 561	3 701	101	204	2 335
Schleicher	6	D	D	(8)	D	1	31.4	12.5	-.1	4 238	2 757	40	122	641
Scurry	36	9 476	89.6	418	2 987	6	243.8	73.8	49.0	4 181	2 785	29	112	568
Shackelford	8	1 783	D	65	464	2	59.9	15.2	46.9	4 727	3 549	82	189	384
Shelby	23	8 487	D	243	2 045	11	283.0	132.1	68.4	5 823	3 794	41	172	1 765
Sherman	9	797	D	46	210	1	48.8	38.8	68.7	13 378	2 568	60	99	2 610
Smith	294	175 142	89.0	5 834	47 777	51	2 055.8	697.7	75.7	4 111	2 965	220	273	637
Somervell	21	6 061	53.7	197	1 924	2	49.7	20.2	100.5	3 056	2 457	28	136	412
Starr	35	10 854	96.7	326	2 444	7	247.5	193.0	119.4	3 411	1 471	86	213	1 522
Stephens	20	5 639	86.1	158	1 335	4	141.3	40.2	53.2	4 132	3 231	95	119	584
Sterling	4	659	100.0	19	160	1	20.1	7.1	105.6	5 346	2 172	32	180	2 492
Stonewall	6	590	D	23	138	1	22.3	12.2	28.5	7 104	3 998	50	238	539
Sutton	11	4 677	65.1	151	1 377	2	55.5	11.4	-4.7	2 641	1 952	20	94	393
Swisher	12	D	D	(6)	D	5	115.1	60.2	47.0	7 292	2 985	31	153	752
Tarrant	2 330	1 821 451	88.2	49 749	499 783	283	12 063.1	6 302.0	5.5	4 559	2 020	1 605	546	377
Taylor	269	151 575	88.4	5 497	41 757	38	1 282.8	742.5	40.2	6 063	3 105	507	1 714	667
Terrell	2	D	D	(8)	D	1	14.2	11.2	46.8	9 306	3 417	36	468	5 067
Terry	24	7 879	87.7	272	2 068	3	164.3	87.2	73.3	6 822	3 018	28	122	941
Throckmorton	2	D	D	(8)	D	3	29.6	11.6	38.2	6 855	4 086	67	289	676
Titus	41	21 071	92.2	689	5 534	9	377.7	101.2	53.4	3 993	2 896	32	212	799
Tom Green	192	110 830	88.2	3 763	32 660	29	935.7	542.3	54.2	5 301	2 957	200	1 306	689
Travis	1 643	1 322 581	76.9	36 951	375 538	155	7 507.1	5 729.2	82.2	7 880	2 010	454	601	4 781
Trinity	15	7 479	25.9	213	2 519	3	75.4	74.9	88.8	5 895	4 531	40	167	1 099
Tyler	17	D	D	(6)	D	7	115.7	90.0	65.0	4 391	3 533	25	109	694
Upshur	28	11 356	95.7	371	2 936	9	338.1	139.6	81.2	3 822	2 957	27	97	703
Upton	8	D	D	(7)	D	2	36.0	14.8	58.4	4 154	2 786	28	99	506
Uvalde	54	20 584	73.6	636	5 678	6	305.6	110.5	65.5	4 249	2 583	19	191	1 179
Val Verde	88	33 284	76.2	1 046	8 536	6	255.0	310.9	67.6	7 036	2 337	1 077	2 306	1 270

[1] Includes only establishments with payroll. [2] Includes full-service restaurants, limited-service eating places, special food services, and drinking places (alcoholic beverages). [3] For pay period including March 12. [4] As of June 30. Covers all FDIC-insured commercial banks and savings institutions. [5] Based on resident population estimated as of July 1, 1999. [6] 100 to 249 employees. [7] 20 to 99 employees. [8] 0 to 19 employees.

Sources: Accommodation and Foodservices—U.S. Census Bureau, 1997 Economic Census, ECON[97] Report Series CD-ROM, CD-EC97-1, Disc 1E, issued February 2001 (related Internet site <http://www.census.gov/epcd/www/97EC72.HTM>). Banking—U.S. Federal Deposit Insurance Corporation and Office of Thrift Supervision, "1999 Bank and Thrift Branch Office Data Book: Summary of Deposits," national and 6 regional data books (related Internet site <http://www2.fdic.gov/sod/>). Federal Funds and Grants—U.S. Census Bureau, County Aggregate files for each state, <http://www.census.gov/govs/www/cffr99.html>, (accessed: August 2000).

[Includes U.S., states, and 3,142 counties/county equivalents defined as of January 1, 1992. For changes to these areas since January 1, 1992, see appendix B. Geographic Information]

County	Accommodation and foodservices[1] (NAICS 72), 1997				Banking,[4] 1999		Federal funds and grants, 1999							
		Sales								Per capita[5] (dollars)				
												By selected type—		
	Estab-lishments	Total ($1,000)	Percent from food-services[2]	Paid employ-ees[3]	Annual payroll ($1,000)	Offices	Deposits (mil. dol.)	Total expenditures or obligations (mil. dol.)	Percent change, 1990–1999	Total	Direct payments for individuals	Procure-ment contract awards	Salaries and wages	Grant awards
TEXAS—Con.														
Van Zandt	54	19 422	D	586	5 258	14	321.2	187.4	99.4	4 173	3 334	26	101	630
Victoria	155	79 600	86.6	2 711	21 748	18	1 108.5	315.6	90.5	3 845	2 526	63	138	943
Walker	77	45 377	87.6	1 545	12 857	8	393.6	165.2	69.5	3 005	2 046	34	179	726
Waller	40	17 976	87.6	722	4 512	8	142.1	109.7	76.7	3 908	2 234	197	120	1 061
Ward	23	5 765	D	198	1 659	3	94.6	52.6	101.4	4 579	2 674	27	105	1 729
Washington	60	23 441	79.6	767	6 143	9	572.0	120.9	72.0	4 157	2 957	28	138	989
Webb	253	144 733	77.9	4 350	37 361	21	3 337.2	721.2	134.2	3 733	1 536	105	456	1 623
Wharton	59	24 816	91.6	780	5 988	19	603.4	205.4	77.9	5 100	2 901	32	125	1 023
Wheeler	17	D	D	(6)	D	5	85.0	43.3	66.9	8 148	4 423	61	237	2 575
Wichita	277	159 579	D	5 225	47 058	31	1 349.3	979.9	78.6	7 642	3 367	707	2 626	875
Wilbarger	37	10 827	82.2	444	3 377	7	241.7	78.3	53.0	5 709	3 709	43	191	780
Willacy	20	5 702	91.7	194	1 432	3	63.2	96.0	78.2	4 887	2 163	99	86	1 563
Williamson	287	154 954	92.7	4 499	41 932	52	1 359.8	743.9	216.0	3 088	1 499	1 208	79	242
Wilson	26	D	D	(7)	D	8	198.2	96.2	94.8	2 958	2 174	45	76	516
Winkler	13	2 357	100.0	100	746	3	73.4	28.2	59.5	3 643	3 035	41	78	474
Wise	53	23 384	82.8	861	6 691	16	406.5	120.3	86.5	2 575	2 017	59	118	335
Wood	59	16 838	D	599	4 344	19	435.0	170.7	82.4	4 956	4 067	43	142	627
Yoakum	19	D	D	(6)	D	5	87.7	40.3	75.0	5 163	2 169	18	79	487
Young	38	9 952	83.7	353	2 659	8	308.8	85.9	57.1	4 892	3 808	36	138	692
Zapata	21	7 199	69.8	188	1 554	2	140.4	42.9	81.1	3 754	2 451	14	121	1 135
Zavala	12	2 744	D	66	548	3	35.0	54.2	66.6	4 557	2 230	18	47	1 847
UTAH	3 785	2 313 309	71.8	74 481	650 041	561	19 248.8	9 238.7	41.7	4 338	2 053	595	690	936
Beaver	34	10 290	64.3	462	3 217	3	48.6	24.0	66.8	4 002	2 638	97	238	980
Box Elder	61	26 038	90.1	1 063	8 512	9	251.3	564.7	–24.4	13 200	2 255	9 803	226	647
Cache	112	50 548	85.4	1 991	13 194	21	662.5	248.4	33.2	2 845	1 517	385	181	711
Carbon	54	16 879	73.1	641	4 326	9	194.1	160.4	156.3	7 675	3 198	3 020	349	1 097
Daggett	5	3 996	D	72	1 599	–	–	8.4	29.5	11 650	3 370	908	3 556	3 799
Davis	269	152 742	91.0	5 785	43 366	51	1 076.8	1 216.8	24.4	5 083	1 895	818	2 109	258
Duchesne	30	8 506	54.2	274	1 882	5	102.1	47.3	61.2	3 205	2 239	61	220	651
Emery	19	4 688	D	108	1 323	4	52.6	49.9	100.0	4 518	2 115	983	193	1 199
Garfield	46	22 431	10.7	425	7 557	3	33.8	23.5	42.4	5 493	3 014	846	1 020	583
Grand	82	38 349	51.8	1 141	9 938	3	74.6	33.2	45.0	4 053	2 367	114	970	598
Iron	82	41 969	54.9	1 349	12 616	10	221.9	91.7	99.2	3 114	2 085	116	456	438
Juab	22	6 794	74.4	292	1 972	3	46.1	26.2	78.1	3 364	2 242	137	131	716
Kane	34	14 003	34.9	328	3 739	3	67.4	23.0	107.2	3 737	3 006	107	389	226
Millard	24	6 044	76.0	328	1 842	3	84.7	61.6	136.8	4 959	2 208	186	334	2 037
Morgan	9	1 871	100.0	89	483	2	32.0	17.9	65.9	2 491	2 216	32	84	134
Piute	3	533	D	38	205	1	7.8	8.4	47.3	5 662	3 232	222	204	1 911
Rich	14	2 169	46.1	42	632	1	10.7	6.1	41.2	3 200	2 137	120	309	479
Salt Lake	1 572	1 202 189	72.2	35 518	334 186	237	11 768.8	3 505.4	60.3	4 123	1 811	424	558	1 311
San Juan	38	19 974	D	382	3 891	5	53.6	77.5	106.4	5 700	1 654	41	447	3 344
Sanpete	40	7 104	94.0	439	1 839	9	129.7	68.6	78.0	3 108	2 071	204	151	647
Sevier	43	15 666	D	628	4 359	6	157.1	69.4	75.2	3 720	2 704	46	406	538
Summit	131	105 051	51.8	3 481	33 827	16	352.6	65.7	211.6	2 372	980	160	201	1 024
Tooele	43	16 002	69.7	475	3 763	6	105.2	226.2	–32.6	6 319	2 642	1 569	1 616	482
Uintah	52	18 081	77.0	657	4 752	4	126.1	82.2	77.6	3 168	1 879	118	594	559
Utah	393	229 366	79.8	8 290	64 592	74	1 876.0	737.5	59.6	2 125	1 385	74	152	503
Wasatch	36	19 702	52.5	682	6 674	4	102.3	40.0	–4.3	2 905	1 599	195	145	936
Washington	195	113 218	58.4	3 580	31 645	26	660.9	285.9	145.8	3 347	2 624	64	404	232
Wayne	22	4 009	40.1	113	758	1	12.4	11.1	10.2	4 641	2 508	204	1 277	584
Weber	320	155 097	87.4	5 808	43 352	42	936.8	1 000.1	42.0	5 392	3 052	354	1 215	764
VERMONT	1 932	910 188	57.4	27 088	277 161	261	7 523.4	3 114.3	75.1	5 245	2 722	465	508	1 488
Addison	88	32 443	62.3	948	10 965	15	343.7	121.3	52.5	3 422	2 042	364	194	750
Bennington	163	76 600	49.8	2 044	21 309	19	540.1	159.4	66.4	4 431	3 043	223	195	952
Caledonia	72	24 363	81.0	767	6 897	19	442.0	129.0	93.3	4 476	2 860	50	211	1 332
Chittenden	392	207 684	76.9	6 211	61 059	52	1 910.2	777.7	84.6	5 403	2 083	1 444	717	1 138
Essex	21	D	D	(8)	D	1	18.2	31.9	55.9	4 808	3 107	190	509	971
Franklin	93	25 085	81.2	854	7 074	14	443.3	189.1	82.3	4 257	2 223	199	817	961
Grand Isle	21	D	D	(8)	D	2	37.8	23.6	79.3	3 703	2 579	69	187	803
Lamoille	112	122 228	24.1	3 415	36 534	12	245.9	83.7	86.8	3 816	2 452	44	174	1 125
Orange	58	20 837	54.3	626	6 368	14	228.1	101.1	83.4	3 626	2 411	69	194	926
Orleans	68	23 771	57.1	867	7 381	11	334.9	120.8	66.9	4 739	2 927	70	369	1 307
Rutland	234	108 628	58.1	3 358	31 713	22	781.3	286.5	64.6	4 590	3 045	70	278	1 174
Washington	176	63 007	76.7	2 200	20 192	25	805.5	463.7	91.9	8 237	2 877	91	345	4 893
Windham	218	106 065	49.4	3 194	36 632	22	659.2	165.1	57.1	3 870	2 723	108	217	797
Windsor	216	92 567	46.5	2 458	28 922	33	733.4	315.5	63.7	5 690	3 046	302	1 311	994

[1] Includes only establishments with payroll.   [2] Includes full-service restaurants, limited-service eating places, special food services, and drinking places (alcoholic beverages).   [3] For pay period including March 12.   [4] As of June 30. Covers all FDIC-insured commercial banks and savings institutions.   [5] Based on resident population estimated as of July 1, 1999.   [6] 100 to 249 employees.   [7] 250 to 499 employees.   [8] 20 to 99 employees.

Sources: Accommodation and Foodservices—U.S. Census Bureau, 1997 Economic Census, ECON97 Report Series CD-ROM, CD-EC97-1, Disc 1E, issued February 2001 (related Internet site <http://www.census.gov/epcd/www/97EC72.HTM>).   Banking—U.S. Federal Deposit Insurance Corporation and Office of Thrift Supervision, "1999 Bank and Thrift Branch Office Data Book: Summary of Deposits," national and 6 regional data books (related Internet site <http://www2.fdic.gov/sod/>).   Federal Funds and Grants—U.S. Census Bureau, County Aggregate files for each state, <http://www.census.gov/govs/www/cffr99.html>, (accessed: August 2000).

Table B–12. Counties — **Accommodation and Foodservices, Banking, and Federal Funds**–Con.

[Includes U.S., states, and 3,142 counties/county equivalents defined as of January 1, 1992. For changes to these areas since January 1, 1992, see appendix B. Geographic Information]

County	Accommodation and foodservices[1] (NAICS 72), 1997					Banking,[4] 1999		Federal funds and grants, 1999						
		Sales								Per capita[5] (dollars)				
												By selected type—		
	Establishments	Total ($1,000)	Percent from foodservices[2]	Paid employees[3]	Annual payroll ($1,000)	Offices	Deposits (mil. dol.)	Total expenditures or obligations (mil. dol.)	Percent change, 1990–1999	Total	Direct payments for individuals	Procurement contract awards	Salaries and wages	Grant awards
VIRGINIA	12 343	8 281 218	74.4	233 639	2 320 695	2 442	79 684.8	57 842.2	58.4	8 416	3 052	2 771	1 753	691
Accomack	100	32 888	63.9	892	9 046	15	376.2	276.8	59.6	8 618	3 812	2 540	1 185	969
Albemarle	140	114 802	D	3 054	35 103	21	417.6	187.9	111.5	2 345	1 791	45	45	457
Alleghany	15	6 901	46.1	199	2 251	–	–	31.5	81.8	2 590	1 236	112	25	1 211
Amelia	7	2 248	D	78	571	3	71.5	37.6	108.9	3 547	2 496	49	136	745
Amherst	44	19 302	97.9	615	4 918	11	243.3	102.8	66.0	3 387	2 609	276	88	403
Appomattox	19	5 555	79.6	185	1 462	4	140.5	45.9	64.6	3 450	2 643	30	154	593
Arlington	473	617 686	52.5	11 365	164 556	68	4 441.9	5 669.1	55.5	32 423	3 070	13 745	14 746	833
Augusta	66	32 969	73.3	1 112	10 007	14	199.6	144.9	74.8	2 369	1 862	37	90	352
Bath	16	2 633	28.4	81	919	2	42.5	25.8	66.7	5 246	3 869	68	348	942
Bedford	27	D	D	(6)	D	8	140.2	178.4	103.6	3 101	2 663	73	99	246
Dland	3	D	D	(7)	D	2	28.8	26.4	70.1	3 891	3 127	96	135	501
Botetourt	34	27 573	50.0	723	7 558	12	230.7	92.4	92.4	3 165	2 579	152	105	311
Brunswick	12	D	D	(8)	D	5	123.9	74.6	68.4	4 066	3 008	56	124	825
Buchanan	25	9 755	D	304	2 644	12	357.2	157.8	69.9	5 543	4 549	86	106	799
Buckingham	4	D	D	(9)	D	4	70.0	51.2	64.2	3 471	2 416	24	87	910
Campbell	55	D	D	(10)	D	12	401.8	166.1	-6.2	3 298	2 025	71	118	1 060
Caroline	28	11 903	D	292	3 210	7	201.8	88.9	43.3	4 027	2 852	230	509	350
Carroll	41	15 570	74.3	498	4 006	5	191.0	92.8	30.9	3 336	2 587	25	88	615
Charles City	6	D	D	(9)	D	1	15.4	22.3	83.9	3 082	2 213	24	134	567
Charlotte	13	3 084	D	117	1 048	6	112.5	69.9	109.6	5 627	3 927	669	191	777
Chesterfield	326	222 535	81.7	6 966	61 701	82	1 546.3	414.1	95.9	1 634	1 260	48	84	240
Clarke	20	D	D	(8)	D	3	113.1	40.7	16.9	3 173	2 491	221	137	268
Craig	4	D	D	(9)	D	2	48.0	20.7	117.3	4 186	2 743	885	200	333
Culpeper	52	21 990	88.9	629	5 851	11	374.2	116.3	73.8	3 464	2 731	47	191	448
Cumberland	4	420	100.0	19	145	3	33.6	26.9	58.1	3 419	2 233	56	84	987
Dickenson	13	2 979	91.8	99	777	5	128.2	100.9	90.1	6 035	4 457	375	124	1 030
Dinwiddie	16	5 913	88.8	154	1 338	6	148.3	80.8	91.0	3 149	2 225	284	73	503
Essex	23	12 422	D	356	3 822	7	171.6	44.5	70.6	4 875	3 868	79	137	503
Fairfax	1 523	1 368 846	71.8	31 596	382 562	241	12 412.1	10 257.1	125.2	10 846	2 310	7 338	933	254
Fauquier	70	47 643	71.6	1 415	13 936	21	685.9	190.4	38.5	3 449	2 101	803	160	357
Floyd	14	D	D	(8)	D	3	159.4	44.2	71.5	3 333	2 698	69	156	384
Fluvanna	9	4 961	D	107	1 533	2	35.4	64.3	114.4	3 278	2 848	25	91	304
Franklin	52	16 425	86.9	560	4 783	21	655.4	140.7	94.8	3 112	2 523	36	121	405
Frederick	72	45 561	79.8	1 317	12 769	16	200.9	112.8	85.9	1 994	1 726	26	43	191
Giles	17	6 097	91.3	187	1 668	9	171.9	75.9	62.0	4 651	3 655	36	128	824
Gloucester	43	19 272	90.3	686	5 124	11	267.2	123.7	29.6	3 489	3 030	36	113	289
Goochland	15	3 879	D	173	1 098	3	80.0	46.4	116.4	2 630	2 042	28	81	432
Grayson	14	1 840	83.4	65	555	6	150.4	61.2	58.4	3 718	2 779	87	111	707
Greene	10	4 546	D	134	1 250	3	62.6	37.3	92.2	2 542	2 025	20	119	364
Greensville	14	6 552	D	221	1 757	–	–	20.7	40.8	1 827	1 159	9	9	507
Halifax	61	23 721	88.4	773	5 922	12	406.0	181.8	152.0	4 924	3 170	583	140	962
Hanover	110	68 999	84.4	2 053	19 177	36	801.1	229.7	114.7	2 690	2 293	90	95	165
Henrico	458	350 647	76.9	9 892	96 796	84	3 128.9	454.9	91.7	1 860	1 501	51	138	167
Henry	73	31 600	85.9	1 105	8 387	15	415.3	157.0	64.3	2 822	2 406	28	64	320
Highland	6	972	D	50	274	2	60.4	11.6	59.3	4 693	3 863	57	204	534
Isle of Wight	34	D	D	(10)	D	6	193.9	107.7	79.4	3 634	2 840	133	147	402
James City	77	74 627	49.1	1 715	21 016	24	521.9	93.3	244.2	2 030	1 617	49	24	332
King and Queen	2	D	D	(7)	D	1	8.0	25.7	36.7	3 923	2 940	52	131	501
King George	18	D	D	(8)	D	3	90.3	596.1	107.9	33 716	2 711	14 747	15 990	207
King William	10	3 852	100.0	136	1 089	6	173.0	42.7	72.3	3 271	2 525	61	132	388
Lancaster	25	17 433	D	452	6 153	12	261.7	82.0	57.3	7 222	6 417	117	197	416
Lee	18	5 665	D	200	1 539	13	290.3	256.8	192.9	10 780	4 121	5 072	108	1 441
Loudoun	212	154 769	82.1	3 877	45 825	49	1 208.8	750.4	169.7	4 802	1 415	1 830	1 415	112
Louisa	20	8 856	79.1	320	2 565	6	181.0	87.2	84.4	3 485	2 845	29	103	478
Lunenburg	5	998	100.0	41	295	5	125.1	48.8	19.3	4 141	3 124	165	113	680
Madison	12	5 694	D	126	1 656	2	76.4	44.1	68.8	3 489	2 540	71	241	561
Mathews	8	D	D	(8)	D	2	89.1	52.6	-9.8	5 684	4 799	343	250	273
Mecklenburg	66	29 144	77.7	1 086	8 261	15	483.1	164.4	89.6	5 306	3 628	708	189	739
Middlesex	22	8 754	D	265	2 269	8	129.0	52.1	76.6	5 335	4 523	39	132	412
Montgomery	150	96 059	84.2	3 446	26 059	33	794.4	314.5	-16.9	4 085	2 019	341	184	1 533
Nelson	21	23 565	D	708	8 300	4	78.5	68.1	26.7	4 803	3 775	175	211	622
New Kent	14	4 799	D	121	1 457	2	64.6	43.9	98.7	3 323	2 818	36	120	304
Northampton	29	15 597	71.4	408	4 030	7	145.5	128.6	163.8	10 042	3 845	4 448	204	1 294
Northumberland	16	3 148	87.1	115	1 071	7	178.0	62.7	78.1	5 375	4 560	43	128	439
Nottoway	29	9 738	84.9	391	2 452	8	237.5	90.3	60.1	5 905	3 856	271	1 109	623
Orange	34	14 614	D	478	3 862	11	262.1	121.8	76.1	4 729	4 063	62	114	453
Page	49	21 892	45.5	543	5 842	9	233.4	102.2	76.0	4 411	3 062	622	289	417
Patrick	22	D	D	(8)	D	8	193.4	65.4	69.3	3 531	2 822	110	126	453
Pittsylvania	56	19 716	88.8	608	5 596	11	221.5	186.8	73.6	3 292	2 281	141	87	733
Powhatan	9	3 920	D	124	919	4	112.5	44.9	63.3	2 005	1 710	35	123	122

[1] Includes only establishments with payroll. [2] Includes full-service restaurants, limited-service eating places, special food services, and drinking places (alcoholic beverages). [3] For pay period including March 12. [4] As of June 30. Covers all FDIC-insured commercial banks and savings institutions. [5] Based on resident population estimated as of July 1, 1999. [6] 250 to 499 employees. [7] 0 to 19 employees. [8] 100 to 249 employees. [9] 20 to 99 employees. [10] 500 to 999 employees.

Sources: Accommodation and Foodservices—U.S. Census Bureau, 1997 Economic Census, ECON97 Report Series CD-ROM, CD-EC97-1, Disc 1E, issued February 2001 (related Internet site <http://www.census.gov/epcd/www/97EC72.HTM>). Banking—U.S. Federal Deposit Insurance Corporation and Office of Thrift Supervision, "1999 Bank and Thrift Branch Office Data Book: Summary of Deposits," national and 6 regional data books (related Internet site <http://www2.fdic.gov/sod/>). Federal Funds and Grants—U.S. Census Bureau, County Aggregate files for each state, <http://www.census.gov/govs/www/cffr99.html>, (accessed: August 2000).

[Includes U.S., states, and 3,142 counties/county equivalents defined as of January 1, 1992. For changes to these areas since January 1, 1992, see appendix B. Geographic Information]

County	Accommodation and foodservices[1] (NAICS 72), 1997					Banking,[4] 1999		Federal funds and grants, 1999						
		Sales						Total expenditures or obligations (mil. dol.)	Percent change, 1990–1999	Per capita[5] (dollars)				
											By selected type—			
	Establishments	Total ($1,000)	Percent from food-services[2]	Paid employees[3]	Annual payroll ($1,000)	Offices	Deposits (mil. dol.)			Total	Direct payments for individuals	Procurement contract awards	Salaries and wages	Grant awards
VIRGINIA—Con.														
Prince Edward	44	27 935	D	1 056	7 565	13	260.7	80.7	65.2	4 194	3 245	51	204	639
Prince George	27	20 903	65.9	674	5 214	5	134.5	419.1	43.0	14 546	1 920	2 301	10 139	151
Prince William	364	265 962	89.1	7 882	72 576	50	898.7	1 205.8	91.2	4 452	1 720	1 057	1 452	219
Pulaski	54	21 488	87.9	749	5 368	10	232.6	134.7	58.2	3 915	3 302	39	93	470
Rappahannock	13	8 716	83.7	206	2 862	2	30.5	30.5	53.7	3 982	3 298	82	203	364
Richmond	11	D	D	(6)	D	17	427.4	43.4	253.6	4 968	3 421	569	143	632
Roanoke	89	43 595	71.9	1 302	12 406	28	698.9	125.1	24.6	1 542	1 341	21	29	147
Rockbridge	44	19 889	45.3	525	5 667	4	75.2	62.5	77.5	3 196	1 935	241	119	871
Rockingham	79	54 188	D	1 706	14 354	20	450.9	178.3	75.1	2 826	2 187	211	140	252
Russell	29	9 733	93.0	339	2 657	12	279.5	139.9	84.2	4 869	3 668	111	111	929
Scott	18	D	D	(7)	D	9	189.8	115.3	66.2	5 123	3 793	30	178	1 054
Shenandoah	72	30 670	71.0	1 160	9 278	20	546.7	137.9	58.5	3 926	3 286	52	206	348
Smyth	47	16 455	D	526	4 356	12	384.6	164.6	31.4	5 034	3 300	729	140	830
Southampton	13	4 115	D	147	1 196	7	86.4	65.2	62.5	3 690	2 477	61	117	703
Spotsylvania	89	61 905	76.2	1 741	16 759	15	352.0	105.2	85.0	1 204	1 060	9	26	102
Stafford	95	57 335	80.0	1 809	14 870	13	263.3	213.7	125.3	2 294	1 790	187	91	221
Surry	5	D	D	(6)	D	2	27.0	25.8	78.9	3 984	2 865	40	177	633
Sussex	14	6 775	D	236	1 994	7	129.0	61.9	99.1	5 012	3 396	54	254	1 128
Tazewell	66	32 456	93.2	1 091	8 670	29	633.9	247.7	63.3	5 345	4 483	38	139	679
Warren	61	25 624	76.5	763	6 979	12	259.8	103.6	68.1	3 383	2 694	181	255	247
Washington	84	48 508	81.6	1 680	14 330	22	621.0	189.7	93.4	3 810	2 642	113	97	933
Westmoreland	37	9 663	81.7	253	2 634	6	146.7	91.1	57.6	5 602	4 616	46	196	590
Wise	49	20 487	D	688	5 642	16	384.9	258.5	73.9	6 432	4 311	1 092	176	830
Wythe	65	38 446	57.8	1 275	10 120	15	327.1	118.9	53.0	4 486	3 582	49	195	621
York	93	77 882	70.6	2 303	20 741	15	266.8	308.7	27.1	5 282	3 043	436	1 549	252
Independent Cities														
Alexandria	310	308 321	66.4	6 616	92 349	47	2 239.3	2 374.0	44.4	20 223	5 581	9 627	4 174	794
Bedford	24	D	D	(7)	D	5	230.2	53.7	86.7	8 039	7 174	312	328	215
Bristol	52	D	D	(8)	D	17	423.1	126.0	53.8	7 541	5 622	199	823	834
Buena Vista	11	4 374	D	162	1 390	3	78.6	28.9	65.1	4 471	3 631	34	204	598
Charlottesville	179	121 519	77.7	3 521	34 729	36	1 193.2	507.7	87.1	13 792	4 114	3 486	1 840	4 300
Chesapeake	305	187 381	86.6	6 321	51 614	59	1 066.1	797.2	65.9	3 932	2 640	521	453	300
Clifton Forge	12	D	D	(9)	D	3	116.6	30.4	56.0	7 240	6 454	44	207	529
Colonial Heights	63	40 782	D	1 431	10 937	11	323.8	95.2	76.3	5 866	5 465	49	166	179
Covington	16	6 739	D	209	1 758	5	238.8	62.6	39.9	9 147	7 684	60	467	928
Danville	114	65 745	88.2	2 159	18 829	37	1 054.1	260.4	51.7	5 126	4 084	44	182	791
Emporia	24	16 198	72.2	490	4 447	9	199.3	42.7	59.7	7 534	6 071	56	229	1 169
Fairfax	150	108 000	88.4	3 029	29 391	27	1 177.2	2 094.4	356.8	101 192	13 578	82 201	2 053	3 224
Falls Church	68	D	D	(10)	D	16	598.4	966.7	64.1	97 215	12 311	50 733	21 835	12 283
Franklin	18	10 096	D	321	2 492	7	153.8	59.5	60.6	7 307	5 461	85	149	1 568
Fredericksburg	141	91 993	83.6	2 748	24 414	32	910.1	239.8	91.6	12 738	10 226	1 354	673	464
Galax	28	D	D	(7)	D	10	253.9	55.5	68.6	8 554	7 175	86	358	927
Hampton	229	149 855	77.2	5 002	41 096	33	674.8	1 704.2	50.1	12 422	3 692	3 216	4 749	745
Harrisonburg	109	70 224	83.5	2 318	18 951	28	754.7	103.3	58.3	3 027	2 385	139	227	268
Hopewell	46	D	D	(10)	D	7	219.8	268.6	245.8	11 851	4 222	6 835	91	657
Lexington	57	27 378	65.8	787	6 919	7	226.1	54.9	88.6	7 463	5 526	135	562	1 231
Lynchburg	173	110 800	83.6	3 808	30 899	42	1 359.9	531.9	−37.9	8 320	3 922	2 864	663	843
Manassas	74	D	D	(8)	D	22	640.5	606.6	21.9	18 109	3 245	13 016	637	1 128
Manassas Park	5	3 246	100.0	136	1 170	–	–	10.0	−16.4	1 265	144	214	106	800
Martinsville	46	25 116	92.6	768	6 625	11	545.7	124.4	71.0	8 293	6 646	465	243	933
Newport News	312	170 072	82.3	5 464	47 733	48	1 230.2	1 863.8	−41.8	10 404	3 028	4 310	2 529	492
Norfolk	539	299 445	80.9	9 980	85 057	69	2 258.5	5 110.0	43.3	22 623	3 354	6 715	11 457	1 016
Norton	23	D	D	(7)	D	5	142.9	38.4	32.5	9 580	6 389	222	1 310	1 588
Petersburg	83	34 227	75.3	1 194	10 148	20	576.6	278.2	82.9	8 087	5 892	510	274	1 337
Poquoson	20	4 336	100.0	193	1 185	2	62.4	23.7	−36.8	2 045	1 906	3	71	64
Portsmouth	137	58 713	88.6	2 040	15 791	20	666.0	1 360.2	31.4	13 837	4 265	2 401	6 281	833
Radford	34	14 285	71.7	567	3 632	11	244.9	88.9	93.8	5 671	2 710	2 120	414	422
Richmond	551	304 206	75.6	9 087	91 363	88	7 037.7	2 852.9	55.7	15 039	6 336	924	2 314	5 303
Roanoke	325	203 403	76.5	6 380	58 743	58	3 089.5	742.6	37.2	7 954	4 982	1 058	961	892
Salem	86	45 222	86.9	1 751	13 185	20	557.6	206.5	64.3	8 592	4 595	388	3 279	296
South Boston	X	X	X	X	X	X	X	X	X	X	X	X	X	X
Staunton	72	34 360	78.6	1 029	9 419	16	512.7	128.4	61.1	5 243	4 370	45	283	535
Suffolk	62	32 827	88.2	1 027	8 880	21	399.9	323.4	99.9	4 991	2 974	1 013	217	719
Virginia Beach	888	576 268	74.1	18 145	163 311	114	2 726.3	2 424.0	53.9	5 592	2 737	690	2 002	157
Waynesboro	51	26 114	81.2	838	7 658	10	247.5	93.9	69.8	4 871	4 365	48	134	302
Williamsburg	140	204 834	37.4	4 581	55 530	3	38.2	195.0	44.0	15 602	11 688	1 366	1 626	892
Winchester	99	57 968	86.3	1 713	18 382	30	692.5	154.5	71.4	6 875	4 555	1 009	879	420

[1] Includes only establishments with payroll. [2] Includes full-service restaurants, limited-service eating places, special food services, and drinking places (alcoholic beverages). [3] For pay period including March 12. [4] As of June 30. Covers all FDIC-insured commercial banks and savings institutions. [5] Based on resident population estimated as of July 1, 1999. [6] 20 to 99 employees. [7] 250 to 499 employees. [8] 1,000 to 2,499 employees. [9] 100 to 249 employees. [10] 500 to 999 employees.

Sources: Accommodation and Foodservices—U.S. Census Bureau, 1997 Economic Census, ECON97 Report Series CD-ROM, CD-EC97-1, Disc 1E, issued February 2001 (related Internet site <http://www.census.gov/epcd/www/97EC72.HTM>). Banking—U.S. Federal Deposit Insurance Corporation and Office of Thrift Supervision, "1999 Bank and Thrift Branch Office Data Book: Summary of Deposits," national and 6 regional data books (related Internet site <http://www2.fdic.gov/sod/>). Federal Funds and Grants—U.S. Census Bureau, County Aggregate files for each state, <http://www.census.gov/govs/www/cffr99.html>, (accessed: August 2000).

[Includes U.S., states, and 3,142 counties/county equivalents defined as of January 1, 1992. For changes to these areas since January 1, 1992, see appendix B. Geographic Information]

County	Accommodation and foodservices[1] (NAICS 72), 1997					Banking,[4] 1999		Federal funds and grants, 1999						
		Sales								Per capita[5] (dollars)				
												By selected type—		
	Estab-lishments	Total ($1,000)	Percent from food-services[2]	Paid employ-ees[3]	Annual payroll ($1,000)	Offices	Deposits (mil. dol.)	Total expenditures or obligations (mil. dol.)	Percent change, 1990–1999	Total	Direct payments for individuals	Procure-ment contract awards	Salaries and wages	Grant awards
WASHINGTON	13 124	7 001 716	79.8	195 157	1 965 223	1 633	57 817.3	31 993.1	59.2	5 558	2 792	802	846	994
Adams	37	12 185	89.1	387	3 038	11	122.9	101.6	104.9	6 667	1 932	717	128	1 908
Asotin	40	16 125	76.8	516	4 948	7	165.1	90.6	72.7	4 270	3 152	100	132	689
Benton	256	136 138	84.3	4 223	36 808	36	954.0	1 884.6	40.1	13 672	2 176	10 582	383	463
Chelan	240	98 751	61.1	2 946	27 072	26	755.6	269.3	-3.9	4 427	2 875	165	465	870
Clallam	214	75 925	73.3	2 104	19 591	26	856.0	361.8	74.0	5 593	4 248	205	404	709
Clark	506	271 705	86.4	8 570	76 760	80	2 087.5	1 111.8	92.2	3 306	2 106	289	392	481
Columbia	12	D	D	(6)	D	4	56.5	35.1	112.7	8 441	3 445	673	574	915
Cowlitz	214	97 069	85.6	3 208	28 745	20	469.4	384.1	82.2	4 178	2 875	289	141	868
Douglas	46	21 610	85.7	733	6 283	10	201.6	111.6	71.1	3 265	2 160	93	174	381
Ferry	21	5 056	82.6	126	1 070	1	14.5	33.9	115.2	4 722	2 563	104	712	1 310
Franklin	87	34 568	70.2	1 105	9 304	13	235.9	182.6	71.5	3 904	1 974	202	476	927
Garfield	3	D	D	(7)	D	3	37.9	25.1	80.1	10 742	4 206	888	1 566	27
Grant	170	58 848	72.5	1 930	15 256	24	438.8	294.9	77.5	4 095	2 381	251	399	704
Grays Harbor	238	74 192	73.7	2 150	20 292	32	743.9	336.1	55.0	5 009	3 578	221	170	1 025
Island	123	44 619	78.7	1 423	12 082	24	566.4	576.3	55.1	7 842	2 926	619	3 964	326
Jefferson	99	35 627	58.4	1 118	10 480	9	238.6	142.3	72.4	5 318	4 098	100	301	814
King	4 462	3 163 076	73.8	76 111	896 990	461	27 035.9	8 828.7	43.9	5 303	2 358	1 075	678	1 150
Kitsap	400	180 343	90.7	6 003	50 634	60	1 385.6	2 239.0	45.7	9 465	3 023	999	4 916	517
Kittitas	125	45 622	77.9	1 431	13 031	10	306.1	123.4	87.9	3 853	2 573	56	211	975
Klickitat	48	9 537	84.1	297	2 872	7	164.5	79.9	53.0	4 092	2 810	161	218	663
Lewis	196	62 902	87.8	1 919	17 526	24	603.1	315.0	69.8	4 591	3 352	99	188	929
Lincoln	33	4 229	91.4	154	1 085	10	178.9	93.8	109.8	9 607	3 775	92	322	873
Mason	98	29 913	83.9	953	7 802	10	285.0	231.0	101.6	4 588	3 708	69	101	691
Okanogan	122	42 433	65.8	1 192	12 449	14	283.1	192.9	64.7	5 019	2 916	508	467	1 063
Pacific	110	26 917	75.9	818	7 612	13	217.3	152.2	102.8	7 327	4 429	1 919	252	708
Pend Oreille	27	4 827	85.3	167	1 361	4	80.0	57.1	86.5	4 924	3 268	85	319	1 192
Pierce	1 220	604 564	93.0	18 833	169 718	163	4 449.7	3 715.1	62.2	5 394	2 784	371	1 501	724
San Juan	99	40 096	37.7	778	13 118	7	215.5	49.9	69.0	3 870	3 344	115	233	170
Skagit	278	118 246	82.0	3 619	31 503	44	1 133.4	401.9	75.7	3 972	3 024	94	172	645
Skamania	17	4 406	50.8	221	1 179	3	43.9	52.7	117.7	5 356	1 888	2 398	691	377
Snohomish	1 112	559 785	90.2	16 740	154 356	153	4 302.6	1 911.8	113.2	3 204	1 924	279	486	506
Spokane	906	454 192	86.1	14 490	128 971	101	3 237.7	1 980.0	60.9	4 832	2 976	230	759	820
Stevens	82	23 484	75.3	689	5 409	7	207.9	159.0	80.6	3 961	2 602	224	363	736
Thurston	406	192 960	87.4	6 076	56 569	55	1 424.8	570.7	59.5	7 645	3 113	110	209	4 001
Wahkiakum	13	1 481	100.0	50	435	2	27.5	16.2	-14.5	4 217	3 528	66	189	408
Walla Walla	113	42 788	87.0	1 482	12 020	17	684.2	275.1	61.5	5 109	2 979	177	633	774
Whatcom	430	195 847	83.4	5 951	52 895	59	1 682.1	670.9	-3.7	4 185	2 343	872	263	682
Whitman	110	30 911	74.9	1 196	7 643	28	376.5	235.6	79.2	6 138	2 110	230	311	1 804
Yakima	411	178 615	84.5	5 371	47 826	55	1 547.4	884.7	66.4	4 007	2 270	241	281	1 166
WEST VIRGINIA	3 290	1 633 164	77.0	51 529	462 334	616	20 888.8	11 028.1	64.0	6 103	3 821	346	504	1 378
Barbour	22	D	D	(8)	D	4	176.4	80.4	66.7	5 030	3 442	56	141	1 385
Berkeley	129	67 640	75.6	1 947	17 024	21	565.0	484.8	125.6	6 655	2 843	1 121	1 944	719
Boone	22	8 269	88.8	259	2 355	6	215.5	129.0	61.7	4 905	3 641	58	178	1 017
Braxton	32	14 348	D	444	3 962	7	144.9	83.8	104.0	6 344	3 492	43	200	2 603
Brooke	58	D	D	(9)	D	8	302.2	100.6	51.6	3 887	3 286	23	94	482
Cabell	253	140 895		4 933	39 332	31	1 356.1	569.6	47.8	6 088	4 138	186	528	1 202
Calhoun	5	3 869	D	88	716	2	55.2	44.2	69.4	5 536	3 459	37	139	1 893
Clay	7	488	D	12	58	3	58.7	56.2	64.8	5 299	3 470	36	128	1 659
Doddridge	4	D	D	(6)	D	2	74.4	26.6	50.4	3 572	2 427	29	102	1 008
Fayette	65	27 864	84.1	918	8 468	17	414.4	291.7	55.2	6 235	4 559	59	304	1 300
Gilmer	11	2 548	85.0	92	612	2	72.1	135.9	477.0	19 020	3 560	13 558	177	1 714
Grant	21	4 365	79.1	166	1 014	5	180.2	55.0	74.2	4 938	2 877	401	232	1 379
Greenbrier	78	118 391	D	2 098	41 828	12	410.7	196.0	68.6	5 550	3 908	288	173	1 171
Hampshire	32	11 150	44.1	311	3 307	7	201.4	114.9	169.2	5 918	2 981	1 848	128	906
Hancock	84	D	D	(9)	D	13	404.9	164.2	51.7	4 867	4 242	40	114	455
Hardy	21	7 525	88.5	341	1 992	6	178.2	58.1	92.0	4 849	2 818	143	216	1 623
Harrison	151	73 049	87.2	2 340	20 576	34	801.2	400.6	52.7	5 696	3 834	257	774	812
Jackson	36	20 076	80.5	637	5 205	10	303.5	125.9	98.9	4 451	3 097	473	152	708
Jefferson	82	37 569	83.7	1 114	10 205	16	460.0	208.5	109.0	4 933	2 772	631	786	693
Kanawha	420	280 726	82.5	8 287	75 852	63	2 852.3	1 573.6	66.9	7 897	4 050	245	703	2 856
Lewis	30	12 374	79.6	341	3 280	5	197.9	89.3	47.6	5 114	3 649	42	188	1 213
Lincoln	11	D	D	(6)	D	6	92.0	116.9	83.6	5 232	3 406	28	106	1 681
Logan	63	24 045	91.5	751	6 121	13	394.9	240.4	62.1	5 983	4 506	41	168	1 264
McDowell	17	5 608	D	176	1 447	12	1 028.2	250.5	64.8	8 549	5 558	434	161	2 390

[1] Includes only establishments with payroll. [2] Includes full-service restaurants, limited-service eating places, special food services, and drinking places (alcoholic beverages). [3] For pay period including March 12. [4] As of June 30. Covers all FDIC-insured commercial banks and savings institutions. [5] Based on resident population estimated as of July 1, 1999. [6] 20 to 99 employees. [7] 0 to 19 employees. [8] 100 to 249 employees. [9] 500 to 999 employees.

Sources: Accommodation and Foodservices—U.S. Census Bureau, 1997 Economic Census, ECON[97] Report Series CD-ROM, CD-EC97-1, Disc 1E, issued February 2001 (related Internet site <http://www.census.gov/epcd/www/97EC72.HTM>). Banking—U.S. Federal Deposit Insurance Corporation and Office of Thrift Supervision, "1999 Bank and Thrift Branch Office Data Book: Summary of Deposits," national and 6 regional data books (related Internet site <http://www2.fdic.gov/sod/>). Federal Funds and Grants—U.S. Census Bureau, County Aggregate files for each state, <http://www.census.gov/govs/www/cffr99.html>, (accessed: August 2000).

Table B–12. Counties — Accommodation and Foodservices, Banking, and Federal Funds–Con.

[Includes U.S., states, and 3,142 counties/county equivalents defined as of January 1, 1992. For changes to these areas since January 1, 1992, see appendix B. Geographic Information]

County	Accommodation and foodservices[1] (NAICS 72), 1997 — Establishments	Sales Total ($1,000)	Sales Percent from foodservices[2]	Paid employees[3]	Annual payroll ($1,000)	Banking,[4] 1999 Offices	Banking Deposits (mil. dol.)	Federal funds and grants, 1999 Total expenditures or obligations (mil. dol.)	Percent change, 1990–1999	Per capita[5] (dollars) Total	By selected type— Direct payments for individuals	Procurement contract awards	Salaries and wages	Grant awards
WEST VIRGINIA—Con.														
Marion	96	36 893	87.3	1 295	10 499	17	561.9	345.2	67.1	6 170	4 091	879	188	992
Marshall	61	19 609	D	661	5 481	10	287.6	144.7	52.3	4 137	3 288	25	146	661
Mason	30	7 574	D	307	2 101	7	247.6	120.2	-3.1	4 620	3 249	205	290	838
Mercer	100	64 283	82.8	2 010	17 110	19	758.0	366.9	55.1	5 721	4 353	48	229	1 079
Mineral	48	13 154	D	486	3 399	10	213.2	135.2	20.0	4 994	3 579	623	117	649
Mingo	42	10 801	72.5	346	3 089	12	409.9	199.5	44.6	6 337	4 149	228	149	1 785
Monongalia	207	95 533	76.4	3 795	28 400	25	895.0	426.2	70.2	5 535	2 538	829	999	1 141
Monroe	13	D	D	(6)	D	5	101.7	83.5	61.4	6 276	3 965	75	966	1 233
Morgan	20	11 807	D	375	4 218	5	149.0	56.2	36.2	4 047	3 457	32	99	450
Nicholas	45	18 595	76.1	590	5 311	9	282.1	135.8	74.3	4 934	3 613	50	192	1 074
Ohio	148	60 250	D	2 136	17 541	25	994.1	300.2	53.8	6 291	4 045	299	493	1 399
Pendleton	11	2 685	D	105	661	3	118.7	53.4	107.2	6 640	3 207	647	1 334	1 380
Pleasants	11	3 646	D	127	1 083	4	89.0	29.8	-68.7	3 964	3 216	30	107	605
Pocahontas	29	40 294	D	1 011	11 039	3	107.8	94.5	45.2	10 419	3 686	392	269	6 043
Preston	30	6 703	83.8	244	1 747	12	297.6	142.8	86.8	4 788	3 279	152	213	1 130
Putnam	67	32 165	89.5	1 050	8 493	11	557.6	154.9	83.7	2 983	2 245	37	151	542
Raleigh	140	84 361	77.2	2 489	23 290	26	894.7	474.2	69.8	6 006	4 087	194	874	839
Randolph	62	23 579	79.9	876	6 579	11	317.6	185.8	59.5	6 484	3 590	68	412	2 393
Ritchie	10	2 177	D	97	509	7	98.1	70.9	136.2	6 763	3 250	2 092	154	1 258
Roane	14	4 528	D	133	1 270	5	192.5	75.8	81.4	4 918	3 241	30	138	1 486
Summers	18	7 367	D	202	2 158	4	127.7	86.8	79.2	6 263	3 851	190	148	2 065
Taylor	15	3 635	D	119	893	3	87.3	68.5	57.2	4 459	3 296	70	165	908
Tucker	28	11 757	D	326	3 475	5	85.5	41.7	76.4	5 551	3 397	100	347	1 700
Tyler	15	D	D	(6)	D	4	72.1	37.8	71.0	3 890	2 887	32	128	830
Upshur	42	13 728	90.6	552	4 218	7	223.9	102.1	58.6	4 334	3 102	70	196	956
Wayne	49	12 384	D	443	3 429	8	244.2	224.3	125.9	5 359	2 848	64	917	1 527
Webster	12	D	D	(6)	D	4	48.0	62.0	70.4	6 176	4 090	60	106	1 915
Wetzel	42	12 280	95.0	420	3 585	13	215.4	92.8	56.8	5 093	3 765	68	158	1 095
Wirt	4	607	D	13	117	2	29.4	26.9	-36.6	4 674	3 096	190	137	1 233
Wood	198	110 746	87.8	3 767	32 139	27	1 048.9	490.6	76.1	5 682	3 488	160	964	1 059
Wyoming	29	8 156	D	267	1 848	8	192.3	157.4	72.1	5 831	4 325	52	186	1 263
WISCONSIN	13 253	5 649 870	79.1	190 520	1 550 660	2 071	72 446.0	22 603.8	49.2	4 305	2 667	273	288	922
Adams	42	14 606	48.8	416	3 997	5	130.8	86.4	75.3	4 611	2 581	53	1 049	804
Ashland	73	20 810	77.6	753	5 653	9	220.7	89.4	39.1	5 457	3 357	461	410	1 191
Barron	146	39 482	84.8	1 395	10 400	22	632.3	181.2	55.4	4 110	2 750	72	169	925
Bayfield	92	22 161	47.1	620	5 459	10	130.4	72.1	60.2	4 693	2 886	223	312	1 175
Brown	533	283 359	79.7	10 183	81 884	71	3 253.9	731.8	55.1	3 380	2 035	533	261	511
Buffalo	45	D	D	(7)	D	10	215.8	66.2	54.8	4 633	2 594	268	411	979
Burnett	66	D	D	(7)	D	8	146.8	69.6	38.7	4 664	3 242	207	123	991
Calumet	75	24 902	98.9	932	6 417	14	351.5	81.0	44.9	2 076	1 487	34	210	216
Chippewa	132	34 329	87.8	1 322	8 496	26	541.4	201.1	19.4	3 675	2 565	87	185	718
Clark	66	D	D	(8)	D	22	393.2	128.2	44.4	3 837	2 623	67	162	752
Columbia	190	62 272	68.4	1 717	15 080	28	690.5	248.7	93.4	4 802	2 888	1 008	194	519
Crawford	54	15 748	79.2	614	4 340	12	292.0	71.8	48.9	4 346	2 705	84	218	1 126
Dane	993	554 110	81.2	18 607	156 853	143	5 984.3	2 510.0	60.1	5 857	2 057	205	510	3 014
Dodge	165	41 572	92.4	1 637	10 659	36	904.0	203.1	40.0	2 432	1 858	39	115	276
Door	243	96 428	52.7	1 796	25 141	18	455.7	122.9	-58.0	4 539	3 332	108	511	491
Douglas	178	50 860	80.8	1 818	13 119	14	385.5	205.8	33.7	4 790	3 272	157	195	1 122
Dunn	107	33 437	84.5	1 383	9 417	27	289.8	124.0	53.5	3 163	1 982	57	127	771
Eau Claire	247	115 948	82.4	4 932	34 571	30	882.2	400.2	73.1	4 460	2 419	93	237	748
Florence	16	D	D	(9)	D	3	40.6	18.8	49.7	3 656	2 806	19	145	644
Fond du Lac	227	92 949	89.0	3 584	25 595	33	1 230.5	332.0	55.6	3 502	2 648	95	136	487
Forest	35	D	D	(9)	D	7	101.6	55.5	56.3	5 737	3 416	302	404	1 409
Grant	139	34 669	86.7	1 431	8 541	33	792.8	199.3	52.7	4 041	2 687	94	179	738
Green	92	29 102	91.8	1 182	8 312	18	626.1	110.7	55.9	3 270	2 371	36	140	388
Green Lake	62	20 049	61.8	707	5 730	13	333.9	79.0	40.3	4 039	3 034	91	153	506
Iowa	52	D	D	(8)	D	14	228.5	76.0	74.9	3 348	1 883	55	192	810
Iron	53	11 310	D	440	2 722	2	52.3	33.3	36.5	5 291	3 941	81	198	1 052
Jackson	52	17 066	76.3	685	4 460	9	165.3	76.8	52.3	4 308	2 648	39	161	1 253
Jefferson	187	52 775	90.8	2 098	13 902	28	848.7	251.1	54.0	3 391	2 568	60	141	503
Juneau	86	34 176	48.0	979	10 099	14	286.7	125.6	35.8	5 212	3 258	664	440	710
Kenosha	340	133 310	91.5	4 546	37 065	37	1 137.3	467.3	50.1	3 194	2 367	197	107	497
Kewaunee	53	11 561	88.1	512	2 788	12	290.7	95.3	109.6	4 775	2 534	1 447	171	398
La Crosse	300	141 879	82.1	5 533	41 428	36	1 258.4	378.1	47.5	3 691	2 421	326	261	642

[1] Includes only establishments with payroll. [2] Includes full-service restaurants, limited-service eating places, special food services, and drinking places (alcoholic beverages). [3] For pay period including March 12. [4] As of June 30. Covers all FDIC-insured commercial banks and savings institutions. [5] Based on resident population estimated as of July 1, 1999. [6] 20 to 99 employees. [7] 250 to 499 employees. [8] 500 to 999 employees. [9] 100 to 249 employees.

Sources: Accommodation and Foodservices—U.S. Census Bureau, 1997 Economic Census, ECON97 Report Series CD-ROM, CD-EC97-1, Disc 1E, issued February 2001 (related Internet site <http://www.census.gov/epcd/www/97EC72.HTM>). Banking—U.S. Federal Deposit Insurance Corporation and Office of Thrift Supervision, "1999 Bank and Thrift Branch Office Data Book: Summary of Deposits," national and 6 regional data books (related Internet site <http://www2.fdic.gov/sod/>). Federal Funds and Grants—U.S. Census Bureau, County Aggregate files for each state, <http://www.census.gov/govs/www/cffr99.html>, (accessed: August 2000).

Table B–12. Counties — **Accommodation and Foodservices, Banking, and Federal Funds**–Con.

[Includes U.S., states, and 3,142 counties/county equivalents defined as of January 1, 1992. For changes to these areas since January 1, 1992, see appendix B. Geographic Information]

County	Estab-lishments	Sales Total ($1,000)	Percent from food-services[2]	Paid employ-ees[3]	Annual payroll ($1,000)	Offices	Deposits (mil. dol.)	Total expenditures or obligations (mil. dol.)	Percent change, 1990–1999	Per capita Total	Direct payments for individuals	Procure-ment contract awards	Salaries and wages	Grant awards
WISCONSIN—Con.														
Lafayette	36	5 537	100.0	256	1 476	11	286.7	62.2	44.8	3 882	2 369	41	164	531
Langlade	75	18 833	83.6	677	5 212	8	155.7	99.6	45.5	4 842	3 185	251	133	1 186
Lincoln	98	21 303	86.6	894	6 274	13	296.8	119.1	54.1	3 976	3 002	32	142	762
Manitowoc	179	59 367	83.9	2 512	16 363	30	1 033.6	288.6	47.2	3 488	2 766	41	128	452
Marathon	276	105 188	88.8	3 779	29 733	49	1 746.6	391.2	62.0	3 165	2 156	88	238	610
Marinette	140	36 184	85.0	1 386	9 915	19	548.1	241.6	99.8	5 616	3 242	1 371	205	736
Marquette	59	D	D	(6)	D	8	141.9	77.8	90.3	5 068	3 712	406	170	617
Menominee	9	D	D	(7)	D	–	–	35.9	55.8	7 126	1 685	1 186	66	4 182
Milwaukee	1 839	1 014 424	85.3	31 402	282 700	278	18 601.6	4 534.0	32.8	5 003	3 057	129	595	1 190
Monroe	110	35 828	81.3	1 186	9 305	18	388.6	258.6	-4.6	6 511	2 934	579	1 964	871
Oconto	107	26 175	92.6	953	6 335	14	272.5	119.4	62.0	3 473	2 442	65	144	677
Oneida	209	61 619	71.6	1 903	16 873	17	535.2	170.4	50.4	4 727	3 594	60	337	720
Outagamie	361	192 103	81.6	6 755	53 490	70	1 903.8	416.9	58.4	2 631	2 001	50	124	391
Ozaukee	182	74 987	90.4	2 900	22 021	36	1 202.2	235.5	30.9	2 871	2 272	276	103	192
Pepin	26	D	D	(8)	D	4	122.8	33.2	53.5	4 538	2 818	470	175	691
Pierce	102	24 302	97.4	994	6 107	15	401.3	103.9	53.0	2 883	2 001	42	155	495
Polk	118	26 367	85.7	904	6 996	21	458.9	138.7	50.4	3 522	2 561	57	174	577
Portage	202	86 245	71.2	3 337	24 615	24	725.1	212.4	63.6	3 266	2 107	157	180	752
Price	42	D	D	(6)	D	9	176.0	70.6	42.5	4 540	3 269	54	302	858
Racine	360	154 746	88.9	5 324	42 190	65	2 134.0	626.2	45.3	3 371	2 508	90	120	626
Richland	32	D	D	(6)	D	9	225.1	72.9	49.4	4 107	2 499	38	148	1 207
Rock	343	151 195	87.7	5 295	41 309	48	1 506.6	569.5	48.0	3 768	2 415	454	122	677
Rusk	42	D	D	(6)	D	7	139.7	71.9	50.8	4 760	3 029	45	191	1 376
St. Croix	142	52 862	80.9	1 962	15 284	28	550.5	153.0	66.2	2 539	1 654	58	129	542
Sauk	241	123 575	59.3	3 276	32 913	32	920.0	199.3	45.8	3 672	2 549	294	148	514
Sawyer	109	24 337	66.8	613	6 054	10	244.1	86.4	51.4	5 325	3 198	262	211	1 594
Shawano	109	32 939	77.7	1 147	8 575	18	466.3	165.1	56.6	4 215	2 659	106	146	1 126
Sheboygan	237	105 915	69.5	3 714	29 104	36	1 542.5	372.5	57.2	3 382	2 447	350	106	435
Taylor	39	D	D	(7)	D	9	288.3	69.1	66.0	3 589	2 339	166	204	718
Trempealeau	85	17 086	91.9	713	4 852	17	338.9	120.8	60.7	4 527	2 751	129	221	1 078
Vernon	66	D	D	(7)	D	17	326.3	114.8	54.7	4 144	2 659	46	179	1 041
Vilas	188	69 921	34.2	1 451	17 335	11	310.0	104.8	47.8	4 829	3 630	170	151	864
Walworth	276	168 117	55.1	5 518	53 074	38	1 067.7	254.8	59.5	2 944	2 305	49	116	359
Washburn	80	17 646	72.5	521	4 325	9	181.6	90.6	54.0	5 748	3 970	163	407	1 132
Washington	217	93 676	93.0	3 737	25 699	45	1 374.0	286.7	70.7	2 477	1 066	32	121	314
Waukesha	635	372 650	80.5	11 945	104 414	151	5 066.5	1 170.6	106.0	3 266	2 164	724	132	226
Waupaca	139	41 776	84.9	1 583	11 127	24	622.6	221.9	50.4	4 365	3 153	155	162	772
Waushara	70	D	D	(6)	D	11	201.5	90.6	60.9	4 153	3 135	39	144	710
Winnebago	341	153 734	85.3	5 832	43 406	41	1 511.0	710.0	21.5	4 715	2 391	1 649	213	411
Wood	191	65 320	84.7	2 468	17 272	37	1 137.4	302.6	67.5	3 970	2 910	149	140	722
WYOMING	1 751	808 887	56.9	24 950	218 995	166	6 453.5	2 916.2	57.6	6 081	2 740	415	854	1 946
Albany	104	45 111	73.5	1 922	12 780	8	272.2	130.5	53.6	4 490	2 280	190	369	1 645
Big Horn	32	4 838	81.5	215	1 532	6	144.4	64.6	79.2	5 764	3 202	435	356	1 597
Campbell	77	41 905	71.9	1 346	11 107	7	375.4	86.1	182.4	2 629	1 166	953	136	284
Carbon	85	25 843	62.1	781	6 800	6	178.7	122.7	101.7	7 949	2 676	2 779	498	1 977
Converse	45	12 667	73.9	474	3 296	3	127.1	36.5	35.6	2 940	2 111	46	221	404
Crook	27	4 622	D	120	1 116	3	71.6	41.0	106.1	7 091	2 481	281	373	3 577
Fremont	152	39 875	72.1	1 397	11 367	12	313.3	177.3	72.7	4 899	2 807	190	495	1 354
Goshen	35	8 994	83.2	369	2 348	6	186.2	67.8	72.8	5 356	2 999	54	328	1 224
Hot Springs	31	7 150	48.0	234	1 776	3	66.1	25.3	41.5	5 648	4 439	57	238	897
Johnson	35	9 720	57.3	305	3 068	4	156.8	28.2	-14.7	4 112	3 154	105	407	384
Laramie	183	106 270	75.7	3 930	31 065	21	645.6	780.7	63.4	9 898	3 218	726	2 744	3 090
Lincoln	53	11 501	60.0	369	2 715	7	154.3	56.3	110.5	4 019	2 353	86	326	1 211
Natrona	172	78 970	78.0	2 924	21 782	15	1 334.9	280.2	49.2	4 436	2 768	120	575	954
Niobrara	18	3 605	77.4	107	833	2	40.7	12.8	-12.4	4 771	3 374	54	374	642
Park	130	90 032	27.0	1 283	21 706	12	406.4	132.0	54.7	5 177	2 779	680	1 013	613
Platte	40	9 124	71.5	352	2 438	6	132.8	48.4	52.9	5 616	3 376	102	566	1 102
Sheridan	88	36 776	62.5	1 199	10 461	7	419.8	138.7	48.0	5 527	3 441	89	963	992
Sublette	46	7 588	74.2	178	1 807	2	49.5	22.1	100.6	3 810	2 190	127	654	834
Sweetwater	109	61 266	D	1 838	17 464	12	497.5	132.3	70.0	3 364	1 832	87	315	1 117
Teton	180	166 268	27.8	4 303	43 843	8	509.6	47.3	29.4	3 254	1 669	275	783	519
Uinta	50	24 249	74.6	829	6 530	8	150.1	43.2	70.5	2 128	1 537	29	150	402
Washakie	35	8 364	77.0	320	2 100	5	127.2	49.5	92.8	5 793	3 040	146	727	1 736
Weston	24	4 149	66.1	155	1 061	3	93.5	38.4	-16.6	6 004	3 069	1 144	318	1 401

Table headers (span groups): **Accommodation and foodservices[1] (NAICS 72), 1997** (Establishments, Sales Total, Percent from food-services, Paid employees, Annual payroll). **Banking,[4] 1999** (Offices, Deposits). **Federal funds and grants, 1999** (Total expenditures or obligations; Percent change 1990–1999; Per capita[5] (dollars) — By selected type—: Total, Direct payments for individuals, Procurement contract awards, Salaries and wages, Grant awards).

[1] Includes only establishments with payroll. [2] Includes full-service restaurants, limited-service eating places, special food services, and drinking places (alcoholic beverages). [3] For pay period including March 12. [4] As of June 30. Covers all FDIC-insured commercial banks and savings institutions. [5] Based on resident population estimated as of July 1, 1999. [6] 250 to 499 employees. [7] 500 to 999 employees. [8] 100 to 249 employees.

Sources: Accommodation and Foodservices—U.S. Census Bureau, 1997 Economic Census, ECON97 Report Series CD-ROM, CD-EC97-1, Disc 1E, issued February 2001 (related Internet site <http://www.census.gov/epcd/www/97EC72.HTM>). Banking—U.S. Federal Deposit Insurance Corporation and Office of Thrift Supervision, "1999 Bank and Thrift Branch Office Data Book: Summary of Deposits," national and 6 regional data books (related Internet site <http://www2.fdic.gov/sod/>). Federal Funds and Grants—U.S. Census Bureau, County Aggregate files for each state, <http://www.census.gov/govs/www/cffr99.html>, (accessed: August 2000).

Table B–13. Counties — Government Programs, Employment, and Finances

[Includes U.S., states, and 3,142 counties/county equivalents defined as of January 1, 1992. For changes to these areas since January 1, 1992, see appendix B. Geographic Information]

County	Social Security Program beneficiaries, December 1999 — Total: Number	Percent change, 1990–1999	Rate[1]	Retired workers	Supplemental Security Income Program recipients, December 1999	Government employment, 1998 — Federal: Civilian	Military	State and local	Local government employment, full-time equivalent, March 1997	Local government finances, 1996–1997 — General revenue: Total (mil. dol.)	Taxes: Total (mil. dol.)	Per capita[2]	Percent property	Direct general expenditure (mil. dol.)
UNITED STATES	43 521 432	11.9	160	27 251 862	6 555 989	2 808 000	2 098 000	17 042 000	10 227 429	747 030.3	284 397.7	1 062	73.3	723 603.9
ALABAMA	810 196	14.3	185	444 171	160 292	53 249	42 064	288 880	175 369	8 918.4	2 474.0	573	36.5	8 853.0
Autauga	6 572	37.6	152	3 535	1 196	86	261	1 786	1 143	58.0	13.8	333	25.1	72.6
Baldwin	27 152	43.0	200	17 225	2 656	265	841	7 663	5 169	282.3	71.8	558	37.7	309.4
Barbour	5 310	15.7	199	2 800	1 751	62	177	1 999	1 186	55.0	10.1	376	31.3	52.6
Bibb	3 707	18.2	189	1 730	908	76	117	1 026	898	39.0	4.3	231	34.4	37.8
Blount	8 452	50.0	178	4 530	1 162	94	287	1 581	1 267	67.7	10.4	232	65.2	66.5
Bullock	2 469	9.2	218	1 205	949	42	70	726	560	18.0	3.0	261	44.6	15.5
Butler	4 801	2.1	223	2 625	1 347	45	135	1 073	924	37.8	7.6	351	35.1	38.2
Calhoun	23 828	14.6	204	12 990	4 422	4 953	3 881	7 422	5 393	301.6	51.1	436	28.6	293.8
Chambers	7 889	-1.6	217	5 005	1 409	58	228	1 532	1 129	46.6	11.1	303	33.4	58.5
Cherokee	4 928	37.8	225	2 810	723	48	135	1 020	858	30.7	7.3	336	46.3	30.9
Chilton	6 966	18.7	185	3 520	1 256	66	229	1 465	1 021	45.7	11.7	321	51.1	53.2
Choctaw	3 451	10.6	222	1 625	999	32	99	620	558	25.4	4.1	257	61.5	26.1
Clarke	5 926	11.9	206	2 950	1 722	94	177	1 876	1 044	50.5	11.9	415	31.8	48.4
Clay	3 298	14.5	235	1 870	521	46	87	1 041	831	46.2	2.3	167	42.9	36.6
Cleburne	2 859	18.1	198	1 555	491	80	89	693	403	22.7	2.8	200	64.6	21.7
Coffee	8 332	23.5	198	4 855	1 490	148	263	2 218	1 905	69.3	19.5	463	34.7	66.3
Colbert	12 161	17.6	231	6 395	1 820	1 457	328	4 014	3 018	146.0	23.5	443	31.9	152.0
Conecuh	3 350	11.3	244	1 690	878	45	94	842	480	17.2	3.2	230	69.3	17.1
Coosa	2 618	23.2	224	1 390	525	25	72	433	310	13.5	2.3	201	54.1	12.9
Covington	9 030	4.1	240	5 605	1 584	147	234	2 063	1 386	61.5	13.5	361	32.2	63.7
Crenshaw	3 211	5.5	236	1 820	832	46	85	599	504	17.9	2.3	169	54.3	19.7
Cullman	15 325	15.4	203	8 695	2 474	257	465	3 453	2 363	144.3	24.8	335	30.5	135.1
Dale	8 286	19.7	169	4 440	1 755	3 004	4 343	2 791	1 843	75.6	18.5	376	35.6	78.6
Dallas	10 000	2.0	214	5 015	4 786	159	290	3 014	1 898	83.2	25.8	548	35.6	75.2
DeKalb	13 368	25.6	227	7 235	2 312	171	362	2 571	1 927	84.9	18.5	321	32.5	84.8
Elmore	10 270	20.9	162	5 740	1 828	131	384	3 143	2 008	87.0	13.9	231	36.6	88.5
Escambia	7 675	12.1	209	4 100	1 418	75	236	2 774	1 450	79.3	11.8	322	36.5	74.0
Etowah	23 333	7.4	226	12 090	4 267	308	646	5 086	3 497	184.1	58.4	563	27.2	176.3
Fayette	4 285	22.8	237	2 465	790	51	112	1 312	857	29.0	3.5	195	38.4	31.4
Franklin	6 712	6.5	226	3 515	1 237	93	184	1 791	950	54.7	7.8	263	51.8	45.3
Geneva	6 036	13.1	242	3 525	1 208	72	155	1 359	1 098	34.7	5.8	232	40.7	38.1
Greene	2 167	8.4	222	980	975	33	61	731	565	21.0	2.5	249	46.8	19.7
Hale	3 210	-2.4	190	1 565	1 203	60	104	907	708	27.2	2.6	159	48.0	28.3
Henry	3 617	14.1	229	2 095	777	50	98	756	752	31.3	3.9	249	40.2	32.8
Houston	16 524	26.5	192	9 530	3 431	344	534	6 690	5 468	312.7	54.4	639	32.9	315.6
Jackson	10 279	12.1	199	5 650	1 921	458	318	3 244	2 251	126.1	17.7	348	34.6	122.3
Jefferson	124 174	-.6	189	67 255	21 856	9 305	4 536	49 243	27 566	1 671.5	730.5	1 106	37.9	1 626.9
Lamar	3 768	13.2	235	2 300	658	45	98	615	443	30.3	5.0	314	36.5	29.0
Lauderdale	18 047	16.5	214	10 005	2 552	324	531	5 999	4 111	261.0	59.4	708	61.9	241.7
Lawrence	5 942	28.9	176	3 040	1 254	90	207	1 384	1 046	55.9	5.5	165	47.8	56.8
Lee	13 498	37.2	132	7 775	2 559	331	726	12 233	4 240	272.4	53.8	546	31.2	269.9
Limestone	10 211	33.0	162	5 570	1 788	1 448	386	4 143	2 346	106.2	14.3	235	29.7	116.0
Lowndes	2 466	22.4	189	1 075	1 040	28	81	718	540	22.1	2.5	193	45.2	20.1
Macon	4 028	4.1	175	2 155	1 282	1 287	156	1 232	1 147	40.5	10.8	468	34.7	37.1
Madison	37 069	34.3	132	22 705	5 439	13 817	3 131	19 355	12 539	501.6	183.1	672	38.8	573.7
Marengo	4 631	11.1	200	2 390	1 550	78	162	1 728	1 283	61.0	9.9	421	48.9	71.8
Marion	6 627	11.7	218	3 730	1 048	75	192	1 502	968	45.9	9.7	313	30.6	42.8
Marshall	15 474	3.3	192	8 615	3 070	340	498	4 971	3 206	132.7	33.7	421	27.8	124.6
Mobile	68 689	11.9	172	36 290	13 763	2 477	3 261	24 677	13 794	758.5	278.8	700	29.7	719.4
Monroe	4 794	12.4	200	2 565	1 068	57	149	1 437	1 123	41.6	6.9	284	46.4	46.1
Montgomery	35 824	11.3	166	20 430	9 288	6 832	6 363	24 329	7 872	379.7	151.6	696	24.3	365.5
Morgan	19 437	16.9	177	11 065	3 026	289	679	6 691	4 764	286.2	56.4	521	44.4	297.3
Perry	2 799	15.2	222	1 355	1 208	30	87	616	610	23.1	2.7	216	48.2	22.7
Pickens	4 600	5.3	219	2 515	1 497	58	131	946	1 159	41.2	4.9	235	46.0	41.0
Pike	5 487	.9	193	3 005	1 798	93	183	2 385	1 117	43.8	11.2	394	29.2	51.8
Randolph	4 845	9.2	239	2 990	856	48	124	1 388	785	32.5	6.6	330	62.8	33.2
Russell	9 528	9.2	190	5 325	2 023	97	312	2 367	2 277	107.8	24.0	473	33.8	97.1
St. Clair	10 356	44.1	162	5 330	1 350	104	384	2 165	1 643	78.5	21.0	347	34.9	76.9
Shelby	16 753	83.5	114	9 440	1 438	257	872	4 830	3 902	190.1	79.1	583	40.8	174.6
Sumter	2 862	3.3	183	1 380	1 250	43	98	1 410	600	28.5	6.7	422	51.7	28.2
Talladega	16 785	13.6	217	8 230	4 003	527	475	4 628	3 009	116.1	25.1	327	35.4	121.1
Tallapoosa	9 162	14.8	227	5 480	1 683	98	252	1 933	1 719	74.7	16.0	398	38.9	75.1
Tuscaloosa	27 081	19.5	168	14 610	5 697	1 477	1 025	18 547	8 927	476.7	64.7	405	51.2	431.0
Walker	16 097	3.6	226	7 620	3 264	197	440	3 277	2 141	100.8	26.4	373	29.7	104.1
Washington	3 590	24.0	202	1 655	882	40	110	989	891	35.3	7.3	413	76.2	35.5
Wilcox	2 981	1.6	222	1 250	1 849	85	84	796	645	31.2	3.4	252	37.9	38.3
Winston	5 177	15.8	212	2 645	1 124	91	150	1 032	1 334	43.1	5.7	238	40.4	44.2

[1] Per 1,000 resident population estimated as of July 1, 1999. [2] Based on resident population estimated as of July 1, 1997.

Sources: Social Security Program—U.S. Social Security Administration, OASDI Beneficiaries by State and County - December 1999, <http://www.ssa.gov/statistics/oasdi_sc/1999/oasdi_sc99.pdf> (accessed: 7 March 2001) for 1999 – annual publication of same title for 1990. Supplemental Security Income Program—U.S. Social Security Administration, SSI Recipients by State and County, <http://www.ssa.gov/statistics/ssi_st_cty/1999/ssi_st_cty.pdf> (accessed: November 2000). Government employment, 1998—U.S. Bureau of Economic Analysis, "Regional Economic Information System (REIS) 1969-1998" on CD-ROM (related Internet site <http://www.bea.doc.gov/bea/regional/data.htm>). Local government employment, 1997—U.S. Census Bureau, 1997 Census of Governments, Compendium of Public Employment, <http://www.census.gov/govs/apes/97coar2.dat> (accessed: 14 January 2000). Local government finances—U.S. Census Bureau, 1997 Census of Governments, Compendium of Government Finances, <http://www.census.gov/prod/gc97/gc974-5.pdf> (accessed: 16 February 2001).

Table B–13. Counties — Government Programs, Employment, and Finances–Con.

[Includes U.S., states, and 3,142 counties/county equivalents defined as of January 1, 1992. For changes to these areas since January 1, 1992, see appendix B. Geographic Information]

County	Social Security Program beneficiaries, December 1999				Supplemental Security Income Program recipients, December 1999	Government employment, 1998			Local government employment, full-time equivalent, March 1997	Local government finances, 1996–1997				
	Total			Retired workers		Federal		State and local		General revenue				Direct general expenditure (mil. dol.)
	Number	Percent change, 1990–1999	Rate[1]			Civilian	Military			Total (mil. dol.)	Taxes			
											Total (mil. dol.)	Per capita[2]	Percent property	
ALASKA	51 320	52.5	83	29 287	8 165	17 041	22 707	53 138	23 132	2 464.6	792.5	1 302	80.1	2 453.1
Aleutians East	90	NA	41	55	(3)	20	17	220	145	16.3	5.0	2 174	19.1	15.0
Aleutians West	158	NA	40	85	[3]16	55	56	422	353	34.0	14.6	3 572	29.9	32.5
Anchorage	19 490	56.9	76	11 340	3 791	9 954	10 753	17 745	7 869	747.0	234.7	934	89.4	796.1
Bethel	1 187	NA	73	440	[4]364	124	120	2 138	481	35.6	3.4	212	–	33.6
Bristol Bay	106	–35.8	100	65	5	46	10	315	104	10.6	2.7	2 484	53.4	10.9
Denali	94	–	50	55	(5)	189	134	115	71	6.0	1.7	849	11.7	5.2
Dillingham	434	NA	95	195	[6]98	51	34	534	193	13.4	1.8	406	–	15.3
Fairbanks North Star	5 858	37.7	69	3 425	846	3 302	7 723	6 504	2 554	261.4	58.7	705	90.6	268.4
Haines	336	26.8	147	235	23	12	17	166	111	10.5	4.2	1 801	45.8	9.6
Juneau	2 682	31.1	89	1 620	345	840	428	5 841	1 573	160.4	50.1	1 654	46.2	148.0
Kenai Peninsula	5 375	66.9	110	3 175	643	401	456	3 767	1 794	181.6	62.9	1 315	60.5	177.8
Ketchikan Gateway	1 510	21.3	107	970	165	273	313	1 504	684	90.1	22.2	1 515	47.6	63.0
Kodiak Island	858	51.9	60	535	100	169	976	947	633	60.0	13.1	891	48.1	58.6
Lake and Peninsula	170	NA	97	85	(6)	48	13	115	201	17.8	4.3	2 515	33.1	20.5
Matanuska-Susitna	5 429	96.3	94	3 035	598	136	424	2 761	1 630	147.2	41.0	761	81.2	135.8
Nome	865	50.4	97	350	174	80	91	1 271	341	34.0	4.1	461	31.7	40.1
North Slope	524	80.7	74	205	36	28	54	1 921	1 918	335.6	224.1	31 019	99.9	325.0
Northwest Arctic	642	52.9	96	220	79	59	51	849	536	47.9	1.9	286	–	45.0
Prince of Wales-Outer Ketchikan	508	51.6	76	310	50	98	53	[6]43	109	20.6	2.1	296	15.8	20.4
Sitka	892	37.2	109	585	82	204	244	842	319	45.5	9.1	1 069	35.0	35.8
Skagway-Yakutat-Angoon	395	21.5	93	235	43	176	NA	417	233	17.3	3.3	700	37.0	19.0
Southeast Fairbanks	651	141.1	111	375	102	325	352	369	1	.2	Z	1	100.0	.2
Valdez-Cordova	881	39.8	86	530	101	130	180	1 032	431	112.3	19.7	1 906	88.5	114.5
Wade Hampton	666	53.1	96	230	192	34	51	1 058	170	6.4	.6	91	14.9	6.8
Wrangell-Petersburg	848	31.5	125	575	48	190	77	649	445	39.0	6.5	943	36.0	41.7
Yukon-Koyukuk	605	NA	98	310	[7]259	97	45	993	233	13.9	.8	120	31.0	14.3
ARIZONA	772 631	30.8	162	502 824	79 490	44 070	32 672	266 516	165 331	11 241.3	3 825.0	840	71.3	11 031.2
Apache	7 951	30.5	116	3 375	4 385	2 060	169	3 549	2 652	174.4	33.5	482	89.4	162.6
Cochise	21 074	28.8	187	13 145	2 283	3 933	5 868	5 713	4 918	259.3	71.2	638	84.0	238.3
Coconino	11 960	5.0	104	6 600	2 969	2 787	295	11 154	4 536	277.5	94.2	828	68.7	259.4
Gila	13 052	24.7	266	8 270	1 118	472	121	2 589	2 122	116.4	41.0	850	78.7	99.1
Graham	4 994	15.3	156	2 795	842	322	78	2 648	1 392	76.4	12.6	402	64.3	81.0
Greenlee	1 280	–2.7	142	725	104	39	23	544	446	29.5	8.2	873	89.4	30.5
La Paz	4 221	48.6	284	2 900	345	140	37	924	759	47.5	10.6	717	84.2	44.1
Maricopa	415 642	28.9	145	274 955	37 567	18 714	12 677	144 715	91 349	6 771.3	2 329.4	863	68.1	6 553.6
Mohave	38 833	56.3	289	26 900	2 341	478	321	5 543	4 737	283.3	121.7	948	81.1	271.2
Navajo	13 276	48.7	135	6 965	4 176	1 356	238	5 089	3 932	237.3	54.4	574	75.1	229.0
Pima	140 261	26.2	175	90 140	14 018	8 619	7 728	56 163	30 313	1 850.7	671.3	862	76.0	1 972.0
Pinal	30 507	48.5	200	19 215	3 345	778	361	12 443	6 289	371.0	123.1	861	81.5	361.8
Santa Cruz	5 181	22.3	132	3 120	1 206	834	94	1 894	1 511	87.4	24.6	661	83.6	92.7
Yavapai	43 160	49.9	282	30 005	2 278	1 139	375	6 812	4 646	322.9	135.5	939	72.0	301.9
Yuma	21 227	33.1	157	13 710	2 457	2 399	4 287	6 736	5 729	336.4	93.8	727	66.7	334.0
ARKANSAS	517 826	10.2	203	294 498	87 732	20 728	19 178	158 504	90 806	4 424.0	1 343.7	532	60.1	4 277.2
Arkansas	4 315	–8.8	208	2 470	757	175	117	1 182	944	40.3	11.7	565	51.9	39.9
Ashley	5 019	1.4	207	2 570	1 020	84	138	1 212	942	43.2	12.3	505	58.0	43.2
Baxter	12 882	14.7	351	9 015	737	164	205	1 312	1 040	40.7	16.8	465	62.6	45.2
Benton	27 883	26.5	201	18 370	1 763	393	757	5 309	4 225	204.5	79.9	613	57.9	195.6
Boone	8 266	17.4	260	4 625	975	234	180	2 342	1 631	82.3	14.1	445	53.6	74.6
Bradley	2 914	–3.7	255	1 525	505	36	65	734	678	33.8	7.2	628	74.8	30.0
Calhoun	1 274	20.8	225	640	171	12	32	604	173	9.2	4.2	729	90.9	8.0
Carroll	5 265	23.4	234	3 385	424	109	127	902	939	39.4	12.4	553	57.0	42.3
Chicot	3 056	–6.3	206	1 590	1 173	44	84	1 193	838	35.9	6.0	394	73.6	34.3
Clark	4 407	–6.3	206	2 600	616	103	124	1 986	669	30.1	11.5	518	48.7	28.2
Clay	4 638	–7.5	272	2 655	803	66	97	857	847	23.4	5.6	323	72.1	20.8
Cleburne	6 567	27.0	282	4 165	610	107	129	756	577	25.0	8.1	358	75.5	24.3
Cleveland	1 674	15.4	196	885	253	17	48	353	302	9.9	1.9	232	80.5	10.1
Columbia	5 851	.4	237	3 095	1 238	56	141	1 794	1 102	44.7	7.3	289	79.9	47.5
Conway	4 805	12.9	242	2 695	878	66	112	1 123	756	49.3	31.6	1 585	90.1	25.8
Craighead	13 200	12.8	170	7 490	2 508	437	444	5 252	2 470	110.0	36.3	476	64.7	111.5
Crawford	9 916	31.4	193	4 950	1 600	89	284	1 788	1 515	70.4	15.7	317	75.6	71.2
Crittenden	7 835	3.0	156	3 795	2 802	113	282	2 531	2 043	90.2	25.3	511	42.6	84.0
Cross	3 693	1.0	191	1 905	984	61	110	1 113	748	35.2	7.1	368	70.7	32.9
Dallas	2 225	–5.3	249	1 130	517	26	51	477	372	13.9	3.2	351	76.0	14.4
Desha	2 946	–7.8	198	1 500	828	102	85	1 177	737	40.0	8.2	539	73.1	38.3

[1] Per 1,000 resident population estimated as of July 1, 1999. [2] Based on resident population estimated as of July 1, 1997. [3] Aleutians East Borough included with Aleutians West Census Area; data not available separately. [4] Bethel Census Area excludes part of old Kuskokwim Census Division not available separately from Yukon-Koyukuk Census Area. [5] Denali Borough included with Yukon-Koyukuk Census Area; data not available separately. [6] Lake and Peninsula Borough included with Dillingham Census Area; data not available separately. [7] Yukon-Koyukuk Census Area includes part of old Kuskokwim Census Division now in Bethel Census Area as well as Denali Borough.

Sources: Social Security Program—U.S. Social Security Administration, OASDI Beneficiaries by State and County - December 1999, <http://www.ssa.gov/statistics/oasdi_sc/1999/oasdi_sc99.pdf> (accessed: 7 March 2001) for 1999 – annual publication of same title for 1990. Supplemental Security Income Program—U.S. Social Security Administration, SSI Recipients by State and County, <http://www.ssa.gov/statistics/ssi_st_cty/1999/ssi_st_cty.pdf> (accessed: November 2000). Government employment, 1998—U.S. Bureau of Economic Analysis, "Regional Economic Information System (REIS) 1969-1998" on CD-ROM (related Internet site <http://www.bea.doc.gov/bea/regional/data.htm>). Local government employment, 1997—U.S. Census Bureau, 1997 Census of Governments, Compendium of Public Employment, <http://www.census.gov/govs/apes/97coar2.dat> (accessed: 14 January 2000). Local government finances—U.S. Census Bureau, 1997 Census of Governments, Compendium of Government Finances, <http://www.census.gov/prod/gc97/gc974-5.pdf> (accessed: 16 February 2001).

[Includes U.S., states, and 3,142 counties/county equivalents defined as of January 1, 1992. For changes to these areas since January 1, 1992, see appendix B. Geographic Information]

County	Social Security Program beneficiaries, December 1999 — Total Number	Percent change, 1990–1999	Rate[1]	Retired workers	Supplemental Security Income Program recipients, December 1999	Government employment, 1998 — Federal Civilian	Federal Military	State and local	Local government employment, full-time equivalent, March 1997	Local government finances, 1996–1997 — General revenue Total (mil. dol.)	Taxes Total (mil. dol.)	Per capita[2]	Percent property	Direct general expenditure (mil. dol.)
ARKANSAS—Con.														
Drew	3 296	4.3	189	1 790	638	100	99	1 609	803	39.6	7.9	447	54.2	36.2
Faulkner	11 324	31.1	141	6 675	1 517	202	448	5 086	1 914	99.6	27.8	363	75.7	107.7
Franklin	3 829	11.8	228	1 985	551	164	273	807	557	21.8	5.8	349	87.4	20.1
Fulton	3 341	28.0	303	1 825	495	37	62	499	385	17.2	3.0	276	67.2	16.3
Garland	23 891	9.9	283	15 945	2 526	590	476	3 442	2 299	123.7	48.8	589	54.9	117.0
Grant	2 834	21.9	177	1 505	294	34	90	815	658	26.3	5.9	377	95.2	25.0
Greene	7 489	13.0	206	4 125	1 222	85	204	1 514	1 262	52.3	13.7	385	42.1	50.3
Hempstead	4 376	.5	198	2 485	812	106	125	1 473	931	30.1	7.3	331	58.1	29.6
Hot Spring	6 477	14.4	222	3 670	779	65	164	1 666	954	59.5	10.8	377	67.4	56.5
Howard	2 923	-5.4	214	1 660	449	70	77	750	513	23.9	7.3	532	57.8	21.2
Independence	7 423	14.4	224	4 100	1 185	213	187	1 657	1 208	65.8	17.5	535	69.8	65.1
Izard	3 911	8.9	298	2 335	457	37	74	810	368	14.4	3.9	298	77.9	14.8
Jackson	4 246	-19.8	242	2 325	893	56	100	911	614	29.6	8.4	469	58.5	25.2
Jefferson	14 494	-3.1	179	7 730	3 762	1 609	516	6 134	2 891	146.4	47.6	580	59.3	148.3
Johnson	4 864	14.9	228	2 570	875	110	121	854	840	42.2	10.2	482	62.6	41.4
Lafayette	1 976	2.6	223	1 005	584	36	50	482	401	16.0	3.7	412	72.3	14.1
Lawrence	4 421	-6.5	255	2 415	934	75	98	1 200	930	33.7	5.6	323	53.8	32.3
Lee	2 486	-6.4	196	1 185	1 104	56	70	891	437	15.3	2.8	195	72.2	15.6
Lincoln	2 248	12.1	156	1 155	574	31	81	1 255	418	15.3	2.8	195	72.2	15.6
Little River	2 697	4.1	206	1 530	434	50	75	816	493	25.5	9.0	678	56.4	31.3
Logan	5 359	7.7	254	2 770	832	134	119	1 172	666	26.3	6.2	291	67.8	28.8
Lonoke	7 723	25.6	150	4 125	1 030	103	283	1 894	1 598	69.3	17.7	360	57.3	67.3
Madison	3 087	23.7	232	1 660	404	55	75	516	428	19.4	4.8	368	56.6	25.8
Marion	4 121	24.7	277	2 480	467	39	84	547	557	17.8	5.0	348	67.0	16.6
Miller	7 004	2.8	178	3 875	1 505	79	226	1 892	1 420	68.8	19.3	489	62.7	66.9
Mississippi	9 481	-2.5	190	4 870	3 267	140	287	3 000	2 224	100.3	25.7	510	40.5	90.6
Monroe	2 362	-13.3	236	1 260	745	45	58	555	416	17.8	4.3	420	64.6	15.6
Montgomery	2 236	23.2	256	1 365	279	68	49	438	267	12.2	2.5	291	64.1	9.9
Nevada	2 181	-2.9	218	1 185	497	33	57	535	393	19.7	4.0	398	67.0	19.6
Newton	2 072	27.1	252	935	499	58	46	455	225	10.7	1.7	204	58.6	9.9
Ouachita	6 845	-3.4	249	3 695	1 429	151	158	1 452	1 670	62.7	10.6	378	72.3	58.9
Perry	2 109	14.0	218	1 120	388	39	54	432	287	25.2	9.4	995	16.2	22.4
Phillips	5 814	-14.0	215	2 720	2 695	76	154	1 879	1 201	49.8	11.9	431	60.6	46.5
Pike	2 585	10.2	247	1 475	309	79	60	640	409	18.2	4.5	429	70.9	20.9
Poinsett	5 539	1.9	225	2 805	1 435	73	140	1 269	945	36.7	9.4	381	60.4	33.7
Polk	4 711	3.1	240	2 785	588	102	111	990	673	26.7	6.0	308	59.7	28.0
Pope	10 143	23.2	193	5 445	1 775	321	299	2 886	1 626	85.0	35.4	691	48.3	72.9
Prairie	2 178	21.0	235	1 165	320	40	53	403	324	12.6	3.8	406	68.6	12.1
Pulaski	57 780	6.6	165	33 435	10 204	9 094	6 553	37 793	14 781	775.2	288.0	825	58.1	779.2
Randolph	4 381	16.8	245	2 435	652	41	100	892	529	20.7	5.1	287	57.0	21.6
St. Francis	5 228	-9.0	188	2 705	2 302	441	159	1 944	1 160	46.8	11.0	387	51.4	48.8
Saline	13 860	90.8	177	8 375	997	83	437	3 724	2 268	154.3	26.7	352	70.9	121.4
Scott	2 749	17.7	258	1 365	377	79	60	384	338	19.4	2.0	184	66.5	17.0
Searcy	2 396	7.0	308	1 235	528	42	44	471	230	10.7	2.8	358	81.5	9.3
Sebastian	20 512	10.9	193	11 420	2 859	1 059	601	4 818	3 401	194.1	82.5	779	52.0	174.2
Sevier	2 817	.1	192	1 585	336	79	83	796	497	19.8	5.0	344	66.2	19.3
Sharp	5 357	2.5	313	3 290	696	54	96	763	484	23.5	6.3	377	66.0	22.7
Stone	3 144	37.6	280	1 700	570	65	63	598	354	15.1	5.3	480	69.5	15.8
Union	10 422	-2.0	232	5 515	1 989	200	257	2 414	1 624	72.3	24.8	548	49.8	68.9
Van Buren	4 876	21.1	311	3 105	513	48	88	635	446	16.8	4.3	280	77.7	16.4
Washington	22 124	19.2	151	12 740	2 655	1 214	800	11 280	4 073	241.7	87.7	611	59.8	252.4
White	12 679	13.1	195	7 330	1 895	161	364	2 720	1 874	109.3	23.8	377	60.3	104.9
Woodruff	2 015	-9.0	231	1 025	609	44	50	538	374	15.4	2.9	319	70.8	15.5
Yell	4 739	7.3	251	2 425	774	169	108	1 111	620	36.8	5.9	310	87.6	36.0
CALIFORNIA	4 105 728	12.0	124	2 621 878	1 065 323	268 568	230 324	1 881 006	1 194 169	109 714.6	28 850.0	895	67.9	105 593.7
Alameda	161 957	4.0	114	102 035	47 685	12 755	4 491	103 466	59 236	5 664.3	1 742.3	1 270	59.5	5 336.5
Alpine	129	-4.4	111	85	21	12	(3)	156	119	12.2	3.1	2 564	72.9	11.5
Amador	7 783	18.6	228	5 335	510	99	67	2 534	1 006	69.6	25.4	759	84.2	66.1
Butte	40 913	4.7	210	25 845	8 784	555	395	13 192	7 280	568.4	112.7	584	71.7	587.8
Calaveras	9 291	26.7	232	6 190	924	135	80	2 050	1 068	101.2	31.4	803	88.2	92.0
Colusa	2 824	3.4	150	1 675	514	71	37	1 262	1 050	72.1	16.7	909	81.5	68.6
Contra Costa	124 282	19.2	133	78 990	21 147	6 389	2 264	36 847	28 643	3 041.2	858.2	954	74.8	3 053.5
Del Norte	5 065	17.1	191	2 850	1 580	145	66	2 807	1 534	88.1	13.5	495	72.8	78.8
El Dorado	25 368	20.1	157	16 800	2 443	743	317	7 410	5 999	454.3	126.7	819	81.2	454.2

[1] Per 1,000 resident population estimated as of July 1, 1999.   [2] Based on resident population estimated as of July 1, 1997.   [3] Less than 10 employees.

Sources: Social Security Program—U.S. Social Security Administration, OASDI Beneficiaries by State and County - December 1999, <http://www.ssa.gov/statistics/oasdi_sc/1999/oasdi_sc99.pdf> (accessed: 7 March 2001) for 1999 – annual publication of same title for 1990.   Supplemental Security Income Program—U.S. Social Security Administration, SSI Recipients by State and County, <http://www.ssa.gov/statistics/ssi_st_cty/1999/ssi_st_cty.pdf> (accessed: November 2000).   Government employment, 1998—U.S. Bureau of Economic Analysis, "Regional Economic Information System (REIS) 1969-1998" on CD-ROM (related Internet site <http://www.bea.doc.gov/bea/regional/data.htm>).   Local government employment, 1997—U.S. Census Bureau, 1997 Census of Governments, Compendium of Public Employment, <http://www.census.gov/govs/apes/97coar2.dat> (accessed: 14 January 2000).   Local government finances—U.S. Census Bureau, 1997 Census of Governments, Compendium of Government Finances, <http://www.census.gov/prod/gc97/gc974-5.pdf> (accessed: 16 February 2001).

Table B–13. Counties — Government Programs, Employment, and Finances-Con.

[Includes U.S., states, and 3,142 counties/county equivalents defined as of January 1, 1992. For changes to these areas since January 1, 1992, see appendix B. Geographic Information]

County	Social Security Program beneficiaries, December 1999 — Total — Number	Total — Percent change, 1990–1999	Total — Rate[1]	Retired workers	Supplemental Security Income Program recipients, December 1999	Government employment, 1998 — Federal — Civilian	Federal — Military	State and local	Local government employment, full-time equivalent, March 1997	Local government finances, 1996–1997 — General revenue — Total (mil. dol.)	Taxes — Total (mil. dol.)	Taxes — Per capita[2]	Taxes — Percent property	Direct general expenditure (mil. dol.)
CALIFORNIA—Con.														
Fresno	98 708	12.3	129	59 135	35 589	9 446	1 597	45 727	33 793	2 675.5	482.9	643	70.5	2 603.4
Glenn	4 686	3.3	178	2 825	909	273	53	1 741	2 002	99.2	16.7	636	79.3	94.3
Humboldt	22 041	9.3	182	12 385	5 681	842	440	9 523	5 273	377.2	81.9	668	76.3	385.5
Imperial	20 995	22.1	145	11 860	8 093	1 603	553	11 701	7 693	519.5	81.0	570	74.8	509.2
Inyo	4 178	-3.6	233	2 855	472	340	36	1 910	1 086	101.1	34.0	1 860	66.9	105.3
Kern	86 395	17.7	134	48 170	25 204	9 314	5 637	38 818	26 459	2 258.2	475.7	762	81.7	2 088.7
Kings	12 735	17.5	103	6 980	3 791	1 133	4 927	8 139	4 266	325.1	53.7	470	71.8	318.1
Lake	14 979	.9	270	9 375	3 257	142	117	3 102	2 560	170.7	35.9	655	83.7	170.1
Lassen	4 132	-6.2	125	2 435	866	925	90	4 192	1 526	95.0	17.7	529	81.9	89.6
Los Angeles	976 169	3.5	105	633 035	352 418	55 490	21 671	485 747	341 941	33 586.2	8 143.3	892	64.1	30 966.1
Madera	17 953	21.6	154	10 975	4 131	322	230	7 025	3 621	295.4	64.8	576	80.6	291.4
Marin	35 878	14.0	152	25 225	3 457	1 037	702	12 348	6 956	673.8	287.2	1 225	75.7	736.7
Mariposa	3 871	28.2	248	2 585	275	586	32	1 019	937	53.9	16.4	1 054	59.9	55.9
Mendocino	15 870	9.8	189	9 475	3 534	285	194	5 419	3 975	313.8	72.7	873	77.4	305.7
Merced	25 912	23.7	129	14 975	8 695	447	397	11 662	9 650	764.1	102.0	526	79.4	735.7
Modoc	2 118	10.6	230	1 305	345	248	19	1 129	800	51.5	7.6	789	86.7	50.6
Mono	1 012	29.7	96	720	101	174	266	1 006	723	59.3	26.8	2 578	70.4	54.2
Monterey	48 130	17.0	129	30 260	8 791	5 214	6 018	23 061	14 583	1 447.3	319.6	891	66.2	1 443.4
Napa	20 598	2.2	170	13 755	2 012	473	239	8 173	4 263	325.9	130.8	1 109	74.8	328.3
Nevada	19 933	27.7	217	13 615	1 610	466	183	4 343	3 107	263.4	73.1	813	82.6	233.5
Orange	298 165	19.9	108	200 680	54 464	13 070	11 475	122 560	74 364	7 095.0	2 392.0	897	71.2	6 913.1
Placer	37 431	49.5	156	24 905	3 947	603	470	12 620	8 487	710.8	240.0	1 089	71.8	667.0
Plumas	4 656	14.7	229	3 030	673	381	41	1 926	865	98.0	20.4	997	85.7	96.4
Riverside	227 873	25.0	149	151 340	39 239	6 393	3 084	72 301	49 579	4 524.7	1 073.4	746	74.0	4 299.8
Sacramento	159 695	17.5	135	95 505	49 222	15 379	5 132	150 261	51 112	3 850.7	882.2	765	65.4	3 723.4
San Benito	5 317	24.7	104	3 455	820	143	98	2 386	1 674	245.9	42.2	905	70.7	227.2
San Bernardino	190 420	18.4	114	111 490	51 653	10 993	18 034	79 192	57 115	5 011.2	1 086.7	675	73.1	5 176.1
San Diego	363 677	15.0	129	236 900	75 860	42 919	104 495	150 058	91 393	8 204.5	2 084.2	766	71.0	8 304.9
San Francisco	104 180	-5.7	140	70 290	46 371	19 698	1 766	70 081	40 951	4 194.8	1 298.5	1 752	52.3	4 245.5
San Joaquin	75 275	15.2	134	44 340	24 220	4 283	1 141	29 290	22 168	1 709.9	354.1	656	70.2	1 701.5
San Luis Obispo	43 194	17.2	182	28 645	5 093	656	490	18 268	8 321	675.9	248.9	1 076	79.6	662.3
San Mateo	92 223	7.3	131	64 145	12 909	3 670	1 552	25 686	20 923	2 114.5	870.7	1 252	69.5	1 913.9
Santa Barbara	59 943	14.6	153	38 960	8 876	3 944	4 093	26 460	15 316	1 210.2	347.8	899	75.4	1 159.3
Santa Clara	166 188	15.1	101	111 030	40 863	12 508	4 466	75 306	53 744	5 450.4	2 060.5	1 271	64.5	5 224.0
Santa Cruz	30 997	1.0	126	19 750	5 330	538	488	16 185	9 944	804.9	228.5	957	66.2	811.9
Shasta	35 144	19.3	214	20 465	7 912	1 194	330	10 104	6 626	535.0	115.6	711	77.4	515.7
Sierra	736	-6.8	221	490	87	86	(3)	531	267	27.0	4.7	1 390	89.1	24.6
Siskiyou	10 554	5.4	242	6 570	2 157	721	88	3 320	2 189	155.6	26.8	604	77.2	149.0
Solano	45 764	33.8	119	27 050	10 033	4 172	8 157	19 746	11 944	1 155.2	277.3	747	69.2	1 129.7
Sonoma	69 430	12.4	158	45 405	9 374	1 821	1 424	24 012	15 333	1 276.7	384.6	902	74.1	1 343.4
Stanislaus	61 973	17.2	142	36 225	18 002	1 241	856	22 055	13 966	1 342.0	254.6	607	68.2	1 290.4
Sutter	12 413	22.9	158	7 360	2 958	179	155	3 911	2 623	212.9	49.4	646	77.5	219.4
Tehama	11 739	17.7	217	7 095	2 363	249	108	2 936	2 144	147.6	30.6	568	77.3	144.7
Trinity	3 088	13.9	239	1 790	563	226	26	1 127	1 283	63.9	6.5	491	84.9	62.5
Tulare	48 112	6.8	134	28 085	15 490	1 196	713	23 673	16 620	1 467.5	190.2	543	67.6	1 428.0
Tuolumne	12 698	18.7	236	8 570	1 509	365	107	3 877	1 884	152.5	37.7	720	80.8	146.2
Ventura	92 555	23.4	124	59 795	13 809	8 700	6 883	31 576	24 052	2 111.5	628.3	870	77.2	2 050.1
Yolo	18 995	24.8	122	11 565	4 602	2 341	320	21 673	5 245	445.1	121.8	804	61.4	458.1
Yuba	9 316	3.0	156	5 145	3 476	1 235	3 205	4 376	2 888	193.2	38.0	632	84.9	191.0
COLORADO	522 116	23.8	129	321 477	54 685	53 973	42 580	270 700	153 146	11 434.3	4 809.8	1 236	61.7	11 101.4
Adams	39 285	13.8	119	23 075	5 009	3 373	1 474	14 830	9 861	774.0	329.1	1 042	61.9	709.3
Alamosa	1 996	11.5	137	1 045	547	150	44	1 831	637	40.4	12.7	877	60.0	48.0
Arapahoe	50 010	49.4	104	31 940	3 381	2 564	2 367	25 364	14 990	1 242.0	615.4	1 330	69.5	1 393.6
Archuleta	1 552	60.0	162	990	109	49	27	441	337	29.8	12.8	1 502	64.3	25.4
Baca	1 152	8.7	267	675	124	43	13	742	532	18.8	4.9	1 127	89.3	22.1
Bent	1 022	3.8	176	565	212	512	17	469	390	22.5	3.9	716	94.2	21.6
Boulder	27 173	17.6	99	17 275	2 373	2 649	915	22 832	7 146	654.1	368.1	1 408	63.5	677.0
Chaffee	3 404	29.2	218	2 285	197	98	45	1 401	769	42.8	14.9	997	66.2	40.3
Cheyenne	413	4.6	185	250	16	20	(3)	306	197	14.0	4.5	1 990	92.6	13.2
Clear Creek	933	62.3	102	570	42	39	27	587	366	23.0	14.1	1 582	83.4	23.1
Conejos	1 598	11.7	198	830	471	45	24	581	507	22.9	4.1	528	82.2	21.8
Costilla	989	33.6	277	485	274	14	11	396	298	14.0	4.4	1 228	93.2	14.9
Crowley	759	-3.3	171	395	162	15	13	509	152	7.9	2.5	589	65.2	8.0
Custer	690	56.8	192	435	33	13	10	208	166	6.5	3.0	902	80.5	6.6

[1] Per 1,000 resident population estimated as of July 1, 1999. [2] Based on resident population estimated as of July 1, 1997. [3] Less than 10 employees.

Sources: Social Security Program—U.S. Social Security Administration, OASDI Beneficiaries by State and County - December 1999, <http://www.ssa.gov/statistics/oasdi_sc/1999/oasdi_sc99.pdf> (accessed: 7 March 2001) for 1999 – annual publication of same title for 1990. Supplemental Security Income Program—U.S. Social Security Administration, SSI Recipients by State and County, <http://www.ssa.gov/statistics/ssi_st_cty/1999/ssi_st_cty.pdf> (accessed: November 2000). Government employment, 1998—U.S. Bureau of Economic Analysis, "Regional Economic Information System (REIS) 1969-1998" on CD-ROM (related Internet site <http://www.bea.doc.gov/bea/regional/data.htm>). Local government employment, 1997—U.S. Census Bureau, 1997 Census of Governments, Compendium of Public Employment, <http://www.census.gov/govs/apes/97coar2.dat> (accessed: 14 January 2000). Local government finances—U.S. Census Bureau, 1997 Census of Governments, Compendium of Government Finances, <http://www.census.gov/prod/gc97/gc974-5.pdf> (accessed: 16 February 2001).

[Includes U.S., states, and 3,142 counties/county equivalents defined as of January 1, 1992. For changes to these areas since January 1, 1992, see appendix B. Geographic Information]

County	Social Security Program beneficiaries, December 1999				Supplemental Security Income Program recipients, December 1999	Government employment, 1998			Local government employment, full-time equivalent, March 1997	Local government finances, 1996–1997				
	Total					Federal		State and local		General revenue				
						Civilian	Military				Taxes			
	Number	Percent change, 1990–1999	Rate¹	Retired workers						Total (mil. dol.)	Total (mil. dol.)	Per capita²	Percent property	Direct general expenditure (mil. dol.)
COLORADO—Con.														
Delta	6 722	13.7	247	4 250	526	194	80	1 689	1 283	71.5	17.9	692	62.5	71.1
Denver	76 213	-3.6	152	47 635	13 716	15 836	2 863	51 732	24 844	2 460.9	947.2	1 897	39.6	2 168.5
Dolores	436	17.8	232	250	24	12	(3)	170	134	6.0	1.7	990	96.1	5.7
Douglas	9 353	225.3	60	6 075	161	155	425	5 632	3 497	351.9	153.4	1 209	71.6	368.2
Eagle	1 548	62.1	44	970	94	140	101	2 218	1 657	149.6	92.1	2 881	59.6	151.1
Elbert	1 637	85.0	83	975	5 670	34	56	800	535	32.5	12.0	686	91.8	31.2
El Paso	59 588	37.4	119	35 455	40	10 213	29 134	26 203	19 057	1 178.8	379.5	791	62.2	1 134.1
Fremont	8 518	13.6	191	5 130	866	1 183	132	3 819	1 186	68.5	22.7	526	64.6	66.4
Garfield	4 954	25.3	122	3 075	307	296	118	2 825	1 732	104.7	50.9	1 350	71.0	112.2
Gilpin	429	99.5	96	260	7	(3)	13	322	260	32.7	17.7	4 459	49.0	26.5
Grand	1 204	36.8	115	850	52	119	30	903	573	45.7	23.1	2 358	66.1	42.3
Gunnison	1 186	29.6	94	780	61	160	38	1 396	597	42.2	22.7	1 849	60.2	60.5
Hinsdale	111	85.0	150	80	3	(3)	(3)	62	46	3.4	1.7	2 454	57.9	3.0
Huerfano	1 686	12.0	248	955	317	19	21	434	543	23.1	8.0	1 185	86.6	21.6
Jackson	271	23.2	176	165	15	33	(3)	151	132	5.4	2.0	1 289	81.3	5.5
Jefferson	60 906	51.5	120	40 035	3 139	8 884	1 522	22 700	15 883	1 002.1	496.0	1 000	74.7	1 019.0
Kiowa	330	-13.2	202	205	27	17	(3)	240	268	12.8	4.3	2 593	94.7	12.3
Kit Carson	1 457	7.9	197	825	80	46	22	747	545	25.4	7.9	1 099	83.0	27.1
Lake	711	.9	111	400	49	54	19	620	951	50.9	19.8	3 141	91.9	61.0
La Plata	5 227	19.1	127	3 280	400	371	122	3 258	1 755	101.4	57.5	1 434	65.9	102.2
Larimer	29 628	30.0	125	18 995	1 872	2 069	728	20 876	8 242	708.1	250.2	1 110	67.0	575.4
Las Animas	3 333	.7	227	1 775	679	72	44	1 618	1 162	38.2	10.1	702	74.6	40.4
Lincoln	974	6.4	172	585	70	30	17	857	278	22.5	5.9	1 048	71.8	19.8
Logan	3 744	8.7	209	2 195	319	74	54	1 797	1 034	59.7	19.7	1 087	70.5	64.0
Mesa	22 241	28.4	193	14 145	2 118	1 170	341	6 556	4 194	246.8	97.9	884	56.6	232.8
Mineral	159	127.1	219	100	3	(3)	(3)	85	61	4.6	2.3	3 499	49.5	4.4
Moffat	1 705	30.7	134	980	146	148	38	1 045	571	66.7	25.9	2 100	77.0	64.9
Montezuma	4 310	31.2	190	2 530	421	339	68	1 445	1 126	72.6	20.4	916	72.3	68.4
Montrose	6 305	20.9	201	3 980	530	290	93	2 245	1 590	107.4	28.8	953	61.1	104.1
Morgan	4 185	8.7	165	2 480	346	133	76	2 119	1 282	69.3	28.7	1 145	80.7	74.7
Otero	4 270	3.0	207	2 400	920	117	62	1 877	1 072	56.4	11.7	559	54.8	63.2
Ouray	549	52.5	158	385	17	(3)	10	271	168	11.7	5.1	1 580	69.8	11.7
Park	1 376	105.4	97	835	41	60	40	644	550	29.2	12.6	998	95.5	33.9
Phillips	844	-18.8	200	520	57	29	13	482	356	14.1	4.2	977	87.5	14.2
Pitkin	1 065	85.2	80	760	20	95	40	1 543	1 063	113.0	63.0	4 646	50.1	93.5
Prowers	2 326	5.5	169	1 310	376	54	41	1 491	852	36.5	10.3	752	59.9	35.8
Pueblo	27 314	12.9	199	14 775	4 923	706	408	10 269	5 707	301.7	112.1	846	61.2	294.9
Rio Blanco	937	25.8	151	555	58	73	19	952	589	39.7	16.0	2 541	91.3	39.0
Rio Grande	2 570	24.5	223	1 480	366	118	34	821	548	35.5	11.5	1 013	58.4	34.6
Routt	1 333	27.0	74	850	54	129	53	1 413	884	62.3	40.4	2 333	62.1	59.0
Saguache	613	-25.7	99	355	164	62	18	568	338	21.0	4.0	681	91.1	18.0
San Juan	78	-13.3	149	40	2	(3)	(3)	71	48	3.9	2.0	3 642	50.4	4.0
San Miguel	318	27.2	58	185	12	31	16	540	332	36.5	22.2	4 169	69.6	38.7
Sedgwick	744	.5	288	490	42	19	(3)	302	257	11.3	3.4	1 310	87.0	13.1
Summit	1 068	111.5	54	750	25	70	56	1 536	1 201	107.0	73.2	3 967	44.7	108.1
Teller	2 424	70.7	114	1 485	89	44	62	974	783	50.4	21.9	1 105	58.7	47.0
Washington	977	2.3	224	560	49	61	14	418	322	16.0	6.3	1 367	94.6	15.9
Weld	21 204	24.1	128	12 285	2 283	547	488	10 606	6 087	380.3	154.2	991	74.2	382.1
Yuma	2 026	15.1	215	1 210	126	51	28	861	623	29.8	13.4	1 433	91.6	31.4
CONNECTICUT	567 637	7.8	173	394 490	47 669	22 175	16 986	185 623	104 338	8 526.0	4 965.5	1 519	98.7	8 309.0
Fairfield	134 127	7.2	159	94 945	10 368	4 483	2 069	38 097	27 830	2 349.9	1 564.8	1 877	98.6	2 311.0
Hartford	153 062	5.6	184	107 160	15 703	7 385	2 155	58 715	27 104	2 193.5	1 259.4	1 522	98.9	2 140.6
Litchfield	31 846	11.3	175	22 455	1 170	389	444	7 371	4 943	395.4	255.6	1 416	98.8	367.2
Middlesex	25 331	14.8	167	18 060	1 176	324	368	8 707	4 314	358.1	216.6	1 456	99.1	343.2
New Haven	144 187	4.5	182	98 850	13 829	6 543	2 095	39 880	24 022	2 064.9	1 105.2	1 395	98.8	2 042.3
New London	42 758	13.0	174	28 385	3 053	2 625	9 258	13 885	8 522	657.4	332.3	1 328	97.8	633.4
Tolland	17 958	38.1	135	12 615	546	208	338	12 730	4 115	270.4	141.3	1 081	99.0	260.2
Windham	18 350	9.6	174	12 010	1 794	218	259	6 238	3 488	236.5	90.3	862	98.8	211.1
DELAWARE	128 935	23.5	171	83 720	11 849	5 407	8 946	49 245	18 865	1 434.3	412.5	561	82.9	1 419.7
Kent	19 488	30.9	155	12 105	2 483	1 733	4 558	13 462	3 498	220.2	37.8	308	90.9	217.4
New Castle	73 895	17.1	152	46 845	6 953	3 215	3 424	29 705	11 602	942.9	306.6	641	81.3	932.6
Sussex	35 546	35.9	253	24 765	2 391	459	964	6 078	3 765	271.1	68.1	508	85.2	269.8
DISTRICT OF COLUMBIA	73 176	-5.4	141	46 809	20 009	183 932	23 335	41 950	46 246	5 279.0	2 637.4	4 988	26.5	4 335.8
District of Columbia	73 176	-5.4	141	46 809	20 009	183 932	23 335	41 950	46 246	5 279.0	2 637.4	4 988	26.5	4 335.8

¹ Per 1,000 resident population estimated as of July 1, 1999.   ² Based on resident population estimated as of July 1, 1997.   ³ Less than 10 employees.

Sources: Social Security Program—U.S. Social Security Administration, OASDI Beneficiaries by State and County - December 1999, <http://www.ssa.gov/statistics/oasdi_sc/1999/oasdi_sc99.pdf> (accessed: 7 March 2001) for 1999 – annual publication of same title for 1990.   Supplemental Security Income Program—U.S. Social Security Administration, SSI Recipients by State and County, <http://www.ssa.gov/statistics/ssi_st_cty/1999/ssi_st_cty.pdf> (accessed: November 2000).   Government employment, 1998—U.S. Bureau of Economic Analysis, "Regional Economic Information System (REIS) 1969-1998" on CD-ROM (related Internet site <http://www.bea.doc.gov/bea/regional/data.htm>).   Local government employment, 1997—U.S. Census Bureau, 1997 Census of Governments, Compendium of Public Employment, <http://www.census.gov/govs/apes/97coar2.dat> (accessed: 14 January 2000).   Local government finances—U.S. Census Bureau, 1997 Census of Governments, Compendium of Government Finances, <http://www.census.gov/prod/gc97/gc974-5.pdf> (accessed: 16 February 2001).

Table B–13. Counties — Government Programs, Employment, and Finances-Con.

[Includes U.S., states, and 3,142 counties/county equivalents defined as of January 1, 1992. For changes to these areas since January 1, 1992, see appendix B. Geographic Information]

County	Social Security Program beneficiaries, December 1999				Supplemental Security Income Program recipients, December 1999	Government employment, 1998			Local government employment, full-time equivalent, March 1997	Local government finances, 1996–1997				
	Total			Retired workers		Federal		State and local		General revenue				Direct general expenditure (mil. dol.)
	Number	Percent change, 1990–1999	Rate[1]			Civilian	Military			Total (mil. dol.)	Taxes			
											Total (mil. dol.)	Per capita[2]	Percent property	
FLORIDA	3 139 437	18.4	208	2 121 056	366 966	119 348	111 309	823 269	543 525	41 196.5	14 647.4	998	78.8	40 665.5
Alachua	27 667	13.7	139	16 540	4 777	2 937	632	36 357	8 678	469.0	135.7	687	84.9	478.9
Baker	3 208	39.8	151	1 530	458	71	48	2 591	691	52.2	8.7	418	70.5	50.2
Bay	26 885	30.9	182	15 930	3 413	3 030	4 452	6 836	6 634	460.6	108.1	739	64.2	471.9
Bradford	3 192	-5.8	128	1 835	710	37	56	2 447	906	49.8	9.1	371	66.6	43.2
Brevard	110 416	43.0	235	74 715	7 552	5 541	3 574	19 592	15 688	992.6	330.2	719	79.4	963.2
Broward	277 697	2.5	181	191 915	26 211	7 008	3 749	73 771	55 161	4 746.9	1 714.5	1 161	79.0	4 631.4
Calhoun	2 390	20.1	192	1 255	501	24	28	952	425	22.5	4.3	350	68.5	23.3
Charlotte	49 853	41.8	364	37 375	1 433	259	305	4 839	3 687	268.9	131.5	994	75.6	238.4
Citrus	42 890	31.3	369	31 315	1 656	194	257	3 632	2 941	196.8	83.4	749	92.0	197.6
Clay	19 464	67.4	138	11 725	1 207	324	313	4 575	3 890	245.5	71.6	535	75.2	233.3
Collier	54 803	51.1	265	39 895	1 923	579	451	8 491	6 758	502.7	285.7	1 481	86.1	529.5
Columbia	10 718	40.0	199	6 125	2 219	1 050	119	3 913	2 034	116.0	26.8	519	63.2	112.8
Dade	311 644	13.1	143	207 040	113 801	18 213	6 970	118 867	87 062	7 614.5	2 454.4	1 151	75.5	7 840.1
DeSoto	6 072	15.3	246	3 870	721	55	56	2 883	957	53.3	15.3	619	75.8	51.3
Dixie	3 206	43.1	248	1 805	549	17	29	1 041	480	25.1	5.3	418	77.4	24.4
Duval	106 161	13.6	144	62 690	17 911	17 172	28 570	33 558	23 788	1 764.1	611.2	837	75.3	1 817.7
Escambia	50 645	26.2	179	29 635	8 331	7 004	14 190	16 195	9 925	659.9	178.9	639	62.9	634.7
Flagler	16 519	102.7	336	12 330	515	90	107	1 889	1 235	90.5	44.0	980	89.9	78.4
Franklin	2 257	23.7	226	1 415	436	23	23	656	438	23.5	11.0	1 089	88.7	22.5
Gadsden	8 356	6.7	190	4 560	2 612	117	99	5 668	1 590	78.6	15.9	360	74.6	87.9
Gilchrist	2 544	51.0	181	1 435	376	28	31	1 064	421	28.1	5.0	376	79.4	28.0
Glades	1 816	96.3	209	1 230	108	11	19	364	285	16.5	6.8	800	90.1	16.2
Gulf	2 956	28.0	218	1 665	382	15	30	1 148	555	33.3	11.6	862	91.0	32.6
Hamilton	2 220	19.0	174	1 115	578	33	29	1 397	652	56.8	27.8	2 229	43.6	63.2
Hardee	4 019	10.0	191	2 365	850	50	47	1 733	1 001	54.0	17.8	846	82.7	51.3
Hendry	4 847	45.1	165	2 795	695	110	66	2 388	1 428	101.2	29.4	1 006	82.9	105.2
Hernando	47 364	30.6	369	34 130	1 975	291	288	4 836	3 912	311.5	134.6	1 085	94.2	297.2
Highlands	28 829	19.9	385	21 145	1 971	292	170	3 576	2 568	156.3	55.9	744	77.8	151.6
Hillsborough	154 169	19.2	164	93 870	25 476	11 153	7 614	57 304	37 347	2 752.7	851.5	936	77.5	2 691.0
Holmes	4 454	32.2	237	2 285	728	61	42	1 280	611	35.3	5.1	277	67.8	32.5
Indian River	33 838	13.0	338	24 625	1 280	342	224	4 468	3 555	350.9	133.0	1 358	81.6	322.4
Jackson	9 742	12.0	219	5 275	2 101	495	109	5 547	2 416	125.3	18.7	420	55.7	123.5
Jefferson	2 486	18.4	190	1 445	675	29	29	936	461	24.3	6.1	470	73.2	24.0
Lafayette	1 113	53.5	172	620	132	15	14	637	241	12.8	2.3	372	89.1	13.0
Lake	62 066	29.0	296	45 425	3 675	502	492	8 139	5 478	348.0	129.1	663	73.6	326.9
Lee	111 884	22.0	279	80 865	5 812	1 821	942	23 544	16 564	1 548.2	458.5	1 188	87.9	1 483.3
Leon	24 597	19.8	114	15 630	3 886	1 693	628	52 108	9 973	585.2	191.1	892	67.3	578.7
Levy	8 535	50.0	264	5 115	976	76	97	1 742	1 293	61.0	18.0	579	77.3	56.8
Liberty	1 095	17.1	163	560	230	49	15	729	225	12.0	2.3	340	75.9	11.7
Madison	3 594	11.4	201	1 985	1 091	50	40	1 459	895	43.3	7.6	434	63.5	41.5
Manatee	66 430	17.8	273	47 810	3 415	1 143	569	9 924	8 166	586.6	222.9	948	83.9	585.5
Marion	76 666	37.9	312	53 730	5 888	649	549	13 640	7 572	411.8	119.9	509	88.2	414.7
Martin	36 630	22.1	310	26 865	1 284	281	265	4 751	3 357	296.6	161.0	1 415	88.7	283.9
Monroe	12 897	27.2	161	8 985	1 161	1 268	1 555	4 779	4 229	297.6	141.3	1 746	76.9	268.6
Nassau	9 694	68.6	171	5 640	810	602	125	2 428	1 806	115.4	41.7	772	82.1	105.5
Okaloosa	27 432	46.0	161	16 990	2 383	6 513	15 163	7 276	5 770	354.9	108.4	647	84.7	346.3
Okeechobee	7 216	4.1	223	4 360	884	75	70	1 745	1 429	65.2	20.6	667	71.4	65.9
Orange	117 109	20.8	143	70 875	19 526	7 316	5 218	48 715	33 139	2 574.5	932.6	1 188	75.8	2 573.3
Osceola	26 263	47.3	174	15 680	2 395	254	328	6 882	5 478	372.6	143.3	1 017	69.0	403.8
Palm Beach	261 377	20.0	249	191 870	13 416	5 731	2 409	47 726	34 775	3 140.0	1 523.2	1 501	84.0	3 022.8
Pasco	102 877	6.1	311	72 055	6 144	652	736	11 419	7 965	549.0	174.7	549	89.6	524.4
Pinellas	223 134	-5.2	254	155 290	15 090	6 027	2 983	35 840	28 611	2 106.4	886.1	1 015	75.2	2 020.6
Polk	104 868	22.2	229	68 610	12 109	1 409	1 030	25 237	16 728	896.4	274.6	615	82.6	892.9
Putnam	17 005	20.5	242	10 075	2 604	158	159	4 477	3 477	240.0	98.9	1 412	93.4	153.1
St. Johns	23 742	45.9	198	15 785	1 735	404	270	5 421	5 568	243.8	99.4	891	87.1	230.4
St. Lucie	50 275	45.9	276	34 575	4 505	483	460	8 809	7 451	471.1	182.2	1 027	89.8	504.9
Santa Rosa	18 320	71.6	151	10 830	1 543	783	1 564	4 576	3 062	201.0	59.2	520	78.1	198.9
Sarasota	102 522	-.1	334	76 030	3 216	838	695	11 286	10 853	970.3	328.7	1 095	79.1	915.1
Seminole	50 530	52.2	141	32 085	4 472	1 400	792	12 689	10 211	709.8	297.4	866	71.9	720.2
Sumter	15 895	98.2	372	11 400	1 267	776	91	2 055	1 479	66.2	18.6	459	65.9	72.4
Suwannee	8 122	31.0	246	4 775	1 100	120	74	1 538	1 128	58.1	14.7	460	70.1	57.1
Taylor	3 960	17.7	208	2 220	743	36	42	1 451	872	44.9	16.3	872	70.1	46.2
Union	1 459	32.0	115	755	300	19	28	2 401	395	28.3	2.9	231	69.3	25.0
Volusia	113 866	15.0	268	78 100	8 491	1 262	976	19 576	13 890	1 122.4	362.7	872	80.2	1 074.2
Wakulla	3 130	50.8	163	1 855	472	74	42	1 244	715	40.0	8.2	444	77.0	43.0
Walton	7 304	56.9	192	4 295	905	170	116	2 038	1 309	82.1	42.0	1 147	78.6	79.2
Washington	4 478	16.5	217	2 420	839	44	46	2 194	1 241	61.9	8.1	402	73.1	56.5

[1] Per 1,000 resident population estimated as of July 1, 1999.   [2] Based on resident population estimated as of July 1, 1997.

Sources: Social Security Program—U.S. Social Security Administration, OASDI Beneficiaries by State and County - December 1999, <http://www.ssa.gov/statistics/oasdi_sc/1999/oasdi_sc99.pdf> (accessed: 7 March 2001) for 1999 – annual publication of same title for 1990. Supplemental Security Income Program—U.S. Social Security Administration, SSI Recipients by State and County, <http://www.ssa.gov/statistics/ssi_st_cty/1999/ssi_st_cty.pdf> (accessed: November 2000). Government employment, 1998—U.S. Bureau of Economic Analysis, "Regional Economic Information System (REIS) 1969-1998" on CD-ROM (related Internet site <http://www.bea.doc.gov/bea/regional/data.htm>). Local government employment, 1997—U.S. Census Bureau, 1997 Census of Governments, Compendium of Public Employment, <http://www.census.gov/govs/apes/97coar2.dat> (accessed: 14 January 2000). Local government finances—U.S. Census Bureau, 1997 Census of Governments, Compendium of Government Finances, <http://www.census.gov/prod/gc97/gc974-5.pdf> (accessed: 16 February 2001).

Table B–13. Counties — Government Programs, Employment, and Finances–Con.

[Includes U.S., states, and 3,142 counties/county equivalents defined as of January 1, 1992. For changes to these areas since January 1, 1992, see appendix B. Geographic Information]

County	Social Security Program beneficiaries, December 1999 — Total — Number	Percent change, 1990–1999	Rate¹	Retired workers	Supplemental Security Income Program recipients, December 1999	Government employment, 1998 — Federal — Civilian	Military	State and local	Local government employment, full-time equivalent, March 1997	Local government finances, 1996–1997 — General revenue — Total (mil. dol.)	Taxes — Total (mil. dol.)	Per capita²	Percent property	Direct general expenditure (mil. dol.)
GEORGIA	1 073 388	21.5	138	620 139	196 959	93 207	94 817	491 328	324 480	19 321.4	7 273.0	972	67.5	18 353.7
Appling	3 055	23.9	183	1 560	768	46	64	1 190	1 147	55.1	18.1	1 105	70.0	51.8
Atkinson	1 187	1.5	163	550	424	19	28	380	285	11.8	4.2	593	60.6	11.2
Bacon	1 926	18.2	186	995	552	30	40	572	714	31.5	6.7	649	61.0	32.5
Baker	681	44.9	188	360	217	11	14	203	219	6.5	2.4	654	82.2	6.6
Baldwin	6 715	20.9	159	3 480	1 420	70	171	8 286	2 064	144.5	29.3	699	52.5	124.5
Banks	2 261	82.3	172	1 325	252	15	49	474	337	17.7	9.2	736	52.8	16.7
Barrow	5 962	25.6	142	3 380	1 207	126	156	1 977	1 496	65.9	28.2	725	65.5	69.9
Bartow	10 921	39.5	146	6 245	1 371	171	277	3 827	3 134	141.5	55.7	804	71.1	149.9
Ben Hill	3 283	2.9	188	1 810	855	36	67	1 490	1 127	51.0	13.5	779	59.4	49.1
Berrien	2 930	16.7	177	1 520	704	42	63	741	731	28.2	10.4	654	58.3	27.1
Bibb	27 915	1.3	180	15 445	6 946	1 475	739	9 930	6 109	377.6	168.9	1 082	59.8	364.8
Bleckley	2 118	10.6	187	1 220	437	32	43	942	561	26.3	6.4	582	60.3	24.7
Brantley	2 412	61.3	174	1 055	474	26	69	658	562	19.7	6.7	501	72.1	19.4
Brooks	3 251	23.6	202	1 760	741	38	62	841	628	24.1	7.8	494	70.2	25.0
Bryan	2 763	31.6	113	1 425	501	45	91	1 213	967	38.9	16.0	690	68.1	36.9
Bulloch	6 814	22.6	134	3 890	1 484	141	205	4 836	2 459	96.2	30.1	603	59.9	105.7
Burke	3 700	10.4	159	1 875	1 095	60	88	1 485	1 278	148.0	35.1	1 562	85.1	145.1
Butts	3 030	21.4	165	1 740	524	38	69	1 212	517	31.1	13.8	802	64.6	29.9
Calhoun	1 117	-18.8	226	595	442	22	19	733	378	11.6	3.6	703	65.9	11.7
Camden	3 680	64.3	78	1 795	576	2 590	5 820	2 239	1 738	83.1	31.7	695	60.3	82.2
Candler	1 849	18.1	207	1 020	532	24	35	659	496	29.5	5.7	644	57.5	25.3
Carroll	13 301	21.1	157	7 630	2 335	209	322	5 147	3 847	134.7	47.6	587	53.0	138.0
Catoosa	8 250	67.7	158	4 990	663	72	195	1 814	2 636	138.6	22.9	464	64.8	149.2
Charlton	1 624	24.9	172	760	365	48	51	562	439	25.6	6.9	740	75.0	22.1
Chatham	37 935	5.6	168	22 510	6 612	2 664	5 077	14 464	10 266	663.3	301.0	1 335	64.7	641.6
Chattahoochee	376	.3	23	175	119	(3)	13 328	193	131	5.9	1.6	101	31.7	5.3
Chattooga	4 930	6.3	216	2 970	826	36	88	1 496	994	38.0	11.9	519	62.5	44.3
Cherokee	12 919	70.7	91	7 895	883	232	519	4 441	3 860	211.7	78.8	620	74.5	216.9
Clarke	11 023	8.1	122	6 585	2 375	1 551	673	15 226	5 663	360.9	85.3	941	66.2	319.8
Clay	831	33.0	236	460	234	69	13	245	138	5.8	2.5	711	60.0	5.6
Clayton	21 453	30.0	100	11 015	3 710	2 093	840	11 642	8 969	419.5	178.2	870	66.4	421.7
Clinch	1 282	12.0	192	565	465	19	26	580	349	21.8	6.7	1 015	74.9	20.0
Cobb	53 993	36.4	93	34 415	5 324	2 633	3 359	30 180	15 350	1 114.2	556.0	1 009	72.4	1 232.6
Coffee	5 545	18.7	159	2 710	1 479	115	132	2 135	1 947	65.6	24.8	734	54.5	66.1
Colquitt	7 303	5.2	179	4 135	1 811	104	155	3 205	2 406	111.9	22.0	555	64.1	113.7
Columbia	9 653	86.9	103	5 645	832	90	351	2 839	2 591	141.7	59.6	672	68.3	136.8
Cook	2 889	14.9	190	1 530	674	32	58	803	621	25.7	9.3	634	55.2	26.6
Coweta	10 858	39.2	121	6 460	1 521	182	328	3 223	2 637	143.8	69.9	865	64.6	141.4
Crawford	1 382	53.6	133	700	278	11	41	454	375	15.4	5.6	522	77.3	14.8
Crisp	3 857	.7	187	2 140	1 220	58	80	1 499	1 670	49.2	18.7	910	54.7	44.9
Dade	2 553	30.9	166	1 360	385	19	58	568	479	20.3	8.6	586	49.8	19.3
Dawson	1 889	40.4	118	1 115	284	27	57	629	423	27.6	12.7	907	69.8	26.7
Decatur	5 070	7.8	187	2 765	1 417	63	104	2 512	1 650	86.9	22.3	837	49.5	80.3
De Kalb	68 998	11.4	116	40 885	11 685	10 767	2 920	29 116	27 693	1 883.8	632.1	1 071	76.5	1 628.3
Dodge	3 559	10.5	196	1 890	935	46	70	1 926	1 068	41.7	7.5	412	64.1	42.2
Dooly	2 182	14.2	209	1 185	584	52	40	960	596	23.3	8.9	851	72.7	22.6
Dougherty	15 516	9.9	165	8 710	4 801	2 839	1 109	8 157	7 624	263.8	97.5	1 020	57.4	258.3
Douglas	10 097	43.2	111	5 790	1 053	156	346	3 626	2 786	155.3	72.7	839	64.9	155.5
Early	2 483	8.2	205	1 350	740	49	47	751	690	26.1	9.0	739	58.3	27.7
Echols	318	32.5	125	175	69	(3)	(3)	170	125	5.0	1.9	778	86.5	4.9
Effingham	4 542	82.0	118	2 175	572	58	141	1 825	1 453	67.7	22.1	630	71.9	72.2
Elbert	4 422	13.8	228	2 400	997	147	75	1 435	1 122	46.2	11.1	580	62.8	44.1
Emanuel	4 654	6.7	221	2 425	1 499	98	81	1 946	1 251	60.1	12.6	599	58.9	61.2
Evans	2 010	25.2	199	1 055	497	57	38	619	514	20.7	6.5	667	53.4	20.6
Fannin	4 965	29.3	262	2 835	762	67	72	789	602	28.5	11.0	603	55.1	26.3
Fayette	10 023	86.3	108	6 600	391	182	342	3 728	2 830	165.5	86.5	1 017	79.5	180.2
Floyd	17 628	12.2	206	10 475	2 692	240	341	5 971	5 023	315.1	79.3	936	59.0	295.9
Forsyth	8 273	90.8	86	5 265	547	138	332	2 628	1 845	134.6	74.7	978	64.4	154.2
Franklin	4 320	14.7	224	2 605	710	48	74	945	1 402	56.4	13.2	710	54.1	55.2
Fulton	88 033	5.0	118	51 355	21 146	23 204	4 555	77 637	37 077	3 271.3	1 537.1	2 124	65.2	2 511.1
Gilmer	4 179	54.8	211	2 475	643	75	72	867	708	29.8	12.1	671	72.9	28.4
Glascock	582	8.8	229	370	92	11	10	157	103	4.0	1.5	601	80.7	3.9
Glynn	12 997	17.2	191	7 755	1 725	1 168	278	5 804	4 203	283.1	78.6	1 181	63.2	272.2
Gordon	6 992	28.8	167	4 060	953	93	158	1 992	1 601	78.0	22.5	559	61.2	76.1
Grady	4 275	15.5	198	2 295	1 065	41	83	1 191	1 145	38.3	11.7	545	66.5	40.8
Greene	3 015	32.2	214	1 720	580	38	53	866	669	26.5	12.2	916	67.9	25.1

¹ Per 1,000 resident population estimated as of July 1, 1999.   ² Based on resident population estimated as of July 1, 1997.   ³ Less than 10 employees.

Sources: Social Security Program—U.S. Social Security Administration, OASDI Beneficiaries by State and County - December 1999, <http://www.ssa.gov/statistics/oasdi_sc/1999/oasdi_sc99.pdf> (accessed: 7 March 2001) for 1999 – annual publication of same title for 1990.   Supplemental Security Income Program—U.S. Social Security Administration, SSI Recipients by State and County, <http://www.ssa.gov/statistics/ssi_st_cty/1999/ssi_st_cty.pdf> (accessed: November 2000).   Government employment, 1998—U.S. Bureau of Economic Analysis, "Regional Economic Information System (REIS) 1969-1998" on CD-ROM (related Internet site <http://www.bea.doc.gov/bea/regional/data.htm>).   Local government employment, 1997—U.S. Census Bureau, 1997 Census of Governments, Compendium of Public Employment, <http://www.census.gov/govs/apes/97coar2.dat> (accessed: 14 January 2000).   Local government finances—U.S. Census Bureau, 1997 Census of Governments, Compendium of Government Finances, <http://www.census.gov/prod/gc97/gc974-5.pdf> (accessed: 16 February 2001).

[Includes U.S., states, and 3,142 counties/county equivalents defined as of January 1, 1992. For changes to these areas since January 1, 1992, see appendix B. Geographic Information]

County	Social Security Program beneficiaries, December 1999				Supplemental Security Income Program recipients, December 1999	Government employment, 1998			Local government employment, full-time equivalent, March 1997	Local government finances, 1996–1997				
	Total			Retired workers		Federal		State and local		General revenue				Direct general expenditure (mil. dol.)
	Number	Percent change, 1990–1999	Rate[1]			Civilian	Military			Total (mil. dol.)	Taxes			
											Total (mil. dol.)	Per capita[2]	Percent property	
GEORGIA—Con.														
Gwinnett	39 864	93.0	73	24 525	3 410	3 626	2 018	18 497	16 107	1 219.1	493.6	986	84.5	1 225.0
Habersham	6 297	28.0	194	4 015	828	132	123	2 481	1 376	76.7	19.6	626	68.2	75.5
Hall	18 381	27.5	149	11 460	2 146	456	461	6 953	4 708	258.8	115.0	993	61.4	261.8
Hancock	1 905	18.7	211	965	550	15	35	889	575	32.1	8.1	904	85.2	26.2
Haralson	4 875	24.7	194	2 830	782	51	95	1 361	937	50.5	13.7	566	62.5	53.6
Harris	3 613	37.6	160	2 210	437	56	86	931	670	41.5	16.8	756	70.9	38.7
Hart	4 758	43.5	215	3 080	615	99	84	985	691	40.1	12.2	566	68.7	39.0
Heard	1 735	44.0	165	940	307	15	39	543	432	20.6	7.8	783	72.6	20.7
Henry	12 410	78.8	109	7 400	1 127	836	404	3 713	3 033	158.7	84.1	860	74.6	162.7
Houston	13 059	40.6	121	7 380	2 201	11 505	4 671	6 254	4 788	255.6	54.7	527	80.0	256.0
Irwin	1 902	23.9	207	1 025	398	29	35	679	423	16.1	5.9	659	77.3	15.8
Jackson	6 349	19.2	163	3 690	1 155	107	145	2 026	1 468	83.6	26.3	723	59.9	89.0
Jasper	1 947	52.1	184	1 155	265	23	39	664	545	18.5	7.8	793	74.3	17.6
Jeff Davis	2 504	16.7	197	1 270	500	30	49	768	669	33.8	9.1	718	48.0	33.0
Jefferson	3 630	4.8	203	1 910	1 228	46	69	1 058	906	36.7	10.1	567	72.6	37.6
Jenkins	1 623	-1.9	193	900	513	25	33	576	455	18.7	5.1	600	60.3	19.0
Johnson	1 728	9.0	208	960	481	17	32	739	314	13.3	4.1	494	65.5	14.4
Jones	3 194	78.4	137	1 690	351	30	89	787	616	30.8	10.8	476	65.8	31.1
Lamar	2 814	21.0	187	1 715	405	37	57	866	542	24.0	8.7	599	74.0	25.0
Lanier	1 129	29.0	162	585	279	13	27	344	273	10.5	3.2	471	64.6	10.5
Laurens	8 226	13.1	187	4 555	1 980	906	169	3 042	2 213	94.1	24.0	554	60.4	116.7
Lee	2 208	58.8	95	1 180	323	37	88	1 110	658	36.4	12.1	553	74.5	39.4
Liberty	3 961	50.6	66	1 895	1 021	3 226	15 923	2 656	2 047	111.4	40.1	667	49.5	92.1
Lincoln	1 727	19.9	207	1 005	285	19	32	441	334	13.3	4.4	537	67.4	14.2
Long	930	75.5	107	445	166	11	33	410	243	11.5	3.9	465	84.5	10.6
Lowndes	11 982	11.5	140	6 705	2 855	975	4 097	8 132	5 181	296.8	68.8	813	41.9	285.1
Lumpkin	2 850	60.6	144	1 685	438	73	275	1 263	537	30.3	13.5	742	69.0	33.0
McDuffie	3 674	15.2	168	2 010	858	43	127	1 417	992	54.3	14.5	673	53.9	47.7
McIntosh	1 958	22.8	194	1 025	407	25	39	675	384	16.4	7.4	749	59.1	17.7
Macon	2 085	-2.8	159	1 085	780	31	51	945	526	29.5	10.4	780	66.8	30.7
Madison	4 316	26.8	171	2 425	800	46	94	890	720	30.4	10.7	442	66.6	32.1
Marion	979	28.0	144	480	290	36	26	408	345	13.2	3.3	499	64.6	14.3
Meriwether	4 105	8.5	178	2 390	1 010	47	89	1 736	1 121	40.6	14.6	639	67.3	38.2
Miller	1 330	6.4	211	775	312	24	25	449	346	11.1	4.2	666	76.5	11.0
Mitchell	4 060	12.0	191	2 150	1 206	77	82	1 960	1 246	46.9	11.4	542	72.8	52.0
Monroe	3 355	41.0	167	1 920	473	44	76	1 449	890	61.9	23.0	1 186	69.8	59.6
Montgomery	1 429	13.0	182	710	391	25	30	410	238	9.7	3.2	414	61.1	9.5
Morgan	2 743	27.0	178	1 700	398	40	58	870	618	34.3	13.6	934	66.6	34.4
Murray	4 719	51.3	139	2 455	789	100	126	1 234	1 112	50.7	18.0	564	60.3	52.3
Muscogee	29 567	11.2	162	17 255	5 686	5 769	4 761	11 932	8 433	420.3	182.5	999	59.0	395.0
Newton	8 921	33.9	147	5 310	1 550	120	224	2 531	2 141	133.1	40.4	732	66.1	133.9
Oconee	2 904	41.7	118	1 800	312	90	92	1 064	631	37.2	16.9	731	73.6	43.1
Oglethorpe	1 995	58.3	173	1 130	325	15	44	435	352	17.8	5.7	507	74.5	17.6
Paulding	7 013	86.3	88	3 820	665	81	284	2 677	2 071	123.4	39.7	577	67.1	125.9
Peach	3 914	24.1	157	2 075	892	94	102	1 949	431	47.7	16.3	683	61.1	47.0
Pickens	4 043	53.7	192	2 535	411	50	76	969	594	33.6	12.4	665	72.9	37.6
Pierce	2 866	17.7	181	1 435	710	46	61	737	582	24.4	8.4	545	64.1	26.1
Pike	2 169	23.2	166	1 345	304	29	49	542	359	16.3	6.1	499	70.5	15.5
Polk	7 511	6.8	205	4 145	1 402	72	140	1 752	1 468	63.0	22.9	638	63.3	61.8
Pulaski	1 731	1.8	207	990	416	17	32	827	316	15.9	5.5	662	72.1	17.0
Putnam	3 425	55.7	188	2 150	419	79	68	1 007	626	45.5	16.7	989	66.5	50.7
Quitman	610	8.9	249	345	189	(³)	10	119	75	4.8	1.4	572	80.7	4.5
Rabun	3 332	29.4	243	2 095	446	63	52	751	573	27.6	12.3	928	79.2	29.0
Randolph	1 661	-4.5	207	820	527	26	30	783	671	25.7	4.3	538	59.6	26.4
Richmond	31 116	12.9	164	16 630	6 816	5 976	10 102	22 142	7 798	431.8	153.7	802	50.4	442.1
Rockdale	8 602	54.3	125	5 400	874	132	263	2 976	2 914	137.6	65.7	981	77.8	176.1
Schley	615	10.8	156	325	147	(³)	15	168	101	6.2	2.0	529	79.3	6.5
Screven	2 930	9.5	203	1 560	874	43	56	954	644	32.0	9.4	652	68.8	31.6
Seminole	2 051	13.9	209	1 150	525	25	38	490	307	16.3	5.4	559	58.7	16.7
Spalding	10 283	9.3	178	6 060	1 951	128	222	3 847	2 351	125.3	45.9	798	60.9	127.9
Stephens	5 849	12.5	231	3 520	982	69	98	1 606	1 143	45.4	19.6	776	65.0	48.3
Stewart	1 097	-1.6	204	585	366	13	21	304	230	10.3	3.1	572	80.2	10.6
Sumter	5 250	4.8	167	3 010	1 462	133	121	3 055	2 000	118.0	23.0	731	56.9	111.7
Talbot	1 278	7.8	183	700	370	16	27	305	208	10.6	4.3	621	77.7	10.4
Taliaferro	453	-6.6	235	260	128	(³)	(³)	100	60	2.9	1.6	833	86.3	2.3
Tattnall	3 442	2.6	180	1 825	1 056	31	73	2 561	649	31.5	10.7	559	65.1	31.6

[1] Per 1,000 resident population estimated as of July 1, 1999. [2] Based on resident population estimated as of July 1, 1997. [3] Less than 10 employees.

[Includes U.S., states, and 3,142 counties/county equivalents defined as of January 1, 1992. For changes to these areas since January 1, 1992, see appendix B. Geographic Information]

County	Social Security Program beneficiaries, December 1999 — Total — Number	Percent change, 1990–1999	Rate[1]	Retired workers	Supplemental Security Income Program recipients, December 1999	Government employment, 1998 — Federal — Civilian	Military	State and local	Local government employment, full-time equivalent, March 1997	Local government finances, 1996–1997 — General revenue — Total (mil. dol.)	Taxes — Total (mil. dol.)	Per capita[2]	Percent property	Direct general expenditure (mil. dol.)
GEORGIA—Con.														
Taylor	1 593	-.7	192	830	571	24	32	530	358	15.4	4.3	532	58.9	15.5
Telfair	2 549	-.2	223	1 350	651	40	45	1 006	465	25.8	7.8	681	58.7	22.9
Terrell	2 043	5.9	182	1 105	676	72	43	555	480	22.3	7.1	639	58.6	22.2
Thomas	8 422	6.8	196	4 715	2 151	191	167	3 672	2 268	90.8	19.5	457	57.2	95.6
Tift	6 193	6.9	167	3 510	1 446	196	141	3 979	2 287	144.3	27.3	747	52.5	163.8
Toombs	4 834	8.3	186	2 565	1 533	68	100	1 320	1 333	52.2	14.3	559	37.8	51.2
Towns	2 794	49.0	318	1 915	248	21	33	342	282	9.7	3.7	454	61.3	10.3
Treutlen	1 236	2.6	208	650	393	14	23	372	237	10.5	2.4	402	70.8	10.4
Troup	10 561	-1.4	180	6 470	2 265	151	227	4 989	3 784	196.3	44.5	763	70.7	201.7
Turner	1 710	-2.8	185	955	497	30	35	476	471	19.8	7.0	766	66.3	19.5
Twiggs	1 991	43.2	195	835	445	11	39	526	332	16.5	6.9	708	72.8	15.6
Union	4 581	64.5	266	3 035	470	75	64	1 115	706	38.2	9.4	598	59.1	37.8
Upson	5 856	6.5	216	3 590	848	52	104	1 644	1 447	41.5	15.9	587	71.0	42.4
Walker	11 884	3.7	189	7 040	1 684	142	243	2 698	2 217	95.5	29.0	467	60.9	92.4
Walton	7 603	26.5	130	4 635	1 334	113	210	2 680	2 102	107.5	34.5	671	77.8	105.1
Ware	6 933	4.9	197	3 655	1 907	151	136	3 313	3 101	88.4	28.6	803	52.1	89.5
Warren	1 323	16.1	218	715	328	18	23	295	221	12.0	4.4	731	69.2	11.1
Washington	3 718	11.2	184	1 930	1 019	51	77	2 196	767	55.3	18.3	915	64.8	62.9
Wayne	4 534	22.0	177	2 420	923	370	98	2 198	1 488	89.1	17.7	707	75.4	66.5
Webster	420	27.3	191	245	97	12	(3)	138	96	4.0	1.3	576	89.3	3.9
Wheeler	1 084	7.9	223	545	334	12	19	332	236	8.5	2.1	419	61.4	9.2
White	3 827	53.7	210	2 440	403	40	67	878	542	31.3	16.5	980	61.8	40.2
Whitfield	12 631	17.0	152	7 745	1 727	180	316	4 846	3 439	314.5	85.5	1 053	75.7	267.8
Wilcox	1 497	-.2	202	820	459	29	28	640	272	13.3	4.0	549	71.7	14.4
Wilkes	2 446	5.7	232	1 475	544	41	41	855	707	34.3	8.5	800	67.3	32.5
Wilkinson	1 947	5.2	178	960	358	20	42	545	416	19.4	9.8	905	64.6	18.4
Worth	3 636	37.5	162	1 985	769	43	87	1 143	901	35.4	11.2	500	67.4	36.2
HAWAII	178 000	19.8	150	125 755	20 417	30 127	55 253	80 967	14 319	1 449.2	760.7	640	79.8	1 440.5
Hawaii	25 232	23.6	177	16 500	2 918	961	1 339	9 511	2 009	178.0	102.2	726	84.6	195.8
Honolulu	126 024	19.9	146	90 700	15 358	28 274	52 170	60 501	9 421	996.0	526.9	603	78.5	972.6
Kalawao	3	-98.1	52	5	–	(4)	(4)	(4)	X	X	X	X	X	X
Kauai	9 415	11.5	167	6 675	813	385	628	3 674	1 023	94.0	39.8	707	82.5	84.6
Maui	17 325	22.5	142	11 875	1 310	4507	41 116	47 281	1 866	181.1	91.9	772	80.7	187.5
IDAHO	190 674	21.2	152	120 373	17 813	12 728	9 768	86 918	46 035	2 631.0	758.5	627	93.8	2 689.4
Ada	34 885	27.8	123	22 685	3 396	4 475	1 321	20 636	7 059	529.1	205.2	769	92.3	559.5
Adams	869	36.9	229	565	46	119	17	270	186	10.4	2.0	532	95.8	9.0
Bannock	9 472	20.1	126	5 780	1 291	520	340	7 800	3 288	177.4	39.1	529	95.4	169.9
Bear Lake	1 223	6.8	186	765	84	50	29	520	261	19.5	4.3	659	96.4	18.4
Benewah	1 829	24.0	202	1 030	170	73	41	645	458	26.0	5.6	627	96.2	24.5
Bingham	6 078	17.6	144	3 765	605	311	186	2 879	1 785	90.8	18.8	453	96.1	91.4
Blaine	1 762	46.2	102	1 200	46	90	77	1 184	948	65.8	27.5	1 599	85.0	65.9
Boise	916	59.3	172	570	50	152	23	335	239	15.5	3.9	766	97.5	15.6
Bonner	6 747	28.8	187	4 035	504	272	157	1 859	1 094	62.4	20.5	590	95.7	60.5
Bonneville	11 450	27.6	140	7 210	1 192	722	360	4 397	3 525	154.0	45.4	567	95.8	156.4
Boundary	1 876	35.5	188	1 105	171	128	44	688	496	24.7	4.3	438	98.7	22.0
Butte	569	3.5	189	360	49	51	15	201	242	12.3	2.7	864	99.8	11.7
Camas	152	-5.0	176	95	7	20	(3)	87	69	2.7	.7	815	96.3	3.0
Canyon	18 276	18.5	147	11 510	2 420	341	535	5 569	3 697	187.4	53.7	461	93.6	210.2
Caribou	1 277	20.5	176	790	57	45	33	570	469	24.7	6.9	946	92.5	26.3
Cassia	3 448	13.2	160	2 290	313	159	95	1 343	882	46.5	12.1	563	95.3	50.7
Clark	121	-10.4	133	80	7	40	(3)	124	67	3.6	.9	1 013	94.7	3.6
Clearwater	2 065	29.9	221	1 180	175	269	41	961	327	30.2	5.6	594	96.3	31.4
Custer	817	21.0	200	515	58	127	18	324	222	9.6	2.8	667	96.0	9.0
Elmore	2 706	27.9	106	1 700	220	1 029	4 257	1 236	979	44.0	9.8	399	95.5	50.0
Franklin	1 711	7.3	151	1 095	105	35	49	719	310	21.3	3.8	354	97.1	23.8
Fremont	2 037	18.1	171	1 315	129	132	53	838	447	26.0	7.4	628	93.9	29.8
Gem	3 042	14.1	201	2 035	202	91	66	676	520	23.7	5.7	391	85.3	23.9
Gooding	2 698	9.2	196	1 820	197	61	61	954	618	28.0	7.3	541	97.8	26.3
Idaho	3 547	27.1	236	2 065	328	467	67	931	568	31.5	5.8	383	95.7	32.7
Jefferson	2 575	14.2	129	1 565	166	49	85	1 010	713	34.4	7.6	399	94.1	34.0
Jerome	2 925	9.3	162	1 920	290	54	80	819	623	30.7	7.8	445	97.4	28.8

[1] Per 1,000 resident population estimated as of July 1, 1999. [2] Based on resident population estimated as of July 1, 1997. [3] Less than 10 employees. [4] Kalawao County included with Maui County; data not available separately.

Sources: Social Security Program—U.S. Social Security Administration, OASDI Beneficiaries by State and County - December 1999, <http://www.ssa.gov/statistics/oasdi_sc/1999/oasdi_sc99.pdf> (accessed: 7 March 2001) for 1999 – annual publication of same title for 1990. Supplemental Security Income Program—U.S. Social Security Administration, SSI Recipients by State and County, <http://www.ssa.gov/statistics/ssi_st_cty/1999/ssi_st_cty.pdf> (accessed: November 2000). Government employment, 1998—U.S. Bureau of Economic Analysis, "Regional Economic Information System (REIS) 1969-1998" on CD-ROM (related Internet site <http://www.bea.doc.gov/bea/regional/data.htm>). Local government employment, 1997—U.S. Census Bureau, 1997 Census of Governments, Compendium of Public Employment, <http://www.census.gov/govs/apes/97coar2.dat> (accessed: 14 January 2000). Local government finances—U.S. Census Bureau, 1997 Census of Governments, Compendium of Government Finances, <http://www.census.gov/prod/gc97/gc974-5.pdf> (accessed: 16 February 2001).

Table B–13. Counties — Government Programs, Employment, and Finances–Con.

[Includes U.S., states, and 3,142 counties/county equivalents defined as of January 1, 1992. For changes to these areas since January 1, 1992, see appendix B. Geographic Information]

County	Social Security Program beneficiaries, December 1999 — Total — Number	Total — Percent change, 1990–1999	Total — Rate[1]	Retired workers	Supplemental Security Income Program recipients, December 1999	Government employment, 1998 — Federal — Civilian	Federal — Military	State and local	Local government employment, full-time equivalent, March 1997	Local government finances, 1996–1997 — General revenue — Total (mil. dol.)	Taxes — Total (mil. dol.)	Taxes — Per capita[2]	Taxes — Percent property	Direct general expend-iture (mil. dol.)
IDAHO—Con.														
Kootenai	18 139	38.3	173	11 170	1 478	651	453	6 466	4 440	212.8	73.7	746	91.8	204.9
Latah	4 134	9.8	127	2 620	232	234	189	6 173	798	64.2	20.3	612	97.1	65.5
Lemhi	1 818	13.3	228	1 135	135	269	36	541	277	18.6	3.1	389	95.5	17.1
Lewis	1 078	-2.4	273	605	137	38	18	366	243	13.6	3.1	761	99.0	15.4
Lincoln	802	40.7	209	535	48	98	17	376	231	9.6	2.5	649	95.5	9.1
Madison	2 150	21.5	87	1 370	143	51	105	1 453	810	52.2	8.7	352	94.5	51.7
Minidoka	3 211	1.0	158	2 085	296	74	90	1 320	1 070	60.6	8.8	429	97.2	61.2
Nez Perce	7 874	20.8	213	4 960	734	200	165	2 872	1 238	77.1	32.8	892	95.1	81.2
Oneida	783	16.0	193	510	50	31	18	366	163	11.5	2.7	675	91.2	13.4
Owyhee	1 586	26.4	152	975	136	31	46	589	397	21.0	3.9	388	97.5	20.4
Payette	3 772	14.3	181	2 450	368	46	91	993	683	33.8	9.7	482	91.0	31.7
Power	1 017	16.9	121	630	66	29	37	644	418	25.3	8.3	1 007	99.2	25.9
Shoshone	3 495	3.2	256	1 880	378	131	62	1 115	768	34.8	8.5	611	97.5	36.0
Teton	675	25.0	118	450	24	41	24	358	241	12.2	2.7	518	94.0	13.0
Twin Falls	11 118	8.6	177	7 430	1 017	579	278	4 327	3 165	186.4	36.0	586	94.3	190.9
Valley	1 661	39.6	211	1 095	75	286	36	744	486	37.0	10.3	1 274	95.9	35.7
Washington	2 285	11.5	222	1 425	203	57	45	640	515	28.0	6.1	610	97.2	27.8
ILLINOIS	1 816 192	3.6	150	1 170 184	251 058	95 718	58 239	715 325	459 893	33 167.7	15 718.2	1 309	80.9	31 001.6
Adams	14 053	-.5	210	9 455	1 133	314	153	4 128	2 644	133.4	39.8	590	86.3	124.9
Alexander	2 242	-12.4	226	1 215	664	39	22	583	369	21.4	4.6	456	69.0	18.4
Bond	3 261	7.1	190	1 985	235	351	36	635	463	23.8	6.9	402	93.8	23.8
Boone	5 617	27.9	142	3 785	205	75	88	1 459	985	66.2	32.7	862	96.5	58.5
Brown	1 053	-8.8	152	640	91	38	15	494	208	10.2	3.1	459	89.3	9.0
Bureau	7 337	-4.6	208	4 875	259	149	80	2 303	1 796	91.4	27.1	758	97.9	90.2
Calhoun	1 177	-8.0	242	705	97	31	11	257	207	13.7	2.1	415	92.6	13.3
Carroll	3 699	6.4	222	2 430	189	419	40	827	581	30.7	13.3	785	94.3	27.7
Cass	2 679	-6.2	202	1 625	204	77	30	799	469	26.5	9.2	696	84.2	24.2
Champaign	20 542	14.4	121	12 975	2 195	1 356	453	30 021	5 840	370.8	150.3	882	87.4	350.1
Christian	8 141	8.3	227	5 005	579	95	78	1 745	1 457	66.2	22.3	621	98.7	61.4
Clark	3 755	-3.0	227	2 335	259	55	37	792	612	29.2	9.2	561	87.7	27.7
Clay	3 386	-1.9	237	2 055	321	57	33	859	625	29.8	6.6	457	94.3	27.8
Clinton	6 376	25.6	179	3 855	308	112	80	2 275	781	47.9	16.4	464	88.8	44.1
Coles	8 610	1.4	166	5 530	987	143	122	6 122	2 037	112.6	37.7	723	92.4	100.7
Cook	736 250	-1.6	142	480 760	156 340	49 579	12 108	292 547	228 240	17 557.6	8 846.2	1 705	73.7	16 014.4
Crawford	4 396	-3.1	211	2 710	265	64	47	1 335	913	48.6	12.3	583	99.1	45.5
Cumberland	2 133	2.1	192	1 340	170	35	25	483	376	20.6	6.5	583	98.5	25.7
DeKalb	10 640	8.7	122	7 060	421	226	197	10 860	2 593	188.4	98.2	1 157	84.5	170.3
De Witt	3 231	4.9	194	2 010	222	54	38	1 237	893	49.7	25.5	1 525	99.3	44.1
Douglas	3 894	30.5	196	2 485	169	66	45	811	571	32.5	15.5	780	82.9	29.5
DuPage	109 021	25.7	122	75 855	5 319	5 208	2 001	40 591	24 912	2 325.3	1 360.3	1 564	88.5	2 197.7
Edgar	4 218	-6.1	216	2 615	403	70	44	1 143	691	37.3	12.5	631	94.8	34.5
Edwards	1 621	2.9	236	1 040	83	24	16	268	197	11.4	2.8	392	93.6	9.8
Effingham	6 042	5.8	179	3 765	390	178	77	1 794	1 140	59.3	18.7	559	98.2	57.8
Fayette	4 455	-.1	202	2 710	478	74	50	1 267	754	33.1	9.3	419	98.7	28.2
Ford	3 114	.5	222	2 030	137	55	32	738	529	33.1	13.1	930	88.7	28.9
Franklin	9 786	-4.8	242	5 495	1 318	239	91	1 910	1 296	68.2	15.1	372	96.0	64.2
Fulton	8 621	-4.3	223	5 340	590	112	88	2 415	1 706	85.0	24.2	624	95.1	78.7
Gallatin	1 595	-1.2	242	870	259	29	15	296	213	12.5	3.4	509	90.6	11.4
Greene	3 401	-3.5	216	2 015	349	60	35	723	573	26.2	6.8	434	91.3	24.4
Grundy	5 803	10.0	156	3 720	104	112	83	1 803	1 290	92.6	56.0	1 546	95.9	91.6
Hamilton	2 080	-6.7	242	1 260	233	40	19	625	489	23.7	4.0	463	82.5	21.3
Hancock	4 431	-8.7	211	2 875	248	90	48	1 186	851	42.0	15.0	711	96.4	40.5
Hardin	1 197	6.9	244	630	156	12	11	303	210	7.9	.9	177	97.2	7.4
Henderson	1 637	7.0	191	1 100	90	44	19	441	339	15.3	5.0	575	96.9	14.8
Henry	10 074	1.2	194	6 570	410	162	117	3 104	1 911	113.1	32.2	625	94.2	103.4
Iroquois	6 988	4.8	224	4 435	343	117	71	1 431	991	57.6	23.5	748	97.7	55.6
Jackson	8 085	.3	133	4 780	1 415	334	156	12 478	2 095	111.4	30.6	500	85.1	101.2
Jasper	2 133	-1.9	202	1 300	155	46	24	674	418	19.7	8.7	819	89.8	20.3
Jefferson	7 466	-2.1	191	4 515	869	165	85	2 015	1 699	92.1	27.6	706	74.1	78.1
Jersey	4 099	26.1	190	2 430	240	52	48	1 082	718	45.8	7.9	371	90.1	42.4
Jo Daviess	4 961	11.0	230	3 425	139	83	49	1 141	852	48.7	21.4	988	89.5	45.2
Johnson	2 471	7.2	182	1 435	283	81	30	978	320	14.4	3.0	229	99.8	13.3
Kane	36 703	-7.4	91	24 650	3 568	1 829	886	21 576	14 241	1 061.6	569.6	1 492	93.5	1 108.3

[1] Per 1,000 resident population estimated as of July 1, 1999.   [2] Based on resident population estimated as of July 1, 1997.

Sources: Social Security Program—U.S. Social Security Administration, OASDI Beneficiaries by State and County - December 1999, <http://www.ssa.gov/statistics/oasdi_sc/1999/oasdi_sc99.pdf> (accessed: 7 March 2001) for 1999 – annual publication of same title for 1990.   Supplemental Security Income Program—U.S. Social Security Administration, SSI Recipients by State and County, <http://www.ssa.gov/statistics/ssi_st_cty/1999/ssi_st_cty.pdf> (accessed: November 2000).   Government employment, 1998—U.S. Bureau of Economic Analysis, "Regional Economic Information System (REIS) 1969-1998" on CD-ROM (related Internet site <http://www.bea.doc.gov/bea/regional/data.htm>).   Local government employment, 1997—U.S. Census Bureau, 1997 Census of Governments, Compendium of Public Employment, <http://www.census.gov/govs/apes/97coar2.dat> (accessed: 14 January 2000).   Local government finances—U.S. Census Bureau, 1997 Census of Governments, Compendium of Government Finances, <http://www.census.gov/prod/gc97/gc974-5.pdf> (accessed: 16 February 2001).

[Includes U.S., states, and 3,142 counties/county equivalents defined as of January 1, 1992. For changes to these areas since January 1, 1992, see appendix B. Geographic Information]

County	Social Security Program beneficiaries, December 1999 — Total — Number	Total — Percent change, 1990–1999	Rate[1]	Retired workers	Supple-mental Security Income Program recipients, December 1999	Government employment, 1998 — Federal — Civilian	Federal — Military	State and local	Local government employment, full-time equivalent, March 1997	Local government finances, 1996–1997 — General revenue — Total (mil. dol.)	Taxes — Total (mil. dol.)	Taxes — Per capita[2]	Percent property	Direct general expend-iture (mil. dol.)
ILLINOIS—Con.														
Kankakee	18 487	2.4	180	10 735	2 660	337	231	6 035	3 331	226.5	80.9	792	90.9	208.2
Kendall	5 968	73.7	111	4 010	100	85	117	1 903	1 355	88.3	52.4	1 051	93.0	86.6
Knox	11 475	–.2	207	7 410	1 139	209	125	3 273	2 200	119.8	36.1	649	79.6	116.5
Lake	66 559	23.2	108	44 295	1 043	6 292	25 792	28 836	20 218	1 642.5	967.2	1 617	92.3	1 600.4
La Salle	22 942	–.3	208	15 345	4 382	361	249	5 864	3 538	222.1	98.0	891	96.1	213.1
Lawrence	3 838	–5.2	253	2 230	344	52	35	974	677	24.0	5.5	356	92.8	21.7
Lee	6 788	4.0	190	4 360	477	99	81	2 433	1 424	77.0	29.3	814	95.7	71.3
Livingston	7 389	5.4	186	4 740	435	116	90	3 012	1 465	87.7	36.4	915	98.7	88.3
Logan	5 865	–.3	185	3 615	374	116	71	2 271	876	56.5	24.3	774	99.0	48.1
McDonough	5 930	9.3	168	3 855	476	107	82	6 390	1 655	93.5	20.1	567	98.4	84.2
McHenry	26 884	22.7	109	18 265	936	555	545	9 844	7 168	482.6	268.3	1 136	92.0	511.6
McLean	18 198	9.4	125	11 950	1 257	935	330	12 380	3 953	285.2	149.2	1 053	85.2	266.4
Macon	22 153	3.3	196	14 010	2 930	354	269	6 064	3 851	265.8	79.6	698	94.4	249.4
Macoupin	10 487	–4.0	214	6 370	846	152	110	2 437	1 250	78.5	26.3	538	81.2	73.3
Madison	48 037	6.4	185	28 540	4 538	783	613	15 561	8 237	534.1	179.6	694	89.1	512.1
Marion	8 483	–7.2	203	5 070	1 068	213	95	2 403	1 679	116.0	25.1	595	91.0	104.6
Marshall	2 846	6.2	219	1 855	102	43	29	400	374	19.8	8.6	666	97.1	18.1
Mason	3 879	6.1	231	2 325	282	65	38	1 124	755	49.0	16.2	960	92.5	48.5
Massac	3 544	2.9	230	2 065	462	51	35	869	666	32.6	7.1	457	94.7	30.9
Menard	2 171	10.5	171	1 355	111	37	28	737	532	25.3	8.0	639	99.1	24.2
Mercer	3 528	11.3	200	2 245	141	73	40	1 180	888	41.0	10.6	603	96.5	36.8
Monroe	4 403	22.1	161	2 835	158	62	60	1 201	610	46.0	15.2	587	86.9	42.3
Montgomery	6 638	–2.7	212	4 075	574	117	71	1 907	1 006	56.7	20.2	643	87.5	52.7
Morgan	7 323	4.8	208	4 495	824	111	80	2 340	1 222	56.4	21.7	605	90.1	53.2
Moultrie	2 962	–8.9	203	1 940	122	40	33	596	460	20.7	8.9	616	99.7	20.4
Ogle	8 547	13.6	168	5 720	264	160	114	2 416	2 019	120.6	63.6	1 268	96.0	117.6
Peoria	32 791	–2.3	181	20 750	4 706	1 584	453	9 068	6 490	393.1	146.4	803	77.2	371.5
Perry	4 527	2.7	212	2 715	363	56	48	1 176	784	30.1	6.6	308	91.8	28.4
Piatt	2 965	–	178	1 880	114	55	37	897	558	36.6	14.7	894	97.5	35.2
Pike	4 048	–8.8	235	2 515	349	76	39	938	683	32.3	9.9	573	91.8	32.0
Pope	980	16.7	204	570	112	97	12	286	150	5.9	1.6	342	94.2	5.7
Pulaski	1 729	–9.0	237	970	392	69	16	807	311	14.8	2.1	295	91.0	14.4
Putnam	1 182	3.7	202	795	54	25	13	296	214	10.3	3.9	668	98.7	9.8
Randolph	6 616	–2.7	197	4 180	431	108	76	2 877	1 327	75.4	15.4	455	82.4	68.7
Richland	3 769	4.3	226	2 345	351	67	38	1 840	1 063	75.3	8.0	473	97.9	76.1
Rock Island	28 311	–.1	192	18 475	2 656	6 388	507	8 700	5 642	335.7	119.4	806	89.2	306.9
St. Clair	42 991	1.2	165	25 020	8 546	4 599	6 368	11 852	8 808	605.5	164.8	625	78.1	569.3
Saline	6 513	–2.6	250	3 530	1 145	133	59	1 888	1 029	59.5	15.1	575	98.7	57.2
Sangamon	33 580	6.0	176	20 750	4 551	2 153	452	27 077	7 565	396.5	166.8	871	87.6	376.6
Schuyler	1 612	–.8	215	1 030	94	31	17	502	368	20.5	5.3	688	89.9	20.2
Scott	1 139	5.0	203	680	70	21	13	347	330	11.6	3.3	586	96.5	12.0
Shelby	4 379	–8.5	195	2 715	286	111	51	1 044	647	36.8	15.2	671	89.1	33.6
Stark	1 538	2.9	245	980	64	33	14	309	223	14.7	7.0	1 111	98.1	14.1
Stephenson	9 932	3.9	204	6 970	716	142	112	2 570	1 819	103.6	37.5	764	97.1	112.3
Tazewell	23 794	10.1	183	15 610	1 494	519	289	6 245	4 267	287.4	105.4	818	91.8	268.1
Union	4 039	–.6	224	2 290	740	65	41	1 990	1 016	45.6	7.2	398	98.5	44.0
Vermilion	17 648	–1.4	211	10 720	2 583	1 576	191	4 479	3 084	186.8	51.5	608	94.5	169.5
Wabash	2 649	1.5	212	1 670	208	38	29	771	616	40.1	9.5	750	90.8	36.8
Warren	3 238	–17.0	171	2 085	296	78	43	984	835	44.7	12.9	679	94.3	38.1
Washington	3 072	–.4	202	1 870	105	63	35	933	567	31.6	9.3	605	86.6	26.0
Wayne	3 874	–2.7	228	2 415	268	70	38	830	626	28.8	8.0	470	87.2	26.0
White	4 119	–8.7	265	2 485	410	65	35	1 141	617	37.1	8.9	567	79.6	34.3
Whiteside	12 510	5.9	210	7 785	867	191	136	3 579	2 475	192.0	43.1	717	93.4	188.0
Will	50 244	36.1	105	31 400	3 407	814	1 055	20 751	12 801	908.5	465.8	1 047	85.1	905.0
Williamson	12 807	8.6	208	7 690	1 350	1 196	137	3 901	1 964	145.7	36.2	591	83.9	141.1
Winnebago	46 078	10.0	172	30 045	5 037	1 143	609	12 612	9 282	617.1	271.4	1 016	95.6	612.8
Woodford	5 735	16.4	161	3 840	146	76	80	1 631	1 228	67.0	30.9	886	95.7	57.0
INDIANA	986 207	8.0	166	619 639	88 314	38 659	21 888	357 365	220 747	14 293.6	5 623.5	958	90.5	13 512.6
Adams	5 232	5.8	158	3 600	208	71	116	1 840	1 427	81.1	23.3	713	93.3	75.7
Allen	48 932	9.6	155	31 820	4 341	2 243	1 114	15 540	9 790	673.0	326.6	1 047	92.2	610.5
Bartholomew	11 537	15.9	165	7 180	948	231	245	5 077	3 695	252.6	78.7	1 143	88.3	230.2
Benton	1 853	–8.7	190	1 160	93	33	34	594	474	23.6	11.2	1 158	93.2	21.4
Blackford	2 951	6.3	212	1 885	177	31	49	750	701	43.6	11.8	841	90.2	31.7
Boone	6 805	23.5	152	4 620	273	98	153	1 954	1 660	117.4	44.9	1 043	81.1	97.8
Brown	2 748	102.8	172	1 810	70	18	56	717	536	28.0	12.7	814	84.4	23.8
Carroll	3 637	24.1	182	2 410	94	68	70	767	627	41.9	21.6	1 087	91.3	41.9
Cass	7 401	4.8	190	4 730	577	117	135	3 354	2 203	104.6	29.4	758	88.1	101.9

[1] Per 1,000 resident population estimated as of July 1, 1999.   [2] Based on resident population estimated as of July 1, 1997.

Sources: Social Security Program—U.S. Social Security Administration, OASDI Beneficiaries by State and County - December 1999, <http://www.ssa.gov/statistics/oasdi_sc/1999/oasdi_sc99.pdf> (accessed: 7 March 2001) for 1999 – annual publication of same title for 1990. Supplemental Security Income Program—U.S. Social Security Administration, SSI Recipients by State and County, <http://www.ssa.gov/statistics/ssi_st_cty/1999/ssi_st_cty.pdf> (accessed: November 2000). Government employment, 1998—U.S. Bureau of Economic Analysis, "Regional Economic Information System (REIS) 1969-1998" on CD-ROM (related Internet site <http://www.bea.doc.gov/bea/regional/data.htm>). Local government employment, 1997—U.S. Census Bureau, 1997 Census of Governments, Compendium of Public Employment, <http://www.census.gov/govs/apes/97coar2.dat> (accessed: 14 January 2000). Local government finances—U.S. Census Bureau, 1997 Census of Governments, Compendium of Government Finances, <http://www.census.gov/prod/gc97/gc974-5.pdf> (accessed: 16 February 2001).

Table B–13. Counties — Government Programs, Employment, and Finances–Con.

[Includes U.S., states, and 3,142 counties/county equivalents defined as of January 1, 1992. For changes to these areas since January 1, 1992, see appendix B. Geographic Information]

County	Social Security Program beneficiaries, December 1999 — Total — Number	Total — Percent change, 1990–1999	Total — Rate[1]	Retired workers	Supplemental Security Income Program recipients, December 1999	Government employment, 1998 — Federal — Civilian	Federal — Military	State and local	Local government employment, full-time equivalent, March 1997	Local government finances, 1996–1997 — General revenue — Total (mil. dol.)	Taxes — Total (mil. dol.)	Taxes — Per capita[2]	Taxes — Percent property	Direct general expenditure (mil. dol.)
INDIANA—Con.														
Clark	16 520	14.8	174	9 585	1 651	2 569	330	5 201	4 169	257.8	77.2	828	98.5	229.7
Clay	5 486	-2.6	204	3 280	486	83	93	1 214	965	59.3	19.3	728	89.2	62.8
Clinton	5 729	-.9	174	3 750	366	78	116	1 484	1 294	83.8	27.3	823	89.1	82.2
Crawford	2 202	6.4	205	1 115	280	32	37	474	401	19.8	5.7	545	98.5	17.2
Daviess	5 067	3.4	174	3 090	444	87	101	1 483	1 155	63.9	16.5	571	85.0	64.3
Dearborn	7 532	20.7	157	4 520	449	80	165	2 054	1 745	127.3	37.3	803	91.3	114.6
Decatur	4 428	7.9	172	2 795	298	70	89	1 215	1 002	60.2	19.3	759	88.6	54.9
De Kalb	5 931	13.4	149	3 865	325	88	138	1 718	1 309	108.4	36.1	928	88.4	102.4
Delaware	21 422	6.1	186	13 065	2 659	413	418	9 633	3 597	214.2	86.0	730	91.6	202.7
Dubois	6 403	13.4	160	4 140	249	110	139	1 790	1 248	78.6	34.0	870	90.3	78.2
Elkhart	25 196	15.9	144	16 890	2 042	292	604	6 815	6 339	350.5	161.4	945	86.1	341.2
Fayette	5 452	4.4	211	3 215	512	55	91	1 382	1 237	59.2	25.4	971	76.9	59.9
Floyd	11 671	9.3	162	6 955	1 247	169	252	4 968	3 164	194.3	45.4	635	97.3	191.5
Fountain	3 794	-4.4	206	2 345	284	60	64	831	660	33.9	13.6	745	88.7	31.6
Franklin	4 033	41.5	182	2 445	251	49	76	837	483	31.3	11.1	518	81.9	26.8
Fulton	4 101	10.1	196	2 750	203	53	72	1 068	798	50.2	15.6	767	90.2	45.8
Gibson	6 404	3.5	199	3 985	372	87	113	1 087	988	61.2	25.5	796	99.4	58.8
Grant	14 945	8.6	207	9 325	1 501	1 067	255	3 224	2 836	150.9	65.1	894	86.6	132.8
Greene	6 447	3.0	194	3 825	553	83	117	1 817	1 312	71.1	19.9	601	83.7	68.1
Hamilton	16 815	58.0	98	11 300	607	342	569	7 180	5 770	406.0	189.8	1 224	81.3	366.8
Hancock	8 130	36.8	146	5 365	281	105	191	2 942	2 359	138.9	40.5	762	84.8	145.1
Harrison	5 745	19.2	162	3 175	464	116	122	1 549	1 198	61.8	18.0	528	90.0	58.4
Hendricks	12 267	41.7	124	8 275	333	158	333	5 398	3 395	241.4	82.7	898	84.5	208.4
Henry	10 396	5.5	215	6 490	760	102	171	3 195	2 398	127.6	34.4	704	85.1	123.5
Howard	15 494	8.7	185	10 025	1 523	321	293	5 361	3 775	282.0	104.5	1 247	92.1	239.1
Huntington	6 633	1.0	177	4 565	308	86	130	1 857	1 620	66.7	26.2	704	87.1	65.9
Jackson	7 554	8.7	183	4 585	667	110	143	2 151	1 564	108.9	32.8	802	88.2	100.2
Jasper	4 978	18.0	169	3 025	236	78	102	1 619	1 287	81.0	30.0	1 050	92.1	70.9
Jay	4 342	-1.8	200	2 830	301	46	76	1 119	973	52.9	14.8	682	87.3	53.8
Jefferson	5 928	7.6	186	3 460	663	93	110	2 213	951	60.5	23.2	740	98.9	53.6
Jennings	4 667	18.6	166	2 430	410	61	97	1 931	655	38.7	11.3	415	83.5	35.7
Johnson	15 581	26.5	138	10 530	703	340	383	4 973	3 618	210.2	80.1	750	85.4	212.9
Knox	8 072	-1.3	207	4 760	998	182	139	5 166	2 724	159.7	27.0	683	99.3	170.4
Kosciusko	11 471	16.8	161	7 670	520	181	249	2 631	2 367	190.2	69.2	983	91.1	177.4
Lagrange	4 147	20.4	122	2 770	146	63	117	1 223	833	61.9	29.1	884	89.8	52.3
Lake	84 261	1.5	175	48 705	10 632	2 117	1 685	26 306	18 342	1 396.2	639.4	1 328	98.5	1 297.5
La Porte	18 807	4.4	171	12 130	1 451	223	399	7 378	4 297	268.9	117.3	1 070	89.5	230.2
Lawrence	8 829	12.1	193	5 380	811	157	160	2 351	1 937	160.2	33.6	740	85.7	132.5
Madison	26 390	5.6	201	16 950	2 477	341	416	6 371	4 875	244.0	93.9	711	88.4	259.5
Marion	126 806	.4	156	78 850	16 687	13 234	3 803	59 052	32 090	2 329.5	1 031.6	1 266	88.9	2 348.1
Marshall	7 630	11.9	165	5 155	307	97	159	2 039	1 447	90.3	40.8	900	90.4	80.8
Martin	2 040	2.3	197	1 230	209	3 862	99	475	347	20.7	8.2	777	88.1	17.1
Miami	5 801	7.7	173	3 625	543	789	123	1 814	1 696	92.6	28.2	848	91.9	85.4
Monroe	14 442	21.0	124	9 530	1 249	406	420	19 245	3 104	209.9	83.6	721	82.2	192.0
Montgomery	6 818	6.0	186	4 375	482	104	127	1 804	1 376	89.3	47.4	1 307	90.2	68.4
Morgan	9 638	21.5	144	5 965	628	122	229	2 520	2 317	119.7	39.1	605	83.5	116.2
Newton	2 374	11.2	160	1 500	115	42	52	742	590	32.1	13.0	883	91.2	29.8
Noble	6 861	14.9	159	4 350	365	88	149	2 051	1 818	107.7	36.6	872	88.8	92.5
Ohio	899	4.5	165	535	46	14	19	296	199	12.2	3.5	638	61.3	12.3
Orange	3 841	7.3	194	2 260	418	47	69	1 040	783	43.7	10.6	547	87.0	41.4
Owen	3 552	27.3	172	2 145	207	41	71	819	543	31.2	11.8	582	87.4	27.3
Parke	3 295	3.5	195	1 955	323	60	59	1 102	504	30.1	12.2	737	89.5	25.0
Perry	3 709	-1.7	194	2 390	280	83	68	1 442	792	47.2	13.1	678	78.6	42.9
Pike	2 573	4.8	198	1 440	258	38	45	606	207	33.4	10.6	827	99.1	31.0
Porter	20 838	28.1	141	12 640	1 061	463	512	7 953	6 450	429.0	146.2	1 014	95.7	393.6
Posey	4 479	12.3	170	2 675	334	81	94	1 172	941	62.1	32.4	1 226	99.8	59.5
Pulaski	2 726	7.5	202	1 635	169	46	46	941	736	39.9	13.3	998	91.5	39.2
Putnam	5 656	18.0	163	3 705	377	83	121	2 490	1 551	81.4	28.5	841	89.9	81.9
Randolph	5 656	1.5	206	3 625	358	82	97	1 496	1 297	62.2	18.3	664	83.2	61.7
Ripley	4 452	-7.1	161	2 630	335	83	95	1 199	897	52.4	22.0	812	85.0	42.9
Rush	3 382	2.5	186	2 145	199	57	64	1 182	841	41.4	14.3	778	89.1	37.1
St. Joseph	44 819	-1.0	173	30 725	3 962	1 160	959	12 676	8 570	544.7	204.9	794	97.7	539.3
Scott	4 341	7.3	185	2 200	722	60	80	1 189	956	51.1	14.7	643	76.2	49.1
Shelby	6 977	18.0	160	4 445	463	140	152	2 064	1 653	108.8	29.5	683	85.9	99.5
Spencer	3 525	8.0	166	2 205	219	79	73	901	686	44.7	23.9	1 149	98.4	36.4
Starke	4 770	21.4	202	2 610	425	55	84	929	1 068	56.5	14.6	615	94.3	50.0
Steuben	5 311	4.2	167	3 540	281	74	110	1 478	1 021	64.8	31.4	1 012	90.0	55.1
Sullivan	4 293	-3.0	199	2 445	364	69	67	2 073	954	56.5	17.0	795	99.7	54.5
Switzerland	1 536	12.5	171	880	169	28	31	399	344	14.5	4.6	531	91.0	14.6
Tippecanoe	16 888	8.3	119	11 095	1 185	523	526	19 356	3 393	242.6	112.5	812	87.6	226.6

[1] Per 1,000 resident population estimated as of July 1, 1999. [2] Based on resident population estimated as of July 1, 1997.

Sources: Social Security Program—U.S. Social Security Administration, OASDI Beneficiaries by State and County - December 1999, <http://www.ssa.gov/statistics/oasdi_sc/1999/oasdi_sc99.pdf> (accessed: 7 March 2001) for 1999 – annual publication of same title for 1990. Supplemental Security Income Program—U.S. Social Security Administration, SSI Recipients by State and County, <http://www.ssa.gov/statistics/ssi_st_cty/1999/ssi_st_cty.pdf> (accessed: November 2000). Government employment, 1998—U.S. Bureau of Economic Analysis, "Regional Economic Information System (REIS) 1969-1998" on CD-ROM (related Internet site <http://www.bea.doc.gov/bea/regional/data.htm>). Local government employment, 1997—U.S. Census Bureau, 1997 Census of Governments, Compendium of Public Employment, <http://www.census.gov/govs/apes/97coar2.dat> (accessed: 14 January 2000). Local government finances—U.S. Census Bureau, 1997 Census of Governments, Compendium of Government Finances, <http://www.census.gov/prod/gc97/gc974-5.pdf> (accessed: 16 February 2001).

Table B–13. Counties — **Government Programs, Employment, and Finances**–Con.

[Includes U.S., states, and 3,142 counties/county equivalents defined as of January 1, 1992. For changes to these areas since January 1, 1992, see appendix B. Geographic Information]

County	Social Security Program beneficiaries, December 1999				Supplemental Security Income Program recipients, December 1999	Government employment, 1998			Local government employment, full-time equivalent, March 1997	Local government finances, 1996–1997				
	Total			Retired workers		Federal		State and local		General revenue				Direct general expenditure (mil. dol.)
	Number	Percent change, 1990–1999	Rate¹			Civilian	Military			Total (mil. dol.)	Taxes			
											Total (mil. dol.)	Per capita²	Percent property	
INDIANA—Con.														
Tipton	3 017	11.1	181	2 040	147	36	59	1 119	902	51.0	14.5	881	87.2	48.7
Union	1 156	5.1	158	695	98	16	25	402	292	16.9	7.3	996	91.3	13.9
Vanderburgh	33 991	1.4	202	21 450	3 676	919	601	8 707	4 906	367.0	153.0	909	84.5	349.3
Vermillion	3 464	–1.2	204	2 050	253	51	67	686	854	35.8	18.4	1 086	99.7	32.4
Vigo	19 728	–2.3	189	12 180	2 471	1 222	391	7 854	3 581	176.5	74.8	707	98.7	199.4
Wabash	7 108	7.5	206	4 695	409	87	121	1 955	1 577	86.7	25.4	730	86.1	86.7
Warren	1 549	27.0	186	1 005	78	24	29	353	342	16.7	7.1	860	85.5	15.0
Warrick	7 451	21.0	142	4 525	472	125	181	1 607	1 362	101.5	51.1	1 003	91.9	89.4
Washington	4 830	23.4	171	2 650	530	59	98	1 317	1 019	56.0	13.9	512	81.6	51.2
Wayne	15 060	2.9	212	9 510	1 564	165	251	4 754	2 743	148.3	61.3	853	88.8	139.1
Wells	4 542	11.3	169	3 075	144	61	94	1 491	921	63.5	19.8	741	87.4	64.0
White	4 886	–2.1	191	3 200	242	74	89	1 430	1 094	72.7	32.0	1 276	90.9	68.2
Whitley	5 123	6.2	166	3 480	156	80	107	1 343	1 230	59.5	27.2	908	89.5	50.0
IOWA	537 366	2.5	187	348 253	40 484	20 040	13 979	212 503	112 667	7 291.4	2 509.1	879	92.4	7 069.7
Adair	1 869	–3.7	232	1 235	82	35	38	537	277	16.5	6.5	795	96.8	16.5
Adams	1 167	–1.5	265	725	108	30	21	258	174	8.7	3.6	807	99.6	8.3
Allamakee	3 220	–.6	229	2 155	177	75	66	934	512	34.6	11.3	804	93.4	31.6
Appanoose	3 433	–4.6	255	2 040	425	78	64	699	486	28.4	8.9	659	97.7	27.2
Audubon	1 874	–3.9	276	1 240	91	37	32	446	320	15.1	6.0	878	98.7	15.2
Benton	4 714	10.5	183	2 935	224	73	120	1 409	799	44.7	16.1	643	99.3	42.1
Black Hawk	22 879	Z	191	14 590	2 722	561	593	10 899	4 254	342.2	104.2	858	85.7	323.1
Boone	5 254	6.7	200	3 370	289	112	124	2 044	977	59.1	18.8	720	84.8	55.8
Bremer	4 406	–1.1	188	2 850	195	66	110	1 321	1 035	60.2	18.6	798	94.5	55.6
Buchanan	3 796	–5.8	179	2 345	289	118	100	1 520	762	42.2	13.7	646	93.3	38.9
Buena Vista	4 140	–7.4	213	2 660	261	79	92	1 469	859	57.3	16.9	858	92.0	56.5
Butler	3 641	–3.3	235	2 230	149	57	74	708	446	25.8	10.2	646	96.1	25.0
Calhoun	2 985	–5.1	264	1 855	146	50	54	808	610	29.4	11.3	987	99.8	28.1
Carroll	4 710	–3.3	219	2 935	257	99	102	1 154	704	43.4	17.1	792	98.1	43.2
Cass	3 649	–5.1	251	2 340	297	84	69	1 266	555	50.6	13.4	912	98.2	53.2
Cedar	3 519	9.3	195	2 310	117	119	85	913	738	37.9	15.0	835	96.5	35.9
Cerro Gordo	10 274	2.2	225	6 725	732	180	219	2 820	1 822	115.8	41.9	904	85.5	115.2
Cherokee	3 193	2.7	244	2 045	129	58	62	1 042	522	32.5	10.8	805	95.5	30.4
Chickasaw	2 954	3.5	220	1 820	145	58	63	668	454	26.3	9.3	691	99.0	24.8
Clarke	1 875	2.7	227	1 235	130	37	39	645	429	24.4	7.7	930	99.1	24.1
Clay	3 722	3.7	216	2 420	200	83	83	1 319	1 063	64.4	14.2	805	97.7	60.7
Clayton	4 346	–.5	234	2 760	300	112	88	1 146	737	41.9	15.2	810	89.0	39.0
Clinton	10 126	–1.2	204	6 600	873	143	235	2 645	1 662	110.7	43.4	865	85.2	105.0
Crawford	3 587	–1.2	218	2 155	225	100	78	1 041	712	40.6	12.2	743	97.4	39.8
Dallas	5 537	3.0	145	3 725	283	105	174	1 873	1 447	82.9	31.3	875	97.8	88.4
Davis	1 664	–8.3	195	1 035	144	41	40	577	476	23.8	5.0	591	98.7	23.2
Decatur	1 940	–4.4	233	1 250	212	46	39	618	408	21.4	5.7	699	96.5	20.8
Delaware	3 324	10.8	180	2 030	240	65	88	1 055	801	48.2	14.5	788	91.1	49.1
Des Moines	8 538	1.6	204	5 790	816	201	202	2 343	1 659	107.0	35.6	847	87.3	102.3
Dickinson	4 105	9.0	252	2 780	150	59	77	1 008	779	43.2	16.9	1 053	96.4	41.6
Dubuque	16 313	4.3	185	10 695	1 300	297	440	3 440	2 629	195.7	72.6	823	83.5	188.8
Emmet	2 510	–6.2	236	1 600	132	49	51	815	465	43.0	8.1	741	95.0	43.7
Fayette	4 913	.6	228	3 075	363	92	103	1 220	808	44.7	16.2	741	92.8	43.0
Floyd	4 100	1.1	252	2 505	289	61	77	1 012	750	46.2	13.3	806	96.8	41.1
Franklin	2 600	1.6	241	1 645	108	49	51	716	541	28.1	10.2	936	91.0	28.2
Fremont	1 918	–9.7	249	1 235	126	39	37	453	331	18.9	7.5	956	93.3	17.4
Greene	2 643	–.5	264	1 700	173	44	47	880	637	32.3	9.7	962	97.5	32.5
Grundy	2 865	4.2	233	1 880	54	42	57	685	598	36.9	12.7	1 034	96.6	34.8
Guthrie	2 945	1.6	254	1 965	133	63	55	739	516	28.5	10.3	894	98.2	27.3
Hamilton	3 571	.9	225	2 405	181	61	75	1 221	656	50.9	15.9	989	96.5	53.4
Hancock	2 591	–1.5	215	1 625	128	53	57	706	448	30.7	11.1	925	92.5	28.9
Hardin	4 554	–6.9	251	2 955	212	82	87	1 726	727	53.1	17.5	947	90.9	52.5
Harrison	3 259	Z	214	2 010	246	85	72	810	614	47.1	14.6	953	94.1	46.2
Henry	3 706	–2.3	184	2 450	221	71	94	1 699	1 008	54.3	15.2	765	87.8	54.3
Howard	2 419	–3.2	253	1 495	125	39	46	759	537	27.8	9.5	977	88.7	27.3
Humboldt	2 532	–1.9	248	1 595	124	62	49	688	377	27.2	9.4	908	98.2	26.6
Ida	1 974	–.8	249	1 225	73	40	37	441	308	16.8	6.5	808	97.1	18.4
Iowa	3 200	2.4	204	2 200	98	69	73	884	589	35.0	13.3	860	81.1	33.4
Jackson	4 271	2.4	212	2 710	320	87	95	1 160	873	48.1	13.8	689	86.9	46.4
Jasper	7 358	6.6	201	4 950	406	111	169	2 515	1 449	101.0	30.0	838	94.6	98.3
Jefferson	2 714	–1.5	162	1 785	243	86	81	1 019	633	35.6	10.6	620	94.7	34.9
Johnson	10 455	21.6	101	6 885	930	1 585	507	25 901	2 690	199.1	84.8	832	92.7	215.8
Jones	3 975	9.1	198	2 550	180	61	96	1 297	647	34.1	13.0	637	95.7	35.2
Keokuk	2 790	–9.0	246	1 705	196	64	54	543	489	26.7	9.6	834	96.9	25.0

¹ Per 1,000 resident population estimated as of July 1, 1999. ² Based on resident population estimated as of July 1, 1997.

Sources: Social Security Program—U.S. Social Security Administration, OASDI Beneficiaries by State and County - December 1999, <http://www.ssa.gov/statistics/oasdi_sc/1999/oasdi_sc99.pdf> (accessed: 7 March 2001) for 1999 – annual publication of same title for 1990. Supplemental Security Income Program—U.S. Social Security Administration, SSI Recipients by State and County, <http://www.ssa.gov/statistics/ssi_st_cty/1999/ssi_st_cty.pdf> (accessed: November 2000). Government employment, 1998—U.S. Bureau of Economic Analysis, "Regional Economic Information System (REIS) 1969-1998" on CD-ROM (related Internet site <http://www.bea.doc.gov/bea/regional/data.htm>). Local government employment, 1997—U.S. Census Bureau, 1997 Census of Governments, Compendium of Public Employment, <http://www.census.gov/govs/apes/97coar2.dat> (accessed: 14 January 2000). Local government finances—U.S. Census Bureau, 1997 Census of Governments, Compendium of Government Finances, <http://www.census.gov/prod/gc97/gc974-5.pdf> (accessed: 16 February 2001).

Table B–13. Counties — **Government Programs, Employment, and Finances**-Con.

[Includes U.S., states, and 3,142 counties/county equivalents defined as of January 1, 1992. For changes to these areas since January 1, 1992, see appendix B. Geographic Information]

County	Social Security Program beneficiaries, December 1999				Supplemental Security Income Program recipients, December 1999	Government employment, 1998			Local government employment, full-time equivalent, March 1997	Local government finances, 1996–1997				
	Total			Retired workers		Federal		State and local		General revenue				Direct general expenditure (mil. dol.)
	Number	Percent change, 1990–1999	Rate[1]			Civilian	Military			Total (mil. dol.)	Taxes			
											Total (mil. dol.)	Per capita[2]	Percent property	
IOWA—Con.														
Kossuth	4 338	5.3	246	2 710	205	81	84	1 092	806	43.5	15.0	837	94.2	42.7
Lee	7 599	−.5	198	4 875	715	111	217	2 255	1 364	83.1	30.9	798	83.9	76.8
Linn	29 962	12.3	162	20 550	2 164	1 099	869	10 292	7 203	464.3	175.0	964	95.9	447.7
Louisa	2 153	5.5	180	1 390	120	61	56	670	556	38.9	11.4	962	98.5	37.5
Lucas	2 216	−1.5	243	1 445	216	40	43	689	461	25.6	6.6	724	96.4	24.1
Lyon	2 539	1.8	211	1 590	70	45	57	566	424	24.8	8.8	739	92.9	28.3
Madison	2 551	2.7	181	1 650	142	52	65	783	529	34.5	10.1	733	96.8	35.7
Mahaska	4 508	Z	205	2 945	386	78	103	1 106	812	52.4	17.2	787	90.1	54.6
Marion	6 115	7.5	194	3 900	338	897	148	1 462	1 140	56.2	21.2	682	95.6	60.8
Marshall	8 004	−.3	206	5 360	510	138	183	3 080	1 584	102.3	35.0	904	98.3	97.9
Mills	2 642	7.0	180	1 485	304	53	68	1 555	571	27.8	10.9	759	98.4	24.8
Mitchell	2 600	−6.6	234	1 695	95	50	52	639	444	31.2	9.3	837	90.6	28.8
Monona	2 640	−3.1	262	1 630	171	55	48	609	421	22.8	9.0	889	90.0	22.3
Monroe	1 949	−1.8	243	1 230	171	35	38	493	300	20.7	5.4	673	99.0	20.3
Montgomery	2 937	−2.3	251	1 900	186	60	56	925	672	38.9	9.9	833	97.4	35.0
Muscatine	6 991	2.4	170	4 550	454	124	194	2 819	2 173	119.7	37.2	910	86.6	109.9
O'Brien	3 760	−.9	257	2 265	210	65	70	1 085	772	43.0	13.9	926	93.0	41.0
Osceola	1 590	−5.9	230	960	71	31	33	323	213	13.1	5.3	751	96.1	12.5
Page	4 131	−3.8	241	2 745	347	73	81	1 425	698	42.1	13.6	785	89.8	45.6
Palo Alto	2 508	−6.6	253	1 550	192	51	47	1 000	591	30.3	9.7	963	97.1	32.4
Plymouth	4 864	4.5	196	3 100	171	80	117	1 253	925	55.5	17.3	701	98.0	58.3
Pocahontas	2 248	−9.0	256	1 410	106	46	41	641	370	21.4	7.2	817	98.4	21.6
Polk	52 872	8.4	145	35 310	5 186	5 867	2 015	25 390	14 378	1 045.8	401.6	1 127	95.2	959.6
Pottawattamie	15 032	9.9	174	9 375	1 468	222	407	4 751	3 311	210.0	76.5	897	84.1	211.3
Poweshiek	3 805	1.9	204	2 615	171	65	89	921	612	35.1	12.8	674	98.4	34.9
Ringgold	1 440	1.1	269	950	125	36	25	455	259	19.8	5.1	955	99.0	18.9
Sac	2 972	−6.8	253	1 915	125	54	56	707	480	24.8	9.6	809	99.3	22.0
Scott	24 192	6.9	152	15 535	2 781	1 057	749	7 476	5 886	400.1	152.0	964	86.0	392.3
Shelby	3 123	5.0	244	2 020	171	59	61	909	674	41.0	12.1	925	98.0	40.9
Sioux	5 646	5.5	180	3 530	226	106	147	1 711	887	64.4	20.4	653	91.0	63.8
Story	9 368	8.4	124	6 580	458	974	389	17 987	3 363	229.1	62.2	830	86.8	218.2
Tama	4 012	.8	226	2 535	174	88	84	944	593	37.9	13.7	778	96.8	36.8
Taylor	1 841	−10.2	262	1 175	129	47	34	445	325	16.1	5.0	698	93.0	15.9
Union	2 774	−9.0	220	1 740	278	88	59	1 182	575	52.1	10.5	844	99.0	51.6
Van Buren	1 060	.6	248	1 260	167	45	07	600	450	22.0	5.2	859	90.0	24.3
Wapello	8 308	−1.7	234	5 040	1 090	145	167	2 615	1 702	105.3	30.0	846	97.8	104.4
Warren	5 954	28.6	147	4 010	184	116	189	1 727	1 252	72.8	25.8	648	97.3	74.7
Washington	4 396	1.3	208	2 950	230	74	99	1 238	853	50.8	15.9	762	96.5	47.6
Wayne	1 885	−11.5	286	1 180	174	44	31	506	315	18.8	4.4	648	97.2	19.4
Webster	8 849	−2.2	228	5 715	755	296	184	2 586	1 463	98.8	34.9	903	97.7	93.1
Winnebago	2 661	−5.3	222	1 795	130	53	56	734	578	30.4	11.3	938	93.5	28.3
Winneshiek	3 864	2.9	185	2 520	192	91	99	1 703	1 083	67.1	17.1	821	88.0	67.8
Woodbury	17 692	−6.9	174	11 205	1 861	820	488	5 350	3 772	258.5	90.1	884	91.7	256.9
Worth	1 763	−4.7	230	1 120	73	39	37	346	285	14.2	6.3	808	98.7	13.9
Wright	3 501	−4.5	252	2 220	177	76	66	944	737	42.9	16.2	1 147	98.2	40.6
KANSAS	435 613	6.9	164	281 732	36 298	26 060	29 108	215 634	118 302	6 597.1	2 529.8	967	80.9	6 540.0
Allen	3 246	.8	225	1 985	297	65	71	1 494	777	34.1	11.4	784	81.1	32.7
Anderson	1 946	−4.8	240	1 260	94	38	39	550	478	16.3	6.5	808	93.3	15.3
Atchison	3 225	−2.1	191	2 130	298	56	83	1 157	716	32.0	12.0	712	77.1	31.0
Barber	1 374	−6.5	262	895	76	29	26	680	446	19.7	7.6	1 417	92.3	20.7
Barton	5 923	2.7	207	3 920	371	93	135	2 317	1 373	69.9	27.0	929	80.6	71.0
Bourbon	3 616	2.3	241	2 320	355	102	75	1 126	768	33.4	10.4	684	84.7	33.4
Brown	2 490	−8.5	228	1 605	219	69	54	855	457	24.1	8.2	743	84.7	22.0
Butler	9 326	28.5	149	6 025	429	127	303	4 555	2 804	140.2	43.0	708	90.0	138.1
Chase	662	−7.4	232	430	37	29	14	268	191	7.3	3.1	1 058	96.1	7.1
Chautauqua	1 277	2.6	299	795	101	19	21	288	213	9.4	3.5	804	90.4	9.5
Cherokee	4 640	−2.3	207	2 610	613	58	110	1 284	925	37.9	10.1	447	81.4	37.0
Cheyenne	927	.8	287	595	25	19	16	298	190	7.5	3.1	962	90.5	7.3
Clark	566	−11.6	242	385	29	15	12	404	260	12.8	4.6	1 917	92.1	12.1
Clay	2 089	−10.7	233	1 350	105	38	45	838	448	29.6	7.0	762	81.9	29.6
Cloud	2 792	−8.9	279	1 910	154	69	49	907	582	31.9	9.7	954	86.3	34.4
Coffey	1 918	1.8	219	1 220	140	43	43	1 226	730	61.1	39.6	4 527	99.7	45.1
Comanche	550	−15.4	281	365	17	(3)	10	315	244	7.8	3.3	1 647	97.2	8.8
Cowley	7 230	.3	196	4 585	711	104	178	3 332	2 227	112.9	29.1	778	85.8	111.9
Crawford	7 375	−9.3	203	4 415	866	127	183	4 560	1 953	76.2	26.1	714	66.2	74.5
Decatur	1 020	−1.4	303	680	37	26	17	315	195	9.4	3.9	1 119	88.1	8.8
Dickinson	4 149	−.9	211	2 755	255	111	97	1 507	968	46.1	13.9	703	79.8	45.6

[1] Per 1,000 resident population estimated as of July 1, 1999.   [2] Based on resident population estimated as of July 1, 1997.   [3] Less than 10 employees.

Sources: Social Security Program—U.S. Social Security Administration, OASDI Beneficiaries by State and County - December 1999, <http://www.ssa.gov/statistics/oasdi_sc/1999/oasdi_sc99.pdf> (accessed: 7 March 2001) for 1999 – annual publication of same title for 1990.   Supplemental Security Income Program—U.S. Social Security Administration, SSI Recipients by State and County, <http://www.ssa.gov/statistics/ssi_st_cty/1999/ssi_st_cty.pdf> (accessed: November 2000).   Government employment, 1998—U.S. Bureau of Economic Analysis, "Regional Economic Information System (REIS) 1969-1998" on CD-ROM (related Internet site <http://www.bea.doc.gov/bea/regional/data.htm>).   Local government employment, 1997—U.S. Census Bureau, 1997 Census of Governments, Compendium of Public Employment, <http://www.census.gov/govs/apes/97coar2.dat> (accessed: 14 January 2000).   Local government finances—U.S. Census Bureau, 1997 Census of Governments, Compendium of Government Finances, <http://www.census.gov/prod/gc97/gc974-5.pdf> (accessed: 16 February 2001).

[Includes U.S., states, and 3,142 counties/county equivalents defined as of January 1, 1992. For changes to these areas since January 1, 1992, see appendix B. Geographic Information]

County	Social Security Program beneficiaries, December 1999 — Total — Number	Percent change, 1990–1999	Rate[1]	Retired workers	Supplemental Security Income Program recipients, December 1999	Government employment, 1998 — Federal — Civilian	Military	State and local	Local government employment, full-time equivalent, March 1997	Local government finances, 1996–1997 — General revenue — Total (mil. dol.)	Taxes Total (mil. dol.)	Per capita[2]	Percent property	Direct general expenditure (mil. dol.)
KANSAS—Con.														
Doniphan	1 689	−5.1	212	1 045	144	39	38	757	519	26.1	6.4	818	87.8	25.8
Douglas	10 026	22.5	102	6 300	943	561	497	14 074	3 242	214.2	76.4	805	78.1	203.8
Edwards	853	−14.3	260	550	40	25	16	292	209	9.6	4.9	1 446	95.7	9.8
Elk	991	−3.3	293	620	63	23	16	435	388	17.6	3.0	883	93.2	17.3
Ellis	4 697	4.7	178	3 020	330	157	129	3 328	1 043	50.2	22.6	849	87.1	49.1
Ellsworth	1 505	−5.0	242	1 035	62	29	31	810	371	20.2	7.7	1 215	92.7	19.7
Finney	3 690	8.7	99	2 105	409	161	179	2 705	1 968	99.9	44.0	1 222	80.9	99.6
Ford	4 195	1.3	142	2 750	346	217	144	2 312	1 284	76.8	31.3	1 075	76.8	71.0
Franklin	4 539	5.8	181	2 860	436	92	121	1 700	1 185	60.8	17.2	702	78.1	58.8
Geary	3 510	18.2	141	2 095	466	1 948	10 229	2 250	1 543	75.8	17.7	706	70.4	81.1
Gove	766	.8	253	495	20	21	15	435	214	14.7	3.7	1 206	92.4	13.7
Graham	865	4.8	277	585	47	27	16	419	288	13.0	4.9	1 509	99.2	12.9
Grant	975	20.4	124	575	88	28	39	783	443	33.3	24.3	3 093	96.6	27.3
Gray	882	3.2	158	555	32	22	27	784	306	15.4	6.8	1 238	94.4	15.4
Greeley	313	6.1	190	200	7	12	(3)	199	110	5.4	3.2	1 871	96.0	5.3
Greenwood	2 123	−7.1	267	1 370	179	51	40	521	346	16.9	6.8	852	90.4	15.6
Hamilton	552	−.5	233	360	25	13	11	347	117	8.8	5.7	2 477	95.0	8.5
Harper	1 691	−7.6	268	1 115	86	39	31	895	606	26.0	7.5	1 147	93.5	24.2
Harvey	5 774	11.0	169	4 025	287	82	168	1 760	1 304	69.7	24.8	730	78.0	67.3
Haskell	575	23.7	142	340	22	19	19	472	333	19.8	10.4	2 585	97.0	16.7
Hodgeman	470	9.3	210	300	5	15	11	334	152	10.1	3.5	1 566	91.8	9.9
Jackson	2 500	12.1	205	1 570	95	62	59	914	559	27.7	7.0	580	89.5	28.3
Jefferson	3 152	17.6	174	2 020	120	72	89	1 345	837	39.7	12.0	668	87.5	38.2
Jewell	1 158	−3.1	306	740	52	36	19	478	284	10.2	4.1	1 029	94.0	9.5
Johnson	51 259	28.5	116	35 630	2 012	4 029	2 107	20 814	15 868	1 046.2	541.1	1 292	79.4	1 078.5
Kearny	631	17.9	153	375	41	19	20	626	363	22.9	16.4	3 920	98.9	18.5
Kingman	1 990	10.6	230	1 265	65	45	42	591	347	16.4	8.0	932	98.1	16.2
Kiowa	867	−6.8	259	600	50	22	17	403	199	9.7	5.2	1 515	95.6	9.5
Labette	4 946	−2.0	216	3 090	608	89	113	2 787	1 545	68.3	12.0	517	87.0	62.5
Lane	539	1.7	248	330	22	13	11	329	242	7.5	3.6	1 634	95.4	7.3
Leavenworth	8 544	25.8	119	5 400	497	3 155	3 555	3 642	2 268	113.8	34.7	492	84.7	114.6
Lincoln	967	−9.6	290	635	39	36	16	436	182	11.7	4.0	1 187	94.5	11.6
Linn	2 223	4.9	239	1 410	142	40	45	714	428	25.3	13.9	1 533	97.6	25.0
Logan	744	1.9	253	485	26	23	15	396	293	11.5	4.0	1 319	94.7	12.7
Lyon	4 987	4.7	148	3 140	482	147	166	4 240	2 014	108.2	24.5	719	82.2	103.6
McPherson	6 174	12.7	214	4 375	220	96	140	1 793	1 212	63.5	26.2	919	86.3	68.5
Marion	3 224	5.4	238	2 145	127	69	66	1 079	566	26.3	8.0	583	87.2	25.2
Marshall	2 696	−7.7	247	1 740	172	69	54	808	606	27.0	9.0	806	96.9	27.2
Meade	925	−.5	210	610	29	14	22	529	306	22.2	7.7	1 748	94.7	16.7
Miami	4 219	18.0	156	2 630	340	75	130	1 894	1 067	49.1	14.8	563	76.0	45.4
Mitchell	1 685	−8.7	242	1 155	66	40	34	794	475	20.0	6.7	959	84.9	19.8
Montgomery	8 583	−6.8	233	5 390	928	154	181	2 512	1 817	99.2	31.7	853	75.0	94.8
Morris	1 524	4.0	247	1 025	67	36	30	507	269	11.3	4.4	702	89.4	11.2
Morton	594	8.0	170	370	33	20	17	630	479	25.2	12.6	3 695	95.9	21.3
Nemaha	2 481	−4.6	244	1 635	133	66	50	716	436	21.9	7.5	738	89.8	21.4
Neosho	3 704	−5.6	223	2 285	338	63	82	1 571	1 070	57.6	12.4	737	83.7	56.7
Ness	963	−10.0	270	655	39	35	18	526	263	16.0	6.0	1 665	98.1	16.0
Norton	1 378	−11.4	245	895	61	33	28	911	385	18.8	5.4	923	93.2	17.9
Osage	3 244	7.8	189	2 105	215	94	84	1 146	637	32.5	8.9	520	95.7	30.8
Osborne	1 278	−11.9	278	870	46	31	23	407	201	9.6	3.5	743	94.1	7.3
Ottawa	1 285	−3.7	218	855	66	25	29	462	334	17.4	5.2	893	87.9	15.7
Pawnee	1 621	−5.2	225	1 065	105	58	36	1 829	447	19.7	6.9	942	89.1	19.3
Phillips	1 568	−5.8	263	955	85	39	30	784	310	18.9	5.5	900	97.2	19.3
Pottawatomie	3 001	12.2	158	1 945	147	60	91	1 359	1 043	57.4	25.8	1 409	94.7	52.1
Pratt	2 131	7.1	224	1 400	95	44	47	1 120	591	26.6	10.6	1 097	93.0	27.2
Rawlins	852	4.5	282	540	38	20	15	368	176	9.4	4.8	1 514	61.5	8.2
Reno	13 088	7.2	205	8 665	1 024	255	309	4 945	2 853	144.5	57.5	913	82.8	148.8
Republic	1 721	−9.4	288	1 160	66	40	30	653	364	16.7	6.9	1 123	90.0	16.3
Rice	2 414	−5.5	236	1 565	114	53	51	989	484	26.4	9.9	947	92.6	25.9
Riley	5 465	9.2	86	3 675	457	593	322	10 837	1 888	92.3	35.8	554	75.6	100.3
Rooks	1 457	−6.3	259	935	64	29	28	720	404	20.8	6.7	1 169	97.9	21.7
Rush	1 075	−7.7	319	685	46	29	17	398	286	12.7	5.1	1 492	99.2	12.6
Russell	2 077	−4.3	278	1 355	139	39	37	681	599	27.1	8.4	1 099	94.5	29.9
Saline	9 361	7.5	182	6 100	846	325	252	3 656	2 481	110.8	40.6	786	70.3	112.2
Scott	950	−3.6	192	605	45	19	25	508	211	12.8	5.9	1 190	89.4	12.9
Sedgwick	65 598	11.9	145	42 910	7 143	4 795	4 808	23 149	14 895	961.5	342.5	780	70.0	983.2
Seward	2 457	10.2	122	1 485	256	98	98	2 062	1 540	87.9	25.9	1 297	73.3	90.8
Shawnee	29 378	13.1	172	18 615	3 567	2 979	1 066	19 323	7 669	423.2	175.0	1 033	78.8	418.7
Sheridan	638	2.1	239	410	24	16	13	337	149	9.5	3.7	1 349	98.8	9.5

[1] Per 1,000 resident population estimated as of July 1, 1999.　[2] Based on resident population estimated as of July 1, 1997.　[3] Less than 10 employees.

Sources: Social Security Program—U.S. Social Security Administration, OASDI Beneficiaries by State and County - December 1999, <http://www.ssa.gov/statistics/oasdi_sc/1999/oasdi_sc99.pdf> (accessed: 7 March 2001) for 1999 – annual publication of same title for 1990. Supplemental Security Income Program—U.S. Social Security Administration, SSI Recipients by State and County, <http://www.ssa.gov/statistics/ssi_st_cty/1999/ssi_st_cty.pdf> (accessed: November 2000). Government employment, 1998—U.S. Bureau of Economic Analysis, "Regional Economic Information System (REIS) 1969-1998" on CD-ROM (related Internet site <http://www.bea.doc.gov/bea/regional/data.htm>). Local government employment, 1997—U.S. Census Bureau, 1997 Census of Governments, Compendium of Public Employment, <http://www.census.gov/govs/apes/97coar2.dat> (accessed: 14 January 2000). Local government finances—U.S. Census Bureau, 1997 Census of Governments, Compendium of Government Finances, <http://www.census.gov/prod/gc97/gc974-5.pdf> (accessed: 16 February 2001).

[Includes U.S., states, and 3,142 counties/county equivalents defined as of January 1, 1992. For changes to these areas since January 1, 1992, see appendix B. Geographic Information]

County	Social Security Program beneficiaries, December 1999				Supplemental Security Income Program recipients, December 1999	Government employment, 1998			Local government employment, full-time equivalent, March 1997	Local government finances, 1996–1997					
	Total			Retired workers		Federal		State and local		General revenue					Direct general expenditure (mil. dol.)
	Number	Percent change, 1990–1999	Rate[1]			Civilian	Military			Total (mil. dol.)	Taxes				
											Total (mil. dol.)	Per capita[2]	Percent property		
KANSAS–Con.															
Sherman	1 348	−1.6	207	820	103	58	32	713	501	20.3	6.5	993	86.6	19.9
Smith	1 413	−5.8	309	930	54	41	22	320	222	11.1	4.4	949	96.8	10.3
Stafford	1 224	−13.5	245	795	60	36	24	656	420	20.9	8.4	1 651	94.2	17.5
Stanton	366	20.0	164	230	11	(3)	11	305	232	12.6	8.5	3 703	98.4	11.2
Stevens	965	19.1	179	555	39	24	26	733	345	25.4	19.1	3 558	97.7	20.6
Sumner	4 790	−.6	176	2 995	289	94	132	1 890	1 145	62.1	18.3	681	90.4	59.3
Thomas	1 430	1.8	180	915	82	53	39	1 086	543	28.6	8.8	1 075	92.0	30.8
Trego	898	−4.0	275	595	37	19	16	448	192	13.2	3.7	1 119	98.3	12.4
Wabaunsee	1 419	12.6	216	880	66	32	33	498	290	13.6	4.4	657	93.2	13.9
Wallace	365	12.3	203	250	10	10	(3)	207	113	5.7	2.4	1 345	98.6	5.5
Washington	1 920	−9.6	297	1 255	92	56	32	816	404	26.6	9.5	1 434	95.4	26.7
Wichita	478	2.8	185	320	17	21	13	271	231	8.8	3.4	1 239	94.6	8.0
Wilson	2 523	−.1	244	1 585	223	45	50	903	611	28.1	7.4	715	94.7	27.1
Woodson	1 094	−7.7	280	725	79	20	19	266	185	7.5	3.2	805	97.2	7.1
Wyandotte	25 039	−5.8	165	14 845	4 446	2 519	747	14 916	8 010	494.3	168.0	1 100	71.5	480.1
KENTUCKY	729 134	12.8	184	375 154	172 253	36 894	47 221	245 003	134 740	6 772.7	2 076.7	531	53.6	6 871.3
Adair	3 687	19.1	224	1 840	1 196	47	57	744	957	22.8	4.5	274	72.1	21.6
Allen	3 498	17.4	208	1 945	828	40	57	694	545	23.5	6.1	376	55.7	21.2
Anderson	2 900	28.9	154	1 680	307	34	64	733	493	24.1	7.6	422	73.0	25.0
Ballard	1 831	−13.2	215	1 000	252	34	29	387	297	13.8	2.5	294	73.3	13.7
Barren	7 918	18.6	212	4 400	1 741	126	128	1 918	1 198	55.6	16.8	457	56.7	56.2
Bath	2 318	25.3	216	1 140	943	33	37	531	342	14.0	2.2	208	73.3	13.1
Bell	7 223	1.4	249	2 405	3 408	151	101	1 665	1 262	46.6	11.2	376	56.1	49.7
Boone	9 973	47.2	120	5 585	915	842	277	3 566	2 116	135.2	65.0	854	54.2	145.5
Bourbon	3 557	11.9	184	2 095	636	46	67	953	591	29.9	10.1	521	50.5	30.4
Boyd	10 910	5.0	223	5 500	2 271	564	173	2 927	1 784	83.0	25.5	513	61.3	89.3
Boyle	5 406	16.3	198	3 200	1 029	85	94	1 760	950	42.3	15.5	574	53.3	40.3
Bracken	1 611	3.6	190	805	302	29	29	367	279	10.9	2.4	285	75.7	15.1
Breathitt	3 559	28.3	226	1 010	2 505	64	54	1 013	619	22.9	3.7	239	52.7	23.8
Breckinridge	3 666	15.8	207	1 935	790	76	61	757	573	23.6	4.4	257	75.4	23.7
Bullitt	7 814	74.4	128	4 035	846	56	206	1 939	1 360	64.1	17.7	306	77.3	72.6
Butler	2 457	16.2	204	1 110	599	34	41	679	427	20.1	5.0	422	35.4	24.1
Caldwell	3 155	4.8	236	1 880	536	54	46	805	557	30.5	4.4	330	39.9	27.9
Calloway	6 550	6.9	197	4 010	727	84	116	4 674	1 770	43.1	11.7	353	69.8	42.7
Campbell	14 419	3.3	165	8 460	1 892	233	303	4 807	2 533	118.2	52.6	601	58.2	115.7
Carlisle	1 317	7.1	245	770	178	22	18	213	156	6.1	1.2	219	71.9	6.4
Carroll	2 015	8.9	206	1 090	464	34	33	650	344	70.2	5.7	593	55.6	71.0
Carter	5 097	10.3	188	2 180	1 821	72	93	1 210	942	34.8	5.5	206	66.0	34.3
Casey	3 222	19.3	216	1 450	1 316	34	51	595	499	21.4	2.9	199	77.3	21.7
Christian	9 648	8.5	134	5 465	2 150	4 033	23 969	3 377	1 752	84.5	22.3	305	42.4	82.5
Clark	5 824	23.5	179	3 170	1 127	118	111	1 367	1 182	59.1	18.0	570	44.6	57.0
Clay	4 479	12.5	197	1 385	3 714	398	79	1 363	863	31.2	4.2	187	52.3	34.1
Clinton	2 420	19.5	256	1 120	1 105	27	32	494	357	12.1	1.6	176	71.9	12.3
Crittenden	2 183	7.5	228	1 110	353	35	33	393	316	11.6	2.6	276	57.7	12.1
Cumberland	1 774	10.5	258	885	715	17	24	349	425	9.9	2.8	414	68.6	9.7
Daviess	17 512	10.1	192	10 540	2 724	292	346	6 901	3 385	189.8	43.6	480	62.4	186.5
Edmonson	2 391	39.4	206	1 150	508	224	39	430	401	11.6	2.0	182	73.7	11.7
Elliott	1 303	46.4	199	460	524	(3)	23	289	272	11.3	1.3	198	73.7	11.9
Estill	3 035	1.3	196	1 340	1 247	25	54	688	473	21.0	3.4	218	58.8	24.9
Fayette	33 463	16.9	137	20 180	5 529	4 309	887	27 315	9 313	487.9	218.7	913	43.2	402.2
Fleming	2 781	14.0	204	1 400	750	49	47	837	534	26.9	3.6	269	67.5	26.0
Floyd	10 368	7.8	240	3 010	3 618	135	150	2 437	1 205	60.6	11.6	268	73.3	64.3
Franklin	9 730	12.2	209	5 405	2 740	467	182	15 525	1 525	67.9	28.9	624	47.7	62.0
Fulton	1 933	−20.9	259	1 040	570	35	42	590	391	16.9	3.4	448	57.5	16.8
Gallatin	1 037	12.1	139	525	232	32	25	288	245	18.6	2.2	328	72.8	18.1
Garrard	2 786	23.8	194	1 510	523	32	48	791	550	22.6	3.8	280	65.6	23.9
Grant	3 542	21.9	170	1 710	622	58	71	905	608	26.8	5.7	289	69.5	27.1
Graves	8 337	2.0	230	4 870	1 420	168	124	1 598	1 040	43.0	13.0	364	50.0	44.9
Grayson	5 015	10.5	210	2 565	1 337	59	82	1 477	691	31.5	7.4	320	48.7	31.4
Green	2 679	16.2	253	1 375	708	28	37	643	572	19.3	2.4	228	68.8	17.6
Greenup	6 499	31.8	177	2 890	1 420	71	128	1 426	1 218	56.8	15.7	424	89.4	63.8
Hancock	1 367	18.9	152	745	210	23	31	415	327	17.2	6.2	694	31.6	15.5
Hardin	12 759	25.8	139	6 725	2 416	5 069	9 804	5 582	3 404	211.7	31.8	354	58.5	212.2
Harlan	9 219	13.3	269	2 665	3 188	114	121	2 150	1 400	63.0	9.2	262	75.5	62.0
Harrison	3 407	9.2	193	1 910	632	59	61	782	608	24.8	7.0	406	43.7	26.1
Hart	3 439	13.5	204	1 675	1 087	42	58	671	438	17.6	4.0	240	63.2	17.2

[1] Per 1,000 resident population estimated as of July 1, 1999. [2] Based on resident population estimated as of July 1, 1997. [3] Less than 10 employees.

Sources: Social Security Program—U.S. Social Security Administration, OASDI Beneficiaries by State and County - December 1999, <http://www.ssa.gov/statistics/oasdi_sc/1999/oasdi_sc99.pdf> (accessed: 7 March 2001) for 1999 – annual publication of same title for 1990. Supplemental Security Income Program—U.S. Social Security Administration, SSI Recipients by State and County, <http://www.ssa.gov/statistics/ssi_st_cty/1999/ssi_st_cty.pdf> (accessed: November 2000). Government employment, 1998—U.S. Bureau of Economic Analysis, "Regional Economic Information System (REIS) 1969-1998" on CD-ROM (related Internet site <http://www.bea.doc.gov/bea/regional/data.htm>). Local government employment, 1997—U.S. Census Bureau, 1997 Census of Governments, Compendium of Public Employment, <http://www.census.gov/govs/apes/97coar2.dat> (accessed: 14 January 2000). Local government finances—U.S. Census Bureau, 1997 Census of Governments, Compendium of Government Finances, <http://www.census.gov/prod/gc97/gc974-5.pdf> (accessed: 16 February 2001).

Table B–13. Counties — Government Programs, Employment, and Finances–Con.

[Includes U.S., states, and 3,142 counties/county equivalents defined as of January 1, 1992. For changes to these areas since January 1, 1992, see appendix B. Geographic Information]

County	Social Security Program beneficiaries, December 1999				Supple-mental Security Income Program recipients, December 1999	Government employment, 1998			Local government employment, full-time equivalent, March 1997	Local government finances, 1996–1997				
	Total			Retired workers		Federal		State and local		General revenue				Direct general expend-iture (mil. dol.)
	Number	Percent change, 1990–1999	Rate[1]			Civilian	Military			Total (mil. dol.)	Taxes			
											Total (mil. dol.)	Per capita[2]	Percent prop-erty	
KENTUCKY—Con.														
Henderson	8 248	10.9	186	4 665	1 328	134	154	2 321	1 945	84.5	19.7	443	57.2	81.1
Henry	2 700	1.3	180	1 450	513	60	51	603	483	19.6	5.7	388	70.9	20.4
Hickman	1 243	16.7	242	700	186	25	18	233	171	7.1	1.4	271	65.4	7.4
Hopkins	9 768	5.3	212	4 870	1 781	372	161	2 771	1 887	74.7	19.1	413	65.0	80.0
Jackson	2 632	13.9	202	995	1 494	37	45	711	512	16.6	2.2	169	65.9	15.7
Jefferson	122 947	3.1	183	73 805	18 889	7 136	2 538	39 565	23 421	1 438.0	609.2	907	47.6	1 529.1
Jessamine	5 128	41.7	137	2 830	850	71	127	1 893	1 047	53.8	21.0	581	60.2	56.8
Johnson	5 171	8.3	215	1 910	1 867	80	83	1 439	971	44.0	10.1	419	63.9	41.1
Kenton	21 832	2.3	148	12 595	3 229	3 752	509	5 900	4 082	330.3	106.0	725	56.8	365.9
Knott	3 623	23.7	202	985	1 830	53	62	866	653	26.4	5.0	281	85.1	27.0
Knox	6 397	24.5	200	2 240	3 687	168	113	1 744	1 254	43.2	6.3	200	71.3	38.8
Larue	2 672	12.7	203	1 430	472	45	45	551	384	15.8	3.3	257	78.9	15.2
Laurel	9 821	43.4	189	4 115	3 169	316	176	2 287	1 711	63.2	16.6	331	49.1	63.8
Lawrence	3 222	22.0	204	1 150	1 341	45	54	716	540	21.2	3.4	222	72.0	21.9
Lee	1 774	15.2	222	665	908	25	28	462	298	14.4	1.6	202	66.0	12.8
Leslie	3 172	42.2	234	785	1 444	38	47	708	455	20.4	3.7	272	81.3	18.4
Letcher	6 234	15.7	239	1 815	2 266	76	91	1 345	972	35.8	6.9	260	78.4	33.5
Lewis	2 566	7.4	190	1 155	987	20	47	558	411	16.8	2.3	167	74.5	23.5
Lincoln	4 451	7.3	197	2 220	1 517	54	78	899	725	27.3	4.4	199	73.4	30.3
Livingston	2 240	9.3	236	1 125	304	79	33	373	268	9.4	2.4	256	78.5	9.3
Logan	5 262	8.5	200	2 875	1 068	72	91	1 188	903	32.6	8.7	335	54.7	34.3
Lyon	1 851	29.9	230	1 085	175	34	28	700	208	7.4	2.3	284	73.0	8.8
McCracken	13 616	4.1	211	7 885	2 187	713	239	3 778	2 244	105.1	40.6	627	47.0	108.9
McCreary	3 417	11.3	204	1 125	2 075	124	58	796	818	24.8	2.1	124	72.7	26.9
McLean	2 071	3.0	209	1 110	285	39	34	475	324	15.2	2.7	274	62.5	13.9
Madison	9 909	24.0	146	5 310	2 502	617	245	5 693	1 591	100.2	30.4	464	43.7	91.9
Magoffin	2 618	20.6	187	780	1 553	22	48	752	527	21.5	2.8	200	71.1	20.3
Marion	3 444	7.8	201	1 795	1 141	53	59	781	557	25.4	6.5	381	53.1	24.4
Marshall	7 067	18.1	234	4 220	583	90	105	1 549	960	39.5	15.2	510	52.0	39.6
Martin	2 906	24.7	244	665	1 361	18	42	653	555	20.9	3.7	299	79.2	20.7
Mason	3 398	-.4	202	2 010	680	59	59	1 012	824	48.9	11.8	694	51.9	49.9
Meade	3 354	63.2	115	1 575	493	38	100	765	638	27.8	5.7	203	68.0	28.7
Menifee	1 292	37.4	220	535	516	61	20	327	206	7.9	1.5	262	69.6	7.6
Mercer	4 221	11.8	203	2 490	673	50	72	836	696	29.6	10.0	489	50.1	30.5
Metcalfe	2 201	12.0	229	1 115	719	32	33	558	323	11.9	2.8	297	48.9	10.7
Monroe	2 790	11.6	250	1 280	1 097	39	39	840	514	15.1	3.0	263	51.9	15.2
Montgomery	4 159	18.0	192	2 135	1 137	73	73	983	821	41.8	9.4	454	53.9	42.1
Morgan	2 506	17.4	183	1 005	1 035	36	47	1 122	484	18.4	2.4	180	58.7	17.5
Muhlenberg	7 256	9.9	227	3 250	1 396	587	111	1 575	984	39.7	7.7	241	78.2	39.2
Nelson	6 171	19.4	167	3 355	1 033	87	124	1 364	1 092	50.2	12.6	359	73.0	62.0
Nicholas	1 460	4.3	205	805	396	17	24	339	216	9.6	2.7	382	61.6	9.0
Ohio	4 834	9.4	218	2 420	948	92	76	1 415	921	37.7	6.3	288	62.9	36.6
Oldham	4 403	51.0	96	2 575	333	70	154	2 872	1 218	50.3	20.5	473	80.6	51.8
Owen	1 721	15.9	165	985	375	25	36	440	313	12.1	2.8	275	78.9	11.6
Owsley	1 184	.8	220	455	1 049	15	19	326	223	7.8	.7	133	82.3	7.7
Pendleton	2 244	14.5	161	1 100	390	30	47	571	545	18.2	3.1	226	74.9	23.1
Perry	6 955	18.4	226	2 020	3 107	157	108	2 451	1 251	58.6	11.4	366	66.1	67.8
Pike	16 685	14.0	233	4 590	4 980	293	250	3 259	1 581	111.6	27.8	384	54.9	114.4
Powell	2 564	68.7	193	1 025	920	42	45	756	491	18.8	2.6	207	42.2	18.9
Pulaski	13 027	29.4	228	6 185	3 873	191	196	3 598	1 978	77.7	21.7	388	55.5	78.2
Robertson	420	-4.5	185	210	110	(3)	(3)	136	58	2.9	.5	251	87.8	3.0
Rockcastle	3 142	28.8	197	1 400	1 198	34	55	720	575	19.0	2.5	160	72.2	19.7
Rowan	3 490	21.2	157	1 685	1 106	94	82	2 819	595	27.6	8.1	369	41.0	26.4
Russell	4 164	29.5	257	1 910	1 463	60	56	1 020	579	28.3	4.8	295	67.1	27.7
Scott	4 084	16.5	127	2 345	775	59	106	1 585	1 186	88.6	23.2	786	40.1	98.3
Shelby	4 833	22.4	158	2 825	655	83	103	1 361	951	40.4	16.9	586	67.0	39.5
Simpson	2 914	8.1	176	1 745	480	38	57	879	663	29.5	7.5	467	57.9	28.2
Spencer	1 582	38.8	152	810	228	27	33	398	291	11.6	2.5	273	78.0	13.0
Taylor	5 395	21.9	235	2 855	1 395	84	80	1 437	1 141	57.3	7.2	317	64.9	54.3
Todd	2 216	3.6	196	1 195	455	39	39	494	383	15.6	2.8	249	58.1	14.9
Trigg	2 979	18.9	237	1 770	407	155	43	627	380	17.7	4.1	336	69.5	16.7
Trimble	1 386	24.3	175	720	219	17	26	268	227	29.0	2.8	381	82.6	32.5
Union	2 973	4.7	180	1 535	356	52	57	669	590	22.4	5.4	327	68.2	22.3
Warren	13 937	12.2	159	7 945	2 772	774	310	6 718	2 828	146.5	54.7	632	47.6	144.4
Washington	2 323	11.7	210	1 280	517	36	38	455	296	12.9	3.4	314	54.7	12.2
Wayne	4 252	22.5	222	1 860	1 982	37	66	942	767	24.5	3.8	203	70.0	22.7
Webster	2 962	-6.1	220	1 525	462	43	47	688	590	35.3	7.0	515	79.4	32.8
Whitley	7 538	-.9	209	3 185	3 090	100	125	1 982	1 297	55.1	9.4	264	55.2	53.2
Wolfe	1 684	19.9	224	610	1 234	31	26	442	320	11.7	1.2	164	49.3	9.8
Woodford	3 387	26.9	149	2 125	325	44	79	974	738	36.1	16.6	745	47.4	36.5

[1] Per 1,000 resident population estimated as of July 1, 1999.   [2] Based on resident population estimated as of July 1, 1997.   [3] Less than 10 employees.

Sources: Social Security Program—U.S. Social Security Administration, OASDI Beneficiaries by State and County - December 1999, <http://www.ssa.gov/statistics/oasdi_sc/1999/oasdi_sc99.pdf> (accessed: 7 March 2001) for 1999 – annual publication of same title for 1990.   Supplemental Security Income Program—U.S. Social Security Administration, SSI Recipients by State and County, <http://www.ssa.gov/statistics/ssi_st_cty/1999/ssi_st_cty.pdf> (accessed: November 2000).   Government employment, 1998—U.S. Bureau of Economic Analysis, "Regional Economic Information System (REIS) 1969-1998" on CD-ROM (related Internet site <http://www.bea.doc.gov/bea/regional/data.htm>).   Local government employment, 1997—U.S. Census Bureau, 1997 Census of Governments, Compendium of Public Employment, <http://www.census.gov/govs/apes/97coar2.dat> (accessed: 14 January 2000).   Local government finances—U.S. Census Bureau, 1997 Census of Governments, Compendium of Government Finances, <http://www.census.gov/prod/gc97/gc974-5.pdf> (accessed: 16 February 2001).

[Includes U.S., states, and 3,142 counties/county equivalents defined as of January 1, 1992. For changes to these areas since January 1, 1992, see appendix B. Geographic Information]

County	Social Security Program beneficiaries, December 1999 — Total — Number	Percent change, 1990–1999	Rate[1]	Retired workers	Supplemental Security Income Program recipients, December 1999	Government employment, 1998 — Federal — Civilian	Military	State and local	Local government employment, full-time equivalent, March 1997	Local government finances, 1996–1997 — General revenue — Total (mil. dol.)	Taxes — Total (mil. dol.)	Per capita[2]	Percent property	Direct general expenditure (mil. dol.)
LOUISIANA	702 105	7.7	161	352 364	168 025	35 309	41 812	324 870	169 976	9 650.3	3 760.4	864	37.5	9 197.5
Acadia	10 651	6.1	184	4 510	3 037	110	319	3 176	2 473	78.2	24.6	428	40.2	80.1
Allen	4 176	5.9	172	1 860	929	718	132	1 495	926	38.4	10.3	432	51.4	34.7
Ascension	8 720	24.4	118	3 925	1 559	114	396	3 343	2 407	169.6	75.8	1 083	37.2	157.6
Assumption	3 886	10.2	167	1 565	1 037	32	127	1 169	835	37.7	11.7	514	46.3	32.6
Avoyelles	8 068	4.2	198	3 490	2 968	94	226	2 994	1 227	60.1	14.5	355	25.3	57.5
Beauregard	5 149	5.0	160	2 560	990	113	177	1 634	1 536	75.6	24.8	778	51.5	76.8
Bienville	3 338	−7.5	212	1 765	901	53	87	780	576	29.8	12.8	807	58.0	26.6
Bossier	13 168	36.2	141	7 650	2 090	1 952	5 903	6 269	4 470	235.4	75.8	811	30.0	213.7
Caddo	42 734	.6	177	24 820	9 748	2 707	1 342	18 969	10 788	559.8	259.7	1 065	49.1	531.5
Calcasieu	29 833	8.9	165	14 855	4 786	621	1 005	12 267	7 344	480.0	238.5	1 331	33.7	453.8
Caldwell	1 880	−5.1	180	910	476	36	57	749	329	14.2	4.3	416	44.3	13.0
Cameron	1 336	40.6	149	695	120	32	50	930	430	33.9	16.9	1 891	98.1	29.9
Catahoula	2 324	11.2	213	1 100	679	58	61	692	314	17.7	4.7	422	44.8	19.8
Claiborne	3 392	2.2	202	1 930	831	49	94	1 596	979	38.4	7.2	422	53.9	40.4
Concordia	3 924	7.8	191	1 970	1 163	82	115	1 505	875	28.1	7.9	384	31.4	30.9
De Soto	4 913	4.8	195	2 490	1 294	55	138	1 423	917	59.3	17.8	712	51.6	60.3
East Baton Rouge	52 004	9.6	132	27 805	10 273	2 349	2 265	48 026	14 399	794.9	391.9	994	32.0	812.2
East Carroll	1 582	−15.2	181	780	780	27	49	874	357	21.1	8.2	912	65.2	19.4
East Feliciana	2 986	9.6	141	1 395	902	43	116	3 100	499	20.2	6.1	294	38.3	19.2
Evangeline	7 021	1.1	205	2 660	3 049	67	188	2 252	1 207	46.0	12.5	366	40.9	45.3
Franklin	4 191	9.0	191	2 160	1 435	59	122	1 400	823	26.3	6.9	313	25.1	25.4
Grant	3 380	14.0	176	1 485	742	95	113	1 041	648	22.7	3.7	197	55.2	20.7
Iberia	11 982	5.0	163	5 405	2 871	132	407	4 315	2 674	154.5	44.8	620	30.4	148.2
Iberville	5 135	4.6	164	2 435	1 503	227	172	3 069	1 253	84.5	51.7	1 661	31.4	72.2
Jackson	3 273	−.1	212	1 765	610	32	86	990	743	22.1	8.5	542	39.7	21.2
Jefferson	71 325	12.3	159	39 210	12 758	1 583	2 578	22 865	17 691	1 257.1	539.0	1 195	25.1	1 100.3
Jefferson Davis	5 868	.1	187	2 740	1 198	78	175	1 726	1 338	60.1	19.0	600	46.1	61.7
Lafayette	24 503	22.6	131	12 570	520	992	1 043	11 024	5 855	266.9	121.6	660	22.7	250.2
Lafourche	14 886	21.9	166	6 115	4 784	147	514	6 977	4 261	217.2	51.0	578	37.9	194.8
La Salle	2 918	−3.1	213	1 330	2 560	34	75	1 048	857	37.9	7.7	558	56.3	33.6
Lincoln	5 590	1.5	136	3 145	1 247	114	242	5 845	1 461	58.3	22.8	549	38.5	57.8
Livingston	11 468	33.4	126	5 380	1 637	119	487	3 714	2 974	107.2	30.0	351	34.0	108.5
Madison	2 190	−.5	169	1 060	886	51	71	995	486	21.1	5.4	415	38.2	19.9
Morehouse	6 152	−2.8	197	3 110	1 929	70	174	1 617	1 317	70.8	19.3	609	41.0	68.8
Natchitoches	6 009	−4.6	162	2 955	2 047	191	212	3 990	2 034	92.9	24.1	649	46.6	91.2
Orleans	77 174	−8.6	167	39 485	27 786	13 082	6 081	44 814	20 873	1 235.2	510.8	1 089	40.5	1 121.7
Ouachita	22 231	6.3	152	12 330	4 932	493	819	11 821	6 093	289.6	136.3	928	38.1	298.7
Plaquemines	3 686	19.7	141	1 750	849	623	893	2 414	1 693	91.4	38.3	1 477	53.6	97.4
Pointe Coupee	3 768	2.8	161	1 810	1 160	67	130	1 359	744	45.2	13.5	574	57.8	45.4
Rapides	22 583	7.1	178	11 155	6 272	2 180	704	11 222	4 963	251.4	113.8	901	41.8	242.7
Red River	1 857	9.6	196	930	563	37	53	610	453	16.2	4.8	497	46.4	17.1
Richland	3 983	−3.8	189	2 100	1 302	112	116	1 233	1 131	54.3	8.7	414	52.0	49.4
Sabine	5 021	8.0	211	2 515	1 052	47	132	1 243	880	35.1	11.0	465	46.5	32.9
St. Bernard	12 550	10.5	192	6 615	1 730	122	365	3 020	1 975	83.4	36.5	551	33.9	92.5
St. Charles	6 103	21.9	125	2 955	946	179	287	2 760	2 012	173.9	96.4	2 025	60.6	160.4
St. Helena	2 340	109.9	244	1 030	538	11	57	755	332	17.9	3.1	322	51.5	18.0
St. James	3 398	16.8	160	1 520	593	61	117	1 597	1 237	71.9	29.6	1 414	61.1	68.4
St. John the Baptist	5 566	34.9	131	2 370	1 298	98	234	1 788	1 436	68.1	32.9	785	45.6	67.3
St. Landry	16 727	2.8	199	6 840	6 413	199	463	5 300	2 895	157.5	34.6	416	37.7	161.1
St. Martin	7 710	24.8	162	3 190	1 993	61	263	2 207	1 626	68.9	18.9	403	53.6	69.8
St. Mary	9 608	7.5	169	4 215	2 292	142	397	3 661	2 391	153.2	53.7	943	34.7	139.0
St. Tammany	26 441	42.4	137	14 290	3 378	589	1 048	10 756	2 506	416.9	143.6	779	42.5	418.0
Tangipahoa	14 948	.5	152	6 795	5 356	268	538	10 032	4 128	248.2	54.5	571	24.9	259.2
Tensas	1 264	−13.1	193	655	519	22	37	562	345	11.2	3.1	460	46.6	10.6
Terrebonne	17 206	13.4	164	6 685	3 900	268	602	5 920	3 830	290.7	77.6	753	35.5	270.6
Union	4 286	2.3	193	2 255	818	86	122	993	870	29.9	8.4	384	40.5	26.8
Vermilion	9 827	7.1	188	4 505	1 754	147	288	3 094	2 505	130.0	33.5	649	50.2	119.3
Vernon	5 675	12.8	110	2 750	1 094	2 758	7 940	2 744	2 237	72.8	19.4	376	32.1	80.6
Washington	9 277	1.2	215	4 265	2 939	104	238	3 375	1 800	78.9	23.9	554	36.7	75.4
Webster	9 000	−1.2	210	4 860	1 727	113	236	1 947	1 315	66.7	25.0	586	33.0	71.8
West Baton Rouge	3 049	17.0	149	1 450	660	71	115	1 401	763	58.0	26.2	1 283	45.7	54.9
West Carroll	2 603	.5	214	1 335	647	40	67	753	426	16.4	4.3	357	37.5	17.0
West Feliciana	1 249	25.5	90	625	351	16	74	2 701	586	55.9	9.7	729	31.2	56.0
Winn	3 014	1.7	172	1 480	693	71	98	929	628	23.5	7.1	397	33.4	25.8

[1] Per 1,000 resident population estimated as of July 1, 1999.   [2] Based on resident population estimated as of July 1, 1997.

Sources: Social Security Program—U.S. Social Security Administration, OASDI Beneficiaries by State and County - December 1999, <http://www.ssa.gov/statistics/oasdi_sc/1999/oasdi_sc99.pdf> (accessed: 7 March 2001) for 1999 – annual publication of same title for 1990. Supplemental Security Income Program—U.S. Social Security Administration, SSI Recipients by State and County, <http://www.ssa.gov/statistics/ssi_st_cty/1999/ssi_st_cty.pdf> (accessed: November 2000). Government employment, 1998—U.S. Bureau of Economic Analysis, "Regional Economic Information System (REIS) 1969-1998" on CD-ROM (related Internet site <http://www.bea.doc.gov/bea/regional/data.htm>). Local government employment, 1997—U.S. Census Bureau, 1997 Census of Governments, Compendium of Public Employment, <http://www.census.gov/govs/apes/97coar2.dat> (accessed: 14 January 2000). Local government finances—U.S. Census Bureau, 1997 Census of Governments, Compendium of Government Finances, <http://www.census.gov/prod/gc97/gc974-5.pdf> (accessed: 16 February 2001).

Table B–13. Counties — **Government Programs, Employment, and Finances**–Con.

[Includes U.S., states, and 3,142 counties/county equivalents defined as of January 1, 1992. For changes to these areas since January 1, 1992, see appendix B. Geographic Information]

County	Social Security Program beneficiaries, December 1999				Supplemental Security Income Program recipients, December 1999	Government employment, 1998			Local government employment, full-time equivalent, March 1997	Local government finances, 1996–1997				
	Total			Retired workers		Federal		State and local		General revenue				Direct general expenditure (mil. dol.)
	Number	Percent change, 1990–1999	Rate[1]			Civilian	Military			Total (mil. dol.)	Taxes			
											Total (mil. dol.)	Per capita[2]	Percent property	
MAINE	246 214	14.6	196	150 290	29 365	13 021	10 838	79 403	46 260	2 743.3	1 535.2	1 233	96.4	2 585.2
Androscoggin	20 708	8.8	204	12 825	3 109	366	519	4 628	3 572	207.6	111.1	1 100	95.8	204.2
Aroostook	17 589	13.0	232	9 780	2 991	759	458	4 889	3 550	183.2	72.3	929	95.6	176.0
Cumberland	45 116	12.7	176	28 450	4 720	3 079	4 245	16 706	9 335	611.2	364.6	1 446	97.5	553.8
Franklin	5 981	21.1	208	3 680	692	91	147	1 794	1 096	72.9	40.9	1 411	98.7	71.8
Hancock	10 486	13.5	211	6 820	739	408	717	2 720	1 677	107.2	70.1	1 413	95.8	106.9
Kennebec	24 156	19.3	210	14 080	3 429	1 608	590	13 903	4 013	223.1	122.5	1 059	96.9	211.8
Knox	8 403	8.8	220	5 490	830	119	274	2 300	1 171	75.8	57.5	1 518	96.3	71.0
Lincoln	7 546	17.3	236	5 005	494	101	184	1 585	1 288	80.6	57.5	1 816	96.4	71.4
Oxford	11 990	14.6	221	7 215	1 233	167	273	2 732	2 112	129.2	79.8	1 484	96.7	125.9
Penobscot	27 029	15.7	187	15 015	4 080	1 414	741	11 893	5 399	315.8	137.6	949	94.6	294.3
Piscataquis	3 987	10.3	221	2 380	435	61	93	1 066	860	51.9	18.9	1 029	96.3	52.0
Sagadahoc	5 708	34.8	157	3 485	392	371	466	1 530	1 265	72.6	44.5	1 255	98.6	67.6
Somerset	9 683	7.8	184	5 650	1 619	158	266	2 617	2 382	119.7	65.3	1 248	96.9	114.6
Waldo	6 949	17.2	188	4 120	921	109	185	1 488	1 160	69.3	41.3	1 145	95.0	61.1
Washington	8 217	10.8	232	5 025	1 139	306	318	2 299	1 227	73.8	38.2	1 063	95.0	67.7
York	32 659	20.2	184	21 265	2 493	3 904	1 362	7 253	6 153	349.5	213.3	1 228	95.3	334.8
MARYLAND	704 867	15.7	136	456 463	86 748	153 567	51 984	303 307	171 635	12 632.0	6 206.5	1 219	58.1	12 361.1
Allegany	16 057	-3.0	226	9 745	1 804	577	270	5 425	2 592	167.3	51.3	706	64.2	177.5
Anne Arundel	59 403	30.0	124	38 850	4 406	33 940	15 423	24 606	13 149	1 002.6	574.2	1 222	55.6	1 004.1
Baltimore	130 891	20.3	181	88 185	9 762	15 582	2 742	36 633	19 886	1 526.6	870.0	1 208	54.8	1 459.6
Calvert	8 132	47.9	110	5 175	676	129	314	2 603	2 093	163.0	88.1	1 271	69.4	154.5
Caroline	5 385	9.6	181	3 505	667	80	112	1 224	993	55.0	20.9	708	63.5	53.0
Carroll	20 640	20.3	135	14 110	1 040	326	573	6 261	4 170	288.7	152.6	1 038	58.9	267.4
Cecil	11 785	27.9	140	6 925	1 044	1 696	312	2 943	2 663	154.3	71.6	886	65.1	158.7
Charles	11 754	50.6	97	6 980	1 323	2 503	876	4 743	3 798	255.0	112.5	976	61.8	253.4
Dorchester	6 512	1.7	219	4 640	846	132	123	1 495	1 085	65.9	25.2	843	69.4	70.6
Frederick	22 772	38.1	119	14 940	1 308	2 509	1 968	8 169	6 296	391.4	193.2	1 056	70.0	371.5
Garrett	5 544	23.5	189	3 145	675	78	111	1 377	1 060	68.7	26.9	914	63.4	66.4
Harford	27 346	47.7	125	17 800	1 815	8 015	3 830	8 695	6 614	400.7	206.7	973	70.8	419.2
Howard	20 568	83.2	85	13 725	1 456	665	895	12 922	7 686	525.1	328.3	1 434	61.7	541.4
Kent	5 058	20.0	265	3 560	307	72	72	820	603	36.5	19.6	1 033	55.7	36.1
Montgomery	92 577	22.1	109	64 800	9 750	41 289	7 242	37 104	30 915	2 584.5	1 501.9	1 812	68.8	2 502.8
Prince George's	73 362	28.0	94	44 555	9 821	24 279	9 383	52 322	24 971	1 927.7	842.0	1 094	54.3	1 840.8
Queen Anne's	5 635	25.5	138	3 855	341	89	150	1 694	1 389	88.3	44.9	1 153	55.4	89.4
St. Mary's	8 876	25.2	100	5 470	1 068	6 594	3 366	3 820	2 200	163.0	70.4	824	58.4	164.9
Somerset	4 467	1.3	184	2 955	626	67	120	2 702	621	41.9	11.7	479	52.7	43.7
Talbot	7 779	12.7	232	5 655	503	566	126	1 305	857	64.3	39.0	1 192	64.9	58.8
Washington	22 327	12.8	175	14 495	2 013	950	771	6 942	3 909	237.6	104.0	817	53.1	232.8
Wicomico	13 579	9.1	171	9 270	1 601	346	304	5 517	2 635	160.1	70.8	895	64.1	164.4
Worcester	11 364	39.9	260	8 480	689	222	191	2 624	2 017	126.6	82.7	1 963	61.0	128.4
Independent City														
Baltimore city	113 044	-14.4	179	65 640	33 004	12 861	2 710	71 361	29 433	2 137.2	698.2	1 062	71.5	2 101.7
MASSACHUSETTS	1 046 655	7.9	169	684 047	166 825	54 691	24 278	360 422	213 917	15 350.4	6 814.3	1 114	67.7	13 649.6
Barnstable	60 572	19.7	285	43 390	3 681	1 859	1 317	10 894	6 994	522.1	331.0	1 613	97.0	534.0
Berkshire	29 794	3.1	225	19 860	3 623	456	433	7 239	4 751	303.3	129.8	969	95.9	293.0
Bristol	97 981	6.5	188	63 470	18 395	1 209	1 898	24 124	17 429	1 091.3	400.1	778	96.6	1 034.5
Dukes	2 646	22.5	188	1 795	171	41	45	1 121	781	63.2	40.2	2 957	98.3	60.2
Essex	121 293	8.5	172	79 585	20 361	4 444	2 344	32 806	23 562	1 592.7	719.9	1 037	96.1	1 567.2
Franklin	12 898	7.5	182	8 095	1 871	181	228	4 552	2 617	168.4	69.9	987	98.1	150.5
Hampden	85 187	4.0	194	53 550	20 030	5 338	1 526	26 706	17 858	1 178.9	373.1	847	98.5	1 124.1
Hampshire	22 414	11.6	149	14 800	2 096	1 278	498	14 465	4 919	277.1	115.6	769	98.0	273.2
Middlesex	218 977	9.5	153	148 225	25 115	13 344	6 634	64 488	44 965	3 181.5	1 844.5	1 302	97.0	2 972.8
Nantucket	1 175	19.9	143	830	43	53	56	582	586	42.7	25.8	3 447	92.0	42.3
Norfolk	105 532	11.0	164	71 570	8 324	1 344	2 110	28 917	19 688	1 404.2	797.8	1 247	97.7	1 340.4
Plymouth	72 397	18.5	153	44 970	8 887	4 597	1 573	22 728	14 581	1 014.7	493.0	1 068	97.7	950.4
Suffolk	90 052	-6.0	140	53 255	35 253	17 484	3 178	74 102	31 506	2 940.7	871.5	1 357	93.9	1 825.0
Worcester	125 728	7.6	170	80 645	18 768	3 063	2 438	47 698	23 680	1 569.7	602.0	831	97.8	1 482.0

[1] Per 1,000 resident population estimated as of July 1, 1999.   [2] Based on resident population estimated as of July 1, 1997.

Sources: Social Security Program—U.S. Social Security Administration, OASDI Beneficiaries by State and County - December 1999, <http://www.ssa.gov/statistics/oasdi_sc/1999/oasdi_sc99.pdf> (accessed: 7 March 2001) for 1999 – annual publication of same title for 1990.   Supplemental Security Income Program—U.S. Social Security Administration, SSI Recipients by State and County, <http://www.ssa.gov/statistics/ssi_st_cty/1999/ssi_st_cty.pdf> (accessed: November 2000).   Government employment, 1998—U.S. Bureau of Economic Analysis, "Regional Economic Information System (REIS) 1969-1998" on CD-ROM (related Internet site <http://www.bea.doc.gov/bea/regional/data.htm>).   Local government employment, 1997—U.S. Census Bureau, 1997 Census of Governments, Compendium of Public Employment, <http://www.census.gov/govs/apes/97coar2.dat> (accessed: 14 January 2000).   Local government finances—U.S. Census Bureau, 1997 Census of Governments, Compendium of Government Finances, <http://www.census.gov/prod/gc97/gc974-5.pdf> (accessed: 16 February 2001).

Table B–13. Counties — Government Programs, Employment, and Finances–Con.

[Includes U.S., states, and 3,142 counties/county equivalents defined as of January 1, 1992. For changes to these areas since January 1, 1992, see appendix B. Geographic Information]

County	Social Security Program beneficiaries, December 1999 — Total Number	Percent change, 1990–1999	Rate[1]	Retired workers	Supplemental Security Income Program recipients, December 1999	Government employment, 1998 — Federal Civilian	Military	State and local	Local government employment, full-time equivalent, March 1997	Local government finances, 1996–1997 — General revenue Total (mil. dol.)	Taxes Total (mil. dol.)	Per capita[2]	Percent property	Direct general expenditure (mil. dol.)
MICHIGAN	1 620 377	8.7	164	996 670	209 957	56 255	21 763	577 804	332 671	26 844.5	6 760.6	691	89.1	27 426.6
Alcona	3 760	10.8	337	2 485	242	40	22	380	279	19.4	7.1	649	99.8	17.3
Alger	2 262	5.5	224	1 455	205	84	20	519	375	23.0	5.0	499	96.7	22.8
Allegan	15 363	21.9	149	9 685	1 115	186	202	4 304	2 855	199.5	43.7	434	97.5	209.4
Alpena	7 378	−.6	241	4 290	853	99	61	3 031	1 896	150.2	16.0	522	97.5	149.1
Antrim	5 361	23.2	244	3 645	335	55	43	1 240	731	59.1	20.4	974	97.4	62.1
Arenac	3 943	1.0	238	2 420	429	50	33	764	502	32.4	7.0	429	97.9	32.9
Baraga	1 857	−6.2	214	1 085	209	28	17	792	292	32.3	3.7	436	98.3	28.8
Barry	8 961	33.7	164	5 960	542	101	108	1 867	1 512	92.2	18.1	333	98.1	107.4
Bay	21 409	7.9	195	12 870	2 295	278	238	6 152	4 707	315.6	73.9	669	97.3	317.0
Benzie	3 533	29.4	232	2 385	215	40	43	666	463	35.6	13.6	950	97.7	34.8
Berrien	30 952	−1.0	194	19 860	4 753	442	335	8 313	6 005	378.2	91.7	572	97.0	378.0
Branch	8 036	10.4	183	5 220	668	105	87	3 508	2 426	137.6	15.3	350	95.0	133.3
Calhoun	26 045	5.8	184	16 030	3 807	3 342	325	7 641	5 321	387.1	87.3	626	83.2	428.8
Cass	9 312	31.7	186	6 025	825	90	99	2 157	1 513	89.8	19.4	390	97.9	90.6
Charlevoix	4 937	12.2	197	3 390	298	64	112	1 624	1 117	70.8	25.2	1 044	98.1	79.6
Cheboygan	6 238	30.1	258	4 210	469	69	124	1 082	749	57.0	16.0	681	98.4	59.7
Chippewa	6 516	8.4	172	4 100	695	345	207	4 214	1 297	85.1	16.2	429	98.3	88.8
Clare	7 867	14.0	263	4 785	1 033	59	59	1 439	1 152	70.2	14.9	515	98.0	74.1
Clinton	9 135	46.0	143	5 935	428	295	427	1 805	1 492	112.7	23.9	380	96.1	127.1
Crawford	3 039	34.2	213	1 925	249	136	28	796	441	27.4	9.4	678	97.9	32.9
Delta	8 505	7.1	219	5 130	762	226	79	2 122	1 350	94.9	18.5	475	99.3	95.1
Dickinson	6 238	.9	232	3 965	416	627	55	2 069	1 383	101.5	18.7	688	96.5	100.8
Eaton	15 412	57.8	152	10 080	755	229	206	5 588	2 884	188.8	43.9	468	96.3	231.2
Emmet	5 512	8.0	190	3 635	571	104	58	1 598	1 043	97.4	30.1	1 062	97.6	103.4
Genesee	73 637	11.1	168	42 600	12 563	1 409	870	22 930	15 354	1 411.0	232.5	534	96.8	1 400.4
Gladwin	6 657	20.7	259	4 280	609	55	50	983	720	46.2	11.7	469	97.3	50.9
Gogebic	4 992	−11.7	293	3 125	473	165	34	1 370	851	62.3	9.9	566	98.9	61.7
Grand Traverse	13 269	11.6	176	8 920	1 104	465	271	4 696	3 200	210.9	52.0	713	95.8	236.2
Gratiot	7 408	4.5	185	4 620	1 011	112	80	2 074	1 339	87.9	13.8	346	97.8	89.9
Hillsdale	8 332	13.1	177	5 150	811	109	93	2 488	1 307	97.7	15.3	330	96.9	94.5
Houghton	7 189	−9.0	203	4 300	752	146	106	4 347	1 030	101.9	13.1	367	98.0	110.0
Huron	8 944	3.2	253	5 735	705	101	75	2 084	1 360	95.3	22.6	641	97.9	94.5
Ingham	36 777	−.6	129	21 830	6 595	2 337	694	45 594	11 765	833.1	207.8	724	86.1	887.2
Ionia	8 368	9.2	125	5 270	806	117	123	4 224	2 193	123.7	21.6	327	97.8	141.6
Iosco	7 944	17.3	300	5 215	563	112	60	1 711	1 063	76.9	17.6	689	98.2	78.1
Iron	4 051	−8.3	316	2 620	279	57	26	1 408	536	45.4	8.2	632	98.5	42.0
Isabella	7 849	22.4	133	4 710	1 179	143	122	6 434	1 460	118.3	18.8	326	93.5	128.0
Jackson	27 285	9.5	173	17 295	3 380	439	312	9 123	4 755	339.1	58.3	375	84.9	368.7
Kalamazoo	35 883	14.7	156	23 540	4 332	1 619	464	16 906	7 573	557.7	145.4	633	96.7	596.2
Kalkaska	3 150	38.5	199	1 920	330	29	31	722	629	32.9	11.1	722	97.5	34.6
Kent	76 971	7.3	140	49 620	10 588	3 050	1 112	23 355	17 775	1 403.0	370.7	685	83.0	1 520.5
Keweenaw	576	−12.7	269	375	35	72	(³)	94	49	4.8	.8	402	96.2	4.7
Lake	3 103	14.9	292	1 960	504	65	21	409	289	14.8	6.4	633	94.5	16.3
Lapeer	11 550	39.1	129	7 065	643	157	176	4 484	2 085	160.5	29.8	343	89.9	155.0
Leelanau	4 406	55.7	227	3 120	119	145	38	658	512	36.1	16.1	856	97.2	39.1
Lenawee	17 357	9.4	174	10 015	1 608	231	196	5 495	3 024	208.0	38.8	396	90.6	206.5
Livingston	17 371	59.5	115	11 140	596	243	291	4 844	3 601	294.5	65.6	462	94.7	293.8
Luce	1 451	−7.3	215	910	210	20	13	1 090	457	41.8	2.8	428	98.5	42.1
Mackinac	2 990	18.4	269	1 875	220	60	64	933	636	41.3	12.8	1 156	96.9	44.8
Macomb	133 969	16.3	169	86 485	7 812	6 797	1 889	27 433	22 222	1 826.4	518.6	662	96.4	1 840.9
Manistee	5 918	9.0	250	3 875	465	97	51	1 485	994	83.4	13.5	581	97.3	80.5
Marquette	11 432	8.0	182	7 025	1 006	307	136	6 313	2 715	176.0	35.8	576	97.0	187.5
Mason	6 082	14.9	217	3 985	595	99	71	1 730	1 169	79.8	22.6	814	90.3	76.7
Mecosta	7 197	23.8	177	4 740	817	92	81	4 241	1 426	89.3	17.8	451	89.9	108.3
Menominee	5 395	−.5	221	3 365	409	75	49	1 470	761	50.7	10.7	439	98.3	49.4
Midland	13 423	32.2	164	8 275	1 020	169	164	3 578	2 481	220.9	74.1	912	98.4	214.8
Missaukee	2 917	27.9	206	1 830	231	30	28	562	407	27.5	5.9	429	94.9	29.3
Monroe	23 469	24.6	162	13 760	1 804	255	286	5 927	4 389	350.5	102.7	723	96.7	345.6
Montcalm	10 654	8.3	174	6 605	1 309	143	120	3 104	2 153	138.3	27.8	466	98.6	150.3
Montmorency	3 569	7.3	356	2 310	250	15	20	434	270	19.1	5.5	554	98.4	18.0
Muskegon	31 821	6.3	189	18 405	4 954	392	333	8 870	6 385	489.7	81.2	489	87.1	550.7
Newaygo	8 870	30.0	191	5 390	885	90	91	2 457	1 899	111.4	18.5	411	98.6	129.0
Oakland	166 309	11.4	141	106 575	14 105	5 276	2 352	50 431	36 662	3 238.2	1 143.7	977	95.0	3 429.1

[1] Per 1,000 resident population estimated as of July 1, 1999. [2] Based on resident population estimated as of July 1, 1997. [3] Less than 10 employees.

Sources: Social Security Program—U.S. Social Security Administration, OASDI Beneficiaries by State and County - December 1999, <http://www.ssa.gov/statistics/oasdi_sc/1999/oasdi_sc99.pdf> (accessed: 7 March 2001) for 1999 – annual publication of same title for 1990. Supplemental Security Income Program—U.S. Social Security Administration, SSI Recipients by State and County, <http://www.ssa.gov/statistics/ssi_st_cty/1999/ssi_st_cty.pdf> (accessed: November 2000). Government employment, 1998—U.S. Bureau of Economic Analysis, "Regional Economic Information System (REIS) 1969-1998" on CD-ROM (related Internet site <http://www.bea.doc.gov/bea/regional/data.htm>). Local government employment, 1997—U.S. Census Bureau, 1997 Census of Governments, Compendium of Public Employment, <http://www.census.gov/govs/apes/97coar2.dat> (accessed: 14 January 2000). Local government finances—U.S. Census Bureau, 1997 Census of Governments, Compendium of Government Finances, <http://www.census.gov/prod/gc97/gc974-5.pdf> (accessed: 16 February 2001).

[Includes U.S., states, and 3,142 counties/county equivalents defined as of January 1, 1992. For changes to these areas since January 1, 1992, see appendix B. Geographic Information]

County	Social Security Program beneficiaries, December 1999			Retired workers	Supplemental Security Income Program recipients, December 1999	Government employment, 1998			Local government employment, full-time equivalent, March 1997	Local government finances, 1996–1997				Direct general expenditure (mil. dol.)
	Total					Federal		State and local		General revenue				
	Number	Percent change, 1990–1999	Rate[1]			Civilian	Military			Total (mil. dol.)	Taxes			
											Total (mil. dol.)	Per capita[2]	Percent property	
MICHIGAN—Con.														
Oceana	5 322	14.1	214	3 305	663	68	49	1 313	822	64.6	12.9	521	99.4	74.8
Ogemaw	5 627	21.1	265	3 480	588	57	42	1 256	889	39.3	9.1	437	94.4	37.9
Ontonagon	2 323	1.7	303	1 415	207	53	16	660	354	20.4	4.8	595	97.8	21.8
Osceola	4 895	4.8	220	3 005	655	64	44	1 157	878	53.2	11.0	499	98.3	58.5
Oscoda	2 390	31.7	269	1 430	184	41	18	379	250	16.9	4.5	512	97.9	14.2
Otsego	4 422	25.4	195	2 910	331	199	45	1 068	719	53.7	19.3	885	97.9	54.6
Ottawa	30 283	23.7	132	20 365	1 595	487	516	12 058	6 645	501.1	127.9	580	96.7	560.7
Presque Isle	4 165	11.7	285	2 600	336	53	29	715	500	28.2	10.4	721	99.1	28.1
Roscommon	8 428	14.6	358	5 630	619	38	47	1 408	968	63.8	21.9	943	98.0	60.1
Saginaw	38 617	7.2	185	22 595	6 780	1 340	441	9 600	7 589	527.6	100.4	476	82.0	529.1
St. Clair	26 335	11.5	163	16 370	2 465	457	386	6 377	4 838	392.1	105.8	672	92.1	402.0
St. Joseph	11 016	10.0	179	7 170	1 005	124	122	3 602	2 406	165.1	28.5	466	98.1	164.4
Sanilac	9 165	11.2	211	5 750	690	120	85	2 317	1 510	102.1	18.3	429	97.2	108.4
Schoolcraft	2 201	2.1	250	1 395	239	57	18	746	440	33.5	4.6	534	98.8	33.4
Shiawassee	11 889	12.2	164	7 305	1 262	144	144	3 498	2 369	154.2	21.7	300	96.0	157.2
Tuscola	10 437	11.9	179	6 270	1 014	149	117	3 512	2 211	128.9	19.9	343	96.1	135.0
Van Buren	13 339	6.8	176	8 325	1 845	163	150	4 811	3 194	215.0	40.9	543	97.1	222.3
Washtenaw	32 886	17.1	107	20 770	3 422	2 727	672	61 774	10 233	797.2	277.5	927	96.5	855.3
Wayne	340 462	–4.1	162	191 560	77 229	17 380	4 769	109 636	75 620	7 205.9	1 785.6	839	75.9	6 878.6
Wexford	6 059	15.0	205	3 710	689	145	59	1 725	955	77.3	14.7	506	96.1	78.0
MINNESOTA	728 088	8.8	152	476 167	63 632	33 229	20 084	328 799	188 845	15 010.8	4 507.6	962	94.7	15 262.1
Aitkin	4 332	14.6	303	3 000	281	47	57	743	545	35.3	11.9	857	99.0	36.0
Anoka	29 486	96.8	99	18 660	1 570	238	1 187	13 185	10 967	769.2	225.2	786	96.5	786.2
Becker	6 085	5.7	204	3 885	515	198	119	1 829	1 082	68.3	16.2	554	98.1	85.4
Beltrami	6 162	15.0	157	3 750	996	302	158	3 691	1 805	106.3	20.7	534	98.5	112.8
Benton	4 454	35.8	128	2 600	287	54	139	1 264	930	63.4	17.6	523	98.4	63.8
Big Stone	1 640	–11.6	294	1 060	110	38	23	574	429	38.2	4.6	812	99.0	32.0
Blue Earth	8 682	Z	161	5 440	881	369	224	5 001	1 980	148.0	47.1	878	97.7	152.8
Brown	5 779	–1.0	215	3 750	241	74	110	1 538	1 065	73.3	18.2	668	98.8	79.2
Carlton	6 140	3.4	195	3 800	456	83	125	2 796	1 487	93.6	22.4	727	98.7	97.4
Carver	6 512	41.6	97	4 340	195	198	262	3 810	2 275	226.0	75.6	1 198	96.1	240.9
Cass	6 566	25.3	243	4 425	542	244	107	1 778	1 184	75.6	27.4	1 060	99.5	74.0
Chippewa	2 841	–5.6	218	1 835	135	46	53	961	687	42.5	10.5	804	98.9	48.4
Chisago	5 734	18.2	136	3 800	290	109	166	1 894	1 778	98.6	25.8	651	95.0	106.9
Clay	7 771	8.7	150	4 920	731	115	209	4 446	1 804	143.8	28.1	544	99.3	144.3
Clearwater	1 708	–11.7	210	1 080	244	30	34	814	686	26.5	7.7	927	99.7	27.2
Cook	1 026	21.4	215	750	34	114	19	447	391	25.5	7.1	1 489	85.1	29.3
Cottonwood	3 149	–2.5	264	2 030	213	57	49	875	643	41.8	10.3	851	99.7	42.7
Crow Wing	11 638	14.8	221	7 815	899	153	209	4 172	2 210	147.4	45.2	884	97.5	152.6
Dakota	33 609	72.4	96	22 365	1 697	1 551	1 391	15 071	10 923	899.7	306.5	916	96.6	920.0
Dodge	2 573	3.1	148	1 665	126	40	70	1 058	820	51.7	12.4	725	98.3	59.9
Douglas	7 097	9.0	227	4 745	406	120	126	2 555	1 132	108.6	23.9	780	98.3	101.8
Faribault	4 068	–7.3	250	2 700	206	58	66	1 018	646	52.1	12.9	785	99.5	47.5
Fillmore	4 688	–7.4	227	3 115	210	78	84	1 235	696	55.9	10.7	517	98.5	58.4
Freeborn	7 603	5.2	241	4 990	421	90	128	1 460	1 001	78.4	19.4	613	91.0	77.4
Goodhue	7 779	4.1	179	5 310	355	122	175	2 689	1 783	135.9	52.4	1 227	99.5	144.4
Grant	1 655	–6.2	272	1 040	73	25	25	371	306	21.4	6.1	986	98.8	21.9
Hennepin	145 409	–.9	137	98 925	18 169	13 748	4 904	80 682	41 965	3 859.5	1 435.9	1 361	92.6	3 874.1
Houston	3 708	2.3	190	2 460	217	73	79	947	689	44.8	9.4	491	97.8	45.8
Hubbard	4 230	19.0	248	2 820	297	40	69	1 009	720	44.6	12.4	746	98.3	43.9
Isanti	4 341	30.8	141	2 815	226	71	122	1 729	1 100	69.7	18.2	615	96.9	65.0
Itasca	9 569	14.7	217	5 745	757	195	178	3 041	2 232	170.1	43.2	991	99.5	169.5
Jackson	2 448	–4.4	215	1 590	108	30	47	929	694	40.8	10.9	938	99.6	40.8
Kanabec	2 610	13.5	181	1 680	186	47	57	840	681	40.3	6.9	491	98.4	41.9
Kandiyohi	7 448	10.1	182	4 715	629	186	167	4 194	1 408	154.1	26.9	656	97.3	161.4
Kittson	1 292	–11.2	250	830	63	52	22	333	275	22.0	7.8	1 454	99.2	20.7
Koochiching	3 310	1.4	222	1 925	244	131	63	982	710	45.7	11.2	737	98.3	52.8
Lac qui Parle	2 120	–7.6	271	1 340	102	34	33	692	656	33.7	7.1	879	99.6	32.8
Lake	2 373	20.2	220	1 560	88	33	43	893	634	40.0	9.7	904	98.9	42.0
Lake of the Woods	972	9.2	210	665	55	21	22	292	196	17.0	3.4	741	98.7	13.8
Le Sueur	4 437	–1.2	174	3 065	231	61	103	1 283	916	59.4	15.2	607	98.5	63.0
Lincoln	1 751	–11.6	273	1 125	96	27	26	335	267	17.1	4.6	690	99.7	16.3
Lyon	4 529	–4.8	187	2 785	306	131	99	2 710	942	84.2	19.7	807	98.4	84.3
McLeod	5 849	4.9	169	3 895	228	81	138	2 702	1 931	132.5	21.3	633	97.6	129.3
Mahnomen	1 128	–1.5	222	655	125	18	21	339	434	26.6	4.8	940	99.8	27.0
Marshall	2 381	–5.5	236	1 500	111	64	42	616	572	40.3	9.5	902	99.6	39.4
Martin	5 291	–.8	243	3 385	328	69	89	1 333	997	58.5	16.3	736	98.5	57.0
Meeker	4 243	1.9	195	2 785	218	69	88	1 192	1 083	72.0	15.8	736	98.8	79.0

[1] Per 1,000 resident population estimated as of July 1, 1999.   [2] Based on resident population estimated as of July 1, 1997.

Sources: Social Security Program—U.S. Social Security Administration, OASDI Beneficiaries by State and County - December 1999, <http://www.ssa.gov/statistics/oasdi_sc/1999/oasdi_sc99.pdf> (accessed: 7 March 2001) for 1999 – annual publication of same title for 1990.   Supplemental Security Income Program—U.S. Social Security Administration, SSI Recipients by State and County, <http://www.ssa.gov/statistics/ssi_st_cty/1999/ssi_st_cty.pdf> (accessed: November 2000).   Government employment, 1998—U.S. Bureau of Economic Analysis, "Regional Economic Information System (REIS) 1969-1998" on CD-ROM (related Internet site <http://www.bea.doc.gov/bea/regional/data.htm>).   Local government employment, 1997—U.S. Census Bureau, 1997 Census of Governments, Compendium of Public Employment, <http://www.census.gov/govs/apes/97coar2.dat> (accessed: 14 January 2000).   Local government finances—U.S. Census Bureau, 1997 Census of Governments, Compendium of Government Finances, <http://www.census.gov/prod/gc97/gc974-5.pdf> (accessed: 16 February 2001).

[Includes U.S., states, and 3,142 counties/county equivalents defined as of January 1, 1992. For changes to these areas since January 1, 1992, see appendix B. Geographic Information]

County	Social Security Program beneficiaries, December 1999				Supplemental Security Income Program recipients, December 1999	Government employment, 1998			Local government employment, full-time equivalent, March 1997	Local government finances, 1996–1997				
	Total			Retired workers		Federal		State and local		General revenue				Direct general expenditure (mil. dol.)
	Number	Percent change, 1990–1999	Rate[1]			Civilian	Military			Total (mil. dol.)	Taxes			
											Total (mil. dol.)	Per capita[2]	Percent property	
MINNESOTA—Con.														
Mille Lacs	4 860	8.8	228	3 180	322	62	85	1 301	1 045	61.9	16.3	786	98.6	61.5
Morrison	6 287	6.9	206	3 855	499	355	124	1 717	1 105	80.1	16.5	543	97.8	83.4
Mower	9 007	–5.3	242	5 815	642	150	150	2 278	1 300	111.2	21.8	588	98.3	106.2
Murray	2 376	3.8	250	1 465	94	39	39	562	390	29.6	7.1	740	99.5	30.2
Nicollet	3 990	16.3	136	2 645	203	47	120	2 342	809	58.4	15.0	503	96.7	57.5
Nobles	4 343	–5.7	227	2 720	303	93	78	1 684	1 113	74.3	13.6	691	97.9	74.4
Norman	1 877	–3.0	250	1 185	106	39	31	537	474	31.1	7.0	918	98.7	30.3
Olmsted	16 461	26.5	138	11 600	1 363	913	477	6 401	3 820	308.3	102.9	898	90.5	312.3
Otter Tail	12 977	10.2	233	8 545	753	225	223	3 446	2 101	146.3	33.5	617	98.0	154.9
Pennington	2 532	–4.8	187	1 620	201	79	55	1 261	888	42.2	9.9	723	97.0	41.2
Pine	5 346	22.6	217	3 445	414	323	97	1 445	1 063	60.1	15.2	643	98.6	66.4
Pipestone	2 326	–12.4	233	1 415	163	49	41	855	455	26.8	7.4	732	98.8	29.8
Polk	6 331	–8.0	206	4 165	470	118	125	2 703	1 333	109.7	23.8	745	96.4	118.9
Pope	2 742	3.1	252	1 825	123	34	44	722	520	33.3	7.2	659	98.8	32.2
Ramsey	70 651	–5.5	145	46 785	11 604	5 140	2 141	49 996	23 277	2 036.3	602.3	1 242	92.6	2 046.3
Red Lake	919	–15.7	219	560	48	21	17	277	238	14.5	2.6	604	98.8	17.5
Redwood	3 790	–9.0	231	2 280	200	63	67	1 299	733	62.7	14.9	894	97.9	57.7
Renville	3 823	–6.6	227	2 440	170	61	69	1 198	562	49.5	13.0	765	99.7	58.1
Rice	7 935	13.8	144	5 270	520	135	219	3 571	1 445	156.4	31.8	593	97.1	170.4
Rock	2 376	7.8	247	1 475	88	35	39	838	497	33.4	6.3	639	99.0	32.4
Roseau	2 470	–2.2	154	1 625	153	62	65	846	844	61.2	9.5	586	99.4	61.8
St. Louis	39 962	–.9	207	24 775	4 252	2 118	903	16 878	8 604	710.6	160.2	823	91.1	698.5
Scott	7 128	45.3	86	4 575	249	253	320	3 335	2 145	178.3	67.6	886	93.8	201.6
Sherburne	6 111	56.1	96	3 925	341	169	245	2 846	1 892	145.0	51.3	885	97.7	147.6
Sibley	2 992	.7	203	1 945	105	39	59	811	568	39.4	10.2	699	98.7	37.1
Stearns	18 659	12.7	143	11 530	1 416	1 496	525	9 582	5 486	379.1	100.0	780	94.1	371.2
Steele	5 436	2.8	170	3 635	247	78	129	1 648	1 248	84.2	20.1	640	97.2	85.0
Stevens	1 920	–4.7	193	1 190	121	78	41	1 296	409	26.0	6.4	635	99.3	25.0
Swift	2 544	–12.4	224	1 625	169	52	44	898	385	39.1	7.6	700	98.8	40.4
Todd	4 826	4.3	199	2 965	468	77	97	1 275	1 092	70.0	14.5	605	99.0	77.2
Traverse	1 265	2.0	304	805	42	22	17	429	317	17.2	4.0	931	94.1	19.6
Wabasha	4 104	–1.2	194	2 680	184	62	85	1 141	947	60.5	14.0	676	98.5	57.7
Wadena	3 245	1.2	245	2 000	363	48	53	1 433	759	46.5	7.6	582	99.0	46.5
Waseca	3 470	2.7	187	2 340	177	263	74	1 234	811	53.6	14.2	767	97.6	59.0
Washington	19 412	91.9	96	12 895	696	250	796	8 255	6 161	448.3	156.2	814	95.2	467.3
Watonwan	2 573	2.1	223	1 625	125	48	46	720	505	30.4	8.7	746	99.4	31.4
Wilkin	1 386	–4.4	190	840	66	28	30	387	391	25.9	6.2	834	99.0	29.5
Winona	8 000	2.2	167	5 245	571	146	196	3 587	1 262	101.2	27.2	563	93.8	100.9
Wright	10 686	26.0	122	6 825	499	178	345	4 242	2 908	218.5	68.3	822	97.1	229.5
Yellow Medicine	2 730	–11.5	241	1 690	145	47	46	1 175	586	50.0	9.8	844	99.6	50.0
MISSISSIPPI	505 731	12.2	183	265 231	131 379	26 375	35 509	197 560	122 256	5 740.6	1 345.3	492	91.8	5 781.0
Adams	7 558	3.7	225	4 025	1 991	134	247	2 181	1 153	97.3	19.6	567	90.4	88.3
Alcorn	8 163	22.8	247	4 200	1 949	96	224	2 201	1 942	104.5	12.3	375	91.0	105.7
Amite	2 699	5.4	194	1 345	776	64	94	403	375	15.0	3.5	253	92.0	14.1
Attala	4 603	.7	251	2 490	1 216	65	126	985	727	43.0	7.7	416	94.6	41.7
Benton	1 687	3.8	209	885	567	21	56	293	234	9.9	2.7	333	99.7	9.1
Bolivar	7 098	–6.6	178	3 360	3 844	102	276	3 535	2 243	88.6	16.8	415	95.8	86.6
Calhoun	3 847	19.7	258	1 955	958	43	101	773	476	22.6	4.8	319	92.0	21.4
Carroll	2 156	33.5	216	1 155	539	27	68	298	236	11.5	3.2	320	98.6	10.1
Chickasaw	4 425	18.8	244	2 245	1 199	51	123	831	716	24.9	6.1	336	96.2	26.3
Choctaw	1 757	14.1	188	885	531	65	64	515	478	19.6	2.6	276	92.7	16.2
Claiborne	1 942	6.4	167	885	896	30	80	1 537	522	51.3	2.6	224	96.4	48.8
Clarke	4 010	18.8	217	2 125	843	39	125	736	595	26.5	7.2	399	90.4	23.2
Clay	4 166	18.7	192	2 155	1 181	85	148	877	793	29.9	8.4	391	87.1	32.9
Coahoma	6 036	–4.0	194	2 915	2 838	88	213	2 122	2 167	64.7	13.7	435	97.0	65.8
Copiah	5 756	2.1	199	2 950	1 783	71	198	2 010	1 144	48.6	11.5	400	94.3	49.8
Covington	3 827	9.8	214	1 880	1 117	68	122	878	812	34.0	6.6	374	95.1	31.5
DeSoto	13 308	67.2	130	7 605	1 491	135	663	3 348	2 771	110.6	42.4	459	92.6	116.1
Forrest	12 192	–3.5	163	6 505	2 830	705	715	10 739	5 530	283.2	42.0	570	90.3	299.0
Franklin	1 794	2.5	220	880	423	62	57	509	321	14.5	3.1	373	98.8	12.7
George	3 411	11.7	169	1 610	584	46	134	1 096	591	20.6	5.3	281	90.4	20.3
Greene	1 889	22.7	150	900	458	16	80	1 077	357	12.9	3.2	258	92.1	12.8
Grenada	4 665	9.5	208	2 450	1 347	236	153	1 621	846	62.1	10.5	469	92.4	62.5
Hancock	7 605	43.5	183	4 255	1 078	1 549	465	1 941	1 561	80.6	19.2	487	92.7	75.8
Harrison	30 286	15.7	170	16 590	5 974	6 510	12 164	11 008	8 163	488.5	136.1	772	78.4	510.1
Hinds	39 595	1.0	161	22 045	10 283	4 630	1 904	31 991	12 978	527.0	185.2	748	93.8	532.3
Holmes	3 847	–15.5	178	1 755	2 431	64	147	1 108	967	41.8	8.0	371	93.1	42.1
Humphreys	2 224	–4.5	198	1 015	1 185	32	78	621	447	19.9	4.7	417	91.2	21.8
Issaquena	289	52.1	177	140	95	(3)	11	97	51	1.9	1.0	584	96.6	3.7

[1] Per 1,000 resident population estimated as of July 1, 1999. [2] Based on resident population estimated as of July 1, 1997. [3] Less than 10 employees.

Sources: Social Security Program—U.S. Social Security Administration, OASDI Beneficiaries by State and County - December 1999, <http://www.ssa.gov/statistics/oasdi_sc/1999/oasdi_sc99.pdf> (accessed: 7 March 2001) for 1999 – annual publication of same title for 1990. Supplemental Security Income Program—U.S. Social Security Administration, SSI Recipients by State and County, <http://www.ssa.gov/statistics/ssi_st_cty/1999/ssi_st_cty.pdf> (accessed: November 2000). Government employment, 1998—U.S. Bureau of Economic Analysis, "Regional Economic Information System (REIS) 1969-1998" on CD-ROM (related Internet site <http://www.bea.doc.gov/bea/regional/data.htm>). Local government employment, 1997—U.S. Census Bureau, 1997 Census of Governments, Compendium of Public Employment, <http://www.census.gov/govs/apes/97coar2.dat> (accessed: 14 January 2000). Local government finances—U.S. Census Bureau, 1997 Census of Governments, Compendium of Government Finances, <http://www.census.gov/prod/gc97/gc974-5.pdf> (accessed: 16 February 2001).

[Includes U.S., states, and 3,142 counties/county equivalents defined as of January 1, 1992. For changes to these areas since January 1, 1992, see appendix B. Geographic Information]

County	Social Security Program beneficiaries, December 1999 — Total — Number	Total — Percent change, 1990–1999	Rate[1]	Retired workers	Supplemental Security Income Program recipients, December 1999	Government employment, 1998 — Federal — Civilian	Federal — Military	State and local	Local government employment, full-time equivalent, March 1997	Local government finances, 1996–1997 — General revenue — Total (mil. dol.)	Taxes — Total (mil. dol.)	Taxes — Per capita[2]	Taxes — Percent prop-erty	Direct general expend-iture (mil. dol.)
MISSISSIPPI—Con.														
Itawamba	4 494	22.1	213	2 620	622	52	144	917	883	51.8	10.0	474	99.5	51.7
Jackson	20 899	36.1	157	11 000	2 456	886	2 976	9 055	4 763	379.4	90.9	704	91.7	417.9
Jasper	3 623	-.3	200	1 715	1 183	62	121	860	607	28.4	6.3	358	93.2	27.2
Jefferson	1 866	14.8	223	650	906	23	63	630	473	15.5	3.3	388	96.2	19.3
Jefferson Davis	2 987	10.6	217	1 370	839	30	95	729	756	16.9	4.0	290	97.8	16.4
Jones	13 466	.1	214	6 955	3 145	244	434	6 066	3 838	169.4	27.7	437	91.7	173.9
Kemper	2 225	13.8	212	1 165	660	36	72	524	463	24.5	4.9	471	98.0	23.6
Lafayette	4 973	30.7	142	2 755	958	288	266	5 332	1 003	45.6	12.2	355	93.8	44.9
Lamar	5 462	46.4	143	2 945	901	48	252	1 354	1 083	48.7	13.2	368	97.0	50.3
Lauderdale	14 430	1.4	190	8 230	3 780	899	2 012	5 825	3 510	144.2	40.1	524	92.1	129.5
Lawrence	3 527	16.6	270	1 690	743	56	89	719	625	23.4	7.0	543	98.1	22.8
Leake	4 446	6.2	227	2 245	1 147	87	133	681	729	22.5	5.1	263	99.6	22.5
Lee	13 913	20.6	185	7 785	2 700	489	556	4 547	2 586	137.9	43.6	592	96.5	125.9
Leflore	6 537	-10.0	178	3 390	3 096	184	258	3 616	2 311	106.9	18.1	484	95.9	104.6
Lincoln	6 886	15.6	214	3 610	1 410	102	217	1 457	1 083	44.5	12.1	383	95.1	44.2
Lowndes	9 235	7.9	153	5 110	2 567	904	1 815	3 351	2 999	103.5	30.8	503	92.1	111.5
Madison	9 806	46.8	132	5 210	2 286	190	498	3 244	2 145	124.4	32.8	462	93.8	116.5
Marion	5 943	3.4	224	2 910	1 472	61	181	1 407	1 124	48.8	8.2	310	93.8	44.4
Marshall	5 827	12.2	180	2 835	2 045	114	221	1 163	1 003	61.3	9.9	309	91.5	59.4
Monroe	8 285	26.4	217	4 570	1 536	154	262	1 585	1 398	61.0	12.0	314	98.0	61.6
Montgomery	2 861	-.5	231	1 550	868	37	85	769	568	24.8	4.4	355	91.3	25.0
Neshoba	5 563	27.0	201	2 975	1 269	507	189	1 274	1 285	28.3	6.8	252	88.2	27.0
Newton	4 999	.1	230	2 750	1 208	84	147	1 749	844	43.9	6.9	320	91.9	43.4
Noxubee	2 556	9.0	205	1 135	1 339	47	85	672	598	23.8	4.3	351	91.4	22.2
Oktibbeha	5 114	6.2	129	2 760	1 783	364	279	7 861	1 671	77.9	15.6	394	90.9	81.8
Panola	6 859	21.2	202	3 280	2 262	122	229	2 016	1 106	51.5	12.7	388	92.5	51.6
Pearl River	9 706	39.3	202	4 900	1 567	99	321	2 467	1 821	72.7	17.2	378	95.7	70.9
Perry	2 609	45.8	217	1 200	558	25	81	715	687	63.6	4.7	395	94.0	62.2
Pike	7 695	.1	203	3 990	2 386	139	260	3 332	2 582	113.3	15.8	415	95.9	111.7
Pontotoc	4 733	13.9	184	2 555	864	60	174	918	901	30.2	7.0	282	96.3	32.9
Prentiss	5 131	8.2	209	2 845	1 135	56	166	1 476	1 255	55.6	8.2	339	99.0	64.5
Quitman	2 068	-10.1	211	930	1 150	32	68	417	407	19.7	4.1	422	87.7	21.0
Rankin	16 092	55.0	143	8 875	2 128	539	751	8 497	2 864	174.1	50.9	476	92.8	201.3
Scott	4 874	-3.4	196	2 515	1 500	214	171	1 100	702	38.1	9.5	377	86.2	39.9
Sharkey	1 134	-10.7	173	550	572	36	45	436	75	12.3	3.4	511	97.0	12.3
Simpson	5 015	9.0	198	2 545	1 313	51	173	1 645	934	38.9	8.4	333	91.5	40.9
Smith	3 824	34.4	248	1 915	708	62	105	571	514	19.9	4.7	309	91.3	18.8
Stone	2 666	19.6	198	1 340	509	82	90	1 037	1 245	73.0	15.7	1 223	99.1	71.4
Sunflower	5 165	-.5	155	2 440	2 179	72	237	4 223	1 675	72.1	13.4	389	92.6	71.9
Tallahatchie	3 288	17.2	225	1 435	1 478	56	102	840	719	23.2	4.4	294	91.2	22.7
Tate	4 087	12.1	167	2 120	999	82	164	1 535	1 276	52.9	10.9	463	94.1	51.4
Tippah	4 852	10.6	230	2 380	1 402	60	144	996	898	36.4	6.0	286	97.0	36.9
Tishomingo	4 867	10.1	260	2 645	937	68	128	667	553	23.8	4.9	263	86.7	22.4
Tunica	1 431	-9.4	180	605	705	21	55	547	451	43.3	6.2	775	87.3	31.7
Union	5 248	16.2	218	2 875	929	60	163	988	1 063	32.5	8.0	340	89.4	32.2
Walthall	2 856	5.0	201	1 430	959	24	98	725	624	26.6	4.3	301	92.2	28.4
Warren	8 034	2.1	163	4 445	2 004	2 348	368	2 602	1 976	99.7	38.3	778	91.4	93.2
Washington	11 325	-4.5	176	5 610	5 036	493	463	4 138	6 336	167.1	33.0	503	92.2	159.2
Wayne	3 895	11.3	189	1 720	1 296	35	139	1 164	1 026	49.0	4.9	241	95.1	49.3
Webster	2 938	30.0	276	1 500	584	41	72	408	354	15.8	3.3	319	97.9	14.0
Wilkinson	1 979	-5.1	219	960	902	11	63	560	354	15.6	3.8	417	95.1	15.2
Winston	4 115	2.9	214	2 210	1 002	48	133	729	622	36.2	5.5	284	86.0	38.9
Yalobusha	3 192	-.4	253	1 630	1 007	97	85	671	667	25.6	4.0	322	91.6	22.1
Yazoo	5 292	4.1	210	2 650	1 882	355	175	1 422	1 025	44.5	11.8	466	94.7	43.9
MISSOURI	993 174	8.7	182	611 577	111 040	58 899	37 557	351 621	201 609	11 391.4	4 779.4	884	58.4	11 314.6
Adair	4 120	4.0	170	2 525	538	88	112	2 689	846	38.8	12.6	517	50.9	38.7
Andrew	2 625	15.9	168	1 630	147	44	70	651	485	19.9	6.4	415	79.4	20.3
Atchison	1 558	-10.5	222	940	98	38	32	425	308	14.5	6.2	875	82.4	14.1
Audrain	5 370	.2	229	3 405	355	86	106	2 494	910	37.2	14.1	600	61.6	38.2
Barry	7 419	6.4	224	4 455	706	152	150	1 652	1 322	48.4	16.3	498	75.1	49.3
Barton	2 651	4.0	218	1 655	245	43	55	797	495	16.1	6.3	527	66.4	16.4
Bates	3 937	5.5	245	2 290	312	62	71	1 021	549	20.3	6.6	417	78.4	20.1
Benton	5 220	23.4	301	3 240	414	107	77	776	565	23.7	6.7	405	71.6	22.5
Bollinger	2 564	10.0	217	1 415	337	35	52	406	344	13.5	4.6	404	79.3	13.7
Boone	15 818	24.8	122	9 625	1 781	1 971	616	26 701	4 022	223.9	93.9	734	58.0	227.4
Buchanan	16 644	-4.5	204	10 485	2 055	519	378	5 683	2 849	149.4	65.2	797	51.6	154.7
Butler	9 855	12.4	244	5 270	2 223	517	184	2 754	1 532	61.2	22.8	564	52.1	66.6
Caldwell	1 945	-7.4	218	1 175	139	41	40	570	397	14.8	3.8	432	83.0	14.0
Callaway	6 372	17.0	168	3 835	523	183	182	3 929	1 055	56.5	26.2	709	50.6	57.7

[1] Per 1,000 resident population estimated as of July 1, 1999.   [2] Based on resident population estimated as of July 1, 1997.

Sources: Social Security Program—U.S. Social Security Administration, OASDI Beneficiaries by State and County - December 1999, <http://www.ssa.gov/statistics/oasdi_sc/1999/oasdi_sc99.pdf> (accessed: 7 March 2001) for 1999 – annual publication of same title for 1990.   Supplemental Security Income Program—U.S. Social Security Administration, SSI Recipients by State and County, <http://www.ssa.gov/statistics/ssi_st_cty/1999/ssi_st_cty.pdf> (accessed: November 2000).   Government employment, 1998—U.S. Bureau of Economic Analysis, "Regional Economic Information System (REIS) 1969-1998" on CD-ROM (related Internet site <http://www.bea.doc.gov/bea/regional/data.htm>).   Local government employment, 1997—U.S. Census Bureau, 1997 Census of Governments, Compendium of Public Employment, <http://www.census.gov/govs/apes/97coar2.dat> (accessed: 14 January 2000).   Local government finances—U.S. Census Bureau, 1997 Census of Governments, Compendium of Government Finances, <http://www.census.gov/prod/gc97/gc974-5.pdf> (accessed: 16 February 2001).

[Includes U.S., states, and 3,142 counties/county equivalents defined as of January 1, 1992. For changes to these areas since January 1, 1992, see appendix B. Geographic Information]

County	Social Security Program beneficiaries, December 1999 Total Number	Total Percent change, 1990–1999	Total Rate[1]	Retired workers	Supplemental Security Income Program recipients, December 1999	Government employment, 1998 Federal Civilian	Federal Military	State and local	Local government employment, full-time equivalent, March 1997	Local government finances, 1996–1997 General revenue Total (mil. dol.)	Taxes Total (mil. dol.)	Taxes Per capita[2]	Taxes Percent property	Direct general expenditure (mil. dol.)
MISSOURI—Con.														
Camden	8 912	48.3	258	6 180	418	67	153	1 605	1 307	55.5	25.7	773	51.8	57.7
Cape Girardeau	11 655	9.3	173	7 400	1 241	398	310	5 240	2 055	94.7	44.6	676	48.4	94.8
Carroll	2 482	-9.9	246	1 475	230	55	46	625	416	16.7	6.0	591	78.3	17.4
Carter	1 541	10.9	245	775	326	69	29	393	242	8.9	2.0	319	84.3	9.1
Cass	12 302	46.8	148	7 870	482	246	838	3 160	2 827	145.1	49.9	639	73.3	146.2
Cedar	3 766	1.8	281	2 340	363	57	60	788	532	24.6	5.6	429	69.5	23.7
Chariton	2 135	.9	250	1 345	153	53	39	460	325	12.3	4.6	525	80.0	12.7
Christian	7 976	65.8	155	4 835	633	102	221	1 616	1 294	58.3	20.5	437	73.2	59.3
Clark	1 533	5.4	208	895	115	37	34	559	434	16.2	4.1	540	83.8	16.4
Clay	25 720	21.5	143	16 925	1 301	314	1 238	10 394	8 258	529.7	161.7	929	66.9	495.8
Clinton	3 076	-2.3	158	1 935	245	66	86	807	570	26.2	8.9	475	73.7	25.9
Cole	11 077	11.7	159	6 895	873	516	313	19 494	1 851	105.1	52.0	755	61.2	104.5
Cooper	3 163	1.4	196	2 055	211	53	80	1 395	754	25.3	7.8	484	62.1	25.5
Crawford	5 014	22.1	224	2 910	503	36	100	837	708	22.9	7.8	353	69.4	21.4
Dade	2 069	7.2	261	1 280	170	35	36	612	456	13.3	3.3	417	74.1	14.5
Dallas	3 510	24.2	225	1 930	391	38	69	613	361	15.1	4.6	307	59.6	16.4
Daviess	1 829	-3.0	227	1 140	122	53	35	520	381	16.9	4.4	564	80.2	14.2
DeKalb	2 061	28.0	183	1 275	87	33	50	1 505	281	11.2	3.5	312	79.9	10.6
Dent	3 684	4.4	258	2 145	539	85	64	917	602	20.4	6.1	433	67.1	21.1
Douglas	3 139	33.9	253	1 750	429	51	56	435	352	11.8	3.1	255	76.4	11.3
Dunklin	7 957	-3.6	245	4 135	2 362	106	148	1 595	1 198	47.5	14.4	439	77.7	46.9
Franklin	15 938	12.0	171	9 700	1 334	232	415	3 778	2 743	131.8	58.2	641	65.0	134.9
Gasconade	3 557	1.9	238	2 390	180	50	67	951	674	29.2	9.5	639	68.2	28.8
Gentry	1 995	-4.1	290	1 135	137	44	31	419	314	42.6	4.0	580	84.4	11.4
Greene	41 043	17.9	181	25 175	4 884	2 190	1 063	14 105	7 560	384.5	161.1	714	55.7	372.6
Grundy	2 586	-4.8	255	1 550	235	55	46	921	640	23.9	5.6	549	67.8	24.5
Harrison	2 319	-6.3	276	1 440	213	52	38	724	508	22.0	5.9	703	76.6	20.8
Henry	5 554	1.7	261	3 320	617	88	96	1 459	1 502	33.8	13.1	623	66.3	33.7
Hickory	3 051	26.1	350	1 945	198	43	39	292	337	12.6	3.5	410	84.0	12.6
Holt	1 420	-10.4	255	800	99	40	25	322	206	9.5	4.2	752	66.0	9.0
Howard	1 916	-10.0	198	1 255	217	40	44	486	366	15.6	5.4	552	71.3	15.3
Howell	9 501	18.9	263	5 320	1 363	112	163	2 173	1 466	57.4	15.8	444	66.4	53.7
Iron	2 792	-1.3	255	1 475	456	28	49	563	501	19.1	7.6	693	79.3	18.6
Jackson	107 428	3.3	164	68 370	12 504	17 192	3 213	43 180	29 649	1 962.8	904.0	1 382	47.7	1 988.2
Jasper	20 219	2.7	202	11 735	2 879	347	451	5 842	3 865	183.4	68.6	693	51.7	190.8
Jefferson	27 034	44.3	136	15 155	1 897	419	884	7 046	4 755	257.6	103.1	535	70.1	258.7
Johnson	6 067	20.5	126	3 650	554	863	3 189	4 755	1 707	66.3	21.3	450	64.4	65.6
Knox	1 124	-6.3	261	675	125	40	20	387	275	10.8	2.8	637	73.4	10.3
Laclede	6 408	13.5	204	3 625	875	83	140	1 300	1 103	41.4	14.7	482	55.5	39.6
Lafayette	6 701	4.3	204	4 270	432	110	154	2 114	1 079	48.4	16.8	516	60.9	50.5
Lawrence	7 575	17.4	226	4 545	695	82	150	1 651	1 313	59.6	19.2	585	51.7	58.5
Lewis	2 073	-7.7	203	1 275	171	63	46	594	449	17.0	4.3	427	77.4	17.4
Lincoln	5 725	32.1	152	3 395	424	116	165	1 574	1 334	75.7	16.9	478	66.9	75.7
Linn	3 328	-9.3	240	2 150	299	66	62	846	605	28.2	8.2	591	61.2	30.0
Livingston	3 283	-4.1	234	2 055	331	104	64	1 070	626	25.7	8.9	622	55.1	25.7
McDonald	3 710	23.3	184	1 955	525	64	90	680	479	21.1	5.4	272	70.6	21.0
Macon	3 615	-7.2	234	2 295	266	80	69	1 595	933	38.1	8.7	571	64.7	38.3
Madison	2 949	1.7	253	1 680	372	29	52	746	324	24.2	4.1	353	80.1	25.6
Maries	1 798	23.6	213	1 115	138	13	38	348	290	10.3	3.5	417	80.0	10.4
Marion	6 006	-1.6	217	3 630	832	85	125	1 869	1 295	51.0	18.0	646	61.0	51.5
Mercer	979	-.6	247	590	74	22	18	254	174	7.9	2.7	676	86.8	8.4
Miller	4 582	3.2	203	2 830	487	54	101	1 005	892	36.3	14.5	644	79.9	40.4
Mississippi	3 099	-4.9	232	1 605	700	45	61	716	555	32.8	9.5	708	56.5	27.4
Moniteau	2 553	1.7	192	1 680	141	43	60	1 056	446	17.7	6.3	474	80.0	18.0
Monroe	2 042	-2.1	223	1 230	157	79	41	734	515	21.3	5.6	623	72.3	20.7
Montgomery	2 697	-2.1	223	1 635	206	54	55	621	419	16.1	5.7	487	61.2	16.4
Morgan	4 898	17.5	259	3 220	367	49	83	876	465	17.3	7.2	397	74.4	17.2
New Madrid	4 205	2.7	211	2 085	1 074	63	92	1 031	887	32.5	13.0	636	77.0	33.6
Newton	9 503	33.4	191	5 755	640	139	222	1 930	1 363	64.6	20.4	421	67.6	59.3
Nodaway	3 594	-8.0	175	2 210	274	98	94	2 556	705	34.0	13.0	620	67.5	34.4
Oregon	2 604	2.9	253	1 330	536	31	46	478	384	12.1	3.2	320	71.9	12.3
Osage	2 251	6.4	180	1 485	110	40	56	623	295	13.1	4.5	360	83.1	13.9
Ozark	2 741	24.9	275	1 565	393	27	45	483	341	12.0	3.6	368	74.7	12.3
Pemiscot	4 657	-6.7	220	2 215	1 797	87	97	1 951	998	37.1	9.7	449	66.9	36.5
Perry	3 408	-1.8	196	2 175	261	58	79	941	648	33.9	8.8	502	68.8	37.1
Pettis	7 743	6.7	209	4 795	894	141	168	2 723	1 300	108.3	24.0	650	57.9	110.2
Phelps	7 474	12.7	192	4 380	951	549	293	5 216	2 090	123.2	18.9	493	52.5	120.3
Pike	3 600	7.0	219	2 100	344	85	74	1 593	822	31.4	9.1	565	71.4	33.6
Platte	8 313	49.9	116	5 410	326	333	319	2 623	1 820	104.0	48.4	704	76.9	116.6
Polk	5 067	4.5	197	2 965	637	80	115	1 537	1 207	63.7	9.2	364	69.3	61.6

[1] Per 1,000 resident population estimated as of July 1, 1999.   [2] Based on resident population estimated as of July 1, 1997.

Sources: Social Security Program—U.S. Social Security Administration, OASDI Beneficiaries by State and County - December 1999, <http://www.ssa.gov/statistics/oasdi_sc/1999/oasdi_sc99.pdf> (accessed: 7 March 2001) for 1999 – annual publication of same title for 1990.   Supplemental Security Income Program—U.S. Social Security Administration, SSI Recipients by State and County, <http://www.ssa.gov/statistics/ssi_st_cty/1999/ssi_st_cty.pdf> (accessed: November 2000).   Government employment, 1998—U.S. Bureau of Economic Analysis, "Regional Economic Information System (REIS) 1969-1998" on CD-ROM (related Internet site <http://www.bea.doc.gov/bea/regional/data.htm>).   Local government employment, 1997—U.S. Census Bureau, 1997 Census of Governments, Compendium of Public Employment, <http://www.census.gov/govs/apes/97coar2.dat> (accessed: 14 January 2000).   Local government finances—U.S. Census Bureau, 1997 Census of Governments, Compendium of Government Finances, <http://www.census.gov/prod/gc97/gc974-5.pdf> (accessed: 16 February 2001).

Table B–13. Counties — Government Programs, Employment, and Finances–Con.

[Includes U.S., states, and 3,142 counties/county equivalents defined as of January 1, 1992. For changes to these areas since January 1, 1992, see appendix B. Geographic Information]

County	Social Security Program beneficiaries, December 1999 — Total — Number	Percent change, 1990–1999	Rate[1]	Retired workers	Supplemental Security Income Program recipients, December 1999	Government employment, 1998 — Federal — Civilian	Military	State and local	Local government employment, full-time equivalent, March 1997	Local government finances, 1996–1997 — General revenue — Total (mil. dol.)	Taxes — Total (mil. dol.)	Per capita[2]	Percent property	Direct general expenditure (mil. dol.)
MISSOURI—Con.														
Pulaski	4 871	16.5	127	2 700	754	1 959	7 801	1 683	1 413	55.9	11.9	313	71.7	52.3
Putnam	1 363	−7.0	280	765	159	26	22	433	254	8.9	2.7	545	79.8	9.3
Ralls	1 724	24.0	188	1 035	102	53	40	381	233	8.6	3.2	362	63.4	8.7
Randolph	4 373	−5.7	183	2 605	595	83	109	1 944	1 072	47.1	17.1	712	60.5	54.9
Ray	3 991	18.6	168	2 360	204	63	107	1 208	952	48.7	12.0	516	70.4	46.6
Reynolds	1 683	15.7	254	805	303	23	30	465	339	9.9	4.1	609	93.9	11.5
Ripley	3 625	14.5	256	1 925	765	56	64	636	481	18.9	5.7	409	90.8	17.8
St. Charles	33 179	60.5	118	21 265	1 383	562	1 232	10 087	7 353	481.6	246.6	934	66.7	532.6
St. Clair	2 707	23.3	292	1 590	243	34	41	674	505	22.6	3.2	349	83.7	22.9
Ste. Genevieve	3 338	20.3	191	2 060	193	36	79	869	414	30.8	9.1	532	68.2	33.3
St. Francois	12 255	12.0	220	6 660	1 833	130	251	4 374	1 953	83.2	25.0	457	62.1	88.9
St. Louis	175 021	8.4	176	117 125	11 121	5 952	4 562	48 433	28 869	2 001.6	1 188.8	1 187	65.2	2 002.2
Saline	4 933	−9.1	217	3 065	544	103	103	2 261	902	42.0	13.3	584	63.3	39.3
Schuyler	994	−21.7	225	600	132	32	20	293	217	7.7	2.1	474	83.5	7.6
Scotland	1 132	−11.2	230	670	113	29	22	548	403	14.2	2.9	586	76.7	12.4
Scott	8 385	6.2	207	4 390	1 634	117	182	2 132	1 594	66.6	21.8	540	65.7	61.4
Shannon	1 898	22.1	229	945	365	68	37	428	234	6.8	1.6	200	71.5	7.3
Shelby	1 684	−10.9	253	995	136	46	31	593	354	13.2	3.8	554	78.3	12.8
Stoddard	7 131	5.9	241	4 055	1 141	165	134	1 278	939	41.7	14.5	490	78.1	42.3
Stone	6 964	47.7	253	4 810	393	39	121	933	768	29.2	11.7	443	78.7	31.0
Sullivan	1 550	−15.3	226	945	235	49	32	455	326	12.7	3.9	578	83.7	12.9
Taney	8 724	21.3	246	5 770	588	105	156	1 481	1 240	72.2	43.0	1 263	40.0	80.1
Texas	4 907	1.3	218	2 815	795	91	101	1 284	1 530	90.6	33.3	1 488	31.2	121.6
Vernon	4 420	1.1	227	2 650	641	92	88	1 762	935	46.6	11.0	573	60.1	47.8
Warren	4 357	37.4	171	2 785	203	54	111	865	568	25.9	12.9	545	63.0	25.8
Washington	4 230	28.2	181	1 960	927	68	104	1 547	905	36.0	7.4	326	66.2	38.3
Wayne	3 914	11.2	300	2 085	755	88	59	594	520	15.4	4.9	384	59.5	14.9
Webster	5 405	20.4	180	2 980	650	80	131	1 140	788	32.2	8.1	284	72.8	30.8
Worth	645	−13.4	281	380	42	21	10	198	177	5.0	1.1	477	65.0	5.0
Wright	4 614	10.9	231	2 535	806	56	88	960	808	30.7	7.0	362	70.6	29.9
Independent City														
St. Louis city	65 731	−21.5	197	38 470	18 452	17 456	2 452	26 827	20 456	1 446.8	554.4	1 609	41.1	1 289.5
MONTANA	155 072	12.6	176	95 734	13 723	12 647	8 474	61 856	32 676	1 821.7	622.2	708	94.8	1 799.4
Beaverhead	1 527	10.3	174	1 000	116	193	50	741	494	33.4	9.8	1 098	98.6	26.0
Big Horn	1 482	7.8	118	780	298	448	71	749	524	28.8	9.0	714	98.0	29.6
Blaine	1 117	3.9	158	660	147	193	40	482	462	19.5	4.9	691	97.7	18.7
Broadwater	948	39.4	228	605	58	37	23	174	146	7.3	3.2	784	97.2	7.2
Carbon	1 938	5.3	203	1 285	95	67	53	464	390	18.0	6.2	655	95.4	18.5
Carter	296	−10.3	204	180	14	19	(3)	122	112	3.3	1.7	1 159	98.7	3.4
Cascade	14 468	11.1	185	9 075	1 440	1 474	3 896	3 791	2 607	135.0	42.8	542	95.1	141.8
Chouteau	1 154	3.5	228	700	48	35	29	470	289	21.7	7.9	1 515	97.2	21.4
Custer	2 479	4.4	209	1 600	230	331	68	837	473	27.6	6.9	572	96.4	25.6
Daniels	554	−7.7	282	355	24	27	11	164	256	8.4	2.6	1 245	98.5	8.6
Dawson	1 761	4.2	203	1 120	65	44	50	836	474	23.7	7.2	799	97.9	22.8
Deer Lodge	2 377	−8.8	245	1 445	222	82	56	896	297	15.8	4.9	491	95.2	16.6
Fallon	613	5.7	212	400	28	18	17	268	198	14.7	3.1	1 024	97.9	12.8
Fergus	2 768	1.0	227	1 750	195	151	69	906	481	22.5	8.5	679	97.3	22.2
Flathead	13 220	20.7	182	8 015	1 001	839	405	3 290	2 333	134.6	52.9	737	91.9	125.9
Gallatin	7 271	21.6	114	4 825	383	543	365	7 352	1 625	105.3	37.6	614	90.1	107.6
Garfield	265	−17.2	187	160	12	23	(3)	111	87	3.4	1.4	968	98.2	3.6
Glacier	1 615	1.9	128	905	397	424	70	804	809	36.5	7.6	602	97.8	39.9
Golden Valley	236	7.3	225	140	13	(3)	(3)	79	61	3.1	1.4	1 391	97.8	3.2
Granite	596	11.4	224	360	27	42	15	239	169	8.3	3.1	1 154	98.2	8.4
Hill	2 462	2.2	144	1 395	338	127	104	1 393	718	39.2	11.9	680	97.3	37.5
Jefferson	1 555	29.6	150	925	112	61	57	773	332	17.6	7.2	731	97.9	18.0
Judith Basin	445	−4.3	195	280	14	37	13	168	130	5.9	2.9	1 257	98.3	5.5
Lake	4 971	19.2	192	2 985	502	137	144	1 129	897	42.8	13.0	512	97.9	41.9
Lewis and Clark	9 132	20.2	169	5 740	801	1 354	306	7 154	1 799	104.6	37.5	703	94.6	103.2
Liberty	415	10.7	184	235	4	24	13	221	211	10.1	3.1	1 332	98.7	9.6
Lincoln	4 258	38.9	226	2 280	451	551	105	903	785	32.1	8.3	443	96.9	32.5
McCone	379	−22.7	197	250	22	20	11	149	85	4.6	2.4	1 183	98.4	4.8
Madison	1 445	19.9	209	980	34	76	39	415	360	19.4	7.7	1 118	85.3	19.0
Meagher	479	19.8	270	295	23	28	10	131	84	4.1	2.3	1 253	98.2	4.3
Mineral	840	20.9	217	515	73	65	21	250	192	12.1	3.8	1 007	98.2	11.9
Missoula	12 437	16.8	139	7 450	1 528	1 281	515	7 687	3 052	157.4	74.9	843	96.5	149.2
Musselshell	1 050	10.5	231	620	80	17	26	234	100	9.4	2.5	554	97.2	8.6
Park	2 519	1.2	158	1 650	208	[4]82	[4]89	[4]665	684	26.9	9.0	560	95.8	27.0
Petroleum	94	−6.0	186	65	4	(3)	(3)	60	26	2.3	.5	963	96.8	2.9

[1] Per 1,000 resident population estimated as of July 1, 1999. [2] Based on resident population estimated as of July 1, 1997. [3] Less than 10 employees. [4] Yellowstone National Park County included with Park County; data not available separately.

Sources: Social Security Program—U.S. Social Security Administration, OASDI Beneficiaries by State and County - December 1999, <http://www.ssa.gov/statistics/oasdi_sc/1999/oasdi_sc99.pdf> (accessed: 7 March 2001) for 1999 – annual publication of same title for 1990. Supplemental Security Income Program—U.S. Social Security Administration, SSI Recipients by State and County, <http://www.ssa.gov/statistics/ssi_st_cty/1999/ssi_st_cty.pdf> (accessed: November 2000). Government employment, 1998—U.S. Bureau of Economic Analysis, "Regional Economic Information System (REIS) 1969-1998" on CD-ROM (related Internet site <http://www.bea.doc.gov/bea/regional/data.htm>). Local government employment, 1997—U.S. Census Bureau, 1997 Census of Governments, Compendium of Public Employment, <http://www.census.gov/govs/apes/97coar2.dat> (accessed: 14 January 2000). Local government finances—U.S. Census Bureau, 1997 Census of Governments, Compendium of Government Finances, <http://www.census.gov/prod/gc97/gc974-5.pdf> (accessed: 16 February 2001).

[Includes U.S., states, and 3,142 counties/county equivalents defined as of January 1, 1992. For changes to these areas since January 1, 1992, see appendix B. Geographic Information]

County	Social Security Program beneficiaries, December 1999				Supplemental Security Income Program recipients, December 1999	Government employment, 1998			Local government employment, full-time equivalent, March 1997	Local government finances, 1996–1997				
	Total					Federal		State and local		General revenue				Direct general expenditure (mil. dol.)
						Civilian	Military				Taxes			
	Number	Percent change, 1990–1999	Rate[1]	Retired workers						Total (mil. dol.)	Total (mil. dol.)	Per capita[2]	Percent property	
MONTANA—Con.														
Phillips	1 008	−1.2	215	600	113	53	27	367	308	15.3	4.4	903	97.3	16.2
Pondera	1 330	7.3	213	830	106	43	36	437	313	15.1	4.7	723	96.7	15.9
Powder River	350	6.1	197	235	13	17	10	216	127	10.7	2.7	1 437	95.7	7.7
Powell	1 179	5.3	170	765	80	74	39	968	269	10.8	3.9	554	95.5	11.8
Prairie	322	−15.3	237	205	11	12	(3)	170	112	6.5	1.5	1 162	98.2	6.2
Ravalli	7 316	30.8	204	4 535	444	464	198	1 251	1 021	46.0	16.7	483	96.5	46.1
Richland	1 975	5.6	196	1 130	123	73	57	611	392	24.4	6.7	654	97.6	22.6
Roosevelt	1 817	2.4	167	1 010	277	227	62	795	806	38.6	7.5	675	98.2	37.6
Rosebud	1 298	18.0	132	705	167	187	56	584	513	54.1	11.7	1 147	98.9	52.7
Sanders	2 404	26.2	235	1 410	208	145	57	528	384	20.4	8.2	803	97.6	20.2
Sheridan	1 127	−8.0	275	730	42	73	24	293	222	11.4	3.6	848	98.0	11.1
Silver Bow	7 295	−4.8	215	4 410	817	322	209	2 119	793	64.5	23.8	693	87.8	76.7
Stillwater	1 487	15.3	179	950	83	34	45	381	240	15.2	6.6	845	97.2	14.9
Sweet Grass	722	−2.4	201	465	17	33	19	277	173	7.4	2.3	676	97.4	7.5
Teton	1 344	−.1	209	805	74	61	36	425	415	18.7	5.6	891	93.4	19.0
Toole	938	.3	202	600	63	70	27	563	396	23.8	5.9	1 218	97.2	20.7
Treasure	189	8.0	220	125	8	(3)	(3)	80	47	2.2	1.1	1 340	98.5	2.3
Valley	1 792	6.0	220	1 160	155	134	46	582	360	21.6	8.0	960	98.3	22.1
Wheatland	467	.4	205	315	27	41	13	153	105	5.2	2.7	1 141	98.0	5.3
Wibaux	255	−	228	150	15	(3)	(3)	92	79	3.6	1.5	1 314	98.7	4.0
Yellowstone	21 288	17.0	167	13 570	1 856	1 713	728	6 857	3 859	246.8	83.5	663	92.3	238.8
Yellowstone National Park	X	X	X	X	–	(4)	(4)	(4)	X	X	X	X	X	X
NEBRASKA	282 661	5.5	170	183 101	21 054	15 840	15 873	129 070	75 377	4 250.2	1 944.2	1 174	81.7	4 088.8
Adams	5 798	1.0	198	3 845	399	112	130	2 492	1 940	89.3	40.4	1 363	88.0	82.2
Antelope	1 708	−.7	236	1 095	69	39	32	519	401	17.3	8.6	1 175	90.8	18.7
Arthur	109	45.3	265	65	11	(3)	(3)	41	34	1.7	1.2	2 843	98.2	1.7
Banner	132	38.9	159	75	1	(3)	(3)	65	60	2.0	1.4	2 233	94.2	2.0
Blaine	92	−16.4	160	55	6	25	(3)	67	41	2.0	1.4	2 233	94.2	2.0
Boone	1 466	−5.4	231	925	62	38	28	565	248	21.1	8.7	1 349	90.7	23.7
Box Butte	1 953	2.5	154	1 260	141	60	57	955	591	35.2	12.2	937	82.5	33.6
Boyd	730	−15.6	290	415	37	17	11	277	148	8.8	3.2	1 191	89.7	8.1
Brown	924	−2.2	264	610	41	21	16	400	234	11.5	4.4	1 232	93.6	12.0
Buffalo	5 944	6.7	148	3 880	332	156	178	3 253	1 308	84.7	41.0	1 005	81.5	84.2
Burt	2 015	−.5	255	1 300	115	38	35	615	405	22.6	10.7	1 349	85.5	21.8
Butler	1 957	−3.6	227	1 240	78	53	38	543	330	25.2	12.7	1 469	95.5	27.2
Cass	3 707	12.3	149	2 395	136	77	108	1 036	766	42.7	21.3	891	94.8	45.4
Cedar	2 168	−1.0	226	1 345	65	97	43	654	396	21.5	8.9	906	88.5	19.7
Chase	1 021	.1	240	670	47	25	19	546	330	16.9	8.0	1 883	92.2	17.0
Cherry	1 327	1.7	210	820	105	51	28	484	272	19.8	8.1	1 268	90.2	20.4
Cheyenne	2 097	1.5	222	1 335	130	50	42	737	556	32.0	16.3	1 706	80.1	30.8
Clay	1 557	−10.0	219	975	64	160	32	684	429	20.6	12.2	1 703	93.9	19.5
Colfax	1 956	−25.5	183	1 230	65	76	47	581	383	19.8	8.7	828	89.5	20.0
Cuming	2 349	5.6	235	1 530	72	55	44	650	459	21.8	11.1	1 107	91.8	20.3
Custer	2 966	−3.9	251	1 870	146	52	53	891	691	31.1	17.1	1 411	92.7	31.0
Dakota	2 829	5.4	148	1 710	261	84	83	835	578	29.8	12.0	645	93.3	28.7
Dawes	1 677	1.3	190	1 075	114	141	40	978	391	17.5	7.9	880	77.2	18.5
Dawson	4 078	−1.3	175	2 645	243	104	102	1 808	1 267	83.0	30.2	1 303	84.1	79.7
Deuel	583	−2.0	293	390	19	14	(3)	195	153	8.8	4.6	2 264	89.2	8.5
Dixon	1 294	−11.7	203	835	51	39	28	402	333	15.4	6.7	1 053	91.5	19.6
Dodge	7 751	4.8	220	5 035	320	129	157	2 560	1 346	112.1	35.0	996	85.5	116.1
Douglas	63 652	3.8	143	41 475	7 316	5 726	2 542	30 119	19 751	1 131.3	571.6	1 296	73.1	1 023.9
Dundy	577	−11.9	265	370	27	16	10	232	193	10.1	3.9	1 675	90.7	9.1
Fillmore	1 608	−4.6	233	1 010	68	38	31	756	445	20.6	10.3	1 491	96.6	21.9
Franklin	1 067	−6.4	290	670	62	31	16	293	236	11.3	5.4	1 427	90.6	10.4
Frontier	624	−7.6	198	380	22	17	14	357	183	8.9	5.0	1 569	94.0	9.2
Furnas	1 539	−13.5	284	965	85	40	24	598	341	18.9	9.5	1 748	94.3	17.3
Gage	5 572	.1	245	3 495	425	108	100	2 234	854	51.3	19.1	838	94.9	52.7
Garden	669	−7.7	323	470	23	22	(3)	300	214	12.5	6.7	3 031	95.3	12.3
Garfield	593	−1.2	294	370	25	10	(3)	157	126	5.3	1.9	921	90.6	5.2
Gosper	635	30.9	281	425	18	15	10	167	80	6.2	4.5	1 996	60.7	5.8
Grant	184	11.5	258	115	7	(3)	(3)	90	63	2.9	2.1	2 802	94.5	3.1
Greeley	700	−6.0	249	460	35	15	13	279	187	10.5	4.3	1 473	94.6	10.3
Hall	8 920	3.8	172	5 840	729	607	230	3 625	2 003	118.2	53.6	1 042	79.3	117.1
Hamilton	1 845	15.7	193	1 150	55	36	42	573	331	23.8	11.7	1 237	97.8	18.8
Harlan	966	−1.4	263	695	41	38	17	267	153	9.0	2.9	764	90.3	9.4
Hayes	190	22.6	178	115	8	13	(3)	81	56	3.0	2.0	1 826	97.2	3.0
Hitchcock	865	−1.1	257	520	41	16	15	361	201	9.1	3.5	1 036	91.2	10.4
Holt	2 688	3.4	226	1 615	202	58	53	831	465	26.0	13.7	1 128	85.4	26.0

[1] Per 1,000 resident population estimated as of July 1, 1999. [2] Based on resident population estimated as of July 1, 1997. [3] Less than 10 employees. [4] Yellowstone National Park County included with Park County; data not available separately.

Sources: Social Security Program—U.S. Social Security Administration, OASDI Beneficiaries by State and County - December 1999, <http://www.ssa.gov/statistics/oasdi_sc/1999/oasdi_sc99.pdf> (accessed: 7 March 2001) for 1999 – annual publication of same title for 1990. Supplemental Security Income Program—U.S. Social Security Administration, SSI Recipients by State and County, <http://www.ssa.gov/statistics/ssi_st_cty/1999/ssi_st_cty.pdf> (accessed: November 2000). Government employment, 1998—U.S. Bureau of Economic Analysis, "Regional Economic Information System (REIS) 1969-1998" on CD-ROM (related Internet site <http://www.bea.doc.gov/bea/regional/data.htm>). Local government employment, 1997—U.S. Census Bureau, 1997 Census of Governments, Compendium of Public Employment, <http://www.census.gov/govs/apes/97coar2.dat> (accessed: 14 January 2000). Local government finances—U.S. Census Bureau, 1997 Census of Governments, Compendium of Government Finances, <http://www.census.gov/prod/gc97/gc974-5.pdf> (accessed: 16 February 2001).

[Includes U.S., states, and 3,142 counties/county equivalents defined as of January 1, 1992. For changes to these areas since January 1, 1992, see appendix B. Geographic Information]

County	Social Security Program beneficiaries, December 1999				Supplemental Security Income Program recipients, December 1999	Government employment, 1998			Local government employment, full-time equivalent, March 1997	Local government finances, 1996–1997				
	Total			Retired workers		Federal		State and local		General revenue				Direct general expenditure (mil. dol.)
	Number	Percent change, 1990–1999	Rate¹			Civilian	Military			Total (mil. dol.)	Taxes			
											Total (mil. dol.)	Per capita²	Percent property	
NEBRASKA—Con.														
Hooker	238	−10.2	345	170	6	(³)	(³)	93	84	3.3	1.8	2 490	91.1	3.2
Howard	1 332	−1.3	204	855	61	32	28	440	429	17.5	7.1	1 101	89.8	16.6
Jefferson	2 168	−7.4	262	1 425	132	39	37	507	430	20.8	10.9	1 300	88.8	21.4
Johnson	1 196	−5.1	263	800	39	38	20	424	298	15.8	6.1	1 334	91.3	15.5
Kearney	1 285	−5.5	187	820	84	31	30	512	378	22.0	10.9	1 619	90.1	19.7
Keith	1 980	9.4	223	1 360	106	34	38	564	419	22.5	12.8	1 490	70.2	22.8
Keya Paha	237	7.7	249	140	9	(³)	(³)	69	39	2.1	1.4	1 446	96.3	2.1
Kimball	1 039	11.7	258	665	41	18	18	372	253	13.0	5.1	1 273	87.4	12.9
Knox	2 497	−5.4	276	1 525	189	55	41	1 014	456	24.2	10.2	1 086	89.1	22.3
Lancaster	32 171	13.6	135	21 635	3 066	2 577	1 093	26 604	10 027	605.8	273.3	1 171	78.9	588.9
Lincoln	5 589	3.9	165	3 460	585	239	148	2 402	1 435	97.2	48.5	1 447	83.1	86.6
Logan	173	−11.3	193	100	8	(³)	(³)	80	57	2.6	1.4	1 534	93.1	2.3
Loup	162	35.0	248	95	7	(³)	(³)	55	44	1.8	1.1	1 639	95.1	1.6
McPherson	121	5.2	221	70	9	(³)	(³)	36	25	1.2	.8	1 444	97.3	1.2
Madison	6 308	2.0	185	4 085	468	241	153	3 193	1 718	96.5	40.2	1 156	81.6	106.2
Merrick	1 783	6.1	221	1 085	89	36	36	571	422	27.3	11.4	1 400	88.7	26.1
Morrill	1 150	−2.1	217	710	90	24	24	488	271	20.7	8.7	1 602	91.5	18.3
Nance	1 000	5.3	246	615	71	19	18	391	181	8.3	3.8	903	90.2	10.3
Nemaha	1 674	−3.2	220	1 075	112	40	34	1 546	367	21.9	7.9	1 017	86.8	21.2
Nuckolls	1 508	−3.3	294	990	62	35	23	389	267	12.6	5.4	1 011	89.4	12.4
Otoe	3 296	2.2	223	2 240	143	63	65	1 034	625	35.4	20.3	1 400	74.7	32.3
Pawnee	989	−7.1	320	680	56	25	14	254	201	11.6	4.1	1 284	93.3	10.9
Perkins	719	−9.6	224	485	23	20	14	384	411	17.9	5.8	1 773	97.6	16.4
Phelps	2 077	7.9	211	1 370	108	42	44	793	531	24.2	14.1	1 415	87.3	24.8
Pierce	1 605	−5.3	202	960	59	35	35	469	360	22.1	9.8	1 238	78.9	20.5
Platte	5 328	17.7	175	3 595	246	125	136	2 397	3 439	86.2	31.3	1 022	87.7	57.3
Polk	1 306	−1.8	237	885	36	24	25	474	332	16.8	8.9	1 592	91.6	17.2
Red Willow	2 534	8.5	224	1 705	178	68	50	1 016	485	29.2	10.7	942	90.8	23.8
Richardson	2 511	−7.7	269	1 580	180	49	42	597	441	17.5	8.5	898	91.6	17.2
Rock	430	−6.5	254	275	24	(³)	(³)	231	94	7.3	3.5	1 974	94.9	7.0
Saline	2 764	−4.9	211	1 785	99	70	57	1 162	689	39.0	14.0	1 076	85.7	40.7
Sarpy	10 924	134.7	89	6 945	379	2 468	8 428	4 187	3 025	204.2	89.1	752	82.4	223.6
Saunders	3 481	.9	181	2 210	148	104	85	1 189	724	39.6	18.1	942	92.8	39.4
Scotts Bluff	8 198	8.8	227	5 100	850	172	159	2 683	1 883	106.5	39.3	1 083	84.9	107.4
Seward	2 879	7.4	175	1 895	85	59	72	943	574	36.9	20.3	1 255	93.6	34.2
Sheridan	1 565	−7.4	244	1 050	86	30	28	766	575	21.9	6.9	1 048	80.4	20.5
Sherman	919	−.1	265	600	43	21	15	287	154	8.9	4.4	1 238	94.8	9.0
Sioux	242	61.3	170	160	3	17	(³)	85	58	2.9	1.7	1 157	95.4	2.9
Stanton	944	30.2	155	555	31	21	27	331	147	8.0	3.1	504	93.9	8.3
Thayer	1 760	−6.4	285	1 135	85	37	28	638	352	20.1	9.3	1 478	95.9	20.7
Thomas	199	−5.2	246	120	11	14	(³)	84	37	2.3	1.2	1 494	94.5	2.1
Thurston	1 198	−2.6	170	670	192	145	32	591	432	21.7	4.1	563	94.0	19.6
Valley	1 260	−6.0	278	810	80	33	20	653	470	21.5	6.8	1 438	87.1	17.6
Washington	2 858	18.6	152	1 945	82	52	82	1 476	526	39.2	20.7	1 127	87.3	43.9
Wayne	1 597	9.0	174	1 045	77	39	41	1 048	341	18.9	8.1	855	83.5	19.5
Webster	1 184	−9.6	301	735	63	29	18	299	222	12.4	4.7	1 177	93.2	13.1
Wheeler	199	2.1	215	125	7	(³)	(³)	72	46	2.4	1.6	1 741	98.8	2.5
York	2 998	3.9	208	1 990	106	60	64	1 024	631	44.4	18.7	1 280	92.3	35.7
NEVADA	271 205	61.2	150	183 219	24 395	14 155	11 329	96 433	56 607	5 169.5	1 522.8	909	61.5	5 356.3
Churchill	3 625	26.7	155	2 335	275	740	1 154	1 271	887	65.3	11.6	510	81.4	62.2
Clark	180 506	73.6	148	121 845	17 729	8 426	8 944	54 990	34 534	3 420.1	1 030.1	932	55.4	3 652.8
Douglas	7 248	90.7	193	5 300	176	97	78	1 764	1 323	105.6	38.5	1 068	76.1	96.2
Elko	3 459	43.8	76	2 070	328	367	97	3 280	1 628	141.1	25.3	556	80.1	141.9
Esmeralda	229	63.6	204	140	20	(³)	(³)	106	102	4.6	1.5	1 303	96.9	4.5
Eureka	247	45.3	133	160	16	(³)	(³)	248	194	18.3	9.7	5 230	97.0	22.3
Humboldt	1 685	39.3	94	1 045	179	140	38	1 143	1 005	73.0	15.7	896	81.7	64.1
Lander	591	39.1	88	335	71	82	15	473	335	30.0	6.8	936	95.0	32.8
Lincoln	857	36.0	203	550	54	33	(³)	586	239	16.8	2.9	698	92.5	15.7
Lyon	6 527	51.6	207	4 395	379	57	63	1 351	1 026	67.2	16.9	585	79.8	67.6
Mineral	1 221	25.9	236	780	109	96	16	428	349	27.1	4.2	745	84.6	27.0
Nye	8 160	227.1	275	5 720	348	181	72	1 391	1 171	87.9	21.4	792	86.1	84.6
Pershing	639	20.6	133	390	59	13	11	673	368	24.5	6.0	1 253	86.2	23.4
Storey	569	191.8	190	395	15	(³)	(³)	197	177	12.4	5.1	1 751	78.2	9.4
Washoe	44 480	30.8	139	30 045	3 897	3 178	692	18 633	10 535	874.3	293.3	957	69.6	870.2
White Pine	1 600	14.3	163	975	125	186	21	1 038	503	32.8	7.3	719	89.6	30.2
Independent City														
Carson City city	9 557	16.3	191	6 735	558	542	107	8 861	2 231	168.6	26.7	548	72.4	151.5

¹ Per 1,000 resident population estimated as of July 1, 1999. ² Based on resident population estimated as of July 1, 1997. ³ Less than 10 employees.

Sources: Social Security Program—U.S. Social Security Administration, OASDI Beneficiaries by State and County - December 1999, <http://www.ssa.gov/statistics/oasdi_sc/1999/oasdi_sc99.pdf> (accessed: 7 March 2001) for 1999 – annual publication of same title for 1990. Supplemental Security Income Program—U.S. Social Security Administration, SSI Recipients by State and County, <http://www.ssa.gov/statistics/ssi_st_cty/1999/ssi_st_cty.pdf> (accessed: November 2000). Government employment, 1998—U.S. Bureau of Economic Analysis, "Regional Economic Information System (REIS) 1969-1998" on CD-ROM (related Internet site <http://www.bea.doc.gov/bea/regional/data.htm>). Local government employment, 1997—U.S. Census Bureau, 1997 Census of Governments, Compendium of Public Employment, <http://www.census.gov/govs/apes/97coar2.dat> (accessed: 14 January 2000). Local government finances—U.S. Census Bureau, 1997 Census of Governments, Compendium of Government Finances, <http://www.census.gov/prod/gc97/gc974-5.pdf> (accessed: 16 February 2001).

Table B–13. Counties — **Government Programs, Employment, and Finances**–Con.

[Includes U.S., states, and 3,142 counties/county equivalents defined as of January 1, 1992. For changes to these areas since January 1, 1992, see appendix B. Geographic Information]

County	Social Security Program beneficiaries, December 1999				Supplemental Security Income Program recipients, December 1999	Government employment, 1998			Local government employment, full-time equivalent, March 1997	Local government finances, 1996–1997				
	Total			Retired workers		Federal		State and local		General revenue				Direct general expenditure (mil. dol.)
	Number	Percent change, 1990–1999	Rate[1]			Civilian	Military			Total (mil. dol.)	Taxes			
											Total (mil. dol.)	Per capita[2]	Percent property	
NEW HAMPSHIRE	195 065	20.7	162	129 909	11 445	8 083	4 374	68 780	38 830	2 539.4	1 836.7	1 566	98.8	2 454.8
Belknap	11 604	23.4	216	8 000	649	229	185	3 157	2 190	138.3	99.5	1 907	99.6	129.0
Carroll	9 637	27.5	240	6 645	400	129	138	2 249	1 556	108.7	79.7	2 057	98.7	101.6
Cheshire	12 967	11.5	179	8 850	733	200	252	4 449	2 622	175.7	120.9	1 683	99.3	165.4
Coos	8 332	8.1	255	5 295	552	151	115	2 308	1 385	96.4	59.2	1 785	98.2	80.2
Grafton	14 204	18.2	181	9 530	730	680	282	5 756	3 146	204.9	149.8	1 922	98.8	194.0
Hillsborough	53 311	20.5	145	35 220	3 548	3 963	1 315	14 420	10 947	716.7	518.3	1 449	98.4	678.5
Merrimack	22 052	13.4	170	14 450	1 487	868	450	13 371	4 432	264.4	190.6	1 506	99.2	275.7
Rockingham	37 916	33.0	138	25 300	1 480	1 421	1 102	10 915	7 805	538.9	418.9	1 571	99.1	564.4
Strafford	16 843	20.6	152	11 155	1 204	332	395	9 394	3 332	213.5	148.5	1 365	98.5	187.0
Sullivan	8 191	22.8	203	5 460	653	110	140	2 761	1 415	82.0	51.3	1 289	98.2	79.0
NEW JERSEY	1 322 550	7.6	162	902 780	145 376	65 637	30 205	491 838	298 363	24 746.9	12 988.6	1 613	98.4	24 199.8
Atlantic	41 903	7.0	175	28 170	4 981	2 508	704	17 301	10 573	880.9	477.6	2 022	98.6	991.4
Bergen	149 015	4.9	174	109 320	8 256	3 156	2 070	37 858	29 330	2 628.6	1 691.6	1 987	98.9	2 557.7
Burlington	65 497	28.7	154	44 040	4 085	5 949	6 338	21 003	15 254	1 072.7	529.6	1 262	98.4	1 116.5
Camden	79 824	2.0	159	50 620	11 954	3 377	1 219	30 211	21 933	1 865.9	677.5	1 342	98.7	1 762.3
Cape May	24 814	7.3	253	17 145	1 559	362	1 423	7 990	5 569	428.4	252.1	2 574	97.9	432.4
Cumberland	25 380	–.6	181	15 870	4 435	759	339	11 204	6 713	463.2	121.7	863	98.7	434.9
Essex	113 365	–3.8	152	72 670	25 479	9 402	1 823	63 285	27 489	2 428.2	1 222.5	1 628	96.0	2 329.5
Gloucester	38 487	23.2	154	24 245	2 874	542	597	14 956	10 048	669.6	293.1	1 192	98.5	674.8
Hudson	77 834	–3.4	141	50 225	21 451	8 293	1 483	35 769	16 770	1 636.7	666.5	1 204	98.5	1 485.4
Hunterdon	15 314	27.2	123	10 585	637	377	295	6 653	3 934	343.7	230.2	1 909	98.8	365.9
Mercer	55 409	4.5	166	36 935	7 990	3 140	842	48 380	14 322	1 212.4	560.9	1 700	98.7	1 164.8
Middlesex	107 531	14.2	150	74 350	9 385	3 395	1 855	47 869	26 594	1 983.6	1 136.3	1 606	98.2	1 950.5
Monmouth	94 020	8.8	154	63 555	6 710	8 967	4 410	29 477	22 900	1 895.4	1 053.5	1 765	97.8	1 844.0
Morris	61 933	21.0	134	44 305	3 250	5 148	1 184	22 676	16 714	1 445.7	921.3	2 027	99.1	1 435.7
Ocean	131 208	16.3	264	97 185	4 613	2 987	1 823	20 082	15 459	1 213.5	699.3	1 450	98.8	1 217.4
Passaic	72 123	.1	149	47 870	13 447	1 890	1 171	23 763	14 424	1 223.5	624.7	1 296	98.8	1 145.9
Salem	12 491	10.7	194	7 910	1 165	185	156	3 936	3 013	239.0	83.4	1 279	97.7	235.4
Somerset	36 732	27.1	128	26 170	1 790	2 598	682	12 406	9 158	774.9	523.5	1 894	98.7	756.6
Sussex	17 805	19.6	123	11 250	1 376	370	345	6 553	5 338	410.6	229.1	1 615	99.1	391.0
Union	85 142	–2.6	171	59 095	8 667	1 958	1 209	25 312	18 998	1 616.8	831.7	1 671	98.6	1 584.2
Warren	16 706	7.1	167	11 260	1 110	274	237	5 154	3 830	313.5	162.5	1 657	99.1	323.7
NEW MEXICO	270 658	23.6	156	158 310	45 911	29 867	18 427	138 207	69 941	3 850.4	881.0	511	55.1	3 900.0
Bernalillo	79 967	19.6	153	49 140	11 164	13 476	6 330	43 440	19 920	1 290.2	345.2	657	60.1	1 308.3
Catron	825	47.3	288	505	73	117	10	217	174	7.1	1.0	368	94.7	8.1
Chaves	11 646	7.0	187	7 025	1 980	377	230	4 495	2 947	167.8	25.7	411	39.3	159.1
Cibola	3 601	98.4	134	1 750	623	396	93	1 551	899	43.5	6.7	257	42.9	41.5
Colfax	2 981	18.1	218	1 830	381	53	48	1 370	646	39.7	9.1	666	52.3	38.4
Curry	6 552	16.6	150	3 665	1 364	995	3 549	2 341	1 941	87.7	16.7	359	42.4	91.5
DeBaca	631	–1.4	267	390	83	15	(3)	231	121	6.1	.8	320	67.8	6.2
Dona Ana	23 065	36.0	135	13 600	4 818	3 608	670	14 177	8 036	371.2	61.6	370	54.2	387.8
Eddy	10 246	7.6	193	5 770	1 394	479	189	2 869	2 500	116.9	30.1	567	48.1	118.9
Grant	6 544	25.8	209	3 870	700	237	111	2 943	1 557	84.6	12.0	382	53.1	80.5
Guadalupe	933	24.4	232	470	249	24	14	362	268	13.3	2.2	501	50.5	13.3
Harding	264	–5.7	309	175	22	16	(3)	87	65	4.2	.5	556	67.9	4.1
Hidalgo	995	14.4	165	555	182	57	22	465	319	20.0	3.1	491	72.3	20.1
Lea	9 332	11.3	169	5 125	1 427	117	198	3 284	2 581	139.3	37.9	677	50.9	132.1
Lincoln	3 996	44.8	238	2 655	303	123	58	1 025	786	49.0	14.2	884	63.0	46.7
Los Alamos	2 165	25.9	118	1 560	47	209	70	9 635	1 261	62.1	11.6	636	40.8	61.0
Luna	5 484	15.9	225	3 525	760	179	85	1 379	1 082	43.7	7.1	301	54.0	42.6
McKinley	7 053	18.5	105	3 190	3 676	2 382	238	3 966	2 803	135.2	24.3	361	53.9	155.3
Mora	1 119	27.2	226	560	337	37	17	291	198	13.2	1.7	354	58.1	13.0
Otero	9 040	46.9	167	5 490	1 062	2 114	4 535	2 754	1 727	85.5	17.0	307	52.3	86.0
Quay	2 402	8.9	243	1 440	414	75	35	987	472	23.5	4.9	483	45.2	24.2
Rio Arriba	6 897	25.1	181	3 235	1 820	423	133	2 612	1 459	72.6	13.6	362	53.3	72.5
Roosevelt	2 925	1.7	168	1 700	558	62	64	1 804	696	29.4	4.5	246	48.4	28.6
Sandoval	12 122	53.2	134	7 455	1 350	370	310	3 113	2 471	121.4	31.0	360	53.7	132.0
San Juan	14 362	29.6	131	7 440	3 263	1 644	376	5 799	4 749	281.4	67.4	651	60.6	308.1
San Miguel	4 848	17.2	170	2 465	1 849	157	102	3 849	1 279	70.7	13.4	467	64.2	73.1
Santa Fe	17 286	36.4	139	10 720	1 824	1 245	441	13 751	3 820	232.7	75.0	617	39.6	256.5
Sierra	3 962	10.5	360	2 650	461	116	39	744	404	19.7	3.5	316	73.4	22.7
Socorro	2 479	30.8	150	1 275	662	222	58	1 976	560	26.8	4.0	245	55.2	27.6
Taos	4 951	34.2	183	2 700	1 054	270	95	1 584	1 153	58.3	12.9	485	47.3	63.0
Torrance	2 274	38.7	139	1 150	390	82	54	966	856	40.1	6.8	463	78.5	41.5
Union	982	6.2	252	590	95	55	14	336	237	12.7	1.9	462	49.6	12.1
Valencia	8 708	23.7	134	4 625	1 482	135	228	3 804	1 954	80.8	13.8	221	65.7	89.6

[1] Per 1,000 resident population estimated as of July 1, 1999. [2] Based on resident population estimated as of July 1, 1997. [3] Less than 10 employees.

Sources: Social Security Program—U.S. Social Security Administration, OASDI Beneficiaries by State and County - December 1999, <http://www.ssa.gov/statistics/oasdi_sc/1999/oasdi_sc99.pdf> (accessed: 7 March 2001) for 1999 – annual publication of same title for 1990. Supplemental Security Income Program—U.S. Social Security Administration, SSI Recipients by State and County, <http://www.ssa.gov/statistics/ssi_st_cty/1999/ssi_st_cty.pdf> (accessed: November 2000). Government employment, 1998—U.S. Bureau of Economic Analysis, "Regional Economic Information System (REIS) 1969-1998" on CD-ROM (related Internet site <http://www.bea.doc.gov/bea/regional/data.htm>). Local government employment, 1997—U.S. Census Bureau, 1997 Census of Governments, Compendium of Public Employment, <http://www.census.gov/govs/apes/97coar2.dat> (accessed: 14 January 2000). Local government finances—U.S. Census Bureau, 1997 Census of Governments, Compendium of Government Finances, <http://www.census.gov/prod/gc97/gc974-5.pdf> (accessed: 16 February 2001).

Table B–13. Counties — Government Programs, Employment, and Finances–Con.

[Includes U.S., states, and 3,142 counties/county equivalents defined as of January 1, 1992. For changes to these areas since January 1, 1992, see appendix B. Geographic Information]

County	Social Security Program beneficiaries, December 1999				Supplemental Security Income Program recipients, December 1999	Government employment, 1998			Local government employment, full-time equivalent, March 1997	Local government finances, 1996–1997				
	Total			Retired workers		Federal		State and local		General revenue				Direct general expend-iture (mil. dol.)
	Number	Percent change, 1990–1999	Rate[1]			Civilian	Military			Total (mil. dol.)	Taxes			
											Total (mil. dol.)	Per capita[2]	Percent property	
NEW YORK	2 966 658	4.8	163	1 919 252	608 986	138 893	57 885	1 242 103	860 168	86 743.9	40 603.8	2 238	59.4	80 961.2
Albany	52 049	7.3	178	34 795	6 184	6 479	991	62 955	12 328	1 003.4	540.9	1 837	66.8	957.5
Allegany	9 495	11.2	188	5 915	1 466	145	103	3 594	2 163	162.2	57.5	1 131	78.5	177.7
Bronx	159 296	–3.3	133	94 710	82 023	8 456	2 491	15 809	(3)	(3)	(3)	(3)	(3)	177.7
Broome	43 282	2.8	222	28 720	5 181	843	414	17 000	9 747	679.9	314.4	1 587	74.0	650.0
Cattaraugus	16 578	3.1	196	10 420	2 645	232	180	7 185	4 065	303.8	112.9	1 326	70.4	301.4
Cayuga	14 567	–.3	178	9 705	1 911	186	166	5 397	3 174	239.4	93.9	1 139	71.8	249.3
Chautauqua	29 528	.3	215	19 130	4 052	414	283	9 312	6 389	483.0	189.6	1 360	79.6	490.8
Chemung	19 317	2.0	211	12 280	2 795	444	198	6 922	3 672	284.8	107.2	1 158	71.4	281.7
Chenango	10 436	10.3	206	6 565	1 527	124	103	3 732	2 519	176.0	74.1	1 436	87.1	170.4
Clinton	13 630	22.8	171	7 785	2 474	524	163	7 389	3 669	255.3	93.7	1 171	72.1	170.4
Columbia	12 955	8.8	206	8 535	1 709	191	129	4 000	2 671	202.3	102.9	1 626	78.4	247.3
Cortland	8 291	9.6	173	5 325	1 255	99	98	3 404	2 079	158.4	63.7	1 322	65.9	152.3
Delaware	11 087	17.9	239	7 000	1 242	157	93	4 136	2 595	197.1	76.5	1 647	89.7	202.8
Dutchess	45 759	17.2	171	28 230	4 943	1 443	539	20 265	10 190	866.8	462.0	1 753	79.7	862.9
Erie	189 698	1.6	205	119 755	25 209	9 100	2 295	63 083	40 450	3 231.0	1 413.2	1 499	69.9	3 190.4
Essex	7 884	4.8	210	4 975	1 011	389	76	3 800	1 645	144.6	75.0	1 990	82.7	143.9
Franklin	9 645	8.1	199	5 430	1 693	151	98	6 011	2 518	167.8	58.8	1 198	83.0	170.3
Fulton	11 427	1.7	216	7 620	1 628	112	109	4 089	2 607	201.8	71.3	1 335	81.9	216.5
Genesee	11 284	3.8	187	7 450	1 028	577	124	4 686	3 003	260.1	82.5	1 353	72.4	247.9
Greene	10 050	10.0	208	6 445	1 080	112	97	3 711	1 923	154.2	83.4	1 750	81.4	146.1
Hamilton	1 404	9.7	271	1 030	108	15	11	617	472	29.9	22.5	4 344	91.8	29.6
Herkimer	14 065	–.1	222	9 335	1 720	136	136	4 528	3 230	204.9	79.9	1 229	78.8	215.8
Jefferson	17 677	4.2	161	10 655	2 778	2 834	10 891	7 868	4 552	362.1	125.0	1 112	74.9	359.4
Kings	293 361	–8.6	129	182 020	142 108	8 778	5 023	23 909	3399 397	345 887.1	319 368.2	32 623	338.1	340 418.6
Lewis	4 945	16.6	181	2 955	640	65	56	2 061	1 580	106.8	30.7	1 113	85.0	104.0
Livingston	10 415	13.1	158	6 730	1 020	165	134	6 668	2 599	189.8	74.2	1 129	80.4	181.2
Madison	11 579	12.9	163	7 310	1 280	162	144	4 016	2 719	204.7	85.0	1 200	86.6	217.1
Monroe	124 773	7.3	175	83 515	17 040	3 105	1 540	42 922	30 294	2 629.4	1 206.5	1 681	72.6	2 615.4
Montgomery	13 061	–1.5	259	9 000	1 451	119	103	2 935	2 386	176.4	61.6	1 202	78.2	185.5
Nassau	237 187	7.7	182	162 615	16 304	7 094	2 990	71 876	55 117	5 981.3	4 027.2	3 099	81.8	6 158.5
New York	208 346	1.6	134	145 380	76 948	32 214	3 362	421 912	(3)	(3)	(3)	(3)	(3)	(3)
Niagara	45 866	5.0	212	28 490	4 862	1 166	458	11 366	9 166	807.0	323.9	1 476	76.5	790.7
Oneida	50 611	1.0	220	31 540	7 406	2 198	601	20 369	10 644	827.8	325.9	1 402	72.7	809.1
Onondaga	82 654	7.7	181	54 255	10 994	4 332	1 269	35 494	21 747	1 571.2	706.1	1 533	74.8	1 621.3
Ontario	17 582	13.5	176	11 790	1 665	1 225	203	6 729	4 603	342.9	157.9	1 584	74.5	336.6
Orange	48 536	16.1	145	28 960	6 290	5 516	6 449	19 429	13 473	1 503.0	553.4	1 694	80.1	1 488.2
Orleans	7 654	12.5	170	4 825	902	92	90	4 299	1 786	129.0	48.3	1 076	76.9	121.8
Oswego	21 282	13.1	172	12 080	2 882	243	268	8 830	6 312	452.0	213.6	1 713	92.9	447.0
Otsego	12 056	6.3	199	7 755	1 516	171	124	4 344	2 769	172.2	71.8	1 183	82.8	169.9
Putnam	12 232	34.0	129	7 855	735	208	189	3 575	3 286	294.9	204.2	2 215	88.6	285.6
Queens	293 793	–1.9	147	199 545	72 888	12 923	4 132	20 298	(3)	(3)	(3)	(3)	(3)	(3)
Rensselaer	26 868	5.8	177	17 625	3 104	395	337	9 691	6 516	531.7	208.5	1 363	78.6	554.3
Richmond	67 026	20.7	162	39 170	10 828	1 264	1 144	5 455	(3)	(3)	(3)	(3)	(3)	(3)
Rockland	43 193	25.3	152	28 440	4 950	668	570	18 319	10 829	1 184.5	761.3	2 735	80.3	1 117.3
St. Lawrence	20 867	7.5	185	11 750	3 757	501	253	10 135	4 964	368.5	124.5	1 095	76.8	357.4
Saratoga	30 445	24.1	152	19 560	2 583	388	1 667	10 867	7 287	534.7	285.2	1 457	76.3	500.1
Schenectady	30 425	–6.4	211	20 210	3 693	727	368	9 221	5 997	471.9	229.7	1 571	78.2	468.5
Schoharie	6 026	7.3	188	3 720	742	93	66	2 574	1 518	101.5	43.1	1 335	82.9	104.1
Schuyler	3 917	27.4	204	2 420	492	56	39	1 034	696	51.4	19.4	1 019	80.9	47.1
Seneca	6 759	13.5	212	4 350	737	223	70	2 197	1 292	99.3	39.2	1 218	75.9	93.7
Steuben	19 872	6.3	203	12 315	2 867	955	199	6 865	5 028	368.7	128.4	1 305	73.4	371.8
Suffolk	226 005	22.1	163	140 110	21 705	12 696	3 023	83 523	52 203	5 486.0	3 377.9	2 484	80.5	5 398.3
Sullivan	15 224	4.8	220	9 140	2 747	222	140	5 681	3 977	312.2	156.8	2 254	86.5	306.1
Tioga	9 385	26.3	180	5 985	973	173	113	2 443	2 186	150.1	54.4	1 039	81.8	140.0
Tompkins	11 949	10.7	122	7 925	1 557	315	216	5 814	3 980	293.8	136.1	1 399	73.0	282.6
Ulster	31 868	16.9	190	19 750	4 299	464	351	12 625	7 143	596.9	335.1	2 007	81.9	574.4
Warren	13 007	14.3	212	8 265	1 460	268	132	4 070	3 195	219.5	117.9	1 924	73.4	213.4
Washington	10 921	8.1	182	6 850	1 422	136	123	4 918	3 067	197.6	74.6	1 236	84.3	189.6
Wayne	17 422	20.2	182	10 660	2 067	199	193	6 675	4 329	315.9	126.2	1 334	82.0	301.2
Westchester	147 711	5.3	163	104 635	14 563	6 022	1 820	54 302	39 330	4 215.4	2 548.0	2 842	82.7	4 128.7
Wyoming	7 266	10.4	164	4 555	657	113	89	4 138	2 192	133.8	43.0	971	75.8	130.5
Yates	5 129	6.9	209	3 365	585	76	49	1 031	900	66.2	35.1	1 454	85.9	57.7

[1] Per 1,000 resident population estimated as of July 1, 1999.   [2] Based on resident population estimated as of July 1, 1997.   [3] Bronx, New York, Queens, and Richmond Counties included with Kings County; data not available separately.

Sources: Social Security Program—U.S. Social Security Administration, OASDI Beneficiaries by State and County - December 1999, <http://www.ssa.gov/statistics/oasdi_sc/1999/oasdi_sc99.pdf> (accessed: 7 March 2001) for 1999 – annual publication of same title for 1990.   Supplemental Security Income Program—U.S. Social Security Administration, SSI Recipients by State and County, <http://www.ssa.gov/statistics/ssi_st_cty/1999/ssi_st_cty.pdf> (accessed: November 2000).   Government employment, 1998—U.S. Bureau of Economic Analysis, "Regional Economic Information System (REIS) 1969-1998" on CD-ROM (related Internet site <http://www.bea.doc.gov/bea/regional/data.htm>).   Local government employment, 1997—U.S. Census Bureau, 1997 Census of Governments, Compendium of Public Employment, <http://www.census.gov/govs/apes/97coar2.dat> (accessed: 14 January 2000).   Local government finances—U.S. Census Bureau, 1997 Census of Governments, Compendium of Government Finances, <http://www.census.gov/prod/gc97/gc974-5.pdf> (accessed: 16 February 2001).

Table B–13. Counties — Government Programs, Employment, and Finances–Con.

[Includes U.S., states, and 3,142 counties/county equivalents defined as of January 1, 1992. For changes to these areas since January 1, 1992, see appendix B. Geographic Information]

County	Social Security Program beneficiaries, December 1999 — Total — Number	Total — Percent change, 1990–1999	Total — Rate[1]	Retired workers	Supplemental Security Income Program recipients, December 1999	Government employment, 1998 — Federal — Civilian	Federal — Military	State and local	Local government employment, full-time equivalent, March 1997	Local government finances, 1996–1997 — General revenue — Total (mil. dol.)	Taxes — Total (mil. dol.)	Taxes — Per capita[2]	Taxes — Percent property	Direct general expenditure (mil. dol.)
NORTH CAROLINA......	1 322 399	23.1	173	813 306	191 841	61 370	120 100	533 782	293 505	18 300.2	5 062.8	682	75.2	17 582.4
Alamance..............	24 606	14.6	203	16 805	2 364	271	371	5 789	3 938	226.3	61.3	519	74.4	222.7
Alexander.............	5 238	28.7	164	3 335	527	54	97	1 245	862	41.1	11.1	364	63.8	36.8
Alleghany.............	2 612	12.3	265	1 650	381	49	31	489	355	17.7	5.4	554	73.4	16.3
Anson.................	5 098	7.0	210	2 860	1 036	63	76	2 305	1 440	85.5	11.4	470	76.3	83.7
Ashe..................	5 731	19.8	236	3 490	1 040	76	75	1 045	681	31.4	10.3	430	67.7	28.6
Avery.................	3 483	15.5	220	2 220	533	51	49	943	587	29.2	11.5	735	75.0	27.6
Beaufort..............	10 258	20.2	227	5 765	1 891	132	138	2 909	1 957	116.0	24.1	545	72.6	116.3
Bertie................	5 129	19.6	252	2 515	1 561	101	64	1 125	736	39.1	7.7	376	74.3	34.4
Bladen................	6 844	28.3	221	3 445	1 907	119	95	2 270	1 469	85.9	16.8	548	76.4	87.4
Brunswick.............	16 831	65.4	236	10 670	1 901	344	260	3 401	2 108	149.7	63.1	958	79.6	139.4
Buncombe.............	41 331	17.1	211	26 290	4 436	2 654	665	12 449	7 247	427.7	144.1	749	74.1	425.6
Burke.................	15 626	17.5	188	9 990	1 833	151	257	7 881	2 868	144.5	35.8	438	86.1	136.4
Cabarrus..............	20 647	6.5	165	14 020	1 809	248	373	8 866	4 050	227.4	76.3	656	78.0	219.8
Caldwell..............	14 218	25.8	186	8 955	1 385	131	236	3 866	2 834	130.4	30.9	409	72.2	131.1
Camden...............	1 341	24.2	195	810	136	12	21	337	237	12.0	3.2	483	73.7	11.4
Carteret..............	12 635	38.0	210	8 235	1 091	252	414	3 948	1 911	146.5	41.4	697	70.0	161.1
Caswell...............	4 347	30.3	194	2 435	811	51	69	1 587	838	32.4	8.3	374	67.4	31.1
Catawba..............	24 621	24.8	183	16 830	1 956	548	413	7 973	5 982	358.8	83.4	640	73.9	346.1
Chatham..............	8 947	46.4	192	6 020	714	131	141	1 905	1 310	74.4	27.4	610	76.7	82.9
Cherokee.............	6 436	26.1	278	3 870	1 009	148	71	1 191	876	40.7	10.3	460	61.3	44.3
Chowan...............	3 460	10.7	242	2 110	550	38	44	843	643	27.5	7.7	544	72.4	29.2
Clay..................	2 443	26.9	279	1 545	286	24	27	410	248	12.8	3.8	460	67.7	12.7
Cleveland.............	19 234	21.6	205	11 905	2 575	203	288	5 074	4 597	239.4	46.0	500	75.6	234.0
Columbus.............	12 281	20.3	232	5 735	3 803	147	164	3 351	2 311	109.6	23.8	454	74.0	106.2
Craven...............	16 610	30.4	186	10 485	2 511	6 253	8 537	7 490	3 314	267.0	42.5	483	70.1	278.1
Cumberland...........	35 129	36.1	124	18 260	7 271	10 355	45 494	19 320	13 429	709.7	158.4	555	72.9	735.1
Currituck.............	2 882	24.0	157	1 745	258	47	56	952	623	40.7	19.9	1 158	73.5	40.5
Dare.................	5 155	52.3	174	3 460	249	221	238	2 204	1 373	84.3	44.6	1 598	70.5	82.1
Davidson.............	25 278	34.5	177	16 510	2 272	184	439	5 995	4 682	214.6	59.3	426	70.0	216.8
Davie................	6 218	30.8	190	4 095	533	56	100	1 340	909	58.4	15.0	481	73.7	61.4
Duplin...............	9 096	22.1	210	4 905	2 093	154	134	3 054	1 826	93.6	21.2	495	74.1	84.0
Durham..............	28 979	13.6	142	18 220	4 271	4 513	683	13 366	8 021	634.3	202.0	1 010	81.8	620.2
Edgecombe...........	11 232	–1.0	205	5 935	3 152	497	172	4 386	2 050	104.3	26.9	484	78.5	94.4
Forsyth..............	50 065	12.8	173	33 650	5 359	1 173	901	15 335	10 607	895.3	400.2	1 400	78.5	722.8
Franklin.............	7 127	30.8	156	3 890	1 636	75	139	2 086	1 297	71.2	22.1	507	74.7	71.9
Gaston...............	34 017	15.1	184	21 500	3 884	387	573	8 473	6 970	382.4	108.2	591	79.4	394.9
Gates................	2 163	17.2	212	1 180	350	32	31	594	311	16.6	4.1	415	74.2	10.0
Graham..............	1 938	17.8	255	1 050	360	76	24	468	301	14.6	3.5	455	68.5	13.0
Granville.............	8 111	23.2	182	4 425	1 502	737	133	6 263	1 312	90.9	19.3	458	71.1	81.1
Greene...............	3 154	42.1	170	1 735	695	59	57	1 331	570	28.4	6.6	365	69.5	27.2
Guilford..............	63 774	15.2	163	43 045	7 031	4 322	1 268	26 134	15 412	940.2	346.5	906	80.9	918.8
Halifax...............	13 958	15.0	250	6 785	4 602	132	175	4 974	2 949	133.8	30.5	540	76.4	139.7
Harnett..............	12 464	30.0	148	6 940	2 209	119	264	4 326	2 560	169.5	31.7	393	69.2	150.8
Haywood.............	13 463	26.0	259	8 280	1 451	137	160	3 344	2 536	158.3	32.4	635	74.9	161.2
Henderson............	22 919	19.5	279	15 825	1 604	224	251	4 430	3 582	204.4	45.1	564	72.1	188.0
Hertford.............	5 158	11.3	235	2 740	1 519	73	69	1 702	1 163	50.9	11.9	535	73.0	48.6
Hoke................	4 249	71.7	136	2 120	891	46	95	2 016	1 072	47.8	11.2	382	72.4	44.7
Hyde................	1 172	1.9	201	640	266	44	18	756	280	13.8	4.3	793	77.0	12.6
Iredell...............	20 154	24.6	171	13 390	1 909	257	353	6 216	3 553	186.6	57.0	522	70.3	177.1
Jackson..............	5 852	24.0	193	3 580	750	69	95	3 689	936	52.1	17.7	597	67.1	47.3
Johnston.............	17 648	27.1	150	9 445	3 558	197	331	5 503	4 161	227.5	56.0	548	70.9	230.8
Jones................	2 220	27.2	238	1 195	426	23	29	519	367	17.0	4.1	434	75.6	16.3
Lee..................	9 632	18.2	195	5 845	1 263	161	153	2 697	2 115	104.1	29.9	620	78.3	104.8
Lenoir...............	12 861	6.2	219	7 335	2 925	335	183	6 605	2 667	140.4	32.2	546	73.5	159.6
Lincoln..............	9 727	28.5	165	6 205	973	105	180	2 893	1 599	92.6	30.4	531	73.7	86.1
McDowell............	8 434	20.0	208	5 230	1 085	98	124	2 385	1 089	61.5	17.0	432	66.9	56.8
Macon...............	8 223	25.4	284	5 565	788	237	88	1 250	927	47.1	18.9	683	72.6	42.1
Madison.............	4 072	16.5	215	2 305	891	71	58	888	645	27.5	7.3	397	74.2	26.0
Martin...............	5 510	9.4	211	3 020	1 434	89	81	2 022	1 528	88.9	15.9	605	76.7	84.3
Mecklenburg.........	77 568	22.2	120	49 900	8 929	4 870	2 067	45 215	30 729	2 651.2	668.8	1 089	75.6	2 475.2
Mitchell.............	3 724	14.6	252	2 180	639	62	46	1 142	629	30.0	6.9	469	68.3	29.0
Montgomery..........	4 469	7.0	184	2 785	832	82	75	1 584	905	49.3	12.5	521	78.2	48.4
Moore...............	19 595	32.1	269	13 525	1 444	159	222	3 858	2 491	144.4	43.3	618	72.9	148.3
Nash................	15 121	41.8	164	8 480	3 128	88	283	5 544	5 281	280.2	47.0	524	76.1	282.9
New Hanover.........	27 602	33.7	183	17 355	3 659	855	648	12 922	5 322	543.3	117.5	800	70.2	553.5
Northampton.........	5 525	17.7	260	2 870	1 472	56	66	1 533	845	41.3	10.5	494	81.2	38.3
Onslow..............	14 257	50.6	100	7 970	2 330	5 281	37 705	6 845	5 574	222.6	48.8	345	63.9	241.9

[1] Per 1,000 resident population estimated as of July 1, 1999.　[2] Based on resident population estimated as of July 1, 1997.

Sources: Social Security Program—U.S. Social Security Administration, OASDI Beneficiaries by State and County - December 1999, <http://www.ssa.gov/statistics/oasdi_sc/1999/oasdi_sc99.pdf> (accessed: 7 March 2001) for 1999 – annual publication of same title for 1990. Supplemental Security Income Program—U.S. Social Security Administration, SSI Recipients by State and County, <http://www.ssa.gov/statistics/ssi_st_cty/1999/ssi_st_cty.pdf> (accessed: November 2000). Government employment, 1998—U.S. Bureau of Economic Analysis, "Regional Economic Information System (REIS) 1969-1998" on CD-ROM (related Internet site <http://www.bea.doc.gov/bea/regional/data.htm>). Local government employment, 1997—U.S. Census Bureau, 1997 Census of Governments, Compendium of Public Employment, <http://www.census.gov/govs/apes/97coar.dat> (accessed: 14 January 2000). Local government finances—U.S. Census Bureau, 1997 Census of Governments, Compendium of Government Finances, <http://www.census.gov/prod/gc97/gc974-5.pdf> (accessed: 16 February 2001).

Table B-13. Counties — Government Programs, Employment, and Finances-Con.

[Includes U.S., states, and 3,142 counties/county equivalents defined as of January 1, 1992. For changes to these areas since January 1, 1992, see appendix B. Geographic Information]

County	Social Security Program beneficiaries, December 1999				Supplemental Security Income Program recipients, December 1999	Government employment, 1998			Local government employment, full-time equivalent, March 1997	Local government finances, 1996–1997				
	Total					Federal				General revenue				
											Taxes			
	Number	Percent change, 1990–1999	Rate[1]	Retired workers		Civilian	Military	State and local		Total (mil. dol.)	Total (mil. dol.)	Per capita[2]	Percent property	Direct general expenditure (mil. dol.)
NORTH CAROLINA–Con.														
Orange	12 534	27.1	112	8 315	1 201	345	423	26 173	3 749	213.3	95.0	876	83.1	204.5
Pamlico	3 086	44.9	251	1 925	360	32	60	702	509	28.3	7.0	574	76.9	26.2
Pasquotank	6 398	11.5	180	3 825	1 155	640	696	4 706	2 506	130.8	17.3	492	69.3	137.1
Pender	7 682	43.1	191	4 455	1 128	80	123	2 196	1 087	61.5	21.8	574	74.8	60.3
Perquimans	2 850	20.0	252	1 735	419	41	35	612	434	22.1	5.6	510	78.4	22.4
Person	6 747	21.8	199	4 065	1 024	66	105	1 992	1 398	75.3	21.7	655	77.2	72.2
Pitt	18 889	23.8	148	10 375	4 825	373	404	17 018	5 129	615.5	64.9	521	73.9	532.4
Polk	5 115	25.4	303	3 540	276	41	52	752	591	23.7	8.1	485	77.9	22.9
Randolph	21 839	29.3	177	14 700	1 827	191	377	5 461	3 580	188.0	54.2	454	72.7	196.3
Richmond	9 874	22.5	216	5 125	2 011	126	144	3 028	1 826	89.0	21.5	469	72.9	82.2
Robeson	20 913	19.5	179	9 780	7 417	550	360	7 843	4 874	224.3	47.1	412	69.6	218.7
Rockingham	18 953	10.9	210	12 000	2 812	175	280	4 294	3 320	168.9	48.2	537	77.2	159.3
Rowan	23 374	27.2	185	15 130	2 178	1 716	391	5 732	4 091	213.5	61.6	498	75.9	215.0
Rutherford	13 243	17.5	215	8 395	1 678	129	189	3 336	2 162	115.9	28.3	470	70.9	112.2
Sampson	11 259	26.6	213	6 160	2 207	136	163	3 761	2 171	101.5	23.9	463	74.4	98.8
Scotland	6 964	34.4	194	3 455	1 693	55	111	1 953	1 627	73.8	20.0	563	74.1	72.6
Stanly	11 402	14.0	202	7 480	1 016	155	175	2 885	2 462	106.4	26.7	482	74.6	102.4
Stokes	7 179	52.7	164	4 210	812	82	135	1 620	1 252	59.6	17.2	404	69.7	57.2
Surry	14 822	13.1	218	9 400	1 921	177	208	4 470	3 106	125.8	33.6	506	67.8	125.8
Swain	3 012	23.7	244	1 695	400	338	38	793	373	18.2	3.7	308	56.3	18.4
Transylvania	7 813	28.9	271	5 265	585	169	88	1 216	866	45.6	18.8	674	75.3	44.1
Tyrrell	889	2.8	226	520	198	15	12	382	191	9.5	2.3	619	80.1	9.9
Union	15 056	52.9	131	9 560	1 283	202	342	5 377	3 401	191.0	59.4	561	76.1	166.4
Vance	8 938	20.8	210	4 705	2 284	104	131	3 278	1 889	106.3	21.3	512	71.7	106.9
Wake	62 502	31.6	106	39 320	7 651	4 203	2 429	61 473	18 447	1 333.0	477.3	865	73.9	1 217.2
Warren	3 989	16.5	212	2 120	1 118	46	57	1 285	775	35.6	9.7	535	77.7	34.4
Washington	3 065	12.5	228	1 600	682	52	42	1 212	752	33.3	6.2	452	75.4	31.9
Watauga	6 053	27.0	146	3 930	714	113	133	4 900	1 237	82.5	24.8	610	70.4	71.4
Wayne	19 699	21.5	176	10 680	4 527	1 455	4 592	8 236	4 102	200.0	47.0	420	69.3	186.8
Wilkes	12 726	23.1	200	7 635	1 967	200	195	4 233	2 128	120.4	28.6	459	66.6	119.0
Wilson	14 206	21.8	206	8 060	2 939	203	212	5 707	3 134	167.4	43.8	645	76.3	161.6
Yadkin	7 054	25.2	200	4 455	737	76	109	1 516	1 052	55.7	14.9	431	69.5	52.6
Yancey	4 361	25.9	259	2 580	765	75	52	789	687	26.1	6.9	419	67.2	25.5
NORTH DAKOTA	114 171	1.4	180	69 430	8 264	8 985	13 097	49 267	21 221	1 363.0	515.1	804	89.8	1 319.7
Adams	707	−7.0	267	425	32	19	22	162	103	6.3	2.4	876	97.9	6.2
Barnes	2 808	−8.8	237	1 740	157	93	97	964	344	22.6	8.7	725	97.8	20.8
Benson	1 268	−14.6	187	710	184	124	56	325	274	14.1	4.0	586	98.0	12.8
Billings	144	25.2	135	80	6	39	(3)	78	68	5.3	.9	775	95.6	4.7
Bottineau	1 761	−9.2	243	1 085	61	64	59	518	276	16.7	6.5	881	97.7	16.5
Bowman	832	−2.1	255	510	36	21	27	226	148	8.1	2.4	725	98.1	8.3
Burke	695	−21.5	317	420	24	58	18	174	122	7.0	3.3	1 417	97.0	7.0
Burleigh	10 880	25.9	161	6 815	915	919	544	7 359	2 116	127.5	50.2	757	82.7	117.6
Cass	14 973	16.0	126	9 295	1 216	2 053	989	8 277	3 033	237.5	97.6	849	83.4	234.7
Cavalier	1 297	−7.4	269	760	44	39	41	298	202	16.1	8.3	1 617	97.5	17.1
Dickey	1 371	−10.1	242	885	85	32	46	284	152	10.0	4.6	820	99.3	10.7
Divide	635	−15.3	277	415	20	30	19	145	96	7.2	3.4	1 406	97.9	8.7
Dunn	715	−.7	207	420	48	30	29	231	149	8.4	2.9	791	99.0	7.8
Eddy	766	−8.3	274	435	39	29	23	170	110	10.5	4.4	1 531	98.7	8.5
Emmons	1 257	−3.7	292	750	53	31	35	233	171	14.9	6.1	1 395	99.5	14.9
Foster	926	−5.5	245	580	28	29	31	228	132	10.6	4.7	1 261	98.9	9.0
Golden Valley	473	−14.0	265	300	5	12	15	138	103	6.6	2.6	1 341	98.0	7.0
Grand Forks	7 768	1.4	120	4 825	557	1 282	3 955	8 070	2 036	139.4	54.9	790	78.9	136.8
Grant	822	−8.7	288	485	63	32	24	160	118	5.5	2.5	825	99.1	5.8
Griggs	747	−17.9	269	485	36	28	23	165	84	10.2	5.9	2 052	99.0	10.5
Hettinger	860	−6.0	303	480	29	27	24	192	140	7.2	3.2	1 097	99.7	7.4
Kidder	736	−5.6	263	405	36	30	23	162	111	13.5	6.1	2 100	100.0	11.8
LaMoure	1 289	−7.9	274	765	51	43	39	279	242	24.0	7.7	1 574	98.7	28.3
Logan	708	−13.7	312	400	43	23	19	140	92	4.7	2.0	847	99.3	4.6
McHenry	1 599	−8.9	268	930	88	72	49	368	231	11.9	4.4	708	95.9	11.7
McIntosh	1 278	−7.7	376	775	54	25	28	190	141	7.3	2.8	797	99.4	7.1
McKenzie	979	−2.6	177	590	80	71	46	377	287	17.6	4.2	740	97.6	17.9
McLean	2 319	−5.5	241	1 405	126	129	79	680	402	20.9	4.8	496	98.4	20.4
Mercer	1 557	3.5	169	890	67	47	76	581	359	31.1	8.4	890	98.4	31.7
Morton	4 595	12.1	187	2 715	326	118	199	1 368	852	48.9	17.1	701	98.4	48.9
Mountrail	1 456	−7.0	223	845	126	109	54	423	339	18.7	5.4	807	97.9	17.3
Nelson	1 134	−16.9	310	725	42	36	30	219	162	10.4	5.5	1 428	99.3	9.6
Oliver	373	24.3	173	210	6	(3)	18	126	87	12.8	1.0	473	90.7	13.1
Pembina	1 932	−9.5	231	1 210	98	124	98	532	365	19.5	8.1	942	96.4	19.1
Pierce	1 216	−8.2	265	765	61	32	37	209	150	8.7	4.1	873	92.5	7.4

[1] Per 1,000 resident population estimated as of July 1, 1999. [2] Based on resident population estimated as of July 1, 1997. [3] Less than 10 employees.

Sources: Social Security Program—U.S. Social Security Administration, OASDI Beneficiaries by State and County - December 1999, <http://www.ssa.gov/statistics/oasdi_sc/1999/oasdi_sc99.pdf> (accessed: 7 March 2001) for 1999 – annual publication of same title for 1990. Supplemental Security Income Program—U.S. Social Security Administration, SSI Recipients by State and County, <http://www.ssa.gov/statistics/ssi_st_cty/1999/ssi_st_cty.pdf> (accessed: November 2000). Government employment, 1998—U.S. Bureau of Economic Analysis, "Regional Economic Information System (REIS) 1969-1998" on CD-ROM (related Internet site <http://www.bea.doc.gov/bea/regional/data.htm>). Local government employment, 1997—U.S. Census Bureau, 1997 Census of Governments, Compendium of Public Employment, <http://www.census.gov/govs/apes/97coar2.dat> (accessed: 14 January 2000). Local government finances—U.S. Census Bureau, 1997 Census of Governments, Compendium of Government Finances, <http://www.census.gov/prod/gc97/gc974-5.pdf> (accessed: 16 February 2001).

[Includes U.S., states, and 3,142 counties/county equivalents defined as of January 1, 1992. For changes to these areas since January 1, 1992, see appendix B. Geographic Information]

County	Social Security Program beneficiaries, December 1999 — Total — Number	Percent change, 1990–1999	Rate[1]	Retired workers	Supplemental Security Income Program recipients, December 1999	Government employment, 1998 — Federal — Civilian	Military	State and local	Local government employment, full-time equivalent, March 1997	Local government finances, 1996–1997 — General revenue — Total (mil. dol.)	Taxes — Total (mil. dol.)	Per capita[2]	Percent property	Direct general expenditure (mil. dol.)
NORTH DAKOTA—Con.														
Ramsey	2 702	–5.7	226	1 725	222	185	98	1 142	438	25.8	10.0	813	89.6	22.8
Ransom	1 293	–9.9	226	810	50	39	47	436	211	12.4	5.0	867	94.5	10.5
Renville	637	–11.5	228	375	12	23	23	178	148	7.9	3.1	1 090	96.4	9.2
Richland	3 135	–2.6	175	1 835	142	81	148	1 328	550	34.5	13.1	712	98.9	35.1
Rolette	1 922	5.9	135	1 005	626	588	115	683	569	27.7	4.4	314	93.0	26.5
Sargent	905	–10.4	211	525	41	49	36	213	146	9.6	4.1	930	99.4	8.7
Sheridan	522	–12.3	314	305	36	16	14	109	66	3.6	1.3	750	99.2	3.1
Sioux	356	–9.9	86	140	185	164	34	184	186	6.8	1.2	292	99.9	5.4
Slope	162	54.3	183	110	6	(3)	(3)	36	28	3.8	.6	699	91.8	2.6
Stark	4 453	8.9	198	2 525	374	157	185	1 696	706	41.5	14.0	618	85.3	39.4
Steele	549	–2.0	252	360	16	21	18	123	89	5.1	2.8	1 243	98.4	4.9
Stutsman	4 570	.2	217	2 850	451	207	170	1 683	684	40.6	16.1	765	88.7	42.3
Towner	739	–14.6	250	450	25	23	24	156	133	7.3	3.2	1 053	99.0	7.3
Traill	1 825	–10.1	213	1 185	44	44	69	645	279	21.0	8.3	966	97.5	19.6
Walsh	2 944	–10.2	220	1 845	104	72	110	1 343	464	26.9	12.0	875	95.8	25.6
Ward	8 884	9.7	152	5 475	692	1 304	4 913	3 597	1 783	97.1	33.7	570	85.6	86.4
Wells	1 468	–11.6	288	865	99	37	42	289	207	10.6	4.4	847	96.4	9.3
Williams	4 224	7.9	214	2 515	287	110	163	1 375	737	39.1	16.4	810	92.2	39.3
OHIO	1 893 896	5.0	168	1 146 261	242 752	83 126	36 706	683 434	421 092	29 022.3	12 647.7	1 128	65.9	27 841.2
Adams	5 367	8.3	187	2 540	1 793	77	74	1 516	1 419	71.9	26.5	935	83.2	96.3
Allen	19 747	3.9	185	12 125	2 500	469	281	6 690	4 077	220.8	88.2	817	65.4	216.4
Ashland	8 640	11.8	166	5 570	464	114	135	2 778	1 540	99.4	41.5	811	71.0	97.1
Ashtabula	18 808	2.2	182	11 140	2 432	258	276	5 016	3 495	221.8	74.7	725	75.9	208.8
Athens	7 817	–2.8	127	4 095	2 157	240	174	10 015	2 266	129.9	39.4	642	75.9	124.2
Auglaize	7 745	–2.3	164	4 880	366	95	121	2 736	1 546	94.7	35.6	759	67.0	88.0
Belmont	16 286	–2.4	229	9 255	1 899	167	178	3 951	2 386	130.6	42.8	597	69.4	125.1
Brown	6 803	19.8	164	3 505	876	89	105	1 927	1 556	103.7	21.4	532	79.7	92.7
Butler	47 993	16.9	144	27 520	5 244	558	875	18 661	9 643	667.4	283.0	863	74.5	673.3
Carroll	5 139	48.1	175	3 035	300	50	75	898	681	38.0	10.8	373	85.1	37.0
Champaign	6 408	12.3	166	3 680	501	82	98	1 781	1 394	83.6	29.1	765	65.6	86.7
Clark	26 675	1.2	184	15 425	3 590	629	379	7 133	5 442	304.5	118.4	812	68.0	301.2
Clermont	25 093	53.2	140	14 095	2 081	311	453	6 462	5 079	369.0	144.7	837	83.7	362.7
Clinton	7 033	18.6	173	3 880	657	146	103	2 880	2 516	118.0	30.8	779	72.1	111.4
Columbiana	21 795	–1.1	196	12 670	2 643	572	288	4 613	3 296	207.3	67.8	609	77.6	194.6
Coshocton	7 055	8.5	195	4 050	731	105	93	1 554	1 315	76.7	35.9	992	77.4	74.1
Crawford	9 308	4.3	198	5 730	947	88	122	2 034	1 650	94.5	36.0	762	76.6	98.6
Cuyahoga	256 341	–5.7	187	166 445	39 905	17 306	4 154	84 516	66 998	4 879.9	2 262.7	1 629	59.0	4 560.4
Darke	9 861	6.5	182	6 155	651	125	140	2 129	1 663	93.9	36.5	672	68.1	89.2
Defiance	6 682	8.4	169	3 955	610	109	103	1 927	1 394	114.2	38.5	963	73.4	94.4
Delaware	11 293	60.2	109	7 210	599	230	238	4 327	2 618	174.9	86.6	958	82.2	192.7
Erie	14 663	11.3	188	9 395	1 141	193	210	4 975	3 183	216.5	96.3	1 225	75.6	209.0
Fairfield	18 231	23.6	144	10 970	1 625	258	321	6 552	3 324	229.3	90.9	748	70.8	224.5
Fayette	4 893	3.3	172	2 780	752	57	73	1 479	1 193	61.1	17.4	609	71.3	61.4
Franklin	131 066	7.2	128	78 515	22 744	13 392	3 285	100 541	37 346	3 039.4	1 557.1	1 530	61.8	2 960.1
Fulton	6 829	3.7	162	4 325	362	109	108	2 455	1 394	88.3	44.9	1 083	66.7	87.0
Gallia	6 088	10.7	183	2 955	1 704	79	86	1 924	1 045	74.5	20.6	623	90.5	72.3
Geauga	12 522	77.5	140	8 550	434	137	229	3 466	2 561	177.9	97.1	1 110	86.5	178.4
Greene	20 623	43.3	138	12 575	1 748	12 006	3 485	9 809	4 841	314.9	130.0	890	74.9	306.8
Guernsey	8 297	2.4	203	4 685	1 296	119	106	2 458	1 355	78.4	31.0	764	71.8	70.8
Hamilton	140 673	–3.9	167	86 995	21 174	9 948	2 336	54 245	33 668	2 664.9	1 282.5	1 506	64.7	2 535.0
Hancock	11 238	10.9	162	7 295	711	178	179	2 988	2 340	143.8	63.4	924	71.5	150.3
Hardin	5 333	1.8	168	3 100	557	86	82	1 603	1 202	53.1	19.6	618	59.5	51.5
Harrison	3 574	–2.1	222	1 955	405	62	41	874	589	38.0	15.4	956	54.8	36.0
Henry	5 155	8.1	173	3 190	284	78	77	1 841	1 089	72.9	26.7	892	77.5	71.3
Highland	7 544	7.9	184	4 185	1 018	107	104	1 972	1 264	87.5	19.1	480	66.9	83.9
Hocking	4 891	17.1	168	2 625	741	54	75	1 583	848	65.3	15.9	554	68.1	62.8
Holmes	3 604	24.3	94	2 125	261	78	98	1 393	972	54.2	22.2	596	93.2	49.0
Huron	9 504	–.7	157	5 700	929	140	156	2 580	2 037	144.4	64.3	1 072	46.9	123.5
Jackson	6 082	5.1	186	2 905	1 541	71	84	1 405	1 070	54.8	11.9	367	83.1	53.2
Jefferson	17 693	–2.7	240	9 520	2 399	264	193	3 715	2 863	135.4	52.4	689	85.8	132.7
Knox	9 516	8.0	177	5 640	864	112	137	2 656	1 679	94.0	37.0	702	74.1	89.7
Lake	39 254	14.0	173	26 120	1 673	510	596	11 081	8 799	618.8	336.2	1 487	73.0	562.3
Lawrence	12 685	8.5	197	5 835	3 812	151	166	3 544	2 752	110.9	22.9	355	70.2	113.6
Licking	22 355	18.6	164	13 360	2 263	530	367	6 573	4 652	299.5	126.1	968	70.7	283.7
Logan	7 687	–.6	164	4 680	614	143	123	2 126	1 655	98.1	40.2	876	81.9	94.9
Lorain	45 169	9.6	160	27 425	4 703	1 178	738	13 065	9 696	671.9	292.7	1 038	68.1	641.0
Lucas	75 571	–.9	169	45 385	14 458	2 140	1 230	29 864	16 869	1 323.9	587.8	1 304	58.9	1 362.5
Madison	5 607	8.1	136	3 315	468	93	107	2 962	1 367	87.7	33.8	830	76.9	76.5
Mahoning	56 895	–4.0	225	34 020	7 609	1 576	678	15 600	8 776	546.2	215.5	837	70.9	520.5

[1] Per 1,000 resident population estimated as of July 1, 1999.   [2] Based on resident population estimated as of July 1, 1997.   [3] Less than 10 employees.

Sources: Social Security Program—U.S. Social Security Administration, OASDI Beneficiaries by State and County - December 1999, <http://www.ssa.gov/statistics/oasdi_sc/1999/oasdi_sc99.pdf> (accessed: 7 March 2001) for 1999 – annual publication of same title for 1990. Supplemental Security Income Program—U.S. Social Security Administration, SSI Recipients by State and County, <http://www.ssa.gov/statistics/ssi_st_cty/1999/ssi_st_cty.pdf> (accessed: November 2000). Government employment, 1998—U.S. Bureau of Economic Analysis, "Regional Economic Information System (REIS) 1969-1998" on CD-ROM (related Internet site <http://www.bea.doc.gov/bea/regional/data.htm>). Local government employment, 1997—U.S. Census Bureau, 1997 Census of Governments, Compendium of Public Employment, <http://www.census.gov/govs/apes/97coar2.dat> (accessed: 14 January 2000). Local government finances—U.S. Census Bureau, 1997 Census of Governments, Compendium of Government Finances, <http://www.census.gov/prod/gc97/gc974-5.pdf> (accessed: 16 February 2001).

[Includes U.S., states, and 3,142 counties/county equivalents defined as of January 1, 1992. For changes to these areas since January 1, 1992, see appendix B. Geographic Information]

County	Social Security Program beneficiaries, December 1999				Supple-mental Security Income Program recipients, December 1999	Government employment, 1998			Local government employment, full-time equivalent, March 1997	Local government finances, 1996–1997				
	Total					Federal				General revenue				
											Taxes			
	Number	Percent change, 1990–1999	Rate[1]	Retired workers		Civilian	Military	State and local		Total (mil. dol.)	Total (mil. dol.)	Per capita[2]	Percent prop-erty	Direct general expend-iture (mil. dol.)
OHIO—Con.														
Marion	11 687	8.3	175	6 455	1 892	172	168	5 870	2 710	147.0	50.7	753	70.2	140.2
Medina	19 887	29.7	135	12 675	868	304	372	5 791	4 651	316.0	135.7	959	85.1	301.8
Meigs	4 436	3.4	185	2 050	1 027	77	62	1 137	850	40.4	9.2	384	80.6	42.0
Mercer	7 391	9.3	180	4 700	361	98	106	2 536	1 681	99.3	31.7	775	71.4	99.6
Miami	16 958	8.0	172	10 575	1 210	227	255	4 399	3 612	218.8	92.9	951	68.8	213.5
Monroe	3 155	7.7	204	1 615	462	63	40	887	743	30.5	12.4	814	87.1	31.4
Montgomery	98 187	1.8	174	58 985	13 466	6 437	4 411	29 629	24 622	1 722.2	741.8	1 297	60.2	1 612.0
Morgan	2 876	16.9	198	1 520	448	45	37	654	571	26.3	7.5	518	78.7	25.7
Morrow	4 766	36.2	148	2 595	390	56	81	1 395	1 015	51.0	15.3	493	79.7	47.1
Muskingum	16 271	1.8	192	9 230	2 619	311	219	4 595	3 326	188.7	66.9	793	66.3	173.2
Noble	2 295	22.7	155	1 220	238	28	32	1 058	452	23.8	6.6	459	84.3	21.1
Ottawa	8 606	9.0	208	5 465	301	166	142	2 039	1 562	107.1	52.6	1 291	83.7	105.2
Paulding	3 433	8.6	171	1 920	303	55	52	1 146	692	46.1	11.7	580	77.3	42.3
Perry	5 946	1.0	174	2 930	859	74	88	1 678	1 234	58.0	12.2	357	81.0	54.2
Pickaway	7 406	17.8	139	4 225	875	91	138	4 171	2 043	123.1	37.0	703	74.2	118.7
Pike	5 334	26.4	191	2 600	1 495	66	72	1 665	943	65.4	12.6	459	85.7	62.2
Portage	21 199	19.2	140	12 960	1 775	306	410	14 195	5 495	393.2	138.7	922	69.9	390.5
Preble	7 331	19.5	169	4 250	437	101	111	1 928	1 460	117.3	32.7	761	61.1	107.7
Putnam	5 573	6.6	158	3 480	269	81	91	1 984	1 381	74.8	23.2	661	66.1	71.3
Richland	23 577	5.5	182	14 680	2 623	702	330	7 788	5 059	297.1	120.7	930	67.1	291.3
Ross	11 821	8.9	156	6 200	2 621	1 385	196	4 841	2 418	137.7	51.0	681	62.4	135.7
Sandusky	11 017	13.8	178	6 680	808	125	160	3 254	2 408	138.1	56.8	910	65.7	128.5
Scioto	16 017	−2.4	199	9 705	5 638	194	207	5 374	2 599	166.0	35.7	439	72.7	157.3
Seneca	11 007	−5.4	184	6 470	921	142	156	3 084	1 922	107.4	43.5	722	63.9	105.2
Shelby	7 489	15.0	156	4 540	547	101	122	2 528	1 226	110.1	47.8	1 012	61.7	93.7
Stark	70 509	−1.2	189	43 935	6 702	1 216	965	17 725	13 207	787.5	328.9	880	69.6	763.5
Summit	94 581	4.4	176	59 135	11 053	2 749	1 415	30 212	19 301	1 499.6	727.6	1 356	62.3	1 414.2
Trumbull	45 426	8.6	202	27 500	4 546	504	583	10 561	7 544	470.7	193.4	851	69.3	468.1
Tuscarawas	16 705	4.6	188	9 950	1 477	219	229	4 635	3 163	186.2	77.1	875	66.0	178.4
Union	4 951	25.0	121	2 905	311	73	102	2 617	1 605	103.6	36.3	933	86.0	92.6
Van Wert	5 828	15.1	194	3 725	316	72	78	1 337	1 025	57.3	22.6	745	72.3	55.6
Vinton	1 991	5.1	161	920	502	23	31	789	503	24.8	5.2	432	86.5	24.3
Warren	18 985	40.9	124	11 225	1 195	274	376	6 521	4 084	290.8	143.4	1 024	76.4	286.8
Washington	12 197	5.2	194	6 955	1 671	260	163	3 132	2 223	121.1	54.5	857	69.0	118.9
Wayne	17 118	10.9	154	10 550	1 403	263	284	6 872	4 675	314.4	98.7	901	72.5	282.4
Williams	6 542	3.3	173	4 255	396	95	98	2 120	1 450	84.7	35.0	922	65.3	77.5
Wood	16 094	16.0	134	9 865	953	236	330	13 172	4 141	273.7	138.1	1 167	63.7	260.4
Wyandot	4 161	.9	182	2 555	248	66	59	1 242	1 093	62.2	16.3	721	74.6	58.1
OKLAHOMA	586 802	10.3	175	357 236	72 665	44 493	41 819	227 140	129 462	6 625.4	2 065.3	623	53.0	6 516.8
Adair	3 754	11.9	183	1 910	946	45	101	1 099	878	34.2	4.9	245	87.0	33.3
Alfalfa	1 442	−16.2	245	935	58	46	30	465	236	9.0	2.9	484	73.5	9.6
Atoka	2 754	16.9	206	1 540	597	74	66	1 132	409	19.5	4.5	333	68.9	20.2
Beaver	1 133	−1.5	188	715	44	32	30	527	336	19.9	7.7	1 300	86.4	16.8
Beckham	3 866	−4.4	195	2 280	537	55	97	934	734	36.2	15.5	803	62.0	33.8
Blaine	2 445	−4.3	238	1 465	220	79	52	915	843	25.4	4.4	415	74.0	26.4
Bryan	7 485	3.6	214	4 350	1 368	120	173	2 541	1 300	47.8	11.9	346	50.1	48.8
Caddo	6 090	−5.4	199	3 525	927	415	154	1 904	1 453	59.7	12.9	418	64.4	57.2
Canadian	10 149	54.0	117	6 350	525	621	855	4 054	3 125	130.1	41.5	492	68.4	136.5
Carter	9 575	4.8	215	5 650	1 466	127	222	2 707	1 918	78.0	27.3	615	53.6	88.3
Cherokee	6 671	17.6	169	3 815	1 074	479	195	3 958	1 615	80.6	10.1	261	41.6	77.5
Choctaw	3 705	−5.7	247	1 940	1 043	65	75	965	748	24.5	4.4	292	40.7	24.6
Cimarron	733	2.5	251	455	35	19	19	351	198	13.3	2.3	763	76.7	13.7
Cleveland	22 314	63.1	110	13 830	1 932	766	1 114	18 652	6 955	376.5	97.9	495	60.3	369.1
Coal	1 363	−.5	222	785	270	25	30	351	269	12.7	4.6	747	86.3	11.0
Comanche	14 722	18.3	138	8 425	2 110	3 810	14 303	7 818	6 132	265.5	49.1	452	48.2	259.6
Cotton	1 425	−8.1	216	865	152	33	33	397	273	9.4	1.8	274	60.2	10.0
Craig	3 298	−6.0	228	1 930	471	60	72	1 896	770	25.4	8.3	577	46.4	25.2
Creek	11 924	55.3	175	6 870	998	118	334	2 762	2 292	100.0	27.4	414	62.9	90.8
Custer	4 359	1.8	170	2 745	527	161	127	2 774	1 348	61.2	19.0	745	61.8	57.1
Delaware	7 680	34.4	220	4 695	835	67	170	1 258	1 114	41.1	13.3	393	63.2	42.5
Dewey	1 175	−20.1	242	690	94	40	25	518	374	17.8	3.1	629	70.5	16.1
Ellis	1 043	−8.1	249	675	56	25	21	435	237	11.8	4.1	968	82.1	9.7
Garfield	11 528	5.5	202	7 285	1 157	381	1 430	3 675	2 179	99.1	35.9	632	51.1	98.5
Garvin	6 661	−1.8	249	3 915	952	93	135	2 350	1 104	55.9	12.1	450	59.3	55.1
Grady	7 776	15.8	169	4 645	926	101	229	2 611	1 799	87.6	16.9	371	62.6	87.1
Grant	1 289	−10.5	246	805	74	37	27	363	279	12.3	4.5	837	91.1	13.7
Greer	1 579	−14.6	247	995	198	27	32	890	270	15.6	2.4	365	72.6	16.1
Harmon	817	−16.2	245	490	151	23	17	335	182	6.4	1.2	351	68.3	6.8
Harper	1 011	1.1	282	640	42	27	18	406	197	9.6	2.7	759	79.3	8.6

[1] Per 1,000 resident population estimated as of July 1, 1999.   [2] Based on resident population estimated as of July 1, 1997.

Sources: Social Security Program—U.S. Social Security Administration, OASDI Beneficiaries by State and County - December 1999, <http://www.ssa.gov/statistics/oasdi_sc/1999/oasdi_sc99.pdf> (accessed: 7 March 2001) for 1999 – annual publication of same title for 1990.   Supplemental Security Income Program—U.S. Social Security Administration, SSI Recipients by State and County, <http://www.ssa.gov/statistics/ssi_st_cty/1999/ssi_st_cty.pdf> (accessed: November 2000).   Government employment, 1998—U.S. Bureau of Economic Analysis, "Regional Economic Information System (REIS) 1969-1998" on CD-ROM (related Internet site <http://www.bea.doc.gov/bea/regional/data.htm>).   Local government employment, 1997—U.S. Census Bureau, 1997 Census of Governments, Compendium of Public Employment, <http://www.census.gov/govs/apes/97coar2.dat> (accessed: 14 January 2000).   Local government finances—U.S. Census Bureau, 1997 Census of Governments, Compendium of Government Finances, <http://www.census.gov/prod/gc97/gc974-5.pdf> (accessed: 16 February 2001).

[Includes U.S., states, and 3,142 counties/county equivalents defined as of January 1, 1992. For changes to these areas since January 1, 1992, see appendix B. Geographic Information]

County	Social Security Program beneficiaries, December 1999				Supple-mental Security Income Program recipients, December 1999	Government employment, 1998			Local government employment, full-time equivalent, March 1997	Local government finances, 1996–1997				
	Total					Federal		State and local		General revenue				Direct general expend-iture (mil. dol.)
						Civilian	Military			Total (mil. dol.)	Taxes			
	Number	Percent change, 1990–1999	Rate[1]	Retired workers							Total (mil. dol.)	Per capita[2]	Percent prop-erty	
OKLAHOMA—Con.														
Haskell	2 848	5.3	249	1 590	505	66	57	753	601	18.6	3.0	266	43.5	17.6
Hughes	3 417	–5.1	243	2 010	513	45	70	937	704	44.8	5.3	374	61.6	42.0
Jackson	4 319	–.5	152	2 605	691	1 633	2 194	2 294	1 853	88.6	13.1	463	52.2	87.1
Jefferson	1 804	–6.8	277	1 045	240	41	33	461	402	16.7	3.9	593	83.0	15.4
Johnston	2 360	13.2	229	1 310	393	50	51	807	415	17.2	3.3	323	79.4	17.5
Kay	10 379	–2.4	223	6 485	783	191	232	2 782	2 067	81.1	29.2	625	65.5	86.4
Kingfisher	2 663	10.3	197	1 610	166	59	67	774	605	26.9	9.7	717	65.1	24.8
Kiowa	2 627	–14.6	250	1 525	395	60	53	894	548	19.7	4.4	410	58.7	20.8
Latimer	2 566	46.6	251	1 465	286	23	51	1 603	660	31.1	11.2	1 091	90.5	30.3
Le Flore	9 429	6.5	202	4 860	2 039	219	232	3 090	1 535	73.2	15.3	330	60.2	71.4
Lincoln	5 963	15.7	187	3 515	603	82	156	1 234	985	43.0	10.6	342	55.0	41.7
Logan	5 113	24.6	168	3 245	381	70	154	1 856	913	45.5	9.0	301	64.2	47.9
Love	1 779	11.9	207	1 120	183	24	42	387	349	10.6	2.3	266	62.4	10.8
McClain	4 444	32.7	166	2 675	331	65	130	1 351	1 021	55.7	18.2	706	69.9	47.2
McCurtain	6 886	5.9	198	3 500	1 728	151	173	2 273	1 469	56.2	12.4	359	67.6	56.4
McIntosh	5 217	13.5	271	3 200	678	37	95	879	653	27.0	7.3	389	46.7	26.0
Major	1 769	3.5	231	1 085	83	41	39	427	295	14.8	3.4	431	70.6	14.9
Marshall	3 211	11.5	259	2 060	397	25	61	703	398	21.1	5.5	460	63.3	23.0
Mayes	7 898	44.5	206	4 740	799	73	187	2 102	1 160	45.5	14.1	382	48.8	45.0
Murray	2 853	7.7	229	1 765	303	90	61	1 184	798	22.2	4.9	400	57.5	21.1
Muskogee	13 932	1.9	199	8 205	2 279	1 395	348	5 330	2 578	194.4	50.8	728	56.1	192.7
Noble	2 158	3.8	190	1 285	184	51	57	825	587	21.4	8.6	763	89.0	21.2
Nowata	2 468	3.3	245	1 455	216	35	50	460	324	14.3	2.9	293	61.4	13.5
Okfuskee	2 558	.9	228	1 450	565	37	57	797	487	18.4	4.4	389	76.3	18.8
Oklahoma	99 111	6.7	156	63 900	13 456	23 748	10 743	47 667	21 651	1 385.1	562.2	891	42.8	1 318.5
Okmulgee	7 988	–.8	206	4 535	1 331	136	193	2 184	1 383	64.1	12.7	331	44.1	62.5
Osage	7 873	78.5	183	4 625	441	203	236	1 769	928	42.7	9.1	214	59.1	43.4
Ottawa	7 966	–3.4	258	4 750	979	133	155	1 983	1 376	54.6	17.4	568	72.3	54.5
Pawnee	3 499	18.4	211	2 030	290	183	82	714	576	22.6	5.1	312	57.2	22.9
Payne	9 128	6.6	140	5 665	1 000	275	344	13 915	2 993	155.2	34.2	527	55.9	152.3
Pittsburg	9 687	10.1	223	5 745	1 486	1 190	219	3 235	2 260	101.0	20.8	485	35.0	102.2
Pontotoc	7 404	3.9	213	4 250	1 141	248	172	2 528	1 322	102.3	19.7	569	41.2	97.8
Pottawatomie	11 549	10.0	184	6 910	1 508	184	310	2 832	2 171	122.5	28.4	464	50.8	118.5
Pushmataha	2 914	5.4	252	1 610	615	38	58	945	617	19.3	2.9	250	51.7	17.7
Roger Mills	838	–3.7	233	505	60	39	18	398	157	5.9	1.7	481	82.5	5.8
Rogers	10 461	91.9	148	6 395	605	456	339	2 921	2 700	79.8	29.8	450	64.4	70.1
Seminole	5 667	–1.6	231	3 135	938	122	123	1 511	988	48.8	9.8	391	65.6	48.3
Sequoyah	7 767	26.5	205	4 060	1 568	143	203	1 972	1 521	52.0	8.6	232	54.2	52.8
Stephens	10 143	6.3	235	6 355	826	103	216	2 006	1 536	62.9	17.0	392	57.0	70.6
Texas	2 634	–1.5	144	1 640	184	71	93	1 607	899	35.3	11.1	618	60.2	35.5
Tillman	2 206	–9.8	234	1 340	317	49	47	658	561	18.3	3.7	383	68.1	18.4
Tulsa	84 250	.3	154	53 590	9 421	4 233	2 728	28 040	20 194	1 254.5	493.4	920	51.0	1 268.3
Wagoner	8 248	81.9	147	4 915	644	80	275	1 293	1 018	40.3	10.7	197	51.3	39.7
Washington	10 952	6.2	230	7 175	737	115	236	2 067	1 710	83.0	32.9	694	59.2	74.2
Washita	2 663	1.1	228	1 590	202	53	59	734	518	25.9	7.0	603	81.1	25.8
Woods	1 990	–7.4	244	1 335	99	43	42	1 130	549	17.9	7.3	878	76.7	16.3
Woodward	3 430	8.9	185	2 155	241	114	92	1 785	860	36.9	11.8	635	50.7	35.9
OREGON	553 547	12.4	167	366 633	50 623	29 971	12 704	213 424	117 999	9 528.2	3 120.2	962	81.2	9 377.6
Baker	3 974	8.3	244	2 585	317	312	56	965	599	36.7	9.7	589	87.6	36.3
Benton	9 669	24.8	125	6 650	582	658	339	10 280	2 551	158.2	64.3	830	86.0	138.9
Clackamas	47 238	28.1	140	31 995	2 456	2 004	1 338	13 070	10 234	760.2	280.6	849	90.9	803.8
Clatsop	7 123	3.8	202	4 680	626	185	470	2 432	1 404	115.1	43.8	1 237	83.5	109.2
Columbia	7 236	17.2	159	4 560	420	82	151	1 869	1 567	117.7	39.5	907	85.4	112.3
Coos	15 480	11.8	251	9 885	1 543	389	420	4 879	3 118	230.4	46.6	745	88.1	229.9
Crook	3 626	26.6	205	2 405	218	349	59	806	552	43.8	10.2	602	91.7	52.8
Curry	7 197	26.8	340	5 140	366	126	103	1 068	788	63.1	14.7	697	86.9	59.1
Deschutes	19 796	34.5	179	13 425	1 166	815	360	5 581	3 598	259.4	107.5	1 058	82.3	251.4
Douglas	23 513	21.8	231	15 205	1 786	1 552	404	5 515	4 027	251.4	62.5	615	87.8	250.5
Gilliam	460	16.5	222	315	24	(3)	(3)	216	126	11.5	2.8	1 417	98.2	10.4
Grant	1 692	11.0	215	1 140	140	355	27	762	527	53.5	6.7	842	69.2	49.1
Harney	1 512	16.8	207	980	129	227	24	698	437	29.7	4.6	663	89.7	27.8
Hood River	3 168	7.6	159	2 295	189	161	66	1 230	819	51.1	11.9	620	91.6	47.5
Jackson	36 763	22.6	209	24 485	2 699	1 752	596	8 586	5 346	386.3	123.7	725	87.1	398.7
Jefferson	3 311	47.2	196	2 190	285	161	56	1 181	927	51.6	11.2	678	88.4	56.9
Josephine	19 611	11.7	262	13 040	1 570	334	253	3 425	2 220	159.4	37.5	512	88.2	169.3
Klamath	12 440	18.6	196	7 890	1 255	920	221	3 696	2 230	262.4	41.9	668	87.1	234.1
Lake	1 790	23.4	250	1 190	138	297	24	636	451	25.4	6.2	856	90.2	25.8
Lane	54 650	16.8	174	35 345	5 074	2 042	1 099	22 585	11 459	846.7	256.5	824	83.6	859.7
Lincoln	11 214	13.9	249	7 725	707	242	216	3 221	2 159	175.7	64.2	1 413	83.4	173.3

[1] Per 1,000 resident population estimated as of July 1, 1999.   [2] Based on resident population estimated as of July 1, 1997.   [3] Less than 10 employees.

Sources: Social Security Program—U.S. Social Security Administration, OASDI Beneficiaries by State and County - December 1999, <http://www.ssa.gov/statistics/oasdi_sc/1999/oasdi_sc99.pdf> (accessed: 7 March 2001) for 1999 – annual publication of same title for 1990.   Supplemental Security Income Program—U.S. Social Security Administration, SSI Recipients by State and County, <http://www.ssa.gov/statistics/ssi_st_cty/1999/ssi_st_cty.pdf> (accessed: November 2000).   Government employment, 1998—U.S. Bureau of Economic Analysis, "Regional Economic Information System (REIS) 1969-1998" on CD-ROM (related Internet site <http://www.bea.doc.gov/bea/regional/data.htm>).   Local government employment, 1997—U.S. Census Bureau, 1997 Census of Governments, Compendium of Public Employment, <http://www.census.gov/govs/apes/97coar2.dat> (accessed: 14 January 2000).   Local government finances—U.S. Census Bureau, 1997 Census of Governments, Compendium of Government Finances, <http://www.census.gov/prod/gc97/gc974-5.pdf> (accessed: 16 February 2001).

Table B–13. Counties — Government Programs, Employment, and Finances–Con.

[Includes U.S., states, and 3,142 counties/county equivalents defined as of January 1, 1992. For changes to these areas since January 1, 1992, see appendix B. Geographic Information]

County	Social Security Program beneficiaries, December 1999				Supplemental Security Income Program recipients, December 1999	Government employment, 1998			Local government employment, full-time equivalent, March 1997	Local government finances, 1996–1997				
	Total			Retired workers		Federal		State and local		General revenue				Direct general expenditure (mil. dol.)
	Number	Percent change, 1990–1999	Rate[1]			Civilian	Military			Total (mil. dol.)	Taxes		Percent property	
											Total (mil. dol.)	Per capita[2]		
OREGON—Con.														
Linn	19 664	11.7	187	12 370	1 768	341	356	5 876	4 097	257.9	78.5	758	89.5	275.4
Malheur	5 450	3.1	192	3 485	618	192	97	2 942	1 458	85.9	16.4	578	86.5	88.5
Marion	45 103	1.6	165	30 190	4 548	1 473	929	30 018	9 899	666.4	198.5	749	89.8	681.5
Morrow	1 522	46.3	145	980	110	69	45	726	619	39.8	13.5	1 412	90.3	45.8
Multnomah	91 005	-10.7	144	59 390	14 463	11 731	2 596	49 962	26 304	2 776.0	1 000.1	1 593	68.1	2 573.2
Polk	10 772	54.3	173	7 300	705	120	209	3 017	1 386	77.2	21.5	359	92.2	86.4
Sherman	386	-14.2	216	260	26	84	(3)	176	105	8.7	2.3	1 257	97.2	8.8
Tillamook	6 294	16.0	258	4 335	364	133	116	1 558	1 015	75.2	21.9	901	90.7	73.0
Umatilla	11 022	4.0	165	7 265	1 116	765	230	4 580	2 716	167.4	42.3	657	90.2	175.4
Union	4 552	11.8	183	2 880	453	221	84	2 322	896	57.1	14.6	583	89.7	54.7
Wallowa	1 770	9.9	244	1 175	119	137	25	600	414	28.0	7.9	1 055	95.1	25.1
Wasco	4 897	7.5	210	3 250	395	338	78	1 555	1 111	79.2	21.4	926	91.1	76.1
Washington	46 502	34.1	114	31 725	3 391	808	1 360	13 832	10 221	935.0	377.5	965	86.8	932.8
Wheeler	458	27.2	294	315	15	(3)	(3)	174	90	5.9	1.7	1 035	86.5	5.2
Yamhill	12 679	20.8	152	8 580	770	581	279	3 385	2 529	179.1	55.3	693	87.7	179.0
PENNSYLVANIA	2 332 589	4.3	194	1 522 467	277 998	111 517	45 066	601 726	365 556	30 375.9	12 502.3	1 040	70.4	29 086.6
Adams	15 324	24.9	175	10 885	838	456	292	3 955	1 988	152.1	69.1	807	70.1	165.9
Allegheny	266 152	-3.3	212	171 070	29 506	15 280	4 960	59 794	43 929	4 146.8	1 679.1	1 311	74.2	3 893.0
Armstrong	16 522	-6.1	226	9 335	2 112	247	247	2 951	2 163	140.3	54.8	747	82.9	128.4
Beaver	41 495	5.8	227	25 080	3 767	404	622	8 112	5 804	461.3	148.2	799	80.6	456.1
Bedford	10 396	11.9	209	6 445	1 060	139	167	2 157	1 338	86.5	28.8	584	78.8	93.6
Berks	67 868	7.2	189	48 700	5 353	1 186	1 223	17 757	11 661	864.2	394.0	1 113	79.0	871.4
Blair	24 269	5.4	187	15 430	4 070	967	442	7 320	3 859	240.9	78.2	598	71.9	234.7
Bradford	12 819	11.5	206	8 025	1 755	202	212	2 952	2 237	157.8	40.5	650	74.3	151.4
Bucks	91 191	28.0	154	61 900	4 964	1 508	1 985	19 196	16 563	1 357.6	708.6	1 216	84.3	1 395.1
Butler	30 470	13.5	177	18 225	2 998	1 454	577	7 342	4 306	330.9	131.7	780	77.0	338.2
Cambria	37 035	-4.3	241	21 665	4 307	1 119	653	8 413	5 482	357.0	96.1	610	77.4	341.9
Cameron	1 446	2.2	260	995	128	17	19	386	205	13.2	4.7	825	84.4	13.3
Carbon	13 566	6.1	231	8 905	926	133	200	2 615	1 853	118.7	49.8	847	77.0	112.0
Centre	16 988	19.0	129	11 310	1 533	476	543	30 627	3 227	219.3	92.8	701	67.1	207.5
Chester	59 717	30.8	139	40 685	3 063	1 966	1 424	16 901	10 366	895.2	491.5	1 182	81.5	936.0
Clarion	8 335	10.6	200	4 765	1 088	115	141	3 343	1 381	81.7	24.9	596	76.5	89.1
Clearfield	17 529	8.8	217	10 745	2 067	265	274	4 449	2 248	154.1	53.0	655	78.6	144.1
Clinton	7 765	7.5	211	5 070	863	141	125	2 486	1 232	89.0	29.5	798	77.6	84.0
Columbia	12 911	-.3	203	8 770	1 206	163	217	4 166	1 836	113.9	45.5	710	69.4	113.4
Crawford	18 003	7.5	202	11 175	2 452	278	303	4 208	2 216	165.9	54.8	614	80.0	168.9
Cumberland	35 247	13.8	167	25 430	1 550	7 029	1 511	10 666	5 816	408.2	209.5	1 009	68.1	411.7
Dauphin	42 605	6.3	173	29 370	4 807	2 892	890	38 288	9 226	715.5	267.3	1 088	71.4	749.5
Delaware	100 508	3.0	186	67 645	7 669	2 270	1 878	21 132	14 528	1 266.5	614.0	1 129	90.5	1 320.7
Elk	7 572	5.2	220	5 220	503	106	117	1 315	897	64.2	26.2	752	70.4	63.5
Erie	50 979	2.9	184	32 635	7 192	1 596	982	14 038	7 519	604.4	212.1	759	78.8	619.1
Fayette	34 120	-1.0	237	18 005	7 895	501	500	4 992	2 941	220.9	60.7	418	75.6	211.9
Forest	1 524	13.3	309	940	146	63	17	351	182	11.4	5.9	1 193	74.6	10.5
Franklin	24 347	22.6	189	16 905	1 942	2 733	440	5 343	3 202	197.1	80.1	628	74.2	188.1
Fulton	2 638	17.0	180	1 650	315	36	49	706	382	26.3	9.3	644	81.2	23.6
Greene	8 332	-.8	198	4 275	1 695	132	137	2 544	1 168	81.6	35.5	840	85.3	86.7
Huntingdon	8 430	9.3	188	5 400	1 051	132	150	2 871	1 039	66.2	22.7	507	78.1	66.3
Indiana	16 980	2.1	193	9 845	2 443	278	315	6 730	2 366	149.2	52.6	590	76.7	144.4
Jefferson	9 973	.9	216	6 320	1 222	128	156	1 924	1 197	76.4	26.4	569	75.1	81.3
Juniata	4 019	13.7	181	2 625	380	79	75	582	414	24.2	7.8	356	63.8	22.5
Lackawanna	50 112	-4.7	243	33 385	5 231	1 154	712	9 912	5 851	435.9	182.8	869	70.4	454.4
Lancaster	77 435	17.2	168	55 355	6 215	1 631	1 541	16 671	10 882	867.9	395.6	872	77.7	940.7
Lawrence	22 552	-4.3	239	13 705	2 795	482	321	4 087	2 328	178.5	59.8	628	76.3	171.3
Lebanon	23 639	13.8	201	16 835	1 561	2 274	444	4 679	3 362	229.8	94.3	805	75.7	231.5
Lehigh	59 937	14.4	200	41 475	5 535	1 375	1 043	14 010	9 388	801.5	322.8	1 082	78.5	813.3
Luzerne	77 596	-1.8	249	51 740	7 436	3 431	1 099	14 715	8 576	614.6	254.8	803	73.8	625.6
Lycoming	23 814	1.3	204	15 855	2 968	662	402	5 478	3 249	249.2	97.0	821	67.7	235.2
McKean	10 141	-2.5	221	6 530	1 497	586	157	2 295	1 638	108.7	33.0	707	77.3	115.9
Mercer	27 205	4.4	224	16 500	3 129	299	412	5 342	3 318	212.4	74.1	607	74.0	217.6
Mifflin	9 889	9.9	211	6 310	1 300	110	159	1 608	1 040	70.1	26.1	556	73.8	65.7
Monroe	23 397	36.9	182	15 065	1 435	3 250	444	6 431	3 705	266.3	167.2	1 363	89.0	284.6
Montgomery	127 476	10.0	176	90 255	5 891	4 655	3 759	28 122	18 791	1 776.1	980.0	1 373	82.3	1 768.5
Montour	3 735	5.4	213	2 510	383	39	60	1 347	548	40.2	14.0	786	65.1	41.9
Northampton	51 191	2.4	197	35 510	3 826	1 353	874	10 968	8 154	634.4	284.9	1 106	78.5	650.2
Northumberland	22 793	-.7	245	14 920	2 312	217	317	4 333	2 752	188.3	51.3	539	60.9	188.3
Perry	6 424	13.1	145	4 130	494	97	150	1 689	1 203	72.2	30.4	689	64.8	65.2
Philadelphia	265 422	-9.7	187	163 690	82 305	36 094	5 542	80 275	63 945	6 504.6	2 309.7	1 591	36.1	5 281.0
Pike	8 750	81.7	212	5 920	355	124	136	1 688	890	59.7	37.7	962	95.3	62.0
Potter	3 920	8.6	229	2 540	482	48	58	1 007	528	40.5	13.3	779	82.6	35.6

[1] Per 1,000 resident population estimated as of July 1, 1999. [2] Based on resident population estimated as of July 1, 1997. [3] Less than 10 employees.

Sources: Social Security Program—U.S. Social Security Administration, OASDI Beneficiaries by State and County - December 1999, <http://www.ssa.gov/statistics/oasdi_sc/1999/oasdi_sc99.pdf> (accessed: 7 March 2001) for 1999 – annual publication of same title for 1990. Supplemental Security Income Program—U.S. Social Security Administration, SSI Recipients by State and County, <http://www.ssa.gov/statistics/ssi_st_cty/1999/ssi_st_cty.pdf> (accessed: November 2000). Government employment, 1998—U.S. Bureau of Economic Analysis, "Regional Economic Information System (REIS) 1969-1998" on CD-ROM (related Internet site <http://www.bea.doc.gov/bea/regional/data.htm>). Local government employment, 1997—U.S. Census Bureau, 1997 Census of Governments, Compendium of Public Employment, <http://www.census.gov/govs/apes/97coar2.dat> (accessed: 14 January 2000). Local government finances—U.S. Census Bureau, 1997 Census of Governments, Compendium of Government Finances, <http://www.census.gov/prod/gc97/gc974-5.pdf> (accessed: 16 February 2001).

Table B–13. Counties — Government Programs, Employment, and Finances-Con.

[Includes U.S., states, and 3,142 counties/county equivalents defined as of January 1, 1992. For changes to these areas since January 1, 1992, see appendix B. Geographic Information]

County	Social Security Program beneficiaries, December 1999 — Total Number	Percent change, 1990–1999	Rate[1]	Retired workers	Supplemental Security Income Program recipients, December 1999	Government employment, 1998 — Federal Civilian	Military	State and local	Local government employment, full-time equivalent, March 1997	General revenue Total (mil. dol.)	Taxes Total (mil. dol.)	Per capita[2]	Percent property	Direct general expenditure (mil. dol.)
PENNSYLVANIA—Con.														
Schuylkill	36 518	-6.0	245	24 245	2 871	722	501	6 453	3 621	271.8	89.4	591	70.1	260.8
Snyder	6 935	11.8	183	4 475	537	93	129	2 497	872	57.2	24.3	636	60.5	62.2
Somerset	17 607	5.1	220	10 540	2 002	231	271	4 173	2 015	137.3	47.9	595	78.7	150.9
Sullivan	1 956	24.6	324	1 315	114	27	21	356	206	12.9	6.6	1 090	88.0	12.5
Susquehanna	8 844	15.7	210	5 685	817	123	143	1 809	1 400	80.7	28.8	684	90.1	84.0
Tioga	8 998	12.3	216	5 655	1 128	169	141	2 864	1 427	86.3	27.5	663	78.5	87.3
Union	6 514	14.8	161	4 595	423	1 589	145	2 198	782	58.0	25.4	622	64.7	56.5
Venango	13 341	10.3	232	7 575	1 959	190	195	3 775	2 070	135.8	40.7	701	77.8	134.4
Warren	9 612	8.1	221	6 250	764	231	148	2 560	1 206	88.7	31.9	722	71.3	89.2
Washington	46 489	1.8	227	27 710	5 074	635	701	9 111	5 379	389.1	160.3	779	78.9	407.8
Wayne	11 665	17.4	253	7 805	774	132	153	2 206	1 392	103.2	54.6	1 208	95.4	95.3
Westmoreland	82 671	6.6	223	50 955	7 533	1 123	1 258	15 084	10 061	760.1	299.8	802	79.6	731.5
Wyoming	5 192	14.1	177	3 245	463	75	98	1 109	1 017	54.8	23.2	791	79.9	53.0
York	63 727	14.8	169	44 730	5 185	3 805	1 689	12 262	9 189	730.7	307.6	829	74.0	674.9
RHODE ISLAND	190 681	5.4	192	129 804	26 837	10 591	9 676	54 934	29 102	2 130.8	1 234.5	1 251	98.6	1 996.7
Bristol	10 131	19.7	206	7 295	407	114	329	1 682	1 327	103.3	55.4	1 130	98.7	98.6
Kent	32 734	11.2	202	22 345	2 818	688	1 006	8 006	4 420	345.5	225.1	1 395	98.3	315.5
Newport	14 815	12.6	178	10 090	1 348	4 246	3 901	3 240	2 969	190.1	117.1	1 411	96.6	172.5
Providence	113 553	.4	198	76 610	21 024	5 015	3 641	31 465	16 912	1 241.1	676.3	1 177	99.1	1 148.7
Washington	19 431	19.4	159	13 455	1 209	528	799	10 541	3 474	250.8	160.6	1 348	98.3	261.5
SOUTH CAROLINA	672 353	24.2	173	398 766	108 198	29 258	56 340	278 278	143 952	7 907.3	2 421.1	639	86.0	7 776.0
Abbeville	5 090	24.4	206	3 135	594	48	142	1 351	675	32.8	11.7	478	88.2	32.8
Aiken	24 580	25.6	182	14 885	3 580	921	772	6 247	3 927	216.3	70.7	531	90.4	207.0
Allendale	1 937	-1.9	171	1 040	782	27	66	1 477	660	21.4	8.0	698	85.7	20.2
Anderson	32 960	22.3	202	20 140	3 196	386	927	9 890	4 223	222.1	83.3	525	86.9	223.3
Bamberg	3 117	15.2	191	1 750	839	42	95	1 269	926	27.0	8.6	520	85.5	25.2
Barnwell	3 861	9.4	177	2 140	1 157	51	125	1 677	1 057	55.0	9.5	438	86.9	48.2
Beaufort	22 116	70.6	196	14 925	1 856	2 153	11 430	5 769	3 536	239.1	101.8	949	90.5	251.1
Berkeley	17 376	77.8	122	8 720	2 817	342	793	6 434	3 910	183.1	51.8	386	93.3	188.2
Calhoun	2 521	35.9	177	1 390	524	34	81	938	434	21.5	9.5	687	97.7	20.1
Charleston	46 905	18.2	147	27 885	8 466	8 520	10 282	31 744	11 395	762.7	298.6	953	71.2	703.6
Cherokee	9 592	30.6	192	5 540	1 129	94	283	2 032	1 675	117.1	30.0	617	88.9	82.4
Chester	6 662	13.5	191	3 880	901	70	198	2 487	1 690	63.2	23.0	680	86.9	60.1
Chesterfield	7 972	16.7	192	4 265	1 774	97	237	1 963	1 367	60.3	19.1	469	89.8	60.7
Clarendon	6 293	27.6	204	3 390	1 809	71	177	1 952	1 416	62.6	12.2	397	90.5	54.7
Colleton	7 692	26.1	204	3 930	1 943	105	215	2 097	1 534	60.2	23.7	638	86.8	62.0
Darlington	12 151	21.4	182	6 635	2 833	120	382	2 937	2 221	99.5	36.0	548	93.5	93.2
Dillon	5 521	9.4	186	2 790	2 120	86	171	1 458	1 112	45.1	9.4	317	69.2	48.5
Dorchester	13 138	44.5	145	6 910	2 252	179	508	4 716	3 056	131.9	39.7	459	89.5	142.8
Edgefield	3 519	27.7	176	2 015	758	321	115	1 030	657	34.4	11.2	569	90.2	34.4
Fairfield	4 238	11.8	188	2 460	929	43	129	1 460	924	52.9	30.2	1 354	98.6	52.6
Florence	20 582	13.2	164	11 245	5 969	707	721	11 233	4 123	208.8	62.9	506	67.1	194.3
Georgetown	11 747	33.1	214	6 740	1 646	98	340	3 786	2 364	122.9	45.4	867	93.5	114.2
Greenville	60 099	13.2	167	37 980	7 106	1 722	2 076	21 976	14 010	1 037.3	250.7	718	87.7	1 005.8
Greenwood	12 772	10.9	200	8 260	1 618	199	366	6 235	2 306	205.0	35.1	555	92.9	175.6
Hampton	4 005	11.4	210	1 990	1 102	376	111	1 180	1 124	42.6	12.9	678	85.9	42.3
Horry	38 717	58.4	217	25 220	4 270	433	1 008	9 429	6 403	409.2	165.7	979	80.5	444.0
Jasper	2 480	4.4	144	1 265	634	41	98	1 076	624	27.2	10.5	617	81.3	29.0
Kershaw	9 762	18.5	198	5 690	1 416	111	280	3 193	2 329	128.1	26.6	556	92.8	126.9
Lancaster	10 552	18.3	177	6 305	1 323	102	339	2 421	2 552	82.3	28.1	486	78.0	77.4
Laurens	13 056	24.3	206	7 275	1 925	103	370	4 251	2 146	107.4	23.9	383	92.5	107.4
Lee	3 553	31.6	175	1 895	1 123	43	117	865	853	27.4	8.2	407	85.9	24.7
Lexington	29 733	43.7	142	18 450	2 990	497	1 183	11 300	8 857	576.2	134.9	673	94.5	575.7
McCormick	2 272	50.0	237	1 410	360	90	55	963	366	14.4	4.5	474	88.7	15.2
Marion	6 450	3.3	187	3 445	2 005	87	199	2 549	2 132	109.3	16.5	474	77.4	100.2
Marlboro	5 844	5.1	198	2 935	1 832	81	170	1 742	1 082	46.2	12.0	405	75.4	50.5
Newberry	7 234	3.9	210	4 550	1 010	147	198	1 997	1 509	54.2	19.4	566	94.8	51.9
Oconee	14 470	34.9	222	9 245	1 177	163	369	3 338	1 955	96.5	49.8	786	96.1	100.7
Orangeburg	17 029	11.4	195	9 570	4 712	234	522	7 130	4 705	220.0	51.7	590	91.1	229.2
Pickens	17 735	29.5	164	11 250	1 420	224	489	7 489	2 547	124.7	43.6	416	80.7	126.1
Richland	42 876	13.2	140	25 160	7 381	7 797	11 747	52 685	13 222	766.6	160.9	534	83.7	813.6
Saluda	3 194	22.8	188	1 975	585	44	98	826	452	20.3	5.7	335	86.8	18.7
Spartanburg	45 758	19.4	183	27 025	6 087	513	1 433	15 126	11 266	408.1	159.2	650	90.9	397.0
Sumter	16 585	24.4	148	9 280	4 350	1 206	5 499	5 588	3 375	161.8	50.9	457	82.4	157.4
Union	7 070	18.3	233	4 050	938	94	176	2 268	1 386	74.1	16.1	527	93.7	69.7
Williamsburg	7 090	20.5	192	3 355	2 367	98	214	2 213	1 352	62.2	13.1	353	94.1	64.4
York	24 461	29.0	155	15 370	2 469	338	890	8 491	4 517	266.5	124.6	829	94.4	252.9

[1] Per 1,000 resident population estimated as of July 1, 1999.   [2] Based on resident population estimated as of July 1, 1997.

Sources: Social Security Program—U.S. Social Security Administration, OASDI Beneficiaries by State and County - December 1999, <http://www.ssa.gov/statistics/oasdi_sc/1999/oasdi_sc99.pdf> (accessed: 7 March 2001) for 1999 - annual publication of same title for 1990. Supplemental Security Income Program—U.S. Social Security Administration, SSI Recipients by State and County, <http://www.ssa.gov/statistics/ssi_st_cty/1999/ssi_st_cty.pdf> (accessed: November 2000). Government employment, 1998—U.S. Bureau of Economic Analysis, "Regional Economic Information System (REIS) 1969-1998" on CD-ROM (related Internet site <http://www.bea.doc.gov/bea/regional/data.htm>). Local government employment, 1997—U.S. Census Bureau, 1997 Census of Governments, Compendium of Public Employment, <http://www.census.gov/govs/apes/97coar2.dat> (accessed: 14 January 2000). Local government finances—U.S. Census Bureau, 1997 Census of Governments, Compendium of Government Finances, <http://www.census.gov/prod/gc97/gc974-5.pdf> (accessed: 16 February 2001).

[Includes U.S., states, and 3,142 counties/county equivalents defined as of January 1, 1992. For changes to these areas since January 1, 1992, see appendix B. Geographic Information]

County	Social Security Program beneficiaries, December 1999				Supplemental Security Income Program recipients, December 1999	Government employment, 1998			Local government employment, full-time equivalent, March 1997	Local government finances, 1996–1997					
	Total			Retired workers		Federal		State and local		General revenue					Direct general expenditure (mil. dol.)
	Number	Percent change, 1990–1999	Rate[1]			Civilian	Military			Total (mil. dol.)	Taxes				
											Total (mil. dol.)	Per capita[2]	Percent property		
SOUTH DAKOTA	135 165	5.4	184	84 435	12 756	10 767	8 260	50 252	26 567	1 419.0	695.1	951	76.7		1 400.2
Aurora...................	736	2.2	245	445	38	23	21	322	138	5.9	2.6	875	87.2		5.5
Beadle	3 956	–1.6	238	2 535	345	370	123	1 034	628	34.9	16.0	894	75.0		36.9
Bennett................	543	3.4	164	285	172	30	24	361	234	9.2	2.4	733	82.3		8.9
Bon Homme	1 780	–2.7	248	1 125	83	35	55	558	277	15.7	6.7	904	86.7		14.1
Brookings.............	3 628	3.1	140	2 385	213	139	197	4 887	1 204	62.2	21.4	818	81.8		63.9
Brown	6 999	4.6	199	4 490	524	540	254	2 453	1 173	63.5	34.0	953	72.2		64.6
Brule	1 102	.6	200	710	83	41	40	350	253	11.4	5.6	1 012	83.3		10.7
Buffalo	231	32.0	130	90	106	128	12	(3)	9	.4	.3	152	96.3		.4
Butte	1 871	13.7	214	1 105	167	57	64	518	404	17.8	6.4	716	79.3		17.5
Campbell	511	–7.1	277	290	27	10	14	112	85	3.6	1.7	862	92.0		3.3
Charles Mix	1 925	–.3	209	1 150	270	190	67	511	354	16.8	7.2	766	89.2		15.8
Clark	1 099	–6.5	256	720	67	28	31	221	159	7.3	4.0	908	90.7		7.1
Clay...................	1 688	–6.5	129	1 110	108	54	113	2 986	387	18.4	10.1	764	78.6		19.7
Codington	4 643	4.8	183	2 945	349	172	182	1 445	990	48.1	25.7	1 009	67.4		52.9
Corson	632	–11.0	154	330	221	114	30	242	217	7.8	1.9	448	81.3		6.9
Custer................	1 613	26.5	230	1 010	102	190	49	544	248	12.8	6.6	961	82.5		12.2
Davison	3 820	1.3	214	2 435	378	114	129	1 075	799	33.0	16.6	935	65.2		34.6
Day	1 760	–12.4	285	1 140	128	68	46	373	242	13.3	5.5	852	90.3		12.8
Deuel	1 116	–2.1	251	680	54	36	32	234	138	6.6	3.6	785	86.3		6.3
Dewey	740	8.8	123	380	313	353	42	257	194	8.1	2.2	384	80.3		7.4
Douglas	875	–2.8	250	505	51	29	25	164	103	5.3	2.7	759	79.7		4.9
Edmunds	1 076	–5.2	257	690	47	24	30	366	304	11.9	4.3	1 021	93.1		11.2
Fall River	2 067	6.8	303	1 295	185	542	51	526	251	15.8	7.2	1 039	83.7		13.9
Faulk	716	–11.1	286	455	43	20	18	164	143	4.9	2.6	1 020	93.4		4.4
Grant	1 790	–4.0	225	1 135	109	44	58	388	278	17.4	8.9	1 102	90.5		17.2
Gregory	1 402	–3.6	286	845	130	39	35	292	243	10.8	4.7	935	83.6		10.4
Haakon	462	–2.7	200	285	24	18	17	149	118	7.5	2.8	1 159	83.0		7.5
Hamlin	1 211	–3.5	224	760	64	34	38	447	356	13.5	5.8	1 073	90.1		17.3
Hand..................	984	7.0	238	635	40	22	30	206	78	7.8	4.8	1 158	89.0		7.6
Hanson	559	4.5	185	355	23	11	21	135	107	4.6	2.2	760	88.6		4.4
Harding...............	248	–4.6	171	135	9	23	11	116	83	3.6	1.9	1 251	81.9		3.5
Hughes................	2 687	13.1	174	1 730	255	339	110	3 284	570	27.6	14.4	940	78.7		29.5
Hutchinson............	2 314	–2.2	287	1 410	91	43	57	464	317	16.5	8.2	1 012	89.7		15.0
Hyde	423	–8.0	267	270	27	(3)	11	102	71	3.4	1.9	1 174	85.0		3.2
Jackson	463	11.6	157	265	90	90	21	131	91	3.6	1.6	569	78.4		3.5
Jerauld	652	–10.1	307	440	36	24	16	161	117	5.0	2.2	994	90.1		5.1
Jones	264	–2.2	219	185	9	11	(3)	100	71	2.9	1.6	1 286	82.8		2.5
Kingsbury.............	1 628	–6.4	284	1 050	78	45	41	281	267	11.5	5.6	955	90.1		11.0
Lake	2 274	–2.4	213	1 480	149	64	80	972	269	21.5	9.7	907	87.5		19.4
Lawrence	4 117	15.6	193	2 545	270	207	161	1 708	678	53.4	25.4	1 146	79.5		51.5
Lincoln	2 957	32.0	137	1 915	93	49	146	714	482	29.0	14.2	729	89.8		27.9
Lyman................	708	11.5	187	395	80	73	27	173	126	5.6	2.9	748	85.5		5.5
McCook	1 292	–9.3	233	800	63	34	40	282	218	11.2	5.7	1 008	86.0		10.8
McPherson	931	–6.0	346	545	45	18	20	171	144	5.6	3.3	1 181	92.9		5.7
Marshall	1 150	–2.5	254	760	55	31	33	326	238	8.4	4.5	973	83.6		8.1
Meade	3 352	17.8	157	1 965	271	1 219	157	861	628	27.1	13.5	617	80.9		27.2
Mellette...............	319	8.1	156	170	119	14	14	157	113	5.3	1.4	681	84.1		4.8
Miner.................	742	–23.5	276	495	32	22	20	163	115	6.5	3.5	1 221	86.1		5.9
Minnehaha.............	21 218	9.5	149	13 575	1 832	2 100	1 057	6 388	4 009	276.2	166.5	1 200	67.4		259.6
Moody................	1 180	–6.3	183	725	62	164	46	322	282	13.1	5.7	874	88.6		12.6
Pennington	14 401	29.0	163	8 870	1 594	1 260	3 559	5 287	3 415	192.8	91.5	1 052	71.2		193.4
Perkins	975	–5.8	281	595	77	34	25	294	159	9.0	3.7	1 055	89.9		8.6
Potter	800	–6.4	282	520	33	28	20	181	143	8.8	4.0	1 349	91.5		8.2
Roberts...............	2 098	–6.5	214	1 315	243	143	70	530	412	16.8	6.7	671	88.9		16.7
Sanborn	642	–13.8	240	410	39	15	20	163	111	4.6	1.9	690	86.1		4.2
Shannon...............	1 113	21.0	89	365	1 018	531	87	335	318	10.3	.6	49	59.4		9.0
Spink.................	1 874	–7.2	252	1 110	170	51	54	971	370	18.9	8.3	1 089	86.4		17.9
Stanley	434	18.9	150	280	20	(3)	21	137	102	5.8	3.1	1 063	81.5		5.6
Sully	326	20.7	220	210	11	11	10	129	125	3.8	2.6	1 698	88.7		3.5
Todd..................	713	1.1	75	305	578	265	66	562	421	16.1	1.7	184	69.0		15.2
Tripp	1 469	1.0	222	905	148	41	48	395	281	11.3	5.5	810	85.6		12.8
Turner................	2 032	–4.6	235	1 300	94	42	62	440	291	13.7	7.1	822	89.0		14.2
Union	2 156	–6.9	173	1 375	92	46	87	604	476	25.8	13.6	1 145	84.2		29.4
Walworth	1 525	14.7	272	980	149	43	40	397	231	10.9	4.7	839	81.7		9.8
Yankton	3 968	8.4	187	2 625	265	196	150	1 511	631	34.4	18.7	896	74.4		36.0
Ziebach	181	–2.2	84	90	84	(3)	16	111	78	2.9	.9	404	80.4		2.9

[1] Per 1,000 resident population estimated as of July 1, 1999.   [2] Based on resident population estimated as of July 1, 1997.   [3] Less than 10 employees.

Sources: Social Security Program—U.S. Social Security Administration, OASDI Beneficiaries by State and County - December 1999, <http://www.ssa.gov/statistics/oasdi_sc/1999/oasdi_sc99.pdf> (accessed: 7 March 2001) for 1999 – annual publication of same title for 1990.   Supplemental Security Income Program—U.S. Social Security Administration, SSI Recipients by State and County, <http://www.ssa.gov/statistics/ssi_st_cty/1999/ssi_st_cty.pdf> (accessed: November 2000).   Government employment, 1998—U.S. Bureau of Economic Analysis, "Regional Economic Information System (REIS) 1969-1998" on CD-ROM (related Internet site <http://www.bea.doc.gov/bea/regional/data.htm>).   Local government employment, 1997—U.S. Census Bureau, 1997 Census of Governments, Compendium of Public Employment, <http://www.census.gov/govs/apes/97coar2.dat> (accessed: 14 January 2000).   Local government finances—U.S. Census Bureau, 1997 Census of Governments, Compendium of Government Finances, <http://www.census.gov/prod/gc97/gc974-5.pdf> (accessed: 16 February 2001).

Table B–13. Counties — **Government Programs, Employment, and Finances**–Con.

[Includes U.S., states, and 3,142 counties/county equivalents defined as of January 1, 1992. For changes to these areas since January 1, 1992, see appendix B. Geographic Information]

County	Social Security Program beneficiaries, December 1999				Supplemental Security Income Program recipients, December 1999	Government employment, 1998			Local government employment, full-time equivalent, March 1997	Local government finances, 1996–1997				
	Total			Retired workers		Federal		State and local		General revenue				Direct general expenditure (mil. dol.)
	Number	Percent change, 1990–1999	Rate¹			Civilian	Military			Total (mil. dol.)	Taxes			
											Total (mil. dol.)	Per capita²	Percent property	
TENNESSEE	970 895	17.7	177	558 215	166 435	50 308	23 782	329 985	194 274	11 286.5	4 009.8	746	58.2	11 575.0
Anderson	15 657	11.6	221	8 815	2 352	1 231	284	3 688	2 608	118.4	38.5	539	76.6	140.0
Bedford	6 379	11.6	183	4 065	820	93	137	1 920	1 325	67.8	16.9	493	72.8	77.8
Benton	4 098	17.3	248	2 430	476	72	65	740	523	22.6	6.2	384	54.5	21.6
Bledsoe	1 962	36.7	179	1 105	388	17	43	1 049	389	15.5	2.9	277	65.6	14.1
Blount	19 801	19.4	193	11 320	2 341	235	417	5 024	3 729	222.1	63.0	632	59.9	206.6
Bradley	14 616	28.8	174	8 515	2 217	256	333	4 657	3 525	190.1	47.6	579	49.5	187.8
Campbell	9 726	22.0	253	4 090	2 988	84	152	2 123	1 277	76.2	17.5	462	56.5	73.1
Cannon	2 557	34.2	209	1 555	307	30	48	411	372	16.3	3.8	317	69.8	14.6
Carroll	7 256	5.2	246	4 435	974	89	116	1 235	996	42.9	12.1	419	59.2	52.8
Carter	11 977	32.8	225	6 390	1 910	108	212	2 106	1 682	73.1	26.6	501	62.0	69.2
Cheatham	4 565	47.5	126	2 505	401	83	141	1 203	1 114	47.9	14.8	430	63.4	44.5
Chester	2 905	26.6	196	1 705	394	32	59	743	379	18.5	5.3	368	56.6	16.7
Claiborne	6 982	28.6	235	2 870	2 180	67	118	1 863	1 225	48.7	9.2	320	60.9	47.3
Clay	1 809	38.6	249	935	453	48	29	376	287	12.3	2.7	372	82.3	14.3
Cocke	7 158	31.6	222	3 510	1 969	69	127	1 364	967	43.5	10.9	343	62.5	48.8
Coffee	9 470	15.6	204	5 865	1 343	376	289	2 755	1 833	76.5	22.9	505	59.4	84.3
Crockett	3 199	5.8	227	1 895	533	50	56	608	624	21.4	6.2	451	57.9	20.2
Cumberland	12 657	62.8	279	8 230	1 412	90	176	1 616	1 277	59.7	20.6	478	46.8	54.9
Davidson	80 496	5.9	152	49 890	12 274	8 353	2 705	38 449	19 587	1 487.5	693.4	1 294	52.5	1 603.0
Decatur	2 994	25.8	278	1 840	379	34	43	699	466	17.4	3.7	340	50.4	14.3
DeKalb	3 485	17.1	215	2 050	679	40	63	677	611	20.0	4.9	309	69.8	17.2
Dickson	7 219	18.3	168	4 240	939	99	168	2 067	1 426	67.1	24.7	604	54.2	66.8
Dyer	7 418	6.2	202	4 095	1 471	113	146	2 332	1 921	65.1	20.8	570	51.5	78.8
Fayette	5 256	61.5	167	2 880	1 150	61	121	1 458	841	36.1	10.7	365	72.2	34.0
Fentress	3 919	27.9	240	1 875	1 174	35	64	782	463	20.5	5.7	360	50.8	20.4
Franklin	8 118	27.8	215	4 990	1 003	151	149	1 525	1 156	51.3	20.0	535	63.2	46.2
Gibson	11 354	.2	236	7 150	1 613	163	194	2 332	1 838	93.2	31.4	653	62.2	96.9
Giles	5 775	11.2	199	3 460	781	77	115	1 266	746	40.8	13.8	483	69.8	41.5
Grainger	3 895	18.0	193	1 800	1 010	55	79	651	457	22.7	4.7	243	62.3	20.2
Greene	13 921	23.2	229	7 760	2 669	232	241	3 377	1 862	86.6	34.9	589	47.5	85.6
Grundy	3 218	24.5	229	1 550	890	24	56	617	458	20.0	4.2	301	73.8	19.3
Hamblen	11 529	31.9	213	6 215	1 916	170	216	2 922	1 692	90.2	40.4	753	50.3	93.1
Hamilton	55 655	10.8	189	34 760	7 781	6 472	1 218	19 408	8 982	976.3	264.1	895	71.3	1 000.3
Hancock	1 388	10.2	205	565	681	11	27	304	202	11.0	1.3	105	84.6	11.2
Hardeman	5 149	11.3	211	2 665	1 616	65	99	1 802	971	38.7	9.2	381	59.5	37.8
Hardin	6 000	28.9	238	3 330	1 133	111	99	1 454	996	47.4	9.5	382	63.2	42.6
Hawkins	10 456	34.8	209	4 985	1 857	265	198	1 963	1 671	69.2	23.1	475	65.3	64.1
Haywood	3 676	5.2	189	2 025	1 141	52	78	1 039	805	33.9	10.0	508	62.9	34.4
Henderson	4 786	2.5	193	2 740	785	57	97	1 028	829	34.1	9.3	389	41.5	29.6
Henry	7 689	7.4	256	4 750	920	120	136	2 025	1 264	77.8	15.7	528	52.1	76.3
Hickman	3 897	20.1	183	2 150	553	62	82	1 245	496	32.2	6.6	331	67.6	29.8
Houston	1 742	14.6	221	990	298	17	31	430	268	11.1	2.6	337	66.2	11.1
Humphreys	3 701	19.2	215	2 170	478	395	68	901	597	32.8	10.3	611	60.3	29.0
Jackson	2 447	38.2	254	1 295	520	27	38	376	337	13.1	3.3	348	69.3	13.2
Jefferson	8 519	28.2	189	4 780	1 264	119	174	1 871	1 443	56.0	16.9	400	60.1	54.0
Johnson	3 846	14.8	230	1 970	940	42	67	607	452	21.4	5.2	316	72.8	19.7
Knox	63 456	14.8	169	37 815	9 705	3 958	1 558	31 424	12 052	691.5	368.3	986	53.2	771.7
Lake	1 459	-5.6	179	810	423	21	33	663	242	10.2	2.4	295	62.7	10.9
Lauderdale	4 874	-3.1	201	2 550	1 365	66	96	1 699	881	41.7	8.7	362	75.2	40.2
Lawrence	8 325	10.9	210	4 575	1 373	114	157	1 801	1 402	57.7	20.4	522	52.4	58.0
Lewis	2 274	26.7	204	1 215	321	24	43	536	295	15.4	3.5	322	57.5	13.7
Lincoln	6 305	12.4	212	3 945	866	68	118	2 334	1 581	62.7	13.2	452	57.2	64.8
Loudon	8 609	34.0	216	5 495	920	168	155	1 447	1 191	54.3	17.7	464	73.4	51.4
McMinn	9 824	23.0	212	5 675	1 526	138	184	2 140	1 794	90.9	24.3	529	66.8	88.9
McNairy	5 819	9.3	239	3 190	1 307	91	96	1 197	679	36.5	6.6	277	74.7	34.9
Macon	3 764	27.8	203	2 055	682	38	72	864	578	26.4	7.6	428	53.2	29.8
Madison	15 085	7.8	174	8 900	2 889	539	345	9 842	5 763	365.3	72.3	852	56.9	395.3
Marion	5 383	26.4	200	2 565	970	77	107	941	793	37.4	11.6	440	53.6	34.4
Marshall	4 655	15.9	176	2 750	517	60	105	1 195	1 002	40.3	17.0	662	64.9	37.6
Maury	11 535	14.4	164	6 575	1 687	215	277	5 032	3 351	211.4	36.4	533	61.9	224.4
Meigs	2 105	35.4	208	1 025	438	20	40	400	312	12.6	2.3	242	68.3	15.6
Monroe	7 911	31.3	222	4 165	1 617	97	139	1 293	1 033	46.5	13.9	409	51.1	48.4
Montgomery	14 674	36.8	113	8 310	2 251	539	515	6 985	4 566	266.3	76.8	618	53.3	260.3
Moore	907	48.7	176	610	90	(³)	21	796	177	5.4	.6	112	61.7	6.9
Morgan	4 483	71.1	240	2 060	616	39	75	1 486	578	24.0	6.4	345	81.3	21.4
Obion	6 736	2.5	209	3 985	1 066	115	129	1 489	1 061	55.5	21.5	672	48.9	52.4

¹ Per 1,000 resident population estimated as of July 1, 1999. ² Based on resident population estimated as of July 1, 1997. ³ Less than 10 employees.

Sources: Social Security Program—U.S. Social Security Administration, OASDI Beneficiaries by State and County - December 1999, <http://www.ssa.gov/statistics/oasdi_sc/1999/oasdi_sc99.pdf> (accessed: 7 March 2001) for 1999 – annual publication of same title for 1990. Supplemental Security Income Program—U.S. Social Security Administration, SSI Recipients by State and County, <http://www.ssa.gov/statistics/ssi_st_cty/1999/ssi_st_cty.pdf> (accessed: November 2000). Government employment, 1998—U.S. Bureau of Economic Analysis, "Regional Economic Information System (REIS) 1969-1998" on CD-ROM (related Internet site <http://www.bea.doc.gov/bea/regional/data.htm>). Local government employment, 1997—U.S. Census Bureau, 1997 Census of Governments, Compendium of Public Employment, <http://www.census.gov/govs/apes/97coar2.dat> (accessed: 14 January 2000). Local government finances—U.S. Census Bureau, 1997 Census of Governments, Compendium of Government Finances, <http://www.census.gov/prod/gc97/gc974-5.pdf> (accessed: 16 February 2001).

[Includes U.S., states, and 3,142 counties/county equivalents defined as of January 1, 1992. For changes to these areas since January 1, 1992, see appendix B. Geographic Information]

County	Social Security Program beneficiaries, December 1999				Supplemental Security Income Program recipients, December 1999	Government employment, 1998			Local government employment, full-time equivalent, March 1997	Local government finances, 1996–1997				
	Total					Federal				General revenue				
								State and local			Taxes			Direct general expenditure (mil. dol.)
	Number	Percent change, 1990–1999	Rate¹	Retired workers		Civilian	Military			Total (mil. dol.)	Total (mil. dol.)	Per capita²	Percent property	
TENNESSEE—Con.														
Overton	4 483	21.8	228	2 415	926	50	78	1 041	641	27.9	5.9	308	60.4	24.9
Perry	1 836	22.4	243	1 030	244	18	30	331	260	11.9	3.5	473	72.4	10.8
Pickett	1 300	46.9	276	745	238	(³)	18	271	191	8.5	1.7	374	66.0	8.1
Polk	3 729	18.6	247	1 895	550	70	59	691	406	19.2	5.9	405	65.7	16.5
Putnam	11 811	17.7	198	6 875	1 899	253	241	7 536	2 649	147.7	30.6	524	58.9	159.2
Rhea	5 758	21.7	205	3 345	1 157	940	111	1 376	1 001	51.4	10.6	384	60.6	50.2
Roane	11 352	17.3	227	6 445	1 933	521	199	3 506	1 881	98.7	26.5	532	62.6	89.3
Robertson	8 614	35.8	157	4 955	956	93	211	2 454	1 494	76.8	28.0	543	60.2	77.2
Rutherford	18 820	42.5	110	10 755	2 133	1 899	668	9 583	4 526	283.8	121.0	757	60.2	268.2
Scott	4 402	21.8	218	1 540	1 685	74	80	1 208	907	35.3	7.7	390	60.5	31.4
Sequatchie	1 994	44.0	184	1 045	362	11	41	446	343	14.5	4.0	395	65.4	16.1
Sevier	12 661	48.7	192	7 475	1 380	271	257	3 411	2 060	162.1	79.0	1 258	23.9	145.4
Shelby	121 822	5.5	140	68 590	31 654	14 732	4 714	56 345	34 851	2 121.2	804.3	930	59.5	2 229.9
Smith	3 264	12.7	195	1 845	534	111	65	658	411	21.7	5.6	349	59.5	21.7
Stewart	2 710	24.9	230	1 510	406	512	46	547	299	15.6	2.8	253	70.1	16.9
Sullivan	34 126	17.2	227	19 355	4 470	512	602	6 968	4 958	247.2	120.1	799	65.1	245.5
Sumner	18 950	39.2	150	11 405	2 096	443	494	5 260	4 379	200.0	75.7	621	61.6	174.7
Tipton	7 505	47.9	155	3 920	1 392	105	188	1 969	1 636	70.2	20.5	445	65.3	69.6
Trousdale	1 418	23.3	203	845	265	48	27	315	216	10.9	3.0	443	72.6	9.6
Unicoi	3 916	19.2	226	2 110	684	86	69	930	579	41.8	7.2	417	65.1	41.8
Union	3 500	83.7	211	1 625	640	21	65	538	449	19.4	3.9	244	72.1	26.4
Van Buren	989	31.9	197	565	183	(³)	20	234	164	8.2	1.9	372	64.6	8.7
Warren	7 597	15.4	209	4 455	1 452	117	144	1 701	1 323	52.9	18.4	515	58.6	49.5
Washington	20 022	13.8	195	11 500	2 947	1 906	423	8 759	3 104	160.0	69.0	680	61.0	173.6
Wayne	3 275	27.2	200	1 735	513	30	66	900	591	25.0	5.2	316	62.8	22.6
Weakley	6 651	6.8	202	4 230	746	135	135	3 161	1 105	46.4	13.6	416	59.0	46.6
White	5 198	15.4	227	3 115	913	57	90	1 021	738	27.7	7.6	342	65.8	33.7
Williamson	12 494	58.2	101	8 045	690	275	468	5 052	4 580	268.9	119.8	1 076	65.2	259.8
Wilson	12 182	41.5	141	7 365	1 235	159	334	2 961	2 152	112.1	46.6	572	55.5	107.4
TEXAS	2 575 745	17.4	129	1 516 987	408 084	184 577	165 408	1 308 218	850 380	46 587.8	20 537.1	1 061	79.6	45 113.0
Anderson	7 878	–1.1	151	4 495	1 185	132	139	5 766	2 088	72.1	32.5	623	79.8	68.3
Andrews	2 154	17.4	157	1 155	254	23	37	1 166	696	49.5	31.0	2 224	94.9	43.3
Angelina	14 148	8.4	182	7 450	2 245	400	206	5 839	3 810	172.8	53.6	702	71.5	181.2
Aransas	4 993	44.1	216	3 260	407	26	61	968	694	34.4	19.7	874	84.4	31.8
Archer	1 556	26.5	188	950	88	20	23	496	322	16.4	7.0	852	78.6	15.1
Armstrong	445	–2.2	203	280	16	(³)	(³)	138	98	3.7	1.6	716	82.5	3.7
Atascosa	5 780	55.2	154	2 820	813	51	97	1 940	1 883	70.0	20.5	580	80.9	72.4
Austin	4 021	–4.3	169	2 460	380	105	63	1 264	949	43.4	19.9	866	81.8	50.0
Bailey	1 226	.1	183	725	163	34	18	573	510	22.3	5.8	850	86.1	22.2
Bandera	3 205	52.3	193	2 045	187	18	42	636	526	20.2	10.6	711	87.3	18.8
Bastrop	6 446	9.3	123	3 895	841	377	134	2 897	2 182	97.8	29.1	595	84.9	84.7
Baylor	1 255	–7.7	307	790	122	20	11	255	312	8.7	3.2	777	86.2	8.1
Bee	4 157	11.6	151	2 155	912	49	74	3 791	1 516	66.9	14.7	528	77.3	67.9
Bell	25 129	19.3	113	14 745	3 499	7 911	42 418	14 341	11 228	537.2	150.4	678	72.8	507.3
Bexar	181 159	18.6	132	103 060	35 770	36 470	36 234	87 053	63 625	3 093.4	1 152.0	862	82.6	3 080.6
Blanco	1 736	–13.2	204	1 135	95	80	22	367	312	13.7	6.0	724	84.8	12.0
Borden	99	65.0	129	60	4	(³)	(³)	88	69	5.7	4.6	6 080	99.0	4.9
Bosque	3 976	–4.9	238	2 610	287	69	44	859	659	32.0	9.6	573	85.2	30.3
Bowie	15 258	8.7	183	8 695	2 617	3 446	239	5 652	3 723	170.6	58.5	700	69.3	165.9
Brazoria	26 251	24.9	112	15 250	2 761	442	653	13 543	8 785	460.1	246.4	1 104	89.4	453.4
Brazos	12 789	27.6	95	7 680	1 721	970	462	28 534	4 877	246.1	125.8	952	75.3	273.9
Brewster	1 526	14.7	174	1 005	180	175	24	1 401	574	30.6	6.1	689	77.0	30.0
Briscoe	437	–24.7	239	240	41	14	(³)	123	87	3.4	1.6	831	87.3	2.6
Brooks	1 542	7.1	183	745	628	99	23	525	402	17.2	7.6	902	90.4	16.8
Brown	7 678	.1	208	4 650	1 001	111	99	2 748	1 808	75.9	24.8	676	76.2	73.8
Burleson	3 337	15.1	214	2 020	424	53	42	792	776	28.0	14.1	916	84.6	28.7
Burnet	7 353	30.3	216	4 900	484	65	85	1 810	1 316	65.7	27.1	879	82.1	66.1
Caldwell	4 841	12.2	148	2 830	793	60	86	1 660	1 265	53.4	12.9	411	80.9	57.2
Calhoun	3 477	20.7	170	2 005	406	43	95	1 339	1 169	72.9	33.3	1 614	88.7	71.0
Callahan	2 801	11.4	217	1 755	245	30	34	650	566	22.5	7.1	555	83.1	21.9
Cameron	41 056	17.6	125	22 555	15 888	1 893	942	21 352	15 256	726.9	157.7	496	74.6	693.2
Camp	2 367	–1.6	216	1 400	402	30	29	482	434	19.7	8.5	779	85.2	19.1
Carson	1 133	–5.2	168	710	70	198	18	427	314	14.3	10.1	1 515	92.8	14.5
Cass	6 978	10.7	228	3 785	970	73	82	2 055	1 846	79.0	24.7	804	86.3	71.6
Castro	1 281	9.0	155	685	159	25	22	721	511	19.6	6.3	754	82.3	18.0

¹ Per 1,000 resident population estimated as of July 1, 1999.   ² Based on resident population estimated as of July 1, 1997.   ³ Less than 10 employees.

Sources: Social Security Program—U.S. Social Security Administration, OASDI Beneficiaries by State and County - December 1999, <http://www.ssa.gov/statistics/oasdi_sc/1999/oasdi_sc99.pdf> (accessed: 7 March 2001) for 1999 – annual publication of same title for 1990.   Supplemental Security Income Program—U.S. Social Security Administration, SSI Recipients by State and County, <http://www.ssa.gov/statistics/ssi_st_cty/1999/ssi_st_cty.pdf> (accessed: November 2000).   Government employment, 1998—U.S. Bureau of Economic Analysis, "Regional Economic Information System (REIS) 1969-1998" on CD-ROM (related Internet site <http://www.bea.doc.gov/bea/regional/data.htm>).   Local government employment, 1997—U.S. Census Bureau, 1997 Census of Governments, Compendium of Public Employment, <http://www.census.gov/govs/apes/97coar2.dat> (accessed: 14 January 2000).   Local government finances—U.S. Census Bureau, 1997 Census of Governments, Compendium of Government Finances, <http://www.census.gov/prod/gc97/gc974-5.pdf> (accessed: 16 February 2001).

[Includes U.S., states, and 3,142 counties/county equivalents defined as of January 1, 1992. For changes to these areas since January 1, 1992, see appendix B. Geographic Information]

County	Social Security Program beneficiaries, December 1999				Supplemental Security Income Program recipients, December 1999	Government employment, 1998			Local government employment, full-time equivalent, March 1997	Local government finances, 1996–1997				
	Total			Retired workers		Federal		State and local		General revenue				Direct general expenditure (mil. dol.)
	Number	Percent change, 1990–1999	Rate[1]			Civilian	Military			Total (mil. dol.)	Taxes			
											Total (mil. dol.)	Per capita[2]	Percent property	
TEXAS—Con.														
Chambers	3 321	60.0	138	1 815	317	52	63	1 413	1 162	69.2	50.0	2 148	94.3	56.4
Cherokee	8 821	12.1	202	5 285	1 099	82	114	3 996	1 549	64.5	22.0	514	80.1	64.6
Childress	1 312	–14.8	174	815	158	37	20	1 131	494	18.5	3.6	473	73.9	19.4
Clay	2 112	21.0	201	1 335	112	28	28	520	431	36.9	6.6	634	92.4	37.0
Cochran	706	4.6	187	370	122	17	10	411	368	16.3	8.9	2 271	94.4	15.9
Coke	906	–6.1	270	610	55	16	(3)	407	316	11.9	4.1	1 202	91.6	11.3
Coleman	2 771	–3.8	293	1 695	291	43	25	765	605	22.9	5.4	553	77.3	23.7
Collin	30 678	86.4	67	19 490	2 328	788	1 140	18 638	12 576	849.2	539.4	1 347	85.2	877.3
Collingsworth	783	–14.4	247	465	109	22	(3)	300	278	10.5	2.4	720	84.6	10.7
Colorado	4 546	8.6	239	2 860	469	59	51	1 012	897	41.4	16.1	854	85.2	38.3
Comal	13 556	37.1	177	8 980	809	172	195	3 519	2 876	134.4	71.5	1 015	82.8	139.6
Comanche	3 568	3.1	263	2 320	318	54	36	849	670	34.9	7.4	546	86.3	30.5
Concho	629	–5.4	210	375	90	25	(3)	255	192	15.9	3.3	1 062	83.8	7.7
Cooke	6 299	14.5	189	4 010	476	71	87	2 483	1 873	93.3	25.8	786	77.0	89.2
Coryell	5 910	30.9	80	3 365	542	314	207	5 733	2 119	104.4	24.5	334	74.1	88.8
Cottle	554	–9.9	293	365	67	17	(3)	160	129	4.9	1.8	907	80.8	4.8
Crane	593	2.2	138	305	67	(3)	12	384	323	30.6	26.9	6 033	97.3	18.5
Crockett	653	12.6	149	370	91	(3)	12	399	453	18.7	12.6	2 809	97.4	16.1
Crosby	1 406	–2.0	199	775	210	24	19	532	448	17.5	5.2	711	85.5	17.2
Culberson	435	22.5	144	255	80	54	(3)	286	238	8.8	4.2	1 344	86.8	8.3
Dallam	933	–30.9	141	560	128	27	18	825	398	15.7	7.4	1 153	79.9	15.1
Dallas	222 989	12.6	108	137 445	32 223	27 913	7 182	112 224	84 583	5 985.1	3 078.1	1 526	72.3	5 515.7
Dawson	2 740	–1.4	190	1 555	518	60	39	1 292	891	38.1	15.3	1 037	87.1	36.6
Deaf Smith	2 699	2.0	144	1 530	523	49	51	1 366	1 240	36.1	11.3	588	84.4	35.9
Delta	1 190	–7.8	239	725	199	25	13	315	263	11.9	3.4	687	84.8	15.0
Denton	27 849	62.9	69	16 715	2 103	1 321	1 028	21 068	10 966	536.0	308.6	848	83.9	572.5
DeWitt	4 435	3.5	230	2 575	653	48	52	2 205	1 226	54.5	11.9	606	86.2	53.6
Dickens	655	–22.5	301	400	106	16	(3)	179	161	7.0	2.5	1 123	69.6	8.3
Dimmit	1 810	2.8	175	925	716	95	28	945	715	32.2	7.3	701	79.1	27.7
Donley	969	–7.3	253	620	83	18	10	406	270	16.0	2.9	770	79.7	16.1
Duval	2 432	3.9	178	1 065	885	66	36	1 238	1 247	40.7	13.8	1 017	87.2	44.1
Eastland	4 674	–11.6	267	2 865	474	63	47	1 382	1 155	49.9	9.9	559	78.5	47.6
Ector	17 827	12.9	144	9 550	2 807	214	336	9 105	6 592	415.2	115.8	943	75.3	407.7
Edwards	509	39.5	139	295	102	17	10	184	224	9.1	3.9	1 076	91.6	8.0
Ellis	13 518	14.0	126	8 275	1 586	207	275	4 589	3 624	180.3	82.4	819	83.0	183.5
El Paso	81 877	23.7	117	44 655	21 250	8 643	11 908	43 448	32 709	1 581.8	507.8	741	77.0	1 542.0
Erath	5 012	1.0	159	3 125	396	88	84	2 904	1 093	55.0	22.1	706	74.0	54.5
Falls	3 552	–5.5	206	2 065	688	404	46	1 549	680	26.9	7.8	440	76.8	27.4
Fannin	6 222	2.9	217	3 935	694	551	75	1 808	1 036	44.1	13.5	485	82.3	47.2
Fayette	5 848	7.6	273	3 750	467	80	57	1 413	870	37.3	21.5	1 023	87.9	34.1
Fisher	1 113	–7.6	266	685	101	27	11	359	275	14.3	4.3	998	91.0	14.0
Floyd	1 459	–5.9	180	825	187	38	22	652	556	20.9	5.4	658	86.1	20.5
Foard	459	–10.9	281	280	42	10	(3)	125	114	8.4	1.7	974	88.7	4.9
Fort Bend	24 375	114.8	69	13 400	2 505	458	897	16 477	9 820	586.7	339.4	1 060	89.4	617.0
Franklin	2 187	66.3	220	1 415	127	16	26	351	314	22.5	7.8	811	85.8	20.6
Freestone	3 554	14.8	201	2 225	365	38	47	1 165	698	33.4	17.5	999	88.6	33.9
Frio	2 236	31.1	140	1 060	552	27	42	1 289	750	46.9	9.0	570	81.7	49.5
Gaines	1 859	13.4	126	980	301	35	40	1 151	874	57.3	35.7	2 427	96.9	48.9
Galveston	34 549	15.0	139	20 705	3 995	918	1 027	28 121	13 097	701.8	395.5	1 632	88.3	693.2
Garza	901	–6.6	200	545	106	17	12	322	270	13.1	7.2	1 532	89.4	12.1
Gillespie	5 279	13.2	259	3 650	205	78	53	909	655	32.5	17.8	901	78.2	30.4
Glasscock	114	8.6	79	70	11	(3)	(3)	147	91	6.9	5.8	4 073	97.0	5.5
Goliad	1 390	20.3	195	795	196	19	19	424	329	13.9	8.8	1 287	93.4	13.3
Gonzales	3 867	1.6	220	2 245	710	71	47	1 206	1 047	43.1	10.9	622	87.7	37.7
Gray	4 983	–3.4	214	3 135	413	65	63	1 534	951	41.9	23.8	1 007	87.0	48.0
Grayson	20 501	8.3	198	12 925	1 948	337	274	5 296	5 564	217.3	85.6	850	80.7	230.0
Gregg	20 428	2.7	181	11 915	2 969	361	302	6 596	6 017	256.6	130.5	1 161	76.1	265.4
Grimes	3 172	–4.5	132	1 820	602	45	62	1 818	850	33.3	15.4	676	84.1	36.5
Guadalupe	12 639	37.1	153	7 710	1 370	177	214	4 196	3 440	116.9	47.7	615	82.4	119.2
Hale	5 836	–1.2	160	3 220	864	127	97	2 635	1 977	82.0	27.4	752	70.3	76.1
Hall	968	–14.7	269	575	124	30	10	357	342	10.3	3.8	1 046	83.8	9.4
Hamilton	2 162	–9.7	284	1 430	181	33	20	511	271	13.6	4.4	578	80.2	13.2
Hansford	967	6.3	179	560	59	19	14	532	330	24.4	13.2	2 464	94.1	16.1
Hardeman	1 181	–17.1	269	705	127	23	12	431	399	14.8	6.5	1 386	84.0	15.0
Hardin	7 798	15.8	157	4 330	773	76	129	2 239	1 977	78.2	26.3	541	89.4	79.6
Harris	311 064	18.7	96	180 290	58 061	24 479	9 568	193 988	131 371	8 382.5	4 158.1	1 320	78.8	8 120.3

[1] Per 1,000 resident population estimated as of July 1, 1999. [2] Based on resident population estimated as of July 1, 1997. [3] Less than 10 employees.

Sources: Social Security Program—U.S. Social Security Administration, OASDI Beneficiaries by State and County - December 1999, <http://www.ssa.gov/statistics/oasdi_sc/1999/oasdi_sc99.pdf> (accessed: 7 March 2001) for 1999 – annual publication of same title for 1990. Supplemental Security Income Program—U.S. Social Security Administration, SSI Recipients by State and County, <http://www.ssa.gov/statistics/ssi_st_cty/1999/ssi_st_cty.pdf> (accessed: November 2000). Government employment, 1998—U.S. Bureau of Economic Analysis, "Regional Economic Information System (REIS) 1969-1998" on CD-ROM (related Internet site <http://www.bea.doc.gov/bea/regional/data.htm>). Local government employment, 1997—U.S. Census Bureau, 1997 Census of Governments, Compendium of Public Employment, <http://www.census.gov/govs/apes/97coar2.dat> (accessed: 14 January 2000). Local government finances—U.S. Census Bureau, 1997 Census of Governments, Compendium of Government Finances, <http://www.census.gov/prod/gc97/gc974-5.pdf> (accessed: 16 February 2001).

[Includes U.S., states, and 3,142 counties/county equivalents defined as of January 1, 1992. For changes to these areas since January 1, 1992, see appendix B. Geographic Information]

County	Social Security Program beneficiaries, December 1999 — Total — Number	Total — Percent change, 1990–1999	Total — Rate[1]	Retired workers	Supplemental Security Income Program recipients, December 1999	Government employment, 1998 — Federal — Civilian	Federal — Military	State and local	Local government employment, full-time equivalent, March 1997	Local government finances, 1996–1997 — General revenue — Total (mil. dol.)	Taxes — Total (mil. dol.)	Taxes — Per capita[2]	Taxes — Percent property	Direct general expenditure (mil. dol.)
TEXAS—Con.														
Harrison	9 940	9.0	166	5 530	1 698	129	159	2 918	2 350	102.5	50.4	848	95.5	94.7
Hartley	518	172.6	98	310	18	11	14	459	96	4.1	2.6	510	86.8	4.4
Haskell	1 777	–9.3	298	1 085	163	38	16	457	359	14.8	5.6	912	85.6	14.7
Hays	9 576	40.0	103	5 850	1 159	141	243	8 894	3 357	167.7	70.2	820	77.8	185.0
Hemphill	560	2.8	161	345	24	16	(3)	351	315	15.9	10.6	2 954	93.6	16.8
Henderson	16 273	66.6	230	10 435	1 138	99	183	2 795	2 289	112.7	47.6	708	81.8	110.7
Hidalgo	61 566	23.5	115	34 085	25 552	2 698	1 395	35 353	25 685	1 209.7	282.0	559	76.3	1 107.0
Hill	6 956	7.0	224	4 305	665	92	81	1 923	1 323	68.4	20.9	695	70.4	75.8
Hockley	3 746	13.0	160	1 930	470	57	63	1 719	1 632	88.8	36.8	1 546	94.2	84.2
Hood	9 091	58.8	235	6 210	406	90	99	1 536	1 398	69.0	27.5	765	83.8	67.9
Hopkins	6 240	10.7	204	3 765	672	99	81	1 914	1 423	69.2	21.1	700	78.3	65.2
Houston	5 102	–.5	230	2 995	874	91	58	2 062	826	32.6	12.6	576	81.4	30.2
Howard	6 056	.8	191	3 560	901	813	85	2 867	1 900	90.2	32.3	1 006	77.9	88.2
Hudspeth	462	81.2	143	240	73	77	(3)	290	187	12.5	3.3	1 032	91.1	10.6
Hunt	13 057	14.1	182	7 920	1 684	312	243	5 774	3 935	165.1	51.2	745	79.2	167.8
Hutchinson	4 779	–4.1	202	2 850	333	72	64	1 694	1 606	60.3	27.4	1 146	82.3	62.3
Irion	315	5.0	186	180	27	(3)	(3)	122	92	5.9	4.5	2 655	95.9	3.7
Jack	1 638	7.4	219	995	100	19	20	525	447	19.5	7.1	974	83.9	18.2
Jackson	2 672	3.0	196	1 465	281	38	36	1 009	837	44.4	13.8	1 011	84.9	41.2
Jasper	7 317	14.0	218	3 940	1 096	82	89	2 033	1 687	74.4	29.4	884	84.7	64.8
Jeff Davis	392	5.9	162	260	48	28	(3)	210	97	3.9	1.8	826	89.2	4.1
Jefferson	44 395	–.1	184	24 725	6 509	2 525	770	16 321	9 623	552.9	332.6	1 378	75.7	564.0
Jim Hogg	958	8.2	193	480	277	63	13	437	368	12.5	6.3	1 275	95.9	12.1
Jim Wells	6 673	6.4	166	3 295	1 861	92	142	2 118	1 625	76.4	24.0	603	70.5	70.4
Johnson	16 186	24.4	132	9 505	1 476	223	314	4 800	3 632	184.3	70.6	620	85.7	204.2
Jones	3 540	–.3	188	2 150	374	91	52	2 545	1 037	43.1	10.0	533	78.4	39.1
Karnes	2 821	.2	187	1 530	646	37	33	1 701	723	33.7	9.9	649	82.8	28.5
Kaufman	10 665	–10.4	157	6 600	1 483	168	175	4 262	2 665	122.6	43.7	685	81.9	120.3
Kendall	4 188	35.3	192	2 780	167	49	56	1 136	853	38.4	23.4	1 146	86.8	40.8
Kenedy	52	–25.7	119	30	7	(3)	(3)	81	55	2.7	2.6	6 035	98.7	.9
Kent	244	6.1	286	155	15	(3)	(3)	193	85	11.9	10.7	12 289	98.9	5.3
Kerr	12 147	21.1	281	8 405	613	646	115	2 713	1 512	66.9	35.8	852	78.0	60.2
Kimble	1 034	10.0	244	665	99	17	11	320	265	13.4	3.0	711	79.2	13.4
King	40	33.3	126	25	3	(3)	(3)	53	60	3.7	3.1	8 945	95.5	2.5
Kinney	887	32.4	256	595	138	66	(3)	231	179	6.8	2.3	677	85.0	6.4
Kleberg	4 153	11.9	140	2 205	884	671	716	3 641	1 419	67.6	26.0	860	82.6	66.8
Knox	1 082	–14.8	264	640	157	40	11	419	353	20.2	3.7	848	84.4	17.7
Lamar	9 752	3.7	212	5 905	1 658	162	122	2 852	2 123	84.8	34.6	759	84.1	85.1
Lamb	3 120	–1.9	211	1 745	433	47	39	995	759	41.3	17.3	1 166	90.6	36.8
Lampasas	3 147	18.8	178	1 870	344	45	47	881	643	27.3	8.4	483	79.2	31.2
La Salle	987	9.1	165	500	297	45	16	502	274	15.9	4.1	692	84.0	15.4
Lavaca	5 116	–11.1	273	3 205	573	58	50	845	694	24.6	12.1	647	85.3	24.9
Lee	2 721	23.7	183	1 600	234	33	40	1 179	631	25.2	11.6	790	84.6	30.7
Leon	3 723	2.6	250	2 310	488	49	38	689	584	25.7	14.3	991	87.4	23.8
Liberty	10 015	9.3	149	5 180	1 485	119	173	3 799	2 219	99.2	44.2	687	84.8	98.3
Limestone	4 890	–1.7	237	2 810	792	61	56	2 924	1 000	51.9	28.3	1 366	91.5	42.9
Lipscomb	643	–6.1	213	365	28	23	(3)	321	259	10.9	7.2	2 406	93.7	10.0
Live Oak	1 962	35.8	194	1 175	263	329	27	626	505	20.2	13.3	1 316	92.9	21.2
Llano	5 305	20.2	383	3 695	202	35	36	887	445	33.5	14.7	1 119	91.9	32.9
Loving	14	–6.7	124	10	–	(3)	–	16	16	1.3	1.1	10 190	98.7	1.9
Lubbock	33 512	14.9	147	19 955	4 762	1 206	657	21 124	8 460	643.4	179.0	778	75.6	565.6
Lynn	1 223	1.9	184	645	184	29	18	530	406	17.9	5.6	848	89.4	17.3
McCulloch	2 073	–8.5	236	1 265	288	32	23	676	579	23.5	5.6	643	76.8	22.3
McLennan	33 971	4.8	166	20 645	4 659	3 220	579	11 831	8 524	606.8	162.8	804	71.8	585.9
McMullen	156	24.8	195	95	13	(3)	(3)	110	76	5.3	4.4	5 511	96.3	3.1
Madison	2 312	19.2	195	1 410	271	25	32	1 169	406	18.7	7.2	611	77.3	16.7
Marion	2 521	25.1	229	1 455	401	37	29	427	364	14.2	7.0	658	64.2	12.9
Martin	791	10.6	159	435	110	22	13	381	335	15.7	6.8	1 372	92.4	15.0
Mason	982	–.8	269	625	98	16	10	257	184	7.3	2.6	717	89.1	7.5
Matagorda	7 104	31.8	188	4 125	844	92	101	2 781	2 205	141.0	79.7	2 105	95.6	111.9
Maverick	6 478	26.9	133	3 190	3 419	389	128	3 128	2 462	113.6	14.8	317	74.6	115.7
Medina	5 843	45.9	155	3 285	560	59	100	2 578	1 726	59.8	18.3	510	78.4	54.9
Menard	615	–8.9	272	370	79	(3)	(3)	205	116	8.1	3.1	1 303	70.6	7.3
Midland	16 322	30.0	138	10 075	1 765	558	318	7 594	6 326	370.5	123.7	1 053	77.3	357.5
Milam	5 069	2.2	209	2 985	653	66	64	1 239	904	43.2	18.4	763	82.9	43.0
Mills	1 364	1.8	289	875	164	23	13	328	268	9.5	2.5	536	84.3	9.6

[1] Per 1,000 resident population estimated as of July 1, 1999.   [2] Based on resident population estimated as of July 1, 1997.   [3] Less than 10 employees.

Sources: Social Security Program—U.S. Social Security Administration, OASDI Beneficiaries by State and County - December 1999, <http://www.ssa.gov/statistics/oasdi_sc/1999/oasdi_sc99.pdf> (accessed: 7 March 2001) for 1999 – annual publication of same title for 1990.   Supplemental Security Income Program—U.S. Social Security Administration, SSI Recipients by State and County, <http://www.ssa.gov/statistics/ssi_st_cty/1999/ssi_st_cty.pdf> (accessed: November 2000).   Government employment, 1998—U.S. Bureau of Economic Analysis, "Regional Economic Information System (REIS) 1969-1998" on CD-ROM (related Internet site <http://www.bea.doc.gov/bea/regional/data.htm>).   Local government employment, 1997—U.S. Census Bureau, 1997 Census of Governments, Compendium of Public Employment, <http://www.census.gov/govs/apes/97coar2.dat> (accessed: 14 January 2000).   Local government finances—U.S. Census Bureau, 1997 Census of Governments, Compendium of Government Finances, <http://www.census.gov/prod/gc97/gc974-5.pdf> (accessed: 16 February 2001).

Table B–13. Counties — Government Programs, Employment, and Finances–Con.

[Includes U.S., states, and 3,142 counties/county equivalents defined as of January 1, 1992. For changes to these areas since January 1, 1992, see appendix B. Geographic Information]

County	Social Security Program beneficiaries, December 1999 Total Number	Percent change, 1990–1999	Rate[1]	Retired workers	Supplemental Security Income Program recipients, December 1999	Government employment, 1998 Federal Civilian	Military	State and local	Local government employment, full-time equivalent, March 1997	Local government finances, 1996–1997 General revenue Total (mil. dol.)	Taxes Total (mil. dol.)	Per capita[2]	Percent property	Direct general expenditure (mil. dol.)
TEXAS—Con.														
Mitchell	1 844	-9.6	210	1 110	228	27	26	1 332	431	22.5	10.7	1 226	88.9	22.3
Montague	4 797	4.2	256	2 950	400	65	49	1 235	974	46.9	10.7	583	81.6	40.3
Montgomery	33 066	60.8	115	19 550	3 175	499	723	10 577	9 061	472.9	245.3	951	89.2	466.3
Moore	2 524	13.2	128	1 410	191	76	52	1 358	1 089	34.3	23.5	1 222	92.6	41.1
Morris	3 129	-.7	238	1 820	429	31	37	683	570	24.2	14.2	1 071	84.8	23.4
Motley	379	-15.8	288	225	43	11	(3)	101	78	2.6	1.3	998	87.7	2.4
Nacogdoches	9 096	2.8	162	5 225	1 530	187	157	4 563	2 664	149.5	36.2	639	71.7	149.9
Navarro	8 364	-1.3	200	5 020	1 354	114	111	2 833	1 935	94.9	33.3	809	74.0	98.9
Newton	2 468	9.9	172	1 195	493	26	38	678	576	22.6	8.1	560	89.0	20.0
Nolan	3 376	-2.7	208	1 955	413	49	44	1 758	1 192	48.5	17.2	1 046	83.2	46.1
Nueces	44 740	13.1	142	24 595	8 833	5 451	3 899	21 162	15 037	875.2	343.0	1 087	80.4	789.4
Ochiltree	1 249	4.5	144	735	92	32	23	649	508	23.3	10.6	1 202	87.1	23.6
Oldham	361	1.7	163	220	30	(3)	(3)	262	160	6.5	2.7	1 221	84.9	6.2
Orange	14 964	17.6	176	7 995	1 510	134	236	4 180	3 198	192.5	85.3	1 009	82.8	190.6
Palo Pinto	5 546	9.4	212	3 355	427	61	68	1 753	1 375	67.7	22.9	895	77.0	71.2
Panola	4 422	9.6	192	2 420	572	74	61	1 374	1 177	60.3	33.6	1 460	98.0	54.9
Parker	12 452	59.3	146	7 760	542	161	218	3 692	2 875	181.7	46.5	591	83.1	149.0
Parmer	1 529	12.0	148	825	162	62	27	801	637	20.6	7.5	726	83.1	20.1
Pecos	2 152	13.9	134	1 200	439	47	42	1 863	795	70.4	44.5	2 744	94.1	65.5
Polk	14 858	77.9	283	10 240	1 140	76	134	2 532	1 325	68.1	31.3	658	83.2	66.5
Potter	16 486	-15.5	151	9 740	2 636	1 861	324	10 171	8 809	357.1	146.5	1 351	73.2	350.8
Presidio	1 379	23.7	154	735	628	182	23	521	376	13.4	3.5	427	75.7	17.3
Rains	1 940	56.5	217	1 200	158	16	23	331	243	11.2	5.2	631	84.2	9.7
Randall	13 908	90.8	140	9 070	483	45	265	4 399	1 197	44.9	24.5	251	88.5	44.9
Reagan	462	3.8	120	250	41	13	11	362	292	14.4	7.8	1 843	93.2	12.9
Real	886	40.6	325	545	110	(3)	(3)	220	94	6.1	2.0	763	85.2	5.7
Red River	3 398	-8.4	248	2 025	594	47	36	793	757	35.4	7.2	522	82.1	30.2
Reeves	2 170	5.1	155	1 135	544	67	38	1 236	1 128	50.9	12.3	847	82.6	45.0
Refugio	1 694	3.0	219	950	242	42	21	627	514	23.0	11.8	1 491	89.3	20.7
Roberts	144	2.9	156	85	4	10	(3)	89	73	4.3	3.8	3 858	97.2	2.9
Robertson	3 299	-.3	209	1 925	598	43	41	930	841	33.2	16.0	1 035	93.1	32.4
Rockwall	4 357	113.6	110	2 880	186	70	99	1 395	1 214	61.3	35.9	1 008	88.3	67.3
Runnels	2 802	-3.2	247	1 625	300	46	31	841	886	31.2	7.6	666	87.2	27.8
Rusk	8 707	10.7	190	5 095	1 000	108	122	2 035	1 509	80.2	32.0	710	80.1	70.3
Sabine	3 472	.1	329	2 085	365	61	28	494	413	19.6	5.8	550	78.4	15.0
San Augustine	2 400	15.7	297	1 310	476	24	21	475	366	13.8	3.8	470	77.2	13.4
San Jacinto	4 304	63.3	191	2 495	498	40	58	713	532	27.4	13.2	635	90.7	27.4
San Patricio	9 863	10.6	138	5 130	1 898	352	3 360	3 556	3 062	131.1	54.4	786	89.9	128.0
San Saba	1 380	.7	237	875	190	26	15	655	278	11.2	3.4	567	81.4	11.4
Schleicher	547	8.3	186	310	77	11	(3)	279	252	10.4	5.0	1 642	93.7	9.6
Scurry	3 159	.8	179	1 845	341	42	48	1 811	1 167	40.7	17.2	950	83.3	40.1
Shackelford	739	-3.4	230	430	47	14	(3)	217	156	6.9	3.1	955	88.0	8.2
Shelby	5 278	-3.9	233	2 895	954	90	60	1 183	1 003	41.7	11.0	489	82.7	39.8
Sherman	392	-.8	135	230	17	12	(3)	273	191	9.3	5.9	2 042	93.3	8.6
Smith	30 245	14.9	178	18 940	3 661	936	456	10 877	6 234	303.6	133.3	805	75.1	294.7
Somervell	1 000	42.9	151	615	96	13	17	542	393	79.1	72.0	11 630	99.3	27.5
Starr	6 234	42.3	110	2 830	3 224	286	148	3 847	3 248	118.3	25.4	467	86.7	120.9
Stephens	2 063	-.3	212	1 290	218	25	26	757	386	26.2	9.3	935	82.7	25.8
Sterling	203	4.1	153	120	26	(3)	(3)	157	99	5.4	4.8	3 520	96.9	4.9
Stonewall	479	-3.2	279	275	41	12	(3)	195	154	5.7	3.4	1 879	91.7	5.7
Sutton	672	20.0	156	390	98	10	12	430	320	13.9	8.7	1 956	90.7	12.6
Swisher	1 692	-1.3	205	980	150	35	22	736	511	20.9	6.2	737	84.1	22.2
Tarrant	149 871	20.3	108	90 935	17 160	13 515	4 661	68 401	54 468	3 083.5	1 568.7	1 183	78.5	3 105.9
Taylor	20 667	10.3	169	12 385	2 618	1 506	4 970	8 559	5 206	239.9	97.6	803	74.2	238.0
Terrell	221	2.8	184	135	31	11	(3)	115	72	5.1	3.9	3 316	95.4	3.9
Terry	2 336	7.2	183	1 295	342	37	34	1 153	900	36.3	14.2	1 093	90.5	36.6
Throckmorton	423	-16.2	250	260	36	12	(3)	192	115	4.2	1.8	1 073	91.8	4.6
Titus	4 272	-7.4	169	2 490	576	126	68	2 614	1 950	113.3	25.8	1 029	77.8	109.6
Tom Green	17 826	13.1	174	10 800	2 232	1 323	3 252	7 584	4 264	173.9	74.3	726	76.4	183.1
Travis	68 799	26.0	95	41 875	9 433	9 074	2 099	95 770	30 507	1 772.2	986.2	1 425	76.4	1 627.9
Trinity	3 647	18.2	287	2 295	450	50	33	662	514	25.9	8.4	674	87.9	24.4
Tyler	4 713	13.2	230	2 610	544	48	54	1 481	898	34.3	11.1	548	87.8	34.3
Upshur	7 350	24.7	201	4 215	767	62	95	1 500	1 242	50.3	18.8	529	86.7	47.4
Upton	660	13.8	186	340	71	(3)	10	457	410	22.8	16.6	4 365	97.6	20.8
Uvalde	4 407	13.4	169	2 480	987	120	68	2 434	2 026	94.5	14.4	565	71.4	93.1
Val Verde	6 148	19.0	139	3 365	2 119	1 666	1 441	2 980	2 460	87.4	20.0	466	72.7	86.7

[1] Per 1,000 resident population estimated as of July 1, 1999. [2] Based on resident population estimated as of July 1, 1997. [3] Less than 10 employees.

Sources: Social Security Program—U.S. Social Security Administration, OASDI Beneficiaries by State and County - December 1999, <http://www.ssa.gov/statistics/oasdi_sc/1999/oasdi_sc99.pdf> (accessed: 7 March 2001) for 1999 – annual publication of same title for 1990. Supplemental Security Income Program—U.S. Social Security Administration, SSI Recipients by State and County, <http://www.ssa.gov/statistics/ssi_st_cty/1999/ssi_st_cty.pdf> (accessed: November 2000). Government employment, 1998—U.S. Bureau of Economic Analysis, "Regional Economic Information System (REIS) 1969-1998" on CD-ROM (related Internet site <http://www.bea.doc.gov/bea/regional/data.htm>). Local government employment, 1997—U.S. Census Bureau, 1997 Census of Governments, Compendium of Public Employment, <http://www.census.gov/govs/apes/97coar2.dat> (accessed: 14 January 2000). Local government finances—U.S. Census Bureau, 1997 Census of Governments, Compendium of Government Finances, <http://www.census.gov/prod/gc97/gc974-5.pdf> (accessed: 16 February 2001).

Table B–13. Counties — Government Programs, Employment, and Finances–Con.

[Includes U.S., states, and 3,142 counties/county equivalents defined as of January 1, 1992. For changes to these areas since January 1, 1992, see appendix B. Geographic Information]

County	Social Security Program beneficiaries, December 1999 Total — Number	Percent change, 1990–1999	Rate[1]	Retired workers	Supplemental Security Income Program recipients, December 1999	Government employment, 1998 Federal — Civilian	Military	State and local	Local government employment, full-time equivalent, March 1997	Local government finances, 1996–1997 General revenue Total (mil. dol.)	Taxes Total (mil. dol.)	Per capita[2]	Percent property	Direct general expenditure (mil. dol.)
TEXAS—Con.														
Van Zandt	9 875	21.5	220	6 345	853	91	117	1 820	1 492	65.6	23.3	542	84.0	67.2
Victoria	12 895	15.2	157	7 245	1 846	234	220	6 067	4 863	255.2	85.8	1 064	78.2	239.3
Walker	6 321	8.8	115	3 920	799	192	152	12 091	2 045	167.1	28.0	515	73.3	149.6
Waller	3 719	25.4	132	2 215	487	55	84	2 987	1 178	51.3	23.9	895	86.5	57.2
Ward	2 104	7.9	183	1 120	290	28	31	1 180	618	31.4	16.5	1 404	91.7	32.4
Washington	6 132	9.1	211	3 695	858	67	77	2 757	1 741	80.2	27.0	940	91.5	85.0
Webb	18 521	25.1	96	9 305	8 043	1 761	501	12 491	9 564	516.1	128.1	710	77.7	514.7
Wharton	7 194	1.1	179	4 080	1 104	102	107	3 074	2 197	97.2	37.6	939	82.1	106.1
Wheeler	1 363	-12.6	256	825	123	29	14	525	426	20.1	10.3	1 938	93.1	17.6
Wichita	20 811	3.8	162	12 830	2 447	2 568	7 802	9 050	5 067	224.2	100.2	779	79.3	228.0
Wilbarger	3 037	-11.2	216	1 870	409	66	36	2 514	932	52.3	16.6	1 167	91.1	50.5
Willacy	3 045	16.0	155	1 565	1 122	36	63	1 341	1 082	41.7	11.4	585	84.2	40.3
Williamson	21 308	58.7	88	13 470	1 681	370	595	10 573	8 870	421.8	227.0	1 079	89.2	449.3
Wilson	4 509	42.9	139	2 460	590	52	83	1 552	1 203	47.6	13.8	458	87.7	48.5
Winkler	1 387	.1	179	700	185	12	21	652	572	27.0	13.5	1 714	93.0	25.5
Wise	6 653	31.6	142	3 955	402	76	117	2 101	1 473	65.1	28.3	666	89.2	65.4
Wood	8 688	13.6	252	5 685	762	80	91	1 666	1 224	62.2	26.3	774	86.5	55.1
Yoakum	1 161	18.5	149	630	102	16	21	738	642	39.1	29.7	3 706	96.9	29.7
Young	4 322	3.8	246	2 740	373	49	47	1 355	1 134	36.7	12.4	704	78.0	33.8
Zapata	1 630	2.2	143	865	442	34	31	906	688	25.9	17.3	1 550	98.7	26.5
Zavala	1 952	4.1	164	1 030	869	12	32	873	687	22.6	6.1	514	65.7	23.4
UTAH	234 587	22.5	110	148 879	19 999	30 620	16 037	145 215	63 884	4 554.1	1 532.4	742	71.6	4 386.0
Beaver	924	9.3	154	615	51	31	32	561	296	23.8	4.9	837	81.1	17.1
Box Elder	5 641	25.6	132	3 705	267	220	231	1 929	1 342	85.1	27.5	669	80.4	87.5
Cache	8 159	17.2	93	5 295	437	298	488	8 109	2 114	137.6	39.0	454	67.0	132.3
Carbon	3 792	10.4	181	2 055	360	167	114	2 034	815	52.1	13.7	657	76.5	53.3
Daggett	141	22.6	197	100	3	70	(3)	131	65	3.9	1.2	1 639	86.4	3.5
Davis	20 855	50.4	87	13 655	1 175	9 844	5 329	9 802	6 926	430.4	125.7	554	73.3	412.6
Duchesne	2 209	29.9	150	1 205	215	83	79	1 527	851	55.2	9.5	663	80.9	55.7
Emery	1 577	31.4	143	880	139	47	60	863	617	67.2	22.0	2 019	92.7	65.5
Garfield	898	15.1	210	595	29	151	23	348	198	14.1	3.5	829	65.5	13.3
Grand	1 410	18.0	172	890	98	201	44	545	391	27.0	9.3	1 152	58.3	30.4
Iron	3 882	35.7	132	2 460	302	294	156	3 073	891	63.6	22.7	819	73.5	62.1
Juab	1 094	9.4	140	690	85	18	41	559	362	21.5	5.4	744	83.3	20.9
Kane	1 336	42.1	217	900	59	72	34	530	314	24.9	5.9	977	62.4	23.4
Millard	1 868	13.6	150	1 205	130	81	67	902	607	48.8	28.3	2 307	94.7	39.1
Morgan	738	35.4	102	480	18	11	38	330	233	13.2	3.9	571	78.1	13.0
Piute	339	2.7	228	210	20	(3)	(3)	112	82	4.2	.7	520	83.7	3.8
Rich	309	28.8	161	215	11	12	10	176	125	6.6	2.3	1 277	88.4	6.6
Salt Lake	90 959	13.1	107	58 100	8 713	8 685	4 973	69 282	25 158	1 905.0	719.5	855	68.6	1 797.4
San Juan	1 438	25.6	106	715	686	210	75	1 313	678	46.7	9.2	682	81.6	38.8
Sanpete	3 292	18.4	149	2 050	227	73	117	2 112	845	47.7	9.5	453	72.3	48.7
Sevier	3 365	28.2	180	2 110	206	167	101	1 339	649	41.0	10.1	562	72.2	39.7
Summit	1 917	63.1	69	1 220	55	85	214	1 656	1 067	99.0	54.1	2 110	76.4	125.7
Tooele	3 522	28.1	98	2 150	234	1 815	256	1 458	1 183	95.4	18.3	582	75.6	86.0
Uintah	3 487	45.9	134	1 990	355	398	140	1 363	1 244	76.6	18.2	716	79.1	76.1
Utah	30 774	21.7	89	18 300	2 860	1 002	1 849	18 209	8 830	615.9	185.8	564	71.5	590.3
Wasatch	1 635	26.7	119	1 025	74	55	72	772	535	31.9	11.3	883	79.1	27.9
Washington	16 000	77.7	187	11 200	655	451	447	3 803	2 269	158.7	52.7	664	70.3	157.8
Wayne	449	-.2	188	275	17	100	13	168	100	6.4	1.2	509	70.8	6.7
Weber	22 569	14.9	122	14 585	2 449	5 973	1 022	12 209	5 097	350.5	116.8	640	72.0	350.7
VERMONT	102 729	17.3	173	64 531	12 520	5 478	4 501	39 543	17 841	1 157.9	720.7	1 224	98.8	1 112.0
Addison	5 269	20.2	149	3 330	622	134	263	1 634	982	69.3	44.8	1 287	99.5	72.1
Bennington	7 770	16.3	216	5 170	818	132	269	1 830	1 035	74.0	47.9	1 328	99.0	62.6
Caledonia	5 625	14.1	195	3 405	763	110	215	1 775	750	55.5	30.8	1 079	99.6	49.7
Chittenden	18 758	27.9	130	11 930	2 075	1 694	1 103	10 554	3 978	277.0	177.9	1 256	97.3	276.8
Essex	1 482	23.0	223	855	163	70	49	290	117	11.6	6.2	947	98.0	9.0
Franklin	6 237	15.8	140	3 535	1 142	681	329	2 132	1 449	75.1	36.4	836	99.1	64.0
Grand Isle	1 146	28.8	180	725	94	19	47	229	123	10.7	8.5	1 385	99.1	7.5
Lamoille	3 498	19.2	159	2 155	452	72	162	1 440	736	42.3	27.5	1 286	99.5	43.2
Orange	4 687	23.7	168	2 960	530	97	209	1 667	610	53.4	31.4	1 133	99.5	48.2
Orleans	5 421	22.1	213	3 145	863	196	189	1 421	850	46.0	24.1	954	98.5	40.9
Rutland	12 986	11.6	208	8 075	1 809	379	468	4 190	2 111	120.2	73.8	1 180	99.1	116.5
Washington	10 346	10.2	184	6 450	1 380	311	457	6 754	1 743	111.7	65.5	1 165	99.6	115.6
Windham	8 072	17.1	189	5 245	826	187	319	2 426	1 420	98.1	70.8	1 648	99.4	94.8
Windsor	11 428	12.1	206	7 550	965	1 396	422	3 201	1 937	113.1	74.9	1 357	99.2	110.8

[1] Per 1,000 resident population estimated as of July 1, 1999. [2] Based on resident population estimated as of July 1, 1997. [3] Less than 10 employees.

Sources: Social Security Program—U.S. Social Security Administration, OASDI Beneficiaries by State and County - December 1999, <http://www.ssa.gov/statistics/oasdi_sc/1999/oasdi_sc99.pdf> (accessed: 7 March 2001) for 1999 – annual publication of same title for 1990. Supplemental Security Income Program—U.S. Social Security Administration, SSI Recipients by State and County, <http://www.ssa.gov/statistics/ssi_st_cty/1999/ssi_st_cty.pdf> (accessed: November 2000). Government employment, 1998—U.S. Bureau of Economic Analysis, "Regional Economic Information System (REIS) 1969-1998" on CD-ROM (related Internet site <http://www.bea.doc.gov/bea/regional/data.htm>). Local government employment, 1997—U.S. Census Bureau, 1997 Census of Governments, Compendium of Public Employment, <http://www.census.gov/govs/apes/97coar2.dat> (accessed: 14 January 2000). Local government finances—U.S. Census Bureau, 1997 Census of Governments, Compendium of Government Finances, <http://www.census.gov/prod/gc97/gc974-5.pdf> (accessed: 16 February 2001).

[Includes U.S., states, and 3,142 counties/county equivalents defined as of January 1, 1992. For changes to these areas since January 1, 1992, see appendix B. Geographic Information]

County	Social Security Program beneficiaries, December 1999 — Total — Number	Percent change, 1990–1999	Rate[1]	Retired workers	Supplemental Security Income Program recipients, December 1999	Government employment, 1998 — Federal — Civilian	Military	State and local	Local government employment, full-time equivalent, March 1997	Local government finances, 1996–1997 — General revenue — Total (mil. dol.)	Taxes — Total (mil. dol.)	Per capita[2]	Percent property	Direct general expenditure (mil. dol.)
VIRGINIA	1 008 033	20.8	147	614 617	131 989	163 596	164 865	450 499	253 219	15 415.7	7 200.6	1 069	72.6	16 054.0
Accomack	7 969	8.7	248	5 205	1 319	679	376	1 679	1 236	63.8	25.0	778	77.0	66.0
Albemarle	11 216	57.2	140	7 660	745	[3]1 233	[3]691	[3]23 650	2 685	134.4	78.4	1 010	72.9	141.0
Alleghany	2 337	463.1	192	1 290	196	[4]104	[4]91	[4]1 601	703	33.0	12.5	1 021	82.0	31.5
Amelia	2 020	39.3	191	1 215	302	25	40	496	296	15.9	5.1	496	76.3	14.5
Amherst	5 760	22.8	190	3 570	690	51	116	2 932	781	39.6	14.5	486	68.6	42.8
Appomattox	2 795	28.8	210	1 710	360	49	51	746	429	18.5	6.3	485	69.8	17.6
Arlington	16 601	−4.7	95	11 850	1 974	32 302	16 742	9 038	8 034	939.6	347.4	1 995	69.9	1 154.8
Augusta	11 483	58.7	188	7 340	652	[5]302	[5]402	[5]8 244	1 852	93.1	36.7	615	66.0	98.6
Bath	1 090	.5	221	700	105	49	19	340	234	13.9	9.4	1 920	93.1	13.0
Bedford	9 974	37.8	173	6 410	706	[6]171	[6]240	[6]2 154	1 565	72.8	27.3	491	82.6	76.2
Bland	1 468	16.0	216	740	164	16	26	567	150	10.7	2.5	374	80.4	8.2
Botetourt	5 176	45.8	177	3 225	286	59	111	1 117	793	42.6	19.7	699	71.8	40.7
Brunswick	3 726	18.5	203	2 200	680	42	65	1 370	533	24.4	7.9	477	77.4	24.1
Buchanan	9 283	32.5	326	1 960	1 775	63	112	1 847	915	49.6	18.7	636	57.1	51.9
Buckingham	2 892	35.1	196	1 675	497	44	57	1 053	464	19.2	4.8	330	79.7	20.0
Campbell	9 584	43.0	190	5 945	935	[7]994	[7]462	[7]6 526	1 644	74.0	27.0	539	74.8	71.2
Caroline	3 851	33.0	174	2 260	346	298	128	1 011	713	32.5	13.5	624	76.6	30.2
Carroll	6 488	33.8	233	3 765	840	[8]90	[8]135	[8]2 183	761	35.4	10.2	368	70.8	33.6
Charles City	1 250	53.4	173	735	140	20	27	348	253	16.3	7.8	1 120	42.5	15.6
Charlotte	3 159	9.5	254	1 830	639	59	47	747	409	18.9	5.8	477	82.0	17.1
Chesterfield	28 938	113.4	114	17 865	2 348	3 441	953	14 798	9 108	509.3	257.0	1 040	78.1	531.4
Clarke	2 023	16.9	158	1 365	150	35	50	638	438	20.0	11.7	918	85.5	18.1
Craig	998	43.6	202	540	115	29	19	185	150	6.5	2.0	405	78.3	5.9
Culpeper	5 435	17.8	162	3 345	644	107	128	2 461	1 081	55.5	26.1	804	75.5	60.9
Cumberland	1 671	38.7	212	990	249	14	30	357	269	14.4	3.9	498	78.9	15.2
Dickenson	5 090	24.3	304	1 370	1 036	44	65	871	551	33.3	8.6	500	67.2	32.4
Dinwiddie	4 261	54.4	166	2 410	797	[9]299	[9]306	[9]8 551	685	38.9	14.3	571	78.7	45.0
Essex	2 174	11.8	238	1 370	242	23	35	403	281	14.8	7.2	782	71.5	15.8
Fairfax	75 911	117.1	80	52 275	6 548	[10]35 169	[10]7 037	[10]48 524	31 688	2 373.5	1 537.6	1 676	79.1	2 474.1
Fauquier	6 831	27.9	124	4 365	451	172	210	2 641	2 036	104.8	66.4	1 255	81.6	99.0
Floyd	2 831	21.5	213	1 685	241	52	51	456	325	16.3	6.6	507	76.2	14.1
Fluvanna	3 438	57.0	175	2 395	254	37	72	910	438	23.2	10.0	560	84.8	20.5
Franklin	9 153	45.3	202	5 540	874	109	173	1 534	1 351	59.4	24.1	548	72.6	63.1
Frederick	8 059	54.2	142	5 295	545	[11]473	[11]308	[11]4 166	1 849	97.4	46.7	857	76.3	97.8
Giles	4 012	5.4	240	2 180	527	50	63	788	640	26.0	10.2	634	79.2	25.2
Gloucester	5 224	25.1	147	3 215	514	88	136	2 385	1 196	52.9	23.2	674	76.8	55.0
Goochland	2 723	65.0	154	1 830	204	26	69	1 191	447	24.3	14.2	833	81.0	22.3
Grayson	4 369	30.2	266	2 685	562	34	62	572	452	19.8	5.5	333	75.2	19.4
Greene	1 980	47.2	135	1 190	213	50	54	678	503	24.3	8.2	614	78.7	21.8
Greensville	2 040	105.0	180	1 160	353	[12]30	[12]65	[12]1 853	490	22.1	5.5	500	75.1	25.9
Halifax	8 694	45.1	235	4 935	1 273	105	143	1 978	1 219	57.6	18.8	510	63.2	64.3
Hanover	11 784	38.6	138	8 080	536	146	318	3 829	2 495	130.3	74.5	940	76.9	153.2
Henrico	39 017	66.7	159	26 435	1 790	797	957	11 747	8 407	522.3	267.3	1 108	69.3	551.5
Henry	12 582	29.8	226	7 660	1 084	[13]148	[13]277	[13]3 656	1 622	77.7	28.3	505	64.5	83.5
Highland	641	.9	258	400	41	10	10	148	105	4.6	1.8	704	84.5	6.8
Isle of Wight	5 027	37.5	170	2 975	547	99	113	1 133	853	50.0	27.8	972	79.7	46.5
James City	7 883	335.5	172	5 495	212	[14]289	[14]548	[14]7 415	616	78.2	56.4	1 304	75.9	30.0
King and Queen	1 216	4.4	186	745	168	17	190	257	235	11.6	4.5	685	89.9	12.5
King George	1 913	47.7	108	1 170	176	3 763	847	673	541	24.5	11.3	671	77.9	23.9
King William	2 205	21.2	169	1 370	176	24	49	623	475	24.3	12.5	1 001	83.8	22.4
Lancaster	3 747	5.0	330	2 610	222	43	44	456	378	18.8	8.8	783	83.8	16.8
Lee	6 586	11.3	276	2 375	1 951	49	92	1 226	872	36.9	8.3	347	69.5	36.1
Loudoun	11 104	81.1	71	7 270	575	3 953	574	7 265	4 464	294.1	194.5	1 449	81.7	312.2
Louisa	4 440	21.6	177	2 660	578	44	96	1 087	713	41.1	23.8	998	93.3	39.6
Lunenburg	2 696	19.3	229	1 635	497	28	47	864	406	17.0	5.4	442	78.8	15.5
Madison	2 214	17.5	175	1 415	259	80	49	459	354	16.1	7.0	557	79.6	15.7
Mathews	2 286	5.3	247	1 515	128	32	64	329	248	12.3	6.5	718	86.0	10.1
Mecklenburg	7 830	14.1	253	4 780	1 315	135	120	2 282	1 066	45.6	15.2	489	64.0	43.6
Middlesex	2 761	19.5	283	1 865	202	24	37	795	284	13.2	7.2	749	81.4	11.8
Montgomery	9 410	22.4	122	5 640	1 009	[15]378	[15]405	[15]14 626	2 350	110.8	43.2	572	68.7	111.1
Nelson	3 076	14.6	217	1 895	386	57	54	532	343	21.0	10.7	778	81.1	19.6
New Kent	1 848	22.8	140	1 155	137	30	51	517	418	21.7	9.7	772	85.7	18.5
Northampton	3 340	4.0	261	2 210	706	47	70	1 155	736	70.6	8.8	690	75.8	137.2
Northumberland	3 530	25.8	303	2 465	179	30	45	415	308	16.9	8.7	760	86.5	17.2
Nottoway	3 300	4.3	216	2 010	586	275	59	1 776	479	25.7	7.6	504	68.6	23.7
Orange	5 608	20.7	218	3 855	536	57	98	1 763	807	40.3	18.1	725	81.4	40.1
Page	4 815	20.2	208	2 910	553	166	89	968	721	34.3	10.3	452	73.6	32.2
Patrick	4 152	30.6	224	2 585	522	44	71	650	469	21.5	7.2	394	69.5	22.6
Pittsylvania	13 703	42.2	241	8 215	1 805	[16]260	[16]419	[16]5 723	1 584	71.3	23.2	411	72.7	79.3
Powhatan	2 611	63.2	117	1 630	212	45	85	2 039	500	26.3	14.5	705	68.6	27.8

[1] Per 1,000 resident population estimated as of July 1, 1999. [2] Based on resident population estimated as of July 1, 1997. [3] Independent city of Charlottesville included with Albemarle County. [4] Independent cities of Clifton Forge and Covington included with Alleghany County. [5] Independent cities of Staunton and Waynesboro included with Augusta County. [6] Independent city of Bedford included with Bedford County. [7] Independent city of Lynchburg included with Campbell County. [8] Independent city of Galax included with Carroll County. [9] Independent cities of Colonial Heights and Petersburg included with Dinwiddie County. [10] Independent cities of Fairfax and Falls Church included with Fairfax County. [11] Independent city of Winchester included with Frederick County. [12] Independent city of Emporia included with Greensville County. [13] Independent city of Martinsville included with Henry County. [14] Independent city of Williamsburg included with James City County. [15] Independent city of Radford included with Montgomery County. [16] Independent city of Danville included with Pittsylvania County.

Sources: Social Security Program—U.S. Social Security Administration, OASDI Beneficiaries by State and County - December 1999, <http://www.ssa.gov/statistics/oasdi_sc/1999/oasdi_sc99.pdf> (accessed: 7 March 2001) for 1999 – annual publication of same title for 1990. Supplemental Security Income Program—U.S. Social Security Administration, SSI Recipients by State and County, <http://www.ssa.gov/statistics/ssi_st_cty/1999/ssi_st_cty.pdf> (accessed: November 2000). Government employment, 1998—U.S. Bureau of Economic Analysis, "Regional Economic Information System (REIS) 1969-1998" on CD-ROM (related Internet site <http://www.bea.doc.gov/bea/regional/data.htm>). Local government employment, 1997—U.S. Census Bureau, 1997 Census of Governments, Compendium of Public Employment, <http://www.census.gov/govs/apes/97coar2.dat> (accessed: 14 January 2000). Local government finances—U.S. Census Bureau, 1997 Census of Governments, Compendium of Government Finances, <http://www.census.gov/prod/gc97/gc974-5.pdf> (accessed: 16 February 2001).

Table B–13. Counties — Government Programs, Employment, and Finances–Con.

[Includes U.S., states, and 3,142 counties/county equivalents defined as of January 1, 1992. For changes to these areas since January 1, 1992, see appendix B. Geographic Information]

County	Social Security Program beneficiaries, December 1999				Supplemental Security Income Program recipients, December 1999	Government employment, 1998			Local government employment, full-time equivalent, March 1997	Local government finances, 1996–1997					
	Total			Retired workers		Federal		State and local		General revenue					Direct general expenditure (mil. dol.)
	Number	Percent change, 1990–1999	Rate[1]			Civilian	Military			Total (mil. dol.)	Taxes				
											Total (mil. dol.)	Per capita[2]	Percent property		
VIRGINIA—Con.															
Prince Edward	3 535	−1.5	184	2 180	842	77	74	1 804	506	27.3	10.4	549	55.6	30.3
Prince George	3 353	97.2	116	1 945	285	[3]3 834	[3]5 605	[3]2 443	949	46.8	16.1	571	80.8	70.6
Prince William	17 317	134.0	64	10 065	1 938	[4]4 217	[4]6 609	[4]14 108	8 052	589.9	309.1	1 208	77.8	588.4
Pulaski	7 695	19.3	224	4 360	1 052	60	134	2 025	1 151	64.6	19.6	571	69.3	64.4
Rappahannock	1 268	8.8	165	795	112	43	28	285	253	9.6	5.5	768	83.6	9.9
Richmond	1 748	2.8	200	1 125	194	23	34	835	224	13.3	4.7	550	74.0	11.4
Roanoke	15 442	159.1	190	10 325	477	[5]2 133	[5]409	[5]6 389	2 813	156.7	86.2	1 062	74.3	156.3
Rockbridge	3 964	48.5	203	2 475	346	[6]154	[6]162	[6]2 470	633	30.9	13.1	685	66.5	35.8
Rockingham	13 890	53.9	220	9 315	813	[7]352	[7]383	[7]8 164	2 107	102.9	39.5	623	81.9	105.7
Russell	8 057	35.9	280	2 700	1 614	59	113	1 464	826	45.7	12.2	419	67.3	46.7
Scott	6 020	9.5	267	2 740	1 577	62	88	978	776	31.5	8.2	360	70.5	30.5
Shenandoah	7 339	13.0	209	5 095	514	156	134	1 489	1 062	49.5	25.5	747	73.3	44.5
Smyth	7 794	11.5	238	4 295	1 297	97	127	2 667	1 220	49.6	15.1	458	62.9	55.0
Southampton	3 445	27.4	195	1 945	545	[8]65	[8]102	[8]2 351	569	26.7	9.4	530	89.4	29.1
Spotsylvania	9 515	151.1	109	5 620	611	[9]300	[9]410	[9]6 281	2 249	136.6	72.3	898	73.7	135.8
Stafford	6 963	76.1	75	4 200	476	155	1 910	3 563	2 689	150.6	75.3	878	80.7	152.9
Surry	1 172	7.0	181	665	150	16	25	473	373	17.0	12.5	1 940	97.2	15.8
Sussex	2 290	−2.1	186	1 290	538	55	38	943	388	21.8	6.4	637	81.7	28.3
Tazewell	10 692	−2.8	231	4 215	2 152	123	181	3 185	1 382	68.3	22.2	474	68.5	66.5
Warren	4 994	19.6	163	3 155	422	163	117	1 165	901	44.6	20.7	691	77.4	44.4
Washington	11 366	43.5	228	6 160	1 736	[10]395	[10]260	[10]3 971	1 337	67.9	26.5	539	64.7	60.6
Westmoreland	3 822	8.0	235	2 505	366	72	63	653	518	27.1	10.8	662	86.5	26.3
Wise	10 124	7.2	252	3 485	2 517	[11]276	[11]166	[11]3 151	1 378	73.8	25.9	659	49.8	73.5
Wythe	6 329	8.7	239	3 510	961	117	102	1 938	970	46.5	15.7	595	56.0	45.1
York	7 086	118.4	121	4 640	270	[12]1 067	[12]1 942	[12]3 108	2 021	107.3	52.5	926	74.3	121.5
Independent Cities															
Alexandria	11 145	−45.6	95	7 645	2 585	7 437	3 263	8 247	4 458	355.7	216.4	1 904	72.0	340.6
Bedford	1 882	−3.0	282	1 225	236	[13]	[13]	[13]	162	43.7	17.8	2 831	57.7	44.1
Bristol	4 595	−16.6	275	2 755	827	[10]	[10]	[10]	775	12.0	4.1	241	70.5	10.9
Buena Vista	1 398	−8.3	216	810	204	[6]	[6]	[6]	242	83.6	44.3	6 777	62.7	92.4
Charlottesville	6 027	−11.2	164	3 875	1 057	[14]	[14]	[14]	1 750	547.0	221.5	5 855	68.9	583.8
Chesapeake	23 633	44.6	117	13 840	2 583	1 170	1 979	12 616	8 625	2.9	1.9	10	37.9	3.5
Clifton Forge	993	−19.9	236	570	216	[15]	[15]	[15]	64	35.2	23.4	5 375	55.1	31.8
Colonial Heights	3 752	11.3	231	2 530	230	[16]	[16]	[16]	576	14.5	7.5	457	68.6	13.5
Covington	1 815	−48.0	265	1 025	274	[15]	[15]	[15]	298	106.7	32.2	4 559	55.8	119.6
Danville	11 555	−13.4	227	7 520	2 353	[17]	[17]	[17]	2 572	60.2	45.3	864	57.0	33.9
Emporia	1 488	−30.0	263	860	367	[18]	[18]	[18]	105	34.9	24.1	4 098	67.3	32.7
Fairfax	2 445	−58.2	118	1 705	886	[19]	[19]	[19]	332	19.3	7.6	371	61.2	20.7
Falls Church	1 315	−80.8	132	935	361	[19]	[19]	[19]	611	63.8	30.3	3 178	55.6	68.2
Franklin	1 974	−14.0	243	1 145	578	[8]	[8]	[8]	590	17.6	6.8	777	46.4	13.2
Fredericksburg	3 476	−39.4	185	2 245	487	[9]	[9]	[9]	1 233	299.3	125.3	5 980	67.3	290.2
Galax	1 936	−33.1	299	1 190	436	[20]	[20]	[20]	278	58.8	31.7	4 744	47.5	58.0
Hampton	19 807	24.8	144	11 785	2 406	8 146	9 219	8 560	5 116	69.4	24.3	175	75.3	62.4
Harrisonburg	2 109	−54.5	62	1 350	497	[7]	[7]	[7]	1 002	10.7	4.2	126	63.4	13.7
Hopewell	4 420	2.9	195	2 610	746	[3]	[3]	[3]	1 123	159.2	68.6	3 051	99.4	151.4
Lexington	1 748	−13.5	238	1 155	216	[6]	[6]	[6]	210	36.6	12.7	1 749	56.9	40.5
Lynchburg	13 973	−9.4	219	8 785	1 970	[21]	[21]	[21]	2 773	396.2	171.0	2 626	68.2	428.8
Manassas	2 666	NA	80	1 550	[22]457	[4]	[4]	[4]	1 042	812.3	245.3	7 622	58.6	836.5
Manassas Park	663	NA	84	345	[22]	[4]	[4]	[4]	286	9.0	3.6	482	41.6	8.9
Martinsville	5 055	−11.9	337	3 065	540	[23]	[23]	[23]	791	174.8	30.5	1 965	64.9	152.5
Newport News	23 800	17.5	133	13 795	4 191	5 013	8 949	10 491	8 299	245.9	85.2	487	66.8	298.4
Norfolk	32 319	−.4	143	19 035	7 688	15 744	57 727	20 245	14 200	34.3	19.8	84	77.0	25.8
Norton	1 491	7.3	372	565	282	[11]	[11]	[11]	191	746.1	276.1	67 862	66.3	803.6
Petersburg	7 812	−16.0	227	4 355	2 282	[16]	[16]	[16]	2 833	272.3	114.3	3 244	56.9	259.2
Poquoson	1 479	57.3	128	975	2	[12]	[12]	[12]	407	43.1	19.4	1 711	59.5	39.2
Portsmouth	17 878	3.6	182	10 445	4 266	10 181	5 149	6 147	5 144	120.7	48.9	492	72.3	134.5
Radford	1 979	−21.5	126	1 285	198	[24]	[24]	[24]	401	952.8	437.8	27 933	68.1	908.1
Richmond	34 245	−32.0	181	21 385	8 447	6 959	1 292	41 045	10 014	42.7	20.1	105	67.1	40.0
Roanoke	18 867	−22.2	202	11 340	3 791	1 698	402	6 257	4 574	41.9	18.4	194	33.3	106.2
Salem	5 013	−9.1	209	3 285	373	[5]	[5]	[5]	1 179	68.5	29.4	1 221	47.5	70.4
South Boston	X	X	X	X	523	X	X	X	X	X	X	X	X	X
Staunton	5 488	−10.0	224	3 600	624	[25]	[25]	[25]	977	7.8	4.4	180	60.9	7.9
Suffolk	10 487	20.7	162	5 950	2 166	196	272	3 931	2 294	11.2	6.4	105	49.8	10.0
Virginia Beach	45 174	48.8	104	27 350	4 544	4 874	21 552	19 060	16 205	57.7	33.0	77	60.4	73.7
Waynesboro	4 587	−1.1	238	2 925	450	[25]	[25]	[25]	718	76.6	40.7	2 115	77.0	69.9
Williamsburg	2 336	−56.0	187	1 595	221	[26]	[26]	[26]	1 519	22.4	9.0	740	79.8	22.3
Winchester	4 585	−2.9	204	3 030	577	[27]	[27]	[27]	1 407	20.5	10.6	472	83.7	18.8

[1] Per 1,000 resident population estimated as of July 1, 1999. [2] Based on resident population estimated as of July 1, 1997. [3] Independent city of Hopewell included with Prince George County. [4] Independent cities of Manassas and Manassas Park included with Prince William County. [5] Independent city of Salem included with Roanoke County. [6] Independent cities of Buena Vista and Lexington included with Rockbridge County. [7] Independent city of Harrisonburg included with Rockingham County. [8] Independent city of Franklin included with Southampton County. [9] Independent city of Fredericksburg included with Spotsylvania County. [10] Independent city of Bristol included with Washington County. [11] Independent city of Norton included with Wise County. [12] Independent city of Poquoson included with York County. [13] Independent city of Bedford included with Bedford County. [14] Independent city of Charlottesville included with Albemarle County. [15] Independent cities of Clifton Forge and Covington included with Alleghany County. [16] Independent cities of Colonial Heights and Petersburg included with Dinwiddie County. [17] Independent city of Danville included with Pittsylvania County. [18] Independent city of Emporia included with Greensville County. [19] Independent cities of Fairfax and Falls Church included with Fairfax County. [20] Independent city of Galax included with Carroll County. [21] Independent city of Lynchburg included with Campbell County. [22] Independent city of Manassas Park included with independent city of Manassas. [23] Independent city of Martinsville included with Henry County. [24] Independent city of Radford included with Montgomery County. [25] Independent cities of Staunton and Waynesboro included with Augusta County. [26] Independent city of Williamsburg included with James City County. [27] Independent city of Winchester included with Frederick County.

Sources: Social Security Program—U.S. Social Security Administration, OASDI Beneficiaries by State and County - December 1999, <http://www.ssa.gov/statistics/oasdi_sc/1999/oasdi_sc99.pdf> (accessed: 7 March 2001) for 1999 — annual publication of same title for 1990. Supplemental Security Income Program—U.S. Social Security Administration, SSI Recipients by State and County, <http://www.ssa.gov/statistics/ssi_st_cty/1999/ssi_st_cty.pdf> (accessed: November 2000). Government employment, 1998—U.S. Bureau of Economic Analysis, "Regional Economic Information System (REIS) 1969-1998" on CD-ROM (related Internet site <http://www.bea.doc.gov/bea/regional/data.htm>). Local government employment, 1997—U.S. Census Bureau, 1997 Census of Governments, Compendium of Public Employment, <http://www.census.gov/govs/apes/97coar2.dat> (accessed: 14 January 2000). Local government finances—U.S. Census Bureau, 1997 Census of Governments, Compendium of Government Finances, <http://www.census.gov/prod/gc97/gc974-5.pdf> (accessed: 16 February 2001).

[Includes U.S., states, and 3,142 counties/county equivalents defined as of January 1, 1992. For changes to these areas since January 1, 1992, see appendix B. Geographic Information]

County	Social Security Program beneficiaries, December 1999				Supplemental Security Income Program recipients, December 1999	Government employment, 1998			Local government employment, full-time equivalent, March 1997	Local government finances, 1996–1997				
	Total			Retired workers		Federal		State and local		General revenue				Direct general expenditure (mil. dol.)
	Number	Percent change, 1990–1999	Rate[1]			Civilian	Military			Total (mil. dol.)	Taxes			
											Total (mil. dol.)	Per capita[2]	Percent property	
WASHINGTON	825 281	15.5	143	535 485	98 067	66 840	73 524	388 621	185 152	16 138.7	5 167.5	922	63.5	15 729.7
Adams	2 215	7.5	145	1 315	262	47	57	1 376	783	59.9	11.6	758	76.9	59.9
Asotin	4 373	18.0	206	2 685	558	66	79	892	572	53.7	9.9	473	75.1	51.0
Benton	18 969	27.9	138	11 925	1 632	815	518	8 906	6 119	499.3	94.8	701	63.2	391.1
Chelan	11 364	10.8	187	7 955	921	711	224	5 300	2 753	175.1	52.1	875	68.2	160.3
Clallam	17 163	18.8	265	11 725	1 234	468	489	4 895	2 619	209.5	40.4	635	72.3	181.9
Clark	41 678	26.1	124	26 445	5 132	2 471	1 224	15 754	8 262	731.2	225.4	709	73.6	728.2
Columbia	952	1.8	229	600	115	54	15	464	336	20.6	2.6	621	77.2	22.2
Cowlitz	16 803	13.0	183	10 195	2 123	271	341	5 406	2 901	237.8	69.8	771	66.3	261.8
Douglas	4 958	18.0	145	3 320	379	138	125	1 590	1 122	81.0	18.0	545	80.9	67.1
Ferry	1 251	44.6	174	715	153	152	27	566	367	19.3	2.9	396	75.2	19.2
Franklin	5 235	7.2	112	3 250	767	461	173	3 470	1 707	142.0	32.8	718	63.9	136.1
Garfield	593	4.0	254	350	32	109	(3)	263	220	11.9	1.7	728	81.1	12.0
Grant	11 208	21.8	156	7 200	1 424	272	269	5 615	4 034	250.4	44.2	641	71.9	236.1
Grays Harbor	14 600	5.4	218	8 890	2 016	226	289	4 773	2 677	190.1	50.1	737	55.0	195.6
Island	9 738	23.4	133	6 795	576	1 444	7 890	2 981	1 704	111.5	31.9	448	68.2	112.8
Jefferson	6 844	34.3	256	4 895	366	166	107	1 707	970	78.8	21.1	819	72.8	77.4
King	212 070	5.8	127	144 185	27 387	20 754	7 441	125 004	56 081	5 839.3	2 283.7	1 397	57.5	5 733.4
Kitsap	30 023	28.3	127	19 140	3 502	14 620	13 716	11 204	5 926	487.9	153.2	658	75.0	484.3
Kittitas	4 951	21.9	155	3 330	390	164	131	3 993	1 142	85.7	20.5	654	59.9	86.3
Klickitat	3 601	17.1	184	2 250	390	115	72	1 486	916	64.0	9.6	509	76.5	63.5
Lewis	14 250	15.3	208	8 650	1 558	322	253	4 627	2 366	175.7	48.0	710	62.5	172.6
Lincoln	2 296	9.6	235	1 425	145	73	36	1 219	730	54.4	9.2	954	83.2	54.3
Mason	11 012	35.2	219	7 370	904	113	185	3 226	1 689	130.2	32.0	645	71.8	114.4
Okanogan	7 601	17.6	198	4 820	956	799	142	3 041	1 871	123.3	21.7	567	70.0	116.8
Pacific	6 005	15.3	289	4 065	519	61	160	1 569	919	65.9	15.6	744	60.3	64.3
Pend Oreille	2 252	18.8	194	1 310	384	109	43	835	634	49.3	10.5	930	78.7	44.8
Pierce	92 616	19.2	134	56 680	14 084	9 703	23 385	37 740	21 210	1 692.8	516.1	778	71.0	1 662.9
San Juan	2 786	22.7	216	2 070	76	64	46	844	426	36.8	16.2	1 334	68.3	35.1
Skagit	18 830	17.1	186	12 550	1 566	416	372	7 559	4 047	356.7	77.8	801	70.3	359.8
Skamania	1 384	52.9	141	840	142	215	36	581	370	26.8	3.7	387	74.8	23.1
Snohomish	72 525	33.5	122	47 140	6 907	2 322	7 631	28 391	16 260	1 440.6	460.5	813	65.6	1 424.0
Spokane	65 247	8.2	159	41 105	8 591	4 300	5 173	25 695	11 717	934.8	295.3	728	62.4	911.1
Stevens	7 339	48.9	183	4 295	842	397	147	2 028	1 055	75.0	15.4	391	69.8	70.5
Thurston	31 292	27.2	152	19 805	3 201	977	845	31 475	6 456	496.3	103.0	619	70.3	474.1
Wahkiakum	877	14.6	228	565	42	14	14	229	156	12.6	2.7	706	70.1	10.8
Walla Walla	9 545	8.4	177	6 385	872	883	201	3 877	1 575	125.2	33.4	624	72.0	130.0
Whatcom	24 441	24.1	152	15 740	2 580	841	605	9 867	4 230	363.0	129.3	835	66.7	323.2
Whitman	4 496	2.3	117	2 860	276	274	161	8 140	1 348	107.3	23.9	621	69.3	105.1
Yakima	31 888	2.8	144	20 635	5 049	1 433	893	12 033	6 882	523.2	116.2	537	64.2	552.6
WEST VIRGINIA	390 558	5.5	216	198 667	70 972	21 583	9 662	118 538	59 926	3 379.8	925.9	510	82.5	3 270.5
Barbour	3 487	5.5	218	1 690	829	44	82	752	532	26.8	3.3	207	83.0	25.8
Berkeley	11 512	26.7	158	6 860	1 427	2 974	383	3 002	1 866	106.5	33.1	479	86.2	108.2
Boone	5 900	11.4	224	2 145	1 278	95	131	1 403	1 040	59.4	18.0	681	96.5	58.4
Braxton	3 138	11.5	238	1 460	812	57	66	763	519	23.0	3.5	268	91.2	22.3
Brooke	5 765	16.9	223	3 275	395	44	130	995	689	37.7	13.7	524	87.6	37.4
Cabell	19 993	–5.0	214	11 275	3 903	1 119	507	6 538	2 989	180.6	66.4	697	73.6	175.6
Calhoun	1 874	–1.1	235	850	608	21	40	364	246	10.5	1.7	213	97.4	13.8
Clay	2 260	4.9	213	915	706	28	53	563	342	17.1	2.5	236	97.9	17.0
Doddridge	1 515	28.9	203	790	251	14	38	308	244	10.3	3.0	411	98.7	10.1
Fayette	12 139	3.3	259	5 320	2 359	290	240	3 345	1 398	71.5	20.1	420	87.3	70.1
Gilmer	1 627	7.0	228	805	378	27	36	715	207	10.5	3.2	456	96.0	10.7
Grant	2 290	19.0	206	1 265	428	62	56	919	737	44.0	5.8	520	97.9	46.0
Greenbrier	8 086	5.5	229	4 125	1 444	129	177	2 140	972	56.7	11.6	326	91.8	52.9
Hampshire	3 988	32.9	205	2 325	693	45	95	1 087	539	22.7	5.5	293	96.5	23.2
Hancock	8 056	–2.9	239	4 640	601	76	170	1 366	1 102	61.7	22.9	667	81.5	58.7
Hardy	2 473	13.4	206	1 460	423	72	59	530	295	18.0	4.8	408	94.6	19.6
Harrison	15 843	–3.6	225	8 660	2 722	4 236	357	3 575	2 319	139.5	48.5	683	80.4	134.7
Jackson	6 004	23.2	212	3 105	1 010	81	140	1 354	928	49.5	14.3	516	90.9	47.1
Jefferson	6 363	25.0	151	3 905	613	620	207	2 317	1 073	54.6	21.8	535	92.8	49.3
Kanawha	44 899	–.8	225	24 985	6 558	2 463	1 106	18 776	7 479	421.7	169.3	833	72.9	398.7
Lewis	4 030	–.4	231	2 155	953	65	87	1 427	532	24.1	6.5	371	92.1	23.3
Lincoln	4 813	17.8	215	1 775	1 875	49	111	889	597	32.1	5.5	247	98.8	30.2
Logan	9 762	–2.3	243	3 485	2 274	132	206	2 003	1 253	63.5	16.3	395	93.1	62.2
McDowell	9 033	–12.2	308	2 525	3 610	97	150	1 949	1 101	47.0	10.1	329	88.2	45.6

[1] Per 1,000 resident population estimated as of July 1, 1999.   [2] Based on resident population estimated as of July 1, 1997.   [3] Less than 10 employees.

Sources: Social Security Program—U.S. Social Security Administration, OASDI Beneficiaries by State and County - December 1999, <http://www.ssa.gov/statistics/oasdi_sc/1999/oasdi_sc99.pdf> (accessed: 7 March 2001) for 1999 - annual publication of same title for 1990.   Supplemental Security Income Program—U.S. Social Security Administration, SSI Recipients by State and County, <http://www.ssa.gov/statistics/ssi_st_cty/1999/ssi_st_cty.pdf> (accessed: November 2000).   Government employment, 1998—U.S. Bureau of Economic Analysis, "Regional Economic Information System (REIS) 1969-1998" on CD-ROM (related Internet site <http://www.bea.doc.gov/bea/regional/data.htm>).   Local government employment, 1997—U.S. Census Bureau, 1997 Census of Governments, Compendium of Public Employment, <http://www.census.gov/govs/apes/97coar2.dat> (accessed: 14 January 2000).   Local government finances—U.S. Census Bureau, 1997 Census of Governments, Compendium of Government Finances, <http://www.census.gov/prod/gc97/gc974-5.pdf> (accessed: 16 February 2001).

[Includes U.S., states, and 3,142 counties/county equivalents defined as of January 1, 1992. For changes to these areas since January 1, 1992, see appendix B. Geographic Information]

County	Social Security Program beneficiaries, December 1999 — Total — Number	Total — Percent change, 1990–1999	Total — Rate¹	Retired workers	Supplemental Security Income Program recipients, December 1999	Government employment, 1998 — Federal — Civilian	Federal — Military	State and local	Local government employment, full-time equivalent, March 1997	Local government finances, 1996–1997 — General revenue — Total (mil. dol.)	Taxes — Total (mil. dol.)	Taxes — Per capita²	Taxes — Percent property	Direct general expenditure (mil. dol.)
WEST VIRGINIA—Con.														
Marion	13 135	–5.5	235	7 515	1 711	180	282	4 012	1 702	174.8	27.7	487	84.2	171.4
Marshall	6 930	3.4	198	4 015	713	75	193	1 928	1 085	78.2	21.5	607	85.8	77.4
Mason	5 477	16.4	211	2 695	1 101	175	130	1 248	813	46.1	13.0	501	93.3	45.4
Mercer	15 447	3.0	241	7 185	3 236	296	321	4 463	2 782	151.9	24.8	384	78.2	159.4
Mineral	4 957	6.5	183	2 860	595	72	134	1 419	795	45.9	10.0	369	92.7	46.2
Mingo	7 490	7.5	238	2 180	2 511	99	160	1 482	1 085	58.8	17.2	530	89.4	55.1
Monongalia	11 112	9.0	144	6 410	1 421	1 393	415	14 887	2 081	126.2	44.2	569	81.3	123.0
Monroe	3 098	–8.2	233	1 600	698	230	66	477	326	13.5	2.3	175	92.7	13.4
Morgan	3 054	30.5	220	1 940	285	25	68	763	438	27.3	5.8	428	94.5	27.7
Nicholas	6 380	14.0	232	2 730	1 138	124	138	1 685	1 152	64.9	12.5	454	74.6	64.3
Ohio	11 836	–5.7	248	7 540	1 322	457	243	3 592	1 936	89.5	29.2	600	65.4	78.9
Pendleton	1 847	9.0	230	1 090	305	173	227	353	230	12.3	2.0	254	95.1	11.8
Pleasants	1 534	–1.0	204	860	202	14	37	502	295	31.4	7.9	1 052	96.4	31.3
Pocahontas	2 217	6.8	245	1 145	336	75	46	763	396	18.4	3.3	360	79.8	19.6
Preston	6 120	10.1	205	3 055	1 095	90	149	1 540	838	38.4	7.5	251	94.4	38.3
Putnam	8 125	38.5	156	4 285	883	168	256	2 080	1 321	77.2	23.0	456	94.1	75.2
Raleigh	18 490	2.0	234	7 885	3 216	1 414	596	3 609	2 261	146.2	36.0	455	77.9	122.5
Randolph	6 033	6.8	211	3 070	1 383	292	144	1 816	746	43.2	6.9	241	80.1	42.5
Ritchie	2 385	2.4	228	1 275	486	31	52	500	334	13.9	3.6	351	98.0	14.0
Roane	3 564	14.8	231	1 715	844	36	77	643	483	21.8	3.9	254	88.1	21.8
Summers	2 864	15.0	207	1 320	817	40	66	757	317	16.6	2.6	189	76.0	16.6
Taylor	3 002	16.6	195	1 560	620	45	77	1 086	487	28.0	5.7	369	87.4	26.8
Tucker	1 819	15.5	242	1 000	215	67	38	660	249	15.0	3.4	445	86.0	14.2
Tyler	2 104	24.5	217	1 165	245	26	49	506	404	20.5	5.3	528	97.2	17.7
Upshur	4 700	9.8	200	2 395	991	112	118	1 189	657	32.9	5.9	250	91.0	35.1
Wayne	8 668	31.5	207	4 050	2 226	944	210	2 192	1 229	71.9	17.2	408	93.7	67.8
Webster	2 474	4.8	247	925	781	22	51	627	339	15.2	3.5	339	94.1	15.0
Wetzel	4 169	–.1	229	2 150	738	55	91	1 107	878	48.6	10.9	589	85.8	44.6
Wirt	1 196	17.8	208	585	263	15	28	261	179	8.5	1.6	288	96.3	8.2
Wood	18 400	8.8	213	10 665	2 601	1 901	436	4 092	3 951	210.6	45.3	520	78.8	201.7
Wyoming	7 076	14.3	262	2 000	1 780	97	137	1 219	1 138	43.2	11.0	397	93.5	42.7
WISCONSIN	890 588	6.2	170	591 942	86 544	29 494	19 338	344 990	201 633	15 575.4	5 438.6	1 046	94.6	15 921.8
Adams	4 859	75.1	259	3 390	326	359	65	725	517	39.2	15.8	866	94.3	46.6
Ashland	3 515	–9.1	214	2 210	394	175	58	1 317	737	55.1	11.4	693	90.9	57.1
Barron	9 460	4.2	215	6 120	889	158	156	3 193	1 751	123.6	31.5	722	91.0	127.3
Bayfield	3 366	18.5	219	2 285	240	139	65	898	607	46.8	15.4	1 016	94.2	44.8
Brown	30 592	12.2	141	19 460	2 881	985	814	12 264	7 804	633.5	208.0	971	97.5	645.2
Buffalo	2 926	2.0	205	1 905	241	180	50	773	537	34.9	8.8	621	94.0	35.7
Burnett	4 126	27.7	277	2 885	268	40	52	718	497	36.8	12.5	860	93.8	39.1
Calumet	5 485	38.9	141	3 625	181	110	135	1 206	1 265	66.7	20.6	541	97.9	72.4
Chippewa	10 529	6.0	192	6 585	866	215	194	3 479	1 819	128.7	32.3	595	90.8	127.2
Clark	6 548	–2.6	196	4 190	554	113	117	1 973	1 475	100.2	20.1	610	98.3	103.4
Columbia	9 694	–1.9	187	6 810	524	191	181	3 190	2 209	152.0	51.8	1 027	92.4	166.5
Crawford	3 497	4.1	212	2 265	380	72	58	832	617	45.2	11.5	698	91.0	48.5
Dane	50 483	14.4	118	34 145	5 282	4 261	1 576	67 772	15 814	1 241.6	558.9	1 324	92.9	1 294.3
Dodge	14 253	23.9	171	9 785	566	188	294	4 203	2 167	188.9	58.6	712	92.4	198.1
Door	6 443	12.8	238	4 545	231	82	146	1 524	1 035	79.8	38.8	1 444	93.4	86.9
Douglas	7 652	–5.0	178	4 635	1 083	119	153	3 189	2 141	161.7	47.5	1 101	92.4	156.8
Dunn	5 852	7.6	149	3 635	598	95	138	4 389	1 503	106.5	26.7	690	92.9	116.9
Eau Claire	14 667	5.4	163	9 390	1 651	375	315	7 710	3 364	268.4	77.8	872	96.4	268.8
Florence	1 139	31.7	222	785	91	21	18	286	200	14.3	4.1	780	98.7	13.5
Fond du Lac	16 606	3.4	175	11 315	1 073	247	335	5 164	3 673	263.9	87.6	928	97.8	265.2
Forest	2 369	6.2	245	1 560	201	123	34	658	435	28.2	8.0	838	94.6	32.9
Grant	10 046	1.2	204	6 605	812	170	174	4 714	2 322	151.0	36.2	735	98.7	153.1
Green	5 960	8.2	176	4 070	297	95	118	1 800	1 331	86.2	26.2	790	97.7	94.2
Green Lake	4 505	–1.1	230	3 155	214	63	69	1 005	666	55.4	20.7	1 070	97.4	55.1
Iowa	3 660	17.1	161	2 420	208	86	79	1 296	931	57.1	19.9	900	93.3	62.7
Iron	1 944	7.1	309	1 290	134	22	22	325	268	21.0	6.3	976	92.8	19.3
Jackson	3 608	3.2	202	2 330	398	54	63	1 341	881	55.6	12.6	715	92.9	58.7
Jefferson	12 710	1.5	172	8 195	709	192	260	3 800	2 927	196.3	65.5	893	93.0	198.4
Juneau	5 477	12.6	227	3 650	489	265	85	1 443	1 008	68.8	17.4	729	92.1	70.8
Kenosha	22 580	9.3	154	14 265	2 223	286	534	7 791	5 246	444.2	169.0	1 182	93.7	451.2
Kewaunee	3 702	–.9	185	2 380	171	79	70	931	662	51.0	14.7	746	98.5	53.3
La Crosse	16 698	7.5	163	11 350	1 770	498	379	8 351	4 463	315.8	97.9	959	90.6	328.7

¹ Per 1,000 resident population estimated as of July 1, 1999. ² Based on resident population estimated as of July 1, 1997.

Sources: Social Security Program—U.S. Social Security Administration, OASDI Beneficiaries by State and County - December 1999, <http://www.ssa.gov/statistics/oasdi_sc/1999/oasdi_sc99.pdf> (accessed: 7 March 2001) for 1999 - annual publication of same title for 1990. Supplemental Security Income Program—U.S. Social Security Administration, SSI Recipients by State and County, <http://www.ssa.gov/statistics/ssi_st_cty/1999/ssi_st_cty.pdf> (accessed: November 2000). Government employment, 1998—U.S. Bureau of Economic Analysis, "Regional Economic Information System (REIS) 1969-1998" on CD-ROM (related Internet site <http://www.bea.doc.gov/bea/regional/data.htm>). Local government employment, 1997—U.S. Census Bureau, 1997 Census of Governments, Compendium of Public Employment, <http://www.census.gov/govs/apes/97coar2.dat> (accessed: 14 January 2000). Local government finances—U.S. Census Bureau, 1997 Census of Governments, Compendium of Government Finances, <http://www.census.gov/prod/gc97/gc974-5.pdf> (accessed: 16 February 2001).

Table B-13. Counties — Government Programs, Employment, and Finances–Con.

[Includes U.S., states, and 3,142 counties/county equivalents defined as of January 1, 1992. For changes to these areas since January 1, 1992, see appendix B. Geographic Information]

County	Social Security Program beneficiaries, December 1999				Supplemental Security Income Program recipients, December 1999	Government employment, 1998			Local government employment, full-time equivalent, March 1997	Local government finances, 1996–1997					
	Total			Retired workers		Federal		State and local		General revenue					Direct general expenditure (mil. dol.)
	Number	Percent change, 1990–1999	Rate[1]			Civilian	Military			Total (mil. dol.)	Taxes				
											Total (mil. dol.)	Per capita[2]	Percent property		
WISCONSIN—Con.														
Lafayette	3 142	10.6	196	2 030	188	62	57	1 144	989	60.5	15.3	939	99.1	63.9
Langlade	4 855	4.1	236	3 275	418	50	72	1 189	803	58.7	17.5	850	93.0	61.9
Lincoln	6 334	2.3	211	4 185	376	72	105	1 800	1 179	84.1	22.7	770	93.4	87.6
Manitowoc	16 517	1.7	200	11 355	991	187	306	4 102	3 143	190.5	52.5	640	96.9	209.4
Marathon	20 031	12.2	162	13 050	1 820	514	437	6 702	5 640	372.6	114.2	934	92.1	396.3
Marinette	9 755	-.2	227	6 350	742	123	208	2 128	1 516	113.6	30.6	712	97.9	115.9
Marquette	3 993	10.9	260	2 870	215	53	53	689	516	32.0	12.3	824	94.6	43.4
Menominee	706	33.2	140	390	143	(3)	17	359	287	19.6	2.6	530	99.2	18.8
Milwaukee	156 602	-8.1	173	100 765	31 641	9 079	3 671	53 672	39 715	3 478.1	1 206.8	1 315	93.5	3 284.5
Monroe	6 953	4.3	175	4 490	683	2 468	246	2 083	1 464	103.6	26.3	671	90.8	105.8
Oconto	7 025	15.3	204	4 570	452	115	120	1 585	991	82.9	20.0	601	92.8	87.0
Oneida	9 219	10.1	256	6 445	540	256	127	2 399	1 696	114.6	58.1	1 632	94.0	114.9
Outagamie	22 209	9.5	140	14 535	1 471	371	551	7 800	5 896	483.9	166.8	1 081	97.5	490.2
Ozaukee	12 513	24.1	153	8 980	272	162	286	3 429	2 404	202.6	101.6	1 259	94.3	245.4
Pepin	1 511	-8.7	207	965	115	29	25	521	398	25.1	6.5	912	95.1	28.8
Pierce	4 770	-1.3	132	3 120	263	105	126	3 288	1 401	100.3	27.0	768	94.3	108.8
Polk	7 611	7.0	193	5 165	485	146	137	2 214	1 602	116.6	30.8	806	93.7	124.9
Portage	9 545	17.5	147	6 395	766	205	234	5 426	2 215	163.0	52.8	817	91.0	163.1
Price	3 749	-1.2	241	2 450	303	127	56	966	668	44.5	11.9	756	94.0	43.2
Racine	31 059	2.3	167	20 160	3 391	418	658	8 367	6 083	476.4	154.5	835	97.6	477.1
Richland	3 627	2.6	204	2 295	341	59	63	1 110	777	47.3	11.5	644	92.9	48.8
Rock	25 326	9.1	168	16 730	2 708	341	532	8 201	5 951	445.3	124.8	831	97.6	462.0
Rusk	3 491	1.3	231	2 235	373	56	54	1 231	900	62.0	9.7	637	84.8	65.7
St. Croix	7 490	28.3	124	4 950	365	152	208	3 026	1 840	146.1	47.2	822	91.8	154.2
Sauk	10 068	10.2	185	6 830	641	155	188	2 968	2 313	154.7	54.1	1 020	89.1	174.3
Sawyer	3 700	4.1	228	2 555	357	71	57	1 027	586	42.3	15.7	980	91.7	48.4
Shawano	8 309	2.1	212	5 500	547	113	137	1 985	1 324	93.9	24.8	643	92.7	114.6
Sheboygan	19 618	1.0	178	13 730	1 235	234	400	5 784	4 786	334.0	107.5	979	97.8	352.3
Taylor	3 583	7.8	186	2 305	246	82	68	857	727	52.4	11.0	568	98.3	54.5
Trempealeau	5 661	-3.6	212	3 675	497	127	93	1 799	1 441	91.2	20.7	783	95.1	96.1
Vernon	5 859	1.8	211	3 765	553	110	96	1 684	883	73.1	17.3	635	98.3	76.9
Vilas	6 219	21.9	287	4 675	239	73	75	941	679	52.7	28.7	1 360	94.1	59.6
Walworth	14 412	13.9	167	9 965	710	203	301	6 193	3 811	268.5	110.9	1 315	92.1	280.3
Washburn	4 150	5.6	263	2 770	371	128	54	1 152	646	44.3	16.7	1 095	94.8	44.3
Washington	16 700	26.1	144	11 675	542	1 112	402	4 713	3 512	268.6	112.9	1 004	96.8	278.9
Waukesha	53 090	34.6	148	37 520	1 587	883	1 248	15 334	10 796	948.0	495.8	1 423	96.9	996.7
Waupaca	10 844	.1	213	7 365	685	143	178	3 175	2 015	133.5	40.9	818	93.5	142.8
Waushara	5 481	16.7	251	3 750	344	65	76	963	718	48.5	18.3	853	94.7	55.3
Winnebago	25 249	8.2	168	17 190	1 779	575	540	10 361	4 890	400.6	133.8	894	97.1	430.4
Wood	14 638	1.4	192	9 665	1 104	205	269	4 363	3 560	226.5	71.5	943	97.7	221.9
WYOMING	74 688	20.6	156	47 617	5 783	7 034	6 349	48 207	27 423	1 619.6	485.1	1 011	78.0	1 622.6
Albany	3 270	15.1	113	2 185	271	235	195	5 944	1 562	97.3	14.5	490	48.6	88.5
Big Horn	2 343	8.5	209	1 480	188	97	71	1 220	853	44.9	11.1	998	66.6	43.8
Campbell	2 726	54.9	83	1 500	190	85	202	3 072	2 180	128.1	76.6	2 390	87.1	134.2
Carbon	2 418	18.8	157	1 515	152	143	97	1 747	986	58.1	21.1	1 343	80.2	53.7
Converse	1 819	29.0	147	1 140	99	69	77	1 107	786	39.2	14.7	1 188	84.2	41.5
Crook	1 017	26.3	176	640	35	77	36	560	378	16.5	5.7	977	85.6	15.0
Fremont	6 603	22.5	182	4 125	747	422	224	3 136	1 767	100.9	24.3	674	83.8	99.0
Goshen	2 639	11.1	209	1 660	196	93	80	1 257	649	34.8	8.2	634	64.6	33.9
Hot Springs	1 261	7.3	282	815	71	15	29	532	370	13.0	6.0	1 279	85.5	18.9
Johnson	1 630	43.0	238	1 140	47	62	42	689	428	30.1	5.7	849	78.7	22.5
Laramie	11 595	25.9	147	7 380	1 112	2 422	3 820	8 667	4 192	251.1	42.9	546	66.1	248.6
Lincoln	2 253	26.9	161	1 545	80	111	86	1 221	826	59.3	18.4	1 328	89.7	61.4
Natrona	11 189	19.9	177	7 180	1 143	642	398	4 443	3 188	170.5	31.4	494	57.7	176.6
Niobrara	593	5.9	221	375	34	25	17	341	203	11.5	2.8	1 047	79.7	10.6
Park	4 787	22.1	188	3 210	223	785	161	2 373	1 576	73.3	21.3	830	92.4	72.1
Platte	1 907	17.7	221	1 240	82	99	54	860	430	27.3	6.9	812	80.0	26.3
Sheridan	5 036	11.9	201	3 245	341	625	157	2 227	1 594	84.6	15.3	609	51.8	83.5
Sublette	936	32.8	161	645	19	92	43	465	314	20.8	12.5	2 216	96.4	21.6
Sweetwater	4 151	14.2	106	2 470	325	260	248	3 695	2 361	170.4	73.8	1 856	86.3	189.3
Teton	1 493	45.0	103	1 065	66	393	88	1 440	908	84.5	31.0	2 231	58.5	76.6
Uinta	1 961	42.6	97	1 060	208	77	127	1 920	1 061	67.2	29.6	1 459	87.2	69.9
Washakie	1 656	10.8	194	1 125	93	145	54	663	401	20.4	6.2	724	93.6	19.5
Weston	1 395	24.0	218	865	58	60	43	628	410	16.1	4.9	754	78.0	15.8

[1] Per 1,000 resident population estimated as of July 1, 1999. [2] Based on resident population estimated as of July 1, 1997.

Sources: Social Security Program—U.S. Social Security Administration, OASDI Beneficiaries by State and County - December 1999, <http://www.ssa.gov/statistics/oasdi_sc/1999/oasdi_sc99.pdf> (accessed: 7 March 2001) for 1999 – annual publication of same title for 1990. Supplemental Security Income Program—U.S. Social Security Administration, SSI Recipients by State and County, <http://www.ssa.gov/statistics/ssi_st_cty/1999/ssi_st_cty.pdf> (accessed: November 2000). Government employment, 1998—U.S. Bureau of Economic Analysis, "Regional Economic Information System (REIS) 1969-1998" on CD-ROM (related Internet site <http://www.bea.doc.gov/bea/regional/data.htm>). Local government employment, 1997—U.S. Census Bureau, 1997 Census of Governments, Compendium of Public Employment, <http://www.census.gov/govs/apes/97coar2.dat> (accessed: 14 January 2000). Local government finances—U.S. Census Bureau, 1997 Census of Governments, Compendium of Government Finances, <http://www.census.gov/prod/gc97/gc974-5.pdf> (accessed: 16 February 2001).

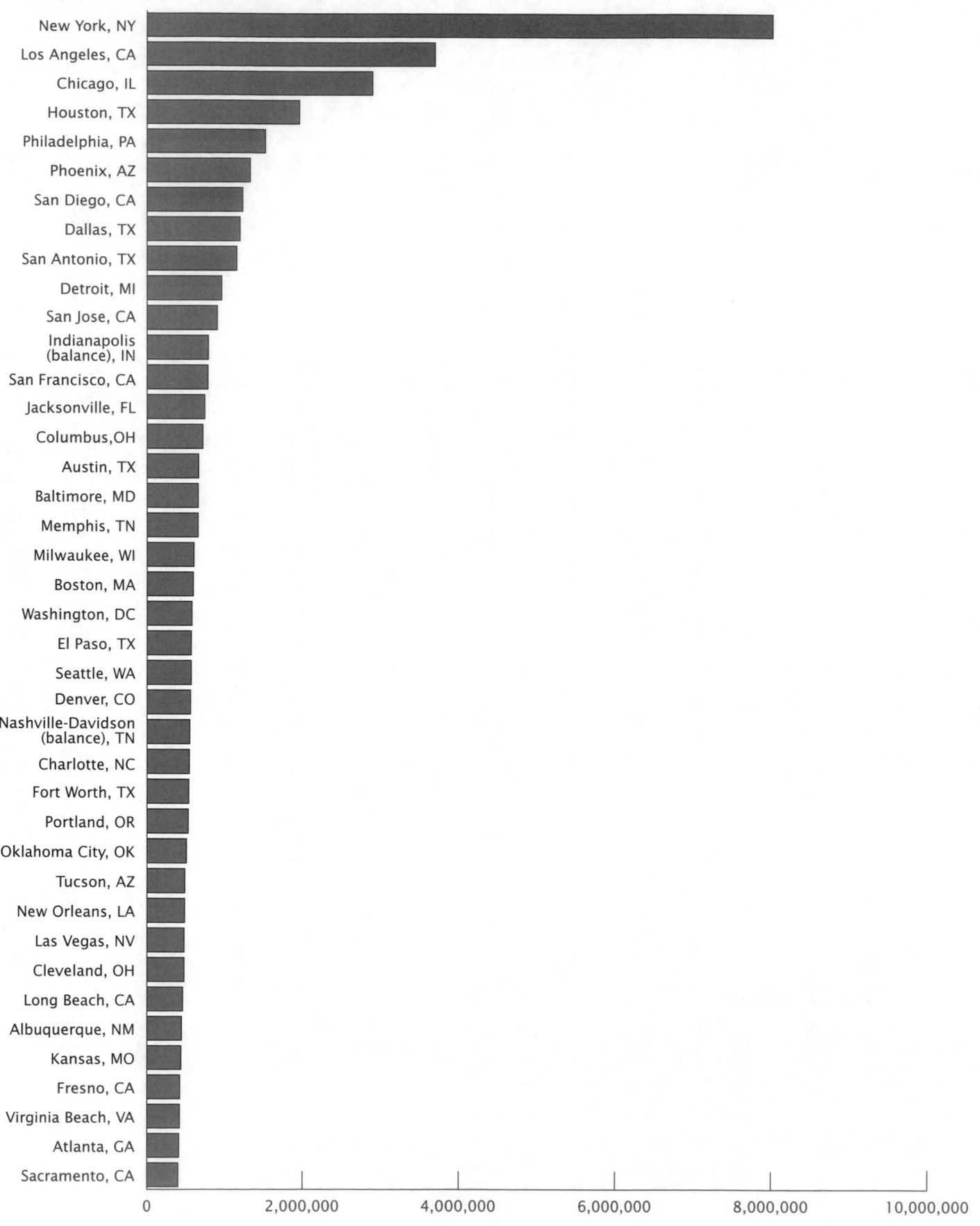

Figure 3.
Top 40 Cities by Population in the United States: 2000

U.S. Census Bureau, County and City Data Book: 2000

Cities

Table C

Page

You may visit us on the Web at
http://www.census.gov/statab/www/ccdb.html

Cities

Table C

Table C–1. Cities — **Area and Population**

[Includes states and 1,070 incorporated places of 25,000 or more population as of April 1, 1990 in all states except Hawaii which has no incorporated places recognized by the Census Bureau. For Hawaii, 8 census designated places (CDPs) of 25,000 or more population as of April 1, 1990 are included. Also included are the 5 boroughs of New York city. For more information on these areas, see appendix B. Geographic Information]

State and place code[1]	City	Land area,[2] 2000 (sq. miles)	2000 Number	2000 Rank[3]	2000 Per square mile	1990[4] Number	1990 Rank[5]	1980	Net change 1990–2000	Net change 1980–1990	Percent change 1990–2000	Percent change 1980–1990	Hispanic or Latino,[6] 2000 Number	Hispanic or Latino,[6] 2000 Percent
01 00000	ALABAMA	50 744.0	4 447 100	X	87.6	4 040 389	X	3 894 025	406 711	146 364	10.1	3.8	75 830	1.7
01 01852	Anniston city............	45.4	24 276	1 070	534.7	27 295	1 001	29 135	−3 019	−1 840	−11.1	−6.3	409	1.7
01 03076	Auburn city.............	39.1	42 987	696	1 099.4	34 620	778	28 471	8 367	6 149	24.2	21.6	666	1.5
01 05980	Bessemer city...........	40.7	29 672	986	729.0	33 616	809	31 729	−3 944	1 887	−11.7	5.9	338	1.1
01 07000	Birmingham city.........	149.9	242 820	71	1 619.9	265 940	60	284 413	−23 120	−18 473	−8.7	−6.5	3 764	1.6
01 20104	Decatur city.............	53.4	53 929	547	1 009.9	50 139	519	42 002	3 790	8 137	7.6	19.4	3 040	5.6
01 21184	Dothan city.............	86.6	57 737	491	666.7	55 333	445	48 750	2 404	6 583	4.3	13.5	764	1.3
01 26896	Florence city............	24.9	36 264	830	1 456.4	36 608	740	37 029	−344	−421	−.9	−1.1	487	1.3
01 28696	Gadsden city............	36.0	38 978	777	1 082.7	43 498	607	47 565	−4 520	−4 067	−10.4	−8.6	1 039	2.7
01 35896	Hoover city.............	43.1	62 742	438	1 455.7	41 089	647	18 996	21 653	22 093	52.7	116.3	2 380	3.8
01 37000	Huntsville city..........	174.0	158 216	127	909.3	160 372	109	142 513	−2 156	17 859	−1.3	12.5	3 225	2.0
01 50000	Mobile city.............	117.9	198 915	91	1 687.2	198 417	78	200 452	498	−2 035	.3	−1.0	2 828	1.4
01 51000	Montgomery city.........	155.4	201 568	87	1 297.1	190 831	84	177 857	10 737	12 974	5.6	7.3	2 484	1.2
01 59472	Phenix City city.........	24.6	28 265	1 010	1 149.0	25 739	1 053	26 928	2 526	−1 189	9.8	−4.4	421	1.5
01 62496	Prichard city............	25.4	28 633	1 001	1 127.3	33 711	807	39 541	−5 078	−5 830	−15.1	−14.7	162	.6
01 77256	Tuscaloosa city..........	56.2	77 906	338	1 386.2	79 242	277	75 211	−1 336	4 031	−1.7	5.4	1 092	1.4
02 00000	ALASKA	571 951.3	626 932	X	1.1	550 043	X	401 851	76 889	148 192	14.0	36.9	25 852	4.1
02 03000	Anchorage city..........	1 697.2	260 283	65	153.4	226 338	69	174 431	33 945	51 907	15.0	29.8	14 799	5.7
02 24230	Fairbanks city...........	31.9	30 224	968	947.5	30 952	886	22 645	−728	8 307	−2.4	36.7	1 854	6.1
02 36400	Juneau city.............	2 716.7	30 711	960	11.3	26 752	1 024	19 528	3 959	7 224	14.8	37.0	1 040	3.4
04 00000	ARIZONA	113 634.6	5 130 632	X	45.2	3 665 339	X	2 716 546	1 465 293	948 793	40.0	34.9	1 295 617	25.3
04 12000	Chandler city...........	57.9	176 581	114	3 049.8	90 703	228	29 673	85 878	61 030	94.7	205.7	37 059	21.0
04 23620	Flagstaff city............	63.6	52 894	558	831.7	45 857	573	34 743	7 037	11 114	15.3	32.0	8 500	16.1
04 27040	Gilbert town............	43.0	109 697	204	2 551.1	30 003	918	5 717	79 694	24 286	265.6	424.8	13 026	11.9
04 27820	Glendale city............	55.7	218 812	80	3 928.4	150 867	119	97 172	67 945	53 695	45.0	55.3	54 343	24.8
04 46000	Mesa city..............	125.0	396 375	42	3 171.0	290 212	53	152 404	106 163	137 808	36.6	90.4	78 281	19.7
04 54050	Peoria city.............	138.2	108 364	210	784.1	51 154	503	12 171	57 210	38 983	111.8	320.3	16 699	15.4
04 55000	Phoenix city	474.9	1 321 045	6	2 781.7	988 983	10	789 704	332 062	199 279	33.6	25.2	449 972	34.1
04 57380	Prescott city	37.1	33 938	885	914.8	27 126	1 011	19 865	6 812	7 261	25.1	36.6	2 773	8.2
04 65000	Scottsdale city..........	184.2	202 705	86	1 100.5	130 086	141	88 622	72 619	41 464	55.8	46.8	14 111	7.0
04 66820	Sierra Vista city.........	153.5	37 775	799	246.1	33 281	822	24 937	4 494	8 344	13.5	33.5	5 971	15.8
04 73000	Tempe city	40.1	158 625	126	3 955.7	142 056	126	106 919	16 569	35 137	11.7	32.9	28 473	17.9
04 77000	Tucson city	194.7	486 699	30	2 499.7	417 139	34	330 537	69 560	86 602	16.7	26.2	173 868	35.7
04 85540	Yuma city	106.7	77 515	340	726.5	59 932	402	42 481	17 583	17 451	29.3	41.1	35 400	45.7
05 00000	ARKANSAS	52 068.2	2 673 400	X	51.3	2 350 624	X	2 286 357	322 776	64 267	13.7	2.8	86 866	3.2
05 15190	Conway city............	35.0	43 167	693	1 233.3	28 579	959	20 375	14 588	8 204	51.0	40.3	983	2.3
05 23290	Fayetteville city	43.4	58 047	487	1 337.5	42 754	621	36 608	15 293	6 146	35.8	16.8	2 821	4.9
05 24550	Fort Smith city..........	50.3	80 268	321	1 595.8	72 803	309	71 626	7 465	1 177	10.3	1.6	7 048	8.8
05 33460	Hot Springs city.........	32.9	35 750	841	1 086.6	33 580	810	35 781	2 170	−2 201	6.5	−6.2	1 358	3.8
05 34750	Jacksonville city.........	26.4	29 916	977	1 133.2	29 165	939	27 589	751	1 576	2.6	5.7	1 012	3.4
05 35710	Jonesboro city..........	79.6	55 515	527	697.4	47 008	558	31 530	8 507	15 478	18.1	49.1	1 297	2.3
05 41000	Little Rock city	116.2	183 133	110	1 576.0	177 086	99	159 151	6 047	17 935	3.4	11.3	4 889	2.7
05 50450	North Little Rock city	44.8	60 433	458	1 349.0	62 838	381	64 388	−2 405	−1 550	−3.8	−2.4	1 463	2.4
05 55310	Pine Bluff city..........	45.6	55 085	532	1 208.0	57 074	429	56 636	−1 989	438	−3.5	.8	452	.8
05 66080	Springdale city..........	31.3	45 798	654	1 463.2	30 229	915	23 458	15 519	6 821	51.3	29.1	9 005	19.7
05 74540	West Memphis city	26.5	27 666	1 025	1 044.0	28 463	962	28 138	−797	325	−2.8	1.2	279	1.0
06 00000	CALIFORNIA	155 959.3	33 871 648	X	217.2	29 811 427	X	23 667 764	4 060 221	6 143 663	13.6	26.0	10 966 556	32.4
06 00562	Alameda city	10.8	72 259	368	6 690.6	73 888	304	63 852	−1 629	10 036	−2.2	15.7	6 725	9.3
06 00884	Alhambra city	7.6	85 804	293	11 290.0	82 090	266	64 767	3 714	17 323	4.5	26.7	30 453	35.5
06 02000	Anaheim city	48.9	328 014	55	6 707.9	266 625	59	219 494	61 389	47 131	23.0	21.5	153 374	46.8
06 02252	Antioch city	26.9	90 532	271	3 365.5	62 179	386	42 683	28 353	19 496	45.6	45.7	20 024	22.1
06 02364	Apple Valley town	73.3	54 239	543	740.0	46 119	567	(7)	8 120	X	17.6	X	10 067	18.6
06 02462	Arcadia city............	11.0	53 054	554	4 823.1	48 440	538	45 993	4 614	2 447	9.5	5.3	5 629	10.6
06 03386	Azusa city.............	8.9	44 712	676	5 023.8	40 831	653	29 380	3 881	11 451	9.5	39.0	28 522	63.8
06 03526	Bakersfield city.........	113.1	247 057	69	2 184.4	183 959	91	105 611	63 098	78 348	34.3	74.2	80 170	32.5
06 03666	Baldwin Park city........	6.7	75 837	351	11 319.0	69 373	336	50 554	6 464	18 819	9.3	37.2	59 660	78.7
06 04870	Bell city...............	2.5	36 664	819	14 665.6	34 220	793	25 450	2 444	8 770	7.1	34.5	33 328	90.9
06 04982	Bellflower city..........	6.1	72 878	364	11 947.2	61 824	391	53 441	11 054	8 383	17.9	15.7	31 503	43.2
06 04996	Bell Gardens city........	2.5	44 054	683	17 621.6	42 199	629	34 117	1 855	8 082	4.4	23.7	41 132	93.4
06 06000	Berkeley city...........	10.5	102 743	227	9 785.0	102 847	194	103 328	−104	−481	−.1	−.5	10 001	9.7
06 06308	Beverly Hills city	5.7	33 784	893	5 927.0	31 935	863	32 646	1 849	−711	5.8	−2.2	1 565	4.6

[1] Federal Information Processing Standards (FIPS) codes for states and places defined as of January 1990.   [2] Dry land and land temporarily or partially covered by water.   [3] Based on 1,078 places (1,070 incorporated places and the 8 CDPs in Hawaii). When places share the same rank, the next lower rank is omitted.   [4] Includes count resolution corrections through 1997 and adjustments based on Census 2000 dress rehearsal results and boundary changes reported as legally effective as of January 1, 1998.   [5] Based on 1,071 places (1,070 incorporated places and Honolulu CDP in Hawaii). When places share the same rank, the next lower rank is omitted.   [6] Persons of Hispanic or Latino origin may be of any race.   [7] Not incorporated as of January 1, 1980.

Sources: Land Area—U.S. Census Bureau, Census of Population and Housing, Census 2000 Redistricting Data (Public Law 94-171) Summary Files (related Internet site <http://www.census.gov/dmd/www/2kresult.html>).   2000 Population—U.S. Census Bureau, 2000 Census of Population and Housing, "Census 2000 Profiles of General Demographic Characteristics" data files, published May 2001, related Internet site <http://www.census.gov/mp/www/pub/2000cen/mscen01.html>.   1990 Population—U.S. Census Bureau, "(SU-99-7) Population Estimates for Places (Sorted Alphabetically Within State): Annual Time Series, July 1, 1990 to July 1, 1999 (includes April 1, 1990 Population Estimates Base)," published 20 October 2000, <http://www.census.gov/population/estimates/metro-city/placebyst/SC99T7_US.txt>.   1980 Population—U.S. Census Bureau, 1990 Census of Population and Housing, "Population and Housing Unit Counts," CPH-2-1 through CPH-2-52.

Table C–1. Cities — **Area and Population**–Con.

[Includes states and 1,070 incorporated places of 25,000 or more population as of April 1, 1990 in all states except Hawaii which has no incorporated places recognized by the Census Bureau. For Hawaii, 8 census designated places (CDPs) of 25,000 or more population as of April 1, 1990 are included. Also included are the 5 boroughs of New York city. For more information on these areas, see appendix B. Geographic Information]

State and place code[1]	City	Land area,[2] 2000 (sq. miles)	Population (April 1) 2000 Number	2000 Rank[3]	2000 Per square mile	1990[4] Number	1990[4] Rank[5]	1980	Net change 1990–2000	Net change 1980–1990	Percent change 1990–2000	Percent change 1980–1990	Hispanic or Latino,[6] 2000 Number	Hispanic or Latino,[6] 2000 Percent
	CALIFORNIA—Con.													
06 08100	Brea city	10.5	35 410	850	3 372.4	32 865	838	27 913	2 545	4 952	7.7	17.7	7 205	20.3
06 08786	Buena Park city	10.6	78 282	335	7 385.1	68 555	339	64 165	9 727	4 390	14.2	6.8	26 221	33.5
06 08954	Burbank city	17.3	100 316	238	5 798.6	93 626	220	84 625	6 690	9 001	7.1	10.6	24 953	24.9
06 09066	Burlingame city	4.3	28 158	1 012	6 548.4	26 753	1 023	26 173	1 405	580	5.3	2.2	2 995	10.6
06 10046	Camarillo city	18.9	57 077	498	3 019.9	52 331	487	37 797	4 746	14 534	9.1	38.5	8 869	15.5
06 10340	Campbell city	5.6	38 138	793	6 810.4	35 901	751	26 843	2 237	9 058	6.2	33.7	5 083	13.3
06 11194	Carlsbad city	37.4	78 247	336	2 092.2	62 995	379	35 490	15 252	27 505	24.2	77.5	9 170	11.7
06 11530	Carson city	18.8	89 730	276	4 772.9	84 097	262	81 221	5 633	2 876	6.7	3.5	31 332	34.9
06 12048	Cathedral City city	19.2	42 647	703	2 221.2	30 584	906	(7)	12 063	X	39.4	X	21 312	50.0
06 12524	Ceres city	6.9	34 609	874	5 015.8	26 842	1 019	13 281	7 767	13 561	28.9	102.1	13 115	37.9
06 12552	Cerritos city	8.6	51 488	573	5 987.0	53 294	473	53 020	-1 806	274	-3.4	.5	5 349	10.4
06 13014	Chico city	27.7	59 954	467	2 164.4	44 328	596	26 716	15 626	17 612	35.3	65.9	7 351	12.3
06 13210	Chino city	21.1	67 168	406	3 183.3	59 652	406	40 165	7 516	19 487	12.6	48.5	31 830	47.4
06 13392	Chula Vista city	48.9	173 556	120	3 549.2	135 243	132	83 927	38 313	51 316	28.3	61.1	86 073	49.6
06 13756	Claremont city	13.1	33 998	884	2 595.3	33 049	830	31 028	949	2 021	2.9	6.5	5 221	15.4
06 14218	Clovis city	17.1	68 468	394	4 004.0	50 731	514	33 021	17 737	17 710	35.0	53.6	13 876	20.3
06 14890	Colton city	15.1	47 662	626	3 156.4	39 546	678	21 310	8 116	18 236	20.5	85.6	28 934	60.7
06 15044	Compton city	10.1	93 493	258	9 256.7	90 298	230	81 350	3 195	8 948	3.5	11.0	53 143	56.8
06 16000	Concord city	30.1	121 780	177	4 045.8	111 197	169	103 763	10 583	7 434	9.5	7.2	26 560	21.8
06 16350	Corona city	35.1	124 966	170	3 560.3	76 181	294	37 791	48 785	38 390	64.0	101.6	44 569	35.7
06 16378	Coronado city	7.7	24 100	1 072	3 129.9	26 557	1 032	18 790	-2 457	7 767	-9.3	41.3	2 369	9.8
06 16532	Costa Mesa city	15.6	108 724	209	6 969.5	96 849	210	82 562	11 875	14 287	12.3	17.3	34 523	31.8
06 16742	Covina city	7.0	46 837	638	6 691.0	43 230	609	32 746	3 607	10 484	8.3	32.0	18 871	40.3
06 17568	Culver City city	5.1	38 816	781	7 611.0	38 889	693	38 139	-73	750	-.2	2.0	9 199	23.7
06 17610	Cupertino city	10.9	50 546	585	4 637.2	40 419	662	34 297	10 127	6 122	25.1	17.8	2 010	4.0
06 17750	Cypress city	6.6	46 229	649	7 004.4	42 655	623	40 738	3 574	1 917	8.4	4.7	7 235	15.7
06 17918	Daly City city	7.6	103 621	223	13 634.3	92 213	226	78 519	11 408	13 694	12.4	17.4	23 072	22.3
06 17946	Dana Point city	6.6	35 110	859	5 319.7	31 724	869	(7)	3 386	X	10.7	X	5 440	15.5
06 17988	Danville city	18.1	41 715	715	2 304.7	31 246	878	(7)	10 469	X	33.5	X	1 945	4.7
06 18100	Davis city	10.5	60 308	461	5 743.6	46 831	560	36 640	13 477	10 191	28.8	27.8	5 793	9.6
06 19192	Diamond Bar city	14.8	56 287	511	3 803.2	53 611	469	(7)	2 676	X	5.0	X	10 393	18.5
06 19766	Downey city	12.4	107 323	212	8 655.1	91 478	227	82 602	15 845	8 876	17.3	10.7	62 089	57.9
06 21712	El Cajon city	14.6	94 869	252	6 497.9	88 983	235	73 892	5 886	15 091	6.6	20.4	21 313	22.5
06 21782	El Centro city	9.6	37 835	798	3 941.1	32 989	831	23 996	4 846	8 993	14.7	37.5	28 219	74.6
06 22230	El Monte city	9.6	115 965	192	12 079.7	100 154	100	70 404	15 811	29 750	9.2	33.5	83 945	72.4
06 22678	Encinitas city	19.1	58 014	488	3 037.4	55 823	439	(7)	2 191	X	3.9	X	8 584	14.8
06 22804	Escondido city	36.3	133 559	160	3 679.3	109 026	176	64 355	24 533	44 671	22.5	69.4	51 693	38.7
06 23042	Eureka city	9.5	26 128	1 057	2 750.3	26 885	1 017	24 153	-757	2 732	-2.8	11.3	2 031	7.8
06 23182	Fairfield city	37.7	96 178	246	2 551.1	78 763	280	58 099	17 415	20 664	22.1	35.6	18 050	18.8
06 24638	Folsom city	21.7	51 884	567	2 391.0	29 801	923	11 003	22 083	18 798	74.1	170.8	4 914	9.5
06 24680	Fontana city	36.1	128 929	163	3 571.4	87 868	238	36 804	41 061	51 064	46.7	138.7	74 424	57.7
06 25338	Foster City city	3.8	28 803	997	7 579.7	28 160	973	23 287	643	4 873	2.3	20.9	1 531	5.3
06 25380	Fountain Valley city	8.9	54 978	533	6 177.3	53 784	465	55 080	1 194	-1 296	2.2	-2.4	5 870	10.7
06 26000	Fremont city	76.7	203 413	85	2 652.1	173 359	100	131 945	30 054	41 414	17.3	31.4	27 409	13.5
06 27000	Fresno city	104.4	427 652	37	4 096.3	355 444	48	217 491	72 208	137 953	20.3	63.4	170 520	39.9
06 28000	Fullerton city	22.2	126 003	189	5 675.8	113 419	164	102 246	12 584	11 173	11.1	10.9	38 014	30.2
06 28168	Gardena city	5.8	57 746	490	9 956.2	52 322	488	45 165	5 424	7 157	10.4	15.8	18 372	31.8
06 29000	Garden Grove city	18.0	165 196	124	9 177.6	143 660	124	123 307	21 536	20 353	15.0	16.5	53 608	32.5
06 29504	Gilroy city	15.9	41 464	720	2 607.8	31 561	870	21 641	9 903	9 920	31.4	45.8	22 298	53.8
06 30000	Glendale city	30.6	194 973	98	6 371.7	180 060	95	139 060	14 913	41 000	8.3	29.5	38 452	19.7
06 30014	Glendora city	19.1	49 415	599	2 587.2	48 009	543	38 500	1 406	9 509	2.9	24.7	10 740	21.7
06 31960	Hanford city	13.1	41 686	716	3 182.1	30 481	911	20 958	11 205	9 523	36.8	45.4	16 116	38.7
06 32548	Hawthorne city	6.1	84 112	302	13 788.9	71 349	324	56 437	12 763	14 912	17.9	26.4	37 227	44.3
06 33000	Hayward city	44.3	140 030	150	3 160.9	114 640	159	93 585	25 390	21 055	22.1	22.5	47 850	34.2
06 33182	Hemet city	25.6	58 812	479	2 297.3	46 487	562	22 531	12 325	23 956	26.5	106.3	13 585	23.1
06 33434	Hesperia city	67.3	62 582	440	929.9	50 819	513	(7)	11 763	X	23.1	X	18 400	29.4
06 33588	Highland city	13.6	44 605	677	3 279.8	34 538	784	(7)	10 067	X	29.1	X	16 342	36.6
06 36000	Huntington Beach city	26.4	189 594	101	7 181.6	182 899	92	170 505	6 695	12 394	3.7	7.3	27 798	14.7
06 36056	Huntington Park city	3.0	61 348	450	20 449.3	56 125	436	45 932	5 223	10 193	9.3	22.2	58 636	95.6
06 36294	Imperial Beach city	4.3	26 992	1 037	6 277.2	26 493	1 034	22 689	499	3 804	1.9	16.8	10 818	40.1
06 36448	Indio city	26.7	49 116	608	1 839.6	37 691	722	21 611	11 425	16 080	30.3	74.4	37 028	75.4
06 36546	Inglewood city	9.1	112 580	200	12 371.4	110 454	173	94 162	2 126	16 292	1.9	17.3	51 829	46.0
06 36770	Irvine city	46.2	143 072	146	3 096.8	111 416	168	62 134	31 656	49 282	28.4	79.3	10 539	7.4
06 39248	Laguna Niguel city	14.7	61 891	444	4 210.3	45 003	584	(7)	16 888	X	37.5	X	6 425	10.4
06 39290	La Habra city	7.3	58 974	476	8 078.6	51 343	500	45 232	7 631	6 111	14.9	13.5	28 922	49.0
06 39892	Lakewood city	9.4	79 345	329	8 441.0	73 565	306	74 511	5 780	-946	7.9	-1.3	18 071	22.8
06 40004	La Mesa city	9.3	54 749	536	5 887.0	52 982	478	50 308	1 767	2 674	3.3	5.3	7 402	13.5
06 40032	La Mirada city	7.8	46 783	641	5 997.8	40 455	660	40 986	6 328	-531	15.6	-1.3	15 657	33.5

[1] Federal Information Processing Standards (FIPS) codes for states and places defined as of January 1990.   [2] Dry land and land temporarily or partially covered by water.   [3] Based on 1,078 places (1,070 incorporated places and the 8 CDPs in Hawaii). When places share the same rank, the next lower rank is omitted.   [4] Includes count resolution corrections through 1997 and adjustments based on Census 2000 dress rehearsal results and boundary changes reported as legally effective as of January 1, 1998.   [5] Based on 1,071 places (1,070 incorporated places and Honolulu CDP in Hawaii). When places share the same rank, the next lower rank is omitted.   [6] Persons of Hispanic or Latino origin may be of any race.   [7] Not incorporated as of January 1, 1980.

Sources: Land Area—U.S. Census Bureau, Census of Population and Housing, Census 2000 Redistricting Data (Public Law 94-171) Summary Files (related Internet site <http://www.census.gov/dmd/www/2kresult.html>).   2000 Population—U.S. Census Bureau, 2000 Census of Population and Housing, "Census 2000 Profiles of General Demographic Characteristics" data files, published May 2001, related Internet site <http://www.census.gov/mp/www/pub/2000cen/mscen01.html>.   1990 Population—U.S. Census Bureau, "(SU-99-7) Population Estimates for Places (Sorted Alphabetically Within State): Annual Time Series, July 1, 1990 to July 1, 1999 (includes April 1, 1990 Population Estimates Base)," published 20 October 2000, <http://www.census.gov/population/estimates/metro-city/placebyst/SC99T7_US.txt>.   1980 Population—U.S. Census Bureau, 1990 Census of Population and Housing, "Population and Housing Unit Counts," CPH-2-1 through CPH-2-52.

Table C–1. Cities — **Area and Population**–Con.

[Includes states and 1,070 incorporated places of 25,000 or more population as of April 1, 1990 in all states except Hawaii which has no incorporated places recognized by the Census Bureau. For Hawaii, 8 census designated places (CDPs) of 25,000 or more population as of April 1, 1990 are included. Also included are the 5 boroughs of New York city. For more information on these areas, see appendix B. Geographic Information]

State and place code[1]	City	Land area,[2] 2000 (sq. miles)	Population (April 1) 2000 Number	2000 Rank[3]	2000 Per square mile	1990[4] Number	1990[4] Rank[5]	1980	Net change 1990–2000	Net change 1980–1990	Percent change 1990–2000	Percent change 1980–1990	Hispanic or Latino,[6] 2000 Number	Hispanic or Latino,[6] 2000 Percent
	CALIFORNIA—Con.													
06 40130	Lancaster city	94.0	118 718	184	1 263.0	98 445	208	48 027	20 273	50 418	20.6	105.0	28 644	24.1
06 40340	La Puente city	3.5	41 063	730	11 732.3	36 842	735	30 882	4 221	5 960	11.5	19.3	34 122	83.1
06 40830	La Verne city	8.3	31 638	936	3 811.8	30 847	893	23 508	791	7 339	2.6	31.2	7 315	23.1
06 40886	Lawndale city	2.0	31 711	933	15 855.5	27 345	999	23 460	4 366	3 885	16.0	16.6	16 515	52.1
06 41992	Livermore city	23.9	73 345	361	3 068.8	57 352	426	48 349	15 993	9 003	27.9	18.6	10 541	14.4
06 42202	Lodi city	12.2	56 999	500	4 672.0	51 671	495	35 221	5 328	16 450	10.3	46.7	15 464	27.1
06 42524	Lompoc city	11.6	41 103	729	3 543.4	37 732	720	26 267	3 371	11 465	8.9	43.6	15 337	37.3
06 43000	Long Beach city	50.4	461 522	34	9 157.2	429 870	32	361 498	31 652	68 372	7.4	18.9	165 092	35.8
06 43280	Los Altos city	6.4	27 693	1 024	4 327.0	26 540	1 033	25 769	1 153	771	4.3	3.0	822	3.0
06 44000	Los Angeles city	469.1	3 694 820	2	7 876.4	3 485 499	2	2 968 528	209 321	516 971	6.0	17.4	1 719 073	46.5
06 44112	Los Gatos town	10.7	28 592	1 004	2 672.1	27 381	997	26 906	1 211	475	4.4	1.8	1 491	5.2
06 44574	Lynwood city	4.9	69 845	384	14 254.1	61 971	387	48 289	7 874	13 682	12.7	28.3	57 503	82.3
06 45022	Madera city	12.3	43 207	692	3 512.8	29 428	933	21 732	13 779	7 696	46.8	35.4	29 274	67.8
06 45400	Manhattan Beach city	3.9	33 852	890	8 680.0	32 330	851	31 542	1 522	788	4.7	2.5	1 756	5.2
06 45484	Manteca city	15.9	49 258	605	3 098.0	41 718	639	24 925	7 540	16 793	18.1	67.4	12 363	25.1
06 45778	Marina city	8.7	25 101	1 068	2 885.2	26 415	1 037	20 647	−1 314	5 768	−5.0	27.9	5 822	23.2
06 46114	Martinez city	12.3	35 866	838	2 915.9	33 563	813	22 582	2 303	10 981	6.9	48.6	3 660	10.2
06 46492	Maywood city	1.2	28 083	1 013	23 402.5	28 061	978	21 810	22	6 251	.1	28.7	27 051	96.3
06 46870	Menlo Park city	10.1	30 785	958	3 048.0	28 934	945	26 438	1 851	2 496	6.4	9.4	4 803	15.6
06 46898	Merced city	19.9	63 893	427	3 210.7	56 673	431	36 423	7 220	20 250	12.7	55.6	26 425	41.4
06 47766	Milpitas city	13.6	62 698	439	4 610.1	50 955	507	37 820	11 743	13 135	23.0	34.7	10 417	16.6
06 48256	Mission Viejo city	18.7	93 102	259	4 978.7	80 313	273	(7)	12 789	X	15.9	X	11 266	12.1
06 48354	Modesto city	35.8	188 856	102	5 275.3	166 430	106	106 963	22 426	59 467	13.5	55.6	48 310	25.6
06 48648	Monrovia city	13.7	36 929	812	2 695.5	35 541	756	30 531	1 388	5 010	3.9	16.4	13 012	35.2
06 48788	Montclair city	5.1	33 049	907	6 480.2	28 515	961	22 628	4 534	5 887	15.9	26.0	19 823	60.0
06 48816	Montebello city	8.2	62 150	443	7 579.3	59 563	409	52 929	2 587	6 634	4.3	12.5	46 347	74.6
06 48872	Monterey city	8.4	29 674	985	3 532.6	32 567	844	27 558	−2 893	5 009	−8.9	18.2	3 222	10.9
06 48914	Monterey Park city	7.6	60 051	465	7 901.4	60 582	398	54 338	−531	6 244	−.9	11.5	17 359	28.9
06 49138	Moorpark city	19.0	31 415	943	1 653.4	25 579	1 058	(7)	5 836	X	22.8	X	8 735	27.8
06 49270	Moreno Valley city	51.2	142 381	148	2 780.9	118 756	154	(7)	23 625	X	19.9	X	54 689	38.4
06 49670	Mountain View city	12.1	70 708	378	5 843.6	66 731	351	58 655	3 977	8 076	6.0	13.8	12 911	18.3
06 50258	Napa city	17.7	72 585	367	4 100.8	62 447	385	50 879	10 138	11 568	16.2	22.7	19 475	26.8
06 50398	National City city	7.4	54 260	542	7 332.4	54 311	459	48 772	−51	5 539	−.1	11.4	32 053	59.1
06 50916	Newark city	14.0	42 471	705	3 033.6	37 862	715	32 126	4 609	5 736	12.2	17.9	12 145	28.6
06 51182	Newport Beach city	14.8	70 032	383	4 731.9	66 761	349	62 556	3 271	4 205	4.9	6.7	3 301	4.7
06 52526	Norwalk city	9.7	103 298	225	10 649.3	94 195	218	84 901	9 103	9 294	9.7	10.9	64 965	62.9
06 52582	Novato city	27.7	47 630	627	1 719.5	47 521	551	43 916	109	3 605	.2	8.2	6 229	13.1
06 53000	Oakland city	56.1	399 484	41	7 120.9	399 886	35	339 337	−402	60 549	−.1	17.8	87 467	21.9
06 53322	Oceanside city	40.6	161 029	125	3 966.2	128 579	142	76 698	32 450	51 881	25.2	67.6	48 691	30.2
06 53896	Ontario city	49.8	158 007	128	3 172.8	133 270	136	88 820	24 737	44 450	18.6	50.0	94 610	59.9
06 53980	Orange city	23.4	128 821	164	5 505.2	110 641	172	91 450	18 180	19 191	16.4	21.0	41 434	32.2
06 54652	Oxnard city	25.3	170 358	122	6 733.5	142 458	125	108 195	27 900	34 263	19.6	31.7	112 807	66.2
06 54806	Pacifica city	12.6	38 390	787	3 046.8	37 677	723	36 866	713	811	1.9	2.2	5 609	14.6
06 55156	Palmdale city	105.0	116 670	190	1 111.1	77 296	288	12 277	39 374	65 019	50.9	529.6	43 991	37.7
06 55254	Palm Springs city	94.2	42 807	699	454.4	40 326	666	32 359	2 481	7 967	6.2	24.6	10 155	23.7
06 55282	Palo Alto city	23.7	58 598	482	2 472.5	55 813	440	55 225	2 785	588	5.0	1.1	2 722	4.6
06 55520	Paradise town	18.2	26 408	1 049	1 451.0	25 524	1 059	22 571	884	2 953	3.5	13.1	1 127	4.3
06 55618	Paramount city	4.7	55 266	530	11 758.7	47 577	549	36 407	7 689	11 170	16.2	30.7	39 945	72.3
06 56000	Pasadena city	23.1	133 936	159	5 798.1	131 735	139	118 072	2 201	13 663	1.7	11.6	44 734	33.4
06 56784	Petaluma city	13.8	54 548	540	3 952.8	43 975	599	33 834	10 573	10 141	24.0	30.0	7 985	14.6
06 56924	Pico Rivera city	8.3	63 428	432	7 641.9	59 186	414	53 387	4 242	5 799	7.2	10.9	56 000	88.3
06 57456	Pittsburg city	15.6	56 769	502	3 639.0	47 785	546	33 465	8 984	14 320	18.8	42.8	18 287	32.2
06 57526	Placentia city	6.6	46 488	645	7 043.6	41 065	649	35 041	5 423	6 024	13.2	17.2	14 460	31.1
06 57764	Pleasant Hill city	7.1	32 837	910	4 624.9	31 897	864	25 547	940	6 350	2.9	24.9	2 767	8.4
06 57792	Pleasanton city	21.7	63 654	429	2 933.4	51 112	504	35 160	12 542	15 952	24.5	45.4	5 011	7.9
06 58072	Pomona city	22.8	149 473	137	6 555.8	132 328	138	92 742	17 145	39 586	13.0	42.7	96 370	64.5
06 58240	Porterville city	14.0	39 615	764	2 829.6	29 817	922	19 707	9 798	10 110	32.9	51.3	19 589	49.4
06 58520	Poway city	39.2	48 044	622	1 225.6	43 415	608	(7)	4 629	X	10.7	X	4 974	10.4
06 59451	Rancho Cucamonga city	37.4	127 743	167	3 415.6	101 385	198	55 250	26 358	46 135	26.0	83.5	35 491	27.8
06 59514	Rancho Palos Verdes city	13.7	41 145	727	3 003.3	41 831	637	36 577	−686	5 254	−1.6	14.4	2 339	5.7
06 59920	Redding city	58.4	80 865	318	1 384.7	67 697	343	42 103	13 168	25 594	19.5	60.8	4 393	5.4
06 59962	Redlands city	35.5	63 591	430	1 791.3	63 161	377	43 619	430	19 542	.7	44.8	15 304	24.1
06 60018	Redondo Beach city	6.3	63 261	434	10 041.4	60 640	396	57 102	2 621	3 538	4.3	6.2	8 524	13.5
06 60102	Redwood City city	19.5	75 402	353	3 866.8	66 126	357	54 951	9 276	11 175	14.0	20.3	23 557	31.2
06 60466	Rialto city	21.9	91 873	265	4 195.1	72 791	310	37 862	19 082	34 929	26.2	92.3	47 050	51.2
06 60620	Richmond city	30.0	99 216	240	3 307.2	85 926	249	74 676	13 290	11 250	15.5	15.1	26 319	26.5
06 60704	Ridgecrest city	21.1	24 927	1 069	1 181.4	28 341	967	15 929	−3 414	12 412	−12.0	77.9	3 001	12.0
06 62000	Riverside city	78.1	255 166	67	3 267.2	226 582	68	170 591	28 584	55 991	12.6	32.8	97 315	38.1
06 62546	Rohnert Park city	6.4	42 236	708	6 599.4	36 147	743	22 965	6 089	13 182	16.8	57.4	5 731	13.6

[1] Federal Information Processing Standards (FIPS) codes for states and places defined as of January 1990. [2] Dry land and land temporarily or partially covered by water. [3] Based on 1,078 places (1,070 incorporated places and the 8 CDPs in Hawaii). When places share the same rank, the next lower rank is omitted. [4] Includes count resolution corrections through 1997 and adjustments based on Census 2000 dress rehearsal results and boundary changes reported as legally effective as of January 1, 1998. [5] Based on 1,071 places (1,070 incorporated places and Honolulu CDP in Hawaii). When places share the same rank, the next lower rank is omitted. [6] Persons of Hispanic or Latino origin may be of any race. [7] Not incorporated as of January 1, 1980.

Sources: Land Area—U.S. Census Bureau, Census of Population and Housing, Census 2000 Redistricting Data (Public Law 94-171) Summary Files (related Internet site <http://www.census.gov/dmd/www/2kresult.html>). 2000 Population—U.S. Census Bureau, 2000 Census of Population and Housing, "Census 2000 Profiles of General Demographic Characteristics" data files, published May 2001, related Internet site <http://www.census.gov/mp/www/pub/2000cen/mscen01.html>. 1990 Population—U.S. Census Bureau, "(SU-99-7) Population Estimates for Places (Sorted Alphabetically Within State): Annual Time Series, July 1, 1990 to July 1, 1999 (includes April 1, 1990 Population Estimates Base)," published 20 October 2000, <http://www.census.gov/population/estimates/metro-city/placebyst/SC99T7_US.txt>. 1980 Population—U.S. Census Bureau, 1990 Census of Population and Housing, "Population and Housing Unit Counts," CPH-2-1 through CPH-2-52.

Table C–1. Cities — **Area and Population**–Con.

[Includes states and 1,070 incorporated places of 25,000 or more population as of April 1, 1990 in all states except Hawaii which has no incorporated places recognized by the Census Bureau. For Hawaii, 8 census designated places (CDPs) of 25,000 or more population as of April 1, 1990 are included. Also included are the 5 boroughs of New York city. For more information on these areas, see appendix B. Geographic Information]

State and place code[1]	City	Land area,[2] 2000 (sq. miles)	Population (April 1)											
			2000			1990[4]		1980	Net change		Percent change		Hispanic or Latino,[6] 2000	
			Number	Rank[3]	Per square mile	Number	Rank[5]		1990–2000	1980–1990	1990–2000	1980–1990	Number	Percent
	CALIFORNIA—Con.													
06 62896	Rosemead city	5.1	53 505	549	10 491.2	51 647	496	42 604	1 858	9 043	3.6	21.2	22 097	41.3
06 62938	Roseville city	30.5	79 921	323	2 620.4	44 744	589	24 347	35 177	20 397	78.6	83.8	9 225	11.5
06 64000	Sacramento city	97.2	407 018	40	4 187.4	395 100	37	275 741	11 918	119 359	3.0	43.3	87 974	21.6
06 64224	Salinas city	19.0	151 060	134	7 950.5	108 863	177	80 479	42 197	28 384	38.8	35.3	96 880	64.1
06 65000	San Bernardino city	58.8	185 401	108	3 153.1	171 209	103	118 794	14 192	52 415	8.3	44.1	88 022	47.5
06 65028	San Bruno city	5.5	40 165	751	7 302.7	38 825	694	35 417	1 340	3 408	3.5	9.6	9 686	24.1
06 65042	San Buenaventura (Ventura) city	21.1	100 916	235	4 782.7	93 628	219	73 774	7 288	19 854	7.8	26.9	24 573	24.3
06 65070	San Carlos city	5.9	27 718	1 023	4 698.0	26 218	1 044	24 710	1 500	1 508	5.7	6.1	2 133	7.7
06 65084	San Clemente city	17.6	49 936	592	2 837.3	41 154	646	27 325	8 782	13 829	21.3	50.6	7 933	15.9
06 66000	San Diego city	324.3	1 223 400	7	3 772.4	1 111 031	6	875 538	112 369	235 493	10.1	26.9	310 752	25.4
06 66070	San Dimas city	15.5	34 980	864	2 256.8	32 815	839	24 014	2 165	8 801	6.6	36.6	8 163	23.3
06 67000	San Francisco city	46.7	776 733	13	16 632.4	723 959	14	678 974	52 774	44 985	7.3	6.6	109 504	14.1
06 67042	San Gabriel city	4.1	39 804	759	9 708.3	36 609	739	30 072	3 195	6 537	8.7	21.7	12 223	30.7
06 68000	San Jose city	174.9	894 943	11	5 116.9	783 324	11	629 400	111 619	153 924	14.2	24.5	269 989	30.2
06 68028	San Juan Capistrano city	14.2	33 826	892	2 382.1	26 163	1 046	18 959	7 663	7 204	29.3	38.0	11 206	33.1
06 68084	San Leandro city	13.1	79 452	327	6 065.0	68 202	342	63 952	11 250	4 250	16.5	6.6	15 939	20.1
06 68154	San Luis Obispo city	10.7	44 174	681	4 128.4	41 946	633	34 252	2 228	7 694	5.3	22.5	5 147	11.7
06 68196	San Marcos city	23.8	54 977	534	2 310.0	39 343	681	17 479	15 634	21 864	39.7	125.1	20 271	36.9
06 68252	San Mateo city	12.2	92 482	262	7 580.5	85 866	250	77 640	6 616	8 226	7.7	10.6	18 973	20.5
06 68294	San Pablo city	2.6	30 215	969	11 621.2	25 078	1 066	19 750	5 137	5 328	20.5	27.0	13 490	44.6
06 68364	San Rafael city	16.6	56 063	515	3 377.3	48 401	540	44 700	7 662	3 701	15.8	8.3	13 070	23.3
06 68378	San Ramon city	11.6	44 722	675	3 855.3	35 280	761	(7)	9 442	X	26.8	X	3 238	7.2
06 69000	Santa Ana city	27.1	337 977	51	12 471.5	294 309	52	204 023	43 668	90 286	14.8	44.3	257 097	76.1
06 69070	Santa Barbara city	19.0	92 325	263	4 859.2	85 489	252	74 414	6 836	11 075	8.0	14.9	32 330	35.0
06 69084	Santa Clara city	18.4	102 361	228	5 563.1	93 349	221	87 700	9 012	5 649	9.7	6.4	16 364	16.0
06 69088	Santa Clarita city	47.8	151 088	133	3 160.8	123 610	149	(7)	27 478	X	22.2	X	30 968	20.5
06 69112	Santa Cruz city	12.5	54 593	539	4 367.4	49 889	521	41 483	4 704	8 406	9.4	20.3	9 491	17.4
06 69196	Santa Maria city	19.3	77 423	342	4 011.6	61 907	389	39 685	15 516	22 222	25.1	56.0	46 196	59.7
06 70000	Santa Monica city	8.3	84 084	303	10 130.6	86 916	244	88 314	–2 832	–1 398	–3.3	–1.6	11 304	13.4
06 70042	Santa Paula city	4.6	28 598	1 003	6 217.0	24 940	1 070	20 658	3 658	4 282	14.7	20.7	20 360	71.2
06 70098	Santa Rosa city	40.1	147 595	140	3 680.7	120 499	152	82 658	27 096	37 841	22.5	45.8	28 318	19.2
06 70224	Santee city	16.1	52 975	556	3 290.4	52 710	481	(7)	265	X	.5	X	6 016	11.4
06 70280	Saratoga city	12.1	29 843	981	2 466.4	28 082	977	29 261	1 761	–1 179	6.3	–4.0	936	3.1
06 70686	Seal Beach city	11.5	24 157	1 071	2 100.6	25 063	1 067	25 975	–906	–912	–3.6	–3.5	1 554	6.4
06 70742	Seaside city	8.8	31 696	935	3 601.8	38 921	691	36 567	–7 225	2 354	–18.6	6.4	10 929	34.5
06 72016	Simi Valley city	39.2	111 351	202	2 840.6	100 311	200	77 500	11 040	22 811	11.0	29.4	18 729	16.8
06 73080	South Gate city	7.4	96 375	245	13 023.6	86 249	247	66 784	10 126	19 465	11.7	29.1	88 669	92.0
06 73262	South San Francisco city	9.0	60 552	456	6 728.0	54 442	456	49 393	6 110	5 049	11.2	10.2	19 282	31.8
06 73962	Stanton city	3.1	37 403	806	12 065.5	30 325	912	23 723	7 078	6 602	23.3	27.8	18 285	48.9
06 75000	Stockton city	54.7	243 771	70	4 456.5	211 495	75	148 283	32 276	63 212	15.3	42.6	79 217	32.5
06 77000	Sunnyvale city	21.9	131 760	161	6 016.4	117 311	156	106 618	14 449	10 693	12.3	10.0	20 390	15.5
06 78120	Temecula city	26.3	57 716	492	2 194.5	27 177	1 007	(7)	30 539	X	112.4	X	10 974	19.0
06 78148	Temple City city	4.0	33 377	902	8 344.3	31 096	881	28 972	2 281	2 124	7.3	7.3	6 836	20.5
06 78582	Thousand Oaks city	54.9	117 005	188	2 131.2	104 000	190	77 072	13 005	26 928	12.5	34.9	15 328	13.1
06 80000	Torrance city	20.5	137 946	155	6 729.1	133 243	137	129 881	4 703	3 362	3.5	2.6	17 637	12.8
06 80238	Tracy city	21.0	56 929	501	2 710.9	34 401	787	18 428	22 528	15 973	65.5	86.7	15 765	27.7
06 80644	Tulare city	16.6	43 994	684	2 650.2	33 805	803	22 530	10 189	11 275	30.1	50.0	20 058	45.6
06 80812	Turlock city	13.3	55 810	521	4 196.2	43 076	614	26 287	12 734	16 789	29.6	63.9	16 422	29.4
06 80854	Tustin city	11.4	67 504	402	5 921.4	49 518	527	32 248	17 986	17 270	36.3	53.6	23 110	34.2
06 81204	Union City city	19.3	66 869	408	3 464.7	53 773	466	39 406	13 096	14 367	24.4	36.5	16 020	24.0
06 81344	Upland city	15.1	68 393	395	4 529.3	63 335	375	47 647	5 058	15 688	8.0	32.9	18 830	27.5
06 81554	Vacaville city	27.1	88 625	279	3 270.3	71 564	320	43 367	17 061	28 197	23.8	65.0	15 847	17.9
06 81666	Vallejo city	30.2	116 760	189	3 866.2	110 835	171	80 303	5 925	30 532	5.3	38.0	18 591	15.9
06 82590	Victorville city	72.8	64 029	426	879.5	50 469	515	14 220	13 560	36 249	26.9	254.9	21 426	33.5
06 82954	Visalia city	28.6	91 565	267	3 201.6	76 522	289	49 729	15 043	26 793	19.7	53.9	32 619	35.6
06 82996	Vista city	18.7	89 857	274	4 805.2	71 872	316	35 834	17 985	36 038	25.0	100.6	34 990	38.9
06 83332	Walnut city	9.0	30 004	975	3 333.8	29 132	941	12 478	872	16 654	3.0	133.5	5 803	19.3
06 83346	Walnut Creek city	19.9	64 296	423	3 231.0	61 114	394	54 033	3 182	7 081	5.2	13.1	3 851	6.0
06 83668	Watsonville city	6.4	44 265	680	6 916.4	33 911	799	23 662	10 354	10 249	30.5	43.3	33 254	75.1
06 84200	West Covina city	16.1	105 080	220	6 526.7	95 915	214	80 292	9 165	15 623	9.6	19.5	48 051	45.7
06 84410	West Hollywood city	1.9	35 716	842	18 797.9	35 810	752	(7)	–94	X	–.3	X	3 142	8.8
06 84550	Westminster city	10.1	88 207	282	8 733.4	79 190	278	71 133	9 017	8 057	11.4	11.3	19 138	21.7
06 84816	West Sacramento city	20.9	31 615	938	1 512.7	29 299	935	(7)	2 316	X	7.9	X	9 470	30.0
06 85292	Whittier city	14.6	83 680	305	5 731.5	77 761	286	68 558	5 919	9 203	7.6	13.4	46 765	55.9
06 86328	Woodland city	10.3	49 151	607	4 771.9	40 391	663	30 235	8 760	10 156	21.7	33.6	19 084	38.8
06 86832	Yorba Linda city	19.4	58 918	478	3 037.0	52 536	483	28 254	6 382	24 282	12.1	85.9	6 044	10.3
06 86972	Yuba City city	9.4	36 758	817	3 910.4	29 072	942	18 736	7 686	10 336	26.4	55.2	9 029	24.6
06 87042	Yucaipa city	27.8	41 207	725	1 482.3	32 987	832	(7)	8 220	X	24.9	X	7 561	18.3

[1] Federal Information Processing Standards (FIPS) codes for states and places defined as of January 1990.　[2] Dry land and land temporarily or partially covered by water.　[3] Based on 1,078 places (1,070 incorporated places and the 8 CDPs in Hawaii). When places share the same rank, the next lower rank is omitted.　[4] Includes count resolution corrections through 1997 and adjustments based on Census 2000 dress rehearsal results and boundary changes reported as legally effective as of January 1, 1998.　[5] Based on 1,071 places (1,070 incorporated places and Honolulu CDP in Hawaii). When places share the same rank, the next lower rank is omitted.　[6] Persons of Hispanic or Latino origin may be of any race.　[7] Not incorporated as of January 1, 1980.

Sources: Land Area—U.S. Census Bureau, Census of Population and Housing, Census 2000 Redistricting Data (Public Law 94-171) Summary Files (related Internet site <http://www.census.gov/dmd/www/2kresult.html>). 2000 Population—U.S. Census Bureau, 2000 Census of Population and Housing, "Census 2000 Profiles of General Demographic Characteristics" data files, published May 2001, related Internet site <http://www.census.gov/mp/www/pub/2000cen/mscen01.html>. 1990 Population—U.S. Census Bureau, "(SU-99-7) Population Estimates for Places (Sorted Alphabetically Within State): Annual Time Series, July 1, 1990 to July 1, 1999 (includes April 1, 1990 Population Estimates Base)," published 20 October 2000, <http://www.census.gov/population/estimates/metro-city/placebyst/SC99T7_US.txt>. 1980 Population—U.S. Census Bureau, 1990 Census of Population and Housing, "Population and Housing Unit Counts," CPH-2-1 through CPH-2-52.

Table C–1. Cities — **Area and Population**–Con.

[Includes states and 1,070 incorporated places of 25,000 or more population as of April 1, 1990 in all states except Hawaii which has no incorporated places recognized by the Census Bureau. For Hawaii, 8 census designated places (CDPs) of 25,000 or more population as of April 1, 1990 are included. Also included are the 5 boroughs of New York city. For more information on these areas, see appendix B. Geographic Information]

State and place code[1]	City	Land area,[2] 2000 (sq. miles)	Population (April 1) 2000 Number	2000 Rank[3]	2000 Per square mile	1990[4] Number	1990[4] Rank[5]	1980	Net change 1990–2000	Net change 1980–1990	Percent change 1990–2000	Percent change 1980–1990	Hispanic or Latino,[6] 2000 Number	Hispanic or Latino,[6] 2000 Percent
08 00000	COLORADO	103 717.5	4 301 261	X	41.5	3 294 473	X	2 889 735	1 006 788	404 738	30.6	14.0	735 601	17.1
08 03455	Arvada city	32.7	102 153	231	3 123.9	89 786	232	84 576	12 367	5 210	13.8	6.2	10 031	9.8
08 04000	Aurora city	142.5	276 393	61	1 939.6	221 855	73	158 588	54 538	63 267	24.6	39.9	54 764	19.8
08 07850	Boulder city	24.4	94 673	253	3 880.0	86 098	248	76 685	8 575	9 413	10.0	12.3	7 801	8.2
08 16000	Colorado Springs city	185.7	360 890	48	1 943.4	283 112	54	215 105	77 778	68 007	27.5	31.6	43 330	12.0
08 20000	Denver city	153.4	554 636	24	3 615.6	467 549	28	492 686	87 087	–25 137	18.6	–5.1	175 704	31.7
08 24785	Englewood city	6.6	31 727	931	4 807.1	29 905	919	30 021	1 822	–116	6.1	–.4	4 140	13.0
08 27425	Fort Collins city	46.5	118 652	185	2 551.7	88 899	236	65 092	29 753	23 807	33.5	36.6	10 402	8.8
08 31660	Grand Junction city	30.8	41 986	713	1 363.2	34 447	786	27 956	7 539	6 491	21.9	23.2	4 561	10.9
08 32155	Greeley city	29.9	76 930	346	2 572.9	60 489	399	53 006	16 441	7 483	27.2	14.1	22 683	29.5
08 43000	Lakewood city	41.6	144 126	144	3 464.6	126 156	146	113 808	17 970	12 348	14.2	10.8	20 949	14.5
08 45255	Littleton city	13.5	40 340	748	2 988.1	33 789	804	28 631	6 551	5 158	19.4	18.0	3 408	8.4
08 45970	Longmont city	21.8	71 093	377	3 261.1	52 214	489	42 942	18 879	9 272	36.2	21.6	13 558	19.1
08 46465	Loveland city	24.6	50 608	583	2 057.2	37 511	727	30 215	13 097	7 296	34.9	24.1	4 337	8.6
08 54330	Northglenn city...........	7.4	31 575	939	4 266.9	27 287	1 002	29 847	4 288	–2 560	15.7	–8.6	6 399	20.3
08 62000	Pueblo city	45.1	102 121	232	2 264.3	99 009	205	101 686	3 112	–2 677	3.1	–2.6	45 066	44.1
08 77290	Thornton city	26.9	82 384	310	3 062.6	55 146	448	42 054	27 238	13 092	49.4	31.1	17 583	21.3
08 83835	Westminster city	31.5	100 940	234	3 204.4	74 176	303	50 211	26 764	23 965	36.1	47.7	15 369	15.2
08 84440	Wheat Ridge city	9.1	32 913	908	3 616.8	29 420	934	30 293	3 493	–873	11.9	–2.9	4 434	13.5
09 00000	CONNECTICUT	4 844.8	3 405 565	X	702.9	3 287 116	X	3 107 564	118 449	179 552	3.6	5.8	320 323	9.4
09 08000	Bridgeport city	16.0	139 529	152	8 720.6	141 555	127	142 546	–2 026	–991	–1.4	–.7	44 478	31.9
09 08420	Bristol city................	26.5	60 062	463	2 266.5	60 618	397	57 370	–556	3 248	–.9	5.7	3 166	5.3
09 18430	Danbury city	42.1	74 848	356	1 777.9	65 584	361	60 470	9 264	5 114	14.1	8.5	11 791	15.8
09 37000	Hartford city	17.3	121 578	179	7 027.6	137 289	131	136 392	–15 711	897	–11.4	.7	49 260	40.5
09 46450	Meriden city	23.7	58 244	486	2 457.6	59 440	411	57 118	–1 196	2 322	–2.0	4.1	12 296	21.1
09 47290	Middletown city	40.9	43 167	693	1 055.4	42 774	619	39 040	393	3 734	.9	9.6	2 287	5.3
09 47515	Milford city (remainder)	22.3	50 594	584	2 268.8	48 139	542	49 101	2 455	–962	5.1	–2.0	1 691	3.3
09 49880	Naugatuck borough	16.4	30 989	952	1 889.6	30 621	903	26 456	368	4 165	1.2	15.7	1 386	4.5
09 50370	New Britain city	13.3	71 538	373	5 378.8	75 481	297	73 840	–3 943	1 641	–5.2	2.2	19 138	26.8
09 52000	New Haven city	18.9	123 626	175	6 541.1	130 191	140	126 089	–6 565	4 102	–5.0	3.3	26 443	21.4
09 52280	New London city	5.5	25 671	1 063	4 667.5	28 566	960	28 842	–2 895	–276	–10.1	–1.0	5 061	19.7
09 55990	Norwalk city	22.8	82 951	308	3 638.2	78 335	283	77 767	4 616	568	5.9	.7	12 966	15.6
09 56200	Norwich city	28.3	36 117	833	1 276.2	37 777	719	38 074	–1 660	–297	–4.4	–.8	2 208	6.1
09 68100	Shelton city...............	30.6	38 101	794	1 245.1	35 394	759	31 314	2 707	4 080	7.6	13.0	1 326	3.5
09 73000	Stamford city	37.7	117 083	187	3 105.6	108 107	182	102 466	8 976	5 641	8.3	5.5	19 635	16.8
09 76500	Torrington city	39.8	35 202	856	884.5	33 724	806	30 987	1 478	2 737	4.4	8.8	1 162	3.3
09 80000	Waterbury city	28.6	107 271	213	3 750.7	108 213	181	103 266	–942	4 947	–.9	4.8	23 354	21.8
09 82800	West Haven city	10.8	52 360	566	4 848.1	54 299	460	53 184	–1 939	1 115	–3.6	2.1	4 757	9.1
10 00000	DELAWARE............	1 953.6	783 600	X	401.1	666 168	X	594 338	117 432	71 830	17.6	12.1	37 277	4.8
10 21200	Dover city	22.4	32 135	924	1 434.6	28 775	954	23 507	3 360	5 268	11.7	22.4	1 327	4.1
10 50670	Newark city...............	8.9	28 547	1 006	3 207.5	26 870	1 018	25 247	1 677	1 623	6.2	6.4	721	2.5
10 77580	Wilmington city	10.8	72 664	366	6 728.1	71 526	321	70 195	1 138	1 331	1.6	1.9	7 148	9.8
11 00000	DISTRICT OF COLUMBIA .	61.4	572 059	X	9 316.9	606 900	X	638 432	–34 841	–31 532	–5.7	–4.9	44 953	7.9
11 50000	Washington city...........	61.4	572 059	21	9 316.9	606 900	19	638 432	–34 841	–31 532	–5.7	–4.9	44 953	7.9
12 00000	FLORIDA	53 926.8	15 982 378	X	296.4	12 938 071	X	9 746 961	3 044 307	3 191 110	23.5	32.7	2 682 715	16.8
12 00950	Altamonte Springs city	8.9	41 200	726	4 629.2	35 160	763	21 105	6 040	14 055	17.2	66.6	6 563	15.9
12 07300	Boca Raton city	27.2	74 764	357	2 748.7	62 866	380	49 447	11 898	13 419	18.9	27.1	6 359	8.5
12 07875	Boynton Beach city	15.9	60 389	459	3 798.1	47 047	557	35 624	13 342	11 423	28.4	32.1	5 564	9.2
12 07950	Bradenton city	12.1	49 504	597	4 091.2	43 665	605	30 228	5 839	13 437	13.4	44.5	5 574	11.3
12 10275	Cape Coral city	105.2	102 286	230	972.3	75 172	298	32 103	27 114	43 069	36.1	134.2	8 521	8.3
12 12875	Clearwater city............	25.3	108 787	208	4 299.9	97 217	209	85 170	11 570	12 047	11.9	14.1	9 754	9.0
12 13275	Coconut Creek city	11.5	43 566	689	3 788.3	27 241	1 005	6 288	16 325	20 953	59.9	333.2	5 076	11.7
12 14250	Coral Gables city..........	13.1	42 249	707	3 225.1	41 428	644	43 241	821	–1 813	2.0	–4.2	19 703	46.6
12 14400	Coral Springs city	23.9	117 549	186	4 918.4	79 137	279	37 349	38 412	41 788	48.5	111.9	18 233	15.5
12 16475	Davie town	33.4	75 720	352	2 267.1	51 515	499	20 500	24 205	31 015	47.0	151.3	14 270	18.8
12 16525	Daytona Beach city	58.7	64 112	425	1 092.2	62 622	384	54 176	1 490	8 446	2.4	15.6	2 232	3.5
12 16725	Deerfield Beach city	13.4	64 583	422	4 819.6	47 162	556	39 193	17 421	7 969	36.9	20.3	5 643	8.7
12 17100	Delray Beach city	15.4	60 020	466	3 897.4	47 748	547	34 329	12 272	13 419	25.7	39.1	4 184	7.0
12 18575	Dunedin city	10.4	35 691	843	3 431.8	35 053	765	30 203	638	4 850	1.8	16.1	1 192	3.3
12 24000	Fort Lauderdale city	31.7	152 397	130	4 807.5	148 779	120	153 279	3 618	–4 500	2.4	–2.9	14 406	9.5

[1] Federal Information Processing Standards (FIPS) codes for states and places defined as of January 1990. [2] Dry land and land temporarily or partially covered by water. [3] Based on 1,078 places (1,070 incorporated places and the 8 CDPs in Hawaii). When places share the same rank, the next lower rank is omitted. [4] Includes count resolution corrections through 1997 and adjustments based on Census 2000 dress rehearsal results and boundary changes reported as legally effective as of January 1, 1998. [5] Based on 1,071 places (1,070 incorporated places and Honolulu CDP in Hawaii). When places share the same rank, the next lower rank is omitted. [6] Persons of Hispanic or Latino origin may be of any race.

Sources: Land Area—U.S. Census Bureau, Census of Population and Housing, Census 2000 Redistricting Data (Public Law 94-171) Summary Files (related Internet site <http://www.census.gov/dmd/www/2kresult.html>). 2000 Population—U.S. Census Bureau, 2000 Census of Population and Housing, "Census 2000 Profiles of General Demographic Characteristics" data files, published May 2001, related Internet site <http://www.census.gov/mp/www/pub/2000cen/mscen01.html>. 1990 Population—U.S. Census Bureau, "(SU-99-7) Population Estimates for Places (Sorted Alphabetically Within State): Annual Time Series, July 1, 1990 to July 1, 1999 (includes April 1, 1990 Population Estimates Base)," published 20 October 2000, <http://www.census.gov/population/estimates/metro-city/placebyst/SC99T7_US.txt>. 1980 Population—U.S. Census Bureau, 1990 Census of Population and Housing, "Population and Housing Unit Counts," CPH-2-1 through CPH-2-52.

Table C–1. Cities — **Area and Population**–Con.

[Includes states and 1,070 incorporated places of 25,000 or more population as of April 1, 1990 in all states except Hawaii which has no incorporated places recognized by the Census Bureau. For Hawaii, 8 census designated places (CDPs) of 25,000 or more population as of April 1, 1990 are included. Also included are the 5 boroughs of New York city. For more information on these areas, see appendix B. Geographic Information]

State and place code[1]	City	Land area,[2] 2000 (sq. miles)	Population (April 1) 2000 Number	2000 Rank[3]	2000 Per square mile	1990[4] Number	1990[4] Rank[5]	1980	Net change 1990–2000	Net change 1980–1990	Percent change 1990–2000	Percent change 1980–1990	Hispanic or Latino,[6] 2000 Number	Hispanic or Latino,[6] 2000 Percent
	FLORIDA—Con.													
12 24125	Fort Myers city	31.8	48 208	618	1 516.0	44 645	591	36 638	3 563	8 007	8.0	21.9	6 984	14.5
12 24300	Fort Pierce city	14.7	37 516	804	2 552.1	37 519	726	33 802	−3	3 717	Z	11.0	5 629	15.0
12 25175	Gainesville city.............	48.2	95 447	249	1 980.2	92 602	224	81 371	2 845	11 231	3.1	13.8	6 112	6.4
12 28450	Hallandale city	4.2	34 282	878	8 162.4	30 116	917	36 517	4 166	−6 401	13.8	−17.5	6 447	18.8
12 30000	Hialeah city...............	19.2	226 419	75	11 792.7	187 905	88	145 254	38 514	42 651	20.5	29.4	204 543	90.3
12 32000	Hollywood city	27.3	139 357	153	5 104.7	122 793	150	121 323	16 564	1 470	13.5	1.2	31 392	22.5
12 32275	Homestead city	14.3	31 909	927	2 231.4	28 387	965	20 668	3 522	7 719	12.4	37.3	16 537	51.8
12 35006	Jacksonville city (remainder)	757.7	735 617	14	970.9	635 042	16	540 920	100 575	94 122	15.8	17.4	30 594	4.2
12 36950	Kissimmee city.............	16.7	47 814	625	2 863.1	30 648	900	15 487	17 166	15 161	56.0	97.9	19 954	41.7
12 38250	Lakeland city	45.8	70 452	333	1 712.9	71 043	327	47 406	7 409	23 637	10.4	49.9	5 032	6.4
12 39075	Lake Worth city	5.6	35 133	858	6 273.8	28 840	952	27 048	6 293	1 792	21.8	6.6	10 437	29.7
12 39425	Largo city	15.7	69 371	386	4 418.5	66 596	353	57 958	2 775	8 638	4.2	14.9	2 902	4.2
12 39525	Lauderdale Lakes city	3.6	31 705	934	8 806.9	27 914	983	25 426	3 791	2 488	13.6	9.8	1 755	5.5
12 39550	Lauderhill city	7.3	57 585	494	7 888.4	49 067	531	37 271	8 518	11 796	17.4	31.6	3 995	6.9
12 43125	Margate city	8.8	53 909	548	6 126.0	43 179	611	35 900	10 730	7 279	24.9	20.3	8 238	15.3
12 43975	Melbourne city	30.2	71 382	374	2 363.6	60 450	400	46 536	10 932	13 914	18.1	29.9	3 958	5.5
12 45000	Miami city	35.7	362 470	47	10 153.2	359 790	46	346 681	2 680	13 109	.7	3.8	238 351	65.8
12 45025	Miami Beach city	7.0	87 933	284	12 561.9	92 296	225	96 298	−4 363	−4 002	−4.7	−4.2	47 000	53.4
12 45975	Miramar city	29.5	72 739	365	2 465.7	41 229	645	32 813	31 510	8 416	76.4	25.6	21 374	29.4
12 49425	North Lauderdale city	3.9	32 264	921	8 272.8	26 812	1 022	18 653	5 452	8 159	20.3	43.7	6 816	21.1
12 49450	North Miami city	8.5	59 880	468	7 044.7	50 156	518	42 566	9 724	7 590	19.4	17.8	13 869	23.2
12 49475	North Miami Beach city	5.0	40 786	735	8 157.2	35 030	769	36 553	5 756	−1 523	16.4	−4.2	12 245	30.0
12 50575	Oakland Park city	6.3	30 966	954	4 915.2	25 645	1 055	22 944	5 321	2 701	20.7	11.8	5 556	17.9
12 50750	Ocala city	38.6	45 943	652	1 190.2	42 773	620	37 170	3 170	5 603	7.4	15.1	2 636	5.7
12 53000	Orlando city	93.5	185 951	104	1 988.8	163 435	108	128 291	22 516	35 144	13.8	27.4	32 510	17.5
12 53150	Ormond Beach city	25.7	36 301	828	1 412.5	31 460	874	21 436	4 841	10 024	15.4	46.8	797	2.2
12 54000	Palm Bay city	63.6	79 413	328	1 248.6	62 664	382	18 560	16 749	44 104	26.7	237.6	6 850	8.6
12 54700	Panama City city	20.5	36 417	823	1 776.4	35 039	768	33 346	1 378	1 693	3.9	5.1	1 060	2.9
12 55775	Pembroke Pines city.......	33.1	137 427	157	4 151.9	65 454	363	35 776	71 973	29 678	110.0	83.0	38 700	28.2
12 55925	Pensacola city	22.7	56 255	514	2 478.2	59 268	413	57 619	−3 013	1 649	−5.1	2.9	1 167	2.1
12 56975	Pinellas Park city..........	14.7	45 658	658	3 106.0	43 968	600	32 811	1 690	11 157	3.8	34.0	2 856	6.3
12 57425	Plantation city	21.7	82 904	309	3 021.0	66 110	359	48 653	16 010	17 400	25.4	35.9	10 000	10.1
12 58050	Pompano Beach city.......	20.6	78 191	337	3 795.7	72 375	312	52 618	5 816	19 757	8.0	37.5	7 770	9.9
12 58575	Port Orange city	24.7	45 823	653	1 855.2	36 933	733	18 756	8 890	18 177	24.1	96.9	1 151	2.5
12 58715	Port St. Lucie city	75.5	88 769	278	1 175.7	55 759	441	14 690	33 010	41 069	59.2	279.6	6 677	7.5
12 60975	Riviera Beach city	8.3	29 884	979	3 600.5	27 362	998	26 489	2 522	873	9.2	3.3	1 348	4.5
12 63000	St. Petersburg city	59.6	248 232	68	4 165.0	240 368	65	238 647	7 864	1 721	3.3	.7	10 502	4.2
12 63650	Sanford city	19.1	38 291	789	2 004.8	32 528	847	23 176	5 763	9 352	17.7	40.4	3 974	10.4
12 64175	Sarasota city	14.9	52 715	562	3 537.9	51 041	506	48 868	1 674	2 173	3.3	4.4	6 283	11.9
12 69700	Sunrise city	18.2	85 779	294	4 713.1	66 212	354	39 681	19 567	26 531	29.6	66.9	14 655	17.1
12 70600	Tallahassee city...........	95.7	150 624	135	1 573.9	125 448	147	81 548	25 176	43 900	20.1	53.8	6 309	4.2
12 70675	Tamarac city	11.4	55 588	525	4 876.1	44 469	594	29 376	11 119	15 093	25.0	51.4	8 274	14.9
12 71000	Tampa city	112.1	303 447	57	2 706.9	280 026	55	271 577	22 621	9 249	8.1	3.4	58 522	19.3
12 71900	Titusville city..............	21.3	40 670	738	1 909.4	39 619	676	31 910	1 051	7 709	2.7	24.2	1 430	3.5
12 76600	West Palm Beach city	55.1	82 103	312	1 490.1	66 837	348	63 305	15 266	3 532	22.8	5.6	14 955	18.2
13 00000	GEORGIA	57 906.1	8 186 453	X	141.4	6 478 149	X	5 462 982	1 708 304	1 015 167	26.4	18.6	435 227	5.3
13 01052	Albany city	55.5	76 939	345	1 386.3	78 350	282	74 425	−1 411	3 925	−1.8	5.3	950	1.2
13 03432	Athens city	[7]117.8	[7]100 266	[7]239	[7]851.2	[7]86 520	[7]245	42 549	[7]13 746	X	[7]15.9	X	[7]6 402	[7]6.4
13 04000	Atlanta city	131.7	416 474	39	3 162.3	393 760	38	425 022	22 714	−31 262	5.8	−7.4	18 720	4.5
13 04196	Augusta city	[8]302.1	[8]195 182	[8]97	[8]646.1	[8]186 177	[8]90	47 532	[8]9 005	X	[8]4.8	X	[8]5 447	[8]2.8
13 19030	Columbus city (remainder) .	216.1	185 781	106	859.7	178 685	96	169 441	7 096	9 244	4.0	5.5	8 368	4.5
13 25720	East Point city	13.8	39 595	765	2 869.2	34 450	785	37 486	5 145	−3 036	14.9	−8.1	2 998	7.6
13 44340	La Grange city	29.0	25 998	1 059	896.5	25 591	1 057	24 204	407	1 387	1.6	5.7	635	2.4
13 49000	Macon city	55.8	97 255	243	1 742.9	106 590	185	116 896	−9 335	−10 306	−8.8	−8.8	1 166	1.2
13 49756	Marietta city	21.9	58 748	480	2 682.6	45 475	578	30 821	13 273	14 654	29.2	47.5	9 947	16.9
13 66668	Rome city	29.4	34 980	864	1 189.8	32 037	860	28 915	2 943	3 122	9.2	10.8	3 620	10.3
13 67284	Roswell city	38.0	79 334	330	2 087.7	48 834	533	23 337	30 500	25 497	62.5	109.3	8 421	10.6
13 69000	Savannah city	74.7	131 510	162	1 760.5	137 628	130	141 654	−6 118	−4 026	−4.4	−2.8	2 938	2.2
13 71492	Smyrna city...............	13.9	40 999	731	2 949.6	33 510	815	20 312	7 489	13 198	22.3	65.0	5 659	13.8
13 78800	Valdosta city..............	29.9	43 724	688	1 462.3	41 073	648	37 596	2 651	3 477	6.5	9.2	954	2.2
13 80508	Warner Robins city	22.8	48 804	610	2 140.5	45 985	569	39 893	2 819	6 092	6.1	15.3	1 856	3.8

[1] Federal Information Processing Standards (FIPS) codes for states and places defined as of January 1990. [2] Dry land and land temporarily or partially covered by water. [3] Based on 1,078 places (1,070 incorporated places and the 8 CDPs in Hawaii). When places share the same rank, the next lower rank is omitted. [4] Includes count resolution corrections through 1997 and adjustments based on Census 2000 dress rehearsal results and boundary changes reported as legally effective as of January 1, 1998. [5] Based on 1,071 places (1,070 incorporated places and Honolulu CDP in Hawaii). When places share the same rank, the next lower rank is omitted. [6] Persons of Hispanic or Latino origin may be of any race. [7] Data are for Athens-Clarke County (balance), GA; Athens city (1990 land area - 16.6 square miles; 1990 population - 45,734) merged with Clarke County effective January 14, 1991. [8] Data are for Augusta-Richmond County (balance), GA; Augusta city (1990 land area - 19.7 square miles; 1990 population - 44,639) merged with Richmond County effective January 1, 1996.

Sources: Land Area—U.S. Census Bureau, Census of Population and Housing, Census 2000 Redistricting Data (Public Law 94-171) Summary Files (related Internet site <http://www.census.gov/dmd/www/2kresult.html>). 2000 Population—U.S. Census Bureau, 2000 Census of Population and Housing, "Census 2000 Profiles of General Demographic Characteristics" data files, published May 2001, related Internet site <http://www.census.gov/mp/www/pub/2000cen/mscen01.html>. 1990 Population—U.S. Census Bureau, "(SU-99-7) Population Estimates for Places (Sorted Alphabetically Within State): Annual Time Series, July 1, 1990 to July 1, 1999 (includes April 1, 1990 Population Estimates Base)," published 20 October 2000, <http://www.census.gov/population/estimates/metro-city/placebyst/SC99T7_US.txt>. 1980 Population—U.S. Census Bureau, 1990 Census of Population and Housing, "Population and Housing Unit Counts," CPH-2-1 through CPH-2-52.

Table C–1. Cities — **Area and Population**–Con.

[Includes states and 1,070 incorporated places of 25,000 or more population as of April 1, 1990 in all states except Hawaii which has no incorporated places recognized by the Census Bureau. For Hawaii, 8 census designated places (CDPs) of 25,000 or more population as of April 1, 1990 are included. Also included are the 5 boroughs of New York city. For more information on these areas, see appendix B. Geographic Information]

State and place code[1]	City	Land area,[2] 2000 (sq. miles)	Population (April 1)										Hispanic or Latino,[6] 2000	
			2000			1990[4]		1980	Net change		Percent change			
			Number	Rank[3]	Per square mile	Number	Rank[5]		1990–2000	1980–1990	1990–2000	1980–1990	Number	Percent
15 00000	HAWAII	6 422.6	1 211 537	X	188.6	1 108 229	X	964 691	103 308	143 538	9.3	14.9	87 699	7.2
15 14650	Hilo CDP	54.3	40 759	736	750.6	NA	NA	35 269	NA	NA	NA	NA	3 579	8.8
15 17000	Honolulu CDP	85.7	371 657	46	4 336.7	376 937	41	365 048	–5 280	11 889	–1.4	3.3	16 229	4.4
15 23150	Kailua CDP	6.6	36 513	821	5 532.3	NA	NA	35 812	NA	NA	NA	NA	2 228	6.1
15 28250	Kaneohe CDP	6.6	34 970	866	5 298.5	NA	NA	29 919	NA	NA	NA	NA	2 523	7.2
15 51050	Mililani Town CDP.......	3.9	28 608	1 002	7 335.4	NA	NA	21 365	NA	NA	NA	NA	2 222	7.8
15 62600	Pearl City CDP	5.0	30 976	953	6 195.2	NA	NA	42 575	NA	NA	NA	NA	1 753	6.0
15 77750	Waimalu CDP	5.9	29 371	991	4 978.1	NA	NA	(7)	NA	NA	NA	NA	1 753	6.0
15 79700	Waipahu CDP	2.6	33 108	904	12 733.8	NA	NA	29 139	NA	NA	NA	NA	2 016	6.1
16 00000	IDAHO...............	82 747.2	1 293 953	X	15.6	1 006 734	X	944 127	287 219	62 607	28.5	6.6	101 690	7.9
16 08830	Boise City city	63.8	185 787	105	2 912.0	135 150	133	102 249	50 637	32 901	37.5	32.2	8 410	4.5
16 39700	Idaho Falls city	17.1	50 730	581	2 966.7	44 235	597	39 739	6 495	4 496	14.7	11.3	3 641	7.2
16 46540	Lewiston city	16.5	30 904	957	1 873.0	28 309	969	27 986	2 595	323	9.2	1.2	590	1.9
16 56260	Nampa city	19.9	51 867	569	2 606.4	29 899	921	25 112	21 968	4 787	73.5	19.1	9 282	17.9
16 64090	Pocatello city	28.2	51 466	575	1 825.0	46 091	568	46 340	5 375	–249	11.7	–.5	2 544	4.9
16 82810	Twin Falls city	12.0	34 469	876	2 872.4	28 095	975	26 209	6 374	1 886	22.7	7.2	3 066	8.9
17 00000	ILLINOIS..............	55 583.6	12 419 293	X	223.4	11 430 602	X	11 427 409	988 691	3 193	8.6	Z	1 530 262	12.3
17 00243	Addison village	9.4	35 914	837	3 820.6	32 125	858	29 826	3 789	2 299	11.8	7.7	10 198	28.4
17 01114	Alton city	15.6	30 496	963	1 954.9	33 135	825	34 171	–2 639	–1 036	–8.0	–3.0	454	1.5
17 02154	Arlington Heights village ...	16.4	76 031	349	4 636.0	74 739	299	66 116	1 292	8 623	1.7	13.0	3 393	4.5
17 03012	Aurora city	38.5	142 990	147	3 714.0	100 279	201	81 293	42 711	18 986	42.6	23.4	46 557	32.6
17 04845	Belleville city	18.9	41 410	721	2 191.0	43 058	615	41 580	–1 648	1 478	–3.8	3.6	677	1.6
17 05573	Berwyn city	3.9	54 016	546	13 850.3	45 538	576	46 849	8 478	–1 311	18.6	–2.8	20 543	38.0
17 06613	Bloomington city	22.5	64 808	421	2 880.4	52 655	482	44 189	12 153	8 466	23.1	19.2	2 150	3.3
17 07133	Bolingbrook village	20.5	56 321	510	2 747.4	41 028	650	37 261	15 293	3 767	37.3	10.1	7 371	13.1
17 09447	Buffalo Grove village	9.2	42 909	698	4 664.0	36 653	738	22 230	6 256	14 423	17.1	64.9	1 425	3.3
17 09642	Burbank city	4.2	27 902	1 017	6 643.3	27 580	992	28 462	322	–882	1.2	–3.1	3 095	11.1
17 10487	Calumet City city	7.3	39 071	771	5 352.2	37 712	721	39 697	1 359	–1 985	3.6	–5.0	4 242	10.9
17 11163	Carbondale city	11.9	20 681	1 078	1 737.9	27 438	995	26 414	–6 757	1 024	–24.6	3.9	630	3.0
17 11332	Carol Stream village	8.9	40 438	744	4 543.6	31 785	867	15 472	8 653	16 313	27.2	105.4	4 055	10.0
17 12385	Champaign city	17.0	67 518	401	3 971.6	64 399	367	58 267	3 119	6 132	4.8	10.5	2 724	4.0
17 14000	Chicago city	227.1	2 896 016	3	12 752.2	2 783 660	3	3 005 072	112 356	–221 412	4.0	–7.4	753 644	26.0
17 14026	Chicago Heights city.......	9.6	32 776	911	3 414.2	33 070	828	37 026	–294	–3 956	–.9	–10.7	7 790	23.8
17 14351	Cicero town	5.8	85 616	296	14 761.4	67 355	346	61 232	18 261	6 123	27.1	10.0	66 299	77.4
17 18563	Danville city	17.0	33 904	886	1 994.4	35 045	767	38 985	–1 141	–3 940	–3.3	–10.1	1 549	4.6
17 18823	Decatur city	41.6	81 860	314	1 967.8	85 424	254	93 939	–3 564	–8 515	–4.2	–9.1	978	1.2
17 19161	DeKalb city	12.6	39 018	775	3 096.7	36 044	747	33 157	2 974	2 887	8.3	8.7	3 527	9.0
17 19642	Des Plaines city	14.4	58 720	481	4 077.8	54 917	449	53 568	3 803	1 349	6.9	2.5	8 229	14.0
17 20591	Downers Grove village	14.2	48 724	611	3 431.3	47 493	552	42 259	1 231	5 234	2.6	12.4	1 747	3.6
17 22255	East St. Louis city	14.1	31 542	940	2 237.0	40 865	652	55 200	–9 323	–14 335	–22.8	–26.0	230	.7
17 23074	Elgin city	25.0	94 487	255	3 779.5	77 353	287	63 668	17 134	13 685	22.2	21.5	32 430	34.3
17 23256	Elk Grove Village village ...	11.0	34 727	872	3 157.0	33 487	817	28 679	1 240	4 808	3.7	16.8	2 165	6.2
17 23620	Elmhurst city	10.3	42 762	700	4 151.7	41 929	634	44 276	833	–2 347	2.0	–5.3	1 717	4.0
17 24582	Evanston city	7.7	74 239	359	9 641.4	73 234	307	73 706	1 005	–472	1.4	–.6	4 539	6.1
17 27884	Freeport city	11.4	26 443	1 048	2 319.6	26 210	1 045	26 266	233	–56	.9	–.2	561	2.1
17 28326	Galesburg city	16.9	33 706	895	1 994.4	33 748	805	35 305	–42	–1 557	–.1	–4.4	1 688	5.0
17 29730	Glendale Heights village ...	5.4	31 765	929	5 882.4	27 610	990	23 251	4 155	4 359	15.0	18.7	5 842	18.4
17 29938	Glenview village	13.5	41 847	714	3 099.8	39 288	684	32 060	2 559	7 228	6.5	22.5	1 702	4.1
17 30926	Granite City city	16.7	31 301	948	1 874.3	33 132	826	36 815	–1 831	–3 683	–5.5	–10.0	894	2.9
17 32746	Hanover Park village	6.8	38 278	790	5 629.1	32 910	836	28 719	5 368	4 191	16.3	14.6	10 233	26.7
17 33383	Harvey city	6.2	30 000	976	4 838.7	30 283	914	35 810	–283	–5 527	–.9	–15.4	3 834	12.8
17 34722	Highland Park city........	12.4	31 365	944	2 529.4	30 561	907	30 599	804	–38	2.6	–.1	2 792	8.9
17 35411	Hoffman Estates village	19.7	49 495	598	2 512.4	46 367	565	37 272	3 128	9 095	6.7	24.4	5 198	10.5
17 38570	Joliet city	38.1	106 221	217	2 788.0	78 585	281	77 956	27 636	629	35.2	.8	19 552	18.4
17 38934	Kankakee city	12.3	27 491	1 027	2 235.0	27 972	981	29 633	–481	–1 661	–1.7	–5.6	2 544	9.3
17 42028	Lansing village........	6.8	28 332	1 009	4 166.5	28 221	972	29 039	111	–818	.4	–2.8	1 624	5.7
17 44407	Lombard village	9.7	42 322	706	4 363.1	40 113	670	36 879	2 209	3 234	5.5	8.8	2 012	4.8
17 47774	Maywood village	2.7	26 987	1 038	9 995.2	27 147	1 010	27 998	–160	–851	–.6	–3.0	2 843	10.5
17 49867	Moline city	15.6	43 768	687	2 805.6	44 046	598	46 407	–278	–2 361	–.6	–5.1	5 212	11.9
17 51089	Mount Prospect village.....	10.2	56 265	513	5 516.2	53 081	475	52 634	3 184	447	6.0	.8	6 620	11.8
17 51622	Naperville city	35.4	128 358	165	3 625.9	86 958	243	42 601	41 400	44 357	47.6	104.1	4 160	3.2
17 53000	Niles village	5.9	30 068	973	5 096.3	28 794	953	30 363	1 274	–1 569	4.4	–5.2	1 512	5.0
17 53234	Normal town	13.6	45 386	663	3 337.2	40 134	669	35 672	5 252	4 462	13.1	12.5	1 162	2.6
17 53481	Northbrook village	12.9	33 435	900	2 591.9	32 743	841	30 778	692	1 965	2.1	6.4	616	1.8
17 53559	North Chicago city........	7.8	35 918	836	4 604.9	35 989	749	38 774	–71	–2 785	–.2	–7.2	6 552	18.2
17 54638	Oak Forest city	5.6	28 051	1 014	5 009.1	27 109	1 012	25 040	942	2 069	3.5	8.3	1 645	5.9

[1] Federal Information Processing Standards (FIPS) codes for states and places defined as of January 1990.   [2] Dry land and land temporarily or partially covered by water.   [3] Based on 1,078 places (1,070 incorporated places and the 8 CDPs in Hawaii). When places share the same rank, the next lower rank is omitted.   [4] Includes count resolution corrections through 1997 and adjustments based on Census 2000 dress rehearsal results and boundary changes reported as legally effective as of January 1, 1998.   [5] Based on 1,071 places (1,070 incorporated places and Honolulu CDP in Hawaii). When places share the same rank, the next lower rank is omitted.   [6] Persons of Hispanic or Latino origin may be of any race.   [7] Not incorporated as of January 1, 1980.

Sources: Land Area—U.S. Census Bureau, Census of Population and Housing, Census 2000 Redistricting Data (Public Law 94-171) Summary Files (related Internet site <http:// www.census.gov/dmd/www/2kresult.html>).   2000 Population—U.S. Census Bureau, 2000 Census of Population and Housing, "Census 2000 Profiles of General Demographic Characteristics" data files, published May 2001, related Internet site <http://www.census.gov/mp/www/pub/2000cen/mscen01.html>.   1990 Population—U.S. Census Bureau, "(SU-99-7) Population Estimates for Places (Sorted Alphabetically Within State): Annual Time Series, July 1, 1990 to July 1, 1999 (includes April 1, 1990 Population Estimates Base)," published 20 October 2000, <http://www.census.gov/population/ estimates/metro-city/placebyst/SC99T7_US.txt>.   1980 Population—U.S. Census Bureau, 1990 Census of Population and Housing, "Population and Housing Unit Counts," CPH-2-1 through CPH-2-52.

Table C–1. Cities — **Area and Population**–Con.

[Includes states and 1,070 incorporated places of 25,000 or more population as of April 1, 1990 in all states except Hawaii which has no incorporated places recognized by the Census Bureau. For Hawaii, 8 census designated places (CDPs) of 25,000 or more population as of April 1, 1990 are included. Also included are the 5 boroughs of New York city. For more information on these areas, see appendix B. Geographic Information]

State and place code[1]	City	Land area,[2] 2000 (sq. miles)	Population (April 1)											
			2000			1990[4]			Net change		Percent change		Hispanic or Latino,[6] 2000	
			Number	Rank[3]	Per square mile	Number	Rank[5]	1980	1990–2000	1980–1990	1990–2000	1980–1990	Number	Percent
	ILLINOIS—Con.													
17 54820	Oak Lawn village	8.6	55 245	531	6 423.8	56 316	435	60 590	–1 071	–4 274	–1.9	–7.1	2 942	5.3
17 54885	Oak Park village	4.7	52 524	564	11 175.3	53 610	470	54 887	–1 086	–1 277	–2.0	–2.3	2 374	4.5
17 56640	Orland Park village	19.1	51 077	578	2 674.2	37 885	712	23 045	13 192	14 840	34.8	64.4	1 874	3.7
17 57225	Palatine village	13.0	65 479	417	5 036.8	49 791	523	32 171	15 688	17 620	31.5	54.8	9 247	14.1
17 57875	Park Ridge city	7.0	37 775	799	5 396.4	37 360	729	38 704	415	–1 344	1.1	–3.5	1 113	2.9
17 58447	Pekin city	13.1	33 857	889	2 584.5	32 228	854	33 967	1 629	–1 739	5.1	–5.1	445	1.3
17 59000	Peoria city	44.4	112 936	199	2 543.6	113 822	163	124 160	–886	–10 338	–.8	–8.3	2 839	2.5
17 62367	Quincy city	14.6	40 366	747	2 764.8	40 523	657	42 554	–157	–2 031	–.4	–4.8	381	.9
17 65000	Rockford city	56.0	150 115	136	2 680.6	143 942	123	139 712	6 173	4 230	4.3	3.0	15 278	10.2
17 65078	Rock Island city	15.9	39 684	760	2 495.8	40 537	656	46 821	–853	–6 284	–2.1	–13.4	2 341	5.9
17 68003	Schaumburg village	19.0	75 386	354	3 967.7	68 678	338	53 355	6 708	15 323	9.8	28.7	3 988	5.3
17 70122	Skokie village	10.0	63 348	433	6 334.8	59 431	412	60 278	3 917	–847	6.6	–1.4	3 620	5.7
17 72000	Springfield city	54.0	111 454	201	2 064.0	107 265	183	100 054	4 189	7 211	3.9	7.2	1 337	1.2
17 73157	Streamwood village	7.3	36 407	824	4 987.3	31 461	873	23 456	4 946	8 005	15.7	34.1	6 108	16.8
17 75484	Tinley Park village	15.0	48 401	617	3 226.7	37 846	716	26 178	10 555	11 668	27.9	44.6	1 998	4.1
17 77005	Urbana city	10.5	36 395	825	3 466.2	37 182	730	35 978	–787	1 204	–2.1	3.3	1 288	3.5
17 79293	Waukegan city	23.0	87 901	285	3 821.8	69 621	334	67 653	18 280	1 968	26.3	2.9	39 396	44.8
17 81048	Wheaton city	11.2	55 416	529	4 947.9	52 057	491	43 043	3 359	9 014	6.5	20.9	2 023	3.7
17 81087	Wheeling village	8.4	34 496	875	4 106.7	29 477	930	23 266	5 019	6 211	17.0	26.7	7 135	20.7
17 82075	Wilmette village	5.4	27 651	1 026	5 120.6	26 829	1 021	28 221	822	–1 392	3.1	–4.9	574	2.1
17 83245	Woodridge village	8.3	30 934	956	3 727.0	26 590	1 030	21 763	4 344	4 827	16.3	22.2	2 839	9.2
18 00000	INDIANA	35 866.9	6 080 485	X	169.5	5 544 156	X	5 490 210	536 329	53 946	9.7	1.0	214 536	3.5
18 01468	Anderson city	40.0	59 734	469	1 493.4	59 494	410	64 695	240	–5 201	.4	–8.0	1 235	2.1
18 05860	Bloomington city	19.7	69 291	388	3 517.3	63 504	373	52 663	5 787	10 841	9.1	20.6	1 722	2.5
18 10342	Carmel city	17.8	37 733	801	2 119.8	26 428	1 036	18 272	11 305	8 156	42.8	44.6	649	1.7
18 14734	Columbus city	25.9	39 059	773	1 508.1	34 250	790	30 614	4 809	3 636	14.0	11.9	1 096	2.8
18 19486	East Chicago city	12.0	32 414	918	2 701.2	33 860	800	39 786	–1 446	–5 926	–4.3	–14.9	16 728	51.6
18 20728	Elkhart city	21.4	51 874	568	2 424.0	44 681	590	41 305	7 193	3 376	16.1	8.2	7 678	14.8
18 22000	Evansville city	40.7	121 582	178	2 987.3	126 172	145	130 496	–4 590	–4 324	–3.6	–3.3	1 392	1.1
18 25000	Fort Wayne city	79.0	205 727	84	2 604.1	202 995	76	172 391	2 732	30 604	1.3	17.8	11 884	5.8
18 27000	Gary city	50.2	102 746	226	2 046.7	116 587	157	151 968	–13 841	–35 381	–11.9	–23.3	5 065	4.9
18 29898	Greenwood city	14.3	36 037	835	2 520.1	27 153	1 009	19 327	8 884	7 826	32.7	40.5	687	1.9
18 31000	Hammond city	22.9	83 048	307	3 626.6	84 248	261	93 714	–1 200	–9 466	–1.4	10.1	17 473	21.0
18 36003	Indianapolis city (remainder)	361.5	781 870	12	2 162.8	731 726	13	700 807	50 144	30 919	6.9	4.4	30 636	3.9
18 40392	Kokomo city	16.2	46 113	650	2 846.5	45 189	581	47 808	924	–2 619	2.0	–5.5	1 204	2.6
18 40788	Lafayette city	20.1	56 397	507	2 805.8	49 762	524	43 011	6 635	6 751	13.3	15.7	5 136	9.1
18 42426	Lawrence city	20.1	38 915	779	1 936.1	26 353	1 039	25 591	12 562	762	47.7	3.0	1 840	4.7
18 46908	Marion city	13.3	31 320	947	2 354.9	33 052	829	35 874	–1 732	–2 822	–5.2	–7.9	1 128	3.6
18 48528	Merrillville town	33.3	30 560	962	917.7	27 987	979	27 677	2 573	310	9.2	1.1	2 950	9.7
18 48798	Michigan City city	19.6	32 900	909	1 678.6	33 989	795	36 850	–1 089	–2 861	–3.2	–7.8	1 035	3.1
18 49932	Mishawaka city	15.7	46 557	643	2 965.4	43 138	612	40 201	3 419	2 937	7.9	7.3	1 297	2.8
18 51876	Muncie city	24.2	67 430	403	2 786.4	71 828	318	77 216	–4 398	–5 388	–6.1	–7.0	971	1.4
18 52326	New Albany city	14.6	37 603	803	2 575.5	38 317	706	37 103	–714	1 214	–1.9	3.3	512	1.4
18 61092	Portage city	25.5	33 496	899	1 313.6	29 256	938	27 409	4 240	1 847	14.5	6.7	3 330	9.9
18 64260	Richmond city	23.2	39 124	769	1 686.4	39 738	674	41 349	–614	–1 611	–1.5	–3.9	796	2.0
18 71000	South Bend city	38.7	107 789	211	2 785.2	106 055	187	109 727	1 734	–3 672	1.6	–3.3	9 110	8.5
18 75428	Terre Haute city	31.2	59 614	471	1 910.7	57 461	424	61 125	2 153	–3 664	3.7	–6.0	942	1.6
18 82862	West Lafayette city	5.5	28 778	998	5 232.4	26 266	1 041	21 247	2 512	5 019	9.6	23.6	920	3.2
19 00000	IOWA	55 869.4	2 926 324	X	52.4	2 776 831	X	2 913 808	149 493	–136 977	5.4	–4.7	82 473	2.8
19 01855	Ames city	21.6	50 731	580	2 348.7	47 362	554	45 775	3 369	1 587	7.1	3.5	1 002	2.0
19 06355	Bettendorf city	21.2	31 275	950	1 475.2	27 844	985	27 381	3 431	463	12.3	1.7	772	2.5
19 09550	Burlington city	14.1	26 839	1 042	1 903.5	27 439	994	29 529	–600	–2 090	–2.2	–7.1	554	2.1
19 11755	Cedar Falls city	28.3	36 145	832	1 277.2	33 857	801	36 322	2 288	–2 465	6.8	–6.8	389	1.1
19 12000	Cedar Rapids city	63.1	120 758	181	1 913.8	108 854	178	110 243	11 904	–1 389	10.9	–1.3	2 065	1.7
19 14430	Clinton city	35.6	27 772	1 021	780.1	29 537	928	32 828	–1 765	–3 291	–6.0	–10.0	466	1.7
19 16860	Council Bluffs city	37.4	58 268	484	1 558.0	54 773	454	56 449	3 495	–1 676	6.4	–3.0	2 594	4.5
19 19000	Davenport city	62.8	98 359	241	1 566.2	95 722	216	103 264	2 637	–7 542	2.8	–7.3	5 268	5.4
19 21000	Des Moines city	75.8	198 682	92	2 621.1	193 333	81	191 003	5 349	2 330	2.8	1.2	13 138	6.6
19 22395	Dubuque city	26.5	57 686	493	2 176.8	57 753	421	62 374	–67	–4 621	–.1	–7.4	911	1.6
19 28515	Fort Dodge city	14.6	25 136	1 067	1 721.6	26 297	1 040	29 423	–1 161	–3 126	–4.4	–10.6	739	2.9
19 38595	Iowa City city	24.2	62 220	441	2 571.1	59 780	404	50 508	2 440	9 272	4.1	18.4	1 833	2.9
19 49755	Marshalltown city	18.0	26 009	1 058	1 444.9	25 347	1 063	26 938	662	–1 591	2.6	–5.9	3 265	12.6
19 50160	Mason City city	25.8	29 172	994	1 130.7	29 289	936	30 144	–117	–855	–.4	–2.8	1 005	3.4
19 73335	Sioux City city	54.8	85 013	299	1 551.3	80 682	272	82 003	4 331	–1 321	5.4	–1.6	9 257	10.9
19 82425	Waterloo city	60.7	68 747	392	1 132.6	66 732	350	75 985	2 015	–9 253	3.0	–12.2	1 806	2.6
19 83910	West Des Moines city	26.8	46 403	646	1 731.5	32 193	856	21 894	14 210	10 299	44.1	47.0	1 404	3.0

[1] Federal Information Processing Standards (FIPS) codes for states and places defined as of January 1990. [2] Dry land and land temporarily or partially covered by water. [3] Based on 1,078 places (1,070 incorporated places and the 8 CDPs in Hawaii). When places share the same rank, the next lower rank is omitted. [4] Includes count resolution corrections through 1997 and adjustments based on Census 2000 dress rehearsal results and boundary changes reported as legally effective as of January 1, 1998. [5] Based on 1,071 places (1,070 incorporated places and Honolulu CDP in Hawaii). When places share the same rank, the next lower rank is omitted. [6] Persons of Hispanic or Latino origin may be of any race.

Sources: Land Area—U.S. Census Bureau, Census of Population and Housing, Census 2000 Redistricting Data (Public Law 94-171) Summary Files (related Internet site <http://www.census.gov/dmd/www/2kresult.html>). 2000 Population—U.S. Census Bureau, 2000 Census of Population and Housing, "Census 2000 Profiles of General Demographic Characteristics" data files, published May 2001, related Internet site <http://www.census.gov/mp/www/pub/2000cen/mscen01.html>. 1990 Population—U.S. Census Bureau, "(SU-99-7) Population Estimates for Places (Sorted Alphabetically Within State): Annual Time Series, July 1, 1990 to July 1, 1999 (includes April 1, 1990 Population Estimates Base)," published 20 October 2000, <http://www.census.gov/population/estimates/metro-city/placebyst/SC99T7_US.txt>. 1980 Population—U.S. Census Bureau, 1990 Census of Population and Housing, "Population and Housing Unit Counts," CPH-2-1 through CPH-2-52.

Table C–1. Cities — **Area and Population**–Con.

[Includes states and 1,070 incorporated places of 25,000 or more population as of April 1, 1990 in all states except Hawaii which has no incorporated places recognized by the Census Bureau. For Hawaii, 8 census designated places (CDPs) of 25,000 or more population as of April 1, 1990 are included. Also included are the 5 boroughs of New York city. For more information on these areas, see appendix B. Geographic Information]

State and place code[1]	City	Land area,[2] 2000 (sq. miles)	Population (April 1) 2000 Number	2000 Rank[3]	2000 Per square mile	1990[4] Number	1990 Rank[5]	1980	Net change 1990–2000	Net change 1980–1990	Percent change 1990–2000	Percent change 1980–1990	Hispanic or Latino,[6] 2000 Number	Percent
20 00000	KANSAS...............	81 814.9	2 688 418	X	32.9	2 477 588	X	2 364 236	210 830	113 352	8.5	4.8	188 252	7.0
20 21275	Emporia city	9.9	26 760	1 044	2 703.0	25 621	1 056	25 287	1 139	334	4.4	1.3	5 752	21.5
20 33625	Hutchinson city	21.1	40 787	734	1 933.0	39 328	682	40 284	1 459	–956	3.7	–2.4	3 130	7.7
20 36000	Kansas City city	124.3	146 866	142	1 181.5	151 344	118	161 148	–4 478	–9 804	–3.0	–6.1	24 639	16.8
20 38900	Lawrence city	28.1	80 098	322	2 850.5	65 992	360	52 738	14 106	13 254	21.4	25.1	2 921	3.6
20 39000	Leavenworth city	23.5	35 420	849	1 507.2	38 714	699	33 656	–3 294	5 058	–8.5	15.0	1 800	5.1
20 39350	Lenexa city	34.3	40 238	750	1 173.1	34 247	791	18 639	5 991	15 608	17.5	83.7	1 598	4.0
20 44250	Manhattan city	15.0	44 831	673	2 988.7	43 084	613	32 644	1 747	10 440	4.1	32.0	1 564	3.5
20 52575	Olathe city	54.2	92 962	260	1 715.2	63 442	374	37 258	29 520	26 184	46.5	70.3	5 060	5.4
20 53775	Overland Park city	56.7	149 080	139	2 629.3	111 798	167	81 784	37 282	30 014	33.3	36.7	5 620	3.8
20 62700	Salina city	22.7	45 679	657	2 012.3	42 561	624	41 843	3 118	718	7.3	1.7	3 067	6.7
20 64500	Shawnee city	41.7	47 996	623	1 151.0	37 884	713	29 653	10 112	8 231	26.7	27.8	2 093	4.4
20 71000	Topeka city	56.0	122 377	176	2 185.3	120 847	151	118 690	1 530	2 157	1.3	1.8	10 847	8.9
20 79000	Wichita city	135.8	344 284	50	2 535.2	308 652	51	279 838	35 632	28 814	11.5	10.3	33 112	9.6
21 00000	KENTUCKY	39 728.2	4 041 769	X	101.7	3 686 892	X	3 660 324	354 877	26 568	9.6	.7	59 939	1.5
21 08902	Bowling Green city	35.4	49 296	604	1 392.5	42 278	626	40 450	7 018	1 828	16.6	4.5	2 011	4.1
21 17848	Covington city	13.1	43 370	690	3 310.7	43 635	606	49 585	–265	–5 950	–.6	–12.0	600	1.4
21 28900	Frankfort city	14.7	27 741	1 022	1 887.1	26 967	1 015	25 973	774	994	2.9	3.8	411	1.5
21 35866	Henderson city	15.0	27 373	1 030	1 824.9	26 143	1 049	24 834	1 230	1 309	4.7	5.3	347	1.3
21 37918	Hopkinsville city	24.0	30 089	972	1 253.7	30 137	916	27 318	–48	2 819	–.2	10.3	508	1.7
21 46027	Lexington-Fayette	284.5	260 512	64	915.7	225 366	70	204 165	35 146	21 201	15.6	10.4	8 561	3.3
21 48000	Louisville city	62.1	256 231	66	4 126.1	269 838	58	298 694	–13 607	–28 856	–5.0	–9.7	4 755	1.9
21 58620	Owensboro city	17.4	54 067	545	3 107.3	53 720	467	54 450	347	–730	.6	–1.3	557	1.0
21 58836	Paducah city	19.5	26 307	1 052	1 349.1	27 404	996	29 315	–1 097	–1 911	–4.0	–6.5	362	1.4
22 00000	LOUISIANA	43 561.8	4 468 976	X	102.6	4 221 826	X	4 206 116	247 150	15 710	5.9	.4	107 738	2.4
22 00975	Alexandria city	26.4	46 342	647	1 755.4	49 499	528	51 648	–3 157	–2 149	–6.4	–4.2	456	1.0
22 05000	Baton Rouge city.......	76.8	227 818	74	2 966.4	222 342	72	220 394	5 476	1 948	2.5	.9	3 918	1.7
22 08920	Bossier City city	40.8	56 461	506	1 383.8	53 129	474	50 817	3 332	2 312	6.3	4.5	2 232	4.0
22 36255	Houma city	14.0	32 393	919	2 313.8	30 797	895	32 602	1 596	–1 805	5.2	–5.5	571	1.8
22 39475	Kenner city	15.1	70 517	380	4 670.0	72 134	313	66 382	–1 617	5 752	–2.2	8.7	9 602	13.6
22 40735	Lafayette city	47.6	110 257	203	2 316.3	102 529	195	80 584	7 728	21 945	7.5	27.2	2 071	1.9
22 41155	Lake Charles city........	40.2	71 757	372	1 785.0	71 508	322	75 226	249	–3 718	.3	–4.9	1 007	1.4
22 51410	Monroe city	28.7	53 107	552	1 850.4	54 779	453	57 597	–1 672	–2 818	–3.1	–4.9	534	1.0
22 54035	New Iberia city	10.6	32 623	916	3 077.6	32 143	857	32 766	480	–623	1.5	–1.9	487	1.5
22 55000	New Orleans city	180.6	484 674	31	2 683.7	496 938	24	557 927	–12 264	–60 989	–2.5	–10.9	14 826	3.1
22 70000	Shreveport city	103.1	200 145	88	1 941.3	198 402	79	206 989	1 743	–8 587	.9	–4.1	3 106	1.6
23 00000	MAINE.................	30 861.6	1 274 923	X	41.3	1 227 928	X	1 125 043	46 995	102 885	3.8	9.1	9 360	.7
23 02795	Bangor city	34.4	31 473	941	914.9	34 590	781	31 643	–3 117	2 947	–9.0	9.3	329	1.0
23 38740	Lewiston city	34.1	35 690	844	1 046.6	39 790	673	40 481	–4 100	–691	–10.3	–1.7	448	1.3
23 60545	Portland city	21.2	64 249	424	3 030.6	63 106	378	61 572	1 143	1 534	1.8	2.5	974	1.5
24 00000	MARYLAND............	9 773.8	5 296 486	X	541.9	4 780 753	X	4 216 933	515 733	563 820	10.8	13.4	227 916	4.3
24 01600	Annapolis city	6.7	35 838	839	5 349.0	32 527	849	31 740	3 311	787	10.2	2.5	2 301	6.4
24 04000	Baltimore city	80.8	651 154	17	8 058.8	736 014	12	786 741	–84 860	–50 727	–11.5	–6.4	11 061	1.7
24 08775	Bowie city	16.1	50 269	589	3 122.3	37 830	717	33 695	12 439	4 135	32.9	12.3	1 468	2.9
24 30325	Frederick city	20.4	52 767	560	2 586.6	40 504	658	28 086	12 263	12 418	30.3	44.2	2 533	4.8
24 31175	Gaithersburg city	10.1	52 613	563	5 209.2	39 567	677	26 424	13 046	13 143	33.0	49.7	10 398	19.8
24 36075	Hagerstown city	10.7	36 687	818	3 428.7	35 939	750	34 132	748	1 807	2.1	5.3	649	1.8
24 67675	Rockville city	13.4	47 388	630	3 536.4	45 181	582	43 811	2 207	1 370	4.9	3.1	5 529	11.7
25 00000	MASSACHUSETTS	7 840.0	6 349 097	X	809.8	6 016 425	X	5 737 093	332 672	279 332	5.5	4.9	428 729	6.8
25 02690	Attleboro city	27.5	42 068	711	1 529.7	38 394	704	34 196	3 674	4 198	9.6	12.3	1 805	4.3
25 05595	Beverly city...........	16.6	39 862	757	2 401.3	38 155	709	37 655	1 707	500	4.5	1.3	720	1.8
25 07000	Boston city	48.4	589 141	20	12 172.3	574 289	20	562 994	14 852	11 295	2.6	2.0	85 089	14.4
25 09000	Brockton city	21.5	94 304	256	4 386.2	92 781	222	95 172	1 523	–2 391	1.6	–2.5	7 552	8.0
25 11000	Cambridge city.........	6.4	101 355	233	15 836.7	95 860	215	95 322	5 495	538	5.7	.6	7 455	7.4
25 13205	Chelsea city	2.2	35 080	861	15 945.5	28 716	958	25 431	6 364	3 285	22.2	12.9	16 984	48.4
25 13660	Chicopee city	22.9	54 653	538	2 386.6	56 650	432	55 112	–1 997	1 538	–3.5	2.8	4 790	8.8
25 21990	Everett city	3.4	38 037	795	11 187.4	35 711	754	37 195	2 326	–1 484	6.5	–4.0	3 617	9.5
25 23000	Fall River city	31.0	91 938	264	2 965.7	92 760	223	92 574	–822	186	–.9	.2	3 040	3.3
25 23875	Fitchburg city	27.8	39 102	770	1 406.5	41 667	641	39 580	–2 565	2 087	–6.2	5.3	5 882	15.0
25 26150	Gloucester city.........	26.0	30 273	966	1 164.3	28 723	957	27 768	1 550	955	5.4	3.4	449	1.5
25 29405	Haverhill city	33.3	58 969	477	1 770.8	51 090	505	46 865	7 879	4 225	15.4	9.0	5 174	8.8

[1] Federal Information Processing Standards (FIPS) codes for states and places defined as of January 1990.   [2] Dry land and land temporarily or partially covered by water.   [3] Based on 1,078 places (1,070 incorporated places and the 8 CDPs in Hawaii). When places share the same rank, the next lower rank is omitted.   [4] Includes count resolution corrections through 1997 and adjustments based on Census 2000 dress rehearsal results and boundary changes reported as legally effective as of January 1, 1998.   [5] Based on 1,071 places (1,070 incorporated places and Honolulu CDP in Hawaii). When places share the same rank, the next lower rank is omitted.   [6] Persons of Hispanic or Latino origin may be of any race.

Sources: Land Area—U.S. Census Bureau, Census of Population and Housing, Census 2000 Redistricting Data (Public Law 94-171) Summary Files (related Internet site <http://www.census.gov/dmd/www/2kresult.html>).   2000 Population—U.S. Census Bureau, 2000 Census of Population and Housing, "Census 2000 Profiles of General Demographic Characteristics" data files, published May 2001, related Internet site <http://www.census.gov/mp/www/pub/2000cen/mscen01.html>.   1990 Population—U.S. Census Bureau, "(SU-99-7) Population Estimates for Places (Sorted Alphabetically Within State): Annual Time Series, July 1, 1990 to July 1, 1999 (includes April 1, 1990 Population Estimates Base)," published 20 October 2000, <http://www.census.gov/population/estimates/metro-city/placebyst/SC99T7_US.txt>.   1980 Population—U.S. Census Bureau, 1990 Census of Population and Housing, "Population and Housing Unit Counts," CPH-2-1 through CPH-2-52.

Table C–1. Cities — **Area and Population**–Con.

[Includes states and 1,070 incorporated places of 25,000 or more population as of April 1, 1990 in all states except Hawaii which has no incorporated places recognized by the Census Bureau. For Hawaii, 8 census designated places (CDPs) of 25,000 or more population as of April 1, 1990 are included. Also included are the 5 boroughs of New York city. For more information on these areas, see appendix B. Geographic Information]

State and place code[1]	City	Land area,[2] 2000 (sq. miles)	Population (April 1) 2000 Number	2000 Rank[3]	2000 Per square mile	1990[4] Number	1990[4] Rank[5]	1980	Net change 1990–2000	Net change 1980–1990	Percent change 1990–2000	Percent change 1980–1990	Hispanic or Latino,[6] 2000 Number	Hispanic or Latino,[6] 2000 Percent
	MASSACHUSETTS— Con.													
25 30840	Holyoke city	21.3	39 838	758	1 870.3	43 707	603	44 678	−3 869	−971	−8.9	−2.2	16 485	41.4
25 34550	Lawrence city	7.0	72 043	370	10 291.9	69 995	331	63 175	2 048	6 820	2.9	10.8	43 019	59.7
25 35075	Leominster city	28.9	41 303	722	1 429.2	37 864	714	34 508	3 439	3 356	9.1	9.7	4 544	11.0
25 37000	Lowell city	13.8	105 167	218	7 620.8	103 428	193	92 418	1 739	11 010	1.7	11.9	14 734	14.0
25 37490	Lynn city	10.8	89 050	277	8 245.4	81 311	269	78 471	7 739	2 840	9.5	3.6	16 383	18.4
25 37875	Malden city	5.1	56 340	509	11 047.1	53 916	462	53 386	2 424	530	4.5	1.0	2 696	4.8
25 38715	Marlborough city	21.1	36 255	831	1 718.2	31 833	866	30 617	4 422	1 216	13.9	4.0	2 196	6.1
25 39835	Medford city	8.1	55 765	522	6 884.6	57 282	428	58 076	−1 517	−794	−2.6	−1.4	1 443	2.6
25 40115	Melrose city	4.7	27 134	1 035	5 773.2	28 112	974	30 055	−978	−1 943	−3.5	−6.5	283	1.0
25 45000	New Bedford city	20.1	93 768	257	4 665.1	98 476	207	98 478	−4 708	−2	−4.8	Z	9 576	10.2
25 45560	Newton city	18.1	83 829	304	4 631.4	82 585	265	83 622	1 244	−1 037	1.5	−1.2	2 111	2.5
25 46330	Northampton city	34.5	28 978	996	839.9	29 283	937	29 286	−305	−3	−1.0	Z	1 518	5.2
25 52490	Peabody city	16.4	48 129	619	2 934.7	47 176	555	45 976	953	1 200	2.0	2.6	1 651	3.4
25 53960	Pittsfield city	40.7	45 793	655	1 125.1	48 792	534	51 974	−2 999	−3 182	−6.1	−6.1	934	2.0
25 55745	Quincy city	16.8	88 025	283	5 239.6	84 977	257	84 743	3 048	234	3.6	.3	1 835	2.1
25 56585	Revere city	5.9	47 283	634	8 014.1	42 783	618	42 423	4 500	360	10.5	.8	4 465	9.4
25 59105	Salem city	8.1	40 407	745	4 988.5	38 129	710	38 276	2 278	−147	6.0	−.4	4 541	11.2
25 62535	Somerville city	4.1	77 478	341	18 897.1	76 302	292	77 372	1 176	−1 070	1.5	−1.4	6 786	8.8
25 67000	Springfield city	32.1	152 082	131	4 737.8	156 964	114	152 319	−4 882	4 645	−3.1	3.0	41 343	27.2
25 69170	Taunton city	46.6	55 976	518	1 201.2	49 881	522	45 001	6 095	4 880	12.2	10.8	2 198	3.9
25 72600	Waltham city	12.7	59 226	474	4 663.5	57 876	420	58 200	1 350	−324	2.3	−.6	5 031	8.5
25 76030	Westfield city	46.6	40 072	754	859.9	38 479	702	36 465	1 593	2 014	4.1	5.5	2 008	5.0
25 81035	Woburn city	12.7	37 258	809	2 933.7	36 093	744	36 626	1 165	−533	3.2	−1.5	1 152	3.1
25 82000	Worcester city	37.6	172 648	121	4 591.7	169 636	104	161 799	3 012	7 837	1.8	4.8	26 155	15.1
26 00000	MICHIGAN	56 803.8	9 938 444	X	175.0	9 295 287	X	9 262 044	643 157	33 243	6.9	.4	323 877	3.3
26 01380	Allen Park city	7.0	29 376	990	4 196.6	31 085	882	34 196	−1 709	−3 111	−5.5	−9.1	1 389	4.7
26 03000	Ann Arbor city	27.0	114 024	195	4 223.1	110 168	174	107 969	3 856	2 199	3.5	2.0	3 814	3.3
26 05920	Battle Creek city	42.8	53 364	551	1 246.8	53 450	471	35 724	−86	17 726	−.2	49.6	2 475	4.6
26 06020	Bay City city	10.4	36 817	815	3 540.1	38 752	697	41 593	−1 935	−2 841	−5.0	−6.8	2 473	6.7
26 12060	Burton city	23.5	30 308	965	1 289.7	27 476	993	29 976	2 832	−2 500	10.3	−8.3	705	2.3
26 21000	Dearborn city	24.4	97 775	242	4 007.2	89 119	234	90 660	8 656	−1 541	9.7	−1.7	2 931	3.0
26 21020	Dearborn Heights city	11.7	58 264	485	4 979.8	60 720	395	67 706	−2 456	−6 986	−4.0	−10.3	1 974	3.4
26 22000	Detroit city	138.8	951 270	10	6 853.5	1 027 946	7	1 203 368	−76 676	−175 422	−7.5	−14.6	47 167	5.0
26 23920	East Detroit city	5.1	34 077	881	6 681.8	35 275	762	38 280	−1 198	−3 005	−3.4	−7.9	453	1.3
26 24120	East Lansing city	11.2	46 525	644	4 154.0	50 943	508	51 392	−4 418	−449	−8.7	−.9	1 252	2.7
26 27440	Farmington Hills city	33.3	82 111	311	2 465.8	74 611	301	58 056	7 500	16 555	10.1	28.5	1 211	1.5
26 27880	Ferndale city	3.9	22 105	1 076	5 667.9	25 044	1 068	26 227	−2 939	−1 183	−11.7	−4.5	399	1.8
26 29000	Flint city	33.6	124 943	171	3 718.5	141 367	128	159 611	−16 424	−18 244	−11.6	−11.4	3 742	3.0
26 31420	Garden City city	5.9	30 047	974	5 092.7	32 045	859	35 640	−1 998	−3 595	−6.2	−10.1	611	2.0
26 34000	Grand Rapids city	44.6	197 800	93	4 435.0	189 673	86	181 843	8 127	7 830	4.3	4.3	25 818	13.1
26 38640	Holland city	16.6	35 048	863	2 111.3	30 869	891	26 281	4 179	4 588	13.5	17.5	7 783	22.2
26 40680	Inkster city	6.3	30 115	971	4 780.2	30 956	884	35 190	−841	−4 234	−2.7	−12.0	482	1.6
26 41420	Jackson city	11.1	36 316	827	3 271.7	37 570	725	39 739	−1 254	−2 169	−3.3	−5.5	1 469	4.0
26 42160	Kalamazoo city	24.7	77 145	344	3 123.3	80 290	274	79 722	−3 145	568	−3.9	.7	3 304	4.3
26 42820	Kentwood city	21.0	45 255	666	2 155.0	37 826	718	30 438	7 429	7 388	19.6	24.3	1 757	3.9
26 46000	Lansing city	35.0	119 128	183	3 403.7	126 932	144	130 414	−7 804	−3 482	−6.1	−2.7	11 886	10.0
26 47800	Lincoln Park city	5.9	40 008	755	6 781.0	41 980	631	45 105	−1 972	−3 125	−4.7	−6.9	2 556	6.4
26 49000	Livonia city	35.7	100 545	237	2 816.4	100 864	199	104 814	−319	−3 950	−.3	−3.8	1 731	1.7
26 50560	Madison Heights city	7.2	31 101	951	4 319.6	32 199	855	35 375	−1 098	−3 176	−3.4	−9.0	502	1.6
26 53780	Midland city	33.2	41 685	717	1 255.6	38 906	692	37 269	2 779	1 637	7.1	4.4	802	1.9
26 56320	Muskegon city	14.4	40 105	752	2 785.1	40 355	664	40 823	−250	−468	−.6	−1.1	2 560	6.4
26 59440	Novi city	30.5	47 386	631	1 553.6	32 979	834	22 525	14 407	10 454	43.7	46.4	855	1.8
26 59920	Oak Park city	5.0	29 793	982	5 958.6	30 590	905	31 537	−797	−947	−2.6	−3.0	381	1.3
26 65440	Pontiac city	20.0	66 337	412	3 316.9	71 136	326	76 715	−4 799	−5 579	−6.7	−7.3	8 463	12.8
26 65560	Portage city	32.2	44 897	672	1 394.3	41 025	651	38 157	3 872	2 868	9.4	7.5	868	1.9
26 65820	Port Huron city	8.1	32 338	920	3 992.3	33 701	808	33 981	−1 363	−280	−4.0	−.8	1 383	4.3
26 69035	Rochester Hills city	32.8	68 825	390	2 098.3	61 884	390	(7)	6 941	X	11.2	X	1 576	2.3
26 69800	Roseville city	9.8	48 129	619	4 911.1	51 270	501	54 311	−3 141	−3 041	−6.1	−5.6	722	1.5
26 70040	Royal Oak city	11.8	60 062	463	5 090.0	64 212	370	70 893	−4 150	−6 681	−6.5	−9.4	781	1.3
26 70520	Saginaw city	17.4	61 799	447	3 551.7	69 502	335	77 508	−7 703	−8 006	−11.1	−10.3	7 259	11.7
26 70760	St. Clair Shores city	11.5	63 096	436	5 486.6	68 300	340	76 210	−5 204	−7 910	−7.6	−10.4	745	1.2
26 74900	Southfield city	26.2	78 296	334	2 988.4	75 706	295	75 568	2 590	138	3.4	.2	934	1.2
26 74960	Southgate city	6.9	30 136	970	4 367.5	30 756	897	32 058	−620	−1 302	−2.0	−4.1	1 198	4.0
26 76460	Sterling Heights city	36.6	124 471	173	3 400.8	117 814	155	108 999	6 657	8 815	5.7	8.1	1 665	1.3
26 79000	Taylor city	23.6	65 868	415	2 791.0	70 809	328	77 568	−4 941	−6 759	−7.0	−8.7	2 131	3.2
26 80700	Troy city	33.5	80 959	317	2 416.7	72 884	308	67 102	8 075	5 782	11.1	8.6	1 184	1.5
26 84000	Warren city	34.3	138 247	154	4 030.5	145 080	122	161 134	−6 833	−16 054	−4.7	−10.0	1 868	1.4
26 86000	Westland city	20.4	86 602	289	4 245.2	84 457	259	84 603	2 145	−146	2.5	−.2	2 138	2.5
26 88900	Wyandotte city	5.3	28 006	1 015	5 284.2	30 772	896	34 006	−2 766	−3 234	−9.0	−9.5	816	2.9
26 88940	Wyoming city	24.4	69 368	387	2 843.0	63 672	372	59 616	5 696	4 056	8.9	6.8	6 704	9.7

[1] Federal Information Processing Standards (FIPS) codes for states and places defined as of January 1990. [2] Dry land and land temporarily or partially covered by water. [3] Based on 1,078 places (1,070 incorporated places and the 8 CDPs in Hawaii). When places share the same rank, the next lower rank is omitted. [4] Includes count resolution corrections through 1997 and adjustments based on Census 2000 dress rehearsal results and boundary changes reported as legally effective as of January 1, 1998. [5] Based on 1,071 places (1,070 incorporated places and Honolulu CDP in Hawaii). When places share the same rank, the next lower rank is omitted. [6] Persons of Hispanic or Latino origin may be of any race. [7] Not incorporated as of January 1, 1980.

Sources: Land Area—U.S. Census Bureau, Census of Population and Housing, Census 2000 Redistricting Data (Public Law 94-171) Summary Files (related Internet site <http://www.census.gov/dmd/www/2kresult.html>). 2000 Population—U.S. Census Bureau, 2000 Census of Population and Housing, "Census 2000 Profiles of General Demographic Characteristics" data files, published May 2001, related Internet site <http://www.census.gov/mp/www/pub/2000cen/msccen01.html>. 1990 Population—U.S. Census Bureau, "(SU-99-7) Population Estimates for Places (Sorted Alphabetically Within State): Annual Time Series, July 1, 1990 to July 1, 1999 (includes April 1, 1990 Population Estimates Base)," published 20 October 2000, <http://www.census.gov/population/estimates/metro-city/placebyst/SC99T7_US.txt>. 1980 Population—U.S. Census Bureau, 1990 Census of Population and Housing, "Population and Housing Unit Counts," CPH-2-1 through CPH-2-52.

Table C–1. Cities — **Area and Population**–Con.

[Includes states and 1,070 incorporated places of 25,000 or more population as of April 1, 1990 in all states except Hawaii which has no incorporated places recognized by the Census Bureau. For Hawaii, 8 census designated places (CDPs) of 25,000 or more population as of April 1, 1990 are included. Also included are the 5 boroughs of New York city. For more information on these areas, see appendix B. Geographic Information]

State and place code[1]	City	Land area,[2] 2000 (sq. miles)	Population (April 1) 2000 Number	2000 Rank[3]	2000 Per square mile	1990[4] Number	1990[4] Rank[5]	1980	Net change 1990–2000	Net change 1980–1990	Percent change 1990–2000	Percent change 1980–1990	Hispanic or Latino,[6] 2000 Number	Hispanic or Latino,[6] 2000 Percent
27 00000	MINNESOTA	79 610.1	4 919 479	X	61.8	4 375 665	X	4 075 970	543 814	299 695	12.4	7.4	143 382	2.9
27 01900	Apple Valley city	17.3	45 527	659	2 631.6	34 608	779	21 818	10 919	12 790	31.6	58.6	912	2.0
27 06382	Blaine city	33.9	44 942	669	1 325.7	38 925	690	28 558	6 017	10 367	15.5	36.3	773	1.7
27 06616	Bloomington city	35.5	85 172	298	2 399.2	86 292	246	81 831	−1 120	4 461	−1.3	5.5	2 290	2.7
27 07948	Brooklyn Center city	7.9	29 172	994	3 692.7	28 881	947	31 230	291	−2 349	1.0	−7.5	823	2.8
27 07966	Brooklyn Park city	26.1	67 388	404	2 581.9	56 366	434	43 332	11 022	13 034	19.6	30.1	1 944	2.9
27 08794	Burnsville city	24.9	60 220	462	2 418.5	51 249	502	35 674	8 971	15 575	17.5	43.7	1 725	2.9
27 13114	Coon Rapids city	22.7	61 607	449	2 714.0	52 970	479	35 826	8 637	17 144	16.3	47.9	933	1.5
27 17000	Duluth city	68.0	86 918	286	1 278.2	85 446	253	92 811	1 472	−7 365	1.7	−7.9	921	1.1
27 17288	Eagan city	32.3	63 557	431	1 967.7	47 416	553	20 700	16 141	26 716	34.0	129.1	1 424	2.2
27 18116	Eden Prairie city	32.4	54 901	535	1 694.5	39 309	683	16 263	15 592	23 046	39.7	141.7	862	1.6
27 18188	Edina city	15.7	47 425	629	3 020.7	45 947	570	46 073	1 478	−126	3.2	−.3	539	1.1
27 22814	Fridley city	10.2	27 449	1 028	2 691.1	28 336	968	30 228	−887	−1 892	−3.1	−6.3	704	2.6
27 39878	Mankato city	15.2	32 427	917	2 133.4	31 957	862	28 646	470	3 311	1.5	11.6	719	2.2
27 40166	Maple Grove city	32.9	50 365	587	1 530.9	38 796	696	20 525	11 569	18 271	29.8	89.0	534	1.1
27 40382	Maplewood city	17.3	34 947	868	2 020.1	30 558	908	26 990	4 389	3 568	14.4	13.2	779	2.2
27 43000	Minneapolis city	54.9	382 618	45	6 969.4	368 284	43	370 951	14 334	−2 667	3.9	−.7	29 175	7.6
27 43252	Minnetonka city	27.1	51 301	577	1 893.0	48 375	541	38 683	2 926	9 692	6.0	25.1	657	1.3
27 43864	Moorhead city	13.4	32 177	922	2 401.3	32 542	846	29 998	−365	2 544	−1.1	8.5	1 439	4.5
27 51730	Plymouth city	32.9	65 894	414	2 002.9	50 892	510	31 615	15 002	19 277	29.5	61.0	1 079	1.6
27 54214	Richfield city	6.9	34 439	877	4 991.2	35 699	755	37 851	−1 260	−2 152	−3.5	−5.7	2 158	6.3
27 54880	Rochester city	39.6	85 806	292	2 166.8	71 590	319	57 906	14 216	13 684	19.9	23.6	2 565	3.0
27 55852	Roseville city	13.2	33 690	896	2 552.3	33 317	820	35 820	373	−2 503	1.1	−7.0	664	2.0
27 56896	St. Cloud city	30.2	59 107	475	1 957.2	55 859	438	42 566	3 248	13 293	5.8	31.2	784	1.3
27 57220	St. Louis Park city	10.7	44 126	682	4 123.9	43 932	601	42 931	194	1 001	.4	2.3	1 294	2.9
27 58000	St. Paul city	52.8	287 151	59	5 438.5	272 235	57	270 230	14 916	2 005	5.5	.7	22 715	7.9
27 71032	Winona city	18.2	27 069	1 036	1 487.3	26 567	1 031	25 075	502	1 492	1.9	6.0	365	1.3
28 00000	MISSISSIPPI	46 907.0	2 844 658	X	60.6	2 575 475	X	2 520 770	269 183	54 705	10.5	2.2	39 569	1.4
28 06220	Biloxi city	38.0	50 644	582	1 332.7	46 327	566	49 311	4 317	−2 984	9.3	−6.1	1 848	3.6
28 29180	Greenville city	26.9	41 633	718	1 547.7	45 667	574	40 613	−4 034	5 054	−8.8	12.4	297	.7
28 29700	Gulfport city	56.9	71 127	376	1 250.0	64 735	365	39 676	6 392	25 059	9.9	63.2	1 814	2.6
28 31020	Hattiesburg city	49.3	44 779	674	908.3	45 221	580	40 829	−442	4 392	−1.0	10.8	630	1.4
28 36000	Jackson city	104.9	184 256	109	1 756.5	196 575	80	202 895	−12 319	−6 320	−6.3	−3.1	1 451	.8
28 46640	Meridian city	45.1	39 968	756	886.2	42 017	630	46 577	−2 049	−4 560	−4.9	−9.8	433	1.1
28 55360	Pascagoula city	15.2	26 200	1 054	1 723.7	26 087	1 050	29 318	113	−3 231	.4	−11.0	1 019	3.9
28 74840	Tupelo city	51.1	34 211	879	669.5	30 867	892	23 905	3 344	6 962	10.8	29.1	484	1.4
29 00000	MISSOURI	68 885.9	5 595 211	X	81.2	5 116 901	X	4 916 766	478 310	200 135	9.3	4.1	118 592	2.1
29 06652	Blue Springs city	18.2	48 080	621	2 641.8	40 354	665	25 936	7 726	14 418	19.1	55.6	1 329	2.8
29 11242	Cape Girardeau city	24.3	35 349	851	1 454.7	34 929	773	34 361	420	568	1.2	1.7	388	1.1
29 13600	Chesterfield city...........	31.5	46 802	640	1 485.8	42 351	625	(7)	4 451	X	10.5	X	726	1.6
29 15670	Columbia city	53.1	84 531	300	1 591.9	69 831	332	62 061	14 700	7 770	21.1	12.5	1 733	2.1
29 24778	Florissant city	11.4	50 497	586	4 429.6	53 886	463	55 721	−3 389	−1 835	−6.3	−3.3	753	1.5
29 27190	Gladstone city	8.0	26 365	1 050	3 295.6	26 221	1 043	24 990	144	1 231	.5	4.9	938	3.6
29 35000	Independence city	78.3	113 288	198	1 446.8	112 402	166	111 797	886	605	.8	.5	4 175	3.7
29 37000	Jefferson City city	27.3	39 636	763	1 451.9	35 758	753	33 619	3 878	2 139	10.8	6.4	616	1.6
29 37592	Joplin city	31.4	45 504	660	1 449.2	41 508	643	39 126	3 996	2 382	9.6	6.1	1 144	2.5
29 38000	Kansas City city	313.5	441 545	36	1 408.4	435 121	31	448 028	6 424	−12 907	1.5	−2.9	30 604	6.9
29 39044	Kirkwood city	9.2	27 324	1 032	2 970.0	28 287	970	27 739	−963	548	−3.4	2.0	298	1.1
29 41248	Lee's Summit city	59.5	70 700	379	1 188.2	46 483	563	28 741	24 217	17 742	52.1	61.7	1 394	2.0
29 46586	Maryland Heights city	21.4	25 756	1 061	1 203.6	25 496	1 060	(7)	260	X	1.0	X	599	2.3
29 60788	Raytown city.............	9.9	30 388	964	3 069.5	30 684	899	31 831	−296	−1 147	−1.0	−3.6	712	2.3
29 64082	St. Charles city	20.4	60 321	460	2 956.9	50 835	512	37 379	9 486	13 456	18.7	36.0	1 187	2.0
29 64550	St. Joseph city	43.8	73 990	360	1 689.3	72 065	314	76 691	1 925	−4 626	2.7	−6.0	1 929	2.6
29 65000	St. Louis city	61.9	348 189	49	5 625.0	396 685	36	452 801	−48 496	−56 116	−12.2	−12.4	7 022	2.0
29 65126	St. Peters city	21.2	51 381	576	2 423.6	41 697	640	15 700	9 684	25 997	23.2	165.6	768	1.5
29 70000	Springfield city	73.2	151 580	132	2 070.8	141 115	129	133 116	10 465	7 999	7.4	6.0	3 501	2.3
29 75220	University City city.........	5.9	37 428	805	6 343.7	39 876	671	42 690	−2 448	−2 814	−6.1	−6.6	583	1.6

[1] Federal Information Processing Standards (FIPS) codes for states and places defined as of January 1990.   [2] Dry land and land temporarily or partially covered by water.   [3] Based on 1,078 places (1,070 incorporated places and the 8 CDPs in Hawaii). When places share the same rank, the next lower rank is omitted.   [4] Includes count resolution corrections through 1997 and adjustments based on Census 2000 dress rehearsal results and boundary changes reported as legally effective as of January 1, 1998.   [5] Based on 1,071 places (1,070 incorporated places and Honolulu CDP in Hawaii). When places share the same rank, the next lower rank is omitted.   [6] Persons of Hispanic or Latino origin may be of any race.   [7] Not incorporated as of January 1, 1980.

Sources: Land Area—U.S. Census Bureau, Census of Population and Housing, Census 2000 Redistricting Data (Public Law 94-171) Summary Files (related Internet site <http://www.census.gov/dmd/www/2kresult.html>).   2000 Population—U.S. Census Bureau, 2000 Census of Population and Housing, "Census 2000 Profiles of General Demographic Characteristics" data files, published May 2001, related Internet site <http://www.census.gov/mp/www/pub/2000cen/mscen01.html>.   1990 Population—U.S. Census Bureau, "(SU-99-7) Population Estimates for Places (Sorted Alphabetically Within State): Annual Time Series, July 1, 1990 to July 1, 1999 (includes April 1, 1990 Population Estimates Base)," published 20 October 2000, <http://www.census.gov/population/estimates/metro-city/placebyst/SC99T7_US.txt>.   1980 Population—U.S. Census Bureau, 1990 Census of Population and Housing, "Population and Housing Unit Counts," CPH-2-1 through CPH-2-52.

Table C–1. Cities — **Area and Population**–Con.

[Includes states and 1,070 incorporated places of 25,000 or more population as of April 1, 1990 in all states except Hawaii which has no incorporated places recognized by the Census Bureau. For Hawaii, 8 census designated places (CDPs) of 25,000 or more population as of April 1, 1990 are included. Also included are the 5 boroughs of New York city. For more information on these areas, see appendix B. Geographic Information]

State and place code[1]	City	Land area,[2] 2000 (sq. miles)	Population (April 1) 2000 Number	2000 Rank[3]	2000 Per square mile	1990[4] Number	1990 Rank[5]	1980	Net change 1990–2000	Net change 1980–1990	Percent change 1990–2000	Percent change 1980–1990	Hispanic or Latino,[6] 2000 Number	Percent
30 00000	MONTANA	145 552.4	902 195	X	6.2	799 065	X	786 690	103 130	12 375	12.9	1.6	18 081	2.0
30 06550	Billings city	33.7	89 847	275	2 666.1	81 469	268	66 818	8 378	14 651	10.3	21.9	3 758	4.2
30 11397	Butte-Silver Bow (remainder)	716.1	33 892	887	47.3	33 252	823	37 205	640	–3 953	1.9	–10.6	927	2.7
30 32800	Great Falls city	19.5	56 690	503	2 907.2	55 376	444	56 884	1 314	–1 508	2.4	–2.7	1 354	2.4
30 50200	Missoula city	23.8	57 053	499	2 397.2	48 430	539	33 351	8 623	15 079	17.8	45.2	1 004	1.8
31 00000	NEBRASKA	76 872.4	1 711 263	X	22.3	1 578 417	X	1 569 825	132 846	8 592	8.4	.5	94 425	5.5
31 03950	Bellevue city	13.3	44 382	679	3 337.0	39 101	685	21 813	5 281	17 288	13.5	79.3	2 609	5.9
31 19595	Grand Island city	21.5	42 940	697	1 997.2	39 383	680	33 180	3 557	6 203	9.0	18.7	6 845	15.9
31 28000	Lincoln city	74.6	225 581	76	3 023.9	192 722	82	171 932	32 859	20 790	17.0	12.1	8 154	3.6
31 37000	Omaha city	115.7	390 007	44	3 370.8	357 807	47	313 939	32 200	43 868	9.0	14.0	29 397	7.5
32 00000	NEVADA	109 826.0	1 998 257	X	18.2	1 201 675	X	800 508	796 582	401 167	66.3	50.1	393 970	19.7
32 09700	Carson City	143.4	52 457	565	365.8	40 443	661	32 022	12 014	8 421	29.7	26.3	7 466	14.2
32 31900	Henderson city	79.7	175 381	116	2 200.5	65 109	364	24 363	110 272	40 746	169.4	167.2	18 785	10.7
32 40000	Las Vegas city	113.3	478 434	32	4 222.7	259 834	63	164 674	218 600	95 160	84.1	57.8	112 962	23.6
32 51800	North Las Vegas city	78.5	115 488	194	1 471.2	47 956	544	42 739	67 532	5 217	140.8	12.2	43 435	37.6
32 60600	Reno city	69.1	180 480	112	2 611.9	134 747	134	100 756	45 733	33 991	33.9	33.7	34 616	19.2
32 68400	Sparks city	23.9	66 346	411	2 776.0	53 834	464	40 780	12 512	13 054	23.2	32.0	13 068	19.7
33 00000	NEW HAMPSHIRE	8 968.1	1 235 786	X	137.8	1 109 252	X	920 610	126 534	188 642	11.4	20.5	20 489	1.7
33 14200	Concord city	64.3	40 687	737	632.8	36 882	734	30 400	3 805	6 482	10.3	21.3	591	1.5
33 18820	Dover city	26.7	26 884	1 040	1 006.9	25 391	1 062	22 377	1 493	3 014	5.9	13.5	306	1.1
33 45140	Manchester city	33.0	107 006	214	3 242.6	99 217	204	90 936	7 789	8 281	7.9	9.1	4 944	4.6
33 50260	Nashua city	30.9	86 605	288	2 802.8	79 767	276	67 865	6 838	11 902	8.6	17.5	5 388	6.2
33 62900	Portsmouth city	15.6	20 784	1 077	1 332.3	26 160	1 048	26 254	–5 376	–94	–20.6	–.4	280	1.3
33 65140	Rochester city	45.2	28 461	1 008	629.7	26 691	1 027	21 560	1 770	5 131	6.6	23.8	255	.9
34 00000	NEW JERSEY	7 417.3	8 414 350	X	1 134.4	7 747 750	X	7 365 011	666 600	382 739	8.6	5.2	1 117 191	13.3
34 02080	Atlantic City city	11.3	40 517	741	3 585.6	37 957	711	40 199	2 560	–2 242	6.7	–5.6	10 107	24.9
34 03500	Bayonne city	5.6	61 842	415	11 043.2	61 464	392	65 047	378	–3 583	.6	–5.5	11 015	17.8
34 10000	Camden city	8.8	79 904	324	9 080.0	87 460	240	84 910	–7 556	2 550	–8.6	3.0	31 019	38.8
34 13690	Clifton city	11.3	78 672	332	6 962.1	72 008	315	74 388	6 664	–2 380	9.3	–3.2	15 608	19.8
34 19390	East Orange city	3.9	69 824	385	17 903.6	73 621	305	77 878	–3 797	–4 257	–5.2	–5.5	3 284	4.7
34 21000	Elizabeth city	12.2	120 568	182	9 882.6	110 138	175	106 201	10 430	3 937	9.5	3.7	59 627	49.5
34 22470	Fair Lawn borough	5.2	31 637	937	6 084.0	30 523	909	32 229	1 114	–1 706	3.6	–5.3	1 744	5.5
34 24420	Fort Lee borough	2.5	35 461	848	14 184.4	31 894	865	32 449	3 567	–555	11.2	–1.7	2 791	7.9
34 25770	Garfield city	2.1	29 786	983	14 183.8	26 727	1 025	26 803	3 059	–76	11.4	–.3	5 989	20.1
34 28680	Hackensack city	4.1	42 677	701	10 409.0	37 087	731	36 039	5 590	1 048	15.1	2.9	11 061	25.9
34 32250	Hoboken city	1.3	38 577	784	29 674.6	33 392	818	42 460	5 185	–9 068	15.5	–21.4	7 783	20.2
34 36000	Jersey City city	14.9	240 055	72	16 111.1	228 475	67	223 532	11 580	4 943	5.1	2.2	67 952	28.3
34 36510	Kearny town	9.1	40 513	742	4 452.0	34 874	775	35 735	5 639	–861	16.2	–2.4	11 075	27.3
34 40350	Linden city	10.8	39 394	768	3 647.6	36 732	736	37 836	2 662	–1 104	7.2	–2.9	5 674	14.4
34 41310	Long Branch city	5.2	31 340	945	6 026.9	28 764	955	29 819	2 576	–1 055	9.0	–3.5	6 477	20.7
34 46680	Millville city	42.3	26 847	1 041	634.7	26 263	1 042	24 815	584	1 448	2.2	5.8	2 998	11.2
34 51000	Newark city	23.8	273 546	63	11 493.5	275 291	56	329 248	–1 745	–53 957	–.6	–16.4	80 622	29.5
34 51210	New Brunswick city	5.2	48 573	614	9 341.0	41 643	642	41 442	6 930	201	16.6	.5	18 947	39.0
34 55950	Paramus borough	10.5	25 737	1 062	2 451.1	24 946	1 069	26 474	791	–1 528	3.2	–5.8	1 253	4.9
34 56550	Passaic city	3.1	67 861	400	21 890.6	58 676	415	52 463	9 185	6 213	15.7	11.8	42 387	62.5
34 57000	Paterson city	8.4	149 222	138	17 764.5	158 019	112	137 970	–8 797	20 049	–5.6	14.5	74 774	50.1
34 58200	Perth Amboy city	4.8	47 303	633	9 854.8	41 868	636	38 951	5 435	2 917	13.0	7.5	33 033	69.8
34 59190	Plainfield city	6.0	47 829	624	7 971.5	46 556	561	45 555	1 273	1 001	2.7	2.2	12 033	25.2
34 61530	Rahway city	4.0	26 500	1 046	6 625.0	25 314	1 065	26 723	1 186	–1 409	4.7	–5.3	3 675	13.9
34 65790	Sayreville borough	15.9	40 377	746	2 539.4	35 431	758	29 969	4 946	5 462	14.0	18.2	2 942	7.3
34 74000	Trenton city	7.7	85 403	297	11 091.3	88 549	237	92 124	–3 146	–3 575	–3.6	–3.9	18 391	21.5
34 74630	Union City city	1.3	67 088	407	51 606.2	58 051	419	55 593	9 037	2 458	15.6	4.4	55 226	82.3
34 76070	Vineland city	68.7	56 271	512	819.1	54 742	455	53 753	1 529	989	2.8	1.8	16 880	30.0
34 79040	Westfield town	6.7	29 644	987	4 424.5	28 868	948	30 447	776	–1 579	2.7	–5.2	836	2.8
34 79610	West New York town	1.0	45 768	656	45 768.0	38 719	698	39 194	7 049	–475	18.2	–1.2	36 038	78.7

[1] Federal Information Processing Standards (FIPS) codes for states and places defined as of January 1990.   [2] Dry land and land temporarily or partially covered by water.   [3] Based on 1,078 places (1,070 incorporated places and the 8 CDPs in Hawaii). When places share the same rank, the next lower rank is omitted.   [4] Includes count resolution corrections through 1997 and adjustments based on Census 2000 dress rehearsal results and boundary changes reported as legally effective as of January 1, 1998.   [5] Based on 1,071 places (1,070 incorporated places and Honolulu CDP in Hawaii). When places share the same rank, the next lower rank is omitted.   [6] Persons of Hispanic or Latino origin may be of any race.

Sources: Land Area—U.S. Census Bureau, Census of Population and Housing, Census 2000 Redistricting Data (Public Law 94-171) Summary Files (related Internet site <http://www.census.gov/dmd/www/2kresult.html>).   2000 Population—U.S. Census Bureau, 2000 Census of Population and Housing, "Census 2000 Profiles of General Demographic Characteristics" data files, published May 2001, related Internet site <http://www.census.gov/mp/www/pub/2000cen/mscen01.html>.   1990 Population—U.S. Census Bureau, "(SU-99-7) Population Estimates for Places (Sorted Alphabetically Within State): Annual Time Series, July 1, 1990 to July 1, 1999 (includes April 1, 1990 Population Estimates Base)," published 20 October 2000, <http://www.census.gov/population/estimates/metro-city/placebyst/SC99T7_US.txt>.   1980 Population—U.S. Census Bureau, 1990 Census of Population and Housing, "Population and Housing Unit Counts," CPH-2-1 through CPH-2-52.

Table C–1. Cities — Area and Population–Con.

[Includes states and 1,070 incorporated places of 25,000 or more population as of April 1, 1990 in all states except Hawaii which has no incorporated places recognized by the Census Bureau. For Hawaii, 8 census designated places (CDPs) of 25,000 or more population as of April 1, 1990 are included. Also included are the 5 boroughs of New York city. For more information on these areas, see appendix B. Geographic Information]

State and place code[1]	City	Land area,[2] 2000 (sq. miles)	Population (April 1) 2000 Number	Rank[3]	Per square mile	1990[4] Number	Rank[5]	1980	Net change 1990–2000	1980–1990	Percent change 1990–2000	1980–1990	Hispanic or Latino,[6] 2000 Number	Percent
35 00000	NEW MEXICO	121 355.5	1 819 046	X	15.0	1 515 069	X	1 303 302	303 977	211 767	20.1	16.2	765 386	42.1
35 01780	Alamogordo city	19.3	35 582	845	1 843.6	27 986	980	24 024	7 596	3 962	27.1	16.5	11 383	32.0
35 02000	Albuquerque city	180.6	448 607	35	2 484.0	386 988	40	332 920	61 619	54 068	15.9	16.2	179 075	39.9
35 16420	Clovis city	22.4	32 667	913	1 458.3	31 366	876	31 194	1 301	172	4.1	.6	10 924	33.4
35 25800	Farmington city	26.6	37 844	797	1 422.7	34 588	782	31 222	3 256	3 366	9.4	10.8	6 684	17.7
35 32520	Hobbs city	18.9	28 657	1 000	1 516.2	29 445	932	29 153	−788	292	−2.7	1.0	12 088	42.2
35 39380	Las Cruces city	52.1	74 267	358	1 425.5	62 648	383	45 086	11 619	17 562	18.5	39.0	38 421	51.7
35 63530	Rio Rancho city	73.4	51 765	571	705.2	32 551	845	(7)	19 214	X	59.0	X	14 329	27.7
35 64930	Roswell city	28.9	45 293	664	1 567.2	44 480	592	39 676	813	4 804	1.8	12.1	20 084	44.3
35 70500	Santa Fe city	37.3	62 203	442	1 667.6	57 605	423	49 160	4 598	8 445	8.0	17.2	29 744	47.8
36 00000	NEW YORK	47 213.8	18 976 457	X	401.9	17 990 778	X	17 558 165	985 679	432 613	5.5	2.5	2 867 583	15.1
36 01000	Albany city	21.4	95 658	248	4 470.0	100 070	202	101 727	−4 412	−1 657	−4.4	−1.6	5 349	5.6
36 03078	Auburn city	8.4	28 574	1 005	3 401.7	31 470	872	32 548	−2 896	−1 078	−9.2	−3.3	806	2.8
36 06607	Binghamton city	10.4	47 380	632	4 555.8	53 689	468	55 860	−6 309	−2 171	−11.8	−3.9	1 849	3.9
36 11000	Buffalo city	40.6	292 648	58	7 208.1	327 931	50	357 870	−35 283	−29 939	−10.8	−8.4	22 076	7.5
36 24229	Elmira city	7.3	30 940	955	4 238.4	33 833	802	35 327	−2 893	−1 494	−8.6	−4.2	970	3.1
36 27485	Freeport village	4.6	43 783	686	9 518.0	39 820	672	38 272	3 963	1 548	10.0	4.0	14 648	33.5
36 33139	Hempstead village	3.7	56 554	505	15 284.9	45 899	572	40 404	10 655	5 495	23.2	13.6	17 991	31.8
36 38077	Ithaca city	5.5	29 287	993	5 324.9	29 547	926	28 732	−260	815	−.9	2.8	1 555	5.3
36 38264	Jamestown city	9.0	31 730	930	3 525.6	35 050	766	35 775	−3 320	−725	−9.5	−2.0	1 567	4.9
36 42554	Lindenhurst village	3.8	27 819	1 020	7 320.8	26 886	1 016	26 919	933	−33	3.5	−.1	1 813	6.5
36 43335	Long Beach city	2.1	35 462	847	16 886.7	33 518	814	34 073	1 944	−555	5.8	−1.6	4 540	12.8
36 49121	Mount Vernon city	4.4	68 381	396	15 541.1	67 039	347	66 713	1 342	326	2.0	.5	7 083	10.4
36 50034	Newburgh city	3.8	28 259	1 011	7 436.6	26 468	1 035	23 438	1 791	3 030	6.8	12.9	10 257	36.3
36 50617	New Rochelle city	10.4	72 182	369	6 940.6	67 368	345	70 794	4 814	−3 426	7.1	−4.8	14 492	20.1
36 51000	New York city	303.3	8 008 278	1	26 403.8	7 322 564	1	7 071 639	685 714	250 925	9.4	3.5	2 160 554	27.0
36 ...	Bronx borough	42.0	1 332 650	X	31 729.8	1 203 789	X	1 168 972	128 861	34 817	10.7	3.0	644 705	48.4
36 ...	Brooklyn borough	70.6	2 465 326	X	34 919.6	2 300 664	X	2 231 028	164 662	69 636	7.2	3.1	487 878	19.8
36 ...	Manhattan borough	23.0	1 537 195	X	66 834.6	1 487 536	X	1 428 285	49 659	59 251	3.3	4.1	417 816	27.2
36 ...	Queens borough	109.2	2 229 379	X	20 415.6	1 951 598	X	1 891 325	277 781	60 273	14.2	3.2	556 605	25.0
36 ...	Staten Island borough ...	58.5	443 728	X	7 585.1	378 977	X	352 029	64 751	26 948	17.1	7.7	53 550	12.1
36 51055	Niagara Falls city	14.1	55 593	524	3 942.8	61 957	388	71 384	−6 364	−9 427	−10.3	−13.2	1 114	2.0
36 53682	North Tonawanda city	10.1	33 262	903	3 293.3	34 992	770	35 760	−1 730	−768	−4.9	−2.1	362	1.1
36 59641	Poughkeepsie city	5.1	29 871	980	5 857.1	28 860	950	29 757	1 011	−897	3.5	−3.0	3 177	10.6
36 63000	Rochester city	35.8	219 773	79	6 138.9	230 872	66	241 741	−11 099	−10 869	−4.8	−4.5	28 032	12.8
36 63418	Rome city	74.9	34 950	867	466.6	44 439	595	43 826	−9 489	613	−21.4	1.4	1 648	4.7
36 65255	Saratoga Springs city	28.4	26 186	1 055	922.0	25 474	1 061	23 906	712	1 568	2.8	6.6	485	1.9
36 65508	Schenectady city	10.8	61 821	446	5 724.2	65 554	362	67 972	−3 733	−2 418	−5.7	−3.6	3 632	5.9
36 73000	Syracuse city	25.1	147 306	141	5 868.8	163 855	107	170 105	−16 549	−6 250	−10.1	−3.7	7 768	5.3
36 75484	Troy city	10.4	49 170	606	4 727.9	54 801	452	56 638	−5 631	−1 837	−10.3	−3.2	2 131	4.3
36 76540	Utica city	16.3	60 651	454	3 720.9	68 722	337	75 632	−8 071	−6 910	−11.7	−9.1	3 510	5.8
36 76705	Valley Stream village	3.4	36 368	826	10 696.5	33 966	797	35 769	2 402	−1 803	7.1	−5.0	4 463	12.3
36 78608	Watertown city	9.0	26 705	1 045	2 967.2	29 519	929	27 861	−2 814	1 658	−9.5	6.0	960	3.6
36 81677	White Plains city	9.8	53 077	553	5 416.0	48 737	536	46 999	4 340	1 738	8.9	3.7	12 476	23.5
36 84000	Yonkers city	18.1	196 086	95	10 833.5	188 185	87	195 351	7 901	−7 166	4.2	−3.7	50 852	25.9
37 00000	NORTH CAROLINA	48 710.9	8 049 313	X	165.2	6 632 448	X	5 880 095	1 416 865	752 353	21.4	12.8	378 963	4.7
37 02140	Asheville city	40.9	68 889	389	1 684.3	66 184	355	54 022	2 705	12 162	4.1	22.5	2 589	3.8
37 09060	Burlington city	21.3	44 917	670	2 108.8	40 822	654	37 266	4 095	3 556	10.0	9.5	4 525	10.1
37 10740	Cary town	42.1	94 536	254	2 245.5	45 497	577	21 763	49 039	23 734	107.8	109.1	4 047	4.3
37 11800	Chapel Hill town	19.8	48 715	612	2 460.4	38 346	705	32 421	10 369	5 925	27.0	18.3	1 564	3.2
37 12000	Charlotte city	242.3	540 828	26	2 232.1	426 984	33	315 474	113 844	111 510	26.7	35.3	39 800	7.4
37 14100	Concord city	51.6	55 977	517	1 084.8	37 661	724	16 942	18 316	20 719	48.6	122.3	4 369	7.8
37 19000	Durham city	94.6	187 035	103	1 977.1	148 450	121	101 149	38 585	47 301	26.0	46.8	16 012	8.6
37 22920	Fayetteville city	58.8	121 015	180	2 058.1	112 644	165	59 507	8 371	53 137	7.4	89.3	6 862	5.7
37 25580	Gastonia city	46.1	66 277	413	1 437.7	59 757	405	47 218	6 520	12 539	10.9	26.6	3 613	5.5
37 26880	Goldsboro city	24.8	39 043	774	1 574.3	44 966	585	31 871	−5 923	13 095	−13.2	41.1	1 052	2.7
37 28000	Greensboro city	104.7	223 891	77	2 138.4	191 591	83	155 642	32 300	35 949	16.9	23.1	9 742	4.4
37 28080	Greenville city	25.6	60 476	457	2 362.3	49 366	529	35 740	11 110	13 626	22.5	38.1	1 244	2.1
37 31060	Hickory city	28.1	37 222	810	1 324.6	29 474	931	20 757	7 748	8 717	26.3	42.0	2 863	7.7
37 31400	High Point city	49.0	85 839	290	1 751.8	69 763	333	63 479	16 076	6 284	23.0	9.9	4 197	4.9
37 34200	Jacksonville city	44.5	66 715	409	1 499.2	78 080	284	18 237	−11 365	59 843	−14.6	328.1	6 702	10.0

[1] Federal Information Processing Standards (FIPS) codes for states and places defined as of January 1990. [2] Dry land and land temporarily or partially covered by water. [3] Based on 1,078 places (1,070 incorporated places and the 8 CDPs in Hawaii). When places share the same rank, the next lower rank is omitted. [4] Includes count resolution corrections through 1997 and adjustments based on Census 2000 dress rehearsal results and boundary changes reported as legally effective as of January 1, 1998. [5] Based on 1,071 places (1,070 incorporated places and Honolulu CDP in Hawaii). When places share the same rank, the next lower rank is omitted. [6] Persons of Hispanic or Latino origin may be of any race. [7] Not incorporated as of January 1, 1980.

Sources: Land Area—U.S. Census Bureau, Census of Population and Housing, Census 2000 Redistricting Data (Public Law 94-171) Summary Files (related Internet site <http://www.census.gov/dmd/www/2kresult.html>). 2000 Population—U.S. Census Bureau, 2000 Census of Population and Housing, "Census 2000 Profiles of General Demographic Characteristics" data files, published May 2001, related Internet site <http://www.census.gov/mp/www/pub/2000cen/mscen01.html>. 1990 Population—U.S. Census Bureau, "(SU-99-7) Population Estimates for Places (Sorted Alphabetically Within State): Annual Time Series, July 1, 1990 to July 1, 1999 (includes April 1, 1990 Population Estimates Base)," published 20 October 2000, <http://www.census.gov/population/estimates/metro-city/placebyst/SC99T7_US.txt>. 1980 Population—U.S. Census Bureau, 1990 Census of Population and Housing, "Population and Housing Unit Counts," CPH-2-1 through CPH-2-52.

Table C–1. Cities — **Area and Population**–Con.

[Includes states and 1,070 incorporated places of 25,000 or more population as of April 1, 1990 in all states except Hawaii which has no incorporated places recognized by the Census Bureau. For Hawaii, 8 census designated places (CDPs) of 25,000 or more population as of April 1, 1990 are included. Also included are the 5 boroughs of New York city. For more information on these areas, see appendix B. Geographic Information]

State and place code[1]	City	Land area,[2] 2000 (sq. miles)	Population (April 1)											
			2000			1990[4]		1980	Net change		Percent change		Hispanic or Latino,[6] 2000	
			Number	Rank[3]	Per square mile	Number	Rank[5]		1990–2000	1980–1990	1990–2000	1980–1990	Number	Percent
	NORTH CAROLINA— Con.													
37 35200	Kannapolis city	29.9	36 910	813	1 234.4	32 404	850	(7)	4 506	X	13.9	X	2 337	6.3
37 35920	Kinston city	16.7	23 688	1 075	1 418.4	25 883	1 052	25 234	-2 195	649	-8.5	2.6	269	1.1
37 55000	Raleigh city	114.6	276 093	62	2 409.2	220 425	74	150 255	55 668	70 170	25.3	46.7	19 308	7.0
37 57500	Rocky Mount city	35.6	55 893	520	1 570.0	54 339	458	41 526	1 554	12 813	2.9	30.9	1 033	1.8
37 74440	Wilmington city	41.0	75 838	350	1 849.7	56 067	437	44 000	19 771	12 067	35.3	27.4	1 991	2.6
37 74540	Wilson city	23.3	44 405	678	1 905.8	39 056	687	34 424	5 349	4 632	13.7	13.5	3 237	7.3
37 75000	Winston-Salem city	108.9	185 776	107	1 705.9	167 254	105	131 885	18 522	35 369	11.1	26.8	16 043	8.6
38 00000	NORTH DAKOTA	68 975.9	642 200	X	9.3	638 800	X	652 717	3 400	-13 917	.5	-2.1	7 786	1.2
38 07200	Bismarck city	26.9	55 532	526	2 064.4	50 005	520	44 485	5 527	5 520	11.1	12.4	415	.7
38 25700	Fargo city	37.9	90 599	270	2 390.5	74 195	302	61 383	16 404	12 812	22.1	20.9	1 167	1.3
38 32060	Grand Forks city	19.2	49 321	603	2 568.8	49 563	526	43 765	-242	5 798	-.5	13.2	921	1.9
38 53380	Minot city	14.6	36 567	820	2 504.6	34 746	776	32 843	1 821	1 903	5.2	5.8	539	1.5
39 00000	OHIO	40 948.4	11 353 140	X	277.3	10 847 115	X	10 797 603	506 025	49 512	4.7	.5	217 123	1.9
39 01000	Akron city	62.1	217 074	81	3 495.6	223 182	71	237 177	-6 108	-13 995	-2.7	-5.9	2 513	1.2
39 03828	Barberton city	9.0	27 899	1 018	3 099.9	27 821	986	29 751	78	-1 930	.3	-6.5	179	.6
39 04720	Beavercreek city	26.4	37 984	796	1 438.8	33 579	811	31 589	4 405	1 990	13.1	6.3	433	1.1
39 07972	Bowling Green city	10.2	29 636	988	2 905.5	28 867	949	25 728	769	3 139	2.7	12.2	1 031	3.5
39 09680	Brunswick city	12.5	33 388	901	2 671.0	28 440	964	28 104	4 948	336	17.4	1.2	454	1.4
39 12000	Canton city	20.5	80 806	319	3 941.8	84 047	263	93 077	-3 241	-9 030	-3.9	-9.7	1 006	1.2
39 15000	Cincinnati city	78.0	331 285	54	4 247.2	364 553	45	385 409	-33 268	-20 856	-9.1	-5.4	4 230	1.3
39 16000	Cleveland city	77.6	478 403	33	6 165.0	505 450	23	573 822	-27 047	-68 372	-5.4	-11.9	34 728	7.3
39 16014	Cleveland Heights city	8.1	49 958	591	6 167.7	54 087	461	56 438	-4 129	-2 351	-7.6	-4.2	791	1.6
39 18000	Columbus city	210.3	711 470	15	3 383.1	636 323	15	565 021	75 147	71 302	11.8	12.6	17 471	2.5
39 19778	Cuyahoga Falls city	25.5	49 374	600	1 936.2	48 867	532	43 890	507	4 977	1.0	11.3	309	.6
39 21000	Dayton city	55.8	166 179	123	2 978.1	182 393	93	193 536	-16 214	-11 143	-8.9	-5.8	2 626	1.6
39 23380	East Cleveland city	3.1	27 217	1 033	8 779.7	33 092	827	36 957	-5 875	-3 865	-17.8	-10.5	207	.8
39 25256	Elyria city	19.9	55 953	519	2 811.7	56 628	433	57 538	-675	-910	-1.2	-1.6	1 553	2.8
39 25704	Euclid city	10.7	52 717	561	4 926.8	54 864	451	59 999	-2 147	-5 135	-3.9	-8.6	604	1.1
39 25914	Fairborn city	13.1	32 052	926	2 446.7	30 953	885	29 702	1 099	1 251	3.6	4.2	542	1.7
39 25970	Fairfield city	21.0	42 097	710	2 004.6	39 704	675	30 777	2 393	8 927	6.0	29.0	646	1.5
39 27018	Findlay city	17.2	38 967	778	2 265.5	36 037	748	35 594	2 930	443	8.1	1.2	1 539	3.9
39 29106	Gahanna city	12.4	32 636	915	2 631.9	24 009	1 071	18 001	8 627	6 008	35.9	33.4	430	1.3
39 29428	Garfield Heights city	7.2	30 734	959	4 268.6	31 736	868	34 938	-1 002	-3 202	-3.2	-9.2	388	1.3
39 33012	Hamilton city	21.6	60 690	453	2 809.7	61 345	393	63 189	-655	-1 844	-1.1	-2.9	1 566	2.6
39 36610	Huber Heights city	21.0	38 212	792	1 819.6	38 675	701	35 480	-463	3 195	-1.2	9.0	635	1.7
39 39872	Kent city	8.7	27 906	1 016	3 207.6	28 852	951	26 164	-946	2 688	-3.3	10.3	357	1.3
39 40040	Kettering city	18.7	57 502	496	3 075.0	60 410	401	61 186	-2 908	-776	-4.8	-1.3	640	1.1
39 41664	Lakewood city	5.5	56 646	504	10 299.3	59 649	407	61 963	-3 003	-2 314	-5.0	-3.7	1 269	2.2
39 41720	Lancaster city	18.1	35 335	852	1 952.2	34 570	783	34 953	765	-383	2.2	-1.1	291	.8
39 43554	Lima city	12.8	40 081	753	3 131.3	45 140	583	47 827	-5 059	-2 687	-11.2	-5.6	789	2.0
39 44856	Lorain city	24.0	68 652	393	2 860.5	71 326	325	75 416	-2 674	-4 090	-3.7	-5.4	14 438	21.0
39 47138	Mansfield city	29.9	49 346	601	1 650.4	50 925	509	53 927	-1 579	-3 002	-3.1	-5.6	605	1.2
39 47306	Maple Heights city	5.2	26 156	1 056	5 030.0	27 089	1 013	29 735	-933	-2 646	-3.4	-8.9	316	1.2
39 47754	Marion city	11.3	35 318	853	3 125.5	36 227	742	37 040	-909	-813	-2.5	-2.2	474	1.3
39 48244	Massillon city	16.7	31 325	946	1 875.7	31 136	880	30 557	189	579	.6	1.9	301	1.0
39 49056	Mentor city	26.8	50 278	508	1 876.0	47 539	550	42 065	2 739	5 474	5.8	13.0	363	.7
39 49840	Middletown city	25.7	51 605	572	2 008.0	51 863	493	43 719	-258	8 144	-.5	18.6	460	.9
39 54040	Newark city	19.6	46 279	648	2 361.2	44 902	586	41 200	1 377	3 702	3.1	9.0	390	.8
39 56882	North Olmsted city	11.6	34 113	880	2 940.8	34 206	794	36 486	-93	-2 280	-.3	-6.2	575	1.7
39 61000	Parma city	20.0	85 655	295	4 282.8	87 650	239	92 548	-1 995	-4 898	-2.3	-5.3	1 323	1.5
39 66390	Reynoldsburg city	10.6	32 069	925	3 025.4	26 162	1 047	20 661	5 907	5 501	22.6	26.6	578	1.8
39 70380	Sandusky city	10.0	27 844	1 019	2 784.4	29 571	925	31 360	-1 727	-1 789	-5.8	-5.7	859	3.1
39 71682	Shaker Heights city	6.3	29 405	989	4 667.5	30 928	888	32 487	-1 523	-1 559	-4.9	-4.8	339	1.2
39 74118	Springfield city	22.5	65 358	418	2 904.8	70 718	329	72 563	-5 360	-1 845	-7.6	-2.5	770	1.2
39 74944	Stow city	17.1	32 139	923	1 879.5	27 652	989	25 303	4 487	2 349	16.2	9.3	291	.9
39 75098	Strongsville city	24.6	43 858	685	1 782.8	35 305	760	28 577	8 553	6 728	24.2	23.5	557	1.3
39 77000	Toledo city	80.6	313 619	56	3 891.1	332 832	49	354 635	-19 213	-21 803	-5.8	-6.1	17 141	5.5
39 79002	Upper Arlington city	9.8	33 686	897	3 437.3	34 292	789	35 648	-606	-1 356	-1.8	-3.8	330	1.0
39 80892	Warren city	16.1	46 832	639	2 908.8	50 890	511	56 629	-4 058	-5 739	-8.0	-10.1	485	1.0
39 83342	Westerville city	12.4	35 318	853	2 848.2	30 901	889	23 414	4 417	7 487	14.3	32.0	379	1.1
39 83622	Westlake city	15.9	31 719	932	1 994.9	27 014	1 014	19 483	4 705	7 531	17.4	38.7	402	1.3
39 88000	Youngstown city	33.9	82 026	313	2 419.6	95 695	217	115 511	-13 669	-19 816	-14.3	-17.2	4 282	5.2
39 88084	Zanesville city	11.2	25 586	1 064	2 284.5	27 226	1 006	28 655	-1 640	-1 429	-6.0	-5.0	202	.8

[1] Federal Information Processing Standards (FIPS) codes for states and places defined as of January 1990. [2] Dry land and land temporarily or partially covered by water. [3] Based on 1,078 places (1,070 incorporated places and the 8 CDPs in Hawaii). When places share the same rank, the next lower rank is omitted. [4] Includes count resolution corrections through 1997 and adjustments based on Census 2000 dress rehearsal results and boundary changes reported as legally effective as of January 1, 1998. [5] Based on 1,071 places (1,070 incorporated places and Honolulu CDP in Hawaii). When places share the same rank, the next lower rank is omitted. [6] Persons of Hispanic or Latino origin may be of any race. [7] Not incorporated as of January 1, 1980.

Sources: Land Area—U.S. Census Bureau, Census of Population and Housing, Census 2000 Redistricting Data (Public Law 94-171) Summary Files (related Internet site <http://www.census.gov/dmd/www/2kresult.html>). 2000 Population—U.S. Census Bureau, 2000 Census of Population and Housing, "Census 2000 Profiles of General Demographic Characteristics" data files, published May 2001, related Internet site <http://www.census.gov/mp/www/pub/2000cen/mscen01.html>. 1990 Population—U.S. Census Bureau, "(SU-99-7) Population Estimates for Places (Sorted Alphabetically Within State): Annual Time Series, July 1, 1990 to July 1, 1999 (includes April 1, 1990 Population Estimates Base)," published 20 October 2000, <http://www.census.gov/population/estimates/metro-city/placebyst/SC99T7_US.txt>. 1980 Population—U.S. Census Bureau, 1990 Census of Population and Housing, "Population and Housing Unit Counts," CPH-2-1 through CPH-2-52.

Table C–1. Cities — **Area and Population**–Con.

[Includes states and 1,070 incorporated places of 25,000 or more population as of April 1, 1990 in all states except Hawaii which has no incorporated places recognized by the Census Bureau. For Hawaii, 8 census designated places (CDPs) of 25,000 or more population as of April 1, 1990 are included. Also included are the 5 boroughs of New York city. For more information on these areas, see appendix B. Geographic Information]

State and place code[1]	City	Land area,[2] 2000 (sq. miles)	Population (April 1)						Net change		Percent change		Hispanic or Latino,[6] 2000	
			2000			1990[4]								
			Number	Rank[3]	Per square mile	Number	Rank[5]	1980	1990–2000	1980–1990	1990–2000	1980–1990	Number	Percent
40 00000	OKLAHOMA	68 667.1	3 450 654	X	50.3	3 145 576	X	3 025 487	305 078	120 089	9.7	4.0	179 304	5.2
40 04450	Bartlesville city	21.1	34 748	870	1 646.8	34 332	788	34 568	416	−236	1.2	−.7	1 049	3.0
40 09050	Broken Arrow city	45.0	74 859	355	1 663.5	58 294	418	35 761	16 565	22 533	28.4	63.0	2 664	3.6
40 23200	Edmond city	85.1	68 315	398	802.8	52 354	485	34 637	15 961	17 717	30.5	51.2	1 881	2.8
40 23950	Enid city	74.0	47 045	637	635.7	45 348	579	50 363	1 697	−5 015	3.7	−10.0	2 232	4.7
40 41850	Lawton city	75.1	92 757	261	1 235.1	80 950	271	80 054	11 807	896	14.6	1.1	8 719	9.4
40 48350	Midwest City city	24.6	54 088	544	2 198.7	52 345	486	49 559	1 743	2 786	3.3	5.6	2 192	4.1
40 49200	Moore city	21.7	41 138	728	1 895.8	40 236	668	35 063	902	5 173	2.2	14.8	2 098	5.1
40 50050	Muskogee city	37.3	38 310	788	1 027.1	38 231	708	40 011	79	−1 780	.2	−4.4	1 258	3.3
40 52500	Norman city	177.0	95 694	247	540.6	80 255	275	68 020	15 439	12 235	19.2	18.0	3 723	3.9
40 55000	Oklahoma City city	607.0	506 132	29	833.8	444 605	30	404 014	61 527	40 591	13.8	10.0	51 368	10.1
40 59850	Ponca City city	18.1	25 919	1 060	1 432.0	26 637	1 029	26 238	−718	399	−2.7	1.5	1 149	4.4
40 66800	Shawnee city	42.3	28 692	999	678.3	27 165	1 008	26 506	1 527	659	5.6	2.5	781	2.7
40 70300	Stillwater city	27.8	39 065	772	1 405.2	36 692	737	38 268	2 373	−1 576	6.5	−4.1	976	2.5
40 75000	Tulsa city	182.6	393 049	43	2 152.5	367 167	44	360 919	25 882	6 248	7.0	1.7	28 111	7.2
41 00000	OREGON	95 996.8	3 421 399	X	35.6	2 842 337	X	2 633 156	579 062	209 181	20.4	7.9	275 314	8.0
41 01000	Albany city	15.9	40 852	733	2 569.3	33 230	824	26 511	7 622	6 719	22.9	25.3	2 489	6.1
41 05350	Beaverton city	16.3	76 129	348	4 670.5	54 364	457	31 962	21 765	22 402	40.0	70.1	8 463	11.1
41 15800	Corvallis city	13.6	49 322	602	3 626.6	44 804	587	40 960	4 518	3 844	10.1	9.4	2 820	5.7
41 23850	Eugene city	40.5	137 893	156	3 404.8	113 913	162	105 664	23 980	8 249	21.1	7.8	6 843	5.0
41 31250	Gresham city	22.2	90 205	273	4 063.3	68 234	341	33 005	21 971	35 229	32.2	106.7	10 732	11.9
41 34100	Hillsboro city	21.6	70 186	381	3 249.4	38 983	689	27 664	31 203	11 319	80.0	40.9	13 262	18.9
41 40550	Lake Oswego city	10.3	35 278	855	3 425.0	30 624	902	22 527	4 654	8 097	15.2	35.9	820	2.3
41 47000	Medford city	21.7	63 154	435	2 910.3	48 774	535	39 746	14 380	9 028	29.5	22.7	5 841	9.2
41 59000	Portland city	134.3	529 121	28	3 939.8	486 083	27	368 148	43 038	117 935	8.9	32.0	36 058	6.8
41 64900	Salem city	45.7	136 924	158	2 996.1	108 846	179	89 091	28 078	19 755	25.8	22.2	19 973	14.6
41 69600	Springfield city	14.4	52 864	559	3 671.1	44 787	588	41 621	8 077	3 166	18.0	7.6	3 651	6.9
41 73650	Tigard city	10.9	41 223	724	3 781.9	30 288	913	14 799	10 935	15 489	36.1	104.7	3 686	8.9
42 00000	PENNSYLVANIA	44 816.6	12 281 054	X	274.0	11 882 842	X	11 864 720	398 212	18 122	3.4	.2	394 088	3.2
42 02000	Allentown city	17.7	106 632	215	6 024.4	105 473	188	103 758	1 159	1 715	1.1	1.7	26 058	24.4
42 02184	Altoona city	9.8	49 523	596	5 053.4	52 385	484	57 078	−2 862	−4 693	−5.5	−8.2	367	.7
42 06064	Bethel Park borough	11.7	33 556	898	2 868.0	33 952	798	34 755	−396	−803	−1.2	−2.3	164	.5
42 06088	Bethlehem city	19.3	71 329	375	3 695.8	71 855	317	70 419	−526	1 436	−.7	2.0	13 002	18.2
42 13208	Chester city	4.8	36 854	814	7 677.9	41 973	632	45 794	−5 119	−3 821	−12.2	−8.3	1 986	5.4
42 21648	Easton city	4.6	26 263	1 053	6 107.7	26 369	1 038	26 027	−106	342	−.4	1.3	2 570	9.8
42 24000	Erie city	22.0	103 717	222	4 714.4	108 717	180	119 123	−5 000	−10 406	−4.6	−8.7	4 572	4.4
42 32800	Harrisburg city	8.1	48 950	609	6 043.2	51 964	492	53 264	−3 014	−1 300	−5.8	−2.4	5 724	11.7
42 38288	Johnstown city	5.8	23 906	1 074	4 121.7	28 087	976	35 496	−4 181	−7 409	−14.9	−20.9	380	1.6
42 41216	Lancaster city	7.4	56 348	508	7 614.6	55 720	442	54 725	628	995	1.1	1.8	17 331	30.8
42 46256	McKeesport city	5.0	24 040	1 073	4 808.0	26 000	1 051	31 012	−1 960	−5 012	−7.5	−16.2	361	1.5
42 52330	Municipality of Monroeville borough	19.8	29 349	992	1 482.3	29 152	940	30 977	197	−1 825	.7	−5.9	225	.8
42 53368	New Castle city	8.5	26 309	1 051	3 095.2	28 365	966	33 621	−2 056	−5 256	−7.2	−15.6	199	.8
42 54656	Norristown borough	3.5	31 282	949	8 937.7	30 496	910	34 684	786	−4 188	2.6	−12.1	3 282	10.5
42 60000	Philadelphia city	135.1	1 517 550	5	11 232.8	1 585 577	5	1 688 210	−68 027	−102 633	−4.3	−6.1	128 928	8.5
42 61000	Pittsburgh city	55.6	334 563	52	6 017.3	370 139	42	423 959	−35 576	−53 820	−9.6	−12.7	4 425	1.3
42 61536	Plum borough	28.6	26 940	1 039	942.0	25 664	1 054	25 390	1 276	274	5.0	1.1	167	.6
42 63624	Reading city	9.8	81 207	316	8 286.4	77 864	285	78 686	3 343	−822	4.3	−1.0	30 302	37.3
42 69000	Scranton city	25.2	76 415	347	3 032.3	81 914	267	88 117	−5 499	−6 203	−6.7	−7.0	1 999	2.6
42 73808	State College borough	4.5	38 420	786	8 537.8	38 988	688	36 130	−568	2 858	−1.5	7.9	1 159	3.0
42 85152	Wilkes-Barre city	8.9	43 123	695	6 341.6	47 653	548	51 551	−4 530	−3 898	−9.5	−7.6	683	1.6
42 85312	Williamsport city	8.9	30 706	961	3 450.1	32 270	853	33 401	−1 564	−1 131	−4.8	−3.4	340	1.1
42 87048	York city	5.2	40 862	732	7 858.1	42 205	628	44 619	−1 343	−2 414	−3.2	−5.4	7 026	17.2
44 00000	RHODE ISLAND	1 044.9	1 048 319	X	1 003.3	1 003 464	X	947 154	44 855	56 310	4.5	5.9	90 820	8.7
44 19180	Cranston city	28.6	79 269	331	2 771.6	76 275	293	71 992	2 994	4 283	3.9	5.9	3 613	4.6
44 22960	East Providence city	13.4	48 688	613	3 633.4	50 439	516	50 980	−1 751	−541	−3.5	−1.1	922	1.9
44 49960	Newport city	7.9	26 475	1 047	3 351.3	28 462	963	29 259	−1 987	−797	−7.0	−2.7	1 467	5.5
44 54640	Pawtucket city	8.7	72 958	363	8 386.0	72 395	311	71 204	563	1 191	.8	1.7	10 141	13.9
44 59000	Providence city	18.5	173 618	119	9 384.8	160 281	110	156 804	13 337	3 477	8.3	2.2	52 146	30.0
44 74300	Warwick city	35.5	85 808	291	2 417.1	85 324	256	87 123	484	−1 799	.6	−2.1	1 372	1.6
44 80780	Woonsocket city	7.7	43 224	691	5 613.5	44 479	593	45 914	−1 255	−1 435	−2.8	−3.1	4 030	9.3

[1] Federal Information Processing Standards (FIPS) codes for states and places defined as of January 1990. [2] Dry land and land temporarily or partially covered by water. [3] Based on 1,078 places (1,070 incorporated places and the 8 CDPs in Hawaii). When places share the same rank, the next lower rank is omitted. [4] Includes count resolution corrections through 1997 and adjustments based on Census 2000 dress rehearsal results and boundary changes reported as legally effective as of January 1, 1998. [5] Based on 1,071 places (1,070 incorporated places and Honolulu CDP in Hawaii). When places share the same rank, the next lower rank is omitted. [6] Persons of Hispanic or Latino origin may be of any race.

Sources: Land Area—U.S. Census Bureau, Census of Population and Housing, Census 2000 Redistricting Data (Public Law 94-171) Summary Files (related Internet site <http://www.census.gov/dmd/www/2kresult.html>). 2000 Population—U.S. Census Bureau, 2000 Census of Population and Housing, "Census 2000 Profiles of General Demographic Characteristics" data files, published May 2001, related Internet site <http://www.census.gov/mp/www/pub/2000cen/mscen01.html>. 1990 Population—U.S. Census Bureau, "(SU-99-7) Population Estimates for Places (Sorted Alphabetically Within State): Annual Time Series, July 1, 1990 to July 1, 1999 (includes April 1, 1990 Population Estimates Base)," published 20 October 2000, <http://www.census.gov/population/estimates/metro-city/placebyst/SC99T7_US.txt>. 1980 Population—U.S. Census Bureau, 1990 Census of Population and Housing, "Population and Housing Unit Counts," CPH-2-1 through CPH-2-52.

Table C–1. Cities — **Area and Population**–Con.

[Includes states and 1,070 incorporated places of 25,000 or more population as of April 1, 1990 in all states except Hawaii which has no incorporated places recognized by the Census Bureau. For Hawaii, 8 census designated places (CDPs) of 25,000 or more population as of April 1, 1990 are included. Also included are the 5 boroughs of New York city. For more information on these areas, see appendix B. Geographic Information]

State and place code[1]	City	Land area,[2] 2000 (sq. miles)	Population (April 1)											
			2000			1990[4]		1980	Net change		Percent change		Hispanic or Latino,[6] 2000	
			Number	Rank[3]	Per square mile	Number	Rank[5]		1990–2000	1980–1990	1990–2000	1980–1990	Number	Percent
45 00000	SOUTH CAROLINA	30 109.5	4 012 012	X	133.2	3 486 310	X	3 120 729	525 702	365 581	15.1	11.7	95 076	2.4
45 01360	Anderson city	13.8	25 514	1 066	1 848.8	26 649	1 028	27 546	−1 135	−897	−4.3	−3.3	377	1.5
45 13330	Charleston city	97.0	96 650	244	996.4	90 620	229	69 779	6 030	20 841	6.7	29.9	1 462	1.5
45 16000	Columbia city	125.2	116 278	191	928.7	114 462	160	101 229	1 816	13 233	1.6	13.1	3 520	3.0
45 25810	Florence city	17.7	30 248	967	1 708.9	30 881	890	29 842	−633	1 039	−2.0	3.5	229	.8
45 30850	Greenville city	26.1	56 002	516	2 145.7	58 548	416	58 242	−2 546	306	−4.3	.5	1 927	3.4
45 48535	Mount Pleasant town	41.9	47 609	628	1 136.3	31 072	883	14 464	16 537	16 608	53.2	114.8	635	1.3
45 50875	North Charleston city	58.5	79 641	325	1 361.4	85 384	255	62 479	−5 743	22 905	−6.7	36.7	3 163	4.0
45 61405	Rock Hill city	31.0	49 765	593	1 605.3	42 894	617	35 327	6 871	7 567	16.0	21.4	1 236	2.5
45 68290	Spartanburg city	19.2	39 673	761	2 066.3	43 673	604	43 826	−4 000	−153	−9.2	−.3	706	1.8
45 70405	Sumter city	26.6	39 643	762	1 490.3	43 181	610	24 921	−3 538	18 260	−8.2	73.3	938	2.4
46 00000	SOUTH DAKOTA	75 884.6	754 844	X	9.9	696 004	X	690 768	58 840	5 236	8.5	.8	10 903	1.4
46 52980	Rapid City city	44.6	59 607	472	1 336.5	55 162	447	46 492	4 445	8 670	8.1	18.6	1 650	2.8
46 59020	Sioux Falls city..........	56.3	123 975	174	2 202.0	101 461	197	81 343	22 514	20 118	22.2	24.7	3 087	2.5
47 00000	TENNESSEE...........	41 217.1	5 689 283	X	138.0	4 877 203	X	4 591 023	812 080	286 180	16.7	6.2	123 838	2.2
47 03440	Bartlett town	19.1	40 543	740	2 122.7	27 927	982	17 170	12 616	10 757	45.2	62.6	462	1.1
47 14000	Chattanooga city	135.2	155 554	129	1 150.5	152 828	116	169 514	2 726	−16 686	1.8	−9.8	3 281	2.1
47 15160	Clarksville city	94.9	103 455	224	1 090.1	76 508	290	54 777	26 947	21 731	35.2	39.7	6 241	6.0
47 15400	Cleveland city	24.9	37 192	811	1 493.7	32 528	847	26 415	4 664	6 113	14.3	23.1	1 066	2.9
47 16540	Columbia city	29.6	33 055	906	1 116.7	28 924	946	26 571	4 131	2 353	14.3	8.9	1 554	4.7
47 28960	Germantown city	17.6	37 348	807	2 122.0	32 984	833	21 467	4 364	11 517	13.2	53.6	407	1.1
47 33280	Hendersonville city	27.3	40 620	739	1 487.9	32 671	842	26 561	7 949	6 110	24.3	23.0	696	1.7
47 37640	Jackson city	49.5	59 643	470	1 204.9	51 626	497	49 258	8 017	2 368	15.5	4.8	1 289	2.2
47 38320	Johnson City city	39.3	55 469	528	1 411.4	51 732	494	39 753	3 737	11 979	7.2	30.1	1 048	1.9
47 39560	Kingsport city	44.1	44 905	671	1 018.3	42 238	627	32 027	2 667	10 211	6.3	31.9	471	1.0
47 40000	Knoxville city	92.7	173 890	117	1 875.8	173 186	101	175 045	704	−1 859	.4	−1.1	2 751	1.6
47 48000	Memphis city	279.3	650 100	18	2 327.6	618 894	18	646 174	31 206	−27 280	5.0	−4.2	19 317	3.0
47 51560	Murfreesboro city	39.0	68 816	391	1 764.5	45 592	575	32 845	23 224	12 747	50.9	38.8	2 430	3.5
47 52006	Nashville-Davidson (remainder)	473.3	545 524	25	1 152.6	488 188	26	455 651	57 336	32 537	11.7	7.1	25 774	4.7
47 55120	Oak Ridge city	85.5	27 387	1 029	320.3	27 327	1 000	27 662	60	−335	.2	−1.2	529	1.9
48 00000	TEXAS	261 797.1	20 851 820	X	79.6	16 986 335	X	14 225 513	3 865 485	2 760 822	22.8	19.4	6 669 666	32.0
48 01000	Abilene city.............	105.1	115 930	193	1 103.0	106 925	184	98 315	9 005	8 610	8.4	8.8	22 548	19.4
48 03000	Amarillo city	89.9	173 627	118	1 931.3	157 861	113	149 230	15 766	8 631	10.0	5.8	37 947	21.9
48 04000	Arlington city	95.8	332 969	53	3 475.7	261 999	61	160 113	70 970	101 886	27.1	63.6	60 817	18.3
48 05000	Austin city	251.5	656 562	16	2 610.6	494 290	25	345 890	162 272	148 400	32.8	42.9	200 579	30.5
48 06128	Baytown city	32.7	66 430	410	2 031.5	64 274	368	56 923	2 156	7 351	3.4	12.9	22 748	34.2
48 07000	Beaumont city	85.0	113 866	196	1 339.6	114 417	161	118 102	−551	−3 685	−.5	−3.1	9 028	7.9
48 07132	Bedford city	10.0	47 152	636	4 715.2	43 742	602	20 821	3 410	22 921	7.8	110.1	3 403	7.2
48 10768	Brownsville city	80.4	139 722	151	1 737.8	115 143	158	84 997	24 579	30 146	21.3	35.5	127 535	91.3
48 10912	Bryan city	43.3	65 660	416	1 516.4	55 215	446	44 337	10 445	10 878	18.9	24.5	18 271	27.8
48 13024	Carrollton city	30.5	109 576	205	3 002.1	82 501	264	40 505	26 986	41 996	32.7	103.5	21 400	19.5
48 15976	College Station city	40.3	67 890	399	1 684.6	52 984	477	37 272	14 906	15 712	28.1	42.2	6 759	10.0
48 16432	Conroe city	37.8	36 811	816	973.8	28 991	944	18 034	7 820	10 957	27.0	60.8	12 006	32.6
48 17000	Corpus Christi city	154.6	277 454	60	1 794.7	258 439	64	232 134	19 015	26 305	7.4	11.3	150 737	54.3
48 19000	Dallas city	342.5	1 188 580	8	3 470.3	1 006 646	8	904 599	181 934	102 047	18.1	11.3	422 587	35.6
48 19624	Deer Park city	10.4	28 520	1 007	2 742.3	27 581	991	22 648	939	4 933	3.4	21.8	4 341	15.2
48 19792	Del Rio city	15.4	33 867	888	2 199.2	31 209	879	30 034	2 658	1 175	8.5	3.9	27 446	81.0
48 19972	Denton city	61.5	80 537	320	1 309.5	66 693	352	48 063	13 844	18 630	20.8	38.8	13 188	16.4
48 20092	DeSoto city	21.6	37 646	802	1 742.9	30 613	904	15 538	7 033	15 075	23.0	97.0	2 750	7.3
48 21628	Duncanville city	11.3	36 081	834	3 193.0	34 955	771	27 781	1 126	7 174	3.2	25.8	5 522	15.3
48 22660	Edinburg city	37.4	48 465	615	1 295.9	34 593	780	24 075	13 872	10 518	40.1	43.7	42 981	88.7
48 24000	El Paso city	249.1	563 662	22	2 262.8	515 652	22	425 259	48 010	90 393	9.3	21.3	431 875	76.6
48 24768	Euless city	16.3	46 005	651	2 822.4	38 288	707	24 002	7 717	14 286	20.2	59.5	6 125	13.3
48 27000	Fort Worth city	292.5	534 694	27	1 828.0	448 181	29	385 164	86 513	63 017	19.3	16.4	159 368	29.8
48 28068	Galveston city	46.2	57 247	497	1 239.1	59 606	408	61 902	−2 359	−2 296	−4.0	−3.7	14 753	25.8
48 29000	Garland city	57.1	215 768	82	3 778.8	180 844	94	138 857	34 924	41 987	19.3	30.2	55 192	25.6
48 30464	Grand Prairie city	71.4	127 427	168	1 784.7	99 496	203	71 462	27 931	28 034	28.1	39.2	42 038	33.0
48 30644	Grapevine city	32.3	42 059	712	1 302.1	29 545	927	11 801	12 514	17 744	42.4	150.4	4 860	11.6
48 31928	Haltom City city	12.4	39 018	775	3 146.6	32 760	840	29 014	6 258	3 746	19.1	12.9	7 771	19.9
48 32372	Harlingen city	34.1	57 564	495	1 688.1	47 818	545	43 543	9 746	4 275	20.4	9.8	41 881	72.8
48 35000	Houston city............	579.4	1 953 631	4	3 371.8	1 697 873	4	1 595 138	255 758	102 735	15.1	6.4	730 865	37.4
48 35528	Huntsville city	30.9	35 078	862	1 135.2	30 942	887	23 936	4 136	7 006	13.4	29.3	5 689	16.2
48 35576	Hurst city	9.9	36 273	829	3 663.9	33 308	821	31 420	2 965	1 888	8.9	6.0	3 999	11.0
48 37000	Irving city	67.2	191 615	100	2 851.4	155 130	115	109 943	36 485	45 187	23.5	41.1	59 838	31.2
48 39148	Killeen city	35.3	86 911	287	2 462.1	63 936	371	46 296	22 975	17 640	35.9	38.1	15 469	17.8

[1] Federal Information Processing Standards (FIPS) codes for states and places defined as of January 1990.   [2] Dry land and land temporarily or partially covered by water.   [3] Based on 1,078 places (1,070 incorporated places and the 8 CDPs in Hawaii). When places share the same rank, the next lower rank is omitted.   [4] Includes count resolution corrections through 1997 and adjustments based on Census 2000 dress rehearsal results and boundary changes reported as legally effective as of January 1, 1998.   [5] Based on 1,071 places (1,070 incorporated places and Honolulu CDP in Hawaii). When places share the same rank, the next lower rank is omitted.   [6] Persons of Hispanic or Latino origin may be of any race.

Sources: Land Area—U.S. Census Bureau, Census of Population and Housing, Census 2000 Redistricting Data (Public Law 94-171) Summary Files (related Internet site <http://www.census.gov/dmd/www/2kresult.html>).   2000 Population—U.S. Census Bureau, 2000 Census of Population and Housing, "Census 2000 Profiles of General Demographic Characteristics" data files, published May 2001, related Internet site <http://www.census.gov/mp/www/pub/2000cen/mscen01.html>.   1990 Population—U.S. Census Bureau, "(SU-99-7) Population Estimates for Places (Sorted Alphabetically Within State): Annual Time Series, July 1, 1990 to July 1, 1999 (includes April 1, 1990 Population Estimates Base)," published 20 October 2000, <http://www.census.gov/population/estimates/metro-city/placebyst/SC99T7_US.txt>.   1980 Population—U.S. Census Bureau, 1990 Census of Population and Housing, "Population and Housing Unit Counts," CPH-2-1 through CPH-2-52.

Table C–1. Cities — **Area and Population**–Con.

[Includes states and 1,070 incorporated places of 25,000 or more population as of April 1, 1990 in all states except Hawaii which has no incorporated places recognized by the Census Bureau. For Hawaii, 8 census designated places (CDPs) of 25,000 or more population as of April 1, 1990 are included. Also included are the 5 boroughs of New York city. For more information on these areas, see appendix B. Geographic Information]

State and place code[1]	City	Land area,[2] 2000 (sq. miles)	Population (April 1) 2000 Number	Rank[3]	Per square mile	1990[4] Number	Rank[5]	1980	Net change 1990–2000	1980–1990	Percent change 1990–2000	1980–1990	Hispanic or Latino,[6] 2000 Number	Percent
	TEXAS—Con.													
48 39352	Kingsville city	13.8	25 575	1 065	1 853.3	25 344	1 064	28 808	231	–3 464	.9	–12.0	17 151	67.1
48 41440	La Porte city	18.9	31 880	928	1 686.8	27 902	984	14 062	3 978	13 840	14.3	98.4	6 520	20.5
48 41464	Laredo city	78.5	176 576	115	2 249.4	125 029	148	91 449	51 547	33 580	41.2	36.7	166 216	94.1
48 41980	League City city	51.2	45 444	661	887.6	29 903	920	16 578	15 541	13 325	52.0	80.4	6 130	13.5
48 42508	Lewisville city	36.8	77 737	339	2 112.4	46 375	564	24 273	31 362	22 102	67.6	91.1	13 799	17.8
48 43888	Longview city	54.7	73 344	362	1 340.8	70 535	330	62 762	2 809	7 773	4.0	12.4	7 564	10.3
48 45000	Lubbock city	114.8	199 564	89	1 738.4	186 770	89	174 361	12 794	12 409	6.9	7.1	54 786	27.5
48 45072	Lufkin city	26.7	32 709	912	1 225.1	30 641	901	28 562	2 068	2 079	6.7	7.3	5 754	17.6
48 45384	McAllen city	46.0	106 414	216	2 313.3	85 623	251	66 281	20 791	19 342	24.3	29.2	85 427	80.3
48 47892	Mesquite city	43.4	124 523	172	2 869.2	101 753	196	67 053	22 770	34 700	22.4	51.8	19 500	15.7
48 48072	Midland city	66.6	94 996	250	1 426.4	89 393	233	70 525	5 603	18 868	6.3	26.8	27 543	29.0
48 48768	Mission city	24.1	45 408	662	1 884.1	30 847	893	22 653	14 561	8 194	47.2	36.2	36 794	81.0
48 48804	Missouri City city	29.7	52 913	557	1 781.6	36 262	741	24 423	16 651	11 839	45.9	48.5	5 755	10.9
48 50256	Nacogdoches city	25.2	29 914	978	1 187.1	31 256	877	27 149	–1 342	4 107	–4.3	15.1	3 236	10.8
48 50820	New Braunfels city	29.2	36 494	822	1 249.8	27 744	988	22 402	8 750	5 342	31.5	23.8	12 599	34.5
48 52356	North Richland Hills city	18.2	55 635	523	3 056.9	45 910	571	30 592	9 725	15 318	21.2	50.1	5 276	9.5
48 53388	Odessa city	36.8	90 943	269	2 471.3	89 808	231	90 027	1 135	–219	1.3	–.2	37 671	41.4
48 56000	Pasadena city	44.2	141 674	149	3 205.3	119 389	153	112 560	22 285	6 829	18.7	6.1	68 348	48.2
48 57200	Pharr city	20.8	46 660	642	2 243.3	34 954	772	21 381	11 706	13 573	33.5	63.5	42 282	90.6
48 58016	Plano city	71.6	222 030	78	3 101.0	128 507	143	72 331	93 523	56 176	72.8	77.7	22 357	10.1
48 58820	Port Arthur city	82.9	57 755	489	696.7	58 373	417	61 251	–618	–2 878	–1.1	–4.7	10 081	17.5
48 61796	Richardson city	28.6	91 802	266	3 209.9	74 640	300	72 496	17 162	2 144	23.0	3.0	9 420	10.3
48 63500	Round Rock city	26.1	61 136	452	2 342.4	31 559	871	12 740	29 577	18 819	93.7	147.7	13 511	22.1
48 64472	San Angelo city	55.9	88 439	280	1 582.1	84 955	258	73 240	3 484	11 715	4.1	16.0	29 321	33.2
48 65000	San Antonio city	407.6	1 144 646	9	2 808.3	997 434	9	785 940	147 212	211 494	14.8	26.9	671 394	58.7
48 65600	San Marcos city	18.2	34 733	871	1 908.4	29 072	942	23 420	5 661	5 652	19.5	24.1	12 676	36.5
48 67496	Sherman city	38.6	35 082	860	908.9	32 286	852	30 413	2 796	1 873	8.7	6.2	4 260	12.1
48 72176	Temple city	65.4	54 514	541	833.5	48 715	537	42 354	5 799	6 361	11.9	15.0	9 716	17.8
48 72368	Texarkana city	25.6	34 782	869	1 358.7	33 578	812	31 271	1 204	2 307	3.6	7.4	1 012	2.9
48 72392	Texas City city	62.4	41 521	719	665.4	40 810	655	41 201	711	–391	1.7	–.9	8 520	20.5
48 74144	Tyler city	49.3	83 650	306	1 696.8	75 669	296	70 508	7 981	5 161	10.5	7.3	13 234	15.8
48 75428	Victoria city	33.0	60 603	455	1 836.5	55 437	443	50 695	5 166	4 742	9.3	9.4	26 012	42.9
48 76000	Waco city	84.2	113 726	197	1 350.7	103 924	191	101 261	9 802	2 663	9.4	2.6	26 885	23.6
48 79000	Wichita Falls city	70.7	104 197	221	1 473.8	96 746	211	94 201	7 451	2 545	7.7	2.7	14 570	14.0
49 00000	UTAH	82 143.7	2 233 169	X	27.2	1 722 850	X	1 461 037	510 319	261 813	29.6	17.9	201 559	9.0
49 07690	Bountiful city	13.5	41 301	723	3 059.3	38 400	703	32 877	2 901	5 523	7.6	16.8	1 197	2.9
49 43660	Layton city	20.7	58 474	483	2 824.8	41 900	635	22 862	16 574	19 038	39.6	83.3	4 068	7.0
49 45860	Logan city	16.5	42 670	702	2 586.1	32 903	837	26 844	9 767	6 059	29.7	22.6	3 509	8.2
49 53230	Murray city	9.6	34 024	883	3 544.2	31 399	875	25 750	2 625	5 649	8.4	21.9	2 549	7.5
49 55980	Ogden city	26.6	77 226	343	2 903.2	64 271	369	64 407	12 955	–136	20.2	–.2	18 253	23.6
49 57300	Orem city	18.4	84 324	301	4 582.8	67 538	344	52 399	16 786	15 139	24.9	28.9	7 217	8.6
49 62470	Provo city	39.6	105 166	219	2 655.7	87 136	241	74 111	18 030	13 025	20.7	17.6	11 013	10.5
49 65330	St. George city	64.4	49 663	594	771.2	28 754	956	11 350	20 909	17 404	72.7	153.3	3 337	6.7
49 67000	Salt Lake City city	109.1	181 743	111	1 665.8	159 952	111	163 034	21 791	–3 082	13.6	–1.9	34 254	18.8
49 67550	Sandy city	22.3	88 418	281	3 964.9	76 325	291	52 210	12 093	24 115	15.8	46.2	3 875	4.4
49 82950	West Jordan city	30.9	68 336	397	2 211.5	43 028	616	27 325	25 308	15 703	58.8	57.5	6 882	10.1
49 83445	West Valley City city	35.4	108 896	207	3 076.2	86 999	242	(7)	21 897	X	25.2	X	20 126	18.5
50 00000	VERMONT	9 249.6	608 827	X	65.8	562 758	X	511 456	46 069	51 302	8.2	10.0	5 504	.9
50 10675	Burlington city	10.6	38 889	780	3 668.8	39 071	686	37 712	–182	1 359	–.5	3.6	546	1.4
51 00000	VIRGINIA	39 594.1	7 078 515	X	178.8	6 189 197	X	5 346 797	889 318	842 400	14.4	15.8	329 540	4.7
51 01000	Alexandria city	15.2	128 283	166	8 439.7	111 183	170	103 217	17 100	7 966	15.4	7.7	18 882	14.7
51 07784	Blacksburg town	19.4	39 573	766	2 039.8	34 922	774	30 638	4 651	4 284	13.3	14.0	920	2.3
51 14968	Charlottesville city	10.3	45 049	668	4 373.7	40 470	659	39 916	4 579	554	11.3	1.4	1 102	2.4
51 16000	Chesapeake city	340.7	199 184	90	584.6	151 982	117	114 486	47 202	37 496	31.1	32.8	4 076	2.0
51 21344	Danville city	43.1	48 411	616	1 123.2	53 056	476	45 642	–4 645	7 414	–8.8	16.2	612	1.3
51 35000	Hampton city	51.8	146 437	143	2 827.0	133 773	135	122 617	12 664	11 156	9.5	9.1	4 153	2.8
51 35624	Harrisonburg city	17.6	40 468	743	2 299.3	30 707	898	19 671	9 761	11 036	31.8	56.1	3 580	8.8
51 47672	Lynchburg city	49.4	65 269	419	1 321.2	66 120	358	66 743	–851	–623	–1.3	–.9	878	1.3
51 48952	Manassas city	9.9	35 135	857	3 549.0	27 757	987	15 438	7 378	12 319	26.6	79.8	5 316	15.1
51 56000	Newport News city	68.3	180 150	113	2 637.6	171 477	102	144 903	8 673	26 574	5.1	18.3	7 595	4.2
51 57000	Norfolk city	53.7	234 403	73	4 365.0	261 250	62	266 979	–26 847	–5 729	–10.3	–2.1	8 915	3.8
51 61832	Petersburg city	22.9	33 740	894	1 473.4	37 071	732	41 055	–3 331	–3 984	–9.0	–9.7	463	1.4

[1] Federal Information Processing Standards (FIPS) codes for states and places defined as of January 1990.   [2] Dry land and land temporarily or partially covered by water.   [3] Based on 1,078 places (1,070 incorporated places and the 8 CDPs in Hawaii). When places share the same rank, the next lower rank is omitted.   [4] Includes count resolution corrections through 1997 and adjustments based on Census 2000 dress rehearsal results and boundary changes reported as legally effective as of January 1, 1998.   [5] Based on 1,071 places (1,070 incorporated places and Honolulu CDP in Hawaii). When places share the same rank, the next lower rank is omitted.   [6] Persons of Hispanic or Latino origin may be of any race.   [7] Not incorporated as of January 1, 1980.

Sources: Land Area—U.S. Census Bureau, Census of Population and Housing, Census 2000 Redistricting Data (Public Law 94-171) Summary Files (related Internet site <http://www.census.gov/dmd/www/2kresult.html>).   2000 Population—U.S. Census Bureau, 2000 Census of Population and Housing, "Census 2000 Profiles of General Demographic Characteristics" data files, published May 2001, related Internet site <http://www.census.gov/mp/www/pub/2000cen/mscen01.html>.   1990 Population—U.S. Census Bureau, "(SU-99-7) Population Estimates for Places (Sorted Alphabetically Within State): Annual Time Series, July 1, 1990 to July 1, 1999 (includes April 1, 1990 Population Estimates Base)," published 20 October 2000, <http://www.census.gov/population/estimates/metro-city/placebyst/SC99T7_US.txt>.   1980 Population—U.S. Census Bureau, 1990 Census of Population and Housing, "Population and Housing Unit Counts," CPH-2-1 through CPH-2-52.

Table C–1. Cities — **Area and Population**–Con.

[Includes states and 1,070 incorporated places of 25,000 or more population as of April 1, 1990 in all states except Hawaii which has no incorporated places recognized by the Census Bureau. For Hawaii, 8 census designated places (CDPs) of 25,000 or more population as of April 1, 1990 are included. Also included are the 5 boroughs of New York city. For more information on these areas, see appendix B. Geographic Information]

State and place code[1]	City	Land area,[2] 2000 (sq. miles)	Population (April 1) 2000 Number	Rank[3]	Per square mile	1990[4] Number	Rank[5]	1980	Net change 1990–2000	1980–1990	Percent change 1990–2000	1980–1990	Hispanic or Latino,[6] 2000 Number	Percent
	VIRGINIA—Con.													
51 64000	Portsmouth city	33.2	100 565	236	3 029.1	103 910	192	104 577	−3 345	−667	−3.2	−.6	1 748	1.7
51 67000	Richmond city	60.1	197 790	94	3 291.0	202 713	77	219 214	−4 923	−16 501	−2.4	−7.5	5 074	2.6
51 68000	Roanoke city	42.9	94 911	251	2 212.4	96 487	213	100 220	−1 576	−3 733	−1.6	−3.7	1 405	1.5
51 76432	Suffolk city	400.0	63 677	428	159.2	52 143	490	47 621	11 534	4 522	22.1	9.5	809	1.3
51 82000	Virginia Beach city	248.3	425 257	38	1 712.7	393 089	39	262 199	32 168	130 890	8.2	49.9	17 770	4.2
53 00000	WASHINGTON	66 544.1	5 894 121	X	88.6	4 866 669	X	4 132 353	1 027 452	734 316	21.1	17.8	441 509	7.5
53 03180	Auburn city	21.3	40 314	749	1 892.7	34 245	792	26 417	6 069	7 828	17.7	29.6	3 019	7.5
53 05210	Bellevue city.............	30.7	109 569	206	3 569.0	98 628	206	73 903	10 941	24 725	11.1	33.5	5 827	5.3
53 05280	Bellingham city	25.6	67 171	405	2 623.9	53 359	472	45 794	13 812	7 565	25.9	16.5	3 111	4.6
53 07695	Bremerton city	22.7	37 259	808	1 641.4	39 546	678	36 208	−2 287	3 338	−5.8	9.2	2 457	6.6
53 20750	Edmonds city	8.9	39 515	767	4 439.9	38 801	695	27 679	714	11 122	1.8	40.2	1 312	3.3
53 22640	Everett city	32.5	91 488	268	2 815.0	71 486	323	54 413	20 002	17 073	28.0	31.4	6 539	7.1
53 35275	Kennewick city	22.9	54 693	537	2 388.3	42 735	622	34 397	11 958	8 338	28.0	24.2	8 503	15.5
53 35415	Kent city	28.0	79 524	326	2 840.1	59 810	403	22 961	19 714	36 849	33.0	160.5	6 466	8.1
53 35940	Kirkland city.............	10.7	45 054	667	4 210.7	40 305	667	18 785	4 749	21 520	11.8	114.6	1 852	4.1
53 40245	Longview city	13.7	34 660	873	2 529.9	31 979	861	31 052	2 681	927	8.4	3.0	2 017	5.8
53 40840	Lynnwood city	7.6	33 847	891	4 453.6	29 690	924	22 641	4 157	7 049	14.0	31.1	2 356	7.0
53 51300	Olympia city	16.7	42 514	704	2 545.7	33 985	796	27 447	8 529	6 538	25.1	23.8	1 863	4.4
53 57535	Redmond city	15.9	45 256	665	2 846.3	36 090	745	23 318	9 166	12 772	25.4	54.8	2 538	5.6
53 57745	Renton city	17.0	50 052	590	2 944.2	41 814	638	31 031	8 238	10 783	19.7	34.7	3 818	7.6
53 58235	Richland city.............	34.8	38 708	782	1 112.3	32 935	835	33 578	5 773	−643	17.5	−1.9	1 826	4.7
53 63000	Seattle city	83.9	563 374	23	6 714.8	516 332	21	493 846	47 042	22 486	9.1	4.6	29 719	5.3
53 67000	Spokane city	57.8	195 629	96	3 384.6	178 120	97	171 300	17 509	6 820	9.8	4.0	5 857	3.0
53 70000	Tacoma city	50.1	193 556	99	3 863.4	177 341	98	158 501	16 215	18 840	9.1	11.9	13 262	6.9
53 74060	Vancouver city	42.8	143 560	145	3 354.2	104 531	189	42 834	39 029	61 697	37.3	144.0	9 035	6.3
53 75775	Walla Walla city	10.8	29 686	984	2 748.7	27 280	1 004	25 618	2 406	1 662	8.8	6.5	5 170	17.4
53 80010	Yakima city..............	20.1	71 845	371	3 574.4	64 586	366	49 826	7 259	14 760	11.2	29.6	24 213	33.7
54 00000	WEST VIRGINIA	24 077.7	1 808 344	X	75.1	1 793 477	X	1 950 186	14 867	−156 709	.8	−8.0	12 279	.7
54 14600	Charleston city...........	31.6	53 421	550	1 690.5	57 691	422	63 968	−4 270	−6 277	−7.4	−9.8	432	.8
54 39460	Huntington city...........	15.9	51 475	574	3 237.4	54 865	450	63 684	−3 390	−8 819	−6.2	−13.8	437	.8
54 55756	Morgantown city	9.8	26 809	1 043	2 735.6	28 272	971	27 605	−1 463	667	−5.2	2.4	412	1.5
54 62140	Parkersburg city	11.8	33 099	905	2 805.0	34 728	777	39 944	−1 629	−5 218	−4.7	−13.1	269	.8
54 86452	Wheeling city	13.9	31 419	942	2 260.4	35 446	757	43 070	−4 027	−7 624	−11.4	−17.7	181	.6
55 00000	WISCONSIN	54 310.1	5 363 675	X	98.8	4 891 954	X	4 705 642	471 721	186 312	9.6	4.0	192 921	3.6
55 02375	Appleton city	20.9	70 087	382	3 353.4	66 137	356	58 913	3 950	7 224	6.0	12.3	1 775	2.5
55 06500	Beloit city	16.4	35 775	840	2 181.4	36 085	746	35 207	−310	878	−.9	2.5	3 257	9.1
55 10025	Brookfield city	27.2	38 649	783	1 420.9	35 156	764	34 035	3 493	1 121	9.9	3.3	453	1.2
55 22300	Eau Claire city	30.3	61 704	448	2 036.4	57 316	427	51 509	4 388	5 807	7.7	11.3	619	1.0
55 26275	Fond du Lac city	16.9	42 203	709	2 497.2	38 690	700	35 863	3 513	2 827	9.1	7.9	1 232	2.9
55 31000	Green Bay city	43.9	102 313	229	2 330.6	96 697	212	87 899	5 616	8 798	5.8	10.0	7 294	7.1
55 31175	Greenfield city	11.5	35 476	846	3 084.9	33 337	819	31 353	2 139	1 984	6.4	6.3	1 376	3.9
55 37825	Janesville city............	27.5	59 498	473	2 163.6	52 733	480	51 071	6 765	1 662	12.8	3.3	1 569	2.6
55 39225	Kenosha city	23.8	90 352	272	3 796.3	81 030	270	77 685	9 322	3 345	11.5	4.3	9 003	10.0
55 40775	La Crosse city	20.1	51 818	570	2 578.0	51 544	498	48 347	274	3 197	.5	6.6	592	1.1
55 48000	Madison city	68.7	208 054	83	3 028.4	190 816	85	170 616	17 238	20 200	9.0	11.8	8 512	4.1
55 48500	Manitowoc city	16.9	34 053	882	2 015.0	32 644	843	32 547	1 409	97	4.3	.3	859	2.5
55 51000	Menomonee Falls village ...	33.3	32 647	914	980.4	26 836	1 020	27 845	5 811	−1 009	21.7	−3.6	377	1.2
55 53000	Milwaukee city	96.1	596 974	19	6 212.0	628 300	17	636 297	−31 326	−7 997	−5.0	−1.3	71 646	12.0
55 56375	New Berlin city	36.8	38 220	791	1 038.6	33 504	816	30 529	4 716	2 975	14.1	9.7	595	1.6
55 60500	Oshkosh city	23.6	62 916	437	2 665.9	56 774	430	49 620	6 142	7 154	10.8	14.4	1 062	1.7
55 66000	Racine city	15.5	81 855	315	5 281.0	84 420	260	85 725	−2 565	−1 305	−3.0	−1.5	11 422	14.0
55 72975	Sheboygan city	13.9	50 792	579	3 654.1	49 718	525	48 085	1 074	1 633	2.2	3.4	3 034	6.0
55 78650	Superior city	36.9	27 368	1 031	741.7	27 286	1 003	29 571	82	−2 285	.3	−7.7	226	.8
55 84250	Waukesha city	21.6	64 825	420	3 001.2	57 450	425	50 365	7 375	7 085	12.8	14.1	5 563	8.6
55 84475	Wausau city	16.5	38 426	785	2 328.8	37 376	728	32 426	1 050	4 950	2.8	15.3	398	1.0
55 84675	Wauwatosa city	13.2	47 271	635	3 581.1	49 341	530	51 308	−2 070	−1 967	−4.2	−3.8	813	1.7
55 85300	West Allis city............	11.3	61 254	451	5 420.7	63 205	376	63 982	−1 951	−777	−3.1	−1.2	2 155	3.5
56 00000	WYOMING	97 100.4	493 782	X	5.1	453 589	X	469 557	40 193	−15 968	8.9	−3.4	31 669	6.4
56 13150	Casper city	23.9	49 644	595	2 077.2	46 843	559	51 016	2 801	−4 173	6.0	−8.2	2 656	5.4
56 13900	Cheyenne city	21.1	53 011	555	2 512.4	50 209	517	47 283	2 802	2 926	5.6	6.2	6 646	12.5
56 45050	Laramie city	11.1	27 204	1 034	2 450.8	26 695	1 026	24 410	509	2 285	1.9	9.4	2 161	7.9

[1] Federal Information Processing Standards (FIPS) codes for states and places defined as of January 1990. [2] Dry land and land temporarily or partially covered by water. [3] Based on 1,078 places (1,070 incorporated places and the 8 CDPs in Hawaii). When places share the same rank, the next lower rank is omitted. [4] Includes count resolution corrections through 1997 and adjustments based on Census 2000 dress rehearsal results and boundary changes reported as legally effective as of January 1, 1998. [5] Based on 1,071 places (1,070 incorporated places and Honolulu CDP in Hawaii). When places share the same rank, the next lower rank is omitted. [6] Persons of Hispanic or Latino origin may be of any race.

Sources: Land Area—U.S. Census Bureau, Census of Population and Housing, Census 2000 Redistricting Data (Public Law 94-171) Summary Files (related Internet site <http://www.census.gov/dmd/www/2kresult.html>). 2000 Population—U.S. Census Bureau, 2000 Census of Population and Housing, "Census 2000 Profiles of General Demographic Characteristics" data files, published May 2001, related Internet site <http://www.census.gov/mp/www/pub/2000cen/mscen01.html>. 1990 Population—U.S. Census Bureau, "(SU-99-7) Population Estimates for Places (Sorted Alphabetically Within State): Annual Time Series, July 1, 1990 to July 1, 1999 (includes April 1, 1990 Population Estimates Base)," published 20 October 2000, <http://www.census.gov/population/estimates/metro-city/placebyst/SC99T7_US.txt>. 1980 Population—U.S. Census Bureau, 1990 Census of Population and Housing, "Population and Housing Unit Counts," CPH-2-1 through CPH-2-52.

Table C–2. Cities — Population by Age, Sex, and Race

[Includes states and 1,070 incorporated places of 25,000 or more population as of April 1, 1990 in all states except Hawaii which has no incorporated places recognized by the Census Bureau. For Hawaii, 8 census designated places (CDPs) of 25,000 or more population as of April 1, 1990 are included. Also included are the 5 boroughs of New York city. For more information on these areas, see appendix B. Geographic Information]

City	Population by age, 2000 (April 1) Percent— Under 5 years	5 to 17 years	18 to 24 years	25 to 44 years	45 to 64 years	65 to 74 years	75 to 84 years	85 years and over	Median age (years)	Males per 100 females, 2000 (April 1)	Population by race, 2000 (April 1) One race White	Black or African American	American Indian and Alaska Native	Asian	Native Hawaiian and Other Pacific Islander	Some other race[1]	Two or more races[2]
ALABAMA	6.7	18.6	9.9	29.0	22.8	7.1	4.4	1.5	35.8	93.3	3 162 808	1 155 930	22 430	31 346	1 409	28 998	44 179
Anniston city	6.6	17.0	8.7	25.7	23.3	9.4	6.9	2.4	39.3	83.9	11 825	11 821	66	189	18	148	209
Auburn city	4.1	11.2	44.6	21.9	11.7	3.2	2.3	.9	22.6	99.4	33 553	7 217	82	1 422	17	244	452
Bessemer city	7.7	19.1	9.6	26.1	21.1	8.2	5.9	2.3	35.9	82.9	8 584	20 638	82	52	5	90	221
Birmingham city	6.8	18.2	11.1	30.0	20.4	6.7	4.8	1.9	34.3	85.7	58 457	178 372	422	1 942	87	1 513	2 027
Decatur city	6.8	18.6	8.8	29.6	23.1	7.0	4.6	1.4	36.3	92.4	40 714	10 548	312	376	68	1 195	716
Dothan city	6.9	18.6	8.4	28.3	23.3	7.6	5.0	2.0	37.2	88.4	38 873	17 385	160	491	11	265	552
Florence city	5.8	15.7	13.7	25.7	21.7	8.7	6.5	2.3	36.9	84.0	28 428	6 963	86	226	12	197	352
Gadsden city	6.6	16.5	9.5	25.3	22.0	9.7	7.9	2.5	39.0	85.2	24 434	13 252	118	208	32	477	457
Hoover city	6.6	18.2	7.9	32.6	23.8	5.8	3.7	1.3	36.2	95.1	54 997	4 248	99	1 812	21	881	684
Huntsville city	6.2	17.0	10.7	29.3	23.4	7.7	4.4	1.2	36.7	92.8	101 998	47 792	857	3 519	88	1 047	2 915
Mobile city	7.3	19.2	10.8	28.0	21.0	6.9	5.0	1.8	34.3	87.8	100 251	92 068	487	3 022	52	1 046	1 989
Montgomery city	7.1	18.9	12.1	29.8	20.3	6.1	4.2	1.5	32.9	88.4	96 085	100 048	500	2 146	71	748	1 970
Phenix City city	7.1	19.2	9.6	28.7	21.2	8.0	4.6	1.6	35.1	86.2	14 964	12 710	65	149	6	157	214
Prichard city	7.8	23.6	11.4	24.6	21.0	6.0	4.1	1.4	31.8	84.1	4 059	24 203	87	33	6	20	225
Tuscaloosa city	5.7	14.1	24.5	25.4	18.5	6.3	4.0	1.5	28.4	90.8	42 143	33 287	127	1 162	19	490	678
ALASKA	7.6	22.8	9.1	32.5	22.3	3.6	1.7	.4	32.4	107.0	434 534	21 787	98 043	25 116	3 309	9 997	34 146
Anchorage city	7.7	21.5	9.6	33.9	21.9	3.4	1.6	.4	32.4	102.4	188 009	15 199	18 941	14 433	2 423	5 703	15 575
Fairbanks city	9.6	19.8	14.7	32.8	16.4	3.6	2.3	.7	27.6	105.3	20 150	3 370	2 994	821	164	740	1 985
Juneau city	6.5	20.9	8.1	32.8	25.7	3.5	2.0	.6	35.3	101.5	22 969	248	3 496	1 438	116	323	2 121
ARIZONA	7.5	19.2	10.0	29.5	20.9	7.1	4.6	1.3	34.2	99.7	3 873 611	158 873	255 879	92 236	6 733	596 774	146 526
Chandler city	9.1	20.7	8.6	38.0	17.8	3.4	1.8	.6	31.2	99.7	136 296	6 151	2 121	7 453	251	18 993	5 316
Flagstaff city	6.7	17.6	21.7	30.5	18.2	3.1	1.7	.5	26.8	98.3	41 214	927	5 284	660	65	3 201	1 543
Gilbert town	10.3	23.9	7.4	37.8	16.9	2.4	1.1	.3	30.1	99.8	94 043	2 639	676	3 937	134	5 233	3 035
Glendale city	8.5	21.6	10.8	31.9	19.9	4.0	2.5	.9	30.8	99.6	165 293	10 270	3 181	6 003	293	26 188	7 584
Mesa city	8.2	19.1	11.2	29.7	18.4	6.7	5.1	1.5	32.0	98.2	323 655	9 977	6 572	5 917	932	38 271	11 051
Peoria city	7.4	21.0	6.7	30.6	19.8	6.9	5.0	2.5	35.6	92.5	92 050	3 012	734	2 077	120	7 686	2 685
Phoenix city	8.7	20.3	10.9	33.2	18.8	4.4	2.8	.9	30.7	103.5	938 853	67 416	26 696	26 449	1 766	216 589	43 276
Prescott city	3.7	12.1	11.2	18.9	27.3	13.8	9.8	3.1	47.8	96.9	31 538	171	432	283	21	941	552
Scottsdale city	5.2	14.2	6.6	30.4	26.9	9.2	5.8	1.8	41.0	93.2	186 883	2 501	1 240	3 964	167	4 603	3 347
Sierra Vista city	7.7	18.1	13.0	29.2	19.9	7.1	4.1	.9	32.0	100.7	27 706	4 115	313	1 347	174	2 285	1 835
Tempe city	5.7	14.1	21.3	33.2	18.5	3.9	2.4	.9	28.8	106.9	122 952	5 801	3 186	7 531	455	13 464	5 236
Tucson city	7.2	17.3	13.8	30.5	19.2	6.0	4.4	1.5	32.1	96.0	341 424	21 057	11 038	11 959	796	81 988	18 437
Yuma city	8.7	20.9	11.9	27.1	17.5	7.4	5.1	1.4	31.2	99.1	52 968	2 491	1 168	1 164	145	16 557	3 022
ARKANSAS	6.8	18.7	9.8	28.1	22.7	7.4	4.8	1.7	36.0	95.3	2 138 598	418 950	17 808	20 220	1 668	40 412	35 744
Conway city	6.9	16.4	22.4	29.2	16.1	4.3	3.3	1.4	27.3	90.6	36 272	5 232	155	541	14	421	532
Fayetteville city	6.5	13.4	25.7	29.9	15.8	4.1	3.2	1.4	26.9	103.0	50 212	2 969	730	1 484	90	1 158	1 404
Fort Smith city	7.6	17.8	9.8	29.3	21.8	6.7	5.1	1.9	35.3	94.1	61 798	6 943	1 358	3 682	43	4 040	2 404
Hot Springs city	5.9	14.3	8.2	25.4	23.0	10.7	8.6	3.9	42.4	88.4	28 194	6 030	196	284	17	363	666
Jacksonville city	9.5	19.5	12.8	33.2	17.6	4.7	2.1	.5	29.5	100.4	20 617	7 406	151	592	38	340	772
Jonesboro city	6.7	16.2	16.6	28.1	20.5	6.2	4.0	1.6	31.8	92.1	47 394	6 259	175	462	16	583	626
Little Rock city	7.1	17.6	10.0	31.7	22.0	5.7	4.3	1.6	34.5	89.2	100 848	74 003	500	3 032	64	2 348	2 338
North Little Rock city	7.1	18.3	9.0	28.4	22.5	7.3	5.6	1.7	36.5	87.7	37 801	20 535	249	356	20	712	760
Pine Bluff city	7.4	20.1	12.2	26.9	19.7	6.6	5.0	2.1	33.1	89.7	17 793	36 275	91	404	23	104	395
Springdale city	9.3	19.7	10.7	31.4	18.7	5.2	3.7	1.3	31.0	98.5	37 380	377	431	772	712	5 079	1 047
West Memphis city	8.5	23.0	9.8	28.2	20.1	5.4	3.7	1.3	31.3	86.6	11 663	15 473	59	148	5	141	177
CALIFORNIA	7.3	20.0	9.9	31.6	20.5	5.6	3.8	1.3	33.3	99.3	20 170 059	2 263 882	333 346	3 697 513	116 961	5 682 241	1 607 646
Alameda city	5.6	15.9	7.0	33.6	24.6	6.5	4.9	1.8	38.3	92.3	41 148	4 488	484	18 894	434	2 380	4 431
Alhambra city	6.2	16.1	9.7	34.0	20.7	6.4	4.7	2.0	35.0	89.1	25 758	1 437	614	40 520	86	13 947	3 442
Anaheim city	9.2	21.0	10.5	33.5	17.7	4.4	2.8	1.0	30.3	100.1	179 627	8 735	3 041	39 311	1 393	79 427	16 480
Antioch city	8.6	23.6	8.2	32.4	19.8	4.1	2.5	.8	32.3	96.0	59 148	8 824	843	6 697	360	8 352	6 308
Apple Valley town	7.1	24.4	7.8	25.2	21.7	7.9	4.7	1.1	35.4	93.8	41 449	4 277	530	1 198	123	4 296	2 366
Arcadia city	4.6	18.7	7.5	27.2	26.5	7.5	5.8	2.2	40.5	88.7	24 180	601	132	24 091	42	2 209	1 799
Azusa city	9.3	21.6	15.5	31.5	15.3	3.9	2.3	.7	27.1	97.5	23 406	1 688	585	2 747	77	13 646	2 563
Bakersfield city	8.8	23.9	10.1	29.9	18.6	4.5	3.1	1.1	30.1	94.6	152 849	22 641	3 454	10 708	298	46 151	10 956
Baldwin Park city	9.7	25.3	11.9	30.6	16.4	3.6	2.0	.6	26.9	100.0	30 472	1 219	1 096	8 826	112	30 718	3 394
Bell city	10.8	24.5	12.9	32.2	14.1	3.0	1.7	.7	25.9	102.0	17 764	468	470	391	22	15 798	1 751
Bellflower city	9.5	22.3	10.3	32.0	17.4	4.3	3.1	1.0	29.7	95.1	33 593	9 540	667	7 062	511	17 766	3 739
Bell Gardens city	11.4	28.0	12.9	31.5	12.2	2.4	1.2	.4	23.8	102.5	21 180	429	730	270	45	19 329	2 071
Berkeley city	4.0	10.1	21.6	31.8	22.3	4.9	3.9	1.5	32.5	96.5	60 797	14 007	467	16 837	146	4 764	5 725
Beverly Hills city	3.7	16.2	6.3	29.3	26.8	8.1	6.7	2.7	41.3	83.5	28 736	597	43	2 383	10	508	1 507

[1] Includes all other responses not included in the other five race categories shown. Also includes write-in entries such as multiracial, mixed, interracial, or a Hispanic/Latino group. [2] Refers to combinations of two or more of the six race categories shown under one race.

Source: Population by Age, Sex, and Race—U.S. Census Bureau; 2000 Census of Population and Housing, "Census 2000 Profiles of General Demographic Characteristics" data files, published May 2001, related Internet site <http://www.census.gov/mp/www/pub/2000cen/mscen01.html>.

Table C–2. Cities — **Population by Age, Sex, and Race**–Con.

[Includes states and 1,070 incorporated places of 25,000 or more population as of April 1, 1990 in all states except Hawaii which has no incorporated places recognized by the Census Bureau. For Hawaii, 8 census designated places (CDPs) of 25,000 or more population as of April 1, 1990 are included. Also included are the 5 boroughs of New York city. For more information on these areas, see appendix B. Geographic Information]

City	Population by age, 2000 (April 1) Percent—								Median age (years)	Males per 100 females, 2000 (April 1)	Population by race, 2000 (April 1) One race						Two or more races[2]
	Under 5 years	5 to 17 years	18 to 24 years	25 to 44 years	45 to 64 years	65 to 74 years	75 to 84 years	85 years and over			White	Black or African American	American Indian and Alaska Native	Asian	Native Hawaiian and Other Pacific Islander	Some other race[1]	
CALIFORNIA—Con.																	
Brea city	6.1	19.6	8.5	30.4	24.1	6.4	3.8	1.1	36.4	95.3	27 384	447	184	3 218	77	2 748	1 352
Buena Park city	8.1	21.4	9.7	32.3	19.2	5.5	3.0	.8	32.0	98.3	41 479	3 000	750	16 490	397	11 893	4 273
Burbank city	5.7	16.5	7.7	35.4	21.8	6.0	5.0	1.9	36.4	94.1	72 409	2 066	549	9 181	142	9 908	6 061
Burlingame city	5.6	13.6	5.5	36.9	23.2	6.5	6.0	2.7	38.4	91.5	21 648	296	65	3 881	135	1 019	1 114
Camarillo city	6.6	18.7	6.5	28.5	22.7	7.2	7.2	2.5	38.9	93.9	46 036	856	299	4 129	114	3 605	2 038
Campbell city	6.5	15.0	7.6	40.2	20.9	5.0	3.4	1.3	35.2	98.6	27 758	964	248	5 402	88	1 859	1 819
Carlsbad city	6.4	16.9	6.2	31.9	24.6	7.1	5.5	1.4	38.9	95.8	67 723	753	329	3 315	155	3 636	2 336
Carson city	6.9	21.5	9.9	28.5	22.5	6.6	3.2	.9	33.7	93.3	23 049	22 804	505	19 987	2 680	16 137	4 568
Cathedral City city	8.8	22.3	8.8	30.6	17.3	6.7	4.3	1.1	32.0	102.7	27 845	1 169	440	1 575	32	9 834	1 752
Ceres city	8.6	25.7	10.1	30.0	17.5	4.7	2.7	.7	29.4	97.0	22 324	951	485	1 743	130	7 061	1 915
Cerritos city	4.7	19.8	8.8	25.8	31.3	6.1	2.9	.6	39.3	94.8	13 851	3 432	142	30 091	96	1 930	1 946
Chico city	6.0	15.1	27.0	26.8	15.2	3.9	4.0	2.0	25.9	96.4	49 377	1 215	782	2 524	115	3 390	2 551
Chino city	7.2	21.3	12.3	34.2	19.2	3.3	2.0	.6	30.9	124.3	37 412	5 250	628	3 308	139	17 169	3 262
Chula Vista city	7.8	20.9	9.4	31.6	19.3	6.0	3.9	1.1	33.0	94.3	95 553	8 022	1 352	19 063	1 013	38 404	10 149
Claremont city	4.3	16.3	18.6	22.8	23.3	7.1	5.4	2.0	35.8	88.6	24 983	1 692	189	3 912	45	1 769	1 408
Clovis city	7.6	23.1	9.2	30.4	20.4	4.7	3.3	1.3	32.8	92.3	51 914	1 302	1 025	4 441	108	6 502	3 176
Colton city	10.0	24.9	11.9	31.5	15.2	3.7	2.1	.6	26.8	97.2	20 343	5 246	600	2 521	108	16 425	2 419
Compton city	10.4	28.1	11.5	28.7	14.4	4.2	2.2	.5	25.0	96.3	15 625	37 690	656	237	985	34 911	3 389
Concord city	7.1	18.2	9.0	32.8	22.2	5.7	3.8	1.3	35.1	97.6	86 114	3 706	929	11 438	612	11 752	7 229
Corona city	9.8	23.6	8.9	35.1	16.8	3.2	1.9	.6	29.9	98.0	77 514	8 031	1 086	9 425	387	21 894	6 629
Coronado city	4.0	12.0	20.2	29.3	18.7	6.9	6.7	2.2	34.2	139.8	20 341	1 241	159	896	72	757	634
Costa Mesa city	7.1	16.1	11.2	39.0	18.1	4.6	2.9	1.0	32.0	105.0	75 542	1 520	845	7 501	656	18 018	4 642
Covina city	7.4	20.7	9.5	31.1	20.4	6.0	3.8	1.1	33.5	92.0	29 084	2 354	420	4 598	97	8 047	2 237
Culver City city	5.5	15.4	6.6	33.3	25.3	7.0	5.2	1.7	39.1	87.5	22 994	4 644	277	4 667	80	3 945	2 207
Cupertino city	6.1	20.6	5.2	33.0	24.1	5.8	3.8	1.4	38.0	99.5	25 342	347	101	22 462	67	639	1 588
Cypress city	6.0	21.0	7.9	30.2	24.4	6.6	3.2	.8	36.7	94.9	30 332	1 280	274	9 618	184	2 515	2 026
Daly City city	6.0	16.4	10.5	32.2	22.8	6.9	4.0	1.2	35.4	96.8	26 836	4 720	456	52 522	940	11 735	6 412
Dana Point city	5.6	15.0	7.1	31.4	28.0	7.4	4.5	1.1	39.8	100.1	30 633	288	201	884	36	2 080	988
Danville city	7.1	21.5	4.2	27.7	29.3	5.3	3.6	1.4	39.9	94.1	36 000	382	86	3 756	48	381	1 062
Davis city	4.6	14.0	30.9	27.1	16.7	3.3	2.5	.9	25.2	91.2	42 256	1 417	407	10 576	144	2 572	2 936
Diamond Bar city	5.7	21.3	8.8	29.6	27.2	4.7	2.3	.5	36.5	96.0	23 103	2 680	185	24 066	67	3 818	2 368
Downey city	8.0	21.2	9.8	31.2	18.8	5.3	4.4	1.3	31.6	94.6	57 395	4 028	929	8 308	236	31 180	5 247
El Cajon city	8.2	19.7	11.2	31.3	18.3	5.6	4.2	1.5	31.9	95.2	70 206	5 090	941	2 643	352	9 950	5 687
El Centro city	8.1	26.3	9.7	28.9	18.5	5.5	3.1	.8	30.0	96.6	17 728	1 195	369	1 324	37	15 771	1 411
El Monte city	10.0	24.1	12.1	31.5	15.4	4.0	2.2	.7	27.1	102.1	41 360	889	1 596	21 465	140	45 544	4 971
Encinitas city	5.9	17.2	7.2	33.4	25.9	4.9	3.9	1.7	37.9	99.2	50 241	340	267	1 798	69	3 645	1 654
Escondido city	8.8	20.9	10.4	31.4	17.5	4.9	4.3	1.8	31.2	98.4	90 578	3 009	1 646	5 957	311	25 636	6 422
Eureka city	5.7	16.6	11.6	28.9	23.5	6.5	5.1	2.1	36.6	98.1	21 544	427	1 101	928	86	709	1 333
Fairfield city	8.5	21.3	11.1	31.3	18.8	5.0	3.1	.9	31.1	99.1	54 063	14 446	744	10 471	899	8 431	7 124
Folsom city	6.9	17.3	6.6	39.0	21.4	4.4	3.3	1.1	35.9	123.4	40 415	3 109	302	3 731	100	2 446	1 781
Fontana city	10.3	27.5	10.3	34.2	14.7	2.7	1.5	.5	26.2	98.5	58 006	15 255	1 450	5 618	427	41 185	6 988
Foster City city	5.9	15.3	5.9	35.3	27.6	6.1	3.1	.9	38.1	96.8	17 087	602	34	9 368	167	355	1 190
Fountain Valley city	6.0	17.5	7.9	30.1	27.2	6.6	3.3	1.4	38.1	95.6	35 196	611	252	14 165	220	2 172	2 362
Fremont city	7.4	18.3	7.7	36.8	21.4	4.9	2.7	.8	34.5	101.1	96 968	6 310	1 048	75 165	819	11 230	11 873
Fresno city	9.1	23.8	11.8	28.8	17.2	4.7	3.3	1.2	28.5	96.6	214 556	35 763	6 763	48 028	583	99 898	22 061
Fullerton city	7.0	18.2	11.5	32.3	19.8	5.9	4.1	1.4	32.9	97.7	77 977	2 861	865	20 259	296	18 666	5 079
Gardena city	7.5	18.3	8.7	32.3	20.9	7.0	4.2	1.2	34.4	95.1	13 755	15 010	367	15 489	424	9 784	2 917
Garden Grove city	7.9	20.5	9.2	33.4	19.3	5.5	3.1	.9	32.3	100.2	77 443	2 168	1 260	51 078	1 081	25 362	6 804
Gilroy city	9.4	23.1	10.0	32.7	18.0	3.7	2.3	.8	29.9	99.3	24 426	745	661	1 810	105	11 499	2 218
Glendale city	5.7	16.7	8.4	32.2	23.1	7.2	4.8	1.9	37.5	91.3	123 960	2 468	629	31 424	163	16 715	19 614
Glendora city	6.3	21.3	7.6	29.1	23.2	6.7	4.4	1.5	36.9	93.2	39 681	740	321	3 064	38	3 579	1 992
Hanford city	8.7	22.9	9.8	29.6	18.6	5.2	3.7	1.5	30.9	95.9	26 704	2 090	569	1 190	74	8 669	2 390
Hawthorne city	10.1	21.6	11.3	34.9	16.1	3.5	2.1	.6	28.7	92.6	24 618	27 775	629	5 660	721	20 320	4 389
Hayward city	7.9	18.9	10.9	33.4	18.8	5.2	3.7	1.2	31.9	98.5	60 146	15 374	1 177	26 579	2 679	23 539	10 536
Hemet city	6.5	16.0	7.2	20.6	16.6	12.8	14.3	5.9	44.6	84.5	47 335	1 527	708	872	79	6 225	2 066
Hesperia city	7.9	24.9	9.3	27.4	19.6	6.1	3.9	1.0	32.0	97.3	46 485	2 522	796	670	122	9 051	2 936
Highland city	9.5	26.1	9.0	30.0	19.0	4.0	2.0	.5	29.3	95.4	25 089	5 403	581	2 740	152	8 307	2 333
Huntington Beach city	6.2	16.1	8.4	34.9	24.0	5.9	3.5	1.0	36.0	100.4	150 194	1 527	1 224	17 709	456	11 019	7 465
Huntington Park city	10.4	25.4	13.0	32.3	13.8	3.1	1.6	.5	25.6	100.3	25 412	478	620	489	38	31 328	2 983
Imperial Beach city	8.4	21.1	13.9	32.3	16.8	4.4	2.6	.5	28.6	99.7	16 805	1 421	298	1 767	163	4 796	1 742
Indio city	10.4	24.9	11.1	29.4	15.2	5.2	3.1	.8	27.3	101.2	23 903	1 361	510	742	49	20 638	1 913
Inglewood city	9.1	23.3	10.2	31.9	18.5	4.1	2.2	.8	29.6	90.3	21 505	53 060	773	1 280	410	30 823	4 729
Irvine city	5.6	17.9	14.4	32.3	22.6	3.9	2.5	.8	33.1	93.8	87 354	2 068	257	42 672	194	3 627	6 900
Laguna Niguel city	7.0	19.6	6.0	32.9	25.7	5.1	3.0	.8	37.5	94.9	51 682	776	180	4 784	73	2 155	2 241
La Habra city	8.4	20.7	10.3	31.7	18.2	5.4	4.0	1.4	31.5	97.1	37 153	926	564	3 498	127	13 953	2 753
Lakewood city	7.1	20.5	8.1	31.1	21.4	6.1	4.8	1.0	35.3	93.9	49 724	5 825	473	10 716	489	8 012	4 106
La Mesa city	5.7	14.1	9.9	32.9	20.3	7.1	6.8	3.2	37.3	89.3	44 148	2 660	364	2 238	217	2 782	2 340
La Mirada city	6.3	19.9	10.7	28.5	20.8	7.7	4.8	1.3	35.4	93.3	30 155	903	350	6 963	125	6 379	1 908

[1] Includes all other responses not included in the other five race categories shown. Also includes write-in entries such as multiracial, mixed, interracial, or a Hispanic/Latino group. [2] Refers to combinations of two or more of the six race categories shown under one race.

Source: Population by Age, Sex, and Race—U.S. Census Bureau; 2000 Census of Population and Housing, "Census 2000 Profiles of General Demographic Characteristics" data files, published May 2001, related Internet site <http://www.census.gov/mp/www/pub/2000cen/mscen01.html>.

Table C–2. Cities — **Population by Age, Sex, and Race**–Con.

[Includes states and 1,070 incorporated places of 25,000 or more population as of April 1, 1990 in all states except Hawaii which has no incorporated places recognized by the Census Bureau. For Hawaii, 8 census designated places (CDPs) of 25,000 or more population as of April 1, 1990 are included. Also included are the 5 boroughs of New York city. For more information on these areas, see appendix B. Geographic Information]

City	Population by age, 2000 (April 1) Percent— Under 5 years	5 to 17 years	18 to 24 years	25 to 44 years	45 to 64 years	65 to 74 years	75 to 84 years	85 years and over	Median age (years)	Males per 100 females, 2000 (April 1)	Population by race, 2000 (April 1) One race White	Black or African American	American Indian and Alaska Native	Asian	Native Hawaiian and Other Pacific Islander	Some other race[1]	Two or more races[2]
CALIFORNIA—Con.																	
Lancaster city	8.0	24.3	9.5	31.3	18.2	4.6	3.0	1.0	31.1	103.1	74 573	19 009	1 213	4 523	278	13 190	5 932
La Puente city	9.0	24.8	11.6	31.0	15.9	4.7	2.4	.6	27.7	100.1	16 060	804	524	2 940	68	18 535	2 132
La Verne city	5.8	19.4	9.7	27.4	24.5	6.6	4.8	1.8	32.7	92.7	24 379	1 016	203	2 278	55	2 348	1 359
Lawndale city	9.3	22.6	10.2	35.8	16.4	3.5	1.7	.4	29.3	102.3	13 394	3 998	313	3 055	289	8 584	2 078
Livermore city	7.7	20.4	7.1	35.1	22.1	4.3	2.5	.8	35.0	100.0	60 070	1 148	444	4 251	208	3 915	3 309
Lodi city	7.9	20.3	9.6	28.1	19.8	6.5	5.5	2.3	34.1	95.3	42 421	344	494	2 881	68	7 972	2 819
Lompoc city	8.0	22.0	8.9	33.3	18.5	5.3	3.1	.9	32.2	113.0	27 050	3 017	651	1 605	133	6 446	2 201
Long Beach city	8.4	20.8	10.9	32.9	18.0	4.4	3.4	1.2	30.8	96.6	208 410	68 618	3 881	55 591	5 605	95 107	24 310
Los Altos city	5.9	17.8	3.5	24.5	29.1	9.0	7.8	2.6	44.2	93.1	22 250	130	48	4 271	45	183	766
Los Angeles city	7.7	18.8	11.1	34.1	18.6	5.1	3.4	1.2	31.6	99.4	1 734 036	415 195	29 412	369 254	5 915	949 720	191 288
Los Gatos town	5.0	16.2	4.3	31.5	27.7	7.4	5.3	2.6	41.2	90.4	24 784	226	87	2 173	21	366	935
Lynwood city	10.6	27.4	13.1	31.2	13.5	2.4	1.3	.5	24.4	104.6	23 481	9 451	839	533	269	32 225	3 047
Madera city	10.7	24.7	12.5	28.3	14.9	4.7	3.0	1.1	26.2	102.8	20 804	1 665	1 207	618	44	16 425	2 444
Manhattan Beach city	6.5	15.8	4.1	37.5	25.7	5.9	3.7	.9	37.7	101.5	30 124	208	70	2 043	41	415	951
Manteca city	7.5	24.1	8.8	30.5	19.8	4.9	3.2	1.1	32.5	96.3	36 534	1 406	643	1 733	179	5 693	3 070
Marina city	5.7	15.6	14.0	38.4	18.4	5.2	2.3	.4	32.3	133.8	10 979	3 600	186	4 084	528	3 718	2 006
Martinez city	5.6	17.1	7.3	32.6	27.3	5.4	3.7	1.1	38.6	98.5	29 064	1 201	264	2 378	84	1 181	1 694
Maywood city	11.4	25.6	13.2	32.6	13.0	2.5	1.3	.5	24.2	104.1	12 073	102	320	101	37	14 177	1 273
Menlo Park city	6.6	15.3	6.2	34.7	21.4	6.7	6.3	2.9	37.4	94.0	22 274	2 163	136	2 201	389	2 635	987
Merced city	9.2	25.5	11.4	27.4	17.1	4.9	3.3	1.2	27.8	95.6	33 481	4 044	818	7 267	133	14 813	3 337
Milpitas city	7.2	17.5	9.5	38.0	20.9	4.6	2.0	.5	33.4	110.8	19 353	2 295	388	32 482	393	4 687	3 100
Mission Viejo city	6.9	20.2	6.6	30.5	24.9	5.5	3.9	1.4	37.5	95.7	77 418	1 067	348	7 199	174	3 553	3 343
Modesto city	7.6	22.5	9.6	28.9	20.3	5.6	4.0	1.5	32.7	94.1	131 414	7 499	2 335	11 388	951	24 066	11 203
Monrovia city	8.0	19.3	8.0	34.0	20.2	5.0	3.9	1.5	33.7	92.2	23 237	3 202	323	2 594	48	5 765	1 760
Montclair city	8.9	24.3	10.7	30.4	17.4	4.4	2.8	1.1	29.0	99.6	14 796	2 112	319	2 688	101	11 442	1 591
Montebello city	8.1	20.5	10.4	30.3	18.2	6.7	4.4	1.3	31.4	92.4	29 098	559	767	7 232	51	21 040	3 403
Monterey city	5.0	11.6	13.1	33.8	21.7	6.7	5.7	2.5	36.1	96.8	23 985	749	170	2 205	86	1 159	1 320
Monterey Park city	5.6	15.7	8.4	30.2	22.2	9.6	6.6	1.7	38.4	92.4	12 786	226	391	37 125	37	7 474	2 012
Moorpark city	8.1	26.1	8.6	32.3	20.4	2.7	1.5	.4	31.5	99.6	23 378	476	149	1 770	46	4 381	1 215
Moreno Valley city	8.8	28.0	10.5	29.5	17.7	3.4	1.7	.4	27.1	95.8	66 689	28 310	1 343	8 427	733	28 584	8 295
Mountain View city	6.0	11.9	8.3	43.4	19.8	5.3	4.0	1.3	34.6	106.8	45 090	1 789	273	14 613	182	5 884	2 877
Napa city	6.8	19.0	8.5	29.6	22.4	6.2	5.3	2.3	36.1	96.4	58 302	381	657	1 241	117	9 181	2 706
National City city	8.1	22.0	14.0	29.0	15.8	6.0	3.9	1.2	28.7	102.4	19 070	3 026	513	10 077	478	18 181	2 915
Newark city	7.2	20.0	9.5	34.3	21.2	4.9	2.4	.6	33.1	101.4	22 179	1 705	273	9 047	426	5 839	3 002
Newport Beach city	4.0	11.7	6.5	33.0	27.2	8.8	6.7	2.1	41.6	97.9	64 583	371	179	2 804	83	792	1 921
Norwalk city	8.6	23.5	10.7	30.5	17.6	5.1	3.1	.8	29.7	97.9	46 303	4 774	1 201	11 924	404	33 829	4 863
Novato city	5.9	17.2	6.4	29.9	27.5	6.6	4.6	1.8	39.6	93.6	39 414	948	246	2 479	82	2 587	1 874
Oakland city	7.1	17.9	9.7	34.0	20.9	5.2	3.8	1.5	33.3	93.2	125 013	142 460	2 655	60 851	2 002	46 592	19 911
Oceanside city	7.6	20.0	10.2	31.0	17.6	6.7	5.5	1.4	33.3	98.0	106 866	10 189	1 370	8 896	2 042	23 342	8 324
Ontario city	9.7	24.7	11.2	32.4	16.1	3.3	2.0	.7	27.6	100.6	75 575	11 864	1 682	6 125	587	53 807	8 367
Orange city	7.4	19.3	9.9	33.3	20.5	5.4	3.2	1.1	33.2	100.8	90 822	2 056	1 010	12 000	296	17 804	4 833
Oxnard city	8.9	22.8	11.8	31.0	17.3	4.7	2.7	.7	28.9	104.6	71 688	6 446	2 143	12 581	698	68 753	8 049
Pacifica city	5.7	17.5	7.7	32.8	26.6	5.8	3.2	.8	37.6	97.2	26 684	1 254	190	5 868	263	1 605	2 526
Palmdale city	9.3	28.7	8.5	31.1	16.8	3.4	1.7	.4	28.2	96.6	63 905	16 913	1 198	4 468	224	23 858	6 104
Palm Springs city	4.7	12.3	6.1	24.2	26.4	12.9	9.7	3.7	46.9	107.8	33 531	1 681	401	1 639	59	4 188	1 308
Palo Alto city	5.1	16.1	4.9	32.4	25.9	7.1	6.1	2.3	40.2	95.8	44 391	1 184	122	10 090	84	827	1 900
Paradise town	4.3	16.1	5.6	21.2	25.3	11.3	11.5	4.4	46.6	87.3	24 751	51	283	275	31	320	697
Paramount city	11.0	25.9	12.0	31.9	14.0	2.9	1.7	.5	25.6	96.3	19 177	7 508	586	1 851	464	23 040	2 640
Pasadena city	6.9	16.2	9.3	34.9	20.6	5.8	4.4	1.9	34.5	95.7	71 469	19 319	952	13 399	132	21 444	7 221
Petaluma city	6.6	19.6	7.2	31.5	24.1	5.2	4.3	1.6	37.1	95.6	45 906	632	294	2 135	93	3 317	2 171
Pico Rivera city	8.2	22.7	10.5	29.7	17.8	6.3	3.8	1.0	30.6	96.4	31 360	450	859	1 681	78	25 551	3 449
Pittsburg city	8.3	22.5	10.4	31.2	19.4	4.5	2.7	1.0	30.9	96.6	24 712	10 724	423	7 179	491	9 144	4 096
Placentia city	7.4	19.6	9.5	32.0	22.4	5.4	2.9	.8	33.2	98.2	31 500	821	386	5 190	82	6 843	1 666
Pleasant Hill city	6.1	15.3	7.2	32.4	25.8	6.2	5.1	2.0	39.0	94.2	26 852	504	155	3 096	90	763	1 377
Pleasanton city	6.8	21.4	5.5	33.4	25.3	4.3	2.5	.9	36.9	96.6	51 203	876	210	7 444	85	1 495	2 341
Pomona city	9.4	25.2	13.0	30.5	15.5	3.5	2.1	.8	26.5	102.4	62 419	14 398	1 883	10 762	311	52 213	7 487
Porterville city	9.5	24.8	10.8	28.0	17.5	4.4	3.5	1.5	28.6	96.4	21 690	506	684	1 835	61	12 959	1 880
Poway city	6.0	24.7	7.1	28.1	25.5	4.5	3.0	1.1	36.9	97.0	39 807	800	231	3 584	133	1 571	1 918
Rancho Cucamonga city	7.0	22.9	9.9	33.2	21.0	3.5	2.0	.5	32.2	100.1	84 987	10 059	855	7 656	341	16 931	6 914
Rancho Palos Verdes city	4.9	18.1	4.7	23.0	30.7	11.1	6.0	1.6	44.7	93.7	27 660	815	62	10 676	41	497	1 394
Redding city	6.6	19.5	9.7	26.4	22.2	7.5	5.9	2.1	36.7	92.0	71 727	851	1 802	2 386	94	1 324	2 681
Redlands city	6.2	20.0	10.7	27.9	22.7	5.9	4.7	2.0	35.1	89.4	46 858	2 739	597	3 257	146	7 204	2 790
Redondo Beach city	5.7	13.1	6.1	43.1	23.6	4.7	2.9	.8	36.7	101.5	49 735	1 592	295	5 756	224	2 762	2 897
Redwood City city	7.5	15.7	8.4	37.4	20.9	4.7	4.0	1.5	34.8	101.2	52 008	1 916	384	6 715	663	10 535	3 181
Rialto city	9.5	28.2	10.4	29.1	16.4	3.9	2.0	.6	26.4	95.6	36 168	20 464	965	2 271	392	26 824	4 789
Richmond city	7.7	20.0	9.9	31.4	21.2	5.2	3.6	1.1	32.8	94.6	31 117	35 777	639	12 198	498	13 754	5 233
Ridgecrest city	7.4	21.7	8.5	28.1	23.0	6.6	3.7	1.0	35.5	99.6	20 446	879	270	967	144	1 229	992
Riverside city	8.0	22.1	12.9	30.0	18.0	4.6	3.3	1.1	29.8	97.1	151 377	18 906	2 779	14 501	991	53 591	13 021
Rohnert Park city	6.3	19.0	14.8	32.0	19.8	3.9	3.2	1.1	31.5	94.1	33 907	833	329	2 356	177	2 417	2 217

[1] Includes all other responses not included in the other five race categories shown. Also includes write-in entries such as multiracial, mixed, interracial, or a Hispanic/Latino group. [2] Refers to combinations of two or more of the six race categories shown under one race.

Source: Population by Age, Sex, and Race—U.S. Census Bureau; 2000 Census of Population and Housing, "Census 2000 Profiles of General Demographic Characteristics" data files, published May 2001, related Internet site <http://www.census.gov/mp/www/pub/2000cen/mscen01.html>.

Table C–2. Cities — **Population by Age, Sex, and Race**–Con.

[Includes states and 1,070 incorporated places of 25,000 or more population as of April 1, 1990 in all states except Hawaii which has no incorporated places recognized by the Census Bureau. For Hawaii, 8 census designated places (CDPs) of 25,000 or more population as of April 1, 1990 are included. Also included are the 5 boroughs of New York city. For more information on these areas, see appendix B. Geographic Information]

City	Population by age, 2000 (April 1) Percent—								Median age (years)	Males per 100 females, 2000 (April 1)	Population by race, 2000 (April 1) One race						Two or more races[2]
	Under 5 years	5 to 17 years	18 to 24 years	25 to 44 years	45 to 64 years	65 to 74 years	75 to 84 years	85 years and over			White	Black or African American	American Indian and Alaska Native	Asian	Native Hawaiian and Other Pacific Islander	Some other race[1]	
CALIFORNIA—Con.																	
Rosemead city	7.5	20.0	10.5	31.7	19.7	6.1	3.4	1.2	32.3	96.4	14 217	363	456	26 090	34	10 535	1 810
Roseville city	7.3	19.5	7.0	30.8	21.0	7.5	5.2	1.7	36.4	92.0	68 756	1 047	559	3 442	157	3 141	2 819
Sacramento city	7.1	20.2	10.4	30.7	20.2	5.7	4.3	1.5	32.8	94.5	196 549	62 968	5 300	67 635	3 861	44 627	26 078
Salinas city	9.3	22.8	11.8	33.7	15.5	3.8	2.4	.9	28.5	113.7	68 218	4 943	1 903	9 390	407	58 466	7 733
San Bernardino city	9.8	25.4	11.0	29.6	16.0	4.3	3.0	1.0	27.6	96.7	83 849	30 425	2 591	7 772	680	50 286	9 798
San Bruno city	6.1	16.9	8.2	34.5	23.1	6.1	4.0	1.2	36.3	97.4	23 156	807	189	7 506	1 156	4 346	3 005
San Buenaventura (Ventura) city	6.6	18.5	7.8	31.5	22.8	6.3	4.9	1.7	36.8	96.9	79 511	1 421	1 173	3 028	175	11 245	4 363
San Carlos city	7.0	15.1	4.3	33.0	26.2	6.5	5.6	2.2	39.9	92.6	23 434	209	53	2 182	110	664	1 066
San Clemente city	6.5	17.6	7.2	31.5	24.1	6.9	4.8	1.4	38.0	102.4	43 905	385	307	1 317	69	2 552	1 401
San Diego city	6.7	17.3	12.4	34.0	19.1	5.4	3.9	1.2	32.5	101.7	736 207	96 216	7 543	166 968	5 853	151 532	59 081
San Dimas city	5.9	19.7	8.9	28.1	25.5	5.8	4.4	1.7	37.3	92.2	26 116	1 156	243	3 286	73	2 569	1 537
San Francisco city	4.1	10.5	9.1	40.5	22.3	6.9	4.9	1.8	36.5	103.4	385 728	60 515	3 458	239 565	3 844	50 368	33 255
San Gabriel city	6.7	16.8	8.6	33.3	21.1	6.3	4.8	2.3	35.6	92.2	13 294	420	331	19 470	39	4 921	1 329
San Jose city	7.6	18.8	9.9	35.4	20.0	4.7	2.7	.9	32.6	103.3	425 017	31 349	6 865	240 375	3 584	142 691	45 062
San Juan Capistrano city	7.2	20.9	7.8	27.3	23.7	6.2	4.9	1.9	36.4	96.9	26 543	265	363	651	38	4 806	1 160
San Leandro city	6.3	15.9	7.8	32.0	22.0	7.4	6.4	2.2	37.7	93.1	40 754	7 849	609	18 242	683	6 737	4 578
San Luis Obispo city	3.4	10.8	33.6	23.7	16.5	5.0	5.0	2.1	26.2	105.8	37 155	644	287	2 331	58	2 130	1 569
San Marcos city	8.8	20.3	9.4	32.3	17.3	5.4	4.7	1.7	32.1	98.4	37 051	1 099	453	2 567	130	11 212	2 465
San Mateo city	6.1	14.3	7.2	35.1	22.2	6.7	5.8	2.5	37.5	95.6	61 251	2 397	447	13 961	1 517	8 260	4 649
San Pablo city	9.1	22.6	10.9	31.8	16.9	4.1	3.2	1.4	29.5	96.5	9 555	5 539	271	4 945	154	7 688	2 063
San Rafael city	5.8	13.7	8.1	33.3	24.8	6.5	5.4	2.5	38.5	98.2	42 472	1 257	312	3 133	95	6 256	2 538
San Ramon city	7.4	18.9	5.8	35.7	26.2	3.4	2.0	.7	36.5	97.3	34 354	862	160	6 680	95	968	1 603
Santa Ana city	10.3	23.9	12.8	34.1	13.5	3.1	1.8	.6	26.5	107.7	144 425	5 749	4 013	29 778	1 160	137 360	15 492
Santa Barbara city	5.6	14.1	13.8	32.3	20.4	5.8	5.3	2.7	34.6	97.0	68 355	1 636	990	2 554	126	15 110	3 554
Santa Clara city	6.5	13.4	11.3	39.1	19.1	5.6	3.9	1.2	33.4	103.6	56 903	2 341	542	29 966	437	7 102	5 070
Santa Clarita city	7.8	22.5	8.1	33.6	20.8	3.8	2.5	.8	33.4	98.0	120 157	3 122	886	7 923	220	12 896	5 884
Santa Cruz city	4.9	12.5	20.5	32.6	21.0	4.0	3.2	1.3	31.7	99.2	42 984	945	469	2 677	72	4 990	2 456
Santa Maria city	9.0	22.6	11.6	29.5	15.9	5.6	4.3	1.5	29.2	103.2	44 962	1 449	1 360	3 673	138	21 691	4 150
Santa Monica city	4.1	10.5	6.1	40.1	24.8	6.4	5.4	2.6	39.3	93.0	65 832	3 176	396	6 100	86	5 019	3 475
Santa Paula city	8.8	22.6	10.9	29.7	17.3	5.3	3.9	1.5	29.6	103.7	15 795	118	404	200	54	10 688	1 339
Santa Rosa city	6.5	17.8	9.5	30.0	22.3	5.9	5.7	2.3	36.2	95.4	114 527	3 177	2 099	5 675	382	15 180	6 555
Santee city	6.7	21.5	8.4	32.9	21.6	4.7	3.4	.8	34.8	93.2	45 929	783	429	1 350	216	2 134	2 134
Saratoga city	5.4	20.7	4.0	23.8	29.9	9.1	5.6	1.5	43.2	96.5	20 111	115	46	8 679	25	171	898
Seal Beach city	3.2	10.1	4.0	21.5	23.7	13.1	16.8	7.6	54.1	78.3	21 477	347	73	1 386	43	309	522
Seaside city	9.7	20.6	11.1	34.4	15.8	5.2	2.7	.6	29.5	103.7	15 599	3 997	331	3 197	410	5 834	2 328
Simi Valley city	7.3	21.1	7.9	32.9	23.1	4.5	2.4	.7	34.7	97.9	90 561	1 401	780	7 052	154	7 235	4 168
South Gate city	10.1	25.5	12.5	31.6	14.9	2.9	1.9	.7	26.0	98.3	40 136	923	901	804	114	49 112	4 385
South San Francisco city	6.5	17.8	9.2	32.0	22.0	7.0	4.4	1.2	35.7	98.3	26 671	1 707	362	17 510	944	9 091	4 267
Stanton city	9.3	21.1	10.5	33.3	16.2	4.9	3.1	1.6	30.0	102.4	18 541	848	397	5 780	344	9 616	1 877
Stockton city	8.6	23.8	11.0	27.4	18.9	5.2	3.7	1.4	29.8	95.0	105 446	27 417	2 727	48 506	981	42 208	16 486
Sunnyvale city	7.0	13.4	7.7	41.3	19.9	5.7	3.8	1.1	34.3	105.9	70 193	2 927	608	42 524	428	9 474	5 606
Temecula city	8.9	25.8	7.8	33.3	17.2	4.4	2.2	.5	31.3	97.6	45 555	1 974	497	2 728	174	4 276	2 512
Temple City city	5.7	18.3	8.1	28.9	25.1	6.6	5.3	2.1	38.6	90.7	16 266	307	148	12 980	19	2 496	1 161
Thousand Oaks city	6.7	19.3	7.1	29.9	25.9	5.8	3.8	1.6	37.7	96.4	99 563	1 241	627	6 873	124	5 274	3 303
Torrance city	5.7	17.3	6.8	32.4	23.8	7.5	4.9	1.6	38.7	94.7	81 605	3 022	560	39 462	481	6 307	6 509
Tracy city	9.4	25.0	7.5	35.0	16.7	3.3	2.2	.9	30.9	100.2	37 127	3 117	518	4 633	315	7 445	3 774
Tulare city	9.6	25.0	10.5	28.7	16.8	4.9	3.3	1.1	28.5	94.4	24 804	2 209	616	890	54	12 798	2 623
Turlock city	8.1	21.8	11.4	28.9	18.1	5.6	4.3	1.9	30.9	92.8	40 370	798	523	2 518	153	8 460	2 988
Tustin city	8.6	18.2	9.3	38.1	18.6	4.1	2.3	.7	31.8	95.9	39 639	1 970	448	10 058	203	12 113	3 073
Union City city	7.3	20.5	9.8	32.7	21.6	4.6	2.6	.9	32.8	98.9	20 198	4 479	356	29 016	610	7 709	4 501
Upland city	7.0	20.3	9.6	29.2	23.1	5.9	3.7	1.2	34.5	92.5	45 966	5 164	518	4 969	101	8 437	3 238
Vacaville city	6.6	20.3	9.0	35.4	20.3	4.5	2.9	.8	33.9	118.4	63 909	8 880	856	3 706	403	5 970	4 901
Vallejo city	7.2	20.4	9.0	29.6	22.6	5.6	4.2	1.4	34.9	93.9	41 996	27 655	767	28 205	1 276	9 196	7 665
Victorville city	8.6	25.6	8.6	28.6	17.4	6.2	4.0	1.0	30.7	93.9	39 091	7 630	713	2 226	129	10 408	3 832
Visalia city	8.1	23.2	9.6	28.5	19.7	5.3	4.0	1.5	31.7	93.2	63 654	1 754	1 235	4 683	117	16 293	3 829
Vista city	8.6	21.1	11.4	32.7	16.2	4.8	3.8	1.4	30.3	99.8	57 750	3 814	895	3 323	607	19 168	4 300
Walnut city	4.9	22.9	9.8	27.2	28.4	4.3	2.1	.5	37.2	96.7	8 513	1 259	72	16 728	24	2 296	1 112
Walnut Creek city	4.4	13.2	5.2	27.1	24.8	9.8	10.6	5.0	45.1	85.8	53 937	688	210	6 017	94	1 263	2 087
Watsonville city	9.3	24.7	11.8	30.5	15.1	4.2	3.1	1.3	27.4	101.0	19 036	334	768	1 455	53	20 328	2 291
West Covina city	7.6	20.9	10.0	30.5	20.6	5.8	3.6	.9	32.7	94.4	46 086	6 696	823	23 849	226	22 295	5 105
West Hollywood city	1.6	4.0	6.3	48.6	22.3	8.0	6.5	2.6	39.4	123.4	30 868	1 104	129	1 350	41	1 026	1 198
Westminster city	7.3	18.7	8.8	32.6	21.5	6.6	3.6	1.0	34.1	99.9	40 392	871	535	33 629	406	8 991	3 383
West Sacramento city	7.7	22.1	9.1	27.7	20.7	7.0	4.4	1.2	34.0	97.6	20 548	811	555	2 282	184	5 056	2 179
Whittier city	7.8	20.5	10.0	30.6	18.6	5.8	5.1	1.7	32.8	94.6	52 876	1 019	1 105	2 770	126	21 588	4 196
Woodland city	8.1	21.7	9.6	30.3	19.9	4.9	3.9	1.7	32.4	96.2	32 851	631	718	1 851	136	10 566	2 398
Yorba Linda city	6.0	23.3	7.3	28.4	27.3	4.5	2.5	.6	37.4	96.6	48 015	688	220	6 537	56	1 593	1 809
Yuba City city	8.1	20.9	10.7	29.4	18.7	6.0	4.3	1.9	31.8	95.5	24 611	1 035	643	3 284	107	5 281	1 797
Yucaipa city	6.5	22.0	7.6	27.2	21.2	7.0	5.8	2.6	36.8	93.5	35 113	369	445	486	55	3 314	1 425

[1] Includes all other responses not included in the other five race categories shown. Also includes write-in entries such as multiracial, mixed, interracial, or a Hispanic/Latino group.   [2] Refers to combinations of two or more of the six race categories shown under one race.

Source: Population by Age, Sex, and Race—U.S. Census Bureau; 2000 Census of Population and Housing, "Census 2000 Profiles of General Demographic Characteristics" data files, published May 2001, related Internet site <http://www.census.gov/mp/www/pub/2000cen/mscen01.html>.

Table C-2. Cities — **Population by Age, Sex, and Race**—Con.

[Includes states and 1,070 incorporated places of 25,000 or more population as of April 1, 1990 in all states except Hawaii which has no incorporated places recognized by the Census Bureau. For Hawaii, 8 census designated places (CDPs) of 25,000 or more population as of April 1, 1990 are included. Also included are the 5 boroughs of New York city. For more information on these areas, see appendix B. Geographic Information]

City	Under 5 years	5 to 17 years	18 to 24 years	25 to 44 years	45 to 64 years	65 to 74 years	75 to 84 years	85 years and over	Median age (years)	Males per 100 females, 2000 (April 1)	White	Black or African American	American Indian and Alaska Native	Asian	Native Hawaiian and Other Pacific Islander	Some other race[1]	Two or more races[2]
COLORADO	6.9	18.7	10.0	32.6	22.2	5.3	3.3	1.1	34.3	101.4	3 560 005	165 063	44 241	95 213	4 621	309 931	122 187
Arvada city	6.4	19.8	7.8	30.4	24.9	6.2	3.4	1.1	37.2	96.0	92 999	672	665	2 215	68	3 146	2 388
Aurora city	8.1	19.5	10.1	34.7	20.2	4.1	2.6	.8	31.7	98.1	190 311	37 104	2 248	12 066	501	22 485	11 678
Boulder city	4.1	10.7	25.9	33.0	18.4	3.7	2.8	1.3	29.0	106.8	83 627	1 154	450	3 806	48	3 318	2 270
Colorado Springs city.......	7.5	19.0	10.3	32.8	20.8	5.1	3.4	1.1	33.6	97.8	291 095	23 677	3 175	10 179	764	18 091	13 909
Denver city..............	6.8	15.1	10.7	36.1	20.0	5.5	4.2	1.5	33.1	102.1	362 180	61 649	7 290	15 611	648	86 464	20 794
Englewood city	5.8	14.5	9.6	35.9	20.0	5.6	5.8	2.8	36.2	98.1	27 846	463	416	591	30	1 582	799
Fort Collins city	5.9	15.6	22.1	31.5	17.0	3.8	2.9	1.2	28.2	100.9	106 347	1 213	715	2 948	143	4 281	3 005
Grand Junction city	5.6	15.6	11.9	26.3	22.8	8.3	6.8	2.8	38.8	95.1	38 533	251	395	320	52	1 600	835
Greeley city	7.5	18.2	19.0	27.3	18.0	4.9	3.7	1.5	28.5	96.1	61 853	672	639	885	106	10 591	2 184
Lakewood city	6.1	16.2	9.6	32.4	23.6	6.5	4.2	1.5	36.5	97.5	125 611	2 128	1 599	3 918	117	7 028	3 725
Littleton city	5.7	17.6	8.2	30.1	24.2	7.2	5.3	1.7	38.6	94.5	37 021	466	293	670	24	1 078	788
Longmont city	7.8	20.1	8.5	33.1	21.3	4.6	3.3	1.3	34.0	97.9	60 255	385	687	1 252	43	6 907	1 564
Loveland city	7.0	19.9	7.8	30.6	22.1	6.3	4.6	1.6	36.0	96.1	46 990	188	349	419	15	1 624	1 023
Northglenn city	7.3	19.4	9.9	32.9	20.3	6.7	2.6	.8	33.2	100.1	26 221	481	361	970	47	2 568	927
Pueblo city	6.7	18.4	10.3	26.6	21.4	8.2	6.1	2.2	36.5	93.9	77 830	2 465	1 766	683	63	15 526	3 788
Thornton city	8.8	21.2	9.6	36.0	18.8	3.2	1.8	.7	30.8	99.0	68 137	1 206	924	2 063	87	7 380	2 587
Westminster city	7.3	19.6	9.6	36.0	21.0	3.8	2.1	.6	32.6	100.2	84 983	1 237	745	5 534	77	5 575	2 789
Wheat Ridge city	6.1	15.1	7.6	29.3	22.9	7.8	7.7	3.4	40.0	89.9	29 361	275	309	450	38	1 642	838
CONNECTICUT	6.6	18.2	8.0	30.3	23.2	6.8	5.1	1.9	37.4	93.9	2 780 355	309 843	9 639	82 313	1 366	147 201	74 848
Bridgeport city	8.2	20.3	11.2	30.5	18.4	5.5	4.4	1.6	31.4	91.2	62 822	42 925	664	4 536	148	20 659	7 775
Bristol city	6.3	16.9	7.2	32.5	22.2	7.3	5.6	2.0	37.6	93.6	55 014	1 612	132	884	18	1 443	959
Danbury city	6.5	15.1	10.2	35.4	21.7	5.6	3.9	1.5	35.2	96.2	56 853	5 060	214	4 082	26	5 653	2 960
Hartford city	8.3	21.8	12.6	29.8	18.0	4.9	3.3	1.3	29.7	91.4	33 705	46 264	659	1 971	135	32 230	6 614
Meriden city	7.1	18.6	8.1	30.2	21.9	6.6	5.5	1.9	36.2	94.0	46 734	3 754	229	796	11	5 036	1 684
Middletown city	6.5	15.2	8.3	35.1	21.5	6.2	5.0	2.2	36.3	93.3	34 540	5 291	99	1 155	21	857	1 204
Milford city (remainder)	6.0	16.4	5.9	31.7	25.0	7.5	5.8	1.7	39.4	93.6	47 332	965	65	1 193	17	447	575
Naugatuck borough	6.9	19.9	7.3	33.1	21.0	5.4	4.7	1.6	35.5	94.7	28 435	882	82	522	5	491	572
New Britain city	6.6	17.5	12.5	28.9	18.6	6.9	6.6	2.2	33.9	91.9	49 634	7 794	264	1 687	43	9 388	2 728
New Haven city............	7.1	18.4	16.4	31.2	16.7	4.8	3.8	1.6	29.3	91.8	53 723	46 181	535	4 819	79	13 460	4 829
New London city	6.7	16.2	17.6	29.6	17.9	5.6	4.7	1.8	31.2	95.5	16 299	4 784	225	544	21	2 343	1 455
Norwalk city	6.9	15.2	7.0	35.5	22.6	6.9	4.4	1.5	36.6	95.3	61 339	12 663	174	2 699	40	3 591	2 445
Norwich city	6.4	17.7	8.9	30.2	21.5	7.3	6.0	2.1	36.9	90.5	30 029	2 469	437	758	10	998	1 416
Shelton city	6.2	17.4	5.8	30.0	25.7	7.3	5.4	2.2	39.8	93.8	35 984	428	57	791	1	341	499
Stamford city	6.9	15.2	7.4	35.0	21.7	7.1	4.8	1.9	36.4	93.7	81 718	18 019	243	5 856	46	7 608	3 593
Torrington city	6.0	17.1	6.4	31.0	22.0	7.5	7.0	3.0	39.1	93.9	32 749	757	70	643	7	460	516
Waterbury city	7.6	18.9	8.9	29.9	19.7	6.7	6.0	2.3	34.9	89.9	72 018	17 500	453	1 615	61	11 698	3 926
West Haven city	6.2	16.9	9.7	31.2	21.8	6.9	5.6	1.7	36.4	91.3	38 824	8 530	128	1 525	27	1 867	1 459
DELAWARE	6.6	18.3	9.6	30.2	22.4	7.2	4.4	1.3	36.0	94.4	584 773	150 666	2 731	16 259	283	15 855	13 033
Dover city................	6.7	16.9	15.7	27.9	19.5	6.7	4.7	1.9	32.9	88.9	17 655	11 961	146	1 016	12	503	842
Newark city	3.0	9.5	43.6	19.8	14.9	4.6	3.4	1.1	22.6	85.2	24 919	1 714	45	1 161	14	245	449
Wilmington city	6.8	19.0	9.8	32.0	19.8	6.1	4.7	1.8	33.7	91.3	25 811	41 001	185	473	20	3 750	1 424
DISTRICT OF COLUMBIA ..	5.7	14.4	12.7	33.1	21.9	6.3	4.4	1.6	34.6	89.0	176 101	343 312	1 713	15 189	348	21 950	13 446
Washington city	5.7	14.4	12.7	33.1	21.9	6.3	4.4	1.6	34.6	89.0	176 101	343 312	1 713	15 189	348	21 950	13 446
FLORIDA	5.9	16.9	8.3	28.6	22.7	9.1	6.4	2.1	38.7	95.3	12 465 029	2 335 505	53 541	266 256	8 625	477 107	376 315
Altamonte Springs city......	5.9	14.5	10.8	37.1	21.0	5.3	3.9	1.5	33.8	92.6	32 642	4 004	138	1 213	18	1 972	1 213
Boca Raton city............	4.7	14.2	8.1	26.4	26.7	9.8	7.3	2.7	42.9	95.1	67 851	2 810	123	1 489	29	1 041	1 421
Boynton Beach city	5.7	14.1	6.4	28.1	19.8	11.0	10.1	4.7	41.8	87.9	42 487	13 822	133	918	30	1 428	1 571
Bradenton city	6.1	15.4	7.7	25.3	19.9	10.4	10.3	4.7	41.5	90.3	38 682	7 481	145	392	23	1 934	847
Cape Coral city	5.5	17.1	5.8	26.8	25.3	10.5	7.1	2.0	41.6	94.1	95 133	2 046	260	938	56	2 253	1 600
Clearwater city	5.2	14.0	8.0	27.6	23.8	9.7	8.2	3.6	41.8	91.8	91 223	10 651	346	1 782	75	2 700	2 010
Coconut Creek city.........	6.2	11.8	5.6	31.3	18.6	9.5	13.1	4.0	41.3	86.8	37 588	2 685	56	1 033	23	1 245	936
Coral Gables city	4.9	12.5	13.9	29.0	23.9	7.5	6.0	2.2	38.1	87.6	38 798	1 394	55	708	15	629	650
Coral Springs city	6.9	23.8	7.9	32.3	23.1	3.1	1.9	1.0	33.8	94.9	95 860	10 766	208	4 152	79	3 520	2 964
Davie town...............	6.7	19.7	8.2	33.4	22.6	5.4	3.1	.9	35.5	95.1	65 916	3 454	187	2 111	30	2 168	1 854
Daytona Beach city	5.0	12.6	16.6	25.6	20.5	9.4	7.6	2.8	37.2	99.7	39 963	20 994	206	1 112	41	670	1 126
Deerfield Beach city	4.8	10.8	6.5	28.4	20.2	10.8	11.8	6.7	44.6	87.2	49 894	10 339	108	896	20	1 521	1 805
Delray Beach city	5.0	13.2	6.3	27.1	22.4	10.8	10.8	4.3	43.8	91.2	39 908	15 981	102	651	49	933	2 396
Dunedin city.............	3.8	11.8	5.4	24.5	24.6	12.9	11.6	5.4	48.2	84.4	33 864	714	80	397	12	227	397
Fort Lauderdale city	5.3	14.1	7.7	32.8	24.8	7.8	5.4	2.1	39.3	110.0	97 941	44 010	344	1 565	74	2 684	5 779

[1] Includes all other responses not included in the other five race categories shown. Also includes write-in entries such as multiracial, mixed, interracial, or a Hispanic/Latino group.   [2] Refers to combinations of two or more of the six race categories shown under one race.

Source: Population by Age, Sex, and Race—U.S. Census Bureau; 2000 Census of Population and Housing, "Census 2000 Profiles of General Demographic Characteristics" data files, published May 2001, related Internet site <http://www.census.gov/mp/www/pub/2000cen/mscen01.html>.

Table C–2. Cities — **Population by Age, Sex, and Race**–Con.

[Includes states and 1,070 incorporated places of 25,000 or more population as of April 1, 1990 in all states except Hawaii which has no incorporated places recognized by the Census Bureau. For Hawaii, 8 census designated places (CDPs) of 25,000 or more population as of April 1, 1990 are included. Also included are the 5 boroughs of New York city. For more information on these areas, see appendix B. Geographic Information]

City	Population by age, 2000 (April 1) — Percent								Median age (years)	Males per 100 females, 2000 (April 1)	Population by race, 2000 (April 1) — One race						Two or more races[2]
	Under 5 years	5 to 17 years	18 to 24 years	25 to 44 years	45 to 64 years	65 to 74 years	75 to 84 years	85 years and over			White	Black or African American	American Indian and Alaska Native	Asian	Native Hawaiian and Other Pacific Islander	Some other race[1]	
FLORIDA—Con.																	
Fort Myers city	8.1	18.2	11.4	30.4	17.6	6.2	5.0	3.1	32.4	97.6	27 166	16 095	181	471	49	2 745	1 501
Fort Pierce city	7.6	19.6	9.8	26.1	19.5	8.7	6.7	2.1	35.4	97.4	18 585	15 326	122	298	30	2 011	1 144
Gainesville city	4.6	13.2	29.4	26.7	16.4	4.8	3.7	1.3	26.4	95.7	65 243	22 181	235	4 282	30	1 392	2 084
Hallandale city	4.0	9.2	5.3	22.9	22.8	14.7	14.1	7.0	52.7	85.6	26 484	5 493	78	344	14	958	911
Hialeah city	5.8	17.2	8.2	29.4	22.9	9.5	5.2	1.9	37.7	92.7	199 276	5 453	304	906	53	12 380	8 047
Hollywood city	5.9	15.4	7.0	31.3	23.1	8.0	6.2	3.2	39.2	94.1	109 190	16 853	381	2 757	117	5 507	4 552
Homestead city	10.6	22.5	12.8	31.2	15.0	4.2	2.7	.9	27.2	107.1	19 465	7 194	159	243	27	3 140	1 681
Jacksonville city (remainder)	7.3	19.4	9.7	32.3	21.0	5.5	3.6	1.2	33.8	93.9	474 307	213 514	2 474	20 427	448	9 816	14 631
Kissimmee city	7.8	19.2	12.0	34.9	18.5	4.5	2.4	.7	30.6	98.1	32 139	4 775	247	1 614	46	6 765	2 228
Lakeland city	6.2	15.2	10.3	24.7	20.6	10.6	9.0	3.4	39.7	86.8	57 677	16 682	217	1 050	46	1 379	1 401
Lake Worth city	7.1	15.8	10.6	32.6	19.6	6.3	5.3	2.6	35.2	108.9	22 877	6 627	273	262	37	3 362	1 695
Largo city	4.2	11.4	6.1	25.1	23.0	13.4	11.8	4.9	47.5	87.0	64 314	1 869	237	1 171	58	688	1 034
Lauderdale Lakes city	7.6	20.1	8.7	26.9	18.9	7.1	6.2	4.6	35.7	81.1	7 596	21 476	38	328	19	603	1 645
Lauderhill city	7.5	19.1	8.7	30.3	18.3	6.2	6.6	3.3	34.9	84.5	19 482	33 840	67	910	35	926	2 325
Margate city	6.0	14.9	6.5	29.2	21.7	7.9	9.3	4.5	40.4	89.5	42 478	6 268	139	1 497	31	1 549	1 947
Melbourne city	5.4	15.3	9.3	28.4	21.9	9.7	7.4	2.6	39.8	94.3	60 339	6 658	245	1 657	47	858	1 578
Miami city	5.9	15.9	8.8	30.3	22.1	9.9	5.8	2.3	37.7	98.9	241 470	80 858	810	2 376	130	19 644	17 182
Miami Beach city	3.9	9.5	7.8	38.2	21.3	8.8	7.1	3.4	39.0	105.0	76 276	3 548	206	1 202	39	3 557	3 105
Miramar city	8.7	22.3	8.6	35.4	18.7	3.8	1.9	.5	31.8	90.8	31 704	31 498	118	2 202	72	3 431	3 714
North Lauderdale city	8.0	21.8	10.7	35.2	17.4	3.2	2.6	1.1	30.5	94.0	16 137	11 343	94	1 006	21	1 893	1 770
North Miami city	8.1	20.0	11.3	31.8	19.6	4.8	3.0	1.4	31.8	92.7	20 842	32 867	191	1 152	28	1 893	2 907
North Miami Beach city	7.1	20.2	9.4	30.9	21.1	5.5	4.1	1.7	34.5	91.6	19 040	15 895	119	1 646	27	1 882	2 177
Oakland Park city	6.7	14.1	9.0	38.7	21.3	5.4	3.6	1.2	35.8	109.1	20 432	7 013	70	600	41	1 379	1 431
Ocala city	5.9	17.3	9.3	26.2	20.9	9.0	7.9	3.5	39.0	89.7	33 474	10 174	167	559	9	831	729
Orlando city	6.6	15.4	10.7	37.3	18.6	5.7	4.2	1.5	32.9	94.0	113 611	49 933	638	4 982	150	10 060	6 577
Ormond Beach city	4.2	15.0	4.5	22.4	26.5	13.3	10.5	3.6	47.5	87.8	34 223	1 000	62	522	7	112	375
Palm Bay city	6.1	20.4	7.6	29.6	21.5	8.7	4.9	1.1	37.2	95.2	64 755	8 983	281	1 354	37	1 894	2 109
Panama City city	6.1	16.9	9.6	29.8	21.6	7.8	5.9	2.3	37.2	94.4	26 819	7 813	231	564	28	274	688
Pembroke Pines city	7.1	18.5	6.4	33.5	19.3	7.0	6.3	1.8	36.5	87.3	103 870	18 210	255	5 163	68	5 086	4 775
Pensacola city	5.7	17.2	8.9	26.9	24.0	8.9	6.4	1.9	39.4	88.5	36 514	17 203	291	998	35	306	908
Pinellas Park city	5.5	15.8	6.7	29.2	22.2	9.5	8.1	2.9	40.2	91.2	40 652	952	176	1 941	10	910	1 014
Plantation city	6.0	17.1	7.1	32.0	24.7	6.2	4.7	2.2	37.9	90.6	64 967	11 426	143	2 390	37	1 655	2 316
Pompano Beach city	5.3	12.5	7.4	29.1	22.5	9.9	9.0	4.5	42.2	97.3	52 989	19 897	186	636	22	1 602	2 859
Port Orange city	4.5	15.3	5.9	24.9	25.7	12.4	8.7	2.6	44.6	91.0	43 803	722	121	523	10	245	399
Port St. Lucie city	5.8	18.5	5.9	28.1	22.8	10.5	6.7	1.6	39.9	94.5	78 011	6 295	200	1 101	31	1 570	1 561
Riviera Beach city	7.1	22.1	8.0	25.8	22.0	8.3	5.2	1.5	35.6	91.0	8 297	20 264	43	296	15	330	639
St. Petersburg city	5.7	15.8	7.7	30.2	23.1	8.1	6.4	2.8	39.3	91.2	177 133	55 502	769	6 640	130	2 661	5 397
Sanford city	7.5	19.3	10.7	32.5	19.4	5.5	3.9	1.1	32.5	99.0	22 872	12 308	174	403	21	1 628	885
Sarasota city	5.3	13.1	9.2	27.9	22.5	9.6	8.5	3.9	41.1	94.6	40 542	8 447	186	536	26	1 969	1 009
Sunrise city	6.4	18.5	7.3	31.7	18.4	6.5	7.8	3.4	36.6	87.9	59 597	17 557	156	2 642	61	2 967	2 799
Tallahassee city	5.2	12.2	29.7	27.9	16.8	4.1	3.1	1.1	26.3	89.5	91 007	51 569	376	3 617	82	1 457	2 516
Tamarac city	4.4	9.0	5.3	23.5	20.1	14.4	16.9	6.4	52.9	80.9	45 625	5 845	99	823	20	1 617	1 559
Tampa city	6.8	17.9	10.0	32.3	20.5	6.4	4.6	1.5	34.7	95.3	194 871	79 118	1 155	6 527	281	12 646	8 849
Titusville city	5.7	17.3	6.9	26.2	23.2	11.2	7.1	2.5	41.0	90.8	34 080	5 142	160	383	16	296	593
West Palm Beach city	6.1	15.3	9.8	31.5	21.4	7.6	5.5	3.0	36.7	97.3	47 696	26 446	274	1 197	133	3 568	2 789
GEORGIA	7.3	19.2	10.2	32.4	21.3	5.3	3.2	1.1	33.4	96.8	5 327 281	2 349 542	21 737	173 170	4 246	196 289	114 188
Albany city	7.8	20.0	13.0	27.7	19.6	6.3	4.1	1.4	31.1	85.3	25 553	49 855	160	459	22	346	544
Athens city	[3]5.2	[3]12.6	[3]31.6	[3]27.3	[3]15.3	[3]4.1	[3]2.9	[3]1.0	[3]25.3	[3]95.4	[3]64 878	[3]27 442	[3]210	[3]3 158	[3]45	[3]3 115	[3]1 418
Atlanta city	6.4	15.9	13.3	35.2	19.4	5.0	3.3	1.4	31.9	99.8	138 352	255 689	765	8 046	173	8 272	5 177
Augusta city	[4]7.1	[4]19.6	[4]12.0	[4]29.9	[4]20.4	[4]6.0	[4]3.7	[4]1.1	[4]32.3	[4]93.2	[4]87 651	[4]98 320	[4]536	[4]2 976	[4]238	[4]1 993	[4]3 468
Columbus city (remainder)	7.3	19.5	11.9	29.8	19.7	6.5	3.9	1.3	32.6	94.7	93 466	81 466	711	2 863	269	3 532	3 474
East Point city	8.7	20.6	11.9	31.3	19.5	4.1	2.9	1.0	30.0	89.5	6 376	30 949	80	244	36	1 348	562
La Grange city	7.7	20.7	11.0	26.9	19.2	6.8	5.5	2.2	32.8	85.4	12 796	12 353	47	212	26	319	245
Macon city	7.8	19.2	11.3	27.5	20.0	7.1	5.3	1.8	33.6	79.7	34 482	60 740	188	628	28	443	746
Marietta city	7.9	14.5	14.1	39.4	15.7	3.7	3.3	1.3	30.0	101.3	33 185	17 330	188	1 744	51	4 694	1 556
Rome city	6.7	17.5	12.1	27.7	20.1	7.6	5.9	2.3	34.6	90.2	22 081	9 677	135	496	56	1 962	573
Roswell city	6.9	17.5	8.2	35.1	24.7	4.0	2.6	.9	35.2	100.0	64 666	6 773	160	2 964	23	3 237	1 511
Savannah city	7.0	18.6	13.2	28.5	19.5	6.5	5.0	1.8	32.3	89.3	51 108	75 072	303	1 997	92	1 224	1 714
Smyrna city	6.9	12.6	10.8	43.8	17.6	4.4	2.9	1.1	32.0	95.3	24 368	11 147	170	1 606	14	2 709	985
Valdosta city	7.7	18.4	18.4	27.2	17.8	5.4	3.7	1.3	28.2	86.2	20 860	21 201	102	610	13	394	544
Warner Robins city	7.2	20.3	9.6	31.9	20.2	6.4	3.6	.8	33.3	94.2	30 504	15 663	148	875	34	603	977

[1] Includes all other responses not included in the other five race categories shown. Also includes write-in entries such as multiracial, mixed, interracial, or a Hispanic/Latino group. [2] Refers to combinations of two or more of the six race categories shown under one race. [3] Data are for Athens-Clarke County (balance), GA; Athens city (1990 land area - 16.6 square miles; 1990 population - 45,734) merged with Clarke County effective January 14, 1991. [4] Data are for Augusta-Richmond County (balance), GA; Augusta city (1990 land area - 19.7 square miles; 1990 population - 44,639) merged with Richmond County effective January 1, 1996.

Source: Population by Age, Sex, and Race—U.S. Census Bureau; 2000 Census of Population and Housing, "Census 2000 Profiles of General Demographic Characteristics" data files, published May 2001, related Internet site <http://www.census.gov/mp/www/pub/2000cen/mscen01.html>.

Table C–2. Cities — **Population by Age, Sex, and Race**–Con.

[Includes states and 1,070 incorporated places of 25,000 or more population as of April 1, 1990 in all states except Hawaii which has no incorporated places recognized by the Census Bureau. For Hawaii, 8 census designated places (CDPs) of 25,000 or more population as of April 1, 1990 are included. Also included are the 5 boroughs of New York city. For more information on these areas, see appendix B. Geographic Information]

City	Population by age, 2000 (April 1) Percent— Under 5 years	5 to 17 years	18 to 24 years	25 to 44 years	45 to 64 years	65 to 74 years	75 to 84 years	85 years and over	Median age (years)	Males per 100 females, 2000 (April 1)	One race White	Black or African American	American Indian and Alaska Native	Asian	Native Hawaiian and Other Pacific Islander	Some other race[1]	Two or more races[2]
HAWAII	6.5	18.0	9.5	29.9	22.9	7.0	4.8	1.4	36.2	101.0	294 102	22 003	3 535	503 868	113 539	15 147	259 343
Hilo CDP	5.6	19.0	10.3	24.4	23.9	8.5	6.1	2.2	38.6	95.9	6 976	183	137	15 610	5 348	385	12 120
Honolulu CDP	5.1	14.1	8.9	29.9	24.1	8.7	6.9	2.2	39.7	96.6	73 093	6 038	689	207 588	25 457	3 318	55 474
Kailua CDP	5.7	18.4	7.2	28.6	26.3	7.6	4.9	1.2	39.1	97.9	16 008	277	109	7 709	2 947	338	9 125
Kaneohe CDP	5.8	18.8	8.2	29.0	23.4	8.3	4.8	1.7	38.0	96.1	7 166	285	69	13 456	3 999	237	9 758
Mililani Town CDP	5.8	21.4	9.2	28.4	28.1	4.6	2.1	.4	36.2	99.7	5 829	879	54	13 426	1 303	381	6 736
Pearl City CDP	5.1	13.7	13.7	27.2	23.2	10.5	5.4	1.3	37.0	115.2	5 340	838	83	16 547	1 904	437	5 827
Waimalu CDP	5.4	16.0	9.5	31.5	27.5	6.3	3.2	.6	37.8	102.6	5 017	684	76	16 248	1 655	324	5 367
Waipahu CDP	6.9	19.6	9.5	26.8	21.5	8.6	5.2	2.0	35.5	97.6	1 566	308	46	21 774	4 077	285	5 052
IDAHO	7.5	21.0	10.7	28.0	21.5	5.9	4.0	1.4	33.2	100.5	1 177 304	5 456	17 645	11 889	1 308	54 742	25 609
Boise City city	7.1	18.3	11.7	32.3	20.6	4.8	3.8	1.5	32.8	98.1	171 204	1 437	1 300	3 870	302	3 241	4 433
Idaho Falls city	8.2	22.1	10.1	27.6	20.9	5.8	4.0	1.4	32.3	97.9	46 717	315	385	533	32	1 932	816
Lewiston city	5.9	17.3	10.7	26.7	22.3	8.0	6.6	2.4	37.9	95.3	29 403	92	491	236	25	159	498
Nampa city	10.5	20.4	12.5	30.3	15.0	5.0	4.4	1.8	28.5	96.0	43 281	206	490	484	92	5 833	1 481
Pocatello city	8.3	18.3	16.7	27.4	18.9	5.2	3.9	1.3	28.8	96.9	47 513	369	693	590	103	1 120	1 078
Twin Falls city	7.8	18.6	12.1	26.2	20.2	6.7	5.7	2.6	33.8	92.5	31 633	76	255	377	39	1 280	809
ILLINOIS	7.1	19.1	9.8	30.6	21.5	6.2	4.3	1.5	34.7	95.9	9 125 471	1 876 875	31 006	423 603	4 610	722 712	235 016
Addison village	7.6	18.6	11.3	32.0	22.1	5.3	2.5	.7	32.2	103.2	27 076	902	127	2 850	5	4 091	863
Alton city	7.2	18.5	9.1	29.1	20.0	7.3	6.0	2.7	35.4	88.4	22 056	7 538	55	115	3	207	522
Arlington Heights village	6.0	17.1	6.0	29.8	25.0	7.9	5.7	2.4	39.7	92.6	68 854	728	58	4 548	30	907	906
Aurora city	10.6	21.2	10.2	35.9	15.9	3.1	2.2	.9	29.3	101.5	97 340	15 817	511	4 370	47	20 762	4 143
Belleville city	6.2	17.3	9.0	30.3	20.1	7.8	6.4	3.0	37.2	88.9	33 754	6 421	108	336	28	171	592
Berwyn city	7.9	18.3	9.6	31.7	19.0	6.0	5.4	2.0	33.8	95.0	39 667	702	239	1 400	14	10 040	1 954
Bloomington city	7.4	17.6	12.5	33.3	19.3	5.0	3.6	1.4	32.4	94.1	55 032	5 602	115	1 958	28	919	1 154
Bolingbrook village	9.5	22.7	8.4	35.2	19.9	2.4	1.4	.5	31.0	99.6	36 330	11 494	130	3 591	36	3 182	1 558
Buffalo Grove village	6.6	22.3	5.3	32.2	24.6	5.2	3.0	.9	37.4	93.6	38 059	325	24	3 618	6	389	488
Burbank city	5.9	19.3	9.9	28.0	22.8	7.7	5.0	1.3	36.9	95.5	25 299	73	47	490	6	1 102	885
Calumet City city	7.7	21.0	8.6	30.7	19.2	6.3	5.1	1.3	33.7	86.8	15 137	20 673	97	207	21	2 097	839
Carbondale city	5.0	10.8	35.4	27.1	12.5	4.1	3.5	1.8	24.7	106.2	13 665	4 785	45	1 379	16	294	497
Carol Stream village	8.2	22.7	9.1	36.6	17.6	2.6	2.1	.9	31.3	97.1	31 749	1 716	71	4 531	4	1 534	833
Champaign city	5.0	12.8	31.7	26.7	15.4	4.5	3.0	1.0	25.3	102.7	49 398	10 543	159	4 611	23	1 307	1 477
Chicago city	7.5	18.7	11.2	33.4	18.9	5.5	3.6	1.2	31.5	94.2	1 215 315	1 065 009	10 290	125 974	1 788	393 203	84 437
Chicago Heights city	9.2	22.5	10.2	28.0	18.3	6.4	4.2	1.2	30.6	94.8	14 756	12 421	146	144	12	4 411	886
Cicero town	10.9	23.7	12.7	31.9	13.6	3.4	2.8	.9	26.4	105.8	41 327	956	759	828	38	38 277	3 431
Danville city	7.1	17.8	9.5	27.7	21.3	7.9	6.4	2.4	36.6	99.3	23 796	8 261	72	406	10	708	651
Decatur city	6.7	17.3	11.1	26.0	22.5	8.2	6.0	2.2	37.2	87.9	63 519	15 940	141	540	15	354	1 351
De Kalb city	5.4	11.6	39.2	23.8	12.0	3.8	3.0	1.4	23.1	97.9	31 015	3 543	94	1 804	49	1 696	817
Des Plaines city	5.9	16.5	7.5	29.2	23.8	8.3	6.2	2.7	39.7	93.6	49 586	594	151	4 492	13	2 726	1 158
Downers Grove village	6.2	18.5	6.6	29.3	25.0	6.5	5.6	2.3	39.1	92.4	43 924	936	55	2 782	6	488	533
East St. Louis city	8.6	24.2	9.7	24.6	20.3	7.1	4.0	1.4	31.2	81.5	387	30 829	59	24	9	59	175
Elgin city	9.2	19.8	10.7	33.6	18.2	4.2	3.2	1.1	30.9	99.9	66 600	6 427	382	3 668	58	14 537	2 815
Elk Grove Village village	6.0	18.9	7.4	31.8	24.2	7.0	3.7	1.1	37.7	95.0	29 874	490	33	3 051	15	797	467
Elmhurst city	7.0	18.6	7.0	28.5	23.0	7.1	6.3	2.6	38.7	92.5	39 940	400	24	1 568	8	416	406
Evanston city	5.8	14.4	16.4	32.0	20.6	5.1	3.8	2.0	32.5	89.0	48 429	16 704	140	4 524	64	2 116	2 262
Freeport city	6.6	17.8	8.5	27.8	21.2	8.1	6.9	3.1	37.9	87.1	21 623	3 651	51	257	10	265	586
Galesburg city	5.7	15.4	11.8	27.0	22.0	8.4	6.8	2.9	38.1	100.3	28 390	3 437	74	346	8	830	621
Glendale Heights village	8.0	18.9	11.5	36.8	19.9	3.1	1.5	.4	30.5	104.2	20 263	1 537	95	6 345	25	2 576	924
Glenview village	6.5	19.1	5.2	25.3	27.9	8.6	5.7	1.7	41.3	92.5	35 817	665	41	4 207	7	532	578
Granite City city	6.0	18.7	8.3	29.2	21.5	8.5	6.1	1.8	37.6	92.5	29 653	622	141	147	7	297	434
Hanover Park village	8.8	22.7	10.9	35.0	18.5	2.6	1.2	.3	29.7	106.3	26 077	2 348	109	4 574	6	3 967	1 197
Harvey city	9.6	25.5	10.8	26.7	18.8	5.0	2.8	.8	27.9	92.2	3 005	23 871	79	114	16	2 382	533
Highland Park city	7.4	19.6	4.6	25.5	27.8	8.5	5.1	1.4	40.6	95.9	28 606	559	24	716	4	1 086	370
Hoffman Estates village	7.2	20.9	8.7	33.9	22.6	3.9	1.9	.9	33.6	99.2	36 837	2 166	86	7 461	12	1 857	1 076
Joliet city	9.3	20.2	10.1	33.1	16.3	5.1	4.2	1.8	31.0	98.2	73 633	19 294	301	1 215	22	9 532	2 224
Kankakee city	8.3	21.1	9.7	28.7	18.7	5.9	5.1	2.3	32.3	91.8	13 998	11 291	75	87	7	1 511	522
Lansing village	6.4	17.9	7.8	29.1	23.1	8.0	6.2	1.4	38.4	90.1	24 295	3 029	36	203	13	437	319
Lombard village	6.1	16.8	7.9	33.4	21.2	6.4	5.5	2.6	36.7	94.3	36 829	1 141	62	2 982	7	606	695
Maywood village	8.0	23.7	10.4	27.7	20.6	6.0	2.6	1.0	30.7	87.9	2 625	22 308	34	80	1	1 500	439
Moline city	6.5	17.6	9.2	27.8	23.6	7.7	5.8	1.9	37.9	91.5	38 682	1 351	87	607	11	2 222	808
Mount Prospect village	6.6	16.4	8.2	31.3	22.7	8.5	5.1	1.2	37.2	98.9	45 338	1 026	110	6 292	28	2 332	1 139
Naperville city	8.4	23.4	6.4	33.7	21.9	3.1	2.2	.9	34.2	95.9	109 346	3 887	154	12 380	24	967	1 600
Niles village	3.8	12.9	6.9	24.0	24.8	12.4	10.5	4.9	46.8	87.5	25 022	139	27	3 812	4	502	562
Normal town	4.9	12.6	38.1	23.1	13.7	3.9	2.7	1.0	23.0	88.6	39 745	3 499	68	1 001	18	421	634
Northbrook village	5.7	19.8	4.4	21.8	29.7	9.9	6.5	2.3	44.1	93.4	29 830	190	13	2 958	3	119	322
North Chicago city	8.0	16.1	34.7	27.5	9.2	2.5	1.6	.4	22.0	156.3	17 140	13 024	301	1 289	53	2 750	1 361
Oak Forest city	6.7	19.3	9.1	31.0	24.7	5.2	3.2	.8	35.6	99.3	25 353	1 021	42	744	4	468	419

[1] Includes all other responses not included in the other five race categories shown. Also includes write-in entries such as multiracial, mixed, interracial, or a Hispanic/Latino group. [2] Refers to combinations of two or more of the six race categories shown under one race.

Source: Population by Age, Sex, and Race—U.S. Census Bureau; 2000 Census of Population and Housing, "Census 2000 Profiles of General Demographic Characteristics" data files, published May 2001, related Internet site <http://www.census.gov/mp/www/pub/2000cen/mscen01.html>.

Table C–2. Cities — Population by Age, Sex, and Race—Con.

[Includes states and 1,070 incorporated places of 25,000 or more population as of April 1, 1990 in all states except Hawaii which has no incorporated places recognized by the Census Bureau. For Hawaii, 8 census designated places (CDPs) of 25,000 or more population as of April 1, 1990 are included. Also included are the 5 boroughs of New York city. For more information on these areas, see appendix B. Geographic Information]

City	Population by age, 2000 (April 1) Percent— Under 5 years	5 to 17 years	18 to 24 years	25 to 44 years	45 to 64 years	65 to 74 years	75 to 84 years	85 years and over	Median age (years)	Males per 100 females, 2000 (April 1)	White	Black or African American	American Indian and Alaska Native	Asian	Native Hawaiian and Other Pacific Islander	Some other race[1]	Two or more races[2]
ILLINOIS—Con.																	
Oak Lawn village	5.4	16.6	7.2	26.2	22.9	10.5	8.7	2.6	41.5	88.3	51 570	673	92	953	5	905	1 047
Oak Park village	6.9	17.3	6.7	35.2	24.4	4.5	3.4	1.6	36.0	86.9	36 124	11 788	81	2 178	16	857	1 480
Orland Park village	5.4	19.0	7.1	24.8	27.3	8.9	6.0	1.5	41.4	91.7	47 772	374	34	1 770	18	530	579
Palatine village	7.3	17.5	8.5	35.8	22.0	5.0	2.8	1.0	34.3	99.2	54 381	1 407	147	4 953	27	3 327	1 237
Park Ridge city	5.8	18.7	5.5	24.5	25.8	9.6	7.3	2.7	42.5	90.1	36 031	90	24	1 004	18	329	279
Pekin city	6.5	16.7	9.3	30.4	21.4	8.1	5.6	2.0	37.1	96.5	32 434	863	125	139	4	62	230
Peoria city	7.4	18.3	12.0	27.2	20.8	6.8	5.4	2.0	33.8	89.9	78 254	27 992	229	2 629	42	1 355	2 435
Quincy city	5.9	17.4	10.0	25.8	20.9	8.5	7.8	3.6	38.4	88.3	37 550	1 879	75	216	5	147	494
Rockford city	7.7	18.9	9.2	29.7	20.4	6.7	5.4	2.1	34.4	93.1	109 303	26 072	474	3 301	67	7 200	3 698
Rock Island city	6.4	16.5	13.1	25.7	21.9	7.6	6.1	2.6	36.4	89.5	30 609	6 814	113	299	26	955	868
Schaumburg village	6.0	15.9	8.3	36.3	24.0	4.7	3.5	1.4	35.3	94.8	59 391	2 526	77	10 697	43	1 307	1 345
Skokie village	5.2	17.8	7.0	25.0	25.5	9.2	7.6	2.7	41.9	90.1	43 661	2 854	109	13 483	16	1 178	2 047
Springfield city	6.6	17.4	8.8	29.8	23.0	7.0	5.3	2.1	36.9	88.6	90 287	17 096	231	1 620	34	525	1 661
Streamwood village	8.7	19.4	8.2	37.3	20.3	3.8	1.8	.5	32.5	100.3	28 225	1 398	106	3 145	12	2 570	951
Tinley Park village	6.6	20.0	8.1	31.0	23.5	5.7	4.1	.9	36.5	93.8	45 092	931	63	1 153	9	539	614
Urbana city	4.4	10.5	36.2	26.4	13.2	4.2	3.5	1.7	24.6	111.3	24 389	5 218	64	5 181	14	639	890
Waukegan city	9.6	20.6	12.1	33.4	16.4	4.2	2.8	1.0	29.0	103.1	44 073	16 890	471	3 146	57	20 185	3 079
Wheaton city	6.3	19.8	10.5	28.8	23.4	5.4	4.1	1.7	35.8	94.9	49 791	1 565	63	2 687	11	571	728
Wheeling village	6.6	16.8	9.4	35.2	21.8	5.3	3.4	1.6	34.5	96.8	26 452	843	80	3 193	25	3 168	735
Wilmette village	7.1	22.6	3.6	21.7	27.8	8.6	6.2	2.4	42.2	91.8	24 791	156	10	2 255	4	117	318
Woodridge village	7.6	19.7	9.2	36.0	22.2	3.3	1.6	.4	32.8	99.0	23 289	2 482	49	3 485	6	962	661
INDIANA	7.0	18.9	10.1	29.5	22.1	6.5	4.4	1.5	35.2	96.3	5 320 022	510 034	15 815	59 126	2 005	97 811	75 672
Anderson city	6.9	16.3	11.2	27.6	21.3	8.0	6.4	2.2	36.1	90.0	48 978	8 886	187	292	9	516	866
Bloomington city	4.1	8.6	42.3	24.6	12.6	3.8	3.0	1.1	23.3	94.4	60 301	2 940	199	3 644	49	763	1 395
Carmel city	7.9	22.4	4.8	29.9	25.3	5.1	3.2	1.5	37.2	94.4	34 951	555	52	1 651	17	173	334
Columbus city	7.4	18.3	8.0	29.5	23.0	6.9	5.0	1.8	36.4	92.8	35 668	1 057	50	1 260	19	542	463
East Chicago city	9.1	21.4	11.1	26.8	18.3	7.4	4.6	1.3	30.8	91.7	11 843	11 695	166	66	26	7 774	844
Elkhart city	9.4	19.0	11.1	31.7	18.0	5.2	4.1	1.4	30.8	96.9	37 077	7 649	225	608	35	4 750	1 530
Evansville city	6.4	16.3	11.5	28.6	21.0	7.7	6.2	2.3	36.5	88.8	104 858	13 275	257	870	55	598	1 669
Fort Wayne city	7.8	19.2	10.7	30.2	19.7	6.0	4.6	1.8	32.8	94.0	155 231	35 752	806	3 205	86	5 993	4 654
Gary city	8.4	21.5	10.1	25.1	22.2	7.5	4.1	1.2	33.6	84.6	12 245	86 340	213	140	24	2 023	1 761
Greenwood city	7.7	17.6	9.6	32.1	20.7	5.8	4.7	1.9	34.1	91.9	34 790	159	67	490	15	250	266
Hammond city	8.1	19.2	9.8	30.1	19.8	6.5	5.1	1.4	33.9	95.3	60 089	12 102	339	383	64	7 741	2 330
Indianapolis city (remainder)	7.4	18.3	10.2	32.9	20.3	5.8	3.9	1.3	33.5	93.7	540 212	199 412	1 985	11 161	322	15 921	12 857
Kokomo city	7.8	17.1	9.4	29.0	22.2	7.2	5.3	1.9	35.7	89.6	39 242	4 770	177	525	12	539	848
Lafayette city	7.0	16.2	14.2	31.3	19.3	5.9	4.7	1.5	31.7	97.7	50 143	1 816	210	689	24	2 601	914
Lawrence city	9.1	20.9	7.7	36.2	18.0	4.5	2.7	1.0	32.4	95.2	30 581	6 036	117	699	30	723	729
Marion city	6.5	16.7	12.5	26.0	21.3	8.3	6.3	2.4	36.3	88.6	24 942	4 878	147	214	7	449	683
Merrillville town	6.6	18.0	8.7	29.4	22.2	6.9	5.9	2.3	37.0	91.2	21 286	6 987	100	460	6	1 035	686
Michigan City city	7.6	17.4	9.6	30.8	20.6	6.9	5.4	1.8	35.2	101.8	22 848	8 657	86	167	6	361	775
Mishawaka city	7.1	16.9	11.8	30.7	19.4	6.5	5.4	2.1	33.5	89.7	42 636	1 659	200	649	22	494	897
Muncie city	5.8	13.9	24.6	24.2	18.3	6.4	4.9	1.7	28.9	89.9	57 799	7 397	183	534	62	451	1 004
New Albany city	6.9	17.2	9.6	29.2	21.8	7.6	5.8	2.0	36.6	88.5	33 844	2 607	118	159	14	252	609
Portage city	7.2	18.9	9.4	29.9	22.8	6.0	4.4	1.4	35.4	94.2	30 992	485	90	215	19	1 072	623
Richmond city	6.8	16.6	11.0	27.5	21.6	8.1	6.1	2.2	36.3	88.7	33 951	3 469	107	312	22	425	838
South Bend city	8.3	19.0	10.4	29.3	18.2	6.8	5.7	2.3	32.7	91.1	71 195	26 522	440	1 292	69	5 250	3 021
Terre Haute city	6.2	15.2	18.7	26.6	18.5	6.5	6.0	2.3	32.1	97.3	51 422	5 827	202	696	25	304	1 138
West Lafayette city	2.5	7.9	54.6	16.9	10.3	3.1	3.0	1.7	22.3	133.5	23 985	684	45	3 263	9	336	456
IOWA	6.4	18.6	10.2	27.6	22.2	7.2	5.4	2.2	36.6	96.3	2 748 640	61 853	8 989	36 635	1 009	37 420	31 778
Ames city	4.4	10.2	40.0	23.7	13.9	3.9	2.7	1.1	23.6	109.3	44 308	1 343	75	3 906	22	388	689
Bettendorf city	6.2	20.1	6.7	28.0	26.6	6.5	4.4	1.5	38.7	94.3	29 715	494	67	444	4	214	337
Burlington city	6.6	17.9	8.9	26.7	22.7	7.9	6.7	2.6	37.9	90.9	24 581	1 354	89	177	11	242	385
Cedar Falls city	4.4	13.6	30.6	20.5	19.0	5.4	4.5	2.0	26.0	88.5	34 389	568	55	583	8	148	394
Cedar Rapids city	7.1	17.3	10.8	30.7	20.9	6.4	4.8	1.8	34.7	95.0	110 931	4 481	306	2 135	78	670	2 157
Clinton city	6.6	18.0	9.1	26.8	22.5	8.0	6.6	2.5	38.3	91.3	26 049	893	90	225	3	141	371
Council Bluffs city	7.2	18.8	10.3	29.7	20.8	7.2	4.6	1.5	34.6	93.7	55 213	614	263	344	15	1 054	765
Davenport city	7.4	18.8	10.7	30.1	20.9	6.0	4.5	1.7	33.6	94.7	82 311	9 093	368	1 967	24	2 279	2 317
Des Moines city	7.5	17.3	10.6	31.8	20.4	6.0	4.5	1.8	33.8	93.8	163 494	16 025	705	6 946	95	6 987	4 430
Dubuque city	6.2	17.4	11.8	26.5	21.6	7.7	6.1	2.7	36.9	90.0	55 466	700	112	390	65	400	553
Fort Dodge city	6.8	17.5	10.7	25.2	21.2	8.2	7.1	3.3	38.0	90.5	23 243	952	52	214	6	328	341
Iowa City city	4.6	11.6	32.8	28.1	15.9	3.5	2.5	1.0	25.4	96.2	54 334	2 333	191	3 509	27	778	1 048
Marshalltown city	6.7	17.8	8.9	26.0	23.0	8.1	6.7	2.8	38.4	98.0	22 574	348	96	271	17	2 228	475
Mason City city	6.2	17.3	10.2	26.7	21.7	8.4	6.6	2.8	38.2	90.0	27 829	342	52	226	3	313	407
Sioux City city	7.9	19.2	11.0	28.5	20.2	6.6	4.9	1.9	33.4	95.4	72 460	2 047	1 661	2 396	33	4 479	1 937
Waterloo city	7.0	17.6	10.6	27.5	22.0	7.3	5.8	2.3	35.9	92.2	56 103	9 529	150	587	34	989	1 355
West Des Moines city	7.7	16.9	9.7	35.5	20.3	5.3	3.5	1.0	33.0	92.0	42 995	868	61	1 280	16	585	598

[1] Includes all other responses not included in the other five race categories shown. Also includes write-in entries such as multiracial, mixed, interracial, or a Hispanic/Latino group. [2] Refers to combinations of two or more of the six race categories shown under one race.

Source: Population by Age, Sex, and Race—U.S. Census Bureau; 2000 Census of Population and Housing, "Census 2000 Profiles of General Demographic Characteristics" data files, published May 2001, related Internet site <http://www.census.gov/mp/www/pub/2000cen/mscen01.html>.

Table C–2. Cities — **Population by Age, Sex, and Race**–Con.

[Includes states and 1,070 incorporated places of 25,000 or more population as of April 1, 1990 in all states except Hawaii which has no incorporated places recognized by the Census Bureau. For Hawaii, 8 census designated places (CDPs) of 25,000 or more population as of April 1, 1990 are included. Also included are the 5 boroughs of New York city. For more information on these areas, see appendix B. Geographic Information]

City	Population by age, 2000 (April 1) Percent—									Males per 100 females, 2000 (April 1)	Population by race, 2000 (April 1) One race						
	Under 5 years	5 to 17 years	18 to 24 years	25 to 44 years	45 to 64 years	65 to 74 years	75 to 84 years	85 years and over	Median age (years)		White	Black or African American	American Indian and Alaska Native	Asian	Native Hawaiian and Other Pacific Islander	Some other race[1]	Two or more races[2]
KANSAS	7.0	19.5	10.3	28.6	21.4	6.5	4.8	1.9	35.2	97.7	2 313 944	154 198	24 936	46 806	1 313	90 725	56 496
Emporia city..............	7.3	18.0	19.4	27.2	17.0	4.8	4.2	2.1	28.4	95.6	21 041	793	128	712	1	3 411	674
Hutchinson city	6.6	16.6	11.0	27.8	21.2	7.8	6.5	2.6	37.1	101.7	36 125	1 747	267	242	15	1 490	901
Kansas City city	8.1	20.4	10.6	29.5	19.8	6.1	4.1	1.4	32.3	95.6	81 910	44 240	1 103	2 527	56	12 645	4 385
Lawrence city	5.4	13.1	30.7	28.5	15.1	3.6	2.7	.9	25.3	98.8	67 122	4 078	2 344	3 030	56	1 086	2 382
Leavenworth city	8.2	19.5	8.8	34.8	19.0	4.9	3.6	1.3	34.1	112.4	27 192	5 781	270	523	59	609	986
Lenexa city	6.4	19.3	9.5	32.0	24.2	3.5	3.0	2.0	35.1	95.8	36 013	1 312	152	1 459	12	644	646
Manhattan city	4.6	11.2	39.2	24.0	13.2	3.6	2.9	1.3	23.5	106.4	39 130	2 179	214	1 764	33	582	929
Olathe city	9.4	21.5	9.2	36.7	18.1	2.8	1.7	.7	30.8	99.4	82 393	3 440	402	2 549	44	2 457	1 677
Overland Park city	7.1	19.0	7.0	32.5	23.0	5.8	4.1	1.5	36.3	93.8	135 137	3 801	401	5 703	52	1 852	2 134
Salina city	7.1	18.8	10.0	28.7	21.1	7.1	5.2	2.0	35.3	95.8	40 090	1 630	256	896	21	1 728	1 058
Shawnee city	7.7	19.1	7.8	34.2	22.7	5.0	2.7	.8	34.8	96.9	43 362	1 422	149	1 273	13	897	880
Topeka city	7.0	17.2	9.9	28.9	21.9	7.4	5.6	2.1	36.3	92.4	96 093	14 332	1 603	1 340	50	4 969	3 990
Wichita city	8.0	19.1	10.1	30.7	20.2	6.0	4.4	1.4	33.4	97.1	258 900	39 325	3 986	13 647	198	17 566	10 662
KENTUCKY..............	6.6	18.0	9.9	30.0	23.0	6.8	4.3	1.4	35.9	95.6	3 640 889	295 994	8 616	29 744	1 460	22 623	42 443
Bowling Green city	6.0	14.2	23.5	26.9	17.5	5.9	4.4	1.7	28.6	93.7	39 842	6 267	111	959	61	1 065	991
Covington city	7.8	18.0	10.0	33.3	19.0	5.9	4.3	1.7	33.1	95.9	37 752	4 397	105	147	15	272	682
Frankfort city	6.2	15.4	11.7	30.3	22.4	7.0	5.1	1.8	35.9	91.1	22 704	4 078	35	260	8	213	443
Henderson city	6.7	16.9	9.2	29.5	22.5	7.8	5.6	1.8	37.0	89.3	23 885	2 883	48	110	2	159	286
Hopkinsville city	7.4	19.0	9.7	28.3	20.8	7.6	5.1	2.2	35.1	87.9	19 875	9 302	69	229	26	178	410
Lexington-Fayette.........	6.2	15.1	14.6	33.2	20.9	5.3	3.5	1.2	33.0	96.5	211 120	35 116	507	6 407	83	3 165	4 114
Louisville city	6.6	17.0	10.4	30.4	21.0	7.3	5.4	2.0	35.8	89.7	161 261	84 586	578	3 705	111	1 709	4 281
Owensboro city	6.8	17.4	9.8	27.4	22.4	8.2	5.9	2.2	37.4	87.6	48 999	3 728	66	276	12	295	691
Paducah city	6.5	16.0	8.5	26.2	22.5	8.8	7.8	3.6	39.9	83.4	19 145	6 353	66	169	20	144	410
LOUISIANA	7.1	20.2	10.6	28.9	21.6	6.3	3.9	1.3	34.0	93.8	2 856 161	1 451 944	25 477	54 758	1 240	31 131	48 265
Alexandria city............	7.3	20.8	9.2	26.2	21.4	7.5	5.6	2.1	35.6	83.5	19 740	25 371	116	577	20	107	411
Baton Rouge city	6.8	17.6	17.5	27.2	19.4	5.8	4.2	1.4	30.4	90.5	104 117	113 953	405	5 972	76	1 113	2 182
Bossier City city	8.0	20.2	11.0	30.4	19.4	6.1	3.7	1.2	32.1	94.5	40 335	12 840	322	976	60	813	1 115
Houma city..............	7.4	20.5	9.8	29.2	20.8	6.6	4.3	1.4	34.3	94.8	21 851	8 461	1 116	230	6	221	508
Kenner city..............	7.0	20.3	9.4	30.5	23.9	5.2	2.8	.9	34.5	92.5	48 038	15 900	279	2 002	41	2 679	1 578
Lafayette city.............	6.4	18.6	13.3	29.5	20.9	6.3	3.6	1.3	33.1	93.1	75 232	31 434	272	1 584	26	641	1 068
Lake Charles city	6.9	18.6	11.5	26.9	21.4	7.7	5.2	1.8	35.3	90.9	36 042	33 599	167	770	18	338	823
Monroe city	7.6	22.0	15.0	25.1	17.5	6.2	4.7	1.9	29.1	84.1	19 535	32 462	68	558	16	132	336
New Iberia city	8.2	21.6	9.7	26.8	20.4	6.8	4.8	1.8	33.6	87.8	18 593	12 533	70	862	7	166	392
New Orleans city	6.9	19.8	11.4	29.3	20.9	6.0	4.2	1.5	33.1	88.2	135 956	325 947	991	10 972	109	4 498	6 201
Shreveport city	7.1	19.8	10.7	27.4	21.1	6.9	5.0	2.0	34.3	87.4	93 394	101 679	619	1 590	66	893	1 904
MAINE	5.5	18.1	8.1	29.1	24.8	7.5	5.0	1.8	38.6	94.8	1 236 014	6 760	7 098	9 111	382	2 911	12 647
Bangor city..............	5.7	15.5	12.4	30.3	22.0	6.7	5.2	2.2	36.1	89.5	29 888	320	309	364	18	123	451
Lewiston city	5.6	15.2	12.6	26.9	22.0	8.3	6.7	2.8	37.6	90.9	34 172	383	100	301	11	130	593
Portland city.............	5.1	13.6	10.7	36.1	20.6	6.3	5.3	2.3	35.7	91.8	58 638	1 665	302	1 982	36	431	1 195
MARYLAND	6.7	18.9	8.5	31.4	23.1	6.1	4.0	1.3	36.0	93.4	3 391 308	1 477 411	15 423	210 929	2 303	95 525	103 587
Annapolis city	6.7	15.0	9.3	33.4	23.7	6.3	4.4	1.3	35.7	90.0	22 457	11 267	60	650	11	796	597
Baltimore city............	6.4	18.4	10.9	29.9	21.2	6.9	4.8	1.5	35.0	87.4	205 982	418 951	2 097	9 985	222	4 363	9 554
Bowie city..............	7.5	19.4	5.7	34.9	23.0	5.7	2.9	.9	36.3	91.5	31 492	15 500	150	1 482	17	470	1 158
Frederick city............	7.5	17.7	9.3	35.2	19.0	5.3	4.3	1.7	33.8	90.9	40 651	7 777	154	1 664	32	1 191	1 298
Gaithersburg city	8.2	16.8	9.0	37.7	20.0	3.5	2.9	1.8	33.6	95.1	30 625	7 680	188	7 241	33	4 535	2 311
Hagerstown city	7.9	17.6	9.0	31.0	20.1	6.8	5.6	2.0	34.8	87.8	31 532	3 722	90	354	15	304	670
Rockville city	6.3	17.1	7.0	32.1	24.4	6.8	4.6	1.7	37.8	95.2	32 120	4 317	160	7 030	15	2 265	1 481
MASSACHUSETTS......	6.3	17.4	9.1	31.3	22.4	6.7	5.0	1.8	36.5	93.0	5 367 286	343 454	15 015	238 124	2 489	236 724	146 005
Attleboro city	7.0	18.4	6.8	34.0	21.0	6.4	4.7	1.8	36.1	94.5	38 410	691	67	1 367	15	765	753
Beverly city	6.3	15.4	9.0	30.9	22.8	7.2	5.8	2.6	38.3	89.7	38 257	413	70	511	12	207	392
Boston city..............	5.4	14.3	16.2	35.8	17.8	5.3	3.7	1.4	31.1	92.8	320 944	149 202	2 365	44 284	366	46 102	25 878
Brockton city	7.3	20.6	9.1	30.5	20.8	5.8	4.2	1.7	34.0	92.1	57 989	16 811	338	2 066	34	9 728	7 338
Cambridge city	4.1	9.2	21.2	38.6	17.8	4.6	3.3	1.2	30.4	96.1	69 022	12 079	290	12 036	77	3 230	4 621
Chelsea city.............	8.1	19.2	10.6	34.6	16.3	5.4	4.0	1.8	31.3	100.9	20 328	2 544	170	1 647	32	8 049	2 310
Chicopee city	5.5	17.2	8.5	28.8	22.5	8.5	7.2	1.9	38.7	90.7	49 089	1 244	107	474	57	2 679	1 003
Everett city..............	5.9	15.7	8.9	34.8	19.9	7.5	5.4	1.9	35.6	91.0	30 321	2 386	120	1 236	26	1 898	2 050
Fall River city............	6.4	17.8	9.2	29.8	20.0	7.6	6.8	2.5	35.7	87.7	83 815	2 283	172	1 987	25	1 311	2 345
Fitchburg city............	6.7	19.1	11.6	28.8	19.2	6.7	5.7	2.2	34.1	91.3	32 007	1 426	138	1 668	13	2 652	1 198
Gloucester city	5.8	16.2	6.5	29.9	26.1	8.3	5.3	2.0	40.1	92.0	29 361	186	37	218	7	152	312
Haverhill city	7.4	18.3	7.7	33.5	20.4	5.9	4.9	2.0	35.5	90.3	52 878	1 419	129	801	18	2 536	1 188

[1] Includes all other responses not included in the other five race categories shown. Also includes write-in entries such as multiracial, mixed, interracial, or a Hispanic/Latino group. [2] Refers to combinations of two or more of the six race categories shown under one race.

Source: Population by Age, Sex, and Race—U.S. Census Bureau; 2000 Census of Population and Housing, "Census 2000 Profiles of General Demographic Characteristics" data files, published May 2001, related Internet site <http://www.census.gov/mp/www/pub/2000cen/mscen01.html>.

Table C–2. Cities — **Population by Age, Sex, and Race**–Con.

[Includes states and 1,070 incorporated places of 25,000 or more population as of April 1, 1990 in all states except Hawaii which has no incorporated places recognized by the Census Bureau. For Hawaii, 8 census designated places (CDPs) of 25,000 or more population as of April 1, 1990 are included. Also included are the 5 boroughs of New York city. For more information on these areas, see appendix B. Geographic Information]

City	Population by age, 2000 (April 1)									Males per 100 females, 2000 (April 1)	Population by race, 2000 (April 1)							
	Percent–								Median age (years)		One race							Two or more races[2]
	Under 5 years	5 to 17 years	18 to 24 years	25 to 44 years	45 to 64 years	65 to 74 years	75 to 84 years	85 years and over			White	Black or African American	American Indian and Alaska Native	Asian	Native Hawaiian and Other Pacific Islander	Some other race[1]	
MASSACHUSETTS—Con.																	
Holyoke city	7.9	21.5	9.0	26.8	19.2	6.7	6.0	2.9	34.0	88.1	26 197	1 476	151	324	48	10 521	1 121
Lawrence city	9.0	23.0	11.1	30.3	16.7	4.4	3.8	1.6	29.5	91.6	35 044	3 516	583	1 910	71	26 418	4 501
Leominster city	7.1	18.4	7.2	32.4	21.3	6.8	5.2	1.7	36.3	92.6	35 982	1 529	63	1 006	24	1 785	914
Lowell city	7.3	19.6	11.9	32.5	17.9	5.4	4.0	1.4	31.4	97.1	72 145	4 423	256	17 371	38	6 813	4 121
Lynn city	7.3	19.7	9.1	31.0	20.1	6.3	4.8	1.7	34.2	93.7	60 452	9 394	332	5 730	79	8 744	4 319
Malden city	5.8	14.1	8.5	36.9	20.8	7.0	4.9	1.9	35.7	92.8	40 618	4 592	80	7 882	33	1 184	1 951
Marlborough city	7.0	16.2	7.0	36.7	21.5	5.8	4.0	1.7	36.1	97.2	31 796	787	72	1 364	13	1 186	1 037
Medford city	4.9	13.1	11.0	32.6	21.2	8.1	6.7	2.5	37.5	88.2	48 209	3 401	63	2 157	17	633	1 285
Melrose city	6.7	15.3	5.4	32.0	24.2	7.0	6.1	2.6	39.1	88.7	25 820	255	26	546	6	109	372
New Bedford city	6.7	18.2	9.5	28.8	20.2	7.7	6.6	2.4	35.9	89.1	73 950	4 112	579	614	44	8 915	5 554
Newton city	5.2	16.0	10.3	28.2	25.2	7.1	5.6	2.5	38.7	86.8	73 831	1 653	61	6 434	29	598	1 223
Northampton city	4.1	12.9	15.4	29.9	23.9	5.9	5.5	2.4	37.3	75.6	26 083	602	86	906	15	697	589
Peabody city	5.8	16.4	6.2	29.4	24.7	9.1	6.3	2.0	40.3	91.9	45 204	466	57	667	7	883	845
Pittsfield city	5.9	17.2	6.9	28.3	23.0	8.8	7.1	2.7	39.6	90.6	42 395	1 674	65	533	20	354	752
Quincy city	5.1	12.4	8.1	36.1	22.1	8.0	6.0	2.3	37.6	91.0	70 066	1 947	142	13 546	20	751	1 553
Revere city	5.8	15.2	7.9	32.6	21.8	8.3	6.2	2.1	37.6	93.6	39 884	1 364	124	2 146	35	1 942	1 788
Salem city	5.6	14.6	10.4	33.4	21.9	6.9	5.4	1.8	36.4	86.5	34 497	1 274	87	807	19	2 724	999
Somerville city	4.5	10.3	15.9	42.6	16.2	5.2	3.8	1.4	31.1	94.9	59 635	5 035	171	4 990	50	3 840	3 757
Springfield city	7.6	21.3	11.4	28.3	18.8	6.1	4.8	1.5	31.9	89.4	85 329	31 960	569	2 916	143	25 016	6 149
Taunton city	7.1	17.8	8.0	33.2	21.0	6.3	4.9	1.6	35.7	92.5	51 315	1 534	92	334	18	1 448	1 235
Waltham city	4.7	10.8	16.8	34.4	20.2	6.6	4.8	1.7	34.2	97.2	49 145	2 614	95	4 318	38	1 896	1 120
Westfield city	5.9	17.9	12.6	28.0	21.9	6.6	5.2	1.8	35.8	93.7	37 881	365	90	329	19	850	538
Woburn city	5.8	15.3	6.9	34.9	21.8	8.6	5.1	1.6	37.7	95.6	33 744	697	36	1 806	19	535	421
Worcester city	6.5	17.1	13.3	30.3	18.6	6.3	5.6	2.2	33.4	92.4	133 124	11 892	769	8 402	96	12 504	5 861
MICHIGAN	6.8	19.4	9.4	29.8	22.4	6.5	4.4	1.4	35.5	96.2	7 966 053	1 412 742	58 479	176 510	2 692	129 552	192 416
Allen Park city	5.3	16.8	6.5	28.2	22.2	9.2	9.3	2.4	41.0	91.0	28 083	214	106	238	7	354	374
Ann Arbor city	5.0	11.7	26.8	31.2	17.3	4.1	2.8	1.0	28.1	97.7	85 151	10 070	332	13 566	41	1 384	3 480
Battle Creek city	7.3	19.9	8.7	29.5	21.0	6.7	5.1	1.8	34.7	91.9	39 838	9 501	411	1 033	6	1 126	1 449
Bay City city	7.0	18.5	9.4	30.5	20.5	6.5	5.7	1.9	35.2	92.9	33 575	1 003	272	195	3	910	859
Burton city	7.3	20.1	8.4	32.0	21.0	6.5	3.7	1.0	34.6	95.8	27 910	1 075	230	224	8	244	617
Dearborn city	8.3	19.6	8.3	29.2	19.1	6.5	6.8	2.2	34.5	99.0	84 931	1 248	258	1 441	14	710	9 173
Dearborn Heights city	6.4	16.1	7.5	29.5	21.7	9.0	7.2	1.0	38.0	93.2	53 395	1 236	216	1 306	4	470	1 637
Detroit city	8.0	23.1	9.7	29.5	19.3	5.6	3.7	1.2	30.9	89.1	116 599	775 772	3 140	9 268	251	24 199	22 041
East Detroit city	6.4	18.1	7.6	32.3	19.2	7.7	7.0	1.8	36.6	94.3	31 395	1 601	143	296	2	93	547
East Lansing city	2.5	6.5	58.6	16.4	9.9	2.5	2.2	1.3	21.7	92.7	37 645	3 441	155	3 819	38	442	985
Farmington Hills city	6.0	17.1	6.7	31.3	24.6	7.0	5.4	2.0	38.6	93.8	68 107	5 699	142	6 188	15	376	1 584
Ferndale city	5.7	14.7	9.1	41.2	19.7	4.7	3.6	1.4	33.5	99.5	20 218	757	121	292	5	141	571
Flint city	9.0	21.6	10.3	29.4	19.2	5.8	3.6	1.1	30.8	88.6	51 710	66 560	798	547	19	1 384	3 925
Garden City city	6.2	18.9	7.6	32.6	21.2	8.5	4.2	.8	36.5	97.4	28 904	332	120	215	2	91	383
Grand Rapids city	8.3	18.8	13.1	31.5	16.7	5.2	4.5	1.9	30.4	95.8	133 116	40 373	1 454	3 195	238	13 115	6 309
Holland city	8.0	18.2	17.5	27.4	15.5	5.4	5.4	2.8	29.2	90.0	27 399	888	202	1 247	10	4 348	954
Inkster city	8.0	21.8	9.2	30.3	19.8	6.1	3.8	.9	31.8	91.3	7 571	20 330	124	1 031	3	224	832
Jackson city	9.1	20.6	9.8	30.4	18.2	5.6	4.6	1.8	31.3	91.0	26 825	7 154	203	186	14	601	1 333
Kalamazoo city	6.2	14.1	27.6	26.8	15.2	4.5	3.8	1.8	26.1	93.1	54 593	15 924	445	1 847	50	1 836	2 450
Kentwood city	7.7	18.9	10.4	33.7	19.5	5.0	3.8	1.1	32.4	93.2	36 599	4 115	207	2 550	18	644	1 122
Lansing city	8.2	18.6	11.4	32.7	19.3	5.2	3.5	1.1	31.4	92.3	77 766	26 095	953	3 367	62	5 410	5 475
Lincoln Park city	6.9	17.4	8.5	32.7	20.4	7.1	5.8	1.2	35.5	95.7	37 312	824	213	204	2	728	725
Livonia city	5.6	18.2	6.3	28.7	24.3	8.9	6.0	2.0	40.2	94.0	95 975	951	223	1 951	14	318	1 113
Madison Heights city	6.2	15.9	8.1	35.4	20.2	8.0	4.8	1.4	36.1	95.8	27 866	567	138	1 547	8	142	833
Midland city	6.5	19.4	10.2	27.9	22.2	6.8	5.2	1.9	36.2	92.0	38 924	760	122	1 123	24	236	496
Muskegon city	7.6	18.1	11.6	32.2	18.0	5.5	5.0	1.9	32.3	109.6	24 309	12 701	418	183	12	1 078	1 404
Novi city	7.4	20.2	6.7	35.7	21.9	4.3	2.9	.9	35.2	96.9	41 349	908	89	4 106	8	223	703
Oak Park city	6.8	21.4	8.0	29.8	21.8	5.9	4.9	1.3	34.6	88.0	13 989	13 690	52	648	5	179	1 230
Pontiac city	8.9	21.7	10.3	32.3	18.3	4.7	2.8	1.0	30.0	94.8	25 934	31 791	382	1 591	26	4 291	2 322
Portage city	6.9	19.5	8.5	29.9	23.4	6.5	4.1	1.2	35.8	92.1	40 746	1 676	135	1 187	10	315	828
Port Huron city	7.8	19.2	9.7	29.6	19.6	6.5	5.2	2.3	34.0	90.7	28 034	2 504	281	179	4	428	908
Rochester Hills city	6.5	19.4	6.7	30.1	26.6	5.5	3.7	1.5	38.1	95.0	61 084	1 667	139	4 652	20	322	941
Roseville city	6.5	16.6	8.2	33.0	20.2	7.9	6.0	1.5	36.2	93.8	44 968	1 252	201	785	15	154	754
Royal Oak city	5.2	12.6	7.5	38.8	21.0	6.7	6.3	1.9	36.9	95.3	56 941	927	157	939	32	228	838
Saginaw city	8.6	23.0	9.9	28.3	18.7	5.8	4.2	1.4	30.7	87.2	29 056	26 735	302	205	10	3 619	1 872
St. Clair Shores city	5.1	15.1	6.2	28.8	23.1	11.1	8.3	2.4	42.0	90.9	61 135	435	175	531	14	111	695
Southfield city	5.6	16.0	7.9	30.6	24.8	6.8	5.7	2.7	38.3	84.9	30 406	42 454	157	2 416	24	498	2 341
Southgate city	5.4	16.1	8.3	30.6	23.3	8.4	6.4	1.4	38.5	93.0	28 224	635	151	502	13	256	355
Sterling Heights city	6.2	17.9	8.5	30.4	25.2	5.8	4.3	1.6	37.0	96.0	112 899	1 614	260	6 123	45	418	3 112
Taylor city	7.5	19.7	9.3	31.0	21.5	6.7	3.3	.9	33.9	93.2	56 731	5 763	448	1 072	21	492	1 341
Troy city	6.2	20.0	6.7	29.8	27.1	5.8	3.5	1.0	38.1	98.1	66 627	1 694	125	10 730	18	292	1 473
Warren city	6.4	16.6	7.6	30.8	21.4	9.1	6.4	1.8	37.9	95.6	126 205	3 697	494	4 275	30	467	3 079
Westland city	6.9	16.3	9.0	33.9	20.6	7.0	4.6	1.7	35.2	92.6	75 527	5 867	396	2 437	28	582	1 765
Wyandotte city	5.6	17.1	8.3	31.6	21.7	7.6	6.7	1.5	38.0	96.0	26 976	146	136	92	8	202	446
Wyoming city	8.0	20.0	10.9	33.7	18.0	5.1	3.4	.9	31.2	97.5	58 491	3 362	406	2 025	27	3 260	1 797

[1] Includes all other responses not included in the other five race categories shown. Also includes write-in entries such as multiracial, mixed, interracial, or a Hispanic/Latino group. [2] Refers to combinations of two or more of the six race categories shown under one race.

Source: Population by Age, Sex, and Race—U.S. Census Bureau; 2000 Census of Population and Housing, "Census 2000 Profiles of General Demographic Characteristics" data files, published May 2001, related Internet site <http://www.census.gov/mp/www/pub/2000cen/mscen01.html>.

Table C–2. Cities — Population by Age, Sex, and Race—Con.

[Includes states and 1,070 incorporated places of 25,000 or more population as of April 1, 1990 in all states except Hawaii which has no incorporated places recognized by the Census Bureau. For Hawaii, 8 census designated places (CDPs) of 25,000 or more population as of April 1, 1990 are included. Also included are the 5 boroughs of New York city. For more information on these areas, see appendix B. Geographic Information]

City	Population by age, 2000 (April 1) Percent— Under 5 years	5 to 17 years	18 to 24 years	25 to 44 years	45 to 64 years	65 to 74 years	75 to 84 years	85 years and over	Median age (years)	Males per 100 females, 2000 (April 1)	Population by race, 2000 (April 1) One race White	Black or African American	American Indian and Alaska Native	Asian	Native Hawaiian and Other Pacific Islander	Some other race[1]	Two or more races[2]
MINNESOTA	6.7	19.5	9.6	30.4	21.8	6.0	4.3	1.7	35.4	98.1	4 400 282	171 731	54 967	141 968	1 979	65 810	82 742
Apple Valley city	7.2	22.5	7.2	33.1	24.4	3.3	1.6	.7	34.5	95.6	41 798	870	130	1 542	17	399	771
Blaine city	7.8	21.3	8.7	34.8	22.0	3.7	1.4	.2	32.7	100.2	42 002	387	281	1 142	10	335	785
Bloomington city	5.3	15.3	8.0	29.4	26.3	8.7	5.2	1.8	40.1	93.4	75 055	2 917	296	4 339	29	1 068	1 468
Brooklyn Center city	6.7	18.3	9.6	30.1	19.8	8.3	5.4	1.7	35.3	94.9	20 825	4 110	253	2 565	4	434	981
Brooklyn Park city	8.1	20.7	9.7	34.9	20.9	3.7	1.6	.3	31.9	98.7	48 145	9 659	381	6 214	44	1 004	1 941
Burnsville city	7.1	19.1	10.1	34.0	22.5	4.4	2.2	.7	33.0	97.3	52 717	2 452	277	2 456	46	855	1 417
Coon Rapids city	7.5	21.2	8.9	33.3	21.7	4.6	2.2	.6	33.3	94.8	57 430	1 346	410	984	8	366	1 063
Duluth city	5.4	15.9	16.2	26.1	21.3	6.5	6.3	2.7	35.4	93.4	80 532	1 415	2 122	993	25	251	1 580
Eagan city	8.1	21.9	7.4	38.2	20.2	2.7	1.2	.2	32.8	96.9	55 949	2 166	164	3 372	66	613	1 227
Eden Prairie city	7.8	22.6	6.2	35.6	22.9	3.0	1.5	.4	34.2	96.3	49 771	1 253	114	2 644	17	276	826
Edina city	5.4	17.5	4.4	23.6	26.5	10.1	9.3	3.3	44.5	84.6	44 712	546	62	1 418	14	165	508
Fridley city	6.7	15.9	10.2	31.0	24.4	7.7	3.3	.9	36.3	97.8	24 334	939	224	794	18	337	803
Mankato city	4.9	12.0	32.5	23.9	15.4	4.9	4.4	2.0	25.3	96.7	30 011	616	110	911	31	306	442
Maple Grove city	7.4	23.3	6.6	34.8	23.7	2.6	1.3	.2	34.4	98.0	47 717	528	119	1 267	16	169	549
Maplewood city	6.5	18.2	7.7	30.0	22.6	7.4	5.5	2.1	37.8	91.5	30 994	1 236	193	1 586	24	256	658
Minneapolis city	6.6	15.4	14.4	36.6	17.9	4.0	3.4	1.7	31.2	101.0	249 186	68 818	8 378	23 455	289	15 798	16 694
Minnetonka city	5.3	17.8	6.0	28.5	28.4	7.2	5.2	1.6	40.8	91.8	48 426	767	101	1 174	15	291	527
Moorhead city	5.8	16.8	23.1	24.2	17.2	5.8	4.8	2.1	28.7	88.4	29 628	247	625	410	14	676	577
Plymouth city	7.0	20.1	7.4	33.0	25.0	4.8	2.3	.5	36.1	97.1	60 200	1 783	217	2 495	9	328	862
Richfield city	6.0	14.2	9.3	33.4	20.7	7.1	7.3	2.0	37.1	96.2	27 981	2 289	248	1 826	14	1 173	908
Rochester city	7.5	18.3	9.1	33.4	20.3	5.5	4.1	1.9	34.3	94.6	75 088	3 064	258	4 830	33	996	1 537
Roseville city	4.6	13.7	11.1	26.8	23.6	9.2	7.9	3.2	41.0	87.0	30 150	945	108	1 646	28	256	557
St. Cloud city	5.5	15.2	24.1	27.6	17.3	5.2	3.7	1.4	28.2	101.8	54 229	1 402	425	1 839	37	345	830
St. Louis Park city	6.0	12.7	8.7	37.7	20.2	6.1	6.0	2.6	35.7	90.3	39 232	1 930	198	1 417	25	563	761
St. Paul city	7.6	19.5	12.5	32.0	18.0	4.6	3.9	1.8	31.0	93.6	192 444	33 637	3 259	35 488	203	11 021	11 099
Winona city	4.5	13.5	27.5	22.2	18.0	5.8	5.4	3.0	28.8	88.7	25 573	306	61	718	4	128	279
MISSISSIPPI	7.2	20.1	10.9	28.4	21.4	6.5	4.0	1.5	33.8	93.4	1 746 099	1 033 809	11 652	18 626	667	13 784	20 021
Biloxi city	7.3	16.9	14.3	30.3	19.2	6.7	4.1	1.2	32.5	101.9	36 177	9 643	248	2 590	58	725	1 203
Greenville city	8.6	22.8	10.1	26.3	20.5	6.0	4.0	1.8	31.5	85.4	12 039	28 976	29	295	6	83	205
Gulfport city	7.1	18.9	11.1	30.4	21.1	6.5	3.9	1.0	33.6	98.2	44 229	23 848	305	891	65	622	1 167
Hattiesburg city	6.7	14.8	24.4	26.3	16.0	5.5	4.3	2.0	27.1	85.3	22 365	21 200	68	547	9	231	359
Jackson city	7.8	20.7	12.4	29.1	19.1	5.5	3.9	1.5	31.0	86.9	51 208	130 151	236	1 056	24	344	1 237
Meridian city	7.6	19.6	9.9	26.6	19.7	7.8	6.3	2.5	34.6	84.0	17 580	21 729	67	238	13	112	229
Pascagoula city	7.8	19.0	12.0	28.9	20.4	6.5	4.0	1.4	32.6	101.8	17 594	7 590	47	253	6	437	273
Tupelo city	7.5	20.0	8.1	30.5	21.4	6.1	4.3	2.0	34.9	88.7	23 744	9 676	35	301	5	160	290
MISSOURI	6.6	18.9	9.6	29.1	22.3	7.0	4.7	1.8	36.1	94.6	4 748 083	629 391	25 076	61 595	3 178	45 827	82 061
Blue Springs city	7.4	22.1	8.7	31.9	22.8	3.9	2.4	.8	33.1	95.8	44 801	1 410	206	465	55	397	746
Cape Girardeau city	5.4	15.2	18.4	25.6	19.9	6.9	5.9	2.7	33.6	89.5	30 865	3 288	138	400	13	151	494
Chesterfield city	5.6	19.1	5.9	25.0	29.7	7.3	4.9	2.5	41.8	91.6	42 730	872	56	2 603	9	184	348
Columbia city	5.8	14.0	26.7	28.7	16.2	4.1	3.2	1.4	26.8	91.8	68 923	9 173	331	3 636	30	684	1 754
Florissant city	6.5	18.1	8.2	29.9	20.0	9.0	6.3	1.8	37.1	89.5	43 257	5 810	101	308	15	261	745
Gladstone city	5.4	15.6	8.6	28.2	26.4	8.8	5.5	1.6	40.0	92.5	24 585	540	136	332	36	301	435
Independence city	6.6	17.3	8.7	28.9	23.0	8.1	5.6	1.8	37.8	91.6	104 081	2 939	721	788	523	1 617	2 619
Jefferson City city	5.8	15.0	11.0	32.1	22.0	6.7	5.1	2.2	36.5	105.3	32 303	5 828	150	488	20	246	601
Joplin city	7.1	16.1	13.5	27.3	20.3	7.4	6.0	2.3	34.7	90.4	41 609	1 217	694	339	17	448	1 180
Kansas City city	7.2	18.2	9.7	32.5	20.6	6.2	4.1	1.4	34.0	93.3	267 931	137 879	2 122	8 182	493	14 158	10 780
Kirkwood city	6.0	17.4	5.9	27.6	24.9	8.1	7.3	2.7	41.1	84.1	24 800	1 932	29	222	10	75	256
Lee's Summit city	8.0	21.1	6.6	33.1	20.9	4.7	3.4	2.1	35.1	91.9	65 874	2 454	257	698	44	367	1 006
Maryland Heights city	5.9	15.6	9.8	37.2	22.0	5.6	3.0	.9	34.2	97.7	21 983	1 436	52	1 832	9	182	262
Raytown city	5.8	16.7	7.8	27.9	22.5	9.5	7.4	2.4	39.8	88.7	25 594	3 567	132	233	47	260	555
St. Charles city	6.2	17.1	12.0	30.5	22.0	6.4	4.3	1.5	35.4	96.3	56 270	2 097	160	612	22	441	719
St. Joseph city	6.4	17.7	11.6	28.6	20.3	7.2	5.8	2.3	35.6	95.6	67 981	3 722	340	351	19	512	1 065
St. Louis city	6.7	19.0	10.6	30.9	19.1	6.6	5.0	2.1	33.7	88.6	152 666	178 266	950	6 891	94	2 783	6 539
St. Peters city	7.4	22.5	7.4	33.5	21.3	4.4	2.8	.6	34.2	95.0	48 427	1 440	105	632	4	224	549
Springfield city	5.9	14.0	17.4	28.0	19.8	7.0	6.2	2.3	33.5	92.9	138 987	4 961	1 142	2 060	136	1 332	2 962
University City city	6.1	15.7	11.3	31.1	22.4	6.8	4.5	2.0	35.4	84.1	18 437	16 974	61	1 065	11	208	672

[1] Includes all other responses not included in the other five race categories shown. Also includes write-in entries such as multiracial, mixed, interracial, or a Hispanic/Latino group.   [2] Refers to combinations of two or more of the six race categories shown under one race.

Source: Population by Age, Sex, and Race—U.S. Census Bureau; 2000 Census of Population and Housing, "Census 2000 Profiles of General Demographic Characteristics" data files, published May 2001, related Internet site <http://www.census.gov/mp/www/pub/2000cen/mscen01.html>.

Table C–2. Cities — **Population by Age, Sex, and Race**–Con.

[Includes states and 1,070 incorporated places of 25,000 or more population as of April 1, 1990 in all states except Hawaii which has no incorporated places recognized by the Census Bureau. For Hawaii, 8 census designated places (CDPs) of 25,000 or more population as of April 1, 1990 are included. Also included are the 5 boroughs of New York city. For more information on these areas, see appendix B. Geographic Information]

City	Population by age, 2000 (April 1) Percent—								Median age (years)	Males per 100 females, 2000 (April 1)	Population by race, 2000 (April 1) One race						Two or more races[2]
	Under 5 years	5 to 17 years	18 to 24 years	25 to 44 years	45 to 64 years	65 to 74 years	75 to 84 years	85 years and over			White	Black or African American	American Indian and Alaska Native	Asian	Native Hawaiian and Other Pacific Islander	Some other race[1]	
MONTANA.............	6.1	19.4	9.5	27.2	24.4	6.9	4.8	1.7	37.5	99.3	817 229	2 692	56 068	4 691	470	5 315	15 730
Billings city...............	6.5	17.5	10.1	28.7	22.3	7.2	5.5	2.1	36.8	92.7	82 539	495	3 088	533	38	1 300	1 854
Butte-Silver Bow (remainder)	5.7	17.9	9.6	26.7	23.9	7.8	6.1	2.3	38.9	97.8	32 325	53	675	147	21	200	471
Great Falls city...........	6.4	18.5	9.0	27.7	22.7	7.7	5.7	2.2	37.8	94.2	50 996	540	2 888	485	49	341	1 391
Missoula city.............	5.3	14.4	20.7	29.4	19.8	4.7	4.1	1.6	30.3	98.8	53 387	207	1 341	703	57	290	1 068
NEBRASKA.............	6.8	19.5	10.2	28.5	21.5	6.8	4.8	2.0	35.3	97.2	1 533 261	68 541	14 896	21 931	836	47 845	23 953
Bellevue city	7.1	20.3	10.2	31.0	21.8	6.0	2.8	.7	33.5	98.3	38 092	2 719	223	938	49	1 235	1 126
Grand Island city	7.8	19.1	9.5	28.6	20.8	6.9	5.3	2.0	34.8	98.1	37 237	180	143	562	71	4 139	608
Lincoln city	6.7	16.3	16.4	30.7	19.5	5.2	3.8	1.4	31.3	99.2	201 322	6 960	1 537	7 048	141	4 081	4 492
Omaha city	7.2	18.4	11.0	30.8	20.7	6.1	4.2	1.5	33.5	95.0	305 745	51 917	2 616	6 773	228	15 250	7 478
NEVADA.............	7.3	18.3	9.0	31.5	23.0	6.6	3.5	.9	35.0	103.9	1 501 886	135 477	26 420	90 266	8 426	159 354	76 428
Carson City	6.3	17.1	7.9	28.9	24.9	7.8	5.6	1.5	38.7	106.9	44 744	946	1 259	930	76	3 391	1 111
Henderson city	6.8	18.3	7.9	32.5	24.4	6.4	3.1	.7	35.9	98.4	148 181	6 590	1 236	6 983	728	5 549	6 114
Las Vegas city............	7.7	18.2	8.8	32.0	21.7	7.1	3.6	.8	34.5	103.3	334 230	49 570	3 570	22 879	2 145	46 643	19 397
North Las Vegas city	10.4	23.6	9.6	34.3	16.4	3.7	1.6	.5	28.8	104.3	64 591	21 970	943	3 740	610	18 224	5 410
Reno city	7.0	16.2	11.8	31.5	22.2	6.1	4.1	1.3	34.5	104.6	139 793	4 651	2 271	9 555	1 004	16 712	6 494
Sparks city	7.4	19.5	9.2	31.6	22.1	5.6	3.5	1.1	34.5	97.7	52 001	1 591	780	3 308	330	6 041	2 295
NEW HAMPSHIRE	6.1	18.9	8.4	30.9	23.8	6.3	4.2	1.5	37.1	96.8	1 186 851	9 035	2 964	15 931	371	7 420	13 214
Concord city	5.8	17.3	8.3	33.0	22.0	5.8	5.1	2.8	37.0	98.1	38 863	421	120	598	13	139	533
Dover city................	5.7	15.2	11.2	34.0	20.3	6.5	5.0	2.3	35.5	92.4	25 396	301	53	635	15	93	391
Manchester city	6.7	17.0	9.5	33.4	20.5	6.1	5.1	1.7	34.9	95.9	98 178	2 246	326	2 487	38	1 880	1 851
Nashua city	6.5	18.1	8.1	33.5	22.2	6.1	4.1	1.4	35.8	97.6	77 291	1 740	275	3 363	29	2 642	1 265
Portsmouth city...........	4.9	12.3	7.2	36.2	23.2	7.8	5.8	2.6	38.5	94.5	19 443	442	44	508	5	59	283
Rochester city	6.8	18.5	7.7	31.5	22.1	7.3	4.7	1.5	36.7	94.6	27 640	149	62	248	9	74	279
NEW JERSEY...........	6.7	18.1	8.0	31.2	22.7	6.8	4.8	1.6	36.7	94.3	6 104 705	1 141 821	19 492	480 276	3 329	450 972	213 755
Atlantic City city	7.5	18.2	8.9	31.0	20.2	7.3	5.0	1.8	34.7	96.1	10 809	17 892	193	1 213	24	5 575	1 811
Bayonne city	5.8	16.3	8.2	30.7	22.5	8.0	6.8	1.8	38.1	89.9	48 631	3 416	106	2 562	30	4 611	2 486
Camden city	9.1	25.5	12.0	29.5	16.3	4.5	2.4	.7	27.2	94.3	13 454	42 628	435	1 958	59	18 239	3 131
Clifton city	6.0	15.6	7.7	30.7	22.5	7.9	7.1	2.6	38.8	91.4	59 960	2 277	192	5 066	27	7 553	3 597
East Orange city...........	7.9	20.2	9.8	30.1	20.8	6.3	3.7	1.3	33.0	81.9	2 683	62 462	177	302	51	1 496	2 653
Elizabeth city	7.7	18.6	10.8	33.7	19.3	5.2	3.5	1.3	32.6	98.0	67 250	24 090	580	2 830	55	18 702	7 061
Fair Lawn borough	5.3	17.5	6.0	26.9	25.6	8.9	7.6	2.2	41.8	90.6	28 960	234	13	1 558	1	434	437
Fort Lee borough	5.3	12.2	5.1	32.6	24.7	10.2	7.4	2.5	41.6	87.7	22 253	615	25	11 146	20	600	802
Garfield city	6.1	16.3	9.6	33.2	20.8	6.7	5.8	1.6	35.6	95.0	24 456	887	99	800	2	2 414	1 128
Hackensack city	5.8	12.4	8.6	38.4	22.3	6.3	4.4	1.8	36.2	98.7	22 451	10 518	191	3 181	23	4 144	2 169
Hoboken city	3.2	7.3	15.3	51.7	13.5	4.6	3.5	1.0	30.4	103.9	31 178	1 644	60	1 661	21	2 942	1 071
Jersey City city	6.9	17.8	10.7	35.1	19.7	5.2	3.4	1.2	32.4	95.3	81 637	67 994	1 071	38 881	181	36 280	14 011
Kearny town	5.7	15.7	10.7	35.7	21.3	5.6	4.0	1.2	34.7	106.6	30 687	1 609	148	2 228	27	4 068	1 746
Linden city	6.0	16.5	8.2	30.4	22.7	7.5	6.6	2.2	38.0	90.4	26 031	8 981	56	925	15	1 923	1 463
Long Branch city	7.0	16.8	10.2	32.4	20.8	6.6	4.7	1.6	34.7	94.3	21 320	5 847	113	513	15	2 220	1 312
Millville city..............	7.0	21.0	8.6	28.8	21.7	6.5	4.9	1.5	35.0	89.5	20 438	4 025	139	216	8	1 384	637
Newark city	7.8	20.2	12.1	32.0	18.7	5.3	3.0	1.0	30.8	94.2	72 537	146 250	1 005	3 263	135	38 430	11 926
New Brunswick city	7.0	13.1	34.0	28.1	11.3	3.2	2.5	.8	23.6	98.4	23 701	11 185	224	2 584	40	8 780	2 059
Paramus borough..........	5.2	18.1	5.5	24.7	25.0	10.5	7.8	3.2	42.9	94.4	20 380	291	12	4 434	3	229	388
Passaic city	9.6	21.2	12.5	31.6	16.9	4.2	2.8	1.1	28.6	99.5	24 044	9 385	531	3 740	29	26 709	3 423
Paterson city	8.4	21.4	11.2	32.0	18.7	4.6	2.8	.9	30.5	94.4	45 913	49 095	901	2 831	84	41 184	9 214
Perth Amboy city	8.0	20.4	11.4	31.6	18.3	5.1	3.9	1.3	31.2	98.2	21 951	4 749	330	723	60	16 834	2 656
Plainfield city	7.9	19.6	10.2	32.6	20.5	5.0	3.0	1.2	32.8	95.7	10 258	29 550	195	447	46	5 156	2 177
Rahway city	6.3	17.6	7.8	32.0	21.8	7.2	5.7	1.6	37.1	91.2	15 950	7 173	42	950	14	1 489	882
Sayreville borough	6.7	16.8	7.3	34.2	22.5	6.5	4.7	1.2	36.5	96.3	30 875	3 481	53	4 265	8	855	840
Trenton city	7.6	20.1	10.1	31.9	18.9	5.8	4.2	1.4	32.2	97.6	27 802	44 465	300	716	199	9 190	2 731
Union City city	7.4	17.9	11.0	34.3	19.4	5.9	3.0	1.1	32.5	100.6	39 167	2 442	467	1 441	54	18 911	4 606
Vineland city	6.2	19.5	8.3	29.0	22.9	6.9	5.3	1.9	36.5	92.0	37 964	7 664	304	655	43	7 881	1 760
Westfield town............	8.0	20.4	4.0	29.6	24.5	6.6	5.1	1.8	38.6	92.1	26 675	1 151	27	1 208	3	185	395
West New York town	6.7	15.6	10.9	34.1	19.9	7.3	4.1	1.3	34.0	96.4	27 503	1 626	305	1 339	15	11 515	3 465

[1] Includes all other responses not included in the other five race categories shown. Also includes write-in entries such as multiracial, mixed, interracial, or a Hispanic/Latino group.   [2] Refers to combinations of two or more of the six race categories shown under one race.

Source: Population by Age, Sex, and Race—U.S. Census Bureau; 2000 Census of Population and Housing, "Census 2000 Profiles of General Demographic Characteristics" data files, published May 2001, related Internet site <http://www.census.gov/mp/www/pub/2000cen/mscen01.html>.

Table C–2. Cities — **Population by Age, Sex, and Race**–Con.

[Includes states and 1,070 incorporated places of 25,000 or more population as of April 1, 1990 in all states except Hawaii which has no incorporated places recognized by the Census Bureau. For Hawaii, 8 census designated places (CDPs) of 25,000 or more population as of April 1, 1990 are included. Also included are the 5 boroughs of New York city. For more information on these areas, see appendix B. Geographic Information]

City	Under 5 years	5 to 17 years	18 to 24 years	25 to 44 years	45 to 64 years	65 to 74 years	75 to 84 years	85 years and over	Median age (years)	Males per 100 females, 2000 (April 1)	White	Black or African American	American Indian and Alaska Native	Asian	Native Hawaiian and Other Pacific Islander	Some other race[1]	Two or more races[2]
	Population by age, 2000 (April 1) — Percent—										Population by race, 2000 (April 1) — One race						
NEW MEXICO	7.2	20.8	9.8	28.4	22.2	6.5	3.9	1.3	34.6	96.7	1 214 253	34 343	173 483	19 255	1 503	309 882	66 327
Alamogordo city	7.6	21.0	9.2	29.7	19.9	7.4	4.1	1.2	33.5	97.6	26 812	1 985	374	545	59	4 295	1 512
Albuquerque city	6.9	17.7	10.6	30.9	21.9	6.1	4.4	1.5	34.9	94.4	321 179	13 854	17 444	10 068	452	66 292	19 318
Clovis city	8.3	21.7	9.4	28.1	19.5	6.7	4.5	1.8	33.1	92.5	23 293	2 392	332	528	41	4 895	1 186
Farmington city	7.6	21.7	9.9	28.5	21.5	5.8	3.8	1.1	33.6	96.2	26 771	316	6 419	197	24	2 942	1 175
Hobbs city	8.1	22.3	10.3	28.0	19.4	6.7	3.9	1.3	32.1	100.2	18 203	1 945	308	123	12	6 997	1 069
Las Cruces city	7.0	18.1	16.0	26.9	19.0	7.1	4.5	1.5	31.2	94.3	51 248	1 738	1 289	863	55	16 031	3 043
Rio Rancho city	7.5	21.7	7.0	32.0	20.1	5.7	4.6	1.5	35.1	94.2	40 563	1 376	1 226	758	89	5 618	2 135
Roswell city	7.4	21.1	9.9	24.9	20.6	7.8	6.0	2.2	35.2	93.1	32 141	1 117	578	293	23	9 643	1 498
Santa Fe city	5.4	14.9	8.9	29.0	28.0	7.3	4.8	1.8	39.8	91.7	47 459	409	1 373	791	49	9 508	2 614
NEW YORK	6.5	18.2	9.3	30.7	22.3	6.7	4.5	1.6	35.9	93.1	12 893 689	3 014 385	82 461	1 044 976	8 818	1 341 946	590 182
Albany city	5.6	14.3	19.3	29.2	18.1	5.9	5.0	2.4	31.4	90.6	60 383	26 915	301	3 116	34	2 060	2 849
Auburn city	6.3	16.5	9.3	30.3	19.8	7.2	7.5	3.1	36.9	99.0	25 307	2 170	84	162	6	403	442
Binghamton city	6.1	15.5	13.2	26.6	21.0	7.7	7.0	2.9	36.7	89.9	39 412	3 987	121	1 579	18	810	1 453
Buffalo city	7.1	19.2	11.3	29.3	19.6	6.8	5.0	1.7	33.6	88.6	159 300	108 951	2 250	4 093	120	10 755	7 179
Elmira city	7.0	18.1	13.0	29.9	18.2	6.5	5.5	1.8	33.4	101.2	25 379	4 039	120	151	9	425	817
Freeport village	6.9	19.5	9.1	32.1	22.0	5.7	3.4	1.4	34.6	92.6	18 791	14 258	201	604	24	7 537	2 368
Hempstead village	7.9	18.4	16.3	31.4	17.5	4.3	2.7	1.4	29.4	91.6	14 515	29 678	298	745	33	8 605	2 680
Ithaca city	2.5	6.8	53.8	20.1	10.6	2.8	2.4	1.1	22.0	102.6	21 663	1 965	114	3 998	16	546	985
Jamestown city	7.6	18.3	9.1	28.1	20.9	7.5	6.0	2.5	36.2	91.0	29 040	1 075	204	141	16	570	684
Lindenhurst village	6.9	19.8	7.1	34.0	21.1	6.3	3.9	.9	35.8	94.5	26 213	233	32	382	3	469	487
Long Beach city	4.9	13.7	6.6	34.4	23.8	7.6	5.6	3.5	39.6	92.7	29 860	2 190	75	822	29	1 683	803
Mount Vernon city	7.1	18.3	8.3	31.1	22.4	6.5	4.5	2.0	35.8	82.3	19 577	40 743	219	1 448	43	3 316	3 035
Newburgh city	9.8	23.4	12.7	28.8	16.1	4.5	3.4	1.3	27.8	90.0	11 962	9 314	201	215	16	5 119	1 432
New Rochelle city	6.8	17.3	8.7	29.5	22.2	7.6	5.3	2.6	37.0	90.7	49 001	13 848	141	2 334	35	4 535	2 288
New York city	6.8	17.5	10.0	32.9	21.2	6.2	4.0	1.5	34.2	90.0	3 576 385	2 129 762	41 289	787 047	5 430	1 074 406	393 959
Bronx borough	8.2	21.6	10.6	30.7	18.8	5.3	3.3	1.4	31.2	87.0	398 003	475 007	11 371	40 120	1 383	329 724	77 042
Brooklyn borough	7.4	19.5	10.3	30.8	20.6	6.1	4.0	1.4	33.1	88.4	1 015 728	898 350	10 117	185 818	1 465	248 557	105 291
Manhattan borough	4.9	11.8	10.2	38.3	22.6	6.4	4.0	1.7	35.7	90.3	835 610	267 302	7 617	144 538	1 069	217 383	63 676
Queens borough	6.4	16.4	9.6	33.1	21.7	6.6	4.5	1.6	35.4	92.9	982 725	446 189	11 077	391 500	1 331	260 387	136 170
Staten Island borough	6.7	18.8	8.5	30.9	23.4	6.3	3.9	1.4	35.9	93.6	344 319	42 914	1 107	25 071	182	18 355	11 780
Niagara Falls city	6.4	18.3	8.6	27.7	20.5	8.7	7.5	2.4	38.0	87.9	42 370	10 409	911	394	26	378	1 105
North Tonawanda city	5.7	18.1	8.6	28.9	23.1	8.2	5.9	1.5	38.4	94.6	32 549	98	114	177	2	95	227
Poughkeepsie city	7.6	18.3	12.2	29.2	19.0	6.6	5.0	2.0	32.7	91.7	15 785	10 666	117	485	14	1 579	1 225
Rochester city	7.8	20.3	11.6	32.2	18.1	4.5	3.7	1.7	30.8	91.6	106 161	84 717	1 033	4 943	104	14 452	8 363
Rome city	5.9	16.3	8.5	29.9	22.3	7.8	7.0	2.4	38.2	105.1	30 704	2 650	93	309	6	473	715
Saratoga Springs city	5.3	14.0	15.5	27.5	23.4	6.1	5.5	2.7	36.3	90.4	24 493	815	63	271	8	168	368
Schenectady city	7.0	17.3	11.6	29.7	19.1	6.6	6.1	2.5	34.8	91.5	47 460	9 132	222	1 239	24	1 559	2 185
Syracuse city	6.9	18.0	16.8	27.9	17.5	5.8	5.1	2.0	30.5	88.9	94 663	37 336	1 670	4 961	72	3 284	5 320
Troy city	6.4	15.7	17.6	28.5	18.1	6.5	5.2	2.0	31.7	98.0	39 443	5 612	140	1 717	20	1 083	1 155
Utica city	6.7	17.4	10.0	26.8	20.2	8.1	7.5	3.2	37.0	88.7	48 166	7 838	170	1 341	29	1 309	1 798
Valley Stream village	5.8	17.7	7.7	29.1	23.4	8.2	6.2	1.8	39.0	91.4	28 654	2 714	54	2 496	17	1 509	924
Watertown city	7.8	18.2	10.4	29.6	18.5	6.8	5.9	2.9	34.0	90.5	23 801	1 321	144	309	30	446	654
White Plains city	6.2	15.0	7.5	32.5	23.6	7.6	5.1	2.4	38.1	89.8	34 465	8 444	182	2 389	37	5 502	2 058
Yonkers city	7.0	17.3	8.8	30.6	21.2	7.7	5.4	1.9	35.8	88.6	118 007	32 575	861	9 526	98	26 349	8 670
NORTH CAROLINA	6.7	17.7	10.0	31.1	22.5	6.6	4.1	1.3	35.3	96.0	5 804 656	1 737 545	99 551	113 689	3 983	186 629	103 260
Asheville city	5.4	14.2	10.3	28.7	23.1	8.6	7.2	2.5	39.2	87.8	53 701	12 129	240	635	39	1 054	1 091
Burlington city	6.5	17.2	8.9	29.0	21.4	8.5	6.3	2.2	36.9	88.7	29 766	11 252	154	766	16	2 316	647
Cary town	8.1	21.0	6.6	38.6	20.4	3.1	1.7	.5	33.7	99.2	77 683	5 813	251	7 643	28	1 392	1 726
Chapel Hill town	3.6	11.5	37.1	24.5	15.3	3.9	3.0	1.1	24.0	82.1	37 973	5 565	203	3 497	12	563	902
Charlotte city	7.1	17.6	10.4	36.2	19.9	4.7	3.1	1.0	32.7	96.1	315 061	176 964	1 863	18 418	283	19 242	8 997
Concord city	7.9	18.3	8.9	33.6	20.2	5.6	4.1	1.4	33.6	95.5	44 128	8 450	168	684	14	1 874	659
Durham city	7.2	15.8	14.1	35.6	18.1	4.6	3.5	1.3	31.0	92.5	85 126	81 937	575	6 815	71	8 875	3 636
Fayetteville city	7.5	17.9	12.7	31.2	19.7	6.5	3.5	1.0	31.9	91.9	59 007	51 338	1 331	2 653	264	3 062	3 360
Gastonia city	7.0	17.9	8.8	30.5	22.0	7.3	4.9	1.6	35.6	89.6	46 513	16 981	137	773	19	1 167	687
Goldsboro city	7.1	17.9	11.4	29.8	20.0	7.3	5.0	1.4	34.3	96.9	16 803	20 397	168	562	30	444	639
Greensboro city	6.3	15.9	14.1	31.6	20.2	6.1	4.2	1.6	33.0	89.2	124 243	83 728	989	6 357	89	4 647	3 838
Greenville city	5.6	13.3	28.7	28.2	15.5	4.6	3.1	1.1	26.0	86.2	37 133	20 649	181	1 098	26	611	778
Hickory city	6.9	16.3	11.2	30.7	21.3	7.0	4.8	1.8	34.6	92.8	28 747	5 243	70	1 450	24	1 146	542
High Point city	7.5	18.5	9.3	31.8	21.0	6.1	4.1	1.6	34.4	91.5	51 985	27 275	392	2 872	17	1 950	1 348
Jacksonville city	9.6	14.6	36.3	25.9	8.8	2.8	1.5	.4	22.4	156.2	42 655	15 987	503	1 380	126	3 614	2 450

[1] Includes all other responses not included in the other five race categories shown. Also includes write-in entries such as multiracial, mixed, interracial, or a Hispanic/Latino group. [2] Refers to combinations of two or more of the six race categories shown under one race.

Source: Population by Age, Sex, and Race—U.S. Census Bureau; 2000 Census of Population and Housing, "Census 2000 Profiles of General Demographic Characteristics" data files, published May 2001, related Internet site <http://www.census.gov/mp/www/pub/2000cen/mscen01.html>.

Table C–2. Cities — **Population by Age, Sex, and Race**–Con.

[Includes states and 1,070 incorporated places of 25,000 or more population as of April 1, 1990 in all states except Hawaii which has no incorporated places recognized by the Census Bureau. For Hawaii, 8 census designated places (CDPs) of 25,000 or more population as of April 1, 1990 are included. Also included are the 5 boroughs of New York city. For more information on these areas, see appendix B. Geographic Information]

City	Under 5 years	5 to 17 years	18 to 24 years	25 to 44 years	45 to 64 years	65 to 74 years	75 to 84 years	85 years and over	Median age (years)	Males per 100 females, 2000 (April 1)	White	Black or African American	American Indian and Alaska Native	Asian	Native Hawaiian and Other Pacific Islander	Some other race[1]	Two or more races[2]
NORTH CAROLINA— Con.																	
Kannapolis city	7.0	17.1	9.0	30.4	20.8	7.6	6.0	2.0	36.0	93.7	28 695	6 072	125	319	5	1 265	429
Kinston city	6.4	18.0	7.3	24.9	24.5	10.1	6.9	1.9	40.8	81.8	8 354	14 837	37	135	11	156	158
Raleigh city	6.3	14.5	15.9	36.6	18.4	4.4	2.9	1.0	30.9	98.0	174 786	76 756	981	9 327	118	8 946	5 179
Rocky Mount city	7.0	20.7	8.9	28.5	21.9	6.7	4.9	1.4	35.2	85.2	22 874	31 314	195	394	12	507	597
Wilmington city	5.3	13.1	17.2	28.5	20.6	7.7	5.8	1.9	34.1	87.5	53 516	19 579	266	682	67	868	860
Wilson city	7.4	18.6	9.8	28.9	21.8	7.1	4.8	1.6	35.1	88.0	20 723	21 106	136	257	8	1 728	447
Winston-Salem city	6.7	16.6	11.7	30.4	20.9	7.0	4.9	1.8	34.6	88.7	103 243	68 924	567	2 108	67	7 965	2 902
NORTH DAKOTA	6.1	18.9	11.4	27.2	21.6	7.1	5.3	2.3	36.2	99.6	593 181	3 916	31 329	3 606	230	2 540	7 398
Bismarck city	6.0	17.5	11.1	29.1	22.4	7.0	4.7	2.0	36.5	93.9	52 634	156	1 884	251	15	95	497
Fargo city	6.4	14.8	19.2	31.1	18.5	5.0	3.5	1.6	30.1	100.0	85 321	922	1 119	1 482	40	400	1 315
Grand Forks city	5.9	15.5	22.9	27.7	18.3	4.7	3.6	1.5	28.3	102.0	46 040	426	1 357	472	28	288	710
Minot city	6.6	16.6	13.3	27.4	20.7	7.2	5.6	2.6	35.0	93.1	34 074	490	1 008	226	25	181	563
OHIO	6.6	18.8	9.3	29.3	22.7	7.0	4.8	1.6	36.2	94.4	9 645 453	1 301 307	24 486	132 633	2 749	88 627	157 885
Akron city	7.2	18.1	10.5	30.3	20.3	6.7	5.2	1.6	34.2	91.4	145 924	61 827	575	3 257	48	940	4 503
Barberton city	7.7	17.1	8.4	28.3	21.2	8.5	6.7	2.1	37.2	87.5	25 787	1 488	74	102	2	66	380
Beavercreek city	5.2	20.1	6.3	26.9	29.3	7.0	4.0	1.2	40.5	97.7	35 495	540	63	1 330	8	117	431
Bowling Green city	3.7	9.4	46.6	19.5	13.2	3.7	2.8	1.2	22.4	87.9	27 219	837	62	543	5	537	433
Brunswick city	7.3	20.5	8.1	32.7	23.2	4.9	2.7	.7	34.6	96.5	32 418	246	44	286	8	126	260
Canton city	7.8	18.8	9.8	29.1	20.2	6.8	5.4	2.1	34.4	87.5	60 164	16 999	396	257	24	492	2 474
Cincinnati city	7.2	17.3	12.9	31.6	18.7	6.0	4.4	1.9	32.1	89.4	175 492	142 176	709	5 132	130	2 093	5 553
Cleveland city	8.1	20.4	9.5	30.4	19.0	6.6	4.4	1.5	33.0	90.0	198 510	243 939	1 458	6 444	178	17 173	10 701
Cleveland Heights city	6.2	17.7	9.2	31.6	23.6	6.2	4.2	1.3	35.2	87.5	26 229	20 873	81	1 280	5	338	1 152
Columbus city	7.5	16.7	14.0	35.1	17.9	4.7	3.1	1.1	30.6	94.6	483 332	174 065	2 090	24 495	367	8 292	18 829
Cuyahoga Falls city	6.5	15.9	7.9	32.0	21.5	8.1	6.3	1.7	37.2	90.3	47 300	923	99	520	6	75	451
Dayton city	7.1	18.0	14.2	29.0	19.6	6.4	4.4	1.2	32.4	93.1	88 676	71 668	500	1 075	63	1 160	3 037
East Cleveland city	7.4	22.3	9.0	26.6	21.4	7.8	4.0	1.5	33.9	79.6	1 240	25 418	59	61	4	45	390
Elyria city	7.9	18.7	8.9	30.2	21.3	6.6	4.7	1.6	34.8	92.4	45 517	7 928	150	340	11	532	1 475
Euclid city	6.3	16.0	6.8	30.7	21.0	8.3	8.0	2.9	38.9	84.0	34 985	16 116	62	493	13	184	864
Fairborn city	6.0	15.1	18.4	29.3	19.7	6.9	3.9	.8	31.3	94.7	27 976	2 010	127	1 064	20	169	686
Fairfield city	6.3	18.0	9.5	32.3	23.2	6.1	3.6	1.0	35.2	94.9	37 830	2 557	66	948	15	215	476
Findlay city	7.0	16.8	11.9	28.7	21.4	6.7	5.3	2.1	35.1	91.3	36 513	546	74	686	10	648	490
Gahanna city	6.8	22.1	6.5	31.7	24.3	4.9	3.0	.8	36.5	94.2	28 216	2 657	65	1 062	9	156	471
Garfield Heights city	6.3	17.7	7.3	29.3	20.7	8.3	8.0	2.2	38.3	87.6	24 807	5 164	48	286	3	132	294
Hamilton city	7.5	18.3	9.8	29.9	20.2	7.5	5.2	1.6	34.9	92.6	53 975	4 581	173	275	23	889	774
Huber Heights city	7.3	20.1	8.6	31.1	23.7	6.0	2.7	.6	34.4	95.0	32 433	3 737	106	832	23	223	858
Kent city	5.0	11.4	40.0	23.0	13.1	3.7	2.9	.9	22.9	84.6	24 018	2 541	53	599	9	124	562
Kettering city	5.8	16.7	7.5	29.4	22.3	9.3	7.0	2.0	38.9	90.5	54 757	955	105	795	14	189	687
Lakewood city	5.9	15.1	9.5	37.2	20.1	5.7	4.6	1.9	34.2	92.9	52 723	1 116	139	800	15	349	1 504
Lancaster city	7.7	16.9	9.3	29.0	21.2	8.0	5.8	2.2	35.9	89.9	34 409	214	107	166	13	62	364
Lima city	8.1	19.0	11.5	28.7	19.4	6.6	4.8	1.8	32.9	100.6	27 776	10 614	124	205	4	388	970
Lorain city	8.0	20.4	9.0	28.2	20.5	7.2	5.2	1.5	34.4	90.2	47 848	10 943	304	227	24	6 565	2 741
Mansfield city	7.2	16.7	9.3	29.7	21.7	7.7	5.8	2.0	36.4	98.5	37 885	9 695	137	311	20	275	1 023
Maple Heights city	6.3	19.4	6.7	30.9	20.1	7.9	6.8	1.8	37.4	87.8	13 509	11 598	33	452	6	124	434
Marion city	7.0	18.2	9.3	30.8	21.5	6.9	4.8	1.6	35.2	102.3	31 926	2 475	69	192	4	227	425
Massillon city	6.6	18.7	7.9	28.1	22.5	8.2	5.9	2.0	37.6	92.6	27 622	2 942	71	79	1	108	502
Mentor city	6.0	19.9	6.5	29.0	26.3	6.6	4.4	1.2	38.9	94.2	48 920	324	24	597	16	91	306
Middletown city	7.2	17.8	9.3	29.2	21.6	7.8	5.4	1.7	36.2	91.4	44 886	5 467	128	190	18	185	731
Newark city	7.5	17.8	9.4	29.2	21.1	7.2	5.5	2.2	35.9	89.7	43 560	1 435	140	278	14	155	697
North Olmsted city	5.5	18.2	7.3	27.6	26.5	8.2	5.1	1.6	39.9	93.3	32 055	346	43	936	4	155	574
Parma city	5.8	16.5	7.0	29.6	21.5	9.0	8.3	2.3	39.4	91.2	81 948	905	118	1 349	17	384	934
Reynoldsburg city	7.1	19.5	8.0	31.9	23.4	6.0	3.3	.8	35.4	91.0	27 261	3 347	86	541	15	238	581
Sandusky city	7.2	18.6	9.2	28.5	21.4	7.5	5.5	2.1	36.2	89.4	20 745	5 870	80	73	4	270	802
Shaker Heights city	6.2	20.0	5.3	27.4	25.5	7.9	5.6	2.1	39.6	83.6	17 624	10 030	19	928	4	147	653
Springfield city	7.5	18.0	11.5	27.0	20.7	7.1	5.9	2.2	34.5	89.3	51 007	11 909	223	455	14	354	1 396
Stow city	6.6	19.4	7.4	31.1	23.5	6.1	4.3	1.6	36.9	93.8	30 596	495	35	615	4	95	299
Strongsville city	6.2	20.0	6.2	28.5	27.6	6.4	3.9	1.0	39.1	95.3	41 304	551	21	1 406	4	122	450
Toledo city	7.3	18.9	11.0	29.8	19.8	6.6	4.9	1.6	33.2	91.9	220 261	73 854	970	3 233	76	7 166	8 059
Upper Arlington city	5.5	19.4	4.4	25.1	27.1	9.0	7.2	2.4	42.6	89.2	31 906	200	35	1 185	3	90	267
Warren city	7.9	18.4	8.6	27.3	21.0	8.3	6.4	2.1	36.3	86.8	33 690	11 802	62	195	16	142	925
Westerville city	6.1	20.8	9.1	27.1	26.5	5.4	3.6	1.5	37.8	90.3	33 035	1 131	46	549	10	127	420
Westlake city	5.1	17.7	5.6	26.8	26.6	7.6	7.1	3.5	42.0	89.4	29 477	301	18	1 332	5	106	480
Youngstown city	7.1	18.7	10.1	26.4	20.3	6.8	6.7	2.1	36.4	91.9	41 737	35 937	246	267	29	1 797	2 013
Zanesville city	8.1	18.6	9.5	27.8	20.5	7.4	5.9	2.3	34.8	85.3	21 870	2 753	102	59	5	107	690

[1] Includes all other responses not included in the other five race categories shown. Also includes write-in entries such as multiracial, mixed, interracial, or a Hispanic/Latino group. [2] Refers to combinations of two or more of the six race categories shown under one race.

Source: Population by Age, Sex, and Race—U.S. Census Bureau; 2000 Census of Population and Housing, "Census 2000 Profiles of General Demographic Characteristics" data files, published May 2001, related Internet site <http://www.census.gov/mp/www/pub/2000cen/mscen01.html>.

Table C–2. Cities — Population by Age, Sex, and Race–Con.

[Includes states and 1,070 incorporated places of 25,000 or more population as of April 1, 1990 in all states except Hawaii which has no incorporated places recognized by the Census Bureau. For Hawaii, 8 census designated places (CDPs) of 25,000 or more population as of April 1, 1990 are included. Also included are the 5 boroughs of New York city. For more information on these areas, see appendix B. Geographic Information]

City	Population by age, 2000 (April 1) Percent—								Median age (years)	Males per 100 females, 2000 (April 1)	Population by race, 2000 (April 1) One race						Two or more races[2]
	Under 5 years	5 to 17 years	18 to 24 years	25 to 44 years	45 to 64 years	65 to 74 years	75 to 84 years	85 years and over			White	Black or African American	American Indian and Alaska Native	Asian	Native Hawaiian and Other Pacific Islander	Some other race[1]	
OKLAHOMA	6.8	19.0	10.3	28.3	22.3	7.0	4.5	1.7	35.5	96.6	2 628 434	260 968	273 230	46 767	2 372	82 898	155 985
Bartlesville city	6.2	18.8	8.1	24.8	23.7	9.1	7.1	2.4	40.0	90.3	28 524	1 112	2 496	332	6	353	1 925
Broken Arrow city	8.0	22.9	7.7	32.3	21.6	4.3	2.4	.8	33.3	95.1	63 886	2 793	3 007	1 425	39	912	2 797
Edmond city	7.0	20.5	11.3	29.6	22.8	4.7	2.8	1.3	33.6	93.7	59 144	2 760	1 554	2 225	53	617	1 962
Enid city	6.9	17.8	9.6	27.7	21.5	7.9	5.9	2.6	37.2	93.1	41 015	1 840	999	472	271	1 112	1 336
Lawton city	8.4	19.5	15.3	31.4	16.3	5.2	3.0	1.1	28.9	108.8	56 897	21 388	3 534	2 285	407	3 675	4 571
Midwest City city	7.3	19.1	10.7	28.8	20.8	7.1	4.9	1.1	34.2	91.4	37 568	10 573	1 887	892	66	835	2 267
Moore city	7.7	21.8	9.3	32.5	21.5	4.6	2.0	.6	32.0	93.7	34 814	1 201	1 704	667	20	720	2 012
Muskogee city	7.5	18.2	9.7	25.8	21.4	7.9	6.6	2.9	36.9	88.8	23 414	6 856	4 727	343	8	601	2 361
Norman city	5.9	15.3	21.4	29.1	19.3	4.8	3.1	1.1	29.3	101.0	78 812	4 080	4 262	3 342	48	1 313	3 837
Oklahoma City city	7.3	18.2	10.7	30.8	21.5	6.1	4.0	1.4	34.0	95.6	346 226	77 810	17 743	17 595	360	26 705	19 693
Ponca City city	7.2	19.1	8.5	25.5	22.1	8.4	6.6	2.6	38.2	90.7	21 818	774	1 626	181	8	540	972
Shawnee city	7.4	16.9	15.2	25.5	19.6	7.5	5.6	2.3	33.3	92.7	22 101	1 164	3 679	273	14	208	1 253
Stillwater city	4.7	10.5	38.2	24.4	13.6	3.7	3.2	1.7	23.9	102.7	32 220	1 681	1 519	1 974	14	345	1 312
Tulsa city	7.2	17.6	10.9	29.9	21.5	6.6	4.6	1.6	34.5	93.5	275 488	60 794	18 551	7 150	202	13 564	17 300
OREGON	6.5	18.2	9.6	29.1	23.7	6.4	4.7	1.7	36.3	98.4	2 961 623	55 662	45 211	101 350	7 976	144 832	104 745
Albany city	7.6	18.8	9.6	29.3	21.9	5.6	5.1	2.0	34.6	94.5	37 453	217	500	465	86	1 084	1 047
Beaverton city	7.2	17.7	10.6	35.2	20.3	4.0	3.4	1.5	32.6	97.5	59 615	1 324	507	7 349	272	4 211	2 851
Corvallis city	4.9	12.8	28.4	27.0	16.8	4.4	3.9	1.7	27.0	99.2	42 433	570	376	3 168	141	1 244	1 390
Eugene city	5.3	15.0	17.3	28.5	21.8	5.3	4.8	2.0	33.0	96.0	121 546	1 729	1 281	4 916	294	3 003	5 124
Gresham city	8.0	19.6	11.1	30.3	21.2	4.7	3.6	1.5	32.5	97.8	74 619	1 707	848	3 007	243	6 335	3 446
Hillsboro city	9.3	19.0	11.4	37.0	17.0	3.1	2.2	.9	29.7	105.6	54 391	858	577	4 585	177	7 285	2 313
Lake Oswego city	4.9	19.8	6.1	26.8	31.0	5.7	4.3	1.4	41.2	92.9	32 149	226	113	1 612	58	250	870
Medford city	7.0	18.8	8.6	27.3	21.8	7.2	6.7	2.7	37.0	92.0	56 834	313	677	720	163	2 442	2 005
Portland city	6.1	15.0	10.3	34.7	22.4	5.3	4.5	1.7	35.2	97.8	412 241	35 115	5 587	33 470	1 993	18 760	21 955
Salem city	7.4	18.0	11.4	30.1	20.6	5.5	4.9	2.1	33.6	100.9	113 746	1 750	2 064	3 304	643	10 820	4 597
Springfield city	8.2	19.0	11.1	31.4	19.9	4.9	3.9	1.5	32.1	95.8	47 386	374	730	588	162	1 632	1 992
Tigard city	7.7	17.8	9.0	34.1	21.4	4.5	4.2	1.4	34.5	96.0	35 195	468	253	2 298	220	1 552	1 237
PENNSYLVANIA	5.9	17.9	8.9	28.6	23.1	7.9	5.8	1.9	38.0	93.4	10 484 203	1 224 612	18 348	219 813	3 417	188 437	142 224
Allentown city	7.1	17.6	11.2	29.8	19.1	7.1	5.9	2.1	34.5	91.8	77 361	8 370	356	2 421	78	14 260	3 786
Altoona city	6.3	16.6	10.9	27.3	22.0	8.2	6.6	2.0	37.4	88.3	47 545	1 231	51	156	8	121	411
Bethel Park borough	5.3	18.4	5.0	26.8	26.5	9.6	6.7	1.9	42.1	91.9	32 584	343	10	371	9	45	194
Bethlehem city	5.4	15.5	14.4	26.6	20.1	8.1	7.4	2.4	36.2	91.5	58 382	2 596	183	1 585	24	6 732	1 827
Chester city	8.4	21.4	13.0	26.8	18.6	6.0	4.5	1.3	30.6	89.1	6 980	27 897	75	226	4	1 116	556
Easton city	6.2	17.1	16.3	29.9	18.6	5.8	4.4	1.8	32.0	97.4	20 610	3 338	63	437	28	965	822
Erie city	7.2	18.2	11.6	28.5	19.2	7.1	6.2	2.1	34.1	90.8	83 550	14 724	232	776	42	1 991	2 402
Harrisburg city	8.1	20.1	9.2	31.0	20.8	5.7	3.7	1.4	33.0	88.7	15 527	26 841	183	1 384	35	3 199	1 781
Johnstown city	6.0	15.3	7.9	25.8	23.0	10.2	8.9	2.9	41.5	84.4	20 627	2 561	31	68	12	147	460
Lancaster city	7.9	19.6	13.9	30.5	17.7	5.3	3.9	1.3	30.4	95.2	34 683	7 939	247	1 386	47	9 826	2 220
McKeesport city	6.9	18.5	7.5	24.8	21.3	9.1	8.5	3.3	39.7	84.8	17 406	5 881	66	30	2	141	514
Municipality of Monroeville borough	4.9	15.4	6.2	27.4	25.8	10.0	7.7	2.6	42.6	88.5	25 118	2 432	41	1 294	13	89	362
New Castle city	6.7	17.1	8.1	26.1	21.3	9.2	8.6	2.9	39.4	85.3	22 829	2 839	28	46	2	78	487
Norristown borough	6.9	18.2	10.5	32.6	20.1	6.2	4.3	1.3	33.7	94.9	16 992	10 887	63	926	10	1 443	961
Philadelphia city	6.5	18.8	11.1	29.3	20.3	7.1	5.2	1.8	34.2	86.8	683 267	655 824	4 073	67 654	729	72 429	33 574
Pittsburgh city	5.3	14.6	14.8	28.6	20.3	7.9	6.4	2.1	35.5	90.7	226 258	90 750	628	9 195	111	2 218	5 403
Plum borough	6.3	18.5	6.1	31.1	24.8	7.1	4.5	1.6	38.4	95.4	25 754	743	23	231	7	45	137
Reading city	8.7	21.3	11.7	28.9	17.0	6.1	4.6	1.7	30.6	93.3	48 059	9 947	356	1 296	32	18 125	3 392
Scranton city	5.3	15.5	12.3	25.5	21.2	9.0	8.2	3.0	38.8	87.0	71 480	2 304	85	823	15	890	818
State College borough	1.8	3.9	65.5	16.2	6.7	2.5	2.4	.9	21.8	108.7	32 392	1 417	58	3 368	50	529	606
Wilkes-Barre city	4.9	15.0	12.6	26.1	20.8	9.5	8.0	3.1	38.8	93.2	39 801	2 193	48	342	14	228	497
Williamsport city	6.0	16.5	18.0	26.7	19.4	6.4	5.1	1.9	32.4	97.7	25 827	3 910	111	175	4	147	532
York city	8.0	20.4	11.4	30.1	19.1	5.5	4.0	1.4	31.3	93.0	24 416	10 270	172	574	28	3 839	1 563
RHODE ISLAND	6.1	17.5	10.2	29.6	22.0	7.0	5.5	2.0	36.7	92.5	891 191	46 908	5 121	23 665	567	52 616	28 251
Cranston city	5.3	16.3	7.7	31.5	22.0	8.0	7.0	2.3	39.0	95.9	70 703	2 926	236	2 599	33	1 528	1 244
East Providence city	5.4	16.3	7.4	29.4	22.6	8.8	7.3	2.9	39.6	86.8	42 111	2 445	225	559	23	1 361	1 964
Newport city	5.8	13.9	14.6	31.5	21.4	6.2	4.8	1.9	34.9	92.9	22 272	2 053	225	353	23	638	911
Pawtucket city	6.7	18.1	9.1	31.3	19.9	7.2	5.8	1.9	35.4	90.2	55 004	5 334	217	621	42	7 841	3 899
Providence city	7.3	18.8	18.9	28.6	15.9	4.9	3.9	1.6	28.1	91.7	94 666	25 243	1 975	10 432	270	30 477	10 555
Warwick city	5.4	16.5	6.7	30.1	24.3	8.3	6.6	2.1	40.0	90.8	81 695	996	213	1 281	15	506	1 102
Woonsocket city	7.6	18.2	9.2	30.0	19.7	7.0	6.0	2.3	34.8	91.2	35 935	1 920	139	1 755	14	2 102	1 359

[1] Includes all other responses not included in the other five race categories shown. Also includes write-in entries such as multiracial, mixed, interracial, or a Hispanic/Latino group. [2] Refers to combinations of two or more of the six race categories shown under one race.

Source: Population by Age, Sex, and Race—U.S. Census Bureau; 2000 Census of Population and Housing, "Census 2000 Profiles of General Demographic Characteristics" data files, published May 2001, related Internet site <http://www.census.gov/mp/www/pub/2000cen/mscen01.html>.

Table C–2. Cities — **Population by Age, Sex, and Race**–Con.

[Includes states and 1,070 incorporated places of 25,000 or more population as of April 1, 1990 in all states except Hawaii which has no incorporated places recognized by the Census Bureau. For Hawaii, 8 census designated places (CDPs) of 25,000 or more population as of April 1, 1990 are included. Also included are the 5 boroughs of New York city. For more information on these areas, see appendix B. Geographic Information]

City	Population by age, 2000 (April 1) Percent— Under 5 years	5 to 17 years	18 to 24 years	25 to 44 years	45 to 64 years	65 to 74 years	75 to 84 years	85 years and over	Median age (years)	Males per 100 females, 2000 (April 1)	Population by race, 2000 (April 1) One race White	Black or African American	American Indian and Alaska Native	Asian	Native Hawaiian and Other Pacific Islander	Some other race[1]	Two or more races[2]
SOUTH CAROLINA	6.6	18.6	10.2	29.6	23.0	6.7	4.1	1.3	35.4	94.5	2 695 560	1 185 216	13 718	36 014	1 628	39 926	39 950
Anderson city	6.7	15.5	10.7	26.3	20.4	8.8	8.2	3.5	38.0	82.3	16 105	8 678	55	199	9	173	295
Charleston city	5.4	14.6	17.2	28.8	20.5	6.7	5.2	1.6	33.2	89.9	60 964	32 864	145	1 197	55	518	907
Columbia city	5.6	14.5	22.9	30.1	16.6	5.0	4.0	1.3	28.6	96.2	57 236	53 465	296	2 008	104	1 582	1 587
Florence city	6.4	18.6	8.7	28.2	23.0	7.4	5.7	2.0	36.8	82.8	16 020	13 541	54	352	4	63	214
Greenville city	5.6	14.3	13.8	31.3	20.5	6.4	5.9	2.1	34.6	89.9	34 788	19 008	77	709	35	766	619
Mount Pleasant town	7.5	17.6	6.5	35.3	22.8	5.3	3.7	1.4	35.9	92.0	42 928	3 453	80	562	10	187	389
North Charleston city	8.0	19.8	13.4	32.0	17.7	5.0	3.1	.9	29.9	98.1	35 651	39 348	349	1 263	75	1 417	1 538
Rock Hill city	7.0	18.0	14.8	30.5	18.4	5.1	4.3	1.9	31.0	84.5	29 230	18 578	248	690	13	509	497
Spartanburg city	6.5	18.7	12.2	26.6	20.6	7.1	6.1	2.3	34.7	79.6	18 707	19 658	73	528	22	303	382
Sumter city	8.1	19.7	12.5	28.2	17.9	6.4	5.2	1.9	31.9	89.2	19 655	18 357	93	505	28	445	560
SOUTH DAKOTA	6.8	20.1	10.3	27.3	21.2	7.0	5.2	2.1	35.6	98.5	669 404	4 685	62 283	4 378	261	3 677	10 156
Rapid City city	7.0	18.3	11.8	28.7	20.9	6.7	4.7	1.8	34.8	96.2	50 266	579	6 046	594	35	434	1 653
Sioux Falls city	7.3	17.9	11.8	32.4	19.6	5.6	4.0	1.5	33.0	97.2	113 938	2 226	2 627	1 479	68	1 521	2 116
TENNESSEE	6.6	18.0	9.6	30.2	23.2	6.7	4.2	1.4	35.9	94.9	4 563 310	932 809	15 152	56 662	2 205	56 036	63 109
Bartlett town	6.6	22.4	6.8	30.0	25.5	5.2	2.7	.7	36.6	95.4	37 476	1 971	112	502	18	151	313
Chattanooga city	6.1	16.3	10.8	28.8	22.8	7.8	5.3	2.1	36.8	89.3	92 874	56 086	446	2 396	164	1 571	2 017
Clarksville city	9.0	19.8	13.6	34.7	15.6	4.2	2.3	.8	28.8	100.9	70 254	24 030	560	2 233	262	2 705	3 411
Cleveland city	6.5	15.5	15.4	27.6	21.2	7.2	4.9	1.8	34.0	89.5	33 102	2 608	86	359	12	481	544
Columbia city	7.5	18.3	9.8	28.6	21.0	7.4	5.4	2.0	35.7	89.9	24 669	6 984	92	137	9	680	484
Germantown city	5.2	22.8	5.8	23.5	33.5	5.7	3.0	.6	41.3	95.0	34 712	869	60	1 306	13	62	326
Hendersonville city	6.6	19.2	7.8	31.5	24.8	5.7	3.3	1.1	36.2	94.9	37 749	1 673	108	447	12	266	365
Jackson city	7.2	18.6	12.8	28.7	19.5	6.4	4.8	2.0	32.8	87.4	32 883	25 091	92	470	6	525	576
Johnson City city	5.5	14.3	13.7	28.1	22.5	7.9	5.6	2.4	36.9	91.1	49 973	3 549	143	678	12	382	732
Kingsport city	5.7	16.0	6.5	26.2	25.3	9.5	7.9	2.9	41.9	84.1	41 906	1 897	106	356	10	153	477
Knoxville city	5.9	13.7	16.8	29.5	19.6	6.9	5.4	2.1	33.4	90.0	138 611	28 171	541	2 525	60	1 257	2 725
Memphis city	7.8	20.1	10.8	30.7	19.7	5.6	3.9	1.4	31.9	89.8	223 728	399 208	1 217	9 482	239	9 438	6 788
Murfreesboro city	6.5	16.2	20.5	30.8	17.3	4.6	3.0	1.2	28.7	98.7	54 947	9 560	192	1 853	18	1 295	951
Nashville-Davidson (remainder)	6.7	15.5	11.9	34.3	20.8	5.8	3.8	1.4	33.9	93.8	359 581	146 235	1 639	12 992	400	13 677	11 000
Oak Ridge city	4.0	17.7	6.6	23.6	26.3	9.7	9.9	2.5	43.4	88.1	23 815	2 239	83	576	6	209	459
TEXAS	7.8	20.4	10.5	31.1	20.2	5.5	3.3	1.1	32.3	98.6	14 799 505	2 404 566	118 362	562 319	14 434	2 438 001	514 633
Abilene city	7.1	18.5	15.3	28.9	18.2	6.3	4.2	1.6	31.1	102.0	90 502	10 215	642	1 543	81	10 117	2 830
Amarillo city	8.0	19.9	10.2	28.8	20.5	6.7	4.4	1.6	33.5	92.4	134 563	10 358	1 346	3 563	64	19 663	4 070
Arlington city	8.3	20.0	11.0	35.7	18.9	3.6	1.9	.6	30.7	100.0	225 379	45 727	1 817	20 015	475	29 763	9 793
Austin city	7.1	15.4	16.6	37.1	17.1	3.5	2.3	.9	29.6	105.8	429 100	65 956	3 889	30 960	469	106 538	19 650
Baytown city	8.7	21.3	11.2	29.4	19.5	4.9	3.7	1.3	30.6	94.4	45 088	8 888	337	651	51	9 578	1 837
Beaumont city	7.1	20.0	10.4	28.0	21.2	6.8	4.8	1.8	34.5	90.7	52 826	52 206	269	2 827	46	4 038	1 654
Bedford city	5.9	16.6	9.7	32.9	26.1	4.8	2.7	1.1	36.2	93.0	41 320	1 722	239	1 708	119	1 151	893
Brownsville city	9.9	24.8	11.2	27.5	17.2	5.4	3.1	1.0	27.7	89.0	114 083	575	580	752	46	20 486	3 200
Bryan city	8.0	19.0	18.1	29.8	15.8	4.5	3.3	1.5	27.6	99.2	42 452	11 635	265	1 084	52	8 747	1 425
Carrollton city	7.9	20.3	8.0	37.1	21.5	3.2	1.6	.5	33.0	98.1	78 758	6 862	503	11 944	75	8 451	2 983
College Station city	4.5	10.0	51.2	21.3	9.4	1.9	1.2	.4	21.9	104.3	54 673	3 698	206	4 951	44	3 036	1 282
Conroe city	8.7	19.4	13.4	31.6	17.3	4.9	3.3	1.4	29.4	101.2	26 193	4 097	149	348	18	4 926	1 080
Corpus Christi city	7.8	20.4	10.6	29.2	21.0	6.1	3.8	1.2	33.2	95.6	198 714	12 969	1 766	3 551	212	51 552	8 690
Dallas city	8.3	18.2	11.8	35.3	17.7	4.5	3.0	1.1	30.5	101.6	604 209	307 957	6 472	32 118	590	204 883	32 351
Deer Park city	6.3	22.7	9.4	30.3	23.9	4.6	2.2	.5	34.7	98.7	25 672	374	118	321	37	1 496	502
Del Rio city	8.6	23.1	8.8	27.6	20.2	6.5	3.9	1.3	31.7	94.0	26 105	409	236	166	20	6 024	907
Denton city	6.2	14.5	25.0	30.8	15.7	3.8	2.8	1.3	26.8	96.7	60 900	7 344	464	2 731	43	7 126	1 929
DeSoto city	7.0	21.1	7.6	30.2	24.8	4.9	3.1	1.3	36.1	88.7	18 382	17 142	118	484	13	964	543
Duncanville city	6.5	21.6	8.5	27.7	26.1	5.7	3.1	.8	35.8	90.0	23 055	8 934	117	717	31	2 466	761
Edinburg city	9.8	23.2	13.1	29.8	15.9	4.8	2.6	.8	27.2	95.3	35 533	281	230	315	19	10 986	1 101
El Paso city	8.5	22.6	10.0	29.1	19.2	6.2	3.4	1.0	31.1	90.4	413 061	17 586	4 601	6 321	583	102 320	19 190
Euless city	7.4	17.5	9.8	39.7	19.7	3.8	1.5	.5	32.2	98.6	34 743	2 987	294	3 288	856	2 475	1 362
Fort Worth city	8.5	19.8	11.3	32.7	18.2	5.0	3.5	1.2	30.9	97.3	319 159	108 310	3 144	14 105	341	75 100	14 535
Galveston city	6.6	16.7	11.3	29.8	21.8	7.5	4.7	1.6	35.5	93.4	33 582	14 592	243	1 839	42	5 571	1 378
Garland city	8.2	21.6	9.6	33.0	20.5	4.2	2.3	.6	31.7	98.3	140 835	25 609	1 284	15 806	141	25 862	6 231
Grand Prairie city	8.9	21.7	10.1	34.1	18.8	3.7	2.1	.5	30.5	98.0	78 970	17 242	982	5 632	74	20 265	4 262
Grapevine city	7.4	21.9	7.5	36.6	21.9	2.5	1.7	.6	34.3	100.5	37 081	1 001	232	1 075	31	1 927	712
Haltom City city	8.2	18.9	10.2	32.9	19.4	5.8	3.6	1.0	32.3	100.8	29 973	1 088	285	3 010	45	3 600	1 017
Harlingen city	9.1	21.7	9.6	26.5	18.0	7.5	5.5	2.0	31.8	90.8	45 290	528	301	506	16	9 435	1 488
Houston city	8.2	19.2	11.2	33.8	19.1	4.8	2.7	.9	30.9	99.7	962 610	494 496	8 568	103 694	1 182	321 603	61 478
Huntsville city	4.6	10.9	30.8	16.3	4.4	2.9	1.2		28.3	152.9	23 075	9 169	117	391	24	1 724	578
Hurst city	7.2	18.2	8.3	30.3	23.6	7.4	3.9	1.1	36.6	94.6	31 189	1 499	231	663	106	1 886	699
Irving city	8.1	17.0	11.9	39.4	17.4	3.7	1.9	.5	30.3	104.0	123 019	19 583	1 244	15 784	248	25 608	6 129
Killeen city	10.1	19.8	16.0	35.7	13.6	3.2	1.4	.3	26.7	100.7	39 788	29 109	680	3 759	787	7 814	4 974

[1] Includes all other responses not included in the other five race categories shown. Also includes write-in entries such as multiracial, mixed, interracial, or a Hispanic/Latino group. [2] Refers to combinations of two or more of the six race categories shown under one race.

Source: Population by Age, Sex, and Race—U.S. Census Bureau; 2000 Census of Population and Housing, "Census 2000 Profiles of General Demographic Characteristics" data files, published May 2001, related Internet site <http://www.census.gov/mp/www/pub/2000cen/mscen01.html>.

Table C–2. Cities — **Population by Age, Sex, and Race**–Con.

[Includes states and 1,070 incorporated places of 25,000 or more population as of April 1, 1990 in all states except Hawaii which has no incorporated places recognized by the Census Bureau. For Hawaii, 8 census designated places (CDPs) of 25,000 or more population as of April 1, 1990 are included. Also included are the 5 boroughs of New York city. For more information on these areas, see appendix B. Geographic Information]

City	Population by age, 2000 (April 1) Percent—								Median age (years)	Males per 100 females, 2000 (April 1)	Population by race, 2000 (April 1) One race						Two or more races[2]
	Under 5 years	5 to 17 years	18 to 24 years	25 to 44 years	45 to 64 years	65 to 74 years	75 to 84 years	85 years and over			White	Black or African American	American Indian and Alaska Native	Asian	Native Hawaiian and Other Pacific Islander	Some other race[1]	
TEXAS—Con.																	
Kingsville city	8.0	18.9	17.3	27.1	18.3	5.6	3.5	1.5	28.4	99.7	18 185	1 111	160	443	17	4 811	848
La Porte city	7.9	21.8	8.9	32.7	21.8	3.9	2.1	.9	32.6	98.5	25 946	1 993	154	359	25	2 717	686
Laredo city	10.5	25.0	11.4	29.5	15.8	4.4	2.5	.9	26.9	92.2	145 267	652	784	820	47	24 611	4 395
League City city	8.1	21.3	6.6	35.9	22.2	3.4	1.7	.8	34.4	99.0	38 170	2 311	168	1 439	24	2 404	928
Lewisville city	9.1	17.5	11.8	41.2	16.1	2.5	1.4	.4	29.8	99.9	60 015	5 747	544	3 028	25	6 468	1 910
Longview city	7.4	19.4	10.8	28.7	20.4	6.9	4.7	1.7	34.0	93.0	51 417	16 214	369	609	16	3 608	1 111
Lubbock city	7.2	17.8	17.9	27.6	18.4	5.9	3.8	1.4	29.7	94.6	145 426	17 292	1 118	3 078	65	28 571	4 014
Lufkin city	8.0	19.0	10.6	27.3	20.1	7.1	5.5	2.5	34.0	88.9	19 599	8 693	84	451	6	3 373	503
McAllen city	8.7	22.1	10.5	29.3	18.9	5.6	3.7	1.2	30.5	90.1	83 491	647	429	2 059	41	16 864	2 883
Mesquite city	7.7	22.8	9.2	33.9	19.3	4.3	2.1	.7	31.9	93.0	91 572	16 585	750	4 665	65	8 009	2 877
Midland city	7.5	22.4	9.0	28.2	20.6	6.9	4.1	1.4	34.1	92.2	71 735	7 948	602	956	29	11 862	1 864
Mission city	9.2	22.9	9.8	26.8	17.1	7.4	5.5	1.3	30.5	91.1	35 249	168	174	288	3	8 465	1 061
Missouri City city	7.3	23.5	7.0	31.0	25.7	3.5	1.5	.4	35.5	94.0	23 435	20 290	107	5 610	21	2 360	1 090
Nacogdoches city	5.8	14.4	30.9	22.3	15.4	5.2	4.1	1.8	24.4	87.7	19 736	7 495	102	337	32	1 748	464
New Braunfels city	7.1	18.6	8.5	28.4	20.6	7.6	6.5	2.8	36.2	91.9	30 763	501	201	211	11	3 988	819
North Richland Hills city	7.1	20.2	9.0	32.6	22.3	5.0	3.0	.9	34.7	96.8	49 224	1 501	303	1 475	93	1 885	1 154
Odessa city	8.0	21.8	10.6	27.8	20.0	6.5	4.0	1.3	32.3	93.2	66 781	5 347	702	797	37	14 611	2 668
Pasadena city	9.3	22.3	11.4	31.2	17.9	4.5	2.7	.7	29.2	99.8	101 219	2 316	957	2 589	58	30 173	4 362
Pharr city	10.6	24.2	11.3	26.3	15.8	6.8	4.1	1.0	27.4	90.9	37 075	110	335	109	13	8 068	950
Plano city	8.3	20.4	7.0	36.5	22.9	2.9	1.5	.5	34.1	99.3	173 761	11 155	803	22 594	98	8 565	5 054
Port Arthur city	7.8	20.8	9.7	26.2	19.9	7.7	5.8	2.1	34.6	91.1	22 528	25 240	260	3 404	9	5 127	1 187
Richardson city	6.7	18.1	8.7	32.7	23.9	5.9	3.1	1.0	35.8	97.6	69 209	5 675	409	10 709	58	3 351	2 391
Round Rock city	9.7	22.2	8.5	38.8	16.3	2.3	1.4	.8	30.1	99.1	46 927	4 718	305	1 767	59	5 792	1 568
San Angelo city	7.1	18.8	13.8	26.9	19.6	6.9	5.0	2.0	32.8	92.1	68 183	4 185	579	844	70	12 344	2 234
San Antonio city	8.1	20.5	10.8	30.8	19.4	5.6	3.6	1.2	31.7	93.5	774 708	78 120	9 584	17 934	1 067	221 362	41 871
San Marcos city	4.9	10.4	41.9	24.8	10.7	3.3	2.6	1.3	23.3	96.8	25 200	1 921	227	426	38	5 914	1 007
Sherman city	7.2	17.3	13.1	27.8	19.3	6.9	5.9	2.4	34.0	92.1	27 526	3 938	468	372	12	1 847	919
Temple city	7.8	18.5	9.2	28.6	20.0	7.1	6.1	2.7	35.2	91.7	38 030	8 988	280	833	50	5 030	1 303
Texarkana city	7.1	18.9	10.0	27.6	20.7	7.3	6.0	2.5	35.7	89.0	20 583	12 885	119	254	17	498	426
Texas City city	6.8	19.9	9.6	27.8	22.4	7.3	4.7	1.4	35.5	89.4	25 224	11 407	207	365	20	3 417	881
Tyler city	7.4	18.7	11.7	26.9	20.0	7.3	5.5	2.5	34.1	88.1	51 795	22 275	287	806	32	7 076	1 379
Victoria city	7.9	20.9	9.7	28.0	21.0	6.6	4.4	1.6	33.9	92.6	43 140	4 599	312	612	24	10 490	1 426
Waco city	7.6	17.8	20.3	25.0	16.0	6.2	5.1	2.2	27.9	91.4	69 119	25 754	576	1 567	61	14 084	2 565
Wichita Falls city	7.1	17.5	15.2	29.3	18.6	6.5	4.3	1.5	31.9	106.2	78 258	12 920	897	2 288	103	6 656	3 075
UTAH	9.4	22.8	14.2	28.1	17.0	4.5	3.0	1.0	27.1	100.4	1 992 975	17 657	29 684	37 108	15 145	93 405	47 195
Bountiful city	8.0	21.7	11.6	23.9	20.5	7.8	5.0	1.6	32.5	94.4	39 469	98	113	474	133	461	553
Layton city	10.3	24.7	12.1	30.3	16.8	3.5	1.8	.4	26.8	101.7	52 573	943	307	1 216	159	1 804	1 472
Logan city	9.5	13.9	34.3	25.5	9.7	3.1	2.6	1.4	23.5	92.1	37 947	272	361	1 537	125	1 740	688
Murray city	7.5	19.8	13.3	28.6	19.5	6.0	4.3	1.1	31.0	95.7	31 153	336	213	624	112	942	644
Ogden city	9.8	18.9	14.6	29.0	16.3	5.3	4.5	1.5	28.6	102.3	61 016	1 785	927	1 105	133	9 997	2 263
Orem city	10.6	24.8	17.4	25.8	14.5	3.6	2.4	.9	23.9	98.7	76 567	280	615	1 226	721	3 073	1 842
Provo city	8.7	13.6	40.2	23.2	8.6	2.8	2.1	.8	22.9	92.6	93 094	486	846	1 924	882	5 368	2 566
St. George city	8.6	19.7	13.7	22.0	16.8	9.8	7.3	2.2	31.4	94.5	45 823	120	812	282	293	1 426	907
Salt Lake City city	7.9	15.7	15.2	33.4	16.7	4.9	4.4	1.7	30.0	102.6	143 933	3 433	2 442	6 579	3 437	15 482	6 437
Sandy city	7.9	26.5	11.1	27.5	21.8	2.8	1.7	.7	29.1	100.9	82 685	445	311	1 916	275	1 326	1 460
West Jordan city	11.3	26.5	12.2	32.1	14.8	1.9	1.0	.3	25.0	100.8	60 653	434	385	1 393	644	3 250	1 577
West Valley City city	10.6	23.1	12.9	30.7	17.4	3.4	1.6	.4	26.8	102.3	85 172	1 247	1 273	4 671	3 157	9 528	3 848
VERMONT	5.6	18.6	9.3	29.0	24.8	6.7	4.4	1.6	37.7	96.1	589 208	3 063	2 420	5 217	141	1 443	7 335
Burlington city	4.6	11.7	25.4	31.0	16.8	5.0	3.7	1.8	29.2	93.2	35 883	693	182	1 031	8	211	881
VIRGINIA	6.5	18.0	9.6	31.6	23.0	6.1	3.9	1.2	35.7	96.3	5 120 110	1 390 293	21 172	261 025	3 946	138 900	143 069
Alexandria city	6.2	10.6	9.2	43.5	21.5	4.4	3.3	1.3	34.4	93.5	76 702	28 915	355	7 249	112	9 467	5 483
Blacksburg town	2.9	6.7	57.4	18.9	9.2	2.6	1.8	.6	21.9	127.0	33 394	1 738	45	3 087	22	355	932
Charlottesville city	4.4	10.8	33.8	25.8	15.2	5.1	3.6	1.3	25.6	87.5	31 337	10 009	49	2 223	15	458	958
Chesapeake city	7.2	21.6	8.2	32.3	21.7	5.1	3.1	.8	34.7	94.4	133 193	56 823	770	3 673	101	1 400	3 224
Danville city	6.0	17.3	8.0	25.5	23.6	9.7	7.4	2.5	40.5	83.5	26 075	21 352	81	291	14	219	379
Hampton city	6.3	17.9	12.6	32.5	20.4	5.8	3.6	.9	34.0	98.3	72 556	65 428	616	2 694	136	1 505	3 502
Harrisonburg city	4.7	10.7	40.9	21.2	13.2	4.3	3.6	1.4	22.6	90.0	34 334	2 394	76	1 257	10	1 355	1 042
Lynchburg city	5.8	16.3	15.5	25.3	20.8	7.5	6.1	2.7	35.1	84.2	43 487	19 382	169	838	28	413	952
Manassas city	8.6	21.0	9.8	35.8	19.4	3.1	1.7	.6	31.3	103.5	25 316	4 535	128	1 206	31	2 773	1 146
Newport News city	7.9	19.6	11.5	32.2	18.8	5.4	3.6	1.0	32.0	93.8	96 383	70 388	752	4 195	214	3 225	4 993
Norfolk city	7.1	17.0	18.2	29.9	16.9	5.5	4.1	1.2	29.6	104.6	113 358	103 387	1 071	6 593	251	3 923	5 820
Petersburg city	6.4	18.7	8.9	27.5	22.9	8.0	5.6	2.0	36.9	84.2	6 249	26 643	67	236	9	198	338

[1] Includes all other responses not included in the other five race categories shown. Also includes write-in entries such as multiracial, mixed, interracial, or a Hispanic/Latino group. [2] Refers to combinations of two or more of the six race categories shown under one race.

Source: Population by Age, Sex, and Race—U.S. Census Bureau; 2000 Census of Population and Housing, "Census 2000 Profiles of General Demographic Characteristics" data files, published May 2001, related Internet site <http://www.census.gov/mp/www/pub/2000cen/mscen01.html>.

Table C–2. Cities — **Population by Age, Sex, and Race**–Con.

[Includes states and 1,070 incorporated places of 25,000 or more population as of April 1, 1990 in all states except Hawaii which has no incorporated places recognized by the Census Bureau. For Hawaii, 8 census designated places (CDPs) of 25,000 or more population as of April 1, 1990 are included. Also included are the 5 boroughs of New York city. For more information on these areas, see appendix B. Geographic Information]

City	Under 5 years	5 to 17 years	18 to 24 years	25 to 44 years	45 to 64 years	65 to 74 years	75 to 84 years	85 years and over	Median age (years)	Males per 100 females, 2000 (April 1)	White	Black or African American	American Indian and Alaska Native	Asian	Native Hawaiian and Other Pacific Islander	Some other race[1]	Two or more races[2]
VIRGINIA—Con.																	
Portsmouth city	7.1	18.6	11.1	29.1	20.3	6.8	5.4	1.5	34.5	93.5	46 096	50 899	478	775	67	618	1 632
Richmond city	6.3	15.6	13.1	31.7	20.1	6.5	4.9	1.8	33.9	87.1	75 744	113 108	479	2 471	157	2 948	2 883
Roanoke city	6.5	16.1	8.2	30.5	22.3	7.8	6.3	2.3	37.6	88.3	65 848	25 380	190	1 096	23	685	1 689
Suffolk city	7.3	20.6	7.1	31.1	22.5	6.3	3.9	1.2	36.0	91.4	34 271	27 718	191	491	15	233	758
Virginia Beach city	7.2	20.3	10.0	34.3	19.8	4.9	2.7	.8	32.7	98.0	303 681	80 593	1 619	20 869	416	6 402	11 677
WASHINGTON	6.7	19.0	9.5	30.8	22.8	5.7	4.1	1.4	35.3	99.1	4 821 823	190 267	93 301	322 335	23 953	228 923	213 519
Auburn city	7.7	18.9	9.5	31.6	20.7	5.7	4.5	1.4	34.1	98.5	33 382	977	1 024	1 410	204	1 477	1 840
Bellevue city	5.6	15.5	7.8	32.6	25.0	7.1	4.9	1.4	38.2	98.4	81 441	2 183	356	19 056	257	2 785	3 491
Bellingham city	5.2	12.5	23.8	26.5	19.6	5.3	4.9	2.3	30.4	92.6	59 031	655	997	2 853	116	1 450	2 069
Bremerton city	8.1	16.4	15.5	30.3	17.2	5.1	5.3	2.2	30.9	103.7	27 932	2 793	726	2 061	345	956	2 446
Edmonds city............	5.0	15.6	7.0	27.4	28.3	8.8	6.0	1.9	42.0	89.8	34 666	530	317	2 199	102	497	1 204
Everett city	7.8	17.3	12.3	33.3	18.9	4.7	4.0	1.6	32.2	103.5	74 152	3 061	1 423	5 773	330	2 865	3 884
Kennewick city	8.4	21.2	10.3	29.3	20.6	5.2	3.8	1.2	32.3	98.3	45 355	624	507	1 161	59	5 142	1 845
Kent city	8.4	19.3	10.3	35.0	19.6	4.0	2.5	.8	31.8	98.4	56 307	6 547	777	7 489	608	3 525	4 271
Kirkland city	5.5	13.0	9.3	38.1	23.9	5.0	3.7	1.5	36.1	94.8	38 420	717	238	3 512	89	761	1 317
Longview city............	7.1	18.8	8.9	27.1	22.6	6.8	5.9	2.7	36.6	93.2	30 967	248	610	753	45	1 025	1 012
Lynnwood city	7.1	17.3	10.4	32.1	21.3	6.0	4.0	1.8	34.9	95.0	25 138	1 110	346	4 696	136	948	1 473
Olympia city	5.4	16.0	11.9	30.4	22.9	5.8	5.3	2.3	36.0	91.5	36 246	805	553	2 473	125	713	1 599
Redmond city	6.4	15.1	9.5	37.9	21.9	3.9	3.4	2.1	34.0	100.4	35 868	687	203	5 893	82	1 114	1 409
Renton city	7.0	14.8	10.2	36.9	20.8	4.9	4.0	1.4	34.0	98.9	34 105	4 238	358	6 692	250	2 122	2 287
Richland city	6.6	20.6	7.5	27.1	25.4	6.7	4.7	1.4	37.7	96.0	34 662	530	293	1 571	41	718	893
Seattle city	4.7	10.9	11.9	38.6	21.9	5.2	4.8	2.0	35.4	99.5	394 889	47 541	5 659	73 910	2 804	13 423	25 148
Spokane city	7.0	17.8	11.1	29.6	20.5	6.2	5.5	2.3	34.7	93.0	175 018	4 052	3 444	4 399	372	1 727	6 617
Tacoma city	7.0	18.8	10.4	31.6	20.3	5.4	4.5	1.9	33.9	95.2	133 704	21 757	3 794	14 656	1 798	5 695	12 152
Vancouver city	8.0	18.7	9.8	32.1	20.6	5.2	4.0	1.5	33.1	96.9	121 752	3 593	1 399	6 470	779	4 112	5 455
Walla Walla city	6.0	16.8	15.2	27.5	19.5	6.2	6.0	2.9	33.8	108.4	24 875	765	313	368	68	2 451	846
Yakima city	8.9	20.5	10.8	27.6	18.2	5.9	5.5	2.7	31.4	95.7	49 409	1 433	1 435	860	102	15 787	2 819
WEST VIRGINIA	5.6	16.6	9.5	27.7	25.2	8.2	5.3	1.8	38.9	94.6	1 718 777	57 232	3 606	9 434	400	3 107	15 788
Charleston city	5.5	15.1	9.4	27.0	25.3	8.6	6.6	2.6	40.8	87.3	43 072	9 049	127	979	16	158	1 021
Huntington city	4.9	12.9	17.5	24.9	21.8	8.7	7.0	2.3	36.7	88.7	46 127	3 858	101	422	25	155	787
Morgantown city	3.0	8.1	44.7	20.4	13.5	4.8	4.1	1.5	23.1	104.7	23 990	1 113	45	1 113	13	138	397
Parkersburg city	5.6	15.6	9.1	27.1	23.7	9.1	7.2	2.5	39.9	87.6	31 894	579	67	138	18	71	332
Wheeling city............	4.9	15.7	9.1	24.3	24.5	10.1	8.5	3.0	42.4	84.1	29 133	1 567	31	287	9	51	341
WISCONSIN	6.4	19.1	9.7	29.5	22.2	6.6	4.7	1.8	36.0	97.6	4 769 857	304 460	47 228	88 763	1 630	84 842	66 895
Appleton city	6.9	20.5	9.7	31.8	19.7	5.5	4.0	1.7	33.8	96.7	64 116	695	401	3 231	21	733	890
Beloit city	7.7	20.0	11.5	28.5	19.3	6.3	4.8	1.9	32.7	92.1	27 034	5 497	135	415	24	1 652	1 018
Brookfield city	5.4	21.4	4.6	23.2	27.8	9.6	6.0	2.0	42.5	93.7	36 407	321	35	1 479	7	87	313
Eau Claire city............	5.8	15.9	22.1	26.1	18.2	5.5	4.7	1.7	29.4	90.7	57 657	429	337	2 259	23	209	790
Fond du Lac city	6.5	17.6	10.7	29.4	20.4	6.5	5.9	2.9	35.7	88.7	39 496	783	243	640	6	535	526
Green Bay city	7.2	18.3	11.6	31.7	19.5	5.7	4.4	1.7	33.2	97.2	87 841	1 407	3 355	3 845	36	3 809	2 020
Greenfield city	4.5	14.4	8.1	24.3	24.3	9.3	8.2	3.0	41.7	88.4	33 247	348	155	802	7	464	453
Janesville city	7.0	19.2	8.3	31.2	21.4	6.8	4.4	1.7	35.3	95.6	56 682	748	146	573	19	605	725
Kenosha city	7.5	19.7	10.1	31.5	19.0	5.9	4.6	1.7	33.6	96.7	75 566	6 943	398	893	40	4 366	2 146
La Crosse city	4.8	14.0	24.4	24.9	17.0	6.6	5.7	2.6	30.1	89.0	47 454	806	266	2 410	18	185	679
Madison city	5.2	12.7	21.4	32.2	19.3	4.6	3.4	1.3	30.6	96.6	174 689	12 155	759	12 065	77	3 474	4 835
Manitowoc city	6.2	18.0	8.2	27.9	21.4	8.2	7.3	3.0	38.6	93.9	31 713	202	188	1 283	25	306	336
Menomonee Falls village ...	6.6	18.4	5.4	30.5	23.4	8.9	4.9	1.8	39.2	96.4	31 504	479	53	288	7	78	238
Milwaukee city............	8.0	20.7	12.2	30.2	18.1	5.5	4.0	1.4	30.6	91.6	298 379	222 933	5 212	17 571	301	36 428	16 150
New Berlin city	6.0	18.8	6.4	29.0	27.1	7.6	3.9	1.2	39.8	96.9	36 631	169	82	883	6	173	276
Oshkosh city	5.4	15.3	18.1	29.7	18.3	6.0	4.8	2.3	32.4	99.9	58 339	1 376	326	1 908	17	334	616
Racine city	8.0	20.7	9.9	30.0	19.2	6.0	4.6	1.6	33.1	95.0	56 408	16 634	328	497	42	5 841	2 105
Sheboygan city	7.0	18.6	9.2	30.0	19.4	6.9	6.2	2.6	35.4	96.0	44 507	436	242	3 290	18	1 447	852
Superior city	6.0	16.7	12.9	27.9	21.6	6.4	6.2	2.5	35.9	92.4	25 797	186	611	230	10	72	462
Waukesha city	7.4	17.3	10.8	33.6	20.2	5.0	3.8	1.8	33.4	95.6	59 133	831	216	1 407	23	2 144	1 071
Wausau city............	6.2	19.2	9.6	27.5	20.4	7.3	6.8	3.0	36.5	92.5	33 010	208	228	4 383	15	117	465
Wauwatosa city............	6.5	16.8	5.5	31.2	21.9	7.4	7.0	3.7	39.1	86.3	44 422	965	128	918	31	254	553
West Allis city	5.8	15.7	8.4	32.3	20.5	7.5	7.1	2.7	37.8	93.0	57 600	818	428	812	12	720	864
WYOMING	6.3	19.8	10.1	28.1	24.0	6.3	4.0	1.4	36.2	101.2	454 670	3 722	11 133	2 771	302	12 301	8 883
Casper city...............	6.6	19.3	10.5	27.7	22.3	7.3	4.8	1.5	36.1	95.0	46 680	428	495	245	10	1 011	775
Cheyenne city	6.5	18.5	8.8	29.7	22.8	7.0	5.0	1.8	36.6	95.3	46 707	1 472	430	561	59	2 356	1 426
Laramie city	5.1	12.4	31.8	25.8	16.8	4.0	3.1	1.0	25.3	107.0	24 704	337	241	522	16	787	597

[1] Includes all other responses not included in the other five race categories shown. Also includes write-in entries such as multiracial, mixed, interracial, or a Hispanic/Latino group.   [2] Refers to combinations of two or more of the six race categories shown under one race.

Source: Population by Age, Sex, and Race—U.S. Census Bureau; 2000 Census of Population and Housing, "Census 2000 Profiles of General Demographic Characteristics" data files, published May 2001, related Internet site <http://www.census.gov/mp/www/pub/2000cen/mscen01.html>.

Table C–3. Cities — **Group Quarters Population and Households**

[Includes states and 1,070 incorporated places of 25,000 or more population as of April 1, 1990 in all states except Hawaii which has no incorporated places recognized by the Census Bureau. For Hawaii, 8 census designated places (CDPs) of 25,000 or more population as of April 1, 1990 are included. Also included are the 5 boroughs of New York city. For more information on these areas, see appendix B. Geographic Information]

City	Group quarters population, 2000[1] Number	Institutionalized population[2]	Households, 2000 (April 1) Number	Percent change, 1990–2000	Persons per household	Percent— One-person	Percent— With 1 or more persons under 18 years	Percent— With 1 or more persons 65 years and over	Family households (families) Number	Percent with own children under 18 years	Married-couple Number	Percent with own children[3]	Female householder[4] Number	Percent with own children[3]	Nonfamily households Number	Percent change, 1990–2000
ALABAMA	114 720	65 363	1 737 080	15.3	2.49	26.1	36.1	24.1	1 215 968	46.2	906 916	43.1	246 466	57.2	521 112	29.3
Anniston city	670	558	10 447	-3.3	2.26	34.8	29.3	32.9	6 416	39.5	3 968	32.2	2 088	53.5	4 031	13.3
Auburn city	3 855	177	18 421	37.0	2.12	36.8	19.9	10.4	7 238	47.4	5 269	46.9	1 416	57.0	11 183	41.3
Bessemer city	629	594	11 537	-8.3	2.52	29.0	37.6	31.5	7 873	44.7	3 995	38.2	3 364	54.4	3 664	-1.9
Birmingham city	8 852	3 902	98 782	-6.3	2.37	34.4	33.3	24.4	59 287	46.1	30 705	40.4	24 346	55.3	39 495	3.2
Decatur city	923	621	21 824	14.1	2.43	28.9	34.6	23.5	14 752	47.0	11 067	42.8	2 919	61.9	7 072	29.5
Dothan city	1 127	1 030	23 685	14.5	2.39	28.4	34.8	24.9	16 028	46.6	11 589	41.3	3 648	63.3	7 657	27.3
Florence city	1 477	736	15 820	6.1	2.20	33.8	28.4	28.0	9 560	42.9	6 905	37.5	2 212	60.6	6 260	26.5
Gadsden city	1 430	878	16 456	-6.0	2.28	33.9	29.5	34.9	10 253	39.9	6 664	33.5	2 980	54.9	6 203	7.3
Hoover city	491	454	25 191	56.8	2.47	25.9	34.7	18.0	17 407	48.3	14 960	47.4	1 817	58.3	7 784	67.8
Huntsville city	5 575	1 666	66 742	5.8	2.29	32.3	30.6	22.8	41 742	44.2	30 350	39.2	9 151	60.3	25 000	24.1
Mobile city	6 180	2 727	78 480	4.0	2.46	30.2	35.3	25.1	50 764	47.8	32 253	42.7	15 655	59.6	27 716	13.3
Montgomery city	10 187	2 870	78 384	12.0	2.44	30.1	36.2	22.1	51 084	49.3	33 224	44.3	15 001	61.1	27 300	24.2
Phenix City city	674	609	11 517	18.2	2.40	30.4	36.1	25.7	7 569	48.2	4 538	41.4	2 545	60.9	3 948	36.0
Prichard city	733	423	9 841	-11.5	2.84	23.4	45.5	25.6	7 269	49.2	3 225	42.3	3 545	57.0	2 572	1.4
Tuscaloosa city	8 102	1 934	31 381	6.5	2.22	35.2	27.2	20.8	16 931	44.3	10 995	38.7	4 933	58.5	14 450	15.3
ALASKA	19 349	4 824	221 600	17.3	2.74	23.5	42.9	11.9	152 337	58.1	116 318	54.4	23 937	72.0	69 263	23.5
Anchorage city	7 014	1 915	94 822	14.7	2.67	23.4	41.6	11.0	64 131	57.5	48 421	53.6	10 884	72.0	30 691	17.1
Fairbanks city	1 899	327	11 075	1.7	2.56	27.4	42.4	12.8	7 187	61.6	5 230	56.8	1 395	75.8	3 888	7.4
Juneau city	678	229	11 543	16.6	2.60	24.4	39.6	12.1	7 638	55.5	5 910	51.4	1 213	69.2	3 905	19.3
ARIZONA	109 850	63 768	1 901 327	38.9	2.64	24.8	35.4	24.5	1 287 367	47.2	986 303	43.5	210 781	61.4	613 960	43.2
Chandler city	782	478	62 377	98.1	2.82	19.3	44.0	11.7	45 382	56.5	35 857	54.7	6 576	66.3	16 995	118.0
Flagstaff city	2 853	177	19 306	33.9	2.59	23.2	35.5	10.8	11 604	54.6	8 487	49.8	2 247	70.0	7 702	53.6
Gilbert town	66	54	35 405	277.4	3.10	12.7	53.2	8.4	28 915	62.2	24 613	61.7	2 934	66.4	6 490	245.8
Glendale city	2 857	1 014	75 700	41.0	2.85	21.3	43.7	15.5	54 384	55.5	40 477	52.6	9 652	65.7	21 316	40.3
Mesa city	3 949	2 189	146 643	36.0	2.68	24.2	36.3	24.3	99 856	49.0	77 267	45.6	15 548	63.3	46 787	39.4
Peoria city	1 514	873	39 184	114.7	2.73	20.5	40.4	26.3	29 299	50.5	24 282	47.9	3 558	63.4	9 885	135.8
Phoenix city	22 468	12 948	465 834	25.9	2.79	25.4	39.7	16.8	307 243	54.1	218 516	51.8	59 949	62.8	158 591	27.8
Prescott city	2 044	862	15 098	31.5	2.11	32.1	20.1	39.4	8 998	30.4	7 351	24.3	1 191	58.4	6 130	41.0
Scottsdale city	1 677	479	90 669	57.5	2.22	30.8	24.1	25.9	54 458	37.7	44 972	34.4	6 823	55.1	36 211	66.8
Sierra Vista city	2 575	259	14 196	21.6	2.48	25.1	37.3	22.1	9 997	49.6	8 026	43.9	1 474	74.8	4 199	38.9
Tempe city	5 242	406	63 602	14.5	2.41	28.5	26.9	12.9	33 654	46.2	24 404	43.9	6 155	57.5	29 948	26.9
Tucson city	19 182	7 942	192 891	18.6	2.42	32.3	32.5	21.9	112 515	49.7	76 546	45.1	26 678	61.4	80 376	22.4
Yuma city	3 144	1 065	26 649	38.2	2.79	21.7	42.4	27.5	19 618	52.8	15 081	48.2	3 480	69.7	7 031	42.6
ARKANSAS	73 908	45 152	1 042 696	17.0	2.49	25.6	35.6	25.3	732 261	45.7	566 401	41.9	126 561	60.7	310 435	29.6
Conway city	4 037	533	16 039	70.0	2.44	26.1	34.9	16.1	10 172	52.1	7 858	48.7	1 793	67.1	5 867	73.7
Fayetteville city	5 350	1 420	23 798	40.9	2.21	34.0	27.2	12.9	12 126	50.0	8 971	45.9	2 278	67.4	11 672	56.1
Fort Smith city	1 990	1 632	32 398	9.3	2.42	30.7	33.8	23.5	20 647	48.3	15 274	43.9	3 989	63.4	11 751	19.2
Hot Springs city	1 586	1 086	16 096	11.1	2.12	38.4	25.1	36.2	9 066	39.0	6 473	32.9	1 997	57.8	7 030	19.9
Jacksonville city	1 204	41	10 890	10.5	2.64	22.0	43.4	15.3	8 006	54.6	6 000	50.2	1 590	68.9	2 884	39.1
Jonesboro city	2 575	712	22 219	23.6	2.38	27.5	32.7	20.6	14 360	46.6	10 856	43.1	2 715	61.6	7 859	38.9
Little Rock city	4 915	2 774	77 352	6.6	2.30	33.8	31.8	20.0	46 490	47.5	31 290	42.0	12 441	61.7	30 862	13.9
North Little Rock city	520	403	25 542	2.2	2.35	32.0	32.4	25.7	16 128	45.8	10 691	38.1	4 493	64.0	9 414	14.5
Pine Bluff city	3 821	2 644	19 956	-4.4	2.57	29.2	38.8	26.6	13 354	49.2	7 732	42.0	4 742	61.6	6 602	4.8
Springdale city	574	509	16 149	41.3	2.80	22.0	42.2	20.4	11 852	52.9	9 391	51.1	1 701	62.6	4 297	49.3
West Memphis city	514	462	10 051	1.7	2.70	24.8	43.0	21.4	7 132	51.7	4 057	44.4	2 527	63.8	2 919	18.7
CALIFORNIA	819 754	413 656	11 502 870	10.8	2.87	23.5	39.7	22.3	7 920 049	52.0	5 877 084	50.9	1 448 510	57.6	3 582 821	10.5
Alameda city	1 077	469	30 226	3.9	2.35	32.2	30.0	22.7	17 858	46.9	13 198	45.3	3 454	54.2	12 368	7.2
Alhambra city	1 923	971	29 111	3.1	2.88	22.5	37.2	26.7	20 669	46.7	14 055	48.7	4 775	45.8	8 442	-5.3
Anaheim city	3 796	1 290	96 969	10.7	3.34	18.1	47.7	19.3	73 502	56.8	54 586	57.5	12 735	57.2	23 467	-3.1
Antioch city	416	262	29 338	37.1	3.07	15.9	50.7	16.7	23 173	58.6	17 696	57.1	3 967	64.8	6 165	28.0
Apple Valley town	363	176	18 557	19.0	2.90	18.0	43.4	27.8	14 358	50.2	10 721	45.2	2 627	65.6	4 199	38.3
Arcadia city	581	419	19 149	4.3	2.74	22.3	37.7	29.5	14 143	47.7	11 068	48.7	2 284	46.2	5 006	-5.1
Azusa city	1 949	69	12 549	-.8	3.41	18.7	49.6	19.0	9 294	58.7	6 237	60.5	2 148	57.3	3 255	-8.1
Bakersfield city	3 813	2 018	83 441	33.6	2.92	21.5	46.5	18.6	60 959	58.2	43 486	54.8	12 956	68.4	22 482	24.8
Baldwin Park city	606	278	16 961	2.1	4.44	8.1	65.8	20.5	15 069	62.9	10 654	67.1	2 963	55.2	1 892	-18.7
Bell city	538	97	8 918	-1.1	4.05	11.0	64.7	16.8	7 616	67.5	5 168	71.6	1 636	62.8	1 302	-32.9
Bellflower city	623	253	23 367	2.0	3.09	21.1	48.5	19.7	17 117	59.6	10 980	59.0	4 444	63.7	6 250	-15.7
Bell Gardens city	456	301	9 466	2.4	4.61	7.4	74.2	13.0	8 511	74.8	5 689	78.2	1 851	73.1	955	-17.0
Berkeley city	5 822	246	44 955	3.5	2.16	38.1	19.8	17.7	18 646	42.8	12 972	41.0	4 253	49.9	26 309	6.8
Beverly Hills city	39	1	15 035	3.2	2.24	38.2	25.6	29.5	8 263	44.3	6 584	42.9	1 223	54.0	6 772	3.5

[1] As of April 1. [2] Includes people under formally authorized, supervised care or custody in institutions at the time of enumeration (such as correctional institutions, nursing homes, and juvenile institutions). [3] Under 18 years. [4] No husband present.

Sources: Group Quarters Population—U.S. Census Bureau; 2000 Census of Population and Housing, "Census 2000 Profiles of General Demographic Characteristics" data files, published May 2001 (related Internet site <http://www.census.gov/mp/www/pub/2000cen/mscen01.html>). Households, 2000—U.S. Census Bureau; 2000 Census of Population and Housing, "Census 2000 Profiles of General Demographic Characteristics" data files, published May 2001 (related Internet site <http://www.census.gov/mp/www/pub/2000cen/mscen01.html>). Households, 1990—U.S. Census Bureau, 1990 Census of Population and Housing, Summary Tape File (STF) 1C on CD-ROM (related Internet site <http://homer.ssd.census.gov/cdrom/lookup>).

Table C–3. Cities — **Group Quarters Population and Households**–Con.

[Includes states and 1,070 incorporated places of 25,000 or more population as of April 1, 1990 in all states except Hawaii which has no incorporated places recognized by the Census Bureau. For Hawaii, 8 census designated places (CDPs) of 25,000 or more population as of April 1, 1990 are included. Also included are the 5 boroughs of New York city. For more information on these areas, see appendix B. Geographic Information]

City	Group quarters population, 2000[1] Number	Institutionalized population[2]	Households, 2000 (April 1) Number	Percent change, 1990–2000	Persons per household	Percent— One-person	With 1 or more persons under 18 years	With 1 or more persons 65 years and over	Family households (families) Number	Percent with own children under 18 years	Married-couple Number	Percent with own children[3]	Female householder[4] Number	Percent with own children[3]	Nonfamily households Number	Percent change, 1990–2000
CALIFORNIA—Con.																
Brea city	128	22	13 067	6.9	2.70	23.0	37.4	22.6	9 301	48.5	7 398	47.9	1 375	53.5	3 766	4.6
Buena Park city	934	325	23 332	5.1	3.32	14.4	48.6	22.1	18 733	53.6	13 771	55.0	3 452	51.3	4 599	-5.5
Burbank city	826	476	41 608	5.9	2.39	31.8	30.8	23.3	24 362	48.6	17 797	48.1	4 792	52.5	17 246	8.0
Burlingame city	486	428	12 511	1.5	2.21	35.6	25.5	23.2	6 954	43.4	5 640	43.2	967	45.1	5 557	-2.2
Camarillo city	939	393	21 438	18.4	2.62	24.1	35.6	31.8	15 240	46.4	12 790	44.5	1 751	57.1	6 198	44.2
Campbell city	290	106	15 920	4.0	2.38	30.4	30.1	16.9	9 121	48.8	6 787	48.0	1 602	52.2	6 799	4.7
Carlsbad city	787	535	31 521	26.1	2.46	24.8	32.3	23.4	20 894	46.3	17 129	44.1	2 701	58.2	10 627	29.6
Carson city	1 210	242	24 648	3.5	3.59	14.2	49.0	28.3	20 243	47.7	14 463	50.8	4 244	40.4	4 405	.5
Cathedral City city	145	–	14 027	28.5	3.03	23.2	43.4	27.6	9 628	57.3	7 117	55.7	1 675	65.2	4 399	16.6
Ceres city	99	57	10 435	21.6	3.31	14.1	53.9	20.0	8 532	59.5	6 239	59.0	1 641	63.4	1 903	10.0
Cerritos city	93	30	15 390	2.4	3.34	8.9	46.0	23.7	13 657	46.1	11 369	47.9	1 670	39.0	1 733	11.6
Chico city	3 063	497	23 476	51.4	2.42	29.3	28.9	16.4	11 641	54.7	8 079	49.2	2 644	70.2	11 835	40.1
Chino city	7 816	7 634	17 304	10.7	3.43	14.1	53.7	17.3	14 102	58.1	10 817	59.1	2 238	57.0	3 202	4.7
Chula Vista city	1 079	647	57 705	20.7	2.99	19.5	45.3	24.5	43 549	53.9	32 144	53.6	8 571	57.1	14 156	8.3
Claremont city	5 104	465	11 281	7.7	2.56	24.9	33.9	29.1	7 810	45.2	6 286	43.3	1 172	56.1	3 471	20.2
Clovis city	480	253	24 347	33.3	2.79	22.3	44.8	19.0	17 665	57.4	13 251	55.1	3 219	64.4	6 682	28.4
Colton city	264	123	14 520	7.8	3.26	19.4	53.0	15.8	10 904	62.0	7 012	61.8	2 835	65.5	3 616	-6.9
Compton city	650	93	22 327	Z	4.16	13.2	62.2	22.4	18 613	60.8	10 566	56.6	6 190	56.0	3 714	.2
Concord city	1 354	706	44 020	5.0	2.74	23.2	37.7	20.7	30 322	49.9	22 613	48.7	5 399	55.7	13 698	6.5
Corona city	632	431	37 839	58.2	3.29	14.4	53.8	13.9	30 391	61.7	24 156	62.2	4 230	62.4	7 448	53.9
Coronado city	6 540	456	7 734	5.6	2.27	30.9	28.0	32.6	4 935	42.3	4 179	39.9	574	55.2	2 799	3.9
Costa Mesa city	3 270	1 268	39 206	4.6	2.69	28.1	32.0	17.0	22 766	50.3	16 762	50.3	4 028	53.1	16 440	2.6
Covina city	602	279	15 971	2.8	2.89	20.8	42.9	22.7	11 762	52.2	8 247	50.8	2 596	56.5	4 209	-6.2
Culver City city	524	241	16 611	2.8	2.31	34.5	28.4	23.0	9 513	45.7	6 782	43.5	2 129	54.0	7 098	7.8
Cupertino city	448	377	18 204	18.5	2.75	19.6	43.2	20.9	13 613	55.6	11 624	57.0	1 428	50.1	4 591	2.4
Cypress city	321	5	15 654	9.6	2.93	17.6	43.0	23.2	12 243	49.7	9 387	49.3	2 082	52.0	3 411	16.0
Daly City city	790	502	30 775	0.1	3.04	10.1	40.7	20.0	23 009	45.4	18 705	40.0	4 304	30.8	7 080	3.1
Dana Point city	242	95	14 456	13.8	2.41	26.0	28.2	22.1	9 286	40.8	7 432	37.7	1 273	53.9	5 170	17.4
Danville city	464	94	14 816	33.9	2.78	15.5	43.4	18.8	11 865	52.7	10 472	51.8	1 049	59.4	2 951	51.4
Davis city	2 970	254	22 948	28.0	2.50	25.0	27.5	12.3	11 291	53.6	8 784	52.1	1 874	63.4	11 657	23.7
Diamond Bar city	118	51	17 651	4.4	3.18	12.5	48.1	17.7	14 801	52.9	12 052	54.2	1 957	50.8	2 850	–
Downey city	1 765	1 423	33 989	3.0	3.11	19.1	46.3	25.0	25 997	54.6	18 404	54.7	5 361	57.2	7 992	-15.8
El Cajon city	2 483	1 429	34 199	4.0	2.70	24.1	40.3	20.9	23 163	54.7	15 715	50.7	5 461	65.0	11 036	7.3
El Centro city	887	749	11 439	18.7	3.23	18.8	53.1	23.0	8 908	60.8	6 162	59.2	2 136	66.5	2 531	21.0
El Monte city	1 270	623	27 034	3.5	4.24	10.9	61.4	21.4	22 995	62.7	15 413	66.7	4 988	59.6	4 039	-14.5
Encinitas city	559	415	22 830	9.9	2.52	25.7	32.8	18.1	14 283	49.5	11 432	47.7	2 011	58.6	8 547	13.7
Escondido city	1 765	696	43 817	11.6	3.01	22.4	42.6	23.6	31 162	54.9	23 626	52.9	5 133	63.9	12 655	4.6
Eureka city	1 355	487	10 957	-1.6	2.26	35.3	28.6	24.0	5 886	48.0	3 818	39.4	1 532	65.6	5 071	12.3
Fairfield city	4 229	1 886	30 870	21.4	2.98	17.0	47.9	18.6	24 018	55.4	18 031	53.3	4 378	63.2	6 852	23.2
Folsom city	6 944	3 228	17 196	96.4	2.61	21.8	40.8	18.5	12 527	53.7	10 609	51.9	1 379	63.4	4 669	112.7
Fontana city	499	218	34 014	28.9	3.78	10.9	63.9	13.5	29 022	67.5	21 273	68.9	5 264	66.1	4 992	-2.5
Foster City city	87	67	11 613	3.6	2.47	23.6	32.0	18.0	7 928	44.7	6 699	44.3	889	49.8	3 685	-3.8
Fountain Valley city	512	169	18 162	4.3	3.00	16.0	38.6	23.6	14 227	43.8	11 511	44.8	1 903	41.9	3 935	15.3
Fremont city	1 759	755	68 237	13.4	2.96	16.5	43.5	17.5	52 228	52.5	42 757	53.7	6 307	50.3	16 009	8.9
Fresno city	8 187	4 527	140 079	15.0	2.99	23.3	44.8	20.5	97 923	57.8	64 622	55.0	24 652	65.5	42 156	10.7
Fullerton city	2 770	884	43 609	6.7	2.83	23.5	36.3	22.4	29 625	48.5	22 575	48.4	4 794	51.9	13 984	5.5
Gardena city	804	556	20 324	12.1	2.80	25.5	38.3	24.8	14 031	48.5	9 038	47.7	3 670	54.0	6 293	8.7
Garden Grove city	2 234	788	45 791	2.8	3.56	15.2	48.4	24.2	36 460	53.4	27 354	56.6	5 936	47.2	9 331	-11.7
Gilroy city	430	219	11 869	24.8	3.46	14.3	53.4	17.2	9 590	59.0	7 222	58.9	1 685	60.9	2 279	19.1
Glendale city	2 864	1 715	71 805	4.7	2.68	25.7	35.4	26.8	49 636	47.7	37 566	50.3	8 508	43.8	22 169	-6.7
Glendora city	1 007	786	16 819	3.0	2.88	19.1	42.2	24.7	12 861	50.4	10 106	50.1	2 043	51.7	3 958	6.6
Hanford city	848	718	13 931	28.3	2.93	20.6	46.3	21.4	10 383	56.7	7 502	52.9	2 141	68.3	3 548	25.9
Hawthorne city	500	308	28 536	5.2	2.93	24.5	48.5	13.6	19 775	63.0	11 025	61.6	6 713	67.6	8 761	-15.0
Hayward city	2 138	755	44 804	11.7	3.08	20.9	42.5	22.2	31 931	52.0	22 555	52.7	6 503	53.1	12 873	2.9
Hemet city	1 679	919	25 252	45.2	2.26	34.4	25.4	50.5	15 187	38.2	11 385	31.3	2 835	59.8	10 065	41.8
Hesperia city	331	196	19 966	20.6	3.12	16.5	48.2	24.6	15 775	53.9	11 758	50.9	2 760	63.2	4 191	27.5
Highland city	240	8	13 478	19.1	3.29	15.4	53.5	16.4	10 780	59.9	7 421	58.2	2 556	65.1	2 698	4.2
Huntington Beach city	792	496	73 657	6.9	2.56	24.3	31.4	19.4	47 716	44.7	37 371	43.4	7 082	50.9	25 941	11.2
Huntington Park city	181	16	14 860	6.9	4.12	10.9	65.2	16.7	12 663	68.5	8 237	72.8	3 018	64.9	2 197	-14.1
Imperial Beach city	666	–	9 272	2.1	2.84	21.4	44.6	16.8	6 449	57.8	4 187	53.2	1 678	67.8	2 823	14.6
Indio city	856	551	13 871	29.1	3.48	16.0	54.9	22.8	11 073	60.4	7 753	59.4	2 311	65.9	2 798	12.0
Inglewood city	1 370	745	36 805	1.9	3.02	25.3	48.6	16.7	25 851	60.8	14 167	61.9	9 147	61.6	10 954	-5.8
Irvine city	7 112	103	51 199	27.2	2.66	22.8	37.5	15.2	34 380	53.6	27 543	53.5	5 019	58.3	16 819	33.6
Laguna Niguel city	303	41	23 217	35.2	2.65	20.6	39.6	16.7	16 793	52.6	13 984	51.3	2 054	61.2	6 424	34.6
La Habra city	595	252	18 947	4.6	3.08	21.0	43.6	23.0	14 013	53.2	10 331	53.1	2 566	54.6	4 934	-5.7
Lakewood city	194	112	26 853	2.9	2.95	18.4	42.8	25.7	20 550	49.7	15 525	50.8	3 596	47.1	6 303	3.2
La Mesa city	1 046	820	24 186	4.2	2.22	34.2	26.7	26.7	13 386	44.6	9 624	41.1	2 807	54.3	10 800	9.8
La Mirada city	1 639	222	14 580	14.5	3.10	17.3	42.5	31.5	11 523	47.3	9 343	49.2	1 512	37.8	3 057	27.5

[1] As of April 1. [2] Includes people under formally authorized, supervised care or custody in institutions at the time of enumeration (such as correctional institutions, nursing homes, and juvenile institutions). [3] Under 18 years. [4] No husband present.

Sources: Group Quarters Population—U.S. Census Bureau; 2000 Census of Population and Housing, "Census 2000 Profiles of General Demographic Characteristics" data files, published May 2001 (related Internet site <http://www.census.gov/mp/www/pub/2000cen/mscen01.html>). Households, 2000—U.S. Census Bureau; 2000 Census of Population and Housing, "Census 2000 Profiles of General Demographic Characteristics" data files, published May 2001 (related Internet site <http://www.census.gov/mp/www/pub/2000cen/mscen01.html>). Households, 1990—U.S. Census Bureau, 1990 Census of Population and Housing, Summary Tape File (STF) 1C on CD-ROM (related Internet site <http://homer.ssd.census.gov/cdrom/lookup>).

Table C–3. Cities — **Group Quarters Population and Households**–Con.

[Includes states and 1,070 incorporated places of 25,000 or more population as of April 1, 1990 in all states except Hawaii which has no incorporated places recognized by the Census Bureau. For Hawaii, 8 census designated places (CDPs) of 25,000 or more population as of April 1, 1990 are included. Also included are the 5 boroughs of New York city. For more information on these areas, see appendix B. Geographic Information]

City	Group quarters population, 2000[1] Number	Institutionalized population[2]	Households, 2000 (April 1) Number	Percent change, 1990–2000	Persons per household	Percent— One-person	With 1 or more persons under 18 years	With 1 or more persons 65 years and over	Family households (families) Number	Percent with own children under 18 years	Married-couple Number	Percent with own children[3]	Female householder[4] Number	Percent with own children[3]	Nonfamily households Number	Percent change, 1990–2000
CALIFORNIA—Con.																
Lancaster city	7 015	6 402	38 224	16.2	2.92	22.1	47.1	18.9	27 684	59.0	18 899	55.0	6 515	69.1	10 540	19.3
La Puente city	32	–	9 461	4.9	4.34	10.1	61.1	25.0	8 182	57.8	5 711	62.3	1 690	50.1	1 279	-3.4
La Verne city	708	159	11 070	3.1	2.79	19.6	38.8	26.9	8 344	47.1	6 639	46.5	1 271	49.3	2 726	5.7
Lawndale city	86	–	9 555	3.6	3.31	18.8	51.1	15.2	7 025	61.9	4 377	64.6	1 818	61.1	2 530	-16.4
Livermore city	201	128	26 123	26.5	2.80	18.8	42.9	15.2	19 512	53.8	15 953	52.6	2 440	59.8	6 611	25.0
Lodi city	1 024	683	20 692	8.9	2.71	25.4	39.0	26.3	14 349	51.6	10 695	48.2	2 522	64.6	6 343	11.2
Lompoc city	3 439	3 245	13 059	4.4	2.88	23.5	45.1	21.4	9 310	57.6	6 660	54.2	1 928	67.5	3 749	6.6
Long Beach city	10 181	3 378	163 088	2.6	2.77	29.6	38.8	18.3	99 663	57.3	64 009	54.9	26 319	65.6	63 425	-2.5
Los Altos city	419	297	10 462	6.4	2.61	18.7	34.9	32.7	8 026	43.8	7 264	43.9	561	41.4	2 436	14.9
Los Angeles city	82 597	30 446	1 275 412	4.8	2.83	28.5	37.6	20.6	798 719	53.5	534 991	54.0	185 486	56.5	476 693	4.0
Los Gatos town	702	553	11 988	6.3	2.33	29.7	28.6	23.7	7 303	44.7	6 104	42.9	865	54.8	4 685	12.6
Lynwood city	2 200	1 622	14 395	1.7	4.70	7.7	72.6	14.4	12 943	70.6	8 716	75.2	2 959	64.8	1 452	-31.1
Madera city	438	201	11 978	30.8	3.57	16.8	54.0	22.6	9 435	61.5	6 438	60.0	2 102	67.7	2 543	15.4
Manhattan Beach city	14	–	14 474	3.4	2.34	29.3	29.2	18.1	8 392	48.5	7 206	48.0	846	52.2	6 082	.8
Manteca city	477	288	16 368	21.8	2.98	18.6	48.0	19.7	12 485	56.7	9 362	54.6	2 128	63.9	3 883	37.1
Marina city	6 307	4 087	6 745	-14.7	2.79	21.4	40.2	21.5	4 812	49.7	3 445	46.2	1 018	61.1	1 933	46.2
Martinez city	1 350	1 217	14 300	14.3	2.41	27.4	32.5	17.9	9 204	46.6	7 058	44.5	1 576	55.2	5 096	19.8
Maywood city	94	90	6 469	-.4	4.33	8.4	70.0	14.0	5 698	71.4	3 934	75.4	1 093	69.4	771	-16.3
Menlo Park city	952	625	12 387	4.8	2.41	32.1	28.4	26.1	7 120	46.3	5 739	45.2	1 053	52.8	5 267	2.8
Merced city	1 370	810	20 435	11.8	3.06	22.6	47.2	21.5	14 632	60.0	9 645	56.3	3 726	69.5	5 803	16.4
Milpitas city	3 174	3 116	17 132	21.5	3.47	11.5	48.5	19.1	14 002	52.7	11 146	55.3	1 859	46.4	3 130	17.0
Mission Viejo city	1 065	32	32 449	28.9	2.84	17.3	41.8	20.5	25 204	51.1	21 452	50.8	2 629	55.4	7 245	46.0
Modesto city	3 208	1 853	64 959	12.1	2.86	22.5	42.9	22.4	46 642	53.9	33 451	50.9	9 525	63.0	18 317	14.0
Monrovia city	293	93	13 502	2.0	2.71	26.0	39.3	21.2	9 091	52.6	6 263	51.8	2 085	55.8	4 411	-1.8
Montclair city	612	181	8 800	3.1	3.69	15.0	54.8	20.9	7 053	59.2	4 955	61.0	1 431	56.2	1 747	-7.3
Montebello city	309	277	18 844	1.2	3.28	17.1	46.5	29.6	14 865	50.9	9 697	51.9	3 793	51.9	3 979	-5.7
Monterey city	2 842	300	12 600	-.7	2.13	37.0	23.5	24.8	6 478	42.3	4 981	39.5	1 061	52.1	6 122	13.9
Monterey Park city	277	85	19 564	.3	3.06	17.3	36.0	39.0	15 246	40.2	10 829	42.5	3 083	38.3	4 318	.4
Moorpark city	12	5	8 994	18.0	3.49	9.9	57.9	12.0	7 703	63.9	6 474	64.5	876	62.6	1 291	8.9
Moreno Valley city	697	6	39 225	12.2	3.61	11.0	60.4	14.9	33 363	63.5	24 174	62.6	6 715	67.9	5 862	12.1
Mountain View city	504	307	31 242	4.2	2.25	35.6	23.7	17.1	15 909	43.1	12 490	43.0	2 273	46.0	15 333	5.3
Napa city	1 459	689	26 978	12.8	2.64	26.8	35.8	26.3	17 940	49.5	13 684	46.7	3 005	59.5	9 038	16.5
National City city	3 343	215	15 018	1.7	3.39	16.7	51.7	27.3	11 802	56.8	7 563	56.7	3 164	60.6	3 216	-4.5
Newark city	89	–	12 992	8.1	3.26	14.1	45.8	19.0	10 345	50.5	8 077	51.6	1 507	49.6	2 647	10.3
Newport Beach city	940	427	33 071	7.2	2.09	35.3	19.0	25.9	16 979	35.1	14 063	32.7	2 004	47.8	16 092	12.0
Norwalk city	1 349	961	26 887	2.1	3.79	12.7	55.1	24.5	22 522	55.7	16 171	59.0	4 476	48.9	4 365	-7.9
Novato city	982	618	18 524	1.6	2.52	25.2	33.9	22.9	12 419	47.9	9 770	45.4	1 907	59.5	6 105	15.2
Oakland city	7 175	2 894	150 790	4.3	2.60	32.5	33.5	20.9	86 347	50.0	51 332	48.4	26 707	55.9	64 443	6.2
Oceanside city	1 280	181	56 488	20.9	2.83	22.7	38.6	27.4	39 285	50.3	30 553	47.8	6 226	60.8	17 203	32.1
Ontario city	1 141	428	43 525	8.1	3.60	15.1	55.9	16.0	34 699	62.0	24 769	63.3	6 741	60.8	8 826	-2.3
Orange city	5 332	3 297	40 930	11.3	3.02	19.5	40.8	20.9	30 168	50.3	23 375	50.4	4 743	51.8	10 762	10.5
Oxnard city	2 597	503	43 576	10.9	3.85	14.6	53.4	22.7	34 959	57.5	25 882	58.8	6 143	56.9	8 617	1.6
Pacifica city	181	142	13 994	4.9	2.73	21.2	35.9	19.9	9 654	46.4	7 482	46.1	1 537	47.8	4 340	21.7
Palmdale city	94	3	34 285	56.2	3.40	13.9	59.2	14.7	28 105	66.6	20 500	65.8	5 538	70.8	6 180	42.7
Palm Springs city	696	279	20 516	10.2	2.05	41.6	18.3	39.3	9 464	35.3	6 967	30.2	1 742	51.8	11 052	29.3
Palo Alto city	668	433	25 216	4.2	2.30	32.6	28.3	25.5	14 593	47.0	12 228	46.3	1 757	51.7	10 623	–
Paradise town	620	317	11 591	4.9	2.22	32.0	25.3	42.1	7 244	36.7	5 644	30.5	1 198	58.0	4 347	18.3
Paramount city	320	300	13 972	7.5	3.93	14.6	62.6	15.4	11 334	67.9	7 166	70.6	3 030	66.0	2 638	-11.2
Pasadena city	3 518	1 333	51 844	3.3	2.52	33.7	30.3	22.4	29 858	47.1	21 362	46.6	6 251	51.0	21 986	7.8
Petaluma city	740	321	19 932	24.1	2.70	22.6	39.1	21.2	14 014	52.0	11 028	50.8	2 105	57.0	5 918	25.0
Pico Rivera city	350	335	16 468	2.9	3.83	12.8	54.1	29.9	13 872	51.7	9 664	54.6	2 927	46.4	2 596	-7.2
Pittsburg city	506	179	17 741	13.4	3.17	18.0	48.4	19.0	13 479	55.6	9 308	55.1	3 058	58.4	4 262	11.7
Placentia city	303	89	15 037	12.5	3.07	16.0	41.8	19.8	11 691	48.7	9 253	49.4	1 683	47.4	3 346	11.6
Pleasant Hill city	460	305	13 753	5.8	2.35	29.1	29.8	22.0	8 398	45.9	6 659	44.8	1 245	50.1	5 355	12.2
Pleasanton city	235	161	23 311	26.1	2.72	19.3	42.5	14.8	17 395	54.7	14 841	54.3	1 826	58.8	5 916	31.3
Pomona city	5 041	1 906	37 855	3.9	3.82	15.4	56.6	18.3	29 798	63.2	20 698	65.4	6 178	61.3	8 057	-10.0
Porterville city	1 632	1 123	11 884	24.0	3.20	19.1	52.1	21.3	9 170	61.6	6 310	58.3	2 099	71.2	2 714	6.9
Poway city	426	354	15 467	11.4	3.08	12.6	50.0	17.7	12 874	56.5	10 641	55.4	1 629	62.6	2 593	17.1
Rancho Cucamonga city	3 626	1 858	40 863	21.5	3.04	16.8	48.8	14.3	31 827	57.4	24 609	56.6	5 229	61.8	9 036	20.9
Rancho Palos Verdes city	509	166	15 256	2.1	2.66	16.8	34.3	32.7	12 223	40.7	10 798	40.5	1 036	43.3	3 033	15.8
Redding city	2 377	1 216	32 103	23.0	2.44	27.6	34.8	26.9	20 994	48.8	15 435	42.0	4 176	68.0	11 109	32.0
Redlands city	1 966	541	23 593	7.3	2.61	26.0	36.9	23.3	16 027	49.3	11 933	46.1	3 065	59.5	7 566	13.8
Redondo Beach city	187	96	28 566	6.9	2.21	33.1	25.2	14.8	15 242	43.7	11 601	42.0	2 558	52.8	13 324	6.5
Redwood City city	1 927	1 481	28 060	10.1	2.62	27.1	33.9	19.7	17 902	49.1	13 810	48.5	2 784	54.6	10 158	8.1
Rialto city	804	265	24 659	12.6	3.69	13.4	60.5	18.2	20 523	63.5	14 204	63.8	4 589	64.3	4 136	-4.0
Richmond city	1 628	953	34 625	5.7	2.82	26.2	40.0	21.3	23 042	50.7	14 023	49.9	6 947	54.4	11 583	5.8
Ridgecrest city	309	89	9 826	-5.1	2.51	27.6	37.8	20.9	6 689	51.5	5 128	45.5	1 126	72.2	3 137	4.6
Riverside city	7 798	2 881	82 005	8.7	3.02	21.5	44.5	20.0	58 155	56.2	41 214	55.0	12 151	60.7	23 850	11.3
Rohnert Park city	1 101	–	15 503	15.6	2.65	24.0	38.0	17.2	9 799	55.5	7 239	54.0	1 841	61.2	5 704	25.8

[1] As of April 1.   [2] Includes people under formally authorized, supervised care or custody in institutions at the time of enumeration (such as correctional institutions, nursing homes, and juvenile institutions).   [3] Under 18 years.   [4] No husband present.

Sources: Group Quarters Population—U.S. Census Bureau; 2000 Census of Population and Housing, "Census 2000 Profiles of General Demographic Characteristics" data files, published May 2001 (related Internet site <http://www.census.gov/mp/www/pub/2000cen/mscen01.html>).   Households, 2000—U.S. Census Bureau; 2000 Census of Population and Housing, "Census 2000 Profiles of General Demographic Characteristics" data files, published May 2001 (related Internet site <http://www.census.gov/mp/www/pub/2000cen/mscen01.html>).   Households, 1990—U.S. Census Bureau, 1990 Census of Population and Housing, Summary Tape File (STF) 1C on CD-ROM (related Internet site <http://homer.ssd.census.gov/cdrom/lookup>).

Table C–3. Cities — Group Quarters Population and Households–Con.

[Includes states and 1,070 incorporated places of 25,000 or more population as of April 1, 1990 in all states except Hawaii which has no incorporated places recognized by the Census Bureau. For Hawaii, 8 census designated places (CDPs) of 25,000 or more population as of April 1, 1990 are included. Also included are the 5 boroughs of New York city. For more information on these areas, see appendix B. Geographic Information]

City	Group quarters population, 2000[1]		Households, 2000 (April 1)			Percent—			By type—							
									Family households (families)		Married-couple		Female householder[4]		Nonfamily households	
	Number	Institutionalized population[2]	Number	Percent change, 1990–2000	Persons per household	One-person	With 1 or more persons under 18 years	With 1 or more persons 65 years and over	Number	Percent with own children under 18 years	Number	Percent with own children[3]	Number	Percent with own children[3]	Number	Percent change, 1990–2000
CALIFORNIA—Con.																
Rosemead city	612	387	13 913	1.5	3.80	12.6	51.2	29.5	11 628	52.2	8 068	57.5	2 416	45.7	2 285	-7.6
Roseville city	928	713	30 783	85.4	2.57	23.1	37.7	25.0	21 849	49.9	17 573	46.7	3 106	63.8	8 934	101.0
Sacramento city	9 002	4 831	154 581	7.0	2.57	32.0	34.2	22.1	91 137	51.2	59 302	47.4	23 790	61.1	63 444	11.1
Salinas city	10 805	8 756	38 298	14.8	3.66	17.1	54.6	19.9	30 008	62.8	22 058	63.2	5 687	64.8	8 290	-.7
San Bernardino city	5 849	3 765	56 330	3.4	3.19	21.1	50.1	20.1	41 099	60.5	25 315	58.4	11 890	66.0	15 231	-5.5
San Bruno city	221	122	14 677	.3	2.72	25.5	34.7	22.1	9 917	46.5	7 601	46.9	1 644	45.8	4 760	-5.2
San Buenaventura (Ventura) city	2 370	1 376	38 524	8.8	2.56	26.5	35.0	23.8	25 244	48.9	18 953	46.2	4 517	57.7	13 280	12.8
San Carlos city	183	145	11 455	3.7	2.40	25.7	31.0	24.4	7 608	44.7	6 468	44.1	824	48.2	3 847	8.8
San Clemente city	292	62	19 395	16.1	2.56	23.4	32.7	23.4	13 015	46.0	10 777	44.2	1 517	56.5	6 380	12.6
San Diego city	45 818	6 637	450 691	11.0	2.61	28.0	33.4	20.5	271 398	50.1	201 213	48.7	51 248	57.5	179 293	14.6
San Dimas city	1 209	372	12 163	11.1	2.78	21.0	39.1	22.7	8 985	48.1	7 019	46.9	1 405	53.1	3 178	20.0
San Francisco city	19 757	4 200	329 700	7.9	2.30	38.6	19.4	23.9	145 186	37.7	104 310	38.6	29 202	38.6	184 514	12.7
San Gabriel city	755	681	12 587	3.0	3.10	18.2	40.5	27.5	9 567	47.0	6 805	50.0	1 915	43.8	3 020	-6.7
San Jose city	10 864	3 846	276 598	10.5	3.20	18.4	43.0	19.1	203 681	52.0	155 000	53.4	32 256	51.6	72 917	9.9
San Juan Capistrano city	426	305	10 930	21.2	3.06	19.7	39.9	27.9	8 196	49.2	6 850	49.4	931	47.2	2 734	19.7
San Leandro city	827	517	30 642	5.2	2.57	28.5	32.4	29.9	19 817	44.5	14 437	44.4	3 903	46.8	10 825	.1
San Luis Obispo city	1 862	362	18 639	10.0	2.27	32.7	18.7	19.5	7 696	42.9	5 840	40.1	1 347	55.5	10 943	17.5
San Marcos city	148	15	18 111	33.0	3.03	20.3	42.1	26.2	13 212	53.5	10 609	52.8	1 736	57.7	4 899	32.9
San Mateo city	1 316	609	37 338	5.2	2.44	31.6	28.3	26.9	22 310	43.4	17 509	43.3	3 392	45.6	15 028	7.0
San Pablo city	465	367	9 051	4.0	3.29	22.5	50.5	20.7	6 490	61.4	4 027	64.2	1 786	61.0	2 561	-9.3
San Rafael city	2 020	1 083	22 371	10.2	2.42	32.1	27.9	24.4	12 776	45.2	9 901	43.0	2 011	57.5	9 595	12.5
San Ramon city	85	47	16 944	31.9	2.63	21.1	39.2	11.8	12 143	52.8	10 468	51.8	1 194	60.3	4 801	42.8
Santa Ana city	5 624	3 482	73 002	1.9	4.55	12.7	60.9	18.4	59 784	65.0	44 205	69.5	9 845	56.2	13 218	-23.3
Santa Barbara city	4 517	477	35 605	3.7	2.47	32.9	26.9	24.9	18 954	45.7	14 163	43.9	3 376	53.4	16 651	4.4
Santa Clara city	2 787	459	38 526	5.4	2.58	25.9	30.6	20.1	24 100	43.8	18 633	44.7	3 659	44.5	14 426	.2
Santa Clarita city	1 393	370	50 787	32.0	2.95	18.7	47.1	15.8	38 222	59.0	30 987	58.7	4 969	62.4	12 565	31.6
Santa Cruz city	4 634	373	20 442	12.8	2.44	29.3	27.0	16.8	10 401	49.4	7 562	45.8	1 962	61.4	10 041	20.4
Santa Maria city	2 162	1 438	22 146	11.2	3.40	20.0	47.3	26.5	16 654	56.3	12 499	55.2	2 954	62.1	5 492	9.6
Santa Monica city	2 516	941	44 497	-.8	1.83	51.2	16.8	20.0	16 783	42.0	12 216	39.6	3 318	51.9	27 714	3.5
Santa Paula city	243	129	8 136	6.2	3.49	17.2	50.4	27.1	6 433	54.8	4 806	56.3	1 089	56.7	1 703	1.4
Santa Rosa city	3 806	1 558	56 036	22.6	2.57	27.8	33.6	26.0	35 117	49.4	26 265	46.1	6 189	59.8	20 919	25.0
Santee city	1 043	899	18 470	3.9	2.81	18.2	44.5	18.7	14 018	53.9	10 660	51.9	2 396	61.2	4 452	10.7
Saratoga city	251	215	10 450	4.0	2.83	14.3	40.2	30.4	8 602	47.0	7 835	47.7	517	40.8	1 848	3.4
Seal Beach city	254	213	13 048	-2.4	1.83	48.8	14.6	54.2	5 884	30.6	4 981	28.6	690	39.9	7 164	.4
Seaside city	103	28	9 833	-7.6	3.21	18.1	48.0	20.6	7 399	56.1	5 386	57.3	1 371	52.2	2 434	2.5
Simi Valley city	800	163	36 421	13.8	3.04	14.7	46.2	17.1	28 952	53.5	23 258	53.0	3 890	55.1	7 469	19.9
South Gate city	141	61	23 213	3.5	4.15	10.4	65.4	18.0	20 063	67.4	13 843	71.2	4 269	61.5	3 150	-24.0
South San Francisco city	443	148	19 677	6.3	3.05	19.9	40.0	28.4	14 650	47.3	10 977	49.6	2 596	42.3	5 027	4.9
Stanton city	518	278	10 767	4.5	3.43	21.5	47.2	23.5	7 804	57.6	5 410	60.9	1 595	53.9	2 963	-8.4
Stockton city	5 316	1 739	78 556	14.2	3.04	22.9	46.0	22.7	56 186	57.1	37 779	54.5	13 559	65.0	22 370	10.9
Sunnyvale city	875	499	52 539	8.8	2.49	27.1	30.0	18.8	32 664	44.4	26 287	44.9	4 315	45.9	19 875	4.9
Temecula city	22	–	18 293	100.4	3.15	12.6	55.1	15.8	15 162	63.2	12 592	61.9	1 835	69.5	3 131	68.2
Temple City city	511	413	11 338	2.6	2.90	19.7	40.1	28.0	8 661	47.8	6 435	49.1	1 625	46.7	2 677	-8.0
Thousand Oaks city	1 951	270	41 793	14.6	2.75	19.6	39.4	21.4	31 162	50.0	26 063	49.3	3 634	54.0	10 631	21.6
Torrance city	1 249	686	54 542	3.7	2.51	27.5	33.5	25.1	36 276	46.8	28 437	46.8	5 624	48.2	18 266	5.7
Tracy city	345	153	17 620	57.2	3.21	14.4	55.7	14.7	14 308	63.7	11 450	63.2	1 886	66.1	3 312	27.8
Tulare city	447	214	13 543	24.7	3.22	16.7	51.7	21.7	10 758	58.3	7 573	55.3	2 315	67.3	2 785	16.8
Turlock city	2 080	504	18 408	25.3	2.92	21.2	43.7	23.8	13 434	55.2	10 088	53.7	2 409	62.4	4 974	23.8
Tustin city	418	35	23 831	30.0	2.82	24.1	39.5	15.0	16 055	54.6	11 961	54.5	2 922	58.2	7 776	29.3
Union City city	342	215	18 642	18.7	3.57	11.3	51.7	20.7	15 700	53.8	12 418	55.9	2 267	49.0	2 942	6.4
Upland city	585	316	24 551	6.4	2.76	21.1	40.0	21.1	17 868	49.9	13 055	46.8	3 510	60.0	6 683	6.8
Vacaville city	9 218	9 149	28 105	24.2	2.83	19.2	45.3	18.1	20 962	55.6	16 027	52.1	3 496	67.8	7 143	33.4
Vallejo city	1 745	819	39 601	5.9	2.90	22.7	42.3	23.7	28 245	51.1	19 452	49.1	6 550	57.3	11 356	11.3
Victorville city	670	406	20 893	46.7	3.03	19.4	48.9	24.6	15 883	57.7	11 346	54.5	3 373	67.8	5 010	37.8
Visalia city	1 622	893	30 883	18.3	2.91	20.7	44.6	22.0	22 901	55.4	16 948	51.6	4 359	68.2	7 982	17.9
Vista city	2 266	1 262	28 877	13.8	3.03	20.5	44.2	20.9	20 783	56.1	15 498	53.8	3 665	64.5	8 094	17.3
Walnut city	40	24	8 260	5.3	3.63	5.8	55.3	18.5	7 580	55.1	6 367	58.1	820	42.6	680	2.4
Walnut Creek city	964	513	30 301	6.9	2.09	38.0	21.9	38.1	16 551	38.2	13 838	36.3	2 035	49.4	13 750	12.3
Watsonville city	553	223	11 381	20.6	3.84	17.6	54.9	23.9	8 865	63.1	6 405	64.1	1 871	62.5	2 516	1.7
West Covina city	808	195	31 411	4.4	3.32	14.8	48.0	24.7	25 261	52.1	18 293	53.8	4 967	50.2	6 150	1.9
West Hollywood city	230	–	23 120	2.4	1.53	60.5	6.4	21.0	5 211	25.9	3 798	22.7	1 011	38.7	17 909	6.9
Westminster city	552	203	26 406	5.3	3.32	16.9	43.2	27.0	20 403	48.9	15 409	51.0	3 277	46.4	6 003	-2.8
West Sacramento city	206	112	11 404	3.2	2.75	27.1	39.1	26.3	7 600	51.9	5 159	48.9	1 754	60.8	3 804	-.9
Whittier city	2 348	1 159	28 271	2.3	2.88	22.4	41.7	25.7	20 470	52.2	14 852	51.3	4 047	55.9	7 801	-1.2
Woodland city	790	451	16 751	18.0	2.89	21.0	44.2	21.1	12 285	54.7	9 187	52.8	2 168	61.7	4 466	17.1
Yorba Linda city	135	6	19 252	14.8	3.05	12.4	47.2	17.1	16 096	53.5	13 917	53.6	1 589	54.2	3 156	23.3
Yuba City city	916	701	13 290	25.6	2.70	26.5	40.4	22.7	8 947	54.5	6 329	50.0	1 907	67.4	4 343	20.9
Yucaipa city	572	430	15 193	14.1	2.67	25.3	38.9	29.8	10 679	50.4	8 234	47.8	1 769	59.6	4 514	5.9

[1] As of April 1. [2] Includes people under formally authorized, supervised care or custody in institutions at the time of enumeration (such as correctional institutions, nursing homes, and juvenile institutions). [3] Under 18 years. [4] No husband present.

Sources: Group Quarters Population—U.S. Census Bureau; 2000 Census of Population and Housing, "Census 2000 Profiles of General Demographic Characteristics" data files, published May 2001 (related Internet site <http://www.census.gov/mp/www/pub/2000cen/mscen01.html>).   Households, 2000—U.S. Census Bureau; 2000 Census of Population and Housing, "Census 2000 Profiles of General Demographic Characteristics" data files, published May 2001 (related Internet site <http://www.census.gov/mp/www/pub/2000cen/mscen01.html>).   Households, 1990—U.S. Census Bureau, 1990 Census of Population and Housing, Summary Tape File (STF) 1C on CD-ROM (related Internet site <http://homer.ssd.census.gov/cdrom/lookup>).

Table C–3. Cities — **Group Quarters Population and Households**–Con.

[Includes states and 1,070 incorporated places of 25,000 or more population as of April 1, 1990 in all states except Hawaii which has no incorporated places recognized by the Census Bureau. For Hawaii, 8 census designated places (CDPs) of 25,000 or more population as of April 1, 1990 are included. Also included are the 5 boroughs of New York city. For more information on these areas, see appendix B. Geographic Information]

City	Group quarters population, 2000[1] Number	Group quarters Institutionalized population[2]	Households, 2000 (April 1) Number	Percent change, 1990-2000	Persons per household	Percent— One-person	Percent— With 1 or more persons under 18 years	Percent— With 1 or more persons 65 years and over	Family households (families) Number	Family households (families) Percent with own children under 18 years	Married-couple Number	Married-couple Percent with own children[3]	Female householder[4] Number	Female householder[4] Percent with own children[3]	Nonfamily households Number	Nonfamily households Percent change, 1990-2000
COLORADO	102 955	52 741	1 658 238	29.3	2.53	26.3	35.3	17.7	1 084 461	50.1	858 671	47.2	158 979	64.2	573 777	34.0
Arvada city	751	143	39 019	19.2	2.60	23.1	36.8	20.1	27 759	48.1	22 435	45.3	3 778	61.2	11 260	40.2
Aurora city	2 089	1 411	105 625	18.5	2.60	27.4	38.5	14.3	68 866	54.5	49 517	51.2	13 889	66.6	36 759	18.2
Boulder city	7 479	1 144	39 596	14.2	2.20	33.7	21.0	13.1	16 802	47.2	13 166	43.9	2 581	65.0	22 794	21.2
Colorado Springs city	7 153	3 665	141 516	27.7	2.50	27.0	36.5	17.1	93 049	51.7	72 840	48.0	14 945	67.6	48 467	33.3
Denver city	12 719	6 216	239 235	13.4	2.27	39.3	26.3	19.3	119 300	46.6	83 016	43.2	25 923	58.7	119 935	17.7
Englewood city	728	622	14 392	8.6	2.15	37.9	25.9	20.4	7 469	45.4	5 277	40.7	1 553	58.4	6 923	20.0
Fort Collins city	6 055	903	45 882	36.2	2.45	26.0	30.4	13.8	25 780	51.6	20 592	49.1	3 638	66.4	20 102	42.6
Grand Junction city	2 180	823	17 865	39.5	2.23	33.2	27.6	28.8	10 549	43.2	8 240	38.0	1 671	62.6	7 316	29.9
Greeley city	4 221	1 177	27 647	22.1	2.63	25.6	35.9	19.1	17 683	51.7	13 452	48.2	2 983	66.0	9 964	20.1
Lakewood city	3 800	2 721	60 531	17.2	2.32	30.7	29.7	19.6	36 474	45.4	27 294	40.5	6 522	62.7	24 057	34.1
Littleton city	611	541	17 313	24.5	2.29	33.3	29.9	23.3	10 384	46.7	8 195	43.1	1 592	62.7	6 929	44.0
Longmont city	615	420	26 667	36.3	2.64	23.7	39.4	17.0	18 458	53.3	14 562	50.2	2 686	66.5	8 209	44.7
Loveland city	361	295	19 741	40.5	2.55	23.4	37.4	21.8	14 037	49.7	11 347	45.5	1 931	70.1	5 704	53.9
Northglenn city	163	163	11 610	18.1	2.71	23.0	38.0	19.3	8 204	47.8	6 226	45.0	1 372	57.9	3 406	35.2
Pueblo city	3 894	2 942	40 307	5.2	2.44	30.0	33.6	29.2	26 115	46.0	17 938	40.0	6 096	61.0	14 192	17.3
Thornton city	550	490	28 882	51.6	2.83	18.7	45.8	11.1	21 528	56.7	16 686	54.5	3 314	66.8	7 354	59.5
Westminster city	487	380	38 343	37.8	2.62	23.7	38.4	12.4	26 024	52.6	20 544	50.7	3 698	62.2	12 319	53.2
Wheat Ridge city	844	505	14 559	10.8	2.20	35.4	27.2	28.6	8 311	43.9	6 025	38.1	1 659	61.3	6 248	19.1
CONNECTICUT	107 939	55 256	1 301 670	5.8	2.53	26.4	34.7	25.1	881 170	47.6	676 467	45.4	157 411	57.9	420 500	14.9
Bridgeport city	3 596	1 919	50 307	–3.9	2.70	29.0	39.5	24.2	32 730	52.7	17 618	48.0	12 095	61.8	17 577	–3.4
Bristol city	771	588	24 886	3.9	2.38	28.9	31.6	25.1	16 179	45.5	12 350	42.4	2 870	57.6	8 707	19.9
Danbury city	3 128	2 010	27 183	12.8	2.64	26.2	33.4	21.2	17 880	46.1	13 894	46.1	2 846	50.9	9 303	19.4
Hartford city	5 355	2 290	44 986	–12.6	2.58	33.2	40.0	19.8	27 189	56.9	11 355	46.3	13 332	67.9	17 797	–13.3
Meriden city	1 141	875	22 951	–1.2	2.49	28.9	34.0	24.6	14 960	48.1	10 414	42.9	3 479	63.2	7 991	7.5
Middletown city	1 874	1 427	18 554	10.3	2.23	35.0	27.7	21.2	10 393	45.9	7 659	41.4	2 157	61.7	8 161	24.8
Milford city (remainder)	537	420	20 138	11.2	2.49	26.3	31.5	26.6	13 619	43.4	11 019	43.2	1 946	45.2	6 519	26.5
Naugatuck borough	220	194	11 829	4.4	2.60	24.9	38.6	22.2	8 297	51.8	6 306	49.6	1 515	61.7	3 532	15.2
New Britain city	3 071	897	28 558	–5.3	2.40	33.1	31.3	27.5	16 942	47.7	10 459	45.4	5 064	63.5	11 616	2.1
New Haven city	10 599	2 662	47 094	–3.9	2.40	36.1	33.4	20.2	25 852	53.4	12 942	44.7	10 784	66.0	21 242	1.4
New London city	2 706	247	10 181	–5.0	2.26	37.8	30.7	21.7	5 386	52.1	3 095	42.5	1 814	68.2	4 795	1.9
Norwalk city	865	527	32 711	7.0	2.51	28.2	31.6	23.3	20 963	44.5	15 662	43.6	3 994	54.2	11 748	16.1
Norwich city	749	388	15 091	.5	2.34	32.0	31.6	25.8	9 074	48.2	6 140	41.1	2 264	65.7	6 017	17.8
Shelton city	561	541	14 190	13.9	2.65	21.8	34.9	26.7	10 540	44.2	8 932	44.1	1 212	48.3	3 650	33.7
Stamford city	1 753	891	45 399	8.2	2.54	28.7	31.3	25.3	28 951	44.9	22 006	44.8	5 240	49.4	16 448	16.5
Torrington city	834	653	14 743	6.2	2.33	32.1	30.3	28.4	9 130	45.9	7 035	42.5	1 518	59.1	5 613	19.1
Waterbury city	2 214	1 562	42 622	–1.3	2.46	31.4	34.5	26.5	26 911	49.4	16 534	42.6	8 137	63.8	15 711	6.7
West Haven city	1 259	449	21 090	–.9	2.42	31.0	31.7	25.4	13 123	45.8	8 838	42.3	3 290	56.5	7 967	9.9
DELAWARE	24 583	11 510	298 736	20.7	2.54	25.0	35.4	23.9	204 590	46.5	153 136	42.8	38 986	58.9	94 146	31.4
Dover city	3 118	842	12 340	24.6	2.35	31.4	33.6	23.0	7 500	49.4	4 983	41.4	2 061	67.1	4 840	46.5
Newark city	6 727	141	8 989	20.4	2.43	27.2	22.3	20.4	4 497	41.4	3 640	39.8	643	51.2	4 492	34.5
Wilmington city	4 228	2 785	28 617	.2	2.39	37.1	33.2	24.3	15 881	48.9	7 621	40.8	6 814	58.8	12 736	4.3
DISTRICT OF COLUMBIA	35 562	7 964	248 338	–.5	2.16	43.8	24.6	21.5	114 166	43.0	56 631	36.6	47 032	52.2	134 172	5.2
Washington city	35 562	7 964	248 338	–.5	2.16	43.8	24.6	21.5	114 166	43.0	56 631	36.6	47 032	52.2	134 172	5.2
FLORIDA	388 945	248 350	6 337 929	23.4	2.46	26.6	31.3	30.7	4 210 760	42.3	3 192 266	38.1	759 000	57.7	2 127 169	31.1
Altamonte Springs city	428	419	18 821	22.0	2.17	36.1	26.9	16.5	10 016	46.6	6 977	41.6	2 266	60.6	8 805	29.9
Boca Raton city	2 806	548	31 848	21.1	2.26	29.5	25.3	31.5	20 004	38.4	16 916	36.0	2 248	56.5	11 844	29.3
Boynton Beach city	1 091	912	26 210	29.2	2.26	33.0	24.9	40.3	15 684	37.1	11 909	32.1	2 853	54.7	10 526	44.0
Bradenton city	1 586	1 415	21 379	13.3	2.24	34.1	26.1	39.2	12 721	38.6	9 302	30.9	2 595	61.7	8 658	24.3
Cape Coral city	591	550	40 768	37.0	2.49	19.7	32.1	32.9	30 210	39.8	24 962	35.9	3 775	59.2	10 558	61.4
Clearwater city	3 863	1 457	48 449	9.8	2.17	35.5	24.1	33.0	27 439	38.3	20 197	31.8	5 476	59.8	21 010	20.3
Coconut Creek city	197	113	20 093	48.0	2.16	32.5	23.4	40.0	12 037	36.8	9 923	33.8	1 540	51.2	8 056	61.5
Coral Gables city	3 510	97	16 793	8.6	2.31	31.5	25.4	28.6	10 251	39.6	8 261	40.1	1 529	40.2	6 542	12.2
Coral Springs city	567	305	39 522	46.3	2.96	15.2	50.8	12.9	31 309	61.0	24 256	59.3	5 263	70.8	8 213	39.7
Davie town	97	33	28 682	60.2	2.64	22.3	39.4	18.8	19 774	53.2	14 855	51.5	3 610	60.8	8 908	72.9
Daytona Beach city	5 097	1 492	28 605	3.8	2.06	39.4	21.4	30.7	13 842	37.2	8 604	26.4	4 137	58.2	14 763	7.8
Deerfield Beach city	1 168	659	31 392	35.8	2.02	40.3	18.5	43.0	16 056	31.9	11 995	27.2	3 015	48.3	15 336	47.1
Delray Beach city	530	304	26 787	25.2	2.22	35.3	21.8	41.2	15 091	33.5	11 352	28.4	2 727	51.6	11 696	41.7
Dunedin city	943	209	17 258	8.6	2.01	37.9	19.6	42.0	9 546	32.9	7 569	27.6	1 527	54.7	7 712	24.3
Fort Lauderdale city	5 559	3 979	68 468	3.1	2.14	40.3	22.5	25.5	32 996	40.7	22 037	34.4	7 862	56.6	35 472	9.8

[1] As of April 1. [2] Includes people under formally authorized, supervised care or custody in institutions at the time of enumeration (such as correctional institutions, nursing homes, and juvenile institutions). [3] Under 18 years. [4] No husband present.

Sources: Group Quarters Population—U.S. Census Bureau; 2000 Census of Population and Housing, "Census 2000 Profiles of General Demographic Characteristics" data files, published May 2001 (related Internet site <http://www.census.gov/mp/www/pub/2000cen/mscen01.html>). Households, 2000—U.S. Census Bureau; 2000 Census of Population and Housing, "Census 2000 Profiles of General Demographic Characteristics" data files, published May 2001 (related Internet site <http://www.census.gov/mp/www/pub/2000cen/mscen01.html>). Households, 1990—U.S. Census Bureau, 1990 Census of Population and Housing, Summary Tape File (STF) 1C on CD-ROM (related Internet site <http://homer.ssd.census.gov/cdrom/lookup>).

Table C–3. Cities — **Group Quarters Population and Households**–Con.

[Includes states and 1,070 incorporated places of 25,000 or more population as of April 1, 1990 in all states except Hawaii which has no incorporated places recognized by the Census Bureau. For Hawaii, 8 census designated places (CDPs) of 25,000 or more population as of April 1, 1990 are included. Also included are the 5 boroughs of New York city. For more information on these areas, see appendix B. Geographic Information]

City	Group quarters population, 2000[1]		Households, 2000 (April 1)													
						Percent—			By type—							
									Family households (families)		Married-couple		Female householder[4]		Nonfamily households	
	Number	Institu-tionalized population[2]	Number	Percent change, 1990–2000	Persons per house-hold	One-person	With 1 or more persons under 18 years	With 1 or more persons 65 years and over	Number	Per-cent with own chil-dren under 18 years	Number	Per-cent with own chil-dren[3]	Number	Per-cent with own chil-dren[3]	Number	Percent change, 1990–2000
FLORIDA—Con.																
Fort Myers city	2 307	2 205	19 107	5.3	2.40	33.8	33.0	25.0	10 735	51.4	6 171	41.4	3 517	68.9	8 372	11.4
Fort Pierce city	705	8	14 407	1.7	2.56	31.1	33.1	32.4	8 821	45.9	5 195	37.0	2 775	63.0	5 586	13.4
Gainesville city	11 507	1 989	37 279	16.8	2.25	32.6	24.7	18.0	18 343	45.3	12 098	39.9	4 972	60.4	18 936	30.3
Hallandale city	368	133	18 051	5.3	1.88	45.2	14.4	50.0	8 706	26.0	6 470	19.2	1 639	48.3	9 345	8.1
Hialeah city	3 652	2 304	70 704	19.1	3.15	14.7	43.3	35.8	57 482	44.6	40 553	44.7	12 296	48.3	13 222	28.1
Hollywood city	1 751	858	59 673	12.8	2.31	34.4	27.8	29.5	34 462	43.1	24 789	39.4	7 076	55.0	25 211	20.4
Homestead city	575	432	10 095	8.4	3.10	20.9	48.4	16.8	7 153	60.2	4 037	56.1	2 258	73.2	2 942	4.0
Jacksonville city (remainder)	15 317	6 579	284 499	17.9	2.53	26.2	37.9	19.6	190 533	50.6	132 756	46.5	45 477	61.9	93 966	23.9
Kissimmee city	461	321	17 121	51.3	2.77	20.9	41.6	15.5	11 809	54.2	8 081	50.6	2 701	65.0	5 312	50.2
Lakeland city	3 710	1 247	33 509	13.0	2.23	32.9	26.5	35.4	20 361	38.6	14 575	30.5	4 588	61.3	13 148	25.4
Lake Worth city	761	645	13 828	10.1	2.49	33.6	29.8	24.7	7 694	46.8	5 104	43.8	1 594	59.1	6 134	7.8
Largo city	1 786	922	34 041	6.6	1.99	38.5	18.5	41.7	18 380	31.4	14 235	25.3	3 049	54.0	15 661	20.0
Lauderdale Lakes city	350	337	12 099	1.1	2.59	30.1	36.5	34.5	7 745	50.1	4 435	41.9	2 687	63.9	4 354	-9.0
Lauderhill city	842	210	22 810	7.9	2.49	31.0	35.8	29.2	14 289	50.8	8 542	43.1	4 589	65.4	8 521	7.9
Margate city	345	247	22 714	20.0	2.36	30.8	28.1	37.3	14 331	40.9	11 150	38.6	2 309	50.8	8 383	32.1
Melbourne city	3 064	1 451	30 788	22.8	2.22	32.9	26.8	31.0	18 257	40.5	13 532	35.2	3 538	56.8	12 531	34.1
Miami city	11 611	8 333	134 198	3.0	2.61	30.4	31.6	33.3	83 281	42.4	49 139	40.2	25 029	49.4	50 917	10.2
Miami Beach city	1 336	796	46 194	-6.3	1.87	48.7	15.5	27.8	18 342	35.2	12 654	32.5	3 936	46.2	27 852	-1.7
Miramar city	28	–	23 058	60.2	3.15	14.3	53.1	15.7	18 663	59.6	12 992	59.8	4 411	61.3	4 395	32.5
North Lauderdale city	–	–	10 799	19.0	2.99	19.6	46.4	16.0	7 815	58.5	5 054	56.0	2 087	66.7	2 984	34.1
North Miami city	1 255	547	20 541	2.1	2.85	26.9	42.2	19.3	13 587	56.9	8 012	55.5	4 125	62.6	6 954	-13.9
North Miami Beach city	426	386	13 987	.1	2.89	23.9	42.1	24.2	9 803	53.6	6 202	52.6	2 729	58.6	4 184	-14.9
Oakland Park city	440	13	13 502	11.6	2.26	35.1	27.2	17.6	6 935	47.7	4 356	43.8	1 801	60.7	6 567	11.6
Ocala city	3 260	2 537	18 646	7.2	2.29	33.0	30.1	32.8	11 282	44.3	7 626	36.2	2 970	62.9	7 364	17.7
Orlando city	4 041	2 489	80 883	23.1	2.25	35.0	27.9	18.7	42 357	46.8	26 190	40.1	12 456	60.9	38 526	33.6
Ormond Beach city	766	571	15 629	23.0	2.27	27.1	25.3	41.7	10 533	34.9	8 713	31.9	1 369	49.2	5 096	34.9
Palm Bay city	390	263	30 336	30.0	2.60	21.8	37.5	26.7	21 767	47.4	16 698	43.1	3 704	63.0	8 569	47.1
Panama City city	2 351	2 091	14 819	5.5	2.30	32.2	30.8	27.2	9 039	45.2	6 200	38.8	2 287	61.5	5 780	17.3
Pembroke Pines city	1 288	1 261	51 989	94.6	2.62	24.1	38.5	29.6	36 835	51.1	29 321	50.2	5 771	56.8	15 154	89.4
Pensacola city	496	342	24 524	2.3	2.27	32.9	28.4	28.8	14 676	41.1	9 741	35.8	4 101	53.9	9 848	14.9
Pinellas Park city	802	484	19 444	6.9	2.31	30.2	28.8	33.0	12 157	41.1	9 055	35.3	2 248	57.5	7 287	22.9
Plantation city	475	417	33 244	25.5	2.48	25.8	33.1	23.3	22 191	46.3	17 297	44.2	3 735	55.6	11 053	41.6
Pompano Beach city	3 239	2 647	35 197	9.5	2.13	38.6	20.6	36.8	18 444	33.2	13 154	27.1	3 821	51.5	16 753	22.2
Port Orange city	504	414	19 574	30.8	2.32	25.7	27.3	37.3	13 234	36.6	10 701	32.7	1 880	53.8	6 340	45.2
Port St. Lucie city	574	331	33 909	64.0	2.60	18.2	34.7	32.8	25 750	41.7	20 940	37.8	3 387	59.9	8 159	115.6
Riviera Beach city	313	137	11 387	10.2	2.60	27.6	35.6	29.0	7 525	44.4	4 225	33.0	2 681	62.7	3 862	19.6
St. Petersburg city	6 502	3 297	109 663	3.7	2.20	35.6	27.2	28.0	61 584	42.7	42 054	36.8	15 145	57.0	48 079	9.1
Sanford city	1 696	1 302	14 237	17.5	2.57	27.0	37.2	22.0	9 172	49.3	5 628	43.9	2 740	60.9	5 065	23.8
Sarasota city	3 122	1 870	23 427	2.7	2.12	38.3	22.6	33.9	12 076	48.3	8 280	30.5	2 892	58.2	11 351	14.4
Sunrise city	1 066	771	33 308	26.6	2.54	27.2	36.1	31.5	22 243	50.1	16 203	47.8	4 592	50.2	11 065	36.8
Tallahassee city	13 157	3 720	63 217	25.3	2.17	34.7	24.1	13.9	29 462	46.8	19 003	41.3	8 336	61.0	33 755	39.4
Tamarac city	609	310	27 423	19.7	2.00	36.3	16.9	52.4	15 734	26.8	12 282	22.1	2 583	44.9	11 689	37.7
Tampa city	8 918	3 000	124 758	8.7	2.36	33.7	31.5	23.0	71 220	48.4	45 356	43.5	20 084	59.3	53 538	16.8
Titusville city	825	638	17 200	6.1	2.32	29.9	29.8	33.7	11 094	41.3	8 243	34.5	2 174	62.2	6 106	23.9
West Palm Beach city	3 635	970	34 769	20.8	2.26	37.6	25.9	25.7	18 270	42.7	11 910	36.2	4 732	58.3	16 499	28.7
GEORGIA	233 822	126 023	3 006 369	27.0	2.65	23.6	39.1	18.8	2 111 647	49.8	1 548 800	47.3	435 410	59.3	894 722	36.9
Albany city	4 237	1 614	28 620	2.5	2.54	28.8	37.9	23.1	18 883	49.0	10 473	41.2	7 201	60.8	9 737	22.5
Athens city	[5]8 141	[5]1 140	[5]39 239	X	[5]2.35	[5]29.9	[5]25.2	[5]14.6	[5]19 333	[5]45.3	[5]12 678	[5]40.9	[5]5 225	[5]59.3	[5]19 906	X
Atlanta city	28 947	8 938	168 147	8.0	2.30	38.5	27.4	18.3	83 182	45.4	41 199	37.5	34 761	56.9	84 965	23.1
Augusta city	[6]10 870	[6]3 193	[6]72 307	X	[6]2.55	[6]27.9	[6]38.5	[6]21.2	[6]48 234	[6]50.2	[6]29 982	[6]44.6	[6]15 071	[6]61.4	[6]24 073	X
Columbus city (remainder)	9 107	3 249	69 599	6.0	2.54	26.7	39.2	22.7	47 560	50.7	31 106	46.3	13 628	60.0	22 039	18.7
East Point city	438	149	14 553	8.8	2.69	27.4	40.9	16.0	9 433	53.2	4 183	46.4	4 200	61.6	5 120	13.3
La Grange city	895	429	10 022	2.6	2.50	30.1	37.9	26.3	6 503	49.9	3 666	43.5	2 355	61.1	3 519	9.7
Macon city	3 595	1 668	38 444	-6.6	2.44	31.7	35.5	26.6	24 214	47.7	12 679	38.5	9 878	60.4	14 230	2.5
Marietta city	1 561	483	23 895	20.3	2.39	32.8	30.7	14.1	13 020	50.9	8 461	46.8	3 304	65.8	10 875	14.6
Rome city	2 114	1 422	13 320	10.9	2.47	30.9	34.0	28.9	8 438	45.9	5 489	42.6	2 265	55.3	4 882	14.8
Roswell city	628	53	30 207	66.1	2.61	23.1	36.5	13.5	20 923	49.9	17 245	48.9	2 610	60.7	9 284	88.9
Savannah city	5 497	2 120	51 375	-1.1	2.45	31.4	34.1	25.8	31 367	46.8	18 106	40.8	11 125	57.3	20 008	13.2
Smyrna city	466	66	18 372	23.8	2.21	37.5	25.2	13.0	9 499	43.5	6 648	39.9	2 096	57.8	8 873	18.2
Valdosta city	1 952	475	16 692	18.0	2.50	28.4	35.3	20.2	10 232	50.5	6 366	44.2	3 261	63.0	6 460	44.4
Warner Robins city	409	292	19 550	16.9	2.48	28.1	37.8	19.2	13 088	51.2	9 044	44.7	3 253	67.5	6 462	38.4

[1] As of April 1.　[2] Includes people under formally authorized, supervised care or custody in institutions at the time of enumeration (such as correctional institutions, nursing homes, and juvenile institutions).　[3] Under 18 years.　[4] No husband present.　[5] Data are for Athens-Clarke County (balance), GA; Athens city (1990 land area - 16.6 square miles; 1990 population - 45,734) merged with Clarke County effective January 14, 1991.　[6] Data are for Augusta-Richmond County (balance), GA; Augusta city (1990 land area - 19.7 square miles; 1990 population - 44,639) merged with Richmond County effective January 1, 1996.

Sources: Group Quarters Population—U.S. Census Bureau; 2000 Census of Population and Housing, "Census 2000 Profiles of General Demographic Characteristics" data files, published May 2001 (related Internet site <http://www.census.gov/mp/www/pub/2000cen/mscen01.html>). Households, 2000—U.S. Census Bureau; 2000 Census of Population and Housing, "Census 2000 Profiles of General Demographic Characteristics" data files, published May 2001 (related Internet site <http://www.census.gov/mp/www/pub/2000cen/mscen01.html>). Households, 1990—U.S. Census Bureau, 1990 Census of Population and Housing, Summary Tape File (STF) 1C on CD-ROM (related Internet site <http://homer.ssd.census.gov/cdrom/lookup>).

Table C–3. Cities — Group Quarters Population and Households–Con.

[Includes states and 1,070 incorporated places of 25,000 or more population as of April 1, 1990 in all states except Hawaii which has no incorporated places recognized by the Census Bureau. For Hawaii, 8 census designated places (CDPs) of 25,000 or more population as of April 1, 1990 are included. Also included are the 5 boroughs of New York city. For more information on these areas, see appendix B. Geographic Information]

City	Group quarters population, 2000[1] Number	Group quarters population, 2000[1] Institutionalized population[2]	Households, 2000 (April 1) Number	Percent change, 1990–2000	Persons per house-hold	Percent— One-person	Percent— With 1 or more persons under 18 years	Percent— With 1 or more persons 65 years and over	By type— Family households (families) Number	By type— Family households Percent with own children under 18 years	Married-couple Number	Married-couple Percent with own children[3]	Female householder[4] Number	Female householder[4] Percent with own children[3]	Nonfamily households Number	Nonfamily households Percent change, 1990–2000
HAWAII	35 782	7 690	403 240	13.2	2.92	21.9	37.9	27.4	287 068	45.0	216 077	44.8	49 923	47.3	116 172	25.2
Hilo CDP	1 391	479	14 577	9.4	2.70	24.1	36.1	31.7	10 105	44.2	7 073	40.2	2 216	55.4	4 472	23.9
Honolulu CDP	11 286	3 039	140 337	4.3	2.57	29.7	28.0	32.3	87 374	38.0	63 809	38.5	16 994	38.8	52 963	11.3
Kailua CDP	69	5	12 229	3.3	2.98	16.6	38.8	29.0	9 324	42.1	7 244	42.2	1 495	41.0	2 905	35.9
Kaneohe CDP	499	276	10 976	3.4	3.14	15.4	40.5	31.4	8 680	41.4	6 627	41.8	1 499	41.3	2 296	30.0
Mililani Town CDP	4	–	9 010	2.7	3.17	10.6	48.1	16.5	7 694	50.4	6 342	50.3	919	54.2	1 316	21.5
Pearl City CDP	2 727	117	8 921	.5	3.17	14.9	34.3	38.9	7 289	30.9	5 700	31.5	1 096	29.2	1 632	60.9
Waimalu CDP	90	1	10 524	1.5	2.78	21.0	34.0	19.7	7 518	40.8	5 887	40.2	1 163	45.1	3 006	12.1
Waipahu CDP	1 134	27	7 566	Z	4.23	11.1	50.6	42.0	6 430	42.6	4 521	43.5	1 368	43.9	1 136	18.3
IDAHO	31 496	17 717	469 645	30.2	2.69	22.4	38.7	21.5	335 588	50.8	276 511	47.8	40 849	66.3	134 057	37.5
Boise City city	4 013	2 569	74 438	46.4	2.44	28.0	34.3	17.5	46 493	52.0	36 271	48.3	7 422	66.5	27 945	55.1
Idaho Falls city	946	672	18 793	17.3	2.65	25.3	39.7	21.2	13 173	53.5	10 610	50.1	1 908	69.0	5 620	20.2
Lewiston city	662	405	12 795	11.1	2.36	27.9	31.0	27.8	8 277	44.3	6 566	39.3	1 185	64.1	4 518	20.2
Nampa city	1 844	688	18 090	77.1	2.77	22.6	43.3	21.3	13 016	56.5	10 065	53.5	2 063	68.3	5 074	61.4
Pocatello city	1 663	280	19 334	12.5	2.58	25.0	36.7	19.1	12 966	51.4	10 177	48.3	2 037	64.9	6 368	16.6
Twin Falls city	1 167	575	13 274	26.8	2.51	26.8	35.4	25.0	8 864	49.3	6 866	44.6	1 464	65.7	4 410	37.6
ILLINOIS	321 781	174 727	4 591 779	9.3	2.63	26.8	36.2	23.2	3 105 513	48.8	2 353 892	47.3	563 718	56.0	1 486 266	16.4
Addison village	201	–	11 649	8.6	3.07	16.9	41.6	19.3	9 095	49.1	7 303	49.2	1 186	54.4	2 554	10.8
Alton city	942	633	12 518	-3.5	2.36	33.3	32.9	27.4	7 650	48.0	4 924	40.5	2 174	63.2	4 868	8.0
Arlington Heights village	919	793	30 763	6.8	2.44	29.0	30.3	27.2	20 531	43.7	17 972	44.0	1 925	44.5	10 232	25.3
Aurora city	1 889	1 015	46 489	37.9	3.04	20.6	47.8	13.5	34 227	60.0	26 279	60.1	5 565	64.0	12 262	30.3
Belleville city	1 476	1 304	17 603	-.8	2.27	35.1	30.7	27.5	10 415	47.9	7 390	43.1	2 372	61.5	7 188	7.8
Berwyn city	181	140	19 702	2.1	2.73	29.4	36.7	28.4	12 931	50.3	9 251	52.8	2 531	46.1	6 771	-7.4
Bloomington city	2 447	555	26 642	24.0	2.34	32.8	32.4	17.7	15 724	51.9	12 342	48.7	2 572	66.9	10 918	24.7
Bolingbrook village	279	270	17 416	40.6	3.22	14.2	52.1	10.1	14 246	58.7	11 587	59.0	1 901	60.2	3 170	51.1
Buffalo Grove village	236	234	15 708	17.8	2.72	22.1	43.6	17.1	11 663	57.5	10 366	57.6	1 040	58.0	4 045	21.9
Burbank city	117	71	9 317	1.6	2.98	18.9	38.4	31.4	7 263	44.1	5 662	47.1	1 129	34.8	2 054	15.7
Calumet City city	22	–	15 139	-1.9	2.58	29.8	39.2	25.7	10 014	52.3	5 798	47.7	3 384	60.4	5 125	-.7
Carbondale city	840	489	9 981	3.9	1.99	43.5	18.3	13.2	3 489	48.7	2 204	40.9	1 009	67.8	6 492	9.2
Carol Stream village	85	83	13 872	22.4	2.91	21.1	47.4	13.0	10 137	62.1	8 285	63.0	1 333	62.1	3 735	26.9
Champaign city	7 239	307	27 071	12.0	2.23	36.6	23.9	15.2	12 450	47.9	9 313	43.7	2 449	64.3	14 621	20.4
Chicago city	59 547	27 323	1 061 928	3.6	2.67	32.6	34.3	21.5	632 558	48.4	372 970	48.1	200 963	62.6	429 370	9.2
Chicago Heights city	644	236	10 703	-2.1	3.00	22.9	44.3	26.2	7 821	52.2	4 812	49.0	2 383	60.3	2 882	7.1
Cicero town	198	190	23 115	-.3	3.70	17.5	56.1	20.1	18 109	64.8	12 971	70.0	3 164	57.7	5 006	-29.2
Danville city	2 522	2 361	13 327	-3.4	2.35	33.9	31.9	30.4	8 155	46.2	5 602	38.6	2 011	63.7	5 172	5.3
Decatur city	3 448	1 590	34 086	.2	2.30	32.7	30.5	27.6	21 088	44.5	15 021	36.8	4 806	66.5	12 998	13.4
De Kalb city	7 374	380	13 081	23.9	2.42	29.6	27.3	15.8	6 572	51.5	4 844	47.5	1 227	69.4	6 509	28.6
Des Plaines city	1 000	858	22 362	11.9	2.58	28.5	31.4	31.4	15 074	43.2	12 251	44.4	2 006	39.7	7 288	31.8
Downers Grove village	768	381	18 979	7.5	2.53	27.4	33.5	26.3	13 017	46.9	11 215	47.5	1 358	45.7	5 962	22.4
East St. Louis city	272	182	11 178	-14.4	2.80	27.8	42.9	28.2	7 664	48.5	2 450	34.7	4 542	57.4	3 514	-6.2
Elgin city	1 908	1 145	31 543	17.4	2.94	23.3	42.9	18.1	22 399	55.8	17 209	55.4	3 549	62.5	9 144	16.0
Elk Grove Village village	221	149	13 278	10.6	2.60	25.6	35.0	22.2	9 294	47.8	7 748	48.2	1 144	47.9	3 984	36.0
Elmhurst city	1 591	851	15 627	3.3	2.63	24.6	35.4	28.2	11 233	47.2	9 693	48.4	1 163	42.0	4 394	25.1
Evanston city	6 964	559	29 651	6.1	2.27	36.3	27.7	19.2	15 963	47.2	11 987	44.5	3 226	57.4	13 688	11.0
Freeport city	730	548	11 222	3.5	2.29	33.7	30.7	29.2	6 849	46.5	5 059	39.5	1 414	68.5	4 373	10.0
Galesburg city	4 079	2 561	13 237	-.3	2.24	34.6	28.9	31.3	7 896	44.1	5 777	36.7	1 636	67.1	5 341	8.7
Glendale Heights village	16	6	10 791	12.3	2.94	22.8	41.7	11.6	7 595	54.3	5 992	55.6	1 071	53.5	3 196	29.3
Glenview village	532	316	15 464	15.9	2.67	20.7	36.6	28.3	11 879	46.4	10 496	46.3	1 065	49.5	3 585	25.6
Granite City city	294	209	12 773	-1.8	2.43	29.4	33.2	28.9	8 462	45.2	6 079	40.6	1 752	57.2	4 311	10.9
Hanover Park village	66	26	11 105	10.5	3.44	13.5	53.3	11.1	9 108	59.9	7 151	61.7	1 310	58.8	1 997	16.0
Harvey city	362	154	8 990	-.7	3.30	20.7	50.3	21.7	6 759	52.0	3 273	49.1	2 863	57.3	2 231	-.1
Highland Park city	196	–	11 521	4.5	2.71	19.5	38.1	28.3	8 918	47.7	8 055	47.2	664	54.5	2 603	19.5
Hoffman Estates village	263	263	17 034	7.0	2.89	19.9	43.3	13.8	12 730	55.3	10 537	55.7	1 627	58.3	4 304	13.2
Joliet city	4 494	3 566	36 182	35.1	2.81	24.7	42.6	22.0	25 404	55.3	18 795	55.0	4 828	59.2	10 778	30.9
Kankakee city	1 447	1 252	10 020	-3.6	2.60	31.5	38.9	25.9	6 272	54.9	3 647	46.9	2 123	68.2	3 748	-3.4
Lansing village	–	–	11 416	4.9	2.48	27.9	32.7	29.0	7 774	44.5	6 088	42.9	1 301	52.0	3 642	23.6
Lombard village	1 341	688	16 487	9.6	2.49	28.7	31.4	23.9	10 720	45.8	8 893	46.4	1 298	44.8	5 767	25.2
Maywood village	189	–	7 937	-1.2	3.38	19.1	49.4	24.6	6 151	46.7	3 230	46.2	2 396	49.8	1 786	2.4
Moline city	350	290	18 492	1.2	2.35	31.9	31.0	26.4	11 603	46.0	9 018	41.5	1 931	64.2	6 889	8.1
Mount Prospect village	66	5	21 585	6.4	2.60	25.1	32.2	28.0	15 163	43.4	12 887	44.2	1 563	42.4	6 422	12.4
Naperville city	1 986	943	43 751	50.3	2.89	18.8	48.1	12.0	33 644	61.5	30 256	61.6	2 600	63.1	10 107	60.4
Niles village	1 350	1 163	12 002	11.4	2.39	30.6	23.5	44.5	7 941	33.1	6 482	34.5	1 024	28.3	4 061	33.9
Normal town	8 584	428	15 157	27.8	2.43	26.6	28.4	14.9	8 187	50.5	6 429	46.2	1 415	69.0	6 970	41.4
Northbrook village	751	515	12 203	7.1	2.68	18.9	36.4	33.4	9 682	44.7	8 821	44.6	652	47.2	2 521	26.1
North Chicago city	12 282	1 691	7 661	7.3	3.09	21.8	51.8	14.3	5 575	63.6	3 715	64.8	1 448	65.0	2 086	29.5
Oak Forest city	534	485	9 785	10.4	2.81	20.7	39.5	18.6	7 335	49.2	5 972	50.4	952	45.1	2 450	31.6

[1] As of April 1. [2] Includes people under formally authorized, supervised care or custody in institutions at the time of enumeration (such as correctional institutions, nursing homes, and juvenile institutions). [3] Under 18 years. [4] No husband present.

Sources: Group Quarters Population—U.S. Census Bureau; 2000 Census of Population and Housing, "Census 2000 Profiles of General Demographic Characteristics" data files, published May 2001 (related Internet site <http://www.census.gov/mp/www/pub/2000cen/mscen01.html>). Households, 2000—U.S. Census Bureau; 2000 Census of Population and Housing, "Census 2000 Profiles of General Demographic Characteristics" data files, published May 2001 (related Internet site <http://www.census.gov/mp/www/pub/2000cen/mscen01.html>). Households, 1990—U.S. Census Bureau, 1990 Census of Population and Housing, Summary Tape File (STF) 1C on CD-ROM (related Internet site <http://homer.ssd.census.gov/cdrom/lookup>).

Table C–3. Cities — **Group Quarters Population and Households**–Con.

[Includes states and 1,070 incorporated places of 25,000 or more population as of April 1, 1990 in all states except Hawaii which has no incorporated places recognized by the Census Bureau. For Hawaii, 8 census designated places (CDPs) of 25,000 or more population as of April 1, 1990 are included. Also included are the 5 boroughs of New York city. For more information on these areas, see appendix B. Geographic Information]

City	Group quarters population, 2000[1] Number	Institutionalized population[2]	Households, 2000 (April 1) Number	Percent change, 1990–2000	Persons per household	Percent— One-person	Percent— With 1 or more persons under 18 years	Percent— With 1 or more persons 65 years and over	Family households (families) Number	Percent with own children under 18 years	Married-couple Number	Married-couple Percent with own children[3]	Female householder[4] Number	Female householder Percent with own children[3]	Nonfamily households Number	Nonfamily households Percent change, 1990–2000
ILLINOIS—Con.																
Oak Lawn village	490	471	22 220	3.5	2.46	30.9	28.1	39.1	14 555	39.4	11 559	41.1	2 245	33.4	7 665	24.7
Oak Park village	379	225	23 079	2.1	2.26	37.0	31.3	16.8	12 980	52.4	9 716	51.5	2 676	57.0	10 099	9.3
Orland Park village	437	411	18 675	54.4	2.71	20.6	33.9	30.2	14 356	41.9	12 387	42.6	1 471	39.5	4 319	100.5
Palatine village	217	144	25 518	68.3	2.56	27.5	33.9	16.6	16 592	49.5	13 596	49.5	2 119	54.2	8 926	92.8
Park Ridge city	667	494	14 219	5.6	2.61	24.1	33.5	34.8	10 466	43.9	9 015	44.9	1 134	39.2	3 753	20.4
Pekin city	2 209	2 001	13 380	2.3	2.37	29.5	33.7	27.4	8 806	47.2	6 778	41.6	1 525	67.1	4 574	10.6
Peoria city	5 428	1 795	45 199	.5	2.38	33.2	32.0	24.5	27 334	48.0	18 789	50.1	6 993	68.0	17 865	8.0
Quincy city	2 364	1 618	16 546	2.9	2.30	33.7	30.9	28.0	10 106	46.8	7 658	41.4	1 923	65.1	6 440	8.0
Rockford city	4 326	2 945	59 158	7.9	2.46	30.7	34.8	24.5	37 348	49.9	25 929	43.8	8 779	66.1	21 810	18.7
Rock Island city	2 435	632	16 148	-.6	2.31	34.5	29.7	28.3	9 547	44.7	6 650	37.2	2 294	63.9	6 601	8.4
Schaumburg village	436	430	31 799	15.3	2.36	32.3	29.7	16.7	19 308	46.7	15 857	46.3	2 582	52.0	12 491	25.6
Skokie village	1 139	722	23 223	2.3	2.68	23.6	34.1	36.9	17 044	43.9	14 041	44.7	2 295	42.7	6 179	9.4
Springfield city	2 556	1 515	48 621	8.0	2.24	36.1	29.7	23.5	27 973	47.7	20 006	42.0	6 266	63.6	20 648	13.3
Streamwood village	225	211	12 095	21.8	2.99	17.3	43.8	13.1	9 411	52.3	7 768	53.1	1 116	52.2	2 684	72.3
Tinley Park village	717	644	17 478	37.9	2.73	23.1	38.4	21.7	12 788	49.8	10 749	50.6	1 507	47.9	4 690	60.8
Urbana city	5 735	618	14 327	8.5	2.14	36.6	21.6	16.1	6 224	46.3	4 618	40.8	1 249	67.8	8 103	23.1
Waukegan city	2 090	1 011	27 787	13.2	3.09	24.2	45.1	18.3	19 445	57.8	13 764	57.4	4 050	63.2	8 342	10.2
Wheaton city	4 200	1 710	19 377	9.0	2.64	24.5	37.8	19.4	13 720	51.8	11 892	51.9	1 410	54.3	5 657	22.3
Wheeling village	370	366	13 280	6.5	2.57	30.1	33.6	18.7	8 454	49.5	6 780	50.1	1 192	51.2	4 826	5.2
Wilmette village	223	126	10 039	3.3	2.73	21.1	41.2	32.3	7 727	52.8	6 913	53.0	645	51.5	2 312	15.8
Woodridge village	86	–	11 382	18.3	2.71	23.5	40.4	11.1	8 088	53.9	6 495	53.5	1 192	60.3	3 294	25.4
INDIANA	178 154	90 885	2 336 306	13.1	2.53	25.9	35.7	22.5	1 602 501	47.9	1 251 458	44.4	259 372	61.8	733 805	25.4
Anderson city	2 179	856	25 274	4.0	2.28	33.1	30.6	28.6	15 422	44.2	10 458	36.3	3 816	62.4	9 852	16.2
Bloomington city	14 005	873	26 468	26.1	2.09	39.1	18.9	14.6	10 454	45.4	7 733	39.6	2 072	65.8	16 014	36.2
Carmel city	521	454	13 597	49.2	2.74	18.9	44.1	14.5	10 571	55.5	9 420	54.5	899	64.8	3 026	52.7
Columbus city	814	781	15 985	24.4	2.39	29.1	34.1	20.1	10 500	40.1	8 290	44.2	1 761	63.6	5 122	33.1
East Chicago city	192	106	11 707	-3.4	2.75	28.6	41.4	28.2	7 941	52.4	4 075	48.2	3 122	61.0	3 766	4.2
Elkhart city	658	292	20 072	14.6	2.55	30.3	37.2	20.6	12 506	53.6	8 208	46.8	3 074	69.6	7 566	19.5
Evansville city	4 720	2 463	52 273	-1.3	2.24	35.1	29.4	26.6	30 512	45.6	21 328	39.5	7 168	61.9	21 761	9.8
Fort Wayne city	5 036	2 865	83 333	19.7	2.41	32.6	34.4	21.5	50 638	51.8	34 920	46.0	12 135	67.3	32 695	26.9
Gary city	849	535	38 244	-6.6	2.66	28.9	39.4	26.4	25 618	46.6	11 568	36.4	11 829	57.7	12 626	6.6
Greenwood city	577	439	14 931	40.9	2.37	29.9	34.3	20.1	9 596	50.5	7 610	46.7	1 474	67.6	5 335	57.0
Hammond city	394	116	32 026	-.4	2.58	29.7	35.8	25.6	20 895	48.8	13 755	45.6	5 411	57.7	11 131	9.7
Indianapolis city (remainder)	17 908	11 375	320 107	9.6	2.39	32.0	33.3	19.4	192 754	49.6	129 907	44.3	48 219	62.6	127 353	22.1
Kokomo city	694	556	20 273	8.6	2.24	35.2	31.3	24.1	12 195	47.4	8 559	40.2	2 850	66.2	8 078	25.0
Lafayette city	709	524	24 060	33.1	2.31	33.2	29.5	19.8	13 670	47.5	10 217	42.9	2 458	64.6	10 390	52.3
Lawrence city	286	263	14 853	40.0	2.60	24.8	42.8	14.9	10 332	57.3	7 740	54.2	1 937	69.5	4 521	34.8
Marion city	2 631	1 119	12 462	-1.8	2.30	33.8	31.2	28.7	7 632	44.8	5 244	36.2	1 832	63.9	4 830	12.1
Merrillville town	555	432	11 678	16.7	2.57	26.1	35.7	27.3	8 125	46.3	6 179	45.2	1 469	52.9	3 553	48.1
Michigan City city	2 661	2 585	12 550	-.1	2.41	30.9	34.9	25.9	7 903	48.6	5 018	41.1	2 271	63.6	4 647	8.4
Mishawaka city	1 305	354	20 248	12.5	2.23	35.8	30.7	23.3	11 649	49.0	8 131	42.5	2 623	66.0	8 599	23.5
Muncie city	6 201	1 036	27 322	.5	2.24	34.1	26.5	23.8	14 597	44.3	9 953	37.1	3 559	61.6	12 725	13.6
New Albany city	680	615	15 959	8.6	2.31	30.8	32.5	25.5	10 059	47.0	6 787	40.4	2 567	62.1	5 900	24.7
Portage city	406	358	12 746	21.2	2.60	23.9	38.2	21.8	9 017	49.0	6 847	46.3	1 550	58.1	3 729	48.6
Richmond city	1 832	859	16 287	4.5	2.29	33.0	30.9	28.1	9 918	45.6	7 020	38.6	2 259	63.3	6 369	18.3
South Bend city	2 817	1 662	42 908	1.5	2.45	32.5	34.1	26.1	25 956	50.4	16 733	44.0	7 296	64.4	16 952	10.5
Terre Haute city	7 401	2 873	22 870	6.4	2.28	34.9	30.2	27.1	13 025	47.7	8 915	41.3	3 193	62.8	9 845	16.3
West Lafayette city	5 138	215	10 462	14.3	2.26	32.7	15.5	14.2	3 591	43.4	2 887	44.4	457	48.6	6 871	22.0
IOWA	104 169	50 256	1 149 276	8.0	2.46	27.2	33.3	25.4	769 684	46.9	633 254	43.4	98 270	65.5	379 592	17.3
Ames city	9 122	186	18 085	15.8	2.30	28.5	22.9	14.2	8 969	44.9	7 587	43.3	962	61.9	9 116	24.5
Bettendorf city	294	180	12 474	17.0	2.48	26.0	35.5	21.9	8 714	48.6	7 418	45.9	1 005	67.7	3 760	38.1
Burlington city	633	475	11 102	1.1	2.36	31.0	31.6	28.3	7 110	45.5	5 354	39.3	1 336	65.9	3 992	9.1
Cedar Falls city	4 694	524	12 833	9.8	2.45	25.5	28.1	20.9	7 561	45.7	6 279	42.1	968	68.3	5 272	30.9
Cedar Rapids city	3 369	1 407	49 820	14.1	2.36	30.2	31.8	21.7	30 824	48.3	24 127	43.8	4 974	66.6	18 996	25.6
Clinton city	787	326	11 427	-2.1	2.36	30.2	32.5	28.0	7 360	46.8	5 591	41.2	1 334	65.7	4 067	9.1
Council Bluffs city	1 329	858	22 889	8.3	2.49	27.9	35.1	23.9	15 089	48.0	10 690	42.5	3 262	62.7	7 800	20.8
Davenport city	2 877	1 471	39 124	5.2	2.44	29.5	34.7	21.1	24 811	50.1	18 002	44.2	5 240	67.8	14 313	14.6
Des Moines city	6 537	2 670	80 504	2.6	2.39	31.9	32.4	21.7	48 710	48.8	35 156	44.2	10 121	62.7	31 794	7.8
Dubuque city	4 167	1 047	22 560	5.2	2.37	31.0	31.5	26.4	14 313	47.2	11 338	43.7	2 258	63.8	8 247	20.6
Fort Dodge city	1 165	815	10 470	-.3	2.29	33.8	30.9	28.4	6 376	47.6	4 808	41.6	1 190	67.5	4 094	10.6
Iowa City city	6 110	462	25 202	14.8	2.23	33.8	22.4	12.7	11 200	47.8	8 868	45.2	1 677	63.2	14 002	26.0
Marshalltown city	1 224	1 146	10 175	2.0	2.44	29.7	32.3	27.3	6 598	46.2	5 137	40.6	1 101	67.0	3 577	8.0
Mason City city	1 125	616	12 368	2.8	2.27	33.5	30.1	28.6	7 513	46.8	5 860	41.4	1 276	66.1	4 855	11.6
Sioux City city	2 674	1 172	32 054	5.1	2.57	27.7	36.2	24.3	21 101	50.7	15 752	46.3	3 906	66.2	10 953	12.7
Waterloo city	1 551	819	28 169	4.2	2.39	30.0	31.8	25.7	17 744	46.0	12 971	39.9	3 752	65.5	10 425	14.5
West Des Moines city	299	220	19 826	52.8	2.33	30.5	31.6	15.9	11 920	50.5	9 907	47.9	1 524	66.9	7 906	73.2

[1] As of April 1. [2] Includes people under formally authorized, supervised care or custody in institutions at the time of enumeration (such as correctional institutions, nursing homes, and juvenile institutions). [3] Under 18 years. [4] No husband present.

Sources: Group Quarters Population—U.S. Census Bureau; 2000 Census of Population and Housing, "Census 2000 Profiles of General Demographic Characteristics" data files, published May 2001 (related Internet site <http://www.census.gov/mp/www/pub/2000cen/mscen01.html>).   Households, 2000—U.S. Census Bureau; 2000 Census of Population and Housing, "Census 2000 Profiles of General Demographic Characteristics" data files, published May 2001 (related Internet site <http://www.census.gov/mp/www/pub/2000cen/mscen01.html>).   Households, 1990—U.S. Census Bureau, 1990 Census of Population and Housing, Summary Tape File (STF) 1C on CD-ROM (related Internet site <http://homer.ssd.census.gov/cdrom/lookup>).

Table C–3. Cities — **Group Quarters Population and Households**–Con.

[Includes states and 1,070 incorporated places of 25,000 or more population as of April 1, 1990 in all states except Hawaii which has no incorporated places recognized by the Census Bureau. For Hawaii, 8 census designated places (CDPs) of 25,000 or more population as of April 1, 1990 are included. Also included are the 5 boroughs of New York city. For more information on these areas, see appendix B. Geographic Information]

City	Group quarters population, 2000[1]		Households, 2000 (April 1)													
						Percent—			By type—							
									Family households (families)							Nonfamily households
											Married-couple		Female householder[4]			
	Number	Institutionalized population[2]	Number	Percent change, 1990–2000	Persons per household	One-person	With 1 or more persons under 18 years	With 1 or more persons 65 years and over	Number	Percent with own children under 18 years	Number	Percent with own children[3]	Number	Percent with own children[3]	Number	Percent change, 1990–2000
KANSAS	81 950	45 396	1 037 891	9.9	2.51	27.0	35.5	23.3	701 547	49.2	567 924	45.9	96 661	64.9	336 344	17.6
Emporia city..............	1 465	318	10 253	5.1	2.47	31.1	33.9	20.1	6 041	53.5	4 656	49.0	965	71.3	4 212	8.5
Hutchinson city	2 974	2 711	16 335	4.3	2.31	31.7	31.1	28.5	10 338	45.6	8 060	40.0	1 685	65.9	5 997	11.8
Kansas City city	1 348	872	55 500	–2.9	2.62	29.2	37.5	22.9	36 226	49.8	22 878	44.8	10 108	61.1	19 274	4.3
Lawrence city	7 957	437	31 388	28.0	2.30	30.6	26.4	12.7	15 737	50.0	11 914	46.1	2 746	66.6	15 651	35.0
Leavenworth city..........	4 103	3 462	12 035	4.9	2.60	27.1	42.2	19.7	8 219	57.3	6 376	54.1	1 394	70.7	3 816	21.1
Lenexa city	670	668	15 574	22.5	2.54	24.3	36.3	13.4	10 554	51.8	8 932	50.0	1 184	63.8	5 020	40.5
Manhattan city	5 794	369	16 949	15.4	2.30	30.5	23.7	13.8	8 259	46.6	6 708	44.5	1 122	63.8	8 690	28.0
Olathe city	1 595	742	32 314	50.7	2.83	18.4	47.1	9.8	24 627	59.2	20 622	57.9	2 894	69.4	7 687	63.2
Overland Park city	1 588	1 433	59 703	32.9	2.47	27.4	35.1	19.0	39 718	50.9	33 908	49.7	4 423	60.5	19 985	42.6
Salina city	1 367	685	18 523	7.1	2.39	30.1	33.8	24.0	11 878	49.2	9 220	44.0	1 951	67.3	6 645	13.6
Shawnee city.............	248	198	18 522	27.2	2.58	22.7	38.1	15.2	13 234	50.8	11 165	49.5	1 519	60.2	5 288	30.4
Topeka city	4 078	3 336	52 190	4.5	2.27	35.0	30.7	24.4	30 682	47.6	21 795	41.0	6 841	65.6	21 508	14.6
Wichita city	4 877	3 196	139 087	12.9	2.44	31.2	34.8	21.0	87 818	50.8	65 817	46.9	16 166	64.6	51 269	17.7
KENTUCKY.............	114 804	62 057	1 590 647	15.3	2.47	26.0	35.5	22.8	1 104 398	46.8	857 944	43.7	187 957	58.8	486 249	33.7
Bowling Green city	5 489	1 101	19 277	20.7	2.27	33.5	28.9	21.3	10 697	47.1	7 424	41.7	2 528	63.1	8 580	33.0
Covington city	1 120	842	18 257	5.4	2.31	36.5	32.5	21.7	10 125	51.9	6 257	46.9	3 008	62.8	8 132	19.8
Frankfort city	1 331	594	12 314	11.6	2.14	37.6	29.1	24.5	6 949	46.9	4 791	40.9	1 733	61.8	5 365	31.7
Henderson city	808	677	11 693	10.9	2.27	32.1	32.5	25.7	7 386	47.1	5 319	41.3	1 651	63.2	4 307	31.1
Hopkinsville city	999	894	12 174	6.8	2.39	29.7	35.7	26.0	8 125	48.5	5 488	41.7	2 211	64.7	4 049	19.9
Lexington-Fayette..........	12 723	4 722	108 288	21.0	2.29	31.7	29.6	17.3	62 955	46.9	47 074	43.4	12 477	60.3	45 333	36.9
Louisville city	8 527	3 664	111 414	–1.5	2.22	37.9	29.5	25.1	61 374	46.7	35 171	38.9	21 380	59.8	50 040	9.6
Owensboro city	2 223	1 103	22 659	4.6	2.29	33.3	31.7	27.6	14 091	46.3	10 132	41.3	3 154	61.3	8 568	18.9
Paducah city	1 212	1 132	11 825	–1.1	2.12	39.3	27.8	31.1	6 648	44.5	4 354	36.6	1 918	61.2	5 177	12.0
LOUISIANA	135 965	90 002	1 656 053	10.5	2.62	25.3	39.2	22.5	1 156 438	49.5	809 498	46.2	275 075	58.7	499 615	22.0
Alexandria city............	1 782	1 281	17 816	–1.8	2.50	30.4	37.4	27.1	11 727	48.4	6 865	42.0	4 141	59.7	6 089	8.3
Baton Rouge city	12 453	3 406	88 973	6.8	2.42	31.7	32.7	21.2	52 661	47.6	31 890	42.6	16 935	58.1	36 312	18.3
Bossier City city	1 695	852	21 197	11.4	2.58	24.7	40.4	20.3	14 894	52.4	10 676	47.5	3 356	67.1	6 303	29.4
Houma city	800	681	11 634	9.2	2.72	24.1	40.8	24.8	8 279	49.8	5 754	47.2	1 939	56.7	3 355	23.4
Kenner city..............	698	437	25 652	2.4	2.72	23.2	41.0	17.9	18 467	50.5	13 059	48.5	4 172	57.3	7 185	11.5
Lafayette city	4 438	1 966	43 506	19.8	2.43	29.4	34.2	19.6	27 116	50.2	19 095	46.0	6 333	62.6	16 390	27.0
Lake Charles city	3 570	2 208	27 974	4.3	2.44	30.0	34.9	26.3	18 027	47.3	11 645	41.0	5 220	61.3	9 947	17.3
Monroe city	3 706	1 373	19 421	1.5	2.54	31.3	37.8	24.9	12 157	51.7	6 479	43.4	4 916	63.4	7 264	11.2
New Iberia city	932	467	11 756	5.5	2.70	25.2	41.9	25.7	8 330	51.7	5 300	46.7	2 405	62.8	3 426	17.2
New Orleans city	17 641	9 772	188 251	Z	2.48	33.2	35.3	22.6	112 977	48.7	58 013	43.0	46 171	57.2	75 274	7.2
Shreveport city	5 391	3 476	78 662	4.0	2.48	30.8	35.4	25.2	50 442	47.0	30 108	40.5	16 938	58.4	28 220	16.9
MAINE	34 912	13 091	518 200	11.4	2.39	27.0	32.4	24.7	340 685	46.2	272 152	41.4	49 022	66.0	177 515	29.9
Bangor city..............	2 360	789	13 713	2.4	2.12	37.6	27.7	22.2	7 179	49.8	4 942	42.2	1 757	68.2	6 534	21.2
Lewiston city	2 543	764	15 290	–3.4	2.17	35.9	27.3	27.6	8 658	44.8	6 255	35.9	1 811	70.8	6 632	17.4
Portland city..............	2 443	924	29 714	5.2	2.08	40.1	22.9	21.2	13 547	46.9	9 545	41.3	3 127	63.0	16 167	19.5
MARYLAND	134 056	69 318	1 980 859	13.3	2.61	25.0	37.3	21.7	1 359 318	48.7	994 549	46.4	279 876	56.9	621 541	23.5
Annapolis city	706	212	15 303	8.8	2.30	32.9	28.1	20.9	8 676	43.2	5 598	36.0	2 502	59.8	6 627	13.3
Baltimore city............	25 753	12 634	257 996	–6.7	2.42	34.9	32.7	25.5	147 154	44.7	68 771	37.4	64 448	53.3	110 842	6.9
Bowie city...............	471	327	18 188	41.1	2.74	19.7	40.9	17.9	13 567	50.5	10 920	50.0	2 007	54.5	4 621	91.6
Frederick city.............	2 110	969	20 891	33.3	2.42	30.0	35.1	18.5	12 787	52.7	9 271	49.4	2 665	64.4	8 104	41.7
Gaithersburg city	623	268	19 621	29.1	2.65	27.8	37.5	15.5	12 580	54.3	9 529	54.0	2 192	59.3	7 041	29.6
Hagerstown city	829	412	15 849	5.2	2.26	35.4	32.5	23.9	9 086	51.5	5 827	41.6	2 524	70.2	6 763	18.2
Rockville city	1 642	1 269	17 247	10.1	2.65	23.8	35.3	23.9	12 002	47.5	9 759	47.2	1 647	52.5	5 245	21.2
MASSACHUSETTS......	221 216	88 453	2 443 580	8.7	2.51	28.0	32.9	24.7	1 576 696	47.5	1 197 917	45.8	289 944	56.4	866 884	18.4
Attleboro city	831	609	16 019	13.0	2.57	25.7	35.6	22.3	10 921	48.9	8 582	46.6	1 698	60.1	5 098	26.6
Beverly city	2 170	774	15 750	6.4	2.39	29.9	30.6	25.6	9 907	45.8	7 890	45.1	1 534	52.0	5 843	19.1
Boston city..............	35 077	8 481	239 528	4.8	2.31	37.1	25.6	18.9	115 096	47.2	65 747	42.9	39 366	57.9	124 432	10.6
Brockton city	1 876	1 367	33 675	2.5	2.74	26.6	39.1	23.2	22 748	51.8	14 148	47.4	6 693	62.8	10 927	12.4
Cambridge city...........	14 663	505	42 615	8.1	2.03	41.4	18.9	16.9	17 595	42.6	12 408	39.0	4 116	56.6	25 020	14.6
Chelsea city..............	953	878	11 888	12.7	2.87	28.8	40.7	21.8	7 614	56.8	4 388	54.8	2 384	64.7	4 274	6.0
Chicopee city............	1 006	310	23 117	2.2	2.32	32.7	28.8	30.5	14 139	43.4	9 859	38.0	3 293	58.6	8 978	22.6
Everett city..............	231	214	15 435	6.2	2.45	31.3	30.2	26.8	9 551	44.6	6 459	43.8	2 343	50.4	5 884	15.2
Fall River city............	1 891	1 472	38 759	3.9	2.32	34.2	32.2	28.2	23 558	49.3	15 613	42.3	6 391	66.5	15 201	21.2
Fitchburg city	1 745	567	14 943	–2.7	2.50	30.3	33.7	26.1	9 363	49.4	6 437	43.6	2 189	65.3	5 580	7.4
Gloucester city	360	265	12 592	8.7	2.38	30.7	29.6	26.8	7 896	44.0	6 141	41.4	1 334	55.7	4 696	19.5
Haverhill city	1 397	851	22 976	17.4	2.51	28.6	35.4	22.5	14 858	51.0	10 801	48.0	3 090	61.6	8 118	31.0

[1] As of April 1. [2] Includes people under formally authorized, supervised care or custody in institutions at the time of enumeration (such as correctional institutions, nursing homes, and juvenile institutions). [3] Under 18 years. [4] No husband present.

Sources: Group Quarters Population—U.S. Census Bureau; 2000 Census of Population and Housing, "Census 2000 Profiles of General Demographic Characteristics" data files, published May 2001 (related Internet site <http://www.census.gov/mp/www/pub/2000cen/mscen01.html>). Households, 2000—U.S. Census Bureau; 2000 Census of Population and Housing, "Census 2000 Profiles of General Demographic Characteristics" data files, published May 2001 (related Internet site <http://www.census.gov/mp/www/pub/2000cen/mscen01.html>). Households, 1990—U.S. Census Bureau, 1990 Census of Population and Housing, Summary Tape File (STF) 1C on CD-ROM (related Internet site <http://homer.ssd.census.gov/cdrom/lookup>).

Table C–3. Cities — **Group Quarters Population and Households**–Con.

[Includes states and 1,070 incorporated places of 25,000 or more population as of April 1, 1990 in all states except Hawaii which has no incorporated places recognized by the Census Bureau. For Hawaii, 8 census designated places (CDPs) of 25,000 or more population as of April 1, 1990 are included. Also included are the 5 boroughs of New York city. For more information on these areas, see appendix B. Geographic Information]

City	Group quarters population, 2000[1] Number	Institu-tionalized population[2]	Households, 2000 (April 1) Number	Percent change, 1990–2000	Persons per house-hold	Percent— One-person	With 1 or more persons under 18 years	With 1 or more persons 65 years and over	Family households (families) Number	Per-cent with own chil-dren under 18 years	Married-couple Number	Per-cent with own chil-dren[3]	Female householder[4] Number	Per-cent with own chil-dren[3]	Nonfamily households Number	Percent change, 1990–2000
MASSACHUSETTS—Con.																
Holyoke city	1 381	1 188	14 967	−5.6	2.57	30.9	36.9	27.0	9 478	52.5	5 464	43.2	3 313	68.8	5 489	7.3
Lawrence city	1 044	801	24 463	.8	2.90	25.5	46.0	21.4	16 905	60.0	8 964	53.1	6 281	71.3	7 558	2.5
Leominster city	394	296	16 491	11.2	2.48	27.9	35.1	24.3	10 902	49.8	8 170	45.9	2 056	64.1	5 589	25.9
Lowell city	3 841	1 120	37 887	2.3	2.67	29.0	37.4	21.1	23 982	53.8	15 202	50.2	6 602	63.8	13 905	8.9
Lynn city	1 344	738	33 511	6.2	2.62	31.0	36.0	25.2	21 033	51.8	13 313	47.3	5 883	63.8	12 478	9.1
Malden city	605	379	23 009	5.0	2.42	32.2	27.7	25.1	13 570	43.0	9 843	43.3	2 819	47.3	9 439	11.3
Marlborough city	489	346	14 501	19.3	2.47	28.4	32.3	19.9	9 285	47.4	7 473	46.5	1 311	54.2	5 216	27.1
Medford city	2 204	536	22 067	1.1	2.43	28.7	25.5	30.7	13 494	38.5	10 058	39.5	2 603	39.7	8 573	16.6
Melrose city	329	291	10 982	.4	2.44	29.7	30.4	28.6	7 108	44.4	5 869	46.2	951	39.2	3 874	9.2
New Bedford city	1 986	1 507	38 178	−1.6	2.40	31.6	34.1	29.0	24 083	49.4	15 099	41.6	7 209	65.2	14 095	15.4
Newton city	5 578	621	31 201	5.9	2.51	25.5	32.3	28.0	20 485	47.3	17 209	48.1	2 500	46.4	10 716	11.7
Northampton city	3 602	1 090	11 880	6.4	2.14	37.3	24.3	21.6	5 878	46.2	4 355	41.9	1 200	61.2	6 002	16.7
Peabody city	720	535	18 581	5.8	2.55	25.4	32.2	31.3	12 981	42.5	10 384	42.6	1 940	45.4	5 600	21.2
Pittsfield city	1 267	910	19 704	−1.1	2.26	34.0	29.4	30.0	11 822	45.4	8 451	39.5	2 589	63.3	7 882	15.2
Quincy city	1 586	780	38 883	9.0	2.22	37.6	22.6	27.6	20 534	39.2	15 031	39.5	4 081	42.3	18 349	23.7
Revere city	318	255	19 463	11.6	2.41	32.7	28.3	29.6	11 865	41.8	8 137	40.1	2 710	50.1	7 598	20.9
Salem city	1 160	162	17 492	10.7	2.24	34.9	26.2	24.5	9 707	43.6	6 790	38.6	2 319	58.3	7 785	21.9
Somerville city	2 515	316	31 555	4.1	2.38	31.0	20.9	19.3	14 668	40.5	10 155	43.2	3 251	44.8	16 887	18.2
Springfield city	5 533	1 648	57 130	−1.1	2.57	30.2	37.9	24.5	36 394	53.0	19 837	43.7	13 616	67.6	20 736	7.7
Taunton city	820	592	22 045	17.0	2.50	28.2	35.1	23.4	14 476	49.1	10 583	46.1	2 952	59.1	7 569	33.6
Waltham city	5 991	749	23 207	12.0	2.29	34.2	22.0	23.6	12 455	37.8	9 590	38.6	2 059	38.8	10 752	26.2
Westfield city	2 468	511	14 797	7.0	2.54	25.9	34.3	25.3	10 012	46.6	7 836	44.2	1 573	58.3	4 785	21.9
Woburn city	244	100	14 997	11.2	2.47	28.7	29.0	27.4	9 652	41.6	7 422	41.5	1 640	45.1	5 345	25.9
Worcester city	11 107	2 893	67 028	4.9	2.41	33.0	31.6	25.1	39 228	49.6	25 685	44.8	10 448	63.3	27 800	16.8
MICHIGAN	249 889	126 132	3 785 661	10.7	2.56	26.2	35.6	22.8	2 575 699	48.0	1 947 710	44.8	473 802	59.9	1 209 962	23.4
Allen Park city	306	295	11 974	−.5	2.43	28.2	29.8	35.5	8 202	40.1	6 591	41.0	1 182	37.1	3 772	22.1
Ann Arbor city	12 389	519	45 693	9.7	2.22	35.5	24.1	14.4	21 708	48.5	17 288	46.5	3 411	59.5	23 985	17.4
Battle Creek city	1 522	1 075	21 348	−.5	2.43	31.6	35.5	24.5	13 360	51.7	8 947	44.5	3 429	68.3	7 988	8.1
Bay City city	585	197	15 208	−2.3	2.38	32.9	32.9	25.6	9 316	49.4	6 449	44.0	2 228	62.2	5 892	8.9
Burton city	110	–	11 699	12.0	2.58	25.3	38.5	21.5	8 164	50.2	6 061	46.0	1 493	63.9	3 535	28.2
Dearborn city	401	224	36 770	3.7	2.65	30.9	33.4	31.2	23 851	48.3	18 740	50.4	3 469	45.3	12 919	11.0
Dearborn Heights city	687	527	23 276	−.7	2.47	28.0	30.1	33.1	15 771	40.6	12 265	41.3	2 507	38.6	7 505	20.5
Detroit city	19 701	10 509	336 428	−10.1	2.77	29.7	41.5	22.8	218 483	52.2	89 660	46.9	106 386	58.8	117 945	−9.1
East Detroit city	79	–	13 595	1.1	2.50	28.8	33.0	31.2	8 961	45.8	6 613	47.2	1 669	43.1	4 634	31.4
East Lansing city	14 573	229	14 390	6.6	2.22	36.2	16.8	13.6	5 090	45.4	3 970	42.9	819	61.3	9 300	23.4
Farmington Hills city	1 313	547	33 559	14.8	2.41	29.6	30.7	23.9	21 822	45.4	18 782	45.1	2 201	49.8	11 737	29.4
Ferndale city	102	69	9 872	.1	2.23	35.2	25.5	16.8	5 108	45.3	3 534	43.3	1 131	51.9	4 764	34.1
Flint city	2 559	1 013	48 744	−9.6	2.51	31.9	38.9	21.2	30 258	54.0	14 125	43.4	13 408	65.8	18 486	−.5
Garden City city	18	2	11 479	2.4	2.62	24.0	35.8	26.1	8 234	45.3	6 426	45.2	1 289	45.4	3 245	38.0
Grand Rapids city	9 694	4 415	73 217	6.1	2.57	30.8	35.3	20.8	44 370	52.8	29 474	48.3	11 538	65.7	28 847	20.3
Holland city	3 006	520	11 971	13.2	2.67	26.8	36.8	25.1	7 928	52.1	6 154	48.6	1 289	66.7	4 043	31.2
Inkster city	252	77	11 169	−.3	2.67	27.9	39.4	22.8	7 465	49.5	3 799	43.4	2 991	58.6	3 704	4.1
Jackson city	1 104	599	14 210	−3.5	2.48	32.0	37.7	22.0	8 666	55.2	5 084	46.0	2 832	69.6	5 544	.7
Kalamazoo city	9 539	1 285	29 413	Z	2.30	34.8	27.3	18.2	14 358	50.9	8 996	41.8	4 311	70.4	15 055	15.1
Kentwood city	362	180	18 477	21.2	2.43	30.9	35.1	17.3	11 523	53.4	8 929	50.4	1 996	65.8	6 954	28.6
Lansing city	872	502	49 505	−2.2	2.39	33.2	33.5	17.6	28 373	52.4	17 715	45.1	8 405	66.7	21 132	10.0
Lincoln Park city	128	116	16 204	−.3	2.46	29.3	33.5	26.2	10 575	46.3	7 495	45.4	2 156	47.8	5 629	18.5
Livonia city	1 891	1 181	38 089	6.1	2.59	22.9	34.1	29.3	28 081	44.0	23 938	44.5	3 037	42.9	10 008	36.3
Madison Heights city	160	139	13 299	3.5	2.33	33.8	29.5	25.2	8 001	44.8	6 011	44.2	1 403	49.5	5 298	21.8
Midland city	1 220	459	16 743	13.0	2.42	28.6	34.3	23.7	10 996	50.5	9 111	47.3	1 459	67.8	5 747	26.1
Muskegon city	4 827	4 459	14 569	−1.4	2.42	34.4	35.2	24.4	8 535	53.1	4 836	43.5	2 941	68.1	6 034	9.9
Novi city	267	202	18 726	47.5	2.52	28.1	37.4	14.4	12 324	55.2	10 525	55.2	1 333	57.8	6 402	73.4
Oak Park city	23	–	11 104	2.0	2.68	26.6	38.8	25.3	7 596	50.3	4 886	49.7	2 164	53.4	3 508	21.8
Pontiac city	1 441	647	24 234	−2.2	2.68	29.4	40.6	18.0	15 276	53.8	7 624	47.2	6 101	63.3	8 958	10.8
Portage city	415	120	18 138	17.3	2.45	27.2	35.7	20.2	12 139	51.0	9 863	47.4	1 766	67.7	5 999	42.9
Port Huron city	839	441	12 961	−1.5	2.43	31.9	35.5	25.1	8 044	52.2	5 164	44.1	2 263	69.0	4 917	11.6
Rochester Hills city	783	280	26 315	17.7	2.59	24.0	36.8	19.6	18 967	49.5	16 534	49.0	1 780	55.3	7 348	39.1
Roseville city	184	153	19 976	2.2	2.40	30.8	31.2	27.8	12 723	44.8	9 267	44.2	2 539	47.7	7 253	28.9
Royal Oak city	506	223	28 880	1.9	2.06	40.8	21.6	22.9	14 447	40.8	11 512	40.8	2 170	43.5	14 433	29.7
Saginaw city	1 438	746	23 182	−11.4	2.60	29.5	40.5	22.3	15 105	54.4	7 617	42.9	6 338	68.7	8 077	−4.7
St. Clair Shores city	484	372	27 434	.8	2.28	32.7	26.2	36.0	17 287	38.3	13 581	38.6	2 748	38.4	10 147	27.5
Southfield city	1 223	673	33 987	5.8	2.27	36.2	28.6	25.5	19 774	43.4	13 671	40.7	4 870	52.0	14 213	14.9
Southgate city	198	171	12 836	5.8	2.33	32.3	29.1	28.8	8 043	42.7	6 317	41.8	1 242	46.6	4 793	28.0
Sterling Heights city	1 198	672	46 319	13.4	2.66	24.1	34.8	22.1	33 392	45.7	27 959	46.0	3 955	46.6	12 927	39.8
Taylor city	695	580	24 776	−.3	2.63	23.1	38.9	20.7	17 751	48.7	12 064	43.9	4 313	61.3	7 025	23.5
Troy city	235	–	30 018	14.7	2.69	22.8	38.0	20.5	21 874	50.6	19 352	51.5	1 816	47.4	8 144	23.8
Warren city	1 302	1 002	55 551	1.7	2.47	28.8	30.5	30.4	36 714	42.0	27 603	40.8	6 518	47.1	18 837	29.4
Westland city	942	848	36 533	10.3	2.34	32.6	31.3	23.1	22 244	47.0	16 222	44.8	4 432	54.0	14 289	30.3
Wyandotte city	94	41	11 816	−4.1	2.36	31.9	30.7	28.4	7 422	44.0	5 470	43.1	1 410	46.9	4 394	10.0
Wyoming city	358	87	26 536	9.8	2.60	26.6	38.4	17.8	17 540	54.0	13 168	51.2	3 175	65.2	8 996	24.3

[1] As of April 1. [2] Includes people under formally authorized, supervised care or custody in institutions at the time of enumeration (such as correctional institutions, nursing homes, and juvenile institutions). [3] Under 18 years. [4] No husband present.

Sources: Group Quarters Population—U.S. Census Bureau; 2000 Census of Population and Housing, "Census 2000 Profiles of General Demographic Characteristics" data files, published May 2001 (related Internet site <http://www.census.gov/mp/www/pub/2000cen/mscen01.html>). Households, 2000—U.S. Census Bureau; 2000 Census of Population and Housing, "Census 2000 Profiles of General Demographic Characteristics" data files, published May 2001 (related Internet site <http://www.census.gov/mp/www/pub/2000cen/mscen01.html>). Households, 1990—U.S. Census Bureau, 1990 Census of Population and Housing, Summary Tape File (STF) 1C on CD-ROM (related Internet site <http://homer.ssd.census.gov/cdrom/lookup>).

Table C–3. Cities — **Group Quarters Population and Households**–Con.

[Includes states and 1,070 incorporated places of 25,000 or more population as of April 1, 1990 in all states except Hawaii which has no incorporated places recognized by the Census Bureau. For Hawaii, 8 census designated places (CDPs) of 25,000 or more population as of April 1, 1990 are included. Also included are the 5 boroughs of New York city. For more information on these areas, see appendix B. Geographic Information]

City	Group quarters population, 2000[1]		Households, 2000 (April 1)			Percent—			By type—							
									Family households (families)		Married-couple		Female householder[4]		Nonfamily households	
	Number	Institutionalized population[2]	Number	Percent change, 1990–2000	Persons per household	One-person	With 1 or more persons under 18 years	With 1 or more persons 65 years and over	Number	Percent with own children under 18 years	Number	Percent with own children[3]	Number	Percent with own children[3]	Number	Percent change, 1990–2000
MINNESOTA	135 883	63 058	1 895 127	15.0	2.52	26.9	34.8	21.3	1 255 141	49.9	1 018 245	46.9	168 782	66.0	639 986	23.7
Apple Valley city	237	192	16 344	46.6	2.77	19.3	44.2	10.4	12 399	56.1	10 413	54.3	1 472	67.1	3 945	107.9
Blaine city	103	–	15 898	24.0	2.82	17.0	44.0	11.2	12 176	53.7	9 709	51.9	1 768	63.9	3 722	58.7
Bloomington city	1 326	727	36 400	5.5	2.30	29.6	26.6	24.9	22 768	40.2	18 650	37.1	2 987	57.8	13 632	25.2
Brooklyn Center city	387	183	11 430	1.8	2.52	28.2	32.4	27.2	7 382	45.9	5 297	40.6	1 537	62.7	4 048	31.2
Brooklyn Park city	218	15	24 432	19.8	2.75	22.0	41.8	11.5	17 354	55.1	13 343	52.9	2 962	66.9	7 078	26.4
Burnsville city	343	131	23 687	23.8	2.53	24.8	35.7	12.8	15 631	51.6	12 503	48.4	2 361	68.3	8 056	48.8
Coon Rapids city	362	184	22 578	29.4	2.71	20.1	41.5	14.1	16 574	53.3	12 939	50.1	2 757	68.6	6 004	82.6
Duluth city	6 561	2 154	35 500	2.7	2.26	34.5	28.1	25.4	19 918	47.3	14 708	41.4	4 057	66.7	15 582	13.5
Eagan city	165	–	23 773	36.4	2.67	23.0	42.4	8.2	16 435	59.6	13 753	58.4	2 007	69.1	7 338	51.5
Eden Prairie city	174	77	20 457	41.6	2.68	22.0	43.3	9.3	14 579	59.7	12 530	58.2	1 576	72.2	5 878	52.2
Edina city	290	262	20 996	5.7	2.24	34.0	27.2	36.6	12 878	43.2	11 303	42.1	1 226	52.8	8 118	20.0
Fridley city	218	53	11 328	3.8	2.40	26.8	30.2	19.8	7 323	43.6	5 504	37.9	1 319	63.9	4 005	30.6
Mankato city	3 839	328	12 367	10.2	2.31	32.2	24.6	19.4	6 056	48.2	4 540	43.5	1 085	67.9	6 311	18.1
Maple Grove city	68	–	17 532	39.9	2.87	15.8	47.3	8.5	13 951	58.2	12 179	57.3	1 319	66.1	3 581	78.4
Maplewood city	817	337	13 758	19.7	2.48	27.0	33.5	25.2	9 191	47.3	7 268	44.5	1 449	61.4	4 567	49.7
Minneapolis city	18 064	5 701	162 352	1.0	2.25	40.3	25.0	15.2	73 939	49.6	47 049	44.3	19 991	64.2	88 413	6.5
Minnetonka city	635	345	21 393	14.5	2.37	27.3	30.0	22.8	14 090	44.2	12 118	42.4	1 459	56.9	7 303	36.5
Moorhead city	3 836	524	11 660	5.4	2.43	29.2	32.7	23.0	7 036	52.1	5 515	47.3	1 148	73.6	4 624	13.7
Plymouth city	1 450	935	24 820	35.2	2.60	21.8	38.7	13.9	17 654	53.1	15 188	51.6	1 874	65.6	7 166	54.2
Richfield city	488	241	15 073	–3.1	2.25	33.7	26.2	26.1	8 731	42.0	6 535	38.6	1 589	57.3	6 342	9.3
Rochester city	2 879	1 559	34 116	22.2	2.43	29.7	34.0	18.7	21 478	51.8	17 672	48.9	2 883	67.5	12 638	24.7
Roseville city	1 642	702	14 598	7.6	2.20	33.6	23.2	30.6	8 600	37.8	7 183	35.2	1 054	53.6	5 998	32.0
St. Cloud city	4 724	1 661	22 652	26.4	2.40	30.2	28.6	17.5	12 263	50.4	9 374	46.1	2 131	67.7	10 389	29.3
St. Louis Park city	914	541	20 782	4.3	2.08	37.9	23.0	21.1	10 562	43.2	8 172	40.1	1 793	58.2	10 220	16.6
St. Paul city	11 196	3 240	112 109	1.7	2.46	35.9	31.6	18.9	60 999	53.5	40 524	49.2	15 627	66.0	51 110	7.1
Winona city	3 653	566	10 301	10.4	2.27	35.2	25.3	24.0	5 324	46.2	4 163	42.2	868	63.8	4 977	23.1
MISSISSIPPI	95 414	50 826	1 046 434	14.8	2.63	24.6	39.6	23.7	747 159	48.6	520 844	45.0	180 705	58.8	299 275	26.3
Biloxi city	3 270	520	19 588	17.7	2.42	30.1	34.7	23.0	12 386	49.7	8 731	45.0	2 745	64.0	7 202	31.5
Greenville city	719	575	14 784	–3.5	2.77	25.8	43.4	24.4	10 419	50.9	5 590	43.7	4 097	60.4	4 365	5.9
Gulfport city	3 424	1 512	26 943	70.6	2.51	27.7	37.1	21.7	17 653	49.0	11 472	43.7	4 906	60.4	9 290	72.0
Hattiesburg city	5 136	1 409	17 295	8.7	2.29	34.4	29.4	20.8	9 396	46.5	5 386	38.5	3 363	60.0	7 899	17.5
Jackson city	7 201	2 485	67 841	–5.6	2.61	28.9	39.4	21.4	44 488	51.4	23 993	45.7	17 178	60.4	23 353	1.3
Meridian city	1 855	1 356	15 966	–1.3	2.39	33.2	35.1	28.6	10 033	49.6	5 777	41.4	3 726	62.6	5 933	8.0
Pascagoula city	1 327	455	9 878	1.1	2.52	27.0	38.4	23.1	6 724	50.7	4 406	44.0	1 853	66.7	3 154	11.8
Tupelo city	1 114	905	13 395	14.4	2.47	28.0	38.3	20.7	9 105	51.3	6 468	46.8	2 170	64.4	4 290	26.7
MISSOURI	162 058	90 430	2 194 594	11.9	2.48	27.3	34.7	24.0	1 476 516	47.4	1 140 866	43.6	253 760	61.7	718 078	21.1
Blue Springs city	246	206	17 286	27.8	2.77	18.1	45.1	13.7	13 361	55.0	10 900	52.4	1 808	66.5	3 925	58.6
Cape Girardeau city	3 070	983	14 380	7.0	2.24	33.6	27.8	24.1	8 293	44.6	6 304	40.1	1 567	61.1	6 087	17.6
Chesterfield city	1 073	1 070	18 060	37.7	2.53	26.3	34.2	23.4	13 110	45.7	11 834	44.7	977	55.0	4 950	83.8
Columbia city	8 459	595	33 689	30.4	2.26	33.1	27.6	14.7	17 295	50.7	12 861	45.8	3 464	68.8	16 394	33.3
Florissant city	781	557	20 399	6.4	2.44	28.8	33.4	29.0	13 687	45.8	10 168	42.7	2 697	55.7	6 712	41.6
Gladstone city	279	230	11 484	9.0	2.27	29.9	28.0	24.4	7 389	39.9	5 856	35.9	1 180	57.5	4 095	36.2
Independence city	1 140	590	47 390	4.6	2.37	30.1	31.4	26.2	30 544	43.6	22 710	38.5	5 852	59.2	16 846	22.4
Jefferson City city	4 734	3 993	15 794	11.5	2.21	36.1	29.6	23.8	9 203	48.0	7 014	42.9	1 701	66.3	6 591	20.8
Joplin city	1 906	676	19 101	9.3	2.28	32.4	30.3	25.8	11 511	45.7	8 472	39.8	2 347	63.0	7 590	15.2
Kansas City city	9 096	4 958	183 981	3.6	2.35	34.1	31.7	20.7	107 402	48.2	69 998	42.6	29 425	61.2	76 579	11.5
Kirkwood city	341	250	11 763	4.9	2.29	33.5	29.6	29.7	7 256	45.3	5 945	44.2	1 054	51.2	4 507	24.2
Lee's Summit city	779	746	26 417	49.8	2.65	22.0	42.5	18.8	19 488	55.2	16 402	53.0	2 345	68.4	6 929	45.6
Maryland Heights city	344	324	11 302	6.0	2.25	33.8	27.6	14.7	6 420	45.4	5 001	43.0	1 076	56.8	4 882	13.5
Raytown city	552	518	12 855	1.2	2.32	30.3	30.2	31.0	8 307	42.0	6 245	36.7	1 618	59.3	4 548	22.0
St. Charles city	2 641	771	24 210	11.7	2.38	29.6	32.1	20.9	15 321	47.6	11 970	43.5	2 479	63.5	8 889	21.2
St. Joseph city	4 618	3 159	29 026	2.2	2.39	30.4	33.1	27.3	18 463	47.3	13 545	42.1	3 726	62.4	10 563	13.2
St. Louis city	10 632	4 667	147 076	–10.8	2.30	40.3	30.1	24.9	76 976	48.6	38 470	41.5	31 359	58.3	70 100	–5.3
St. Peters city	146	127	18 435	21.1	2.78	20.3	44.7	15.7	13 939	56.0	11 573	54.7	1 780	64.2	4 496	67.2
Springfield city	11 019	3 122	64 691	12.8	2.17	35.3	26.2	24.2	35 682	43.5	26 299	37.5	7 037	61.6	29 009	27.5
University City city	409	238	16 453	–.6	2.25	34.2	27.6	22.4	9 119	42.7	5 974	39.9	2 677	50.2	7 334	16.9

[1] As of April 1.   [2] Includes people under formally authorized, supervised care or custody in institutions at the time of enumeration (such as correctional institutions, nursing homes, and juvenile institutions).   [3] Under 18 years.   [4] No husband present.

Sources: Group Quarters Population—U.S. Census Bureau; 2000 Census of Population and Housing, "Census 2000 Profiles of General Demographic Characteristics" data files, published May 2001 (related Internet site <http://www.census.gov/mp/www/pub/2000cen/mscen01.html>).   Households, 2000—U.S. Census Bureau; 2000 Census of Population and Housing, "Census 2000 Profiles of General Demographic Characteristics" data files, published May 2001 (related Internet site <http://www.census.gov/mp/www/pub/2000cen/mscen01.html>).   Households, 1990—U.S. Census Bureau, 1990 Census of Population and Housing, Summary Tape File (STF) 1C on CD-ROM (related Internet site <http://homer.ssd.census.gov/cdrom/lookup>).

Table C–3. Cities — **Group Quarters Population and Households**–Con.

[Includes states and 1,070 incorporated places of 25,000 or more population as of April 1, 1990 in all states except Hawaii which has no incorporated places recognized by the Census Bureau. For Hawaii, 8 census designated places (CDPs) of 25,000 or more population as of April 1, 1990 are included. Also included are the 5 boroughs of New York city. For more information on these areas, see appendix B. Geographic Information]

City	Group quarters population, 2000[1] Number	Institutionalized population[2]	Households, 2000 (April 1) Number	Percent change, 1990–2000	Persons per household	Percent— One-person	Percent— With 1 or more persons under 18 years	Percent— With 1 or more persons 65 years and over	Family households (families) Number	Percent with own children under 18 years	Married-couple Number	Percent with own children[3]	Female householder[4] Number	Percent with own children[3]	Nonfamily households Number	Percent change, 1990–2000
MONTANA..............	24 762	12 068	358 667	17.1	2.45	27.4	33.3	23.4	237 407	47.1	192 067	42.9	32 016	66.2	121 260	28.3
Billings city................	2 683	1 572	37 525	13.1	2.32	31.3	31.2	24.5	23 142	47.3	17 729	42.3	4 045	65.1	14 383	23.0
Butte-Silver Bow (remainder).............	1 092	715	14 135	3.5	2.32	32.8	30.1	27.6	8 736	45.1	6 746	41.2	1 481	59.7	5 399	12.7
Great Falls city............	1 531	1 272	23 834	5.3	2.31	31.9	32.1	25.9	14 838	48.4	11 289	42.1	2 657	70.0	8 996	17.2
Missoula city..............	3 286	487	24 141	36.6	2.23	33.6	26.2	17.8	12 327	48.3	9 148	42.8	2 405	66.3	11 814	53.2
NEBRASKA..............	50 818	26 011	666 184	10.6	2.49	27.6	34.5	23.7	443 411	49.1	360 996	45.9	60 343	65.8	222 773	19.2
Bellevue city	223	101	16 937	48.2	2.61	23.2	38.2	18.1	11 948	50.3	9 382	46.3	1 914	66.8	4 989	68.4
Grand Island city	1 091	770	16 426	7.8	2.55	27.1	36.6	24.0	11 034	51.1	8 703	46.7	1 716	70.3	5 392	9.6
Lincoln city	11 643	3 689	90 485	20.0	2.36	30.4	31.0	18.3	53 580	49.8	41 927	46.3	8 592	66.2	36 905	29.3
Omaha city	10 581	5 760	156 738	17.1	2.42	31.9	32.6	20.7	94 933	49.6	68 611	45.7	20 394	62.7	61 805	25.5
NEVADA	33 675	22 173	751 165	61.1	2.62	24.9	35.3	21.3	498 333	47.9	373 201	44.5	83 482	60.7	252 832	59.1
Carson City	3 223	3 102	20 171	26.9	2.44	27.8	32.7	27.6	13 256	45.4	10 080	40.6	2 217	60.8	6 915	31.1
Henderson city	1 026	741	66 331	185.5	2.63	20.3	36.0	19.2	47 111	46.5	37 386	43.1	6 635	60.5	19 220	225.9
Las Vegas city	8 185	5 416	176 750	77.2	2.66	25.0	35.7	22.7	117 466	48.0	85 359	44.6	21 637	59.8	59 284	69.8
North Las Vegas city	1 338	1 223	34 018	134.2	3.36	13.6	53.6	14.2	27 119	59.9	19 500	59.4	5 168	64.0	6 899	102.7
Reno city	4 496	1 633	73 904	29.0	2.38	32.6	30.3	20.6	41 647	49.0	29 957	44.8	7 817	63.6	32 257	26.7
Sparks city...............	623	551	24 601	19.6	2.67	24.3	38.7	20.0	16 637	52.1	12 309	49.7	2 940	60.8	7 964	19.3
NEW HAMPSHIRE	35 539	13 784	474 606	15.4	2.53	24.4	35.5	21.5	323 651	48.9	262 438	45.9	42 952	63.5	150 955	27.3
Concord city	3 267	2 819	16 281	14.5	2.30	32.7	32.2	22.1	9 630	51.7	7 215	46.2	1 857	70.3	6 651	22.3
Dover city	757	646	11 573	11.9	2.26	31.0	28.0	20.8	6 496	46.9	4 920	42.3	1 195	63.3	5 077	24.2
Manchester city	2 602	1 442	44 247	9.7	2.36	31.7	31.4	21.9	26 114	49.8	18 843	45.2	5 193	64.3	18 133	19.3
Nashua city	1 403	639	34 614	11.5	2.46	28.3	33.5	20.6	22 083	49.5	17 079	46.2	3 606	62.0	12 531	23.6
Portsmouth city	607	377	9 875	–4.4	2.04	38.9	21.3	23.4	4 862	40.5	3 730	36.0	850	59.1	5 013	24.7
Rochester city	293	221	11 434	11.9	2.46	25.7	35.2	23.1	7 648	49.1	5 819	43.3	1 302	68.6	3 786	31.0
NEW JERSEY...........	194 821	110 169	3 064 645	9.7	2.68	24.5	36.6	25.9	2 154 539	47.6	1 638 322	47.4	387 012	50.9	910 106	17.7
Atlantic City city	1 475	332	15 848	.7	2.46	37.2	33.2	28.0	8 708	50.5	3 934	43.5	3 681	60.4	7 140	–5.4
Bayonne city	142	–	25 545	.9	2.42	32.8	30.5	31.3	16 022	45.2	10 942	45.2	3 846	48.7	9 523	8.5
Camden city	4 375	3 454	24 177	–9.2	3.12	22.5	51.8	19.9	17 434	58.5	6 319	52.0	9 126	65.0	6 743	–10.5
Clifton city	386	244	30 244	4.1	2.59	27.9	31.3	33.9	20 352	42.9	15 517	44.7	3 467	40.1	9 892	6.3
East Orange city	1 304	925	26 024	–4.4	2.63	33.0	39.5	23.3	16 079	51.6	6 769	46.2	7 490	57.9	9 945	–8.2
Elizabeth city	2 916	2 313	40 482	3.5	2.91	24.6	41.5	22.3	28 170	52.7	17 386	53.1	7 728	55.9	12 312	.1
Fair Lawn borough	168	139	11 806	2.7	2.67	21.3	35.0	35.3	8 906	44.3	7 497	45.7	1 065	38.3	2 900	11.2
Fort Lee borough	34	–	16 544	8.6	2.14	39.0	23.6	33.0	9 402	39.7	7 729	40.7	1 232	39.4	7 142	10.5
Garfield city	70	–	11 250	2.8	2.64	27.4	33.3	28.8	7 426	46.2	5 231	48.5	1 557	44.3	3 824	.1
Hackensack city	1 662	990	18 113	10.0	2.26	39.8	24.9	21.7	9 549	41.6	6 303	39.9	2 353	49.4	8 564	11.5
Hoboken city	1 288	158	19 418	29.1	1.92	41.8	12.9	14.5	6 842	32.3	4 619	27.8	1 742	45.8	12 576	58.6
Jersey City city	3 377	1 563	88 632	7.6	2.67	29.2	35.9	20.1	55 636	49.5	32 236	48.5	17 912	55.3	32 996	14.5
Kearny town	2 520	2 423	13 539	8.6	2.81	21.8	37.7	24.2	9 809	47.7	7 284	49.3	1 783	46.4	3 730	11.8
Linden city	253	246	15 052	4.8	2.60	27.9	33.1	31.8	10 087	43.3	7 030	44.5	2 298	42.7	4 965	12.2
Long Branch city	205	70	12 594	9.1	2.47	34.1	30.8	24.0	7 248	46.4	4 644	43.1	2 006	57.8	5 346	17.7
Millville city	258	123	10 043	4.2	2.65	25.1	39.6	25.5	7 011	50.2	4 671	44.8	1 797	62.3	3 032	9.8
Newark city	12 773	7 451	91 382	–.2	2.85	26.6	43.0	20.9	61 999	51.9	28 334	48.7	26 801	58.3	29 383	1.6
New Brunswick city	6 446	109	13 057	2.7	3.23	24.3	35.0	18.6	7 202	52.7	3 866	53.3	2 349	55.6	5 855	1.8
Paramus borough..........	1 507	1 244	8 082	3.9	3.00	14.4	39.4	37.0	6 779	44.1	5 924	45.9	644	32.9	1 303	23.2
Passaic city	579	200	19 458	3.9	3.46	20.3	49.0	21.7	14 456	56.5	8 497	58.6	4 232	57.3	5 002	–5.7
Paterson city	3 821	2 139	44 710	1.7	3.25	20.4	49.2	21.9	33 351	54.8	17 631	54.0	12 001	58.4	11 359	1.4
Perth Amboy city	702	379	14 562	2.5	3.20	20.6	46.2	24.0	10 768	54.5	6 489	53.5	3 063	57.9	3 794	–6.1
Plainfield city	907	550	15 137	–.1	3.10	21.1	44.6	21.1	10 898	49.3	5 952	47.8	3 711	52.9	4 239	.1
Rahway city	160	118	10 028	4.2	2.63	28.0	34.4	28.7	6 727	44.7	4 682	44.5	1 563	47.4	3 301	17.9
Sayreville borough	246	194	14 955	17.3	2.68	22.3	36.8	24.3	10 923	47.0	8 597	48.2	1 660	45.4	4 032	33.3
Trenton city	4 401	3 301	29 437	–4.3	2.75	29.7	39.6	25.4	18 695	51.0	8 524	46.0	7 965	58.2	10 742	.6
Union City city	355	181	22 872	11.0	2.92	23.0	41.4	22.3	16 067	52.1	9 696	52.1	4 410	57.7	6 805	12.9
Vineland city	2 402	1 052	19 930	6.4	2.70	23.7	38.6	27.5	14 201	47.6	9 730	43.8	3 347	56.9	5 729	20.4
Westfield town.............	267	177	10 622	3.2	2.77	19.3	41.9	25.6	8 181	52.9	7 222	54.1	757	45.4	2 441	14.3
West New York town	28	–	16 719	16.0	2.74	27.5	35.1	27.6	11 042	47.1	6 997	47.5	2 822	50.4	5 677	25.0

[1] As of April 1. [2] Includes people under formally authorized, supervised care or custody in institutions at the time of enumeration (such as correctional institutions, nursing homes, and juvenile institutions). [3] Under 18 years. [4] No husband present.

Sources: Group Quarters Population—U.S. Census Bureau; 2000 Census of Population and Housing, "Census 2000 Profiles of General Demographic Characteristics" data files, published May 2001 (related Internet site <http://www.census.gov/mp/www/pub/2000cen/mscen01.html>).   Households, 2000—U.S. Census Bureau; 2000 Census of Population and Housing, "Census 2000 Profiles of General Demographic Characteristics" data files, published May 2001 (related Internet site <http://www.census.gov/mp/www/pub/2000cen/mscen01.html>).   Households, 1990—U.S. Census Bureau, 1990 Census of Population and Housing, Summary Tape File (STF) 1C on CD-ROM (related Internet site <http://homer.ssd.census.gov/cdrom/lookup>).

Table C–3. Cities — **Group Quarters Population and Households**–Con.

[Includes states and 1,070 incorporated places of 25,000 or more population as of April 1, 1990 in all states except Hawaii which has no incorporated places recognized by the Census Bureau. For Hawaii, 8 census designated places (CDPs) of 25,000 or more population as of April 1, 1990 are included. Also included are the 5 boroughs of New York city. For more information on these areas, see appendix B. Geographic Information]

City	Group quarters population, 2000 [1] Number	Institutionalized population [2]	Households, 2000 (April 1) Number	Percent change, 1990–2000	Persons per house-hold	Percent— One-person	With 1 or more persons under 18 years	With 1 or more persons 65 years and over	Family households (families) Number	Percent with own children under 18 years	Married-couple Number	Percent with own children [3]	Female householder [4] Number	Percent with own children [3]	Nonfamily households Number	Percent change, 1990–2000
NEW MEXICO	36 307	19 178	677 971	24.9	2.63	25.4	38.6	22.4	466 515	50.4	341 818	46.1	89 622	62.6	211 456	39.8
Alamogordo city	426	364	13 704	30.7	2.57	25.2	39.2	23.1	9 728	51.1	7 618	46.3	1 610	69.4	3 976	40.9
Albuquerque city	9 344	4 043	183 236	19.1	2.40	30.5	33.3	20.7	112 623	49.2	79 915	44.4	23 626	62.3	70 613	30.0
Clovis city...............	596	500	12 458	6.7	2.57	26.8	39.9	23.8	8 598	52.6	6 200	46.4	1 862	69.8	3 860	22.3
Farmington city	509	348	13 982	16.7	2.67	22.6	41.3	20.0	10 099	52.5	7 599	47.7	1 730	68.0	3 883	29.6
Hobbs city...............	1 333	1 226	10 040	–2.0	2.72	23.4	43.8	24.2	7 373	54.2	5 436	49.6	1 466	68.1	2 667	4.3
Las Cruces city	2 399	1 147	29 184	22.6	2.46	27.9	33.8	23.4	18 130	49.0	12 355	42.4	4 409	65.5	11 054	35.8
Rio Rancho city	418	257	18 995	62.9	2.70	20.8	43.0	21.7	14 112	54.2	11 283	52.0	1 962	63.1	4 883	101.3
Roswell city	1 192	554	17 068	5.4	2.58	27.1	38.5	30.5	11 747	50.1	8 380	44.3	2 535	65.2	5 321	17.5
Santa Fe city.............	1 474	415	27 569	21.0	2.20	36.4	26.8	23.1	14 982	44.4	10 373	38.8	3 334	57.9	12 587	42.2
NEW YORK.............	580 461	262 262	7 056 860	6.3	2.61	28.1	35.0	25.0	4 639 387	48.1	3 289 514	46.4	1 038 176	55.2	2 417 473	12.4
Albany city	9 902	2 046	40 709	–3.4	2.11	41.9	24.3	21.7	18 397	48.7	10 301	38.5	6 558	65.3	22 312	2.3
Auburn city	2 620	2 200	11 411	–4.4	2.27	36.3	30.3	30.2	6 536	49.1	4 255	42.2	1 682	64.9	4 875	9.0
Binghamton city	1 244	911	21 089	–6.8	2.19	40.3	25.5	28.6	10 419	47.2	6 666	40.0	2 920	62.9	10 670	3.5
Buffalo city	11 126	5 203	122 720	–10.1	2.29	37.7	32.1	23.7	67 053	52.3	33 888	43.4	27 387	64.6	55 667	–4.3
Elmira city	3 732	2 514	11 475	–7.7	2.37	34.5	34.3	26.4	6 701	53.2	4 052	43.8	2 106	69.8	4 774	3.1
Freeport village	637	375	13 504	2.0	3.20	21.2	43.5	24.5	9 917	49.6	6 713	50.3	2 399	50.5	3 587	–.1
Hempstead village	4 741	1 001	15 188	4.1	3.41	20.8	48.1	20.5	11 175	52.6	5 926	52.8	4 100	55.0	4 013	–5.0
Ithaca city	7 417	180	10 287	7.0	2.13	43.3	15.3	13.2	2 958	49.3	1 951	49.6	803	65.3	7 329	15.4
Jamestown city	735	341	13 558	–5.0	2.29	35.0	31.8	26.8	7 901	50.5	5 301	41.3	1 971	71.7	5 657	5.9
Lindenhurst village	125	–	9 061	5.4	3.06	17.0	43.5	25.1	7 081	50.6	5 619	53.3	1 070	41.5	1 980	29.7
Long Beach city	1 714	900	14 923	9.8	2.26	36.7	24.1	24.6	8 106	39.8	5 964	38.7	1 610	45.7	6 817	19.8
Mount Vernon city	748	539	25 729	2.2	2.63	30.0	36.6	25.5	16 669	48.0	9 487	45.5	5 910	53.6	9 060	8.3
Newburgh city	1 105	193	9 144	1.5	2.97	27.1	46.4	21.9	6 078	60.2	3 122	55.8	2 324	67.8	3 066	2.4
New Rochelle city.........	2 116	1 108	26 189	3.4	2.68	28.0	35.7	28.9	17 541	48.8	13 235	50.1	3 277	47.7	8 648	3.9
New York city	182 430	75 870	3 021 588	7.2	2.59	31.9	34.0	23.6	1 853 223	48.4	1 124 305	47.4	576 354	54.2	1 168 365	7.7
Bronx borough	47 235	27 904	463 212	9.2	2.78	27.4	43.8	21.6	315 090	56.0	145 537	51.7	140 620	63.2	148 122	9.3
Brooklyn borough	39 299	15 582	880 727	6.3	2.75	27.8	38.2	24.4	584 120	50.1	339 957	49.5	195 988	55.0	296 607	8.7
Manhattan borough	59 837	12 422	738 644	3.1	2.00	48.0	19.7	20.4	301 970	41.8	186 023	38.2	92 994	51.4	436 674	5.1
Queens borough	26 873	14 928	782 664	8.7	2.81	25.6	35.9	26.8	537 991	45.8	366 876	47.8	125 089	45.5	244 673	6.7
Staten Island borough	9 186	5 034	156 341	19.8	2.78	23.2	38.5	23.5	114 052	49.1	85 912	49.6	21 663	51.5	42 289	34.4
Niagara Falls city	806	505	24 099	–7.2	2.27	35.9	30.8	31.2	14 258	47.0	8 717	39.5	4 422	61.9	9 841	2.1
North Tonawanda city	99	79	13 671	.3	2.43	29.5	31.9	28.3	8 987	46.0	6 949	43.2	1 519	56.5	4 684	16.9
Poughkeepsie city	985	559	12 014	1.2	2.40	35.4	32.4	25.1	6 557	51.9	3 581	42.4	2 372	67.2	5 457	9.0
Rochester city	9 422	3 991	88 999	–4.9	2.36	37.1	33.9	17.8	47 165	56.7	22 298	45.0	20 713	70.4	41 834	.4
Rome city...............	3 498	3 152	13 653	–13.3	2.30	33.2	30.3	30.2	8 332	46.1	5 820	38.1	1 901	66.0	5 321	7.3
Saratoga Springs city.......	2 300	442	10 784	11.3	2.21	35.0	26.9	24.0	5 982	45.6	4 652	42.0	1 035	59.1	4 802	20.0
Schenectady city	3 265	1 128	26 265	–5.3	2.23	38.6	29.8	26.2	14 054	50.9	8 398	41.9	4 384	66.5	12 211	3.0
Syracuse city	10 989	2 267	59 482	–8.4	2.29	38.2	30.5	22.6	30 351	53.8	16 349	43.3	11 455	69.2	29 131	–3.5
Troy city................	3 988	846	19 996	–3.7	2.26	36.6	29.3	24.2	10 729	50.4	6 520	41.6	3 256	66.7	9 267	4.9
Utica city...............	3 404	1 714	25 100	–11.5	2.28	37.4	29.5	30.8	14 224	47.6	8 923	40.4	4 235	63.1	10 876	–6.4
Valley Stream village	55	–	12 484	5.3	2.91	20.2	37.2	34.6	9 599	44.0	7 681	46.4	1 436	36.1	2 885	18.4
Watertown city	1 097	741	11 036	–3.4	2.32	34.5	33.9	25.0	6 503	54.1	4 487	47.4	1 566	71.0	4 533	12.6
White Plains city	1 414	651	20 921	7.7	2.47	33.4	29.6	26.9	12 704	44.3	9 566	45.0	2 356	45.1	8 217	7.9
Yonkers city.............	2 320	869	74 351	3.1	2.61	29.2	34.0	29.0	49 290	46.7	32 885	44.1	12 775	56.4	25 061	9.2
NORTH CAROLINA......	253 881	106 659	3 132 013	24.4	2.49	25.4	35.3	21.8	2 158 869	46.1	1 645 346	43.0	389 997	58.3	973 144	38.0
Asheville city	3 211	1 363	30 690	13.6	2.14	36.8	25.0	29.1	16 737	40.7	11 692	34.6	3 989	57.0	13 953	29.1
Burlington city	1 111	749	18 280	9.9	2.40	30.3	32.5	27.8	11 750	45.1	8 248	40.7	2 721	58.9	6 530	20.7
Cary town...............	569	497	34 906	106.4	2.69	21.0	42.9	9.7	25 146	57.9	22 079	57.2	2 208	67.4	9 760	109.0
Chapel Hill town	9 247	345	17 808	29.2	2.22	31.2	23.4	15.1	8 139	49.1	6 453	46.0	1 339	66.4	9 669	37.9
Charlotte city	12 228	5 081	215 449	35.5	2.45	29.5	34.0	15.7	132 378	49.9	93 970	47.1	29 483	60.9	83 071	48.1
Concord city	1 346	756	20 962	94.0	2.61	23.6	38.5	19.8	14 979	49.2	11 680	47.1	2 403	58.8	5 983	78.3
Durham city	9 373	2 341	74 981	33.9	2.37	31.9	32.3	16.5	43 558	49.3	28 625	44.9	11 954	62.3	31 423	35.3
Fayetteville city	3 962	1 481	48 414	63.3	2.42	28.2	36.1	19.5	31 682	48.6	21 658	42.9	8 261	62.3	16 732	81.7
Gastonia city	1 479	1 176	25 945	23.6	2.50	26.5	35.3	23.9	17 709	44.9	12 278	41.1	4 220	55.9	8 236	39.6
Goldsboro city	3 901	2 704	14 630	9.0	2.40	30.5	36.4	25.4	9 466	49.6	6 009	43.1	2 988	62.2	5 164	29.1
Greensboro city	11 307	1 902	92 394	23.3	2.30	32.6	30.5	19.9	53 930	47.1	36 802	42.6	13 510	60.5	38 464	33.6
Greenville city	5 590	413	25 204	48.1	2.18	35.4	25.6	14.3	12 003	48.3	7 761	42.4	3 479	63.0	13 201	66.0
Hickory city	1 164	400	15 372	30.3	2.35	32.2	31.0	23.2	9 369	45.7	6 851	42.5	1 885	57.7	6 003	35.3
High Point city	2 303	949	33 519	21.8	2.49	27.2	36.8	21.8	22 523	49.0	15 730	44.9	5 463	62.1	10 996	27.4
Jacksonville city	18 053	383	17 175	57.3	2.83	16.6	51.9	12.5	13 536	62.8	10 961	60.7	2 117	72.5	3 639	50.2

[1] As of April 1. [2] Includes people under formally authorized, supervised care or custody in institutions at the time of enumeration (such as correctional institutions, nursing homes, and juvenile institutions). [3] Under 18 years. [4] No husband present.

Sources: Group Quarters Population—U.S. Census Bureau; 2000 Census of Population and Housing, "Census 2000 Profiles of General Demographic Characteristics" data files, published May 2001 (related Internet site <http://www.census.gov/mp/www/pub/2000cen/mscen01.html>). Households, 2000—U.S. Census Bureau; 2000 Census of Population and Housing, "Census 2000 Profiles of General Demographic Characteristics" data files, published May 2001 (related Internet site <http://www.census.gov/mp/www/pub/2000cen/mscen01.html>). Households, 1990—U.S. Census Bureau, 1990 Census of Population and Housing, Summary Tape File (STF) 1C on CD-ROM (related Internet site <http://homer.ssd.census.gov/cdrom/lookup>).

Table C–3. Cities — Group Quarters Population and Households–Con.

[Includes states and 1,070 incorporated places of 25,000 or more population as of April 1, 1990 in all states except Hawaii which has no incorporated places recognized by the Census Bureau. For Hawaii, 8 census designated places (CDPs) of 25,000 or more population as of April 1, 1990 are included. Also included are the 5 boroughs of New York city. For more information on these areas, see appendix B. Geographic Information]

City	Group quarters population, 2000[1] Number	Institutionalized population[2]	Households, 2000 (April 1) Number	Percent change, 1990–2000	Persons per household	Percent— One-person	Percent— With 1 or more persons under 18 years	Percent— With 1 or more persons 65 years and over	Family households (families) Number	Percent with own children under 18 years	Married-couple Number	Married-couple Percent with own children[3]	Female householder[4] Number	Female householder Percent with own children[3]	Nonfamily households Number	Percent change, 1990–2000
NORTH CAROLINA—Con.																
Kannapolis city	502	486	14 804	23.2	2.46	26.5	34.2	27.3	10 147	43.8	7 466	40.5	2 001	55.7	4 657	31.5
Kinston city	1 167	884	9 829	-1.6	2.29	34.5	32.7	33.1	6 073	45.3	3 506	35.7	2 230	61.2	3 756	10.1
Raleigh city	17 316	4 935	112 608	31.2	2.30	33.1	28.8	14.4	61 327	48.6	44 468	45.3	12 868	62.7	51 281	36.5
Rocky Mount city	1 164	420	21 435	13.6	2.55	27.4	38.0	24.4	14 682	48.0	9 288	43.1	4 483	58.5	6 753	19.6
Wilmington city	3 589	725	34 359	45.9	2.10	36.6	23.1	24.2	17 360	40.4	11 494	32.3	4 824	59.7	16 999	76.1
Wilson city	1 645	992	17 296	19.6	2.47	29.4	36.4	23.8	11 324	48.3	7 267	43.6	3 332	60.0	5 972	25.1
Winston-Salem city	9 114	3 145	76 247	27.3	2.32	33.4	31.6	23.5	46 206	46.2	30 615	40.2	12 679	60.8	30 041	27.0
NORTH DAKOTA	23 631	9 688	257 152	6.8	2.41	29.3	32.7	24.7	166 150	48.4	137 433	45.1	20 148	67.7	91 002	22.0
Bismarck city	1 728	1 334	23 185	20.0	2.32	31.0	31.3	22.5	14 435	48.5	11 605	44.7	2 146	66.6	8 750	37.9
Fargo city	4 015	817	39 268	30.2	2.20	34.6	27.4	16.0	20 724	50.1	16 407	46.8	3 078	68.1	18 544	44.6
Grand Forks city	3 817	566	19 677	6.2	2.31	31.4	29.9	17.0	11 054	51.1	8 504	46.2	1 960	71.6	8 623	19.4
Minot city	1 310	518	15 520	11.1	2.27	32.5	30.0	24.5	9 265	48.0	7 239	43.0	1 552	68.2	6 255	24.2
OHIO	299 121	172 368	4 445 773	8.8	2.49	27.3	34.5	23.8	2 993 023	47.1	2 285 798	43.6	536 878	60.2	1 452 750	21.8
Akron city	4 908	2 259	90 116	.2	2.35	33.1	32.0	24.2	53 716	47.8	33 812	41.0	15 949	61.7	36 400	9.1
Barberton city	394	319	11 523	4.0	2.39	30.1	32.8	30.0	7 449	45.6	5 178	40.2	1 774	60.1	4 074	16.7
Beavercreek city	555	453	14 071	20.3	2.66	17.5	36.9	20.6	11 094	44.7	9 949	43.5	817	58.1	2 977	53.9
Bowling Green city	6 951	356	10 266	20.7	2.21	34.3	21.3	14.3	4 438	46.8	3 407	41.6	765	68.6	5 828	27.6
Brunswick city	255	185	11 883	31.6	2.79	17.7	42.1	16.2	9 277	50.4	7 758	49.2	1 100	58.5	2 606	89.7
Canton city	3 042	1 555	32 489	-2.9	2.39	33.0	34.0	25.3	19 772	49.3	12 050	41.5	6 199	63.5	12 717	6.5
Cincinnati city	13 436	6 502	148 095	-4.0	2.15	42.8	28.3	20.5	72 496	51.4	39 414	40.8	27 480	66.7	75 599	5.5
Cleveland city	13 434	6 962	190 638	-4.6	2.44	35.2	35.0	24.0	111 998	51.0	54 244	42.7	47 295	61.6	78 640	2.3
Cleveland Heights city	261	157	20 913	-.5	2.38	32.6	30.2	20.7	12 174	46.1	8 622	43.7	2 954	54.5	8 739	11.9
Columbus city	17 659	5 412	301 534	17.3	2.30	34.1	30.9	15.4	165 380	51.1	108 708	45.8	43 780	64.1	136 154	27.8
Cuyahoga Falls city	399	316	21 655	6.2	2.26	32.6	28.7	26.4	13 307	44.0	10 467	40.8	2 187	56.8	8 348	22.2
Dayton city	10 829	3 336	67 409	-7.2	2.30	36.8	31.8	22.8	37 615	48.9	20 339	40.7	13 895	60.2	29 794	2.6
East Cleveland city	449	339	11 210	-16.1	2.39	38.0	35.2	24.7	6 419	49.8	2 380	34.7	3 398	61.4	4 791	-6.9
Elyria city	934	864	22 409	4.6	2.46	28.5	35.6	23.6	14 827	48.3	10 398	42.5	3 394	64.2	7 582	24.7
Euclid city	626	507	24 353	-2.2	2.14	39.7	27.2	30.9	13 484	45.0	8 831	40.6	3 711	56.3	10 869	5.7
Fairborn city	1 031	87	13 615	7.4	2.28	31.0	28.8	20.0	8 018	45.3	5 831	39.3	1 689	63.4	5 597	26.3
Fairfield city	654	411	16 960	10.9	2.44	26.6	34.8	17.8	11 361	48.4	9 113	44.9	1 646	65.2	5 599	29.3
Findlay city	1 505	636	15 905	12.7	2.36	30.2	31.5	22.7	10 006	46.5	7 848	41.3	1 582	66.3	5 899	30.0
Gahanna city	221	211	11 990	26.8	2.70	20.9	42.4	16.8	8 930	54.3	7 480	53.3	1 098	60.9	3 060	62.3
Garfield Heights city	421	268	12 452	-.2	2.43	30.0	32.1	32.6	8 212	43.8	5 794	42.3	1 902	48.8	4 240	17.6
Hamilton city	1 340	1 014	24 188	.8	2.45	29.3	35.4	25.9	15 862	48.0	11 003	42.7	3 710	61.1	8 326	15.5
Huber Heights city	199	91	14 392	6.5	2.64	20.5	40.0	17.8	10 773	49.4	8 441	45.9	1 728	62.5	3 619	39.6
Kent city	5 725	92	9 772	10.9	2.27	32.4	27.2	15.9	4 801	52.5	3 205	44.1	1 295	72.7	4 971	24.6
Kettering city	435	341	25 657	-1.7	2.22	33.4	28.5	28.7	15 715	44.0	12 506	39.8	2 446	61.4	9 942	11.4
Lakewood city	772	411	26 693	-1.1	2.09	43.6	24.5	19.6	12 556	49.0	9 084	46.6	2 594	59.3	14 137	9.4
Lancaster city	450	415	14 852	6.2	2.35	30.3	32.9	27.6	9 568	47.3	7 107	42.2	1 922	62.5	5 284	21.3
Lima city	2 741	2 177	15 410	-5.5	2.42	32.1	35.8	25.2	9 567	51.3	5 748	41.7	3 039	68.4	5 843	10.9
Lorain city	723	529	26 434	.9	2.57	27.4	37.4	26.0	17 981	48.9	11 533	41.0	5 083	65.4	8 453	16.0
Mansfield city	3 346	2 871	20 182	-.1	2.28	34.8	30.9	27.6	12 035	45.8	8 174	38.1	3 062	63.9	8 147	11.4
Maple Heights city	224	189	10 489	-.6	2.47	29.9	34.6	29.5	6 969	46.4	4 743	44.1	1 781	52.4	3 520	20.6
Marion city	2 204	2 112	13 551	2.8	2.44	29.3	35.3	25.1	8 826	48.6	6 269	42.8	1 909	62.3	4 725	17.3
Massillon city	853	697	12 677	4.7	2.40	29.6	33.0	28.7	8 324	45.4	6 056	40.6	1 750	58.8	4 353	16.4
Mentor city	476	324	18 797	12.4	2.65	20.5	37.6	22.7	14 235	47.3	11 957	46.7	1 678	51.3	4 562	34.8
Middletown city	578	488	21 469	16.9	2.38	29.6	33.4	25.9	13 930	46.2	9 851	40.5	3 132	61.3	7 539	37.3
Newark city	926	808	19 312	8.5	2.35	31.5	33.5	25.2	12 103	49.2	8 787	43.0	2 589	66.7	7 209	19.9
North Olmsted city	316	272	13 517	6.8	2.50	26.5	31.5	26.3	9 361	42.7	7 763	42.3	1 168	45.7	4 156	29.5
Parma city	1 224	1 145	35 126	1.3	2.40	29.2	29.4	32.8	23 333	41.6	18 498	41.0	3 594	45.2	11 793	23.8
Reynoldsburg city	103	91	12 844	28.7	2.49	25.8	37.2	18.5	8 807	50.7	6 782	46.8	1 578	64.5	4 042	40.9
Sandusky city	473	322	11 851	-1.7	2.31	34.9	32.4	25.8	7 036	48.7	4 585	40.7	1 942	65.2	4 815	9.8
Shaker Heights city	198	133	12 220	-3.4	2.39	30.2	34.4	27.2	8 037	48.9	6 123	46.8	1 580	56.6	4 183	5.0
Springfield city	2 820	1 304	26 254	-3.6	2.38	32.2	33.6	26.7	16 212	48.5	10 637	41.3	4 364	63.1	10 042	7.9
Stow city	540	463	12 317	22.1	2.57	23.7	36.8	20.2	8 747	48.8	7 364	48.4	1 037	58.5	3 570	51.3
Strongsville city	329	258	16 209	32.0	2.69	19.9	37.4	21.0	12 389	46.9	10 947	46.6	1 040	51.8	3 820	61.7
Toledo city	6 895	2 636	128 925	-1.5	2.38	32.8	33.1	23.3	77 378	49.6	49 255	42.6	22 138	64.1	51 547	10.8
Upper Arlington city	314	314	13 985	.2	2.39	28.2	32.5	30.4	9 512	46.9	8 266	45.4	962	57.9	4 473	12.8
Warren city	1 161	1 039	19 288	-5.1	2.37	32.9	33.2	29.2	12 035	47.3	7 411	38.5	3 746	63.7	7 253	8.5
Westerville city	1 558	575	12 663	24.4	2.67	20.9	40.8	18.6	9 550	52.1	8 211	50.2	1 054	65.9	3 113	45.5
Westlake city	1 266	1 091	12 826	25.0	2.37	32.0	29.3	27.2	8 195	44.6	7 171	44.1	739	50.2	4 631	49.2
Youngstown city	4 994	3 498	32 171	-13.1	2.39	34.0	32.3	32.3	19 729	44.3	10 691	35.7	7 363	57.8	12 448	1.8
Zanesville city	663	519	10 572	-2.3	2.36	33.4	34.0	27.1	6 438	50.4	4 068	41.7	1 905	66.9	4 134	6.3

[1] As of April 1. [2] Includes people under formally authorized, supervised care or custody in institutions at the time of enumeration (such as correctional institutions, nursing homes, and juvenile institutions). [3] Under 18 years. [4] No husband present.

Sources: Group Quarters Population—U.S. Census Bureau; 2000 Census of Population and Housing, "Census 2000 Profiles of General Demographic Characteristics" data files, published May 2001 (related Internet site <http://www.census.gov/mp/www/pub/2000cen/mscen01.html>). Households, 2000—U.S. Census Bureau; 2000 Census of Population and Housing, "Census 2000 Profiles of General Demographic Characteristics" data files, published May 2001 (related Internet site <http://www.census.gov/mp/www/pub/2000cen/mscen01.html>). Households, 1990—U.S. Census Bureau, 1990 Census of Population and Housing, Summary Tape File (STF) 1C on CD-ROM (related Internet site <http://homer.ssd.census.gov/cdrom/lookup>).

Table C-3. Cities — **Group Quarters Population and Households**–Con.

[Includes states and 1,070 incorporated places of 25,000 or more population as of April 1, 1990 in all states except Hawaii which has no incorporated places recognized by the Census Bureau. For Hawaii, 8 census designated places (CDPs) of 25,000 or more population as of April 1, 1990 are included. Also included are the 5 boroughs of New York city. For more information on these areas, see appendix B. Geographic Information]

City	Group quarters population, 2000[1] Number	Institutionalized population[2]	Households, 2000 (April 1) Number	Percent change, 1990–2000	Persons per household	Percent— One-person	Percent— With 1 or more persons under 18 years	Percent— With 1 or more persons 65 years and over	Family households (families) Number	Family households Percent with own children under 18 years	Married-couple Number	Married-couple Percent with own children[3]	Female householder[4] Number	Female householder Percent with own children[3]	Nonfamily households Number	Nonfamily households Percent change, 1990–2000
OKLAHOMA	112 375	66 746	1 342 293	11.3	2.49	26.7	35.7	23.8	921 750	47.2	717 611	43.4	152 575	61.9	420 543	19.9
Bartlesville city	552	285	14 565	3.9	2.35	29.5	32.2	30.9	9 830	44.7	7 996	40.2	1 411	65.2	4 735	16.3
Broken Arrow city	517	476	26 159	35.8	2.84	15.7	47.7	14.2	21 167	56.2	17 801	54.2	2 547	68.6	4 992	61.2
Edmond city	1 869	460	25 256	34.7	2.63	20.6	40.9	15.6	18 597	53.4	15 634	51.1	2 300	68.8	6 659	49.4
Enid city	1 725	1 221	18 955	4.1	2.39	29.1	33.6	27.0	12 565	46.6	9 779	41.7	2 120	64.0	6 390	9.7
Lawton city	9 784	3 082	31 778	7.5	2.61	24.6	43.3	18.9	22 521	55.9	16 434	51.9	4 851	68.5	9 257	22.6
Midwest City city	478	436	22 161	8.7	2.42	28.6	35.5	22.8	14 761	47.7	10 233	41.0	3 661	64.1	7 400	24.3
Moore city	263	190	14 848	9.4	2.75	18.2	45.5	14.7	11 565	53.7	8 973	50.5	1 968	66.0	3 283	42.1
Muskogee city	1 274	922	15 523	2.9	2.39	31.8	33.3	29.9	9 951	45.7	7 009	40.7	2 386	58.8	5 572	11.0
Norman city	6 071	1 123	38 834	21.7	2.31	30.3	29.7	15.3	22 560	47.7	17 507	45.0	3 703	60.5	16 274	26.9
Oklahoma City city	13 133	8 455	204 434	14.4	2.41	30.7	34.1	20.3	129 360	48.7	93 647	44.1	27 006	63.3	75 074	20.4
Ponca City city	587	392	10 636	-.9	2.38	30.0	33.9	28.9	7 025	47.1	5 457	41.9	1 185	67.3	3 611	6.6
Shawnee city	1 753	379	11 311	9.4	2.38	30.4	33.4	27.7	7 306	46.1	5 230	40.5	1 628	61.2	4 005	11.7
Stillwater city	5 902	288	15 604	10.1	2.13	34.6	22.1	14.4	7 317	44.5	5 630	41.2	1 197	61.9	8 287	17.0
Tulsa city	10 433	4 722	165 743	6.6	2.31	33.9	31.4	21.5	99 094	47.7	71 441	42.5	21 319	63.8	66 649	13.5
OREGON	77 491	37 901	1 333 723	20.9	2.51	26.1	33.4	22.9	877 671	46.8	692 532	42.8	130 782	63.6	456 052	29.4
Albany city	687	492	16 108	36.7	2.49	26.1	35.9	22.9	10 809	49.6	8 233	43.9	1 877	67.9	5 299	34.7
Beaverton city	917	287	30 821	39.5	2.44	29.7	34.0	15.3	18 656	53.4	14 433	51.1	3 005	64.5	12 165	47.3
Corvallis city	4 887	322	19 630	17.2	2.26	31.5	25.1	16.9	9 969	47.2	8 002	44.0	1 421	64.8	9 661	24.7
Eugene city	6 086	1 672	58 110	25.6	2.27	31.7	27.5	19.8	31 297	48.0	23 565	42.4	5 665	67.0	26 813	34.0
Gresham city	1 128	714	33 327	29.7	2.67	24.3	39.1	18.3	22 683	53.1	16 978	49.6	4 007	65.8	10 644	39.5
Hillsboro city	950	796	25 079	95.2	2.76	23.4	40.6	12.7	17 083	55.7	13 723	53.6	2 259	69.1	7 996	151.1
Lake Oswego city	163	76	14 769	18.3	2.38	27.9	32.9	19.4	9 665	48.9	8 295	47.2	1 023	62.1	5 104	29.4
Medford city	1 285	670	25 093	33.0	2.47	27.7	34.1	28.3	16 518	48.1	12 612	42.1	2 945	68.6	8 575	37.7
Portland city	14 992	5 454	223 737	19.5	2.30	34.6	27.0	19.7	118 447	46.2	85 277	42.4	24 102	58.5	105 290	26.4
Salem city	8 884	6 360	50 676	23.8	2.53	28.3	34.9	22.8	32 336	50.7	24 197	46.2	5 873	67.0	18 340	22.4
Springfield city	635	93	20 514	17.6	2.55	25.4	38.4	18.2	13 479	53.8	9 373	47.6	2 942	69.7	7 035	20.2
Tigard city	221	107	16 507	36.9	2.48	26.7	35.4	17.8	10 739	51.5	8 590	48.5	1 525	68.1	5 768	43.9
PENNSYLVANIA	433 301	213 790	4 777 003	6.3	2.48	27.7	32.6	27.8	3 208 388	44.6	2 467 673	42.3	554 693	53.7	1 568 615	17.1
Allentown city	4 996	2 260	42 032	-1.7	2.42	33.1	32.0	27.3	25 127	48.3	16 565	41.3	6 350	63.8	16 905	3.8
Altoona city	1 930	439	20 059	-3.0	2.37	31.6	31.3	30.0	12 583	45.3	8 937	41.1	2 763	55.3	7 476	10.0
Bethel Park borough	382	271	13 362	5.3	2.48	26.1	31.5	30.9	9 539	42.4	8 286	42.6	963	42.8	3 823	33.8
Bethlehem city	5 652	1 275	28 116	3.1	2.34	32.3	28.7	30.9	17 090	43.3	12 410	38.1	3 590	59.3	11 026	19.4
Chester city	2 977	1 364	12 814	-11.9	2.64	31.2	40.0	25.4	8 126	51.5	3 181	42.3	4 113	59.5	4 688	-1.8
Easton city	2 760	927	9 544	1.6	2.46	31.6	34.0	22.9	5 738	50.7	3 599	46.5	1 581	60.7	3 806	12.6
Erie city	5 854	2 356	40 938	-2.8	2.39	33.4	32.4	27.3	24 493	48.8	15 641	42.4	6 893	62.6	16 445	7.4
Harrisburg city	1 252	565	20 561	-4.5	2.32	39.3	33.6	20.0	10 912	53.7	4 817	41.3	5 022	65.4	9 649	-.4
Johnstown city	440	92	11 134	-11.2	2.11	41.5	25.0	35.7	6 049	41.3	3 795	34.2	1 748	54.9	5 085	1.2
Lancaster city	3 690	1 666	20 933	-1.2	2.52	33.1	35.8	20.4	12 156	54.4	6 991	46.2	3 980	68.0	8 777	1.4
McKeesport city	1 325	794	9 655	-8.4	2.35	33.9	32.1	33.2	5 973	46.2	3 349	37.2	2 119	60.3	3 682	-2.8
Municipality of Monroeville borough	940	474	12 376	4.6	2.30	30.8	27.5	30.2	8 044	39.7	6 518	38.1	1 201	49.3	4 332	23.4
New Castle city	999	725	10 727	-5.7	2.36	33.5	30.2	35.5	6 722	43.1	4 419	37.6	1 818	55.6	4 005	5.1
Norristown borough	995	848	12 028	-1.3	2.52	32.7	33.5	22.0	7 148	48.3	4 053	43.8	2 378	58.5	4 880	-2.7
Philadelphia city	54 731	20 411	590 071	-2.2	2.48	33.8	33.1	27.0	352 331	46.2	189 291	42.2	131 332	53.1	237 740	5.6
Pittsburgh city	22 814	8 191	143 739	-6.3	2.17	39.4	24.8	28.2	74 104	42.5	44 776	36.6	23 683	54.6	69 635	5.5
Plum borough	233	44	10 270	13.3	2.60	21.5	35.8	23.9	7 691	45.6	6 530	45.0	869	50.7	2 579	49.5
Reading city	2 125	261	30 113	-4.1	2.63	31.7	38.1	25.1	18 423	55.0	10 349	47.5	6 084	66.7	11 690	-4.5
Scranton city	4 876	1 560	31 303	-4.1	2.29	36.7	26.5	35.2	18 112	42.2	12 460	39.7	4 323	50.1	13 191	8.1
State College borough	10 725	198	12 024	9.9	2.30	33.5	11.0	12.2	3 303	38.3	2 694	36.9	404	52.5	8 721	18.2
Wilkes-Barre city	3 674	2 212	17 961	-7.6	2.20	39.0	25.3	35.5	9 877	41.9	6 563	38.5	2 511	51.2	8 084	3.7
Williamsport city	2 597	514	12 219	-2.9	2.30	35.1	30.2	25.1	6 728	49.7	4 260	40.4	1 893	66.3	5 491	13.1
York city	887	167	16 137	-4.4	2.48	33.1	35.4	21.1	9 249	53.8	4 997	42.9	3 319	68.7	6 888	2.0
RHODE ISLAND	38 816	13 801	408 424	8.1	2.47	28.6	32.9	26.3	265 398	47.0	196 757	43.6	52 609	60.3	143 026	20.1
Cranston city	4 659	4 051	30 954	5.5	2.41	29.4	30.9	31.5	20 238	43.8	15 244	42.4	3 858	50.6	10 716	18.1
East Providence city	755	659	20 530	2.9	2.33	32.4	29.4	31.7	12 850	43.3	9 500	40.4	2 611	54.2	7 680	18.9
Newport city	2 082	245	11 566	3.3	2.11	39.4	24.6	21.6	5 646	46.8	3 734	38.5	1 578	66.9	5 920	20.1
Pawtucket city	657	422	30 047	1.1	2.41	32.3	33.2	26.6	18 520	49.6	11 923	43.5	5 040	64.3	11 527	9.3
Providence city	13 648	1 491	62 389	5.9	2.56	32.3	35.5	21.3	35 859	46.3	19 883	49.3	12 769	69.6	26 530	11.1
Warwick city	991	650	35 517	6.2	2.39	29.8	29.8	29.5	22 971	42.4	18 012	41.0	3 628	48.4	12 546	23.3
Woonsocket city	1 075	742	17 750	1.0	2.37	32.7	33.4	25.1	10 768	51.4	6 994	42.0	2 883	72.5	6 982	14.6

[1] As of April 1. [2] Includes people under formally authorized, supervised care or custody in institutions at the time of enumeration (such as correctional institutions, nursing homes, and juvenile institutions). [3] Under 18 years. [4] No husband present.

Sources: Group Quarters Population—U.S. Census Bureau; 2000 Census of Population and Housing, "Census 2000 Profiles of General Demographic Characteristics" data files, published May 2001 (related Internet site <http://www.census.gov/mp/www/pub/2000cen/mscen01.html>). Households, 2000—U.S. Census Bureau; 2000 Census of Population and Housing, "Census 2000 Profiles of General Demographic Characteristics" data files, published May 2001 (related Internet site <http://www.census.gov/mp/www/pub/2000cen/mscen01.html>). Households, 1990—U.S. Census Bureau, 1990 Census of Population and Housing, Summary Tape File (STF) 1C on CD-ROM (related Internet site <http://homer.ssd.census.gov/cdrom/lookup>).

Table C–3. Cities — **Group Quarters Population and Households**–Con.

[Includes states and 1,070 incorporated places of 25,000 or more population as of April 1, 1990 in all states except Hawaii which has no incorporated places recognized by the Census Bureau. For Hawaii, 8 census designated places (CDPs) of 25,000 or more population as of April 1, 1990 are included. Also included are the 5 boroughs of New York city. For more information on these areas, see appendix B. Geographic Information]

City	Group quarters population, 2000[1] Number	Institutionalized population[2]	Households, 2000 (April 1) Number	Percent change, 1990–2000	Persons per household	Percent— One-person	With 1 or more persons under 18 years	With 1 or more persons 65 years and over	Family households (families) Number	Percent with own children under 18 years	Married-couple Number	Percent with own children[3]	Female householder[4] Number	Percent with own children[3]	Nonfamily households Number	Percent change, 1990–2000
SOUTH CAROLINA	135 037	60 533	1 533 854	21.9	2.53	25.0	36.5	22.6	1 072 822	46.2	783 142	42.6	226 958	57.7	461 032	39.8
Anderson city	1 890	1 007	10 641	1.3	2.22	36.0	29.2	32.0	6 304	42.9	3 922	35.5	1 991	57.7	4 337	12.2
Charleston city	5 510	455	40 791	32.6	2.23	33.7	26.7	23.3	22 159	42.8	14 676	38.2	6 206	55.3	18 632	53.6
Columbia city	22 990	6 053	42 245	24.5	2.21	37.0	28.7	20.3	22 136	48.5	13 304	42.3	7 456	61.0	20 109	34.8
Florence city	1 155	779	11 925	7.7	2.44	29.5	35.0	25.5	7 878	45.6	4 994	42.3	2 470	53.4	4 047	14.1
Greenville city	4 495	1 121	24 382	1.2	2.11	40.8	25.4	24.6	12 573	43.2	7 984	37.5	3 776	56.6	11 809	16.5
Mount Pleasant town	665	569	19 025	61.4	2.47	24.1	35.4	16.8	12 852	50.2	10 831	48.9	1 583	59.6	6 173	68.2
North Charleston city	4 958	2 282	29 783	26.7	2.51	28.6	39.1	16.9	18 980	53.9	10 722	46.0	6 792	67.3	10 803	41.5
Rock Hill city	3 118	721	18 750	27.8	2.49	27.5	36.7	19.8	12 100	49.8	7 809	45.4	3 435	60.7	6 650	46.8
Spartanburg city	2 428	409	15 989	–4.3	2.33	34.0	33.5	27.1	9 717	47.6	5 436	38.1	3 683	61.9	6 272	5.9
Sumter city	2 221	322	14 564	14.3	2.57	27.3	39.9	25.7	10 052	51.5	6 698	49.2	2 806	58.0	4 512	45.4
SOUTH DAKOTA	28 418	14 387	290 245	12.0	2.50	27.6	34.8	25.0	194 330	49.0	157 391	45.2	26 205	67.3	95 915	21.8
Rapid City city	2 233	841	23 969	13.3	2.39	29.4	33.3	22.6	15 211	49.1	11 203	42.6	3 020	69.5	8 758	28.4
Sioux Falls city	4 802	2 746	49 731	25.0	2.40	29.8	33.7	19.1	30 801	51.8	24 064	47.7	4 965	69.7	18 930	34.2
TENNESSEE	147 946	83 397	2 232 905	20.5	2.48	25.8	35.2	22.5	1 547 835	45.7	1 173 960	42.5	287 899	57.6	685 070	35.5
Bartlett town	327	313	13 773	62.9	2.92	12.1	46.9	17.1	11 811	51.3	10 272	50.9	1 193	54.8	1 962	140.1
Chattanooga city	5 826	2 763	65 499	5.3	2.29	33.5	29.3	26.1	39 650	41.7	25 687	35.6	11 308	55.5	25 849	18.2
Clarksville city	4 080	897	36 969	45.3	2.69	21.1	44.5	14.2	26 965	56.6	20 834	53.5	4 832	69.1	10 004	67.5
Cleveland city	2 151	646	15 037	25.4	2.33	30.4	31.3	23.7	9 511	44.8	7 006	40.6	1 955	59.6	5 526	48.9
Columbia city	928	863	13 059	15.9	2.46	27.8	36.4	25.0	8 807	48.0	6 106	43.6	2 133	60.6	4 252	28.6
Germantown city	34	29	13 220	23.4	2.82	14.6	42.7	18.2	11 064	49.3	10 010	48.5	811	56.5	2 156	66.0
Hendersonville city	229	224	15 823	38.3	2.55	22.3	38.2	18.4	11 572	48.8	9 377	46.2	1 697	61.0	4 251	88.8
Jackson city	3 150	1 185	23 503	22.4	2.40	30.3	35.8	23.0	15 141	49.8	9 748	42.8	4 549	65.0	8 362	32.9
Johnson City city	3 373	1 176	23 720	20.6	2.20	33.9	27.2	25.4	14 013	42.3	10 465	38.2	2 747	57.2	9 707	37.2
Kingsport city	1 167	923	19 662	25.8	2.22	32.5	29.0	31.6	12 638	41.3	9 539	37.0	2 493	55.8	7 024	40.0
Knoxville city	11 034	2 738	76 650	9.5	2.12	38.3	25.6	23.2	40 193	43.6	27 039	37.7	10 527	58.3	36 457	24.0
Memphis city	17 226	11 067	250 721	9.1	2.52	30.5	36.9	21.1	158 458	49.6	85 458	43.4	59 665	59.8	92 263	21.3
Murfreesboro city	4 648	1 280	26 511	54.9	2.42	28.3	33.1	15.7	15 748	51.6	11 609	48.3	3 147	66.1	10 763	60.6
Nashville-Davidson (remainder)	24 084	10 232	227 403	14.5	2.29	33.8	29.9	19.1	131 100	46.0	88 978	41.3	33 112	58.9	96 303	30.4
Oak Ridge city	423	282	12 062	2.5	2.24	32.7	29.0	33.0	7 701	42.0	5 992	37.1	1 341	61.1	4 361	14.8
TEXAS	561 109	374 704	7 393 354	21.8	2.74	23.7	40.9	19.9	5 247 794	51.9	3 989 741	50.2	937 589	60.2	2 145 560	24.2
Abilene city	10 932	5 832	41 570	8.3	2.53	26.6	37.6	23.0	28 081	50.6	21 628	46.6	4 935	64.9	13 489	21.3
Amarillo city	2 309	1 625	67 699	10.7	2.53	27.7	37.5	22.7	45 768	50.2	34 269	46.4	8 651	63.1	21 931	16.0
Arlington city	2 448	954	124 686	23.9	2.65	24.7	41.0	11.6	85 000	55.7	64 371	53.5	14 744	67.8	39 686	23.2
Austin city	20 130	6 799	265 649	38.3	2.40	32.8	29.7	11.7	141 589	50.3	101 098	48.6	28 563	60.9	124 060	42.0
Baytown city	631	443	23 483	4.7	2.80	23.0	43.9	19.9	17 020	54.0	12 434	51.4	3 339	63.6	6 463	10.7
Beaumont city	3 069	2 045	44 361	2.3	2.50	29.5	36.3	25.0	29 113	48.5	19 291	43.8	8 030	60.4	15 248	10.3
Bedford city	533	519	20 251	15.2	2.30	31.6	31.0	13.7	12 517	46.9	10 092	43.5	1 792	63.0	7 734	35.4
Brownsville city	1 691	1 454	38 174	45.0	3.62	13.7	58.0	25.4	32 188	59.4	22 645	61.4	7 983	56.3	5 986	34.3
Bryan city	2 622	2 241	23 759	14.8	2.65	26.1	35.9	18.4	14 877	51.6	10 510	48.9	3 337	63.0	8 882	21.5
Carrollton city	589	375	39 136	28.5	2.78	20.1	43.8	10.3	28 932	55.9	23 517	55.3	3 864	64.1	10 204	31.7
College Station city	10 703	217	24 691	38.1	2.32	27.1	22.2	6.7	10 368	50.1	7 954	50.8	1 678	57.6	14 323	38.4
Conroe city	862	774	13 145	31.2	2.73	27.2	39.9	20.0	8 726	53.2	6 242	50.8	1 775	64.3	4 419	45.3
Corpus Christi city	5 332	2 536	98 791	10.4	2.75	23.2	41.4	22.3	70 465	50.6	50 253	48.1	15 214	58.1	28 326	18.9
Dallas city	21 164	15 899	451 833	12.4	2.58	32.9	34.9	16.4	266 789	51.3	175 252	50.1	67 435	58.9	185 044	11.2
Deer Park city	303	89	9 615	9.0	2.93	14.0	47.6	15.4	7 939	52.8	6 426	50.8	1 110	61.9	1 676	37.4
Del Rio city	528	433	10 778	13.9	3.09	18.7	49.0	26.7	8 513	53.2	6 391	52.3	1 700	57.4	2 265	19.7
Denton city	7 842	2 463	30 895	20.1	2.35	31.5	28.6	13.9	16 407	49.2	12 307	47.0	2 933	61.8	14 488	19.7
DeSoto city	434	423	13 709	27.5	2.71	20.6	43.4	16.9	10 464	51.8	8 060	48.7	1 936	64.5	3 245	52.2
Duncanville city	90	63	12 896	3.1	2.79	17.6	42.8	19.3	10 234	48.4	7 648	44.8	2 070	60.1	2 662	8.6
Edinburg city	1 779	1 525	14 183	67.4	3.29	15.4	53.2	20.7	11 412	58.8	8 073	59.3	2 695	59.2	2 771	68.4
El Paso city	5 129	3 248	182 063	13.4	3.07	19.2	48.6	24.2	141 071	54.7	99 400	54.4	33 608	57.6	40 992	21.3
Euless city	213	166	19 218	24.3	2.38	31.0	34.1	10.0	11 634	52.2	8 700	48.8	2 092	67.2	7 584	39.1
Fort Worth city	14 754	9 513	195 078	15.9	2.67	28.6	39.2	19.0	127 530	53.1	89 370	51.6	28 582	59.7	67 548	16.6
Galveston city	2 364	1 250	23 842	–1.3	2.30	35.6	30.3	24.8	13 744	45.6	8 730	40.4	4 019	57.2	10 098	4.2
Garland city	1 037	557	73 241	15.9	2.93	19.8	45.7	15.2	55 415	54.9	41 541	53.9	10 018	61.8	17 826	22.2
Grand Prairie city	420	377	43 791	25.3	2.90	20.7	45.9	13.6	32 333	56.0	24 048	54.2	6 009	63.8	11 458	30.8
Grapevine city	212	211	15 712	43.2	2.66	22.2	43.9	9.2	11 318	58.5	9 260	56.8	1 470	72.6	4 394	54.6
Haltom City city	126	126	14 922	17.0	2.61	27.1	37.9	20.1	9 998	50.3	7 378	48.4	1 791	57.0	4 924	24.7
Harlingen city	1 590	1 174	19 021	23.5	2.94	20.9	43.8	30.1	14 358	51.1	10 576	49.0	3 088	58.3	4 663	34.5
Houston city	33 256	18 819	717 945	16.4	2.67	29.6	37.8	17.0	457 549	52.0	310 066	51.4	109 723	57.6	260 396	13.6
Huntsville city	11 377	8 904	10 266	30.7	2.31	30.8	28.0	18.2	5 474	47.4	3 801	42.3	1 279	64.6	4 792	26.7
Hurst city	231	217	14 076	10.1	2.56	22.4	36.7	22.0	10 265	45.9	8 054	42.8	1 628	59.2	3 811	23.0
Irving city	1 073	468	76 241	20.6	2.50	31.3	34.4	11.3	46 168	51.6	33 613	49.5	8 527	63.3	30 073	23.2
Killeen city	310	255	32 447	39.6	2.67	22.3	45.3	9.5	22 984	59.4	17 504	54.7	4 347	76.6	9 463	61.9

[1] As of April 1. [2] Includes people under formally authorized, supervised care or custody in institutions at the time of enumeration (such as correctional institutions, nursing homes, and juvenile institutions). [3] Under 18 years. [4] No husband present.

Sources: Group Quarters Population—U.S. Census Bureau; 2000 Census of Population and Housing, "Census 2000 Profiles of General Demographic Characteristics" data files, published May 2001 (related Internet site <http://www.census.gov/mp/www/pub/2000cen/mscen01.html>).   Households, 2000—U.S. Census Bureau; 2000 Census of Population and Housing, "Census 2000 Profiles of General Demographic Characteristics" data files, published May 2001 (related Internet site <http://www.census.gov/mp/www/pub/2000cen/mscen01.html>).   Households, 1990—U.S. Census Bureau, 1990 Census of Population and Housing, Summary Tape File (STF) 1C on CD-ROM (related Internet site <http://homer.ssd.census.gov/cdrom/lookup>).

Table C–3. Cities — **Group Quarters Population and Households**–Con.

[Includes states and 1,070 incorporated places of 25,000 or more population as of April 1, 1990 in all states except Hawaii which has no incorporated places recognized by the Census Bureau. For Hawaii, 8 census designated places (CDPs) of 25,000 or more population as of April 1, 1990 are included. Also included are the 5 boroughs of New York city. For more information on these areas, see appendix B. Geographic Information]

City	Group quarters population, 2000[1]		Households, 2000 (April 1)												
						Percent—			By type—						
									Family households (families)						Nonfamily households
											Married-couple		Female householder[4]		
	Number	Institutionalized population[2]	Number	Percent change, 1990–2000	Persons per household	One-person	With 1 or more persons under 18 years	With 1 or more persons 65 years and over	Number	Percent with own children under 18 years	Number	Percent with own children[3]	Number	Percent with own children[3]	Number	Percent change, 1990–2000
TEXAS—Con.																
Kingsville city.............	1 180	279	8 943	4.9	2.73	23.5	39.1	21.5	6 136	50.2	4 390	47.7	1 333	60.2	2 807	14.7
La Porte city	235	38	10 928	19.5	2.90	17.4	47.5	13.9	8 575	55.1	6 862	53.5	1 242	61.5	2 353	38.0
Laredo city	3 044	1 929	46 852	46.3	3.70	12.7	59.9	21.6	39 983	61.3	29 054	64.8	8 747	54.7	6 869	45.4
League City city	390	357	16 189	52.9	2.78	18.4	45.0	11.2	12 471	55.4	10 586	53.5	1 331	67.2	3 718	61.9
Lewisville city	361	127	30 043	69.9	2.58	25.2	38.6	8.1	19 815	54.8	15 704	53.2	2 890	66.3	10 228	89.9
Longview city	2 496	1 601	28 363	4.3	2.50	27.9	37.0	24.2	19 109	49.2	13 880	44.9	4 119	62.9	9 254	11.6
Lubbock city	8 456	2 653	77 527	12.1	2.47	28.3	33.9	20.0	48 547	48.3	35 343	44.8	9 975	60.6	28 980	22.7
Lufkin city	1 122	824	12 247	9.1	2.58	27.9	37.6	26.9	8 361	48.2	6 051	45.1	1 806	58.4	3 886	15.3
McAllen city	986	811	33 151	33.1	3.18	17.9	48.9	23.2	26 092	54.9	19 568	55.4	5 314	56.1	7 059	43.3
Mesquite city	700	643	43 926	22.5	2.82	20.6	47.1	14.7	32 898	57.5	24 776	55.9	6 134	64.4	11 028	33.3
Midland city	1 422	1 042	35 674	7.6	2.62	25.8	41.3	22.6	25 209	53.7	19 746	50.8	4 252	65.1	10 465	12.6
Mission city	110	105	13 766	65.6	3.29	15.3	49.4	32.0	11 385	52.4	8 921	52.0	1 998	56.3	2 381	82.7
Missouri City city	141	14	17 069	47.9	3.09	11.9	52.0	12.3	14 645	56.6	11 987	56.5	2 135	58.3	2 424	63.3
Nacogdoches city	4 133	486	11 220	–.8	2.30	33.5	28.4	20.3	5 932	47.9	4 000	43.2	1 538	63.1	5 288	1.3
New Braunfels city	1 178	819	13 558	35.6	2.60	24.8	37.0	29.2	9 599	47.2	7 508	44.3	1 565	58.9	3 959	47.4
North Richland Hills city	269	202	20 793	23.0	2.66	20.4	40.9	16.5	15 416	51.3	12 445	49.4	2 141	61.6	5 377	35.5
Odessa city	1 837	1 563	33 661	2.5	2.65	25.7	42.2	22.7	23 707	53.9	17 369	49.9	4 894	65.7	9 954	11.3
Pasadena city	1 050	865	47 031	11.9	2.99	20.4	47.5	17.1	35 183	57.7	26 251	56.9	6 140	63.5	11 848	6.0
Pharr city	21	–	12 798	47.8	3.64	13.3	55.3	30.3	10 878	55.4	8 210	56.2	2 166	55.4	1 920	66.7
Plano city	1 124	531	80 875	82.3	2.73	20.2	43.7	9.7	60 578	56.1	52 029	55.4	6 069	64.6	20 297	133.5
Port Arthur city	734	497	21 839	–2.2	2.61	29.4	38.3	30.3	14 665	49.4	9 310	45.1	4 300	60.6	7 174	3.3
Richardson city	809	548	35 191	29.3	2.59	22.9	35.8	17.4	24 778	47.9	20 459	46.4	3 139	58.8	10 413	81.5
Round Rock city	550	438	21 076	99.4	2.87	18.1	50.1	8.4	15 931	62.9	12 752	61.2	2 328	72.9	5 145	113.2
San Angelo city	3 955	1 123	34 006	10.9	2.48	28.8	36.0	25.5	22 414	49.1	16 827	45.1	4 259	62.3	11 592	25.1
San Antonio city	23 180	11 682	405 474	24.1	2.77	25.1	40.9	21.1	280 828	51.9	194 872	50.1	66 438	58.0	124 646	29.6
San Marcos city	5 528	793	12 660	28.5	2.31	31.0	22.4	13.3	5 385	45.1	3 534	44.0	1 278	52.6	7 275	36.3
Sherman city	1 770	940	13 739	10.3	2.42	30.4	34.5	26.3	8 824	48.1	6 420	43.9	1 843	61.5	4 915	19.0
Temple city	1 994	1 578	21 543	18.7	2.44	29.9	35.5	26.0	14 110	49.0	10 424	44.3	2 932	65.1	7 433	24.7
Texarkana city...........	1 911	1 597	13 569	8.8	2.42	29.9	36.1	26.1	8 947	47.8	5 773	41.2	2 621	62.3	4 622	13.5
Texas City city...........	922	871	15 479	2.4	2.62	24.8	39.1	25.0	10 967	46.7	7 517	42.8	2 679	56.9	4 512	11.5
Tyler city...............	3 053	1 811	32 525	10.7	2.48	30.2	34.5	26.3	21 064	47.6	15 197	43.8	4 723	60.3	11 461	14.0
Victoria city.............	1 222	951	22 129	11.9	2.68	24.5	40.7	24.2	15 756	50.7	11 596	46.7	3 158	64.4	6 373	19.5
Waco city...............	8 443	3 430	42 279	7.1	2.49	31.1	33.6	23.9	24 794	50.3	16 241	45.2	6 861	62.8	17 485	12.0
Wichita Falls city...........	10 951	5 273	37 970	7.0	2.46	28.7	36.4	23.8	25 003	50.2	18 875	46.2	4 686	64.8	12 967	19.8
UTAH	40 480	19 467	701 281	30.5	3.13	17.8	45.8	18.6	535 294	56.0	442 931	55.5	65 941	61.2	165 987	31.3
Bountiful city	564	429	13 341	19.6	3.05	16.7	41.2	27.9	10 766	47.3	9 250	46.5	1 185	52.7	2 575	39.1
Layton city	99	6	18 282	43.6	3.19	15.2	51.8	12.8	14 769	60.5	12 323	59.6	1 773	67.7	3 513	58.0
Logan city	2 138	372	13 902	26.0	2.92	17.9	35.1	13.8	9 174	50.6	7 663	49.4	1 069	61.2	4 728	24.3
Murray city	90	84	12 673	8.2	2.68	24.6	36.9	21.7	8 720	49.6	6 749	48.0	1 431	56.3	3 953	9.0
Ogden city	2 356	1 011	27 384	13.0	2.73	26.2	38.9	22.5	18 405	52.4	13 261	49.9	3 586	62.2	8 979	9.6
Orem city	751	624	23 382	33.0	3.57	12.4	52.0	16.8	19 085	59.8	16 142	61.0	2 216	57.4	4 297	81.5
Provo city	7 572	879	29 192	22.6	3.34	11.8	36.4	13.8	19 948	49.4	16 628	50.5	2 289	49.8	9 244	26.2
St. George city	859	399	17 367	83.8	2.81	19.4	36.5	34.4	13 041	45.3	11 050	42.3	1 497	66.5	4 326	101.8
Salt Lake City city	4 573	1 134	71 461	7.2	2.48	33.2	29.6	20.4	39 830	48.5	29 360	47.2	7 298	57.2	31 631	7.9
Sandy city	524	322	25 737	32.5	3.42	11.6	54.2	12.0	21 786	60.6	18 767	60.4	2 201	64.2	3 951	101.4
West Jordan city	396	237	18 897	69.6	3.60	10.2	61.1	8.1	16 240	66.7	13 614	66.8	1 888	68.6	2 657	91.4
West Valley City city	495	200	32 253	24.4	3.36	14.7	52.4	13.5	25 932	58.6	19 775	58.3	4 243	62.4	6 321	30.2
VERMONT..............	20 760	5 663	240 634	14.2	2.44	26.2	33.6	22.5	157 763	48.4	126 413	44.2	22 272	66.4	82 871	26.0
Burlington city	4 022	485	15 885	8.2	2.19	35.6	22.7	16.9	7 055	48.0	4 990	41.3	1 592	67.7	8 830	14.5
VIRGINIA...............	231 398	111 484	2 699 173	17.8	2.54	25.1	35.9	20.9	1 847 796	47.7	1 426 044	45.3	320 290	58.3	851 377	28.5
Alexandria city.............	1 901	1 439	61 889	16.2	2.04	43.4	20.5	13.8	27 749	41.4	19 905	38.5	5 700	54.4	34 140	17.2
Blacksburg town	8 444	188	13 162	17.8	2.37	26.6	17.0	9.7	4 779	44.8	3 773	43.1	697	60.0	8 383	28.5
Charlottesville city	6 832	374	16 851	5.3	2.27	34.9	23.0	18.7	7 626	45.3	4 927	37.3	2 215	62.9	9 225	18.6
Chesapeake city	4 114	3 205	69 900	34.5	2.79	18.0	45.3	18.1	54 158	52.9	41 702	50.8	9 797	61.8	15 742	50.1
Danville city.............	1 679	1 078	20 607	–5.1	2.27	33.9	30.6	33.0	12 931	41.7	8 083	34.0	4 036	56.9	7 676	6.7
Hampton city	12 468	9 341	53 887	8.5	2.49	26.6	36.8	20.5	35 911	48.8	24 907	43.6	8 834	62.6	17 976	24.1
Harrisonburg city	7 194	898	13 133	27.4	2.53	28.3	25.3	18.1	6 442	47.5	4 778	43.4	1 217	61.8	6 691	44.4
Lynchburg city............	6 551	1 703	25 477	1.3	2.30	32.7	30.9	28.1	15 588	45.4	10 597	39.1	4 066	60.6	9 889	12.8
Manassas city	861	747	11 757	24.0	2.92	21.1	45.5	11.3	8 437	58.9	6 556	58.0	1 324	64.8	3 320	39.6
Newport News city	5 833	2 064	69 686	9.0	2.50	27.0	39.3	19.0	46 358	54.5	31 084	48.0	12 473	67.5	23 328	24.7
Norfolk city..............	23 289	3 000	86 210	–3.7	2.45	30.2	34.9	21.9	51 915	50.3	31 813	44.4	16 218	62.2	34 295	7.7
Petersburg city	906	589	13 799	–6.3	2.38	32.2	33.8	27.4	8 508	44.7	4 150	34.0	3 604	57.4	5 291	–1.9

[1] As of April 1.   [2] Includes people under formally authorized, supervised care or custody in institutions at the time of enumeration (such as correctional institutions, nursing homes, and juvenile institutions).   [3] Under 18 years.   [4] No husband present.

Sources: Group Quarters Population—U.S. Census Bureau; 2000 Census of Population and Housing, "Census 2000 Profiles of General Demographic Characteristics" data files, published May 2001 (related Internet site <http://www.census.gov/mp/www/pub/2000cen/mscen01.html>).   Households, 2000—U.S. Census Bureau; 2000 Census of Population and Housing, "Census 2000 Profiles of General Demographic Characteristics" data files, published May 2001 (related Internet site <http://www.census.gov/mp/www/pub/2000cen/mscen01.html>).   Households, 1990—U.S. Census Bureau, 1990 Census of Population and Housing, Summary Tape File (STF) 1C on CD-ROM (related Internet site <http://homer.ssd.census.gov/cdrom/lookup>).

Table C–3. Cities — **Group Quarters Population and Households**–Con.

[Includes states and 1,070 incorporated places of 25,000 or more population as of April 1, 1990 in all states except Hawaii which has no incorporated places recognized by the Census Bureau. For Hawaii, 8 census designated places (CDPs) of 25,000 or more population as of April 1, 1990 are included. Also included are the 5 boroughs of New York city. For more information on these areas, see appendix B. Geographic Information]

City	Group quarters population, 2000[1] Number	Group quarters population, 2000[1] Institutionalized population[2]	Households, 2000 (April 1) Number	Percent change, 1990–2000	Persons per household	Percent— One-person	Percent— With 1 or more persons under 18 years	Percent— With 1 or more persons 65 years and over	Family households (families) Number	Family households (families) Percent with own children under 18 years	Married-couple Number	Married-couple Percent with own children[3]	Female householder[4] Number	Female householder[4] Percent with own children[3]	Nonfamily households Number	Nonfamily households Percent change, 1990–2000
VIRGINIA—Con.																
Portsmouth city	4 814	1 798	38 170	-1.5	2.51	27.5	36.6	26.6	25 482	45.9	15 704	39.9	7 977	57.6	12 688	12.8
Richmond city	11 236	3 179	84 549	-.9	2.21	37.6	27.7	23.0	43 649	44.8	22 898	35.5	17 269	58.2	40 900	6.1
Roanoke city	2 538	1 698	42 003	2.4	2.20	35.9	29.1	26.6	24 255	44.1	15 574	37.3	6 939	58.5	17 748	15.0
Suffolk city	979	874	23 283	25.7	2.69	20.2	41.7	22.7	17 730	48.1	12 833	45.4	3 908	57.3	5 553	27.7
Virginia Beach city	7 683	2 794	154 455	13.9	2.70	20.4	42.1	16.4	110 953	54.0	85 982	51.4	19 135	64.9	43 502	30.4
WASHINGTON	136 382	57 218	2 271 398	21.3	2.53	26.2	35.2	20.4	1 499 127	49.5	1 181 995	45.8	224 618	65.4	772 271	27.1
Auburn city	593	218	16 108	20.6	2.47	29.1	35.8	19.9	10 055	52.6	7 044	46.6	2 151	68.4	6 053	26.2
Bellevue city	791	209	45 836	28.2	2.37	28.4	28.9	21.8	29 069	43.3	24 280	41.9	3 432	54.5	16 767	35.4
Bellingham city	4 593	1 071	27 999	32.1	2.24	33.0	24.5	20.6	13 990	46.2	10 512	40.5	2 567	67.3	14 009	44.1
Bremerton city	2 586	401	15 096	2.6	2.30	35.4	32.7	22.0	8 469	53.8	5 801	46.4	2 012	70.9	6 627	11.7
Edmonds city	352	174	16 904	33.9	2.32	29.0	27.9	27.1	10 815	40.7	8 798	37.9	1 474	54.1	6 089	55.3
Everett city	4 203	882	36 325	26.7	2.40	31.7	34.4	18.1	21 616	53.6	15 276	48.1	4 552	68.8	14 709	32.1
Kennewick city	594	490	20 786	29.3	2.60	26.1	40.3	19.2	14 177	55.1	10 700	49.8	2 537	72.6	6 609	31.7
Kent city	698	165	31 113	91.5	2.53	28.5	38.0	13.9	19 591	56.4	14 036	51.8	3 976	72.3	11 522	70.8
Kirkland city	848	279	20 736	20.5	2.13	35.6	24.6	15.2	11 035	43.8	8 704	40.1	1 685	59.5	9 701	35.2
Longview city	861	549	14 066	9.3	2.40	30.1	33.7	25.6	8 938	48.6	6 539	41.0	1 737	70.9	5 128	16.6
Lynnwood city	522	47	13 328	17.6	2.50	29.3	34.5	20.7	8 335	51.4	6 175	48.9	1 533	60.9	4 993	22.5
Olympia city	1 312	893	18 670	24.9	2.21	35.2	28.6	20.8	9 968	50.2	7 396	44.4	1 942	69.5	8 702	35.7
Redmond city	833	347	19 102	35.0	2.33	30.4	29.8	13.9	11 347	47.9	9 336	45.8	1 450	61.3	7 755	56.8
Renton city	401	312	21 708	19.2	2.29	34.0	29.1	17.4	12 234	47.5	8 881	42.7	2 340	64.4	9 474	24.9
Richland city	135	80	15 549	18.1	2.48	27.2	35.8	22.8	10 687	49.6	8 700	44.8	1 439	71.9	4 862	17.4
Seattle city	26 655	6 860	258 499	9.2	2.08	40.8	19.6	19.0	113 400	40.8	84 648	38.2	20 916	52.3	145 099	17.3
Spokane city	6 152	2 693	81 512	8.5	2.32	33.9	31.7	23.4	47 256	50.7	33 704	44.5	10 134	67.2	34 256	11.5
Tacoma city	6 731	3 033	76 152	8.9	2.45	31.7	34.3	21.5	45 924	51.2	31 699	45.8	10 580	65.1	30 228	12.4
Vancouver city	2 082	1 345	56 628	181.2	2.50	27.6	36.0	19.1	36 308	52.1	26 808	47.1	6 867	68.3	20 320	133.9
Walla Walla city	3 829	2 825	10 596	6.9	2.44	31.9	33.1	29.2	6 523	49.7	4 919	44.1	1 164	68.6	4 073	7.5
Yakima city	2 139	1 669	26 498	22.7	2.63	30.3	37.7	27.1	16 836	54.1	11 717	47.8	3 760	71.0	9 662	22.8
WEST VIRGINIA	43 147	24 009	736 481	7.0	2.40	27.1	31.8	27.3	504 055	42.3	397 499	39.5	79 120	53.5	232 426	23.4
Charleston city	1 670	833	24 505	-3.2	2.11	38.9	25.8	28.5	13 616	42.6	9 533	36.8	3 319	58.2	10 889	8.1
Huntington city	2 866	977	22 955	-2.0	2.12	37.6	23.2	29.8	12 230	38.7	8 475	34.5	3 005	50.4	10 725	11.7
Morgantown city	4 329	181	10 782	12.5	2.08	37.3	15.8	18.9	4 188	38.6	3 138	37.3	758	47.5	6 594	25.7
Parkersburg city	870	516	14 467	Z	2.23	34.0	27.8	30.9	8 769	41.2	6 248	35.6	1 958	56.7	5 698	12.8
Wheeling city	1 622	584	13 719	-8.8	2.17	38.3	25.6	35.1	7 808	41.2	5 731	37.1	1 667	52.8	5 911	.3
WISCONSIN	155 958	79 073	2 084 544	14.4	2.50	26.8	33.9	23.0	1 386 815	48.0	1 108 597	44.5	200 300	64.4	697 729	27.6
Appleton city	2 405	1 035	26 864	8.2	2.52	27.6	36.3	20.1	17 665	53.2	14 476	50.5	2 328	67.2	9 199	21.7
Beloit city	1 410	349	13 370	5.3	2.57	27.5	37.9	24.1	8 908	51.1	5 956	43.7	2 223	69.0	4 462	8.0
Brookfield city	652	481	13 891	16.3	2.74	16.7	37.4	30.1	11 220	44.7	10 160	44.6	761	46.9	2 671	69.2
Eau Claire city	4 641	862	24 016	13.7	2.38	30.0	29.0	21.2	13 567	49.1	10 664	44.7	2 241	67.5	10 449	26.2
Fond du Lac city	2 686	1 974	16 638	13.7	2.38	30.9	32.3	24.6	10 285	49.5	8 046	45.0	1 627	68.8	6 353	28.9
Green Bay city	2 695	1 164	41 591	8.4	2.40	31.6	32.5	20.1	24 652	51.7	18 350	46.5	4 512	70.5	16 939	21.6
Greenfield city	922	606	15 697	13.9	2.20	34.6	24.1	30.5	9 163	38.6	7 428	36.6	1 258	47.9	6 534	36.6
Janesville city	921	512	23 894	17.2	2.45	27.4	35.0	21.9	15 743	49.6	12 213	44.6	2 502	69.0	8 151	30.9
Kenosha city	2 980	1 457	34 411	15.0	2.54	28.4	37.1	22.5	22 546	52.1	16 214	47.7	4 775	65.8	11 865	29.8
La Crosse city	4 806	998	21 110	5.7	2.23	37.0	23.3	24.7	10 214	45.5	7 625	39.9	1 969	64.2	10 896	20.6
Madison city	12 833	2 456	89 019	15.1	2.19	35.3	23.3	15.1	42 458	46.3	32 953	42.4	6 943	64.1	46 561	26.4
Manitowoc city	960	788	14 235	8.3	2.32	32.5	30.0	29.4	8 811	46.2	6 981	41.4	1 297	66.7	5 424	17.0
Menomonee Falls village	243	211	12 844	30.8	2.52	23.7	33.5	27.7	9 298	44.8	8 163	44.0	829	49.6	3 546	73.1
Milwaukee city	16 403	6 464	232 188	-3.5	2.50	33.5	34.8	20.6	135 189	52.4	74 794	44.5	48 918	65.9	96 999	6.6
New Berlin city	219	130	14 495	23.9	2.62	19.0	35.2	22.3	11 040	44.6	9 853	44.3	821	50.5	3 455	68.7
Oshkosh city	7 342	3 516	24 082	14.9	2.31	32.4	28.8	23.1	13 653	48.2	10 657	43.7	2 194	66.9	10 429	26.9
Racine city	1 872	1 541	31 449	-1.0	2.54	29.4	37.7	22.9	20 405	52.3	13 271	45.5	5 618	67.5	11 044	13.4
Sheboygan city	1 207	937	20 779	5.5	2.39	32.2	31.3	25.8	12 795	48.3	10 022	43.6	1 958	68.0	7 984	20.8
Superior city	1 125	419	11 609	5.5	2.26	34.2	29.8	25.2	6 696	48.3	4 791	41.3	1 426	68.8	4 913	20.8
Waukesha city	2 445	1 213	25 663	20.9	2.43	29.0	34.1	18.5	16 288	51.2	12 872	48.0	2 519	66.3	9 375	37.6
Wausau city	1 290	847	15 678	6.5	2.37	33.6	29.3	28.3	9 336	46.7	7 314	42.4	1 489	63.1	6 342	23.4
Wauwatosa city	983	833	20 388	2.7	2.27	33.9	29.2	29.7	12 314	46.9	10 193	45.9	1 612	53.1	8 074	22.7
West Allis city	922	596	27 604	3.0	2.19	37.3	27.2	27.1	15 367	45.8	11 361	41.8	2 928	59.8	12 237	22.8
WYOMING	14 083	7 861	193 608	14.7	2.48	26.3	35.0	20.8	130 497	48.5	106 179	44.3	16 837	68.9	63 111	28.8
Casper city	1 226	554	20 343	9.9	2.38	29.1	34.1	22.7	13 139	49.3	10 084	43.3	2 265	70.7	7 204	22.3
Cheyenne city	991	651	22 324	10.3	2.33	31.3	32.7	22.8	14 174	47.9	10 985	42.7	2 373	67.8	8 150	22.8
Laramie city	2 362	133	11 336	9.0	2.19	33.2	24.3	13.7	5 608	46.4	4 339	42.5	903	65.0	5 728	21.6

[1] As of April 1. [2] Includes people under formally authorized, supervised care or custody in institutions at the time of enumeration (such as correctional institutions, nursing homes, and juvenile institutions). [3] Under 18 years. [4] No husband present.

Sources: Group Quarters Population—U.S. Census Bureau; 2000 Census of Population and Housing, "Census 2000 Profiles of General Demographic Characteristics" data files, published May 2001 (related Internet site <http://www.census.gov/mp/www/pub/2000cen/mscen01.html>). Households, 2000—U.S. Census Bureau; 2000 Census of Population and Housing, "Census 2000 Profiles of General Demographic Characteristics" data files, published May 2001 (related Internet site <http://www.census.gov/mp/www/pub/2000cen/mscen01.html>). Households, 1990—U.S. Census Bureau, 1990 Census of Population and Housing, Summary Tape File (STF) 1C on CD-ROM (related Internet site <http://homer.ssd.census.gov/cdrom/lookup>).

Table C–4. Cities — **Housing, Crime, and Labor Force**

[Includes states and 1,070 incorporated places of 25,000 or more population as of April 1, 1990 in all states except Hawaii which has no incorporated places recognized by the Census Bureau. For Hawaii, 8 census designated places (CDPs) of 25,000 or more population as of April 1, 1990 are included. Also included are the 5 boroughs of New York city. For more information on these areas, see appendix B. Geographic Information]

City	Housing, 2000 Total units	Percent change, 1990–2000	Occupied units Number	Percent owner–occupied	Serious crimes known to police[1] Number 1999 Total	Violent[2]	Property[3]	1998	Rate[4] 1999	1998	Civilian labor force, 2000 Total	Percent change, 1999–2000	Unemployment Total	Rate[5]
ALABAMA	1 963 711	17.6	1 737 080	72.5	192 819	21 421	171 398	200 065	4 412	4 597	2 154 273	.6	99 092	4.6
Anniston city	12 787	5.7	10 447	59.5	NA	NA	NA	NA	NA	NA	11 034	−1.4	1 234	11.2
Auburn city	20 043	36.6	18 421	40.9	2 031	124	1 907	2 132	5 004	5 448	17 918	2.5	607	3.4
Bessemer city	12 790	−7.2	11 537	59.2	3 586	388	3 198	4 065	11 580	12 961	14 120	1.0	809	5.7
Birmingham city	111 927	−4.9	98 782	53.7	20 710	2 843	17 867	22 533	8 148	8 685	129 888	1.0	6 444	5.0
Decatur city	23 950	16.0	21 824	63.8	3 656	283	3 373	3 666	6 657	6 709	28 248	1.1	1 250	4.4
Dothan city	25 920	16.8	23 685	62.9	3 423	342	3 081	NA	5 974	NA	29 943	1.0	1 473	4.9
Florence city	17 707	11.3	15 820	58.5	1 703	121	1 582	2 044	4 338	5 191	19 300	1.1	1 478	7.7
Gadsden city	18 797	−1.8	16 456	63.6	NA	NA	NA	NA	NA	NA	18 865	.6	1 609	8.5
Hoover city	27 150	59.3	25 191	66.0	NA	NA	NA	NA	NA	NA	26 930	.9	330	1.2
Huntsville city	73 670	8.6	66 742	61.6	12 949	1 492	11 457	11 716	7 328	6 767	98 939	1.7	2 901	2.9
Mobile city	86 187	4.1	78 480	59.3	15 417	1 288	14 129	18 357	6 338	7 486	102 936	1.0	6 065	5.9
Montgomery city	86 787	13.2	78 384	61.9	15 407	1 583	13 824	13 908	7 788	7 031	100 744	.8	3 799	3.8
Phenix City city	13 250	22.5	11 517	52.7	1 289	146	1 143	1 468	4 693	5 295	13 807	.5	622	4.5
Prichard city	11 336	−13.0	9 841	58.4	NA	NA	NA	NA	NA	NA	12 123	.2	807	6.7
Tuscaloosa city	34 857	11.7	31 381	47.7	10 986	843	10 143	11 276	13 123	13 425	43 172	1.0	1 504	3.5
ALASKA	260 978	12.2	221 600	62.5	27 008	3 909	23 099	29 331	4 363	4 777	321 964	1.0	21 296	6.6
Anchorage city	100 368	6.6	94 822	60.1	12 950	1 685	11 265	13 364	5 024	5 256	144 117	1.1	6 750	4.7
Fairbanks city	12 357	−1.4	11 075	34.9	1 511	361	1 150	1 681	4 498	5 025	15 965	−.5	1 121	7.0
Juneau city	12 282	15.5	11 543	63.7	NA	NA	NA	NA	NA	NA	17 129	−.5	839	4.9
ARIZONA	2 189 189	31.9	1 901 327	68.0	281 735	26 334	255 401	306 985	5 897	6 575	2 346 997	−.5	91 223	3.9
Chandler city	66 592	90.4	62 377	73.6	7 972	360	7 612	8 490	4 858	5 617	70 194	−.4	1 387	2.0
Flagstaff city	21 396	31.2	19 306	48.2	4 588	297	4 291	4 954	7 912	8 645	32 788	2.3	1 468	4.5
Gilbert town	37 007	247.3	35 405	84.9	3 555	104	3 451	3 276	3 910	4 816	21 692	−.4	401	1.8
Glendale city	79 667	30.1	75 700	64.8	13 309	1 226	12 083	13 021	6 721	6 757	110 031	−.5	2 909	2.6
Mesa city	175 701	25.1	146 643	66.4	22 732	2 132	20 600	25 322	6 168	6 945	201 744	−.4	4 511	2.2
Peoria city	42 573	94.0	39 184	84.3	3 759	236	3 523	3 263	4 219	4 058	32 394	−.4	657	2.0
Phoenix city	495 832	17.5	465 834	60.7	94 641	10 199	84 442	104 734	7 720	8 545	720 895	−.5	20 990	2.9
Prescott city	17 144	28.0	15 098	65.2	1 776	134	1 642	NA	5 084	NA	17 169	1.0	532	3.1
Scottsdale city	104 974	52.1	90 669	69.6	8 588	392	8 196	9 934	4 294	5 248	104 256	−.4	1 978	1.9
Sierra Vista city	15 685	21.3	14 196	52.2	1 391	71	1 320	1 622	3 570	4 163	13 922	−.6	482	3.5
Tempe city	67 068	9.1	63 602	51.0	14 087	872	13 215	15 282	8 211	8 882	119 106	−.4	2 683	2.3
Tucson city	209 609	14.3	192 891	53.4	42 380	4 307	38 073	45 296	8 992	9 685	238 565	−.3	7 519	3.2
Yuma city	34 475	51.9	26 649	63.5	NA	NA	NA	NA	NA	NA	34 459	−.6	6 698	19.4
ARKANSAS	1 173 043	17.2	1 042 696	69.4	103 131	10 848	92 283	108 713	4 043	4 283	1 238 151	.7	54 930	4.4
Conway city	17 289	70.5	16 039	55.1	1 841	88	1 753	2 098	4 677	5 633	19 305	.7	712	3.7
Fayetteville city	25 467	35.2	23 798	42.2	2 849	191	2 658	2 551	5 318	4 771	30 093	2.7	708	2.4
Fort Smith city	35 341	6.9	32 398	56.3	4 977	454	4 523	5 203	6 546	6 797	40 899	.6	1 369	3.3
Hot Springs city	18 813	7.2	16 096	57.3	3 619	254	3 365	3 664	9 485	9 897	15 205	−.1	736	4.8
Jacksonville city	11 890	9.2	10 890	47.3	1 513	165	1 348	1 528	5 219	5 221	12 496	.5	698	5.6
Jonesboro city	24 263	24.2	22 219	57.7	2 601	183	2 418	2 909	4 952	5 432	30 128	1.4	1 112	3.7
Little Rock city	84 793	4.7	77 352	57.4	17 392	1 845	15 547	18 515	9 891	10 497	100 448	.4	3 599	3.6
North Little Rock city	27 567	1.1	25 542	57.5	5 942	536	5 406	6 294	9 988	10 383	31 921	.4	1 183	3.7
Pine Bluff city	22 484	−3.0	19 956	58.8	4 929	1 124	3 805	5 430	9 258	10 044	23 810	−.2	1 907	8.0
Springdale city	16 962	41.3	16 149	60.4	1 520	131	1 389	1 463	3 754	3 712	21 209	2.7	423	2.0
West Memphis city	11 022	4.9	10 051	56.0	1 497	221	1 276	1 660	5 603	6 113	13 555	.7	546	4.0
CALIFORNIA	12 214 549	9.2	11 502 870	56.9	1 261 164	207 879	1 053 285	1 418 674	3 805	4 343	17 090 815	3.0	845 192	4.9
Alameda city	31 644	3.7	30 226	47.9	2 933	249	2 684	3 576	3 673	4 588	41 009	3.0	868	2.1
Alhambra city	30 069	1.6	29 111	39.2	2 042	269	1 773	2 495	2 392	2 927	43 387	2.2	1 902	4.4
Anaheim city	99 719	7.0	96 969	50.0	10 104	1 639	8 465	10 438	3 374	3 495	166 882	2.8	4 922	2.9
Antioch city	30 116	31.1	29 338	71.0	2 500	519	1 981	3 293	3 026	4 180	37 171	2.9	1 351	3.6
Apple Valley town	20 163	20.9	18 557	70.0	2 006	216	1 790	2 255	3 503	4 007	24 421	4.9	1 238	5.1
Arcadia city	19 970	2.5	19 149	62.3	1 406	138	1 268	1 596	2 763	3 102	25 933	2.4	678	2.6
Azusa city	13 013	−1.7	12 549	50.5	1 222	159	1 063	1 386	2 826	3 228	22 284	2.1	1 347	6.0
Bakersfield city	88 262	33.4	83 441	60.5	11 207	859	10 348	12 348	5 253	5 870	100 444	2.3	8 372	8.3
Baldwin Park city	17 430	1.5	16 961	61.0	1 421	238	1 183	1 380	1 946	1 896	32 641	2.0	2 013	6.2
Bell city	9 215	−2.0	8 918	30.9	938	327	611	777	2 626	2 173	15 238	1.7	1 391	9.1
Bellflower city	24 247	.5	23 367	40.3	2 526	501	2 025	3 035	3 914	4 710	33 992	2.2	1 452	4.3
Bell Gardens city	9 788	2.5	9 466	23.8	1 391	363	1 028	1 626	3 089	3 617	18 004	1.7	1 783	9.9
Berkeley city	46 875	2.5	44 955	42.7	8 343	842	7 501	9 274	7 606	8 764	65 045	2.9	1 776	2.7
Beverly Hills city	15 856	.8	15 035	43.4	1 408	157	1 251	1 619	4 283	4 908	18 526	2.4	507	2.7

[1] Data on serious crimes have not been adjusted for underreporting; this may affect comparability over time or among geographic areas. [2] Includes murder and nonnegligent manslaughter, forcible rape, robbery, and aggravated assault. [3] Includes burglary, larceny-theft, and motor vehicle theft. [4] Per 100,000 resident population provided by the U.S. Federal Bureau of Investigation. [5] Civilian unemployed as a percent of total civilian labor force.

Sources: Housing, 2000—U.S. Census Bureau, 2000 Census of Population and Housing, "Census 2000 Profiles of General Demographic Characteristics" data files, published May 2001 (related Internet site <http://www.census.gov/mp/www/pub/2000cen/mscen01.html>). Housing, 1990—U.S. Census Bureau, "1990 Census of Population and Housing, Summary Tape File (STF) 1C" on CD-ROM (related Internet site <http://homer.ssd.census.gov/cdrom/lookup>). Serious Crimes Known to Police—U.S. Federal Bureau of Investigation, Uniform Crime Reporting Program, "Crime in the United States," annual <http://www.fbi.gov/ucr/Cius_99/99crime/99c2_01.pdf> (accessed: 20 October 2000) and <http://www.fbi.gov/ucr/Cius_98/98crime/98cius05.pdf> (accessed: 9 December 1999). Civilian Labor Force—U.S. Bureau of Labor Statistics, Local Area Unemployment Statistics, 2000 data published 2 May 2001, 1999 data published 30 May 2001 <ftp://ftp.bls.gov/pub/time.series/la/> (related Internet site <http://www.bls.gov/lauhome.htm>).

Table C–4. Cities — **Housing, Crime, and Labor Force**–Con.

[Includes states and 1,070 incorporated places of 25,000 or more population as of April 1, 1990 in all states except Hawaii which has no incorporated places recognized by the Census Bureau. For Hawaii, 8 census designated places (CDPs) of 25,000 or more population as of April 1, 1990 are included. Also included are the 5 boroughs of New York city. For more information on these areas, see appendix B. Geographic Information]

City	Housing, 2000				Serious crimes known to police[1]						Civilian labor force, 2000			
			Occupied units		Number				Rate[4]				Unemployment	
					1999									
	Total units	Percent change, 1990–2000	Number	Percent owner-occupied	Total	Violent[2]	Property[3]	1998	1999	1998	Total	Percent change, 1999–2000	Total	Rate[5]
CALIFORNIA—Con.														
Brea city	13 327	5.4	13 067	64.2	1 460	98	1 362	1 675	4 046	4 658	22 033	2.8	382	1.7
Buena Park city	23 826	2.7	23 332	57.1	1 902	259	1 643	2 447	2 555	3 288	41 526	2.8	1 254	3.0
Burbank city	42 847	4.0	41 608	43.5	2 813	311	2 502	3 160	2 846	3 210	55 816	2.3	2 066	3.7
Burlingame city	12 869	-.3	12 511	47.9	907	60	847	1 071	3 181	3 767	17 466	3.4	184	1.1
Camarillo city	21 946	17.2	21 438	73.5	1 128	101	1 027	1 263	1 873	2 151	30 195	3.6	1 082	3.6
Campbell city	16 286	2.7	15 920	48.2	1 214	200	1 014	1 501	3 098	3 813	26 989	4.3	386	1.4
Carlsbad city	33 798	24.1	31 521	67.4	2 187	201	1 986	2 281	2 884	3 208	40 233	3.2	963	2.4
Carson city	25 337	3.7	24 648	77.9	3 391	733	2 658	3 549	3 813	4 025	46 450	2.1	2 430	5.2
Cathedral City city	17 893	17.5	14 027	65.2	1 503	150	1 353	1 430	3 936	3 799	20 757	5.0	1 011	4.9
Ceres city	10 773	18.7	10 435	66.2	2 124	169	1 955	2 191	6 556	6 852	14 495	1.8	1 511	10.4
Cerritos city	15 607	1.6	15 390	83.5	2 583	212	2 371	3 137	4 725	5 737	30 868	2.4	819	2.7
Chico city	24 386	49.7	23 476	40.4	2 394	184	2 210	2 653	5 029	5 666	22 718	2.0	1 529	6.7
Chino city	17 898	10.9	17 304	68.7	2 197	305	1 892	2 547	3 292	3 836	33 237	5.0	1 135	3.4
Chula Vista city	59 495	19.4	57 705	57.4	7 009	1 024	5 985	8 150	4 303	5 209	73 567	3.2	2 328	3.2
Claremont city	11 559	6.7	11 281	66.7	957	73	884	1 071	2 794	3 136	18 404	2.4	559	3.0
Clovis city	25 250	33.7	24 347	60.4	2 423	146	2 277	2 660	3 733	4 120	33 812	3.0	3 008	8.9
Colton city	15 680	6.2	14 520	52.0	1 961	193	1 768	2 139	4 326	4 815	23 448	4.9	1 441	6.1
Compton city	23 795	2.4	22 327	56.3	4 864	1 502	3 362	4 860	5 195	5 200	36 522	1.6	3 885	10.6
Concord city	45 083	3.1	44 020	62.6	6 566	636	5 930	6 801	5 498	5 735	74 809	3.1	1 875	2.5
Corona city	39 271	48.0	37 839	67.5	3 638	295	3 343	4 076	3 178	3 926	55 475	5.0	2 499	4.5
Coronado city	9 494	3.8	7 734	51.6	561	35	526	608	2 133	2 298	8 808	3.2	177	2.0
Costa Mesa city	40 406	2.0	39 206	40.5	3 608	319	3 289	3 956	3 474	3 792	68 676	2.8	1 506	2.2
Covina city	16 364	1.6	15 971	58.4	1 968	233	1 735	1 858	4 359	4 116	24 724	2.3	957	3.9
Culver City city	17 130	1.1	16 611	54.4	1 333	201	1 132	1 525	3 309	3 808	24 291	2.4	723	3.0
Cupertino city	18 682	16.4	18 204	63.6	1 046	76	970	1 164	2 286	2 650	28 951	4.4	332	1.1
Cypress city	16 028	8.9	15 654	69.4	1 158	109	1 049	1 205	2 383	2 479	27 597	2.8	654	2.4
Daly City city	31 311	3.8	30 775	59.8	2 528	258	2 270	2 779	2 511	2 774	57 021	3.1	1 187	2.1
Dana Point city	15 682	6.9	14 456	62.0	726	51	675	757	2 077	2 162	21 237	2.8	426	2.0
Danville city	15 130	32.0	14 816	89.1	587	15	572	694	1 437	1 751	21 106	3.2	274	1.3
Davis city	23 617	29.2	22 948	44.6	1 646	203	1 443	1 700	2 982	3 156	34 637	2.5	1 136	3.3
Diamond Bar city	17 959	1.7	17 651	82.6	931	143	788	1 101	1 685	1 995	32 399	2.4	829	2.6
Downey city	34 759	1.3	33 989	51.8	3 645	381	3 264	4 146	3 836	4 371	50 010	2.3	1 968	3.9
El Cajon city	35 190	2.1	34 199	40.5	3 855	573	3 282	4 818	4 031	5 084	49 071	3.2	1 790	3.6
El Centro city	12 263	20.5	11 439	50.2	2 398	365	2 033	2 265	6 326	5 927	17 731	5.3	4 518	25.5
El Monte city	27 758	2.2	27 034	41.0	3 324	988	2 336	3 920	2 934	3 496	49 449	2.0	3 404	6.9
Encinitas city	23 843	7.8	22 830	64.2	1 390	182	1 208	1 506	2 285	2 528	38 417	3.2	774	2.0
Escondido city	45 050	7.2	43 817	53.2	4 802	607	4 195	5 670	3 925	4 740	63 727	3.2	1 972	3.1
Eureka city	11 637	-1.2	10 957	46.5	2 153	148	2 005	2 591	8 289	9 746	13 335	.2	851	6.4
Fairfield city	31 792	20.6	30 870	59.7	4 517	476	4 041	4 878	4 954	5 566	43 131	3.4	2 006	4.7
Folsom city	17 968	90.8	17 196	76.3	891	74	817	1 244	1 949	2 960	14 447	3.3	405	2.8
Fontana city	35 908	22.2	34 014	68.1	3 561	803	2 758	4 006	3 197	3 750	49 327	4.9	2 268	4.6
Foster City city	12 009	2.2	11 613	61.5	451	25	426	555	1 460	1 822	20 463	3.3	263	1.3
Fountain Valley city	18 473	2.5	18 162	74.7	1 697	114	1 583	1 886	2 951	3 271	35 293	2.8	734	2.1
Fremont city	69 452	11.3	68 237	64.5	5 966	423	5 543	7 323	2 878	3 805	111 028	3.0	2 251	2.0
Fresno city	149 025	15.2	140 079	50.6	28 833	4 008	24 825	32 075	7 137	7 934	200 007	3.3	25 725	12.9
Fullerton city	44 771	4.2	43 609	53.9	4 002	317	3 685	4 482	3 234	3 608	72 822	2.8	1 785	2.5
Gardena city	21 041	10.5	20 324	47.3	2 613	605	2 008	2 533	4 801	4 680	28 675	2.2	1 224	4.3
Garden Grove city	46 703	1.6	45 791	59.6	5 480	709	4 771	5 623	3 570	3 646	84 560	2.8	2 794	3.3
Gilroy city	12 152	24.4	11 869	61.2	1 739	344	1 395	2 075	4 542	5 882	18 556		624	3.4
Glendale city	73 713	2.2	71 805	38.4	4 990	529	4 461	5 346	2 657	2 846	98 345	2.2	4 968	5.1
Glendora city	17 145	1.6	16 819	73.6	1 080	106	974	1 140	2 137	2 172	26 754	2.3	829	3.1
Hanford city	14 721	26.8	13 931	59.0	1 789	139	1 650	NA	4 746	NA	16 895	6.2	2 076	12.3
Hawthorne city	29 629	1.4	28 536	25.9	3 564	1 108	2 456	4 310	4 785	5 797	41 732	2.2	2 099	5.0
Hayward city	45 922	8.8	44 804	53.2	5 995	871	5 124	7 122	4 585	5 713	64 629	2.9	1 935	3.0
Hemet city	29 401	49.3	25 252	64.6	2 579	374	2 205	2 812	4 816	5 286	15 045	5.1	1 162	7.7
Hesperia city	21 348	23.0	19 966	72.3	1 810	175	1 635	2 179	2 863	3 503	25 068	4.9	1 455	5.8
Highland city	14 858	18.3	13 478	66.6	1 661	225	1 436	1 892	3 895	4 557	19 520	4.9	1 095	5.6
Huntington Beach city	75 662	4.0	73 657	60.6	4 863	396	4 467	5 907	2 454	2 996	126 107	2.8	2 401	1.9
Huntington Park city	15 335	5.6	14 860	27.4	2 429	536	1 893	2 648	4 113	4 538	26 812	1.7	2 534	9.5
Imperial Beach city	9 739	2.2	9 272	30.0	862	173	689	1 085	2 955	3 758	12 614	3.1	649	5.1
Indio city	16 909	29.8	13 871	56.2	2 252	330	1 922	2 370	4 930	5 230	23 155	5.1	1 792	7.7
Inglewood city	38 648	-.2	36 805	36.3	4 377	1 349	3 028	5 069	3 865	4 479	57 916	1.9	4 257	7.4
Irvine city	53 711	27.2	51 199	60.0	3 374	168	3 206	3 593	2 437	2 719	71 683	2.8	1 260	1.8
Laguna Niguel city	23 885	26.4	23 217	75.0	741	67	674	770	1 362	1 441	29 740	2.9	443	1.5
La Habra city	19 441	4.1	18 947	56.6	1 434	156	1 278	1 787	2 603	3 220	31 527	2.8	920	2.9
Lakewood city	27 310	1.9	26 853	72.0	2 555	353	2 202	3 176	3 304	4 129	41 306	2.3	1 295	3.1
La Mesa city	24 943	3.3	24 186	47.2	2 073	199	1 874	2 302	3 649	4 077	32 982	3.2	808	2.4
La Mirada city	14 811	10.9	14 580	82.0	1 098	202	896	1 162	2 431	2 599	22 801	2.3	753	3.3

[1] Data on serious crimes have not been adjusted for underreporting; this may affect comparability over time or among geographic areas. [2] Includes murder and nonnegligent manslaughter, forcible rape, robbery, and aggravated assault. [3] Includes burglary, larceny-theft, and motor vehicle theft. [4] Per 100,000 resident population provided by the U.S. Federal Bureau of Investigation. [5] Civilian unemployed as a percent of total civilian labor force.

Sources: Housing, 2000—U.S. Census Bureau, 2000 Census of Population and Housing, "Census 2000 Profiles of General Demographic Characteristics" data files, published May 2001 (related Internet site <http://www.census.gov/mp/www/pub/2000cen/mscen01.html>). Housing, 1990—U.S. Census Bureau, "1990 Census of Population and Housing, Summary Tape File (STF) 1C" on CD-ROM (related Internet site <http://homer.ssd.census.gov/cdrom/lookup>). Serious Crimes Known to Police—U.S. Federal Bureau of Investigation, Uniform Crime Reporting Program, "Crime in the United States," annual <http://www.fbi.gov/ucr/Cius_99/99crime/00c2_01.pdf> (accessed: 20 October 2000) and <http://www.fbi.gov/ucr/Cius_98/98cius05.pdf> (accessed: 9 December 1999). Civilian Labor Force—U.S. Bureau of Labor Statistics, Local Area Unemployment Statistics, 2000 data published 2 May 2001, 1999 data published 30 May 2001 <ftp://ftp.bls.gov/pub/time.series/la/> (related Internet site <http://www.bls.gov/lauhome.htm>).

Table C–4. Cities — **Housing, Crime, and Labor Force**–Con.

[Includes states and 1,070 incorporated places of 25,000 or more population as of April 1, 1990 in all states except Hawaii which has no incorporated places recognized by the Census Bureau. For Hawaii, 8 census designated places (CDPs) of 25,000 or more population as of April 1, 1990 are included. Also included are the 5 boroughs of New York city. For more information on these areas, see appendix B. Geographic Information]

City	Housing, 2000 Total units	Percent change, 1990–2000	Occupied units Number	Percent owner-occupied	Serious crimes known to police[1] Number 1999 Total	Violent[2]	Property[3]	1998	Rate[4] 1999	1998	Civilian labor force, 2000 Total	Percent change, 1999–2000	Unemployment Total	Rate[5]
CALIFORNIA—Con.														
Lancaster city	41 745	15.3	38 224	61.4	4 107	1 116	2 991	5 368	3 415	4 553	48 330	2.1	2 463	5.1
La Puente city	9 660	4.0	9 461	60.9	1 027	320	707	1 141	2 613	2 911	18 105	2.0	1 222	6.7
La Verne city	11 286	1.6	11 070	77.5	726	77	649	777	2 212	2 383	17 149	2.4	488	2.8
Lawndale city	9 869	.9	9 555	33.2	989	291	698	1 283	3 362	4 413	15 786	2.1	866	5.5
Livermore city	26 610	23.8	26 123	72.2	1 815	124	1 691	1 893	2 475	2 857	36 065	3.0	730	2.0
Lodi city	21 378	8.7	20 692	54.6	2 815	342	2 473	3 052	4 939	5 426	30 683	3.5	1 992	6.5
Lompoc city	13 621	2.7	13 059	51.6	1 690	188	1 502	1 798	4 046	4 281	18 317	2.6	929	5.1
Long Beach city	171 632	.7	163 088	41.0	18 154	3 257	14 897	19 078	4 152	4 437	222 371	2.2	11 078	5.0
Los Altos city	10 727	6.1	10 462	85.6	369	48	321	396	1 302	1 393	16 910	4.4	202	1.2
Los Angeles city	1 337 706	2.9	1 275 412	38.6	167 495	46 840	120 655	183 706	4 589	5 072	1 906 860	2.0	116 240	6.1
Los Gatos town	12 367	4.6	11 988	65.3	724	55	669	711	2 450	2 402	19 784	4.4	241	1.2
Lynwood city	14 987	3.2	14 395	47.1	2 598	1 013	1 585	2 758	4 041	4 301	26 031	1.7	2 396	9.2
Madera city	12 521	31.4	11 978	52.7	2 370	525	1 845	2 751	6 374	7 434	17 695	2.9	3 008	17.0
Manhattan Beach city	15 034	2.3	14 474	65.1	1 236	82	1 154	1 252	3 589	3 696	22 248	2.5	378	1.7
Manteca city	16 937	21.1	16 368	63.0	1 950	152	1 798	2 247	4 052	4 793	23 403	3.5	1 646	7.0
Marina city	8 537	3.3	6 745	45.8	477	46	431	600	2 706	2 424	11 605	2.2	733	6.3
Martinez city	14 597	12.5	14 300	68.8	1 024	67	957	1 320	2 926	3 821	21 546	3.1	474	2.2
Maywood city	6 701	.3	6 469	29.4	587	133	454	739	2 047	2 571	13 302	1.8	1 199	9.0
Menlo Park city	12 714	3.8	12 387	57.0	885	98	787	953	2 899	3 149	16 795	3.4	205	1.2
Merced city	21 532	13.5	20 435	46.5	4 069	440	3 629	4 523	6 754	7 569	25 887	1.1	3 706	14.3
Milpitas city	17 364	20.0	17 132	69.8	2 250	233	2 017	2 256	3 651	3 752	32 479	3.9	668	2.1
Mission Viejo city	32 985	25.0	32 449	81.4	1 328	118	1 210	1 490	1 371	1 702	45 619	2.8	694	1.5
Modesto city	67 179	10.4	64 959	58.7	10 048	992	9 056	12 349	5 441	6 737	94 431	1.8	8 732	9.2
Monrovia city	13 957	.1	13 502	47.9	1 025	171	854	1 042	2 697	2 743	20 244	2.2	912	4.5
Montclair city	9 066	1.7	8 800	60.6	1 871	215	1 656	2 167	6 070	7 031	17 535	4.9	827	4.7
Montebello city	19 416	1.2	18 844	47.5	2 244	342	1 902	2 520	3 654	4 102	29 674	2.2	1 452	4.9
Monterey city	13 382	-.9	12 600	38.5	1 441	214	1 227	1 785	4 566	6 151	17 339	2.2	606	3.5
Monterey Park city	20 209	-.4	19 564	54.0	1 399	203	1 196	1 832	2 205	2 903	30 294	2.2	1 351	4.5
Moorpark city	9 094	14.9	8 994	82.1	399	53	346	386	1 311	1 301	16 205	3.6	553	3.4
Moreno Valley city	41 431	9.2	39 225	71.1	5 101	948	4 153	7 587	3 476	5 196	77 740	5.1	4 562	5.9
Mountain View city	32 432	3.0	31 242	41.5	2 370	377	1 993	2 484	3 235	3 430	51 618	4.3	701	1.4
Napa city	27 776	11.5	26 978	60.6	1 964	221	1 743	2 714	2 909	4 063	36 801	3.7	1 356	3.7
National City city	15 422	1.2	15 018	35.0	3 008	555	2 453	3 122	5 391	5 938	22 470	3.1	1 246	5.5
Newark city	13 150	7.0	12 992	70.6	1 778	138	1 640	2 000	4 063	4 886	23 827	2.9	614	2.6
Newport Beach city	37 288	7.0	33 071	55.7	2 139	125	2 014	2 527	2 911	3 510	46 049	2.8	724	1.6
Norwalk city	27 554	1.1	26 887	65.8	3 248	719	2 529	3 554	3 283	3 480	47 707	2.2	2 303	4.8
Novato city	18 994	1.1	18 524	67.6	1 225	154	1 071	1 382	2 481	2 811	27 892	3.4	419	1.5
Oakland city	157 508	1.8	150 790	41.4	31 073	5 754	25 319	36 863	8 370	9 794	192 683	2.5	9 070	4.7
Oceanside city	59 581	16.6	56 488	62.1	5 229	942	4 287	5 917	3 382	3 938	67 397	3.2	2 452	3.6
Ontario city	45 182	6.2	43 525	57.6	7 712	1 006	6 706	8 328	5 164	5 604	81 088	4.9	3 694	4.6
Orange city	41 904	10.2	40 930	62.6	3 628	475	3 153	3 592	2 888	2 899	70 746	2.4	1 706	2.4
Oxnard city	45 166	9.5	43 576	57.3	5 907	850	5 057	6 378	3 765	4 107	83 486	3.4	5 452	6.5
Pacifica city	14 245	3.7	13 994	68.6	647	135	512	891	1 568	2 170	24 882	3.3	316	1.3
Palmdale city	37 096	52.0	34 285	71.0	3 867	954	2 913	4 792	3 805	4 413	34 904	2.2	1 756	5.0
Palm Springs city	30 823	1.0	20 516	60.8	3 048	619	2 429	3 205	6 836	7 136	27 550	5.0	1 160	4.2
Palo Alto city	26 048	3.4	25 216	57.2	2 083	94	1 989	2 502	3 474	4 184	39 724	4.5	396	1.0
Paradise town	12 374	6.4	11 591	70.9	878	101	777	1 002	3 356	3 838	10 350	2.0	563	5.4
Paramount city	14 591	6.3	13 972	42.9	2 525	436	2 089	3 077	4 867	5 944	22 674	1.9	1 643	7.2
Pasadena city	54 132	2.1	51 844	45.8	4 985	826	4 159	5 889	3 650	4 308	73 761	2.2	3 374	4.6
Petaluma city	20 304	22.7	19 932	70.1	1 561	125	1 436	1 986	3 022	3 980	30 309	3.5	648	2.1
Pico Rivera city	16 807	3.0	16 468	70.4	1 638	437	1 201	2 080	2 660	3 403	28 617	2.0	1 763	6.2
Pittsburg city	18 300	9.5	17 741	62.8	2 311	271	2 040	2 773	4 314	5 285	27 482	2.9	1 062	3.9
Placentia city	15 326	11.6	15 037	69.0	932	135	797	1 147	1 948	2 477	26 839	2.8	608	2.3
Pleasant Hill city	14 034	2.8	13 753	63.5	1 249	105	1 144	1 970	3 695	5 936	22 290	3.2	385	1.7
Pleasanton city	23 968	23.8	23 311	73.4	1 595	44	1 551	1 819	2 455	3 099	34 362	3.1	506	1.5
Pomona city	39 598	2.9	37 855	57.3	6 610	1 446	5 164	6 383	4 802	4 649	63 810	2.0	4 243	6.6
Porterville city	12 691	26.0	11 884	56.4	1 703	177	1 526	2 050	4 714	5 815	15 552	2.3	2 844	18.3
Poway city	15 714	9.2	15 467	77.7	923	103	820	879	1 852	1 806	26 893	3.2	512	1.9
Rancho Cucamonga city	42 134	15.9	40 863	70.2	3 824	268	3 556	3 705	3 139	3 097	66 977	5.0	2 008	3.0
Rancho Palos Verdes city	15 709	1.6	15 256	81.6	433	58	375	596	1 000	1 381	23 302	2.5	392	1.7
Redding city	33 802	24.1	32 103	56.7	3 382	369	3 013	4 258	4 276	5 448	35 635	3.2	2 454	6.9
Redlands city	24 790	6.9	23 593	60.4	2 350	330	2 020	2 785	3 441	4 071	36 852	5.0	1 113	3.0
Redondo Beach city	29 543	4.7	28 566	49.5	2 038	166	1 872	2 115	3 184	3 327	43 962	2.4	1 079	2.5
Redwood City city	28 921	7.7	28 060	53.0	2 404	253	2 151	2 577	3 226	3 531	42 464	3.3	616	1.5
Rialto city	26 045	9.3	24 659	68.4	3 410	588	2 822	3 528	4 004	4 178	40 441	4.9	2 060	5.1
Richmond city	36 044	4.4	34 625	53.3	7 119	1 225	5 894	7 525	7 506	8 007	49 530	2.7	2 599	5.2
Ridgecrest city	11 309	.5	9 826	63.0	647	136	511	637	2 123	2 032	17 302	2.3	1 038	6.0
Riverside city	85 974	7.1	82 005	56.6	11 665	2 064	9 601	12 373	4 386	4 682	155 523	5.0	8 439	5.4
Rohnert Park city	15 808	13.6	15 503	58.4	1 610	90	1 520	1 820	3 871	4 477	25 926	3.5	769	3.0

[1] Data on serious crimes have not been adjusted for underreporting; this may affect comparability over time or among geographic areas.   [2] Includes murder and nonnegligent manslaughter, forcible rape, robbery, and aggravated assault.   [3] Includes burglary, larceny-theft, and motor vehicle theft.   [4] Per 100,000 resident population provided by the U.S. Federal Bureau of Investigation.   [5] Civilian unemployed as a percent of total civilian labor force.

Sources: Housing, 2000—U.S. Census Bureau, 2000 Census of Population and Housing, "Census 2000 Profiles of General Demographic Characteristics" data files, published May 2001 (related Internet site <http://www.census.gov/mp/www/pub/2000cen/mscen01.html>).   Housing, 1990—U.S. Census Bureau, "1990 Census of Population and Housing, Summary Tape File (STF) 1C" on CD-ROM (related Internet site <http://homer.ssd.census.gov/cdrom/lookup>).   Serious Crimes Known to Police—U.S. Federal Bureau of Investigation, Uniform Crime Reporting Program, "Crime in the United States," annual <http://www.fbi.gov/ucr/Cius_99/99crime/99c2_01.pdf> (accessed: 20 October 2000) and <http://www.fbi.gov/ucr/Cius_98/98crime/98cius05.pdf> (accessed: 9 December 1999). Civilian Labor Force—U.S. Bureau of Labor Statistics, Local Area Unemployment Statistics, 2000 data published 2 May 2001, 1999 data published 30 May 2001 <ftp://ftp.bls.gov/pub/time.series/la/> (related Internet site <http://www.bls.gov/lauhome.htm>).

Table C–4. Cities — **Housing, Crime, and Labor Force**–Con.

[Includes states and 1,070 incorporated places of 25,000 or more population as of April 1, 1990 in all states except Hawaii which has no incorporated places recognized by the Census Bureau. For Hawaii, 8 census designated places (CDPs) of 25,000 or more population as of April 1, 1990 are included. Also included are the 5 boroughs of New York city. For more information on these areas, see appendix B. Geographic Information]

City	Housing, 2000 Total units	Percent change, 1990–2000	Occupied units Number	Percent owner-occupied	Serious crimes known to police[1] Number 1999 Total	Violent[2]	Property[3]	1998	Rate[4] 1999	1998	Civilian labor force, 2000 Total	Percent change, 1999–2000	Unemployment Total	Rate[5]
CALIFORNIA—Con.														
Rosemead city	14 345	1.5	13 913	48.8	1 511	375	1 136	1 824	2 800	3 396	24 180	2.1	1 483	6.1
Roseville city	31 925	79.5	30 783	69.5	2 696	259	2 437	2 704	3 711	4 122	32 811	3.3	1 104	3.4
Sacramento city	163 957	6.9	154 581	50.1	27 110	3 084	24 026	31 620	6 611	8 219	204 130	3.3	10 612	5.2
Salinas city	39 659	14.7	38 298	50.1	6 298	1 155	5 143	6 374	5 110	5 449	63 718	2.3	8 055	12.6
San Bernardino city	63 535	8.0	56 330	52.4	11 909	2 020	9 889	13 792	6 297	7 328	84 008	4.9	5 812	6.9
San Bruno city	14 980	−1.3	14 677	63.0	1 018	62	956	1 270	2 465	3 074	24 690	3.3	387	1.6
San Buenaventura (Ventura) city	39 803	6.6	38 524	58.7	2 989	334	2 655	3 828	2 995	3 766	57 777	3.6	2 051	3.5
San Carlos city	11 691	3.1	11 455	72.7	582	62	520	631	2 042	2 223	17 447	3.4	159	.9
San Clemente city	20 653	10.3	19 395	62.4	822	76	746	890	1 742	1 896	25 740	2.8	502	2.0
San Diego city	469 689	8.8	450 691	49.5	49 587	7 411	42 176	54 421	4 004	4 514	644 191	3.2	19 631	3.0
San Dimas city	12 503	8.9	12 163	73.7	733	129	604	872	2 111	2 539	19 131	2.4	471	2.5
San Francisco city	346 527	5.5	329 700	35.0	43 322	6 555	36 767	46 139	5 725	6 224	435 211	3.4	12 201	2.8
San Gabriel city	12 909	1.4	12 587	47.6	922	202	720	1 164	2 394	3 030	19 352	2.2	864	4.5
San Jose city	281 841	8.7	276 598	61.8	25 784	5 088	20 696	30 382	2 944	3 532	509 304	3.8	11 943	2.3
San Juan Capistrano city	11 320	17.8	10 930	78.9	569	76	493	702	1 809	2 340	15 481	2.8	298	1.9
San Leandro city	31 334	3.8	30 642	60.6	4 294	511	3 783	4 456	5 689	6 213	39 315	2.9	1 016	2.6
San Luis Obispo city	19 306	8.0	18 639	41.9	1 928	115	1 813	2 225	4 426	5 106	25 097	3.3	812	3.2
San Marcos city	18 862	30.3	18 111	66.0	1 589	189	1 400	1 543	3 158	3 171	21 748	3.2	624	2.9
San Mateo city	38 249	3.6	37 338	53.9	2 581	278	2 303	3 012	2 787	3 256	56 050	3.3	907	1.6
San Pablo city	9 340	−.8	9 051	49.1	2 201	326	1 875	2 423	8 048	8 982	12 945	2.7	732	5.7
San Rafael city	22 948	8.6	22 371	53.8	1 767	333	1 434	2 009	3 411	3 898	29 712	3.2	700	2.4
San Ramon city	17 552	29.7	16 944	71.3	887	59	828	921	2 059	2 237	25 848	3.2	385	1.5
Santa Ana city	74 588	−.5	73 002	49.3	11 167	1 828	9 339	11 525	3 597	3 687	168 378	2.7	7 714	4.6
Santa Barbara city	37 076	2.3	35 605	42.0	2 919	523	2 396	3 385	3 320	3 829	52 747	2.7	1 632	3.1
Santa Clara city	39 630	4.6	38 526	46.1	3 068	262	2 806	3 485	3 013	3 442	67 814	4.0	1 266	1.9
Santa Clarita city	52 442	27.5	50 787	74.7	2 673	488	2 185	2 900	2 074	2 273	67 212	2.4	1 698	2.5
Santa Cruz city	21 504	11.1	20 442	46.6	2 614	382	2 232	2 875	4 874	5 488	31 638	1.6	1 558	4.9
Santa Maria city	22 847	8.1	22 146	55.9	2 538	316	2 222	2 988	3 672	4 345	30 983	2.6	1 642	5.3
Santa Monica city	47 863	.2	44 497	29.8	4 883	628	4 255	5 380	5 376	5 966	55 942	2.3	1 944	3.5
Santa Paula city	8 341	3.5	8 136	57.7	864	163	701	1 118	3 186	4 107	14 070	3.4	1 029	7.3
Santa Rosa city	57 578	20.6	56 036	58.5	5 410	522	4 888	6 868	4 202	5 472	74 318	3.5	1 904	2.6
Santee city	18 833	3.1	18 470	71.0	1 344	154	1 190	1 357	2 294	2 356	31 906	3.2	805	2.5
Saratoga city	10 649	3.2	10 450	90.0	369	17	352	356	1 217	1 178	17 817	4.4	212	1.2
Seal Beach city	14 267	−1.0	13 048	76.4	584	81	503	518	2 200	1 941	12 323	2.8	191	1.5
Seaside city	11 005	−2.1	9 833	44.0	1 017	223	794	1 373	3 547	4 177	16 792	2.3	1 378	8.2
Simi Valley city	37 272	12.6	36 421	77.6	1 647	116	1 531	1 788	1 469	1 625	68 247	3.5	2 678	3.9
South Gate city	24 269	5.8	23 213	46.9	2 903	664	2 239	3 213	3 237	3 577	40 278	1.9	3 203	8.0
South San Francisco city	20 138	5.5	19 677	62.5	1 596	142	1 454	1 924	2 674	3 270	32 860	3.2	663	2.0
Stanton city	11 011	2.4	10 767	48.9	1 001	139	862	1 196	2 986	3 548	18 146	2.7	823	4.5
Stockton city	82 042	13.1	78 556	51.6	16 546	2 808	13 738	17 526	6 791	7 311	107 445	3.5	11 156	10.4
Sunnyvale city	53 753	5.8	52 539	47.6	2 655	200	2 455	3 000	2 053	2 337	86 006	4.1	1 447	1.7
Temecula city	19 099	79.2	18 293	73.4	1 405	190	1 215	1 638	3 128	4 021	19 268	5.0	658	3.4
Temple City city	11 674	1.1	11 338	63.1	537	124	413	632	1 652	1 955	16 906	2.3	562	3.3
Thousand Oaks city	42 958	13.8	41 793	75.3	1 831	156	1 675	1 997	1 540	1 713	69 512	3.6	2 619	3.8
Torrance city	55 967	1.9	54 542	56.0	4 611	443	4 168	5 130	3 304	3 696	80 529	2.4	2 300	2.9
Tracy city	18 087	48.6	17 620	72.2	1 962	115	1 847	2 046	4 059	4 435	20 806	3.5	1 526	7.3
Tulare city	14 253	26.0	13 543	60.5	2 750	424	2 326	2 697	6 621	6 613	17 719	2.8	2 354	13.3
Turlock city	19 095	24.0	18 408	55.8	2 913	294	2 619	2 936	5 712	5 837	24 128	1.8	2 196	9.1
Tustin city	25 501	32.1	23 831	49.6	2 263	261	2 002	2 406	3 465	3 741	31 942	2.8	825	2.6
Union City city	18 877	16.1	18 642	71.3	2 594	314	2 280	2 812	3 989	4 707	32 051	3.0	697	2.2
Upland city	25 467	4.0	24 551	58.9	2 951	391	2 560	3 126	4 288	4 542	42 711	5.0	1 367	3.2
Vacaville city	28 696	21.3	28 105	66.7	2 337	312	2 025	2 462	2 763	2 956	39 974	3.5	1 370	3.4
Vallejo city	41 219	3.3	39 601	63.2	7 304	1 297	6 007	7 563	6 454	6 741	62 003	3.4	2 916	4.7
Victorville city	22 498	44.0	20 893	65.1	3 127	315	2 812	3 348	4 472	4 865	20 221	4.9	1 325	6.6
Visalia city	32 654	20.3	30 883	62.7	5 004	753	4 251	5 711	5 522	6 369	42 685	3.0	4 296	10.1
Vista city	29 814	8.7	28 877	54.2	2 742	414	2 328	3 432	3 340	4 247	39 508	3.2	1 351	3.4
Walnut city	8 395	3.8	8 260	88.9	511	89	422	607	1 619	1 931	16 473	2.4	509	3.1
Walnut Creek city	31 425	4.9	30 301	68.3	2 201	123	2 078	3 014	3 373	4 649	38 225	3.2	674	1.8
Watsonville city	11 695	18.0	11 381	48.1	1 831	339	1 492	2 175	5 411	6 484	16 932	.7	2 021	11.9
West Covina city	32 058	3.0	31 411	66.5	4 265	421	3 844	4 702	4 226	4 544	53 062	2.3	1 903	3.6
West Hollywood city	24 110	1.2	23 120	21.6	1 985	333	1 652	2 228	5 386	5 989	24 911	2.1	1 275	5.1
Westminster city	26 940	4.2	26 406	60.2	3 575	368	3 207	3 376	4 192	3 963	46 868	2.8	1 424	3.0
West Sacramento city	12 133	4.1	11 404	54.5	1 809	546	1 263	2 042	5 994	6 678	16 475	2.5	937	5.7
Whittier city	28 977	.8	28 271	57.8	2 391	277	2 114	2 537	2 978	3 161	41 227	2.3	1 444	3.5
Woodland city	17 120	15.5	16 751	58.5	1 306	230	1 076	1 625	2 952	3 738	26 713	2.5	1 277	4.8
Yorba Linda city	19 567	12.8	19 252	84.7	862	70	792	885	1 412	1 473	33 684	2.9	479	1.4
Yuba City city	13 912	25.7	13 290	47.4	2 094	179	1 915	2 027	6 255	6 046	15 779	3.0	2 372	15.0
Yucaipa city	16 112	12.9	15 193	74.2	842	83	759	997	2 256	2 694	16 870	5.0	544	3.2

[1] Data on serious crimes have not been adjusted for underreporting; this may affect comparability over time or among geographic areas. [2] Includes murder and nonnegligent manslaughter, forcible rape, robbery, and aggravated assault. [3] Includes burglary, larceny-theft, and motor vehicle theft. [4] Per 100,000 resident population provided by the U.S. Federal Bureau of Investigation. [5] Civilian unemployed as a percent of total civilian labor force.

Sources: Housing, 2000—U.S. Census Bureau, 2000 Census of Population and Housing, "Census 2000 Profiles of General Demographic Characteristics" data files, published May 2001 (related Internet site <http://www.census.gov/mp/www/pub/2000cen/mscen01.html>). Housing, 1990—U.S. Census Bureau, "1990 Census of Population and Housing, Summary Tape File (STF) 1C" on CD-ROM (related Internet site <http://homer.ssd.census.gov/cdrom/lookup>). Serious Crimes Known to Police—U.S. Federal Bureau of Investigation, Uniform Crime Reporting Program, "Crime in the United States," annual <http://www.fbi.gov/ucr/Cius_99/99crime/99c2_01.pdf> (accessed: 20 October 2000) and <http://www.fbi.gov/ucr/Cius_98/98crime/98cius05.pdf> (accessed: 9 December 1999). Civilian Labor Force—U.S. Bureau of Labor Statistics, Local Area Unemployment Statistics, 2000 data published 2 May 2001, 1999 data published 30 May 2001 <ftp://ftp.bls.gov/pub/time.series/la/> (related Internet site <http://www.bls.gov/lauhome.htm>).

Table C–4. Cities — **Housing, Crime, and Labor Force**–Con.

[Includes states and 1,070 incorporated places of 25,000 or more population as of April 1, 1990 in all states except Hawaii which has no incorporated places recognized by the Census Bureau. For Hawaii, 8 census designated places (CDPs) of 25,000 or more population as of April 1, 1990 are included. Also included are the 5 boroughs of New York city. For more information on these areas, see appendix B. Geographic Information]

City	Housing, 2000				Serious crimes known to police[1]						Civilian labor force, 2000			
			Occupied units		Number				Rate[4]				Unemployment	
					1999									
	Total units	Percent change, 1990–2000	Number	Percent owner-occupied	Total	Violent[2]	Property[3]	1998	1999	1998	Total	Percent change, 1999–2000	Total	Rate[5]
COLORADO	1 808 037	22.4	1 658 238	67.3	164 813	13 811	151 002	178 197	4 063	4 487	2 275 545	.5	62 501	2.7
Arvada city	39 733	15.0	39 019	75.7	3 487	65	3 422	–	3 497	–	62 345	.6	1 453	2.3
Aurora city	109 260	9.4	105 625	63.9	14 303	1 481	12 822	14 529	5 588	5 536	161 998	.7	3 627	2.2
Boulder city	40 726	12.3	39 596	49.5	3 924	186	3 738	4 899	4 243	5 200	70 071	3.2	1 832	2.6
Colorado Springs city	148 690	19.5	141 516	60.8	18 937	1 933	17 004	20 922	5 374	5 848	191 965	-.2	6 201	3.2
Denver city	251 435	4.9	239 235	52.5	26 786	2 909	23 877	27 027	5 256	5 306	277 881	.7	8 468	3.0
Englewood city	14 916	.1	14 392	52.2	2 268	208	2 060	2 241	7 028	6 825	20 978	.7	491	2.3
Fort Collins city	47 755	35.1	45 882	57.0	4 849	389	4 460	4 903	4 359	4 520	68 835	1.6	2 182	3.2
Grand Junction city	18 784	37.1	17 865	62.6	2 659	162	2 497	2 983	6 308	8 286	17 499	-.2	797	4.6
Greeley city	28 972	20.8	27 647	58.4	3 631	265	3 366	3 997	5 047	5 567	39 820	.1	1 356	3.4
Lakewood city	62 422	12.1	60 531	60.9	6 811	336	6 475	NA	4 871	NA	90 926	.6	1 958	2.2
Littleton city	18 084	22.4	17 313	62.1	1 225	77	1 148	1 516	2 921	3 687	24 125	.7	524	2.2
Longmont city	27 394	33.8	26 667	65.6	NA	NA	NA	3 349	NA	5 542	38 870	3.1	1 211	3.1
Loveland city	20 299	38.0	19 741	69.4	NA	NA	NA	1 924	NA	4 114	27 159	1.6	767	2.8
Northglenn city	12 051	15.4	11 610	67.4	1 419	97	1 322	1 475	4 647	4 847	20 228	.8	431	2.1
Pueblo city	43 121	5.5	40 307	65.6	6 724	1 092	5 632	6 701	6 135	6 514	45 947	-3.1	2 060	4.5
Thornton city	29 573	41.0	28 882	77.7	3 824	333	3 491	4 134	5 050	5 904	39 454	.7	864	2.2
Westminster city	39 318	31.6	38 343	69.7	4 181	198	3 983	4 427	4 278	4 581	55 775	.7	979	1.8
Wheat Ridge city	14 931	5.7	14 559	54.6	NA	NA	NA	1 799	NA	5 820	19 126	.6	432	2.3
CONNECTICUT	1 385 975	4.9	1 301 670	66.8	111 236	11 342	99 894	123 971	3 389	3 787	1 746 489	2.2	39 345	2.3
Bridgeport city	54 367	-5.0	50 307	43.2	8 285	1 820	6 465	9 053	6 015	6 527	60 332	.2	2 565	4.3
Bristol city	26 125	4.5	24 886	61.9	1 520	238	1 282	1 646	2 563	2 769	31 779	2.1	764	2.4
Danbury city	28 519	9.9	27 183	58.3	2 268	112	2 156	2 339	3 437	3 556	36 672	2.5	662	1.8
Hartford city	50 644	-9.7	44 986	24.6	10 261	1 485	8 776	NA	7 783	NA	52 723	1.7	2 554	4.8
Meriden city	24 631	-.8	22 951	59.9	2 201	352	1 849	NA	3 875	NA	30 607	3.4	952	3.1
Middletown city	19 697	8.8	18 554	51.3	1 333	49	1 284	1 490	3 047	3 413	24 206	2.4	567	2.3
Milford city (remainder)	21 145	9.3	20 138	77.5	2 077	82	1 995	2 162	4 142	4 499	[6]26 157	[6]1.1	[6]544	[6]2.1
Naugatuck borough	12 341	3.4	11 829	66.5	609	67	542	653	2 010	2 152	16 693	1.0	486	2.9
New Britain city	31 164	-3.6	28 558	42.7	3 963	340	3 623	5 042	5 608	7 072	33 998	1.6	1 330	3.9
New Haven city	52 941	-2.1	47 094	29.6	12 009	1 917	10 092	13 255	9 725	10 622	58 075	3.5	1 889	3.3
New London city	11 560	-3.4	10 181	37.9	1 267	240	1 027	1 504	5 295	5 999	13 196	1.6	433	3.3
Norwalk city	33 753	4.7	32 711	62.0	NA	NA	NA	3 603	NA	4 602	49 642	1.9	853	1.7
Norwich city	16 600	.8	15 091	52.5	1 246	150	1 096	1 554	3 558	4 327	18 923	1.4	542	2.9
Shelton city	14 707	13.3	14 190	81.8	602	20	582	701	1 586	1 878	20 175	1.2	457	2.3
Stamford city	47 317	6.9	45 399	56.7	3 448	373	3 075	4 491	3 107	4 064	67 565	2.2	1 168	1.7
Torrington city	16 147	6.5	14 743	64.6	777	53	724	684	2 250	1 967	18 272	-1.4	435	2.4
Waterbury city	46 827	-.8	42 622	47.6	6 360	585	5 775	7 187	6 023	6 748	52 067	.3	1 908	3.7
West Haven city	22 336	-1.5	21 090	55.2	2 107	94	2 013	2 348	4 070	4 498	28 835	3.1	725	2.5
DELAWARE	343 072	18.3	298 736	72.3	36 456	5 534	30 922	39 902	4 835	5 363	409 058	5.0	16 247	4.0
Dover city	13 195	25.8	12 340	52.3	–	-2 355	2 355	–	–	–	17 640	4.4	742	4.2
Newark city	9 294	18.2	8 989	54.5	–	-1 117	1 117	–	–	–	14 429	4.4	399	2.8
Wilmington city	32 138	2.9	28 617	50.1	–	-5 564	5 564	NA	–	NA	35 014	4.8	1 859	5.3
DISTRICT OF COLUMBIA	274 845	-1.3	248 338	40.8	41 868	8 448	33 420	46 210	8 067	8 836	278 875	-.7	16 112	5.8
Washington city	274 845	-1.3	248 338	40.8	41 868	8 448	33 420	46 210	8 067	8 836	278 875	-.7	16 112	5.8
FLORIDA	7 302 947	19.7	6 337 929	70.1	937 718	129 044	808 674	1 027 123	6 206	6 886	7 490 307	1.8	268 808	3.6
Altamonte Springs city	19 992	16.6	18 821	41.8	2 143	168	1 975	2 217	5 386	5 542	30 916	1.8	750	2.4
Boca Raton city	37 547	13.6	31 848	75.6	3 243	192	3 051	3 959	4 461	5 553	39 951	2.6	1 121	2.8
Boynton Beach city	30 643	20.0	26 210	72.8	4 958	520	4 438	5 786	9 129	10 956	26 215	2.4	1 180	4.5
Bradenton city	24 887	12.5	21 379	61.7	3 387	347	3 040	NA	7 106	NA	25 529	2.7	666	2.6
Cape Coral city	45 653	32.4	40 768	80.0	2 985	247	2 738	NA	3 231	NA	41 530	1.7	1 046	2.5
Clearwater city	56 802	5.5	48 449	62.1	6 920	1 037	5 883	7 382	6 731	7 215	56 689	2.7	1 524	2.7
Coconut Creek city	22 182	40.6	20 093	75.5	1 220	102	1 118	1 203	3 217	3 401	15 110	1.6	659	4.4
Coral Gables city	17 849	7.8	16 793	65.8	3 407	186	3 221	3 735	8 231	9 161	23 662	1.2	648	2.7
Coral Springs city	41 337	38.8	39 522	65.0	3 918	304	3 614	4 273	3 461	3 906	53 553	1.8	1 435	2.7
Davie town	31 284	57.3	28 682	76.5	3 878	304	3 574	4 033	6 151	6 615	33 534	1.7	1 090	3.3
Daytona Beach city	33 345	3.7	28 605	47.3	6 741	1 200	5 541	8 257	10 215	12 281	30 233	.3	1 153	3.8
Deerfield Beach city	37 343	29.7	31 392	70.2	2 062	234	1 828	2 374	3 997	4 616	25 452	1.7	850	3.3
Delray Beach city	31 702	15.2	26 787	69.7	5 009	707	4 302	5 773	9 221	10 936	26 667	2.1	1 645	6.2
Dunedin city	19 952	8.4	17 258	71.4	1 200	111	1 089	1 198	3 385	3 369	18 194	2.7	395	2.2
Fort Lauderdale city	80 862	-.5	68 468	55.4	14 309	1 571	12 738	18 260	9 188	11 575	95 449	1.6	4 471	4.7

[1] Data on serious crimes have not been adjusted for underreporting; this may affect comparability over time or among geographic areas. [2] Includes murder and nonnegligent manslaughter, forcible rape, robbery, and aggravated assault. [3] Includes burglary, larceny-theft, and motor vehicle theft. [4] Per 100,000 resident population provided by the U.S. Federal Bureau of Investigation. [5] Civilian unemployed as a percent of total civilian labor force. [6] Data are for consolidated city of Milford; data for Milford city (remainder) not available.

Sources: Housing, 2000—U.S. Census Bureau, 2000 Census of Population and Housing, "Census 2000 Profiles of General Demographic Characteristics" data files, published May 2001 (related Internet site <http://www.census.gov/mp/www/pub/2000cen/mscen01.html>). Housing, 1990—U.S. Census Bureau, "1990 Census of Population and Housing, Summary Tape File (STF) 1C" on CD-ROM (related Internet site <http://homer.ssd.census.gov/cdrom/lookup>). Serious Crimes Known to Police—U.S. Federal Bureau of Investigation, Uniform Crime Reporting Program, "Crime in the United States," annual <http://www.fbi.gov/ucr/Cius_99/99crime/99c2_01.pdf> (accessed: 20 October 2000) and <http://www.fbi.gov/ucr/Cius_98/98crime/98cius05.pdf> (accessed: 9 December 1999). Civilian Labor Force—U.S. Bureau of Labor Statistics, Local Area Unemployment Statistics, 2000 data published 2 May 2001, 1999 data published 30 May 2001 <ftp://ftp.bls.gov/pub/time.series/la/> (related Internet site <http://www.bls.gov/lauhome.htm>).

Table C–4. Cities — Housing, Crime, and Labor Force–Con.

[Includes states and 1,070 incorporated places of 25,000 or more population as of April 1, 1990 in all states except Hawaii which has no incorporated places recognized by the Census Bureau. For Hawaii, 8 census designated places (CDPs) of 25,000 or more population as of April 1, 1990 are included. Also included are the 5 boroughs of New York city. For more information on these areas, see appendix B. Geographic Information]

City	Housing, 2000 Total units	Percent change, 1990–2000	Occupied units Number	Percent owner-occupied	Serious crimes known to police[1] Number 1999 Total	Violent[2]	Property[3]	1998	Rate[4] 1999	1998	Civilian labor force, 2000 Total	Percent change, 1999–2000	Unemployment Total	Rate[5]
FLORIDA—Con.														
Fort Myers city	21 836	2.1	19 107	39.7	5 978	1 082	4 896	6 063	12 913	12 766	26 246	1.7	952	3.6
Fort Pierce city	17 170	−.5	14 407	53.2	3 926	963	2 963	5 126	10 664	13 388	18 369	.5	2 366	12.9
Gainesville city	40 105	15.9	37 279	47.7	7 638	921	6 717	9 498	8 138	10 641	47 749	.1	1 076	2.3
Hallandale city	25 022	.9	18 051	66.6	2 437	469	1 968	1 324	7 695	4 088	13 196	1.5	677	5.1
Hialeah city	72 142	16.0	70 704	50.7	14 922	1 792	13 130	16 776	6 968	8 024	105 163	.9	5 802	5.5
Hollywood city	68 426	8.1	59 673	62.2	9 743	945	8 798	11 017	7 396	8 289	73 729	1.6	3 128	4.2
Homestead city	11 162	3.6	10 095	36.0	3 590	670	2 920	4 313	12 189	18 355	13 116	1.0	655	5.0
Jacksonville city (remainder)	308 826	15.6	284 499	63.2	50 238	7 265	42 973	54 725	7 152	7 782	[6]392 748	[6]3.0	[6]12 913	[6]3.3
Kissimmee city	19 642	44.4	17 121	44.9	4 064	488	3 576	4 188	10 408	10 863	27 336	2.0	879	3.2
Lakeland city	38 980	11.6	33 509	60.3	6 798	589	6 209	8 849	9 043	11 707	35 708	2.1	1 543	4.3
Lake Worth city	15 861	1.5	13 828	52.4	3 388	356	3 032	4 091	11 486	13 797	17 532	2.3	845	4.8
Largo city	40 261	4.0	34 041	67.4	3 072	337	2 735	3 425	4 576	5 095	35 992	2.7	785	2.2
Lauderdale Lakes city	14 325	2.9	12 099	62.2	1 488	274	1 214	1 935	5 202	6 616	14 430	1.5	760	5.3
Lauderhill city	25 751	−2.0	22 810	59.4	3 082	473	2 609	3 172	5 987	6 041	30 027	1.7	1 165	3.9
Margate city	24 740	14.3	22 714	80.1	1 800	228	1 572	1 980	3 466	3 767	24 817	1.7	917	3.7
Melbourne city	33 678	20.0	30 788	62.1	5 064	764	4 300	5 492	7 238	7 866	31 460	.9	1 220	3.9
Miami city	148 388	2.7	134 198	34.9	NA	NA	NA	44 922	NA	12 045	181 589	.7	13 941	7.7
Miami Beach city	59 723	−4.3	46 194	36.6	14 359	1 400	12 959	15 189	14 604	15 729	44 673	.8	2 755	6.2
Miramar city	25 905	69.9	23 058	80.1	2 690	349	2 341	2 912	4 641	5 499	27 649	1.7	925	3.3
North Lauderdale city	11 444	16.8	10 799	63.7	1 284	198	1 086	1 623	4 303	5 523	19 022	1.7	668	3.5
North Miami city	22 281	.8	20 541	50.5	4 867	810	4 057	5 258	9 462	10 142	28 930	.9	1 644	5.7
North Miami Beach city	15 350	−3.0	13 987	61.8	2 424	258	2 166	2 554	6 730	7 177	18 960	1.0	819	4.3
Oakland Park city	14 509	4.6	13 502	50.7	2 962	346	2 616	3 552	10 267	12 148	19 762	1.7	634	3.2
Ocala city	20 501	5.3	18 646	57.2	5 499	738	4 761	5 617	11 540	11 969	22 935	1.2	904	3.9
Orlando city	88 486	20.5	80 883	40.8	24 995	3 922	21 073	25 421	13 618	14 004	116 520	1.7	3 179	2.7
Ormond Beach city	17 258	21.6	15 629	81.7	1 486	95	1 391	1 556	4 437	4 677	14 195	.4	282	2.0
Palm Bay city	32 902	25.2	30 336	75.3	3 573	669	2 904	4 220	4 552	5 452	33 840	.9	1 185	3.5
Panama City city	16 548	3.9	14 819	57.8	2 515	201	2 314	3 036	6 288	8 200	17 444	−1.5	1 219	7.0
Pembroke Pines city	55 296	87.2	51 989	80.2	4 373	290	4 083	4 289	3 742	4 100	41 436	1.8	1 012	2.4
Pensacola city	26 995	2.4	24 524	63.3	3 256	438	2 818	3 757	5 523	6 129	26 944	.9	1 170	4.3
Pinellas Park city	21 843	6.1	19 444	75.1	2 984	277	2 707	2 973	6 667	6 615	25 139	2.7	587	2.3
Plantation city	34 999	19.0	33 244	71.7	5 012	276	4 736	5 252	6 076	6 424	46 666	1.8	1 268	2.7
Pompano Beach city	44 496	4.2	35 197	62.8	6 578	969	5 609	7 475	8 545	9 644	41 749	1.6	1 852	4.4
Port Orange city	21 102	24.0	19 574	82.1	1 013	34	979	1 158	2 324	2 714	17 856	.4	385	2.2
Port St. Lucie city	36 785	51.7	33 909	83.3	2 350	240	2 110	2 595	2 923	3 309	31 481	1.8	1 858	5.9
Riviera Beach city	14 220	1.0	11 387	59.2	4 427	560	3 867	5 941	14 542	19 940	16 372	1.9	1 276	7.8
St. Petersburg city	124 618	−.7	109 663	63.5	21 078	4 010	17 068	22 833	8 815	9 469	137 861	2.7	4 004	2.9
Sanford city	15 623	12.9	14 237	55.4	4 121	584	3 537	3 648	11 008	9 841	21 785	1.7	692	3.2
Sarasota city	26 898	−.3	23 427	58.4	3 711	589	3 122	4 617	7 178	8 800	31 926	2.5	821	2.6
Sunrise city	35 661	21.7	33 308	73.8	5 023	315	4 708	6 162	6 172	7 642	38 682	1.7	1 313	3.4
Tallahassee city	68 417	23.9	63 217	43.8	12 905	1 952	10 953	14 507	9 323	10 380	83 805	1.3	2 447	2.9
Tamarac city	29 750	13.8	27 423	79.9	1 427	112	1 315	1 767	2 661	3 329	21 295	1.6	866	4.1
Tampa city	135 776	4.7	124 758	55.0	32 016	6 603	25 413	35 960	10 929	12 189	179 096	2.9	5 785	3.2
Titusville city	19 178	5.5	17 200	68.0	2 352	400	1 952	2 285	5 590	5 328	20 635	.9	688	3.3
West Palm Beach city	40 461	15.7	34 769	52.0	11 913	1 354	10 559	12 803	15 410	15 512	45 317	2.2	2 526	5.6
GEORGIA	3 281 737	24.4	3 006 369	67.5	400 968	41 585	359 383	417 479	5 149	5 463	4 173 274	2.3	154 398	3.7
Albany city	32 062	4.8	28 620	47.4	6 452	596	5 856	6 527	8 164	8 183	35 256	−.8	2 635	7.5
Athens city	[7]41 633	X	[7]39 239	[7]41.5	76 814	[7]463	76 351	76 407	[7]7 464	[7]8 059	[8]46 256	[8]1.0	[8]1 231	[8]2.7
Atlanta city	186 925	2.3	168 147	43.7	55 477	11 226	44 251	58 129	13 489	14 032	226 790	2.7	11 474	5.1
Augusta city	[9]80 481	X	[9]72 307	[9]57.5	NA	NA	NA	NA	NA	NA	[10]80 429	10.9	[10]4 668	[10]5.8
Columbus city (remainder)	75 940	7.5	69 599	56.4	12 345	988	11 357	12 272	6 648	6 598	[11]86 436	[11]1.6	[11]4 286	[11]5.0
East Point city	15 637	−.2	14 553	45.4	3 518	308	3 210	4 001	10 253	11 349	21 387	2.8	997	4.7
La Grange city	11 000	.5	10 022	46.8	2 098	118	1 980	2 664	8 198	10 235	13 719	.4	776	5.7
Macon city	44 341	−2.5	38 444	50.1	12 353	1 061	11 292	12 750	10 602	10 962	49 574	.5	2 917	5.9
Marietta city	25 227	8.9	23 895	37.6	3 200	302	2 898	3 809	6 114	7 144	35 096	2.8	1 150	3.3
Rome city	14 508	10.8	13 320	53.0	3 336	611	2 725	3 370	10 594	11 417	15 368	−.8	731	4.8
Roswell city	31 300	54.1	30 207	67.0	NA	NA	NA	2 587	NA	4 519	34 885	2.9	485	1.4
Savannah city	57 437	−2.3	51 375	50.3	11 279	1 240	10 039	11 597	8 405	8 328	63 798	.9	2 889	4.5
Smyrna city	19 633	16.7	18 372	50.1	2 360	194	2 166	NA	6 451	NA	28 481	2.9	679	2.4
Valdosta city	18 907	21.1	16 692	47.7	NA	NA	NA	5 300	NA	12 399	23 008	2.9	1 550	6.7
Warner Robins city	21 688	19.9	19 550	57.5	NA	NA	NA	3 950	NA	8 301	25 256	.2	908	3.6

[1] Data on serious crimes have not been adjusted for underreporting; this may affect comparability over time or among geographic areas. [2] Includes murder and nonnegligent manslaughter, forcible rape, robbery, and aggravated assault. [3] Includes burglary, larceny-theft, and motor vehicle theft. [4] Per 100,000 resident population provided by the U.S. Federal Bureau of Investigation. [5] Civilian unemployed as a percent of total civilian labor force. [6] Data are for consolidated city of Jacksonville; data for Jacksonville (remainder) not available. [7] Data are for Athens-Clarke County (balance), GA; Athens city (1990 land area - 16.6 square miles; 1990 population - 45,734) merged with Clarke County effective January 14, 1991. [8] Data are for consolidated city of Athens-Clarke County; for information on Athens city, see previous footnote. [9] Data are for Augusta-Richmond County (balance), GA; Augusta city (1990 land area - 19.7 square miles; 1990 population - 44,639) merged with Richmond County effective January 1, 1996. [10] Data are for consolidated city of Augusta-Richmond County; for information on Augusta city, see previous footnote. [11] Data are for consolidated city of Columbus; data for Columbus city (remainder) not available.

Sources: Housing, 2000—U.S. Census Bureau, 2000 Census of Population and Housing, "Census 2000 Profiles of General Demographic Characteristics" data files, published May 2001 (related Internet site <http://www.census.gov/mp/www/pub/2000cen/mscen01.html>). Housing, 1990—U.S. Census Bureau, "1990 Census of Population and Housing, Summary Tape File (STF) 1C" on CD-ROM (related Internet site <http://homer.ssd.census.gov/cdrom/lookup>). Serious Crimes Known to Police—U.S. Federal Bureau of Investigation, Uniform Crime Reporting Program, "Crime in the United States," annual <http://www.fbi.gov/ucr/Cius_99/99crime/99c2_01.pdf> (accessed: 20 October 2000) and <http://www.fbi.gov/ucr/Cius_98/98crime/98cius05.pdf> (accessed: 9 December 1999). Civilian Labor Force—U.S. Bureau of Labor Statistics, Local Area Unemployment Statistics, 2000 data published 2 May 2001, 1999 data published 30 May 2001 <ftp://ftp.bls.gov/pub/time.series/la/> (related Internet site <http://www.bls.gov/lauhome.htm>).

Table C–4. Cities — Housing, Crime, and Labor Force–Con.

[Includes states and 1,070 incorporated places of 25,000 or more population as of April 1, 1990 in all states except Hawaii which has no incorporated places recognized by the Census Bureau. For Hawaii, 8 census designated places (CDPs) of 25,000 or more population as of April 1, 1990 are included. Also included are the 5 boroughs of New York city. For more information on these areas, see appendix B. Geographic Information]

City	Housing, 2000				Serious crimes known to police[1]						Civilian labor force, 2000			
			Occupied units		Number				Rate[4]				Unemployment	
					1999									
	Total units	Percent change, 1990–2000	Number	Percent owner-occupied	Total	Violent[2]	Property[3]	1998	1999	1998	Total	Percent change, 1999–2000	Total	Rate[5]
HAWAII	460 542	18.1	403 240	56.5	57 324	2 785	54 539	63 623	4 837	5 333	595 432	.4	25 517	4.3
Hilo CDP	16 026	13.4	14 577	60.9	NA	NA	NA	NA	NA	NA	NA	NA	NA	NA
Honolulu CDP	158 663	8.8	140 337	46.9	[6]42 678	[6]2 198	[6]40 480	[6]47 453	[6]4 925	[6]5 425	[6]423 493	[6].1	[6]15 892	[6]3.8
Kailua CDP	12 780	4.5	12 229	69.7	(6)	(6)	(6)	(6)	(6)	(6)	(6)	(6)	(6)	(6)
Kaneohe CDP	11 472	5.7	10 976	68.1	(6)	(6)	(6)	(6)	(6)	(6)	(6)	(6)	(6)	(6)
Mililani Town CDP	9 280	4.3	9 010	75.9	(6)	(6)	(6)	(6)	(6)	(6)	(6)	(6)	(6)	(6)
Pearl City CDP	9 181	2.0	8 921	68.7	(6)	(6)	(6)	(6)	(6)	(6)	(6)	(6)	(6)	(6)
Waimalu CDP	10 999	3.6	10 524	62.1	(6)	(6)	(6)	(6)	(6)	(6)	(6)	(6)	(6)	(6)
Waipahu CDP	8 033	3.8	7 566	53.4	(6)	(6)	(6)	(6)	(6)	(6)	(6)	(6)	(6)	(6)
IDAHO	527 824	27.7	469 645	72.4	39 429	3 066	36 363	45 653	3 149	3 715	657 712	1.0	31 914	4.9
Boise City city	77 850	46.1	74 438	64.0	7 649	494	7 155	8 482	4 760	5 333	108 178	3.0	3 174	2.9
Idaho Falls city	19 771	17.4	18 793	68.3	2 406	183	2 223	3 003	4 908	6 087	28 702	.3	1 004	3.5
Lewiston city	13 394	11.1	12 795	66.8	1 312	36	1 276	1 554	4 242	5 020	19 356	-2.7	707	3.7
Nampa city	19 379	80.1	18 090	69.5	2 567	126	2 441	2 587	6 007	6 545	19 966	3.0	968	4.8
Pocatello city	20 627	9.9	19 334	66.2	1 684	130	1 554	2 072	3 115	3 948	28 282	.8	1 388	4.9
Twin Falls city	14 162	28.6	13 274	62.5	2 152	153	1 999	2 734	6 344	8 278	16 683	-.9	776	4.7
ILLINOIS	4 885 615	8.4	4 591 779	67.3	546 561	88 838	457 723	586 923	4 507	4 873	6 419 316	.6	279 433	4.4
Addison village	11 805	7.1	11 649	68.4	NA	NA	NA	NA	NA	NA	20 779	1.1	902	4.3
Alton city	13 894	-2.2	12 518	65.4	NA	NA	NA	NA	NA	NA	14 034	1.1	941	6.7
Arlington Heights village	31 725	4.3	30 763	76.7	NA	NA	NA	NA	NA	NA	45 363	.8	1 094	2.4
Aurora city	48 797	37.0	46 489	70.1	[7]5 692	[7]778	4 914	[7]5 966	[7]4 532	[7]4 921	70 236	1.3	3 271	4.7
Belleville city	19 142	.3	17 603	60.2	NA	NA	NA	NA	NA	NA	20 718	.8	1 677	8.1
Berwyn city	20 691	3.2	19 702	61.5	NA	NA	NA	NA	NA	NA	22 818	1.1	1 083	4.7
Bloomington city	28 431	25.6	26 642	63.1	NA	NA	NA	NA	NA	NA	40 532	3.0	1 111	2.7
Bolingbrook village	17 884	38.8	17 416	85.2	NA	NA	NA	NA	NA	NA	32 514	.9	1 216	3.7
Buffalo Grove village	16 166	16.6	15 708	87.1	NA	NA	NA	NA	NA	NA	26 191	.8	572	2.2
Burbank city	9 518	2.4	9 317	83.0	NA	NA	NA	NA	NA	NA	14 890	.9	558	3.7
Calumet City city	15 947	-3.9	15 139	63.3	NA	NA	NA	NA	NA	NA	19 193	1.5	1 168	6.1
Carbondale city	10 968	5.3	9 981	28.7	NA	NA	NA	NA	NA	NA	12 791	.3	422	3.3
Carol Stream village	14 200	17.4	13 872	70.5	NA	NA	NA	NA	NA	NA	22 770	.8	640	2.8
Champaign city	28 556	9.8	27 071	47.4	NA	NA	NA	NA	NA	NA	38 896	1.8	919	2.4
Chicago city	1 152 868	1.8	1 061 928	43.8	[7]227 381	[7]53 906	173 475	[7]249 932	[7]8 060	[7]9 085	1 341 836	1.0	75 077	5.6
Chicago Heights city	11 444	-1.5	10 703	62.8	NA	NA	NA	NA	NA	NA	14 744	1.5	1 114	7.6
Cicero town	24 640	-.8	23 115	55.2	NA	NA	NA	NA	NA	NA	33 727	1.3	2 335	6.9
Danville city	14 886	-2.9	13 327	62.5	NA	NA	NA	NA	NA	NA	15 023	-.1	1 294	8.6
Decatur city	37 239	-.6	34 086	66.4	NA	NA	NA	NA	NA	NA	42 380	.4	2 546	6.0
De Kalb city	13 619	24.8	13 081	41.9	NA	NA	NA	NA	NA	NA	22 078	.8	636	2.9
Des Plaines city	22 851	11.4	22 362	79.3	NA	NA	NA	NA	NA	NA	34 166	.9	1 422	4.2
Downers Grove village	19 477	7.2	18 979	79.2	NA	NA	NA	NA	NA	NA	30 071	.6	751	2.5
East St. Louis city	12 899	-17.4	11 178	52.9	NA	NA	NA	NA	NA	NA	11 388	-.3	1 018	8.9
Elgin city	32 665	16.9	31 543	70.2	NA	NA	NA	NA	NA	NA	50 377	1.1	2 777	5.5
Elk Grove Village village	13 513	8.8	13 278	76.7	NA	NA	NA	NA	NA	NA	21 528	1.0	577	2.7
Elmhurst city	16 147	4.3	15 627	83.3	NA	NA	NA	NA	NA	NA	25 319	.8	599	2.4
Evanston city	30 817	5.7	29 651	52.7	NA	NA	NA	NA	NA	NA	42 713	.7	1 426	3.3
Freeport city	12 471	6.4	11 222	68.2	NA	NA	NA	NA	NA	NA	12 985	-2.7	1 069	8.2
Galesburg city	14 133	-1.3	13 237	64.3	NA	NA	NA	NA	NA	NA	16 665	-.7	805	4.8
Glendale Heights village	11 105	8.8	10 791	70.1	NA	NA	NA	NA	NA	NA	19 107	1.0	669	3.5
Glenview village	15 853	15.2	15 464	88.0	NA	NA	NA	NA	NA	NA	22 354	1.1	548	2.5
Granite City city	14 022	1.0	12 773	70.5	NA	NA	NA	NA	NA	NA	15 174	1.1	1 064	7.0
Hanover Park village	11 343	9.0	11 105	82.3	NA	NA	NA	NA	NA	NA	21 755	.8	874	4.0
Harvey city	10 158	-1.2	8 990	56.4	NA	NA	NA	NA	NA	NA	12 629	1.6	1 189	9.4
Highland Park city	11 934	4.4	11 521	82.1	NA	NA	NA	NA	NA	NA	17 400	.9	323	1.9
Hoffman Estates village	17 387	4.7	17 034	76.5	NA	NA	NA	NA	NA	NA	29 889	.7	762	2.5
Joliet city	38 176	31.4	36 182	70.4	NA	NA	NA	NA	NA	NA	46 292	.9	2 966	6.4
Kankakee city	10 965	-3.6	10 020	53.4	NA	NA	NA	NA	NA	NA	12 031	-.1	964	8.0
Lansing village	11 748	5.0	11 416	75.3	NA	NA	NA	NA	NA	NA	15 999	1.0	573	3.6
Lombard village	17 019	7.4	16 487	74.9	NA	NA	NA	NA	NA	NA	25 842	1.0	784	3.0
Maywood village	8 475	-.8	7 937	62.8	NA	NA	NA	NA	NA	NA	12 843	.5	1 004	7.8
Moline city	19 487	1.3	18 492	67.3	NA	NA	NA	NA	NA	NA	22 726	-.8	1 119	4.9
Mount Prospect village	21 952	4.8	21 585	71.5	NA	NA	NA	NA	NA	NA	33 059	.8	831	2.5
Naperville city	45 651	47.7	43 751	79.7	[7]2 268	[7]60	2 208	[7]2 346	[7]1 825	[7]2 139	70 445	.8	1 700	2.4
Niles village	12 256	10.9	12 002	76.5	NA	NA	NA	NA	NA	NA	16 326	.8	474	2.9
Normal town	15 683	27.5	15 157	55.2	NA	NA	NA	NA	NA	NA	29 617	2.7	602	2.0
Northbrook village	12 492	7.0	12 203	91.7	NA	NA	NA	NA	NA	NA	18 514	.8	395	2.1
North Chicago city	8 377	5.7	7 661	36.3	NA	NA	NA	NA	NA	NA	9 064	1.4	834	9.2
Oak Forest city	10 022	10.6	9 785	81.7	NA	NA	NA	NA	NA	NA	16 985	1.0	562	3.3

[1] Data on serious crimes have not been adjusted for underreporting; this may affect comparability over time or among geographic areas. [2] Includes murder and nonnegligent manslaughter, forcible rape, robbery, and aggravated assault. [3] Includes burglary, larceny-theft, and motor vehicle theft. [4] Per 100,000 resident population provided by the U.S. Federal Bureau of Investigation. [5] Civilian unemployed as a percent of total civilian labor force. [6] Data for Honolulu CDP are for Honolulu City/County which includes all CDPs listed except Hilo which is in Maui County. [7] Excludes rape.

Sources: Housing, 2000—U.S. Census Bureau, 2000 Census of Population and Housing, "Census 2000 Profiles of General Demographic Characteristics" data files, published May 2001 (related Internet site <http://www.census.gov/mp/www/pub/2000cen/mscen01.html>). Housing, 1990—U.S. Census Bureau, "1990 Census of Population and Housing, Summary Tape File (STF) 1C" on CD-ROM (related Internet site <http://homer.ssd.census.gov/cdrom/lookup>). Serious Crimes Known to Police—U.S. Federal Bureau of Investigation, Uniform Crime Reporting Program, "Crime in the United States," annual <http://www.fbi.gov/ucr/Cius_99/99crime/99c2_01.pdf> (accessed: 20 October 2000) and <http://www.fbi.gov/ucr/Cius_98/98crime/98cius05.pdf> (accessed: 9 December 1999). Civilian Labor Force—U.S. Bureau of Labor Statistics, Local Area Unemployment Statistics, 2000 data published 2 May 2001, 1999 data published 30 May 2001 <ftp://ftp.bls.gov/pub/time.series/la/> (related Internet site <http://www.bls.gov/lauhome.htm>).

Table C–4. Cities — **Housing, Crime, and Labor Force**–Con.

[Includes states and 1,070 incorporated places of 25,000 or more population as of April 1, 1990 in all states except Hawaii which has no incorporated places recognized by the Census Bureau. For Hawaii, 8 census designated places (CDPs) of 25,000 or more population as of April 1, 1990 are included. Also included are the 5 boroughs of New York city. For more information on these areas, see appendix B. Geographic Information]

City	Housing, 2000				Serious crimes known to police[1]							Civilian labor force, 2000			
			Occupied units		Number				Rate[4]					Unemployment	
					1999										
	Total units	Percent change, 1990–2000	Number	Percent owner-occupied	Total	Violent[2]	Property[3]	1998	1999	1998		Total	Percent change, 1999–2000	Total	Rate[5]
ILLINOIS—Con.															
Oak Lawn village	22 846	4.6	22 220	82.9	NA	NA	NA	NA	NA	NA		30 817	.8	979	3.2
Oak Park village	23 723	.6	23 079	56.3	NA	NA	NA	NA	NA	NA		33 394	.9	910	2.7
Orland Park village	19 045	52.6	18 675	91.1	NA	NA	NA	NA	NA	NA		28 365	.8	755	2.7
Palatine village	26 223	65.4	25 518	69.3	NA	NA	NA	NA	NA	NA		33 979	.8	1 204	3.5
Park Ridge city	14 646	6.0	14 219	87.6	NA	NA	NA	NA	NA	NA		20 967	.8	447	2.1
Pekin city	14 038	1.9	13 380	67.2	NA	NA	NA	NA	NA	NA		17 136	–.4	900	5.3
Peoria city	49 125	1.8	45 199	59.7	[6]10 266	[6]972	9 294	[6]10 971	[6]9 173	[6]9 673		56 995	Z	2 722	4.8
Quincy city	18 043	2.9	16 546	66.4	NA	NA	NA	NA	NA	NA		21 325	–1.6	893	4.2
Rockford city	63 570	9.3	59 158	61.1	[6]13 031	[6]1 282	11 749	[6]13 709	[6]0 009	[6]9 390		78 356	.5	5 276	6.7
Rock Island city	17 542	–2.0	16 148	65.1	NA	NA	NA	NA	NA	NA		18 827	–.6	982	5.2
Schaumburg village	33 093	12.2	31 799	69.4	NA	NA	NA	NA	NA	NA		49 471	.7	1 228	2.5
Skokie village	23 702	2.3	23 223	75.2	NA	NA	NA	NA	NA	NA		32 540	.7	837	2.6
Springfield city	53 733	10.7	48 621	62.8	[6]8 207	[6]1 087	7 120	[6]7 986	[6]6 961	[6]6 985		62 162	.4	2 624	4.2
Streamwood village	12 371	19.8	12 095	89.6	NA	NA	NA	NA	NA	NA		22 362	.8	822	3.7
Tinley Park village	18 037	36.4	17 478	84.9	NA	NA	NA	NA	NA	NA		25 810	.7	746	2.9
Urbana city	15 311	9.3	14 327	37.0	NA	NA	NA	NA	NA	NA		21 473	1.7	571	2.7
Waukegan city	29 243	13.3	27 787	56.5	NA	NA	NA	NA	NA	NA		41 099	1.9	2 763	6.7
Wheaton city	19 881	6.7	19 377	74.1	NA	NA	NA	NA	NA	NA		32 249	.7	645	2.0
Wheeling village	13 697	5.4	13 280	66.6	NA	NA	NA	NA	NA	NA		19 842	.8	623	3.1
Wilmette village	10 319	2.7	10 039	86.8	NA	NA	NA	NA	NA	NA		13 882	.7	223	1.6
Woodridge village	11 708	14.8	11 382	67.2	NA	NA	NA	NA	NA	NA		19 109	.7	535	2.8
INDIANA	2 532 319	12.7	2 336 306	71.4	223 808	22 261	201 547	245 952	3 766	4 169		3 084 135	.3	100 203	3.2
Anderson city	27 643	4.9	25 274	63.8	NA	NA	NA	3 191	NA	5 386		29 740	2.4	1 245	4.2
Bloomington city	28 400	28.9	26 468	35.3	2 669	154	2 515	2 829	4 072	4 204		31 452	–.8	785	2.5
Carmel city	14 107	46.3	13 597	79.1	833	12	821	919	1 965	2 367		23 197	2.5	280	1.2
Columbus city	17 162	27.5	15 985	64.9	1 907	50	1 857	NA	5 870	NA		18 859	–1.6	486	2.6
East Chicago city	13 261	–1.7	11 707	44.6	NA	NA	NA	NA	NA	NA		12 786	–1.4	1 017	8.0
Elkhart city	21 688	13.3	20 072	53.5	4 668	258	4 410	NA	10 610	NA		26 904	1.8	1 025	3.8
Evansville city	57 065	–1.9	52 273	60.0	6 214	472	5 742	7 812	5 024	6 302		67 522	–.2	2 538	3.8
Fort Wayne city	90 915	17.8	83 333	61.6	12 388	923	11 465	14 163	6 621	7 570		98 013	.2	3 729	3.8
Gary city	43 630	–7.3	38 244	55.8	6 603	930	5 673	7 487	6 043	6 702		44 797	–1.3	4 220	9.4
Greenwood city	16 042	40.7	14 931	62.5	1 389	54	1 335	1 464	4 126	4 641		20 284	2.4	273	1.3
Hammond city	34 139	.6	32 026	63.2	6 170	907	5 263	6 633	7 831	8 228		38 498	–1.7	1 869	4.9
Indianapolis city (remainder)	352 429	10.1	320 107	58.6	[7]40 398	[7]7 714	[7]32 684	[7]47 534	[7]5 322	[7]6 257		414 779	2.4	12 343	3.0
Kokomo city	22 292	9.6	20 273	61.1	2 679	192	2 487	2 874	5 890	6 259		22 134	–.6	891	4.0
Lafayette city	25 602	32.9	24 060	52.9	NA	NA	NA	3 096	NA	6 933		26 226	–.3	588	2.2
Lawrence city	16 292	40.2	14 853	75.8	919	43	876	1 138	2 640	3 471		15 406	2.4	407	2.6
Marion city	13 820	–1.3	12 462	62.1	NA	NA	NA	2 461	NA	8 215		13 105	–2.3	840	6.4
Merrillville town	12 303	19.2	11 678	70.6	1 272	60	1 212	1 051	4 130	3 415		13 992	–1.9	309	2.2
Michigan City city	14 221	1.6	12 550	61.1	2 144	159	1 985	2 849	6 523	8 602		16 218	.3	854	5.3
Mishawaka city	21 572	13.4	20 248	56.8	4 120	216	3 904	4 270	9 026	9 397		24 575	.2	794	3.2
Muncie city	30 305	1.3	27 322	55.8	NA	NA	NA	NA	NA	NA		33 675	–2.4	1 427	4.2
New Albany city	17 098	9.7	15 959	59.3	2 443	178	2 265	2 325	6 338	5 976		21 499	1.6	766	3.6
Portage city	13 375	23.1	12 746	72.5	1 253	60	1 193	1 367	3 766	4 134		15 952	–1.8	665	4.2
Richmond city	17 647	4.2	16 287	58.7	2 499	148	2 351	NA	6 688	NA		18 794	–3.7	887	4.7
South Bend city	46 349	1.3	42 908	63.1	8 820	784	8 036	9 168	8 806	8 901		55 328	.8	2 587	4.7
Terre Haute city	25 636	6.5	22 870	59.5	4 814	150	4 664	5 013	8 956	9 225		25 203	.8	1 473	5.8
West Lafayette city	10 819	14.3	10 462	32.2	NA	NA	NA	NA	NA	NA		13 822	–.3	410	3.0
IOWA	1 232 511	7.8	1 149 276	72.3	92 497	8 034	84 463	100 188	3 224	3 501		1 563 063	–.6	40 922	2.6
Ames city	18 757	16.8	18 085	46.1	NA	NA	NA	1 053	NA	2 199		29 521	.2	674	2.3
Bettendorf city	13 044	17.9	12 474	77.3	936	96	840	969	2 942	3 104		16 993	.2	341	2.0
Burlington city	11 985	1.8	11 102	70.2	1 392	186	1 206	1 501	5 171	5 608		14 357	.3	552	3.8
Cedar Falls city	13 271	10.0	12 833	64.3	1 088	99	989	1 206	3 126	3 466		20 099	–.5	514	2.6
Cedar Rapids city	52 240	14.9	49 820	69.0	7 024	379	6 645	NA	6 116	NA		73 275	1.2	1 443	2.0
Clinton city	12 412	–1.4	11 427	69.3	NA	NA	NA	NA	NA	NA		14 508	–1.4	622	4.3
Council Bluffs city	24 340	9.4	22 889	65.0	5 162	522	4 640	5 519	9 145	9 826		31 300	2.3	829	2.6
Davenport city	41 350	2.5	39 124	65.2	7 589	1 386	6 203	7 091	7 817	7 262		52 053	.1	1 761	3.4
Des Moines city	85 067	2.1	80 504	64.7	11 679	745	10 934	14 202	6 104	7 309		121 042	.5	3 104	2.6
Dubuque city	23 819	6.4	22 560	67.5	1 927	130	1 797	2 175	3 404	3 792		32 032	Z	1 185	3.7
Fort Dodge city	11 168	–.4	10 470	66.4	1 822	131	1 691	1 798	7 347	7 297		12 631	–1.7	389	3.1
Iowa City city	26 083	16.1	25 202	46.5	2 031	396	1 635	2 485	3 327	4 036		42 036	1.6	919	2.2
Marshalltown city	10 857	2.1	10 175	70.1	1 356	212	1 144	1 431	5 368	5 620		12 979	–1.6	347	2.7
Mason City city	13 029	2.8	12 368	67.4	2 261	125	2 136	2 119	7 854	7 290		15 620	–1.3	426	2.7
Sioux City city	33 816	5.1	32 054	66.2	6 407	707	5 700	6 352	7 729	7 582		43 573	–.9	1 299	3.0
Waterloo city	29 499	1.6	28 169	67.1	4 080	312	3 768	4 526	6 389	6 979		33 984	–.8	1 251	3.7
West Des Moines city	20 815	52.3	19 826	62.1	1 561	63	1 498	1 631	3 678	4 012		21 973	.4	319	1.5

[1] Data on serious crimes have not been adjusted for underreporting; this may affect comparability over time or among geographic areas. [2] Includes murder and nonnegligent manslaughter, forcible rape, robbery, and aggravated assault. [3] Includes burglary, larceny-theft, and motor vehicle theft. [4] Per 100,000 resident population provided by the U.S. Federal Bureau of Investigation. [5] Civilian unemployed as a percent of total civilian labor force. [6] Excludes rape. [7] Data are for consolidated city of Indianapolis; data for Indianapolis city (remainder) not available.

Sources: Housing, 2000—U.S. Census Bureau, 2000 Census of Population and Housing, "Census 2000 Profiles of General Demographic Characteristics" data files, published May 2001 (related Internet site <http://www.census.gov/mp/www/pub/2000cen/mscen01.html>). Housing, 1990—U.S. Census Bureau, "1990 Census of Population and Housing, Summary Tape File (STF) 1C" on CD-ROM (related Internet site <http://homer.ssd.census.gov/cdrom/lookup>). Serious Crimes Known to Police—U.S. Federal Bureau of Investigation, Uniform Crime Reporting Program, "Crime in the United States," annual <http://www.fbi.gov/ucr/Cius_99/99crime/99c2_01.pdf> (accessed: 20 October 2000) and <http://www.fbi.gov/ucr/Cius_98/98crime/98cius05.pdf> (accessed: 9 December 1999). Civilian Labor Force—U.S. Bureau of Labor Statistics, Local Area Unemployment Statistics, 2000 data published 2 May 2001, 1999 data published 30 May 2001 <ftp://ftp.bls.gov/pub/time.series/la/> (related Internet site <http://www.bls.gov/lauhome.htm>).

Table C–4. Cities — **Housing, Crime, and Labor Force**–Con.

[Includes states and 1,070 incorporated places of 25,000 or more population as of April 1, 1990 in all states except Hawaii which has no incorporated places recognized by the Census Bureau. For Hawaii, 8 census designated places (CDPs) of 25,000 or more population as of April 1, 1990 are included. Also included are the 5 boroughs of New York city. For more information on these areas, see appendix B. Geographic Information]

City	Housing, 2000 Total units	Percent change, 1990–2000	Occupied units Number	Percent owner–occupied	Number 1999 Total	Violent[2]	Property[3]	1998	Rate[4] 1999	1998	Civilian labor force, 2000 Total	Percent change, 1999–2000	Unemployment Total	Rate[5]
KANSAS	1 131 200	8.3	1 037 891	69.2	117 803	10 159	107 644	127 737	4 439	4 859	1 411 024	-1.6	52 323	3.7
Emporia city	11 019	2.7	10 253	53.6	NA	NA	NA	NA	NA	NA	14 094	-3.1	548	3.9
Hutchinson city	17 693	3.1	16 335	64.7	NA	NA	NA	NA	NA	NA	20 091	-3.5	827	4.1
Kansas City city	61 446	-4.7	55 500	62.0	NA	NA	NA	NA	NA	NA	70 626	.3	5 067	7.2
Lawrence city	32 761	26.5	31 388	45.9	NA	NA	NA	NA	NA	NA	44 178	-1.8	1 919	4.3
Leavenworth city	12 936	2.9	12 035	50.8	NA	NA	NA	NA	NA	NA	29 351	-.4	1 179	4.0
Lenexa city	16 378	21.4	15 574	62.7	NA	NA	NA	NA	NA	NA	27 145	-.7	619	2.3
Manhattan city	17 690	13.7	16 949	42.9	NA	NA	NA	NA	NA	NA	21 062	-.9	689	3.3
Olathe city	33 343	48.2	32 314	71.5	NA	NA	NA	NA	NA	NA	47 568	-.6	1 305	2.7
Overland Park city	62 586	30.3	59 703	68.3	NA	NA	NA	NA	NA	NA	87 790	-.7	1 892	2.2
Salina city	19 599	6.5	18 523	66.1	NA	NA	NA	NA	NA	NA	30 570	-1.1	863	2.8
Shawnee city	19 086	25.4	18 522	74.4	NA	NA	NA	NA	NA	NA	30 076	-.6	844	2.8
Topeka city	56 435	3.2	52 190	60.7	13 350	1 108	12 242	15 500	11 115	12 773	65 900	-.3	2 912	4.4
Wichita city	152 119	12.6	139 087	61.6	20 977	1 927	19 050	23 303	6 313	7 079	178 585	-2.0	8 299	4.6
KENTUCKY	1 750 927	16.2	1 590 647	70.8	114 003	11 908	102 095	113 725	2 878	2 889	1 981 868	.8	81 752	4.1
Bowling Green city	21 290	21.7	19 277	47.0	2 898	363	2 535	3 245	6 426	7 206	25 244	.5	261	1.0
Covington city	20 448	7.0	18 257	49.3	NA	NA	NA	NA	NA	NA	19 326	1.0	644	3.3
Frankfort city	13 422	13.0	12 314	52.0	NA	NA	NA	NA	NA	NA	14 766	.6	472	3.2
Henderson city	12 652	11.4	11 693	57.3	NA	NA	NA	NA	NA	NA	14 383	.4	667	4.6
Hopkinsville city	13 260	8.4	12 174	57.9	NA	NA	NA	NA	NA	NA	16 314	3.1	601	3.7
Lexington-Fayette	116 167	18.9	108 288	55.3	14 842	1 913	12 929	13 616	6 102	5 636	146 703	1.1	2 711	1.8
Louisville city	121 275	-2.2	111 414	52.5	15 317	2 216	13 101	17 896	5 965	6 005	130 741	1.3	4 786	3.7
Owensboro city	24 302	5.3	22 659	60.2	2 566	118	2 448	2 576	4 719	4 691	29 468	.1	1 444	4.9
Paducah city	13 221	.5	11 825	52.9	1 962	186	1 776	2 198	7 534	8 200	11 689	-.1	284	2.4
LOUISIANA	1 847 181	7.6	1 656 053	67.9	251 252	32 033	219 219	266 435	5 747	6 098	2 029 566	-1.1	112 475	5.5
Alexandria city	19 806	-2.7	17 816	57.4	4 973	490	4 483	5 341	10 850	11 510	22 542	-.8	1 648	7.3
Baton Rouge city	97 388	.3	88 973	52.2	21 323	2 233	19 090	24 291	10 072	11 235	120 150	1.0	5 899	4.9
Bossier City city	23 026	5.6	21 197	60.0	4 202	494	3 708	3 815	7 414	6 762	27 723	-1.9	1 329	4.8
Houma city	12 514	9.0	11 634	67.7	2 762	458	2 304	2 959	9 211	9 653	15 042	-.3	671	4.5
Kenner city	27 378	.4	25 662	60.8	4 305	403	3 902	4 574	6 005	6 330	38 728	-1.6	1 668	4.3
Lafayette city	46 865	16.1	43 506	58.3	8 617	816	7 801	8 806	7 579	8 243	55 594	-1.9	2 548	4.6
Lake Charles city	31 429	5.3	27 974	57.6	5 119	572	4 547	5 562	7 229	7 721	37 133	-2.7	2 294	6.2
Monroe city	21 278	-1.5	19 421	49.6	7 162	1 002	6 160	7 986	13 349	14 551	24 296	.8	1 481	6.1
New Iberia city	12 880	3.7	11 756	62.6	830	86	744	825	2 539	2 508	14 651	-3.3	1 237	8.4
New Orleans city	215 091	-4.6	188 251	46.5	35 761	5 931	29 830	40 811	7 677	8 662	194 237	-1.5	11 071	5.7
Shreveport city	86 802	-.8	78 662	59.0	18 296	1 968	16 328	18 510	9 709	9 669	93 651	-1.5	5 057	5.4
MAINE	651 901	11.0	518 200	71.6	36 024	1 406	34 618	37 826	2 875	3 041	688 754	2.8	24 153	3.5
Bangor city	14 587	1.5	13 713	47.5	NA	NA	NA	2 139	NA	6 776	18 408	3.4	524	2.8
Lewiston city	16 470	-3.8	15 290	47.2	NA	NA	NA	1 814	NA	4 943	22 115	3.9	673	3.0
Portland city	31 862	1.8	29 714	42.5	NA	NA	NA	3 657	NA	5 751	37 594	2.7	801	2.1
MARYLAND	2 145 283	13.4	1 980 859	67.7	254 420	38 447	215 973	275 527	4 919	5 366	2 804 827	1.1	108 284	3.9
Annapolis city	16 165	6.0	15 303	51.7	2 639	488	2 151	2 904	7 802	8 580	21 444	.5	1 082	5.0
Baltimore city	300 477	-1.1	257 996	50.3	NA	NA	NA	72 497	NA	10 947	293 059	1.2	23 782	8.1
Bowie city	18 718	43.3	18 188	85.0	NA	NA	NA	NA	NA	NA	24 226	1.5	518	2.1
Frederick city	22 106	33.1	20 891	55.6	2 543	519	2 024	2 475	5 319	5 200	27 293	1.4	738	2.7
Gaithersburg city	20 674	28.7	19 621	52.6	NA	NA	NA	NA	NA	NA	26 562	1.3	618	2.3
Hagerstown city	17 089	4.4	15 849	41.9	1 751	213	1 538	1 870	5 098	5 320	20 274	.3	675	3.3
Rockville city	17 786	9.5	17 247	67.7	NA	NA	NA	NA	NA	NA	27 918	1.3	617	2.2
MASSACHUSETTS	2 621 989	6.0	2 443 580	61.7	201 460	34 023	167 437	211 203	3 263	3 436	3 236 597	-1.4	85 610	2.6
Attleboro city	16 554	10.0	16 019	63.8	1 289	129	1 160	1 382	3 244	3 510	21 386	-2.2	634	3.0
Beverly city	16 275	4.0	15 750	60.0	706	25	681	837	1 800	2 144	21 478	-1.3	390	1.8
Boston city	251 935	.4	239 528	32.2	35 078	7 263	27 815	34 981	6 288	6 251	292 277	-1.1	8 495	2.9
Brockton city	34 837	-1.5	33 675	54.6	5 223	982	4 241	5 094	5 580	5 428	44 858	-2.6	1 618	3.6
Cambridge city	44 725	6.5	42 615	32.3	4 362	544	3 818	4 362	4 651	4 616	54 202	-1.0	846	1.6
Chelsea city	12 337	6.6	11 888	28.9	1 703	445	1 258	1 775	6 181	6 420	12 113	-2.2	477	3.9
Chicopee city	24 424	3.1	23 117	59.3	3 174	1 192	1 982	3 263	5 846	5 961	26 146	-2.1	874	3.3
Everett city	15 908	3.2	15 435	41.4	1 025	219	806	1 137	2 922	3 220	18 173	-1.6	554	3.0
Fall River city	41 857	3.7	38 759	34.9	4 027	577	3 450	4 012	4 422	4 381	41 440	-2.9	2 057	5.0
Fitchburg city	16 002	-4.0	14 943	51.6	2 314	485	1 829	2 475	5 757	6 125	17 375	-2.6	692	4.0
Gloucester city	13 958	6.3	12 592	59.7	539	72	467	623	1 809	2 104	15 839	-1.3	602	3.8
Haverhill city	23 737	11.3	22 976	60.2	NA	NA	NA	2 408	NA	4 413	28 805	-1.2	878	3.0

[1] Data on serious crimes have not been adjusted for underreporting; this may affect comparability over time or among geographic areas. [2] Includes murder and nonnegligent manslaughter, forcible rape, robbery, and aggravated assault. [3] Includes burglary, larceny-theft, and motor vehicle theft. [4] Per 100,000 resident population provided by the U.S. Federal Bureau of Investigation. [5] Civilian unemployed as a percent of total civilian labor force.

Sources: Housing, 2000–U.S. Census Bureau, 2000 Census of Population and Housing, "Census 2000 Profiles of General Demographic Characteristics" data files, published May 2001 (related Internet site <http://www.census.gov/mp/www/pub/2000cen/mscen01.html>). Housing, 1990–U.S. Census Bureau, "1990 Census of Population and Housing, Summary Tape File (STF) 1C" on CD-ROM (related Internet site <http://homer.ssd.census.gov/cdrom/lookup>). Serious Crimes Known to Police–U.S. Federal Bureau of Investigation, Uniform Crime Reporting Program, "Crime in the United States," annual <http://www.fbi.gov/ucr/Cius_99/99crime/99c2_01.pdf> (accessed: 20 October 2000) and <http://www.fbi.gov/ucr/Cius_98/98crime/98cius05.pdf> (accessed: 9 December 1999). Civilian Labor Force–U.S. Bureau of Labor Statistics, Local Area Unemployment Statistics, 2000 data published 2 May 2001, 1999 data published 30 May 2001 <ftp://ftp.bls.gov/pub/time.series/la/> (related Internet site <http://www.bls.gov/lauhome.htm>).

Table C–4. Cities — Housing, Crime, and Labor Force–Con.

[Includes states and 1,070 incorporated places of 25,000 or more population as of April 1, 1990 in all states except Hawaii which has no incorporated places recognized by the Census Bureau. For Hawaii, 8 census designated places (CDPs) of 25,000 or more population as of April 1, 1990 are included. Also included are the 5 boroughs of New York city. For more information on these areas, see appendix B. Geographic Information]

City	Housing, 2000				Serious crimes known to police[1]						Civilian labor force, 2000			
			Occupied units		Number				Rate[4]				Unemployment	
					1999									
	Total units	Percent change, 1990–2000	Number	Percent owner-occupied	Total	Violent[2]	Property[3]	1998	1999	1998	Total	Percent change, 1999–2000	Total	Rate[5]
MASSACHUSETTS—Con.														
Holyoke city	16 210	-4.2	14 967	41.5	2 810	407	2 403	2 828	6 829	6 795	15 538	-2.3	648	4.2
Lawrence city	25 601	-4.9	24 463	32.2	–	3 849	3 849	NA	–	NA	27 626	-2.2	1 764	6.4
Leominster city	16 976	9.3	16 491	57.9	1 573	72	1 501	1 512	3 894	3 797	20 241	-2.8	657	3.2
Lowell city	39 468	-2.1	37 887	43.0	3 307	789	2 518	4 005	3 257	3 933	51 078	.6	1 675	3.3
Lynn city	34 637	-.1	33 511	45.6	4 455	967	3 488	NA	5 470	NA	37 818	-1.4	1 282	3.4
Malden city	23 634	1.8	23 009	43.3	1 741	477	1 264	NA	3 292	NA	29 129	-1.5	726	2.5
Marlborough city	14 903	14.4	14 501	61.0	669	87	582	754	2 001	2 267	19 736	-1.4	444	2.2
Medford city	22 687	.2	22 067	58.6	1 463	201	1 262	1 464	2 602	2 583	30 591	-1.2	630	2.1
Melrose city	11 248	-.4	10 982	67.0	352	10	342	442	1 280	1 598	14 895	-1.2	281	1.9
New Bedford city	41 511	-.6	38 178	43.8	NA	NA	NA	3 907	NA	4 000	39 399	-2.0	2 575	6.5
Newton city	32 112	5.3	31 201	69.5	1 391	73	1 318	1 336	1 723	1 651	46 442	-1.0	626	1.3
Northampton city	12 405	5.6	11 880	53.5	680	99	581	763	2 360	2 624	15 212	-2.0	288	1.9
Peabody city	18 898	3.6	18 581	71.2	1 447	111	1 336	1 531	2 927	3 129	26 970	-1.4	561	2.1
Pittsfield city	21 366	.4	19 704	60.8	1 530	109	1 421	1 509	3 346	3 254	20 309	-3.3	730	3.6
Quincy city	40 093	6.3	38 883	49.0	2 739	230	2 509	2 669	3 179	3 096	49 018	-1.0	1 279	2.6
Revere city	20 181	7.8	19 463	50.0	1 630	316	1 314	1 671	3 895	3 995	20 931	-1.5	702	3.4
Salem city	18 175	5.9	17 492	49.1	1 388	116	1 272	1 306	3 603	3 397	20 957	-1.5	533	2.5
Somerville city	32 477	2.2	31 555	30.6	1 976	170	1 806	2 303	2 655	3 070	43 805	-1.2	763	1.7
Springfield city	61 172	-.2	57 130	49.9	11 951	2 876	9 075	13 728	8 031	9 121	62 294	-2.3	2 749	4.4
Taunton city	22 908	13.0	22 045	61.2	1 636	230	1 406	1 650	3 099	3 152	27 446	-.9	872	3.2
Waltham city	23 880	9.9	23 207	46.0	1 101	99	1 002	1 349	1 872	2 338	34 020	-1.0	698	2.1
Westfield city	15 441	6.7	14 797	67.8	1 101	303	798	1 204	2 917	3 195	18 569	-2.2	519	2.8
Woburn city	15 391	9.1	14 997	61.2	881	38	843	801	2 366	2 169	22 104	-1.4	423	1.9
Worcester city	70 723	2.0	67 028	43.3	9 739	1 745	7 994	10 074	5 821	5 972	75 548	-2.5	2 467	3.3
MICHIGAN	4 234 279	10.0	3 785 661	73.8	426 596	56 709	369 887	459 720	4 325	4 683	5 201 404	1.1	185 356	3.6
Allen Park city	12 254	.2	11 974	87.9	690	56	634	955	2 162	3 040	15 808	1.3	258	1.6
Ann Arbor city	47 218	7.3	45 693	45.3	4 008	362	3 646	4 747	3 628	4 291	69 929	1.0	969	1.4
Battle Creek city	23 525	1.2	21 348	65.8	4 854	626	4 228	4 953	6 351	9 121	26 523	.4	1 328	5.0
Bay City city	16 259	-.7	15 208	69.5	1 925	220	1 705	1 979	5 399	5 404	18 274	-.5	1 016	5.6
Burton city	12 348	13.9	11 699	80.8	1 959	171	1 788	2 151	7 160	7 830	12 185	-2.6	742	6.1
Dearborn city	38 981	5.6	36 770	73.4	6 225	779	5 446	NA	6 757	NA	44 523	1.3	832	1.9
Dearborn Heights city	23 913	-.1	23 278	85.4	2 020	150	1 004	2 247	6 062	6 655	32 385	1.3	570	1.8
Detroit city	375 096	-8.5	336 428	54.9	101 561	21 976	79 585	117 911	10 416	11 791	402 383	.9	26 359	6.6
East Detroit city	13 965	2.1	13 595	88.0	1 523	227	1 296	NA	4 439	NA	20 408	1.3	550	2.7
East Lansing city	15 321	6.4	14 390	32.0	NA	NA	NA	1 798	NA	3 725	29 388	1.1	876	3.0
Farmington Hills city	34 858	11.8	33 559	66.9	2 231	198	2 033	2 817	2 783	3 488	50 562	1.2	757	1.5
Ferndale city	10 243	.4	9 872	70.8	968	103	865	1 351	3 939	5 459	15 484	1.1	411	2.7
Flint city	55 464	-5.6	48 744	58.8	14 576	3 096	11 480	16 216	11 018	11 973	52 751	-2.7	5 026	9.5
Garden City city	11 719	3.0	11 479	86.2	727	39	688	833	2 209	2 577	18 050	1.3	318	1.8
Grand Rapids city	77 960	5.8	73 217	59.7	NA	NA	NA	14 502	NA	7 619	118 283	2.2	5 156	4.4
Holland city	12 533	11.5	11 971	67.1	1 404	128	1 276	1 343	4 203	3 939	22 196	2.1	684	3.1
Inkster city	12 013	-.3	11 169	58.0	1 784	337	1 447	1 814	5 698	5 855	14 073	1.1	617	4.4
Jackson city	15 241	-2.9	14 210	57.6	2 814	364	2 450	2 722	7 960	7 506	18 672	2.0	857	4.6
Kalamazoo city	31 798	1.0	29 413	47.7	5 516	739	4 777	5 461	7 201	7 014	43 123	.1	1 848	4.3
Kentwood city	19 507	19.4	18 477	61.0	1 950	95	1 855	2 028	4 586	4 796	28 318	2.3	565	2.0
Lansing city	53 159	-1.4	49 505	57.5	7 635	1 188	6 447	9 122	5 945	7 242	67 523	1.1	2 262	3.3
Lincoln Park city	16 821	.3	16 204	79.1	2 161	209	1 952	2 496	5 087	5 922	21 578	1.3	509	2.4
Livonia city	38 658	5.5	38 089	88.8	3 098	203	2 895	3 926	3 042	3 737	58 342	1.3	776	1.3
Madison Heights city	13 623	3.0	13 299	70.1	1 496	94	1 402	1 715	4 674	5 211	20 723	1.1	598	2.9
Midland city	17 773	15.1	16 743	69.7	879	59	820	1 113	2 190	2 757	22 849	.5	510	2.2
Muskegon city	15 999	-.1	14 569	56.9	3 996	412	3 584	3 558	10 193	8 906	18 838	2.1	1 146	6.1
Novi city	19 649	44.9	18 726	71.1	1 460	55	1 405	1 883	3 246	4 270	22 583	1.2	367	1.6
Oak Park city	11 370	.2	11 104	74.8	1 230	145	1 085	865	4 137	2 856	17 912	1.1	467	2.6
Pontiac city	26 336	-1.0	24 234	52.8	4 617	1 281	3 336	6 237	6 668	8 757	34 463	.6	2 212	6.4
Portage city	18 880	17.0	18 138	68.9	1 852	93	1 759	1 917	4 217	4 403	25 764	.2	465	1.8
Port Huron city	14 003	-.2	12 961	57.2	1 543	199	1 344	1 741	4 761	5 206	17 556	1.3	977	5.6
Rochester Hills city	27 263	15.8	26 315	79.1	NA	NA	NA	NA	NA	NA	40 191	1.2	684	1.7
Roseville city	20 519	2.5	19 976	75.2	1 919	131	1 788	2 561	3 717	4 943	31 911	1.3	1 228	3.8
Royal Oak city	29 942	2.7	28 880	70.1	2 074	145	1 929	2 214	3 211	3 373	43 655	1.2	795	1.8
Saginaw city	25 639	-8.4	23 182	63.6	4 292	1 118	3 174	4 964	6 731	7 619	27 595	-.2	2 046	7.4
St. Clair Shores city	28 208	1.0	27 434	85.8	1 663	123	1 540	2 108	2 506	3 256	42 147	1.3	1 204	2.9
Southfield city	35 698	1.8	33 987	54.1	5 390	678	4 712	6 332	7 143	8 224	49 819	1.1	1 211	2.4
Southgate city	13 361	6.9	12 836	70.6	1 368	226	1 142	1 342	4 206	4 270	17 229	1.3	313	1.8
Sterling Heights city	47 547	12.4	46 319	79.0	3 787	273	3 514	4 575	3 031	3 814	79 572	1.4	2 026	2.5
Taylor city	25 905	2.4	24 776	70.8	3 992	326	3 666	4 559	5 476	6 340	36 774	1.2	998	2.7
Troy city	30 872	13.5	30 018	77.3	2 433	99	2 334	3 018	3 054	3 774	48 724	1.3	645	1.3
Warren city	57 249	1.9	55 551	80.4	NA	NA	NA	9 051	NA	6 487	89 074	1.3	3 256	3.7
Westland city	38 077	10.3	36 533	62.7	3 027	278	2 749	5 033	3 494	5 545	50 107	1.3	938	1.9
Wyandotte city	12 303	-4.0	11 816	73.0	821	31	790	965	2 563	3 036	15 272	1.2	374	2.4
Wyoming city	27 506	9.8	26 536	67.6	2 650	233	2 417	2 925	3 841	4 345	45 613	2.3	1 376	3.0

[1] Data on serious crimes have not been adjusted for underreporting; this may affect comparability over time or among geographic areas. [2] Includes murder and nonnegligent manslaughter, forcible rape, robbery, and aggravated assault. [3] Includes burglary, larceny-theft, and motor vehicle theft. [4] Per 100,000 resident population provided by the U.S. Federal Bureau of Investigation. [5] Civilian unemployed as a percent of total civilian labor force.

Sources: Housing, 2000—U.S. Census Bureau, 2000 Census of Population and Housing, "Census 2000 Profiles of General Demographic Characteristics" data files, published May 2001 (related Internet site <http://www.census.gov/mp/www/pub/2000cen/mscen01.html>). Housing, 1990—U.S. Census Bureau, "1990 Census of Population and Housing, Summary Tape File (STF) 1C" on CD-ROM (related Internet site <http://homer.ssd.census.gov/cdrom/lookup>). Serious Crimes Known to Police—U.S. Federal Bureau of Investigation, Uniform Crime Reporting Program, "Crime in the United States," annual <http://www.fbi.gov/ucr/Cius_99/99crime/99c2_01.pdf> (accessed: 20 October 2000) and <http://www.fbi.gov/ucr/Cius_98/98crime/98cius05.pdf> (accessed: 9 December 1999). Civilian Labor Force—U.S. Bureau of Labor Statistics, Local Area Unemployment Statistics, 2000 data published 2 May 2001, 1999 data published 30 May 2001 <ftp://ftp.bls.gov/pub/time.series/la/> (related Internet site <http://www.bls.gov/lauhome.htm>).

Table C–4. Cities — Housing, Crime, and Labor Force–Con.

[Includes states and 1,070 incorporated places of 25,000 or more population as of April 1, 1990 in all states except Hawaii which has no incorporated places recognized by the Census Bureau. For Hawaii, 8 census designated places (CDPs) of 25,000 or more population as of April 1, 1990 are included. Also included are the 5 boroughs of New York city. For more information on these areas, see appendix B. Geographic Information]

City	Housing, 2000 Total units	Percent change, 1990–2000	Occupied units Number	Percent owner-occupied	Serious crimes 1999 Total	Violent[2]	Property[3]	1998	Rate[4] 1999	1998	Civilian labor force 2000 Total	Percent change, 1999–2000	Unemployment Total	Rate[5]
MINNESOTA	2 065 946	11.8	1 895 127	74.6	171 802	13 085	158 717	191 197	3 597	4 046	2 738 685	1.3	89 540	3.3
Apple Valley city	16 536	43.3	16 344	88.0	1 144	38	1 106	1 254	2 492	2 831	28 682	1.3	595	2.1
Blaine city	16 169	22.7	15 898	90.5	2 144	96	2 048	2 498	4 719	5 627	28 957	1.4	716	2.5
Bloomington city	37 104	3.6	36 400	70.6	4 802	221	4 581	5 155	5 513	5 901	57 227	1.3	1 291	2.3
Brooklyn Center city	11 598	−1.0	11 430	68.7	2 348	90	2 258	2 356	8 342	8 308	16 386	1.5	496	3.0
Brooklyn Park city	24 846	16.8	24 432	73.4	3 102	290	2 812	3 148	4 863	5 092	41 093	1.3	1 101	2.7
Burnsville city	24 261	19.8	23 687	68.1	2 305	98	2 207	2 471	3 844	4 197	40 080	1.2	848	2.1
Coon Rapids city	22 828	26.1	22 578	80.4	2 636	90	2 546	2 957	4 096	4 587	39 366	1.3	968	2.5
Duluth city	36 994	2.7	35 500	64.1	3 742	309	3 433	4 085	4 558	4 832	44 577	1.6	1 921	4.3
Eagan city	24 390	32.2	23 773	75.0	1 723	70	1 653	1 691	2 840	2 862	40 208	1.2	741	1.8
Eden Prairie city	21 026	36.5	20 457	78.3	1 609	35	1 574	1 463	3 167	3 047	31 982	1.3	680	2.1
Edina city	21 669	3.3	20 996	76.5	1 339	25	1 314	1 475	2 887	3 158	25 682	1.1	487	1.9
Fridley city	11 504	.8	11 328	67.7	1 765	109	1 656	1 777	6 243	6 207	18 273	1.3	506	2.8
Mankato city	12 759	9.2	12 367	52.9	1 910	55	1 855	1 828	6 140	5 806	20 924	1.4	543	2.6
Maple Grove city	17 745	36.8	17 532	92.7	1 211	48	1 163	1 406	2 553	3 090	31 080	1.3	620	2.0
Maplewood city	14 004	15.5	13 758	75.7	NA	NA	NA	1 983	NA	5 771	20 183	1.6	489	2.4
Minneapolis city	168 606	−2.4	162 352	51.4	30 737	4 943	25 794	34 621	8 635	9 561	206 217	1.2	6 594	3.2
Minnetonka city	22 228	10.5	21 393	75.7	1 515	39	1 476	1 562	2 942	3 086	32 976	1.1	641	1.9
Moorhead city	12 180	5.8	11 660	63.7	889	72	817	1 282	2 659	3 808	19 562	−.3	436	2.2
Plymouth city	25 258	28.8	24 820	76.5	1 659	57	1 602	1 709	2 669	2 821	40 184	1.3	816	2.0
Richfield city	15 357	−4.6	15 073	67.6	1 566	124	1 442	1 694	4 552	4 887	21 237	1.3	502	2.4
Rochester city	35 346	22.0	34 116	71.0	2 719	173	2 546	2 838	3 442	3 674	50 740	2.9	1 413	2.8
Roseville city	14 917	4.9	14 598	67.5	1 798	52	1 746	1 934	5 162	5 596	20 964	1.2	400	1.9
St. Cloud city	23 249	23.5	22 652	55.9	NA	NA	NA	3 034	NA	5 851	37 983	2.1	1 324	3.5
St. Louis Park city	21 140	2.2	20 782	63.6	1 713	52	1 661	1 696	3 999	3 928	28 193	1.0	529	1.9
St. Paul city	115 713	−1.6	112 109	54.8	18 368	2 208	16 160	20 265	7 064	7 720	140 457	1.4	4 935	3.5
Winona city	10 666	10.2	10 301	60.9	985	22	963	1 188	4 030	4 766	14 711	1.7	575	3.9
MISSISSIPPI	1 161 953	15.0	1 046 434	72.3	118 231	9 671	108 560	120 647	4 270	4 384	1 326 349	4.6	75 285	5.7
Biloxi city	22 115	17.2	19 588	48.9	5 234	336	4 898	4 735	10 996	9 667	20 027	3.3	964	4.8
Greenville city	16 251	−1.5	14 784	55.8	NA	NA	NA	5 436	NA	12 596	18 335	4.1	1 730	9.4
Gulfport city	29 559	62.1	26 943	58.7	5 387	251	5 136	5 528	8 268	8 428	32 833	4.5	1 630	5.0
Hattiesburg city	19 258	9.0	17 295	44.6	3 535	176	3 359	3 920	7 200	8 074	22 839	6.4	1 141	5.0
Jackson city	75 678	−4.7	67 841	58.0	20 072	2 080	17 992	20 674	10 568	10 690	101 128	5.7	5 333	5.3
Meridian city	17 890	.8	15 966	56.3	2 088	242	1 846	2 237	5 156	5 446	18 542	3.9	1 214	6.5
Pascagoula city	10 931	−1.1	9 878	56.8	3 107	197	2 910	2 293	11 370	8 376	15 421	5.3	1 046	6.8
Tupelo city	14 551	18.0	13 395	62.2	2 446	126	2 320	2 875	6 832	8 021	21 100	5.9	666	3.2
MISSOURI	2 442 017	11.0	2 194 594	70.3	250 363	27 353	223 010	262 506	4 579	4 826	2 929 827	3.1	101 447	3.5
Blue Springs city	17 733	24.5	17 286	74.2	2 356	523	1 833	2 080	5 274	4 606	24 649	5.0	515	2.1
Cape Girardeau city	15 827	8.2	14 380	57.3	2 556	68	2 488	2 326	7 141	6 489	20 995	1.5	732	3.5
Chesterfield city	18 738	33.7	18 060	77.9	1 121	45	1 076	1 075	2 422	2 348	21 078	3.9	291	1.4
Columbia city	35 916	30.4	33 689	47.3	4 019	333	3 686	4 403	5 065	5 592	50 565	2.7	672	1.3
Florissant city	21 027	6.2	20 399	76.8	1 351	41	1 310	1 556	2 855	3 062	29 365	3.9	629	2.1
Gladstone city	11 919	7.6	11 484	68.6	1 009	48	961	1 100	3 578	3 845	19 616	4.8	315	1.6
Independence city	50 213	4.0	47 390	67.8	8 245	632	7 613	8 813	7 019	7 904	67 353	5.1	2 049	3.0
Jefferson City city	16 987	10.0	15 794	58.6	1 612	126	1 486	1 853	4 592	5 053	22 241	2.3	555	2.5
Joplin city	21 328	10.1	19 101	57.6	3 316	123	3 193	2 870	7 393	6 459	24 807	.8	894	3.6
Kansas City city	202 334	.3	183 981	57.7	51 640	7 766	43 874	53 727	11 631	12 000	265 879	5.0	10 535	4.0
Kirkwood city	12 306	5.2	11 763	77.1	444	22	422	552	1 647	3 225	15 141	3.9	288	1.9
Lee's Summit city	27 311	45.6	26 417	75.6	1 769	70	1 699	2 078	2 641	3 289	28 610	5.0	561	2.0
Maryland Heights city	11 846	3.3	11 302	62.6	1 119	40	1 079	1 240	4 742	5 113	17 703	3.9	288	1.6
Raytown city	13 309	.7	12 855	73.9	1 061	45	1 016	1 319	3 719	4 434	18 684	5.0	404	2.2
St. Charles city	25 283	8.8	24 210	64.6	1 891	130	1 761	2 274	3 233	3 866	43 485	4.0	952	2.2
St. Joseph city	31 752	1.5	29 026	64.8	4 507	262	4 245	4 907	6 438	6 950	35 623	1.5	1 326	3.7
St. Louis city	176 354	−9.5	147 076	46.9	47 711	7 611	40 100	51 459	13 998	14 952	156 738	3.9	10 400	6.6
St. Peters city	18 776	19.0	18 435	85.4	1 856	115	1 741	1 870	3 670	3 705	35 159	4.0	676	1.9
Springfield city	69 650	11.5	64 691	53.7	11 499	552	10 947	NA	8 003	NA	86 866	5.7	2 288	2.6
University City city	17 485	−1.2	16 453	57.8	2 683	168	2 515	2 344	7 240	–	23 018	3.9	920	4.0

[1] Data on serious crimes have not been adjusted for underreporting; this may affect comparability over time or among geographic areas. [2] Includes murder and nonnegligent manslaughter, forcible rape, robbery, and aggravated assault. [3] Includes burglary, larceny-theft, and motor vehicle theft. [4] Per 100,000 resident population provided by the U.S. Federal Bureau of Investigation. [5] Civilian unemployed as a percent of total civilian labor force.

Sources: Housing, 2000—U.S. Census Bureau, 2000 Census of Population and Housing, "Census 2000 Profiles of General Demographic Characteristics" data files, published May 2001 (related Internet site <http://www.census.gov/mp/www/pub/2000cen/mscen01.html>). Housing, 1990—U.S. Census Bureau, "1990 Census of Population and Housing, Summary Tape File (STF) 1C" on CD-ROM (related Internet site <http://homer.ssd.census.gov/cdrom/lookup>). Serious Crimes Known to Police—U.S. Federal Bureau of Investigation, Uniform Crime Reporting Program, "Crime in the United States," annual <http://www.fbi.gov/ucr/Cius_99/99crime/99c2_01.pdf> (accessed: 20 October 2000) and <http://www.fbi.gov/ucr/Cius_98/98crime/98cius05.pdf> (accessed: 9 December 1999). Civilian Labor Force—U.S. Bureau of Labor Statistics, Local Area Unemployment Statistics, 2000 data published 2 May 2001, 1999 data published 30 May 2001 <ftp://ftp.bls.gov/pub/time.series/la/> (related Internet site <http://www.bls.gov/lauhome.htm>).

Table C–4. Cities — **Housing, Crime, and Labor Force**–Con.

[Includes states and 1,070 incorporated places of 25,000 or more population as of April 1, 1990 in all states except Hawaii which has no incorporated places recognized by the Census Bureau. For Hawaii, 8 census designated places (CDPs) of 25,000 or more population as of April 1, 1990 are included. Also included are the 5 boroughs of New York city. For more information on these areas, see appendix B. Geographic Information]

City	Housing, 2000				Serious crimes known to police[1]						Civilian labor force, 2000			
			Occupied units		Number				Rate[4]				Unemployment	
					1999									
	Total units	Percent change, 1990–2000	Number	Percent owner-occupied	Total	Violent[2]	Property[3]	1998	1999	1998	Total	Percent change, 1999–2000	Total	Rate[5]
MONTANA............	412 633	14.3	358 667	69.1	35 937	1 823	34 114	35 822	4 070	4 071	479 132	1.1	23 524	4.9
Billings city..............	39 293	9.3	37 525	64.0	4 735	197	4 538	NA	5 132	NA	52 731	1.1	1 954	3.7
Butte-Silver Bow (remainder)............	15 833	4.3	14 135	70.1	NA	NA	NA	NA	NA	NA	[6]16 866	[6]–3.1	[6]1 038	[6]6.2
Great Falls city...........	25 250	4.5	23 834	63.0	3 812	126	3 686	NA	6 742	NA	27 702	.1	1 447	5.2
Missoula city.............	25 225	36.4	24 141	50.2	4 052	258	3 794	NA	7 736	NA	30 562	2.9	1 121	3.7
NEBRASKA...........	722 668	9.4	666 184	67.4	68 444	7 167	61 277	73 259	4 108	4 405	924 298	1.4	27 537	3.0
Bellevue city.............	17 439	45.8	16 937	66.1	1 479	26	1 453	1 387	3 351	3 157	19 604	2.1	498	2.5
Grand Island city.........	17 421	9.9	16 426	62.7	2 735	130	2 605	3 629	6 594	8 754	24 787	.2	776	3.1
Lincoln city..............	95 199	20.4	90 485	58.0	13 399	1 218	12 181	14 226	6 276	6 711	131 041	1.6	3 596	2.7
Omaha city..............	165 731	15.4	156 738	59.6	26 245	4 613	21 632	26 409	7 048	7 171	207 009	2.3	7 171	3.5
NEVADA	827 457	59.5	751 165	60.9	84 185	10 311	73 874	92 250	4 654	5 280	986 052	4.7	39 978	4.1
Carson City	21 283	28.0	20 171	63.1	NA	NA	NA	NA	NA	NA	22 739	1.6	765	3.4
Henderson city	71 149	180.1	66 331	70.5	5 509	507	5 002	6 539	3 483	4 855	59 660	6.0	2 009	3.4
Las Vegas city..........	190 724	73.9	176 750	59.1	[7]47 828	[7]6 133	[7]41 695	[7]53 115	[7]5 185	[7]5 846	243 256	5.9	9 957	4.1
North Las Vegas city	36 600	131.1	34 018	70.1	6 048	1 198	4 850	6 022	6 198	6 953	37 430	5.7	2 685	7.2
Reno city	79 453	29.4	73 904	47.5	9 416	857	8 559	10 075	5 566	6 075	94 274	3.0	3 093	3.3
Sparks city	26 025	20.2	24 601	59.7	3 302	246	3 056	3 222	5 107	5 077	37 781	3.1	1 040	2.8
NEW HAMPSHIRE	547 024	8.6	474 606	69.7	27 406	1 159	26 247	28 675	2 282	2 420	685 511	2.6	19 191	2.8
Concord city	16 881	7.5	16 281	51.4	NA	NA	NA	NA	NA	NA	22 438	3.1	458	2.0
Dover city................	11 924	5.5	11 573	51.2	NA	NA	NA	NA	NA	NA	15 277	4.1	321	2.1
Manchester city	45 892	3.5	44 247	46.0	4 085	224	3 861	4 018	3 936	3 876	59 154	3.5	1 451	2.5
Nashua city	35 387	6.0	34 614	56.9	NA	NA	NA	NA	NA	NA	48 767	2.8	1 410	2.9
Portsmouth city	10 186	–10.4	9 875	50.0	NA	NA	NA	933	NA	3 629	13 059	4.1	267	2.0
Rochester city...........	11 836	6.9	11 434	66.8	967	52	915	1 155	3 423	4 095	14 738	4.5	445	3.0
NEW JERSEY...........	3 310 275	7.6	3 064 645	65.6	276 873	–779 077	1 055 950	296 527	3 400	3 654	4 187 899	–.4	157 410	3.8
Atlantic City city.........	20 219	–6.5	15 848	28.9	8 526	619	7 907	8 786	22 322	22 580	19 362	–3.2	1 914	9.9
Bayonne city.............	26 826	1.4	25 545	40.0	1 409	197	1 212	1 342	2 300	2 199	30 076	Z	1 139	3.8
Camden city	29 769	–1.2	24 177	46.1	7 269	1 811	5 458	8 499	8 670	9 977	31 379	–2.8	3 579	11.4
Clifton city	31 060	3.5	30 244	60.9	2 506	171	2 335	2 501	3 278	3 459	37 330	–1.5	1 216	3.3
East Orange city	28 485	–1.7	26 024	26.6	5 052	1 188	3 864	5 382	7 233	7 614	34 586	–1.0	2 199	6.4
Elizabeth city............	42 838	3.7	40 482	29.7	7 079	927	6 152	8 138	6 375	7 319	54 858	–1.0	3 583	6.5
Fair Lawn borough	12 006	2.1	11 806	80.0	508	35	473	514	1 628	1 643	15 387	–1.1	401	2.6
Fort Lee borough	17 446	3.6	16 544	56.2	777	52	725	912	2 278	2 717	16 616	–1.2	551	3.3
Garfield city	11 698	2.1	11 250	40.2	740	44	696	794	2 705	2 896	13 752	–1.5	609	4.4
Hackensack city	18 945	7.0	18 113	32.4	1 561	168	1 393	1 667	4 114	4 390	21 302	–1.4	861	4.0
Hoboken city	19 915	14.3	19 418	22.6	1 346	137	1 209	1 225	4 021	3 664	19 701	Z	777	3.9
Jersey City city..........	93 648	3.2	88 632	28.2	13 400	3 280	10 120	13 242	5 745	5 731	110 937	–.9	7 827	7.1
Kearny town	13 872	3.3	13 539	48.0	1 511	122	1 389	1 611	4 249	4 547	18 507	Z	737	4.0
Linden city	15 567	4.4	15 052	58.7	1 621	148	1 473	2 109	4 342	5 668	18 787	–.5	817	4.3
Long Branch city..........	13 983	2.6	12 594	42.4	1 326	153	1 173	1 505	4 571	5 109	15 834	–.2	866	5.5
Millville city..............	10 652	4.9	10 043	63.9	1 434	187	1 247	1 590	5 421	5 998	12 550	–2.4	781	6.2
Newark city	100 141	–2.3	91 382	23.8	21 149	4 867	16 282	23 045	7 881	8 560	109 868	–1.3	8 885	8.1
New Brunswick city	13 893	2.5	13 057	26.3	2 989	327	2 662	3 255	7 131	7 715	23 892	.3	1 319	5.5
Paramus borough..........	8 209	4.0	8 082	90.7	2 777	85	2 692	2 907	10 602	11 226	12 565	–1.1	320	2.5
Passaic city	20 194	2.9	19 458	27.0	3 184	669	2 515	3 147	5 217	5 441	27 521	–2.7	2 126	7.7
Paterson city	47 169	2.2	44 710	31.5	6 553	1 210	5 343	6 588	4 406	4 323	65 094	–2.7	5 075	7.8
Perth Amboy city	15 236	1.5	14 562	40.5	1 802	275	1 527	1 854	4 227	4 319	23 214	Z	1 590	6.8
Plainfield city	16 180	.7	15 137	50.1	2 965	650	2 315	2 997	6 366	6 419	25 311	–.8	1 434	5.7
Rahway city..............	10 381	3.9	10 028	62.7	827	88	739	1 027	3 253	4 033	13 826	–.3	480	3.5
Sayreville borough	15 235	14.1	14 955	67.7	874	74	800	1 026	2 289	2 704	21 687	1.0	534	2.5
Trenton city	33 843	.8	29 437	45.5	6 287	1 253	5 034	5 960	7 415	6 932	40 881	.5	2 688	6.6
Union City city...........	23 741	5.1	22 872	18.2	2 375	321	2 054	2 254	4 107	3 910	29 229	–.9	2 070	7.1
Vineland city	20 958	7.2	19 930	66.2	3 161	387	2 774	3 402	5 677	6 053	25 754	–2.5	1 802	7.0
Westfield town...........	10 819	2.2	10 622	81.7	390	7	383	515	1 327	1 752	15 697	Z	302	1.9
West New York town	17 360	9.9	16 719	19.9	1 472	172	1 300	1 763	3 858	4 636	19 570	–.5	1 085	5.5

[1] Data on serious crimes have not been adjusted for underreporting; this may affect comparability over time or among geographic areas. [2] Includes murder and nonnegligent manslaughter, forcible rape, robbery, and aggravated assault. [3] Includes burglary, larceny-theft, and motor vehicle theft. [4] Per 100,000 resident population provided by the U.S. Federal Bureau of Investigation. [5] Civilian unemployed as a percent of total civilian labor force. [6] Data are for consolidated city of Butte-Silver Bow; data for Butte-Silver Bow (remainder) not available. [7] Data are for area covered by Las Vegas Metropolitan Police Jurisdiction.

Sources: Housing, 2000–U.S. Census Bureau, 2000 Census of Population and Housing, "Census 2000 Profiles of General Demographic Characteristics" data files, published May 2001 (related Internet site <http://www.census.gov/mp/www/pub/2000cen/mscen01.html>). Housing, 1990–U.S. Census Bureau, "1990 Census of Population and Housing, Summary Tape File (STF) 1C" on CD-ROM (related Internet site <http://homer.ssd.census.gov/cdrom/lookup>). Serious Crimes Known to Police–U.S. Federal Bureau of Investigation, Uniform Crime Reporting Program, "Crime in the United States," annual <http://www.fbi.gov/ucr/Cius_99/99crime/99c2_01.pdf> (accessed: 20 October 2000) and <http://www.fbi.gov/ucr/Cius_98/98crime/98cius05.pdf> (accessed: 9 December 1999). Civilian Labor Force–U.S. Bureau of Labor Statistics, Local Area Unemployment Statistics, 2000 data published 2 May 2001, 1999 data published 30 May 2001 <ftp://ftp.bls.gov/pub/time.series/la/> (related Internet site <http://www.bls.gov/lauhome.htm>).

Table C–4. Cities — Housing, Crime, and Labor Force–Con.

[Includes states and 1,070 incorporated places of 25,000 or more population as of April 1, 1990 in all states except Hawaii which has no incorporated places recognized by the Census Bureau. For Hawaii, 8 census designated places (CDPs) of 25,000 or more population as of April 1, 1990 are included. Also included are the 5 boroughs of New York city. For more information on these areas, see appendix B. Geographic Information]

City	Housing, 2000				Serious crimes known to police[1]						Civilian labor force, 2000			
			Occupied units		Number				Rate[4]				Unemployment	
					1999									
	Total units	Percent change, 1990–2000	Number	Percent owner-occupied	Total	Violent[2]	Property[3]	1998	1999	1998	Total	Percent change, 1999–2000	Total	Rate[5]
NEW MEXICO	780 579	23.5	677 971	70.0	103 740	14 520	89 220	116 711	5 962	6 719	832 835	2.9	40 400	4.9
Alamogordo city	15 920	33.0	13 704	60.7	1 078	91	987	1 504	3 801	5 164	11 460	−.4	492	4.3
Albuquerque city...........	198 465	18.9	183 236	60.4	41 034	5 255	35 779	45 648	9 766	10 806	241 454	4.1	7 595	3.1
Clovis city..............	14 269	9.9	12 458	62.3	2 519	536	1 983	NA	7 763	NA	14 748	.2	581	3.9
Farmington city	15 077	14.9	13 982	68.4	1 818	308	1 510	2 777	4 650	7 198	21 653	1.3	951	4.4
Hobbs city	11 968	−2.9	10 040	67.9	1 628	346	1 282	1 975	5 985	7 034	12 808	3.6	640	5.0
Las Cruces city	31 682	23.4	29 184	58.1	6 458	541	5 917	7 041	8 472	9 131	35 850	3.9	2 225	6.2
Rio Rancho city...........	20 209	64.0	18 995	81.5	1 543	169	1 374	1 360	3 078	2 819	24 904	4.2	608	2.4
Roswell city	19 327	5.9	17 068	68.4	NA	NA	NA	NA	NA	NA	18 624	−1.8	1 218	6.5
Santa Fe city	30 533	23.7	27 569	58.2	NA	NA	NA	NA	NA	NA	38 185	3.2	928	2.4
NEW YORK............	7 679 307	6.3	7 056 860	53.0	596 743	107 147	489 596	652 202	3 279	3 588	8 941 082	.7	407 769	4.6
Albany city	45 288	−2.0	40 709	37.6	7 475	897	6 578	7 392	7 917	7 165	52 211	−.9	2 083	4.0
Auburn city	12 637	−.4	11 411	51.9	1 259	59	1 200	1 256	4 315	4 212	13 322	−1.7	757	5.7
Binghamton city	23 971	−2.7	21 089	43.0	2 355	163	2 192	2 581	5 030	5 398	22 914	−.9	1 118	4.9
Buffalo city..............	145 574	−4.2	122 720	43.5	20 679	3 243	17 436	22 321	6 869	7 232	138 445	−2.4	11 181	8.1
Elmira city	12 895	−3.1	11 475	48.3	NA	NA	NA	1 773	NA	5 558	13 499	−3.0	995	7.4
Freeport village	13 819	1.2	13 504	65.2	1 279	234	1 045	1 573	3 197	3 902	22 492	−.5	713	3.2
Hempstead village	15 579	3.1	15 188	43.2	1 916	550	1 366	1 463	4 098	3 127	27 084	−.7	1 230	4.5
Ithaca city	10 736	6.6	10 287	26.0	NA	NA	NA	1 063	NA	3 702	14 500	−1.0	440	3.0
Jamestown city	15 027	−2.8	13 558	51.3	1 301	126	1 175	NA	4 040	NA	15 651	−.7	826	5.3
Lindenhurst village	9 277	4.9	9 061	80.6	NA	NA	NA	NA	NA	NA	14 914	−.8	528	3.5
Long Beach city	16 128	5.0	14 923	53.4	NA	NA	NA	637	NA	1 849	17 825	−.6	656	3.7
Mount Vernon city	27 048	3.1	25 729	36.5	NA	NA	NA	NA	NA	NA	32 812	−1.4	1 561	4.8
Newburgh city	10 476	4.8	9 144	30.7	1 417	346	1 071	1 256	5 420	4 735	12 226	−1.3	816	6.7
New Rochelle city.........	26 995	2.3	26 189	50.3	NA	NA	NA	2 199	NA	3 247	34 849	−1.2	1 142	3.3
New York city	3 200 912	7.0	3 021 588	30.2	299 523	78 984	220 539	323 150	4 032	4 392	3 560 924	3.2	203 561	5.7
Bronx borough	490 659	11.3	463 212	19.6	NA	NA	NA	NA	NA	NA	479 000	3.4	34 856	7.3
Brooklyn borough	930 866	6.5	880 727	27.1	NA	NA	NA	NA	NA	NA	995 580	3.1	67 313	6.8
Manhattan borough	798 144	1.7	738 644	20.1	NA	NA	NA	NA	NA	NA	856 133	3.5	42 230	4.9
Queens borough	817 250	8.6	782 664	42.8	NA	NA	NA	NA	NA	NA	1 024 481	3.1	49 275	4.8
Staten Island borough	163 993	17.4	156 341	63.8	NA	NA	NA	NA	NA	NA	205 730	3.3	9 887	4.8
Niagara Falls city	27 837	−2.8	24 099	57.6	NA	NA	NA	NA	NA	NA	27 275	−2.2	2 510	9.2
North Tonawanda city	14 425	3.0	13 671	68.7	662	20	642	732	2 007	2 171	18 086	−1.9	861	4.8
Poughkeepsie city	13 153	.3	12 014	36.8	1 471	173	1 298	1 479	5 310	5 273	12 821	−.5	655	5.1
Rochester city............	99 789	−1.3	88 999	40.2	16 100	1 522	14 578	18 713	7 415	8 449	111 980	−1.2	7 499	6.7
Rome city...............	16 272	−2.3	13 653	57.1	746	38	708	844	1 873	2 076	16 742	−.3	669	4.0
Saratoga Springs city.......	11 584	7.7	10 784	55.8	766	37	729	898	3 043	3 542	13 570	−.8	519	3.8
Schenectady city	30 272	.1	26 265	44.7	NA	NA	NA	3 463	NA	5 509	30 477	−1.0	1 526	5.0
Syracuse city..............	68 192	−4.6	59 482	40.3	8 868	1 439	7 429	9 949	5 819	6 422	72 517	−.9	4 046	5.6
Troy city	23 093	1.0	19 996	40.1	NA	NA	NA	NA	NA	NA	25 616	−1.0	1 420	5.5
Utica city	29 186	−6.2	25 100	48.8	2 811	202	2 609	3 185	4 732	5 232	29 542	−.4	1 607	5.4
Valley Stream village	12 688	4.3	12 484	80.3	NA	NA	NA	NA	NA	NA	17 348	−.5	535	3.1
Watertown city	12 450	.4	11 036	43.0	937	66	871	1 023	3 371	3 583	12 003	−1.8	1 031	8.6
White Plains city	21 576	4.2	20 921	52.2	2 485	190	2 295	2 282	4 970	4 572	26 383	−1.2	842	3.2
Yonkers city..............	77 589	2.7	74 351	43.2	6 033	915	5 118	7 185	3 169	3 756	89 742	−1.3	3 718	4.1
NORTH CAROLINA......	3 523 944	25.0	3 132 013	69.4	395 971	41 474	354 497	401 615	5 175	5 322	3 958 354	2.3	144 079	3.6
Asheville city	33 567	13.0	30 690	56.8	5 346	556	4 790	5 005	8 366	7 628	34 148	1.9	1 177	3.4
Burlington city	19 567	10.6	18 280	59.4	3 094	304	2 790	3 150	7 530	7 575	23 830	2.0	724	3.0
Cary town................	36 863	104.7	34 906	72.8	1 991	71	1 920	2 145	2 393	2 699	39 169	3.1	426	1.1
Chapel Hill town	18 976	27.8	17 808	42.9	2 856	194	2 662	2 865	6 761	6 272	24 516	3.2	381	1.6
Charlotte city............	230 434	35.2	215 449	57.5	53 413	8 138	45 275	52 502	8 830	8 852	292 024	4.7	8 028	2.7
Concord city	22 485	93.6	20 962	67.6	1 809	143	1 666	2 133	5 155	6 218	18 472	4.8	530	2.9
Durham city	80 797	33.3	74 981	48.9	17 709	2 016	15 693	16 433	11 379	10 641	86 669	3.2	2 263	2.6
Fayetteville city	53 565	68.9	48 414	53.3	8 762	723	8 039	9 038	11 181	11 156	37 388	1.9	1 581	4.2
Gastonia city	27 857	25.5	25 945	56.7	−	−6 245	6 245	7 503	−	12 961	30 747	7.1	2 067	6.7
Goldsboro city	16 372	14.1	14 630	42.5	3 275	406	2 869	3 728	7 897	8 976	14 431	.6	745	5.2
Greensboro city	99 305	23.5	92 394	54.0	15 531	1 820	13 711	17 653	7 741	8 807	116 731	2.1	3 594	3.1
Greenville city	28 145	55.9	25 204	39.3	5 390	495	4 895	6 412	9 326	11 370	28 092	−1.1	1 626	5.8
Hickory city	16 571	30.5	15 372	55.0	2 775	194	2 581	3 261	8 683	10 380	17 422	2.0	537	3.1
High Point city	35 952	22.3	33 519	59.0	6 883	872	6 011	6 998	8 919	9 169	41 460	2.2	1 494	3.6
Jacksonville city	18 312	55.1	17 175	39.2	2 805	225	2 580	2 621	4 046	3 687	13 050	−.8	457	3.5

[1] Data on serious crimes have not been adjusted for underreporting; this may affect comparability over time or among geographic areas. [2] Includes murder and nonnegligent manslaughter, forcible rape, robbery, and aggravated assault. [3] Includes burglary, larceny-theft, and motor vehicle theft. [4] Per 100,000 resident population provided by the U.S. Federal Bureau of Investigation. [5] Civilian unemployed as a percent of total civilian labor force.

Sources: Housing, 2000—U.S. Census Bureau, 2000 Census of Population and Housing, "Census 2000 Profiles of General Demographic Characteristics" data files, published May 2001 (related Internet site <http://www.census.gov/mp/www/pub/2000cen/mscen01.html>). Housing, 1990—U.S. Census Bureau, "1990 Census of Population and Housing, Summary Tape File (STF) 1C" on CD-ROM (related Internet site <http://homer.ssd.census.gov/cdrom/lookup>). Serious Crimes Known to Police—U.S. Federal Bureau of Investigation, Uniform Crime Reporting Program, "Crime in the United States," annual <http://www.fbi.gov/ucr/Cius_99/99crime/99c2_01.pdf> (accessed: 20 October 2000) and <http://www.fbi.gov/ucr/Cius_98/98crime/98cius05.pdf> (accessed: 9 December 1999). Civilian Labor Force—U.S. Bureau of Labor Statistics, Local Area Unemployment Statistics, 2000 data published 2 May 2001, 1999 data published 30 May 2001 <ftp://ftp.bls.gov/pub/time.series/la/> (related Internet site <http://www.bls.gov/lauhome.htm>).

Table C–4. Cities — Housing, Crime, and Labor Force–Con.

[Includes states and 1,070 incorporated places of 25,000 or more population as of April 1, 1990 in all states except Hawaii which has no incorporated places recognized by the Census Bureau. For Hawaii, 8 census designated places (CDPs) of 25,000 or more population as of April 1, 1990 are included. Also included are the 5 boroughs of New York city. For more information on these areas, see appendix B. Geographic Information]

City	Housing, 2000 Total units	Percent change, 1990–2000	Occupied units Number	Occupied units Percent owner-occupied	Serious crimes known to police[1] Number 1999 Total	Violent[2]	Property[3]	Number 1998	Rate[4] 1999	Rate[4] 1998	Civilian labor force, 2000 Total	Percent change, 1999–2000	Unemployment Total	Rate[5]
NORTH CAROLINA— Con.														
Kannapolis city	15 941	25.4	14 804	66.7	NA	NA	NA	1 040	NA	2 803	18 519	5.6	910	4.9
Kinston city	11 229	3.7	9 829	52.0	2 257	253	2 004	2 549	9 098	9 923	11 570	-.8	918	7.9
Raleigh city	120 699	30.3	112 608	51.6	18 672	2 031	16 641	17 985	7 099	7 023	174 525	3.2	3 162	1.8
Rocky Mount city	24 167	19.8	21 435	55.0	5 250	579	4 671	5 842	9 101	10 797	24 248	-.5	1 679	6.9
Wilmington city	38 678	46.1	34 359	48.6	7 866	774	7 092	6 899	11 400	10 649	35 902	4.0	1 540	4.3
Wilson city	18 660	21.3	17 296	51.0	3 276	355	2 921	3 815	8 040	9 315	19 337	1.0	1 700	8.8
Winston-Salem city	82 593	25.8	76 247	55.8	16 894	2 213	14 681	16 243	10 141	10 337	78 650	2.1	2 839	3.6
NORTH DAKOTA........	289 677	4.8	257 152	66.6	15 172	424	14 748	17 105	2 393	2 681	338 822	.6	10 106	3.0
Bismarck city	24 217	20.9	23 185	63.4	1 961	32	1 929	2 242	3 655	4 243	33 068	1.0	719	2.2
Fargo city	41 200	29.9	39 268	47.1	2 886	118	2 768	2 965	3 339	3 502	53 303	1.5	890	1.7
Grand Forks city	20 838	6.4	19 677	50.7	2 336	64	2 272	2 896	4 971	5 858	28 295	1.6	731	2.6
Minot city	16 475	9.5	15 520	62.4	1 087	29	1 058	1 602	3 103	4 541	19 124	2.3	541	2.8
OHIO	4 783 051	9.4	4 445 773	69.1	449 880	35 616	414 264	485 066	3 996	4 327	5 782 649	.5	236 536	4.1
Akron city	97 315	1.0	90 116	59.4	15 829	2 125	13 704	NA	7 307	NA	114 063	.2	6 399	5.6
Barberton city	12 163	3.7	11 523	65.1	1 433	105	1 328	1 380	5 266	5 037	13 338	.2	719	5.4
Beavercreek city	14 769	21.6	14 071	84.5	1 565	39	1 526	1 720	3 895	5 534	19 347	.1	419	2.2
Bowling Green city	10 667	19.0	10 266	42.2	1 091	33	1 058	1 110	3 853	3 862	17 256	Z	658	3.8
Brunswick city	12 251	29.7	11 883	80.6	NA	NA	NA	NA	NA	NA	19 286	.5	720	3.7
Canton city...............	35 502	-2.8	32 489	59.7	NA	NA	NA	6 482	NA	7 988	38 355	1.0	2 515	6.6
Cincinnati city	166 012	-1.8	148 095	39.0	21 469	2 475	18 994	25 345	6 355	7 350	173 116	.7	8 834	5.1
Cleveland city	215 856	-3.8	190 638	48.5	33 573	6 049	27 524	34 593	6 743	6 981	206 022	.5	18 011	8.7
Cleveland Heights city	21 798	-.3	20 913	62.1	1 068	23	1 045	1 024	1 987	1 896	29 047	.6	837	2.9
Columbus city	327 175	17.7	301 534	49.1	61 292	5 755	55 537	62 608	9 102	9 468	397 407	1.8	11 300	2.8
Cuyahoga Falls city	22 727	6.9	21 655	65.7	1 795	130	1 665	1 744	3 581	3 089	28 836	.3	802	2.8
Dayton city...............	77 321	-3.8	67 409	52.8	15 997	1 789	14 208	18 021	9 512	10 476	76 362	Z	4 998	6.5
East Cleveland city........	13 491	-11.1	11 210	35.5	NA	NA	NA	NA	NA	NA	14 337	.5	1 454	10.1
Elyria city	23 841	5.8	22 409	64.6	NA	NA	NA	NA	NA	NA	30 710	.9	1 692	5.5
Euclid city...............	26 123	-1.7	24 353	59.5	2 367	116	2 251	2 614	4 654	5 009	27 509	.6	978	3.6
Fairborn city.............	14 419	8.5	13 615	51.7	1 476	82	1 394	1 345	4 682	4 402	16 243	.2	742	4.6
Fairfield city	17 789	9.3	16 960	65.4	2 097	146	1 951	2 117	5 000	4 959	30 034	1.7	617	2.1
Findlay city	17 152	14.3	15 905	64.8	NA	NA	NA	NA	NA	NA	23 878	2.3	774	3.2
Gahanna city	12 390	24.9	11 990	77.7	951	45	906	972	2 999	3 081	17 130	1.8	307	1.8
Garfield Heights city........	12 998	Z	12 452	79.9	NA	NA	NA	NA	NA	NA	15 472	.6	550	3.6
Hamilton city	25 913	2.2	24 188	60.7	4 860	663	4 197	4 969	7 830	7 936	35 418	1.6	1 608	4.5
Huber Heights city	14 938	4.4	14 392	72.0	1 567	64	1 503	1 577	4 218	4 072	20 265	Z	595	2.9
Kent city	10 435	12.5	9 772	37.8	966	75	891	1 050	3 585	3 842	16 940	.4	763	4.5
Kettering city	26 936	-.6	25 657	66.6	2 329	98	2 231	2 373	4 054	4 099	32 010	Z	601	1.9
Lakewood city	28 416	-.4	26 693	45.2	1 504	83	1 421	1 423	2 690	2 567	33 685	.6	984	2.9
Lancaster city	15 891	7.7	14 852	59.4	1 858	37	1 821	NA	4 908	NA	21 631	1.5	734	3.4
Lima city	17 631	-5.5	15 410	56.8	2 948	372	2 576	3 536	6 927	8 263	19 216	1.3	1 429	7.4
Lorain city	28 231	2.5	26 434	61.2	2 241	215	2 026	2 530	3 241	3 603	33 151	1.1	2 470	7.5
Mansfield city	22 267	1.6	20 182	57.6	3 391	176	3 215	3 501	6 780	6 875	22 684	-1.4	1 619	7.1
Maple Heights city	10 935	1.3	10 489	83.8	700	55	645	NA	2 755	NA	13 684	.6	432	3.2
Marion city	14 713	3.3	13 551	63.5	NA	NA	NA	2 256	NA	6 784	16 450	.2	852	5.2
Massillon city	13 567	5.9	12 677	69.0	NA	NA	NA	NA	NA	NA	14 644	1.1	758	5.2
Mentor city	19 301	12.4	18 797	87.5	1 408	56	1 352	1 707	2 848	3 384	28 492	.3	870	3.1
Middletown city	23 144	19.4	21 469	60.1	3 123	116	3 007	3 199	6 400	6 579	27 874	1.6	1 247	4.5
Newark city	20 625	8.7	19 312	58.2	NA	NA	NA	2 748	NA	5 545	23 780	1.6	1 109	4.7
North Olmsted city	14 059	7.5	13 517	79.7	NA	NA	NA	NA	NA	NA	18 650	.6	391	2.1
Parma city	36 414	2.3	35 126	77.5	NA	NA	NA	NA	NA	NA	44 629	.6	960	2.2
Reynoldsburg city..........	13 434	26.9	12 849	65.1	1 147	56	1 091	1 075	3 875	3 671	17 765	1.8	264	1.5
Sandusky city	13 323	-.7	11 851	56.5	1 912	92	1 820	2 512	6 746	8 656	16 107	1.1	1 028	6.4
Shaker Heights city	12 982	-2.9	12 220	64.9	895	53	842	821	3 170	2 827	16 698	.6	393	2.4
Springfield city...........	29 309	-.9	26 254	57.2	6 665	940	5 725	6 595	10 122	9 825	30 562	.3	1 777	5.8
Stow city.................	12 852	22.8	12 317	72.1	663	24	639	741	2 105	2 388	16 901	.4	323	1.9
Strongsville city	16 863	28.7	16 209	82.7	1 184	20	1 164	1 163	2 855	2 834	19 828	.6	425	2.1
Toledo city	139 871	-1.6	128 925	59.8	23 228	2 158	21 070	25 571	7 410	8 046	160 249	-.2	9 199	5.7
Upper Arlington city	14 432	.4	13 985	81.3	760	30	730	811	2 388	2 452	20 358	1.8	179	.9
Warren city	21 279	-2.3	19 288	58.4	NA	NA	NA	NA	NA	NA	22 336	-1.3	1 765	7.9
Westerville city	13 143	24.9	12 663	79.2	NA	NA	NA	1 093	NA	3 221	19 256	1.8	230	1.2
Westlake city	13 648	23.9	12 826	74.8	425	24	401	517	1 423	1 731	14 340	.6	258	1.8
Youngstown city	37 159	-8.9	32 177	64.0	6 372	888	5 484	6 886	7 496	7 925	34 260	-1.1	3 373	9.8
Zanesville city	11 662	-.9	10 572	54.6	NA	NA	NA	2 018	NA	7 347	12 984	2.7	1 129	8.7

[1] Data on serious crimes have not been adjusted for underreporting; this may affect comparability over time or among geographic areas. [2] Includes murder and nonnegligent manslaughter, forcible rape, robbery, and aggravated assault. [3] Includes burglary, larceny-theft, and motor vehicle theft. [4] Per 100,000 resident population provided by the U.S. Federal Bureau of Investigation. [5] Civilian unemployed as a percent of total civilian labor force.

Sources: Housing, 2000—U.S. Census Bureau, 2000 Census of Population and Housing, "Census 2000 Profiles of General Demographic Characteristics" data files, published May 2001 (related Internet site <http://www.census.gov/mp/www/pub/2000cen/mscen01.html>). Housing, 1990—U.S. Census Bureau, "1990 Census of Population and Housing, Summary Tape File (STF) 1C" on CD-ROM (related Internet site <http://homer.ssd.census.gov/cdrom/lookup>). Serious Crimes Known to Police—U.S. Federal Bureau of Investigation, Uniform Crime Reporting Program, "Crime in the United States," annual <http://www.fbi.gov/ucr/Cius_99/99crime/99c2_01.pdf> (accessed: 20 October 2000) and <http://www.fbi.gov/ucr/Cius_98/98crime/98cius05.pdf> (accessed: 9 December 1999). Civilian Labor Force—U.S. Bureau of Labor Statistics, Local Area Unemployment Statistics, 2000 data published 2 May 2001, 1999 data published 30 May 2001 <ftp://ftp.bls.gov/pub/time.series/la/> (related Internet site <http://www.bls.gov/lauhome.htm>).

Table C–4. Cities — Housing, Crime, and Labor Force–Con.

[Includes states and 1,070 incorporated places of 25,000 or more population as of April 1, 1990 in all states except Hawaii which has no incorporated places recognized by the Census Bureau. For Hawaii, 8 census designated places (CDPs) of 25,000 or more population as of April 1, 1990 are included. Also included are the 5 boroughs of New York city. For more information on these areas, see appendix B. Geographic Information]

City	Housing, 2000				Serious crimes known to police[1]						Civilian labor force, 2000			
			Occupied units		Number				Rate[4]				Unemployment	
					1999									
	Total units	Percent change, 1990–2000	Number	Percent owner-occupied	Total	Violent[2]	Property[3]	1998	1999	1998	Total	Percent change, 1999–2000	Total	Rate[5]
OKLAHOMA	1 514 400	7.7	1 342 293	68.4	157 286	17 066	140 220	167 479	4 684	5 004	1 648 017	−.4	50 048	3.0
Bartlesville city	16 091	1.2	14 565	70.4	1 627	114	1 513	1 540	4 819	4 515	13 308	−2.5	460	3.5
Broken Arrow city	27 085	32.6	26 159	78.7	2 020	161	1 859	1 939	2 774	2 746	35 458	−.3	650	1.8
Edmond city	26 380	28.1	25 256	72.8	1 758	73	1 685	2 098	2 697	3 277	31 701	.3	454	1.4
Enid city	21 255	−2.0	18 955	67.2	3 064	263	2 801	3 532	6 751	7 679	20 702	−4.2	660	3.2
Lawton city	36 433	5.2	31 778	54.7	4 794	433	4 361	5 605	5 891	6 785	31 707	−1.7	1 064	3.4
Midwest City city	23 853	4.4	22 161	61.2	2 723	160	2 563	3 170	5 022	5 793	27 945	.2	732	2.6
Moore city	15 801	6.6	14 848	75.8	1 440	106	1 334	1 724	3 167	3 774	26 395	.1	408	1.5
Muskogee city	17 517	−.9	15 523	61.9	2 804	285	2 519	3 207	7 280	8 377	17 285	−2.9	633	3.7
Norman city	41 547	16.5	38 834	55.2	3 313	149	3 164	3 806	3 550	4 107	52 661	.1	1 084	2.1
Oklahoma City city	228 149	7.4	204 434	59.4	44 153	4 071	40 082	46 722	9 319	10 077	253 091	.2	6 738	2.7
Ponca City city	11 871	−3.4	10 636	68.1	1 637	93	1 544	1 870	6 290	7 131	11 970	−3.0	629	5.3
Shawnee city	12 651	7.4	11 311	59.9	1 988	127	1 861	2 083	7 336	7 684	12 419	Z	455	3.7
Stillwater city	16 827	6.7	15 604	41.8	1 383	95	1 288	1 585	3 556	4 058	23 591	1.4	282	1.2
Tulsa city	179 405	1.8	165 743	55.6	28 303	4 447	23 856	28 296	7 396	7 326	219 949	−.5	6 685	3.0
OREGON	1 452 709	21.7	1 333 723	64.3	165 866	12 432	153 434	185 323	5 002	5 647	1 802 889	2.4	87 486	4.9
Albany city	17 374	41.0	16 108	59.5	2 668	67	2 601	3 239	6 800	8 315	17 582	−.7	1 092	6.2
Beaverton city	32 500	34.9	30 821	47.7	3 151	216	2 935	3 226	5 021	4 926	45 940	2.8	1 385	3.0
Corvallis city	20 909	20.8	19 630	44.9	2 244	97	2 147	2 231	4 424	4 601	24 594	1.1	634	2.6
Eugene city	61 444	28.0	58 110	51.8	10 222	650	9 572	11 463	7 889	9 013	69 941	2.2	3 213	4.6
Gresham city	35 309	30.9	33 327	54.9	5 009	341	4 668	5 150	5 831	6 203	44 095	2.8	1 428	3.2
Hillsboro city	27 211	103.9	25 079	52.3	2 680	195	2 485	2 978	4 340	5 479	28 392	2.7	925	3.3
Lake Oswego city	15 741	20.1	14 769	70.6	769	32	737	944	2 193	2 634	23 030	2.9	529	2.3
Medford city	26 297	33.6	25 093	57.3	3 822	203	3 619	4 799	6 618	8 331	30 584	3.4	1 540	5.0
Portland city	237 307	19.6	223 737	55.8	41 399	6 294	35 105	46 067	8 134	9 424	280 226	2.5	12 853	4.6
Salem city	53 817	26.3	50 676	57.1	9 631	287	9 344	10 583	7 423	8 375	66 381	2.5	3 713	5.6
Springfield city	21 500	18.6	20 514	53.6	4 841	115	4 726	5 246	9 453	10 324	26 264	2.1	1 503	5.7
Tigard city	17 369	37.9	16 507	58.3	2 530	103	2 427	2 878	6 782	7 794	24 302	2.7	775	3.2
PENNSYLVANIA	5 249 750	6.3	4 777 003	71.3	373 452	50 431	323 021	392 788	3 114	3 273	5 971 913	−.1	249 922	4.2
Allentown city	45 960	.7	42 032	53.0	5 561	660	4 901	6 022	5 523	5 887	50 489	−.2	2 107	4.2
Altoona city	21 681	−4.5	20 059	65.9	2 035	152	1 883	1 945	4 137	3 900	23 225	−.3	1 298	5.6
Bethel Park borough	13 871	6.7	13 362	79.9	318	23	295	329	968	988	18 148	Z	512	2.8
Bethlehem city	29 631	4.0	28 116	58.1	2 555	227	2 328	2 569	3 685	3 655	33 136	.1	1 251	3.8
Chester city	14 976	−9.3	12 814	47.7	3 385	1 282	2 103	4 206	8 421	10 429	16 200	−1.2	938	5.8
Easton city	10 545	2.3	9 544	48.5	1 498	230	1 268	NA	5 910	NA	11 940	.4	512	4.3
Erie city	44 971	−1.0	40 938	56.2	3 929	450	3 479	4 635	3 830	4 420	49 429	.5	2 775	5.6
Harrisburg city	24 314	−1.1	20 561	42.3	2 963	575	2 388	NA	5 989	NA	23 830	−.2	1 131	4.7
Johnstown city	12 802	−12.7	11 134	50.0	954	120	834	948	3 155	3 659	9 489	.8	823	8.7
Lancaster city	23 024	2.5	20 933	46.6	NA	NA	NA	NA	NA	NA	25 349	.8	891	3.5
McKeesport city	11 124	−11.3	9 655	60.0	1 333	255	1 078	1 206	5 777	5 221	8 653	−.8	514	5.9
Municipality of Monroeville borough	13 159	4.1	12 376	69.7	945	109	836	NA	3 381	NA	17 141	−.2	503	2.9
New Castle city	11 709	−6.0	10 727	64.6	1 152	157	995	1 357	4 403	5 078	10 199	1.4	846	8.3
Norristown borough	13 531	3.4	12 028	48.1	1 987	315	1 672	2 265	6 680	7 522	15 459	−.5	636	4.1
Philadelphia city	661 958	−1.9	590 071	59.3	104 658	23 031	81 627	106 078	7 291	7 319	628 687	−.3	38 573	6.1
Pittsburgh city	163 366	−4.0	143 739	52.1	21 253	3 046	18 207	21 492	6 124	5 964	159 459	−.3	6 478	4.1
Plum borough	10 624	14.4	10 270	79.8	309	14	295	371	1 168	1 413	15 700	−.5	443	2.8
Reading city	34 314	.1	30 113	51.0	5 901	886	5 015	6 291	7 898	8 275	33 970	.3	1 973	5.8
Scranton city	35 336	−.1	31 303	54.5	NA	NA	NA	NA	NA	NA	34 907	Z	1 540	4.4
State College borough	12 488	7.4	12 024	22.8	1 207	51	1 156	NA	2 303	NA	16 204	Z	177	1.1
Wilkes-Barre city	20 294	−2.1	17 961	53.5	2 089	194	1 895	2 126	4 881	4 841	20 580	.2	1 094	5.3
Williamsport city	13 524	1.5	12 219	44.8	1 665	90	1 575	1 819	5 574	5 996	13 493	−.3	832	6.2
York city	18 534	.7	16 137	46.8	NA	NA	NA	3 235	NA	7 889	18 088	.2	971	5.4
RHODE ISLAND	439 837	6.1	408 424	60.0	35 497	2 840	32 657	34 756	3 582	3 518	504 800	.1	20 586	4.1
Cranston city	32 068	5.1	30 954	66.9	2 124	136	1 988	2 104	2 843	2 845	37 338	−.1	1 502	4.0
East Providence city	21 309	2.4	20 530	58.9	1 027	89	938	NA	2 140	NA	24 982	.3	1 168	4.7
Newport city	13 226	1.0	11 566	41.9	1 592	150	1 442	1 814	6 542	7 473	12 174	2.9	494	4.1
Pawtucket city	31 819	.6	30 047	44.4	3 043	281	2 762	2 701	4 453	3 930	35 396	Z	1 647	4.7
Providence city	67 915	1.7	62 389	34.6	12 156	1 141	11 015	11 190	8 027	7 393	67 998	Z	3 683	5.4
Warwick city	37 085	5.5	35 517	72.7	2 770	162	2 608	2 911	3 286	3 450	44 520	Z	1 630	3.7
Woonsocket city	18 757	.1	17 750	35.0	1 064	122	942	1 056	2 587	2 538	19 570	−.5	869	4.4

[1] Data on serious crimes have not been adjusted for underreporting; this may affect comparability over time or among geographic areas. [2] Includes murder and nonnegligent manslaughter, forcible rape, robbery, and aggravated assault. [3] Includes burglary, larceny-theft, and motor vehicle theft. [4] Per 100,000 resident population provided by the U.S. Federal Bureau of Investigation. [5] Civilian unemployed as a percent of total civilian labor force.

Sources: Housing, 2000—U.S. Census Bureau, 2000 Census of Population and Housing, "Census 2000 Profiles of General Demographic Characteristics" data files, published May 2001 (related Internet site <http://www.census.gov/mp/www/pub/2000cen/mscen01.html>). Housing, 1990—U.S. Census Bureau, "1990 Census of Population and Housing, Summary Tape File (STF) 1C" on CD-ROM (related Internet site <http://homer.ssd.census.gov/cdrom/lookup>). Serious Crimes Known to Police—U.S. Federal Bureau of Investigation, Uniform Crime Reporting Program, "Crime in the United States," annual <http://www.fbi.gov/ucr/Cius_99/99crime/99c2_01.pdf> (accessed: 20 October 2000) and <http://www.fbi.gov/ucr/Cius_98/98crime/98cius05.pdf> (accessed: 9 December 1999). Civilian Labor Force—U.S. Bureau of Labor Statistics, Local Area Unemployment Statistics, 2000 data published 2 May 2001, 1999 data published 30 May 2001 <ftp://ftp.bls.gov/pub/time.series/la/> (related Internet site <http://www.bls.gov/lauhome.htm>).

Table C–4. Cities — **Housing, Crime, and Labor Force**–Con.

[Includes states and 1,070 incorporated places of 25,000 or more population as of April 1, 1990 in all states except Hawaii which has no incorporated places recognized by the Census Bureau. For Hawaii, 8 census designated places (CDPs) of 25,000 or more population as of April 1, 1990 are included. Also included are the 5 boroughs of New York city. For more information on these areas, see appendix B. Geographic Information]

City	Housing, 2000				Serious crimes known to police[1]						Civilian labor force, 2000			
			Occupied units		Number				Rate[4]				Unemployment	
					1999									
	Total units	Percent change, 1990–2000	Number	Percent owner-occupied	Total	Violent[2]	Property[3]	1998	1999	1998	Total	Percent change, 1999–2000	Total	Rate[5]
SOUTH CAROLINA......	1 753 670	23.1	1 533 854	72.2	206 907	32 920	173 987	221 607	5 324	5 777	1 985 249	1.1	76 504	3.9
Anderson city	12 068	4.9	10 641	53.4	1 945	290	1 655	2 177	7 357	7 975	14 027	1.4	542	3.9
Charleston city	44 563	29.8	40 791	51.1	6 879	876	6 003	7 617	7 802	10 411	46 684	3.9	1 433	3.1
Columbia city............	46 142	25.0	42 245	45.6	–	–2 038	2 038	11 344	–	9 835	48 220	–.1	1 874	3.9
Florence city	13 090	11.0	11 925	61.4	3 771	621	3 150	3 613	12 615	11 630	15 819	–.5	873	5.5
Greenville city	27 295	3.2	24 382	47.0	5 266	755	4 511	5 871	9 211	9 968	35 009	1.6	856	2.4
Mount Pleasant town	20 197	62.3	19 025	74.0	1 672	110	1 562	1 647	3 994	4 668	20 497	4.1	234	1.1
North Charleston city	33 631	26.4	29 783	46.4	7 975	1 424	6 551	7 402	11 566	11 996	32 687	3.8	1 313	4.0
Rock Hill city	20 287	29.4	18 750	53.4	NA	NA	NA	3 185	NA	6 911	27 981	2.7	1 369	4.9
Spartanburg city	17 696	–1.4	15 989	49.8	3 805	623	3 182	5 441	9 172	12 547	23 420	.9	1 111	4.7
Sumter city	16 032	17.5	14 564	53.1	NA	NA	NA	2 940	NA	7 497	16 038	1.0	815	5.1
SOUTH DAKOTA.......	323 208	10.5	290 245	68.2	19 386	1 227	18 159	19 366	2 645	2 624	401 151	.4	9 145	2.3
Rapid City city	25 096	11.4	23 969	59.3	3 224	226	2 998	3 128	5 644	5 409	32 932	2.4	639	1.9
Sioux Falls city	51 680	24.3	49 731	61.1	4 378	365	4 013	3 915	3 780	3 464	75 965	2.5	1 213	1.6
TENNESSEE	2 439 443	20.4	2 232 905	69.9	257 413	38 111	219 302	273 420	4 694	5 034	2 798 336	–.6	110 174	3.9
Bartlett town	14 021	59.2	13 773	92.2	NA	NA	NA	1 000	NA	2 763	16 253	–.7	210	1.3
Chattanooga city..........	72 108	3.6	65 499	54.9	16 099	2 700	13 399	15 960	10 788	10 468	76 619	Z	2 643	3.4
Clarksville city	40 041	44.9	36 969	57.5	3 656	504	3 152	4 988	3 695	5 058	41 994	1.0	1 460	3.5
Cleveland city	16 431	25.9	15 037	51.8	1 797	196	1 601	1 952	5 020	5 698	16 542	–2.7	631	3.8
Columbia city...........	14 322	18.0	13 059	63.5	2 345	346	1 999	NA	7 288	NA	18 919	–1.8	712	3.8
Germantown city	13 676	22.9	13 220	89.0	757	29	728	771	1 995	2 396	19 055	–.7	231	1.2
Hendersonville city	16 507	32.4	15 823	71.4	1 008	88	920	1 041	2 585	2 707	23 634	.4	535	2.3
Jackson city	25 501	23.0	23 503	56.7	5 340	897	4 443	5 711	10 346	11 111	31 701	1.8	1 233	3.9
Johnson City city	25 730	21.1	23 720	57.2	3 093	369	2 724	3 164	5 367	5 546	26 866	–1.4	1 081	4.0
Kingsport city	21 796	30.2	19 662	64.8	2 580	336	2 244	2 590	6 211	6 147	16 678	–2.2	632	3.8
Knoxville city	84 981	11.2	76 650	51.2	9 469	1 392	8 077	10 165	5 665	5 965	92 863	–.4	2 780	3.0
Memphis city	271 552	9.2	250 721	55.8	51 033	8 602	42 431	53 214	8 368	8 807	316 652	–.5	15 166	4.8
Murfreesboro city	28 815	54.0	26 511	52.1	3 548	422	3 126	3 468	6 014	6 132	37 743	.6	1 403	3.7
Nashville-Davidson (remainder)	242 451	10.4	227 403	54.5	46 456	8 405	38 051	53 249	8 884	10 160	[6]305 847	[6].2	[6]8 855	[6]2.9
Oak Ridge city...........	13 417	5.7	12 062	68.4	NA	NA	NA	1 557	NA	5 549	14 488	–.7	408	2.8
TEXAS	8 157 575	16.4	7 393 354	63.8	1 008 567	112 306	896 261	1 010 062	5 032	5 112	10 324 527	1.0	437 488	4.2
Abilene city	45 618	2.7	41 570	58.6	4 980	495	4 485	5 573	4 535	5 052	51 178	–3.1	1 915	3.7
Amarillo city	72 408	5.6	67 699	63.3	13 528	1 221	12 307	13 280	7 789	7 639	94 271	–.3	3 583	3.8
Arlington city	130 628	15.8	124 686	54.7	19 407	1 951	17 456	19 520	6 242	6 380	192 666	2.1	5 267	2.7
Austin city	276 842	27.5	265 649	44.8	40 041	2 965	37 076	39 193	7 145	7 002	390 409	4.1	8 632	2.2
Baytown city	26 203	4.7	23 483	59.6	3 253	273	2 980	3 383	4 675	4 816	35 502	.5	1 754	4.9
Beaumont city	48 815	–.4	44 361	59.9	10 082	1 323	8 759	9 294	9 048	8 245	56 921	–.7	4 269	7.5
Bedford city	21 113	12.0	20 251	55.0	1 651	122	1 529	1 547	3 246	3 068	34 478	2.1	658	1.9
Brownsville city	42 323	46.0	38 174	61.2	8 650	783	7 867	7 860	6 184	5 727	48 804	2.4	4 913	10.1
Bryan city..............	25 703	11.7	23 759	50.8	4 103	387	3 716	4 056	6 883	6 772	36 303	1.3	560	1.5
Carrollton city	40 458	22.6	39 136	65.7	3 581	239	3 342	3 911	3 514	3 862	72 166	2.7	1 373	1.9
College Station city	26 054	31.3	24 691	30.6	2 422	124	2 298	2 531	3 997	4 189	30 452	1.3	487	1.6
Conroe city	14 378	25.0	13 145	47.3	2 080	244	1 836	2 392	5 800	6 632	21 884	.8	735	3.4
Corpus Christi city	107 831	7.6	98 791	59.6	20 375	2 485	17 890	22 510	7 136	7 833	129 749	–1.2	8 083	6.2
Dallas city	484 117	4.0	451 833	43.2	104 944	15 435	89 509	100 594	9 616	9 236	679 572	2.6	27 367	4.0
Deer Park city	9 921	8.7	9 615	79.3	543	30	513	607	1 751	1 949	17 403	.7	566	3.3
Del Rio city	11 895	11.3	10 778	64.6	1 840	131	1 709	1 719	5 184	4 871	14 951	–.4	1 083	7.2
Denton city.............	32 716	13.6	30 895	41.9	3 297	323	2 974	3 568	4 225	4 565	57 924	2.9	1 709	3.0
DeSoto city	14 069	20.8	13 709	72.2	1 412	129	1 283	1 461	3 901	4 049	21 661	2.7	484	2.2
Duncanville city	13 290	–.5	12 896	71.7	1 605	152	1 453	1 601	4 376	4 312	24 205	2.7	603	2.5
Edinburg city	16 031	74.1	14 183	61.7	3 636	254	3 382	3 526	8 833	8 902	17 547	4.9	2 113	12.0
El Paso city	193 663	14.8	182 063	61.4	36 135	4 280	31 855	35 787	5 792	5 730	255 875	–1.0	20 194	7.9
Euless city	20 136	17.6	19 218	43.8	1 624	112	1 512	1 692	3 538	3 917	30 294	2.1	681	2.2
Fort Worth city	211 035	8.5	195 078	55.9	37 354	4 246	33 108	35 491	7 488	7 129	276 551	2.1	11 491	4.2
Galveston city	30 017	–2.9	23 842	43.6	5 262	468	4 794	5 310	8 708	8 600	31 282	–3.4	2 408	7.7
Garland city	75 300	8.2	73 241	65.6	8 851	495	8 356	8 870	4 511	4 526	125 398	2.7	3 348	2.7
Grand Prairie city	46 425	19.9	43 791	61.2	6 698	465	6 233	6 972	5 826	6 187	65 604	2.5	2 138	3.3
Grapevine city	16 486	38.5	15 712	65.0	1 571	56	1 515	1 383	3 843	3 554	21 757	2.1	364	1.7
Haltom City city	15 716	12.0	14 922	59.5	NA	NA	NA	1 694	NA	4 593	21 419	2.1	655	3.1
Harlingen city...........	23 008	29.3	19 021	61.1	3 834	350	3 484	3 838	6 493	6 492	26 886	3.0	1 671	6.2
Houston city............	782 009	7.7	717 945	45.8	131 774	21 517	110 257	127 817	7 271	7 112	1 027 064	.5	52 265	5.1
Huntsville city	11 508	26.0	10 266	43.5	1 329	165	1 164	1 247	4 132	4 204	12 574	–.4	287	2.3
Hurst city	14 729	6.7	14 076	66.1	2 005	119	1 886	2 136	5 304	5 638	24 167	2.1	720	3.0
Irving city	80 293	13.0	76 241	37.2	9 212	737	8 475	9 454	5 095	5 180	116 835	2.7	3 340	2.9
Killeen city	35 343	33.7	32 447	46.4	5 010	529	4 481	5 304	6 119	6 659	27 673	.2	1 434	5.2

[1] Data on serious crimes have not been adjusted for underreporting; this may affect comparability over time or among geographic areas. [2] Includes murder and nonnegligent manslaughter, forcible rape, robbery, and aggravated assault. [3] Includes burglary, larceny-theft, and motor vehicle theft. [4] Per 100,000 resident population provided by the U.S. Federal Bureau of Investigation. [5] Civilian unemployed as a percent of total civilian labor force. [6] Data are for consolidated city of Nashville-Davidson; data for Nashville-Davidson (remainder) not available.

Sources: Housing, 2000–U.S. Census Bureau, 2000 Census of Population and Housing, "Census 2000 Profiles of General Demographic Characteristics" data files, published May 2001 (related Internet site <http://www.census.gov/mp/www/pub/2000cen/mscen01.html>). Housing, 1990–U.S. Census Bureau, "1990 Census of Population and Housing, Summary Tape File (STF) 1C" on CD-ROM (related Internet site <http://homer.ssd.census.gov/cdrom/lookup>). Serious Crimes Known to Police–U.S. Federal Bureau of Investigation, Uniform Crime Reporting Program, "Crime in the United States," annual <http://www.fbi.gov/ucr/Cius_99/99crime/99c2_01.pdf> (accessed: 20 October 2000) and <http://www.fbi.gov/ucr/Cius_98/98crime/98cius05.pdf> (accessed: 9 December 1999). Civilian Labor Force–U.S. Bureau of Labor Statistics, Local Area Unemployment Statistics, 2000 data published 2 May 2001, 1999 data published 30 May 2001 <ftp://ftp.bls.gov/pub/time.series/la/> (related Internet site <http://www.bls.gov/lauhome.htm>).

Table C–4. Cities — **Housing, Crime, and Labor Force**–Con.

[Includes states and 1,070 incorporated places of 25,000 or more population as of April 1, 1990 in all states except Hawaii which has no incorporated places recognized by the Census Bureau. For Hawaii, 8 census designated places (CDPs) of 25,000 or more population as of April 1, 1990 are included. Also included are the 5 boroughs of New York city. For more information on these areas, see appendix B. Geographic Information]

City	Housing, 2000 Total units	Percent change, 1990–2000	Occupied units Number	Percent owner-occupied	Serious crimes Number 1999 Total	Violent[2]	Property[3]	1998	Rate[4] 1999	1998	Civilian labor force 2000 Total	Percent change, 1999–2000	Unemployment Total	Rate[5]
TEXAS—Con.														
Kingsville city.............	10 427	3.2	8 943	55.0	1 535	138	1 397	1 619	6 002	6 298	10 449	–4.0	566	5.4
La Porte city..............	11 720	17.6	10 928	77.2	677	53	624	647	2 022	1 965	17 373	.7	557	3.2
Laredo city...............	50 319	48.0	46 852	64.4	13 292	829	12 463	13 135	7 454	7 571	69 428	2.1	4 711	6.8
League City city...........	17 280	51.8	16 189	77.0	1 078	48	1 030	1 197	2 436	2 865	18 446	–2.9	486	2.6
Lewisville city............	31 764	61.0	30 043	53.9	NA	NA	NA	3 237	NA	4 947	45 892	2.8	829	1.8
Longview city.............	30 726	1.4	28 363	58.3	4 787	393	4 394	4 950	6 244	6 469	39 455	–1.4	2 387	6.0
Lubbock city..............	84 066	8.0	77 527	55.8	12 852	2 394	10 458	12 299	6 634	6 270	104 734	.4	2 762	2.6
Lufkin city...............	13 402	7.3	12 247	60.0	2 402	226	2 176	2 402	7 121	7 056	15 755	.5	763	4.8
McAllen city..............	37 922	32.6	33 151	63.3	7 906	376	7 530	8 003	7 296	7 379	50 536	5.1	4 908	9.7
Mesquite city.............	46 245	17.8	43 926	65.5	6 152	441	5 711	5 898	5 291	5 109	69 341	2.7	1 791	2.6
Midland city..............	39 855	3.6	35 674	66.1	3 651	359	3 292	4 050	3 613	4 002	50 282	–2.3	2 350	4.7
Mission city..............	17 723	66.3	13 766	74.9	2 692	51	2 641	2 794	6 621	7 048	14 439	5.0	1 660	11.5
Missouri City city.........	17 481	41.6	17 069	90.8	1 426	98	1 328	1 289	2 254	2 175	32 521	.8	626	1.9
Nacogdoches city..........	12 329	.6	11 220	43.5	1 758	128	1 630	1 020	5 635	3 186	14 293	–.1	557	3.9
New Braunfels city........	14 896	34.6	13 558	64.4	2 379	72	2 307	2 241	6 421	6 233	20 214	.9	495	2.4
North Richland Hills city	21 600	19.2	20 793	67.1	2 246	115	2 131	2 321	4 053	4 203	33 464	2.1	798	2.4
Odessa city...............	37 966	.6	33 661	64.1	4 782	560	4 222	5 647	5 148	6 072	44 765	–4.2	2 833	6.3
Pasadena city.............	50 367	5.9	47 031	56.1	6 333	669	5 664	6 390	4 660	4 711	70 088	.5	3 214	4.6
Pharr city................	16 537	49.9	12 798	73.2	3 004	289	2 715	3 012	6 998	7 100	16 224	4.6	2 618	16.1
Plano city................	86 078	81.7	80 875	68.8	7 895	794	7 101	8 182	3 546	3 894	141 265	2.7	2 423	1.7
Port Arthur city...........	24 713	–4.0	21 839	62.2	2 907	426	2 481	3 122	4 248	4 517	25 406	–1.0	3 120	12.3
Richardson city............	36 530	27.1	35 191	64.4	3 644	267	3 377	3 427	4 176	4 076	56 334	2.7	1 230	2.2
Round Rock city...........	21 766	86.1	21 076	65.3	1 053	91	962	1 130	1 711	1 997	35 203	4.2	458	1.3
San Angelo city...........	37 699	8.9	34 006	60.8	4 414	361	4 053	5 095	4 932	5 655	42 096	–1.2	1 425	3.4
San Antonio city...........	433 122	18.5	405 474	58.1	76 777	6 340	70 437	77 408	6 793	7 032	532 099	1.2	20 437	3.8
San Marcos city...........	13 340	22.1	12 660	30.2	1 462	139	1 323	2 099	3 650	5 658	23 264	3.9	798	3.4
Sherman city.............	14 926	4.7	13 739	56.4	2 240	182	2 058	2 302	6 486	6 747	16 931	–1.0	686	4.1
Temple city..............	23 511	13.5	21 543	55.9	3 185	196	2 989	3 466	6 352	6 606	27 515	.4	645	2.3
Texarkana city............	15 105	5.5	13 569	58.7	2 249	275	1 974	2 636	7 042	8 033	14 287	–1.5	865	6.1
Texas City city...........	16 715	.2	15 479	63.3	4 177	462	3 715	4 196	9 691	9 632	21 118	–3.4	1 469	7.0
Tyler city................	35 337	7.5	32 525	56.2	NA	NA	NA	6 123	NA	7 238	45 635	1.6	2 097	4.6
Victoria city..............	24 192	11.0	22 129	60.8	3 375	442	2 933	3 283	5 377	5 264	32 081	Z	1 206	3.8
Waco city................	45 819	1.6	42 279	46.4	NA	NA	NA	9 535	NA	8 589	51 519	–.2	2 184	4.2
Wichita Falls city..........	41 916	3.8	37 970	57.8	–	–4 896	4 896	5 891	–	5 811	45 486	–2.0	1 920	4.2
UTAH	768 594	28.4	701 281	71.5	105 999	5 869	100 130	115 624	4 976	5 506	1 104 208	1.7	35 837	3.2
Bountiful city	13 819	20.3	13 341	77.7	1 123	160	963	NA	2 739	NA	25 533	1.7	600	2.3
Layton city...............	19 145	42.2	18 282	74.5	NA	NA	NA	NA	NA	NA	28 602	1.6	889	3.1
Logan city................	14 692	28.4	13 902	44.0	NA	NA	NA	NA	NA	NA	21 960	.4	683	3.1
Murray city...............	13 327	7.9	12 673	66.7	NA	NA	NA	NA	NA	NA	22 180	1.8	449	2.0
Ogden city...............	29 763	9.4	27 384	61.2	5 390	425	4 965	6 067	7 990	8 909	40 135	1.5	2 414	6.0
Orem city................	24 166	34.5	23 382	67.1	3 857	52	3 805	4 005	4 817	4 806	42 097	3.1	900	2.1
Provo city................	30 374	23.6	29 192	42.6	3 602	140	3 462	3 739	3 216	3 592	61 330	2.9	1 779	2.9
St. George city............	21 083	79.2	17 367	67.9	NA	NA	NA	NA	NA	NA	24 562	4.8	866	3.5
Salt Lake City city.........	77 054	4.5	71 461	51.2	18 268	1 257	17 011	19 337	10 320	10 828	110 195	1.6	3 841	3.5
Sandy city...............	26 579	32.2	25 737	84.3	3 216	189	3 027	3 778	3 197	3 856	46 856	1.8	1 034	2.2
West Jordan city	19 597	68.4	18 897	81.9	2 532	93	2 439	2 481	4 105	4 159	26 423	1.7	601	2.3
West Valley City city	33 488	22.4	32 253	72.6	7 587	449	7 138	7 368	7 527	7 176	58 176	1.5	2 294	3.9
VERMONT.............	294 382	8.5	240 634	70.6	16 735	676	16 059	18 552	2 817	3 139	331 574	–1.3	9 657	2.9
Burlington city	16 395	5.9	15 885	41.5	2 000	142	1 858	2 505	5 141	6 345	23 284	–.6	541	2.3
VIRGINIA..............	2 904 192	16.3	2 699 173	68.1	231 886	21 626	210 260	248 576	3 374	3 660	3 609 703	2.3	79 801	2.2
Alexandria city............	64 251	10.3	61 889	40.0	5 682	388	5 294	6 060	4 746	5 162	77 542	4.5	1 193	1.5
Blacksburg town...........	13 732	15.8	13 162	30.4	797	54	743	883	2 340	2 547	15 927	2.2	345	2.2
Charlottesville city	17 591	4.8	16 851	40.8	2 343	368	1 975	2 700	6 057	7 063	18 769	3.6	370	2.0
Chesapeake city...........	72 672	30.4	69 900	74.9	NA	NA	NA	8 411	NA	4 264	107 001	1.0	2 310	2.2
Danville city..............	23 108	–.8	20 607	58.1	2 631	230	2 401	2 549	5 111	4 955	25 090	–.2	1 315	5.2
Hampton city	57 311	6.9	53 887	58.6	5 868	481	5 387	7 360	4 233	5 267	66 325	.3	1 897	2.9
Harrisonburg city..........	13 689	25.6	13 133	39.0	1 469	153	1 316	1 438	4 342	4 255	18 758	1.0	202	1.1
Lynchburg city............	27 640	1.5	25 477	58.5	2 781	298	2 483	3 208	4 197	4 869	30 163	2.0	639	2.1
Manassas city.............	12 114	18.4	11 757	69.8	1 190	84	1 106	NA	3 328	NA	19 651	4.8	237	1.2
Newport News city	74 117	6.3	69 686	52.4	10 242	1 492	8 750	9 496	5 666	5 355	84 294	.2	2 379	2.8
Norfolk city..............	94 416	–4.4	86 210	45.5	NA	NA	NA	16 188	NA	6 998	83 647	.4	3 518	4.2
Petersburg city	15 955	–1.5	13 799	51.5	NA	NA	NA	3 341	NA	9 705	15 717	.9	581	3.7

[1] Data on serious crimes have not been adjusted for underreporting; this may affect comparability over time or among geographic areas.   [2] Includes murder and nonnegligent manslaughter, forcible rape, robbery, and aggravated assault.   [3] Includes burglary, larceny-theft, and motor vehicle theft.   [4] Per 100,000 resident population provided by the U.S. Federal Bureau of Investigation.   [5] Civilian unemployed as a percent of total civilian labor force.

Sources: Housing, 2000—U.S. Census Bureau, 2000 Census of Population and Housing, "Census 2000 Profiles of General Demographic Characteristics" data files, published May 2001 (related Internet site <http://www.census.gov/mp/www/pub/2000cen/mscen01.html>).   Housing, 1990—U.S. Census Bureau, "1990 Census of Population and Housing, Summary Tape File (STF) 1C" on CD-ROM (related Internet site <http://homer.ssd.census.gov/cdrom/lookup>).   Serious Crimes Known to Police—U.S. Federal Bureau of Investigation, Uniform Crime Reporting Program, "Crime in the United States," annual <http://www.fbi.gov/ucr/Cius_99/99crime/99c2_01.pdf> (accessed: 20 October 2000) and <http://www.fbi.gov/ucr/Cius_98/98crime/98cius05.pdf> (accessed: 9 December 1999).   Civilian Labor Force—U.S. Bureau of Labor Statistics, Local Area Unemployment Statistics, 2000 data published 2 May 2001, 1999 data published 30 May 2001 <ftp://ftp.bls.gov/pub/time.series/la/> (related Internet site <http://www.bls.gov/lauhome.htm>).

Table C–4. Cities — **Housing, Crime, and Labor Force**–Con.

[Includes states and 1,070 incorporated places of 25,000 or more population as of April 1, 1990 in all states except Hawaii which has no incorporated places recognized by the Census Bureau. For Hawaii, 8 census designated places (CDPs) of 25,000 or more population as of April 1, 1990 are included. Also included are the 5 boroughs of New York city. For more information on these areas, see appendix B. Geographic Information]

City	Housing, 2000 Total units	Percent change, 1990–2000	Occupied units Number	Percent owner-occupied	Number 1999 Total	Violent[2]	Property[3]	1998	Rate[4] 1999	1998	Civilian labor force, 2000 Total	Percent change, 1999–2000	Unemployment Total	Rate[5]
VIRGINIA—Con.														
Portsmouth city	41 605	−1.6	38 170	58.6	6 921	887	6 034	7 944	6 912	7 917	44 349	.6	1 858	4.2
Richmond city	92 282	−2.0	84 549	46.1	15 564	2 244	13 320	17 684	7 920	9 114	95 188	2.0	2 763	2.9
Roanoke city	45 257	2.0	42 003	56.3	4 709	652	4 057	5 364	4 963	5 649	49 349	1.5	1 079	2.2
Suffolk city	24 704	23.5	23 283	72.2	3 056	389	2 667	3 125	4 816	5 077	30 817	.6	806	2.6
Virginia Beach city	162 277	10.4	154 455	65.6	16 089	1 044	15 045	17 665	3 676	4 050	213 269	1.0	4 681	2.2
WASHINGTON	2 451 075	20.6	2 271 398	64.6	302 509	21 716	280 793	333 799	5 256	5 867	3 045 244	−1.0	157 714	5.2
Auburn city	16 767	20.0	16 108	54.2	3 886	226	3 660	3 930	10 210	10 523	21 100	−.5	900	4.3
Bellevue city	48 396	29.3	45 836	61.5	4 652	129	4 523	4 570	4 419	4 826	61 751	−.6	1 618	2.6
Bellingham city	29 474	33.3	27 999	48.2	4 414	192	4 222	4 736	7 048	7 550	34 918	−.9	1 972	5.6
Bremerton city	16 631	6.0	15 096	41.4	2 673	359	2 314	2 759	6 681	6 447	15 892	−.3	1 402	8.8
Edmonds city	17 508	35.2	16 904	68.1	1 181	45	1 136	1 249	3 528	3 712	24 228	−.8	789	3.3
Everett city	38 512	25.1	36 325	46.0	5 847	492	5 355	6 321	6 521	7 419	48 722	−.6	3 087	6.3
Kennewick city	22 043	28.1	20 786	59.7	3 156	182	2 974	3 670	6 199	7 006	26 836	.2	1 975	7.4
Kent city	32 488	85.8	31 113	48.8	5 453	292	5 161	5 782	11 959	13 195	27 321	−.5	1 023	3.7
Kirkland city	21 831	20.9	20 736	57.0	1 505	71	1 434	1 680	3 253	3 739	29 950	−.6	893	3.0
Longview city	15 225	13.3	14 066	57.8	3 082	148	2 934	3 519	9 012	10 175	16 026	−1.9	1 297	8.1
Lynnwood city	13 808	16.3	13 328	53.0	2 415	83	2 332	2 778	7 246	8 430	22 495	−.7	1 017	4.5
Olympia city	19 738	23.9	18 670	50.3	2 571	129	2 442	3 003	6 484	7 453	21 834	−2.9	1 081	5.0
Redmond city	20 248	35.2	19 102	55.1	1 695	88	1 607	1 558	3 800	3 604	26 080	−.7	644	2.5
Renton city	22 676	17.8	21 708	50.0	3 548	247	3 301	4 019	7 388	8 673	29 029	−.5	1 154	4.0
Richland city	16 458	18.6	15 549	66.3	1 141	59	1 082	1 272	3 024	3 319	21 676	−.1	1 152	5.3
Seattle city	270 524	8.6	258 499	48.4	49 760	4 166	45 594	52 870	9 165	9 825	357 756	−.5	15 187	4.2
Spokane city	87 941	10.1	81 512	58.8	14 976	1 372	13 604	17 664	8 042	9 314	100 454	−1.3	6 346	6.3
Tacoma city	81 102	7.9	76 152	54.7	17 373	2 351	15 022	19 319	9 549	10 480	99 328	−.7	6 071	6.1
Vancouver city	60 039	185.6	56 628	52.9	6 727	596	6 131	5 500	9 043	8 713	73 610	−1.3	4 118	5.6
Walla Walla city	11 400	7.1	10 596	59.1	1 989	146	1 843	2 433	6 844	8 414	13 012	−2.9	1 054	8.1
Yakima city	28 643	24.7	26 498	53.2	6 543	344	6 199	7 220	9 954	10 824	31 117	−2.5	3 341	10.7
WEST VIRGINIA	844 623	8.1	736 481	75.2	49 161	6 336	42 825	46 130	2 721	2 547	824 578	1.0	45 626	5.5
Charleston city	27 131	3.5	24 505	58.1	4 977	581	4 396	5 752	9 048	10 268	30 643	1.9	1 382	4.5
Huntington city	25 888	−2.9	22 955	54.6	NA	NA	NA	3 326	NA	6 243	23 510	.7	1 042	5.7
Morgantown city	11 721	12.5	10 782	41.7	NA	NA	NA	1 059	NA	3 967	13 148	3.2	351	2.7
Parkersburg city	16 100	−1.5	14 467	62.0	1 187	79	1 108	1 526	3 751	4 695	16 875	2.2	929	5.5
Wheeling city	15 706	−8.3	13 719	62.7	NA	NA	NA	1 282	NA	3 893	16 888	1.1	588	3.5
WISCONSIN	2 321 144	12.9	2 084 544	68.4	173 062	12 908	160 154	185 093	3 296	3 543	2 934 931	1.6	103 769	3.5
Appleton city	27 736	8.6	26 864	68.7	1 743	97	1 646	NA	2 647	NA	43 683	2.4	1 395	3.2
Beloit city	14 262	1.6	13 370	61.9	1 709	87	1 622	NA	4 836	NA	17 521	2.3	1 242	7.1
Brookfield city	14 208	15.9	13 891	89.9	1 169	32	1 137	NA	3 081	NA	21 022	.4	441	2.1
Eau Claire city	24 895	13.8	24 016	57.3	2 435	134	2 301	NA	4 092	NA	34 699	1.1	1 345	3.9
Fond du Lac city	17 519	15.4	16 638	61.7	1 621	38	1 583	NA	4 060	NA	22 330	1.3	863	3.9
Green Bay city	43 123	8.6	41 591	56.0	4 268	344	3 924	4 749	4 342	4 566	60 512	2.3	2 500	4.1
Greenfield city	16 203	13.3	15 697	59.5	1 333	36	1 297	NA	3 844	NA	19 278	.5	438	2.3
Janesville city	25 083	18.6	23 894	68.2	3 280	136	3 144	NA	5 517	NA	32 436	1.4	1 674	5.2
Kenosha city	36 004	15.4	34 411	62.2	3 078	434	2 644	NA	3 486	NA	48 312	1.8	2 314	4.8
La Crosse city	22 233	6.4	21 110	50.9	2 072	70	2 002	NA	4 200	NA	28 019	2.5	1 172	4.2
Madison city	92 394	15.4	89 019	47.7	7 882	706	7 176	8 349	3 746	4 149	129 260	1.7	2 379	1.8
Manitowoc city	15 007	9.3	14 235	67.6	1 413	23	1 390	NA	4 251	NA	16 997	1.6	710	4.2
Menomonee Falls village	13 140	30.8	12 844	77.4	596	21	575	NA	1 889	NA	19 203	.4	369	1.9
Milwaukee city	249 225	−2.0	232 188	45.3	46 061	6 061	40 000	46 144	7 929	7 843	266 573	1.5	17 848	6.7
New Berlin city	14 921	23.3	14 495	81.3	579	25	554	NA	1 547	NA	23 912	.6	507	2.1
Oshkosh city	25 420	16.5	24 082	57.5	2 151	123	2 028	NA	3 692	NA	38 103	2.6	1 178	3.1
Racine city	33 414	.8	31 449	60.3	5 199	472	4 727	NA	6 378	NA	37 444	.2	2 817	7.5
Sheboygan city	21 762	5.7	20 779	61.1	2 139	71	2 068	NA	4 310	NA	27 526	3.0	766	2.8
Superior city	12 196	4.4	11 609	61.7	1 656	91	1 565	NA	6 070	NA	14 435	2.3	641	4.4
Waukesha city	26 856	21.7	25 663	56.5	1 443	92	1 351	NA	2 316	NA	38 720	.7	1 361	3.5
Wausau city	16 668	8.8	15 678	61.7	1 415	96	1 319	NA	3 872	NA	20 647	2.6	917	4.4
Wauwatosa city	20 917	3.1	20 388	67.8	2 205	127	2 078	NA	4 784	NA	23 204	.7	620	2.7
West Allis city	28 708	4.4	27 604	58.1	2 719	113	2 606	NA	4 510	NA	31 348	.7	1 039	3.3
WYOMING	223 854	10.1	193 608	70.0	16 583	1 115	15 468	18 315	3 455	3 808	266 945	1.9	10 377	3.9
Casper city	21 872	.8	20 343	66.9	2 170	145	2 025	2 457	4 507	5 025	26 044	1.5	1 053	4.0
Cheyenne city	23 782	8.8	22 324	66.0	2 302	90	2 212	2 503	4 271	4 640	28 947	3.2	829	2.9
Laramie city	11 994	8.3	11 336	47.5	811	64	747	930	3 248	3 591	16 013	2.0	249	1.6

[1] Data on serious crimes have not been adjusted for underreporting; this may affect comparability over time or among geographic areas.   [2] Includes murder and nonnegligent manslaughter, forcible rape, robbery, and aggravated assault.   [3] Includes burglary, larceny-theft, and motor vehicle theft.   [4] Per 100,000 resident population provided by the U.S. Federal Bureau of Investigation.   [5] Civilian unemployed as a percent of total civilian labor force.

Sources: Housing, 2000—U.S. Census Bureau, 2000 Census of Population and Housing, "Census 2000 Profiles of General Demographic Characteristics" data files, published May 2001 (related Internet site <http://www.census.gov/mp/www/pub/2000cen/mscen01.html>). Housing, 1990—U.S. Census Bureau, "1990 Census of Population and Housing, Summary Tape File (STF) 1C" on CD-ROM (related Internet site <http://homer.ssd.census.gov/cdrom/lookup>). Serious Crimes Known to Police—U.S. Federal Bureau of Investigation, Uniform Crime Reporting Program, "Crime in the United States," annual <http://www.fbi.gov/ucr/Cius_99/99crime/99c2_01.pdf> (accessed: 20 October 2000) and <http://www.fbi.gov/ucr/Cius_98/98crime/98cius05.pdf> (accessed: 9 December 1999). Civilian Labor Force—U.S. Bureau of Labor Statistics, Local Area Unemployment Statistics, 2000 data published 2 May 2001, 1999 data published 30 May 2001 <ftp://ftp.bls.gov/pub/time.series/la/> (related Internet site <http://www.bls.gov/lauhome.htm>).

Table C–5. Cities — Manufacturing and Wholesale Trade

[Includes states and 1,070 incorporated places of 25,000 or more population as of April 1, 1990 in all states except Hawaii which has no incorporated places recognized by the Census Bureau. For Hawaii, 8 census designated places (CDPs) of 25,000 or more population as of April 1, 1990 are included. Also included are the 5 boroughs of New York city. For more information on these areas, see appendix B. Geographic Information]

| City | Manufacturing (NAICS 31-33), 1997 | | | | | | | | Wholesale trade[3] (NAICS 42), 1997 | | | | | |
| | Establishments | | All employees | | Production workers | | Value added by manufacture (mil. dol.) | Value of shipments (mil. dol.) | Estab-lishments | Sales | | Paid employees[4] | Annual payroll (mil. dol.) | Operating expenses (mil. dol.) |
	Total	Percent with 20 or more employ-ees	Number[1]	Annual payroll (mil. dol.)	Number[2]	Wages (mil. dol.)				Total (mil. dol.)	Merchant whole-salers (mil. dol.)			
ALABAMA	5 444	38.4	352 618	10 187.8	275 637	6 928.4	29 221.5	67 970.1	6 315	40 986.3	26 045.8	79 229	2 394.7	4 844.9
Anniston city	61	52.5	4 995	122.0	3 907	84.1	355.6	749.2	61	593.9	D	873	25.7	67.4
Auburn city	28	42.9	1 708	34.8	1 468	22.9	149.9	270.3	26	D	D	(5)	D	D
Bessemer city	45	42.2	2 164	70.0	1 759	52.8	162.2	367.9	70	922.7	819.7	1 423	47.8	88.8
Birmingham city	382	40.8	19 057	621.0	13 056	366.4	1 239.1	3 179.5	736	6 744.4	4 906.2	14 656	494.1	965.2
Decatur city	124	40.3	8 495	291.1	6 713	196.4	1 218.5	3 219.0	138	868.5	742.8	1 785	51.9	106.6
Dothan city	102	38.2	8 269	212.8	6 600	145.9	622.2	1 311.0	180	643.2	519.3	1 918	49.1	100.0
Florence city	83	36.1	6 049	140.9	5 078	102.8	345.8	743.8	72	349.0	333.8	1 842	43.6	87.9
Gadsden city	67	31.3	6 067	217.5	4 638	141.3	568.3	1 241.0	70	283.2	217.6	1 031	28.3	66.3
Hoover city	NA	NA	NA	NA	NA	NA	NA	NA	126	1 767.6	447.0	1 240	57.1	103.4
Huntsville city	240	36.7	25 793	1 014.6	16 081	568.3	2 668.6	6 694.3	361	2 828.5	1 689.4	3 968	143.7	279.8
Mobile city	213	31.0	11 631	445.0	8 713	307.0	968.8	1 907.4	491	2 669.0	1 945.7	6 314	195.4	383.1
Montgomery city	190	38.9	10 312	269.0	7 234	165.0	901.2	1 798.7	365	2 701.0	D	4 733	141.0	280.9
Phenix City city	34	41.2	2 566	91.6	2 128	68.5	477.1	864.2	17	91.2	D	453	11.6	27.9
Prichard city	22	31.8	1 038	40.2	778	29.7	129.1	340.1	27	147.7	D	476	15.5	26.5
Tuscaloosa city	89	37.1	6 020	179.1	4 763	124.0	415.7	1 058.9	117	516.6	400.3	1 153	37.2	66.3
ALASKA	488	20.9	10 770	331.2	8 805	238.2	1 159.3	3 305.0	784	2 989.8	2 148.8	6 860	256.8	507.9
Anchorage city	187	13.9	2 022	62.9	1 459	38.8	157.8	322.3	434	1 989.1	1 393.4	4 748	181.4	351.8
Fairbanks city	NA	NA	NA	NA	NA	NA	NA	NA	51	178.3	D	590	21.8	39.7
Juneau city	NA	NA	NA	NA	NA	NA	NA	NA	33	96.3	87.8	196	8.2	17.6
ARIZONA	4 917	27.9	193 616	6 753.6	121 994	3 000.1	26 898.9	43 030.3	6 689	45 899.1	26 412.6	80 155	2 748.9	5 311.0
Chandler city	135	37.0	9 668	352.0	6 425	164.9	3 984.8	4 744.3	162	1 254.0	D	1 952	59.2	128.9
Flagstaff city	62	14.5	1 798	67.7	902	22.8	307.4	505.2	80	505.0	D	739	18.2	40.7
Gilbert town	78	24.4	2 228	57.4	1 771	41.5	150.8	311.5	74	119.1	84.8	301	9.4	20.6
Glendale city	156	25.0	6 398	244.0	3 598	94.8	649.6	1 075.9	160	848.8	486.9	2 130	57.3	124.4
Mesa city	258	21.3	13 921	530.7	7 718	186.0	2 404.7	3 367.1	347	1 280.8	1 006.5	2 797	109.0	210.3
Peoria city	34	17.6	558	13.8	439	9.4	30.3	54.3	25	37.6	D	113	3.3	8.7
Phoenix city	1 706	32.6	69 401	2 532.4	43 093	1 069.3	10 283.8	14 649.6	2 447	21 996.9	10 751.2	37 073	1 383.9	2 570.0
Prescott city	65	20.0	1 509	36.7	1 221	25.5	106.4	178.0	47	113.6	D	302	7.8	16.8
Scottsdale city	257	18.7	8 254	192.1	3 865	87.9	756.3	1 128.2	634	2 749.3	1 459.7	3 997	164.0	344.2
Sierra Vista city	NA	NA	NA	NA	NA	NA	NA	NA	15	D	D	(5)	D	D
Tempe city	498	33.3	24 105	865.2	15 432	404.8	3 345.3	5 414.8	659	9 609.2	7 040.4	10 322	370.2	727.8
Tucson city	520	26.7	20 152	841.2	10 438	237.7	1 767.5	3 483.6	615	1 801.0	1 308.3	6 532	190.1	361.6
Yuma city	36	25.0	2 481	44.5	2 255	36.0	136.5	348.1	65	207.9	D	635	19.8	38.6
ARKANSAS	3 316	37.6	230 153	5 778.4	187 493	4 192.7	19 346.8	45 186.0	3 619	27 515.4	14 409.6	41 385	1 136.6	2 271.9
Conway city	67	41.8	7 242	183.1	5 653	129.4	570.8	1 205.9	54	D	149.0	(6)	D	D
Fayetteville city	68	42.6	5 962	144.2	4 791	105.0	449.0	948.9	88	6 024.6	D	1 202	43.7	95.9
Fort Smith city	206	45.1	20 817	521.5	17 070	384.7	1 786.2	3 949.8	219	660.3	612.7	1 942	52.1	110.1
Hot Springs city	66	27.3	2 756	68.2	1 914	40.5	180.3	610.0	71	D	D	(5)	D	D
Jacksonville city	32	50.0	1 995	53.7	1 553	33.6	127.7	309.5	17	D	D	(6)	D	D
Jonesboro city	97	40.2	6 234	170.7	4 922	115.8	469.3	1 126.9	111	458.1	381.7	1 342	30.6	61.3
Little Rock city	251	37.8	12 570	365.9	9 303	223.7	977.1	2 458.0	555	4 550.3	2 911.8	10 270	332.1	622.7
North Little Rock city	91	36.3	4 073	110.4	2 975	71.2	582.3	1 095.8	219	4 712.8	1 310.2	3 255	91.6	188.5
Pine Bluff city	75	48.0	(7)	D	D	D	D	D	69	D	D	(6)	D	D
Springdale city	106	36.8	(7)	D	D	D	D	D	163	673.2	D	1 775	51.4	98.7
West Memphis city	33	51.5	(8)	D	D	D	D	D	41	281.9	D	477	14.5	31.6
CALIFORNIA	49 418	30.9	1 809 667	65 762.8	1 181 865	31 140.0	300.0	31 700.0	57 841	548 864.5	342 227.7	757 294	29 875.0	64 165.6
Alameda city	56	30.4	2 298	127.3	1 132	40.0	578.7	1 009.1	68	353.4	D	538	24.5	45.8
Alhambra city	125	28.8	3 248	81.8	2 658	55.7	175.9	308.5	427	747.1	676.2	1 972	46.3	106.5
Anaheim city	896	35.6	38 330	1 358.7	24 360	628.0	3 402.5	6 019.8	962	15 533.1	4 215.7	12 779	457.4	955.5
Antioch city	38	21.1	577	20.2	412	11.9	61.3	117.7	32	85.6	D	273	9.1	18.6
Apple Valley town	NA	NA	NA	NA	NA	NA	NA	NA	21	14.8	9.1	109	2.0	4.3
Arcadia city	72	20.8	971	29.0	689	15.4	151.0	201.2	309	569.8	459.1	1 131	30.2	69.0
Azusa city	126	42.1	5 017	197.7	2 974	71.4	488.7	905.9	56	412.9	396.6	939	26.6	63.1
Bakersfield city	160	18.1	4 560	107.9	3 631	69.1	217.8	416.0	291	2 747.6	2 189.5	3 891	144.2	286.8
Baldwin Park city	141	24.8	2 854	68.5	2 146	40.7	147.0	232.1	152	744.9	738.4	1 323	40.7	88.6
Bell city	29	37.9	940	28.8	624	12.6	69.0	177.3	71	591.7	564.7	1 287	39.2	88.5
Bellflower city	NA	NA	NA	NA	NA	NA	NA	NA	44	62.6	D	316	6.9	14.2
Bell Gardens city	70	37.1	1 672	42.2	1 252	26.5	81.4	163.3	35	147.1	D	319	7.9	17.2
Berkeley city	199	26.6	5 247	212.8	3 390	98.6	656.5	996.6	136	438.2	D	1 389	61.0	142.1
Beverly Hills city	64	6.3	501	10.9	351	6.1	21.7	45.1	186	1 136.9	D	1 256	60.1	119.9

[1] Average number of production workers plus the number of other (nonproduction) employees for the pay period including March 12. [2] Average number of production workers for the pay periods including the 12th of March, May, August, and November. [3] Includes only establishments with payroll. [4] For pay period including March 12. [5] 100 to 249 employees. [6] 500 to 999 employees. [7] 5,000 to 9,999 employees. [8] 1,000 to 2,499 employees.

Sources: Manufacturing—U.S. Census Bureau, 1997 Economic Census – Manufacturing, generated by Statistical Compendia Branch, using American Factfinder at <http://www.census.gov/>, (June 2000) [related Internet site <http://www.census.gov/epcd/www/97EC31.HTM>]. Wholesale Trade—U.S. Census Bureau, 1997 Economic Census, individual state .pdf files from <http://www.census.gov/epcd/www/97EC42.HTM> (accessed June 2000) and ECON97 Report Series CD-ROM, CD-EC97-1, Disc 1E, issued February 2001.

Table C–5. Cities — **Manufacturing and Wholesale Trade**–Con.

[Includes states and 1,070 incorporated places of 25,000 or more population as of April 1, 1990 in all states except Hawaii which has no incorporated places recognized by the Census Bureau. For Hawaii, 8 census designated places (CDPs) of 25,000 or more population as of April 1, 1990 are included. Also included are the 5 boroughs of New York city. For more information on these areas, see appendix B. Geographic Information]

City	Manufacturing (NAICS 31-33), 1997								Wholesale trade[3] (NAICS 42), 1997					
	Establishments		All employees		Production workers		Value added by manu-facture (mil. dol.)	Value of ship-ments (mil. dol.)	Estab-lishments	Sales		Paid em-ployees[4]	Annual payroll (mil. dol.)	Operating expenses (mil. dol.)
	Total	Percent with 20 or more employ-ees	Number[1]	Annual payroll (mil. dol.)	Number[2]	Wages (mil. dol.)				Total (mil. dol.)	Merchant whole-salers (mil. dol.)			
CALIFORNIA—Con.														
Brea city	187	36.9	8 461	316.5	5 140	140.1	603.2	1 145.1	235	2 455.1	1 916.1	2 926	121.4	390.7
Buena Park city	126	43.7	7 108	227.8	4 980	128.5	676.0	1 358.5	157	1 322.6	1 070.2	2 150	74.7	195.2
Burbank city	298	31.5	9 355	306.9	6 746	172.3	725.8	1 131.2	261	5 069.4	3 753.1	3 956	162.2	375.6
Burlingame city	83	31.3	2 286	90.9	1 550	48.5	237.2	408.5	244	2 062.5	1 645.4	1 597	70.2	146.2
Camarillo city	173	41.6	8 487	296.9	5 520	143.7	875.6	1 513.5	128	632.8	553.1	1 892	82.1	172.2
Campbell city	156	19.2	3 307	133.6	2 152	64.3	352.0	613.5	120	1 523.4	D	2 129	125.6	245.4
Carlsbad city	205	45.4	12 384	458.0	7 251	184.0	1 482.2	2 418.9	266	2 140.3	885.9	4 290	174.8	341.5
Carson city	321	42.7	13 958	477.5	9 576	259.8	2 235.2	5 207.9	338	5 176.5	4 938.5	7 029	273.5	643.4
Cathedral City city	NA	NA	NA	NA	NA	NA	NA	NA	35	52.5	44.7	250	7.9	16.0
Ceres city	32	28.1	835	24.0	597	13.4	67.7	131.1	20	D	D	(5)	D	D
Cerritos city	117	53.0	5 463	169.4	3 820	94.8	348.0	801.1	276	3 940.4	3 193.1	5 313	201.6	420.8
Chico city	107	25.2	2 455	63.1	1 834	40.0	195.3	403.7	109	469.1	424.1	1 300	44.3	87.6
Chino city	259	38.2	9 897	245.8	7 629	161.4	621.2	1 294.7	217	1 296.1	1 012.1	2 830	107.0	213.2
Chula Vista city	158	25.3	5 626	210.9	4 164	108.4	390.0	1 029.2	265	681.3	637.3	1 717	46.0	108.3
Claremont city	29	44.8	1 309	58.0	819	21.1	100.9	177.6	29	91.1	74.7	210	7.9	18.1
Clovis city	55	23.6	2 320	56.0	1 593	29.4	117.5	259.4	44	89.1	D	219	5.6	10.6
Colton city	54	38.9	1 668	45.4	1 225	26.3	139.7	278.2	60	279.4	144.1	846	27.3	51.6
Compton city	179	54.7	8 188	215.3	6 267	128.5	563.0	1 108.1	135	1 325.1	1 068.9	3 114	108.7	230.9
Concord city	145	21.4	2 554	97.6	1 380	42.3	167.8	353.3	203	1 264.6	520.5	1 677	68.7	160.2
Corona city	291	39.9	10 424	313.2	7 934	194.4	859.5	1 817.4	220	2 396.6	1 793.8	2 958	102.7	250.6
Coronado city	NA	NA	NA	NA	NA	NA	NA	NA	18	31.1	12.8	82	1.8	4.5
Costa Mesa city	310	26.5	11 091	429.6	6 085	150.0	986.0	1 757.6	373	7 388.3	4 658.9	5 888	289.9	608.3
Covina city	119	23.5	3 226	114.5	2 362	58.9	236.6	359.5	97	333.2	270.8	652	20.4	47.7
Culver City city	119	31.1	2 789	76.1	2 142	41.0	160.3	253.7	201	1 638.7	D	3 449	160.4	351.5
Cupertino city	49	20.4	2 626	112.9	809	27.9	188.4	295.1	92	1 935.2	D	1 464	117.9	254.9
Cypress city	40	40.0	1 341	41.8	966	21.5	132.7	200.4	99	5 099.8	4 670.7	6 044	230.9	1 147.8
Daly City city	NA	NA	NA	NA	NA	NA	NA	NA	47	209.7	D	550	21.4	40.3
Dana Point city	NA	NA	NA	NA	NA	NA	NA	NA	46	136.8	D	143	5.1	10.4
Danville city	NA	NA	NA	NA	NA	NA	NA	NA	75	328.4	158.3	286	13.2	24.9
Davis city	NA	NA	NA	NA	NA	NA	NA	NA	27	29.5	D	93	4.1	6.4
Diamond Bar city	NA	NA	NA	NA	NA	NA	NA	NA	174	1 241.9	D	1 100	31.3	68.4
Downey city	102	29.4	7 464	372.8	2 630	84.2	841.6	1 419.0	98	635.1	202.4	1 112	43.5	77.5
El Cajon city	187	32.1	6 102	194.1	4 319	117.0	390.3	654.3	116	369.2	351.8	1 262	34.0	68.8
El Centro city	NA	NA	NA	NA	NA	NA	NA	NA	47	137.5	117.8	334	0.0	18.8
El Monte city	238	37.4	8 068	211.8	6 081	129.0	484.3	882.2	314	2 389.6	D	3 461	129.8	285.0
Encinitas city	NA	NA	NA	NA	NA	NA	NA	NA	81	234.6	D	461	17.0	34.4
Escondido city	190	27.4	4 330	114.5	2 678	62.2	296.4	563.8	171	377.2	294.7	1 172	38.9	76.9
Eureka city	44	18.2	686	20.6	551	15.1	61.8	128.5	56	166.3	139.6	587	17.3	38.0
Fairfield city	53	39.6	2 955	121.7	2 158	75.8	561.8	1 036.1	60	913.8	D	1 016	37.1	76.0
Folsom city	23	30.4	648	26.2	417	16.5	44.6	79.2	23	D	D	(6)	D	D
Fontana city	111	48.6	4 811	153.9	3 605	89.5	460.8	1 128.7	69	1 925.2	D	2 432	64.6	141.2
Foster City city	26	42.3	1 866	115.8	945	51.8	297.9	563.4	97	862.6	461.8	1 595	98.2	163.0
Fountain Valley city	111	25.2	2 645	84.6	2 153	61.3	737.1	1 302.2	157	1 951.1	1 671.4	1 429	63.4	133.8
Fremont city	464	47.2	34 623	1 593.4	20 938	800.9	4 280.6	10 765.3	656	15 406.2	9 590.6	10 975	477.3	954.8
Fresno city	412	31.1	15 225	395.1	10 466	233.4	1 298.2	3 099.8	655	3 934.0	2 854.7	8 209	269.4	550.4
Fullerton city	228	38.6	10 916	375.8	8 238	254.2	1 202.0	2 217.1	225	2 331.2	845.8	3 596	134.9	256.2
Gardena city	NA	NA	NA	NA	NA	NA	NA	NA	198	606.8	552.3	1 708	51.2	113.2
Garden Grove city	354	24.3	9 710	269.5	7 393	154.1	1 158.1	2 255.3	240	1 469.9	1 357.0	3 031	101.4	220.5
Gilroy city	61	29.5	2 538	76.7	1 960	49.2	145.9	426.9	43	D	D	(7)	D	D
Glendale city	329	29.8	7 280	217.7	5 006	121.2	511.0	784.7	315	1 057.6	737.0	2 813	101.1	183.5
Glendora city	53	20.8	1 321	49.3	877	22.0	131.4	194.4	50	392.6	D	546	22.8	70.2
Hanford city	27	25.9	1 672	62.6	1 412	48.5	113.9	376.3	27	114.5	D	218	4.7	11.6
Hawthorne city	114	34.2	5 719	234.6	3 831	116.7	793.9	1 006.6	55	218.9	D	821	28.2	53.2
Hayward city	385	39.2	11 817	430.1	7 948	226.8	1 036.3	2 287.2	598	5 283.1	3 131.4	9 655	364.3	716.8
Hemet city	25	28.0	972	19.9	821	11.7	69.1	106.5	19	49.1	49.1	87	3.3	7.2
Hesperia city	66	24.2	1 212	26.3	1 007	17.4	68.4	157.6	38	98.2	D	187	4.9	9.3
Highland city	NA	NA	NA	NA	NA	NA	NA	NA	6	25.1	25.1	148	3.0	7.5
Huntington Beach city	417	25.2	14 927	594.8	8 714	246.8	906.3	2 377.3	477	2 484.3	1 257.1	4 819	171.6	345.7
Huntington Park city	163	38.0	5 042	133.5	3 908	86.5	301.7	575.4	58	374.8	D	1 167	35.9	69.0
Imperial Beach city	308	64.6	25 655	815.8	18 319	443.9	2 335.2	4 888.4	6	6.6	6.6	34	.5	1.3
Indio city	NA	NA	NA	NA	NA	NA	NA	NA	33	D	D	(5)	D	D
Inglewood city	74	28.4	2 554	79.7	1 800	45.5	204.9	384.3	102	509.8	445.0	1 455	48.9	90.0
Irvine city	479	52.2	34 067	1 319.0	21 417	589.8	4 143.4	8 500.6	894	29 723.1	17 756.6	17 641	881.0	2 167.1
Laguna Niguel city	NA	NA	NA	NA	NA	NA	NA	NA	102	462.7	109.0	337	14.3	30.9
La Habra city	87	19.5	1 371	39.4	979	23.1	95.4	155.0	67	175.2	D	479	14.8	32.1
Lakewood city	NA	NA	NA	NA	NA	NA	NA	NA	43	58.6	D	315	7.4	14.5
La Mesa city	NA	NA	NA	NA	NA	NA	NA	NA	36	70.3	62.8	222	7.5	14.0
La Mirada city	74	52.7	4 323	132.1	3 489	89.7	360.4	757.0	114	2 521.4	1 916.7	2 755	118.2	271.7

[1] Average number of production workers plus the number of other (nonproduction) employees for the pay period including March 12. [2] Average number of production workers for the pay periods including the 12th of March, May, August, and November. [3] Includes only establishments with payroll. [4] For pay period including March 12. [5] 250 to 499 employees. [6] 100 to 249 employees. [7] 500 to 999 employees.

Sources: Manufacturing—U.S. Census Bureau, 1997 Economic Census – Manufacturing, generated by Statistical Compendia Branch, using American Factfinder at <http://www.census.gov/>, (June 2000) [related Internet site <http://www.census.gov/epcd/www/97EC31.HTM>]. Wholesale Trade—U.S. Census Bureau, 1997 Economic Census, individual state .pdf files from <http://www.census.gov/epcd/www/97EC42.HTM> (accessed June 2000) and ECON97 Report Series CD-ROM, CD-EC97-1, Disc 1E, issued February 2001.

Table C–5. Cities — Manufacturing and Wholesale Trade–Con.

[Includes states and 1,070 incorporated places of 25,000 or more population as of April 1, 1990 in all states except Hawaii which has no incorporated places recognized by the Census Bureau. For Hawaii, 8 census designated places (CDPs) of 25,000 or more population as of April 1, 1990 are included. Also included are the 5 boroughs of New York city. For more information on these areas, see appendix B. Geographic Information]

City	Manufacturing (NAICS 31-33), 1997								Wholesale trade[3] (NAICS 42), 1997					
	Establishments		All employees		Production workers		Value added by manufacture (mil. dol.)	Value of shipments (mil. dol.)	Establishments	Sales		Paid employees[4]	Annual payroll (mil. dol.)	Operating expenses (mil. dol.)
	Total	Percent with 20 or more employees	Number[1]	Annual payroll (mil. dol.)	Number[2]	Wages (mil. dol.)				Total (mil. dol.)	Merchant wholesalers (mil. dol.)			
CALIFORNIA—Con.														
Lancaster city	NA	NA	NA	NA	NA	NA	NA	NA	61	198.1	183.8	652	17.2	36.1
La Puente city	NA	NA	NA	NA	NA	NA	NA	NA	18	D	D	(5)	D	D
La Verne city	43	37.2	1 062	35.0	791	20.7	105.8	188.6	45	220.7	193.2	340	11.3	27.7
Lawndale city	NA	NA	NA	NA	NA	NA	NA	NA	22	D	D	(5)	D	D
Livermore city	112	32.1	2 897	89.7	2 030	52.6	211.0	499.5	129	1 133.7	874.6	1 708	74.4	145.0
Lodi city	99	28.3	3 149	88.6	2 644	65.1	220.2	475.3	58	415.4	399.9	1 050	30.3	53.4
Lompoc city	NA	NA	NA	NA	NA	NA	NA	NA	17	D	D	(6)	D	D
Long Beach city	332	27.7	27 548	1 400.3	15 443	557.3	2 239.0	8 786.9	402	8 218.0	6 745.1	5 257	200.8	420.1
Los Altos city	NA	NA	NA	NA	NA	NA	NA	NA	51	D	D	(5)	D	D
Los Angeles city	7 222	27.4	186 758	5 302.8	137 467	2 909.9	14 314.9	27 378.2	8 327	49 609.3	38 497.2	87 405	3 065.1	6 699.2
Los Gatos town	61	21.3	1 055	50.2	731	19.3	80.5	136.4	65	272.6	D	440	24.2	46.8
Lynwood city	62	51.6	2 516	56.6	2 007	36.3	119.9	289.0	44	259.6	D	747	23.3	46.5
Madera city	38	39.5	1 260	33.9	863	19.6	90.5	190.9	33	D	D	(7)	D	D
Manhattan Beach city	NA	NA	NA	NA	NA	NA	NA	NA	54	403.3	D	442	27.1	73.2
Manteca city	NA	NA	NA	NA	NA	NA	NA	NA	23	D	D	(5)	D	D
Marina city	NA	NA	NA	NA	NA	NA	NA	NA	9	18.7	D	59	1.9	3.8
Martinez city	33	21.2	(8)	D	D	D	D	D	41	654.3	D	446	20.1	45.9
Maywood city	31	29.0	514	9.1	446	6.6	19.9	32.7	16	54.3	54.3	164	4.7	8.4
Menlo Park city	78	56.4	6 371	369.8	3 053	108.7	950.1	1 478.0	68	779.9	D	1 674	107.2	173.3
Merced city	42	42.9	2 326	64.3	1 762	44.9	208.6	457.3	37	416.7	D	576	18.7	37.2
Milpitas city	202	53.0	27 550	1 364.6	12 846	449.5	4 486.7	7 129.6	224	3 747.0	3 202.5	4 470	206.3	492.4
Mission Viejo city	46	15.2	1 466	70.3	634	27.8	151.3	272.3	142	465.7	317.7	783	38.5	68.2
Modesto city	137	30.7	7 462	265.5	4 677	116.2	946.5	2 124.8	164	870.5	820.6	2 111	66.9	123.5
Monrovia city	130	39.2	5 150	199.4	2 969	89.9	395.6	725.6	109	282.7	257.1	1 020	32.9	70.3
Montclair city	72	13.9	854	19.9	699	13.0	40.9	95.0	57	129.2	D	499	14.1	27.2
Montebello city	112	38.4	4 850	133.7	3 421	74.8	367.8	642.2	123	1 474.6	731.2	1 929	77.0	166.5
Monterey city	61	21.3	1 317	44.1	745	17.2	80.2	159.6	56	1 460.5	D	1 324	49.7	106.1
Monterey Park city	79	27.8	1 841	43.9	1 318	23.9	106.1	170.4	268	864.8	675.8	1 656	44.3	92.4
Moorpark city	52	34.6	2 578	79.4	1 576	34.6	221.2	370.2	56	242.3	195.6	773	31.4	60.2
Moreno Valley city	19	26.3	1 095	20.8	631	15.0	58.0	143.7	25	47.0	D	80	2.5	5.4
Mountain View city	235	33.2	20 837	1 298.7	7 926	352.6	6 251.6	9 372.0	180	2 612.0	D	5 479	283.5	461.4
Napa city	104	19.2	2 694	84.7	1 805	41.0	400.5	591.2	84	202.5	176.2	568	17.0	35.7
National City city	100	22.0	1 744	45.1	1 321	27.6	133.6	342.7	119	814.1	589.1	1 302	39.9	82.0
Newark city	84	44.0	2 989	124.1	2 179	70.6	337.1	597.5	83	683.9	597.7	1 410	56.6	131.6
Newport Beach city	109	16.5	5 136	255.6	2 563	69.6	1 295.2	1 481.8	289	2 642.8	697.3	7 136	140.7	232.0
Norwalk city	75	25.3	1 234	28.9	922	18.2	73.1	159.9	84	610.1	D	815	28.7	74.5
Novato city	82	24.4	1 669	65.2	947	25.4	122.5	263.1	111	423.1	334.3	981	34.9	78.7
Oakland city	574	27.4	13 913	426.2	9 664	242.9	1 196.8	2 048.1	526	3 553.2	2 396.7	7 662	285.6	541.7
Oceanside city	157	32.5	3 749	97.5	2 934	59.0	256.3	416.5	125	925.6	D	1 694	42.1	100.1
Ontario city	420	42.6	16 296	483.4	12 703	312.4	1 692.6	3 257.5	371	5 425.5	4 179.8	7 262	251.6	631.5
Orange city	338	32.8	10 463	309.4	7 545	162.9	767.5	1 452.6	403	4 685.5	2 357.8	5 751	228.2	440.7
Oxnard city	172	40.7	6 935	220.8	5 242	130.3	749.0	1 440.7	174	795.9	735.0	2 255	80.6	179.7
Pacifica city	NA	NA	NA	NA	NA	NA	NA	NA	7	7.3	D	14	.6	1.4
Palmdale city	44	9.1	(9)	D	D	D	D	D	36	71.7	D	268	8.4	17.0
Palm Springs city	37	24.3	734	22.5	470	8.5	73.8	107.6	40	D	D	(7)	D	D
Palo Alto city	114	28.9	7 983	362.6	5 766	231.8	1 825.3	2 232.0	104	1 019.1	D	1 382	126.5	223.5
Paradise town	NA	NA	NA	NA	NA	NA	NA	NA	8	D	D	(10)	D	D
Paramount city	268	32.1	6 401	199.4	4 813	125.6	450.6	1 081.7	200	888.6	764.4	2 752	83.4	161.1
Pasadena city	151	24.5	2 877	87.4	1 931	44.2	207.6	389.0	200	2 219.5	906.2	2 492	108.6	232.6
Petaluma city	119	39.5	4 998	249.8	2 730	82.4	665.3	1 403.7	113	579.8	D	1 948	60.5	142.4
Pico Rivera city	81	51.9	3 122	89.0	2 269	46.3	259.4	518.5	86	620.1	528.0	1 532	51.9	105.7
Pittsburg city	46	34.8	2 362	118.3	1 651	81.6	616.9	1 503.1	31	147.4	D	378	14.6	37.2
Placentia city	134	32.1	3 438	85.9	2 468	49.8	288.9	447.2	129	477.6	378.3	1 264	45.6	88.4
Pleasant Hill city	NA	NA	NA	NA	NA	NA	NA	NA	35	153.9	D	338	15.3	29.1
Pleasanton city	100	21.0	1 759	77.1	989	31.5	188.2	328.4	253	13 939.1	2 978.8	5 868	331.2	610.0
Pomona city	253	33.6	9 792	301.9	6 435	149.0	742.6	1 551.4	229	1 184.8	1 018.0	2 982	87.3	190.9
Porterville city	35	22.9	1 045	28.1	874	21.0	97.0	161.4	23	150.5	D	398	6.3	15.3
Poway city	52	21.2	1 397	41.2	1 023	21.5	104.3	227.6	60	263.4	169.7	530	20.3	44.4
Rancho Cucamonga city	243	42.0	9 913	311.7	7 625	196.2	977.3	2 009.1	219	1 529.4	821.7	2 594	86.3	186.3
Rancho Palos Verdes city	NA	NA	NA	NA	NA	NA	NA	NA	46	110.7	D	101	5.6	11.2
Redding city	110	11.8	1 351	38.0	912	20.6	77.3	166.2	152	436.3	D	1 311	40.5	83.0
Redlands city	54	24.1	1 803	41.3	1 526	29.4	99.9	196.1	37	161.2	123.4	496	16.3	31.0
Redondo Beach city	40	12.5	(9)	D	D	D	D	D	77	366.7	169.5	552	23.2	53.7
Redwood City city	98	30.6	4 606	238.6	2 179	68.7	632.3	930.1	128	1 099.4	D	1 376	72.6	140.7
Rialto city	66	31.8	1 935	50.2	1 493	32.7	140.2	299.0	50	924.3	D	553	21.3	44.6
Richmond city	137	30.7	4 640	207.8	3 280	133.3	985.5	2 979.0	105	690.9	397.7	1 396	47.6	114.0
Ridgecrest city	NA	NA	NA	NA	NA	NA	NA	NA	4	D	D	(10)	D	D
Riverside city	289	29.1	10 901	322.4	7 732	195.2	789.1	1 687.2	267	1 723.0	918.9	3 395	104.9	213.7
Rohnert Park city	48	18.8	781	27.6	480	10.5	80.9	136.2	35	D	D	(7)	D	D

[1] Average number of production workers plus the number of other (nonproduction) employees for the pay period including March 12. [2] Average number of production workers for the pay periods including the 12th of March, May, August, and November. [3] Includes only establishments with payroll. [4] For pay period including March 12. [5] 100 to 249 employees. [6] 20 to 99 employees. [7] 250 to 499 employees. [8] 1,000 to 2,499 employees. [9] 5,000 to 9,999 employees. [10] 0 to 19 employees.

Sources: Manufacturing—U.S. Census Bureau, 1997 Economic Census – Manufacturing, generated by Statistical Compendia Branch, using American Factfinder at <http://www.census.gov/>, (June 2000) [related Internet site <http://www.census.gov/epcd/www/97EC31.HTM>]. Wholesale Trade—U.S. Census Bureau, 1997 Economic Census, individual state .pdf files from <http://www.census.gov/epcd/www/97EC42.HTM> (accessed June 2000) and ECON97 Report Series CD-ROM, CD-EC97-1, Disc 1E, issued February 2001.

Table C–5. Cities — Manufacturing and Wholesale Trade–Con.

[Includes states and 1,070 incorporated places of 25,000 or more population as of April 1, 1990 in all states except Hawaii which has no incorporated places recognized by the Census Bureau. For Hawaii, 8 census designated places (CDPs) of 25,000 or more population as of April 1, 1990 are included. Also included are the 5 boroughs of New York city. For more information on these areas, see appendix B. Geographic Information]

City	Manufacturing (NAICS 31-33), 1997								Wholesale trade[3] (NAICS 42), 1997					
	Establishments		All employees		Production workers		Value added by manu-facture (mil. dol.)	Value of ship-ments (mil. dol.)	Sales					
	Total	Percent with 20 or more employ-ees	Number[1]	Annual payroll (mil. dol.)	Number[2]	Wages (mil. dol.)			Estab-lishments	Total (mil. dol.)	Merchant whole-salers (mil. dol.)	Paid em-ployees[4]	Annual payroll (mil. dol.)	Operating expenses (mil. dol.)

City	Total	Pct 20+	Number[1]	Ann. payroll	Number[2]	Wages	Value added	Value shipments	Estab.	Total	Merchant	Paid emp[4]	Ann. payroll	Oper. exp.
CALIFORNIA—Con.														
Rosemead city	82	23.2	1 759	38.1	1 380	24.5	86.3	149.6	100	668.4	290.2	(5)	D	D
Roseville city	57	21.1	(6)	D	D	D	D	D	77	D	D	1 520	66.1	122.5
Sacramento city	423	30.0	15 763	579.1	10 275	279.8	1 965.4	3 582.7	594	5 538.2	3 403.6	10 553	369.9	765.6
Salinas city	97	24.7	2 752	96.0	1 994	57.7	345.1	641.6	200	2 308.0	1 922.4	3 802	145.6	284.6
San Bernardino city	150	34.0	4 140	106.1	3 208	69.8	269.1	589.5	150	1 050.2	932.8	2 728	88.0	169.5
San Bruno city	NA	NA	NA	NA	NA	NA	NA	NA	35	452.9	D	244	10.8	41.8
San Buenaventura (Ventura) city	157	24.2	3 126	90.9	2 439	57.1	225.0	374.7	201	639.9	515.5	2 816	98.2	200.0
San Carlos city	148	29.1	3 712	144.4	2 659	93.9	339.9	561.6	129	671.4	427.6	1 504	57.1	111.1
San Clemente city	91	20.9	1 452	49.3	973	24.7	100.2	189.3	144	748.4	385.8	1 293	48.7	101.2
San Diego city	1 444	28.9	65 599	2 562.7	37 155	1 026.1	6 680.4	14 315.4	2 178	18 478.4	11 334.8	33 766	1 634.8	3 003.4
San Dimas city	99	26.3	2 382	73.1	1 678	39.9	183.1	321.7	102	1 271.8	951.6	970	34.0	67.2
San Francisco city	1 247	24.8	25 037	642.4	19 500	392.8	1 998.4	3 978.9	1 900	12 219.1	8 973.1	17 677	779.8	1 501.5
San Gabriel city	54	25.9	628	11.0	490	6.9	22.6	36.5	156	195.5	D	599	12.8	29.1
San Jose city	1 225	33.3	86 726	4 263.5	39 798	1 320.4	14 933.2	26 808.1	1 423	27 076.8	16 276.7	25 578	1 398.6	2 899.5
San Juan Capistrano city	44	27.3	1 108	40.7	709	17.2	125.7	176.6	66	212.3	129.2	391	14.1	27.5
San Leandro city	257	34.6	9 002	310.7	6 524	182.8	1 027.7	2 260.6	324	2 533.4	1 193.2	4 402	176.1	399.2
San Luis Obispo city	78	20.5	1 521	43.9	993	19.8	125.0	195.0	69	161.6	D	554	14.4	32.7
San Marcos city	227	32.6	5 981	172.1	4 070	91.5	500.0	872.1	155	495.5	401.5	1 843	63.8	122.5
San Mateo city	77	5.2	531	18.4	335	10.4	39.3	67.5	156	1 840.2	828.0	2 138	179.4	370.6
San Pablo city	NA	NA	NA	NA	NA	NA	NA	NA	13	11.5	11.5	41	.8	1.8
San Rafael city	149	12.8	1 809	58.3	1 171	28.1	129.6	223.2	221	754.6	534.0	1 775	66.1	131.6
San Ramon city	NA	NA	NA	NA	NA	NA	NA	NA	162	7 459.8	2 880.4	2 759	175.5	295.7
Santa Ana city	961	32.3	30 246	878.1	22 469	491.8	2 343.8	4 052.4	571	4 113.4	2 181.3	8 899	357.2	707.0
Santa Barbara city	155	19.4	2 204	68.7	1 278	28.4	146.8	262.6	157	379.8	286.5	1 145	35.2	76.2
Santa Clara city	711	35.4	46 029	2 398.9	25 363	941.8	7 469.2	12 884.0	593	20 791.0	5 497.2	13 779	892.0	1 607.8
Santa Clarita city	66	16.7	1 136	39.5	800	23.0	101.9	164.3	75	392.6	304.1	576	37.4	106.6
Santa Cruz city	122	21.3	2 969	101.2	1 622	46.3	498.4	866.8	92	170.1	D	888	23.7	42.0
Santa Maria city	86	25.6	2 608	63.7	1 906	34.4	283.5	452.4	117	451.7	330.2	1 350	43.7	117.1
Santa Monica city	147	20.4	4 065	141.0	2 469	71.5	330.0	560.6	234	3 792.3	3 263.4	2 608	124.3	311.5
Santa Paula city	NA	NA	NA	NA	NA	NA	NA	NA	32	265.1	D	765	19.4	50.8
Santa Rosa city	203	22.2	9 598	418.2	6 678	236.9	1 199.6	1 784.1	182	716.2	618.6	2 088	71.3	133.8
Santee city	127	26.0	2 356	61.1	1 564	32.3	132.4	216.9	63	106.6	94.1	418	11.2	26.6
Saratoga city	NA	NA	NA	NA	NA	NA	NA	NA	48	D	D	(7)	D	D
Seal Beach city	10	40.0	(8)	D	D	D	D	D	26	161.8	D	159	9.6	15.0
Seaside city	NA	NA	NA	NA	NA	NA	NA	NA	15	23.6	23.6	123	2.9	5.6
Simi Valley city	157	29.3	4 709	170.5	2 952	73.0	646.6	1 208.3	146	843.9	D	2 050	76.9	144.7
South Gate city	200	38.0	7 603	214.9	6 088	146.1	591.7	1 330.9	86	1 327.5	D	1 417	41.1	94.0
South San Francisco city	193	39.9	10 151	485.9	5 524	149.3	1 478.0	2 011.2	472	4 778.9	3 365.0	7 370	302.0	721.9
Stanton city	64	17.2	1 251	31.4	955	19.8	66.7	117.2	39	127.9	91.3	732	18.7	38.6
Stockton city	191	37.7	8 783	256.7	6 900	181.8	774.6	1 809.8	262	2 949.0	2 512.9	4 027	125.9	280.0
Sunnyvale city	438	46.8	43 471	2 683.0	15 750	561.8	7 469.5	11 208.6	386	7 425.4	4 379.7	8 677	574.6	1 239.4
Temecula city	107	29.9	4 321	145.6	2 904	70.9	843.0	1 113.4	77	579.6	510.4	973	37.4	78.1
Temple City city	NA	NA	NA	NA	NA	NA	NA	NA	75	90.7	D	311	5.9	12.1
Thousand Oaks city	137	28.5	4 172	158.9	2 156	57.7	342.7	602.0	202	6 480.3	D	1 997	96.3	219.6
Torrance city	328	34.8	16 065	719.9	10 890	401.0	1 849.3	4 364.1	618	14 366.0	D	7 802	405.3	1 554.9
Tracy city	48	45.8	2 527	77.5	2 063	54.8	264.4	651.2	30	219.5	D	299	9.7	25.1
Tulare city	35	45.7	1 797	61.0	1 428	44.0	206.3	1 331.8	40	135.9	D	478	12.4	23.6
Turlock city	69	42.0	3 636	93.0	3 009	69.5	409.9	857.2	53	166.4	D	409	12.5	24.4
Tustin city	141	34.0	6 771	282.5	4 470	132.2	833.8	1 446.3	232	2 236.2	1 254.5	3 233	139.6	291.3
Union City city	93	41.9	3 696	128.1	2 640	78.5	360.6	677.5	179	2 722.5	2 250.3	4 640	186.2	359.1
Upland city	95	22.1	1 510	40.1	1 044	21.7	99.1	224.1	108	191.3	138.4	579	16.0	37.0
Vacaville city	58	29.3	2 382	71.1	1 952	46.6	217.8	355.8	35	110.2	D	392	9.9	18.4
Vallejo city	40	20.0	682	23.0	470	14.4	84.1	198.2	32	220.4	D	387	12.8	32.9
Victorville city	29	17.2	773	27.8	616	20.2	128.1	216.3	29	63.6	D	227	8.3	15.2
Visalia city	87	36.8	3 873	106.7	3 033	75.4	373.4	821.2	137	1 050.8	D	1 344	44.4	102.7
Vista city	153	35.3	5 607	148.9	3 903	79.8	390.3	743.9	110	426.5	399.1	1 592	48.7	102.6
Walnut city	48	18.8	665	23.0	455	10.0	77.3	146.7	247	1 278.7	D	1 212	33.7	86.3
Walnut Creek city	45	15.6	1 417	63.5	617	18.7	239.2	355.1	121	2 546.0	353.6	1 276	69.3	152.3
Watsonville city	81	38.3	3 482	87.0	2 498	50.2	268.4	555.6	57	750.6	590.6	1 641	57.2	111.8
West Covina city	42	26.2	1 312	47.3	817	22.1	122.2	184.9	59	114.2	68.6	199	6.0	12.8
West Hollywood city	NA	NA	NA	NA	NA	NA	NA	NA	135	457.9	225.3	862	34.3	85.4
Westminster city	128	14.8	1 984	43.7	1 644	28.8	96.1	168.5	86	202.6	158.3	585	15.4	35.3
West Sacramento city	68	25.0	2 487	91.5	1 386	40.1	342.4	712.9	154	3 109.2	D	4 361	145.5	283.2
Whittier city	76	34.2	2 733	69.4	2 108	40.8	158.1	298.3	90	660.4	D	696	29.0	57.6
Woodland city	65	35.4	2 309	77.6	1 769	48.5	205.4	484.6	74	1 561.0	1 504.1	2 953	92.8	191.0
Yorba Linda city	72	18.1	1 523	70.6	844	22.9	116.9	205.8	157	1 700.6	343.0	4 351	65.0	128.8
Yuba City city	35	14.3	759	27.2	569	17.0	116.0	234.1	48	181.5	121.4	390	14.1	27.7
Yucaipa city	NA	NA	NA	NA	NA	NA	NA	NA	23	72.1	D	208	4.7	10.1

[1] Average number of production workers plus the number of other (nonproduction) employees for the pay period including March 12.   [2] Average number of production workers for the pay periods including the 12th of March, May, August, and November.   [3] Includes only establishments with payroll.   [4] For pay period including March 12.   [5] 500 to 999 employees.   [6] 5,000 to 9,999 employees.   [7] 100 to 249 employees.   [8] 1,000 to 2,499 employees.

Sources: Manufacturing—U.S. Census Bureau, 1997 Economic Census – Manufacturing, generated by Statistical Compendia Branch, using American Factfinder at <http://www.census.gov/>, (June 2000) [related Internet site <http://www.census.gov/epcd/www/97EC31.HTM>].   Wholesale Trade—U.S. Census Bureau, 1997 Economic Census, individual state .pdf files from <http://www.census.gov/epcd/www/97EC42.HTM> (accessed June 2000) and ECON97 Report Series CD-ROM, CD-EC97-1, Disc 1E, issued February 2001.

Table C–5. Cities — **Manufacturing and Wholesale Trade**–Con.

[Includes states and 1,070 incorporated places of 25,000 or more population as of April 1, 1990 in all states except Hawaii which has no incorporated places recognized by the Census Bureau. For Hawaii, 8 census designated places (CDPs) of 25,000 or more population as of April 1, 1990 are included. Also included are the 5 boroughs of New York city. For more information on these areas, see appendix B. Geographic Information]

City	Manufacturing (NAICS 31-33), 1997								Wholesale trade[3] (NAICS 42), 1997					
	Establishments		All employees		Production workers		Value added by manufacture (mil. dol.)	Value of shipments (mil. dol.)	Establishments	Sales		Paid employees[4]	Annual payroll (mil. dol.)	Operating expenses (mil. dol.)
	Total	Percent with 20 or more employees	Number[1]	Annual payroll (mil. dol.)	Number[2]	Wages (mil. dol.)				Total (mil. dol.)	Merchant wholesalers (mil. dol.)			
COLORADO	5 480	23.1	173 069	6 176.8	115 308	3 177.7	20 673.0	40 012.8	7 383	60 310.4	27 610.4	88 364	3 282.0	6 213.5
Arvada city	106	19.8	3 022	100.6	1 821	40.0	251.6	432.0	122	282.1	D	1 075	30.2	59.8
Aurora city	139	16.5	2 360	75.3	1 579	39.5	172.7	342.4	289	4 326.8	2 205.4	4 800	189.1	379.4
Boulder city	282	25.5	9 940	415.7	5 374	168.6	1 002.8	1 758.8	251	1 598.3	1 337.8	2 548	100.1	200.5
Colorado Springs city	418	24.2	17 439	565.9	11 638	299.4	2 600.9	4 204.3	417	1 205.2	993.5	5 911	200.8	356.3
Denver city	976	29.6	26 320	816.2	18 087	456.2	2 525.0	4 867.8	1 681	16 177.1	7 593.4	26 604	972.8	1 846.9
Englewood city	200	27.0	4 684	145.2	3 168	80.0	351.1	617.2	220	4 291.7	2 562.8	3 278	137.6	287.6
Fort Collins city	124	29.8	8 117	351.8	3 676	116.7	1 099.5	2 334.6	110	D	(5)	D	D	D
Grand Junction city	113	27.4	3 212	91.0	2 321	55.4	241.2	446.0	141	390.4	298.1	1 123	32.7	60.8
Greeley city	71	38.0	5 073	120.0	4 209	89.2	376.3	1 926.5	107	442.2	309.2	1 098	33.9	66.7
Lakewood city	125	12.0	1 720	72.1	1 152	28.8	278.4	359.0	221	957.5	382.5	1 326	53.3	101.4
Littleton city	67	19.4	1 860	60.0	1 328	37.9	165.1	279.0	114	875.4	189.4	1 093	43.9	81.4
Longmont city	152	27.6	4 688	136.6	3 399	77.8	305.4	556.7	79	1 751.6	D	1 519	81.3	133.9
Loveland city	66	31.8	5 214	225.2	2 748	96.3	734.9	1 260.8	62	186.4	91.9	611	18.0	35.5
Northglenn city	42	21.4	616	17.4	441	10.5	47.3	102.8	26	59.7	D	145	4.1	15.2
Pueblo city	70	28.6	2 818	96.2	2 188	71.2	264.7	578.4	90	360.3	D	890	24.0	47.2
Thornton city	26	23.1	1 587	44.5	969	19.1	122.1	279.3	47	557.6	493.0	438	18.8	43.5
Westminster city	70	18.6	2 450	95.7	1 581	52.5	203.4	659.3	94	272.5	D	688	26.9	45.2
Wheat Ridge city	58	19.0	1 413	53.1	1 060	34.6	145.8	295.2	66	268.3	142.3	648	18.1	31.9
CONNECTICUT	5 844	33.0	252 330	10 452.1	153 045	4 895.3	27 295.2	46 938.2	5 283	76 167.9	54 110.8	77 716	3 595.3	7 560.0
Bridgeport city	249	30.1	10 340	375.0	6 677	195.7	758.0	1 424.4	131	601.2	D	1 665	63.7	131.8
Bristol city	158	38.0	4 542	159.0	3 328	100.0	361.1	580.5	58	251.9	D	839	32.1	60.0
Danbury city	130	40.0	6 556	281.0	3 814	123.3	731.7	1 302.0	125	904.0	328.8	2 150	69.9	142.0
Hartford city	112	30.4	2 183	60.6	1 555	33.6	130.7	254.5	171	3 038.6	1 110.2	4 575	214.5	431.3
Meriden city	103	33.0	4 353	162.9	2 637	73.0	378.8	751.2	67	220.4	167.0	745	25.1	45.4
Middletown city	58	50.0	5 256	222.0	3 774	145.2	705.7	1 662.2	51	220.3	195.5	672	22.8	46.8
Milford city (remainder)	[6]206	[6]25.7	[6]6 100	[6]258.8	[6]3 871	[6]135.3	[6]720.4	[6]1 104.5	[6]153	[6]776.7	[6]676.5	[6]1 925	[6]80.7	[6]162.4
Naugatuck borough	NA	NA	NA	NA	NA	NA	NA	NA	22	152.2	D	372	13.0	24.1
New Britain city	141	34.0	5 329	193.2	3 903	124.1	497.7	845.0	41	279.0	248.5	575	24.0	55.3
New Haven city	106	39.6	4 177	147.2	2 804	80.5	413.8	750.6	130	737.6	490.4	1 399	50.9	95.9
New London city	NA	NA	NA	NA	NA	NA	NA	NA	22	63.8	D	223	8.3	16.4
Norwalk city	170	30.6	6 713	297.7	3 604	121.1	889.9	1 420.5	210	4 028.5	955.8	4 143	338.1	692.6
Norwich city	48	31.3	1 403	44.8	882	23.3	139.0	254.5	29	175.8	D	480	15.2	27.2
Shelton city	77	45.5	4 923	211.8	2 607	88.5	441.2	728.6	47	921.7	805.6	1 111	54.0	106.2
Stamford city	183	25.7	6 126	229.6	2 996	106.6	1 644.8	2 515.3	354	22 164.2	18 192.0	5 992	430.8	1 131.3
Torrington city	83	41.0	3 770	118.7	2 795	75.9	240.5	443.8	52	209.8	D	603	23.9	46.1
Waterbury city	219	35.6	6 433	220.9	4 940	148.5	531.4	1 085.3	113	494.9	459.9	1 462	51.7	109.4
West Haven city	62	35.5	5 258	276.5	1 544	41.7	1 116.3	1 623.1	57	490.0	407.9	1 000	41.5	76.3
DELAWARE	675	34.4	41 084	1 474.3	28 959	899.8	5 389.5	13 397.3	906	12 585.5	2 943.2	13 509	619.5	1 262.7
Dover city	29	31.0	3 902	111.5	2 114	78.3	845.9	1 338.5	40	D	D	(7)	D	D
Newark city	52	44.2	(8)	D	D	D	D	D	52	D	D	(5)	D	D
Wilmington city	102	27.5	(9)	D	D	D	D	D	106	1 158.1	D	1 736	70.1	122.3
DISTRICT OF COLUMBIA	200	17.5	2 858	101.1	1 926	60.9	170.8	320.2	348	3 918.6	1 091.0	5 008	223.0	411.3
Washington city	200	17.5	2 858	101.1	1 926	60.9	170.8	320.2	348	3 918.6	1 091.0	5 008	223.0	411.3
FLORIDA	15 992	22.7	433 149	13 185.1	291 452	6 826.0	40 213.4	77 477.5	31 214	187 079.9	121 260.1	296 139	9 678.2	20 378.7
Altamonte Springs city	NA	NA	NA	NA	NA	NA	NA	NA	152	897.2	569.7	1 137	51.0	95.8
Boca Raton city	175	18.9	4 828	211.2	2 644	56.6	300.4	639.0	525	4 325.7	3 450.9	6 440	322.1	649.7
Boynton Beach city	65	20.0	(9)	D	D	D	D	D	92	171.1	131.5	498	14.4	27.7
Bradenton city	34	23.5	(9)	D	D	D	D	D	37	98.3	D	219	6.5	14.1
Cape Coral city	77	7.8	549	12.9	427	8.9	24.8	46.5	94	D	95.6	(10)	D	D
Clearwater city	182	18.1	3 191	84.8	1 888	39.1	198.0	342.9	301	1 020.3	598.1	2 173	65.6	124.6
Coconut Creek city	NA	NA	NA	NA	NA	NA	NA	NA	41	61.1	D	85	3.9	8.6
Coral Gables city	NA	NA	NA	NA	NA	NA	NA	NA	268	4 723.1	2 059.8	1 981	117.7	229.5
Coral Springs city	82	13.4	1 186	34.5	838	17.6	70.6	139.8	259	915.1	724.7	2 588	88.7	217.0
Davie town	111	15.3	1 447	39.0	1 077	24.0	85.2	156.1	267	1 406.1	D	2 285	56.1	134.8
Daytona Beach city	63	23.8	1 931	44.4	1 338	25.5	102.9	200.4	90	393.2	170.1	1 028	27.6	75.9
Deerfield Beach city	100	30.0	2 511	78.4	1 706	42.5	174.2	333.9	211	6 510.8	D	3 391	153.8	439.1
Delray Beach city	67	9.0	613	18.2	439	11.2	44.6	84.4	120	231.5	175.4	569	19.2	40.7
Dunedin city	NA	NA	NA	NA	NA	NA	NA	NA	41	81.8	54.3	217	8.4	16.6
Fort Lauderdale city	352	21.0	7 546	247.2	4 526	108.0	543.4	1 001.7	761	6 347.6	2 627.2	8 279	336.0	693.2

[1] Average number of production workers plus the number of other (nonproduction) employees for the pay period including March 12. [2] Average number of production workers for the pay periods including the 12th of March, May, August, and November. [3] Includes only establishments with payroll. [4] For pay period including March 12. [5] 500 to 999 employees. [6] Data are for consolidated city of Milford; data for Milford city (remainder) not available. [7] 100 to 249 employees. [8] 5,000 to 9,999 employees. [9] 2,500 to 4,999 employees. [10] 250 to 499 employees.

Sources: Manufacturing—U.S. Census Bureau, 1997 Economic Census – Manufacturing, generated by Statistical Compendia Branch, using American Factfinder at <http://www.census.gov/>, (June 2000) [related Internet site <http://www.census.gov/epcd/www/97EC31.HTM>]. Wholesale Trade—U.S. Census Bureau, 1997 Economic Census, individual state .pdf files from <http://www.census.gov/epcd/www/97EC42.HTM> (accessed June 2000) and ECON97 Report Series CD-ROM, CD-EC97-1, Disc 1E, issued February 2001.

Table C–5. Cities — Manufacturing and Wholesale Trade–Con.

[Includes states and 1,070 incorporated places of 25,000 or more population as of April 1, 1990 in all states except Hawaii which has no incorporated places recognized by the Census Bureau. For Hawaii, 8 census designated places (CDPs) of 25,000 or more population as of April 1, 1990 are included. Also included are the 5 boroughs of New York city. For more information on these areas, see appendix B. Geographic Information]

| City | Manufacturing (NAICS 31-33), 1997 | | | | | | | | Wholesale trade[3] (NAICS 42), 1997 | | | | | |
| | Establishments | | All employees | | Production workers | | Value added by manufacture (mil. dol.) | Value of shipments (mil. dol.) | Sales | | | Paid employees[4] | Annual payroll (mil. dol.) | Operating expenses (mil. dol.) |
	Total	Percent with 20 or more employees	Number[1]	Annual payroll (mil. dol.)	Number[2]	Wages (mil. dol.)			Establishments	Total (mil. dol.)	Merchant wholesalers (mil. dol.)			
FLORIDA—Con.														
Fort Myers city	95	22.1	1 743	47.9	1 267	29.5	179.3	296.7	207	557.6	359.8	2 258	65.2	124.2
Fort Pierce city	NA	NA	NA	NA	NA	NA	NA	NA	59	260.3	122.1	899	19.1	39.0
Gainesville city	85	25.9	1 688	57.7	1 170	33.8	162.9	414.3	138	620.9	408.8	1 296	40.8	83.6
Hallandale city	55	21.8	733	18.7	557	11.3	43.8	78.3	90	121.7	115.5	524	12.1	27.6
Hialeah city	690	27.8	18 397	425.4	13 798	253.2	939.1	1 822.3	576	1 114.6	1 057.3	4 040	99.0	202.5
Hollywood city	169	24.3	3 498	92.6	2 539	52.3	461.9	769.6	361	1 191.1	674.8	2 408	80.0	166.5
Homestead city	NA	NA	NA	NA	NA	NA	NA	NA	35	D	D	(5)	D	D
Jacksonville city (remainder)	723	32.0	27 933	935.6	19 768	555.3	3 878.4	7 203.4	1 328	16 397.3	9 460.1	21 599	750.2	1 546.1
Kissimmee city	32	31.3	526	15.1	397	10.5	37.8	79.5	43	D	D	(5)	D	D
Lakeland city	81	33.3	4 007	127.5	2 843	72.1	349.5	652.3	164	2 191.2	D	2 468	65.1	133.9
Lake Worth city	46	15.2	523	10.8	379	6.8	22.3	40.3	69	D	D	(5)	D	D
Largo city	138	18.8	2 544	60.6	1 849	35.6	136.0	229.8	179	526.0	418.2	1 593	46.4	97.1
Lauderdale Lakes city	NA	NA	NA	NA	NA	NA	NA	NA	19	D	D	(6)	D	D
Lauderhill city	NA	NA	NA	NA	NA	NA	NA	NA	51	63.6	50.6	193	4.9	9.9
Margate city	NA	NA	NA	NA	NA	NA	NA	NA	97	195.8	173.6	381	10.3	24.4
Melbourne city	91	22.0	4 435	160.6	2 055	43.8	737.6	1 282.6	142	388.1	267.8	1 124	38.5	78.2
Miami city	575	15.1	7 490	188.8	5 643	122.9	546.6	1 021.7	1 810	7 178.4	6 655.3	12 885	388.8	900.0
Miami Beach city	NA	NA	NA	NA	NA	NA	NA	NA	136	255.9	222.4	470	12.5	28.1
Miramar city	36	27.8	729	25.1	472	11.9	73.4	124.9	84	712.8	529.8	1 479	57.9	119.2
North Lauderdale city	NA	NA	NA	NA	NA	NA	NA	NA	13	8.8	D	27	.6	1.4
North Miami city	63	11.1	529	10.3	415	7.2	24.3	44.6	108	183.1	158.9	574	16.2	39.2
North Miami Beach city	48	14.6	647	16.0	409	8.6	42.5	100.9	96	180.7	D	379	11.3	27.6
Oakland Park city	166	11.4	1 855	48.8	1 370	28.7	99.2	193.8	223	489.7	415.5	1 500	49.2	91.7
Ocala city	138	34.8	7 680	185.3	5 370	113.5	510.9	1 023.1	198	680.8	D	2 243	54.6	118.5
Orlando city	281	30.2	12 168	522.5	5 592	145.7	1 553.7	2 390.5	676	4 389.2	3 109.5	9 637	315.3	581.3
Ormond Beach city	47	27.7	1 039	26.4	689	15.9	56.1	100.1	58	207.6	D	622	17.9	39.7
Palm Bay city	61	29.5	8 325	358.6	2 468	72.5	544.8	1 171.6	46	117.5	113.2	264	11.0	21.8
Panama City city	63	23.8	2 255	74.8	1 668	48.1	247.8	514.8	88	246.5	D	686	18.1	38.7
Pembroke Pines city	54	11.1	632	15.7	517	8.5	54.2	80.0	135	233.3	147.1	417	13.9	29.9
Pensacola city	75	24.0	1 865	62.9	1 365	41.9	226.6	475.7	151	552.8	433.2	1 992	53.9	100.8
Pinellas Park city	190	30.5	7 653	209.6	5 154	111.1	630.2	1 136.3	115	391.7	304.0	1 234	33.0	70.4
Plantation city	53	15.1	(7)	D	D	D	D	D	229	629.3	236.2	878	35.0	69.1
Pompano Beach city	284	28.2	6 711	187.8	4 776	106.8	436.6	783.8	503	2 386.7	2 016.4	5 616	177.8	385.4
Port Orange city	NA	NA	NA	NA	NA	NA	NA	NA	38	62.0	52.2	207	5.6	10.9
Port St. Lucie city	NA	NA	NA	NA	NA	NA	NA	NA	44	32.9	28.2	153	3.8	8.7
Riviera Beach city	73	30.1	1 439	42.1	984	24.5	127.3	213.2	101	1 088.9	982.7	1 627	55.3	111.9
St. Petersburg city	203	23.6	7 389	227.1	4 091	96.6	650.4	1 237.3	293	2 221.3	1 159.6	3 147	112.5	245.6
Sanford city	61	41.0	2 270	50.2	1 732	29.5	124.8	253.6	84	249.6	D	1 046	28.1	53.3
Sarasota city	89	12.4	1 529	35.5	1 119	18.9	85.6	136.6	123	329.3	253.7	890	23.9	49.8
Sunrise city	71	16.9	2 405	50.6	1 029	26.0	104.4	201.3	246	1 728.5	676.0	2 713	123.1	233.2
Tallahassee city	102	19.6	(8)	D	D	D	D	D	204	602.2	476.0	2 181	62.6	121.0
Tamarac city	NA	NA	NA	NA	NA	NA	NA	NA	95	433.5	D	706	24.9	59.5
Tampa city	463	27.2	13 213	364.2	9 147	214.8	1 125.6	2 442.1	1 048	15 906.4	7 562.5	18 497	630.9	1 251.1
Titusville city	46	19.6	614	12.3	495	8.0	29.3	49.9	29	42.3	D	186	4.0	7.2
West Palm Beach city	154	17.5	7 014	402.8	2 457	81.5	1 886.4	2 269.2	188	1 356.4	D	1 897	68.4	256.8
GEORGIA	9 083	36.3	533 830	15 534.1	410 713	10 173.4	55 550.1	11 100.0	13 978	163 782.6	69 922.1	191 087	7 519.7	15 252.1
Albany city	76	43.4	(9)	D	D	D	D	D	171	971.2	836.7	2 151	63.8	122.7
Athens city	[10]90	[10]37.8	[10]9 388	[10]234.9	[10]7 520	[10]168.5	[10]577.4	[10]1 368.5	[10]81	D	[10]225.7	(8)	D	D
Atlanta city	499	35.7	21 497	688.7	15 058	406.4	3 093.9	5 822.0	1 164	17 285.9	6 022.8	15 406	636.9	1 287.5
Augusta city	[11]132	[11]45.5	(12)	D	D	D	D	D	[11]245	[11]756.9	[11]649.2	[11]2 262	[11]168.8	[11]136.6
Columbus city (remainder)	[13]158	[13]47.5	(12)	D	D	D	D	D	[13]208	[13]1 316.5	D	[13]2 884	[13]91.3	[13]211.3
East Point city	41	34.1	1 199	40.6	925	26.9	122.7	286.7	39	396.0	D	673	17.0	48.9
La Grange city	70	65.7	8 540	257.6	6 597	160.3	651.2	1 634.0	42	189.3	176.7	397	12.9	29.7
Macon city	154	34.4	10 650	419.5	8 038	295.6	3 709.1	5 388.6	210	984.0	723.7	2 776	81.8	156.3
Marietta city	158	26.6	4 886	169.1	3 440	92.7	462.4	924.1	342	2 719.7	1 479.6	4 471	190.6	365.2
Rome city	88	45.5	5 342	154.1	4 301	102.1	425.5	1 070.6	76	309.9	D	795	25.5	49.2
Roswell city	58	8.6	759	24.7	550	16.6	85.6	164.3	309	6 033.5	1 415.4	2 912	151.9	320.5
Savannah city	131	19.8	4 579	139.3	2 993	73.7	450.5	1 279.7	220	1 487.2	1 009.9	2 737	90.9	170.5
Smyrna city	50	18.0	1 032	36.6	728	20.3	75.9	136.8	117	3 411.0	D	1 906	82.4	146.4
Valdosta city	70	44.3	4 816	118.9	3 699	77.3	366.1	1 272.4	109	408.0	D	1 027	27.5	54.0
Warner Robins city	34	14.7	(14)	D	D	D	D	D	31	184.1	D	310	10.5	18.4

[1] Average number of production workers plus the number of other (nonproduction) employees for the pay period including March 12.   [2] Average number of production workers for the pay periods including the 12th of March, May, August, and November.   [3] Includes only establishments with payroll.   [4] For pay period including March 12.   [5] 250 to 499 employees.   [6] 20 to 99 employees.   [7] 2,500 to 4,999 employees.   [8] 1,000 to 2,499 employees.   [9] 5,000 to 9,999 employees.   [10] Data are for consolidated city of Athens-Clarke County; Athens city (1990 land area - 16.6 square miles; 1990 population - 45,734) merged with Clarke County effective January 14, 1991.   [11] 10,000 to 24,999 employees.   [12] Data are for Augusta-Richmond County (balance), GA; Augusta city (1990 land area - 19.7 square miles; 1990 population - 44,639) merged with Richmond County effective January 1, 1996.   [13] Data are for consolidated city of Columbus; data for Columbus city (remainder) not available.   [14] 500 to 999 employees.

Sources: Manufacturing—U.S. Census Bureau, 1997 Economic Census – Manufacturing, generated by Statistical Compendia Branch, using American Factfinder at <http://www.census.gov/>, (June 2000) [related Internet site <http://www.census.gov/epcd/www/97EC31.HTM>].   Wholesale Trade—U.S. Census Bureau, 1997 Economic Census, individual state .pdf files from <http://www.census.gov/epcd/www/97EC42.HTM> (accessed June 2000) and ECON97 Report Series CD-ROM, CD-EC97-1, Disc 1E, issued February 2001.

Table C–5. Cities — **Manufacturing and Wholesale Trade**–Con.

[Includes states and 1,070 incorporated places of 25,000 or more population as of April 1, 1990 in all states except Hawaii which has no incorporated places recognized by the Census Bureau. For Hawaii, 8 census designated places (CDPs) of 25,000 or more population as of April 1, 1990 are included. Also included are the 5 boroughs of New York city. For more information on these areas, see appendix B. Geographic Information]

City	Manufacturing (NAICS 31-33), 1997								Wholesale trade[3] (NAICS 42), 1997					
	Establishments		All employees		Production workers					Sales				
	Total	Percent with 20 or more employees	Number[1]	Annual payroll (mil. dol.)	Number[2]	Wages (mil. dol.)	Value added by manufacture (mil. dol.)	Value of shipments (mil. dol.)	Establishments	Total (mil. dol.)	Merchant wholesalers (mil. dol.)	Paid employees[4]	Annual payroll (mil. dol.)	Operating expenses (mil. dol.)
HAWAII	921	17.3	15 109	405.0	9 899	231.6	1 262.4	3 192.5	1 872	7 147.5	5 088.7	18 532	576.0	1 213.5
Hilo CDP	58	13.8	716	17.5	431	8.6	34.5	80.2	87	314.2	240.1	811	22.0	49.4
Honolulu CDP	491	18.3	7 639	187.7	4 898	105.9	446.9	904.9	1 114	4 537.5	2 987.4	11 332	354.2	749.6
Kailua CDP	NA	NA	NA	NA	NA	NA	NA	NA	26	58.4	27.8	81	3.9	7.2
Kaneohe CDP	NA	NA	NA	NA	NA	NA	NA	NA	22	23.1	13.3	84	1.9	4.1
Mililani Town CDP	NA	NA	NA	NA	NA	NA	NA	NA	14	37.5	D	115	6.3	10.6
Pearl City CDP	NA	NA	NA	NA	NA	NA	NA	NA	37	176.1	D	517	14.8	30.6
Waimalu CDP	NA	NA	NA	NA	NA	NA	NA	NA	18	10.0	D	86	1.5	3.0
Waipahu CDP	NA	NA	NA	NA	NA	NA	NA	NA	60	364.7	356.4	1 246	41.3	81.7
IDAHO	1 647	25.4	66 184	2 099.8	50 362	1 277.2	6 393.1	16 952.9	1 980	10 127.8	6 081.3	22 828	628.0	1 303.0
Boise City city	210	26.2	16 823	753.4	10 931	348.7	1 990.8	5 780.6	367	4 637.4	1 430.4	5 235	200.1	390.5
Idaho Falls city	79	22.8	2 107	44.9	1 581	29.6	110.6	217.8	125	572.0	487.7	1 529	38.9	75.7
Lewiston city	44	15.9	(5)	D	D	D	D	D	55	183.1	D	557	14.7	28.4
Nampa city	71	36.6	5 798	179.9	4 515	117.9	936.8	3 008.7	70	377.1	332.3	890	23.8	56.1
Pocatello city	52	32.7	2 315	70.4	1 717	27.9	208.1	385.7	89	270.6	244.2	883	24.2	47.5
Twin Falls city	64	26.6	2 400	51.8	1 989	35.9	177.3	512.1	109	330.7	267.4	1 190	26.9	62.4
ILLINOIS	17 953	36.6	887 350	31 837.9	629 423	18 713.8	95 287.3	300.0	21 951	275 968.4	142 923.4	325 752	13 324.5	27 788.0
Addison village	388	39.7	10 598	346.9	7 638	200.4	820.7	1 461.1	257	2 649.9	1 330.5	4 566	182.1	337.3
Alton city	31	29.0	1 716	66.1	1 340	48.8	76.6	358.4	27	79.2	D	327	11.6	20.3
Arlington Heights village	120	30.8	10 976	645.6	5 238	256.6	902.9	3 052.9	326	4 427.1	1 148.7	3 664	192.3	372.2
Aurora city	148	45.3	8 759	387.4	5 784	213.8	1 415.1	2 743.1	140	5 262.0	D	2 212	93.8	242.8
Belleville city	60	25.0	2 239	65.7	1 626	34.6	159.0	307.7	42	D	D	(6)	D	D
Berwyn city	22	18.2	585	23.6	333	11.0	47.1	79.5	29	98.1	D	141	4.7	9.1
Bloomington city	59	37.3	(7)	D	D	D	D	D	109	566.6	298.4	1 137	50.5	95.9
Bolingbrook village	21	38.1	2 453	153.8	845	34.8	530.1	807.9	54	1 102.0	D	1 076	34.9	80.9
Buffalo Grove village	54	38.9	3 889	138.3	2 710	76.7	337.9	652.1	190	2 784.6	2 068.9	2 251	111.8	228.3
Burbank city	NA	NA	NA	NA	NA	NA	NA	NA	9	7.2	7.2	61	1.2	3.0
Calumet City city	19	42.1	757	23.4	481	13.8	78.0	155.3	20	D	D	375	D	D
Carbondale city	NA	NA	NA	NA	NA	NA	NA	NA	19	42.6	29.4	173	4.7	9.1
Carol Stream village	91	53.8	5 123	190.8	3 534	103.7	503.5	973.3	103	4 950.8	3 456.3	3 552	157.4	292.6
Champaign city	67	31.3	2 846	74.8	2 081	47.6	219.2	393.2	76	689.0	D	1 414	38.3	68.9
Chicago city	3 195	35.2	130 372	4 178.4	95 706	2 572.1	13 497.8	26 745.9	3 312	31 971.1	19 255.2	50 029	1 970.1	4 053.7
Chicago Heights city	71	43.7	4 061	149.0	3 003	97.4	419.3	982.5	51	371.9	290.5	890	25.6	49.7
Cicero town	123	49.6	5 613	190.7	4 219	120.6	499.9	973.2	45	403.7	D	669	29.5	59.5
Danville city	60	48.3	4 864	160.5	3 819	115.8	507.5	1 363.4	60	1 004.0	955.8	1 802	55.1	100.6
Decatur city	98	38.8	(8)	D	D	D	271.3	535.3	129	3 119.0	2 988.3	1 609	50.6	102.4
De Kalb city	47	44.7	2 648	71.2	1 790	40.7	271.3	535.3	20	D	D	(9)	D	D
Des Plaines city	164	47.6	12 021	411.0	8 025	221.6	989.0	1 849.6	224	4 724.2	1 812.4	5 611	258.4	475.2
Downers Grove village	104	32.7	5 174	203.0	3 330	107.6	426.8	692.7	171	3 195.4	999.1	3 009	143.0	264.0
East St. Louis city	22	22.7	564	20.9	413	15.6	63.8	134.9	23	D	D	(6)	D	D
Elgin city	175	52.6	9 955	345.8	7 337	215.9	909.0	1 779.0	169	2 158.1	1 671.9	2 985	129.4	253.0
Elk Grove Village village	550	45.6	23 239	864.4	16 670	508.8	2 109.3	3 916.5	621	8 110.0	4 185.3	10 899	479.7	965.6
Elmhurst city	85	42.4	2 882	103.1	1 927	56.3	226.6	421.0	197	2 264.9	1 142.0	6 605	341.4	667.0
Evanston city	67	35.8	2 310	74.4	1 233	31.0	167.5	321.7	95	403.3	295.7	992	30.0	53.6
Freeport city	40	40.0	7 645	280.7	5 377	180.5	595.6	1 058.2	25	80.1	80.1	230	5.6	12.4
Galesburg city	48	45.8	(10)	D	D	D	D	D	42	210.5	196.3	527	14.5	29.4
Glendale Heights village	48	64.6	2 304	87.7	1 514	42.0	190.1	327.2	79	1 337.5	948.9	2 417	96.7	194.0
Glenview village	68	22.1	1 481	54.2	964	31.9	102.2	222.9	146	866.8	654.2	1 753	77.3	142.5
Granite City city	28	57.1	5 632	234.5	4 714	184.8	813.9	1 857.1	36	859.5	382.3	578	19.2	42.9
Hanover Park village	NA	NA	NA	NA	NA	NA	NA	NA	26	333.7	D	558	26.0	53.5
Harvey city	48	41.7	2 361	110.4	1 452	49.9	315.5	699.2	30	277.7	D	659	26.5	46.8
Highland Park city	44	13.6	(5)	D	D	D	D	D	106	1 106.1	496.1	410	22.0	66.4
Hoffman Estates village	23	26.1	971	45.6	500	17.5	104.6	191.2	107	1 790.1	713.5	1 094	67.9	130.2
Joliet city	104	38.5	7 268	323.6	5 562	215.2	1 304.4	3 814.8	89	214.2	201.7	935	28.7	53.1
Kankakee city	32	62.5	2 502	96.0	1 893	69.5	288.2	673.5	40	205.9	D	403	13.6	32.5
Lansing village	34	23.5	870	29.7	568	13.3	93.3	171.4	42	307.9	288.5	575	22.9	64.2
Lombard village	102	18.6	1 718	62.2	1 333	40.9	146.4	246.3	180	3 228.9	1 329.5	3 003	137.2	252.0
Maywood village	28	32.1	603	19.1	452	12.1	41.9	74.0	10	21.3	21.3	68	1.7	3.4
Moline city	61	26.2	2 150	89.7	1 463	56.8	237.8	500.4	73	766.8	D	1 072	43.6	79.0
Mount Prospect village	46	37.0	3 457	134.8	1 200	37.0	270.7	553.4	136	3 162.7	1 189.5	2 164	109.9	274.8
Naperville city	84	31.0	2 334	80.4	1 658	47.1	193.3	348.9	310	12 942.4	1 619.3	3 398	192.8	374.2
Niles village	102	52.9	6 376	242.4	3 939	128.1	588.4	1 023.3	95	661.9	D	2 178	72.5	152.5
Normal town	19	31.6	(5)	D	D	D	D	D	35	D	D	(5)	D	D
Northbrook village	123	35.0	4 672	161.1	3 262	91.4	474.9	840.3	375	3 172.5	1 917.1	4 107	190.8	391.1
North Chicago city	28	42.9	1 606	51.7	1 202	31.5	130.0	356.6	22	269.7	D	777	37.9	58.0
Oak Forest city	22	22.7	519	16.1	397	9.4	46.9	85.7	31	173.7	D	323	12.4	20.9

[1] Average number of production workers plus the number of other (nonproduction) employees for the pay period including March 12. [2] Average number of production workers for the pay periods including the 12th of March, May, August, and November. [3] Includes only establishments with payroll. [4] For pay period including March 12. [5] 500 to 999 employees. [6] 250 to 499 employees. [7] 2,500 to 4,999 employees. [8] 10,000 to 24,999 employees. [9] 100 to 249 employees. [10] 5,000 to 9,999 employees.

Sources: Manufacturing—U.S. Census Bureau, 1997 Economic Census – Manufacturing, generated by Statistical Compendia Branch, using American Factfinder at <http://www.census.gov/>, (June 2000) [related Internet site <http://www.census.gov/epcd/www/97EC31.HTM>]. Wholesale Trade—U.S. Census Bureau, 1997 Economic Census, individual state .pdf files from <http://www.census.gov/epcd/www/97EC42.HTM> (accessed June 2000) and ECON97 Report Series CD-ROM, CD-EC97-1, Disc 1E, issued February 2001.

Table C–5. Cities — **Manufacturing and Wholesale Trade**–Con.

[Includes states and 1,070 incorporated places of 25,000 or more population as of April 1, 1990 in all states except Hawaii which has no incorporated places recognized by the Census Bureau. For Hawaii, 8 census designated places (CDPs) of 25,000 or more population as of April 1, 1990 are included. Also included are the 5 boroughs of New York city. For more information on these areas, see appendix B. Geographic Information]

City	Manufacturing (NAICS 31-33), 1997								Wholesale trade[3] (NAICS 42), 1997					
	Establishments		All employees		Production workers		Value added by manufacture (mil. dol.)	Value of shipments (mil. dol.)	Establishments	Sales		Paid employees[4]	Annual payroll (mil. dol.)	Operating expenses (mil. dol.)
	Total	Percent with 20 or more employees	Number[1]	Annual payroll (mil. dol.)	Number[2]	Wages (mil. dol.)				Total (mil. dol.)	Merchant wholesalers (mil. dol.)			
ILLINOIS—Con.														
Oak Lawn village	31	25.8	527	17.5	349	9.1	30.7	57.1	39	71.2	D	139	3.9	7.6
Oak Park village	43	14.0	679	22.3	512	14.4	49.0	82.8	57	146.1	110.2	242	9.4	15.9
Orland Park village	55	12.7	2 195	92.4	1 082	36.3	360.0	477.7	72	148.3	120.8	459	16.2	30.4
Palatine village	76	27.6	2 830	91.9	2 136	54.9	258.0	453.6	167	689.3	235.7	799	36.4	67.5
Park Ridge city	NA	NA	NA	NA	NA	NA	NA	NA	108	605.4	150.1	457	18.1	32.2
Pekin city	28	35.7	–	D	D	D	D	D	28	D	D	375	D	D
Peoria city	113	43.4	5 666	197.3	3 473	108.0	541.5	1 381.6	231	5 321.3	D	3 831	138.6	277.9
Quincy city	57	29.8	2 995	96.6	2 092	48.9	405.8	774.0	82	403.4	D	1 175	34.0	66.3
Rockford city	477	41.5	26 100	998.8	17 445	555.4	2 524.9	4 467.4	320	1 812.5	1 286.7	4 838	167.6	341.2
Rock Island city	58	34.5	1 927	47.7	1 567	33.7	137.4	238.5	80	543.6	527.0	1 728	53.9	97.8
Schaumburg village	190	27.4	8 709	404.8	3 760	117.7	920.4	1 448.1	431	12 007.5	D	9 640	536.1	1 059.7
Skokie village	212	33.0	9 083	310.1	6 352	165.6	1 176.8	1 815.5	234	6 222.6	3 791.8	3 921	230.0	524.3
Springfield city	84	34.5	2 850	82.2	1 989	47.1	211.9	462.9	162	963.3	819.9	2 370	80.0	149.5
Streamwood village	45	15.6	918	36.8	625	19.1	84.2	148.4	32	93.9	41.0	184	7.3	13.7
Tinley Park village	33	33.3	1 140	40.2	820	26.7	104.7	197.1	41	172.7	114.7	350	12.9	30.5
Urbana city	33	36.4	(5)	D	D	D	D	D	32	D	D	(5)	D	D
Waukegan city	95	33.7	6 037	213.6	4 193	119.8	453.5	986.8	73	1 016.1	292.1	2 423	94.6	316.7
Wheaton city	34	11.8	508	19.0	381	10.5	37.7	63.1	115	408.2	106.2	369	15.1	29.9
Wheeling village	NA	NA	NA	NA	NA	NA	NA	NA	203	1 473.3	1 030.4	3 111	134.3	265.9
Wilmette village	NA	NA	NA	NA	NA	NA	NA	NA	47	214.6	92.3	134	6.8	12.1
Woodridge village	16	37.5	741	30.5	465	16.7	92.3	192.6	33	536.7	483.7	1 109	41.0	113.2
INDIANA	9 303	42.4	625 692	22 121.4	478 248	14 956.5	67 210.9	11 300.0	8 896	66 350.1	38 354.0	112 705	3 737.8	7 412.2
Anderson city	59	33.9	8 999	456.0	7 458	370.7	717.7	1 769.1	60	247.7	176.8	885	23.1	43.1
Bloomington city	61	27.9	5 013	159.4	4 577	136.7	641.8	1 751.3	72	284.5	D	868	26.7	55.6
Carmel city	53	28.3	1 304	44.2	845	22.3	77.7	177.8	175	2 788.6	494.5	1 670	90.4	156.0
Columbus city	96	52.1	11 647	366.2	8 854	252.2	1 055.1	2 273.1	81	588.1	516.9	698	22.4	45.9
East Chicago city	51	62.7	16 068	812.4	11 666	559.4	2 405.1	4 894.2	60	953.8	D	1 115	39.0	82.6
Elkhart city	349	50.7	17 947	554.5	13 772	349.8	1 481.1	3 023.5	168	1 147.6	976.4	2 457	80.3	151.5
Evansville city	213	39.4	15 029	528.1	9 543	280.8	2 148.0	3 446.0	296	1 480.3	D	4 051	123.3	236.9
Fort Wayne city	390	39.7	22 830	846.3	15 779	498.4	2 043.4	4 258.9	531	4 041.7	2 657.6	8 532	281.3	535.9
Gary city	62	46.8	10 066	511.3	8 125	418.4	1 802.5	3 377.4	65	534.5	D	1 480	52.1	99.0
Greenwood city	45	22.2	1 013	36.1	605	17.2	78.8	289.6	61	552.5	D	501	19.7	37.9
Hammond city	76	52.6	4 195	171.4	3 241	110.6	556.3	1 468.0	95	961.1	D	1 366	44.5	86.6
Indianapolis city (remainder)	1 093	36.3	59 135	2 525.5	41 838	1 565.4	11 048.2	17 918.8	1 860	D	D	(6)	D	D
Kokomo city	NA	NA	NA	NA	NA	NA	NA	NA	73	553.3	D	601	22.3	44.4
Lafayette city	71	50.7	(7)	D	D	D	D	D	83	218.2	185.1	1 027	26.3	52.8
Lawrence city	30	26.7	626	19.6	502	12.1	30.3	61.9	34	110.7	D	346	11.0	22.7
Marion city	56	51.8	8 037	356.6	6 841	288.3	642.3	1 537.0	43	118.8	D	431	13.4	31.9
Merrillville town	35	37.1	641	17.7	447	10.2	44.8	82.1	63	284.0	187.9	681	24.3	38.8
Michigan City city	69	58.0	4 621	153.3	3 055	85.9	516.9	946.9	55	248.0	173.9	726	22.7	46.8
Mishawaka city	128	37.5	5 253	162.9	3 846	100.0	360.3	636.5	87	667.0	580.1	1 278	41.4	71.1
Muncie city	109	49.5	7 185	302.4	5 283	191.8	614.3	1 305.6	80	444.0	D	1 151	37.6	74.9
New Albany city	100	54.0	6 779	188.2	5 440	130.8	634.3	1 168.7	69	D	209.5	(8)	D	D
Portage city	22	40.9	2 172	112.6	1 623	85.0	359.4	1 124.5	27	364.5	D	612	18.3	44.0
Richmond city	95	64.2	8 093	250.1	6 519	174.5	660.7	1 500.2	68	1 148.3	D	1 362	45.7	89.6
South Bend city	200	42.0	10 066	361.8	6 627	190.8	956.5	1 850.1	250	2 191.4	1 741.4	4 759	155.5	309.3
Terre Haute city	92	45.7	5 998	200.3	4 552	137.6	788.4	1 398.4	114	592.3	D	1 390	36.6	81.6
West Lafayette city	20	25.0	(5)	D	D	D	D	D	9	D	D	(9)	D	D
IOWA	3 749	37.7	235 880	7 573.3	175 933	4 936.1	28 673.3	62 413.7	5 399	35 453.7	25 728.6	63 596	1 820.1	3 746.2
Ames city	44	36.4	2 344	75.3	1 563	39.6	568.1	824.1	50	129.6	78.0	380	10.8	20.8
Bettendorf city	28	46.4	1 127	34.3	845	23.0	72.8	130.9	78	516.4	293.9	665	26.3	46.0
Burlington city	37	56.8	4 089	142.0	3 109	101.9	295.0	891.2	33	152.2	134.6	330	7.9	17.1
Cedar Falls city	50	44.0	1 911	61.5	1 398	39.0	162.4	261.7	38	420.6	D	723	22.3	43.2
Cedar Rapids city	164	44.5	21 491	890.3	10 796	363.8	3 517.3	6 194.2	285	1 986.5	1 552.2	4 914	139.7	254.7
Clinton city	28	50.0	3 649	126.9	2 886	89.8	909.7	1 780.1	36	77.4	D	277	6.0	12.8
Council Bluffs city	41	53.7	(10)	D	D	D	D	D	68	836.3	D	1 155	36.0	78.0
Davenport city	121	37.2	6 380	248.0	4 460	156.1	1 363.2	2 984.9	252	2 372.4	868.6	3 458	111.8	263.7
Des Moines city	234	31.2	11 168	375.8	8 073	235.9	1 027.8	2 841.7	408	2 459.9	1 709.6	6 500	221.1	394.0
Dubuque city	86	52.3	(11)	D	D	D	D	D	97	656.2	606.0	1 164	32.3	64.6
Fort Dodge city	44	34.1	1 976	61.3	1 194	34.0	634.1	911.3	53	D	D	(8)	D	D
Iowa City city	48	20.8	2 945	102.7	2 341	76.2	1 769.5	2 339.2	38	D	D	(12)	D	D
Marshalltown city	38	39.5	(11)	D	D	D	D	D	39	D	D	(12)	D	D
Mason City city	37	54.1	3 308	88.8	2 475	60.2	252.2	677.9	55	344.1	299.0	657	19.1	35.7
Sioux City city	94	55.3	6 018	160.2	4 290	96.8	477.0	1 853.7	188	D	868.0	(5)	D	D
Waterloo city	93	48.4	11 413	487.4	8 402	338.5	2 082.7	4 848.1	102	389.1	355.0	1 750	49.3	92.1
West Des Moines city	43	37.2	1 390	43.6	991	24.5	114.0	194.6	118	3 625.2	D	1 665	68.3	132.4

[1] Average number of production workers plus the number of other (nonproduction) employees for the pay period including March 12.   [2] Average number of production workers for the pay periods including the 12th of March, May, August, and November.   [3] Includes only establishments with payroll.   [4] For pay period including March 12.   [5] 1,000 to 2,499 employees.   [6] 25,000 to 49,999 employees.   [7] 10,000 to 24,999 employees.   [8] 500 to 999 employees.   [9] 20 to 99 employees.   [10] 2,500 to 4,999 employees.   [11] 5,000 to 9,999 employees.   [12] 250 to 499 employees.

Sources: Manufacturing—U.S. Census Bureau, 1997 Economic Census – Manufacturing, generated by Statistical Compendia Branch, using American Factfinder at <http://www.census.gov/>, (June 2000) [related Internet site <http://www.census.gov/epcd/www/97EC31.HTM>].   Wholesale Trade—U.S. Census Bureau, 1997 Economic Census, individual state .pdf files from <http://www.census.gov/epcd/www/97EC42.HTM> (accessed June 2000) and ECON97 Report Series CD-ROM, CD-EC97-1, Disc 1E, issued February 2001.

Table C–5. Cities — Manufacturing and Wholesale Trade—Con.

[Includes states and 1,070 incorporated places of 25,000 or more population as of April 1, 1990 in all states except Hawaii which has no incorporated places recognized by the Census Bureau. For Hawaii, 8 census designated places (CDPs) of 25,000 or more population as of April 1, 1990 are included. Also included are the 5 boroughs of New York city. For more information on these areas, see appendix B. Geographic Information]

City	Manufacturing (NAICS 31-33), 1997								Wholesale trade[3] (NAICS 42), 1997					
	Establishments		All employees		Production workers		Value added by manufacture (mil. dol.)	Value of shipments (mil. dol.)	Establishments	Sales		Paid employees[4]	Annual payroll (mil. dol.)	Operating expenses (mil. dol.)
	Total	Percent with 20 or more employees	Number[1]	Annual payroll (mil. dol.)	Number[2]	Wages (mil. dol.)				Total (mil. dol.)	Merchant wholesalers (mil. dol.)			
KANSAS	3 309	34.8	193 742	6 532.5	141 169	4 052.5	17 650.6	46 296.4	5 085	42 209.9	23 579.8	59 954	1 946.8	3 921.6
Emporia city	30	53.3	(5)	D	D	D	D	D	35	182.9	D	535	13.3	25.0
Hutchinson city	47	40.4	2 365	71.2	1 707	46.5	232.0	364.0	60	345.4	D	955	28.8	56.2
Kansas City city	249	43.8	14 624	623.8	11 438	456.7	2 826.7	7 562.1	293	3 864.7	3 425.2	6 566	216.5	462.3
Lawrence city	56	35.7	3 439	86.2	2 691	57.0	325.2	541.6	77	207.0	D	644	18.7	33.6
Leavenworth city	NA	NA	NA	NA	NA	NA	NA	NA	13	D	D	(6)	D	D
Lenexa city	NA	NA	NA	NA	NA	NA	NA	NA	383	3 410.9	1 624.5	6 605	248.5	476.7
Manhattan city	NA	NA	NA	NA	NA	NA	NA	NA	41	141.7	127.1	517	12.7	23.4
Olathe city	117	32.5	4 902	181.4	2 877	82.5	523.7	842.3	181	1 536.1	938.2	3 333	130.5	239.5
Overland Park city	106	19.8	1 632	50.7	1 132	27.8	115.6	226.4	513	12 533.4	3 647.7	5 130	244.3	453.5
Salina city	68	36.8	5 496	160.7	4 545	120.1	329.7	985.3	81	421.4	D	989	28.4	54.6
Shawnee city	42	28.6	(7)	D	D	D	D	D	75	376.5	188.2	593	18.7	37.0
Topeka city	124	33.9	(5)	D	D	D	D	D	177	706.5	D	1 900	56.7	107.2
Wichita city	496	38.9	52 170	2 158.6	34 386	1 183.1	4 011.1	8 579.6	682	4 005.0	D	8 221	274.3	538.6
KENTUCKY	4 218	40.6	288 405	9 198.1	223 868	6 251.6	38 337.6	86 636.1	5 051	37 242.9	23 683.8	69 309	2 071.2	4 190.9
Bowling Green city	88	46.6	(5)	D	D	D	148.3	321.1	128	1 276.6	D	1 795	50.3	120.5
Covington city	45	35.6	1 491	40.7	1 262	29.0	266.1	504.5	35	159.3	D	312	11.2	20.4
Frankfort city	28	42.9	2 760	79.1	2 256	58.0	557.8	504.5	26	D	D	(8)	D	D
Henderson city	62	58.1	6 189	193.0	4 991	138.8	784.6	1 557.8	59	D	474.0	(7)	D	D
Hopkinsville city	48	47.9	4 406	114.5	3 579	79.1	329.4	775.0	66	4 181.5	2 659.7	6 529	203.8	390.1
Lexington-Fayette	283	32.5	17 403	654.0	10 380	275.0	2 147.7	4 313.9	492	4 181.5	2 659.7	6 529	203.8	390.1
Louisville city	456	44.3	29 078	1 076.2	21 525	718.7	9 820.0	17 225.4	677	8 597.4	3 766.9	14 614	488.2	870.2
Owensboro city	86	45.3	(5)	D	D	D	D	D	105	564.7	D	1 272	33.6	95.1
Paducah city	40	55.0	1 634	51.9	1 228	33.3	152.6	300.9	112	D	D	(7)	D	D
LOUISIANA	3 545	33.0	165 777	6 054.5	123 566	3 967.7	29 066.9	80 424.0	6 390	46 972.3	34 931.9	76 350	2 375.2	4 827.7
Alexandria city	32	31.3	(7)	D	D	D	D	D	101	427.5	342.0	1 255	32.5	65.9
Baton Rouge city	265	26.4	5 598	201.2	3 751	104.7	547.4	1 444.6	594	2 925.2	1 810.1	7 871	283.0	563.8
Bossier City city	57	38.6	1 915	45.4	1 545	31.2	87.1	211.4	77	1 111.3	D	1 023	28.2	65.2
Houma city	57	28.1	2 086	74.5	1 673	52.7	157.9	269.5	102	429.7	393.7	1 276	38.6	73.5
Kenner city	68	16.2	1 693	45.6	1 264	29.6	88.9	161.2	170	D	D	(7)	D	D
Lafayette city	125	22.4	3 434	89.1	2 250	47.3	258.7	538.4	321	1 864.0	1 638.1	4 159	137.4	253.1
Lake Charles city	66	28.8	(10)	D	D	D	D	D	141	533.0	D	2 039	56.0	101.9
Monroe city	58	48.3	3 061	76.1	2 079	41.8	182.4	408.0	139	680.8	573.2	1 867	56.9	116.5
New Iberia city	51	31.4	1 427	46.8	1 098	32.8	100.5	209.0	82	279.8	232.8	1 139	36.2	64.8
New Orleans city	261	29.5	10 453	362.2	7 022	226.5	1 064.6	2 305.0	484	2 450.5	1 718.5	6 086	210.2	405.8
Shreveport city	177	32.2	(5)	D	D	D	D	D	422	1 723.0	1 083.4	5 186	154.9	292.6
MAINE	1 812	28.3	82 288	2 591.1	62 647	1 746.0	6 530.6	14 097.6	1 726	7 305.6	6 051.1	19 932	616.2	1 231.5
Bangor city	46	26.1	(7)	D	D	D	D	D	92	620.5	D	1 600	49.2	102.3
Lewiston city	79	35.4	(10)	D	D	D	D	D	60	D	D	(9)	D	D
Portland city	119	23.5	3 905	107.0	2 729	69.5	319.2	624.9	233	1 477.5	1 239.3	3 538	113.0	218.8
MARYLAND	3 996	30.4	163 992	5 840.5	109 564	3 249.2	18 721.6	36 505.9	6 283	54 906.7	31 714.9	92 458	3 656.3	7 019.8
Annapolis city	NA	NA	NA	NA	NA	NA	NA	NA	89	419.0	212.9	646	28.6	57.9
Baltimore city	688	39.7	30 216	1 006.2	21 898	636.2	4 452.9	9 822.2	792	6 171.2	4 215.8	14 152	499.2	957.4
Bowie city	NA	NA	NA	NA	NA	NA	NA	NA	26	D	D	(8)	D	D
Frederick city	79	41.8	3 097	100.3	2 078	50.9	221.4	505.1	123	634.0	509.7	2 088	68.4	121.4
Gaithersburg city	42	31.0	1 993	89.8	1 035	39.8	206.0	318.0	76	D	D	(7)	D	D
Hagerstown city	64	35.9	3 361	96.9	2 604	64.7	347.5	593.1	79	301.6	D	967	28.3	56.3
Rockville city	68	19.1	1 438	52.9	932	27.0	102.6	166.2	131	2 937.3	D	2 656	150.0	268.9
MASSACHUSETTS	9 554	34.7	417 135	16 379.0	257 050	7 734.8	44 337.8	77 876.6	9 993	112 792.4	61 530.3	146 827	6 484.8	12 686.7
Attleboro city	143	37.8	9 714	333.5	6 375	147.9	704.8	1 412.0	40	172.1	D	394	16.7	33.5
Beverly city	83	31.3	3 861	168.1	1 862	58.3	469.1	726.1	46	210.8	109.1	331	18.0	41.4
Boston city	536	29.7	18 944	671.5	12 521	353.1	2 424.5	3 941.5	770	7 574.9	4 633.8	9 857	437.2	822.9
Brockton city	121	31.4	3 009	92.0	2 260	55.2	217.6	378.0	84	604.2	562.9	1 666	58.1	121.2
Cambridge city	106	39.6	3 050	98.1	1 707	45.6	357.0	585.2	145	1 457.9	984.7	3 696	183.4	360.9
Chelsea city	62	45.2	2 084	66.0	1 352	33.7	163.1	341.4	116	D	D	(7)	D	D
Chicopee city	109	42.2	4 974	184.6	3 427	95.8	560.8	990.0	57	D	D	(7)	D	D
Everett city	77	35.1	2 216	82.1	1 574	43.7	172.0	297.0	75	925.6	D	1 269	59.8	111.8
Fall River city	199	44.7	12 366	337.3	9 909	223.1	720.2	1 364.5	87	419.0	D	1 079	27.4	51.9
Fitchburg city	89	36.0	3 896	145.3	2 626	78.1	349.7	653.6	45	D	D	(9)	D	D
Gloucester city	64	37.5	3 948	137.2	2 689	84.1	419.1	846.8	66	227.8	202.6	318	11.0	22.7
Haverhill city	119	41.2	3 885	130.8	2 793	73.1	260.2	545.9	71	157.7	D	703	19.4	36.9

[1] Average number of production workers plus the number of other (nonproduction) employees for the pay period including March 12. [2] Average number of production workers for the pay periods including the 12th of March, May, August, and November. [3] Includes only establishments with payroll. [4] For pay period including March 12. [5] 5,000 to 9,999 employees. [6] 20 to 99 employees. [7] 1,000 to 2,499 employees. [8] 100 to 249 employees. [9] 500 to 999 employees. [10] 2,500 to 4,999 employees.

Sources: Manufacturing—U.S. Census Bureau, 1997 Economic Census – Manufacturing, generated by Statistical Compendia Branch, using American Factfinder at <http://www.census.gov/>, (June 2000) [related Internet site <http://www.census.gov/epcd/www/97EC31.HTM>]. Wholesale Trade—U.S. Census Bureau, 1997 Economic Census, individual state .pdf files from <http://www.census.gov/epcd/www/97EC42.HTM> (accessed June 2000) and ECON97 Report Series CD-ROM, CD-EC97-1, Disc 1E, issued February 2001.

Table C–5. Cities — **Manufacturing and Wholesale Trade**–Con.

[Includes states and 1,070 incorporated places of 25,000 or more population as of April 1, 1990 in all states except Hawaii which has no incorporated places recognized by the Census Bureau. For Hawaii, 8 census designated places (CDPs) of 25,000 or more population as of April 1, 1990 are included. Also included are the 5 boroughs of New York city. For more information on these areas, see appendix B. Geographic Information]

| City | Manufacturing (NAICS 31-33), 1997 | | | | | | | | Wholesale trade[3] (NAICS 42), 1997 | | | | | |
| | Establishments | | All employees | | Production workers | | Value added by manu-facture (mil. dol.) | Value of ship-ments (mil. dol.) | Estab-lishments | Sales | | Paid em-ployees[4] | Annual payroll (mil. dol.) | Operating expenses (mil. dol.) |
	Total	Percent with 20 or more employ-ees	Number[1]	Annual payroll (mil. dol.)	Number[2]	Wages (mil. dol.)				Total (mil. dol.)	Merchant whole-salers (mil. dol.)			
MASSACHUSETTS—Con.														
Holyoke city	88	47.7	4 223	139.0	2 811	76.9	410.9	886.8	47	245.6	D	765	24.3	44.7
Lawrence city	120	39.2	6 252	207.9	4 560	119.4	608.0	1 052.4	72	344.5	D	1 119	37.1	72.8
Leominster city	135	40.7	6 003	196.3	4 698	127.8	548.0	1 256.0	56	408.7	311.3	602	22.4	50.9
Lowell city	101	49.5	5 709	193.3	3 540	95.7	454.9	888.1	88	353.9	D	1 159	41.5	72.7
Lynn city	67	38.8	6 870	325.2	4 182	166.6	788.1	2 101.8	61	419.5	191.7	856	31.4	62.0
Malden city	63	38.1	1 929	63.8	1 198	31.6	163.0	309.2	48	463.8	425.4	845	29.8	56.2
Marlborough city	90	41.1	4 959	258.0	2 115	69.0	1 102.6	1 592.9	104	2 244.5	1 762.7	3 725	201.3	359.5
Medford city	52	15.4	924	24.9	578	12.1	66.3	98.3	64	386.2	222.1	1 146	40.2	92.1
Melrose city	37	29.7	1 400	47.0	1 055	29.1	88.1	195.2	18	67.3	67.3	238	5.8	11.5
New Bedford city	151	42.4	9 839	273.8	7 526	172.4	650.6	1 259.9	146	782.7	D	2 111	59.4	131.3
Newton city	87	31.0	2 999	110.2	1 801	50.4	282.3	542.6	175	1 857.5	861.0	2 587	109.0	215.4
Northampton city	39	43.6	1 471	46.3	1 020	24.3	133.5	264.5	22	D	D	(5)	D	D
Peabody city	98	36.7	4 028	164.5	2 183	60.7	370.5	690.1	109	2 689.7	2 177.0	2 817	132.4	258.9
Pittsfield city	59	37.3	(6)	D	D	D	D	D	51	D	D	(7)	D	D
Quincy city	72	16.7	753	25.9	481	14.2	54.2	127.3	89	384.8	287.1	859	28.0	56.7
Revere city	NA	NA	NA	NA	NA	NA	NA	NA	30	D	D	(5)	D	D
Salem city	70	25.7	1 733	54.9	1 074	26.8	120.8	190.2	49	175.3	144.0	456	20.7	42.6
Somerville city	83	19.3	2 574	96.2	1 803	55.7	244.8	433.0	80	352.0	D	1 020	35.0	64.9
Springfield city	174	32.2	7 199	258.9	5 075	153.9	665.7	1 161.1	166	1 989.4	1 060.4	2 524	116.4	201.6
Taunton city	71	53.5	4 465	174.4	3 421	125.9	396.1	709.0	73	644.5	521.1	1 364	56.2	100.7
Waltham city	161	36.6	7 431	351.5	4 113	142.9	622.3	1 217.2	158	4 387.3	2 311.9	4 158	279.2	465.7
Westfield city	105	34.3	3 786	132.6	2 748	82.3	321.1	634.7	51	765.3	722.4	879	23.9	56.0
Woburn city	195	31.8	5 778	226.8	3 677	105.4	526.2	876.7	288	2 780.6	1 943.7	4 495	216.5	433.3
Worcester city	278	41.4	13 475	528.5	8 780	260.4	1 210.5	2 139.5	216	803.4	D	2 085	70.0	143.7
MICHIGAN	16 045	35.9	833 429	34 418.9	630 390	23 486.0	93 809.5	21 000.0	13 936	159 432.3	70 982.0	189 057	7 629.6	15 704.7
Allen Park city	20	20.0	(8)	D	D	D	D	D	30	272.4	D	399	27.0	52.3
Ann Arbor city	131	26.7	4 330	160.0	2 826	78.9	347.3	599.8	174	1 399.0	921.1	1 767	80.6	150.3
Battle Creek city	81	49.4	10 194	409.4	7 955	304.3	1 726.9	3 337.7	59	1 139.7	D	976	37.5	102.4
Bay City city	79	39.2	4 174	198.3	3 325	146.9	317.9	794.7	63	409.2	D	938	27.0	55.4
Burton city	41	36.6	(9)	D	D	D	D	D	31	136.3	D	560	17.7	27.9
Dearborn city	119	36.1	13 098	764.4	10 422	591.7	2 440.4	5 533.8	156	1 104.2	685.8	1 822	78.4	147.5
Dearborn Heights city	NA	NA	NA	NA	NA	NA	NA	NA	30	101.6	80.4	237	8.4	15.6
Detroit city	825	31.4	47 487	2 312.2	37 202	1 715.4	6 445.9	19 778.5	740	14 616.4	4 655.4	12 878	541.3	1 055.2
East Detroit city	NA	NA	NA	NA	NA	NA	NA	NA	27	D	D	(5)	D	D
East Lansing city	NA	NA	NA	NA	NA	NA	NA	NA	22	D	D	(7)	D	D
Farmington Hills city	155	40.0	5 109	225.3	2 884	92.6	476.8	993.8	416	7 318.4	2 489.6	5 457	266.7	530.0
Ferndale city	89	33.7	2 278	85.1	1 430	44.9	199.5	403.7	69	289.5	153.3	808	31.0	65.9
Flint city	94	35.1	(10)	D	D	D	D	D	139	728.3	527.1	1 970	62.0	121.5
Garden City city	NA	NA	NA	NA	NA	NA	NA	NA	18	24.1	24.1	139	4.2	8.0
Grand Rapids city	459	40.7	30 971	1 309.1	21 313	740.0	3 124.0	5 140.1	485	4 426.2	2 930.2	8 890	345.5	620.8
Holland city	117	49.6	16 130	615.7	10 931	332.0	1 757.1	3 246.8	64	549.2	470.4	1 011	35.3	76.0
Inkster city	NA	NA	NA	NA	NA	NA	NA	NA	8	27.0	D	79	3.0	5.6
Jackson city	143	36.4	4 453	149.8	3 290	93.6	425.9	826.2	100	633.6	451.6	1 311	52.1	96.2
Kalamazoo city	153	39.9	7 499	253.8	4 770	139.4	699.0	1 450.5	155	687.3	549.3	2 389	84.8	161.3
Kentwood city	99	53.5	9 998	332.1	7 346	202.7	859.8	1 550.8	121	3 354.0	2 641.4	3 845	142.9	251.9
Lansing city	131	39.7	(11)	D	D	D	D	D	190	933.4	D	3 186	103.9	192.5
Lincoln Park city	NA	NA	NA	NA	NA	NA	NA	NA	22	40.0	40.0	187	5.2	10.3
Livonia city	350	32.0	17 012	826.7	13 244	592.8	1 810.4	4 243.0	424	6 430.2	3 327.7	8 691	337.7	633.4
Madison Heights city	227	37.9	6 683	282.2	4 732	171.5	586.8	1 060.2	141	2 722.8	989.6	2 960	152.0	278.2
Midland city	49	22.4	5 289	278.9	2 923	135.7	760.5	1 671.1	54	240.4	169.1	478	19.6	42.4
Muskegon city	108	43.5	6 918	236.7	4 757	145.9	630.6	1 231.0	53	237.7	D	669	22.3	45.4
Novi city	87	34.5	2 448	104.4	1 752	68.3	204.1	378.8	163	2 851.9	1 955.9	3 940	185.1	323.1
Oak Park city	78	33.3	1 632	63.4	961	33.9	122.0	208.1	91	627.7	505.4	1 178	44.3	87.6
Pontiac city	58	34.5	8 474	378.7	7 434	314.1	1 526.6	4 570.2	76	D	266.0	(8)	D	D
Portage city	78	42.3	5 667	239.4	4 137	162.4	400.7	902.3	83	692.7	222.5	2 431	94.7	276.6
Port Huron city	74	45.9	5 789	184.8	4 193	119.1	519.1	1 355.6	30	173.1	83.5	285	11.4	26.1
Rochester Hills city	140	50.0	7 936	285.9	5 934	174.3	638.1	1 264.0	175	1 302.5	339.3	1 405	66.9	124.9
Roseville city	202	41.1	6 582	257.1	5 117	175.3	551.8	930.5	78	383.6	361.4	973	39.0	68.9
Royal Oak city	98	21.4	2 397	96.3	1 788	56.4	274.3	531.4	118	590.0	D	915	37.8	70.7
Saginaw city	78	44.9	7 667	420.8	6 118	337.1	738.3	2 289.5	76	317.9	D	1 182	39.0	70.4
St. Clair Shores city	68	17.6	2 756	76.7	1 867	49.9	158.4	335.0	86	605.4	149.1	548	23.5	39.8
Southfield city	115	28.7	4 564	211.7	3 393	124.1	326.8	748.8	440	15 374.8	3 243.7	6 838	426.0	838.2
Southgate city	NA	NA	NA	NA	NA	NA	NA	NA	17	D	39.6	(5)	D	D
Sterling Heights city	314	35.4	21 628	1 241.7	17 743	977.8	2 423.2	6 777.9	155	952.0	724.8	2 409	106.0	194.0
Taylor city	90	38.9	2 662	94.2	2 029	56.7	225.5	652.4	86	1 872.1	D	1 931	66.3	147.5
Troy city	396	36.9	11 872	470.9	7 968	251.4	898.3	1 678.0	521	11 690.9	2 336.9	7 489	384.1	734.9
Warren city	518	35.9	23 404	1 157.2	18 803	875.5	2 210.4	8 065.3	274	2 802.5	1 220.6	4 379	169.5	296.6
Westland city	79	29.1	2 533	91.5	1 842	55.9	199.4	402.6	76	280.8	208.3	738	27.9	49.4
Wyandotte city	49	36.7	2 227	96.0	1 101	32.8	175.8	511.1	31	59.5	D	286	9.4	17.3
Wyoming city	185	43.8	11 933	539.2	9 513	414.8	965.4	2 055.0	223	3 330.3	2 906.8	7 193	272.5	502.3

[1] Average number of production workers plus the number of other (nonproduction) employees for the pay period including March 12. [2] Average number of production workers for the pay periods including the 12th of March, May, August, and November. [3] Includes only establishments with payroll. [4] For pay period including March 12. [5] 100 to 249 employees. [6] 2,500 to 4,999 employees. [7] 250 to 499 employees. [8] 1,000 to 2,499 employees. [9] 500 to 999 employees. [10] 25,000 to 49,999 employees. [11] 10,000 to 24,999 employees.

Sources: Manufacturing—U.S. Census Bureau, 1997 Economic Census – Manufacturing, generated by Statistical Compendia Branch, using American Factfinder at <http://www.census.gov/>, (June 2000) [related Internet site <http://www.census.gov/epcd/www/97EC31.HTM>]. Wholesale Trade—U.S. Census Bureau, 1997 Economic Census, individual state .pdf files from <http://www.census.gov/epcd/www/97EC42.HTM> (accessed June 2000) and ECON97 Report Series CD-ROM, CD-EC97-1, Disc 1E, issued February 2001.

Table C–5. Cities — **Manufacturing and Wholesale Trade**–Con.

[Includes states and 1,070 incorporated places of 25,000 or more population as of April 1, 1990 in all states except Hawaii which has no incorporated places recognized by the Census Bureau. For Hawaii, 8 census designated places (CDPs) of 25,000 or more population as of April 1, 1990 are included. Also included are the 5 boroughs of New York city. For more information on these areas, see appendix B. Geographic Information]

| City | Manufacturing (NAICS 31-33), 1997 | | | | | | | Wholesale trade[3] (NAICS 42), 1997 | | | | | |
| | Establishments | | All employees | | Production workers | | Value added by manu-facture (mil. dol.) | Value of ship-ments (mil. dol.) | Sales | | | | | |
	Total	Percent with 20 or more employ-ees	Number[1]	Annual payroll (mil. dol.)	Number[2]	Wages (mil. dol.)			Estab-lishments	Total (mil. dol.)	Merchant whole-salers (mil. dol.)	Paid em-ployees[4]	Annual payroll (mil. dol.)	Operating expenses (mil. dol.)
MINNESOTA	8 091	33.7	382 530	13 126.1	260 158	7 250.1	36 629.9	76 244.9	9 348	99 444.5	56 577.7	131 787	5 024.0	10 030.4
Apple Valley city	NA	NA	NA	NA	NA	NA	NA	NA	49	245.7	51.0	244	12.9	26.7
Blaine city	134	20.9	3 147	106.2	2 321	71.9	240.8	368.3	59	316.5	D	964	33.0	64.5
Bloomington city	209	29.7	10 538	420.8	5 738	160.2	783.6	1 655.5	485	10 687.5	3 723.0	8 222	402.2	741.7
Brooklyn Center city	44	38.6	1 723	66.6	1 159	35.4	148.0	242.3	54	329.1	223.6	540	20.1	37.2
Brooklyn Park city	109	35.8	5 406	226.8	2 782	88.8	416.1	860.9	97	580.1	452.4	1 270	52.7	101.7
Burnsville city	113	31.9	4 055	148.1	2 170	53.2	384.6	723.6	225	1 605.0	953.9	2 563	88.5	202.4
Coon Rapids city	61	37.7	2 613	102.8	1 970	64.7	220.5	379.1	39	172.3	137.0	456	19.7	32.3
Duluth city	97	25.8	2 751	88.9	1 937	56.3	286.3	534.2	129	778.7	D	1 611	49.3	106.5
Eagan city	85	42.4	4 169	169.5	2 762	101.1	1 114.6	3 294.1	163	2 059.3	1 323.4	3 496	144.7	263.9
Eden Prairie city	146	42.5	9 873	412.6	4 982	170.2	917.4	1 528.6	319	5 447.1	3 122.5	6 208	303.0	604.5
Edina city	93	21.5	3 007	109.4	2 038	59.0	289.2	479.4	300	5 783.3	1 016.1	2 906	145.7	288.9
Fridley city	159	43.4	9 797	382.5	6 127	195.9	866.1	1 673.7	94	817.6	551.1	1 593	61.3	120.7
Mankato city	62	51.6	3 721	116.6	2 577	70.8	340.3	1 476.4	74	415.5	D	1 179	32.9	57.2
Maple Grove city	105	32.4	5 685	227.8	3 831	118.5	616.2	1 028.2	95	1 252.8	336.6	1 606	86.2	135.7
Maplewood city	32	28.1	712	21.6	453	13.4	46.2	110.2	41	126.1	107.8	421	12.1	27.6
Minneapolis city	699	34.2	25 906	951.1	17 446	512.1	2 106.6	3 953.5	841	13 527.1	7 672.0	14 152	644.3	1 197.2
Minnetonka city	118	35.6	7 462	296.9	4 046	114.1	971.6	1 457.8	288	7 374.9	2 594.8	4 016	189.6	382.2
Moorhead city	26	30.8	926	29.1	786	23.1	44.6	205.3	36	220.1	D	507	12.0	21.4
Plymouth city	207	48.8	12 651	498.1	7 163	229.5	1 138.2	2 096.5	350	6 950.7	3 973.4	11 437	412.4	751.3
Richfield city	NA	NA	NA	NA	NA	NA	NA	NA	37	110.1	45.2	322	11.6	14.7
Rochester city	64	42.2	(5)	D	D	D	D	D	88	443.4	427.8	843	28.6	50.8
Roseville city	88	47.7	5 238	196.0	2 816	81.1	248.8	604.9	151	1 227.2	654.2	2 334	89.6	154.4
St. Cloud city	75	45.3	7 189	194.0	5 689	137.5	499.3	981.7	98	985.2	D	2 835	100.4	167.6
St. Louis Park city	113	32.7	4 241	159.9	2 594	74.4	388.4	707.5	229	2 204.8	680.9	2 817	118.5	207.8
St. Paul city	375	35.7	20 215	737.5	13 968	440.5	2 873.9	5 536.6	456	4 075.5	2 616.5	7 746	323.5	827.1
Winona city	83	49.4	5 992	170.7	4 104	96.3	426.0	921.5	57	360.7	347.2	508	13.4	28.5
MISSISSIPPI	3 008	42.6	227 800	5 599.4	182 630	3 905.8	17 088.5	39 658.3	3 173	18 445.2	13 925.7	36 520	1 012.1	2 143.3
Biloxi city	36	27.8	(6)	D	D	D	D	D	44	175.3	D	551	14.0	31.0
Greenville city	49	51.0	4 313	105.3	3 684	80.6	416.8	904.0	55	333.9	321.1	610	19.9	35.5
Gulfport city	67	23.9	1 885	50.4	1 429	34.1	115.3	259.3	98	286.1	D	1 147	27.6	54.9
Hattiesburg city	62	37.1	4 625	103.4	3 406	64.5	387.5	942.4	93	1 119.3	D	1 266	28.4	70.4
Jackson city	173	37.0	9 337	236.9	7 121	158.2	828.7	1 709.3	404	2 828.5	D	6 820	218.4	408.6
Meridian city	70	44.3	(5)	D	D	D	D	D	94	942.1	786.7	1 770	48.0	94.6
Pascagoula city	39	33.3	(7)	D	D	D	D	D	30	173.1	D	271	8.6	14.7
Tupelo city	109	45.0	8 813	231.3	7 225	171.7	664.5	1 470.7	156	670.7	511.8	1 721	46.5	99.1
MISSOURI	7 497	33.3	371 448	11 647.1	270 297	7 197.3	43 186.1	93 115.5	9 522	91 411.9	47 744.0	125 929	4 639.8	9 354.1
Blue Springs city	41	19.5	978	28.2	698	15.0	74.3	127.5	61	195.0	154.1	372	12.7	27.8
Cape Girardeau city	52	34.6	3 602	111.3	2 957	84.6	721.4	1 246.9	111	539.0	501.9	1 183	31.9	63.4
Chesterfield city	42	28.6	1 489	47.8	1 092	28.4	108.1	207.7	243	3 024.1	635.4	2 023	98.0	218.1
Columbia city	62	37.1	4 277	120.7	3 456	83.5	739.5	1 376.1	106	596.4	350.9	1 466	44.5	95.3
Florissant city	NA	NA	NA	NA	NA	NA	NA	NA	48	95.1	55.2	415	11.7	26.3
Gladstone city	NA	NA	NA	NA	NA	NA	NA	NA	22	31.0	D	101	2.8	6.3
Independence city	108	28.7	3 711	129.1	2 692	85.3	521.8	812.5	106	410.8	325.9	981	30.2	69.2
Jefferson City city	39	30.8	3 603	114.9	2 958	86.8	610.1	1 046.8	83	D	782.9	(8)	D	D
Joplin city	108	37.0	5 585	148.2	4 252	101.8	391.0	849.8	142	651.9	574.9	1 495	38.6	76.5
Kansas City city	575	36.0	27 888	998.5	17 573	512.4	4 235.4	7 155.5	898	12 630.3	5 667.3	1 379 562	702.2	1 379.6
Kirkwood city	41	39.0	1 272	41.1	936	23.5	74.9	136.5	97	286.6	157.6	637	22.4	40.6
Lee's Summit city	77	22.1	2 577	72.1	1 636	47.0	296.1	456.7	101	907.8	D	975	31.0	65.8
Maryland Heights city	132	42.4	4 858	171.6	3 047	82.4	487.5	980.3	258	2 687.7	1 888.1	4 975	187.6	331.8
Raytown city	33	39.4	663	17.5	508	10.3	32.2	58.0	53	342.5	D	487	22.6	54.6
St. Charles city	83	31.3	2 565	78.7	1 926	50.5	187.4	360.2	109	354.2	236.8	1 055	31.2	62.3
St. Joseph city	91	52.7	(5)	D	D	D	D	D	139	1 106.3	D	1 556	42.9	94.9
St. Louis city	802	39.0	33 836	1 243.6	23 100	723.4	5 088.6	8 605.5	902	10 582.9	5 698.4	16 599	646.4	1 321.6
St. Peters city	69	30.4	3 822	126.4	3 130	87.6	1 227.4	1 489.7	67	666.2	589.7	594	19.6	38.1
Springfield city	310	32.9	18 260	488.3	13 285	305.0	1 670.8	3 673.5	488	4 908.2	3 572.1	8 326	249.7	461.8
University City city	NA	NA	NA	NA	NA	NA	NA	NA	54	180.3	147.5	615	20.7	39.0

[1] Average number of production workers plus the number of other (nonproduction) employees for the pay period including March 12.   [2] Average number of production workers for the pay periods including the 12th of March, May, August, and November.   [3] Includes only establishments with payroll.   [4] For pay period including March 12.   [5] 5,000 to 9,999 employees.   [6] 500 to 999 employees.   [7] 10,000 to 24,999 employees.   [8] 2,500 to 4,999 employees.

Sources: Manufacturing—U.S. Census Bureau, 1997 Economic Census – Manufacturing, generated by Statistical Compendia Branch, using American Factfinder at <http://www.census.gov/>, (June 2000) [related Internet site <http://www.census.gov/epcd/www/97EC31.HTM>].   Wholesale Trade—U.S. Census Bureau, 1997 Economic Census, individual state .pdf files from <http://www.census.gov/epcd/www/97EC42.HTM> (accessed June 2000) and ECON97 Report Series CD-ROM, CD-EC97-1, Disc 1E, issued February 2001.

Table C–5. Cities — **Manufacturing and Wholesale Trade**–Con.

[Includes states and 1,070 incorporated places of 25,000 or more population as of April 1, 1990 in all states except Hawaii which has no incorporated places recognized by the Census Bureau. For Hawaii, 8 census designated places (CDPs) of 25,000 or more population as of April 1, 1990 are included. Also included are the 5 boroughs of New York city. For more information on these areas, see appendix B. Geographic Information]

City	Manufacturing (NAICS 31-33), 1997								Wholesale trade[3] (NAICS 42), 1997					
	Establishments		All employees		Production workers		Value added by manu-facture (mil. dol.)	Value of ship-ments (mil. dol.)		Sales				
	Total	Percent with 20 or more employ-ees	Number[1]	Annual payroll (mil. dol.)	Number[2]	Wages (mil. dol.)			Estab-lishments	Total (mil. dol.)	Merchant whole-salers (mil. dol.)	Paid em-ployees[4]	Annual payroll (mil. dol.)	Operating expenses (mil. dol.)
MONTANA.............	1 160	15.4	19 611	560.1	14 988	394.0	1 732.2	4 866.3	1 574	7 596.8	6 045.5	14 356	371.6	765.3
Billings city...............	141	13.5	(5)	D	D	D	D	D	314	2 295.1	1 798.6	4 128	121.1	234.3
Butte-Silver Bow (remainder)	NA	NA	NA	NA	NA	NA	NA	NA	[6]55	[6]192.0	D	[6]534	[6]10.7	[6]21.7
Great Falls city	64	20.3	853	22.1	630	14.2	54.9	221.2	110	996.2	939.8	1 013	27.3	53.0
Missoula city	94	12.8	1 103	28.1	877	21.5	65.4	151.0	145	515.4	494.4	1 675	42.7	85.8
NEBRASKA............	1 960	31.2	106 690	3 040.5	84 085	2 132.7	10 822.7	27 859.2	3 157	38 015.4	17 741.8	41 002	1 170.2	2 461.1
Bellevue city	10	50.0	1 070	20.9	479	9.8	87.0	146.1	12	3.4	D	15	.3	.7
Grand Island city	59	28.8	5 107	139.1	4 296	110.2	414.5	1 714.9	94	D	D	(5)	D	D
Lincoln city...............	234	35.9	(7)	D	D	D	D	D	270	D	D	(8)	D	D
Omaha city	497	33.6	24 767	787.2	19 192	548.2	2 939.1	6 528.1	932	10 907.3	6 257.2	15 973	533.0	1 081.5
NEVADA	1 615	25.3	37 849	1 178.0	26 247	677.2	3 298.1	6 361.8	2 253	12 806.9	8 185.7	27 251	918.5	1 865.4
Carson City	186	25.3	4 157	120.8	3 011	70.5	297.3	514.5	88	222.4	D	557	18.7	39.0
Henderson city	60	35.0	3 131	96.8	2 380	66.7	544.1	939.1	85	301.2	196.3	729	21.7	46.6
Las Vegas city............	274	17.9	3 884	114.1	2 748	65.9	273.0	493.8	500	2 208.8	1 651.5	6 266	209.2	429.3
North Las Vegas city	74	32.4	2 071	63.0	1 583	40.5	195.7	363.6	91	735.5	584.5	1 903	67.5	135.2
Reno city	192	25.0	6 086	191.6	3 700	86.7	446.7	1 076.3	286	3 043.4	D	3 487	118.6	274.0
Sparks city	182	36.3	4 477	136.2	3 120	77.8	390.1	684.6	290	2 376.7	1 610.8	5 391	188.2	371.2
NEW HAMPSHIRE	2 328	32.5	98 934	3 361.4	68 942	1 935.5	11 320.1	19 813.1	2 033	11 371.1	7 618.2	22 631	875.0	1 731.7
Concord city	56	50.0	3 016	89.6	2 294	50.5	216.1	372.7	63	268.7	243.6	848	28.8	73.4
Dover city................	58	39.7	3 300	111.4	1 713	44.3	291.8	525.2	44	114.9	D	329	9.2	16.4
Manchester city	191	33.0	8 952	289.7	6 141	151.7	705.8	1 394.5	226	1 368.2	1 023.2	3 185	115.0	214.3
Nashua city	179	32.4	11 164	521.2	7 803	301.5	1 255.9	1 990.4	160	1 527.4	816.2	2 028	102.3	178.1
Portsmouth city	50	32.0	1 497	46.2	1 048	27.4	159.6	279.3	101	1 263.7	931.1	1 270	58.4	115.0
Rochester city	38	42.1	2 694	74.8	1 741	32.8	808.5	1 218.0	26	88.8	D	829	20.1	41.9
NEW JERSEY...........	11 812	32.4	409 788	15 430.2	275 840	8 152.1	50 101.7	97 060.8	17 812	227 309.0	129 415.1	266 944	11 886.1	26 750.7
Atlantic City city	NA	NA	NA	NA	NA	NA	NA	NA	24	63.5	63.5	203	7.0	12.5
Bayonne city	52	36.5	1 747	60.6	1 038	28.3	243.9	556.1	57	1 081.0	D	1 127	45.7	121.8
Camden city	81	33.3	2 757	117.6	1 533	46.4	340.5	557.8	92	480.5	D	1 184	40.8	87.2
Clifton city...............	211	41.7	9 631	374.9	6 761	205.5	932.6	1 780.5	215	2 579.4	705.6	2 474	104.8	186.6
East Orange city	NA	NA	NA	NA	NA	NA	NA	NA	17	D	D	(9)	D	D
Elizabeth city	129	35.7	5 983	191.0	4 646	123.1	544.7	1 143.6	158	2 119.1	2 012.3	3 181	120.3	240.8
Fair Lawn borough	62	48.4	3 146	116.4	2 319	70.0	346.4	589.3	83	1 264.7	D	715	31.1	78.4
Fort Lee borough	NA	NA	NA	NA	NA	NA	NA	NA	250	4 332.1	2 295.9	1 942	119.2	248.8
Garfield city	105	31.4	3 293	90.8	2 627	58.4	293.5	521.4	61	D	D	(10)	D	D
Hackensack city	140	19.3	2 551	85.2	1 842	46.0	191.2	391.7	279	2 434.3	1 210.3	2 902	131.5	279.3
Hoboken city	69	34.8	1 655	47.5	1 252	25.8	120.6	311.0	83	742.6	D	575	25.7	53.1
Jersey City city	190	36.8	5 770	179.8	4 276	110.2	534.6	1 039.2	278	2 510.8	2 234.6	5 701	202.7	392.0
Kearny town	69	39.1	2 068	62.7	1 485	35.7	180.4	361.9	98	539.9	D	1 231	56.3	114.2
Linden city	164	39.6	8 202	364.1	6 059	236.0	1 951.3	6 332.5	131	1 861.6	D	1 475	56.8	130.1
Long Branch city	24	12.5	505	15.2	337	7.0	31.1	58.5	41	523.2	D	394	14.7	27.4
Millville city..............	52	42.3	4 684	154.4	3 667	113.8	344.7	609.5	25	D	D	(11)	D	D
Newark city	439	39.2	14 960	491.9	10 693	290.9	1 817.3	3 353.1	426	2 319.3	1 669.4	5 393	192.0	386.6
New Brunswick city	78	29.5	3 689	114.0	2 008	71.6	497.1	689.9	63	249.1	227.7	908	28.8	57.6
Paramus borough..........	32	21.9	1 541	70.8	687	24.7	124.6	238.2	167	2 943.1	1 267.0	2 785	157.9	365.3
Passaic city	144	37.5	4 687	108.6	3 715	71.2	237.9	433.2	95	296.4	292.1	919	29.4	57.1
Paterson city	340	33.5	8 436	277.2	6 219	155.6	929.4	1 748.4	211	1 105.6	843.9	2 804	104.4	208.8
Perth Amboy city	53	34.0	2 408	85.9	1 823	57.3	220.4	865.6	62	514.8	D	871	32.8	66.6
Plainfield city	42	26.2	1 128	30.9	836	18.2	64.6	154.9	35	97.9	D	381	11.3	25.2
Rahway city..............	68	38.2	3 316	167.4	1 954	73.6	636.1	1 153.8	56	444.9	D	912	38.1	90.5
Sayreville borough	24	29.2	2 272	101.2	1 777	71.9	540.4	860.7	48	117.6	111.3	335	12.0	24.9
Trenton city	89	34.8	2 790	104.7	1 898	59.7	185.7	370.8	81	314.8	D	987	32.9	62.2
Union City city	133	15.8	1 563	29.4	1 304	20.1	61.8	102.3	88	166.2	D	509	15.8	34.9
Vineland city	105	49.5	6 223	186.9	4 788	124.8	494.4	913.0	123	542.7	466.6	1 184	38.8	79.2
Westfield town............	NA	NA	NA	NA	NA	NA	NA	NA	53	327.2	275.1	280	20.4	42.7
West New York town	172	15.7	1 970	34.3	1 590	23.6	73.1	142.2	64	160.7	D	413	14.8	32.3

[1] Average number of production workers plus the number of other (nonproduction) employees for the pay period including March 12. [2] Average number of production workers for the pay periods including the 12th of March, May, August, and November. [3] Includes only establishments with payroll. [4] For pay period including March 12. [5] 1,000 to 2,499 employees. [6] Data are for consolidated city of Butte-Silver Bow; data for Butte-Silver Bow (remainder) not available. [7] 10,000 to 24,999 employees. [8] 2,500 to 4,999 employees. [9] 100 to 249 employees. [10] 500 to 999 employees. [11] 250 to 499 employees.

Sources: Manufacturing—U.S. Census Bureau, 1997 Economic Census – Manufacturing, generated by Statistical Compendia Branch, using American Factfinder at <http://www.census.gov/>, (June 2000) [related Internet site <http://www.census.gov/epcd/www/97EC31.HTM>]. Wholesale Trade—U.S. Census Bureau, 1997 Economic Census, individual state .pdf files from <http://www.census.gov/epcd/www/97EC42.HTM> (accessed June 2000) and ECON[97] Report Series CD-ROM, CD-EC97-1, Disc 1E, issued February 2001.

Table C–5. Cities — **Manufacturing and Wholesale Trade**–Con.

[Includes states and 1,070 incorporated places of 25,000 or more population as of April 1, 1990 in all states except Hawaii which has no incorporated places recognized by the Census Bureau. For Hawaii, 8 census designated places (CDPs) of 25,000 or more population as of April 1, 1990 are included. Also included are the 5 boroughs of New York city. For more information on these areas, see appendix B. Geographic Information]

| City | Manufacturing (NAICS 31-33), 1997 | | | | | | | | Wholesale trade[3] (NAICS 42), 1997 | | | | | |
| | Establishments | | All employees | | Production workers | | Value added by manufacture (mil. dol.) | Value of shipments (mil. dol.) | | Sales | | | | |
	Total	Percent with 20 or more employees	Number[1]	Annual payroll (mil. dol.)	Number[2]	Wages (mil. dol.)			Establishments	Total (mil. dol.)	Merchant wholesalers (mil. dol.)	Paid employees[4]	Annual payroll (mil. dol.)	Operating expenses (mil. dol.)
NEW MEXICO	1 593	18.4	39 664	1 135.8	29 334	721.4	13 440.2	17 906.1	2 182	7 397.6	5 400.6	21 344	601.1	1 201.7
Alamogordo city	18	27.8	562	10.1	520	8.6	46.0	92.1	17	25.2	D	94	2.0	3.9
Albuquerque city	592	21.8	(5)	D	D	D	D	D	919	3 630.1	D	10 636	330.3	634.9
Clovis city	NA	NA	NA	NA	NA	NA	NA	NA	33	95.3	82.0	268	5.9	13.1
Farmington city	47	14.9	695	16.9	552	11.0	46.4	74.1	115	276.8	203.3	1 002	28.5	61.1
Hobbs city	NA	NA	NA	NA	NA	NA	NA	NA	85	253.8	201.8	708	20.6	43.5
Las Cruces city	65	21.5	1 433	28.6	1 196	21.3	106.2	253.4	79	194.2	159.2	656	17.8	39.8
Rio Rancho city	30	43.3	–	D	D	D	D	D	19	216.6	D	348	8.7	15.3
Roswell city	40	25.0	(6)	D	D	D	D	D	61	196.9	D	514	12.0	25.8
Santa Fe city	136	8.1	1 155	23.7	834	15.3	55.5	95.2	146	319.7	274.1	1 207	37.7	75.7
NEW YORK	23 908	28.0	785 891	26 515.8	538 186	14 695.8	76 999.8	11 400.0	37 499	319 697.6	217 216.8	414 249	17 185.8	37 754.1
Albany city	86	24.4	1 933	62.6	1 412	36.4	157.3	420.5	164	1 438.6	836.4	2 401	90.4	171.1
Auburn city	64	42.2	3 087	92.6	2 344	61.6	275.9	556.3	44	131.5	D	424	12.1	25.1
Binghamton city	79	45.6	5 994	199.6	4 173	99.1	718.1	1 266.4	80	305.7	197.5	1 018	26.6	58.0
Buffalo city	466	36.3	20 307	748.4	14 499	462.9	2 491.3	4 527.2	468	3 273.0	2 314.5	7 225	235.5	490.8
Elmira city	30	53.3	2 531	70.3	1 488	37.6	221.9	334.5	46	136.6	121.9	552	15.1	30.2
Freeport village	122	33.6	3 330	92.7	2 354	51.0	175.7	392.4	120	350.6	D	969	30.6	57.2
Hempstead village	38	31.6	674	20.3	482	11.2	44.9	84.1	58	191.9	D	547	21.0	39.8
Ithaca city	61	27.9	2 775	97.0	2 007	60.6	247.0	515.3	42	166.9	D	268	9.2	19.1
Jamestown city	83	43.4	5 056	150.2	3 776	90.2	405.3	666.9	65	172.1	D	583	15.3	29.7
Lindenhurst village	68	13.2	802	20.5	624	13.5	49.1	82.0	65	310.4	304.7	389	12.2	27.2
Long Beach city	NA	NA	NA	NA	NA	NA	NA	NA	26	29.3	8.2	23	1.1	2.6
Mount Vernon city	147	36.1	4 405	142.3	3 015	74.1	287.1	602.1	123	673.5	479.2	1 708	65.0	135.3
Newburgh city	48	29.2	1 467	28.5	1 179	18.6	59.2	116.9	57	199.7	D	683	21.5	43.2
New Rochelle city	61	23.0	1 167	36.8	866	21.2	84.2	138.9	147	614.1	500.2	1 221	55.8	123.4
New York city	10 569	24.0	207 975	5 504.1	149 269	3 101.5	13 876.0	27 735.8	18 482	182 107.1	128 818.7	185 407	8 614.3	19 861.0
Bronx borough	527	30.7	12 941	319.6	9 928	202.1	725.5	1 252.3	755	5 373.6	D	10 728	389.9	791.4
Brooklyn borough	2 672	23.2	48 589	1 139.9	37 284	718.3	3 014.6	5 725.5	2 953	11 371.6	10 591.2	25 838	742.8	1 583.3
Manhattan borough	5 165	23.2	93 784	2 551.8	63 917	1 336.4	6 420.9	14 028.9	11 629	151 792.8	102 916.5	119 913	6 473.4	15 323.3
Queens borough	2 043	26.5	50 505	1 433.2	36 736	806.8	3 566.3	6 412.8	2 787	12 942.0	9 764.4	27 165	952.6	2 026.1
Staten Island borough	162	12.3	2 156	59.6	1 404	37.8	148.8	316.2	358	627.1	D	1 763	55.5	137.0
Niagara Falls city	69	43.5	3 942	183.7	2 722	114.0	684.0	1 234.0	60	204.4	D	708	16.8	37.4
North Tonawanda city	61	42.6	2 131	72.6	1 531	42.7	300.9	522.2	38	D	D	(7)	D	D
Poughkeepsie city	38	39.5	(8)	D	D	D	D	D	50	D	D	(9)	D	D
Rochester city	533	37.7	51 405	2 218.8	31 693	1 198.6	7 098.4	12 269.7	441	5 193.4	1 596.7	7 349	308.2	563.4
Rome city	49	42.9	2 278	72.9	1 579	44.3	148.1	547.5	24	31.4	31.4	146	3.5	7.3
Saratoga Springs city	28	32.1	1 782	59.5	1 443	46.3	174.9	374.0	28	188.3	158.1	294	8.8	18.6
Schenectady city	66	27.3	3 401	154.9	2 592	109.2	568.6	1 302.9	57	425.5	391.6	1 060	41.3	73.9
Syracuse city	163	33.7	10 193	409.5	5 800	183.1	1 111.9	1 958.1	262	1 529.4	798.6	3 569	124.9	226.8
Troy city	41	34.1	1 727	53.2	749	20.7	77.1	196.9	55	201.7	151.8	482	13.5	26.3
Utica city	102	31.4	4 095	118.7	2 732	60.5	251.5	509.2	94	448.8	D	1 341	37.7	72.6
Valley Stream village	NA	NA	NA	NA	NA	NA	NA	NA	52	168.3	D	554	15.4	30.7
Watertown city	41	36.6	1 855	56.0	1 198	30.2	138.8	279.9	139	3 222.7	2 186.9	1 781	127.4	425.1
White Plains city	NA	NA	NA	NA	NA	NA	NA	NA	228	1 037.6	986.4	2 460	84.2	176.8
Yonkers city	131	26.0	4 074	132.6	3 114	79.3	274.6	742.6	228	1 037.6	986.4	2 460	84.2	176.8
NORTH CAROLINA	11 306	40.9	773 548	21 297.9	601 190	14 061.0	78 638.0	11 500.0	12 284	98 080.1	48 386.9	157 774	5 574.1	11 039.1
Asheville city	142	33.8	6 168	164.7	4 631	107.6	628.6	1 405.3	211	777.0	503.3	2 134	64.8	122.4
Burlington city	110	52.7	8 811	208.6	7 241	147.7	600.5	1 435.6	89	332.4	245.0	1 080	35.6	68.8
Cary town	8	37.5	1 620	80.0	1 221	57.6	137.0	364.5	132	1 728.9	1 147.8	1 260	57.9	114.1
Chapel Hill town	65	23.1	2 767	89.3	2 102	53.8	217.4	384.7	33	254.9	D	123	5.2	11.8
Charlotte city	787	31.1	31 811	1 058.5	20 279	565.4	3 235.2	6 504.0	2 150	30 244.7	9 287.9	32 325	1 319.9	2 479.1
Concord city	78	41.0	6 253	225.4	4 667	148.2	5 678.5	6 968.6	74	691.7	D	1 000	28.7	52.3
Durham city	123	30.1	(10)	D	D	D	D	D	182	1 652.9	1 113.9	2 736	80.4	159.8
Fayetteville city	78	46.2	9 100	295.1	7 503	223.2	1 107.2	2 170.0	140	549.5	355.4	1 653	45.8	89.3
Gastonia city	211	37.9	12 666	360.0	10 120	261.5	1 193.6	2 385.8	127	726.9	368.1	1 197	41.8	79.1
Goldsboro city	64	42.2	4 644	116.1	3 294	72.3	305.2	579.8	101	738.2	D	1 799	47.8	91.9
Greensboro city	411	38.4	21 305	711.5	14 979	416.7	3 497.3	5 903.6	783	9 531.0	3 738.8	14 701	629.7	1 398.8
Greenville city	60	38.3	4 006	143.5	2 646	76.3	1 330.2	1 827.6	122	527.2	359.4	1 196	30.2	74.6
Hickory city	253	49.4	17 501	441.1	14 497	320.5	965.3	2 235.8	194	1 990.6	1 679.5	4 048	127.8	223.4
High Point city	288	46.5	17 182	465.0	13 076	298.2	972.2	2 247.9	315	1 885.4	1 009.4	2 996	102.7	239.2
Jacksonville city	NA	NA	NA	NA	NA	NA	NA	NA	28	36.4	D	156	3.7	7.9

[1] Average number of production workers plus the number of other (nonproduction) employees for the pay period including March 12.   [2] Average number of production workers for the pay periods including the 12th of March, May, August, and November.   [3] Includes only establishments with payroll.   [4] For pay period including March 12.   [5] 10,000 to 24,999 employees.   [6] 1,000 to 2,499 employees.   [7] 500 to 999 employees.   [8] 2,500 to 4,999 employees.   [9] 250 to 499 employees.   [10] 5,000 to 9,999 employees.

Sources: Manufacturing—U.S. Census Bureau, 1997 Economic Census – Manufacturing, generated by Statistical Compendia Branch, using American Factfinder at <http://www.census.gov/>, (June 2000) [related Internet site <http://www.census.gov/epcd/www/97EC31.HTM>].   Wholesale Trade—U.S. Census Bureau, 1997 Economic Census, individual state .pdf files from <http://www.census.gov/epcd/www/97EC42.HTM> (accessed June 2000) and ECON⁹⁷ Report Series CD-ROM, CD-EC97-1, Disc 1E, issued February 2001.

Table C–5. Cities — **Manufacturing and Wholesale Trade**–Con.

[Includes states and 1,070 incorporated places of 25,000 or more population as of April 1, 1990 in all states except Hawaii which has no incorporated places recognized by the Census Bureau. For Hawaii, 8 census designated places (CDPs) of 25,000 or more population as of April 1, 1990 are included. Also included are the 5 boroughs of New York city. For more information on these areas, see appendix B. Geographic Information]

| City | Manufacturing (NAICS 31-33), 1997 | | | | | | | | Wholesale trade[3] (NAICS 42), 1997 | | | | | |
| | Establishments | | All employees | | Production workers | | Value added by manu- facture (mil. dol.) | Value of ship- ments (mil. dol.) | Estab- lishments | Sales | | Paid em- ployees[4] | Annual payroll (mil. dol.) | Operating expenses (mil. dol.) |
	Total	Percent with 20 or more employ- ees	Number[1]	Annual payroll (mil. dol.)	Number[2]	Wages (mil. dol.)				Total (mil. dol.)	Merchant whole- salers (mil. dol.)			
NORTH CAROLINA— Con.														
Kannapolis city	21	19.0	(5)	D	D	D	D	D	16	D	D	(6)	D	D
Kinston city	51	47.1	3 832	98.1	2 796	56.1	345.2	904.5	50	357.7	181.5	1 017	18.1	34.1
Raleigh city	328	23.8	7 954	241.5	5 580	131.7	1 057.5	2 147.1	778	8 296.7	2 999.4	11 873	553.2	1 009.6
Rocky Mount city	65	47.7	7 886	220.3	6 006	153.9	767.3	1 475.0	99	896.0	832.8	1 744	58.6	127.4
Wilmington city	139	29.5	5 257	202.0	3 933	136.7	700.9	1 241.1	209	994.0	647.0	2 748	74.1	150.5
Wilson city	70	42.9	7 534	238.5	6 095	159.7	833.8	2 821.1	93	422.1	240.7	1 075	29.1	63.9
Winston-Salem city	241	39.0	17 789	583.0	14 025	407.0	2 444.5	4 449.7	331	2 543.7	1 490.8	4 649	149.8	294.3
NORTH DAKOTA	704	26.7	21 956	604.8	16 364	386.9	1 802.4	5 115.9	1 604	8 618.4	7 464.2	16 992	454.4	934.3
Bismarck city	48	22.9	(7)	D	D	D	D	D	134	591.2	D	1 472	42.0	83.4
Fargo city	133	36.1	5 206	131.2	3 721	78.4	493.4	1 057.5	246	2 168.8	1 805.2	4 603	148.5	271.2
Grand Forks city	43	23.3	1 536	33.7	1 275	26.1	131.6	231.9	97	D	380.2	(7)	D	D
Minot city	41	22.0	(8)	D	D	D	D	D	62	D	D	(8)	D	D
OHIO	17 974	38.4	984 201	35 950.5	730 170	23 561.0	11 000.0	21 300.0	17 322	160 415.6	76 172.9	254 226	9 192.2	18 406.0
Akron city	370	33.2	12 822	451.8	7 762	228.3	1 130.0	2 020.4	334	2 808.5	1 599.7	4 956	175.7	345.1
Barberton city	77	40.3	4 140	122.5	3 241	77.9	233.2	535.5	42	122.2	96.9	401	15.0	28.1
Beavercreek city	31	29.0	826	31.4	446	12.0	76.3	167.7	41	287.2	D	289	12.0	21.3
Bowling Green city	41	48.8	3 107	96.6	2 296	62.0	255.7	429.8	23	63.3	D	164	4.4	9.3
Brunswick city	29	48.3	658	21.0	485	12.6	48.4	93.6	44	155.8	129.3	464	13.3	26.8
Canton city	182	38.5	13 120	461.9	10 384	334.8	1 745.1	3 233.5	141	1 072.0	598.8	2 493	75.1	133.8
Cincinnati city	604	38.7	28 917	1 021.8	18 157	554.9	3 778.7	6 540.2	705	10 660.8	4 071.7	15 388	671.6	1 230.7
Cleveland city	1 270	34.8	44 400	1 662.2	31 573	1 008.5	4 128.6	8 675.8	921	7 155.4	4 894.7	16 936	622.5	1 242.0
Cleveland Heights city	NA	NA	NA	NA	NA	NA	NA	NA	27	52.7	15.0	58	1.7	5.4
Columbus city	685	35.3	32 243	1 173.3	22 784	725.1	4 498.7	8 409.3	1 092	13 539.2	6 608.0	24 483	1 002.5	2 098.7
Cuyahoga Falls city	88	39.8	3 220	111.4	2 263	60.3	315.1	531.9	79	157.2	D	530	16.8	31.2
Dayton city	NA	NA	NA	NA	NA	NA	NA	NA	287	3 296.5	1 307.9	5 256	209.5	418.1
East Cleveland city	NA	NA	NA	NA	NA	NA	NA	NA	12	D	21.4	(9)	D	D
Elyria city	132	43.9	7 704	260.2	5 644	162.1	858.7	1 610.8	65	183.1	135.7	647	19.0	39.0
Euclid city	108	38.9	8 223	326.0	4 778	166.5	725.7	1 627.6	72	1 342.3	D	2 532	174.3	285.4
Fairborn city	14	57.1	779	27.0	574	16.9	83.3	139.5	15	138.1	D	253	8.3	12.8
Fairfield city	84	39.3	3 096	95.9	2 232	59.1	245.0	492.8	93	1 279.9	958.9	1 683	60.5	114.6
Findlay city	66	45.5	7 559	271.5	5 475	172.2	696.9	1 397.3	61	336.0	288.5	607	17.8	34.4
Gahanna city	28	25.0	517	16.1	305	7.1	36.5	74.4	49	278.9	151.3	421	19.3	34.1
Garfield Heights city	48	37.5	1 502	48.1	1 050	28.1	102.5	189.3	51	810.2	634.0	1 487	71.4	177.1
Hamilton city	86	39.5	3 717	136.9	2 659	89.3	363.0	692.2	75	890.5	D	1 404	51.2	93.5
Huber Heights city	34	35.3	(7)	D	D	D	D	D	21	160.1	153.6	295	13.1	25.2
Kent city	72	43.1	2 412	70.2	1 807	42.2	155.1	343.0	28	61.0	D	189	6.1	12.0
Kettering city	51	33.3	5 025	269.9	3 781	167.7	457.1	831.9	73	595.4	D	924	43.1	78.2
Lakewood city	41	24.4	1 128	44.1	777	27.4	103.8	182.1	62	255.7	D	617	22.8	55.6
Lancaster city	78	28.2	4 282	134.0	3 313	90.6	366.5	625.1	40	97.7	D	364	12.2	24.2
Lima city	48	37.5	3 856	209.3	3 110	161.2	623.3	1 743.7	89	436.2	D	1 197	32.8	64.9
Lorain city	64	32.8	7 745	340.4	6 498	256.8	3 215.7	6 869.5	40	199.0	D	877	23.6	44.7
Mansfield city	126	43.7	7 844	265.4	5 962	181.1	644.0	1 256.5	96	445.3	293.5	1 344	36.2	73.6
Maple Heights city	31	22.6	576	19.0	464	12.5	31.4	77.9	27	250.5	151.3	709	20.3	39.7
Marion city	48	47.9	2 723	92.6	1 877	54.5	300.4	784.9	32	84.7	D	287	8.8	21.6
Massillon city	64	50.0	4 737	144.7	3 732	93.7	273.2	975.6	33	833.3	767.5	1 158	45.5	84.6
Mentor city	244	40.2	8 617	274.8	6 225	156.0	870.7	1 450.4	138	477.5	397.8	1 828	56.8	107.0
Middletown city	71	53.5	7 187	353.0	5 542	269.4	2 808.0	3 662.9	40	302.2	D	876	29.0	62.6
Newark city	49	36.7	4 017	133.4	3 276	99.6	441.9	770.2	43	178.5	D	447	14.8	29.9
North Olmsted city	NA	NA	NA	NA	NA	NA	NA	NA	57	D	D	(10)	D	D
Parma city	58	22.4	5 002	278.8	4 327	233.0	388.1	972.8	73	290.8	223.9	981	34.1	57.6
Reynoldsburg city	15	26.7	591	16.0	488	11.9	95.8	213.0	33	147.9	88.5	432	8.9	19.8
Sandusky city	66	53.0	5 206	223.4	4 000	162.6	303.5	799.0	47	147.8	D	498	15.1	27.3
Shaker Heights city	NA	NA	NA	NA	NA	NA	NA	NA	34	337.0	D	245	8.8	15.8
Springfield city	115	47.0	(7)	D	D	D	D	D	69	657.6	D	1 126	30.5	65.0
Stow city	72	38.9	2 527	89.4	1 694	49.4	179.5	342.5	46	451.2	D	727	23.7	45.6
Strongsville city	76	46.1	3 286	122.7	2 178	68.3	340.2	650.9	85	632.2	362.5	1 516	62.8	136.4
Toledo city	462	36.1	25 446	1 101.0	20 604	848.4	2 764.9	9 282.3	487	3 692.8	2 767.8	7 731	259.5	513.7
Upper Arlington city	NA	NA	NA	NA	NA	NA	NA	NA	48	242.9	43.7	366	12.3	24.2
Warren city	69	42.0	12 471	629.7	9 738	467.2	1 097.9	3 247.4	62	265.2	D	728	19.2	33.6
Westerville city	37	27.0	1 206	49.8	745	20.3	99.6	191.5	74	831.9	D	963	35.1	62.9
Westlake city	55	34.5	1 662	54.8	1 141	33.0	145.7	308.7	174	2 050.2	820.2	2 482	123.6	261.7
Youngstown city	148	33.1	4 658	166.5	3 392	108.1	413.6	954.0	153	702.1	D	2 251	69.5	126.7
Zanesville city	53	39.6	4 194	112.2	3 507	83.7	356.5	599.0	41	337.3	265.1	813	22.0	45.6

[1] Average number of production workers plus the number of other (nonproduction) employees for the pay period including March 12. [2] Average number of production workers for the pay periods including the 12th of March, May, August, and November. [3] Includes only establishments with payroll. [4] For pay period including March 12. [5] 2,500 to 4,999 employees. [6] 20 to 99 employees. [7] 1,000 to 2,499 employees. [8] 500 to 999 employees. [9] 100 to 249 employees. [10] 250 to 499 employees.

Sources: Manufacturing—U.S. Census Bureau, 1997 Economic Census – Manufacturing, generated by Statistical Compendia Branch, using American Factfinder at <http://www.census.gov/>, (June 2000) [related Internet site <http://www.census.gov/epcd/www/97EC31.HTM>]. Wholesale Trade—U.S. Census Bureau, 1997 Economic Census, individual state .pdf files from <http://www.census.gov/epcd/www/97EC42.HTM> (accessed June 2000) and ECON97 Report Series CD-ROM, CD-EC97-1, Disc 1E, issued February 2001.

Table C–5. Cities — **Manufacturing and Wholesale Trade**–Con.

[Includes states and 1,070 incorporated places of 25,000 or more population as of April 1, 1990 in all states except Hawaii which has no incorporated places recognized by the Census Bureau. For Hawaii, 8 census designated places (CDPs) of 25,000 or more population as of April 1, 1990 are included. Also included are the 5 boroughs of New York city. For more information on these areas, see appendix B. Geographic Information]

City	Manufacturing (NAICS 31-33), 1997								Wholesale trade[3] (NAICS 42), 1997					
	Establishments		All employees		Production workers		Value added by manu-facture (mil. dol.)	Value of ship-ments (mil. dol.)	Estab-lishments	Sales		Paid em-ployees[4]	Annual payroll (mil. dol.)	Operating expenses (mil. dol.)
	Total	Percent with 20 or more employ-ees	Number[1]	Annual payroll (mil. dol.)	Number[2]	Wages (mil. dol.)				Total (mil. dol.)	Merchant whole-salers (mil. dol.)			
OKLAHOMA	4 087	29.1	164 060	4 963.2	122 705	3 229.5	17 233.7	37 453.2	5 191	32 132.3	20 292.5	59 641	1 756.1	3 612.6
Bartlesville city	31	12.9	930	40.2	560	13.3	86.5	139.7	28	24.1	D	112	2.4	4.6
Broken Arrow city	129	31.8	4 191	136.8	2 753	72.2	340.7	614.9	113	420.4	D	1 218	42.5	79.1
Edmond city..............	39	20.5	929	23.2	581	13.2	56.5	91.0	96	156.0	67.9	399	11.9	22.1
Enid city	54	18.5	(5)	D	D	D	D	D	96	D	410.6	(5)	D	D
Lawton city..............	45	24.4	(6)	D	D	D	D	D	80	173.2	D	751	15.9	29.6
Midwest City city	18	33.3	(7)	D	NA	NA	D	D	28	D	D	(8)	D	D
Moore city	NA	NA	NA	NA	NA	NA	NA	NA	40	93.5	D	350	6.7	15.9
Muskogee city............	61	29.5	3 476	117.4	2 953	94.2	475.8	760.7	65	231.7	195.9	830	21.2	41.5
Norman city	83	20.5	2 442	71.6	1 811	42.7	331.9	679.6	79	397.6	345.8	987	27.0	52.2
Oklahoma City city	759	30.8	38 354	1 251.1	27 355	793.7	4 451.9	9 658.1	1 307	14 323.2	6 465.4	19 128	572.8	1 255.6
Ponca City city	45	37.8	(5)	D	D	D	D	D	32	145.7	D	226	6.3	19.0
Shawnee city.............	41	29.3	2 799	96.3	2 268	72.0	272.4	545.5	25	D	D	(8)	D	D
Stillwater city.............	28	32.1	2 195	68.4	1 655	45.4	438.9	814.6	30	135.1	D	399	8.8	30.7
Tulsa city	872	32.2	29 436	986.6	19 670	553.7	2 656.9	5 526.1	1 237	8 372.1	6 806.6	16 094	577.7	1 102.5
OREGON..............	5 768	29.0	213 111	7 095.3	158 506	4 545.8	25 077.2	47 666.0	5 943	53 679.1	38 230.9	74 790	2 578.7	5 192.5
Albany city	68	33.8	3 538	124.2	2 691	79.1	345.1	630.7	55	214.6	NA	731	21.7	NA
Beaverton city	135	33.3	9 717	383.4	5 200	148.9	1 336.4	2 310.1	271	5 353.3	NA	3 919	189.0	NA
Corvallis city	119	22.7	3 422	87.4	2 776	58.9	225.8	496.3	29	45.4	NA	387	7.4	NA
Eugene city	340	26.5	9 524	277.1	6 647	162.6	614.9	1 330.3	356	1 687.8	NA	3 977	125.2	NA
Gresham city	82	30.5	5 338	183.2	4 026	143.2	476.8	795.6	64	507.8	NA	722	23.5	NA
Hillsboro city	173	31.8	8 734	339.4	5 874	178.7	788.2	1 977.3	83	325.5	NA	1 007	41.7	NA
Lake Oswego city..........	54	24.1	1 083	36.3	651	16.6	70.0	127.8	166	2 076.1	NA	1 448	70.5	NA
Medford city	74	20.3	2 007	61.9	1 489	40.2	132.5	344.8	149	462.5	NA	1 216	38.3	NA
Portland city	1 144	30.2	39 059	1 310.6	29 273	873.6	3 465.3	7 385.1	1 700	23 728.9	NA	26 464	948.6	NA
Salem city	224	33.9	7 085	211.4	5 331	122.1	644.9	1 226.0	171	694.8	NA	2 083	60.3	NA
Springfield city............	87	31.0	3 334	123.3	2 624	88.4	373.0	915.3	53	242.0	NA	642	15.7	NA
Tigard city	110	33.6	3 706	125.5	2 421	65.1	290.0	566.4	246	3 212.5	NA	3 515	157.4	NA
PENNSYLVANIA	17 128	37.1	826 521	27 641.3	597 544	17 045.1	86 212.1	11 600.0	17 138	159 354.2	80 673.7	237 567	8 588.2	17 081.0
Allentown city	238	31.9	8 310	325.0	6 059	184.1	3 362.3	4 060.0	203	1 531.9	708.6	2 749	92.2	195.3
Altoona city	68	33.8	2 622	62.7	2 041	41.1	253.1	424.7	85	1 090.2	933.8	2 011	61.7	173.9
Bethel Park borough	49	18.4	527	15.7	334	7.9	28.7	71.3	56	157.2	97.4	483	15.7	28.4
Bethlehem city	109	48.6	6 650	237.3	4 279	127.0	527.2	1 063.1	111	858.8	307.0	1 344	55.4	97.8
Chester city	34	58.8	2 372	101.3	1 831	72.4	534.4	782.6	30	96.2	96.2	311	10.3	17.3
Easton city	53	43.4	3 748	112.4	3 028	81.9	430.3	639.5	46	624.2	D	1 235	52.6	95.1
Erie city	203	45.3	10 286	357.2	7 180	225.7	937.8	1 789.0	128	487.4	441.3	1 861	57.8	114.2
Harrisburg city	58	41.4	2 299	69.9	1 731	48.7	223.4	478.9	91	2 544.3	2 209.3	3 726	110.2	201.4
Johnstown city	49	40.8	4 264	112.4	2 659	71.6	348.9	989.4	43	281.5	D	932	29.8	61.7
Lancaster city	108	40.7	9 758	382.2	7 699	266.8	1 148.2	2 038.5	97	420.9	333.5	953	29.4	56.4
McKeesport city	24	37.5	827	30.7	602	20.6	67.1	111.0	29	95.9	95.9	357	8.5	19.2
Municipality of Monroeville borough	26	30.8	687	19.6	422	9.5	43.0	82.2	81	331.7	171.3	824	31.8	60.6
New Castle city............	89	39.3	2 483	76.0	1 860	48.0	201.3	436.9	51	231.5	D	515	14.3	30.1
Norristown borough	63	39.7	1 517	48.8	998	25.7	113.4	196.6	77	549.7	D	1 416	50.9	96.8
Philadelphia city	1 342	32.0	47 928	1 582.4	33 884	926.0	3 997.5	11 098.1	1 403	12 004.0	7 486.7	22 298	848.4	1 629.6
Pittsburgh city	479	28.6	13 924	471.6	9 652	289.2	1 183.7	2 395.0	742	12 543.4	4 195.0	12 740	517.2	990.5
Plum borough	36	30.6	1 523	48.1	929	20.9	104.4	194.2	46	257.2	D	515	20.7	50.5
Reading city	160	43.8	16 969	737.4	12 458	463.2	1 893.3	3 654.2	95	583.5	459.0	1 851	61.0	116.6
Scranton city	124	41.1	4 567	114.1	3 516	70.2	340.4	591.2	130	464.3	D	1 835	44.8	91.5
State College borough	38	50.0	2 140	66.0	1 371	34.4	173.0	251.8	29	69.0	D	384	10.0	18.9
Wilkes-Barre city..........	69	42.0	3 390	81.3	2 479	52.3	241.4	422.4	77	417.8	289.5	1 379	35.9	70.7
Williamsport city	72	51.4	6 023	182.7	4 605	110.6	587.7	1 284.3	58	238.7	D	1 181	28.8	62.9
York city	123	50.4	9 253	332.3	6 618	191.8	1 257.2	1 924.0	98	549.1	266.4	1 612	48.1	142.7
RHODE ISLAND........	2 535	27.8	75 599	2 288.6	52 889	1 279.8	5 484.2	10 482.0	1 590	7 602.7	5 058.1	18 762	635.2	1 276.1
Cranston city	252	31.3	7 160	213.3	4 980	111.3	523.3	949.0	153	961.9	837.6	2 776	97.3	212.0
East Providence city	133	36.1	4 397	129.2	3 016	69.5	328.5	555.5	128	966.4	518.4	1 981	75.6	142.4
Newport city..............	NA	NA	NA	NA	NA	NA	NA	NA	31	89.5	D	119	4.3	10.0
Pawtucket city	205	40.5	9 766	294.3	6 755	165.5	682.5	1 535.2	92	231.7	213.4	953	27.8	60.6
Providence city	570	23.2	12 465	337.1	8 814	197.0	739.9	1 294.1	295	1 462.4	954.4	3 589	125.9	221.6
Warwick city	260	25.8	6 751	206.0	4 674	112.6	611.0	1 154.8	206	782.6	571.8	1 924	66.6	126.3
Woonsocket city	84	33.3	2 700	80.5	2 043	52.9	169.2	317.3	45	161.6	110.5	683	19.6	36.3

[1] Average number of production workers plus the number of other (nonproduction) employees for the pay period including March 12. [2] Average number of production workers for the pay periods including the 12th of March, May, August, and November. [3] Includes only establishments with payroll. [4] For pay period including March 12. [5] 1,000 to 2,499 employees. [6] 2,500 to 4,999 employees. [7] 500 to 999 employees. [8] 100 to 249 employees.

Sources: Manufacturing—U.S. Census Bureau, 1997 Economic Census – Manufacturing, generated by Statistical Compendia Branch, using American Factfinder at <http://www.census.gov/>, (June 2000) [related Internet site <http://www.census.gov/epcd/www/97EC31.HTM>]. Wholesale Trade—U.S. Census Bureau, 1997 Economic Census, individual state .pdf files from <http://www.census.gov/epcd/www/97EC42.HTM> (accessed June 2000) and ECON97 Report Series CD-ROM, CD-EC97-1, Disc 1E, issued February 2001.

Table C–5. Cities — Manufacturing and Wholesale Trade–Con.

[Includes states and 1,070 incorporated places of 25,000 or more population as of April 1, 1990 in all states except Hawaii which has no incorporated places recognized by the Census Bureau. For Hawaii, 8 census designated places (CDPs) of 25,000 or more population as of April 1, 1990 are included. Also included are the 5 boroughs of New York city. For more information on these areas, see appendix B. Geographic Information]

| | Manufacturing (NAICS 31-33), 1997 | | | | | | | | Wholesale trade[3] (NAICS 42), 1997 | | | | | |
| | Establishments | | All employees | | Production workers | | | | | Sales | | | | |
City	Total	Percent with 20 or more employees	Number[1]	Annual payroll (mil. dol.)	Number[2]	Wages (mil. dol.)	Value added by manufacture (mil. dol.)	Value of shipments (mil. dol.)	Establishments	Total (mil. dol.)	Merchant wholesalers (mil. dol.)	Paid employees[4]	Annual payroll (mil. dol.)	Operating expenses (mil. dol.)
SOUTH CAROLINA......	4 450	42.1	346 142	10 369.4	267 548	6 856.0	33 657.8	70 797.0	5 035	34 179.8	19 994.2	58 910	1 866.8	3 763.1
Anderson city	73	43.8	9 005	285.6	7 057	196.5	962.6	2 141.4	57	241.9	100.5	685	17.0	36.8
Charleston city	84	15.5	1 985	65.7	1 435	43.1	362.3	602.9	111	455.6	235.1	1 064	34.9	67.0
Columbia city...........	105	31.4	7 137	253.4	5 185	156.6	763.8	1 648.3	276	1 584.9	940.1	3 637	136.6	272.8
Florence city	52	40.4	4 653	148.6	3 107	76.2	343.3	701.2	93	D	D	(5)	D	D
Greenville city	159	40.3	14 641	504.2	11 402	350.3	1 956.0	4 021.7	288	6 613.6	D	3 975	162.4	327.4
Mount Pleasant town	NA	NA	NA	NA	NA	NA	NA	NA	52	161.2	49.4	178	7.5	14.0
North Charleston city	108	37.0	5 292	188.6	3 667	109.6	573.7	1 237.0	203	2 237.3	D	3 211	107.6	210.0
Rock Hill city	75	48.0	4 658	151.9	3 380	90.3	420.3	901.1	100	415.4	282.7	1 137	41.5	73.1
Spartanburg city	93	43.0	8 867	311.4	7 080	223.1	754.6	2 339.5	105	D	D	(5)	D	D
Sumter city	59	57.6	10 009	234.4	8 857	180.9	810.6	1 522.3	56	D	D	(0)	D	D
SOUTH DAKOTA........	888	32.9	46 539	1 162.6	33 230	707.4	3 880.9	12 305.5	1 402	7 874.2	6 181.7	15 509	389.8	794.3
Rapid City city	109	27.5	3 513	77.3	2 621	46.6	268.0	756.2	144	633.9	605.7	1 897	54.2	103.7
Sioux Falls city	133	39.1	11 605	301.9	8 550	193.9	580.0	2 995.2	313	2 073.5	1 611.3	5 146	157.5	296.1
TENNESSEE	7 407	39.2	483 823	14 351.9	375 121	9 468.8	44 355.2	98 503.1	8 234	82 626.4	47 023.5	120 228	3 975.4	8 044.6
Bartlett town	31	29.0	1 327	29.5	1 088	20.7	59.1	242.8	50	D	D	(6)	D	D
Chattanooga city...........	389	42.4	23 272	739.9	17 293	470.9	1 844.9	4 091.4	602	3 688.8	2 597.5	8 378	255.1	507.5
Clarksville city	70	38.6	6 047	169.5	5 104	125.7	688.7	1 190.7	86	D	D	(7)	D	D
Cleveland city	122	40.2	11 978	322.0	10 174	232.1	1 440.8	2 618.5	73	1 616.1	D	2 213	47.1	102.6
Columbia city.............	42	35.7	(5)	D	D	D	D	D	43	205.2	D	556	16.1	34.7
Germantown city	NA	NA	NA	NA	NA	NA	NA	NA	66	1 417.2	487.8	472	28.3	56.9
Hendersonville city	62	16.1	1 917	52.7	1 333	28.5	78.7	307.2	71	218.2	160.8	437	16.4	32.2
Jackson city	123	51.2	(8)	D	D	D	D	D	143	702.1	D	1 975	55.1	106.6
Johnson City city	101	57.4	8 801	211.5	7 022	146.1	444.7	1 074.1	126	1 086.4	960.5	1 843	47.4	97.3
Kingsport city	61	27.9	(8)	D	D	D	D	D	102	464.7	D	1 167	31.1	71.0
Knoxville city	318	34.6	14 827	394.5	11 352	253.7	1 060.6	2 429.9	671	4 595.8	2 819.7	8 791	309.0	567.3
Memphis city	688	39.4	32 938	1 104.8	22 128	618.2	3 593.5	8 888.5	1 470	24 961.4	11 265.6	27 381	948.4	1 878.8
Murfreesboro city	87	42.5	5 660	170.8	4 359	117.5	661.3	1 415.5	92	477.6	270.9	935	28.3	53.1
Nashville-Davidson (remainder)	721	35.1	(9)	D	D	D	D	D	1 377	16 474.9	8 989.6	25 290	938.6	1 860.1
Oak Ridge city.............	59	35.6	5 669	247.3	2 277	78.0	774.5	897.3	30	52.7	D	180	6.1	10.3
TEXAS	21 808	31.1	959 665	32 760.8	663 929	18 163.1	11 200.0	400.0	33 346	323 111.7	170 652.6	425 750	15 504.9	31 787.8
Abilene city	106	23.6	2 798	74.0	1 900	40.2	519.3	977.5	200	653.2	D	1 861	50.5	106.9
Amarillo city	176	25.0	(10)	D	D	D	D	D	307	1 466.5	1 177.9	3 565	115.7	222.2
Arlington city	323	31.6	13 408	481.6	9 335	294.9	1 374.8	2 909.8	519	4 614.2	1 971.8	6 347	226.9	470.7
Austin city	596	27.7	46 780	1 892.1	21 199	677.1	10 541.9	13 235.1	1 065	8 086.0	4 199.2	16 673	661.5	1 195.8
Baytown city	44	45.5	(11)	D	D	D	D	D	46	D	D	(6)	D	D
Beaumont city	131	30.5	5 882	250.9	4 083	158.1	1 210.5	5 041.5	271	1 379.4	1 043.3	3 246	107.6	208.5
Bedford city	24	12.5	(7)	D	D	D	D	D	84	335.6	87.3	332	17.8	31.1
Brownsville city	110	26.4	6 511	123.6	5 235	80.5	443.3	963.3	220	585.7	550.6	1 952	37.3	83.8
Bryan city	73	24.7	2 527	63.4	1 863	37.9	134.6	309.3	90	278.4	D	1 097	28.8	62.4
Carrollton city	227	46.7	13 714	532.5	9 569	256.5	1 362.4	2 502.0	431	14 382.2	3 587.6	7 788	312.8	675.3
College Station city	NA	NA	NA	NA	NA	NA	NA	NA	22	79.5	D	368	7.8	12.5
Conroe city	91	36.3	2 544	86.4	1 772	49.6	321.5	806.8	103	D	D	(5)	D	D
Corpus Christi city	205	26.8	(10)	D	D	D	D	D	453	1 656.2	1 262.2	4 708	144.5	278.7
Dallas city	1 762	34.3	77 920	2 884.1	48 530	1 337.3	9 756.2	15 722.9	3 470	35 859.7	16 483.1	49 621	2 128.0	3 971.7
Deer Park city	31	58.1	4 364	260.7	2 650	154.7	4 599.8	7 583.0	31	157.0	D	529	24.1	41.5
Del Rio city	NA	NA	NA	NA	NA	NA	NA	NA	30	54.5	45.4	291	5.1	11.5
Denton city	73	30.1	4 187	143.7	3 313	105.4	519.9	1 350.0	101	796.3	710.3	1 152	32.0	69.1
DeSoto city	NA	NA	NA	NA	NA	NA	NA	NA	42	68.0	56.5	194	6.3	12.9
Duncanville city.............	40	30.0	2 452	50.3	1 744	30.7	146.6	237.3	51	132.6	92.0	309	9.9	26.8
Edinburg city	26	50.0	2 134	32.5	1 817	24.4	236.1	471.5	45	204.9	181.7	1 145	15.9	32.1
El Paso city	599	34.2	33 212	716.2	26 525	482.3	3 115.9	7 602.1	950	5 954.5	4 571.9	10 705	300.9	679.7
Euless city	41	39.0	1 060	31.0	711	17.3	68.4	107.1	69	294.5	124.3	606	25.1	41.3
Fort Worth city	821	36.5	56 215	2 337.9	31 800	964.9	5 885.3	11 198.3	843	9 968.1	5 451.2	14 840	524.9	1 176.4
Galveston city	32	15.6	592	15.8	538	13.5	24.1	76.8	55	212.3	D	606	16.5	31.4
Garland city	377	37.4	16 285	556.5	9 809	233.2	1 467.0	2 944.6	283	2 727.3	1 926.5	4 671	170.5	323.7
Grand Prairie city	232	41.8	12 709	464.0	9 277	286.7	1 121.5	2 014.2	326	5 025.1	3 348.6	6 538	236.1	546.6
Grapevine city	36	33.3	1 539	47.6	929	23.0	139.5	310.4	60	425.5	D	411	21.7	43.4
Haltom City city	138	31.2	3 292	89.7	2 355	52.3	183.1	361.3	116	431.6	375.4	1 305	42.4	79.1
Harlingen city	65	32.3	4 480	86.1	3 872	67.7	229.2	562.4	96	359.9	233.3	1 170	27.4	52.9
Houston city.............	2 969	30.8	104 218	3 599.3	72 361	2 024.0	13 318.8	32 595.8	5 750	99 680.2	56 283.4	82 917	3 389.1	7 101.9
Huntsville city	NA	NA	NA	NA	NA	NA	NA	NA	25	D	D	(12)	D	D
Hurst city	43	23.3	716	17.5	522	12.5	48.6	104.7	63	183.4	121.7	416	14.6	27.8
Irving city	240	30.4	11 146	435.9	7 072	190.9	1 256.8	2 590.9	522	2 890.4	5 735.7	16 195	741.9	1 651.3
Killeen city	NA	NA	NA	NA	NA	NA	NA	NA	25	54.3	D	206	3.9	8.3

[1] Average number of production workers plus the number of other (nonproduction) employees for the pay period including March 12. [2] Average number of production workers for the pay periods including the 12th of March, May, August, and November. [3] Includes only establishments with payroll. [4] For pay period including March 12. [5] 1,000 to 2,499 employees. [6] 250 to 499 employees. [7] 500 to 999 employees. [8] 10,000 to 24,999 employees. [9] 25,000 to 49,999 employees. [10] 5,000 to 9,999 employees. [11] 2,500 to 4,999 employees. [12] 100 to 249 employees.

Sources: Manufacturing—U.S. Census Bureau, 1997 Economic Census – Manufacturing, generated by Statistical Compendia Branch, using American Factfinder at <http://www.census.gov/>, (June 2000) [related Internet site <http://www.census.gov/epcd/www/97EC31.HTM>]. Wholesale Trade—U.S. Census Bureau, 1997 Economic Census, individual state .pdf files from <http://www.census.gov/epcd/www/97EC42.HTM> (accessed June 2000) and ECON97 Report Series CD-ROM, CD-EC97-1, Disc 1E, issued February 2001.

Table C–5. Cities — **Manufacturing and Wholesale Trade**–Con.

[Includes states and 1,070 incorporated places of 25,000 or more population as of April 1, 1990 in all states except Hawaii which has no incorporated places recognized by the Census Bureau. For Hawaii, 8 census designated places (CDPs) of 25,000 or more population as of April 1, 1990 are included. Also included are the 5 boroughs of New York city. For more information on these areas, see appendix B. Geographic Information]

City	Manufacturing (NAICS 31-33), 1997								Wholesale trade[3] (NAICS 42), 1997					
	Establishments		All employees		Production workers		Value added by manufacture (mil. dol.)	Value of shipments (mil. dol.)	Estab-lishments	Sales		Paid employees[4]	Annual payroll (mil. dol.)	Operating expenses (mil. dol.)
	Total	Percent with 20 or more employees	Number[1]	Annual payroll (mil. dol.)	Number[2]	Wages (mil. dol.)				Total (mil. dol.)	Merchant wholesalers (mil. dol.)			
TEXAS—Con.														
Kingsville city	NA	NA	NA	NA	NA	NA	NA	NA	9	D	D	(5)	D	D
La Porte city	35	51.4	2 442	132.5	1 568	78.1	785.4	1 819.1	38	144.4	D	378	16.5	34.5
Laredo city	86	17.4	(6)	D	D	D	D	D	335	D	1 039.9	(6)	D	D
League City city	NA	NA	NA	NA	NA	NA	NA	NA	31	49.9	D	161	4.5	8.4
Lewisville city	85	32.9	5 347	219.5	3 155	88.6	617.9	930.8	95	773.7	425.1	1 348	43.6	87.4
Longview city	135	40.7	10 208	374.8	7 476	236.4	1 249.7	3 074.3	245	847.9	671.8	2 772	87.5	173.2
Lubbock city	210	27.6	6 357	182.3	4 331	86.8	828.9	1 465.0	446	3 705.7	2 869.9	6 118	170.6	366.5
Lufkin city	52	30.8	5 006	120.1	4 347	96.5	283.2	763.2	59	193.3	D	919	22.6	42.4
McAllen city	100	29.0	3 709	69.5	2 779	43.1	260.8	511.4	295	966.8	650.3	2 443	54.6	110.5
Mesquite city	72	31.9	3 338	111.1	2 395	68.1	739.7	1 147.3	88	1 384.1	D	1 505	48.8	116.3
Midland city	73	16.4	901	32.4	461	10.0	77.5	119.1	223	1 304.9	1 197.4	1 921	67.5	126.6
Mission city	27	18.5	1 176	22.1	1 050	18.5	88.4	177.9	36	96.7	89.0	264	6.0	13.9
Missouri City city	18	33.3	675	28.3	480	17.2	75.1	163.4	33	35.8	D	117	4.2	7.8
Nacogdoches city	36	50.0	3 101	92.5	2 507	67.8	232.8	719.6	37	118.3	D	355	10.0	22.4
New Braunfels city	59	39.0	3 525	86.2	2 726	54.1	274.8	449.9	65	301.5	173.0	506	16.8	40.8
North Richland Hills city	33	27.3	1 980	59.4	1 478	29.3	233.1	405.3	57	218.4	135.4	270	11.0	27.0
Odessa city	120	23.3	1 886	62.1	1 366	38.6	201.8	758.9	234	738.8	578.6	2 279	73.7	143.0
Pasadena city	100	39.0	5 905	270.7	4 111	155.5	1 435.0	4 893.4	110	589.6	271.0	1 583	56.5	97.9
Pharr city	NA	NA	NA	NA	NA	NA	NA	NA	55	201.6	D	713	14.0	30.1
Plano city	124	23.4	8 614	448.6	4 460	151.0	1 478.6	2 547.5	443	5 038.9	1 724.8	4 766	194.4	398.0
Port Arthur city	33	42.4	3 915	234.9	2 799	159.3	1 454.4	6 712.2	33	355.0	D	1 053	34.5	70.2
Richardson city	179	28.5	11 246	444.5	5 049	121.5	1 883.4	3 350.5	478	8 145.8	1 757.9	10 306	565.8	1 163.7
Round Rock city	69	43.5	(7)	D	D	D	D	D	70	433.2	286.5	767	27.9	52.4
San Angelo city	85	30.6	4 323	101.8	3 480	72.7	353.6	803.4	141	346.5	D	1 282	29.6	61.8
San Antonio city	953	27.4	32 870	911.6	23 027	494.2	2 552.0	5 199.7	1 650	12 097.5	7 864.7	23 198	756.4	1 488.2
San Marcos city	42	45.2	1 972	54.0	1 305	26.5	122.9	245.7	35	D	D	(8)	D	D
Sherman city	58	37.9	6 992	274.4	5 265	159.9	1 681.1	2 672.0	67	206.6	151.2	569	15.7	35.2
Temple city	59	54.2	5 515	183.0	4 332	131.6	596.1	1 164.7	76	1 271.7	D	2 081	69.5	114.0
Texarkana city	49	30.6	2 717	90.3	2 097	61.2	289.9	608.3	102	879.6	802.0	1 411	44.5	76.7
Texas City city	27	51.9	5 408	327.2	3 569	213.1	1 632.2	8 922.0	40	109.0	D	223	9.0	15.1
Tyler city	115	33.0	9 228	339.0	7 143	237.1	996.1	2 068.8	186	990.8	504.9	2 189	71.3	140.7
Victoria city	60	23.3	2 765	111.0	2 040	76.5	569.2	1 195.5	125	D	325.3	(6)	D	D
Waco city	177	46.9	14 884	444.3	10 629	268.9	1 987.8	3 608.3	210	1 481.1	1 265.5	2 956	82.1	170.6
Wichita Falls city	121	25.6	6 090	206.0	4 731	148.6	570.3	1 069.6	176	391.2	306.6	1 771	41.0	81.7
UTAH	2 860	30.1	119 140	3 726.1	84 129	2 218.7	11 343.5	24 014.4	3 277	21 271.9	13 618.2	44 312	1 420.4	2 763.4
Bountiful city	37	18.9	504	12.3	375	8.8	27.0	54.1	51	95.9	58.6	221	6.7	13.9
Layton city	NA	NA	NA	NA	NA	NA	NA	NA	41	121.1	76.9	401	8.3	27.4
Logan city	79	38.0	5 455	124.5	3 628	78.1	283.9	909.8	53	74.9	73.3	409	8.1	15.8
Murray city	148	19.6	2 680	61.9	2 032	37.1	136.9	247.3	186	967.7	366.9	2 103	64.1	115.4
Ogden city	130	34.6	13 226	410.9	10 339	313.5	1 546.5	2 696.5	127	504.5	381.9	1 654	45.5	86.3
Orem city	99	28.3	2 359	61.3	1 688	36.8	142.0	272.6	103	481.7	456.8	1 047	31.4	68.6
Provo city	93	31.2	3 367	79.8	2 440	52.6	191.4	346.7	91	1 748.9	1 688.9	3 704	114.1	262.0
St. George city	60	33.3	1 377	35.5	1 043	24.5	107.6	191.3	66	216.8	204.0	559	16.4	35.9
Salt Lake City city	512	36.9	25 306	813.8	15 769	401.9	2 306.2	4 894.8	714	7 718.7	4 899.7	13 524	471.1	883.1
Sandy city	92	21.7	2 662	82.1	1 838	40.0	187.8	309.5	147	412.4	174.4	1 070	24.7	48.9
West Jordan city	76	39.5	2 567	91.1	1 920	58.1	156.0	433.5	53	262.3	170.7	626	17.7	39.8
West Valley City city	170	34.7	6 627	230.8	4 163	105.7	637.8	1 199.4	185	1 670.6	739.7	3 139	124.1	226.2
VERMONT	1 226	27.7	42 533	1 459.6	29 318	758.0	4 044.6	7 803.0	941	4 731.4	4 109.5	10 987	330.6	740.3
Burlington city	55	25.5	(6)	D	D	D	D	D	58	331.5	D	678	24.6	44.5
VIRGINIA	5 986	34.1	370 595	11 557.8	279 682	7 412.2	43 563.0	83 814.0	7 868	61 046.7	34 446.6	106 365	3 784.4	7 276.7
Alexandria city	114	20.2	1 907	59.4	1 230	33.8	194.8	328.1	137	899.6	395.0	1 830	75.1	146.6
Blacksburg town	23	30.4	1 910	57.8	1 501	42.6	149.3	225.3	8	D	D	(9)	D	D
Charlottesville city	67	28.4	(10)	D	D	D	D	D	81	265.9	D	954	29.7	63.2
Chesapeake city	132	34.1	4 558	147.0	2 967	80.9	336.7	1 085.0	246	1 768.2	1 069.1	3 833	115.7	233.6
Danville city	47	48.9	(11)	D	D	D	D	D	55	211.8	D	964	22.6	42.7
Hampton city	80	28.8	4 636	123.4	3 636	81.3	422.7	971.0	94	370.7	D	1 073	31.3	57.2
Harrisonburg city	38	47.4	3 687	102.6	2 985	73.9	254.3	725.8	62	749.2	D	971	25.5	88.8
Lynchburg city	117	44.4	12 535	481.1	8 365	257.1	1 602.6	3 096.4	100	504.6	298.1	1 292	43.8	86.3
Manassas city	34	32.4	2 822	188.5	582	20.2	594.7	791.6	59	626.3	524.7	1 008	41.0	66.8
Newport News city	131	33.6	24 707	898.4	19 157	574.7	1 653.6	3 300.5	132	604.2	482.9	1 634	50.3	99.3
Norfolk city	199	34.2	10 996	402.2	8 838	303.4	2 789.7	5 737.3	324	2 914.6	2 003.5	5 845	183.9	361.9
Petersburg city	43	46.5	2 553	72.4	1 771	39.1	145.4	409.6	35	139.2	D	538	16.8	32.0

[1] Average number of production workers plus the number of other (nonproduction) employees for the pay period including March 12. [2] Average number of production workers for the pay periods including the 12th of March, May, August, and November. [3] Includes only establishments with payroll. [4] For pay period including March 12. [5] 20 to 99 employees. [6] 1,000 to 2,499 employees. [7] 5,000 to 9,999 employees. [8] 250 to 499 employees. [9] 100 to 249 employees. [10] 2,500 to 4,999 employees. [11] 10,000 to 24,999 employees.

Sources: Manufacturing—U.S. Census Bureau, 1997 Economic Census - Manufacturing, generated by Statistical Compendia Branch, using American Factfinder at <http://www.census.gov/>, (June 2000) [related Internet site <http://www.census.gov/epcd/www/97EC31.HTM>]. Wholesale Trade—U.S. Census Bureau, 1997 Economic Census, individual state .pdf files from <http://www.census.gov/epcd/www/97EC42.HTM> (accessed June 2000) and ECON97 Report Series CD-ROM, CD-EC97-1, Disc 1E, issued February 2001.

Table C–5. Cities — **Manufacturing and Wholesale Trade**–Con.

[Includes states and 1,070 incorporated places of 25,000 or more population as of April 1, 1990 in all states except Hawaii which has no incorporated places recognized by the Census Bureau. For Hawaii, 8 census designated places (CDPs) of 25,000 or more population as of April 1, 1990 are included. Also included are the 5 boroughs of New York city. For more information on these areas, see appendix B. Geographic Information]

| | Manufacturing (NAICS 31-33), 1997 | | | | | | | | Wholesale trade[3] (NAICS 42), 1997 | | | | | |
| City | Establishments | | All employees | | Production workers | | Value added by manufacture (mil. dol.) | Value of shipments (mil. dol.) | Establishments | Sales | | Paid employees[4] | Annual payroll (mil. dol.) | Operating expenses (mil. dol.) |
	Total	Percent with 20 or more employees	Number[1]	Annual payroll (mil. dol.)	Number[2]	Wages (mil. dol.)				Total (mil. dol.)	Merchant wholesalers (mil. dol.)			
VIRGINIA—Con.														
Portsmouth city	71	21.1	1 812	52.0	1 341	33.6	143.6	368.7	63	167.3	141.1	712	23.6	44.5
Richmond city	325	36.6	21 879	941.2	14 775	539.5	8 229.6	11 748.3	464	5 979.5	3 318.3	7 572	283.5	539.0
Roanoke city	152	38.2	8 489	242.9	5 819	144.1	1 213.4	2 156.3	299	1 292.7	796.5	3 768	121.0	229.9
Suffolk city	52	44.2	2 257	63.8	1 920	48.6	539.6	1 103.5	61	822.5	344.6	1 305	43.7	87.2
Virginia Beach city	236	20.3	5 806	139.3	3 913	82.1	380.4	967.2	479	1 922.8	1 506.5	5 642	159.4	300.6
WASHINGTON	7 801	27.7	328 511	13 004.1	213 330	7 046.4	30 434.8	78 852.5	10 039	75 397.8	47 863.7	118 810	4 376.0	8 684.1
Auburn city	167	23.4	13 946	605.2	9 598	438.1	1 205.7	1 875.8	135	1 409.5	1 099.9	2 935	90.0	185.5
Bellevue city	163	17.8	2 740	93.3	1 754	48.4	281.2	681.8	579	11 707.9	2 784.3	6 532	316.2	584.8
Bellingham city	130	24.6	3 457	91.5	2 562	61.9	235.2	583.9	154	570.4	506.0	1 264	38.9	91.1
Bremerton city	NA	NA	NA	NA	NA	NA	NA	NA	24	86.9	D	289	10.0	20.0
Edmonds city	NA	NA	NA	NA	NA	NA	NA	NA	70	325.1	D	316	11.4	23.1
Everett city	130	36.9	(5)	D	D	D	D	D	144	592.6	500.1	1 570	56.1	119.8
Kennewick city	46	8.7	(6)	D	D	D	D	D	59	193.2	176.8	419	11.3	25.1
Kent city	295	43.1	26 894	1 274.8	12 515	396.2	2 503.7	3 997.4	454	5 480.1	3 619.6	9 062	346.8	713.9
Kirkland city	93	22.6	1 941	63.2	1 366	34.8	194.1	315.8	206	2 421.9	720.0	2 341	135.7	223.8
Longview city	46	37.0	2 556	115.2	1 908	80.3	336.9	824.3	46	108.0	103.3	488	12.9	24.1
Lynnwood city	61	23.0	1 526	40.8	1 084	23.4	75.0	145.9	87	726.1	274.4	835	29.7	57.6
Olympia city	47	31.9	1 368	47.3	1 118	36.6	155.7	387.0	74	204.8	118.7	647	23.7	39.5
Redmond city	227	38.3	11 807	448.5	6 686	173.2	1 297.9	2 183.7	344	4 405.2	3 439.5	4 489	202.9	546.8
Renton city	70	34.3	(5)	D	D	D	D	D	126	1 709.3	1 114.3	3 117	121.8	204.2
Richland city	28	17.9	1 449	65.6	980	32.3	138.6	294.2	22	D	D	(7)	D	D
Seattle city	1 213	28.7	33 935	1 132.7	22 619	651.0	2 723.0	5 021.1	1 860	16 085.6	11 685.5	23 635	978.1	1 887.5
Spokane city	315	28.3	6 862	210.0	4 435	121.0	447.4	927.5	521	2 709.8	1 845.5	7 028	214.1	394.2
Tacoma city	276	37.7	10 894	363.5	8 320	250.4	1 037.1	2 625.6	318	2 819.6	2 296.1	4 790	181.7	352.6
Vancouver city	193	38.3	13 073	494.0	10 504	355.3	1 316.8	2 515.9	248	1 237.4	717.4	2 277	86.5	188.3
Walla Walla city	43	20.9	1 137	31.2	928	21.8	95.6	154.7	56	D	180.7	(8)	D	D
Yakima city	102	33.3	4 624	124.0	3 513	85.7	320.1	747.7	152	1 047.5	911.4	2 984	87.5	166.4
WEST VIRGINIA	1 505	34.4	72 813	2 460.7	55 643	1 658.9	9 311.0	18 293.3	1 956	10 290.4	6 503.4	23 805	681.1	1 396.6
Charleston city	44	31.8	2 152	85.5	1 427	53.4	113.8	278.2	179	1 386.6	757.2	2 738	84.0	161.3
Huntington city	72	44.4	5 111	176.3	3 781	124.0	569.7	1 034.8	136	551.4	445.4	1 803	50.0	100.3
Morgantown city	20	30.0	(9)	D	D	D	D	D	36	D	54.1	(8)	D	D
Parkersburg city	30	26.7	1 103	31.6	872	22.8	67.9	113.6	78	350.0	D	917	23.9	51.7
Wheeling city	53	35.8	(9)	D	D	D	D	D	89	1 361.1	D	1 694	47.1	98.5
WISCONSIN	9 936	39.3	562 479	18 766.4	416 254	11 952.6	54 947.1	11 100.0	8 025	57 192.9	35 760.6	110 309	3 764.9	7 173.4
Appleton city	120	42.5	8 235	314.7	5 399	178.1	949.9	2 168.1	94	583.2	510.1	1 631	56.7	100.9
Beloit city	52	42.3	4 896	198.9	3 398	115.0	666.9	1 257.5	17	185.9	D	288	13.7	31.6
Brookfield city	90	32.2	2 873	102.5	2 058	64.8	244.1	456.6	226	1 541.1	536.1	3 092	141.5	233.0
Eau Claire city	93	37.6	4 353	115.6	3 358	76.5	369.9	623.5	100	754.4	536.9	1 629	52.3	103.7
Fond du Lac city	93	39.8	7 301	297.4	5 015	183.0	888.8	1 609.5	66	361.7	D	848	27.2	56.5
Green Bay city	200	41.5	16 692	695.3	12 174	406.4	1 768.4	4 634.5	201	1 316.0	746.7	2 733	88.9	186.9
Greenfield city	NA	NA	NA	NA	NA	NA	NA	NA	36	D	D	(8)	D	D
Janesville city	104	38.5	12 380	504.2	10 247	395.1	3 016.1	8 390.6	68	1 270.6	1 248.5	1 829	60.4	137.1
Kenosha city	126	38.1	5 949	280.6	4 661	211.0	533.4	1 287.7	66	208.6	109.5	853	27.3	53.9
La Crosse city	91	36.3	7 001	246.2	4 728	137.5	367.4	1 110.3	92	1 746.4	D	2 701	88.7	149.5
Madison city	228	34.6	11 464	370.4	8 407	240.7	1 344.5	2 573.9	324	1 621.6	1 278.2	4 530	149.1	289.4
Manitowoc city	88	56.8	9 202	280.1	7 213	189.3	819.4	1 478.9	34	192.3	D	370	15.3	32.7
Menomonee Falls village	211	47.4	9 784	354.1	6 613	199.0	745.8	1 476.3	151	1 051.2	654.3	1 762	74.2	145.8
Milwaukee city	848	37.9	46 467	1 643.5	32 625	967.2	4 168.5	8 392.4	753	8 379.2	3 971.2	14 029	531.4	1 007.0
New Berlin city	150	52.0	6 647	259.0	4 721	149.0	732.6	1 299.8	166	1 064.5	817.4	2 918	107.1	193.7
Oshkosh city	114	57.0	8 692	291.8	6 352	189.5	718.8	1 860.5	72	323.1	226.1	1 078	32.7	64.7
Racine city	219	36.1	9 065	322.3	6 388	187.6	1 118.6	1 845.0	101	2 300.4	D	1 974	67.7	149.4
Sheboygan city	99	55.6	7 887	260.6	6 595	149.3	664.0	1 415.6	57	712.8	677.8	1 173	38.1	60.8
Superior city	45	24.4	(9)	D	D	D	D	D	48	D	D	(6)	D	D
Waukesha city	195	40.5	9 902	394.2	6 539	230.9	1 361.2	2 578.4	203	3 554.5	1 317.6	2 738	114.7	193.6
Wausau city	83	45.8	8 190	228.8	6 401	150.8	564.7	1 192.1	71	306.1	280.7	873	27.8	54.0
Wauwatosa city	81	29.6	7 766	342.8	4 912	204.6	877.7	1 388.8	140	1 773.5	1 495.2	2 622	89.9	183.0
West Allis city	145	30.3	7 537	226.4	5 315	130.0	422.2	864.7	128	578.4	389.4	1 797	66.2	112.5
WYOMING	503	17.9	8 448	256.4	6 426	174.8	1 031.1	2 955.1	800	2 547.1	1 995.0	5 761	161.9	323.7
Casper city	NA	NA	NA	NA	NA	NA	NA	NA	122	687.1	620.6	921	25.6	54.3
Cheyenne city	35	40.0	(9)	D	D	D	D	D	56	178.2	165.4	457	13.4	25.1
Laramie city	NA	NA	NA	NA	NA	NA	NA	NA	19	81.5	81.5	101	2.3	5.5

[1] Average number of production workers plus the number of other (nonproduction) employees for the pay period including March 12.   [2] Average number of production workers for the pay periods including the 12th of March, May, August, and November.   [3] Includes only establishments with payroll.   [4] For pay period including March 12.   [5] 25,000 to 49,999 employees.   [6] 500 to 999 employees.   [7] 100 to 249 employees.   [8] 250 to 499 employees.   [9] 1,000 to 2,499 employees.

Sources: Manufacturing—U.S. Census Bureau, 1997 Economic Census – Manufacturing, generated by Statistical Compendia Branch, using American Factfinder at <http://www.census.gov/>, (June 2000) [related Internet site <http://www.census.gov/epcd/www/97ECON31.HTM>].   Wholesale Trade—U.S. Census Bureau, 1997 Economic Census, individual state .pdf files from <http://www.census.gov/epcd/www/97EC42.HTM> (accessed June 2000) and ECON97 Report Series CD-ROM, CD-EC97-1, Disc 1E, issued February 2001.

Table C–6. Cities — Retail Trade and Accommodation and Foodservices

[Includes states and 1,070 incorporated places of 25,000 or more population as of April 1, 1990 in all states except Hawaii which has no incorporated places recognized by the Census Bureau. For Hawaii, 8 census designated places (CDPs) of 25,000 or more population as of April 1, 1990 are included. Also included are the 5 boroughs of New York city. For more information on these areas, see appendix B. Geographic Information]

City	Retail trade[1] (NAICS 44-45), 1997								Accommodation and foodservices[1] (NAICS 72), 1997				
	Sales						Annual payroll		Sales				
			Per capita[2]		Percent from general merchandise stores								Annual payroll ($1,000)
	Establishments	Total ($1,000)	Amount (dollars)	Percent of national average		Paid employees[3]	Total ($1,000)	Per paid employee (dollars)	Establishments	Total ($1,000)	Percent from foodservices[4]	Paid employees[3]	
ALABAMA	20 163	36 623 327	8 477	92.2	15.5	231 665	3 381 730	14 598	6 955	3 881 782	84.0	134 719	1 059 642
Anniston city	273	521 531	19 752	214.9	D	3 220	47 642	14 796	86	48 255	91.9	1 683	12 705
Auburn city	198	385 089	9 534	103.7	D	2 851	37 213	13 053	125	76 317	79.0	3 013	20 152
Bessemer city	209	518 997	16 487	179.4	D	2 773	45 093	16 261	52	33 261	89.7	1 459	9 280
Birmingham city	1 150	3 085 494	12 219	133.0	8.0	16 618	294 707	17 734	524	346 844	81.1	10 504	99 636
Decatur city	410	921 937	16 833	183.2	D	4 920	74 212	15 084	137	86 492	85.9	3 117	25 277
Dothan city	547	1 199 204	20 750	225.8	D	7 148	116 047	16 235	176	111 045	D	3 527	28 297
Florence city	353	710 047	18 159	197.6	25.9	5 049	68 694	13 605	109	59 597	95.8	2 242	17 396
Gadsden city	290	503 504	11 991	130.5	22.7	3 148	45 244	14 372	102	56 698	D	1 953	15 698
Hoover city	203	874 235	15 263	166.1	8.2	4 812	81 998	17 040	90	60 314	91.2	1 916	17 196
Huntsville city	945	2 268 581	12 989	141.3	D	14 647	219 335	14 975	400	282 135	79.8	8 853	76 572
Mobile city	1 140	2 573 227	12 838	139.7	16.8	17 003	261 239	15 364	482	301 597	81.2	10 102	84 826
Montgomery city	1 091	2 425 286	12 261	133.4	D	15 619	232 273	14 871	411	277 289	D	9 983	76 471
Phenix City city	127	181 111	6 482	70.5	D	1 470	18 587	12 644	60	30 364	92.2	882	7 868
Prichard city	77	71 147	2 099	22.8	3.2	566	8 797	15 542	26	D	D	(5)	D
Tuscaloosa city	577	1 250 922	14 899	162.1	D	8 496	122 289	14 394	252	171 577	80.5	6 355	47 354
ALASKA	2 866	6 251 372	10 268	111.7	20.0	32 502	670 465	20 628	1 763	1 065 459	68.5	20 587	301 523
Anchorage city	1 001	3 114 874	12 392	134.8	22.5	15 115	319 285	21 124	640	573 955	71.1	11 364	165 792
Fairbanks city	248	726 964	22 506	244.9	D	3 356	77 202	23 004	121	86 658	65.9	1 989	23 437
Juneau city	173	312 748	10 323	112.3	33.2	1 807	37 191	20 582	94	57 721	69.8	1 117	16 123
ARIZONA	16 283	43 960 933	9 657	105.1	13.0	232 050	4 223 879	18 202	9 094	6 634 744	66.5	184 382	1 823 706
Chandler city	283	1 190 697	7 870	85.6	D	5 528	127 136	22 999	207	130 247	82.9	3 846	35 905
Flagstaff city	367	784 611	13 916	151.4	D	5 011	79 029	15 771	268	179 708	60.5	5 144	46 991
Gilbert town	110	362 737	4 827	52.5	D	1 870	39 230	20 979	44	24 256	D	783	6 331
Glendale city	598	2 311 884	12 219	133.1	19.8	11 308	203 316	17 980	293	187 017	96.9	6 042	51 116
Mesa city	1 405	4 348 728	12 319	134.0	18.1	23 747	420 169	17 694	577	411 391	81.9	12 355	108 857
Peoria city	149	454 486	5 660	61.6	15.4	2 558	46 610	18 221	74	35 432	D	1 128	10 006
Phoenix city	3 807	11 407 585	9 643	104.9	10.8	58 531	1 123 223	19 190	2 224	2 009 068	64.9	50 283	555 256
Prescott city	251	513 746	15 016	163.4	14.5	2 822	52 483	18 598	140	64 124	78.8	2 037	17 322
Scottsdale city	1 232	3 614 557	19 509	212.3	D	16 189	342 417	21 151	564	723 767	D	18 406	211 906
Sierra Vista city	145	371 375	9 747	106.1	D	2 321	37 129	15 997	77	38 448	81.6	1 455	10 062
Tempe city	728	3 491 855	21 233	231.0	D	13 575	295 266	21 751	514	345 367	85.2	10 694	95 879
Tucson city	2 079	5 370 201	11 707	127.4	15.4	30 607	547 728	17 896	1 152	704 694	79.9	23 793	199 153
Yuma city	300	697 945	11 101	120.8	D	4 376	66 246	15 138	175	97 925	79.0	3 289	24 638
ARKANSAS	12 600	21 643 695	8 575	93.3	18.4	132 335	1 904 412	14 391	4 663	2 179 696	81.9	73 397	589 917
Conway city	248	526 241	13 263	144.3	D	3 111	47 827	15 374	91	60 967	D	2 125	16 752
Fayetteville city	401	790 006	13 827	150.5	29.3	5 711	79 910	13 992	222	110 663	82.0	3 881	31 419
Fort Smith city	599	1 282 639	17 016	185.2	D	8 197	121 416	14 812	239	133 079	88.8	4 463	36 614
Hot Springs city	399	807 600	21 361	232.4	19.7	4 583	69 260	15 112	175	107 075	D	3 544	33 198
Jacksonville city	109	239 819	8 298	90.3	20.8	1 394	22 533	16 164	52	27 325	89.3	893	6 860
Jonesboro city	410	770 309	15 071	164.0	D	5 146	73 849	14 351	118	D	D	(6)	D
Little Rock city	1 101	2 590 542	14 787	160.9	15.9	15 944	236 869	14 856	490	328 995	76.5	10 389	95 837
North Little Rock city	466	1 328 519	21 899	238.3	D	7 671	121 918	15 893	186	126 002	83.5	4 378	34 428
Pine Bluff city	349	653 485	12 273	133.5	17.3	4 359	65 956	15 131	118	D	D	(7)	D
Springdale city	278	614 957	14 909	162.2	D	3 463	58 805	16 981	124	66 199	73.8	2 099	17 869
West Memphis city	151	402 238	14 872	161.8	D	2 170	26 976	12 431	65	45 627	72.3	1 307	11 688
CALIFORNIA	106 357	263 118 346	8 167	88.9	13.1	1 354 797	26 362 691	19 459	62 629	42 312 641	73.8	1 054 106	11 455 306
Alameda city	204	408 550	5 449	59.3	8.8	2 329	48 539	20 841	165	66 856	94.8	1 908	17 884
Alhambra city	249	983 162	11 814	128.6	18.0	3 672	75 989	20 694	172	91 017	87.9	2 627	24 179
Anaheim city	963	2 773 742	9 467	103.0	10.4	13 119	278 206	21 206	689	818 622	42.6	18 054	222 930
Antioch city	197	500 123	6 352	69.1	D	2 898	51 432	17 747	109	54 136	98.4	1 501	13 498
Apple Valley town	68	146 590	2 641	28.7	D	960	14 588	15 196	41	17 197	97.4	612	4 241
Arcadia city	283	509 747	10 269	111.7	22.9	4 000	59 830	14 958	134	84 372	81.6	2 232	21 022
Azusa city	89	306 971	7 359	80.1	D	1 226	26 722	21 796	63	31 389	96.0	894	7 838
Bakersfield city	918	2 382 176	11 115	120.9	D	12 207	230 005	18 842	472	272 641	86.5	7 956	72 796
Baldwin Park city	125	204 462	2 870	31.2	13.8	1 041	21 243	20 406	60	32 616	90.4	839	7 632
Bell city	62	102 140	2 939	32.0	D	483	10 272	21 267	50	25 465	94.1	684	5 514
Bellflower city	169	439 420	6 969	75.8	D	2 116	40 989	19 371	88	38 892	92.1	1 057	8 840
Bell Gardens city	80	104 030	2 371	25.8	D	584	9 519	16 300	37	15 700	88.2	382	3 311
Berkeley city	536	1 238 700	11 589	126.1	D	6 313	131 907	20 895	369	199 441	78.1	4 742	57 238
Beverly Hills city	414	1 377 369	42 935	467.2	D	5 910	170 765	28 894	188	297 902	D	6 230	92 677

[1] Includes only establishments with payroll. [2] Based on resident population estimated as of July 1, 1997. [3] For pay period including March 12. [4] Foodservices and drinking places (NAICS 722) includes full-service restaurants, limited-service eating places, special food services, and drinking places (alcoholic beverages). [5] 250 to 499 employees. [6] 2,500 to 4,999 employees. [7] 1,000 to 2,499 employees.

Sources: Retail Trade—U.S. Census Bureau, 1997 Economic Census, ECON97 Report Series CD-ROM, CD-EC97-1, Disc 1D issued July 2000 and Disc 1E issued February 2001 (related Internet site <http://www.census.gov/epcd/www/97EC44.HTM>). Accommodation and Foodservices—U.S. Census Bureau, 1997 Economic Census, ECON97 Report Series CD-ROM, Disc 1E issued February 2001 (related Internet site <http://www.census.gov/epcd/www/97EC72.HTM>).

[Includes states and 1,070 incorporated places of 25,000 or more population as of April 1, 1990 in all states except Hawaii which has no incorporated places recognized by the Census Bureau. For Hawaii, 8 census designated places (CDPs) of 25,000 or more population as of April 1, 1990 are included. Also included are the 5 boroughs of New York city. For more information on these areas, see appendix B. Geographic Information]

	Retail trade[1] (NAICS 44-45), 1997								Accommodation and foodservices[1] (NAICS 72), 1997				
		Sales				Annual payroll				Sales			
			Per capita[2]		Percent from general mer-chandise stores						Percent from food-services[4]		
City	Estab-lishments	Total ($1,000)	Amount (dollars)	Percent of national average		Paid employees[3]	Total ($1,000)	Per paid employee (dollars)	Estab-lishments	Total ($1,000)		Paid employees[3]	Annual payroll ($1,000)
CALIFORNIA—Con.													
Brea city	296	765 511	21 851	237.8	20.9	5 094	75 623	14 846	103	85 039	D	2 393	21 898
Buena Park city	235	966 606	13 360	145.4	10.3	3 793	88 459	23 322	119	102 000	76.0	2 750	27 912
Burbank city	381	1 306 063	13 440	146.2	D	5 981	110 629	18 497	237	201 162	81.8	4 766	53 009
Burlingame city	192	546 304	19 484	212.0	D	2 282	59 251	25 965	123	287 426	47.5	4 988	83 817
Camarillo city	249	607 888	10 424	113.4	6.9	3 110	58 922	18 946	112	69 671	86.6	1 846	17 557
Campbell city	216	712 631	18 516	201.5	D	3 342	66 979	20 042	122	87 617	92.5	2 124	24 245
Carlsbad city	355	1 120 511	15 955	173.6	D	4 855	106 709	21 979	166	186 544	D	4 176	50 434
Carson city	216	949 459	10 946	119.1	D	4 505	100 005	22 199	118	63 607	87.8	1 606	15 677
Cathedral City city	169	574 017	15 362	167.2	D	2 421	52 620	21 735	86	32 439	92.1	957	8 276
Ceres city	81	222 736	6 929	75.4	29.5	1 350	20 891	15 475	43	20 400	D	566	4 765
Cerritos city	279	1 934 276	36 245	394.4	15.3	7 822	159 802	20 430	99	72 877	D	1 972	21 638
Chico city	420	987 820	19 486	212.0	D	5 812	97 658	16 803	210	94 142	91.6	3 754	26 041
Chino city	184	554 203	8 643	94.0	17.1	2 963	55 598	18 764	89	56 949	96.5	1 816	14 863
Chula Vista city	546	1 276 637	8 204	89.3	D	7 502	125 657	16 750	281	157 461	85.2	4 376	40 002
Claremont city	97	321 626	9 500	103.4	D	1 251	26 669	21 318	70	40 018	89.1	1 235	11 461
Clovis city	262	852 988	13 339	145.1	D	4 319	78 355	18 142	133	D	D	(5)	D
Colton city	103	327 592	7 680	83.6	D	1 682	33 120	19 691	75	33 543	96.0	1 021	8 553
Compton city	148	375 190	4 121	44.8	4.5	1 811	33 468	18 480	63	23 386	98.1	687	5 535
Concord city	481	1 654 950	14 328	155.9	D	7 295	164 337	22 527	218	141 786	87.2	3 621	38 204
Corona city	270	1 066 373	10 095	109.8	D	4 513	95 986	21 269	136	77 756	96.5	2 311	19 666
Coronado city	75	64 786	2 242	24.4	NA	529	8 457	15 987	70	126 226	34.4	2 236	36 948
Costa Mesa city	693	2 343 258	23 014	250.4	14.4	12 297	251 847	20 480	316	283 106	69.9	6 655	75 527
Covina city	177	537 892	12 217	132.9	D	2 632	52 267	19 858	106	63 348	67.9	1 603	15 978
Culver City city	341	884 909	22 516	245.0	D	4 970	97 614	19 641	153	118 899	67.9	2 491	33 520
Cupertino city	248	509 180	11 443	124.5	D	3 355	55 023	16 400	138	109 434	89.0	2 657	30 548
Cypress city	100	310 563	6 558	71.4	D	1 254	25 691	20 487	89	48 523	81.5	1 400	12 350
Daly City city	240	524 883	5 301	57.7	11.9	3 214	52 316	16 278	115	82 444	96.8	2 049	21 389
Dana Point city	114	306 294	9 049	98.5	D	1 295	27 646	21 348	72	140 508	D	2 515	34 752
Danville city	139	352 762	8 942	97.3	D	1 599	31 070	19 431	99	D	D	(5)	D
Davis city	139	324 611	6 055	65.9	NA	1 885	37 392	19 837	118	57 147	91.8	1 930	14 325
Diamond Bar city	102	204 334	3 802	41.4	D	1 031	17 368	16 846	69	35 224	95.4	1 021	9 115
Downey city	295	1 001 140	11 451	124.6	16.6	4 694	103 603	22 071	183	116 639	93.0	2 964	29 961
El Cajon city	497	1 211 804	13 094	142.5	14.2	6 539	123 631	18 907	211	103 415	93.1	2 819	25 393
El Centro city	172	417 681	10 744	116.9	D	2 393	42 961	17 953	96	42 979	81.7	1 294	10 927
El Monte city	245	1 335 284	12 156	132.3	4.5	3 320	96 574	29 089	128	53 219	97.4	1 317	11 726
Encinitas city	224	493 401	8 403	91.4	D	2 525	50 587	20 034	148	73 438	88.8	2 207	20 682
Escondido city	600	1 765 602	14 960	162.8	D	9 390	185 984	19 807	234	124 234	86.7	3 526	33 075
Eureka city	271	539 732	20 970	228.2	D	3 173	53 874	16 979	146	64 704	69.7	1 951	17 085
Fairfield city	336	940 907	10 615	115.5	D	5 090	92 986	18 268	133	79 540	87.2	2 346	20 243
Folsom city	162	444 942	10 443	113.6	D	2 134	41 588	19 488	103	D	D	(5)	D
Fontana city	209	773 617	7 257	79.0	D	4 001	75 074	18 764	119	55 762	96.3	1 530	13 465
Foster City city	60	246 874	8 210	89.3	D	1 171	23 871	20 385	62	51 172	60.8	1 206	13 443
Fountain Valley city	218	632 180	11 262	122.5	9.6	3 242	57 411	17 709	129	74 838	D	1 996	18 368
Fremont city	440	1 705 061	8 612	93.7	10.3	6 544	152 053	23 235	290	176 772	87.5	4 612	44 178
Fresno city	1 546	3 589 549	9 028	98.2	15.2	19 850	362 824	18 278	801	433 607	86.0	13 929	119 901
Fullerton city	292	938 604	7 765	84.5	14.2	4 361	88 007	20 180	199	136 970	85.2	3 792	37 038
Gardena city	175	439 316	8 124	88.4	D	2 196	44 086	20 076	162	67 990	93.2	1 734	16 817
Garden Grove city	413	1 247 852	8 289	90.2	14.2	5 618	116 343	20 709	278	138 132	81.6	3 868	36 493
Gilroy city	273	664 777	18 615	202.6	D	3 118	60 054	19 260	83	48 250	89.3	1 147	10 413
Glendale city	725	1 844 206	10 035	109.2	10.7	9 426	188 131	19 959	305	191 671	87.0	4 932	51 553
Glendora city	133	341 514	6 909	75.2	D	1 758	34 712	19 745	78	39 196	95.3	1 149	10 361
Hanford city	184	414 553	11 304	123.0	D	2 512	41 187	16 396	91	40 739	96.9	1 256	10 307
Hawthorne city	187	528 441	7 259	79.0	D	2 581	49 117	19 030	98	57 775	93.2	1 272	12 428
Hayward city	438	1 460 620	11 452	124.6	9.1	6 541	147 610	22 567	236	112 925	87.6	2 959	27 900
Hemet city	221	561 743	10 341	112.5	D	3 349	60 008	17 918	106	44 482	95.8	1 332	11 186
Hesperia city	129	200 236	3 260	35.5	D	1 161	21 361	18 399	68	26 690	96.6	873	7 146
Highland city	50	109 094	2 669	29.0	D	578	9 202	15 920	35	D	D	(6)	D
Huntington Beach city	601	1 700 614	8 798	95.7	8.5	8 063	160 624	19 921	378	237 890	83.3	6 467	64 305
Huntington Park city	173	296 213	5 137	55.9	3.3	1 658	30 924	18 651	74	D	D	(7)	D
Imperial Beach city	43	34 053	1 207	13.1	D	254	3 519	13 854	47	13 946	88.4	430	3 675
Indio city	136	327 036	7 309	79.5	D	1 752	32 292	18 432	74	42 021	72.8	1 050	9 525
Inglewood city	231	527 864	4 729	51.5	22.6	2 567	47 163	18 373	127	74 055	84.0	1 694	15 946
Irvine city	400	1 368 514	10 359	112.7	14.0	6 137	137 085	22 337	301	338 647	73.9	8 073	91 610
Laguna Niguel city	146	526 811	10 051	109.4	30.5	2 911	50 209	17 248	109	D	D	(5)	D
La Habra city	158	392 210	7 266	79.1	D	2 378	43 616	18 341	98	49 844	D	1 526	12 858
Lakewood city	250	637 007	8 453	92.0	18.5	4 211	66 136	15 706	147	91 652	97.8	2 837	23 536
La Mesa city	281	872 093	15 824	172.2	17.9	4 491	84 567	18 830	152	120 910	96.1	3 516	35 198
La Mirada city	95	287 743	6 505	70.8	D	1 394	29 025	20 821	72	44 282	D	1 084	11 022

[1] Includes only establishments with payroll. [2] Based on resident population estimated as of July 1, 1997. [3] For pay period including March 12. [4] Foodservices and drinking places (NAICS 722) includes full-service restaurants, limited-service eating places, special food services, and drinking places (alcoholic beverages). [5] 1,000 to 2,499 employees. [6] 250 to 499 employees. [7] 500 to 999 employees.

Sources: Retail Trade—U.S. Census Bureau, 1997 Economic Census, ECON97 Report Series CD-ROM, CD-EC97-1, Disc 1D issued July 2000 and Disc 1E issued February 2001 (related Internet site <http://www.census.gov/epcd/www/97EC44.HTM>). Accommodation and Foodservices—U.S. Census Bureau, 1997 Economic Census, ECON97 Report Series CD-ROM, Disc 1E issued February 2001 (related Internet site <http://www.census.gov/epcd/www/97EC72.HTM>).

[Includes states and 1,070 incorporated places of 25,000 or more population as of April 1, 1990 in all states except Hawaii which has no incorporated places recognized by the Census Bureau. For Hawaii, 8 census designated places (CDPs) of 25,000 or more population as of April 1, 1990 are included. Also included are the 5 boroughs of New York city. For more information on these areas, see appendix B. Geographic Information]

City	Retail trade[1] (NAICS 44-45), 1997								Accommodation and foodservices[1] (NAICS 72), 1997				
	Sales					Paid employees[3]	Annual payroll		Sales			Paid employees[3]	Annual payroll ($1,000)
	Estab-lishments	Total ($1,000)	Per capita[2]		Percent from general mer-chandise stores		Total ($1,000)	Per paid employee (dollars)	Estab-lishments	Total ($1,000)	Percent from food-services[4]		
			Amount (dollars)	Percent of national average									
CALIFORNIA—Con.													
Lancaster city	326	715 792	5 971	65.0	6.8	3 906	75 480	19 324	149	92 754	87.4	2 722	23 087
La Puente city	100	228 227	5 958	64.8	3.3	1 125	19 945	17 729	57	20 698	97.4	521	4 592
La Verne city	84	212 821	6 644	72.3	15.7	1 229	21 118	17 183	43	25 160	D	744	6 346
Lawndale city	96	303 881	10 616	115.5	D	1 108	21 836	19 708	46	22 917	89.3	594	5 843
Livermore city	188	593 720	8 502	92.5	D	2 931	55 405	18 903	119	64 767	81.4	1 755	15 609
Lodi city	218	529 718	9 667	105.2	D	2 970	53 802	18 115	124	51 124	95.3	1 561	12 778
Lompoc city	111	245 730	5 960	64.9	D	1 439	23 904	16 612	77	37 723	65.8	1 109	8 898
Long Beach city	998	1 939 912	4 533	49.3	7.9	11 047	197 427	17 872	679	446 575	77.3	11 593	120 992
Los Altos city	115	163 621	5 872	63.9	D	920	20 013	21 753	60	47 482	84.6	1 250	13 344
Los Angeles city	10 639	22 932 763	6 434	70.0	10.6	118 117	2 342 874	19 835	6 223	4 526 693	77.0	103 746	1 250 259
Los Gatos town	199	484 879	16 663	181.3	D	2 216	53 555	24 167	120	79 392	93.9	2 282	23 431
Lynwood city	83	179 910	2 872	31.3	.4	925	17 072	18 456	56	20 993	98.2	478	4 403
Madera city	141	302 469	8 390	91.3	D	1 918	31 509	16 428	64	D	D	(5)	D
Manhattan Beach city	159	612 273	18 221	198.3	23.4	2 794	51 091	18 286	126	121 852	74.2	2 782	33 569
Manteca city	147	359 291	7 606	82.8	D	1 996	36 196	18 134	80	D	D	(6)	D
Marina city	41	59 861	3 511	38.2	D	475	6 708	14 122	29	13 930	75.4	341	3 060
Martinez city	78	281 676	7 918	86.2	D	1 224	27 880	22 778	77	27 914	D	802	7 361
Maywood city	47	86 713	3 072	33.4	D	572	8 934	15 619	27	12 347	100.0	278	2 567
Menlo Park city	139	558 083	18 388	200.1	NA	1 930	49 794	25 800	84	67 737	74.5	1 361	17 818
Merced city	265	674 665	11 499	125.1	D	3 722	65 821	17 684	129	55 244	89.2	1 755	13 732
Milpitas city	318	804 482	13 478	146.7	9.8	4 934	89 154	18 069	194	148 296	74.7	3 859	37 422
Mission Viejo city	256	774 997	8 183	89.0	D	3 702	67 721	18 293	130	73 504	D	2 184	18 434
Modesto city	704	1 765 712	9 720	105.8	D	10 008	177 079	17 694	335	182 821	85.8	5 949	48 428
Monrovia city	141	553 209	14 923	162.4	D	2 617	48 306	18 459	73	56 654	80.9	1 502	15 825
Montclair city	290	709 913	23 720	258.1	D	5 363	84 807	15 813	73	D	D	(6)	D
Montebello city	242	629 975	10 511	114.4	D	3 468	62 235	17 946	119	57 363	98.2	1 614	13 953
Monterey city	264	380 976	12 059	131.2	D	2 785	44 501	15 979	205	236 680	45.3	4 733	62 813
Monterey Park city	169	275 250	4 470	48.6	D	1 683	26 151	15 538	129	84 158	92.3	2 040	22 780
Moorpark city	33	77 859	2 641	28.7	NA	452	9 513	21 046	26	D	D	(7)	D
Moreno Valley city	277	691 220	4 819	52.4	D	3 997	74 948	18 751	129	66 602	95.0	2 149	17 984
Mountain View city	296	977 592	13 828	150.5	D	4 458	98 788	22 160	221	173 669	84.4	3 463	41 376
Napa city	319	648 828	9 793	106.6	D	3 712	69 594	18 748	189	111 325	72.8	2 720	30 481
National City city	324	1 052 263	18 372	199.9	12.8	5 030	105 686	21 011	148	63 746	94.6	1 844	16 503
Newark city	218	626 840	15 035	163.6	D	3 470	60 185	17 344	103	74 621	65.6	1 684	17 574
Newport Beach city	440	1 140 188	16 044	174.6	D	5 947	125 089	21 034	341	374 238	67.8	8 474	107 818
Norwalk city	172	630 111	6 516	70.9	23.7	2 810	57 397	20 426	118	64 398	86.8	1 651	14 781
Novato city	192	543 750	11 285	122.8	D	2 619	59 468	22 706	111	50 963	90.7	1 359	13 458
Oakland city	1 030	2 146 503	5 861	63.8	D	10 190	213 132	20 916	738	436 339	73.9	9 390	121 341
Oceanside city	388	781 180	5 192	56.5	18.3	4 916	82 394	16 760	239	126 103	93.9	3 893	33 945
Ontario city	461	1 769 058	12 241	133.2	D	7 653	152 056	19 869	210	217 038	72.8	4 760	58 814
Orange city	484	1 227 329	10 091	109.8	8.7	5 519	123 810	22 433	247	171 635	79.6	4 335	45 646
Oxnard city	487	1 398 691	9 209	100.2	D	6 821	135 780	19 906	221	166 934	79.6	4 492	47 092
Pacifica city	70	127 263	3 143	34.2	D	721	12 063	16 731	62	24 936	97.3	575	6 019
Palmdale city	208	542 953	5 074	55.2	10.3	2 852	53 312	18 693	111	74 575	91.0	2 286	19 198
Palm Springs city	225	438 099	10 157	110.5	D	2 759	49 069	17 785	221	197 792	48.9	4 982	57 449
Palo Alto city	307	1 337 719	22 769	247.8	D	6 097	139 863	22 940	249	241 028	81.3	5 221	72 624
Paradise town	84	120 913	4 703	51.2	D	859	13 297	15 480	52	16 342	95.6	658	4 273
Paramount city	115	230 158	4 533	49.3	22.9	1 515	24 533	16 193	55	21 704	100.0	559	4 854
Pasadena city	567	1 553 081	11 631	126.6	17.1	8 330	160 943	19 321	365	313 709	77.9	8 055	92 951
Petaluma city	276	618 586	12 319	134.0	D	3 307	65 661	19 855	138	64 108	88.9	2 010	17 310
Pico Rivera city	108	303 857	5 089	55.4	10.8	1 554	33 778	21 736	71	37 340	96.0	1 004	9 004
Pittsburg city	111	368 971	7 107	77.3	19.3	2 158	38 567	17 872	66	30 250	D	864	8 249
Placentia city	110	334 568	7 391	80.4	D	1 525	38 135	25 007	77	47 317	D	1 250	11 132
Pleasant Hill city	159	382 202	11 638	126.6	24.3	2 383	36 187	15 185	72	49 098	D	1 268	12 218
Pleasanton city	349	1 068 161	17 297	188.2	20.0	5 665	107 476	18 972	187	152 455	75.5	3 699	40 663
Pomona city	269	599 474	4 445	48.4	5.9	3 216	63 634	19 787	165	94 456	86.1	2 603	23 842
Porterville city	165	340 611	9 733	105.9	22.9	2 097	35 107	16 742	79	35 421	93.2	1 143	7 978
Poway city	139	442 784	9 216	100.3	15.3	2 036	38 891	19 102	80	39 513	94.5	1 086	10 218
Rancho Cucamonga city	233	708 931	5 992	65.2	28.1	3 947	70 487	17 858	153	D	D	(8)	D
Rancho Palos Verdes city	49	109 722	2 590	28.2	D	595	10 751	18 069	34	26 225	D	694	6 386
Redding city	501	1 128 293	14 362	156.3	D	6 513	115 615	17 751	254	120 491	74.2	3 849	31 605
Redlands city	208	560 804	8 390	91.3	D	3 313	60 442	18 244	119	59 116	95.6	1 865	16 101
Redondo Beach city	287	538 537	8 546	93.0	D	3 968	62 782	15 822	161	126 071	77.0	3 122	34 771
Redwood City city	256	1 097 195	15 110	164.4	14.3	4 199	104 493	24 885	173	130 434	76.2	3 138	35 239
Rialto city	115	313 889	3 782	41.2	D	1 708	28 985	16 970	64	32 510	D	1 152	8 024
Richmond city	224	453 732	4 921	53.5	D	2 510	45 627	18 178	83	29 828	91.8	947	7 449
Ridgecrest city	97	202 958	6 639	72.2	23.2	1 388	20 807	14 991	48	24 933	82.3	897	6 775
Riverside city	800	2 279 336	8 949	97.4	13.6	11 452	219 703	19 185	397	208 300	89.8	6 281	56 660
Rohnert Park city	108	390 755	9 748	106.1	D	2 203	40 694	18 472	75	60 117	74.8	1 798	16 457

[1] Includes only establishments with payroll. [2] Based on resident population estimated as of July 1, 1997. [3] For pay period including March 12. [4] Foodservices and drinking places (NAICS 722) includes full-service restaurants, limited-service eating places, special food services, and drinking places (alcoholic beverages). [5] 500 to 999 employees. [6] 1,000 to 2,499 employees. [7] 250 to 499 employees. [8] 2,500 to 4,999 employees.

Sources: Retail Trade—U.S. Census Bureau, 1997 Economic Census, ECON97 Report Series CD-ROM, CD-EC97-1, Disc 1D issued July 2000 and Disc 1E issued February 2001 (related Internet site <http://www.census.gov/epcd/www/97EC44.HTM>). Accommodation and Foodservices—U.S. Census Bureau, 1997 Economic Census, ECON97 Report Series CD-ROM, Disc 1E issued February 2001 (related Internet site <http://www.census.gov/epcd/www/97EC72.HTM>).

[Includes states and 1,070 incorporated places of 25,000 or more population as of April 1, 1990 in all states except Hawaii which has no incorporated places recognized by the Census Bureau. For Hawaii, 8 census designated places (CDPs) of 25,000 or more population as of April 1, 1990 are included. Also included are the 5 boroughs of New York city. For more information on these areas, see appendix B. Geographic Information]

City	Retail trade[1] (NAICS 44-45), 1997								Accommodation and foodservices[1] (NAICS 72), 1997				
		Sales					Annual payroll			Sales			
			Per capita[2]		Percent from general merchandise stores						Percent from food-services[4]		
	Establishments	Total ($1,000)	Amount (dollars)	Percent of national average		Paid employees[3]	Total ($1,000)	Per paid employee (dollars)	Establishments	Total ($1,000)		Paid employees[3]	Annual payroll ($1,000)
CALIFORNIA—Con.													
Rosemead city	134	190 051	3 611	39.3	8.4	1 155	18 057	15 634	103	42 977	78.4	1 159	10 125
Roseville city	279	1 545 866	23 122	251.6	13.3	5 514	134 668	24 423	167	102 015	85.8	3 185	27 223
Sacramento city	1 296	3 039 615	7 555	82.2	13.7	18 093	329 744	18 225	880	531 078	74.0	14 904	143 840
Salinas city	496	1 332 541	11 207	121.9	D	7 173	146 324	20 399	226	105 349	88.6	3 118	27 194
San Bernardino city	640	1 903 908	10 302	112.1	18.2	9 571	181 032	18 915	322	177 479	93.6	5 345	47 731
San Bruno city	138	656 572	16 241	176.7	36.2	2 833	57 941	20 452	59	38 123	77.9	971	10 216
San Buenaventura (Ventura) city	483	1 249 786	12 692	138.1	10.4	6 334	128 162	20 234	251	166 394	77.7	4 544	47 045
San Carlos city	142	315 907	11 380	123.8	D	1 503	36 403	24 220	83	32 023	95.4	755	9 142
San Clemente city	173	286 739	6 220	67.7	D	1 587	27 546	17 357	117	56 795	73.9	1 269	14 285
San Diego city	4 128	10 018 185	8 371	91.1	11.1	54 308	1 020 345	18 788	2 781	2 610 320	58.6	61 236	707 681
San Dimas city	101	210 677	6 131	66.7	D	1 295	22 285	17 208	59	39 475	84.0	1 156	10 049
San Francisco city	3 841	6 795 006	9 170	99.8	9.6	39 693	830 599	20 926	3 264	3 283 495	50.7	60 178	956 602
San Gabriel city	173	306 743	8 290	90.2	D	1 475	26 730	18 122	134	57 237	97.8	1 535	15 234
San Jose city	2 169	6 905 044	8 109	88.2	13.9	34 278	700 491	20 436	1 478	981 340	78.6	23 699	249 453
San Juan Capistrano city	122	326 924	10 960	119.3	D	1 427	32 402	22 706	58	33 259	D	932	9 067
San Leandro city	351	1 116 667	15 320	166.7	D	5 952	113 940	19 143	170	79 294	94.5	2 256	21 950
San Luis Obispo city	319	606 062	14 272	155.3	D	3 845	62 781	16 328	173	114 427	65.0	3 535	30 852
San Marcos city	229	525 120	10 688	116.3	D	2 275	48 656	21 387	92	48 495	98.1	1 555	14 005
San Mateo city	400	1 082 809	11 852	129.0	D	6 247	120 732	19 326	235	148 703	81.3	3 428	43 983
San Pablo city	139	315 209	11 961	130.2	D	1 552	31 733	20 447	60	29 431	D	788	6 963
San Rafael city	411	1 075 186	21 199	230.7	9.2	4 637	115 716	24 955	199	93 973	85.6	2 443	23 935
San Ramon city	143	380 038	8 763	95.4	D	1 962	38 748	19 749	99	D	D	(5)	D
Santa Ana city	876	2 302 616	7 575	82.4	14.5	11 543	232 101	20 108	454	264 451	91.2	6 519	66 990
Santa Barbara city	655	1 220 392	14 212	154.6	D	7 589	143 310	18 884	386	295 136	64.1	7 570	85 169
Santa Clara city	414	1 758 653	17 789	193.6	9.4	6 703	187 604	27 988	309	316 310	59.6	6 513	82 618
Santa Clarita city	297	736 605	5 707	62.1	16.1	3 720	66 850	17 970	151	80 814	98.1	2 432	22 562
Santa Cruz city	282	578 918	11 211	122.0	D	3 626	62 313	17 185	216	124 484	80.7	3 339	33 928
Santa Maria city	353	810 501	11 956	130.1	D	4 928	89 519	18 165	146	79 071	81.2	2 593	22 811
Santa Monica city	726	2 200 324	24 921	271.2	4.9	8 018	190 021	23 699	376	463 602	67.9	9 917	127 310
Santa Paula city	72	124 400	4 701	51.2	D	515	7 426	14 419	38	12 816	95.6	396	3 091
Santa Rosa city	758	2 118 799	16 091	175.1	D	10 653	220 455	20 694	344	177 104	90.4	5 177	47 698
Santee city	125	401 538	7 139	77.7	37.2	2 234	40 103	17 951	70	D	D	(6)	D
Saratoga city	64	102 701	3 445	37.5	NA	569	12 073	21 218	43	28 820	89.6	557	7 284
Seal Beach city	75	123 045	4 752	51.7	D	749	12 921	17 251	62	41 304	D	1 149	11 264
Seaside city	83	353 343	12 944	140.8	D	1 204	32 505	26 998	54	35 790	60.7	953	9 588
Simi Valley city	279	852 368	7 831	85.2	15.7	3 806	68 994	18 128	157	92 652	90.0	2 789	23 815
South Gate city	154	361 145	4 128	44.9	D	1 738	31 951	18 384	98	36 625	93.5	966	8 090
South San Francisco city	187	585 904	10 068	109.6	D	2 558	56 574	22 116	152	221 878	77.4	3 819	64 366
Stanton city	96	238 912	7 332	79.8	D	1 136	21 568	18 986	75	29 937	84.6	785	7 204
Stockton city	742	1 771 380	7 523	81.9	D	9 842	178 164	18 102	398	197 734	87.5	5 902	51 532
Sunnyvale city	373	1 659 757	13 111	142.7	D	6 319	150 335	23 791	293	226 471	70.6	4 987	59 840
Temecula city	211	687 692	17 007	185.1	D	2 817	63 008	22 367	107	75 266	85.6	2 274	20 937
Temple City city	89	142 382	4 505	49.0	D	1 033	14 918	14 441	46	D	D	(6)	D
Thousand Oaks city	504	1 706 440	14 963	162.8	9.7	7 185	153 149	21 315	234	179 928	89.8	5 150	47 702
Torrance city	794	3 023 276	22 224	241.8	13.6	12 773	265 019	20 748	401	296 682	81.6	7 760	79 618
Tracy city	196	400 953	8 480	92.3	D	2 464	38 357	15 567	88	43 822	93.0	1 368	10 783
Tulare city	154	315 517	7 763	84.5	16.5	2 095	35 412	16 903	73	27 258	86.1	786	6 420
Turlock city	166	352 643	7 036	76.6	D	1 898	34 596	18 228	87	35 901	91.8	1 146	9 175
Tustin city	235	1 691 653	27 491	299.1	7.4	4 916	138 307	28 134	143	97 895	94.9	2 877	26 854
Union City city	88	510 879	8 296	90.3	D	2 227	49 597	22 271	69	25 135	D	648	5 871
Upland city	224	528 405	7 948	86.5	11.6	2 684	54 295	20 229	114	D	D	(5)	D
Vacaville city	302	701 460	8 467	92.1	D	3 830	66 991	17 486	121	77 029	93.2	2 260	20 521
Vallejo city	279	791 025	7 092	77.2	19.6	4 187	83 227	19 877	172	73 287	87.7	2 225	18 695
Victorville city	304	839 923	12 378	134.7	26.2	4 766	80 969	16 989	143	83 814	88.4	2 588	22 810
Visalia city	436	1 042 924	11 714	127.5	D	6 124	100 744	16 451	204	123 455	82.7	3 751	31 739
Vista city	233	665 633	8 361	91.0	21.3	3 212	61 462	19 135	127	48 258	94.7	1 380	11 723
Walnut city	60	91 433	2 963	32.2	NA	553	9 866	17 841	30	D	D	(7)	D
Walnut Creek city	339	1 240 911	19 432	211.4	7.9	5 859	132 784	22 663	197	156 569	79.6	3 719	42 110
Watsonville city	142	302 065	8 440	91.8	D	1 551	31 518	20 321	81	32 909	91.1	908	7 998
West Covina city	297	972 756	9 946	108.2	19.9	5 218	88 274	16 917	146	82 083	93.9	2 285	23 669
West Hollywood city	324	571 210	15 715	171.0	D	2 794	69 242	24 782	184	205 445	78.6	4 676	61 638
Westminster city	444	1 051 857	12 556	136.6	8.5	5 042	92 986	18 442	206	81 170	95.2	2 288	20 235
West Sacramento city	101	215 748	7 177	78.1	D	1 098	22 973	20 923	66	30 530	81.8	910	7 879
Whittier city	247	618 093	7 839	85.3	10.5	3 181	64 613	20 312	142	78 626	98.0	2 488	20 371
Woodland city	165	406 528	9 443	102.8	D	2 372	43 613	18 387	83	38 136	91.0	1 157	9 814
Yorba Linda city	116	371 257	6 246	68.0	D	1 726	34 114	19 765	68	49 696	D	1 573	13 365
Yuba City city	231	528 785	15 357	167.1	30.6	3 273	54 747	16 727	79	39 411	D	1 269	11 375
Yucaipa city	79	108 607	3 013	32.8	D	646	10 697	16 559	40	19 081	98.8	627	4 982

[1] Includes only establishments with payroll. [2] Based on resident population estimated as of July 1, 1997. [3] For pay period including March 12. [4] Foodservices and drinking places (NAICS 722) includes full-service restaurants, limited-service eating places, special food services, and drinking places (alcoholic beverages). [5] 1,000 to 2,499 employees. [6] 500 to 999 employees. [7] 100 to 249 employees.

Sources: Retail Trade—U.S. Census Bureau, 1997 Economic Census, ECON97 Report Series CD-ROM, CD-EC97-1, Disc 1D issued July 2000 and Disc 1E issued February 2001 (related Internet site <http://www.census.gov/epcd/www/97EC44.HTM>). Accommodation and Foodservices—U.S. Census Bureau, 1997 Economic Census, ECON97 Report Series CD-ROM, Disc 1E issued February 2001 (related Internet site <http://www.census.gov/epcd/www/97EC72.HTM>).

[Includes states and 1,070 incorporated places of 25,000 or more population as of April 1, 1990 in all states except Hawaii which has no incorporated places recognized by the Census Bureau. For Hawaii, 8 census designated places (CDPs) of 25,000 or more population as of April 1, 1990 are included. Also included are the 5 boroughs of New York city. For more information on these areas, see appendix B. Geographic Information]

City	Retail trade[1] (NAICS 44-45), 1997								Accommodation and foodservices[1] (NAICS 72), 1997				
	Sales					Annual payroll			Sales				
			Per capita[2]		Percent from general merchandise stores						Percent from food-services[4]		Annual payroll ($1,000)
	Estab-lishments	Total ($1,000)	Amount (dollars)	Percent of national average		Paid employees[3]	Total ($1,000)	Per paid employee (dollars)	Estab-lishments	Total ($1,000)		Paid employees[3]	
COLORADO	18 299	40 536 034	10 417	113.4	12.8	225 647	4 163 312	18 451	10 073	6 710 540	68.7	195 262	1 939 282
Arvada city	294	660 054	6 775	73.7	D	4 106	70 212	17 100	150	D	D	(5)	D
Aurora city	842	2 335 862	9 452	102.9	18.7	13 348	230 695	17 283	424	278 300	87.4	8 844	76 815
Boulder city	699	1 544 857	16 865	183.5	8.1	9 587	169 808	17 712	364	273 643	80.3	8 098	79 387
Colorado Springs city	1 644	4 669 333	13 845	150.7	D	25 565	466 503	18 248	830	703 765	62.5	19 478	200 061
Denver city	2 410	5 600 934	11 217	122.1	8.7	30 080	628 027	20 879	1 564	1 335 200	69.7	33 749	385 979
Englewood city	275	941 099	29 442	320.4	D	3 427	82 548	24 088	96	D	D	(6)	D
Fort Collins city	603	1 437 014	13 341	145.2	15.6	8 644	141 512	16 371	312	191 417	86.9	6 767	54 764
Grand Junction city	467	965 910	23 580	256.6	22.4	5 179	94 381	18 224	180	102 773	80.4	3 697	30 036
Greeley city	297	764 779	10 937	119.0	21.1	4 511	75 260	16 684	153	70 465	92.6	2 654	19 336
Lakewood city	654	1 801 584	13 291	144.6	13.6	9 359	179 371	19 166	318	202 648	91.0	6 244	60 224
Littleton city	360	1 598 963	39 946	434.7	10.7	7 383	145 065	19 649	139	D	D	(5)	D
Longmont city	300	776 367	13 077	142.3	D	4 269	76 813	17 993	140	82 584	87.4	2 460	22 903
Loveland city	264	613 525	13 401	145.8	D	3 101	52 292	16 863	103	53 943	92.1	1 728	13 602
Northglenn city	106	268 046	9 044	98.4	D	1 276	27 156	21 282	49	39 162	D	1 128	10 884
Pueblo city	532	1 117 209	10 846	118.0	D	6 586	114 505	17 386	280	131 645	85.5	4 547	35 308
Thornton city	158	729 217	10 481	114.0	25.0	4 013	80 005	19 936	109	85 213	77.0	2 616	23 505
Westminster city	372	1 093 437	11 588	126.1	D	6 483	104 563	16 129	170	117 954	90.2	3 812	33 941
Wheat Ridge city	198	589 250	19 659	213.9	D	2 747	57 604	20 970	99	54 223	84.1	1 707	15 517
CONNECTICUT	14 574	34 938 893	10 690	116.3	9.5	186 935	3 634 321	19 442	6 903	3 746 560	83.5	96 556	1 062 812
Bridgeport city	342	665 835	4 844	52.7	D	3 755	81 577	21 725	163	D	D	(6)	D
Bristol city	215	556 087	9 369	101.9	5.0	2 741	50 710	18 501	98	D	D	(6)	D
Danbury city	497	1 715 454	26 204	285.1	D	8 262	166 596	20 164	181	111 418	85.5	2 803	30 040
Hartford city	419	764 793	5 908	64.3	1.6	3 644	87 001	23 875	313	172 757	85.9	4 733	50 409
Meriden city	256	570 108	10 032	109.2	20.6	3 678	59 558	16 193	106	49 591	76.0	1 232	12 293
Middletown city	148	377 567	8 694	94.6	D	2 020	40 027	19 815	103	44 503	96.7	1 094	11 973
Milford city (remainder)	[7]342	[7]1 133 329	[7]22 827	[7]248.4	[7]18.8	[7]5 645	[7]106 017	[7]18 781	[7]168	[7]98 958	[7]87.2	[7]2 647	[7]25 632
Naugatuck borough	77	186 878	6 187	67.3	D	1 139	18 634	16 360	42	D	D	(8)	D
New Britain city	203	435 704	6 154	67.0	4.7	2 068	42 787	20 690	95	D	D	(6)	D
New Haven city	390	506 235	4 100	44.6	10.4	3 377	64 390	19 067	262	137 827	86.3	3 327	37 822
New London city	146	428 606	16 039	174.5	D	1 799	43 825	24 361	95	48 109	77.3	1 392	14 028
Norwalk city	411	1 792 016	23 017	250.5	3.5	7 133	180 726	25 337	202	93 161	90.2	1 944	25 719
Norwich city	181	468 533	13 078	142.3	13.4	2 749	47 834	17 401	78	47 877	67.2	1 379	13 393
Shelton city	94	381 193	10 192	110.9	D	1 626	30 747	18 910	74	40 901	D	862	10 163
Stamford city	545	1 798 099	16 313	177.5	8.1	6 973	186 705	26 775	281	198 374	70.5	3 980	54 995
Torrington city	201	454 467	13 152	143.1	12.3	2 531	43 527	17 198	72	30 929	90.0	866	8 638
Waterbury city	481	982 016	9 329	101.5	18.5	5 527	96 401	17 442	198	83 880	D	2 472	23 389
West Haven city	140	277 239	5 330	58.0	7.0	1 479	28 431	19 223	97	42 628	93.8	1 238	12 062
DELAWARE	3 736	8 236 970	11 206	121.9	13.5	47 116	798 702	16 952	1 605	1 008 954	85.3	26 969	280 815
Dover city	310	802 879	25 441	276.8	D	5 026	77 155	15 351	134	82 260	79.9	2 689	22 248
Newark city	204	760 828	27 297	297.0	5.1	3 796	70 130	18 475	123	111 236	75.2	2 829	26 597
Wilmington city	354	708 463	9 840	107.1	D	3 674	71 733	19 524	219	155 900	72.3	3 798	50 504
DISTRICT OF COLUMBIA	2 075	2 788 831	5 274	57.4	6.3	19 608	351 473	17 925	1 700	2 263 498	52.2	42 650	701 354
Washington city	2 075	2 788 831	5 274	57.4	6.3	19 608	351 473	17 925	1 700	2 263 498	52.2	42 650	701 354
FLORIDA	66 643	151 191 241	10 297	112.0	13.0	841 814	14 169 511	16 832	28 999	24 165 336	63.5	608 834	6 239 469
Altamonte Springs city	407	896 642	22 964	249.9	23.1	6 342	94 838	14 954	156	167 197	78.3	4 756	47 508
Boca Raton city	744	1 438 245	20 013	217.8	14.9	9 092	163 784	18 014	297	279 048	66.9	5 635	61 521
Boynton Beach city	219	405 005	7 626	83.0	16.9	2 757	42 246	15 323	101	63 046	94.8	2 001	18 078
Bradenton city	241	519 620	11 000	119.7	D	3 294	50 051	15 195	104	55 163	83.8	1 652	13 240
Cape Coral city	300	515 287	5 736	62.4	D	3 747	52 933	14 127	122	60 009	84.0	1 787	16 466
Clearwater city	775	2 535 489	25 606	278.6	13.6	11 505	222 944	19 378	401	339 322	51.5	7 830	84 137
Coconut Creek city	55	420 367	11 807	128.5	NA	1 016	27 529	27 095	19	5 307	100.0	116	1 261
Coral Gables city	315	795 216	18 529	201.6	D	3 652	75 589	20 698	172	153 320	62.2	3 701	47 305
Coral Springs city	417	949 979	8 672	94.4	D	6 395	92 320	14 436	179	109 937	95.9	3 218	27 464
Davie town	303	684 335	10 456	113.8	16.9	3 690	71 610	19 407	138	D	D	(5)	D
Daytona Beach city	546	1 466 874	22 572	245.6	17.2	7 481	126 665	16 932	321	247 196	D	7 016	62 615
Deerfield Beach city	278	885 761	17 571	191.2	D	4 340	81 820	18 853	140	105 009	73.5	2 438	25 493
Delray Beach city	344	1 467 277	27 855	303.1	7.1	4 265	102 438	24 018	138	84 195	90.5	2 233	21 789
Dunedin city	129	175 366	4 922	53.6	1.1	1 346	20 035	14 885	77	31 979	D	916	7 915
Fort Lauderdale city	1 203	3 192 205	20 941	227.9	4.7	13 080	287 878	22 009	698	941 545	47.1	19 971	221 852

[1] Includes only establishments with payroll. [2] Based on resident population estimated as of July 1, 1997. [3] For pay period including March 12. [4] Foodservices and drinking places (NAICS 722) includes full-service restaurants, limited-service eating places, special food services, and drinking places (alcoholic beverages). [5] 2,500 to 4,999 employees. [6] 1,000 to 2,499 employees. [7] Data are for consolidated city of Milford; data for Milford city (remainder) not available. [8] 250 to 499 employees.

Sources: Retail Trade—U.S. Census Bureau, 1997 Economic Census, ECON97 Report Series CD-ROM, CD-EC97-1, Disc 1D issued July 2000 and Disc 1E issued February 2001 (related Internet site <http://www.census.gov/epcd/www/97EC44.HTM>). Accommodation and Foodservices—U.S. Census Bureau, 1997 Economic Census, ECON97 Report Series CD-ROM, Disc 1E issued February 2001 (related Internet site <http://www.census.gov/epcd/www/97EC72.HTM>).

Table C–6. Cities — Retail Trade and Accommodation and Foodservices–Con.

[Includes states and 1,070 incorporated places of 25,000 or more population as of April 1, 1990 in all states except Hawaii which has no incorporated places recognized by the Census Bureau. For Hawaii, 8 census designated places (CDPs) of 25,000 or more population as of April 1, 1990 are included. Also included are the 5 boroughs of New York city. For more information on these areas, see appendix B. Geographic Information]

City	Retail trade[1] (NAICS 44-45), 1997								Accommodation and foodservices[1] (NAICS 72), 1997				
		Sales				Annual payroll				Sales			
			Per capita[2]		Percent from general merchandise stores								
	Estab-lishments	Total ($1,000)	Amount (dollars)	Percent of national average		Paid employees[3]	Total ($1,000)	Per paid employee (dollars)	Estab-lishments	Total ($1,000)	Percent from food-services[4]	Paid employees[3]	Annual payroll ($1,000)
FLORIDA—Con.													
Fort Myers city	614	1 695 053	37 133	404.1	D	8 593	160 236	18 647	213	145 062	76.4	4 338	38 052
Fort Pierce city	257	430 999	11 577	126.0	D	2 844	39 937	14 043	113	53 839	88.8	1 751	14 276
Gainesville city	498	1 098 307	11 678	127.1	10.2	6 521	104 773	16 067	273	140 158	82.7	4 610	36 152
Hallandale city	134	263 009	8 642	94.0	D	1 932	29 137	15 081	67	46 033	86.1	1 610	13 257
Hialeah city	945	1 530 907	7 187	78.2	12.8	10 430	151 235	14 500	268	129 718	92.5	3 248	31 247
Hollywood city	556	1 234 895	9 475	103.1	6.0	6 758	121 621	17 997	320	163 385	74.4	4 871	44 573
Homestead city	122	302 982	11 800	128.4	D	1 636	27 788	16 985	67	32 771	86.8	990	8 185
Jacksonville city (remainder)	2 883	7 623 835	11 078	120.5	D	41 368	720 136	17 408	1 286	828 899	83.9	25 909	220 472
Kissimmee city	309	531 730	13 993	152.3	2.5	3 517	52 314	14 875	205	480 166	27.7	6 281	80 171
Lakeland city	621	1 559 950	21 074	229.3	19.8	9 559	148 566	15 542	222	160 414	83.7	5 146	42 830
Lake Worth city	183	274 606	9 455	102.9	D	1 519	26 393	17 375	78	32 930	95.6	852	9 241
Largo city	382	626 517	9 384	102.1	15.9	4 358	66 126	15 173	176	89 803	96.0	2 854	21 841
Lauderdale Lakes city	78	142 072	4 926	53.6	D	713	13 167	18 467	27	11 576	100.0	326	2 991
Lauderhill city	159	534 124	10 496	114.2	3.1	1 884	33 267	17 658	63	D	D	(5)	D
Margate city	198	848 128	16 594	180.6	D	3 187	68 220	21 406	97	D	D	(6)	D
Melbourne city	446	1 137 473	16 589	180.5	16.4	6 394	111 609	17 455	182	96 758	89.1	3 407	28 080
Miami city	2 533	3 681 547	9 907	107.8	9.8	21 675	362 469	16 723	912	764 781	63.3	16 953	202 656
Miami Beach city	466	504 226	5 165	56.2	5.3	3 680	62 070	16 867	466	550 993	45.1	12 714	160 255
Miramar city	115	341 126	6 222	67.7	D	2 063	29 333	14 219	44	15 592	100.0	425	3 367
North Lauderdale city	48	121 160	4 114	44.8	D	950	11 686	12 301	36	14 045	100.0	431	3 310
North Miami city	235	705 758	13 766	149.8	D	3 402	83 177	24 449	107	66 638	98.5	1 952	16 737
North Miami Beach city	217	541 384	15 252	166.0	22.9	2 775	47 802	17 226	74	32 842	100.0	911	8 350
Oakland Park city	275	517 406	18 594	202.3	D	2 719	53 595	19 711	115	70 707	82.1	1 729	17 462
Ocala city	602	1 470 399	31 825	346.3	14.4	8 560	136 686	15 968	203	141 173	89.0	4 763	38 978
Orlando city	1 406	3 786 451	21 489	233.8	7.6	18 296	334 308	18 272	581	753 526	64.1	18 872	213 964
Ormond Beach city	170	257 122	7 448	81.0	D	2 231	30 222	13 546	113	70 539	80.5	2 485	19 810
Palm Bay city	150	307 062	4 019	43.7	D	2 174	28 116	12 933	80	35 485	93.6	1 152	9 428
Panama City city	415	916 873	23 089	251.2	D	5 461	88 633	16 230	175	129 543	D	3 471	33 341
Pembroke Pines city	375	1 650 665	15 226	165.7	14.8	7 362	125 841	17 093	190	134 349	D	4 009	34 386
Pensacola city	470	991 449	16 748	182.2	D	6 415	93 888	14 636	183	130 514	95.8	4 156	35 342
Pinellas Park city	241	1 530 801	34 427	374.6	6.0	5 235	104 923	20 043	92	60 404	93.7	1 565	14 115
Plantation city	441	1 137 370	14 143	153.9	D	6 511	109 855	16 872	164	136 098	80.1	3 601	35 482
Pompano Beach city	587	1 571 822	20 897	227.4	13.1	6 828	140 074	20 515	229	124 878	72.5	3 035	34 098
Port Orange city	109	207 527	4 718	51.3	D	1 572	21 785	13 858	66	40 729	94.7	1 403	11 415
Port St. Lucie city	185	359 607	4 602	50.1	D	2 477	35 445	14 310	92	75 962	D	1 828	18 828
Riviera Beach city	114	157 296	5 429	59.1	D	847	17 921	21 158	41	33 120	D	741	8 205
St. Petersburg city	933	2 128 709	9 034	98.3	13.2	12 942	208 233	16 090	432	268 769	76.6	7 827	76 215
Sanford city	303	628 435	17 426	189.6	32.0	3 960	57 663	14 561	81	51 350	93.4	1 594	13 818
Sarasota city	512	931 609	18 265	198.7	13.0	5 601	93 854	16 757	241	183 456	68.2	4 628	49 483
Sunrise city	448	1 355 242	16 976	184.7	18.6	7 971	133 747	16 779	163	115 914	90.2	3 065	27 782
Tallahassee city	864	1 721 163	12 732	138.5	20.0	13 270	188 473	14 203	401	268 859	83.1	8 819	69 761
Tamarac city	208	350 840	6 776	73.7	9.5	2 516	38 359	15 246	102	D	D	(6)	D
Tampa city	1 792	4 756 721	16 571	180.3	9.2	25 054	428 869	17 118	842	782 839	66.7	20 303	212 272
Titusville city	182	386 464	9 257	100.7	27.8	2 602	37 100	14 258	80	52 844	86.1	2 005	15 811
West Palm Beach city	615	1 968 520	26 049	283.4	11.3	9 261	188 350	20 338	294	222 982	77.8	5 797	60 116
GEORGIA	33 073	72 212 484	9 646	105.0	12.9	420 676	6 943 559	16 506	13 829	9 689 927	76.7	274 322	2 695 138
Albany city	548	1 134 755	14 671	159.6	18.9	7 595	112 610	14 827	188	116 619	D	3 688	31 173
Athens city	[7]540	[7]1 118 808	[7]12 336	[7]134.2		[7]7 760	[7]110 334	[7]14 218	[7]240	[7]125 546	[7]89.9	[7]4 371	[7]33 769
Atlanta city	2 044	4 229 777	10 546	114.8	13.4	26 738	491 061	18 366	1 361	1 604 798	62.3	37 792	478 728
Augusta city	[8]896	[8]1 894 150	[8]10 092	[8]109.8	[8]17.4	[8]12 213	[8]187 934	[8]15 388	[8]395	[8]255 062	[8]79.0	[8]8 284	[8]70 289
Columbus city (remainder)	[9]845	[9]1 950 857	[9]10 675	[9]116.2		[9]11 718	[9]186 553	[9]15 920	[9]365	D	D	(10)	D
East Point city	91	155 415	4 633	50.4	11.8	1 160	16 805	14 487	48	45 276	64.5	1 084	12 613
La Grange city	202	445 583	17 692	192.5	D	2 809	43 497	15 485	59	31 287	88.6	1 026	7 853
Macon city	765	1 630 245	14 382	156.5	D	10 586	159 476	15 065	273	174 961	84.8	5 786	47 265
Marietta city	409	1 948 249	38 565	419.6	D	7 391	167 125	22 612	235	163 217	76.0	4 203	45 431
Rome city	343	707 023	21 665	235.7	D	4 389	65 812	14 995	118	78 874	94.1	2 246	20 215
Roswell city	321	1 298 754	22 864	248.8	D	4 720	118 375	25 079	151	115 835	84.7	3 072	33 552
Savannah city	962	1 894 348	14 212	154.6	17.7	12 394	188 813	15 234	413	334 571	70.2	9 619	90 061
Smyrna city	226	927 176	25 621	278.8	14.0	4 820	81 041	16 813	142	109 484	94.2	3 028	30 657
Valdosta city	379	758 210	17 782	193.5	D	4 892	72 705	14 862	138	83 040	87.1	2 787	23 589
Warner Robins city	238	607 077	12 546	136.5	D	3 790	58 024	15 310	120	69 478	89.6	2 510	18 576

[1] Includes only establishments with payroll.   [2] Based on resident population estimated as of July 1, 1997.   [3] For pay period including March 12.   [4] Foodservices and drinking places (NAICS 722) includes full-service restaurants, limited-service eating places, special food services, and drinking places (alcoholic beverages).   [5] 500 to 999 employees.   [6] 1,000 to 2,499 employees.   [7] Data are for consolidated city of Athens-Clarke County; Athens city (1990 land area - 16.6 square miles; 1990 population - 45,734) merged with Clarke County effective January 14, 1991.   [8] Data are for Augusta-Richmond County (balance), GA; Augusta city (1990 land area - 19.7 square miles; 1990 population - 44,639) merged with Richmond County effective January 1, 1996.   [9] Data are for consolidated city of Columbus; data for Columbus city (remainder) not available.   [10] 5,000 to 9,999 employees.

Sources: Retail Trade—U.S. Census Bureau, 1997 Economic Census, ECON97 Report Series CD-ROM, CD-EC97-1, Disc 1D issued July 2000 and Disc 1E issued February 2001 (related Internet site <http://www.census.gov/epcd/www/97EC44.HTM>).   Accommodation and Foodservices—U.S. Census Bureau, 1997 Economic Census, ECON97 Report Series CD-ROM, Disc 1E issued February 2001 (related Internet site <http://www.census.gov/epcd/www/97EC72.HTM>).

Table C–6. Cities — **Retail Trade and Accommodation and Foodservices**–Con.

[Includes states and 1,070 incorporated places of 25,000 or more population as of April 1, 1990 in all states except Hawaii which has no incorporated places recognized by the Census Bureau. For Hawaii, 8 census designated places (CDPs) of 25,000 or more population as of April 1, 1990 are included. Also included are the 5 boroughs of New York city. For more information on these areas, see appendix B. Geographic Information]

City	Retail trade[1] (NAICS 44-45), 1997								Accommodation and foodservices[1] (NAICS 72), 1997				
		Sales				Annual payroll				Sales			
			Per capita[2]		Percent from general mer-chandise stores						Percent from food-services[4]		
	Estab-lishments	Total ($1,000)	Amount (dollars)	Percent of national average		Paid employees[3]	Total ($1,000)	Per paid employee (dollars)	Estab-lishments	Total ($1,000)		Paid employees[3]	Annual payroll ($1,000)
HAWAII	5 088	11 317 752	9 516	103.5	20.1	64 218	1 161 805	18 092	3 081	5 007 899	39.6	88 083	1 507 538
Hilo CDP	261	552 226	NA	NA	D	3 696	63 033	17 054	116	64 725	83.9	1 881	18 517
Honolulu CDP	2 258	5 483 510	13 899	151.2	22.0	27 812	534 745	19 227	1 503	2 603 981	D	42 549	733 432
Kailua CDP	104	227 863	NA	NA	D	1 758	27 505	15 646	83	D	D	(5)	D
Kaneohe CDP	137	371 808	NA	NA	D	2 171	37 739	17 383	60	36 854	100.0	1 009	9 527
Mililani Town CDP	50	176 798	NA	NA	D	1 181	19 549	16 553	27	D	D	(6)	D
Pearl City CDP	50	239 662	NA	NA	D	1 062	18 809	17 711	42	27 917	100.0	734	7 201
Waimalu CDP	84	251 665	NA	NA	D	1 259	27 022	21 463	43	39 766	93.2	884	10 181
Waipahu CDP	119	378 262	NA	NA	D	1 908	39 561	20 734	77	48 675	100.0	1 287	12 569
IDAHO	5 848	11 649 609	9 623	104.7	13.1	63 732	1 079 700	16 941	2 980	1 233 215	72.5	42 087	345 955
Boise City city	939	2 505 929	15 289	166.4	15.6	12 880	229 964	17 854	512	316 780	71.9	10 148	89 122
Idaho Falls city	398	790 013	16 301	177.4	22.1	4 758	76 885	16 159	171	88 917	D	3 345	25 596
Lewiston city	220	453 557	14 814	161.2	D	2 749	47 241	17 185	97	41 954	80.8	1 415	12 297
Nampa city	216	563 159	13 662	148.7	11.3	2 664	49 048	18 411	96	46 104	92.1	1 701	12 293
Pocatello city	239	538 384	10 359	112.7	D	2 809	48 777	17 365	133	56 429	83.6	2 031	15 416
Twin Falls city	299	726 726	21 875	238.0	D	4 013	65 642	16 357	125	58 330	D	2 160	17 087
ILLINOIS	44 568	108 002 177	8 992	97.8	13.0	610 790	10 596 015	17 348	23 984	14 826 805	79.4	397 300	4 018 697
Addison village	123	800 995	23 723	258.1	D	2 754	63 875	23 194	53	39 212	D	990	8 682
Alton city	207	392 637	12 345	134.3	22.8	2 404	36 791	15 304	99	57 081	90.6	1 821	14 979
Arlington Heights village	326	1 302 532	17 138	186.5	D	4 970	92 690	18 650	147	124 203	81.5	2 953	32 514
Aurora city	463	1 171 494	9 686	105.4	20.1	7 942	120 960	15 230	192	110 327	97.6	3 122	29 144
Belleville city	231	543 398	13 102	142.6	D	3 073	55 416	18 033	132	61 815	97.7	2 260	17 011
Berwyn city	147	272 766	6 268	68.2	D	1 578	27 767	17 596	101	D	D	(5)	D
Bloomington city	364	905 082	15 354	167.1	D	5 300	85 580	16 147	192	124 650	78.9	4 221	37 116
Bolingbrook village	102	456 938	8 558	93.1	D	2 786	43 913	15 762	57	34 367	D	988	8 749
Buffalo Grove village	123	357 626	8 518	92.7	D	1 705	40 876	23 974	74	D	D	1 750	D
Burbank city	91	290 246	10 451	113.7	11.2	1 794	26 030	14 509	69	D	D	(6)	D
Calumet City city	194	715 069	19 344	210.5	D	4 775	72 080	15 095	106	51 439	100.0	1 674	12 824
Carbondale city	206	443 443	16 200	176.3	D	3 170	44 549	14 053	107	52 084	89.4	1 945	14 132
Carol Stream village	80	299 722	7 987	86.9	D	1 349	26 587	19 709	50	29 546	D	864	7 763
Champaign city	379	825 342	12 633	137.5	30.1	6 227	82 633	13 270	252	152 111	83.9	5 728	42 486
Chicago city	7 885	13 882 143	4 944	53.8	9.3	86 703	1 553 157	17 914	5 148	4 481 917	68.7	92 348	1 194 059
Chicago Heights city	93	308 693	9 677	105.3	D	1 165	26 351	22 619	54	23 504	100.0	762	6 189
Cicero town	133	347 429	5 018	54.6	D	1 869	32 303	17 284	89	37 797	90.0	914	9 324
Danville city	214	434 167	13 006	141.5	27.6	3 212	44 190	13 758	116	53 323	88.1	1 893	15 455
Decatur city	372	882 553	10 787	117.4	18.2	5 334	87 790	16 459	196	D	D	(7)	D
De Kalb city	130	297 885	7 772	84.6	D	2 153	32 054	14 888	94	45 379	84.0	1 719	11 121
Des Plaines city	197	562 568	9 914	107.9	D	2 592	51 803	19 986	144	104 574	77.9	2 408	26 764
Downers Grove village	267	1 591 557	31 226	339.8	3.7	5 969	135 104	22 634	117	126 394	78.6	3 415	35 128
East St. Louis city	73	71 156	1 874	20.4	D	617	8 624	13 977	37	18 637	D	476	4 081
Elgin city	226	862 846	9 830	107.0	D	3 887	82 415	21 203	129	76 391	91.3	2 019	20 163
Elk Grove Village village	152	550 134	15 756	171.4	D	3 039	68 237	22 454	85	63 616	71.4	1 442	16 622
Elmhurst city	188	850 386	19 566	212.9	D	2 898	73 993	25 532	83	D	D	(5)	D
Evanston city	292	746 034	10 404	113.2	D	4 370	87 095	19 930	177	110 101	91.8	2 491	30 070
Freeport city	135	346 342	13 118	142.7	D	2 155	34 916	16 202	78	31 376	D	1 108	7 512
Galesburg city	198	409 268	12 349	134.4	D	3 304	45 859	13 880	104	D	D	(5)	D
Glendale Heights village	63	332 760	11 058	120.3	D	1 390	29 729	21 388	43	D	D	(6)	D
Glenview village	166	515 574	12 766	138.9	D	1 909	45 369	23 766	104	76 329	79.4	1 842	21 732
Granite City city	110	250 151	7 911	86.1	17.8	1 456	22 664	15 566	72	28 603	96.7	937	7 524
Hanover Park village	76	157 625	4 379	47.6	D	1 094	18 512	16 921	47	23 305	100.0	626	6 030
Harvey city	66	141 132	4 792	52.1	1.9	777	15 817	20 356	38	13 656	D	504	3 633
Highland Park city	180	570 536	18 265	198.7	D	2 419	52 427	21 673	71	41 576	D	968	10 911
Hoffman Estates village	104	332 845	6 838	74.4	D	1 657	36 663	22 126	83	72 057	90.7	1 653	18 371
Joliet city	405	1 281 511	14 078	153.2	D	7 042	119 905	17 027	191	107 948	88.1	3 300	28 083
Kankakee city	115	212 321	7 784	84.7	2.4	1 289	24 520	19 022	69	26 545	94.0	900	7 233
Lansing village	158	472 884	16 455	179.1	16.4	3 073	48 069	15 642	75	46 272	81.4	1 331	12 518
Lombard village	282	858 235	20 082	218.5	D	5 138	91 278	17 765	95	87 597	83.7	2 231	24 271
Maywood village	45	90 322	3 472	37.8	NA	332	7 016	21 133	33	19 303	D	363	4 738
Moline city	325	805 453	18 600	202.4	22.8	5 164	81 608	15 803	163	90 515	89.2	3 304	25 670
Mount Prospect village	232	573 081	10 633	115.7	D	4 285	66 184	15 446	101	D	D	(5)	D
Naperville city	396	1 506 671	13 305	144.8	D	7 212	143 268	19 865	233	184 752	84.7	4 972	53 044
Niles village	234	1 147 863	38 975	424.1	D	5 190	91 163	17 565	102	59 862	98.2	1 774	16 446
Normal town	152	398 215	8 994	97.9	26.8	2 843	39 809	14 002	93	60 164	81.9	2 250	16 750
Northbrook village	269	723 048	21 796	237.2	D	4 258	86 207	20 246	112	75 087	80.6	1 602	21 115
North Chicago city	37	69 204	1 950	21.2	D	343	11 280	32 886	56	31 289	D	934	8 928
Oak Forest city	58	155 303	5 439	59.2	NA	549	14 313	26 071	36	16 101	D	532	4 458

[1] Includes only establishments with payroll. [2] Based on resident population estimated as of July 1, 1997. [3] For pay period including March 12. [4] Foodservices and drinking places (NAICS 722) includes full-service restaurants, limited-service eating places, special food services, and drinking places (alcoholic beverages). [5] 1,000 to 2,499 employees. [6] 500 to 999 employees. [7] 2,500 to 4,999 employees.

Sources: Retail Trade—U.S. Census Bureau, 1997 Economic Census, ECON97 Report Series CD-ROM, CD-EC97-1, Disc 1D issued July 2000 and Disc 1E issued February 2001 (related Internet site <http://www.census.gov/epcd/www/97EC44.HTM>). Accommodation and Foodservices—U.S. Census Bureau, 1997 Economic Census, ECON97 Report Series CD-ROM, Disc 1E issued February 2001 (related Internet site <http://www.census.gov/epcd/www/97EC72.HTM>).

[Includes states and 1,070 incorporated places of 25,000 or more population as of April 1, 1990 in all states except Hawaii which has no incorporated places recognized by the Census Bureau. For Hawaii, 8 census designated places (CDPs) of 25,000 or more population as of April 1, 1990 are included. Also included are the 5 boroughs of New York city. For more information on these areas, see appendix B. Geographic Information]

City	Retail trade[1] (NAICS 44-45), 1997								Accommodation and foodservices[1] (NAICS 72), 1997				
	Sales					Annual payroll			Sales				
			Per capita[2]		Percent from general mer-chandise stores						Percent from food-services[4]		
	Estab-lishments	Total ($1,000)	Amount (dollars)	Percent of national average		Paid employees[3]	Total ($1,000)	Per paid employee (dollars)	Estab-lishments	Total ($1,000)		Paid employees[3]	Annual payroll ($1,000)
ILLINOIS—Con.													
Oak Lawn village	239	1 039 908	17 977	195.6	D	4 298	91 954	21 395	96	74 442	79.8	2 205	20 190
Oak Park village	181	240 011	4 461	48.5	NA	1 624	26 681	16 429	81	49 325	D	1 458	14 574
Orland Park village	374	1 244 862	25 257	274.8	D	7 389	117 777	15 940	127	98 708	95.2	2 676	26 217
Palatine village	217	554 475	10 470	113.9	D	2 943	54 564	18 540	115	69 458	88.3	1 887	17 577
Park Ridge city	117	304 975	8 187	89.1	D	1 432	28 961	20 224	61	25 863	D	755	6 332
Pekin city	152	463 828	13 896	151.2	D	2 429	41 542	17 103	75	34 597	96.1	1 319	10 029
Peoria city	566	1 501 043	13 418	146.0	21.8	9 434	149 294	15 825	344	203 361	79.9	6 592	59 127
Quincy city	275	607 123	14 921	162.4	D	4 308	62 007	14 393	117	62 876	84.8	2 098	17 536
Rockford city	679	1 875 304	12 882	140.2	15.8	11 718	185 939	15 868	347	223 700	84.7	6 904	61 146
Rock Island city	128	201 082	5 133	55.9	7.3	1 365	19 970	14 630	92	33 632	D	1 178	8 289
Schaumburg village	523	2 262 588	30 108	327.6	D	12 331	227 513	18 450	210	239 171	73.5	5 836	62 683
Skokie village	413	981 588	16 772	182.5	8.9	7 088	118 689	16 745	138	101 010	86.7	2 572	27 815
Springfield city	618	1 634 307	14 029	152.7	17.4	9 812	154 700	15 766	373	209 886	83.0	6 820	61 959
Streamwood village	64	163 669	4 656	50.7	D	891	12 446	13 969	38	24 224	100.0	612	6 294
Tinley Park village	130	494 039	10 868	118.3	D	2 456	44 126	17 967	62	34 878	D	1 037	9 431
Urbana city	109	287 308	8 002	87.1	D	1 836	30 413	16 565	104	62 887	67.6	2 038	18 380
Waukegan city	288	735 232	9 788	106.5	12.4	4 373	78 212	17 885	152	79 477	82.0	2 101	19 715
Wheaton city	217	513 343	9 265	100.8	D	2 919	51 744	17 727	84	62 163	98.8	2 007	16 554
Wheeling village	101	366 651	12 282	133.6	D	1 707	31 749	18 599	57	D	D	1 750	D
Wilmette village	133	240 988	9 236	100.5	D	1 571	26 984	17 176	45	D	D	(5)	D
Woodridge village	64	203 268	6 929	75.4	41.9	1 308	19 274	14 735	25	15 265	100.0	466	4 472
INDIANA	24 954	57 241 650	9 748	106.1	15.4	337 867	5 273 772	15 609	11 705	6 646 318	84.1	215 710	1 865 305
Anderson city	346	832 981	14 140	153.9	D	5 079	76 964	15 153	160	116 439	92.5	4 055	32 780
Bloomington city	443	1 010 635	15 012	163.4	D	6 424	91 420	14 231	275	165 763	D	6 020	45 135
Carmel city	184	720 897	17 713	192.7	D	3 663	69 878	19 077	79	57 737	73.1	1 636	16 334
Columbus city	286	566 771	15 405	167.6	19.6	3 941	55 552	14 096	110	88 636	82.1	2 721	24 582
East Chicago city	60	83 592	2 669	29.0	D	610	10 615	17 402	57	15 963	100.0	494	3 633
Elkhart city	330	920 216	20 966	228.1	11.6	5 168	82 479	15 960	184	94 545	87.6	3 093	26 882
Evansville city	870	2 092 622	16 961	184.6	D	13 665	211 332	15 477	396	D	D	(6)	D
Fort Wayne city	1 058	2 859 613	14 470	157.5	D	17 653	283 019	16 032	506	350 945	87.3	11 413	103 025
Gary city	218	359 778	3 223	35.1	D	2 361	30 807	13 048	120	43 741	98.5	1 465	11 372
Greenwood city	258	728 471	22 122	240.7	D	4 847	70 073	14 457	107	66 388	94.4	2 419	19 296
Hammond city	251	556 297	7 023	76.4	6.6	3 388	51 969	15 339	164	71 280	89.5	2 024	17 326
Indianapolis city (remainder)	3 395	10 228 013	13 751	149.6	12.2	56 279	982 670	17 461	1 742	1 448 463	77.2	41 447	411 422
Kokomo city	346	878 729	19 236	209.3	25.5	5 564	81 506	14 649	160	109 577	D	3 637	29 926
Lafayette city	410	1 060 413	21 642	235.5	19.2	6 608	100 760	15 248	152	94 671	96.7	3 092	27 623
Lawrence city	116	241 350	7 274	79.2	D	1 418	25 552	18 020	52	23 176	D	802	6 642
Marion city	233	524 913	16 976	184.7	16.6	3 131	46 199	14 755	92	54 903	92.1	1 901	15 267
Merrillville town	308	965 622	30 853	335.7	D	5 485	87 472	15 947	134	118 222	73.3	3 640	33 483
Michigan City city	299	562 417	16 983	184.8	20.9	3 759	57 084	15 186	106	55 101	86.6	1 679	15 003
Mishawaka city	393	1 479 915	32 353	352.0	D	8 081	116 763	14 449	164	104 799	93.8	3 655	29 845
Muncie city	406	863 284	12 508	136.1	D	5 648	83 693	14 818	174	109 194	93.8	4 337	30 362
New Albany city	174	265 714	6 572	71.5	D	1 886	29 958	15 884	87	44 473	D	1 408	12 764
Portage city	80	197 229	5 986	65.1	D	1 185	17 512	14 778	56	28 061	86.5	951	8 024
Richmond city	249	585 737	15 015	163.4	20.3	3 582	54 629	15 251	103	63 587	88.1	2 158	18 442
South Bend city	440	939 137	9 245	100.6	D	6 597	98 551	14 939	257	142 757	80.9	4 868	40 760
Terre Haute city	411	1 963 782	36 356	395.6	5.7	7 586	129 831	17 115	217	126 796	89.5	4 308	36 240
West Lafayette city	79	188 356	6 770	73.7	D	1 660	17 181	10 350	86	47 004	76.9	1 860	13 507
IOWA	14 695	26 723 822	9 362	101.9	13.0	175 694	2 633 445	14 989	6 830	2 762 766	80.3	99 148	769 461
Ames city	246	510 771	10 589	115.2	D	3 922	54 641	13 932	168	78 997	D	3 173	21 673
Bettendorf city	124	252 151	8 079	87.9	D	1 821	28 942	15 893	72	49 544	D	1 712	15 769
Burlington city	132	259 339	9 703	105.6	14.4	2 108	31 028	14 719	89	D	D	(7)	D
Cedar Falls city	180	429 489	12 444	135.4	D	2 611	41 396	15 854	99	47 940	D	2 182	15 313
Cedar Rapids city	640	1 638 612	14 278	155.4	D	10 952	171 961	15 701	350	209 802	81.6	6 760	59 512
Clinton city	153	321 529	11 326	123.2	D	1 883	34 327	18 230	91	32 061	D	1 184	8 985
Council Bluffs city	287	717 237	12 697	138.2	D	4 400	67 466	15 333	146	174 218	D	3 338	45 119
Davenport city	545	1 416 166	14 499	157.8	D	8 810	147 506	16 743	262	166 989	83.6	5 707	48 520
Des Moines city	897	2 103 922	10 964	119.3	12.2	13 577	231 621	17 060	514	293 686	76.6	9 234	86 705
Dubuque city	382	734 277	12 802	139.3	D	5 537	80 420	14 524	179	80 056	83.2	3 220	23 748
Fort Dodge city	216	374 436	14 739	160.4	24.6	2 932	40 515	13 818	78	35 483	D	1 274	10 273
Iowa City city	333	775 216	12 747	138.7	D	5 448	79 797	14 647	178	89 167	83.8	3 743	25 494
Marshalltown city	155	294 996	11 410	124.2	17.5	2 296	31 824	13 861	70	27 282	D	981	7 905
Mason City city	218	519 718	17 883	194.6	D	3 451	47 375	13 728	88	39 062	90.3	1 495	11 108
Sioux City city	469	1 049 676	12 568	136.8	D	7 174	108 345	15 102	214	103 159	87.6	3 544	28 389
Waterloo city	347	807 785	12 623	137.4	D	6 030	88 457	14 669	163	82 060	87.1	3 120	22 236
West Des Moines city	274	608 203	14 408	156.8	D	5 081	68 427	13 467	118	78 440	D	2 641	24 807

[1] Includes only establishments with payroll.   [2] Based on resident population estimated as of July 1, 1997.   [3] For pay period including March 12.   [4] Foodservices and drinking places (NAICS 722) includes full-service restaurants, limited-service eating places, special food services, and drinking places (alcoholic beverages).   [5] 500 to 999 employees.   [6] 5,000 to 9,999 employees.   [7] 1,000 to 2,499 employees.

Sources: Retail Trade—U.S. Census Bureau, 1997 Economic Census, ECON[97] Report Series CD-ROM, CD-EC97-1, Disc 1D issued July 2000 and Disc 1E issued February 2001 (related Internet site <http://www.census.gov/epcd/www/97EC44.HTM>).   Accommodation and Foodservices—U.S. Census Bureau, 1997 Economic Census, ECON[97] Report Series CD-ROM, Disc 1E issued February 2001 (related Internet site <http://www.census.gov/epcd/www/97EC72.HTM>).

[Includes states and 1,070 incorporated places of 25,000 or more population as of April 1, 1990 in all states except Hawaii which has no incorporated places recognized by the Census Bureau. For Hawaii, 8 census designated places (CDPs) of 25,000 or more population as of April 1, 1990 are included. Also included are the 5 boroughs of New York city. For more information on these areas, see appendix B. Geographic Information]

City	Retail trade[1] (NAICS 44-45), 1997								Accommodation and foodservices[1] (NAICS 72), 1997				
		Sales				Annual payroll				Sales			Annual payroll ($1,000)
			Per capita[2]		Percent from general merchandise stores								
	Establishments	Total ($1,000)	Amount (dollars)	Percent of national average		Paid employees[3]	Total ($1,000)	Per paid employee (dollars)	Establishments	Total ($1,000)	Percent from foodservices[4]	Paid employees[3]	Annual payroll ($1,000)
KANSAS	12 271	22 571 918	8 627	93.9	15.3	140 412	2 191 057	15 604	5 677	2 685 732	83.9	91 173	757 095
Emporia city...............	163	274 344	10 951	119.2	D	1 870	26 629	14 240	96	36 164	D	1 593	9 731
Hutchinson city............	238	510 316	12 996	141.4	13.2	2 966	50 680	17 087	103	56 728	85.8	1 927	14 607
Kansas City city	404	851 044	6 009	65.4	D	4 622	83 285	18 019	212	102 620	D	2 962	28 736
Lawrence city	413	731 454	9 617	104.6	15.3	5 420	77 808	14 356	222	117 862	81.3	4 511	33 611
Leavenworth city	128	271 966	6 899	75.1	D	1 638	24 346	14 863	63	27 630	91.2	1 104	8 288
Lenexa city	226	634 375	16 675	181.4	18.4	3 574	70 737	19 792	89	69 687	79.1	1 994	19 194
Manhattan city	294	484 394	11 508	125.2	18.0	3 570	47 784	13 385	153	75 321	74.7	3 003	21 180
Olathe city	319	1 106 948	13 471	146.6	D	4 695	97 779	20 826	128	79 178	93.8	2 785	23 661
Overland Park city	745	2 208 676	16 375	178.2	D	13 018	222 555	17 096	340	316 733	70.2	8 788	93 765
Salina city	302	663 450	14 958	162.8	21.2	4 285	62 746	14 643	127	66 109	D	2 357	20 046
Shawnee city..............	165	459 060	10 413	113.3	D	2 439	44 248	18 142	77	D	D	(5)	D
Topeka city	706	1 559 833	12 599	137.1	21.0	10 166	160 221	15 760	353	D	D	(6)	D
Wichita city	1 580	3 834 486	11 670	127.0	D	22 657	381 940	16 857	852	528 052	81.5	15 891	151 056
KENTUCKY.............	17 369	33 332 675	8 530	92.8	16.1	212 189	3 128 099	14 742	6 546	4 056 107	83.3	129 442	1 140 617
Bowling Green city	458	1 048 182	23 196	252.4	D	6 764	96 276	14 234	182	134 013	82.2	4 306	39 540
Covington city	173	310 066	7 638	83.1	D	1 869	32 404	17 338	133	87 499	83.5	2 283	24 258
Frankfort city	179	381 993	14 170	154.2	19.3	2 893	34 949	12 081	85	D	D	(5)	D
Henderson city	192	415 386	15 588	169.6	D	2 203	36 112	16 392	75	40 808	88.6	1 392	11 753
Hopkinsville city	241	405 996	12 728	138.5	D	2 498	39 647	15 871	72	42 392	D	1 713	14 881
Lexington-Fayette..........	1 251	3 133 071	13 078	142.3	D	20 363	308 747	15 162	610	508 106	72.2	15 216	146 858
Louisville city	1 166	2 069 021	8 061	87.7	11.4	15 744	239 986	15 243	648	507 595	74.8	15 529	147 741
Owensboro city	393	656 069	12 075	131.4	D	4 356	63 376	14 549	121	87 395	78.7	2 865	23 197
Paducah city	432	914 252	34 582	376.3	28.5	5 688	81 756	14 373	167	117 480	D	3 808	33 273
LOUISIANA.............	17 863	35 807 894	8 229	89.5	16.2	224 412	3 307 929	14 740	7 151	5 259 921	69.4	147 016	1 408 910
Alexandria city............	362	777 586	16 722	182.0	26.5	5 064	76 303	15 068	138	80 700	79.0	2 717	22 239
Baton Rouge city	1 408	3 382 504	15 745	171.3	14.3	20 737	328 884	15 860	594	409 481	84.1	13 431	113 590
Bossier City city	305	761 727	13 297	144.7	23.0	4 370	67 023	15 337	150	292 693	D	5 379	67 864
Houma city...............	246	437 482	13 563	147.6	D	3 088	42 444	13 745	86	41 843	97.5	1 262	13 210
Kenner city...............	350	968 897	13 501	146.9	D	5 765	86 461	14 998	160	148 442	68.6	3 712	35 446
Lafayette city.............	818	2 104 278	18 261	198.7	D	12 689	198 915	15 676	329	250 893	D	8 380	73 317
Lake Charles city	483	1 019 815	14 072	153.1	22.1	6 705	96 416	14 380	183	239 520	43.6	6 092	59 700
Monroe city	470	1 058 130	19 825	215.7	23.2	6 314	94 446	14 958	172	116 891	84.5	3 734	29 459
New Iberia city	214	505 347	15 244	165.9	D	2 748	43 328	15 767	71	29 561	D	1 186	7 691
New Orleans city	1 871	2 771 305	5 908	64.3	9.5	20 405	315 558	15 465	1 105	1 371 830	49.4	32 081	377 486
Shreveport city	930	2 056 451	10 827	117.8	D	12 010	198 309	16 512	374	219 333	85.6	7 150	61 237
MAINE	7 074	12 737 087	10 229	111.3	10.9	72 897	1 164 153	15 970	3 716	1 510 182	70.5	39 657	429 143
Bangor city...............	335	999 684	30 180	328.4	D	5 340	87 873	16 456	144	88 426	76.6	2 709	27 186
Lewiston city	202	593 116	16 349	177.9	6.4	2 548	40 067	15 725	77	32 171	85.8	1 032	9 673
Portland city..............	422	1 292 308	20 875	227.1	3.9	5 380	97 479	18 119	275	147 378	78.5	4 084	42 402
MARYLAND	19 798	46 428 206	9 116	99.2	12.5	274 260	4 913 952	17 917	9 049	5 972 467	81.2	161 273	1 644 729
Annapolis city	466	1 032 947	31 595	343.8	4.4	6 238	111 326	17 846	166	169 246	68.6	4 426	49 497
Baltimore city.............	2 256	3 438 384	5 229	56.9	D	23 159	414 701	17 907	1 328	849 854	72.1	20 021	231 966
Bowie city................	104	339 142	8 374	91.1	D	2 284	35 456	15 524	44	33 350	100.0	1 031	9 130
Frederick city.............	464	1 308 226	27 724	301.7	D	7 724	132 734	17 185	178	123 205	85.6	3 687	33 434
Gaithersburg city	333	1 340 111	29 359	319.5	D	6 573	128 742	19 586	144	129 504	70.8	3 327	35 097
Hagerstown city	305	689 739	19 639	213.7	17.9	4 123	62 438	15 144	124	78 475	75.2	2 604	22 286
Rockville city	305	983 574	21 199	230.7	D	4 250	97 397	22 917	183	104 948	80.1	2 703	28 140
MASSACHUSETTS......	26 209	58 578 048	9 579	104.2	10.1	335 736	5 894 813	17 558	14 827	9 282 541	78.4	227 898	2 579 922
Attleboro city	158	476 335	12 133	132.0	D	2 973	38 830	13 061	81	53 865	96.3	1 697	15 001
Beverly city	146	350 524	9 027	98.2	D	1 820	34 222	18 803	79	33 273	97.1	909	8 815
Boston city...............	2 262	4 255 687	7 656	83.3	6.5	26 624	472 016	17 729	1 908	2 049 540	66.0	39 844	576 264
Brockton city	359	932 387	10 022	109.1	9.6	5 414	106 418	19 656	150	88 176	93.3	2 658	24 910
Cambridge city	538	1 113 354	11 905	129.5	D	7 290	124 614	17 094	413	404 274	63.5	7 766	111 890
Chelsea city..............	98	241 404	8 781	95.5	D	1 260	24 648	19 562	62	D	D	(7)	D
Chicopee city.............	183	382 771	7 060	76.8	20.2	2 372	33 991	14 330	125	52 751	88.3	1 608	14 010
Everett city...............	85	123 901	3 543	38.6	1.5	595	11 390	19 143	55	D	D	(8)	D
Fall River city	349	592 374	6 544	71.2	6.0	3 408	61 074	17 921	181	78 334	98.2	2 276	20 919
Fitchburg city.............	170	349 761	8 687	94.5	13.5	2 011	39 198	19 492	101	46 930	D	1 370	12 694
Gloucester city	123	227 566	7 720	84.0	D	1 300	23 657	18 198	101	42 352	72.3	1 031	12 958
Haverhill city	158	420 748	7 741	84.2	D	2 202	39 322	17 857	123	D	D	(5)	D

[1] Includes only establishments with payroll. [2] Based on resident population estimated as of July 1, 1997. [3] For pay period including March 12. [4] Foodservices and drinking places (NAICS 722) includes full-service restaurants, limited-service eating places, special food services, and drinking places (alcoholic beverages). [5] 1,000 to 2,499 employees. [6] 5,000 to 9,999 employees. [7] 500 to 999 employees. [8] 250 to 499 employees.

Sources: Retail Trade—U.S. Census Bureau, 1997 Economic Census, ECON97 Report Series CD-ROM, CD-EC97-1, Disc 1D issued July 2000 and Disc 1E issued February 2001 (related Internet site <http://www.census.gov/epcd/www/97EC44.HTM>). Accommodation and Foodservices—U.S. Census Bureau, 1997 Economic Census, ECON97 Report Series CD-ROM, Disc 1E issued February 2001 (related Internet site <http://www.census.gov/epcd/www/97EC72.HTM>).

Table C–6. Cities — Retail Trade and Accommodation and Foodservices–Con.

[Includes states and 1,070 incorporated places of 25,000 or more population as of April 1, 1990 in all states except Hawaii which has no incorporated places recognized by the Census Bureau. For Hawaii, 8 census designated places (CDPs) of 25,000 or more population as of April 1, 1990 are included. Also included are the 5 boroughs of New York city. For more information on these areas, see appendix B. Geographic Information]

| City | Retail trade[1] (NAICS 44-45), 1997 | | | | | | | | Accommodation and foodservices[1] (NAICS 72), 1997 | | | | |
| | Sales | | | | | Annual payroll | | | Sales | | | | Annual payroll ($1,000) |
	Estab-lishments	Total ($1,000)	Per capita[2] Amount (dollars)	Percent of national average	Percent from general merchandise stores	Paid employees[3]	Total ($1,000)	Per paid employee (dollars)	Estab-lishments	Total ($1,000)	Percent from food-services[4]	Paid employees[3]	
MASSACHUSETTS—Con.													
Holyoke city	218	451 310	10 967	119.3	D	3 305	46 823	14 167	81	39 735	D	1 153	10 019
Lawrence city	158	328 440	4 763	51.8	D	1 255	29 921	23 841	84	D	D	(5)	D
Leominster city	209	494 228	12 498	136.0	D	3 166	45 426	14 348	95	42 466	94.4	1 344	11 582
Lowell city	256	472 409	4 661	50.7	D	2 514	44 091	17 538	174	D	D	(6)	D
Lynn city	213	429 785	5 315	57.8	9.0	2 658	43 897	16 515	132	D	D	(6)	D
Malden city	161	364 628	6 915	75.2	D	1 869	31 932	17 085	90	36 628	92.5	946	9 602
Marlborough city	219	494 256	14 892	162.0	14.9	3 074	58 954	19 178	115	80 028	73.8	2 024	23 397
Medford city	185	547 441	9 787	106.5	14.5	2 918	50 314	17 243	87	42 597	100.0	1 201	11 379
Melrose city	73	130 195	4 756	51.8	D	818	14 158	17 308	30	13 907	100.0	364	3 819
New Bedford city	325	499 444	5 252	57.1	D	3 273	52 196	15 947	209	70 739	D	2 019	17 393
Newton city	390	978 074	12 193	132.7	D	5 701	113 889	19 977	163	172 123	84.7	3 699	49 147
Northampton city	206	379 955	13 300	144.7	D	2 525	41 542	16 452	97	57 894	84.7	1 873	17 377
Peabody city	282	886 418	18 222	198.3	18.0	4 899	86 393	17 635	135	97 855	79.4	2 408	27 389
Pittsfield city	243	527 854	11 481	124.9	D	3 362	56 028	16 665	125	61 616	82.7	2 083	17 993
Quincy city	271	822 544	9 594	104.4	D	5 146	83 960	16 316	201	115 200	97.3	2 943	30 871
Revere city	140	302 783	7 273	79.1	D	1 882	31 273	16 617	84	D	D	(6)	D
Salem city	172	292 709	7 668	83.4	D	1 880	32 142	17 097	116	51 549	96.6	1 556	14 928
Somerville city	208	558 967	7 512	81.7	7.6	3 307	53 003	16 028	155	D	D	(6)	D
Springfield city	565	1 123 304	7 547	82.1	11.5	7 313	120 120	16 426	280	148 049	83.1	4 826	43 982
Taunton city	252	417 177	7 972	86.7	25.0	3 261	44 477	13 639	101	D	D	(6)	D
Waltham city	258	587 461	10 200	111.0	14.3	3 185	64 812	20 349	173	123 724	77.7	2 880	31 004
Westfield city	152	335 752	8 938	97.3	12.8	2 191	32 163	14 680	73	29 825		1 095	7 799
Woburn city	223	754 286	20 373	221.7	6.1	3 640	86 172	23 674	78	74 750	65.0	1 550	18 112
Worcester city	722	1 530 515	9 186	100.0	6.0	8 854	157 272	17 763	417	201 548	88.8	6 243	55 116
MICHIGAN	39 564	93 706 078	9 576	104.2	16.1	529 441	8 922 347	16 852	18 958	10 158 693	84.8	320 014	2 835 825
Allen Park city	104	115 375	3 558	38.7	D	852	13 498	15 843	62	34 486	D	1 276	8 674
Ann Arbor city	647	1 369 549	12 498	136.0	D	9 645	154 390	16 007	344	273 748	80.7	8 266	75 855
Battle Creek city	266	632 692	11 924	129.7	28.6	3 825	58 153	15 203	162	91 402	88.7	3 033	26 917
Bay City city	221	400 102	11 154	121.4	D	2 081	36 584	17 580	111	41 327	D	1 629	11 143
Burton city	228	513 522	18 838	205.0	34.0	3 754	56 250	14 984	82	43 226	97.5	1 445	12 060
Dearborn city	557	1 752 492	10 861	216.1	D	9 607	170 861	17 785	267	221 277	59.4	5 771	61 976
Dearborn Heights city	187	391 642	6 694	72.8	D	2 455	38 846	15 823	104	57 033	100.0	1 814	14 315
Detroit city	2 253	3 188 731	3 269	35.6	2.5	17 886	289 126	16 165	1 108	575 961	86.5	15 426	150 444
East Detroit city	137	325 695	9 439	102.7	D	1 671	32 536	19 471	36	D	D	(5)	D
East Lansing city	119	304 028	6 377	69.4	D	2 471	32 321	13 080	113	62 860	79.1	2 372	16 962
Farmington Hills city	328	1 100 432	13 813	150.3	D	4 696	104 190	22 187	181	131 372	86.0	3 779	38 245
Ferndale city	109	341 430	13 883	151.1	D	1 363	32 888	24 129	50	20 010	D	615	5 135
Flint city	531	864 639	6 470	70.4	4.4	5 157	86 346	16 743	266	112 853	96.0	3 824	29 750
Garden City city	111	392 147	11 837	128.8	D	1 300	31 475	24 212	54	26 353	100.0	740	6 139
Grand Rapids city	795	2 018 108	10 754	117.0	6.0	11 558	214 833	18 555	386	262 643	73.9	8 134	78 454
Holland city	230	612 317	18 226	198.3	D	3 525	58 708	16 655	87	57 273	82.0	2 258	19 078
Inkster city	55	86 682	2 724	29.6	D	470	7 898	16 804	28	8 941	79.6	164	1 950
Jackson city	237	567 488	15 853	172.5	D	3 671	56 338	15 347	111	57 854	97.0	1 769	14 637
Kalamazoo city	337	727 222	9 428	102.6	D	4 265	70 523	16 535	206	112 121	89.5	4 217	33 796
Kentwood city	267	855 438	20 345	221.4	D	5 718	84 409	14 762	102	84 700	85.6	2 798	24 709
Lansing city	523	1 486 621	11 621	126.5	17.8	8 178	150 244	18 372	260	159 815	83.0	5 620	47 739
Lincoln Park city	159	352 517	8 182	89.0	D	2 644	35 905	13 580	79	D	D	(6)	D
Livonia city	644	1 591 215	15 756	171.4	D	9 668	167 704	17 346	266	213 621	80.1	6 399	57 096
Madison Heights city	193	717 761	22 413	243.9	19.0	3 744	66 377	17 729	102	77 932	83.4	2 250	19 643
Midland city	256	584 715	14 357	156.2	D	3 673	59 356	16 160	93	67 984	D	2 330	20 532
Muskegon city	176	413 045	10 349	112.6	D	2 571	42 463	16 516	82	D	D	(6)	D
Novi city	323	1 177 759	26 730	290.9	D	6 100	105 404	17 279	96	90 871	D	2 778	28 735
Oak Park city	182	401 852	13 558	147.5	D	2 510	55 221	22 000	45	22 355	D	743	5 884
Pontiac city	228	502 329	7 282	79.2	3.3	2 548	44 588	17 499	130	D	D	(6)	D
Portage city	338	878 591	20 238	220.2	40.1	6 404	85 880	13 410	110	78 598	94.6	2 752	23 438
Port Huron city	168	375 655	11 595	126.2	.5	1 936	40 282	20 807	69	38 433	D	1 143	10 258
Rochester Hills city	240	968 282	14 407	156.8	D	4 340	92 345	21 278	103	76 673	96.4	2 592	22 425
Roseville city	293	966 290	18 639	202.8	30.6	5 807	91 208	15 707	111	83 202	91.0	2 563	22 269
Royal Oak city	297	773 883	11 916	129.7	D	4 193	85 433	20 375	143	106 984	96.2	3 071	32 866
Saginaw city	206	260 567	4 061	44.2	D	1 898	30 485	16 062	123	55 531	94.0	1 928	15 238
St. Clair Shores city	234	547 807	8 204	89.3	D	3 306	58 358	17 652	128	D	D	(6)	D
Southfield city	566	1 987 669	26 345	286.7	D	8 925	182 610	20 461	283	195 608	74.4	4 739	54 488
Southgate city	171	888 685	27 439	298.6	19.1	3 836	70 312	18 330	74	D	D	(6)	D
Sterling Heights city	495	1 598 878	12 886	140.2	28.8	9 680	160 011	16 530	202	126 314	91.5	4 083	36 663
Taylor city	343	1 036 976	14 010	152.4	25.3	6 038	102 263	16 937	154	84 416	93.5	2 789	22 921
Troy city	607	2 410 805	30 434	331.2	17.3	12 184	226 858	18 619	225	202 424	77.8	5 330	57 288
Warren city	563	1 730 709	12 044	131.1	7.3	8 524	172 001	20 178	301	193 252	87.3	5 435	51 404
Westland city	335	1 160 469	13 377	145.6	30.2	6 533	101 185	15 488	154	94 132	100.0	3 022	25 091
Wyandotte city	107	122 215	3 752	40.8	NA	753	13 349	17 728	68	26 768	D	901	7 198
Wyoming city	308	934 568	13 754	149.7	17.1	5 510	101 418	18 406	131	78 140	91.7	2 557	21 916

[1] Includes only establishments with payroll. [2] Based on resident population estimated as of July 1, 1997. [3] For pay period including March 12. [4] Foodservices and drinking places (NAICS 722) includes full-service restaurants, limited-service eating places, special food services, and drinking places (alcoholic beverages). [5] 500 to 999 employees. [6] 1,000 to 2,499 employees.

Sources: Retail Trade—U.S. Census Bureau, 1997 Economic Census, ECON97 Report Series CD-ROM, CD-EC97-1, Disc 1D issued July 2000 and Disc 1E issued February 2001 (related Internet site <http://www.census.gov/epcd/www/97EC44.HTM>). Accommodation and Foodservices—U.S. Census Bureau, 1997 Economic Census, ECON97 Report Series CD-ROM, Disc 1E issued February 2001 (related Internet site <http://www.census.gov/epcd/www/97EC72.HTM>).

Table C–6. Cities — Retail Trade and Accommodation and Foodservices–Con.

[Includes states and 1,070 incorporated places of 25,000 or more population as of April 1, 1990 in all states except Hawaii which has no incorporated places recognized by the Census Bureau. For Hawaii, 8 census designated places (CDPs) of 25,000 or more population as of April 1, 1990 are included. Also included are the 5 boroughs of New York city. For more information on these areas, see appendix B. Geographic Information]

City	Retail trade[1] (NAICS 44-45), 1997								Accommodation and foodservices[1] (NAICS 72), 1997				
	Sales				Paid employees[3]	Annual payroll			Sales			Paid employees[3]	Annual payroll ($1,000)
	Estab-lishments	Total ($1,000)	Per capita[2]		Percent from general mer-chandise stores		Total ($1,000)	Per paid employee (dollars)	Estab-lishments	Total ($1,000)	Percent from food-services[4]		
			Amount (dollars)	Percent of national average									
MINNESOTA	20 888	48 097 982	10 260	111.6	12.9	282 413	4 528 536	16 035	9 982	5 934 155	74.4	179 487	1 688 779
Apple Valley city	112	529 336	11 927	129.8	D	2 761	46 487	16 837	37	33 796	D	1 011	9 009
Blaine city	199	504 432	11 506	125.2	D	3 100	45 540	14 690	52	43 946	D	1 568	12 724
Bloomington city	587	2 078 983	24 200	263.3	11.7	12 036	201 297	16 725	246	383 294	D	9 049	106 736
Brooklyn Center city	133	675 022	24 233	263.7	D	3 435	57 994	16 883	45	44 491	74.6	1 456	14 113
Brooklyn Park city	154	1 220 100	19 757	215.0	10.0	4 656	93 634	20 110	68	D	D	(5)	D
Burnsville city	372	1 272 873	21 726	236.4	D	7 850	123 398	15 719	108	92 248	88.2	3 101	26 972
Coon Rapids city	151	573 715	9 174	99.8	D	3 412	49 275	14 442	77	53 680	85.4	1 705	15 467
Duluth city	536	1 037 130	12 658	137.7	20.2	7 277	110 779	15 223	241	156 271	76.8	4 872	43 101
Eagan city	140	555 125	9 502	103.4	16.7	3 251	57 423	17 663	102	82 735	83.1	2 541	26 577
Eden Prairie city	188	676 415	14 575	158.6	19.1	3 597	61 850	17 195	106	85 879	82.6	2 189	24 552
Edina city	377	1 182 862	25 805	280.8	D	8 123	132 554	16 318	89	D	D	(5)	D
Fridley city	107	482 453	17 359	188.9	D	2 863	47 030	16 427	45	28 224	D	1 145	8 767
Mankato city	266	702 447	22 465	244.5	D	4 823	66 059	13 697	111	62 353	94.2	2 295	17 126
Maple Grove city	97	277 628	6 057	65.9	D	1 569	24 859	15 844	55	42 142	D	1 552	12 469
Maplewood city	254	854 634	25 079	272.9	D	4 936	77 497	15 700	87	64 133	91.6	2 249	18 796
Minneapolis city	1 333	2 343 990	6 588	71.7	10.1	15 860	287 715	18 141	921	828 882	68.2	20 653	246 773
Minnetonka city	352	1 157 626	22 662	246.6	D	7 410	116 502	15 722	110	108 444	77.4	2 804	32 927
Moorhead city	138	361 624	10 822	117.8	D	2 113	28 657	13 562	65	32 179	89.2	1 349	9 655
Plymouth city	165	1 460 423	24 086	262.1	D	4 057	109 482	26 986	72	107 399	D	2 130	31 574
Richfield city	148	438 704	12 955	141.0	D	2 746	46 234	16 837	52	45 433	95.0	1 414	12 615
Rochester city	505	1 312 809	16 947	184.4	D	8 698	126 770	14 575	247	196 743	D	5 624	56 412
Roseville city	350	1 210 650	35 399	385.2	D	8 031	122 886	15 301	103	102 315	92.5	3 362	31 082
St. Cloud city	373	1 065 252	18 443	200.7	D	6 530	99 068	15 171	142	100 472	80.7	3 759	27 517
St. Louis Park city	232	671 498	15 754	171.4	21.4	3 851	69 671	18 092	89	66 540	83.4	2 255	20 605
St. Paul city	872	1 907 304	7 398	80.5	D	12 246	225 698	18 430	599	350 907	88.8	10 532	105 541
Winona city	173	313 623	12 208	132.8	D	2 135	30 377	14 228	85	40 033	D	1 501	10 638
MISSISSIPPI	12 791	20 774 508	7 605	82.8	17.3	138 372	1 935 338	13 986	4 050	3 064 753	55.7	84 834	814 454
Biloxi city	259	403 177	8 542	92.9	D	3 162	44 938	14 212	144	183 215	38.8	4 911	51 793
Greenville city	252	413 236	9 645	105.0	23.7	3 048	41 621	13 655	80	44 726	79.7	1 400	11 673
Gulfport city	395	861 529	13 219	143.8	20.6	4 958	77 839	15 700	156	87 357	81.7	3 017	23 006
Hattiesburg city	385	818 709	16 984	184.8	24.8	5 542	78 686	14 198	161	101 078	83.9	3 502	26 486
Jackson city	968	2 595 633	14 084	153.3	D	15 841	265 659	16 770	396	293 346	80.2	9 427	85 027
Meridian city	434	753 034	18 131	197.3	D	5 009	72 778	14 529	138	85 802	D	2 777	23 544
Pascagoula city	186	499 830	18 341	199.6	12.0	2 632	41 540	15 783	59	35 992	85.5	1 272	9 858
Tupelo city	431	895 168	24 845	270.3	D	5 785	84 673	14 637	134	78 283	D	2 662	21 672
MISSOURI	24 181	51 269 881	9 482	103.2	15.2	297 556	4 945 014	16 619	11 150	6 780 812	74.7	203 849	1 933 340
Blue Springs city	171	534 311	11 322	123.2	D	2 833	51 153	18 056	83	52 008	87.2	1 868	14 940
Cape Girardeau city	359	780 584	21 564	234.6	D	4 893	72 991	14 917	103	76 986	D	2 468	21 454
Chesterfield city	218	380 525	8 594	93.5	D	3 564	47 472	13 320	78	D	D	(5)	D
Columbia city	491	1 270 791	16 000	174.8	D	7 836	116 742	14 898	278	173 580	83.6	5 731	46 644
Florissant city	227	688 246	13 428	146.1	21.2	4 432	68 731	15 508	131	D	D	(5)	D
Gladstone city	104	317 239	11 283	122.8	D	1 828	31 277	17 110	52	D	D	(5)	D
Independence city	507	1 278 361	11 028	120.0	20.2	8 120	127 979	15 761	221	143 062	93.6	4 577	41 474
Jefferson City city	260	693 986	19 091	207.7	20.1	4 191	64 375	15 360	118	80 647	73.4	2 619	23 563
Joplin city	438	970 577	21 721	236.4	30.9	6 287	89 816	14 286	187	116 076	86.2	4 118	33 919
Kansas City city	1 843	5 773 028	13 247	144.1	12.4	27 774	510 953	18 397	1 053	1 042 546	58.5	26 879	312 300
Kirkwood city	140	437 889	15 899	173.0	D	1 994	44 949	22 542	55	30 235	D	1 113	9 601
Lee's Summit city	195	475 341	7 383	80.3	D	2 709	46 320	17 099	89	53 589	D	1 798	15 640
Maryland Heights city	127	717 342	29 663	322.8	D	3 459	80 014	23 132	75	126 677	36.8	3 097	38 790
Raytown city	137	498 701	16 366	178.1	D	2 804	49 174	17 537	60	25 437	100.0	921	7 066
St. Charles city	300	650 021	11 195	121.8	D	3 815	61 261	16 058	176	113 572	93.1	3 783	31 878
St. Joseph city	382	777 625	11 107	120.9	D	4 733	71 165	15 036	189	94 250	D	3 133	26 101
St. Louis city	1 241	2 361 726	6 856	74.6	D	14 511	282 422	19 463	954	686 612	73.4	18 843	195 758
St. Peters city	308	1 000 784	19 694	214.3	D	5 619	95 685	17 029	111	64 978	D	2 492	19 198
Springfield city	1 106	2 937 427	20 365	221.6	19.1	16 060	266 669	16 605	545	335 789	D	11 243	96 160
University City city	105	164 070	4 334	47.2	D	1 366	20 618	15 094	67	D	D	(6)	D

[1] Includes only establishments with payroll.　[2] Based on resident population estimated as of July 1, 1997.　[3] For pay period including March 12.　[4] Foodservices and drinking places (NAICS 722) includes full-service restaurants, limited-service eating places, special food services, and drinking places (alcoholic beverages).　[5] 1,000 to 2,499 employees.　[6] 500 to 999 employees.

Sources: Retail Trade—U.S. Census Bureau, 1997 Economic Census, ECON97 Report Series CD-ROM, CD-EC97-1, Disc 1D issued July 2000 and Disc 1E issued February 2001 (related Internet site <http://www.census.gov/epcd/www/97EC44.HTM>). Accommodation and Foodservices—U.S. Census Bureau, 1997 Economic Census, ECON97 Report Series CD-ROM, Disc 1E issued February 2001 (related Internet site <http://www.census.gov/epcd/www/97EC72.HTM>).

Table C–6. Cities — **Retail Trade and Accommodation and Foodservices**–Con.

[Includes states and 1,070 incorporated places of 25,000 or more population as of April 1, 1990 in all states except Hawaii which has no incorporated places recognized by the Census Bureau. For Hawaii, 8 census designated places (CDPs) of 25,000 or more population as of April 1, 1990 are included. Also included are the 5 boroughs of New York city. For more information on these areas, see appendix B. Geographic Information]

City	Retail trade[1] (NAICS 44-45), 1997							Accommodation and foodservices[1] (NAICS 72), 1997				
		Sales				Annual payroll			Sales			
			Per capita[2]		Percent from general merchandise stores							
	Estab-lishments	Total ($1,000)	Amount (dollars)	Percent of national average		Paid employees[3]	Total ($1,000)	Per paid employee (dollars)	Estab-lishments	Total ($1,000)	Percent from food-services[4]	Paid employees[3]	Annual payroll ($1,000)
MONTANA..............	5 042	7 779 112	8 853	96.3	14.7	48 337	746 459	15 443	3 280	1 199 251	71.8	38 551	325 510
Billings city...............	642	1 431 996	15 617	169.9	D	8 103	133 831	16 516	303	186 219	78.6	6 137	53 726
Butte-Silver Bow (remainder)	[5]220	[5]333 086	[5]9 691	[5]105.5	D	[5]2 147	[5]32 042	[5]14 924	[5]130	[5]47 814	[5]79.9	[5]1 354	[5]12 286
Great Falls city	389	782 903	13 833	150.5	D	4 895	79 836	16 310	223	95 818	D	3 277	26 978
Missoula city	463	989 962	17 194	187.1	D	6 166	97 136	15 753	259	129 673	77.8	4 322	36 363
NEBRASKA.............	8 295	16 529 333	9 981	108.6	13.3	102 684	1 554 621	15 140	4 070	1 726 647	83.5	61 048	488 208
Bellevue city	124	379 155	8 689	94.5	17.7	2 335	34 605	14 820	78	35 104	88.6	1 196	10 058
Grand Island city	307	658 478	15 797	171.9	D	4 256	63 589	14 941	139	67 747	82.5	2 702	20 184
Lincoln city	952	2 197 539	10 388	113.0	16.3	15 326	225 224	14 696	518	309 710	D	10 856	89 225
Omaha city	1 786	5 479 272	14 366	156.3	11.7	33 724	572 296	16 970	960	590 837	D	18 796	176 094
NEVADA...............	6 222	18 220 790	10 874	118.3	13.5	89 452	1 798 249	20 103	3 633	15 323 751	12.8	241 682	4 665 524
Carson City	262	678 405	13 942	151.7	D	3 383	66 080	19 533	133	93 051	51.0	2 404	27 726
Henderson city	321	1 252 566	9 153	99.6	D	5 824	113 609	19 507	167	206 841	47.6	3 736	55 002
Las Vegas city............	1 516	5 811 508	14 860	161.7	9.5	24 600	535 734	21 778	872	2 283 705	23.3	43 124	836 121
North Las Vegas city	138	433 905	4 900	53.3	7.2	2 277	39 734	17 450	53	127 609	D	2 276	37 429
Reno city	928	2 865 817	17 802	193.7	D	14 619	294 198	20 124	566	1 407 604	17.0	26 478	462 853
Sparks city...............	256	640 186	10 552	114.8	D	3 559	71 166	19 996	117	253 548	18.0	5 118	71 812
NEW HAMPSHIRE	6 645	15 812 027	13 477	146.6	13.1	84 170	1 421 994	16 894	3 033	1 544 942	76.4	43 996	450 258
Concord city	331	943 649	24 538	267.0	D	4 578	75 745	16 545	119	73 468	90.0	2 266	21 612
Dover city.................	119	270 120	10 364	112.8	D	1 603	27 629	17 236	61	D	D	(6)	D
Manchester city	561	1 547 567	15 268	166.1	D	7 594	140 505	18 502	231	140 316	89.4	4 121	38 422
Nashua city	492	1 848 842	22 633	246.3	15.7	9 611	161 187	16 771	183	131 867	79.1	3 714	39 634
Portsmouth city	273	881 012	34 537	375.8	9.4	3 784	66 995	17 705	154	123 979	67.5	2 978	35 469
Rochester city	143	371 169	13 336	145.1	D	2 154	35 404	16 436	61	24 569	95.0	761	6 688
NEW JERSEY	34 837	79 914 892	9 922	108.0	10.2	420 724	7 926 020	18 839	16 975	13 416 088	53.6	252 031	3 610 740
Atlantic City city	255	296 544	7 803	84.9	D	1 832	31 755	17 334	205	4 717 149	D	48 506	1 246 014
Bayonne city	224	232 060	3 824	41.6	1.3	1 588	31 766	20 004	114	D	(7)	(7)	D
Camden city	158	241 676	2 867	31.2	2.1	1 212	24 052	19 845	84	25 214	97.8	583	5 757
Clifton city	286	767 762	10 175	110.7	14.0	4 075	78 976	19 381	142	D	D	(6)	D
East Orange city	131	149 114	2 130	23.2	1.9	939	16 961	18 063	59	37 221	92.6	955	9 411
Elizabeth city	396	723 755	6 549	71.3	D	3 947	65 121	16 499	227	117 876	52.9	2 132	30 013
Fair Lawn borough	116	241 669	7 818	85.1	NA	1 199	24 068	20 073	59	22 456	D	566	6 105
Fort Lee borough	158	300 728	9 054	98.5	D	1 588	28 868	18 179	96	53 608	67.6	1 062	15 015
Garfield city	81	137 545	5 054	55.0	D	817	17 356	21 244	48	12 196	100.0	305	3 130
Hackensack city	284	719 764	19 118	208.0	D	3 895	82 094	21 077	108	D	D	(6)	D
Hoboken city	152	129 982	3 896	42.4	D	974	12 678	13 016	132	46 912	98.7	1 150	12 581
Jersey City city	809	1 535 952	6 662	72.5	16.0	8 787	144 562	16 452	345	121 303	93.0	2 789	32 506
Kearny town	131	237 337	6 731	73.2	D	1 550	28 468	18 366	74	D	D	(7)	D
Linden city	195	502 364	13 621	148.2	16.8	2 303	50 339	21 858	103	39 229	85.5	987	11 110
Long Branch city...........	73	147 487	5 044	54.9	D	785	15 131	19 275	77	39 180	D	941	12 546
Millville city................	100	257 659	9 698	105.5	D	1 621	26 438	16 310	44	14 326	D	408	3 833
Newark city	832	912 814	3 419	37.2	3.1	5 920	101 539	17 152	454	335 022	67.0	5 346	88 512
New Brunswick city	136	149 717	3 595	39.1	D	1 208	18 540	15 348	131	67 298	D	1 614	19 508
Paramus borough..........	623	2 438 341	95 218	1 036.1	21.6	13 648	249 347	18 270	128	98 384	91.4	2 306	25 365
Passaic city	218	440 088	7 209	78.4	D	1 961	38 497	19 631	68	19 299	98.2	418	4 360
Paterson city	382	409 303	2 752	29.9	4.7	2 513	48 108	19 144	154	39 932	D	861	10 287
Perth Amboy city	152	215 462	5 120	55.7	.9	1 302	21 753	16 707	71	18 869	D	448	3 765
Plainfield city	122	136 265	2 947	32.1	1.1	813	15 987	19 664	46	D	D	(7)	D
Rahway city	86	166 144	6 584	71.6	NA	609	13 319	21 870	66	24 544	96.3	572	6 307
Sayreville borough	104	243 006	6 376	69.4	D	1 673	24 758	14 799	45	15 505	91.2	414	3 828
Trenton city	240	353 873	4 165	45.3	D	2 039	41 104	20 159	187	51 783	98.0	1 131	13 259
Union City city	319	264 986	4 617	50.2	1.0	1 504	25 542	16 983	143	D	D	(7)	D
Vineland city	308	643 751	11 522	125.4	D	3 680	69 585	18 909	100	44 810	D	1 531	12 307
Westfield town	170	234 291	8 021	87.3	D	1 338	25 793	19 277	64	D	D	(7)	D
West New York town	217	150 398	3 918	42.6	3.5	1 028	17 029	16 565	66	17 548	100.0	502	4 177

[1] Includes only establishments with payroll.   [2] Based on resident population estimated as of July 1, 1997.   [3] For pay period including March 12.   [4] Foodservices and drinking places (NAICS 722) includes full-service restaurants, limited-service eating places, special food services, and drinking places (alcoholic beverages).   [5] Data are for consolidated city of Butte-Silver Bow; data for Butte-Silver Bow (remainder) not available.   [6] 1,000 to 2,499 employees.   [7] 500 to 999 employees.

Sources: Retail Trade—U.S. Census Bureau, 1997 Economic Census, ECON97 Report Series CD-ROM, CD-EC97-1, Disc 1D issued July 2000 and Disc 1E issued February 2001 (related Internet site <http://www.census.gov/epcd/www/97EC44.HTM>).   Accommodation and Foodservices—U.S. Census Bureau, 1997 Economic Census, ECON97 Report Series CD-ROM, Disc 1E issued February 2001 (related Internet site <http://www.census.gov/epcd/www/97EC72.HTM>).

[Includes states and 1,070 incorporated places of 25,000 or more population as of April 1, 1990 in all states except Hawaii which has no incorporated places recognized by the Census Bureau. For Hawaii, 8 census designated places (CDPs) of 25,000 or more population as of April 1, 1990 are included. Also included are the 5 boroughs of New York city. For more information on these areas, see appendix B. Geographic Information]

City	Retail trade[1] (NAICS 44-45), 1997								Accommodation and foodservices[1] (NAICS 72), 1997				
	Sales					Annual payroll			Sales				
			Per capita[2]		Percent from general mer-chandise stores						Percent from food-services[4]		Annual payroll ($1,000)
	Estab-lishments	Total ($1,000)	Amount (dollars)	Percent of national average		Paid employees[3]	Total ($1,000)	Per paid employee (dollars)	Estab-lishments	Total ($1,000)		Paid employees[3]	
NEW MEXICO	7 421	14 984 454	8 697	94.6	14.2	86 300	1 455 458	16 865	3 827	2 146 558	73.1	67 203	599 757
Alamogordo city	164	287 616	9 940	108.2	D	1 996	28 541	14 299	73	29 281	80.9	1 068	7 696
Albuquerque city...........	2 004	5 914 566	14 052	152.9	D	30 720	568 707	18 513	1 083	814 460	74.2	24 795	229 258
Clovis city................	221	330 548	9 717	105.7	D	2 352	33 289	14 153	79	45 652	85.8	1 605	13 024
Farmington city	359	806 932	21 069	229.3	D	4 854	79 017	16 279	121	79 754	79.6	2 783	21 690
Hobbs city	175	336 095	12 112	131.8	D	1 914	34 763	18 162	78	33 512	D	1 152	8 947
Las Cruces city	407	955 616	12 715	138.4	D	5 655	89 148	15 764	208	103 209	82.3	3 396	27 192
Rio Rancho city...........	64	292 401	6 005	65.3	D	1 505	28 259	18 777	48	25 796	85.9	829	6 899
Roswell city	243	384 278	8 079	87.9	20.1	2 542	37 745	14 849	106	51 523	79.1	1 859	13 722
Santa Fe city	782	1 368 273	20 042	218.1	D	7 504	143 057	19 064	329	288 942	57.6	7 045	84 493
NEW YORK............	75 241	139 303 944	7 678	83.5	11.4	805 208	14 329 825	17 796	38 051	21 680 529	74.5	473 481	6 104 432
Albany city	492	1 074 159	11 222	122.1	13.2	6 830	113 178	16 571	365	152 166	83.5	4 395	41 072
Auburn city	183	412 063	13 861	150.8	16.7	2 671	41 361	15 485	94	34 325	88.0	1 266	10 001
Binghamton city	202	452 300	9 468	103.0	D	3 239	45 209	13 958	157	64 793	78.8	2 278	18 895
Buffalo city	916	1 243 881	4 087	44.5	6.6	10 187	154 348	15 151	678	252 259	86.5	8 280	70 506
Elmira city	119	234 800	7 394	80.5	D	1 685	23 775	14 110	80	D	D	(5)	D
Freeport village	162	431 116	10 807	117.6	D	1 964	39 875	20 303	71	27 193	88.8	586	8 123
Hempstead village	208	570 329	12 311	134.0	.4	1 584	43 118	27 221	53	30 780	D	709	8 102
Ithaca city	273	491 018	16 617	180.8	D	3 581	52 797	14 744	213	81 308	80.3	2 718	23 332
Jamestown city	149	425 097	12 840	139.7	16.8	2 638	38 955	14 767	96	26 106	76.0	897	6 866
Lindenhurst village	102	170 403	6 455	70.2	D	991	20 404	20 589	65	24 779	96.9	684	6 150
Long Beach city	93	88 353	2 576	28.0	D	549	9 981	18 180	43	12 482	100.0	269	3 235
Mount Vernon city	240	303 495	4 534	49.3	1.2	1 739	37 959	21 828	63	15 782	100.0	376	3 896
Newburgh city	121	197 724	7 549	82.1	16.6	1 277	21 763	17 042	62	D	D	(5)	D
New Rochelle city.........	256	609 360	9 033	98.3	D	2 581	50 969	19 748	123	D	D	1 750	D
New York city	28 456	41 912 167	5 677	61.8	10.2	232 494	4 731 064	20 349	13 728	11 008 676	67.6	182 518	3 122 961
Bronx borough	3 110	3 434 878	2 884	31.4	D	21 641	352 543	16 291	1 067	371 580	95.2	8 264	95 747
Brooklyn borough	6 994	7 983 578	3 523	38.3	8.2	45 941	821 809	17 888	2 221	734 498	97.0	15 748	188 129
Manhattan borough	11 222	19 502 446	12 652	137.7	11.4	102 965	2 447 153	23 767	7 219	8 318 219	59.5	127 621	2 423 407
Queens borough	5 933	8 755 996	4 416	48.1	8.3	48 425	890 129	18 382	2 668	1 344 780	88.4	25 458	360 360
Staten Island borough	1 197	2 235 269	5 562	60.5	D	13 522	219 430	16 228	553	239 599	97.8	5 427	55 318
Niagara Falls city	255	438 881	7 632	83.0	D	3 437	44 988	13 089	222	104 779	D	3 254	28 379
North Tonawanda city	103	134 578	4 042	44.0	D	1 159	15 250	13 158	60	12 414	100.0	477	3 300
Poughkeepsie city	172	195 607	7 058	76.8	D	1 475	23 694	16 064	91	39 849	84.9	894	9 731
Rochester city	756	1 140 792	5 204	56.6	9.5	8 251	131 868	15 982	516	222 521	81.8	6 498	63 928
Rome city	164	321 591	7 960	86.6	24.1	2 177	29 927	13 747	85	28 205	92.6	957	7 884
Saratoga Springs city......	183	374 996	14 718	160.2	D	2 348	35 855	15 270	121	87 717	64.7	2 107	26 357
Schenectady city	235	338 427	5 446	59.3	D	2 169	35 462	16 349	182	51 527	89.7	1 453	14 345
Syracuse city.............	708	1 346 770	8 784	95.6	10.8	8 860	147 387	16 635	414	167 851	83.6	5 253	50 680
Troy city	168	330 158	6 381	69.4	D	2 258	34 292	15 187	127	46 086	92.1	1 590	13 645
Utica city	218	346 480	5 770	62.8	D	2 461	35 988	14 623	149	50 402	75.1	1 625	14 101
Valley Stream village	251	586 848	17 297	188.2	D	2 873	51 238	17 834	89	41 684	D	1 133	10 434
Watertown city	273	519 384	18 383	200.0	26.2	3 743	52 603	14 054	122	57 196	88.3	1 642	15 073
White Plains city	497	1 176 712	23 620	257.0	17.7	6 946	133 364	19 200	180	113 779	D	2 103	29 221
Yonkers city..............	620	1 533 440	8 042	87.5	14.2	8 171	144 804	17 722	249	102 239	90.3	2 103	25 152
NORTH CAROLINA......	35 563	72 356 763	9 740	106.0	11.9	416 287	6 697 393	16 088	14 579	8 624 993	80.2	262 848	2 393 158
Asheville city	794	1 762 033	26 629	289.8	D	10 637	170 788	16 056	356	267 980	68.4	7 242	81 386
Burlington city	419	829 438	19 872	216.2	14.9	5 403	82 275	15 228	151	103 738	86.9	3 553	28 281
Cary town................	410	1 218 289	14 792	161.0	D	7 311	108 225	14 803	187	132 829	86.3	3 765	37 486
Chapel Hill town	223	480 604	11 254	122.5	D	3 347	58 352	17 434	211	130 131	69.4	3 566	38 031
Charlotte city	2 306	6 830 312	13 742	149.5	D	35 463	662 534	18 682	1 277	1 008 690	71.7	27 598	279 106
Concord city	228	667 019	14 491	157.7	16.8	3 734	61 336	16 426	89	66 398	91.5	1 915	18 027
Durham city	909	1 833 087	10 674	116.1	D	12 206	195 667	16 030	386	295 920	70.2	7 800	81 865
Fayetteville city	755	2 089 880	19 238	209.3	18.5	12 055	193 376	16 041	354	246 779	84.5	8 134	67 216
Gastonia city	442	1 128 102	18 362	199.8	18.1	6 895	103 301	14 982	166	106 974	91.5	3 346	29 085
Goldsboro city	371	812 362	17 826	194.0	20.2	4 996	70 478	14 107	125	73 027	D	2 553	19 929
Greensboro city	1 294	3 389 981	17 144	186.6	11.0	19 942	350 023	17 552	653	489 267	78.4	15 531	142 712
Greenville city	474	1 144 520	20 138	219.1	D	6 729	105 325	15 652	198	138 670	D	4 854	38 063
Hickory city	493	1 291 339	40 271	438.2	18.6	7 484	122 209	16 329	195	127 523	88.4	4 498	37 351
High Point city	501	1 173 907	15 583	169.6	D	6 575	117 551	17 878	184	97 129	96.0	3 023	27 930
Jacksonville city	321	758 356	11 089	120.7	16.5	4 561	69 214	15 175	137	76 746	84.8	2 729	20 424

[1] Includes only establishments with payroll. [2] Based on resident population estimated as of July 1, 1997. [3] For pay period including March 12. [4] Foodservices and drinking places (NAICS 722) includes full-service restaurants, limited-service eating places, special food services, and drinking places (alcoholic beverages). [5] 500 to 999 employees.

Sources: Retail Trade—U.S. Census Bureau, 1997 Economic Census, ECON97 Report Series CD-ROM, CD-EC97-1, Disc 1D issued July 2000 and Disc 1E issued February 2001 (related Internet site <http://www.census.gov/epcd/www/97EC44.HTM>). Accommodation and Foodservices—U.S. Census Bureau, 1997 Economic Census, ECON97 Report Series CD-ROM, Disc 1E issued February 2001 (related Internet site <http://www.census.gov/epcd/www/97EC72.HTM>).

[Includes states and 1,070 incorporated places of 25,000 or more population as of April 1, 1990 in all states except Hawaii which has no incorporated places recognized by the Census Bureau. For Hawaii, 8 census designated places (CDPs) of 25,000 or more population as of April 1, 1990 are included. Also included are the 5 boroughs of New York city. For more information on these areas, see appendix B. Geographic Information]

City	Retail trade[1] (NAICS 44-45), 1997								Accommodation and foodservices[1] (NAICS 72), 1997				
	Sales					Annual payroll			Sales				Annual payroll ($1,000)
			Per capita[2]		Percent from general merchandise stores								
	Estab-lishments	Total ($1,000)	Amount (dollars)	Percent of national average		Paid employees[3]	Total ($1,000)	Per paid employee (dollars)	Estab-lishments	Total ($1,000)	Percent from food-services[4]	Paid employees[3]	
NORTH CAROLINA—Con.													
Kannapolis city	189	350 876	10 196	110.9	15.8	2 223	33 344	15 000	58	30 977	D	909	8 350
Kinston city	258	462 018	18 277	198.9	13.0	2 935	42 017	14 316	75	46 458	89.9	1 517	13 197
Raleigh city	1 618	4 568 535	17 856	194.3	10.2	22 689	414 455	18 267	780	606 205	80.9	16 886	171 332
Rocky Mount city	392	825 342	14 281	155.4	12.4	4 833	76 388	15 806	118	81 171	79.7	2 549	22 073
Wilmington city	743	1 952 231	31 735	345.3	12.9	9 566	163 592	17 101	289	203 495	80.3	6 562	56 914
Wilson city	319	663 138	16 387	178.3	12.4	3 975	60 428	15 202	115	76 225	90.7	2 463	20 503
Winston-Salem city	1 101	2 769 234	16 403	178.5	14.6	15 734	260 432	16 552	479	327 724	85.0	10 328	93 995
NORTH DAKOTA	3 569	6 702 134	10 457	113.8	13.9	40 685	616 136	15 144	1 827	684 930	77.7	26 330	188 982
Bismarck city	356	808 435	14 782	160.8	D	5 081	81 952	16 129	149	95 685	D	3 444	27 551
Fargo city	486	1 588 856	18 614	202.5	D	9 166	152 958	16 688	242	178 660	72.5	6 616	51 464
Grand Forks city	312	889 197	17 998	195.8	D	5 345	77 454	14 491	152	88 444	D	3 941	26 051
Minot city	292	711 704	19 774	215.2	D	4 534	69 821	15 399	131	67 998	D	2 678	19 752
OHIO	44 521	102 938 830	9 181	99.9	14.6	630 098	9 924 531	15 751	22 631	12 410 978	86.6	401 206	3 444 193
Akron city	908	1 731 690	8 023	87.3	12.4	11 912	192 477	16 158	489	223 929	96.0	7 364	62 555
Barberton city	93	123 804	4 499	49.0	D	873	12 635	14 473	57	22 508	D	692	5 766
Beavercreek city	230	707 378	18 650	202.9	D	4 947	64 836	13 106	69	D	D	(5)	D
Bowling Green city	124	262 503	9 244	100.6	19.6	1 895	23 679	12 496	87	39 657	87.4	1 808	11 001
Brunswick city	102	307 848	9 680	105.3	D	1 285	24 932	19 402	48	21 350	90.8	824	6 025
Canton city	391	775 748	9 688	105.4	13.3	5 050	78 762	15 596	208	100 121	90.8	3 620	26 996
Cincinnati city	1 334	3 016 965	8 871	96.5	6.4	18 093	308 689	17 061	829	564 120	77.4	16 006	158 053
Cleveland city	1 607	2 378 305	4 751	51.7	4.2	15 454	276 668	17 903	1 099	674 440	73.2	17 757	176 852
Cleveland Heights city	154	278 705	5 183	56.4	D	1 594	28 812	18 075	83	D	D	(5)	D
Columbus city	2 717	8 595 454	12 852	139.8	17.1	51 028	897 662	17 592	1 508	1 160 046	79.2	32 807	334 746
Cuyahoga Falls city	207	760 299	15 436	168.0	5.4	3 683	64 699	17 567	123	79 810	D	2 695	23 531
Dayton city	529	1 045 209	6 072	66.1	16.2	6 801	113 724	16 722	327	180 698	80.7	5 098	47 967
East Cleveland city	69	54 292	1 791	19.5	D	515	6 711	13 031	29	14 063	D	454	3 752
Elyria city	272	705 629	12 499	136.0	D	4 415	66 093	14 970	124	68 638	88.5	2 278	17 552
Euclid city	169	314 673	6 080	66.2	D	2 418	32 516	13 447	83	D	D	(6)	D
Fairborn city	101	224 369	6 829	74.3	6.6	1 328	18 992	14 020	70	50 630	74.8	1 656	14 620
Fairfield city	182	710 553	16 873	183.6	D	3 254	60 575	18 616	81	48 531	97.1	1 727	13 638
Findlay city	259	569 301	14 913	162.3	D	3 665	52 285	14 266	143	74 718	88.2	2 766	22 336
Gahanna city	89	189 239	6 371	69.3	D	1 296	17 601	13 581	64	38 232	100.0	1 272	11 493
Garfield Heights city	78	179 943	6 108	66.5	D	1 287	18 562	14 423	54	D	D	(6)	D
Hamilton city	233	375 273	6 076	66.1	12.7	2 755	40 251	14 610	130	62 053	93.2	2 184	16 978
Huber Heights city	129	276 577	6 662	72.5	D	2 150	26 132	12 154	79	45 248	95.2	1 524	12 519
Kent city	74	338 132	12 622	137.3	D	1 215	26 281	21 630	84	33 331	92.2	1 328	9 931
Kettering city	228	756 013	12 892	140.3	16.8	4 821	71 191	14 767	115	D	D	(7)	D
Lakewood city	155	300 560	5 346	58.2	D	1 767	30 868	17 469	112	41 300	92.8	1 356	10 659
Lancaster city	270	540 002	14 863	161.7	D	3 868	57 859	14 958	100	66 322	92.8	2 249	18 410
Lima city	188	361 876	8 347	90.8	D	2 143	33 516	15 640	93	43 702	93.9	1 427	11 721
Lorain city	175	314 930	4 531	49.3	D	2 148	29 514	13 740	99	D	D	(5)	D
Mansfield city	273	486 581	9 308	101.3	3.8	3 186	53 133	16 677	143	74 029	90.7	2 289	20 331
Maple Heights city	135	197 879	7 721	84.0	D	1 750	23 014	13 151	47	19 251	100.0	575	4 976
Marion city	156	397 677	10 730	116.8	31.1	2 482	37 350	15 048	67	41 598	D	1 395	10 832
Massillon city	128	296 622	9 621	104.7	12.5	1 831	28 069	15 330	79	30 980	96.9	1 107	7 460
Mentor city	401	1 316 314	25 836	281.1	D	7 492	120 605	16 098	127	86 464	97.9	3 338	24 867
Middletown city	193	327 027	6 137	66.8	17.9	2 232	33 532	15 023	97	69 484	93.1	2 370	19 994
Newark city	192	323 258	7 098	77.2	D	2 038	32 932	16 159	102	40 607	97.2	1 335	11 079
North Olmsted city	324	935 636	28 997	315.5	D	5 444	76 903	14 126	117	72 263	90.7	2 617	20 628
Parma city	366	794 053	9 485	103.2	17.8	5 440	80 811	14 855	189	76 247	99.8	2 778	20 355
Reynoldsburg city	101	151 668	5 142	56.0	25.4	1 214	16 636	13 703	75	33 572	91.9	1 043	9 023
Sandusky city	224	419 714	14 696	159.9	D	3 016	43 351	14 374	123	104 935	D	2 853	28 798
Shaker Heights city	89	203 876	6 972	75.9	D	1 187	19 578	16 494	38	22 599	100.0	779	6 092
Springfield city	328	724 226	10 924	118.9	21.3	4 983	70 569	14 162	169	95 036	91.8	3 258	26 277
Stow city	99	266 386	8 640	94.0	D	1 971	29 165	14 797	44	23 598	100.0	886	6 194
Strongsville city	226	511 280	12 967	141.1	30.3	4 434	57 386	12 942	95	51 437	92.8	2 151	13 355
Toledo city	1 281	2 513 079	8 013	87.2	D	18 732	280 365	14 967	737	424 039	89.9	13 187	112 286
Upper Arlington city	124	156 683	4 886	53.2	D	1 511	21 348	14 128	53	29 550	100.0	1 016	9 173
Warren city	281	761 250	15 525	168.9	8.7	4 639	82 118	17 702	137	67 946	89.2	2 415	18 360
Westerville city	136	283 708	8 315	90.5	D	1 989	28 073	14 114	62	D	D	(5)	D
Westlake city	148	400 992	13 443	146.3	D	2 532	41 359	16 335	70	61 512	80.2	1 936	16 873
Youngstown city	347	487 362	5 717	62.2	2.4	3 442	56 266	16 347	177	79 304	96.2	2 467	19 854
Zanesville city	266	506 950	18 676	203.2	D	3 226	46 608	14 448	105	61 388	93.5	2 097	16 904

[1] Includes only establishments with payroll. [2] Based on resident population estimated as of July 1, 1997. [3] For pay period including March 12. [4] Foodservices and drinking places (NAICS 722) includes full-service restaurants, limited-service eating places, special food services, and drinking places (alcoholic beverages). [5] 1,000 to 2,499 employees. [6] 500 to 999 employees. [7] 2,500 to 4,999 employees.

Sources: Retail Trade—U.S. Census Bureau, 1997 Economic Census, ECON[97] Report Series CD-ROM, CD-EC97-1, Disc 1D issued July 2000 and Disc 1E issued February 2001 (related Internet site <http://www.census.gov/epcd/www/97EC44.HTM>). Accommodation and Foodservices—U.S. Census Bureau, 1997 Economic Census, ECON[97] Report Series CD-ROM, Disc 1E issued February 2001 (related Internet site <http://www.census.gov/epcd/www/97EC72.HTM>).

[Includes states and 1,070 incorporated places of 25,000 or more population as of April 1, 1990 in all states except Hawaii which has no incorporated places recognized by the Census Bureau. For Hawaii, 8 census designated places (CDPs) of 25,000 or more population as of April 1, 1990 are included. Also included are the 5 boroughs of New York city. For more information on these areas, see appendix B. Geographic Information]

City	Retail trade[1] (NAICS 44-45), 1997								Accommodation and foodservices[1] (NAICS 72), 1997				
	Sales					Paid employees[3]	Annual payroll		Sales			Paid employees[3]	Annual payroll ($1,000)
	Establishments	Total ($1,000)	Per capita[2]		Percent from general merchandise stores		Total ($1,000)	Per paid employee (dollars)	Establishments	Total ($1,000)	Percent from foodservices[4]		
			Amount (dollars)	Percent of national average									
OKLAHOMA	14 352	27 065 555	8 166	88.9	16.7	161 613	2 406 936	14 893	6 534	3 151 332	86.7	105 934	856 753
Bartlesville city	183	409 761	12 159	132.3	D	2 431	36 644	15 074	83	47 088	D	1 443	13 071
Broken Arrow city	217	616 020	8 660	94.2	10.3	2 956	48 508	16 410	101	49 324	92.2	1 789	14 023
Edmond city	274	522 632	8 151	88.7	D	3 549	50 355	14 189	124	76 863	96.2	2 603	22 157
Enid city	282	488 596	10 813	117.7	20.7	3 333	46 929	14 080	117	51 583	89.6	1 889	14 600
Lawton city	392	664 420	8 128	88.4	30.4	5 005	65 486	13 084	179	89 061	D	3 391	25 037
Midwest City city	220	742 700	13 692	149.0	D	4 401	60 824	13 820	98	56 250	85.7	1 973	15 960
Moore city	114	237 530	5 295	57.6	D	1 592	22 290	14 001	68	31 742	D	1 107	8 679
Muskogee city	281	505 616	13 200	143.6	18.8	3 221	48 001	14 903	109	54 885	D	1 959	14 226
Norman city	399	968 019	10 531	114.6	D	5 268	82 526	15 666	225	139 902	D	4 779	38 586
Oklahoma City city	2 145	5 337 019	11 399	124.0	11.9	28 167	490 819	17 425	1 071	684 238	83.1	21 553	188 787
Ponca City city	158	280 467	10 707	116.5	D	1 963	26 978	13 743	62	29 486	91.2	1 054	7 807
Shawnee city	221	358 314	13 195	143.6	D	2 535	33 887	13 368	111	69 986	93.7	2 439	19 241
Stillwater city	193	370 554	9 642	104.9	D	2 639	34 220	12 967	114	56 006	D	2 398	15 609
Tulsa city	1 905	5 100 458	13 448	146.3	16.8	28 474	484 133	17 003	1 035	643 859	84.3	19 183	172 625
OREGON	14 467	33 396 849	10 297	112.0	16.8	178 349	3 308 810	18 552	8 371	4 388 304	77.3	124 506	1 237 426
Albany city	198	461 919	12 190	132.6	D	2 773	45 391	16 369	98	50 932	93.0	1 633	14 558
Beaverton city	399	1 584 596	24 439	265.9	8.5	6 830	146 020	21 379	200	146 151	78.5	3 738	41 706
Corvallis city	236	413 695	8 362	91.0	D	2 792	46 724	16 735	177	78 776	D	2 545	22 028
Eugene city	826	2 036 420	16 020	174.3	18.8	11 203	209 426	18 694	453	235 054	84.8	7 369	68 319
Gresham city	277	905 415	10 795	117.5	14.5	4 397	79 599	18 103	166	105 041	94.9	3 321	30 288
Hillsboro city	225	884 291	15 628	170.1	13.2	3 704	78 598	21 220	130	82 290	84.6	2 613	23 055
Lake Oswego city	151	251 365	7 150	77.8	D	1 357	28 346	20 889	88	46 985	85.1	1 404	12 809
Medford city	499	1 306 888	22 425	244.0	23.7	6 687	121 577	18 181	213	119 029	79.8	3 634	35 272
Portland city	2 621	6 190 396	12 302	133.9	15.3	34 060	683 869	20 078	1 681	1 135 725	75.6	28 862	323 061
Salem city	665	1 826 172	14 507	157.9	24.1	10 054	181 907	18 093	335	186 081	88.9	5 642	52 386
Springfield city	248	504 643	10 059	109.5	22.9	3 141	47 578	15 147	136	82 035	77.9	2 369	22 185
Tigard city	335	1 429 402	38 349	417.3	32.0	7 330	139 695	19 058	130	88 391	95.5	2 541	25 482
PENNSYLVANIA	50 208	109 948 462	9 150	99.6	11.5	650 144	10 561 877	16 245	24 465	12 227 177	80.9	365 158	3 364 117
Allentown city	452	1 037 130	10 203	111.0	5.1	5 234	99 617	19 033	230	132 145	89.0	3 665	36 534
Altoona city	326	814 406	16 247	176.8	27.8	5 126	71 456	13 940	152	65 758	96.0	2 419	17 633
Bethel Park borough	122	335 809	10 060	109.5	D	2 087	31 413	15 052	64	D	D	(5)	D
Bethlehem city	228	486 177	6 932	75.4	6.2	2 856	49 926	17 481	182	81 092	85.1	2 120	21 723
Chester city	79	156 228	3 879	42.2	1.3	657	16 010	24 368	51	12 708	D	335	3 060
Easton city	129	167 157	6 512	70.9	D	1 071	19 296	18 017	89	33 758	89.9	884	9 555
Erie city	494	772 261	7 432	80.9	14.8	5 859	83 270	14 212	238	81 011	93.2	2 926	21 508
Harrisburg city	229	591 289	11 871	129.2	D	2 977	57 589	19 345	174	71 148	75.9	1 958	18 508
Johnstown city	149	227 926	8 823	96.0	D	1 632	23 083	14 144	78	22 248	D	680	5 659
Lancaster city	311	750 162	14 034	152.7	D	4 582	82 495	18 004	129	68 444	D	1 932	19 244
McKeesport city	80	168 491	7 195	78.3	D	779	14 099	18 099	41	10 890	100.0	386	2 723
Municipality of Monroeville borough	335	1 173 663	41 529	451.9	D	7 123	108 889	15 287	109	98 450	78.6	3 260	28 308
New Castle city	176	379 265	14 291	155.5	D	2 650	38 837	14 655	86	34 336	89.4	1 333	9 226
Norristown borough	106	225 493	7 607	82.8	1.3	1 337	25 764	19 270	68	D	D	(6)	D
Philadelphia city	4 782	8 118 245	5 592	60.8	9.3	51 398	887 136	17 260	2 989	1 691 565	75.2	38 521	461 137
Pittsburgh city	1 544	2 734 082	7 922	86.2	9.3	19 790	311 268	15 729	1 065	677 310	75.3	19 012	188 160
Plum borough	60	103 385	3 918	42.6	NA	673	10 639	15 808	29	13 044	100.0	470	3 768
Reading city	310	502 845	6 719	73.1	.6	2 919	55 703	19 083	164	D	D	(5)	D
Scranton city	473	902 795	11 922	129.7	20.5	6 503	91 517	14 073	201	86 563	88.5	2 913	22 446
State College borough	271	424 458	10 649	115.9	D	3 665	43 215	11 791	139	84 117	67.5	2 908	22 248
Wilkes-Barre city	319	894 007	20 520	223.3	D	5 659	80 763	14 272	143	73 705	85.3	2 487	20 206
Williamsport city	175	320 955	10 520	114.5	D	2 081	34 387	16 524	98	24 671	D	854	6 380
York city	190	338 424	8 378	91.2	D	1 861	38 766	20 831	111	D	D	(5)	D
RHODE ISLAND	4 169	7 505 754	7 605	82.8	10.2	45 747	752 150	16 442	2 617	1 220 865	85.0	34 162	340 552
Cranston city	305	689 385	9 226	100.4	7.2	4 031	61 300	15 207	162	D	D	(5)	D
East Providence city	189	393 118	8 177	89.0	D	2 134	39 181	18 360	108	D	D	(5)	D
Newport city	247	200 509	8 114	88.3	D	1 442	21 303	14 773	182	144 394	55.6	2 938	43 099
Pawtucket city	233	434 732	6 375	69.4	7.0	2 489	49 692	19 965	122	D	D	(5)	D
Providence city	611	772 588	5 116	55.7	D	5 155	92 169	17 880	443	237 634	85.9	6 216	63 710
Warwick city	519	1 446 620	17 252	187.7	23.7	8 920	137 496	15 414	232	154 969	81.6	4 899	43 735
Woonsocket city	152	245 013	5 867	63.8	D	1 806	24 145	13 369	89	D	D	(5)	D

[1] Includes only establishments with payroll.   [2] Based on resident population estimated as of July 1, 1997.   [3] For pay period including March 12.   [4] Foodservices and drinking places (NAICS 722) includes full-service restaurants, limited-service eating places, special food services, and drinking places (alcoholic beverages).   [5] 1,000 to 2,499 employees.   [6] 250 to 499 employees.

Sources: Retail Trade—U.S. Census Bureau, 1997 Economic Census, ECON97 Report Series CD-ROM, CD-EC97-1, Disc 1D issued July 2000 and Disc 1E issued February 2001 (related Internet site <http://www.census.gov/epcd/www/97EC44.HTM>).   Accommodation and Foodservices—U.S. Census Bureau, 1997 Economic Census, ECON97 Report Series CD-ROM, Disc 1E issued February 2001 (related Internet site <http://www.census.gov/epcd/www/97EC72.HTM>).

Table C–6. Cities — Retail Trade and Accommodation and Foodservices–Con.

[Includes states and 1,070 incorporated places of 25,000 or more population as of April 1, 1990 in all states except Hawaii which has no incorporated places recognized by the Census Bureau. For Hawaii, 8 census designated places (CDPs) of 25,000 or more population as of April 1, 1990 are included. Also included are the 5 boroughs of New York city. For more information on these areas, see appendix B. Geographic Information]

City	Retail trade¹ (NAICS 44-45), 1997								Accommodation and foodservices¹ (NAICS 72), 1997				
	Sales					Annual payroll			Sales				
			Per capita²		Percent from general merchandise stores								
	Estab-lishments	Total ($1,000)	Amount (dollars)	Percent of national average		Paid employees³	Total ($1,000)	Per paid employee (dollars)	Estab-lishments	Total ($1,000)	Percent from food-services⁴	Paid employees³	Annual payroll ($1,000)
SOUTH CAROLINA	18 481	33 634 264	8 874	96.6	13.0	209 256	3 107 153	14 849	7 775	4 835 839	75.0	150 621	1 313 837
Anderson city	378	718 728	27 187	295.8	D	5 272	69 635	13 208	130	87 279	93.0	2 792	23 358
Charleston city	793	1 351 186	15 810	172.0	14.2	9 394	137 807	14 670	388	346 439	64.8	9 484	97 561
Columbia city	827	1 917 275	17 100	186.1	14.3	11 608	190 534	16 414	387	242 406	81.4	7 826	69 729
Florence city	415	926 913	30 084	327.4	19.4	5 954	89 618	15 052	162	113 047	75.7	3 838	31 457
Greenville city	812	2 011 148	34 810	378.8	14.8	12 028	186 833	15 533	342	237 982	76.3	7 560	68 260
Mount Pleasant town	234	357 169	8 621	93.8	D	2 625	37 980	14 469	103	72 765	86.0	2 181	19 809
North Charleston city	507	1 341 364	15 817	172.1	14.8	7 214	125 741	17 430	211	135 116	78.2	4 297	35 143
Rock Hill city	330	699 073	15 050	163.8	13.4	4 249	64 138	15 095	134	92 202	86.2	3 179	24 441
Spartanburg city	440	1 017 128	24 409	265.6	19.2	6 349	96 419	15 186	194	109 801	95.3	4 282	31 943
Sumter city	340	654 117	14 352	156.2	13.8	4 355	62 758	14 411	107	65 264	D	2 148	17 730
SOUTH DAKOTA	4 311	11 707 133	16 018	174.3	8.2	45 867	689 586	15 034	2 259	888 148	69.6	30 136	234 413
Rapid City city	486	1 040 585	17 969	195.5	D	6 368	102 051	16 026	234	135 522	69.1	4 643	37 559
Sioux Falls city	696	1 913 556	16 842	183.3	D	11 676	184 798	15 827	352	214 997	79.3	7 691	61 833
TENNESSEE	24 808	50 813 221	9 448	102.8	15.3	304 452	4 810 252	15 800	9 604	6 790 159	74.7	197 881	1 880 279
Bartlett town	144	466 658	12 950	140.9	D	3 110	44 425	14 285	53	D	D	(5)	D
Chattanooga city	1 150	2 707 050	18 115	197.1	14.6	16 191	267 954	16 550	528	366 660	80.4	10 682	103 640
Clarksville city	485	1 143 300	11 928	129.8	22.3	6 674	105 401	15 793	221	D	D	(6)	D
Cleveland city	355	721 578	20 433	222.3	D	3 937	63 928	16 238	130	80 207	D	2 476	21 299
Columbia city	247	527 981	16 515	179.7	D	3 119	51 665	16 565	81	48 261	D	1 836	13 136
Germantown city	186	367 976	10 093	109.8	D	3 200	37 749	11 797	61	D	D	(5)	D
Hendersonville city	139	238 483	6 217	67.6	14.3	1 552	23 629	15 225	61	34 841	82.9	1 135	10 369
Jackson city	547	1 152 252	21 793	237.1	D	7 771	110 011	14 157	177	137 083	83.8	4 079	36 940
Johnson City city	435	1 012 868	17 515	190.6	D	6 118	91 933	15 027	160	125 220	D	4 131	36 049
Kingsport city	415	996 042	23 154	251.9	D	5 841	92 426	15 824	155	115 012	86.2	3 545	32 990
Knoxville city	1 431	4 031 085	23 349	254.1	14.2	22 302	386 463	17 329	586	405 919	85.7	12 873	117 189
Memphis city	2 535	6 358 313	10 382	113.0	D	37 267	635 388	17 050	1 071	920 588	D	25 344	254 879
Murfreesboro city	433	1 187 877	20 849	226.9	D	6 874	113 831	16 560	171	150 962	87.5	4 785	44 601
Nashville-Davidson (remainder)	2 823	7 255 431	14 176	154.3	D	40 576	730 325	17 999	1 331	1 455 324	61.9	35 854	409 191
Oak Ridge city	192	455 424	16 621	180.9	D	2 625	41 132	15 669	79	48 132	84.6	1 504	13 329
TEXAS	74 105	182 516 112	9 430	102.6	14.2	950 848	16 197 114	17 034	34 160	22 698 848	80.1	638 333	6 175 414
Abilene city	586	1 223 129	11 290	122.9	D	6 820	112 375	16 477	246	143 927	88.7	5 225	39 500
Amarillo city	910	2 195 974	12 891	140.3	19.0	11 528	195 432	16 953	442	247 937	85.1	7 732	67 141
Arlington city	1 152	3 806 714	12 717	138.4	13.0	18 925	368 195	19 455	548	521 876	87.0	13 989	139 313
Austin city	2 604	7 561 447	13 332	145.1	11.1	40 259	749 700	18 622	1 491	1 215 725	77.6	33 899	348 782
Baytown city	268	755 044	10 966	119.3	21.5	4 289	69 211	16 137	124	72 340	90.7	1 960	18 765
Beaumont city	656	1 674 358	15 200	165.4	18.2	9 662	150 713	15 599	265	181 992	86.2	5 794	49 145
Bedford city	141	448 941	9 026	98.2	D	2 039	36 321	17 813	82	67 587	79.9	1 850	18 459
Brownsville city	518	984 988	6 903	75.1	D	6 661	91 511	13 738	221	105 280	84.8	3 035	26 407
Bryan city	281	657 492	11 245	122.4	D	3 555	58 482	16 451	115	53 105	D	1 743	14 436
Carrollton city	320	1 230 476	12 471	135.7	D	5 405	124 842	23 098	164	105 976	95.2	2 974	28 789
College Station city	268	653 540	10 977	119.4	D	4 342	62 056	14 292	156	117 411	78.1	3 909	33 707
Conroe city	360	1 146 718	31 320	340.8	D	5 170	91 956	17 786	98	73 656	96.1	1 963	19 643
Corpus Christi city	1 183	2 666 643	9 484	103.2	D	16 289	255 674	15 696	647	382 466	86.7	11 822	102 002
Dallas city	4 365	12 435 991	11 742	127.8	10.7	60 881	1 266 110	20 796	2 374	2 354 804	69.3	58 031	663 222
Deer Park city	73	111 966	3 661	39.8	NA	768	11 421	14 871	30	17 083	100.0	485	4 317
Del Rio city	166	275 489	7 933	86.3	19.5	1 777	25 032	14 087	80	31 841	D	1 010	8 199
Denton city	374	966 833	12 815	139.4	18.8	5 476	87 175	15 919	171	110 895	88.6	3 395	30 624
DeSoto city	88	256 346	7 233	78.7	D	1 287	22 334	17 354	47	40 202	D	1 109	11 620
Duncanville city	126	365 796	10 156	110.5	16.4	2 015	34 905	17 323	57	40 759	83.2	1 231	11 523
Edinburg city	99	254 126	5 934	64.6	D	1 699	22 215	13 075	78	34 443	87.3	1 034	8 337
El Paso city	2 006	4 588 038	7 650	83.2	D	28 171	420 228	14 917	1 040	687 231	D	18 828	189 596
Euless city	83	191 257	4 477	48.7	D	1 076	16 585	15 414	54	35 027	89.3	871	9 099
Fort Worth city	1 856	4 703 291	9 697	105.5	12.2	23 572	449 187	19 056	881	614 727	82.5	17 152	172 620
Galveston city	252	361 980	6 016	65.5	D	2 777	37 848	13 629	190	141 364	68.2	4 240	41 157
Garland city	543	1 426 830	7 457	81.1	21.7	7 133	135 455	18 990	301	165 638	90.9	4 471	42 351
Grand Prairie city	305	920 031	8 316	90.5	D	4 760	92 858	19 508	151	88 001	90.4	2 236	21 556
Grapevine city	206	573 709	14 565	158.5	D	2 205	48 229	21 873	92	180 785	97.9	3 629	51 784
Haltom City city	149	291 853	8 104	88.2	6.7	1 527	28 190	18 461	52	26 472	94.9	664	6 416
Harlingen city	326	611 366	10 934	119.0	D	4 106	59 030	14 377	126	77 121	86.2	2 269	21 039
Houston city	7 871	21 778 420	12 050	131.1	11.6	112 989	2 078 293	18 394	3 902	3 398 870	76.2	83 796	903 385
Huntsville city	157	371 132	11 568	125.9	D	2 122	30 725	14 479	73	43 985	D	1 477	12 151
Hurst city	282	685 235	18 718	203.7	D	4 233	69 847	16 501	84	39 413	D	1 262	10 571
Irving city	651	3 255 940	18 346	199.6	7.2	13 102	277 352	21 169	397	575 303	40.8	11 448	140 230
Killeen city	329	660 294	8 321	90.5	7.1	3 879	61 165	15 768	174	90 548	86.2	3 022	23 859

¹ Includes only establishments with payroll.   ² Based on resident population estimated as of July 1, 1997.   ³ For pay period including March 12.   ⁴ Foodservices and drinking places (NAICS 722) includes full-service restaurants, limited-service eating places, special food services, and drinking places (alcoholic beverages).   ⁵ 1,000 to 2,499 employees.   ⁶ 2,500 to 4,999 employees.

Sources: Retail Trade—U.S. Census Bureau, 1997 Economic Census, ECON97 Report Series CD-ROM, CD-EC97-1, Disc 1D issued July 2000 and Disc 1E issued February 2001 (related Internet site <http://www.census.gov/epcd/www/97EC44.HTM>).   Accommodation and Foodservices—U.S. Census Bureau, 1997 Economic Census, ECON97 Report Series CD-ROM, Disc 1E issued February 2001 (related Internet site <http://www.census.gov/epcd/www/97EC72.HTM>).

Table C–6. Cities — Retail Trade and Accommodation and Foodservices–Con.

[Includes states and 1,070 incorporated places of 25,000 or more population as of April 1, 1990 in all states except Hawaii which has no incorporated places recognized by the Census Bureau. For Hawaii, 8 census designated places (CDPs) of 25,000 or more population as of April 1, 1990 are included. Also included are the 5 boroughs of New York city. For more information on these areas, see appendix B. Geographic Information]

City	Retail trade[1] (NAICS 44-45), 1997								Accommodation and foodservices[1] (NAICS 72), 1997				
		Sales				Annual payroll				Sales			
			Per capita[2]		Percent from general merchandise stores						Percent from food-services[4]		Annual payroll ($1,000)
	Establishments	Total ($1,000)	Amount (dollars)	Percent of national average		Paid employees[3]	Total ($1,000)	Per paid employee (dollars)	Establishments	Total ($1,000)		Paid employees[3]	
TEXAS—Con.													
Kingsville city	105	209 249	8 261	89.9	D	1 385	19 698	14 222	66	27 978	D	923	7 575
La Porte city	72	212 046	6 559	71.4	D	977	18 307	18 738	46	19 528	D	660	5 234
Laredo city	723	1 520 800	8 907	96.9	19.9	9 027	138 538	15 347	249	144 243	77.8	4 341	37 261
League City city	116	279 765	6 713	73.0	.5	1 339	25 492	19 038	46	34 151	D	966	9 355
Lewisville city	402	1 412 380	21 288	231.6	D	6 554	124 968	19 067	134	122 244	92.2	3 713	34 981
Longview city	583	1 252 368	16 716	181.9	22.3	7 436	121 744	16 372	213	128 021	89.0	3 927	36 974
Lubbock city	992	2 519 755	13 132	142.9	17.5	13 893	226 644	16 314	488	321 145	89.0	10 760	84 271
Lufkin city	291	626 555	18 874	205.4	19.5	3 824	57 850	15 128	102	56 770	85.6	1 781	16 443
McAllen city	757	1 665 654	15 479	168.4	25.8	10 916	165 858	15 194	253	188 575	83.6	6 005	50 020
Mesquite city	476	1 572 815	13 903	151.3	22.0	8 899	147 311	16 554	168	148 396	94.5	4 278	40 487
Midland city	516	1 199 378	12 234	133.1	17.4	6 500	105 634	16 251	225	D	(5)	D
Mission city	136	314 862	7 538	82.0	D	1 963	28 819	14 681	70	30 789	89.5	923	7 957
Missouri City city	85	145 273	2 478	27.0	D	1 163	14 998	12 896	39	17 898	D	531	4 384
Nacogdoches city	230	431 004	13 761	149.7	D	2 749	40 354	14 680	78	53 998	85.4	1 789	14 857
New Braunfels city	262	583 993	16 509	179.6	D	2 979	51 916	17 427	128	72 724	83.1	2 162	20 707
North Richland Hills city	236	993 857	18 402	200.2	D	4 647	87 304	18 787	91	76 796	95.1	2 570	21 263
Odessa city	489	1 063 435	11 849	128.9	21.8	5 614	98 209	17 494	217	117 913	D	3 704	32 383
Pasadena city	422	878 176	6 658	72.4	23.5	5 739	88 073	15 346	174	108 643	95.1	3 081	28 759
Pharr city	160	208 835	4 731	51.5	12.0	1 587	21 929	13 818	48	25 125	91.1	678	5 850
Plano city	804	3 167 182	15 243	165.9	D	14 928	290 930	19 489	347	298 845	89.8	8 108	83 884
Port Arthur city	215	399 558	7 034	76.5	10.7	2 585	38 996	15 085	86	44 497	83.0	1 265	12 164
Richardson city	417	1 597 735	19 224	209.2	5.0	6 096	141 511	23 214	205	149 728	81.2	3 633	39 394
Round Rock city	162	D	D	D	D	(5)	D	D	102	77 242	92.9	2 130	21 489
San Angelo city	446	874 840	9 913	107.9	20.0	5 246	82 757	15 775	184	108 613	88.0	3 706	32 010
San Antonio city	3 848	9 723 633	8 691	94.6	14.9	55 174	947 044	17 165	2 237	1 844 063	74.2	50 503	509 411
San Marcos city	285	599 107	16 158	175.8	D	3 449	50 489	14 639	131	74 580	88.9	2 444	20 633
Sherman city	250	749 092	22 847	248.6	D	4 231	67 784	16 021	95	63 589	89.4	1 921	17 635
Temple city	305	729 980	13 681	148.9	D	4 196	71 288	16 990	130	77 511	87.0	2 497	20 834
Texarkana city	331	768 324	23 503	255.7	27.1	4 263	69 595	16 325	102	70 174	D	2 081	17 146
Texas City city	184	460 039	10 867	118.2	D	3 127	42 544	13 605	82	42 828	92.7	1 471	11 453
Tyler city	643	1 692 885	20 585	224.0	D	8 822	154 273	17 487	228	152 513	90.8	5 027	41 581
Victoria city	379	846 331	14 001	152.4	21.8	4 913	77 946	15 865	147	78 535	86.4	2 680	21 502
Waco city	601	1 393 686	12 866	140.0	D	8 053	128 122	15 910	276	177 367	87.5	5 511	48 291
Wichita Falls city	514	1 070 132	10 755	117.0	19.7	6 450	96 385	14 943	234	D	D	(5)	D
UTAH	7 656	19 964 601	9 666	105.2	12.8	114 474	1 856 875	16 221	3 785	2 313 309	71.8	74 481	650 041
Bountiful city	142	510 156	12 319	134.0	D	2 425	45 718	18 853	57	26 576	D	1 026	7 611
Layton city	208	676 924	12 672	137.9	21.4	3 631	58 035	15 983	94	66 135	94.1	2 520	18 649
Logan city	248	500 765	12 254	133.3	10.9	3 895	53 767	13 804	85	41 924	83.4	1 561	10 470
Murray city	343	1 418 924	42 726	464.9	D	6 445	128 463	19 932	95	62 134	D	2 186	18 248
Ogden city	408	922 832	13 455	146.4	D	6 090	94 676	15 546	183	84 036	90.6	3 153	24 249
Orem city	420	1 170 297	14 607	158.9	16.7	7 352	116 234	15 810	104	60 730	97.8	2 273	16 101
Provo city	252	638 116	5 985	65.1	D	3 782	60 874	16 096	142	105 848	67.2	3 759	31 558
St. George city	332	784 462	17 258	187.8	D	4 151	68 423	16 483	133	83 902	63.0	2 961	24 440
Salt Lake City city	1 039	3 040 974	17 723	192.9	7.9	15 539	278 543	17 925	639	573 280	63.4	15 664	157 594
Sandy city	312	915 580	9 320	101.4	17.7	5 647	90 795	16 078	140	88 869	89.9	2 960	24 661
West Jordan city	97	330 730	5 545	60.3	18.4	2 173	32 763	15 077	61	30 688	100.0	1 054	8 349
West Valley City city	273	1 173 727	11 814	128.6	11.7	5 727	97 217	16 975	107	66 200	100.0	1 986	18 660
VERMONT	4 093	5 898 646	10 020	109.0	7.5	36 306	603 345	16 618	1 932	910 188	57.4	27 088	277 161
Burlington city	261	354 888	9 225	100.4	D	3 041	42 637	14 021	136	66 391	D	1 862	19 103
VIRGINIA	29 032	62 569 924	9 293	101.1	13.8	379 039	6 202 575	16 364	12 343	8 281 218	74.4	233 639	2 320 695
Alexandria city	593	1 507 569	13 261	144.3	D	7 746	159 960	20 651	310	308 321	66.4	6 616	92 349
Blacksburg town	127	191 317	5 657	61.6	D	1 773	21 209	11 962	72	42 850	D	1 689	11 582
Charlottesville city	360	730 271	19 304	210.1	D	4 345	73 214	16 850	179	121 519	77.7	3 521	34 729
Chesapeake city	779	1 993 340	10 171	110.7	21.4	12 554	184 481	14 695	305	187 381	86.6	6 321	51 614
Danville city	334	585 472	11 159	121.4	17.7	3 787	56 903	15 026	114	65 745	88.2	2 159	18 829
Hampton city	514	1 638 883	11 804	128.4	18.5	9 930	150 547	15 161	229	149 855	77.2	5 002	41 096
Harrisonburg city	308	690 756	20 570	223.8	21.0	4 161	64 000	15 381	109	70 224	83.5	2 318	18 951
Lynchburg city	446	1 228 549	18 869	205.3	15.3	7 209	115 781	16 061	173	110 800	83.6	3 808	30 899
Manassas city	230	647 495	20 115	218.9	16.2	3 355	64 917	19 349	74	D	D	(6)	D
Newport News city	681	1 488 616	8 516	92.7	13.1	9 284	143 575	15 465	312	170 072	82.3	5 464	47 733
Norfolk city	918	1 900 364	8 069	87.8	15.0	12 628	207 305	16 416	539	299 445	80.9	9 980	85 057
Petersburg city	189	290 027	8 229	89.5	D	1 764	29 521	16 735	83	34 227	75.3	1 194	10 148

[1] Includes only establishments with payroll.   [2] Based on resident population estimated as of July 1, 1997.   [3] For pay period including March 12.   [4] Foodservices and drinking places (NAICS 722) includes full-service restaurants, limited-service eating places, special food services, and drinking places (alcoholic beverages).   [5] 2,500 to 4,999 employees.   [6] 1,000 to 2,499 employees.

Sources: Retail Trade—U.S. Census Bureau, 1997 Economic Census, ECON97 Report Series CD-ROM, CD-EC97-1, Disc 1D issued July 2000 and Disc 1E issued February 2001 (related Internet site <http://www.census.gov/epcd/www/97EC44.HTM>). Accommodation and Foodservices—U.S. Census Bureau, 1997 Economic Census, ECON97 Report Series CD-ROM, Disc 1E issued February 2001 (related Internet site <http://www.census.gov/epcd/www/97EC72.HTM>).

[Includes states and 1,070 incorporated places of 25,000 or more population as of April 1, 1990 in all states except Hawaii which has no incorporated places recognized by the Census Bureau. For Hawaii, 8 census designated places (CDPs) of 25,000 or more population as of April 1, 1990 are included. Also included are the 5 boroughs of New York city. For more information on these areas, see appendix B. Geographic Information]

City	Retail trade[1] (NAICS 44-45), 1997								Accommodation and foodservices[1] (NAICS 72), 1997				
	Sales					Annual payroll			Sales				
			Per capita[2]		Percent from general merchandise stores								
	Establishments	Total ($1,000)	Amount (dollars)	Percent of national average		Paid employees[3]	Total ($1,000)	Per paid employee (dollars)	Establishments	Total ($1,000)	Percent from foodservices[4]	Paid employees[3]	Annual payroll ($1,000)
VIRGINIA—Con.													
Portsmouth city	295	468 443	4 712	51.3	3.5	3 291	51 216	15 562	137	58 713	88.6	2 040	15 791
Richmond city	1 013	1 738 092	9 112	99.2	D	11 579	193 461	16 708	551	304 206	75.6	9 087	91 363
Roanoke city	792	1 843 734	19 422	211.3	D	12 425	191 252	15 393	325	203 403	76.5	6 380	58 743
Suffolk city	212	379 979	6 214	67.6	D	2 697	37 957	14 074	62	32 827	88.2	1 027	8 880
Virginia Beach city	1 621	3 342 718	7 754	84.4	13.6	21 987	337 224	15 337	888	576 268	74.1	18 145	163 311
WASHINGTON	22 841	52 472 866	9 363	101.9	14.2	283 653	5 385 915	18 988	13 124	7 001 716	79.8	195 157	1 965 223
Auburn city	207	931 393	25 089	273.0	D	4 494	92 912	20 675	112	55 309	94.0	1 894	15 453
Bellevue city	789	2 745 930	26 682	290.3	8.5	13 580	266 165	19 600	332	272 504	64.8	6 369	73 924
Bellingham city	502	1 126 837	18 414	200.4	D	6 902	115 296	16 705	265	112 319	88.6	3 818	31 983
Bremerton city	182	463 615	11 183	121.7	2.3	2 149	48 337	22 493	108	49 399	91.5	1 613	13 587
Edmonds city	160	361 162	8 934	97.2	D	1 788	38 458	21 509	93	41 895	88.9	1 174	11 503
Everett city	473	1 339 960	15 763	171.5	D	6 518	133 474	20 478	263	143 481	90.9	4 184	37 687
Kennewick city	378	890 689	17 806	193.8	D	5 236	83 843	16 013	141	77 173	88.9	2 339	20 207
Kent city	315	929 931	14 243	155.0	11.7	4 399	94 383	21 456	181	96 227	88.1	2 744	25 685
Kirkland city	250	1 012 900	22 823	248.3	D	3 984	86 055	21 600	168	150 070	76.2	3 838	45 224
Longview city	224	554 530	16 179	176.1	16.8	3 019	56 431	18 692	94	45 735	94.8	1 642	13 254
Lynnwood city	404	1 374 893	41 497	451.5	20.0	7 637	139 394	18 252	151	107 092	82.6	3 160	29 249
Olympia city	371	853 474	21 498	233.9	D	4 670	86 528	18 528	202	106 940	84.4	3 426	32 859
Redmond city	271	543 617	12 473	135.7	D	3 061	65 227	21 309	134	79 724	91.4	2 062	22 329
Renton city	228	1 417 454	31 315	340.8	6.3	4 662	121 095	25 975	165	84 390	90.6	2 468	24 029
Richland city	131	202 997	5 442	59.2	D	1 338	21 826	16 312	79	47 169	75.0	1 483	13 382
Seattle city	2 698	6 146 245	11 520	125.4	10.8	34 886	717 700	20 573	2 110	1 551 882	72.2	34 222	446 260
Spokane city	1 054	2 389 810	12 859	139.9	14.0	13 757	263 037	19 120	570	306 953	86.5	9 881	88 986
Tacoma city	832	2 180 286	12 367	134.6	D	11 432	226 609	19 822	426	221 379	93.5	6 754	62 251
Vancouver city	440	1 298 357	11 513	125.3	16.3	6 900	137 871	19 981	254	136 954	85.9	4 169	39 852
Walla Walla city	190	348 449	12 084	131.5	17.5	2 233	38 904	17 422	96	38 246	D	1 287	10 675
Yakima city	443	1 053 672	14 743	160.4	17.2	6 123	107 143	17 498	219	115 821	81.9	3 445	31 863
WEST VIRGINIA	8 082	14 057 933	7 743	84.3	16.2	90 087	1 309 316	14 534	3 290	1 633 164	77.0	51 529	462 334
Charleston city	466	061 786	17 197	187.1	17.7	7 135	102 231	14 328	210	147 649	75.2	3 967	38 850
Huntington city	313	637 535	11 956	130.1	14.5	4 091	65 371	15 979	187	102 095	88.3	3 573	28 645
Morgantown city	267	505 453	17 212	187.3	D	3 650	54 882	15 036	150	72 448	78.7	2 726	21 019
Parkersburg city	291	617 080	18 653	203.0	D	3 667	58 464	15 943	129	69 094	92.0	2 367	19 588
Wheeling city	223	354 337	10 620	115.6	D	2 342	39 200	16 738	130	51 629	89.3	1 837	14 980
WISCONSIN	21 717	50 520 463	9 715	105.7	13.4	305 255	4 826 217	15 810	13 253	5 649 870	79.1	190 520	1 550 660
Appleton city	329	691 009	10 316	112.3	12.5	4 683	73 915	15 784	168	94 020	D	3 336	28 067
Beloit city	141	385 650	10 681	116.2	D	1 994	32 276	16 187	91	37 823	D	1 360	10 944
Brookfield city	349	939 422	24 672	268.5	D	6 557	94 027	14 340	99	93 921	60.0	2 519	24 485
Eau Claire city	372	1 007 484	16 854	183.4	D	6 849	95 264	13 909	200	108 403	81.1	4 659	32 866
Fond du Lac city	270	635 930	15 503	168.7	D	4 084	61 501	15 059	134	69 261	87.5	2 525	19 420
Green Bay city	515	1 395 544	13 986	152.2	D	8 419	135 825	16 133	286	137 897	86.0	5 153	40 123
Greenfield city	184	707 771	20 589	224.0	13.0	4 012	65 785	16 397	74	58 379	D	2 176	17 289
Janesville city	310	992 098	16 603	180.7	D	5 461	98 410	18 021	154	88 345	87.1	3 107	24 186
Kenosha city	313	699 744	7 904	86.0	D	4 549	66 426	14 602	207	78 632	95.6	2 787	21 774
La Crosse city	336	905 274	17 986	195.7	D	5 685	90 902	15 990	208	98 294	78.8	3 799	29 189
Madison city	1 078	2 761 009	13 136	142.9	16.2	18 263	282 450	15 466	602	390 803	80.2	12 763	110 857
Manitowoc city	162	357 289	10 726	116.7	24.9	2 411	34 397	14 267	92	38 202	78.9	1 480	10 618
Menomonee Falls village	152	535 126	17 330	188.6	D	3 142	56 112	17 859	56	24 452	D	868	7 439
Milwaukee city	1 700	3 381 213	5 785	62.9	9.5	22 655	360 593	15 917	1 144	615 393	82.3	17 852	172 600
New Berlin city	92	213 576	5 791	63.0	D	1 481	24 250	16 374	54	D	D	(5)	D
Oshkosh city	332	841 471	13 987	152.2	D	4 744	83 297	17 558	177	93 479	81.6	3 591	27 334
Racine city	362	709 968	8 585	93.4	D	5 297	70 114	13 237	166	78 439	94.7	2 653	21 772
Sheboygan city	210	523 933	10 427	113.5	D	3 565	54 687	15 340	136	49 289	92.0	1 809	13 252
Superior city	128	309 213	11 181	121.7	D	1 884	28 583	15 171	111	37 622	79.8	1 447	10 469
Waukesha city	242	970 793	15 678	170.6	D	4 556	82 636	18 138	127	79 908	83.3	2 688	23 304
Wausau city	251	745 891	20 051	218.2	D	5 060	77 456	15 308	101	39 655	90.2	1 496	11 516
Wauwatosa city	289	942 936	20 320	221.1	D	6 903	121 384	17 584	114	81 951	84.3	2 559	23 108
West Allis city	311	1 013 531	16 878	183.7	D	5 485	93 209	16 993	159	D	D	(6)	D
WYOMING	2 939	4 530 537	9 438	102.7	14.7	26 934	426 666	15 841	1 751	808 887	56.9	24 950	218 995
Casper city	346	595 158	12 195	132.7	D	3 702	59 570	16 091	138	69 899	77.6	2 644	19 748
Cheyenne city	308	761 402	14 198	154.5	19.3	4 496	71 894	15 991	156	90 414	80.3	3 423	26 881
Laramie city	158	332 558	13 030	141.8	D	1 607	26 888	16 732	92	42 471	D	1 866	11 969

[1] Includes only establishments with payroll. [2] Based on resident population estimated as of July 1, 1997. [3] For pay period including March 12. [4] Foodservices and drinking places (NAICS 722) includes full-service restaurants, limited-service eating places, special food services, and drinking places (alcoholic beverages). [5] 500 to 999 employees. [6] 2,500 to 4,999 employees.

Sources: Retail Trade—U.S. Census Bureau, 1997 Economic Census, ECON97 Report Series CD-ROM, CD-EC97-1, Disc 1D issued July 2000 and Disc 1E issued February 2001 (related Internet site <http://www.census.gov/epcd/www/97EC44.HTM>).   Accommodation and Foodservices—U.S. Census Bureau, 1997 Economic Census, ECON97 Report Series CD-ROM, Disc 1E issued February 2001 (related Internet site <http://www.census.gov/epcd/www/97EC72.HTM>).

Table C–7. Cities — **Government Finances and Climate**

[Includes states and 1,070 incorporated places of 25,000 or more population as of April 1, 1990 in all states except Hawaii which has no incorporated places recognized by the Census Bureau. For Hawaii, 8 census designated places (CDPs) of 25,000 or more population as of April 1, 1990 are included. Also included are the 5 boroughs of New York city. For more information on these areas, see appendix B. Geographic Information]

	City government finances, 1996-1997									Climate[2]						
	General revenue				General expenditure					Average daily temperature (degrees Fahrenheit)						
			Taxes				By selected function, percent from—									
City	Total ($1,000)	Per capita[1] (dollars)	Total ($1,000)	Per capita[1] (dollars)	Total ($1,000)	Per capita[1] (dollars)	Police protection	Sewerage and solid waste management	Highways	January	July	January[3]	July[4]	Annual precipitation (inches)	Heating degree days[5]	Cooling degree days[6]
ALABAMA	X	X	X	X	X	X	X	X	X	X	X	X	X	X	X	X
Anniston city	28 149	1 066	20 414	773	26 911	1 019	17.8	3.6	11.2	42.0	79.6	31.6	90.2	52.88	2 854	1 787
Auburn city	34 297	849	21 644	536	28 687	710	12.3	18.7	4.4	43.1	79.2	32.7	89.3	56.47	2 612	1 865
Bessemer city	20 465	650	15 143	481	26 060	828	23.0	22.3	3.8	41.7	79.7	30.5	91.4	59.11	2 893	1 777
Birmingham city	311 272	1 233	211 906	839	316 478	1 253	16.0	3.6	7.2	41.5	79.8	31.3	89.9	54.58	2 918	1 797
Decatur city	139 724	2 551	29 956	547	128 107	2 339	5.0	11.7	2.7	38.8	79.0	29.2	89.0	57.18	3 323	1 651
Dothan city	49 935	864	34 480	597	47 017	814	16.2	19.5	5.4	48.2	80.0	37.2	91.0	55.61	1 903	2 204
Florence city	NA	NA	NA	NA	NA	NA	NA	NA	NA	38.7	79.7	29.0	90.3	53.85	3 325	1 736
Gadsden city	47 385	1 129	33 663	802	45 733	1 089	16.6	12.0	9.6	39.1	78.9	28.7	89.5	55.31	3 317	1 610
Hoover city	51 950	907	47 538	830	49 340	861	15.6	8.5	2.2	41.5	79.8	31.3	89.9	54.58	2 918	1 797
Huntsville city	195 301	1 118	111 887	641	176 454	1 010	12.3	23.4	10.2	38.8	79.0	29.2	89.0	57.18	3 323	1 651
Mobile city	226 813	1 132	144 592	721	197 097	983	13.9	16.7	9.2	49.9	82.3	40.0	91.3	63.96	1 702	2 627
Montgomery city	132 928	672	101 434	513	128 130	648	19.6	10.3	18.6	46.1	81.3	35.8	91.1	53.43	2 224	2 212
Phenix City city	NA	NA	NA	NA	NA	NA	NA	NA	NA	45.7	81.9	35.2	91.8	51.00	2 261	2 284
Prichard city	13 614	402	8 211	242	10 655	314	23.3	18.0	12.0	49.9	82.3	40.0	91.3	63.96	1 702	2 627
Tuscaloosa city	53 911	642	19 621	234	50 489	601	16.4	17.6	6.3	42.8	81.1	32.4	91.1	54.90	2 661	2 070
ALASKA	X	X	X	X	X	X	X	X	X	X	X	X	X	X	X	X
Anchorage city	741 105	2 948	234 712	934	790 618	3 145	5.1	3.4	7.7	14.9	58.4	8.4	65.2	15.91	10 570	–
Fairbanks city	54 656	1 692	8 656	268	47 547	1 472	11.2	11.7	10.4	10.1	62.5	18.5	72.3	10.87	13 940	84
Juneau city	146 885	4 848	50 123	1 654	135 444	4 471	5.1	3.2	5.2	24.2	56.0	19.0	63.9	54.31	8 897	–
ARIZONA	X	X	X	X	X	X	X	X	X	X	X	X	X	X	X	X
Chandler city	153 653	1 016	46 269	306	130 588	863	18.9	29.2	14.5	51.9	90.2	38.1	104.8	9.04	1 490	3 476
Flagstaff city	60 629	1 075	23 336	414	48 259	856	14.8	12.2	13.9	28.7	66.3	15.2	81.9	22.80	7 131	145
Gilbert town	62 273	829	25 614	341	52 853	703	11.4	37.7	8.6	51.9	90.2	38.1	104.8	9.04	1 490	3 476
Glendale city	169 574	897	58 310	309	145 270	769	16.2	17.0	11.2	53.6	93.5	41.2	105.9	7.66	1 350	4 162
Mesa city	265 657	753	78 292	222	324 862	920	23.0	15.9	10.7	52.9	91.2	39.5	105.5	8.50	1 366	3 635
Peoria city	79 178	986	29 581	368	64 843	808	11.8	18.6	6.5	53.6	93.5	41.2	105.9	7.66	1 350	4 162
Phoenix city	1 381 111	1 167	461 425	390	1 291 768	1 092	16.7	11.0	5.8	53.6	93.5	41.2	105.9	7.66	1 350	4 162
Prescott city	44 199	1 292	16 952	495	30 691	897	13.8	25.0	15.3	36.2	73.1	21.9	88.1	19.63	4 995	631
Scottsdale city	263 663	1 423	129 584	699	259 898	1 403	11.8	8.9	9.8	53.6	93.5	41.2	105.9	7.66	1 350	4 162
Sierra Vista city	25 947	681	8 618	226	25 396	667	15.0	8.2	9.9	45.1	78.5	26.8	93.5	18.63	2 928	1 441
Tempe city	193 541	1 177	86 973	529	144 899	881	18.4	11.2	11.3	52.6	90.6	37.8	106.7	8.88	1 464	3 530
Tucson city	485 964	1 059	181 124	395	426 890	931	14.8	6.0	12.4	51.3	86.6	38.6	99.4	12.00	1 678	2 954
Yuma city	58 634	933	19 334	308	67 820	1 079	19.0	14.9	19.8	56.5	93.7	44.2	106.6	3.17	927	4 305
ARKANSAS	X	X	X	X	X	X	X	X	X	X	X	X	X	X	X	X
Conway city	21 467	541	7 097	179	23 320	588	15.3	17.0	6.2	39.0	81.4	27.9	93.1	49.36	3 147	1 917
Fayetteville city	39 315	688	14 537	254	42 696	747	12.0	33.7	9.2	34.0	78.7	22.9	89.3	44.04	4 141	1 401
Fort Smith city	56 714	752	29 653	393	49 480	656	13.0	19.8	32.1	36.9	81.5	25.5	93.0	40.90	3 478	1 894
Hot Springs city	38 454	1 017	16 471	436	34 253	906	22.9	21.9	10.3	39.3	81.7	28.5	93.3	56.52	3 181	1 958
Jacksonville city	51 431	1 780	2 109	73	51 179	1 771	4.3	6.3	3.0	38.5	81.4	29.4	91.5	49.25	3 228	1 916
Jonesboro city	23 048	451	2 982	58	24 390	477	15.0	31.3	18.1	36.6	81.7	27.9	92.3	47.19	3 504	1 940
Little Rock city	191 280	1 092	32 493	185	227 906	1 301	12.9	13.6	12.5	39.1	81.9	29.1	92.4	50.86	3 155	2 005
North Little Rock city	43 253	713	5 489	90	50 659	835	23.1	15.9	8.3	38.5	81.4	29.4	91.5	49.25	3 228	1 916
Pine Bluff city	36 836	692	12 669	238	37 141	698	20.1	24.4	8.7	40.0	81.8	29.6	92.4	52.36	3 016	2 050
Springdale city	23 670	574	6 415	156	38 858	942	10.6	42.8	9.6	34.0	78.7	22.9	89.3	44.04	4 141	1 401
West Memphis city	20 566	760	6 916	256	20 186	746	18.4	22.4	6.8	37.0	81.1	27.4	90.9	50.77	3 438	1 871
CALIFORNIA	X	X	X	X	X	X	X	X	X	X	X	X	X	X	X	X
Alameda city	70 846	945	36 256	484	83 394	1 112	17.3	2.0	14.8	49.9	62.1	43.3	70.0	24.30	2 902	115
Alhambra city	56 756	682	28 263	340	57 246	688	24.2	10.1	8.5	55.7	75.2	41.7	89.2	17.90	1 433	1 427
Anaheim city	321 427	1 097	138 444	473	360 560	1 231	15.0	9.1	6.8	57.4	72.6	45.6	82.6	12.27	1 238	1 175
Antioch city	54 569	693	17 274	219	58 309	741	19.6	2.6	36.1	44.5	73.8	35.9	90.8	12.80	2 837	1 066
Apple Valley town	17 550	316	6 110	110	17 179	310	25.0	31.0	13.9	44.2	79.3	30.0	97.4	5.51	3 127	1 525
Arcadia city	34 999	705	22 203	447	35 830	722	24.1	.9	11.7	55.7	75.2	41.7	89.2	17.90	1 433	1 427
Azusa city	39 943	958	19 397	465	28 831	691	27.1	5.5	7.1	55.8	75.0	43.6	89.0	19.37	1 453	1 394
Bakersfield city	148 184	691	63 303	295	150 911	704	20.8	17.1	15.4	47.8	84.1	38.6	98.5	5.72	2 182	2 365
Baldwin Park city	27 913	392	13 931	196	26 951	378	31.1	–	22.2	55.7	75.2	41.7	89.2	17.90	1 433	1 427
Bell city	17 140	493	8 912	256	15 643	450	24.4	6.2	15.0	58.3	74.3	48.9	84.0	14.77	1 154	1 537
Bellflower city	20 342	323	11 711	186	19 234	305	35.5	–	20.9	55.9	73.1	44.9	82.7	11.80	1 430	1 201
Bell Gardens city	20 638	470	10 083	230	21 218	484	34.2	.9	12.3	58.3	74.3	48.9	84.0	14.77	1 154	1 537
Berkeley city	168 541	1 577	72 072	674	178 264	1 668	14.8	16.3	6.9	49.9	62.1	43.3	70.0	24.30	2 902	115
Beverly Hills city	126 096	3 931	69 694	2 173	129 554	4 038	16.8	12.7	7.8	57.2	70.4	46.5	79.2	13.06	1 391	986

[1] Based on resident population estimated as of July 1, 1997. [2] Represents normal values for the 30-year period, 1961–1990. [3] Average daily minimum. [4] Average daily maximum. [5] One heating degree day is accumulated for each whole degree that the mean daily temperature is below 65 degrees Fahrenheit. [6] One cooling degree day is accumulated for each whole degree that the mean daily temperature is above 65 degrees Fahrenheit.

Sources: City Government Finances—U.S. Census Bureau, 1997 Census of Governments, Volume 4, Government Finances, GC97(4)-4, Finances of Municipal and Township Governments, issued September 2000 (related Internet site <http://www.census.gov/govs/www/cog.html>). 1997 Population for Government Finances calculations—U.S. Census Bureau, Population Estimates for Places: Annual Time Series, July 1, 1990 to July 1, 1999 (SU-99-7), published 20 October 2000, <http://www.census.gov/estimates/metro-city/placesbyst/SC99T7_US.txt>. Climate: U.S. National Oceanic and Atmospheric Administration (NOAA), National Climatic Data Center (NCDC), Climatography of the United States, Number 81, published January 1992 (related Internet site <http://lwf.ncdc.noaa.gov/oa/climate/normals/usnormals.html>).

Table C–7. Cities — **Government Finances and Climate**–Con.

[Includes states and 1,070 incorporated places of 25,000 or more population as of April 1, 1990 in all states except Hawaii which has no incorporated places recognized by the Census Bureau. For Hawaii, 8 census designated places (CDPs) of 25,000 or more population as of April 1, 1990 are included. Also included are the 5 boroughs of New York city. For more information on these areas, see appendix B. Geographic Information]

City	City government finances, 1996-1997 General revenue Total ($1,000)	Per capita[1] (dollars)	Taxes Total ($1,000)	Taxes Per capita[1] (dollars)	General expenditure Total ($1,000)	Per capita[1] (dollars)	By selected function, percent from— Police protection	Sewerage and solid waste management	Highways	Climate[2] Average daily temperature (degrees Fahrenheit) January	July	January[3]	July[4]	Annual precipitation (inches)	Heating degree days[5]	Cooling degree days[6]
CALIFORNIA—Con.																
Brea city	62 860	1 794	32 632	931	69 465	1 983	18.7	2.9	7.2	57.4	72.6	45.6	82.6	12.27	1 238	1 175
Buena Park city	44 621	617	25 300	350	42 503	587	27.6	5.1	23.0	57.4	72.6	45.6	82.6	12.27	1 238	1 175
Burbank city	150 275	1 546	69 708	717	162 775	1 675	14.0	7.7	10.4	54.5	75.6	41.3	90.2	15.87	1 609	1 424
Burlingame city	37 674	1 344	24 520	875	38 756	1 382	14.6	8.4	11.8	48.7	62.7	41.8	71.6	19.70	3 016	145
Camarillo city	36 471	625	14 017	240	34 281	588	28.2	23.5	17.2	55.3	66.1	44.2	74.4	14.38	1 992	416
Campbell city	29 931	778	18 369	477	28 739	747	21.8	.5	10.2	49.4	69.5	40.6	82.4	14.42	2 387	594
Carlsbad city	95 061	1 354	36 661	522	74 766	1 065	15.1	3.9	10.3	54.5	67.6	44.1	73.5	10.93	2 010	555
Carson city	63 130	728	37 680	434	60 551	698	18.3	—	14.4	56.1	69.7	45.3	78.8	13.57	1 568	794
Cathedral City city	40 454	1 083	25 215	675	50 621	1 355	11.2	—	25.6	56.4	92.0	42.5	108.7	5.31	985	4 014
Ceres city	13 803	429	7 053	219	10 940	340	35.4	18.3	12.3	45.6	77.1	37.4	94.2	12.10	2 605	1 401
Cerritos city	81 333	1 524	43 027	806	77 398	1 450	7.7	2.7	13.1	55.9	73.1	44.9	82.7	11.80	1 430	1 201
Chico city	42 265	834	23 235	458	51 311	1 012	14.7	3.8	.1	44.0	77.4	34.5	94.2	26.32	2 953	1 360
Chino city	49 764	776	19 319	301	49 771	776	24.2	22.4	12.0	54.3	74.6	40.7	90.4	16.62	1 713	1 273
Chula Vista city	119 256	766	50 573	325	112 458	723	17.9	9.6	10.1	55.3	68.2	45.3	73.1	9.34	1 798	638
Claremont city	22 523	665	10 606	313	20 602	609	26.8	14.4	12.3	54.3	74.6	40.7	90.4	16.62	1 713	1 273
Clovis city	50 934	797	22 230	348	45 244	708	21.3	25.0	14.7	45.7	81.9	37.4	98.6	10.60	2 556	1 967
Colton city	33 480	785	14 987	351	36 731	861	19.7	8.3	3.2	53.6	79.4	40.3	97.0	15.42	1 719	1 804
Compton city	89 006	978	40 497	445	83 040	912	20.6	4.9	15.6	56.1	69.7	45.3	78.8	13.57	1 568	794
Concord city	103 415	895	45 775	396	95 392	826	23.2	9.3	8.8	44.5	73.8	35.9	90.8	12.80	2 837	1 066
Corona city	95 255	902	40 313	382	98 311	931	18.1	21.7	6.2	53.9	75.4	40.5	92.1	11.83	1 747	1 339
Coronado city	31 829	1 102	15 028	520	37 341	1 292	13.2	6.8	18.6	57.4	71.0	48.9	76.2	9.90	1 256	984
Costa Mesa city	67 865	667	46 132	453	74 559	732	32.2	1.4	16.1	55.2	67.1	46.8	71.8	10.85	1 866	500
Covina city	36 073	819	19 793	450	33 493	761	26.2	4.2	9.6	54.3	74.6	40.7	90.4	16.62	1 713	1 273
Culver City city	95 225	2 423	52 768	1 343	93 588	2 381	17.2	14.1	5.9	57.2	70.4	46.5	79.2	13.06	1 391	986
Cupertino city	32 412	728	19 070	429	27 851	626	15.5	6.2	10.5	49.4	69.5	40.6	82.4	14.42	2 387	594
Cypress city	29 574	624	17 229	364	22 047	466	34.0	.6	22.6	57.4	72.6	45.6	82.6	12.27	1 238	1 175
Daly City city	66 463	671	23 531	238	59 911	605	20.0	12.5	8.0	48.7	62.7	41.8	71.6	19.70	3 016	145
Dana Point city	17 480	516	11 718	346	14 262	421	32.6	.2	25.0	53.7	72.6	41.5	75.8	12.19	2 157	493
Danville city	18 636	472	10 131	257	17 916	454	18.2	1.9	17.4	46.1	71.6	35.5	89.8	14.21	2 909	780
Davis city	53 703	1 002	22 613	422	51 442	900	11.2	21.7	11.4	44.5	74.1	36.0	92.7	10.10	2 011	1 041
Diamond Bar city	16 127	300	6 758	126	11 302	210	33.8	.7	21.6	54.3	74.6	40.7	90.4	16.62	1 713	1 273
Downey city	50 228	542	26 664	288	50 589	546	31.5	.9	12.4	58.3	74.3	48.9	84.0	14.77	1 154	1 537
El Cajon city	49 378	534	25 439	275	48 467	524	26.2	15.1	12.8	56.6	72.5	44.6	83.4	12.80	1 400	1 110
El Centro city	69 463	1 787	10 344	266	67 751	1 743	5.9	8.1	6.6	54.6	91.3	39.3	107.5	2.71	1 156	3 741
El Monte city	51 456	468	31 531	287	49 185	448	28.0	—	12.8	55.7	75.2	41.7	89.2	17.90	1 433	1 427
Encinitas city	33 484	570	18 012	307	28 009	477	19.3	.1	21.8	54.5	67.6	44.1	73.5	10.93	2 010	555
Escondido city	80 340	681	36 919	313	79 241	671	20.7	11.7	14.4	55.2	70.5	43.1	81.3	13.04	1 802	868
Eureka city	25 752	1 001	13 165	512	23 518	914	23.8	10.5	9.4	48.0	57.0	41.5	61.8	37.53	4 496	—
Fairfield city	87 734	990	41 786	471	79 641	898	15.0	.2	15.9	45.5	72.0	36.2	88.5	21.38	2 767	898
Folsom city	60 634	1 423	30 630	719	61 444	1 442	8.7	10.6	21.2	45.6	77.2	37.7	94.2	23.91	2 683	1 422
Fontana city	88 989	835	49 506	464	86 629	813	17.7	5.4	10.4	56.0	78.6	44.5	94.8	15.63	1 478	1 922
Foster City city	48 592	1 618	25 068	834	43 907	1 400	11.5	5.2	4.7	48.7	68.7	38.0	83.4	19.70	2 563	486
Fountain Valley city	36 257	646	21 394	381	36 545	651	24.2	14.0	15.9	57.4	72.6	45.6	82.6	12.27	1 238	1 175
Fremont city	132 000	667	82 726	418	137 927	697	21.1	.9	11.0	49.0	66.7	41.1	76.1	13.73	2 578	410
Fresno city	318 027	800	110 469	278	318 433	801	19.6	28.3	7.5	45.7	81.9	37.4	98.6	10.60	2 556	1 967
Fullerton city	71 656	593	37 948	314	69 019	571	31.7	10.5	12.0	57.4	72.6	45.6	82.6	12.27	1 238	1 175
Gardena city	36 706	679	24 277	449	37 548	694	29.8	—	9.5	56.1	69.7	45.3	78.8	13.57	1 568	794
Garden Grove city	88 417	587	36 786	244	89 785	596	24.7	—	12.6	57.4	72.6	45.6	82.6	12.27	1 238	1 175
Gilroy city	44 762	1 253	17 749	497	35 772	1 002	23.6	23.1	13.1	47.4	70.9	35.6	88.3	19.77	2 668	719
Glendale city	168 532	917	70 506	384	162 156	882	19.9	14.5	8.9	54.5	75.6	41.3	90.2	15.87	1 609	1 424
Glendora city	23 594	477	11 877	240	22 925	464	28.6	13.4	10.8	54.3	74.6	40.7	90.4	16.62	1 713	1 273
Hanford city	25 833	704	9 205	251	23 568	643	18.0	30.1	12.0	43.9	78.8	34.3	95.9	7.95	2 816	1 551
Hawthorne city	65 388	898	27 919	383	55 973	769	37.9	16.2	7.3	56.8	69.1	47.8	75.3	12.01	1 458	727
Hayward city	96 279	755	50 237	394	110 813	869	20.9	12.5	20.4	49.0	66.7	41.1	76.1	13.73	2 578	410
Hemet city	28 995	534	14 301	263	31 353	577	22.3	16.7	16.9	50.2	77.6	39.3	96.2	17.33	2 432	1 451
Hesperia city	15 811	257	7 414	121	21 856	356	20.1	—	26.8	44.2	79.3	30.0	97.4	5.51	3 127	1 525
Highland city	11 756	288	4 707	115	13 308	326	23.2	—	33.5	53.6	79.4	40.3	97.0	15.42	1 719	1 804
Huntington Beach city	138 039	714	72 459	375	128 232	663	27.3	6.7	11.6	55.2	67.1	46.8	71.8	10.85	1 866	500
Huntington Park city	36 442	632	15 925	276	36 325	630	30.8	.5	6.9	58.3	74.3	48.9	84.0	14.77	1 154	1 537
Imperial Beach city	12 431	440	3 752	133	11 767	417	24.0	24.6	18.9	55.3	68.2	45.3	73.1	9.34	1 798	638
Indio city	22 805	510	10 745	240	27 069	605	21.9	1.5	6.4	56.4	92.0	42.5	108.7	5.31	985	4 014
Inglewood city	140 310	1 257	47 868	429	150 913	1 352	26.9	9.5	7.5	56.8	69.1	47.8	75.3	12.01	1 458	727
Irvine city	111 449	844	61 317	464	103 614	784	22.8	3.8	25.8	54.5	71.6	41.4	83.7	11.81	1 784	973
Laguna Niguel city	15 591	297	8 890	170	12 909	246	35.1	—	29.5	53.7	67.2	41.5	75.8	12.19	2 157	493
La Habra city	34 374	637	15 130	280	32 347	599	25.8	7.0	11.8	57.4	72.6	45.6	82.6	12.27	1 238	1 175
Lakewood city	37 466	497	19 440	258	27 315	362	24.3	9.8	11.9	55.9	73.1	44.9	82.7	11.80	1 430	1 201
La Mesa city	30 140	547	13 723	249	28 582	519	21.8	16.1	7.6	56.6	72.5	44.6	83.4	12.80	1 400	1 110
La Mirada city	30 175	682	18 103	409	24 882	562	16.4	—	13.5	57.4	72.6	45.6	82.6	12.27	1 238	1 175

[1] Based on resident population estimated as of July 1, 1997.   [2] Represents normal values for the 30-year period, 1961–1990.   [3] Average daily minimum.   [4] Average daily maximum.   [5] One heating degree day is accumulated for each whole degree that the mean daily temperature is below 65 degrees Fahrenheit.   [6] One cooling degree day is accumulated for each whole degree that the mean daily temperature is above 65 degrees Fahrenheit.

Sources: City Government Finances—U.S. Census Bureau, 1997 Census of Governments, Volume 4, Government Finances, GC97(4)-4, Finances of Municipal and Township Governments, issued September 2000 (related Internet site <http://www.census.gov/govs/www/cog.html>).   1997 Population for Government Finances calculations—U.S. Census Bureau, Population Estimates for Places: Annual Time Series, July 1, 1990 to July 1, 1999 (SU-99-7), published 20 October 2000, <http://www.census.gov/estimates/metro-city/placesbyst/SC99T7_US.txt>.   Climate: U.S. National Oceanic and Atmospheric Administration (NOAA), National Climatic Data Center (NCDC), Climatography of the United States, Number 81, published January 1992 (related Internet site <http://lwf.ncdc.noaa.gov/oa/climate/normals/usnormals.html>).

Table C–7. Cities — **Government Finances and Climate**–Con.

[Includes states and 1,070 incorporated places of 25,000 or more population as of April 1, 1990 in all states except Hawaii which has no incorporated places recognized by the Census Bureau. For Hawaii, 8 census designated places (CDPs) of 25,000 or more population as of April 1, 1990 are included. Also included are the 5 boroughs of New York city. For more information on these areas, see appendix B. Geographic Information]

City	City government finances, 1996-1997									Climate[2]						
	General revenue				General expenditure					Average daily temperature (degrees Fahrenheit)						
			Taxes				By selected function, percent from—									
	Total ($1,000)	Per capita[1] (dollars)	Total ($1,000)	Per capita[1] (dollars)	Total ($1,000)	Per capita[1] (dollars)	Police protection	Sewerage and solid waste management	Highways	January	July	January[3]	July[4]	Annual precipitation (inches)	Heating degree days[5]	Cooling degree days[6]
CALIFORNIA—Con.																
Lancaster city	90 699	757	42 474	354	92 687	773	15.3	.1	17.2	45.1	80.7	31.9	97.1	6.92	2 948	1 720
La Puente city	8 315	217	3 895	102	6 943	181	46.9	1.0	8.4	55.7	75.2	41.7	89.2	17.90	1 433	1 427
La Verne city	22 708	709	10 908	341	19 372	605	26.6	1.3	15.0	54.3	74.6	40.7	90.4	16.62	1 713	1 273
Lawndale city	11 134	389	6 915	242	7 465	261	43.0	–	8.9	56.1	69.7	45.3	78.8	13.57	1 568	794
Livermore city	65 487	938	26 733	383	64 853	929	16.3	11.1	17.0	46.1	71.6	35.5	89.8	14.21	2 909	780
Lodi city	35 965	656	14 346	262	41 193	752	19.5	9.1	12.6	45.1	73.9	36.4	91.4	17.11	2 809	1 020
Lompoc city	25 140	610	8 454	205	23 596	572	18.4	31.3	15.4	52.9	62.9	40.1	72.9	13.95	2 651	265
Long Beach city	905 438	2 116	180 538	422	962 407	2 249	12.3	7.1	4.7	55.9	73.1	44.9	82.7	11.80	1 430	1 201
Los Altos city	19 698	707	8 737	314	25 151	903	16.0	13.2	7.1	47.5	66.4	37.7	78.4	14.96	2 911	297
Los Angeles city	4 706 326	1 320	1 988 838	558	4 935 452	1 385	18.1	11.6	3.1	58.3	74.3	48.9	84.0	14.77	1 154	1 537
Los Gatos town	20 978	721	13 183	453	17 047	586	35.3	3.2	11.0	49.4	69.5	40.6	82.4	14.42	2 387	594
Lynwood city	32 369	517	16 833	269	36 370	581	13.1	9.0	12.4	58.3	74.3	48.9	84.0	14.77	1 154	1 537
Madera city	22 188	615	8 496	236	22 637	628	18.3	19.0	14.0	44.7	79.7	35.5	97.8	11.15	2 741	1 632
Manhattan Beach city	31 661	942	17 103	509	28 831	858	31.7	12.4	11.1	56.8	69.1	47.8	75.3	12.01	1 458	727
Manteca city	27 593	584	12 815	271	26 793	567	19.9	22.3	16.4	45.0	77.7	37.0	94.4	13.95	2 707	1 470
Marina city	NA	NA	NA	NA	NA	NA	NA	NA	NA	51.7	60.0	43.3	68.1	18.72	3 125	55
Martinez city	20 554	578	9 011	253	18 425	518	27.0	.4	38.3	49.9	63.2	42.0	71.0	22.20	2 574	199
Maywood city	7 224	256	3 881	137	6 561	232	55.8	–	16.7	58.3	74.3	48.9	84.0	14.77	1 154	1 537
Menlo Park city	35 217	1 160	21 385	705	34 576	1 139	19.1	3.3	7.4	47.5	66.4	37.7	78.4	14.96	2 911	297
Merced city	42 465	724	16 175	276	48 699	830	19.8	17.9	4.3	45.1	78.6	35.7	96.9	12.01	2 692	1 500
Milpitas city	70 309	1 178	44 463	745	69 055	1 157	17.5	10.5	28.8	49.4	69.5	40.6	82.4	14.42	2 387	594
Mission Viejo city	35 481	375	23 795	251	40 131	424	17.2	–	18.9	54.5	71.6	41.4	83.7	11.81	1 784	973
Modesto city	111 671	615	50 869	280	114 669	631	24.9	15.3	12.3	45.6	77.1	37.4	94.2	12.10	2 605	1 401
Monrovia city	29 355	792	17 561	474	29 629	799	25.9	3.2	7.1	55.8	75.0	43.6	89.0	19.37	1 453	1 394
Montclair city	26 464	884	18 041	603	26 430	883	24.7	13.0	8.9	54.3	74.6	40.7	90.4	16.62	1 713	1 273
Montebello city	58 001	968	32 050	535	43 207	721	27.9	4.0	2.8	58.3	74.3	48.9	84.0	14.77	1 154	1 537
Monterey city	55 200	1 747	29 133	922	47 183	1 494	14.8	1.0	12.2	51.7	60.0	43.3	68.1	18.72	3 125	55
Monterey Park city	36 670	595	18 563	301	37 775	613	25.6	9.1	9.3	55.7	75.2	41.7	89.2	17.90	1 433	1 427
Moorpark city	14 534	493	6 177	209	13 530	459	21.2	.8	31.0	54.6	67.8	41.2	80.8	17.39	2 039	569
Moreno Valley city	59 535	415	27 955	195	67 108	468	34.7	–	17.1	53.6	76.9	41.2	93.7	10.00	1 796	1 500
Mountain View city	111 396	1 576	56 555	800	114 305	1 617	9.9	17.8	6.0	47.5	66.4	37.7	78.4	14.96	2 911	297
Napa city	48 641	734	23 521	355	43 683	659	18.8	5.6	12.0	47.1	67.9	37.2	82.1	25.12	2 844	456
National City city	34 554	603	19 784	345	30 317	529	29.2	10.8	8.0	57.4	71.0	48.9	76.2	9.90	1 256	984
Newark city	26 044	625	15 159	364	26 256	630	30.6	.7	12.7	49.0	66.7	41.1	76.1	13.73	2 578	410
Newport Beach city	86 639	1 219	50 597	712	88 395	1 244	24.7	6.8	17.8	55.2	67.1	46.8	71.8	10.85	1 866	500
Norwalk city	45 070	466	20 396	211	46 628	482	18.0	.4	7.9	55.9	73.1	44.9	82.7	11.80	1 430	1 201
Novato city	25 172	522	12 848	267	32 573	676	22.4	–	7.1	46.4	67.0	36.8	82.5	24.60	3 050	335
Oakland city	700 872	1 914	240 389	656	786 921	2 149	12.6	2.3	4.5	49.9	62.1	43.3	70.0	24.30	2 902	115
Oceanside city	136 126	905	33 549	223	135 532	901	16.9	22.6	11.3	54.5	67.6	44.1	73.5	10.93	2 010	555
Ontario city	147 993	1 024	68 179	472	175 401	1 214	17.8	10.4	7.3	54.3	74.6	40.7	90.4	16.62	1 713	1 273
Orange city	83 953	690	44 802	368	81 902	673	24.4	9.0	13.6	57.4	72.6	45.6	82.6	12.27	1 238	1 175
Oxnard city	110 278	726	42 274	278	123 829	815	17.5	29.5	10.6	55.3	66.1	44.2	74.4	14.38	1 992	416
Pacifica city	22 200	548	8 397	207	28 833	712	15.2	33.4	12.6	48.7	62.7	41.8	71.6	19.70	3 016	145
Palmdale city	63 439	593	38 568	360	83 017	776	10.8	–	15.9	45.1	80.7	31.9	97.1	6.92	2 948	1 720
Palm Springs city	73 241	1 698	35 395	821	77 321	1 793	14.9	6.2	12.6	56.4	92.0	42.5	108.7	5.31	985	4 014
Palo Alto city	114 261	1 945	41 574	708	114 156	1 943	11.3	30.5	10.7	47.5	66.4	37.7	78.4	14.96	2 911	297
Paradise town	8 392	326	4 898	190	6 785	264	31.5	–	13.9	45.4	77.2	36.9	90.8	52.71	3 214	1 342
Paramount city	31 768	626	15 778	311	30 781	606	20.9	–	11.3	55.9	73.1	44.9	82.7	11.80	1 430	1 201
Pasadena city	224 564	1 682	94 948	711	225 163	1 686	13.3	3.4	6.0	55.8	75.0	43.6	89.0	19.37	1 453	1 394
Petaluma city	40 463	806	22 394	446	45 801	912	16.4	12.9	22.1	46.4	67.0	36.8	82.5	24.60	3 050	335
Pico Rivera city	38 399	643	17 157	287	32 170	539	16.4	–	5.0	58.3	74.3	48.9	84.0	14.77	1 154	1 537
Pittsburg city	48 516	934	21 254	409	49 215	948	16.4	1.4	10.0	44.5	73.8	35.9	90.8	12.80	2 837	1 066
Placentia city	23 977	530	13 636	301	26 471	585	23.7	6.1	14.3	57.4	72.6	45.6	82.6	12.27	1 238	1 175
Pleasant Hill city	19 353	589	10 345	315	18 494	563	29.1	–	23.6	44.5	73.8	35.9	90.8	12.80	2 837	1 066
Pleasanton city	67 976	1 101	39 087	633	78 054	1 264	13.5	10.0	12.1	46.1	71.6	35.5	89.8	14.21	2 909	780
Pomona city	119 194	884	59 326	440	116 658	865	23.1	7.2	7.3	54.3	74.6	40.7	90.4	16.62	1 713	1 273
Porterville city	24 307	695	9 329	267	24 580	702	16.2	23.8	7.8	46.4	81.8	36.4	98.3	11.03	2 374	1 998
Poway city	56 154	1 169	23 326	486	72 797	1 515	5.7	5.7	7.0	56.6	72.5	44.6	83.4	12.80	1 400	1 110
Rancho Cucamonga city	89 201	754	54 382	460	92 693	783	22.4	–	15.0	56.0	78.6	44.5	94.8	15.63	1 478	1 922
Rancho Palos Verdes city	22 578	533	8 213	194	19 723	466	12.6	.7	20.1	56.1	69.7	45.3	78.8	13.57	1 568	794
Redding city	81 723	1 040	28 547	363	81 966	1 043	14.5	18.4	13.0	45.5	81.5	35.7	98.3	33.30	2 855	1 797
Redlands city	44 250	662	21 816	326	46 125	690	18.2	19.6	11.1	52.8	78.4	39.6	95.8	12.80	1 875	1 673
Redondo Beach city	63 391	1 006	32 006	508	63 159	1 002	21.3	3.2	5.7	56.8	69.1	47.8	75.3	12.01	1 458	727
Redwood City city	80 508	1 109	46 987	647	79 004	1 088	11.9	14.6	14.6	48.7	66.7	38.9	83.4	19.74	2 563	486
Rialto city	40 828	492	18 792	226	50 524	609	27.6	12.1	9.7	53.6	79.4	40.3	97.0	15.42	1 719	1 804
Richmond city	132 204	1 434	66 167	718	136 554	1 481	20.8	8.3	14.6	49.9	63.2	42.0	71.0	22.20	2 574	199
Ridgecrest city	15 211	498	8 525	279	11 915	390	23.9	4.7	8.9	44.9	84.3	29.9	102.9	4.49	2 724	2 231
Riverside city	223 149	876	76 224	299	207 201	814	20.6	14.3	12.0	53.9	77.9	40.5	94.4	9.58	1 678	1 651
Rohnert Park city	28 564	713	9 258	231	34 929	871	16.1	35.7	8.4	47.4	67.6	37.0	83.8	30.30	2 883	489

[1] Based on resident population estimated as of July 1, 1997.   [2] Represents normal values for the 30-year period, 1961–1990.   [3] Average daily minimum.   [4] Average daily maximum.   [5] One heating degree day is accumulated for each whole degree that the mean daily temperature is below 65 degrees Fahrenheit.   [6] One cooling degree day is accumulated for each whole degree that the mean daily temperature is above 65 degrees Fahrenheit.

Sources: City Government Finances—U.S. Census Bureau, 1997 Census of Governments, Volume 4, Government Finances, GC97(4)-4, Finances of Municipal and Township Governments, issued September 2000 (related Internet site <http://www.census.gov/govs/www/cog.html>).   1997 Population for Government Finances calculations—U.S. Census Bureau, Population Estimates for Places: Annual Time Series, July 1, 1990 to July 1, 1999 (SU-99-7), published 20 October 2000, <http://www.census.gov/estimates/metro-city/placesbyst/SC99T7_US.txt>.   Climate: U.S. National Oceanic and Atmospheric Administration (NOAA), National Climatic Data Center (NCDC), Climatography of the United States, Number 81, published January 1992 (related Internet site <http://lwf.ncdc.noaa.gov/oa/climate/normals/usnormals.html>).

Table C–7. Cities — Government Finances and Climate–Con.

[Includes states and 1,070 incorporated places of 25,000 or more population as of April 1, 1990 in all states except Hawaii which has no incorporated places recognized by the Census Bureau. For Hawaii, 8 census designated places (CDPs) of 25,000 or more population as of April 1, 1990 are included. Also included are the 5 boroughs of New York city. For more information on these areas, see appendix B. Geographic Information]

City	City government finances, 1996-1997 — General revenue — Total ($1,000)	Per capita[1] (dollars)	Taxes — Total ($1,000)	Per capita[1] (dollars)	General expenditure — Total ($1,000)	Per capita[1] (dollars)	By selected function, percent from — Police protection	Sewerage and solid waste management	Highways	Climate[2] — Average daily temperature (degrees Fahrenheit) — January	July	January[3]	July[4]	Annual precipitation (inches)	Heating degree days[5]	Cooling degree days[6]
CALIFORNIA—Con.																
Rosemead city	20 761	394	10 334	196	16 852	320	28.3	.3	9.3	55.7	75.2	41.7	89.2	17.90	1 433	1 427
Roseville city	100 205	1 499	41 102	615	87 777	1 313	15.9	16.8	11.0	45.6	77.2	37.7	94.2	23.91	2 683	1 422
Sacramento city	403 145	1 002	182 824	454	337 664	839	23.0	12.1	10.0	45.2	75.7	37.7	93.2	17.52	2 749	1 237
Salinas city	69 886	588	38 158	321	72 527	610	25.0	4.4	12.5	50.5	62.5	40.0	71.1	12.44	2 964	181
San Bernardino city	182 539	988	71 940	389	200 591	1 085	16.8	12.3	7.6	53.6	79.4	40.3	97.0	15.42	1 719	1 804
San Bruno city	35 040	867	12 786	316	31 362	776	18.0	8.7	7.4	48.7	62.7	41.8	71.6	19.70	3 016	145
San Buenaventura (Ventura) city	79 596	808	34 636	352	80 709	820	18.7	8.6	18.2	55.3	66.1	44.2	74.4	14.38	1 992	416
San Carlos city	33 628	1 211	12 094	436	35 525	1 280	12.4	10.1	3.9	48.7	68.7	38.9	83.4	19.74	2 563	486
San Clemente city	38 680	839	13 484	292	38 965	845	16.3	8.4	24.8	53.7	67.2	41.5	75.8	12.19	2 157	493
San Diego city	1 420 878	1 187	442 684	370	1 529 193	1 278	13.0	31.3	6.5	57.4	71.0	48.9	76.2	9.90	1 256	984
San Dimas city	16 492	480	9 829	286	16 334	475	23.1	.1	17.9	54.3	74.6	40.7	90.4	16.62	1 713	1 273
San Francisco city	3 480 314	4 697	1 079 961	1 457	3 594 316	4 851	7.8	4.2	1.2	51.1	59.1	45.8	64.6	19.71	3 005	65
San Gabriel city	16 348	442	9 940	269	16 222	438	31.4	–	10.0	55.7	75.2	41.7	89.2	17.90	1 433	1 427
San Jose city	917 531	1 078	424 714	499	850 551	999	16.3	19.1	6.2	49.4	69.5	40.6	82.4	14.42	2 387	594
San Juan Capistrano city	23 330	782	13 141	441	18 643	625	17.9	12.4	14.0	53.7	67.2	41.5	75.8	12.19	2 157	493
San Leandro city	71 455	980	40 451	555	69 390	952	18.2	15.2	14.8	49.9	62.1	43.3	70.0	24.30	2 902	115
San Luis Obispo city	38 935	917	18 905	445	36 204	853	17.3	10.5	15.0	52.5	65.2	41.5	78.1	23.46	2 498	335
San Marcos city	40 131	817	25 723	524	36 747	748	14.2	–	11.7	55.2	70.5	43.1	81.3	13.04	1 802	868
San Mateo city	72 606	795	39 921	437	70 088	767	19.8	17.2	12.3	48.7	68.7	38.9	83.4	19.74	2 563	486
San Pablo city	21 719	824	12 876	489	21 231	806	31.5	–	18.1	49.9	63.2	42.0	71.0	22.20	2 574	199
San Rafael city	49 604	978	24 340	480	52 594	1 037	18.2	–	14.8	48.8	67.7	40.6	81.6	35.74	2 581	449
San Ramon city	41 550	958	25 539	589	42 899	989	17.5	.2	24.9	46.1	71.6	35.5	89.8	14.21	2 909	780
Santa Ana city	217 955	717	108 437	357	255 947	842	28.4	6.3	9.5	57.4	72.6	45.6	82.6	12.27	1 238	1 175
Santa Barbara city	118 073	1 375	47 613	554	111 485	1 298	15.5	4.8	10.3	52.0	65.4	40.3	73.9	16.25	2 438	289
Santa Clara city	171 918	1 739	70 200	710	145 802	1 475	13.6	17.8	8.5	49.4	69.5	40.6	82.4	14.42	2 387	594
Santa Clarita city	65 464	507	32 845	254	50 719	393	21.5	.9	25.8	54.5	75.6	41.3	90.2	15.87	1 609	1 424
Santa Cruz city	90 653	1 756	32 506	629	91 187	1 766	14.6	32.6	7.6	49.9	63.5	38.8	75.7	28.99	2 969	148
Santa Maria city	50 934	751	19 058	281	54 984	811	18.3	35.9	13.0	51.1	63.1	38.3	73.3	12.36	2 984	169
Santa Monica city	210 573	2 385	103 419	1 171	176 755	2 002	20.0	10.5	7.6	57.2	65.5	49.6	69.3	13.21	1 019	440
Santa Paula city	11 014	416	4 843	183	12 790	483	24.0	21.0	15.0	54.6	67.8	41.2	80.8	17.39	2 039	569
Santa Rosa city	130 857	994	50 010	380	138 618	1 053	16.2	25.8	12.8	47.4	67.6	37.0	83.8	30.30	2 883	489
Santee city	24 250	431	14 057	250	23 346	415	26.3	–	16.5	56.6	72.5	44.6	83.4	12.80	1 400	1 110
Saratoga city	14 700	493	6 271	210	12 705	426	22.6	–	18.2	49.4	69.5	40.6	82.4	14.42	2 387	594
Seal Beach city	18 107	699	10 711	414	16 519	638	32.1	8.0	8.7	55.9	73.1	44.9	82.7	11.80	1 430	1 201
Seaside city	18 450	676	11 895	436	12 558	460	33.9	1.6	10.0	51.7	60.0	43.3	68.1	18.72	3 125	55
Simi Valley city	71 452	656	31 307	288	60 584	557	25.3	14.4	11.5	54.6	67.8	41.2	80.8	17.39	2 039	569
South Gate city	44 565	509	16 599	190	43 440	497	29.4	8.8	14.3	58.3	74.3	48.9	84.0	14.77	1 154	1 537
South San Francisco city	68 795	1 182	31 208	536	70 567	1 213	13.2	13.6	10.2	48.7	62.7	41.8	71.6	19.70	3 016	145
Stanton city	13 824	424	8 136	250	12 545	385	38.6	1.1	15.2	57.4	72.6	45.6	82.6	12.27	1 238	1 175
Stockton city	166 757	708	72 512	308	186 398	792	25.2	12.6	6.8	45.0	77.7	37.0	94.4	13.95	2 707	1 470
Sunnyvale city	147 336	1 164	59 695	472	146 561	1 158	13.3	27.4	8.4	49.4	69.5	40.6	82.4	14.42	2 387	594
Temecula city	33 030	817	22 654	560	39 801	984	11.3	–	25.7	53.9	75.4	40.5	92.1	11.83	1 747	1 339
Temple City city	10 343	327	4 710	149	7 539	239	29.1	.6	13.3	55.7	75.2	41.7	89.2	17.90	1 433	1 427
Thousand Oaks city	88 457	776	46 231	405	83 715	734	14.7	12.3	20.3	55.3	66.1	44.2	74.4	14.38	1 992	416
Torrance city	166 674	1 225	90 154	663	140 867	1 036	25.3	4.6	5.4	56.1	69.7	45.3	78.8	13.57	1 568	794
Tracy city	47 408	1 003	12 290	260	57 766	1 222	11.6	19.4	19.6	45.2	76.2	36.7	92.1	11.85	2 659	1 321
Tulare city	27 140	668	10 848	267	30 286	745	15.9	42.0	7.8	45.4	80.4	37.0	96.0	10.15	2 511	1 762
Turlock city	26 271	524	10 689	213	29 425	587	26.4	29.3	11.9	45.6	77.1	37.4	94.2	12.10	2 605	1 401
Tustin city	38 813	631	25 022	407	43 665	710	27.0	–	12.3	54.5	71.6	41.4	83.7	11.81	1 784	973
Union City city	36 709	596	19 923	324	35 307	573	27.0	–	9.2	49.0	66.7	41.1	76.1	13.73	2 578	410
Upland city	45 685	687	16 084	242	53 291	802	18.5	22.8	10.3	54.3	74.6	40.7	90.4	16.62	1 713	1 273
Vacaville city	81 685	986	34 657	418	78 171	944	15.2	11.6	13.6	45.2	75.2	36.1	94.1	23.84	2 764	1 154
Vallejo city	109 794	984	29 266	262	107 982	968	19.4	2.1	9.9	49.9	63.2	42.0	71.0	22.20	2 574	199
Victorville city	41 126	606	19 446	287	36 259	534	18.1	19.2	22.6	44.2	79.3	30.0	97.4	5.51	3 127	1 525
Visalia city	68 129	765	23 699	266	60 457	679	18.4	21.9	3.1	45.4	80.4	37.0	96.0	10.15	2 511	1 762
Vista city	61 928	778	35 974	452	62 512	785	12.3	10.0	26.5	55.2	70.5	43.1	81.3	13.04	1 802	868
Walnut city	27 593	894	18 519	600	25 582	829	9.5	–	10.1	54.3	74.6	40.7	90.4	16.62	1 713	1 273
Walnut Creek city	44 268	693	25 652	402	43 699	684	25.1	–	15.2	44.5	73.8	35.9	90.8	12.80	2 837	1 066
Watsonville city	49 038	1 370	17 665	494	51 334	1 434	12.3	31.1	3.9	49.4	61.8	38.3	71.3	21.73	3 213	107
West Covina city	62 127	635	33 439	342	61 182	626	25.5	1.7	14.9	55.7	75.2	41.7	89.2	17.90	1 433	1 427
West Hollywood city	41 497	1 142	22 681	624	37 424	1 030	24.3	5.2	15.3	58.3	74.3	48.9	84.0	14.77	1 154	1 537
Westminster city	38 671	462	23 320	278	41 346	494	39.1	–	14.3	57.4	72.6	45.6	82.6	12.27	1 238	1 175
West Sacramento city	52 550	1 748	22 324	743	62 211	2 069	13.4	11.8	29.7	45.2	75.7	37.7	93.2	17.52	2 749	1 237
Whittier city	52 441	665	20 801	264	44 918	570	34.0	11.9	13.5	55.7	75.2	41.7	89.2	17.90	1 433	1 427
Woodland city	28 745	668	17 302	402	27 342	635	22.6	9.0	13.9	44.5	76.9	35.9	96.3	19.43	2 777	1 387
Yorba Linda city	44 061	741	24 336	409	48 381	814	12.2	–	20.5	57.4	72.6	45.6	82.6	12.27	1 238	1 175
Yuba City city	21 237	617	11 230	326	28 805	837	18.4	18.1	14.2	45.6	78.8	37.2	96.0	21.04	2 524	1 607
Yucaipa city	10 379	288	5 104	142	6 365	177	42.2	–	20.5	52.8	78.4	39.6	95.8	12.80	1 875	1 673

[1] Based on resident population estimated as of July 1, 1997. [2] Represents normal values for the 30-year period, 1961–1990. [3] Average daily minimum. [4] Average daily maximum. [5] One heating degree day is accumulated for each whole degree that the mean daily temperature is below 65 degrees Fahrenheit. [6] One cooling degree day is accumulated for each whole degree that the mean daily temperature is above 65 degrees Fahrenheit.

Sources: City Government Finances—U.S. Census Bureau, 1997 Census of Governments, Volume 4, Government Finances, GC97(4)-4, Finances of Municipal and Township Governments, issued September 2000 (related Internet site <http://www.census.gov/govs/www/cog.html>). 1997 Population for Government Finances calculations—U.S. Census Bureau, Population Estimates for Places: Annual Time Series, July 1, 1990 to July 1, 1999 (SU-99-7), published 20 October 2000, <http://www.census.gov/estimates/metro-city/placesbyst/SC99T7_US.txt>. Climate: U.S. National Oceanic and Atmospheric Administration (NOAA), National Climatic Data Center (NCDC), Climatography of the United States, Number 81, published January 1992 (related Internet site <http://lwf.ncdc.noaa.gov/oa/climate/normals/usnormals.html>).

Table C–7. Cities — **Government Finances and Climate**–Con.

[Includes states and 1,070 incorporated places of 25,000 or more population as of April 1, 1990 in all states except Hawaii which has no incorporated places recognized by the Census Bureau. For Hawaii, 8 census designated places (CDPs) of 25,000 or more population as of April 1, 1990 are included. Also included are the 5 boroughs of New York city. For more information on these areas, see appendix B. Geographic Information]

City	City government finances, 1996-1997									Climate[2]						
	General revenue				General expenditure					Average daily temperature (degrees Fahrenheit)						
			Taxes				By selected function, percent from—									
	Total ($1,000)	Per capita[1] (dollars)	Total ($1,000)	Per capita[1] (dollars)	Total ($1,000)	Per capita[1] (dollars)	Police protection	Sewerage and solid waste management	Highways	January	July	January[3]	July[4]	Annual precipitation (inches)	Heating degree days[5]	Cooling degree days[6]
COLORADO	X	X	X	X	X	X	X	X	X	X	X	X	X	X	X	X
Arvada city	74 267	762	39 211	402	63 033	647	15.7	8.8	20.2	30.2	71.9	17.1	85.7	15.86	6 158	554
Aurora city	208 386	843	124 875	505	193 643	784	21.6	9.6	7.4	29.7	73.5	16.1	88.2	15.40	6 020	679
Boulder city	119 599	1 306	81 574	891	112 036	1 223	12.4	5.8	14.0	32.6	73.0	19.9	87.5	18.58	5 554	649
Colorado Springs city	453 379	1 344	104 689	310	379 453	1 125	12.8	4.4	10.8	28.8	70.8	16.1	84.4	16.24	6 415	419
Denver city	1 636 995	3 278	501 438	1 004	1 635 204	3 275	6.9	5.1	3.6	29.7	73.5	16.1	88.2	15.40	6 020	679
Englewood city	38 692	1 210	20 712	648	36 426	1 140	14.9	12.7	11.2	29.7	73.5	16.1	88.2	15.40	6 020	679
Fort Collins city	115 905	1 076	64 786	601	110 030	1 022	12.6	12.0	22.2	27.7	71.5	14.1	85.5	15.07	6 368	479
Grand Junction city	41 873	1 022	24 140	589	43 619	1 065	17.7	6.7	18.1	25.0	78.8	14.5	93.6	8.64	5 548	1 183
Greeley city	49 843	713	29 552	423	53 881	771	17.1	18.5	13.7	26.1	73.5	12.3	89.1	13.97	6 306	645
Lakewood city	NA	NA	NA	NA	NA	NA	NA	NA	NA	30.2	71.9	17.1	85.7	15.86	6 158	554
Littleton city	35 891	897	18 420	460	33 104	827	15.3	14.1	10.6	30.2	71.9	17.1	85.7	15.86	6 158	554
Longmont city	58 701	989	33 603	566	59 036	994	14.1	19.2	15.6	26.6	72.4	11.7	88.7	13.60	6 443	562
Loveland city	39 693	867	16 194	354	40 076	875	16.9	13.6	13.3	27.7	71.5	14.1	85.5	15.07	6 368	479
Northglenn city	20 448	690	11 546	390	20 604	695	21.7	21.1	14.1	29.7	73.5	16.1	88.2	15.40	6 020	679
Pueblo city	68 427	664	41 166	400	61 330	595	17.2	7.0	14.0	29.8	77.1	14.2	93.0	11.19	5 413	973
Thornton city	60 997	877	37 883	544	49 298	709	16.1	18.9	20.0	29.7	73.5	16.1	88.2	15.40	6 020	679
Westminster city	103 095	1 093	49 457	524	85 039	901	12.0	5.4	16.6	30.2	71.9	17.1	85.7	15.86	6 158	554
Wheat Ridge city	19 872	663	14 210	474	19 670	656	32.6	–	15.3	30.2	71.9	17.1	85.7	15.86	6 158	554
CONNECTICUT	X	X	X	X	X	X	X	X	X	X	X	X	X	X	X	X
Bridgeport city	421 634	3 067	163 417	1 189	407 231	2 962	7.2	6.5	1.0	28.9	73.7	21.9	81.7	41.66	5 537	724
Bristol city	127 858	2 154	70 989	1 196	128 975	2 173	6.7	6.2	3.7	24.6	73.7	15.8	85.0	44.14	6 151	677
Danbury city	145 903	2 229	90 348	1 380	142 650	2 179	6.7	2.4	3.6	23.8	71.3	13.2	83.6	44.50	6 492	486
Hartford city	523 503	4 044	184 862	1 428	534 538	4 130	6.3	2.8	3.6	24.6	73.7	15.8	85.0	44.14	6 151	677
Meriden city	127 853	2 250	64 728	1 139	147 808	2 601	4.7	3.9	1.9	27.1	72.8	19.2	83.3	49.72	5 945	633
Middletown city	115 976	2 671	54 611	1 258	115 673	2 664	6.7	14.8	6.7	27.1	72.8	19.2	83.3	49.72	5 945	633
Milford city (remainder)	[7]120 385	[7]2 514	[7]90 192	[7]1 884	[7]117 641	[7]2 457	[7]5.5	[7]8.2	[7]3.9	28.9	73.7	21.9	81.7	41.66	5 537	724
Naugatuck borough	67 549	2 236	32 744	1 084	64 166	2 124	4.8	.2	4.1	27.1	72.8	19.2	83.3	49.72	5 945	633
New Britain city	159 593	2 254	75 110	1 061	130 063	1 837	6.5	7.1	2.2	24.6	73.7	15.8	85.0	44.14	6 151	677
New Haven city	449 131	3 638	147 783	1 197	458 898	3 717	5.1	3.7	2.9	28.9	73.7	21.9	81.7	41.66	5 537	724
New London city	70 784	2 649	24 349	911	73 909	2 766	9.9	9.0	8.3	27.7	71.4	18.5	80.7	48.16	5 951	472
Norwalk city	196 840	2 528	154 851	1 988	163 425	2 098	7.8	.1	12.0	27.5	72.9	17.9	83.5	46.80	5 865	613
Norwich city	96 652	2 698	40 981	1 144	107 884	3 011	5.6	7.0	2.7	27.6	72.2	17.5	82.7	50.01	5 869	551
Shelton city	63 645	1 702	48 070	1 285	64 800	1 732	4.6	5.3	3.8	28.9	73.7	21.9	81.7	41.66	5 537	724
Stamford city	308 902	2 802	242 382	2 199	332 620	3 018	6.3	3.7	2.2	27.4	72.6	17.6	84.4	49.43	5 778	613
Torrington city	70 883	2 051	43 321	1 254	64 415	1 864	6.9	9.7	4.6	23.6	70.7	13.5	82.0	49.28	6 636	418
Waterbury city	254 180	2 415	115 952	1 102	231 815	2 202	9.3	5.7	2.0	27.1	72.8	19.2	83.3	49.72	5 945	633
West Haven city	NA	NA	NA	NA	NA	NA	NA	NA	NA	28.9	73.7	21.9	81.7	41.66	5 537	724
DELAWARE	X	X	X	X	X	X	X	X	X	X	X	X	X	X	X	X
Dover city	18 017	571	8 100	257	23 431	742	37.6	29.9	7.9	33.8	77.2	25.0	87.7	44.14	4 337	1 199
Newark city	12 860	461	4 216	151	17 015	610	23.3	30.0	7.2	31.3	76.0	22.3	87.2	42.61	4 825	1 033
Wilmington city	106 297	1 476	58 798	817	101 981	1 417	20.7	25.1	1.5	30.6	76.4	22.4	85.6	40.84	4 937	1 046
DISTRICT OF COLUMBIA	X	X	X	X	X	X	X	X	X	34.6	80.0	26.8	88.5	38.63	4 047	1 549
Washington city	5 040 012	9 532	2 637 408	4 988	4 517 675	8 544	6.2	3.8	2.6	34.6	80.0	26.8	88.5	38.63	4 047	1 549
FLORIDA	X	X	X	X	X	X	X	X	X	X	X	X	X	X	X	X
Altamonte Springs city	38 162	977	18 351	470	32 615	835	20.0	16.8	6.8	59.7	82.3	48.6	91.5	48.11	686	3 381
Boca Raton city	100 698	1 401	53 112	739	104 680	1 457	12.5	7.3	8.9	66.2	82.5	56.8	91.2	59.15	262	4 038
Boynton Beach city	57 576	1 084	26 110	492	47 115	887	20.8	22.9	1.8	65.1	82.2	55.7	89.9	60.75	323	3 891
Bradenton city	28 811	610	10 857	230	25 178	533	18.6	25.1	4.7	60.2	81.4	49.0	90.8	53.71	678	3 186
Cape Coral city	106 072	1 181	31 632	352	66 991	746	14.2	5.9	11.0	63.8	82.8	53.2	91.1	53.37	418	3 855
Clearwater city	115 709	1 169	51 240	517	117 775	1 189	19.6	16.9	8.2	59.9	82.1	50.0	90.2	43.92	726	3 396
Coconut Creek city	19 833	557	10 997	309	17 174	482	32.2	14.7	8.4	66.2	82.5	56.8	91.2	59.15	262	4 038
Coral Gables city	73 018	1 701	40 743	949	81 321	1 895	29.7	12.2	4.8	67.2	82.6	59.2	89.0	55.91	200	4 198
Coral Springs city	62 732	573	35 868	327	63 588	580	28.4	8.0	7.6	66.2	82.5	56.8	91.2	59.15	262	4 038
Davie town	34 908	533	23 625	361	34 699	530	37.1	–	8.4	67.2	82.6	57.9	90.1	60.64	205	4 124
Daytona Beach city	67 177	1 034	25 970	400	63 123	971	27.2	16.0	7.7	57.5	81.2	46.9	89.8	47.89	909	2 919
Deerfield Beach city	46 142	915	18 154	360	43 270	858	13.8	25.2	4.5	66.2	82.5	56.8	91.2	59.15	262	4 038
Delray Beach city	56 126	1 065	31 127	591	63 675	1 209	20.9	8.4	5.1	66.2	82.5	56.8	91.2	59.15	262	4 038
Dunedin city	36 965	1 038	12 596	354	35 674	1 001	9.4	25.9	4.2	59.9	82.1	50.0	90.2	43.92	726	3 396
Fort Lauderdale city	183 874	1 206	93 938	616	180 020	1 181	30.0	8.0	4.1	67.2	82.6	57.9	90.1	60.64	205	4 124

[1] Based on resident population estimated as of July 1, 1997. [2] Represents normal values for the 30-year period, 1961–1990. [3] Average daily minimum. [4] Average daily maximum. [5] One heating degree day is accumulated for each whole degree that the mean daily temperature is below 65 degrees Fahrenheit. [6] One cooling degree day is accumulated for each whole degree that the mean daily temperature is above 65 degrees Fahrenheit. [7] Data are for consolidated city of Milford; data for Milford city (remainder) not available.

Sources: City Government Finances—U.S. Census Bureau, 1997 Census of Governments, Volume 4, Government Finances, GC97(4)-4, Finances of Municipal and Township Governments, issued September 2000 (related Internet site <http://www.census.gov/govs/www/cog.html>). 1997 Population for Government Finances calculations—U.S. Census Bureau, Population Estimates for Places: Annual Time Series, July 1, 1990 to July 1, 1999 (SU-99-7), published 20 October 2000, <http://www.census.gov/estimates/metro-city/placesbyst/SC99T7_US.txt>. Climate: U.S. National Oceanic and Atmospheric Administration (NOAA), National Climatic Data Center (NCDC), Climatography of the United States, Number 81, published January 1992 (related Internet site <http://lwf.ncdc.noaa.gov/oa/climate/normals/usnormals.html>).

Table C–7. Cities — **Government Finances and Climate**–Con.

[Includes states and 1,070 incorporated places of 25,000 or more population as of April 1, 1990 in all states except Hawaii which has no incorporated places recognized by the Census Bureau. For Hawaii, 8 census designated places (CDPs) of 25,000 or more population as of April 1, 1990 are included. Also included are the 5 boroughs of New York city. For more information on these areas, see appendix B. Geographic Information]

City	City government finances, 1996-1997									Climate[2]						
	General revenue				General expenditure					Average daily temperature (degrees Fahrenheit)						
			Taxes				By selected function, percent from—									
	Total ($1,000)	Per capita[1] (dollars)	Total ($1,000)	Per capita[1] (dollars)	Total ($1,000)	Per capita[1] (dollars)	Police protection	Sewerage and solid waste management	Highways	January	July	January[3]	July[4]	Annual precipitation (inches)	Heating degree days[5]	Cooling degree days[6]
FLORIDA—Con.																
Fort Myers city	76 580	1 678	23 504	515	68 635	1 504	16.4	12.7	5.6	63.8	82.8	53.2	91.1	53.37	418	3 855
Fort Pierce city	32 377	870	11 044	297	30 376	816	23.6	24.6	6.6	62.5	81.4	51.6	90.4	50.06	490	3 441
Gainesville city	75 143	799	22 413	238	86 483	920	20.6	16.5	5.8	53.7	80.7	42.5	90.7	51.81	1 316	2 570
Hallandale city	36 489	1 199	15 728	517	34 448	1 132	23.8	17.4	3.9	67.2	82.6	57.9	90.1	60.64	205	4 124
Hialeah city	146 430	687	78 621	369	139 232	654	19.2	25.2	4.7	66.3	82.4	56.8	89.8	63.01	273	4 012
Hollywood city	125 317	962	56 310	432	117 503	902	30.6	19.5	7.3	67.2	82.6	57.9	90.1	60.64	205	4 124
Homestead city	NA	NA	NA	NA	NA	NA	NA	NA	NA	65.3	81.1	54.5	90.1	58.74	277	3 603
Jacksonville city (remainder)	[7]898 617	[7]1 306	[7]379 304	[7]551	[7]1 018 943	[7]1 481	[7]9.8	[7]13.0	[7]3.9	52.4	81.6	40.5	91.4	51.32	1 434	2 551
Kissimmee city	36 305	955	13 340	351	29 965	789	24.3	4.7	19.3	61.0	81.7	48.7	91.4	46.11	603	3 324
Lakeland city	95 020	1 284	18 447	249	104 828	1 416	15.5	20.9	5.7	61.1	82.5	50.4	92.2	47.54	588	3 546
Lake Worth city	34 373	1 183	10 252	353	32 760	1 128	23.1	24.6	6.2	65.1	82.2	55.7	89.9	60.75	323	3 891
Largo city	55 774	835	20 864	312	58 259	873	16.0	23.2	1.9	59.9	82.1	50.0	90.2	43.92	726	3 396
Lauderdale Lakes city	NA	NA	NA	NA	NA	NA	NA	NA	NA	67.2	82.6	57.9	90.1	60.64	205	4 124
Lauderhill city	20 048	394	12 484	245	21 909	431	20.9	18.2	4.1	67.2	82.6	57.9	90.1	60.64	205	4 124
Margate city	25 097	491	16 812	329	25 357	496	30.1	–	2.9	66.2	82.5	56.8	91.2	59.15	262	4 038
Melbourne city	58 106	847	21 096	308	43 538	635	27.0	13.7	9.3	60.9	81.1	50.7	90.0	45.49	644	3 193
Miami city	379 681	1 022	193 105	520	416 376	1 120	23.9	10.2	4.6	67.2	82.6	59.2	89.0	55.91	200	4 198
Miami Beach city	246 303	2 523	99 625	1 020	204 519	2 095	18.8	11.1	1.5	68.1	82.6	62.3	86.9	45.35	139	4 157
Miramar city	35 855	654	17 057	311	36 735	670	25.7	21.0	3.1	66.3	82.4	56.8	89.8	63.01	273	4 012
North Lauderdale city	14 521	493	6 420	218	13 143	446	34.2	18.3	5.2	66.2	82.5	56.8	91.2	59.15	262	4 038
North Miami city	47 585	928	15 326	299	44 257	863	37.3	17.0	4.1	66.3	82.4	56.8	89.8	63.01	273	4 012
North Miami Beach city	46 312	1 305	17 763	500	45 114	1 271	24.0	22.5	6.1	68.1	82.6	62.3	86.9	45.35	139	4 157
Oakland Park city	28 508	1 024	11 640	418	27 348	983	24.5	33.5	1.8	67.2	82.6	57.9	90.1	60.64	205	4 124
Ocala city	40 824	884	12 256	265	54 624	1 182	21.7	15.8	14.9	57.5	81.5	45.1	92.2	51.59	930	3 046
Orlando city	319 620	1 814	102 517	582	276 975	1 572	20.1	14.9	7.5	59.7	82.3	48.6	91.5	48.11	686	3 381
Ormond Beach city	29 172	845	11 296	327	24 930	722	16.8	29.9	8.0	57.5	81.2	46.9	89.8	47.89	909	2 919
Palm Bay city	37 692	493	21 558	282	34 486	451	25.7	6.8	17.2	60.9	81.1	50.7	90.0	45.49	644	3 193
Panama City city	32 998	831	15 663	394	29 164	734	18.8	10.1	11.7	50.7	80.8	39.1	90.0	65.06	1 681	2 409
Pembroke Pines city	74 207	684	38 060	351	104 619	965	14.2	5.7	2.7	66.3	82.4	56.8	89.8	63.01	273	4 012
Pensacola city	70 881	1 197	28 034	474	76 113	1 286	14.5	6.1	7.3	50.6	82.1	41.4	89.9	62.25	1 617	2 636
Pinellas Park city	32 232	725	17 573	395	30 398	684	20.6	10.5	14.9	60.7	83.1	52.9	89.8	48.62	603	3 626
Plantation city	50 213	624	30 646	381	45 075	560	36.7	10.3	5.4	67.2	82.6	57.9	90.1	60.64	205	4 124
Pompano Beach city	84 053	1 117	45 209	601	80 169	1 066	30.6	13.8	2.7	66.2	82.5	56.8	91.2	59.15	262	4 038
Port Orange city	28 672	652	9 401	214	25 675	584	16.4	17.6	7.4	57.5	81.2	46.9	89.8	47.89	909	2 919
Port St. Lucie city	38 942	498	16 507	211	42 825	548	21.8	18.9	10.9	62.5	81.4	51.6	90.4	50.06	490	3 441
Riviera Beach city	31 938	1 102	17 977	620	28 789	994	27.6	9.0	6.3	65.1	82.2	55.7	89.9	60.75	323	3 891
St. Petersburg city	265 431	1 126	93 995	399	246 401	1 046	19.8	16.8	6.1	60.7	83.1	52.9	89.8	48.62	603	3 626
Sanford city	26 366	731	11 594	321	23 804	660	21.2	11.3	16.0	58.2	81.5	46.8	91.6	48.81	831	3 004
Sarasota city	79 870	1 566	35 898	704	69 786	1 368	24.4	20.3	7.4	60.2	81.4	49.0	90.8	53.71	678	3 186
Sunrise city	86 741	1 087	34 922	437	92 637	1 160	14.0	27.0	2.9	67.2	82.6	57.9	90.1	60.64	205	4 124
Tallahassee city	178 764	1 322	47 269	350	194 251	1 437	14.0	22.8	9.3	50.5	81.3	38.1	91.3	65.71	1 705	2 518
Tamarac city	30 683	593	13 489	261	25 598	494	24.4	13.9	7.4	66.2	82.5	56.8	91.2	59.15	262	4 038
Tampa city	347 068	1 209	141 193	492	322 735	1 124	23.9	21.7	6.3	59.9	82.1	50.0	90.2	43.92	726	3 396
Titusville city	25 547	612	10 743	257	22 031	528	24.5	14.8	9.2	58.6	81.3	47.3	91.4	54.07	803	3 057
West Palm Beach city	102 061	1 351	55 705	737	90 897	1 203	26.6	7.2	5.4	65.1	82.2	55.7	89.9	60.75	323	3 891
GEORGIA	X	X	X	X	X	X	X	X	X	X	X	X	X	X	X	X
Albany city	62 676	810	21 467	278	62 702	811	15.5	20.1	3.0	46.5	80.8	33.8	91.9	51.48	2 205	2 206
Athens city	[8]120 827	[8]1 350	[8]53 607	[8]599	[8]105 440	[8]1 178	[8]17.4	[8]13.5	[8]5.7	41.8	79.6	32.0	89.6	49.74	2 893	1 709
Atlanta city	813 869	2 029	241 153	601	887 683	2 213	11.2	14.6	5.3	41.0	78.8	31.5	88.0	50.77	2 991	1 667
Augusta city	[9]199 732	[9]1 064	[9]104 271	[9]556	[9]190 316	[9]1 014	[9]12.5	[9]10.1	[9]8.6	43.9	80.8	32.0	91.7	44.66	2 565	1 948
Columbus city (remainder)	[10]192 283	[10]1 055	[10]125 500	[10]689	[10]182 377	[10]1 001	[10]13.8	[10]9.0	[10]6.1	45.7	81.9	35.2	91.8	51.00	2 261	2 284
East Point city	25 741	767	9 037	269	26 831	800	23.5	16.8	4.4	41.0	78.8	31.5	88.0	50.77	2 991	1 667
La Grange city	83 109	3 300	3 616	144	87 456	3 473	4.6	6.6	2.2	43.4	79.0	31.9	90.1	54.52	2 667	1 696
Macon city	83 000	732	30 184	266	84 606	746	18.5	6.2	5.1	45.4	81.2	34.2	91.9	44.63	2 334	2 125
Marietta city	60 106	1 190	22 810	452	75 356	1 492	10.6	10.4	7.3	41.0	78.8	31.5	88.0	50.77	2 991	1 667
Rome city	31 061	952	13 228	405	29 392	901	14.1	24.6	11.2	38.4	76.9	27.0	87.3	55.33	3 467	1 337
Roswell city	45 273	797	19 786	348	46 041	811	13.7	11.4	10.4	41.0	78.8	31.5	88.0	50.77	2 991	1 667
Savannah city	155 804	1 169	55 160	414	165 445	1 241	14.7	20.1	7.6	48.9	81.8	38.1	91.1	49.22	1 847	2 365
Smyrna city	28 903	799	13 946	385	32 047	886	32.2	18.0	5.8	41.0	78.8	31.5	88.0	50.77	2 991	1 667
Valdosta city	30 141	707	13 400	314	31 780	745	19.9	17.1	20.9	48.0	80.7	36.7	92.1	52.24	1 844	2 350
Warner Robins city	24 763	512	12 221	253	26 838	555	20.6	23.1	6.9	45.4	81.2	34.2	91.9	44.63	2 334	2 125

[1] Based on resident population estimated as of July 1, 1997. [2] Represents normal values for the 30-year period, 1961–1990. [3] Average daily minimum. [4] Average daily maximum. [5] One heating degree day is accumulated for each whole degree that the mean daily temperature is below 65 degrees Fahrenheit. [6] One cooling degree day is accumulated for each whole degree that the mean daily temperature is above 65 degrees Fahrenheit. [7] Data are for consolidated city of Jacksonville; data for Jacksonville city (remainder) not available. [8] Data are for consolidated city of Athens-Clarke County; Athens city (1990 land area - 16.6 square miles; 1990 population - 45,734) merged with Clarke County effective January 14, 1991. [9] Data are for consolidated city of Augusta-Richmond County; Augusta city (1990 land area - 19.7 square miles; 1990 population - 44,639) merged with Richmond County effective January 1, 1996. [10] Data are for consolidated city of Columbus; data for Columbus city (remainder) not available.

Sources: City Government Finances—U.S. Census Bureau, 1997 Census of Governments, Volume 4, Government Finances, GC97(4)-4, Finances of Municipal and Township Governments, issued September 2000 (related Internet site <http://www.census.gov/govs/www/cog.html>).   1997 Population for Government Finances calculations—U.S. Census Bureau, Population Estimates for Places: Annual Time Series, July 1, 1990 to July 1, 1999 (SU-99-7), published 20 October 2000, <http://www.census.gov/estimates/metro-city/placesbyst/SC99T7_US.txt>.   Climate: U.S. National Oceanic and Atmospheric Administration (NOAA), National Climatic Data Center (NCDC), Climatography of the United States, Number 81, published January 1992 (related Internet site <http://lwf.ncdc.noaa.gov/oa/climate/normals/usnormals.html>).

Table C-7. Cities — **Government Finances and Climate**–Con.

[Includes states and 1,070 incorporated places of 25,000 or more population as of April 1, 1990 in all states except Hawaii which has no incorporated places recognized by the Census Bureau. For Hawaii, 8 census designated places (CDPs) of 25,000 or more population as of April 1, 1990 are included. Also included are the 5 boroughs of New York city. For more information on these areas, see appendix B. Geographic Information]

| | City government finances, 1996-1997 | | | | | | | | | Climate[2] | | | | | | |
| | General revenue | | Taxes | | General expenditure | | By selected function, percent from— | | | Average daily temperature (degrees Fahrenheit) | | | | | | |
City	Total ($1,000)	Per capita[1] (dollars)	Total ($1,000)	Per capita[1] (dollars)	Total ($1,000)	Per capita[1] (dollars)	Police protection	Sewerage and solid waste management	Highways	January	July	January[3]	July[4]	Annual precipitation (inches)	Heating degree days[5]	Cooling degree days[6]
HAWAII	X	X	X	X	X	X	X	X	X	X	X	X	X	X	X	X
Hilo CDP	NA	NA	NA	NA	NA	NA	NA	NA	NA	71.7	75.8	63.6	83.0	129.19	–	3 284
Honolulu CDP	[7]975 403	[7]1 117	[7]526 880	[7]603	[7]958 090	[7]1 097	[7]13.6	[7]20.2	[7]2.6	71.4	78.9	62.4	87.7	21.53	–	3 845
Kailua CDP	([7])	([7])	([7])	([7])	([7])	([7])	([7])	([7])	([7])	71.3	77.0	65.5	82.2	79.91	–	3 482
Kaneohe CDP...........	([7])	([7])	([7])	([7])	([7])	([7])	([7])	([7])	([7])	71.3	77.0	65.5	82.2	79.91	–	3 482
Mililani Town CDP	([7])	([7])	([7])	([7])	([7])	([7])	([7])	([7])	([7])	71.4	78.9	62.4	87.7	21.53	–	3 845
Pearl City CDP	([7])	([7])	([7])	([7])	([7])	([7])	([7])	([7])	([7])	71.4	78.9	62.4	87.7	21.53	–	3 845
Waimalu CDP	([7])	([7])	([7])	([7])	([7])	([7])	([7])	([7])	([7])	71.4	78.9	62.4	87.7	21.53	–	3 845
Waipahu CDP	([7])	([7])	([7])	([7])	([7])	([7])	([7])	([7])	([7])	71.4	78.9	62.4	87.7	21.53	–	3 845
IDAHO	X	X	X	X	X	X	X	X	X	X	X	X	X	X	X	X
Boise City city	130 946	799	49 566	302	137 594	839	12.5	25.9	.4	29.0	74.0	21.6	90.2	12.11	5 861	754
Idaho Falls city	35 036	723	13 118	271	37 716	778	17.6	15.9	6.9	18.2	68.6	10.0	86.0	10.88	8 063	305
Lewiston city	24 624	804	9 829	321	25 325	827	12.9	23.0	14.6	33.6	74.1	27.6	89.0	12.43	5 270	814
Nampa city..............	23 848	579	7 588	184	24 844	603	15.6	17.5	8.5	29.0	74.0	21.6	90.2	12.11	5 861	754
Pocatello city	30 964	596	12 787	246	28 150	542	16.8	21.0	10.6	23.3	70.6	14.4	88.1	12.14	7 180	421
Twin Falls city	NA	NA	NA	NA	NA	NA	NA	NA	NA	26.9	68.8	18.6	85.0	10.40	6 769	329
ILLINOIS	X	X	X	X	X	X	X	X	X	X	X	X	X	X	X	X
Addison village	26 446	783	5 480	162	30 682	909	19.0	13.3	13.7	21.0	73.2	12.9	83.7	35.82	6 536	752
Alton city	28 374	892	5 204	164	25 716	809	15.6	13.6	11.0	27.0	78.5	17.9	88.4	38.43	5 214	1 346
Arlington Heights village	52 814	695	25 871	340	44 900	591	21.2	–	4.3	21.0	73.2	12.9	83.7	35.82	6 536	752
Aurora city	NA	NA	NA	NA	NA	NA	NA	NA	NA	19.7	73.1	10.7	84.2	36.88	6 699	702
Belleville city	28 665	691	15 457	373	26 852	647	16.9	23.6	7.5	29.9	77.4	20.3	89.4	38.37	4 774	1 271
Berwyn city	26 621	612	13 806	317	28 398	653	19.2	14.4	13.2	21.0	73.2	12.9	83.7	35.82	6 536	752
Bloomington city	46 611	791	25 860	439	49 625	842	21.7	8.7	14.9	23.9	75.9	15.4	86.7	37.10	5 759	1 117
Bolingbrook village	39 098	732	16 873	316	39 920	748	19.8	10.6	25.9	19.7	73.1	10.7	84.2	36.88	6 699	702
Buffalo Grove village	32 093	764	8 683	207	28 442	677	21.3	12.7	11.6	21.0	73.2	12.9	83.7	35.82	6 536	752
Burbank city	14 885	536	8 437	304	13 699	493	24.3	–	6.1	22.4	75.1	14.9	84.4	37.38	6 176	940
Calumet City city	25 559	691	8 535	231	32 926	891	15.9	3.0	16.8	23.7	74.1	15.2	85.5	36.82	6 043	857
Carbondale city...........	23 356	853	3 670	134	22 535	823	17.2	10.2	5.8	29.5	77.6	19.1	89.0	44.40	4 865	1 271
Carol Stream village........	18 234	486	6 486	173	20 197	538	20.7	7.2	34.0	21.0	73.2	12.9	83.7	35.82	6 536	752
Champaign city	NA	NA	NA	NA	NA	NA	NA	NA	NA	23.8	75.0	16.0	85.3	39.71	5 854	985
Chicago city.............	4 172 926	1 486	1 742 104	620	4 144 017	1 476	20.7	7.2	10.2	22.4	75.1	14.9	84.4	37.38	6 176	940
Chicago Heights city	27 855	873	15 751	494	30 759	964	18.8	13.8	5.7	20.6	73.7	12.2	83.8	37.12	6 541	780
Cicero town	NA	NA	NA	NA	NA	NA	NA	NA	NA	22.4	75.1	14.9	84.4	37.38	6 176	940
Danville city	23 366	700	6 762	203	25 096	752	22.2	8.7	5.9	25.1	75.2	16.1	86.8	40.18	5 610	1 005
Decatur city	50 081	612	11 995	147	54 244	663	21.9	1.6	16.6	25.2	76.2	16.0	87.9	40.16	5 522	1 120
De Kalb city	NA	NA	NA	NA	NA	NA	NA	NA	NA	17.7	73.0	8.9	83.8	36.35	7 034	682
Des Plaines city	43 045	759	20 203	356	43 449	766	18.5	5.7	17.6	21.0	73.2	12.9	83.7	35.82	6 536	752
Downers Grove village	34 630	679	9 583	188	33 106	650	19.0	3.0	15.2	21.0	73.2	12.9	83.7	35.82	6 536	752
East St. Louis city..........	33 327	878	8 262	218	31 644	834	23.4	8.7	12.8	28.4	78.4	18.9	89.6	37.86	5 001	1 329
Elgin city.................	83 317	949	24 295	277	84 491	963	29.3	6.1	14.9	18.3	71.9	9.3	82.7	35.19	7 084	603
Elk Grove Village village	32 909	943	16 736	479	32 789	939	19.9	5.1	16.0	21.0	73.2	12.9	83.7	35.82	6 536	752
Elmhurst city	40 404	930	12 468	287	33 817	778	19.9	12.4	24.9	21.0	73.2	12.9	83.7	35.82	6 536	752
Evanston city............	80 720	1 226	44 269	617	121 929	1 700	10.2	44.8	2.8	21.0	73.2	12.9	83.7	35.82	6 536	752
Freeport city	17 033	645	3 118	118	15 656	593	16.6	26.9	12.1	17.1	72.9	7.8	84.2	33.08	7 169	645
Galesburg city...........	25 421	767	8 731	263	25 193	760	16.3	6.0	12.2	21.1	75.1	12.5	85.3	36.55	6 314	925
Glendale Heights village	21 580	717	5 918	197	17 683	588	20.4	8.9	18.8	21.0	73.2	12.9	83.7	35.82	6 536	752
Glenview village	35 970	891	14 918	369	35 766	886	15.7	5.7	12.6	21.0	73.2	12.9	83.7	35.82	6 536	752
Granite City city	NA	NA	NA	NA	NA	NA	NA	NA	NA	28.4	78.4	18.9	89.6	37.86	5 001	1 329
Hanover Park village	14 444	401	8 753	243	11 085	308	35.2	–	24.7	21.0	73.2	12.9	83.7	35.82	6 536	752
Harvey city..............	NA	NA	NA	NA	NA	NA	NA	NA	NA	20.6	73.7	12.2	83.8	37.12	6 541	780
Highland Park city	42 896	1 373	21 250	680	41 599	1 332	12.3	1.8	19.5	21.0	73.2	12.9	83.7	35.82	6 536	752
Hoffman Estates village.....	47 408	974	28 646	589	50 178	1 031	16.4	2.6	7.1	18.3	71.9	9.3	82.7	35.19	7 084	603
Joliet city..............	100 438	1 103	53 972	593	88 850	976	17.9	7.6	15.1	20.7	73.8	11.8	84.6	36.26	6 463	776
Kankakee city	25 077	919	8 436	309	23 386	857	17.5	23.6	10.7	21.1	74.6	12.3	85.2	35.31	6 322	921
Lansing village	20 773	723	4 383	153	21 705	755	21.2	10.2	9.9	23.7	74.1	15.2	85.5	36.82	6 043	857
Lombard village	31 579	739	11 055	259	32 472	760	15.7	3.4	7.4	21.0	73.2	12.9	83.7	35.82	6 536	752
Maywood village	NA	NA	NA	NA	NA	NA	NA	NA	NA	21.0	73.2	12.9	83.7	35.82	6 536	752
Moline city	31 194	720	13 773	318	31 467	727	19.3	12.6	9.9	19.9	75.2	11.3	85.9	39.08	6 474	911
Mount Prospect village	NA	NA	NA	NA	NA	NA	NA	NA	NA	21.0	73.2	12.9	83.7	35.82	6 536	752
Naperville city	96 005	848	36 785	325	85 485	755	18.7	11.7	23.3	19.7	73.1	10.7	84.2	36.88	6 699	702
Niles village	25 664	871	19 351	657	27 822	945	16.4	5.0	1.7	21.0	73.2	12.9	83.7	35.82	6 536	752
Normal town	28 822	651	8 354	189	26 760	604	12.5	3.6	17.4	23.9	75.9	15.4	86.7	37.10	5 759	1 117
Northbrook village	NA	NA	NA	NA	NA	NA	NA	NA	NA	21.0	73.2	12.9	83.7	35.82	6 536	752
North Chicago city	12 629	356	4 575	129	9 660	272	37.1	10.6	9.0	19.3	71.2	10.8	81.1	34.20	7 136	542
Oak Forest city	12 081	423	5 452	191	11 797	413	26.4	2.7	13.9	20.6	73.7	12.2	83.8	37.12	6 541	780

[1] Based on resident population estimated as of July 1, 1997. [2] Represents normal values for the 30-year period, 1961–1990. [3] Average daily minimum. [4] Average daily maximum. [5] One heating degree day is accumulated for each whole degree that the mean daily temperature is below 65 degrees Fahrenheit. [6] One cooling degree day is accumulated for each whole degree that the mean daily temperature is above 65 degrees Fahrenheit. [7] Data for Honolulu CDP are for Honolulu City/County which includes all CDPs listed except Hilo which is in Maui County.

Sources: City Government Finances—U.S. Census Bureau, 1997 Census of Governments, Volume 4, Government Finances, GC97(4)-4, Finances of Municipal and Township Governments, issued September 2000 (related Internet site <http://www.census.gov/govs/www/cog.html>). 1997 Population for Government Finances calculations—U.S. Census Bureau, Population Estimates for Places: Annual Time Series, July 1, 1990 to July 1, 1999 (SU-99-7), published 20 October 2000, <http://www.census.gov/estimates/metro-city/placesbyst/SC99T7_US.txt>. Climate: U.S. National Oceanic and Atmospheric Administration (NOAA), National Climatic Data Center (NCDC), Climatography of the United States, Number 81, published January 1992 (related Internet site <http://lwf.ncdc.noaa.gov/oa/climate/normals/usnormals.html>).

Table C-7. Cities — **Government Finances and Climate**—Con.

[Includes states and 1,070 incorporated places of 25,000 or more population as of April 1, 1990 in all states except Hawaii which has no incorporated places recognized by the Census Bureau. For Hawaii, 8 census designated places (CDPs) of 25,000 or more population as of April 1, 1990 are included. Also included are the 5 boroughs of New York city. For more information on these areas, see appendix B. Geographic Information]

City	City government finances, 1996-1997									Climate[2]						
	General revenue				General expenditure					Average daily temperature (degrees Fahrenheit)						
			Taxes				By selected function, percent from—									
	Total ($1,000)	Per capita[1] (dollars)	Total ($1,000)	Per capita[1] (dollars)	Total ($1,000)	Per capita[1] (dollars)	Police pro-tection	Sewerage and solid waste manage-ment	High-ways	January	July	January[3]	July[4]	Annual precip-itation (inches)	Heating degree days[5]	Cooling degree days[6]
ILLINOIS—Con.																
Oak Lawn village	34 400	595	11 108	192	30 333	524	28.1	10.1	8.8	22.4	75.1	14.9	84.4	37.38	6 176	940
Oak Park village	44 168	821	22 764	423	45 140	839	21.8	4.4	10.6	22.4	75.1	14.9	84.4	37.38	6 176	940
Orland Park village	34 081	691	6 719	136	29 718	603	24.5	15.5	6.6	20.6	73.7	12.2	83.8	37.12	6 541	780
Palatine village	32 589	615	13 104	247	31 019	586	24.0	14.0	8.5	21.0	73.2	12.9	83.7	35.82	6 536	752
Park Ridge city	25 322	680	16 649	447	23 704	636	18.8	12.1	13.4	21.0	73.2	12.9	83.7	35.82	6 536	752
Pekin city	23 033	690	5 140	154	20 463	613	17.0	11.7	10.4	21.6	75.5	13.2	85.7	36.25	6 148	982
Peoria city	100 872	902	41 834	374	103 359	924	14.3	5.0	11.6	21.6	75.5	13.2	85.7	36.25	6 148	982
Quincy city	31 624	777	7 913	194	29 428	723	16.6	16.1	16.5	23.9	76.7	15.6	86.8	39.66	5 763	1 106
Rockford city	109 623	753	41 164	283	106 919	734	21.2	8.4	17.7	18.2	73.2	9.8	83.8	36.28	6 969	702
Rock Island city	41 156	1 051	12 769	326	35 800	914	17.5	8.4	12.4	19.9	75.2	11.3	85.9	39.08	6 474	911
Schaumburg village	61 700	821	42 306	563	57 761	769	24.9	2.1	18.1	21.0	73.2	12.9	83.7	35.82	6 536	752
Skokie village	45 292	774	24 109	412	59 172	1 011	12.7	5.1	6.9	21.0	73.2	12.9	83.7	35.82	6 536	752
Springfield city	82 729	710	27 276	234	83 190	714	21.7	5.9	14.0	24.2	76.5	15.9	86.9	35.25	5 688	1 141
Streamwood village	16 451	468	8 395	239	14 689	418	29.1	–	27.7	18.3	71.9	9.3	82.7	35.19	7 084	603
Tinley Park village	22 807	502	8 627	190	17 906	394	32.3	5.6	17.7	20.6	73.7	12.2	83.8	37.12	6 541	780
Urbana city	24 659	687	13 130	366	26 426	736	20.7	7.4	18.5	23.8	75.0	16.0	85.3	39.71	5 854	985
Waukegan city	57 669	768	21 535	287	57 669	768	22.7	7.6	18.7	19.3	71.2	10.8	81.1	34.20	7 136	542
Wheaton city	34 031	614	12 708	229	31 262	564	18.7	7.4	13.4	21.1	73.9	12.3	86.0	36.68	6 354	818
Wheeling village	20 169	676	6 646	223	19 632	658	25.7	3.4	15.2	21.0	73.2	12.9	83.7	35.82	6 536	752
Wilmette village	20 950	803	10 311	395	22 080	846	17.7	28.9	16.5	21.0	73.2	12.9	83.7	35.82	6 536	752
Woodridge village	16 937	577	5 225	178	20 397	695	20.8	1.0	12.7	19.7	73.1	10.7	84.2	36.88	6 699	702
INDIANA	X	X	X	X	X	X	X	X	X	X	X	X	X	X	X	X
Anderson city	44 350	753	22 218	377	52 299	888	14.8	17.0	6.1	24.8	73.5	17.4	83.7	38.47	5 916	812
Bloomington city	48 640	723	19 151	284	45 850	681	8.7	30.9	9.6	27.3	75.8	18.1	85.9	43.14	5 309	1 068
Carmel city	32 153	790	16 261	400	25 772	633	19.7	13.9	7.9	25.5	75.4	17.2	85.5	39.94	5 615	1 014
Columbus city	32 654	888	10 437	284	29 010	789	12.0	17.7	8.2	22.0	72.1	13.6	83.6	37.50	6 576	644
East Chicago city	72 156	2 304	32 279	1 031	64 181	2 049	9.8	20.5	5.9	23.7	74.1	15.2	85.5	36.82	6 043	857
Elkhart city	39 579	902	18 113	413	35 951	819	16.6	19.0	6.5	23.3	72.9	16.1	82.9	39.14	6 331	728
Evansville city	110 263	894	38 137	309	85 072	690	19.7	16.8	5.3	30.1	78.4	21.2	89.1	43.14	4 708	1 376
Fort Wayne city	110 514	559	44 745	226	109 947	556	22.0	13.4	9.6	22.9	74.0	15.3	84.6	34.75	6 273	824
Gary city	NA	NA	NA	NA	NA	NA	NA	NA	NA	23.7	74.1	15.2	85.5	36.82	6 043	857
Greenwood city	18 330	557	4 474	136	18 755	570	14.2	22.8	5.8	25.5	75.4	17.2	85.5	39.94	5 615	1 014
Hammond city	88 247	1 114	31 135	393	91 760	1 158	12.9	21.1	6.4	23.7	74.1	15.2	85.5	36.82	6 043	857
Indianapolis city (remainder)	[7]1 187 803	[7]1 597	[7]520 689	[7]700	[7]1 222 878	[7]1 644	[7]8.3	[7]7.6	[7]5.2	25.5	75.4	17.2	85.5	39.94	5 615	1 014
Kokomo city	43 383	950	19 877	435	42 660	934	14.0	18.6	9.4	22.1	73.1	13.6	84.4	39.89	6 429	770
Lafayette city	39 210	800	16 627	339	33 520	684	14.6	16.3	10.5	22.5	73.5	13.9	84.4	36.05	6 228	806
Lawrence city	12 134	366	4 986	150	11 987	361	20.1	19.7	12.9	25.5	75.4	17.2	85.5	39.94	5 615	1 014
Marion city	21 965	710	10 394	336	20 080	649	18.8	17.1	9.0	23.1	73.3	14.7	84.4	37.56	6 260	760
Merrillville town	8 901	284	5 099	163	8 589	274	27.6	–	13.0	23.7	74.1	15.2	85.5	36.82	6 043	857
Michigan City city	34 661	1 047	12 614	381	32 475	981	11.4	40.1	5.0	23.7	74.1	15.2	85.5	36.82	6 043	857
Mishawaka city	25 086	548	11 768	257	25 825	565	14.7	13.5	7.6	23.3	72.9	16.1	82.9	39.14	6 331	728
Muncie city	37 738	547	17 851	259	37 484	543	13.5	31.6	6.5	23.6	74.4	15.7	84.4	37.88	6 027	878
New Albany city	23 522	582	8 750	216	21 797	539	18.0	27.4	8.2	31.7	77.2	23.2	87.0	44.39	4 514	1 288
Portage city	21 384	649	6 132	186	16 613	504	13.4	21.1	10.4	23.7	74.1	15.2	85.5	36.82	6 043	857
Richmond city	29 581	758	11 016	282	29 923	767	15.3	20.8	7.1	24.9	73.1	15.9	84.5	39.95	5 963	759
South Bend city	NA	NA	NA	NA	NA	NA	NA	NA	NA	23.3	72.9	16.1	82.9	39.14	6 331	728
Terre Haute city	36 737	680	17 594	326	33 897	628	12.3	14.3	6.2	25.3	75.6	16.2	86.6	41.19	5 581	1 025
West Lafayette city	15 938	573	6 689	240	11 955	430	18.5	30.6	8.1	23.8	74.9	15.8	86.0	35.80	5 940	935
IOWA	X	X	X	X	X	X	X	X	X	X	X	X	X	X	X	X
Ames city	117 054	2 427	13 771	285	110 397	2 289	3.8	6.6	7.9	18.2	74.2	8.8	85.3	32.94	6 776	816
Bettendorf city	30 564	979	13 436	430	30 984	993	10.8	6.3	28.3	19.9	75.2	11.3	85.9	39.08	6 474	911
Burlington city	21 428	802	9 363	350	21 813	816	13.8	14.3	20.4	21.8	75.7	13.1	85.8	36.06	6 158	992
Cedar Falls city	58 218	1 687	12 459	361	50 340	1 459	5.2	6.3	18.4	14.6	73.1	5.4	83.9	33.70	7 406	702
Cedar Rapids city	136 745	1 192	48 780	425	134 293	1 170	15.8	22.4	13.0	17.6	74.2	9.2	84.6	33.72	6 924	788
Clinton city	25 176	887	11 631	410	26 246	925	13.7	9.6	28.6	20.3	75.1	11.3	86.1	35.21	6 324	941
Council Bluffs city	54 998	974	28 760	509	60 998	1 080	10.3	28.9	14.8	21.1	76.9	10.9	87.9	29.86	6 300	1 072
Davenport city	100 475	1 029	42 918	439	100 843	1 032	4.3	10.2	20.7	19.9	75.2	11.3	85.9	39.08	6 474	911
Des Moines city	236 720	1 234	100 304	523	220 912	1 151	13.1	22.5	8.6	19.4	76.6	10.7	86.7	33.12	6 497	1 036
Dubuque city	60 697	1 058	23 319	407	66 127	1 153	9.0	14.5	17.2	15.9	72.3	7.7	82.4	38.36	7 327	593
Fort Dodge city	NA	NA	NA	NA	NA	NA	NA	NA	NA	16.2	73.8	6.6	85.1	33.93	7 261	768
Iowa City city	66 989	1 102	20 873	343	71 341	1 173	7.2	35.5	13.9	20.6	76.3	11.5	87.5	36.31	6 227	1 047
Marshalltown city	18 976	734	9 319	360	19 397	750	15.8	29.5	15.9	16.9	73.3	7.2	84.8	34.43	7 170	695
Mason City city	24 511	843	11 309	389	19 721	679	15.0	13.1	14.9	13.2	72.5	4.2	83.6	32.74	7 837	623
Sioux City city	93 041	1 114	36 800	441	100 457	1 203	10.1	8.9	10.9	17.7	75.7	7.7	86.5	25.86	6 893	907
Waterloo city	88 416	1 382	32 848	513	94 734	1 480	8.9	29.9	16.2	14.6	73.1	5.4	83.9	33.70	7 406	702
West Des Moines city	40 930	970	22 349	529	37 067	878	12.0	10.8	25.4	19.4	76.6	10.7	86.7	33.12	6 497	1 036

[1] Based on resident population estimated as of July 1, 1997. [2] Represents normal values for the 30-year period, 1961–1990. [3] Average daily minimum. [4] Average daily maximum. [5] One heating degree day is accumulated for each whole degree that the mean daily temperature is below 65 degrees Fahrenheit. [6] One cooling degree day is accumulated for each whole degree that the mean daily temperature is above 65 degrees Fahrenheit. [7] Data are for consolidated city of Indianapolis; data for Indianapolis city (remainder) not available.

Sources: City Government Finances—U.S. Census Bureau, 1997 Census of Governments, Volume 4, Government Finances, GC97(4)-4, Finances of Municipal and Township Governments, issued September 2000 (related Internet site <http://www.census.gov/govs/www/cog.html>). 1997 Population for Government Finances calculations—U.S. Census Bureau, Population Estimates for Places: Annual Time Series, July 1, 1990 to July 1, 1999 (SU-99-7), published 20 October 2000, <http://www.census.gov/estimates/metro-city/placesbyst/SC99T7_US.txt>. Climate: U.S. National Oceanic and Atmospheric Administration (NOAA), National Climatic Data Center (NCDC), Climatography of the United States, Number 81, published January 1992 (related Internet site <http://lwf.ncdc.noaa.gov/oa/climate/normals/usnormals.html>).

Table C–7. Cities — Government Finances and Climate—Con.

[Includes states and 1,070 incorporated places of 25,000 or more population as of April 1, 1990 in all states except Hawaii which has no incorporated places recognized by the Census Bureau. For Hawaii, 8 census designated places (CDPs) of 25,000 or more population as of April 1, 1990 are included. Also included are the 5 boroughs of New York city. For more information on these areas, see appendix B. Geographic Information]

City	City government finances, 1996-1997 General revenue Total ($1,000)	Per capita[1] (dollars)	Taxes Total ($1,000)	Per capita[1] (dollars)	General expenditure Total ($1,000)	Per capita[1] (dollars)	By selected function, percent from— Police protection	Sewerage and solid waste management	Highways	Climate[2] Average daily temperature (degrees Fahrenheit) January	July	January[3]	July[4]	Annual precipitation (inches)	Heating degree days[5]	Cooling degree days[6]
KANSAS	X	X	X	X	X	X	X	X	X	X	X	X	X	X	X	X
Emporia city	NA	NA	NA	NA	NA	NA	NA	NA	NA	28.7	79.3	17.9	91.3	36.84	4 856	1 414
Hutchinson city	30 783	784	14 872	379	28 075	715	14.3	17.6	8.3	28.1	80.7	16.4	93.6	29.22	5 103	1 489
Kansas City city	220 579	1 557	64 604	456	209 023	1 476	13.5	6.1	6.2	25.7	78.5	16.7	88.7	37.62	5 393	1 288
Lawrence city	102 785	1 351	21 916	288	98 210	1 291	7.9	6.7	4.7	29.2	80.3	19.2	91.3	39.28	4 734	1 565
Leavenworth city	20 900	530	10 329	262	22 845	579	12.3	10.7	21.3	27.0	78.5	16.7	90.1	40.54	5 192	1 313
Lenexa city	46 720	1 228	22 648	595	45 354	1 192	13.3	.5	21.5	28.0	78.2	18.3	88.7	39.56	5 029	1 308
Manhattan city	25 977	617	10 876	258	31 192	741	14.9	22.0	5.3	27.8	80.0	17.3	91.4	33.82	5 043	1 478
Olathe city	76 185	927	25 090	305	68 924	839	12.8	13.8	14.3	28.0	78.2	18.3	88.7	39.56	5 029	1 308
Overland Park city	86 587	642	54 624	405	85 875	637	20.2	–	30.6	28.0	78.2	18.3	88.7	39.56	5 029	1 308
Salina city	40 056	903	9 894	223	36 995	834	9.3	9.8	6.4	28.1	80.9	17.6	92.6	29.82	5 101	1 534
Shawnee city	28 427	645	12 510	284	27 702	628	19.0	8.1	32.1	28.0	78.2	18.3	88.7	39.56	5 029	1 308
Topeka city	132 795	1 073	63 376	512	134 577	1 087	14.4	11.5	11.5	26.7	78.5	16.3	89.3	35.23	5 265	1 304
Wichita city	323 567	985	80 319	244	340 708	1 037	11.5	13.0	19.7	29.5	81.4	19.2	92.8	29.33	4 791	1 628
KENTUCKY	X	X	X	X	X	X	X	X	X	X	X	X	X	X	X	X
Bowling Green city	51 477	1 139	24 948	552	46 988	1 040	12.3	9.0	9.0	32.9	77.9	23.6	88.7	50.93	4 328	1 370
Covington city	50 221	1 237	23 466	578	45 295	1 116	18.5	4.3	11.1	28.1	75.1	19.5	85.5	41.33	5 248	996
Frankfort city	21 226	787	11 776	437	18 542	688	15.4	18.0	7.4	29.8	75.5	19.4	87.3	42.52	5 002	1 038
Henderson city	21 326	800	7 160	269	20 192	758	14.1	24.2	6.8	32.2	77.8	23.4	88.6	44.80	4 323	1 393
Hopkinsville city	21 935	688	10 691	335	19 502	611	14.3	17.7	8.2	32.0	77.7	22.1	89.5	50.79	4 437	1 365
Lexington-Fayette	296 712	1 239	121 046	505	204 090	852	15.6	1.2	9.5	30.8	75.8	22.4	85.8	44.55	4 783	1 140
Louisville city	320 114	1 247	169 262	659	310 767	1 211	14.5	4.5	6.8	31.7	77.2	23.2	87.0	44.39	4 514	1 288
Owensboro city	44 518	819	14 826	273	44 360	816	13.4	10.7	6.6	32.2	77.9	23.1	89.3	46.65	4 334	1 415
Paducah city	37 128	1 404	18 699	707	34 754	1 315	14.4	18.4	9.7	32.6	78.8	23.5	89.0	49.31	4 279	1 475
LOUISIANA	X	X	X	X	X	X	X	X	X	X	X	X	X	X	X	X
Alexandria city	49 167	1 057	23 396	503	56 028	1 205	14.3	23.0	7.6	46.8	82.4	36.4	92.5	58.50	2 003	2 477
Baton Rouge city	481 029	2 239	267 704	1 246	500 109	2 328	12.6	18.6	9.8	49.8	82.3	39.6	91.4	60.89	1 669	2 690
Bossier City city	107 621	1 879	37 019	646	90 267	1 576	9.0	5.5	3.3	45.1	82.7	34.8	93.0	46.11	2 264	2 368
Houma city	NA	NA	NA	NA	NA	NA	NA	NA	NA	52.1	81.6	42.0	90.4	62.91	1 429	2 668
Kenner city	58 629	817	17 669	246	47 153	657	22.6	13.6	10.6	51.3	81.9	41.8	90.6	61.88	1 513	2 655
Lafayette city	99 318	862	54 445	472	87 353	758	11.4	14.9	11.3	50.6	82.1	41.2	90.6	58.36	1 587	2 673
Lake Charles city	60 339	833	43 177	596	61 123	843	10.9	8.9	10.3	50.4	82.2	41.1	90.8	54.84	1 616	2 650
Monroe city	79 826	1 496	48 730	913	76 876	1 440	10.4	11.1	21.4	44.2	82.3	34.6	92.4	51.48	2 407	2 323
New Iberia city	17 204	519	11 446	345	18 046	544	16.0	35.3	11.9	50.4	81.7	40.5	90.7	59.56	1 609	2 596
New Orleans city	755 967	1 612	332 675	709	703 178	1 499	9.9	12.2	2.7	51.3	81.9	41.8	90.6	61.88	1 513	2 655
Shreveport city	217 241	1 144	123 210	649	187 586	988	13.5	14.7	6.4	45.1	82.7	34.8	93.0	46.11	2 264	2 368
MAINE	X	X	X	X	X	X	X	X	X	X	X	X	X	X	X	X
Bangor city	97 647	2 948	34 436	1 040	83 472	2 520	5.3	3.2	6.3	17.5	68.2	8.2	78.1	41.23	7 930	251
Lewiston city	67 278	1 854	38 064	1 049	63 534	1 751	5.5	11.8	.5	20.2	70.7	11.1	80.7	45.30	7 244	398
Portland city	171 560	2 771	88 814	1 435	177 315	2 864	4.5	6.1	4.9	20.8	68.6	11.4	78.8	44.34	7 378	268
MARYLAND	X	X	X	X	X	X	X	X	X	X	X	X	X	X	X	X
Annapolis city	38 305	1 172	19 502	597	40 454	1 237	17.2	23.2	10.4	33.6	77.6	24.6	87.6	41.81	4 382	1 271
Baltimore city	1 952 997	2 970	698 167	1 062	1 842 018	2 801	11.1	7.8	7.5	31.8	77.0	23.4	87.2	40.76	4 707	1 137
Bowie city	19 748	488	8 732	216	17 048	421	2.1	28.4	9.9	33.6	77.6	24.6	87.6	41.81	4 382	1 271
Frederick city	44 308	939	18 849	399	43 062	913	18.0	12.8	17.9	31.4	74.7	23.1	85.3	40.25	4 810	925
Gaithersburg city	24 664	540	13 020	285	20 732	454	21.6	5.8	12.6	30.7	74.7	21.4	85.8	41.11	5 093	889
Hagerstown city	29 818	849	12 187	347	32 117	914	20.6	23.2	7.1	28.7	74.9	20.3	85.8	38.60	5 293	909
Rockville city	42 580	918	18 636	402	36 533	787	7.9	13.4	10.7	30.7	74.7	21.4	85.8	41.11	5 093	889
MASSACHUSETTS	X	X	X	X	X	X	X	X	X	X	X	X	X	X	X	X
Attleboro city	66 379	1 691	30 307	772	74 359	1 894	5.0	13.5	3.0	25.9	71.2	15.5	82.3	46.68	6 346	457
Beverly city	68 845	1 773	42 736	1 101	64 944	1 673	6.9	9.9	3.6	28.6	73.5	21.6	81.8	41.51	5 641	678
Boston city	1 995 395	3 590	802 253	1 443	1 859 248	3 345	11.2	7.6	3.4	28.6	73.5	21.6	81.8	41.51	5 641	678
Brockton city	200 705	2 157	67 487	725	177 309	1 906	6.6	6.7	3.4	26.9	71.2	16.9	82.2	45.50	6 225	461
Cambridge city	246 643	2 637	162 111	1 733	246 660	2 637	6.8	4.1	2.8	28.6	73.5	21.6	81.8	41.51	5 641	678
Chelsea city	89 104	3 241	20 239	736	95 917	3 489	5.0	2.3	2.6	28.6	73.5	21.6	81.8	41.51	5 641	678
Chicopee city	95 079	1 754	39 112	721	92 683	1 709	6.0	5.5	4.1	26.8	74.1	17.6	85.4	43.88	5 754	751
Everett city	75 642	2 163	46 484	1 329	74 266	2 124	7.6	2.6	5.3	28.6	73.5	21.6	81.8	41.51	5 641	678
Fall River city	174 005	1 922	39 534	437	161 832	1 788	11.4	4.6	2.8	30.6	73.5	23.4	81.3	47.34	5 426	729
Fitchburg city	76 863	1 909	23 601	586	73 917	1 836	6.4	6.7	3.8	23.4	71.3	13.4	81.5	47.02	6 698	485
Gloucester city	60 720	2 060	36 163	1 227	65 487	2 221	5.9	10.8	4.3	28.6	73.5	21.6	81.8	41.51	5 641	678
Haverhill city	139 687	2 570	43 966	809	139 401	2 565	4.7	3.9	1.9	24.7	72.5	15.2	83.8	44.43	6 413	575

[1] Based on resident population estimated as of July 1, 1997. [2] Represents normal values for the 30-year period, 1961–1990. [3] Average daily minimum. [4] Average daily maximum. [5] One heating degree day is accumulated for each whole degree that the mean daily temperature is below 65 degrees Fahrenheit. [6] One cooling degree day is accumulated for each whole degree that the mean daily temperature is above 65 degrees Fahrenheit.

Sources: City Government Finances—U.S. Census Bureau, 1997 Census of Governments, Volume 4, Government Finances, GC97(4)-4, Finances of Municipal and Township Governments, issued September 2000 (related Internet site <http://www.census.gov/govs/www/cog.html>).   1997 Population for Government Finances calculations—U.S. Census Bureau, Population Estimates for Places: Annual Time Series, July 1, 1990 to July 1, 1999 (SU-99-7), published 20 October 2000, <http://www.census.gov/estimates/metro-city/placesbyst/SC99T7_US.txt>.   Climate: U.S. National Oceanic and Atmospheric Administration (NOAA), National Climatic Data Center (NCDC), Climatography of the United States, Number 81, published January 1992 (related Internet site <http://lwf.ncdc.noaa.gov/oa/climate/normals/usnormals.html>).

Table C–7. Cities — **Government Finances and Climate**–Con.

[Includes states and 1,070 incorporated places of 25,000 or more population as of April 1, 1990 in all states except Hawaii which has no incorporated places recognized by the Census Bureau. For Hawaii, 8 census designated places (CDPs) of 25,000 or more population as of April 1, 1990 are included. Also included are the 5 boroughs of New York city. For more information on these areas, see appendix B. Geographic Information]

City	General revenue Total ($1,000)	General revenue Per capita[1] (dollars)	Taxes Total ($1,000)	Taxes Per capita[1] (dollars)	General expenditure Total ($1,000)	General expenditure Per capita[1] (dollars)	Police protection	Sewerage and solid waste management	Highways	January	July	January[3]	July[4]	Annual precipitation (inches)	Heating degree days[5]	Cooling degree days[6]
MASSACHUSETTS—Con.																
Holyoke city	135 268	3 287	30 237	735	132 840	3 228	10.8	4.5	3.0	26.8	74.1	17.6	85.4	43.88	5 754	751
Lawrence city	179 296	2 600	30 180	438	156 355	2 267	4.5	4.9	2.5	24.7	72.5	15.4	82.6	42.80	6 322	555
Leominster city	64 165	1 623	31 110	787	59 121	1 495	6.7	11.8	4.6	23.4	71.3	13.4	81.5	47.02	6 698	485
Lowell city	224 878	2 219	62 565	617	214 278	2 114	6.4	5.5	1.6	24.3	73.3	14.7	84.8	42.07	6 339	610
Lynn city	179 383	2 218	52 205	646	168 302	2 081	5.9	4.8	4.0	28.6	73.5	21.6	81.8	41.51	5 641	678
Malden city	93 226	1 768	41 247	782	95 998	1 820	6.2	2.9	3.1	28.6	73.5	21.6	81.8	41.51	5 641	678
Marlborough city	65 486	1 973	47 730	1 438	58 556	1 764	7.5	7.9	6.9	23.4	71.3	13.4	81.5	47.02	6 698	485
Medford city	93 747	1 676	52 158	932	90 728	1 622	7.7	4.2	3.0	28.6	73.5	21.6	81.8	41.51	5 641	678
Melrose city	49 870	1 822	28 808	1 052	49 072	1 793	5.8	10.4	3.0	28.6	73.5	21.6	81.8	41.51	5 641	678
New Bedford city	210 146	2 210	53 435	562	190 458	2 003	6.9	13.6	2.8	30.6	73.5	23.4	81.3	47.34	5 426	729
Newton city	196 984	2 456	147 955	1 845	198 058	2 469	4.9	3.6	5.3	28.6	73.5	21.6	81.8	41.51	5 641	678
Northampton city	49 638	1 737	23 730	831	54 150	1 895	5.4	3.7	4.5	23.6	71.8	12.2	84.6	42.50	6 404	522
Peabody city	90 232	1 855	44 293	911	89 714	1 844	5.9	4.3	4.2	24.5	71.0	14.3	82.7	46.64	6 573	425
Pittsfield city	90 327	1 965	38 045	827	92 844	2 019	5.5	6.8	3.4	21.4	68.9	11.0	81.5	43.47	7 060	293
Quincy city	241 729	2 820	88 897	1 037	256 437	2 991	6.2	3.5	2.7	27.4	71.5	18.5	81.5	47.69	6 072	450
Revere city	75 411	1 811	37 196	893	82 283	1 976	6.4	3.0	3.2	28.6	73.5	21.6	81.8	41.51	5 641	678
Salem city	80 664	2 113	44 180	1 157	75 795	1 986	7.1	3.4	2.8	28.6	73.5	21.6	81.8	41.51	5 641	678
Somerville city	124 827	1 678	50 414	678	138 773	1 865	7.0	2.2	4.0	28.6	73.5	21.6	81.8	41.51	5 641	678
Springfield city	437 167	2 937	101 506	682	458 397	3 080	5.6	7.0	1.1	26.8	74.1	17.6	85.4	43.88	5 754	751
Taunton city	88 460	1 690	36 831	704	95 296	1 821	6.6	3.6	4.1	25.9	71.2	15.5	82.3	46.68	6 346	457
Waltham city	115 807	2 011	78 009	1 354	106 665	1 852	8.2	10.8	5.1	28.6	73.5	21.6	81.8	41.51	5 641	678
Westfield city	73 296	1 951	30 969	824	73 680	1 962	5.0	5.8	4.9	26.8	74.1	17.6	85.4	43.88	5 754	751
Woburn city	68 547	1 851	45 068	1 217	66 365	1 792	7.6	2.6	5.8	24.5	71.0	14.3	82.7	46.64	6 573	425
Worcester city	378 128	2 269	128 757	773	365 857	2 196	6.7	4.4	3.7	22.8	69.7	15.0	79.3	47.75	6 979	333
MICHIGAN	X	X	X	X	X	X	X	X	X	X	X	X	X	X	X	X
Allen Park city	27 366	844	12 003	370	24 634	760	13.8	25.0	14.1	22.9	72.9	15.5	83.8	32.71	6 500	677
Ann Arbor city	126 293	1 153	50 053	457	115 809	1 057	10.9	14.0	8.0	23.2	73.0	16.2	83.7	32.81	6 379	713
Battle Creek city	86 260	1 626	36 791	693	118 539	2 234	9.9	9.8	11.1	22.5	71.7	14.9	83.2	35.70	6 677	575
Bay City city	34 645	966	12 176	339	33 077	922	16.4	21.4	19.3	22.0	72.2	14.7	84.1	29.51	6 763	599
Burton city	12 684	465	4 207	154	13 279	487	24.0	29.3	16.3	21.5	70.6	14.2	81.5	30.28	6 979	483
Dearborn city	NA	NA	NA	NA	NA	NA	NA	NA	NA	22.9	72.9	15.5	83.8	32.71	6 500	677
Dearborn Heights city	42 620	728	14 893	255	41 155	703	20.8	29.0	15.1	22.9	72.9	15.5	83.8	32.71	6 500	677
Detroit city	1 971 322	2 021	635 718	652	1 788 987	1 834	16.8	18.8	8.6	24.7	74.2	18.7	83.3	32.09	6 167	805
East Detroit city	25 059	726	10 143	294	24 123	699	20.1	20.9	11.9	24.7	74.2	18.7	83.3	32.09	6 167	805
East Lansing city	32 642	685	9 750	204	39 623	831	15.9	26.1	8.1	20.1	70.5	12.4	81.9	29.68	7 228	458
Farmington Hills city	57 346	720	29 982	376	52 478	659	21.4	5.2	14.3	22.2	72.4	14.8	83.8	30.56	6 653	647
Ferndale city	NA	NA	NA	NA	NA	NA	NA	NA	NA	24.7	74.2	18.7	83.3	32.09	6 167	805
Flint city	395 256	2 958	54 748	410	376 125	2 814	7.4	4.4	2.6	21.5	70.6	14.2	81.5	30.28	6 979	483
Garden City city	28 482	860	8 443	255	28 724	867	12.4	17.6	9.7	22.9	72.9	15.5	83.8	32.71	6 500	677
Grand Rapids city	188 559	1 005	71 170	379	194 714	1 038	15.7	13.2	9.8	21.8	71.6	14.7	82.8	36.04	6 973	534
Holland city	35 209	1 048	10 778	321	39 490	1 175	9.5	16.1	19.1	23.3	70.8	16.8	81.9	36.25	6 747	529
Inkster city	18 205	572	6 337	199	18 185	571	19.6	24.9	17.2	22.9	72.3	15.6	83.3	32.62	6 569	626
Jackson city	34 208	956	13 790	385	35 151	982	19.0	14.5	20.1	21.5	72.2	14.3	83.2	29.73	6 791	621
Kalamazoo city	101 640	1 318	26 221	340	97 728	1 267	23.7	20.5	12.9	23.7	73.5	16.4	84.9	37.03	6 230	764
Kentwood city	18 828	448	7 991	190	18 660	444	22.9	7.0	19.2	21.8	71.6	14.7	82.8	36.04	6 973	534
Lansing city	166 050	1 298	58 283	456	169 274	1 323	9.8	12.9	5.7	20.9	70.8	13.3	82.6	30.62	7 101	490
Lincoln Park city	32 851	762	13 485	313	28 419	660	23.8	22.0	13.5	22.9	72.9	15.5	83.8	32.71	6 500	677
Livonia city	NA	NA	NA	NA	NA	NA	NA	NA	NA	22.9	72.9	15.5	83.8	32.71	6 500	677
Madison Heights city	31 912	997	14 388	449	33 191	1 036	19.3	37.2	9.3	24.7	74.2	18.7	83.3	32.09	6 167	805
Midland city	44 206	1 085	20 885	513	36 725	902	11.3	17.1	13.9	22.0	72.2	14.7	84.1	29.51	6 763	599
Muskegon city	32 941	825	12 394	311	40 073	1 004	15.0	17.1	19.2	23.3	70.3	17.7	80.3	32.56	6 924	431
Novi city	37 027	840	17 597	399	43 683	991	14.9	20.4	22.1	21.0	71.0	13.6	81.4	29.95	7 064	515
Oak Park city	30 782	1 039	12 120	409	29 956	1 011	23.6	20.6	7.1	24.7	74.2	18.7	83.3	32.09	6 167	805
Pontiac city	98 581	1 429	38 034	551	97 781	1 417	15.6	9.2	7.5	22.2	72.4	14.8	83.8	30.56	6 653	647
Portage city	42 612	981	17 331	399	33 026	760	16.4	16.8	15.8	23.7	73.5	16.4	84.9	37.03	6 230	764
Port Huron city	31 270	965	14 063	434	42 072	1 299	12.4	23.0	10.6	22.4	71.7	15.4	81.5	30.34	6 898	544
Rochester Hills city	47 120	701	17 657	263	55 555	827	15.5	38.5	12.2	22.2	72.4	14.8	83.8	30.56	6 653	647
Roseville city	39 033	753	15 852	306	38 825	749	21.0	24.5	17.1	24.7	74.2	18.7	83.3	32.09	6 167	805
Royal Oak city	55 191	850	24 090	371	51 216	789	15.8	22.0	6.7	24.7	74.2	18.7	83.3	32.09	6 167	805
Saginaw city	71 978	1 122	21 807	340	71 218	1 110	18.0	18.2	9.6	22.7	73.0	15.7	84.4	30.89	6 538	675
St. Clair Shores city	47 962	718	18 161	272	46 724	700	18.5	31.0	12.1	24.7	73.5	17.4	83.7	33.23	6 185	737
Southfield city	95 360	1 264	44 321	587	93 205	1 235	15.6	17.1	9.7	22.2	72.4	14.8	83.8	30.56	6 653	647
Southgate city	25 341	782	11 611	358	22 990	710	18.9	25.8	15.6	22.9	72.3	15.6	83.3	32.62	6 569	626
Sterling Heights city	78 536	633	38 945	314	80 749	651	22.4	10.2	12.6	23.1	71.3	16.7	81.3	31.36	6 777	526
Taylor city	61 743	834	30 326	410	55 386	748	13.8	.6	17.1	22.9	72.3	15.6	83.3	32.62	6 569	626
Troy city	NA	NA	NA	NA	NA	NA	NA	NA	NA	22.2	72.4	14.8	83.8	30.56	6 653	647
Warren city	123 085	857	57 872	403	116 564	811	19.9	23.3	10.8	24.7	74.2	18.7	83.3	32.09	6 167	805
Westland city	57 865	667	20 430	236	58 040	669	16.8	32.1	12.9	22.9	72.3	15.6	83.3	32.62	6 569	626
Wyandotte city	NA	NA	NA	NA	NA	NA	NA	NA	NA	22.9	72.9	15.5	83.8	32.71	6 500	677
Wyoming city	43 232	636	16 013	236	51 627	760	17.1	22.6	17.7	21.8	71.6	14.7	82.8	36.04	6 973	534

[1] Based on resident population estimated as of July 1, 1997. [2] Represents normal values for the 30-year period, 1961–1990. [3] Average daily minimum. [4] Average daily maximum. [5] One heating degree day is accumulated for each whole degree that the mean daily temperature is below 65 degrees Fahrenheit. [6] One cooling degree day is accumulated for each whole degree that the mean daily temperature is above 65 degrees Fahrenheit.

Sources: City Government Finances—U.S. Census Bureau, 1997 Census of Governments, Volume 4, Government Finances, GC97(4)-4, Finances of Municipal and Township Governments, issued September 2000 (related Internet site <http://www.census.gov/govs/www/cog.html>).   1997 Population for Government Finances calculations—U.S. Census Bureau, Population Estimates for Places: Annual Time Series, July 1, 1990 to July 1, 1999 (SU-99-7), published 20 October 2000, <http://www.census.gov/estimates/metro-city/placesbyst/SC99T7_US.txt>.   Climate: U.S. National Oceanic and Atmospheric Administration (NOAA), National Climatic Data Center (NCDC), Climatography of the United States, Number 81, published January 1992 (related Internet site <http://lwf.ncdc.noaa.gov/oa/climate/normals/usnormals.html>).

Table C–7. Cities — Government Finances and Climate–Con.

[Includes states and 1,070 incorporated places of 25,000 or more population as of April 1, 1990 in all states except Hawaii which has no incorporated places recognized by the Census Bureau. For Hawaii, 8 census designated places (CDPs) of 25,000 or more population as of April 1, 1990 are included. Also included are the 5 boroughs of New York city. For more information on these areas, see appendix B. Geographic Information]

City	City government finances, 1996-1997									Climate[2]						
	General revenue				General expenditure					Average daily temperature (degrees Fahrenheit)				Annual precip- itation (inches)	Heating degree days[5]	Cooling degree days[6]
			Taxes				By selected function, percent from—									
	Total ($1,000)	Per capita[1] (dollars)	Total ($1,000)	Per capita[1] (dollars)	Total ($1,000)	Per capita[1] (dollars)	Police pro- tection	Sewerage and solid waste manage- ment	High- ways	January	July	January[3]	July[4]			
MINNESOTA	X	X	X	X	X	X	X	X	X	X	X	X	X	X	X	X
Apple Valley city	32 564	734	10 864	245	23 816	537	16.1	16.8	22.3	11.3	72.4	.9	84.5	32.42	8 048	590
Blaine city	25 390	579	8 160	186	20 369	465	13.7	20.3	3.8	11.8	73.6	2.8	84.0	28.32	7 981	682
Bloomington city	100 725	1 172	50 596	589	76 133	886	12.6	11.8	12.9	11.8	73.6	2.8	84.0	28.32	7 981	682
Brooklyn Center city	28 836	1 035	9 268	333	31 888	1 145	12.6	18.1	19.1	11.8	73.6	2.8	84.0	28.32	7 981	682
Brooklyn Park city	51 603	836	23 280	377	63 628	1 030	11.3	22.8	12.2	11.8	73.6	2.8	84.0	28.32	7 981	682
Burnsville city	57 533	982	15 549	265	52 682	899	10.7	7.2	16.7	11.8	73.6	2.8	84.0	28.32	7 981	682
Coon Rapids city	45 992	735	12 379	198	39 222	627	10.0	11.6	5.8	11.8	73.6	2.8	84.0	28.32	7 981	682
Duluth city	131 627	1 606	29 322	358	118 960	1 452	9.3	10.8	16.7	7.0	66.1	-2.2	77.1	30.00	9 818	180
Eagan city	41 896	717	13 952	239	34 934	598	15.8	11.9	7.8	11.8	73.6	2.8	84.0	28.32	7 981	682
Eden Prairie city	47 858	1 031	17 743	382	38 512	830	10.3	21.3	8.9	11.8	73.6	2.8	84.0	28.32	7 981	682
Edina city	38 695	844	17 703	386	36 566	798	11.8	13.1	14.9	11.8	73.6	2.8	84.0	28.32	7 981	682
Fridley city	21 255	765	7 722	278	18 930	681	17.3	21.4	16.0	11.8	73.6	2.8	84.0	28.32	7 981	682
Mankato city	32 648	1 044	10 265	328	37 384	1 196	9.0	15.6	21.7	11.7	73.1	1.2	84.7	29.51	8 005	670
Maple Grove city	41 456	905	13 511	295	42 981	938	8.2	9.2	46.9	11.8	73.6	2.8	84.0	28.32	7 981	682
Maplewood city	31 881	936	9 395	276	30 549	896	12.2	16.1	5.8	11.8	73.6	2.8	84.0	28.32	7 981	682
Minneapolis city	663 709	1 865	225 405	633	667 682	1 876	10.8	8.9	5.0	11.8	73.6	2.8	84.0	28.32	7 981	682
Minnetonka city	33 007	646	16 020	314	34 235	670	14.3	14.4	12.1	11.8	73.6	2.8	84.0	28.32	7 981	682
Moorhead city	30 357	908	3 059	92	36 346	1 088	10.6	19.9	16.0	5.9	71.1	-3.6	83.4	19.45	9 254	537
Plymouth city	45 156	745	16 442	271	38 915	642	11.9	14.3	31.5	11.8	73.6	2.8	84.0	28.32	7 981	682
Richfield city	30 119	889	10 444	308	23 516	694	19.0	12.3	7.2	11.8	73.6	2.8	84.0	28.32	7 981	682
Rochester city	73 532	949	27 251	352	71 013	917	13.8	10.1	13.3	11.5	70.9	2.6	81.8	29.66	8 250	472
Roseville city	36 142	1 057	14 426	422	29 466	862	10.4	11.3	13.4	11.8	73.6	2.8	84.0	28.32	7 981	682
St. Cloud city	67 357	1 166	16 891	292	63 947	1 107	10.0	12.3	17.4	8.1	70.1	-2.4	82.6	27.43	8 928	415
St. Louis Park city	58 512	1 373	14 366	337	58 369	1 369	8.3	10.9	4.4	11.8	73.6	2.8	84.0	28.32	7 981	682
St. Paul city	466 228	1 808	107 757	418	433 134	1 680	11.4	9.4	14.6	11.8	73.6	2.8	84.0	28.32	7 981	682
Winona city	NA	NA	NA	NA	NA	NA	NA	NA	NA	14.1	73.2	4.0	85.0	32.57	7 694	662
MISSISSIPPI	X	X	X	X	X	X	X	X	X	X	X	X	X	X	X	X
Biloxi city	55 720	1 181	23 730	503	43 214	916	19.7	16.6	18.9	51.0	82.3	42.3	90.0	61.76	1 507	2 666
Greenville city	26 727	624	6 637	155	25 916	605	21.5	25.3	9.7	41.2	81.9	31.0	92.5	53.38	2 778	2 153
Gulfport city	181 631	2 787	21 331	327	184 778	2 835	5.3	3.7	1.9	50.7	82.3	41.2	91.3	62.72	1 551	2 645
Hattiesburg city	37 360	775	12 703	264	38 447	798	14.9	19.0	10.7	46.0	81.3	34.3	91.8	60.58	2 180	2 265
Jackson city	154 677	839	52 129	283	148 665	807	15.1	12.7	12.9	44.1	81.5	32.7	92.4	55.37	2 467	2 215
Meridian city	31 422	757	11 876	286	25 293	609	18.4	15.9	10.8	45.0	81.0	33.4	92.1	56.71	2 444	2 138
Pascagoula city	18 833	691	5 949	218	19 291	708	18.2	22.1	19.0	48.9	82.1	39.3	90.3	63.72	1 761	2 617
Tupelo city	38 688	1 074	8 542	237	33 287	924	16.8	9.0	29.9	39.9	80.6	30.9	90.7	55.87	3 079	1 908
MISSOURI	X	X	X	X	X	X	X	X	X	X	X	X	X	X	X	X
Blue Springs city	22 487	476	12 793	271	21 349	452	19.6	11.0	17.7	25.7	78.5	16.7	88.7	37.62	5 393	1 288
Cape Girardeau city	32 029	885	17 638	487	29 578	817	13.0	27.4	11.8	31.7	79.6	22.6	90.2	46.31	4 386	1 543
Chesterfield city	17 988	406	6 265	141	23 215	524	18.5	3.2	33.8	29.3	79.8	20.8	89.3	37.51	4 758	1 534
Columbia city	60 965	770	26 283	332	62 946	795	13.2	19.4	11.2	27.6	77.4	18.5	88.6	39.05	5 212	1 189
Florissant city	16 307	318	4 972	97	15 429	301	35.6	—	22.6	29.3	79.8	20.8	89.3	37.51	4 758	1 534
Gladstone city	14 701	523	9 031	321	14 693	523	20.9	8.9	22.9	25.7	78.5	16.7	88.7	37.62	5 393	1 288
Independence city	57 597	497	28 150	243	62 643	540	27.4	14.4	7.2	25.7	78.5	16.7	88.7	37.62	5 393	1 288
Jefferson City city	30 358	835	17 957	494	28 241	777	17.3	14.4	25.2	27.4	77.4	15.3	90.1	38.43	5 302	1 175
Joplin city	31 344	701	18 529	415	40 165	899	10.6	32.2	11.5	32.3	80.0	22.7	90.2	43.23	4 303	1 560
Kansas City city	723 705	1 661	412 824	947	783 866	1 799	13.4	8.1	5.6	25.7	78.5	16.7	88.7	37.62	5 393	1 288
Kirkwood city	14 356	521	5 424	197	18 173	660	19.4	7.3	11.8	29.3	79.8	20.8	89.3	37.51	4 758	1 534
Lee's Summit city	50 286	781	22 472	349	38 152	593	18.3	14.9	12.9	28.0	78.3	17.5	90.2	39.84	4 993	1 316
Maryland Heights city	NA	NA	NA	NA	NA	NA	NA	NA	NA	29.3	79.8	20.8	89.3	37.51	4 758	1 534
Raytown city	12 164	399	6 764	222	12 175	400	26.0	17.7	16.7	25.7	78.5	16.7	88.7	37.62	5 393	1 288
St. Charles city	51 930	894	34 425	593	48 789	840	18.6	5.6	15.3	27.5	77.6	17.2	89.2	37.74	5 179	1 226
St. Joseph city	50 941	728	27 267	389	57 055	815	10.9	21.9	12.0	24.6	78.1	14.7	88.9	35.69	5 590	1 254
St. Louis city	655 677	1 903	373 357	1 084	630 766	1 831	17.6	3.0	2.3	28.4	78.4	18.9	89.6	37.86	5 001	1 329
St. Peters city	29 991	590	19 164	377	31 033	611	12.4	12.4	32.2	27.5	77.6	17.2	89.2	37.74	5 179	1 226
Springfield city	137 301	952	58 149	403	126 360	876	11.6	16.5	13.7	31.1	78.1	20.4	89.6	43.04	4 638	1 320
University City city	21 020	555	7 573	200	21 651	572	22.4	10.8	12.1	29.3	79.8	20.8	89.3	37.51	4 758	1 534

[1] Based on resident population estimated as of July 1, 1997.   [2] Represents normal values for the 30-year period, 1961–1990.   [3] Average daily minimum.   [4] Average daily maximum.   [5] One heating degree day is accumulated for each whole degree that the mean daily temperature is below 65 degrees Fahrenheit.   [6] One cooling degree day is accumulated for each whole degree that the mean daily temperature is above 65 degrees Fahrenheit.

Sources: City Government Finances—U.S. Census Bureau, 1997 Census of Governments, Volume 4, Government Finances, GC97(4)-4, Finances of Municipal and Township Governments, issued September 2000 (related Internet site <http://www.census.gov/govs/www/cog.html>).   1997 Population for Government Finances calculations—U.S. Census Bureau, Population Estimates for Places: Annual Time Series, July 1, 1990 to July 1, 1999 (SU-99-7), published 20 October 2000, <http://www.census.gov/estimates/metro-city/placesbyst/SC99T7_US.txt>.   Climate: U.S. National Oceanic and Atmospheric Administration (NOAA), National Climatic Data Center (NCDC), Climatography of the United States, Number 81, published January 1992 (related Internet site <http://lwf.ncdc.noaa.gov/oa/climate/normals/usnormals.html>).

Table C-7. Cities — **Government Finances and Climate**–Con.

[Includes states and 1,070 incorporated places of 25,000 or more population as of April 1, 1990 in all states except Hawaii which has no incorporated places recognized by the Census Bureau. For Hawaii, 8 census designated places (CDPs) of 25,000 or more population as of April 1, 1990 are included. Also included are the 5 boroughs of New York city. For more information on these areas, see appendix B. Geographic Information]

City	City government finances, 1996-1997									Climate[2]						
	General revenue				General expenditure					Average daily temperature (degrees Fahrenheit)				Annual precipitation (inches)	Heating degree days[5]	Cooling degree days[6]
			Taxes				By selected function, percent from—									
	Total ($1,000)	Per capita[1] (dollars)	Total ($1,000)	Per capita[1] (dollars)	Total ($1,000)	Per capita[1] (dollars)	Police protection	Sewerage and solid waste management	Highways	January	July	January[3]	July[4]			
MONTANA	X	X	X	X	X	X	12.9	15.1	7.4	22.8	72.5	13.7	86.7	15.08	7 164	652
Billings city	64 285	701	17 208	188	56 739	619	12.9	15.1	7.4	22.8	72.5	13.7	86.7	15.08	7 164	652
Butte-Silver Bow (remainder)	[7]33 457	[7]992	[7]12 021	[7]357	[7]42 885	[7]1 272	[7]9.4	[7]6.7	[7]6.9	16.8	62.9	5.0	80.1	12.10	9 517	110
Great Falls city	31 538	557	9 130	161	31 533	557	12.8	11.5	8.3	21.2	68.2	11.6	83.3	15.21	7 741	388
Missoula city	27 475	477	12 974	225	30 471	529	15.1	10.3	7.2	22.7	66.8	15.4	83.4	13.46	7 792	280
NEBRASKA	X	X	X	X	X	X	19.1	22.7	15.7	21.1	76.9	10.9	87.9	29.86	6 300	1 072
Bellevue city	23 999	550	14 026	321	21 033	482	19.1	22.7	15.7	21.1	76.9	10.9	87.9	29.86	6 300	1 072
Grand Island city	40 351	968	15 100	362	31 890	765	12.9	16.2	15.3	21.9	76.7	11.1	88.5	24.90	6 421	997
Lincoln city	228 993	1 082	77 358	366	212 426	1 004	7.8	9.4	9.9	21.3	78.2	10.1	90.0	28.26	6 278	1 134
Omaha city	270 904	710	175 826	461	268 168	703	16.8	14.1	17.3	21.1	76.9	10.9	87.9	29.86	6 300	1 072
NEVADA	X	X	X	X	X	X	7.8	2.8	4.8	33.6	69.9	20.7	89.5	10.87	5 691	401
Carson City	118 769	2 441	15 436	317	103 891	2 135	7.8	2.8	4.8	33.6	69.9	20.7	89.5	10.87	5 691	401
Henderson city	137 037	1 001	33 681	246	142 365	1 040	11.5	15.1	5.5	45.5	91.1	33.6	105.9	4.13	2 407	3 201
Las Vegas city	433 846	1 109	102 206	261	384 733	984	14.9	11.5	12.5	45.5	91.1	33.6	105.9	4.13	2 407	3 201
North Las Vegas city	88 900	1 004	20 633	233	85 253	963	21.1	9.1	9.8	45.5	91.1	33.6	105.9	4.13	2 407	3 201
Reno city	158 237	983	61 888	384	153 732	955	23.8	9.0	11.6	32.9	71.6	20.7	91.9	7.53	5 674	508
Sparks city	55 678	918	21 462	354	68 048	1 122	14.1	15.2	9.7	32.9	71.6	20.7	91.9	7.53	5 674	508
NEW HAMPSHIRE	X	X	X	X	X	X	12.6	10.4	11.0	18.6	69.5	7.4	82.4	36.37	7 554	328
Concord city	36 294	944	21 568	561	35 661	927	12.6	10.4	11.0	18.6	69.5	7.4	82.4	36.37	7 554	328
Dover city	48 281	1 852	34 034	1 306	48 172	1 848	6.3	8.7	3.2	22.2	69.8	11.0	82.9	43.00	7 002	347
Manchester city	181 621	1 792	119 577	1 180	179 626	1 772	6.9	4.8	7.8	18.6	69.5	7.4	82.4	43.00	7 110	382
Nashua city	150 344	1 840	117 665	1 440	150 844	1 847	6.4	5.6	4.4	21.4	70.2	10.0	82.4	42.18	7 002	347
Portsmouth city	53 355	2 092	34 095	1 337	49 442	1 938	9.6	10.3	4.6	22.2	69.8	11.0	82.9	42.18	7 002	347
Rochester city	48 679	1 749	37 220	1 337	38 413	1 000	6.5	6.9	6.4	21.5	70.2	10.4	83.2	46.85	7 052	397
NEW JERSEY	X	X	X	X	X	X	X	X	X	30.9	74.7	21.4	84.5	40.29	5 169	826
Atlantic City city	NA	NA	NA	NA	NA	NA	NA	NA	NA	30.9	74.7	21.4	84.5	40.29	5 169	826
Bayonne city	NA	NA	NA	NA	NA	NA	NA	NA	NA	29.5	74.9	23.3	82.2	43.50	5 362	874
Camden city	NA	NA	NA	NA	NA	NA	NA	NA	NA	31.8	76.6	23.7	86.6	45.56	4 725	1 085
Clifton city	NA	NA	NA	NA	NA	NA	NA	NA	NA	28.3	74.9	19.4	85.9	49.79	5 486	838
East Orange city	NA	NA	NA	NA	NA	NA	NA	NA	NA	30.6	77.8	23.4	87.0	43.97	4 888	1 201
Elizabeth city	129 608	1 173	49 254	446	129 712	1 174	19.5	15.2	4.9	30.6	77.8	23.4	87.0	43.97	4 888	1 201
Fair Lawn borough	NA	NA	NA	NA	NA	NA	NA	NA	NA	28.3	74.9	19.4	85.9	49.79	5 486	838
Fort Lee borough	NA	NA	NA	NA	NA	NA	NA	NA	NA	29.5	74.9	23.3	82.2	43.50	5 362	874
Garfield city	NA	NA	NA	NA	NA	NA	NA	NA	NA	28.3	74.9	19.4	85.9	49.79	5 486	838
Hackensack city	NA	NA	NA	NA	NA	NA	NA	NA	NA	28.3	74.9	19.4	85.9	49.79	5 486	838
Hoboken city	66 952	2 007	20 229	606	58 536	1 754	15.6	6.3	1.1	29.5	74.9	23.3	82.2	43.50	5 362	874
Jersey City city	NA	NA	NA	NA	NA	NA	NA	NA	NA	29.5	74.9	23.3	82.2	43.50	5 362	874
Kearny town	NA	NA	NA	NA	NA	NA	NA	NA	NA	30.6	77.8	23.4	87.0	43.97	4 888	1 201
Linden city	NA	NA	NA	NA	NA	NA	NA	NA	NA	30.6	77.8	23.4	87.0	43.97	4 888	1 201
Long Branch city	NA	NA	NA	NA	NA	NA	NA	NA	NA	30.6	73.7	22.3	82.3	47.13	5 253	746
Millville city	NA	NA	NA	NA	NA	NA	NA	NA	NA	31.1	75.9	22.5	85.3	42.28	4 946	983
Newark city	522 827	1 959	151 830	569	492 506	1 845	16.9	11.0	1.8	30.6	77.8	23.4	87.0	43.97	4 888	1 201
New Brunswick city	103 563	2 487	39 416	946	104 999	2 521	9.1	5.5	1.1	29.0	74.6	20.6	84.9	47.02	5 340	804
Paramus borough	NA	NA	NA	NA	NA	NA	NA	NA	NA	28.3	74.9	19.4	85.9	49.79	5 486	838
Passaic city	NA	NA	NA	NA	NA	NA	NA	NA	NA	28.3	74.9	19.4	85.9	49.79	5 486	838
Paterson city	156 081	1 049	67 445	453	156 240	1 051	18.7	16.5	4.9	29.0	74.6	20.6	84.9	47.02	5 340	804
Perth Amboy city	46 210	1 098	17 300	411	45 284	1 076	19.7	27.4	2.7	29.4	75.0	21.5	86.4	49.00	5 227	891
Plainfield city	46 341	1 002	24 893	538	42 739	924	21.1	5.0	7.6	30.6	77.8	23.4	87.0	43.97	4 888	1 201
Rahway city	NA	NA	NA	NA	NA	NA	NA	NA	NA	30.6	77.8	23.4	87.0	43.97	4 888	1 201
Sayreville borough	NA	NA	NA	NA	NA	NA	NA	NA	NA	29.0	74.6	20.6	84.9	47.02	5 340	804
Trenton city	297 181	3 498	76 381	899	294 386	3 465	9.5	6.3	.8	29.6	75.4	20.5	87.3	45.43	5 172	937
Union City city	146 501	2 553	46 980	819	141 008	2 457	8.1	3.4	.7	29.5	74.9	23.3	82.2	43.50	5 362	874
Vineland city	42 460	760	14 105	252	42 549	762	16.3	1.1	13.3	31.1	75.9	22.5	85.3	42.28	4 946	983
Westfield town	20 233	693	11 366	389	22 922	785	20.3	8.9	6.2	29.7	74.8	20.3	86.6	48.75	5 239	841
West New York town	94 747	2 468	36 227	944	98 812	2 574	7.5	4.6	1.6	29.5	74.9	23.3	82.2	43.50	5 362	874

[1] Based on resident population estimated as of July 1, 1997. [2] Represents normal values for the 30-year period, 1961–1990. [3] Average daily minimum. [4] Average daily maximum. [5] One heating degree day is accumulated for each whole degree that the mean daily temperature is below 65 degrees Fahrenheit. [6] One cooling degree day is accumulated for each whole degree that the mean daily temperature is above 65 degrees Fahrenheit. [7] Data are for consolidated city of Butte-Silver Bow; data for Butte-Silver Bow (remainder) not available.

Sources: City Government Finances—U.S. Census Bureau, 1997 Census of Governments, Volume 4, Government Finances, GC97(4)-4, Finances of Municipal and Township Governments, issued September 2000 (related Internet site <http://www.census.gov/govs/www/cog.html>). 1997 Population for Government Finances calculations—U.S. Census Bureau, Population Estimates for Places: Annual Time Series, July 1, 1990 to July 1, 1999 (SU-99-7), published 20 October 2000, <http://www.census.gov/estimates/metro-city/placesbyst/SC99T7_US.txt>. Climate: U.S. National Oceanic and Atmospheric Administration (NOAA), National Climatic Data Center (NCDC), Climatography of the United States, Number 81, published January 1992 (related Internet site <http://lwf.ncdc.noaa.gov/oa/climate/normals/usnormals.html>).

Table C–7. Cities — **Government Finances and Climate**–Con.

[Includes states and 1,070 incorporated places of 25,000 or more population as of April 1, 1990 in all states except Hawaii which has no incorporated places recognized by the Census Bureau. For Hawaii, 8 census designated places (CDPs) of 25,000 or more population as of April 1, 1990 are included. Also included are the 5 boroughs of New York city. For more information on these areas, see appendix B. Geographic Information]

City	City government finances, 1996-1997									Climate[2]						
	General revenue				General expenditure					Average daily temperature (degrees Fahrenheit)				Annual precipitation (inches)	Heating degree days[5]	Cooling degree days[6]
			Taxes				By selected function, percent from—									
	Total ($1,000)	Per capita[1] (dollars)	Total ($1,000)	Per capita[1] (dollars)	Total ($1,000)	Per capita[1] (dollars)	Police protection	Sewerage and solid waste management	Highways	January	July	January[3]	July[4]			
NEW MEXICO	X	X	X	X	X	X	X	X	X	X	X	X	X	X	X	X
Alamogordo city	23 148	800	8 747	302	23 413	809	17.1	14.7	14.3	42.6	80.4	28.3	94.9	12.74	2 908	1 764
Albuquerque city	618 284	1 469	168 389	400	623 247	1 481	12.7	12.1	8.2	34.2	78.5	21.7	92.5	8.88	4 425	1 244
Clovis city	19 879	584	8 525	251	21 201	623	19.4	18.6	13.9	36.5	76.9	22.3	90.5	17.51	4 068	1 156
Farmington city	78 016	2 037	16 056	419	80 852	2 111	8.4	8.1	9.6	28.6	75.0	15.7	92.3	8.26	5 495	803
Hobbs city	29 963	1 080	9 782	353	28 908	1 042	29.0	10.4	16.1	42.5	79.8	28.0	92.8	16.78	2 851	1 790
Las Cruces city	49 555	659	21 564	287	63 150	840	12.5	14.1	14.5	41.8	80.4	26.4	94.2	9.40	3 155	1 618
Rio Rancho city	NA	NA	NA	NA	NA	NA	NA	NA	NA	34.2	78.5	21.7	92.5	8.88	4 425	1 244
Roswell city	NA	NA	NA	NA	NA	NA	NA	NA	NA	39.5	80.7	24.7	94.6	12.58	3 267	1 776
Santa Fe city	102 835	1 506	35 704	523	116 637	1 708	8.6	16.1	14.9	30.4	69.0	13.7	84.9	16.37	6 138	324
NEW YORK	X	X	X	X	X	X	X	X	X	X	X	X	X	X	X	X
Albany city	125 125	1 307	39 461	412	117 391	1 226	20.2	9.3	6.4	20.6	71.8	11.0	84.0	36.17	6 894	507
Auburn city	32 302	1 087	8 814	296	39 904	1 342	8.6	30.2	8.2	23.1	71.5	15.1	81.7	36.57	6 782	501
Binghamton city	51 260	1 073	18 795	393	52 257	1 094	13.5	15.2	9.3	21.1	69.2	14.3	78.6	36.99	7 273	337
Buffalo city	836 751	2 749	117 340	386	931 026	3 059	6.1	4.7	3.6	23.6	71.1	17.0	80.2	38.58	6 747	477
Elmira city	28 509	898	8 621	271	29 472	928	14.5	3.7	9.9	22.8	69.7	13.4	82.7	33.32	6 982	373
Freeport village	29 291	734	17 575	441	34 736	871	26.7	9.7	6.9	31.2	75.5	24.9	82.8	41.59	5 027	921
Hempstead village	37 446	808	26 795	578	47 222	1 019	21.8	5.2	7.6	31.0	74.4	25.0	82.6	44.68	5 316	853
Ithaca city	36 152	1 223	15 380	520	34 369	1 163	14.0	13.0	7.9	21.5	68.6	12.9	79.8	35.40	7 207	288
Jamestown city	47 588	1 437	10 410	314	54 449	1 645	7.0	7.7	4.3	24.3	70.5	17.8	78.7	45.82	6 591	461
Lindenhurst village	8 942	339	5 699	216	8 996	341	–	9.7	15.3	31.2	75.5	24.9	82.8	41.59	5 027	921
Long Beach city	44 142	1 287	20 980	612	50 662	1 477	19.7	13.6	8.3	31.2	75.5	24.9	82.8	41.59	5 027	921
Mount Vernon city	59 230	885	34 506	515	57 533	860	18.6	6.8	2.5	28.7	74.1	19.7	85.7	46.01	5 470	779
Newburgh city	30 467	1 163	9 816	375	29 758	1 136	19.9	14.5	7.2	27.4	75.2	19.3	86.5	47.51	5 550	896
New Rochelle city	83 244	1 234	47 541	705	92 749	1 375	16.4	4.4	5.1	28.7	74.1	19.7	85.7	46.01	5 470	779
New York city	43 756 189	5 927	19 368 172	2 623	41 433 578	5 612	6.9	5.3	2.9	31.5	76.8	25.3	85.2	47.25	4 805	1 096
Bronx borough	NA	NA	NA	NA	NA	NA	NA	NA	NA	31.5	76.8	25.3	85.2	47.25	4 805	1 096
Brooklyn borough	NA	NA	NA	NA	NA	NA	NA	NA	NA	31.6	76.8	25.2	84.7	44.98	4 809	1 084
Manhattan borough	NA	NA	NA	NA	NA	NA	NA	NA	NA	31.5	76.8	25.3	85.2	47.25	4 805	1 096
Queens borough	NA	NA	NA	NA	NA	NA	NA	NA	NA	31.3	76.4	25.5	83.9	42.12	4 910	1 052
Staten Island borough	NA	NA	NA	NA	NA	NA	NA	NA	NA	30.7	75.5	23.1	85.0	47.24	5 009	945
Niagara Falls city	95 252	1 656	28 438	495	97 299	1 692	10.8	15.7	3.8	23.6	71.1	17.0	80.2	38.58	6 747	477
North Tonawanda city	31 611	950	14 509	436	32 590	979	10.6	18.2	10.2	23.6	71.1	17.0	80.2	38.58	6 747	477
Poughkeepsie city	41 630	1 502	11 836	427	36 282	1 309	15.9	15.6	5.2	23.8	72.2	14.2	83.8	40.72	6 391	566
Rochester city	640 540	2 922	152 892	698	674 114	3 075	6.8	2.6	3.0	23.6	70.2	16.3	80.7	31.96	6 734	425
Rome city	47 084	1 165	18 946	469	45 296	1 121	9.9	11.8	13.7	20.1	70.2	12.7	80.3	45.09	7 305	423
Saratoga Springs city	25 989	1 020	8 637	339	27 640	1 085	13.2	14.5	8.9	20.1	71.1	9.3	84.1	40.88	6 998	452
Schenectady city	64 886	1 044	20 162	324	66 570	1 071	14.5	17.6	9.2	21.8	71.7	13.2	82.6	36.46	6 881	537
Syracuse city	352 966	2 302	31 544	206	391 420	2 553	6.4	2.3	4.0	22.4	70.4	14.2	81.7	38.93	6 834	438
Troy city	62 862	1 215	16 070	311	65 684	1 270	11.2	5.7	4.4	21.3	73.0	11.6	83.8	36.18	6 758	599
Utica city	62 298	1 037	25 894	431	75 191	1 252	11.6	6.9	4.1	20.1	70.2	12.7	80.3	45.09	7 305	423
Valley Stream village	18 413	543	15 192	448	18 851	556	.9	21.3	14.2	31.2	75.5	24.9	82.8	41.59	5 027	921
Watertown city	33 727	1 194	8 466	300	32 226	1 141	12.5	9.4	10.5	17.9	68.6	8.3	79.6	32.04	7 753	299
White Plains city	102 745	2 062	64 682	1 298	94 330	1 893	18.9	7.2	6.6	27.2	73.3	20.2	82.1	48.92	5 832	691
Yonkers city	450 423	2 362	242 720	1 273	476 545	2 499	8.6	2.1	3.1	28.7	74.1	19.7	85.7	46.01	5 470	779
NORTH CAROLINA	X	X	X	X	X	X	X	X	X	X	X	X	X	X	X	X
Asheville city	71 798	1 085	24 600	372	63 610	961	16.6	15.8	12.5	35.7	72.8	24.8	83.0	47.59	4 308	787
Burlington city	38 516	923	11 259	270	33 901	812	18.4	27.4	8.3	37.5	78.2	27.0	88.9	44.96	3 680	1 408
Cary town	77 772	944	33 830	411	44 430	539	11.4	22.4	5.2	38.9	78.1	28.8	88.0	41.43	3 457	1 417
Chapel Hill town	38 914	911	15 512	363	31 753	744	19.4	8.2	5.4	37.2	76.8	25.7	88.7	46.02	3 802	1 233
Charlotte city	718 125	1 445	207 659	418	527 233	1 061	16.7	10.2	9.1	39.3	79.3	29.6	88.9	43.09	3 341	1 582
Concord city	43 468	944	14 541	316	42 804	930	11.3	22.8	7.0	38.5	78.8	27.2	90.0	45.70	3 497	1 541
Durham city	182 639	1 063	54 824	319	144 122	839	18.3	24.8	10.0	37.1	77.1	25.1	88.8	48.10	3 867	1 278
Fayetteville city	102 460	943	27 400	252	91 162	839	27.6	21.4	10.5	40.3	79.4	29.1	89.7	46.72	3 169	1 623
Gastonia city	55 044	896	14 383	234	67 418	1 097	14.6	18.5	20.2	39.8	78.2	29.1	88.9	46.63	3 338	1 464
Goldsboro city	28 364	622	7 656	168	24 944	547	19.2	17.0	19.8	41.0	79.8	30.5	89.9	49.27	3 040	1 689
Greensboro city	222 116	1 123	88 486	448	206 968	1 047	18.1	15.2	10.1	36.7	76.9	26.6	86.9	42.62	3 865	1 253
Greenville city	42 147	742	13 270	233	40 966	721	20.2	25.5	9.4	40.6	78.8	29.6	89.5	49.00	3 129	1 561
Hickory city	48 902	1 525	16 382	511	47 479	1 481	10.6	17.4	21.2	37.7	76.8	27.8	86.6	49.38	3 728	1 258
High Point city	86 069	1 142	30 100	400	75 463	1 002	14.8	21.7	7.5	38.9	77.9	29.0	88.3	44.52	3 420	1 400
Jacksonville city	31 592	462	7 096	104	30 218	442	17.2	24.6	9.7	44.9	79.5	35.0	86.8	54.75	2 506	1 815

[1] Based on resident population estimated as of July 1, 1997.   [2] Represents normal values for the 30-year period, 1961–1990.   [3] Average daily minimum.   [4] Average daily maximum.   [5] One heating degree day is accumulated for each whole degree that the mean daily temperature is below 65 degrees Fahrenheit.   [6] One cooling degree day is accumulated for each whole degree that the mean daily temperature is above 65 degrees Fahrenheit.

Sources: City Government Finances—U.S. Census Bureau, 1997 Census of Governments, Volume 4, Government Finances, GC97(4)-4, Finances of Municipal and Township Governments, issued September 2000 (related Internet site <http://www.census.gov/govs/www/cog.html>).   1997 Population for Government Finances calculations—U.S. Census Bureau, Population Estimates for Places: Annual Time Series, July 1, 1990 to July 1, 1999 (SU-99-7), published 20 October 2000, <http://www.census.gov/estimates/metro-city/placesbyst/SC99T7_US.txt>.   Climate: U.S. National Oceanic and Atmospheric Administration (NOAA), National Climatic Data Center (NCDC), Climatography of the United States, Number 81, published January 1992 (related Internet site <http://lwf.ncdc.noaa.gov/oa/climate/normals/usnormals.html>).

Table C–7. Cities — **Government Finances and Climate**–Con.

[Includes states and 1,070 incorporated places of 25,000 or more population as of April 1, 1990 in all states except Hawaii which has no incorporated places recognized by the Census Bureau. For Hawaii, 8 census designated places (CDPs) of 25,000 or more population as of April 1, 1990 are included. Also included are the 5 boroughs of New York city. For more information on these areas, see appendix B. Geographic Information]

City	City government finances, 1996-1997									Climate[2]						
	General revenue				General expenditure					Average daily temperature (degrees Fahrenheit)						
			Taxes				By selected function, percent from—									
	Total ($1,000)	Per capita[1] (dollars)	Total ($1,000)	Per capita[1] (dollars)	Total ($1,000)	Per capita[1] (dollars)	Police protection	Sewerage and solid waste management	Highways	January	July	January[3]	July[4]	Annual precipitation (inches)	Heating degree days[5]	Cooling degree days[6]
NORTH CAROLINA—Con.																
Kannapolis city	15 284	444	5 963	173	13 382	389	28.9	22.2	10.3	38.5	78.8	27.2	90.0	45.70	3 497	1 541
Kinston city	30 232	1 196	5 754	228	25 703	1 017	5.3	18.4	5.7	40.6	78.1	29.5	89.0	51.20	3 196	1 465
Raleigh city	240 515	940	97 413	381	193 741	757	15.6	14.5	11.8	38.8	78.6	28.9	88.3	44.97	3 397	1 493
Rocky Mount city	43 382	751	12 100	209	43 326	750	17.0	22.8	11.0	39.9	78.4	29.4	88.9	45.69	3 321	1 447
Wilmington city	66 583	1 082	17 983	292	50 545	822	17.8	18.8	6.4	44.9	80.1	34.4	88.5	54.27	2 470	1 926
Wilson city	40 204	993	10 408	257	34 293	847	15.5	23.5	7.0	39.4	78.5	28.4	89.4	46.96	3 371	1 519
Winston-Salem city	247 241	1 464	67 347	399	175 881	1 042	17.8	24.3	9.4	38.9	77.9	29.0	88.3	44.52	3 420	1 400
NORTH DAKOTA	X	X	X	X	X	X	X	X	X	X	X	X	X	X	X	X
Bismarck city	50 790	929	17 375	318	44 775	819	11.5	9.5	16.5	9.2	70.4	-1.7	84.4	15.47	8 968	488
Fargo city	74 548	873	24 674	289	76 280	894	6.6	6.7	3.5	5.9	71.1	-3.6	83.4	19.45	9 254	537
Grand Forks city	46 245	936	17 371	352	48 030	972	9.0	14.9	7.3	4.3	69.1	-5.3	81.6	18.34	9 733	453
Minot city	NA	NA	NA	NA	NA	NA	NA	NA	NA	9.0	69.9	.4	82.0	18.57	9 193	492
OHIO	X	X	X	X	X	X	X	X	X	X	X	X	X	X	X	X
Akron city	270 489	1 253	144 234	668	264 020	1 223	14.3	16.2	10.8	24.8	71.9	16.9	82.3	36.82	6 160	625
Barberton city	22 190	806	10 142	369	21 425	779	15.9	14.6	13.3	24.8	71.9	16.9	82.3	36.82	6 160	625
Beavercreek city	11 941	315	6 711	177	13 893	366	34.0	–	20.3	26.0	74.2	17.9	84.9	36.64	5 708	886
Bowling Green city	20 956	738	10 631	374	22 211	782	22.5	29.6	8.9	22.7	73.0	14.4	84.6	32.77	6 482	694
Brunswick city	14 368	452	6 992	220	11 445	360	19.3	16.4	14.0	24.8	71.9	16.9	82.3	36.63	6 201	621
Canton city	79 468	992	39 386	492	77 109	963	17.7	15.1	10.4	24.8	71.9	16.9	82.3	36.82	6 160	625
Cincinnati city	658 243	1 935	286 112	841	647 941	1 905	11.7	24.1	9.6	29.8	76.4	21.2	86.6	40.70	4 928	1 135
Cleveland city	684 844	1 368	338 280	676	643 289	1 285	22.8	6.1	7.0	24.8	71.9	17.6	82.4	36.63	6 201	621
Cleveland Heights city	42 481	790	25 815	480	38 633	718	15.1	9.2	9.7	24.8	71.9	17.6	82.4	36.63	6 201	621
Columbus city	770 215	1 152	383 671	574	757 294	1 132	20.1	18.9	8.9	26.4	73.2	18.5	83.7	38.09	5 708	797
Cuyahoga Falls city	40 253	817	18 527	376	41 361	840	30.1	23.3	7.2	24.8	71.9	16.9	82.3	36.82	6 160	625
Dayton city	257 346	1 495	120 677	701	269 522	1 566	16.8	9.5	9.6	26.0	74.2	17.9	84.9	36.64	5 708	886
East Cleveland city	19 936	658	9 443	312	17 324	572	23.6	25.1	4.9	24.8	71.9	17.6	82.4	36.63	6 201	621
Elyria city	48 036	851	24 597	436	45 138	800	19.8	19.0	13.7	26.2	73.3	17.9	85.0	35.95	5 818	779
Euclid city	49 785	962	28 097	543	47 559	919	16.4	23.0	7.0	24.8	71.9	17.6	82.4	36.63	6 201	621
Fairborn city	20 335	619	7 683	234	18 576	565	21.0	20.3	1.7	26.0	74.2	17.9	84.9	36.64	5 708	886
Fairfield city	30 157	716	14 722	350	26 578	631	18.1	17.6	18.6	26.1	73.9	15.8	86.2	41.79	5 791	830
Findlay city	25 500	668	12 112	317	27 801	728	19.8	23.4	12.9	23.6	72.8	16.5	82.7	34.26	6 302	720
Gahanna city	NA	NA	NA	NA	NA	NA	NA	NA	NA	26.4	73.2	18.5	83.7	38.09	5 708	797
Garfield Heights city	20 590	699	13 194	448	17 791	604	21.4	11.2	7.2	24.8	71.9	17.6	82.4	36.63	6 201	621
Hamilton city	73 747	1 194	22 950	372	63 380	1 026	11.4	34.4	6.7	26.1	73.9	15.8	86.2	41.79	5 791	830
Huber Heights city	19 822	477	10 815	260	21 014	506	21.9	13.0	11.8	26.0	74.2	17.9	84.9	36.64	5 708	886
Kent city	19 314	721	10 109	377	23 316	870	9.5	12.7	18.8	24.8	71.9	16.9	82.3	36.82	6 160	625
Kettering city	47 525	810	28 174	480	38 390	655	20.2	1.0	21.0	26.0	74.2	17.9	84.9	36.64	5 708	886
Lakewood city	41 731	742	23 002	409	36 311	646	14.9	17.9	4.9	24.8	71.9	17.6	82.4	36.63	6 201	621
Lancaster city	26 925	741	10 344	285	27 085	746	18.8	23.9	8.7	25.4	72.8	16.0	84.7	36.32	5 988	724
Lima city	28 995	669	14 837	342	27 396	632	21.8	31.3	4.1	23.6	73.6	15.2	84.4	35.94	6 253	810
Lorain city	45 583	656	22 361	322	42 131	606	22.1	12.9	6.1	26.2	73.3	17.9	85.0	35.95	5 818	779
Mansfield city	41 289	790	21 990	421	39 614	758	19.8	4.2	19.8	24.5	72.1	16.8	82.1	39.66	6 258	666
Maple Heights city	18 477	721	10 742	419	17 883	698	16.8	25.7	8.2	24.8	71.9	17.6	82.4	36.63	6 201	621
Marion city	28 613	772	10 301	278	27 038	730	15.7	27.2	8.9	23.4	72.6	14.3	84.5	36.91	6 407	692
Massillon city	NA	NA	NA	NA	NA	NA	NA	NA	NA	24.8	71.9	16.9	82.3	36.82	6 160	625
Mentor city	41 156	808	27 633	542	37 918	744	17.5	1.4	19.3	26.6	71.9	19.3	81.2	35.93	5 929	636
Middletown city	NA	NA	NA	NA	NA	NA	NA	NA	NA	26.6	74.3	17.5	85.5	39.26	5 694	897
Newark city	NA	NA	NA	NA	NA	NA	NA	NA	NA	26.7	73.2	18.2	85.0	41.48	5 657	767
North Olmsted city	34 383	1 066	17 167	532	30 164	935	11.9	12.6	22.2	24.8	71.9	17.6	82.4	36.63	6 201	621
Parma city	44 955	537	29 978	358	46 444	555	20.3	1.8	21.0	24.8	71.9	17.6	82.4	36.63	6 201	621
Reynoldsburg city	12 721	431	6 266	212	12 711	431	27.5	22.2	21.8	26.4	73.2	18.5	83.7	38.09	5 708	797
Sandusky city	20 361	713	11 457	401	20 381	714	15.3	15.0	6.0	24.8	73.6	17.5	82.4	34.05	6 131	752
Shaker Heights city	36 322	1 242	23 953	819	37 340	1 277	17.4	11.6	11.6	24.8	71.9	17.6	82.4	36.63	6 201	621
Springfield city	NA	NA	NA	NA	NA	NA	NA	NA	NA	24.3	72.2	15.3	83.7	38.31	6 254	649
Stow city	16 126	523	12 260	398	12 757	414	19.8	.9	15.1	24.8	71.9	16.9	82.3	36.82	6 160	625
Strongsville city	NA	NA	NA	NA	NA	NA	NA	NA	NA	24.8	71.9	17.6	82.4	36.63	6 201	621
Toledo city	289 807	924	162 946	520	300 942	960	19.1	15.9	6.2	22.5	72.1	14.9	83.4	32.97	6 579	610
Upper Arlington city	24 824	774	16 471	514	21 212	662	19.2	10.4	9.0	26.4	73.2	18.5	83.7	38.09	5 708	797
Warren city	42 369	864	16 390	334	55 436	1 131	9.5	14.6	7.1	24.4	70.5	15.3	83.2	36.11	6 402	491
Westerville city	33 896	993	17 362	509	32 364	948	14.5	15.7	17.0	25.9	73.2	16.5	85.5	39.32	5 719	786
Westlake city	32 049	1 074	18 989	637	26 828	899	12.3	9.4	14.0	24.8	71.9	17.6	82.4	36.63	6 201	621
Youngstown city	69 648	817	29 997	352	72 106	846	18.2	16.4	7.9	23.6	70.3	16.4	81.3	37.32	6 544	497
Zanesville city	NA	NA	NA	NA	NA	NA	NA	NA	NA	26.8	72.7	18.3	83.5	39.42	5 714	716

[1] Based on resident population estimated as of July 1, 1997. [2] Represents normal values for the 30-year period, 1961–1990. [3] Average daily minimum. [4] Average daily maximum. [5] One heating degree day is accumulated for each whole degree that the mean daily temperature is below 65 degrees Fahrenheit. [6] One cooling degree day is accumulated for each whole degree that the mean daily temperature is above 65 degrees Fahrenheit.

Sources: City Government Finances—U.S. Census Bureau, 1997 Census of Governments, Volume 4, Government Finances, GC97(4)-4, Finances of Municipal and Township Governments, issued September 2000 (related Internet site <http://www.census.gov/govs/www/cog.html>). 1997 Population for Government Finances calculations—U.S. Census Bureau, Population Estimates for Places: Annual Time Series, July 1, 1990 to July 1, 1999 (SU-99-7), published 20 October 2000, <http://www.census.gov/estimates/metro-city/placesbyst/SC99T7_US.txt>. Climate: U.S. National Oceanic and Atmospheric Administration (NOAA), National Climatic Data Center (NCDC), Climatography of the United States, Number 81, published January 1992 (related Internet site <http://lwf.ncdc.noaa.gov/oa/climate/normals/usnormals.html>).

Table C–7. Cities — **Government Finances and Climate**–Con.

[Includes states and 1,070 incorporated places of 25,000 or more population as of April 1, 1990 in all states except Hawaii which has no incorporated places recognized by the Census Bureau. For Hawaii, 8 census designated places (CDPs) of 25,000 or more population as of April 1, 1990 are included. Also included are the 5 boroughs of New York city. For more information on these areas, see appendix B. Geographic Information]

City	General revenue — Total ($1,000)	General revenue — Per capita[1] (dollars)	Taxes — Total ($1,000)	Taxes — Per capita[1] (dollars)	General expenditure — Total ($1,000)	General expenditure — Per capita[1] (dollars)	Police protection	Sewerage and solid waste management	Highways	Temp January	Temp July	January[3]	July[4]	Annual precipitation (inches)	Heating degree days[5]	Cooling degree days[6]
OKLAHOMA	X	X	X	X	X	X	X	X	X	X	X	X	X	X	X	X
Bartlesville city	26 636	790	14 775	438	23 506	698	14.5	26.3	9.3	34.7	82.1	22.5	94.7	35.91	3 777	1 868
Broken Arrow city	32 463	456	19 414	273	30 211	425	19.2	21.6	10.0	35.2	83.3	24.9	93.7	40.59	3 691	2 017
Edmond city	34 708	541	16 763	261	41 810	652	16.2	13.9	12.1	35.9	82.0	25.2	93.4	33.36	3 659	1 859
Enid city	36 792	814	17 032	377	37 848	838	10.3	31.2	9.2	35.1	83.3	24.7	95.2	32.35	3 788	2 008
Lawton city	41 168	504	25 045	306	37 664	461	24.1	17.2	7.0	36.8	83.5	23.7	95.8	29.27	3 457	2 069
Midwest City city	104 838	1 933	19 935	367	92 185	1 699	7.7	4.5	3.2	35.9	82.0	25.2	93.4	33.36	3 659	1 859
Moore city	19 300	430	10 855	242	23 765	530	13.8	6.7	4.5	35.9	82.0	25.2	93.4	33.36	3 659	1 859
Muskogee city	84 636	2 210	16 550	432	83 137	2 170	5.4	3.7	4.9	37.3	82.2	26.6	93.8	41.74	3 413	1 937
Norman city	147 441	1 604	29 571	322	138 922	1 511	6.7	6.9	6.5	37.8	82.2	25.6	94.8	35.41	3 295	1 967
Oklahoma City city	511 487	1 092	287 971	615	440 971	942	19.8	12.3	8.6	35.9	82.0	25.2	93.4	33.36	3 659	1 859
Ponca City city	19 911	760	8 299	317	23 487	897	13.0	14.0	5.9	32.4	82.5	22.1	93.8	34.24	4 226	1 865
Shawnee city	41 869	1 542	12 266	452	37 871	1 395	6.8	4.7	8.0	38.3	82.0	25.9	94.9	38.27	3 222	1 954
Stillwater city	61 518	1 601	13 524	352	56 919	1 481	8.7	7.0	4.3	33.6	81.6	21.4	93.1	33.85	4 028	1 755
Tulsa city	480 358	1 267	203 926	538	511 706	1 349	12.9	20.8	2.8	35.2	83.3	24.9	93.7	40.59	3 691	2 017
OREGON	X	X	X	X	X	X	X	X	X	X	X	X	X	X	X	X
Albany city	34 374	907	14 895	393	30 041	793	15.1	10.2	24.6	38.3	64.3	31.6	78.4	66.42	5 287	172
Beaverton city	38 525	594	16 407	253	29 197	450	25.5	6.2	18.8	38.9	65.8	32.5	79.7	37.57	5 011	232
Corvallis city	47 031	951	22 541	456	37 983	768	17.4	17.8	9.9	39.3	65.6	33.0	80.2	42.70	4 923	203
Eugene city	155 505	1 223	61 801	486	147 502	1 160	15.3	12.3	5.4	40.8	67.3	35.2	81.7	49.37	4 546	300
Gresham city	55 071	657	28 580	341	79 869	952	14.9	13.9	5.2	39.6	68.2	33.7	79.9	36.30	4 522	371
Hillsboro city	64 110	1 133	27 380	484	41 872	740	14.7	29.7	10.8	38.9	65.8	32.5	79.7	37.57	5 011	232
Lake Oswego city	35 589	1 012	22 194	631	34 873	992	11.1	11.7	17.2	39.6	68.2	33.7	79.9	36.30	4 522	371
Medford city	47 581	816	25 393	436	40 589	696	23.2	17.9	14.1	38.1	72.9	30.4	90.5	18.86	4 611	725
Portland city	645 402	1 283	320 837	638	686 370	1 364	14.5	26.8	10.0	39.6	68.2	33.7	79.9	36.30	4 522	371
Salem city	116 728	927	53 518	425	113 328	900	14.6	17.3	15.8	39.6	66.3	32.7	81.6	39.16	4 927	247
Springfield city	NA	NA	NA	NA	NA	NA	NA	NA	NA	40.8	67.3	35.2	81.7	49.37	4 546	300
Tigard city	24 107	647	15 136	406	17 548	471	27.0	5.5	17.2	38.9	65.8	32.5	79.7	37.57	5 011	232
PENNSYLVANIA	X	X	X	X	X	X	X	X	X	X	X	X	X	X	X	X
Allentown city	75 009	738	32 544	320	69 764	686	17.2	20.2	10.2	26.6	74.1	18.8	84.5	43.52	5 785	773
Altoona city	20 909	417	10 675	213	20 589	411	19.6	.3	14.6	26.0	71.3	19.1	81.5	36.81	6 140	582
Bethel Park borough	15 430	462	7 957	238	15 488	464	20.5	23.1	14.8	26.1	72.1	18.5	82.6	36.85	5 968	654
Bethlehem city	51 538	735	20 819	297	62 183	887	11.9	22.4	4.0	26.6	74.1	18.8	84.5	43.52	5 785	773
Chester city	NA	NA	NA	NA	NA	NA	NA	NA	NA	32.4	78.3	26.4	87.3	42.45	4 586	1 291
Easton city	24 204	943	6 031	235	24 723	963	12.0	24.2	4.1	26.6	74.1	18.8	84.5	43.52	5 785	773
Erie city	78 075	751	30 320	292	76 188	733	22.5	19.0	8.7	25.4	71.3	18.2	79.9	41.53	6 279	550
Harrisburg city	64 830	1 302	17 291	347	79 578	1 598	13.9	15.9	8.9	28.6	75.7	21.2	85.8	40.50	5 347	962
Johnstown city	NA	NA	NA	NA	NA	NA	NA	NA	NA	28.0	73.2	19.6	85.9	47.75	5 649	739
Lancaster city	39 500	739	14 049	263	42 255	790	18.8	25.6	4.6	27.9	74.1	19.2	84.9	41.22	5 584	780
McKeesport city	NA	NA	NA	NA	NA	NA	NA	NA	NA	26.1	72.1	18.5	82.6	36.85	5 968	654
Municipality of Monroeville borough	21 253	752	15 170	537	NA	NA	NA	NA	NA	26.1	72.1	18.5	82.6	36.85	5 968	654
New Castle city	13 927	525	7 710	291	12 267	462	14.4	13.6	9.0	24.1	70.6	15.0	83.2	37.38	6 542	489
Norristown borough	18 547	626	11 641	393	17 053	575	26.2	7.1	9.1	29.8	75.9	21.4	86.5	44.38	5 114	1 022
Philadelphia city	3 722 582	2 564	1 715 305	1 182	3 445 451	2 373	11.8	7.3	2.9	30.4	76.7	22.8	86.1	41.41	4 954	1 101
Pittsburgh city	483 814	1 402	247 412	717	493 928	1 431	12.9	4.9	6.8	26.1	72.1	18.5	82.6	36.85	5 968	654
Plum borough	6 332	240	4 159	158	8 031	304	22.7	9.3	26.2	26.1	72.1	18.5	82.6	36.85	5 968	654
Reading city	55 607	743	23 051	308	52 446	701	19.3	10.8	5.3	26.6	74.0	17.0	85.1	44.71	5 796	759
Scranton city	46 556	615	30 698	405	50 772	670	19.5	5.3	11.2	24.7	71.7	17.5	81.8	36.18	6 291	539
State College borough	20 151	506	6 071	152	18 408	462	20.7	31.8	7.3	24.7	71.3	16.7	82.0	37.48	6 364	529
Wilkes-Barre city	29 960	688	17 536	403	27 371	628	18.5	8.8	9.0	24.7	71.7	17.5	81.8	36.18	6 291	539
Williamsport city	16 596	544	8 923	292	17 438	572	20.2	1.5	8.8	25.2	72.3	17.1	83.1	40.72	6 087	622
York city	35 759	885	11 960	296	42 284	1 047	15.0	20.8	5.1	29.0	74.5	19.4	86.9	40.40	5 256	860
RHODE ISLAND	X	X	X	X	X	X	X	X	X	X	X	X	X	X	X	X
Cranston city	162 105	2 169	105 083	1 406	148 092	1 982	10.1	8.1	3.5	27.9	72.7	19.1	82.1	45.53	5 884	606
East Providence city	82 875	1 724	53 861	1 120	79 888	1 662	8.2	7.3	3.0	27.9	72.7	19.1	82.1	45.53	5 884	606
Newport city	NA	NA	NA	NA	NA	NA	NA	NA	NA	30.3	70.7	22.6	78.3	44.81	5 659	464
Pawtucket city	118 819	1 742	60 561	888	115 471	1 693	9.5	.1	2.9	27.9	72.7	19.1	82.1	45.53	5 884	606
Providence city	389 984	2 582	179 767	1 190	358 727	2 375	7.3	1.5	.8	27.9	72.7	19.1	82.1	45.53	5 884	606
Warwick city	180 762	2 156	132 931	1 585	176 445	2 104	6.1	4.6	2.2	27.9	72.7	19.1	82.1	45.53	5 884	606
Woonsocket city	81 114	1 942	38 591	924	86 620	2 074	6.1	6.7	1.8	27.9	72.7	19.1	82.1	45.53	5 884	606

[1] Based on resident population estimated as of July 1, 1997.   [2] Represents normal values for the 30-year period, 1961–1990.   [3] Average daily minimum.   [4] Average daily maximum.   [5] One heating degree day is accumulated for each whole degree that the mean daily temperature is below 65 degrees Fahrenheit.   [6] One cooling degree day is accumulated for each whole degree that the mean daily temperature is above 65 degrees Fahrenheit.

Sources: City Government Finances—U.S. Census Bureau, 1997 Census of Governments, Volume 4, Government Finances, GC97(4)-4, Finances of Municipal and Township Governments, issued September 2000 (related Internet site <http://www.census.gov/govs/www/cog.html>).   1997 Population for Government Finances calculations—U.S. Census Bureau, Population Estimates for Places: Annual Time Series, July 1, 1990 to July 1, 1999 (SU-99-7), published 20 October 2000, <http://www.census.gov/estimates/metro-city/placesbyst/SC99T7_US.txt>.   Climate: U.S. National Oceanic and Atmospheric Administration (NOAA), National Climatic Data Center (NCDC), Climatography of the United States, Number 81, published January 1992 (related Internet site <http://lwf.ncdc.noaa.gov/oa/climate/normals/usnormals.html>).

Table C–7. Cities — **Government Finances and Climate**–Con.

[Includes states and 1,070 incorporated places of 25,000 or more population as of April 1, 1990 in all states except Hawaii which has no incorporated places recognized by the Census Bureau. For Hawaii, 8 census designated places (CDPs) of 25,000 or more population as of April 1, 1990 are included. Also included are the 5 boroughs of New York city. For more information on these areas, see appendix B. Geographic Information]

City	City government finances, 1996-1997 General revenue Total ($1,000)	Per capita[1] (dollars)	Taxes Total ($1,000)	Per capita[1] (dollars)	General expenditure Total ($1,000)	Per capita[1] (dollars)	By selected function, percent from— Police protection	Sewerage and solid waste management	Highways	Climate[2] Average daily temperature (degrees Fahrenheit) January	July	January[3]	July[4]	Annual precipitation (inches)	Heating degree days[5]	Cooling degree days[6]
SOUTH CAROLINA	X	X	X	X	X	X	X	X	X	X	X	X	X	X	X	X
Anderson city	18 753	709	8 506	322	19 277	729	16.6	19.7	6.6	42.1	79.8	32.2	89.9	46.38	2 891	1 807
Charleston city	123 277	1 442	56 847	665	94 608	1 107	17.1	17.7	2.3	47.8	81.5	37.7	90.2	51.53	2 013	2 266
Columbia city	110 127	982	43 006	384	98 781	881	17.2	20.4	6.1	43.8	80.8	32.1	91.6	49.91	2 649	1 966
Florence city	20 297	659	10 761	349	17 731	575	23.3	17.4	7.5	43.8	80.6	33.4	90.4	43.84	2 585	1 993
Greenville city	62 516	1 082	37 436	648	55 349	958	18.3	8.9	5.5	40.1	78.2	30.0	88.2	51.27	3 272	1 473
Mount Pleasant town	25 933	626	13 877	335	20 061	484	20.2	28.1	3.0	47.8	81.5	37.7	90.2	51.53	2 013	2 266
North Charleston city	50 358	594	27 863	329	52 932	624	26.5	6.0	3.1	47.8	81.5	37.7	90.2	51.53	2 013	2 266
Rock Hill city	22 455	483	11 920	257	31 348	675	16.9	9.2	3.7	40.9	79.1	30.9	89.2	48.65	3 054	1 624
Spartanburg city	34 022	816	16 346	392	25 116	603	23.2	12.8	11.9	41.9	79.4	31.5	90.6	49.87	2 887	1 688
Sumter city	19 068	418	8 575	188	17 526	385	26.5	22.1	3.9	44.0	80.0	32.4	91.1	48.14	2 609	1 888
SOUTH DAKOTA	X	X	X	X	X	X	X	X	X	X	X	X	X	X	X	X
Rapid City city	59 685	1 031	29 247	505	69 778	1 205	9.9	16.7	4.0	22.3	72.2	10.7	86.2	16.64	7 301	611
Sioux Falls city	103 784	913	62 427	549	93 559	823	10.7	8.6	19.3	13.8	74.3	3.3	86.3	23.86	7 809	744
TENNESSEE	X	X	X	X	X	X	X	X	X	X	X	X	X	X	X	X
Bartlett town	24 663	684	9 196	255	26 023	722	28.8	10.2	15.8	39.7	82.6	30.9	92.3	52.10	3 082	2 118
Chattanooga city	NA	NA	NA	NA	NA	NA	NA	NA	NA	37.4	78.7	28.0	89.0	53.46	3 587	1 544
Clarksville city	47 916	500	13 635	142	36 742	383	21.0	12.0	12.3	34.0	78.1	23.3	90.0	50.75	4 159	1 417
Cleveland city	NA	NA	NA	NA	NA	NA	NA	NA	NA	36.5	76.6	25.8	88.0	54.65	3 884	1 236
Columbia city	24 107	754	5 972	187	20 643	646	17.7	30.6	11.3	34.4	77.1	23.2	88.8	54.26	4 206	1 281
Germantown city	29 110	798	11 572	317	31 491	864	13.5	11.7	5.0	39.7	82.6	30.9	92.3	52.10	3 082	2 118
Hendersonville city	15 838	413	7 813	204	15 482	404	23.1	13.7	17.1	36.2	79.3	26.5	89.5	47.30	3 729	1 616
Jackson city	NA	NA	NA	NA	NA	NA	NA	NA	NA	37.0	80.1	27.3	90.9	52.88	3 540	1 744
Johnson City city	103 082	1 783	25 273	437	106 317	1 839	6.4	11.7	10.5	34.0	74.4	24.3	84.6	40.72	4 406	972
Kingsport city	87 928	2 044	23 422	544	77 531	1 802	7.4	7.4	5.0	36.1	75.8	26.4	87.1	43.79	3 901	1 167
Knoxville city	194 249	1 125	100 738	583	241 617	1 399	10.4	17.7	12.9	36.0	76.6	26.0	87.1	47.14	3 937	1 266
Memphis city	1 164 973	1 902	228 537	373	1 187 872	1 940	11.1	7.0	4.3	39.7	82.6	30.9	92.3	52.10	3 082	2 118
Murfreesboro city	82 169	1 442	20 928	367	74 961	1 316	8.7	10.0	6.1	35.2	77.9	24.5	89.3	53.17	3 992	1 405
Nashville-Davidson (remainder)	[7]1 337 743	[7]2 614	[7]690 549	[7]1 349	[7]1 355 766	[7]2 649	[7]6.9	[7]7.2	[7]2.9	36.2	79.3	26.5	89.5	47.30	3 729	1 616
Oak Ridge city	55 193	2 014	12 029	439	60 341	2 202	5.2	9.7	6.1	35.0	75.8	25.1	86.7	53.77	4 183	1 156
TEXAS	X	X	X	X	X	X	X	X	X	X	X	X	X	X	X	X
Abilene city	68 722	634	41 359	382	65 533	605	16.3	11.8	11.3	42.8	84.0	30.8	95.2	24.40	2 584	2 451
Amarillo city	109 328	642	49 757	292	110 309	648	15.6	14.5	17.9	35.1	78.6	21.2	91.7	19.56	4 258	1 354
Arlington city	183 615	613	103 234	345	175 963	588	20.9	14.1	14.7	43.4	85.3	32.7	96.5	33.70	2 407	2 603
Austin city	631 273	1 113	253 841	448	629 427	1 110	12.2	11.9	6.2	48.8	84.5	38.6	95.0	31.88	1 688	3 016
Baytown city	48 648	707	25 870	376	51 808	752	22.1	12.3	12.5	50.5	83.1	40.6	91.4	51.85	1 550	2 809
Beaumont city	94 463	858	63 427	576	104 479	948	17.6	9.3	16.4	49.6	82.3	39.5	91.9	55.58	1 677	2 581
Bedford city	NA	NA	NA	NA	NA	NA	NA	NA	NA	43.4	85.3	32.7	96.5	33.70	2 407	2 603
Brownsville city	57 557	403	24 981	175	62 651	439	18.4	12.5	8.7	59.4	84.5	49.9	93.3	26.61	635	3 888
Bryan city	41 390	708	18 556	317	42 355	724	14.1	20.7	7.4	48.5	83.6	38.7	93.8	39.08	1 788	2 776
Carrollton city	79 815	809	49 614	503	63 246	641	16.9	10.9	16.9	43.4	85.3	32.7	96.5	33.70	2 407	2 603
College Station city	39 936	671	21 847	367	43 979	739	10.4	21.2	5.3	48.5	83.6	38.7	93.8	39.08	1 788	2 776
Conroe city	26 711	730	19 073	521	22 304	609	19.1	12.7	8.5	48.8	83.1	37.9	94.0	47.33	1 774	2 676
Corpus Christi city	202 632	721	90 284	321	165 241	588	21.5	11.2	6.1	55.1	84.1	45.3	93.3	30.13	1 016	3 439
Dallas city	1 452 293	1 371	575 291	543	1 194 426	1 128	15.7	13.9	6.7	44.6	85.9	34.5	95.7	36.08	2 259	2 763
Deer Park city	14 759	483	14 387	470	13 012	425	24.7	12.2	5.3	52.2	83.5	42.9	92.3	50.83	1 371	3 012
Del Rio city	NA	NA	NA	NA	NA	NA	NA	NA	NA	50.2	85.2	38.5	96.2	18.24	1 506	3 142
Denton city	59 305	786	24 581	326	51 999	689	16.8	21.7	9.2	41.9	83.2	30.3	94.0	37.27	2 665	2 225
DeSoto city	28 561	806	13 746	388	41 139	1 161	8.9	5.0	2.7	44.6	85.9	34.5	95.7	36.08	2 259	2 763
Duncanville city	21 604	600	11 896	330	24 140	670	19.1	27.8	12.6	44.6	85.9	34.5	95.7	36.08	2 259	2 763
Edinburg city	NA	NA	NA	NA	NA	NA	NA	NA	NA	58.5	85.4	48.5	95.8	22.83	693	4 076
El Paso city	355 240	592	181 190	302	316 830	528	22.7	12.6	6.6	42.8	82.3	29.4	96.1	8.81	2 708	2 094
Euless city	25 039	586	12 937	303	46 876	1 097	11.5	7.9	2.1	43.4	85.3	32.7	96.5	33.70	2 407	2 603
Fort Worth city	482 390	995	239 755	494	433 457	894	19.7	21.9	11.7	43.4	85.3	32.7	96.5	33.70	2 407	2 603
Galveston city	71 633	1 191	28 330	471	60 559	1 007	11.3	11.7	4.2	52.7	83.3	47.1	87.3	42.28	1 263	2 994
Garland city	128 881	674	58 414	305	130 304	681	17.3	17.8	20.2	44.6	85.9	34.5	95.7	36.08	2 259	2 763
Grand Prairie city	91 456	827	45 991	416	79 619	720	19.4	15.9	7.0	43.4	85.3	32.7	96.5	33.70	2 407	2 603
Grapevine city	49 956	1 268	24 364	619	75 451	1 915	6.8	4.5	15.1	41.6	83.7	30.0	94.9	33.68	2 683	2 328
Haltom City city	16 167	449	9 982	277	15 282	424	31.7	20.9	6.7	43.4	85.3	32.7	96.5	33.70	2 407	2 603
Harlingen city	45 075	806	17 178	307	43 952	786	12.6	18.9	8.1	57.3	83.9	46.7	94.4	27.53	813	3 662
Houston city	1 733 823	959	891 815	493	1 907 215	1 055	19.9	20.8	8.7	52.2	83.5	42.9	92.3	50.83	1 371	3 012
Huntsville city	13 520	421	6 435	201	11 780	367	18.7	20.7	14.4	47.6	83.3	37.6	94.4	44.96	1 862	2 654
Hurst city	25 945	709	18 844	515	41 193	1 125	14.1	9.3	8.1	43.4	85.3	32.7	96.5	33.70	2 407	2 603
Irving city	132 310	746	89 040	502	139 708	787	12.2	17.5	11.2	44.6	85.9	34.5	95.7	36.08	2 259	2 763
Killeen city	37 631	474	21 062	265	32 729	412	23.8	21.6	8.1	45.4	84.0	34.5	95.2	34.87	2 153	2 623

[1] Based on resident population estimated as of July 1, 1997. [2] Represents normal values for the 30-year period, 1961–1990. [3] Average daily minimum. [4] Average daily maximum. [5] One heating degree day is accumulated for each whole degree that the mean daily temperature is below 65 degrees Fahrenheit. [6] One cooling degree day is accumulated for each whole degree that the mean daily temperature is above 65 degrees Fahrenheit. [7] Data are for consolidated city of Nashville-Davidson; data for Nashville-Davidson (remainder) not available.

Sources: City Government Finances—U.S. Census Bureau, 1997 Census of Governments, Volume 4, Government Finances, GC97(4)-4, Finances of Municipal and Township Governments, issued September 2000 (related Internet site <http://www.census.gov/govs/www/cog.html>). 1997 Population for Government Finances calculations—U.S. Census Bureau, Population Estimates for Places: Annual Time Series, July 1, 1990 to July 1, 1999 (SU-99-7), published 20 October 2000, <http://www.census.gov/estimates/metro-city/placesbyst/SC99T7_US.txt>. Climate: U.S. National Oceanic and Atmospheric Administration (NOAA), National Climatic Data Center (NCDC), Climatography of the United States, Number 81, published January 1992 (related Internet site <http://lwf.ncdc.noaa.gov/oa/climate/normals/usnormals.html>).

Table C–7. Cities — **Government Finances and Climate**–Con.

[Includes states and 1,070 incorporated places of 25,000 or more population as of April 1, 1990 in all states except Hawaii which has no incorporated places recognized by the Census Bureau. For Hawaii, 8 census designated places (CDPs) of 25,000 or more population as of April 1, 1990 are included. Also included are the 5 boroughs of New York city. For more information on these areas, see appendix B. Geographic Information]

City	City government finances, 1996-1997									Climate[2]						
	General revenue				General expenditure					Average daily temperature (degrees Fahrenheit)						
			Taxes				By selected function, percent from—									
	Total ($1,000)	Per capita[1] (dollars)	Total ($1,000)	Per capita[1] (dollars)	Total ($1,000)	Per capita[1] (dollars)	Police protection	Sewerage and solid waste management	Highways	January	July	January[3]	July[4]	Annual precipitation (inches)	Heating degree days[5]	Cooling degree days[6]
TEXAS—Con.																
Kingsville city	11 064	437	6 457	255	10 547	416	22.7	31.2	—	56.4	84.3	44.7	95.0	27.60	911	3 590
La Porte city	26 277	813	10 933	338	23 262	720	18.2	13.7	8.5	52.2	83.5	42.9	92.3	50.83	1 371	3 012
Laredo city	197 446	1 156	36 755	215	182 256	1 067	9.5	6.4	13.6	54.4	86.9	42.9	98.8	21.42	1 025	3 915
League City city	25 848	620	16 837	404	26 011	624	15.1	11.7	17.0	52.2	83.5	42.9	92.3	50.83	1 371	3 012
Lewisville city	45 787	690	29 989	452	37 625	567	20.0	16.6	11.7	41.9	83.2	30.3	94.0	37.27	2 665	2 225
Longview city	49 111	656	33 439	446	53 549	715	17.8	15.2	15.8	44.0	82.6	32.7	93.2	47.27	2 433	2 249
Lubbock city	165 342	862	51 083	266	123 211	642	17.2	19.5	9.4	38.8	80.0	24.6	91.9	18.65	3 431	1 689
Lufkin city	26 368	794	16 329	492	24 773	746	18.3	19.2	24.0	47.6	82.8	36.9	93.2	42.40	1 951	2 551
McAllen city	88 653	824	39 736	369	38 888	361	25.7	6.3	4.9	58.5	85.4	48.5	95.8	22.83	693	4 076
Mesquite city	75 233	665	45 641	403	90 041	796	18.0	10.6	14.2	44.6	85.9	34.5	95.7	36.08	2 259	2 763
Midland city	71 682	731	36 849	376	72 911	744	15.6	24.5	6.2	43.6	81.4	28.5	94.6	15.21	2 570	2 132
Mission city	NA	NA	NA	NA	NA	NA	NA	NA	NA	57.1	85.5	45.8	96.7	22.82	829	3 985
Missouri City city	16 578	283	14 048	240	21 340	364	28.7	11.7	16.4	52.2	83.5	42.9	92.3	50.83	1 371	3 012
Nacogdoches city	18 903	604	10 311	329	20 707	661	13.3	28.7	2.5	47.6	82.8	36.9	93.2	42.40	1 951	2 551
New Braunfels city	NA	NA	NA	NA	NA	NA	NA	NA	NA	48.2	83.7	36.5	95.3	34.27	1 790	2 791
North Richland Hills city	37 630	697	24 518	454	20 125	373	29.1	—	8.0	43.4	85.3	32.7	96.5	33.70	2 407	2 603
Odessa city	55 768	621	24 115	269	52 520	585	23.1	17.9	12.0	42.5	82.0	28.5	95.4	14.96	2 751	2 163
Pasadena city	73 520	557	47 079	357	65 031	493	26.9	10.8	7.9	52.2	83.5	42.9	92.3	50.83	1 371	3 012
Pharr city	NA	NA	NA	NA	NA	NA	NA	NA	NA	58.5	85.4	48.5	95.8	22.83	693	4 076
Plano city	153 252	738	96 920	466	148 889	717	13.0	16.1	11.2	43.4	85.3	32.7	96.5	33.70	2 407	2 603
Port Arthur city	35 635	627	13 501	238	46 426	817	16.9	17.9	12.2	50.9	82.8	41.5	91.9	57.18	1 499	2 764
Richardson city	101 182	1 217	53 597	645	96 151	1 157	16.4	15.4	8.7	44.6	85.9	34.5	95.7	36.08	2 259	2 763
Round Rock city	28 890	508	18 849	331	26 615	468	17.4	7.4	14.8	48.8	84.5	38.6	95.0	31.88	1 688	3 016
San Angelo city	47 102	534	27 442	311	46 519	527	23.5	7.7	9.9	43.7	82.7	30.6	96.2	20.45	2 414	2 400
San Antonio city	776 859	694	317 163	283	856 914	766	17.8	13.1	9.1	49.3	85.0	37.9	95.0	30.98	1 644	2 996
San Marcos city	24 064	649	12 068	325	35 685	962	11.7	14.2	14.6	48.1	83.2	36.2	94.7	34.55	1 818	2 712
Sherman city	28 427	867	15 551	474	21 095	643	19.9	19.6	9.1	40.5	83.3	29.8	94.6	40.39	2 890	2 209
Temple city	42 129	790	22 561	423	41 747	782	15.2	11.4	7.8	45.4	84.0	34.5	95.2	34.87	2 153	2 623
Texarkana city	28 715	878	15 035	460	27 567	843	17.6	21.0	8.0	44.5	82.8	35.0	93.0	46.89	2 295	2 380
Texas City city	NA	NA	NA	NA	NA	NA	NA	NA	NA	52.7	83.3	47.1	87.3	42.28	1 263	2 994
Tyler city	62 913	765	29 301	356	54 258	660	20.5	14.2	9.5	46.4	83.2	35.0	95.2	39.74	2 105	2 490
Victoria city	42 662	706	25 064	415	34 800	576	22.9	14.9	11.9	52.7	84.1	42.5	93.5	37.41	1 296	3 118
Waco city	96 184	888	46 700	431	90 399	835	16.5	16.6	9.7	45.2	85.6	34.2	96.8	31.96	2 179	2 816
Wichita Falls city	64 410	647	33 858	340	67 082	674	16.5	16.0	8.7	39.8	85.0	27.6	97.2	28.90	3 042	2 340
UTAH	X	X	X	X	X	X	X	X	X	X	X	X	X	X	X	X
Bountiful city	16 235	392	8 343	201	20 997	507	37.5	11.0	10.4	27.9	77.9	19.3	92.2	16.18	5 765	1 047
Layton city	25 125	470	12 986	243	23 925	448	19.2	20.4	20.0	28.6	76.2	19.6	92.0	22.09	5 799	927
Logan city	25 848	632	9 329	228	27 658	677	12.6	22.3	9.6	23.6	73.0	15.5	86.7	19.52	6 854	623
Murray city	25 608	771	15 165	457	23 913	720	25.9	6.7	19.5	27.9	77.9	19.3	92.2	16.18	5 765	1 047
Ogden city	57 041	832	31 162	454	49 078	716	11.2	12.4	8.0	28.9	77.8	19.8	92.3	22.59	5 557	1 096
Orem city	38 235	477	21 182	264	38 538	481	15.1	16.0	18.6	28.0	74.5	18.3	90.2	17.04	5 907	745
Provo city	48 021	450	23 569	221	56 144	527	15.2	7.5	4.0	28.0	74.5	18.3	90.2	17.04	5 907	745
St. George city	33 739	742	14 552	320	32 465	714	12.9	18.5	11.8	32.2	73.5	19.8	88.8	18.23	5 452	687
Salt Lake City city	314 397	1 832	120 961	705	275 808	1 607	12.4	7.7	10.4	27.9	77.9	19.3	92.2	16.18	5 765	1 047
Sandy city	38 171	389	23 870	243	42 347	431	17.6	5.7	17.5	27.9	77.9	19.3	92.2	16.18	5 765	1 047
West Jordan city	26 285	441	13 528	227	26 384	442	20.4	12.8	9.1	27.9	77.9	19.3	92.2	16.18	5 765	1 047
West Valley City city	43 513	438	26 850	270	85 076	856	10.5	.9	8.0	27.9	77.9	19.3	92.2	16.18	5 765	1 047
VERMONT	X	X	X	X	X	X	X	X	X	X	X	X	X	X	X	X
Burlington city	NA	NA	NA	NA	NA	NA	NA	NA	NA	16.3	70.5	7.5	81.2	34.47	7 771	388
VIRGINIA	X	X	X	X	X	X	X	X	X	X	X	X	X	X	X	X
Alexandria city	367 733	3 235	216 416	1 904	347 959	3 061	7.8	7.2	5.9	34.6	80.0	26.8	88.5	38.63	4 047	1 549
Blacksburg town	15 944	471	4 845	143	14 785	437	21.0	20.0	5.6	29.6	70.6	19.0	82.3	40.91	5 574	514
Charlottesville city	82 635	2 184	44 299	1 171	91 876	2 429	7.5	5.8	4.9	34.5	76.4	25.5	86.7	47.29	4 224	1 156
Chesapeake city	424 519	2 166	221 506	1 130	474 748	2 422	4.5	3.4	8.7	39.1	78.2	30.9	86.4	44.64	3 495	1 422
Danville city	106 729	2 034	32 198	614	119 583	2 279	5.0	8.5	5.4	36.1	78.0	25.4	89.6	43.18	3 944	1 381
Hampton city	294 788	2 123	125 304	902	284 720	2 051	6.2	5.3	2.5	39.1	78.2	30.9	86.4	44.64	3 495	1 422
Harrisonburg city	57 748	1 720	31 685	944	59 537	1 773	5.1	19.5	8.0	31.3	74.3	20.5	86.7	35.24	4 908	876
Lynchburg city	159 195	2 445	68 557	1 053	152 091	2 336	5.4	6.0	7.9	34.2	75.6	24.7	86.0	40.88	4 340	1 048
Manassas city	76 444	2 375	40 685	1 264	72 058	2 239	7.8	9.0	4.5	33.0	77.2	22.9	88.7	36.13	4 447	1 198
Newport News city	397 609	2 275	170 964	978	428 770	2 453	7.1	4.8	5.3	39.1	78.2	30.9	86.4	44.64	3 495	1 422
Norfolk city	687 807	2 920	245 339	1 042	703 367	2 986	6.3	4.3	3.1	39.1	78.2	30.9	86.4	44.64	3 495	1 422
Petersburg city	NA	NA	NA	NA	NA	NA	NA	NA	NA	38.6	78.9	27.8	90.3	43.53	3 408	1 533

[1] Based on resident population estimated as of July 1, 1997.   [2] Represents normal values for the 30-year period, 1961–1990.   [3] Average daily minimum.   [4] Average daily maximum.   [5] One heating degree day is accumulated for each whole degree that the mean daily temperature is below 65 degrees Fahrenheit.   [6] One cooling degree day is accumulated for each whole degree that the mean daily temperature is above 65 degrees Fahrenheit.

Sources: City Government Finances—U.S. Census Bureau, 1997 Census of Governments, Volume 4, Government Finances, GC97(4)-4, Finances of Municipal and Township Governments, issued September 2000 (related Internet site <http://www.census.gov/govs/www/cog.html>).   1997 Population for Government Finances calculations—U.S. Census Bureau, Population Estimates for Places: Annual Time Series, July 1, 1990 to July 1, 1999 (SU-99-7), published 20 October 2000, <http://www.census.gov/estimates/metro-city/placesbyst/SC99T7_US.txt>.   Climate: U.S. National Oceanic and Atmospheric Administration (NOAA), National Climatic Data Center (NCDC), Climatography of the United States, Number 81, published January 1992 (related Internet site <http://lwf.ncdc.noaa.gov/oa/climate/normals/usnormals.html>).

Table C–7. Cities — **Government Finances and Climate**–Con.

[Includes states and 1,070 incorporated places of 25,000 or more population as of April 1, 1990 in all states except Hawaii which has no incorporated places recognized by the Census Bureau. For Hawaii, 8 census designated places (CDPs) of 25,000 or more population as of April 1, 1990 are included. Also included are the 5 boroughs of New York city. For more information on these areas, see appendix B. Geographic Information]

City	City government finances, 1996-1997									Climate[2]						
	General revenue				General expenditure					Average daily temperature (degrees Fahrenheit)						
			Taxes				By selected function, percent from—									
	Total ($1,000)	Per capita[1] (dollars)	Total ($1,000)	Per capita[1] (dollars)	Total ($1,000)	Per capita[1] (dollars)	Police protection	Sewerage and solid waste management	Highways	January	July	January[3]	July[4]	Annual precipitation (inches)	Heating degree days[5]	Cooling degree days[6]
VIRGINIA—Con.																
Portsmouth city	243 566	2 450	85 180	857	256 018	2 575	4.8	5.1	3.2	39.1	78.2	30.9	86.4	44.64	3 495	1 422
Richmond city	726 991	3 811	276 113	1 447	779 892	4 088	5.7	8.2	2.3	35.7	78.0	25.7	88.4	43.16	3 963	1 348
Roanoke city	264 943	2 791	114 334	1 204	251 990	2 654	5.2	6.3	3.6	34.5	75.6	25.0	86.4	41.13	4 360	1 052
Suffolk city	120 682	1 974	48 942	800	134 486	2 199	4.2	6.3	3.3	39.1	78.2	30.9	86.4	44.64	3 495	1 422
Virginia Beach city	859 871	1 995	437 768	1 015	823 900	1 911	5.6	4.6	2.6	39.1	78.2	30.9	86.4	44.64	3 495	1 422
WASHINGTON	X	X	X	X	X	X	X	X	X	X	X	X	X	X	X	X
Auburn city...............	52 678	1 419	23 618	636	41 200	1 110	17.1	22.7	14.2	39.7	64.7	33.1	78.0	39.39	4 996	139
Bellevue city	153 110	1 488	90 875	883	144 391	1 403	10.4	11.2	16.0	40.1	65.2	35.2	75.2	37.19	4 908	190
Bellingham city	67 623	1 105	33 925	554	57 013	932	12.9	10.9	15.0	37.6	62.2	31.8	70.9	36.17	5 609	51
Bremerton city	33 340	804	15 734	380	37 342	901	13.3	28.1	8.5	39.1	64.1	33.7	75.0	51.65	5 119	134
Edmonds city	28 141	696	12 854	318	23 477	581	17.9	5.5	12.9	40.1	65.2	35.2	75.2	37.19	4 908	190
Everett city	116 247	1 368	67 553	795	117 922	1 387	12.5	12.0	11.0	39.1	62.9	33.3	72.2	36.51	5 311	80
Kennewick city	43 364	867	20 248	405	41 729	834	13.0	7.6	34.4	33.1	74.7	26.1	90.3	7.49	4 895	830
Kent city	85 459	1 309	40 952	627	93 798	1 437	10.9	14.9	11.1	39.7	64.7	33.1	78.0	39.39	4 996	139
Kirkland city	46 849	1 056	25 129	566	47 986	1 081	10.1	24.4	11.3	40.1	65.2	35.2	75.2	37.19	4 908	190
Longview city	31 939	932	15 521	453	33 185	968	17.1	18.4	14.6	39.0	63.8	32.7	76.4	46.54	5 094	132
Lynnwood city	46 235	1 395	20 134	608	51 071	1 541	9.0	6.0	42.3	40.1	65.2	35.2	75.2	37.19	4 908	190
Olympia city	61 799	1 557	26 087	657	53 029	1 336	11.7	19.8	5.8	38.0	62.9	31.6	76.5	50.59	5 655	101
Redmond city	62 051	1 424	33 513	769	57 439	1 318	8.9	20.9	22.1	40.1	65.2	35.2	75.2	37.19	4 908	190
Renton city	80 189	1 772	38 281	846	74 074	1 636	12.6	19.9	19.7	40.1	65.2	35.2	75.2	37.19	4 908	190
Richland city	39 916	1 070	16 045	430	52 824	1 416	6.6	11.0	19.3	33.4	74.4	25.9	89.4	6.99	4 882	822
Seattle city	940 112	1 762	474 018	888	1 117 867	2 095	12.6	17.2	9.4	40.1	65.2	35.2	75.2	37.19	4 908	190
Spokane city	192 095	1 034	77 400	416	188 979	1 017	12.2	28.8	7.7	27.1	68.8	20.8	83.1	16.49	6 842	398
Tacoma city	243 556	1 381	97 245	552	236 589	1 342	15.7	24.3	8.4	40.1	65.2	35.2	75.2	37.19	4 908	190
Vancouver city	83 638	742	33 869	300	83 388	739	10.1	18.1	8.1	38.1	64.6	31.2	77.1	41.30	5 196	183
Walla Walla city	25 992	901	7 926	275	29 110	1 010	9.1	28.4	13.1	34.1	75.1	28.4	89.4	19.49	4 958	889
Yakima city	59 352	830	28 768	403	63 036	882	16.1	20.5	13.3	29.7	69.9	21.8	86.7	7.97	5 967	458
WEST VIRGINIA	X	X	X	X	X	X	X	X	X	X	X	X	X	X	X	X
Charleston city	79 960	1 430	42 068	752	77 749	1 390	13.1	10.8	5.3	32.1	75.1	23.0	85.7	42.53	4 646	1 031
Huntington city	42 387	795	18 096	339	42 259	793	13.8	13.4	4.7	32.0	74.7	23.2	84.3	41.49	4 665	1 005
Morgantown city	23 466	799	9 345	318	21 247	724	14.3	27.1	7.2	29.0	72.9	20.8	83.2	41.21	5 363	785
Parkersburg city	89 199	2 696	9 980	302	86 769	2 623	4.0	5.3	4.0	29.9	74.4	21.7	84.2	41.51	5 063	953
Wheeling city.............	26 596	797	11 755	352	19 876	596	17.6	22.8	10.7	27.7	73.3	17.6	85.4	40.81	5 598	788
WISCONSIN	X	X	X	X	X	X	X	X	X	X	X	X	X	X	X	X
Appleton city	73 087	1 091	26 380	394	63 095	942	13.7	19.1	17.2	15.5	71.9	7.2	81.9	30.75	7 693	539
Beloit city	43 903	1 216	7 802	216	42 296	1 171	17.2	17.3	13.4	17.6	72.7	8.8	83.7	33.05	7 161	636
Brookfield city	40 109	1 053	19 038	500	34 967	918	15.6	22.6	16.3	19.9	73.6	12.3	84.3	31.11	6 804	725
Eau Claire city	51 962	869	14 324	240	55 338	926	14.1	13.4	20.6	10.7	71.5	.8	83.2	31.61	8 330	507
Fond du Lac city	37 848	923	13 936	340	36 820	898	14.7	17.3	20.2	16.1	72.0	7.9	82.0	29.39	7 541	562
Green Bay city	104 976	1 052	32 447	325	107 026	1 073	15.3	18.3	20.0	14.3	69.7	5.8	80.5	28.83	8 089	381
Greenfield city	27 969	814	14 744	429	23 172	674	23.9	12.2	15.7	18.9	70.9	11.6	79.9	32.93	7 324	479
Janesville city	51 115	855	14 757	247	58 268	975	12.1	17.5	15.7	17.6	72.7	8.8	83.7	33.05	7 161	636
Kenosha city	76 559	865	28 443	321	74 829	845	18.6	13.8	11.0	20.0	69.7	11.7	78.7	33.21	7 195	410
La Crosse city	56 764	1 128	17 155	341	57 166	1 136	13.2	10.6	12.7	14.4	73.5	5.3	84.5	30.55	7 491	692
Madison city	233 354	1 110	92 701	441	212 306	1 010	15.6	12.4	10.7	16.0	71.0	7.2	82.4	30.88	7 673	485
Manitowoc city	32 650	980	7 447	224	32 519	976	12.9	16.1	19.0	17.9	69.8	9.7	80.1	29.11	7 597	374
Menomonee Falls village ...	34 106	1 105	14 983	485	40 370	1 307	12.5	30.4	19.3	18.9	70.9	11.6	79.9	32.93	7 324	479
Milwaukee city	697 923	1 194	164 954	282	720 567	1 233	21.6	15.3	8.0	19.9	73.6	12.3	84.3	31.11	6 804	725
New Berlin city	28 045	760	11 495	312	63 412	1 719	8.5	20.5	8.3	19.8	73.6	12.3	83.0	32.33	6 795	708
Oshkosh city	54 395	904	14 958	249	50 687	843	13.7	15.0	21.6	14.8	71.8	5.4	82.5	31.15	7 852	522
Racine city	96 362	1 165	33 365	403	88 778	1 073	24.2	13.4	11.4	19.4	71.0	11.2	79.7	34.37	7 167	509
Sheboygan city	47 782	951	16 184	322	48 649	968	14.8	15.6	15.2	20.3	70.9	12.8	80.4	31.19	7 087	472
Superior city	40 405	1 461	9 032	327	34 307	1 241	13.2	14.4	14.9	10.0	65.9	-.1	77.5	28.91	9 483	206
Waukesha city............	52 847	853	25 883	418	54 704	883	16.1	16.1	17.6	18.6	72.3	10.8	82.8	32.55	7 117	600
Wausau city	37 084	997	12 202	328	35 912	965	14.4	12.5	23.2	12.0	70.0	2.8	80.8	32.82	8 427	402
Wauwatosa city	44 736	964	24 269	523	51 205	1 103	18.1	19.4	16.4	19.9	73.6	12.3	84.3	31.11	6 804	725
West Allis city	58 432	973	24 582	409	58 955	982	20.8	13.1	16.2	19.8	73.6	12.3	83.0	32.33	6 795	708
WYOMING	X	X	X	X	X	X	X	X	X	X	X	X	X	X	X	X
Casper city...............	49 768	1 020	3 072	63	41 878	858	15.4	20.4	9.6	22.4	70.8	12.0	87.6	12.52	7 682	445
Cheyenne city	46 837	873	5 164	96	39 939	745	13.4	14.2	21.5	26.5	68.4	15.2	82.2	14.40	7 326	285
Laramie city	25 143	985	1 721	67	23 401	917	10.8	14.6	44.6	20.0	64.1	8.0	80.4	10.88	9 008	74

[1] Based on resident population estimated as of July 1, 1997. [2] Represents normal values for the 30-year period, 1961–1990. [3] Average daily minimum. [4] Average daily maximum. [5] One heating degree day is accumulated for each whole degree that the mean daily temperature is below 65 degrees Fahrenheit. [6] One cooling degree day is accumulated for each whole degree that the mean daily temperature is above 65 degrees Fahrenheit.

Sources: City Government Finances—U.S. Census Bureau, 1997 Census of Governments, Volume 4, Government Finances, GC97(4)-4, Finances of Municipal and Township Governments, issued September 2000 (related Internet site <http://www.census.gov/govs/www/cog.html>). 1997 Population for Government Finances calculations—U.S. Census Bureau, Population Estimates for Places: Annual Time Series, July 1, 1990 to July 1, 1999 (SU-99-7), published 20 October 2000, <http://www.census.gov/estimates/metro-city/placesbyst/SC99T7_US.txt>. Climate: U.S. National Oceanic and Atmospheric Administration (NOAA), National Climatic Data Center (NCDC), Climatography of the United States, Number 81, published January 1992 (related Internet site <http://lwf.ncdc.noaa.gov/oa/climate/normals/usnormals.html>).

Places/MCDs

Table D

Page

You may visit us on the Web at
http://www.census.gov/statab/www/ccdb.html

Table D

Places/MCDs

Table D-1. Places — Area and Population

[Includes incorporated places and census designated places (CDPs) of 2,500 or more population as of April 1, 2000. Codes shown are two-digit Federal Information Processing Standards (FIPS) state codes and five-digit FIPS place codes. Place names and codes are those in effect as of January 1, 2000. County refers to the county (or counties) in which the place is located. IC in this column = independent city, a county equivalent. If a place is located in more than one county, counties are listed in alphabetic order]

State and place code	Place	County	Land area, 2000 (sq. mi.)	Population, 2000 (April 1) By race— One race Total	White	Black or African American	American Indian and Alaska Native	Asian	Native Hawaiian and Other Pacific Islander	Some other race	Two or more races	Hispanic or Latino (of any race)	18 years and over
01 00000	ALABAMA		50,744.0	4,447,100	3,162,808	1,155,930	22,430	31,346	1,409	28,998	44,179	75,830	3,323,678
01 00124	Abbeville city	Henry	15.6	2,987	1,692	1,193	-	2	-	85	15	105	2,302
01 00460	Adamsville city	Jefferson	19.6	4,965	3,763	1,133	20	7	1	8	33	26	3,818
01 00820	Alabaster city	Shelby	20.5	22,619	19,839	2,250	71	144	4	156	155	348	16,343
01 00988	Albertville city	Marshall	26.0	17,247	14,859	353	54	45	17	1,687	232	2,773	12,760
01 01132	Alexander City city	Tallapoosa	38.8	15,008	10,589	4,258	19	42	3	23	74	67	11,372
01 01180	Alexandria CDP	Calhoun	11.1	3,692	3,265	360	10	22	4	9	22	24	2,682
01 01228	Aliceville city	Pickens	4.5	2,567	829	1,708	3	8	-	-	19	10	1,792
01 01708	Andalusia city	Covington	18.9	8,794	6,501	2,152	32	24	2	16	67	69	6,750
01 01852	Anniston city	Calhoun	45.4	24,276	11,825	11,821	66	189	18	148	209	409	18,546
01 02116	Arab city	Cullman, Marshall	12.8	7,174	7,051	13	35	28	-	12	35	47	5,461
01 02956	Athens city	Limestone	39.3	18,967	14,741	3,464	76	134	3	365	184	922	14,425
01 03004	Atmore city	Escambia	8.3	7,676	3,798	3,555	185	36	4	28	70	56	5,646
01 03028	Attalla city	Etowah	6.7	6,592	5,533	872	23	12	-	108	44	164	5,029
01 03076	Auburn city	Lee	39.1	42,987	33,553	7,217	82	1,422	17	244	452	666	36,383
01 04660	Bay Minette city	Baldwin	8.0	7,820	5,030	2,617	47	34	1	33	58	80	5,807
01 05980	Bessemer city	Jefferson	40.7	29,672	8,584	20,638	82	52	5	90	221	338	21,724
01 07000	Birmingham city	Jefferson, Shelby	149.9	242,820	58,457	178,372	422	1,942	87	1,513	2,027	3,764	182,013
01 07912	Boaz city	Etowah, Marshall	12.2	7,411	6,929	97	35	33	3	223	91	369	5,708
01 09136	Brent city	Bibb	8.7	4,024	1,969	2,013	3	8	-	20	11	39	3,176
01 09208	Brewton city	Escambia	11.3	5,498	3,167	2,212	23	27	-	29	40	61	4,191
01 09328	Bridgeport city	Jackson	3.1	2,728	2,394	219	39	3	-	10	63	36	2,072
01 09400	Brighton city	Jefferson	1.4	3,640	328	3,244	14	1	1	32	20	63	2,711
01 11248	Cahaba Heights CDP	Jefferson	2.0	5,203	4,992	61	11	75	-	19	45	39	4,299
01 11416	Calera city	Chilton, Shelby	12.9	3,158	2,445	629	6	17	2	21	38	60	2,314
01 13264	Center Point CDP	Jefferson	8.0	22,784	16,610	5,521	63	126	7	233	224	507	16,726
01 13648	Centre city	Cherokee	11.0	3,216	2,827	322	12	4	-	10	41	31	2,590
01 13720	Chalkville CDP	Jefferson	2.9	3,829	3,688	89	9	18	2	3	20	22	2,688
01 14104	Chelsea town	Shelby	10.0	2,949	2,854	23	26	5	1	17	23	24	2,085
01 14392	Chickasaw city	Mobile	4.4	6,364	5,657	517	86	15	1	19	69	73	4,859
01 14464	Childersburg city	Shelby, Talladega	7.7	4,927	3,393	1,465	16	3	1	13	36	30	3,598
01 15064	Citronelle city	Mobile	24.4	3,659	2,816	681	101	5	1	9	46	30	2,624
01 15136	Clanton city	Chilton	20.3	7,800	6,030	1,561	23	26	1	101	58	206	5,943
01 15256	Clay CDP	Jefferson	10.3	4,947	4,846	35	15	20	-	6	25	20	3,430
01 16768	Columbiana city	Shelby	15.2	3,316	2,606	650	8	5	1	22	24	66	2,457
01 18970	Cullman city	Cullman	18.3	13,995	13,496	50	34	63	6	148	198	679	10,947
01 19336	Dadeville city	Tallapoosa	16.0	3,212	1,710	1,448	8	9	-	12	25	26	2,395
01 19360	Daleville city	Dale	13.5	4,653	2,987	1,180	35	170	10	102	169	183	3,429
01 19648	Daphne city	Baldwin	13.5	16,581	14,148	2,048	50	101	1	72	161	254	12,342
01 20104	Decatur city	Limestone, Morgan	53.4	53,929	40,714	10,548	312	376	68	1,195	716	3,040	40,236
01 20296	Demopolis city	Marengo	12.2	7,540	3,600	3,838	7	15	-	36	44	74	5,349
01 21184	Dothan city	Dale, Henry, Houston	86.6	57,737	38,873	17,385	160	491	11	265	552	764	43,061
01 23296	Elba city	Coffee	15.4	4,185	2,675	1,435	27	1	1	8	38	43	3,194
01 24184	Enterprise city	Coffee, Dale	31.0	21,178	15,167	4,861	101	339	33	270	407	821	15,806
01 24568	Eufaula city	Barbour	59.4	13,908	7,967	5,621	40	65	5	120	90	213	9,926
01 24808	Evergreen city	Conecuh	15.2	3,630	1,678	1,916	7	7	1	3	18	30	2,612
01 25120	Fairfield city	Jefferson	3.5	12,381	1,102	11,171	7	19	2	21	59	73	9,070
01 25240	Fairhope city	Baldwin	11.0	12,480	11,259	972	25	77	5	26	116	130	9,784
01 25840	Fayette city	Fayette	8.6	4,922	3,708	1,151	6	14	-	15	28	47	3,870
01 26896	Florence city	Lauderdale	24.9	36,264	28,428	6,963	86	226	12	197	352	487	28,496
01 26992	Foley city	Baldwin	14.3	7,590	5,654	1,659	45	42	3	100	87	352	5,836
01 27088	Forestdale CDP	Jefferson	6.9	10,509	5,556	4,826	17	37	-	18	55	48	8,116
01 27616	Fort Payne city	DeKalb	55.9	12,938	10,767	586	103	71	21	1,088	302	1,574	9,915
01 27640	Fort Rucker CDP	Dale	10.9	6,052	4,147	1,097	57	124	45	319	263	707	3,914
01 28552	Fultondale city	Jefferson	12.3	6,595	6,041	352	42	25	-	66	69	105	5,147
01 28696	Gadsden city	Etowah	36.0	38,978	24,434	13,252	118	208	32	477	457	1,039	29,994
01 29056	Gardendale city	Jefferson	17.9	11,626	11,299	172	20	62	2	16	55	75	9,122
01 29464	Geneva city	Geneva	14.9	4,388	3,691	622	14	2	1	20	38	48	3,337
01 29992	Glencoe city	Calhoun, Etowah	16.1	5,152	4,994	89	15	9	1	5	39	18	4,009
01 31024	Grand Bay CDP	Mobile	8.7	3,918	3,487	348	9	31	2	5	36	34	2,832
01 31348	Grayson Valley CDP	Jefferson	2.3	5,447	5,151	194	15	31	-	5	51	38	4,025
01 31720	Greensboro city	Hale	2.4	2,731	1,046	1,663	1	-	-	-	21	24	1,949
01 31912	Greenville city	Butler	21.2	7,228	3,664	3,492	20	26	-	4	22	62	5,290
01 32272	Gulf Shores city	Baldwin	18.4	5,044	4,920	11	22	15	2	20	54	62	4,216
01 32416	Guntersville city	Marshall	23.6	7,395	6,520	631	36	30	1	70	107	212	5,736
01 32704	Haleyville city	Marion, Winston	7.4	4,182	3,965	62	7	5	-	112	31	130	3,240
01 32848	Hamilton city	Marion	36.1	6,786	6,135	515	22	33	2	33	46	116	5,442
01 32968	Hanceville city	Cullman	4.1	2,951	2,747	136	18	2	1	22	25	68	2,425
01 33448	Hartselle city	Morgan	14.9	12,019	11,087	620	76	37	2	40	157	155	8,949
01 33472	Harvest CDP	Madison	12.4	3,054	2,338	573	39	34	-	6	64	30	2,180
01 33808	Hazel Green CDP	Madison	10.0	3,805	3,560	101	50	19	1	12	62	67	2,615
01 33856	Headland city	Henry	16.0	3,523	2,379	1,102	7	3	-	1	31	7	2,611
01 33976	Heflin city	Cleburne	11.8	3,002	2,578	355	7	10	-	23	29	58	2,331
01 34024	Helena city	Jefferson, Shelby	17.1	10,296	9,601	515	21	67	2	36	54	103	7,340
01 35392	Hokes Bluff city	Etowah	11.6	4,149	4,107	4	9	3	-	10	16	19	3,198
01 35704	Holt CDP	Tuscaloosa	3.2	4,103	2,120	1,930	18	1	-	5	29	61	2,972
01 35800	Homewood city	Jefferson	8.3	25,043	19,972	3,831	49	643	7	250	291	702	19,955
01 35896	Hoover city	Jefferson, Shelby	43.1	62,742	54,997	4,248	99	1,812	21	881	684	2,380	47,200

U.S. Census Bureau, County and City Data Book: 2000

[Includes incorporated places and census designated places (CDPs) of 2,500 or more population as of April 1, 2000. Codes shown are two-digit Federal Information Processing Standards (FIPS) state codes and five-digit FIPS place codes. Place names and codes are those in effect as of January 1, 2000. County refers to the county (or counties) in which the place is located. IC in this column = independent city, a county equivalent. If a place is located in more than one county, counties are listed in alphabetic order]

State and place code	Place	County	Land area, 2000 (sq. mi.)	Population, 2000 (April 1) By race— One race								Hispanic or Latino (of any race)	18 years and over
				Total	White	Black or African American	American Indian and Alaska Native	Asian	Native Hawaiian and Other Pacific Islander	Some other race	Two or more races		
01 00000	ALABAMA—Con.												
01 36448	Hueytown city	Jefferson	11.6	15,364	12,877	2,380	22	20	-	12	53	72	11,958
01 36592	Huguley CDP	Chambers	8.8	2,953	2,178	743	3	2	-	3	24	30	2,191
01 37000	Huntsville city	Limestone, Madison	174.0	158,216	101,998	47,792	857	3,519	88	1,047	2,915	3,225	121,601
01 37864	Irondale city	Jefferson	9.0	9,813	7,035	2,481	14	93	2	95	93	263	7,448
01 38152	Jackson city	Clarke	15.1	5,419	3,274	2,086	14	20	-	11	14	35	3,977
01 38272	Jacksonville city	Calhoun	8.3	8,404	6,404	1,696	29	108	6	65	96	157	7,005
01 38416	Jasper city	Walker	26.9	14,052	11,825	1,965	29	74	3	75	81	189	10,973
01 40648	Ladonia CDP	Russell	3.2	3,229	2,965	169	21	7	-	10	57	47	2,395
01 40672	La Fayette city	Chambers	8.9	3,234	1,037	2,176	1	5	-	7	8	23	2,471
01 40806	Lake Purdy CDP	Shelby	3.0	5,799	5,023	451	22	240	1	27	35	199	4,564
01 41296	Lanett city	Chambers	5.4	7,897	3,582	4,231	9	17	-	8	50	63	5,848
01 41968	Leeds city	Jefferson, St. Clair, Shelby	22.3	10,455	8,571	1,663	36	50	8	42	85	140	7,892
01 43120	Lincoln city	Talladega	21.3	4,577	3,291	1,238	14	3	-	3	28	32	3,530
01 43720	Livingston city	Sumter	7.1	3,297	1,247	2,004	5	6	-	10	25	47	2,432
01 44728	Luverne city	Crenshaw	12.4	2,635	1,851	749	2	4	1	3	25	18	2,028
01 45784	Madison city	Limestone, Madison	23.2	29,329	23,506	3,812	185	1,029	18	197	582	675	20,445
01 46768	Marion city	Perry	10.6	3,511	1,273	2,193	9	3	3	9	21	34	2,545
01 47740	Meadowbrook CDP	Shelby	2.5	4,697	4,429	135	2	98	-	3	30	31	3,250
01 48112	Meridianville CDP	Madison	15.7	4,117	3,566	387	44	30	2	8	80	29	2,983
01 48376	Midfield city	Jefferson	2.6	5,626	2,210	3,347	5	24	2	6	32	8	4,004
01 48712	Millbrook city	Autauga, Elmore	9.5	10,386	8,294	1,777	57	59	2	58	139	150	7,097
01 50000	Mobile city	Mobile	117.9	198,915	100,251	92,068	487	3,022	52	1,046	1,989	2,828	146,144
01 50192	Monroeville city	Monroe	13.1	6,862	3,643	3,077	26	40	-	10	66	62	4,962
01 50312	Montevallo city	Shelby	7.6	4,825	3,500	1,249	19	19	3	7	28	76	3,944
01 51000	Montgomery city	Montgomery	155.4	201,568	96,085	100,048	500	2,146	71	748	1,970	2,484	149,276
01 51096	Moody town	St. Clair	23.9	8,053	7,577	307	34	18	-	30	87	88	5,944
01 51216	Moores Mill CDP	Madison	13.9	5,178	4,019	962	68	41	1	5	82	51	3,733
01 51600	Moulton city	Lawrence	5.9	3,260	2,602	489	90	11	-	3	65	27	2,584
01 51696	Mountain Brook city	Jefferson	12.2	20,604	20,324	63	9	134	4	25	45	119	14,763
01 52344	Mount Olive CDP	Jefferson	9.5	3,957	3,882	3	13	2	-	-	57	31	3,028
01 53016	Muscle Shoals city	Colbert	12.2	11,924	10,002	1,689	45	67	-	37	84	138	8,968
01 54168	New Hope city	Madison	8.8	2,539	2,407	10	46	6	-	17	53	24	1,878
01 55200	Northport city	Tuscaloosa	14.6	19,435	13,820	5,058	37	155	30	199	136	374	14,600
01 57000	Oneonta city	Blount	15.3	5,576	4,788	413	27	11	-	248	89	738	4,375
01 57048	Opelika city	Lee	52.8	23,498	12,932	10,079	45	218	2	63	159	252	17,008
01 57120	Opp city	Covington	17.1	6,607	5,498	1,038	22	15	-	5	29	45	5,069
01 57144	Orange Beach city	Baldwin	10.4	3,784	3,588	14	26	8	-	77	71	105	3,154
01 57576	Oxford city	Calhoun, Talladega	18.2	14,592	12,762	1,442	55	91	4	114	124	281	10,978
01 57648	Ozark city	Dale	34.2	15,119	10,323	4,279	102	106	8	69	232	314	11,352
01 58848	Pelham city	Shelby	38.0	14,369	12,935	571	51	241	-	405	166	923	10,687
01 58896	Pell City city	St. Clair	24.6	9,565	7,978	1,471	15	21	2	25	53	120	7,275
01 59472	Phenix City city	Lee, Russell	24.6	28,265	14,964	12,710	65	149	6	157	214	421	20,837
01 59640	Piedmont city	Calhoun, Cherokee	9.8	5,120	4,545	480	5	4	1	22	63	51	3,982
01 60648	Pinson CDP	Jefferson	7.0	5,033	4,522	419	16	20	1	17	38	114	3,610
01 61008	Pleasant Grove city	Jefferson	8.8	9,983	8,453	1,442	19	15	-	16	38	28	7,545
01 62328	Prattville city	Autauga, Elmore	23.2	24,303	20,193	3,505	103	156	12	129	205	416	17,382
01 62496	Prichard city	Mobile	25.4	28,633	4,059	24,203	87	33	6	20	225	162	19,628
01 63288	Rainbow City city	Etowah	25.1	8,428	7,846	296	29	122	-	43	92	122	6,491
01 63336	Rainsville city	DeKalb	19.9	4,499	4,369	4	20	4	4	49	49	98	3,435
01 63576	Red Bay city	Franklin	9.8	3,374	3,268	49	7	-	-	21	29	27	2,641
01 65040	Roanoke city	Randolph	18.8	6,563	3,868	2,610	4	17	-	22	42	78	4,858
01 65208	Robertsdale city	Baldwin	5.5	3,782	3,565	125	27	9	-	16	40	73	2,719
01 67056	Russellville city	Franklin	13.2	8,971	7,115	1,009	31	11	24	676	105	1,134	6,798
01 67608	Saks CDP	Calhoun	12.1	10,698	9,037	1,375	42	75	8	56	105	177	8,153
01 68160	Saraland city	Mobile	21.9	12,288	10,875	1,102	69	56	1	46	139	144	9,418
01 68352	Satsuma city	Mobile	6.5	5,687	5,330	287	31	14	-	9	16	33	4,210
01 68736	Scottsboro city	Jackson	47.3	14,762	13,449	788	150	79	4	83	209	221	11,393
01 69120	Selma city	Dallas	13.9	20,512	5,901	14,293	21	114	2	46	135	138	14,915
01 69180	Selmont-West Selmont CDP	Dallas	3.3	3,502	277	3,199	5	3	-	1	17	30	2,232
01 69648	Sheffield city	Colbert	6.6	9,652	6,873	2,530	38	27	4	55	125	145	7,367
01 71136	Smiths CDP	Lee	71.2	21,756	18,448	2,756	82	84	2	161	223	453	15,133
01 71832	Southside city	Calhoun, Etowah	18.9	7,036	6,903	43	16	17	-	9	48	47	5,339
01 71976	Spanish Fort city	Baldwin	6.4	5,423	5,078	237	20	40	-	14	34	51	4,003
01 72600	Springville town	St. Clair	6.4	2,521	2,283	195	4	7	4	-	28	6	1,893
01 73848	Sumiton city	Jefferson, Walker	5.3	2,665	2,484	96	9	4	1	16	55	19	2,096
01 74352	Sylacauga city	Talladega	18.5	12,616	8,727	3,647	33	37	7	50	115	123	9,456
01 74592	Talladega city	Talladega	23.9	15,143	8,503	6,402	27	46	3	56	106	136	11,267
01 74688	Tallassee city	Elmore, Tallapoosa	9.6	4,934	3,964	869	17	15	1	9	59	53	3,724
01 74976	Tarrant city	Jefferson	6.4	7,022	5,557	1,315	26	10	1	59	54	120	5,313
01 75768	Theodore CDP	Mobile	11.9	6,811	4,843	1,742	42	88	-	28	68	94	4,871
01 75960	Thomasville city	Clarke	8.7	4,649	2,433	2,151	4	15	-	24	22	42	3,329
01 76320	Tillmans Corner CDP	Mobile	17.5	15,685	14,676	495	95	148	1	63	207	192	11,617
01 76920	Troy city	Pike	26.2	13,935	8,207	5,373	36	96	2	61	160	181	10,782
01 76944	Trussville city	Jefferson, St. Clair	22.2	12,924	12,507	191	42	55	1	48	80	109	9,378
01 77256	Tuscaloosa city	Tuscaloosa	56.2	77,906	42,143	33,287	127	1,162	19	490	678	1,092	62,466
01 77280	Tuscumbia city	Colbert	7.3	7,856	5,971	1,768	23	11	-	16	67	76	6,221
01 77304	Tuskegee city	Macon	15.5	11,846	307	11,310	22	82	1	20	104	81	9,164

Table D-1. Places — **Area and Population**—Con.

[Includes incorporated places and census designated places (CDPs) of 2,500 or more population as of April 1, 2000. Codes shown are two-digit Federal Information Processing Standards (FIPS) state codes and five-digit FIPS place codes. Place names and codes are those in effect as of January 1, 2000. County refers to the county (or counties) in which the place is located. IC in this column = independent city, a county equivalent. If a place is located in more than one county, counties are listed in alphabetic order]

State and place code	Place	County	Land area, 2000 (sq. mi.)	Population, 2000 (April 1)									
					By race—							Hispanic or Latino (of any race)	18 years and over
					One race						Two or more races		
				Total	White	Black or African American	American Indian and Alaska Native	Asian	Native Hawaiian and Other Pacific Islander	Some other race			
01 00000	ALABAMA—Con.												
01 77580	Underwood-Petersville CDP	Lauderdale	6.0	3,137	2,970	129	6	11	-	3	18	17	2,435
01 77880	Union Springs city	Bullock	6.9	3,670	837	2,731	12	18	1	33	38	251	2,554
01 78204	Valley city	Chambers	9.7	9,198	6,454	2,647	12	32	-	10	43	77	6,990
01 78552	Vestavia Hills city	Jefferson, Shelby	14.6	24,476	23,119	454	27	604	24	85	163	334	18,156
01 79944	Warrior city	Blount, Jefferson	7.9	3,169	2,637	488	13	5	-	1	25	10	2,445
01 80352	Weaver city	Calhoun	2.6	2,619	2,280	227	12	31	9	15	45	60	1,941
01 81084	West End-Cobb Town CDP	Calhoun	4.1	3,924	3,049	785	24	2	1	12	51	35	3,030
01 81720	Wetumpka city	Elmore	8.5	5,726	3,882	1,661	23	23	4	79	54	133	4,673
01 82992	Winfield city	Fayette, Marion	16.2	4,540	4,293	191	9	10	-	9	28	54	3,482
01 84096	York city	Sumter	7.1	2,854	591	2,235	2	2	1	1	22	31	1,985
02 00000	ALASKA		571,951.3	626,932	434,534	21,787	98,043	25,116	3,309	9,997	34,146	25,852	436,215
02 03000	Anchorage municipality	Anchorage	1,697.2	260,283	188,009	15,199	18,941	14,433	2,423	5,703	15,575	14,799	184,412
02 05200	Barrow city	North Slope	18.4	4,581	1,000	46	2,620	431	62	32	390	153	2,901
02 06520	Bethel city	Bethel	43.8	5,471	1,468	51	3,380	157	9	28	378	93	3,528
02 07070	Big Lake CDP	Matanuska-Susitna	131.9	2,635	2,296	9	193	7	1	23	106	52	1,910
02 09710	Butte CDP	Matanuska-Susitna	40.3	2,561	2,369	13	74	3	2	13	87	32	1,780
02 16750	College CDP	Fairbanks North Star	18.7	11,402	8,876	355	1,020	364	9	124	654	396	8,361
02 21370	Eielson AFB CDP	Fairbanks North Star	52.0	5,400	4,412	506	34	115	9	116	208	314	3,195
02 24230	Fairbanks city	Fairbanks North Star	31.9	30,224	20,150	3,370	2,994	821	164	740	1,985	1,854	21,324
02 28200	Gateway CDP	Matanuska-Susitna	16.3	2,952	2,605	21	118	27	4	29	148	71	1,933
02 33140	Homer city	Kenai Peninsula	10.6	3,946	3,573	13	167	36	4	29	124	95	2,857
02 36400	Juneau city and borough	Juneau	2,716.7	30,711	22,969	248	3,496	1,438	116	323	2,121	1,040	22,294
02 37250	Kalifornsky CDP	Kenai Peninsula	69.2	5,846	5,247	14	269	39	5	35	237	115	4,017
02 38420	Kenai city	Kenai Peninsula	29.9	6,942	5,745	34	607	115	16	78	347	265	4,665
02 38970	Ketchikan city	Ketchikan Gateway	3.4	7,922	5,340	59	1,394	543	16	41	529	268	5,797
02 40645	Knik-Fairview CDP	Matanuska-Susitna	69.8	7,049	6,198	47	403	53	6	55	287	214	4,664
02 40950	Kodiak city	Kodiak Island	3.5	6,334	2,939	44	663	2,010	59	276	343	541	4,488
02 41830	Kotzebue city	Northwest Arctic	27.0	3,082	600	10	2,194	56	2	24	196	36	1,855
02 42832	Lakes CDP	Matanuska-Susitna	13.6	6,706	6,001	40	307	36	6	37	279	131	4,484
02 47735	Meadow Lakes CDP	Matanuska-Susitna	67.0	4,819	4,234	26	261	29	10	28	231	145	3,208
02 54050	Nikiski CDP	Kenai Peninsula	69.6	4,327	3,771	5	327	31	22	36	135	57	2,876
02 54920	Nome city	Nome	12.5	3,505	1,328	30	1,789	54	2	15	287	72	2,387
02 58660	Palmer city	Matanuska-Susitna	3.8	4,533	3,669	93	371	48	15	52	285	159	3,008
02 60310	Petersburg city	Wrangell-Petersburg	43.9	3,224	2,632	10	232	89	6	60	195	92	2,263
02 68560	Seward city	Kenai Peninsula	14.4	2,830	2,041	69	472	52	5	25	166	68	2,210
02 70540	Sitka city and borough	Sitka	2,874.0	8,835	6,052	28	1,641	335	31	83	665	290	6,436
02 71640	Soldotna city	Kenai Peninsula	6.9	3,759	3,310	11	187	65	14	48	124	121	2,575
02 73070	Sterling CDP	Kenai Peninsula	77.3	4,705	4,361	17	153	25	5	28	116	57	3,266
02 75077	Tanaina CDP	Matanuska-Susitna	27.1	4,993	4,388	27	233	30	1	69	245	172	3,205
02 80770	Unalaska city	Aleutians West	111.0	4,283	1,893	157	330	1,312	24	399	168	551	3,659
02 82200	Valdez city	Valdez-Cordova	222.0	4,036	3,375	17	290	88	18	57	191	160	2,838
02 83080	Wasilla city	Matanuska-Susitna	11.7	5,469	4,674	32	287	72	7	72	325	201	3,632
04 00000	ARIZONA		113,634.6	5,130,632	3,873,611	158,873	255,879	92,236	6,733	596,774	146,526	1,295,617	3,763,685
04 00870	Ajo CDP	Pima	28.1	3,705	2,916	9	255	11	3	339	172	1,392	2,942
04 02830	Apache Junction city	Maricopa, Pinal	34.2	31,814	29,478	194	316	166	23	991	646	2,801	25,299
04 03530	Arizona City CDP	Pinal	6.1	4,385	3,751	50	96	17	3	353	115	726	3,374
04 04720	Avondale city	Maricopa	41.3	35,883	22,704	1,866	459	678	52	8,727	1,397	16,589	23,595
04 04880	Avra Valley CDP	Pima	22.1	5,038	4,233	91	84	19	2	486	123	1,044	3,451
04 05770	Benson city	Cochise	35.7	4,711	4,208	34	61	22	6	268	112	935	3,790
04 06015	Big Park CDP	Yavapai	4.5	5,245	5,012	19	19	32	1	80	82	356	4,577
04 06260	Bisbee city	Cochise	4.8	6,090	5,123	28	74	30	4	674	157	2,094	4,772
04 06610	Black Canyon City CDP	Yavapai	20.0	2,697	2,585	4	33	5	1	20	49	92	2,225
04 07940	Buckeye town	Maricopa	145.8	6,537	4,742	220	112	29	5	1,264	165	2,396	4,330
04 08220	Bullhead City city	Mohave	45.2	33,769	28,896	340	452	339	25	2,787	930	6,807	26,175
04 09690	Camp Verde town	Yavapai	42.6	9,451	8,038	33	691	21	13	444	211	1,034	7,186
04 10180	Carefree town	Maricopa	8.8	2,927	2,880	7	1	13	-	10	16	78	2,554
04 10530	Casa Grande city	Pinal	48.2	25,224	16,371	1,077	1,238	294	25	5,321	898	9,871	17,427
04 10670	Casas Adobes CDP	Pima	22.6	54,011	47,889	891	355	1,180	33	2,414	1,249	7,434	41,572
04 11160	Catalina CDP	Pima	13.9	7,025	5,986	38	101	28	11	682	179	1,663	5,094
04 11230	Catalina Foothills CDP	Pima	44.5	53,794	49,140	653	265	1,744	50	931	1,011	4,062	43,090
04 11300	Cave Creek town	Maricopa	28.2	3,728	3,541	11	7	16	2	97	54	263	2,949
04 11720	Central Heights-Midland City CDP	Gila	1.7	2,694	2,348	1	28	6	6	248	57	685	1,975
04 12000	Chandler city	Maricopa	57.9	176,581	136,296	6,151	2,121	7,453	251	18,993	5,316	37,059	123,956
04 12770	Chinle CDP	Apache	16.0	5,366	343	10	4,898	9	2	32	72	98	3,009
04 12840	Chino Valley town	Yavapai	18.6	7,835	7,370	18	74	12	6	203	152	766	5,756
04 13890	Clarkdale town	Yavapai	7.3	3,422	2,892	10	233	12	2	185	88	404	2,685
04 14380	Clifton town	Greenlee	14.9	2,596	1,742	25	59	1	-	694	75	1,450	1,757
04 14870	Colorado City town	Mohave	10.5	3,334	3,229	6	-	3	7	30	59	97	1,320
04 15500	Coolidge city	Pinal	5.0	7,786	4,504	646	438	56	4	1,836	302	3,052	5,228
04 15920	Cornville CDP	Yavapai	13.2	3,335	3,109	13	28	20	2	90	73	304	2,518
04 16410	Cottonwood city	Yavapai	10.7	9,179	7,824	45	144	38	3	887	238	1,884	7,030

Table D-1. Places — **Area and Population**—Con.

[Includes incorporated places and census designated places (CDPs) of 2,500 or more population as of April 1, 2000. Codes shown are two-digit Federal Information Processing Standards (FIPS) state codes and five-digit FIPS place codes. Place names and codes are those in effect as of January 1, 2000. County refers to the county (or counties) in which the place is located. IC in this column = independent city, a county equivalent. If a place is located in more than one county, counties are listed in alphabetic order]

State and place code	Place	County	Land area, 2000 (sq. mi.)	Population, 2000 (April 1) Total	By race— One race White	Black or African American	American Indian and Alaska Native	Asian	Native Hawaiian and Other Pacific Islander	Some other race	Two or more races	Hispanic or Latino (of any race)	18 years and over
04 00000	ARIZONA—Con.												
04 16485	Cottonwood-Verde Village CDP	Yavapai	8.8	10,610	9,663	34	132	49	6	471	255	1,186	8,000
04 19145	Dewey-Humboldt CDP	Yavapai	22.9	6,295	6,070	14	37	21	2	94	57	328	5,236
04 20050	Douglas city	Cochise	7.7	14,312	9,045	70	155	63	12	4,552	415	12,306	9,514
04 20505	Drexel-Alvernon CDP	Pima	0.9	4,192	2,372	215	83	23	3	1,320	176	2,434	2,841
04 20540	Drexel Heights CDP	Pima	19.7	23,849	13,867	625	815	195	23	7,460	864	14,327	16,238
04 20960	Eagar town	Apache	11.3	4,033	3,512	17	135	5	14	198	152	564	2,572
04 22220	El Mirage city	Maricopa	9.7	7,609	5,042	250	65	29	4	1,992	227	5,084	4,808
04 22360	Eloy city	Pinal	71.7	10,375	5,468	552	465	124	11	3,266	489	7,717	6,874
04 23620	Flagstaff city	Coconino	63.6	52,894	41,214	927	5,284	660	65	3,201	1,543	8,500	40,060
04 23760	Florence town	Pinal	8.3	17,054	9,741	1,563	753	141	9	4,568	279	6,041	15,760
04 23960	Flowing Wells CDP	Pima	3.4	15,050	12,674	134	219	99	8	1,372	544	3,290	11,224
04 24460	Fort Defiance CDP	Apache	6.1	4,061	184	7	3,771	12	1	9	77	55	2,436
04 25030	Fortuna Foothills CDP	Yuma	40.0	20,478	18,443	91	143	107	15	1,348	331	2,609	18,068
04 25300	Fountain Hills town	Maricopa	18.2	20,235	19,478	119	99	180	12	133	214	618	16,486
04 27400	Gilbert town	Maricopa	43.0	109,697	94,043	2,639	676	3,937	134	5,233	3,035	13,026	72,215
04 27820	Glendale city	Maricopa	55.7	218,812	165,293	10,270	3,181	6,003	293	26,188	7,584	54,343	152,950
04 28030	Globe city	Gila	18.0	7,486	5,809	86	232	84	3	1,092	180	2,449	5,555
04 28120	Gold Camp CDP	Pinal	22.3	6,029	5,800	18	40	29	4	82	56	213	5,281
04 28195	Golden Valley CDP	Mohave	28.0	4,515	4,244	23	43	33	7	82	83	363	3,504
04 28380	Goodyear city	Maricopa	116.5	18,911	14,775	983	200	323	16	2,056	558	3,933	14,713
04 29710	Green Valley CDP	Pima	26.2	17,283	16,997	31	32	57	9	63	94	394	17,013
04 30270	Guadalupe town	Maricopa	0.8	5,228	913	56	2,310	7	11	1,632	299	3,782	3,285
04 32310	Heber-Overgaard CDP	Navajo	7.0	2,722	2,583	2	63	4	3	39	28	165	2,133
04 33280	Holbrook city	Navajo	15.4	4,917	2,915	116	1,180	51	-	412	243	1,148	3,164
04 36475	Kachina Village CDP	Coconino	1.2	2,664	2,370	9	114	8	1	127	35	259	1,972
04 36990	Kayenta CDP	Navajo	13.2	4,922	317	10	4,514	6	2	8	65	46	2,737
04 37620	Kingman city	Mohave	30.0	20,069	18,051	111	398	288	28	685	508	1,856	15,048
04 39370	Lake Havasu City city	Mohave	43.0	41,938	39,568	129	291	245	41	1,051	613	3,298	33,787
04 39720	Lake Montezuma CDP	Yavapai	12.0	3,344	3,096	3	78	6	-	93	68	243	2,690
04 41330	Litchfield Park city	Maricopa	3.1	3,810	3,508	53	15	110	8	57	59	209	2,909
04 44270	Marana town	Pima	72.7	13,556	11,094	392	286	334	20	1,014	416	2,663	9,930
04 46000	Mesa city	Maricopa	125.0	396,375	323,655	9,977	6,572	5,917	932	38,271	11,051	78,281	287,998
04 47400	Mohave Valley CDP	Mohave	45.3	13,694	12,433	62	320	129	16	447	287	1,640	10,328
04 49270	New Kingman-Butler CDP	Mohave	14.6	14,810	13,514	65	250	63	17	444	457	1,374	11,004
04 49360	New River CDP	Maricopa	70.8	10,740	10,296	45	64	49	5	134	147	521	7,948
04 49640	Nogales city	Santa Cruz	20.8	20,878	16,249	78	120	67	15	3,751	598	19,539	13,650
04 51180	Oracle CDP	Pinal	11.4	3,563	2,744	5	54	3	7	615	135	1,365	2,622
04 51600	Oro Valley town	Pima	31.8	29,700	27,652	315	122	570	35	543	463	2,218	23,308
04 51810	Page city	Coconino	16.6	6,809	4,584	27	1,817	46	13	110	212	320	4,631
04 52930	Paradise Valley town	Maricopa	15.5	13,664	13,063	100	27	276	5	54	139	364	10,267
04 53070	Parker town	LaPaz	22.0	3,140	1,948	59	725	27	5	234	142	935	2,110
04 53210	Parker Strip CDP	LaPaz	7.1	3,302	3,057	19	66	27	-	73	60	299	2,775
04 53560	Paulden CDP	Yavapai	62.7	3,420	3,146	18	81	7	4	98	66	535	2,341
04 53700	Payson town	Gila	19.5	13,620	12,905	36	257	72	7	183	160	708	10,881
04 54050	Peoria city	Maricopa, Yavapai	138.2	108,364	92,050	3,012	734	2,077	120	7,686	2,685	16,699	77,623
04 55000	Phoenix city	Maricopa	474.9	1,321,045	938,853	67,416	26,696	26,449	1,766	216,589	43,276	449,972	938,610
04 55300	Picture Rocks CDP	Pima	55.6	8,139	7,295	47	114	31	6	438	208	1,120	5,698
04 55980	Pinetop-Lakeside town	Navajo	11.3	3,582	3,194	37	82	12	1	165	91	407	2,670
04 57380	Prescott city	Yavapai	37.1	33,938	31,538	171	432	283	21	941	552	2,773	28,551
04 57450	Prescott Valley town	Yavapai	31.7	23,535	21,441	114	227	129	34	1,081	509	2,617	17,236
04 58010	Quartzsite town	LaPaz	36.3	3,354	3,169	8	39	9	2	87	40	169	3,163
04 58150	Queen Creek town	Maricopa, Pinal	25.8	4,316	3,545	15	23	14	3	617	99	1,294	2,788
04 60186	Rio Rico Northeast CDP	Santa Cruz	31.6	3,164	2,218	11	28	46	6	751	104	2,124	2,079
04 60188	Rio Rico Northwest CDP	Santa Cruz	16.1	2,882	1,811	20	21	35	1	931	63	2,516	1,680
04 60192	Rio Rico Southwest CDP	Santa Cruz	19.2	2,777	1,970	12	27	20	3	668	77	2,364	1,665
04 62000	Safford city	Graham	7.9	9,232	6,940	130	93	86	4	1,713	266	3,667	6,442
04 62140	Sahuarita town	Pima	15.2	3,242	2,848	19	35	32	-	240	68	784	2,413
04 62350	St. Johns city	Apache	6.6	3,269	2,631	12	204	9	1	298	114	758	2,109
04 62910	San Carlos CDP	Gila	8.8	3,716	169	9	3,442	11	-	9	76	97	2,150
04 63470	San Luis city	Yuma	26.4	15,322	9,007	452	224	25	3	5,265	346	13,657	9,873
04 63540	San Manuel CDP	Pinal	20.9	4,375	3,021	17	60	15	3	1,084	175	2,022	2,949
04 65000	Scottsdale city	Maricopa	184.2	202,705	186,883	2,501	1,240	3,964	167	4,603	3,347	14,111	163,540
04 65350	Sedona city	Coconino, Yavapai	18.6	10,192	9,394	50	46	96	9	437	160	907	8,791
04 65490	Sells CDP	Pima	9.4	2,799	79	1	2,696	6	-	5	12	91	1,827
04 66470	Show Low city	Navajo	27.9	7,695	6,848	21	302	50	6	312	156	795	5,447
04 66820	Sierra Vista city	Cochise	153.5	37,775	27,706	4,115	313	1,347	174	2,285	1,835	5,971	28,020
04 66845	Sierra Vista Southeast CDP	Cochise	112.3	14,348	12,121	315	193	259	66	806	588	2,308	10,467
04 67800	Snowflake town	Navajo	30.8	4,460	3,891	12	309	22	3	134	89	359	2,769
04 68080	Somerton city	Yuma	1.3	7,266	3,235	27	47	25	1	3,714	217	6,915	4,443
04 68850	South Tucson city	Pima	1.0	5,490	2,386	127	502	22	3	2,264	186	4,460	3,760
04 70240	Summit CDP	Pima	10.1	3,702	2,439	19	82	5	1	961	195	2,349	2,414
04 70320	Sun City CDP	Maricopa	14.5	38,309	37,710	196	48	115	10	63	167	383	38,142
04 70355	Sun City West CDP	Maricopa	11.1	26,344	26,005	129	14	97	10	18	71	154	26,318
04 70530	Sun Lakes CDP	Maricopa	5.2	11,936	11,741	93	16	38	1	12	35	112	11,916
04 71300	Superior town	Pinal	1.9	3,254	2,365	15	53	11	3	750	57	2,248	2,378
04 71510	Surprise city	Maricopa	69.5	30,848	26,521	806	134	329	16	2,427	615	7,184	24,713
04 72000	Tanque Verde CDP	Pima	32.9	16,195	15,269	113	90	211	18	220	274	1,180	12,097

Table D-1. Places — **Area and Population**—Con.

[Includes incorporated places and census designated places (CDPs) of 2,500 or more population as of April 1, 2000. Codes shown are two-digit Federal Information Processing Standards (FIPS) state codes and five-digit FIPS place codes. Place names and codes are those in effect as of January 1, 2000. County refers to the county (or counties) in which the place is located. IC in this column = independent city, a county equivalent. If a place is located in more than one county, counties are listed in alphabetic order]

| State and place code | Place | County | Land area, 2000 (sq. mi.) | Population, 2000 (April 1) By race— One race | | | | | | | Two or more races | Hispanic or Latino (of any race) | 18 years and over |
				Total	White	Black or African American	American Indian and Alaska Native	Asian	Native Hawaiian and Other Pacific Islander	Some other race			
04 00000	ARIZONA—Con.												
04 72420	Taylor town	Navajo	24.6	3,176	2,826	17	168	4	2	87	72	292	1,901
04 73000	Tempe city	Maricopa	40.1	158,625	122,952	5,801	3,186	7,531	455	13,464	5,236	28,473	127,144
04 73420	Thatcher town	Graham	4.4	4,022	3,408	31	74	21	3	397	88	786	2,912
04 73700	Three Points CDP	Pima	44.5	5,273	3,723	37	134	21	6	1,168	184	2,151	3,598
04 74190	Tolleson city	Maricopa	5.6	4,974	2,597	71	61	23	8	2,029	185	3,878	3,360
04 74975	Tortolita CDP	Pima	11.9	3,740	3,460	28	30	28	-	99	95	460	2,709
04 76010	Tuba City CDP	Coconino	8.9	8,225	450	13	7,568	18	3	52	121	194	4,708
04 77000	Tucson city	Pima	194.7	486,699	341,424	21,057	11,038	11,959	796	81,988	18,437	173,868	367,082
04 77035	Tucson Estates CDP	Pima	35.1	9,755	8,178	67	162	28	2	1,121	197	2,316	7,859
04 82530	Whiteriver CDP	Navajo	17.8	5,220	158	2	4,964	2	-	16	78	99	2,903
04 82740	Wickenburg town	Maricopa	11.5	5,082	4,663	14	60	19	6	230	90	560	4,069
04 83090	Willcox city	Cochise	6.0	3,733	2,798	26	60	31	2	658	158	1,557	2,636
04 83160	Williams city	Coconino	43.5	2,842	2,192	82	49	38	1	404	76	919	1,995
04 83388	Williamson CDP	Yavapai	57.6	3,776	3,659	4	15	11	4	30	53	133	3,108
04 83720	Window Rock CDP	Apache	5.2	3,059	97	5	2,920	13	1	2	21	44	1,948
04 83930	Winslow city	Navajo	12.3	9,520	5,004	493	2,234	98	9	1,284	398	2,746	6,685
04 85400	Youngtown town	Maricopa	1.3	3,010	2,676	41	15	18	8	218	34	383	2,711
04 85540	Yuma city	Yuma	106.7	77,515	52,968	2,491	1,168	1,164	145	16,557	3,022	35,400	54,585
05 00000	ARKANSAS		52,068.2	2,673,400	2,138,598	418,950	17,808	20,220	1,668	40,412	35,744	86,866	1,993,031
05 00970	Alma city	Crawford	4.8	4,160	3,938	71	65	4	5	31	46	154	2,824
05 01870	Arkadelphia city	Clark	7.3	10,912	7,527	2,893	58	141	6	147	140	283	8,940
05 02380	Ashdown city	Little River	7.1	4,781	3,005	1,630	50	11	1	23	61	46	3,520
05 02590	Atkins city	Pope	6.1	2,878	2,793	25	20	5	-	9	26	26	2,144
05 02740	Augusta city	Woodruff	2.0	2,665	1,364	1,279	3	-	-	2	17	10	1,911
05 03280	Bald Knob city	White	4.5	3,210	2,886	195	20	19	1	39	50	102	2,338
05 03640	Barling city	Sebastian	21.9	4,176	3,635	58	78	213	1	85	106	166	3,069
05 04030	Batesville city	Independence	10.4	9,445	8,635	439	27	110	7	132	95	236	7,363
05 04600	Beebe city	White	4.3	4,930	4,480	289	23	31	2	27	78	66	3,651
05 04840	Bella Vista CDP	Benton	65.6	16,582	16,228	30	115	45	1	33	130	168	14,544
05 05290	Benton city	Saline	17.9	21,906	20,368	894	86	123	10	165	260	417	16,366
05 05320	Bentonville city	Benton	21.2	19,730	17,939	174	262	473	7	528	347	1,198	13,910
05 05560	Berryville city	Carroll	4.4	4,433	4,025	2	31	21	-	296	58	868	3,286
05 07330	Blytheville city	Mississippi	20.6	18,272	8,249	9,528	35	109	12	87	252	239	12,805
05 07720	Booneville city	Logan	4.1	4,117	3,978	2	46	11	2	7	71	36	2,965
05 08950	Brinkley city	Monroe	5.5	3,940	1,934	1,913	7	8	2	12	64	44	2,719
05 09460	Bryant city	Saline	9.1	9,764	9,361	149	33	103	-	36	82	103	7,039
05 10300	Cabot city	Lonoke	19.1	15,261	14,736	50	61	135	6	75	198	286	10,452
05 10720	Camden city	Ouachita	16.5	13,154	6,430	6,499	32	49	3	26	115	76	9,708
05 13300	Charleston city	Franklin	4.2	2,965	2,834	2	19	10	-	44	56	61	2,204
05 13472	Cherokee Village city	Fulton, Sharp	19.9	4,648	4,515	8	30	11	1	5	78	29	3,922
05 14140	Clarksville city	Johnson	18.0	7,719	6,762	267	34	36	2	475	143	1,178	5,878
05 15190	Conway city	Faulkner	35.0	43,167	36,272	5,232	155	541	14	421	532	983	33,117
05 15460	Corning city	Clay	3.2	3,679	3,597	12	22	9	-	4	35	14	2,821
05 16240	Crossett city	Ashley	5.8	6,097	3,628	2,379	4	28	1	18	39	67	4,484
05 17380	Dardanelle city	Yell	3.1	4,228	3,181	196	23	18	4	704	102	908	3,153
05 18490	De Queen city	Sevier	5.6	5,765	3,828	350	137	12	6	1,330	102	2,225	4,016
05 18520	Dermott city	Chicot	2.8	3,292	831	2,412	5	10	-	2	32	25	2,336
05 18790	De Witt city	Arkansas	2.6	3,552	2,768	743	6	8	-	7	20	19	2,680
05 19990	Dumas city	Desha	3.0	5,238	1,918	3,144	4	26	-	105	41	167	3,660
05 20320	Earle city	Crittenden	3.3	3,036	712	2,284	6	13	-	3	18	16	1,924
05 20470	East End CDP	Saline	20.1	5,623	5,391	49	37	49	3	18	76	72	4,042
05 21070	El Dorado city	Union	16.3	21,530	11,552	9,512	43	152	3	83	185	224	15,874
05 21730	England city	Lonoke	1.9	2,972	1,947	986	11	3	-	3	22	25	2,166
05 22180	Eudora city	Chicot	3.1	2,819	393	2,382	1	5	-	13	25	39	1,907
05 23170	Farmington city	Washington	4.8	3,605	3,389	23	63	9	-	34	87	79	2,498
05 23290	Fayetteville city	Washington	43.4	58,047	50,212	2,969	730	1,484	90	1,158	1,404	2,821	46,468
05 24220	Fordyce city	Dallas	6.6	4,799	2,383	2,383	9	20	-	36	18	57	3,431
05 24430	Forrest City city	St. Francis	16.3	14,774	5,247	9,002	28	110	-	45	342	1,221	10,705
05 24550	Fort Smith city	Sebastian	50.3	80,268	61,798	6,943	1,358	3,682	43	4,040	2,404	7,048	59,862
05 26710	Gibson CDP	Pulaski	8.2	4,678	4,033	416	41	27	1	54	106	123	3,405
05 27700	Gosnell city	Mississippi	1.7	3,968	3,179	601	17	40	-	74	57	137	2,584
05 28270	Gravel Ridge CDP	Pulaski	1.9	3,232	2,604	458	21	35	1	36	77	95	2,364
05 28510	Greenbrier city	Faulkner	7.7	3,042	2,962	18	14	2	-	11	35	30	2,120
05 28600	Green Forest city	Carroll	2.3	2,717	2,243	11	29	13	10	336	75	902	1,940
05 28780	Greenwood city	Sebastian	9.2	7,112	6,837	17	109	31	-	13	105	110	4,861
05 29500	Hamburg city	Ashley	3.4	3,039	1,833	1,022	11	4	3	110	56	199	2,191
05 30460	Harrison city	Boone	10.2	12,152	11,816	14	90	62	2	75	93	186	9,409
05 30640	Haskell city	Saline	4.6	2,645	2,356	232	19	6	-	5	27	36	2,069
05 31090	Heber Springs city	Cleburne	7.0	6,432	6,297	15	28	25	2	14	51	116	5,051
05 31180	Helena city	Phillips	8.9	6,323	1,934	4,295	8	38	-	11	37	46	4,265
05 33190	Hope city	Hempstead	10.0	10,616	5,065	4,583	40	32	3	704	189	1,431	7,544
05 33400	Hot Springs city	Garland	32.9	35,750	28,194	6,030	196	284	17	363	666	1,358	28,513
05 33482	Hot Springs Village CDP	Garland, Saline	37.9	8,397	8,227	79	12	16	-	17	46	85	7,841
05 33580	Hoxie city	Lawrence	4.0	2,817	2,765	13	11	-	2	8	18	42	2,032
05 34750	Jacksonville city	Pulaski	26.4	29,916	20,617	7,406	151	592	38	340	772	1,012	21,239

Table D-1. Places — **Area and Population**—Con.

[Includes incorporated places and census designated places (CDPs) of 2,500 or more population as of April 1, 2000. Codes shown are two-digit Federal Information Processing Standards (FIPS) state codes and five-digit FIPS place codes. Place names and codes are those in effect as of January 1, 2000. County refers to the county (or counties) in which the place is located. IC in this column = independent city, a county equivalent. If a place is located in more than one county, counties are listed in alphabetic order]

State and place code	Place	County	Land area, 2000 (sq. mi.)	Population, 2000 (April 1) Total	By race—One race White	Black or African American	American Indian and Alaska Native	Asian	Native Hawaiian and Other Pacific Islander	Some other race	Two or more races	Hispanic or Latino (of any race)	18 years and over
05 00000	ARKANSAS—Con.												
05 35710	Jonesboro city	Craighead	79.6	55,515	47,394	6,259	175	462	16	583	626	1,297	42,790
05 38170	Lake Village city	Chicot	2.1	2,823	1,150	1,585	6	32	-	16	34	39	1,996
05 40120	Little Flock city	Benton	7.6	2,585	2,151	23	44	146	11	152	58	413	1,870
05 41000	Little Rock city	Pulaski	116.2	183,133	100,848	74,003	500	3,032	64	2,348	2,338	4,889	137,898
05 41420	Lonoke city	Lonoke	4.3	4,287	3,142	1,003	33	14	2	42	51	79	3,159
05 41720	Lowell city	Benton	6.3	5,013	4,445	39	44	136	49	205	95	448	3,573
05 42770	McGehee city	Desha	6.4	4,570	2,592	1,897	26	11	2	10	32	68	3,269
05 43460	Magnolia city	Columbia	9.3	10,858	6,324	4,276	24	71	2	52	109	116	8,232
05 43610	Malvern city	Hot Spring	7.4	9,021	6,149	2,585	32	26	6	48	175	114	6,763
05 43820	Manila city	Mississippi	3.2	3,055	3,000	1	12	2	-	8	32	33	2,264
05 44120	Marianna city	Lee	3.6	5,181	1,266	3,841	8	29	-	15	22	54	3,401
05 44180	Marion city	Crittenden	13.4	8,901	7,473	1,258	23	53	-	44	50	128	6,226
05 44210	Marked Tree city	Poinsett	2.3	2,800	1,830	898	3	8	-	35	26	58	2,057
05 44600	Maumelle city	Pulaski	8.8	10,557	9,760	516	53	82	1	43	102	187	7,701
05 45170	Mena city	Polk	6.7	5,637	5,463	11	49	15	3	28	68	123	4,337
05 46580	Monticello city	Drew	10.7	9,146	5,941	2,983	14	64	1	53	90	118	6,786
05 46970	Morrilton city	Conway	8.2	6,550	5,134	1,144	52	22	1	90	107	221	4,889
05 47390	Mountain Home city	Baxter	10.6	11,012	10,758	20	52	41	3	29	109	132	9,065
05 47540	Mountain View city	Stone	6.8	2,876	2,789	-	27	-	1	9	50	49	2,295
05 48560	Nashville city	Howard	4.6	4,878	2,925	1,620	12	60	1	214	46	341	3,533
05 49580	Newport city	Jackson	13.0	7,811	5,200	2,481	21	26	1	22	60	88	6,280
05 50200	North Crossett CDP	Ashley	10.3	3,581	3,140	373	9	7	5	26	21	73	2,594
05 50450	North Little Rock city	Pulaski	44.8	60,433	37,801	20,535	249	356	20	712	760	1,463	45,025
05 52580	Osceola city	Mississippi	7.8	8,875	4,206	4,529	9	22	-	36	73	119	6,020
05 52970	Ozark city	Franklin	7.2	3,525	3,401	5	24	5	8	38	44	90	2,638
05 53390	Paragould city	Greene	30.8	22,017	21,527	31	93	48	5	123	190	292	16,549
05 53480	Paris city	Logan	4.5	3,707	3,525	74	15	4	-	41	48	80	2,823
05 53555	Parkers-Iron Springs CDP	Pulaski	9.3	3,499	2,976	398	14	18	-	26	67	58	2,766
05 55130	Piggott city	Clay	5.2	3,894	3,839	9	7	-	-	7	32	30	3,034
05 55310	Pine Bluff city	Jefferson	45.6	55,085	17,793	36,275	91	404	23	104	395	452	39,971
05 55610	Piney CDP	Garland	6.5	3,988	3,710	90	46	7	4	54	77	132	2,981
05 56540	Pocahontas city	Randolph	7.4	6,518	6,340	72	29	5	-	13	59	58	4,970
05 57170	Prairie Grove city	Washington	2.1	2,540	2,414	13	38	12	1	17	45	52	1,841
05 57260	Prescott city	Nevada	6.5	3,686	1,965	1,640	14	3	-	43	21	65	2,739
05 60110	Rockwell CDP	Garland	3.2	3,024	2,937	25	12	8	-	4	38	26	2,382
05 60410	Rogers city	Benton	33.5	38,829	33,296	184	407	556	29	3,660	697	7,490	27,398
05 61670	Russellville city	Pope	25.9	23,682	21,251	1,232	171	279	6	403	340	773	18,093
05 62210	Salem CDP	Saline	3.4	2,789	2,734	9	13	5	-	10	18	30	2,100
05 63020	Searcy city	White	14.7	18,928	17,080	1,249	58	94	4	206	237	390	15,197
05 63710	Sheridan city	Grant	4.0	3,872	3,769	37	11	6	2	22	25	37	2,855
05 63800	Sherwood city	Pulaski	13.8	21,511	18,574	2,182	93	205	13	178	266	442	16,251
05 64370	Siloam Springs city	Benton	10.6	10,843	9,240	53	465	90	9	615	371	1,518	8,027
05 66080	Springdale city	Benton, Washington	31.3	45,798	37,380	377	431	772	712	5,079	1,047	9,005	32,511
05 67490	Stuttgart city	Arkansas	6.2	9,745	6,233	3,361	24	57	1	20	49	79	7,209
05 68810	Texarkana city	Miller	31.8	26,448	17,437	8,199	126	131	8	161	386	472	19,603
05 70010	Trumann city	Poinsett	4.8	6,889	6,496	278	19	14	1	31	50	56	5,041
05 71480	Van Buren city	Crawford	15.1	18,986	16,589	312	373	535	-	602	575	1,147	13,358
05 72380	Waldron city	Scott	5.0	3,508	3,172	5	32	4	-	251	44	537	2,566
05 72890	Walnut Ridge city	Lawrence	11.6	4,925	4,779	29	25	6	-	-	86	21	3,872
05 73130	Ward city	Lonoke	3.9	2,580	2,511	5	20	10	-	4	30	50	1,730
05 73310	Warren city	Bradley	6.9	6,442	3,508	2,628	12	5	1	246	42	327	4,896
05 74450	West Helena city	Phillips	4.4	8,689	2,847	5,708	20	33	2	29	50	88	5,729
05 74540	West Memphis city	Crittenden	26.5	27,666	11,663	15,473	59	148	5	141	177	279	18,938
05 75170	White Hall city	Jefferson	6.8	4,732	4,379	220	23	62	-	16	32	49	3,433
05 77090	Wynne city	Cross	8.2	8,615	5,678	2,784	13	41	-	23	76	89	6,140
06 00000	CALIFORNIA		155,959.3	33,871,648	20,170,059	2,263,882	333,346	3,697,513	116,961	5,682,241	1,607,646	10,966,556	24,621,819
06 00296	Adelanto city	San Bernardino	53.5	18,130	9,147	2,377	292	290	32	4,819	1,173	8,299	11,244
06 00394	Agoura Hills city	Los Angeles	8.2	20,537	17,858	272	51	1,335	21	429	571	1,407	14,282
06 00562	Alameda city	Alameda	10.8	72,259	41,148	4,488	484	18,894	434	2,380	4,431	6,725	56,725
06 00618	Alamo CDP	Contra Costa	20.6	15,626	14,119	74	34	935	18	100	346	616	11,313
06 00674	Albany city	Alameda	1.7	16,444	10,078	675	64	4,126	22	521	958	1,312	12,686
06 00884	Alhambra city	Los Angeles	7.6	85,804	25,758	1,437	614	40,520	86	13,947	3,442	30,453	66,631
06 00947	Aliso Viejo CDP	Orange	10.2	40,166	31,395	828	158	4,413	88	1,411	1,873	4,680	29,699
06 01150	Alondra Park CDP	Los Angeles	1.1	8,622	3,584	1,088	70	1,407	36	1,900	537	3,526	6,076
06 01192	Alpine CDP	San Diego	26.9	13,143	11,931	109	154	260	27	376	286	1,343	9,725
06 01290	Altadena CDP	Los Angeles	8.7	42,610	20,156	13,388	247	1,807	56	4,340	2,616	8,690	31,289
06 01360	Alta Sierra CDP	Nevada	8.4	6,522	6,257	19	37	48	6	42	113	270	5,107
06 01444	Alturas city	Modoc	2.2	2,892	2,484	9	127	21	3	140	108	344	2,061
06 01458	Alum Rock CDP	Santa Clara	1.1	13,479	5,950	301	230	1,172	53	4,972	801	9,029	9,359
06 01640	American Canyon city	Napa	4.1	9,774	5,786	717	80	1,579	126	845	641	1,731	6,998
06 02000	Anaheim city	Orange	48.9	328,014	179,627	8,735	3,041	39,311	1,393	79,427	16,480	153,374	229,050
06 02042	Anderson city	Shasta	6.4	9,022	7,805	56	373	160	11	210	407	659	6,175
06 02132	Angels City city	Calaveras	3.0	3,004	2,798	6	55	14	1	43	87	243	2,275
06 02168	Angwin CDP	Napa	4.9	3,148	2,379	103	15	324	14	171	142	404	2,664
06 02252	Antioch city	Contra Costa	26.9	90,532	59,148	8,824	843	6,697	360	8,352	6,308	20,024	61,314
06 02364	Apple Valley town	San Bernardino	73.3	54,239	41,449	4,277	530	1,198	123	4,296	2,366	10,067	37,124
06 02378	Aptos CDP	Santa Cruz	7.0	9,396	8,492	53	61	225	10	234	321	655	7,587

Table D-1. Places — **Area and Population**—Con.

[Includes incorporated places and census designated places (CDPs) of 2,500 or more population as of April 1, 2000. Codes shown are two-digit Federal Information Processing Standards (FIPS) state codes and five-digit FIPS place codes. Place names and codes are those in effect as of January 1, 2000. County refers to the county (or counties) in which the place is located. IC in this column = independent city, a county equivalent. If a place is located in more than one county, counties are listed in alphabetic order]

State and place code	Place	County	Land area, 2000 (sq. mi.)	Population, 2000 (April 1) Total	By race— One race White	Black or African American	American Indian and Alaska Native	Asian	Native Hawaiian and Other Pacific Islander	Some other race	Two or more races	Hispanic or Latino (of any race)	18 years and over
06 00000	CALIFORNIA—Con.												
06 02462	Arcadia city	Los Angeles	11.0	53,054	24,180	601	132	24,091	42	2,209	1,799	5,629	40,700
06 02476	Arcata city	Humboldt	9.2	16,651	14,072	259	442	378	34	581	885	1,202	14,100
06 02553	Arden-Arcade CDP	Sacramento	18.9	96,025	74,285	5,779	920	4,664	411	4,972	4,994	11,501	75,471
06 02700	Armona CDP	Kings	1.9	3,239	1,822	139	78	43	8	971	178	1,574	2,094
06 02770	Arnold CDP	Calaveras	14.8	4,218	4,012	10	40	21	5	30	100	141	3,423
06 02812	Aromas CDP	Monterey, San Benito	4.7	2,797	2,216	5	37	73	2	308	156	641	1,950
06 02868	Arroyo Grande city	San Luis Obispo	5.7	15,851	14,020	99	71	489	28	597	547	1,770	12,154
06 02896	Artesia city	Los Angeles	1.6	16,380	7,236	582	127	4,490	89	3,025	831	6,272	11,929
06 02924	Arvin city	Kern	4.8	12,956	5,836	140	189	143	15	6,031	602	11,341	7,769
06 02980	Ashland CDP	Alameda	1.8	20,793	8,115	4,186	269	3,091	237	3,346	1,549	6,753	14,876
06 03064	Atascadero city	San Luis Obispo	26.7	26,411	23,451	623	247	336	30	842	882	2,783	19,639
06 03092	Atherton town	San Mateo	4.9	7,194	6,141	50	12	704	30	72	185	200	5,491
06 03162	Atwater city	Merced	5.4	23,113	13,252	1,153	293	1,254	83	5,659	1,419	9,594	15,041
06 03204	Auburn city	Placer	7.4	12,462	11,641	57	104	165	12	189	294	744	9,560
06 03209	August CDP	San Joaquin	1.3	7,808	4,008	103	237	253	42	2,665	500	4,370	5,203
06 03274	Avalon city	Los Angeles	2.8	3,127	2,240	23	32	19	7	637	169	1,437	2,178
06 03302	Avenal city	Kings	19.1	14,674	5,259	1,850	139	57	8	6,952	409	9,667	11,464
06 03344	Avocado Heights CDP	Los Angeles	2.7	15,148	7,790	223	176	1,381	16	5,008	554	11,776	10,470
06 03386	Azusa city	Los Angeles	8.9	44,712	23,406	1,688	585	2,747	77	13,646	2,563	28,522	30,932
06 03526	Bakersfield city	Kern	113.1	247,057	152,849	22,641	3,454	10,708	298	46,151	10,956	80,170	166,374
06 03666	Baldwin Park city	Los Angeles	6.7	75,837	30,472	1,219	1,096	8,826	112	30,718	3,394	59,660	49,360
06 03820	Banning city	Riverside	23.1	23,562	15,124	2,014	593	1,268	30	3,505	1,028	7,119	17,332
06 04030	Barstow city	San Bernardino	33.6	21,119	12,059	2,450	510	650	200	3,886	1,364	7,708	14,615
06 04415	Bay Point CDP	Contra Costa	9.3	21,534	9,960	2,736	226	2,400	184	4,345	1,683	8,321	14,379
06 04503	Bayview-Montalvin CDP	Contra Costa	0.6	5,004	2,388	599	55	695	38	963	266	1,761	3,558
06 04541	Baywood-Los Osos CDP	San Luis Obispo	7.6	14,351	12,667	92	99	655	10	358	470	1,292	11,246
06 04576	Beale AFB CDP	Yuba	10.1	5,115	3,659	549	58	266	30	260	293	573	3,184
06 04734	Bear Valley Springs CDP	Kern	41.5	4,232	3,804	58	13	30	3	125	199	332	3,109
06 04758	Beaumont city	Riverside	27.2	11,384	7,751	331	265	189	8	2,314	526	4,122	7,632
06 04870	Bell city	Los Angeles	2.5	36,664	17,764	468	470	391	22	15,798	1,751	33,328	23,712
06 04982	Bellflower city	Los Angeles	6.1	72,878	33,593	9,540	667	7,062	511	17,766	3,739	31,503	49,665
06 04996	Bell Gardens city	Los Angeles	2.5	44,054	21,180	429	730	270	45	19,329	2,071	41,132	26,659
06 05108	Belmont city	San Mateo	4.5	25,123	18,889	422	72	3,878	136	659	1,067	2,090	20,278
06 05290	Benicia city	Solano	12.9	26,865	21,195	1,295	162	2,031	78	712	1,392	2,424	19,582
06 06000	Berkeley city	Alameda	10.5	102,743	60,797	14,007	467	16,837	146	4,764	5,725	10,001	88,230
06 06028	Bermuda Dunes CDP	Riverside	3.2	6,229	5,245	129	38	171	4	429	213	1,215	4,761
06 06308	Beverly Hills city	Los Angeles	5.7	33,784	28,736	597	43	2,383	10	508	1,507	1,565	27,033
06 06406	Big Bear City CDP	San Bernardino	3.5	5,779	5,148	36	75	26	4	218	272	747	4,250
06 06434	Big Bear Lake city	San Bernardino	6.3	5,438	4,958	37	53	41	2	194	153	745	4,211
06 06798	Bishop city	Inyo	1.8	3,575	3,025	7	73	45	1	232	192	621	2,711
06 06933	Blackhawk-Camino Tassajara CDP	Contra Costa	9.3	10,048	7,747	232	18	1,686	14	75	276	391	7,132
06 07064	Bloomington CDP	San Bernardino	6.0	19,318	10,437	778	346	215	38	6,666	838	12,436	12,285
06 07218	Blythe city	Riverside	24.2	12,155	6,735	1,014	174	168	24	3,499	541	5,571	8,029
06 07379	Bonadelle Ranchos-Madera Ranchos CDP	Madera	11.6	7,300	6,236	102	87	83	6	560	226	1,376	5,179
06 07414	Bonita CDP	San Diego	4.9	12,401	8,928	386	70	1,059	38	1,320	600	3,779	9,379
06 07498	Bonsall CDP	San Diego	13.5	3,401	2,857	29	13	94	4	331	73	729	2,611
06 07596	Borrego Springs CDP	San Diego	42.5	2,535	2,100	25	11	6	-	333	60	822	2,069
06 07624	Bostonia CDP	San Diego	1.9	15,169	12,106	604	137	225	54	1,182	861	2,523	10,876
06 07652	Boulder Creek CDP	Santa Cruz	4.2	4,081	3,683	24	45	70	8	89	162	232	3,119
06 07848	Boyes Hot Springs CDP	Sonoma	1.1	6,665	4,998	28	48	61	6	1,216	308	2,777	4,764
06 08058	Brawley city	Imperial	5.8	22,052	11,638	540	244	288	41	8,349	952	16,280	14,454
06 08100	Brea city	Orange	10.5	35,410	27,384	447	184	3,218	77	2,748	1,352	7,205	26,328
06 08142	Brentwood city	Contra Costa	11.6	23,302	17,201	579	143	666	73	3,387	1,253	6,565	15,659
06 08172	Bret Harte CDP	Stanislaus	0.6	5,161	2,082	59	99	32	1	2,617	271	3,926	3,186
06 08310	Brisbane city	San Mateo	3.3	3,597	2,624	38	24	524	22	180	185	550	2,959
06 08338	Broadmoor CDP	San Mateo	0.4	4,026	1,978	74	18	1,409	45	262	240	729	3,093
06 08758	Buellton city	Santa Barbara	1.6	3,828	3,120	21	44	42	8	468	125	985	2,792
06 08786	Buena Park city	Orange	10.6	78,282	41,479	3,000	750	16,490	397	11,893	4,273	26,221	55,261
06 08954	Burbank city	Los Angeles	17.3	100,316	72,409	2,066	549	9,181	142	9,908	6,061	24,953	77,979
06 08968	Burbank CDP	Santa Clara	0.4	5,239	3,328	154	44	353	30	1,038	292	2,259	3,939
06 09066	Burlingame city	San Mateo	4.3	28,158	21,648	296	65	3,881	135	1,019	1,114	2,995	22,756
06 09122	Burney CDP	Shasta	5.2	3,217	2,830	3	221	21	2	69	71	192	2,325
06 09353	Bystrom CDP	Stanislaus	1.1	4,518	2,449	116	76	140	22	1,514	201	2,540	3,058
06 09598	Calabasas city	Los Angeles	13.1	20,033	17,412	236	27	1,544	9	262	543	949	14,296
06 09710	Calexico city	Imperial	6.2	27,109	12,621	134	181	492	6	12,739	936	25,832	17,645
06 09780	California City city	Kern	203.6	8,385	5,718	1,075	131	313	27	623	498	1,422	5,807
06 09864	Calimesa city	Riverside	15.6	7,139	6,363	42	47	76	7	385	219	1,008	5,584
06 09878	Calipatria city	Imperial	3.7	7,289	2,361	1,554	53	46	2	3,109	164	4,180	6,100
06 09892	Calistoga city	Napa	2.6	5,190	3,978	17	51	51	1	914	178	1,978	3,982
06 10046	Camarillo city	Ventura	18.9	57,077	46,036	856	299	4,129	114	3,605	2,038	8,869	42,658
06 10074	Cambria CDP	San Luis Obispo	8.6	6,232	5,676	22	62	72	8	251	141	874	5,210
06 10088	Cambrian Park CDP	Santa Clara	0.6	3,258	2,765	13	34	134	7	141	164	379	2,420
06 10256	Cameron Park CDP	El Dorado	7.4	14,549	13,421	92	129	209	18	273	407	975	10,608
06 10345	Campbell city	Santa Clara	5.6	38,138	27,758	964	248	5,402	88	1,859	1,819	5,083	29,919
06 10559	Camp Pendleton North CDP	San Diego	9.0	8,197	5,500	869	132	231	28	1,057	380	1,854	6,547

Table D-1. Places — **Area and Population**—Con.

[Includes incorporated places and census designated places (CDPs) of 2,500 or more population as of April 1, 2000. Codes shown are two-digit Federal Information Processing Standards (FIPS) state codes and five-digit FIPS place codes. Place names and codes are those in effect as of January 1, 2000. County refers to the county (or counties) in which the place is located. IC in this column = independent city, a county equivalent. If a place is located in more than one county, counties are listed in alphabetic order]

State and place code	Place	County	Land area, 2000 (sq. mi.)	Total	White	Black or African American	American Indian and Alaska Native	Asian	Native Hawaiian and Other Pacific Islander	Some other race	Two or more races	Hispanic or Latino (of any race)	18 years and over
06 00000	CALIFORNIA—Con.												
06 10561	Camp Pendleton South CDP	San Diego	3.8	8,854	5,522	1,266	142	337	62	953	572	1,691	5,771
06 10928	Canyon Lake city	Riverside	4.0	9,952	9,248	81	35	153	11	181	243	848	7,374
06 11040	Capitola city	Santa Cruz	1.6	10,033	8,412	117	57	401	20	555	471	1,267	8,187
06 11194	Carlsbad city	San Diego	37.4	78,247	67,723	753	329	3,315	155	3,636	2,336	9,170	60,007
06 11250	Carmel-by-the-Sea city	Monterey	1.1	4,081	3,860	18	13	92	6	37	55	120	3,678
06 11324	Carmel Valley Village CDP	Monterey	19.1	4,700	4,345	18	18	89	5	128	97	273	3,732
06 11390	Carmichael CDP	Sacramento	10.8	49,742	43,083	1,338	412	1,780	136	1,041	1,952	3,479	38,144
06 11446	Carpinteria city	Santa Barbara	2.7	14,194	10,418	84	140	338	26	2,568	620	6,175	10,559
06 11530	Carson city	Los Angeles	18.8	89,730	23,049	22,804	505	19,987	2,680	16,137	4,568	31,332	64,245
06 11656	Casa Conejo CDP	Ventura	0.5	3,180	2,717	32	9	108	12	201	101	502	2,282
06 11691	Casa de Oro-Mount Helix CDP	San Diego	6.8	18,874	15,800	966	114	399	61	785	749	2,142	14,530
06 11964	Castro Valley CDP	Alameda	14.4	57,292	40,587	2,946	336	7,757	254	2,355	3,057	6,984	43,698
06 11978	Castroville CDP	Monterey	1.0	6,724	2,458	71	70	219	7	3,574	325	5,802	4,231
06 12048	Cathedral City city	Riverside	19.2	42,647	27,845	1,169	440	1,575	32	9,834	1,752	21,312	29,380
06 12132	Cayucos CDP	San Luis Obispo	3.1	2,943	2,761	7	11	37	1	62	64	200	2,448
06 12524	Ceres city	Stanislaus	6.9	34,609	22,324	951	485	1,743	130	7,061	1,915	13,115	22,718
06 12552	Cerritos city	Los Angeles	8.6	51,488	13,851	3,432	142	30,091	96	1,930	1,946	5,349	38,878
06 12669	Channel Islands Beach CDP	Ventura	0.4	3,142	2,840	35	14	60	7	92	94	292	2,574
06 12734	Charter Oak CDP	Los Angeles	0.9	9,027	5,895	431	115	830	13	1,266	477	3,302	6,354
06 12902	Cherryland CDP	Alameda	1.2	13,837	7,319	1,360	161	1,151	178	2,776	892	5,774	10,104
06 12916	Cherry Valley CDP	Riverside	8.2	5,891	5,308	37	70	66	9	255	146	788	4,784
06 13014	Chico city	Butte	27.7	59,954	49,377	1,215	782	2,524	115	3,390	2,551	7,351	47,281
06 13210	Chino city	San Bernardino	21.1	67,168	37,412	5,250	628	3,308	139	17,169	3,262	31,830	48,040
06 13214	Chino Hills city	San Bernardino	44.8	66,787	37,656	3,697	375	14,744	85	7,062	3,168	17,151	44,841
06 13294	Chowchilla city	Madera	7.1	11,127	7,061	1,142	289	147	29	1,798	661	3,138	8,653
06 13392	Chula Vista city	San Diego	48.9	173,556	95,553	8,022	1,352	19,063	1,013	38,404	10,149	86,073	123,692
06 13560	Citrus CDP	Los Angeles	0.9	10,581	5,542	343	163	712	5	3,293	523	6,861	7,088
06 13588	Citrus Heights city	Sacramento	14.3	85,071	72,001	2,442	860	2,423	288	3,032	4,025	8,539	63,611
06 13756	Claremont city	Los Angeles	13.1	33,998	24,983	1,692	189	3,912	45	1,769	1,408	5,221	26,967
06 13882	Clayton city	Contra Costa	3.9	10,762	9,465	120	20	579	11	166	401	681	7,911
06 13945	Clearlake city	Lake	10.2	13,142	10,823	684	354	149	21	480	631	1,449	9,755
06 14190	Cloverdale city	Sonoma	2.5	6,831	5,323	12	106	71	5	1,045	269	1,823	4,968
06 14218	Clovis city	Fresno	17.1	68,468	51,914	1,302	1,025	4,441	108	6,502	3,176	13,876	47,471
06 14260	Coachella city	Riverside	20.8	22,724	8,810	103	191	71	7	12,854	688	22,132	13,454
06 14274	Coalinga city	Fresno	5.9	11,668	6,687	276	177	193	28	3,769	538	5,811	7,793
06 14890	Colton city	San Bernardino	15.1	47,662	20,343	5,246	600	2,521	108	16,425	2,419	28,934	31,007
06 14946	Colusa city	Colusa	1.7	5,402	3,709	16	95	79	42	1,258	203	2,253	3,773
06 14974	Commerce city	Los Angeles	6.6	12,568	5,625	98	199	136	10	5,900	600	11,765	8,316
06 15044	Compton city	Los Angeles	10.1	93,493	15,625	37,690	656	237	985	34,911	3,389	53,143	57,500
06 16000	Concord city	Contra Costa	30.1	121,780	86,114	3,706	929	11,438	612	11,752	7,229	26,560	90,937
06 16224	Corcoran city	Kings	6.4	14,458	4,927	2,054	206	103	12	6,711	445	8,618	10,931
06 16322	Corning city	Tehama	2.9	6,741	5,021	35	147	36	6	1,174	322	1,943	4,548
06 16350	Corona city	Riverside	35.1	124,966	77,514	8,031	1,086	9,425	387	21,894	6,629	44,569	83,233
06 16378	Coronado city	San Diego	7.7	24,100	20,341	1,241	159	896	72	757	634	2,369	20,251
06 16462	Corte Madera town	Marin	3.2	9,100	7,977	80	29	553	17	118	326	436	6,974
06 16532	Costa Mesa city	Orange	15.6	108,724	75,542	1,520	845	7,501	656	18,018	4,642	34,523	83,452
06 16560	Cotati city	Sonoma	1.9	6,471	5,407	151	58	233	15	285	322	810	4,807
06 16580	Coto de Caza CDP	Orange	7.9	13,057	11,668	96	19	674	19	216	365	868	8,470
06 16630	Cottonwood CDP	Shasta	2.4	2,960	2,555	7	95	90	1	99	113	278	2,010
06 16651	Country Club CDP	San Joaquin	1.9	9,462	6,467	335	135	579	13	1,114	819	2,719	6,868
06 16742	Covina city	Los Angeles	7.0	46,837	29,084	2,354	420	4,598	97	8,047	2,237	18,871	33,691
06 17022	Crescent City city	Del Norte	1.8	4,006	3,138	21	244	185	5	171	242	441	2,800
06 17030	Crescent City North CDP	Del Norte	1.9	4,028	3,163	33	274	193	4	169	192	363	2,780
06 17106	Crest CDP	San Diego	6.4	2,716	2,523	9	22	19	7	51	85	213	1,991
06 17162	Crestline CDP	San Bernardino	10.9	10,218	8,996	81	115	60	19	509	438	1,069	7,380
06 17274	Crockett CDP	Contra Costa	5.0	3,194	2,718	100	30	83	-	136	127	371	2,603
06 17498	Cudahy city	Los Angeles	1.1	24,208	10,443	300	310	178	42	11,634	1,301	22,790	14,543
06 17568	Culver City city	Los Angeles	5.1	38,816	22,996	4,644	277	4,667	80	3,945	2,207	9,199	30,720
06 17610	Cupertino city	Santa Clara	10.9	50,546	25,342	347	101	22,462	67	639	1,588	2,010	37,083
06 17708	Cutler CDP	Tulare	0.8	4,491	1,547	17	53	37	-	2,633	204	4,322	2,812
06 17722	Cutten CDP	Humboldt	1.3	2,933	2,579	22	90	44	11	62	125	176	2,248
06 17750	Cypress city	Orange	6.6	46,229	30,332	1,280	274	9,618	184	2,515	2,026	7,235	33,735
06 17918	Daly City city	San Mateo	7.6	103,621	26,836	4,720	456	52,522	940	11,735	6,412	23,072	80,343
06 17946	Dana Point city	Orange	6.6	35,110	30,633	288	201	884	36	2,080	988	5,440	27,878
06 17988	Danville town	Contra Costa	18.1	41,715	36,000	382	86	3,756	48	381	1,062	1,945	29,798
06 18100	Davis city	Yolo	10.5	60,308	42,256	1,417	407	10,576	144	2,572	2,936	5,793	49,072
06 18153	Day Valley CDP	Santa Cruz	19.0	3,587	3,098	23	41	60	-	245	120	519	2,672
06 18352	Del Aire CDP	Los Angeles	1.0	9,012	5,675	377	58	728	72	1,597	505	3,751	6,465
06 18394	Delano city	Kern	10.1	38,824	10,157	2,115	352	6,165	22	18,276	1,737	26,584	26,206
06 18464	Delhi CDP	Merced	4.6	8,022	4,279	136	80	209	7	2,767	544	4,448	5,051
06 18506	Del Mar city	San Diego	1.7	4,389	4,132	11	15	126	5	25	75	170	3,791
06 18590	Del Monte Forest CDP	Monterey	8.0	4,531	4,140	18	12	238	8	40	75	106	3,950

Table D-1. Places — **Area and Population**—Con.

[Includes incorporated places and census designated places (CDPs) of 2,500 or more population as of April 1, 2000. Codes shown are two-digit Federal Information Processing Standards (FIPS) state codes and five-digit FIPS place codes. Place names and codes are those in effect as of January 1, 2000. County refers to the county (or counties) in which the place is located. IC in this column = Independent city, a county equivalent. If a place is located in more than one county, counties are listed in alphabetic order]

State and place code	Place	County	Land area, 2000 (sq. mi.)	Population, 2000 (April 1) Total	By race— One race White	Black or African American	American Indian and Alaska Native	Asian	Native Hawaiian and Other Pacific Islander	Some other race	Two or more races	Hispanic or Latino (of any race)	18 years and over
06 00000	CALIFORNIA—Con.												
06 18856	Denair CDP	Stanislaus	2.0	3,446	2,709	9	50	8	1	529	140	915	2,421
06 18996	Desert Hot Springs city	Riverside	23.3	16,582	11,306	1,014	238	326	14	2,717	967	6,699	11,063
06 19192	Diamond Bar city	Los Angeles	14.8	56,287	23,103	2,680	185	24,066	67	3,818	2,368	10,393	41,104
06 19220	Diamond Springs CDP	El Dorado	5.9	4,888	4,407	5	109	24	3	219	121	416	3,701
06 19318	Dinuba city	Tulare	3.4	16,844	8,816	60	215	442	23	6,398	890	12,647	10,821
06 19339	Discovery Bay CDP	Contra Costa	8.1	8,981	7,865	165	75	160	16	355	345	937	6,781
06 19402	Dixon city	Solano	6.6	16,103	11,354	311	160	501	48	2,877	852	5,414	10,947
06 19406	Dixon Lane-Meadow Creek CDP	Inyo	3.4	2,702	2,469	2	35	18	-	101	77	271	2,018
06 19612	Dos Palos city	Merced	1.5	4,581	2,985	190	63	28	-	1,155	160	2,482	2,980
06 19766	Downey city	Los Angeles	12.4	107,323	57,395	4,028	929	8,308	236	31,180	5,247	62,089	75,966
06 19990	Duarte city	Los Angeles	6.7	21,486	11,178	1,952	201	2,711	24	4,296	1,124	9,326	15,429
06 20018	Dublin city	Alameda	12.6	29,973	20,793	3,024	220	3,101	95	1,576	1,164	4,059	23,691
06 20270	Durham CDP	Butte	81.8	5,220	4,812	7	41	32	6	187	135	469	3,755
06 20438	Earlimart CDP	Tulare	2.0	6,583	1,272	54	87	532	3	4,294	341	5,760	3,801
06 20550	East Compton CDP	Los Angeles	0.5	9,286	2,293	1,841	65	14	109	4,664	300	7,164	5,586
06 20598	East Foothills CDP	Santa Clara	2.3	8,133	5,504	230	81	876	13	915	514	2,333	6,298
06 20697	East Hemet CDP	Riverside	3.2	14,823	11,864	228	210	154	13	1,763	591	3,692	9,962
06 20746	East La Mirada CDP	Los Angeles	1.1	9,538	7,181	171	73	348	13	1,286	466	3,640	6,916
06 20802	East Los Angeles CDP	Los Angeles	7.4	124,283	48,788	490	1,603	962	70	67,122	5,248	120,307	81,334
06 20907	East Oakdale CDP	Stanislaus	5.6	2,742	2,503	10	51	45	2	57	74	187	2,047
06 20956	East Palo Alto city	San Mateo	2.5	29,506	7,962	6,796	246	657	2,252	10,248	1,345	17,346	19,187
06 20984	East Pasadena CDP	Los Angeles	1.3	6,045	3,367	154	48	1,211	3	872	390	2,130	4,558
06 21012	East Porterville CDP	Tulare	3.1	6,730	3,082	46	188	179	26	2,902	307	4,249	4,182
06 21061	East Richmond Heights CDP	Contra Costa	0.6	3,357	2,153	468	22	360	18	131	205	358	2,719
06 21096	East San Gabriel CDP	Los Angeles	1.6	14,512	6,175	269	92	5,873	13	1,469	621	3,413	11,070
06 21600	Edwards AFB CDP	Kern	17.2	5,909	4,296	616	49	257	31	321	339	690	3,778
06 21712	El Cajon city	San Diego	14.6	94,869	70,206	5,090	941	2,643	352	9,950	5,687	21,313	68,438
06 21782	El Centro city	Imperial	9.6	37,835	17,728	1,195	369	1,324	37	15,771	1,411	28.219	25.119
06 21796	El Cerrito city	Contra Costa	3.6	23,171	13,391	1,978	116	5,649	59	708	1,270	1,838	19,479
06 21810	El Cerrito CDP	Riverside	3.0	4,590	3,260	102	42	57	21	910	198	1,708	3,154
06 21880	El Dorado Hills CDP	El Dorado	17.9	18,016	16,234	139	83	740	30	247	543	896	12,043
06 21936	El Granada CDP	San Mateo	5.4	5,724	4,820	32	60	163	11	390	248	900	4,192
06 22020	Elk Grove CDP	Sacramento	15.2	59,984	35,464	5,110	562	10,553	355	3,865	4,075	8,398	40,221
06 22230	El Monte city	Los Angeles	9.6	115,965	41,360	889	1,596	21,465	140	45,544	4,971	83,945	76,460
06 22300	El Paso de Robles (Paso Robles) city	San Luis Obispo	17.3	24,297	18,393	806	316	458	34	3,325	965	6,735	17,057
06 22370	El Rio CDP	Ventura	1.6	6,193	2,948	78	156	86	21	2,631	273	4,791	4,150
06 22412	El Segundo city	Los Angeles	5.5	16,033	13,405	187	75	1,028	47	562	729	1,765	12,394
06 22454	El Sobrante CDP	Contra Costa	3.1	12,260	7,399	1,491	82	1,532	35	855	866	1,910	9,230
06 22510	El Verano CDP	Sonoma	1.1	3,954	3,275	12	39	54	3	352	219	922	2,900
06 22587	Emerald Lake Hills CDP	San Mateo	1.2	3,899	3,488	22	7	201	8	53	120	202	3,012
06 22594	Emeryville city	Alameda	1.2	6,882	3,096	1,339	34	1,760	17	288	348	616	6,099
06 22622	Empire CDP	Stanislaus	1.6	3,903	2,573	21	57	71	8	961	212	1,674	2,668
06 22678	Encinitas city	San Diego	19.1	58,014	50,241	340	267	1,798	69	3,645	1,654	8,584	44,637
06 22790	Escalon city	San Joaquin	2.0	5,963	5,082	34	57	65	11	520	194	1,125	4,120
06 22804	Escondido city	San Diego	36.3	133,559	90,578	3,009	1,646	5,957	311	25,636	6,422	51,693	93,872
06 23042	Eureka city	Homboldt	9.5	26,128	21,544	427	1,101	928	86	709	1,333	2,031	20,287
06 23126	Exeter city	Tulare	2.2	9,168	6,393	63	135	119	4	2,127	327	3,507	6,075
06 23168	Fairfax town	Marin	2.1	7,319	6,689	85	35	144	12	112	242	418	5,914
06 23182	Fairfield city	Solano	37.7	96,178	54,063	14,446	744	10,471	899	8,431	7,124	18,050	67,519
06 23294	Fair Oaks CDP	Sacramento	9.9	28,008	24,659	514	165	1,182	44	499	945	1,767	21,634
06 23350	Fairview CDP	Alameda	2.8	9,470	5,234	1,939	53	964	66	582	632	1,433	7,186
06 23462	Fallbrook CDP	San Diego	17.5	29,100	20,888	415	263	447	87	5,868	1,132	10,853	20,593
06 23616	Farmersville city	Tulare	1.9	8,737	3,701	35	154	100	3	4,224	520	6,292	5,383
06 23973	Fetters Hot Springs-Agua Caliente CDP	Sonoma	0.4	2,505	2,068	24	28	30	4	218	133	749	1,821
06 24092	Fillmore city	Ventura	2.8	13,643	7,304	44	192	132	18	5,394	559	9,090	9,230
06 24134	Firebaugh city	Fresno	2.8	5,743	2,504	66	78	50	1	2,786	258	5,026	3,486
06 24477	Florence-Graham CDP	Los Angeles	3.6	60,197	14,778	7,908	590	70	56	33,950	2,845	51,712	36,137
06 24498	Florin CDP	Sacramento	5.6	27,653	11,502	5,185	346	5,407	241	3,033	1,939	5,760	18,741
06 24638	Folsom city	Sacramento	21.7	51,884	40,415	3,109	302	3,731	100	2,446	1,781	4,914	39,327
06 24680	Fontana city	San Bernardino	36.1	128,929	58,006	15,255	1,450	5,618	427	41,185	6,988	74,424	80,135
06 24722	Foothill Farms CDP	Sacramento	2.3	17,426	12,162	2,155	231	757	93	1,024	1,004	2,523	12,348
06 24730	Foothill Ranch CDP	Orange	2.8	10,899	8,107	209	32	1,631	31	368	521	1,183	7,461
06 24764	Ford City CDP	Kern	1.5	3,512	2,827	22	64	45	22	408	124	771	2,409
06 25058	Fort Bragg city	Mendocino	2.7	7,026	5,583	73	130	62	10	847	321	1,596	5,295
06 25296	Fortuna city	Humboldt	4.8	10,497	9,278	47	305	102	18	415	332	1,097	7,763
06 25338	Foster City city	San Mateo	3.8	28,803	17,087	602	34	9,368	167	355	1,190	1,531	22,705
06 25380	Fountain Valley city	Orange	8.9	54,978	35,196	611	252	14,165	220	2,172	2,362	5,870	42,073
06 25436	Fowler city	Fresno	2.0	3,979	1,953	82	64	222	3	1,500	155	2,677	2,669
06 25576	Freedom CDP	Santa Cruz	1.3	6,000	2,665	29	112	201	13	2,623	357	4,165	4,154
06 26000	Fremont city	Alameda	76.7	203,413	96,968	6,310	1,048	75,165	819	11,230	11,873	27,409	150,961
06 26028	French Camp CDP	San Joaquin	3.1	4,109	1,816	492	33	183	19	1,320	246	1,847	3,102
06 27000	Fresno city	Fresno	104.4	427,652	214,556	35,763	6,763	48,028	583	99,898	22,061	170,520	286,861
06 28000	Fullerton city	Orange	22.2	126,000	77,977	2,861	865	20,259	296	18,666	5,079	38,014	94,320
06 28112	Galt city	Sacramento	5.9	19,472	13,726	225	204	553	31	3,616	1,117	6,465	12,762
06 28168	Gardena city	Los Angeles	5.8	57,746	13,755	15,010	367	15,489	424	9,784	2,917	18,372	42,832

[Includes incorporated places and census designated places (CDPs) of 2,500 or more population as of April 1, 2000. Codes shown are two-digit Federal Information Processing Standards (FIPS) state codes and five-digit FIPS place codes. Place names and codes are those in effect as of January 1, 2000. County refers to the county (or counties) in which the place is located. IC in this column = independent city, a county equivalent. If a place is located in more than one county, counties are listed in alphabetic order]

State and place code	Place	County	Land area, 2000 (sq. mi.)	Population, 2000 (April 1)									
					By race—							Hispanic or Latino (of any race)	18 years and over
					One race						Two or more races		
				Total	White	Black or African American	American Indian and Alaska Native	Asian	Native Hawaiian and Other Pacific Islander	Some other race			
06 00000	CALIFORNIA—Con.												
06 28182	Garden Acres CDP	San Joaquin	2.6	9,747	5,364	100	193	372	23	3,083	612	5,174	6,386
06 29000	Garden Grove city	Orange	18.0	165,196	77,443	2,168	1,260	51,078	1,081	25,362	6,804	53,608	118,178
06 29504	Gilroy city	Santa Clara	15.9	41,464	24,426	745	661	1,810	105	11,499	2,218	22,298	27,963
06 29644	Glen Avon CDP	Riverside	7.4	14,853	9,029	566	228	332	29	4,025	644	7,006	10,278
06 30000	Glendale city	Los Angeles	30.6	194,973	123,960	2,468	629	31,424	163	16,715	19,614	38,452	151,347
06 30014	Glendora city	Los Angeles	19.1	49,415	39,681	740	321	3,064	38	3,579	1,992	10,740	35,766
06 30282	Golden Hills CDP	Kern	12.3	7,434	6,188	97	63	107	6	586	387	1,228	4,925
06 30345	Gold River CDP	Sacramento	2.7	8,023	6,357	103	21	1,219	11	85	227	327	6,036
06 30378	Goleta CDP	Santa Barbara	26.3	55,204	43,397	703	451	3,548	60	5,098	1,947	12,326	42,454
06 30392	Gonzales city	Monterey	1.4	7,525	2,617	60	106	154	13	4,213	362	6,474	4,683
06 30658	Grand Terrace city	San Bernardino	3.5	11,626	8,575	537	84	653	36	1,133	608	2,954	8,566
06 30693	Granite Bay CDP	Placer	21.6	19,388	17,720	131	113	684	16	211	513	910	13,428
06 30703	Granite Hills CDP	San Diego	2.9	3,246	2,973	47	22	32	4	97	71	236	2,459
06 30798	Grass Valley city	Nevada	4.1	10,922	10,038	29	146	115	8	181	405	717	8,375
06 30994	Greenfield city	Monterey	1.7	12,583	4,989	148	150	97	19	6,537	643	11,055	7,760
06 31260	Gridley city	Butte	1.6	5,382	3,583	17	83	187	1	1,295	216	2,079	3,764
06 31375	Groveland-Big Oak Flat CDP	Tuolumne	28.5	3,388	3,138	22	54	24	3	36	111	167	2,800
06 31393	Grover Beach city	San Luis Obispo	2.3	13,067	10,421	135	221	490	39	1,206	555	2,941	9,721
06 31414	Guadalupe city	Santa Barbara	1.4	5,659	2,577	40	105	333	9	2,190	405	4,781	3,642
06 31568	Gustine city	Merced	1.6	4,698	3,395	34	46	71	3	891	258	1,648	3,277
06 31596	Hacienda Heights CDP	Los Angeles	11.4	53,122	21,797	825	380	19,174	64	8,819	2,063	20,320	39,688
06 31708	Half Moon Bay city	San Mateo	6.5	11,842	9,150	463	52	402	14	1,307	454	2,751	9,215
06 31960	Hanford city	Kings	13.1	41,686	26,704	2,090	569	1,190	74	8,669	2,390	16,116	28,505
06 32044	Harbison Canyon CDP	San Diego	10.0	3,645	3,305	17	65	42	4	81	131	390	2,646
06 32506	Hawaiian Gardens city	Los Angeles	1.0	14,779	5,651	657	189	1,300	109	6,156	717	10,869	9,343
06 32548	Hawthorne city	Los Angeles	6.1	84,112	24,618	27,775	629	5,660	721	20,320	4,389	37,227	57,485
06 33000	Hayward city	Alameda	44.3	140,030	60,146	15,374	1,177	26,579	2,679	23,539	10,536	47,850	102,531
06 33056	Healdsburg city	Sonoma	3.8	10,722	8,566	54	193	80	6	1,441	382	3,090	7,934
06 33084	Heber CDP	Imperial	1.5	2,988	1,026	19	18	8	-	1,848	69	2,914	1,947
06 33182	Hemet city	Riverside	25.6	58,812	47,335	1,527	708	872	79	6,225	2,066	13,585	45,543
06 33308	Hercules city	Contra Costa	6.5	19,488	5,453	3,659	49	8,327	90	872	1,038	2,106	14,302
06 33364	Hermosa Beach city	Los Angeles	1.4	18,566	16,632	150	74	817	41	312	540	1,253	16,339
06 33434	Hesperia city	San Bernardino	67.3	62,582	46,485	2,522	796	670	122	9,051	2,936	18,400	42,086
06 33532	Hidden Meadows CDP	San Diego	8.5	3,463	3,241	31	12	59	4	41	75	203	3,031
06 33559	Hidden Valley Lake CDP	Lake	10.9	3,777	3,506	27	39	28	7	67	103	255	2,719
06 33574	Highgrove CDP	Riverside	1.1	3,445	1,861	148	39	82	17	1,157	141	1,952	2,190
06 33588	Highland city	San Bernardino	13.6	44,605	25,089	5,403	581	2,740	152	8,307	2,333	16,342	28,730
06 33633	Highlands-Baywood Park CDP	San Mateo	1.8	4,210	2,970	60	16	853	10	94	207	250	3,186
06 33798	Hillsborough town	San Mateo	6.2	10,825	7,772	54	7	2,602	25	76	289	304	8,110
06 33861	Hilmar-Irwin CDP	Merced	3.9	4,807	3,746	17	16	115	-	317	596	595	3,415
06 34120	Hollister city	San Benito	6.6	34,413	20,341	469	390	965	63	10,312	1,873	18,949	22,499
06 34246	Holtville city	Imperial	1.1	5,612	3,051	35	47	47	4	2,197	231	4,144	3,639
06 34302	Home Gardens CDP	Riverside	1.1	9,461	4,533	320	125	432	21	3,606	424	6,293	6,142
06 34316	Homeland CDP	Riverside	3.3	3,710	2,966	29	40	19	4	515	137	1,102	2,855
06 34904	Hughson city	Stanislaus	1.1	3,980	2,738	24	57	44	5	967	145	1,545	2,647
06 34928	Humboldt Hill CDP	Humboldt	4.2	3,246	2,846	29	106	60	10	65	130	197	2,503
06 36000	Huntington Beach city	Orange	26.4	189,594	150,194	1,527	1,224	17,709	456	11,019	7,465	27,798	147,411
06 36056	Huntington Park city	Los Angeles	3.0	61,348	25,412	478	620	489	38	31,328	2,983	58,636	39,379
06 36084	Huron city	Fresno	1.3	6,306	1,284	20	62	25	8	4,715	192	6,197	3,840
06 36203	Idyllwild-Pine Cove CDP	Riverside	13.8	3,504	3,209	20	35	23	2	72	143	286	2,808
06 36280	Imperial city	Imperial	3.9	7,560	4,425	201	57	205	13	2,336	323	4,619	4,890
06 36294	Imperial Beach city	San Diego	4.3	26,992	16,805	1,421	298	1,767	163	4,796	1,742	10,818	19,044
06 36434	Indian Wells city	Riverside	13.2	3,816	3,676	15	8	57	3	18	39	113	3,526
06 36448	Indio city	Riverside	26.7	49,116	23,903	1,361	510	742	49	20,638	1,913	37,028	31,798
06 36546	Inglewood city	Los Angeles	9.1	112,580	21,505	53,060	773	1,280	410	30,823	4,729	51,829	76,143
06 36613	Interlaken CDP	Santa Cruz	9.7	7,328	3,802	74	94	410	5	2,563	380	4,551	4,962
06 36672	Ione city	Amador	4.7	7,129	4,128	1,271	164	120	12	1,292	142	1,437	5,859
06 36770	Irvine city	Orange	46.2	143,072	87,354	2,068	257	42,672	194	3,627	6,900	10,539	109,517
06 36868	Isla Vista CDP	Santa Barbara	2.1	18,344	12,748	385	118	2,121	42	1,864	1,066	3,671	16,771
06 36910	Ivanhoe CDP	Tulare	2.0	4,474	2,121	20	70	28	2	1,809	424	3,407	2,781
06 36980	Jackson city	Amador	3.5	3,989	3,731	20	55	23	3	74	83	258	3,193
06 37106	Jamestown CDP	Tuolumne	3.1	3,017	2,760	3	67	36	8	58	85	286	2,323
06 37120	Jamul CDP	San Diego	16.5	5,920	5,113	126	23	182	14	215	247	815	4,162
06 37554	Joshua Tree CDP	San Bernardino	6.1	4,207	3,634	74	66	47	26	194	166	520	3,051
06 38044	Kelseyville CDP	Lake	3.2	2,928	2,254	4	78	26	-	427	139	842	2,095
06 38065	Kennedy CDP	San Joaquin	1.2	3,275	953	301	51	344	8	1,449	169	2,208	2,026
06 38086	Kensington CDP	Contra Costa	1.1	4,936	4,036	126	12	522	8	45	194	172	4,064
06 38114	Kentfield CDP	Marin	3.0	6,351	6,004	22	11	136	7	29	142	141	4,763
06 38226	Kerman city	Fresno	2.2	8,551	3,634	31	167	709	2	3,624	384	5,552	5,532
06 38422	Keyes CDP	Stanislaus	2.9	4,575	2,836	27	91	149	12	1,264	196	1,882	2,970
06 38520	King City city	Monterey	3.7	11,094	4,669	65	116	136	15	5,598	495	8,922	7,138
06 38548	Kings Beach CDP	Placer	3.4	4,037	2,827	29	76	16	1	953	135	1,955	2,908
06 38562	Kingsburg city	Fresno	2.3	9,199	6,617	41	62	252	13	1,804	410	3,166	6,435
06 39003	La Canada Flintridge city	Los Angeles	8.7	20,318	15,142	73	36	4,180	9	206	672	976	14,269
06 39045	La Crescenta-Montrose CDP	Los Angeles	3.4	18,532	13,516	96	67	3,462	8	498	885	1,837	13,620

Table D-1. Places — **Area and Population**—Con.

[Includes incorporated places and census designated places (CDPs) of 2,500 or more population as of April 1, 2000. Codes shown are two-digit Federal Information Processing Standards (FIPS) state codes and five-digit FIPS place codes. Place names and codes are those in effect as of January 1, 2000. County refers to the county (or counties) in which the place is located. IC in this column = independent city, a county equivalent. If a place is located in more than one county, counties are listed in alphabetic order]

				Population, 2000 (April 1)									
					By race—								
					One race								
State and place code	Place	County	Land area, 2000 (sq. mi.)	Total	White	Black or African American	American Indian and Alaska Native	Asian	Native Hawaiian and Other Pacific Islander	Some other race	Two or more races	Hispanic or Latino (of any race)	18 years and over
06 00000	CALIFORNIA—Con.												
06 39108	Ladera Heights CDP	Los Angeles	2.9	6,568	1,318	4,647	18	190	6	91	298	222	5,206
06 39122	Lafayette city	Contra Costa	15.2	23,908	20,754	131	53	1,967	21	194	788	945	17,722
06 39173	Laguna CDP	Sacramento	6.7	34,309	20,275	3,329	228	6,171	122	1,881	2,303	4,984	22,703
06 39178	Laguna Beach city	Orange	8.8	23,727	21,826	190	86	494	20	524	587	1,570	19,976
06 39220	Laguna Hills city	Orange	6.3	31,178	23,954	429	138	3,181	47	2,241	1,188	5,113	23,004
06 39248	Laguna Niguel city	Orange	14.7	61,891	51,682	776	180	4,784	73	2,155	2,241	6,425	45,433
06 39257	Laguna West-Lakeside CDP	Sacramento	2.1	8,414	4,580	877	27	1,766	38	440	686	1,111	5,974
06 39259	Laguna Woods city	Orange	3.2	16,507	15,866	41	20	412	9	31	128	340	16,414
06 39290	La Habra city	Orange	7.3	58,974	37,153	926	564	3,498	127	13,953	2,753	28,922	41,822
06 39304	La Habra Heights city	Los Angeles	6.2	5,712	4,136	69	19	1,051	6	221	210	779	4,312
06 39444	Lake Arrowhead CDP	San Bernardino	11.4	8,934	8,083	50	79	91	10	346	275	1,211	6,351
06 39486	Lake Elsinore city	Riverside	33.8	28,928	18,981	1,501	374	592	87	5,880	1,513	11,007	18,509
06 39496	Lake Forest city	Orange	12.5	58,707	44,629	1,073	295	5,693	120	4,408	2,489	10,913	42,884
06 39570	Lake Isabella CDP	Kern	22.1	3,315	2,998	2	63	27	2	83	140	224	2,552
06 39598	Lakeland Village CDP	Riverside	2.3	5,626	4,445	100	92	55	5	715	214	1,743	3,885
06 39612	Lake Los Angeles CDP	Los Angeles	13.0	11,523	7,030	1,396	172	115	19	2,158	633	3,869	6,924
06 39690	Lake of the Pines CDP	Nevada	1.5	3,956	3,816	6	24	33	3	29	45	126	3,050
06 39710	Lakeport city	Lake	2.7	4,820	4,276	36	96	72	8	168	164	552	3,639
06 39724	Lake San Marcos CDP	San Diego	1.8	4,138	3,884	11	6	72	5	102	58	237	3,894
06 39766	Lakeside CDP	San Diego	5.7	19,560	17,571	146	216	248	55	641	683	2,254	13,885
06 39885	Lake Wildwood CDP	Nevada	3.1	4,868	4,699	11	19	38	1	9	91	111	4,072
06 39892	Lakewood city	Los Angeles	9.4	79,345	49,724	5,825	473	10,716	489	8,012	4,106	18,071	57,487
06 40004	La Mesa city	San Diego	9.3	54,749	44,148	2,660	364	2,238	217	2,782	2,340	7,402	43,897
06 40032	La Mirada city	Los Angeles	7.8	46,783	30,155	903	350	6,963	125	6,379	1,908	15,657	34,528
06 40088	Lamont CDP	Kern	4.6	13,296	5,917	371	204	138	11	6,132	523	11,814	8,160
06 40130	Lancaster city	Los Angeles	94.0	118,718	74,573	19,009	1,213	4,523	278	13,190	5,932	28,644	80,329
06 40256	La Palma city	Orange	1.8	15,408	6,632	710	48	6,900	45	534	539	1,736	11,743
06 40326	La Presa CDP	San Diego	5.6	32,721	16,428	4,739	288	3,215	370	5,349	2,332	10,813	22,475
06 40340	La Puente city	Los Angeles	3.5	41,063	16,060	804	524	2,940	68	18,535	2,132	34,122	27,178
06 40354	La Quinta city	Riverside	31.8	23,694	18,602	336	171	446	21	3,282	836	7,584	16,789
06 40410	La Riviera CDP	Sacramento	1.8	10,273	7,444	872	65	819	59	436	578	1,165	8,235
06 40426	Larkfield-Wikiup CDP	Sonoma	4.6	7,479	6,514	77	83	253	9	246	297	798	5,372
06 40438	Larkspur city	Marin	3.1	12,014	10,963	96	26	466	15	131	317	515	10,048
06 40526	Las Flores CDP	Orange	2.0	5,625	4,397	106	26	575	5	237	279	668	3,804
06 40592	Las Lomas CDP	Monterey	1.1	3,078	1,504	25	43	43	7	1,353	103	2,583	1,982
06 40704	Lathrop city	San Joaquin	16.4	10,445	5,319	469	126	1,395	56	2,205	875	4,031	6,806
06 40830	La Verne city	Los Angeles	8.3	31,638	24,379	1,016	203	2,278	55	2,348	1,359	7,315	23,663
06 40886	Lawndale city	Los Angeles	2.0	31,711	13,394	3,998	313	3,055	289	8,584	2,078	16,515	21,609
06 41124	Lemon Grove city	San Diego	3.8	24,918	14,859	3,010	273	1,433	209	3,364	1,770	7,107	18,032
06 41152	Lemoore city	Kings	8.5	19,712	11,687	1,435	313	1,649	65	3,420	1,143	6,013	12,884
06 41166	Lemoore Station CDP	Kings	4.2	5,749	3,546	630	75	550	44	514	390	968	3,712
06 41180	Lennox CDP	Los Angeles	1.1	22,950	7,275	952	234	189	319	12,923	1,058	20,602	14,008
06 41194	Lenwood CDP	San Bernardino	2.5	3,222	2,153	173	72	27	22	584	191	1,201	2,141
06 41474	Lincoln city	Placer	18.3	11,205	8,924	49	141	121	16	1,509	445	2,911	7,843
06 41558	Lincoln Village CDP	San Joaquin	0.7	4,216	3,344	123	44	180	1	284	240	801	2,993
06 41572	Linda CDP	Yuba	5.6	13,474	7,393	423	391	2,476	28	1,838	925	2,984	8,433
06 41712	Lindsay city	Tulare	2.4	10,297	4,616	59	155	109	15	4,970	373	8,029	6,385
06 41922	Live Oak CDP	Santa Cruz	3.2	16,628	12,905	227	169	636	18	1,840	833	3,655	12,725
06 41936	Live Oak city	Sutter	1.9	6,229	3,094	98	118	600	4	2,032	283	3,028	4,172
06 41992	Livermore city	Alameda	23.9	73,345	60,070	1,148	444	4,251	208	3,915	3,309	10,541	52,705
06 42006	Livingston city	Merced	3.5	10,473	3,825	77	97	1,513	8	4,350	603	7,521	6,526
06 42104	Lockeford CDP	San Joaquin	8.4	3,179	2,461	8	33	45	12	511	109	784	2,295
06 42202	Lodi city	San Joaquin	12.2	56,999	42,421	344	494	2,881	68	7,972	2,819	15,464	40,908
06 42370	Loma Linda city	San Bernardino	7.3	18,681	10,121	1,347	92	4,555	33	1,403	1,130	3,050	14,581
06 42468	Lomita city	Los Angeles	1.9	20,046	13,263	838	141	2,287	105	2,163	1,249	5,252	14,933
06 42524	Lompoc city	Santa Barbara	11.6	41,103	27,050	3,017	651	1,605	133	6,446	2,201	15,337	28,793
06 43000	Long Beach city	Los Angeles	50.4	461,522	208,410	68,618	3,881	55,591	5,605	95,107	24,310	165,092	326,883
06 43140	Loomis town	Placer	7.3	6,260	5,575	12	60	202	11	126	274	430	4,459
06 43224	Los Alamitos city	Orange	4.0	11,536	8,879	369	67	1,095	38	619	469	1,848	8,624
06 43280	Los Altos city	Santa Clara	6.4	27,693	22,250	130	48	4,271	45	183	766	822	21,132
06 43294	Los Altos Hills town	Santa Clara	8.6	7,902	5,922	47	7	1,667	7	36	216	170	6,041
06 44000	Los Angeles city	Los Angeles	469.1	3,694,820	1,734,036	415,195	29,412	369,254	5,915	949,720	191,288	1,719,073	2,713,509
06 44028	Los Banos city	Merced	8.0	25,869	15,161	1,100	350	606	85	6,960	1,607	13,048	16,780
06 44112	Los Gatos town	Santa Clara	10.7	28,592	24,784	226	87	2,173	21	366	935	1,491	22,540
06 44378	Loyola CDP	Santa Clara	1.7	3,478	2,752	12	5	554	2	38	115	136	2,674
06 44399	Lucas Valley-Marinwood CDP	Marin	5.6	6,357	5,646	51	14	380	6	72	188	267	4,667
06 44406	Lucerne CDP	Lake	6.1	2,870	2,522	48	90	12	3	98	97	245	2,273
06 44574	Lynwood city	Los Angeles	4.9	69,845	23,481	9,451	839	533	269	32,225	3,047	57,503	43,276
06 44826	McFarland city	Kern	2.1	9,618	2,740	307	157	66	8	5,889	451	8,239	6,241
06 44910	McKinleyville CDP	Humboldt	20.9	13,599	11,918	52	620	145	8	226	630	589	10,014
06 45022	Madera city	Madera	12.3	43,207	20,804	1,665	1,207	618	44	16,425	2,444	29,274	27,902
06 45050	Madera Acres CDP	Madera	7.6	7,741	4,657	276	168	120	4	2,124	392	3,939	5,056
06 45120	Magalia CDP	Butte	14.1	10,569	9,944	43	127	62	10	109	274	516	8,258
06 45246	Malibu city	Los Angeles	19.9	12,575	11,558	113	27	313	12	210	342	689	10,108
06 45358	Mammoth Lakes town	Mono	24.8	7,093	5,902	29	35	90	9	876	152	1,575	5,499
06 45400	Manhattan Beach city	Los Angeles	3.9	33,852	30,124	208	70	2,043	41	415	951	1,756	26,316

Table D-1. Places — Area and Population—Con.

[Includes incorporated places and census designated places (CDPs) of 2,500 or more population as of April 1, 2000. Codes shown are two-digit Federal Information Processing Standards (FIPS) state codes and five-digit FIPS place codes. Place names and codes are those in effect as of January 1, 2000. County refers to the county (or counties) in which the place is located. IC in this column = independent city, a county equivalent. If a place is located in more than one county, counties are listed in alphabetic order]

State and place code	Place	County	Land area, 2000 (sq. mi.)	Population, 2000 (April 1)									
					By race—							Hispanic or Latino (of any race)	18 years and over
					One race						Two or more races		
				Total	White	Black or African American	American Indian and Alaska Native	Asian	Native Hawaiian and Other Pacific Islander	Some other race			
06 00000	CALIFORNIA—Con.												
06 45484	Manteca city	San Joaquin	15.9	49,258	36,534	1,406	643	1,733	179	5,693	3,070	12,363	33,691
06 45778	Marina city	Monterey	8.7	25,101	10,979	3,600	186	4,084	528	3,718	2,006	5,822	19,745
06 45806	Marina del Rey CDP	Los Angeles	0.9	8,176	6,742	383	13	671	13	106	248	437	7,654
06 46114	Martinez city	Contra Costa	12.3	35,866	29,064	1,201	264	2,378	84	1,181	1,694	3,660	27,738
06 46170	Marysville city	Yuba	3.5	12,268	8,704	589	282	735	23	1,239	696	2,152	8,893
06 46436	Mayflower Village CDP	Los Angeles	0.7	5,081	3,373	60	35	841	9	526	237	1,352	3,825
06 46492	Maywood city	Los Angeles	1.2	28,083	12,073	102	320	101	37	14,177	1,273	27,051	17,691
06 46632	Meadow Vista CDP	Placer	5.4	3,096	2,980	2	25	12	6	8	63	112	2,306
06 46660	Mecca CDP	Riverside	1.3	5,402	1,302	6	55	40	-	3,817	182	5,295	3,250
06 46702	Meiners Oaks CDP	Ventura	1.4	3,750	3,117	16	41	34	3	404	135	866	2,629
06 46828	Mendota city	Fresno	1.9	7,890	2,156	52	103	57	13	4,980	529	7,468	5,217
06 46870	Menlo Park city	San Mateo	10.1	30,785	22,274	2,163	136	2,201	389	2,635	987	4,803	24,048
06 46884	Mentone CDP	San Bernardino	6.2	7,803	5,811	368	86	232	16	970	320	1,956	5,411
06 46898	Merced city	Merced	19.9	63,893	33,481	4,044	818	7,267	133	14,813	3,337	26,425	41,732
06 47486	Millbrae city	San Mateo	3.2	20,718	13,061	165	47	5,651	238	745	811	2,376	16,456
06 47710	Mill Valley city	Marin	4.7	13,600	12,435	135	34	563	29	89	315	472	10,718
06 47766	Milpitas city	Santa Clara	13.6	62,698	19,353	2,295	388	32,482	393	4,687	3,100	10,417	47,261
06 47976	Mira Loma CDP	Riverside	6.4	17,617	11,281	233	229	162	43	4,978	691	8,513	11,625
06 48046	Mira Monte CDP	Ventura	4.2	7,177	6,414	38	56	82	6	360	221	951	5,370
06 48147	Mission Canyon CDP	Santa Barbara	1.6	2,610	2,444	11	4	34	1	57	59	173	2,168
06 48186	Mission Hills CDP	Santa Barbara	1.2	3,142	2,489	113	46	92	11	239	152	640	2,207
06 48256	Mission Viejo city	Orange	18.7	93,102	77,418	1,067	348	7,199	174	3,553	3,343	11,266	67,829
06 48354	Modesto city	Stanislaus	35.8	188,856	131,414	7,499	2,335	11,388	951	24,066	11,203	48,310	132,071
06 48452	Mojave CDP	Kern	58.4	3,836	2,591	214	51	77	5	695	203	1,086	2,591
06 48641	Mono Vista CDP	Tuolumne	3.1	3,072	2,890	14	24	13	3	50	78	229	2,225
06 48648	Monrovia city	Los Angeles	13.7	36,929	23,237	3,202	323	2,594	48	5,765	1,760	13,012	26,822
06 48760	Montara CDP	San Mateo	3.9	2,950	2,632	30	4	108	5	64	107	267	2,200
06 48788	Montclair city	San Bernardino	5.1	33,049	14,796	2,112	319	2,688	101	11,442	1,591	19,823	22,101
06 48816	Montebello city	Los Angeles	8.2	62,150	29,098	559	767	7,232	51	21,040	3,403	46,347	44,374
06 48844	Montecito CDP	Santa Barbara	9.3	10,000	9,403	48	31	129	21	214	154	519	8,163
06 48872	Monterey city	Monterey	8.4	29,674	23,985	749	170	2,205	86	1,159	1,320	3,222	24,747
06 48914	Monterey Park city	Los Angeles	7.6	60,051	12,786	226	391	37,125	37	7,474	2,012	17,359	47,283
06 48956	Monte Sereno city	Santa Clara	1.6	3,483	2,912	6	2	428	1	37	97	125	2,513
06 49138	Moorpark city	Ventura	19.0	31,415	23,378	476	149	1,770	46	4,381	1,215	8,735	20,674
06 49180	Morada CDP	San Joaquin	3.0	3,726	3,050	26	25	243	17	230	135	489	2,835
06 49194	Moraga town	Contra Costa	9.3	16,290	13,212	165	25	2,026	14	237	611	775	12,595
06 49270	Moreno Valley city	Riverside	51.2	142,381	66,689	28,310	1,343	8,427	733	28,584	8,295	54,689	89,969
06 49278	Morgan Hill city	Santa Clara	11.7	33,556	24,296	573	362	2,020	77	4,505	1,723	9,229	23,310
06 49362	Morro Bay city	San Luis Obispo	5.2	10,350	9,257	70	98	187	9	424	305	1,183	8,784
06 49670	Mountain View city	Santa Clara	12.1	70,708	45,090	1,789	273	14,613	182	5,884	2,877	12,911	58,012
06 49684	Mountain View Acres CDP	San Bernardino	1.6	2,521	1,614	254	32	56	4	404	157	868	1,733
06 49852	Mount Shasta city	Siskiyou	3.7	3,621	3,323	55	16	59	5	77	86	211	2,753
06 50076	Murrieta city	Riverside	28.4	44,282	36,152	1,500	293	1,775	98	2,553	1,911	7,739	29,363
06 50090	Murrieta Hot Springs CDP	Riverside	1.3	2,948	2,708	46	19	57	1	50	67	239	2,709
06 50132	Muscoy CDP	San Bernardino	2.9	8,919	3,809	687	188	85	54	3,628	468	5,912	5,360
06 50188	Myrtletown CDP	Humboldt	2.1	4,459	3,984	35	127	62	3	50	198	204	3,410
06 50258	Napa city	Napa	17.7	72,585	58,302	381	657	1,241	117	9,181	2,706	19,475	53,915
06 50398	National City city	San Diego	7.4	54,260	19,070	3,026	513	10,077	478	18,181	2,915	32,053	37,918
06 50734	Needles city	San Bernardino	29.8	4,830	3,761	78	338	69	6	308	270	887	3,498
06 50874	Nevada City city	Nevada	2.1	3,001	2,829	13	41	22	1	22	73	104	2,411
06 50916	Newark city	Alameda	14.0	42,471	22,179	1,705	273	9,047	426	5,839	3,002	12,145	30,896
06 51140	Newman city	Stanislaus	1.4	7,093	4,310	89	94	131	5	2,051	413	3,648	4,591
06 51182	Newport Beach city	Orange	14.8	70,032	64,583	371	179	2,804	83	792	1,220	3,301	59,018
06 51186	Newport Coast CDP	Orange	7.0	2,671	2,085	7	4	483	-	8	84	112	2,014
06 51294	Nice CDP	Lake	2.2	2,509	2,190	54	123	11	6	46	79	217	1,929
06 51474	Nipomo CDP	San Luis Obispo	11.4	12,626	9,582	76	167	182	7	2,021	591	4,362	8,748
06 51560	Norco city	Riverside	14.1	24,157	19,915	1,481	182	280	33	1,538	728	5,504	18,744
06 51637	North Auburn CDP	Placer	7.6	11,847	10,632	84	139	212	11	442	327	1,091	9,211
06 51820	North El Monte CDP	Los Angeles	0.4	3,703	2,213	28	10	969	2	378	103	936	2,852
06 51840	North Fair Oaks CDP	San Mateo	1.2	15,440	7,813	296	130	468	203	5,858	672	10,741	10,768
06 51924	North Highlands CDP	Sacramento	12.8	44,187	30,006	4,920	616	2,515	240	2,708	3,182	6,695	30,537
06 51990	North Lakeport CDP	Lake	3.7	2,879	2,555	33	60	12	4	141	74	380	2,179
06 52526	Norwalk city	Los Angeles	9.7	103,298	46,303	4,774	1,201	11,924	404	33,829	4,863	64,965	70,111
06 52582	Novato city	Marin	27.7	47,630	39,414	948	246	2,479	82	2,587	1,874	6,229	36,633
06 52624	Nuevo CDP	Riverside	5.4	4,135	3,125	86	40	54	1	698	131	1,215	2,797
06 52694	Oakdale city	Stanislaus	5.0	15,503	12,995	74	169	183	18	1,437	627	3,109	11,015
06 52726	Oakhurst CDP	Madera	5.9	2,868	2,513	13	84	30	3	173	52	285	2,304
06 53000	Oakland city	Alameda	56.1	399,484	125,013	142,460	2,655	60,851	2,002	46,592	19,911	87,467	299,725
06 53070	Oakley city	Contra Costa	12.4	25,619	19,342	876	227	733	75	2,711	1,655	6,399	16,780
06 53182	Oak View CDP	Ventura	1.9	4,199	3,593	24	70	38	2	349	123	819	3,022
06 53294	Oceano CDP	San Luis Obispo	1.5	7,260	4,990	81	94	131	2	1,581	381	3,240	5,121
06 53322	Oceanside city	San Diego	40.6	161,029	106,866	10,189	1,370	8,896	2,042	23,342	8,324	48,691	116,573
06 53448	Oildale CDP	Kern	6.4	27,885	24,814	95	611	93	18	1,337	917	2,828	19,649
06 53476	Ojai city	Ventura	4.4	7,862	6,919	47	39	124	13	492	228	1,245	5,901
06 53714	Olivehurst CDP	Yuba	5.0	11,061	7,443	183	406	560	19	1,717	733	2,760	7,353
06 53896	Ontario city	San Bernardino	49.8	158,007	75,575	11,864	1,682	6,125	587	53,807	8,367	94,610	103,703
06 53924	Opal Cliffs CDP	Santa Cruz	0.8	6,458	5,481	63	50	142	9	414	299	808	5,265

Table D-1. Places — **Area and Population**—Con.

[Includes incorporated places and census designated places (CDPs) of 2,500 or more population as of April 1, 2000. Codes shown are two-digit Federal Information Processing Standards (FIPS) state codes and five-digit FIPS place codes. Place names and codes are those in effect as of January 1, 2000. County refers to the county (or counties) in which the place is located. IC in this column = independent city, a county equivalent. If a place is located in more than one county, counties are listed in alphabetic order]

State and place code	Place	County	Land area, 2000 (sq. mi.)	Total	White	Black or African American	American Indian and Alaska Native	Asian	Native Hawaiian and Other Pacific Islander	Some other race	Two or more races	Hispanic or Latino (of any race)	18 years and over
06 00000	CALIFORNIA—Con.												
06 53980	Orange city	Orange	23.4	128,821	90,822	2,056	1,010	12,000	296	17,804	4,833	41,434	94,480
06 54008	Orange Cove city	Fresno	1.5	7,722	2,591	24	187	115	-	4,544	261	6,996	4,603
06 54092	Orangevale CDP	Sacramento	10.0	26,705	23,906	301	277	656	50	450	1,065	1,816	19,609
06 54120	Orcutt CDP	Santa Barbara	11.3	28,830	24,990	403	265	924	24	1,127	1,097	4,165	21,056
06 54232	Orinda city	Contra Costa	12.6	17,599	15,246	82	26	1,626	7	112	500	560	13,035
06 54274	Orland city	Glenn	2.5	6,281	4,263	37	98	119	11	1,514	239	2,340	4,236
06 54358	Orosi CDP	Tulare	2.5	7,318	2,153	26	67	747	2	3,917	406	6,000	4,696
06 54386	Oroville city	Butte	12.3	13,004	10,043	524	511	825	34	362	705	1,073	9,096
06 54388	Oroville East CDP	Butte	20.7	8,680	7,868	57	277	80	16	121	261	396	6,936
06 54652	Oxnard city	Ventura	25.3	170,358	71,688	6,446	2,143	12,581	698	68,753	8,049	112,807	116,242
06 54764	Pacheco CDP	Contra Costa	0.7	3,562	2,951	79	28	264	8	105	127	421	2,833
06 54806	Pacifica city	San Mateo	12.6	38,390	26,684	1,254	190	5,868	263	1,605	2,526	5,609	29,500
06 54848	Pacific Grove city	Monterey	2.9	15,522	13,665	177	86	698	41	276	579	1,108	12,756
06 55044	Pajaro CDP	Monterey	0.9	3,384	1,453	16	56	51	12	1,634	162	3,189	2,045
06 55086	Palermo CDP	Butte	39.0	5,720	4,461	33	337	137	7	450	295	892	4,102
06 55156	Palmdale city	Los Angeles	105.0	116,670	63,905	16,913	1,198	4,468	224	23,858	6,104	43,991	72,352
06 55184	Palm Desert city	Riverside	24.4	41,155	35,739	495	187	1,056	40	2,666	972	7,031	34,025
06 55254	Palm Springs city	Riverside	94.2	42,807	33,531	1,681	401	1,639	59	4,188	1,308	10,155	35,532
06 55282	Palo Alto city	Santa Clara	23.7	58,598	44,391	1,184	122	10,090	84	827	1,900	2,722	46,192
06 55380	Palos Verdes Estates city	Los Angeles	4.8	13,340	10,448	132	18	2,286	16	80	360	378	10,246
06 55520	Paradise town	Butte	18.2	26,408	24,751	51	283	275	31	320	697	1,127	21,022
06 55618	Paramount city	Los Angeles	4.7	55,266	19,177	7,508	586	1,851	464	23,040	2,640	39,945	34,893
06 55751	Parksdale CDP	Madera	1.8	2,688	863	81	85	2	5	1,449	203	2,198	1,611
06 55837	Parkway-South Sacramento CDP	Sacramento	4.8	36,468	13,895	6,067	562	6,339	235	6,572	2,798	12,402	23,509
06 55856	Parlier city	Fresno	1.6	11,145	3,748	65	216	91	5	6,623	397	10,807	6,916
06 56000	Pasadena city	Los Angeles	23.1	133,936	71,469	19,319	952	13,399	132	21,444	7,221	44,734	102,980
06 56112	Patterson city	Stanislaus	2.9	11,606	6,459	219	171	244	49	3,661	803	6,611	7,381
06 56350	Pedley CDP	Riverside	5.1	11,207	7,492	105	416	416	25	2,065	587	3,840	7,511
06 56700	Perris city	Riverside	31.4	36,189	14,909	5,748	529	995	121	11,781	2,106	20,322	21,857
06 56784	Petaluma city	Sonoma	13.8	54,548	45,906	632	294	2,135	93	3,317	2,171	7,985	40,270
06 56871	Phoenix Lake-Cedar Ridge CDP	Tuolumne	25.2	5,123	4,839	18	58	35	8	56	109	256	3,936
06 56924	Pico Rivera city	Los Angeles	8.3	63,428	31,360	450	859	1,681	78	25,551	3,449	56,000	43,784
06 56938	Piedmont city	Alameda	1.7	10,952	8,607	136	12	1,754	4	69	370	325	7,639
06 57204	Pine Hills CDP	Humboldt	10.2	3,108	2,785	17	81	50	9	34	132	143	2,330
06 57288	Pinole city	Contra Costa	5.2	19,039	10,356	2,115	108	4,134	70	1,107	1,149	2,618	14,272
06 57414	Pismo Beach city	San Luis Obispo	3.6	8,551	7,811	51	61	250	5	141	232	589	7,244
06 57456	Pittsburg city	Contra Costa	15.6	56,769	24,712	10,724	423	7,179	491	9,144	4,096	18,287	39,270
06 57512	Pixley CDP	Tulare	3.1	2,586	850	109	45	5	2	1,457	118	1,763	1,555
06 57526	Placentia city	Orange	6.6	46,488	31,500	821	386	5,190	82	6,843	1,666	14,460	33,920
06 57540	Placerville city	El Dorado	5.0	9,610	8,511	22	122	85	12	556	302	1,212	7,150
06 57582	Planada CDP	Merced	2.1	4,369	1,061	30	79	23	1	2,967	208	4,024	2,674
06 57764	Pleasant Hill city	Contra Costa	7.1	32,837	26,852	504	155	3,096	90	763	1,377	2,767	25,828
06 57792	Pleasanton city	Alameda	21.7	63,654	51,203	876	210	7,444	85	1,495	2,341	5,011	45,702
06 58030	Pollock Pines CDP	El Dorado	5.8	4,728	4,421	1	56	33	14	67	136	248	3,540
06 58072	Pomona city	Los Angeles	22.8	149,473	62,419	14,398	1,883	10,762	311	52,213	7,487	96,370	97,731
06 58240	Porterville city	Tulare	14.0	39,615	21,690	506	684	1,835	61	12,959	1,880	19,589	26,045
06 58296	Port Hueneme city	Ventura	4.4	21,845	12,510	1,324	369	1,383	110	4,772	1,377	8,960	15,814
06 58356	Portola Hills CDP	Orange	1.3	6,391	5,407	104	19	432	8	169	252	641	4,290
06 58380	Portola Valley town	San Mateo	9.2	4,462	4,146	18	11	178	2	43	64	149	3,441
06 58520	Poway city	San Diego	39.2	48,044	39,807	800	231	3,584	133	1,571	1,918	4,974	33,303
06 58870	Prunedale CDP	Monterey	46.1	16,432	12,648	209	170	592	28	1,914	871	3,781	12,135
06 59052	Quartz Hill CDP	Los Angeles	3.8	9,890	8,057	494	112	182	24	605	416	1,511	6,878
06 59346	Ramona CDP	San Diego	15.3	15,691	12,647	122	208	122	43	1,971	578	3,921	10,803
06 59426	Rancho Calaveras CDP	Calaveras	8.5	4,182	3,723	36	52	62	5	117	187	424	3,000
06 59444	Rancho Cordova CDP	Sacramento	22.5	55,060	36,704	6,245	521	4,537	300	3,151	3,602	7,100	39,440
06 59451	Rancho Cucamonga city	San Bernardino	37.4	127,743	84,987	10,059	855	7,656	341	16,931	6,914	35,491	89,598
06 59500	Rancho Mirage city	Riverside	24.3	13,249	12,280	118	26	165	15	479	166	1,251	11,887
06 59506	Rancho Murieta CDP	Sacramento	11.9	4,193	3,817	81	15	114	3	45	118	194	3,403
06 59514	Rancho Palos Verdes city	Los Angeles	13.7	41,145	27,660	815	62	10,676	41	497	1,394	2,339	31,688
06 59550	Rancho San Diego CDP	San Diego	8.9	20,155	16,857	656	112	838	56	663	973	2,177	14,657
06 59584	Rancho Santa Fe CDP	San Diego	6.8	3,252	3,035	15	5	90	2	70	35	173	2,410
06 59587	Rancho Santa Margarita city	Orange	12.3	47,214	38,523	826	199	3,492	97	2,119	1,958	6,139	31,359
06 59892	Red Bluff city	Tehama	7.4	13,147	11,397	81	294	211	9	759	396	1,799	9,370
06 59920	Redding city	Shasta	58.4	80,865	71,727	851	1,802	2,386	94	1,324	2,681	4,393	59,750
06 59962	Redlands city	San Bernardino	35.5	63,591	46,858	2,739	597	3,257	146	7,204	2,790	15,304	46,940
06 60018	Redondo Beach city	Los Angeles	6.3	63,261	49,735	1,592	295	5,756	224	2,762	2,897	8,524	51,371
06 60102	Redwood City city	San Mateo	19.5	75,402	52,008	1,916	384	6,715	663	10,535	3,181	23,557	57,911
06 60242	Reedley city	Fresno	4.4	20,756	10,743	89	251	906	15	7,830	922	14,028	14,083
06 60466	Rialto city	San Bernardino	21.9	91,873	36,168	20,464	965	2,271	392	26,824	4,789	47,050	57,247
06 60606	Richgrove CDP	Tulare	0.5	2,723	439	2	22	165	6	2,028	61	2,493	1,539
06 60620	Richmond city	Contra Costa	30.0	99,216	31,117	35,777	639	12,198	498	13,754	5,233	26,319	71,722
06 60704	Ridgecrest city	Kern	21.1	24,927	20,446	879	270	967	144	1,229	992	3,001	17,676
06 60706	Ridgemark CDP	San Benito	2.7	2,741	2,460	18	22	64	1	81	95	333	2,174
06 60900	Rio Dell city	Humboldt	1.9	3,174	2,718	5	123	12	1	182	133	343	2,277
06 60928	Rio del Mar CDP	Santa Cruz	3.0	9,198	8,438	56	49	237	15	172	231	594	7,435

Table D-1. Places — **Area and Population**—Con.

[Includes incorporated places and census designated places (CDPs) of 2,500 or more population as of April 1, 2000. Codes shown are two-digit Federal Information Processing Standards (FIPS) state codes and five-digit FIPS place codes. Place names and codes are those in effect as of January 1, 2000. County refers to the county (or counties) in which the place is located. IC in this column = independent city, a county equivalent. If a place is located in more than one county, counties are listed in alphabetic order]

State and place code	Place	County	Land area, 2000 (sq. mi.)	Population, 2000 (April 1) Total	White	Black or African American	American Indian and Alaska Native	Asian	Native Hawaiian and Other Pacific Islander	Some other race	Two or more races	Hispanic or Latino (of any race)	18 years and over
06 00000	CALIFORNIA—Con.												
06 60942	Rio Linda CDP	Sacramento	5.5	10,466	8,691	233	153	282	50	511	546	1,162	7,242
06 60984	Rio Vista city	Solano	6.8	4,571	4,038	54	42	73	1	187	176	522	3,430
06 61026	Ripon city	San Joaquin	4.1	10,146	8,575	35	62	153	28	893	400	1,843	6,901
06 61068	Riverbank city	Stanislaus	3.1	15,826	10,579	242	227	208	20	3,803	747	7,266	10,458
06 62000	Riverside city	Riverside	78.1	255,166	151,377	18,906	2,779	14,501	991	53,591	13,021	97,315	178,462
06 62364	Rocklin city	Placer	16.2	36,330	32,086	330	291	1,510	70	701	1,342	2,874	25,436
06 62490	Rodeo CDP	Contra Costa	7.4	8,717	4,550	1,398	113	1,398	44	625	589	1,489	6,159
06 62546	Rohnert Park city	Sonoma	6.4	42,236	33,907	833	329	2,356	177	2,417	2,217	5,731	31,562
06 62644	Rolling Hills Estates city	Los Angeles	3.6	7,676	5,673	89	25	1,557	6	76	250	366	5,809
06 62700	Rollingwood CDP	Contra Costa	0.2	2,900	961	302	32	690	13	711	191	1,225	1,935
06 62756	Romoland CDP	Riverside	3.0	2,764	1,494	69	48	9	5	1,013	126	1,530	1,802
06 62826	Rosamond CDP	Kern	52.2	14,349	10,333	950	189	432	33	1,671	741	3,684	9,633
06 62854	Rosedale CDP	Kern	37.9	8,445	7,514	103	103	115	3	363	244	929	5,637
06 62868	Roseland CDP	Sonoma	1.1	6,369	3,672	171	169	337	32	1,602	386	2,753	4,355
06 62896	Rosemead city	Los Angeles	5.1	53,505	14,217	363	456	26,090	34	10,535	1,810	22,097	38,776
06 62910	Rosemont CDP	Sacramento	4.3	22,904	14,771	2,496	259	2,559	93	1,216	1,510	3,023	16,692
06 62938	Roseville city	Placer	30.5	79,921	68,756	1,047	559	3,442	157	3,141	2,819	9,225	58,537
06 63050	Rossmoor CDP	Orange	1.6	10,298	9,153	80	35	589	10	140	291	687	7,547
06 63218	Rowland Heights CDP	Los Angeles	9.0	48,553	14,206	1,268	221	24,432	150	6,228	2,048	13,748	35,945
06 63260	Rubidoux CDP	Riverside	9.2	29,180	15,107	2,137	416	654	85	9,342	1,439	15,843	18,687
06 63316	Running Springs CDP	San Bernardino	4.0	5,125	4,495	24	87	47	5	208	259	570	3,722
06 64000	Sacramento city	Sacramento	97.2	407,018	196,549	62,968	5,300	67,635	3,861	44,627	26,078	87,974	295,728
06 64140	St. Helena city	Napa	4.7	5,950	4,900	26	27	42	10	786	159	1,691	4,456
06 64210	Salida CDP	Stanislaus	5.0	12,560	8,628	424	161	595	31	1,964	757	3,902	8,038
06 64224	Salinas city	Monterey	19.0	151,060	68,218	4,943	1,903	9,390	407	58,466	7,733	96,880	102,671
06 64420	San Andreas CDP	Calaveras	8.7	2,615	2,408	2	40	19	-	51	95	166	1,981
06 64434	San Anselmo town	Marin	2.7	12,378	11,341	130	50	361	15	118	363	513	9,679
06 64462	San Antonio Heights CDP	San Bernardino	1.4	3,122	2,666	42	22	191	1	96	104	327	2,361
06 65000	San Bernardino city	San Bernardino	58.8	185,401	83,849	30,425	2,591	7,772	680	50,286	9,798	88,022	120,221
06 65028	San Bruno city	San Mateo	5.5	40,165	23,156	807	189	7,506	1,156	4,346	3,005	9,686	30,936
06 65042	San Buenaventura (Ventura) city	Ventura	21.1	100,916	79,511	1,421	1,173	3,028	175	11,245	4,363	24,573	75,654
06 65070	San Carlos city	San Mateo	5.9	27,718	23,434	209	53	2,182	110	664	1,066	2,133	21,595
06 65084	San Clemente city	Orange	17.6	49,936	43,905	385	307	1,317	69	2,552	1,401	7,933	37,903
06 66000	San Diego city	San Diego	324.3	1,223,400	736,207	96,216	7,543	166,968	5,853	151,532	59,081	310,752	929,492
06 66004	San Diego Country Estates CDP	San Diego	17.0	9,262	8,606	67	45	104	25	159	256	713	6,331
06 66070	San Dimas city	Los Angeles	15.5	34,980	26,116	1,156	243	3,286	73	2,569	1,537	8,163	26,046
06 66140	San Fernando city	Los Angeles	2.4	23,564	10,076	231	399	264	26	11,629	939	21,038	15,455
06 67000	San Francisco city	San Francisco	46.7	776,733	385,728	60,515	3,458	239,565	3,844	50,368	33,255	109,504	663,931
06 67042	San Gabriel city	Los Angeles	4.1	39,804	13,294	420	331	19,470	39	4,921	1,329	12,223	30,449
06 67056	Sanger city	Fresno	4.7	18,931	9,376	80	228	371	16	8,170	690	15,319	12,474
06 67112	San Jacinto city	Riverside	24.9	23,779	16,488	630	556	267	38	4,641	1,159	9,583	16,328
06 67126	San Joaquin city	Fresno	1.0	3,270	1,159	7	51	118	-	1,757	178	3,008	1,922
06 67143	San Joaquin Hills CDP	Orange	1.2	2,959	2,544	18	2	282	4	41	68	98	2,316
06 68000	San Jose city	Santa Clara	174.9	894,943	425,017	31,349	6,865	240,375	3,584	142,691	45,062	269,989	658,819
06 68028	San Juan Capistrano city	Orange	14.2	33,826	26,543	265	363	651	38	4,806	1,160	11,206	24,326
06 68084	San Leandro city	Alameda	13.1	79,452	40,754	7,849	609	18,242	683	6,737	4,578	15,939	61,798
06 68112	San Lorenzo CDP	Alameda	2.8	21,898	13,865	616	195	3,389	105	2,369	1,359	5,398	16,390
06 68154	San Luis Obispo city	San Luis Obispo	10.7	44,174	37,155	644	287	2,331	58	2,130	1,569	5,147	37,911
06 68196	San Marcos city	San Diego	23.8	54,977	37,051	1,099	453	2,567	130	11,212	2,465	20,271	38,972
06 68224	San Marino city	Los Angeles	3.8	12,945	6,177	33	6	6,286	10	135	298	571	9,520
06 68238	San Martin CDP	Santa Clara	5.5	4,230	2,769	35	69	259	10	887	201	1,667	3,034
06 68252	San Mateo city	San Mateo	12.2	92,482	61,251	2,397	447	13,961	1,517	8,260	4,649	18,973	73,648
06 68294	San Pablo city	Contra Costa	2.6	30,215	9,555	5,539	271	4,945	154	7,688	2,063	13,490	20,635
06 68364	San Rafael city	Marin	16.6	56,063	42,472	1,257	312	3,133	95	6,256	2,538	13,070	45,126
06 68378	San Ramon city	Contra Costa	11.6	44,722	34,354	862	160	6,680	95	968	1,603	3,238	32,961
06 69000	Santa Ana city	Orange	27.1	337,977	144,425	5,749	4,013	29,778	1,160	137,360	15,492	257,097	222,470
06 69070	Santa Barbara city	Santa Barbara	19.0	92,325	68,355	1,636	990	2,554	126	15,110	3,554	32,330	74,070
06 69084	Santa Clara city	Santa Clara	18.4	102,361	56,903	2,341	542	29,966	437	7,102	5,070	16,364	81,966
06 69088	Santa Clarita city	Los Angeles	47.8	151,088	120,157	3,122	886	7,923	220	12,896	5,884	30,968	105,314
06 69112	Santa Cruz city	Santa Cruz	12.5	54,593	42,984	945	469	2,677	72	4,990	2,456	9,491	45,130
06 69154	Santa Fe Springs city	Los Angeles	8.8	17,438	8,932	679	250	688	35	6,102	752	12,447	12,371
06 69196	Santa Maria city	Santa Barbara	19.3	77,423	44,962	1,449	1,360	3,673	138	21,691	4,150	46,196	52,953
06 70000	Santa Monica city	Los Angeles	8.3	84,084	65,832	3,176	396	6,100	86	5,019	3,475	11,304	71,770
06 70042	Santa Paula city	Ventura	4.6	28,598	15,795	118	404	200	54	10,688	1,339	20,360	19,608
06 70098	Santa Rosa city	Sonoma	40.1	147,595	114,527	3,177	2,099	5,675	382	15,180	6,555	28,318	111,790
06 70154	Santa Venetia CDP	Marin	3.8	4,298	3,510	93	30	257	8	215	185	518	3,519
06 70182	Santa Ynez CDP	Santa Barbara	7.8	4,584	4,210	8	56	59	1	141	109	422	3,385
06 70224	Santee city	San Diego	16.1	52,975	45,929	783	429	1,350	216	2,134	2,134	6,016	38,011
06 70280	Saratoga city	Santa Clara	12.1	29,843	20,111	115	46	8,679	25	171	696	936	22,079
06 70364	Sausalito city	Marin	1.9	7,330	6,718	48	21	306	18	52	167	244	6,786
06 70588	Scotts Valley city	Santa Cruz	4.6	11,385	10,090	55	46	526	21	245	402	729	8,446
06 70686	Seal Beach city	Orange	11.5	24,157	21,477	347	73	1,386	43	309	522	1,554	20,940
06 70742	Seaside city	Monterey	8.8	31,696	15,599	3,997	331	3,197	410	5,834	2,328	10,929	22,121
06 70770	Sebastopol city	Sonoma	1.9	7,774	6,985	51	61	118	8	300	251	720	5,938
06 70784	Sedco Hills CDP	Riverside	1.6	3,078	2,274	101	61	35	1	495	111	1,118	2,152
06 70882	Selma city	Fresno	4.3	19,444	8,536	146	304	619	6	8,962	871	13,952	13,017
06 71084	Shackelford CDP	Stanislaus	0.8	5,170	2,592	73	110	49	7	1,997	342	3,522	3,227

U.S. Census Bureau, County and City Data Book: 2000

[Includes incorporated places and census designated places (CDPs) of 2,500 or more population as of April 1, 2000. Codes shown are two-digit Federal Information Processing Standards (FIPS) state codes and five-digit FIPS place codes. Place names and codes are those in effect as of January 1, 2000. County refers to the county (or counties) in which the place is located. IC in this column = independent city, a county equivalent. If a place is located in more than one county, counties are listed in alphabetic order]

State and place code	Place	County	Land area, 2000 (sq. mi.)	Population, 2000 (April 1)									
				By race—									
				One race							Two or more races	Hispanic or Latino (of any race)	18 years and over
				Total	White	Black or African American	American Indian and Alaska Native	Asian	Native Hawaiian and Other Pacific Islander	Some other race			
06 00000	CALIFORNIA—Con.												
06 71106	Shafter city	Kern	18.0	12,736	5,670	204	159	40	18	6,159	486	8,667	8,069
06 71225	Shasta Lake city	Shasta	10.9	9,008	7,911	65	399	32	8	180	413	557	6,417
06 71554	Shingle Springs CDP	El Dorado	5.2	2,643	2,423	10	34	43	4	35	94	175	1,866
06 71806	Sierra Madre city	Los Angeles	3.0	10,578	9,077	121	37	592	11	319	421	1,054	8,579
06 71876	Signal Hill city	Los Angeles	2.2	9,333	4,245	1,212	55	1,539	194	1,510	578	2,707	6,873
06 72016	Simi Valley city	Ventura	39.2	111,351	90,561	1,401	780	7,052	154	7,235	4,168	18,729	79,672
06 72506	Solana Beach city	San Diego	3.5	12,979	11,293	65	54	449	18	725	375	1,922	10,654
06 72520	Soledad city	Monterey	4.2	11,263	3,593	129	195	265	9	6,596	476	9,779	7,129
06 72576	Solvang city	Santa Barbara	2.5	5,332	4,705	23	35	56	2	294	217	1,059	4,162
06 72646	Sonoma city	Sonoma	2.7	9,128	8,562	33	31	155	5	147	195	625	7,434
06 72674	Sonora city	Tuolumne	3.0	4,423	4,041	30	66	54	6	88	138	372	3,522
06 72688	Soquel CDP	Santa Cruz	1.1	5,081	4,214	80	32	203	9	314	229	711	3,832
06 72996	South El Monte city	Los Angeles	2.9	21,144	8,586	80	332	1,783	39	9,300	1,024	18,190	14,057
06 73080	South Gate city	Los Angeles	7.4	96,375	40,136	923	901	804	114	49,112	4,385	88,669	62,097
06 73108	South Lake Tahoe city	El Dorado	10.1	23,609	17,878	178	228	1,419	40	2,946	920	6,294	17,669
06 73178	South Oroville CDP	Butte	4.5	7,695	5,314	375	306	980	4	291	425	769	4,995
06 73220	South Pasadena city	Los Angeles	3.4	24,292	14,653	738	83	6,456	20	1,257	1,085	3,903	18,804
06 73262	South San Francisco city	San Mateo	9.0	60,552	26,671	1,707	362	17,510	944	9,091	4,267	19,282	45,886
06 73276	South San Gabriel CDP	Los Angeles	0.8	7,595	2,333	30	89	3,292	15	1,514	322	3,491	5,695
06 73290	South San Jose Hills CDP	Los Angeles	1.5	20,218	7,837	376	312	1,322	71	9,371	929	16,868	13,227
06 73430	South Whittier CDP	Los Angeles	5.4	55,193	28,958	812	678	1,669	142	20,074	2,860	38,256	36,949
06 73461	South Woodbridge CDP	San Joaquin	0.4	2,825	2,153	4	28	137	1	388	114	774	1,878
06 73472	South Yuba City CDP	Sutter	3.2	12,651	8,090	212	115	2,904	29	778	523	1,501	8,897
06 73696	Spring Valley CDP	San Diego	7.2	26,663	18,153	2,730	204	1,276	139	2,520	1,641	5,726	18,900
06 73794	Squaw Valley CDP	Fresno	56.7	2,691	2,377	37	64	15	6	130	62	327	2,059
06 73906	Stanford CDP	Santa Clara	2.7	13,315	8,042	653	96	3,405	21	486	612	1,193	12,356
06 73962	Stanton city	Orange	3.1	37,403	18,541	848	397	5,780	344	9,616	1,877	18,285	26,026
06 75000	Stockton city	San Joaquin	54.7	243,771	105,446	27,417	2,727	48,506	981	42,208	16,486	79,217	164,687
06 75280	Strathmore CDP	Tulare	1.4	2,584	1,175	6	28	36	-	1,231	108	1,771	1,588
06 75315	Strawberry CDP	Marin	1.4	5,302	4,431	106	12	483	7	80	183	253	4,308
06 75630	Suisun City city	Solano	4.0	26,118	11,606	5,044	189	4,621	268	2,225	2,165	4,652	17,619
06 75826	Sun City CDP	Riverside	7.8	17,773	15,930	378	91	211	26	730	407	2,187	15,246
06 76022	Sunnyslope CDP	Riverside	1.4	4,437	2,560	172	70	101	5	1,356	173	2,356	2,911
06 77000	Sunnyvale city	Santa Clara	21.9	131,760	70,193	2,927	608	42,524	428	9,474	5,606	20,390	104,863
06 77364	Susanville city	Lassen	5.9	13,541	10,295	1,692	431	155	120	469	379	2,109	10,839
06 77378	Sutter CDP	Sutter	3.0	2,885	2,448	8	73	19	-	181	156	358	1,891
06 77574	Taft city	Kern	15.1	6,400	5,322	126	54	81	28	665	124	995	4,761
06 77805	Tamalpais-Homestead Valley CDP	Marin	5.0	10,691	9,626	101	22	533	11	94	304	409	8,538
06 77924	Tara Hills CDP	Contra Costa	0.8	5,332	2,760	770	35	754	29	669	315	1,273	3,941
06 78092	Tehachapi city	Kern	9.6	10,957	6,264	1,512	148	81	17	2,610	325	3,583	8,931
06 78120	Temecula city	Riverside	26.3	57,716	45,555	1,974	497	2,728	174	4,276	2,512	10,974	37,684
06 78148	Temple City city	Los Angeles	4.0	33,377	16,266	307	148	12,980	19	2,496	1,161	6,836	25,381
06 78162	Templeton CDP	San Luis Obispo	4.7	4,687	4,235	55	33	43	4	170	147	554	3,109
06 78288	Terra Bella CDP	Tulare	1.7	3,466	1,000	19	57	124	-	2,120	146	2,910	2,150
06 78470	Thermalito CDP	Butte	12.8	6,045	4,699	28	176	635	12	180	315	465	4,227
06 78582	Thousand Oaks city	Ventura	54.9	117,005	99,563	1,241	627	6,873	124	5,274	3,303	15,328	86,617
06 78596	Thousand Palms CDP	Riverside	4.0	5,120	3,828	37	47	38	13	993	164	2,231	3,808
06 78666	Tiburon town	Marin	4.5	8,666	7,879	75	19	383	10	65	235	317	6,767
06 78680	Tierra Buena CDP	Sutter	3.4	4,587	3,479	59	55	527	8	271	188	487	3,362
06 80000	Torrance city	Los Angeles	20.5	137,946	81,605	3,022	560	39,462	481	6,307	6,509	17,637	106,206
06 80238	Tracy city	San Joaquin	21.0	56,929	37,127	3,117	518	4,633	315	7,445	3,774	15,765	37,330
06 80588	Truckee town	Nevada	32.5	13,864	12,254	34	82	120	24	1,050	300	1,773	10,167
06 80644	Tulare city	Tulare	16.6	43,994	24,804	2,209	616	890	54	12,798	2,623	20,058	28,781
06 80812	Turlock city	Stanislaus	13.3	55,810	40,370	798	523	2,518	153	8,460	2,988	16,422	39,154
06 80854	Tustin city	Orange	11.4	67,504	39,639	1,970	448	10,058	203	12,113	3,073	23,110	49,382
06 80868	Tustin Foothills CDP	Orange	6.7	24,044	20,869	134	87	1,695	31	631	597	2,037	18,036
06 80966	Twain Harte CDP	Tuolumne	3.6	2,586	2,411	3	26	19	14	28	85	143	2,033
06 80994	Twentynine Palms city	San Bernardino	54.8	14,764	10,485	1,381	215	563	260	921	939	2,202	10,163
06 81008	Twentynine Palms Base CDP	San Bernardino	1.4	8,413	5,911	873	118	260	24	801	426	1,646	7,116
06 81050	Twin Lakes CDP	Santa Cruz	0.7	5,533	4,362	50	35	127	10	688	261	1,247	4,591
06 81134	Ukiah city	Mendocino	4.7	15,497	12,325	148	587	261	15	1,499	662	2,993	11,383
06 81204	Union City city	Alameda	19.3	66,869	20,198	4,479	356	29,016	610	7,709	4,501	16,020	48,307
06 81344	Upland city	San Bernardino	15.1	68,393	45,966	5,164	518	4,969	101	8,437	3,238	18,830	49,694
06 81554	Vacaville city	Solano	27.1	88,625	63,909	8,880	856	3,706	403	5,970	4,901	15,847	64,704
06 81638	Valinda CDP	Los Angeles	2.0	21,776	8,813	536	258	2,052	41	8,946	1,130	16,271	14,306
06 81666	Vallejo city	Solano	30.2	116,760	41,996	27,655	767	28,205	1,276	9,196	7,665	18,591	84,541
06 81708	Valle Vista CDP	Riverside	3.2	10,488	9,288	130	134	135	16	514	271	1,539	8,151
06 81736	Valley Center CDP	San Diego	29.3	7,323	6,275	38	208	99	14	472	217	1,206	5,159
06 81890	Valley Springs CDP	Calaveras	9.8	2,560	2,241	17	46	35	3	124	94	275	1,863
06 82072	Vandenberg AFB CDP	Santa Barbara	22.1	6,151	4,445	722	33	240	40	305	366	683	3,816
06 82086	Vandenberg Village CDP	Santa Barbara	5.2	5,802	4,905	325	59	174	10	155	174	515	4,523
06 82590	Victorville city	San Bernardino	72.8	64,029	39,091	7,630	713	2,226	129	10,408	3,832	21,426	42,112
06 82667	View Park-Windsor Hills CDP	Los Angeles	1.9	10,958	588	9,641	19	122	7	126	455	297	8,733
06 82744	Villa Park city	Orange	2.1	5,999	4,943	48	26	775	2	56	149	354	4,520
06 82814	Vincent CDP	Los Angeles	1.5	15,097	7,811	403	192	1,035	12	4,801	843	9,724	10,068

Table D-1. Places — **Area and Population**—Con.

[Includes incorporated places and census designated places (CDPs) of 2,500 or more population as of April 1, 2000. Codes shown are two-digit Federal Information Processing Standards (FIPS) state codes and five-digit FIPS place codes. Place names and codes are those in effect as of January 1, 2000. County refers to the county (or counties) in which the place is located. IC in this column = independent city, a county equivalent. If a place is located in more than one county, counties are listed in alphabetic order]

State and place code	Place	County	Land area, 2000 (sq. mi.)	Population, 2000 (April 1) Total	By race— One race White	Black or African American	American Indian and Alaska Native	Asian	Native Hawaiian and Other Pacific Islander	Some other race	Two or more races	Hispanic or Latino (of any race)	18 years and over
06 00000	CALIFORNIA—Con.												
06 82842	Vine Hill CDP	Contra Costa	4.7	3,260	2,448	73	56	74	6	391	212	787	2,382
06 82852	Vineyard CDP	Sacramento	8.1	10,109	6,677	671	68	1,617	53	424	599	1,243	6,822
06 82954	Visalia city	Tulare	28.6	91,565	63,654	1,754	1,235	4,683	117	16,293	3,829	32,619	62,950
06 82996	Vista city	San Diego	18.7	89,857	57,750	3,814	895	3,323	607	19,168	4,300	34,990	63,204
06 83215	Waldon CDP	Contra Costa	0.7	5,133	3,872	105	17	807	13	115	204	317	4,644
06 83332	Walnut city	Los Angeles	9.0	30,004	8,513	1,259	72	16,728	24	2,296	1,112	5,803	21,675
06 83346	Walnut Creek city	Contra Costa	19.9	64,296	53,937	688	210	6,017	94	1,263	2,087	3,851	52,987
06 83402	Walnut Park CDP	Los Angeles	0.7	16,180	7,461	58	145	83	23	7,691	719	15,496	10,774
06 83542	Wasco city	Kern	7.6	21,263	7,366	2,183	217	143	32	10,730	592	14,187	15,427
06 83612	Waterford city	Stanislaus	1.6	6,924	5,002	33	106	52	11	1,384	336	2,454	4,401
06 83668	Watsonville city	Santa Cruz	6.4	44,265	19,036	334	768	1,455	53	20,328	2,291	33,254	29,228
06 83794	Weaverville CDP	Trinity	35.4	3,554	3,251	9	104	25	5	43	117	154	2,693
06 83850	Weed city	Siskiyou	4.9	2,978	2,182	276	58	136	14	164	148	380	2,215
06 83863	Weedpatch CDP	Kern	3.1	2,726	1,319	19	102	7	2	1,127	150	2,431	1,587
06 84116	West Athens CDP	Los Angeles	1.3	9,101	1,174	5,105	53	144	37	2,287	301	3,577	5,908
06 84120	West Bishop CDP	Inyo	8.7	2,807	2,582	2	34	31	1	115	42	216	2,164
06 84144	West Carson CDP	Los Angeles	2.3	21,138	8,876	2,483	139	5,300	254	2,947	1,139	6,223	16,363
06 84186	West Compton CDP	Los Angeles	1.6	5,435	551	3,366	34	48	23	1,222	191	1,837	3,631
06 84200	West Covina city	Los Angeles	16.1	105,080	46,086	6,696	823	23,849	226	22,295	5,105	48,051	75,128
06 84410	West Hollywood city	Los Angeles	1.9	35,716	30,868	1,104	129	1,350	41	1,026	1,198	3,142	33,682
06 84438	Westlake Village city	Los Angeles	5.2	8,368	7,506	69	11	509	6	85	182	386	6,378
06 84536	West Menlo Park CDP	San Mateo	0.5	3,629	3,174	33	7	263	4	34	114	162	2,710
06 84550	Westminster city	Orange	10.1	88,207	40,392	871	535	33,629	406	8,991	3,383	19,138	65,335
06 84578	West Modesto CDP	Stanislaus	1.8	6,096	3,369	203	154	187	22	1,873	288	3,126	4,009
06 84592	Westmont CDP	Los Angeles	1.8	31,623	3,718	18,336	189	120	62	8,150	1,048	12,499	19,655
06 84774	West Puente Valley CDP	Los Angeles	1.7	22,589	9,906	555	257	1,795	40	9,036	1,000	18,416	15,387
06 84816	West Sacramento city	Yolo	20.9	31,615	20,548	811	555	2,282	184	5,056	2,179	9,470	22,185
06 84921	West Whittier-Los Nietos CDP	Los Angeles	2.5	25,129	13,334	144	314	410	51	9,673	1,203	20,874	17,367
06 85292	Whittier city	Los Angeles	14.6	83,680	52,876	1,019	1,105	2,770	126	21,588	4,196	46,765	60,013
06 85446	Wildomar CDP	Riverside	13.2	14,064	11,540	248	126	259	36	1,286	569	3,035	9,822
06 85586	Williams city	Colusa	5.4	3,670	1,668	18	42	42	-	1,670	230	2,613	2,402
06 85600	Willits city	Mendocino	2.8	5,073	4,247	32	179	59	2	359	195	745	3,594
06 85614	Willowbrook CDP	Los Angeles	3.7	34,138	5,482	15,331	245	91	44	11,940	1,005	18,297	21,407
06 85684	Willows city	Glenn	2.9	6,220	4,308	55	140	641	15	765	296	1,446	4,186
06 85880	Wilton CDP	Sacramento	29.6	4,551	3,878	86	55	107	9	165	251	440	3,368
06 85922	Windsor town	Sonoma	6.7	22,744	17,968	178	336	521	32	2,825	884	5,364	15,737
06 85992	Winter Gardens CDP	San Diego	4.5	19,771	17,475	258	197	269	56	794	722	2,424	14,446
06 86034	Winters city	Yolo	2.8	6,125	4,276	41	54	61	17	1,382	294	2,720	4,084
06 86076	Winton CDP	Merced	2.9	8,832	3,911	206	95	473	30	3,621	496	5,493	5,379
06 86244	Woodcrest CDP	Riverside	10.1	8,342	6,760	380	102	292	20	485	303	1,390	5,990
06 86300	Woodlake city	Tulare	2.0	6,651	3,130	22	72	60	3	3,047	317	5,575	4,138
06 86328	Woodland city	Yolo	10.3	49,151	32,851	631	718	1,851	136	10,566	2,398	19,084	34,532
06 86440	Woodside town	San Mateo	11.8	5,352	4,828	20	8	267	6	70	153	232	4,100
06 86594	Wrightwood CDP	San Bernardino	2.2	3,837	3,489	13	25	29	7	105	169	337	2,738
06 86832	Yorba Linda city	Orange	19.4	58,918	48,015	688	220	6,537	56	1,593	1,809	6,044	41,655
06 86878	Yosemite Lakes CDP	Madera	20.9	4,160	3,877	15	41	29	17	95	86	330	3,114
06 86930	Yountville town	Napa	1.6	2,916	2,687	32	17	40	2	82	56	281	2,591
06 86944	Yreka city	Siskiyou	10.0	7,290	6,310	35	440	133	5	124	243	392	5,432
06 86972	Yuba City city	Sutter	9.4	36,758	24,611	1,035	643	3,284	107	5,281	1,797	9,029	26,101
06 87042	Yucaipa city	San Bernardino	27.8	41,207	35,113	369	445	486	55	3,314	1,425	7,561	29,445
06 87056	Yucca Valley town	San Bernardino	40.0	16,865	14,716	379	227	218	51	772	502	1,922	12,630
08 00000	COLORADO		103,717.5	4,301,261	3,560,005	165,063	44,241	95,213	4,621	309,931	122,187	735,601	3,200,466
08 00320	Acres Green CDP	Douglas	0.6	3,205	2,983	20	16	65	-	54	67	173	2,199
08 00870	Air Force Academy CDP	El Paso	10.0	7,526	6,288	433	60	213	19	231	282	654	5,705
08 01090	Alamosa city	Alamosa	4.0	7,960	5,455	112	175	76	21	1,780	341	3,725	6,014
08 02575	Applewood CDP	Jefferson	4.8	7,123	6,738	27	36	87	8	105	122	312	5,541
08 03455	Arvada city	Adams, Jefferson	32.7	102,153	92,999	672	665	2,215	68	3,146	2,388	10,031	75,344
08 03620	Aspen city	Pitkin	3.5	5,914	5,615	26	14	86	5	97	71	363	5,137
08 04000	Aurora city	Adams, Arapahoe, Douglas	142.5	276,393	190,311	37,104	2,248	12,066	501	22,485	11,678	54,764	200,185
08 04110	Avon town	Eagle	8.0	5,561	4,033	44	38	55	3	1,212	176	2,222	4,414
08 04935	Basalt town	Eagle, Pitkin	1.9	2,681	2,454	13	14	34	3	128	35	315	2,049
08 05120	Battlement Mesa CDP	Garfield	8.1	3,497	3,320	14	24	6	4	70	59	247	2,670
08 06172	Berkley CDP	Adams	4.0	10,743	7,825	117	169	506	19	1,676	431	4,643	7,792
08 06255	Berthoud town	Larimer, Weld	4.0	4,839	4,509	11	27	29	3	187	73	390	3,416
08 06970	Black Forest CDP	El Paso	127.5	13,247	12,595	113	88	94	5	117	235	438	9,341
08 07850	Boulder city	Boulder	24.4	94,673	83,627	1,154	450	3,806	48	3,318	2,270	7,801	80,631
08 08675	Brighton city	Adams, Weld	17.1	20,905	16,077	206	308	230	9	3,406	669	7,990	14,929
08 09280	Broomfield city	Adams, Boulder, Jefferson, Weld	27.1	38,272	33,918	352	235	1,585	14	1,230	938	3,471	27,045
08 09555	Brush city	Morgan	2.4	5,117	3,879	20	26	8	2	1,033	149	1,904	3,667
08 10600	Burlington city	Kit Carson	2.1	3,678	2,927	137	20	14	3	544	33	755	2,750
08 11810	Canon City city	Fremont	12.0	15,431	14,374	246	161	83	9	248	310	1,285	11,807
08 12045	Carbondale town	Garfield	2.0	5,196	4,379	34	28	36	1	613	105	1,669	3,839
08 12387	Castle Pines CDP	Douglas	10.2	5,958	5,711	53	20	77	-	34	63	188	4,198

Table D-1. Places — **Area and Population**—Con.

[Includes incorporated places and census designated places (CDPs) of 2,500 or more population as of April 1, 2000. Codes shown are two-digit Federal Information Processing Standards (FIPS) state codes and five-digit FIPS place codes. Place names and codes are those in effect as of January 1, 2000. County refers to the county (or counties) in which the place is located. IC in this column = independent city, a county equivalent. If a place is located in more than one county, counties are listed in alphabetic order]

State and place code	Place	County	Land area, 2000 (sq. mi.)	Population, 2000 (April 1)									
					By race—							Hispanic or Latino (of any race)	18 years and over
					One race						Two or more races		
				Total	White	Black or African American	American Indian and Alaska Native	Asian	Native Hawaiian and Other Pacific Islander	Some other race			
08 00000	COLORADO—Con.												
08 12415	Castle Rock town	Douglas	31.6	20,224	18,980	95	126	222	13	376	412	1,250	13,842
08 12442	Castlewood CDP	Arapahoe	6.1	25,567	23,972	274	58	717	5	214	327	1,098	18,420
08 13845	Cherry Hills Village city	Arapahoe	6.2	5,958	5,723	38	9	90	-	34	64	112	4,085
08 14587	Cimarron Hills CDP	El Paso	6.1	15,194	11,953	1,217	120	387	63	679	775	1,798	10,387
08 15165	Clifton CDP	Mesa	6.8	17,345	15,453	96	246	68	8	992	482	2,448	11,867
08 16000	Colorado Springs city	El Paso	185.7	360,890	291,095	23,677	3,175	10,179	764	18,091	13,909	43,330	265,267
08 16110	Columbine CDP	Arapahoe, Jefferson	6.6	24,095	22,848	114	96	280	28	378	351	1,345	17,587
08 16495	Commerce City city	Adams	25.8	20,991	13,761	428	363	132	11	5,390	906	11,096	14,573
08 17375	Cortez city	Montezuma	5.5	7,977	6,443	21	805	28	3	482	195	1,061	5,850
08 17760	Craig city	Moffat	4.9	9,189	8,505	28	88	39	2	353	174	992	6,572
08 19080	Dacono city	Weld	2.7	3,015	2,323	13	29	30	-	542	78	966	2,135
08 19850	Delta city	Delta	5.3	6,400	5,520	13	57	25	-	636	149	1,442	4,662
08 20000	Denver city	Denver	153.4	554,636	362,180	61,649	7,290	15,611	648	86,464	20,794	175,704	432,870
08 20275	Derby CDP	Adams	1.6	6,423	4,393	98	173	56	6	1,385	312	3,036	4,519
08 22035	Durango city	La Plata	6.8	13,922	12,090	70	767	103	16	574	302	1,436	11,610
08 22200	Eagle town	Eagle	2.4	3,032	2,650	11	19	12	3	276	61	520	2,105
08 22225	Eagle-Vail CDP	Eagle	2.0	2,887	2,767	8	10	13	2	30	57	130	2,345
08 22860	Eaton town	Weld	1.9	2,690	2,451	1	14	21	-	155	48	340	1,920
08 23135	Edgewater city	Jefferson	0.7	5,445	4,077	80	85	71	13	881	238	1,939	4,133
08 23300	Edwards CDP	Eagle	39.7	8,257	6,803	28	33	68	4	1,202	119	2,249	6,159
08 23795	El Jebel CDP	Eagle	6.7	4,488	3,940	4	12	43	1	403	85	1,339	3,116
08 24785	Englewood city	Arapahoe	6.6	31,727	27,846	463	416	591	30	1,582	799	4,140	25,298
08 24950	Erie town	Boulder, Weld	9.5	6,291	5,645	27	41	172	2	256	148	692	4,382
08 25115	Estes Park town	Larimer	5.8	5,413	5,150	17	26	42	3	112	63	301	4,462
08 25280	Evans city	Weld	3.8	9,514	6,763	75	122	68	2	2,136	348	3,813	6,460
08 25390	Evergreen CDP	Jefferson	11.6	9,216	8,972	24	33	57	6	23	101	192	6,826
08 26270	Federal Heights city	Adams	1.8	12,065	9,656	176	166	735	22	941	369	2,729	9,063
08 27040	Florence city	Fremont	4.1	3,653	3,389	11	45	11	-	96	101	572	2,649
08 27370	Fort Carson CDP	El Paso	9.4	10,566	6,630	2,114	176	226	79	839	502	1,626	7,664
08 27425	Fort Collins city	Larimer	40.5	118,052	100,347	1,213	715	2,948	143	4,281	3,005	10,402	93,114
08 27700	Fort Lupton city	Weld	4.0	6,787	4,774	29	92	56	2	1,537	297	3,216	4,454
08 27810	Fort Morgan city	Morgan	4.5	11,034	8,213	31	111	20	27	2,275	357	4,308	7,707
08 27865	Fountain city	El Paso	14.0	15,197	11,409	1,328	215	306	84	1,019	836	2,289	9,956
08 28745	Fruita city	Mesa	5.9	6,478	5,872	24	75	19	2	353	133	773	4,672
08 28800	Fruitvale CDP	Mesa	3.1	6,936	6,479	16	50	43	1	204	143	469	5,153
08 29625	Genesee CDP	Jefferson	6.7	3,699	3,549	8	13	66	3	28	32	101	2,894
08 30340	Glendale city	Arapahoe	0.6	4,547	3,099	441	39	282	7	414	265	1,245	3,942
08 30420	Gleneagle CDP	El Paso	2.5	4,246	3,999	53	6	81	1	34	72	164	2,959
08 30780	Glenwood Springs city	Garfield	4.8	7,736	6,995	18	55	62	4	450	150	1,029	5,950
08 30835	Golden city	Jefferson	9.0	17,159	15,556	176	180	513	10	340	384	1,130	13,675
08 31660	Grand Junction city	Mesa	30.8	41,986	38,533	251	395	320	52	1,600	835	4,561	33,083
08 32155	Greeley city	Weld	29.9	76,930	61,053	672	639	885	106	10,591	2,184	22,683	57,207
08 33035	Greenwood Village city	Arapahoe	8.1	11,035	10,362	126	21	281	5	67	173	344	7,759
08 33502	Gunbarrel CDP	Boulder	6.4	9,435	8,754	127	39	258	13	88	156	362	7,359
08 33640	Gunnison city	Gunnison	3.2	5,409	5,057	42	42	30	3	97	138	374	4,593
08 33695	Gypsum town	Eagle	3.7	3,654	2,970	6	48	8	2	548	72	1,144	2,445
08 36410	Highlands Ranch CDP	Douglas	23.5	70,931	64,375	915	233	2,861	52	1,079	1,416	3,847	47,745
08 39855	Johnstown town	Weld	1.1	3,827	3,261	5	23	13	-	454	71	917	2,663
08 40377	Ken Caryl CDP	Jefferson	9.7	30,887	28,863	220	136	549	23	516	580	2,056	21,485
08 41835	Lafayette city	Boulder	8.9	23,197	19,841	209	170	771	20	1,581	605	3,808	16,823
08 42110	La Junta city	Otero	2.9	7,568	5,617	92	134	65	10	1,387	263	3,300	5,520
08 43000	Lakewood city	Jefferson	41.6	144,126	125,611	2,128	1,599	3,918	117	7,028	3,725	20,949	112,084
08 43110	Lamar city	Prowers	4.2	8,869	6,762	34	131	42	4	1,668	228	3,241	6,284
08 43220	Laporte CDP	Larimer	6.1	2,691	2,489	6	29	12	-	63	92	217	1,998
08 43660	Las Animas city	Bent	1.3	2,758	2,065	25	79	16	-	423	150	1,175	2,006
08 44320	Leadville city	Lake	1.1	2,821	2,356	4	36	9	3	348	65	718	2,226
08 45145	Lincoln Park CDP	Fremont	3.8	3,904	3,722	8	37	9	9	43	76	214	3,004
08 45255	Littleton city	Arapahoe, Douglas, Jefferson	13.5	40,340	37,021	466	293	670	24	1,078	788	3,408	30,959
08 45955	Lone Tree city	Douglas	1.7	4,873	4,461	72	12	180	2	64	82	223	3,496
08 45970	Longmont city	Boulder, Weld	21.8	71,093	60,255	385	687	1,252	43	6,907	1,564	13,558	51,270
08 46355	Louisville city	Boulder	8.5	18,937	17,264	177	102	672	16	347	359	950	13,498
08 46465	Loveland city	Larimer	24.6	50,608	46,990	188	349	419	15	1,624	1,023	4,337	36,994
08 48445	Manitou Springs city	El Paso	3.0	4,980	4,680	25	53	56	6	47	113	182	4,053
08 50480	Milliken town	Weld	5.7	2,888	2,134	9	34	14	-	624	73	1,177	1,873
08 51635	Monte Vista city	Rio Grande	1.9	4,529	2,857	17	73	13	2	1,441	126	2,636	3,189
08 51745	Montrose city	Montrose	11.5	12,344	10,987	54	121	71	9	808	294	2,143	9,391
08 53780	Niwot CDP	Boulder	4.1	4,160	3,932	20	16	90	1	44	57	141	2,976
08 54330	Northglenn city	Adams, Weld	7.4	31,575	26,221	481	361	970	47	2,568	927	6,399	23,129
08 55980	Orchard City town	Delta	11.4	2,880	2,718	2	28	13	2	59	58	228	2,268
08 56035	Orchard Mesa CDP	Mesa	5.4	6,456	6,039	23	55	22	8	214	95	563	4,693
08 56970	Palisade town	Mesa	1.1	2,579	2,422	5	27	13	7	35	70	161	1,953
08 57630	Parker town	Douglas	14.6	23,558	21,814	237	107	402	7	443	548	1,366	15,550
08 58400	Penrose CDP	Fremont	33.3	4,070	3,878	9	36	15	-	70	62	311	2,953
08 60655	Ponderosa Park CDP	Elbert	14.8	3,112	2,968	17	14	15	6	37	55	124	2,202
08 62000	Pueblo city	Pueblo	45.1	102,121	77,830	2,465	1,766	683	63	15,526	3,788	45,066	76,471
08 62220	Pueblo West CDP	Pueblo	77.5	16,899	14,947	141	168	180	12	1,016	435	3,092	11,838
08 63375	Redlands CDP	Mesa	14.9	8,043	7,716	5	33	37	4	125	123	420	6,226

Table D-1. Places — **Area and Population**—Con.

[Includes incorporated places and census designated places (CDPs) of 2,500 or more population as of April 1, 2000. Codes shown are two-digit Federal Information Processing Standards (FIPS) state codes and five-digit FIPS place codes. Place names and codes are those in effect as of January 1, 2000. County refers to the county (or counties) in which the place is located. IC in this column = independent city, a county equivalent. If a place is located in more than one county, counties are listed in alphabetic order]

State and place code	Place	County	Land area, 2000 (sq. mi.)	Population, 2000 (April 1) By race— One race Total	White	Black or African American	American Indian and Alaska Native	Asian	Native Hawaiian and Other Pacific Islander	Some other race	Two or more races	Hispanic or Latino (of any race)	18 years and over
08 00000	COLORADO—Con.												
08 64255	Rifle city	Garfield	4.3	6,784	6,210	30	46	18	3	322	155	1,103	4,689
08 65190	Rocky Ford city	Otero	1.7	4,286	3,104	17	63	32	5	937	128	2,449	3,078
08 66197	Roxborough Park CDP . . .	Douglas	9.7	4,446	4,174	21	21	63	4	76	87	248	3,140
08 67280	Salida city	Chaffee	2.2	5,504	5,100	3	79	21	1	181	119	592	4,324
08 68847	Security-Widefield CDP . .	El Paso	14.5	29,845	22,075	3,145	242	914	168	1,598	1,703	3,763	20,528
08 69645	Sheridan city	Arapahoe	2.2	5,600	4,312	105	123	94	4	702	260	1,821	4,131
08 69810	Sherrelwood CDP	Adams	2.4	17,657	12,715	214	209	596	33	3,183	707	7,032	12,817
08 70525	Silverthorne town	Summit	3.2	3,196	2,626	32	21	24	9	357	127	751	2,458
08 72505	Southglenn CDP	Arapahoe	9.7	43,520	41,172	345	175	796	24	376	632	1,758	32,158
08 73825	Steamboat Springs city . .	Routt	10.1	9,815	9,509	13	32	49	10	72	130	307	7,980
08 73935	Sterling city	Logan	6.9	11,360	10,309	85	90	47	9	636	184	1,613	8,459
08 74080	Stonegate CDP	Douglas	2.0	6,284	5,813	60	32	164	-	72	143	273	3,810
08 74430	Stratmoor CDP	El Paso	2.9	6,650	4,366	816	137	172	18	609	532	1,301	4,483
08 75640	Superior town	Boulder, Jefferson	4.0	9,011	7,825	114	31	674	2	174	191	438	6,358
08 77235	The Pinery CDP	Douglas	8.0	7,253	7,014	25	28	68	6	32	80	228	4,977
08 77290	Thornton city	Adams, Weld	26.9	82,384	68,137	1,206	924	2,063	87	7,380	2,587	17,583	57,636
08 78610	Trinidad city	Las Animas	6.3	9,078	7,260	49	274	39	13	1,100	343	4,364	6,819
08 79100	Twin Lakes CDP	Adams	1.7	6,301	4,853	49	93	216	13	857	220	3,108	4,679
08 80040	Vail town	Eagle	4.5	4,531	4,265	13	22	75	4	65	87	281	4,082
08 82350	Walsenburg city	Huerfano	2.3	4,182	3,136	200	140	17	3	521	165	2,131	3,306
08 83120	Welby CDP	Adams	3.8	12,973	9,271	205	228	153	15	2,507	594	4,792	9,297
08 83230	Wellington town	Larimer	1.8	2,672	2,335	7	28	18	2	220	62	324	1,799
08 83835	Westminster city	Adams, Jefferson	31.5	100,940	84,983	1,237	745	5,534	77	5,575	2,789	15,369	73,830
08 84042	West Pleasant View CDP .	Jefferson	1.5	3,932	3,596	51	39	19	1	99	127	323	3,070
08 84440	Wheat Ridge city	Jefferson	9.1	32,913	29,361	275	309	450	38	1,642	838	4,434	25,926
08 85485	Windsor town	Larimer, Weld	14.6	9,896	9,080	45	73	51	6	422	219	1,039	6,947
08 86090	Woodland Park city	Teller	5.7	6,515	6,182	34	47	57	-	53	142	225	4,658
08 86117	Woodmoor CDP	El Paso	6.3	7,177	6,808	53	24	118	2	44	128	201	4,953
08 86750	Yuma city	Yuma	2.4	3,285	3,002	3	10	1	2	232	35	771	2,352
09 00000	CONNECTICUT		4,844.8	3,405,565	2,780,355	309,843	9,639	82,313	1,366	147,201	74,848	320,323	2,563,877
09 01150	Ansonia city	New Haven	6.0	18,554	15,867	1,562	63	209	3	411	439	1,376	14,065
09 04790	Bethel CDP	Fairfield	4.1	9,137	8,220	147	12	402	2	153	201	423	6,774
09 06050	Blue Hills CDP	Hartford	1.1	3,020	296	2,510	12	37	1	45	119	123	2,244
09 07345	Branford Center CDP	New Haven	1.9	5,735	5,362	71	14	135	12	46	95	218	4,715
09 08000	Bridgeport city	Fairfield	16.0	139,529	62,822	42,925	664	4,536	148	20,659	7,775	44,478	99,857
09 08420	Bristol city	Hartford	26.5	60,062	55,014	1,612	132	884	18	1,443	959	3,166	46,140
09 08770	Broad Brook CDP	Hartford	5.9	3,469	3,183	154	-	53	-	36	43	75	2,575
09 13435	Central Manchester CDP .	Hartford	6.5	30,595	25,456	2,540	64	738	13	1,025	759	2,130	23,434
09 13495	Central Waterford CDP . . .	New London	2.0	2,935	2,690	78	12	67	-	39	49	86	2,341
09 14200	Cheshire Village CDP . . .	New Haven	3.4	5,789	5,511	44	3	171	1	13	46	74	4,395
09 15420	Clinton CDP	Middlesex	2.4	3,516	3,344	22	9	42	1	50	48	237	2,725
09 16120	Collinsville CDP	Hartford	3.1	2,686	2,620	15	2	13	-	8	28	43	2,032
09 16960	Conning Towers-Nautilus Park CDP	New London	5.0	10,241	8,327	985	58	238	33	235	365	635	6,717
09 17835	Coventry Lake CDP	Tolland	2.9	2,914	2,816	17	8	17	1	20	35	48	2,148
09 18430	Danbury city	Fairfield	42.1	74,848	56,853	5,060	214	4,082	26	5,653	2,960	11,791	58,621
09 18780	Danielson borough	Windham	1.1	4,265	3,813	112	26	117	-	78	119	217	3,107
09 18920	Darien CDP	Fairfield	12.9	19,607	18,816	89	8	474	5	58	157	429	13,243
09 19480	Derby city	New Haven	5.0	12,391	11,162	449	20	215	8	312	225	950	9,704
09 20740	Durham CDP	Middlesex	6.3	2,773	2,715	13	2	24	-	7	12	28	2,048
09 22700	East Hartford CDP	Hartford	18.0	49,575	32,071	9,335	167	1,989	18	4,333	1,662	7,552	37,630
09 22980	East Haven CDP	New Haven	12.3	28,189	26,475	396	40	539	4	428	307	1,228	21,934
09 26370	Essex Village CDP	Middlesex	3.5	2,573	2,529	11	2	13	-	3	15	24	2,111
09 31270	Glastonbury Center CDP .	Hartford	4.8	7,157	6,834	63	15	129	-	67	49	184	5,711
09 34180	Groton city	New London	3.2	10,010	7,780	1,019	93	355	5	284	474	773	7,755
09 35020	Guilford Center CDP	New Haven	2.2	2,603	2,526	19	1	24	-	13	21	78	2,094
09 37000	Hartford city	Hartford	17.3	121,578	33,705	46,264	659	1,971	135	32,230	6,614	49,260	85,010
09 37770	Hazardville CDP	Hartford	3.3	4,900	4,677	69	11	69	1	22	51	69	3,711
09 37930	Heritage Village CDP	New Haven	2.3	3,435	3,401	7	1	11	-	3	12	23	3,341
09 39940	Jewett City borough	New London	0.7	3,053	2,811	75	27	44	2	34	60	87	2,324
09 40150	Kensington CDP	Hartford	5.3	8,541	8,233	20	6	198	2	19	63	127	6,587
09 41410	Lake Pocotopaug CDP . . .	Middlesex	2.7	3,169	3,068	30	11	29	1	1	29	32	2,427
09 43790	Long Hill CDP	New London	1.5	3,534	2,794	229	44	267	12	48	140	168	2,973
09 46450	Meriden city	New Haven	23.7	58,244	46,734	3,754	229	796	11	5,036	1,684	12,296	43,278
09 47290	Middletown city	Middlesex	40.9	43,167	34,540	5,291	99	1,155	21	857	1,204	2,287	33,803
09 47515	Milford city (balance)	New Haven	22.3	50,594	47,332	965	65	1,193	17	447	575	1,691	39,250
09 49180	Moosup CDP	Windham	2.3	3,237	3,102	19	22	29	-	31	34	101	2,314
09 49810	Mystic CDP	New London	3.4	4,001	3,832	32	16	54	1	14	52	54	3,332
09 49880	Naugatuck borough	New Haven	16.4	30,989	28,435	882	82	522	5	491	572	1,386	22,664
09 50370	New Britain city	Hartford	13.3	71,538	49,634	7,794	264	1,687	43	9,388	2,728	19,138	54,249
09 52000	New Haven city	New Haven	18.9	123,626	53,723	46,181	535	4,819	79	13,460	4,829	26,443	92,180
09 52210	Newington CDP	Hartford	13.2	29,306	27,103	609	35	824	14	351	370	1,079	23,259
09 52280	New London city	New London	5.5	25,671	16,299	4,784	225	544	21	2,343	1,455	5,061	19,814
09 52560	New Milford CDP	Litchfield	3.4	6,633	6,181	121	18	140	1	56	116	205	5,017
09 53120	Niantic CDP	New London	1.5	3,085	2,981	15	5	38	-	13	33	65	2,459
09 54940	North Haven CDP	New Haven	20.8	23,035	21,418	512	20	775	3	119	188	433	17,833

Table D-1. Places — **Area and Population**—Con.

[Includes incorporated places and census designated places (CDPs) of 2,500 or more population as of April 1, 2000. Codes shown are two-digit Federal Information Processing Standards (FIPS) state codes and five-digit FIPS place codes. Place names and codes are those in effect as of January 1, 2000. County refers to the county (or counties) in which the place is located. IC in this column = independent city, a county equivalent. If a place is located in more than one county, counties are listed in alphabetic order]

State and place code	Place	County	Land area, 2000 (sq. mi.)	Population, 2000 (April 1) Total	By race— One race White	Black or African American	American Indian and Alaska Native	Asian	Native Hawaiian and Other Pacific Islander	Some other race	Two or more races	Hispanic or Latino (of any race)	18 years and over
09 00000	CONNECTICUT—Con.												
09 55725	Northwest Harwinton CDP.	Litchfield	8.7	3,242	3,208	2	3	13	3	5	8	32	2,449
09 55990	Norwalk city	Fairfield	22.8	82,951	61,339	12,663	174	2,699	40	3,591	2,445	12,966	64,641
09 56200	Norwich city	New London	28.3	36,117	30,029	2,469	437	758	10	998	1,416	2,208	27,412
09 56690	Oakville CDP	Litchfield	3.2	8,618	8,249	101	7	97	2	55	107	243	6,484
09 57180	Old Mystic CDP	New London	4.3	3,205	2,888	78	21	110	2	16	90	52	2,380
09 57670	Orange CDP	New Haven	17.2	13,233	12,450	104	11	508	1	43	116	190	9,979
09 58520	Oxoboxo River CDP	New London	4.3	2,938	2,659	47	38	75	-	32	87	103	2,263
09 59140	Pawcatuck CDP	New London	3.7	5,474	5,120	41	38	116	3	38	118	79	4,203
09 60090	Plainfield Village CDP	Windham	1.6	2,638	2,497	39	21	15	-	32	34	62	1,958
09 61870	Portland CDP	Middlesex	4.9	5,534	5,196	178	12	30	3	31	84	127	4,223
09 62745	Putnam District CDP	Windham	3.2	6,746	6,387	102	59	27	4	42	125	155	5,096
09 63900	Ridgefield CDP	Fairfield	6.4	7,212	6,889	39	8	176	1	37	62	163	5,272
09 65230	Rockville CDP	Tolland	1.7	7,708	6,389	597	31	245	2	183	261	556	5,703
09 68100	Shelton city	Fairfield	30.6	38,101	35,984	428	57	791	1	341	499	1,326	29,129
09 68450	Sherwood Manor CDP	Hartford	3.1	5,689	5,488	65	3	61	-	27	45	104	4,403
09 69010	Simsbury Center CDP	Hartford	4.5	5,603	5,378	31	4	122	1	14	53	87	4,072
09 71460	Southwood Acres CDP	Hartford	4.1	8,067	7,783	77	5	67	-	59	76	129	6,080
09 73000	Stamford city	Fairfield	37.7	117,083	81,718	18,019	243	5,856	46	7,608	3,593	19,635	91,187
09 73980	Storrs CDP	Tolland	5.7	10,996	8,918	624	10	1,004	5	187	248	484	10,553
09 74260	Stratford CDP	Fairfield	17.6	49,976	42,361	4,892	82	700	17	1,071	853	3,399	38,470
09 75240	Terryville CDP	Litchfield	2.8	5,360	5,209	46	8	22	-	16	59	63	3,997
09 75940	Thompsonville CDP	Hartford	2.1	8,125	7,313	322	27	131	4	122	206	382	6,050
09 76500	Torrington city	Litchfield	39.8	35,202	32,749	757	70	643	7	460	516	1,162	27,091
09 77270	Trumbull CDP	Fairfield	23.3	34,243	32,194	645	38	815	6	242	303	923	25,330
09 78880	Wallingford Center CDP	New Haven	7.2	17,509	16,221	209	40	382	-	382	275	1,403	13,502
09 80000	Waterbury city	New Haven	28.6	107,271	72,018	17,500	453	1,615	61	11,698	3,926	23,354	78,817
09 80770	Weatogue CDP	Hartford	3.0	2,805	2,683	21	1	66	1	7	26	48	1,954
09 82660	West Hartford CDP	Hartford	22.0	63,589	54,658	3,041	77	3,053	47	1,659	1,054	3,990	49,544
09 82900	West Haven city	New Haven	10.0	52,360	39,824	6,530	120	1,525	27	1,867	1,459	4,757	40,252
09 83570	Westport CDP	Fairfield	20.0	25,749	24,503	292	12	625	5	103	209	602	18,559
09 84970	Wethersfield CDP	Hartford	12.4	26,271	24,481	549	21	416	6	477	321	1,101	20,999
09 85810	Willimantic CDP	Windham	4.4	15,823	11,132	989	94	264	21	2,670	653	4,777	12,247
09 87140	Windsor Locks CDP	Hartford	9.0	12,043	11,136	322	15	309	-	90	171	267	9,194
09 87350	Winsted CDP	Litchfield	4.7	7,321	6,829	112	17	82	1	161	110	204	5,508
10 00000	DELAWARE		1,953.6	783,600	584,773	150,666	2,731	16,259	283	15,855	13,033	37,277	589,013
10 04130	Bear CDP	New Castle	5.7	17,593	11,772	4,714	38	357	4	313	395	968	11,792
10 09850	Brookside CDP	New Castle	3.9	14,806	11,452	2,225	48	386	11	328	356	827	10,843
10 15310	Claymont CDP	New Castle	2.1	9,220	6,550	2,151	30	133	2	150	204	385	6,784
10 21200	Dover city	Kent	22.4	32,135	17,655	11,961	146	1,016	12	503	842	1,327	24,573
10 21387	Dover Base Housing CDP.	Kent	0.7	3,394	2,463	563	26	63	4	95	180	263	2,030
10 23240	Edgemoor CDP	New Castle	1.8	5,992	3,731	2,012	12	69	1	59	108	163	4,304
10 24540	Elsmere town	New Castle	1.0	5,800	4,780	548	13	56	-	296	107	701	4,347
10 29090	Georgetown town	Sussex	4.1	4,643	2,609	969	96	12	2	837	118	1,473	3,465
10 29350	Glasgow CDP	New Castle	9.9	12,840	10,013	2,185	28	299	3	136	176	386	9,080
10 33120	Harrington city	Kent	2.0	3,174	2,386	687	8	14	3	23	53	80	2,180
10 34810	Highland Acres CDP	Kent	1.6	3,379	2,799	387	13	87	-	15	78	87	2,556
10 35850	Hockessin CDP	New Castle	10.0	12,902	11,460	342	9	924	1	58	108	257	9,434
10 41310	Laurel town	Sussex	1.7	3,668	2,038	1,446	13	35	1	44	91	85	2,450
10 41830	Lewes city	Sussex	3.7	2,932	2,560	290	4	30	1	21	26	49	2,532
10 47030	Middletown town	New Castle	6.4	6,161	4,585	1,312	7	48	1	119	89	326	4,258
10 47420	Milford city	Kent, Sussex	5.6	6,732	4,576	1,566	23	70	11	286	200	594	4,898
10 50670	Newark city	New Castle	8.9	28,547	24,919	1,714	45	1,161	14	245	449	721	24,969
10 50800	New Castle city	New Castle	3.0	4,862	3,767	982	12	19	-	41	41	117	3,802
10 52490	North Star CDP	New Castle	6.8	8,277	7,416	207	6	553	2	25	68	97	5,676
10 56490	Pike Creek CDP	New Castle	6.1	19,751	17,440	808	33	1,102	19	124	225	511	15,236
10 64320	Seaford city	Sussex	3.5	6,699	4,290	2,011	25	100	13	115	145	285	4,981
10 67310	Smyrna town	Kent, New Castle	3.7	5,679	4,139	1,273	29	32	4	82	120	194	4,142
10 77580	Wilmington city	New Castle	10.8	72,664	25,811	41,001	185	473	20	3,750	1,424	7,148	53,871
10 77840	Wilmington Manor CDP	New Castle	1.6	8,262	6,554	905	16	70	5	553	159	1,071	6,216
11 00000	DISTRICT OF COLUMBIA		61.4	572,059	176,101	343,312	1,713	15,189	348	21,950	13,446	44,953	457,067
11 50000	Washington city	District of Columbia	61.4	572,059	176,101	343,312	1,713	15,189	348	21,950	13,446	44,953	457,067
12 00000	FLORIDA		53,926.8	15,982,378	12,465,029	2,335,505	53,541	266,256	8,625	477,107	376,315	2,682,715	12,336,038
12 00375	Alachua city	Alachua	28.9	6,098	4,120	1,773	9	68	-	69	59	220	4,405
12 00950	Altamonte Springs city	Seminole	8.9	41,200	32,642	4,004	138	1,213	18	1,972	1,213	6,563	32,788
12 01315	Andover CDP	Miami-Dade	1.7	8,489	1,871	6,025	23	97	2	261	210	1,257	6,246
12 01675	Apollo Beach CDP	Hillsborough	5.7	7,444	6,984	63	30	104	-	157	106	553	6,091
12 01700	Apopka city	Orange	24.0	26,642	19,675	4,145	112	503	24	1,429	754	4,817	19,131
12 01750	Arcadia city	DeSoto	4.0	6,604	4,102	1,855	25	54	1	474	93	1,324	4,677
12 02400	Atlantic Beach city	Duval	3.7	13,368	10,992	1,697	35	279	4	150	211	559	10,365

U.S. Census Bureau, County and City Data Book: 2000

Table D-1. Places — **Area and Population**—Con.

[Includes incorporated places and census designated places (CDPs) of 2,500 or more population as of April 1, 2000. Codes shown are two-digit Federal Information Processing Standards (FIPS) state codes and five-digit FIPS place codes. Place names and codes are those in effect as of January 1, 2000. County refers to the county (or counties) in which the place is located. IC in this column = independent city, a county equivalent. If a place is located in more than one county, counties are listed in alphabetic order]

State and place code	Place	County	Land area, 2000 (sq. mi.)	Population, 2000 (April 1) Total	By race— One race White	Black or African American	American Indian and Alaska Native	Asian	Native Hawaiian and Other Pacific Islander	Some other race	Two or more races	Hispanic or Latino (of any race)	18 years and over
12 00000	FLORIDA—Con.												
12 02550	Auburndale city	Polk	5.2	11,032	8,950	1,353	29	97	5	382	216	894	8,036
12 02681	Aventura city	Miami-Dade	2.7	25,267	23,695	430	18	307	5	366	446	5,218	22,703
12 02750	Avon Park city	Highlands	4.6	8,542	5,031	2,513	27	59	4	713	195	1,598	6,282
12 02850	Azalea Park CDP	Orange	3.2	11,073	7,777	747	55	399	8	1,611	476	4,315	8,211
12 03275	Bal Harbour village	Miami-Dade	0.3	3,305	3,122	54	-	27	3	37	62	760	2,968
12 03675	Bartow city	Polk	11.2	15,340	10,111	4,355	70	141	12	340	311	1,244	11,558
12 03975	Bay Harbor Islands town	Miami-Dade	0.4	5,146	4,694	92	4	63	3	146	144	1,816	4,222
12 04070	Bay Hill CDP	Orange	2.5	5,177	4,406	118	9	493	-	33	118	295	3,807
12 04162	Bayonet Point CDP	Pasco	5.6	23,577	22,832	159	58	141	7	145	235	826	20,063
12 04200	Bay Pines CDP	Pinellas	1.4	3,065	3,001	7	6	14	-	14	23	72	2,581
12 04350	Bayshore Gardens CDP	Manatee	3.6	17,350	15,592	690	66	217	17	406	362	1,426	14,242
12 04650	Beacon Square CDP	Pasco	2.0	7,263	6,923	75	25	59	-	79	102	279	6,074
12 04925	Bee Ridge CDP	Sarasota	3.9	8,744	8,508	68	18	59	-	41	50	255	7,128
12 05025	Bellair-Meadowbrook Terrace CDP	Clay	5.6	16,539	13,024	1,849	89	606	18	424	529	1,112	12,381
12 05075	Belleair town	Pinellas	1.8	4,067	4,000	6	6	16	-	8	31	103	3,407
12 05200	Belle Glade city	Palm Beach	4.6	14,906	4,515	7,555	25	28	6	1,446	1,331	4,110	9,916
12 05300	Belle Isle city	Orange	1.9	5,531	5,219	104	7	69	1	73	58	331	4,278
12 05375	Belleview city	Marion	1.8	3,478	3,170	147	16	20	-	73	52	267	2,774
12 05462	Bellview CDP	Escambia	11.8	21,201	17,100	2,479	230	695	33	143	521	509	15,579
12 06125	Beverly Hills CDP	Citrus	2.8	8,317	7,976	142	16	50	1	32	100	330	7,421
12 06350	Big Coppitt Key CDP	Monroe	1.4	2,595	2,411	28	21	38	2	27	68	435	2,094
12 06425	Big Pine Key CDP	Monroe	9.8	5,032	4,772	55	25	29	1	60	90	338	4,186
12 06600	Biscayne Park village	Miami-Dade	0.6	3,269	2,361	605	22	89	-	82	110	867	2,492
12 06625	Bithlo CDP	Orange	10.7	4,626	4,319	46	42	16	2	99	102	431	3,336
12 06875	Bloomingdale CDP	Hillsborough	7.8	19,839	17,483	1,266	51	445	14	223	357	1,375	13,605
12 07235	Boca Del Mar CDP	Palm Beach	4.0	21,832	20,616	269	12	410	6	231	288	1,782	18,683
12 07285	Boca Pointe CDP	Palm Beach	1.2	3,302	3,257	13	-	20	-	6	6	111	3,149
12 07300	Boca Raton city	Palm Beach	27.2	74,764	67,851	2,810	123	1,489	29	1,041	1,421	6,359	60,629
12 07450	Bonifay city	Holmes	3.6	4,078	2,802	1,040	29	42	1	77	87	168	3,454
12 07525	Bonita Springs city	Lee	35.3	32,797	29,356	118	84	123	28	2,582	506	5,615	28,291
12 07562	Bonnie Lock-Woodsetter North CDP	Broward	0.5	4,275	2,048	1,332	18	113	2	352	410	731	2,992
12 07775	Bowling Green city	Hardee	1.4	2,892	1,650	391	24	10	9	752	56	1,332	1,935
12 07825	Boyette CDP	Hillsborough	6.6	5,895	5,215	318	37	89	4	101	131	481	4,024
12 07875	Boynton Beach city	Palm Beach	15.9	60,389	42,487	13,822	133	918	30	1,428	1,571	5,564	48,399
12 07950	Bradenton city	Manatee	12.1	49,504	38,682	7,481	145	392	23	1,934	847	5,574	38,832
12 08150	Brandon CDP	Hillsborough	28.7	77,895	63,798	7,213	315	1,865	72	2,668	1,964	9,882	56,952
12 08300	Brent CDP	Escambia	10.4	22,257	13,326	7,622	164	508	60	104	473	433	16,959
12 08650	Broadview Park CDP	Broward	1.0	6,798	4,617	1,154	14	132	33	555	293	2,877	4,774
12 08662	Broadview-Pompano Park CDP	Broward	0.6	5,314	3,315	1,006	14	174	-	498	307	1,946	3,590
12 08762	Brookridge CDP	Hernando	2.0	3,279	3,242	5	3	6	-	7	16	31	3,184
12 08800	Brooksville city	Hernando	4.9	7,264	5,443	1,548	26	89	-	79	79	223	5,661
12 08880	Broward Estates CDP	Broward	0.5	3,416	28	3,312	1	10	-	11	54	42	2,333
12 09000	Brownsville CDP	Miami-Dade	2.3	14,393	829	13,131	32	3	2	209	187	1,183	9,359
12 09350	Buckingham CDP	Lee	19.0	3,742	3,525	87	7	19	-	72	32	175	2,961
12 09500	Bunche Park CDP	Miami-Dade	0.8	3,972	54	3,831	3	5	-	25	54	121	2,844
12 09630	Butler Beach CDP	St. Johns	2.5	4,436	4,346	13	8	31	-	18	20	66	3,899
12 09725	Callaway city	Bay	5.7	14,233	10,769	2,251	119	478	12	170	434	509	10,349
12 09875	Campbell CDP	Osceola	1.9	2,677	2,531	25	7	23	2	46	43	119	2,320
12 10250	Cape Canaveral city	Brevard	2.3	8,829	8,359	126	28	150	5	37	124	307	7,827
12 10275	Cape Coral city	Lee	105.2	102,286	95,133	2,046	260	938	56	2,253	1,600	8,521	79,196
12 10650	Carol City CDP	Miami-Dade	7.6	59,443	22,653	30,970	115	324	24	3,287	2,070	24,965	41,036
12 10920	Carver Ranches CDP	Broward	0.7	4,299	94	4,145	7	1	-	24	28	71	2,909
12 11050	Casselberry city	Seminole	6.7	22,629	19,381	1,218	63	430	9	944	584	3,424	17,944
12 11150	Cedar Grove town	Bay	9.4	5,367	4,587	515	39	95	5	30	96	113	3,909
12 11285	Celebration CDP	Osceola	10.7	2,736	2,560	47	7	66	-	28	28	208	1,894
12 11437	Century Village CDP	Palm Beach	1.0	7,616	7,495	33	2	32	6	8	40	228	7,595
12 11557	Chambers Estates CDP	Broward	0.6	3,556	2,776	394	10	65	-	192	119	921	2,568
12 11625	Charlotte Harbor CDP	Charlotte	2.2	3,647	3,416	104	7	47	1	46	26	117	3,306
12 11800	Chattahoochee city	Gadsden	5.5	3,287	1,667	1,536	4	31	1	22	26	84	2,699
12 11912	Cheval CDP	Hillsborough	6.7	7,602	6,527	352	14	381	12	161	155	990	5,841
12 11975	Chipley city	Washington	4.1	3,592	2,437	1,024	46	20	1	8	56	52	2,690
12 12412	Citrus Hills CDP	Citrus	9.8	4,029	3,738	58	13	162	-	18	40	114	3,494
12 12425	Citrus Park CDP	Hillsborough	10.6	20,226	16,484	1,532	71	643	15	929	552	4,0^8	14,395
12 12435	Citrus Ridge CDP	Lake, Orange, Osceola, Polk	46.8	12,015	10,441	429	38	275	10	495	327	1,874	9,619
12 12450	Citrus Springs CDP	Citrus	21.3	4,157	3,895	93	13	27	3	57	69	227	3,409
12 12875	Clearwater city	Pinellas	25.3	108,787	91,223	10,651	346	1,782	75	2,700	2,010	9,754	87,969
12 12925	Clermont city	Lake	10.5	9,333	7,793	1,127	45	83	1	145	139	533	7,453
12 12950	Cleveland CDP	Charlotte	5.5	3,268	3,197	13	11	7	1	16	23	47	2,800
12 13000	Clewiston city	Hendry	4.7	6,460	4,896	706	25	76	-	623	134	2,645	4,539
12 13150	Cocoa city	Brevard	7.5	16,412	10,252	5,298	104	154	38	259	307	809	12,079
12 13175	Cocoa Beach city	Brevard	4.9	12,482	12,062	78	28	134	7	38	135	314	10,955
12 13225	Cocoa West CDP	Brevard	4.3	5,921	3,266	2,421	38	15	7	74	100	209	4,184
12 13275	Coconut Creek city	Broward	11.5	43,566	37,588	2,685	56	1,033	23	1,245	936	5,076	35,727
12 13625	Collier Manor-Cresthaven CDP	Broward	1.2	7,741	6,024	912	36	85	2	375	307	1,260	5,865

[Includes incorporated places and census designated places (CDPs) of 2,500 or more population as of April 1, 2000. Codes shown are two-digit Federal Information Processing Standards (FIPS) state codes and five-digit FIPS place codes. Place names and codes are those in effect as of January 1, 2000. County refers to the county (or counties) in which the place is located. IC in this column = independent city, a county equivalent. If a place is located in more than one county, counties are listed in alphabetic order]

State and place code	Place	County	Land area, 2000 (sq. mi.)	Population, 2000 (April 1) Total	By race— One race White	Black or African American	American Indian and Alaska Native	Asian	Native Hawaiian and Other Pacific Islander	Some other race	Two or more races	Hispanic or Latino (of any race)	18 years and over
12 00000	FLORIDA—Con.												
12 13775	Combee Settlement CDP .	Polk	2.1	5,436	4,779	311	48	35	2	159	102	348	4,100
12 14050	Conway CDP	Orange	3.5	14,394	12,983	368	42	283	8	385	325	1,661	10,585
12 14125	Cooper City city	Broward.	6.3	27,939	24,893	864	44	1,143	11	461	523	4,349	19,184
12 14250	Coral Gables city.	Miami-Dade	13.1	42,249	38,798	1,394	55	708	15	629	650	19,703	34,897
12 14400	Coral Springs city	Broward.	23.9	117,549	95,860	10,766	208	4,152	79	3,520	2,964	18,233	81,499
12 14412	Coral Terrace CDP	Miami-Dade	3.4	24,380	22,687	281	24	130	2	693	563	20,015	19,439
12 14700	Cortez CDP	Manatee	2.2	4,491	4,416	7	9	24	-	7	28	59	4,107
12 14895	Country Club CDP.	Miami-Dade	4.3	36,310	23,072	7,992	82	803	21	2,634	1,706	21,903	26,450
12 15055	Country Walk CDP	Miami-Dade	2.7	10,653	8,267	1,136	11	268	5	533	433	5,980	7,166
12 15475	Crestview city	Okaloosa	12.8	14,766	11,032	2,719	89	337	22	180	387	481	10,453
12 15725	Crystal Lake CDP	Polk	2.7	5,341	4,323	728	40	47	1	131	71	385	3,980
12 15775	Crystal River city	Citrus	5.7	3,485	2,919	449	14	46	2	16	39	106	2,822
12 15962	Cutler CDP	Miami-Dade	6.7	17,390	15,513	679	19	521	5	332	321	4,555	12,262
12 15975	Cutler Ridge CDP	Miami-Dade	4.8	24,781	18,268	3,885	67	428	18	1,184	931	9,107	17,576
12 16050	Cypress Gardens CDP. .	Polk	3.8	8,844	8,321	170	25	149	-	76	103	274	6,944
12 16062	Cypress Lake CDP	Lee.	4.0	12,072	11,669	126	15	75	4	66	117	437	10,659
12 16125	Dade City city	Pasco	3.3	6,188	4,016	1,495	24	37	3	501	112	975	4,563
12 16175	Dade City North CDP. . . .	Pasco	1.8	3,319	1,827	358	16	4	2	988	124	1,875	2,220
12 16325	Dania Beach city.	Broward.	6.1	20,061	14,070	4,763	60	278	6	455	429	2,410	16,056
12 16475	Davie town.	Broward.	33.4	75,720	65,916	3,454	187	2,111	30	2,168	1,854	14,270	55,756
12 16525	Daytona Beach city	Volusia	58.7	64,112	39,963	20,994	206	1,112	41	670	1,126	2,232	52,815
12 16550	Daytona Beach Shores city	Volusia	0.9	4,299	4,152	25	7	74	5	6	30	46	4,115
12 16675	De Bary city	Volusia	18.2	15,559	14,772	296	31	176	1	134	149	645	12,447
12 16725	Deerfield Beach city. . . .	Broward.	13.4	64,583	49,894	10,339	108	896	20	1,521	1,805	5,643	54,520
12 16800	De Funiak Springs city . . .	Walton	11.0	5,089	3,653	1,170	51	26	4	92	93	168	3,890
12 16875	De Land city.	Volusia	15.9	20,904	15,670	4,010	47	170	3	627	377	1,824	16,578
12 17100	Delray Beach city	Palm Beach	15.4	60,020	39,908	15,981	102	651	49	933	2,396	4,184	49,082
12 17200	Deltona city	Volusia	35.8	69,543	58,659	4,848	245	660	36	3,464	1,651	12,747	50,751
12 17300	Desoto Lakes CDP	Sarasota	1.3	3,198	2,990	98	1	33	1	27	48	139	2,541
12 17325	Destin city	Okaloosa	7.5	11,119	10,698	41	44	115	9	41	171	296	8,961
12 17725	Doctor Phillips CDP	Orange	3.4	9,548	8,034	291	6	808	3	185	221	798	7,019
12 17935	Doral CDP	Miami-Dade	13.2	20,438	17,713	543	15	1,039	3	892	773	13,784	15,311
12 18075	Dover CDP	Hillsborough	2.6	2,798	2,074	12	29	17	7	535	124	1,423	1,875
12 18550	Dundee town	Polk	3.9	2,912	2,036	642	4	27	1	162	40	331	2,155
12 18575	Dunedin city	Pinellas	10.4	35,691	33,864	714	80	397	12	227	397	1,192	30,118
12 19206	East Lake CDP.	Pinellas	29.8	29,394	27,886	327	42	679	2	170	288	1,094	22,384
12 19212	East Lake-Orient Park CDP	Hillsborough	4.4	5,703	3,637	1,607	62	35	-	205	157	682	4,052
12 19387	East Perrine CDP	Miami-Dade	2.0	7,079	5,128	1,194	11	169	3	265	309	2,130	5,050
12 19825	Edgewater city	Volusia	10.0	18,668	17,987	263	48	100	2	56	212	365	14,423
12 20050	Eglin AFB CDP.	Okaloosa	3.1	8,082	5,802	1,198	39	239	31	342	431	904	4,570
12 20108	Egypt Lake-Leto CDP . . .	Hillsborough	6.0	32,782	24,946	2,618	122	1,110	17	2,665	1,304	15,015	25,216
12 20275	Elfers CDP	Pasco	3.5	13,161	12,528	126	50	120	4	122	211	595	10,516
12 20375	Ellenton CDP	Manatee	3.7	3,142	2,872	112	18	13	-	87	40	294	2,524
12 20650	El Portal village.	Miami-Dade	0.4	2,505	712	1,537	7	20	-	63	166	482	1,869
12 20825	Englewood CDP	Charlotte, Sarasota	9.8	16,196	15,913	30	40	59	2	65	87	241	14,530
12 20925	Ensley CDP	Escambia.	12.3	18,752	12,546	5,333	172	216	9	120	356	390	14,026
12 21150	Estero CDP	Lee.	21.1	9,503	9,259	61	10	33	1	73	66	303	8,625
12 21350	Eustis city	Lake	8.4	15,106	11,616	2,867	52	95	14	286	176	962	11,696
12 21750	Fairview Shores CDP. . . .	Orange	3.9	13,898	10,853	1,846	50	378	15	437	319	1,310	10,691
12 21945	Feather Sound CDP	Pinellas	4.2	3,597	3,376	75	4	91	1	24	26	146	3,113
12 22100	Fellsmere city	Indian River	5.3	3,813	2,292	255	18	4	2	1,170	72	2,790	2,543
12 22175	Fernandina Beach city . . .	Nassau	10.7	10,549	8,602	1,708	29	62	6	54	88	246	8,416
12 22250	Fern Park CDP.	Seminole	2.1	8,318	7,082	627	35	128	1	255	190	1,067	6,627
12 22275	Ferry Pass CDP	Escambia.	14.1	27,176	22,771	2,882	166	517	12	212	616	740	22,197
12 22550	Flagler Beach city	Flagler, Volusia	3.7	4,954	4,848	26	11	28	1	7	33	91	4,383
12 22775	Floral City CDP.	Citrus	23.3	4,989	4,804	82	18	7	2	19	57	128	3,975
12 22975	Florida City city	Miami-Dade	3.2	7,843	2,278	4,445	26	52	3	554	485	2,519	4,726
12 23050	Florida Ridge CDP	Indian River	10.8	15,217	13,017	1,689	29	103	2	150	227	620	11,782
12 23375	Forest City CDP	Seminole	4.3	12,612	10,761	613	31	429	5	459	314	1,964	9,399
12 24000	Fort Lauderdale city.	Broward.	31.7	152,397	97,941	44,010	344	1,565	74	2,684	5,779	14,406	122,821
12 24100	Fort Meade city	Polk	5.0	5,691	3,847	1,243	23	5	-	524	49	977	4,072
12 24125	Fort Myers city	Lee.	31.8	48,208	27,166	16,095	181	471	49	2,745	1,501	6,984	35,532
12 24150	Fort Myers Beach town . .	Lee.	2.9	6,561	6,380	5	25	19	2	65	65	227	6,064
12 24175	Fort Myers Shores CDP . .	Lee.	2.1	5,793	4,981	213	37	88	4	357	113	1,006	4,242
12 24300	Fort Pierce city	St. Lucie	14.7	37,516	18,585	15,326	122	298	30	2,011	1,144	5,629	27,313
12 24337	Fort Pierce North CDP . . .	St. Lucie	4.5	7,386	1,717	5,344	19	5	11	151	139	406	5,178
12 24387	Fort Pierce South CDP. . .	St. Lucie	4.5	5,672	4,384	745	3	66	3	325	146	998	4,089
12 24475	Fort Walton Beach city . . .	Okaloosa	7.4	19,973	15,746	2,664	90	543	16	243	671	807	15,497
12 24562	Fountainbleau CDP	Miami-Dade	4.4	59,549	50,732	1,214	114	1,057	17	4,044	2,371	51,948	46,016
12 24900	Frostproof city.	Polk	2.5	2,975	2,327	116	25	2	2	427	76	644	2,180
12 24925	Fruit Cove CDP	St. Johns	17.9	16,077	15,235	331	29	259	22	71	130	382	10,882
12 24975	Fruitland Park city	Lake	2.9	3,186	2,838	228	18	42	2	20	38	81	2,296
12 25000	Fruitville CDP	Sarasota	7.0	12,741	12,185	167	22	150	1	109	107	519	9,806
12 25125	Fussels Corner CDP	Polk	7.1	5,313	4,713	289	19	8	2	205	77	305	4,268
12 25175	Gainesville city	Alachua	48.2	95,447	65,243	22,181	235	4,282	30	1,392	2,084	6,112	78,497
12 25655	Gateway CDP.	Lee.	8.6	2,943	2,783	62	4	45	-	23	26	96	2,205

[Includes incorporated places and census designated places (CDPs) of 2,500 or more population as of April 1, 2000. Codes shown are two-digit Federal Information Processing Standards (FIPS) state codes and five-digit FIPS place codes. Place names and codes are those in effect as of January 1, 2000. County refers to the county (or counties) in which the place is located. IC in this column = independent city, a county equivalent. If a place is located in more than one county, counties are listed in alphabetic order]

State and place code	Place	County	Land area, 2000 (sq. mi.)	Total	White	Black or African American	American Indian and Alaska Native	Asian	Native Hawaiian and Other Pacific Islander	Some other race	Two or more races	Hispanic or Latino (of any race)	18 years and over
				Population, 2000 (April 1) — By race — One race									
12 00000	FLORIDA—Con.												
12 25750	Geneva CDP	Seminole	11.4	2,601	2,468	59	22	23	2	8	19	54	1,902
12 25875	Gibsonia CDP	Polk	2.6	4,507	4,191	120	16	34	6	61	79	297	3,413
12 25900	Gibsonton CDP	Hillsborough	12.9	8,752	7,762	119	82	63	3	584	139	1,576	6,149
12 25925	Gifford CDP	Indian River	7.0	7,599	2,941	4,364	12	19	-	149	114	507	5,611
12 25987	Gladeview CDP	Miami-Dade	2.5	14,468	2,545	11,138	31	24	4	359	367	3,084	8,976
12 26100	Glenvar Heights CDP	Miami-Dade	4.2	16,243	14,246	488	31	472	9	555	442	9,008	13,279
12 26300	Golden Gate CDP	Collier	4.0	20,951	16,132	2,126	80	149	25	1,537	902	7,781	14,653
12 26375	Golden Glades CDP	Miami-Dade	4.9	32,623	7,628	21,299	92	592	24	953	2,035	5,753	22,464
12 26460	Golden Lakes CDP	Palm Beach	2.4	6,694	4,614	1,512	27	79	3	214	245	1,073	5,219
12 26475	Goldenrod CDP	Orange, Seminole	2.6	12,871	10,609	712	60	368	12	692	418	2,295	10,115
12 26700	Gonzalez CDP	Escambia	15.3	11,365	10,004	869	91	169	2	47	183	190	8,125
12 26925	Goulding CDP	Escambia	1.2	4,484	1,121	3,249	16	27	1	20	50	69	3,844
12 26950	Goulds CDP	Miami-Dade	3.0	7,453	1,134	5,823	13	40	1	259	183	1,219	4,593
12 27313	Greater Carrollwood CDP	Hillsborough	9.6	33,519	28,320	1,960	82	1,161	17	1,125	854	6,131	25,529
12 27317	Greater Northdale CDP	Hillsborough	7.9	20,461	17,533	1,149	46	750	18	485	480	3,074	15,052
12 27319	Greater Sun Center CDP	Hillsborough	12.5	16,321	16,152	22	13	65	11	23	35	195	16,255
12 27322	Greenacres city	Palm Beach	4.7	27,569	22,939	1,790	96	505	11	1,546	682	5,858	21,801
12 27400	Green Cove Springs city	Clay	6.8	5,378	3,848	1,312	22	29	2	72	93	273	4,101
12 28000	Gulf Breeze city	Santa Rosa	4.8	5,665	5,517	14	31	32	1	10	60	77	4,400
12 28050	Gulf Gate Estates CDP	Sarasota	2.8	11,647	11,235	91	24	94	3	90	110	373	10,097
12 28175	Gulfport city	Pinellas	2.8	12,527	11,199	884	52	67	8	98	219	435	10,548
12 28400	Haines City city	Polk	8.3	13,174	7,229	4,197	69	51	5	1,373	250	3,074	9,597
12 28450	Hallandale city	Broward	4.2	34,282	26,484	5,493	78	344	14	958	911	6,447	29,748
12 28592	Hamptons at Boca Raton CDP	Palm Beach	2.5	11,306	10,718	188	5	166	1	105	123	522	10,104
12 28650	Harbor Bluffs CDP	Pinellas	0.7	2,807	2,724	3	1	44	-	7	28	55	2,265
12 28800	Harbour Heights CDP	Charlotte	2.2	2,873	2,692	82	1	22	2	21	53	110	2,351
12 28925	Harlem CDP	Hendry	1.0	2,730	63	2,604	5	3	-	14	41	72	1,652
12 29320	Heathrow CDP	Seminole	2.8	4,068	3,634	150	5	191	-	40	48	249	3,258
12 29425	Hernando CDP	Citrus	31.5	8,253	7,888	187	24	43	5	14	92	135	6,830
12 30000	Hialeah city	Miami-Dade	19.2	226,419	199,276	5,453	304	906	53	12,380	8,047	204,543	174,402
12 30025	Hialeah Gardens city	Miami-Dade	2.5	19,297	17,060	348	15	154	-	1,027	693	17,324	13,956
12 30200	Highland Beach town	Palm Beach	0.5	3,775	3,712	14	2	14	-	4	29	112	3,628
12 30494	High Point CDP	Hernando	2.9	2,973	2,927	4	3	9	-	16	14	67	2,650
12 30525	High Springs city	Alachua	18.5	3,863	2,952	818	15	13	-	12	53	159	2,881
12 30750	Hilliard town	Nassau	5.5	2,702	2,272	354	19	13	-	-	44	27	1,881
12 30975	Hobe Sound CDP	Martin	5.5	11,376	10,464	659	17	68	3	73	92	253	9,462
12 31025	Holden Heights CDP	Orange	1.3	3,856	2,806	666	12	101	7	155	109	566	3,097
12 31075	Holiday CDP	Pasco	5.4	21,904	20,838	309	60	198	12	186	301	883	18,106
12 31350	Holly Hill city	Volusia	3.9	12,119	10,556	1,087	44	121	3	110	198	447	9,712
12 32000	Hollywood city	Broward	27.3	139,357	109,190	16,853	381	2,757	117	5,507	4,552	31,392	109,687
12 32150	Holmes Beach city	Manatee	1.6	4,966	4,896	6	6	14	4	11	29	82	4,327
12 32275	Homestead city	Miami-Dade	14.3	31,909	19,465	7,194	159	243	27	3,140	1,681	16,537	21,328
12 32400	Homosassa Springs CDP	Citrus	25.8	12,458	12,041	112	85	61	1	27	131	260	9,730
12 32825	Hudson CDP	Pasco	6.4	12,765	12,365	46	28	116	4	54	152	332	11,123
12 32967	Hunters Creek CDP	Orange	4.3	9,369	7,668	485	13	671	2	283	247	1,296	6,918
12 32993	Hutchinson Island South CDP	St. Lucie	4.5	4,846	4,795	7	6	11	-	5	22	43	4,757
12 33250	Immokalee CDP	Collier	8.1	19,763	7,610	3,564	204	39	37	7,048	1,261	14,027	12,858
12 33375	Indialantic town	Brevard	1.0	2,944	2,865	8	4	21	-	17	29	69	2,426
12 33450	Indian Harbour Beach city	Brevard	2.1	8,152	7,777	76	23	128	3	45	100	267	6,641
12 33585	Indian River Estates CDP	St. Lucie	5.5	5,793	5,520	134	11	27	4	43	54	205	4,573
12 33600	Indian River Shores town	Indian River	5.2	3,448	3,404	4	2	23	-	-	15	29	3,278
12 33625	Indian Rocks Beach city	Pinellas	0.9	5,072	4,929	15	9	31	1	15	72	161	4,559
12 33700	Indiantown CDP	Martin	6.0	5,588	2,566	1,173	128	11	54	1,483	173	2,734	3,845
12 33950	Inverness city	Citrus	7.3	6,789	6,234	353	26	39	4	52	81	300	5,663
12 33966	Inverness Highlands South CDP	Citrus	5.6	5,781	5,540	100	20	40	1	33	47	286	4,675
12 34000	Inwood CDP	Polk	1.9	6,925	4,729	1,628	26	70	-	243	229	544	5,083
12 34012	Iona CDP	Lee	7.1	11,756	11,459	48	20	56	1	98	74	463	10,561
12 34132	Islamorada, Village of Islands village	Monroe	7.1	6,846	6,630	31	15	42	6	54	68	460	5,784
12 34400	Ives Estates CDP	Miami-Dade	2.6	17,586	8,986	6,174	30	815	9	662	910	4,234	13,221
12 35000	Jacksonville city	Duval	757.7	735,617	474,307	213,514	2,474	20,427	448	9,816	14,631	30,594	539,278
12 35050	Jacksonville Beach city	Duval	7.7	20,990	19,089	1,011	57	342	9	165	317	628	17,220
12 35300	Jan Phyl Village CDP	Polk	4.7	5,633	4,272	952	13	110	-	132	154	395	3,943
12 35350	Jasmine Estates CDP	Pasco	3.6	18,213	17,204	296	58	160	3	220	272	1,105	14,729
12 35550	Jensen Beach CDP	Martin	7.2	11,100	10,634	250	24	52	4	41	95	307	8,880
12 35800	June Park CDP	Brevard	3.7	4,367	4,230	33	7	53	-	6	38	100	3,442
12 35850	Juno Beach town	Palm Beach	1.4	3,262	3,191	14	4	20	2	11	20	110	2,931
12 35875	Jupiter town	Palm Beach	20.0	39,328	37,307	480	73	442	47	540	439	2,881	31,200
12 35950	Kathleen CDP	Polk	3.3	3,280	3,079	56	14	7	4	84	36	248	2,352
12 36062	Kendale Lakes CDP	Miami-Dade	8.2	56,901	49,492	1,312	74	1,083	14	2,886	2,040	43,574	42,357
12 36100	Kendall CDP	Miami-Dade	16.1	75,226	65,055	3,348	106	2,250	21	2,113	2,333	37,549	57,719
12 36112	Kendall Green CDP	Broward	0.5	3,084	1,215	1,273	7	32	2	127	428	494	2,160
12 36121	Kendall West CDP	Miami-Dade	3.4	38,034	31,708	1,609	73	564	13	2,450	1,617	30,060	26,919
12 36175	Kenneth City town	Pinellas	0.7	4,400	3,874	147	8	213	-	84	74	249	3,583
12 36200	Kensington Park CDP	Sarasota	1.3	3,720	3,208	252	6	52	2	144	56	392	2,918

Table D-1. Places — **Area and Population**—Con.

[Includes incorporated places and census designated places (CDPs) of 2,500 or more population as of April 1, 2000. Codes shown are two-digit Federal Information Processing Standards (FIPS) state codes and five-digit FIPS place codes. Place names and codes are those in effect as of January 1, 2000. County refers to the county (or counties) in which the place is located. IC in this column = independent city, a county equivalent. If a place is located in more than one county, counties are listed in alphabetic order]

State and place code	Place	County	Land area, 2000 (sq. mi.)	Population, 2000 (April 1) Total	By race—One race White	Black or African American	American Indian and Alaska Native	Asian	Native Hawaiian and Other Pacific Islander	Some other race	Two or more races	Hispanic or Latino (of any race)	18 years and over
12 00000	FLORIDA—Con.												
12 36300	Key Biscayne village	Miami-Dade	1.3	10,507	10,030	48	15	97	-	157	160	5,231	7,960
12 36375	Key Largo CDP	Monroe	12.2	11,886	11,218	243	35	56	-	113	221	1,979	9,550
12 36462	Keystone CDP	Hillsborough	36.1	14,627	13,355	512	50	359	7	137	207	1,240	10,651
12 36550	Key West city	Monroe	5.9	25,478	21,642	2,365	99	329	14	474	555	4,215	21,406
12 36812	Kings Point CDP	Palm Beach	1.8	12,207	12,097	33	5	22	1	10	39	138	12,185
12 36950	Kissimmee city	Osceola	16.7	47,814	32,139	4,775	247	1,614	46	6,765	2,228	19,954	34,913
12 37225	Labelle city	Hendry	3.5	4,210	3,085	474	26	14	-	525	86	1,320	3,081
12 37375	Lady Lake town	Lake	6.6	11,828	11,274	383	24	37	7	44	59	217	10,921
12 37500	Laguna Beach CDP	Bay	2.6	2,909	2,765	24	35	39	-	7	39	25	2,418
12 37525	Lake Alfred city	Polk	4.9	3,890	3,044	671	9	31	-	67	68	229	2,860
12 37662	Lake Butler CDP	Orange	12.9	7,062	6,338	241	10	276	2	52	143	330	4,769
12 37775	Lake City city	Columbia	10.6	9,980	5,920	3,739	23	102	8	33	155	281	7,450
12 37800	Lake Clarke Shores town	Palm Beach	1.0	3,451	3,215	36	8	67	8	85	39	639	2,802
12 37850	Lake Forest CDP	Broward	0.7	4,994	3,083	1,119	21	53	6	410	302	1,663	3,494
12 38025	Lake Helen city	Volusia	4.2	2,743	2,387	293	8	8	1	26	20	81	2,132
12 38250	Lakeland city	Polk	45.8	78,452	57,677	16,682	217	1,050	46	1,379	1,401	5,032	61,657
12 38262	Lakeland Highlands CDP	Polk	5.6	12,557	11,830	310	25	208	2	60	122	484	9,134
12 38287	Lake Lorraine CDP	Okaloosa	2.0	7,106	5,877	606	29	229	11	132	222	383	5,437
12 38300	Lake Lucerne CDP	Miami-Dade	2.6	9,132	1,013	7,648	17	15	1	232	206	1,353	6,069
12 38350	Lake Magdalene CDP	Hillsborough	10.6	28,755	24,915	1,698	101	670	9	760	602	3,886	22,289
12 38425	Lake Mary city	Seminole	8.6	11,458	10,236	413	28	439	10	169	163	713	8,399
12 38575	Lake Panasoffkee CDP	Sumter	4.0	3,413	3,311	22	25	16	-	5	34	31	2,888
12 38600	Lake Park town	Palm Beach	2.2	8,721	3,598	4,256	30	252	-	111	474	506	6,404
12 38690	Lake Sarasota CDP	Sarasota	1.4	4,458	4,287	37	22	14	1	46	51	181	3,102
12 38718	Lakes by the Bay CDP	Miami-Dade	4.9	9,055	6,603	1,391	16	252	9	425	359	3,969	6,426
12 38813	Lakeside CDP	Clay	15.2	30,927	26,520	2,199	123	843	26	454	762	1,638	22,152
12 38835	Lakeside Green CDP	Palm Beach	0.5	3,311	2,515	478	4	109	7	87	111	339	2,700
12 38950	Lake Wales city	Polk	13.3	10,194	6,064	3,526	31	52	10	369	142	1,014	7,451
12 39062	Lakewood Park CDP	St. Lucie	6.7	10,458	9,602	552	38	65	6	70	125	266	8,391
12 39075	Lake Worth city	Palm Beach	5.6	35,133	22,877	6,627	273	262	37	3,362	1,695	10,437	27,086
12 39087	Lake Worth Corridor CDP	Palm Beach	3.4	18,663	11,813	2,542	104	221	15	2,976	992	7,613	13,050
12 39200	Land O' Lakes CDP	Pasco	18.6	20,971	19,630	442	54	278	1	252	314	1,836	15,236
12 39375	Lantana town	Palm Beach	2.3	9,437	7,581	1,012	35	78	8	441	282	1,523	7,200
12 39425	Largo city	Pinellas	15.7	69,371	64,314	1,860	237	1,171	58	688	1,034	2,002	58,542
12 39475	Lauderdale-by-the-Sea town	Broward	0.5	2,563	2,472	19	3	23	-	22	24	135	2,359
12 39525	Lauderdale Lakes city	Broward	3.6	31,705	7,596	21,476	38	328	19	603	1,645	1,755	22,924
12 39550	Lauderhill city	Broward	7.3	57,585	19,482	33,840	67	910	35	926	2,325	3,995	42,261
12 39600	Laurel CDP	Sarasota	5.2	8,393	8,035	165	25	64	1	25	78	108	7,352
12 39825	Lecanto CDP	Citrus	27.0	5,161	4,845	153	39	39	1	22	62	140	4,101
12 39875	Leesburg city	Lake	18.7	15,956	10,627	4,646	43	213	1	201	225	657	12,209
12 39925	Lehigh Acres CDP	Lee	94.9	33,430	28,183	2,938	96	280	6	1,261	666	4,466	24,724
12 39950	Leisure City CDP	Miami-Dade	3.4	22,152	14,406	3,987	45	186	7	2,529	992	14,465	14,132
12 39987	Lely CDP	Collier	1.5	3,857	3,757	27	6	17	-	35	15	143	3,545
12 40450	Lighthouse Point city	Broward	2.3	10,767	10,449	46	16	85	1	45	125	450	9,021
12 40875	Live Oak city	Suwannee	7.0	6,480	3,774	2,440	16	51	2	119	78	558	4,754
12 40970	Loch Lomond CDP	Broward	0.2	3,537	1,539	1,074	18	57	8	357	484	871	2,701
12 40985	Lochmoor Waterway Estates CDP	Lee	2.2	3,858	3,692	30	17	54	4	13	48	137	3,151
12 41025	Lockhart CDP	Orange	4.4	12,944	9,552	2,081	75	286	5	545	400	2,083	9,167
12 41150	Longboat Key town	Manatee, Sarasota	4.9	7,603	7,545	5	6	33	1	1	12	51	7,403
12 41250	Longwood city	Seminole	5.3	13,745	11,999	495	36	340	6	536	333	1,519	10,288
12 41562	Lower Grand Lagoon CDP	Bay	2.2	4,082	3,914	48	24	30	3	13	50	125	3,537
12 41775	Lutz CDP	Hillsborough	21.5	17,081	15,794	512	52	245	1	217	260	1,343	12,679
12 41825	Lynn Haven city	Bay	8.2	12,451	10,738	1,164	90	197	15	58	189	202	9,196
12 41950	Macclenny city	Baker	3.3	4,459	3,384	975	16	30	3	20	31	110	3,170
12 42090	McGregor CDP	Lee	2.6	7,136	6,857	60	14	111	-	28	66	208	6,066
12 42400	Madeira Beach city	Pinellas	1.0	4,511	4,378	12	14	26	2	30	49	107	4,139
12 42425	Madison city	Madison	2.5	3,061	1,094	1,911	3	15	1	9	28	66	2,170
12 42575	Maitland city	Orange	4.6	12,019	10,243	1,169	14	262	1	140	190	717	8,953
12 42625	Malabar town	Brevard	10.6	2,622	2,451	73	14	30	3	9	42	69	2,035
12 42850	Mango CDP	Hillsborough	4.6	8,842	7,690	569	51	64	4	212	252	810	6,269
12 43000	Marathon city	Monroe	8.6	10,255	9,341	477	37	49	4	205	142	2,095	8,485
12 43075	Marco Island city	Collier	10.6	14,879	14,594	35	27	86	1	73	63	608	13,253
12 43125	Margate city	Broward	8.8	53,909	42,478	6,268	139	1,497	31	1,549	1,947	8,238	42,664
12 43175	Marianna city	Jackson	8.0	6,230	3,540	2,502	16	46	-	54	72	162	4,569
12 43375	Mary Esther city	Okaloosa	1.5	4,055	3,392	262	39	153	7	49	153	166	3,108
12 43425	Mascotte city	Lake	2.4	2,687	1,801	113	18	13	-	636	106	1,180	1,796
12 43800	Meadow Woods CDP	Orange	11.4	11,286	7,561	1,349	62	273	13	1,503	525	5,964	7,920
12 43925	Medulla CDP	Polk	5.7	6,637	5,610	773	2	41	1	121	89	345	4,883
12 43975	Melbourne city	Brevard	30.2	71,382	60,339	6,658	245	1,657	47	858	1,578	3,958	56,626
12 44000	Melbourne Beach town	Brevard	1.0	3,335	3,252	3	4	33	-	8	35	76	2,666
12 44125	Melrose Park CDP	Broward	0.9	7,114	715	5,880	7	56	2	115	339	277	4,784
12 44175	Memphis CDP	Manatee	3.2	7,264	3,502	3,043	7	22	10	567	113	1,460	5,133
12 44275	Merritt Island CDP	Brevard	17.7	36,090	32,560	1,918	149	597	21	246	599	1,381	28,225
12 45000	Miami city	Miami-Dade	35.7	362,470	241,470	80,858	810	2,376	130	19,644	17,182	238,351	283,673
12 45025	Miami Beach city	Miami-Dade	7.0	87,933	76,276	3,548	206	1,202	39	3,557	3,105	47,000	76,118
12 45050	Miami Gardens CDP	Broward	0.4	2,706	1,484	727	9	62	4	290	130	1,171	1,878

Table D-1. Places — **Area and Population**—Con.

[Includes incorporated places and census designated places (CDPs) of 2,500 or more population as of April 1, 2000. Codes shown are two-digit Federal Information Processing Standards (FIPS) state codes and five-digit FIPS place codes. Place names and codes are those in effect as of January 1, 2000. County refers to the county (or counties) in which the place is located. IC in this column = independent city, a county equivalent. If a place is located in more than one county, counties are listed in alphabetic order]

State and place code	Place	County	Land area, 2000 (sq. mi.)	Population, 2000 (April 1) Total	By race— One race White	Black or African American	American Indian and Alaska Native	Asian	Native Hawaiian and Other Pacific Islander	Some other race	Two or more races	Hispanic or Latino (of any race)	18 years and over
12 00000	FLORIDA—Con.												
12 45100	Miami Lakes CDP	Miami-Dade	6.0	22,676	20,239	635	32	500	6	649	615	15,083	16,977
12 45175	Miami Shores village	Miami-Dade	2.5	10,380	6,753	2,541	11	254	8	289	524	2,257	8,048
12 45200	Miami Springs city	Miami-Dade	2.9	13,712	12,452	280	30	163	5	417	365	8,173	10,578
12 45275	Micco CDP	Brevard	9.4	9,498	9,386	23	14	9	12	17	37	125	8,937
12 45350	Middleburg CDP	Clay	18.3	10,338	9,632	334	74	65	5	66	162	266	7,148
12 45750	Milton city	Santa Rosa	4.4	7,045	5,484	1,124	50	122	12	73	180	243	5,122
12 45775	Mims CDP	Brevard	19.8	9,147	7,919	1,004	58	20	2	24	120	141	6,953
12 45900	Minneola city	Lake	3.1	5,435	4,821	275	15	72	2	160	90	594	3,821
12 45975	Miramar city	Broward	29.5	72,739	31,704	31,498	118	2,202	72	3,431	3,714	21,374	50,154
12 46040	Mission Bay CDP	Palm Beach	0.8	2,926	2,712	41	-	79	4	34	56	289	2,060
12 46500	Monticello city	Jefferson	3.4	2,533	1,192	1,288	3	15	2	11	22	33	1,898
12 47050	Mount Dora city	Lake	4.9	9,418	7,277	1,806	16	65	5	140	109	628	7,486
12 47125	Mount Plymouth CDP	Lake	2.8	2,814	2,559	139	21	33	5	17	40	113	2,105
12 47200	Mulberry city	Polk	3.1	3,230	2,472	645	7	11	-	54	41	143	2,478
12 47550	Myrtle Grove CDP	Escambia	6.6	17,211	12,950	2,322	153	862	51	276	597	740	13,382
12 47625	Naples city	Collier	12.0	20,976	19,402	975	26	70	5	63	435	467	18,687
12 47650	Naples Manor CDP	Collier	0.7	5,186	2,566	852	20	7	5	1,512	224	3,594	3,439
12 47675	Naples Park CDP	Collier	1.2	6,741	6,195	89	9	57	4	309	78	1,184	5,232
12 47700	Naranja CDP	Miami-Dade	1.5	4,034	1,331	2,321	17	56	6	157	146	1,088	2,439
12 47787	Nassau Village-Ratliff CDP	Nassau	14.8	4,667	4,548	18	26	13	-	7	55	45	3,409
12 48100	Neptune Beach city	Duval	2.4	7,270	6,985	53	29	75	4	38	86	152	5,870
12 48200	Newberry city	Alachua	44.9	3,316	2,707	542	8	8	4	17	30	88	2,398
12 48500	New Port Richey city	Pasco	4.5	16,117	15,165	161	86	152	14	235	304	846	13,043
12 48525	New Port Richey East CDP	Pasco	3.6	9,916	9,460	103	22	110	3	66	152	484	7,956
12 48625	New Smyrna Beach city	Volusia	27.7	20,048	18,358	1,257	67	101	7	62	196	301	17,264
12 48750	Niceville city	Okaloosa	10.9	11,684	10,194	535	86	374	13	133	349	434	8,992
12 48875	Nokomis CDP	Sarasota	1.7	3,334	3,257	20	8	10	-	9	30	62	2,763
12 49000	Norland CDP	Miami-Dade	3.6	22,995	2,989	18,285	34	248	1	502	936	2,285	15,606
12 49150	North Andrews Gardens CDP	Broward	1.1	9,656	8,111	466	36	139	3	539	362	2,682	7,116
12 49225	North Bay Village city	Miami-Dade	0.3	6,733	5,461	344	20	227	2	401	278	3,302	5,601
12 49350	North Fort Myers CDP	Lee	52.6	40,214	38,804	375	136	194	22	324	359	1,166	35,014
12 49425	North Lauderdale city	Broward	3.9	32,264	16,137	11,343	94	1,006	21	1,893	1,770	6,816	22,630
12 49450	North Miami city	Miami-Dade	8.5	59,880	20,842	32,867	191	1,152	28	1,893	2,907	13,869	43,065
12 49475	North Miami Beach city	Miami-Dade	5.0	40,786	19,040	15,895	119	1,646	27	1,882	2,177	12,245	29,657
12 49600	North Palm Beach village	Palm Beach	3.6	12,064	11,608	112	11	147	3	60	123	426	10,339
12 49675	North Port city	Sarasota	74.8	22,797	21,127	954	53	115	3	163	382	739	17,480
12 49750	North River Shores CDP	Martin	1.3	3,101	3,034	16	4	19	-	8	20	56	2,548
12 49787	North Sarasota CDP	Sarasota	3.8	6,738	4,303	2,071	18	33	2	200	111	591	5,248
12 49905	North Weeki Wachee CDP	Hernando	7.4	4,253	4,109	42	17	23	1	25	36	200	3,608
12 50575	Oakland Park city	Broward	6.3	30,966	20,432	7,013	70	600	41	1,379	1,431	5,556	24,509
12 50638	Oak Ridge CDP	Orange	4.2	22,349	9,628	6,357	91	1,267	64	3,111	1,831	9,257	15,733
12 50750	Ocala city	Marion	38.6	45,943	33,474	10,174	167	559	9	831	729	2,636	35,297
12 50925	Ocean City CDP	Okaloosa	1.6	5,594	4,698	392	36	181	3	89	195	241	4,425
12 51075	Ocoee city	Orange	13.2	24,391	19,871	1,607	86	714	15	1,517	581	3,707	17,258
12 51100	Odessa CDP	Pasco	5.3	3,173	3,044	21	18	23	1	29	37	216	2,382
12 51125	Ojus CDP	Miami-Dade	2.8	16,642	14,161	1,174	22	290	7	512	476	5,093	13,063
12 51200	Okeechobee city	Okeechobee	4.1	5,376	4,247	581	27	53	6	345	117	842	4,041
12 51350	Oldsmar city	Pinellas	8.9	11,910	10,771	352	35	333	19	154	246	794	8,744
12 51475	Olympia Heights CDP	Miami-Dade	2.7	13,452	12,578	112	14	122	-	331	295	10,268	10,761
12 51650	Opa-locka city	Miami-Dade	4.3	14,951	3,414	10,412	52	31	3	538	501	4,268	9,776
12 51662	Opa-locka North CDP	Miami-Dade	2.2	6,224	1,249	4,667	10	29	2	114	153	1,189	4,484
12 51825	Orange City city	Volusia	6.1	6,604	6,140	242	25	37	4	93	63	339	5,449
12 52125	Orange Park town	Clay	3.9	9,081	7,533	995	47	210	4	131	161	418	7,171
12 53000	Orlando city	Orange	93.5	185,951	113,611	49,933	638	4,982	150	10,060	6,577	32,510	144,987
12 53100	Orlovista CDP	Orange	1.9	6,047	3,562	1,609	36	214	3	393	230	894	4,373
12 53150	Ormond Beach city	Volusia	25.7	36,301	34,223	1,000	62	522	7	112	375	797	29,342
12 53200	Ormond-By-The-Sea CDP	Volusia	2.0	8,430	8,222	28	33	42	8	24	73	194	7,342
12 53425	Osprey CDP	Sarasota	5.5	4,143	4,043	8	6	36	5	15	30	58	3,563
12 53575	Oviedo city	Seminole	15.1	26,316	21,986	2,325	71	637	10	689	598	3,209	17,896
12 53725	Pace CDP	Santa Rosa	9.4	7,393	6,932	98	116	77	3	36	131	140	5,386
12 53800	Pahokee city	Palm Beach	5.4	5,985	1,509	3,355	6	30	-	910	175	1,763	3,686
12 53875	Palatka city	Putnam	7.0	10,033	4,909	4,859	16	44	1	104	100	284	7,160
12 54000	Palm Bay city	Brevard	63.6	79,413	64,755	8,983	281	1,354	37	1,894	2,109	6,850	58,330
12 54025	Palm Beach town	Palm Beach	3.9	10,468	10,049	269	4	56	2	22	66	268	9,479
12 54075	Palm Beach Gardens city	Palm Beach	55.7	35,058	32,878	806	38	754	11	235	336	1,973	28,500
12 54175	Palm City CDP	Martin	14.6	20,097	19,406	217	27	206	1	81	159	556	15,859
12 54200	Palm Coast city	Flagler	50.7	32,732	27,834	3,360	78	497	10	403	550	2,196	26,666
12 54250	Palmetto city	Manatee	4.3	12,571	9,454	1,607	68	45	13	1,104	280	3,358	9,259
12 54300	Palmetto Estates CDP	Miami-Dade	2.1	13,675	5,153	6,669	29	419	2	659	744	3,953	9,414
12 54350	Palm Harbor CDP	Pinellas	17.9	59,248	56,780	574	112	760	14	358	650	2,047	46,928
12 54387	Palm River-Clair Mel CDP	Hillsborough	11.7	17,589	9,556	6,087	93	213	4	1,078	558	3,958	12,054
12 54450	Palm Springs village	Palm Beach	1.6	11,699	9,855	781	39	162	3	557	302	2,929	9,167
12 54500	Palm Springs North CDP	Miami-Dade	0.7	5,460	5,079	42	10	32	-	172	125	3,545	3,965
12 54525	Palm Valley CDP	St. Johns	13.4	19,860	19,034	249	34	257	5	103	178	557	14,896
12 54700	Panama City city	Bay	20.5	36,417	26,819	7,813	231	564	28	274	688	1,060	28,056

[Includes incorporated places and census designated places (CDPs) of 2,500 or more population as of April 1, 2000. Codes shown are two-digit Federal Information Processing Standards (FIPS) state codes and five-digit FIPS place codes. Place names and codes are those in effect as of January 1, 2000. County refers to the county (or counties) in which the place is located. IC in this column = independent city, a county equivalent. If a place is located in more than one county, counties are listed in alphabetic order]

State and place code	Place	County	Land area, 2000 (sq. mi.)	Population, 2000 (April 1)									
					By race—								
					One race							Hispanic or Latino (of any race)	18 years and over
				Total	White	Black or African American	American Indian and Alaska Native	Asian	Native Hawaiian and Other Pacific Islander	Some other race	Two or more races		
12 00000	FLORIDA—Con.												
12 54725	Panama City Beach city . .	Bay	6.9	7,671	7,380	67	41	60	-	26	97	169	6,408
12 55075	Parker city	Bay	1.9	4,623	3,777	524	30	123	3	43	123	116	3,590
12 55125	Parkland city	Broward .	10.2	13,835	12,648	425	16	445	1	129	171	1,152	8,981
12 55540	Pebble Creek CDP	Hillsborough .	3.0	4,824	4,037	294	10	294	4	81	104	450	3,414
12 55650	Pelican Bay CDP	Collier	3.2	5,686	5,641	5	2	27	-	4	7	52	5,493
12 55750	Pembroke Park town . . .	Broward .	1.4	6,299	2,684	3,085	23	43	4	249	211	967	4,601
12 55775	Pembroke Pines city	Broward .	33.1	137,427	103,870	18,210	255	5,163	68	5,086	4,775	38,700	102,222
12 55925	Pensacola city	Escambia .	22.7	56,255	36,514	17,203	291	998	35	306	908	1,167	43,369
12 56150	Perry city	Taylor	9.3	6,847	3,835	2,819	44	33	1	38	77	113	4,902
12 56425	Pierson town	Volusia .	8.1	2,596	2,127	128	7	2	-	298	34	1,621	2,032
12 56500	Pine Castle CDP	Orange	2.6	8,803	6,055	1,127	76	227	18	901	399	3,134	6,434
12 56625	Pinecrest village	Miami-Dade .	7.5	19,055	17,206	327	23	864	2	249	384	5,652	13,064
12 56825	Pine Hills CDP	Orange .	7.7	41,764	14,172	21,473	116	1,205	23	2,449	2,326	5,875	28,018
12 56855	Pine Island Ridge CDP. .	Broward .	0.8	5,199	4,922	63	4	78	1	58	73	537	4,662
12 56975	Pinellas Park city	Pinellas .	14.7	45,658	40,652	952	176	1,941	10	913	1,014	2,856	35,899
12 57025	Pine Manor CDP	Lee	0.4	3,785	2,490	621	26	24	1	483	140	1,642	2,609
12 57058	Pine Ridge CDP	Citrus	25.2	5,490	5,202	142	9	78	1	17	41	155	4,826
12 57250	Pinewood CDP	Miami-Dade .	1.7	16,523	3,182	11,739	41	54	5	594	908	3,775	11,214
12 57407	Placid Lakes CDP	Highlands .	18.3	3,054	2,739	161	24	32	1	60	37	321	2,473
12 57425	Plantation city	Broward .	21.7	82,934	64,967	11,426	143	2,390	37	1,655	2,316	10,860	63,751
12 57450	Plantation CDP	Sarasota .	2.4	4,168	4,111	10	8	13	-	13	13	34	3,978
12 57550	Plant City city	Hillsborough .	22.6	29,915	21,440	4,833	111	267	13	2,723	528	5,211	21,120
12 57900	Poinciana CDP	Osceola .	35.1	13,647	8,884	2,420	66	140	13	1,351	773	5,393	9,000
12 58050	Pompano Beach city	Broward .	20.6	78,191	52,989	19,897	186	636	22	1,602	2,859	7,770	64,321
12 58075	Pompano Beach Highlands CDP.	Broward .	1.3	6,505	5,001	594	47	162	3	338	360	1,462	4,748
12 58087	Pompano Estates CDP. . .	Broward .	0.5	3,367	1,168	1,778	10	12	1	81	317	358	2,261
12 58200	Ponce Inlet town	Volusia .	4.3	2,513	2,456	15	6	18	1	4	13	39	2,258
12 58350	Port Charlotte CDP	Charlotte .	22.3	46,451	41,448	3,033	132	529	22	550	737	2,395	37,772
12 58420	Port La Belle CDP	Hendry .	8.6	3,050	2,145	325	21	20	-	422	117	1,351	2,094
12 58575	Port Orange city	Volusia .	24.7	45,823	43,803	722	121	523	10	245	399	1,151	36,757
12 58600	Port Richey city	Pasco	2.1	3,021	2,904	19	18	33	2	11	34	87	2,573
12 58675	Port St. Joe city	Gulf	3.3	3,644	2,497	1,097	8	8	-	2	32	20	2,785
12 58700	Port St. John CDP	Brevard .	3.8	12,112	10,985	607	57	111	21	100	231	397	8,713
12 58715	Port St. Lucie city	St. Lucie .	75.5	88,769	78,011	6,295	200	1,101	31	1,570	1,561	6,677	67,184
12 58725	Port St. Lucie-River Park CDP	St. Lucie .	2.3	5,175	4,713	247	10	57	1	89	58	332	4,314
12 58727	Port Salerno CDP	Martin .	3.6	10,141	8,975	705	14	69	12	230	136	827	8,123
12 58962	Pretty Bayou CDP	Bay	2.0	3,519	3,309	94	19	47	-	9	41	57	2,840
12 58975	Princeton CDP	Miami-Dade .	7.3	10,090	5,426	3,283	34	138	6	777	426	4,792	6,451
12 59200	Punta Gorda city	Charlotte .	14.2	14,344	13,569	454	24	112	4	84	97	285	13,167
12 59325	Quincy city	Gadsden .	7.6	6,982	2,203	4,479	11	16	-	225	48	481	5,042
12 60225	Richmond Heights CDP . .	Miami-Dade .	1.7	8,479	1,056	7,023	19	70	1	170	140	1,057	6,024
12 60230	Richmond West CDP	Miami-Dade .	4.2	28,082	21,996	2,391	59	644	18	1,822	1,152	19,663	18,851
12 60325	Ridge Manor CDP	Hernando .	8.7	4,108	3,924	76	20	12	-	44	32	118	3,229
12 60475	Ridge Wood Heights CDP.	Sarasota .	1.4	5,028	4,817	39	21	48	3	52	48	216	3,928
12 60950	Riverview CDP	Hillsborough .	9.1	12,035	10,327	1,002	53	160	8	238	247	1,085	8,668
12 60975	Riviera Beach city	Palm Beach .	8.3	29,884	8,297	20,264	43	296	15	330	639	1,348	21,159
12 61412	Rock Island CDP	Broward .	0.6	3,076	52	2,969	5	7	2	6	35	27	2,145
12 61500	Rockledge city	Brevard .	10.7	20,170	16,349	2,952	56	335	17	147	314	662	15,371
12 61937	Rotonda CDP	Charlotte .	11.0	6,574	6,453	29	15	23	-	21	33	88	5,848
12 62100	Royal Palm Beach village .	Palm Beach .	9.9	21,523	16,821	3,059	60	567	9	494	513	2,546	15,368
12 62118	Royal Palm Estates CDP .	Palm Beach .	0.8	3,583	2,502	547	16	46	4	306	162	1,221	2,497
12 62275	Ruskin CDP	Hillsborough .	14.2	8,321	6,714	102	52	36	11	1,236	170	3,056	6,120
12 62425	Safety Harbor city	Pinellas .	4.9	17,203	15,867	712	42	289	8	76	209	628	13,459
12 62500	St. Augustine city	St. Johns .	8.4	11,592	9,414	1,747	48	83	11	102	187	361	9,724
12 62525	St. Augustine Beach city . .	St. Johns .	1.9	4,683	4,533	15	19	54	1	20	41	129	3,963
12 62550	St. Augustine Shores CDP	St. Johns .	3.4	4,922	4,688	100	8	55	4	29	38	152	4,080
12 62562	St. Augustine South CDP .	St. Johns .	1.7	5,035	4,874	48	13	56	1	7	36	142	3,826
12 62625	St. Cloud city	Osceola .	9.2	20,074	18,121	415	94	191	15	824	414	2,681	14,950
12 62675	St. James City CDP	Lee	14.6	4,105	4,062	4	6	11	-	6	16	31	3,814
12 62885	St. Pete Beach city	Pinellas .	2.2	9,929	9,692	66	22	55	3	34	57	249	8,967
12 63000	St. Petersburg city	Pinellas .	59.6	248,232	177,133	55,502	769	6,640	130	2,661	5,397	10,502	194,796
12 63225	Samoset CDP	Manatee .	1.9	3,440	2,168	912	13	4	1	252	90	608	2,335
12 63362	Samsula-Spruce Creek CDP	Volusia .	19.9	4,877	4,737	16	16	40	4	7	57	86	3,917
12 63425	San Carlos Park CDP . . .	Lee	4.9	16,317	15,312	205	55	115	1	377	252	1,329	11,542
12 63450	Sandalfoot Cove CDP . . .	Palm Beach .	3.0	16,582	14,461	657	25	492	9	545	393	2,397	12,882
12 63650	Sanford city	Seminole .	19.1	38,291	22,872	12,308	174	403	21	1,628	805	3,974	26,040
12 63700	Sanibel city	Lee	17.2	6,064	5,942	57	5	20	3	7	30	84	5,454
12 64175	Sarasota city	Sarasota .	14.9	52,715	40,542	8,447	186	536	26	1,969	1,009	6,283	42,992
12 64325	Sarasota Springs CDP . . .	Sarasota .	3.6	15,875	15,185	116	37	118	4	203	212	759	12,303
12 64400	Satellite Beach city	Brevard .	2.4	9,577	9,097	98	17	148	3	64	150	283	7,493
12 64525	Sawgrass CDP	St. Johns .	3.1	4,942	4,819	24	4	47	-	25	23	93	4,233
12 64587	Scott Lake CDP	Miami-Dade .	3.3	14,401	670	13,133	26	59	6	145	362	789	9,894
12 64825	Sebastian city	Indian River .	12.6	16,181	15,155	515	39	120	-	153	199	625	12,915

Table D-1. Places — **Area and Population**—Con.

[Includes incorporated places and census designated places (CDPs) of 2,500 or more population as of April 1, 2000. Codes shown are two-digit Federal Information Processing Standards (FIPS) state codes and five-digit FIPS place codes. Place names and codes are those in effect as of January 1, 2000. County refers to the county (or counties) in which the place is located. IC in this column = independent city, a county equivalent. If a place is located in more than one county, counties are listed in alphabetic order]

State and place code	Place	County	Land area, 2000 (sq. mi.)	Population, 2000 (April 1) Total	White	Black or African American	American Indian and Alaska Native	Asian	Native Hawaiian and Other Pacific Islander	Some other race	Two or more races	Hispanic or Latino (of any race)	18 years and over
12 00000	FLORIDA—Con.												
12 64875	Sebring city	Highlands	5.1	9,667	7,329	1,517	55	72	10	489	195	1,063	7,530
12 64925	Seffner CDP	Hillsborough	3.6	5,467	4,994	178	16	56	-	148	75	449	4,025
12 64975	Seminole city	Pinellas	2.5	10,890	10,521	52	37	93	3	45	139	245	9,609
12 65100	Seminole Manor CDP	Palm Beach	0.4	2,546	1,766	441	12	23	9	206	89	669	1,776
12 65385	Shady Hills CDP	Palm Beach	26.2	7,798	7,551	44	48	14	1	48	92	304	5,705
12 65525	Sharpes CDP	Brevard	3.0	3,415	3,139	121	30	22	-	24	79	80	2,684
12 66000	Siesta Key CDP	Sarasota	2.3	7,150	7,052	7	10	31	1	18	31	112	6,503
12 66175	Silver Springs Shores CDP	Marion	4.8	6,690	4,239	1,903	21	72	-	224	231	808	5,094
12 66425	Sky Lake CDP	Orange	1.3	5,651	3,955	693	19	128	42	526	288	1,960	4,220
12 67163	South Apopka CDP	Orange	2.7	5,800	1,555	3,792	33	4	6	319	91	740	3,777
12 67175	South Bay city	Palm Beach	2.7	3,859	935	2,583	11	10	1	225	94	755	2,817
12 67192	South Beach CDP	Indian River	2.7	3,457	3,393	20	3	35	-	2	4	47	2,982
12 67258	South Bradenton CDP	Manatee	4.5	21,587	19,410	997	68	282	21	469	340	1,870	17,811
12 67270	Southchase CDP	Orange	2.2	4,633	2,746	673	12	424	3	535	240	1,567	3,161
12 67325	South Daytona city	Volusia	3.6	13,177	11,684	1,034	16	159	7	70	207	381	10,504
12 67355	Southeast Arcadia CDP	DeSoto	7.3	6,064	4,441	252	151	22	-	1,097	101	2,773	4,529
12 67425	Southgate CDP	Sarasota	2.0	7,455	7,169	60	16	72	7	55	76	426	6,282
12 67450	South Gate Ridge CDP	Sarasota	1.8	5,655	5,346	43	15	100	3	88	60	295	4,525
12 67462	South Highpoint CDP	Pinellas	2.2	8,839	6,007	2,055	38	320	6	258	155	819	6,993
12 67550	South Miami city	Miami-Dade	2.3	10,741	7,502	2,653	15	150	4	188	229	3,692	8,301
12 67575	South Miami Heights CDP	Miami-Dade	4.9	33,522	18,594	10,163	95	612	8	2,297	1,753	18,829	23,275
12 67675	South Pasadena city	Pinellas	0.7	5,778	5,684	12	2	42	1	12	25	89	5,612
12 67725	South Patrick Shores CDP	Brevard	2.1	8,913	8,061	325	47	186	5	83	206	443	6,775
12 67887	South Sarasota CDP	Sarasota	2.0	5,314	5,100	21	11	62	-	71	49	214	4,352
12 68100	South Venice CDP	Sarasota	6.2	13,539	13,223	54	35	68	2	49	108	236	10,902
12 68275	Springfield city	Bay	4.0	8,810	5,941	2,056	75	375	11	85	267	225	6,311
12 68350	Spring Hill CDP	Hernando	53.1	69,078	64,591	2,073	167	534	15	842	856	4,720	55,637
12 68525	Starke city	Bradford	6.7	5,593	3,750	1,652	12	70	9	36	64	125	4,100
12 68800	Stock Island CDP	Monroe	0.9	4,410	3,526	461	16	48	2	210	147	1,911	3,372
12 68875	Stuart city	Martin	6.3	14,633	12,189	1,804	38	96	5	288	213	920	12,511
12 68950	Sugarmill Woods CDP	Citrus	26.4	6,409	6,264	57	12	52	1	4	19	89	5,823
12 69275	Suncoast Estates CDP	Lee	2.7	4,867	4,632	31	41	11	-	95	57	285	3,476
12 69550	Sunny Isles Beach city	Miami-Dade	1.0	15,315	14,067	311	24	209	1	358	345	5,607	13,588
12 69700	Sunrise city	Broward	18.2	85,779	59,597	17,557	156	2,642	61	2,967	2,799	14,655	64,400
12 69812	Sunset CDP	Miami-Dade	3.6	17,150	15,647	259	19	420	-	427	378	11,952	13,159
12 70075	Surfside town	Miami-Dade	0.5	4,909	4,590	63	2	57	1	74	122	2,137	4,111
12 70275	Sweetwater city	Miami-Dade	0.8	14,226	12,398	126	42	28	2	1,020	610	13,253	10,781
12 70600	Tallahassee city	Leon	95.7	150,624	91,007	51,569	376	3,617	82	1,457	2,516	6,309	124,431
12 70675	Tamarac city	Broward	11.4	55,588	45,625	5,845	99	823	20	1,617	1,559	8,274	48,117
12 70700	Tamiami CDP	Miami-Dade	7.3	54,788	49,619	486	54	324	10	2,659	1,636	47,654	41,443
12 71000	Tampa city	Hillsborough	112.1	303,447	194,871	79,118	1,155	6,527	281	12,646	8,849	58,522	228,681
12 71150	Tarpon Springs city	Pinellas	9.1	21,003	18,918	1,292	61	219	13	171	329	909	16,964
12 71225	Tavares city	Lake	7.1	9,700	8,631	747	29	78	7	101	107	336	8,329
12 71300	Taylor Creek CDP	Okeechobee	4.0	4,289	4,055	11	18	26	2	134	43	221	3,661
12 71400	Temple Terrace city	Hillsborough	6.9	20,918	16,831	2,334	77	541	28	500	607	2,373	16,264
12 71525	Tequesta village	Palm Beach	1.7	5,273	5,166	25	5	37	1	7	32	128	4,268
12 71558	Terra Mar CDP	Broward	0.4	2,631	2,575	15	-	5	-	15	21	133	2,499
12 71567	The Crossings CDP	Miami-Dade	3.7	23,557	20,071	1,094	21	779	11	747	834	13,219	17,461
12 71569	The Hammocks CDP	Miami-Dade	7.9	47,379	37,260	3,259	101	1,540	32	3,097	2,090	30,953	33,973
12 71580	The Meadows CDP	Sarasota	2.3	4,423	4,267	76	3	28	2	18	29	64	4,217
12 71625	The Villages CDP	Sumter	5.2	8,333	8,201	43	8	44	1	5	31	108	8,304
12 71725	Thonotosassa CDP	Hillsborough	16.7	6,091	5,520	301	31	23	2	109	105	383	4,466
12 71741	Three Lakes CDP	Miami-Dade	3.3	6,955	5,042	1,088	8	269	1	285	262	3,322	4,989
12 71800	Tice CDP	Lee	1.1	4,538	3,044	573	30	48	6	639	198	1,853	3,199
12 71825	Tierra Verde CDP	Pinellas	1.5	3,574	3,427	64	7	35	5	17	19	122	3,082
12 71867	Timber Pines CDP	Hernando	2.4	5,840	5,778	22	3	16	-	5	16	37	5,781
12 71900	Titusville city	Brevard	21.3	40,670	34,080	5,142	160	383	16	296	593	1,430	31,337
12 72145	Town 'n' Country CDP	Hillsborough	23.7	72,523	56,913	5,724	262	2,377	60	5,044	2,143	21,010	55,101
12 72325	Treasure Island city	Pinellas	1.6	7,450	7,278	21	21	44	2	32	52	166	6,763
12 72442	Trinity CDP	Pasco	4.7	4,279	4,109	42	-	73	1	18	36	121	3,399
12 72875	Tyndall AFB CDP	Bay	14.6	2,757	2,062	392	13	85	1	78	126	228	1,712
12 73075	Union Park CDP	Orange	3.0	10,191	7,965	503	33	352	6	961	371	2,657	7,657
12 73163	University CDP	Hillsborough	3.9	30,736	15,768	10,469	127	1,111	22	1,957	1,282	5,935	23,723
12 73287	University Park CDP	Miami-Dade	4.1	26,538	23,630	903	17	421	5	897	665	21,945	21,873
12 73312	Upper Grand Lagoon CDP	Bay	8.2	10,889	10,199	154	89	178	10	74	185	267	8,417
12 73675	Valparaiso city	Okaloosa	11.9	6,408	5,176	635	41	171	7	192	186	588	5,330
12 73700	Valrico CDP	Hillsborough	5.6	6,582	5,879	211	32	97	-	235	128	844	4,992
12 73725	Vamo CDP	Sarasota	1.8	5,285	5,121	38	9	58	-	22	37	188	4,575
12 73900	Venice city	Sarasota	9.1	17,764	17,433	97	24	72	5	43	90	195	16,542
12 73950	Venice Gardens CDP	Sarasota	2.5	7,466	7,274	30	6	93	-	11	52	100	6,381
12 74150	Vero Beach city	Indian River	11.1	17,705	16,418	606	35	219	5	247	175	1,025	14,880
12 74200	Vero Beach South CDP	Indian River	10.3	20,362	19,177	467	65	192	15	161	285	686	15,899
12 74494	Villages of Oriole CDP	Palm Beach	1.0	4,758	4,726	14	-	2	2	5	9	30	4,741
12 74498	Villano Beach CDP	St. Johns	1.8	2,533	2,465	12	9	18	-	10	19	35	2,147
12 74512	Villas CDP	Lee	4.7	11,346	10,691	187	19	133	5	151	160	634	9,803

Table D-1. Places — **Area and Population**—Con.

[Includes incorporated places and census designated places (CDPs) of 2,500 or more population as of April 1, 2000. Codes shown are two-digit Federal Information Processing Standards (FIPS) state codes and five-digit FIPS place codes. Place names and codes are those in effect as of January 1, 2000. County refers to the county (or counties) in which the place is located. IC in this column = independent city, a county equivalent. If a place is located in more than one county, counties are listed in alphabetic order]

State and place code	Place	County	Land area, 2000 (sq. mi.)	Population, 2000 (April 1) Total	White	Black or African American	American Indian and Alaska Native	Asian	Native Hawaiian and Other Pacific Islander	Some other race	Two or more races	Hispanic or Latino (of any race)	18 years and over
12 00000	FLORIDA—Con.												
12 74775	Wahneta CDP	Polk	2.4	4,731	3,321	48	27	1	-	1,234	100	2,236	3,129
12 75175	Warm Mineral Springs CDP	Sarasota	2.6	4,811	4,758	16	3	10	-	3	21	39	4,690
12 75200	Warrington CDP	Escambia	6.6	15,207	10,883	3,299	159	316	25	139	386	438	11,301
12 75300	Watertown CDP	Columbia	2.4	2,837	1,899	858	16	7	1	6	50	38	2,129
12 75375	Wauchula city	Hardee	2.6	4,368	3,208	182	25	13	-	823	117	1,722	3,026
12 75612	Wedgefield CDP	Orange	23.4	2,700	2,191	183	2	204	6	76	38	247	2,037
12 75725	Wekiwa Springs CDP	Seminole	8.6	23,169	21,878	343	39	524	6	150	229	1,139	17,287
12 75812	Wellington village	Palm Beach	31.1	38,216	33,918	2,057	49	758	10	702	722	4,395	26,366
12 75875	Wesley Chapel CDP	Pasco	6.1	5,691	4,670	408	12	297	7	143	154	675	4,035
12 75887	Wesley Chapel South CDP	Pasco	11.1	3,245	3,023	47	18	60	-	32	65	206	2,492
12 75912	West and East Lealman CDP	Pinellas	4.7	21,753	19,210	701	132	888	16	360	446	1,067	17,180
12 76050	West Bradenton CDP	Manatee	1.4	4,444	4,313	23	8	41	2	18	39	119	3,316
12 76062	Westchase CDP	Hillsborough	10.7	11,116	9,661	563	11	453	1	239	188	1,322	8,073
12 76075	Westchester CDP	Miami-Dade	4.0	30,271	28,389	186	13	154	1	852	676	25,824	24,601
12 76087	West De Land CDP	Volusia	2.3	3,424	3,037	225	7	19	-	90	46	221	2,557
12 76305	Westgate-Belvedere Homes CDP	Palm Beach	2.1	8,134	5,051	1,956	50	73	6	660	338	2,633	5,626
12 76407	West Ken-Lark CDP	Broward	0.5	3,412	35	3,321	4	3	-	9	40	51	2,269
12 76487	West Little River CDP	Miami-Dade	4.6	32,498	10,572	18,594	86	59	22	1,783	1,382	13,016	23,298
12 76500	West Melbourne city	Brevard	7.8	9,824	9,203	138	13	204	3	119	144	377	8,263
12 76525	West Miami city	Miami-Dade	0.7	5,863	5,393	48	11	27	-	200	184	4,927	4,787
12 76582	Weston city	Broward	23.8	49,286	43,286	1,832	58	1,561	8	1,443	1,098	14,880	33,319
12 76600	West Palm Beach city	Palm Beach	55.1	82,103	47,696	26,446	274	1,197	133	3,568	2,789	14,955	64,581
12 76675	West Pensacola CDP	Escambia	7.4	21,939	12,737	7,391	271	747	42	164	587	571	15,839
12 76700	West Perrine CDP	Miami-Dade	1.7	8,600	1,627	6,313	24	103	6	272	255	1,401	5,687
12 76740	West Samoset CDP	Manatee	1.4	5,507	3,326	1,492	18	46	1	479	145	1,224	3,654
12 76937	West Vero Corridor CDP	Indian River	5.0	7,695	7,558	18	13	31	2	46	27	162	7,160
12 76950	Westview CDP	Miami-Dade	3.1	9,692	1,649	7,330	11	42	13	292	326	1,915	6,665
12 77075	Westwood Lakes CDP	Miami-Dade	1.7	12,005	11,159	95	11	129	-	345	266	9,164	9,472
12 77137	Whiskey Creek CDP	Lee	1.6	4,806	4,641	46	4	34	1	21	59	110	3,989
12 77216	Whisper Walk CDP	Palm Beach	1.0	5,135	4,810	106	2	142	-	27	48	289	4,369
12 77275	White City CDP	St. Lucie	7.1	4,221	3,951	98	12	40	3	48	69	197	3,166
12 77467	Whitfield CDP	Manatee	1.4	2,984	2,813	89	4	21	2	24	31	141	2,450
12 77675	Wildwood city	Sumter	5.2	3,924	2,541	1,292	5	5	-	38	43	95	3,050
12 77735	Williamsburg CDP	Orange	3.7	6,736	6,035	133	7	266	10	145	140	638	6,018
12 77862	Willow Oak CDP	Polk	3.2	4,917	4,114	345	22	24	1	317	94	981	3,497
12 78000	Wilton Manors city	Broward	1.9	12,697	10,058	1,674	31	204	7	224	499	1,228	10,591
12 78025	Wimauma CDP	Hillsborough	8.4	4,246	2,171	315	34	9	12	1,580	125	3,095	2,606
12 78200	Winston CDP	Polk	5.4	9,024	5,711	2,311	55	20	1	714	212	1,372	6,251
12 78250	Winter Garden city	Orange	12.1	14,351	10,993	1,902	51	142	7	925	331	2,511	10,629
12 78275	Winter Haven city	Polk	17.7	26,487	18,941	6,134	50	269	10	496	587	1,309	20,947
12 78300	Winter Park city	Orange	7.3	24,090	20,694	2,534	39	317	6	226	274	1,039	19,626
12 78325	Winter Springs city	Seminole	14.3	31,666	28,098	1,452	59	615	14	799	629	3,330	23,106
12 78700	Woodville CDP	Leon	6.4	3,006	2,385	550	21	4	-	8	38	60	2,250
12 78800	Wright CDP	Okaloosa	5.5	21,697	16,491	3,045	128	738	41	333	921	1,136	16,669
12 78975	Yeehaw Junction CDP	Osceola	5.6	21,778	13,647	2,565	82	584	20	3,806	1,074	11,898	15,447
12 79175	Yulee CDP	Nassau	23.0	8,392	7,601	555	50	40	3	30	113	128	6,075
12 79200	Zellwood CDP	Orange	3.9	2,540	2,378	72	8	1	-	53	28	231	2,258
12 79225	Zephyrhills city	Pasco	6.3	10,833	10,035	302	25	121	3	173	174	545	8,870
12 79231	Zephyrhills North CDP	Pasco	1.1	2,544	2,400	29	17	35	1	27	35	84	2,215
12 79237	Zephyrhills South CDP	Pasco	1.9	4,435	4,260	33	16	16	1	26	83	117	3,916
12 79243	Zephyrhills West CDP	Pasco	2.7	5,242	5,116	12	18	26	1	21	48	109	4,772
13 00000	GEORGIA		57,906.1	8,186,453	5,327,281	2,349,542	21,737	173,170	4,246	196,289	114,188	435,227	6,017,219
13 00408	Acworth city	Cobb	7.1	13,422	10,692	1,696	28	309	3	426	268	812	9,792
13 00436	Adairsville city	Bartow	6.2	2,542	1,845	573	8	35	-	38	43	51	1,800
13 00576	Adel city	Cook	7.9	5,307	2,546	2,596	4	40	5	76	40	201	3,749
13 01052	Albany city	Dougherty	55.5	76,939	25,553	49,855	160	459	22	346	544	950	55,516
13 01612	Alma city	Bacon	5.7	3,236	1,876	1,248	3	16	-	61	32	143	2,377
13 01696	Alpharetta city	Fulton	21.4	34,854	29,150	2,256	68	1,998	7	853	522	1,927	25,427
13 02116	Americus city	Sumter	10.5	17,013	6,644	9,912	39	146	2	153	117	423	12,242
13 03236	Ashburn city	Turner	4.5	4,419	1,440	2,882	4	10	-	73	10	118	3,062
13 03440	Athens-Clarke County (balance)	Clarke	117.8	100,266	64,878	27,442	210	3,158	45	3,115	1,418	6,402	82,460
13 04000	Atlanta city	DeKalb, Fulton	131.7	416,474	138,352	255,689	765	8,046	173	8,272	5,177	18,720	323,470
13 04140	Auburn city	Barrow, Gwinnett	5.3	6,904	6,131	182	21	288	4	154	124	300	4,576
13 04204	Augusta-Richmond County (balance)	Richmond	302.1	195,182	87,651	98,320	536	2,976	238	1,993	3,468	5,447	142,908
13 04252	Austell city	Cobb, Douglas	5.7	5,359	3,506	1,317	24	48	-	343	121	593	3,894
13 04644	Avondale Estates city	DeKalb	1.1	2,609	2,316	225	4	27	-	7	30	40	2,165
13 04896	Bainbridge city	Decatur	17.7	11,722	5,566	5,901	14	75	2	92	72	234	8,435
13 05244	Barnesville city	Lamar	5.7	5,972	2,873	2,978	9	20	2	34	56	101	4,564
13 06016	Baxley city	Appling	7.1	4,150	2,377	1,574	9	25	-	131	34	300	3,004
13 06884	Belvedere Park CDP	DeKalb	5.0	18,945	2,494	15,607	35	178	4	320	307	660	13,251
13 08284	Blackshear city	Pierce	4.3	3,283	2,529	701	10	6	3	14	20	33	2,453

[Includes incorporated places and census designated places (CDPs) of 2,500 or more population as of April 1, 2000. Codes shown are two-digit Federal Information Processing Standards (FIPS) state codes and five-digit FIPS place codes. Place names and codes are those in effect as of January 1, 2000. County refers to the county (or counties) in which the place is located. IC in this column = independent city, a county equivalent. If a place is located in more than one county, counties are listed in alphabetic order]

State and place code	Place	County	Land area, 2000 (sq. mi.)	Population, 2000 (April 1)									
					By race—								
					One race						Two or more races	Hispanic or Latino (of any race)	18 years and over
				Total	White	Black or African American	American Indian and Alaska Native	Asian	Native Hawaiian and Other Pacific Islander	Some other race			
13 00000	GEORGIA—Con.												
13 08536	Blakely city	Early	17.5	5,696	2,184	3,416	11	18	7	23	37	88	3,877
13 08844	Bloomingdale city	Chatham	13.2	2,665	2,434	168	16	12	-	14	21	33	1,948
13 09272	Bonanza CDP	Clayton	1.2	2,904	1,822	889	7	46	1	105	34	158	1,956
13 10132	Bremen city	Carroll, Haralson	8.9	4,579	4,054	437	10	34	-	11	33	40	3,411
13 11560	Brunswick city	Glynn	17.2	15,600	5,680	9,330	42	55	5	270	218	908	11,339
13 11784	Buford city	Gwinnett, Hall	14.7	10,668	8,125	1,422	33	87	4	807	190	1,842	7,842
13 12260	Byron city	Peach	5.8	2,887	2,214	584	11	15	3	16	44	24	2,060
13 12400	Cairo city	Grady	9.3	9,239	4,064	4,740	39	53	2	259	82	467	6,553
13 12456	Calhoun city	Gordon	11.7	10,667	8,311	806	45	107	15	1,238	145	1,821	8,081
13 12624	Camilla city	Mitchell	6.1	5,669	1,831	3,698	7	25	2	71	35	125	3,953
13 12834	Candler-McAfee CDP	DeKalb	7.0	28,294	936	26,926	56	42	3	117	214	264	20,385
13 12988	Canton city	Cherokee	14.3	7,709	6,011	429	70	47	9	992	151	1,829	5,791
13 13492	Carrollton city	Carroll	20.2	19,843	12,399	6,184	44	251	1	571	393	1,120	15,761
13 13688	Cartersville city	Bartow	23.4	15,925	12,187	2,714	44	131	7	598	244	1,160	11,807
13 14500	Cedartown city	Polk	6.8	9,470	6,001	1,913	20	35	11	1,338	152	2,142	7,096
13 14920	Centerville city	Houston	2.8	4,278	3,591	478	16	73	4	43	73	131	3,101
13 15172	Chamblee city	DeKalb	3.1	9,552	4,333	354	87	1,335	31	3,004	408	5,384	7,333
13 15508	Chatsworth city	Murray	4.7	3,531	3,307	41	9	20	1	117	36	229	2,727
13 15585	Chattanooga Valley CDP	Walker	7.5	4,065	3,991	22	12	9	-	13	18	28	3,103
13 16544	Clarkston city	DeKalb	1.1	7,231	1,406	4,025	8	909	3	185	695	333	5,062
13 17328	Cochran city	Bleckley	4.1	4,455	2,464	1,875	4	63	-	21	28	44	3,291
13 17776	College Park city	Clayton, Fulton	9.7	20,382	2,525	16,674	34	125	1	678	345	1,398	14,225
13 19007	Columbus city (balance)	Muscogee	216.1	185,781	93,466	81,466	711	2,863	269	3,532	3,474	8,368	135,902
13 19112	Commerce city	Jackson	8.3	5,292	4,399	780	8	26	-	32	47	82	4,097
13 19280	Conley CDP	Clayton	1.9	6,188	2,125	3,271	19	294	16	375	88	647	4,152
13 19336	Conyers city	Rockdale	11.8	10,689	6,231	3,572	34	278	5	404	165	1,153	7,771
13 19616	Cordele city	Crisp	9.5	11,608	3,703	7,549	7	98	7	138	106	226	7,939
13 19728	Cornelia city	Habersham	3.4	3,674	2,681	350	10	171	14	351	97	704	2,814
13 19830	Country Club Estates CDP	Glynn	4.7	7,594	4,295	2,954	23	83	10	115	114	254	5,602
13 20064	Covington city	Newton	13.8	11,547	5,953	5,259	21	63	5	109	137	331	8,369
13 20932	Cumming city	Forsyth	5.9	4,220	3,776	85	13	11	-	240	95	704	3,263
13 21072	Cuthbert city	Randolph	3.0	3,731	884	2,769	12	12	4	33	17	73	2,734
13 21184	Dacula city	Gwinnett	2.9	3,848	3,516	163	13	59	1	48	48	143	2,724
13 21240	Dahlonega city	Lumpkin	6.4	3,638	3,272	180	16	26	4	93	47	239	3,148
13 21324	Dallas city	Paulding	4.5	5,056	4,337	512	10	40	1	45	111	103	3,621
13 21380	Dalton city	Whitfield	19.8	27,912	18,468	2,153	123	478	15	5,904	771	11,219	20,305
13 21912	Dawson city	Terrell	3.7	5,058	1,087	3,908	3	20	-	5	35	47	3,524
13 22052	Decatur city	DeKalb	4.2	18,147	11,906	5,532	29	298	6	115	261	304	14,519
13 23200	Dock Junction CDP	Glynn	9.5	6,951	4,755	2,020	13	26	9	67	61	211	5,128
13 23368	Donalsonville city	Seminole	4.0	2,796	1,041	1,642	2	13	-	77	21	109	1,977
13 23536	Doraville city	DeKalb	3.6	9,862	4,571	1,457	126	1,250	16	2,034	408	4,284	7,534
13 23872	Douglas city	Coffee	12.9	10,639	5,150	4,823	29	116	5	404	112	736	7,684
13 23900	Douglasville city	Douglas	21.4	20,065	12,809	6,077	63	347	3	339	427	800	14,396
13 24264	Druid Hills CDP	DeKalb	4.2	12,741	10,721	764	21	935	9	82	209	309	11,089
13 24376	Dublin city	Laurens	13.2	15,857	7,222	8,154	31	277	7	46	120	181	11,624
13 24600	Duluth city	Gwinnett	8.8	22,122	15,186	2,623	73	2,851	9	847	533	2,002	16,684
13 24768	Dunwoody CDP	DeKalb	12.1	32,808	27,893	1,452	39	2,552	4	441	427	1,514	26,370
13 25552	Eastman city	Dodge	5.1	5,440	3,279	2,032	13	26	3	63	24	98	3,836
13 25720	East Point city	Fulton	13.8	39,595	6,376	30,949	80	244	36	1,348	562	2,998	27,984
13 26084	Eatonton city	Putnam	20.6	6,764	2,536	4,013	7	28	-	91	89	161	4,833
13 26616	Elberton city	Elbert	4.0	4,743	2,577	2,039	9	29	-	63	26	105	3,485
13 27988	Euharlee city	Bartow	4.6	3,208	2,865	245	16	20	-	36	26	87	2,041
13 28044	Evans CDP	Columbia	9.9	17,727	14,999	1,811	44	476	8	118	271	396	12,693
13 28296	Experiment CDP	Spalding	3.0	3,233	1,471	1,699	5	1	-	17	40	40	2,245
13 28380	Fairburn city	Fulton	7.3	5,464	2,354	2,603	16	39	-	353	99	711	3,975
13 28520	Fair Oaks CDP	Cobb	2.0	8,443	4,286	2,012	61	83	1	1,725	275	3,085	6,270
13 28632	Fairview CDP	Walker	7.5	6,601	6,110	342	23	32	1	16	77	45	4,996
13 28968	Fayetteville city	Fayette	9.9	11,148	8,967	1,557	25	371	1	106	121	310	8,210
13 29528	Fitzgerald city	Ben Hill, Irwin	7.2	8,758	4,140	4,315	16	27	-	200	60	388	6,279
13 30536	Forest Park city	Clayton	9.4	21,447	9,675	8,018	107	1,282	4	1,836	525	4,322	15,459
13 30732	Forsyth city	Monroe	5.0	3,776	1,549	2,176	5	9	2	1	34	60	2,772
13 30795	Fort Benning South CDP	Chattahoochee	8.6	11,737	6,669	3,424	106	244	54	724	516	1,461	8,355
13 30956	Fort Oglethorpe city	Catoosa, Walker	13.0	6,940	6,464	165	13	144	2	39	113	98	5,359
13 31068	Fort Stewart CDP	Liberty	6.6	11,205	5,603	4,118	81	214	46	756	387	1,358	8,144
13 31096	Fort Valley city	Peach	5.3	8,005	1,769	5,976	30	20	4	148	58	350	5,816
13 31908	Gainesville city	Hall	27.1	25,578	16,680	4,023	76	687	34	3,650	428	8,484	19,179
13 32048	Garden City city	Chatham	14.6	11,289	6,115	4,514	54	103	5	262	236	675	8,608
13 32482	Georgetown CDP	Chatham	11.5	10,599	7,714	2,108	41	327	7	182	220	490	7,736
13 33336	Glennville city	Tattnall	6.6	3,641	2,307	1,225	5	26	4	47	27	88	2,677
13 34876	Greensboro city	Greene	5.8	3,238	1,083	2,008	13	10	9	86	29	173	2,289
13 35240	Gresham Park CDP	DeKalb	2.8	9,215	287	8,807	29	2	1	28	61	78	6,333
13 35324	Griffin city	Spalding	14.5	23,451	11,018	11,697	39	233	6	229	229	520	16,726
13 35716	Grovetown city	Columbia	2.9	6,089	4,320	1,214	34	95	17	186	223	563	4,044
13 36276	Hampton city	Henry	4.3	3,857	3,246	516	6	26	-	22	41	67	2,708
13 36416	Hannahs Mill CDP	Upson	4.4	3,267	2,995	209	16	26	-	-	21	47	2,459
13 36472	Hapeville city	Fulton	2.4	6,180	3,196	1,641	38	544	10	611	140	1,348	4,669
13 37144	Hartwell city	Hart	4.6	4,188	2,656	1,460	3	26	1	14	28	42	3,278

[Includes incorporated places and census designated places (CDPs) of 2,500 or more population as of April 1, 2000. Codes shown are two-digit Federal Information Processing Standards (FIPS) state codes and five-digit FIPS place codes. Place names and codes are those in effect as of January 1, 2000. County refers to the county (or counties) in which the place is located. IC in this column = independent city, a county equivalent. If a place is located in more than one county, counties are listed in alphabetic order]

State and place code	Place	County	Land area, 2000 (sq. mi.)	Population, 2000 (April 1)									
					By race—							Hispanic or Latino (of any race)	18 years and over
					One race						Two or more races		
				Total	White	Black or African American	American Indian and Alaska Native	Asian	Native Hawaiian and Other Pacific Islander	Some other race			
13 00000	GEORGIA—Con.												
13 37396	Hawkinsville city	Pulaski	4.4	3,280	1,585	1,612	13	24	12	12	22	39	2,420
13 37564	Hazlehurst city	Jeff Davis	4.7	3,787	2,596	1,048	16	28	-	63	36	130	2,796
13 38040	Hephzibah city	Richmond	19.4	3,880	2,769	973	14	24	6	29	65	76	2,787
13 38964	Hinesville city	Liberty	16.2	30,392	12,613	13,992	143	688	173	1,519	1,264	2,769	20,001
13 39244	Hogansville city	Troup	6.6	2,774	1,530	1,199	5	13	-	8	10	16	1,999
13 39524	Holly Springs city	Cherokee	3.2	3,195	3,029	37	21	24	1	46	37	154	2,234
13 39748	Homerville city	Clinch	2.2	2,803	1,643	1,122	4	3	-	1	30	17	2,092
13 41347	Irondale CDP	Clayton	3.2	7,727	3,619	3,639	38	148	1	118	164	323	5,141
13 41484	Isle of Hope CDP	Chatham	1.9	2,605	2,560	22	-	9	-	7	7	28	1,911
13 41596	Jackson city	Butts	4.7	3,934	2,113	1,741	8	17	1	13	41	50	2,895
13 41988	Jefferson city	Jackson	19.0	3,825	3,077	614	-	46	-	44	44	161	2,752
13 42268	Jesup city	Wayne	16.5	9,279	5,008	3,889	11	65	-	204	102	665	7,129
13 42604	Jonesboro city	Clayton	2.6	3,829	2,398	1,179	8	28	12	132	72	289	2,710
13 43192	Kennesaw city	Cobb	8.4	21,675	17,767	2,146	47	630	4	551	530	1,344	15,662
13 43580	Kings Bay Base CDP	Camden	2.0	2,599	1,882	520	13	21	2	97	64	208	1,957
13 43640	Kingsland city	Camden	16.7	10,506	7,696	2,221	61	162	6	130	230	379	6,849
13 44312	La Fayette city	Walker	8.1	6,702	6,072	478	6	32	1	51	62	72	5,089
13 44340	LaGrange city	Troup	29.0	25,998	12,796	12,353	47	212	26	319	245	635	18,604
13 44508	Lake City city	Clayton	1.8	2,886	1,498	930	27	279	4	92	56	216	2,206
13 44592	Lakeland city	Lanier	3.1	2,730	1,561	1,072	18	13	-	21	45	78	2,004
13 44900	Lakeview CDP	Catoosa, Walker	2.3	4,820	4,672	30	24	37	2	8	47	44	3,739
13 44956	Lakeview Estates CDP	Rockdale	0.5	2,637	1,434	150	20	12	-	929	92	1,684	1,818
13 45488	Lawrenceville city	Gwinnett	13.0	22,397	17,030	3,048	49	709	22	999	540	2,720	16,489
13 45768	Leesburg city	Lee	4.7	2,633	1,621	959	8	24	-	2	19	22	1,841
13 46356	Lilburn city	Gwinnett	6.2	11,307	7,812	1,349	38	1,322	3	544	239	1,495	8,399
13 46580	Lindale CDP	Floyd	5.5	4,088	3,884	73	7	11	-	54	59	112	3,116
13 47196	Loganville city	Gwinnett, Walton	6.0	5,435	4,979	246	14	51	6	67	72	186	3,833
13 47560	Louisville city	Jefferson	3.6	2,712	912	1,788	1	6	-	2	3	10	1,947
13 48232	Lyons city	Toombs	7.5	4,169	2,470	1,350	15	7	1	301	26	628	2,064
13 48288	Mableton CDP	Cobb	20.6	29,733	18,550	8,699	78	417	7	1,380	602	2,915	21,993
13 48624	McDonough city	Henry	7.8	8,493	5,213	2,913	14	118	-	151	84	295	6,253
13 49000	Macon city	Bibb, Jones	55.8	97,255	34,482	60,740	188	628	28	443	746	1,166	71,045
13 49084	McRae city	Telfair	3.4	2,682	1,488	1,145	-	8	-	30	11	42	2,039
13 49196	Madison city	Morgan	8.9	3,636	1,779	1,739	3	36	-	40	39	76	2,686
13 49532	Manchester city	Meriwether, Talbot	5.7	3,988	2,242	1,684	13	26	-	4	19	20	2,874
13 49756	Marietta city	Cobb	21.9	58,748	33,185	17,330	188	1,744	51	4,694	1,556	9,947	45,590
13 50036	Martinez CDP	Columbia	12.6	27,749	23,304	2,225	63	1,554	20	190	393	640	19,613
13 51072	Metter city	Candler	7.3	3,879	2,135	1,590	-	17	-	119	18	204	2,890
13 51394	Midway-Hardwick CDP	Baldwin	4.9	5,135	1,285	3,726	22	33	-	16	53	30	3,678
13 51492	Milledgeville city	Baldwin	20.0	18,757	9,368	8,943	24	290	1	37	94	231	15,764
13 51520	Millen city	Jenkins	3.6	3,492	1,324	2,071	2	6	6	47	36	100	2,502
13 52192	Monroe city	Walton	10.4	11,407	6,239	4,818	24	41	4	144	137	287	8,137
13 52304	Montezuma city	Macon	4.5	3,999	1,121	2,793	8	15	-	28	34	56	2,837
13 52332	Montgomery CDP	Chatham	5.3	4,134	3,646	384	4	25	14	23	38	61	3,072
13 53004	Morrow city	Clayton	2.9	4,882	2,169	1,763	15	630	-	194	111	292	3,689
13 53060	Moultrie city	Colquitt	14.2	14,387	6,619	7,089	48	53	7	430	141	866	10,307
13 53186	Mountain Park CDP	Gwinnett	5.8	11,753	9,655	700	27	1,069	3	117	182	313	8,877
13 54264	Nashville city	Berrien	4.6	4,697	3,567	1,013	13	21	1	43	39	74	3,418
13 55020	Newnan city	Coweta	17.9	16,242	8,783	6,846	33	118	3	259	200	806	11,730
13 55776	Norcross city	Gwinnett	4.1	8,410	4,499	1,751	45	513	3	1,294	305	3,442	6,499
13 56000	North Atlanta CDP	DeKalb	7.7	38,579	23,733	6,773	158	1,881	20	4,878	1,136	10,574	32,569
13 56112	North Decatur CDP	DeKalb	5.0	15,270	12,795	1,227	38	875	9	99	227	429	13,352
13 56168	North Druid Hills CDP	DeKalb	5.0	18,852	15,553	1,376	28	1,269	6	272	348	815	16,994
13 57260	Oakwood city	Hall	3.1	2,689	2,064	281	8	84	3	204	45	556	1,964
13 57428	Ocilla city	Irwin	2.6	3,270	1,271	1,942	3	11	-	28	15	58	2,127
13 58884	Palmetto city	Coweta, Fulton	5.2	3,400	1,612	1,502	21	1	1	183	80	395	2,376
13 59080	Panthersville CDP	DeKalb	3.7	11,791	225	11,360	19	24	6	37	120	140	8,237
13 59724	Peachtree City city	Fayette	23.3	31,580	27,683	1,929	50	1,167	9	291	451	1,184	21,616
13 59976	Pelham city	Mitchell	4.0	4,126	1,719	2,316	10	19	1	32	29	59	2,801
13 60340	Perry city	Houston, Peach	16.4	9,602	5,716	3,570	20	120	4	86	86	178	7,112
13 62104	Pooler city	Chatham	28.6	6,239	5,475	490	11	129	1	21	112	77	4,516
13 62328	Port Wentworth city	Chatham	16.4	3,276	2,707	470	16	34	1	25	23	101	2,572
13 62524	Powder Springs city	Cobb	6.3	12,481	7,225	4,666	25	135	7	215	208	539	8,257
13 63084	Putney CDP	Dougherty	21.5	2,998	2,063	885	4	7	-	15	24	30	2,266
13 63224	Quitman city	Brooks	3.8	4,638	1,437	3,078	6	17	-	49	51	101	3,242
13 63952	Redan CDP	DeKalb	9.6	33,841	1,922	30,886	41	238	11	255	488	603	23,068
13 65044	Richmond Hill city	Bryan	10.1	6,959	5,656	953	42	99	3	89	117	258	4,595
13 65296	Rincon city	Effingham	6.7	4,376	3,342	837	11	38	-	74	74	129	3,087
13 65464	Riverdale city	Clayton	4.3	12,478	2,507	8,413	37	965	10	284	262	600	8,428
13 65968	Robins AFB CDP	Houston	2.7	3,949	2,272	1,271	23	106	17	96	164	195	2,854
13 66276	Rockmart city	Polk	4.3	3,870	3,089	715	4	13	-	15	34	58	2,835
13 66668	Rome city	Floyd	29.4	34,980	22,081	9,677	135	496	56	1,962	573	3,620	26,506
13 67256	Rossville city	Walker	1.8	3,511	3,283	137	20	12	-	17	42	45	2,649
13 67284	Roswell city	Fulton	38.0	79,334	64,666	6,773	160	2,964	23	3,237	1,511	8,421	59,920
13 67984	St. Marys city	Camden	18.8	13,761	10,267	2,751	65	166	10	214	288	614	9,171
13 68040	St. Simons CDP	Glynn	16.6	13,381	12,617	494	22	124	2	38	84	253	10,800
13 68208	Sandersville city	Washington	9.1	6,144	2,443	3,627	7	37	3	2	25	15	4,421
13 68516	Sandy Springs CDP	Fulton	37.7	85,781	66,522	10,332	154	2,820	44	4,240	1,669	8,514	70,518

Table D-1. Places — **Area and Population**—Con.

[Includes incorporated places and census designated places (CDPs) of 2,500 or more population as of April 1, 2000. Codes shown are two-digit Federal Information Processing Standards (FIPS) state codes and five-digit FIPS place codes. Place names and codes are those in effect as of January 1, 2000. County refers to the county (or counties) in which the place is located. IC in this column = independent city, a county equivalent. If a place is located in more than one county, counties are listed in alphabetic order]

				Population, 2000 (April 1)									
					By race—								
					One race								
State and place code	Place	County	Land area, 2000 (sq. mi.)	Total	White	Black or African American	American Indian and Alaska Native	Asian	Native Hawaiian and Other Pacific Islander	Some other race	Two or more races	Hispanic or Latino (of any race)	18 years and over
13 00000	GEORGIA—Con.												
13 69000	Savannah city	Chatham	74.7	131,510	51,108	75,072	303	1,997	92	1,224	1,714	2,938	97,892
13 69392	Scottdale CDP	DeKalb	3.5	9,803	3,637	4,761	19	941	18	167	260	444	7,401
13 71184	Skidaway Island CDP	Chatham	16.4	6,914	6,746	33	1	95	-	11	28	53	6,140
13 71492	Smyrna city	Cobb	13.9	40,999	24,368	11,147	170	1,606	14	2,709	985	5,659	33,007
13 71604	Snellville city	Gwinnett	9.7	15,351	13,761	828	38	311	3	242	168	628	11,274
13 71660	Social Circle city	Newton, Walton	11.2	3,379	1,933	1,396	2	6	1	7	34	50	2,424
13 71772	Soperton city	Treutlen	3.2	2,824	1,318	1,464	1	10	-	11	20	26	2,025
13 73256	Statesboro city	Bulloch	12.5	22,698	12,758	9,136	16	300	12	215	261	487	19,463
13 73704	Stockbridge city	Henry	10.9	9,853	7,058	2,021	27	448	13	142	144	415	7,069
13 73816	Stone Mountain city	DeKalb	1.6	7,145	1,750	4,945	15	140	3	110	182	292	4,842
13 74180	Sugar Hill city	Gwinnett	9.2	11,399	9,998	533	19	189	2	461	197	1,039	8,072
13 74376	Summerville city	Chattooga	4.0	4,556	3,283	1,153	3	7	-	41	69	72	3,448
13 74936	Suwanee city	Gwinnett	9.8	8,725	7,372	557	11	597	1	63	124	276	6,148
13 74964	Swainsboro city	Emanuel	12.4	6,943	3,337	3,449	10	24	1	85	37	141	4,935
13 75160	Sylvania city	Screven	3.8	2,675	1,536	1,112	3	9	-	9	6	25	2,068
13 75188	Sylvester city	Worth	5.7	5,990	2,345	3,592	6	7	1	22	17	54	4,106
13 75300	Tallapoosa city	Haralson	7.4	2,789	2,543	185	6	25	-	2	28	9	2,101
13 76168	Thomaston city	Upson	9.1	9,411	5,905	3,322	26	57	1	50	50	167	7,034
13 76224	Thomasville city	Thomas	14.9	18,162	7,779	10,060	41	96	2	43	141	232	13,285
13 76280	Thomson city	McDuffie	4.0	6,828	2,894	3,843	5	19	2	16	49	87	4,874
13 76476	Tifton city	Tift	8.9	15,060	9,226	4,755	34	247	5	695	98	1,139	11,027
13 76756	Toccoa city	Stephens	8.3	9,323	7,036	2,001	27	63	16	49	131	131	7,238
13 77652	Tucker CDP	DeKalb	12.0	26,532	19,438	3,729	45	2,096	13	717	494	2,047	21,022
13 78036	Tybee Island city	Chatham	2.6	3,392	3,254	64	19	29	-	2	24	43	2,923
13 78044	Tyrone town	Fayette	12.6	3,916	3,696	132	13	39	-	6	30	57	2,843
13 78156	Unadilla city	Dooly	5.2	2,772	957	1,722	6	15	-	46	26	83	2,284
13 78324	Union City city	Fulton	8.6	11,621	2,947	8,057	30	147	3	237	200	607	8,457
13 78800	Valdosta city	Lowndes	29.9	43,724	20,860	21,201	102	610	13	394	544	954	32,317
13 79388	Vidalia city	Montgomery, Toombs	17.3	10,491	6,254	3,869	15	93	-	191	69	340	7,566
13 79444	Vienna city	Dooly	5.3	2,973	823	1,988	6	12	13	112	19	166	2,056
13 79528	Villa Rica city	Carroll, Douglas	12.6	4,134	3,279	740	33	11	1	44	26	90	2,976
13 79612	Vinings CDP	Cobb	3.2	9,677	7,932	1,170	18	357	3	80	117	219	8,631
13 80256	Walthourville city	Liberty	3.8	4,030	1,490	2,219	35	38	14	120	114	257	2,566
13 80508	Warner Robins city	Houston, Peach	22.8	48,804	30,504	15,663	148	875	34	603	977	1,856	35,372
13 80704	Washington city	Wilkes	7.8	4,295	1,634	2,609	3	13	-	2	34	20	3,258
13 80956	Waycross city	Pierce, Ware	11.7	15,333	6,794	8,205	19	95	3	104	113	210	11,296
13 80984	Waynesboro city	Burke	5.5	5,813	2,086	3,636	6	5	-	24	56	70	3,878
13 82132	West Point city	Harris, Troup	4.4	3,382	1,373	1,956	1	30	-	5	17	21	2,389
13 82636	Whitemarsh Island CDP	Chatham	5.9	5,824	4,787	538	15	335	7	59	83	140	4,368
13 83168	Wilmington Island CDP	Chatham	8.4	14,213	13,113	559	17	357	5	50	112	188	10,551
13 83420	Winder city	Barrow	10.8	10,201	7,846	1,838	26	125	3	175	188	385	7,519
13 84176	Woodstock city	Cherokee	8.8	10,050	8,987	508	29	167	2	195	162	496	7,355
15 00000	HAWAII		6,422.6	1,211,537	294,102	22,003	3,535	503,868	113,539	15,147	259,343	87,699	915,770
15 00400	Ahuimanu CDP	Honolulu	1.8	8,506	1,894	81	12	2,953	838	56	2,672	691	6,136
15 00550	Aiea CDP	Honolulu	1.7	9,019	1,466	77	13	5,259	458	69	1,677	493	7,110
15 03850	Captain Cook CDP	Hawaii	12.2	3,206	1,072	7	6	1,014	252	35	820	258	2,366
15 07450	Ewa Beach CDP	Honolulu	1.4	14,650	1,633	96	16	7,199	1,556	151	3,999	1,421	10,377
15 07470	Ewa Gentry CDP	Honolulu	0.3	4,939	750	191	9	2,536	253	51	1,149	429	3,528
15 07485	Ewa Villages CDP	Honolulu	1.0	4,741	166	14	5	3,339	220	36	961	417	3,423
15 09260	Haiku-Pauwela CDP	Maui	15.8	6,578	3,697	34	35	667	461	64	1,620	544	4,867
15 10000	Halawa CDP	Honolulu	2.3	13,891	2,153	254	28	7,070	1,449	116	2,821	905	10,642
15 11650	Hanamaulu CDP	Kauai	1.1	3,272	269	7	5	2,013	188	15	775	221	2,397
15 12400	Hauula CDP	Honolulu	6.0	3,651	614	28	13	209	1,367	35	1,385	358	2,313
15 12500	Hawaiian Beaches CDP	Hawaii	25.4	3,709	1,038	24	18	619	573	39	1,398	580	2,533
15 12600	Hawaiian Paradise Park CDP	Hawaii	15.0	7,051	2,309	30	43	1,539	723	70	2,337	996	4,838
15 13900	Heeia CDP	Honolulu	2.0	4,944	1,269	22	7	2,019	421	38	1,168	239	3,884
15 14200	Hickam Housing CDP	Honolulu	1.2	5,471	3,622	641	31	449	53	223	452	458	3,260
15 14650	Hilo CDP	Hawaii	54.3	40,759	6,976	183	137	15,610	5,348	385	12,120	3,579	30,694
15 15700	Holualoa CDP	Hawaii	14.2	6,107	3,390	36	33	1,045	466	91	1,046	449	4,801
15 17000	Honolulu CDP	Honolulu	85.7	371,657	73,093	6,038	689	207,588	25,457	3,318	55,474	16,229	300,185
15 21200	Kahaluu CDP	Honolulu	1.2	2,935	788	11	2	651	514	29	940	200	2,192
15 22700	Kahului CDP	Maui	15.2	20,146	2,027	49	55	10,803	1,997	296	4,919	1,763	14,957
15 23000	Kailua CDP	Hawaii	35.5	9,870	3,815	45	45	1,804	1,299	190	2,672	1,007	7,172
15 23150	Kailua CDP	Honolulu	6.6	36,513	16,008	277	109	7,709	2,947	338	9,125	2,228	27,699
15 24950	Kalaheo CDP	Kauai	2.9	3,913	1,566	9	6	1,160	153	45	974	451	2,951
15 25400	Kalaoa CDP	Hawaii	39.5	6,794	3,352	24	35	910	703	53	1,717	404	5,063
15 28250	Kaneohe CDP	Honolulu	6.6	34,970	7,166	285	69	13,456	3,999	237	9,758	2,523	26,377
15 28400	Kaneohe Station CDP	Honolulu	4.4	11,827	7,877	1,428	129	631	141	897	724	1,731	8,989
15 28850	Kapaa CDP	Kauai	9.8	9,472	2,634	32	49	3,000	942	95	2,720	896	6,647
15 31100	Kaunakakai CDP	Maui	2.0	2,726	235	1	4	784	836	5	861	152	1,847
15 35600	Kekaha CDP	Kauai	1.0	3,175	506	6	16	1,384	393	31	839	275	2,378
15 36500	Kihei CDP	Maui	10.2	16,749	7,999	124	81	4,140	1,315	265	2,825	1,259	12,547
15 42950	Lahaina CDP	Maui	5.8	9,118	2,411	31	28	3,957	896	199	1,596	644	7,041
15 43250	Laie CDP	Honolulu	1.3	4,585	1,265	16	7	423	1,691	30	1,153	143	3,125
15 43700	Lanai City CDP	Maui	3.6	3,164	419	4	12	1,838	222	10	659	245	2,277
15 45200	Lihue CDP	Kauai	6.3	5,674	1,291	12	13	2,794	365	38	1,161	370	4,378

Table D-1. Places — **Area and Population**—Con.

[Includes incorporated places and census designated places (CDPs) of 2,500 or more population as of April 1, 2000. Codes shown are two-digit Federal Information Processing Standards (FIPS) state codes and five-digit FIPS place codes. Place names and codes are those in effect as of January 1, 2000. County refers to the county (or counties) in which the place is located. IC in this column = independent city, a county equivalent. If a place is located in more than one county, counties are listed in alphabetic order]

State and place code	Place	County	Land area, 2000 (sq. mi.)	Population, 2000 (April 1) Total	By race— One race White	Black or African American	American Indian and Alaska Native	Asian	Native Hawaiian and Other Pacific Islander	Some other race	Two or more races	Hispanic or Latino (of any race)	18 years and over
15 00000	HAWAII—Con.												
15 47300	Maili CDP	Honolulu	1.0	5,943	658	54	14	1,341	1,420	65	2,391	872	3,860
15 47450	Makaha CDP	Honolulu	2.3	7,753	1,473	108	55	1,181	1,698	126	3,112	1,385	5,295
15 47750	Makakilo City CDP	Honolulu	3.1	13,156	3,179	333	26	4,220	1,342	199	3,857	1,327	9,143
15 48050	Makawao CDP	Maui	4.7	6,327	2,565	20	35	1,078	553	99	1,977	755	4,456
15 50750	Maunawili CDP	Honolulu	3.5	4,869	1,783	27	4	1,386	428	27	1,214	282	3,747
15 51050	Mililani Town CDP	Honolulu	3.9	28,608	5,829	879	54	13,426	1,303	381	6,736	2,222	20,830
15 53300	Mountain View CDP	Hawaii	56.6	2,799	723	13	23	618	350	42	1,030	450	1,898
15 53900	Nanakuli CDP	Honolulu	2.5	10,814	616	85	31	1,255	4,348	90	4,389	1,202	6,941
15 54100	Napili-Honokowai CDP	Maui	5.9	6,788	3,640	49	29	1,298	549	282	941	728	5,244
15 62600	Pearl City CDP	Honolulu	5.0	30,976	5,340	838	83	16,547	1,904	437	5,827	2,260	25,147
15 65900	Pukalani CDP	Maui	4.4	7,380	2,507	30	17	2,069	545	74	2,138	681	5,311
15 66800	Pupukea CDP	Honolulu	3.4	4,250	2,378	10	28	619	277	50	888	356	3,246
15 69050	Schofield Barracks CDP	Honolulu	2.7	14,428	8,137	3,154	158	559	238	1,246	936	2,337	9,797
15 72255	Village Park CDP	Honolulu	0.9	9,625	901	216	24	5,573	729	117	2,065	682	6,699
15 72650	Wahiawa CDP	Honolulu	2.1	16,151	1,826	326	52	7,392	1,554	295	4,706	1,777	11,933
15 74000	Waialua CDP	Honolulu	1.3	3,761	577	14	2	1,950	149	39	1,030	246	2,863
15 74450	Waianae CDP	Honolulu	3.4	10,506	982	85	27	2,042	2,864	102	4,404	1,471	6,848
15 75510	Waihee-Waiehu CDP	Maui	4.3	7,310	981	21	10	3,329	1,069	74	1,826	570	4,929
15 76600	Waikoloa Village CDP	Hawaii	19.1	4,806	2,207	23	10	800	442	70	1,254	432	3,371
15 76935	Wailea-Makena CDP	Maui	22.6	5,671	4,293	45	29	597	119	58	530	284	4,725
15 77225	Wailua Homesteads CDP	Kauai	7.0	4,567	1,820	18	20	1,108	361	46	1,194	403	3,368
15 77450	Wailuku CDP	Maui	5.1	12,296	2,233	29	44	5,174	1,439	145	3,232	953	9,383
15 77750	Waimalu CDP	Honolulu	5.9	29,371	5,017	684	76	16,248	1,655	324	5,367	1,753	23,084
15 78050	Waimanalo CDP	Honolulu	0.4	3,664	397	6	5	982	906	12	1,356	380	2,512
15 78200	Waimanalo Beach CDP	Honolulu	1.6	4,271	554	4	10	228	2,024	27	1,424	277	3,129
15 78500	Waimea CDP	Hawaii	38.7	7,028	2,154	23	12	1,426	1,097	51	2,265	548	4,939
15 79700	Waipahu CDP	Honolulu	2.6	33,108	1,566	308	46	21,774	4,077	285	5,052	2,016	24,354
15 79860	Waipio CDP	Honolulu	1.2	11,672	1,683	329	21	6,380	636	100	2,523	789	8,614
15 80000	Waipio Acres CDP	Honolulu	1.0	5,298	999	276	19	1,948	434	112	1,510	622	3,859
15 80600	Wheeler AFB CDP	Honolulu	2.3	2,829	1,613	611	31	113	53	179	229	372	1,788
15 80900	Whitmore Village CDP	Honolulu	0.9	4,057	207	18	4	2,673	265	39	851	308	2,845
16 00000	IDAHO		82,747.2	1,293,953	1,177,304	5,456	17,645	11,889	1,308	54,742	25,609	101,690	924,923
16 01900	American Falls city	Power	1.5	4,111	3,353	6	41	17	1	623	70	1,144	2,725
16 01990	Ammon city	Bonneville	2.9	6,187	5,930	17	27	35	5	101	72	193	3,939
16 07840	Blackfoot city	Bingham	5.4	10,419	9,040	22	261	114	3	660	319	1,372	7,164
16 08830	Boise City city	Ada	63.8	185,787	171,204	1,437	1,300	3,870	302	3,241	4,433	8,410	138,721
16 09370	Bonners Ferry city	Boundary	2.1	2,515	2,406	1	40	13	-	33	22	108	1,838
16 10810	Buhl city	Twin Falls	1.7	3,985	3,459	1	30	29	1	365	100	628	2,849
16 11260	Burley city	Cassia, Minidoka	4.1	9,316	7,263	20	121	43	7	1,598	264	2,488	6,345
16 12250	Caldwell city	Canyon	11.3	25,967	19,493	121	245	216	26	5,110	756	7,307	17,931
16 14680	Chubbuck city	Bannock	3.5	9,700	8,905	34	194	106	4	240	217	522	6,407
16 16750	Coeur d'Alene city	Kootenai	13.1	34,514	33,064	77	267	209	31	216	650	932	25,904
16 23410	Eagle city	Ada	9.2	11,085	10,631	41	52	82	14	65	200	291	7,467
16 25570	Emmett city	Gem	1.8	5,490	4,974	4	41	24	8	318	121	635	3,932
16 28360	Fort Hall CDP	Bannock, Bingham	35.2	3,193	965	1	2,088	10	1	72	56	243	2,084
16 28990	Fruitland city	Payette	1.5	3,805	3,337	2	23	34	1	305	103	682	2,591
16 29620	Garden City city	Ada	4.2	10,624	9,491	50	90	146	12	525	310	1,018	8,047
16 32140	Gooding city	Gooding	1.4	3,384	3,029	5	54	7	-	202	87	501	2,445
16 32950	Grangeville city	Idaho	1.4	3,228	3,110	1	37	9	1	22	48	53	2,395
16 34390	Hailey city	Blaine	3.2	6,200	5,560	16	22	67	3	435	97	741	4,357
16 36370	Hayden city	Kootenai	7.8	9,159	8,801	17	70	50	7	86	128	223	6,629
16 37360	Heyburn city	Minidoka	1.9	2,899	2,172	5	32	15	2	582	91	823	1,956
16 38170	Homedale city	Owyhee	0.9	2,528	1,612	5	25	18	2	773	93	992	1,619
16 39700	Idaho Falls city	Bonneville	17.1	50,730	46,717	315	385	533	32	1,932	816	3,641	35,349
16 41320	Jerome city	Jerome	3.2	7,780	6,727	14	71	18	5	750	195	1,316	5,324
16 43030	Ketchum city	Blaine	3.0	3,003	2,845	-	8	17	5	70	58	147	2,629
16 43570	Kimberly city	Twin Falls	0.8	2,614	2,483	2	24	12	1	41	51	134	1,802
16 44290	Kuna city	Ada	2.4	5,382	5,094	14	39	19	3	102	111	261	3,377
16 46540	Lewiston city	Nez Perce	16.5	30,904	29,403	92	491	236	25	*159	498	590	23,721
16 52120	Meridian city	Ada	11.8	34,919	32,927	164	166	440	42	438	742	1,291	23,158
16 52660	Middleton city	Canyon	1.8	2,978	2,730	9	32	7	7	105	88	304	1,961
16 53920	Montpelier city	Bear Lake	1.8	2,785	2,693	-	17	-	1	55	19	106	1,886
16 54550	Moscow city	Latah	6.2	21,291	19,636	194	170	667	30	206	388	525	17,861
16 54730	Mountain Home city	Elmore	5.2	11,143	9,794	291	105	193	34	380	346	928	7,845
16 54820	Mountain Home AFB CDP	Elmore	9.9	8,894	7,401	614	68	224	18	240	329	575	6,760
16 56260	Nampa city	Canyon	19.9	51,867	43,281	206	490	484	92	5,833	1,481	9,282	35,810
16 59320	Orofino city	Clearwater	2.4	3,247	3,050	12	69	19	3	32	62	73	2,595
16 61300	Payette city	Payette	3.4	7,054	6,167	6	81	61	2	541	196	1,113	4,885
16 64090	Pocatello city	Bannock, Power	28.2	51,466	47,513	369	693	590	103	1,120	1,078	2,544	37,776
16 64810	Post Falls city	Kootenai	9.7	17,247	16,579	31	150	96	11	103	277	439	11,976
16 65260	Preston city	Franklin	6.7	4,682	4,458	4	21	6	3	146	44	236	3,030
16 66340	Rathdrum city	Kootenai	4.8	4,816	4,583	7	46	16	2	47	115	149	3,095
16 67420	Rexburg city	Madison	4.9	17,257	16,429	51	53	114	48	384	178	697	14,092
16 67780	Rigby city	Jefferson	1.0	2,998	2,733	13	26	12	2	169	43	350	1,989

[Includes incorporated places and census designated places (CDPs) of 2,500 or more population as of April 1, 2000. Codes shown are two-digit Federal Information Processing Standards (FIPS) state codes and five-digit FIPS place codes. Place names and codes are those in effect as of January 1, 2000. County refers to the county (or counties) in which the place is located. IC in this column = independent city, a county equivalent. If a place is located in more than one county, counties are listed in alphabetic order]

State and place code	Place	County	Land area, 2000 (sq. mi.)	Population, 2000 (April 1) By race— One race Total	White	Black or African American	American Indian and Alaska Native	Asian	Native Hawaiian and Other Pacific Islander	Some other race	Two or more races	Hispanic or Latino (of any race)	18 years and over
16 00000	IDAHO—Con.												
16 70660	Rupert city	Minidoka	2.0	5,645	4,101	21	66	18	1	1,281	157	1,998	3,883
16 71020	St. Anthony city	Fremont	1.3	3,342	2,976	7	23	22	2	237	75	514	2,232
16 71470	St. Maries city	Benewah	1.1	2,652	2,544	-	46	3	-	5	54	44	1,953
16 71650	Salmon city	Lemhi	1.7	3,122	3,021	6	17	9	-	19	50	68	2,297
16 72100	Sandpoint city	Bonner	3.9	6,835	6,578	8	69	28	3	32	117	168	5,069
16 73450	Shelley city	Bingham	1.3	3,813	3,429	7	26	10	1	257	83	449	2,455
16 75195	Soda Springs city	Caribou	4.5	3,381	3,267	1	3	5	7	40	58	98	2,338
16 82810	Twin Falls city	Twin Falls	12.0	34,469	31,633	76	255	377	39	1,280	809	3,066	25,345
16 86140	Weiser city	Washington	2.3	5,343	4,335	4	43	64	7	744	146	1,224	3,833
17 00000	ILLINOIS		55,583.6	12,419,293	9,125,471	1,876,875	31,006	423,603	4,610	722,712	235,016	1,530,262	9,173,842
17 00113	Abingdon city	Knox	1.5	3,612	3,544	20	9	4	-	6	29	41	2,680
17 00243	Addison village	DuPage	9.4	35,914	27,076	902	127	2,850	5	4,091	863	10,198	26,495
17 00646	Aledo city	Mercer	2.2	3,613	3,553	16	4	11	-	7	22	26	2,768
17 00685	Algonquin village	Kane, McHenry	9.8	23,276	21,939	214	24	546	3	280	270	948	15,647
17 00958	Alorton village	St. Clair	1.8	2,749	43	2,669	4	-	-	7	26	20	1,669
17 01010	Alsip village	Cook	6.4	19,725	16,104	1,991	29	415	6	635	545	1,727	14,510
17 01114	Alton city	Madison	15.6	30,496	22,056	7,538	55	115	3	207	522	454	22,643
17 01270	Amboy city	Lee	1.3	2,561	2,509	20	1	-	-	6	25	55	1,855
17 01543	Anna city	Union	3.4	5,136	4,941	89	13	14	1	21	57	75	4,126
17 01595	Antioch village	Lake	7.4	8,788	8,365	94	31	102	1	95	100	388	6,159
17 01881	Arcola city	Douglas	1.4	2,652	2,371	7	3	21	-	213	37	527	1,971
17 02154	Arlington Heights village	Cook, Lake	16.4	76,031	68,854	728	58	4,548	30	907	906	3,393	58,476
17 02921	Auburn city	Sangamon	3.2	4,317	4,246	13	7	12	-	13	26	33	3,003
17 03012	Aurora city	DuPage, Kane, Kendall, Will	38.5	142,990	97,340	15,817	511	4,370	47	20,762	4,143	46,557	97,625
17 03454	Baldwin village	Randolph	0.7	3,627	1,244	2,135	1	6	6	228	7	282	3,487
17 03844	Barrington village	Cook, Lake	4.6	10,168	9,778	63	13	203	1	32	78	237	7,132
17 03883	Barrington Hills village	Cook, Kane, Lake, McHenry	27.9	3,915	3,692	18	-	153	-	29	23	75	2,924
17 04013	Bartlett village	Cook, DuPage, Kane	14.8	36,706	32,020	725	52	2,871	8	497	533	2,024	25,057
17 04039	Bartonville village	Peoria	8.0	6,310	6,189	25	4	24	1	21	46	61	4,855
17 04078	Batavia city	DuPage, Kane	9.0	23,866	22,245	577	26	321	1	364	332	1,257	16,392
17 04303	Beach Park village	Lake	6.4	10,072	8,592	457	28	150	3	616	226	1,368	7,349
17 04351	Beardstown city	Cass	3.4	5,766	5,233	50	13	19	3	404	44	1,032	4,261
17 04845	Belleville city	St. Clair	18.9	41,410	33,754	6,421	108	336	28	171	592	677	31,701
17 04975	Bellwood village	Cook	2.4	20,535	2,412	16,783	49	197	4	779	311	1,631	14,274
17 05092	Belvidere city	Boone	9.1	20,820	17,600	239	76	94	4	2,408	399	4,179	14,633
17 05248	Bensenville village	Cook, DuPage	6.0	20,703	14,615	579	94	1,318	5	3,438	654	7,690	15,510
17 05300	Benton city	Franklin	5.3	6,880	6,792	20	10	19	-	4	35	35	5,369
17 05404	Berkeley village	Cook	1.4	5,245	3,114	1,455	6	202	1	354	113	814	3,902
17 05573	Berwyn city	Cook	3.9	54,016	39,667	702	239	1,400	14	10,040	1,954	20,543	39,856
17 05599	Bethalto village	Madison	6.6	9,454	9,250	72	21	38	-	31	42	95	7,021
17 06587	Bloomingdale village	DuPage	6.8	21,675	18,505	557	26	1,916	3	325	343	1,074	16,975
17 06613	Bloomington city	McLean	22.5	64,808	55,032	5,602	115	1,958	28	919	1,154	2,150	48,640
17 06704	Blue Island city	Cook	4.0	23,463	12,596	5,655	135	87	8	4,149	833	8,899	16,392
17 07133	Bolingbrook village	DuPage, Will	20.5	56,321	36,330	11,494	130	3,591	36	3,182	1,558	7,371	38,156
17 07419	Boulder Hill CDP	Kendall	1.5	8,169	7,408	156	31	54	1	370	149	802	5,791
17 07471	Bourbonnais village	Kankakee	4.6	15,256	13,839	701	16	365	4	105	226	345	11,370
17 07744	Bradley village	Kankakee	3.8	12,784	12,224	157	27	87	3	153	133	461	9,455
17 07770	Braidwood city	Will	4.6	5,203	5,072	14	5	17	-	41	54	147	3,670
17 07913	Breese city	Clinton	2.3	4,048	3,990	4	2	14	-	22	16	52	2,909
17 08225	Bridgeview village	Cook	4.1	15,335	13,406	126	46	341	-	609	807	1,445	11,523
17 08446	Broadview village	Cook	1.8	8,264	1,815	6,043	13	110	-	126	157	325	6,169
17 08576	Brookfield village	Cook	3.1	19,085	17,850	169	27	237	2	550	250	1,537	14,532
17 09447	Buffalo Grove village	Cook, Lake	9.2	42,909	38,059	325	24	3,618	6	389	488	1,425	30,505
17 09642	Burbank city	Cook	4.2	27,902	25,299	73	47	490	6	1,102	885	3,095	20,886
17 09798	Burnham village	Cook	1.9	4,170	1,451	2,259	9	42	1	316	92	635	3,021
17 09980	Burr Ridge village	Cook, DuPage	6.4	10,408	8,919	102	3	1,138	3	78	165	304	7,641
17 10110	Bushnell city	McDonough	2.0	3,221	3,182	4	6	3	-	14	12	22	2,420
17 10240	Byron city	Ogle	2.5	2,917	2,850	12	4	9	-	9	33	45	2,037
17 10370	Cahokia village	St. Clair	9.6	16,391	9,552	6,342	53	63	5	120	256	369	10,910
17 10383	Cairo city	Alexander	7.1	3,632	1,305	2,241	3	26	1	13	43	27	2,529
17 10487	Calumet City city	Cook	7.3	39,071	15,137	20,673	97	207	21	2,097	839	4,242	27,844
17 10513	Calumet Park village	Cook	1.1	8,516	1,034	7,058	26	6	1	262	129	659	6,020
17 11007	Canton city	Fulton	7.8	15,288	13,696	1,353	22	62	3	67	85	320	12,192
17 11163	Carbondale city	Jackson	11.9	20,681	13,665	4,785	45	1,379	16	294	497	630	17,417
17 11202	Carlinville city	Macoupin	2.4	5,685	5,515	85	14	15	1	13	42	43	4,357
17 11228	Carlyle city	Clinton	3.0	3,406	3,244	116	8	17	1	4	16	28	2,614
17 11293	Carmi city	White	2.5	5,422	5,330	26	19	13	-	3	31	35	4,315
17 11332	Carol Stream village	DuPage	8.9	40,438	31,749	1,716	71	4,531	4	1,534	833	4,055	27,933
17 11358	Carpentersville village	Kane	7.5	30,586	21,031	1,279	197	606	30	6,372	1,071	12,410	20,436
17 11462	Carrollton city	Greene	1.7	2,605	2,573	1	6	8	2	5	10	13	1,987
17 11514	Carterville city	Williamson	4.3	4,616	4,441	52	7	43	1	27	45	52	3,451
17 11527	Carthage city	Hancock	1.6	2,725	2,674	13	13	15	2	1	7	9	2,082
17 11592	Cary village	McHenry	5.3	15,531	14,837	61	24	210	4	285	110	843	10,133
17 11618	Casey city	Clark, Cumberland	2.1	2,942	2,903	13	4	-	-	1	21	7	2,233
17 11644	Caseyville village	St. Clair	6.2	4,310	3,849	338	15	7	-	45	56	152	3,306

Table D-1. Places — **Area and Population**—Con.

[Includes incorporated places and census designated places (CDPs) of 2,500 or more population as of April 1, 2000. Codes shown are two-digit Federal Information Processing Standards (FIPS) state codes and five-digit FIPS place codes. Place names and codes are those in effect as of January 1, 2000. County refers to the county (or counties) in which the place is located. IC in this column = independent city, a county equivalent. If a place is located in more than one county, counties are listed in alphabetic order]

State and place code	Place	County	Land area, 2000 (sq. mi.)	Population, 2000 (April 1)									
					By race—								
					One race							Hispanic or Latino (of any race)	18 years and over
				Total	White	Black or African American	American Indian and Alaska Native	Asian	Native Hawaiian and Other Pacific Islander	Some other race	Two or more races		
17 00000	ILLINOIS—Con.												
17 12164	Centralia city	Clinton, Jefferson, Marion, Washington	7.5	14,136	12,227	1,462	35	103	9	58	242	170	10,707
17 12203	Centreville city	St. Clair	4.3	5,951	201	5,681	8	-	1	8	52	34	3,956
17 12385	Champaign city	Champaign	17.0	67,518	49,398	10,543	159	4,611	23	1,307	1,477	2,724	55,507
17 12476	Channahon village	Grundy, Will	7.2	7,344	7,140	31	8	20	-	70	75	267	4,933
17 12567	Charleston city	Coles	0.0	21,039	19,402	894	51	282	18	105	227	370	18,141
17 12684	Chatham village	Sangamon	5.0	8,583	8,367	66	13	77	-	13	47	66	5,837
17 13139	Chester city	Randolph	5.9	5,185	4,919	186	8	11	2	11	48	39	4,026
17 14000	Chicago city	Cook, DuPage	227.1	2,896,016	1,215,315	1,065,009	10,290	125,974	1,788	393,203	84,437	753,644	2,136,176
17 14026	Chicago Heights city	Cook	9.6	32,776	14,756	12,421	146	144	12	4,411	886	7,790	22,403
17 14065	Chicago Ridge village	Cook	2.2	14,127	12,592	345	32	207	-	277	674	883	10,749
17 14117	Chillicothe city	Peoria	4.9	5,996	5,840	13	10	10	2	65	56	210	4,517
17 14286	Christopher city	Franklin	1.4	2,836	2,797	3	1	8	-	3	24	15	2,218
17 14351	Cicero town	Cook	5.8	85,616	41,327	956	759	828	38	38,277	3,431	66,299	55,968
17 14572	Clarendon Hills village	DuPage	1.7	7,610	7,159	64	1	268	-	32	86	180	5,305
17 15001	Clinton city	De Witt	2.7	7,485	7,269	63	15	14	3	69	52	167	5,588
17 15170	Coal City village	Grundy, Will	2.4	4,797	4,723	6	12	1	1	26	28	91	3,480
17 15235	Coal Valley village	Henry, Rock Island	2.9	3,606	3,500	25	1	15	-	21	44	108	2,713
17 15599	Collinsville city	Madison, St. Clair	13.6	24,707	22,603	1,446	66	147	5	146	294	534	18,969
17 15664	Colona city	Henry	3.5	5,173	4,996	16	13	9	-	88	51	210	3,750
17 15833	Columbia city	Monroe, St. Clair	9.4	7,922	7,805	8	15	27	-	16	51	76	5,867
17 16691	Country Club Hills city	Cook	4.6	16,169	2,346	13,243	24	164	-	88	304	280	11,200
17 16873	Countryside city	Cook	2.7	5,991	5,529	129	6	93	-	131	103	410	4,798
17 17458	Crest Hill city	Will	7.2	13,329	9,912	2,606	26	150	17	425	193	1,174	10,808
17 17497	Crestwood village	Cook	3.1	11,251	10,403	508	14	82	-	117	127	414	8,869
17 17523	Crete village	Will	6.4	7,346	6,351	769	5	55	1	68	97	267	5,531
17 17549	Creve Coeur village	Tazewell	4.1	5,448	5,292	21	29	10	1	44	51	106	4,105
17 17887	Crystal Lake city	McHenry	16.2	38,000	35,746	212	62	747	8	826	399	2,662	25,985
17 17930	Crystal Lawns CDP	Will	1.0	2,933	2,800	19	9	12	-	55	30	174	2,108
17 18563	Danville city	Vermilion	17.0	33,904	23,796	8,261	72	406	10	708	651	1,549	25,474
17 18628	Darien city	DuPage	6.0	22,860	19,225	451	26	2,635	6	222	295	831	17,579
17 18823	Decatur city	Macon	41.6	81,860	63,519	15,940	141	540	15	354	1,351	978	62,231
17 18992	Deerfield village	Cook, Lake	5.5	18,420	17,662	61	7	465	4	79	142	312	12,792
17 19083	Deer Park village	Cook, Lake	3.6	3,102	2,977	18	2	75	1	8	21	47	2,146
17 19161	DeKalb city	DeKalb	12.6	39,018	31,015	3,543	94	1,804	49	1,696	817	3,527	32,406
17 19642	Des Plaines city	Cook	14.4	58,720	49,586	594	151	4,492	13	2,726	1,158	8,229	45,599
17 20149	Dixmoor village	Cook	1.2	3,934	1,212	2,247	10	6	-	373	86	716	2,740
17 20162	Dixon city	Lee	6.3	15,941	13,762	1,671	22	130	8	175	173	685	12,605
17 20292	Dolton village	Cook	4.6	25,614	3,671	21,098	44	144	4	365	288	791	17,425
17 20591	Downers Grove village	DuPage	14.2	48,724	43,924	936	55	2,782	6	488	533	1,747	36,663
17 21254	Dupo village	St. Clair	4.4	3,933	3,823	46	12	10	-	14	28	27	2,940
17 21267	Du Quoin city	Perry	6.9	6,448	5,818	466	23	22	3	23	93	85	4,934
17 21358	Dwight village	Grundy, Livingston	2.6	4,363	4,220	40	2	11	-	51	39	122	3,212
17 21553	East Alton village	Madison	5.5	6,830	6,606	64	17	26	1	12	104	70	5,109
17 21696	East Dundee village	Cook, Kane	2.7	2,955	2,782	29	3	51	-	51	39	116	2,337
17 22073	East Moline city	Rock Island	9.0	20,333	16,274	1,493	71	458	1	1,519	517	3,081	15,307
17 22164	East Peoria city	Tazewell	18.8	22,638	22,031	106	55	150	2	100	194	293	17,571
17 22255	East St. Louis city	St. Clair	14.1	31,542	387	30,829	59	24	9	59	175	230	21,196
17 22697	Edwardsville city	Madison	13.9	21,491	18,847	1,861	60	364	6	62	291	215	16,626
17 22736	Effingham city	Effingham	8.7	12,384	12,110	44	24	73	-	47	86	129	9,297
17 22931	Elburn village	Kane	2.7	2,756	2,703	3	4	9	-	13	24	59	1,970
17 23009	Eldorado city	Saline	2.3	4,534	4,455	16	10	1	1	10	41	54	3,528
17 23074	Elgin city	Cook, Kane	25.0	94,487	66,600	6,427	382	3,668	58	14,537	2,815	32,430	67,063
17 23256	Elk Grove Village village	Cook, DuPage	11.0	34,727	29,874	490	33	3,051	15	797	467	2,165	26,092
17 23620	Elmhurst city	Cook, DuPage	10.3	42,762	39,940	400	24	1,568	8	416	406	1,717	31,821
17 23724	Elmwood Park village	Cook	1.9	25,405	23,255	132	45	530	7	842	594	2,798	19,834
17 23737	El Paso city	McLean, Woodford	1.5	2,695	2,665	4	4	6	-	6	10	19	1,978
17 24543	Eureka city	Woodford	2.7	4,871	4,772	28	18	16	-	8	29	50	3,685
17 24582	Evanston city	Cook	7.7	74,239	48,429	16,704	140	4,524	64	2,116	2,262	4,539	59,238
17 24634	Evergreen Park village	Cook	3.2	20,821	18,388	1,644	29	257	3	258	242	831	15,068
17 24764	Fairbury city	Livingston	1.3	3,968	3,841	16	2	18	-	66	25	103	2,897
17 24816	Fairfield city	Wayne	3.6	5,421	5,334	5	14	34	1	3	30	23	4,308
17 24920	Fairmont CDP	Will	1.6	2,563	927	1,374	6	12	1	162	81	279	1,856
17 25141	Fairview Heights city	St. Clair	11.1	15,034	11,787	2,567	25	321	1	109	224	289	11,522
17 25253	Farmington city	Fulton	1.2	2,601	2,565	3	9	4	-	5	15	25	2,002
17 26454	Flora city	Clay	4.4	5,086	4,972	9	17	57	2	14	15	33	3,891
17 26571	Flossmoor village	Cook	3.6	9,301	6,167	2,522	8	393	-	51	160	223	6,711
17 26710	Ford Heights village	Cook	1.8	3,456	61	3,314	2	4	-	40	35	87	1,892
17 26935	Forest Park village	Cook	2.4	15,688	8,808	4,892	23	1,071	11	440	443	1,230	12,588
17 27442	Fox Lake village	Lake, McHenry	7.3	9,178	8,764	70	22	60	5	141	116	533	7,099
17 27455	Fox Lake Hills CDP	Lake	1.3	2,561	2,465	30	3	15	-	11	37	75	1,867
17 27533	Fox River Grove village	Lake, McHenry	1.7	4,862	4,663	33	6	62	-	55	43	186	3,323
17 27624	Frankfort village	Cook, Will	10.9	10,391	9,753	258	18	221	-	64	77	240	7,411
17 27644	Frankfort Square CDP	Will	2.1	7,766	7,365	99	4	135	-	94	69	312	4,959
17 27702	Franklin Park village	Cook	4.7	19,434	15,401	147	57	481	9	2,840	499	7,399	14,367
17 27806	Freeburg village	St. Clair	3.2	3,872	3,816	6	11	8	4	8	19	43	2,821
17 27884	Freeport city	Stephenson	11.4	26,443	21,623	3,651	51	257	10	265	586	561	19,969
17 28144	Fulton city	Whiteside	2.3	3,881	3,800	23	7	20	-	13	18	49	2,961

[Includes incorporated places and census designated places (CDPs) of 2,500 or more population as of April 1, 2000. Codes shown are two-digit Federal Information Processing Standards (FIPS) state codes and five-digit FIPS place codes. Place names and codes are those in effect as of January 1, 2000. County refers to the county (or counties) in which the place is located. IC in this column = independent city, a county equivalent. If a place is located in more than one county, counties are listed in alphabetic order]

State and place code	Place	County	Land area, 2000 (sq. mi.)	Population, 2000 (April 1) Total	White	Black or African American	American Indian and Alaska Native	Asian	Native Hawaiian and Other Pacific Islander	Some other race	Two or more races	Hispanic or Latino (of any race)	18 years and over
17 00000	ILLINOIS—Con.												
17 28248	Gages Lake CDP	Lake	3.1	10,415	9,574	210	28	325	1	148	129	436	7,267
17 28300	Galena city	Jo Daviess	3.7	3,460	3,375	11	3	11	-	40	20	175	2,814
17 28326	Galesburg city	Knox	16.9	33,706	28,390	3,437	74	346	8	830	621	1,688	26,580
17 28430	Galva city	Henry	1.7	2,758	2,719	7	6	3	-	9	14	54	2,077
17 28846	Geneseo city	Henry	4.0	6,480	6,387	12	6	23	1	18	33	61	4,902
17 28872	Geneva city	Kane	8.4	19,515	18,832	199	11	244	5	114	110	541	13,301
17 28898	Genoa city	DeKalb	1.9	4,169	3,972	6	8	12	1	131	39	444	2,895
17 28963	Georgetown city	Vermilion	1.6	3,628	3,466	99	10	2	-	9	42	43	2,615
17 29119	Gibson city	Ford	2.1	3,373	3,310	20	-	18	-	1	24	22	2,591
17 29236	Gillespie city	Macoupin	1.5	3,412	3,363	11	7	4	2	5	20	25	2,617
17 29639	Glen Carbon village	Madison	7.4	10,425	9,288	726	21	221	4	43	122	156	7,787
17 29652	Glencoe village	Cook	3.8	8,762	8,330	176	4	147	-	23	82	108	5,998
17 29730	Glendale Heights village	DuPage	5.4	31,765	20,263	1,537	95	6,345	25	2,576	924	5,842	23,233
17 29756	Glen Ellyn village	DuPage	6.6	26,999	24,163	575	39	1,280	2	493	447	1,275	19,342
17 29938	Glenview village	Cook	13.5	41,847	35,817	665	41	4,207	7	532	578	1,702	31,137
17 30029	Glenwood village	Cook	2.7	9,000	4,615	4,008	9	56	9	203	100	452	6,718
17 30094	Godfrey village	Madison	34.5	16,286	15,319	658	51	106	1	31	120	159	12,599
17 30471	Goodings Grove CDP	Will	9.4	17,084	16,484	35	2	297	-	100	166	601	11,778
17 30900	Grandwood Park CDP	Lake	1.6	4,521	3,927	187	5	203	-	95	104	252	3,062
17 30926	Granite City city	Madison	16.7	31,301	29,653	622	141	147	7	297	434	894	23,567
17 31121	Grayslake village	Lake	9.4	18,506	16,840	293	35	783	6	314	235	920	12,379
17 31446	Green Oaks village	Lake	4.0	3,572	3,245	62	5	195	-	15	50	94	2,378
17 31589	Greenville city	Bond	5.2	6,955	5,731	1,074	43	33	-	26	48	171	5,848
17 32018	Gurnee village	Lake	13.4	28,834	23,679	1,459	52	2,364	15	621	644	1,738	20,093
17 32434	Hamilton city	Hancock	3.7	3,029	2,974	17	5	13	-	7	13	24	2,335
17 32525	Hampshire village	Kane	4.9	2,900	2,848	3	11	4	-	18	16	70	2,040
17 32746	Hanover Park village	Cook, DuPage	6.8	38,278	26,077	2,348	109	4,574	6	3,967	1,197	10,233	26,228
17 33136	Harrisburg city	Saline	6.2	9,860	8,938	683	27	35	-	54	123	144	7,393
17 33331	Harvard city	McHenry	5.3	7,996	6,097	68	30	114	1	1,500	186	3,023	5,587
17 33383	Harvey city	Cook	6.2	30,000	3,005	23,871	79	114	16	2,382	533	3,834	19,466
17 33435	Harwood Heights village	Cook	0.8	8,297	7,644	26	20	367	2	128	110	484	6,759
17 33513	Havana city	Mason	2.6	3,577	3,523	5	5	19	-	2	23	21	2,730
17 33630	Hawthorn Woods village	Lake	5.4	6,002	5,675	42	1	186	4	34	60	124	3,986
17 33695	Hazel Crest village	Cook	3.4	14,816	2,885	11,308	18	138	3	220	244	494	10,327
17 34163	Henry city	Marshall	1.4	2,540	2,481	13	5	5	-	3	33	16	1,933
17 34358	Herrin city	Williamson	8.2	11,298	10,927	104	39	76	3	35	114	107	8,788
17 34514	Hickory Hills city	Cook	2.8	13,926	12,657	172	32	290	1	331	443	1,129	10,604
17 34670	Highland city	Madison	5.4	8,438	8,320	7	10	41	-	22	38	111	6,288
17 34722	Highland Park city	Lake	12.4	31,365	28,606	559	24	716	4	1,086	370	2,792	22,882
17 34865	Highwood city	Lake	0.6	4,143	3,030	89	24	88	2	712	198	1,584	3,178
17 35047	Hillsboro city	Montgomery	3.6	4,359	4,238	48	14	16	3	17	23	52	3,235
17 35086	Hillside village	Cook	2.1	8,155	4,020	3,008	14	418	5	472	218	1,068	6,140
17 35307	Hinsdale village	Cook, DuPage	4.6	17,349	16,187	136	12	777	4	86	147	414	11,642
17 35411	Hoffman Estates village	Cook, Kane	19.7	49,495	36,837	2,166	86	7,461	12	1,857	1,076	5,198	35,596
17 35866	Hometown city	Cook	0.5	4,467	4,346	-	8	13	-	45	55	171	3,408
17 35879	Homewood village	Cook	5.2	19,543	15,270	3,422	20	307	13	207	304	597	14,245
17 36061	Hoopeston city	Vermilion	3.1	5,965	5,475	49	17	8	-	334	82	500	4,487
17 36750	Huntley village	Kane, McHenry	11.7	5,730	5,440	25	10	122	-	72	61	245	4,395
17 37257	Indian Head Park village	Cook	0.8	3,685	3,535	32	2	73	1	19	23	72	3,120
17 37465	Ingalls Park CDP	Will	1.1	3,082	2,762	91	10	9	-	123	87	398	2,330
17 37608	Inverness village	Cook	6.3	6,749	6,207	45	6	421	6	28	36	128	5,044
17 37894	Island Lake village	Lake, McHenry	2.9	8,153	7,647	40	13	132	1	222	98	679	5,542
17 37907	Itasca village	DuPage	4.9	8,302	7,309	140	22	484	2	143	202	581	6,391
17 38115	Jacksonville city	Morgan	10.1	18,940	17,109	1,261	40	130	2	132	266	291	14,788
17 38414	Jerseyville city	Jersey	4.4	7,984	7,892	7	14	13	-	8	50	43	6,034
17 38479	Johnsburg village	McHenry	5.5	5,391	5,328	7	3	10	-	9	34	82	3,742
17 38544	Johnston City city	Williamson	2.0	3,557	3,524	4	5	2	-	3	19	38	2,746
17 38570	Joliet city	Kendall, Will	38.1	106,221	73,633	19,294	301	1,215	22	9,532	2,224	19,552	74,934
17 38830	Justice village	Cook	2.9	12,193	8,639	2,456	23	213	4	336	523	928	8,745
17 38934	Kankakee city	Kankakee	12.3	27,491	13,998	11,291	75	87	7	1,511	522	2,544	19,391
17 39727	Kewanee city	Henry	6.3	12,944	11,684	476	8	45	2	477	252	790	9,737
17 39883	Kildeer village	Lake	3.5	3,460	3,246	32	-	148	-	13	21	80	2,334
17 40416	Knoxville city	Knox	2.2	3,183	3,138	11	4	2	-	4	24	18	2,430
17 40767	La Grange village	Cook	2.5	15,608	14,206	939	14	156	3	155	135	572	11,167
17 40793	La Grange Park village	Cook	2.3	13,295	12,394	409	14	218	5	121	134	472	10,146
17 40884	Lake Barrington village	Lake	5.3	4,757	4,634	20	9	51	3	7	33	47	3,786
17 40910	Lake Bluff village	Lake	4.1	6,056	5,771	31	2	200	2	14	36	72	4,064
17 41105	Lake Forest city	Lake	16.9	20,059	18,815	271	12	692	26	89	154	376	14,539
17 41183	Lake in the Hills village	McHenry	9.4	23,152	21,206	347	33	770	4	430	362	1,462	15,408
17 41326	Lakemoor village	Lake, McHenry	4.3	2,788	2,585	18	4	51	5	80	45	196	1,931
17 41346	Lake of the Woods CDP	Champaign	2.1	3,026	2,950	24	14	3	-	6	29	23	2,129
17 41586	Lake Villa village	Lake	5.7	5,864	5,450	145	7	96	5	52	109	181	3,982
17 41742	Lake Zurich village	Lake	6.5	18,104	16,711	146	30	691	2	357	167	1,005	11,931
17 42028	Lansing village	Cook	6.8	28,332	24,295	3,029	36	203	13	437	319	1,624	21,445
17 42184	La Salle city	La Salle	6.3	9,796	9,182	125	17	47	3	301	121	805	7,506
17 42405	Lawrenceville city	Lawrence	2.0	4,745	4,643	43	4	11	-	19	25	68	3,794
17 42496	Lebanon city	St. Clair	2.1	3,523	2,764	650	12	17	3	14	63	54	2,789
17 42795	Lemont village	Cook, DuPage, Will	6.5	13,098	12,757	40	19	107	4	87	84	393	9,472

Table D-1. Places — **Area and Population**—Con.

[Includes incorporated places and census designated places (CDPs) of 2,500 or more population as of April 1, 2000. Codes shown are two-digit Federal Information Processing Standards (FIPS) state codes and five-digit FIPS place codes. Place names and codes are those in effect as of January 1, 2000. County refers to the county (or counties) in which the place is located. IC in this column = independent city, a county equivalent. If a place is located in more than one county, counties are listed in alphabetic order]

State and place code	Place	County	Land area, 2000 (sq. mi.)	Population, 2000 (April 1) Total	By race— One race White	Black or African American	American Indian and Alaska Native	Asian	Native Hawaiian and Other Pacific Islander	Some other race	Two or more races	Hispanic or Latino (of any race)	18 years and over
	ILLINOIS—Con.												
17 00000													
17 42834	Lena village	Stephenson	2.1	2,887	2,846	6	1	3	-	9	22	33	2,179
17 42971	Le Roy city	McLean	2.2	3,332	3,307	2	4	3	-	9	7	40	2,425
17 43055	Lewistown city	Fulton	1.8	2,522	2,495	2	5	1	2	5	12	27	1,977
17 43250	Libertyville village	Lake	8.8	20,742	19,121	211	18	949	6	231	206	566	14,868
17 43536	Lincoln city	Logan	5.9	15,369	14,569	434	24	137	4	69	132	183	12,048
17 43666	Lincolnshire village	Lake	4.4	6,108	5,748	31	2	227	4	30	66	153	4,465
17 43744	Lincolnwood village	Cook	2.7	12,359	9,211	47	4	2,605	3	152	337	517	9,524
17 43770	Lindenhurst village	Lake	3.7	12,539	11,640	184	19	377	1	165	153	508	8,735
17 43939	Lisle village	DuPage	6.4	21,182	17,661	736	40	2,073	6	355	311	1,163	16,016
17 43965	Litchfield city	Montgomery	5.1	6,815	6,700	25	12	18	1	15	44	65	5,068
17 44225	Lockport city	Will	7.1	15,191	14,556	168	34	114	1	143	175	660	10,910
17 44407	Lombard village	DuPage	9.7	42,322	36,829	1,141	62	2,982	7	606	695	2,012	32,606
17 44524	Long Grove village	Lake	12.3	6,735	6,116	63	1	456	-	36	63	202	4,608
17 44550	Long Lake CDP	Lake	1.1	3,356	3,132	11	11	24	-	148	30	387	2,344
17 45031	Loves Park city	Boone, Winnebago	14.4	20,044	18,618	467	43	363	5	227	321	655	14,783
17 45421	Lynwood village	Cook	4.9	7,377	3,699	3,349	17	72	-	114	126	337	5,182
17 45434	Lyons village	Cook	2.2	10,255	8,911	103	25	143	4	703	366	1,668	7,775
17 45694	McHenry city	McHenry	11.6	21,501	20,250	75	45	192	8	711	220	1,527	15,364
17 45726	Machesney Park village	Winnebago	12.0	20,759	19,805	284	53	201	7	169	240	584	15,267
17 45824	McLeansboro city	Hamilton	2.3	2,945	2,889	23	1	6	1	5	20	11	2,273
17 45889	Macomb city	McDonough	9.8	18,558	16,467	1,101	29	568	6	128	259	389	16,223
17 45993	Madison city	Madison, St. Clair	7.0	4,545	2,516	1,915	13	5	1	42	53	89	3,190
17 46136	Mahomet village	Champaign	6.9	4,877	4,788	7	5	29	-	19	29	46	3,204
17 46357	Manhattan village	Will	3.4	3,330	3,237	7	4	7	-	39	36	101	2,252
17 46500	Manteno village	Kankakee	3.0	6,414	6,272	17	11	13	1	63	37	181	4,727
17 46786	Marengo city	McHenry	4.0	6,355	5,851	19	17	18	1	352	97	826	4,495
17 46916	Marion city	Williamson	12.8	16,035	14,895	696	39	133	8	70	194	257	12,379
17 47007	Markham city	Cook	5.2	12,620	2,183	9,952	20	75	3	203	184	396	8,663
17 47111	Marquette Heights city	Tazewell	1.6	2,794	2,744	11	2	7	-	11	19	37	1,997
17 47150	Marseilles city	La Salle	8.3	4,655	4,559	4	10	12	-	30	40	89	3,494
17 47163	Marshall city	Clark	3.1	3,771	3,708	11	5	6	4	5	32	18	2,877
17 47397	Maryville village	Madison	4.7	4,651	4,377	161	5	23	2	36	47	93	3,493
17 47423	Mascoutah city	St. Clair	8.6	5,659	5,191	237	20	55	3	48	105	99	4,164
17 47475	Mason City city	Mason	1.0	2,558	2,534	1	2	4	-	7	10	15	1,913
17 47540	Matteson village	Cook, Will	7.1	12,928	4,230	8,098	16	201	-	144	239	436	9,350
17 47553	Mattoon city	Coles	9.3	18,291	17,676	260	33	75	2	75	170	232	14,219
17 47774	Maywood village	Cook	2.7	26,987	2,625	22,308	34	80	1	1,500	439	2,843	18,438
17 48242	Melrose Park village	Cook	4.2	23,171	16,575	676	114	461	3	4,653	689	12,485	16,824
17 48333	Mendota city	La Salle	3.8	7,272	6,499	29	22	33	-	612	77	1,320	5,409
17 48606	Metamora village	Woodford	1.4	2,700	2,675	7	5	2	-	2	9	17	2,057
17 48645	Metropolis city	Massac	5.0	6,482	5,868	493	13	13	-	29	66	48	5,186
17 48892	Midlothian village	Cook	2.8	14,315	12,636	877	22	236	3	322	219	976	10,290
17 49009	Milan village	Rock Island	5.5	5,348	4,945	231	12	24	2	58	76	156	4,102
17 49386	Millstadt village	St. Clair	1.1	2,794	2,757	-	7	7	-	8	15	21	2,132
17 49607	Minooka village	Grundy, Kendall, Will	4.3	3,971	3,893	10	8	12	-	21	27	113	2,703
17 49854	Mokena village	Will	6.0	14,583	14,126	72	10	183	8	92	92	421	9,857
17 49867	Moline city	Rock Island	15.6	43,768	38,682	1,351	87	607	11	2,222	808	5,212	33,242
17 49893	Momence city	Kankakee	1.4	3,171	2,828	137	6	3	-	157	40	361	2,359
17 49945	Monee village	Will	0.1	2,004	2,745	62	2	10	-	55	47	110	2,205
17 50010	Monmouth city	Warren	4.0	9,841	9,125	276	23	46	19	188	164	428	7,576
17 50218	Montgomery village	Kane, Kendall	6.4	5,471	4,887	165	23	44	2	267	83	741	4,138
17 50244	Monticello city	Piatt	3.0	5,138	5,087	4	7	7	1	4	28	41	3,935
17 50491	Morris city	Grundy	6.9	11,928	11,373	41	27	61	3	292	131	828	8,942
17 50530	Morrison city	Whiteside	2.1	4,447	4,342	32	5	9	-	23	36	105	3,496
17 50621	Morton village	Tazewell	12.2	15,198	14,874	20	27	176	1	39	61	122	11,578
17 50647	Morton Grove village	Cook	5.1	22,451	16,606	142	27	4,980	1	261	434	988	17,785
17 50868	Mount Carmel city	Wabash	4.6	7,982	7,798	38	15	41	6	23	61	69	6,099
17 50998	Mount Morris village	Ogle	1.2	3,013	2,927	5	6	13	4	30	28	83	2,295
17 51089	Mount Prospect village	Cook	10.2	56,265	45,338	1,026	110	6,292	28	2,332	1,139	6,620	43,319
17 51180	Mount Vernon city	Jefferson	11.5	16,269	13,706	2,011	27	125	3	77	320	242	12,243
17 51206	Mount Zion village	Macon	3.8	4,845	4,752	12	11	37	-	33	33	12	3,474
17 51349	Mundelein village	Lake	8.6	30,935	24,340	494	87	2,041	23	3,298	652	7,487	21,220
17 51453	Murphysboro city	Jackson	4.8	13,295	10,612	2,101	52	137	12	146	235	361	11,343
17 51622	Naperville city	DuPage, Will	35.4	128,358	109,346	3,887	154	12,380	24	967	1,600	4,160	87,506
17 51700	Nashville city	Washington	2.7	3,147	3,107	5	4	12	3	6	10	25	2,374
17 52142	New Baden village	Clinton, St. Clair	1.3	3,001	2,860	56	5	26	3	19	32	48	2,192
17 52584	New Lenox village	Will	10.1	17,771	17,354	54	11	65	2	150	135	563	11,915
17 52844	Newton city	Jasper	1.9	3,069	3,038	3	-	6	-	7	15	18	2,337
17 53000	Niles village	Cook	5.9	30,068	25,022	139	27	3,812	4	502	562	1,512	25,058
17 53234	Normal town	McLean	13.6	45,386	39,745	3,499	68	1,001	18	421	634	1,162	37,447
17 53377	Norridge village	Cook	1.8	14,582	13,829	15	11	399	1	180	147	553	12,110
17 53442	North Aurora village	Kane	5.2	10,585	9,284	474	22	269	3	352	181	1,025	7,714
17 53455	North Barrington village	Lake	4.4	2,918	2,816	14	-	47	1	10	30	71	2,083
17 53481	Northbrook village	Cook	12.9	33,435	29,830	190	13	2,958	3	119	322	616	24,908
17 53559	North Chicago city	Lake	7.8	35,918	17,140	13,024	301	1,289	53	2,750	1,361	6,552	27,214
17 53663	Northfield village	Cook	3.0	5,389	4,984	28	2	300	-	23	52	90	3,995
17 53871	Northlake city	Cook	3.0	11,878	8,964	285	59	436	6	1,825	303	4,133	8,864
17 54144	North Riverside village	Cook	1.5	6,688	6,066	198	9	175	1	164	75	544	5,645

Table D-1. Places — **Area and Population**—Con.

[Includes incorporated places and census designated places (CDPs) of 2,500 or more population as of April 1, 2000. Codes shown are two-digit Federal Information Processing Standards (FIPS) state codes and five-digit FIPS place codes. Place names and codes are those in effect as of January 1, 2000. County refers to the county (or counties) in which the place is located. IC in this column = independent city, a county equivalent. If a place is located in more than one county, counties are listed in alphabetic order]

State and place code	Place	County	Land area, 2000 (sq. mi.)	Population, 2000 (April 1)									
					By race—								
					One race							Hispanic or Latino (of any race)	18 years and over
				Total	White	Black or African American	American Indian and Alaska Native	Asian	Native Hawaiian and Other Pacific Islander	Some other race	Two or more races		
17 00000	ILLINOIS—Con.												
17 54534	Oak Brook village	Cook, DuPage	8.2	8,702	6,666	119	-	1,750	1	19	147	208	6,996
17 54638	Oak Forest city	Cook	5.6	28,051	25,353	1,021	42	744	4	468	419	1,645	20,755
17 54820	Oak Lawn village	Cook	8.6	55,245	51,570	673	92	953	5	905	1,047	2,942	43,122
17 54885	Oak Park village	Cook	4.7	52,524	36,124	11,788	81	2,178	16	857	1,480	2,374	39,803
17 55249	O'Fallon city	St. Clair	10.9	21,910	18,113	2,627	51	542	15	174	388	488	15,704
17 55353	Oglesby city	La Salle	4.0	3,647	3,578	16	3	12	-	13	25	103	2,816
17 55912	Olney city	Richland	5.8	8,631	8,430	41	14	55	3	28	60	83	6,574
17 55938	Olympia Fields village	Cook	2.8	4,732	2,018	2,466	2	160	1	27	58	86	3,637
17 56484	Oregon city	Ogle	2.0	4,060	3,899	41	6	23	2	36	53	92	3,095
17 56627	Orland Hills village	Cook	1.1	6,779	5,878	346	17	225	-	117	196	409	4,467
17 56640	Orland Park village	Cook, Will	19.1	51,077	47,772	374	34	1,770	18	530	579	1,874	38,639
17 56887	Oswego village	Kendall	6.6	13,326	12,459	239	24	183	4	238	179	665	9,085
17 56926	Ottawa city	La Salle	7.3	18,307	17,440	251	27	152	11	171	255	954	13,741
17 57225	Palatine village	Cook	13.0	65,479	54,381	1,407	147	4,953	27	3,327	1,237	9,247	49,222
17 57381	Palos Heights city	Cook	3.8	11,260	10,853	49	10	232	-	28	88	161	8,981
17 57394	Palos Hills city	Cook	4.2	17,665	15,401	968	19	472	2	277	526	854	14,309
17 57407	Palos Park village	Cook	3.8	4,689	4,556	13	2	81	-	9	28	99	3,672
17 57472	Pana city	Christian	2.7	5,614	5,563	4	8	14	-	3	22	28	4,238
17 57628	Paris city	Edgar	4.8	9,077	8,924	46	19	20	1	23	44	76	6,918
17 57654	Park City city	Lake	1.1	6,637	4,008	500	15	586	10	1,149	369	2,506	4,787
17 57732	Park Forest village	Cook, Will	4.9	23,462	13,003	9,247	53	193	17	362	587	1,169	17,140
17 57875	Park Ridge city	Cook	7.0	37,775	36,031	90	24	1,004	18	329	279	1,113	28,509
17 58174	Pawnee village	Sangamon	1.2	2,647	2,616	4	3	5	-	1	18	8	1,902
17 58239	Paxton city	Ford	2.2	4,525	4,428	13	3	17	-	25	39	74	3,344
17 58447	Pekin city	Peoria, Tazewell	13.1	33,857	32,434	863	125	139	4	62	230	445	25,995
17 59000	Peoria city	Peoria	44.4	112,936	78,254	27,992	229	2,629	42	1,355	2,435	2,839	83,925
17 59026	Peoria Heights village	Peoria, Tazewell, Woodford	2.6	6,635	6,163	229	21	71	-	70	81	126	5,290
17 59052	Peotone village	Will	1.5	3,385	3,315	9	2	16	-	10	33	46	2,441
17 59234	Peru city	La Salle	5.9	9,835	9,488	31	18	109	1	114	74	401	7,675
17 59884	Pinckneyville city	Perry	3.2	5,464	3,893	1,331	9	11	3	206	11	244	4,701
17 60144	Pistakee Highlands CDP	McHenry	1.4	3,812	3,735	5	10	5	-	26	31	126	2,709
17 60222	Pittsfield city	Pike	3.6	4,211	4,145	9	8	15	-	7	27	26	3,312
17 60287	Plainfield village	Will	11.6	13,038	12,497	110	10	163	1	132	125	504	8,881
17 60352	Plano city	Kendall	3.5	5,633	4,638	21	14	17	1	822	120	1,453	3,863
17 61015	Pontiac city	Livingston	5.2	11,864	10,131	1,293	22	51	-	244	123	519	9,147
17 61067	Pontoon Beach village	Madison	8.2	5,620	4,930	499	31	44	1	40	75	108	4,036
17 61314	Posen village	Cook	1.2	4,730	3,703	413	16	11	3	462	122	1,087	3,365
17 61860	Preston Heights CDP	Will	1.5	2,527	783	1,604	14	3	5	70	48	137	1,716
17 61899	Princeton city	Bureau	6.7	7,501	7,337	29	8	47	-	32	48	93	5,832
17 62016	Prospect Heights city	Cook	4.3	17,081	13,223	300	42	746	8	2,361	401	4,711	12,939
17 62367	Quincy city	Adams	14.6	40,366	37,550	1,879	75	216	5	147	494	381	30,938
17 62783	Rantoul village	Champaign	7.2	12,857	9,860	2,170	60	225	7	114	421	346	9,175
17 63043	Red Bud city	Randolph	2.1	3,422	3,378	-	-	11	-	3	30	30	2,629
17 63706	Richton Park village	Cook	3.4	12,533	4,474	7,407	30	192	5	167	258	484	8,921
17 64278	Riverdale village	Cook	3.6	15,055	1,667	13,004	24	29	7	157	167	366	9,401
17 64304	River Forest village	Cook	2.5	11,635	10,396	560	11	364	5	114	185	466	8,537
17 64343	River Grove village	Cook	2.4	10,668	9,841	38	31	217	6	389	146	1,043	8,391
17 64421	Riverside village	Cook	2.0	8,895	8,484	23	7	142	1	140	98	489	6,773
17 64486	Riverton village	Sangamon	2.0	3,048	3,015	3	5	3	-	-	22	28	2,216
17 64538	Riverwoods village	Lake	4.0	3,843	3,617	14	-	173	1	7	31	76	2,773
17 64616	Robbins village	Cook	1.5	6,635	187	6,320	8	5	-	62	53	129	4,490
17 64707	Robinson city	Crawford	3.6	6,822	6,548	79	28	43	1	45	78	118	5,164
17 64746	Rochelle city	Ogle	7.5	9,424	8,181	107	46	87	2	819	182	1,806	6,869
17 64759	Rochester village	Sangamon	2.1	2,893	2,854	8	1	11	1	3	15	20	2,096
17 64928	Rock Falls city	Whiteside	3.3	9,580	8,793	84	43	25	-	451	184	1,106	7,134
17 65000	Rockford city	Winnebago	56.0	150,115	109,303	26,072	474	3,301	67	7,200	3,698	15,278	110,093
17 65078	Rock Island city	Rock Island	15.9	39,684	30,609	6,814	113	299	26	955	868	2,341	30,565
17 65156	Rockton village	Winnebago	3.5	5,296	5,162	37	4	43	2	24	24	81	3,648
17 65338	Rolling Meadows city	Cook	5.5	24,604	20,256	696	67	1,627	7	1,463	488	4,725	18,432
17 65442	Romeoville village	Will	14.5	21,153	17,872	1,137	82	518	5	1,039	500	2,781	15,105
17 65611	Roscoe village	Winnebago	9.2	6,244	5,948	119	14	51	1	46	65	156	4,265
17 65806	Roselle village	Cook, DuPage	5.4	23,115	20,315	383	48	1,685	11	333	340	1,197	17,127
17 65819	Rosemont village	Cook	1.7	4,224	3,347	57	37	186	1	488	108	1,493	3,194
17 65884	Rosewood Heights CDP	Madison	2.1	4,262	4,210	5	10	9	-	9	19	35	3,314
17 66027	Round Lake village	Lake	3.5	5,842	4,782	116	23	112	2	630	177	1,292	4,104
17 66040	Round Lake Beach village	Lake	5.0	25,859	19,227	792	161	534	11	4,387	747	8,084	16,814
17 66066	Round Lake Park village	Lake	3.0	6,038	4,905	104	22	33	1	817	156	1,584	4,359
17 66339	Rushville city	Schuyler	1.6	3,212	3,184	2	3	2	1	7	13	15	2,514
17 66703	St. Charles city	DuPage, Kane	14.0	27,896	26,169	462	39	499	1	463	263	1,535	20,147
17 66950	St. Joseph village	Champaign	1.1	2,912	2,880	3	2	7	-	7	13	25	2,083
17 67236	Salem city	Marion	6.1	7,909	7,682	57	24	91	3	11	41	57	6,050
17 67548	Sandwich city	DeKalb, Kendall	3.0	6,509	6,208	16	15	21	4	168	77	545	4,739
17 67769	Sauk Village village	Cook, Will	3.8	10,411	6,221	3,382	26	69	4	348	361	1,224	6,943
17 67821	Savanna city	Carroll	2.6	3,542	3,333	54	12	8	1	91	43	186	2,704
17 67860	Savoy village	Champaign	1.5	4,476	3,644	202	7	485	2	35	101	95	3,532
17 68003	Schaumburg village	Cook, DuPage	19.0	75,386	59,391	2,526	77	10,697	43	1,307	1,345	3,988	58,902

808   U.S. Census Bureau, County and City Data Book: 2000

Table D-1. Places — **Area and Population**—Con.

[Includes incorporated places and census designated places (CDPs) of 2,500 or more population as of April 1, 2000. Codes shown are two-digit Federal Information Processing Standards (FIPS) state codes and five-digit FIPS place codes. Place names and codes are those in effect as of January 1, 2000. County refers to the county (or counties) in which the place is located. IC in this column = independent city, a county equivalent. If a place is located in more than one county, counties are listed in alphabetic order]

State and place code	Place	County	Land area, 2000 (sq. mi.)	Population, 2000 (April 1) By race— One race Total	White	Black or African American	American Indian and Alaska Native	Asian	Native Hawaiian and Other Pacific Islander	Some other race	Two or more races	Hispanic or Latino (of any race)	18 years and over
17 00000	ILLINOIS—Con.												
17 68081	Schiller Park village	Cook	2.8	11,850	9,596	235	33	609	2	961	414	2,598	9,046
17 68328	Scott AFB CDP	St. Clair	3.8	2,707	2,136	366	9	80	2	49	65	110	1,498
17 69186	Shelbyville city	Shelby	3.7	4,971	4,899	7	9	17	1	13	25	38	3,826
17 69342	Sherman village	Sangamon	3.1	2,871	2,806	9	12	29	2	1	12	15	2,107
17 60524	Shiloh village	St. Clair	10.1	7,643	6,278	1,018	21	137	6	57	126	200	5,529
17 69758	Shorewood village	Will	3.9	7,686	7,126	184	21	102	1	152	100	341	5,394
17 69979	Silvis city	Rock Island	3.6	7,269	6,258	251	34	59	-	473	194	1,044	5,409
17 70122	Skokie village	Cook	10.0	63,348	43,661	2,854	109	13,483	16	1,178	2,047	3,620	48,784
17 70161	Sleepy Hollow village	Kane	2.0	3,553	3,316	23	2	77	1	63	71	134	2,471
17 70564	South Barrington village	Cook	6.6	3,760	3,096	33	2	541	1	20	67	69	2,638
17 70590	South Beloit city	Winnebago	4.0	5,397	4,812	215	34	45	4	188	99	366	3,969
17 70629	South Chicago Heights village	Cook	1.5	3,970	3,142	288	20	42	2	356	120	718	3,095
17 70720	South Elgin village	Kane	6.3	16,100	13,850	415	27	881	2	625	300	1,664	11,412
17 70850	South Holland village	Cook	7.3	22,147	9,975	11,253	37	190	2	428	262	836	16,483
17 70889	South Jacksonville village	Morgan	1.7	3,475	3,382	36	6	23	-	7	21	26	2,765
17 71448	Sparta city	Randolph	9.0	4,486	3,651	702	16	23	-	12	82	61	3,336
17 72000	Springfield city	Sangamon	54.0	111,454	90,287	17,096	231	1,620	34	525	1,661	1,337	84,744
17 72052	Spring Grove village	McHenry	6.2	3,880	3,778	5	6	35	4	14	38	69	2,512
17 72156	Spring Valley city	Bureau	3.9	5,398	5,168	41	9	24	-	92	64	359	4,134
17 72403	Staunton city	Macoupin	2.3	5,030	4,968	5	12	16	2	4	23	37	3,743
17 72520	Steger village	Cook, Will	3.5	9,682	8,482	610	33	47	9	298	203	781	7,260
17 72546	Sterling city	Whiteside	4.7	15,451	13,035	347	63	125	1	1,517	363	2,973	11,571
17 72676	Stickney village	Cook	1.9	6,148	5,581	26	14	67	-	388	72	1,323	4,746
17 72923	Stone Park village	Cook	0.3	5,127	2,768	93	24	104	1	1,992	145	4,057	3,432
17 73157	Streamwood village	Cook	7.3	36,407	28,225	1,398	106	3,145	12	2,570	951	6,108	26,188
17 73170	Streator city	La Salle, Livingston	5.8	14,190	13,378	292	27	70	1	213	209	942	10,520
17 73391	Sugar Grove village	Kane	6.4	3,909	3,747	54	1	20	-	50	37	173	2,641
17 73406	Sullivan city	Moultrie	2.0	4,326	4,269	13	5	7	-	4	28	17	3,339
17 73638	Summit village	Cook	2.1	10,637	6,734	1,282	32	150	2	2,089	348	5,156	7,532
17 74119	Swansea village	St. Clair	5.1	10,579	9,313	909	25	170	8	35	119	163	7,767
17 74223	Sycamore city	DeKalb	5.5	12,020	11,225	329	27	100	2	188	149	513	8,655
17 74574	Taylorville city	Christian	8.1	11,427	11,161	81	22	58	7	35	63	80	8,673
17 75185	Thornton village	Cook	2.3	2,582	2,496	21	3	6	-	22	34	107	1,987
17 75276	Tilton village	Vermilion	3.1	2,976	2,925	5	3	2	-	10	31	32	2,322
17 75484	Tinley Park village	Cook, Will	15.0	48,401	45,092	931	63	1,153	9	539	614	1,998	35,525
17 75614	Tolono village	Champaign	1.9	2,700	2,640	8	14	4	3	10	21	25	1,961
17 75991	Trenton city	Clinton	1.0	2,610	2,570	9	5	14	-	4	8	34	1,963
17 76199	Troy city	Madison	4.2	8,524	8,139	126	27	60	-	32	140	127	5,947
17 76407	Tuscola city	Douglas	2.1	4,448	4,364	14	18	23	1	9	19	47	3,334
17 76935	University Park village	Cook, Will	9.8	6,662	801	5,591	5	22	1	41	201	120	4,389
17 77005	Urbana city	Champaign	10.5	36,395	24,388	5,218	64	5,181	14	639	890	1,288	30,976
17 77317	Vandalia city	Fayette	5.7	6,975	5,829	1,047	9	21	-	35	34	119	5,700
17 77460	Venetian Village CDP	Lake	2.4	3,082	2,921	35	4	25	-	37	60	124	2,191
17 77473	Venice city	Madison	1.9	2,528	139	2,365	9	1	-	-	14	19	1,686
17 77694	Vernon Hills village	Lake	7.4	20,120	16,470	340	21	2,348	6	588	347	1,446	14,249
17 77941	Villa Grove city	Douglas	1.5	2,553	2,504	8	4	2	-	3	32	22	1,887
17 77993	Villa Park village	DuPage	4.7	22,075	19,679	369	39	805	7	806	370	2,770	16,128
17 78149	Virden city	Macoupin, Sangamon	1.7	3,488	3,446	11	14	3	-	2	12	16	2,654
17 78370	Wadsworth village	Lake	8.8	3,083	2,902	53	4	32	-	32	60	109	2,226
17 78929	Warrenville city	DuPage	5.5	13,363	11,910	319	39	459	5	463	168	1,349	9,532
17 79033	Washington city	Tazewell	7.5	10,841	10,663	28	9	46	-	28	67	73	8,020
17 79085	Washington Park village	St. Clair	2.5	5,345	324	4,914	8	7	-	40	52	101	3,365
17 79150	Waterloo city	Monroe	5.6	7,614	7,521	1	22	25	-	13	32	52	5,624
17 79228	Watseka city	Iroquois	2.6	5,670	5,486	35	15	27	-	49	58	148	4,328
17 79267	Wauconda village	Lake	3.9	9,448	8,526	39	25	169	4	600	85	1,125	7,079
17 79293	Waukegan city	Lake	23.0	87,901	44,073	16,890	471	3,146	57	20,185	3,079	39,396	61,348
17 80047	Westchester village	Cook	3.2	16,824	14,494	1,212	11	579	1	334	193	956	13,703
17 80060	West Chicago city	DuPage	13.8	23,469	18,271	395	85	457	7	3,547	707	11,405	16,061
17 80125	West Dundee village	Kane	2.7	5,428	5,098	33	21	120	-	76	80	231	3,908
17 80242	Western Springs village	Cook	2.6	12,493	12,283	23	5	90	-	26	66	212	8,624
17 80333	West Frankfort city	Franklin	4.7	8,196	8,077	11	19	25	-	10	54	63	6,370
17 80645	Westmont village	DuPage	4.9	24,554	19,156	1,321	33	2,935	-	591	518	1,714	19,182
17 80736	West Peoria city	Peoria	1.3	4,762	4,195	406	9	41	-	35	76	66	3,718
17 80931	Westville village	Vermilion	1.6	3,175	3,107	13	6	1	1	12	35	24	2,460
17 81048	Wheaton city	DuPage	11.2	55,416	49,791	1,565	63	2,687	11	571	728	2,023	40,916
17 81087	Wheeling village	Cook, Lake	8.4	34,496	26,452	843	80	3,193	25	3,168	735	7,135	26,420
17 81256	White Hall city	Greene	2.6	2,629	2,587	5	6	1	-	-	10	20	2,020
17 81919	Willowbrook village	DuPage	2.6	8,967	7,589	217	4	898	4	104	151	382	7,341
17 82049	Willow Springs village	Cook	3.9	5,027	4,721	36	6	93	1	54	116	254	3,897
17 82075	Wilmette village	Cook	5.4	27,651	24,791	156	10	2,255	4	117	318	574	19,428
17 82101	Wilmington city	Will	4.2	5,134	4,987	38	18	15	1	31	44	100	3,785
17 82400	Winfield village	DuPage	2.7	8,718	8,160	108	9	258	2	79	102	233	6,092
17 82491	Winnebago village	Winnebago	1.4	2,958	2,903	33	1	9	-	-	12	35	1,944
17 82530	Winnetka village	Cook	3.8	12,419	11,958	31	2	302	-	37	89	156	8,122
17 82686	Winthrop Harbor village	Lake	4.3	6,670	6,256	38	33	127	1	101	114	303	4,844
17 82842	Wonder Lake CDP	McHenry	6.2	7,463	7,181	21	16	44	-	103	98	380	5,298
17 82985	Wood Dale city	DuPage	4.7	13,535	12,076	78	20	439	10	650	262	1,768	10,509

Table D-1. Places — **Area and Population**—Con.

[Includes incorporated places and census designated places (CDPs) of 2,500 or more population as of April 1, 2000. Codes shown are two-digit Federal Information Processing Standards (FIPS) state codes and five-digit FIPS place codes. Place names and codes are those in effect as of January 1, 2000. County refers to the county (or counties) in which the place is located. IC in this column = independent city, a county equivalent. If a place is located in more than one county, counties are listed in alphabetic order]

State and place code	Place	County	Land area, 2000 (sq. mi.)	Population, 2000 (April 1) Total	By race— One race White	Black or African American	American Indian and Alaska Native	Asian	Native Hawaiian and Other Pacific Islander	Some other race	Two or more races	Hispanic or Latino (of any race)	18 years and over
17 00000	ILLINOIS—Con.												
17 83245	Woodridge village	Cook, DuPage, Will	8.3	30,934	23,289	2,482	49	3,485	6	962	661	2,839	22,491
17 83271	Wood River city	Madison	6.1	11,296	11,021	71	31	51	-	40	82	137	8,578
17 83349	Woodstock city	McHenry	10.7	20,151	17,628	214	47	406	-	1,550	306	3,830	14,526
17 83518	Worth village	Cook	2.4	11,047	10,211	176	20	135	2	241	262	669	8,447
17 84038	Yorkville city	Kendall	7.0	6,189	6,003	26	12	24	3	45	76	182	4,332
17 84220	Zion city	Lake	8.2	22,866	13,435	6,196	88	428	16	1,783	920	3,487	15,268
18 00000	INDIANA		35,866.9	6,080,485	5,320,022	510,034	15,815	59,126	2,005	97,811	75,672	214,536	4,506,089
18 00910	Alexandria city	Madison	2.7	6,260	6,141	29	5	7	1	27	50	62	4,522
18 01468	Anderson city	Madison	40.0	59,734	48,978	8,886	187	292	9	516	866	1,235	45,885
18 01666	Angola city	Steuben	4.2	7,344	6,903	60	32	90	3	141	115	286	5,679
18 02620	Attica city	Fountain	1.5	3,491	3,435	1	4	4	-	18	29	53	2,599
18 02674	Auburn city	De Kalb	6.6	12,074	11,797	42	12	50	3	74	96	211	8,883
18 02782	Aurora city	Dearborn	2.8	3,965	3,909	4	13	6	-	10	23	24	2,900
18 02800	Austin town	Scott	2.4	4,724	4,639	3	7	9	-	37	29	72	3,350
18 02908	Avon town	Hendricks	6.4	6,248	5,990	36	16	88	4	45	69	85	4,171
18 03664	Batesville city	Franklin, Ripley	5.8	6,033	5,862	1	8	68	-	55	39	74	4,312
18 04114	Bedford city	Lawrence	11.9	13,768	13,337	109	38	66	1	96	121	173	10,843
18 04204	Beech Grove city	Marion	4.3	14,880	14,321	133	28	120	7	116	155	308	11,132
18 04888	Berne city	Adams	1.8	4,150	4,052	3	3	9	2	43	38	79	3,083
18 05176	Bicknell city	Knox	1.5	3,378	3,315	15	7	5	4	2	30	20	2,522
18 05716	Bloomfield town	Greene	1.4	2,542	2,499	5	2	11	-	8	17	28	2,012
18 05860	Bloomington city	Monroe	19.7	69,291	60,301	2,940	199	3,644	49	763	1,395	1,722	60,503
18 06220	Bluffton city	Wells	6.6	9,536	9,312	32	21	23	7	75	66	224	7,150
18 06616	Boonville city	Warrick	2.9	6,834	6,732	44	14	8	1	2	33	30	5,112
18 07174	Brazil city	Clay	3.3	8,188	8,008	52	30	14	2	23	59	50	6,075
18 07318	Bremen town	Marshall	2.3	4,486	4,101	7	17	14	2	293	52	539	3,262
18 07624	Bright CDP	Dearborn	14.3	5,405	5,320	22	6	5	-	16	36	34	3,693
18 08182	Brookville town	Franklin	1.3	2,652	2,623	1	5	9	-	5	9	14	2,028
18 08416	Brownsburg town	Hendricks	7.3	14,520	14,148	47	25	113	11	51	125	172	10,283
18 08470	Brownstown town	Jackson	1.4	2,978	2,941	3	7	7	3	2	15	18	2,181
18 09532	Butler city	De Kalb	1.8	2,725	2,662	4	5	3	-	34	17	61	1,887
18 10270	Carlisle town	Sullivan	0.5	2,660	1,694	858	24	2	-	42	40	57	2,474
18 10342	Carmel city	Hamilton	17.8	37,733	34,951	555	52	1,651	17	173	334	649	26,325
18 11062	Cedar Lake town	Lake	6.8	9,279	9,038	8	22	19	-	82	110	325	6,634
18 12034	Chandler town	Warrick	1.7	3,094	3,051	11	4	2	2	2	22	18	2,244
18 12124	Charlestown city	Clark	2.3	5,993	5,568	148	16	10	4	166	81	319	4,258
18 12376	Chesterfield town	Delaware, Madison	1.1	2,969	2,922	12	3	9	-	9	14	41	2,250
18 12412	Chesterton town	Porter	8.5	10,488	10,099	46	22	144	2	53	122	347	7,672
18 12628	Cicero town	Hamilton	1.5	4,303	4,212	8	13	12	1	27	30	48	3,169
18 12934	Clarksville town	Clark	10.1	21,400	19,380	1,197	58	200	6	231	328	599	16,465
18 13780	Clinton city	Vermilion	2.2	5,126	5,031	18	19	4	-	8	46	35	3,951
18 14716	Columbia City city	Whitley	5.2	7,077	6,943	23	31	6	2	24	48	85	5,349
18 14734	Columbus city	Bartholomew	25.9	39,059	35,668	1,057	50	1,260	19	542	463	1,096	29,015
18 14932	Connersville city	Fayette	8.1	15,411	14,810	382	18	44	5	20	132	100	11,813
18 15256	Corydon town	Harrison	1.6	2,715	2,641	31	11	3	1	23	5	51	2,168
18 15490	Covington city	Fountain	1.2	2,565	2,533	1	3	10	-	6	12	13	2,028
18 15742	Crawfordsville city	Montgomery	8.4	15,243	14,331	246	47	106	10	364	139	495	11,686
18 16138	Crown Point city	Lake	16.6	19,806	18,879	280	36	195	8	202	206	793	15,352
18 16336	Cumberland town	Hancock, Marion	1.9	5,500	4,686	581	12	97	2	41	81	80	3,850
18 16804	Danville town	Hendricks	6.1	6,418	6,314	22	14	17	1	7	43	68	4,646
18 17074	Decatur city	Adams	4.9	9,528	9,017	23	33	34	6	341	74	733	7,010
18 17614	Delphi city	Carroll	2.6	3,015	2,791	4	6	8	-	177	29	367	2,234
18 17722	De Motte town	Jasper	3.6	3,234	3,202	2	2	2	-	8	18	52	2,426
18 19054	Dunkirk city	Blackford, Jay	1.1	2,646	2,602	8	4	7	2	3	20	17	1,996
18 19072	Dunlap CDP	Elkhart	4.2	5,887	5,398	169	10	55	6	179	70	274	4,191
18 19270	Dyer town	Lake	6.0	13,895	13,258	91	19	222	5	175	125	696	10,263
18 19486	East Chicago city	Lake	12.0	32,414	11,843	11,695	166	66	26	7,774	844	16,728	22,542
18 20404	Edinburgh town	Bartholomew, Johnson, Shelby	2.8	4,505	4,468	6	6	3	1	10	11	48	3,269
18 20728	Elkhart city	Elkhart	21.4	51,874	37,077	7,649	225	608	35	4,750	1,530	7,678	37,139
18 20800	Ellettsville town	Monroe	2.2	5,078	4,866	62	9	37	-	41	63	60	3,551
18 21070	Elwood city	Madison, Tipton	3.5	9,737	9,574	5	12	24	5	66	51	160	7,180
18 22000	Evansville city	Vanderburgh	40.7	121,582	104,858	13,275	257	870	55	598	1,669	1,392	93,949
18 22432	Fairmount town	Grant	1.5	2,992	2,941	5	21	6	-	2	17	13	2,238
18 23278	Fishers town	Hamilton	21.7	37,835	34,910	1,110	44	1,171	7	208	385	764	25,671
18 24286	Fortville town	Hancock	1.2	3,444	3,380	2	2	6	-	25	29	60	2,485
18 25000	Fort Wayne city	Allen	79.0	205,727	155,231	35,752	806	3,205	86	5,993	4,654	11,884	150,153
18 25324	Frankfort city	Clinton	5.1	16,662	15,009	79	27	46	5	1,306	190	2,255	12,164
18 25450	Franklin city	Johnson	11.3	19,463	18,818	229	36	99	10	114	157	254	14,410
18 26386	Garrett city	De Kalb	3.1	5,803	5,656	17	19	29	9	36	37	120	4,135
18 27000	Gary city	Lake	50.2	102,746	12,245	86,340	213	140	24	2,023	1,761	5,065	72,031
18 27054	Gas City city	Grant	3.7	5,940	5,789	18	19	13	4	33	64	90	4,441
18 27372	Georgetown CDP	St. Joseph	1.9	4,497	3,838	345	27	156	3	51	77	122	3,594
18 28386	Goshen city	Elkhart	13.2	29,383	24,431	449	76	324	7	3,526	570	5,679	21,776
18 28800	Granger CDP	St. Joseph	26.2	28,284	26,629	493	35	745	7	73	302	341	19,322
18 29358	Greencastle city	Putnam	5.3	9,880	9,278	264	25	134	8	67	104	141	7,880
18 29448	Greendale city	Dearborn	6.0	4,296	4,206	25	3	21	-	1	40	14	3,298

Table D-1. Places — **Area and Population**—Con.

[Includes incorporated places and census designated places (CDPs) of 2,500 or more population as of April 1, 2000. Codes shown are two-digit Federal Information Processing Standards (FIPS) state codes and five-digit FIPS place codes. Place names and codes are those in effect as of January 1, 2000. County refers to the county (or counties) in which the place is located. IC in this column = independent city, a county equivalent. If a place is located in more than one county, counties are listed in alphabetic order]

State and place code	Place	County	Land area, 2000 (sq. mi.)	Population, 2000 (April 1) Total	By race— One race White	Black or African American	American Indian and Alaska Native	Asian	Native Hawaiian and Other Pacific Islander	Some other race	Two or more races	Hispanic or Latino (of any race)	18 years and over
18 00000	INDIANA—Con.												
18 29520	Greenfield city	Hancock	8.0	14,600	14,341	8	30	78	2	48	93	186	10,927
18 29718	Greensburg city	Decatur	4.8	10,260	10,011	8	16	143	1	10	71	64	7,732
18 29772	Greentown town	Howard	1.0	2,546	2,493	12	8	8	-	7	18	25	1,831
18 29898	Greenwood city	Johnson	14.3	36,037	34,790	159	67	490	15	250	266	687	26,910
18 30042	Griffith town	Lake	7.2	17,334	14,562	1,753	60	140	7	495	317	1,461	12,922
18 30230	Gulivoire Park CDP	St. Joseph	1.4	2,974	2,904	19	-	20	-	9	22	35	2,306
18 31000	Hammond city	Lake	22.9	83,048	60,089	12,102	339	383	64	7,741	2,330	17,473	60,346
18 31216	Hanover town	Jefferson	2.1	2,834	2,737	58	5	9	2	10	13	35	2,046
18 32242	Hartford City city	Blackford	3.7	6,928	6,813	6	26	14	-	15	54	42	5,198
18 32818	Hebron town	Porter	1.5	3,596	3,466	10	4	10	-	46	60	148	2,554
18 33392	Hidden Valley CDP	Dearborn	4.2	4,417	4,321	12	8	22	3	15	36	36	3,178
18 33466	Highland town	Lake	6.9	23,546	22,240	296	36	260	5	425	284	1,557	18,474
18 33484	Highland CDP	Vanderburgh	2.3	4,107	3,997	33	-	48	2	4	23	18	3,031
18 34114	Hobart city	Lake	26.2	25,363	23,773	353	53	136	4	660	384	2,042	19,390
18 35284	Huntingburg city	Dubois	3.6	5,598	5,159	9	13	10	6	356	45	549	4,134
18 35302	Huntington city	Huntington	8.3	17,450	17,072	37	79	78	4	53	127	196	12,881
18 36003	Indianapolis city (balance)	Marion	361.5	781,870	540,212	199,412	1,985	11,161	322	15,921	12,857	30,636	581,253
18 36144	Indian Heights CDP	Howard	0.9	3,274	3,099	93	11	3	-	15	53	80	2,279
18 37782	Jasper city	Dubois	9.2	12,100	11,737	30	10	49	3	186	85	408	9,023
18 38358	Jeffersonville city	Clark	13.6	27,362	22,575	3,742	75	229	22	179	540	493	20,903
18 39402	Kendallville city	Noble	5.1	9,616	9,295	24	15	57	1	132	92	304	6,921
18 40374	Knox city	Starke	3.9	3,721	3,620	4	9	11	1	37	39	85	2,768
18 40392	Kokomo city	Howard	16.2	46,113	39,242	4,770	177	525	12	539	848	1,204	34,599
18 40788	Lafayette city	Tippecanoe	20.1	56,397	50,143	1,816	210	689	24	2,601	914	5,136	43,324
18 40860	Lagrange town	Lagrange	1.7	2,919	2,724	11	1	14	-	137	32	201	2,144
18 41530	Lakes of the Four Seasons CDP	Lake, Porter	2.7	7,291	7,077	9	15	56	1	47	86	284	5,252
18 41535	Lake Station city	Lake	8.3	13,948	12,027	107	70	42	7	1,298	397	2,875	10,172
18 42246	La Porte city	La Porte	11.5	21,621	20,021	416	80	82	1	734	287	1,410	16,334
18 42426	Lawrence city	Marion	20.1	38,915	30,581	6,036	117	699	30	723	729	1,840	27,261
18 42462	Lawrenceburg city	Dearborn	4.9	4,685	4,395	196	7	21	2	15	49	40	3,549
18 42624	Lebanon city	Boone	7.3	14,222	13,891	47	56	53	-	82	93	229	10,425
18 42861	Leo-Cedarville town	Allen	3.7	2,782	2,721	2	8	11	-	8	32	29	1,868
18 43686	Ligonier city	Noble	2.2	4,357	3,191	23	7	18	-	1,076	42	1,451	2,991
18 44190	Linton city	Greene	3.0	5,774	5,676	5	14	14	1	14	50	72	4,464
18 44658	Logansport city	Cass	8.3	19,684	17,674	409	72	177	12	1,108	232	2,476	14,626
18 44910	Loogootee city	Martin	1.6	2,741	2,715	1	3	9	-	1	12	11	2,118
18 45144	Lowell town	Lake	4.1	7,505	7,302	2	29	18	1	84	69	265	5,355
18 45990	Madison city	Jefferson	8.6	12,004	11,357	292	23	100	1	61	170	163	9,419
18 46908	Marion city	Grant	13.3	31,320	24,942	4,878	147	214	7	449	683	1,128	24,031
18 47448	Martinsville city	Morgan	4.5	11,698	11,536	11	31	21	5	29	65	116	8,766
18 48330	Melody Hill CDP	Vanderburgh	1.4	3,066	2,981	48	6	15	-	5	11	21	2,266
18 48528	Merrillville town	Lake	33.3	30,560	21,286	6,987	100	460	6	1,035	686	2,950	23,033
18 48798	Michigan City city	La Porte	19.6	32,900	22,848	8,657	86	167	6	361	775	1,035	24,679
18 48924	Middlebury town	Elkhart	3.4	2,956	2,868	5	4	38	2	8	31	12	2,013
18 49932	Mishawaka city	St. Joseph	15.7	46,557	42,636	1,659	200	649	22	494	897	1,297	35,385
18 49950	Mitchell city	Lawrence	3.4	4,567	4,490	13	5	4	1	6	48	24	3,380
18 50760	Monticello city	White	2.8	5,723	5,230	16	18	34	4	341	80	642	4,333
18 50976	Mooresville town	Morgan	5.5	9,273	9,136	8	28	37	2	17	45	67	6,627
18 51732	Mount Vernon city	Posey	2.5	7,478	7,168	198	12	17	-	19	64	42	5,526
18 51876	Muncie city	Delaware	24.2	67,430	57,799	7,397	183	534	62	451	1,004	971	54,081
18 51912	Munster town	Lake	7.5	21,511	19,851	222	13	965	4	237	219	1,050	16,286
18 52020	Nappanee city	Elkhart, Kosciusko	3.7	6,710	6,407	19	15	23	-	169	77	334	4,720
18 52326	New Albany city	Floyd	14.6	37,603	33,844	2,607	118	159	14	252	609	512	28,570
18 52650	Newburgh town	Warrick	1.4	3,088	3,007	36	1	11	-	10	23	18	2,403
18 52740	New Castle city	Henry	6.0	17,780	17,135	329	40	38	4	73	161	193	13,603
18 52992	New Haven city	Allen	8.2	12,406	12,037	83	41	36	1	54	154	242	9,195
18 53874	New Whiteland town	Johnson	1.2	4,579	4,525	-	13	14	3	6	18	39	3,180
18 54180	Noblesville city	Hamilton	17.9	28,590	27,545	326	58	230	15	179	237	398	20,146
18 54954	North Manchester town	Wabash	3.6	6,260	6,019	58	17	52	4	50	60	109	5,148
18 55098	North Terre Haute CDP	Vigo	3.6	4,606	4,430	118	14	16	-	2	26	46	3,375
18 55116	North Vernon city	Jennings	4.4	6,515	6,285	97	13	26	-	18	76	68	4,725
18 55710	Oakland City city	Gibson	1.1	2,588	2,526	19	5	13	-	11	14	40	2,055
18 55782	Oak Park CDP	Clark	2.2	5,379	4,700	564	8	21	1	14	71	34	4,055
18 57168	Ossian town	Wells	1.5	2,943	2,897	4	3	4	-	13	22	34	2,106
18 57780	Paoli town	Orange	3.8	3,844	3,780	8	9	7	-	7	33	27	2,932
18 58662	Pendleton town	Madison	6.7	3,873	3,806	15	4	18	-	8	22	20	2,879
18 59328	Peru city	Miami	4.6	12,994	12,047	383	197	56	1	72	238	172	9,601
18 59364	Petersburg city	Pike	1.5	2,570	2,546	5	1	1	-	2	15	10	2,016
18 60246	Plainfield town	Hendricks	18.0	18,396	17,496	410	58	168	3	66	195	251	13,495
18 60822	Plymouth city	Marshall	7.0	9,840	8,935	62	44	49	-	609	141	1,475	7,272
18 61092	Portage city	Porter	25.5	33,496	30,992	485	90	215	19	1,072	623	3,330	24,772
18 61164	Porter town	Porter	6.3	4,972	4,780	41	11	29	-	31	80	233	3,566
18 61236	Portland city	Jay	4.1	6,437	6,211	24	7	22	3	116	54	216	4,947
18 62046	Princeton city	Gibson	4.8	8,175	7,469	438	14	103	1	32	118	92	6,205
18 63792	Rensselaer city	Jasper	2.9	5,294	5,185	17	11	5	-	35	41	134	3,957
18 64260	Richmond city	Wayne	23.2	39,124	33,951	3,469	107	312	22	425	838	796	29,956
18 65214	Rochester city	Fulton	4.6	6,414	6,173	29	38	54	-	55	65	119	4,901
18 65520	Rockville town	Parke	1.4	2,765	2,714	4	13	8	-	6	20	23	2,170

U.S. Census Bureau, County and City Data Book: 2000

Table D-1. Places — **Area and Population**—Con.

[Includes incorporated places and census designated places (CDPs) of 2,500 or more population as of April 1, 2000. Codes shown are two-digit Federal Information Processing Standards (FIPS) state codes and five-digit FIPS place codes. Place names and codes are those in effect as of January 1, 2000. County refers to the county (or counties) in which the place is located. IC in this column = independent city, a county equivalent. If a place is located in more than one county, counties are listed in alphabetic order]

State and place code	Place	County	Land area, 2000 (sq. mi.)	Population, 2000 (April 1) Total	White	Black or African American	American Indian and Alaska Native	Asian	Native Hawaiian and Other Pacific Islander	Some other race	Two or more races	Hispanic or Latino (of any race)	18 years and over
18 00000	**INDIANA—Con.**												
18 66006	Roselawn CDP	Jasper, Newton	8.1	3,933	3,827	6	5	11	7	38	39	131	2,779
18 66438	Rushville city	Rush	2.2	5,995	5,782	95	12	51	3	8	44	24	4,487
18 66852	St. John town	Lake	6.7	8,382	8,177	11	14	39	-	63	78	352	6,004
18 67464	Salem city	Washington	3.9	6,172	6,094	2	13	15	-	5	43	26	4,787
18 68220	Schererville town	Lake	13.6	24,851	22,726	533	28	636	11	504	413	1,576	18,820
18 68526	Scottsburg city	Scott	4.8	6,040	5,940	4	17	17	-	16	46	53	4,579
18 68670	Sellersburg town	Clark	4.0	6,071	5,979	15	17	10	1	17	32	63	4,582
18 68832	Seymour city	Jackson	10.8	18,101	16,907	184	55	259	9	531	156	877	13,491
18 69318	Shelbyville city	Shelby	8.9	17,951	17,104	283	27	208	4	162	163	343	13,241
18 69354	Sheridan town	Hamilton	1.3	2,520	2,461	14	3	7	1	8	26	19	1,786
18 69840	Simonton Lake CDP	Elkhart	3.3	4,053	3,841	66	10	63	-	26	47	102	3,055
18 71000	South Bend city	St. Joseph	38.7	107,789	71,195	26,522	440	1,292	69	5,250	3,021	9,110	78,380
18 71288	South Haven CDP	Porter	1.2	5,619	5,442	21	13	14	-	59	70	346	3,985
18 71828	Speedway town	Marion	4.8	12,881	10,712	1,531	36	207	2	155	238	339	10,191
18 71972	Spencer town	Owen	1.3	2,508	2,471	5	-	10	-	6	16	15	1,932
18 74006	Sullivan city	Sullivan	1.9	4,617	4,521	23	17	11	-	6	39	38	3,533
18 74744	Syracuse town	Kosciusko	1.6	3,038	2,848	26	11	17	1	81	54	141	2,237
18 75248	Tell City city	Perry	4.6	7,845	7,739	21	14	18	3	11	39	70	6,127
18 75428	Terre Haute city	Vigo	31.2	59,614	51,422	5,827	202	696	25	304	1,138	942	46,893
18 75986	Tipton city	Tipton	1.9	5,251	5,146	8	9	29	-	14	45	81	4,005
18 76526	Tri-Lakes CDP	Whitley	35.2	3,925	3,881	3	7	12	1	7	14	24	2,898
18 77768	Union City city	Randolph	1.8	3,622	3,406	37	6	8	3	113	49	164	2,708
18 77966	Upland town	Grant	3.9	3,803	3,590	58	26	57	5	26	41	88	3,297
18 78326	Valparaiso city	Porter	10.9	27,428	25,879	440	62	410	5	216	416	917	21,614
18 79208	Vincennes city	Knox	7.1	18,701	17,642	613	47	134	11	90	164	191	14,956
18 79370	Wabash city	Wabash	8.9	11,743	11,373	44	124	60	3	48	91	172	8,890
18 80306	Warsaw city	Kosciusko	10.5	12,415	11,235	175	48	133	2	652	170	1,144	9,184
18 80504	Washington city	Daviess	4.7	11,380	10,845	104	34	44	6	250	97	472	8,479
18 82700	Westfield town	Hamilton	7.6	9,293	8,698	93	37	168	10	173	114	356	6,247
18 82862	West Lafayette city	Tippecanoe	5.5	28,778	23,985	684	45	3,263	9	336	456	920	25,779
18 83816	Whiteland town	Johnson	2.3	3,958	3,897	2	4	14	-	22	19	43	2,685
18 84122	Whiting city	Lake	1.8	5,137	4,488	29	15	47	4	467	87	1,313	3,802
18 84752	Winchester city	Randolph	3.1	5,037	4,952	12	13	15	-	16	29	71	3,919
18 84950	Winona Lake town	Kosciusko	2.9	3,987	3,634	30	1	34	1	229	58	330	2,837
18 86084	Yorktown town	Delaware	3.5	4,785	4,672	46	7	17	-	11	32	35	3,507
18 86372	Zionsville town	Boone	5.8	8,775	8,580	29	10	94	-	28	34	85	5,994
19 00000	**IOWA**		55,869.4	2,926,324	2,748,640	61,853	8,989	36,635	1,009	37,420	31,778	82,473	2,192,686
19 00505	Adel city	Dallas	3.3	3,435	3,358	5	6	14	-	18	34	44	2,455
19 00910	Albia city	Monroe	3.1	3,706	3,629	12	12	23	-	9	21	31	2,774
19 01135	Algona city	Kossuth	4.5	5,741	5,648	5	11	46	1	14	16	41	4,334
19 01630	Altoona city	Polk	7.1	10,345	9,922	95	34	48	42	80	124	171	7,183
19 01855	Ames city	Story	21.6	50,731	44,308	1,343	75	3,906	22	388	689	1,002	43,320
19 01990	Anamosa city	Jones	2.2	5,494	4,983	333	39	28	-	38	73	119	4,413
19 02305	Ankeny city	Polk	16.8	27,117	26,287	206	40	254	7	102	221	293	19,757
19 03520	Atlantic city	Cass	8.1	7,257	7,159	18	9	16	4	30	21	57	5,590
19 05590	Belle Plaine city	Benton	3.2	2,878	2,847	2	1	5	3	2	18	19	2,137
19 05680	Belmond city	Wright	2.9	2,560	2,428	6	3	5	-	101	17	144	1,971
19 06355	Bettendorf city	Scott	21.2	31,275	29,715	494	67	444	4	214	337	772	23,075
19 07030	Bloomfield city	Davis	2.3	2,601	2,563	3	4	5	-	4	22	10	2,061
19 07480	Boone city	Boone	8.9	12,803	12,590	41	28	27	-	45	72	112	9,693
19 09550	Burlington city	Des Moines	14.1	26,839	24,581	1,354	89	177	11	242	385	554	20,266
19 10135	Camanche city	Clinton	8.7	4,215	4,129	23	9	9	1	9	35	29	3,250
19 10765	Carlisle city	Polk, Warren	4.3	3,497	3,429	6	12	7	2	17	24	40	2,532
19 11080	Carroll city	Carroll	5.5	10,106	9,961	18	10	52	-	28	37	58	7,486
19 11215	Carter Lake city	Pottawattamie	1.8	3,248	3,141	8	24	8	-	28	39	94	2,407
19 11755	Cedar Falls city	Black Hawk	28.3	36,145	34,389	568	55	583	8	148	394	389	29,648
19 12000	Cedar Rapids city	Linn	63.1	120,758	110,931	4,481	306	2,135	78	670	2,157	2,065	91,205
19 12315	Centerville city	Appanoose	4.5	5,924	5,767	48	8	22	-	26	53	90	4,542
19 12720	Chariton city	Lucas	3.7	4,573	4,522	7	4	7	-	12	21	40	3,446
19 12765	Charles City city	Floyd	6.2	7,812	7,571	34	12	51	15	62	67	166	6,003
19 13080	Cherokee city	Cherokee	6.4	5,369	5,235	29	12	33	-	29	31	81	4,125
19 13575	Clarinda city	Page	5.2	5,690	5,236	263	37	62	2	29	61	80	4,430
19 13620	Clarion city	Wright	2.7	2,968	2,780	6	7	4	-	164	7	291	2,268
19 14025	Clear Lake city	Cerro Gordo	10.4	8,161	7,915	22	11	75	5	61	72	152	6,288
19 14430	Clinton city	Clinton	35.6	27,772	26,049	893	90	225	3	141	371	466	20,939
19 14520	Clive city	Dallas, Polk	7.2	12,855	11,962	160	10	370	1	161	191	333	9,064
19 16230	Coralville city	Johnson	10.2	15,123	13,152	640	51	786	9	162	323	459	11,808
19 16860	Council Bluffs city	Pottawattamie	37.4	58,268	55,213	614	263	344	15	1,054	765	2,594	43,119
19 17220	Cresco city	Howard	3.3	3,905	3,857	9	6	6	-	1	26	28	2,906
19 17265	Creston city	Union	5.1	7,597	7,455	26	17	26	-	29	44	96	5,879
19 19000	Davenport city	Scott	62.8	98,359	82,311	9,093	368	1,967	24	2,279	2,317	5,268	72,592
19 19405	Decorah city	Winneshiek	6.4	8,172	7,844	92	8	131	1	34	62	106	6,950
19 19945	Denison city	Crawford	6.2	7,339	6,379	117	33	60	1	662	87	1,274	5,430
19 21000	Des Moines city	Polk	75.8	198,682	163,494	16,025	705	6,946	95	6,987	4,430	13,138	149,354
19 21180	De Witt city	Clinton	4.9	5,049	4,954	11	4	32	3	12	33	49	3,686
19 22395	Dubuque city	Dubuque	26.5	57,686	55,466	700	112	390	65	400	553	911	44,049
19 23115	Dyersville city	Delaware, Dubuque	4.6	4,035	3,983	18	-	5	7	2	20	18	2,905

Table D-1. Places — **Area and Population**—Con.

[Includes incorporated places and census designated places (CDPs) of 2,500 or more population as of April 1, 2000. Codes shown are two-digit Federal Information Processing Standards (FIPS) state codes and five-digit FIPS place codes. Place names and codes are those in effect as of January 1, 2000. County refers to the county (or counties) in which the place is located. IC in this column = independent city, a county equivalent. If a place is located in more than one county, counties are listed in alphabetic order]

State and place code	Place	County	Land area, 2000 (sq. mi.)	Population, 2000 (April 1) By race— One race Total	White	Black or African American	American Indian and Alaska Native	Asian	Native Hawaiian and Other Pacific Islander	Some other race	Two or more races	Hispanic or Latino (of any race)	18 years and over
19 00000	IOWA—Con.												
19 23250	Eagle Grove city	Wright	4.0	3,712	3,613	6	2	3	-	50	38	76	2,759
19 24465	Eldora city	Hardin	4.3	3,035	2,898	40	7	21	7	47	15	90	2,131
19 24600	Eldridge city	Scott	9.4	4,159	4,100	10	2	9	-	7	31	67	2,849
19 25590	Emmetsburg city	Palo Alto	3.8	3,958	3,902	3	7	21	-	5	20	33	3,145
19 25860	Estherville city	Emmet	5.2	6,656	6,434	12	11	27	1	126	45	412	5,119
19 25995	Evansdale city	Black Hawk	4.2	4,526	4,365	35	8	25	3	15	75	42	3,371
19 26445	Fairfield city	Jefferson	5.7	9,509	8,972	94	15	241	3	69	115	251	7,254
19 28380	Forest City city	Hancock, Winnebago	4.2	4,362	4,186	25	3	53	1	64	30	142	3,300
19 28515	Fort Dodge city	Webster	14.6	25,136	23,243	952	52	214	6	328	341	739	19,024
19 28605	Fort Madison city	Lee	9.2	10,715	9,926	286	30	65	18	253	137	583	8,183
19 29955	Garner city	Hancock	2.1	2,922	2,892	1	-	11	2	6	10	21	2,169
19 31350	Glenwood city	Mills	2.6	5,358	5,211	33	20	17	-	26	51	79	3,947
19 33060	Grimes city	Dallas, Polk	9.0	5,098	4,955	17	11	45	-	14	56	55	3,433
19 33105	Grinnell city	Poweshiek	5.0	9,105	8,639	95	26	183	9	34	119	143	7,241
19 33195	Grundy Center city	Grundy	2.5	2,596	2,576	1	-	4	-	-	15	14	2,015
19 33960	Hampton city	Franklin	4.3	4,218	3,834	6	11	8	-	324	35	463	3,241
19 34500	Harlan city	Shelby	4.4	5,282	5,192	4	16	25	-	9	36	33	3,958
19 35940	Hiawatha city	Linn	3.5	6,480	6,107	140	20	99	-	24	90	86	4,952
19 37560	Humboldt city	Humboldt	4.6	4,452	4,381	9	2	11	-	29	20	67	3,480
19 38100	Independence city	Buchanan	3.7	6,014	5,892	17	3	46	-	13	43	30	4,488
19 38280	Indianola city	Warren	9.2	12,998	12,728	52	19	66	9	23	101	111	9,908
19 38595	Iowa City city	Johnson	24.2	62,220	54,334	2,333	191	3,509	27	778	1,048	1,833	52,167
19 38640	Iowa Falls city	Hardin	5.0	5,193	5,055	63	8	17	-	22	28	54	4,139
19 39450	Jefferson city	Greene	5.8	4,626	4,532	7	11	18	1	28	29	80	3,529
19 39765	Johnston city	Polk	14.3	8,649	8,320	50	9	173	-	42	55	132	6,082
19 40845	Keokuk city	Lee	9.2	11,427	10,612	446	31	59	1	51	227	125	8,524
19 42015	Knoxville city	Marion	4.4	7,731	7,499	68	24	40	5	22	73	64	5,880
19 44085	Le Claire city	Scott	4.2	2,847	2,782	6	3	12	-	17	27	63	2,088
19 44400	Le Mars city	Plymouth	6.8	9,237	8,982	42	15	28	8	87	75	225	6,722
19 48810	Manchester city	Delaware	4.1	5,257	5,204	5	8	14	2	3	21	43	3,882
19 49215	Maquoketa city	Jackson	3.4	6,112	5,996	10	13	7	21	21	44	60	4,619
19 49395	Marengo city	Iowa	2.1	2,535	2,487	7	1	17	-	7	16	29	1,892
19 49485	Marion city	Linn	12.0	26,294	25,507	157	49	247	9	105	220	289	19,363
19 49755	Marshalltown city	Marshall	18.0	26,009	22,554	348	96	271	17	2,228	475	3,265	19,630
19 50160	Mason City city	Cerro Gordo	25.8	29,172	27,829	342	52	226	3	313	407	1,005	22,296
19 52860	Missouri Valley city	Harrison	3.0	2,992	2,963	1	1	2	-	6	20	21	2,286
19 53625	Monticello city	Jones	3.7	3,607	3,562	7	3	5	-	6	24	42	2,775
19 54705	Mount Pleasant city	Henry	7.7	8,751	7,916	279	28	309	5	64	150	157	6,780
19 54840	Mount Vernon city	Linn	3.5	3,390	3,290	22	8	24	1	14	31	32	2,522
19 55110	Muscatine city	Muscatine	16.8	22,697	20,519	245	83	148	6	1,370	326	2,791	16,716
19 55695	Nevada city	Story	4.2	6,658	6,456	39	9	44	-	36	74	68	5,003
19 56100	New Hampton city	Chickasaw	2.9	3,692	3,641	-	1	17	1	3	29	13	2,840
19 56505	Newton city	Jasper	10.3	15,579	15,197	61	35	94	16	52	124	188	11,903
19 57360	North Liberty city	Johnson	6.8	5,367	5,119	82	9	44	6	42	65	128	3,929
19 57675	Norwalk city	Warren	6.6	6,884	6,729	16	4	39	3	28	65	92	4,611
19 58620	Oelwein city	Fayette	4.8	6,692	6,504	28	13	27	4	43	73	153	5,056
19 59115	Onawa city	Monona	4.9	3,091	3,025	1	36	6	1	1	21	33	2,385
19 59475	Orange City city	Sioux	3.1	5,582	5,443	28	3	54	-	34	20	63	4,317
19 59745	Osage city	Mitchell	2.1	3,451	3,422	6	3	4	-	6	10	25	2,674
19 59835	Osceola city	Clarke	5.8	4,659	4,460	5	9	27	3	128	27	291	3,464
19 59925	Oskaloosa city	Mahaska	6.9	10,938	10,485	127	27	144	4	45	106	138	8,301
19 60465	Ottumwa city	Wapello	15.8	24,998	23,830	318	82	196	5	344	223	691	19,274
19 62040	Pella city	Marion	6.8	9,832	9,470	17	21	232	6	27	59	106	7,706
19 62355	Perry city	Dallas	3.7	7,633	6,323	81	25	57	14	1,007	126	1,873	5,547
19 63525	Pleasant Hill city	Polk	7.8	5,070	4,818	40	14	88	12	57	41	123	3,759
19 66135	Red Oak city	Montgomery	3.7	6,197	6,037	7	31	23	1	69	29	133	4,675
19 68160	Rock Rapids city	Lyon	4.0	2,573	2,551	4	1	9	-	1	7	6	1,969
19 68205	Rock Valley city	Sioux	1.7	2,702	2,661	3	2	9	-	16	11	28	2,016
19 70995	Saylorville CDP	Polk	8.3	3,238	3,117	53	7	27	-	16	18	24	2,435
19 71625	Sergeant Bluff city	Woodbury	2.0	3,321	3,138	30	24	59	-	24	46	63	2,209
19 72390	Sheldon city	O'Brien, Sioux	4.4	4,914	4,790	21	3	38	-	40	22	126	3,756
19 72525	Shenandoah city	Fremont, Page	3.5	5,546	5,430	6	26	12	-	40	32	151	4,302
19 72975	Sibley city	Osceola	1.6	2,796	2,731	6	9	9	1	25	15	62	2,134
19 73290	Sioux Center city	Sioux	5.3	6,002	5,797	9	6	51	2	97	40	280	4,665
19 73335	Sioux City city	Plymouth, Woodbury	54.8	85,013	72,460	2,047	1,661	2,396	33	4,479	1,937	9,257	61,993
19 74280	Spencer city	Clay	10.1	11,317	11,042	16	15	126	5	39	74	162	8,627
19 74415	Spirit Lake city	Dickinson	3.3	4,261	4,218	6	5	2	-	4	26	27	3,212
19 75630	Storm Lake city	Buena Vista	4.0	10,076	8,029	53	17	788	2	962	225	2,121	7,648
19 75675	Story City city	Story	2.4	3,228	3,188	9	6	12	-	4	9	14	2,471
19 77115	Tama city	Tama	3.0	2,731	2,377	11	131	11	-	143	58	263	1,984
19 78285	Tipton city	Cedar	1.8	3,155	3,111	11	1	10	-	2	20	34	2,410
19 78510	Toledo city	Tama	2.3	2,539	2,222	13	148	9	1	74	72	149	1,844
19 79950	Urbandale city	Dallas, Polk	20.7	29,072	27,670	445	26	503	29	148	251	465	21,421
19 81210	Vinton city	Benton	4.3	5,102	5,013	13	9	14	1	11	41	48	3,826
19 82335	Washington city	Washington	4.8	7,047	6,709	40	8	25	3	192	70	332	5,440
19 82425	Waterloo city	Black Hawk	60.7	68,747	56,103	9,529	150	587	34	989	1,355	1,806	51,783
19 82695	Waukee city	Dallas	8.4	5,126	5,032	22	-	29	1	16	26	38	3,566
19 82740	Waukon city	Allamakee	2.9	4,131	4,079	-	4	9	1	6	32	30	3,188

Table D-1. Places — **Area and Population**—Con.

[Includes incorporated places and census designated places (CDPs) of 2,500 or more population as of April 1, 2000. Codes shown are two-digit Federal Information Processing Standards (FIPS) state codes and five-digit FIPS place codes. Place names and codes are those in effect as of January 1, 2000. County refers to the county (or counties) in which the place is located. IC in this column = independent city, a county equivalent. If a place is located in more than one county, counties are listed in alphabetic order]

State and place code	Place	County	Land area, 2000 (sq. mi.)	Population, 2000 (April 1)									
					By race—								
					One race								
				Total	White	Black or African American	American Indian and Alaska Native	Asian	Native Hawaiian and Other Pacific Islander	Some other race	Two or more races	Hispanic or Latino (of any race)	18 years and over
19 00000	IOWA—Con.												
19 82875	Waverly city	Bremer	11.2	8,968	8,709	94	10	78	1	11	65	55	7,041
19 83145	Webster City city	Hamilton	8.6	8,176	7,801	27	21	200	1	39	87	108	6,202
19 83685	West Burlington city	Des Moines	5.0	3,161	2,994	79	2	33	-	18	35	97	2,497
19 83910	West Des Moines city	Dallas, Polk	26.8	46,403	42,995	868	61	1,280	16	585	598	1,404	34,955
19 84315	West Liberty city	Muscatine	1.6	3,332	2,239	10	14	118	-	833	118	1,349	2,340
19 84765	West Union city	Fayette	2.7	2,549	2,483	6	6	18	-	5	31	35	1,973
19 85845	Williamsburg city	Iowa	3.1	2,622	2,569	3	1	6	3	26	14	45	1,865
19 86070	Wilton city	Cedar, Muscatine	1.9	2,829	2,765	6	6	13	-	17	22	57	2,044
19 86250	Windsor Heights city	Polk	1.4	4,805	4,568	83	4	60	3	28	59	76	3,861
19 86520	Winterset city	Madison	3.5	4,768	4,714	3	7	13	-	6	25	28	3,537
20 00000	KANSAS		81,814.9	2,688,418	2,313,944	154,198	24,936	46,806	1,313	90,725	56,496	188,252	1,975,425
20 00125	Abilene city	Dickinson	4.1	6,543	6,250	66	34	25	-	63	105	178	4,926
20 01800	Andover city	Butler	6.8	6,698	6,372	35	37	70	1	69	114	160	4,463
20 02300	Arkansas City city	Cowley	7.5	11,963	10,426	539	322	77	2	233	364	535	8,891
20 02900	Atchison city	Atchison	6.8	10,232	9,061	798	52	42	9	66	204	264	7,602
20 03300	Augusta city	Butler	4.0	8,423	8,092	15	70	30	-	57	159	218	6,063
20 03900	Baldwin City city	Douglas	2.2	3,400	3,183	38	25	21	2	13	118	55	2,539
20 04625	Baxter Springs city	Cherokee	3.1	4,602	4,051	45	232	9	8	22	235	60	3,382
20 05337	Bel Aire city	Sedgwick	2.2	5,836	4,988	427	26	215	1	64	115	176	3,915
20 05775	Beloit city	Mitchell	4.0	4,019	3,896	31	14	15	2	7	54	43	3,041
20 07975	Bonner Springs city	Johnson, Wyandotte	15.8	6,768	6,105	274	57	31	-	183	118	419	4,859
20 09400	Burlington city	Coffey	2.1	2,790	2,677	9	16	19	-	17	52	50	2,064
20 12500	Chanute city	Neosho	6.1	9,411	8,771	134	104	44	4	131	223	366	7,035
20 13625	Clay Center city	Clay	2.6	4,564	4,472	29	15	9	-	3	36	24	3,515
20 14600	Coffeyville city	Montgomery	7.1	11,021	8,350	1,336	548	66	4	180	537	421	8,376
20 14650	Colby city	Thomas	3.3	5,450	5,272	35	21	21	1	55	45	108	4,137
20 15075	Columbus city	Cherokee	2.4	3,396	3,216	11	53	14	-	26	76	69	2,503
20 15200	Concordia city	Cloud	3.4	5,714	5,594	33	14	22	-	8	43	42	4,499
20 17800	Derby city	Sedgwick	7.4	17,807	16,742	237	139	179	25	167	318	533	12,073
20 17850	De Soto city	Johnson	11.3	4,561	4,324	9	43	17	3	77	88	313	3,171
20 18250	Dodge City city	Ford	12.6	25,176	17,983	488	173	596	38	5,241	657	10,793	17,316
20 20000	Edwardsville city	Wyandotte	9.0	4,146	3,745	205	15	10	-	73	98	198	3,068
20 20075	El Dorado city	Butler	6.4	12,057	11,372	165	129	27	8	128	228	353	9,021
20 20500	Ellsworth city	Ellsworth	2.1	2,965	2,621	224	28	15	1	28	48	117	2,452
20 21275	Emporia city	Lyon	9.9	26,760	21,041	793	128	712	1	3,411	674	5,752	19,992
20 21675	Eudora city	Douglas	2.0	4,307	4,086	30	63	21	1	29	77	103	2,984
20 21800	Eureka city	Greenwood	2.0	2,914	2,805	4	23	4	-	28	50	77	2,238
20 22700	Fairway city	Johnson	1.1	3,952	3,801	16	14	49	-	30	42	88	3,088
20 23990	Fort Riley North CDP	Geary, Riley	5.1	8,114	4,865	1,995	100	170	47	514	423	1,052	5,735
20 24000	Fort Scott city	Bourbon	5.4	8,297	7,594	427	77	44	5	33	117	139	6,231
20 24575	Fredonia city	Wilson	2.4	2,600	2,503	10	22	14	2	15	34	65	1,973
20 24850	Frontenac city	Crawford	4.0	2,996	2,927	6	21	2	-	13	27	22	2,293
20 25100	Galena city	Cherokee	4.6	3,287	2,938	25	194	2	-	29	99	59	2,421
20 25325	Garden City city	Finney	8.5	28,451	19,574	425	301	1,009	27	6,338	777	12,492	19,164
20 25425	Gardner city	Johnson	4.9	9,396	8,844	114	46	99	1	118	174	281	6,288
20 25925	Garnett city	Anderson	3.0	3,368	3,266	13	35	9	2	18	25	49	2,546
20 26300	Girard city	Crawford	1.9	2,773	2,688	29	15	3	1	6	31	19	2,085
20 26875	Goodland city	Sherman	4.4	4,948	4,619	21	16	12	6	224	50	447	3,797
20 28300	Great Bend city	Barton	10.6	15,345	13,781	248	66	47	2	886	315	2,025	11,401
20 31100	Hays city	Ellis	7.6	20,013	19,098	159	49	219	5	287	196	527	15,709
20 31125	Haysville city	Sedgwick	3.5	8,502	7,980	45	97	45	1	120	214	272	5,885
20 31400	Herington city	Dickinson, Morris	2.1	2,563	2,455	16	10	13	1	42	26	116	1,949
20 31600	Hesston city	Harvey	2.6	3,509	3,318	52	21	29	-	44	45	101	2,647
20 31675	Hiawatha city	Brown	2.2	3,417	3,124	95	75	5	-	41	77	102	2,582
20 32275	Hillsboro city	Marion	2.0	2,854	2,782	10	10	9	-	16	27	43	2,271
20 32550	Hoisington city	Barton	1.2	2,975	2,848	32	20	-	-	35	40	108	2,236
20 32825	Holton city	Jackson	2.4	3,353	3,123	38	97	7	-	18	70	73	2,571
20 33425	Hugoton city	Stevens	1.8	3,708	3,023	40	25	12	-	538	70	850	2,576
20 33625	Hutchinson city	Reno	21.1	40,787	36,125	1,747	267	242	15	1,490	901	3,130	31,332
20 33875	Independence city	Montgomery	5.0	9,846	8,566	706	114	61	1	108	290	378	7,312
20 34300	Iola city	Allen	4.2	6,302	5,906	178	44	14	-	46	114	114	4,698
20 35750	Junction City city	Geary	7.6	18,886	11,025	5,041	155	724	74	757	1,110	1,569	13,557
20 36000	Kansas City city	Wyandotte	124.3	146,866	81,910	44,240	1,103	2,527	56	12,645	4,385	24,639	104,917
20 36950	Kingman city	Kingman	3.5	3,387	3,308	7	12	17	-	10	33	65	2,494
20 38650	Lansing city	Leavenworth	8.5	9,199	7,447	1,146	112	122	14	123	235	354	7,172
20 38700	Larned city	Pawnee	2.3	4,236	3,851	159	41	32	-	75	78	228	3,240
20 38900	Lawrence city	Douglas	28.1	80,098	67,122	4,078	2,344	3,030	56	1,086	2,382	2,921	65,227
20 39000	Leavenworth city	Leavenworth	23.5	35,420	27,192	5,781	270	523	59	609	986	1,800	25,619
20 39075	Leawood city	Johnson	15.1	27,656	26,326	405	38	603	2	70	212	360	19,316
20 39350	Lenexa city	Johnson	34.3	40,238	36,013	1,312	152	1,459	12	644	646	1,598	29,892
20 39825	Liberal city	Seward	11.1	19,666	12,499	827	141	640	12	4,903	644	8,513	13,439
20 41375	Lindsborg city	McPherson	1.5	3,321	3,223	37	13	10	-	10	28	53	2,639
20 42875	Louisburg city	Miami	3.3	2,576	2,530	8	9	2	1	3	23	27	1,855
20 43525	Lyons city	Rice	2.2	3,732	3,402	73	28	12	4	140	73	449	2,742
20 43950	McPherson city	McPherson	6.1	13,770	13,096	181	50	57	13	167	206	402	10,249
20 44250	Manhattan city	Pottawatomie, Riley	15.0	44,831	39,130	2,179	214	1,764	33	582	929	1,564	37,732
20 45050	Marysville city	Marshall	3.3	3,271	3,207	5	11	16	-	5	27	24	2,527

Table D-1. Places — **Area and Population**—Con.

[Includes incorporated places and census designated places (CDPs) of 2,500 or more population as of April 1, 2000. Codes shown are two-digit Federal Information Processing Standards (FIPS) state codes and five-digit FIPS place codes. Place names and codes are those in effect as of January 1, 2000. County refers to the county (or counties) in which the place is located. IC in this column = independent city, a county equivalent. If a place is located in more than one county, counties are listed in alphabetic order]

State and place code	Place	County	Land area, 2000 (sq. mi.)	Population, 2000 (April 1) Total	By race— One race White	Black or African American	American Indian and Alaska Native	Asian	Native Hawaiian and Other Pacific Islander	Some other race	Two or more races	Hispanic or Latino (of any race)	18 years and over
20 00000	KANSAS—Con.												
20 46000	Merriam city	Johnson	4.3	11,008	9,824	443	46	230	2	215	248	596	8,621
20 47225	Mission city	Johnson	2.5	9,727	8,652	368	32	268	1	197	209	478	8,159
20 47350	Mission Hills city	Johnson	2.0	3,593	3,529	3	1	31	-	6	23	39	2,530
20 49100	Mulvane city	Sedgwick, Sumner	2.3	5,155	4,969	9	51	15	3	31	77	133	3,587
20 49650	Neodesha city	Wilson	1.1	2,848	2,748	10	19	6	-	24	41	60	2,063
20 50475	Newton city	Harvey	9.6	17,190	14,909	395	91	113	5	1,175	502	2,189	12,664
20 51500	Norton city	Norton	1.9	3,012	2,949	1	12	10	1	19	20	61	2,275
20 51810	Oaklawn-Sunview CDP	Sedgwick	0.5	3,135	1,966	280	75	485	1	168	160	356	2,034
20 52575	Olathe city	Johnson	54.2	92,962	82,393	3,440	402	2,549	44	2,457	1,677	5,060	64,285
20 53200	Osage City city	Osage	3.4	3,034	2,922	11	32	2	12	16	39	71	2,213
20 53225	Osawatomie city	Miami	4.4	4,645	4,283	193	22	10	2	35	100	118	3,381
20 53550	Ottawa city	Franklin	6.7	11,921	11,059	275	145	63	1	156	222	496	8,747
20 53775	Overland Park city	Johnson	56.7	149,080	135,137	3,801	401	5,703	52	1,852	2,134	5,620	110,072
20 54250	Paola city	Miami	4.1	5,011	4,682	178	37	15	-	22	77	104	3,605
20 54450	Park City city	Sedgwick	5.6	5,814	5,296	137	80	28	-	189	84	325	3,948
20 54675	Parsons city	Labette	10.4	11,514	9,849	941	129	48	1	219	327	534	8,500
20 55675	Phillipsburg city	Phillips	1.6	2,668	2,602	7	3	25	-	2	29	25	2,024
20 56025	Pittsburg city	Crawford	12.4	19,243	17,266	598	207	374	32	365	401	722	15,240
20 57575	Prairie Village city	Johnson	6.2	22,072	21,222	172	36	249	6	142	245	502	17,174
20 57625	Pratt city	Pratt	7.4	6,570	6,233	66	25	42	2	128	74	227	4,971
20 60825	Roeland Park city	Johnson	1.6	6,817	6,298	134	31	97	7	147	103	453	5,330
20 61250	Rose Hill city	Butler	1.6	3,432	3,326	9	23	14	4	12	44	62	2,138
20 61825	Russell city	Russell	4.9	4,696	4,561	31	27	21	1	14	41	47	3,642
20 62025	Sabetha city	Brown, Nemaha	3.2	2,589	2,531	24	4	5	1	5	19	8	1,983
20 62700	Salina city	Saline	22.7	45,679	40,090	1,630	256	896	21	1,728	1,058	3,067	33,832
20 63600	Scott City city	Scott	2.2	3,855	3,669	5	19	6	-	111	45	280	2,851
20 64500	Shawnee city	Johnson	41.7	47,996	43,362	1,422	149	1,273	13	897	880	2,093	35,139
20 66750	South Hutchinson city	Reno	2.8	2,539	2,373	20	15	6	1	82	42	135	1,988
20 67625	Spring Hill city	Johnson, Miami	3.5	2,727	2,631	22	23	4	1	14	32	76	1,858
20 68200	Sterling city	Rice	1.4	2,642	2,521	40	20	18	-	19	24	46	2,129
20 70800	Tonganoxie city	Leavenworth	3.1	2,728	2,598	32	24	10	7	18	39	62	1,909
20 71000	Topeka city	Shawnee	56.0	122,377	96,093	14,332	1,603	1,340	50	4,969	3,990	10,847	92,672
20 71975	Ulysses city	Grant	2.9	5,960	4,477	17	57	27	-	1,263	119	2,236	4,009
20 73250	Valley Center city	Sedgwick	3.3	4,883	4,726	16	27	18	-	34	62	110	3,448
20 75325	Wamego city	Pottawatomie	1.6	4,246	4,108	31	15	5	-	33	54	80	2,997
20 76475	Wellington city	Sumner	5.7	8,647	7,986	148	107	25	9	223	149	628	6,263
20 79000	Wichita city	Sedgwick	135.8	344,284	258,900	39,325	3,986	13,647	198	17,566	10,662	33,112	250,907
20 79950	Winfield city	Cowley	11.1	12,206	10,748	398	132	456	2	211	259	569	9,166
21 00000	KENTUCKY		39,728.2	4,041,769	3,640,889	295,994	8,616	29,744	1,460	22,623	42,443	59,939	3,046,951
21 00802	Alexandria city	Campbell	5.4	8,286	8,188	2	2	38	-	28	28	63	5,736
21 02368	Ashland city	Boyd	11.1	21,981	21,066	505	26	86	2	49	247	130	17,165
21 03574	Barbourville city	Knox	3.5	3,589	3,388	116	20	9	-	6	50	21	2,795
21 03628	Bardstown city	Nelson	7.2	10,374	8,518	1,563	13	98	1	70	111	143	7,502
21 04654	Beaver Dam city	Ohio	2.5	3,033	2,824	104	5	8	2	52	38	78	2,330
21 05446	Bellevue city	Campbell	0.9	6,480	6,376	14	21	22	1	8	38	57	4,864
21 05824	Benton city	Marshall	3.9	4,197	4,112	26	7	14	1	14	23	38	3,394
21 05842	Berea city	Madison	9.3	9,851	9,106	424	36	86	1	47	151	98	7,724
21 08902	Bowling Green city	Warren	35.4	49,296	39,842	6,267	111	959	61	1,065	991	2,011	39,342
21 09964	Brooks CDP	Bullitt	4.7	2,678	2,606	19	18	6	-	5	24	29	1,987
21 10648	Buckner CDP	Oldham	7.4	4,000	3,230	730	3	10	-	15	12	29	3,428
21 10666	Buechel CDP	Jefferson	2.5	7,272	5,558	1,299	17	103	1	168	126	296	5,646
21 11170	Burlington CDP	Boone	8.4	10,779	10,208	204	31	120	1	101	114	187	7,534
21 12016	Calvert City city	Marshall	13.9	2,701	2,674	-	7	2	-	1	17	10	2,133
21 12160	Campbellsville city	Taylor	6.0	10,498	9,355	918	15	31	4	64	111	123	8,211
21 13024	Carrollton city	Carroll	2.2	3,846	3,615	86	5	7	-	78	55	170	2,960
21 13978	Central City city	Muhlenberg	5.2	5,893	5,190	629	3	14	1	24	32	47	4,707
21 15166	Claryville CDP	Campbell	7.0	2,588	2,565	7	3	3	-	2	8	12	1,911
21 16372	Cold Spring city	Campbell	4.7	3,806	3,743	16	8	18	-	-	21	12	2,885
21 16750	Columbia city	Adair	3.4	4,014	3,628	296	9	24	1	8	48	41	3,290
21 17362	Corbin city	Knox, Whitley	7.4	7,742	7,614	6	14	25	1	13	69	61	5,940
21 17848	Covington city	Kenton	13.1	43,370	37,752	4,397	105	147	15	272	682	600	32,151
21 18352	Crescent Springs city	Kenton	1.4	3,931	3,766	54	2	70	1	5	33	35	2,895
21 18442	Crestview Hills city	Kenton	1.9	2,889	2,728	75	4	50	3	9	20	15	2,343
21 19108	Cumberland city	Harlan	4.6	2,611	2,444	133	13	1	-	1	19	22	1,946
21 19432	Cynthiana city	Harrison	3.3	6,258	5,784	331	10	11	3	51	68	88	4,837
21 19882	Danville city	Boyle	15.8	15,477	12,949	2,015	38	128	6	127	214	229	12,013
21 20224	Dawson Springs city	Caldwell, Hopkins	3.9	2,980	2,912	28	8	9	-	2	21	8	2,293
21 20350	Dayton city	Campbell	1.3	5,966	5,866	27	11	10	1	5	46	35	4,285
21 22204	Douglass Hills city	Jefferson	1.3	5,718	5,105	397	3	101	4	70	38	166	4,436
21 23932	Edgewood city	Kenton	4.2	9,400	9,155	36	-	126	6	28	49	83	6,667
21 24274	Elizabethtown city	Hardin	24.1	22,542	19,395	2,186	67	425	13	127	329	403	16,931
21 24778	Elsmere city	Kenton	2.5	8,139	7,497	445	13	27	4	46	107	124	5,818
21 25300	Erlanger city	Kenton	8.3	16,676	16,023	302	13	119	4	70	145	253	12,281
21 25966	Fairdale CDP	Jefferson	5.7	7,658	7,412	68	29	27	1	27	94	100	5,567
21 27046	Fern Creek CDP	Jefferson	5.8	17,870	15,711	1,396	25	310	6	176	246	369	13,160
21 27802	Flatwoods city	Greenup	4.5	7,605	7,467	29	15	27	-	23	44	44	5,853

Table D-1. Places — **Area and Population**—Con.

[Includes incorporated places and census designated places (CDPs) of 2,500 or more population as of April 1, 2000. Codes shown are two-digit Federal Information Processing Standards (FIPS) state codes and five-digit FIPS place codes. Place names and codes are those in effect as of January 1, 2000. County refers to the county (or counties) in which the place is located. IC in this column = independent city, a county equivalent. If a place is located in more than one county, counties are listed in alphabetic order]

State and place code	Place	County	Land area, 2000 (sq. mi.)	Population, 2000 (April 1) Total	By race— One race White	Black or African American	American Indian and Alaska Native	Asian	Native Hawaiian and Other Pacific Islander	Some other race	Two or more races	Hispanic or Latino (of any race)	18 years and over
21 00000	KENTUCKY—Con.												
21 27856	Flemingsburg city	Fleming	2.6	3,010	2,791	152	3	12	-	13	39	31	2,310
21 27982	Florence city	Boone	9.9	23,551	21,771	629	61	353	15	372	350	896	17,686
21 28486	Fort Campbell North CDP	Christian	4.0	14,338	8,396	3,703	142	248	147	1,019	683	1,985	9,235
21 28540	Fort Knox CDP	Hardin, Meade	20.9	12,377	8,208	2,856	90	204	54	516	449	1,281	8,058
21 28558	Fort Mitchell city	Kenton	3.1	8,089	7,836	80	8	65	2	38	60	69	6,157
21 28594	Fort Thomas city	Campbell	5.7	16,495	16,100	120	23	109	-	36	107	103	12,372
21 28612	Fort Wright city	Kenton	3.5	5,681	5,529	56	3	45	1	12	35	39	4,459
21 28900	Frankfort city	Franklin	14.7	27,741	22,704	4,078	35	260	8	213	443	411	21,747
21 28918	Franklin city	Simpson	7.4	7,996	6,476	1,340	17	61	8	21	73	65	5,979
21 29566	Fulton city	Fulton	2.8	2,775	1,869	816	7	19	-	24	40	40	2,075
21 30700	Georgetown city	Scott	13.7	18,080	16,033	1,449	41	115	1	186	255	360	13,450
21 31114	Glasgow city	Barren	14.7	13,019	11,576	1,074	17	104	9	105	134	186	10,150
21 32523	Graymoor-Devondale city	Jefferson	0.7	2,925	2,644	152	9	71	5	17	27	50	2,347
21 32572	Grayson city	Carter	2.5	3,877	3,812	20	15	11	1	7	11	30	3,028
21 33022	Greenville city	Muhlenberg	4.8	4,398	3,953	385	7	4	-	5	44	13	3,560
21 34966	Harrodsburg city	Mercer	5.3	8,014	7,126	603	11	61	2	91	120	172	5,999
21 35020	Hartford city	Ohio	2.6	2,571	2,489	36	12	6	-	6	22	22	2,002
21 35362	Hazard city	Perry	7.0	4,806	4,338	316	4	99	-	7	42	22	3,755
21 35866	Henderson city	Henderson	15.0	27,373	23,885	2,883	48	110	2	159	286	347	20,929
21 35902	Hendron CDP	McCracken	5.2	4,239	4,052	95	11	28	-	18	35	53	3,328
21 36298	Hickman city	Fulton	3.6	2,560	1,640	895	2	-	-	1	22	13	1,923
21 36604	Highland Heights city	Campbell	2.3	6,554	6,261	139	3	81	1	19	50	47	5,363
21 36730	Highview CDP	Jefferson	6.5	15,161	13,537	1,180	25	117	7	123	172	307	11,617
21 36982	Hillview city	Bullitt	4.2	7,037	6,889	26	33	20	-	8	61	49	5,019
21 37396	Hodgenville city	Larue	1.7	2,874	2,490	324	7	2	-	10	41	34	2,220
21 37918	Hopkinsville city	Christian	24.0	30,089	19,875	9,302	69	229	26	178	410	508	22,141
21 38814	Hurstbourne city	Jefferson	1.9	3,884	3,552	117	4	165	-	9	37	42	3,169
21 39142	Independence city	Kenton	16.8	14,982	14,563	144	27	60	3	54	131	173	10,426
21 39304	Indian Hills city	Jefferson	2.0	2,882	2,758	50	-	46	1	1	26	42	2,201
21 39646	Irvine city	Estill	1.5	2,843	2,822	1	6	-	-	1	13	16	2,192
21 40222	Jeffersontown city	Jefferson	10.0	26,633	23,101	2,305	57	471	7	304	388	677	20,039
21 43480	La Grange city	Oldham	3.7	5,676	5,135	289	10	22	3	132	85	202	4,062
21 43606	Lakeside Park city	Kenton	0.8	2,869	2,775	46	3	8	-	17	20	33	2,210
21 43840	Lancaster city	Garrard	1.8	3,734	3,291	359	3	-	-	42	39	73	2,875
21 44146	Lawrenceburg city	Anderson	3.7	9,014	8,500	370	15	15	1	24	89	100	6,539
21 44344	Lebanon city	Marion	4.4	5,718	4,453	1,139	7	42	-	27	50	59	4,365
21 44686	Leitchfield city	Grayson	8.8	6,139	5,932	96	16	11	1	20	63	59	4,575
21 46027	Lexington-Fayette	Fayette	284.5	260,512	211,120	35,116	507	6,407	83	3,165	4,114	8,561	204,979
21 47476	London city	Laurel	7.7	5,692	5,466	104	19	39	-	6	58	27	4,591
21 48000	Louisville city	Jefferson	62.1	256,231	161,261	84,586	578	3,705	111	1,709	4,281	4,755	195,622
21 48378	Ludlow city	Kenton	0.9	4,409	4,341	17	4	6	-	8	33	33	3,140
21 48558	Lyndon city	Jefferson	3.4	9,369	8,022	854	26	199	5	108	155	262	7,545
21 49368	Madisonville city	Hopkins	17.8	19,307	16,644	2,170	35	99	6	121	232	259	14,692
21 50034	Marion city	Crittenden	3.3	3,196	3,089	56	6	1	-	9	35	27	2,544
21 50556	Massac CDP	McCracken	3.9	3,888	3,686	105	10	33	2	9	43	49	2,930
21 50898	Mayfield city	Graves	6.7	10,349	8,338	1,377	22	38	-	360	214	606	7,934
21 51024	Maysville city	Mason	19.9	8,993	7,734	1,038	13	54	3	45	106	77	6,950
21 51924	Middlesborough city	Bell	7.6	10,384	9,641	509	39	65	4	20	106	82	7,933
21 51978	Middletown city	Jefferson	4.9	5,744	5,192	318	17	83	5	38	91	86	4,318
21 53130	Monticello city	Wayne	6.1	5,981	5,660	145	24	17	-	80	55	177	4,484
21 53418	Morehead city	Rowan	9.2	5,914	5,574	152	9	90	1	7	81	45	4,998
21 53472	Morganfield city	Union	2.1	3,494	2,877	567	1	6	-	6	37	30	2,637
21 53490	Morgantown city	Butler	3.4	2,544	2,430	28	4	8	-	60	14	82	1,960
21 54084	Mount Sterling city	Montgomery	3.4	5,876	5,235	513	13	11	-	44	60	99	4,543
21 54174	Mount Vernon city	Rockcastle	3.2	2,592	2,552	17	4	4	-	1	14	10	2,024
21 54228	Mount Washington city	Bullitt	5.3	8,485	8,337	27	27	13	-	23	58	49	6,028
21 54642	Murray city	Calloway	9.7	14,950	13,180	1,017	31	411	3	102	206	259	12,924
21 55542	Newburg CDP	Jefferson	5.7	20,636	7,873	11,986	55	179	10	181	352	560	14,508
21 55884	Newport city	Campbell	2.7	17,048	15,628	937	49	67	6	115	246	287	12,554
21 56136	Nicholasville city	Jessamine	8.5	19,680	18,313	862	50	56	9	117	273	296	14,129
21 57030	Oakbrook CDP	Boone	3.3	7,726	7,325	142	8	162	-	28	61	82	5,569
21 57090	Oak Grove city	Christian	10.3	7,064	4,360	1,823	73	116	36	278	378	665	4,788
21 57612	Okolona CDP	Jefferson	6.9	17,807	15,717	1,291	47	236	7	205	304	567	13,661
21 58620	Owensboro city	Daviess	17.4	54,067	48,999	3,728	66	276	12	295	691	557	41,024
21 58836	Paducah city	McCracken	19.5	26,307	19,145	6,353	66	169	20	144	410	362	20,384
21 58962	Paintsville city	Johnson	5.3	4,132	4,028	27	8	25	1	4	39	31	3,257
21 59196	Paris city	Bourbon	6.8	9,183	7,735	1,167	15	15	-	124	127	241	6,863
21 59255	Park Hills city	Kenton	0.8	2,977	2,877	49	2	23	-	9	17	18	2,386
21 60852	Pikeville city	Pike	15.4	6,295	5,954	166	11	79	3	16	66	88	4,895
21 61356	Pioneer Village city	Bullitt	1.2	2,555	2,506	7	1	19	-	8	14	15	1,802
21 61752	Pleasure Ridge Park CDP	Jefferson	8.3	25,776	24,330	990	51	112	9	77	207	232	19,633
21 62940	Prestonsburg city	Floyd	10.9	3,612	3,522	12	18	19	-	16	25	37	2,882
21 63138	Princeton city	Caldwell	9.1	6,536	5,830	589	9	18	-	42	48	60	5,060
21 63264	Prospect city	Jefferson, Oldham	4.0	4,657	4,327	158	12	96	1	10	53	30	3,376
21 63372	Providence city	Webster	6.1	3,611	2,958	597	4	3	3	10	36	31	2,731
21 63912	Radcliff city	Hardin	11.5	21,961	13,782	5,632	134	772	90	572	979	1,243	15,560
21 64632	Reidland CDP	McCracken	4.8	4,353	4,265	13	6	31	1	12	25	28	3,377
21 65226	Richmond city	Madison	19.1	27,152	23,976	2,246	80	297	8	116	429	328	22,395

U.S. Census Bureau, County and City Data Book: 2000

Table D-1. Places — **Area and Population**—Con.

[Includes incorporated places and census designated places (CDPs) of 2,500 or more population as of April 1, 2000. Codes shown are two-digit Federal Information Processing Standards (FIPS) state codes and five-digit FIPS place codes. Place names and codes are those in effect as of January 1, 2000. County refers to the county (or counties) in which the place is located. IC in this column = independent city, a county equivalent. If a place is located in more than one county, counties are listed in alphabetic order]

State and place code	Place	County	Land area, 2000 (sq. mi.)	Population, 2000 (April 1) Total	White	Black or African American	American Indian and Alaska Native	Asian	Native Hawaiian and Other Pacific Islander	Some other race	Two or more races	Hispanic or Latino (of any race)	18 years and over
								By race— One race					

State and place code	Place	County	Land area, 2000 (sq. mi.)	Total	White	Black or African American	American Indian and Alaska Native	Asian	Native Hawaiian and Other Pacific Islander	Some other race	Two or more races	Hispanic or Latino (of any race)	18 years and over
21 00000	KENTUCKY—Con.												
21 67458	Russell city	Greenup	4.0	3,645	3,517	26	1	78	-	8	15	30	2,854
21 67512	Russellville city	Logan	10.6	7,149	5,622	1,331	28	26	2	41	99	113	5,454
21 67728	St. Dennis CDP	Jefferson	2.6	9,177	5,850	3,113	27	29	1	44	113	111	6,819
21 67944	St. Matthews city	Jefferson	4.0	15,852	14,317	785	24	416	1	93	216	268	13,160
21 69114	Scottsville city	Allen	5.8	4,327	4,132	142	1	4	1	16	31	35	3,285
21 70050	Shelbyville city	Shelby	7.6	10,085	7,561	1,649	33	53	33	503	253	959	7,423
21 70086	Shepherdsville city	Bullitt	10.5	8,334	8,104	77	29	31	2	10	81	62	5,929
21 70284	Shively city	Jefferson	4.6	15,157	10,195	4,595	39	64	-	118	146	211	11,864
21 71688	Somerset city	Pulaski	11.3	11,352	10,689	416	20	81	-	30	116	112	9,010
21 71976	Southgate city	Campbell	1.4	3,472	3,328	25	9	53	-	24	33	43	2,719
21 72660	Springfield city	Washington	2.5	2,634	1,967	590	-	14	-	21	42	33	2,059
21 73110	Stanford city	Lincoln	3.1	3,430	3,086	278	3	3	-	7	53	47	2,649
21 73164	Stanton city	Powell	2.0	3,029	2,999	13	8	1	-	1	7	22	2,290
21 75738	Taylor Mill city	Kenton	6.3	6,913	6,771	29	12	45	2	10	44	54	5,087
21 77160	Tompkinsville city	Monroe	3.7	2,660	2,380	238	1	-	2	14	25	29	2,077
21 78384	Union city	Boone	3.2	2,893	2,778	16	5	55	1	13	25	24	1,806
21 78942	Valley Station CDP	Jefferson	7.8	22,946	21,951	492	54	91	8	87	263	204	17,145
21 79482	Versailles city	Woodford	2.8	7,511	6,623	651	11	26	1	101	98	322	5,769
21 79698	Villa Hills city	Kenton	3.7	7,948	7,751	36	13	75	-	13	60	67	5,824
21 79734	Vine Grove city	Hardin	5.9	4,169	3,473	443	23	72	13	50	95	126	3,020
21 81858	West Liberty city	Morgan	4.4	3,277	2,603	596	13	7	2	7	49	41	2,945
21 82146	Westwood CDP	Boyd	3.9	4,888	4,800	23	4	18	-	2	41	24	3,865
21 83172	Wilder city	Campbell	3.7	2,624	2,480	60	3	41	-	14	26	25	2,020
21 83334	Williamsburg city	Whitley	4.7	5,143	4,961	89	11	18	1	6	57	34	4,142
21 83406	Williamstown city	Grant, Pendleton	16.0	3,227	3,161	2	4	14	7	26	13	47	2,393
21 83550	Wilmore city	Jessamine	2.6	5,905	5,582	114	8	123	2	19	57	77	4,597
21 83676	Winchester city	Clark	7.6	16,724	14,875	1,477	36	42	1	136	157	268	12,554
21 84567	Woodlawn-Oakdale CDP	McCracken	5.9	4,937	4,668	124	20	20	5	17	83	43	3,696
22 00000	LOUISIANA		43,561.8	4,468,976	2,856,161	1,451,944	25,477	54,758	1,240	31,131	48,265	107,738	3,249,177
22 00100	Abbeville city	Vermilion	5.6	11,887	6,454	4,584	23	654	-	46	126	229	8,356
22 00975	Alexandria city	Rapides	26.4	46,342	19,740	25,371	116	577	20	107	411	456	33,326
22 01885	Amite City town	Tangipahoa	3.9	4,110	1,908	2,130	4	32	-	4	32	58	3,071
22 02550	Arabi CDP	St. Bernard	1.8	8,093	7,760	72	25	66	-	73	97	413	6,635
22 02655	Arcadia town	Bienville	3.0	3,041	1,155	1,842	8	3	-	8	25	49	2,217
22 03810	Avondale CDP	Jefferson	5.4	5,441	3,466	1,102	29	664	-	86	94	261	3,855
22 03985	Baker city	East Baton Rouge	7.9	13,793	6,341	7,222	39	31	1	23	136	119	9,687
22 04055	Ball town	Rapides	8.0	3,681	3,561	58	24	13	1	8	16	52	2,653
22 04685	Bastrop city	Morehouse	8.4	12,988	4,503	8,377	17	20	-	5	66	90	9,085
22 05000	Baton Rouge city	East Baton Rouge	76.8	227,818	104,117	113,953	405	5,972	76	1,113	2,182	3,918	172,121
22 05210	Bayou Cane CDP	Terrebonne	7.6	17,046	14,605	1,673	332	119	4	83	230	400	12,463
22 05525	Bayou Vista CDP	St. Mary	1.8	4,351	3,998	158	45	11	2	59	78	111	3,069
22 06120	Belle Chasse CDP	Plaquemines	25.0	9,848	9,072	417	60	84	2	84	129	232	7,038
22 07100	Berwick town	St. Mary	6.0	4,418	3,828	365	31	32	-	24	138	64	3,105
22 08150	Bogalusa city	Washington	9.5	13,365	7,642	5,508	43	52	-	22	98	100	9,707
22 08920	Bossier City city	Bossier	40.8	56,461	40,335	12,840	322	976	60	813	1,115	2,232	40,528
22 09340	Breaux Bridge city	St. Martin	6.5	7,281	3,629	3,543	8	23	-	20	58	47	5,090
22 09480	Bridge City CDP	Jefferson	4.4	8,323	3,752	3,958	63	328	2	106	114	371	5,497
22 10075	Broussard town	Lafayette, St. Martin	11.4	5,874	4,776	981	29	22	-	23	43	87	4,185
22 10145	Brownfields CDP	East Baton Rouge	4.1	5,222	2,444	2,706	8	24	-	6	34	30	3,872
22 10230	Brownsville-Bawcomville CDP	Ouachita	6.6	7,616	6,649	851	39	5	-	21	51	150	5,617
22 10950	Bunkie city	Avoyelles	2.6	4,662	2,263	2,343	2	13	-	16	25	69	3,250
22 11020	Buras-Triumph CDP	Plaquemines	5.0	3,358	2,407	366	56	413	-	43	73	37	2,341
22 12665	Carencro city	Lafayette	6.1	6,120	3,450	2,582	12	14	-	15	47	67	4,271
22 12840	Carlyss CDP	Calcasieu	12.0	4,049	3,946	34	10	10	1	13	35	48	2,888
22 14100	Chackbay CDP	Lafourche	28.6	4,018	3,796	160	28	11	-	4	19	30	2,912
22 14135	Chalmette CDP	St. Bernard	7.3	32,069	29,725	765	140	578	10	304	547	1,543	24,464
22 14520	Chauvin CDP	Terrebonne	4.7	3,229	3,132	3	64	9	1	1	19	22	2,325
22 15465	Church Point town	Acadia	2.8	4,756	3,209	1,500	8	7	-	20	12	75	3,301
22 15605	Claiborne CDP	Ouachita	10.1	9,830	9,539	155	13	30	1	23	69	106	7,039
22 18125	Covington city	St. Tammany	6.8	8,483	6,570	1,711	28	29	3	21	121	132	6,209
22 18650	Crowley city	Acadia	4.9	14,225	9,649	4,407	22	41	1	33	72	157	10,170
22 18930	Cut Off CDP	Lafourche	14.8	5,635	5,151	63	213	71	-	62	73	120	4,094
22 20190	Delhi town	Richland	2.5	3,066	1,295	1,741	2	3	-	11	14	30	2,247
22 20435	Denham Springs city	Livingston	6.0	8,757	7,407	1,166	22	59	7	15	81	78	6,409
22 20575	DeQuincy city	Calcasieu	3.2	3,398	2,693	648	18	6	-	6	27	28	2,478
22 20610	De Ridder city	Beauregard, Vernon	8.5	9,808	5,964	3,406	56	139	3	56	184	235	7,148
22 20680	Des Allemands CDP	Lafourche, St. Charles	8.7	2,500	2,172	261	7	4	1	21	34	62	1,851
22 20820	Destrehan CDP	St. Charles	6.9	11,260	9,531	1,439	13	117	-	64	96	429	7,615
22 21240	Donaldsonville city	Ascension	2.5	7,605	2,268	5,207	9	9	-	28	34	84	5,166
22 22610	Eastwood CDP	Bossier	6.3	3,374	3,057	207	19	22	1	16	52	66	2,390
22 22722	Eden Isle CDP	St. Tammany	3.4	6,261	5,832	165	33	137	2	20	72	153	5,149
22 22815	Edgard CDP	St. John the Baptist	15.5	2,637	121	2,501	-	-	1	7	7	4	1,862
22 23567	Elmwood CDP	Jefferson	3.7	4,270	3,433	496	15	195	-	62	68	224	3,839
22 24390	Estelle CDP	Jefferson	5.1	15,880	11,963	2,666	131	526	7	301	286	1,143	10,977
22 24565	Eunice city	Acadia, St. Landry	4.7	11,499	7,907	3,439	13	24	2	39	75	128	8,099

Table D-1. Places — **Area and Population**—Con.

[Includes incorporated places and census designated places (CDPs) of 2,500 or more population as of April 1, 2000. Codes shown are two-digit Federal Information Processing Standards (FIPS) state codes and five-digit FIPS place codes. Place names and codes are those in effect as of January 1, 2000. County refers to the county (or counties) in which the place is located. IC in this column = independent city, a county equivalent. If a place is located in more than one county, counties are listed in alphabetic order]

State and place code	Place	County	Land area, 2000 (sq. mi.)	Total	White	Black or African American	American Indian and Alaska Native	Asian	Native Hawaiian and Other Pacific Islander	Some other race	Two or more races	Hispanic or Latino (of any race)	18 years and over
22 00000	LOUISIANA—Con.												
22 25160	Farmerville town	Union	5.5	3,808	1,296	2,419	1	26	1	47	18	65	2,710
22 25440	Ferriday town	Concordia	1.7	3,723	897	2,788	7	10	1	7	13	17	2,531
22 26746	Fort Polk North CDP	Vernon	8.1	3,279	2,062	698	44	68	18	168	221	389	2,092
22 26757	Fort Polk South CDP	Vernon	6.2	11,000	6,470	3,045	101	236	58	584	506	1,290	7,372
22 27155	Franklin city	St. Mary	10.4	8,354	3,966	4,177	53	26	-	25	107	66	5,813
22 27190	Franklinton town	Washington	4.1	3,657	1,719	1,897	4	7	-	-	30	18	2,675
22 28065	Galliano CDP	Lafourche	11.0	7,356	6,792	51	330	59	-	45	79	128	5,331
22 28275	Gardere CDP	East Baton Rouge	3.3	8,992	2,053	6,381	13	193	6	199	147	513	5,960
22 28345	Garyville CDP	St. John the Baptist	20.9	2,775	1,290	1,455	4	4	2	1	19	20	1,921
22 29850	Gonzales city	Ascension	8.4	8,156	5,334	2,549	18	50	1	134	70	295	5,919
22 30515	Grambling town	Lincoln	5.5	4,693	50	4,557	5	7	-	25	49	46	4,065
22 30550	Gramercy town	St. James	2.1	3,066	1,950	1,068	14	3	-	-	31	22	2,189
22 31180	Gray CDP	Terrebonne	11.6	4,958	2,931	1,812	112	18	-	18	67	74	3,338
22 31915	Gretna city	Jefferson	3.5	17,423	9,813	6,191	105	543	8	458	305	1,105	13,268
22 32510	Hahnville CDP	St. Charles	7.8	2,792	1,335	1,421	8	3	-	6	19	32	1,989
22 32755	Hammond city	Tangipahoa	12.8	17,639	9,248	7,972	28	146	3	82	160	277	13,417
22 32930	Harahan city	Jefferson	2.0	9,885	9,594	61	44	37	3	37	109	243	7,827
22 33245	Harvey CDP	Jefferson	6.7	22,226	10,696	9,434	113	1,164	5	453	361	1,186	15,684
22 33420	Haughton town	Bossier	4.2	2,792	2,130	579	10	5	-	13	55	38	1,945
22 33525	Haynesville town	Claiborne	4.9	2,679	1,324	1,333	5	1	1	2	13	22	1,947
22 35870	Homer town	Claiborne	4.6	3,788	1,432	2,322	6	8	-	5	15	34	2,626
22 36255	Houma city	Terrebonne	14.0	32,393	21,851	8,461	1,116	230	6	221	508	571	23,364
22 37270	Inniswold CDP	East Baton Rouge	2.2	4,944	3,979	754	7	114	-	54	36	107	3,679
22 37445	Iowa town	Calcasieu	3.1	2,663	2,101	495	10	2	-	16	39	39	1,866
22 37830	Jackson town	East Feliciana	4.5	4,130	1,923	2,160	6	16	-	3	22	14	3,505
22 38075	Jeanerette city	Iberia	2.2	5,997	2,299	3,580	14	10	1	35	58	86	4,101
22 38145	Jefferson CDP	Jefferson	2.8	11,843	8,509	2,779	31	178	3	196	147	601	9,613
22 38285	Jena town	La Salle	5.4	2,971	2,542	357	20	14	-	15	23	36	2,154
22 38355	Jennings city	Jefferson Davis	10.2	10,986	7,736	3,076	41	32	-	24	77	101	7,820
22 38670	Jonesboro town	Jackson	4.9	3,914	2,114	1,762	6	13	-	1	18	17	2,944
22 39055	Kaplan city	Vermilion	2.3	5,177	4,407	669	9	26	1	11	54	62	3,840
22 39475	Kenner city	Jefferson	15.1	70,517	48,038	15,900	279	2,002	41	2,679	1,578	9,602	51,300
22 40665	Lacombe CDP	St. Tammany	26.7	7,518	5,199	1,903	120	25	3	102	166	194	5,575
22 40735	Lafayette city	Lafayette	47.6	110,257	75,232	31,434	272	1,584	26	641	1,068	2,071	82,617
22 41050	Lake Arthur town	Jefferson Davis	1.9	3,007	2,652	327	2	3	1	-	22	22	2,176
22 41155	Lake Charles city	Calcasieu	40.2	71,757	36,042	33,599	167	770	18	338	823	1,007	53,449
22 41400	Lake Providence town	East Carroll	3.6	5,104	1,001	4,058	9	11	-	8	17	35	3,304
22 42030	Laplace CDP	St. John the Baptist	21.5	27,684	16,904	9,860	90	195	6	306	323	1,021	19,048
22 42135	Larose CDP	Lafourche	11.2	7,306	6,252	413	282	174	-	61	124	184	5,320
22 43010	Leesville city	Vernon	5.5	6,753	3,747	2,386	99	141	38	152	190	332	4,993
22 44900	Lockport town	Lafourche	0.6	2,624	2,512	27	43	11	-	16	15	31	1,946
22 46615	Luling CDP	St. Charles	18.5	11,512	9,437	1,784	30	85	3	73	100	310	8,070
22 46720	Lutcher town	St. James	3.4	3,735	1,864	1,859	2	1	-	2	7	13	2,737
22 48085	Mamou town	Evangeline	1.4	3,566	2,174	1,346	8	2	1	2	33	26	2,557
22 48225	Mandeville city	St. Tammany	6.8	10,489	9,666	502	33	122	6	62	98	255	7,621
22 48365	Mansfield city	De Soto	3.7	5,582	1,905	3,587	7	15	-	26	42	89	3,931
22 48470	Many town	Sabine	3.1	2,889	1,392	1,370	49	14	1	8	55	49	2,123
22 48750	Marksville city	Avoyelles	4.1	5,537	3,155	2,137	155	15	-	6	69	36	3,948
22 48785	Marrero CDP	Jefferson	8.0	36,165	17,111	17,246	141	890	18	258	441	1,127	25,663
22 49800	Meraux CDP	St. Bernard	4.2	10,192	9,449	373	48	166	-	34	122	415	7,399
22 49940	Merrydale CDP	East Baton Rouge	4.3	10,427	907	9,403	9	18	-	21	69	94	6,824
22 50115	Metairie CDP	Jefferson	23.2	146,136	126,445	9,984	394	4,041	34	2,787	2,451	10,595	116,083
22 50885	Minden city	Webster	11.9	13,027	6,037	6,796	41	35	6	27	85	80	9,508
22 51410	Monroe city	Ouachita	28.7	53,107	19,535	32,462	68	558	16	132	336	534	37,349
22 51645	Monticello CDP	East Baton Rouge	2.4	4,763	1,621	3,041	11	47	3	14	26	63	3,262
22 52040	Morgan City city	St. Mary	5.9	12,703	9,055	3,036	116	130	1	150	215	428	9,351
22 52425	Moss Bluff CDP	Calcasieu	15.2	10,535	9,696	621	41	47	1	49	80	169	7,380
22 53545	Natchitoches city	Natchitoches	21.6	17,865	7,810	9,469	122	146	3	121	194	232	13,642
22 54035	New Iberia city	Iberia	10.6	32,623	18,593	12,533	70	862	7	166	392	487	22,898
22 55000	New Orleans city	Orleans	180.6	484,674	135,956	325,947	991	10,972	109	4,498	6,201	14,826	355,266
22 55105	New Roads city	Pointe Coupee	4.5	4,966	1,936	2,946	11	39	-	8	26	31	3,605
22 55525	Norco CDP	St. Charles	3.0	3,579	2,816	688	15	10	-	12	38	72	2,639
22 56540	Oakdale city	Allen	5.1	8,137	5,051	2,843	46	100	1	27	69	994	6,416
22 56855	Oak Hills Place CDP	East Baton Rouge	3.1	7,996	6,593	972	17	282	3	33	96	200	5,767
22 57705	Old Jefferson CDP	East Baton Rouge	3.5	5,631	5,089	320	22	107	4	25	64	88	3,973
22 58045	Opelousas city	St. Landry	7.1	22,860	6,699	15,801	24	73	4	68	191	202	15,934
22 59340	Patterson city	St. Mary	2.5	5,130	2,747	2,220	36	30	-	51	46	99	3,543
22 60075	Pierre Part CDP	Assumption	3.0	3,239	3,214	3	7	-	-	-	15	20	2,356
22 60530	Pineville city	Rapides	11.5	13,829	9,621	3,607	70	263	12	42	214	158	10,722
22 60880	Plaquemine city	Iberville	2.9	7,064	3,480	3,504	12	19	2	6	41	81	5,240
22 61615	Ponchatoula city	Tangipahoa	4.2	5,180	3,222	1,908	10	6	-	8	26	44	3,634
22 61790	Port Allen city	West Baton Rouge	2.1	5,278	2,377	2,849	8	2	1	14	27	53	3,933
22 62070	Port Sulphur CDP	Plaquemines	6.1	3,115	1,412	1,384	219	19	1	28	52	30	2,156
22 62280	Poydras CDP	St. Bernard	4.2	3,886	3,415	336	30	22	2	21	60	203	2,800
22 62647	Prien CDP	Calcasieu	6.9	7,215	6,549	452	20	61	2	47	85	130	5,050
22 63155	Raceland CDP	Lafourche	21.6	10,224	7,278	2,682	98	26	4	66	70	157	7,390
22 63645	Rayne city	Acadia	3.5	8,552	5,606	2,867	9	14	-	16	40	69	6,020
22 63680	Rayville town	Richland	2.3	4,234	1,331	2,848	12	7	-	5	31	21	2,868

[Includes incorporated places and census designated places (CDPs) of 2,500 or more population as of April 1, 2000. Codes shown are two-digit Federal Information Processing Standards (FIPS) state codes and five-digit FIPS place codes. Place names and codes are those in effect as of January 1, 2000. County refers to the county (or counties) in which the place is located. IC in this column = independent city, a county equivalent. If a place is located in more than one county, counties are listed in alphabetic order]

State and place code	Place	County	Land area, 2000 (sq. mi.)	Population, 2000 (April 1)									
					By race—								
					One race							Hispanic or Latino (of any race)	18 years and over
				Total	White	Black or African American	American Indian and Alaska Native	Asian	Native Hawaiian and Other Pacific Islander	Some other race	Two or more races		
22 00000	LOUISIANA—Con.												
22 63855	Red Chute CDP	Bossier	9.3	5,984	5,318	432	44	48	5	45	92	185	4,253
22 64310	Reserve CDP	St. John the Baptist	16.1	9,111	4,024	4,913	17	29	2	55	71	180	6,180
22 65150	River Ridge CDP	Jefferson	2.8	14,588	12,656	1,603	34	114	5	65	111	426	11,283
22 66655	Ruston city	Lincoln	18.1	20,546	11,699	7,997	34	496	5	130	185	266	16,281
22 67250	St. Gabriel town	Iberville	28.7	5,514	1,493	3,969	3	18	1	12	18	62	4,751
22 67600	St. Martinville city	St. Martin	3.0	6,989	2,501	4,392	14	10	-	24	48	73	5,020
22 67740	St. Rose CDP	St. Charles	4.0	6,540	3,612	2,715	21	31	2	78	81	296	4,543
22 68300	Schriever CDP	Terrebonne	14.4	5,880	4,297	1,419	55	30	-	27	52	79	4,141
22 68475	Scott city	Lafayette	8.9	7,870	6,751	910	26	75	1	39	68	102	5,508
22 69225	Shenandoah CDP	East Baton Rouge	6.3	17,070	15,726	755	41	355	2	67	124	276	11,987
22 70000	Shreveport city	Bossier, Caddo	103.1	200,145	93,394	101,679	619	1,590	66	893	1,904	3,106	146,277
22 70805	Slidell city	St. Tammany	11.8	25,695	21,360	3,484	127	184	13	160	367	687	18,769
22 72092	South Vacherie CDP	St. James	15.5	3,543	2,407	1,121	-	1	-	5	9	9	2,602
22 72485	Springhill city	Webster	6.2	5,439	3,997	1,367	11	12	2	14	36	43	4,145
22 73640	Sulphur city	Calcasieu	10.0	20,512	19,165	905	68	76	9	72	217	305	14,947
22 74340	Swartz CDP	Ouachita	13.5	4,247	3,869	289	17	20	-	33	19	69	3,055
22 74690	Tallulah city	Madison	2.7	9,189	2,134	6,872	15	17	2	12	137	195	5,736
22 75180	Terrytown CDP	Jefferson	3.7	25,430	14,216	8,813	130	885	12	690	684	2,206	18,051
22 75425	Thibodaux city	Lafourche	5.5	14,431	9,242	4,872	54	93	3	37	130	148	10,888
22 75740	Timberlane CDP	Jefferson	2.1	11,405	7,494	2,679	82	521	6	356	267	876	8,442
22 78470	Vidalia town	Concordia	2.3	4,543	3,256	1,230	10	18	-	12	17	47	3,298
22 78680	Village St. George CDP	East Baton Rouge	2.2	6,993	4,991	1,656	13	183	1	37	112	232	4,906
22 78715	Ville Platte city	Evangeline	3.1	8,145	3,301	4,779	17	6	-	9	33	100	5,626
22 78820	Vinton town	Calcasieu	4.8	3,338	2,489	778	20	7	3	3	38	30	2,343
22 78855	Violet CDP	St. Bernard	4.1	8,555	4,987	3,317	41	50	1	32	127	367	5,786
22 78890	Vivian town	Caddo	5.2	4,031	2,576	1,378	21	14	-	1	41	29	2,826
22 79100	Waggaman CDP	Jefferson	5.6	9,435	3,955	5,136	46	69	1	122	106	392	6,579
22 79240	Walker town	Livingston	5.8	4,801	4,145	594	11	2	-	11	38	57	3,372
22 80430	Welsh town	Jefferson Davis	6.2	3,380	2,630	709	10	1	1	9	20	37	2,419
22 80815	Westlake city	Calcasieu	2.3	4,668	3,747	838	9	10	-	8	56	83	3,369
22 80920	Westminster CDP	East Baton Rouge	1.1	2,515	2,362	84	3	20	-	13	33	52	1,916
22 80955	West Monroe city	Ouachita	7.7	13,250	9,861	3,108	39	40	6	63	133	196	10,102
22 81165	Westwego city	Jefferson	3.2	10,763	8,089	2,155	101	169	-	98	151	386	7,803
22 82460	Winnfield city	Winn	3.3	5,749	2,776	2,865	22	9	-	9	68	66	4,047
22 82495	Winnsboro city	Franklin	4.1	5,344	2,136	3,128	9	22	1	8	40	32	3,666
22 83002	Woodmere CDP	Jefferson	3.7	13,058	3,255	8,536	33	783	-	256	195	698	8,403
22 83335	Youngsville town	Lafayette	6.7	3,992	3,513	401	21	12	10	20	15	67	2,709
22 83405	Zachary city	East Baton Rouge	23.7	11,275	7,866	3,238	21	52	-	36	62	81	7,887
23 00000	MAINE		30,861.6	1,274,923	1,236,014	6,760	7,098	9,111	382	2,911	12,647	9,360	973,685
23 02060	Auburn city	Androscoggin	59.8	23,203	22,517	137	69	137	12	24	307	169	17,818
23 02100	Augusta city	Kennebec	55.4	18,560	17,856	93	89	250	2	29	241	160	14,757
23 02795	Bangor city	Penobscot	34.4	31,473	29,888	320	309	364	18	123	451	329	24,784
23 02830	Bar Harbor CDP	Hancock	3.1	2,680	2,609	7	6	27	-	4	27	19	2,229
23 03355	Bath city	Sagadahoc	9.1	9,266	8,795	148	54	44	12	63	150	163	6,950
23 03950	Belfast city	Waldo	34.0	6,381	6,225	18	17	18	1	17	85	44	5,048
23 04860	Biddeford city	York	30.0	20,942	20,240	133	83	206	6	37	235	137	16,319
23 06925	Brewer city	Penobscot	15.1	8,987	8,774	30	57	49	2	21	54	57	6,970
23 08395	Brunswick CDP	Cumberland	12.6	14,816	14,104	147	24	282	6	66	187	194	11,636
23 08780	Bucksport CDP	Hancock	11.4	2,970	2,893	1	13	8	2	4	49	34	2,250
23 09585	Calais city	Washington	34.0	3,447	3,337	12	21	24	-	17	36	25	2,691
23 09690	Camden CDP	Knox	3.8	3,934	3,863	12	5	16	-	7	31	33	3,198
23 10320	Cape Neddick CDP	York	3.7	2,997	2,945	8	-	14	3	6	21	27	2,452
23 10565	Caribou city	Aroostook	79.3	8,312	7,998	24	123	76	6	7	78	38	6,445
23 15500	Cumberland Center CDP	Cumberland	4.2	2,596	2,570	4	3	11	-	3	5	11	1,717
23 18230	Dover-Foxcroft CDP	Piscataquis	8.4	2,592	2,499	5	11	21	1	5	50	29	1,973
23 23200	Ellsworth city	Hancock	79.3	6,456	6,313	12	19	27	2	19	64	42	5,039
23 24285	Fairfield CDP	Somerset	1.8	2,569	2,508	6	6	13	-	1	35	5	1,906
23 24740	Farmington CDP	Franklin	4.0	4,098	3,970	15	13	38	-	10	52	35	3,576
23 27085	Gardiner city	Kennebec	15.7	6,198	6,006	24	41	22	3	15	87	50	4,659
23 28205	Gorham CDP	Cumberland	5.4	4,164	4,029	23	25	46	1	6	34	32	3,461
23 30760	Hampden CDP	Penobscot	11.1	4,126	4,038	18	20	25	-	6	19	19	3,006
23 33945	Houlton CDP	Aroostook	7.7	5,270	5,032	18	148	28	5	6	33	26	4,052
23 36500	Kennebunk CDP	York	6.7	4,804	4,723	8	4	23	-	9	37	14	3,728
23 37235	Kittery CDP	York	2.8	4,884	4,594	134	11	39	2	40	64	114	3,805
23 38740	Lewiston city	Androscoggin	34.1	35,690	34,172	383	100	301	11	130	593	448	28,297
23 39440	Lincoln CDP	Penobscot	7.4	2,933	2,883	4	12	15	-	19	7	2,256
23 40105	Lisbon Falls CDP	Androscoggin	3.8	4,420	4,287	28	10	18	3	20	54	47	3,210
23 42485	Madawaska CDP	Aroostook	5.3	3,326	3,263	3	17	22	-	4	17	6	2,705
23 42625	Madison CDP	Somerset	6.4	2,733	2,676	2	5	4	1	-	45	7	2,117
23 45845	Millinocket CDP	Penobscot	5.4	5,190	5,113	5	28	19	-	1	24	12	4,095
23 53685	North Windham CDP	Cumberland	6.9	4,568	4,483	25	18	13	-	1	28	15	3,347
23 53965	Norway CDP	Oxford	5.1	2,623	2,563	11	11	12	1	1	24	10	2,046
23 54525	Oakland CDP	Kennebec	5.4	2,758	2,707	7	7	17	-	2	18	21	2,063
23 55120	Old Orchard Beach CDP	York	7.4	8,856	8,638	50	25	41	3	20	79	90	7,163
23 55225	Old Town city	Penobscot	38.3	8,130	7,693	53	120	149	3	23	89	42	6,503
23 55575	Orono CDP	Penobscot	7.3	8,253	7,700	121	78	212	5	45	92	105	7,374

Table D-1. Places — **Area and Population**—Con.

[Includes incorporated places and census designated places (CDPs) of 2,500 or more population as of April 1, 2000. Codes shown are two-digit Federal Information Processing Standards (FIPS) state codes and five-digit FIPS place codes. Place names and codes are those in effect as of January 1, 2000. County refers to the county (or counties) in which the place is located. IC in this column = independent city, a county equivalent. If a place is located in more than one county, counties are listed in alphabetic order]

State and place code	Place	County	Land area, 2000 (sq. mi.)	Population, 2000 (April 1) Total	By race— One race White	Black or African American	American Indian and Alaska Native	Asian	Native Hawaiian and Other Pacific Islander	Some other race	Two or more races	Hispanic or Latino (of any race)	18 years and over
23 00000	MAINE—Con.												
23 58970	Pittsfield CDP	Somerset	9.4	3,217	3,078	30	12	44	5	2	46	19	2,298
23 60545	Portland city	Cumberland	21.2	64,249	58,638	1,665	302	1,982	36	431	1,195	974	52,177
23 60825	Presque Isle city	Aroostook	75.7	9,511	9,048	34	215	80	3	16	115	62	7,453
23 63590	Rockland city	Knox	12.9	7,609	7,449	19	18	43	2	8	70	43	6,001
23 64255	Rumford CDP	Oxford	7.9	4,795	4,729	6	18	10	-	4	28	30	3,710
23 64675	Saco city	York	38.5	16,822	16,470	54	25	85	15	17	156	97	12,621
23 65725	Sanford CDP	York	5.1	10,133	9,685	60	35	195	1	40	117	130	7,426
23 66110	Scarborough CDP	Cumberland	5.0	3,867	3,718	18	10	77	-	12	32	31	3,003
23 68875	Skowhegan CDP	Somerset	13.4	6,696	6,539	16	30	35	-	11	65	47	5,187
23 70660	South Eliot CDP	York	7.2	3,445	3,392	5	4	17	-	5	22	17	2,608
23 71990	South Portland city	Cumberland	12.0	23,324	22,345	146	78	370	6	73	306	263	18,121
23 72200	South Sanford CDP	York	22.8	4,173	3,976	11	15	119	-	10	42	34	3,091
23 73285	Springvale CDP	York	3.1	3,488	3,320	15	11	75	2	1	64	15	2,564
23 76330	Thomaston CDP	Knox	2.0	2,714	2,636	22	8	18	1	2	27	15	2,208
23 76925	Topsham CDP	Sagadahoc	11.0	6,271	5,923	113	13	93	5	28	96	99	4,511
23 80740	Waterville city	Kennebec	13.6	15,605	14,951	122	88	161	4	66	213	171	12,530
23 82105	Westbrook city	Cumberland	16.9	16,142	15,608	142	43	132	5	46	166	144	12,358
23 86480	Winslow CDP	Kennebec	36.9	7,743	7,592	10	21	27	1	17	75	60	5,875
23 86935	Winthrop CDP	Kennebec	5.6	2,893	2,835	15	10	11	-	2	20	12	2,264
23 87810	Yarmouth CDP	Cumberland	2.6	3,560	3,508	15	1	13	-	8	15	17	2,581
23 88160	York Harbor CDP	York	3.2	3,321	3,259	4	2	19	-	7	30	21	2,594
24 00000	MARYLAND		9,773.8	5,296,486	3,391,308	1,477,411	15,423	210,929	2,303	95,525	103,587	227,916	3,940,314
24 00125	Aberdeen city	Harford	6.4	13,842	8,984	3,790	34	343	13	197	481	477	10,184
24 00175	Aberdeen Proving Ground CDP	Harford	11.4	3,116	1,573	1,078	20	97	39	177	132	349	1,867
24 00250	Accokeek CDP	Prince George's	22.4	7,349	3,172	3,498	38	382	5	71	183	172	5,308
24 00400	Adelphi CDP	Prince George's	3.0	14,998	4,421	5,974	42	1,493	9	2,255	804	3,860	11,591
24 01450	Andrews AFB CDP	Prince George's	6.8	7,925	5,175	1,805	51	251	9	289	345	691	5,148
24 01600	Annapolis city	Anne Arundel	6.7	35,838	22,457	11,267	60	650	11	796	597	2,301	28,064
24 01975	Arbutus CDP	Baltimore	6.5	20,116	17,141	1,261	57	1,228	5	96	328	308	15,642
24 02275	Arnold CDP	Anne Arundel	10.8	23,422	21,429	1,132	43	350	6	138	324	442	16,914
24 02762	Ashton-Sandy Springs CDP	Montgomery	7.6	3,437	2,784	422	8	118	-	43	62	121	2,532
24 02825	Aspen Hill CDP	Montgomery	10.5	50,228	27,929	10,538	164	5,779	31	3,759	2,028	7,757	38,164
24 03800	Ballenger Creek CDP	Frederick	5.6	13,518	11,275	1,362	36	417	5	150	273	424	9,332
24 04000	Baltimore city	Baltimore IC	80.8	651,154	205,982	418,951	2,097	9,985	222	4,363	9,554	11,061	489,801
24 05550	Bel Air town	Harford	2.8	10,080	9,356	441	20	142	3	27	91	123	7,856
24 05825	Bel Air North CDP	Harford	16.4	25,798	24,498	574	31	416	6	69	204	284	17,696
24 05950	Bel Air South CDP	Harford	15.7	39,711	36,373	1,632	64	897	15	260	470	752	28,324
24 06400	Beltsville CDP	Prince George's	6.6	15,690	7,562	5,015	41	1,686	16	850	520	1,544	11,983
24 06615	Bennsville CDP	Charles	17.0	7,325	5,601	1,320	30	170	7	40	157	161	5,267
24 06800	Berlin town	Worcester	2.2	3,491	2,225	1,118	7	53	1	34	53	118	2,580
24 06925	Berwyn Heights town	Prince George's	0.6	2,942	2,112	353	16	252	-	129	80	242	2,328
24 07125	Bethesda CDP	Montgomery	13.1	55,277	47,460	1,476	92	4,376	26	680	1,167	3,000	43,165
24 07850	Bladensburg town	Prince George's	1.0	7,661	1,258	5,433	26	193	4	526	221	1,001	5,544
24 08625	Boonsboro town	Washington	1.5	2,803	2,748	21	3	5	1	4	21	21	2,088
24 08775	Bowie city	Prince George's	16.1	50,269	31,492	15,500	150	1,482	17	470	1,158	1,468	36,739
24 08800	Bowleys Quarters CDP	Baltimore	3.2	6,314	5,787	387	13	41	3	18	65	36	4,763
24 09100	Braddock Heights CDP	Frederick	7.4	4,627	4,450	55	-	47	1	16	58	80	3,469
24 09500	Brentwood town	Prince George's	0.4	2,844	814	1,415	12	60	-	428	115	672	2,018
24 10475	Brooklyn Park CDP	Anne Arundel	3.0	10,938	10,079	461	52	164	4	63	115	174	8,211
24 10500	Brookmont CDP	Montgomery	1.4	3,202	2,957	53	10	119	-	14	49	127	2,377
24 10900	Brunswick city	Frederick	2.1	4,894	4,507	260	12	22	2	9	82	47	3,558
24 10925	Bryans Road CDP	Charles	8.3	4,912	2,562	2,083	70	70	2	34	91	115	3,527
24 11750	Burtonsville CDP	Montgomery	7.8	7,305	3,802	1,857	16	1,287	1	120	222	409	5,115
24 12150	California CDP	St. Mary's	12.9	9,307	7,323	1,370	37	337	3	65	172	255	6,568
24 12350	Calverton CDP	Montgomery, Prince George's	4.7	12,610	5,434	4,295	18	2,083	1	329	450	803	9,454
24 12400	Cambridge city	Dorchester	6.7	10,911	5,210	5,449	18	71	1	67	95	157	8,245
24 12600	Camp Springs CDP	Prince George's	7.3	17,968	3,606	13,346	71	419	12	193	321	439	13,408
24 12912	Cape St. Claire CDP	Anne Arundel	2.0	8,022	7,459	308	9	91	6	52	97	171	5,729
24 13000	Capitol Heights town	Prince George's	0.8	4,138	199	3,842	11	15	-	15	56	36	2,865
24 13312	Carmody Hills-Pepper Mill Village CDP	Prince George's	0.7	4,801	70	4,652	7	7	-	12	53	24	3,389
24 13325	Carney CDP	Baltimore	7.0	28,264	24,112	1,957	47	1,623	16	122	387	428	22,059
24 14125	Catonsville CDP	Baltimore	14.0	39,820	32,762	4,711	88	1,439	15	236	569	743	31,907
24 15925	Chesapeake Beach town	Calvert	2.8	3,180	2,910	168	11	35	-	12	44	45	2,316
24 16062	Chesapeake Ranch Estates-Drum Point CDP	Calvert	6.0	11,503	9,837	1,210	41	98	6	100	211	280	7,558
24 16125	Chester CDP	Queen Anne's	5.3	3,723	3,336	263	5	38	2	22	57	49	2,862
24 16225	Chestertown town	Kent	2.6	4,746	3,534	1,038	7	77	5	19	66	77	4,109
24 16550	Cheverly town	Prince George's	1.3	6,433	2,178	3,653	11	161	2	207	221	435	4,599
24 16620	Chevy Chase town	Montgomery	0.5	2,726	2,590	24	1	60	1	14	36	92	1,948
24 16625	Chevy Chase CDP	Montgomery	2.5	9,381	8,442	345	13	279	6	104	192	444	7,447
24 16875	Chillum CDP	Prince George's	4.0	34,252	4,913	21,468	161	987	29	4,964	1,730	8,108	25,419
24 17900	Clinton CDP	Prince George's	11.8	26,064	5,359	19,207	122	643	5	187	541	494	18,979

820

Table D-1. Places — **Area and Population**—Con.

[Includes incorporated places and census designated places (CDPs) of 2,500 or more population as of April 1, 2000. Codes shown are two-digit Federal Information Processing Standards (FIPS) state codes and five-digit FIPS place codes. Place names and codes are those in effect as of January 1, 2000. County refers to the county (or counties) in which the place is located. IC in this column = independent city, a county equivalent. If a place is located in more than one county, counties are listed in alphabetic order]

State and place code	Place	County	Land area, 2000 (sq. mi.)	Population, 2000 (April 1) Total	By race— One race White	Black or African American	American Indian and Alaska Native	Asian	Native Hawaiian and Other Pacific Islander	Some other race	Two or more races	Hispanic or Latino (of any race)	18 years and over
24 00000	MARYLAND—Con.												
24 18100	Clover Hill CDP	Frederick	1.2	3,260	3,026	50	5	132	-	12	35	58	2,364
24 18150	Cloverly CDP	Montgomery	3.9	7,835	4,820	1,499	31	1,101	-	155	229	402	5,560
24 18250	Cockeysville CDP	Baltimore	11.3	19,388	15,117	1,720	56	1,918	4	197	376	657	15,726
24 18475	Colesville CDP	Montgomery	9.2	19,810	10,961	4,408	45	3,551	4	302	539	948	14,845
24 18750	College Park city	Prince George's	5.4	24,657	16,969	3,929	81	2,474	2	633	569	1,366	22,056
24 19125	Columbia CDP	Howard	27.6	88,254	58,708	18,949	232	6,440	46	1,442	2,437	3,636	65,086
24 19825	Coral Hills CDP	Prince George's	1.5	10,720	385	10,030	53	55	5	48	144	134	7,434
24 20530	Cresaptown-Bel Air CDP	Allegany	7.4	5,884	4,602	1,220	3	30	-	8	21	26	4,875
24 20775	Crisfield city	Somerset	1.6	2,723	1,594	1,020	11	14	1	10	73	45	1,965
24 20875	Crofton CDP	Anne Arundel	5.0	20,091	18,124	1,031	47	469	9	121	290	499	14,340
24 21325	Cumberland city	Allegany	9.1	21,518	19,913	1,088	57	132	4	57	267	150	16,630
24 21475	Damascus CDP	Montgomery	9.6	11,430	10,248	529	28	253	3	146	223	493	7,547
24 21825	Darnestown CDP	Montgomery	16.6	6,378	5,425	252	16	505	2	37	141	206	4,418
24 22050	Deale CDP	Anne Arundel	4.3	4,796	4,407	288	5	21	3	7	65	51	3,530
24 22725	Denton town	Caroline	2.5	2,960	2,121	753	10	11	-	7	58	55	2,271
24 23025	District Heights city	Prince George's	0.9	5,958	548	5,240	7	51	-	12	100	29	4,125
24 23975	Dundalk CDP	Baltimore	13.3	62,306	55,815	4,680	358	460	25	270	698	904	47,415
24 24475	Easton town	Talbot	10.3	11,708	8,401	2,746	20	210	42	176	113	404	9,058
24 24650	East Riverdale CDP	Prince George's	1.6	14,961	4,296	7,477	89	555	21	1,972	551	3,960	10,315
24 24950	Edgemere CDP	Baltimore	10.8	9,248	8,640	480	17	29	17	8	57	61	7,205
24 25150	Edgewood CDP	Harford	17.9	23,378	15,921	5,999	94	383	22	328	631	794	15,856
24 25575	Eldersburg CDP	Carroll	40.1	27,741	26,250	880	60	263	3	73	212	302	19,667
24 25750	Elkridge CDP	Howard	7.9	22,042	17,762	2,114	47	1,427	6	209	477	489	15,614
24 25800	Elkton town	Cecil	8.0	11,893	10,210	1,146	38	139	5	93	262	353	8,400
24 26000	Ellicott City CDP	Howard	32.0	56,397	44,177	4,138	84	6,714	9	313	962	1,209	40,324
24 26600	Essex CDP	Baltimore	9.5	39,078	29,136	8,200	213	458	19	321	731	884	28,893
24 27250	Fairland CDP	Montgomery	5.0	21,738	7,771	9,345	54	3,154	7	636	771	1,461	16,209
24 27700	Fallston CDP	Harford	14.0	8,427	8,202	64	10	93	-	8	50	74	6,255
24 27900	Federalsburg town	Caroline	2.0	2,620	1,544	965	8	17	1	10	75	29	1,814
24 20075	Ferndale CDP	Anne Arundel	4.1	16,056	12,395	2,504	65	529	3	236	324	499	11,966
24 28640	Forest Glen CDP	Montgomery	1.3	7,344	4,797	1,282	30	570	4	366	295	1,047	5,751
24 28725	Forest Heights town	Prince George's	0.5	2,585	346	2,045	3	87	9	45	50	76	1,880
24 29000	Forestville CDP	Prince George's	4.0	12,707	1,339	10,900	37	117	7	77	230	167	9,123
24 29400	Fort Meade CDP	Anne Arundel	6.6	9,882	6,172	2,491	45	294	26	354	500	944	6,033
24 29525	Fort Washington CDP	Prince George's	13.6	23,845	4,460	16,016	86	2,468	15	232	568	548	18,158
24 29712	Fountainhead-Orchard Hills CDP	Washington	3.8	3,844	3,627	88	4	73	1	12	39	61	3,012
24 30325	Frederick city	Frederick	20.4	52,767	40,651	7,777	154	1,664	32	1,191	1,298	2,533	39,509
24 30575	Friendly CDP	Prince George's	6.8	10,938	1,465	8,496	39	619	8	107	204	239	7,944
24 30837	Friendship Village CDP	Montgomery	0.1	4,512	3,786	204	5	365	1	43	108	359	4,245
24 30900	Frostburg city	Allegany	3.1	7,873	7,119	504	18	77	7	39	109	96	6,899
24 30950	Fruitland city	Wicomico	3.5	3,774	2,483	1,152	17	40	-	24	58	70	2,708
24 31175	Gaithersburg city	Montgomery	10.1	52,613	30,625	7,680	188	7,241	33	4,535	2,311	10,398	39,449
24 31625	Garrison CDP	Baltimore	3.1	7,969	6,179	1,362	10	267	1	73	77	181	6,218
24 32025	Germantown CDP	Montgomery	10.8	55,419	34,473	10,600	187	5,456	37	2,338	2,328	5,660	39,416
24 32500	Glenarden city	Prince George's	1.3	6,318	54	6,051	23	41	2	23	124	48	4,067
24 32650	Glen Burnie CDP	Anne Arundel	12.2	38,922	31,569	5,263	135	933	27	304	691	958	29,697
24 33400	Glenn Dale CDP	Prince George's	7.4	12,609	5,092	6,064	32	983	4	116	318	304	8,854
24 33812	Goddard CDP	Prince George's	2.4	5,554	1,663	2,961	23	649	4	84	170	174	4,267
24 33850	Golden Beach CDP	St. Mary's	2.6	2,665	2,524	64	7	20	4	8	38	18	1,925
24 34711	Greater Landover CDP	Prince George's	4.1	22,900	947	21,076	45	120	9	309	394	663	15,269
24 34712	Greater Upper Marlboro CDP	Prince George's	37.2	18,720	3,856	14,134	58	230	7	126	309	338	13,824
24 34775	Greenbelt city	Prince George's	6.0	21,456	8,526	8,871	50	2,586	11	667	745	1,383	16,760
24 34975	Green Haven CDP	Anne Arundel	3.2	17,415	16,014	760	80	229	4	85	243	256	12,122
24 35412	Green Valley CDP	Frederick	20.6	12,262	11,761	152	28	121	5	46	149	207	8,439
24 36075	Hagerstown city	Washington	10.7	36,687	31,532	3,722	90	354	15	304	670	649	27,312
24 36125	Halfway CDP	Washington	4.7	10,065	9,609	214	9	98	12	24	99	110	7,831
24 36500	Hampstead town	Baltimore, Carroll	2.7	5,060	4,948	40	3	26	-	3	40	55	3,305
24 36512	Hampton CDP	Baltimore	5.7	5,004	4,574	74	-	300	1	11	44	74	3,906
24 37600	Havre de Grace city	Harford	4.0	11,331	8,979	1,830	25	146	13	91	247	241	8,339
24 38850	Hillandale CDP	Montgomery, Prince George's	1.2	3,054	1,692	781	14	295	1	179	92	348	2,444
24 38975	Hillcrest Heights CDP	Prince George's	2.4	16,359	750	15,243	20	58	1	52	235	182	12,199
24 39300	Hillsmere Shores CDP	Anne Arundel	1.4	2,977	2,799	59	2	46	-	19	52	49	2,292
24 41250	Hyattsville city	Prince George's	2.1	14,733	5,824	6,045	73	592	6	1,607	586	2,673	11,165
24 41500	Indian Head town	Charles	1.2	3,422	1,904	1,303	61	49	1	16	88	58	2,293
24 42325	Jarrettsville CDP	Harford	8.7	2,756	2,679	32	4	8	-	9	24	15	1,959
24 42550	Jessup CDP	Anne Arundel, Howard	4.2	7,865	2,460	5,327	12	26	2	21	17	81	7,612
24 42875	Joppatowne CDP	Harford	6.9	11,391	9,739	1,174	28	149	6	112	183	236	8,643
24 43200	Kemp Mill CDP	Montgomery	2.4	9,956	6,815	1,523	23	814	9	489	283	1,075	7,455
24 43900	Kettering CDP	Prince George's	5.5	11,008	636	9,975	21	136	-	52	188	105	8,076
24 44350	Kingsville CDP	Baltimore	10.1	4,214	4,105	15	13	41	-	10	30	36	3,184
24 44817	Lake Arbor CDP	Prince George's	3.1	8,533	614	7,572	24	151	2	36	134	140	6,340
24 44975	Lake Shore CDP	Anne Arundel	9.9	13,065	12,559	218	44	95	6	22	121	109	9,885
24 45525	Langley Park CDP	Prince George's	0.8	16,214	6,758	4,290	144	550	31	3,474	967	10,294	11,775
24 45612	Lanham-Seabrook CDP	Prince George's	5.3	18,190	4,845	11,559	55	894	5	342	490	841	13,301
24 45662	Lansdowne-Baltimore Highlands CDP	Baltimore	4.1	15,724	11,903	2,888	56	292	5	274	306	557	11,073

[Includes incorporated places and census designated places (CDPs) of 2,500 or more population as of April 1, 2000. Codes shown are two-digit Federal Information Processing Standards (FIPS) state codes and five-digit FIPS place codes. Place names and codes are those in effect as of January 1, 2000. County refers to the county (or counties) in which the place is located. IC in this column = independent city, a county equivalent. If a place is located in more than one county, counties are listed in alphabetic order]

State and place code	Place	County	Land area, 2000 (sq. mi.)	Population, 2000 (April 1)									
					By race—								
					One race							Hispanic or Latino (of any race)	18 years and over
				Total	White	Black or African American	American Indian and Alaska Native	Asian	Native Hawaiian and Other Pacific Islander	Some other race	Two or more races		
24 00000	MARYLAND—Con.												
24 45750	La Plata town	Charles	6.9	6,551	4,764	1,552	34	102	3	25	71	85	4,868
24 45825	Largo CDP	Prince George's	3.0	8,408	359	7,793	11	66	3	43	133	120	6,282
24 45900	Laurel city	Prince George's	3.8	19,960	10,428	6,887	76	1,376	42	459	692	1,245	15,559
24 46075	La Vale CDP	Allegany	8.1	4,613	4,502	30	2	47	1	6	25	22	3,662
24 46725	Lexington Park CDP	St. Mary's	8.0	11,021	6,612	3,306	42	465	13	199	384	527	7,554
24 47043	Linganore-Bartonsville CDP	Frederick	16.1	12,529	11,667	411	26	169	6	68	182	270	8,260
24 47125	Linthicum CDP	Anne Arundel	4.2	7,539	7,116	133	18	184	11	17	60	67	5,936
24 47450	Lochearn CDP	Baltimore	5.6	25,269	4,674	19,812	77	205	10	123	368	378	18,916
24 47925	Londontowne CDP	Anne Arundel	3.0	7,595	7,283	150	24	37	1	12	88	148	5,812
24 48900	Lutherville-Timonium CDP	Baltimore	7.4	15,814	14,249	509	24	834	1	38	159	193	12,693
24 49950	Manchester town	Carroll	1.9	3,329	3,241	29	8	7	-	8	36	19	2,386
24 50750	Marlow Heights CDP	Prince George's	2.1	6,059	492	5,364	14	62	-	22	105	92	4,380
24 50775	Marlton CDP	Prince George's	6.0	7,798	3,060	4,327	22	122	1	64	202	189	5,571
24 51075	Maryland City CDP	Anne Arundel	2.6	6,814	4,288	1,811	34	359	2	132	188	337	5,007
24 51575	Mayo CDP	Anne Arundel	2.5	3,153	3,037	40	16	21	1	6	32	56	2,365
24 51587	Mays Chapel CDP	Baltimore	3.8	11,427	10,382	98	5	795	1	46	100	151	8,551
24 52300	Middle River CDP	Baltimore	7.7	23,958	19,790	3,165	143	294	8	206	352	461	17,757
24 52425	Middletown town	Frederick	1.7	2,668	2,585	39	2	9	-	6	27	22	1,814
24 52562	Milford Mill CDP	Baltimore	7.0	26,527	4,294	20,971	57	444	4	196	561	483	19,170
24 52975	Mitchellville CDP	Prince George's	5.0	9,611	1,277	7,545	25	378	6	77	303	201	6,970
24 53325	Montgomery Village CDP	Montgomery	6.5	38,051	23,684	6,432	136	4,516	26	1,726	1,531	4,458	27,928
24 53875	Mount Airy town	Carroll, Frederick	3.8	6,425	6,085	166	11	56	-	16	87	86	4,215
24 54275	Mount Rainier city	Prince George's	0.7	8,498	1,717	5,274	28	196	2	905	376	1,555	6,390
24 55050	Naval Academy CDP	Anne Arundel	0.6	4,264	3,714	234	14	126	5	78	93	296	3,924
24 55400	New Carrollton city	Prince George's	1.5	12,589	2,746	8,498	30	605	8	390	312	827	9,080
24 56337	North Bethesda CDP	Montgomery	9.0	38,610	29,822	1,916	112	4,620	20	1,008	1,112	3,680	31,702
24 56450	North East town	Cecil	1.6	2,733	2,564	87	11	24	-	12	35	42	1,935
24 56712	North Kensington CDP	Montgomery	1.5	8,940	5,990	1,190	35	774	6	566	379	1,348	7,067
24 56725	North Laurel CDP	Howard	10.2	20,468	14,619	3,500	66	1,426	16	304	537	818	14,349
24 56875	North Potomac CDP	Montgomery	6.5	23,044	14,896	970	30	6,357	10	250	531	908	15,157
24 58225	Ocean City town	Worcester	4.6	7,173	6,839	179	8	53	1	25	68	89	6,364
24 58275	Ocean Pines CDP	Worcester	6.8	10,496	10,095	215	14	59	-	18	95	96	8,696
24 58300	Odenton CDP	Anne Arundel	12.4	20,534	16,458	2,620	75	628	16	202	535	568	15,004
24 58900	Olney CDP	Montgomery	13.0	31,438	24,849	2,761	79	2,526	14	515	694	1,576	21,628
24 59325	Overlea CDP	Baltimore	3.1	12,148	10,659	1,067	36	218	2	28	138	169	9,370
24 59425	Owings Mills CDP	Baltimore	9.6	20,193	11,268	7,359	49	791	8	242	476	647	15,882
24 59505	Oxon Hill-Glassmanor CDP	Prince George's	9.0	35,355	2,700	30,646	113	984	30	244	638	593	25,262
24 59787	Paramount-Long Meadow CDP	Washington	2.8	2,722	2,549	67	5	66	-	15	20	23	2,090
24 60275	Parkville CDP	Baltimore	4.2	31,118	22,916	6,995	51	586	6	131	433	515	24,012
24 60325	Parole CDP	Anne Arundel	10.3	14,031	12,679	910	30	215	11	48	138	219	12,315
24 60475	Pasadena CDP	Anne Arundel	7.4	12,093	10,890	823	34	178	5	35	128	161	8,867
24 60975	Perry Hall CDP	Baltimore	7.0	28,705	25,486	1,299	33	1,459	8	105	315	430	21,751
24 61150	Perryville town	Cecil	2.5	3,672	3,339	215	10	28	-	20	60	85	2,673
24 61400	Pikesville CDP	Baltimore	12.4	29,123	25,158	2,482	26	1,016	3	147	291	438	23,400
24 62175	Pleasant Hills CDP	Harford	4.4	2,851	2,745	34	4	34	-	7	27	30	2,157
24 62475	Pocomoke City city	Worcester	3.0	4,098	2,079	1,900	19	19	1	14	66	43	2,850
24 62850	Poolesville town	Montgomery	3.9	5,151	4,820	147	25	56	1	36	66	138	3,348
24 63300	Potomac CDP	Montgomery	25.2	44,822	35,615	1,763	50	5,991	4	402	997	2,411	33,053
24 64250	Pumphrey CDP	Anne Arundel	2.4	5,317	4,180	864	24	128	7	28	86	93	4,158
24 64950	Randallstown CDP	Baltimore	10.3	30,870	7,156	22,259	62	683	6	168	536	476	22,740
24 65312	Redland CDP	Montgomery	6.9	16,998	9,355	2,677	59	2,709	8	1,461	729	2,566	11,955
24 65600	Reisterstown CDP	Baltimore	5.0	22,438	16,467	4,127	50	903	16	365	510	986	16,601
24 66400	Riva CDP	Anne Arundel	2.5	3,966	3,737	136	-	48	-	6	39	84	2,931
24 66635	Riverdale Park town	Prince George's	1.6	6,690	2,670	2,576	33	284	8	869	250	1,891	4,773
24 66762	Riverside CDP	Harford	2.4	6,128	4,879	931	24	97	3	72	122	197	4,350
24 66850	Riviera Beach CDP	Anne Arundel	2.7	12,695	12,076	274	38	131	15	48	113	175	9,451
24 67000	Robinwood CDP	Washington	3.8	4,731	4,160	300	9	125	9	47	81	105	3,548
24 67675	Rockville city	Montgomery	13.4	47,388	32,120	4,317	160	7,030	15	2,265	1,481	5,529	36,307
24 68300	Rosaryville CDP	Prince George's	13.7	12,322	4,206	7,340	79	329	13	78	277	261	8,872
24 68400	Rosedale CDP	Baltimore	6.9	19,199	14,343	4,070	47	366	12	100	261	266	14,625
24 68675	Rossmoor CDP	Montgomery	1.1	7,569	6,294	876	3	132	1	137	126	335	7,175
24 68700	Rossville CDP	Baltimore	5.4	11,515	8,130	2,520	33	491	1	143	197	329	8,868
24 69350	St. Charles CDP	Charles	11.8	33,379	21,453	9,571	234	805	23	351	942	1,114	22,807
24 69925	Salisbury city	Wicomico	11.1	23,743	14,414	7,673	55	757	6	348	490	806	18,571
24 70487	Savage-Guilford CDP	Howard	4.9	12,918	8,505	3,015	47	760	6	179	410	468	9,132
24 70850	Seat Pleasant city	Prince George's	0.7	4,885	98	4,725	5	8	-	7	42	32	3,414
24 71050	Selby-on-the-Bay CDP	Anne Arundel	3.2	3,674	3,537	45	6	16	-	10	60	45	2,746
24 71150	Severn CDP	Anne Arundel	14.0	35,076	19,730	12,124	148	1,504	34	477	1,059	1,390	24,464
24 71200	Severna Park CDP	Anne Arundel	12.9	28,507	26,355	939	50	790	12	92	269	338	20,510
24 71450	Shady Side CDP	Anne Arundel	7.3	5,559	4,791	623	26	26	-	22	71	70	4,070
24 72450	Silver Spring CDP	Montgomery	9.4	76,540	35,678	21,482	338	6,293	48	8,844	3,857	17,004	58,973
24 73550	South Gate CDP	Anne Arundel	6.3	28,672	20,341	5,631	101	1,513	26	374	686	899	21,252
24 73600	South Kensington CDP	Montgomery	2.1	7,887	7,262	191	12	223	4	75	120	385	5,985
24 73650	South Laurel CDP	Prince George's	4.3	20,479	7,922	10,178	39	1,148	7	523	662	1,077	15,108
24 74282	Springdale CDP	Prince George's	0.8	2,645	72	2,441	7	46	2	22	55	42	1,828

Table D-1. Places — **Area and Population**—Con.

[Includes incorporated places and census designated places (CDPs) of 2,500 or more population as of April 1, 2000. Codes shown are two-digit Federal Information Processing Standards (FIPS) state codes and five-digit FIPS place codes. Place names and codes are those in effect as of January 1, 2000. County refers to the county (or counties) in which the place is located. IC in this column = independent city, a county equivalent. If a place is located in more than one county, counties are listed in alphabetic order]

State and place code	Place	County	Land area, 2000 (sq. mi.)	Population, 2000 (April 1)									
					By race—								
					One race								
				Total	White	Black or African American	American Indian and Alaska Native	Asian	Native Hawaiian and Other Pacific Islander	Some other race	Two or more races	Hispanic or Latino (of any race)	18 years and over
24 00000	MARYLAND—Con.												
24 75025	Stevensville CDP	Queen Anne's	6.1	5,880	5,520	153	22	67	1	40	77	60	4,025
24 75762	Suitland-Silver Hill CDP	Prince George's	5.6	33,515	1,295	31,172	103	201	9	213	522	625	22,729
24 76550	Sykesville town	Carroll	1.6	4,197	3,867	205	6	68	-	1	50	56	2,852
24 76650	Takoma Park city	Montgomery	2.1	17,299	8,440	5,876	76	754	6	1,287	860	2,494	13,224
24 76725	Taneytown city	Carroll	2.9	5,128	4,923	89	8	24	-	32	52	77	3,378
24 77100	Temple Hills CDP	Prince George's	1.4	7,792	726	6,624	16	109	12	185	120	342	5,488
24 77825	Thurmont town	Frederick	3.0	5,588	5,481	15	15	21	-	15	41	37	4,000
24 78425	Towson CDP	Baltimore	14.0	51,793	45,028	3,901	52	1,936	11	262	603	985	42,779
24 78650	Travilah CDP	Montgomery	14.4	7,442	5,939	259	6	1,020	3	52	163	277	5,249
24 81175	Waldorf CDP	Charles	12.8	22,312	13,634	7,136	121	578	5	196	642	650	15,494
24 81250	Walker Mill CDP	Prince George's	3.2	11,104	274	10,548	41	29	1	25	186	100	7,677
24 81275	Walkersville town	Frederick	4.3	5,192	4,938	101	4	62	-	25	62	85	3,611
24 83025	West Laurel CDP	Prince George's	4.1	4,083	3,449	381	-	148	1	33	71	140	3,090
24 83100	Westminster city	Carroll	5.7	16,731	15,272	919	38	201	6	109	186	297	12,698
24 83225	West Ocean City CDP	Worcester	4.0	3,311	3,180	53	14	22	1	2	39	47	2,656
24 83837	Wheaton-Glenmont CDP	Montgomery	10.2	57,694	28,802	10,862	229	7,018	35	7,648	3,100	14,956	43,313
24 84350	White Marsh CDP	Baltimore	5.3	8,485	7,448	363	27	458	3	78	108	186	6,486
24 84375	White Oak CDP	Montgomery	5.0	20,973	8,509	7,771	70	2,344	21	1,372	886	2,722	15,930
24 86475	Woodlawn CDP	Baltimore	9.6	36,079	13,849	18,581	109	2,243	18	383	896	849	26,438
24 86525	Woodlawn CDP	Prince George's	1.1	6,251	1,091	4,522	24	138	6	304	166	597	4,394
24 86710	Woodmore CDP	Prince George's	12.1	6,077	1,747	3,945	7	179	1	53	145	123	4,333
25 00000	MASSACHUSETTS		7,840.0	6,349,097	5,367,286	343,454	15,015	238,124	2,489	236,724	146,005	428,729	4,849,033
25 00135	Abington CDP	Plymouth	9.9	14,605	14,237	111	17	71	1	47	121	103	10,867
25 00530	Acushnet Center CDP	Bristol	1.5	3,171	3,072	21	10	3	1	23	41	32	2,475
25 00590	Adams CDP	Berkshire	2.3	5,784	5,682	20	7	12	2	21	40	59	4,520
25 00765	Agawam city	Hampden	23.2	28,144	27,217	257	48	275	3	120	224	514	21,931
25 01220	Amesbury CDP	Essex	5.3	12,327	11,941	80	26	74	2	35	169	129	9,191
25 01360	Amherst Center CDP	Hampshire	4.9	17,050	13,810	878	38	1,368	11	422	523	916	15,989
25 01430	Andover CDP	Essex	3.7	7,900	7,413	85	6	248	4	75	69	144	6,099
25 01640	Arlington CDP	Middlesex	5.2	42,389	38,561	719	57	2,107	6	279	660	787	34,605
25 02515	Athol CDP	Worcester	8.3	8,370	8,036	64	35	35	2	59	139	183	6,162
25 02690	Attleboro city	Bristol	27.5	42,068	38,410	691	67	1,367	15	765	753	1,805	31,394
25 03040	Ayer CDP	Middlesex	1.2	2,960	2,614	146	7	78	4	32	79	92	2,313
25 03600	Barnstable Town city	Barnstable	60.0	47,821	43,925	1,309	283	387	18	799	1,100	812	37,323
25 04790	Belchertown CDP	Hampshire	5.0	2,626	2,472	33	6	47	1	22	45	56	1,914
25 04965	Bellingham CDP	Norfolk	5.3	4,497	4,325	54	6	34	3	24	51	64	3,309
25 05105	Belmont CDP	Middlesex	4.7	24,194	22,062	266	31	1,393	2	100	340	440	18,707
25 05595	Beverly city	Essex	16.6	39,862	38,257	413	70	511	12	207	392	720	31,207
25 06170	Bliss Corner CDP	Bristol	2.0	5,466	5,186	38	8	54	-	56	124	51	4,479
25 07000	Boston city	Suffolk	48.4	589,141	320,944	149,202	2,365	44,284	366	46,102	25,878	85,089	472,582
25 07700	Braintree CDP	Norfolk	13.4	33,698	31,677	391	36	1,051	11	216	316	394	26,122
25 08050	Bridgewater CDP	Plymouth	2.2	6,664	5,362	131	4	123	4	941	95	217	5,569
25 09000	Brockton city	Plymouth	21.5	94,304	57,989	16,811	338	2,066	34	9,728	7,338	7,552	68,050
25 09210	Brookline CDP	Norfolk	6.8	57,107	46,304	1,566	71	7,325	16	578	1,247	2,018	47,604
25 09875	Burlington CDP	Middlesex	11.8	22,876	19,836	312	16	2,436	5	74	197	296	17,483
25 10015	Buzzards Bay CDP	Barnstable	2.0	3,549	3,389	36	19	32	-	35	38	37	2,986
25 11000	Cambridge city	Middlesex	6.4	101,355	69,022	12,079	290	12,036	77	3,230	4,621	7,455	87,908
25 13205	Chelsea city	Suffolk	2.2	35,080	20,328	2,544	170	1,647	32	8,049	2,310	16,984	25,512
25 13660	Chicopee city	Hampden	22.9	54,653	49,089	1,244	107	474	57	2,679	1,003	4,790	42,284
25 14430	Clinton CDP	Worcester	1.5	7,884	7,066	183	20	60	5	386	164	873	6,144
25 14570	Cochituate CDP	Middlesex	3.8	6,768	6,152	63	6	422	4	16	105	68	4,925
25 15340	Cordaville CDP	Worcester	1.8	2,515	2,319	20	-	130	3	18	25	44	1,619
25 16285	Danvers CDP	Essex	13.3	25,212	24,638	87	25	281	4	55	122	210	19,370
25 16530	Dedham CDP	Norfolk	10.5	23,464	22,175	362	37	439	10	188	253	567	18,256
25 16740	Dennis CDP	Barnstable	4.9	2,798	2,738	7	3	13	-	9	28	29	2,345
25 16810	Dennis Port CDP	Barnstable	3.1	3,612	3,252	177	13	14	-	63	93	108	2,965
25 18840	East Dennis CDP	Barnstable	4.8	3,299	3,203	26	7	11	-	24	28	55	2,782
25 18980	East Falmouth CDP	Barnstable	5.4	6,615	6,099	193	32	34	1	111	145	116	5,192
25 19330	Easthampton city	Hampshire	13.4	15,994	15,260	102	23	275	1	180	153	336	12,612
25 19400	East Harwich CDP	Barnstable	8.0	4,744	4,585	16	7	18	2	51	65	44	3,823
25 20380	East Sandwich CDP	Barnstable	7.5	3,720	3,671	8	3	13	1	8	16	25	2,839
25 21990	Everett city	Middlesex	3.4	38,037	30,321	2,386	120	1,236	26	1,898	2,050	3,617	29,806
25 23000	Fall River city	Bristol	31.0	91,938	83,815	2,283	172	1,987	25	1,311	2,345	3,040	69,759
25 23070	Falmouth CDP	Barnstable	2.1	4,115	3,908	59	18	38	-	48	44	53	3,600
25 23875	Fitchburg city	Worcester	27.8	39,102	32,007	1,426	138	1,668	13	2,652	1,198	5,852	28,998
25 24190	Forestdale CDP	Barnstable	3.7	3,992	3,871	34	23	20	-	14	30	51	2,644
25 24855	Foxborough CDP	Norfolk	2.9	5,509	5,320	78	7	59	-	16	29	88	4,313
25 24960	Framingham CDP	Middlesex	25.1	66,910	53,373	3,409	116	3,527	27	4,195	2,263	7,265	52,575
25 25100	Franklin city	Norfolk	26.7	29,560	28,364	318	43	491	9	87	248	318	20,595
25 25485	Gardner city	Worcester	22.2	20,770	19,343	476	70	284	16	253	328	848	15,841
25 26150	Gloucester city	Essex	26.0	30,273	29,361	186	37	218	7	152	312	449	23,614
25 27060	Greenfield CDP	Franklin	5.7	13,716	12,774	193	50	168	1	174	356	471	10,747
25 29405	Haverhill city	Essex	33.3	58,969	52,878	1,419	129	801	18	2,536	1,188	5,174	43,817
25 30175	Hingham CDP	Plymouth	3.1	5,352	5,263	8	1	21	-	16	43	25	3,856
25 30420	Holbrook CDP	Norfolk	7.4	10,785	9,908	430	20	162	1	120	144	257	8,305
25 30840	Holyoke city	Hampden	21.3	39,838	26,197	1,476	151	324	48	10,521	1,121	16,485	28,098

U.S. Census Bureau, County and City Data Book: 2000

Table D-1. Places — **Area and Population**—Con.

[Includes incorporated places and census designated places (CDPs) of 2,500 or more population as of April 1, 2000. Codes shown are two-digit Federal Information Processing Standards (FIPS) state codes and five-digit FIPS place codes. Place names and codes are those in effect as of January 1, 2000. County refers to the county (or counties) in which the place is located. IC in this column = independent city, a county equivalent. If a place is located in more than one county, counties are listed in alphabetic order]

State and place code	Place	County	Land area, 2000 (sq. mi.)	Population, 2000 (April 1)									
					By race—								
					One race							Hispanic or Latino (of any race)	18 years and over
				Total	White	Black or African American	American Indian and Alaska Native	Asian	Native Hawaiian and Other Pacific Islander	Some other race	Two or more races		
25 00000	MASSACHUSETTS—Con.												
25 30980	Hopedale CDP	Worcester	1.7	4,158	4,051	21	1	28	-	26	31	54	3,050
25 31050	Hopkinton CDP	Middlesex	1.7	2,628	2,554	9	4	24	2	18	17	54	1,932
25 31575	Hudson CDP	Middlesex	5.7	14,388	13,512	126	21	175	4	236	314	501	11,045
25 31680	Hull CDP	Plymouth	3.0	11,050	10,713	51	34	98	5	51	98	120	8,612
25 32275	Ipswich CDP	Essex	1.7	4,161	4,027	16	6	41	-	23	48	46	3,238
25 33185	Kingston CDP	Plymouth	4.8	5,380	5,192	73	9	30	-	33	43	26	4,074
25 34550	Lawrence city	Essex	7.0	72,043	35,044	3,516	583	1,910	71	26,418	4,501	43,019	49,024
25 35075	Leominster city	Worcester	28.9	41,303	35,982	1,529	63	1,006	24	1,785	914	4,544	30,762
25 35250	Lexington CDP	Middlesex	16.4	30,355	26,146	343	23	3,310	2	102	429	428	22,352
25 36020	Littleton Common CDP	Middlesex	3.5	2,816	2,732	8	2	37	1	7	29	34	2,139
25 36335	Longmeadow CDP	Hampden	9.0	15,633	14,917	108	8	453	9	41	97	170	11,444
25 37000	Lowell city	Middlesex	13.8	105,167	72,145	4,423	256	17,371	38	6,813	4,121	14,734	76,826
25 37490	Lynn city	Essex	10.8	89,050	60,452	9,394	332	5,730	79	8,744	4,319	16,383	64,999
25 37595	Lynnfield CDP	Essex	10.1	11,542	11,165	50	-	222	4	24	77	77	8,676
25 37875	Malden city	Middlesex	5.1	56,340	40,618	4,592	80	7,882	33	1,184	1,951	2,696	45,102
25 38230	Mansfield Center CDP	Bristol	2.9	7,320	6,912	175	17	108	3	37	68	127	5,492
25 38435	Marblehead CDP	Essex	4.5	20,377	19,879	89	16	200	6	38	149	179	15,507
25 38715	Marlborough city	Middlesex	21.1	36,255	31,796	787	72	1,364	13	1,186	1,037	2,196	27,824
25 38820	Marshfield CDP	Plymouth	5.1	4,246	4,154	22	6	19	1	9	35	29	3,214
25 39485	Mattapoisett Center CDP	Plymouth	4.4	2,966	2,851	29	2	27	-	36	21	23	2,298
25 39660	Maynard CDP	Middlesex	5.2	10,433	9,874	108	28	169	-	123	131	290	7,991
25 39730	Medfield CDP	Norfolk	5.0	6,670	6,417	35	5	148	-	16	49	57	4,623
25 39835	Medford city	Middlesex	8.1	55,765	48,209	3,401	63	2,157	17	633	1,285	1,443	45,756
25 40115	Melrose city	Middlesex	4.7	27,134	25,820	255	26	546	6	109	372	283	21,165
25 40710	Methuen city	Essex	22.4	43,789	39,126	591	97	1,040	5	2,131	799	4,221	32,958
25 40885	Middleborough Center CDP	Plymouth	4.1	6,913	6,568	118	21	44	2	45	115	70	5,049
25 41200	Milford CDP	Worcester	10.0	24,230	22,421	344	28	440	17	516	464	1,129	18,350
25 41532	Millis-Clicquot CDP	Norfolk	3.1	4,607	4,461	47	4	54	-	6	35	41	3,416
25 41725	Milton CDP	Norfolk	13.0	26,062	22,252	2,666	17	531	10	164	422	450	19,341
25 43615	Nahant CDP	Essex	1.2	3,632	3,527	14	3	39	2	17	30	39	2,956
25 43755	Nantucket CDP	Nantucket	2.5	3,830	3,164	472	1	35	-	60	98	67	3,292
25 44140	Needham CDP	Norfolk	12.6	28,911	27,412	201	8	1,024	-	73	193	341	21,335
25 45000	New Bedford city	Bristol	20.1	93,768	73,950	4,112	579	614	44	8,915	5,554	9,576	70,441
25 45245	Newburyport city	Essex	8.4	17,189	16,864	73	21	105	2	27	97	151	13,638
25 45560	Newton city	Middlesex	18.1	83,829	73,831	1,653	61	6,434	29	598	1,223	2,111	66,018
25 46225	North Adams city	Berkshire	20.4	14,681	13,946	245	39	117	5	117	212	298	11,399
25 46295	North Amherst CDP	Hampshire	2.1	6,019	4,560	267	15	788	13	187	189	387	5,167
25 46330	Northampton city	Hampshire	34.5	28,978	26,083	602	86	906	15	697	589	1,518	24,061
25 46585	North Attleborough Center CDP	Bristol	5.5	16,796	16,029	189	29	292	4	102	151	284	12,587
25 46785	Northborough CDP	Worcester	3.3	6,257	5,858	43	7	263	5	20	61	76	4,488
25 47100	North Brookfield CDP	Worcester	1.5	2,527	2,466	9	7	-	-	13	32	34	1,849
25 47730	North Falmouth CDP	Barnstable	4.0	3,355	3,219	35	5	28	-	31	37	31	2,656
25 48710	North Pembroke CDP	Plymouth	4.4	2,913	2,829	13	-	29	-	12	30	21	2,057
25 48780	North Plymouth CDP	Plymouth	1.3	3,593	3,358	70	10	21	-	37	97	36	2,714
25 49165	North Scituate CDP	Plymouth	3.9	5,065	4,954	11	2	21	2	47	28	48	3,672
25 49200	North Seekonk CDP	Bristol	1.3	2,598	2,536	11	4	32	-	9	6	27	1,977
25 49700	Northwest Harwich CDP	Barnstable	8.1	4,001	3,766	46	9	3	4	115	58	51	3,221
25 49710	North Westport CDP	Bristol	5.2	4,533	4,427	11	4	29	1	18	43	34	3,583
25 50005	Norton Center CDP	Bristol	1.8	2,618	1,719	41	7	38	-	769	44	91	2,326
25 50285	Norwood CDP	Norfolk	10.5	28,587	25,873	659	27	1,446	4	221	357	473	22,652
25 50862	Ocean Bluff-Brant Rock CDP	Plymouth	2.0	5,100	5,016	15	4	15	-	15	35	27	3,801
25 50880	Ocean Grove CDP	Bristol	0.7	3,012	2,930	13	3	8	-	7	51	11	2,385
25 51230	Orange CDP	Franklin	6.0	3,945	3,782	48	10	24	1	23	57	70	2,814
25 51790	Oxford CDP	Worcester	3.5	5,899	5,743	30	17	27	-	12	70	38	4,504
25 52070	Palmer CDP	Hampden	4.1	3,900	3,718	56	11	40	-	20	55	59	3,028
25 52490	Peabody city	Essex	16.4	48,129	45,204	466	57	667	7	883	845	1,651	37,413
25 52770	Pepperell CDP	Middlesex	2.0	2,517	2,424	17	5	31	-	7	33	18	1,751
25 53680	Pinehurst CDP	Middlesex	3.8	6,941	6,589	71	11	166	2	13	89	90	5,062
25 53960	Pittsfield city	Berkshire	40.7	45,793	42,395	1,674	65	533	20	354	752	934	35,190
25 54275	Plymouth CDP	Plymouth	2.3	7,658	7,184	176	24	72	2	68	132	92	6,093
25 54450	Pocasset CDP	Barnstable	3.7	2,671	2,571	34	14	7	-	14	31	10	2,240
25 55535	Provincetown CDP	Barnstable	1.8	3,192	2,794	239	10	16	-	36	97	67	2,950
25 55745	Quincy city	Norfolk	16.8	88,025	70,066	1,947	142	13,546	20	751	1,553	1,835	72,644
25 55990	Randolph CDP	Norfolk	10.1	30,963	19,455	6,456	70	3,151	11	782	1,038	1,006	23,748
25 56095	Raynham Center CDP	Bristol	4.3	3,633	3,495	38	1	41	3	22	33	27	2,691
25 56165	Reading CDP	Middlesex	9.9	23,708	22,871	86	15	525	6	50	155	200	17,476
25 56585	Revere city	Suffolk	5.9	47,283	39,884	1,364	124	2,146	35	1,942	1,788	4,465	37,363
25 57845	Rockport CDP	Essex	4.0	5,606	5,489	14	8	26	1	21	47	55	4,453
25 58965	Sagamore CDP	Barnstable	3.4	3,544	3,329	57	16	27	1	39	75	59	2,682
25 59105	Salem city	Essex	8.1	40,407	34,497	1,274	87	807	19	2,724	999	4,541	32,250
25 59210	Salisbury CDP	Essex	5.9	4,484	4,360	24	12	22	7	15	44	66	3,510
25 59700	Sandwich CDP	Barnstable	3.6	3,058	2,998	7	4	15	1	14	19	20	2,473
25 60050	Saugus CDP	Essex	11.0	26,078	25,379	114	14	314	10	70	177	254	20,728
25 60295	Scituate CDP	Plymouth	4.1	5,069	4,854	52	3	27	-	67	66	39	3,927
25 60820	Sharon CDP	Norfolk	3.0	5,941	5,490	146	14	184	1	29	77	67	4,112

Table D-1. Places — **Area and Population**—Con.

[Includes incorporated places and census designated places (CDPs) of 2,500 or more population as of April 1, 2000. Codes shown are two-digit Federal Information Processing Standards (FIPS) state codes and five-digit FIPS place codes. Place names and codes are those in effect as of January 1, 2000. County refers to the county (or counties) in which the place is located. IC in this column = independent city, a county equivalent. If a place is located in more than one county, counties are listed in alphabetic order]

State and place code	Place	County	Land area, 2000 (sq. mi.)	Population, 2000 (April 1) Total	By race— One race White	Black or African American	American Indian and Alaska Native	Asian	Native Hawaiian and Other Pacific Islander	Some other race	Two or more races	Hispanic or Latino (of any race)	18 years and over
25 00000	MASSACHUSETTS—Con.												
25 62300	Smith Mills CDP	Bristol	4.7	4,432	4,238	12	12	47	2	58	63	59	3,502
25 62465	Somerset CDP	Bristol	8.1	18,234	17,909	30	22	97	4	28	144	90	14,516
25 62535	Somerville city	Middlesex	4.1	77,478	59,635	5,035	171	4,990	50	3,840	3,757	6,786	65,983
25 62675	South Amherst CDP	Hampshire	4.2	5,039	3,611	353	11	545	6	272	241	495	4,040
25 63305	Southbridge CDP	Worcester	5.3	12,878	10,708	187	55	234	8	1,336	350	3,073	9,580
25 63655	South Dennis CDP	Barnstable	4.6	3,679	3,510	37	22	13	-	33	64	48	2,933
25 63690	South Duxbury CDP	Plymouth	3.0	3,062	3,000	8	7	20	-	2	25	24	2,132
25 66035	South Yarmouth CDP	Barnstable	7.0	11,603	10,993	177	40	73	7	120	193	189	9,615
25 66070	Spencer CDP	Worcester	2.1	6,032	5,886	37	19	17	1	25	47	97	4,561
25 67000	Springfield city	Hampden	32.1	152,082	85,329	31,960	569	2,916	143	25,016	6,149	41,343	108,055
25 67700	Stoneham CDP	Middlesex	6.1	22,219	21,110	197	12	558	9	132	201	397	17,562
25 68680	Swampscott CDP	Essex	3.0	14,412	14,047	106	9	98	3	41	108	183	10,959
25 69170	Taunton city	Bristol	46.6	55,976	51,315	1,534	92	334	18	1,448	1,235	2,198	42,057
25 69730	Three Rivers CDP	Hampden	3.2	2,939	2,863	10	10	4	-	13	39	31	2,206
25 70115	Topsfield CDP	Essex	2.8	2,826	2,774	3	2	16	-	12	19	24	2,062
25 70815	Turners Falls CDP	Franklin	2.0	4,441	4,216	33	15	43	5	35	94	155	3,378
25 72250	Wakefield CDP	Middlesex	7.5	24,804	24,045	111	19	354	2	49	224	204	19,197
25 72460	Walpole CDP	Norfolk	2.9	5,867	5,674	46	4	90	1	9	43	55	4,537
25 72600	Waltham city	Middlesex	12.7	59,226	49,145	2,614	95	4,318	38	1,896	1,120	5,031	50,053
25 72845	Ware CDP	Hampshire	6.2	6,174	5,902	45	15	50	1	63	98	169	4,638
25 73020	Wareham Center CDP	Plymouth	1.5	2,874	2,596	67	14	7	1	78	111	32	2,193
25 73440	Watertown city	Middlesex	4.1	32,986	30,155	572	54	1,276	6	281	642	883	28,327
25 73930	Webster CDP	Worcester	2.9	11,600	10,866	156	46	126	-	224	182	588	8,890
25 74210	Wellesley CDP	Norfolk	10.2	26,613	23,947	426	22	1,691	3	141	383	617	19,938
25 75050	Westborough CDP	Worcester	1.9	3,983	3,759	63	9	78	-	26	48	125	3,108
25 75680	West Concord CDP	Middlesex	3.4	5,632	4,708	328	6	197	1	316	76	348	4,491
25 75820	West Dennis CDP	Barnstable	3.3	2,570	2,455	61	14	8	-	11	21	24	2,237
25 76030	Westfield city	Hampden	46.6	40,072	37,881	365	90	329	19	850	538	2,008	30,534
25 77885	West Springfield CDP	Hampden	16.7	27,899	25,300	572	61	551	10	819	586	1,605	21,360
25 78795	West Yarmouth CDP	Barnstable	6.7	6,460	6,014	131	31	34	1	95	154	108	5,317
25 78900	Weymouth CDP	Norfolk	17.0	53,988	51,229	779	102	843	28	344	663	721	42,132
25 79495	Whitinsville CDP	Worcester	3.6	6,340	6,010	64	18	21	2	75	150	151	4,484
25 79705	Wilbraham CDP	Hampden	5.6	3,544	3,442	37	3	28	3	13	18	50	2,664
25 79950	Williamstown CDP	Berkshire	3.4	4,754	4,130	182	3	228	5	57	149	173	4,200
25 80195	Wilmington CDP	Middlesex	17.1	21,363	20,575	88	17	434	1	90	158	203	15,463
25 80370	Winchendon CDP	Worcester	2.3	4,246	4,044	44	17	36	-	53	52	102	3,017
25 80545	Winchester CDP	Middlesex	6.0	20,810	19,375	142	29	961	3	57	243	211	15,468
25 80965	Winthrop CDP	Suffolk	2.0	18,303	17,286	308	30	210	8	249	212	493	14,890
25 81035	Woburn city	Middlesex	12.7	37,258	33,744	697	36	1,806	19	535	421	1,152	29,396
25 82000	Worcester city	Worcester	37.6	172,648	133,124	11,892	769	8,402	96	12,504	5,861	26,155	131,921
25 82595	Yarmouth Port CDP	Barnstable	6.0	5,395	5,312	14	9	17	1	10	32	38	4,544
26 00000	MICHIGAN		56,803.8	9,938,444	7,966,053	1,412,742	58,479	176,510	2,692	129,552	192,416	323,877	7,342,677
26 00440	Adrian city	Lenawee	7.1	21,574	18,223	760	133	178	4	1,666	610	3,665	16,123
26 00980	Albion city	Calhoun	4.5	9,144	5,582	3,038	33	63	-	147	281	416	6,788
26 01180	Algonac city	St. Clair	1.4	4,613	4,491	7	44	9	1	8	53	47	3,435
26 01260	Allegan city	Allegan	3.8	4,838	4,424	228	12	31	2	65	76	138	3,548
26 01340	Allendale CDP	Ottawa	22.8	11,555	10,771	343	39	103	9	167	123	350	9,162
26 01380	Allen Park city	Wayne	7.0	29,376	28,083	214	106	238	7	354	374	1,389	22,867
26 01540	Alma city	Gratiot	5.4	9,275	8,695	49	48	70	1	238	174	576	7,248
26 01660	Almont village	Lapeer	1.5	2,803	2,678	9	15	10	-	65	26	116	1,954
26 01740	Alpena city	Alpena	8.4	11,304	11,040	47	49	54	1	10	103	67	8,706
26 03000	Ann Arbor city	Washtenaw	27.0	114,024	85,151	10,070	332	13,566	41	1,384	3,480	3,814	94,915
26 04000	Auburn Hills city	Oakland	16.6	19,837	15,061	2,623	64	1,255	8	309	517	892	15,786
26 04740	Bad Axe city	Huron	2.1	3,462	3,378	9	9	20	-	13	33	53	2,625
26 05920	Battle Creek city	Calhoun	42.8	53,364	39,838	9,501	411	1,033	6	1,126	1,449	2,475	38,829
26 06020	Bay City city	Bay	10.4	36,817	33,575	1,003	272	195	3	910	859	2,473	27,429
26 06820	Beecher CDP	Genesee	5.9	12,793	3,583	8,438	75	10	5	246	436	506	8,399
26 06880	Beechwood CDP	Ottawa	1.8	2,963	2,573	36	9	126	1	163	55	399	2,104
26 06900	Belding city	Ionia	4.7	5,877	5,669	23	32	26	1	36	90	177	4,077
26 07020	Belleville city	Wayne	1.1	3,997	3,499	315	16	47	-	38	82	101	3,120
26 07520	Benton Harbor city	Berrien	4.4	11,182	613	10,332	17	15	4	16	185	65	6,756
26 07540	Benton Heights CDP	Berrien	3.8	5,458	1,665	3,582	22	7	-	48	134	79	3,478
26 07660	Berkley city	Oakland	2.6	15,531	14,923	108	38	160	2	62	238	204	11,989
26 08160	Beverly Hills village	Oakland	4.0	10,437	9,728	318	16	193	2	30	150	147	7,873
26 08300	Big Rapids city	Mecosta	4.2	10,849	9,066	1,153	79	243	4	54	250	199	9,197
26 08640	Birmingham city	Oakland	4.8	19,291	18,545	175	28	290	7	36	210	230	15,197
26 09000	Blissfield village	Lenawee	2.1	3,223	3,113	2	1	2	-	84	21	198	2,385
26 09180	Bloomfield Hills city	Oakland	4.9	3,940	3,573	65	4	259	-	10	29	43	3,165
26 09190	Bloomfield Township CDP	Oakland	24.9	43,021	37,730	1,849	35	2,783	23	125	476	595	32,779
26 09820	Boyne City city	Charlevoix	3.9	3,503	3,395	4	40	6	2	14	42	26	2,579
26 10440	Bridgeport CDP	Saginaw	8.3	7,849	5,027	2,244	42	19	-	301	216	808	5,793
26 10620	Brighton city	Livingston	3.6	6,701	6,474	23	28	88	-	26	62	99	5,250
26 11200	Brownlee Park CDP	Calhoun	2.0	2,588	2,358	70	26	17	2	39	76	109	1,871
26 11400	Buchanan city	Berrien	2.4	4,681	4,038	479	22	24	-	28	90	86	3,483
26 11555	Buena Vista CDP	Saginaw	4.5	7,845	1,766	5,434	35	13	1	385	211	770	5,428
26 12060	Burton city	Genesee	23.5	30,308	27,910	1,075	230	224	8	244	617	705	22,001
26 12280	Byron Center CDP	Kent	5.0	3,777	3,699	4	7	23	1	8	35	36	2,550

[Includes incorporated places and census designated places (CDPs) of 2,500 or more population as of April 1, 2000. Codes shown are two-digit Federal Information Processing Standards (FIPS) state codes and five-digit FIPS place codes. Place names and codes are those in effect as of January 1, 2000. County refers to the county (or counties) in which the place is located. IC in this column = independent city, a county equivalent. If a place is located in more than one county, counties are listed in alphabetic order]

State and place code	Place	County	Land area, 2000 (sq. mi.)	Population, 2000 (April 1)									
					By race—							Hispanic or Latino (of any race)	18 years and over
					One race						Two or more races		
				Total	White	Black or African American	American Indian and Alaska Native	Asian	Native Hawaiian and Other Pacific Islander	Some other race			
26 00000	MICHIGAN—Con.												
26 12320	Cadillac city	Wexford	6.8	10,000	9,655	21	92	63	3	28	138	118	7,376
26 13110	Canton CDP	Wayne	36.0	76,366	64,045	3,466	224	6,664	17	489	1,461	1,788	54,196
26 13220	Carleton village	Monroe	1.0	2,562	2,478	1	11	6	-	8	58	48	1,834
26 13420	Caro village	Tuscola	2.4	4,145	3,922	23	42	36	2	81	39	169	3,122
26 13560	Carrollton CDP	Saginaw	3.2	6,602	5,452	605	33	45	1	323	143	711	4,771
26 13880	Cass City village	Tuscola	1.7	2,643	2,582	9	23	13	-	6	10	33	2,002
26 14200	Cedar Springs city	Kent	1.8	3,112	2,983	9	23	14	-	37	46	119	2,137
26 14320	Center Line city	Macomb	1.7	8,531	8,004	264	21	86	-	22	134	129	6,675
26 14780	Charlevoix city	Charlevoix	2.0	2,994	2,842	8	85	6	-	13	40	37	2,348
26 14820	Charlotte city	Eaton	6.0	8,389	8,036	79	46	29	-	90	109	290	6,170
26 15000	Cheboygan city	Cheboygan	6.8	5,295	4,861	27	218	14	1	20	154	76	3,943
26 15020	Chelsea village	Washtenaw	3.3	4,398	4,272	31	12	21	3	17	42	36	3,358
26 15140	Chesaning village	Saginaw	3.1	2,548	2,492	9	6	2	1	19	19	91	1,927
26 15920	Clare city	Clare, Isabella	3.1	3,173	3,089	8	19	16	-	13	28	50	2,389
26 16160	Clawson city	Oakland	2.2	12,732	12,235	102	43	168	-	32	152	145	10,111
26 16510	Clinton CDP	Macomb	28.2	95,648	87,151	4,461	276	1,605	14	391	1,750	1,664	74,266
26 17020	Coldwater city	Branch	8.1	12,697	10,837	1,069	95	117	4	193	382	574	9,856
26 17690	Comstock Northwest CDP	Kalamazoo	3.2	4,472	3,927	336	12	74	-	43	80	94	3,403
26 17700	Comstock Park CDP	Kent	3.9	10,674	9,318	417	82	205	6	355	291	771	8,138
26 18020	Coopersville city	Ottawa	4.8	3,910	3,768	8	25	27	-	50	32	106	2,728
26 18300	Corunna city	Shiawassee	3.1	3,381	3,258	36	22	7	-	19	39	86	2,604
26 19500	Cutlerville CDP	Kent	6.0	15,114	13,441	696	88	248	3	296	342	679	10,972
26 19880	Davison city	Genesee	1.8	5,536	5,340	28	32	20	1	24	91	132	4,186
26 21000	Dearborn city	Wayne	24.4	97,775	84,931	1,248	258	1,441	14	710	9,173	2,931	70,566
26 21020	Dearborn Heights city	Wayne	11.7	58,264	53,395	1,236	216	1,306	4	470	1,637	1,974	45,134
26 22000	Detroit city	Wayne	138.8	951,270	116,599	775,772	3,140	9,268	251	24,199	22,041	47,167	655,561
26 22120	De Witt city	Clinton	2.9	4,702	4,507	48	11	30	1	19	86	120	3,113
26 22880	Dowagiac city	Cass	4.0	6,147	4,730	961	124	35	-	98	199	153	4,422
26 23380	Dundee village	Monroe	3.2	3,522	3,413	23	14	14	-	8	50	42	2,505
26 23500	Durand city	Shiawassee	2.0	3,933	3,813	3	26	3	1	22	65	70	2,865
26 23980	East Grand Rapids city	Kent	2.9	10,764	10,440	105	14	107	-	34	64	92	7,264
26 24020	East Jordan city	Charlevoix	3.1	2,507	2,366	10	44	4	-	19	64	40	1,743
26 24120	East Lansing city	Clinton, Ingham	11.2	46,525	37,645	3,441	155	3,819	38	442	985	1,252	42,325
26 24290	Eastpointe city	Macomb	5.1	34,077	31,395	1,601	143	296	2	93	547	453	25,744
26 24420	East Tawas city	Iosco	2.9	2,951	2,886	1	13	13	2	3	33	22	2,294
26 24500	Eastwood CDP	Kalamazoo	2.0	6,265	4,696	1,207	18	52	3	109	180	226	4,697
26 24540	Eaton Rapids city	Eaton	3.4	5,330	5,123	20	24	29	-	54	80	156	3,678
26 24740	Ecorse city	Wayne	2.7	11,229	5,859	4,555	73	21	2	377	342	1,004	8,104
26 26360	Escanaba city	Delta	12.7	13,140	12,570	14	343	43	3	24	143	87	10,180
26 26420	Essexville city	Bay	1.2	3,766	3,628	20	30	22	-	23	43	78	2,810
26 27160	Fair Plain CDP	Berrien	4.2	7,828	3,842	3,712	36	52	5	69	112	131	5,914
26 27380	Farmington city	Oakland	2.7	10,423	8,929	285	19	1,051	2	29	108	125	8,335
26 27440	Farmington Hills city	Oakland	33.3	82,111	68,107	5,699	142	6,188	15	376	1,584	1,211	63,169
26 27760	Fenton city	Genesee	6.6	10,582	10,185	63	41	100	-	70	123	191	7,897
26 27880	Ferndale city	Oakland	3.9	22,105	20,218	757	121	292	5	141	571	399	17,601
26 27960	Ferrysburg city	Ottawa	3.0	3,040	2,929	18	23	27	-	15	28	39	2,350
26 28360	Flat Rock city	Wayne	6.7	8,488	8,091	121	42	40	-	54	140	229	6,005
26 29000	Flint city	Genesee	33.6	124,943	51,710	66,560	798	547	19	1,384	3,925	3,742	86,702
26 29200	Flushing city	Genesee	4.3	8,348	8,096	53	27	33	3	31	105	134	6,428
26 29580	Forest Hills CDP	Kent	49.4	20,942	19,954	133	41	551	1	71	191	198	14,371
26 30060	Fowlerville village	Livingston	2.3	2,972	2,862	5	40	9	1	11	44	50	2,090
26 30200	Frankenmuth city	Saginaw	2.7	4,838	4,780	13	10	14	-	3	18	46	3,850
26 30340	Franklin village	Oakland	2.7	2,937	2,637	149	3	105	-	10	33	25	2,107
26 30420	Fraser city	Macomb	4.2	15,297	14,787	139	40	142	2	32	155	203	11,592
26 30540	Freeland CDP	Saginaw	6.7	5,147	4,265	671	33	25	3	42	108	163	4,007
26 30700	Fremont city	Newaygo	3.3	4,224	4,080	16	21	42	2	20	43	83	3,087
26 31420	Garden City city	Wayne	5.9	30,047	28,904	332	120	215	2	91	383	611	22,498
26 31720	Gaylord city	Otsego	3.9	3,681	3,552	11	35	11	3	12	57	63	2,763
26 32020	Gibraltar city	Wayne	3.8	4,264	4,125	22	14	17	-	25	61	78	3,263
26 32300	Gladstone city	Delta	5.0	5,032	4,869	7	74	11	4	2	65	21	3,780
26 32320	Gladwin city	Gladwin	2.9	3,001	2,884	7	16	32	-	11	51	45	2,255
26 33280	Grand Blanc city	Genesee	3.8	8,242	7,349	413	22	265	-	48	145	138	6,215
26 33340	Grand Haven city	Ottawa	5.8	11,168	10,760	50	63	97	2	45	151	177	8,918
26 33420	Grand Ledge city	Clinton, Eaton	3.6	7,813	7,526	34	31	45	2	61	114	204	5,768
26 34000	Grand Rapids city	Kent	44.6	197,800	133,116	40,373	1,454	3,195	238	13,115	6,309	25,818	144,319
26 34160	Grandville city	Kent	7.4	16,263	15,440	227	43	189	4	142	218	501	11,733
26 35100	Greenville city	Montcalm	5.7	7,935	7,630	43	43	25	6	92	96	258	5,921
26 35440	Grosse Ile CDP	Wayne	9.6	10,894	10,374	39	37	299	4	32	109	175	8,183
26 35480	Grosse Pointe city	Wayne	1.1	5,670	5,510	45	4	59	1	17	34	83	4,231
26 35520	Grosse Pointe Farms city	Wayne	2.7	9,764	9,528	63	11	110	-	11	41	108	7,177
26 35540	Grosse Pointe Park city	Wayne	2.2	12,443	11,507	367	44	226	4	49	246	217	9,023
26 35560	Grosse Pointe Shores village	Macomb, Wayne	1.1	2,823	2,648	17	7	115	-	12	24	49	2,182
26 35580	Grosse Pointe Woods city	Wayne	3.3	17,080	16,448	108	11	355	-	19	139	167	12,620
26 36280	Hamtramck city	Wayne	2.1	22,976	14,007	3,473	98	2,382	23	262	2,731	300	16,600
26 36300	Hancock city	Houghton	2.5	4,323	4,148	33	40	46	1	10	45	33	3,501
26 36700	Harper Woods city	Wayne	2.6	14,254	12,247	1,460	48	243	1	57	198	224	11,061
26 36810	Harrison CDP	Macomb	14.3	24,461	23,123	604	94	141	10	109	380	362	19,109

Table D-1. Places — **Area and Population**—Con.

[Includes incorporated places and census designated places (CDPs) of 2,500 or more population as of April 1, 2000. Codes shown are two-digit Federal Information Processing Standards (FIPS) state codes and five-digit FIPS place codes. Place names and codes are those in effect as of January 1, 2000. County refers to the county (or counties) in which the place is located. IC in this column = independent city, a county equivalent. If a place is located in more than one county, counties are listed in alphabetic order]

State and place code	Place	County	Land area, 2000 (sq. mi.)	Total	White	Black or African American	American Indian and Alaska Native	Asian	Native Hawaiian and Other Pacific Islander	Some other race	Two or more races	Hispanic or Latino (of any race)	18 years and over
26 00000	MICHIGAN—Con.												
26 37100	Haslett CDP	Ingham	8.3	11,283	10,422	270	34	306	3	82	166	280	8,659
26 37120	Hastings city	Barry	5.2	7,095	6,904	10	33	23	-	41	84	152	5,127
26 37420	Hazel Park city	Oakland	2.8	18,963	17,374	308	170	344	4	112	651	395	13,718
26 38180	Highland Park city	Wayne	3.0	16,746	688	15,648	45	41	3	42	279	95	11,879
26 38460	Hillsdale city	Hillsdale	5.3	8,233	7,947	49	41	68	1	40	87	126	6,382
26 38640	Holland city	Allegan, Ottawa	16.6	35,048	27,309	888	202	1,247	10	4,348	954	7,783	25,886
26 38700	Holly village	Oakland	2.8	6,135	5,837	79	27	25	1	62	104	203	4,476
26 38780	Holt CDP	Ingham	4.3	11,315	10,510	275	57	117	5	108	243	411	8,082
26 39360	Houghton city	Houghton	4.3	7,010	6,256	131	28	476	1	17	101	54	6,172
26 39400	Houghton Lake CDP	Roscommon	5.9	3,749	3,672	13	24	7	1	5	27	34	2,946
26 39540	Howell city	Livingston	4.1	9,232	8,860	29	56	114	17	67	89	199	7,004
26 39800	Hudsonville city	Ottawa	4.1	7,160	6,996	34	19	29	1	28	53	104	4,952
26 40000	Huntington Woods city	Oakland	1.5	6,151	5,964	42	3	87	-	16	39	54	4,517
26 40320	Imlay City city	Lapeer	2.3	3,869	3,430	22	11	51	-	301	54	743	2,773
26 40680	Inkster city	Wayne	6.3	30,115	7,571	20,330	124	1,031	3	224	832	482	21,129
26 40860	Ionia city	Ionia	5.0	10,569	7,512	2,319	111	69	-	225	333	537	8,616
26 40960	Iron Mountain city	Dickinson	7.2	8,154	7,964	16	39	54	1	19	61	87	6,110
26 41060	Ironwood city	Gogebic	6.6	6,293	6,137	6	45	14	-	9	82	52	4,897
26 41220	Ishpeming city	Marquette	8.7	6,686	6,505	4	80	13	-	18	66	54	5,133
26 41340	Ithaca city	Gratiot	4.1	3,098	2,975	7	20	11	-	62	23	163	2,257
26 41420	Jackson city	Jackson	11.1	36,316	26,825	7,154	203	186	14	601	1,333	1,469	25,544
26 41680	Jenison CDP	Ottawa	5.9	17,211	16,701	84	36	147	1	92	150	305	12,236
26 42160	Kalamazoo city	Kalamazoo	24.7	77,145	54,593	15,924	445	1,847	50	1,836	2,450	3,304	61,490
26 42460	Keego Harbor city	Oakland	0.5	2,769	2,605	17	32	29	-	35	51	121	2,080
26 42820	Kentwood city	Kent	21.0	45,255	36,599	4,115	207	2,550	18	644	1,122	1,757	33,233
26 43300	Kingsford city	Dickinson	4.3	5,549	5,429	12	27	18	1	1	61	30	4,143
26 44520	Lake Fenton CDP	Genesee	5.5	4,876	4,734	12	22	32	1	13	62	68	3,727
26 44940	Lake Orion village	Oakland	0.8	2,715	2,655	7	9	8	1	3	32	65	2,163
26 45420	Lambertville CDP	Monroe	6.1	9,299	9,103	31	6	53	62	32	74	167	6,688
26 46000	Lansing city	Eaton, Ingham	35.0	119,128	77,766	26,095	953	3,367	62	5,410	5,475	11,886	87,234
26 46040	Lapeer city	Lapeer	5.5	9,072	8,157	540	43	52	3	99	178	302	6,844
26 46320	Lathrup Village city	Oakland	1.5	4,236	1,992	2,110	4	26	-	9	95	40	3,194
26 47230	Level Park-Oak Park CDP	Calhoun	5.3	3,605	3,302	157	12	21	2	38	73	63	2,690
26 47800	Lincoln Park city	Wayne	5.9	40,008	37,312	824	213	204	2	728	725	2,556	30,276
26 47820	Linden city	Genesee	2.4	2,861	2,799	2	10	14	-	13	23	26	2,147
26 49000	Livonia city	Wayne	35.7	100,545	95,975	951	223	1,951	14	318	1,113	1,731	76,587
26 49540	Lowell city	Kent	2.9	4,013	3,861	23	25	17	5	29	53	86	2,839
26 49640	Ludington city	Mason	3.4	8,357	7,941	81	77	18	-	89	151	347	6,354
26 50560	Madison Heights city	Oakland	7.2	31,101	27,866	567	138	1,547	8	142	833	502	24,234
26 50720	Manistee city	Manistee	3.3	6,586	6,250	22	91	34	2	63	124	145	5,005
26 50760	Manistique city	Schoolcraft	3.2	3,583	3,118	134	185	26	-	10	110	47	2,737
26 51600	Marine City city	St. Clair	2.2	4,652	4,526	4	26	12	-	40	44	64	3,368
26 51900	Marquette city	Marquette	11.4	19,661	18,685	162	343	162	4	43	262	152	16,357
26 51940	Marshall city	Calhoun	5.9	7,459	7,154	24	32	44	-	74	131	236	5,593
26 52080	Marysville city	St. Clair	6.9	9,684	9,508	17	29	42	1	32	55	112	7,324
26 52180	Mason city	Ingham	4.6	6,714	6,444	43	31	48	-	50	98	183	4,994
26 52380	Mattawan village	Van Buren	4.1	2,536	2,388	48	9	8	-	31	52	79	1,775
26 52940	Melvindale city	Wayne	2.8	10,735	9,382	565	80	138	4	257	309	955	8,114
26 53020	Menominee city	Menominee	5.2	9,131	8,889	13	75	29	-	25	100	102	6,951
26 53580	Michigan Center CDP	Jackson	5.2	4,641	4,535	16	20	20	-	12	38	71	3,551
26 53760	Middleville village	Barry	2.1	2,721	2,605	5	12	20	-	32	47	59	1,846
26 53780	Midland city	Bay, Midland	33.2	41,685	38,924	760	122	1,123	24	236	496	802	30,884
26 53920	Milan city	Monroe, Washtenaw	2.2	4,775	4,503	83	17	33	1	82	56	167	3,458
26 53960	Milford village	Oakland	2.4	6,272	6,106	10	24	31	-	22	79	83	4,479
26 55020	Monroe city	Monroe	9.0	22,076	20,060	1,120	53	186	4	199	454	610	16,135
26 55820	Mount Clemens city	Macomb	4.2	17,312	13,121	3,395	127	85	3	132	449	404	13,575
26 55960	Mount Morris city	Genesee	1.2	3,194	2,975	98	19	13	1	20	68	71	2,302
26 56020	Mount Pleasant city	Isabella	7.8	25,946	23,124	951	399	739	17	241	475	646	22,960
26 56200	Munising city	Alger	5.4	2,539	2,380	4	89	17	3	2	44	25	1,995
26 56320	Muskegon city	Muskegon	14.4	40,105	24,309	12,701	418	183	12	1,078	1,404	2,560	29,765
26 56360	Muskegon Heights city	Muskegon	3.2	12,049	2,131	9,370	54	30	3	197	264	424	7,804
26 56860	Negaunee city	Marquette	13.8	4,576	4,422	13	59	10	-	6	66	20	3,554
26 57100	New Baltimore city	Macomb	4.6	7,405	7,175	39	27	35	1	34	94	99	5,521
26 57140	Newberry village	Luce	1.0	2,686	1,878	518	133	18	1	27	111	99	2,197
26 57380	New Haven village	Macomb	2.4	3,071	2,299	582	22	3	-	30	135	117	2,080
26 57760	Niles city	Berrien, Cass	5.8	12,204	10,030	1,509	80	63	10	154	358	485	8,921
26 58640	North Muskegon city	Muskegon	1.8	4,031	3,919	41	8	15	1	14	33	53	3,029
26 58945	Northview CDP	Kent	10.4	14,730	13,902	286	55	159	12	119	197	313	10,584
26 58980	Northville city	Oakland, Wayne	2.0	6,459	6,208	25	12	120	6	38	50	106	4,921
26 59140	Norton Shores city	Muskegon	23.2	22,527	21,317	368	164	189	2	143	344	606	16,942
26 59220	Norway city	Dickinson	8.8	2,959	2,886	-	28	2	4	7	32	23	2,209
26 59440	Novi city	Oakland	30.5	47,386	41,349	908	89	4,106	8	223	703	855	34,317
26 59920	Oak Park city	Oakland	5.0	29,793	13,989	13,690	52	648	5	179	1,230	381	21,402
26 60340	Okemos CDP	Ingham	16.8	22,805	19,159	958	76	1,980	9	139	484	509	17,345
26 61620	Otsego city	Allegan	2.0	3,933	3,819	12	22	15	-	13	52	59	2,830
26 61940	Owosso city	Shiawassee	4.9	15,713	15,244	27	94	59	-	119	170	465	11,420
26 62020	Oxford village	Oakland	1.2	3,540	3,442	21	10	19	-	11	37	94	2,543

Table D-1. Places — **Area and Population**—Con.

[Includes incorporated places and census designated places (CDPs) of 2,500 or more population as of April 1, 2000. Codes shown are two-digit Federal Information Processing Standards (FIPS) state codes and five-digit FIPS place codes. Place names and codes are those in effect as of January 1, 2000. County refers to the county (or counties) in which the place is located. IC in this column = independent city, a county equivalent. If a place is located in more than one county, counties are listed in alphabetic order]

State and place code	Place	County	Land area, 2000 (sq. mi.)	Population, 2000 (April 1) Total	By race—One race White	Black or African American	American Indian and Alaska Native	Asian	Native Hawaiian and Other Pacific Islander	Some other race	Two or more races	Hispanic or Latino (of any race)	18 years and over
26 00000	MICHIGAN—Con.												
26 62980	Paw Paw village	Van Buren	2.7	3,363	3,122	96	28	9	2	40	66	100	2,581
26 63020	Paw Paw Lake CDP	Berrien	5.2	3,944	3,811	23	20	27	2	8	53	54	3,059
26 63200	Pearl Beach CDP	St. Clair	2.1	3,224	3,165	-	13	5	-	11	30	20	2,664
26 63820	Petoskey city	Emmet	5.0	6,080	5,726	20	193	49	1	12	79	71	4,683
26 64740	Plainwell city	Allegan	2.1	3,933	3,806	18	19	14	-	26	50	65	2,891
26 64900	Pleasant Ridge city	Oakland	0.6	2,594	2,505	22	11	23	1	10	22	46	2,024
26 65060	Plymouth city	Wayne	2.2	9,022	8,699	51	32	95	6	27	112	118	7,332
26 65085	Plymouth Township CDP	Wayne	15.9	27,798	25,680	822	76	759	4	110	347	455	21,503
26 65440	Pontiac city	Oakland	20.0	66,337	25,934	31,791	382	1,591	26	4,291	2,322	8,463	46,017
26 65560	Portage city	Kalamazoo	32.2	44,897	40,746	1,676	135	1,187	10	315	828	868	33,026
26 65820	Port Huron city	St. Clair	8.1	32,338	28,034	2,504	281	179	4	428	908	1,383	23,609
26 65860	Portland city	Ionia	2.4	3,789	3,701	19	9	7	-	13	40	50	2,698
26 67620	Redford CDP	Wayne	11.2	51,622	45,418	4,410	222	392	10	295	875	1,044	38,544
26 68380	Richmond city	Macomb, St. Clair	2.9	4,897	4,673	12	15	40	9	91	57	232	3,711
26 68760	River Rouge city	Wayne	2.7	9,917	4,166	5,214	77	16	4	162	278	492	6,823
26 68880	Riverview city	Wayne	4.4	13,272	12,497	276	57	249	2	42	149	327	10,439
26 69020	Rochester city	Oakland	3.9	10,467	9,670	234	26	386	1	25	125	176	8,050
26 69035	Rochester Hills city	Oakland	32.8	68,825	61,084	1,667	139	4,652	20	322	941	1,576	50,951
26 69080	Rockford city	Kent	3.0	4,626	4,450	28	18	42	1	29	58	70	3,060
26 69180	Rockwood city	Wayne	2.7	3,442	3,292	22	34	21	-	33	40	87	2,592
26 69260	Rogers City city	Presque Isle	4.6	3,322	3,270	1	23	9	-	1	18	15	2,645
26 69400	Romeo village	Macomb	2.0	3,721	3,448	162	6	15	4	25	61	102	2,750
26 69420	Romulus city	Wayne	35.9	22,979	15,019	6,891	124	135	20	185	605	463	16,268
26 69520	Roosevelt Park city	Muskegon	1.0	3,890	3,631	122	18	41	2	24	52	76	3,027
26 69800	Roseville city	Macomb	9.8	48,129	44,968	1,252	201	785	15	154	754	722	36,992
26 70040	Royal Oak city	Oakland	11.8	60,062	56,941	927	157	939	32	228	838	781	49,367
26 70520	Saginaw city	Saginaw	17.4	61,799	29,056	26,735	302	205	10	3,619	1,872	7,259	42,264
26 70545	Saginaw Township North CDP	Saginaw	13.5	24,994	22,013	1,338	67	771	-	403	402	1,023	19,831
26 70550	Saginaw Township South CDP	Saginaw	6.9	13,801	12,401	740	35	270	2	174	179	609	10,790
26 70680	St. Clair city	St. Clair	2.8	5,802	5,649	7	14	50	-	8	74	70	4,219
26 70760	St. Clair Shores city	Macomb	11.5	63,096	61,135	435	175	531	14	111	695	745	50,356
26 70800	St. Helen CDP	Roscommon	5.0	2,993	2,947	2	19	3	1	2	19	23	2,385
26 70840	St. Ignace city	Mackinac	2.7	2,678	1,923	8	520	15	1	5	206	24	2,057
26 70940	St. Johns city	Clinton	3.9	7,485	7,159	56	42	46	4	83	95	254	5,488
26 70960	St. Joseph city	Berrien	3.4	8,789	7,937	449	36	210	2	40	115	113	7,119
26 71000	St. Louis city	Gratiot	2.9	4,494	3,730	453	46	14	-	123	128	337	3,568
26 71140	Saline city	Washtenaw	4.6	8,034	7,688	45	26	156	4	26	89	139	5,737
26 71540	Sandusky city	Sanilac	1.9	2,745	2,611	24	4	48	-	37	21	94	2,120
26 71740	Sault Ste. Marie city	Chippewa	14.8	16,542	12,239	1,077	2,270	107	9	77	763	308	13,336
26 72818	Shelby CDP	Macomb	34.7	65,159	61,870	553	158	1,374	12	291	901	1,112	48,940
26 73560	Shields CDP	Saginaw	6.5	6,590	6,375	53	18	34	-	49	61	219	4,981
26 74200	Skidway Lake CDP	Ogemaw	11.3	3,147	3,011	11	53	-	-	1	71	45	2,437
26 74900	Southfield city	Oakland	26.2	78,296	30,406	42,454	157	2,416	24	498	2,341	934	61,420
26 74960	Southgate city	Wayne	6.9	30,136	28,224	635	151	502	13	256	355	1,198	23,652
26 74980	South Haven city	Allegan, Van Buren	3.5	5,021	4,155	644	35	35	-	52	100	117	3,838
26 75100	South Lyon city	Oakland	3.4	10,036	9,703	39	17	109	12	40	116	161	7,545
26 75140	South Monroe CDP	Monroe	2.4	6,370	5,904	187	12	75	1	74	117	154	4,752
26 75420	Sparta village	Kent	2.4	4,159	3,980	26	7	17	-	78	51	149	2,924
26 75700	Springfield city	Calhoun	3.7	5,189	4,478	399	50	71	1	56	134	130	4,029
26 75820	Spring Lake village	Ottawa	1.1	2,514	2,465	8	11	6	-	9	15	33	1,993
26 76460	Sterling Heights city	Macomb	36.6	124,471	112,899	1,614	260	6,123	45	418	3,112	1,665	94,506
26 76960	Sturgis city	St. Joseph	6.0	11,285	10,306	139	39	78	-	540	183	1,499	8,097
26 77700	Swartz Creek city	Genesee	4.0	5,102	4,889	62	18	32	1	22	78	107	3,965
26 79000	Taylor city	Wayne	23.6	65,868	56,731	5,763	448	1,072	21	492	1,341	2,131	47,958
26 79120	Tecumseh city	Lenawee	5.2	8,574	8,218	16	54	59	1	128	98	377	6,312
26 79240	Temperance CDP	Monroe	4.6	7,757	7,610	15	11	41	1	31	48	150	5,636
26 79760	Three Rivers city	St. Joseph	4.5	7,328	6,182	773	30	50	-	125	168	199	5,213
26 80340	Traverse City city	Grand Traverse, Leelanau	8.4	14,532	13,950	95	142	72	5	70	198	242	11,585
26 80420	Trenton city	Wayne	7.3	19,584	18,981	73	81	152	5	45	247	390	15,025
26 80700	Troy city	Oakland	33.5	80,959	66,627	1,694	125	10,730	18	292	1,473	1,184	59,741
26 81540	Utica city	Macomb	1.8	4,577	4,292	42	17	117	-	34	75	96	3,616
26 81740	Vandercook Lake CDP	Jackson	4.6	4,809	4,623	57	26	3	2	27	71	115	3,501
26 81840	Vassar city	Tuscola	2.2	2,823	2,496	233	6	6	-	38	44	83	1,857
26 82960	Walker city	Kent	25.2	21,842	20,643	322	100	213	9	238	317	601	16,191
26 83060	Walled Lake city	Oakland	2.3	6,713	6,400	49	21	114	-	33	96	113	5,282
26 84000	Warren city	Macomb	34.3	138,247	126,205	3,697	494	4,275	30	467	3,079	1,868	106,524
26 84220	Waterford CDP	Oakland	31.3	73,150	67,777	2,114	259	926	9	829	1,236	2,863	56,193
26 84800	Waverly CDP	Eaton	5.7	16,194	13,170	1,732	58	545	8	253	428	739	12,367
26 84880	Wayland city	Allegan	2.9	3,939	3,811	25	36	6	2	25	34	82	2,741
26 84940	Wayne city	Wayne	6.0	19,051	16,072	2,151	117	275	8	82	346	369	14,023
26 85510	West Bloomfield Township CDP	Oakland	27.3	64,862	54,646	3,360	78	5,063	11	246	1,458	905	47,769
26 85700	West Ishpeming CDP	Marquette	3.0	2,792	2,750	5	4	7	-	5	21	14	2,146
26 86000	Westland city	Wayne	20.4	86,602	75,527	5,867	396	2,437	28	582	1,765	2,138	66,445
26 86050	West Monroe CDP	Monroe	1.3	3,893	3,756	38	10	25	-	27	37	69	2,800
26 86380	Westwood CDP	Kalamazoo	2.8	9,122	7,777	966	13	143	1	65	157	125	7,541

Table D-1. Places — **Area and Population**—Con.

[Includes incorporated places and census designated places (CDPs) of 2,500 or more population as of April 1, 2000. Codes shown are two-digit Federal Information Processing Standards (FIPS) state codes and five-digit FIPS place codes. Place names and codes are those in effect as of January 1, 2000. County refers to the county (or counties) in which the place is located. IC in this column = independent city, a county equivalent. If a place is located in more than one county, counties are listed in alphabetic order]

State and place code	Place	County	Land area, 2000 (sq. mi.)	Population, 2000 (April 1)									
					By race—							Hispanic or Latino (of any race)	18 years and over
					One race						Two or more races		
				Total	White	Black or African American	American Indian and Alaska Native	Asian	Native Hawaiian and Other Pacific Islander	Some other race			
26 00000	MICHIGAN—Con.												
26 86780	Whitehall city	Muskegon	3.0	2,884	2,786	22	33	9	-	20	14	60	2,172
26 87060	Whitmore Lake CDP	Livingston, Washtenaw...	4.4	6,574	6,314	61	30	31	8	15	115	96	4,963
26 87420	Williamston city	Ingham	2.5	3,441	3,336	6	11	24	-	24	40	101	2,512
26 88140	Wixom city	Oakland	9.3	13,263	11,990	332	68	378	5	206	284	424	9,963
26 88220	Wolf Lake CDP	Muskegon	3.5	4,455	4,201	46	55	4	-	63	86	188	3,212
26 88260	Wolverine Lake village	Oakland	1.3	4,415	4,316	18	5	26	3	11	36	46	3,290
26 88380	Woodhaven city	Wayne	6.5	12,530	11,680	292	61	205	2	105	185	433	9,450
26 88900	Wyandotte city	Wayne	5.3	28,006	26,976	146	136	92	8	202	446	816	21,663
26 88940	Wyoming city	Kent	24.4	69,368	58,491	3,362	406	2,025	27	3,260	1,797	6,704	49,949
26 89140	Ypsilanti city	Washtenaw	4.4	22,362	13,731	6,838	98	712	15	295	673	552	18,804
26 89260	Zeeland city	Ottawa	3.0	5,805	5,451	34	8	76	1	122	113	269	4,285
27 00000	MINNESOTA		79,610.1	4,919,479	4,400,282	171,731	54,967	141,968	1,979	65,810	82,742	143,382	3,632,585
27 00316	Afton city	Washington	25.2	2,839	2,744	7	-	29	-	11	48	27	2,077
27 00694	Albert Lea city	Freeborn	10.8	18,356	17,034	68	53	147	5	833	216	1,740	14,143
27 00730	Albertville city	Wright	4.4	3,621	3,567	11	8	9	-	3	23	24	2,387
27 00928	Alexandria city	Douglas	8.9	8,820	8,638	37	30	50	5	16	44	71	7,052
27 01486	Andover city	Anoka	34.1	26,588	25,653	143	94	286	4	86	322	278	17,148
27 01684	Annandale city	Wright	2.7	2,684	2,617	10	5	7	-	8	37	26	1,950
27 01720	Anoka city	Anoka	6.7	18,076	16,837	446	190	168	5	93	337	349	13,625
27 01864	Appleton city	Swift	2.0	2,871	1,956	308	45	144	180	69	169	139	2,524
27 01900	Apple Valley city	Dakota	17.3	45,527	41,798	870	130	1,542	17	399	771	912	31,998
27 02026	Arden Hills city	Ramsey	8.9	9,652	8,958	127	19	351	4	52	141	131	7,720
27 02260	Arnold CDP	St. Louis	11.6	3,032	2,967	11	17	7	2	1	27	10	2,200
27 02908	Austin city	Mower	10.8	23,314	21,589	188	43	517	4	720	253	1,426	17,877
27 04042	Baxter city	Crow Wing	17.3	5,555	5,479	1	12	23	-	5	35	34	3,795
27 04114	Bayport city	Washington	1.8	3,162	2,306	569	141	22	-	31	93	101	2,772
27 04618	Becker city	Sherburne	8.7	2,673	2,625	9	12	12	-	2	13	21	1,765
27 04834	Belle Plaine city	Scott	4.1	3,789	3,690	5	15	27	-	17	35	43	2,723
27 05068	Bemidji city	Beltrami	11.8	11,917	10,047	91	1,373	133	4	24	245	136	9,396
27 05212	Benson city	Swift	2.5	3,376	3,311	8	8	8	2	17	22	40	2,582
27 05752	Big Lake city	Sherburne	3.6	6,063	5,863	8	30	26	1	54	81	109	4,093
27 06382	Blaine city	Anoka, Ramsey	33.9	44,942	42,002	387	281	1,142	10	335	785	773	31,851
27 06616	Bloomington city	Hennepin	35.5	85,172	75,055	2,917	296	4,339	29	1,068	1,468	2,290	67,612
27 06688	Blue Earth city	Faribault	3.2	3,621	3,507	6	2	12	7	58	29	150	2,783
27 07300	Brainerd city	Crow Wing	8.0	13,178	12,629	94	190	60	1	34	170	113	9,864
27 07462	Breckenridge city	Wilkin	2.3	3,559	3,474	5	20	6	1	14	39	61	2,613
27 07948	Brooklyn Center city	Hennepin	7.9	29,172	20,825	4,110	253	2,565	4	434	981	823	21,862
27 07966	Brooklyn Park city	Hennepin	26.1	67,388	48,145	9,659	381	6,214	44	1,004	1,941	1,944	47,958
27 08452	Buffalo city	Wright	6.0	10,097	9,768	53	49	68	-	31	128	112	7,147
27 08794	Burnsville city	Dakota	24.9	60,220	52,717	2,452	277	2,456	46	855	1,417	1,725	44,454
27 08154	Byron city	Olmsted	1.4	3,500	3,422	8	8	31	1	16	14	31	2,286
27 09226	Caledonia city	Houston	2.9	2,965	2,916	12	5	9	-	1	22	16	2,205
27 09370	Cambridge city	Isanti	6.2	5,520	5,366	17	37	32	1	14	53	35	4,146
27 09730	Cannon Falls city	Goodhue	4.0	3,795	3,726	7	11	25	-	16	10	41	2,788
27 10648	Centerville city	Anoka	2.2	3,202	3,097	8	14	23	-	12	48	46	2,125
27 10846	Champlin city	Hennepin	8.2	22,193	21,086	314	95	367	4	83	244	250	14,746
27 10918	Chanhassen city	Carver, Hennepin	20.8	20,321	19,284	152	31	576	1	84	193	402	13,295
27 10972	Chaska city	Carver	13.7	17,449	16,351	178	49	291	1	381	198	1,013	11,779
27 11350	Chisago City city	Chisago	2.0	2,622	2,546	14	5	12	2	15	28	42	1,965
27 11386	Chisholm city	St. Louis	4.4	4,960	4,857	5	30	14	1	5	48	36	3,849
27 11494	Circle Pines city	Anoka	1.8	4,663	4,477	11	26	81	-	9	59	45	3,355
27 12160	Cloquet city	Carlton	35.2	11,201	9,880	18	1,047	44	1	15	196	71	8,330
27 12430	Cokato city	Wright	1.3	2,727	2,640	4	7	12	1	34	29	73	1,859
27 12484	Cold Spring city	Stearns	2.1	2,975	2,927	6	2	6	-	21	13	40	2,148
27 12700	Columbia Heights city	Anoka	3.4	18,520	16,184	671	304	640	2	240	479	583	14,670
27 13114	Coon Rapids city	Anoka	22.7	61,607	57,430	1,346	410	984	8	366	1,063	933	43,921
27 13168	Corcoran city	Hennepin	35.8	5,630	5,444	11	11	99	-	21	44	49	3,788
27 13456	Cottage Grove city	Washington	34.0	30,582	28,606	720	125	437	18	277	399	775	20,595
27 13870	Crookston city	Polk	4.9	8,192	7,475	41	126	40	2	380	128	722	6,206
27 14158	Crystal city	Hennepin	5.8	22,698	20,052	953	133	780	4	234	542	570	17,607
27 15022	Dayton city	Hennepin, Wright	23.5	4,699	4,477	30	30	38	-	88	36	129	3,267
27 15148	Deephaven city	Hennepin	2.3	3,853	3,751	11	13	27	2	11	38	35	2,677
27 15454	Delano city	Wright	2.6	3,837	3,767	13	6	11	-	12	28	35	2,550
27 15832	Detroit Lakes city	Becker	7.5	7,348	6,759	31	331	39	1	43	144	88	5,669
27 15976	Dilworth city	Clay	2.0	3,001	2,750	1	54	6	-	126	64	229	2,045
27 17000	Duluth city	St. Louis	68.0	86,918	80,532	1,415	2,122	993	25	251	1,580	921	68,397
27 17288	Eagan city	Dakota	32.3	63,557	55,949	2,166	164	3,372	66	613	1,227	1,424	44,501
27 17486	East Bethel city	Anoka	44.9	10,941	10,673	21	47	49	-	35	116	104	7,428
27 17612	East Grand Forks city	Polk	5.0	7,501	6,824	39	126	25	1	335	151	565	5,339
27 18116	Eden Prairie city	Hennepin	32.4	54,901	49,771	1,253	114	2,644	17	276	826	862	38,182
27 18188	Edina city	Hennepin	15.7	47,425	44,712	546	62	1,418	14	165	508	539	36,587
27 18674	Elk River city	Sherburne	42.7	16,447	15,984	73	61	81	2	79	167	219	11,301
27 19142	Ely city	St. Louis	2.7	3,724	3,607	32	20	7	-	11	47	25	3,061
27 19934	Eveleth city	St. Louis	6.3	3,865	3,729	6	67	16	-	3	44	9	3,032
27 20330	Fairmont city	Martin	14.6	10,889	10,409	48	11	72	3	241	105	324	8,241

Table D-1. Places — **Area and Population**—Con.

[Includes incorporated places and census designated places (CDPs) of 2,500 or more population as of April 1, 2000. Codes shown are two-digit Federal Information Processing Standards (FIPS) state codes and five-digit FIPS place codes. Place names and codes are those in effect as of January 1, 2000. County refers to the county (or counties) in which the place is located. IC in this column = independent city, a county equivalent. If a place is located in more than one county, counties are listed in alphabetic order]

State and place code	Place	County	Land area, 2000 (sq. mi.)	Population, 2000 (April 1)									
					By race—								
					One race							Hispanic or Latino (of any race)	18 years and over
				Total	White	Black or African American	American Indian and Alaska Native	Asian	Native Hawaiian and Other Pacific Islander	Some other race	Two or more races		
27 00000	MINNESOTA—Con.												
27 20420	Falcon Heights city	Ramsey	2.2	5,572	4,327	187	24	833	7	74	120	172	4,374
27 20546	Faribault city	Rice	12.7	20,818	18,710	561	139	382	13	694	319	1,852	15,362
27 20618	Farmington city	Dakota	12.5	12,365	11,824	92	35	180	3	73	158	232	8,157
27 20906	Fergus Falls city	Otter Tail	13.1	13,471	13,069	83	103	77	1	27	111	122	10,366
27 21770	Forest Lake city	Washington	4.2	6,798	6,606	27	27	37	4	13	84	68	5,044
27 22814	Fridley city	Anoka	10.2	27,449	24,334	939	224	794	18	337	803	704	21,270
27 23948	Glencoe city	McLeod	2.7	5,453	5,085	9	15	31	7	282	24	707	3,932
27 24074	Glenwood city	Pope	5.6	2,594	2,566	4	6	-	1	8	9	15	2,051
27 24308	Golden Valley city	Hennepin	10.2	20,281	18,469	728	59	582	6	111	326	357	16,109
27 24524	Goodview city	Winona	1.7	3,373	3,287	13	5	39	-	9	20	32	2,505
27 25118	Grand Rapids city	Itasca	7.3	7,764	7,417	22	150	55	2	30	88	66	6,046
27 25280	Granite Falls city	Chippewa, Yellow Medicine	3.4	3,070	2,835	2	175	5	-	13	40	66	2,330
27 25334	Grant city	Washington	25.7	4,026	3,951	6	3	36	-	18	12	48	2,895
27 25622	Greenfield city	Hennepin	20.4	2,544	2,486	10	6	16	-	5	21	20	1,685
27 26738	Ham Lake city	Anoka	34.5	12,710	12,290	64	49	96	5	47	159	145	8,765
27 27530	Hastings city	Dakota, Washington	10.1	18,204	17,687	79	69	117	7	65	180	207	13,233
27 28682	Hermantown city	St. Louis	34.3	7,448	7,245	27	62	35	4	8	67	47	5,427
27 28790	Hibbing city	St. Louis	181.7	17,071	16,616	79	124	46	1	33	172	116	13,180
27 30140	Hopkins city	Hennepin	4.1	17,145	14,164	890	134	1,015	15	443	484	949	13,785
27 30392	Hugo city	Washington	34.0	6,363	6,182	13	27	91	3	13	34	86	4,369
27 30644	Hutchinson city	McLeod	7.4	13,080	12,588	47	30	120	4	178	113	278	9,469
27 30842	Independence city	Hennepin	32.6	3,236	3,163	3	6	34	1	7	22	28	2,262
27 31040	International Falls city	Koochiching	6.3	6,703	6,388	19	173	15	6	4	98	50	5,140
27 31076	Inver Grove Heights city	Dakota	28.6	29,751	27,312	625	143	597	6	516	552	1,256	21,626
27 31562	Jackson city	Jackson	3.8	3,501	3,292	9	6	141	-	27	26	53	2,684
27 32174	Jordan city	Scott	2.6	3,833	3,606	19	23	7	-	119	59	253	2,548
27 32498	Kasson city	Dodge	2.0	4,398	4,279	17	1	22	-	62	17	101	3,062
27 33866	La Crescent city	Houston, Winona	3.0	4,923	4,805	21	4	43	-	4	46	36	3,580
27 34172	Lake City city	Goodhue, Wabasha	4.2	4,950	4,792	31	20	55	-	14	38	110	3,821
27 34244	Lake Elmo city	Washington	22.8	6,863	6,576	26	20	120	-	37	84	90	4,859
27 35180	Lakeville city	Dakota	36.2	43,128	40,654	553	165	868	10	328	550	835	27,568
27 36746	Le Sueur city	Le Sueur, Sibley	4.5	3,922	3,627	10	6	11	3	230	35	378	2,832
27 37304	Lindstrom city	Chisago	2.3	3,015	2,943	6	11	15	-	17	23	34	2,231
27 37322	Lino Lakes city	Anoka	28.2	16,791	15,726	417	123	192	1	115	217	259	11,140
27 37448	Litchfield city	Meeker	3.8	6,562	6,210	24	18	27	-	241	42	338	4,913
27 37502	Little Canada city	Ramsey	4.0	9,771	8,342	410	57	653	1	88	220	224	7,616
27 37556	Little Falls city	Morrison	6.3	7,719	7,504	38	40	40	5	18	74	81	5,795
27 38060	Long Prairie city	Todd	2.4	3,040	2,829	2	53	3	1	130	22	285	2,269
27 38564	Luverne city	Rock	3.4	4,617	4,491	31	15	27	-	27	26	72	3,520
27 39428	Mahtomedi city	Washington	3.6	7,563	7,312	62	9	51	10	13	106	86	4,943
27 39878	Mankato city	Blue Earth, Le Sueur, Nicollet	15.2	32,427	30,011	616	110	911	31	306	442	719	26,945
27 40166	Maple Grove city	Hennepin	32.9	50,365	47,717	528	119	1,267	16	169	549	534	34,876
27 40382	Maplewood city	Ramsey	17.3	34,947	30,994	1,236	193	1,586	24	256	658	779	26,303
27 40688	Marshall city	Lyon	8.3	12,735	11,634	355	44	194	4	333	171	755	9,687
27 41480	Medina city	Hennepin	25.6	4,005	3,898	19	9	48	1	7	23	33	2,714
27 41570	Melrose city	Stearns	2.8	3,091	2,960	15	2	17	-	78	19	381	2,234
27 41696	Mendota Heights city	Dakota	9.4	11,434	10,938	101	19	204	-	53	119	203	8,282
27 42110	Milaca city	Mille Lacs	3.2	2,580	2,494	3	33	5	-	1	44	25	1,999
27 43000	Minneapolis city	Hennepin	54.9	382,618	249,186	68,818	8,378	23,455	289	15,798	16,694	29,175	298,449
27 43252	Minnetonka city	Hennepin	27.1	51,301	48,426	767	101	1,174	15	291	527	657	39,428
27 43306	Minnetrista city	Hennepin	26.1	4,358	4,230	15	9	64	-	22	18	29	3,081
27 43720	Montevideo city	Chippewa	4.5	5,346	5,191	6	22	18	3	43	63	107	4,034
27 43738	Montgomery city	Le Sueur	1.6	2,794	2,615	9	7	9	-	120	34	273	1,991
27 43774	Monticello city	Wright	6.2	7,868	7,629	26	16	43	-	50	103	160	5,394
27 43864	Moorhead city	Clay	13.4	32,177	29,628	247	625	410	14	676	577	1,439	24,887
27 44044	Mora city	Kanabec	4.1	3,193	3,088	9	41	6	1	8	40	50	2,416
27 44242	Morris city	Stevens	4.3	5,068	4,745	89	62	78	1	32	61	75	4,223
27 44476	Mound city	Hennepin	2.9	9,435	9,080	60	18	123	4	42	108	91	7,183
27 44530	Mounds View city	Ramsey	4.1	12,738	11,547	306	84	398	7	130	266	334	9,449
27 44548	Mountain Iron city	St. Louis	49.4	2,999	2,948	-	23	7	-	4	17	12	2,312
27 45430	New Brighton city	Ramsey	6.6	22,206	19,672	738	137	972	13	186	488	393	17,270
27 45628	New Hope city	Hennepin	5.1	20,873	18,088	1,207	97	669	8	364	440	721	16,418
27 45790	Newport city	Washington	3.7	3,715	3,409	63	34	55	4	72	78	158	2,698
27 45808	New Prague city	Le Sueur, Scott	2.6	4,559	4,479	6	9	16	-	10	39	40	3,164
27 46042	New Ulm city	Brown	8.8	13,594	13,336	15	20	63	4	68	88	171	10,453
27 46798	North Branch city	Chisago	35.7	8,023	7,804	13	39	83	3	17	64	109	5,374
27 46924	Northfield city	Dakota, Rice	7.0	17,147	15,873	154	58	405	9	306	342	982	13,677
27 47068	North Mankato city	Blue Earth, Nicollet	4.7	11,798	11,381	77	28	163	4	52	93	188	8,700
27 47104	North Oaks city	Ramsey	7.3	3,883	3,624	12	6	179	1	22	39	47	2,812
27 47221	North St. Paul city	Ramsey	2.9	11,929	11,077	313	66	201	4	102	166	281	8,794
27 47520	Norwood Young America city	Carver	1.7	3,108	3,049	4	14	13	-	16	12	82	2,195
27 47680	Oakdale city	Washington	11.1	26,653	24,576	611	96	654	2	206	508	732	18,918
27 47690	Oak Grove city	Anoka	33.7	6,903	6,710	35	47	33	-	15	63	41	4,695
27 47914	Oak Park Heights city	Washington	3.0	3,957	3,602	175	36	51	1	25	67	83	3,094
27 48256	Olivia city	Renville	2.3	2,570	2,472	3	3	3	-	66	23	196	1,934
27 48580	Orono city	Hennepin	16.1	7,538	7,367	20	11	71	-	18	51	65	5,476

830

U.S. Census Bureau, County and City Data Book: 2000

[Includes incorporated places and census designated places (CDPs) of 2,500 or more population as of April 1, 2000. Codes shown are two-digit Federal Information Processing Standards (FIPS) state codes and five-digit FIPS place codes. Place names and codes are those in effect as of January 1, 2000. County refers to the county (or counties) in which the place is located. IC in this column = independent city, a county equivalent. If a place is located in more than one county, counties are listed in alphabetic order]

State and place code	Place	County	Land area, 2000 (sq. mi.)	Population, 2000 (April 1)									
					By race—								
					One race								
				Total	White	Black or African American	American Indian and Alaska Native	Asian	Native Hawaiian and Other Pacific Islander	Some other race	Two or more races	Hispanic or Latino (of any race)	18 years and over
27 00000	MINNESOTA—Con.												
27 49138	Otsego city	Wright	29.4	6,389	6,214	16	23	46	-	36	54	81	4,315
27 49300	Owatonna city	Steele	12.6	22,434	21,108	351	29	223	7	430	286	967	16,132
27 49768	Park Rapids city	Hubbard	6.0	3,276	3,144	10	72	12	1	15	22	35	2,505
27 50470	Perham city	Otter Tail	2.6	2,559	2,482	9	26	7	-	17	18	29	1,917
27 51064	Pine City city	Pine	2.8	3,043	2,969	5	29	5	1	5	29	41	2,272
27 51388	Pipestone city	Pipestone	3.9	4,280	4,033	12	126	32	2	15	60	41	3,222
27 51424	Plainview city	Wabasha	2.2	3,190	3,089	1	2	3	-	78	17	164	2,255
27 51730	Plymouth city	Hennepin	32.9	65,894	60,200	1,783	217	2,495	9	328	862	1,079	48,028
27 52522	Princeton city	Mille Lacs, Sherburne	4.4	3,933	3,865	5	15	11	1	14	22	35	2,935
27 52594	Prior Lake city	Scott	13.5	15,917	15,046	122	331	150	7	53	208	177	11,092
27 52630	Proctor city	St. Louis	3.0	2,852	2,752	4	33	15	-	8	40	21	2,167
27 53026	Ramsey city	Anoka	28.8	18,510	17,918	58	84	185	1	52	212	221	12,563
27 53620	Red Wing city	Goodhue	35.4	16,116	15,202	213	357	119	8	85	132	205	12,148
27 53656	Redwood Falls city	Redwood, Renville	4.7	5,459	5,092	12	212	26	2	42	73	105	4,093
27 54214	Richfield city	Hennepin	6.9	34,439	27,981	2,289	248	1,826	14	1,173	908	2,158	27,468
27 54808	Robbinsdale city	Hennepin	2.8	14,123	12,553	811	84	293	1	142	239	282	11,055
27 54880	Rochester city	Olmsted	39.6	85,806	75,088	3,064	258	4,830	33	996	1,537	2,565	63,694
27 55006	Rockford city	Hennepin, Wright	1.7	3,484	3,399	14	18	16	3	5	29	35	2,374
27 55186	Rogers city	Hennepin	5.0	3,588	3,484	13	1	24	-	13	53	35	2,375
27 55546	Roseau city	Roseau	2.4	2,756	2,714	1	14	10	-	2	15	11	2,032
27 55726	Rosemount city	Dakota	33.7	14,619	13,564	297	44	311	-	117	286	268	9,488
27 55852	Roseville city	Ramsey	13.2	33,690	30,150	945	108	1,646	28	256	557	664	27,549
27 56680	St. Anthony city	Hennepin, Ramsey	2.3	8,012	7,257	165	51	361	2	63	113	132	6,573
27 56788	St. Charles city	Winona	3.3	3,295	3,019	32	9	119	3	89	24	163	2,331
27 56896	St. Cloud city	Benton, Sherburne, Stearns	30.2	59,107	54,229	1,402	425	1,839	37	345	830	784	46,829
27 56950	St. Francis city	Anoka	23.3	4,910	4,701	11	36	63	2	13	84	45	3,180
27 57040	St. James city	Watonwan	2.3	4,695	3,908	19	7	24	-	670	67	1,116	3,386
27 57130	St. Joseph city	Stearns	1.9	4,681	4,526	47	10	46	3	18	31	57	3,897
27 57220	St. Louis Park city	Hennepin	10.7	44,126	39,232	1,930	198	1,417	25	563	761	1,294	35,847
27 57346	St. Michael city	Wright	32.6	9,099	8,959	3	15	46	-	15	61	89	5,955
27 58000	St. Paul city	Ramsey	52.8	287,151	192,444	33,637	3,259	35,488	203	11,021	11,099	22,715	209,324
27 58018	St. Paul Park city	Washington	2.4	5,070	4,759	115	17	56	2	50	71	141	3,593
27 58036	St. Peter city	Nicollet	5.4	9,747	9,179	153	42	149	3	122	99	296	7,821
27 58612	Sartell city	Benton, Stearns	5.9	9,641	9,392	28	16	117	1	20	67	84	6,557
27 58648	Sauk Centre city	Stearns	3.7	3,930	3,878	12	5	10	-	10	15	21	2,925
27 58684	Sauk Rapids city	Benton	4.6	10,213	9,918	58	32	80	4	23	98	110	7,347
27 58738	Savage city	Scott	15.9	21,115	19,140	335	52	1,138	5	139	306	345	13,594
27 59350	Shakopee city	Scott	27.0	20,568	18,842	273	193	495	8	440	317	906	14,915
27 59998	Shoreview city	Ramsey	11.2	25,924	24,183	261	56	946	14	113	351	346	19,134
27 60016	Shorewood city	Hennepin	5.3	7,400	7,239	29	2	66	-	14	50	61	5,061
27 60844	Sleepy Eye city	Brown	1.7	3,515	3,305	8	2	12	-	137	51	274	2,532
27 61492	South St. Paul city	Dakota	5.7	20,167	18,680	258	114	165	2	564	384	1,295	15,041
27 61996	Spring Lake Park city	Anoka, Ramsey	2.0	6,772	6,154	86	55	211	1	133	132	229	5,243
27 62104	Spring Valley city	Fillmore	2.5	2,518	2,491	2	6	2	-	1	16	11	1,862
27 62446	Staples city	Todd, Wadena	4.5	3,104	3,026	8	25	11	-	7	27	46	2,261
27 62806	Stewartville city	Olmsted	2.1	5,411	5,254	38	16	28	1	18	56	54	3,777
27 62824	Stillwater city	Washington	6.5	15,143	14,767	48	43	86	3	55	141	148	10,954
27 64570	Thief River Falls city	Pennington	4.8	8,410	8,120	23	80	56	3	52	76	137	6,524
27 65956	Two Harbors city	Lake	3.2	3,613	3,543	2	24	4	-	3	37	22	2,782
27 66460	Vadnais Heights city	Ramsey	7.3	13,069	11,981	194	60	592	-	62	180	210	9,548
27 67036	Victoria city	Carver	7.0	4,025	3,941	11	5	34	-	15	19	40	2,751
27 67288	Virginia city	St. Louis	18.8	9,157	8,715	42	205	50	1	16	128	73	7,415
27 67378	Wabasha city	Wabasha	8.2	2,599	2,546	18	14	4	-	5	12	8	2,026
27 67432	Waconia city	Carver	2.8	6,814	6,614	23	8	44	1	68	56	87	4,777
27 67504	Wadena city	Otter Tail, Wadena	5.2	4,294	4,203	36	12	8	1	7	27	26	3,290
27 67612	Waite Park city	Stearns	7.8	6,568	6,091	47	37	230	3	79	81	132	5,280
27 68296	Waseca city	Waseca	3.8	8,493	8,004	118	30	49	4	212	76	433	6,200
27 68548	Watertown city	Carver	1.7	3,029	2,959	10	6	16	-	13	25	44	2,145
27 68818	Wayzata city	Hennepin	3.2	4,113	3,953	17	13	55	8	31	36	58	3,319
27 69700	West St. Paul city	Dakota	5.0	19,405	16,934	549	121	367	5	946	483	1,937	15,310
27 69970	White Bear Lake city	Ramsey, Washington	8.2	24,325	23,183	262	89	374	13	85	319	425	18,295
27 70420	Willmar city	Kandiyohi	11.8	18,351	16,171	165	84	98	20	1,563	250	2,911	13,540
27 70798	Windom city	Cottonwood	3.6	4,490	4,362	11	15	32	5	38	27	71	3,426
27 71032	Winona city	Winona	18.2	27,069	25,573	306	61	718	4	128	279	365	22,186
27 71428	Woodbury city	Washington	35.0	46,463	41,836	1,168	113	2,329	6	286	725	996	32,245
27 71734	Worthington city	Nobles	7.1	11,283	8,667	215	55	797	15	1,296	238	2,175	8,402
27 72022	Wyoming city	Chisago	2.8	3,048	2,976	12	16	13	2	8	21	22	2,054
27 72238	Zimmerman city	Sherburne	2.8	2,851	2,783	3	7	8	-	10	40	37	1,825
27 72328	Zumbrota city	Goodhue	2.0	2,789	2,688	23	4	18	1	33	22	41	2,046
28 00000	MISSISSIPPI		46,907.0	2,844,658	1,746,099	1,033,809	11,652	18,626	667	13,784	20,021	39,569	2,069,471
28 00180	Aberdeen city	Monroe	10.7	6,415	2,488	3,862	6	25	3	4	27	36	4,505
28 01260	Amory city	Monroe	7.5	6,956	4,859	2,030	8	4	-	11	44	55	5,157
28 02700	Baldwyn city	Lee, Prentiss	11.5	3,321	1,811	1,457	8	-	-	10	35	33	2,431
28 03620	Batesville city	Panola	11.1	7,113	4,014	2,979	4	27	3	58	28	114	5,054
28 03980	Bay St. Louis city	Hancock	6.1	8,209	6,586	1,362	33	91	4	16	117	138	6,198
28 05140	Belzoni city	Humphreys	1.0	2,663	812	1,813	1	17	-	16	4	36	1,805

[Includes incorporated places and census designated places (CDPs) of 2,500 or more population as of April 1, 2000. Codes shown are two-digit Federal Information Processing Standards (FIPS) state codes and five-digit FIPS place codes. Place names and codes are those in effect as of January 1, 2000. County refers to the county (or counties) in which the place is located. IC in this column = independent city, a county equivalent. If a place is located in more than one county, counties are listed in alphabetic order]

State and place code	Place	County	Land area, 2000 (sq. mi.)	Population, 2000 (April 1)									
					By race—							Hispanic or Latino (of any race)	18 years and over
					One race						Two or more races		
				Total	White	Black or African American	American Indian and Alaska Native	Asian	Native Hawaiian and Other Pacific Islander	Some other race			
28 00000	MISSISSIPPI—Con.												
28 06220	Biloxi city	Harrison	38.0	50,644	36,177	9,643	248	2,590	58	725	1,203	1,848	38,370
28 07780	Booneville city	Prentiss	25.7	8,625	6,890	1,595	26	27	-	13	74	61	6,706
28 08300	Brandon city	Rankin	21.3	16,436	14,235	1,954	16	95	10	49	77	213	12,288
28 08820	Brookhaven city	Lincoln	7.3	9,861	4,689	5,020	9	60	-	18	65	78	7,267
28 10140	Byram CDP	Hinds	17.8	7,386	6,328	962	14	35	1	19	27	56	5,390
28 11100	Canton city	Madison	18.6	12,911	2,406	10,368	19	26	-	18	74	56	8,739
28 11780	Carthage city	Leake	9.4	4,637	2,451	2,052	48	20	1	27	38	90	3,428
28 13820	Clarksdale city	Coahoma	13.8	20,645	6,184	14,146	23	120	3	46	123	134	13,850
28 14260	Cleveland city	Bolivar	7.3	13,841	6,907	6,679	17	137	3	35	63	130	10,488
28 14420	Clinton city	Hinds	23.8	23,347	17,492	5,259	24	359	4	60	149	203	17,575
28 15140	Collins city	Covington	7.6	2,683	1,248	1,407	2	2	-	18	6	43	1,951
28 15340	Columbia city	Marion	6.4	6,603	4,131	2,353	26	29	-	12	52	51	5,025
28 15380	Columbus city	Lowndes	21.4	25,944	11,317	14,117	25	144	3	133	205	292	19,198
28 15700	Corinth city	Alcorn	30.5	14,054	10,720	3,035	12	50	17	118	102	243	10,990
28 17060	Crystal Springs city	Copiah	5.4	5,873	2,525	3,275	5	9	-	36	23	72	4,220
28 19100	Diamondhead CDP	Hancock	11.3	5,912	5,637	105	24	52	2	28	64	174	4,801
28 19180	D'Iberville city	Harrison	4.7	7,608	5,950	867	28	535	1	65	162	201	5,553
28 20500	Durant city	Holmes	2.2	2,932	844	2,057	4	9	-	2	16	23	2,027
28 22020	Ellisville city	Jones	5.5	3,465	2,336	1,071	7	6	-	21	24	51	2,690
28 22900	Escatawpa CDP	Jackson	6.5	3,566	2,869	629	11	26	3	2	26	21	2,656
28 25100	Flowood city	Rankin	16.3	4,750	3,796	790	8	90	3	29	34	84	3,634
28 25340	Forest city	Scott	13.0	5,987	2,416	3,046	24	32	4	350	115	761	4,235
28 26300	Fulton city	Itawamba	8.6	3,882	3,249	567	9	20	-	11	26	49	3,158
28 26860	Gautier city	Jackson	12.2	11,681	7,965	3,230	60	150	5	105	166	373	8,358
28 29180	Greenville city	Washington	26.9	41,633	12,039	28,976	29	295	6	83	205	297	28,571
28 29340	Greenwood city	Leflore	9.2	18,425	6,047	12,042	20	168	14	45	89	189	12,710
28 29460	Grenada city	Grenada	30.0	14,879	7,333	7,342	24	75	3	18	84	104	10,794
28 29620	Gulf Hills CDP	Jackson	7.6	5,900	4,817	626	11	344	1	28	73	119	4,408
28 29660	Gulf Park Estates CDP	Jackson	2.7	4,272	3,926	154	16	66	1	32	77	98	2,982
28 29700	Gulfport city	Harrison	56.9	71,127	44,229	23,848	305	891	65	622	1,167	1,814	52,618
28 31020	Hattiesburg city	Forrest, Lamar	49.3	44,779	22,365	21,200	68	547	9	231	359	630	35,141
28 31220	Hazlehurst city	Copiah	4.4	4,400	1,289	3,018	1	21	-	26	45	90	3,162
28 31780	Hernando city	DeSoto	11.3	6,812	5,201	1,463	10	45	-	53	40	207	5,046
28 32082	Hickory Hills CDP	Jackson	5.4	3,046	2,501	436	17	15	-	25	52	76	2,154
28 32900	Hollandale city	Washington	2.2	3,437	552	2,860	-	3	-	-	22	26	2,221
28 33100	Holly Springs city	Marshall	12.7	7,957	1,815	6,062	5	13	2	5	55	47	5,961
28 33700	Horn Lake city	DeSoto	7.2	14,099	11,704	1,729	73	126	6	310	151	603	9,505
28 33900	Houston city	Chickasaw	7.6	4,079	2,443	1,492	11	7	5	110	11	209	2,995
28 34740	Indianola city	Sunflower	8.6	12,066	3,105	8,854	1	55	-	19	32	86	8,095
28 35300	Iuka city	Tishomingo	9.7	3,059	2,788	217	7	5	-	18	24	37	2,463
28 36000	Jackson city	Hinds, Madison, Rankin	104.9	184,256	51,208	130,151	236	1,056	24	344	1,237	1,451	131,713
28 38320	Kosciusko city	Attala	7.5	7,372	3,956	3,286	12	34	-	44	40	78	5,444
28 39520	Latimer CDP	Jackson	16.2	4,288	4,051	91	26	65	2	13	40	51	3,049
28 39640	Laurel city	Jones	15.4	18,393	7,474	10,130	21	60	1	583	124	712	13,255
28 40280	Leland city	Washington	2.1	5,502	1,761	3,687	9	7	-	2	36	41	3,746
28 41680	Long Beach city	Harrison	10.1	17,320	15,154	1,275	67	445	12	117	250	397	12,625
28 42280	Louisville city	Winston	15.1	7,006	3,243	3,675	9	12	-	31	36	116	4,984
28 42840	Lynchburg CDP	DeSoto	3.4	2,959	2,757	59	10	31	3	86	13	122	2,127
28 43280	McComb city	Pike	11.5	13,337	5,354	7,789	9	66	4	51	64	113	9,467
28 44520	Madison city	Madison	13.5	14,692	13,697	719	11	176	4	26	59	102	10,107
28 44600	Magee city	Simpson	4.9	4,200	2,632	1,423	3	11	-	97	34	152	3,035
28 46600	Mendenhall city	Simpson	5.3	2,555	1,820	715	1	3	-	2	14	26	1,898
28 46640	Meridian city	Lauderdale	45.1	39,968	17,580	21,729	67	238	13	112	229	433	29,100
28 48760	Moorhead city	Sunflower	1.3	2,573	526	2,032	-	5	-	7	3	32	1,850
28 49080	Morton city	Scott	6.7	3,482	1,910	1,336	5	4	1	205	21	454	2,514
28 49240	Moss Point city	Jackson	25.0	15,851	4,445	11,184	24	34	4	69	91	159	11,601
28 50440	Natchez city	Adams	13.2	18,464	8,158	10,061	20	71	3	34	117	130	13,579
28 51000	New Albany city	Union	17.1	7,607	4,867	2,509	13	27	-	117	74	215	5,608
28 51720	Newton city	Newton	7.2	3,699	1,624	2,023	5	23	-	7	17	32	2,687
28 53520	Ocean Springs city	Jackson	11.6	17,225	15,113	1,211	69	453	13	108	258	430	12,698
28 53680	Okolona city	Chickasaw	6.3	3,056	1,204	1,822	1	4	-	4	21	32	2,138
28 54040	Olive Branch city	DeSoto	36.2	21,054	18,233	2,379	42	87	1	158	154	307	14,835
28 54840	Oxford city	Lafayette	10.0	11,756	8,818	2,463	14	315	2	42	102	122	10,002
28 55360	Pascagoula city	Jackson	15.2	26,200	17,594	7,590	47	253	6	437	273	1,019	19,159
28 55400	Pass Christian city	Harrison	8.4	6,579	4,336	1,853	41	229	2	41	77	115	5,037
28 55760	Pearl city	Rankin	21.8	21,961	17,828	3,567	49	174	7	171	165	446	16,156
28 55930	Pearl River CDP	Neshoba	30.7	3,156	513	45	2,536	2	-	3	57	34	1,917
28 56800	Petal city	Forrest	9.7	7,579	7,119	336	22	6	-	40	56	109	5,521
28 56960	Philadelphia city	Neshoba	10.6	7,303	4,056	2,930	147	36	6	40	88	110	5,397
28 57160	Picayune city	Pearl River	11.8	10,535	6,534	3,784	40	32	5	19	121	121	7,689
28 59160	Pontotoc city	Pontotoc	9.4	5,253	4,089	1,003	15	12	1	79	54	145	3,903
28 59480	Poplarville city	Pearl River	3.8	2,601	1,933	623	4	13	3	4	21	17	2,038
28 62400	Richland city	Rankin	12.2	6,027	5,543	318	5	91	1	12	57	53	4,383
28 62520	Ridgeland city	Madison	15.9	20,173	15,544	3,719	30	596	8	110	166	313	15,461
28 62600	Ripley city	Tippah	11.5	5,478	4,144	1,090	12	11	1	183	37	269	4,138
28 64200	Ruleville city	Sunflower	2.5	3,234	603	2,612	2	14	-	1	2	28	2,222
28 64680	St. Martin CDP	Jackson	4.4	6,676	5,521	530	35	464	5	28	93	128	4,854
28 64840	Saltillo town	Lee	8.7	3,393	3,187	159	2	16	1	3	25	20	2,479

[Includes incorporated places and census designated places (CDPs) of 2,500 or more population as of April 1, 2000. Codes shown are two-digit Federal Information Processing Standards (FIPS) state codes and five-digit FIPS place codes. Place names and codes are those in effect as of January 1, 2000. County refers to the county (or counties) in which the place is located. IC in this column = independent city, a county equivalent. If a place is located in more than one county, counties are listed in alphabetic order]

				Population, 2000 (April 1)									
					By race—								
					One race						Two or more races	Hispanic or Latino (of any race)	18 years and over
State and place code	Place	County	Land area, 2000 (sq. mi.)	Total	White	Black or African American	American Indian and Alaska Native	Asian	Native Hawaiian and Other Pacific Islander	Some other race			
28 00000	MISSISSIPPI—Con.												
28 66440	Senatobia city	Tate	10.7	6,682	4,546	2,039	8	15	10	16	48	57	5,023
28 67040	Shelby city	Bolivar	2.7	2,926	232	2,665	2	3	-	11	13	29	1,830
28 67435	Shoreline Park CDP	Hancock	7.8	4,058	3,837	81	42	13	-	14	71	79	3,128
28 69280	Southaven city	DeSoto	33.8	28,977	26,175	1,928	93	214	8	328	231	654	21,107
28 70240	Starkville city	Oktibbeha	25.7	21,869	14,128	6,565	32	821	8	141	174	294	17,500
28 74840	Tupelo city	Lee	51.1	34,211	23,744	9,676	35	301	5	160	290	484	24,807
28 76200	Vancleave CDP	Jackson	43.4	4,910	4,478	331	28	13	-	12	48	47	3,459
28 76560	Verona city	Lee	3.7	3,334	1,293	1,923	14	11	-	55	38	74	2,231
28 76720	Vicksburg city	Warren	32.9	26,407	9,982	15,957	40	160	4	107	157	274	18,911
28 78000	Water Valley city	Yalobusha	7.0	3,677	2,128	1,498	12	6	8	7	18	44	2,704
28 78200	Waveland city	Hancock	6.8	6,674	5,698	748	33	100	2	33	60	135	4,936
28 78360	Waynesboro city	Wayne	6.6	5,197	2,159	2,977	11	19	-	13	18	49	3,665
28 78890	West Hattiesburg CDP . . .	Lamar	7.1	6,305	4,721	1,394	4	103	-	18	65	87	4,698
28 79120	West Point city	Clay	20.8	12,145	5,211	6,823	9	27	-	23	52	120	8,640
28 80160	Wiggins city	Stone	10.8	3,849	2,602	1,213	2	6	-	12	14	41	2,754
28 80760	Winona city	Montgomery	13.1	5,482	2,637	2,781	8	27	3	2	24	49	3,955
28 81520	Yazoo City city	Yazoo	10.8	14,550	4,180	10,138	26	85	-	34	87	1,087	10,326
29 00000	MISSOURI		68,885.9	5,595,211	4,748,083	629,391	25,076	61,595	3,178	45,827	82,061	118,592	4,167,519
29 00280	Affton CDP	St. Louis	4.6	20,535	19,841	94	38	266	6	57	233	207	16,043
29 01972	Arnold city	Jefferson	11.2	19,965	19,548	59	42	75	4	53	184	207	14,872
29 02548	Aurora city	Lawrence	5.5	7,014	6,711	18	58	18	-	94	115	190	5,073
29 02674	Ava city	Douglas	3.1	3,021	2,924	4	20	13	1	8	51	41	2,255
29 03160	Ballwin city	St. Louis	9.0	31,283	29,215	468	69	1,022	13	160	336	583	22,834
29 03394	Barnhart CDP	Jefferson	5.1	6,108	5,975	22	8	23	1	21	58	90	4,222
29 04222	Bellefontaine Neighbors city	St. Louis	4.4	11,271	6,056	5,006	22	29	2	35	121	76	8,556
29 04366	Bel-Ridge village	St. Louis	0.8	3,082	541	2,455	7	12	1	4	62	36	2,079
29 04384	Belton city	Cass	13.4	21,730	20,205	621	128	128	17	232	399	1,017	15,212
29 04906	Berkeley city	St. Louis	4.9	10,063	2,077	7,717	26	37	2	43	161	109	6,827
29 05068	Bethany city	Harrison	4.4	3,087	3,056	3	10	6	-	1	11	19	2,461
29 06004	Black Jack city	St. Louis	2.7	6,792	1,787	4,844	9	24	1	24	103	45	4,938
29 06652	Blue Springs city	Jackson	18.2	48,080	44,801	1,410	206	465	55	397	746	1,329	33,884
29 06976	Bolivar city	Polk	6.3	9,143	8,823	79	55	35	4	38	109	128	7,240
29 07102	Bonne Terre city	St. Francois	4.0	4,039	3,977	12	8	2	-	5	35	7	2,945
29 07318	Boonville city	Cooper	6.9	8,202	6,580	1,381	42	34	3	33	129	101	6,591
29 07660	Bowling Green city	Pike	1.9	3,260	2,955	250	4	6	-	7	38	24	2,373
29 07966	Branson city	Stone, Taney	16.2	6,050	5,717	51	52	43	2	89	96	258	4,823
29 08164	Breckenridge Hills city . . .	St. Louis	0.8	4,817	3,174	1,388	10	22	3	102	118	189	3,488
29 08236	Brentwood city	St. Louis	1.9	7,693	7,130	139	15	268	-	25	116	133	6,214
29 08398	Bridgeton city	St. Louis	14.6	15,550	13,446	1,408	32	353	1	108	202	345	12,119
29 08650	Brookfield city	Linn	4.3	4,769	4,623	60	17	7	-	6	56	45	3,622
29 09424	Buckner city	Jackson	1.7	2,725	2,614	3	12	12	7	23	66	54	1,900
29 09514	Buffalo city	Dallas	2.2	2,781	2,695	8	20	1	-	10	47	35	2,088
29 10054	Butler city	Bates	3.9	4,209	4,026	81	18	16	1	23	44	41	3,158
29 10468	California city	Moniteau	3.0	4,005	3,748	26	8	22	-	163	38	303	2,997
29 10810	Camdenton city	Camden	3.5	2,779	2,658	5	25	21	4	14	52	60	2,011
29 10828	Cameron city	Clinton, DeKalb	5.3	8,312	7,057	1,051	50	25	-	21	108	114	6,774
29 11134	Canton city	Lewis	2.3	2,557	2,431	54	7	21	-	14	30	23	2,007
29 11242	Cape Girardeau city	Cape Girardeau, Scott . . .	24.3	35,349	30,865	3,288	138	400	13	151	494	388	28,086
29 11368	Carl Junction city	Jasper	4.9	5,294	5,088	23	67	19	-	18	79	80	3,708
29 11566	Carrollton city	Carroll	4.3	4,122	3,910	127	12	8	-	13	52	47	3,125
29 11656	Carthage city	Jasper	9.5	12,668	10,984	195	133	202	27	842	285	1,589	9,450
29 11692	Caruthersville city	Pemiscot	5.2	6,760	4,467	2,123	9	36	2	47	76	112	4,545
29 11890	Cassville city	Barry	2.8	2,890	2,783	1	21	20	-	32	33	76	2,152
29 11908	Castle Point CDP	St. Louis	0.7	4,559	435	4,042	14	2	-	2	64	19	2,847
29 12898	Centralia city	Audrain, Boone	2.5	3,774	3,665	43	16	3	-	8	39	31	2,709
29 12988	Chaffee city	Scott	1.8	3,044	2,997	2	7	2	-	12	24	36	2,277
29 13366	Charleston city	Mississippi	4.7	4,732	2,513	2,158	2	13	1	7	38	52	3,304
29 13600	Chesterfield city	St. Louis	31.5	46,802	42,730	872	56	2,603	9	184	348	726	35,270
29 13690	Chillicothe city	Livingston	6.5	8,968	8,417	331	37	36	-	31	116	86	6,891
29 14176	Clarkson Valley city	St. Louis	2.7	2,675	2,519	36	5	86	-	3	26	32	1,928
29 14572	Clayton city	St. Louis	2.5	12,825	10,894	997	16	721	4	37	156	191	10,241
29 14986	Clinton city	Henry	9.2	9,311	8,891	165	86	29	-	47	93	96	7,133
29 15670	Columbia city	Boone	53.1	84,531	68,923	9,173	331	3,636	30	684	1,754	1,733	67,852
29 16030	Concord CDP	St. Louis	5.5	16,689	16,347	52	15	138	1	41	95	141	13,259
29 17218	Crestwood city	St. Louis	3.6	11,863	11,437	85	23	172	1	31	114	119	9,493
29 17272	Creve Coeur city	St. Louis	10.1	16,500	14,651	569	35	993	1	91	160	292	13,042
29 17632	Crystal City city	Jefferson	3.7	4,247	3,912	227	11	22	-	3	72	21	3,227
29 17668	Cuba city	Crawford	2.9	3,230	3,155	16	11	10	-	9	29	39	2,352
29 18253	Dardenne Prairie town . . .	St. Charles	4.4	4,384	4,227	73	5	42	3	16	18	42	2,970
29 19018	Dellwood city	St. Louis	1.0	5,255	2,076	3,058	15	34	-	11	61	18	3,595
29 19216	Desloge city	St. Francois	2.7	4,802	4,736	5	20	6	2	6	27	34	3,589
29 19252	De Soto city	Jefferson	3.8	6,375	6,165	109	20	12	1	17	51	65	4,764
29 19270	Des Peres city	St. Louis	4.4	8,592	8,296	68	16	157	3	13	39	71	6,209
29 19396	Dexter city	Stoddard	6.1	7,356	7,158	11	34	13	-	37	103	88	5,614

Table D-1. Places — **Area and Population**—Con.

[Includes incorporated places and census designated places (CDPs) of 2,500 or more population as of April 1, 2000. Codes shown are two-digit Federal Information Processing Standards (FIPS) state codes and five-digit FIPS place codes. Place names and codes are those in effect as of January 1, 2000. County refers to the county (or counties) in which the place is located. IC in this column = independent city, a county equivalent. If a place is located in more than one county, counties are listed in alphabetic order]

State and place code	Place	County	Land area, 2000 (sq. mi.)	Population, 2000 (April 1)									
					By race—								
					One race							Hispanic or Latino (of any race)	18 years and over
				Total	White	Black or African American	American Indian and Alaska Native	Asian	Native Hawaiian and Other Pacific Islander	Some other race	Two or more races		
29 00000	MISSOURI—Con.												
29 21052	East Prairie city	Mississippi	1.3	3,227	3,091	73	21	2	-	9	31	25	2,360
29 21484	Eldon city	Miller	3.4	4,895	4,804	16	15	8	-	15	37	57	3,757
29 21502	El Dorado Springs city	Cedar	3.1	3,775	3,638	4	37	14	4	24	54	51	2,879
29 21898	Ellisville city	St. Louis	4.3	9,104	8,659	144	10	187	-	35	69	106	6,624
29 22834	Eureka city	St. Louis	10.1	7,676	7,475	44	15	63	-	20	59	94	5,231
29 23086	Excelsior Springs city	Clay, Ray	9.8	10,847	10,119	365	54	37	4	65	203	201	7,901
29 23752	Farmington city	St. Francois	9.0	13,924	12,494	1,025	70	102	2	45	186	161	11,298
29 23842	Fayette city	Howard	2.2	2,793	2,211	512	13	6	1	13	37	26	2,294
29 23950	Fenton city	St. Louis	6.1	4,360	4,272	17	7	41	-	8	15	35	3,249
29 23986	Ferguson city	St. Louis	6.2	22,406	10,026	11,743	24	150	4	85	374	228	15,615
29 24094	Festus city	Jefferson	4.8	9,660	9,048	380	29	70	4	36	93	100	7,172
29 24778	Florissant city	St. Louis	11.4	50,497	43,257	5,810	101	308	15	261	745	753	38,035
29 25264	Fort Leonard Wood CDP	Pulaski	97.2	13,666	8,857	2,950	150	327	61	682	639	1,562	9,869
29 25768	Fredericktown city	Madison	4.3	3,928	3,840	8	13	23	-	16	28	27	3,017
29 26110	Frontenac city	St. Louis	2.9	3,483	3,313	28	3	97	-	5	37	33	2,567
29 26182	Fulton city	Callaway	11.3	12,128	9,855	1,872	50	128	3	46	174	132	9,944
29 27190	Gladstone city	Clay	8.0	26,365	24,585	540	136	332	36	301	435	938	20,829
29 27226	Glasgow Village CDP	St. Louis	0.9	5,234	2,978	2,149	3	19	1	16	68	58	3,470
29 27334	Glendale city	St. Louis	1.3	5,767	5,629	51	2	32	-	18	35	65	4,172
29 28090	Grain Valley city	Jackson	4.8	5,160	4,976	29	20	25	8	22	80	128	3,561
29 28324	Grandview city	Jackson	14.7	24,881	14,882	8,346	140	262	24	481	746	1,077	18,116
29 28918	Gray Summit CDP	Franklin	7.4	2,640	2,582	10	6	4	2	10	26	9	1,907
29 29324	Green Park city	St. Louis	1.4	2,666	2,609	-	1	22	2	14	18	32	2,097
29 29494	Greenwood city	Jackson	4.0	3,952	3,757	89	12	18	2	22	52	83	2,662
29 30214	Hannibal city	Marion, Ralls	14.6	17,757	16,090	1,167	63	63	13	44	317	200	13,170
29 30610	Harrisonville city	Cass	8.6	8,946	8,602	87	59	42	1	35	120	126	6,474
29 31132	Hayti city	Pemiscot	2.2	3,207	1,753	1,403	14	6	-	4	27	42	2,242
29 31276	Hazelwood city	St. Louis	15.9	26,206	21,027	4,203	48	312	17	137	462	419	19,758
29 31708	Herculaneum city	Jefferson	3.4	2,805	2,711	73	-	5	-	1	15	18	2,171
29 31762	Hermann city	Gasconade	2.3	2,674	2,642	6	2	2	-	8	14	16	2,075
29 31960	Higginsville city	Lafayette	3.7	4,682	4,287	247	20	25	-	32	71	70	3,518
29 32140	High Ridge CDP	Jefferson	4.0	4,236	4,142	13	5	17	-	6	53	49	3,070
29 32572	Holden city	Johnson	2.4	2,510	2,372	48	27	3	1	4	55	27	1,757
29 32662	Hollister city	Taney	3.7	3,867	3,733	8	44	6	6	30	40	119	2,992
29 32770	Holts Summit city	Callaway	3.3	2,935	2,774	87	25	2	-	8	39	37	2,047
29 34354	Imperial CDP	Jefferson	5.4	4,373	4,282	6	6	15	1	5	58	51	3,164
29 35000	Independence city	Clay, Jackson	78.3	113,288	104,081	2,939	721	788	523	1,617	2,619	4,175	86,240
29 35648	Jackson city	Cape Girardeau	10.1	11,947	11,537	162	33	67	4	23	121	91	8,770
29 37000	Jefferson City city	Callaway, Cole	27.3	39,636	32,303	5,828	150	488	20	246	601	616	31,358
29 37178	Jennings city	St. Louis	3.7	15,469	2,938	12,155	16	59	4	30	217	113	10,769
29 37592	Joplin city	Jasper, Newton	31.4	45,504	41,609	1,217	694	339	17	448	1,180	1,144	34,965
29 38000	Kansas City city	Cass, Clay, Jackson, Platte	313.5	441,545	267,931	137,879	2,122	8,182	493	14,158	10,780	30,604	329,559
29 38072	Kearney city	Clay	6.6	5,472	5,325	22	14	14	4	30	63	92	3,635
29 38306	Kennett city	Dunklin	6.7	11,260	9,508	1,494	25	58	1	41	133	202	8,235
29 39026	Kirksville city	Adair	10.5	16,988	16,034	294	44	328	7	100	181	262	14,346
29 39044	Kirkwood city	St. Louis	9.2	27,324	24,800	1,932	29	222	10	75	256	298	20,923
29 39656	Ladue city	St. Louis	8.6	8,645	8,371	76	9	129	10	11	39	67	6,528
29 40043	Lake St. Louis city	St. Charles	7.5	10,169	9,722	187	25	99	4	41	91	137	7,674
29 40376	Lamar city	Barton	3.8	4,425	4,275	8	27	15	6	15	79	62	3,246
29 41168	Lebanon city	Laclede	13.6	12,155	11,667	110	66	61	4	51	196	201	9,089
29 41348	Lee's Summit city	Cass, Jackson	59.5	70,700	65,874	2,454	257	698	44	367	1,006	1,394	50,087
29 41438	Lemay CDP	St. Louis	4.3	17,215	16,615	175	52	92	2	114	165	349	13,288
29 41870	Lexington city	Lafayette	3.5	4,453	4,053	269	8	22	2	47	52	97	3,332
29 42032	Liberty city	Clay	27.0	26,232	24,592	680	104	160	17	261	418	703	18,979
29 44174	Louisiana city	Pike	3.1	3,863	3,487	221	14	10	5	85	41	152	2,920
29 45326	Macon city	Macon	6.1	5,538	5,138	297	12	13	1	23	54	49	4,282
29 45614	Malden city	Dunklin	6.2	4,782	3,505	1,151	19	18	-	9	80	44	3,480
29 45668	Manchester city	St. Louis	5.0	19,161	17,552	463	17	830	6	77	216	292	13,940
29 45830	Maplewood city	St. Louis	1.5	9,228	7,028	1,470	30	390	6	66	238	205	7,540
29 45866	Marceline city	Chariton, Linn	3.2	2,558	2,512	3	20	5	-	5	13	21	1,876
29 46316	Marshall city	Saline	10.1	12,433	10,699	920	53	48	42	430	241	891	9,363
29 46388	Marshfield city	Webster	4.8	5,720	5,594	11	24	17	-	7	67	100	4,168
29 46586	Maryland Heights city	St. Louis	21.4	25,756	21,983	1,436	52	1,832	9	182	262	599	20,216
29 46640	Maryville city	Nodaway	5.0	10,581	10,134	157	19	154	2	33	82	104	9,103
29 47180	Mehlville CDP	St. Louis	7.4	28,822	27,347	505	37	510	5	99	319	417	22,716
29 47648	Mexico city	Audrain	11.4	11,320	10,051	1,040	30	58	2	32	107	99	8,617
29 49034	Moberly city	Randolph	11.6	11,945	10,812	802	44	77	3	47	160	199	8,987
29 49088	Moline Acres city	St. Louis	0.6	2,662	324	2,277	1	7	1	7	45	8	1,852
29 49196	Monett city	Barry, Lawrence	6.5	7,396	6,616	16	61	46	8	578	71	834	5,437
29 49394	Monroe City city	Marion, Monroe, Ralls	3.1	2,588	2,312	229	1	-	4	9	33	11	1,908
29 50402	Mountain Grove city	Texas, Wright	4.2	4,574	4,457	8	28	4	-	22	55	50	3,398
29 50672	Mount Vernon city	Lawrence	3.4	4,017	3,881	27	37	11	-	22	39	49	3,083
29 50834	Murphy CDP	Jefferson	4.0	9,048	8,844	20	18	39	-	30	97	97	6,649
29 51572	Neosho city	Newton	14.9	10,505	9,559	109	169	41	105	287	235	444	7,752
29 51644	Nevada city	Vernon	8.9	8,607	8,245	89	81	38	4	42	108	111	6,387
29 52076	New Madrid city	New Madrid	4.5	3,334	2,419	883	6	10	-	3	13	23	2,395
29 52616	Nixa city	Christian	6.2	12,124	11,812	56	44	52	2	36	122	153	8,685

[Includes incorporated places and census designated places (CDPs) of 2,500 or more population as of April 1, 2000. Codes shown are two-digit Federal Information Processing Standards (FIPS) state codes and five-digit FIPS place codes. Place names and codes are those in effect as of January 1, 2000. County refers to the county (or counties) in which the place is located. IC in this column = independent city, a county equivalent. If a place is located in more than one county, counties are listed in alphabetic order]

State and place code	Place	County	Land area, 2000 (sq. mi.)	Population, 2000 (April 1)									
					By race—								
					One race								
				Total	White	Black or African American	American Indian and Alaska Native	Asian	Native Hawaiian and Other Pacific Islander	Some other race	Two or more races	Hispanic or Latino (of any race)	18 years and over
29 00000	MISSOURI—Con.												
29 52796	Normandy city	St. Louis	1.8	5,153	1,382	3,436	13	164	3	24	131	66	3,811
29 53102	North Kansas City city	Clay	4.4	4,714	3,888	187	28	202	11	156	242	398	3,866
29 53408	Northwoods city	St. Louis	0.7	4,643	290	4,302	2	6	-	5	38	10	3,526
29 53624	Oak Grove city	Jackson, Lafayette	4.9	5,535	5,373	14	14	23	11	42	58	92	3,773
29 53876	Oakville CDP	St. Louis	16.1	35,309	34,563	86	47	324	6	72	211	365	25,772
29 54038	Odessa city	Lafayette	3.5	4,818	4,070	57	10	5	2	16	47	36	3,459
29 54074	O'Fallon city	St. Charles	22.5	46,169	44,006	1,033	108	342	13	197	470	671	30,757
29 54650	Olivette city	St. Louis	2.8	7,438	5,235	1,629	6	372	1	56	139	117	5,667
29 55244	Osage Beach city	Camden, Miller	9.4	3,662	3,565	28	15	18	-	6	30	44	3,075
29 55550	Overland city	St. Louis	4.4	16,838	14,069	1,885	54	339	5	140	346	368	12,674
29 55640	Owensville city	Gasconade	2.0	2,500	2,461	2	6	4	-	2	25	9	1,856
29 55766	Ozark city	Christian	7.5	9,665	9,313	32	69	29	7	57	158	164	6,872
29 55910	Pacific city	Franklin, St. Louis	5.4	5,482	5,172	160	17	21	2	29	81	59	4,025
29 55964	Pagedale city	St. Louis	1.2	3,616	205	3,330	11	8	-	10	52	36	2,488
29 56036	Palmyra city	Marion	2.2	3,467	3,336	91	8	9	-	1	22	21	2,608
29 56272	Park Hills city	St. Francois	20.0	7,861	7,674	25	21	35	2	32	72	72	5,772
29 56288	Parkville city	Platte	6.9	4,059	3,668	191	21	53	39	33	54	92	2,986
29 56756	Peculiar city	Cass	3.5	2,604	2,531	7	11	9	2	5	39	38	1,777
29 57116	Perryville city	Perry	7.6	7,667	7,473	19	13	101	1	12	48	54	5,782
29 57278	Pevely city	Jefferson	3.3	3,768	3,613	60	14	17	-	11	53	35	2,632
29 57800	Pine Lawn city	St. Louis	0.6	4,204	99	4,034	5	3	-	17	46	16	2,791
29 58178	Platte City city	Platte	3.4	3,866	3,560	129	19	31	-	45	82	108	2,819
29 58394	Pleasant Hill city	Cass	4.5	5,582	5,445	12	19	21	-	25	60	88	3,898
29 58520	Pleasant Valley city	Clay	1.3	3,321	3,124	73	25	20	-	25	54	98	2,516
29 59096	Poplar Bluff city	Butler	11.6	16,651	14,493	1,617	91	86	-	80	284	224	12,604
29 59186	Portageville city	New Madrid, Pemiscot	2.0	3,295	2,702	539	6	10	-	9	29	27	2,397
29 59330	Potosi city	Washington	2.2	2,662	2,545	57	12	4	-	6	38	22	1,952
29 60752	Raymore city	Cass	17.0	11,146	10,620	205	55	74	5	40	147	226	7,915
29 60788	Raytown city	Jackson	9.9	30,388	25,594	3,567	132	233	47	260	555	712	23,535
29 61238	Republic city	Greene	5.6	8,438	8,221	20	47	41	2	20	87	88	6,018
29 61670	Richmond city	Ray	5.8	6,116	5,767	228	16	3	-	23	79	63	4,450
29 61706	Richmond Heights city	St. Louis	2.3	9,602	7,829	1,279	24	307	1	33	129	167	7,755
29 62156	Riverside city	Platte	5.3	2,979	2,522	183	31	69	2	91	81	211	2,315
29 62192	Riverview village	St. Louis	0.8	3,146	1,826	1,250	12	5	-	8	45	51	2,275
29 62660	Rock Hill city	St. Louis	1.1	4,765	3,245	1,304	8	94	1	10	103	61	3,698
29 62912	Rolla city	Phelps	11.3	16,367	14,599	478	76	797	20	120	277	282	13,082
29 63956	St. Ann city	St. Louis	3.1	13,607	11,254	1,557	38	271	2	243	242	560	10,575
29 64082	St. Charles city	St. Charles	20.4	60,321	56,270	2,097	160	612	22	441	719	1,187	46,226
29 64136	St. Clair city	Franklin	3.1	4,390	4,278	33	20	9	-	4	46	31	3,163
29 64180	Ste. Genevieve city	Ste. Genevieve	4.2	4,476	4,300	96	26	14	-	11	29	50	3,496
29 64424	St. James city	Phelps	2.8	3,704	3,474	10	20	11	-	16	173	34	2,762
29 64478	St. John city	St. Louis	1.4	6,871	5,620	961	16	87	-	53	134	163	5,139
29 64550	St. Joseph city	Buchanan	43.8	73,990	67,981	3,722	340	351	19	512	1,065	1,929	56,138
29 65000	St. Louis city	St. Louis IC	61.9	348,189	152,666	178,266	950	6,891	94	2,783	6,539	7,022	258,532
29 65126	St. Peters city	St. Charles	21.2	51,381	48,427	1,440	105	632	4	224	549	768	35,980
29 65144	St. Robert city	Pulaski	7.2	2,760	1,784	560	16	150	11	80	159	169	2,017
29 65234	Salem city	Dent	3.0	4,854	4,711	36	26	8	-	12	61	40	3,669
29 65954	Sappington CDP	St. Louis	2.6	7,287	7,034	47	8	133	-	9	56	75	5,936
29 66044	Savannah city	Andrew	3.1	4,762	4,685	14	18	10	-	12	23	28	3,550
29 66368	Scott City city	Cape Girardeau, Scott	4.6	4,591	4,511	18	17	2	-	6	37	29	3,368
29 66440	Sedalia city	Pettis	12.0	20,339	18,025	1,007	80	81	4	763	379	1,129	15,312
29 67700	Shrewsbury city	St. Louis	1.4	6,644	6,244	98	12	175	1	36	78	112	5,605
29 67870	Sikeston city	New Madrid, Scott	17.9	16,992	12,832	3,800	46	63	-	83	168	204	12,298
29 68420	Smithville city	Clay	13.7	5,514	5,361	12	25	21	6	37	52	108	3,947
29 69266	Spanish Lake CDP	St. Louis	7.4	21,337	9,014	11,691	43	141	6	98	344	220	14,843
29 70000	Springfield city	Christian, Greene	73.2	151,580	138,987	4,961	1,142	2,060	136	1,332	2,962	3,501	121,411
29 71368	Sugar Creek city	Clay, Jackson	8.3	3,839	3,602	31	30	20	17	64	75	156	2,990
29 71440	Sullivan city	Crawford, Franklin	7.7	6,351	6,248	13	13	35	3	13	26	76	4,704
29 71746	Sunset Hills city	St. Louis	9.0	8,267	7,959	89	11	119	-	24	65	73	6,483
29 73420	Tipton city	Moniteau	2.1	3,261	2,658	495	31	14	1	9	53	29	2,713
29 73618	Town and Country city	St. Louis	11.9	10,894	9,822	219	6	690	1	25	131	117	8,407
29 73816	Trenton city	Grundy	5.8	6,216	6,042	35	25	13	1	46	54	133	4,849
29 73942	Troy city	Lincoln	5.9	6,737	6,324	193	26	9	1	54	130	115	4,731
29 74626	Union city	Franklin	8.1	7,757	7,481	111	23	13	-	18	111	77	5,613
29 75220	University City city	St. Louis	5.9	37,428	18,437	16,974	61	1,065	11	208	672	583	29,254
29 75472	Valley Park city	St. Louis	3.0	6,518	5,802	268	6	282	3	62	95	148	4,737
29 75688	Vandalia city	Audrain, Ralls	2.3	2,529	2,198	272	-	12	-	5	42	20	1,929
29 75922	Versailles city	Morgan	2.3	2,565	2,447	55	17	1	-	4	41	27	1,931
29 77092	Warrensburg city	Johnson	8.4	16,340	14,200	1,055	105	456	23	128	373	398	13,394
29 77128	Warrenton city	Warren	7.3	5,281	5,051	90	22	20	2	30	66	68	3,699
29 77416	Washington city	Franklin	8.5	13,243	12,946	112	17	55	-	30	83	88	9,845
29 77992	Waynesville city	Pulaski	6.2	3,507	2,795	385	33	101	4	50	139	109	2,550
29 78118	Webb City city	Jasper	7.4	9,812	9,232	53	130	77	11	112	197	245	6,956
29 78154	Webster Groves city	St. Louis	5.9	23,230	21,108	1,482	39	280	3	73	245	291	17,453
29 78314	Weldon Spring city	St. Charles	7.9	5,270	5,059	96	8	57	2	16	32	58	3,869
29 78442	Wentzville city	St. Charles	14.4	6,896	5,836	829	11	38	4	36	142	103	4,701
29 78928	West Plains city	Howell	12.4	10,866	10,401	79	104	77	7	56	142	179	8,166

Table D-1. Places — **Area and Population**—Con.

[Includes incorporated places and census designated places (CDPs) of 2,500 or more population as of April 1, 2000. Codes shown are two-digit Federal Information Processing Standards (FIPS) state codes and five-digit FIPS place codes. Place names and codes are those in effect as of January 1, 2000. County refers to the county (or counties) in which the place is located. IC in this column = independent city, a county equivalent. If a place is located in more than one county, counties are listed in alphabetic order]

State and place code	Place	County	Land area, 2000 (sq. mi.)	Population, 2000 (April 1)									
					By race—							Hispanic or Latino (of any race)	18 years and over
					One race						Two or more races		
				Total	White	Black or African American	American Indian and Alaska Native	Asian	Native Hawaiian and Other Pacific Islander	Some other race			
29 00000	MISSOURI—Con.												
29 79432	Whiteman AFB CDP	Johnson	5.2	3,814	3,119	371	25	66	17	84	132	219	2,381
29 79820	Wildwood city	St. Louis	66.0	32,884	31,155	534	38	784	2	97	274	454	21,973
29 79882	Willard city	Greene	5.6	3,193	3,121	5	21	3	-	7	36	17	2,156
29 80350	Windsor city	Henry, Pettis	2.4	3,087	2,995	16	20	8	-	11	37	16	2,307
29 80962	Woodson Terrace city	St. Louis	0.8	4,189	3,534	486	6	42	-	52	69	104	3,119
30 00000	MONTANA...........		145,552.4	902,195	817,229	2,692	56,068	4,691	470	5,315	15,730	18,081	672,133
30 01675	Anaconda-Deer Lodge County	Deer Lodge	737.0	9,417	9,028	16	167	34	1	17	154	155	7,295
30 04975	Belgrade city	Gallatin	1.7	5,728	5,527	5	61	17	5	45	68	111	4,024
30 06550	Billings city	Yellowstone	33.7	89,847	82,539	495	3,088	533	38	1,300	1,854	3,758	68,258
30 08950	Bozeman city	Gallatin	12.6	27,509	26,058	92	342	445	18	149	405	438	23,102
30 11397	Butte-Silver Bow (balance)	Silver Bow	716.1	33,892	32,325	53	675	147	21	200	471	927	25,875
30 16600	Columbia Falls city	Flathead	1.5	3,645	3,509	9	45	18	3	15	46	67	2,612
30 17275	Conrad city	Pondera	1.2	2,753	2,636	3	63	5	3	6	37	26	2,028
30 18775	Cut Bank city	Glacier	1.0	3,105	2,563	1	420	7	4	4	106	28	2,220
30 19825	Deer Lodge city	Powell...........	1.4	3,421	3,273	1	35	21	-	21	70	63	2,557
30 20800	Dillon city..........	Beaverhead	1.6	3,752	3,618	13	49	5	-	23	44	73	2,901
30 25075	Evergreen CDP	Flathead	8.0	6,215	5,893	15	125	23	3	47	109	116	4,475
30 31075	Glasgow city........	Valley	1.4	3,253	3,055	4	114	13	-	10	57	35	2,481
30 31450	Glendive city	Dawson	3.3	4,729	4,605	14	57	5	-	17	31	48	3,702
30 32800	Great Falls city	Cascade	19.5	56,690	50,996	540	2,888	485	49	341	1,391	1,354	42,552
30 33775	Hamilton city	Ravalli...........	2.3	3,705	3,565	4	33	29	-	8	66	61	2,956
30 34225	Hardin city	Big Horn	1.4	3,384	2,107	4	1,069	12	-	35	157	187	2,336
30 35050	Havre city	Hill.............	3.5	9,621	8,378	11	867	47	2	49	267	142	7,145
30 35600	Helena city..........	Lewis and Clark ...	14.0	25,780	24,434	59	541	201	18	98	429	430	20,002
30 35634	Helena Valley Southeast CDP	Lewis and Clark	16.2	7,141	6,684	19	204	27	1	35	171	138	4,687
30 35637	Helena Valley West Central CDP .	Lewis and Clark	26.6	6,983	6,759	11	99	17	4	25	68	68	4,952
30 40075	Kalispell city.........	Flathead	5.5	14,223	13,632	40	174	79	6	56	236	220	10,811
30 42700	Laurel city	Yellowstone	1.9	6,255	6,039	10	73	24	1	43	65	151	4,633
30 43375	Lewistown city	Fergus	1.9	5,813	5,611	4	82	20	-	8	88	42	4,474
30 43450	Libby city...........	Lincoln	1.3	2,626	2,508	4	33	16	-	14	51	32	1,995
30 43975	Livingston city........	Park	2.6	6,851	6,604	21	67	34	-	41	84	148	5,295
30 44200	Lockwood CDP	Yellowstone	7.5	4,306	4,007	20	115	15	5	44	100	161	3,018
30 44650	Lolo CDP...........	Missoula	9.5	3,388	3,276	8	30	8	-	7	59	35	2,328
30 47275	Malmstrom AFB CDP	Cascade	5.2	4,544	3,780	299	27	106	7	150	175	356	2,870
30 49525	Miles City city	Custer...........	3.3	8,487	8,209	10	118	24	4	37	85	135	6,402
30 50200	Missoula city	Missoula	23.8	57,053	53,387	207	1,341	703	57	290	1,068	1,004	45,798
30 55675	Orchard Homes CDP ...	Missoula	6.4	5,199	4,957	7	70	67	6	27	65	70	3,941
30 58750	Polson city..........	Lake	2.7	4,041	3,162	6	651	19	3	18	182	91	3,007
30 67450	Shelby city	Toole	3.2	3,216	2,974	8	134	13	-	8	79	40	2,444
30 67900	Sidney city..........	Richland	2.2	4,774	4,574	5	90	15	-	48	42	116	3,501
30 79825	Whitefish city	Flathead	4.4	5,032	4,829	7	56	29	3	36	72	97	3,946
30 81475	Wolf Point city	Roosevelt	0.9	2,663	1,484	1	1,079	27	-	9	63	43	1,837
31 00000	NEBRASKA..........		76,872.4	1,711,263	1,533,261	68,541	14,896	21,931	836	47,845	23,953	94,425	1,261,021
31 00905	Alliance city	Box Butte	4.8	8,959	7,982	44	305	54	1	386	187	801	6,442
31 02655	Auburn city..........	Nemaha	1.5	3,350	3,256	12	9	35	1	10	27	27	2,535
31 02690	Aurora city..........	Hamilton	1.9	4,225	4,137	8	2	18	-	24	36	66	3,067
31 03390	Beatrice city.........	Gage	7.5	12,496	12,184	42	56	41	4	38	131	120	9,575
31 03950	Bellevue city.........	Sarpy	13.3	44,382	38,092	2,719	223	938	49	1,235	1,126	2,609	32,221
31 05350	Blair city	Washington	4.6	7,512	7,319	33	22	25	20	25	68	101	5,645
31 06610	Broken Bow city	Custer...........	1.6	3,491	3,429	6	23	3	-	4	26	28	2,657
31 08535	Central City city	Merrick	2.0	2,998	2,944	12	3	15	1	8	15	39	2,204
31 08605	Chadron city	Dawes	3.6	5,634	5,239	37	186	18	5	64	85	153	4,604
31 08640	Chalco CDP	Sarpy	2.9	10,736	10,225	88	32	116	2	97	176	302	7,173
31 10110	Columbus city	Platte	9.0	20,971	19,753	95	74	100	8	731	210	1,395	15,059
31 11020	Cozad city..........	Dawson	2.1	4,163	3,888	7	18	18	-	159	73	456	3,063
31 11370	Crete city...........	Saline	2.4	6,028	5,213	46	44	197	2	416	110	814	4,590
31 12315	David City city	Butler	1.5	2,597	2,560	4	4	6	3	13	7	26	1,931
31 15080	Elkhorn city	Douglas..........	3.7	6,062	5,986	8	15	20	-	12	21	77	4,139
31 16410	Fairbury city.........	Jefferson.........	1.9	4,262	4,172	6	26	8	1	27	22	79	3,345
31 16655	Falls City city	Richardson........	2.6	4,671	4,447	6	109	10	-	12	87	41	3,514
31 17670	Fremont city.........	Dodge...........	7.4	25,174	23,987	144	78	154	28	576	207	1,085	19,074
31 18580	Gering city..........	Scotts Bluff	3.7	7,751	7,091	10	88	19	3	431	109	1,039	5,845
31 19385	Gothenburg city	Dawson	2.5	3,619	3,524	16	12	6	-	44	17	131	2,638
31 19595	Grand Island city	Hall.............	21.5	42,940	37,237	180	143	562	71	4,139	608	6,845	31,360
31 21415	Hastings city.........	Adams	9.8	24,064	22,474	189	101	485	10	575	230	1,343	18,377
31 22640	Holdrege city	Phelps	3.8	5,636	5,483	8	19	14	-	58	54	175	4,198
31 25055	Kearney city.........	Buffalo	11.0	27,431	26,109	172	105	253	12	460	320	1,118	21,345
31 25475	Kimball city	Kimball	1.5	2,559	2,463	9	27	4	-	10	46	90	1,942
31 26385	La Vista city	Sarpy	2.8	11,699	10,582	344	46	275	12	190	250	485	8,211
31 26910	Lexington city........	Dawson	2.9	10,011	6,427	44	117	110	2	3,081	230	5,121	6,749
31 28000	Lincoln city..........	Lancaster	74.6	225,581	201,322	6,960	1,537	7,048	141	4,081	4,492	8,154	173,675

U.S. Census Bureau, County and City Data Book: 2000

Table D-1. Places — **Area and Population**—Con.

[Includes incorporated places and census designated places (CDPs) of 2,500 or more population as of April 1, 2000. Codes shown are two-digit Federal Information Processing Standards (FIPS) state codes and five-digit FIPS place codes. Place names and codes are those in effect as of January 1, 2000. County refers to the county (or counties) in which the place is located. IC in this column = independent city, a county equivalent. If a place is located in more than one county, counties are listed in alphabetic order]

State and place code	Place	County	Land area, 2000 (sq. mi.)	Population, 2000 (April 1) Total	By race— One race White	Black or African American	American Indian and Alaska Native	Asian	Native Hawaiian and Other Pacific Islander	Some other race	Two or more races	Hispanic or Latino (of any race)	18 years and over
31 00000	NEBRASKA—Con.												
31 29925	McCook city	Red Willow	5.4	7,994	7,784	14	36	14	-	73	73	202	6,065
31 32340	Minden city	Kearney	1.6	2,964	2,924	5	7	3	-	13	12	69	2,225
31 33705	Nebraska City city	Otoe	4.4	7,228	6,939	27	22	27	5	145	63	318	5,361
31 34615	Norfolk city	Madison	10.0	23,516	21,497	272	359	114	8	986	280	1,790	17,432
31 35000	North Platte city	Lincoln	10.5	23,878	22,319	170	154	94	7	787	347	1,596	17,659
31 35875	Offutt AFB CDP	Sarpy	4.2	8,901	6,940	929	61	243	28	316	384	657	5,170
31 35980	Ogallala city	Keith	3.3	4,930	4,755	1	43	11	-	83	37	236	3,625
31 37000	Omaha city	Douglas	115.7	390,007	305,745	51,917	2,616	6,773	228	15,250	7,478	29,397	290,060
31 37105	O'Neill city	Holt	2.4	3,733	3,678	1	16	6	-	15	17	44	2,735
31 38295	Papillion city	Sarpy	4.2	16,363	15,221	402	62	230	4	164	280	478	11,195
31 39345	Plattsmouth city	Cass	2.9	6,887	6,705	21	35	36	1	32	57	138	4,884
31 40605	Ralston city	Douglas	1.7	6,314	5,996	78	10	73	3	100	54	277	4,760
31 44035	Schuyler city	Colfax	2.1	5,371	3,722	6	14	15	13	1,470	131	2,423	3,777
31 44245	Scottsbluff city	Scotts Bluff	5.9	14,732	12,062	65	471	110	6	1,709	309	3,476	10,824
31 44420	Seward city	Seward	3.3	6,319	6,191	29	8	30	-	23	38	62	4,888
31 45295	Sidney city	Cheyenne	6.2	6,282	5,982	11	48	35	3	130	73	371	4,639
31 46030	South Sioux City city	Dakota	4.9	11,925	9,049	102	281	381	11	1,737	364	2,958	8,370
31 49950	Valentine city	Cherry	2.0	2,820	2,600	1	163	16	-	6	34	25	2,088
31 50965	Wahoo city	Saunders	2.1	3,942	3,879	6	12	14	-	12	19	33	2,906
31 51840	Wayne city	Wayne	2.2	5,583	5,379	89	20	19	1	24	51	79	4,706
31 52575	West Point city	Cuming	2.5	3,660	3,368	8	15	6	-	210	53	440	2,740
31 54045	York city	York	5.6	8,081	7,819	60	12	60	9	47	74	126	6,166
32 00000	NEVADA		109,826.0	1,998,257	1,501,886	135,477	26,420	90,266	8,426	159,354	76,428	393,970	1,486,458
32 04900	Battle Mountain CDP	Lander	1.8	2,871	2,334	4	73	14	1	339	106	677	1,901
32 06500	Boulder City city	Clark	202.6	14,966	14,149	107	108	107	24	190	281	650	11,920
32 09700	Carson City	Carson City IC	143.4	52,457	44,744	946	1,259	930	76	3,391	1,111	7,466	40,186
32 14090	Cold Springs CDP	Washoe	17.1	3,834	3,552	45	44	43	4	32	114	167	2,633
32 17500	Dayton CDP	Lyon	31.7	5,907	5,400	21	61	61	9	227	128	520	4,248
32 22500	Elko city	Elko	14.5	16,708	13,894	62	445	187	20	1,609	491	3,528	11,641
32 23500	Ely city	White Pine	7.1	4,041	3,602	13	126	44	14	150	92	499	3,004
32 23770	Enterprise CDP	Clark	48.6	14,676	12,078	464	118	762	80	593	581	1,766	11,673
32 24100	Fallon city	Churchill	3.0	7,536	6,128	154	256	377	28	256	337	745	5,397
32 24900	Fernley CDP	Lyon	35.4	8,543	7,698	39	131	58	17	307	293	758	6,051
32 26300	Gardnerville CDP	Douglas	4.8	3,357	3,019	15	36	43	3	178	63	397	2,597
32 26500	Gardnerville Ranchos CDP	Douglas	14.7	11,054	10,141	30	241	111	14	230	287	830	7,786
32 31300	Hawthorne CDP	Mineral	1.5	3,311	2,797	204	93	40	4	101	72	305	2,552
32 31900	Henderson city	Clark	79.7	175,381	148,181	6,590	1,236	6,983	728	5,549	6,114	18,785	131,369
32 35200	Incline Village-Crystal Bay CDP	Washoe	28.9	9,952	9,053	46	59	156	16	432	190	1,207	8,000
32 35275	Indian Hills CDP	Douglas	9.8	4,407	4,024	10	54	38	-	186	95	418	3,226
32 37190	Johnson Lane CDP	Douglas	21.4	4,837	4,609	6	37	44	4	31	106	212	3,650
32 38000	Kingsbury CDP	Douglas	21.8	2,624	2,448	12	16	56	6	41	45	109	2,168
32 40000	Las Vegas city	Clark	113.3	478,434	334,230	49,570	3,570	22,879	2,145	46,643	19,397	112,962	354,379
32 41000	Laughlin CDP	Clark	88.1	7,076	6,302	199	44	162	13	194	162	747	5,779
32 41825	Lemmon Valley-Golden Valley CDP	Washoe	32.5	6,855	6,198	24	163	81	12	163	214	406	5,058
32 46000	Mesquite city	Clark	15.3	9,389	7,539	61	92	119	7	1,367	204	2,324	6,988
32 47000	Minden CDP	Douglas	4.3	2,836	2,667	2	20	32	3	59	53	187	2,214
32 47880	Moapa Valley CDP	Clark	43.6	5,784	5,345	14	38	15	21	251	100	526	3,845
32 50400	Nellis AFB CDP	Clark	3.1	8,896	6,090	1,276	122	442	65	436	465	1,043	5,924
32 51800	North Las Vegas city	Clark	78.5	115,488	64,591	21,970	943	3,740	610	18,224	5,410	43,435	76,298
32 53800	Pahrump CDP	Nye	297.9	24,631	22,419	321	318	210	92	560	711	1,879	19,143
32 54600	Paradise CDP	Clark	47.1	186,070	134,927	12,260	1,424	12,135	1,097	15,568	8,659	43,663	146,705
32 60600	Reno city	Washoe	69.1	180,480	139,793	4,651	2,271	9,555	1,004	16,712	6,494	34,616	138,651
32 67200	Silver Springs CDP	Lyon	72.4	4,708	4,316	57	86	21	10	69	149	218	3,529
32 68350	Spanish Springs CDP	Washoe	59.5	9,018	8,350	67	107	126	7	155	206	521	6,183
32 68400	Sparks city	Washoe	23.9	66,346	52,001	1,591	780	3,308	330	6,041	2,295	13,068	48,508
32 68550	Spring Creek CDP	Elko	58.7	10,548	9,816	22	166	34	18	240	252	690	6,842
32 68585	Spring Valley CDP	Clark	33.4	117,390	85,224	6,214	701	13,164	567	6,036	5,484	16,165	92,536
32 70900	Summerlin South CDP	Clark	40.8	3,735	2,946	155	22	375	16	106	115	293	2,989
32 71400	Sunrise Manor CDP	Clark	38.2	156,120	102,212	20,117	1,529	8,445	713	15,814	7,290	40,619	109,713
32 71600	Sun Valley CDP	Washoe	15.0	19,461	15,526	429	376	431	121	1,850	728	4,113	13,467
32 73600	Tonopah CDP	Nye	16.2	2,627	2,397	20	37	11	8	74	80	162	1,915
32 79425	Verdi-Mogul CDP	Washoe	24.1	2,949	2,835	15	6	31	-	23	39	97	2,204
32 83730	West Wendover city	Elko	7.5	4,721	3,350	32	107	28	2	1,074	128	2,684	2,881
32 83800	Whitney CDP	Clark	7.5	18,273	13,200	1,247	203	697	82	2,017	827	4,622	13,694
32 84600	Winchester CDP	Clark	4.3	26,958	19,364	1,895	234	1,445	119	2,605	1,296	7,820	21,616
32 84800	Winnemucca city	Humboldt	8.3	7,174	5,984	23	160	64	2	689	252	1,488	5,006
32 85400	Yerington city	Lyon	1.7	2,883	2,437	5	180	11	-	167	83	445	2,172
33 00000	NEW HAMPSHIRE		8,968.1	1,235,786	1,186,851	9,035	2,964	15,931	371	7,420	13,214	20,489	926,224
33 05140	Berlin city	Coos	61.7	10,331	10,150	19	24	38	1	16	83	68	8,130
33 12900	Claremont city	Sullivan	43.1	13,151	12,845	41	43	81	4	16	121	66	10,085
33 14200	Concord city	Merrimack	64.3	40,687	38,863	421	120	598	13	139	533	591	31,292
33 17860	Derry CDP	Rockingham	15.4	22,661	21,659	238	50	253	4	171	286	501	16,080
33 18820	Dover city	Strafford	26.7	26,884	25,396	301	53	635	15	93	391	306	21,282

Table D-1. Places — **Area and Population**—Con.

[Includes incorporated places and census designated places (CDPs) of 2,500 or more population as of April 1, 2000. Codes shown are two-digit Federal Information Processing Standards (FIPS) state codes and five-digit FIPS place codes. Place names and codes are those in effect as of January 1, 2000. County refers to the county (or counties) in which the place is located. IC in this column = independent city, a county equivalent. If a place is located in more than one county, counties are listed in alphabetic order]

State and place code	Place	County	Land area, 2000 (sq. mi.)	Population, 2000 (April 1) Total	White	Black or African American	American Indian and Alaska Native	Asian	Native Hawaiian and Other Pacific Islander	Some other race	Two or more races	Hispanic or Latino (of any race)	18 years and over
33 00000	NEW HAMPSHIRE—Con.												
33 19620	Durham CDP	Strafford	2.7	9,024	8,417	75	26	357	16	29	104	118	8,409
33 21780	East Merrimack CDP	Hillsborough	3.0	3,784	3,606	38	5	78	1	15	41	66	2,927
33 25300	Exeter CDP	Rockingham	4.4	9,759	9,487	45	20	90	-	21	96	75	7,443
33 25940	Farmington CDP	Strafford	6.4	3,468	3,403	-	19	4	-	9	33	38	2,480
33 27380	Franklin city	Merrimack	27.6	8,405	8,161	32	23	43	1	29	116	100	6,238
33 32980	Hampton CDP	Rockingham	5.4	9,126	8,926	17	7	99	5	23	49	81	7,014
33 33780	Hanover CDP	Grafton	4.6	8,162	6,960	184	50	668	7	92	201	259	7,257
33 37220	Hooksett CDP	Merrimack	4.7	3,609	3,477	27	10	57	-	10	28	54	2,704
33 37860	Hudson CDP	Hillsborough	3.1	7,814	7,481	96	20	87	-	64	66	181	5,891
33 38420	Jaffrey CDP	Cheshire	2.5	2,802	2,729	8	7	19	-	-	39	18	2,042
33 39300	Keene city	Cheshire	37.3	22,563	22,034	89	45	153	7	50	185	172	18,147
33 40180	Laconia city	Belknap	20.3	16,411	15,885	90	68	120	4	44	200	162	12,748
33 41300	Lebanon city	Grafton	40.4	12,568	11,862	104	54	335	4	51	158	206	9,732
33 42500	Littleton CDP	Grafton	8.6	4,431	4,259	14	32	40	-	34	52	73	3,337
33 43140	Londonderry CDP	Rockingham	12.2	11,417	11,100	57	17	106	5	24	108	174	7,767
33 45140	Manchester city	Hillsborough	33.0	107,006	98,178	2,246	326	2,487	38	1,880	1,851	4,944	81,648
33 47940	Milford CDP	Hillsborough	5.7	8,293	8,002	82	8	84	1	12	104	88	6,135
33 50260	Nashua city	Hillsborough	30.9	86,605	77,291	1,740	275	3,363	29	2,642	1,265	5,388	65,251
33 52260	Newmarket CDP	Rockingham	1.9	5,124	4,811	43	13	141	-	25	91	102	4,126
33 52500	Newport CDP	Sullivan	10.9	4,008	3,933	9	9	7	-	3	47	18	2,926
33 60500	Peterborough CDP	Hillsborough	4.7	2,944	2,874	12	7	26	1	5	19	23	2,275
33 61220	Pinardville CDP	Hillsborough	1.7	5,779	5,634	13	15	35	1	28	53	64	4,784
33 62580	Plymouth CDP	Grafton	3.7	3,528	3,417	15	3	33	-	18	42	31	3,209
33 62900	Portsmouth city	Rockingham	15.6	20,784	19,443	442	44	508	5	59	283	280	17,219
33 63940	Raymond CDP	Rockingham	4.6	2,839	2,772	11	9	8	-	3	36	26	2,093
33 65140	Rochester city	Strafford	45.2	28,461	27,640	149	62	248	9	74	279	255	21,266
33 69940	Somersworth city	Strafford	9.8	11,477	11,037	66	22	110	1	68	173	185	8,463
33 71220	South Hooksett CDP	Merrimack	5.3	5,282	5,054	42	8	119	3	11	45	73	4,103
33 75140	Suncook CDP	Merrimack	3.7	5,362	5,207	29	18	24	-	6	78	39	4,081
33 77100	Tilton-Northfield CDP	Belknap, Merrimack	3.0	3,231	3,124	3	16	22	-	4	62	19	2,436
33 86340	Wolfeboro CDP	Carroll	7.0	2,979	2,957	5	2	6	-	2	7	32	2,383
34 00000	NEW JERSEY		7,417.3	8,414,350	6,104,705	1,141,821	19,492	480,276	3,329	450,972	213,755	1,117,191	6,326,792
34 00100	Absecon city	Atlantic	5.7	7,638	6,363	459	13	570	-	115	118	288	5,842
34 00675	Allamuchy-Panther Valley CDP	Warren	5.7	3,125	2,997	30	1	65	-	16	16	74	2,589
34 00700	Allendale borough	Bergen	3.1	6,699	6,195	26	4	408	-	31	35	170	4,663
34 01960	Asbury Park city	Monmouth	1.4	16,930	4,194	10,515	55	119	12	1,098	937	2,637	11,811
34 01990	Ashland CDP	Camden	2.9	8,375	7,342	369	18	535	2	49	60	219	6,402
34 02080	Atlantic City city	Atlantic	11.3	40,517	10,809	17,892	193	4,213	24	5,575	1,811	10,107	30,090
34 02110	Atlantic Highlands borough	Monmouth	1.2	4,705	4,440	108	3	58	-	48	48	165	3,700
34 02200	Audubon borough	Camden	1.5	9,182	8,938	48	10	82	1	44	59	139	6,907
34 02350	Avenel CDP	Middlesex	3.4	17,552	9,393	3,451	62	3,318	5	641	682	1,729	13,898
34 02905	Barclay-Kingston CDP	Camden	2.8	10,728	9,371	386	18	734	1	70	148	244	8,183
34 03250	Barrington borough	Camden	1.6	7,084	6,490	295	17	102	3	76	101	201	5,588
34 03580	Bayonne city	Hudson	5.6	61,842	48,631	3,416	106	2,562	30	4,611	2,486	11,015	48,170
34 04120	Beach Haven West CDP	Ocean	2.0	4,444	4,343	16	1	34	4	21	25	97	3,886
34 04180	Beachwood borough	Ocean	2.8	10,375	9,925	101	13	117	6	115	98	438	7,415
34 04240	Beatyestown CDP	Warren	3.0	3,223	2,957	53	1	60	-	85	67	210	2,309
34 04400	Beckett CDP	Gloucester	1.8	4,726	3,739	749	4	99	1	59	75	143	3,106
34 04690	Belleville CDP	Essex	3.3	35,928	24,950	1,926	60	4,062	26	3,532	1,372	8,507	28,082
34 04750	Bellmawr borough	Camden	3.0	11,262	10,450	133	7	344	2	173	153	394	8,922
34 04930	Belmar borough	Monmouth	1.0	6,045	5,533	209	11	62	-	120	110	414	5,007
34 04990	Belvidere town	Warren	1.3	2,771	2,716	14	1	14	-	7	19	64	1,991
34 05170	Bergenfield borough	Bergen	2.9	26,247	16,510	1,812	63	5,357	4	1,698	803	4,474	19,726
34 05350	Berkeley Heights CDP	Union	6.3	13,407	12,019	149	11	1,055	-	82	91	494	9,812
34 05440	Berlin borough	Camden	3.6	6,149	5,784	134	13	104	4	30	80	130	4,636
34 05590	Bernardsville borough	Somerset	12.9	7,345	6,900	18	11	194	-	114	108	439	5,430
34 05740	Beverly city	Burlington	0.6	2,661	1,721	765	3	24	-	38	110	122	1,907
34 06040	Blackwood CDP	Camden	1.2	4,692	4,284	185	5	99	3	56	60	148	3,563
34 06250	Bloomfield CDP	Essex	5.3	47,683	33,421	5,573	91	3,998	31	3,061	1,508	6,901	37,644
34 06340	Bloomingdale borough	Passaic	8.8	7,610	7,271	32	9	167	-	51	80	332	5,914
34 06490	Bogota borough	Bergen	0.8	8,249	6,246	473	12	639	5	558	316	1,759	6,161
34 06610	Boonton town	Morris	2.3	8,496	7,052	337	18	660	1	187	241	582	6,633
34 06670	Bordentown city	Burlington	0.9	3,969	3,225	519	2	76	1	32	114	112	3,139
34 06790	Bound Brook borough	Somerset	1.7	10,155	8,385	256	31	292	7	880	304	3,541	7,950
34 06970	Bradley Beach borough	Monmouth	0.6	4,793	4,225	185	8	70	1	192	112	615	3,931
34 07600	Bridgeton city	Cumberland	6.2	22,771	8,854	9,528	271	159	20	3,112	827	5,576	16,843
34 07750	Brielle borough	Monmouth	1.8	4,893	4,553	172	3	33	-	79	53	162	3,733
34 07810	Brigantine city	Atlantic	6.4	12,594	10,472	496	23	720	6	588	289	1,185	9,973
34 08455	Browns Mills CDP	Burlington	5.4	11,257	7,261	2,568	56	419	8	352	593	1,052	7,961
34 08492	Brownville CDP	Middlesex	0.9	2,660	2,242	123	1	216	-	31	47	156	2,079
34 08620	Budd Lake CDP	Morris	5.9	8,100	7,056	287	6	470	-	119	162	536	5,775
34 08680	Buena borough	Atlantic	7.6	3,873	2,993	296	20	17	1	408	138	916	2,876
34 08920	Burlington city	Burlington	3.0	9,736	6,638	2,592	26	125	1	126	228	332	7,408
34 09040	Butler borough	Morris	2.1	7,420	7,041	46	15	137	1	110	70	379	5,813

838

Table D-1. Places — Area and Population—Con.

[Includes incorporated places and census designated places (CDPs) of 2,500 or more population as of April 1, 2000. Codes shown are two-digit Federal Information Processing Standards (FIPS) state codes and five-digit FIPS place codes. Place names and codes are those in effect as of January 1, 2000. County refers to the county (or counties) in which the place is located. IC in this column = independent city, a county equivalent. If a place is located in more than one county, counties are listed in alphabetic order]

State and place code	Place	County	Land area, 2000 (sq. mi.)	Population, 2000 (April 1) Total	By race— One race White	Black or African American	American Indian and Alaska Native	Asian	Native Hawaiian and Other Pacific Islander	Some other race	Two or more races	Hispanic or Latino (of any race)	18 years and over
34 00000	NEW JERSEY—Con.												
34 09220	Caldwell borough	Essex	1.2	7,584	6,918	172	8	308	5	91	82	352	6,215
34 10000	Camden city	Camden	8.8	79,904	13,454	42,628	435	1,958	59	18,239	3,131	31,019	52,230
34 10270	Cape May city	Cape May	2.5	4,034	3,684	212	8	16	2	51	61	153	3,375
34 10300	Cape May Court House CDP	Cape May	9.0	4,704	3,968	512	9	127	3	19	66	74	3,582
34 10480	Carlstadt borough	Bergen	4.0	5,917	5,260	81	5	366	1	126	78	473	4,790
34 10600	Carneys Point CDP	Salem	8.7	6,914	5,326	1,215	20	60	3	153	137	287	5,322
34 10750	Carteret borough	Middlesex	4.4	20,709	14,239	1,975	49	1,722	7	1,918	799	4,839	15,481
34 11230	Cedar Grove CDP	Essex	4.2	12,300	11,076	368	6	667	3	57	123	393	9,934
34 12100	Chatham borough	Morris	2.4	8,460	8,104	12	5	238	1	42	58	223	6,068
34 12385	Cherry Hill Mall CDP	Camden	3.7	13,238	11,008	668	6	1,196	11	145	204	399	10,258
34 13180	Clark CDP	Union	4.3	14,597	13,956	44	2	402	-	92	101	535	11,562
34 13360	Clayton borough	Gloucester	7.2	7,139	5,656	1,146	30	47	2	68	190	234	5,061
34 13399	Clearbrook Park CDP	Middlesex	0.9	3,053	3,009	25	-	9	-	-	10	21	3,029
34 13420	Clementon borough	Camden	1.9	4,986	4,100	577	11	46	9	117	126	206	3,752
34 13570	Cliffside Park borough	Bergen	1.0	23,007	17,911	422	58	2,772	5	1,144	695	4,177	19,126
34 13630	Cliffwood Beach CDP	Monmouth	0.9	3,538	2,781	532	11	48	-	102	64	346	2,601
34 13690	Clifton city	Passaic	11.3	78,672	59,960	2,277	192	5,066	27	7,553	3,597	15,608	61,700
34 13720	Clinton town	Hunterdon	1.4	2,632	2,423	35	12	98	-	36	28	108	1,938
34 13810	Closter borough	Bergen	3.2	8,383	6,314	78	8	1,807	-	68	108	343	6,038
34 14260	Collingswood borough	Camden	1.8	14,326	12,388	955	48	395	3	346	191	812	11,209
34 14380	Colonia CDP	Middlesex	3.9	17,811	15,317	847	18	1,124	11	227	267	886	13,595
34 14758	Concordia CDP	Middlesex	1.1	3,658	3,612	19	-	17	-	2	8	12	3,643
34 15250	Country Lake Estates CDP	Burlington	1.1	4,012	2,814	813	12	113	2	96	162	354	2,872
34 15670	Cranford CDP	Union	4.8	22,578	21,156	583	9	485	5	151	189	879	17,316
34 15820	Cresskill borough	Bergen	2.1	7,746	6,046	71	3	1,444	-	50	132	309	5,710
34 15910	Crestwood Village CDP	Ocean	4.4	8,392	8,256	64	6	20	-	12	34	94	8,362
34 16630	Dayton CDP	Middlesex	2.1	6,235	3,837	617	14	1,561	3	81	122	321	4,251
34 17530	Demarest borough	Bergen	2.1	4,845	3,744	24	1	981	1	23	71	167	3,444
34 18070	Dover town	Morris	2.7	18,188	12,631	1,242	62	450	5	2,909	889	10,539	13,976
34 18400	Dumont borough	Bergen	2.0	17,503	14,663	261	17	1,918	1	339	304	1,463	13,239
34 18490	Dunellen borough	Middlesex	1.0	6,823	5,736	250	17	243	1	435	141	1,010	5,124
34 18970	East Brunswick CDP	Middlesex	22.0	46,756	36,265	1,321	42	7,607	5	526	990	1,957	34,588
34 19150	East Freehold CDP	Monmouth	3.0	4,936	4,280	182	2	359	1	45	67	190	3,459
34 19390	East Orange city	Essex	3.9	69,824	2,683	62,462	177	302	51	1,496	2,653	3,284	50,188
34 19510	East Rutherford borough	Bergen	3.8	8,716	6,945	324	10	932	4	280	221	928	7,027
34 19840	Eatontown borough	Monmouth	5.9	14,008	10,267	1,626	48	1,305	5	323	434	928	10,796
34 19900	Echelon CDP	Camden	2.8	10,440	7,678	1,057	19	1,385	2	84	215	317	8,373
34 20020	Edgewater borough	Bergen	0.8	7,677	5,153	270	16	1,775	3	226	234	802	6,494
34 20260	Edison CDP	Middlesex	30.1	97,687	58,110	6,728	132	28,597	37	1,973	2,104	6,226	75,365
34 20350	Egg Harbor City city	Atlantic	11.1	4,545	3,036	645	17	57	4	613	173	1,116	3,261
34 21000	Elizabeth city	Union	12.2	120,568	67,250	24,090	580	2,830	55	18,702	7,061	59,627	88,888
34 21300	Elmwood Park borough	Bergen	2.7	18,925	15,619	409	21	1,477	1	841	557	2,535	14,971
34 21450	Emerson borough	Bergen	2.2	7,197	6,450	61	4	568	-	63	51	332	5,527
34 21480	Englewood city	Bergen	4.9	26,203	11,134	10,215	71	1,366	12	2,226	1,179	5,703	19,947
34 21510	Englewood Cliffs borough	Bergen	2.1	5,322	3,557	73	2	1,580	-	38	72	260	4,221
34 21645	Erlton-Ellisburg CDP	Camden	1.9	8,168	7,103	324	9	547	7	75	103	311	6,554
34 22180	Ewing CDP	Mercer	15.3	35,707	24,645	8,863	55	811	22	653	658	1,586	29,263
34 22380	Fairfield CDP	Essex	10.5	7,063	6,754	37	7	199	-	28	38	244	5,506
34 22440	Fair Haven borough	Monmouth	1.7	5,937	5,573	243	2	58	-	13	48	79	3,976
34 22470	Fair Lawn borough	Bergen	5.2	31,637	28,960	234	13	1,558	1	434	437	1,744	24,423
34 22560	Fairview borough	Bergen	0.9	13,255	9,605	226	51	659	4	1,712	998	4,911	10,456
34 22740	Fairview CDP	Monmouth	1.3	3,942	3,781	22	-	78	1	18	42	160	2,855
34 22860	Fanwood borough	Union	1.3	7,174	6,335	369	7	315	2	57	89	268	5,323
34 23700	Flemington borough	Hunterdon	1.1	4,200	3,684	134	13	131	7	132	99	461	3,267
34 23895	Florence-Roebling CDP	Burlington	2.2	8,200	6,976	864	7	171	1	50	131	167	6,097
34 23910	Florham Park borough	Morris	7.4	8,857	8,326	88	1	343	5	34	60	190	6,935
34 24030	Fords CDP	Middlesex	2.6	15,032	10,952	891	17	2,421	-	407	344	1,388	11,655
34 24180	Forked River CDP	Ocean	2.9	4,914	4,785	36	11	16	-	41	25	166	3,735
34 24300	Fort Dix CDP	Burlington	11.2	7,464	4,357	2,660	33	95	9	184	126	1,701	6,451
34 24420	Fort Lee borough	Bergen	2.5	35,461	22,253	615	25	11,146	20	600	802	2,791	29,261
34 24930	Franklin borough	Sussex	4.5	5,160	4,907	32	18	76	-	63	64	228	3,741
34 24990	Franklin Lakes borough	Bergen	9.5	10,422	9,521	96	11	660	1	43	90	286	7,433
34 25200	Freehold borough	Monmouth	2.0	10,976	7,795	1,738	60	269	2	729	383	3,081	8,258
34 25770	Garfield city	Bergen	2.1	29,786	24,456	887	99	800	2	2,414	1,128	5,989	23,124
34 25800	Garwood borough	Union	0.7	4,153	3,983	15	-	55	-	64	36	207	3,322
34 26100	Gibbstown CDP	Gloucester	1.6	3,758	3,632	41	4	26	1	12	42	57	2,893
34 26340	Glassboro borough	Gloucester	9.2	19,068	14,212	3,712	32	441	17	282	372	728	14,859
34 26520	Glendora CDP	Camden	1.1	4,907	4,787	25	8	16	1	21	49	77	3,850
34 26610	Glen Ridge borough	Essex	1.3	7,271	6,484	362	11	243	-	72	99	251	5,039
34 26640	Glen Rock borough	Bergen	2.7	11,546	10,399	209	18	748	2	71	99	314	8,151
34 26820	Gloucester City city	Camden	2.2	11,484	11,155	79	21	78	4	74	73	216	8,435
34 26902	Golden Triangle CDP	Camden	2.9	3,511	2,835	330	5	181	-	73	87	193	2,835
34 27995	Greentree CDP	Camden	4.7	11,536	8,942	698	8	1,710	2	63	113	236	8,373
34 28650	Guttenberg town	Hudson	0.2	10,807	7,022	412	41	789	1	1,775	767	5,871	8,520
34 28680	Hackensack city	Bergen	4.1	42,677	22,451	10,518	191	3,181	23	4,144	2,169	11,061	34,906
34 28710	Hackettstown town	Warren	3.7	10,403	9,389	227	13	303	6	208	257	833	8,043
34 28770	Haddonfield borough	Camden	2.8	11,659	11,247	148	15	131	3	37	78	170	8,488

Table D-1. Places — **Area and Population**—Con.

[Includes incorporated places and census designated places (CDPs) of 2,500 or more population as of April 1, 2000. Codes shown are two-digit Federal Information Processing Standards (FIPS) state codes and five-digit FIPS place codes. Place names and codes are those in effect as of January 1, 2000. County refers to the county (or counties) in which the place is located. IC in this column = independent city, a county equivalent. If a place is located in more than one county, counties are listed in alphabetic order]

State and place code	Place	County	Land area, 2000 (sq. mi.)	Population, 2000 (April 1) Total	By race—One race White	Black or African American	American Indian and Alaska Native	Asian	Native Hawaiian and Other Pacific Islander	Some other race	Two or more races	Hispanic or Latino (of any race)	18 years and over
34 00000	NEW JERSEY—Con.												
34 28800	Haddon Heights borough	Camden	1.6	7,547	7,394	30	8	49	3	20	43	79	5,731
34 29070	Haledon borough	Passaic	1.2	8,252	6,073	585	14	377	2	833	368	1,865	6,144
34 29220	Hamburg borough	Sussex	1.2	3,105	2,892	23	9	71	-	52	58	131	2,274
34 29430	Hammonton town	Atlantic	41.3	12,604	11,073	219	18	144	3	987	160	1,876	9,730
34 30150	Harrington Park borough	Bergen	1.9	4,740	3,959	32	2	695	-	30	22	122	3,384
34 30210	Harrison town	Hudson	1.2	14,424	9,534	142	57	1,715	4	2,302	670	5,333	11,320
34 30420	Hasbrouck Heights borough	Bergen	1.5	11,662	10,247	200	5	776	1	255	178	964	9,076
34 30540	Haworth borough	Bergen	2.0	3,390	2,981	41	-	312	-	25	31	92	2,411
34 30570	Hawthorne borough	Passaic	3.4	18,218	17,080	137	25	344	3	287	342	1,354	14,252
34 30738	Heathcote CDP	Middlesex	2.6	4,755	3,298	521	3	781	-	51	101	207	3,654
34 31320	High Bridge borough	Hunterdon	2.4	3,776	3,634	30	13	54	1	17	27	80	2,732
34 31405	Highland Lake CDP	Sussex	5.0	5,051	4,853	55	4	24	-	62	53	211	3,564
34 31470	Highland Park borough	Middlesex	1.8	13,999	10,087	1,111	16	1,908	12	503	362	1,145	10,955
34 31500	Highlands borough	Monmouth	0.8	5,097	4,847	81	17	51	-	30	71	207	4,140
34 31620	Hightstown borough	Mercer	1.2	5,216	3,992	444	19	119	4	503	135	1,046	4,042
34 31920	Hillsdale borough	Bergen	3.0	10,087	9,321	86	7	512	4	87	70	429	7,465
34 32010	Hillside CDP	Union	2.8	21,747	8,705	10,122	50	751	17	1,144	958	3,153	16,185
34 32250	Hoboken city	Hudson	1.3	38,577	31,178	1,644	60	1,661	21	2,942	1,071	7,783	34,543
34 32310	Ho-Ho-Kus borough	Bergen	1.7	4,060	3,762	24	4	212	8	15	35	80	2,942
34 32415	Holiday City-Berkeley CDP	Ocean	5.8	13,884	13,741	53	1	31	2	7	49	151	13,865
34 32418	Holiday City South CDP	Ocean	1.9	4,047	3,815	206	2	6	-	1	17	39	3,981
34 32910	Hopatcong borough	Sussex	11.0	15,888	14,792	310	18	286	-	226	256	952	11,687
34 34440	Irvington CDP	Essex	3.0	60,695	5,446	49,566	146	669	59	2,234	2,575	5,086	43,691
34 34470	Iselin CDP	Middlesex	3.1	16,698	10,796	1,006	20	4,201	2	292	381	914	13,056
34 34890	Jamesburg borough	Middlesex	0.8	6,025	4,990	532	12	134	-	229	128	606	4,541
34 36000	Jersey City city	Hudson	14.9	240,055	81,637	67,994	1,071	38,881	181	36,280	14,011	67,952	180,652
34 36480	Keansburg borough	Monmouth	1.1	10,732	10,014	229	11	132	7	187	152	853	7,814
34 36510	Kearny town	Hudson	9.1	40,513	30,687	1,609	148	2,228	27	4,068	1,746	11,075	31,814
34 36660	Kendall Park CDP	Middlesex	3.7	9,006	7,143	408	2	1,188	5	87	173	391	6,312
34 36690	Kenilworth borough	Union	2.1	7,675	7,007	184	19	221	-	138	106	663	6,079
34 36810	Keyport borough	Monmouth	1.4	7,568	6,447	531	9	168	3	224	186	839	5,919
34 37110	Kinnelon borough	Morris	17.9	9,365	8,953	54	4	266	9	22	57	218	6,556
34 37770	Lakehurst borough	Ocean	0.9	2,522	2,124	198	16	59	2	69	54	201	1,751
34 38040	Lake Mohawk CDP	Sussex	5.0	9,755	9,451	37	9	108	4	43	103	247	7,057
34 38580	Lakewood CDP	Ocean	7.2	36,065	28,000	4,415	73	345	13	2,002	1,217	6,381	21,151
34 38610	Lambertville city	Hunterdon	1.1	3,868	3,661	75	13	41	2	35	41	120	3,274
34 39120	Laurel Lake CDP	Cumberland	1.8	2,929	2,784	51	12	4	1	24	53	126	2,086
34 39360	Laurence Harbor CDP	Middlesex	2.8	6,227	5,645	222	14	137	3	102	104	427	4,631
34 39390	Lavallette borough	Ocean	0.8	2,665	2,615	7	3	4	-	17	19	43	2,316
34 39420	Lawnside borough	Camden	1.4	2,692	47	2,520	27	14	2	13	69	64	2,065
34 39570	Lawrenceville CDP	Mercer	1.0	4,081	3,596	146	3	257	-	22	57	141	3,095
34 39885	Leisuretowne CDP	Burlington	1.8	2,535	2,496	27	2	3	-	-	7	19	2,530
34 39900	Leisure Village CDP	Ocean	1.2	4,443	4,163	145	1	24	1	54	55	257	4,117
34 39910	Leisure Village East CDP	Ocean	1.6	4,597	4,561	15	-	8	-	1	12	49	4,584
34 39920	Leisure Village West-Pine Lake Park CDP	Ocean	3.8	11,085	10,346	317	20	126	5	131	140	437	9,021
34 39990	Leonardo CDP	Monmouth	0.6	2,823	2,746	15	7	14	3	13	25	137	2,091
34 40020	Leonia borough	Bergen	1.5	8,914	5,860	202	8	2,323	1	285	235	1,135	6,725
34 40290	Lincoln Park borough	Morris	6.7	10,930	9,845	191	13	578	1	142	160	633	8,716
34 40320	Lincroft CDP	Monmouth	5.6	6,255	5,824	52	5	283	-	41	50	159	4,495
34 40350	Linden city	Union	10.8	39,394	26,031	8,981	56	925	15	1,923	1,463	5,674	30,548
34 40440	Lindenwold borough	Camden	3.9	17,414	10,695	4,915	83	614	10	564	533	1,316	13,299
34 40530	Linwood city	Atlantic	3.8	7,172	6,828	76	8	173	-	16	71	130	5,291
34 40650	Little Falls CDP	Passaic	2.8	10,855	10,001	71	7	456	2	144	174	579	8,888
34 40680	Little Ferry borough	Bergen	1.5	10,800	7,426	509	16	1,847	6	621	375	1,641	8,616
34 40770	Little Silver borough	Monmouth	2.8	6,170	5,994	19	10	93	1	12	41	81	4,479
34 40920	Livingston CDP	Essex	13.9	27,391	22,637	328	14	3,982	3	190	237	695	20,107
34 41100	Lodi borough	Bergen	2.3	23,971	18,736	852	40	2,124	8	1,498	713	4,309	18,865
34 41310	Long Branch city	Monmouth	5.2	31,340	21,320	5,847	113	513	15	2,220	1,312	6,477	23,890
34 42120	Lyndhurst CDP	Bergen	4.6	19,383	17,433	119	9	1,046	1	397	378	1,744	15,690
34 42390	McGuire AFB CDP	Burlington	2.1	6,478	4,489	1,225	46	179	8	206	325	564	4,170
34 42510	Madison borough	Morris	4.2	16,530	14,826	496	21	624	38	256	269	987	13,126
34 42540	Madison Park CDP	Middlesex	1.6	6,929	3,905	953	7	1,384	8	289	383	904	5,044
34 42630	Magnolia borough	Camden	1.0	4,409	3,395	785	10	41	1	68	109	179	3,318
34 43050	Manasquan borough	Monmouth	1.4	6,310	6,177	26	7	28	-	30	42	283	4,808
34 43620	Manville borough	Somerset	2.5	10,343	9,928	47	7	136	3	118	104	559	8,203
34 43830	Maplewood CDP	Essex	3.8	23,868	14,030	7,788	31	682	7	373	957	1,248	17,175
34 43890	Margate City city	Atlantic	1.4	8,193	7,843	71	2	128	6	75	68	222	6,935
34 44100	Marlton CDP	Burlington	3.2	10,260	9,369	295	14	429	1	61	91	240	7,852
34 44520	Matawan borough	Monmouth	2.3	8,910	7,337	582	2	712	2	110	165	575	6,900
34 44880	Maywood borough	Bergen	1.3	9,523	8,054	266	7	682	1	315	198	1,115	7,514
34 45210	Medford Lakes borough	Burlington	1.2	4,173	4,103	18	5	20	-	4	23	41	3,106
34 45330	Mendham borough	Morris	6.0	5,097	4,951	23	1	72	3	14	33	125	3,730
34 45495	Mercerville-Hamilton Square CDP	Mercer	7.7	26,419	24,872	384	34	666	2	207	254	671	20,272
34 45510	Merchantville borough	Camden	0.6	3,801	3,265	282	11	80	-	108	55	208	2,825
34 45690	Metuchen borough	Middlesex	2.7	12,840	10,835	681	13	928	-	144	239	508	9,849

U.S. Census Bureau, County and City Data Book: 2000

Table D-1. Places — **Area and Population**—Con.

[Includes incorporated places and census designated places (CDPs) of 2,500 or more population as of April 1, 2000. Codes shown are two-digit Federal Information Processing Standards (FIPS) state codes and five-digit FIPS place codes. Place names and codes are those in effect as of January 1, 2000. County refers to the county (or counties) in which the place is located. IC in this column = independent city, a county equivalent. If a place is located in more than one county, counties are listed in alphabetic order]

State and place code	Place	County	Land area, 2000 (sq. mi.)	Population, 2000 (April 1) Total	White	Black or African American	American Indian and Alaska Native	Asian	Native Hawaiian and Other Pacific Islander	Some other race	Two or more races	Hispanic or Latino (of any race)	18 years and over
34 00000	NEW JERSEY—Con.												
34 45900	Middlesex borough	Middlesex	3.5	13,717	11,970	461	18	570	3	440	255	1,235	10,411
34 46110	Midland Park borough	Bergen	1.6	6,947	6,656	30	4	154	1	53	49	256	5,258
34 46410	Millburn CDP	Essex	9.4	19,765	17,573	217	10	1,660	6	85	214	404	13,789
34 46620	Milltown borough	Middlesex	1.6	7,000	6,570	53	11	215	-	81	70	261	5,399
34 46680	Millville city	Cumberland	42.3	26,847	20,438	4,025	139	216	8	1,384	637	2,998	19,349
34 47130	Monmouth Beach borough	Monmouth	1.1	3,595	3,511	19	-	31	-	12	22	68	2,864
34 47190	Monmouth Junction CDP	Middlesex	1.5	2,721	2,040	193	10	394	-	32	52	113	1,863
34 47490	Montclair CDP	Essex	6.3	38,977	23,297	12,497	73	1,228	14	688	1,180	1,995	29,013
34 47610	Montvale borough	Bergen	4.0	7,034	6,527	31	6	377	-	44	49	217	5,209
34 47700	Moonachie borough	Bergen	1.7	2,754	2,359	26	3	183	-	81	102	349	2,179
34 47895	Moorestown-Lenola CDP	Burlington	7.0	13,860	12,291	964	27	295	1	76	206	274	10,199
34 48030	Morganville CDP	Monmouth	5.9	11,255	9,822	193	1	1,098	5	56	80	331	8,118
34 48210	Morris Plains borough	Morris	2.6	5,236	4,865	70	3	226	5	21	46	141	4,003
34 48300	Morristown town	Morris	2.9	18,544	12,452	3,144	41	700	12	1,572	623	5,034	15,140
34 48480	Mountain Lakes borough	Morris	2.7	4,256	3,960	16	-	220	3	22	35	72	2,738
34 48510	Mountainside borough	Union	4.0	6,602	6,278	62	6	185	4	18	49	199	5,210
34 48690	Mount Arlington borough	Morris	2.1	4,663	4,263	85	9	178	2	59	67	212	3,634
34 48750	Mount Ephraim borough	Camden	0.9	4,495	4,383	18	3	28	1	29	33	89	3,491
34 49560	Mystic Island CDP	Ocean	7.6	8,694	8,391	59	27	46	1	76	94	280	6,773
34 49680	National Park borough	Gloucester	1.0	3,205	3,152	3	8	8	1	17	16	46	2,360
34 49920	Neptune City borough	Monmouth	0.9	5,218	4,351	497	12	142	-	110	106	277	4,096
34 50130	Netcong borough	Morris	0.8	2,580	2,433	31	1	43	-	37	35	184	1,987
34 51000	Newark city	Essex	23.8	273,546	72,537	146,250	1,005	3,263	135	38,430	11,926	80,622	197,127
34 51210	New Brunswick city	Middlesex	5.2	48,573	23,701	11,185	224	2,584	40	8,780	2,059	18,947	38,824
34 51360	New Egypt CDP	Ocean	4.0	2,519	2,315	55	7	32	-	69	41	156	1,810
34 51660	New Milford borough	Bergen	2.3	16,400	12,888	429	19	2,420	4	305	335	1,326	12,895
34 51810	New Providence borough	Union	3.7	11,907	10,689	105	4	905	3	81	120	417	8,771
34 51930	Newton town	Sussex	3.1	8,244	7,582	281	11	162	1	96	111	313	6,271
34 52320	North Arlington borough	Bergen	2.6	15,181	13,603	70	22	852	2	348	284	1,605	12,445
34 52605	North Brunswick Township CDP	Middlesex	12.0	36,287	22,763	5,542	63	5,152	10	1,707	1,050	3,775	27,934
34 52620	North Caldwell borough	Essex	3.0	7,375	5,873	1,070	2	347	-	19	64	159	5,673
34 52650	North Cape May CDP	Cape May	1.4	3,618	3,416	101	16	17	-	27	41	78	2,794
34 52950	Northfield city	Atlantic	3.4	7,725	7,070	205	8	193	6	140	103	338	5,755
34 53040	North Haledon borough	Passaic	3.4	7,920	7,526	114	5	79	-	75	121	308	6,360
34 53205	North Middletown CDP	Monmouth	0.5	3,165	3,000	46	-	45	1	48	25	170	2,185
34 53280	North Plainfield borough	Somerset	2.8	21,103	13,307	2,824	59	1,064	17	2,887	945	6,916	15,664
34 53430	Northvale borough	Bergen	1.3	4,460	3,698	34	3	627	-	52	46	211	3,458
34 53490	North Wildwood city	Cape May	1.8	4,935	4,768	40	4	28	1	38	56	96	4,086
34 53610	Norwood borough	Bergen	2.7	5,751	4,478	48	1	1,092	-	54	78	172	4,269
34 53670	Nutley CDP	Essex	3.4	27,362	24,064	511	15	1,943	10	480	339	1,830	21,396
34 53790	Oakhurst CDP	Monmouth	1.6	4,152	3,990	31	-	95	-	13	23	84	2,979
34 53850	Oakland borough	Bergen	8.6	12,466	11,813	97	8	337	1	87	123	483	9,294
34 53880	Oaklyn borough	Camden	0.6	4,188	4,017	48	9	40	1	35	38	97	3,233
34 54060	Oak Valley CDP	Gloucester	0.7	3,747	3,501	152	10	30	-	10	44	84	2,796
34 54315	Ocean Acres CDP	Ocean	5.9	13,155	12,673	132	17	122	3	71	137	365	9,570
34 54360	Ocean City city	Cape May	6.9	15,378	14,398	663	18	86	10	80	132	306	12,862
34 54480	Ocean Grove CDP	Monmouth	0.4	4,256	3,964	168	4	41	1	39	39	154	3,835
34 54570	Oceanport borough	Monmouth	3.2	5,807	5,558	114	4	46	1	32	52	120	4,384
34 54660	Ogdensburg borough	Sussex	2.3	2,638	2,573	4	1	19	-	7	34	110	1,860
34 54690	Old Bridge CDP	Middlesex	7.1	22,833	19,435	859	31	1,805	6	317	380	1,501	16,545
34 54870	Old Tappan borough	Bergen	3.2	5,482	4,533	33	3	857	-	24	32	151	4,004
34 54990	Oradell borough	Bergen	2.4	8,047	7,248	39	3	651	1	26	79	249	6,020
34 55020	Orange CDP	Essex	2.2	32,868	4,337	24,685	113	415	33	1,712	1,573	4,097	23,760
34 55770	Palisades Park borough	Bergen	1.2	17,073	8,241	235	32	7,016	5	991	553	2,813	13,761
34 55800	Palmyra borough	Burlington	2.0	7,091	5,743	1,017	21	99	3	100	108	229	5,508
34 55950	Paramus borough	Bergen	10.5	25,737	20,380	291	12	4,434	3	229	388	1,253	19,755
34 56130	Park Ridge borough	Bergen	2.6	8,708	8,140	75	12	336	2	64	79	463	6,664
34 56550	Passaic city	Passaic	3.1	67,861	24,044	9,385	531	3,740	29	26,709	3,423	42,387	46,962
34 57000	Paterson city	Passaic	8.4	149,222	45,913	49,095	901	2,831	84	41,184	9,214	74,774	104,785
34 57150	Paulsboro borough	Gloucester	2.0	6,160	3,915	1,949	15	20	6	81	174	268	4,387
34 57540	Pemberton Heights CDP	Burlington	0.9	2,512	1,050	1,165	3	96	-	103	95	291	2,041
34 57600	Pennington borough	Mercer	1.0	2,696	2,560	71	-	27	-	11	27	32	1,922
34 57690	Pennsauken CDP	Camden	10.5	35,737	21,479	8,641	124	1,636	7	2,954	896	5,126	25,925
34 57750	Penns Grove borough	Salem	0.9	4,886	2,387	1,942	18	14	8	397	120	845	3,275
34 57840	Pennsville CDP	Salem	10.5	11,657	11,320	79	19	103	2	44	90	185	8,936
34 58200	Perth Amboy city	Middlesex	4.8	47,303	21,951	4,749	330	723	60	16,834	2,656	33,033	33,831
34 58350	Phillipsburg town	Warren	3.2	15,166	13,928	527	18	126	2	306	259	816	11,128
34 58770	Pine Hill borough	Camden	3.9	10,880	8,355	1,996	30	153	2	132	212	396	7,917
34 59070	Pitman borough	Gloucester	2.3	9,331	9,066	85	11	58	1	21	89	132	6,977
34 59190	Plainfield city	Union	6.0	47,829	10,258	29,550	195	447	46	5,156	2,177	12,033	34,662
34 59640	Pleasantville city	Atlantic	5.8	19,012	4,755	10,969	54	371	5	2,084	774	4,158	13,234
34 59880	Point Pleasant borough	Ocean	3.5	19,306	18,887	56	27	105	2	96	133	465	14,729
34 59910	Point Pleasant Beach borough	Ocean	1.4	5,314	5,098	28	18	54	1	78	37	234	4,292
34 60030	Pomona CDP	Atlantic	2.8	4,019	2,980	323	14	482	1	143	76	301	2,799
34 60090	Pompton Lakes borough	Passaic	3.0	10,640	9,896	129	20	322	1	167	105	611	8,061

[Includes incorporated places and census designated places (CDPs) of 2,500 or more population as of April 1, 2000. Codes shown are two-digit Federal Information Processing Standards (FIPS) state codes and five-digit FIPS place codes. Place names and codes are those in effect as of January 1, 2000. County refers to the county (or counties) in which the place is located. IC in this column = independent city, a county equivalent. If a place is located in more than one county, counties are listed in alphabetical order]

State and place code	Place	County	Land area, 2000 (sq. mi.)	Population, 2000 (April 1) By race— One race Total	White	Black or African American	American Indian and Alaska Native	Asian	Native Hawaiian and Other Pacific Islander	Some other race	Two or more races	Hispanic or Latino (of any race)	18 years and over
34 00000	NEW JERSEY—Con.												
34 60360	Port Monmouth CDP	Monmouth	1.3	3,742	3,581	48	7	16	-	43	47	260	2,718
34 60540	Port Reading CDP	Middlesex	2.2	3,829	3,484	100	-	92	-	68	85	290	2,937
34 60900	Princeton borough	Mercer	1.8	14,203	11,399	908	40	1,060	20	355	421	1,009	12,774
34 60975	Princeton Meadows CDP	Middlesex	2.2	13,436	7,546	1,295	18	4,037	-	230	310	708	10,174
34 60990	Princeton North CDP	Mercer	1.6	4,528	3,693	259	12	269	3	201	91	380	3,483
34 61170	Prospect Park borough	Passaic	0.5	5,779	3,535	789	24	182	4	792	453	2,211	4,070
34 61530	Rahway city	Union	4.0	26,500	15,950	7,173	42	950	14	1,489	882	3,675	20,170
34 61650	Ramblewood CDP	Burlington	3.4	6,003	5,406	287	3	209	-	29	69	122	4,685
34 61680	Ramsey borough	Bergen	5.6	14,351	13,148	112	14	840	1	78	158	420	10,474
34 61725	Ramtown CDP	Monmouth	2.1	5,932	5,516	120	1	130	-	88	77	368	3,792
34 61980	Raritan borough	Somerset	2.0	6,338	5,561	59	5	518	10	104	81	533	4,922
34 62430	Red Bank borough	Monmouth	1.8	11,844	8,077	2,375	41	259	10	797	285	2,027	9,770
34 62910	Ridgefield borough	Bergen	2.6	10,830	8,217	83	9	1,887	4	379	251	1,494	8,465
34 62940	Ridgefield Park village	Bergen	1.7	12,873	10,067	528	28	1,011	4	837	398	2,863	9,995
34 63000	Ridgewood village	Bergen	5.8	24,936	21,899	409	11	2,162	-	148	307	942	17,461
34 63150	Ringwood borough	Passaic	25.2	12,396	11,636	199	179	148	1	83	150	527	8,978
34 63360	River Edge borough	Bergen	1.9	10,946	9,208	116	9	1,379	1	89	144	581	8,312
34 63660	Riverton borough	Burlington	0.7	2,759	2,644	49	3	23	-	8	32	30	2,158
34 63720	River Vale CDP	Bergen	4.1	9,449	8,724	55	-	557	2	41	70	304	6,876
34 64020	Rochelle Park CDP	Bergen	1.0	5,528	4,980	25	2	333	-	112	76	474	4,497
34 64050	Rockaway borough	Morris	2.1	6,473	5,680	91	13	412	2	193	82	608	4,968
34 64590	Roseland borough	Essex	3.6	5,298	4,950	38	2	250	-	23	35	121	4,207
34 64620	Roselle borough	Union	2.6	21,274	7,570	10,917	67	577	15	1,291	837	3,641	15,841
34 64650	Roselle Park borough	Union	1.2	13,281	10,740	322	14	1,214	2	650	339	2,170	10,328
34 64865	Rossmoor CDP	Middlesex	0.9	3,129	3,065	30	3	16	-	2	13	16	3,127
34 65130	Rumson borough	Monmouth	5.2	7,137	6,978	17	4	76	-	26	36	99	4,862
34 65160	Runnemede borough	Camden	2.1	8,533	7,831	321	9	132	1	104	135	306	6,557
34 65280	Rutherford borough	Bergen	2.8	18,110	14,849	489	8	2,054	5	337	368	1,555	14,349
34 65370	Saddle Brook CDP	Bergen	2.7	13,155	11,936	183	5	623	-	223	185	825	10,499
34 65400	Saddle River borough	Bergen	5.0	3,201	2,876	24	-	229	1	26	45	82	2,482
34 65490	Salem city	Salem	2.6	5,857	2,194	3,325	35	14	-	81	208	286	4,044
34 65790	Sayreville borough	Middlesex	15.9	40,377	30,875	3,481	53	4,265	8	855	840	2,942	30,863
34 66090	Scotch Plains CDP	Union	9.1	22,732	17,931	2,568	21	1,648	3	216	345	895	16,967
34 66390	Sea Isle City city	Cape May	2.2	2,835	2,775	8	11	10	1	2	28	30	2,391
34 66450	Seaside Heights borough	Ocean	0.6	3,155	2,838	127	20	27	-	37	106	306	2,419
34 66570	Secaucus town	Hudson	5.9	15,931	12,512	709	18	1,880	7	445	360	1,953	12,866
34 66720	Sewaren CDP	Middlesex	1.0	2,780	2,373	159	5	131	1	76	35	266	2,118
34 66840	Shark River Hills CDP	Monmouth	0.8	3,878	3,777	22	1	31	1	11	35	48	3,014
34 67350	Shrewsbury borough	Monmouth	2.2	3,590	3,468	19	-	60	-	13	30	69	2,485
34 68304	Society Hill CDP	Middlesex	1.4	3,804	1,729	607	9	1,296	-	54	109	192	2,931
34 68340	Somerdale borough	Camden	1.4	5,192	3,912	917	11	168	1	56	127	202	4,033
34 68370	Somerset CDP	Somerset	5.3	23,040	10,124	8,881	59	1,896	11	1,391	678	2,764	17,500
34 68430	Somers Point city	Atlantic	4.0	11,614	9,948	814	29	368	4	261	190	696	8,899
34 68460	Somerville borough	Somerset	2.4	12,423	8,847	1,606	23	913	3	634	397	2,112	9,698
34 68550	South Amboy city	Middlesex	1.6	7,913	7,456	68	15	109	2	135	128	534	5,990
34 68730	South Bound Brook borough	Somerset	0.8	4,492	3,504	349	12	184	2	295	146	1,028	3,437
34 69255	South Orange CDP	Essex	2.9	16,964	10,248	5,309	16	660	5	266	460	837	13,187
34 69390	South Plainfield borough	Middlesex	8.4	21,810	16,956	1,866	49	1,652	1	759	527	1,888	16,325
34 69420	South River borough	Middlesex	2.8	15,322	12,801	929	18	542	8	587	437	1,480	11,793
34 69510	South Toms River borough	Ocean	1.2	3,634	2,637	769	5	25	-	91	107	337	2,467
34 69810	Spotswood borough	Middlesex	2.3	7,880	7,391	122	6	230	1	58	72	345	6,117
34 69900	Springdale CDP	Camden	5.4	14,409	12,639	346	7	1,302	1	16	98	176	10,890
34 70050	Springfield CDP	Union	5.1	14,429	12,946	537	3	676	-	139	128	597	11,463
34 70110	Spring Lake borough	Monmouth	1.3	3,567	3,523	12	-	10	-	4	18	26	2,790
34 70140	Spring Lake Heights borough	Monmouth	1.3	5,227	5,085	58	1	19	1	35	28	111	4,347
34 70380	Stanhope borough	Sussex	1.9	3,584	3,353	48	2	55	3	50	73	145	2,686
34 71220	Stratford borough	Camden	1.6	7,271	6,439	480	9	173	1	63	106	277	5,476
34 71280	Strathmore CDP	Monmouth	1.8	6,740	5,917	222	4	438	-	43	116	315	5,051
34 71385	Succasunna-Kenvil CDP	Morris	6.7	12,569	11,687	168	11	517	-	84	102	487	8,999
34 71430	Summit city	Union	6.1	21,131	18,546	914	19	941	3	360	348	2,150	15,434
34 72390	Teaneck CDP	Bergen	6.1	39,260	22,082	11,298	59	2,798	11	1,633	1,379	4,103	29,139
34 72420	Tenafly borough	Bergen	4.6	13,806	10,601	132	13	2,634	3	193	230	642	9,900
34 73020	Tinton Falls borough	Monmouth	15.6	15,053	11,862	1,963	36	747	2	157	286	707	11,215
34 73110	Toms River CDP	Ocean	39.4	86,327	80,598	1,565	110	2,194	21	849	990	4,010	65,797
34 73140	Totowa borough	Passaic	4.0	9,892	9,239	111	2	224	-	195	121	630	8,085
34 74000	Trenton city	Mercer	7.7	85,403	27,802	44,465	300	716	199	9,190	2,731	18,391	61,757
34 74210	Tuckerton borough	Ocean	3.7	3,517	3,408	14	10	19	-	19	47	109	2,708
34 74270	Turnersville CDP	Gloucester	1.5	3,867	3,584	142	1	96	1	15	28	56	2,713
34 74330	Twin Rivers CDP	Mercer	1.3	7,422	5,659	754	6	464	14	342	183	1,086	5,681
34 74510	Union CDP	Union	9.1	54,405	36,809	10,752	80	4,201	13	1,329	1,221	4,861	42,286
34 74540	Union Beach borough	Monmouth	1.9	6,649	6,280	58	13	82	-	90	126	538	4,713
34 74630	Union City city	Hudson	1.3	67,088	39,167	2,442	467	1,441	54	18,911	4,606	55,226	50,117
34 75140	Upper Saddle River borough	Bergen	5.3	7,741	7,063	72	2	486	1	40	77	169	5,368
34 75620	Ventnor City city	Atlantic	2.1	12,910	9,953	379	24	962	4	1,210	378	2,213	10,328

[Includes incorporated places and census designated places (CDPs) of 2,500 or more population as of April 1, 2000. Codes shown are two-digit Federal Information Processing Standards (FIPS) state codes and five-digit FIPS place codes. Place names and codes are those in effect as of January 1, 2000. County refers to the county (or counties) in which the place is located. IC in this column = independent city, a county equivalent. If a place is located in more than one county, counties are listed in alphabetic order]

State and place code	Place	County	Land area, 2000 (sq. mi.)	Population, 2000 (April 1)									
					By race—								
					One race								
				Total	White	Black or African American	American Indian and Alaska Native	Asian	Native Hawaiian and Other Pacific Islander	Some other race	Two or more races	Hispanic or Latino (of any race)	18 years and over
34 00000	NEW JERSEY—Con.												
34 75800	Verona CDP	Essex	2.8	13,533	12,585	207	3	462	8	96	172	467	10,490
34 76010	Villas CDP	Cape May	4.0	9,064	8,733	108	25	32	3	78	85	218	6,748
34 76070	Vineland city	Cumberland	68.7	56,271	37,964	7,664	304	655	43	7,881	1,760	16,880	41,808
34 76400	Waldwick borough	Bergen	2.1	9,622	8,918	57	4	435	-	126	82	511	7,170
34 76490	Wallington borough	Bergen	1.0	11,583	10,147	309	11	577	2	269	268	776	9,451
34 76700	Wanamassa CDP	Monmouth	1.1	4,551	4,289	58	6	129	8	21	40	136	3,343
34 76730	Wanaque borough	Passaic	8.0	10,266	9,308	155	35	372	3	211	182	554	7,765
34 77270	Washington borough	Warren	2.0	6,712	6,138	261	8	97	1	108	99	280	4,932
34 77510	Washington Township CDP	Bergen	2.9	8,938	8,229	88	4	498	-	39	80	299	6,905
34 77600	Watchung borough	Somerset	6.0	5,613	4,732	189	5	553	5	40	89	168	4,386
34 77870	Wayne CDP	Passaic	23.8	54,069	48,687	895	54	3,066	11	631	725	2,754	41,543
34 78350	West Belmar CDP	Monmouth	0.5	2,606	2,488	24	5	33	7	22	27	67	1,922
34 78500	West Caldwell CDP	Essex	5.0	11,233	10,541	100	4	432	4	68	84	314	8,463
34 79040	Westfield town	Union	6.7	29,644	26,675	1,151	27	1,208	3	185	395	836	21,235
34 79100	West Freehold CDP	Monmouth	5.9	12,498	11,333	308	19	535	3	141	159	673	9,527
34 79310	West Long Branch borough	Monmouth	2.9	8,258	7,781	184	6	100	3	41	143	241	6,458
34 79430	West Milford CDP	Passaic	75.4	26,410	25,110	326	159	269	4	160	382	893	19,222
34 79610	West New York town	Hudson	1.0	45,768	27,503	1,626	305	1,339	15	11,515	3,465	36,038	35,562
34 79790	West Orange CDP	Essex	12.1	44,943	30,359	7,848	63	3,635	17	1,584	1,437	4,514	34,477
34 79820	West Paterson borough	Passaic	3.0	10,987	9,507	347	9	421	4	348	351	1,105	8,834
34 80120	Westville borough	Gloucester	1.0	4,500	4,206	122	6	45	1	58	62	133	3,396
34 80270	Westwood borough	Bergen	2.3	10,999	9,525	629	15	483	1	184	162	660	8,631
34 80390	Wharton borough	Morris	2.2	6,298	5,170	277	28	198	-	454	171	1,462	4,660
34 80630	White Horse CDP	Mercer	3.2	9,373	8,604	358	6	156	-	139	110	372	7,439
34 80750	White Meadow Lake CDP	Morris	4.1	9,052	8,290	146	12	425	-	82	97	426	6,453
34 81170	Wildwood city	Cape May	1.3	5,436	3,835	905	21	26	8	481	160	958	4,038
34 81200	Wildwood Crest borough	Cape May	1.2	3,980	3,776	49	4	19	-	88	44	168	3,255
04 01000	Williamstown CDP	Gloucester	6.2	11,812	10,120	1,223	36	113	7	117	197	339	8,834
34 81890	Woodbine borough	Cape May	8.0	2,716	1,450	880	6	3	-	299	78	577	1,993
34 81950	Woodbridge CDP	Middlesex	3.9	18,309	13,629	1,399	22	2,353	4	542	360	1,801	14,386
34 82120	Woodbury city	Gloucester	2.1	10,307	7,467	2,353	23	102	14	132	216	406	7,754
34 82180	Woodbury Heights borough	Gloucester	1.2	2,988	2,879	46	8	30	-	14	11	37	2,207
34 82300	Woodcliff Lake borough	Bergen	3.3	5,745	5,391	50	2	257	-	11	34	134	4,027
34 82450	Woodlynne borough	Camden	0.2	2,796	1,354	635	16	343	-	324	124	576	1,889
34 82570	Wood-Ridge borough	Bergen	1.1	7,644	6,957	64	6	384	1	135	97	556	6,021
34 82720	Woodstown borough	Salem	1.6	3,136	2,667	405	6	23	-	8	27	49	2,360
34 83080	Wyckoff CDP	Bergen	6.5	16,508	15,607	77	25	611	2	74	112	376	11,837
34 83185	Yardville-Grovoville CDP	Mercer	3.4	9,208	8,572	278	7	184	7	74	86	277	7,027
34 83245	Yorketown CDP	Monmouth	2.4	6,712	6,295	149	3	170	3	22	70	236	4,608
35 00000	NEW MEXICO		121,355.5	1,819,046	1,214,253	34,343	173,483	19,255	1,503	309,882	66,327	765,386	1,310,472
35 01780	Alamogordo city	Otero	19.3	35,582	26,812	1,985	374	545	59	4,295	1,512	11,383	25,386
35 02000	Albuquerque city	Bernalillo	180.6	448,607	321,179	13,854	17,444	10,068	452	66,292	19,318	179,075	338,515
35 03820	Anthony CDP	Dona Ana	3.9	7,904	4,567	21	74	18	11	2,989	224	7,623	4,769
35 05220	Artesia city	Eddy	8.0	10,692	7,725	154	165	21	16	2,305	306	4,809	7,454
35 05780	Aztec city	San Juan	9.7	6,378	5,053	24	594	9	8	480	210	1,226	4,682
35 06270	Bayard city	Grant	0.9	2,534	1,664	8	42	1	-	736	83	2,137	1,795
35 06480	Belen city	Valencia	4.7	6,901	4,658	74	114	12	11	1,752	280	4,735	4,915
35 06970	Bernalillo town	Sandoval	4.6	6,611	3,978	49	259	13	-	2,072	240	4,942	4,559
35 07880	Bloomfield city	San Juan	5.0	6,417	4,003	21	1,072	22	4	1,024	271	1,765	4,338
35 08580	Bosque Farms village	Valencia	3.9	3,931	3,250	24	74	8	-	440	135	1,161	2,907
35 10750	Cannon AFB CDP	Curry	5.3	2,557	1,738	341	18	146	8	155	151	310	2,041
35 12150	Carlsbad city	Eddy	28.4	25,625	19,834	563	321	181	20	4,060	646	9,417	18,668
35 14250	Chaparral CDP	Dona Ana	38.8	6,117	4,324	77	79	26	11	1,308	292	3,945	3,902
35 14950	Chimayo CDP	Rio Arriba, Santa Fe	5.5	2,924	1,421	4	20	2	1	1,311	166	2,656	2,184
35 15720	Clayton town	Union	4.7	2,524	1,902	1	27	4	5	516	70	1,173	1,826
35 16420	Clovis city	Curry	22.4	32,667	23,293	2,392	332	528	41	4,895	1,186	10,924	22,876
35 17960	Corrales village	Bernalillo, Sandoval	10.7	7,334	6,311	42	111	58	2	603	207	1,874	5,528
35 18940	Crownpoint CDP	McKinley	7.1	2,630	231	11	2,343	10	1	6	28	31	1,585
35 20270	Deming city	Luna	9.3	14,116	9,833	173	193	68	1	3,414	434	9,116	9,756
35 21390	Dulce CDP	Rio Arriba	12.9	2,623	90	1	2,378	-	-	114	40	308	1,575
35 22584	El Cerro-Monterey Park CDP	Valencia	9.3	5,483	3,182	44	98	14	8	1,858	279	4,049	3,213
35 22625	Eldorado at Santa Fe CDP	Santa Fe	20.7	5,799	5,281	35	65	49	2	206	161	783	4,428
35 25170	Espanola city	Rio Arriba, Santa Fe	8.4	9,688	6,544	56	277	14	6	2,476	315	8,175	6,991
35 25450	Eunice city	Lea	2.9	2,562	1,819	28	11	3	-	626	75	1,015	1,807
35 25800	Farmington city	San Juan	26.6	37,844	26,771	316	6,419	197	24	2,942	1,175	6,684	26,753
35 28460	Gallup city	McKinley	13.4	20,209	8,106	219	7,404	289	19	2,985	1,187	6,699	13,594
35 30490	Grants city	Cibola	13.7	8,806	4,947	143	1,054	81	11	2,184	386	4,611	6,270
35 32520	Hobbs city	Lea	18.9	28,657	18,203	1,945	308	123	12	6,997	1,069	12,088	19,951
35 36230	Kirtland CDP	San Juan	11.7	6,190	2,685	12	3,029	15	1	264	184	585	3,939
35 36720	La Cienega CDP	Santa Fe	13.3	3,007	1,830	15	43	9	2	938	170	2,129	2,072
35 39380	Las Cruces city	Dona Ana	52.1	74,267	51,248	1,738	1,289	863	55	16,031	3,043	38,421	55,618
35 39940	Las Vegas city	San Miguel	7.5	14,565	7,895	144	285	89	14	5,417	721	12,080	10,723

Table D-1. Places — **Area and Population**—Con.

[Includes incorporated places and census designated places (CDPs) of 2,500 or more population as of April 1, 2000. Codes shown are two-digit Federal Information Processing Standards (FIPS) state codes and five-digit FIPS place codes. Place names and codes are those in effect as of January 1, 2000. County refers to the county (or counties) in which the place is located. IC in this column = independent city, a county equivalent. If a place is located in more than one county, counties are listed in alphabetic order]

State and place code	Place	County	Land area, 2000 (sq. mi.)	Population, 2000 (April 1) Total	By race—One race White	Black or African American	American Indian and Alaska Native	Asian	Native Hawaiian and Other Pacific Islander	Some other race	Two or more races	Hispanic or Latino (of any race)	18 years and over
35 00000	NEW MEXICO—Con.												
35 42180	Lordsburg city	Hidalgo	8.4	3,379	2,727	19	26	17	-	472	118	2,515	2,301
35 42320	Los Alamos CDP	Los Alamos	10.9	11,909	10,614	52	67	532	5	359	280	1,454	8,950
35 42740	Los Chaves CDP	Valencia	10.2	5,033	3,343	30	64	10	1	1,330	255	2,723	3,521
35 43370	Los Lunas village	Valencia	10.0	10,034	6,436	116	263	50	6	2,772	391	5,894	6,910
35 43930	Los Ranchos de Albuquerque village	Bernalillo	4.1	5,092	4,155	25	79	36	3	618	176	1,905	3,873
35 44490	Lovington city	Lea	4.8	9,471	5,668	287	74	45	6	3,101	290	4,936	6,455
35 47220	Meadow Lake CDP	Valencia	9.7	4,491	2,426	57	183	16	3	1,509	297	2,600	2,781
35 52750	North Valley CDP	Bernalillo	7.2	11,923	8,778	124	347	49	7	2,169	449	6,773	8,876
35 56180	Peralta CDP	Valencia	4.4	3,750	2,508	28	85	12	-	909	208	1,923	2,665
35 58070	Placitas CDP	Sandoval	29.9	3,452	2,883	24	45	18	1	361	120	698	2,802
35 59260	Portales city	Roosevelt	6.9	11,131	7,658	254	125	107	10	2,604	373	4,244	8,200
35 62060	Raton city	Colfax	7.3	7,282	5,683	17	116	29	1	1,179	257	4,148	5,455
35 63145	Rio Communities CDP	Valencia	6.1	4,213	3,365	132	54	20	7	476	159	1,561	3,236
35 63460	Rio Rancho city	Bernalillo, Sandoval	73.4	51,765	40,563	1,376	1,226	758	89	5,618	2,135	14,329	36,659
35 64930	Roswell city	Chaves	28.9	45,293	32,141	1,117	578	293	23	9,643	1,498	20,084	32,407
35 65210	Ruidoso village	Lincoln	14.3	7,698	6,736	22	183	24	2	573	158	1,402	6,117
35 70500	Santa Fe city	Santa Fe	37.3	62,203	47,459	409	1,373	791	49	9,508	2,614	29,744	49,589
35 70670	Santa Rosa city	Guadalupe	4.2	2,744	1,577	60	48	24	1	909	125	2,227	2,109
35 70700	Santa Teresa CDP	Dona Ana	11.0	2,607	2,140	31	17	10	6	340	63	1,449	1,883
35 70810	Santo Domingo Pueblo CDP	Sandoval	2.0	2,550	6	-	2,517	-	1	20	6	30	1,607
35 72770	Shiprock CDP	San Juan	15.9	8,156	177	13	7,890	10	1	8	57	105	5,009
35 73260	Silver City town	Grant	10.1	10,545	7,563	91	120	47	5	2,364	355	5,529	7,904
35 73540	Socorro city	Socorro	14.4	8,877	5,873	66	246	199	5	2,063	425	4,838	6,622
35 74520	South Valley CDP	Bernalillo	29.5	39,060	22,337	447	782	128	48	13,658	1,660	30,307	27,401
35 75640	Sunland Park city	Dona Ana	10.6	13,309	9,290	71	108	9	1	3,463	367	12,835	8,324
35 76200	Taos town	Taos	5.4	4,700	3,198	25	193	29	5	1,018	232	2,554	3,621
35 79840	Truth or Consequences city	Sierra	12.7	7,289	6,221	46	129	12	4	682	195	1,994	5,815
35 79910	Tucumcari city	Quay	7.5	5,989	4,544	77	83	72	13	1,024	176	3,079	4,432
35 79980	Tularosa village	Otero	2.1	2,864	1,965	25	122	19	1	616	116	1,606	2,080
35 81030	University Park CDP	Dona Ana	1.6	2,732	1,822	136	153	155	5	341	120	1,015	2,282
35 81590	Vado CDP	Dona Ana	3.0	3,003	1,621	31	45	2	-	1,199	105	2,853	1,826
35 81800	Valencia CDP	Valencia	5.5	4,500	3,099	34	87	30	4	1,038	208	2,235	3,244
35 84740	White Rock CDP	Los Alamos	7.2	6,045	5,607	15	32	162	1	113	115	640	4,379
35 86595	Zuni Pueblo CDP	McKinley	8.8	6,367	135	2	6,178	2	-	19	31	128	4,159
36 00000	NEW YORK		47,213.8	18,976,457	12,893,689	3,014,385	82,461	1,044,976	8,818	1,341,946	590,182	2,867,583	14,286,350
36 00408	Airmont village	Rockland	4.6	7,799	7,035	290	13	275	2	78	106	410	5,620
36 00441	Akron village	Erie	2.0	3,085	3,010	12	43	1	-	4	15	20	2,354
36 01000	Albany city	Albany	21.4	95,658	60,383	26,915	301	3,116	34	2,060	2,849	5,349	76,573
36 01011	Albertson CDP	Nassau	0.7	5,200	4,271	12	1	755	-	66	95	286	4,032
36 01033	Albion village	Orleans	3.0	7,438	5,495	1,354	51	43	6	371	118	693	5,702
36 01088	Alden village	Erie	2.7	2,666	2,632	9	2	15	3	-	5	5	1,965
36 01198	Alfred village	Allegany	1.2	3,954	3,567	174	13	107	1	48	44	108	3,834
36 02044	Amityville village	Suffolk	2.1	9,441	7,963	806	19	121	-	313	219	867	7,375
36 02066	Amsterdam city	Montgomery	5.9	18,355	16,522	399	50	131	4	880	369	2,941	13,895
36 02506	Ardsley village	Westchester	1.3	4,269	3,586	65	4	527	1	31	55	182	3,079
36 02616	Arlington CDP	Dutchess	4.9	12,481	9,611	1,532	23	760	5	234	316	672	10,064
36 02649	Armonk CDP	Westchester	6.1	3,461	3,237	21	2	144	-	14	43	130	2,429
36 03001	Attica village	Genesee, Wyoming	1.7	2,597	2,566	4	9	4	-	3	11	16	1,928
36 03078	Auburn city	Cayuga	8.4	28,574	25,307	2,170	84	162	6	403	442	806	22,066
36 03358	Avon village	Livingston	3.0	2,977	2,849	55	7	24	1	7	34	29	2,148
36 03408	Babylon village	Suffolk	2.4	12,615	11,664	339	13	183	1	188	227	644	9,377
36 04143	Baldwin CDP	Nassau	2.9	23,455	15,442	5,368	76	775	6	1,078	710	2,721	17,338
36 04154	Baldwin Harbor CDP	Nassau	1.2	8,147	6,732	725	9	382	-	147	152	561	6,065
36 04198	Baldwinsville village	Onondaga	3.1	7,053	6,832	53	36	47	2	12	71	56	5,178
36 04253	Ballston Spa village	Saratoga	1.6	5,556	5,352	65	9	29	1	34	67	108	4,228
36 04286	Balmville CDP	Orange	2.1	3,339	2,660	316	1	102	4	163	93	335	2,570
36 04396	Bardonia CDP	Rockland	2.6	4,367	3,823	67	10	344	-	61	62	225	3,266
36 04715	Batavia city	Genesee	5.2	16,256	14,667	883	78	142	4	173	309	399	12,445
36 04759	Bath village	Steuben	2.9	5,641	5,426	78	18	50	1	7	61	51	4,403
36 04913	Bayport CDP	Suffolk	3.7	8,662	8,321	77	6	102	-	71	85	340	6,444
36 04935	Bay Shore CDP	Suffolk	5.3	23,852	16,419	4,091	108	560	7	1,716	951	4,738	17,682
36 05034	Bayville village	Nassau	1.4	7,135	6,850	22	17	117	-	77	52	344	5,451
36 05039	Baywood CDP	Suffolk	2.2	7,571	5,640	727	19	139	5	766	275	1,759	5,511
36 05100	Beacon city	Dutchess	4.8	13,808	9,440	2,713	43	181	-	956	475	2,334	10,065
36 05193	Beaverdam Lake-Salisbury Mills CDP	Orange	2.4	2,779	2,603	64	8	29	1	42	32	149	1,913
36 05738	Bellmore CDP	Nassau	2.5	16,441	15,784	77	20	330	4	85	141	515	12,283
36 06387	Bethpage CDP	Nassau	3.6	16,543	15,578	48	4	494	-	165	254	785	12,790
36 06607	Binghamton city	Broome	10.4	47,380	39,412	3,987	121	1,579	18	810	1,453	1,849	37,174
36 06849	Blasdell village	Erie	1.2	2,718	2,631	6	10	2	-	41	28	94	2,050
36 06860	Blauvelt CDP	Rockland	4.6	5,207	4,604	81	1	382	-	75	64	309	3,875

U.S. Census Bureau, County and City Data Book: 2000

Table D-1. Places — **Area and Population**—Con.

[Includes incorporated places and census designated places (CDPs) of 2,500 or more population as of April 1, 2000. Codes shown are two-digit Federal Information Processing Standards (FIPS) state codes and five-digit FIPS place codes. Place names and codes are those in effect as of January 1, 2000. County refers to the county (or counties) in which the place is located. IC in this column = independent city, a county equivalent. If a place is located in more than one county, counties are listed in alphabetic order]

State and place code	Place	County	Land area, 2000 (sq. mi.)	Population, 2000 (April 1) By race— One race Total	White	Black or African American	American Indian and Alaska Native	Asian	Native Hawaiian and Other Pacific Islander	Some other race	Two or more races	Hispanic or Latino (of any race)	18 years and over
36 00000	NEW YORK—Con.												
36 07069	Blue Point CDP	Suffolk	1.8	4,407	4,249	30	5	47	1	37	38	192	3,228
36 07157	Bohemia CDP	Suffolk	8.7	9,871	9,339	85	5	235	-	82	125	435	7,578
36 08026	Brentwood CDP	Suffolk	10.1	53,917	25,736	9,735	310	1,084	61	13,719	3,272	29,251	37,805
36 08059	Brewerton CDP	Onondaga, Oswego	3.2	3,453	3,347	25	14	20	-	7	40	26	2,450
36 08103	Briarcliff Manor village	Westchester	5.9	7,696	6,983	133	4	419	3	73	81	241	5,634
36 08257	Brighton CDP	Monroe	15.4	35,584	30,635	1,315	35	2,892	10	223	474	831	28,467
36 08323	Brightwaters village	Suffolk	1.0	3,248	3,093	51	2	42	2	21	37	132	2,360
36 08334	Brinckerhoff CDP	Dutchess	1.1	2,734	2,453	123	1	126	-	13	18	150	2,069
36 08466	Brockport village	Monroe	2.2	8,103	7,442	357	22	79	4	80	119	237	6,886
36 08532	Bronxville village	Westchester	1.0	6,543	6,012	75	3	316	4	48	85	192	4,641
36 09000	Brookhaven CDP	Suffolk	6.0	3,570	3,034	361	9	23	1	48	94	228	2,669
36 11000	Buffalo city	Erie	40.6	292,648	159,300	108,951	2,250	4,093	120	10,755	7,179	22,076	215,691
36 11671	Calcium CDP	Jefferson	5.6	3,346	2,252	653	41	55	12	207	126	422	2,009
36 11781	Calverton CDP	Suffolk	28.0	5,704	4,940	437	26	54	2	116	129	346	4,548
36 12144	Canandaigua city	Ontario	4.6	11,264	10,818	172	25	74	7	29	139	115	8,643
36 12188	Canastota village	Madison	3.3	4,425	4,306	41	17	13	-	17	31	50	3,304
36 12331	Canton village	St. Lawrence	3.2	5,882	5,400	264	32	58	-	60	68	113	5,160
36 12419	Carle Place CDP	Nassau	0.9	5,247	4,716	99	1	286	1	77	67	408	4,051
36 12532	Carmel Hamlet CDP	Putnam	8.5	5,650	5,278	88	14	45	1	122	102	446	4,230
36 12683	Carthage village	Jefferson	2.5	3,721	3,398	159	8	39	2	41	74	100	2,668
36 13002	Catskill village	Greene	2.2	4,392	3,575	559	17	27	1	65	148	273	3,272
36 13079	Cayuga Heights village	Tompkins	1.8	3,273	2,806	61	2	293	3	39	69	117	2,772
36 13145	Cazenovia village	Madison	1.6	2,614	2,493	63	10	14	1	7	26	72	2,141
36 13233	Cedarhurst village	Nassau	0.7	6,164	5,593	79	7	190	-	181	114	515	4,617
36 13376	Centereach CDP	Suffolk	8.0	27,285	25,072	539	49	864	2	371	388	1,932	19,903
36 13420	Center Moriches CDP	Suffolk	5.0	6,655	5,991	349	11	66	-	86	152	440	4,983
36 13442	Centerport CDP	Suffolk	2.1	5,446	5,318	12	6	64	-	17	29	117	4,084
36 13552	Central Islip CDP	Suffolk	7.3	31,950	15,269	8,769	167	991	37	5,116	1,601	11,452	22,621
36 13805	Chappaqua CDP	Westchester	9.4	9,468	8,692	89	3	532	2	49	101	241	6,363
36 15000	Cheektowaga CDP	Erie	25.5	79,988	75,487	2,683	135	829	6	220	628	793	63,522
36 15297	Chester village	Orange	2.1	3,445	2,875	266	32	102	-	90	80	350	2,637
36 15400	Chestnut Ridge village	Rockland	4.9	7,829	5,790	1,086	10	528	5	210	200	633	6,052
36 15561	Chittenango village	Madison	2.4	4,855	4,757	22	14	15	-	8	39	36	3,455
36 16628	Cobleskill village	Schoharie	3.3	4,533	4,245	125	11	58	3	30	61	118	3,818
36 16749	Cohoes city	Albany	3.7	15,521	14,767	335	25	106	6	91	191	315	12,037
36 16958	Cold Spring Harbor CDP	Suffolk	3.7	4,975	4,827	21	1	65	-	12	49	98	3,649
36 17332	Colonie village	Albany	3.3	7,916	7,257	280	7	244	2	34	92	126	6,208
36 17530	Commack CDP	Suffolk	12.1	36,367	34,343	231	14	1,367	-	173	239	1,055	26,786
36 17739	Congers CDP	Rockland	3.2	8,303	7,077	147	15	717	9	173	165	634	6,138
36 18146	Copiague CDP	Suffolk	3.2	21,922	17,976	960	42	382	16	1,859	687	4,489	16,824
36 18157	Coram CDP	Suffolk	13.8	34,923	28,757	3,024	93	1,161	7	1,089	792	3,314	26,170
36 18256	Corning city	Steuben	3.1	10,842	10,185	308	37	162	1	26	123	86	8,320
36 18333	Cornwall on Hudson village	Orange	2.0	3,058	2,955	12	9	20	1	26	35	116	2,233
36 18388	Cortland city	Cortland	3.9	18,740	17,937	292	46	107	3	105	250	322	15,308
36 18718	Coxsackie village	Greene	2.2	2,895	2,776	66	8	14	1	7	23	75	2,110
36 19213	Croton-on-Hudson village	Westchester	4.7	7,606	6,961	142	20	157	1	196	129	527	5,649
36 19229	Crown Heights CDP	Dutchess	2.1	2,992	2,481	272	-	131	-	55	53	196	2,117
36 19466	Cutchogue CDP	Suffolk	8.1	2,849	2,674	69	1	15	-	49	41	162	2,237
36 19642	Dannemora village	Clinton	1.2	4,129	2,026	1,567	23	40	-	433	40	770	3,762
36 19664	Dansville village	Livingston	2.4	4,832	4,628	61	11	32	-	63	37	100	3,541
36 19972	Deer Park CDP	Suffolk	6.3	28,316	23,618	2,577	63	814	3	588	653	2,139	21,179
36 20126	Delhi village	Delaware	3.2	2,583	2,267	180	8	47	-	40	41	111	2,243
36 20148	Delmar CDP	Albany	4.4	8,292	8,011	98	10	103	1	21	48	102	6,187
36 20313	Depew village	Erie	5.1	16,629	16,286	105	32	67	2	30	107	122	12,969
36 20687	Dix Hills CDP	Suffolk	15.9	26,024	22,566	846	14	1,916	4	218	460	995	18,619
36 20698	Dobbs Ferry village	Westchester	2.4	10,622	8,572	784	8	803	10	205	240	744	7,863
36 21105	Dunkirk city	Chautauqua	4.5	13,131	10,857	665	68	30	5	1,200	306	2,608	9,807
36 21589	East Aurora village	Erie	2.5	6,673	6,593	13	2	27	-	3	35	46	4,965
36 21809	Eastchester CDP	Westchester	3.3	18,564	16,748	175	12	1,222	4	175	228	661	14,448
36 21985	East Farmingdale CDP	Suffolk	5.4	5,400	3,960	801	8	221	5	244	161	687	3,997
36 22084	East Glenville CDP	Schenectady	7.3	6,064	5,892	62	9	65	2	5	29	73	4,726
36 22106	East Greenbush CDP	Rensselaer	2.6	4,085	3,785	131	6	106	-	10	47	58	2,997
36 22200	East Hampton North CDP	Suffolk	5.6	3,587	2,958	265	3	58	3	213	87	596	2,787
36 22260	East Hills village	Nassau	2.3	6,842	6,359	55	1	330	1	39	57	101	4,799
36 22315	East Islip CDP	Suffolk	4.1	14,078	13,543	80	9	198	3	135	110	547	10,066
36 22480	East Massapequa CDP	Nassau	3.5	19,565	15,812	2,415	40	437	5	484	372	1,466	14,652
36 22502	East Meadow CDP	Nassau	6.3	37,461	31,994	1,617	55	2,503	14	734	589	2,626	28,703
36 22546	East Moriches CDP	Suffolk	5.4	4,550	4,302	72	2	66	11	46	51	235	3,348
36 22612	East Northport CDP	Suffolk	5.9	20,845	19,745	189	26	475	6	146	258	814	15,527
36 22623	East Norwich CDP	Nassau	1.0	2,675	2,560	16	-	66	-	15	18	85	2,051
36 22733	East Patchogue CDP	Suffolk	8.3	20,824	18,633	665	29	405	3	676	413	1,895	16,008
36 22832	East Quogue CDP	Suffolk	10.3	4,265	4,063	30	3	30	1	41	97	230	3,232
36 22865	East Rochester CDP	Monroe	1.4	6,650	6,379	92	17	49	1	24	88	158	5,046
36 22876	East Rockaway village	Nassau	1.0	10,414	9,960	64	3	178	1	113	95	603	7,942
36 22980	East Shoreham CDP	Suffolk	5.1	5,809	5,551	70	7	88	3	46	44	235	4,073
36 23052	East Syracuse village	Onondaga	1.6	3,178	3,021	46	32	8	-	3	68	37	2,319
36 23217	East Williston village	Nassau	0.6	2,503	2,384	9	1	84	2	6	17	59	1,796

[Includes incorporated places and census designated places (CDPs) of 2,500 or more population as of April 1, 2000. Codes shown are two-digit Federal Information Processing Standards (FIPS) state codes and five-digit FIPS place codes. Place names and codes are those in effect as of January 1, 2000. County refers to the county (or counties) in which the place is located. IC in this column = independent city, a county equivalent. If a place is located in more than one county, counties are listed in alphabetic order]

State and place code	Place	County	Land area, 2000 (sq. mi.)	Population, 2000 (April 1)									
					By race—								
					One race								
				Total	White	Black or African American	American Indian and Alaska Native	Asian	Native Hawaiian and Other Pacific Islander	Some other race	Two or more races	Hispanic or Latino (of any race)	18 years and over
36 00000	NEW YORK—Con.												
36 23404	Eden CDP	Erie	5.6	3,579	3,509	21	8	14	1	7	19	18	2,584
36 23965	Ellenville village	Ulster	8.7	4,130	2,852	482	20	65	-	509	202	1,173	2,938
36 24229	Elmira city	Chemung	7.3	30,940	25,379	4,039	120	151	9	425	817	970	23,177
36 24251	Elmira Heights village	Chemung	1.1	4,170	4,046	43	8	21	1	8	43	33	3,144
36 24273	Elmont CDP	Nassau	3.4	32,657	14,878	11,329	142	2,968	27	1,859	1,454	4,672	24,022
36 24295	Elmsford village	Westchester	1.1	4,676	2,609	949	35	424	2	387	270	1,089	3,642
36 24405	Elwood CDP	Suffolk	4.8	10,916	9,390	612	24	611	3	148	128	550	8,072
36 24515	Endicott village	Broome	3.1	13,038	11,949	489	33	255	9	87	216	218	10,190
36 24526	Endwell CDP	Broome	3.7	11,706	11,177	155	10	201	1	55	107	149	9,247
36 25043	Fairmount CDP	Onondaga	3.4	10,795	10,336	139	33	146	3	31	107	115	8,305
36 25076	Fairport village	Monroe	1.6	5,740	5,567	42	7	59	-	12	53	79	4,291
36 25109	Fairview CDP	Dutchess	3.5	5,421	4,394	616	11	121	5	126	148	280	4,083
36 25120	Fairview CDP	Westchester	0.4	2,887	332	2,110	6	81	9	183	166	410	2,117
36 25164	Falconer village	Chautauqua	1.1	2,540	2,485	14	13	7	-	3	18	29	1,930
36 25384	Farmingdale village	Nassau	1.1	8,399	7,310	135	10	311	4	425	204	1,056	6,617
36 25417	Farmingville CDP	Suffolk	4.5	16,458	15,396	204	23	292	-	243	300	1,336	11,796
36 25527	Fayetteville village	Onondaga	1.7	4,190	4,015	26	6	101	-	13	29	48	3,141
36 25857	Firthcliffe CDP	Orange	3.0	4,970	4,689	59	6	55	-	70	91	314	3,629
36 26121	Flanders CDP	Suffolk	12.3	3,646	2,597	725	50	26	-	139	109	502	2,633
36 26264	Floral Park village	Nassau	1.4	15,967	14,938	74	9	620	5	164	157	859	12,063
36 26319	Florida village	Orange	1.9	2,571	2,392	65	13	16	-	48	37	167	1,885
36 26352	Flower Hill village	Nassau	1.6	4,508	3,861	47	1	465	-	44	90	181	3,332
36 26759	Fort Drum CDP	Jefferson	25.3	12,123	7,779	2,398	101	291	84	922	548	1,609	9,109
36 26770	Fort Edward village	Washington	1.8	3,141	3,100	11	6	12	-	-	12	9	2,314
36 26946	Fort Salonga CDP	Suffolk	9.0	9,634	9,329	59	5	165	-	27	49	217	7,139
36 27188	Frankfort village	Herkimer	1.0	2,537	2,479	1	7	4	-	5	41	25	1,947
36 27309	Franklin Square CDP	Nassau	2.9	29,342	26,987	290	33	1,112	3	513	404	2,023	22,893
36 27419	Fredonia village	Chautauqua	5.2	10,706	10,316	109	34	113	2	53	79	181	9,021
36 27485	Freeport village	Nassau	4.6	43,783	18,791	14,258	201	604	24	7,537	2,368	14,648	32,240
36 27815	Fulton city	Oswego	3.8	11,855	11,476	88	44	39	3	104	101	228	8,635
36 28035	Galeville CDP	Onondaga	1.1	4,476	4,107	173	28	68	2	25	73	57	3,624
36 28145	Gang Mills CDP	Steuben	6.5	3,304	2,876	121	5	266	-	5	31	52	2,388
36 28178	Garden City village	Nassau	5.3	21,672	20,418	266	15	715	7	79	172	600	15,924
36 28189	Garden City Park CDP	Nassau	1.0	7,554	5,303	318	21	1,548	2	161	201	611	5,864
36 28200	Garden City South CDP	Nassau	0.4	3,974	3,783	13	-	122	1	30	25	233	3,089
36 28310	Gardnertown CDP	Orange	4.9	4,533	3,846	298	15	71	-	198	105	486	3,288
36 28458	Gates-North Gates CDP	Monroe	4.7	15,138	13,300	929	26	426	5	221	231	497	11,675
36 28618	Geneseo village	Livingston	2.8	7,579	7,028	135	6	250	3	65	92	196	6,927
36 28640	Geneva city	Ontario, Seneca	4.3	13,617	11,101	1,391	34	168	7	461	455	1,157	10,456
36 29113	Glen Cove city	Nassau	6.6	26,622	21,373	1,703	77	1,094	14	1,523	838	5,336	20,979
36 29245	Glen Head CDP	Nassau	1.6	4,625	4,407	23	2	93	3	53	44	213	3,521
36 29333	Glens Falls city	Warren	3.8	14,354	13,857	186	22	61	2	48	178	199	10,850
36 29338	Glens Falls North CDP	Warren	8.1	8,061	7,816	61	9	84	2	23	66	106	6,223
36 29421	Glenwood Landing CDP	Nassau	1.0	3,541	3,377	10	-	92	-	21	41	118	2,613
36 29443	Gloversville city	Fulton	5.1	15,413	14,699	286	30	93	4	85	216	258	11,536
36 29509	Gordon Heights CDP	Suffolk	1.7	3,094	751	1,922	42	59	1	159	160	449	2,004
36 29542	Goshen village	Orange	3.2	5,676	4,968	432	8	88	4	128	48	433	4,408
36 29597	Gouverneur village	St. Lawrence	2.1	4,263	4,024	76	16	17	10	45	75	97	2,992
36 29630	Gowanda village	Cattaraugus, Erie	1.6	2,842	2,657	14	121	10	-	6	34	40	2,173
36 30026	Granville village	Washington	1.6	2,644	2,593	6	6	7	1	11	20	21	1,965
36 30169	Great Neck village	Nassau	1.4	9,538	8,139	269	10	471	4	313	332	875	7,023
36 30191	Great Neck Estates village	Nassau	0.8	2,756	2,555	26	-	133	-	9	33	72	2,014
36 30213	Great Neck Plaza village	Nassau	0.3	6,433	5,861	107	3	194	2	131	135	469	5,686
36 30279	Greece CDP	Monroe	4.3	14,614	13,746	366	26	241	4	105	126	357	11,441
36 30543	Greenlawn CDP	Suffolk	3.7	13,286	10,269	2,027	33	372	4	314	267	905	9,830
36 30642	Greenville CDP	Westchester	2.9	8,648	6,547	208	6	1,708	1	51	127	365	6,478
36 30752	Greenwood Lake village	Orange	2.0	3,411	3,260	26	9	29	1	28	58	172	2,503
36 31445	Halesite CDP	Suffolk	0.9	2,582	2,460	41	2	24	1	20	34	80	2,034
36 31643	Hamburg village	Erie	2.5	10,116	9,978	20	15	40	-	15	48	76	7,447
36 31709	Hamilton village	Madison	2.4	3,509	3,188	102	3	130	2	16	68	80	3,207
36 31896	Hampton Bays CDP	Suffolk	12.0	12,236	11,373	107	16	86	12	452	190	1,529	9,696
36 31918	Hampton Manor CDP	Rensselaer	0.6	2,525	2,408	43	4	43	-	3	24	18	1,900
36 32391	Harris Hill CDP	Erie	4.0	4,881	4,753	25	7	61	3	19	13	40	3,641
36 32402	Harrison village	Westchester	16.8	24,154	21,686	345	21	1,314	2	383	403	1,618	18,238
36 32523	Hartsdale CDP	Westchester	3.2	9,830	7,485	856	19	1,000	4	260	206	939	8,044
36 32710	Hastings-on-Hudson village	Westchester	2.0	7,648	6,867	180	13	317	-	139	132	344	5,736
36 32732	Hauppauge CDP	Suffolk	10.8	20,100	18,743	230	7	721	6	153	240	887	15,268
36 32754	Haverstraw village	Rockland	2.0	10,117	4,656	1,221	37	110	13	3,511	569	5,998	7,226
36 32776	Haviland CDP	Dutchess	3.9	3,710	3,459	108	3	65	-	21	54	83	2,752
36 32842	Hawthorne CDP	Westchester	1.7	5,083	4,734	170	1	75	2	59	42	306	3,718
36 33139	Hempstead village	Nassau	3.7	56,554	14,515	29,678	298	745	33	8,605	2,680	17,991	41,709
36 34118	Heritage Hills CDP	Westchester	2.3	3,683	3,572	32	1	54	-	3	21	40	3,489
36 34121	Herkimer village	Herkimer	2.4	7,498	7,209	92	18	93	1	37	48	103	6,062
36 34198	Herricks CDP	Nassau	0.6	4,076	2,965	12	4	994	4	38	59	170	3,103
36 34286	Hewlett CDP	Nassau	0.9	7,060	6,379	65	6	338	1	197	74	612	5,359
36 34374	Hicksville CDP	Nassau	6.8	41,260	34,891	562	44	3,731	14	1,258	760	3,819	31,959
36 34484	Highland CDP	Ulster	4.7	5,060	4,563	227	6	73	1	90	100	290	3,904

Table D-1. Places — **Area and Population**—Con.

[Includes incorporated places and census designated places (CDPs) of 2,500 or more population as of April 1, 2000. Codes shown are two-digit Federal Information Processing Standards (FIPS) state codes and five-digit FIPS place codes. Place names and codes are those in effect as of January 1, 2000. County refers to the county (or counties) in which the place is located. IC in this column = independent city, a county equivalent. If a place is located in more than one county, counties are listed in alphabetic order]

State and place code	Place	County	Land area, 2000 (sq. mi.)	Population, 2000 (April 1)									
				By race—								Hispanic or Latino (of any race)	18 years and over
				One race							Two or more races		
				Total	White	Black or African American	American Indian and Alaska Native	Asian	Native Hawaiian and Other Pacific Islander	Some other race			
36 00000	NEW YORK—Con.												
36 34495	Highland Falls village....	Orange	1.1	3,678	2,830	469	14	80	7	139	139	389	2,795
36 34517	Highland Mills CDP.....	Orange	1.7	3,468	3,023	176	5	94	2	82	86	314	2,382
36 34693	Hillcrest CDP.........	Rockland	1.3	7,106	1,818	3,632	23	1,044	5	286	298	816	5,210
36 34847	Hilton village.........	Monroe	1.7	5,856	5,663	97	8	33	-	11	44	87	4,025
36 35056	Holbrook CDP.........	Suffolk	6.8	27,512	25,847	363	23	789	12	189	289	1,616	20,437
36 35254	Holtsville CDP........	Suffolk	7.0	17,006	16,049	189	31	296	1	205	235	1,200	12,205
36 35276	Homer village........	Cortland	1.7	3,368	3,299	19	7	12	1	8	22	30	2,565
36 35364	Honeoye Falls village....	Monroe	2.6	2,595	2,521	26	4	20	-	6	18	27	1,968
36 35474	Hoosick Falls village....	Rensselaer	1.7	3,436	3,353	19	14	17	2	11	20	34	2,547
36 35573	Hopewell Junction CDP ..	Dutchess	2.8	2,610	2,408	47	7	102	-	11	35	104	1,830
36 35672	Hornell city..........	Steuben	2.7	9,019	8,634	215	21	51	4	34	60	116	6,521
36 35694	Horseheads village ...	Chemung	3.9	6,452	6,166	84	8	124	1	13	56	59	4,992
36 35710	Horseheads North CDP ..	Chemung	2.3	2,852	2,763	24	4	35	-	1	25	13	2,094
36 35969	Hudson city..........	Columbia	2.2	7,524	4,837	1,807	21	214	1	312	332	633	5,743
36 35980	Hudson Falls village.....	Washington	1.8	6,927	6,782	31	15	17	-	11	71	47	5,179
36 36233	Huntington CDP........	Suffolk	7.5	18,403	17,245	385	21	332	2	210	208	658	14,143
36 37044	Huntington Station CDP ..	Suffolk	5.4	29,910	21,401	3,459	106	924	4	3,002	1,014	6,802	22,206
36 37132	Hurley CDP...........	Ulster	5.5	3,561	3,410	44	4	51	3	2	47	76	2,738
36 37275	Ilion village..........	Herkimer	2.5	8,610	8,382	57	10	18	1	21	121	136	6,317
36 37583	Inwood CDP..........	Nassau	1.7	9,325	4,966	2,412	39	190	2	1,213	503	2,454	6,735
36 37737	Irondequoit CDP.......	Monroe	15.2	52,354	48,707	1,857	79	514	10	533	654	1,602	40,873
36 37803	Irvington village........	Westchester	2.8	6,631	5,879	96	7	461	-	77	111	251	4,764
36 37840	Islandia village........	Suffolk	2.2	3,057	2,251	376	4	185	1	151	89	584	2,303
36 37847	Island Park village.....	Nassau	0.4	4,732	4,214	62	17	51	6	219	163	864	3,657
36 37869	Islip CDP............	Suffolk	5.4	20,575	18,038	1,008	21	425	6	621	456	2,195	14,935
36 38022	Islip Terrace CDP	Suffolk	1.4	5,641	5,405	28	2	84	-	61	61	373	3,976
36 38077	Ithaca city...........	Tompkins	5.5	29,287	21,663	1,965	114	3,998	16	546	985	1,555	26,582
36 38264	Jamestown city........	Chautauqua	9.0	31,730	29,040	1,075	204	141	16	570	684	1,567	23,540
36 38275	Jamestown West CDP ...	Chautauqua	2.6	2,535	2,499	6	4	12	-	3	12	17	1,988
36 38500	Jefferson Valley-Yorktown CDP............	Westchester	6.9	14,891	13,746	347	16	480	1	158	143	699	10,932
36 38539	Jericho CDP..........	Nassau	4.1	13,045	11,266	185	4	1,394	1	67	128	318	9,747
36 38748	Johnson City village.....	Broome	4.4	15,535	13,805	480	29	766	8	131	316	347	12,427
36 38781	Johnstown city........	Fulton	4.9	8,511	8,219	53	27	84	3	35	90	92	6,432
36 38934	Kaser village.........	Rockland	0.2	3,316	3,270	8	-	15	1	-	22	18	1,546
36 39232	Kenmore village	Erie	1.4	16,426	15,909	163	57	95	7	58	137	213	12,605
36 39672	Kings Park CDP	Suffolk	5.9	16,146	15,411	136	21	305	5	100	168	538	12,071
36 39694	Kings Point village......	Nassau	3.3	5,076	4,653	44	4	180	-	33	162	99	3,851
36 39727	Kingston city.........	Ulster	7.4	23,456	18,853	2,995	70	358	1	446	733	1,516	17,849
36 39853	Kiryas Joel village.....	Orange	1.1	13,138	13,009	27	-	3	-	16	83	122	5,581
36 40189	Lackawanna city.......	Erie	6.1	19,064	16,011	1,812	76	59	1	439	666	969	14,387
36 40398	Lake Carmel CDP	Putnam	5.2	8,663	8,110	130	15	73	2	167	136	539	6,320
36 40486	Lake Erie Beach CDP ...	Erie	3.8	4,499	4,391	9	29	4	-	10	56	42	3,251
36 40530	Lake Grove village.....	Suffolk	3.0	10,250	9,359	148	9	505	-	102	127	496	7,554
36 40607	Lakeland CDP	Onondaga	1.5	2,852	2,806	6	5	17	-	-	18	28	2,142
36 40689	Lake Mohegan CDP	Westchester	2.9	5,979	5,067	412	20	174	1	166	139	580	4,258
36 40761	Lake Placid village.....	Essex	1.4	2,638	2,526	18	12	24	15	5	38	24	2,047
36 40838	Lake Ronkonkoma CDP ..	Suffolk	4.9	19,701	18,427	267	30	474	5	247	251	1,153	14,842
36 40937	Lake Success village	Nassau	1.9	2,797	2,208	133	-	424	1	7	24	33	2,236
36 41003	Lakeview CDP	Nassau	1.0	5,607	387	4,763	18	27	-	193	219	389	4,022
36 41069	Lakewood village......	Chautauqua	2.0	3,258	3,177	23	2	22	-	12	22	25	2,538
36 41135	Lancaster village......	Erie	2.7	11,188	11,034	36	29	15	1	20	53	91	8,659
36 41223	Lansing village	Tompkins	4.6	3,417	2,324	175	8	769	2	48	91	121	2,772
36 41333	Larchmont village	Westchester	1.1	6,485	6,111	44	6	183	5	50	86	291	4,582
36 41553	Lawrence village	Nassau	3.8	6,522	6,208	74	1	113	1	65	60	223	4,393
36 42026	Le Roy village........	Genesee	2.7	4,462	4,227	110	17	25	1	10	72	41	3,345
36 42081	Levittown CDP	Nassau	6.9	53,067	49,962	266	36	1,511	10	673	609	3,601	39,423
36 42147	Lewiston village	Niagara	1.1	2,781	2,740	3	15	10	1	1	11	16	2,299
36 42224	Liberty village	Sullivan	2.4	3,975	3,044	552	12	77	-	214	76	565	2,960
36 42279	Lido Beach CDP	Nassau	1.7	2,825	2,715	16	-	45	-	22	27	81	2,208
36 42554	Lindenhurst village.....	Suffolk	3.8	27,819	26,213	233	32	382	3	469	487	1,813	20,387
36 42741	Little Falls city.......	Herkimer	3.8	5,188	5,073	15	17	30	-	3	50	28	4,059
36 42884	Liverpool village	Onondaga	0.8	2,505	2,403	33	5	32	-	9	23	45	1,989
36 43005	Lloyd Harbor village.....	Suffolk	9.4	3,675	3,546	23	2	69	-	8	27	85	2,524
36 43082	Lockport city.........	Niagara	8.5	22,279	20,282	1,287	105	108	2	112	383	460	16,536
36 43192	Locust Valley CDP.....	Nassau	0.9	3,521	3,046	137	1	70	1	200	66	512	2,684
36 43335	Long Beach city.......	Nassau	2.1	35,462	29,860	2,190	75	822	29	1,683	803	4,540	28,885
36 43720	Lowville village.......	Lewis	1.9	3,476	3,360	26	14	29	-	26	21	35	2,579
36 43874	Lynbrook village......	Nassau	2.0	19,911	18,334	183	11	596	-	500	287	1,648	15,438
36 43885	Lyncourt CDP........	Onondaga	1.2	4,268	4,027	121	28	16	2	17	57	40	3,373
36 43962	Lyons village	Wayne	4.1	3,695	3,146	402	7	20	1	50	69	110	2,727
36 44534	Mahopac CDP	Putnam	5.3	8,478	7,996	90	13	103	-	163	113	565	6,337
36 44710	Malone village	Franklin	3.2	6,075	5,928	30	28	31	-	27	31	64	4,675
36 44787	Malverne village	Nassau	1.1	8,934	8,223	154	14	277	-	158	108	537	6,869
36 44831	Mamaroneck village.....	Westchester	3.2	18,752	15,859	778	46	660	12	909	488	3,284	14,398
36 44897	Manhasset CDP	Nassau	2.4	8,362	6,474	1,010	8	577	-	139	154	599	6,336
36 44908	Manhasset Hills CDP ...	Nassau	0.6	3,661	2,577	13	1	990	-	24	56	121	2,776
36 45018	Manlius village	Onondaga	1.8	4,819	4,485	49	11	201	-	10	63	63	3,531

Table D-1. Places — Area and Population—Con.

[Includes incorporated places and census designated places (CDPs) of 2,500 or more population as of April 1, 2000. Codes shown are two-digit Federal Information Processing Standards (FIPS) state codes and five-digit FIPS place codes. Place names and codes are those in effect as of January 1, 2000. County refers to the county (or counties) in which the place is located. IC in this column = independent city, a county equivalent. If a place is located in more than one county, counties are listed in alphabetic order]

State and place code	Place	County	Land area, 2000 (sq. mi.)	Population, 2000 (April 1) By race— One race Total	White	Black or African American	American Indian and Alaska Native	Asian	Native Hawaiian and Other Pacific Islander	Some other race	Two or more races	Hispanic or Latino (of any race)	18 years and over
36 00000	NEW YORK—Con.												
36 45106	Manorhaven village	Nassau	0.5	6,138	4,702	80	16	821	-	317	202	1,197	4,771
36 45139	Manorville CDP	Suffolk	25.4	11,131	10,728	131	13	73	4	83	99	461	8,063
36 45986	Massapequa CDP	Nassau	3.6	22,652	22,067	38	5	287	6	84	165	587	16,863
36 45997	Massapequa Park village	Nassau	2.2	17,499	17,039	38	4	246	4	69	99	525	13,073
36 46019	Massena village	St. Lawrence	4.5	11,209	10,703	40	237	82	4	27	116	133	8,513
36 46074	Mastic CDP	Suffolk	4.5	15,436	13,161	934	265	173	1	554	348	1,875	10,390
36 46085	Mastic Beach CDP	Suffolk	4.2	11,543	10,176	580	56	105	1	305	320	1,222	7,873
36 46140	Mattituck CDP	Suffolk	8.6	4,198	4,056	49	1	22	-	27	43	107	3,222
36 46151	Mattydale CDP	Onondaga	1.9	6,367	6,006	111	55	51	2	43	99	136	4,750
36 46162	Maybrook village	Orange	1.3	3,084	2,554	277	9	37	-	123	84	393	2,077
36 46349	Mechanicstown CDP	Orange	3.3	6,061	4,389	843	27	173	6	418	205	1,205	4,557
36 46360	Mechanicville city	Saratoga	0.8	5,019	4,916	18	5	33	-	22	25	60	3,793
36 46404	Medford CDP	Suffolk	10.5	21,985	19,607	875	56	303	5	683	456	2,373	15,896
36 46415	Medina village	Orleans	3.3	6,415	5,638	485	38	36	2	104	112	246	4,689
36 46514	Melville CDP	Suffolk	11.3	14,533	13,070	300	5	787	10	151	210	540	10,823
36 46536	Menands village	Albany	3.2	3,910	3,275	356	5	170	-	37	67	106	3,187
36 46668	Merrick CDP	Nassau	4.2	22,764	21,666	127	23	510	2	214	222	842	16,499
36 46976	Middle Island CDP	Suffolk	8.3	9,702	8,290	735	24	237	6	186	224	667	7,517
36 47042	Middletown city	Orange	5.1	25,388	17,437	3,840	190	429	7	2,369	1,116	6,375	18,333
36 47306	Miller Place CDP	Suffolk	7.2	10,580	10,237	45	20	143	-	52	83	339	7,382
36 47548	Milton CDP	Saratoga	1.5	2,692	2,623	20	4	9	-	8	28	49	1,948
36 47636	Mineola village	Nassau	1.9	19,234	16,617	199	56	870	8	755	729	2,507	15,350
36 47757	Minoa village	Onondaga	1.2	3,348	3,235	17	14	48	1	7	26	19	2,475
36 47823	Mohawk village	Herkimer	0.9	2,660	2,618	13	4	4	-	6	15	50	2,084
36 47988	Monroe village	Orange	3.4	7,780	7,082	200	31	182	1	177	107	679	5,495
36 48010	Monsey CDP	Rockland	2.2	14,504	13,462	626	5	152	2	101	156	415	7,457
36 48054	Montauk CDP	Suffolk	17.5	3,851	3,352	33	4	32	-	376	54	921	3,081
36 48090	Montebello village	Rockland	4.4	3,688	3,422	101	4	99	-	30	32	109	2,504
36 48142	Montgomery village	Orange	1.4	3,636	3,291	156	6	31	-	95	57	281	2,584
36 48175	Monticello village	Sullivan	4.1	6,512	3,619	1,909	20	139	3	530	292	1,508	4,672
36 48879	Mount Ivy CDP	Rockland	1.5	6,536	5,159	554	28	287	4	290	214	883	4,997
36 48890	Mount Kisco village	Westchester	3.1	9,983	7,766	598	28	423	-	901	267	2,450	7,773
36 48945	Mount Morris village	Livingston	2.0	3,266	3,076	37	9	22	-	82	40	189	2,486
36 49066	Mount Sinai CDP	Suffolk	5.3	8,734	8,314	112	7	130	3	82	86	364	6,110
36 49121	Mount Vernon city	Westchester	4.4	68,381	19,577	40,743	219	1,448	43	3,316	3,035	7,083	51,063
36 49231	Munsey Park village	Nassau	0.5	2,632	2,457	9	-	149	-	2	15	43	1,821
36 49330	Muttontown village	Nassau	6.1	3,412	2,727	62	-	546	-	7	70	78	2,391
36 49363	Myers Corner CDP	Dutchess	4.3	5,546	4,801	239	12	303	3	82	106	350	4,018
36 49407	Nanuet CDP	Rockland	5.4	16,707	11,993	2,228	38	1,620	14	385	429	1,364	12,754
36 49825	Nesconset CDP	Suffolk	3.8	11,992	11,317	115	13	373	8	68	98	403	8,915
36 49891	Newark village	Wayne	5.4	9,682	8,618	482	23	40	5	282	232	714	7,226
36 50034	Newburgh city	Orange	3.8	28,259	11,962	9,314	201	215	16	5,119	1,432	10,257	18,880
36 50067	New Cassel CDP	Nassau	1.5	13,298	4,207	6,292	60	188	6	1,674	871	5,467	9,461
36 50100	New City CDP	Rockland	15.6	34,038	28,963	1,591	28	2,378	7	616	455	1,999	25,305
36 50221	Newfane CDP	Niagara	4.7	3,129	3,058	21	14	5	-	-	31	14	2,319
36 50353	New Hempstead village	Rockland	2.8	4,767	3,335	836	8	346	4	146	92	431	3,064
36 50397	New Hyde Park village	Nassau	0.8	9,523	7,810	54	7	1,276	2	247	127	756	7,421
36 50551	New Paltz village	Ulster	1.7	6,034	4,430	470	16	423	6	504	185	720	5,619
36 50617	New Rochelle city	Westchester	10.4	72,182	49,001	13,848	141	2,334	35	4,535	2,288	14,492	54,831
36 50705	New Square village	Rockland	0.4	4,624	4,483	76	-	41	-	-	24	19	1,826
36 50837	New Windsor CDP	Orange	3.8	9,077	7,784	554	14	128	3	425	169	1,046	6,762
36 51000	New York city	Bronx, Kings, New York, Queens, Richmond	303.3	8,008,278	3,576,385	2,129,762	41,289	787,047	5,430	1,074,406	393,959	2,160,554	6,068,009
36 51011	New York Mills village	Oneida	1.1	3,191	3,134	12	2	11	1	8	23	34	2,596
36 51055	Niagara Falls city	Niagara	14.1	55,593	42,370	10,409	911	394	26	378	1,105	1,114	41,852
36 51275	Niskayuna CDP	Schenectady	1.0	4,892	4,631	51	3	127	4	20	56	77	3,563
36 51396	North Amityville CDP	Suffolk	2.4	16,572	3,091	11,386	183	173	12	939	788	2,242	11,632
36 51440	North Babylon CDP	Suffolk	3.4	17,877	16,456	371	31	373	6	348	292	1,313	13,668
36 51495	North Bay Shore CDP	Suffolk	3.0	14,992	7,269	2,821	95	306	12	3,491	998	7,608	10,534
36 51517	North Bellmore CDP	Nassau	2.6	20,079	18,530	430	13	633	5	205	263	913	14,965
36 51528	North Bellport CDP	Suffolk	4.6	9,007	4,780	2,789	135	178	6	656	463	1,841	5,985
36 51583	North Boston CDP	Erie	4.1	2,680	2,656	2	5	1	-	7	8	24	2,037
36 51915	Northeast Ithaca CDP	Tompkins	1.5	2,655	1,982	160	2	415	-	37	59	106	1,945
36 52078	North Great River CDP	Suffolk	2.3	3,929	3,722	62	2	49	1	50	43	248	2,834
36 53022	North Hills village	Nassau	2.8	4,301	3,502	39	-	681	-	6	73	62	3,677
36 53198	North Lindenhurst CDP	Suffolk	1.9	11,767	10,387	459	23	251	6	411	230	1,372	8,758
36 53253	North Massapequa CDP	Nassau	3.0	19,152	18,639	42	3	221	-	105	142	619	14,478
36 53264	North Merrick CDP	Nassau	1.8	11,844	11,083	127	11	378	6	84	155	436	8,864
36 53275	North New Hyde Park CDP	Nassau	2.0	14,542	11,980	48	21	2,157	3	177	156	707	11,346
36 53319	North Patchogue CDP	Suffolk	2.1	7,825	7,301	113	7	87	1	186	130	686	5,753
36 53396	Northport village	Suffolk	2.3	7,606	7,381	45	4	95	1	23	57	159	5,766
36 53561	North Sea CDP	Suffolk	12.3	4,493	4,255	63	8	43	10	74	40	238	3,572
36 53660	North Syracuse village	Onondaga	2.0	6,862	6,514	93	59	74	2	16	104	68	5,204
36 53682	North Tonawanda city	Niagara	10.1	33,262	32,549	98	114	177	2	95	227	362	25,367
36 53748	North Valley Stream CDP	Nassau	1.9	15,789	7,062	5,854	43	1,426	10	741	653	1,709	11,684
36 53792	North Wantagh CDP	Nassau	1.8	12,156	11,670	55	1	221	1	97	111	556	9,292
36 53852	Northwest Harbor CDP	Suffolk	14.5	3,059	2,768	111	5	32	1	80	62	280	2,287
36 53979	Norwich city	Chenango	2.0	7,355	7,096	102	20	51	-	14	72	50	5,542

Table D-1. Places — **Area and Population**—Con.

[Includes incorporated places and census designated places (CDPs) of 2,500 or more population as of April 1, 2000. Codes shown are two-digit Federal Information Processing Standards (FIPS) state codes and five-digit FIPS place codes. Place names and codes are those in effect as of January 1, 2000. County refers to the county (or counties) in which the place is located. IC in this column = independent city, a county equivalent. If a place is located in more than one county, counties are listed in alphabetic order]

State and place code	Place	County	Land area, 2000 (sq. mi.)	Population, 2000 (April 1) Total	White	Black or African American	American Indian and Alaska Native	Asian	Native Hawaiian and Other Pacific Islander	Some other race	Two or more races	Hispanic or Latino (of any race)	18 years and over
36 00000	NEW YORK—Con.												
36 54056	Noyack CDP	Suffolk	7.0	2,696	2,583	26	3	23	1	39	21	124	2,121
36 54100	Nyack village	Rockland	0.8	6,737	4,299	1,774	14	163	1	179	307	577	5,460
36 54144	Oakdale CDP	Suffolk	3.3	8,075	7,823	118	1	54	-	38	41	243	6,285
36 54441	Oceanside CDP	Nassau	5.0	32,733	31,079	184	22	600	3	518	327	1,931	24,556
36 54485	Ogdensburg city	St. Lawrence	5.1	12,364	10,515	1,227	99	85	7	348	83	769	9,727
36 54551	Old Bethpage CDP	Nassau	4.1	5,400	5,107	64	2	159	-	19	49	104	4,091
36 54705	Old Westbury village	Nassau	8.6	4,228	2,883	602	1	487	-	155	100	302	3,270
36 54716	Olean city	Cattaraugus	5.9	15,347	14,321	532	66	136	4	66	222	190	11,565
36 54837	Oneida city	Madison	22.0	10,987	10,579	88	153	51	2	20	94	92	8,231
36 54881	Oneonta city	Otsego	4.4	13,292	12,204	515	28	183	12	126	224	475	11,483
36 55167	Orangeburg CDP	Rockland	3.1	3,388	2,717	75	5	496	-	42	53	189	2,650
36 55189	Orange Lake CDP	Orange	5.4	6,085	4,886	764	4	89	-	192	150	737	4,523
36 55266	Orchard Park village	Erie	1.3	3,294	3,216	15	7	32	-	5	19	29	2,519
36 55530	Ossining village	Westchester	3.2	24,010	14,520	4,858	115	1,004	3	2,506	1,004	6,654	19,048
36 55574	Oswego city	Oswego	7.7	17,954	17,114	186	59	147	-	193	255	503	13,964
36 55882	Owego village	Tioga	2.5	3,911	3,732	45	18	40	-	13	63	71	2,998
36 55992	Oyster Bay CDP	Nassau	1.2	6,826	6,178	216	19	120	2	148	143	836	5,414
36 56187	Palmyra village	Wayne	1.3	3,490	3,394	17	17	16	-	3	43	22	2,637
36 56660	Patchogue village	Suffolk	2.2	11,919	9,687	464	41	166	2	1,100	459	2,842	9,236
36 56902	Pearl River CDP	Rockland	6.8	15,553	14,796	61	8	491	3	88	106	535	11,618
36 56979	Peekskill city	Westchester	4.3	22,441	12,819	5,732	95	535	13	2,206	1,041	4,920	16,970
36 57001	Pelham village	Westchester	0.8	6,400	5,326	426	6	317	-	158	167	461	4,629
36 57023	Pelham Manor village	Westchester	1.3	5,466	5,037	116	4	153	-	58	98	253	3,842
36 57177	Penn Yan village	Yates	2.3	5,219	5,070	35	14	16	3	17	64	49	3,973
36 57243	Perry village	Wyoming	2.3	3,945	3,843	29	6	14	1	18	34	61	2,926
36 57749	Piermont village	Rockland	0.7	2,607	2,053	123	5	203	-	143	80	303	2,106
36 58409	Plainedge CDP	Nassau	1.4	9,195	8,681	50	9	225	3	125	102	473	6,921
36 58442	Plainview CDP	Nassau	5.7	25,637	23,984	98	4	1,229	1	101	220	658	19,214
36 58574	Plattsburgh city	Clinton	5.0	18,816	17,576	463	98	281	10	128	260	399	15,717
36 58728	Pleasantville village	Westchester	1.8	7,172	6,480	208	13	207	-	124	140	528	5,126
36 58992	Pomona village	Rockland	2.4	2,726	2,155	283	5	181	-	44	58	162	2,117
36 59223	Port Chester village	Westchester	2.4	27,867	16,914	1,949	112	573	11	6,405	1,903	12,884	21,600
36 59311	Port Ewen CDP	Ulster	2.0	3,650	3,409	98	8	49	-	23	63	68	2,727
36 59355	Port Jefferson village	Suffolk	3.0	7,837	7,208	131	3	261	-	133	101	408	6,266
36 59377	Port Jefferson Station CDP	Suffolk	2.6	7,527	6,655	168	12	283	6	272	131	685	5,631
36 59388	Port Jervis city	Orange	2.5	8,860	7,956	399	52	57	2	194	200	660	6,399
36 59520	Port Washington CDP	Nassau	4.2	15,215	13,081	427	17	924	3	480	283	1,704	11,371
36 59531	Port Washington North village	Nassau	0.5	2,700	2,343	31	1	247	-	27	51	170	2,086
36 59564	Potsdam village	St. Lawrence	4.4	9,425	8,633	236	34	366	1	50	105	165	8,362
36 59641	Poughkeepsie city	Dutchess	5.1	29,871	15,785	10,666	117	485	14	1,579	1,225	3,177	22,121
36 60103	Putnam Lake CDP	Putnam	3.9	3,855	3,574	112	3	38	1	42	85	267	2,694
36 60675	Ravena village	Albany	1.3	3,369	3,127	98	9	22	1	33	79	140	2,504
36 60983	Red Oaks Mill CDP	Dutchess	3.5	4,930	4,424	230	7	138	-	74	57	249	3,611
36 61142	Remsenburg-Speonk CDP	Suffolk	5.9	2,675	2,539	47	5	17	17	19	31	140	2,038
36 61148	Rensselaer city	Rensselaer	3.0	7,761	6,916	548	21	85	1	33	157	165	5,824
36 61346	Rhinebeck village	Dutchess	1.6	3,077	2,909	59	5	35	-	35	34	122	2,494
36 61665	Ridge CDP	Suffolk	13.5	13,380	12,442	462	38	120	4	101	213	469	10,270
36 61973	Riverhead CDP	Suffolk	15.1	10,513	7,357	2,504	58	119	8	226	241	949	7,980
36 62066	Riverside CDP	Suffolk	5.1	2,875	1,699	1,023	31	21	-	39	62	278	2,457
36 63000	Rochester city	Monroe	35.8	219,773	106,161	84,717	1,033	4,943	104	14,452	8,363	28,032	158,038
36 63264	Rockville Centre village	Nassau	3.3	24,568	22,327	914	19	348	10	696	254	1,896	18,228
36 63319	Rocky Point CDP	Suffolk	10.3	10,185	9,737	69	16	123	1	81	158	511	7,103
36 63418	Rome city	Oneida	74.9	34,950	30,704	2,650	93	309	6	473	715	1,648	27,224
36 63473	Ronkonkoma CDP	Suffolk	8.2	20,029	18,798	180	12	479	8	224	328	1,269	14,863
36 63506	Roosevelt CDP	Nassau	1.8	15,854	1,263	12,528	73	77	8	1,320	585	2,572	11,024
36 63770	Roslyn village	Nassau	0.6	2,570	2,231	60	2	158	-	52	67	163	2,102
36 63814	Roslyn Heights CDP	Nassau	1.5	6,295	4,975	406	7	630	-	126	151	406	4,615
36 63924	Rotterdam CDP	Schenectady	6.9	20,536	19,935	218	32	113	4	43	191	212	15,843
36 64309	Rye city	Westchester	5.8	14,955	13,401	190	16	971	1	190	186	718	10,503
36 64325	Rye Brook village	Westchester	3.5	8,602	7,910	89	18	366	2	117	100	468	6,407
36 64584	St. James CDP	Suffolk	4.5	13,268	12,918	36	7	164	1	73	69	458	9,835
36 64749	Salamanca city	Cattaraugus	6.0	6,097	5,198	40	716	20	5	11	107	111	4,449
36 64842	Salisbury CDP	Nassau	1.7	12,341	10,728	127	17	1,108	1	198	162	1,056	9,334
36 65035	Sands Point village	Nassau	4.2	2,786	2,461	45	-	230	-	35	15	109	2,025
36 65233	Saranac Lake village	Essex, Franklin	2.8	5,041	4,883	38	16	24	-	13	67	54	3,920
36 65255	Saratoga Springs city	Saratoga	28.4	26,186	24,493	815	63	271	8	168	368	485	21,119
36 65288	Saugerties village	Ulster	1.8	4,955	3,958	602	18	69	1	254	53	587	3,969
36 65409	Sayville CDP	Suffolk	5.5	16,735	16,033	121	7	340	-	80	154	505	12,185
36 65431	Scarsdale village	Westchester	6.6	17,823	14,989	271	3	2,242	3	71	244	467	11,985
36 65508	Schenectady city	Schenectady	10.8	61,821	47,460	9,132	222	1,239	24	1,559	2,185	3,632	46,781
36 65882	Scotchtown CDP	Orange	4.2	8,954	6,839	1,028	23	317	-	416	327	1,317	6,474
36 65893	Scotia village	Schenectady	1.7	7,957	7,698	65	12	87	1	16	78	142	5,871
36 66047	Sea Cliff village	Nassau	1.1	5,066	4,804	85	5	62	1	48	61	241	3,845
36 66058	Seaford CDP	Nassau	2.6	15,791	15,286	49	10	265	3	85	93	586	11,804
36 66102	Searingtown CDP	Nassau	0.9	5,034	3,512	50	5	1,302	-	35	130	144	3,686
36 66212	Selden CDP	Suffolk	4.7	21,861	20,103	410	41	537	4	389	377	1,799	15,663

Table D-1. Places — **Area and Population**—Con.

[Includes incorporated places and census designated places (CDPs) of 2,500 or more population as of April 1, 2000. Codes shown are two-digit Federal Information Processing Standards (FIPS) state codes and five-digit FIPS place codes. Place names and codes are those in effect as of January 1, 2000. County refers to the county (or counties) in which the place is located. IC in this column = independent city, a county equivalent. If a place is located in more than one county, counties are listed in alphabetic order]

State and place code	Place	County	Land area, 2000 (sq. mi.)	Population, 2000 (April 1) Total	White	Black or African American	American Indian and Alaska Native	Asian	Native Hawaiian and Other Pacific Islander	Some other race	Two or more races	Hispanic or Latino (of any race)	18 years and over
36 00000	NEW YORK—Con.												
36 66322	Seneca Falls village	Seneca	4.4	6,861	6,616	50	17	92	-	24	62	81	5,208
36 66481	Setauket-East Setauket CDP	Suffolk	8.5	15,931	13,981	203	27	1,402	6	97	215	546	11,649
36 66993	Sherrill city	Oneida	2.0	3,147	3,084	7	19	19	-	1	17	26	2,322
36 67070	Shirley CDP	Suffolk	11.1	25,395	22,778	845	82	312	8	721	649	2,749	17,478
36 67334	Sidney village	Delaware	2.4	4,068	3,905	37	17	39	1	14	55	62	3,020
36 67411	Silver Creek village	Chautauqua	1.2	2,896	2,800	8	19	3	-	36	30	52	2,075
36 67510	Skaneateles village	Onondaga	1.4	2,616	2,594	2	-	8	-	1	11	8	1,942
36 67638	Sleepy Hollow village	Westchester	2.3	9,212	6,231	482	77	172	8	1,734	508	4,153	6,907
36 67686	Sloan village	Erie	0.8	3,775	3,739	8	5	5	-	6	12	27	3,017
36 67708	Sloatsburg village	Rockland	2.7	3,117	2,835	110	14	78	3	29	48	174	2,302
36 67851	Smithtown CDP	Suffolk	11.9	26,901	25,918	165	11	475	3	143	186	910	19,892
36 68286	Solvay village	Onondaga	1.6	6,845	6,558	46	70	27	4	20	120	162	5,253
36 68374	Sound Beach CDP	Suffolk	2.7	9,807	9,436	62	14	117	7	68	103	341	6,995
36 68462	Southampton village	Suffolk	6.3	3,965	3,187	513	33	63	1	78	90	359	3,190
36 69001	South Farmingdale CDP	Nassau	2.2	15,061	14,008	119	12	479	4	278	161	888	11,283
36 69078	South Glens Falls village	Saratoga	1.3	3,368	3,318	23	3	5	-	4	15	21	2,636
36 69188	South Hempstead CDP	Nassau	0.6	3,188	2,544	386	4	80	-	111	63	303	2,324
36 69199	South Hill CDP	Tompkins	5.9	6,003	5,501	145	8	106	2	107	134	166	5,574
36 69254	South Huntington CDP	Suffolk	3.4	9,465	8,847	80	6	336	-	78	118	356	7,343
36 69386	South Lockport CDP	Niagara	5.7	8,552	7,813	418	41	91	1	46	142	151	6,301
36 69441	South Nyack village	Rockland	0.6	3,473	2,477	557	7	201	1	83	147	240	2,838
36 69452	Southold CDP	Suffolk	10.5	5,465	5,271	51	7	11	1	65	59	148	4,332
36 69606	Southport CDP	Chemung	6.6	7,396	7,114	141	16	22	4	31	68	54	5,708
36 69892	South Valley Stream CDP	Nassau	0.9	5,638	4,178	451	4	764	1	86	154	286	4,222
36 70035	Spackenkill CDP	Dutchess	2.9	4,756	4,133	183	5	317	2	52	64	237	3,461
36 70189	Spencerport village	Monroe	1.4	3,559	3,471	20	11	18	-	9	30	67	2,691
36 70387	Springs CDP	Suffolk	8.5	4,950	4,446	73	10	72	1	191	157	804	3,844
36 70420	Spring Valley village	Rockland	2.1	25,464	9,734	11,200	101	1,415	63	1,358	1,593	3,921	17,291
36 70442	Springville village	Erie	3.7	4,252	4,179	21	9	17	1	8	17	26	3,183
36 71608	Stony Brook CDP	Suffolk	5.7	13,727	12,604	169	5	782	3	35	129	334	10,029
36 71663	Stony Point CDP	Rockland	5.5	11,744	11,069	161	16	163	3	189	143	829	8,703
36 71894	Suffern village	Rockland	2.1	11,006	9,557	388	29	311	10	498	213	1,416	8,793
36 72554	Syosset CDP	Nassau	5.0	18,544	15,810	49	7	2,347	2	104	181	542	13,722
36 73000	Syracuse city	Onondaga	25.1	147,306	94,663	37,336	1,670	4,961	72	3,284	5,320	7,768	110,521
36 73154	Tappan CDP	Rockland	2.8	6,757	5,559	86	8	913	5	100	86	430	5,072
36 73176	Tarrytown village	Westchester	3.0	11,090	8,588	781	24	720	5	587	385	1,793	8,908
36 73352	Terryville CDP	Suffolk	3.2	10,589	9,722	172	11	242	1	283	158	1,007	7,684
36 73583	Thiells CDP	Rockland	1.9	4,758	4,192	185	11	134	-	165	71	602	3,589
36 73605	Thomaston village	Nassau	0.4	2,607	2,114	22	1	357	6	62	45	207	1,996
36 73715	Thornwood CDP	Westchester	3.4	5,980	5,440	141	2	239	4	83	71	347	4,288
36 74166	Tonawanda city	Erie	3.8	16,136	15,826	67	75	63	2	28	75	144	12,279
36 74183	Tonawanda CDP	Erie	17.4	61,729	59,099	940	153	802	8	223	504	802	48,451
36 75121	Town Line CDP	Erie	4.6	2,521	2,503	-	5	4	-	-	8	11	1,918
36 75484	Troy city	Rensselaer	10.4	49,170	39,443	5,612	140	1,717	20	1,083	1,155	2,131	38,305
36 75583	Tuckahoe village	Westchester	0.6	6,211	4,595	628	6	606	1	216	159	549	4,761
36 75671	Tupper Lake village	Franklin	1.8	3,935	3,852	30	12	2	-	4	35	20	2,893
36 76089	Uniondale CDP	Nassau	2.7	23,011	6,207	12,779	81	484	18	2,289	1,153	5,261	16,913
36 76287	University Gardens CDP	Nassau	0.6	4,138	3,338	99	5	550	-	82	64	314	3,199
36 76540	Utica city	Oneida	16.3	60,651	48,166	7,838	170	1,341	29	1,309	1,798	3,510	46,031
36 76584	Vails Gate CDP	Orange	1.0	3,319	2,401	394	13	139	-	238	134	641	2,554
36 76639	Valhalla CDP	Westchester	2.7	5,379	5,156	41	4	114	1	16	47	181	4,125
36 76661	Valley Cottage CDP	Rockland	4.3	9,269	7,615	333	8	909	12	175	217	622	7,331
36 76705	Valley Stream village	Nassau	3.4	36,368	28,654	2,714	54	2,496	17	1,509	924	4,463	27,809
36 77513	Village Green CDP	Onondaga	1.2	3,945	3,817	41	9	29	-	13	36	45	3,119
36 77574	Viola CDP	Rockland	2.7	5,931	5,801	19	3	40	4	27	37	155	3,567
36 77684	Voorheesville village	Albany	2.1	2,705	2,654	10	7	16	-	2	16	22	2,030
36 77772	Wading River CDP	Suffolk	9.8	6,668	6,341	131	3	65	9	54	65	246	4,867
36 77849	Walden village	Orange	2.0	6,164	5,585	236	22	39	1	166	115	576	4,304
36 78036	Walton village	Delaware	1.6	3,070	3,006	10	12	10	-	4	28	42	2,327
36 78146	Wantagh CDP	Nassau	3.8	18,971	18,354	37	7	359	-	65	149	619	13,798
36 78168	Wappingers Falls village	Dutchess	1.1	4,929	4,043	295	13	150	-	278	150	742	3,728
36 78289	Warrensburg CDP	Warren	11.1	3,208	3,156	4	3	14	-	3	28	16	2,405
36 78333	Warsaw village	Wyoming	4.1	3,814	3,698	20	15	41	-	4	36	33	2,906
36 78355	Warwick village	Orange	2.2	6,412	5,935	209	12	40	2	69	145	364	4,725
36 78465	Washingtonville village	Orange	2.5	5,851	5,156	326	13	83	-	177	96	660	3,969
36 78553	Waterloo village	Seneca	2.1	5,111	4,989	42	6	25	-	9	40	60	3,857
36 78608	Watertown city	Jefferson	9.0	26,705	23,801	1,321	144	309	30	446	654	960	19,782
36 78674	Watervliet city	Albany	1.3	10,207	9,390	395	18	137	8	123	136	369	7,790
36 78806	Waverly village	Tioga	2.3	4,607	4,498	29	11	23	-	14	32	57	3,500
36 78960	Webster village	Monroe	2.2	5,216	4,646	214	16	191	-	42	107	109	3,844
36 79092	Wellsville village	Allegheny	2.4	5,171	4,960	34	10	77	-	15	75	47	3,997
36 79174	Wesley Hills village	Rockland	3.4	4,848	4,281	240	3	219	8	51	46	180	3,216
36 79246	West Babylon CDP	Suffolk	7.7	43,452	36,407	4,483	53	825	8	883	793	3,344	32,339
36 79301	West Bay Shore CDP	Suffolk	2.4	4,775	4,518	45	8	105	-	44	55	195	3,664
36 79444	Westbury village	Nassau	2.4	14,263	8,789	3,230	34	673	15	848	674	2,689	11,089
36 79785	West Elmira CDP	Chemung	3.0	5,136	4,926	94	4	74	-	9	29	26	3,947
36 79939	Westfield village	Chautauqua	3.8	3,481	3,345	14	10	20	-	63	29	114	2,577
36 80082	West Glens Falls CDP	Warren	4.6	6,721	6,583	28	18	17	-	15	60	67	4,898

U.S. Census Bureau, County and City Data Book: 2000

Table D-1. Places — **Area and Population**—Con.

[Includes incorporated places and census designated places (CDPs) of 2,500 or more population as of April 1, 2000. Codes shown are two-digit Federal Information Processing Standards (FIPS) state codes and five-digit FIPS place codes. Place names and codes are those in effect as of January 1, 2000. County refers to the county (or counties) in which the place is located. IC in this column = independent city, a county equivalent. If a place is located in more than one county, counties are listed in alphabetic order]

State and place code	Place	County	Land area, 2000 (sq. mi.)	Population, 2000 (April 1)									
					By race—									
					One race									
				Total	White	Black or African American	American Indian and Alaska Native	Asian	Native Hawaiian and Other Pacific Islander	Some other race	Two or more races	Hispanic or Latino (of any race)	18 years and over
36 00000	NEW YORK—Con.												
36 80170	Westhampton CDP	Suffolk	8.8	2,869	2,612	127	8	36	-	23	63	157	2,107
36 80203	West Haverstraw village	Rockland	1.5	10,295	6,676	1,318	57	427	10	1,304	503	3,127	7,474
36 80225	West Hempstead CDP	Nassau	2.7	18,713	15,473	1,111	32	951	4	601	541	1,860	13,808
36 80258	West Hills CDP	Suffolk	5.0	5,607	5,293	50	1	191	-	25	47	135	4,279
36 80302	West Islip CDP	Suffolk	6.2	28,907	28,009	115	16	316	3	146	302	1,018	20,682
36 80423	Westmere CDP	Albany	3.2	7,188	6,379	260	3	440	2	31	64	144	5,672
36 80599	West Nyack CDP	Rockland	2.9	3,282	2,889	65	1	249	-	32	46	183	2,501
36 80747	West Point CDP	Orange	24.3	7,138	5,875	649	36	239	11	117	211	468	5,576
36 80885	West Sayville CDP	Suffolk	1.9	5,003	4,864	20	8	65	-	28	18	105	3,680
36 80907	West Seneca CDP	Erie	21.4	45,943	45,074	213	80	229	4	86	257	405	35,705
36 81127	Westvale CDP	Onondaga	1.3	5,166	5,056	14	19	25	1	10	41	55	3,912
36 81419	Wheatley Heights CDP	Suffolk	1.4	5,013	2,005	2,427	15	171	-	208	187	585	3,496
36 81622	Whitehall village	Washington	4.7	2,667	2,617	6	5	2	-	22	15	44	1,977
36 81677	White Plains city	Westchester	9.8	53,077	34,465	8,444	182	2,389	37	5,502	2,058	12,476	41,815
36 81710	Whitesboro village	Oneida	1.1	3,943	3,852	21	1	13	-	21	35	58	3,025
36 82084	Williamsville village	Erie	1.3	5,573	5,422	38	6	53	-	18	36	60	4,492
36 82117	Williston Park village	Nassau	0.6	7,261	6,551	29	4	507	-	98	72	313	5,571
36 82744	Woodbury CDP	Nassau	5.1	9,010	8,187	88	5	636	1	25	68	128	6,784
36 82942	Woodmere CDP	Nassau	2.6	16,447	15,210	274	4	613	1	198	147	587	11,847
36 83294	Wyandanch CDP	Suffolk	4.4	10,546	1,077	8,196	79	60	3	660	471	1,724	6,793
36 83349	Wynantskill CDP	Rensselaer	2.4	3,018	2,952	16	6	9	1	1	33	13	2,372
36 83426	Yaphank CDP	Suffolk	14.0	5,025	4,277	564	12	52	2	47	71	369	3,926
36 84000	Yonkers city	Westchester	18.1	196,086	118,000	32,575	861	9,526	98	26,349	8,670	50,852	148,372
36 84088	Yorktown Heights CDP	Westchester	5.7	7,972	7,214	192	5	374	1	68	118	446	5,707
36 84099	Yorkville village	Oneida	0.7	2,675	2,628	13	-	13	-	6	15	31	2,072
37 00000	NORTH CAROLINA		48,710.9	8,049,313	5,804,656	1,737,545	99,551	113,689	3,983	186,629	103,260	378,963	6,085,266
37 00160	Aberdeen town	Moore	6.2	3,400	2,483	740	32	11	-	60	44	135	2,649
37 00500	Ahoskie town	Hertford	2.7	4,523	1,677	2,663	77	28	4	29	45	81	3,362
37 00680	Albemarle city	Stanly	15.7	15,680	11,423	3,215	37	653	5	168	179	293	11,605
37 01400	Angier town	Harnett	2.3	3,419	2,305	799	14	32	1	213	55	416	2,550
37 01520	Apex town	Wake	10.5	20,212	17,192	1,526	58	863	12	224	337	648	13,982
37 01720	Archdale city	Guilford, Randolph	7.8	9,014	8,401	248	42	184	1	66	72	163	6,923
37 02080	Asheboro city	Randolph	15.3	21,672	16,577	2,618	110	301	3	1,673	390	4,319	16,447
37 02140	Asheville city	Buncombe	40.9	68,889	53,701	12,129	240	635	39	1,054	1,091	2,589	55,397
37 02840	Ayden town	Pitt	2.3	4,622	2,202	2,289	8	9	2	61	51	102	3,437
37 04015	Bayshore CDP	New Hanover	3.6	2,512	2,425	48	8	14	1	5	11	26	1,879
37 04260	Beaufort town	Carteret	2.7	3,771	2,861	754	4	14	2	90	46	142	3,081
37 04840	Belmont city	Gaston	8.1	8,705	7,346	877	23	259	4	110	86	217	6,724
37 05040	Benson town	Johnston	2.1	2,923	1,684	995	14	13	2	169	46	213	2,118
37 05220	Bessemer City city	Gaston	4.2	5,119	4,274	687	16	30	-	53	59	179	3,806
37 05530	Bethlehem CDP	Alexander	7.6	3,713	3,597	19	1	52	-	26	18	66	2,845
37 06140	Black Mountain town	Buncombe	6.4	7,511	6,823	471	23	65	3	34	92	61	6,079
37 06760	Boiling Spring Lakes city	Brunswick	22.6	2,972	2,810	97	20	10	-	3	32	18	2,317
37 06800	Boiling Springs town	Cleveland	4.3	3,866	3,452	335	5	30	-	16	28	54	3,057
37 07080	Boone town	Watauga	5.8	13,472	12,661	461	40	160	7	62	81	221	12,687
37 07720	Brevard city	Transylvania	4.8	6,789	5,758	783	15	60	5	31	137	77	5,545
37 08110	Brogden CDP	Wayne	2.2	2,907	1,055	1,654	15	10	-	124	49	194	2,091
37 08960	Burgaw town	Pender	3.4	3,337	1,709	1,498	23	4	-	70	33	150	2,709
37 09060	Burlington city	Alamance	21.3	44,917	29,766	11,252	154	766	16	2,316	647	4,525	34,254
37 09360	Butner CDP	Granville	6.6	5,792	2,814	2,622	40	37	-	194	85	264	4,702
37 09530	Cajah's Mountain town	Caldwell	3.1	2,683	2,554	85	5	15	-	14	10	25	2,193
37 10240	Canton town	Haywood	3.8	4,029	3,873	64	23	4	-	38	27	97	3,240
37 10500	Carolina Beach town	New Hanover	2.3	4,701	4,557	56	28	21	-	8	31	36	4,007
37 10620	Carrboro town	Orange	4.5	16,782	12,195	2,273	61	864	1	982	406	2,062	13,598
37 10740	Cary town	Chatham, Wake	42.1	94,536	77,683	5,813	251	7,643	28	1,392	1,726	4,047	67,062
37 11800	Chapel Hill town	Durham, Orange	19.8	48,715	37,973	5,565	203	3,497	12	563	902	1,564	41,369
37 12000	Charlotte city	Mecklenburg	242.3	540,828	315,061	176,964	1,863	18,418	283	19,242	8,997	39,800	407,193
37 12340	Cherryville city	Gaston	4.7	5,361	4,761	513	7	33	-	28	19	123	4,222
37 12480	China Grove town	Rowan	2.0	3,616	3,099	252	10	34	5	195	21	341	2,690
37 12860	Clayton town	Johnston	5.4	6,973	4,995	1,392	11	60	1	440	74	703	5,102
37 12960	Clemmons village	Forsyth	10.7	13,827	12,426	721	12	291	3	243	131	490	10,275
37 13240	Clinton city	Sampson	7.1	8,600	4,565	3,559	83	64	3	243	83	401	6,742
37 14100	Concord city	Cabarrus	51.6	55,977	44,128	8,450	168	684	14	1,874	659	4,369	41,308
37 14340	Conover city	Catawba	10.2	6,604	5,574	557	15	207	2	173	76	517	5,188
37 14700	Cornelius town	Mecklenburg	8.5	11,969	10,969	673	25	148	6	60	88	334	9,288
37 15260	Cramerton town	Gaston	3.6	2,976	2,801	70	15	57	-	6	27	11	2,204
37 15880	Cullowhee CDP	Jackson	3.6	3,579	3,182	259	34	48	3	19	34	47	3,367
37 16180	Dallas town	Gaston	1.7	3,402	2,597	765	4	13	-	2	21	81	2,564
37 16400	Davidson town	Iredell, Mecklenburg	4.9	7,139	6,320	581	11	92	6	69	60	163	5,633
37 18320	Dunn city	Harnett	6.2	9,196	5,017	3,790	89	55	6	118	121	206	6,888
37 19000	Durham city	Durham, Orange, Wake	94.6	187,035	85,126	81,937	575	6,815	71	8,875	3,636	16,012	144,145
37 19420	East Flat Rock CDP	Henderson	3.2	4,151	3,557	128	13	12	-	365	76	621	3,140
37 19800	East Rockingham CDP	Richmond	3.4	3,885	3,187	464	70	25	6	78	55	199	2,937
37 20080	Eden city	Rockingham	15.0	15,908	12,000	3,524	33	49	9	164	129	372	12,229
37 20120	Edenton town	Chowan	5.0	5,394	2,312	2,979	11	34	1	24	33	78	4,116

Table D-1. Places — **Area and Population**—Con.

[Includes incorporated places and census designated places (CDPs) of 2,500 or more population as of April 1, 2000. Codes shown are two-digit Federal Information Processing Standards (FIPS) state codes and five-digit FIPS place codes. Place names and codes are those in effect as of January 1, 2000. County refers to the county (or counties) in which the place is located. IC in this column = independent city, a county equivalent. If a place is located in more than one county, counties are listed in alphabetic order]

State and place code	Place	County	Land area, 2000 (sq. mi.)	Population, 2000 (April 1)									
					By race—								
					One race								
				Total	White	Black or African American	American Indian and Alaska Native	Asian	Native Hawaiian and Other Pacific Islander	Some other race	Two or more races	Hispanic or Latino (of any race)	18 years and over
37 00000	NORTH CAROLINA—Con.												
37 20580	Elizabeth City city	Camden, Pasquotank....	8.9	17,188	6,917	9,729	47	136	2	106	251	258	12,764
37 20600	Elizabethtown town	Bladen	4.6	3,698	1,777	1,811	16	11	1	48	34	94	2,868
37 20620	Elkin town	Surry, Wilkes	6.3	4,109	3,456	297	1	13	1	280	61	552	3,199
37 21100	Elon College town	Alamance	3.4	6,738	5,903	690	3	69	2	33	38	107	5,749
37 21130	Elroy CDP	Wayne	6.4	3,896	2,761	826	8	75	-	157	69	268	2,925
37 21160	Emerald Isle town	Carteret	5.2	3,488	3,372	28	16	22	1	10	39	57	3,032
37 21500	Enochville CDP	Rowan	4.4	2,851	2,736	58	13	17	2	12	13	61	2,212
37 21740	Erwin town	Harnett	4.0	4,537	3,658	724	25	4	-	81	45	188	3,460
37 21880	Etowah CDP	Henderson	4.6	2,766	2,677	47	4	16	4	4	14	24	2,330
37 22360	Fairmont town	Robeson	2.2	2,604	788	1,528	257	6	-	12	13	15	1,941
37 22820	Farmville town	Pitt	3.1	4,302	2,038	2,155	3	10	-	51	45	91	3,272
37 22920	Fayetteville city	Cumberland	58.8	121,015	59,007	51,338	1,331	2,653	264	3,062	3,360	6,862	90,283
37 23600	Flat Rock village	Henderson	7.8	2,565	2,535	12	1	3	-	-	13	30	2,215
37 23760	Fletcher town	Henderson	5.3	4,185	3,917	138	5	53	-	21	51	65	3,187
37 24080	Forest City town	Rutherford	8.2	7,549	5,086	2,176	15	58	10	104	100	281	5,666
37 24198	Forest Oaks CDP	Guilford	5.1	3,241	3,056	147	6	6	-	9	17	11	2,511
37 24260	Fort Bragg CDP	Cumberland	18.9	29,183	16,942	7,368	336	536	255	2,419	1,327	4,603	21,664
37 24640	Franklin town	Macon	3.8	3,490	3,330	69	11	22	1	17	40	105	2,745
37 25300	Fuquay-Varina town	Wake	6.8	7,898	5,578	1,927	32	38	-	232	91	583	5,744
37 25380	Gamewell town	Caldwell	7.9	3,644	3,429	143	9	4	-	36	23	50	2,864
37 25480	Garner town	Wake	12.8	17,757	11,901	4,817	73	197	4	492	273	843	13,315
37 25580	Gastonia city	Gaston	46.1	66,277	46,513	16,981	137	773	19	1,167	687	3,613	49,733
37 25980	Gibsonville town	Alamance, Guilford	2.4	4,372	3,505	679	17	33	-	76	62	119	3,150
37 26460	Glen Raven CDP	Alamance	4.0	2,750	2,105	509	23	4	-	79	30	176	2,061
37 26880	Goldsboro city	Wayne	24.8	39,043	16,803	20,397	168	562	30	444	639	1,052	29,254
37 27280	Graham city	Alamance	8.1	12,833	9,353	2,777	56	94	-	409	144	1,301	9,758
37 27420	Granite Falls town	Caldwell	4.3	4,612	4,246	108	8	18	3	182	47	280	3,485
37 28000	Greensboro city	Guilford	104.7	223,891	124,243	83,728	989	6,357	89	4,647	3,838	9,742	173,991
37 28080	Greenville city	Pitt	25.6	60,476	37,133	20,649	181	1,098	26	611	778	1,244	49,101
37 28900	Half Moon CDP	Onslow	4.3	6,645	4,328	1,626	38	172	11	183	287	446	4,489
37 29160	Hamlet city	Richmond	5.0	6,018	3,722	2,077	97	21	-	29	72	76	4,453
37 29800	Harrisburg town	Cabarrus	6.3	4,493	4,257	145	19	42	-	10	20	37	3,233
37 30120	Havelock city	Craven	16.7	22,442	15,816	4,159	176	570	33	885	803	2,022	16,116
37 30660	Henderson city	Vance	8.2	16,095	5,917	9,524	43	103	4	380	124	826	11,677
37 30720	Hendersonville city	Henderson	6.0	10,420	8,486	1,307	29	76	1	363	158	947	8,410
37 31060	Hickory city	Burke, Caldwell, Catawba.	28.1	37,222	28,747	5,243	70	1,450	24	1,146	542	2,863	28,553
37 31400	High Point city	Davidson, Forsyth, Guilford, Randolph.	49.0	85,839	51,985	27,275	392	2,872	17	1,950	1,348	4,197	63,522
37 31620	Hillsborough town	Orange	4.6	5,446	3,282	1,897	28	31	-	88	120	152	4,017
37 32260	Holly Springs town	Wake	7.5	9,192	7,091	1,714	39	113	1	103	131	278	6,312
37 32640	Hope Mills town	Cumberland	6.1	11,237	8,207	1,979	228	142	24	311	346	719	7,632
37 32980	Hudson town	Caldwell	3.7	3,078	2,998	4	4	25	-	34	13	46	2,462
37 33120	Huntersville town	Mecklenburg	31.1	24,960	22,070	1,865	92	374	13	264	282	968	17,885
37 33320	Icard CDP	Burke	3.9	2,734	2,649	13	4	49	-	5	14	18	2,060
37 33560	Indian Trail town	Union	15.2	11,905	10,822	637	63	114	11	113	145	295	8,345
37 34200	Jacksonville city	Onslow	44.5	66,715	42,655	15,987	503	1,380	126	3,614	2,450	6,702	50,514
37 34260	James City CDP	Craven	8.3	5,420	4,277	983	13	26	1	56	64	106	4,084
37 34300	Jamestown town	Guilford	2.7	3,088	2,711	246	6	74	-	23	28	63	2,336
37 35200	Kannapolis city	Cabarrus, Rowan	29.9	36,910	28,695	6,072	125	319	5	1,265	429	2,337	27,992
37 35600	Kernersville town	Forsyth, Guilford	12.1	17,126	14,404	1,497	55	216	9	742	203	1,261	13,039
37 35720	Kill Devil Hills town	Dare	5.5	5,897	5,685	36	10	35	7	62	62	174	4,664
37 35760	King city	Forsyth, Stokes.	5.2	5,952	5,749	103	8	34	1	20	37	122	4,495
37 35870	Kings Grant CDP	New Hanover	4.6	7,738	6,526	949	40	73	3	62	85	134	5,909
37 35880	Kings Mountain city	Cleveland, Gaston.	8.2	9,693	7,255	2,089	15	175	2	61	96	139	7,242
37 35920	Kinston city	Lenoir	16.7	23,688	8,354	14,837	37	135	11	156	158	269	17,906
37 36060	Kitty Hawk town	Dare	8.2	2,991	2,935	19	7	8	1	6	15	28	2,347
37 36080	Knightdale town	Wake	2.7	5,958	4,043	1,599	21	87	2	121	85	220	4,070
37 36400	La Grange town	Lenoir	2.3	2,844	1,219	1,565	-	10	1	26	23	37	2,174
37 36480	Lake Junaluska CDP	Haywood	5.5	2,675	2,639	10	7	3	-	2	14	36	2,242
37 36511	Lake Norman of Catawba CDP	Catawba	19.1	4,744	4,620	62	19	9	2	11	21	33	3,812
37 36860	Landis town	Rowan	2.5	2,996	2,757	74	7	49	-	76	33	249	2,288
37 37220	Laurinburg city	Scotland	12.4	15,874	8,023	6,835	671	120	5	55	165	168	11,656
37 37760	Lenoir city	Caldwell	16.6	16,793	13,583	2,470	38	112	19	382	189	714	12,954
37 38040	Lewisville town	Forsyth	10.7	8,826	8,218	370	17	118	-	48	55	109	6,460
37 38060	Lexington city	Davidson	17.6	19,953	11,733	5,968	91	511	9	1,201	440	2,135	15,040
37 38100	Liberty town	Randolph	2.6	2,661	1,748	629	19	2	-	215	48	378	1,967
37 38220	Lillington town	Harnett	4.0	2,915	1,596	1,182	23	13	3	63	35	119	2,472
37 38320	Lincolnton city	Lincoln	8.2	9,965	7,977	1,343	33	39	-	414	159	1,491	7,614
37 39280	Long View town	Burke, Catawba	3.5	4,722	3,876	428	4	174	-	152	88	335	3,661
37 39360	Louisburg town	Franklin	2.3	3,111	1,580	1,452	3	17	-	34	25	94	2,498
37 39480	Lowell city	Gaston	2.6	2,662	2,433	172	6	17	-	5	29	35	2,050
37 39700	Lumberton city	Robeson	15.7	20,795	10,094	7,369	2,660	190	7	245	230	686	15,319
37 40660	Maiden town	Catawba, Lincoln.	4.7	3,282	2,627	483	12	27	10	89	34	188	2,571
37 41420	Marion city	McDowell.	3.4	4,943	4,114	521	14	52	2	189	51	348	3,918
37 41540	Mar-Mac CDP	Wayne	4.4	3,004	2,253	587	16	45	-	63	40	95	2,329
37 41740	Masonboro CDP	New Hanover	6.0	11,812	11,058	396	33	156	2	38	129	138	8,406
37 41960	Matthews town	Mecklenburg	14.2	22,127	19,970	1,181	74	523	2	173	204	553	15,644

852   U.S. Census Bureau, County and City Data Book: 2000

Table D-1. Places — **Area and Population**—Con.

[Includes incorporated places and census designated places (CDPs) of 2,500 or more population as of April 1, 2000. Codes shown are two-digit Federal Information Processing Standards (FIPS) state codes and five-digit FIPS place codes. Place names and codes are those in effect as of January 1, 2000. County refers to the county (or counties) in which the place is located. IC in this column = independent city, a county equivalent. If a place is located in more than one county, counties are listed in alphabetic order]

State and place code	Place	County	Land area, 2000 (sq. mi.)	Population, 2000 (April 1)									
					By race—								
					One race							Hispanic or Latino (of any race)	18 years and over
				Total	White	Black or African American	American Indian and Alaska Native	Asian	Native Hawaiian and Other Pacific Islander	Some other race	Two or more races		
37 00000	NORTH CAROLINA—Con.												
37 42020	Maxton town	Robeson, Scotland	2.2	2,551	651	1,635	179	8	4	28	46	41	1,803
37 42240	Mebane city	Alamance, Orange	5.9	7,284	5,638	1,273	17	45	1	210	100	382	5,317
37 43480	Mint Hill town	Mecklenburg	21.2	14,922	13,446	867	107	172	4	159	167	472	11,289
37 43720	Mocksville town	Davie	6.9	4,178	3,181	742	8	28	2	160	57	337	3,198
37 43920	Monroe city	Union	24.6	26,228	15,769	7,287	116	170	9	2,457	420	5,611	19,174
37 44220	Mooresville town	Iredell	14.7	18,823	15,348	2,679	67	312	4	214	199	480	13,415
37 44320	Morehead City town	Carteret	5.1	7,691	6,284	1,075	51	59	3	87	132	180	6,135
37 44400	Morganton city	Burke	18.2	17,310	13,098	2,208	96	344	141	1,149	274	1,931	13,652
37 44520	Morrisville town	Durham, Wake	6.8	5,208	3,982	573	23	472	-	61	97	170	4,133
37 44770	Mountain View CDP	Catawba	4.8	3,768	3,359	225	13	124	6	16	25	49	2,732
37 44800	Mount Airy city	Surry	8.4	8,484	7,240	678	30	216	4	211	105	498	6,655
37 44960	Mount Holly city	Gaston	7.8	9,618	8,276	894	34	240	-	72	102	204	7,369
37 45100	Mount Olive town	Duplin, Wayne	2.5	4,567	1,963	2,480	7	7	5	61	44	145	3,522
37 45720	Murraysville CDP	New Hanover	11.5	7,279	5,800	1,288	14	62	2	20	93	107	5,400
37 45840	Myrtle Grove CDP	New Hanover	6.9	7,125	6,736	253	12	61	8	10	45	66	5,521
37 45880	Nags Head town	Dare	6.5	2,700	2,618	36	4	12	-	13	17	39	2,181
37 46000	Nashville town	Nash	3.0	4,309	2,362	1,857	13	25	-	26	26	54	3,286
37 46340	New Bern city	Craven	25.8	23,128	12,943	9,325	75	148	9	332	296	692	17,593
37 46860	Newport town	Carteret	7.3	3,349	2,784	400	21	43	1	48	52	124	2,524
37 47000	Newton city	Catawba	13.0	12,560	9,744	1,549	54	427	4	581	201	1,196	9,575
37 47880	North Wilkesboro town	Wilkes	5.1	4,116	3,230	572	15	30	20	175	74	464	3,139
37 48345	Oak Island town	Brunswick	8.0	6,571	6,440	28	31	10	-	12	50	49	5,583
37 48480	Oak Ridge town	Guilford	14.7	3,988	3,728	168	11	29	-	25	27	52	2,805
37 48790	Ogden CDP	New Hanover	4.7	5,481	5,293	81	13	33	-	14	47	64	4,102
37 49800	Oxford city	Granville	4.5	8,338	3,651	4,288	17	34	5	283	60	380	6,178
37 51940	Pinehurst village	Moore	14.3	9,706	9,251	317	23	60	2	26	27	101	8,571
37 52220	Pineville town	Mecklenburg	3.6	3,449	2,761	345	7	114	2	138	82	385	2,845
37 52260	Piney Green CDP	Onslow	13.4	11,658	7,547	2,863	87	301	29	364	467	887	8,132
37 52760	Pleasant Garden town	Guilford	15.3	4,714	4,016	530	51	11	1	19	66	77	3,507
37 53040	Plymouth town	Washington	3.9	4,107	1,439	2,591	1	25	-	30	21	54	2,933
37 53360	Pope AFB CDP	Cumberland	2.9	2,583	1,987	365	11	67	8	80	65	159	1,785
37 54580	Raeford city	Hoke	3.8	3,386	1,786	1,386	97	32	1	37	47	141	2,583
37 55000	Raleigh city	Durham, Wake	114.6	276,093	174,786	76,756	981	9,327	118	8,946	5,179	19,308	218,487
37 55080	Randleman city	Randolph	3.6	3,557	3,245	132	12	14	-	100	54	298	2,609
37 55640	Red Oak town	Nash	19.5	2,723	2,469	219	2	7	-	9	17	36	2,013
37 55660	Red Springs town	Hoke, Robeson	2.8	3,493	1,334	1,717	302	12	5	81	42	128	2,584
37 55900	Reidsville city	Rockingham	13.4	14,485	8,260	5,725	31	93	9	195	172	381	11,097
37 56710	River Bend town	Craven	2.5	2,923	2,727	167	3	11	2	1	12	30	2,513
37 56815	River Road CDP	Beaufort	7.1	4,094	2,783	1,074	12	9	6	184	26	402	3,144
37 56900	Roanoke Rapids city	Halifax	7.8	16,957	12,214	4,218	98	240	5	84	98	179	12,425
37 57260	Rockingham city	Richmond	7.3	9,672	6,342	2,892	106	130	6	78	118	203	7,181
37 57500	Rocky Mount city	Edgecombe, Nash	35.6	55,893	22,874	31,314	195	394	12	507	597	1,033	40,429
37 58160	Roxboro city	Person	6.3	8,696	4,355	3,948	50	21	2	225	95	329	6,635
37 58260	Royal Pines CDP	Buncombe	3.0	5,334	5,013	185	7	57	-	20	52	42	4,039
37 58460	Rutherfordton town	Rutherford	4.2	4,131	3,477	562	5	30	-	30	27	53	3,198
37 58730	St. Stephens CDP	Catawba	9.8	9,439	8,379	252	40	263	3	383	119	921	7,117
37 58740	Salem CDP	Burke	4.2	2,923	2,305	465	14	53	13	37	36	64	2,193
37 58860	Salisbury city	Rowan	17.8	26,462	15,163	9,940	74	369	15	509	392	1,138	20,703
37 59280	Sanford city	Lee	24.1	23,220	12,973	6,779	116	246	8	2,771	327	4,419	16,919
37 59540	Sawmills town	Caldwell	6.2	4,921	4,790	27	10	8	1	57	28	116	3,657
37 60060	Seagate CDP	New Hanover	3.5	4,590	4,227	204	12	31	2	58	56	105	3,504
37 60320	Selma town	Johnston	3.2	5,914	2,785	2,385	34	11	5	585	109	1,125	4,264
37 60515	Seven Lakes CDP	Moore	8.2	3,214	3,052	120	7	6	-	4	25	26	2,736
37 61200	Shelby city	Cleveland	18.1	19,477	11,079	7,980	17	109	3	141	148	304	14,600
37 61860	Siler City town	Chatham	4.9	6,966	3,540	1,370	32	41	13	1,847	123	2,740	5,234
37 61950	Silver Lake CDP	New Hanover	6.6	5,788	5,107	463	34	70	6	47	61	125	4,327
37 62520	Smithfield town	Johnston	11.4	11,510	7,212	3,567	49	73	2	477	130	1,140	9,054
37 63120	Southern Pines town	Moore	15.4	10,918	7,729	2,901	39	72	8	87	82	223	8,591
37 63180	South Gastonia CDP	Gaston	6.4	5,433	4,611	654	17	34	-	67	50	102	4,081
37 63470	South Rosemary CDP	Halifax	6.2	2,843	1,403	1,407	8	6	-	4	15	20	2,109
37 63760	Spencer town	Rowan	2.7	3,355	2,358	792	12	16	1	121	55	227	2,565
37 63880	Spindale town	Rutherford	5.5	4,022	2,928	1,000	20	22	-	20	32	58	3,128
37 64180	Spring Lake town	Cumberland	3.7	8,098	2,751	4,139	67	291	30	395	425	963	5,645
37 64420	Stallings town	Union	3.5	3,189	2,821	248	25	11	-	56	28	117	2,338
37 64500	Stanley town	Gaston	2.3	3,053	2,730	257	12	14	1	20	19	25	2,240
37 64740	Statesville city	Iredell	20.5	23,320	13,979	7,433	43	633	4	896	332	1,658	17,622
37 65040	Stokesdale town	Guilford	19.4	3,267	2,963	227	10	22	-	15	30	63	2,411
37 65580	Summerfield town	Guilford	27.1	7,018	6,560	283	31	45	-	39	60	100	5,047
37 66280	Swannanoa CDP	Buncombe	6.4	4,132	3,782	209	19	27	1	50	44	104	2,978
37 66520	Tabor City town	Columbus	2.9	2,509	1,621	825	18	2	3	29	11	55	1,869
37 66700	Tarboro town	Edgecombe	9.7	11,138	6,241	4,393	7	34	-	397	66	662	8,452
37 67420	Thomasville city	Davidson, Randolph	11.1	19,788	13,779	4,731	90	164	-	757	267	1,371	14,737
37 68340	Trent Woods town	Craven	2.9	4,192	4,092	45	-	16	1	25	13	27	3,194
37 68400	Trinity city	Randolph	16.9	6,690	6,225	337	42	36	1	22	27	61	5,188
37 68520	Troy town	Montgomery	3.0	3,430	1,867	1,337	25	39	-	114	48	248	2,690
37 69260	Unionville town	Union	26.2	4,797	4,628	107	9	16	-	23	14	82	3,408
37 69520	Valdese town	Burke	5.4	4,485	4,105	47	10	179	3	101	40	220	3,430
37 70380	Wadesboro town	Anson	3.0	3,552	1,481	2,002	14	16	1	25	13	46	2,590

[Includes incorporated places and census designated places (CDPs) of 2,500 or more population as of April 1, 2000. Codes shown are two-digit Federal Information Processing Standards (FIPS) state codes and five-digit FIPS place codes. Place names and codes are those in effect as of January 1, 2000. County refers to the county (or counties) in which the place is located. IC in this column = independent city, a county equivalent. If a place is located in more than one county, counties are listed in alphabetic order]

State and place code	Place	County	Land area, 2000 (sq. mi.)	Population, 2000 (April 1)									
					By race—							Hispanic or Latino (of any race)	18 years and over
					One race						Two or more races		
				Total	White	Black or African American	American Indian and Alaska Native	Asian	Native Hawaiian and Other Pacific Islander	Some other race			
37 00000	NORTH CAROLINA—Con.												
37 70540	Wake Forest town	Wake	7.8	12,588	10,024	1,987	26	256	1	98	196	262	8,852
37 70660	Walkertown town	Forsyth	5.9	4,009	3,529	401	16	12	-	17	34	56	3,171
37 70720	Wallace town	Duplin, Pender	2.6	3,344	1,861	945	2	8	-	470	58	608	2,555
37 71160	Warsaw town	Duplin	2.8	3,051	1,095	1,542	7	3	18	362	24	481	2,225
37 71220	Washington city	Beaufort	6.5	9,583	4,962	4,360	16	47	2	100	96	261	7,219
37 71460	Waxhaw town	Union	2.8	2,625	2,132	447	8	7	-	4	27	45	1,801
37 71500	Waynesville town	Haywood	7.7	9,232	8,717	306	50	15	7	70	67	186	7,391
37 71680	Weddington town	Mecklenburg, Union	15.8	6,696	6,396	138	18	72	-	28	44	71	4,520
37 71760	Welcome CDP	Davidson	9.3	3,538	3,372	94	3	28	-	13	28	23	2,739
37 71860	Wendell town	Wake	2.0	4,247	2,991	1,022	18	17	2	140	57	251	3,000
37 71900	Wentworth town	Rockingham	14.3	2,779	2,248	470	11	9	-	19	22	37	2,113
37 71940	Wesley Chapel village	Union	8.4	2,549	2,473	36	3	8	1	9	19	48	1,806
37 73660	Whiteville city	Columbus	5.4	5,148	3,115	1,888	33	38	2	29	43	48	3,905
37 74020	Wilkesboro town	Wilkes	5.5	3,159	2,697	310	6	86	-	40	20	130	2,518
37 74220	Williamston town	Martin	3.7	5,843	2,361	3,360	17	27	5	29	44	87	4,279
37 74440	Wilmington city	New Hanover	41.0	75,838	53,516	19,579	266	682	67	868	860	1,991	61,896
37 74540	Wilson city	Wilson	23.3	44,405	20,723	21,106	136	257	8	1,728	447	3,237	32,849
37 75000	Winston-Salem city	Forsyth	108.9	185,776	103,243	68,924	567	2,108	67	7,965	2,902	16,043	142,411
37 75060	Winterville town	Pitt	2.5	4,791	2,838	1,838	17	39	5	19	35	49	3,451
37 75280	Woodfin town	Buncombe	3.5	3,162	2,930	62	11	13	-	104	42	212	2,554
37 75780	Wrightsboro CDP	New Hanover	10.7	4,496	2,877	1,510	28	9	1	25	46	69	3,345
37 75820	Wrightsville Beach town	New Hanover	1.3	2,593	2,544	7	8	14	2	5	13	17	2,363
37 75960	Yadkinville town	Yadkin	2.7	2,818	2,419	184	1	5	-	178	31	530	2,171
37 76220	Zebulon town	Johnston, Wake	3.2	4,046	2,171	1,608	23	41	-	162	41	348	2,901
38 00000	NORTH DAKOTA		68,975.9	642,200	593,181	3,916	31,329	3,606	230	2,540	7,398	7,786	481,351
38 06660	Beulah city	Mercer	2.4	3,152	3,019	1	53	9	20	5	45	15	2,189
38 07200	Bismarck city	Burleigh	26.9	55,532	52,634	156	1,884	251	15	95	497	415	42,458
38 19420	Devils Lake city	Ramsey	6.3	7,222	6,444	16	566	20	-	15	161	40	5,487
38 19620	Dickinson city	Stark	9.5	16,010	15,556	43	192	38	5	52	124	168	12,091
38 25700	Fargo city	Cass	37.9	90,599	85,321	922	1,119	1,482	40	400	1,315	1,167	71,463
38 31820	Grafton city	Walsh	3.4	4,516	4,140	26	61	17	-	212	60	432	3,422
38 32060	Grand Forks city	Grand Forks	19.2	49,321	46,040	426	1,357	472	28	288	710	921	38,756
38 32140	Grand Forks AFB CDP	Grand Forks	8.2	4,832	3,907	406	43	117	15	129	215	289	2,975
38 40580	Jamestown city	Stutsman	12.5	15,527	15,037	56	188	76	7	42	121	185	12,163
38 49900	Mandan city	Morton	10.2	16,718	15,879	34	505	56	2	25	217	130	12,212
38 53380	Minot city	Ward	14.6	36,567	34,074	490	1,008	226	25	181	563	539	28,071
38 53420	Minot AFB CDP	Ward	7.2	7,599	6,014	777	53	216	11	213	315	469	4,843
38 68860	Rugby city	Pierce	1.9	2,939	2,883	-	30	11	-	1	14	13	2,259
38 81180	Valley City city	Barnes	3.3	6,826	6,648	50	51	19	-	13	45	56	5,543
38 82660	Wahpeton city	Richland	5.0	8,586	8,197	53	207	37	3	10	79	65	6,765
38 84780	West Fargo city	Cass	7.3	14,940	14,402	63	156	42	3	100	174	211	10,573
38 86220	Williston city	Williams	7.0	12,512	11,723	21	457	30	2	21	258	154	9,308
39 00000	OHIO		40,948.4	11,353,140	9,645,453	1,301,307	24,486	132,633	2,749	88,627	157,885	217,123	8,464,801
39 00198	Ada village	Hardin	1.9	5,582	5,331	88	7	70	-	17	69	33	4,808
39 01000	Akron city	Summit	62.1	217,074	145,924	61,827	575	3,257	48	940	4,503	2,513	162,108
39 01420	Alliance city	Mahoning, Stark	8.6	23,253	19,884	2,602	39	180	4	96	448	271	17,797
39 01672	Amberley village	Hamilton	3.5	3,425	2,994	303	3	82	-	11	32	18	2,638
39 01742	Amelia village	Clermont	1.4	2,752	2,663	16	2	8	-	20	43	35	1,968
39 01798	Amherst city	Lorain	7.2	11,797	11,424	62	16	86	1	92	116	346	8,733
39 02344	Archbold village	Fulton	4.3	4,290	3,927	20	14	22	-	248	59	533	3,156
39 02568	Ashland city	Ashland	10.4	21,249	20,473	253	28	224	10	67	194	181	16,444
39 02638	Ashtabula city	Ashtabula	7.6	20,962	17,753	2,053	60	84	11	527	474	1,115	15,182
39 02680	Ashville village	Pickaway	1.6	3,174	3,105	6	10	2	-	6	45	34	2,236
39 02736	Athens city	Athens	8.3	21,342	19,028	816	32	954	12	128	372	301	19,922
39 03086	Aurora city	Portage	23.2	13,556	12,969	293	14	168	2	17	93	78	10,066
39 03184	Austintown CDP	Mahoning	11.7	31,627	29,258	1,610	45	186	8	136	384	578	25,019
39 03352	Avon city	Lorain	20.9	11,446	11,105	82	20	118	-	28	93	147	8,282
39 03464	Avon Lake city	Lorain	11.1	18,145	17,656	82	29	175	7	45	151	226	12,904
39 03585	Bainbridge CDP	Geauga	3.4	3,417	3,323	25	3	24	-	11	31	21	2,458
39 03716	Ballville CDP	Sandusky	2.7	3,255	3,086	41	2	24	-	62	40	120	2,546
39 03758	Baltimore village	Fairfield	1.8	2,881	2,851	3	1	5	-	1	20	11	2,128
39 03828	Barberton city	Summit	9.0	27,899	25,787	1,488	74	102	2	66	380	179	20,981
39 03926	Barnesville village	Belmont	1.9	4,225	4,158	30	3	7	-	-	27	11	3,226
39 04416	Bay Village city	Cuyahoga	4.6	16,087	15,773	43	4	116	1	34	116	157	11,924
39 04500	Beachwood city	Cuyahoga	5.3	12,186	10,541	1,106	10	391	2	18	118	95	9,707
39 04720	Beavercreek city	Greene	26.4	37,984	35,495	540	63	1,330	8	117	431	433	28,380
39 04840	Beckett Ridge CDP	Butler	4.9	8,663	7,647	418	16	479	1	24	78	141	6,026
39 04878	Bedford city	Cuyahoga	5.4	14,214	11,231	2,506	24	154	2	67	230	152	11,302
39 04920	Bedford Heights city	Cuyahoga	4.5	11,375	3,173	7,669	23	216	1	61	232	182	8,886
39 05074	Bellaire city	Belmont	1.8	4,892	4,504	279	6	9	1	7	86	15	3,712
39 05102	Bellbrook city	Greene	3.1	7,009	6,812	55	21	69	2	8	42	84	5,044
39 05130	Bellefontaine city	Logan	8.8	13,069	11,869	670	20	122	5	69	314	146	9,397
39 05228	Bellevue city	Erie, Huron, Sandusky	5.1	8,193	8,010	22	12	22	-	67	60	210	6,019

Table D-1. Places — **Area and Population**—Con.

[Includes incorporated places and census designated places (CDPs) of 2,500 or more population as of April 1, 2000. Codes shown are two-digit Federal Information Processing Standards (FIPS) state codes and five-digit FIPS place codes. Place names and codes are those in effect as of January 1, 2000. County refers to the county (or counties) in which the place is located. IC in this column = independent city, a county equivalent. If a place is located in more than one county, counties are listed in alphabetic order]

State and place code	Place	County	Land area, 2000 (sq. mi.)	Population, 2000 (April 1) Total	White	Black or African American	American Indian and Alaska Native	Asian	Native Hawaiian and Other Pacific Islander	Some other race	Two or more races	Hispanic or Latino (of any race)	18 years and over
39 00000	OHIO—Con.												
39 05424	Belpre city	Washington	3.5	6,660	6,394	140	7	28	-	8	83	32	5,271
39 05690	Berea city	Cuyahoga	5.5	18,970	17,353	974	46	170	6	116	305	301	14,892
39 06068	Bethel village	Clermont	1.3	2,637	2,592	3	5	5	-	-	32	19	1,797
39 06278	Bexley city	Franklin	2.4	13,203	12,206	592	22	131	6	62	184	121	9,596
39 06670	Blacklick Estates CDP	Franklin	2.0	9,518	8,254	854	36	102	10	53	209	120	6,726
39 06908	Blanchester village	Clinton, Warren	3.0	4,220	4,165	6	7	15	-	1	26	26	3,076
39 07300	Blue Ash city	Hamilton	7.7	12,513	10,897	627	31	800	2	36	120	122	9,329
39 07426	Bluffton village	Allen, Hancock	3.3	3,896	3,811	30	2	21	-	7	25	46	3,129
39 07454	Boardman CDP	Mahoning	15.9	37,215	35,448	951	33	302	8	155	318	670	29,516
39 07972	Bowling Green city	Wood	10.2	29,636	27,219	837	62	543	5	537	433	1,031	25,756
39 08364	Brecksville city	Cuyahoga	19.6	13,382	12,695	255	4	342	1	14	71	136	10,189
39 08605	Bridgetown North CDP	Hamilton	3.4	12,569	12,368	45	7	66	3	15	65	63	9,362
39 08826	Brimfield CDP	Portage	4.0	3,248	3,131	57	12	6	1	9	32	20	2,347
39 09064	Broadview Heights city	Cuyahoga	13.1	15,967	15,170	126	12	480	1	53	125	147	11,993
39 09246	Brooklyn city	Cuyahoga	4.3	11,586	10,736	196	12	264	1	189	188	449	9,393
39 09288	Brook Park city	Cuyahoga	7.5	21,218	20,048	414	48	268	-	164	276	423	16,389
39 09358	Brookville village	Montgomery	3.4	5,289	5,221	4	7	34	-	11	12	23	4,057
39 09680	Brunswick city	Medina	12.5	33,388	32,418	246	44	286	8	126	260	454	24,129
39 09792	Bryan city	Williams	4.6	8,333	8,019	26	19	59	-	117	93	311	6,267
39 09890	Buckeye Lake village	Fairfield, Licking	2.0	3,049	2,959	19	19	4	-	8	40	17	2,210
39 10030	Bucyrus city	Crawford	7.3	13,224	12,877	103	36	68	2	35	103	130	10,015
39 10352	Burlington CDP	Lawrence	1.4	2,794	2,440	265	7	3	-	13	66	48	2,233
39 10716	Byesville village	Guernsey	1.0	2,574	2,524	5	11	6	1	-	27	17	1,869
39 10800	Cadiz village	Harrison	8.8	3,308	2,901	297	-	13	1	5	91	9	2,569
39 10926	Calcutta CDP	Columbiana	11.7	3,491	3,439	6	2	25	-	3	16	23	2,773
39 10996	Cambridge city	Guernsey	5.6	11,520	10,695	451	38	43	-	54	239	111	8,539
39 11066	Campbell city	Mahoning	3.7	9,460	7,304	1,579	9	20	-	329	219	1,038	7,097
39 11304	Canal Fulton village	Stark	2.4	5,061	4,923	46	8	21	-	9	54	34	3,665
39 11332	Canal Winchester village	Fairfield, Franklin	6.4	4,478	4,281	98	17	30	-	2	50	23	3,269
39 11360	Canfield city	Mahoning	4.6	7,374	7,173	33	3	95	3	24	43	62	5,487
39 12000	Canton city	Stark	20.5	80,806	60,164	16,999	396	257	24	492	2,474	1,006	59,312
39 12112	Carey village	Wyandot	2.0	3,901	3,761	6	4	68	-	33	29	54	2,853
39 12168	Carlisle village	Montgomery, Warren	3.4	5,121	5,038	12	9	15	3	7	37	29	3,765
39 12280	Carrollton village	Carroll	2.4	3,190	3,145	8	6	2	-	2	27	15	2,507
39 12784	Cedarville village	Greene	1.1	3,828	3,639	76	15	31	1	12	54	36	3,430
39 12868	Celina city	Mercer	4.4	10,303	9,998	19	38	69	2	64	113	220	7,497
39 13190	Centerville city	Montgomery	10.2	23,024	21,258	678	29	730	14	61	254	272	18,053
39 13358	Chagrin Falls village	Cuyahoga	2.1	4,024	3,972	2	1	18	-	9	22	36	3,131
39 13484	Champion Heights CDP	Trumbull	3.4	4,727	4,653	31	15	5	-	4	19	30	3,602
39 13554	Chardon village	Geauga	4.6	5,156	5,041	22	1	23	1	5	63	24	3,873
39 13848	Cherry Grove CDP	Hamilton	1.1	4,555	4,376	54	4	75	4	18	24	43	3,190
39 14100	Chesterland CDP	Geauga	4.4	2,646	2,613	13	-	14	-	-	6	18	2,042
39 14128	Cheviot city	Hamilton	1.2	9,015	8,738	71	16	56	1	44	89	100	6,995
39 14184	Chillicothe city	Ross	9.5	21,796	19,445	1,637	74	121	8	76	435	182	16,966
39 14324	Churchill CDP	Trumbull	2.5	2,601	2,283	262	1	11	-	11	33	35	2,036
39 15000	Cincinnati city	Hamilton	78.0	331,285	175,064	142,176	709	5,132	130	2,093	5,553	4,230	250,141
39 15070	Circleville city	Pickaway	6.6	13,485	12,859	342	27	66	8	37	146	111	9,880
39 15644	Clayton city	Montgomery	18.4	13,347	11,631	1,318	20	194	6	40	138	120	9,761
39 16000	Cleveland city	Cuyahoga	77.6	478,403	198,510	243,939	1,458	6,444	178	17,173	10,701	34,728	342,000
39 16014	Cleveland Heights city	Cuyahoga	8.1	49,958	26,229	20,873	81	1,280	5	338	1,152	791	38,033
39 16028	Cleves village	Hamilton	1.6	2,790	2,740	16	4	4	4	2	20	10	1,914
39 16308	Clyde city	Sandusky	4.4	6,064	5,824	9	7	16	2	134	72	285	4,426
39 16532	Coldwater village	Mercer	2.0	4,482	4,437	3	4	6	-	14	18	54	3,142
39 17036	Columbiana village	Columbiana, Mahoning	6.1	5,635	5,571	6	4	10	1	4	39	18	4,564
39 18000	Columbus city	Delaware, Fairfield, Franklin	210.3	711,470	483,332	174,065	2,090	24,495	367	8,292	18,829	17,471	539,602
39 18350	Conneaut city	Ashtabula	26.4	12,485	12,027	140	23	59	6	29	201	132	9,344
39 18812	Cortland city	Trumbull	4.5	6,830	6,667	64	8	26	-	8	57	51	5,147
39 18868	Coshocton city	Coshocton	7.5	11,682	11,220	190	19	92	2	39	120	69	8,969
39 19008	Covedale CDP	Hamilton	2.8	6,360	6,270	22	8	20	-	13	27	41	4,754
39 19050	Covington village	Miami	1.2	2,559	2,528	4	-	1	-	11	15	23	1,947
39 19330	Crestline village	Crawford, Richland	2.9	5,088	4,914	92	9	13	3	11	46	34	3,729
39 19778	Cuyahoga Falls city	Summit	25.5	49,374	47,300	923	99	520	6	75	451	309	38,287
39 20366	Day Heights CDP	Clermont	1.2	2,823	2,752	28	3	7	-	14	19	14	2,100
39 21000	Dayton city	Montgomery	55.8	166,179	88,676	71,668	500	1,075	63	1,160	3,037	2,626	124,447
39 21266	Deer Park city	Hamilton	0.9	5,982	5,774	101	11	41	-	13	42	40	4,679
39 21308	Defiance city	Defiance	10.5	16,465	14,349	567	53	64	8	1,070	354	2,100	12,237
39 21434	Delaware city	Delaware	15.0	25,243	23,435	968	48	211	24	138	419	312	19,018
39 21602	Delphos city	Allen, Van Wert	2.9	6,944	6,849	19	10	13	-	17	36	53	5,086
39 21616	Delta village	Fulton	2.6	2,930	2,811	3	16	3	6	58	33	161	2,090
39 21714	Dennison village	Tuscarawas	1.4	2,992	2,878	49	6	3	3	11	42	30	2,152
39 21742	Dent CDP	Hamilton	6.0	7,612	7,462	52	17	24	2	12	43	32	5,884
39 21868	Devola CDP	Washington	5.1	2,771	2,704	2	-	52	-	2	11	3	2,149
39 22008	Dillonvale CDP	Hamilton	0.9	3,716	3,576	60	9	15	2	14	40	37	2,933
39 22456	Dover city	Tuscarawas	5.3	12,210	11,855	155	30	62	3	25	80	73	9,270
39 22568	Doylestown village	Wayne	1.8	2,799	2,768	4	1	3	-	6	17	17	2,106
39 22674	Dry Run CDP	Hamilton	4.8	6,553	6,322	43	3	123	-	17	45	63	4,312
39 22694	Dublin city	Delaware, Franklin, Union	21.1	31,392	28,146	543	25	2,312	6	62	298	317	21,309

[Includes incorporated places and census designated places (CDPs) of 2,500 or more population as of April 1, 2000. Codes shown are two-digit Federal Information Processing Standards (FIPS) state codes and five-digit FIPS place codes. Place names and codes are those in effect as of January 1, 2000. County refers to the county (or counties) in which the place is located. IC in this column = independent city, a county equivalent. If a place is located in more than one county, counties are listed in alphabetic order]

State and place code	Place	County	Land area, 2000 (sq. mi.)	Population, 2000 (April 1) Total	By race— One race White	Black or African American	American Indian and Alaska Native	Asian	Native Hawaiian and Other Pacific Islander	Some other race	Two or more races	Hispanic or Latino (of any race)	18 years and over
39 00000	OHIO—Con.												
39 23380	East Cleveland city	Cuyahoga	3.1	27,217	1,240	25,418	59	61	4	45	390	207	19,136
39 23618	Eastlake city	Lake	6.4	20,255	19,737	110	32	196	2	30	148	141	15,426
39 23730	East Liverpool city	Columbiana	4.3	13,089	12,153	630	31	11	6	27	231	94	9,543
39 23940	East Palestine city	Columbiana	2.8	4,917	4,842	18	3	7	-	13	34	35	3,694
39 24234	Eaton city	Preble	5.7	8,133	7,972	32	7	45	2	6	69	46	6,182
39 24542	Edgewood CDP	Ashtabula	6.7	4,762	4,608	60	6	34	-	11	43	54	3,737
39 25186	Elmwood Place village	Hamilton	0.3	2,681	2,463	146	15	5	2	18	32	44	1,898
39 25256	Elyria city	Lorain	19.9	55,953	45,517	7,928	150	340	11	532	1,475	1,553	41,086
39 25396	Englewood city	Montgomery	6.6	12,235	11,318	564	26	159	2	46	120	106	9,292
39 25452	Enon village	Clark	1.3	2,638	2,559	15	8	16	-	7	33	27	2,097
39 25704	Euclid city	Cuyahoga	10.7	52,717	34,985	16,116	62	493	13	184	864	604	40,937
39 25802	Evendale village	Hamilton	4.8	3,090	2,666	223	-	166	-	9	26	17	2,213
39 25914	Fairborn city	Greene	13.1	32,052	27,976	2,010	127	1,064	20	169	686	542	25,307
39 25970	Fairfield city	Butler, Hamilton	21.0	42,097	37,830	2,557	56	948	15	215	476	646	31,840
39 26166	Fairlawn city	Summit	4.4	7,307	6,489	447	5	241	1	32	92	79	5,821
39 26306	Fairport Harbor village	Lake	1.0	3,180	3,115	18	3	5	1	4	34	44	2,448
39 26446	Fairview Park city	Cuyahoga	4.7	17,572	16,864	113	18	276	4	64	233	264	13,670
39 27048	Findlay city	Hancock	17.2	38,967	36,513	546	74	686	10	648	490	1,539	29,697
39 27104	Finneytown CDP	Hamilton	4.0	13,492	9,843	3,215	22	149	2	61	200	108	9,762
39 27706	Forest Park city	Hamilton	6.5	19,463	7,142	10,949	22	715	15	192	428	289	14,187
39 27776	Forestville CDP	Hamilton	3.7	10,978	10,508	96	5	244	1	34	90	26	8,002
39 27846	Fort McKinley CDP	Montgomery	1.3	3,989	1,733	2,121	7	14	-	22	92	54	2,894
39 27944	Fort Shawnee village	Allen	7.2	3,855	3,638	118	3	24	1	38	33	64	2,894
39 28014	Fostoria city	Hancock, Seneca, Wood	7.3	13,931	12,165	801	27	67	-	501	370	1,104	10,163
39 28476	Franklin city	Warren	9.1	11,396	11,112	93	14	46	-	37	94	81	8,366
39 28826	Fremont city	Sandusky	7.5	17,375	14,290	1,441	32	41	-	1,016	555	2,140	12,578
39 28966	Fruit Hill CDP	Hamilton	1.3	3,945	3,846	31	12	42	-	1	13	25	2,887
39 29106	Gahanna city	Franklin	12.4	32,636	28,216	2,657	65	1,062	9	156	471	430	23,219
39 29162	Galion city	Crawford	5.0	11,341	11,146	25	35	30	1	40	64	105	8,453
39 29204	Gallipolis city	Gallia	3.6	4,180	3,786	269	18	32	-	8	67	24	3,341
39 29428	Garfield Heights city	Cuyahoga	7.2	30,734	24,807	5,164	48	286	3	132	294	388	23,342
39 29610	Geneva city	Ashtabula	4.0	6,595	6,255	76	10	16	2	119	117	392	5,019
39 29778	Georgetown village	Brown	3.7	3,691	3,571	74	4	11	-	4	27	16	2,756
39 29932	Germantown village	Montgomery	3.6	4,884	4,812	18	5	15	-	4	30	38	3,562
39 30072	Gibsonburg village	Sandusky	2.5	2,506	2,346	8	4	7	-	112	29	208	1,817
39 30198	Girard city	Trumbull	6.1	10,902	10,421	266	28	38	2	22	125	79	8,360
39 30786	Golf Manor village	Hamilton	0.6	3,999	1,369	2,515	2	28	-	15	70	24	2,977
39 31304	Grandview Heights city	Franklin	1.3	6,695	6,422	90	4	67	-	28	84	101	5,041
39 31402	Granville village	Licking	4.0	3,167	3,064	22	9	32	1	5	35	36	2,313
39 31860	Green city	Summit	32.1	22,817	22,250	165	34	178	5	28	157	111	16,871
39 32088	Greenfield city	Highland	1.9	4,906	4,699	108	4	4	6	16	69	34	3,612
39 32158	Greenhills village	Hamilton	1.2	4,103	3,884	110	1	15	-	16	77	49	3,026
39 32298	Greentown CDP	Stark	2.7	3,154	3,065	29	4	24	1	10	21	31	2,123
39 32340	Greenville city	Darke	6.0	13,294	12,937	75	22	70	2	59	129	152	10,275
39 32536	Groesbeck CDP	Hamilton	2.9	7,202	6,620	408	5	48	2	24	95	43	5,210
39 32592	Grove City city	Franklin	13.9	27,075	26,039	418	60	163	3	91	301	318	19,424
39 32606	Groveport village	Franklin	8.0	3,865	3,590	140	24	42	-	22	47	49	2,938
39 33012	Hamilton city	Butler	21.6	60,690	53,975	4,581	173	275	23	889	774	1,566	45,045
39 33838	Harrison city	Hamilton	3.7	7,487	7,351	13	7	29	1	15	71	39	5,245
39 34748	Heath city	Licking	10.4	8,527	8,151	169	28	70	1	27	81	86	6,405
39 35098	Hicksville village	Defiance	2.5	3,649	3,535	5	12	3	-	49	45	121	2,653
39 35252	Highland Heights city	Cuyahoga	5.1	8,082	7,531	112	1	372	-	5	61	36	5,915
39 35476	Hilliard city	Franklin	11.1	24,230	22,489	357	42	844	4	175	319	426	16,442
39 35560	Hillsboro city	Highland	5.2	6,368	5,768	407	13	68	2	24	86	60	4,829
39 36557	Howland Center CDP	Trumbull	4.0	6,481	6,186	108	4	102	1	11	69	52	4,941
39 36582	Hubbard city	Trumbull	3.4	8,284	8,125	76	9	12	1	12	49	38	6,361
39 36610	Huber Heights city	Miami, Montgomery	21.0	38,212	32,433	3,737	106	832	23	223	858	635	27,741
39 36624	Huber Ridge CDP	Franklin	1.1	4,883	4,450	267	10	48	-	22	86	61	3,374
39 36651	Hudson city	Summit	25.6	22,439	21,239	333	20	633	1	44	169	184	14,929
39 37016	Huron city	Erie	4.9	7,958	7,749	56	14	42	-	32	65	130	5,967
39 37240	Independence city	Cuyahoga	9.6	7,109	6,937	41	-	92	-	10	29	58	5,394
39 37464	Ironton city	Lawrence	4.1	11,211	10,463	587	10	28	2	10	111	57	8,762
39 37842	Jackson city	Jackson	7.5	6,184	6,072	27	12	16	2	18	37	53	4,656
39 38500	Jefferson village	Ashtabula	2.3	3,572	3,471	51	9	8	-	5	28	22	2,670
39 39340	Johnstown village	Licking	2.1	3,440	3,388	5	10	5	-	8	24	15	2,545
39 39872	Kent city	Portage	8.7	27,906	24,018	2,541	53	599	9	124	562	357	23,337
39 39886	Kenton city	Hardin	4.5	8,336	8,095	76	23	31	-	27	84	75	6,213
39 39914	Kenwood CDP	Hamilton	2.3	7,423	6,617	379	7	353	-	25	42	131	5,788
39 40040	Kettering city	Greene, Montgomery	18.7	57,502	54,757	955	105	795	14	189	687	640	44,563
39 40642	Kirtland city	Lake	16.6	6,670	6,568	18	10	26	2	2	44	37	5,088
39 41363	Lake Darby CDP	Franklin	3.4	3,727	3,510	71	13	21	1	32	79	58	2,462
39 41454	Lakemore village	Summit	1.5	2,561	2,505	12	9	1	1	4	29	13	1,923
39 41664	Lakewood city	Cuyahoga	5.5	56,646	52,723	1,116	139	800	15	349	1,504	1,269	44,733
39 41720	Lancaster city	Fairfield	18.1	35,335	34,409	214	107	166	13	62	364	291	26,641
39 41755	Landen CDP	Warren	4.7	12,766	11,982	189	12	345	13	99	126	278	9,026
39 42364	Lebanon city	Warren	11.8	16,962	15,432	1,079	54	109	3	62	223	191	12,355
39 42994	Lexington village	Richland	3.7	4,165	4,047	50	2	30	3	18	15	37	2,995
39 43554	Lima city	Allen	12.8	40,081	27,776	10,614	124	205	4	388	970	789	29,192

Table D-1. Places — **Area and Population**—Con.

[Includes incorporated places and census designated places (CDPs) of 2,500 or more population as of April 1, 2000. Codes shown are two-digit Federal Information Processing Standards (FIPS) state codes and five-digit FIPS place codes. Place names and codes are those in effect as of January 1, 2000. County refers to the county (or counties) in which the place is located. IC in this column = independent city, a county equivalent. If a place is located in more than one county, counties are listed in alphabetic order]

State and place code	Place	County	Land area, 2000 (sq. mi.)	Population, 2000 (April 1) By race— One race Total	White	Black or African American	American Indian and Alaska Native	Asian	Native Hawaiian and Other Pacific Islander	Some other race	Two or more races	Hispanic or Latino (of any race)	18 years and over
39 00000	OHIO—Con.												
39 43722	Lincoln Heights village	Hamilton	0.7	4,113	39	4,025	4	1	1	7	36	35	2,705
39 43792	Lincoln Village CDP	Franklin	1.9	9,482	8,641	355	36	54	2	276	118	474	7,257
39 44030	Lisbon village	Columbiana	1.1	2,788	2,725	25	6	6	1	8	17	17	2,094
39 44366	Lockland village	Hamilton	1.2	3,707	2,611	975	10	17	-	35	59	57	2,816
39 44604	Lodi village	Medina	2.1	3,061	3,016	1	11	5	-	2	27	15	2,277
39 44632	Logan city	Hocking	3.1	6,704	6,561	38	26	4	-	1	74	31	5,066
39 44674	London city	Madison	8.5	8,771	7,890	595	26	37	2	37	184	62	6,438
39 44856	Lorain city	Lorain	24.0	68,652	47,848	10,943	304	227	24	6,565	2,741	14,438	49,198
39 44912	Lordstown village	Trumbull	23.1	3,633	3,482	105	3	13	-	4	26	16	2,760
39 45066	Loudonville village	Ashland, Holmes	2.5	2,906	2,875	-	1	6	-	5	19	15	2,192
39 45094	Louisville city	Stark	5.2	8,904	8,773	28	13	26	-	6	58	74	6,492
39 45108	Loveland city	Clermont, Hamilton, Warren	4.6	11,677	11,170	182	6	123	-	49	147	131	8,275
39 45556	Lyndhurst city	Cuyahoga	4.4	15,279	14,778	196	1	182	2	30	90	104	12,245
39 45934	McDonald village	Trumbull	1.7	3,481	3,402	35	9	4	1	7	23	33	2,581
39 45976	Macedonia city	Summit	9.7	9,224	8,433	516	14	169	-	22	70	69	6,757
39 46151	Mack North CDP	Hamilton	3.1	3,529	3,462	28	11	4	-	3	21	25	2,450
39 46162	Mack South CDP	Hamilton	3.7	5,837	5,779	2	5	25	2	2	22	16	4,209
39 46312	Madeira city	Hamilton	3.4	8,923	8,539	115	12	169	-	31	57	69	6,538
39 46480	Madison village	Lake	4.6	2,921	2,873	13	4	6	-	4	21	24	2,155
39 47138	Mansfield city	Richland	29.9	49,346	37,885	9,695	137	311	20	275	1,023	605	37,547
39 47306	Maple Heights city	Cuyahoga	5.2	26,156	13,509	11,598	33	452	6	124	434	316	19,430
39 47600	Mariemont village	Hamilton	0.9	3,408	3,303	34	8	27	4	7	25	35	2,493
39 47628	Marietta city	Washington	8.3	14,515	13,979	157	67	103	8	40	161	114	11,476
39 47754	Marion city	Marion	11.3	35,318	31,926	2,475	69	192	4	227	425	474	26,414
39 48104	Martins Ferry city	Belmont	2.2	7,226	6,734	369	22	3	2	16	80	46	5,605
39 48160	Marysville city	Union	15.5	15,942	14,559	981	25	154	4	39	180	167	11,762
39 48188	Mason city	Warren	17.6	22,016	20,868	354	42	481	2	65	204	213	14,956
39 48244	Massillon city	Stark	16.7	31,325	27,622	2,942	71	79	1	108	502	301	23,403
39 48272	Masury CDP	Trumbull	3.6	2,618	2,477	86	1	5	-	8	41	22	2,001
39 48342	Maumee city	Lucas	9.9	15,237	14,720	160	8	109	5	89	146	277	11,507
39 48468	Mayfield village	Cuyahoga	3.9	3,435	3,244	45	1	123	-	6	16	27	2,722
39 48482	Mayfield Heights city	Cuyahoga	4.2	19,386	17,806	577	5	782	1	34	181	201	16,266
39 48790	Medina city	Medina	11.1	25,139	23,781	697	48	186	7	65	355	252	17,613
39 49056	Mentor city	Lake	26.8	50,278	48,920	324	24	597	16	91	306	363	37,247
39 49098	Mentor-on-the-Lake city	Lake	1.6	8,127	7,895	66	6	53	-	24	83	97	6,130
39 49434	Miamisburg city	Montgomery	11.2	19,489	18,699	310	26	143	7	53	251	165	14,451
39 49644	Middleburg Heights city	Cuyahoga	8.1	15,542	14,708	206	24	351	11	43	199	197	12,795
39 49756	Middleport village	Meigs	1.8	2,525	2,415	60	9	4	-	3	34	14	1,947
39 49840	Middletown city	Butler, Warren	25.7	51,605	44,886	5,467	128	190	18	185	731	460	38,693
39 50176	Milford city	Clermont, Hamilton	3.8	6,284	5,975	209	8	28	2	20	42	57	4,864
39 50372	Millersburg village	Holmes	2.0	3,326	3,222	49	-	3	1	18	33	67	2,502
39 50778	Mineral Ridge CDP	Mahoning, Trumbull	3.3	3,900	3,756	81	4	4	1	24	30	59	2,946
39 50834	Minerva village	Carroll, Columbiana, Stark	2.1	3,934	3,896	2	3	5	-	2	26	19	3,007
39 50904	Mingo Junction village	Jefferson	2.5	3,631	3,462	109	6	1	4	14	35	28	2,865
39 50918	Minster village	Auglaize	1.9	2,794	2,785	-	2	2	-	-	5	3	1,985
39 51058	Mogadore village	Portage, Summit	2.1	3,893	3,842	7	2	6	-	-	36	10	2,930
39 51215	Monfort Heights East CDP	Hamilton	1.4	3,880	3,519	250	8	59	-	10	34	21	2,793
39 51217	Monfort Heights South CDP	Hamilton	3.1	4,466	4,364	32	5	27	-	4	34	23	3,347
39 51310	Monroe city	Butler, Warren	15.5	7,133	6,930	101	7	24	-	16	55	46	5,504
39 51716	Montgomery city	Hamilton	5.3	10,163	9,553	160	5	331	-	10	104	78	7,304
39 51772	Montpelier village	Williams	2.7	4,320	4,174	13	7	64	1	28	33	66	3,137
39 51816	Montrose-Ghent CDP	Summit	9.4	5,261	5,078	46	4	97	-	3	33	30	3,938
39 52010	Moraine city	Montgomery	9.1	6,897	6,175	430	30	138	-	35	89	97	5,148
39 52052	Moreland Hills village	Cuyahoga	7.2	3,298	3,067	100	1	107	-	3	20	22	2,535
39 52612	Mount Carmel CDP	Clermont	1.7	4,308	4,170	36	9	13	-	28	52	52	3,180
39 52738	Mount Gilead village	Morrow	3.2	3,290	3,217	35	4	8	-	10	16	34	2,501
39 52752	Mount Healthy city	Hamilton	1.4	7,149	5,269	1,667	14	35	4	43	117	73	5,433
39 52780	Mount Healthy Heights CDP	Hamilton	0.8	3,450	2,528	805	3	42	-	19	53	34	2,508
39 53032	Mount Repose CDP	Clermont	2.0	4,102	3,980	43	8	28	-	4	39	35	2,923
39 53102	Mount Vernon city	Knox	8.4	14,375	13,895	166	45	78	-	41	150	125	10,962
39 53270	Mulberry CDP	Clermont	1.5	3,139	3,053	29	9	23	1	6	18	23	2,496
39 53312	Munroe Falls city	Summit	2.7	5,314	5,160	49	1	63	3	5	33	37	4,005
39 53550	Napoleon city	Henry	5.6	9,318	8,724	78	32	57	-	328	99	591	6,905
39 53886	Nelsonville city	Athens	5.0	5,230	4,980	125	25	19	-	13	68	65	4,260
39 53970	New Albany village	Franklin	8.9	3,711	3,495	58	12	102	-	13	31	30	2,483
39 54040	Newark city	Licking	19.6	46,279	43,560	1,435	140	278	14	155	697	390	34,543
39 54194	New Bremen village	Auglaize	2.1	2,909	2,859	1	11	15	-	4	19	9	1,991
39 54334	New Carlisle city	Clark	1.9	5,735	5,516	19	15	20	1	96	68	157	4,182
39 54432	Newcomerstown village	Tuscarawas	2.5	4,008	3,841	103	10	3	-	8	43	29	2,963
39 54446	New Concord village	Muskingum	1.5	2,651	2,549	38	3	44	-	2	15	24	2,315
39 54852	New Lebanon village	Montgomery	2.0	4,231	4,166	14	4	7	-	10	30	32	3,031
39 54866	New Lexington city	Perry	2.3	4,689	4,631	8	11	6	2	6	25	18	3,373
39 54908	New London village	Huron	2.1	2,696	2,585	68	-	5	2	8	28	19	1,939
39 55216	New Philadelphia city	Tuscarawas	7.8	17,056	16,525	165	30	84	10	83	159	227	13,130

Table D-1. Places — **Area and Population**—Con.

[Includes incorporated places and census designated places (CDPs) of 2,500 or more population as of April 1, 2000. Codes shown are two-digit Federal Information Processing Standards (FIPS) state codes and five-digit FIPS place codes. Place names and codes are those in effect as of January 1, 2000. County refers to the county (or counties) in which the place is located. IC in this column = independent city, a county equivalent. If a place is located in more than one county, counties are listed in alphabetic order]

State and place code	Place	County	Land area, 2000 (sq. mi.)	Population, 2000 (April 1) Total	White	Black or African American	American Indian and Alaska Native	Asian	Native Hawaiian and Other Pacific Islander	Some other race	Two or more races	Hispanic or Latino (of any race)	18 years and over
39 00000	OHIO—Con.												
39 55650	Newton Falls village	Trumbull	2.3	5,002	4,907	19	21	3	2	12	38	32	3,760
39 55916	Niles city	Trumbull	8.6	20,932	20,090	475	39	69	2	47	210	174	16,273
39 56154	North Baltimore village	Wood	2.2	3,361	3,254	-	12	13	-	38	44	112	2,413
39 56280	Northbrook CDP	Hamilton	1.9	11,076	9,099	1,568	39	107	10	63	190	173	7,899
39 56294	North Canton city	Stark	6.1	16,369	15,862	183	11	170	-	30	113	134	13,211
39 56322	North College Hill city	Hamilton	1.8	10,082	7,682	2,187	23	26	1	47	116	59	7,514
39 56448	Northfield village	Summit	1.1	3,827	3,540	130	9	84	-	24	40	32	2,896
39 56553	Northgate CDP	Hamilton	2.5	8,016	6,911	831	7	105	6	51	105	115	5,822
39 56700	North Kingsville village	Ashtabula	8.9	2,658	2,593	10	6	15	-	11	23	31	2,006
39 56812	North Madison CDP	Lake	4.0	8,451	8,290	10	20	32	-	32	67	120	5,979
39 56882	North Olmsted city	Cuyahoga	11.6	34,113	32,055	346	43	936	4	155	574	575	26,039
39 56938	Northridge CDP	Clark	3.1	6,853	6,701	83	-	24	-	5	40	33	5,276
39 56952	Northridge CDP	Montgomery	2.3	8,487	7,298	1,011	22	7	3	36	110	66	6,103
39 56966	North Ridgeville city	Lorain	23.4	22,338	21,526	192	48	206	1	109	256	445	16,884
39 57008	North Royalton city	Cuyahoga	21.3	28,648	27,553	203	33	570	6	45	238	273	21,694
39 57190	Northwood city	Wood	8.4	5,471	5,197	33	22	54	2	94	69	223	4,004
39 57218	North Zanesville CDP	Muskingum	3.6	3,013	2,882	53	2	45	-	7	24	12	2,315
39 57260	Norton city	Summit, Wayne	20.1	11,523	11,218	154	20	32	4	16	79	47	8,696
39 57302	Norwalk city	Huron	8.3	16,238	15,350	316	35	52	-	302	183	620	11,700
39 57386	Norwood city	Hamilton	3.1	21,675	20,429	509	80	167	4	190	296	401	16,603
39 57582	Oak Harbor village	Ottawa	1.3	2,841	2,788	2	5	11	9	11	15	55	2,095
39 57750	Oakwood village	Cuyahoga	3.5	3,667	1,491	2,062	7	13	1	26	67	51	2,879
39 57764	Oakwood city	Montgomery	2.2	9,215	8,976	44	6	90	3	27	69	111	6,531
39 57834	Oberlin city	Lorain	4.4	8,195	5,894	1,520	40	279	14	99	349	249	6,994
39 57862	Obetz village	Franklin	3.8	3,977	3,727	115	28	6	1	23	77	59	2,868
39 58422	Olmsted Falls city	Cuyahoga	4.1	7,962	7,700	104	3	58	5	22	70	120	5,847
39 58520	Ontario village	Richland	10.9	5,303	4,898	218	2	84	2	30	69	57	3,968
39 58604	Orange village	Cuyahoga	3.8	3,236	2,636	409	2	136	3	8	42	23	2,304
39 58730	Oregon city	Lucas	29.4	19,355	18,369	193	28	136	2	333	294	922	14,690
39 58828	Orrville city	Wayne	5.3	8,551	7,772	507	14	98	1	44	115	110	6,195
39 58982	Ottawa village	Putnam	3.9	4,367	4,120	12	4	19	-	163	49	321	3,198
39 59010	Ottawa Hills village	Lucas	1.9	4,564	4,289	57	4	123	-	21	70	56	3,188
39 59234	Oxford city	Butler	5.9	21,943	20,013	947	38	530	5	105	305	317	20,131
39 59416	Painesville city	Lake	6.0	17,503	13,475	2,264	51	74	1	1,138	500	2,256	12,646
39 59920	Park Layne CDP	Clark	1.5	4,519	4,365	21	17	12	-	17	87	66	3,146
39 61000	Parma city	Cuyahoga	20.0	85,655	81,948	905	118	1,349	17	384	934	1,323	66,570
39 61028	Parma Heights city	Cuyahoga	4.2	21,659	20,523	253	29	505	3	98	248	351	17,521
39 61112	Pataskala city	Licking	28.5	10,249	9,693	303	35	55	1	57	105	104	7,396
39 61252	Paulding village	Paulding	2.3	3,595	3,273	92	8	10	-	137	75	249	2,674
39 61686	Pepper Pike city	Cuyahoga	7.1	6,040	5,432	294	3	251	-	20	40	70	4,614
39 62134	Perry Heights CDP	Stark	2.9	8,900	8,470	247	28	21	-	51	83	128	6,833
39 62148	Perrysburg city	Wood	8.9	16,945	16,156	174	17	300	4	152	142	348	12,037
39 62498	Pickerington city	Fairfield, Franklin	7.4	9,792	9,124	364	8	135	4	40	117	132	6,588
39 62848	Piqua city	Miami	10.7	20,738	19,537	700	69	92	-	56	284	153	15,246
39 63030	Plain City village	Madison, Union	1.8	2,832	2,745	22	4	8	1	21	31	34	2,038
39 63604	Pleasant Run CDP	Hamilton	2.1	5,267	4,669	405	21	101	2	12	57	61	3,722
39 63618	Pleasant Run Farm CDP	Hamilton	1.0	4,731	3,507	1,081	5	65	3	17	53	32	3,248
39 63954	Poland village	Mahoning	1.2	2,866	2,842	7	-	3	-	5	9	28	2,162
39 64136	Portage Lakes CDP	Summit	6.6	9,870	9,652	56	31	31	1	20	79	57	7,843
39 64150	Port Clinton city	Ottawa	2.1	6,391	5,953	152	20	22	2	147	95	384	4,966
39 64304	Portsmouth city	Scioto	10.8	20,909	19,131	1,046	132	127	4	67	402	195	16,306
39 64486	Powell village	Delaware	3.0	6,247	5,890	97	7	186	-	14	53	68	4,006
39 65592	Ravenna city	Portage	5.4	11,771	10,950	520	30	46	2	27	196	107	8,976
39 65732	Reading city	Hamilton	2.9	11,292	10,579	361	18	133	2	58	141	89	8,753
39 66390	Reynoldsburg city	Fairfield, Franklin, Licking	10.6	32,069	27,261	3,347	86	541	15	238	581	578	23,530
39 66530	Richfield village	Summit	8.5	3,286	3,199	16	10	43	1	2	15	8	2,511
39 66894	Richmond Heights city	Cuyahoga	4.4	10,944	7,549	2,612	6	519	4	71	183	173	8,785
39 67356	Rittman city	Medina, Wayne	6.0	6,314	6,196	6	14	24	-	17	57	56	4,640
39 67468	Riverside city	Montgomery	7.9	23,545	21,532	1,003	50	414	11	143	392	364	18,012
39 68056	Rocky River city	Cuyahoga	4.8	20,735	20,077	84	14	276	4	57	223	248	16,392
39 68686	Rossford city	Wood	4.3	6,406	6,167	82	13	52	1	31	60	108	4,780
39 69400	Sabina village	Clinton	1.3	2,780	2,710	17	8	12	-	2	31	32	2,019
39 69470	St. Bernard city	Hamilton	1.5	4,924	4,501	318	9	31	1	21	43	32	3,674
39 69526	St. Clairsville city	Belmont	2.1	5,057	4,778	156	2	69	2	8	42	24	4,054
39 69680	St. Marys city	Auglaize	4.3	8,342	8,133	29	11	82	2	12	73	38	5,979
39 69834	Salem city	Columbiana	5.5	12,197	11,996	63	11	42	3	10	72	66	9,417
39 70380	Sandusky city	Erie	10.0	27,844	20,745	5,870	80	73	4	270	802	859	20,661
39 70422	Sandusky South CDP	Erie	4.3	6,599	5,812	626	13	41	-	13	94	76	5,132
39 71220	Sebring village	Mahoning	2.1	4,912	4,832	23	4	8	1	12	32	38	3,850
39 71416	Seven Hills city	Cuyahoga	5.0	12,080	11,739	18	4	256	-	13	51	92	9,884
39 71640	Shadyside village	Belmont	1.0	3,675	3,647	4	3	2	-	2	17	8	2,954
39 71682	Shaker Heights city	Cuyahoga	6.3	29,405	17,624	10,030	19	928	4	147	653	339	21,698
39 71892	Sharonville city	Butler, Hamilton	9.8	13,804	12,250	666	16	524	3	133	212	317	10,964
39 72060	Sheffield village	Lorain	10.8	2,949	2,680	126	3	24	3	77	36	175	2,174
39 72088	Sheffield Lake city	Lorain	2.5	9,371	9,059	91	38	27	2	57	97	281	6,891
39 72102	Shelby city	Richland	5.0	9,821	9,664	14	18	34	-	36	55	100	7,295
39 72252	Sherwood CDP	Hamilton	1.1	3,907	3,772	24	-	60	1	19	31	50	2,690

Table D-1. Places — Area and Population—Con.

[Includes incorporated places and census designated places (CDPs) of 2,500 or more population as of April 1, 2000. Codes shown are two-digit Federal Information Processing Standards (FIPS) state codes and five-digit FIPS place codes. Place names and codes are those in effect as of January 1, 2000. County refers to the county (or counties) in which the place is located. IC in this column = independent city, a county equivalent. If a place is located in more than one county, counties are listed in alphabetic order]

State and place code	Place	County	Land area, 2000 (sq. mi.)	Population, 2000 (April 1)									
					By race—						Two or more races	Hispanic or Latino (of any race)	18 years and over
					One race								
				Total	White	Black or African American	American Indian and Alaska Native	Asian	Native Hawaiian and Other Pacific Islander	Some other race			
39 00000	OHIO—Con.												
39 72284	Shiloh CDP	Montgomery	3.8	11,272	6,949	3,937	22	78	5	56	225	130	9,323
39 72424	Sidney city	Shelby	10.4	20,211	18,717	618	49	377	21	80	349	262	14,541
39 72494	Silver Lake village	Summit	1.4	3,019	2,966	4	3	21	-	5	20	24	2,334
39 72522	Silverton city	Hamilton	1.1	5,178	2,357	2,605	10	42	2	40	122	60	4,202
39 72928	Solon city	Cuyahoga	20.6	21,802	19,140	1,334	8	1,070	2	37	211	153	15,144
39 73264	South Euclid city	Cuyahoga	4.7	23,537	17,709	5,032	24	353	3	99	317	241	17,643
39 73446	South Lebanon village	Warren	1.7	2,538	2,502	1	5	5	-	8	17	28	1,843
39 73670	South Point village	Lawrence	2.4	3,742	3,589	85	3	6	1	-	58	12	2,877
39 73684	South Russell village	Geauga	3.9	4,022	3,959	14	-	32	-	-	17	29	2,703
39 74076	Springboro city	Montgomery, Warren	8.8	12,380	11,885	123	20	198	4	36	114	124	8,376
39 74104	Springdale city	Hamilton	5.0	10,563	7,223	2,707	12	267	2	158	194	384	8,032
39 74118	Springfield city	Clark	22.5	65,358	51,007	11,909	223	455	14	354	1,396	770	48,646
39 74608	Steubenville city	Jefferson	10.3	19,015	15,127	3,281	42	139	2	100	324	185	14,988
39 74944	Stow city	Summit	17.1	32,139	30,596	495	35	615	4	95	299	291	23,773
39 75014	Streetsboro city	Portage	24.0	12,311	11,744	241	11	169	2	18	126	96	9,320
39 75098	Strongsville city	Cuyahoga	24.6	43,858	41,304	551	21	1,406	4	122	450	557	32,330
39 75126	Struthers city	Mahoning	3.7	11,756	11,360	209	22	22	1	55	87	237	9,015
39 75434	Summerside CDP	Clermont	2.3	5,523	5,309	63	14	56	-	25	56	61	4,045
39 75602	Sunbury village	Delaware	2.5	2,630	2,573	10	10	6	1	6	24	29	1,931
39 75896	Swanton village	Fulton, Lucas	2.4	3,307	3,255	6	6	6	-	20	14	46	2,446
39 76022	Sylvania city	Lucas	5.8	18,670	17,774	186	18	392	1	120	179	304	13,397
39 76106	Tallmadge city	Portage, Summit	14.0	16,390	15,698	341	19	142	5	13	172	94	12,458
39 76568	The Plains CDP	Athens	2.3	2,931	2,759	71	9	32	-	8	52	24	2,243
39 76582	The Village of Indian Hill city	Hamilton	18.5	5,907	5,577	32	5	229	-	9	55	35	4,119
39 76778	Tiffin city	Seneca	6.5	18,135	17,457	264	31	92	3	107	181	380	14,088
39 76876	Tipp City city	Miami	6.2	9,221	8,994	23	21	83	-	36	64	111	6,625
39 77000	Toledo city	Lucas	80.6	313,619	220,261	73,854	970	3,233	76	7,166	8,059	17,141	231,488
39 77112	Toronto city	Jefferson	1.9	5,676	5,540	57	11	12	-	4	52	27	4,380
39 77322	Trenton city	Butler	3.8	8,746	8,592	42	16	25	-	18	53	76	6,161
39 77504	Trotwood city	Montgomery	30.5	27,420	10,600	15,998	88	67	4	119	544	224	20,233
39 77588	Troy city	Miami	9.7	21,999	20,140	1,051	46	366	2	65	329	170	16,364
39 77840	Turpin Hills CDP	Hamilton	3.0	4,960	4,793	31	17	81	-	15	23	53	3,443
39 78050	Twinsburg city	Summit	12.4	17,006	14,783	1,484	19	502	2	53	163	176	12,462
39 78176	Uhrichsville city	Tuscarawas	2.9	5,662	5,525	63	11	7	-	5	51	35	4,052
39 78470	Union city	Miami, Montgomery	4.3	5,574	5,400	51	8	20	1	20	74	66	3,973
39 78736	Uniontown CDP	Stark	2.5	2,802	2,750	9	4	15	-	4	20	14	2,217
39 78932	University Heights city	Cuyahoga	1.8	14,146	10,671	2,916	14	240	6	88	211	221	11,206
39 79002	Upper Arlington city	Franklin	9.8	33,686	31,906	200	35	1,185	3	90	267	330	25,311
39 79044	Upper Sandusky city	Wyandot	5.2	6,533	6,347	12	6	37	-	95	36	177	4,999
39 79072	Urbana city	Champaign	6.8	11,613	10,571	691	39	35	3	56	218	126	8,858
39 79492	Vandalia city	Montgomery	11.8	14,603	14,031	187	19	179	4	51	132	130	11,155
39 79562	Van Wert city	Van Wert	5.9	10,690	10,270	160	12	37	-	116	95	241	8,115
39 79716	Vermilion city	Erie, Lorain	10.8	10,927	10,724	19	10	23	-	37	114	190	8,158
39 79912	Versailles village	Darke	1.7	2,589	2,573	1	3	2	-	3	7	3	1,929
39 80304	Wadsworth city	Medina	9.5	18,437	18,040	72	45	113	2	35	130	125	13,583
39 80486	Walbridge village	Wood	1.7	2,546	2,477	13	8	6	-	18	24	68	1,951
39 80766	Wapakoneta city	Auglaize	5.7	9,474	9,281	18	25	37	5	35	73	82	6,993
39 80892	Warren city	Trumbull	16.1	46,832	33,690	11,802	62	195	16	142	925	485	34,510
39 80990	Warrensville Heights city	Cuyahoga	4.1	15,109	993	13,660	26	138	6	48	238	113	11,246
39 81214	Washington city	Fayette	6.4	13,524	12,783	367	21	111	2	89	151	187	10,143
39 81858	Waterville village	Lucas	3.5	4,828	4,727	7	7	17	-	27	43	65	3,472
39 81928	Wauseon city	Fulton	4.9	7,091	6,578	39	26	58	1	285	104	694	5,026
39 81942	Waverly City city	Pike	3.9	4,433	4,289	51	26	24	2	1	40	17	3,515
39 82418	Waynesville village	Warren	2.3	2,558	2,515	2	6	2	-	4	29	19	1,856
39 82642	Wellington village	Lorain	2.9	4,511	4,382	60	12	6	1	9	41	47	3,286
39 82712	Wellston city	Jackson	7.0	6,078	5,961	22	17	10	-	13	55	37	4,443
39 82740	Wellsville village	Columbiana	1.8	4,133	3,744	288	5	5	1	2	88	16	3,047
39 83111	West Carrollton City city	Montgomery	6.3	13,818	12,794	582	29	163	1	70	179	199	10,748
39 83342	Westerville city	Delaware, Franklin	12.4	35,318	33,035	1,131	46	549	10	127	420	379	25,831
39 83541	West Hill CDP	Trumbull	1.6	2,523	2,208	265	4	9	1	6	30	18	1,944
39 83580	West Jefferson village	Madison	3.3	4,331	4,288	1	7	6	1	4	24	25	3,146
39 83622	Westlake city	Cuyahoga	15.9	31,719	29,477	301	18	1,332	5	106	480	402	24,485
39 83902	West Milton village	Miami	2.4	4,645	4,579	13	8	12	-	8	25	30	3,345
39 84140	West Portsmouth CDP	Scioto	4.7	3,458	3,354	3	51	2	-	5	43	3	2,562
39 84294	West Union village	Adams	2.6	2,903	2,848	7	21	3	2	3	19	13	2,263
39 84588	Wheelersburg CDP	Scioto	5.8	6,471	6,335	18	41	9	1	10	57	29	4,913
39 84742	Whitehall city	Franklin	5.2	19,201	14,285	3,678	74	391	6	233	534	566	14,334
39 84770	Whitehouse village	Lucas	3.5	2,733	2,691	3	3	7	1	17	11	33	2,008
39 84812	White Oak CDP	Hamilton	4.1	13,277	12,464	471	22	145	-	54	121	143	9,763
39 84831	White Oak East CDP	Hamilton	0.8	3,508	3,406	43	8	32	-	9	10	16	2,690
39 84864	White Oak West CDP	Hamilton	1.3	2,932	2,862	33	5	16	-	3	13	5	2,248
39 85036	Wickliffe city	Lake	4.7	13,484	12,860	384	6	106	2	12	114	72	10,768
39 85232	Willard city	Huron	3.5	6,806	6,147	105	13	21	1	416	103	849	4,712
39 85484	Willoughby city	Lake	10.2	22,621	21,822	258	38	261	14	25	203	161	17,842
39 85512	Willoughby Hills city	Lake	10.8	8,595	7,636	556	7	305	-	13	79	60	7,036
39 85638	Willowick city	Lake	2.5	14,361	14,052	107	7	88	-	5	102	102	11,317
39 85792	Wilmington city	Clinton	7.5	11,921	10,807	801	27	77	1	30	178	100	9,092

Table D-1. Places — **Area and Population**—Con.

[Includes incorporated places and census designated places (CDPs) of 2,500 or more population as of April 1, 2000. Codes shown are two-digit Federal Information Processing Standards (FIPS) state codes and five-digit FIPS place codes. Place names and codes are those in effect as of January 1, 2000. County refers to the county (or counties) in which the place is located. IC in this column = independent city, a county equivalent. If a place is located in more than one county, counties are listed in alphabetic order]

				Population, 2000 (April 1)									
					By race—								
					One race								
State and place code	Place	County	Land area, 2000 (sq. mi.)	Total	White	Black or African American	American Indian and Alaska Native	Asian	Native Hawaiian and Other Pacific Islander	Some other race	Two or more races	Hispanic or Latino (of any race)	18 years and over
39 00000	OHIO—Con.												
39 85946	Windham village	Portage	2.1	2,806	2,608	138	6	2	-	5	47	12	1,800
39 86184	Wintersville village	Jefferson	3.5	4,067	3,775	245	1	8	-	1	37	23	3,319
39 86254	Withamsville CDP	Clermont	1.8	3,145	3,064	24	3	25	1	14	14	24	2,374
39 86331	Woodbourne-Hyde Park CDP	Montgomery	4.6	7,910	7,601	80	6	146	-	18	59	63	6,201
39 86366	Woodlawn village	Hamilton	2.6	2,816	763	1,926	3	67	-	25	32	36	2,189
39 86436	Woodsfield village	Monroe	2.0	2,598	2,567	1	5	3	1	7	14	15	2,060
39 86548	Wooster city	Wayne	14.4	24,811	22,972	947	64	383	2	90	353	266	19,360
39 86604	Worthington city	Franklin	5.7	14,125	13,273	241	17	391	1	31	171	138	10,744
39 86660	Wright-Patterson AFB CDP	Greene, Montgomery	11.7	6,656	5,066	1,015	30	153	8	139	245	296	3,826
39 86730	Wyoming city	Hamilton	2.9	8,261	7,231	788	11	112	-	32	87	106	5,735
39 86772	Xenia city	Greene	12.1	24,164	20,128	3,265	83	70	12	128	478	264	17,608
39 86940	Yellow Springs village	Greene	1.9	3,761	2,880	563	19	56	-	27	216	73	3,068
39 88000	Youngstown city	Mahoning, Trumbull	33.9	82,026	41,737	35,937	246	267	29	1,797	2,013	4,282	60,863
39 88084	Zanesville city	Muskingum	11.2	25,586	21,870	2,753	102	59	5	107	690	202	18,732
40 00000	OKLAHOMA		68,667.1	3,450,654	2,628,434	260,968	273,230	46,767	2,372	82,898	155,985	179,304	2,558,294
40 00200	Ada city	Pontotoc	15.7	15,691	11,582	555	2,370	130	12	140	912	453	12,191
40 01700	Altus city	Jackson	16.8	21,447	15,574	2,233	318	295	42	2,214	771	3,699	15,058
40 01800	Alva city	Woods	2.4	5,288	5,023	69	71	41	2	12	70	96	4,288
40 02050	Anadarko city	Caddo	7.1	6,645	2,749	414	2,742	16	2	204	518	608	4,479
40 02250	Antlers city	Pushmataha	2.7	2,552	1,994	47	381	2	-	8	120	45	1,870
40 02600	Ardmore city	Carter	49.1	23,711	17,313	2,672	2,083	234	4	368	1,037	877	17,752
40 03300	Atoka city	Atoka	8.4	2,988	2,177	344	307	8	-	3	149	27	2,256
40 04450	Bartlesville city	Osage, Washington	21.1	34,748	28,524	1,112	2,496	332	6	353	1,925	1,049	26,082
40 05700	Bethany city	Oklahoma	5.2	20,307	17,422	886	583	281	11	442	682	1,178	15,633
40 05800	Bethel Acres town	Pottawatomie	28.2	2,735	2,422	14	162	9	1	12	115	36	1,977
40 06400	Bixby city	Tulsa, Wagoner	24.1	13,336	11,590	125	765	65	2	261	528	530	9,489
40 06600	Blackwell city	Kay	5.4	7,668	6,691	10	317	36	1	243	370	453	5,600
40 06700	Blanchard city	Grady, McClain	11.1	2,816	2,580	9	91	6	-	15	115	68	2,043
40 08900	Bristow city	Creek	3.3	4,325	3,262	368	460	7	-	19	209	87	3,120
40 09050	Broken Arrow city	Tulsa, Wagoner	45.0	74,859	63,886	2,793	3,007	1,425	39	912	2,797	2,664	51,771
40 09100	Broken Bow city	McCurtain	5.0	4,230	2,717	399	753	8	2	87	264	225	2,925
40 12900	Catoosa city	Rogers, Wagoner	7.0	5,449	4,337	27	661	7	2	48	367	188	3,833
40 13500	Chandler city	Lincoln	7.3	2,842	2,267	275	160	11	-	14	115	51	2,111
40 13650	Checotah city	McIntosh	8.9	3,481	2,364	241	554	8	3	14	297	45	2,572
40 13950	Chickasha city	Grady	18.1	15,850	12,870	1,339	750	115	1	241	534	596	11,997
40 14200	Choctaw city	Oklahoma	27.1	9,377	8,327	154	347	58	6	80	405	262	6,953
40 14700	Claremore city	Rogers	12.0	15,873	12,015	316	2,271	70	4	178	1,019	479	11,630
40 15350	Cleveland city	Pawnee	2.6	3,282	2,796	7	294	15	2	11	157	34	2,432
40 15400	Clinton city	Custer, Washita	8.9	8,833	6,088	514	564	69	2	1,203	393	1,677	6,395
40 16350	Collinsville city	Rogers, Tulsa	5.9	4,077	3,382	15	361	16	4	14	285	70	2,978
40 16500	Commerce city	Ottawa	0.8	2,645	1,800	17	353	5	3	309	158	490	1,860
40 17800	Coweta city	Wagoner	7.6	7,139	5,410	291	846	15	1	125	451	271	4,936
40 18850	Cushing city	Payne	7.6	8,371	6,668	588	667	11	-	75	362	226	6,450
40 19450	Davis city	Garvin, Murray	11.0	2,610	2,097	119	278	10	-	13	93	27	1,912
40 19900	Del City city	Oklahoma	7.5	22,128	16,427	3,106	942	349	25	406	873	1,043	16,309
40 20550	Dewey city	Washington	2.5	3,179	2,500	69	350	2	-	53	205	105	2,367
40 21750	Drumright city	Creek, Payne	7.1	2,905	2,453	27	246	1	-	5	173	26	2,164
40 21900	Duncan city	Stephens	38.8	22,505	19,462	915	889	106	10	531	592	1,349	17,081
40 22050	Durant city	Bryan	19.0	13,549	10,702	209	1,663	122	6	213	634	483	10,408
40 23200	Edmond city	Oklahoma	85.1	68,315	59,144	2,760	1,554	2,225	53	617	1,962	1,881	49,531
40 23500	Elk City city	Beckham	14.6	10,510	9,349	322	317	57	3	236	226	626	7,648
40 23700	El Reno city	Canadian	80.0	16,212	12,384	1,273	1,594	103	3	377	478	1,219	12,284
40 23950	Enid city	Garfield	74.0	47,045	41,015	1,840	999	472	271	1,112	1,336	2,232	35,388
40 24650	Eufaula city	McIntosh	6.6	2,639	1,754	196	473	8	1	7	200	32	2,090
40 25100	Fairview city	Major	7.0	2,733	2,644	2	34	3	-	7	43	40	2,073
40 27200	Fort Gibson town	Cherokee, Muskogee	13.4	4,054	2,787	81	801	5	-	103	277	198	2,805
40 27800	Frederick city	Tillman	5.0	4,637	3,155	525	130	20	2	642	163	1,021	3,382
40 29600	Glenpool city	Tulsa	9.3	8,123	6,246	184	1,054	74	1	80	484	271	5,403
40 31600	Grove city	Delaware	9.0	5,131	4,238	4	523	27	2	33	304	88	4,110
40 31700	Guthrie city	Logan	18.7	9,925	7,527	1,565	295	42	2	193	301	376	7,470
40 31750	Guymon city	Texas	7.3	10,472	7,376	88	138	89	18	2,457	306	4,018	7,423
40 32750	Harrah city	Oklahoma	11.9	4,719	4,149	32	296	12	3	16	211	117	3,385
40 33350	Healdton city	Carter	14.1	2,786	2,426	26	208	3	1	24	98	43	2,117
40 33400	Heavener city	Le Flore	4.9	3,201	2,362	20	315	5	-	338	161	721	2,360
40 33750	Henryetta city	Okmulgee	6.0	6,096	4,858	35	750	20	1	48	384	134	4,515
40 35000	Hobart city	Kiowa	2.7	3,997	3,198	327	175	24	4	153	116	356	2,996
40 35400	Holdenville city	Hughes	4.8	4,732	3,552	163	685	13	-	47	272	116	3,562
40 35850	Hominy city	Osage	2.0	2,584	1,661	49	654	4	-	8	208	84	1,823
40 36300	Hugo city	Choctaw	5.5	5,536	3,290	1,140	778	15	1	21	291	89	4,064
40 36750	Idabel city	McCurtain	15.9	6,952	3,962	1,700	726	21	1	234	308	345	4,904
40 37800	Jenks city	Tulsa	14.3	9,557	8,352	151	453	77	2	165	357	394	6,717
40 38350	Jones town	Oklahoma	13.7	2,517	2,219	111	84	4	-	15	84	74	1,887
40 39850	Kingfisher city	Kingfisher	4.1	4,380	3,725	86	250	20	1	175	123	267	3,233
40 41850	Lawton city	Comanche	75.1	92,757	56,897	21,388	3,534	2,285	407	3,675	4,571	8,719	66,943
40 43150	Lindsay city	Garvin	2.3	2,889	2,625	4	142	3	1	22	92	36	2,215

[Includes incorporated places and census designated places (CDPs) of 2,500 or more population as of April 1, 2000. Codes shown are two-digit Federal Information Processing Standards (FIPS) state codes and five-digit FIPS place codes. Place names and codes are those in effect as of January 1, 2000. County refers to the county (or counties) in which the place is located. IC in this column = independent city, a county equivalent. If a place is located in more than one county, counties are listed in alphabetic order]

State and place code	Place	County	Land area, 2000 (sq. mi.)	Population, 2000 (April 1)								
					By race—							
					One race						Hispanic or Latino (of any race)	18 years and over
				Total	White	Black or African American	American Indian and Alaska Native	Asian	Native Hawaiian and Other Pacific Islander	Some other race	Two or more races	
40 00000	OKLAHOMA—Con.											
40 43750	Lone Grove city	Carter	28.1	4,631	3,913	86	366	7	5	24	230	91	3,200
40 44800	McAlester city	Pittsburg	15.7	17,783	13,288	1,544	1,863	70	9	230	779	541	13,836
40 45350	McLoud town	Pottawatomie	18.3	3,548	2,554	287	424	13	35	27	208	98	2,784
40 45750	Madill city	Marshall	2.9	3,410	2,200	206	219	9	1	540	235	715	2,406
40 46050	Mangum city	Greer	1.7	2,924	2,469	197	40	3	-	132	83	246	2,227
40 46600	Marlow city	Stephens	7.1	4,592	4,174	2	275	11	-	12	118	101	3,457
40 48000	Miami city	Ottawa	9.7	13,704	10,329	164	2,100	64	30	128	889	322	10,385
40 48350	Midwest City city	Oklahoma	24.6	54,088	37,568	10,573	1,887	892	66	835	2,267	2,192	39,769
40 49200	Moore city	Cleveland	21.7	41,138	34,814	1,201	1,704	667	20	720	2,012	2,098	29,028
40 49850	Muldrow town	Sequoyah	3.9	3,104	2,160	56	510	9	2	41	326	115	2,233
40 50050	Muskogee city	Muskogee	37.3	38,310	23,414	6,856	4,727	343	8	601	2,361	1,258	28,457
40 50100	Mustang city	Canadian	12.0	13,156	12,055	77	438	66	12	103	405	396	9,267
40 51150	Newcastle city	McClain	49.8	5,434	4,870	10	286	19	1	61	187	135	4,002
40 51250	New Cordell city	Washita	2.5	2,867	2,733	6	60	5	-	27	36	75	2,125
40 51800	Nichols Hills city	Oklahoma	2.0	4,056	3,799	17	56	79	-	24	81	55	3,056
40 52150	Noble city	Cleveland	12.5	5,260	4,750	10	256	13	1	20	210	144	3,758
40 52500	Norman city	Cleveland	177.0	95,694	78,812	4,080	4,262	3,342	48	1,313	3,837	3,723	75,365
40 52900	Nowata city	Nowata	3.1	3,971	2,783	185	636	5	-	15	347	47	2,955
40 53350	Oakhurst CDP	Creek, Tulsa	6.7	2,731	2,213	35	273	15	2	20	173	68	2,058
40 54200	Okemah city	Okfuskee	2.6	3,038	2,099	72	694	3	-	14	156	59	2,205
40 55000	Oklahoma City city	Canadian, Cleveland, Oklahoma, Pottawatomie	607.0	506,132	346,226	77,810	17,743	17,595	360	26,705	19,693	51,368	376,858
40 55150	Okmulgee city	Okmulgee	12.8	13,022	7,663	2,773	1,772	38	3	69	704	238	9,715
40 56650	Owasso city	Rogers, Tulsa	10.0	18,502	16,033	296	932	194	1	309	737	729	12,523
40 57300	Park Hill CDP	Cherokee	34.5	3,936	1,752	30	1,779	3	1	65	306	190	2,546
40 57550	Pauls Valley city	Garvin	8.3	6,256	4,959	331	463	41	4	217	241	471	4,729
40 57600	Pawhuska city	Osage	3.8	3,629	2,358	101	924	9	-	19	218	67	2,621
40 58250	Perry city	Noble	6.1	5,230	4,693	164	175	26	3	29	140	96	3,977
40 58700	Piedmont city	Canadian, Kingfisher	43.8	3,650	3,405	17	106	1	2	31	88	83	2,500
40 59750	Pocola town	Le Flore	30.3	3,994	3,449	133	206	10	1	18	177	75	2,936
40 59850	Ponca City city	Kay, Osage	18.1	25,919	21,818	774	1,626	181	8	540	972	1,149	19,121
40 60350	Poteau city	Le Flore	28.6	7,939	6,521	178	794	30	2	110	304	462	5,987
40 61000	Pryor Creek city	Mayes	6.5	8,659	6,746	25	1,223	54	2	84	525	241	6,401
40 61150	Purcell city	Cleveland, McClain	9.9	5,571	4,546	123	364	16	-	251	271	562	4,075
40 63800	Roland town	Sequoyah	2.6	2,842	2,100	130	319	4	1	22	266	88	1,946
40 65000	Sallisaw city	Sequoyah	12.7	7,989	5,456	108	1,622	23	2	89	689	180	5,864
40 65300	Sand Springs city	Osage, Tulsa	18.7	17,451	14,981	323	1,245	76	3	82	741	360	12,492
40 65400	Sapulpa city	Creek	18.6	19,166	15,514	719	1,666	77	6	189	995	470	14,172
40 65700	Sayre city	Beckham	3.4	4,114	3,085	751	104	17	-	79	78	220	3,513
40 66350	Seminole city	Seminole	13.9	6,899	5,065	274	1,130	22	3	50	355	180	5,074
40 66800	Shawnee city	Pottawatomie	42.3	28,692	22,101	1,164	3,679	273	14	208	1,253	781	21,709
40 67850	Skiatook town	Osage, Tulsa	14.6	5,396	3,848	27	1,012	9	1	21	478	95	3,722
40 67950	Slaughterville town	Cleveland	38.1	3,609	3,064	25	202	6	3	56	253	146	2,551
40 69200	Spencer city	Oklahoma	5.3	3,746	1,496	1,941	106	13	2	19	169	87	2,668
40 70250	Stigler city	Haskell	2.2	2,731	2,151	1	422	9	-	16	132	73	2,014
40 70300	Stillwater city	Payne	27.8	39,065	32,220	1,681	1,519	1,974	14	345	1,312	976	33,123
40 70350	Stilwell city	Adair	3.2	3,276	1,372	16	1,586	7	1	113	181	229	2,294
40 71000	Stroud city	Creek, Lincoln	11.5	2,758	2,309	101	233	15	-	13	87	40	2,055
40 71350	Sulphur city	Murray	6.8	4,794	3,809	65	610	18	2	73	217	230	3,648
40 72100	Tahlequah city	Cherokee	12.0	14,458	8,532	366	3,884	76	5	593	1,002	1,049	11,244
40 72650	Tecumseh city	Pottawatomie	15.0	6,098	4,816	125	785	11	5	28	332	108	4,367
40 73250	The Village city	Oklahoma	2.5	10,157	8,145	1,063	258	194	3	115	379	383	8,108
40 73900	Tishomingo city	Johnston	4.7	3,162	2,312	147	482	14	1	31	175	96	2,378
40 74150	Tonkawa city	Kay	5.6	3,299	2,850	28	183	11	-	101	126	219	2,479
40 75000	Tulsa city	Osage, Rogers, Tulsa	182.6	393,049	275,488	60,794	18,551	7,150	202	13,564	17,300	28,111	295,709
40 75150	Turley CDP	Tulsa	3.7	3,231	2,163	465	357	12	1	27	206	123	2,382
40 75450	Tuttle city	Grady	29.2	4,294	3,922	-	214	7	-	4	147	95	3,146
40 77550	Vinita city	Craig	4.4	6,472	4,357	396	962	18	2	40	697	96	5,069
40 77850	Wagoner city	Wagoner	7.0	7,669	5,405	711	1,013	26	6	54	454	148	5,511
40 78150	Walters city	Cotton	8.1	2,657	2,242	10	272	2	-	27	104	91	1,919
40 78500	Warr Acres city	Oklahoma	2.8	9,735	7,935	759	248	191	5	276	321	748	7,213
40 78950	Watonga city	Blaine	2.7	4,658	2,850	714	384	72	94	228	316	555	3,703
40 79450	Weatherford city	Custer	5.8	9,859	8,593	192	490	127	6	174	277	424	7,906
40 80550	Wewoka city	Seminole	4.8	3,562	1,818	708	764	10	3	37	222	85	2,571
40 81000	Wilburton city	Latimer	3.0	2,972	2,227	40	503	9	1	26	166	70	2,246
40 82150	Woodward city	Woodward	13.1	11,853	10,902	30	232	80	2	386	221	718	8,667
40 82950	Yukon city	Canadian	25.8	21,043	19,135	176	564	394	10	257	507	633	15,215
41 00000	OREGON		95,996.8	3,421,399	2,961,623	55,662	45,211	101,350	7,976	144,832	104,745	275,314	2,574,873
41 01000	Albany city	Benton, Linn	15.9	40,852	37,453	217	500	465	86	1,084	1,047	2,489	30,067
41 01650	Aloha CDP	Washington	7.4	41,741	33,143	563	324	3,208	155	2,796	1,552	5,396	29,291
41 01850	Altamont CDP	Klamath	8.7	19,603	17,378	125	691	150	27	552	680	1,326	14,386
41 03050	Ashland city	Jackson	6.5	19,522	17,873	118	199	365	26	333	608	695	15,846
41 03150	Astoria city	Clatsop	6.1	9,813	8,938	51	112	190	19	262	241	587	7,454
41 03250	Aumsville city	Marion	0.8	3,003	2,605	9	55	14	5	182	133	342	1,910
41 03650	Baker City city	Baker	6.9	9,860	9,381	30	108	55	6	103	177	250	7,442

[Includes incorporated places and census designated places (CDPs) of 2,500 or more population as of April 1, 2000. Codes shown are two-digit Federal Information Processing Standards (FIPS) state codes and five-digit FIPS place codes. Place names and codes are those in effect as of January 1, 2000. County refers to the county (or counties) in which the place is located. IC in this column = independent city, a county equivalent. If a place is located in more than one county, counties are listed in alphabetic order]

				Population, 2000 (April 1)									
				By race—									
				One race							Two or more races	Hispanic or Latino (of any race)	18 years and over
State and place code	Place	County	Land area, 2000 (sq. mi.)	Total	White	Black or African American	American Indian and Alaska Native	Asian	Native Hawaiian and Other Pacific Islander	Some other race			
41 00000	OREGON—Con.												
41 03800	Bandon city	Coos.	2.8	2,833	2,620	7	55	17	3	27	104	78	2,293
41 05350	Beaverton city	Washington	16.3	76,129	59,615	1,324	507	7,349	272	4,211	2,851	8,463	57,132
41 05800	Bend city	Deschutes	32.0	52,029	48,897	145	412	521	42	910	1,102	2,396	39,303
41 07200	Boardman city	Morrow	3.6	2,855	1,577	11	55	20	3	1,106	83	1,431	1,766
41 08650	Brookings city	Curry	2.8	5,447	4,932	11	131	70	7	78	218	258	4,149
41 09800	Burns city	Harney	3.6	3,064	2,866	6	76	16	3	34	63	162	2,267
41 10750	Canby city	Clackamas.	3.8	12,790	11,309	60	98	128	17	956	222	1,985	8,878
41 12050	Cedar Hills CDP	Washington	2.3	8,949	7,453	118	51	428	31	541	327	1,003	6,893
41 12150	Cedar Mill CDP.	Washington	3.7	12,597	10,760	108	52	941	26	340	370	767	9,016
41 12400	Central Point city	Jackson.	3.1	12,493	11,743	31	110	91	24	158	336	527	8,921
41 12800	Chenoweth CDP	Wasco.	6.7	3,412	2,982	6	65	30	10	234	85	372	2,518
41 13425	City of The Dalles city	Wasco.	5.3	12,156	10,677	48	146	117	93	757	318	1,276	9,140
41 13450	Clackamas CDP	Clackamas.	2.1	5,177	4,415	56	34	327	17	140	188	308	3,778
41 15250	Coos Bay city	Coos.	10.6	15,374	13,952	57	349	221	48	207	540	691	11,898
41 15350	Coquille city	Coos.	2.7	4,184	3,876	21	74	15	6	67	125	171	3,224
41 15550	Cornelius city	Washington	1.9	9,652	6,622	73	120	100	27	2,347	363	3,609	6,519
41 15800	Corvallis city	Benton	13.6	49,322	42,433	570	376	3,168	141	1,244	1,390	2,820	40,596
41 15950	Cottage Grove city	Lane	3.3	8,445	7,840	13	102	78	8	131	273	417	6,135
41 16950	Creswell city	Lane.	1.2	3,579	3,186	11	65	19	6	146	146	251	2,460
41 17700	Dallas city	Polk	4.5	12,459	11,621	22	222	69	13	173	339	500	8,987
41 19020	Deschutes River Woods CDP	Deschutes	4.9	4,631	4,433	12	29	16	4	60	77	151	3,273
41 21050	Dundee city	Yamhill	1.4	2,598	2,409	-	22	26	-	86	55	196	1,804
41 21550	Eagle Point city	Jackson.	2.6	4,797	4,469	18	83	19	9	53	146	169	3,235
41 23850	Eugene city	Lane.	40.5	137,893	121,546	1,729	1,281	4,916	294	3,003	5,124	6,843	109,840
41 24250	Fairview city	Multnomah.	3.2	7,561	5,762	230	63	260	28	795	423	1,210	5,435
41 26050	Florence city.	Lane.	4.9	7,263	6,964	20	67	40	10	41	121	172	6,040
41 26200	Forest Grove city	Washington	4.6	17,708	14,425	77	158	374	42	2,017	615	3,065	12,852
41 26750	Four Corners CDP.	Marion.	2.8	13,922	10,968	184	278	258	133	1,584	517	2,513	9,710
41 27825	Garden Home-Whitford CDP	Washington	1.9	6,931	6,362	52	28	220	11	50	208	222	5,471
41 29000	Gladstone city	Clackamas.	2.5	11,438	10,342	82	70	241	33	348	322	700	8,397
41 30550	Grants Pass city	Josephine	7.6	23,003	21,386	76	251	226	27	375	662	1,236	17,013
41 30750	Green CDP	Douglas.	4.5	6,174	5,800	10	74	31	8	97	154	272	4,302
41 31250	Gresham city	Multnomah.	22.2	90,205	74,619	1,707	848	3,007	243	6,335	3,446	10,732	65,354
41 32050	Happy Valley city.	Clackamas.	2.7	4,519	3,949	35	13	400	7	20	95	85	3,100
41 32075	Harbeck-Fruitdale CDP. . .	Josephine	1.6	3,780	3,544	9	48	23	1	82	73	250	2,903
41 32100	Harbor CDP.	Curry	1.9	2,622	2,470	9	57	5	2	24	55	80	2,321
41 32550	Harrisburg city	Linn	1.6	2,795	2,599	3	34	16	-	80	63	159	1,917
41 32850	Hayesville CDP.	Marion.	3.9	18,222	13,997	173	313	638	129	2,277	695	3,601	13,183
41 33700	Hermiston city.	Umatilla.	6.5	13,154	10,382	122	119	208	5	1,982	336	3,168	9,227
41 34100	Hillsboro city.	Washington	21.6	70,186	54,391	858	577	4,585	177	7,285	2,313	13,262	50,293
41 34900	Hood River city.	Hood River.	2.1	5,831	4,713	35	58	67	11	792	155	1,351	4,305
41 36150	Independence city.	Polk	2.3	6,035	4,447	25	90	35	22	1,185	231	1,818	4,195
41 37400	Jennings Lodge CDP. . . .	Clackamas.	1.6	7,036	6,269	61	33	100	9	373	191	758	5,272
41 38000	Junction City city.	Lane.	1.4	4,721	4,306	14	58	28	2	173	140	391	3,441
41 38500	Keizer city	Marion.	7.2	32,203	27,539	242	444	480	66	2,325	1,107	3,950	23,273
41 39700	Klamath Falls city	Klamath.	17.9	19,462	16,566	198	864	256	26	807	745	1,814	14,504
41 40300	Lafayette city	Yamhill	0.9	2,586	2,221	11	42	16	6	216	74	523	1,740
41 40350	La Grande city	Union	4.4	12,327	11,454	84	96	155	111	172	255	342	9,418
41 40550	Lake Oswego city	Clackamas, Multnomah, Washington	10.3	35,278	32,149	226	113	1,612	58	250	870	820	26,539
41 41050	La Pine CDP	Deschutes	29.3	5,799	5,558	5	74	14	6	32	110	129	4,467
41 41650	Lebanon city	Linn.	5.2	12,950	12,170	22	133	124	11	183	307	478	9,457
41 42600	Lincoln City city.	Lincoln	5.3	7,437	6,574	34	232	76	26	224	271	611	5,786
41 45000	McMinnville city.	Yamhill	9.9	26,499	22,892	179	368	331	47	1,924	758	3,879	19,539
41 45250	Madras city	Jefferson	2.2	5,078	3,227	30	312	28	18	1,247	216	1,815	3,399
41 47000	Medford city.	Jackson.	21.7	63,154	56,834	313	677	720	163	2,442	2,005	5,841	46,855
41 47800	Metzger CDP.	Washington	0.7	3,354	2,885	37	31	91	33	147	130	285	2,603
41 48600	Milton-Freewater city . . .	Umatilla.	1.9	6,470	4,758	28	46	29	76	1,348	185	2,055	4,453
41 48650	Milwaukie city.	Clackamas, Multnomah . .	4.8	20,490	18,637	194	193	484	52	327	603	813	15,811
41 49450	Molalla city.	Clackamas.	1.9	5,647	5,003	25	73	28	16	378	124	596	3,851
41 49550	Monmouth city	Polk	1.9	7,741	6,632	71	81	158	57	481	261	753	6,232
41 50150	Mount Angel city	Marion.	1.0	3,121	2,361	14	29	6	3	557	151	869	2,177
41 50235	Mount Hood Village CDP .	Clackamas.	6.9	3,306	3,054	11	55	16	1	96	73	210	2,497
41 50950	Myrtle Creek city	Douglas.	1.8	3,419	3,195	5	73	30	-	23	93	105	2,443
41 52100	Newberg city	Yamhill	5.0	18,064	16,347	64	115	188	31	914	405	1,901	13,069
41 52450	Newport city	Lincoln	8.9	9,532	8,442	43	205	164	20	368	290	854	7,409
41 53000	North Bend city	Coos.	3.9	9,544	8,827	36	171	125	32	98	255	354	7,196
41 53750	Nyssa city	Malheur.	1.1	3,163	1,787	13	25	32	3	1,209	94	1,809	2,034
41 53900	Oak Grove CDP	Clackamas.	2.9	12,808	11,715	72	100	229	13	327	352	755	10,053
41 53988	Oak Hills CDP	Washington	1.5	9,050	7,101	116	39	1,245	21	272	256	527	6,430
41 54100	Oakridge city	Lane.	1.9	3,148	2,914	10	50	8	2	59	105	158	2,395
41 54325	Oatfield CDP	Clackamas.	4.4	15,750	14,716	74	84	314	19	146	397	416	12,098
41 54900	Ontario city	Malheur.	4.5	10,985	7,609	60	97	295	16	2,536	372	3,521	7,632
41 55200	Oregon City city	Clackamas.	8.1	25,754	23,807	150	277	288	28	553	651	1,283	18,808
41 57150	Pendleton city.	Umatilla.	10.1	16,354	14,580	250	412	154	10	602	346	981	12,515
41 57450	Philomath city.	Benton	1.3	3,838	3,579	6	63	46	9	48	87	151	2,520
41 57500	Phoenix city.	Jackson.	1.2	4,060	3,652	35	44	27	7	183	112	361	3,119

Table D-1. Places — **Area and Population**—Con.

[Includes incorporated places and census designated places (CDPs) of 2,500 or more population as of April 1, 2000. Codes shown are two-digit Federal Information Processing Standards (FIPS) state codes and five-digit FIPS place codes. Place names and codes are those in effect as of January 1, 2000. County refers to the county (or counties) in which the place is located. IC in this column = independent city, a county equivalent. If a place is located in more than one county, counties are listed in alphabetic order]

State and place code	Place	County	Land area, 2000 (sq. mi.)	Population, 2000 (April 1) Total	By race— One race White	Black or African American	American Indian and Alaska Native	Asian	Native Hawaiian and Other Pacific Islander	Some other race	Two or more races	Hispanic or Latino (of any race)	18 years and over
41 00000	OREGON—Con.												
41 59000	Portland city	Clackamas, Multnomah, Washington	134.3	529,121	412,241	35,115	5,587	33,470	1,993	18,760	21,955	36,058	417,667
41 59850	Prineville city	Crook	6.7	7,356	6,753	1	110	54	1	331	106	546	5,198
41 60900	Raleigh Hills CDP	Washington	1.5	5,865	5,283	58	18	182	11	196	117	337	4,605
41 61200	Redmond city	Deschutes	10.2	13,481	12,634	12	157	87	22	288	281	739	9,490
41 61250	Redwood CDP	Josephine	4.8	5,844	5,544	18	59	19	4	45	155	215	4,398
41 61300	Reedsport city	Douglas	2.1	4,378	4,112	1	54	19	1	94	97	205	3,474
41 63010	Rockcreek CDP	Washington	2.0	9,404	8,057	79	44	709	26	207	282	431	6,714
41 63650	Roseburg city	Douglas	9.2	20,017	18,728	61	260	198	20	253	497	746	15,367
41 63660	Roseburg North CDP	Douglas	22.8	5,473	5,143	10	58	41	1	66	154	168	4,316
41 64600	St. Helens city	Columbia	4.3	10,019	9,292	34	168	63	15	135	312	406	6,993
41 64900	Salem city	Marion, Polk	45.7	136,924	113,746	1,750	2,064	3,304	643	10,820	4,597	19,973	102,105
41 65250	Sandy city	Clackamas	2.6	5,385	5,057	8	62	40	14	89	115	220	3,719
41 65500	Scappoose city	Columbia	2.5	4,976	4,688	16	58	42	3	27	142	122	3,582
41 65950	Seaside city	Clatsop	3.9	5,900	5,492	20	58	63	17	128	122	381	4,640
41 67050	Sheridan city	Yamhill	1.9	3,570	3,132	12	173	23	3	142	85	274	2,470
41 67100	Sherwood city	Washington	4.1	11,791	10,890	51	60	262	5	208	315	557	8,057
41 67650	Silverton city	Marion	2.7	7,414	6,620	16	82	32	3	486	175	857	5,059
41 69600	Springfield city	Lane	14.4	52,864	47,386	374	730	588	162	1,632	1,992	3,651	38,468
41 70200	Stayton city	Marion	2.7	6,816	6,199	9	102	42	5	262	197	626	4,710
41 71100	Sunnyside CDP	Clackamas	2.6	6,791	5,766	94	47	479	21	144	240	310	5,195
41 71650	Sutherlin city	Douglas	5.2	6,669	6,255	9	115	34	4	73	179	265	4,999
41 71950	Sweet Home city	Linn	5.3	8,016	7,506	20	133	49	12	80	216	248	5,782
41 72500	Talent city	Jackson	1.3	5,589	4,879	30	59	20	6	442	153	693	4,135
41 73650	Tigard city	Washington	10.9	41,223	35,195	468	253	2,298	220	1,552	1,237	3,686	30,692
41 73700	Tillamook city	Tillamook	1.5	4,352	4,028	7	53	31	7	149	77	484	3,080
41 74000	Toledo city	Lincoln	2.2	3,472	3,190	8	117	20	1	18	118	90	2,445
41 74650	Tri-City CDP	Douglas	7.6	3,519	3,300	5	63	18	1	10	122	100	2,628
41 74850	Troutdale city	Multnomah	5.0	13,777	12,061	262	127	571	34	235	487	636	9,633
41 74950	Tualatin city	Clackamas, Washington	7.8	22,791	19,803	181	157	824	84	1,102	640	2,701	16,354
41 75650	Umatilla city	Umatilla	3.5	4,978	3,589	134	67	19	3	1,070	96	1,622	3,433
41 77050	Veneta city	Lane	2.7	2,755	2,560	7	38	18	1	25	106	115	1,847
41 78900	Warrenton city	Clatsop	12.3	4,096	3,790	9	54	72	3	52	116	119	3,008
41 80025	West Haven-Sylvan CDP	Washington	2.7	7,147	6,093	84	36	386	8	76	164	203	5,889
41 80150	West Linn city	Clackamas	7.4	22,261	20,775	120	78	647	18	165	458	638	15,798
41 80900	West Slope CDP	Washington	1.7	6,442	5,714	93	45	277	10	143	160	307	5,075
41 81450	White City CDP	Jackson	1.8	5,466	4,672	10	81	29	5	446	223	902	3,595
41 82800	Wilsonville city	Clackamas, Washington	6.7	13,991	12,655	92	98	311	23	441	371	971	10,555
41 83400	Winston city	Douglas	2.1	4,613	4,363	7	63	24	3	57	96	131	3,284
41 83750	Woodburn city	Marion	5.2	20,100	11,682	90	236	107	15	7,167	803	10,064	14,068
41 83950	Wood Village city	Multnomah	1.0	2,860	2,336	16	37	49	7	282	133	435	2,041
42 00000	PENNSYLVANIA		44,816.6	12,281,054	10,484,203	1,224,612	18,348	219,813	3,417	188,437	142,224	394,088	9,358,833
42 00540	Akron borough	Lancaster	1.3	4,046	3,901	22	9	56	-	32	26	90	3,167
42 00676	Aldan borough	Delaware	0.6	4,313	4,024	187	8	58	-	5	31	40	3,331
42 00820	Aliquippa city	Beaver	4.1	11,734	7,344	4,168	8	21	4	21	168	117	8,972
42 02000	Allentown city	Lehigh	17.7	106,632	77,361	8,370	356	2,421	78	14,260	3,786	26,058	80,238
42 02144	Altamont CDP	Schuylkill	0.9	2,689	1,442	1,107	1	17	-	116	6	206	2,571
42 02184	Altoona city	Blair	9.8	49,523	47,545	1,231	51	156	8	121	411	367	38,165
42 02264	Ambler borough	Montgomery	0.8	6,426	5,352	773	16	159	4	32	90	137	4,919
42 02288	Ambridge borough	Beaver	1.5	7,769	6,657	884	6	35	1	57	129	142	6,085
42 02349	Amity Gardens CDP	Berks	1.0	3,370	3,202	87	2	28	1	9	41	44	2,457
42 02416	Ancient Oaks CDP	Lehigh	2.2	3,161	3,033	22	1	84	-	11	10	52	2,302
42 02608	Annville CDP	Lebanon	1.6	4,518	4,310	49	1	56	5	44	53	81	3,781
42 02832	Archbald borough	Lackawanna	16.8	6,220	6,136	17	10	13	-	1	43	25	4,811
42 02896	Ardmore CDP	Delaware, Montgomery	1.9	12,616	10,536	1,447	15	325	16	75	202	259	10,053
42 03008	Arlington Heights CDP	Monroe	5.3	5,132	4,648	225	10	101	-	80	68	231	3,949
42 03088	Arnold city	Westmoreland	0.7	5,667	4,808	723	10	8	1	15	102	64	4,443
42 03264	Ashland borough	Columbia, Schuylkill	1.7	3,283	3,263	7	-	3	-	2	8	3	2,590
42 03272	Ashley borough	Luzerne	0.9	2,866	2,822	11	1	7	-	3	22	12	2,249
42 03320	Aspinwall borough	Allegheny	0.3	2,960	2,904	8	1	27	-	5	15	30	2,417
42 03392	Athens borough	Bradford	1.8	3,415	3,341	31	5	10	-	8	20	34	2,575
42 03544	Audubon CDP	Montgomery	4.5	6,549	5,754	285	3	395	-	84	28	133	4,688
42 03608	Avalon borough	Allegheny	0.6	5,294	4,925	257	5	24	1	8	74	31	4,333
42 03640	Avoca borough	Luzerne	0.9	2,851	2,830	4	-	4	6	3	4	3	2,246
42 03648	Avon CDP	Lebanon	1.6	2,856	2,711	53	5	21	1	46	19	154	2,323
42 03714	Back Mountain CDP	Luzerne	107.0	26,690	25,209	1,148	27	139	5	47	115	281	20,951
42 03736	Baden borough	Beaver	2.3	4,377	4,315	32	2	6	-	4	18	25	3,615
42 03928	Baldwin borough	Allegheny	5.8	19,999	19,239	483	9	112	1	34	121	129	15,788
42 04032	Bangor borough	Northampton	1.5	5,319	5,205	26	10	17	-	18	43	79	3,845
42 04432	Bath borough	Northampton	0.9	2,678	2,570	40	1	18	-	17	32	47	1,981
42 04688	Beaver borough	Beaver	0.9	4,775	4,605	126	6	13	-	13	12	42	3,858
42 04792	Beaver Falls city	Beaver	2.1	9,920	7,819	1,739	13	62	2	50	235	105	7,750
42 04944	Bedford borough	Bedford	1.1	3,141	3,069	16	2	24	3	4	23	25	2,549
42 05256	Bellefonte borough	Centre	1.8	6,395	6,219	58	7	30	7	22	52	38	5,046
42 05312	Bellevue borough	Allegheny	1.0	8,770	8,188	386	15	57	-	14	110	71	7,058
42 05400	Belmont CDP	Cambria	1.8	2,846	2,793	20	-	12	-	3	18	11	2,391
42 05672	Bentleyville borough	Washington	3.7	2,502	2,421	38	3	1	-	3	36	12	1,938

U.S. Census Bureau, County and City Data Book: 2000

Table D-1. Places — **Area and Population**—Con.

[Includes incorporated places and census designated places (CDPs) of 2,500 or more population as of April 1, 2000. Codes shown are two-digit Federal Information Processing Standards (FIPS) state codes and five-digit FIPS place codes. Place names and codes are those in effect as of January 1, 2000. County refers to the county (or counties) in which the place is located. IC in this column = independent city, a county equivalent. If a place is located in more than one county, counties are listed in alphabetic order]

State and place code	Place	County	Land area, 2000 (sq. mi.)	Total	White	Black or African American	American Indian and Alaska Native	Asian	Native Hawaiian and Other Pacific Islander	Some other race	Two or more races	Hispanic or Latino (of any race)	18 years and over
42 00000	PENNSYLVANIA—Con.												
42 05888	Berwick borough	Columbia	3.1	10,774	10,462	95	30	46	5	66	70	175	8,289
42 06064	Bethel Park borough	Allegheny	11.7	33,556	32,584	343	10	371	9	45	194	164	25,614
42 06088	Bethlehem city	Lehigh, Northampton	19.3	71,329	58,382	2,596	183	1,585	24	6,732	1,827	13,002	56,380
42 06504	Birdsboro borough	Berks	1.4	5,064	4,905	53	6	18	3	32	47	63	3,583
42 06904	Blairsville borough	Indiana	1.4	3,607	3,451	108	4	21	-	2	21	2	2,800
42 06928	Blakely borough	Lackawanna	3.9	7,027	6,909	20	3	32	-	24	39	54	5,635
42 07128	Bloomsburg town	Columbia	4.4	12,375	11,684	322	25	137	5	89	113	215	10,855
42 07224	Blue Bell CDP	Montgomery	5.4	6,395	5,776	155	1	417	-	14	32	73	4,870
42 07368	Boalsburg CDP	Centre	6.2	3,578	3,374	52	3	74	1	12	62	51	2,512
42 07472	Boiling Springs CDP	Cumberland	2.5	2,769	2,713	18	1	16	5	2	14	15	1,991
42 07616	Boothwyn CDP	Delaware	1.2	5,206	4,722	319	5	87	1	21	51	58	4,026
42 07960	Boyertown borough	Berks	0.8	3,940	3,894	8	1	14	-	5	18	29	3,109
42 07976	Brackenridge borough	Allegheny	0.5	3,543	3,367	122	4	8	1	13	28	19	2,817
42 07992	Braddock borough	Allegheny	0.6	2,912	877	1,937	4	7	-	20	67	44	1,996
42 08040	Bradford city	McKean	3.4	9,175	8,968	45	28	48	3	25	58	87	6,840
42 08416	Brentwood borough	Allegheny	1.4	10,466	10,251	56	25	57	1	22	54	72	8,247
42 08434	Bressler-Enhaut-Oberlin CDP	Dauphin	0.6	2,809	2,315	375	6	7	1	49	56	209	2,121
42 08568	Bridgeport borough	Montgomery	0.7	4,371	3,997	117	6	106	-	55	90	168	3,544
42 08624	Bridgeville borough	Allegheny	1.1	5,341	5,023	236	5	20	-	18	39	41	4,379
42 08760	Bristol borough	Bucks	1.6	9,923	8,282	872	15	34	3	447	270	1,144	7,494
42 08819	Brittany Farms-Highlands CDP	Bucks	1.2	3,268	3,137	44	1	33	-	23	30	41	2,581
42 09080	Brookhaven borough	Delaware	1.7	7,985	7,637	161	6	99	-	35	47	90	6,406
42 09224	Brookville borough	Jefferson	3.2	4,230	4,160	11	4	30	-	4	21	20	3,301
42 09248	Broomall CDP	Delaware	2.9	11,046	10,097	70	11	792	-	18	58	69	8,681
42 09432	Brownsville borough	Fayette	1.0	2,804	2,410	320	3	2	-	6	63	23	2,154
42 09738	Bryn Mawr CDP	Montgomery	0.6	4,382	3,443	457	4	320	14	44	100	130	4,016
42 10464	Butler city	Butler	2.7	15,121	14,444	335	21	66	4	79	172	215	11,541
42 10768	California borough	Washington	11.0	5,274	4,954	218	9	39	-	7	47	26	4,708
42 11000	Camp Hill borough	Cumberland	2.1	7,636	7,337	27	12	172	1	19	68	83	6,006
42 11152	Canonsburg borough	Washington	2.3	8,607	7,833	562	5	55	7	16	129	62	6,863
42 11232	Carbondale city	Lackawanna	3.2	9,804	9,662	23	20	23	-	25	51	122	7,539
42 11272	Carlisle borough	Cumberland	5.4	17,970	15,980	1,243	26	288	3	127	303	352	14,635
42 11336	Carnegie borough	Allegheny	1.7	8,389	7,661	467	7	103	4	33	114	83	6,759
42 11348	Carnot-Moon CDP	Allegheny	6.0	10,637	9,607	565	12	286	5	34	128	112	8,717
42 11472	Carroll Valley borough	Adams	5.4	3,291	3,186	20	14	13	-	8	50	26	2,315
42 11680	Castle Shannon borough	Allegheny	1.6	8,556	8,292	115	5	67	1	33	43	84	6,870
42 11720	Catasauqua borough	Lehigh	1.3	6,588	6,298	78	22	39	1	71	79	233	4,939
42 11804	Cecil-Bishop CDP	Washington	2.5	2,585	2,555	8	1	6	-	3	12	19	1,920
42 12224	Centerville borough	Washington	13.2	3,390	3,351	6	5	7	-	8	13	9	2,654
42 12504	Chalfont borough	Bucks	1.6	3,900	3,766	41	3	58	-	2	30	45	2,765
42 12536	Chambersburg borough	Franklin	6.9	17,862	15,439	1,350	33	155	9	550	326	1,140	14,146
42 12704	Charleroi borough	Washington	0.8	4,871	4,643	158	6	14	-	11	39	35	3,872
42 13208	Chester city	Delaware	4.8	36,854	6,980	27,897	75	226	4	1,116	556	1,986	25,885
42 13216	Chesterbrook CDP	Chester	1.6	4,625	4,149	85	8	327	-	24	32	94	3,827
42 13272	Chester Township CDP	Delaware	1.4	4,604	1,046	3,376	12	27	1	44	98	95	3,051
42 13608	Churchill borough	Allegheny	2.2	3,566	3,156	300	5	69	1	10	25	41	2,920
42 13648	Churchville CDP	Bucks	2.0	4,469	4,379	18	-	53	-	2	17	23	3,300
42 13704	Clairton city	Allegheny	2.8	8,491	5,869	2,405	9	14	-	24	170	62	6,615
42 13800	Clarion borough	Clarion	1.5	6,185	5,848	215	5	61	-	9	47	51	5,638
42 13880	Clarks Summit borough	Lackawanna	1.6	5,126	5,010	20	5	58	1	12	20	48	3,980
42 14064	Clearfield borough	Clearfield	1.8	6,631	6,528	48	5	21	-	4	25	22	5,277
42 14264	Clifton Heights borough	Delaware	0.6	6,779	6,387	198	4	102	-	26	62	67	5,031
42 14712	Coatesville city	Chester	1.9	10,838	4,542	5,327	39	57	3	499	371	1,165	7,399
42 15192	Collegeville borough	Montgomery	1.6	8,032	4,966	2,505	8	171	1	316	65	412	6,997
42 15232	Collingdale borough	Delaware	0.9	8,664	7,966	407	25	140	1	21	104	77	6,187
42 15328	Colonial Park CDP	Dauphin	4.7	13,259	11,030	1,293	11	509	2	201	213	414	10,763
42 15384	Columbia borough	Lancaster	2.4	10,311	9,418	456	19	42	5	175	196	463	7,802
42 15755	Conneaut Lakeshore CDP	Crawford	5.2	2,502	2,483	2	-	3	-	-	14	9	2,009
42 15776	Connellsville city	Fayette	2.3	9,146	8,647	359	12	30	-	16	82	49	6,903
42 15848	Conshohocken borough	Montgomery	1.0	7,589	6,821	590	6	64	1	37	70	102	6,011
42 16056	Coopersburg borough	Lehigh	0.9	2,582	2,479	18	2	44	1	12	26	46	2,023
42 16128	Coplay borough	Lehigh	0.6	3,387	3,280	53	3	11	-	18	22	77	2,607
42 16144	Coraopolis borough	Allegheny	1.3	6,131	5,209	762	5	17	1	35	102	60	4,940
42 16256	Cornwall borough	Lebanon	9.8	3,486	3,409	12	7	37	-	11	10	26	2,758
42 16274	Cornwells Heights-Eddington CDP	Bucks	1.0	3,406	3,297	47	4	37	1	6	14	52	2,626
42 16296	Corry city	Erie	6.1	6,834	6,710	20	20	11	1	6	66	62	4,969
42 16448	Coudersport borough	Potter	5.7	2,650	2,571	13	2	43	-	5	16	13	1,979
42 16848	Crafton borough	Allegheny	1.1	6,706	6,404	184	7	40	5	10	56	38	5,260
42 17448	Croydon CDP	Bucks	2.5	9,993	9,323	289	31	128	1	118	103	368	7,535
42 17840	Curwensville borough	Clearfield	2.2	2,650	2,624	9	6	2	-	1	8	8	2,047
42 18048	Dallas borough	Luzerne	2.3	2,557	2,505	12	2	20	-	3	15	17	2,000
42 18072	Dallastown borough	York	0.7	4,087	3,972	32	8	14	5	16	40	73	3,133
42 18136	Danville borough	Montour	1.6	4,897	4,704	38	6	88	-	23	38	56	3,832
42 18152	Darby borough	Delaware	0.8	10,299	3,746	6,179	14	90	7	53	210	98	6,862
42 18164	Darby Township CDP	Delaware	1.4	9,622	5,994	3,498	11	23	3	28	65	86	7,108

U.S. Census Bureau, County and City Data Book: 2000

[Includes incorporated places and census designated places (CDPs) of 2,500 or more population as of April 1, 2000. Codes shown are two-digit Federal Information Processing Standards (FIPS) state codes and five-digit FIPS place codes. Place names and codes are those in effect as of January 1, 2000. County refers to the county (or counties) in which the place is located. IC in this column = independent city, a county equivalent. If a place is located in more than one county, counties are listed in alphabetic order]

State and place code	Place	County	Land area, 2000 (sq. mi.)	Population, 2000 (April 1)									
					By race—							Hispanic or Latino (of any race)	18 years and over
					One race						Two or more races		
				Total	White	Black or African American	American Indian and Alaska Native	Asian	Native Hawaiian and Other Pacific Islander	Some other race			
42 00000	PENNSYLVANIA—Con.												
42 18888	Denver borough	Lancaster	1.3	3,332	3,225	27	-	33	1	22	24	76	2,435
42 18960	Derry borough	Westmoreland	0.8	2,991	2,961	19	1	-	-	2	8	14	2,271
42 19044	Devon-Berwyn CDP	Chester	2.5	5,067	4,675	229	8	121	-	3	31	58	3,913
42 19160	Dickson City borough	Lackawanna	4.7	6,205	6,132	15	4	16	-	13	25	52	4,973
42 19536	Donora borough	Washington	1.9	5,653	4,041	839	8	15	1	18	131	114	4,429
42 19576	Dormont borough	Allegheny	0.7	9,305	8,940	98	16	152	5	18	76	99	7,327
42 19752	Downingtown borough	Chester	2.2	7,589	6,348	819	9	174	3	109	127	268	5,666
42 19784	Doylestown borough	Bucks	2.2	8,227	7,901	107	9	117	6	35	52	99	6,868
42 19920	Drexel Hill CDP	Delaware	3.2	29,364	27,322	581	28	1,130	4	76	223	285	22,223
42 20136	DuBois city	Clearfield	3.3	8,123	7,975	24	8	43	4	7	62	34	6,248
42 20352	Dunmore borough	Lackawanna	8.7	14,018	13,801	69	8	62	2	25	51	123	11,095
42 20424	Dupont borough	Luzerne	1.5	2,719	2,698	12	-	2	-	-	7	3	2,287
42 20432	Duquesne city	Allegheny	1.8	7,332	3,587	3,501	11	10	1	54	168	53	5,258
42 20512	Duryea borough	Luzerne	5.5	4,634	4,581	12	5	16	-	4	16	14	3,748
42 20672	Eagleville CDP	Montgomery	1.6	4,458	2,951	1,202	1	147	14	115	28	184	3,734
42 21200	East Greenville borough	Montgomery	0.5	3,103	3,003	28	4	16	-	28	24	82	2,128
42 21384	East Lansdowne borough	Delaware	0.2	2,586	1,842	530	2	156	-	12	44	32	1,919
42 21400	Eastlawn Gardens CDP	Northampton	1.7	2,832	2,770	8	5	15	-	21	13	40	2,014
42 21608	East Norriton CDP	Montgomery	6.1	13,211	11,730	800	17	507	-	51	106	154	10,728
42 21648	Easton city	Northampton	4.3	26,263	20,610	3,338	63	437	28	965	822	2,570	20,155
42 21688	East Petersburg borough	Lancaster	1.2	4,450	4,229	60	7	49	3	52	50	127	3,333
42 21872	East Stroudsburg borough	Monroe	2.9	9,888	8,681	618	22	154	1	178	234	550	8,109
42 21960	East Uniontown CDP	Fayette	2.0	2,760	2,563	167	1	6	-	8	15	13	2,108
42 22104	East York CDP	York	2.9	8,782	8,299	131	14	211	5	57	65	118	7,135
42 22144	Ebensburg borough	Cambria	1.7	3,091	3,050	11	-	16	-	4	10	16	2,399
42 22264	Economy borough	Beaver	17.7	9,363	9,207	62	9	26	-	12	47	41	7,287
42 22520	Edgewood borough	Allegheny	0.6	3,311	2,951	260	4	49	3	17	27	45	2,735
42 22528	Edgewood CDP	Northumberland	0.5	2,610	2,500	4	1	12	-	4	15	10	2,095
42 22608	Edinboro borough	Erie	2.3	6,950	6,414	309	11	112	2	36	66	69	6,200
42 22672	Edwardsville borough	Luzerne	1.2	4,984	4,756	128	15	15	-	18	52	59	3,852
42 22976	Elim CDP	Cambria	2.0	4,175	4,096	33	4	23	3	4	12	15	3,482
42 23016	Elizabethtown borough	Lancaster	2.6	11,887	11,450	107	21	146	5	54	104	172	9,596
42 23304	Ellwood City borough	Beaver, Lawrence	2.3	8,688	8,533	70	8	20	-	16	41	52	6,729
42 23584	Emmaus borough	Lehigh	2.9	11,313	10,848	79	7	205	3	100	71	171	8,917
42 23600	Emporium borough	Cameron	0.7	2,526	2,485	18	3	2	3	3	12	23	1,908
42 23616	Emsworth borough	Allegheny	0.6	2,598	2,453	93	1	30	-	1	20	11	1,981
42 23744	Enola CDP	Cumberland	1.9	5,627	5,398	50	12	49	-	25	93	83	4,400
42 23832	Ephrata borough	Lancaster	3.6	13,213	12,698	84	35	140	18	109	129	364	10,045
42 24000	Erie city	Erie	22.0	103,717	83,550	14,724	232	776	42	1,991	2,402	4,572	77,375
42 24160	Etna borough	Allegheny	0.7	3,924	3,837	30	14	6	-	6	31	45	3,038
42 24392	Exeter borough	Luzerne	4.7	5,955	5,877	29	8	8	-	2	31	34	4,703
42 24440	Exton CDP	Chester	3.2	4,267	3,758	173	6	258	1	23	48	80	3,503
42 24712	Fairless Hills CDP	Bucks	1.9	8,365	7,687	235	15	242	-	59	127	213	6,289
42 25360	Farrell city	Mercer	2.3	6,050	3,042	2,826	7	12	1	18	144	40	4,504
42 25464	Fayetteville CDP	Franklin	3.3	2,774	2,650	63	7	8	-	7	39	24	2,171
42 25520	Feasterville-Trevose CDP	Bucks	1.3	6,525	6,159	139	3	130	2	27	65	149	4,996
42 25752	Fernway CDP	Butler	5.3	12,188	11,829	129	4	130	1	22	73	77	8,339
42 26280	Fleetwood borough	Berks	1.0	4,018	3,930	11	-	16	-	39	22	69	3,021
42 26376	Flourtown CDP	Montgomery	1.4	4,669	4,376	154	-	86	-	15	38	32	3,572
42 26408	Folcroft borough	Delaware	1.4	6,978	6,551	277	6	66	2	20	56	77	5,106
42 26432	Folsom CDP	Delaware	1.3	8,072	7,790	148	1	86	-	9	38	48	6,235
42 26512	Ford City borough	Armstrong	0.7	3,451	3,257	134	5	6	-	5	44	26	2,700
42 26592	Forest Hills borough	Allegheny	1.6	6,831	6,471	204	2	91	1	13	49	49	5,482
42 26872	Fort Washington CDP	Montgomery	2.7	3,680	3,360	112	3	185	-	4	16	26	2,633
42 26880	Forty Fort borough	Luzerne	1.3	4,579	4,509	23	3	17	-	8	19	24	3,641
42 27008	Fountain Hill borough	Lehigh	0.7	4,614	4,007	176	9	42	-	277	103	495	3,613
42 27120	Fox Chapel borough	Allegheny	7.8	5,436	5,071	30	1	284	2	7	41	37	3,802
42 27207	Fox Run CDP	Butler	2.4	3,044	2,949	22	1	43	2	-	27	20	2,098
42 27232	Frackville borough	Schuylkill	0.6	4,361	4,280	16	3	46	-	11	5	31	3,503
42 27456	Franklin city	Venango	4.6	7,212	6,835	225	6	24	1	22	99	48	5,499
42 27552	Franklin Park borough	Allegheny	13.6	11,364	10,801	116	5	328	22	19	73	61	7,869
42 27744	Freeland borough	Luzerne	0.7	3,643	3,590	4	2	26	-	12	9	35	2,852
42 28144	Fullerton CDP	Lehigh	3.7	14,268	12,284	554	23	788	10	367	242	878	11,466
42 28456	Garden View CDP	Lycoming	1.0	2,679	2,569	30	3	36	-	10	31	12	2,144
42 28600	Gastonville CDP	Washington	2.8	3,002	2,949	23	1	5	-	10	14	29	2,386
42 28720	Geistown borough	Cambria	1.1	2,555	2,496	10	1	35	-	1	12	8	2,015
42 28960	Gettysburg borough	Adams	1.6	7,490	6,401	434	28	96	3	350	178	601	6,273
42 29096	Gilbertsville CDP	Montgomery	3.4	4,242	4,125	33	6	43	1	5	29	19	3,107
42 29232	Girard borough	Erie	2.4	3,164	3,123	12	9	6	-	7	7	19	2,235
42 29432	Glassport borough	Allegheny	1.7	4,993	4,905	28	14	9	3	9	25	41	3,949
42 29720	Glenolden borough	Delaware	1.0	7,476	6,899	301	3	178	1	16	78	88	5,695
42 29808	Glenside CDP	Montgomery	1.3	7,914	7,041	527	8	239	1	21	76	114	5,938
42 30435	Grantley CDP	York	1.7	3,580	3,456	49	1	25	1	20	28	79	3,140
42 30896	Greencastle borough	Franklin	1.6	3,722	3,600	50	7	23	2	13	27	36	2,966
42 31200	Greensburg city	Westmoreland	4.2	15,889	14,845	621	14	112	2	61	234	172	12,682
42 31256	Green Tree borough	Allegheny	2.1	4,719	4,540	25	-	92	-	2	60	31	3,803
42 31328	Greenville borough	Mercer	1.9	6,380	6,146	113	8	52	2	13	46	31	4,994

Table D-1. Places — **Area and Population**—Con.

[Includes incorporated places and census designated places (CDPs) of 2,500 or more population as of April 1, 2000. Codes shown are two-digit Federal Information Processing Standards (FIPS) state codes and five-digit FIPS place codes. Place names and codes are those in effect as of January 1, 2000. County refers to the county (or counties) in which the place is located. IC in this column = independent city, a county equivalent. If a place is located in more than one county, counties are listed in alphabetic order]

State and place code	Place	County	Land area, 2000 (sq. mi.)	Population, 2000 (April 1) Total	White	Black or African American	American Indian and Alaska Native	Asian	Native Hawaiian and Other Pacific Islander	Some other race	Two or more races	Hispanic or Latino (of any race)	18 years and over
42 00000	PENNSYLVANIA—Con.												
42 31656	Grove City borough	Mercer	2.7	8,024	7,809	51	5	87	2	11	59	43	6,681
42 32120	Hamburg borough	Berks	1.9	4,114	4,028	14	5	13	-	20	34	34	3,248
42 32334	Hampton Township CDP	Allegheny	16.0	17,526	17,116	118	8	215	1	21	47	93	12,605
42 32448	Hanover borough	York	3.7	14,535	14,092	75	27	127	8	107	99	298	11,608
42 32616	Harleysville CDP	Montgomery	4.2	8,795	8,258	230	5	197	6	30	69	159	6,267
42 32740	Harmony Township CDP	Beaver	2.9	3,373	3,288	49	-	4	4	7	21	19	2,728
42 32800	Harrisburg city	Dauphin	8.1	48,950	15,527	26,841	183	1,384	35	3,199	1,781	5,724	35,144
42 32868	Harrison Township CDP	Allegheny	7.3	10,934	10,367	404	6	45	-	12	100	60	8,642
42 33000	Harveys Lake borough	Luzerne	5.3	2,888	2,833	4	9	11	1	9	21	22	2,230
42 33088	Hatboro borough	Montgomery	1.4	7,393	7,078	144	10	78	-	43	40	107	5,616
42 33112	Hatfield borough	Montgomery	0.6	2,605	2,141	46	8	314	1	37	58	87	2,001
42 33408	Hazleton city	Luzerne	6.0	23,329	22,092	192	38	152	3	645	207	1,132	18,422
42 33744	Hellertown borough	Northampton	1.3	5,606	5,505	17	4	11	-	38	31	139	4,476
42 34064	Hermitage city	Mercer	29.5	16,157	15,344	500	7	130	1	37	138	107	12,659
42 34144	Hershey CDP	Dauphin	14.4	12,771	11,631	271	8	622	1	62	176	198	10,174
42 34664	Highspire borough	Dauphin	0.7	2,720	2,356	223	3	24	-	59	55	139	2,181
42 35120	Hokendauqua CDP	Lehigh	1.1	3,411	3,280	60	6	29	1	17	18	71	2,695
42 35224	Hollidaysburg borough	Blair	2.4	5,368	5,271	44	9	14	-	3	27	26	4,269
42 35364	Homeacre-Lyndora CDP	Butler	6.7	6,685	6,536	44	2	46	3	9	45	28	5,483
42 35424	Homestead borough	Allegheny	0.6	3,569	1,522	1,831	9	101	1	8	97	22	2,704
42 35520	Honesdale borough	Wayne	4.1	4,874	4,759	32	7	38	-	8	30	92	3,732
42 35800	Horsham CDP	Montgomery	5.5	14,779	13,316	560	28	641	-	89	145	214	11,038
42 36232	Hummelstown borough	Dauphin	1.3	4,360	4,230	14	1	46	3	29	37	66	3,333
42 36368	Huntingdon borough	Huntingdon	3.4	6,918	6,669	97	12	42	-	21	77	46	5,635
42 36772	Imperial-Enlow CDP	Allegheny	4.0	3,514	3,388	58	6	20	1	6	35	17	2,598
42 36816	Indiana borough	Indiana	1.8	14,895	13,630	773	10	281	3	65	133	178	13,671
42 37000	Ingram borough	Allegheny	0.4	3,712	3,542	114	8	20	-	8	20	21	2,870
42 37208	Irwin borough	Westmoreland	0.9	4,366	4,218	44	4	52	1	16	31	29	3,455
42 37784	Jeannette city	Westmoreland	2.4	10,654	9,888	553	9	10	4	20	170	53	8,297
42 37955	Jefferson Hills borough	Allegheny	16.6	9,666	9,353	127	16	105	-	14	51	67	7,346
42 38000	Jenkintown borough	Montgomery	0.6	4,478	4,192	179	2	42	1	22	40	58	3,452
42 38128	Jersey Shore borough	Lycoming	1.2	4,482	4,426	17	6	13	3	5	12	6	3,318
42 38160	Jessup borough	Lackawanna	6.7	4,718	4,657	13	-	13	1	6	28	13	3,709
42 38200	Jim Thorpe borough	Carbon	14.5	4,804	4,725	30	2	13	2	2	30	40	3,793
42 38248	Johnsonburg borough	Elk	3.0	3,003	2,968	1	9	11	1	3	10	39	2,271
42 38288	Johnstown city	Cambria	5.8	23,906	20,627	2,561	31	68	12	147	460	380	18,820
42 38688	Kane borough	McKean	1.6	4,126	4,081	5	4	7	-	10	19	34	3,172
42 39256	Kenhorst borough	Berks	0.6	2,679	2,568	22	1	43	-	28	17	54	2,187
42 39332	Kennedy Township CDP	Allegheny	5.4	7,504	7,402	38	1	36	2	3	22	22	5,969
42 39352	Kennett Square borough	Chester	1.1	5,273	3,880	541	5	86	-	658	103	1,470	3,963
42 39736	King of Prussia CDP	Montgomery	8.4	18,511	15,308	788	30	1,965	7	155	258	354	15,246
42 39784	Kingston borough	Luzerne	2.1	13,855	13,417	106	10	212	1	40	69	111	11,124
42 40040	Kittanning borough	Armstrong	1.0	4,787	4,658	75	11	12	-	4	27	32	3,726
42 40584	Kulpmont borough	Northumberland	0.9	2,985	2,952	14	-	1	-	7	11	16	2,401
42 40608	Kulpsville CDP	Montgomery	3.4	8,005	7,199	302	8	361	-	35	100	120	5,910
42 40656	Kutztown borough	Berks	1.6	5,067	4,915	50	5	45	-	27	25	49	4,440
42 40960	Lake City borough	Erie	1.8	2,811	2,792	-	-	4	-	4	11	17	1,968
42 41216	Lancaster city	Lancaster	7.4	56,348	34,683	7,939	247	1,386	47	9,826	2,220	17,331	40,870
42 41432	Lansdale borough	Montgomery	3.1	16,071	13,725	634	15	1,282	25	118	272	466	12,505
42 41440	Lansdowne borough	Delaware	1.2	11,044	8,311	2,096	10	317	1	47	262	163	8,509
42 41464	Lansford borough	Carbon	1.6	4,230	4,153	15	3	13	3	12	31	60	3,277
42 41608	Larksville borough	Luzerne	4.8	4,694	4,644	13	2	13	-	6	16	33	3,594
42 41680	Latrobe city	Westmoreland	2.3	8,994	8,884	29	7	40	-	6	28	33	7,090
42 41768	Laureldale borough	Berks	0.8	3,759	3,605	28	2	14	1	76	33	204	2,998
42 41944	Lawnton CDP	Dauphin	1.1	3,787	3,033	547	3	67	-	51	86	144	2,840
42 41992	Lawrence Park CDP	Erie	1.9	4,048	3,994	21	1	9	-	7	16	33	3,027
42 42084	Leacock-Leola-Bareville CDP	Lancaster	6.0	6,625	6,012	99	9	309	-	90	106	262	4,817
42 42168	Lebanon city	Lebanon	4.2	24,461	20,915	790	69	249	25	1,983	430	4,019	18,335
42 42472	Lehighton borough	Carbon	1.7	5,537	5,444	19	3	25	5	2	39	37	4,288
42 42596	Leith-Hatfield CDP	Fayette	1.9	2,820	2,737	16	3	44	1	2	17	4	2,218
42 42648	Lemoyne borough	Cumberland	1.6	3,995	3,856	23	3	52	-	22	39	43	3,171
42 42928	Levittown CDP	Bucks	10.2	53,966	50,922	1,321	88	520	22	462	631	1,199	39,728
42 42976	Lewisburg borough	Union	1.0	5,620	5,146	147	10	157	6	56	98	131	5,058
42 43000	Lewistown borough	Mifflin	2.0	8,998	8,774	86	18	26	2	33	59	102	6,917
42 43064	Liberty borough	Allegheny	1.4	2,670	2,616	39	3	3	1	-	8	10	2,132
42 43272	Lima CDP	Delaware	1.5	3,225	3,039	146	1	32	-	-	7	10	2,963
42 43672	Linglestown CDP	Dauphin	3.7	6,414	6,111	136	8	105	1	8	45	67	4,936
42 43720	Linwood CDP	Delaware	0.5	3,374	3,256	61	5	14	-	6	32	45	2,391
42 43747	Lionville-Marchwood CDP	Chester	2.5	6,298	5,814	161	7	234	1	17	64	76	4,744
42 43816	Lititz borough	Lancaster	2.3	9,029	8,779	40	8	79	3	45	75	137	6,949
42 43944	Littlestown borough	Adams	1.6	3,947	3,839	22	4	17	-	20	45	50	2,855
42 44128	Lock Haven city	Clinton	2.5	9,149	8,807	131	14	75	1	39	82	102	7,619
42 44672	Lorane CDP	Berks	1.6	2,994	2,888	59	3	18	1	4	21	40	2,286
42 44824	Lower Allen CDP	Cumberland	2.3	6,619	6,243	169	4	125	1	31	46	112	5,339
42 44864	Lower Burrell city	Westmoreland	11.5	12,608	12,349	117	4	45	2	13	78	56	9,899
42 45568	Luzerne borough	Luzerne	0.7	2,952	2,920	10	-	2	-	6	14	13	2,431

Table D-1. Places — **Area and Population**—Con.

[Includes incorporated places and census designated places (CDPs) of 2,500 or more population as of April 1, 2000. Codes shown are two-digit Federal Information Processing Standards (FIPS) state codes and five-digit FIPS place codes. Place names and codes are those in effect as of January 1, 2000. County refers to the county (or counties) in which the place is located. IC in this column = independent city, a county equivalent. If a place is located in more than one county, counties are listed in alphabetic order]

State and place code	Place	County	Population, 2000 (April 1) Land area, 2000 (sq. mi.)	Total	By race— One race White	Black or African American	American Indian and Alaska Native	Asian	Native Hawaiian and Other Pacific Islander	Some other race	Two or more races	Hispanic or Latino (of any race)	18 years and over
42 00000	PENNSYLVANIA—Con.												
42 45904	McCandless Township CDP	Allegheny	16.5	29,022	27,449	375	15	926	2	41	214	202	22,176
42 45940	McChesneytown-Loyalhanna CDP	Westmoreland	2.3	3,415	3,392	9	1	6	-	-	7	7	2,743
42 46160	McGovern CDP	Washington	1.9	2,538	2,488	40	-	3	-	-	7	13	2,054
42 46256	McKeesport city	Allegheny	5.0	24,040	17,406	5,881	66	30	2	141	514	361	17,929
42 46264	McKees Rocks borough	Allegheny	1.0	6,622	5,477	931	17	45	2	27	123	72	5,024
42 46344	McMurray CDP	Washington	3.1	4,726	4,630	26	1	46	-	7	16	34	3,262
42 46376	McSherrystown borough	Adams	0.5	2,691	2,634	14	6	5	1	8	23	44	2,090
42 46392	Macungie borough	Lehigh	1.0	3,039	2,883	41	2	64	1	25	23	41	2,417
42 46592	Mahanoy City borough	Schuylkill	0.5	4,647	4,591	10	4	10	-	10	22	60	3,656
42 46792	Malvern borough	Chester	1.3	3,059	2,787	117	6	99	-	8	42	47	2,444
42 46888	Manheim borough	Lancaster	1.4	4,784	4,611	30	4	48	1	29	61	81	3,609
42 47000	Manor borough	Westmoreland	2.0	2,796	2,779	3	2	6	-	2	4	24	1,994
42 47080	Mansfield borough	Tioga	1.9	3,411	3,184	142	11	26	-	13	35	34	2,965
42 47152	Maple Glen CDP	Montgomery	3.1	7,042	6,496	149	11	322	-	22	42	103	4,816
42 47424	Marietta borough	Lancaster	0.7	2,689	2,577	67	4	4	1	14	22	51	2,022
42 48000	Masontown borough	Fayette	1.5	3,611	3,368	202	8	1	-	11	21	8	2,780
42 48224	Maytown CDP	Lancaster	3.7	2,604	2,541	18	2	18	-	7	18	51	1,842
42 48336	Meadowood CDP	Butler	1.5	2,912	2,875	21	1	6	-	-	9	4	2,317
42 48360	Meadville city	Crawford	4.4	13,685	12,587	686	24	86	6	46	250	152	11,033
42 48376	Mechanicsburg borough	Cumberland	2.6	9,042	8,768	39	8	104	-	25	98	75	7,095
42 48440	Mechanicsville CDP	Montour	2.0	3,099	2,945	28	1	96	-	14	15	32	2,467
42 48480	Media borough	Delaware	0.7	5,533	4,483	787	8	111	1	36	107	104	4,774
42 48728	Meridian CDP	Butler	2.8	3,794	3,765	7	3	11	3	-	5	14	2,984
42 49128	Middletown borough	Dauphin	2.0	9,242	8,204	678	25	49	4	85	197	294	7,113
42 49144	Middletown CDP	Northampton	2.6	7,378	7,000	153	4	69	-	82	70	318	5,611
42 49184	Midland borough	Beaver	2.0	3,137	2,375	654	14	-	-	28	66	116	2,410
42 49288	Mifflinburg borough	Union	1.8	3,594	3,520	10	0	8	1	12	26	27	2,686
42 49680	Millersburg borough	Dauphin	0.8	2,562	2,524	6	3	13	-	8	8	28	2,033
42 49728	Millersville borough	Lancaster	2.0	7,774	7,187	335	5	87	6	76	78	198	6,930
42 49920	Millvale borough	Allegheny	0.7	4,028	3,907	39	8	7	-	27	40	36	3,082
42 50016	Milton borough	Northumberland	3.5	6,650	6,305	158	8	14	-	63	102	144	5,073
42 50088	Minersville borough	Schuylkill	0.7	4,552	4,484	20	3	8	1	3	33	26	3,577
42 50272	Mohnton borough	Berks	0.9	2,963	2,868	33	2	13	-	26	21	50	2,204
42 50320	Monaca borough	Beaver	2.1	6,286	6,105	122	-	14	-	3	42	38	4,901
42 50344	Monessen city	Westmoreland	2.9	8,669	7,257	1,213	8	20	1	29	141	71	6,969
42 50408	Monongahela city	Washington	1.9	4,761	4,520	155	4	9	-	20	53	34	3,804
42 50672	Montgomeryville CDP	Montgomery	4.8	12,031	10,533	392	7	933	3	48	115	165	8,438
42 50720	Montoursville borough	Lycoming	4.0	4,777	4,730	5	3	16	-	3	20	20	3,661
42 50880	Moosic borough	Lackawanna	6.5	5,575	5,502	16	-	27	-	14	16	30	4,493
42 51144	Morrisville borough	Bucks	1.8	10,023	7,615	1,918	18	120	-	208	144	483	7,545
42 51176	Morton borough	Delaware	0.4	2,715	1,897	664	2	106	-	9	37	31	2,087
42 51384	Mountain Top CDP	Luzerne	68.2	15,269	14,814	82	4	248	-	36	85	165	11,297
42 51496	Mount Carmel borough	Northumberland	0.7	6,390	6,298	4	10	18	1	16	43	57	5,133
42 51656	Mount Joy borough	Lancaster	2.3	6,765	6,475	100	8	34	-	77	71	209	5,158
42 51704	Mount Lebanon CDP	Allegheny	6.1	33,017	31,766	202	23	757	4	61	204	263	24,818
42 51744	Mount Oliver borough	Allegheny	0.3	3,970	3,325	466	9	65	1	27	77	43	3,017
42 51760	Mount Penn borough	Berks	0.4	3,016	2,909	32	1	32	-	15	27	102	2,277
42 51880	Mount Pleasant borough	Westmoreland	1.1	4,728	4,591	79	7	11	-	7	33	15	3,825
42 51912	Mount Pocono borough	Monroe	3.5	2,742	2,247	297	4	25	-	97	72	278	1,987
42 51984	Mount Union borough	Huntingdon	1.1	2,504	2,166	276	1	-	-	8	53	30	1,862
42 52264	Muncy borough	Lycoming	0.8	2,663	2,622	1	2	6	-	8	24	25	2,036
42 52320	Munhall borough	Allegheny	2.3	12,264	11,624	415	2	75	-	35	113	98	9,720
42 52330	Municipality of Monroeville borough	Allegheny	19.8	29,349	25,118	2,432	41	1,294	13	89	362	225	23,370
42 52332	Municipality of Murrysville borough	Westmoreland	36.9	18,872	18,000	116	9	619	2	31	95	106	14,180
42 52488	Myerstown borough	Lebanon	0.9	3,171	3,091	46	-	14	-	7	13	30	2,467
42 52584	Nanticoke city	Luzerne	3.5	10,955	10,828	30	11	28	1	17	40	49	8,799
42 52616	Nanty-Glo borough	Cambria	1.8	3,054	3,036	7	1	-	-	1	9	9	2,399
42 52664	Narberth borough	Montgomery	0.5	4,233	4,031	50	5	96	-	6	45	59	3,289
42 52808	Nazareth borough	Northampton	1.7	6,023	5,930	33	5	24	-	17	14	57	4,806
42 53088	Nesquehoning borough	Carbon	21.2	3,288	3,212	21	8	14	-	10	23	50	2,669
42 53112	Nether Providence Township CDP	Delaware	4.7	13,456	12,121	824	13	315	5	36	142	152	10,033
42 53288	New Brighton borough	Beaver	1.0	6,641	5,730	701	16	13	-	19	162	33	4,922
42 53296	New Britain borough	Bucks	1.3	3,125	2,996	64	2	25	1	8	29	51	2,545
42 53368	New Castle city	Lawrence	8.5	26,309	22,829	2,839	28	46	2	78	487	199	20,043
42 53464	New Cumberland borough	Cumberland	1.7	7,349	7,143	47	7	53	4	30	65	83	5,790
42 53568	New Freedom borough	York	2.1	3,512	3,390	27	5	49	-	3	37	17	2,593
42 53696	New Holland borough	Lancaster	2.1	5,092	4,600	52	4	219	1	131	85	327	3,952
42 53736	New Kensington city	Westmoreland	4.0	14,701	12,915	1,447	18	34	1	54	232	106	11,503
42 54268	Newtown Grant CDP	Bucks	0.8	3,887	3,682	48	3	105	-	13	36	58	2,746
42 54656	Norristown borough	Montgomery	3.5	31,282	16,992	10,887	63	926	10	1,443	961	3,282	23,435
42 54696	Northampton borough	Northampton	2.6	9,405	9,237	33	5	41	-	37	52	164	7,295
42 54816	North Braddock borough	Allegheny	1.5	6,410	3,955	2,263	11	20	3	38	120	80	4,681

[Includes incorporated places and census designated places (CDPs) of 2,500 or more population as of April 1, 2000. Codes shown are two-digit Federal Information Processing Standards (FIPS) state codes and five-digit FIPS place codes. Place names and codes are those in effect as of January 1, 2000. County refers to the county (or counties) in which the place is located. IC in this column = independent city, a county equivalent. If a place is located in more than one county, counties are listed in alphabetic order]

State and place code	Place	County	Land area, 2000 (sq. mi.)	Population, 2000 (April 1)									
					By race—								
					One race							Hispanic or Latino (of any race)	18 years and over
				Total	White	Black or African American	American Indian and Alaska Native	Asian	Native Hawaiian and Other Pacific Islander	Some other race	Two or more races		
42 00000	PENNSYLVANIA—Con.												
42 54872	North Catasauqua borough.	Northampton	0.7	2,814	2,750	13	1	13	2	13	22	51	2,161
42 54952	North East borough	Erie	1.3	4,601	4,493	37	4	4	-	27	36	86	3,335
42 55000	Northern Cambria borough.	Cambria	3.0	4,199	4,170	3	4	10	1	4	7	13	3,275
42 55456	Northumberland borough .	Northumberland	1.6	3,714	3,654	27	5	7	1	15	6	23	2,908
42 55496	North Versailles CDP	Allegheny	8.1	11,125	9,769	1,087	7	85	3	24	150	54	8,910
42 55512	North Wales borough . . .	Montgomery	0.6	3,342	3,018	161	2	70	6	26	59	50	2,447
42 55572	Northwest Harborcreek CDP	Erie	5.0	8,658	8,434	120	8	51	-	10	35	38	6,639
42 55664	Norwood borough	Delaware	0.8	5,985	5,839	66	3	42	-	11	24	44	4,411
42 56088	Oakmont borough	Allegheny	1.6	6,911	6,762	62	7	34	-	12	34	43	5,576
42 56386	O'Hara Township CDP . . .	Allegheny	7.0	8,856	8,435	74	4	269	-	23	51	101	6,585
42 56432	Ohioville borough	Beaver	23.4	3,759	3,652	75	1	3	-	9	19	30	2,820
42 56456	Oil City city	Venango	4.5	11,504	11,256	102	30	33	5	13	65	72	8,534
42 56576	Old Forge borough	Lackawanna	3.5	8,798	8,711	14	3	34	-	11	25	30	7,060
42 56704	Oliver CDP	Fayette	2.2	2,925	2,675	202	7	14	1	3	23	15	2,306
42 56792	Olyphant borough	Lackawanna	5.4	4,978	4,903	23	1	20	2	4	25	27	3,945
42 57024	Oreland CDP	Montgomery	1.4	5,509	4,693	666	12	82	-	19	37	50	4,096
42 57184	Orwigsburg borough	Schuylkill	2.2	3,106	3,035	10	1	34	2	7	17	17	2,403
42 57480	Oxford borough.	Chester	1.9	4,315	3,355	512	4	27	10	319	88	697	3,211
42 57680	Palmer Heights CDP	Northampton	1.2	3,612	3,447	60	4	45	1	33	22	95	2,975
42 57696	Palmerton borough	Carbon	2.5	5,248	5,158	8	9	9	2	24	38	124	4,037
42 57720	Palmyra borough	Lebanon	1.9	7,096	6,863	64	8	65	1	24	71	85	5,522
42 57816	Paoli CDP	Chester	2.0	5,425	4,933	291	5	143	1	21	31	46	4,329
42 58032	Parkesburg borough	Chester	1.2	3,373	3,067	232	5	5	1	38	25	127	2,371
42 58036	Park Forest Village CDP .	Centre.	2.4	8,830	7,486	260	11	806	9	61	197	230	6,829
42 58240	Parkville CDP	York	2.9	6,593	6,402	36	13	64	3	36	39	89	4,852
42 58416	Patterson Township CDP .	Beaver	1.7	3,197	3,114	47	5	2	-	1	28	21	2,491
42 58528	Paxtonia CDP.	Dauphin	2.3	5,254	4,731	287	4	117	2	46	67	93	3,908
42 58696	Pen Argyl borough	Northampton	1.4	3,615	3,536	17	4	20	-	9	29	44	2,649
42 58712	Penbrook borough	Dauphin	0.5	3,044	2,354	464	7	49	-	57	113	140	2,243
42 59040	Penn Hills CDP.	Allegheny	19.0	46,809	34,443	11,347	62	255	5	157	540	297	36,669
42 59120	Pennsburg borough	Montgomery	0.8	2,732	2,660	22	2	13	-	15	20	44	1,995
42 59312	Penn Wynne CDP	Montgomery	1.0	5,382	4,921	197	-	192	-	24	48	67	4,083
42 59384	Perkasie borough	Bucks	2.6	8,828	8,631	52	14	47	-	32	52	120	6,219
42 60000	Philadelphia city	Philadelphia	135.1	1,517,550	683,267	655,824	4,073	67,654	729	72,429	33,574	128,928	1,134,081
42 60008	Philipsburg borough.	Centre.	0.8	3,056	3,007	9	5	12	-	3	20	8	2,375
42 60120	Phoenixville borough	Chester	3.6	14,788	12,857	1,133	22	358	3	173	242	432	11,467
42 60712	Pitcairn borough	Allegheny	0.5	3,689	3,619	16	4	15	-	2	33	20	2,869
42 61000	Pittsburgh city.	Allegheny	55.6	334,563	226,258	90,750	628	9,195	111	2,218	5,403	4,425	268,055
42 61048	Pittston city	Luzerne.	1.6	8,104	7,973	55	7	25	2	14	28	55	6,345
42 61328	Pleasant Hills borough . . .	Allegheny	2.7	8,397	8,149	110	4	90	1	12	31	30	6,547
42 61536	Plum borough.	Allegheny	28.6	26,940	25,754	743	23	231	7	45	137	167	20,247
42 61648	Plymouth borough	Luzerne.	1.1	6,507	6,405	49	10	7	-	14	22	52	4,997
42 61688	Plymouth Meeting CDP . .	Montgomery	3.8	5,593	4,997	190	5	352	-	8	41	51	4,323
42 62048	Portage borough	Cambria	0.7	2,837	2,822	2	1	2	-	1	9	14	2,251
42 62320	Port Vue borough	Allegheny	1.1	4,228	4,175	29	1	1	1	5	16	32	3,346
42 62396	Pottsgrove CDP	Montgomery	2.7	3,266	3,185	29	1	27	1	4	19	20	2,458
42 62416	Pottstown borough	Montgomery	4.8	21,859	17,343	3,291	50	142	19	413	601	990	16,260
42 62432	Pottsville city	Schuylkill	4.2	15,549	14,885	352	19	79	1	82	131	190	12,042
42 62736	Progress CDP	Dauphin	2.8	9,647	7,253	1,830	15	184	5	124	236	276	7,662
42 62792	Prospect Park borough. . .	Delaware	0.7	6,594	6,293	91	8	115	1	26	60	60	4,905
42 62920	Punxsutawney borough . .	Jefferson	3.4	6,271	6,195	14	10	17	-	1	34	47	4,937
42 63048	Quakertown borough	Bucks	2.0	8,931	8,436	107	12	135	5	141	95	257	6,653
42 63268	Radnor Township CDP . . .	Delaware	13.8	30,878	27,652	953	24	1,750	5	190	304	628	24,866
42 63624	Reading city.	Berks	9.8	81,207	48,059	9,947	356	1,296	32	18,125	3,392	30,302	56,913
42 63664	Reamstown CDP.	Lancaster	2.3	3,498	3,331	11	9	78	1	28	40	67	2,498
42 63840	Red Lion borough	York	1.3	6,149	5,972	37	15	25	3	20	77	56	4,605
42 64072	Reiffton CDP	Berks	1.6	2,888	2,805	32	1	32	-	6	12	28	2,251
42 64248	Reserve Township CDP . .	Allegheny	2.0	3,856	3,775	52	7	11	-	6	5	17	2,998
42 64376	Reynoldsville borough . . .	Jefferson	1.4	2,710	2,679	4	10	3	-	-	14	15	1,977
42 64464	Richboro CDP	Bucks	4.4	6,678	6,484	24	-	121	-	1	48	42	4,747
42 64784	Ridgway borough	Elk	2.7	4,591	4,524	8	2	32	-	8	17	24	3,539
42 64832	Ridley Park borough	Delaware	1.1	7,196	6,974	46	1	106	2	15	52	36	5,654
42 65378	Robinson Township CDP .	Allegheny	14.7	12,289	11,705	234	7	251	3	17	72	90	9,488
42 65392	Rochester borough	Beaver	0.6	4,014	3,364	537	9	8	-	23	73	37	3,146
42 65568	Rockledge borough	Montgomery	0.3	2,577	2,525	1	1	25	-	8	17	15	1,970
42 66356	Ross Township CDP	Allegheny	14.4	32,551	31,225	463	27	586	21	65	164	237	26,246
42 66392	Rothsville CDP	Lancaster	2.5	3,017	2,892	10	-	39	-	21	55	88	2,045
42 66576	Royersford borough	Montgomery	0.8	4,246	4,075	83	10	27	-	12	39	50	3,277
42 66864	Rutherford CDP	Dauphin	1.2	3,859	3,382	301	4	67	2	37	66	100	2,971
42 67224	St. Clair borough	Schuylkill	1.2	3,254	3,212	22	3	2	-	7	8	23	2,650
42 67344	St. Marys city	Elk	99.3	14,502	14,321	33	11	61	13	18	45	44	11,008
42 67659	Salunga-Landisville CDP .	Lancaster	3.0	4,771	4,583	51	-	83	-	23	31	78	3,458
42 67712	Sanatoga CDP	Montgomery	3.4	7,734	6,620	886	11	71	3	25	118	117	5,351
42 68096	Sayre borough	Bradford	2.0	5,813	5,634	36	10	73	-	9	51	41	4,426
42 68188	Schlusser CDP	Cumberland	2.9	4,750	4,386	159	11	102	10	33	49	79	3,683
42 68312	Schuylkill Haven borough .	Schuylkill	1.4	5,548	5,394	42	8	39	3	16	46	70	4,269

[Includes incorporated places and census designated places (CDPs) of 2,500 or more population as of April 1, 2000. Codes shown are two-digit Federal Information Processing Standards (FIPS) state codes and five-digit FIPS place codes. Place names and codes are those in effect as of January 1, 2000. County refers to the county (or counties) in which the place is located. IC in this column = independent city, a county equivalent. If a place is located in more than one county, counties are listed in alphabetic order]

				Population, 2000 (April 1)									
					By race—								
					One race								
State and place code	Place	County	Land area, 2000 (sq. mi.)	Total	White	Black or African American	American Indian and Alaska Native	Asian	Native Hawaiian and Other Pacific Islander	Some other race	Two or more races	Hispanic or Latino (of any race)	18 years and over
42 00000	PENNSYLVANIA—Con.												
42 68432	Scottdale borough	Westmoreland	1.2	4,772	4,683	53	5	6	3	4	18	17	3,760
42 68464	Scott Township CDP	Allegheny	4.0	17,288	15,792	198	14	1,067	2	40	175	117	14,072
42 69000	Scranton city	Lackawanna	25.2	76,415	71,480	2,304	85	823	15	890	818	1,999	60,538
42 69216	Selinsgrove borough	Snyder	1.9	5,383	5,096	147	4	49	-	47	40	157	4,595
42 69248	Sellersville borough	Bucks	1.2	4,564	4,441	26	7	16	2	22	50	81	3,304
42 69376	Sewickley borough	Allegheny	1.0	3,902	3,442	376	5	33	1	2	43	42	3,109
42 69596	Shaler Township CDP	Allegheny	11.0	29,757	29,139	122	18	268	7	35	168	155	23,206
42 69600	Shamokin city	Northumberland	0.8	8,009	7,916	10	8	25	1	11	38	52	6,234
42 69715	Shanor-Northvue CDP	Butler	6.7	4,825	4,737	19	1	32	1	12	23	21	3,779
42 69720	Sharon city	Mercer	3.8	16,328	14,114	1,771	29	34	4	37	339	144	12,349
42 69752	Sharon Hill borough	Delaware	0.8	5,468	3,886	1,356	5	83	2	27	109	58	3,945
42 69776	Sharpsburg borough	Allegheny	0.5	3,594	3,369	137	1	23	2	13	49	76	2,873
42 69800	Sharpsville borough	Mercer	1.4	4,500	4,329	104	6	18	-	13	30	41	3,439
42 70056	Shenandoah borough	Schuylkill	1.5	5,624	5,478	19	14	20	2	57	34	155	4,558
42 70248	Shillington borough	Berks	1.0	5,059	4,913	25	5	27	-	38	51	106	3,970
42 70256	Shiloh CDP	York	4.2	10,192	9,722	174	8	151	-	31	106	108	8,081
42 70352	Shippensburg borough	Cumberland, Franklin	2.0	5,586	5,260	192	6	55	1	26	46	64	4,601
42 70568	Shrewsbury borough	York	1.8	3,378	3,293	27	5	26	5	9	13	33	2,511
42 70880	Sinking Spring borough	Berks	1.3	2,639	2,527	28	4	21	-	32	27	72	2,121
42 71008	Skippack CDP	Montgomery	2.5	2,889	2,794	29	13	31	-	6	16	38	2,141
42 71144	Slatington borough	Lehigh	1.3	4,434	4,267	63	9	17	1	34	43	90	3,233
42 71184	Slippery Rock borough	Butler	1.7	3,068	2,801	100	6	101	2	21	37	34	2,806
42 71776	Somerset borough	Somerset	2.7	6,762	6,613	47	6	47	2	13	34	37	5,280
42 71856	Souderton borough	Montgomery	1.1	6,730	6,171	67	13	268	2	125	84	289	5,038
42 72403	South Park Township CDP	Allegheny	9.2	14,340	13,645	460	9	109	6	17	94	79	10,673
42 72648	South Williamsport borough	Lycoming	1.9	6,412	6,331	28	8	13	-	2	30	36	4,903
42 72920	Spring City borough	Chester	0.8	3,305	3,148	64	17	34	2	9	31	39	2,617
42 72960	Springdale borough	Allegheny	0.9	3,828	3,791	11	3	5	-	7	11	8	2,991
42 72994	Springetts Manor-Yorklyn CDP	York	1.1	4,156	3,303	583	5	141	3	77	44	329	3,614
42 73040	Springfield CDP	Delaware	6.4	23,677	22,868	170	13	466	3	29	128	146	17,997
42 73264	Spring House CDP	Montgomery	2.6	3,290	3,076	75	-	118	1	5	15	22	2,590
42 73528	Spry CDP	York	2.6	4,903	4,714	74	6	59	-	7	43	64	3,845
42 73808	State College borough	Centre	4.5	38,420	32,392	1,417	58	3,368	50	529	606	1,159	36,208
42 73888	Steelton borough	Dauphin	1.8	5,858	3,634	1,823	13	38	2	141	207	438	4,172
42 74426	Stonybrook-Wilshire CDP	York	3.4	5,414	5,035	110	9	139	4	41	76	95	4,109
42 74660	Stowe CDP	Montgomery	1.5	3,585	3,200	259	6	32	1	26	61	76	2,703
42 74661	Stowe Township CDP	Allegheny	2.0	6,706	6,065	539	14	11	-	15	62	28	5,374
42 74712	Strasburg borough	Lancaster	1.0	2,800	2,734	16	2	24	-	3	21	12	2,075
42 74888	Stroudsburg borough	Monroe	1.8	5,756	4,985	371	12	109	-	130	149	400	4,538
42 75000	Sugarcreek borough	Venango	37.4	5,331	5,264	17	7	10	-	6	27	15	4,161
42 75248	Summit Hill borough	Carbon	8.9	2,974	2,944	2	3	5	-	2	18	12	2,377
42 75304	Sunbury city	Northumberland	2.1	10,610	10,107	137	15	28	2	203	118	328	8,076
42 75648	Swarthmore borough	Delaware	1.4	6,170	5,298	291	15	339	3	66	158	208	4,904
42 75816	Swissvale borough	Allegheny	1.2	9,653	7,187	2,137	11	88	6	58	166	102	7,724
42 75832	Swoyersville borough	Luzerne	2.2	5,157	5,117	5	3	8	-	4	20	8	4,201
42 76032	Tamaqua borough	Schuylkill	9.8	7,174	7,080	13	6	16	-	18	41	93	5,611
42 76104	Tarentum borough	Allegheny	1.2	4,993	4,683	182	14	30	2	13	69	45	3,895
42 76184	Taylor borough	Lackawanna	5.2	6,475	6,367	22	5	40	-	26	15	41	5,087
42 76304	Telford borough	Bucks, Montgomery	1.0	4,680	4,328	61	1	176	1	53	60	169	3,604
42 76552	Thompsonville CDP	Washington	2.0	3,592	3,525	12	2	29	-	10	14	25	2,718
42 76584	Thorndale CDP	Chester	1.8	3,561	2,943	391	8	83	4	76	56	154	2,631
42 76648	Throop borough	Lackawanna	5.0	4,010	3,969	19	-	5	-	1	16	30	3,167
42 76796	Tinicum Township CDP	Delaware	5.7	4,353	4,226	35	3	19	-	14	56	55	3,339
42 76904	Titusville city	Crawford	2.9	6,146	5,997	74	18	17	-	5	35	52	4,656
42 77168	Towanda borough	Bradford	1.1	3,024	2,914	26	11	36	-	4	33	36	2,266
42 77272	Trafford borough	Allegheny, Westmoreland	1.4	3,236	3,180	22	1	10	-	6	17	13	2,600
42 77304	Trappe borough	Montgomery	2.1	3,210	3,018	77	7	44	-	11	53	38	2,416
42 77335	Treasure Lake CDP	Clearfield	10.7	4,507	4,425	13	3	39	1	7	19	25	3,405
42 77520	Trooper CDP	Montgomery	2.4	6,061	5,564	79	14	341	-	11	52	89	4,296
42 77912	Turtle Creek borough	Allegheny	1.0	6,076	5,633	314	5	37	-	9	78	37	4,857
42 78116	Tyler Run-Queens Gate CDP	York	1.6	2,926	2,748	88	3	50	2	18	17	38	2,475
42 78168	Tyrone borough	Blair	2.0	5,528	5,465	18	6	6	-	8	25	30	4,282
42 78448	Union City borough	Erie	1.9	3,463	3,391	5	11	26	1	8	21	29	2,422
42 78528	Uniontown city	Fayette	2.0	12,422	10,455	1,686	12	50	4	35	180	68	9,820
42 78712	Upland borough	Delaware	0.7	2,977	2,299	586	9	10	-	24	49	62	2,123
42 79260	Upper Providence Township CDP	Delaware	5.6	10,509	9,650	410	8	321	-	31	89	112	7,910
42 79277	Upper St. Clair CDP	Allegheny	9.8	20,053	18,962	136	5	806	5	15	124	157	14,369
42 79640	Valley Green CDP	York	1.4	3,550	3,414	54	1	31	2	15	33	74	2,487
42 79682	Valley View CDP	York	0.8	2,743	2,657	46	1	21	-	2	16	25	2,216
42 79776	Vandergrift borough	Westmoreland	1.2	5,455	5,151	188	11	13	1	9	82	20	4,259
42 80032	Verona borough	Allegheny	0.5	3,124	2,992	96	4	11	-	5	16	10	2,377
42 80218	Village Green-Green Ridge CDP	Delaware	1.8	8,279	8,081	50	2	63	2	21	60	92	6,425

[Includes incorporated places and census designated places (CDPs) of 2,500 or more population as of April 1, 2000. Codes shown are two-digit Federal Information Processing Standards (FIPS) state codes and five-digit FIPS place codes. Place names and codes are those in effect as of January 1, 2000. County refers to the county (or counties) in which the place is located. IC in this column = independent city, a county equivalent. If a place is located in more than one county, counties are listed in alphabetic order]

State and place code	Place	County	Land area, 2000 (sq. mi.)	Population, 2000 (April 1)									
					By race—								
					One race								
				Total	White	Black or African American	American Indian and Alaska Native	Asian	Native Hawaiian and Other Pacific Islander	Some other race	Two or more races	Hispanic or Latino (of any race)	18 years and over
42 00000	PENNSYLVANIA—Con.												
42 80229	Village Shires CDP	Bucks	1.2	4,137	4,017	25	5	39	-	20	31	40	3,214
42 80962	Warminster Heights CDP	Bucks	0.6	4,191	2,739	548	18	166	1	528	191	1,007	2,948
42 81000	Warren city	Warren	2.9	10,259	10,108	21	21	37	2	13	57	40	7,885
42 81328	Washington city	Washington	2.9	15,268	12,501	2,229	23	69	3	93	350	144	12,032
42 81824	Waynesboro borough	Franklin	3.4	9,614	9,153	252	14	48	1	52	94	148	7,396
42 81832	Waynesburg borough	Greene	0.8	4,184	4,056	68	4	24	2	7	23	27	3,404
42 81856	Weatherly borough	Carbon	3.0	2,612	2,585	7	-	2	1	6	11	18	2,012
42 82008	Weigelstown CDP	York	5.8	10,117	9,757	123	22	57	1	76	81	144	7,653
42 82160	Wellsboro borough	Tioga	4.9	3,328	3,266	13	6	30	-	6	7	19	2,631
42 82344	Wesleyville borough	Erie	0.5	3,617	3,498	39	10	8	1	18	43	61	2,737
42 82704	West Chester borough	Chester	1.8	17,861	13,475	3,050	55	261	13	650	357	1,596	15,472
42 83072	West Goshen CDP	Chester	3.2	8,472	7,434	420	8	475	1	64	70	193	6,557
42 83104	West Grove borough	Chester	0.6	2,652	2,088	222	11	-	-	259	72	451	1,826
42 83136	West Hazleton borough	Luzerne	1.6	3,542	3,461	20	2	8	-	36	15	79	2,823
42 83512	West Mifflin borough	Allegheny	14.2	22,464	20,137	1,987	26	56	13	57	188	127	17,631
42 83584	Westmont borough	Cambria	2.4	5,523	5,390	17	5	71	3	7	30	50	4,178
42 83680	West Newton borough	Westmoreland	1.1	3,083	3,006	35	5	7	-	5	25	13	2,426
42 83704	West Norriton CDP	Montgomery	5.9	14,901	13,335	909	11	407	8	72	159	236	12,071
42 83856	West Pittston borough	Luzerne	0.8	5,072	5,040	5	2	2	-	5	18	12	4,060
42 83928	West Reading borough	Berks	0.6	4,049	3,617	163	9	62	1	138	59	315	3,290
42 84144	West View borough	Allegheny	1.0	7,277	7,104	68	5	38	-	13	49	39	5,572
42 84272	West Wyoming borough	Luzerne	3.6	2,833	2,814	5	-	2	1	1	10	7	2,242
42 84280	West Wyomissing CDP	Berks	0.7	3,016	2,879	38	2	16	1	36	44	93	2,463
42 84288	West York borough	York	0.5	4,321	4,051	121	13	7	-	59	70	128	3,231
42 84512	Whitehall borough	Allegheny	3.3	14,444	13,953	205	3	134	2	40	107	96	11,645
42 84704	White Oak borough	Allegheny	6.7	8,437	8,201	157	1	30	1	10	37	34	6,932
42 84856	Whitfield CDP	Berks	0.7	2,952	2,843	15	-	60	-	21	13	54	2,217
42 85152	Wilkes-Barre city	Luzerne	6.8	43,123	39,801	2,193	48	342	14	228	497	683	34,549
42 85168	Wilkes-Barre Township CDP	Luzerne	3.0	3,235	3,006	76	7	117	-	3	26	25	2,657
42 85188	Wilkinsburg borough	Allegheny	2.3	19,196	5,615	12,768	72	156	12	105	468	216	14,711
42 85192	Wilkins Township CDP	Allegheny	2.6	6,917	6,418	303	6	105	4	13	68	31	5,747
42 85312	Williamsport city	Lycoming	8.9	30,706	25,827	3,910	111	175	4	147	532	340	23,805
42 85408	Willow Grove CDP	Montgomery	3.6	16,234	14,378	1,068	14	496	4	78	196	255	12,511
42 85464	Willow Street CDP	Lancaster	5.4	7,258	7,132	27	3	37	-	26	33	86	6,019
42 85592	Wilson borough	Northampton	1.2	7,682	7,211	141	5	120	3	85	117	311	5,771
42 85632	Windber borough	Somerset	2.1	4,395	4,364	-	3	4	1	7	16	25	3,458
42 85664	Wind Gap borough	Northampton	1.4	2,812	2,745	13	1	19	-	15	19	45	2,226
42 86000	Wolfdale CDP	Washington	2.4	2,873	2,797	34	3	4	-	2	33	15	2,294
42 86056	Womelsdorf borough	Berks	0.9	2,599	2,507	17	-	37	-	25	13	57	1,968
42 86112	Woodbourne CDP	Bucks	1.2	3,512	3,289	66	-	112	1	7	37	52	2,259
42 86288	Woodlyn CDP	Delaware	1.6	10,036	8,820	918	15	118	7	34	124	138	7,467
42 86352	Woodside CDP	Bucks	1.0	2,575	2,389	48	1	113	-	5	19	31	1,790
42 86528	Wormleysburg borough	Cumberland	0.9	2,607	2,402	34	4	110	1	8	48	35	2,146
42 86744	Wyncote CDP	Montgomery	0.8	3,046	2,736	243	2	38	3	8	16	24	2,428
42 86776	Wyndmoor CDP	Montgomery	1.7	5,601	4,520	875	11	119	-	19	57	59	4,466
42 86856	Wyoming borough	Luzerne	1.4	3,221	3,205	2	-	2	1	5	6	9	2,601
42 86880	Wyomissing borough	Berks	3.8	8,587	8,137	129	6	163	2	76	74	157	7,021
42 86888	Wyomissing Hills borough	Berks	0.7	2,568	2,399	22	4	94	-	25	24	52	1,985
42 86968	Yeadon borough	Delaware	1.6	11,762	1,830	9,500	25	105	1	48	253	120	8,886
42 87048	York city	York	5.2	40,862	24,416	10,270	172	574	28	3,839	1,563	7,026	29,243
42 87232	Youngwood borough	Westmoreland	1.8	4,138	3,628	482	10	7	-	1	10	98	3,530
42 87272	Zelienople borough	Butler	2.1	4,123	4,037	16	3	27	-	7	33	13	3,254
44 00000	RHODE ISLAND		1,044.9	1,048,319	891,191	46,908	5,121	23,665	567	52,616	28,251	90,820	800,497
44 04960	Barrington CDP	Bristol	8.4	16,819	16,209	115	19	297	-	43	136	177	12,074
44 09460	Bristol CDP	Bristol	10.1	22,469	21,826	140	37	151	10	74	231	289	18,070
44 14140	Central Falls city	Providence	1.2	18,928	10,820	1,101	108	128	8	5,367	1,396	9,041	13,397
44 19180	Cranston city	Providence	28.6	79,269	70,703	2,926	236	2,599	33	1,528	1,244	3,613	62,171
44 20260	Cumberland Hill CDP	Providence	3.3	7,738	7,497	30	2	99	3	41	66	97	5,831
44 22960	East Providence city	Providence	13.4	48,688	42,111	2,445	225	559	23	1,361	1,964	922	38,142
44 31600	Greenville CDP	Providence	5.2	8,626	8,494	24	17	44	2	5	40	50	6,757
44 38980	Kingston CDP	Washington	1.6	5,446	4,664	191	82	249	13	130	117	250	5,116
44 44870	Narragansett Pier CDP	Washington	3.6	3,671	3,452	32	62	38	-	29	58	69	3,184
44 49960	Newport city	Newport	7.9	26,475	22,272	2,053	225	353	23	638	911	1,467	21,276
44 50140	Newport East CDP	Newport	5.7	11,463	10,369	463	42	213	13	98	265	249	8,988
44 51940	North Providence CDP	Providence	5.7	32,411	29,812	859	55	598	7	511	569	1,247	26,475
44 54460	Pascoag CDP	Providence	5.0	4,742	4,663	17	15	13	1	8	25	49	3,486
44 54640	Pawtucket city	Providence	8.7	72,958	55,004	5,334	217	621	42	7,841	3,899	10,141	54,807
44 59000	Providence city	Providence	18.5	173,618	94,666	25,243	1,975	10,432	270	30,477	10,555	52,146	128,341
44 70700	Tiverton CDP	Newport	4.2	7,282	7,121	27	15	36	5	19	59	72	5,805
44 72500	Valley Falls CDP	Providence	3.5	11,599	11,121	96	13	60	-	165	144	457	8,901
44 73130	Wakefield-Peacedale CDP	Washington	4.9	8,468	7,650	170	261	104	-	47	236	132	6,067
44 74300	Warwick city	Kent	35.5	85,808	81,695	996	213	1,281	15	506	1,102	1,372	67,028
44 76820	Westerly CDP	Washington	16.0	17,682	16,736	145	97	424	-	61	219	205	13,664
44 78260	West Warwick CDP	Kent	7.9	29,581	27,740	328	105	420	7	425	556	918	22,949
44 80780	Woonsocket city	Providence	7.7	43,224	35,935	1,920	139	1,755	14	2,102	1,359	4,030	32,069

Table D-1. Places — **Area and Population**—Con.

[Includes incorporated places and census designated places (CDPs) of 2,500 or more population as of April 1, 2000. Codes shown are two-digit Federal Information Processing Standards (FIPS) state codes and five-digit FIPS place codes. Place names and codes are those in effect as of January 1, 2000. County refers to the county (or counties) in which the place is located. IC in this column = independent city, a county equivalent. If a place is located in more than one county, counties are listed in alphabetic order]

State and place code	Place	County	Land area, 2000 (sq. mi.)	Population, 2000 (April 1)									
					By race—								
					One race						Two or more races	Hispanic or Latino (of any race)	18 years and over
				Total	White	Black or African American	American Indian and Alaska Native	Asian	Native Hawaiian and Other Pacific Islander	Some other race			
45 00000	SOUTH CAROLINA.....		30,109.5	4,012,012	2,695,560	1,185,216	13,718	36,014	1,628	39,926	39,950	95,076	3,002,371
45 00100	Abbeville city	Abbeville	5.9	5,840	2,947	2,831	7	15	1	11	28	44	4,250
45 00550	Aiken city	Aiken	16.2	25,337	16,881	7,678	64	324	3	111	276	378	19,451
45 00955	Allendale town	Allendale	3.3	4,052	737	3,243	-	7	7	39	19	91	2,730
45 01360	Anderson city	Anderson	13.8	25,514	16,105	8,678	55	199	9	173	295	377	19,858
45 01450	Andrews town	Georgetown, Williamsburg	2.2	3,068	1,152	1,864	7	-	-	27	18	44	2,133
45 02440	Arial CDP	Pickens	4.9	2,607	2,446	109	2	4	-	25	21	49	1,999
45 03790	Bamberg town	Bamberg	3.5	3,733	1,688	2,000	8	12	-	4	21	18	2,774
45 04060	Barnwell city	Barnwell	7.6	5,035	2,508	2,385	20	53	2	17	50	31	3,603
45 04300	Batesburg-Leesville town .	Lexington, Saluda	7.3	5,517	2,914	2,519	16	11	-	22	35	89	4,054
45 04690	Beaufort city	Beaufort	18.6	12,950	8,988	3,256	41	138	16	257	254	568	10,154
45 05365	Belton city	Anderson	3.9	4,461	3,592	781	17	12	-	15	44	80	3,441
45 05410	Belvedere CDP	Aiken	3.9	5,631	4,189	1,331	5	22	2	29	53	102	4,198
45 05680	Bennettsville city	Marlboro	5.6	9,425	3,280	5,952	80	47	-	10	56	59	7,248
45 05770	Berea CDP	Greenville	7.6	14,158	10,717	2,257	23	207	1	696	257	1,902	10,881
45 06310	Bishopville city	Lee...............	2.4	3,670	1,205	2,416	4	16	-	8	21	48	2,672
45 06490	Blackville town	Barnwell	9.2	2,973	703	2,248	2	6	2	1	11	15	2,105
45 07345	Boiling Springs CDP	Spartanburg	6.8	4,544	4,127	288	11	68	-	23	27	55	3,358
45 09527	Brookdale CDP	Orangeburg	3.6	4,724	45	4,632	8	4	1	10	24	30	3,399
45 10270	Burnettown town	Aiken	4.8	2,720	2,350	323	7	16	-	7	17	20	2,057
45 10360	Burton CDP	Beaufort	11.0	7,180	3,719	2,983	23	95	1	182	177	432	5,000
45 10855	Camden city	Kershaw	9.7	6,682	4,057	2,485	7	30	7	42	54	88	5,226
45 12655	Cayce city	Lexington	10.9	12,150	9,058	2,734	31	131	18	81	97	155	9,634
45 12965	Centerville CDP	Anderson	5.9	5,181	4,688	385	4	56	1	18	29	52	3,933
45 13015	Central town	Pickens	2.4	3,522	2,807	537	11	63	-	75	39	152	2,991
45 13330	Charleston city	Berkeley, Charleston	97.0	96,650	60,964	32,864	145	1,197	55	518	907	1,462	77,333
45 13600	Cheraw town	Chesterfield	4.6	5,524	2,528	2,884	20	45	-	17	30	44	4,062
45 14095	Chester city	Chester	3.2	6,476	2,355	4,032	10	18	2	16	43	54	4,581
45 14000	Clearwater CDP	Aiken	4.3	4,199	3,356	675	25	14	1	70	58	157	3,156
45 14950	Clemson city	Anderson, Pickens	7.4	11,939	9,668	1,359	13	684	3	87	125	217	10,209
45 15295	Clinton city	Laurens	9.1	8,091	4,880	3,073	17	22	2	37	60	77	6,256
45 15355	Clover town	York	2.8	4,014	3,049	844	11	18	3	52	37	78	2,853
45 16000	Columbia city	Lexington, Richland	125.2	116,278	57,236	53,465	296	2,008	104	1,582	1,587	3,520	92,908
45 16405	Conway city	Horry	12.7	11,788	6,580	4,933	25	87	3	75	85	221	8,832
45 18565	Darlington city	Darlington	4.3	6,720	2,856	3,766	11	24	1	34	28	68	5,029
45 19105	Denmark city	Bamberg	3.0	3,328	424	2,859	3	17	-	2	23	25	2,436
45 19285	Dentsville CDP	Richland	7.1	13,009	4,690	7,581	27	330	6	169	206	377	10,202
45 19420	Dillon city	Dillon	4.8	6,316	3,392	2,741	85	47	-	16	35	48	4,574
45 21265	Duncan town	Spartanburg	3.5	2,870	1,885	885	4	19	-	48	29	98	1,923
45 21310	Dunean CDP	Greenville	1.7	4,158	2,827	1,093	13	21	-	128	76	337	3,232
45 21985	Easley city..........	Pickens	10.6	17,754	15,153	2,096	25	93	6	222	159	501	13,575
45 22075	East Gaffney CDP	Cherokee	3.2	3,349	2,600	683	3	11	1	29	22	86	2,521
45 22795	Edgefield town	Edgefield	4.1	4,449	1,727	2,666	22	14	-	8	12	199	3,821
45 22997	Edisto CDP	Orangeburg	5.5	2,632	749	1,831	21	12	-	5	14	20	1,921
45 24370	Fairfax town	Allendale	3.3	3,206	825	2,355	4	4	-	12	6	11	2,604
45 25540	Five Forks CDP	Greenville	7.7	8,064	7,331	372	11	200	1	65	84	188	5,270
45 25810	Florence city	Florence	17.7	30,248	16,020	13,541	54	352	4	63	214	229	22,680
45 26305	Forest Acres city	Richland	4.6	10,558	8,538	1,639	20	123	1	108	129	268	8,453
45 26372	Forestbrook CDP	Horry	3.6	3,391	2,981	308	13	32	-	19	38	62	2,481
45 26890	Fort Mill town	York	4.6	7,587	6,198	1,213	15	37	-	53	71	99	5,230
45 27070	Fountain Inn city	Greenville, Laurens	5.5	6,017	4,061	1,824	8	17	1	47	59	145	4,313
45 28060	Gaffney city	Cherokee	7.9	12,968	6,935	5,730	19	59	4	129	92	257	9,935
45 28375	Gantt CDP..........	Greenville	10.1	13,962	4,728	8,810	20	47	7	196	154	419	10,107
45 28455	Garden City CDP	Horry	5.4	9,357	9,078	94	26	39	9	28	83	105	6,390
45 28870	Georgetown city	Georgetown	6.5	8,950	3,669	5,104	11	28	4	75	59	168	6,390
45 29410	Gloverville CDP	Aiken	3.5	2,805	2,420	306	9	3	-	10	57	34	2,051
45 29815	Goose Creek city	Berkeley, Charleston	31.7	29,208	22,929	4,153	171	776	34	455	690	1,182	20,566
45 30850	Greenville city.......	Greenville	26.1	56,002	34,788	19,008	77	709	35	766	619	1,927	44,826
45 30895	Greenwood city.......	Greenwood	13.7	22,071	11,057	10,044	43	191	15	533	188	1,440	16,619
45 30985	Greer city..........	Greenville, Spartanburg	16.1	16,843	12,361	3,283	37	195	10	744	213	1,377	12,661
45 31885	Hampton town	Hampton	4.5	2,837	1,569	1,204	8	15	-	22	19	23	2,074
45 32065	Hanahan city	Berkeley	10.1	12,937	10,563	1,645	46	264	6	169	244	410	10,226
45 32560	Hartsville city	Darlington	5.0	7,556	4,231	3,209	7	47	2	14	46	63	5,665
45 34045	Hilton Head Island town ..	Beaufort	42.1	33,862	28,893	2,797	49	187	8	1,518	410	3,886	28,004
45 34495	Hollywood town.......	Charleston	20.0	3,946	1,175	2,714	6	4	1	31	15	68	2,781
45 34720	Homeland Park CDP	Anderson	4.8	6,337	4,870	1,324	13	18	-	56	56	93	4,763
45 34810	Honea Path town	Abbeville, Anderson	3.5	3,504	2,769	685	6	7	2	9	26	35	2,739
45 35890	Irmo town	Lexington, Richland	4.1	11,039	8,473	2,225	28	158	9	49	97	157	7,654
45 36115	Isle of Palms city	Charleston	4.5	4,583	4,502	16	7	24	1	6	27	55	3,710
45 38590	Kingstree town	Williamsburg	3.1	3,496	1,187	2,260	2	20	-	6	21	19	2,521
45 39220	Ladson CDP	Berkeley, Charleston	8.6	13,264	9,510	2,926	129	271	9	172	247	394	9,153
45 39310	Lake City city	Florence	4.7	6,478	1,761	4,627	5	22	-	18	45	71	4,551
45 39475	Lake Murray of Richland CDP	Richland	5.8	3,526	3,449	30	2	30	-	3	12	33	2,848
45 39772	Lakewood CDP........	Sumter	7.6	2,603	1,726	818	3	5	1	17	33	27	1,871
45 39785	Lake Wylie CDP	York	3.5	3,061	2,990	32	8	23	-	2	6	25	2,647
45 39895	Lancaster city	Lancaster	5.8	8,177	3,887	4,047	10	72	3	94	64	184	6,066
45 40525	Laurel Bay CDP	Beaufort	4.7	6,625	4,376	1,714	42	96	9	254	134	523	3,792
45 40615	Laurens city	Laurens	10.6	9,916	5,327	4,320	26	16	11	133	83	240	7,441

Table D-1. Places — **Area and Population**—Con.

[Includes incorporated places and census designated places (CDPs) of 2,500 or more population as of April 1, 2000. Codes shown are two-digit Federal Information Processing Standards (FIPS) state codes and five-digit FIPS place codes. Place names and codes are those in effect as of January 1, 2000. County refers to the county (or counties) in which the place is located. IC in this column = independent city, a county equivalent. If a place is located in more than one county, counties are listed in alphabetical order]

State and place code	Place	County	Land area, 2000 (sq. mi.)	Total	White	Black or African American	American Indian and Alaska Native	Asian	Native Hawaiian and Other Pacific Islander	Some other race	Two or more races	Hispanic or Latino (of any race)	18 years and over
45 00000	SOUTH CAROLINA—Con.												
45 41335	Lexington town	Lexington	5.7	9,793	8,214	1,222	18	201	3	66	69	187	7,140
45 41380	Liberty town	Pickens	4.3	3,009	2,616	347	3	2	-	19	22	30	2,317
45 42010	Little River CDP	Horry	10.5	7,027	6,423	478	30	20	3	24	49	72	5,922
45 43000	Lugoff CDP	Kershaw	12.8	6,278	5,183	970	18	34	3	18	52	83	4,457
45 43315	Lyman town	Spartanburg	4.1	2,659	2,438	162	3	7	-	24	25	39	2,089
45 44350	Manning city	Clarendon	2.4	4,025	1,441	2,510	10	25	3	16	20	42	2,905
45 44575	Marion city	Marion	4.3	7,042	2,263	4,663	10	28	-	28	50	72	4,984
45 45115	Mauldin city	Greenville	8.6	15,224	11,304	3,169	45	341	17	149	199	416	11,424
45 47275	Moncks Corner town	Berkeley	4.5	5,952	3,412	2,178	38	33	3	177	111	250	4,230
45 48535	Mount Pleasant town	Charleston	41.9	47,609	42,928	3,453	80	562	10	187	389	635	35,668
45 48805	Mullins city	Marion	3.1	5,029	1,840	3,097	14	34	-	6	38	47	3,642
45 48985	Murrells Inlet CDP	Georgetown	7.3	5,519	5,055	393	9	16	2	11	33	34	4,665
45 49075	Myrtle Beach city	Horry	16.8	22,759	18,472	2,903	95	291	29	540	429	1,062	18,664
45 49570	Newberry town	Newberry	6.6	10,580	5,592	4,376	50	64	13	305	180	1,004	8,110
45 49885	Newport CDP	York	9.0	4,033	3,650	303	25	18	-	16	21	47	2,861
45 50695	North Augusta city	Aiken, Edgefield	17.2	17,574	13,647	3,299	49	207	9	178	185	424	13,143
45 50875	North Charleston city	Charleston, Dorchester	58.5	79,641	35,651	39,348	349	1,263	75	1,417	1,538	3,163	57,445
45 51145	North Hartsville CDP	Darlington	4.9	3,136	2,380	676	15	11	-	41	13	75	2,298
45 51180	Northlake CDP	Anderson	4.2	3,659	3,326	249	6	47	-	6	25	19	2,931
45 51280	North Myrtle Beach city	Horry	13.0	10,974	10,370	253	52	70	15	116	98	259	9,465
45 51720	Oak Grove CDP	Lexington	6.7	8,183	7,238	670	28	84	1	67	95	184	6,203
45 53080	Orangeburg city	Orangeburg	8.3	12,765	3,801	8,618	17	145	5	101	78	165	10,507
45 53845	Pacolet town	Spartansburg	3.0	2,690	1,931	705	7	14	-	6	27	32	2,089
45 54025	Pageland town	Chesterfield	4.4	2,521	1,370	903	6	25	1	182	34	221	1,878
45 54535	Parker CDP	Greenville	6.9	10,760	8,493	1,788	30	32	6	258	153	684	8,094
45 54850	Parris Island CDP	Beaufort	12.2	4,841	3,347	840	40	85	6	345	178	637	4,327
45 55645	Pendleton town	Anderson	3.6	2,966	1,919	981	6	14	-	16	30	45	2,366
45 56140	Pickens town	Pickens	2.5	3,012	2,426	506	2	11	-	32	35	75	2,335
45 56365	Piedmont CDP	Anderson, Greenville	8.6	4,684	4,313	274	9	11	1	5	71	56	3,520
45 58030	Port Royal town	Beaufort	3.9	3,950	2,535	1,152	18	67	4	76	98	169	3,046
45 58165	Powderville CDP	Anderson	13.9	5,362	5,050	233	14	20	3	11	31	61	3,966
45 59110	Red Bank CDP	Lexington	11.9	8,811	7,819	779	31	43	3	82	54	167	6,187
45 59190	Red Hill CDP	Horry	10.9	10,509	9,321	771	62	82	8	128	137	327	8,035
45 60280	Ridgeland town	Jasper	2.4	2,518	1,124	1,238	4	19	-	118	15	192	2,143
45 61405	Rock Hill city	York	31.0	49,765	29,230	18,578	248	690	13	509	497	1,236	37,293
45 62395	St. Andrews CDP	Richland	6.9	21,814	9,392	11,493	55	400	15	181	278	431	17,180
45 63250	Saluda town	Saluda	3.2	3,066	1,495	1,241	7	-	-	305	18	594	2,207
45 63700	Sans Souci CDP	Greenville	3.4	7,836	6,314	990	34	95	10	261	132	599	6,076
45 64240	Saxon CDP	Spartanburg	2.4	3,707	2,160	1,196	10	24	1	228	88	452	2,865
45 65095	Seneca city	Oconee	7.1	7,652	4,845	2,584	24	48	1	50	100	117	5,784
45 65207	Seven Oaks CDP	Lexington	7.8	15,755	11,582	3,388	52	442	9	92	190	298	12,084
45 65680	Shell Point CDP	Beaufort	6.1	2,856	2,215	461	14	46	2	73	45	142	2,029
45 66580	Simpsonville city	Greenville	6.2	14,352	11,867	1,975	33	113	6	176	182	667	10,283
45 67390	Socastee CDP	Horry	13.4	14,295	12,410	1,002	50	300	18	288	227	666	10,816
45 67750	Southern Shops CDP	Spartanburg	3.6	3,707	2,494	547	30	29	-	472	135	930	2,907
45 68177	South Sumter CDP	Sumter	2.7	3,365	301	3,026	7	-	-	5	26	30	2,364
45 68200	Spartanburg city	Spartanburg	19.2	39,673	18,707	19,658	73	528	22	303	382	706	29,663
45 68380	Springdale CDP	Lancaster	4.2	2,864	1,854	752	6	7	4	219	22	269	2,136
45 68425	Springdale town	Lexington	4.0	2,877	2,558	223	19	48	-	7	22	20	2,308
45 70270	Summerville town	Berkelely, Charleston, Dorchester	15.4	27,752	21,421	5,379	129	248	16	186	373	547	19,783
45 70405	Sumter city	Sumter	26.6	39,643	19,655	18,357	93	505	28	445	560	938	28,604
45 70585	Surfside Beach town	Horry	1.9	4,425	4,281	42	22	16	1	22	41	63	3,823
45 71395	Taylors CDP	Greenville	10.9	20,125	16,420	2,856	49	305	7	224	264	586	14,948
45 71417	Tega Cay city	York	2.5	4,044	3,877	86	5	33	4	15	24	37	2,959
45 72430	Travelers Rest city	Greenville	4.4	4,099	3,171	750	11	50	-	69	48	173	2,872
45 73105	Union city	Union	8.0	8,793	4,966	3,704	21	33	1	4	64	60	6,777
45 73465	Valley Falls CDP	Spartanburg	5.2	3,990	3,288	544	11	106	2	14	25	64	3,285
45 73870	Wade Hampton CDP	Greenville	8.8	20,458	17,359	1,652	36	683	13	488	227	1,255	16,580
45 74095	Walhalla city	Oconee	3.7	3,801	3,162	263	12	12	7	291	54	584	2,824
45 74275	Walterboro city	Colleton	5.0	5,153	2,583	2,489	8	15	1	25	32	75	3,870
45 75535	Welcome CDP	Greenville	4.6	6,390	4,840	1,149	26	8	11	283	73	503	4,989
45 75850	West Columbia city	Lexington	6.1	13,064	9,738	2,588	36	223	2	267	210	609	10,610
45 76165	Westminster city	Oconee	3.4	2,743	2,348	324	1	5	-	33	32	68	2,098
45 77672	Wilkinson Heights CDP	Orangeburg	3.0	3,068	105	2,935	10	1	-	12	5	34	2,249
45 77875	Williamston town	Anderson	3.6	3,791	3,063	670	3	4	-	25	26	66	2,927
45 77965	Williston town	Barnwell	8.9	3,307	1,680	1,571	12	-	3	7	34	27	2,381
45 78460	Winnsboro town	Fairfield	3.2	3,599	1,450	2,104	-	11	-	12	22	47	2,597
45 78820	Woodfield CDP	Richland	2.8	9,238	3,713	4,461	43	431	22	340	228	782	6,930
45 79090	Woodruff city	Spartanburg	3.7	4,229	2,898	1,172	7	6	1	69	76	158	3,164
45 79630	York city	York	7.9	6,985	3,802	2,816	41	29	-	255	42	350	5,034
46 00000	SOUTH DAKOTA		75,884.6	754,844	669,404	4,685	62,283	4,378	261	3,677	10,156	10,903	552,195
46 00100	Aberdeen city	Brown	13.0	24,658	23,328	92	782	133	31	48	244	196	19,274
46 04380	Belle Fourche city	Butte	3.2	4,565	4,338	7	87	15	-	58	60	169	3,322
46 06620	Box Elder city	Meade, Pennington	5.8	2,841	2,370	65	159	59	3	20	165	101	1,859
46 06840	Brandon city	Minnehaha	3.8	5,693	5,592	24	22	13	2	5	35	24	3,731

[Includes incorporated places and census designated places (CDPs) of 2,500 or more population as of April 1, 2000. Codes shown are two-digit Federal Information Processing Standards (FIPS) state codes and five-digit FIPS place codes. Place names and codes are those in effect as of January 1, 2000. County refers to the county (or counties) in which the place is located. IC in this column = independent city, a county equivalent. If a place is located in more than one county, counties are listed in alphabetic order]

State and place code	Place	County	Land area, 2000 (sq. mi.)	Population, 2000 (April 1) Total	White	Black or African American	American Indian and Alaska Native	Asian	Native Hawaiian and Other Pacific Islander	Some other race	Two or more races	Hispanic or Latino (of any race)	18 years and over
46 00000	SOUTH DAKOTA—Con.												
46 07580	Brookings city	Brookings	11.9	18,504	17,670	81	184	348	10	49	162	139	15,279
46 09500	Canton city	Lincoln	3.0	3,110	3,030	10	25	18	-	1	26	15	2,235
46 13355	Colonial Pine Hills CDP	Pennington	17.2	2,561	2,466	8	31	23	2	3	28	29	1,731
46 15980	Dell Rapids city	Minnehaha	2.0	2,980	2,941	4	14	6	-	2	13	19	2,133
46 18980	Ellsworth AFB CDP	Meade, Pennington	1.9	4,165	3,424	277	38	95	12	107	212	276	2,649
46 30220	Hot Springs city	Fall River	2.9	4,129	3,636	16	323	15	2	8	129	79	3,137
46 31060	Huron city	Beadle	8.2	11,893	11,408	114	153	50	3	42	123	143	9,116
46 36220	Lead city	Lawrence	2.0	3,027	2,898	7	68	6	-	18	30	82	2,238
46 40220	Madison city	Lake	4.3	6,540	6,354	16	53	50	1	26	40	60	5,148
46 42260	Milbank city	Grant	2.7	3,640	3,601	1	3	13	-	5	17	13	2,735
46 43100	Mitchell city	Davison	9.9	14,558	13,922	47	350	66	4	42	127	112	11,056
46 43180	Mobridge city	Walworth	1.8	3,574	2,842	1	648	8	2	3	70	30	2,705
46 49600	Pierre city	Hughes	13.0	13,876	12,337	28	1,188	64	3	40	216	173	10,102
46 49660	Pine Ridge CDP	Shannon	3.1	3,171	118	3	2,987	1	3	16	43	57	1,685
46 52980	Rapid City city	Pennington	44.6	59,607	50,266	579	6,046	594	35	434	1,653	1,650	44,544
46 53007	Rapid Valley CDP	Pennington	10.1	7,043	6,387	44	282	37	7	28	258	177	4,715
46 53460	Redfield city	Spink	1.7	2,897	2,763	12	87	3	1	6	25	19	2,281
46 59020	Sioux Falls city	Lincoln, Minnehaha	56.3	123,975	113,938	2,226	2,627	1,479	68	1,521	2,116	3,087	92,737
46 59260	Sisseton city	Roberts	1.6	2,572	1,442	3	1,051	7	-	1	68	28	1,819
46 60020	Spearfish city	Lawrence	6.1	8,606	8,204	30	199	31	2	28	112	149	6,861
46 62100	Sturgis city	Meade	3.7	6,442	6,107	13	160	20	-	21	121	113	4,834
46 66700	Vermillion city	Clay	3.8	9,765	8,881	126	329	240	1	36	152	104	8,057
46 69300	Watertown city	Codington	15.2	20,237	19,479	28	333	67	4	144	182	259	15,000
46 72180	Winner city	Tripp	1.5	3,137	2,803	2	287	2	-	3	40	22	2,357
46 73060	Yankton city	Yankton	7.8	13,528	12,764	222	214	68	4	122	134	333	10,358
47 00000	TENNESSEE		41,217.1	5,689,283	4,563,310	932,809	15,152	56,662	2,205	56,036	63,109	123,838	4,290,762
47 00540	Alcoa city	Blount	13.8	7,734	6,276	1,238	15	26	1	60	118	146	6,114
47 00640	Algood town	Putnam	3.8	2,942	2,740	145	2	12	-	7	36	32	2,276
47 01740	Arlington town	Shelby	20.4	2,569	1,907	591	12	16	-	14	29	29	1,899
47 02180	Ashland City town	Cheatham	8.9	3,641	3,424	136	10	9	-	38	24	74	2,728
47 02320	Athens city	McMinn	13.5	13,220	11,413	1,232	31	182	9	177	176	398	10,057
47 02340	Atoka town	Tipton	6.7	3,235	2,843	301	8	17	2	10	54	68	2,203
47 03440	Bartlett city	Shelby	19.1	40,543	37,476	1,971	112	502	18	151	313	462	28,758
47 04620	Belle Meade city	Davidson	3.1	2,943	2,903	10	1	14	-	6	9	21	2,059
47 06640	Bloomingdale CDP	Sullivan	10.3	10,350	10,198	29	33	10	1	18	61	81	8,076
47 06740	Blountville CDP	Sullivan	5.7	2,959	2,900	39	5	6	1	2	6	26	2,460
47 07180	Bolivar city	Hardeman	8.5	5,802	2,456	3,272	4	29	1	4	36	35	4,253
47 08280	Brentwood city	Williamson	34.6	23,445	22,187	442	37	585	-	44	150	259	16,050
47 08540	Bristol city	Sullivan	29.3	24,821	23,617	736	78	158	2	56	174	170	19,581
47 08920	Brownsville city	Haywood	9.1	10,748	3,925	6,526	15	11	8	197	66	388	7,574
47 10560	Camden city	Benton	11.1	3,828	3,563	204	10	9	-	12	30	51	3,058
47 12420	Centerville town	Hickman	10.9	3,793	3,547	181	14	1	-	9	41	34	2,992
47 12460	Central CDP	Carter	4.3	2,717	2,690	5	5	3	-	-	14	13	2,124
47 14000	Chattanooga city	Hamilton, Marion	135.2	155,554	92,874	56,086	446	2,396	164	1,571	2,017	3,281	120,698
47 14980	Church Hill city	Hawkins	8.9	5,916	5,795	77	7	13	-	4	20	24	4,650
47 15160	Clarksville city	Montgomery	94.9	103,455	70,254	24,030	560	2,233	262	2,705	3,411	6,241	73,650
47 15400	Cleveland city	Bradley	24.9	37,192	33,102	2,608	86	359	12	481	544	1,066	29,037
47 15480	Clifton city	Wayne	6.4	2,699	1,611	1,064	3	1	-	12	8	23	2,511
47 15580	Clinton city	Anderson	10.9	9,409	8,983	256	31	36	-	26	77	80	7,379
47 16300	Collegedale city	Hamilton	8.3	6,514	5,621	334	33	196	2	187	141	504	5,227
47 16420	Collierville town	Shelby	24.5	31,872	28,643	2,337	62	467	4	106	253	481	21,218
47 16500	Colonial Heights CDP	Sullivan	6.5	7,067	6,897	62	11	47	2	14	34	51	5,434
47 16540	Columbia city	Maury	29.6	33,055	24,669	6,984	92	137	9	680	484	1,554	24,529
47 16920	Cookeville city	Putnam	21.9	23,923	21,797	697	38	449	50	624	268	1,009	19,628
47 16980	Coopertown town	Robertson	31.9	3,027	2,905	49	12	14	-	18	29	38	2,215
47 17680	Covington city	Tipton	10.3	8,463	4,366	3,939	41	37	4	21	55	67	5,950
47 18540	Crossville city	Cumberland	14.7	8,981	8,713	13	21	31	4	93	106	218	6,954
47 19700	Dayton city	Rhea	6.1	6,180	5,605	325	14	45	2	108	81	193	4,725
47 20620	Dickson city	Dickson	16.5	12,244	10,757	1,081	56	68	-	94	188	238	8,918
47 21540	Dresden town	Weakley	5.3	2,855	2,699	124	1	10	-	4	17	13	2,264
47 22000	Dunlap city	Sequatchie	8.6	4,173	4,126	7	8	10	-	4	18	34	3,142
47 22200	Dyersburg city	Dyer	15.1	17,452	13,208	3,843	36	95	4	93	173	237	12,854
47 22340	Eagleton Village CDP	Blount	3.2	4,883	4,686	109	15	22	-	12	39	54	3,792
47 22440	East Brainerd CDP	Hamilton	8.7	14,132	12,490	1,101	18	319	1	65	138	193	10,247
47 22720	East Ridge city	Hamilton	8.3	20,640	19,262	662	64	347	7	88	210	225	16,609
47 23500	Elizabethton city	Carter	9.2	13,372	12,744	330	22	73	1	65	137	158	10,629
47 24360	Erwin city	Unicoi	3.5	5,610	5,485	3	16	6	-	57	43	112	4,503
47 24480	Etowah city	McMinn	2.8	3,663	3,422	119	14	4	3	40	61	78	2,879
47 24980	Fairfield Glade CDP	Cumberland	21.8	4,885	4,815	26	2	9	2	12	19	21	4,672
47 25090	Fairmount CDP	Hamilton	5.9	2,600	2,568	7	2	12	-	2	9	11	1,848
47 25440	Fairview city	Williamson	14.1	5,800	5,630	38	22	14	-	19	77	86	4,045
47 25760	Farragut town	Knox, Loudon	16.1	17,720	16,635	319	26	560	-	58	122	189	12,993
47 25920	Fayetteville city	Lincoln	7.3	6,994	4,993	1,834	21	21	6	19	100	57	5,512
47 27020	Forest Hills city	Davidson	9.3	4,710	4,528	66	3	65	-	19	29	36	3,493
47 27740	Franklin city	Williamson	30.0	41,842	35,368	4,330	99	674	19	908	444	2,025	30,179

Table D-1. Places — **Area and Population**—Con.

[Includes incorporated places and census designated places (CDPs) of 2,500 or more population as of April 1, 2000. Codes shown are two-digit Federal Information Processing Standards (FIPS) state codes and five-digit FIPS place codes. Place names and codes are those in effect as of January 1, 2000. County refers to the county (or counties) in which the place is located. IC in this column = independent city, a county equivalent. If a place is located in more than one county, counties are listed in alphabetic order]

State and place code	Place	County	Land area, 2000 (sq. mi.)	Total	White	Black or African American	American Indian and Alaska Native	Asian	Native Hawaiian and Other Pacific Islander	Some other race	Two or more races	Hispanic or Latino (of any race)	18 years and over
47 00000	TENNESSEE—Con.												
47 28540	Gallatin city	Sumner	22.0	23,230	18,189	4,081	70	98	16	469	307	801	17,335
47 28800	Gatlinburg city	Sevier	10.1	3,382	3,237	5	19	58	1	29	33	66	2,878
47 28960	Germantown city	Shelby	17.6	37,348	34,712	869	60	1,306	13	62	326	407	26,882
47 29920	Goodlettsville city	Davidson, Sumner	14.0	13,780	11,909	1,354	30	226	2	90	169	204	10,519
47 30960	Greenbrier town	Robertson	6.6	4,940	4,813	33	11	19	-	24	40	63	3,525
47 30980	Greeneville town	Greene	14.0	15,198	13,986	873	29	82	3	134	91	226	11,965
47 31100	Green Hill CDP	Wilson	3.9	7,068	6,684	214	11	51	2	22	84	68	5,259
47 32520	Harriman city	Morgan, Roane	10.0	6,744	6,077	501	15	18	1	12	120	51	5,264
47 32600	Harrison CDP	Hamilton	7.3	7,630	6,454	987	27	53	1	20	88	89	5,729
47 32650	Harrogate-Shawanee CDP	Claiborne	4.2	2,865	2,714	27	12	27	-	5	80	15	2,279
47 33260	Henderson city	Chester	5.7	5,670	4,541	1,013	5	23	-	21	67	86	4,453
47 33320	Hendersonville city	Sumner	27.3	40,620	37,749	1,673	108	447	12	266	365	696	30,140
47 33960	Hickory Withe town	Fayette	28.3	2,574	2,119	418	2	5	1	1	28	32	2,047
47 35160	Hohenwald city	Lewis	4.4	3,754	3,626	78	4	6	-	12	28	42	2,829
47 36460	Humboldt city	Gibson, Madison	9.7	9,467	5,213	4,071	24	6	-	95	58	148	7,191
47 36580	Huntingdon town	Carroll	11.2	4,349	3,502	777	6	5	1	5	53	27	3,337
47 37640	Jackson city	Madison	49.5	59,643	32,883	25,091	92	470	6	525	576	1,289	44,216
47 37820	Jasper town	Marion	9.0	3,214	2,905	236	10	21	1	6	35	39	2,491
47 37960	Jefferson City city	Jefferson	5.3	7,760	6,983	488	34	59	13	89	94	212	6,289
47 38320	Johnson City city	Carter, Sullivan, Washington	39.3	55,469	49,973	3,549	143	678	12	382	732	1,048	44,467
47 38540	Jonesborough town	Washington	4.3	4,168	3,894	231	4	7	-	8	24	34	3,357
47 39560	Kingsport city	Hawkins, Sullivan	44.1	44,905	41,906	1,897	106	356	10	153	477	471	35,165
47 39620	Kingston city	Roane	6.5	5,264	4,935	187	12	26	3	12	89	51	4,183
47 39660	Kingston Springs town	Cheatham	9.8	2,773	2,702	24	10	15	-	11	11	15	1,982
47 40000	Knoxville city	Knox	92.7	173,890	138,611	28,171	541	2,525	60	1,257	2,725	2,751	139,693
47 40160	Lafayette city	Macon	4.4	3,885	3,803	6	13	15	10	20	18	82	3,084
47 40180	La Follette city	Campbell	4.9	7,926	7,759	43	32	14	6	11	61	33	6,185
47 40350	Lakeland city	Shelby	17.6	6,862	6,283	358	9	122	-	34	56	101	5,171
47 40560	Lake Tansi CDP	Cumberland	8.7	2,621	2,579	2	8	8	-	3	21	22	2,123
47 41200	La Vergne city	Rutherford	24.8	18,687	15,790	2,059	81	246	13	239	259	661	12,828
47 41340	Lawrenceburg city	Lawrence	12.6	10,796	10,072	425	46	42	3	91	117	180	8,353
47 41520	Lebanon city	Wilson	29.2	20,235	16,773	2,789	66	165	7	203	232	457	15,394
47 41760	Lenoir City city	Loudon	6.2	6,819	6,301	74	30	8	4	297	105	409	5,111
47 41860	Lewisburg city	Marshall	11.7	10,413	8,326	1,608	20	49	3	297	110	536	7,898
47 41980	Lexington city	Henderson	11.5	7,393	6,247	966	10	19	2	31	118	87	5,619
47 43140	Livingston town	Overton	5.1	3,498	3,431	21	10	6	5	5	20	11	2,799
47 43780	Loudon town	Loudon	9.3	4,476	4,162	144	14	17	-	91	48	145	3,524
47 44382	Lynchburg, Moore County	Moore	129.2	5,740	5,501	156	11	8	-	29	35	45	4,400
47 44940	McKenzie city	Carroll, Henry, Weakley	5.5	5,295	4,384	754	6	18	1	42	90	114	4,143
47 45100	McMinnville city	Warren	10.0	12,749	11,273	529	20	119	7	638	163	868	9,759
47 45320	Madisonville town	Monroe	5.8	3,939	3,680	156	10	13	5	31	44	79	3,033
47 45500	Manchester city	Coffee	11.0	8,294	7,685	324	31	100	-	83	71	272	6,425
47 46240	Martin city	Weakley	12.4	10,515	8,235	1,642	8	434	-	102	94	191	8,756
47 46380	Maryville city	Blount	15.9	23,120	21,637	681	50	358	8	122	264	318	17,604
47 48000	Memphis city	Shelby	279.3	650,100	223,728	399,208	1,217	9,482	239	9,438	6,788	19,317	468,805
47 48360	Middle Valley CDP	Hamilton	12.1	11,854	11,368	222	32	123	3	31	75	95	8,807
47 48660	Milan city	Gibson	8.0	7,664	5,777	1,738	15	19	1	45	69	115	5,835
47 48980	Millersville city	Robertson, Sumner	13.5	5,308	4,989	187	25	34	1	29	43	80	3,828
47 49060	Millington city	Shelby	15.6	10,433	7,383	2,305	75	262	16	147	245	486	7,369
47 49760	Monterey town	Putnam	3.0	2,717	2,413	25	1	5	-	247	26	444	2,046
47 50280	Morristown city	Hamblen, Jefferson	20.9	24,965	20,903	1,870	74	171	26	1,575	346	2,603	19,322
47 50580	Mount Carmel town	Hawkins	6.8	4,795	4,712	26	6	7	2	11	31	28	3,730
47 50780	Mount Juliet city	Wilson	16.2	12,366	11,607	486	48	64	1	36	124	145	8,592
47 51080	Mount Pleasant city	Maury	11.0	4,491	3,369	1,053	15	5	1	11	37	39	3,304
47 51540	Munford town	Tipton	8.0	4,708	4,270	273	13	39	-	30	83	71	3,230
47 51560	Murfreesboro city	Rutherford	39.0	68,816	54,947	9,560	192	1,853	18	1,295	951	2,430	53,199
47 52006	Nashville-Davidson (balance)	Davidson	473.3	545,524	359,581	146,235	1,639	12,992	400	13,677	11,000	25,774	424,855
47 52400	Newbern town	Dyer	4.8	2,988	2,537	384	7	8	1	14	37	37	2,161
47 53000	Newport city	Cocke	5.4	7,242	6,668	388	37	17	2	33	97	95	5,598
47 53140	New Tazewell town	Claiborne	5.3	2,871	2,762	42	13	12	-	22	20	30	2,179
47 53460	Nolensville town	Williamson	9.5	3,099	2,862	198	5	3	-	14	17	41	2,078
47 54700	Oak Grove CDP	Washington	4.6	4,072	3,985	33	17	8	-	6	23	33	3,222
47 54780	Oak Hill city	Davidson	7.9	4,493	4,325	44	5	74	1	12	32	34	3,474
47 55120	Oak Ridge city	Anderson, Roane	85.5	27,387	23,815	2,239	83	576	6	209	459	529	21,242
47 55800	Oliver Springs town	Anderson, Morgan, Roane	5.1	3,303	3,133	115	10	4	1	2	38	12	2,537
47 55860	Oneida town	Scott	10.2	3,615	3,555	1	5	14	-	7	33	11	2,738
47 55900	Ooltewah CDP	Hamilton	7.7	5,681	4,743	678	26	48	1	64	121	110	4,252
47 56720	Paris city	Henry	10.9	9,763	7,526	1,978	10	59	6	38	146	115	7,647
47 58080	Pigeon Forge city	Sevier	11.6	5,083	4,814	33	11	65	3	98	59	188	3,941
47 58240	Pine Crest CDP	Carter	2.2	2,872	2,768	36	11	7	-	7	43	20	2,317
47 59560	Pleasant View city	Cheatham	12.6	2,934	2,871	12	6	3	-	6	36	23	2,007
47 60280	Portland city	Sumner	11.4	8,458	7,995	228	28	16	-	118	73	194	6,082
47 61040	Pulaski city	Giles	6.6	7,871	5,541	2,130	19	67	1	18	95	87	6,133
47 61960	Red Bank city	Hamilton	6.4	12,418	10,879	1,023	64	110	7	148	187	352	9,932
47 63340	Ripley city	Lauderdale	12.8	7,844	4,044	3,672	12	21	-	30	65	84	5,677

Table D-1. Places — **Area and Population**—Con.

[Includes incorporated places and census designated places (CDPs) of 2,500 or more population as of April 1, 2000. Codes shown are two-digit Federal Information Processing Standards (FIPS) state codes and five-digit FIPS place codes. Place names and codes are those in effect as of January 1, 2000. County refers to the county (or counties) in which the place is located. IC in this column = independent city, a county equivalent. If a place is located in more than one county, counties are listed in alphabetic order]

				Population, 2000 (April 1)									
					By race—								
					One race								
State and place code	Place	County	Land area, 2000 (sq. mi.)	Total	White	Black or African American	American Indian and Alaska Native	Asian	Native Hawaiian and Other Pacific Islander	Some other race	Two or more races	Hispanic or Latino (of any race)	18 years and over
47 00000	TENNESSEE—Con.												
47 64440	Rockwood city	Roane	7.9	5,774	5,362	314	15	17	-	12	54	47	4,535
47 64820	Rogersville town	Hawkins	3.3	4,240	3,991	172	6	13	1	28	29	45	3,486
47 66720	Savannah city	Hardin	5.7	6,917	6,211	592	15	20	1	24	54	78	5,365
47 66940	Selmer town	McNairy	9.8	4,541	3,706	723	10	12	-	17	73	70	3,575
47 67120	Sevierville city	Sevier	19.9	11,757	11,244	137	43	109	2	86	136	190	9,155
47 67200	Seymour CDP	Blount, Sevier	12.6	8,850	8,669	32	14	42	-	20	73	77	6,700
47 67760	Shelbyville city	Bedford	15.5	16,105	12,423	2,412	56	112	8	808	286	2,343	12,045
47 68540	Signal Mountain town	Hamilton	6.7	7,429	7,307	16	12	26	-	16	52	63	5,524
47 69320	Smithville city	DeKalb	5.9	3,994	3,768	109	6	4	-	66	41	162	3,079
47 69420	Smyrna town	Rutherford	22.8	25,569	22,303	1,999	73	310	20	464	400	1,101	18,508
47 69560	Soddy-Daisy city	Hamilton	23.0	11,530	11,317	69	28	22	1	20	73	92	8,873
47 69620	Somerville town	Fayette	11.2	2,519	1,510	992	2	2	-	1	12	6	1,906
47 69740	South Cleveland CDP	Bradley	14.6	6,216	5,898	123	9	17	-	57	112	130	4,622
47 69900	South Fulton city	Obion	3.1	2,517	1,988	490	7	3	-	5	24	14	1,941
47 70060	South Pittsburg city	Marion	5.9	3,295	2,657	577	4	9	-	9	39	31	2,503
47 70180	Sparta city	White	6.3	4,599	4,223	243	9	30	6	31	57	53	3,596
47 70500	Springfield city	Robertson	12.2	14,329	10,111	3,712	53	80	5	252	116	995	10,774
47 70580	Spring Hill city	Maury, Williamson	17.7	7,715	6,815	602	25	38	5	140	90	307	5,186
47 70680	Spurgeon CDP	Sullivan, Washington	4.1	3,460	3,390	19	7	6	2	2	34	18	2,689
47 72540	Sweetwater city	McMinn, Monroe	6.9	5,586	5,012	409	8	51	1	23	82	53	4,303
47 75000	Trenton city	Gibson	5.5	4,683	3,052	1,530	4	12	-	46	39	80	3,551
47 75320	Tullahoma city	Coffee, Franklin	22.2	17,994	16,139	1,216	51	181	9	116	282	307	13,423
47 75820	Unicoi town	Unicoi	16.3	3,519	3,440	2	11	8	1	37	20	78	2,734
47 75940	Union City city	Obion	10.7	10,876	8,205	2,316	24	31	14	173	113	371	8,314
47 77900	Walnut Hill CDP	Sullivan	4.7	2,756	2,715	14	7	8	-	-	12	4	2,215
47 78560	Waverly city	Humphreys	8.1	4,028	3,575	383	6	9	-	15	40	47	3,134
47 80200	White House city	Robertson, Sumner	9.0	7,220	7,029	96	18	25	-	22	30	74	4,932
47 80540	Whiteville town	Hardeman	2.4	3,148	1,197	1,918	3	2	-	4	24	24	2,818
47 80760	Wildwood Lake CDP	Bradley	12.0	3,050	2,979	25	2	6	-	18	20	26	2,329
47 81080	Winchester city	Franklin	10.0	7,329	6,194	905	30	38	4	90	82	165	5,672
48 00000	TEXAS		261,797.1	20,851,820	14,799,505	2,404,566	118,362	562,319	14,434	2,438,001	514,633	6,669,666	14,965,061
48 00160	Abernathy city	Hale, Lubbock	1.2	2,839	2,162	70	22	4	-	529	52	1,225	1,985
48 01000	Abilene city	Jones, Taylor	105.1	115,930	90,502	10,215	642	1,543	81	10,117	2,830	22,548	86,207
48 01066	Abram-Perezville CDP	Hidalgo	5.1	5,444	2,568	12	-	3	-	2,656	205	4,442	3,657
48 01240	Addison town	Dallas	4.4	14,166	9,603	1,364	58	1,107	15	1,529	490	3,406	11,902
48 01576	Alamo city	Hidalgo	5.7	14,760	12,341	31	63	13	-	2,026	286	11,528	10,333
48 01600	Alamo Heights city	Bexar	1.8	7,319	6,865	41	24	62	1	206	120	992	5,687
48 01696	Aldine CDP	Harris	8.1	13,979	8,289	816	97	477	10	3,856	434	7,875	9,356
48 01852	Alice city	Jim Wells	11.9	19,010	14,722	164	100	143	16	3,406	459	14,837	13,246
48 01924	Allen city	Collin	26.3	43,554	37,953	1,915	228	1,625	20	1,051	762	3,038	28,344
48 02104	Alpine city	Brewster	4.1	5,786	4,582	77	47	26	4	894	156	2,911	4,382
48 02212	Alton city	Hidalgo	2.1	4,384	3,478	2	14	-	-	834	56	4,292	2,724
48 02218	Alton North CDP	Hidalgo	4.2	5,051	4,621	1	3	4	-	392	30	4,925	2,984
48 02260	Alvarado city	Johnson	3.9	3,288	2,673	235	20	14	-	304	42	607	2,314
48 02272	Alvin city	Brazoria	16.4	21,413	17,618	452	105	170	12	2,329	727	6,014	15,044
48 03000	Amarillo city	Potter, Randall	89.9	173,627	134,563	10,358	1,346	3,563	64	19,663	4,070	37,947	125,204
48 03197	Anderson Mill CDP	Travis, Williamson	1.4	8,953	7,453	364	44	410	14	368	300	1,323	6,479
48 03216	Andrews city	Andrews	4.8	9,652	7,302	197	87	69	3	1,710	284	4,049	6,613
48 03264	Angleton city	Brazoria	10.6	18,130	13,636	2,063	85	203	7	1,746	390	4,205	12,720
48 03372	Anson city	Jones	2.1	2,556	1,938	71	12	19	-	476	40	834	1,833
48 03432	Anthony town	El Paso	6.5	3,850	2,995	149	51	8	1	570	76	3,187	3,053
48 03600	Aransas Pass city	Aransas, Nueces, San Patricio	10.7	8,138	6,558	280	62	37	1	918	282	3,068	5,829
48 04000	Arlington city	Tarrant	95.8	332,969	225,379	45,727	1,817	20,015	475	29,763	9,793	60,817	238,771
48 04462	Atascocita CDP	Harris	27.6	35,757	27,876	4,648	114	874	15	1,444	786	4,297	25,041
48 04504	Athens city	Henderson	14.6	11,297	8,150	2,172	35	72	7	697	164	1,962	8,314
48 04516	Atlanta city	Cass	10.9	5,745	3,914	1,679	30	21	1	28	72	99	4,195
48 05000	Austin city	Travis, Williamson	251.5	656,562	429,100	65,956	3,889	30,960	469	106,538	19,650	200,579	509,014
48 05168	Azle city	Parker, Tarrant	8.2	9,600	9,206	21	63	49	2	135	124	403	7,072
48 05180	Bacliff CDP	Galveston	2.5	6,962	5,754	124	54	208	1	673	148	1,622	4,940
48 05372	Balch Springs city	Dallas	8.1	19,375	12,186	3,589	189	123	5	2,723	560	4,983	12,759
48 05384	Balcones Heights city	Bexar	0.6	3,016	2,301	162	47	34	1	525	146	2,099	2,301
48 05456	Ballinger city	Runnels	3.3	4,243	3,381	91	30	19	-	616	106	1,327	3,101
48 05696	Barrett CDP	Harris	6.5	2,872	248	2,486	10	-	-	83	45	177	2,016
48 05864	Bastrop city	Bastrop	7.3	5,340	3,863	908	39	53	-	375	102	948	3,980
48 05984	Bay City city	Matagorda	8.5	18,667	11,502	3,221	139	165	13	3,143	484	6,484	12,893
48 06128	Baytown city	Chambers, Harris	32.7	66,430	45,088	8,888	337	651	51	9,578	1,837	22,748	46,510
48 07000	Beaumont city	Jefferson	85.0	113,866	52,826	52,206	269	2,827	46	4,038	1,654	9,028	83,014
48 07132	Bedford city	Tarrant	10.0	47,152	41,320	1,722	239	1,708	119	1,151	893	3,403	36,524
48 07192	Beeville city	Bee	6.1	13,129	9,464	377	78	90	6	2,708	406	8,884	9,044
48 07300	Bellaire city	Harris	3.6	15,642	13,939	131	43	993	10	289	237	1,221	11,332
48 07408	Bellmead city	McLennan	6.2	9,214	6,346	1,347	61	52	5	1,214	189	2,195	6,493
48 07432	Bellville city	Austin	2.6	3,794	3,107	443	15	13	-	150	66	454	2,792
48 07492	Belton city	Bell	12.5	14,623	10,627	1,184	93	139	15	2,169	396	3,675	10,694
48 07552	Benbrook city	Tarrant	11.5	20,208	17,844	894	102	433	9	548	378	1,406	15,705
48 08212	Big Lake city	Reagan	1.2	2,885	1,836	95	14	9	-	875	56	1,487	1,878

[Includes incorporated places and census designated places (CDPs) of 2,500 or more population as of April 1, 2000. Codes shown are two-digit Federal Information Processing Standards (FIPS) state codes and five-digit FIPS place codes. Place names and codes are those in effect as of January 1, 2000. County refers to the county (or counties) in which the place is located. IC in this column = independent city, a county equivalent. If a place is located in more than one county, counties are listed in alphabetic order]

State and place code	Place	County	Land area, 2000 (sq. mi.)	Population, 2000 (April 1) Total	By race— One race White	Black or African American	American Indian and Alaska Native	Asian	Native Hawaiian and Other Pacific Islander	Some other race	Two or more races	Hispanic or Latino (of any race)	18 years and over
48 00000	TEXAS—Con.												
48 08236	Big Spring city	Howard	19.1	25,233	19,352	1,339	150	159	4	3,635	594	11,265	19,274
48 08392	Bishop city	Nueces	2.4	3,305	2,780	32	19	4	2	387	81	1,983	2,315
48 08800	Bloomington CDP	Victoria	2.7	2,562	1,360	161	17	2	5	934	83	1,731	1,612
48 09160	Boerne city	Kendall	5.8	6,178	5,854	22	23	10	1	203	65	1,201	4,571
48 09250	Bolivar Peninsula CDP	Galveston	45.2	3,853	3,610	18	31	22	-	108	64	268	3,198
48 09328	Bonham city	Fannin	9.4	9,990	7,619	1,675	84	48	3	422	139	874	8,211
48 09556	Borger city	Hutchinson	8.7	14,302	11,835	523	190	62	4	1,339	349	2,817	10,332
48 09640	Bowie city	Montague	3.8	5,219	5,008	4	38	26	2	64	77	247	3,915
48 09916	Brady city	McCulloch	9.2	5,523	4,496	120	11	7	-	784	105	1,805	3,952
48 10072	Brazoria city	Brazoria	1.9	2,787	2,284	287	16	19	-	150	31	317	1,970
48 10132	Breckenridge city	Stephens	4.2	5,868	4,922	132	20	27	2	662	103	1,211	4,098
48 10156	Brenham city	Washington	8.8	13,507	9,454	2,960	34	251	1	642	165	1,384	10,469
48 10192	Briar CDP	Parker, Tarrant, Wise	20.6	5,350	5,108	25	38	20	-	77	82	237	3,854
48 10252	Bridge City city	Orange	5.1	8,651	8,256	17	65	121	5	110	77	309	6,315
48 10264	Bridgeport city	Wise	3.7	4,309	3,445	114	19	5	2	632	92	1,215	3,015
48 10636	Brookshire city	Waller	3.5	3,450	1,127	1,318	20	13	1	900	71	1,282	2,332
48 10720	Brownfield city	Terry	6.3	9,488	7,074	625	40	24	-	1,373	352	4,360	6,909
48 10768	Brownsville city	Cameron	80.4	139,722	114,083	575	580	752	46	20,486	3,200	127,535	91,323
48 10780	Brownwood city	Brown	12.6	18,813	15,565	1,037	115	112	-	1,594	390	4,014	13,639
48 10897	Brushy Creek CDP	Williamson	8.7	15,371	12,751	627	41	1,047	13	570	322	1,572	9,985
48 10912	Bryan city	Brazos	43.3	65,660	42,452	11,635	265	1,084	52	8,747	1,425	18,271	47,929
48 11224	Bulverde city	Comal	7.6	3,761	3,585	12	12	19	1	68	64	412	2,696
48 11300	Bunker Hill Village city	Harris	1.5	3,654	3,343	9	3	236	1	17	45	128	2,560
48 11368	Burkburnett city	Wichita	9.5	10,927	9,908	315	116	70	8	291	219	677	7,878
48 11428	Burleson city	Johnson, Tarrant	19.6	20,976	20,058	84	109	112	10	306	297	1,135	14,877
48 11464	Burnet city	Burnet	6.8	4,735	3,968	252	57	23	2	368	65	898	3,602
48 11692	Cactus city	Moore	2.0	2,538	620	14	22	7	-	1,808	67	2,439	1,454
48 11836	Caldwell city	Burleson	3.4	3,449	2,457	436	6	3	-	473	74	792	2,457
48 12040	Cameron city	Milam	4.2	5,634	3,757	1,164	34	9	-	573	97	1,502	4,056
48 12045	Cameron Park CDP	Cameron	0.6	5,961	5,189	5	-	7	-	711	49	5,918	3,371
48 12334	Camp Swift CDP	Bastrop	11.9	4,731	3,467	418	55	12	3	620	156	1,792	3,664
48 12496	Canton city	Van Zandt	5.2	3,292	3,099	90	17	11	3	36	36	115	2,586
48 12508	Canutillo CDP	El Paso	3.0	5,129	4,810	31	12	4	-	229	43	4,610	3,307
48 12532	Canyon city	Randall	5.0	12,875	11,372	247	69	264	5	733	185	1,382	9,817
48 12580	Canyon Lake CDP	Comal	144.3	16,870	16,003	53	96	31	5	420	262	1,648	13,090
48 12988	Carrizo Springs city	Dimmit	3.1	5,655	4,257	76	39	62	7	1,065	149	4,932	3,773
48 13024	Carrollton city	Collin, Dallas, Denton	36.5	109,576	78,758	6,862	503	11,944	75	8,451	2,983	21,400	78,613
48 13108	Carthage city	Panola	10.5	6,664	4,975	1,401	31	39	-	132	86	290	4,981
48 13276	Castle Hills city	Bexar	2.5	4,202	3,865	27	8	74	1	153	74	1,206	3,387
48 13312	Castroville city	Medina	2.5	2,664	2,172	3	8	21	2	367	91	959	1,917
48 13492	Cedar Hill city	Dallas, Ellis	35.2	32,093	18,186	10,788	160	636	16	1,564	743	3,822	21,620
48 13552	Cedar Park city	Travis, Williamson	17.0	26,049	22,510	865	88	679	15	1,329	563	3,516	17,317
48 13732	Center city	Shelby	6.2	5,678	2,904	1,943	13	26	-	622	170	1,025	4,186
48 13972	Central Gardens CDP	Jefferson	2.5	4,106	3,945	23	12	20	1	51	54	177	3,049
48 14236	Channelview CDP	Harris	16.2	29,685	18,746	3,867	163	603	19	5,430	857	11,017	19,668
48 14668	Childress city	Childress	8.2	6,778	4,373	1,061	23	23	4	1,161	133	1,516	5,309
48 14920	Cibolo city	Bexar, Guadalupe	5.3	3,035	2,461	187	8	41	3	246	89	577	2,143
48 14927	Cienegas Terrace CDP	Val Verde	3.2	2,878	1,683	17	15	8	-	1,117	38	2,739	1,676
48 14929	Cinco Ranch CDP	Fort Bend, Harris	4.9	11,196	9,843	319	26	742	2	119	145	654	6,913
48 15004	Cisco city	Eastland	4.8	3,851	3,466	149	26	6	2	155	47	385	2,926
48 15160	Clarksville city	Red River	3.0	3,883	2,073	1,638	8	10	-	117	37	283	2,842
48 15364	Cleburne city	Johnson	27.8	26,005	22,448	1,154	122	108	55	1,669	449	5,175	18,743
48 15436	Cleveland city	Liberty	4.8	7,605	4,460	2,063	25	45	-	881	131	1,560	5,522
48 15472	Clifton city	Bosque	1.9	3,542	3,047	119	12	6	-	318	40	667	2,656
48 15628	Cloverleaf CDP	Harris	3.6	23,508	13,816	3,787	139	354	11	4,765	636	10,423	15,583
48 15652	Clute city	Brazoria	5.3	10,424	6,694	798	79	100	1	2,401	351	5,013	7,153
48 15676	Clyde city	Callahan	2.4	3,345	3,221	12	13	6	4	53	36	135	2,385
48 15796	Cockrell Hill city	Dallas	0.6	4,443	1,983	74	46	10	1	2,206	123	3,739	2,819
48 15916	Coleman city	Coleman	6.2	5,127	4,360	151	34	12	-	456	114	868	3,846
48 15976	College Station city	Brazos	40.3	67,890	54,673	3,698	206	4,951	44	3,036	1,282	6,759	58,101
48 15988	Colleyville city	Tarrant	13.1	19,636	18,289	257	76	619	6	115	274	634	13,428
48 16120	Colorado City city	Mitchell	5.3	4,281	3,284	218	23	19	-	626	111	1,552	3,061
48 16168	Columbus city	Colorado	2.8	3,916	2,606	781	14	13	1	412	89	690	3,000
48 16192	Comanche city	Comanche	4.5	4,482	3,586	54	49	10	-	678	105	1,278	3,226
48 16204	Combes town	Cameron	2.5	2,553	2,052	9	33	7	8	385	59	1,948	1,689
48 16240	Commerce city	Hunt	6.5	7,669	5,450	1,594	32	199	16	240	138	587	6,020
48 16432	Conroe city	Montgomery	37.8	36,811	26,193	4,097	149	348	18	4,926	1,080	12,006	26,465
48 16468	Converse city	Bexar	6.3	11,508	7,985	1,499	64	253	16	1,226	465	3,388	7,944
48 16612	Coppell city	Dallas, Denton	14.9	35,958	29,929	1,174	122	3,343	8	675	707	2,490	23,474
48 16624	Copperas Cove city	Bell, Coryell, Lampasas	13.9	29,592	19,340	6,047	257	798	171	1,474	1,505	3,460	20,125
48 16696	Corinth city	Denton	7.9	11,325	10,031	475	75	270	6	255	213	690	7,875
48 17000	Corpus Christi city	Kleburg, Nueces, San Patricio	154.6	277,454	198,714	12,969	1,766	3,551	212	51,552	8,690	150,737	199,392
48 17060	Corsicana city	Navarro	20.7	24,485	14,515	5,775	120	155	114	3,339	467	5,502	17,812
48 17216	Cotulla city	La Salle	2.0	3,614	3,016	23	14	18	-	458	85	3,020	2,398
48 17504	Crandall city	Kaufman	2.8	2,774	2,480	106	17	5	-	127	39	200	1,810
48 17516	Crane city	Crane	1.0	3,191	2,346	96	31	12	-	620	86	1,449	2,150
48 17744	Crockett city	Houston	8.9	7,141	3,466	3,190	26	33	10	341	75	750	5,010

Table D-1. Places — **Area and Population**—Con.

[Includes incorporated places and census designated places (CDPs) of 2,500 or more population as of April 1, 2000. Codes shown are two-digit Federal Information Processing Standards (FIPS) state codes and five-digit FIPS place codes. Place names and codes are those in effect as of January 1, 2000. County refers to the county (or counties) in which the place is located. IC in this column = independent city, a county equivalent. If a place is located in more than one county, counties are listed in alphabetic order]

State and place code	Place	County	Land area, 2000 (sq. mi.)	Population, 2000 (April 1) Total	By race— One race White	Black or African Ameri-can	American Indian and Alaska Native	Asian	Native Hawaiian and Other Pacific Islander	Some other race	Two or more races	Hispanic or Latino (of any race)	18 years and over
48 00000	TEXAS—Con.												
48 17960	Crowley city	Johnson, Tarrant	6.7	7,467	6,950	104	57	36	1	171	148	583	5,159
48 18020	Crystal City city	Zavala	3.6	7,190	4,886	48	28	7	4	2,037	180	6,828	4,680
48 18092	Cuero city	DeWitt	4.9	6,571	4,419	1,098	40	34	-	844	136	2,282	4,791
48 18464	Daingerfield town	Morris	2.4	2,517	1,698	658	14	10	-	96	41	134	1,788
48 18524	Dalhart city	Dallam, Hartley	4.3	7,237	6,183	106	57	23	1	721	146	1,650	5,091
48 19000	Dallas city	Collin, Dallas, Denton, Kaufman, Rockwall	342.5	1,188,580	604,209	307,957	6,472	32,118	590	204,883	32,351	422,587	873,004
48 19432	Dayton city	Liberty	11.0	5,709	4,058	1,124	25	39	2	381	80	601	3,997
48 19528	Decatur city	Wise	7.0	5,201	4,246	103	30	38	-	647	137	1,172	3,785
48 19624	Deer Park city	Harris	10.4	28,520	25,672	374	118	321	37	1,496	502	4,341	20,247
48 19792	Del Rio city	Val Verde	15.4	33,867	26,105	409	236	166	20	6,024	907	27,446	23,117
48 19900	Denison city	Grayson	22.6	22,773	19,134	1,964	380	104	14	499	678	1,190	17,167
48 19972	Denton city	Denton	61.5	80,537	60,900	7,344	464	2,731	43	7,126	1,929	13,188	63,888
48 19984	Denver City town	Gaines, Yoakum	2.5	3,985	2,725	61	31	8	-	1,100	60	1,879	2,734
48 20092	DeSoto city	Dallas	21.6	37,646	18,382	17,142	118	484	13	964	543	2,750	27,034
48 20152	Devine city	Medina	3.1	4,140	3,173	28	32	12	-	767	128	2,163	2,927
48 20308	Diboll city	Angelina	4.8	5,470	2,936	1,320	29	3	3	1,061	118	2,038	3,981
48 20344	Dickinson city	Galveston	9.7	17,093	12,367	1,798	109	206	6	2,191	416	4,256	12,229
48 20428	Dilley city	Frio	2.3	3,674	2,459	382	21	28	-	691	93	2,654	2,650
48 20464	Dimmitt city	Castro	2.1	4,375	3,282	131	74	-	-	792	96	2,491	2,914
48 20734	Doffing CDP	Hidalgo	4.3	4,256	1,462	1	-	-	-	2,763	30	4,222	2,313
48 20884	Donna city	Hidalgo	5.0	14,768	11,233	54	88	27	-	3,012	354	12,886	9,734
48 21484	Dublin city	Erath	3.4	3,754	3,019	9	34	4	1	610	77	1,112	2,538
48 21556	Dumas city	Moore	5.1	13,747	9,361	99	81	160	3	3,675	368	5,876	9,304
48 21628	Duncanville city	Dallas	11.3	36,081	23,055	8,934	117	717	31	2,466	761	5,522	25,941
48 21844	Eagle Lake city	Colorado	2.7	3,664	1,934	857	24	-	1	750	98	1,620	2,569
48 21856	Eagle Mountain CDP	Tarrant	22.3	6,599	6,247	61	35	47	2	84	123	263	5,014
48 21892	Eagle Pass city	Maverick	7.4	22,413	16,302	60	88	171	1	5,089	702	21,269	15,083
48 21904	Early city	Brown	2.6	2,588	2,437	26	9	15	1	84	16	236	1,830
48 22132	Eastland city	Eastland	2.8	3,769	3,454	68	20	5	2	176	44	486	2,802
48 22528	Edcouch city	Hidalgo	0.9	3,342	2,551	21	21	-	-	663	86	3,246	2,102
48 22552	Eden city	Concho	2.4	2,561	2,321	39	9	1	4	166	21	1,317	2,246
48 22588	Edgecliff Village town	Tarrant	1.2	2,550	2,147	217	11	28	-	102	45	309	2,016
48 22660	Edinburg city	Hidalgo	37.4	48,465	35,533	281	230	315	19	10,986	1,101	42,981	32,462
48 22720	Edna city	Jackson	3.9	5,899	3,824	805	29	45	-	1,031	165	1,839	4,174
48 22810	Eidson Road CDP	Maverick	7.1	9,348	7,149	36	63	4	-	1,813	283	9,202	5,529
48 22864	El Campo city	Wharton	7.5	10,945	7,560	1,300	36	31	1	1,823	194	4,234	7,647
48 22905	El Cenizo city	Webb	0.5	3,545	2,862	10	38	2	-	520	113	3,506	1,813
48 22984	Electra city	Wichita	2.4	3,168	2,777	145	35	2	-	136	73	275	2,289
48 23044	Elgin city	Bastrop, Travis	4.7	5,700	3,840	857	51	30	3	740	179	2,635	3,999
48 23164	El Lago city	Harris	0.7	3,075	2,906	24	14	43	2	42	44	155	2,396
48 24000	El Paso city	El Paso	249.1	563,662	413,061	17,586	4,601	6,321	583	102,320	19,190	431,875	388,727
48 24036	Elsa city	Hidalgo	1.5	5,549	4,134	19	25	3	-	1,203	165	5,398	3,626
48 24348	Ennis city	Ellis	18.0	16,045	10,681	2,360	75	46	1	2,556	326	5,325	11,167
48 24768	Euless city	Tarrant	16.3	46,005	34,743	2,987	294	3,288	856	2,475	1,362	6,125	34,523
48 24912	Everman city	Tarrant	2.0	5,836	3,200	1,618	28	83	2	734	171	1,341	4,004
48 25032	Fabens CDP	El Paso	3.7	8,043	5,953	46	64	2	-	1,748	230	7,734	4,882
48 25104	Fairfield city	Freestone	4.5	3,094	2,211	663	8	21	-	144	47	325	2,281
48 25168	Fair Oaks Ranch city	Bexar, Comal, Kendall	7.2	4,695	4,525	18	20	29	3	49	51	371	3,515
48 25224	Fairview town	Collin	8.8	2,644	2,494	7	16	48	-	24	55	103	1,780
48 25368	Falfurrias city	Brooks	2.7	5,297	3,984	13	29	7	6	1,142	116	4,902	3,594
48 25452	Farmers Branch city	Dallas	12.0	27,508	21,560	661	150	804	9	3,579	745	10,241	20,455
48 25488	Farmersville city	Collin	3.2	3,118	2,569	315	13	2	-	165	54	503	2,197
48 26160	Floresville city	Wilson	4.8	5,868	4,185	96	28	20	3	1,343	193	3,756	4,144
48 26232	Flower Mound town	Denton, Tarrant	40.9	50,702	45,753	1,482	178	1,547	27	898	817	2,855	33,039
48 26268	Floydada city	Floyd	2.0	3,676	2,586	152	40	5	-	816	77	1,898	2,516
48 26544	Forest Hill city	Tarrant	4.2	12,949	4,354	7,389	54	147	1	820	184	2,349	9,537
48 26604	Forney city	Kaufman	7.8	5,588	4,678	413	31	11	8	352	95	537	3,796
48 26664	Fort Bliss CDP	El Paso	6.2	8,264	4,802	2,075	110	194	57	738	288	1,596	5,846
48 26736	Fort Hood CDP	Bell, Coryell	14.9	33,711	17,103	10,651	407	719	284	2,938	1,609	5,630	22,477
48 26808	Fort Stockton city	Pecos	5.1	7,846	5,497	70	45	60	1	1,974	199	5,482	5,484
48 27000	Fort Worth city	Denton, Tarrant	292.5	534,694	319,159	108,310	3,144	14,105	341	75,100	14,535	159,368	383,627
48 27102	Four Corners CDP	Fort Bend	2.8	2,954	1,263	560	19	471	1	556	84	1,216	1,869
48 27348	Fredericksburg city	Gillespie	6.6	8,911	8,294	24	24	17	4	454	94	1,515	7,102
48 27420	Freeport city	Brazoria	11.9	12,708	7,822	1,700	71	45	1	2,657	412	6,614	8,172
48 27432	Freer city	Duval	4.0	3,241	2,612	15	22	8	-	482	102	2,508	2,168
48 27540	Fresno CDP	Fort Bend	9.0	6,603	2,929	1,753	27	71	2	1,666	155	3,294	4,222
48 27648	Friendswood city	Galveston, Harris	21.0	29,037	26,158	783	115	695	4	809	473	2,553	20,318
48 27660	Friona city	Parmer	1.4	3,854	2,369	50	29	15	-	1,303	88	2,230	2,574
48 27684	Frisco city	Collin, Denton	69.9	33,714	29,417	1,268	128	791	10	1,464	636	3,716	23,347
48 27984	Gainesville city	Cooke	17.0	15,538	12,550	933	207	85	3	1,413	347	2,714	11,319
48 27996	Galena Park city	Harris	5.0	10,592	6,710	810	60	42	1	2,579	390	7,343	7,013
48 28068	Galveston city	Galveston	46.2	57,247	33,582	14,592	243	1,839	42	5,571	1,378	14,753	43,868
48 29000	Garland city	Collin, Dallas, Rockwall	57.1	215,768	140,835	25,069	1,284	15,806	141	25,862	6,231	55,192	151,435
48 29168	Gatesville city	Coryell	8.7	15,591	9,854	4,210	53	54	8	1,324	88	2,297	13,766
48 29336	Georgetown city	Williamson	22.8	28,339	24,200	960	100	190	15	2,355	519	5,121	21,695
48 29348	George West city	Live Oak	1.9	2,524	2,088	7	10	4	-	363	52	1,464	1,747
48 29432	Giddings city	Lee	5.1	5,105	3,369	677	26	29	-	841	163	1,773	3,509

Table D-1. Places — **Area and Population**—Con.

[Includes incorporated places and census designated places (CDPs) of 2,500 or more population as of April 1, 2000. Codes shown are two-digit Federal Information Processing Standards (FIPS) state codes and five-digit FIPS place codes. Place names and codes are those in effect as of January 1, 2000. County refers to the county (or counties) in which the place is located. IC in this column = independent city, a county equivalent. If a place is located in more than one county, counties are listed in alphabetic order]

State and place code	Place	County	Land area, 2000 (sq. mi.)	Population, 2000 (April 1)									
					By race—								
					One race							Hispanic or Latino (of any race)	18 years and over
				Total	White	Black or African American	American Indian and Alaska Native	Asian	Native Hawaiian and Other Pacific Islander	Some other race	Two or more races		
48 00000	TEXAS—Con.												
48 29564	Gilmer city	Upshur	4.6	4,799	3,643	971	17	4	1	91	72	212	3,583
48 29660	Gladewater city	Gregg, Upshur	11.6	6,078	4,850	980	50	35	1	96	66	213	4,416
48 29840	Glenn Heights city	Dallas, Ellis	7.0	7,224	4,815	1,815	56	28	8	367	135	1,137	4,663
48 30116	Gonzales city	Gonzales	5.1	7,202	4,534	893	53	36	7	1,523	156	3,322	5,062
48 30392	Graham city	Young	5.5	8,716	7,704	108	48	26	7	678	145	1,169	6,452
48 30416	Granbury city	Hood	5.5	5,718	5,406	22	40	30	2	150	68	418	4,516
48 30464	Grand Prairie city	Dallas, Ellis, Tarrant	71.4	127,427	78,970	17,242	982	5,632	74	20,265	4,262	42,038	88,507
48 30476	Grand Saline city	Van Zandt	2.0	3,028	2,784	18	11	4	1	168	42	428	2,188
48 30629	Grape Creek CDP	Tom Green	17.2	3,138	2,880	13	24	3	1	152	65	495	2,233
48 30644	Grapevine city	Dallas, Denton, Tarrant	32.3	42,059	37,081	1,001	232	1,075	31	1,927	712	4,860	29,766
48 30806	Greatwood CDP	Fort Bend	3.9	6,640	5,597	315	9	498	4	91	126	370	4,595
48 30920	Greenville city	Hunt	33.9	23,960	16,702	4,518	116	146	9	1,963	506	3,511	17,489
48 31280	Groesbeck city	Limestone	3.8	4,291	2,513	1,069	16	2	1	599	91	752	3,307
48 31328	Groves city	Jefferson	5.2	15,733	14,704	208	41	260	5	312	203	1,231	11,979
48 31592	Gun Barrel City town	Henderson	5.1	5,145	4,848	57	39	39	-	68	94	185	4,023
48 31904	Hallsville city	Harrison	2.3	2,772	2,582	132	4	10	-	19	25	63	1,852
48 31928	Haltom City city	Tarrant	12.4	39,018	29,973	1,088	285	3,010	45	3,600	1,017	7,771	28,457
48 31952	Hamilton city	Hamilton	2.8	2,977	2,832	2	5	10	-	98	30	201	2,210
48 32312	Harker Heights city	Bell	12.8	17,308	12,269	2,585	135	620	70	1,002	627	2,153	12,047
48 32372	Harlingen city	Cameron	34.1	57,564	45,290	528	301	506	16	9,435	1,488	41,881	39,864
48 32696	Haskell city	Haskell	3.4	3,106	2,495	121	17	3	-	387	83	705	2,322
48 32972	Hearne city	Robertson	4.1	4,690	1,788	2,083	23	8	2	679	107	1,318	3,147
48 32984	Heath city	Rockwall	6.9	4,149	3,950	34	16	56	3	54	36	125	2,838
48 33008	Hebbronville CDP	Jim Hogg	5.9	4,498	3,679	24	40	8	-	666	81	4,073	3,097
48 33146	Helotes city	Bexar	4.2	4,285	3,726	96	19	97	6	211	130	1,135	3,135
48 33200	Hempstead city	Waller	5.0	4,691	1,870	2,038	7	9	1	687	79	1,162	3,318
48 33212	Henderson city	Rusk	11.9	11,273	7,776	2,518	31	53	1	767	127	1,330	8,243
48 33284	Henrietta city	Clay	4.7	3,264	3,130	29	34	-	-	32	39	96	2,407
48 33320	Hereford city	Deaf Smith	5.6	14,597	10,198	257	119	38	17	3,616	352	8,958	9,636
48 33428	Hewitt city	McLennan	6.9	11,085	9,320	853	47	260	7	446	152	1,029	7,767
48 33560	Hidalgo city	Hidalgo	4.4	7,322	6,013	9	21	9	-	1,131	139	7,157	4,465
48 33824	Highland Park town	Dallas	2.2	8,842	8,601	34	12	73	1	68	53	241	6,434
48 33836	Highlands CDP	Harris	6.2	7,089	6,393	114	36	28	2	374	142	922	5,115
48 33848	Highland Village city	Denton	5.5	12,173	11,468	179	49	234	2	97	144	421	8,166
48 34088	Hillsboro city	Hill	9.1	8,232	5,694	1,330	24	46	5	942	191	2,326	5,951
48 34220	Hitchcock city	Galveston	66.5	6,386	3,829	2,095	18	10	2	304	128	877	4,617
48 34628	Hollywood Park town	Bexar	1.5	2,983	2,853	8	8	28	4	33	49	300	2,366
48 34671	Homestead Meadows North CDP	El Paso	16.6	4,232	3,098	18	47	-	6	961	102	3,491	2,681
48 34673	Homestead Meadows South CDP	El Paso	3.3	6,807	4,149	22	30	6	4	2,521	75	6,546	3,935
48 34676	Hondo city	Medina	9.6	7,897	5,791	658	37	20	-	1,203	188	4,732	5,846
48 34736	Hooks city	Bowie	2.1	2,973	2,498	301	29	13	2	43	87	88	2,164
48 34832	Horizon City city	El Paso	5.7	5,233	4,287	91	39	25	6	633	152	3,397	3,445
48 34862	Horseshoe Bay CDP	Burnet, Llano	23.4	3,337	3,211	11	8	26	-	49	32	143	2,984
48 35000	Houston city	Fort Bend, Harris, Montgomery	579.4	1,953,631	962,610	494,496	8,568	103,694	1,182	321,603	61,478	730,865	1,416,973
48 35228	Hudson city	Angelina	4.6	3,792	3,182	150	8	11	-	372	69	647	2,604
48 35348	Humble city	Harris	9.9	14,579	10,094	2,113	99	470	38	1,322	443	3,406	10,498
48 35480	Hunters Creek Village city	Harris	1.9	4,374	4,084	16	6	210	-	20	38	157	3,009
48 35528	Huntsville city	Walker	30.9	35,078	23,075	9,169	117	391	24	1,724	578	5,689	29,790
48 35576	Hurst city	Tarrant	9.9	36,273	31,189	1,499	231	663	106	1,886	699	3,999	27,041
48 35612	Hutchins city	Dallas	8.5	2,805	1,208	1,047	25	7	-	433	85	673	1,996
48 36008	Ingleside city	Nueces, San Patricio	14.4	9,388	7,281	526	83	175	25	956	342	2,601	6,589
48 36104	Iowa Park city	Wichita	3.6	6,431	6,171	17	70	24	2	58	89	230	4,661
48 37000	Irving city	Dallas	67.2	191,615	123,019	19,583	1,244	15,784	248	25,608	6,129	59,838	143,397
48 37156	Jacinto City city	Harris	1.9	10,302	7,024	127	92	24	1	2,644	390	7,767	6,870
48 37168	Jacksboro city	Jack	5.8	4,533	3,715	474	26	14	1	252	51	487	3,550
48 37216	Jacksonville city	Cherokee	14.1	13,868	8,682	3,009	67	94	18	1,764	234	3,195	9,812
48 37420	Jasper city	Jasper	10.3	8,247	3,980	3,621	36	58	2	427	123	706	6,048
48 37612	Jersey Village city	Harris	3.4	6,880	5,960	280	15	350	4	167	104	499	5,364
48 37936	Jollyville CDP	Travis, Williamson	5.9	15,813	12,621	742	49	1,348	3	689	361	1,808	11,280
48 38080	Joshua city	Johnson	6.5	4,528	4,277	12	29	14	-	129	67	358	3,181
48 38116	Jourdanton city	Atascosa	3.5	3,732	2,778	42	36	11	1	762	102	1,973	2,532
48 38248	Junction city	Kimble	2.3	2,618	2,255	1	10	18	-	291	43	759	1,879
48 38452	Karnes City city	Karnes	2.1	3,457	2,459	196	11	20	-	673	98	2,208	2,562
48 38476	Katy city	Fort Bend, Harris, Waller	10.7	11,775	9,889	499	66	59	5	1,018	239	2,797	8,060
48 38488	Kaufman city	Kaufman	6.6	6,490	4,402	835	43	27	-	1,033	150	1,930	4,516
48 38548	Keene city	Johnson	2.8	5,003	3,725	353	38	122	130	467	168	1,293	3,690
48 38632	Keller city	Tarrant	18.4	27,345	25,634	392	106	483	10	324	396	1,234	18,117
48 38860	Kenedy city	Karnes	3.3	3,487	2,526	111	25	25	6	721	73	2,263	2,475
48 38896	Kennedale city	Tarrant	6.0	5,850	5,178	202	44	57	-	251	118	580	4,177
48 39004	Kermit city	Winkler	2.5	5,714	4,151	117	27	14	-	1,287	118	2,733	4,003
48 39040	Kerrville city	Kerr	16.7	20,425	17,543	610	112	117	16	1,674	353	4,643	16,140
48 39124	Kilgore city	Gregg, Rusk	15.4	11,301	8,840	1,394	46	77	3	785	156	1,256	8,517
48 39148	Killeen city	Bell	35.3	86,911	39,788	29,109	680	3,759	787	7,814	4,974	15,469	60,940
48 39304	Kingsland CDP	Llano	9.0	4,584	4,385	6	14	24	1	106	48	270	3,788
48 39352	Kingsville city	Kleberg	13.8	25,575	18,185	1,111	160	443	17	4,811	848	17,151	18,717

Table D-1. Places — **Area and Population**—Con.

[Includes incorporated places and census designated places (CDPs) of 2,500 or more population as of April 1, 2000. Codes shown are two-digit Federal Information Processing Standards (FIPS) state codes and five-digit FIPS place codes. Place names and codes are those in effect as of January 1, 2000. County refers to the county (or counties) in which the place is located. IC in this column = independent city, a county equivalent. If a place is located in more than one county, counties are listed in alphabetic order]

State and place code	Place	County	Land area, 2000 (sq. mi.)	Population, 2000 (April 1)									
					By race—							Hispanic or Latino (of any race)	18 years and over
					One race						Two or more races		
				Total	White	Black or African American	American Indian and Alaska Native	Asian	Native Hawaiian and Other Pacific Islander	Some other race			
48 00000	TEXAS—Con.												
48 39448	Kirby city	Bexar	1.9	8,673	5,574	1,263	46	179	12	1,286	313	3,616	6,048
48 39952	Kyle city	Hays	5.9	5,314	3,363	441	34	22	2	1,246	206	2,780	3,656
48 40036	Lackland AFB CDP	Bexar	4.3	7,123	4,644	1,354	61	259	23	157	625	981	6,744
48 40168	Lacy-Lakeview city	McLennan	3.8	5,764	4,274	858	35	48	6	404	139	940	4,251
48 40204	La Feria city	Cameron	2.0	6,115	4,581	16	26	20	4	1,265	203	4,736	4,246
48 40264	Lago Vista city	Travis	8.7	4,507	4,237	38	12	30	4	110	76	355	3,571
48 40276	La Grange city	Fayette	3.6	4,478	3,326	464	24	31	1	546	86	932	3,347
48 40342	La Homa CDP	Hidalgo	6.9	10,433	9,170	12	2	7	-	1,196	46	10,196	5,926
48 40384	La Joya city	Hidalgo	2.8	3,303	2,112	6	17	16	1	1,096	55	3,210	2,150
48 40516	Lake Dallas city	Denton	2.3	6,166	5,519	205	39	58	1	237	107	606	4,273
48 40576	Lakehills CDP	Bandera	30.3	4,668	4,343	20	35	13	3	167	87	602	3,521
48 40588	Lake Jackson city	Brazoria	19.0	26,386	22,754	1,023	102	660	5	1,370	472	3,879	18,322
48 40984	Lakeway city	Travis	5.8	8,002	7,713	64	10	69	-	69	77	337	6,024
48 41056	Lake Worth city	Tarrant	2.5	4,618	4,073	40	41	44	5	285	130	670	3,439
48 41116	La Marque city	Galveston	14.2	13,682	7,640	4,746	63	64	4	849	316	2,111	10,159
48 41164	Lamesa city	Dawson	4.8	9,952	7,330	420	29	19	-	1,942	212	5,271	6,992
48 41188	Lampasas city	Lampasas	6.2	6,786	5,753	138	48	39	5	683	120	1,568	4,914
48 41212	Lancaster city	Dallas	29.3	25,894	9,744	13,725	126	100	14	1,705	480	3,001	18,004
48 41440	La Porte city	Harris	18.9	31,880	25,946	1,993	154	359	25	2,717	686	6,520	22,412
48 41464	Laredo city	Webb	78.5	176,576	145,267	652	784	820	47	24,611	4,395	166,216	113,914
48 41566	Las Lomas CDP	Starr	0.6	2,684	2,419	-	-	1	-	258	6	2,667	1,478
48 41728	Laureles CDP	Cameron	4.9	3,285	3,208	3	11	-	-	34	29	3,221	1,904
48 41980	League City city	Galveston, Harris	51.2	45,444	38,170	2,311	168	1,439	24	2,404	928	6,130	32,064
48 42016	Leander city	Travis, Williamson	7.5	7,596	6,549	221	70	39	10	527	180	1,211	5,054
48 42388	Leon Valley city	Bexar	3.4	9,239	7,213	256	62	180	14	1,219	295	4,125	7,080
48 42448	Levelland city	Hockley	9.9	12,866	9,050	690	122	23	6	2,691	284	5,045	9,316
48 42508	Lewisville city	Dallas, Denton	36.8	77,737	60,015	5,747	544	3,028	25	6,468	1,910	13,799	57,070
48 42568	Liberty city	Liberty	35.1	8,033	6,068	1,053	32	55	1	743	81	1,191	5,858
48 42820	Lindale town	Smith	4.0	2,954	2,605	204	16	21	-	64	44	132	2,160
48 40012	Little Elm town	Denton	4.9	3,646	2,909	100	20	27	2	510	81	637	2,401
48 43024	Littlefield city	Lamb	6.0	6,507	5,017	350	45	11	3	951	130	2,982	4,599
48 43096	Live Oak city	Bexar	4.7	9,156	7,160	773	71	232	14	575	331	2,469	6,746
48 43132	Livingston town	Polk	8.4	5,433	3,824	1,005	35	45	-	439	85	755	3,929
48 43144	Llano city	Llano	4.4	3,325	3,137	19	22	8	-	113	26	296	2,512
48 43150	Llano Grande CDP	Hidalgo	1.7	3,333	2,663	2	8	12	-	631	17	2,947	2,156
48 43240	Lockhart city	Caldwell	11.2	11,615	7,598	1,473	78	40	7	2,091	328	5,507	8,534
48 43888	Longview city	Gregg, Harrison	54.7	73,344	51,417	16,214	369	609	16	3,608	1,111	7,564	53,738
48 43972	Lopezville CDP	Hidalgo	1.8	4,476	4,089	9	-	2	-	322	54	4,395	2,685
48 44116	Los Fresnos city	Cameron	2.4	4,512	3,698	19	6	1	4	649	135	3,818	2,871
48 44166	Lost Creek CDP	Travis	3.1	4,729	4,360	24	13	231	-	27	74	174	3,192
48 45000	Lubbock city	Lubbock	114.8	199,564	145,426	17,292	1,118	3,078	65	28,571	4,014	54,786	149,863
48 45012	Lucas city	Collin	9.2	2,890	2,787	12	15	8	1	29	38	103	2,017
48 45072	Lufkin city	Angelina	26.7	32,709	19,599	8,693	84	451	6	3,373	503	5,754	23,891
48 45096	Luling city	Caldwell	3.8	5,080	3,317	485	16	21	-	1,122	119	2,236	3,563
48 45120	Lumberton city	Hardin	9.4	8,731	8,525	4	25	18	-	76	83	244	6,188
48 45384	McAllen city	Hidalgo	46.0	106,414	83,491	647	429	2,059	41	16,864	2,883	85,427	73,677
48 45672	McGregor city	Coryell, McLennan	21.8	4,727	3,361	545	48	18	-	681	74	1,289	3,419
48 45744	McKinney city	Collin	58.0	54,369	42,628	3,913	293	811	35	5,562	1,127	9,876	37,542
48 45948	McQueeney CDP	Guadalupe	4.2	2,527	2,214	19	20	6	4	222	42	538	1,943
48 45996	Madisonville city	Madison	4.1	4,159	2,354	1,215	21	17	1	439	112	925	2,922
48 46452	Mansfield city	Ellis, Johnson, Tarrant	36.5	28,031	24,221	1,232	159	346	5	1,590	478	3,574	19,117
48 46500	Manvel city	Brazoria	23.3	3,046	2,779	71	14	17	-	119	46	392	2,259
48 46584	Marble Falls city	Burnet	6.1	4,959	4,255	123	20	21	1	440	99	1,118	3,537
48 46740	Marlin city	Falls	4.5	6,628	2,773	2,948	18	13	1	770	105	1,213	4,428
48 46776	Marshall city	Harrison	29.6	23,935	13,082	9,237	93	132	10	1,155	226	2,069	17,686
48 47040	Mathis city	San Patricio	2.0	5,034	2,710	82	46	21	5	2,018	152	4,556	3,288
48 47100	Mauriceville CDP	Orange	8.5	2,743	2,618	10	18	2	-	69	26	161	1,881
48 47335	Meadows Place city	Fort Bend	0.9	4,912	3,528	299	11	772	5	159	138	563	3,542
48 47406	Medina CDP	Zapata	1.8	2,960	2,426	9	12	6	1	438	68	2,768	1,695
48 47700	Mercedes city	Hidalgo	8.6	13,649	10,840	49	122	9	1	2,313	315	12,286	9,159
48 47796	Merkel town	Taylor	2.0	2,637	2,358	30	16	8	1	167	57	375	1,893
48 47872	Mesquite city	Dallas, Kaufman	43.4	124,523	91,572	16,585	750	4,665	65	8,009	2,877	19,500	86,542
48 47916	Mexia city	Limestone	5.2	6,563	3,669	2,079	15	13	-	700	87	1,175	4,589
48 48072	Midland city	Martin, Midland	66.6	94,996	71,735	7,948	602	956	29	11,862	1,864	27,543	66,591
48 48096	Midlothian city	Ellis	37.7	7,480	6,766	218	39	37	1	295	124	981	5,147
48 48272	Midway North CDP	Hidalgo	2.1	3,946	3,500	6	7	-	-	393	40	3,905	2,258
48 48320	Mila Doce CDP	Hidalgo	3.3	4,907	4,649	-	10	-	-	209	39	4,884	2,754
48 48648	Mineola city	Wood	5.3	4,550	3,512	609	32	12	1	293	91	589	3,354
48 48684	Mineral Wells city	Palo Pinto, Parker	20.5	16,946	13,165	1,487	92	110	1	1,779	312	3,265	12,859
48 48768	Mission city	Hidalgo	24.1	45,408	35,249	168	174	288	3	8,465	1,061	36,794	30,829
48 48772	Mission Bend CDP	Fort Bend, Harris	5.2	30,831	14,281	6,628	96	5,229	25	3,277	1,295	8,343	20,441
48 48804	Missouri City city	Fort Bend, Harris	29.7	52,913	23,435	20,290	107	5,610	21	2,360	1,090	5,755	36,603
48 48936	Monahans city	Ward, Winkler	24.8	6,821	5,409	352	24	24	3	853	156	2,978	4,753
48 49392	Morgan's Point Resort city	Bell	2.6	2,989	2,721	13	13	18	5	174	45	277	2,135
48 49800	Mount Pleasant city	Titus	12.5	13,935	7,901	2,230	77	117	1	3,285	324	5,664	9,593
48 49988	Muleshoe city	Bailey	3.4	4,530	2,866	68	29	9	-	1,431	127	2,416	3,112
48 50100	Murphy city	Collin	5.3	3,099	2,357	295	34	281	-	62	70	153	2,179

[Includes incorporated places and census designated places (CDPs) of 2,500 or more population as of April 1, 2000. Codes shown are two-digit Federal Information Processing Standards (FIPS) state codes and five-digit FIPS place codes. Place names and codes are those in effect as of January 1, 2000. County refers to the county (or counties) in which the place is located. IC in this column = independent city, a county equivalent. If a place is located in more than one county, counties are listed in alphabetic order]

State and place code	Place	County	Land area, 2000 (sq. mi.)	Population, 2000 (April 1) By race— One race							Two or more races	Hispanic or Latino (of any race)	18 years and over
				Total	White	Black or African American	American Indian and Alaska Native	Asian	Native Hawaiian and Other Pacific Islander	Some other race			
48 00000	TEXAS—Con.												
48 50256	Nacogdoches city	Nacogdoches	25.2	29,914	19,736	7,495	102	337	32	1,748	464	3,236	23,857
48 50376	Nassau Bay city	Harris	1.3	4,170	3,738	78	21	163	7	70	93	262	3,532
48 50472	Navasota city	Grimes	6.1	6,789	3,627	2,316	20	31	-	672	123	1,898	4,734
48 50580	Nederland city	Jefferson	5.7	17,422	16,291	155	58	352	7	351	208	1,089	12,862
48 50628	Needville city	Fort Bend	1.7	2,609	1,933	344	7	3	-	267	55	625	1,840
48 50808	New Boston city	Bowie	3.5	4,808	3,822	848	36	13	5	21	63	70	3,528
48 50820	New Braunfels city	Comal, Guadalupe	29.2	36,494	30,763	501	201	211	11	3,988	819	12,599	27,125
48 51366	New Territory CDP	Fort Bend	5.0	13,861	7,979	1,389	31	3,614	6	435	407	1,157	9,034
48 51648	Nocona city	Montague	2.8	3,198	2,993	8	27	11	1	106	52	399	2,347
48 52356	North Richland Hills city	Tarrant	18.2	55,635	49,224	1,501	303	1,475	93	1,885	1,154	5,276	40,484
48 52746	Nurillo CDP	Hidalgo	7.0	5,056	3,840	17	16	-	-	1,063	120	4,889	3,041
48 53190	Oak Ridge North city	Montgomery	1.1	2,991	2,849	38	9	35	-	31	29	160	2,236
48 53388	Odessa city	Ector, Midland	36.8	90,943	66,781	5,347	702	797	37	14,611	2,668	37,671	63,814
48 54000	Olney city	Young	2.1	3,396	3,049	84	27	4	1	156	75	490	2,518
48 54132	Orange city	Orange	20.1	18,643	11,295	6,593	70	218	15	201	251	675	13,539
48 54444	Ovilla city	Dallas, Ellis	5.7	3,405	3,130	166	12	24	1	24	48	114	2,379
48 54552	Ozona CDP	Crockett	4.7	3,436	2,564	28	23	11	1	719	90	2,066	2,394
48 54684	Palacios city	Matagorda	5.0	5,153	2,941	244	35	625	-	1,152	156	2,638	3,327
48 54708	Palestine city	Anderson	17.7	17,598	11,369	4,359	86	139	13	1,391	241	2,619	12,481
48 54780	Palmhurst city	Hidalgo	6.1	4,872	4,125	12	12	19	-	668	36	4,262	2,976
48 54804	Palmview city	Hidalgo	2.4	4,107	2,766	1	5	5	-	1,281	49	3,828	2,580
48 54810	Palmview South CDP	Hidalgo	3.0	6,219	4,895	12	3	5	1	1,232	71	5,297	4,000
48 54912	Pampa city	Gray	8.7	17,887	14,969	689	191	74	5	1,470	489	2,454	13,259
48 54960	Panhandle town	Carson	2.1	2,589	2,412	17	20	2	-	100	38	232	1,829
48 55080	Paris city	Lamar	42.8	25,898	18,884	5,766	245	172	7	403	421	1,068	19,329
48 56000	Pasadena city	Harris	44.2	141,674	101,219	2,316	957	2,589	58	30,173	4,362	68,348	96,947
48 56348	Pearland city	Brazoria, Fort Bend, Harris	39.3	37,640	31,100	2,006	157	1,373	14	2,305	685	6,107	26,785
48 56384	Pearsall city	Frio	4.2	7,157	5,282	28	51	20	1	1,575	200	6,029	4,968
48 56482	Pecan Grove CDP	Fort Bend	8.7	13,551	12,371	446	26	181	-	340	187	1,230	9,026
48 56498	Pecan Plantation CDP	Hood	7.0	3,544	3,477	6	9	15	2	10	25	86	2,898
48 56516	Pecos city	Reeves	7.3	9,501	7,251	233	44	45	1	1,716	211	7,560	6,416
48 56912	Perryton city	Ochiltree	4.4	7,774	6,626	12	76	31	1	863	165	2,653	5,342
48 57176	Pflugerville city	Travis, Williamson	11.3	16,335	12,607	1,545	39	704	14	979	447	2,727	10,685
48 57200	Pharr city	Hidalgo	20.8	46,660	37,075	110	335	109	13	8,068	950	42,282	30,441
48 57476	Pilot Point city	Denton	3.0	3,538	2,942	164	33	6	-	314	79	528	2,480
48 57584	Pinehurst CDP	Montgomery	9.0	4,266	4,004	37	26	9	-	138	52	439	3,013
48 57800	Piney Point Village city	Harris	2.1	3,380	3,017	18	1	284	3	15	42	127	2,482
48 57908	Pittsburg city	Camp	3.3	4,347	2,369	1,216	13	7	2	685	55	1,037	3,043
48 57980	Plainview city	Hale	13.8	22,336	14,118	1,312	253	95	14	5,926	618	11,131	15,401
48 58016	Plano city	Collin, Denton	71.6	222,030	173,761	11,155	803	22,594	98	8,565	5,054	22,357	158,284
48 58280	Pleasanton city	Atascosa	6.4	8,266	6,541	81	80	41	14	1,268	241	4,228	5,756
48 58808	Port Aransas city	Nueces	8.8	3,370	3,165	14	42	29	1	73	46	205	2,733
48 58820	Port Arthur city	Jefferson, Orange	82.9	57,755	22,528	25,240	260	3,404	9	5,127	1,187	10,081	41,206
48 58892	Port Isabel city	Cameron	2.2	4,865	3,876	50	16	12	5	756	150	3,619	3,385
48 58904	Portland city	Nueces, San Patricio	7.0	14,827	12,424	610	84	156	30	1,102	421	3,870	9,989
48 58916	Port Lavaca city	Calhoun	9.8	12,035	8,659	488	56	476	10	2,036	310	6,272	8,390
48 58940	Port Neches city	Jefferson	9.1	13,601	12,887	126	64	214	1	161	148	690	10,127
48 59012	Post city	Garza	3.8	3,708	2,691	203	9	4	-	693	108	1,581	2,689
48 59084	Poteet city	Atascosa	1.5	3,305	2,148	12	9	-	-	995	141	2,936	2,162
48 59336	Prairie View city	Waller	7.2	4,410	153	4,124	8	19	-	60	46	117	4,007
48 59384	Premont city	Jim Wells	1.7	2,772	2,116	15	15	1	1	579	45	2,330	1,897
48 59396	Presidio city	Presidio	2.6	4,167	3,475	4	6	2	1	643	36	3,922	2,615
48 59540	Primera town	Cameron	1.5	2,723	2,222	18	12	1	1	382	87	2,439	1,737
48 59576	Princeton city	Collin	4.3	3,477	3,162	33	34	10	-	159	79	379	2,446
48 59636	Progreso city	Hidalgo	3.0	4,851	4,318	1	5	2	-	501	25	4,803	2,789
48 60044	Quanah city	Hardeman	3.5	3,022	2,540	150	12	13	-	249	58	498	2,262
48 60632	Ranger city	Eastland	7.0	2,584	2,192	174	17	11	-	146	44	349	1,998
48 60836	Raymondville city	Willacy	3.8	9,733	6,804	381	57	10	-	2,267	214	8,432	6,822
48 61196	Red Oak city	Ellis	7.8	4,301	3,698	233	23	38	-	200	109	503	2,987
48 61352	Redwood CDP	Guadalupe	5.9	3,586	1,726	55	32	4	1	1,604	164	3,018	2,185
48 61436	Refugio town	Refugio	1.6	2,941	2,192	394	15	15	3	276	46	1,303	2,155
48 61568	Rendon CDP	Tarrant	24.8	9,022	8,126	371	68	31	3	321	102	706	6,636
48 61592	Reno city	Lamar	3.8	2,767	2,586	78	40	11	-	19	33	61	1,950
48 61796	Richardson city	Collin, Dallas	28.6	91,802	69,209	5,675	409	10,709	58	3,351	2,391	9,420	69,046
48 61844	Richland Hills city	Tarrant	3.1	8,132	7,352	117	50	82	22	330	179	825	6,215
48 61892	Richmond city	Fort Bend	3.7	11,081	5,674	1,501	70	59	8	3,435	334	6,506	7,574
48 61904	Richwood city	Brazoria	1.6	3,012	2,355	256	11	15	2	279	94	704	2,145
48 62138	Rio Bravo city	Webb	0.7	5,553	4,365	19	55	1	1	923	189	5,425	3,007
48 62168	Rio Grande City city	Starr	7.6	11,923	9,893	36	52	132	1	1,491	318	11,433	7,976
48 62384	River Oaks city	Tarrant	2.0	6,985	5,926	28	48	54	7	763	159	1,902	5,101
48 62504	Roanoke city	Denton	6.0	2,810	2,541	38	32	30	2	91	76	304	2,015
48 62588	Robinson city	McLennan	31.6	7,845	7,198	164	30	38	1	335	79	706	5,766
48 62600	Robstown city	Nueces	12.1	12,727	8,523	180	76	19	8	3,452	469	11,848	8,465
48 62672	Rockdale city	Milam	3.1	5,439	3,845	777	19	23	-	665	110	1,193	3,890
48 62804	Rockport city	Aransas	9.4	7,385	6,549	97	37	269	-	251	182	1,440	5,804
48 62828	Rockwall city	Rockwall	22.3	17,976	16,421	539	69	249	6	462	230	1,157	13,040
48 63020	Roma city	Starr	2.8	9,617	8,684	14	19	4	5	746	145	9,477	6,258

[Includes incorporated places and census designated places (CDPs) of 2,500 or more population as of April 1, 2000. Codes shown are two-digit Federal Information Processing Standards (FIPS) state codes and five-digit FIPS place codes. Place names and codes are those in effect as of January 1, 2000. County refers to the county (or counties) in which the place is located. IC in this column = independent city, a county equivalent. If a place is located in more than one county, counties are listed in alphabetic order]

State and place code	Place	County	Land area, 2000 (sq. mi.)	Population, 2000 (April 1)									
					By race—							Hispanic or Latino (of any race)	18 years and over
					One race						Two or more races		
				Total	White	Black or African American	American Indian and Alaska Native	Asian	Native Hawaiian and Other Pacific Islander	Some other race			
48 00000	TEXAS—Con.												
48 63284	Rosenberg city	Fort Bend	21.2	24,043	15,793	2,052	90	91	10	5,331	676	13,215	16,608
48 63360	Rosita North CDP	Maverick	3.1	3,400	2,268	11	33	-	-	1,001	87	3,337	1,943
48 63364	Rosita South CDP	Maverick	7.8	2,574	1,503	5	411	-	3	584	68	2,140	1,420
48 63500	Round Rock city	Travis, Williamson	26.1	61,136	46,927	4,718	305	1,767	59	5,792	1,568	13,511	41,606
48 63572	Rowlett city	Dallas, Rockwall	20.2	44,503	36,406	4,010	220	1,481	25	1,570	791	3,899	29,609
48 63668	Royse City city	Collin, Rockwall	10.2	2,957	2,340	222	14	16	-	282	74	620	2,001
48 63848	Rusk city	Cherokee	6.8	5,085	3,189	1,526	9	49	-	262	50	352	4,203
48 64064	Sachse city	Collin, Dallas	9.7	9,751	8,517	451	63	210	1	329	180	801	6,565
48 64112	Saginaw city	Tarrant	7.5	12,374	10,844	239	113	154	-	753	271	1,823	8,420
48 64268	Salado CDP	Bell	17.0	3,475	3,210	9	22	21	2	179	32	301	2,698
48 64472	San Angelo city	Tom Green	55.9	88,439	68,183	4,185	579	844	70	12,344	2,234	29,321	65,589
48 65000	San Antonio city	Bexar, Comal	407.6	1,144,646	774,708	78,120	9,584	17,934	1,067	221,362	41,871	671,394	817,989
48 65036	San Benito city	Cameron	11.0	23,444	17,854	74	97	58	1	4,802	558	20,380	15,641
48 65048	San Carlos CDP	Hidalgo	1.8	2,650	2,115	8	-	-	-	455	72	2,572	1,574
48 65180	San Diego city	Duval, Jim Wells	1.6	4,753	3,710	13	37	1	2	842	148	4,604	3,191
48 65360	San Elizario CDP	El Paso	9.9	11,046	10,420	17	61	1	1	462	84	10,812	6,374
48 65408	Sanger city	Denton	3.1	4,534	4,039	138	50	6	-	190	111	513	3,147
48 65516	San Juan city	Hidalgo	11.0	26,229	21,293	88	143	23	9	4,177	496	24,950	16,419
48 65564	San Leon CDP	Galveston	4.9	4,365	3,510	35	36	332	5	361	86	627	3,360
48 65600	San Marcos city	Caldwell, Hays	18.2	34,733	25,200	1,921	227	426	38	5,914	1,007	12,676	29,388
48 65648	San Saba town	San Saba	1.8	2,637	2,071	17	46	3	-	457	43	831	1,925
48 65660	Sansom Park city	Tarrant	1.2	4,181	3,397	18	42	24	-	614	86	1,180	2,973
48 65726	Santa Fe city	Galveston	14.0	9,548	9,063	24	55	22	1	281	102	1,029	6,868
48 65768	Santa Rosa town	Cameron	0.6	2,833	1,858	16	27	3	-	849	80	2,710	1,742
48 66089	Scenic Oaks CDP	Bexar	8.3	3,279	3,072	6	11	31	-	112	47	491	2,433
48 66128	Schertz city	Bexar, Comal, Guadalupe	24.7	18,694	15,336	1,228	90	330	34	1,034	642	3,640	13,211
48 66188	Schulenburg city	Fayette	2.4	2,699	2,059	417	8	9	1	163	42	366	2,114
48 66248	Scissors CDP	Hidalgo	1.7	2,805	2,179	1	6	-	-	588	31	2,783	1,597
48 66392	Seabrook city	Chambers, Galveston, Harris	5.7	9,443	8,397	199	48	313	2	261	223	1,017	7,189
48 66428	Seagoville city	Dallas, Kaufman	16.2	10,823	8,524	1,041	81	61	8	842	266	1,905	8,030
48 66464	Sealy city	Austin	6.9	5,248	3,753	673	16	29	-	676	101	1,597	3,665
48 66644	Seguin city	Guadalupe	19.0	22,011	14,397	2,002	134	190	12	4,478	798	11,669	15,979
48 66764	Seminole city	Gaines	3.4	5,910	4,766	117	58	17	1	799	152	2,340	4,022
48 66968	Seymour city	Baylor	2.7	2,908	2,595	133	14	21	3	100	42	304	2,200
48 67082	Shady Hollow CDP	Travis	5.4	5,140	4,609	134	18	137	1	164	77	664	3,558
48 67496	Sherman city	Grayson	38.6	35,082	27,526	3,938	468	372	12	1,847	919	4,260	26,461
48 67832	Silsbee city	Hardin	7.5	6,393	4,210	2,048	11	24	2	54	44	153	4,649
48 68036	Sinton city	San Patricio	2.2	5,676	4,170	206	53	2	5	1,049	191	4,032	3,975
48 68180	Slaton city	Lubbock	5.4	6,109	4,420	474	36	10	5	1,043	121	2,582	4,340
48 68456	Smithville city	Bastrop	3.5	3,901	3,043	567	12	16	-	199	64	602	2,838
48 68624	Snyder city	Scurry	8.6	10,783	8,519	506	61	27	-	1,475	195	3,427	7,787
48 68636	Socorro city	El Paso	17.5	27,152	19,932	96	365	20	4	5,981	754	26,183	17,349
48 68756	Sonora city	Sutton	2.0	2,924	2,169	10	10	7	-	683	45	1,560	2,014
48 68846	South Alamo CDP	Hidalgo	2.0	3,101	3,010	6	-	9	-	52	24	3,051	1,686
48 69020	South Houston city	Harris	3.0	15,833	10,344	165	95	111	8	4,392	718	12,338	10,428
48 69032	Southlake city	Denton, Tarrant	21.9	21,519	20,345	299	53	386	2	175	259	789	13,541
48 69432	Sparks CDP	El Paso	1.3	2,974	2,104	-	5	5	-	836	24	2,958	1,700
48 69476	Spearman city	Hansford	2.1	3,021	2,411	1	22	5	-	536	46	970	2,150
48 69596	Spring CDP	Harris	23.9	36,385	30,203	2,544	186	518	48	2,046	840	5,844	25,098
48 69812	Spring Valley city	Harris	1.3	3,611	3,423	12	18	107	1	25	25	156	2,591
48 69908	Stafford city	Fort Bend, Harris	7.0	15,681	7,362	2,956	67	3,105	9	1,651	531	3,653	11,309
48 69980	Stamford city	Haskell, Jones	6.0	3,636	2,691	288	50	4	-	538	65	979	2,632
48 70040	Stanton city	Martin	1.8	2,556	1,891	73	19	8	-	500	65	1,352	1,662
48 70208	Stephenville city	Erath	10.0	14,921	13,554	219	86	97	8	671	286	1,725	11,895
48 70808	Sugar Land city	Fort Bend	24.1	63,328	41,798	3,294	149	15,072	18	1,470	1,527	5,053	43,590
48 70868	Sullivan City city	Hidalgo	3.6	3,998	2,597	4	1	-	-	1,363	33	3,944	2,458
48 70904	Sulphur Springs city	Hopkins	17.9	14,551	11,570	2,076	101	58	9	537	200	1,191	10,779
48 71156	Sunnyvale town	Dallas	16.7	2,693	2,395	70	19	124	-	60	25	118	1,897
48 71492	Sweeny city	Brazoria	1.9	3,624	2,727	572	37	15	-	217	56	497	2,547
48 71540	Sweetwater city	Nolan	10.0	11,415	8,594	666	66	36	8	1,793	252	3,618	8,212
48 71684	Taft city	San Patricio	1.5	3,396	2,412	113	7	2	1	779	82	2,276	2,258
48 71708	Tahoka city	Lynn	2.4	2,910	2,174	159	40	3	-	476	58	1,303	1,979
48 71948	Taylor city	Williamson	13.5	13,575	9,212	1,929	70	46	7	2,032	279	4,626	9,679
48 71960	Taylor Lake Village city	Harris	1.2	3,694	3,413	100	18	76	5	38	44	169	2,749
48 72020	Teague city	Freestone	3.4	4,557	2,975	1,261	6	9	3	275	28	615	3,651
48 72176	Temple city	Bell	65.4	54,514	38,030	8,988	280	833	50	5,030	1,303	9,716	40,196
48 72284	Terrell city	Kaufman	18.3	13,606	7,532	4,386	49	76	3	1,325	235	2,390	9,733
48 72296	Terrell Hills city	Bexar	1.7	5,019	4,788	26	8	11	1	120	65	586	3,605
48 72368	Texarkana city	Bowie	25.6	34,782	20,583	12,885	119	254	17	498	426	1,012	25,742
48 72392	Texas City city	Chambers, Galveston	62.4	41,521	25,224	11,407	207	365	20	3,417	881	8,520	30,416
48 72530	The Colony city	Denton	13.7	26,531	22,409	1,375	188	447	12	1,405	695	3,519	17,517
48 72656	The Woodlands CDP	Montgomery	23.4	55,649	51,399	973	160	1,556	30	795	736	3,697	37,940
48 73057	Timberwood Park CDP	Bexar	19.0	5,889	5,315	65	27	64	-	255	163	1,193	4,156
48 73316	Tomball city	Harris, Montgomery	10.2	9,089	7,883	446	36	58	5	506	155	1,095	6,793
48 73664	Trinity city	Trinity	3.8	2,721	1,556	922	11	13	-	184	35	297	1,948
48 73710	Trophy Club town	Denton, Tarrant	4.0	6,350	5,933	105	19	112	4	74	103	265	4,531
48 73868	Tulia city	Swisher	3.5	5,117	3,400	430	22	5	1	1,132	127	2,028	3,694

Table D-1. Places — **Area and Population**—Con.

[Includes incorporated places and census designated places (CDPs) of 2,500 or more population as of April 1, 2000. Codes shown are two-digit Federal Information Processing Standards (FIPS) state codes and five-digit FIPS place codes. Place names and codes are those in effect as of January 1, 2000. County refers to the county (or counties) in which the place is located. IC in this column = independent city, a county equivalent. If a place is located in more than one county, counties are listed in alphabetical order]

State and place code	Place	County	Land area, 2000 (sq. mi.)	Total	White	Black or African American	American Indian and Alaska Native	Asian	Native Hawaiian and Other Pacific Islander	Some other race	Two or more races	Hispanic or Latino (of any race)	18 years and over
48 00000	TEXAS—Con.												
48 74144	Tyler city	Smith	49.3	83,650	51,795	22,275	287	806	32	7,076	1,379	13,234	61,812
48 74408	Universal City city	Bexar	5.6	14,849	11,960	954	112	428	40	832	523	3,206	11,179
48 74492	University Park city	Dallas	3.7	23,324	22,002	333	52	520	4	217	196	723	16,754
48 74588	Uvalde city	Uvalde	6.7	14,929	10,938	70	93	72	10	3,302	444	11,268	10,094
48 74924	Van Alstyne city	Collin, Grayson	3.4	2,502	2,262	90	25	4	-	85	36	195	1,817
48 75308	Vernon city	Wilbarger	8.1	11,660	8,900	1,125	80	83	2	1,250	220	2,611	8,558
48 75428	Victoria city	Victoria	33.0	60,603	43,140	4,599	312	612	24	10,490	1,426	26,012	43,163
48 75476	Vidor city	Orange	10.6	11,440	11,135	8	59	22	3	75	138	399	8,383
48 76000	Waco city	McLennan	84.2	113,726	69,119	25,754	576	1,567	61	14,084	2,565	26,885	84,866
48 76096	Wake Village city	Bowie	1.7	5,129	4,245	728	47	24	2	49	34	163	3,808
48 76672	Watauga city	Tarrant	4.2	21,908	19,072	498	140	809	43	857	489	2,335	14,832
48 76816	Waxahachie city	Ellis	40.0	21,426	15,094	3,663	163	85	1	2,000	420	4,229	15,658
48 76864	Weatherford city	Parker	20.9	19,000	17,271	394	163	128	5	771	268	1,943	14,259
48 76948	Webster city	Harris	6.6	9,083	5,890	820	50	520	14	1,433	356	2,474	7,183
48 77196	Wells Branch CDP	Travis	2.5	11,271	8,036	1,088	45	1,081	19	668	334	1,880	9,022
48 77272	Weslaco city	Hidalgo	12.7	26,935	20,179	72	133	308	15	5,638	590	22,560	18,377
48 77332	West city	McLennan	1.6	2,692	2,479	113	15	2	1	48	34	219	2,010
48 77416	West Columbia city	Brazoria	2.6	4,255	2,985	830	17	16	1	333	73	768	3,030
48 77632	West Lake Hills city	Travis	3.7	3,116	2,979	9	9	40	-	22	57	120	2,241
48 77662	West Livingston CDP	Polk	23.9	6,612	4,401	1,979	18	24	-	127	63	972	5,721
48 77728	West Odessa CDP	Ector	62.4	17,799	12,751	131	193	16	11	4,250	447	8,552	11,905
48 77752	West Orange city	Orange	3.2	4,111	3,820	76	14	25	-	98	78	237	3,104
48 77866	West Sharyland CDP	Hidalgo	2.3	2,947	2,515	1	2	-	7	412	10	2,891	1,699
48 77956	West University Place city	Harris	2.0	14,211	13,126	71	10	673	3	128	200	671	9,974
48 78016	Westway CDP	El Paso	1.3	3,829	3,760	18	-	1	-	38	12	3,732	2,250
48 78136	Wharton city	Wharton	7.2	9,237	5,203	2,441	38	66	15	1,310	164	2,871	6,728
48 78388	Whitehouse city	Smith	3.8	5,346	4,979	132	34	46	-	95	60	213	3,612
48 78436	White Oak city	Gregg	9.1	5,624	5,319	109	56	5	1	58	76	180	3,881
48 78532	Whitesboro city	Grayson	3.2	3,760	3,631	7	29	15	1	41	36	111	2,770
48 78544	White Settlement city	Tarrant	4.9	14,831	12,730	600	86	217	11	669	518	2,017	10,781
48 79000	Wichita Falls city	Wichita	70.7	104,197	78,258	12,920	897	2,288	103	6,656	3,075	14,570	78,504
48 79408	Willis city	Montgomery	3.3	3,985	2,442	843	27	19	-	574	80	1,085	2,645
48 79492	Willow Park city	Parker	6.2	2,849	2,744	9	21	13	-	36	26	101	2,056
48 79564	Wills Point city	Van Zandt	3.6	3,496	2,799	457	28	3	-	156	53	382	2,503
48 79576	Wilmer city	Dallas	6.3	3,393	1,625	795	38	2	-	833	100	1,408	2,350
48 79624	Wimberley CDP	Hays	16.1	3,797	3,589	7	30	5	3	113	50	263	2,979
48 79672	Windcrest city	Bexar	1.8	5,105	4,288	420	16	107	10	194	70	762	4,362
48 79676	Windemere CDP	Travis	2.1	6,868	4,372	1,155	22	411	8	682	218	1,585	4,592
48 79792	Winnie CDP	Chambers	4.0	2,914	2,543	155	21	8	-	162	25	295	2,117
48 79816	Winnsboro city	Franklin, Wood	3.7	3,584	3,072	319	27	27	4	98	41	180	2,871
48 79876	Winters city	Runnels	2.2	2,880	2,190	59	27	8	2	535	59	1,130	2,007
48 79922	Wolfforth city	Lubbock	1.5	2,554	2,183	33	4	6	-	308	20	580	1,791
48 80224	Woodway city	McLennan	6.6	8,733	8,184	195	18	163	4	97	72	330	6,648
48 80356	Wylie city	Collin, Dallas, Rockwall	19.4	15,132	13,687	313	106	91	4	650	281	1,580	10,078
48 80560	Yoakum city	DeWitt, Lavaca	4.6	5,731	4,200	681	22	10	3	711	104	1,942	4,063
48 80716	Zapata CDP	Zapata	7.7	4,856	4,075	12	14	3	1	602	149	4,327	3,318
49 00000	UTAH		82,143.7	2,233,169	1,992,975	17,657	29,684	37,108	15,145	93,405	47,195	201,559	1,514,471
49 00540	Alpine city	Utah	7.2	7,146	6,960	13	14	21	12	25	101	114	3,940
49 01310	American Fork city	Utah	7.5	21,941	20,896	35	92	143	53	423	299	1,011	13,533
49 06370	Blanding city	San Juan	2.4	3,162	2,093	2	915	3	1	57	91	128	1,870
49 06810	Bluffdale city	Salt Lake	16.4	4,700	4,557	11	13	11	12	56	40	157	2,757
49 07690	Bountiful city	Davis	13.5	41,301	39,469	98	113	474	133	461	553	1,197	29,055
49 08460	Brigham City city	Box Elder	14.3	17,411	15,890	41	283	134	18	709	336	1,335	11,451
49 10390	Canyon Rim CDP	Salt Lake	2.1	10,428	9,946	56	29	163	33	77	124	250	7,810
49 11320	Cedar City city	Iron	20.1	20,527	18,897	97	519	227	67	339	381	850	14,734
49 11440	Cedar Hills town	Utah	2.0	3,094	3,004	3	9	16	6	16	40	60	1,579
49 11980	Centerville city	Davis	6.0	14,585	14,156	33	23	109	34	88	142	285	9,343
49 13850	Clearfield city	Davis	7.7	25,974	21,605	938	418	731	74	1,256	952	2,747	16,577
49 14290	Clinton city	Davis	5.5	12,585	11,370	127	79	224	39	456	290	1,011	7,834
49 16270	Cottonwood Heights CDP	Salt Lake	6.8	27,569	25,797	193	74	629	88	306	482	846	20,278
49 16395	Cottonwood West CDP	Salt Lake	4.0	18,727	17,431	146	86	441	33	241	349	787	14,896
49 18910	Delta city	Millard	3.2	3,209	3,036	2	31	4	9	101	26	324	1,967
49 20120	Draper city	Salt Lake, Utah	30.3	25,220	23,013	384	189	329	92	684	529	1,469	17,155
49 21550	East Millcreek CDP	Salt Lake	4.5	21,385	20,324	91	31	311	56	231	341	586	15,655
49 23200	Enoch city	Iron	3.3	3,467	3,286	6	85	9	14	37	30	88	2,040
49 23530	Ephraim city	Sanpete	3.6	4,505	4,020	17	17	58	24	309	60	444	3,385
49 24740	Farmington city	Davis	7.8	12,081	11,557	44	74	102	20	155	129	360	7,610
49 24850	Farr West city	Weber	5.8	3,094	3,004	7	12	18	-	27	26	86	2,114
49 27490	Fruit Heights city	Davis	2.2	4,701	4,598	2	6	40	-	26	29	96	3,050
49 31120	Grantsville city	Tooele	17.8	6,015	5,757	5	72	13	6	89	73	268	3,809
49 33540	Harrisville city	Weber	2.7	3,645	3,418	15	15	42	13	85	57	170	2,214
49 34200	Heber city	Wasatch	3.4	7,291	6,877	4	32	21	5	242	110	516	4,728
49 35190	Highland city	Utah	7.0	8,172	7,967	10	11	25	8	60	91	177	4,483
49 36070	Holladay city	Salt Lake	5.3	14,561	13,901	67	27	240	29	81	216	272	10,668
49 36400	Hooper CDP	Weber	11.5	3,926	3,836	6	11	20	4	25	24	81	2,617

Table D-1. Places — **Area and Population**—Con.

[Includes incorporated places and census designated places (CDPs) of 2,500 or more population as of April 1, 2000. Codes shown are two-digit Federal Information Processing Standards (FIPS) state codes and five-digit FIPS place codes. Place names and codes are those in effect as of January 1, 2000. County refers to the county (or counties) in which the place is located. IC in this column = independent city, a county equivalent. If a place is located in more than one county, counties are listed in alphabetic order]

State and place code	Place	County	Land area, 2000 (sq. mi.)	Total	White	Black or African American	American Indian and Alaska Native	Asian	Native Hawaiian and Other Pacific Islander	Some other race	Two or more races	Hispanic or Latino (of any race)	18 years and over
49 00000	UTAH—Con.												
49 37170	Hurricane city	Washington	31.1	8,250	7,911	13	79	21	24	96	106	224	5,541
49 37390	Hyde Park city	Cache	3.2	2,955	2,896	4	2	11	3	14	25	47	1,763
49 37500	Hyrum city	Cache	3.9	6,316	5,595	12	47	11	12	528	111	851	3,764
49 38710	Ivins town	Washington	10.2	4,450	4,181	3	53	15	15	91	92	175	2,979
49 39920	Kanab city	Kane	14.0	3,564	3,449	2	35	9	1	24	44	67	2,533
49 40360	Kaysville city	Davis	10.1	20,351	19,653	63	57	134	37	184	223	606	12,098
49 40470	Kearns CDP	Salt Lake	4.8	33,659	27,525	221	343	568	787	3,306	909	8,604	21,153
49 43440	La Verkin city	Washington	16.1	3,392	3,182	4	43	7	4	65	87	156	2,177
49 43660	Layton city	Davis	20.7	58,474	52,573	943	307	1,216	159	1,804	1,472	4,068	37,962
49 44320	Lehi city	Utah	20.3	19,028	18,206	47	110	89	82	254	240	569	11,227
49 45090	Lindon city	Utah	8.4	8,363	8,001	17	18	58	13	154	102	278	4,772
49 45275	Little Cottonwood Creek Valley CDP	Salt Lake	2.6	7,221	6,924	37	12	92	11	26	119	162	5,090
49 45860	Logan city	Cache	16.5	42,670	37,947	272	361	1,537	125	1,740	688	3,509	32,666
49 47180	Maeser CDP	Uintah	6.5	2,855	2,769	2	29	7	-	31	17	67	1,818
49 47290	Magna CDP	Salt Lake	7.4	22,770	19,642	145	204	136	320	1,775	548	3,416	14,526
49 47730	Manti city	Sanpete	1.9	3,040	2,933	2	48	2	13	15	27	79	1,882
49 47950	Mapleton city	Utah	9.2	5,809	5,681	8	14	20	13	30	43	119	3,480
49 49710	Midvale city	Salt Lake	5.8	27,029	22,283	319	348	500	156	2,691	732	5,613	20,063
49 50150	Millcreek CDP	Salt Lake	4.9	30,377	26,448	476	377	944	194	1,014	924	2,780	23,383
49 50700	Moab city	Grand	3.6	4,779	4,318	17	261	14	4	90	75	308	3,462
49 51910	Morgan city	Morgan	3.2	2,635	2,611	1	1	2	-	8	12	25	1,654
49 52900	Mount Olympus CDP	Salt Lake	3.4	7,103	6,720	15	13	221	2	29	103	126	5,398
49 53010	Mount Pleasant city	Sanpete	2.8	2,707	2,611	-	11	13	4	32	36	72	1,720
49 53230	Murray city	Salt Lake	9.6	34,024	31,153	336	213	624	112	942	644	2,549	24,760
49 54220	Nephi city	Juab	4.2	4,733	4,590	5	30	22	1	46	39	116	2,946
49 54990	North Logan city	Cache	6.9	6,163	5,815	30	17	124	8	85	84	222	3,858
49 55100	North Ogden city	Weber	6.5	15,026	14,412	55	51	118	10	243	137	577	9,736
49 55210	North Salt Lake city	Davis	8.2	8,749	8,102	27	88	131	37	210	154	556	5,957
49 55980	Ogden city	Weber	26.6	77,226	61,016	1,785	927	1,105	133	9,997	2,203	18,253	55,018
49 56800	Oquirrh CDP	Salt Lake	1.7	10,390	9,102	72	43	141	168	642	222	1,307	5,926
49 57300	Orem city	Utah	18.4	84,324	76,567	280	615	1,226	721	3,073	1,842	7,217	54,492
49 58070	Park City city	Summit, Wasatch	9.4	7,371	5,934	31	22	137	1	1,158	88	1,448	5,651
49 58510	Parowan city	Iron	5.8	2,565	2,473	-	10	3	4	46	29	81	1,766
49 58730	Payson city	Utah	6.8	12,716	11,956	16	49	48	30	448	169	864	7,848
49 60710	Plain City city	Weber	3.7	3,489	3,398	1	11	17	1	22	39	71	2,220
49 60930	Pleasant Grove city	Utah	8.7	23,468	22,330	68	90	126	92	410	352	1,069	13,851
49 01150	Pleasant View city	Weber	6.7	5,632	5,368	27	34	27	7	100	69	222	3,790
49 62030	Price city	Carbon	4.2	8,402	7,621	22	115	47	3	357	237	847	6,084
49 62360	Providence city	Cache	2.8	4,377	4,234	6	11	23	4	73	26	90	2,777
49 62470	Provo city	Utah	39.6	105,166	93,094	486	846	1,924	882	5,368	2,566	11,013	81,758
49 63570	Richfield city	Sevier	5.3	6,847	6,464	27	225	18	5	38	70	161	4,424
49 64010	Riverdale city	Weber	4.4	7,656	7,040	113	46	106	23	178	150	488	5,500
49 64340	Riverton city	Salt Lake	12.6	25,011	24,123	54	61	163	59	256	295	793	14,363
49 64670	Roosevelt city	Duchesne	5.3	4,299	3,722	8	350	9	-	75	135	167	2,600
49 65110	Roy city	Weber	7.6	32,885	29,842	383	193	590	37	1,197	643	2,526	21,884
49 65330	St. George city	Washington	64.4	49,663	45,823	120	812	282	293	1,426	907	3,337	35,572
49 65750	Salem city	Utah	5.3	4,372	4,244	3	4	6	12	61	42	122	2,597
49 67000	Salt Lake City city	Salt Lake City	109.1	181,743	143,933	3,433	2,442	6,579	3,437	15,482	6,437	34,254	138,773
49 67440	Sandy city	Salt Lake	22.3	88,418	82,685	445	311	1,916	275	1,326	1,460	3,875	57,957
49 67660	Santa Clara city	Washington	4.9	4,630	4,506	7	14	13	15	22	53	94	2,769
49 67770	Santaquin city	Utah	2.6	4,834	4,425	8	30	8	3	294	66	414	2,787
49 69640	Smithfield city	Cache	4.3	7,261	6,915	9	17	35	3	205	77	366	4,517
49 70850	South Jordan city	Salt Lake	20.9	29,437	28,115	88	30	298	140	380	386	962	17,888
49 70960	South Ogden city	Weber	3.7	14,377	13,157	106	100	209	39	457	309	1,056	10,459
49 71070	South Salt Lake city	Salt Lake	6.9	22,038	16,582	642	662	584	266	2,356	946	4,932	16,751
49 71125	South Snyderville Basin CDP	Summit	10.9	3,636	3,478	5	13	36	3	40	61	125	2,464
49 71180	South Weber city	Davis	4.6	4,260	4,054	21	34	26	1	51	73	169	2,567
49 71290	Spanish Fork city	Utah	13.2	20,246	19,295	41	114	62	58	405	271	861	12,214
49 72280	Springville city	Utah	11.5	20,424	19,317	22	126	72	58	456	373	975	12,793
49 74095	Summit Park CDP	Summit	21.7	6,597	6,292	18	22	58	3	90	114	255	4,457
49 74480	Sunset city	Davis	1.5	5,204	4,521	81	48	143	8	246	157	547	3,622
49 74810	Syracuse city	Davis	8.7	9,398	8,910	40	29	132	19	118	150	343	5,659
49 75360	Taylorsville city	Salt Lake	10.7	57,439	49,139	508	589	1,745	904	3,087	1,467	7,022	39,832
49 76680	Tooele city	Tooele	21.1	22,502	20,468	166	296	126	33	865	548	2,271	14,820
49 77120	Tremonton city	Box Elder	5.2	5,592	5,118	9	25	63	2	292	83	543	3,409
49 80090	Vernal city	Uintah	4.6	7,714	7,291	14	178	26	4	91	110	343	5,226
49 81960	Washington city	Washington	31.5	8,186	7,720	30	140	24	8	176	88	384	5,726
49 82070	Washington Terrace city	Weber	1.9	8,551	7,647	192	49	102	30	336	195	674	6,166
49 82620	Wellsville city	Cache	6.4	2,728	2,654	-	11	4	4	47	8	76	1,684
49 82840	West Bountiful city	Davis	3.0	4,484	4,315	1	16	25	29	37	61	91	2,886
49 82930	West Haven city	Weber	10.2	3,976	3,740	19	19	33	3	91	71	193	2,507
49 82950	West Jordan city	Salt Lake	30.9	68,336	60,653	434	385	1,393	644	3,250	1,577	6,882	42,501
49 83390	West Point city	Davis	7.2	6,033	5,715	25	32	61	2	94	104	243	3,724
49 83470	West Valley City city	Salt Lake	35.4	108,896	85,172	1,247	1,273	4,671	3,157	9,528	3,848	20,126	72,249
49 84050	White City CDP	Salt Lake	0.9	5,988	5,527	28	40	49	49	176	119	440	4,137
49 85370	Woods Cross city	Davis	3.6	6,419	6,018	28	16	45	17	164	131	367	4,107

[Includes incorporated places and census designated places (CDPs) of 2,500 or more population as of April 1, 2000. Codes shown are two-digit Federal Information Processing Standards (FIPS) state codes and five-digit FIPS place codes. Place names and codes are those in effect as of January 1, 2000. County refers to the county (or counties) in which the place is located. IC in this column = independent city, a county equivalent. If a place is located in more than one county, counties are listed in alphabetic order]

State and place code	Place	County	Land area, 2000 (sq. mi.)	Population, 2000 (April 1)									
					By race—								
					One race							Hispanic or Latino (of any race)	18 years and over
				Total	White	Black or African American	American Indian and Alaska Native	Asian	Native Hawaiian and Other Pacific Islander	Some other race	Two or more races		
50 00000	VERMONT.		9,249.6	608,827	589,208	3,063	2,420	5,217	141	1,443	7,335	5,504	461,304
50 03175	Barre city.	Washington	4.0	9,291	9,049	45	35	48	1	30	83	156	7,209
50 04225	Bellows Falls village.	Windham	1.4	3,165	3,079	11	5	16	1	7	46	36	2,340
50 04750	Bennington CDP	Bennington	4.9	9,168	8,899	47	29	93	1	24	75	86	7,071
50 07975	Brattleboro CDP	Windham	9.5	8,289	7,711	112	23	163	2	50	228	148	6,467
50 10675	Burlington city.	Chittenden	10.6	38,889	35,883	693	182	1,031	8	211	881	546	32,558
50 24400	Essex Junction village . . .	Chittenden	4.8	8,591	8,209	59	21	203	-	25	74	98	6,326
50 44275	Middlebury CDP	Addison	13.9	6,252	5,826	87	20	142	1	50	126	155	5,318
50 46000	Montpelier city	Washington	10.2	8,035	7,758	52	19	66	1	31	108	113	6,325
50 48850	Newport city.	Orleans	6.0	5,005	4,812	38	31	31	-	11	82	64	3,896
50 50200	Northfield village	Washington	1.4	3,208	2,996	57	11	62	-	22	60	106	2,726
50 61225	Rutland city	Rutland	7.6	17,292	16,912	76	42	74	9	22	157	156	13,373
50 61675	St. Albans city.	Franklin	2.0	7,650	7,334	30	92	27	2	35	130	69	5,695
50 62125	St. Johnsbury CDP	Caledonia	13.0	6,319	6,081	30	47	41	2	17	101	85	4,911
50 66175	South Burlington city	Chittenden	16.6	15,814	14,831	132	29	530	-	65	225	192	12,399
50 69475	Springfield CDP	Windsor.	2.4	3,938	3,813	15	6	47	3	9	45	46	2,969
50 71650	Swanton village.	Franklin	0.8	2,548	2,325	9	110	25	-	7	72	14	1,916
50 74650	Vergennes city	Addison	2.4	2,741	2,561	55	6	10	1	29	79	80	1,963
50 78850	West Brattleboro CDP . . .	Windham	9.9	3,222	3,102	24	8	30	3	15	40	46	2,482
50 83575	White River Junction CDP.	Windsor.	1.6	2,569	2,480	15	11	18	-	1	44	15	1,946
50 85150	Winooski city	Chittenden	1.4	6,561	5,941	82	34	354	3	35	112	75	5,148
51 00000	VIRGINIA.		39,594.1	7,078,515	5,120,110	1,390,293	21,172	261,025	3,946	138,900	143,069	329,540	5,340,253
51 00148	Abingdon town	Washington	8.3	7,780	7,390	265	10	50	1	15	49	62	6,353
51 01000	Alexandria city	Alexandria IC	15.2	128,283	76,702	28,915	355	7,249	112	9,467	5,483	18,882	106,746
51 01528	Altavista town	Campbell.	4.9	3,425	2,543	841	3	7	-	11	20	32	2,656
51 01912	Annandale CDP	Fairfax.	13.8	54,994	35,473	3,224	165	10,647	41	3,266	2,178	7,966	42,555
51 02112	Aquia Harbour CDP.	Stafford	7.7	7,856	6,752	701	44	100	8	68	183	268	5,495
51 03000	Arlington CDP.	Arlington	25.9	189,453	130,601	17,705	662	16,327	143	15,786	8,229	35,268	158,214
51 03368	Ashland town	Hanover	7.2	6,619	4,947	1,473	24	47	-	45	83	115	5,299
51 04088	Bailey's Crossroads CDP .	Fairfax.	2.1	23,166	11,096	2,514	126	2,865	21	4,340	2,204	8,596	17,836
51 05544	Bedford city	Bedford IC	6.9	6,299	4,745	1,410	15	36	5	15	73	56	4,936
51 05928	Belle Haven CDP	Fairfax.	2.0	6,269	5,402	431	16	142	4	121	153	343	5,188
51 06216	Bellwood CDP	Chesterfield	5.9	5,974	4,132	1,214	48	153	2	260	165	449	4,279
51 06728	Bensley CDP	Chesterfield	2.9	5,435	3,388	1,322	35	239	6	274	171	689	4,049
51 06968	Berryville town	Clarke	1.8	2,963	2,505	403	3	17	-	4	31	39	2,279
51 07480	Big Stone Gap town	Wise	4.9	4,856	4,549	214	7	22	1	18	45	29	3,731
51 07784	Blacksburg town	Montgomery.	19.4	39,573	33,394	1,738	45	3,087	22	355	932	920	35,752
51 07832	Blackstone town	Nottoway	4.5	3,675	1,846	1,705	1	26	-	69	28	88	2,781
51 08152	Bluefield town.	Tazewell	7.6	5,078	4,687	247	16	72	-	6	50	21	4,165
51 08200	Blue Ridge CDP	Botetourt	6.3	3,188	3,039	91	7	16	-	2	33	17	2,392
51 08472	Bon Air CDP.	Chesterfield	8.8	16,213	14,090	1,366	26	410	6	137	178	281	11,896
51 09656	Bridgewater town	Rockingham	2.4	5,203	4,952	129	6	22	-	49	45	160	4,221
51 09816	Bristol city	Bristol IC	12.9	17,367	16,072	967	43	64	2	32	187	169	13,837
51 11032	Buena Vista city	Buena Vista IC	6.8	6,349	5,940	305	19	27	1	5	52	64	4,923
51 11230	Bull Run CDP.	Prince William.	2.7	11,337	7,193	2,151	31	619	9	911	423	1,817	8,334
51 11464	Burke CDP.	Fairfax.	11.5	57,737	42,936	2,910	124	8,462	47	1,370	1,888	4,291	41,629
51 13720	Cave Spring CDP	Roanoke	11.8	24,941	23,186	605	21	738	6	111	274	376	19,439
51 14440	Centreville CDP	Fairfax.	9.7	48,661	33,816	4,322	143	6,934	25	1,776	1,645	4,461	34,832
51 14544	Chamberlayne CDP.	Henrico	3.8	4,380	2,095	2,155	7	49	4	17	53	37	3,651
51 14744	Chantilly CDP.	Fairfax.	11.7	41,041	30,098	2,046	117	6,716	24	826	1,214	2,818	30,342
51 14968	Charlottesville city	Charlottesville IC.	10.3	45,049	31,337	10,009	49	2,223	15	458	958	1,102	38,214
51 16000	Chesapeake city	Chesapeake IC.	340.7	199,184	133,193	56,823	770	3,673	101	1,400	3,224	4,076	141,901
51 16096	Chester CDP	Chesterfield	13.0	17,890	14,541	2,403	78	386	19	188	275	547	12,832
51 16208	Chesterfield Court House CDP	Chesterfield	2.3	3,558	2,499	856	25	52	3	55	68	124	2,698
51 16512	Chincoteague town	Accomack	9.6	4,317	4,184	41	12	12	-	16	52	23	3,541
51 16608	Christiansburg town	Montgomery.	13.9	16,947	15,783	819	36	70	3	81	155	168	12,915
51 17440	Clifton Forge city	Clifton Forge IC	3.1	4,289	3,558	627	4	2	-	21	77	38	3,384
51 17680	Cloverdale CDP	Botetourt	3.1	2,986	2,837	66	3	35	-	24	21	23	2,183
51 18352	Collinsville CDP	Henry	7.9	7,777	6,598	877	11	49	14	154	74	293	6,095
51 18400	Colonial Beach town	Westmoreland	2.6	3,228	2,557	547	3	20	-	53	48	109	2,517
51 18448	Colonial Heights city	Colonial Heights IC . . .	7.5	16,897	15,052	1,059	32	459	14	108	173	274	13,082
51 19728	Covington city.	Covington	5.7	6,303	5,298	828	22	41	1	13	100	40	4,951
51 20560	Crozet CDP	Albemarle	3.7	2,820	2,592	166	2	17	-	10	33	45	2,059
51 20752	Culpeper town	Culpeper	6.7	9,664	6,848	2,290	20	128	1	191	186	440	7,182
51 21088	Dale City CDP	Prince William.	15.0	55,971	31,818	16,099	235	2,840	107	2,392	2,480	5,534	37,667
51 21344	Danville city	Danville IC	43.1	48,411	26,075	21,352	81	291	14	219	379	612	37,139
51 23744	Dumbarton CDP	Henrico	2.1	6,674	4,032	1,931	18	376	1	147	169	273	5,444
51 23760	Dumfries town	Prince William.	1.6	4,937	2,612	1,741	31	53	-	283	217	645	3,211
51 23984	Dunn Loring CDP	Fairfax.	2.0	7,861	5,828	236	23	1,198	1	325	250	776	5,972
51 24496	East Highland Park CDP .	Henrico	9.0	12,488	2,307	9,910	36	49	1	42	143	125	9,346
51 25808	Emporia city	Emporia IC.	6.9	5,665	2,405	3,181	4	30	4	17	24	84	4,240
51 26128	Ettrick CDP	Chesterfield	3.0	5,627	1,209	4,228	18	29	5	56	82	125	4,635
51 26496	Fairfax city	Fairfax IC.	6.3	21,498	15,675	1,090	73	2,617	16	1,326	701	2,932	17,082
51 27200	Falls Church city	Falls Church IC.	2.0	10,377	8,817	340	25	675	7	261	252	876	7,947
51 27264	Falmouth CDP	Stafford	3.1	3,624	3,236	234	8	39	-	22	85	78	2,676

Table D-1. Places — **Area and Population**—Con.

[Includes incorporated places and census designated places (CDPs) of 2,500 or more population as of April 1, 2000. Codes shown are two-digit Federal Information Processing Standards (FIPS) state codes and five-digit FIPS place codes. Place names and codes are those in effect as of January 1, 2000. County refers to the county (or counties) in which the place is located. IC in this column = independent city, a county equivalent. If a place is located in more than one county, counties are listed in alphabetic order]

State and place code	Place	County	Land area, 2000 (sq. mi.)	Population, 2000 (April 1)									
					By race—							Hispanic or Latino (of any race)	18 years and over
					One race						Two or more races		
				Total	White	Black or African American	American Indian and Alaska Native	Asian	Native Hawaiian and Other Pacific Islander	Some other race			
51 00000	VIRGINIA—Con.												
51 27440	Farmville town	Cumberland, Prince Edward	7.0	6,845	4,865	1,758	14	72	18	33	85	86	5,841
51 27968	Fishersville CDP	Augusta	13.1	4,998	4,736	199	6	21	-	4	32	31	3,891
51 28688	Forest CDP	Bedford	14.6	8,006	7,349	452	8	109	1	22	65	76	5,856
51 29008	Fort Belvoir CDP	Fairfax	8.8	7,176	3,996	2,284	39	123	64	364	306	760	3,001
51 29136	Fort Hunt CDP	Fairfax	5.1	12,923	11,997	306	22	331	6	63	198	342	9,713
51 29152	Fort Lee CDP	Prince George	8.4	7,269	2,868	3,420	53	170	29	485	244	830	5,244
51 29552	Franconia CDP	Fairfax	7.1	31,907	22,099	4,329	95	3,419	35	727	1,203	2,337	24,935
51 29600	Franklin city	Franklin IC	8.4	8,346	3,816	4,366	12	65	1	16	70	46	6,247
51 29744	Fredericksburg city	Fredericksburg IC	10.5	19,279	14,108	3,935	65	291	11	494	375	945	15,851
51 29968	Front Royal town	Warren	9.3	13,589	12,000	1,180	38	85	6	90	190	290	10,102
51 30176	Gainesville CDP	Prince William	9.7	4,382	3,890	298	10	60	2	67	55	165	3,311
51 30208	Galax city	Galax IC	8.2	6,837	5,887	428	31	48	1	377	65	757	5,265
51 31200	Glen Allen CDP	Henrico	8.8	12,562	9,412	2,454	52	387	8	101	148	217	9,443
51 31616	Gloucester Point CDP	Gloucester	8.4	9,429	8,220	864	44	120	6	57	118	163	7,127
51 32496	Great Falls CDP	Fairfax	17.9	8,549	7,594	103	12	633	3	37	167	219	6,031
51 33584	Groveton CDP	Fairfax	6.2	21,296	12,491	4,125	66	1,650	21	1,994	949	3,955	16,073
51 35000	Hampton city	Hampton IC	51.8	146,437	72,556	65,428	616	2,694	136	1,505	3,502	4,153	110,940
51 35624	Harrisonburg city	Harrisonburg IC	17.6	40,468	34,334	2,394	76	1,257	10	1,355	1,042	3,580	34,231
51 36648	Herndon town	Fairfax	4.2	21,655	12,535	2,060	91	3,002	10	2,805	1,152	5,633	15,788
51 37032	Highland Springs CDP	Henrico	8.5	15,137	6,733	7,845	94	97	1	121	246	235	10,738
51 37336	Hillsville town	Carroll	5.7	2,607	2,513	5	4	11	-	46	28	87	2,117
51 37880	Hollins CDP	Botetourt, Roanoke	8.7	14,309	12,975	855	26	266	1	56	130	147	11,571
51 38424	Hopewell city	Hopewell IC	10.2	22,354	13,924	7,484	79	180	16	275	396	651	16,389
51 39064	Huntington CDP	Fairfax	0.8	8,325	5,407	1,394	33	584	13	575	319	1,166	7,245
51 39304	Hybla Valley CDP	Fairfax	3.1	16,721	8,357	4,770	97	1,340	10	1,517	630	3,213	12,343
51 39448	Idylwood CDP	Fairfax	2.8	16,005	10,034	1,109	51	3,074	9	1,134	594	2,621	12,852
51 40584	Jefferson CDP	Fairfax	5.1	27,422	16,823	1,245	94	5,253	8	2,895	1,104	6,351	21,459
51 43352	Lake Barcroft CDP	Fairfax	2.5	8,906	6,767	438	23	854	6	431	387	1,311	7,077
51 43424	Lake Monticello CDP	Fluvanna	8.8	6,852	6,445	240	11	35	2	19	100	102	5,235
51 43432	Lake Ridge CDP	Prince William	8.2	30,404	22,615	4,872	73	1,072	39	669	1,064	2,161	21,422
51 43464	Lakeside CDP	Henrico	4.2	11,157	9,613	976	68	160	8	136	196	273	8,905
51 44280	Laurel CDP	Henrico	5.5	14,875	9,666	3,615	49	917	8	310	310	618	11,865
51 44696	Lebanon town	Russell	4.1	3,273	3,127	122	4	-	-	3	17	11	2,626
51 44984	Leesburg town	Loudoun	11.6	28,311	23,580	2,604	53	739	9	716	610	1,667	20,000
51 45512	Lexington city	Lexington IC	2.5	6,867	5,906	713	18	132	1	33	64	109	6,112
51 45784	Lincolnia CDP	Fairfax	2.9	15,788	7,519	2,971	35	2,369	3	1,812	1,079	3,532	11,799
51 45957	Linton Hall CDP	Prince William	8.3	8,620	7,547	577	16	228	11	93	148	343	5,572
51 46328	Loch Lomond CDP	Prince William	0.7	3,411	2,708	239	9	72	2	303	78	481	2,410
51 47064	Lorton CDP	Fairfax	12.4	17,786	8,706	6,165	52	1,357	23	697	786	1,732	13,296
51 47528	Luray town	Page	4.7	4,871	4,503	269	12	16	-	22	49	66	3,793
51 47672	Lynchburg city	Lynchburg IC	49.4	65,269	43,487	19,382	169	838	28	413	952	878	50,812
51 48376	McLean CDP	Fairfax	18.5	38,929	32,918	616	37	4,129	12	267	950	1,564	29,052
51 48520	Madison Heights CDP	Amherst	19.3	11,584	9,012	2,267	77	52	-	67	109	103	9,044
51 48952	Manassas city	Manassas IC	9.9	35,135	25,316	4,535	128	1,206	31	2,773	1,146	5,316	24,748
51 48968	Manassas Park city	Manassas Park IC	2.5	10,290	7,490	1,149	45	418	7	838	343	1,544	7,099
51 49144	Mantua CDP	Fairfax	2.4	7,485	5,897	147	31	1,019	3	219	169	511	5,653
51 49464	Marion town	Smyth	4.2	6,349	5,840	377	15	33	1	24	59	72	5,116
51 49784	Martinsville city	Martinsville IC	11.0	15,416	8,537	6,559	16	72	-	107	125	358	11,938
51 50856	Mechanicsville CDP	Hanover	28.4	30,464	27,660	1,951	130	275	4	149	295	359	22,265
51 51192	Merrifield CDP	Fairfax	2.7	11,170	6,107	663	28	3,344	11	558	459	1,442	9,000
51 52658	Montclair CDP	Prince William	6.0	15,728	12,210	2,314	64	475	32	170	463	709	10,636
51 52904	Montrose CDP	Henrico	3.4	7,018	3,262	3,507	25	71	-	62	91	110	5,096
51 54144	Mount Vernon CDP	Fairfax	7.6	28,582	15,554	7,904	95	1,810	36	1,965	1,218	4,145	21,064
51 55752	Newington CDP	Fairfax	6.6	19,784	13,413	2,538	52	2,307	16	526	932	1,578	14,137
51 56000	Newport News city	Newport News IC	68.3	180,150	96,383	70,388	752	4,195	214	3,225	4,993	7,595	130,625
51 57000	Norfolk city	Norfolk IC	53.7	234,403	113,358	103,387	1,071	6,593	251	3,923	5,820	8,915	178,051
51 57560	North Springfield CDP	Fairfax	2.4	9,173	6,604	335	16	1,480	19	425	294	963	6,959
51 57688	Norton city	Norton IC	7.5	3,904	3,575	240	3	39	5	7	35	34	3,054
51 58472	Oakton CDP	Fairfax	9.7	29,348	21,853	1,407	58	4,060	23	903	1,044	2,831	22,502
51 59496	Orange town	Orange	3.2	4,123	3,168	864	8	14	-	28	41	70	3,194
51 61208	Pearisburg town	Giles	3.1	2,729	2,623	55	2	14	-	12	23	19	2,127
51 61832	Petersburg city	Petersburg IC	22.9	33,740	6,249	26,643	67	236	9	198	338	463	25,256
51 62264	Pimmit Hills CDP	Fairfax	1.5	6,152	4,540	154	28	707	10	460	253	1,025	4,846
51 63768	Poquoson city	Poquoson IC	15.5	11,566	11,134	78	27	182	4	31	110	122	8,464
51 64000	Portsmouth city	Portsmouth IC	33.2	100,565	46,096	50,899	478	775	67	618	1,632	1,748	74,711
51 64880	Pulaski town	Pulaski	7.8	9,473	8,483	734	11	34	8	91	112	191	7,415
51 65008	Purcellville town	Loudoun	2.4	3,584	3,187	267	3	30	1	28	68	82	2,410
51 65136	Quantico Station CDP	Prince William, Stafford	7.2	6,571	4,813	1,052	30	141	10	257	268	616	4,447
51 65392	Radford city	Radford IC	9.8	15,859	13,990	1,284	39	226	4	77	239	184	13,810
51 65744	Raven CDP	Russell, Tazewell	6.8	2,593	2,568	1	2	-	-	-	22	20	1,993
51 66672	Reston CDP	Fairfax	17.2	56,407	41,528	5,145	141	5,427	22	2,323	1,821	5,699	43,713
51 66928	Richlands town	Tazewell	2.6	4,144	4,092	2	5	21	-	8	16	14	3,310
51 67000	Richmond city	Richmond IC	60.1	197,790	75,744	113,108	479	2,471	157	2,948	2,883	5,074	154,612
51 68000	Roanoke city	Roanoke IC	42.9	94,911	65,848	25,380	190	1,096	23	685	1,689	1,405	73,454
51 68496	Rocky Mount town	Franklin	4.6	4,066	3,029	905	11	45	4	20	52	68	3,196
51 68880	Rose Hill CDP	Fairfax	4.6	15,058	11,070	1,434	41	1,277	8	663	565	1,604	11,634
51 70000	Salem city	Salem IC	14.6	24,747	22,738	1,455	32	241	6	61	214	205	19,585

[Includes incorporated places and census designated places (CDPs) of 2,500 or more population as of April 1, 2000. Codes shown are two-digit Federal Information Processing Standards (FIPS) state codes and five-digit FIPS place codes. Place names and codes are those in effect as of January 1, 2000. County refers to the county (or counties) in which the place is located. IC in this column = independent city, a county equivalent. If a place is located in more than one county, counties are listed in alphabetic order]

State and place code	Place	County	Land area, 2000 (sq. mi.)	Population, 2000 (April 1) Total	By race— One race White	Black or African American	American Indian and Alaska Native	Asian	Native Hawaiian and Other Pacific Islander	Some other race	Two or more races	Hispanic or Latino (of any race)	18 years and over
51 00000	VIRGINIA—Con.												
51 71216	Seven Corners CDP	Fairfax.............	0.7	8,701	4,272	581	24	1,787	6	1,407	624	3,533	6,856
51 73200	Smithfield town.......	Isle of Wight.......	9.5	6,324	4,251	1,952	22	26	1	14	58	59	4,618
51 73712	South Boston town	Halifax............	12.2	8,491	4,299	4,012	18	41	-	43	78	123	6,479
51 73904	South Hill town	Mecklenburg	6.3	4,403	2,570	1,736	13	44	-	17	23	69	3,381
51 74470	Spotsylvania Courthouse CDP	Spotsylvania........	8.7	3,833	3,102	577	8	39	-	24	83	107	2,521
51 74592	Springfield CDP	Fairfax.............	9.8	30,417	17,572	2,722	92	6,251	17	2,356	1,407	5,373	23,282
51 75216	Staunton city	Staunton IC........	19.7	23,853	19,866	3,328	52	110	2	125	370	265	19,124
51 76000	Strasburg town	Shenandoah........	3.1	4,017	3,761	180	2	16	2	18	38	57	3,025
51 76272	Stuarts Draft CDP	Augusta............	19.8	8,367	7,971	288	22	17	4	24	41	89	6,104
51 76416	Sudley CDP	Prince William.......	1.6	7,719	5,821	917	37	287	9	394	254	717	5,475
51 76432	Suffolk city	Suffolk IC..........	400.0	63,677	34,271	27,718	191	491	15	233	758	809	45,944
51 77792	Tazewell town.........	Tazewell...........	4.0	4,206	3,734	392	7	22	-	15	36	26	3,423
51 78688	Timberlake CDP	Campbell...........	8.8	10,683	9,735	579	30	183	2	50	104	108	8,262
51 79360	Triangle CDP	Prince William.......	2.6	5,500	3,359	1,558	27	158	6	197	195	408	3,972
51 79560	Tuckahoe CDP	Henrico............	20.6	43,242	38,393	2,499	72	1,484	14	290	490	923	33,189
51 79952	Tysons Corner CDP.....	Fairfax.............	4.9	18,540	13,201	716	25	3,287	13	233	1,065	1,140	15,238
51 80864	Verona CDP	Augusta............	7.0	3,638	3,450	118	8	22	-	5	35	23	2,746
51 81072	Vienna town	Fairfax.............	4.4	14,453	11,722	497	27	1,368	-	392	447	1,068	11,044
51 81280	Vinton town	Roanoke...........	3.2	7,782	7,342	261	8	51	3	46	71	86	6,001
51 82000	Virginia Beach city......	Virginia Beach IC....	248.3	425,257	303,683	80,593	1,619	20,869	416	6,402	11,677	17,770	308,369
51 83136	Warrenton town	Fauquier...........	4.2	6,670	5,339	1,100	16	67	1	42	105	217	5,079
51 83680	Waynesboro city	Waynesboro IC......	15.4	19,520	16,877	1,945	61	112	6	213	306	643	14,856
51 84424	West Gate CDP	Prince William.......	1.2	7,493	4,215	1,287	44	298	8	1,278	363	1,963	5,302
51 84960	West Point town	King William........	5.1	2,866	2,302	485	13	30	-	10	26	50	2,121
51 84976	West Springfield CDP ...	Fairfax.............	6.8	28,378	21,371	1,387	79	3,946	17	724	854	2,081	21,109
51 86160	Williamsburg city.......	Williamsburg IC.....	8.5	11,998	9,543	1,601	32	549	7	90	176	302	10,850
51 86720	Winchester city........	Winchester IC......	9.3	23,585	19,355	2,470	56	375	8	817	504	1,527	18,473
51 87072	Wise town	Wise..............	3.1	3,255	3,100	63	9	37	-	25	21	46	2,614
51 87240	Wolf Trap CDP	Fairfax.............	9.3	14,001	12,104	250	18	1,170	-	90	369	368	9,936
51 87312	Woodbridge CDP	Prince William.......	10.5	31,941	17,996	7,490	177	1,566	54	3,074	1,584	6,091	22,363
51 87712	Woodstock town	Shenandoah........	3.2	3,952	3,621	108	3	7	1	169	43	254	3,138
51 87960	Wyndham CDP........	Henrico	3.6	6,176	5,646	164	6	281	-	14	65	87	3,970
51 88000	Wytheville town........	Wythe.............	14.3	7,804	7,083	561	10	55	2	26	67	64	6,298
51 88176	Yorkshire CDP	Prince William.......	2.4	6,732	5,098	574	28	161	7	561	303	1,270	4,776
53 00000	WASHINGTON........		66,544.1	5,894,121	4,821,823	190,267	93,301	322,335	23,953	228,923	213,519	441,509	4,380,278
53 00100	Aberdeen city	Grays Harbor	10.6	16,461	13,971	77	609	345	23	848	588	1,518	12,053
53 00800	Ahtanum CDP	Yakima............	9.7	4,181	3,795	31	43	19	1	201	91	366	3,088
53 00905	Airway Heights city	Spokane...........	4.9	4,500	3,575	471	144	83	17	70	140	447	3,740
53 01185	Alderwood Manor CDP...	Snohomish.........	4.8	15,329	12,588	249	132	1,505	71	243	541	609	11,026
53 01990	Anacortes city........	Skagit.............	11.8	14,557	13,489	46	166	239	19	215	383	459	11,147
53 02585	Arlington city	Snohomish.........	7.6	11,713	10,543	132	122	258	38	289	331	683	8,018
53 02620	Arlington Heights CDP ...	Snohomish.........	11.3	2,510	2,402	6	10	20	-	23	49	44	1,769
53 02910	Artondale CDP	Pierce.............	10.1	8,630	7,999	66	48	134	24	71	288	272	6,018
53 03180	Auburn city..........	King, Pierce	21.3	40,314	33,382	977	1,024	1,410	204	1,477	1,840	3,019	29,580
53 03736	Bainbridge Island city ...	Kitsap.............	27.6	20,308	18,863	57	125	487	22	152	602	440	14,884
53 04113	Bangor Trident Base CDP.	Kitsap.............	11.0	7,253	5,565	584	93	340	57	284	330	743	5,262
53 04195	Barberton CDP	Clark..............	4.3	4,617	4,327	33	30	101	7	23	96	112	3,301
53 04475	Battle Ground city	Clark..............	3.6	9,296	8,721	46	80	67	10	160	212	385	5,930
53 05210	Bellevue city..........	King...............	30.7	109,569	81,441	2,183	356	19,056	257	2,785	3,491	5,827	86,427
53 05280	Bellingham city........	Whatcom...........	25.6	67,171	59,031	655	997	2,853	116	1,450	2,069	3,111	55,286
53 05560	Benton City city........	Benton	1.7	2,624	2,213	4	30	16	1	279	81	512	1,713
53 06190	Birch Bay CDP	Whatcom...........	15.8	4,961	4,582	52	59	61	7	95	105	221	3,808
53 06330	Black Diamond city	King...............	5.4	3,970	3,709	3	62	40	2	35	119	107	2,840
53 06505	Blaine city	Whatcom...........	5.5	3,770	3,307	45	43	158	25	50	142	164	2,770
53 07170	Bonney Lake city	Pierce.............	5.4	9,687	9,114	58	99	123	7	60	226	298	6,589
53 07380	Bothell city...........	King, Snohomish.....	12.1	30,150	26,316	350	188	1,797	63	531	905	1,338	22,549
53 07695	Bremerton city	Kitsap.............	22.7	37,259	27,932	2,793	726	2,061	345	956	2,446	2,457	28,141
53 07940	Brier city	Snohomish.........	2.1	6,383	5,516	53	42	496	10	62	204	206	4,437
53 08552	Bryn Mawr-Skyway CDP..	King...............	3.2	13,977	6,183	3,541	113	3,050	71	306	713	635	10,790
53 08570	Buckley city	Pierce.............	3.9	4,145	3,887	26	47	32	7	23	123	75	3,050
53 08780	Burbank CDP	Walla Walla	13.3	3,303	2,978	10	27	12	4	192	80	328	2,276
53 08850	Burien city	King...............	7.4	31,881	24,146	1,638	411	2,232	370	1,720	1,364	3,397	24,620
53 08920	Burlington city........	Skagit.............	4.2	6,757	5,101	56	74	119	12	1,193	202	1,707	4,728
53 09365	Camano CDP	Island.............	39.8	13,347	12,761	33	111	87	34	75	246	275	10,134
53 09480	Camas city..........	Clark..............	10.9	12,534	11,532	86	87	428	18	100	283	359	8,628
53 10372	Cascade-Fairwood CDP..	King...............	8.9	34,580	25,227	2,107	206	4,670	160	651	1,559	1,420	25,514
53 10495	Cashmere city	Chelan............	0.9	2,965	2,660	-	16	9	2	243	35	504	2,130
53 10600	Cathcart CDP	Snohomish.........	4.2	3,015	2,839	14	14	24	7	42	75	85	2,103
53 11160	Centralia city	Lewis	7.4	14,742	13,232	65	184	138	44	728	351	1,506	11,029
53 11195	Central Park CDP	Grays Harbor	3.5	2,558	2,401	2	32	31	2	13	77	46	1,964
53 11475	Chehalis city..........	Lewis	5.6	7,057	6,320	95	103	85	17	279	158	558	4,999
53 11615	Chelan city...........	Chelan............	3.8	3,522	3,018	4	54	17	4	325	100	509	2,630
53 11825	Cheney city	Spokane...........	4.1	8,832	7,532	186	117	560	31	151	255	384	7,222
53 12630	Clarkston city.........	Asotin.............	1.9	7,337	6,928	25	118	48	2	58	158	188	5,455
53 12680	Clarkston Heights-Vineland CDP ..	Asotin.............	6.0	6,117	5,939	3	55	19	2	26	73	90	4,505

Table D-1. Places — **Area and Population**—Con.

[Includes incorporated places and census designated places (CDPs) of 2,500 or more population as of April 1, 2000. Codes shown are two-digit Federal Information Processing Standards (FIPS) state codes and five-digit FIPS place codes. Place names and codes are those in effect as of January 1, 2000. County refers to the county (or counties) in which the place is located. IC in this column = independent city, a county equivalent. If a place is located in more than one county, counties are listed in alphabetic order]

State and place code	Place	County	Land area, 2000 (sq. mi.)	Total	White	Black or African American	American Indian and Alaska Native	Asian	Native Hawaiian and Other Pacific Islander	Some other race	Two or more races	Hispanic or Latino (of any race)	18 years and over
53 00000	WASHINGTON—Con.												
53 13365	Clyde Hill city	King	1.1	2,890	2,590	16	5	211	-	17	51	43	2,135
53 13785	Colfax city	Whitman	1.7	2,844	2,678	7	24	59	-	17	59	42	2,177
53 13855	College Place city	Walla Walla	2.4	7,818	6,788	121	36	137	41	491	204	996	6,165
53 14170	Colville city	Stevens	2.4	4,988	4,626	8	108	25	12	44	165	117	3,652
53 14485	Connell city	Franklin	2.9	2,956	1,868	116	33	129	1	636	173	1,226	2,028
53 14940	Cottage Lake CDP	King	22.8	24,330	22,158	154	83	917	11	320	645	721	16,009
53 15150	Country Homes CDP	Spokane	1.7	5,203	4,753	71	66	100	47	38	128	129	4,218
53 15290	Covington city	King	5.8	13,783	12,112	336	140	430	31	248	486	617	9,122
53 16970	Dayton city	Columbia	1.5	2,655	2,458	8	28	13	1	94	53	217	1,971
53 17320	Deer Park city	Spokane	6.4	3,017	2,863	10	41	5	2	32	64	73	2,035
53 17635	Des Moines city	King	6.3	29,267	21,702	2,106	280	2,422	393	972	1,392	1,936	22,304
53 17985	Dishman CDP	Spokane	3.4	10,031	9,322	81	182	133	3	110	200	290	7,568
53 19035	Duvall city	King	2.3	4,616	4,314	21	21	91	2	69	98	172	3,122
53 19420	Eastgate CDP	King	1.3	4,558	3,788	74	26	441	16	90	123	203	3,470
53 19515	East Hill-Meridian CDP	King	8.9	29,308	21,516	1,364	177	4,262	191	498	1,300	1,116	20,441
53 19770	East Port Orchard CDP	Kitsap	2.5	5,116	4,391	89	57	220	66	66	227	237	3,631
53 19857	East Renton Highlands CDP	King	12.6	13,264	12,038	193	114	411	14	134	360	455	9,724
53 20155	East Wenatchee city	Douglas	2.3	5,757	5,129	23	55	36	6	353	155	694	4,209
53 20190	East Wenatchee Bench CDP	Douglas	8.4	13,658	12,256	29	124	83	9	912	245	1,727	9,655
53 20645	Edgewood city	Pierce	8.5	9,089	8,430	56	83	204	22	61	233	215	6,748
53 20750	Edmonds city	Snohomish	8.9	39,515	34,666	530	317	2,199	102	497	1,204	1,312	31,358
53 21205	Elk Plain CDP	Pierce	9.6	15,697	12,647	848	193	636	215	233	925	743	10,540
53 21240	Ellensburg city	Kittitas	6.6	15,414	13,575	181	146	631	25	441	415	976	12,980
53 21450	Elma city	Grays Harbor	1.7	3,049	2,774	18	40	39	8	50	120	111	2,160
53 22045	Enumclaw city	King, Pierce	3.9	11,116	10,477	33	88	87	12	128	291	380	7,871
53 22080	Ephrata city	Grant	10.0	6,808	6,171	27	48	49	8	362	143	701	4,840
53 22118	Erlands Point-Kitsap Lake CDP	Kitsap	1.8	2,723	2,435	58	36	59	16	24	95	96	2,005
53 22255	Esperance CDP	Snohomish	0.7	3,503	3,052	53	31	249	2	18	98	81	2,621
53 22640	Everett city	Snohomish	32.5	91,488	74,152	3,061	1,423	5,773	330	2,865	3,884	6,539	68,509
53 22955	Fairchild AFB CDP	Spokane	6.5	4,357	3,407	344	23	155	16	165	247	371	2,871
53 23165	Fairwood CDP	Spokane	3.6	6,764	6,385	35	63	110	12	32	127	151	4,891
53 23515	Federal Way city	King	21.0	83,259	57,318	6,609	740	10,232	852	3,055	4,453	6,266	59,748
53 23550	Felida CDP	Clark	2.9	5,683	5,236	70	33	168	2	40	134	147	3,902
53 23620	Ferndale city	Whatcom	6.2	8,758	7,431	72	224	213	22	465	331	790	5,910
53 23795	Fife city	Pierce	5.6	4,784	3,283	326	198	311	59	332	275	648	3,549
53 23865	Finley CDP	Benton	11.5	5,770	5,274	2	64	14	7	272	137	519	4,069
53 23970	Fircrest city	Pierce	1.6	5,868	5,132	305	33	158	30	27	183	158	4,515
53 24188	Five Corners CDP	Clark	6.2	12,207	10,821	201	107	487	76	186	329	505	8,523
53 24810	Forks city	Clallam	3.1	3,120	2,542	13	157	47	6	265	91	405	2,170
53 24915	Fort Lewis CDP	Pierce	15.3	19,089	11,537	3,882	259	650	342	1,189	1,230	2,507	12,958
53 25370	Fox Island CDP	Pierce	5.2	2,803	2,637	18	21	46	4	11	66	52	2,038
53 25475	Frederickson CDP	Pierce	7.3	5,758	4,860	183	90	211	49	92	273	257	3,968
53 26735	Gig Harbor city	Pierce	4.4	6,465	6,088	72	41	99	14	35	116	196	5,153
53 26945	Gleed CDP	Yakima	5.4	2,947	2,698	12	14	6	3	149	65	246	2,170
53 27435	Goldendale city	Klickitat	2.4	3,760	3,287	8	174	27	10	153	101	220	2,691
53 27785	Graham CDP	Pierce	21.4	8,739	7,878	112	112	157	44	86	350	246	6,089
53 27925	Grandview city	Yakima	5.4	8,377	4,282	49	79	79	9	3,625	254	5,700	5,343
53 27960	Granger town	Yakima	1.3	2,530	511	-	20	-	-	1,932	67	2,164	1,441
53 28520	Green Acres CDP	Spokane	3.3	5,158	4,909	24	52	37	1	17	118	127	3,777
53 30312	Hazel Dell North CDP	Clark	2.7	9,261	7,806	239	81	207	38	559	331	1,037	6,692
53 30313	Hazel Dell South CDP	Clark	2.2	6,605	5,823	219	55	124	13	144	227	332	4,989
53 30775	Highland CDP	Benton	27.6	3,388	3,130	9	13	23	1	124	88	255	2,294
53 31495	Hobart CDP	King	18.7	6,251	5,945	51	42	57	8	25	123	101	4,551
53 31530	Hockinson CDP	Clark	16.6	5,136	4,929	15	24	33	10	35	90	83	3,445
53 32300	Hoquiam city	Grays Harbor	9.2	9,097	8,125	29	351	107	6	190	289	523	6,606
53 33280	Indianola CDP	Kitsap	4.9	3,026	2,655	16	160	42	10	25	118	83	2,130
53 33380	Inglewood-Finn Hill CDP	King	5.8	22,661	19,666	316	108	1,446	42	297	786	860	16,729
53 33805	Issaquah city	King	8.4	11,212	9,861	99	71	677	12	164	328	555	8,728
53 35065	Kelso city	Cowlitz	8.1	11,895	10,722	98	244	112	25	371	323	824	8,528
53 35170	Kenmore city	King	6.2	18,678	16,194	259	69	1,338	34	231	553	655	14,107
53 35275	Kennewick city	Benton	22.9	54,693	45,355	624	507	1,161	59	5,142	1,845	8,503	38,522
53 35415	Kent city	King	28.0	79,524	56,307	6,547	777	7,489	608	3,525	4,271	6,466	57,513
53 35835	Kingsgate CDP	King	2.3	12,222	9,771	199	75	1,422	29	222	504	690	8,817
53 35940	Kirkland city	King	10.7	45,054	38,420	717	238	3,512	89	761	1,317	1,852	36,732
53 36745	Lacey city	Thurston	15.9	31,226	24,417	1,490	416	2,423	330	676	1,474	1,843	23,000
53 37270	Lake Forest Park city	King	3.5	13,142	11,213	216	56	1,043	15	121	478	294	10,201
53 37287	Lake Goodwin CDP	Snohomish	4.0	3,354	3,173	16	45	24	3	29	64	82	2,437
53 37420	Lakeland North CDP	King	5.3	15,085	12,438	514	161	1,048	75	245	604	537	10,554
53 37430	Lakeland South CDP	King	5.4	11,436	9,599	422	100	697	48	132	438	381	8,277
53 37567	Lake Morton-Berrydale CDP	King	12.5	9,659	8,935	83	77	202	18	105	239	223	6,846
53 37830	Lake Shore CDP	Clark	1.6	6,670	6,162	80	48	164	5	45	166	194	4,825
53 37900	Lake Stevens city	Snohomish	2.2	6,361	5,872	38	58	70	20	57	246	226	4,204
53 38038	Lakewood city	Pierce	17.1	58,211	37,734	7,132	902	5,208	1,070	2,068	4,097	4,941	43,998
53 38815	Lea Hill CDP	King	5.9	10,871	9,366	242	103	486	19	210	445	536	7,444
53 39335	Liberty Lake CDP	Spokane	4.3	4,660	4,366	33	13	121	7	26	94	104	3,304

Table D-1. Places — **Area and Population**—Con.

[Includes incorporated places and census designated places (CDPs) of 2,500 or more population as of April 1, 2000. Codes shown are two-digit Federal Information Processing Standards (FIPS) state codes and five-digit FIPS place codes. Place names and codes are those in effect as of January 1, 2000. County refers to the county (or counties) in which the place is located. IC in this column = independent city, a county equivalent. If a place is located in more than one county, counties are listed in alphabetic order]

State and place code	Place	County	Land area, 2000 (sq. mi.)	Total	White	Black or African American	American Indian and Alaska Native	Asian	Native Hawaiian and Other Pacific Islander	Some other race	Two or more races	Hispanic or Latino (of any race)	18 years and over
53 00000	WASHINGTON—Con.												
53 40245	Longview city	Cowlitz	13.7	34,660	30,967	248	610	753	45	1,025	1,012	2,017	25,665
53 40270	Longview Heights CDP	Cowlitz	4.2	3,513	3,343	14	33	50	3	15	55	63	2,597
53 40805	Lynden city	Whatcom	4.1	9,020	8,395	24	41	204	-	226	130	427	6,479
53 40840	Lynnwood city	Snohomish	7.6	33,847	25,138	1,110	346	4,696	136	948	1,473	2,356	25,583
53 41155	McChord AFB CDP	Pierce	5.8	4,096	3,133	350	30	170	27	130	256	331	2,610
53 42415	Maltby CDP	Snohomish	16.8	8,267	7,781	24	39	197	13	53	160	176	5,910
53 42450	Manchester CDP	Kitsap	2.9	4,958	4,346	65	56	132	46	67	246	187	3,526
53 43062	Maple Heights-Lake Desire CDP	King	4.1	2,569	2,230	33	38	175	5	23	65	70	1,880
53 43150	Maple Valley city	King	5.4	14,209	12,876	158	94	349	22	193	517	506	9,403
53 43491	Marietta-Alderwood CDP	Whatcom	6.0	3,594	3,026	40	138	181	14	102	93	215	2,768
53 43815	Martha Lake CDP	Snohomish	4.8	12,633	10,586	192	100	1,090	29	164	472	467	9,222
53 43955	Marysville city	Snohomish	9.6	25,315	22,331	257	406	967	90	478	786	1,222	17,684
53 44165	Mattawa town	Grant	0.5	2,609	772	5	14	24	-	1,718	76	2,343	1,614
53 44690	Medical Lake city	Spokane	3.4	3,758	3,340	173	53	59	8	38	87	155	2,845
53 44725	Medina city	King	1.4	3,011	2,789	5	8	147	2	10	50	42	2,195
53 45005	Mercer Island city	King	6.4	22,036	18,530	251	35	2,615	16	114	475	410	16,312
53 45495	Midland CDP	Pierce	3.0	7,414	5,272	626	177	426	68	327	518	691	5,273
53 45865	Mill Creek city	Snohomish	3.6	11,525	9,392	163	50	1,457	29	129	305	375	8,719
53 45915	Mill Plain CDP	Clark	6.0	7,400	6,463	120	42	461	8	44	262	197	4,847
53 46020	Milton city	Pierce, King	2.5	5,795	5,235	66	68	164	16	46	200	206	4,358
53 46125	Minnehaha CDP	Clark	2.2	7,689	6,788	169	73	216	48	161	234	315	5,493
53 46215	Mirrormont CDP	King	10.4	3,804	3,577	17	22	52	5	31	100	64	2,779
53 46685	Monroe city	Snohomish	5.8	13,795	11,882	434	182	328	43	553	373	1,332	10,009
53 46895	Montesano city	Grays Harbor	10.3	3,312	3,146	4	62	16	2	6	76	61	2,523
53 47245	Moses Lake city	Grant	10.2	14,953	11,537	253	152	214	10	2,309	478	3,800	10,645
53 47280	Moses Lake North CDP	Grant	6.1	4,232	3,063	212	74	28	2	623	230	1,025	2,518
53 47490	Mountlake Terrace city	Snohomish	4.0	20,362	15,821	514	219	2,167	119	531	991	1,151	15,218
53 47560	Mount Vernon city	Skagit	11.1	26,232	19,789	192	268	676	40	4,494	773	6,589	18,635
53 47630	Mount Vista CDP	Clark	5.2	5,770	5,371	57	25	163	8	27	119	142	4,341
53 47735	Mukilteo city	Snohomish	6.3	18,019	14,787	266	143	1,977	45	204	597	522	12,931
53 48225	Navy Yard City CDP	Kitsap	0.6	2,638	2,027	204	40	138	30	60	139	170	2,024
53 48645	Newcastle city	King	4.5	7,737	5,807	125	35	1,412	19	105	234	223	5,926
53 49415	Normandy Park city	King	2.5	6,392	5,766	73	25	294	15	51	168	156	4,973
53 49485	North Bend city	King	2.9	4,746	4,367	33	49	106	8	69	114	180	3,452
53 49665	North Creek CDP	Snohomish	13.6	25,742	22,659	260	166	1,445	74	369	769	1,137	18,300
53 49992	North Marysville CDP	Snohomish	13.7	21,161	19,011	150	268	708	36	371	617	973	14,615
53 50210	North Yelm CDP	Thurston	3.4	2,793	2,500	27	61	41	21	33	110	112	1,977
53 50360	Oak Harbor city	Island	9.1	19,795	14,833	1,078	242	1,905	152	480	1,105	1,309	13,538
53 50570	Ocean Shores city	Grays Harbor	8.6	3,836	3,546	23	84	47	4	31	101	67	3,192
53 51300	Olympia city	Thurston	16.7	42,514	36,246	805	553	2,473	125	713	1,599	1,863	33,394
53 51340	Omak city	Okanogan	2.9	4,721	3,282	8	718	43	7	473	190	614	3,411
53 51515	Opportunity CDP	Spokane	6.7	25,065	23,440	252	252	324	26	157	614	670	18,633
53 51795	Orchards CDP	Clark	6.9	17,852	15,601	312	157	733	106	328	615	809	11,745
53 52005	Orting city	Pierce	2.7	3,760	3,473	23	37	47	10	48	122	129	2,527
53 52215	Othello city	Adams	3.0	5,847	3,168	31	59	59	5	2,312	213	3,728	3,739
53 52267	Otis Orchards-East Farms CDP	Spokane	8.1	6,318	6,009	11	77	73	3	32	113	123	4,316
53 52495	Pacific city	King, Pierce	2.6	5,527	4,719	79	89	261	11	163	205	358	3,805
53 52765	Paine Field-Lake Stickney CDP	Snohomish	7.4	24,383	19,077	955	313	1,796	121	1,039	1,082	2,065	17,913
53 53335	Parkland CDP	Pierce	7.4	24,053	17,778	1,940	251	1,597	435	496	1,556	1,281	18,044
53 53440	Parkwood CDP	Kitsap	2.6	7,213	6,098	182	88	313	73	106	353	312	5,161
53 53545	Pasco city	Franklin	28.1	32,066	16,919	1,033	248	567	46	12,004	1,249	18,041	20,673
53 54215	Picnic Point-North Lynnwood CDP	Snohomish	7.4	22,953	18,182	504	201	2,531	71	463	1,001	1,097	16,907
53 55365	Port Angeles city	Clallam	10.1	18,397	16,806	127	600	238	32	70	524	430	14,032
53 55400	Port Angeles East CDP	Clallam	3.8	3,053	2,893	8	60	16	5	13	58	65	2,397
53 55620	Port Hadlock-Irondale CDP	Jefferson	6.7	3,476	3,154	11	67	49	3	20	172	87	2,532
53 55785	Port Orchard city	Kitsap	4.0	7,693	6,325	308	115	284	81	106	474	395	5,726
53 55855	Port Townsend city	Jefferson	7.0	8,334	7,773	48	104	106	19	74	210	192	6,697
53 55995	Poulsbo city	Kitsap	3.2	6,813	6,002	69	66	204	29	131	312	330	5,167
53 56170	Prairie Ridge CDP	Pierce	4.3	11,688	10,914	63	137	106	44	92	332	393	7,810
53 56450	Prosser city	Benton	4.3	4,838	3,865	26	44	37	14	731	121	1,421	3,265
53 56625	Pullman city	Whitman	9.0	24,675	20,505	591	165	2,093	93	390	838	953	21,418
53 56695	Puyallup city	Pierce	12.1	33,011	29,010	496	334	1,079	112	640	1,340	1,542	24,010
53 57115	Quincy city	Grant	2.2	5,044	3,226	12	67	26	3	1,567	143	3,264	3,230
53 57430	Raymond city	Pacific	3.8	2,975	2,490	7	81	210	5	94	88	273	2,196
53 57535	Redmond city	King	15.9	45,256	35,868	687	203	5,893	82	1,114	1,409	2,538	35,548
53 57745	Renton city	King	17.0	50,052	34,105	4,238	358	6,692	250	2,122	2,287	3,818	39,139
53 58235	Richland city	Benton	34.8	38,708	34,662	530	293	1,571	41	718	893	1,826	28,178
53 58878	Riverton-Boulevard Park CDP	King	2.7	11,188	6,842	929	162	1,342	192	1,077	644	1,755	8,388
53 61000	Salmon Creek CDP	Clark	6.3	16,767	15,312	211	90	417	23	225	489	806	12,063
53 61115	Sammamish city	King	18.1	34,104	29,950	289	99	2,690	30	206	840	853	22,718
53 62288	SeaTac city	King	10.0	25,496	16,027	2,334	382	2,822	677	1,634	1,620	3,302	19,279
53 63000	Seattle city	King	83.9	563,374	394,889	47,541	5,659	73,910	2,804	13,423	25,148	29,719	475,547

Table D-1. Places — **Area and Population**—Con.

[Includes incorporated places and census designated places (CDPs) of 2,500 or more population as of April 1, 2000. Codes shown are two-digit Federal Information Processing Standards (FIPS) state codes and five-digit FIPS place codes. Place names and codes are those in effect as of January 1, 2000. County refers to the county (or counties) in which the place is located. IC in this column = independent city, a county equivalent. If a place is located in more than one county, counties are listed in alphabetic order]

State and place code	Place	County	Land area, 2000 (sq. mi.)	Population, 2000 (April 1) By race— One race Total	White	Black or African American	American Indian and Alaska Native	Asian	Native Hawaiian and Other Pacific Islander	Some other race	Two or more races	Hispanic or Latino (of any race)	18 years and over
53 00000	WASHINGTON—Con.												
53 63052	Seattle Hill-Silver Firs CDP	Snohomish	14.0	35,311	30,385	408	221	2,658	76	450	1,113	1,065	24,334
53 63210	Sedro-Woolley city	Skagit	3.4	8,658	7,963	22	138	70	11	281	173	626	6,162
53 63280	Selah city	Yakima	4.4	6,310	5,579	38	77	52	5	404	155	697	4,311
53 63385	Sequim city	Clallam	5.3	4,334	4,070	13	50	76	4	40	81	124	3,670
53 63735	Shelton city	Mason	5.6	8,442	7,246	30	230	99	02	487	288	918	6,192
53 63960	Shoreline city	King	11.7	53,025	40,824	1,467	485	7,016	168	799	2,266	2,054	41,105
53 64365	Silverdale CDP	Kitsap	6.9	15,816	12,206	550	132	1,739	168	229	792	690	11,395
53 65170	Snohomish city	Snohomish	2.5	8,494	7,954	43	47	106	10	88	246	330	6,245
53 65922	South Hill CDP	Pierce	18.0	31,623	27,641	766	297	1,061	155	458	1,245	1,307	21,728
53 66255	Spanaway CDP	Pierce	8.3	21,588	15,355	1,966	347	1,368	458	465	1,629	1,185	15,111
53 67000	Spokane city	Spokane	57.8	195,629	175,018	4,052	3,444	4,399	372	1,727	6,617	5,857	147,105
53 67455	Stanwood city	Snohomish	2.0	3,923	3,592	23	37	43	9	99	120	195	2,689
53 67770	Steilacoom town	Pierce	2.1	6,049	4,746	405	51	355	37	100	355	327	4,671
53 68200	Sudden Valley CDP	Whatcom	6.2	4,165	3,842	33	67	82	5	38	98	126	3,188
53 68260	Sultan city	Snohomish	3.0	3,344	3,053	9	40	52	4	52	134	160	2,302
53 68365	Summit CDP	Pierce	5.2	8,041	7,082	173	80	233	28	145	300	300	5,996
53 68435	Sumner city	Pierce	6.7	8,504	7,681	79	120	141	20	206	257	508	6,247
53 68750	Sunnyside city	Yakima	5.9	13,905	5,925	55	87	96	12	7,311	419	10,158	8,603
53 68785	Sunnyslope CDP	Chelan	9.6	2,521	2,324	4	11	33	3	86	60	167	1,830
53 69170	Suquamish CDP	Kitsap	6.8	3,510	2,855	12	337	85	7	45	169	107	2,659
53 70000	Tacoma city	Pierce	50.1	193,556	133,704	21,757	3,794	14,656	1,798	5,695	12,152	13,262	143,666
53 70297	Tanglewilde-Thompson Place CDP	Thurston	1.4	5,670	4,142	399	123	394	60	208	344	516	3,999
53 70315	Tanner CDP	King	6.1	2,966	2,791	11	29	36	4	25	70	68	2,096
53 70805	Terrace Heights CDP	Yakima	7.9	6,447	5,711	54	73	33	1	389	186	713	4,873
53 71960	Toppenish city	Yakima	1.9	8,946	2,816	50	707	33	2	5,005	333	6,774	5,477
53 72170	Town and Country CDP	Spokane	1.4	4,452	4,153	65	68	43	6	31	86	95	3,385
53 72205	Tracyton CDP	Kitsap	1.5	3,267	2,632	120	24	198	32	65	196	118	2,381
53 72310	Trentwood CDP	Spokane	1.8	4,388	4,067	31	47	110	5	31	88	105	3,023
53 72625	Tukwila city	King	8.9	17,181	10,074	2,198	223	1,870	312	1,385	1,119	2,329	13,057
53 72905	Tumwater city	Thurston	10.0	12,698	11,226	176	157	495	46	191	407	518	9,755
53 73290	Union Gap city	Yakima	5.0	5,621	4,058	23	126	32	5	1,134	243	1,662	4,020
53 73307	Union Hill-Novelty Hill CDP	King	24.3	11,265	10,225	88	44	479	7	146	276	389	7,510
53 73465	University Place city	Pierce	8.4	29,933	22,711	2,617	217	2,236	167	403	1,582	1,150	22,157
53 74060	Vancouver city	Clark	42.8	143,560	121,752	3,593	1,399	6,470	779	4,112	5,455	9,035	105,212
53 74305	Vashon CDP	King	37.0	10,123	9,476	46	71	158	6	88	278	259	7,777
53 74585	Venersborg CDP	Clark	10.7	3,274	3,181	6	5	14	2	5	61	61	2,204
53 74725	Veradale CDP	Spokane	3.1	9,387	8,818	99	74	176	5	46	169	218	6,640
53 75775	Walla Walla city	Walla Walla	10.8	29,686	24,875	765	313	368	68	2,451	846	5,170	22,904
53 75905	Waller CDP	Pierce	9.2	9,200	8,188	141	190	192	15	167	307	398	6,954
53 76055	Walnut Grove CDP	Clark	3.8	7,164	6,501	80	57	225	34	85	182	212	5,307
53 76125	Wapato city	Yakima	1.0	4,582	1,169	23	428	70	-	2,638	254	3,492	2,831
53 76160	Warden city	Grant	2.1	2,544	1,057	5	23	8	-	1,376	75	1,827	1,525
53 76405	Washougal city	Clark	5.0	8,595	8,082	37	108	67	10	71	220	216	6,034
53 77105	Wenatchee city	Chelan	6.9	27,856	22,543	109	315	264	36	3,897	692	5,996	20,222
53 77297	West Clarkston-Highland CDP	Asotin	2.7	4,707	4,471	8	68	24	-	38	98	94	3,587
53 77535	West Lake Sammamish CDP	King	1.4	5,937	5,137	64	25	536	5	30	140	113	4,367
53 77542	West Lake Stevens CDP	Snohomish	9.7	18,071	16,447	187	152	354	30	314	587	794	12,237
53 77547	West Longview CDP	Cowlitz	1.6	2,882	2,590	17	54	72	12	53	84	120	2,071
53 77612	West Pasco CDP	Franklin	6.0	4,629	4,147	51	34	54	2	207	134	464	3,399
53 77665	West Richland city	Benton	21.7	8,385	7,813	47	42	138	2	156	187	405	5,644
53 77745	West Side Highway CDP	Cowlitz	2.5	4,565	4,301	12	56	51	-	37	108	91	3,259
53 77885	West Valley CDP	Yakima	7.2	10,433	9,348	86	94	213	14	405	273	910	7,387
53 78225	White Center CDP	King	3.4	20,975	11,527	1,344	422	4,424	545	1,445	1,268	2,513	15,282
53 78365	White Swan CDP	Yakima	103.3	3,033	796	9	1,798	8	1	247	174	485	1,819
53 79590	Woodinville city	King	5.6	9,194	7,724	84	47	674	23	340	302	658	6,747
53 79625	Woodland city	Clark, Cowlitz	2.5	3,780	3,529	13	35	17	4	107	75	278	2,674
53 79825	Woods Creek CDP	Snohomish	12.4	4,502	4,223	6	25	32	10	108	98	207	3,157
53 80010	Yakima city	Yakima	20.1	71,845	49,409	1,433	1,435	860	102	15,787	2,819	24,213	50,704
53 80220	Yelm city	Thurston	5.6	3,289	2,834	59	73	57	38	52	176	176	2,238
54 00000	WEST VIRGINIA		24,077.7	1,808,344	1,718,777	57,232	3,606	9,434	400	3,107	15,788	12,279	1,405,951
54 04276	Barboursville village	Cabell	3.7	3,183	3,112	26	5	19	2	2	17	23	2,567
54 05332	Beckley city	Raleigh	9.2	17,254	12,705	3,949	25	326	3	36	210	128	13,487
54 06940	Bethlehem village	Ohio	3.5	2,651	2,560	31	2	43	-	1	14	10	2,078
54 08308	Blennerhassett CDP	Wood	5.0	3,225	3,175	18	1	16	-	-	15	12	2,448
54 08524	Bluefield city	Mercer	8.7	11,451	8,684	2,535	14	64	1	24	129	60	8,993
54 10180	Bridgeport city	Harrison	8.3	7,306	7,082	91	4	77	-	14	38	94	5,626
54 10420	Brookhaven CDP	Monongalia	9.3	4,734	4,558	49	12	25	5	8	77	38	3,474
54 11188	Buckhannon city	Upshur	2.5	5,725	5,505	115	6	48	1	16	34	55	4,838
54 14600	Charleston city	Kanawha	31.6	53,421	43,072	8,048	127	979	16	158	1,021	432	42,378
54 14610	Charles Town city	Jefferson	1.4	2,907	2,294	510	3	30	1	18	51	74	2,241
54 14775	Cheat Lake CDP	Monongalia	14.4	6,396	6,115	77	6	120	5	3	70	35	4,749
54 15076	Chester city	Hancock	1.0	2,592	2,560	4	-	6	-	8	14	29	2,023
54 15628	Clarksburg city	Harrison	9.5	16,743	15,715	641	21	60	8	74	224	177	13,211

Table D-1. Places — **Area and Population**—Con.

[Includes incorporated places and census designated places (CDPs) of 2,500 or more population as of April 1, 2000. Codes shown are two-digit Federal Information Processing Standards (FIPS) state codes and five-digit FIPS place codes. Place names and codes are those in effect as of January 1, 2000. County refers to the county (or counties) in which the place is located. IC in this column = independent city, a county equivalent. If a place is located in more than one county, counties are listed in alphabetic order]

State and place code	Place	County	Land area, 2000 (sq. mi.)	Population, 2000 (April 1)									
					By race—								
					One race								
				Total	White	Black or African American	American Indian and Alaska Native	Asian	Native Hawaiian and Other Pacific Islander	Some other race	Two or more races	Hispanic or Latino (of any race)	18 years and over
54 00000	WEST VIRGINIA—Con.												
54 18040	Corporation of Ranson town	Jefferson	0.9	2,951	2,414	431	4	11	1	33	57	93	2,180
54 18508	Crab Orchard CDP	Raleigh	2.3	2,761	2,711	25	2	3	1	5	14	17	2,124
54 19108	Cross Lanes CDP	Kanawha	6.5	10,353	9,694	398	22	128	2	10	99	59	7,863
54 19516	Culloden CDP	Cabell, Putnam	3.7	2,940	2,906	9	3	8	-	1	13	7	2,283
54 22564	Dunbar city	Kanawha	2.8	8,154	6,984	874	7	147	1	15	126	45	6,680
54 24580	Elkins city	Randolph	3.2	7,032	6,817	63	21	67	-	22	42	54	5,543
54 26452	Fairmont city	Marion	7.8	19,097	17,217	1,386	49	117	4	39	285	157	15,583
54 27028	Fayetteville town	Fayette	2.9	2,754	2,613	126	4	1	1	5	4	17	2,193
54 28204	Follansbee city	Brooke	1.8	3,115	3,083	2	2	10	'	1	17	8	2,453
54 32716	Grafton city	Taylor	3.7	5,489	5,383	46	15	9	-	3	33	37	4,192
54 37636	Hinton city	Summers	2.3	2,880	2,662	158	15	6	3	2	34	21	2,321
54 38476	Hooverson Heights CDP	Brooke	2.3	2,909	2,877	8	1	5	-	-	18	12	2,300
54 39460	Huntington city	Cabell, Wayne	15.9	51,475	46,127	3,858	101	422	25	155	787	437	42,344
54 39532	Hurricane city	Putnam	3.0	5,222	5,124	35	4	20	-	5	34	28	3,912
54 43180	Kenova city	Wayne	1.2	3,485	3,458	8	6	2	-	1	10	7	2,769
54 43492	Keyser city	Mineral	1.9	5,303	4,802	375	12	21	-	17	76	38	4,244
54 44044	Kingwood city	Preston	2.5	2,944	2,876	30	-	13	-	2	23	10	2,287
54 46636	Lewisburg city	Greenbrier	3.8	3,624	3,288	242	16	19	-	13	46	24	2,980
54 50524	Madison city	Boone	5.6	2,677	2,538	112	1	11	-	2	13	7	2,124
54 52060	Martinsburg city	Berkeley	5.0	14,972	12,561	1,741	60	94	3	188	325	436	11,516
54 55756	Morgantown city	Monongalia	9.8	26,809	23,990	1,113	45	1,113	13	138	397	412	23,846
54 56020	Moundsville city	Marshall	2.9	9,998	9,811	73	13	30	1	10	60	116	7,958
54 56342	Mount Gay-Shamrock CDP	Logan	12.0	2,623	2,372	217	8	3	1	4	18	10	2,031
54 58684	New Martinsville city	Wetzel	2.8	5,984	5,897	3	6	45	2	1	30	26	4,612
54 59068	Nitro city	Kanawha, Putnam	3.7	6,824	6,595	111	17	17	-	27	57	37	5,454
54 60028	Oak Hill city	Fayette	4.8	7,589	7,059	364	24	32	2	18	90	64	6,035
54 61636	Paden City city	Tyler, Wetzel	0.9	2,860	2,841	3	3	3	-	-	10	14	2,195
54 62140	Parkersburg city	Wood	11.8	33,099	31,894	579	67	138	18	71	332	269	26,085
54 62488	Pea Ridge CDP	Cabell	2.3	6,363	6,018	103	15	164	1	4	58	27	5,126
54 63292	Philippi city	Barbour	2.8	2,870	2,720	32	30	25	1	12	50	23	2,270
54 63772	Pinch CDP	Kanawha	3.5	2,811	2,789	4	6	1	-	2	9	14	2,191
54 64228	Pleasant Valley city	Marion	3.3	3,124	3,058	33	2	14	-	-	17	19	2,465
54 64708	Point Pleasant city	Mason	2.4	4,637	4,478	88	7	28	-	4	32	25	3,648
54 65692	Princeton city	Mercer	3.0	6,347	5,841	394	19	27	1	12	53	33	5,181
54 67108	Ravenswood city	Jackson	1.8	4,031	3,952	10	2	30	-	6	31	24	3,081
54 68596	Ripley city	Jackson	3.1	3,263	3,205	2	2	7	-	12	35	21	2,638
54 71212	St. Albans city	Kanawha	3.6	11,567	11,031	329	15	50	-	21	121	73	9,349
54 74356	Sissonville CDP	Kanawha	12.7	4,399	4,329	21	6	1	-	16	26	23	3,424
54 75292	South Charleston city	Kanawha	7.4	13,390	12,165	893	20	108	-	32	172	75	10,827
54 77980	Summersville town	Nicholas	4.2	3,294	3,230	2	3	20	-	17	22	39	2,576
54 79545	Teays Valley CDP	Putnam	7.3	12,704	12,246	119	14	202	2	32	89	98	9,254
54 83500	Vienna city	Wood	3.8	10,861	10,503	103	18	146	2	15	74	54	8,561
54 85156	Weirton city	Brooke, Hancock	17.9	20,411	19,293	787	22	120	3	29	157	138	16,486
54 85228	Welch city	McDowell	3.3	2,683	2,125	517	7	8	-	9	17	28	2,164
54 85324	Wellsburg city	Brooke	0.9	2,891	2,795	58	3	3	-	1	31	7	2,373
54 85972	Weston city	Lewis	1.7	4,317	4,241	8	4	31	-	8	25	20	3,440
54 85996	Westover city	Monongalia	1.3	3,941	3,688	137	8	29	1	10	68	18	3,156
54 86452	Wheeling city	Marshall, Ohio	13.9	31,419	29,133	1,567	31	287	9	51	341	181	24,947
54 87508	Williamson city	Mingo	3.3	3,414	2,851	466	13	34	-	10	40	31	2,730
54 87556	Williamstown city	Wood	1.3	2,996	2,944	6	9	14	-	1	22	20	2,282
55 00000	WISCONSIN		54,310.1	5,363,675	4,769,857	304,460	47,228	88,763	1,630	84,842	66,895	192,921	3,994,919
55 01000	Algoma city	Kewaunee	2.4	3,357	3,304	3	10	2	-	17	21	33	2,650
55 01150	Allouez village	Brown	4.6	15,443	14,218	717	178	130	1	95	104	199	12,023
55 01550	Altoona city	Eau Claire	4.1	6,698	6,423	27	39	77	5	18	109	49	5,072
55 01725	Amery city	Polk	3.0	2,845	2,787	2	20	7	5	9	15	27	2,216
55 02250	Antigo city	Langlade	6.4	8,560	8,326	26	74	25	1	27	81	103	6,458
55 02375	Appleton city	Calumet, Outagamie, Winnebago	20.9	70,087	64,116	695	401	3,231	21	733	890	1,775	50,876
55 03225	Ashland city	Ashland	13.4	8,620	7,773	28	543	42	5	37	192	118	6,703
55 03425	Ashwaubenon village	Brown	12.4	17,634	16,764	114	221	320	4	82	129	202	13,175
55 04400	Baldwin village	St. Croix	2.3	2,667	2,625	4	5	11	-	2	20	11	2,024
55 04625	Baraboo city	Sauk	5.3	10,711	10,402	55	83	56	-	44	71	168	8,045
55 04875	Barron city	Barron	2.8	3,248	3,148	20	5	8	5	34	28	61	2,486
55 05450	Bayside village	Milwaukee, Ozaukee	2.4	4,518	4,263	125	7	82	4	14	23	77	3,469
55 05900	Beaver Dam city	Dodge	5.2	15,169	14,555	66	48	92	7	244	157	640	11,382
55 06362	Bellevue Town CDP	Brown	14.3	11,828	11,284	60	99	160	2	130	93	310	8,644
55 06500	Beloit city	Rock	16.4	35,775	27,034	5,497	135	415	24	1,652	1,018	3,257	25,880
55 06925	Berlin city	Green, Waushara	6.0	5,305	5,077	8	15	41	1	131	32	242	3,972
55 07900	Black River Falls city	Jackson	3.2	3,618	3,378	7	171	4	3	20	35	42	2,867
55 08225	Bloomer city	Chippewa	2.7	3,347	3,318	2	9	3	-	2	13	11	2,544
55 08850	Boscobel city	Grant	2.9	3,047	2,888	114	6	5	-	6	28	36	2,290
55 09725	Brillion city	Calumet	2.6	2,937	2,897	-	21	5	-	5	9	15	2,164
55 09925	Brodhead city	Green	1.6	3,180	3,118	9	1	8	-	17	27	31	2,331

Table D-1. Places — **Area and Population**—Con.

[Includes incorporated places and census designated places (CDPs) of 2,500 or more population as of April 1, 2000. Codes shown are two-digit Federal Information Processing Standards (FIPS) state codes and five-digit FIPS place codes. Place names and codes are those in effect as of January 1, 2000. County refers to the county (or counties) in which the place is located. IC in this column = independent city, a county equivalent. If a place is located in more than one county, counties are listed in alphabetic order]

				Population, 2000 (April 1)									
				Total	By race—							Hispanic or Latino (of any race)	18 years and over
					One race						Two or more races		
State and place code	Place	County	Land area, 2000 (sq. mi.)		White	Black or African American	American Indian and Alaska Native	Asian	Native Hawaiian and Other Pacific Islander	Some other race			
55 00000	WISCONSIN—Con.												
55 10025	Brookfield city	Waukesha	27.2	38,649	36,407	321	35	1,479	7	87	313	453	28,288
55 10375	Brown Deer village	Milwaukee	4.4	12,170	9,984	1,522	31	319	5	80	229	260	9,782
55 11200	Burlington city	Racine, Walworth	6.0	9,936	9,528	37	12	55	-	220	84	462	7,172
55 12400	Camp Lake CDP	Kenosha	4.5	3,255	3,172	12	10	9	-	34	18	92	2,248
55 13375	Cedarburg city	Ozaukee	3.7	10,908	10,708	27	14	80	2	14	63	94	7,939
55 14475	Chilton city	Calumet	3.9	3,708	3,652	14	12	9	-	7	14	32	2,810
55 14575	Chippewa Falls city	Chippewa	10.9	12,925	12,618	39	59	87	1	21	100	82	9,803
55 15725	Clintonville city	Waupaca	4.2	4,736	4,594	11	25	12	-	47	47	102	3,575
55 16450	Columbus city	Columbia, Dodge	4.0	4,479	4,402	16	10	14	1	13	23	44	3,314
55 17175	Cottage Grove village	Dane	2.3	4,059	3,885	74	10	20	-	22	48	73	2,758
55 17775	Cross Plains village	Dane	1.2	3,084	3,047	7	4	5	1	1	19	13	2,204
55 17975	Cudahy city	Milwaukee	4.7	18,429	17,303	175	150	154	6	267	374	872	14,187
55 19350	DeForest village	Dane	4.8	7,368	7,025	109	25	50	10	46	103	161	5,073
55 19400	Delafield city	Waukesha	9.5	6,472	6,326	6	20	37	-	21	62	95	4,749
55 19450	Delavan city	Walworth	6.4	7,956	6,704	91	37	53	6	849	216	1,690	5,644
55 19775	De Pere city	Brown	10.6	20,559	19,883	110	189	155	7	39	176	202	15,518
55 20350	Dodgeville city	Iowa	3.6	4,220	4,138	15	1	25	2	7	32	18	3,132
55 22100	East Troy village	Walworth	3.6	3,564	3,449	6	10	19	-	48	32	105	2,571
55 22300	Eau Claire city	Chippewa, Eau Claire	30.3	61,704	57,657	429	337	2,259	23	209	790	619	48,346
55 22575	Edgerton city	Dane, Rock	3.7	4,933	4,763	10	25	19	-	44	72	188	3,611
55 23300	Elkhorn city	Walworth	7.3	7,305	6,926	34	29	40	2	207	67	448	5,263
55 23525	Ellsworth village	Pierce	3.7	2,909	2,857	-	6	4	-	17	25	33	2,192
55 23575	Elm Grove village	Waukesha	3.3	6,249	6,070	27	7	93	5	25	22	75	4,690
55 24550	Evansville city	Rock	2.2	4,039	3,942	5	17	7	2	26	40	72	2,864
55 24587	Evergreen CDP	Marathon	3.8	3,611	3,546	3	8	40	-	6	8	8	2,505
55 25950	Fitchburg city	Dane	34.8	20,501	16,849	1,771	87	654	8	626	506	1,329	15,602
55 26275	Fond du Lac city	Fond du Lac	16.9	42,203	39,496	783	217	640	6	535	526	1,232	32,009
55 26675	Fort Atkinson city	Jefferson	5.4	11,621	11,167	40	34	70	1	217	92	508	8,805
55 27075	Fox Point village	Milwaukee	2.9	7,012	6,700	85	8	150	1	13	55	74	5,336
55 27300	Franklin city	Milwaukee	34.6	29,494	26,775	1,520	106	619	10	197	267	780	22,592
55 27875	French Island CDP	La Crosse	2.0	4,410	4,255	23	23	48	1	12	48	30	3,362
55 28875	Germantown village	Washington	34.4	18,260	17,498	247	45	292	7	62	109	205	13,315
55 29400	Glendale city	Milwaukee	5.8	13,367	11,597	1,087	31	395	13	66	178	236	10,775
55 30000	Grafton village	Ozaukee	4.0	10,312	10,077	29	25	77	1	38	65	165	7,597
55 31000	Green Bay city	Brown	43.9	102,313	87,841	1,407	3,355	3,845	36	3,809	2,020	7,294	76,281
55 31125	Greendale village	Milwaukee	5.6	14,405	13,855	41	23	296	1	81	108	340	11,183
55 31175	Greenfield city	Milwaukee	11.5	35,476	33,247	348	155	802	7	464	453	1,376	28,773
55 32075	Hales Corners village	Milwaukee	3.2	7,765	7,544	17	38	75	3	44	44	162	6,050
55 33000	Hartford city	Dodge, Washington	6.0	10,905	10,545	29	38	50	5	134	104	326	7,898
55 33100	Hartland village	Waukesha	4.5	7,905	7,723	22	26	38	-	34	62	119	5,560
55 35450	Holmen village	La Crosse	3.2	6,200	5,909	19	20	198	-	16	38	56	4,239
55 35750	Horicon city	Dodge	3.4	3,775	3,684	15	7	7	3	39	20	79	2,772
55 35950	Howard village	Brown, Outagamie	18.0	13,546	13,026	99	122	106	1	43	149	147	9,775
55 36025	Howards Grove village	Sheboygan	2.1	2,792	2,756	1	3	13	-	12	7	21	1,976
55 36250	Hudson city	St. Croix	5.4	8,775	8,588	19	23	40	-	19	86	91	6,628
55 37675	Jackson village	Washington	2.5	4,938	4,865	4	12	10	-	16	31	61	3,586
55 37825	Janesville city	Rock	27.5	59,498	56,682	748	146	573	19	605	725	1,569	43,915
55 37900	Jefferson city	Jefferson	4.5	7,338	6,918	39	40	34	2	223	82	498	5,668
55 38800	Kaukauna city	Outagamie	6.2	12,983	12,396	35	98	288	9	39	118	103	9,383
55 39225	Kenosha city	Kenosha	23.8	90,352	75,566	6,943	398	893	40	4,366	2,146	9,003	65,754
55 39300	Kewaskum village	Washington	1.5	3,274	3,207	9	6	12	-	12	28	30	2,378
55 39350	Kewaunee city	Kewaunee	3.5	2,806	2,757	10	11	6	-	4	18	16	2,151
55 39525	Kiel city	Calumet, Manitowoc	2.4	3,450	3,401	2	8	16	-	8	15	25	2,540
55 39650	Kimberly village	Outagamie	1.9	6,146	5,995	16	44	51	-	10	30	46	4,558
55 40775	La Crosse city	La Crosse	20.1	51,818	47,454	806	266	2,410	18	185	679	592	42,056
55 40850	Ladysmith city	Rusk	3.9	3,932	3,787	58	22	19	5	4	37	30	3,036
55 41450	Lake Geneva city	Walworth	5.0	7,148	6,491	64	8	77	4	369	135	1,054	5,507
55 41675	Lake Mills city	Jefferson	3.4	4,843	4,724	8	12	42	-	20	37	113	3,528
55 41975	Lake Wazeecha CDP	Wood	3.8	2,659	2,614	4	15	21	-	-	5	21	1,899
55 42012	Lake Wisconsin CDP	Columbia, Sauk	12.7	3,493	3,443	5	15	9	-	5	16	19	2,708
55 42250	Lancaster city	Grant	2.8	4,070	4,039	3	-	12	-	4	12	17	3,115
55 44950	Little Chute village	Outagamie	4.1	10,476	10,158	10	57	81	3	89	78	175	7,426
55 45350	Lodi city	Columbia	1.4	2,882	2,832	5	8	7	1	9	20	29	2,115
55 46850	McFarland village	Dane	3.5	6,416	6,237	22	25	44	2	32	54	73	4,539
55 48000	Madison city	Dane	68.7	208,054	174,689	12,155	759	12,065	77	3,474	4,835	8,512	170,793
55 48050	Manitowoc city	Manitowoc	16.9	34,053	31,713	202	188	1,283	25	306	336	859	25,839
55 49300	Marinette city	Marinette	6.8	11,749	11,447	44	76	41	1	34	106	123	8,966
55 49575	Marshall village	Dane	1.7	3,432	3,244	31	25	6	1	100	25	138	2,380
55 49675	Marshfield city	Marathon, Wood	12.7	18,800	18,259	74	44	260	1	41	121	146	14,501
55 50025	Mauston city	Juneau	3.7	3,740	3,601	25	13	44	-	18	39	79	2,835
55 50200	Mayville city	Dodge	3.1	4,902	4,821	4	10	14	-	36	17	71	3,637
55 50425	Medford city	Taylor	3.5	4,350	4,293	5	8	8	-	1	35	25	3,342
55 50825	Menasha city	Calumet, Winnebago	5.3	16,331	15,481	88	99	264	4	225	170	590	12,144
55 51000	Menomonee Falls village	Waukesha	33.3	32,647	31,504	479	53	288	7	78	238	377	24,485
55 51025	Menomonie city	Dunn	12.9	14,937	14,009	114	61	479	2	95	177	170	12,618
55 51150	Mequon city	Ozaukee	46.2	21,823	20,549	492	21	522	6	51	182	261	15,699
55 51250	Merrill city	Lincoln	7.0	10,146	9,920	20	55	43	4	37	67	104	7,583

[Includes incorporated places and census designated places (CDPs) of 2,500 or more population as of April 1, 2000. Codes shown are two-digit Federal Information Processing Standards (FIPS) state codes and five-digit FIPS place codes. Place names and codes are those in effect as of January 1, 2000. County refers to the county (or counties) in which the place is located. IC in this column = independent city, a county equivalent. If a place is located in more than one county, counties are listed in alphabetic order]

State and place code	Place	County	Land area, 2000 (sq. mi.)	Population, 2000 (April 1) By race— One race Total	White	Black or African American	American Indian and Alaska Native	Asian	Native Hawaiian and Other Pacific Islander	Some other race	Two or more races	Hispanic or Latino (of any race)	18 years and over
55 00000	WISCONSIN—Con.												
55 51575	Middleton city	Dane	8.1	15,770	14,521	311	71	419	4	201	243	444	12,186
55 52200	Milton city	Rock	3.2	5,132	5,033	9	7	16	-	25	42	47	3,717
55 53000	Milwaukee city	Milwaukee, Washington, Waukesha	96.1	596,974	298,379	222,933	5,212	17,571	301	36,428	16,150	71,646	425,990
55 53100	Mineral Point city	Iowa	3.0	2,617	2,591	5	1	6	-	4	10	11	1,976
55 53600	Mondovi city	Buffalo	3.8	2,634	2,600	5	8	7	-	14	12	2,016
55 53675	Monona city	Dane	3.4	8,018	7,513	185	27	67	3	105	118	256	6,374
55 53750	Monroe city	Green	4.3	10,843	10,596	38	37	34	-	59	79	158	8,184
55 54500	Mosinee city	Marathon	7.8	4,063	4,014	5	5	9	-	13	17	28	2,996
55 54725	Mount Horeb village	Dane	2.9	5,860	5,759	13	14	18	5	20	31	34	4,173
55 55050	Mukwonago village	Walworth, Waukesha	4.7	6,162	6,052	12	15	22	-	18	43	117	4,589
55 55275	Muskego city	Waukesha	31.2	21,397	20,992	34	46	97	5	76	147	281	15,510
55 55750	Neenah city	Winnebago	8.2	24,507	23,547	84	134	235	1	211	295	495	17,758
55 55800	Neillsville city	Clark	2.8	2,731	2,643	4	30	34	1	7	12	26	2,040
55 55875	Nekoosa city	Wood	3.4	2,590	2,505	3	33	8	-	25	16	47	1,874
55 56375	New Berlin city	Waukesha	36.8	38,220	36,631	169	82	883	6	173	276	595	28,747
55 56800	New Holstein city	Calumet	2.3	3,301	3,251	1	8	8	-	3	30	19	2,553
55 56925	New London city	Outagamie, Waupaca	5.6	7,085	6,847	14	32	36	1	91	64	174	5,280
55 57100	New Richmond city	St. Croix	5.1	6,310	6,193	14	15	22	-	8	58	49	4,650
55 58000	North Fond du Lac village	Fond du Lac	1.9	4,557	4,463	10	10	17	1	13	43	52	3,359
55 58050	North Hudson village	St. Croix	1.3	3,463	3,363	10	13	37	-	4	36	17	2,526
55 58800	Oak Creek city	Milwaukee	28.6	28,456	26,169	519	169	680	1	484	434	1,267	21,349
55 59250	Oconomowoc city	Waukesha	6.7	12,382	12,098	38	35	66	1	58	86	204	9,325
55 59350	Oconto city	Oconto	6.9	4,708	4,604	1	40	8	3	10	42	37	3,495
55 59400	Oconto Falls city	Oconto	2.7	2,843	2,792	4	14	10	-	3	20	12	2,093
55 59650	Okauchee Lake CDP	Waukesha	3.5	3,916	3,861	8	2	6	1	10	28	26	2,966
55 59875	Omro city	Winnebago	2.2	3,177	3,113	6	7	4	-	26	21	88	2,344
55 59925	Onalaska city	La Crosse	9.1	14,839	14,123	93	29	416	-	37	141	141	10,956
55 60100	Oostburg village	Sheboygan	1.9	2,660	2,636	4	2	8	-	4	6	33	1,873
55 60200	Oregon village	Dane	3.1	7,514	7,342	42	14	50	-	14	52	50	5,225
55 60500	Oshkosh city	Winnebago	23.6	62,916	58,339	1,376	326	1,908	17	334	616	1,062	49,871
55 60975	Paddock Lake village	Kenosha	2.0	3,012	2,917	12	5	21	1	28	28	135	2,111
55 61200	Park Falls city	Price	3.5	2,793	2,737	3	12	24	1	2	14	30	2,140
55 61725	Pell Lake CDP	Walworth	3.9	2,988	2,922	14	5	9	-	11	27	64	2,118
55 62175	Peshtigo city	Marinette	3.0	3,357	3,290	4	16	19	1	3	24	25	2,534
55 62240	Pewaukee city	Waukesha	21.8	11,783	11,455	41	9	126	1	52	99	153	9,065
55 62250	Pewaukee village	Waukesha	4.1	8,170	7,859	47	18	147	-	29	70	99	6,360
55 63250	Platteville city	Grant	4.2	9,989	9,604	112	27	140	4	27	75	88	8,554
55 63300	Pleasant Prairie village	Kenosha	33.5	16,136	15,181	234	63	223	4	167	264	544	11,747
55 63525	Plover village	Portage	8.5	10,520	10,185	45	44	100	4	43	99	142	7,489
55 63700	Plymouth city	Sheboygan	4.1	7,781	7,660	18	17	34	-	15	37	86	5,766
55 64100	Portage city	Columbia	8.3	9,728	9,024	379	50	69	5	83	118	330	7,464
55 64450	Port Washington city	Ozaukee	3.8	10,467	10,150	73	39	49	-	63	93	168	7,768
55 65050	Prairie du Chien city	Crawford	5.6	6,018	5,721	217	17	10	1	5	47	53	4,559
55 65100	Prairie du Sac village	Sauk	1.3	3,231	3,171	4	7	10	-	15	24	66	2,334
55 65375	Prescott city	Pierce	2.0	3,764	3,695	8	18	9	-	13	21	46	2,769
55 65675	Pulaski village	Brown, Oconto, Shawano	2.5	3,060	2,979	10	21	22	-	5	23	29	2,196
55 66000	Racine city	Racine	15.5	81,855	56,408	16,634	328	497	42	5,841	2,105	11,422	58,325
55 66800	Reedsburg city	Sauk	5.2	7,827	7,627	13	62	15	1	48	61	124	5,734
55 67200	Rhinelander city	Oneida	7.7	7,735	7,490	30	74	25	9	18	89	56	5,924
55 67320	Rib Mountain CDP	Marathon	12.1	6,059	5,820	10	14	169	-	14	32	37	4,451
55 67350	Rice Lake city	Barron	8.6	8,320	8,063	11	60	54	10	56	66	125	6,364
55 67625	Richland Center city	Richland	4.4	5,114	5,023	8	13	17	-	18	35	47	4,010
55 68175	Ripon city	Fond du Lac	4.2	6,828	6,672	13	11	34	-	59	39	151	5,239
55 68275	River Falls city	Pierce, St. Croix	5.0	12,560	12,129	66	45	128	11	40	141	119	10,310
55 69725	Rothschild village	Marathon	6.5	4,970	4,779	14	14	143	1	4	15	14	3,657
55 70650	St. Francis city	Milwaukee	2.5	8,662	8,122	84	76	91	2	130	157	392	6,987
55 71650	Sauk City village	Sauk	1.5	3,109	3,016	12	7	6	-	45	23	117	2,358
55 71700	Saukville village	Ozaukee	3.0	4,068	3,963	23	6	25	-	13	38	89	2,948
55 72725	Seymour city	Outagamie	2.5	3,335	3,190	5	82	5	2	15	36	40	2,403
55 72925	Shawano city	Shawano	6.0	8,298	7,388	27	654	45	10	46	128	134	6,303
55 72975	Sheboygan city	Sheboygan	13.9	50,792	44,507	436	242	3,290	18	1,447	852	3,034	37,769
55 73025	Sheboygan Falls city	Sheboygan	4.1	6,772	6,640	23	21	20	-	20	48	58	5,153
55 73725	Shorewood village	Milwaukee	1.6	13,763	12,584	332	32	439	5	116	255	345	10,876
55 74400	Slinger village	Washington	3.7	3,901	3,821	10	6	7	2	16	39	54	2,857
55 75125	South Milwaukee city	Milwaukee	4.8	21,256	20,153	222	123	147	9	289	313	852	16,166
55 75325	Sparta city	Monroe	5.5	8,648	8,386	60	29	54	4	49	66	157	6,407
55 75625	Spooner city	Washburn	3.0	2,653	2,546	11	54	1	-	10	31	32	2,015
55 77200	Stevens Point city	Portage	15.3	24,551	22,718	115	112	1,174	23	118	291	395	20,073
55 77675	Stoughton city	Dane	4.0	12,354	11,941	114	36	87	2	44	130	153	8,863
55 77875	Sturgeon Bay city	Door	9.6	9,437	9,175	31	74	35	2	43	77	121	7,218
55 77925	Sturtevant village	Racine	3.1	5,287	4,243	835	61	21	11	44	72	303	4,229
55 78600	Sun Prairie city	Dane	9.5	20,369	18,877	631	60	273	7	199	322	555	14,557
55 78650	Superior city	Douglas	36.9	27,368	25,797	186	611	230	10	72	462	226	21,157
55 78750	Sussex village	Waukesha	6.0	8,828	8,561	66	16	71	4	32	78	147	6,239
55 79475	Thiensville village	Ozaukee	1.1	3,254	3,142	24	2	41	-	6	39	34	2,582
55 80075	Tomah city	Monroe	7.3	8,419	7,994	87	139	56	7	39	97	119	6,249
55 80125	Tomahawk city	Lincoln	7.4	3,770	3,694	2	24	25	1	8	16	29	2,822
55 81250	Twin Lakes village	Kenosha	5.4	5,124	4,988	19	9	29	1	29	49	127	3,737

Table D-1. Places — **Area and Population**—Con.

[Includes incorporated places and census designated places (CDPs) of 2,500 or more population as of April 1, 2000. Codes shown are two-digit Federal Information Processing Standards (FIPS) state codes and five-digit FIPS place codes. Place names and codes are those in effect as of January 1, 2000. County refers to the county (or counties) in which the place is located. IC in this column = independent city, a county equivalent. If a place is located in more than one county, counties are listed in alphabetic order]

State and place code	Place	County	Land area, 2000 (sq. mi.)	Population, 2000 (April 1) Total	White	Black or African American	American Indian and Alaska Native	Asian	Native Hawaiian and Other Pacific Islander	Some other race	Two or more races	Hispanic or Latino (of any race)	18 years and over
55 00000	WISCONSIN—Con.												
55 81325	Two Rivers city	Manitowoc	5.7	12,639	12,100	20	56	281	7	69	106	170	9,408
55 81775	Union Grove village	Racine	1.7	4,322	4,201	12	9	31	-	18	51	102	3,086
55 82600	Verona city	Dane	3.3	7,052	6,873	44	12	47	-	16	60	50	4,838
55 82925	Viroqua city	Vernon	3.3	4,335	4,280	3	7	20	-	8	17	30	3,407
55 83175	Wales village	Waukesha	2.4	2,523	2,488	4	6	6	-	5	14	26	1,758
55 00025	Waterford village	Racine	2.5	4,048	3,973	11	9	8	-	17	30	76	2,900
55 83860	Waterford North CDP	Racine	11.4	4,761	4,688	17	6	10	1	8	31	66	3,399
55 83925	Waterloo city	Jefferson	3.9	3,259	3,072	17	7	10	-	124	29	240	2,370
55 83975	Watertown city	Dodge, Jefferson	10.9	21,598	20,712	55	84	131	7	366	243	1,067	15,987
55 84250	Waukesha city	Waukesha	21.6	64,825	59,133	831	216	1,407	23	2,144	1,071	5,563	48,821
55 84350	Waunakee village	Dane	6.0	8,995	8,821	32	7	46	1	22	66	86	6,108
55 84375	Waupaca city	Waupaca	6.0	5,676	5,464	19	49	14	1	79	50	194	4,236
55 84425	Waupun city	Dodge, Fond du Lac	3.7	10,718	9,224	1,266	97	28	5	55	43	304	8,581
55 84475	Wausau city	Marathon	16.5	38,426	33,010	208	228	4,383	15	117	465	398	28,670
55 84675	Wauwatosa city	Milwaukee	13.2	47,271	44,422	965	128	918	31	254	553	813	36,257
55 85300	West Allis city	Milwaukee	11.3	61,254	57,600	818	428	812	12	720	864	2,155	48,087
55 85350	West Bend city	Washington	12.7	28,152	27,391	96	119	148	2	173	223	519	20,974
55 85875	West Milwaukee village	Milwaukee	1.1	4,201	3,511	147	65	107	3	246	122	504	3,326
55 86025	Weston village	Marathon	21.3	12,079	11,247	36	48	590	2	39	117	84	8,645
55 86275	West Salem village	La Crosse	2.4	4,540	4,451	23	19	20	-	3	24	27	3,177
55 86700	Whitefish Bay village	Milwaukee	2.1	14,163	13,467	139	10	366	8	37	136	221	9,996
55 86925	Whitewater city	Jefferson, Walworth	7.0	13,437	12,395	315	36	197	2	333	159	873	11,781
55 87675	Wind Lake CDP	Racine	5.3	5,202	5,106	16	18	13	3	16	30	88	3,670
55 87725	Windsor CDP	Dane	3.2	2,533	2,435	13	9	30	-	15	31	37	1,848
55 88200	Wisconsin Rapids city	Wood	13.3	18,435	17,337	63	148	638	3	68	178	242	13,876
56 00000	WYOMING		97,100.4	493,782	454,670	3,722	11,133	2,771	302	12,301	8,883	31,669	364,909
56 10005	Duffalo city	Johnson	3.5	3,900	3,762	4	32	2	-	21	79	71	2,998
56 13150	Casper city	Natrona	23.9	49,644	46,680	428	495	245	10	1,011	775	2,656	36,802
56 13900	Cheyenne city	Laramie	21.1	53,011	46,707	1,472	430	561	59	2,356	1,426	6,646	39,798
56 15760	Cody city	Park	9.3	8,835	8,561	9	37	51	4	75	98	196	6,642
56 21125	Douglas city	Converse	5.1	5,288	4,977	3	41	7	1	192	67	351	3,782
56 25620	Evanston city	Uinta	10.2	11,507	10,620	18	122	46	9	477	215	839	7,667
56 29300	Fox Farm-College CDP	Laramie	3.4	3,272	2,897	44	51	9	3	161	107	413	2,373
56 31855	Gillette city	Campbell	13.4	19,646	18,762	39	188	82	20	258	297	774	13,716
56 33740	Green River city	Sweetwater	13.7	11,808	10,879	32	160	38	7	500	192	1,206	8,140
56 40120	Jackson town	Teton	2.8	8,647	7,728	18	67	54	3	659	118	1,024	7,052
56 42005	Kemmerer city	Lincoln	7.4	2,651	2,564	3	13	16	1	31	23	89	1,899
56 44760	Lander city	Fremont	4.4	6,867	6,236	10	411	22	-	48	140	239	5,210
56 45050	Laramie city	Albany	11.1	27,204	24,704	337	241	522	16	787	597	2,161	22,434
56 53400	Mills town	Natrona	1.7	2,591	2,435	12	39	6	1	50	48	102	2,009
56 56215	Newcastle city	Weston	2.5	3,065	2,936	4	44	9	-	31	41	51	2,319
56 62450	Powell city	Park	3.7	5,373	5,128	7	25	21	2	136	54	366	4,243
56 63800	Ranchettes CDP	Laramie	51.4	4,869	4,624	43	42	45	1	68	46	233	3,639
56 63900	Rawlins city	Carbon	7.4	8,538	7,331	69	125	72	8	707	226	1,797	6,317
56 66220	Riverton city	Fremont	9.8	9,310	8,082	16	752	44	3	173	240	660	7,056
56 67235	Rock Springs city	Sweetwater	18.4	18,708	17,164	201	160	191	6	570	416	1,676	13,632
56 69845	Sheridan city	Sheridan	8.5	15,804	15,161	34	154	73	31	134	217	417	12,159
56 71800	South Greeley CDP	Laramie	1.7	4,201	3,565	97	63	14	-	302	160	626	2,851
56 76515	Thermopolis town	Hot Springs	2.4	3,172	3,042	15	54	8	-	16	37	73	2,459
56 77530	Torrington city	Goshen	3.6	5,776	5,400	18	52	17	6	211	72	547	4,428
56 81640	Warren AFB CDP	Laramie	5.0	4,440	3,535	417	22	98	15	195	158	389	3,418
56 83040	Wheatland town	Platte	4.2	3,548	3,406	11	24	12	-	67	28	232	2,739
56 84925	Worland city	Washakie	4.1	5,250	4,697	3	30	44	-	353	123	708	3,875

Source: U.S. Census Bureau, 2000 Census of Population and Housing, *Race and Hispanic or Latino Summary File on CD-ROM*, PL/00-3, issued April 2001 (related Internet site <http://www.census.gov/clo/www/redistricting.html>).

[Includes functioning minor civil divisions [MCDs] of 2,500 or more population as of April 1, 2000 in the following 12 states: CT, ME, MA, MI, MN, NH, NJ, NY, PA, RI, VT, and WI. Codes shown are two-digit Federal Information Processing Standards (FIPS) state codes and five-digit FIPS place codes. Place names and codes are those in effect as of January 1, 2000. County refers to the county in which the MCD is located]

State and place code	MCD	County	Land area, 2000 (sq. mi.)	Population, 2000 (April 1)								Hispanic or Latino (of any race)	18 years and over
					By race—								
					One race						Two or more races		
				Total	White	Black or African American	American Indian and Alaska Native	Asian	Native Hawaiian and Other Pacific Islander	Some other race			
09 00000	CONNECTICUT		4,844.8	3,405,565	2,780,355	309,843	9,639	82,313	1,366	147,201	74,848	320,323	2,563,877
09 01080	Andover town	Tolland	15.5	3,036	2,934	28	10	14	-	21	29	47	2,208
09 01220	Ansonia town	New Haven	6.0	18,554	15,867	1,562	63	209	3	411	439	1,376	14,065
09 01430	Ashford town	Windham	38.8	4,098	3,922	41	11	42	-	18	64	82	3,047
09 02060	Avon town	Hartford	23.1	15,832	15,030	155	8	469	3	45	122	249	11,695
09 02760	Barkhamsted town	Litchfield	36.2	3,494	3,443	2	6	14	-	10	19	31	2,621
09 03250	Beacon Falls town	New Haven	9.8	5,246	5,087	38	4	54	2	21	40	112	3,922
09 04300	Berlin town	Hartford	26.5	18,215	17,674	65	9	300	2	32	133	267	13,719
09 04580	Bethany town	New Haven	21.0	5,040	4,790	92	15	77	5	24	37	102	3,664
09 04720	Bethel town	Fairfield	16.8	18,067	16,692	228	28	641	7	197	274	669	13,142
09 04930	Bethlehem town	Litchfield	19.4	3,422	3,336	9	2	27	1	13	34	22	2,559
09 05910	Bloomfield town	Hartford	26.0	19,587	7,834	10,589	41	252	3	314	554	718	15,389
09 06260	Bolton town	Tolland	14.4	5,017	4,903	33	3	24	2	15	37	83	3,713
09 07310	Branford town	New Haven	22.0	28,683	26,976	386	28	781	18	151	343	737	22,755
09 08070	Bridgeport town	Fairfield	16.0	139,529	62,822	42,925	664	4,536	148	20,659	7,775	44,478	99,857
09 08490	Bristol town	Hartford	26.5	60,062	55,014	1,612	132	884	18	1,443	959	3,166	46,140
09 08980	Brookfield town	Fairfield	19.8	15,664	14,926	119	11	388	-	96	124	372	11,376
09 09190	Brooklyn town	Windham	29.0	7,173	6,686	263	46	37	1	60	80	186	5,474
09 10100	Burlington town	Hartford	29.8	8,190	7,980	48	4	60	5	19	74	110	5,877
09 12130	Canterbury town	Windham	39.9	4,692	4,567	17	13	12	1	14	68	50	3,485
09 12270	Canton town	Hartford	24.6	8,840	8,588	47	4	64	2	43	92	113	6,592
09 14160	Cheshire town	New Haven	32.9	28,543	25,518	1,332	62	751	6	545	329	1,097	21,341
09 14300	Chester town	Middlesex	16.0	3,743	3,623	32	13	31	2	9	33	64	2,910
09 15350	Clinton town	Middlesex	16.3	13,094	12,550	74	38	148	3	134	147	523	9,809
09 15910	Colchester town	New London . . .	49.1	14,551	13,900	200	61	87	2	109	192	280	10,209
09 16400	Columbia town	Tolland	21.4	4,971	4,843	19	4	35	3	28	39	84	3,670
09 17800	Coventry town	Tolland	37.7	11,504	11,153	66	29	70	1	46	139	198	8,390
09 18080	Cromwell town	Middlesex	12.4	12,871	11,980	403	7	159	1	132	189	410	10,094
09 18500	Danbury town	Fairfield	42.1	74,848	56,853	5,060	214	4,082	26	5,653	2,960	11,791	58,621
09 18850	Darien town	Fairfield	12.9	19,607	18,816	89	8	474	5	58	157	429	13,243
09 19130	Deep River town	Middlesex	13.6	4,610	4,359	111	2	37	3	48	50	136	3,491
09 19550	Derby town	New Haven	5.0	12,391	11,162	449	20	215	8	312	225	950	9,704
09 20810	Durham town	Middlesex	23.6	6,627	6,407	76	12	56	-	20	56	102	4,706
09 22070	East Granby town	Hartford	17.5	4,745	4,536	65	6	50	-	31	57	72	3,505
09 22280	East Haddam town	Middlesex	54.3	8,333	8,105	70	23	33	-	38	64	82	6,210
09 22490	East Hampton town	Middlesex	35.6	13,352	12,466	273	26	319	7	59	202	226	10,497
09 22630	East Hartford town	Hartford	18.0	49,575	32,071	9,335	167	1,989	18	4,333	1,662	7,552	37,630
09 22910	East Haven town	New Haven	12.3	28,189	26,475	396	40	539	4	428	307	1,228	21,934
09 23400	East Lyme town	New London . . .	34.0	18,118	15,815	1,154	79	511	8	220	331	832	14,149
09 23890	Easton town	Fairfield	27.4	7,272	7,035	16	3	147	1	30	40	128	5,190
09 24800	East Windsor town	Hartford	26.3	9,818	8,981	402	16	196	4	81	138	207	7,642
09 25360	Ellington town	Tolland	34.1	12,921	12,434	128	21	167	1	57	113	181	9,664
09 25990	Enfield town	Hartford	33.4	45,212	40,573	2,536	89	604	7	708	695	1,691	34,978
09 26270	Essex town	Middlesex	10.4	6,505	6,357	34	6	36	1	23	48	93	5,081
09 26620	Fairfield town	Fairfield	30.0	57,340	54,630	623	32	1,171	16	313	555	1,340	43,731
09 27600	Farmington town	Hartford	28.1	23,641	21,964	366	28	880	1	140	262	517	17,879
09 31240	Glastonbury town	Hartford	51.4	31,876	29,678	489	47	1,084	2	291	285	799	23,345
09 32290	Goshen town	Litchfield	43.7	2,697	2,650	13	4	20	-	-	10	33	2,084
09 32640	Granby town	Hartford	40.7	10,347	10,092	63	24	77	2	24	65	134	7,521
09 33620	Greenwich town	Fairfield	47.8	61,101	55,001	1,017	52	3,165	16	892	958	3,846	45,557
09 33900	Griswold town	New London . . .	34.9	10,807	10,189	151	116	94	5	71	181	210	8,034
09 34250	Groton town	New London . . .	31.3	39,907	33,368	2,774	330	1,330	66	662	1,377	2,001	29,993
09 34950	Guilford town	New Haven	47.1	21,398	20,550	200	10	352	-	88	198	455	15,960
09 35230	Haddam town	Middlesex	44.0	7,157	6,932	74	8	59	2	12	70	76	5,391
09 35650	Hamden town	New Haven	32.8	56,913	43,996	8,840	75	2,007	18	915	1,062	2,425	45,080
09 37070	Hartford town	Hartford	17.3	121,578	33,705	46,264	659	1,971	135	32,230	6,614	49,260	85,010
09 37280	Harwinton town	Litchfield	30.7	5,283	5,214	4	3	27	3	7	25	47	3,959
09 37910	Hebron town	Tolland	36.9	8,610	8,411	50	11	48	3	17	70	92	6,027
09 40290	Kent town	Litchfield	48.5	2,858	2,737	16	22	28	1	20	34	72	2,205
09 40500	Killingly town	Windham	48.5	16,472	15,439	230	84	262	-	127	330	370	12,244
09 40710	Killingworth town	Middlesex	35.3	6,018	5,870	25	4	50	-	15	54	71	4,386
09 42390	Lebanon town	New London . . .	54.1	6,907	6,692	56	27	18	4	34	76	114	4,973
09 42600	Ledyard town	New London . . .	38.1	14,687	12,959	367	515	321	10	124	391	401	10,532
09 43230	Lisbon town	New London . . .	16.3	4,069	3,935	13	17	19	-	15	70	23	3,010
09 43370	Litchfield town	Litchfield	56.1	8,316	8,066	62	19	39	1	38	91	130	6,220
09 44560	Madison town	New Haven	36.2	17,858	17,255	72	11	306	1	45	168	240	12,816
09 44700	Manchester town	Hartford	27.3	54,740	45,307	4,610	107	1,726	18	1,706	1,266	3,579	42,285
09 44910	Mansfield town	Tolland	44.5	20,720	17,387	1,010	41	1,482	10	389	401	893	17,967
09 45820	Marlborough town	Hartford	23.3	5,709	5,567	44	4	40	-	15	39	60	4,147
09 46520	Meriden town	New Haven	23.7	58,244	46,734	3,754	229	796	11	5,036	1,684	12,296	43,278
09 46940	Middlebury town	New Haven	17.8	6,451	6,265	23	4	84	2	17	56	79	4,869
09 47080	Middlefield town	Middlesex	12.7	4,203	4,109	31	1	15	1	18	28	56	3,166
09 47360	Middletown town	Middlesex	40.9	43,167	34,540	5,291	99	1,155	21	857	1,204	2,287	33,803
09 47535	Milford town	New Haven	22.6	52,305	48,967	989	69	1,217	17	460	586	1,750	40,627
09 48620	Monroe town	Fairfield	26.1	19,247	18,453	231	15	292	-	96	160	482	13,654
09 48900	Montville town	New London . . .	42.0	18,546	15,956	1,019	270	350	7	414	530	1,010	14,160
09 49950	Naugatuck town	New Haven	16.4	30,989	28,435	882	82	522	5	491	572	1,386	22,664
09 50440	New Britain town	Hartford	13.3	71,538	49,634	7,794	264	1,687	43	9,388	2,728	19,138	54,249

[Includes functioning minor civil divisions (MCDs) of 2,500 or more population as of April 1, 2000 in the following 12 states: CT, ME, MA, MI, MN, NH, NJ, NY, PA, RI, VT, and WI. Codes shown are two-digit Federal Information Processing Standards (FIPS) state codes and five-digit FIPS place codes. Place names and codes are those in effect as of January 1, 2000. County refers to the county in which the MCD is located]

State and place code	MCD	County	Land area, 2000 (sq. mi.)	Population, 2000 (April 1)									
					By race—							Hispanic or Latino (of any race)	18 years and over
					One race						Two or more races		
				Total	White	Black or African American	American Indian and Alaska Native	Asian	Native Hawaiian and Other Pacific Islander	Some other race			
09 00000	CONNECTICUT—Con.												
09 50580	New Canaan town	Fairfield	22.1	19,395	18,477	201	8	445	1	73	190	338	13,345
09 50860	New Fairfield town	Fairfield	20.5	13,953	13,511	54	5	177	1	72	133	393	9,762
09 51350	New Hartford town	Litchfield	37.0	6,088	5,946	39	3	45	4	12	39	82	4,449
09 52070	New Haven town	New Haven	18.9	123,626	53,723	46,181	535	4,819	79	13,460	4,829	26,443	92,180
09 52140	Newington town	Hartford	13.2	29,306	27,103	609	35	824	14	351	370	1,079	23,259
09 52350	New London town	New London	5.5	25,671	16,299	4,784	225	544	21	2,343	1,455	5,061	19,814
09 52630	New Milford town	Litchfield	61.6	27,121	25,583	383	40	518	7	184	406	751	19,685
09 52980	Newtown town	Fairfield	57.8	25,031	23,815	437	35	351	9	160	224	590	17,699
09 53890	North Branford town	New Haven	24.9	13,906	13,419	165	9	128	3	65	117	250	10,346
09 54030	North Canaan town	Litchfield	19.5	3,350	3,247	40	6	6	-	13	38	79	2,570
09 54870	North Haven town	New Haven	20.8	23,035	21,418	512	20	775	3	119	188	433	17,833
09 55500	North Stonington town	New London	54.3	4,991	4,707	30	103	53	-	11	87	72	3,736
09 56060	Norwalk town	Fairfield	22.8	82,951	61,339	12,663	174	2,699	40	3,591	2,445	12,966	64,641
09 56270	Norwich town	New London	28.3	36,117	30,029	2,469	437	758	10	998	1,416	2,208	27,412
09 57040	Old Lyme town	New London	23.1	7,406	7,211	19	21	86	1	24	44	70	5,627
09 57320	Old Saybrook town	Middlesex	15.0	10,367	9,926	105	8	178	7	47	96	194	8,117
09 57600	Orange town	New Haven	17.2	13,233	12,450	104	11	508	1	43	116	190	9,979
09 58300	Oxford town	New Haven	32.9	9,821	9,594	50	17	65	4	34	57	180	7,158
09 59980	Plainfield town	Windham	42.3	14,619	14,056	114	78	87	4	92	188	384	10,682
09 60120	Plainville town	Hartford	9.8	17,328	16,205	390	29	289	2	206	207	618	13,646
09 60750	Plymouth town	Litchfield	21.7	11,634	11,325	91	18	49	2	37	113	147	8,636
09 61030	Pomfret town	Windham	40.3	3,798	3,693	15	6	28	-	14	42	61	2,785
09 61800	Portland town	Middlesex	23.4	8,732	8,306	213	14	45	3	40	111	171	6,507
09 62150	Preston town	New London	30.9	4,688	4,483	35	39	54	1	24	52	65	3,639
09 62290	Prospect town	New Haven	14.3	8,707	8,386	124	8	63	-	63	63	168	6,535
09 62710	Putnam town	Windham	20.3	9,002	8,581	117	70	34	4	43	153	168	6,879
09 63480	Redding town	Fairfield	31.5	8,270	7,952	62	6	147	-	34	69	122	5,865
09 63970	Ridgefield town	Fairfield	34.4	23,643	22,726	146	22	492	6	85	166	465	16,411
09 65370	Rocky Hill town	Hartford	13.5	17,966	16,205	615	19	713	5	181	228	575	14,432
09 66210	Salem town	New London	29.0	3,858	3,684	32	23	57	-	11	51	47	2,722
09 66420	Salisbury town	Litchfield	57.3	3,977	3,808	66	13	38	-	18	34	61	3,085
09 67610	Seymour town	New Haven	14.6	15,454	14,642	209	32	273	3	161	134	470	11,767
09 67960	Sharon town	Litchfield	58.7	2,968	2,875	28	13	17	-	10	25	58	2,335
09 68170	Shelton town	Fairfield	30.6	38,101	35,984	428	57	791	1	341	499	1,326	29,129
09 68310	Sherman town	Fairfield	21.8	3,827	3,726	21	1	26	3	24	26	66	2,806
09 68940	Simsbury town	Hartford	33.9	23,234	22,142	271	20	493	7	61	240	358	16,376
09 69220	Somers town	Tolland	28.3	10,417	8,643	1,023	57	65	6	417	206	844	8,248
09 69640	Southbury town	New Haven	39.1	18,567	18,073	84	14	214	1	65	116	296	14,339
09 70550	Southington town	Hartford	36.0	39,728	38,317	341	35	414	3	228	390	801	30,258
09 71390	South Windsor town	Hartford	28.0	24,412	22,336	721	45	905	8	162	235	554	17,735
09 71670	Sprague town	New London	13.2	2,971	2,835	21	19	40	2	11	43	33	2,199
09 72090	Stafford town	Tolland	58.0	11,307	10,956	72	29	103	-	57	90	187	8,422
09 73070	Stamford town	Fairfield	37.7	117,083	81,718	18,019	243	5,856	46	7,608	3,593	19,635	91,187
09 73420	Sterling town	Windham	27.2	3,099	2,981	5	22	10	1	5	75	41	2,227
09 73770	Stonington town	New London	38.7	17,906	17,156	112	67	225	9	82	255	233	14,022
09 74190	Stratford town	Fairfield	17.6	49,976	42,361	4,892	82	700	17	1,071	853	3,399	38,470
09 74540	Suffield town	Hartford	42.2	13,552	12,016	942	33	127	6	275	153	576	10,561
09 75730	Thomaston town	Litchfield	12.0	7,503	7,342	45	8	37	-	31	40	109	5,604
09 75870	Thompson town	Windham	46.9	8,878	8,702	37	22	31	2	21	63	67	6,658
09 76290	Tolland town	Tolland	39.7	13,146	12,720	101	10	156	2	51	106	151	9,421
09 76570	Torrington town	Litchfield	39.8	35,202	32,749	757	70	643	7	460	516	1,162	27,091
09 77200	Trumbull town	Fairfield	23.3	34,243	32,194	645	38	815	6	242	303	923	25,330
09 78250	Vernon town	Tolland	17.7	28,063	25,243	1,120	68	745	10	342	535	1,005	21,858
09 78600	Voluntown town	New London	38.9	2,528	2,443	14	25	7	-	10	29	30	1,857
09 78740	Wallingford town	New Haven	39.0	43,026	40,774	441	71	753	-	497	490	1,946	32,700
09 79720	Washington town	Litchfield	38.2	3,596	3,440	23	4	56	-	28	45	77	2,720
09 80070	Waterbury town	New Haven	28.6	107,271	72,018	17,500	453	1,615	61	11,698	3,926	23,354	78,817
09 80280	Waterford town	New London	32.8	19,152	17,699	426	91	481	3	142	310	459	14,967
09 80490	Watertown town	Litchfield	29.2	21,661	20,894	162	27	276	10	103	189	406	16,292
09 81680	Westbrook town	Middlesex	15.7	6,292	6,025	44	8	98	7	45	65	158	4,923
09 82590	West Hartford town	Hartford	22.0	63,589	54,658	3,041	77	3,053	47	1,659	1,054	3,990	49,544
09 82870	West Haven town	New Haven	10.8	52,360	38,824	8,530	128	1,525	27	1,867	1,459	4,757	40,252
09 83430	Weston town	Fairfield	19.8	10,037	9,610	88	11	195	10	25	98	206	6,708
09 83500	Westport town	Fairfield	20.0	25,749	24,503	292	12	625	5	103	209	602	18,559
09 84900	Wethersfield town	Hartford	12.4	26,271	24,481	549	21	416	6	477	321	1,101	20,999
09 85950	Willington town	Tolland	33.3	5,959	5,605	58	7	180	5	37	67	108	4,712
09 86370	Wilton town	Fairfield	26.9	17,633	16,848	106	15	474	2	48	140	269	12,070
09 86440	Winchester town	Litchfield	32.3	10,664	10,071	132	25	99	2	180	156	338	8,180
09 86790	Windham town	Windham	27.1	22,857	16,919	1,156	128	297	28	3,465	864	6,136	17,594
09 87000	Windsor town	Hartford	29.6	28,237	18,387	7,648	45	887	8	590	672	1,405	21,282
09 87070	Windsor Locks town	Hartford	9.0	12,043	11,136	322	15	309	-	90	171	267	9,194
09 87560	Wolcott town	New Haven	20.4	15,215	14,641	189	21	114	6	90	154	273	11,257
09 87700	Woodbridge town	New Haven	18.8	8,983	8,205	135	4	458	2	54	125	138	6,487
09 87910	Woodbury town	Litchfield	36.5	9,198	8,945	49	20	106	6	20	52	152	6,988
09 88190	Woodstock town	Windham	60.5	7,221	7,031	12	21	31	1	32	93	59	5,321

[Includes functioning minor civil divisions (MCDs) of 2,500 or more population as of April 1, 2000 in the following 12 states: CT, ME, MA, MI, MN, NH, NJ, NY, PA, RI, VT, and WI. Codes shown are two-digit Federal Information Processing Standards (FIPS) state codes and five-digit FIPS place codes. Place names and codes are those in effect as of January 1, 2000. County refers to the county in which the MCD is located]

State and place code	MCD	County	Land area, 2000 (sq. mi.)	Population, 2000 (April 1)									
					By race—								
					One race								
				Total	White	Black or African American	American Indian and Alaska Native	Asian	Native Hawaiian and Other Pacific Islander	Some other race	Two or more races	Hispanic or Latino (of any race)	18 years and over
23 00000	MAINE		30,861.6	1,274,923	1,236,014	6,760	7,098	9,111	382	2,911	12,647	9,360	973,685
23 01395	Anson town	Somerset	47.5	2,583	2,540	2	13	1	-	-	27	8	1,930
23 01605	Arundel town	York	23.9	3,571	3,509	5	16	14	2	5	20	18	2,638
23 02865	Bar Harbor town	Hancock	42.2	4,820	4,718	7	10	43	-	4	38	30	3,867
23 04020	Belgrade town	Kennebec	43.3	2,978	2,939	3	3	6	4	1	22	14	2,224
23 04475	Benton town	Kennebec	28.4	2,557	2,523	5	6	3	-	5	15	12	1,922
23 04720	Berwick town	York	37.1	6,353	6,182	23	9	74	2	4	59	34	4,503
23 06050	Boothbay town	Lincoln	22.1	2,960	2,932	1	10	4	-	3	10	15	2,335
23 06260	Bowdoin town	Sagadahoc	43.5	2,727	2,667	7	3	7	2	9	32	21	1,944
23 06365	Bowdoinham town	Sagadahoc	34.4	2,612	2,552	10	11	13	1	-	25	13	1,937
23 07170	Bridgton town	Cumberland	57.3	4,883	4,754	23	13	13	-	11	69	40	3,804
23 07485	Bristol town	Lincoln	35.5	2,644	2,619	3	1	13	-	1	7	6	2,147
23 08430	Brunswick town	Cumberland	46.8	21,172	19,976	362	48	353	12	134	287	344	16,301
23 08815	Bucksport town	Hancock	51.6	4,908	4,813	4	15	8	3	7	58	43	3,679
23 09410	Buxton town	York	40.5	7,452	7,290	31	18	44	9	14	46	41	5,580
23 09725	Camden town	Knox	18.3	5,254	5,166	13	7	21	-	8	39	45	4,221
23 10180	Cape Elizabeth town	Cumberland	14.7	9,068	8,884	29	5	90	5	11	44	45	6,666
23 11125	Casco town	Cumberland	31.3	3,469	3,398	10	13	18	-	4	26	18	2,596
23 12350	Chelsea town	Kennebec	19.5	2,559	2,482	7	25	20	-	2	23	12	1,940
23 12735	China town	Kennebec	49.8	4,106	4,023	6	19	16	1	2	39	26	2,970
23 13470	Clinton town	Kennebec	43.9	3,340	3,276	4	7	2	-	6	45	32	2,452
23 14380	Corinth town	Penobscot	40.2	2,511	2,465	2	16	2	-	12	14	19	1,868
23 15430	Cumberland town	Cumberland	26.1	7,159	7,070	10	7	30	1	9	32	47	4,984
23 17530	Dexter town	Penobscot	35.2	3,890	3,834	12	9	4	1	1	29	25	2,970
23 17740	Dixfield town	Oxford	41.2	2,514	2,471	-	5	13	-	6	19	20	1,842
23 18195	Dover-Foxcroft town	Piscataquis	68.2	4,211	4,081	9	22	22	1	8	68	40	3,162
23 19105	Durham town	Androscoggin	38.1	3,381	3,346	4	5	9	-	3	14	22	2,472
23 22955	Eliot town	York	19.7	5,954	5,861	13	7	21	-	6	46	29	4,416
23 24320	Fairfield town	Somerset	53.8	6,573	6,436	23	22	18	3	3	68	20	4,812
23 24195	Falmouth town	Cumberland	29.0	10,310	10,078	25	12	119	-	18	58	50	7,499
23 24670	Farmingdale town	Kennebec	11.2	2,804	2,733	20	11	14	-	3	23	15	2,125
23 24775	Farmington town	Franklin	55.8	7,410	7,223	15	22	48	2	30	70	61	6,047
23 25615	Fort Fairfield town	Aroostook	76.6	3,579	3,520	7	16	1	1	7	27	27	2,740
23 25755	Fort Kent town	Aroostook	54.2	4,233	4,104	16	32	37	-	12	32	21	3,290
23 26525	Freeport town	Cumberland	34.7	7,800	7,583	33	24	81	3	26	50	58	5,836
23 26910	Fryeburg town	Oxford	58.3	3,083	3,026	10	4	7	-	5	26	36	2,360
23 27645	Glenburn town	Penobscot	27.2	3,964	3,885	11	17	9	-	4	38	13	2,897
23 28240	Gorham town	Cumberland	50.6	14,141	13,797	60	46	90	1	24	123	85	10,479
23 28870	Gray town	Cumberland	43.3	6,820	6,676	29	10	26	5	15	59	40	5,144
23 29255	Greene town	Androscoggin	32.4	4,076	4,014	19	4	12	-	3	24	29	2,992
23 30795	Hampden town	Penobscot	38.1	6,327	6,195	25	22	40	-	11	34	32	4,615
23 31390	Harpswell town	Cumberland	24.2	5,239	5,131	13	18	29	-	12	36	69	4,214
23 32510	Hermon town	Penobscot	35.9	4,437	4,352	7	13	19	1	4	41	23	3,234
23 33490	Holden town	Penobscot	30.9	2,827	2,774	5	15	10	4	11	8	7	2,149
23 33665	Hollis town	York	32.0	4,114	4,065	6	5	6	4	3	25	22	3,012
23 33980	Houlton town	Aroostook	36.7	6,476	6,100	19	274	31	5	6	41	28	4,940
23 35625	Jay town	Franklin	48.5	4,985	4,881	13	23	11	3	5	49	24	3,680
23 36535	Kennebunk town	York	35.1	10,476	10,271	19	12	89	1	19	65	53	7,793
23 36745	Kennebunkport town	York	20.6	3,720	3,664	8	6	18	3	3	18	23	2,958
23 37270	Kittery town	York	17.8	9,543	9,159	170	17	62	2	43	90	143	7,453
23 38425	Lebanon town	York	54.7	5,083	5,006	16	14	13	-	4	30	32	3,627
23 39405	Limington town	York	42.0	3,403	3,346	14	16	6	2	4	15	10	2,471
23 39475	Lincoln town	Penobscot	67.9	5,221	5,135	5	19	21	-	4	37	19	3,953
23 40035	Lisbon town	Androscoggin	23.6	9,077	8,842	59	20	35	9	28	84	67	6,673
23 40175	Litchfield town	Kennebec	37.4	3,110	3,059	2	8	13	-	5	23	25	2,292
23 40770	Livermore Falls town	Androscoggin	19.7	3,227	3,139	16	20	7	-	1	44	33	2,331
23 41750	Lyman town	York	38.9	3,795	3,736	11	10	9	-	4	25	12	2,790
23 42520	Madawaska town	Aroostook	55.7	4,534	4,447	7	20	31	-	4	25	9	3,611
23 42660	Madison town	Somerset	51.8	4,523	4,438	3	13	7	1	3	58	10	3,519
23 44585	Mechanic Falls town	Androscoggin	11.1	3,138	3,052	16	20	19	1	2	28	16	2,288
23 45285	Mexico town	Oxford	23.4	2,959	2,895	7	-	26	-	-	31	8	2,249
23 45670	Milford town	Penobscot	45.6	2,950	2,847	3	39	14	1	12	34	16	2,252
23 45810	Millinocket town	Penobscot	15.9	5,203	5,126	5	28	19	-	1	24	12	4,107
23 46405	Monmouth town	Kennebec	34.1	3,785	3,728	12	16	6	-	1	22	26	2,739
23 48085	Naples town	Cumberland	31.8	3,274	3,215	5	10	10	-	7	27	7	2,467
23 48820	New Gloucester town	Cumberland	47.1	4,803	4,715	11	3	19	5	6	44	27	3,420
23 49065	Newport town	Penobscot	29.5	3,017	2,965	5	11	12	1	1	22	13	2,282
23 49835	Norridgewock town	Somerset	49.8	3,294	3,240	10	15	4	-	6	19	12	2,427
23 50325	North Berwick town	York	38.3	4,293	4,168	28	10	33	2	3	49	26	3,142
23 53860	North Yarmouth town	Cumberland	21.1	3,210	3,167	3	3	19	-	4	14	15	2,241
23 54000	Norway town	Oxford	45.1	4,611	4,511	14	17	17	1	6	45	23	3,574
23 54560	Oakland town	Kennebec	25.7	5,959	5,856	9	14	33	-	5	42	31	4,358
23 55085	Old Orchard Beach town	York	7.4	8,856	8,638	50	25	41	3	20	79	90	7,163
23 55565	Orono town	Penobscot	18.2	9,112	8,523	126	87	218	6	47	105	110	8,028
23 55680	Orrington town	Penobscot	25.4	3,526	3,494	7	4	8	-	1	12	5	2,695
23 56310	Oxford town	Oxford	38.7	3,960	3,876	10	10	11	1	9	43	25	2,912
23 56625	Paris town	Oxford	40.8	4,793	4,692	15	7	44	1	9	25	17	3,753
23 59005	Pittsfield town	Somerset	48.2	4,214	4,057	37	17	46	5	4	48	27	3,038

[Includes functioning minor civil divisions (MCDs) of 2,500 or more population as of April 1, 2000 in the following 12 states: CT, ME, MA, MI, MN, NH, NJ, NY, PA, RI, VT, and WI. Codes shown are two-digit Federal Information Processing Standards (FIPS) state codes and five-digit FIPS place codes. Place names and codes are those in effect as of January 1, 2000. County refers to the county in which the MCD is located]

State and place code	MCD	County	Land area, 2000 (sq. mi.)	Population, 2000 (April 1) Total	By race— One race White	Black or African American	American Indian and Alaska Native	Asian	Native Hawaiian and Other Pacific Islander	Some other race	Two or more races	Hispanic or Latino (of any race)	18 years and over
23 00000	MAINE—Con.												
23 59110	Pittston town	Kennebec	32.2	2,548	2,490	5	19	2	-	6	26	16	1,929
23 60020	Poland town	Androscoggin	42.3	4,866	4,795	16	6	7	4	1	37	15	3,635
23 61945	Raymond town	Cumberland	33.2	4,299	4,230	17	13	11	1	3	24	26	3,165
23 62645	Richmond town	Sagadahoc	30.4	3,298	3,238	14	6	8	2	12	18	28	2,396
23 63660	Rockport town	Knox	21.7	3,209	3,167	5	2	14	-	6	15	24	2,455
23 64290	Rumford town	Oxford	68.6	6,472	6,386	7	21	17	-	4	37	39	4,977
23 64570	Sabattus town	Androscoggin	25.6	4,486	4,409	5	13	10	-	5	44	26	3,318
23 65130	St. George town	Knox	25.6	2,580	2,546	4	6	9	-	1	14	6	2,011
23 65760	Sanford town	York	47.8	20,806	19,907	91	65	431	4	56	252	199	15,258
23 66145	Scarborough town	Cumberland	47.7	16,970	16,518	64	30	197	2	29	130	82	12,571
23 66635	Searsport town	Waldo	28.6	2,641	2,590	7	19	-	-	2	23	5	2,026
23 68385	Sidney town	Kennebec	42.2	3,514	3,471	2	6	10	2	4	19	15	2,564
23 68910	Skowhegan town	Somerset	59.0	8,824	8,609	22	38	48	1	11	95	64	6,753
23 70030	South Berwick town	York	32.1	6,671	6,513	20	20	44	-	18	56	45	4,643
23 73670	Standish town	Cumberland	59.1	9,285	9,107	36	15	22	7	21	77	43	6,939
23 76365	Thomaston town	Knox	10.9	3,748	3,666	23	8	18	1	2	30	16	2,981
23 76960	Topsham town	Sagadahoc	32.0	9,100	8,662	121	21	121	5	40	130	113	6,574
23 77800	Turner town	Androscoggin	59.6	4,972	4,812	5	9	14	2	90	40	138	3,514
23 78570	Van Buren town	Aroostook	33.9	2,631	2,594	3	8	4	-	1	21	19	2,111
23 78745	Vassalboro town	Kennebec	44.3	4,047	3,991	6	9	2	-	7	32	23	2,948
23 79550	Waldoboro town	Lincoln	71.2	4,916	4,848	11	7	21	4	2	23	13	3,670
23 80215	Warren town	Knox	46.4	3,794	3,701	11	29	15	1	2	35	28	2,829
23 80530	Waterboro town	York	55.5	6,214	6,131	7	20	13	-	9	34	42	4,303
23 81475	Wells town	York	57.6	9,400	9,229	22	19	45	1	13	71	60	7,428
23 82945	West Gardiner town	Kennebec	24.6	2,902	2,837	15	8	8	-	10	24	13	2,177
23 85850	Wilton town	Franklin	41.3	4,123	4,018	18	16	33	-	4	34	18	3,048
23 86025	Windham town	Cumberland	46.7	14,904	14,540	73	62	56	2	18	153	66	11,282
23 86515	Winslow town	Kennebec	36.9	7,743	7,592	10	21	27	1	17	75	60	5,875
23 86760	Winterport town	Waldo	35.6	3,602	3,534	7	18	8	2	4	29	14	2,654
23 86970	Winthrop town	Kennebec	31.2	6,232	6,134	20	20	25	2	4	27	33	4,821
23 87075	Wiscasset town	Lincoln	24.6	3,603	3,531	11	6	18	-	11	26	24	2,691
23 87460	Woolwich town	Sagadahoc	35.0	2,810	2,743	10	3	13	-	4	37	23	2,142
23 87845	Yarmouth town	Cumberland	13.3	8,360	8,234	31	3	30	2	18	42	49	6,300
23 87985	York town	York	54.9	12,854	12,643	32	14	63	3	25	74	93	9,919
25 00000	MASSACHUSETTS		7,840.0	6,349,097	5,367,286	343,454	15,015	238,124	2,489	236,724	146,005	428,729	4,849,033
25 00170	Abington town	Plymouth	9.9	14,605	14,237	111	17	71	1	47	121	103	10,867
25 00380	Acton town	Middlesex	20.0	20,331	17,982	142	15	1,758	5	130	299	360	14,339
25 00520	Acushnet town	Bristol	18.5	10,161	9,876	43	17	17	2	79	127	80	7,787
25 00555	Adams town	Berkshire	22.9	8,809	8,635	32	7	21	4	24	86	72	6,832
25 01185	Amesbury town	Essex	12.4	16,450	15,988	105	37	95	4	40	181	156	12,157
25 01325	Amherst town	Hampshire	27.7	34,874	27,665	1,780	74	3,144	33	1,009	1,169	2,159	30,398
25 01465	Andover town	Essex	31.0	31,247	28,621	234	19	1,791	11	262	309	567	22,259
25 01605	Arlington town	Middlesex	5.2	42,389	38,561	719	57	2,107	6	279	660	787	34,605
25 01885	Ashburnham town	Worcester	38.7	5,546	5,416	12	2	34	-	17	65	92	3,940
25 01955	Ashby town	Middlesex	23.8	2,845	2,789	8	6	10	-	3	29	24	2,047
25 02130	Ashland town	Middlesex	12.4	14,674	13,482	262	15	363	4	245	303	428	10,967
25 02480	Athol town	Worcester	32.6	11,299	10,884	74	40	48	3	83	167	222	8,424
25 02760	Auburn town	Worcester	15.4	15,901	15,510	92	18	142	4	37	98	166	12,285
25 02935	Avon town	Norfolk	4.4	4,443	4,152	166	12	41	-	34	38	64	3,442
25 03005	Ayer town	Middlesex	9.0	7,287	6,261	415	19	211	10	166	205	342	5,539
25 03740	Barre town	Worcester	44.3	5,113	4,992	26	5	17	-	15	58	41	3,661
25 04615	Bedford town	Middlesex	13.7	12,595	11,486	208	28	680	-	43	150	227	9,623
25 04825	Belchertown town	Hampshire	52.7	12,968	12,467	105	25	125	6	71	169	204	9,429
25 04930	Bellingham town	Norfolk	18.5	15,314	14,844	140	19	131	5	46	129	184	11,204
25 05070	Belmont town	Middlesex	4.7	24,194	22,062	266	31	1,393	2	100	340	440	18,707
25 05280	Berkley town	Bristol	16.5	5,749	5,561	32	8	21	2	61	64	55	3,998
25 05805	Billerica town	Middlesex	25.9	38,981	36,906	432	39	1,074	16	127	387	600	28,947
25 06015	Blackstone town	Worcester	10.9	8,804	8,574	29	21	67	1	21	91	91	6,361
25 06365	Bolton town	Worcester	19.9	4,148	4,055	8	2	54	1	8	20	33	2,885
25 07175	Bourne town	Barnstable	40.9	18,721	17,732	261	100	132	2	185	309	273	14,630
25 07350	Boxborough town	Middlesex	10.4	4,868	4,324	16	1	413	-	18	96	55	3,381
25 07420	Boxford town	Essex	24.0	7,921	7,713	27	9	96	2	23	51	67	5,370
25 07525	Boylston town	Worcester	16.0	4,008	3,876	27	9	55	-	10	31	23	3,034
25 07665	Braintree town	Norfolk	13.9	33,828	31,784	398	36	1,062	11	216	321	394	26,230
25 07980	Brewster town	Barnstable	23.0	10,094	9,815	77	23	77	3	35	64	107	7,988
25 08085	Bridgewater town	Plymouth	27.5	25,185	21,982	1,017	59	271	5	1,569	282	693	19,420
25 08470	Brimfield town	Hampden	34.7	3,339	3,262	17	12	2	2	24	20	43	2,427
25 09105	Brookfield town	Worcester	15.5	3,051	2,993	6	16	9	-	1	26	18	2,260
25 09175	Brookline town	Norfolk	6.8	57,107	46,304	1,566	71	7,325	16	578	1,247	2,018	47,604
25 09840	Burlington town	Middlesex	11.8	22,876	19,836	312	16	2,436	5	74	197	296	17,483
25 11315	Canton town	Norfolk	18.9	20,775	19,220	598	24	626	5	105	197	296	15,869
25 11525	Carlisle town	Middlesex	15.4	4,717	4,409	8	3	228	2	6	61	56	3,272
25 11665	Carver town	Plymouth	37.5	11,163	10,692	136	11	34	1	107	182	91	8,118
25 12715	Charlton town	Worcester	42.5	11,263	11,047	26	23	52	7	38	70	110	7,887
25 12995	Chatham town	Barnstable	16.2	6,625	6,362	117	12	18	1	61	54	66	5,746
25 13135	Chelmsford town	Middlesex	22.6	33,858	31,520	266	23	1,563	3	177	306	418	25,403
25 13345	Cheshire town	Berkshire	26.9	3,401	3,340	13	3	21	-	2	22	15	2,606

Table D-2. MCDs — **Area and Population**—Con.

[Includes functioning minor civil divisions (MCDs) of 2,500 or more population as of April 1, 2000 in the following 12 states: CT, ME, MA, MI, MN, NH, NJ, NY, PA, RI, VT, and WI. Codes shown are two-digit Federal Information Processing Standards (FIPS) state codes and five-digit FIPS place codes. Place names and codes are those in effect as of January 1, 2000. County refers to the county in which the MCD is located]

State and place code	MCD	County	Land area, 2000 (sq. mi.)	Population, 2000 (April 1) Total	By race—One race White	Black or African American	American Indian and Alaska Native	Asian	Native Hawaiian and Other Pacific Islander	Some other race	Two or more races	Hispanic or Latino (of any race)	18 years and over
25 00000	MASSACHUSETTS—Con.												
25 14395	Clinton town	Worcester	5.7	13,435	11,849	346	29	120	6	799	286	1,558	10,342
25 14640	Cohasset town	Norfolk	9.9	7,261	7,130	13	5	55	2	14	42	50	5,236
25 15060	Concord town	Middlesex	24.9	16,993	15,572	380	16	492	4	361	168	475	12,730
25 16180	Dalton town	Berkshire	21.8	6,892	6,739	35	8	49	-	30	31	70	5,116
25 16250	Danvers town	Essex	13.3	25,212	24,638	87	25	281	4	55	122	210	19,370
25 16425	Dartmouth town	Bristol	61.6	30,666	27,836	326	60	363	10	1,570	502	461	24,404
25 16495	Dedham town	Norfolk	10.5	23,464	22,175	362	37	439	10	188	253	567	18,256
25 16670	Deerfield town	Franklin	32.3	4,750	4,619	23	5	41	-	23	39	74	3,683
25 16775	Dennis town	Barnstable	20.6	15,973	15,173	308	59	59	-	140	234	264	13,276
25 16950	Dighton town	Bristol	22.4	6,175	6,039	33	12	30	1	17	43	66	4,561
25 17300	Douglas town	Worcester	36.4	7,045	6,859	34	9	45	5	20	73	67	4,960
25 17405	Dover town	Norfolk	15.3	5,558	5,290	23	2	202	1	3	37	66	3,804
25 17475	Dracut town	Middlesex	20.9	28,562	27,170	222	27	737	9	123	274	443	21,271
25 17685	Dudley town	Worcester	21.1	10,036	9,718	49	23	74	-	75	97	202	7,556
25 17825	Dunstable town	Middlesex	16.5	2,829	2,758	3	1	43	-	2	22	15	1,948
25 17895	Duxbury town	Plymouth	23.8	14,248	13,934	91	14	92	1	37	79	102	10,036
25 18455	East Bridgewater town	Plymouth	17.2	12,974	12,573	129	22	62	4	43	141	97	9,364
25 19295	Eastham town	Barnstable	14.0	5,453	5,252	81	8	17	2	16	77	45	4,488
25 19645	East Longmeadow town	Hampden	13.0	14,100	13,750	105	6	124	7	34	74	130	10,609
25 20100	Easton town	Bristol	28.4	22,299	20,501	354	10	309	2	920	203	352	16,848
25 21150	Edgartown town	Dukes	27.0	3,779	3,527	67	17	20	2	58	88	44	2,936
25 21850	Essex town	Essex	14.2	3,267	3,218	5	4	14	1	7	18	30	2,475
25 22130	Fairhaven town	Bristol	12.4	16,159	15,565	97	42	71	3	192	189	135	12,653
25 23105	Falmouth town	Barnstable	44.2	32,660	30,502	593	168	300	5	469	623	417	25,896
25 24820	Foxborough town	Norfolk	20.1	16,246	15,774	134	18	199	2	32	87	172	11,948
25 24925	Framingham town	Middlesex	25.1	66,910	53,373	3,409	116	3,527	27	4,195	2,263	7,265	52,575
25 25240	Freetown town	Bristol	36.6	8,472	8,146	61	16	55	1	92	101	62	6,387
25 25625	Georgetown town	Essex	12.9	7,377	7,268	11	10	31	-	23	34	47	5,264
25 26430	Grafton town	Worcester	22.7	14,894	14,286	186	17	216	-	36	150	205	11,050
25 26535	Granby town	Hampshire	27.9	6,132	5,934	31	8	59	1	32	67	74	4,568
25 26815	Great Barrington town	Berkshire	45.2	7,527	7,131	157	12	94	2	53	78	156	5,828
25 27025	Greenfield town	Franklin	21.7	18,168	16,967	244	58	199	3	256	441	644	14,194
25 27480	Groton town	Middlesex	32.8	9,547	9,282	33	12	93	2	26	99	109	6,430
25 27620	Groveland town	Essex	8.9	6,038	5,941	21	8	36	-	5	27	28	4,251
25 27690	Hadley town	Hampshire	23.3	4,793	4,597	36	3	75	-	28	54	80	3,834
25 27795	Halifax town	Plymouth	16.1	7,500	7,360	23	2	20	-	36	59	41	5,594
25 27900	Hamilton town	Essex	14.6	8,315	7,832	39	14	354	4	28	44	82	6,035
25 28075	Hampden town	Hampden	19.6	5,171	5,084	9	10	22	2	14	30	33	3,810
25 28285	Hanover town	Plymouth	15.6	13,164	12,858	73	10	101	1	36	85	90	9,243
25 28495	Hanson town	Plymouth	15.0	9,495	9,176	105	22	33	-	55	104	65	6,813
25 28740	Hardwick town	Worcester	38.6	2,622	2,564	14	4	3	-	5	32	23	1,888
25 28950	Harvard town	Worcester	26.4	5,981	5,484	269	10	118	3	30	67	364	4,391
25 29020	Harwich town	Barnstable	21.0	12,386	11,817	88	23	27	6	252	173	119	10,123
25 29265	Hatfield town	Hampshire	16.0	3,249	3,185	7	4	16	2	19	16	34	2,575
25 30210	Hingham town	Plymouth	22.5	19,882	19,386	79	7	175	3	44	188	149	14,367
25 30455	Holbrook town	Norfolk	7.4	10,785	9,908	430	20	162	1	120	144	257	8,305
25 30560	Holden town	Worcester	35.0	15,621	15,214	76	15	154	1	37	124	150	11,397
25 30700	Holliston town	Middlesex	18.7	13,801	13,346	123	18	165	1	43	105	190	9,660
25 30945	Hopedale town	Worcester	5.2	5,907	5,761	33	1	42	-	30	40	69	4,360
25 31085	Hopkinton town	Middlesex	26.6	13,346	12,856	92	20	221	6	39	112	177	8,929
25 31435	Hubbardston town	Worcester	41.0	3,909	3,846	6	3	19	-	11	24	52	2,694
25 31540	Hudson town	Middlesex	11.5	18,113	17,048	165	23	254	10	254	359	554	13,766
25 31645	Hull town	Plymouth	3.0	11,050	10,713	51	34	98	5	51	98	120	8,612
25 32310	Ipswich town	Essex	32.6	12,987	12,675	51	11	104	1	43	102	135	10,002
25 33220	Kingston town	Plymouth	18.5	11,780	11,427	113	14	51	1	59	115	88	8,544
25 33920	Lakeville town	Plymouth	29.9	9,821	9,555	30	14	58	1	49	114	104	7,126
25 34165	Lancaster town	Worcester	27.7	7,380	6,237	783	14	85	-	114	147	549	5,775
25 34340	Lanesborough town	Berkshire	29.0	2,990	2,911	21	1	24	1	5	27	20	2,274
25 34655	Lee town	Berkshire	26.4	5,985	5,801	37	9	57	1	44	36	149	4,662
25 34795	Leicester town	Worcester	23.4	10,471	10,083	134	32	78	6	32	106	183	7,752
25 34970	Lenox town	Berkshire	21.2	5,077	4,903	66	4	52	2	21	29	97	4,019
25 35215	Lexington town	Middlesex	16.4	30,355	26,146	343	23	3,310	2	102	429	428	22,352
25 35425	Lincoln town	Middlesex	14.4	8,056	7,022	390	31	336	2	107	168	239	5,582
25 35950	Littleton town	Middlesex	16.6	8,184	7,897	28	6	140	2	27	84	79	5,965
25 36300	Longmeadow town	Hampden	9.0	15,633	14,917	108	8	453	9	41	97	170	11,444
25 37175	Ludlow town	Hampden	27.1	21,209	20,315	432	20	125	2	65	250	1,372	16,781
25 37420	Lunenburg town	Worcester	26.4	9,401	9,120	65	19	73	2	24	98	108	6,974
25 37560	Lynnfield town	Essex	10.1	11,542	11,165	50	-	222	4	24	77	77	8,676
25 37995	Manchester-by-the-Sea town	Essex	9.3	5,228	5,169	3	9	20	-	6	21	40	3,978
25 38225	Mansfield town	Bristol	20.5	22,414	21,137	489	46	432	4	96	210	317	15,386
25 38400	Marblehead town	Essex	4.5	20,377	19,879	89	16	200	6	38	149	179	15,507
25 38540	Marion town	Plymouth	14.6	5,123	4,722	81	5	18	4	177	116	28	3,838
25 38855	Marshfield town	Plymouth	28.5	24,324	23,761	131	26	91	4	126	185	163	17,660
25 39100	Mashpee town	Barnstable	23.5	12,946	11,683	365	377	74	3	142	302	212	9,752
25 39450	Mattapoisett town	Plymouth	16.5	6,268	6,049	39	8	41	2	69	60	36	4,772
25 39625	Maynard town	Middlesex	5.2	10,433	9,874	108	28	169	-	123	131	290	7,991
25 39765	Medfield town	Norfolk	14.5	12,273	11,878	62	5	216	1	28	83	110	8,151

[Includes functioning minor civil divisions [MCDs] of 2,500 or more population as of April 1, 2000 in the following 12 states: CT, ME, MA, MI, MN, NH, NJ, NY, PA, RI, VT, and WI. Codes shown are two-digit Federal Information Processing Standards (FIPS) state codes and five-digit FIPS place codes. Place names and codes are those in effect as of January 1, 2000. County refers to the county in which the MCD is located]

State and place code	MCD	County	Land area, 2000 (sq. mi.)	Population, 2000 (April 1) Total	White	Black or African American	American Indian and Alaska Native	Asian	Native Hawaiian and Other Pacific Islander	Some other race	Two or more races	Hispanic or Latino (of any race)	18 years and over
25 00000	MASSACHUSETTS—Con.												
25 39975	Medway town	Norfolk	11.5	12,448	12,139	71	12	120	2	20	84	105	8,483
25 40255	Mendon town	Worcester	18.1	5,286	5,180	21	-	31	-	8	46	51	3,725
25 40430	Merrimac town	Essex	8.5	6,138	6,032	24	7	17	-	18	40	55	4,359
25 40850	Middleborough town	Plymouth	69.6	19,941	19,168	252	51	87	7	114	262	156	14,423
25 41095	Middleton town	Essex	14.0	7,744	7,390	128	4	86	4	21	111	485	5,965
25 41165	Milford town	Worcester	14.6	26,799	24,909	362	29	473	17	534	475	1,168	20,152
25 41340	Millbury town	Worcester	15.7	12,784	12,425	68	19	131	4	30	107	131	9,835
25 41515	Millis town	Norfolk	12.2	7,902	7,660	56	11	90	-	19	66	74	5,774
25 41585	Millville town	Worcester	4.9	2,724	2,662	21	1	5	-	7	28	17	1,875
25 41690	Milton town	Norfolk	13.0	26,062	22,252	2,666	17	531	10	164	422	450	19,341
25 42145	Monson town	Hampden	44.3	8,359	8,166	56	19	26	1	19	72	98	6,251
25 42285	Montague town	Franklin	30.4	8,489	8,076	71	33	79	9	58	163	217	6,540
25 43580	Nahant town	Essex	1.2	3,632	3,527	14	3	39	2	17	30	39	2,956
25 43790	Nantucket town	Nantucket	47.8	9,520	8,363	789	1	61	4	152	150	212	7,692
25 43895	Natick town	Middlesex	15.1	32,170	29,602	525	34	1,242	17	247	503	635	24,769
25 44105	Needham town	Norfolk	12.6	28,911	27,412	201	8	1,024	-	73	193	341	21,335
25 45175	Newbury town	Essex	24.2	6,717	6,604	25	9	30	1	19	29	61	4,897
25 46050	Norfolk town	Norfolk	14.8	10,460	9,306	513	32	123	2	359	125	510	7,611
25 46365	North Andover town	Essex	26.7	27,202	25,481	196	14	1,078	2	201	230	541	20,276
25 46575	North Attleborough town	Bristol	18.6	27,143	26,048	251	33	463	5	122	221	358	19,852
25 46820	Northborough town	Worcester	18.5	14,013	13,033	91	11	708	10	51	109	179	9,881
25 46925	Northbridge town	Worcester	17.2	13,182	12,688	79	22	42	4	131	216	241	9,558
25 47135	North Brookfield town	Worcester	21.1	4,683	4,573	16	12	10	-	17	55	51	3,407
25 47835	Northfield town	Franklin	34.4	2,951	2,907	3	6	6	-	1	28	17	2,175
25 48955	North Reading town	Middlesex	13.3	13,837	13,495	55	6	180	1	33	67	102	10,026
25 49970	Norton town	Bristol	28.7	18,036	16,621	209	24	180	1	806	195	206	13,175
25 50145	Norwell town	Plymouth	20.9	9,765	9,529	36	5	113	-	16	66	62	6,973
25 50250	Norwood town	Norfolk	10.5	28,587	25,873	659	27	1,446	4	221	357	473	22,652
25 50390	Oak Bluffs town	Dukes	7.4	3,713	3,220	160	56	25	-	93	159	44	2,875
25 51265	Orange town	Franklin	35.4	7,518	7,239	80	17	36	1	44	101	124	5,514
25 51440	Orleans town	Barnstable	14.2	6,341	6,187	37	11	34	-	9	63	49	5,468
25 51825	Oxford town	Worcester	26.6	13,352	12,901	116	34	112	3	43	143	263	9,872
25 52105	Palmer town	Hampden	31.5	12,497	12,100	94	29	70	-	55	149	154	9,349
25 52420	Paxton town	Worcester	14.7	4,386	4,241	30	4	47	-	25	39	68	3,338
25 52630	Pembroke town	Plymouth	21.8	16,927	16,569	85	12	86	2	48	125	90	12,081
25 52805	Pepperell town	Middlesex	22.6	11,142	10,826	52	14	80	-	37	133	114	7,728
25 54100	Plainville town	Norfolk	11.1	7,683	7,435	54	-	125	-	19	50	73	5,721
25 54310	Plymouth town	Plymouth	96.5	51,701	49,022	988	131	295	20	481	764	870	38,358
25 54415	Plympton town	Plymouth	14.8	2,637	2,554	26	16	9	-	14	18	11	1,884
25 55395	Princeton town	Worcester	35.4	3,353	3,244	10	11	32	-	21	35	49	2,383
25 55500	Provincetown town	Barnstable	9.7	3,431	3,004	258	11	17	-	37	104	74	3,158
25 55955	Randolph town	Norfolk	10.1	30,963	19,455	6,456	70	3,151	11	782	1,038	1,006	23,748
25 56060	Raynham town	Bristol	20.5	11,739	11,333	122	7	81	3	83	110	97	8,723
25 56130	Reading town	Middlesex	9.9	23,708	22,871	86	15	525	6	50	155	200	17,476
25 56375	Rehoboth town	Bristol	46.5	10,172	9,938	36	31	53	1	26	87	51	7,502
25 57600	Rochester town	Plymouth	33.9	4,581	4,427	29	9	16	-	53	47	17	3,353
25 57775	Rockland town	Plymouth	10.0	17,670	16,753	302	26	190	-	139	260	180	12,996
25 57880	Rockport town	Essex	7.1	7,767	7,591	21	17	35	2	40	61	83	6,113
25 58405	Rowley town	Essex	18.7	5,500	5,411	13	14	25	-	15	22	47	3,961
25 58825	Rutland town	Worcester	35.3	6,353	6,136	66	9	29	-	28	85	84	4,399
25 59245	Salisbury town	Essex	15.4	7,827	7,635	32	24	27	7	20	82	92	5,980
25 59735	Sandwich town	Barnstable	43.0	20,136	19,683	77	62	109	2	65	138	161	14,423
25 60015	Saugus town	Essex	11.0	26,078	25,379	114	14	314	10	70	177	254	20,728
25 60330	Scituate town	Plymouth	17.2	17,863	17,276	88	6	80	2	231	180	148	13,203
25 60645	Seekonk town	Bristol	18.3	13,425	12,964	70	38	127	-	68	158	99	10,033
25 60785	Sharon town	Norfolk	23.3	17,408	15,659	591	23	846	1	74	214	194	12,152
25 61065	Sheffield town	Berkshire	48.1	3,335	3,247	35	10	8	-	18	17	44	2,541
25 61380	Sherborn town	Middlesex	16.0	4,200	4,053	16	2	101	-	11	17	47	2,861
25 61590	Shirley town	Middlesex	15.8	6,373	5,347	428	30	134	5	326	103	437	4,991
25 61800	Shrewsbury town	Worcester	20.7	31,640	28,199	459	37	2,408	4	218	315	504	23,529
25 62430	Somerset town	Bristol	8.1	18,234	17,909	30	22	97	4	28	144	90	14,516
25 62745	Southampton town	Hampshire	28.1	5,387	5,295	11	7	34	-	11	29	47	4,012
25 63165	Southborough town	Worcester	14.1	8,781	8,295	47	6	309	4	44	76	132	5,963
25 63270	Southbridge town	Worcester	20.4	17,214	14,672	246	73	261	11	1,498	453	3,472	12,847
25 64145	South Hadley town	Hampshire	17.7	17,196	16,172	207	20	435	10	132	220	405	13,817
25 65825	Southwick town	Hampden	31.0	8,835	8,606	45	18	33	1	30	102	152	6,490
25 66105	Spencer town	Worcester	32.8	11,691	11,449	69	28	38	2	30	75	156	8,819
25 67385	Sterling town	Worcester	30.5	7,257	7,116	42	7	29	1	20	42	59	5,260
25 67665	Stoneham town	Middlesex	6.1	22,219	21,110	197	12	558	9	132	201	397	17,562
25 67945	Stoughton town	Norfolk	16.0	27,149	24,017	1,548	28	580	13	344	619	419	21,057
25 68050	Stow town	Middlesex	17.6	5,902	5,635	21	11	120	-	20	95	84	4,235
25 68155	Sturbridge town	Worcester	37.4	7,837	7,613	28	21	89	7	24	55	102	5,841
25 68260	Sudbury town	Middlesex	24.4	16,841	15,870	134	5	626	5	39	162	208	11,365
25 68400	Sunderland town	Franklin	14.4	3,777	3,353	89	10	243	3	40	39	89	3,091
25 68610	Sutton town	Worcester	32.4	8,250	8,100	23	11	49	-	22	45	58	5,821
25 68645	Swampscott town	Essex	3.0	14,412	14,047	106	9	98	3	41	108	183	10,959
25 68750	Swansea town	Bristol	23.1	15,901	15,569	60	12	57	1	43	159	96	12,371

Table D-2. MCDs — **Area and Population**—Con.

[Includes functioning minor civil divisions (MCDs) of 2,500 or more population as of April 1, 2000 in the following 12 states: CT, ME, MA, MI, MN, NH, NJ, NY, PA, RI, VT, and WI. Codes shown are two-digit Federal Information Processing Standards (FIPS) state codes and five-digit FIPS place codes. Place names and codes are those in effect as of January 1, 2000. County refers to the county in which the MCD is located]

State and place code	MCD	County	Land area, 2000 (sq. mi.)	Population, 2000 (April 1)									
					By race—							Hispanic or Latino (of any race)	18 years and over
					One race						Two or more races		
				Total	White	Black or African American	American Indian and Alaska Native	Asian	Native Hawaiian and Other Pacific Islander	Some other race			
25 00000	MASSACHUSETTS—Con.												
25 69275	Templeton town	Worcester	32.0	6,799	6,673	24	15	19	-	29	39	98	5,022
25 69415	Tewksbury town	Middlesex	20.7	28,851	27,824	194	36	460	2	118	217	352	21,638
25 69940	Tisbury town	Dukes	6.6	3,755	3,381	111	51	12	-	50	148	39	2,948
25 70150	Topsfield town	Essex	12.7	6,141	6,003	23	2	52	-	21	40	51	4,407
25 70360	Townsend town	Middlesex	32.9	9,198	8,972	67	21	21	2	36	79	108	6,399
25 71025	Tyngsborough town	Middlesex	16.9	11,081	10,597	66	26	275	4	15	110	123	7,721
25 71480	Upton town	Worcester	21.5	5,642	5,492	27	4	55	-	17	47	41	4,001
25 71620	Uxbridge town	Worcester	29.5	11,156	10,937	17	15	68	8	33	78	106	7,899
25 72215	Wakefield town	Middlesex	7.5	24,804	24,045	111	19	354	2	49	224	204	19,197
25 72495	Walpole town	Norfolk	20.5	22,824	21,777	363	24	257	2	256	145	461	16,925
25 72880	Ware town	Hampshire	34.4	9,707	9,366	53	22	58	6	74	128	202	7,307
25 72985	Wareham town	Plymouth	35.8	20,335	17,776	594	109	90	10	1,058	698	292	15,346
25 73090	Warren town	Worcester	27.5	4,776	4,653	20	14	13	-	10	66	42	3,494
25 73790	Wayland town	Middlesex	15.2	13,100	12,080	98	13	699	4	35	171	151	9,341
25 73895	Webster town	Worcester	12.5	16,415	15,564	183	56	156	-	245	211	649	12,599
25 74175	Wellesley town	Norfolk	10.2	26,613	23,947	426	22	1,691	3	141	383	617	19,938
25 74385	Wellfleet town	Barnstable	19.8	2,749	2,655	26	8	10	1	16	33	19	2,259
25 74595	Wenham town	Essex	7.7	4,440	4,344	19	1	60	-	3	13	26	3,464
25 75155	West Boylston town	Worcester	12.9	7,481	6,855	399	12	64	1	47	103	357	5,883
25 75260	West Bridgewater town	Plymouth	15.7	6,634	6,395	63	17	45	-	30	84	67	5,125
25 75400	West Brookfield town	Worcester	20.5	3,804	3,734	12	9	9	2	6	32	40	2,932
25 76030	Westfield city	Hampden	46.6	40,072	37,881	365	90	329	19	850	538	2,008	30,534
25 76135	Westford town	Middlesex	30.6	20,754	19,444	62	13	994	3	62	176	229	14,153
25 77010	Westminster town	Worcester	35.5	6,907	6,734	32	10	79	-	10	42	77	5,057
25 77150	West Newbury town	Essex	13.5	4,149	4,086	8	1	22	-	15	17	27	2,903
25 77255	Weston town	Middlesex	17.0	11,469	10,352	135	6	782	6	49	139	218	8,254
25 77570	Westport town	Bristol	50.0	14,183	13,901	24	20	70	3	53	112	98	11,113
25 77850	West Springfield town	Hampden	16.7	27,899	25,300	572	61	551	10	819	586	1,605	21,360
25 78690	Westwood town	Norfolk	11.0	14,117	13,549	70	6	350	-	00	112	132	10,190
25 78865	Weymouth town	Norfolk	17.0	53,988	51,229	779	102	843	28	344	663	721	42,132
25 79530	Whitman town	Plymouth	7.0	13,882	13,487	90	22	59	2	66	156	122	10,169
25 79740	Wilbraham town	Hampden	22.2	13,473	12,988	161	8	170	8	34	104	189	9,854
25 79985	Williamstown town	Berkshire	46.9	8,424	7,648	229	9	263	10	65	200	233	7,131
25 80230	Wilmington town	Middlesex	17.1	21,363	20,575	88	17	434	1	90	158	203	15,463
25 80405	Winchendon town	Worcester	43.3	9,611	9,223	77	29	60	7	91	124	195	6,704
25 80510	Winchester town	Middlesex	6.0	20,810	19,375	142	29	961	3	57	243	211	15,468
25 80930	Winthrop town	Suffolk	2.0	18,303	17,286	308	30	210	8	249	212	493	14,890
25 82315	Wrentham town	Norfolk	22.2	10,554	10,305	64	13	84	1	34	53	83	7,619
25 82525	Yarmouth town	Barnstable	24.2	24,807	23,623	333	81	132	10	233	395	358	20,537
26 00000	MICHIGAN		56,803.8	9,938,444	7,966,053	1,412,742	58,479	176,510	2,092	129,552	192,416	323,877	7,342,677
26 00200	Acme township	Grand Traverse	25.2	4,332	4,215	10	12	15	-	46	34	91	3,229
26 00240	Ada township	Kent	36.1	9,882	9,444	46	16	232	1	50	93	106	6,657
26 00320	Adams township	Houghton	47.2	2,747	2,544	142	4	15	1	6	35	17	2,054
26 00400	Addison township	Oakland	36.2	6,439	6,252	69	21	15	1	17	64	125	4,559
26 00440	Adrian city	Lenawee	7.1	21,574	18,223	760	133	178	4	1,666	610	3,665	16,123
26 00800	Alaiedon township	Ingham	35.5	3,498	3,142	215	22	49	2	30	38	83	2,739
26 00840	Alamo township	Kalamazoo	36.3	3,820	3,690	37	18	20	-	8	47	34	2,828
26 00940	Albert township	Montmorency	65.8	2,695	2,651	4	7	1	-	9	23	24	2,183
26 01160	Algoma township	Kent	34.9	7,596	7,409	17	22	34	1	55	58	127	5,305
26 01280	Allegan township	Allegan	30.4	4,050	3,930	21	12	11	-	25	51	67	3,001
26 01360	Allendale township	Ottawa	31.3	13,042	12,209	350	45	110	9	187	132	376	10,130
26 01600	Almena township	Van Buren	34.5	4,226	4,065	52	33	12	3	31	30	60	3,089
26 01620	Almer township	Tuscola	34.6	3,023	2,931	6	17	14	-	21	34	80	2,279
26 01640	Almira township	Benzie	33.8	2,811	2,746	6	17	2	-	7	33	32	2,031
26 01680	Almont township	Lapeer	37.0	6,041	5,841	11	23	20	-	90	56	184	4,289
26 01760	Alpena township	Alpena	105.0	9,788	9,630	10	42	41	-	11	54	55	7,576
26 01840	Alpine township	Kent	35.8	13,976	12,515	435	107	211	7	398	303	916	10,487
26 03020	Ann Arbor township	Washtenaw	17.6	4,720	3,833	106	8	641	3	40	89	105	3,723
26 03140	Antwerp township	Van Buren	34.9	10,813	10,115	140	38	56	-	237	227	548	7,577
26 03220	Arbela township	Tuscola	33.4	3,219	3,122	9	21	4	5	16	42	59	2,342
26 03280	Arcadia township	Lapeer	35.3	3,197	3,146	10	4	4	-	17	16	56	2,302
26 03420	Argentine township	Genesee	35.1	6,521	6,339	15	55	12	5	16	79	76	4,584
26 03540	Armada township	Macomb	36.5	5,246	5,144	6	15	6	1	20	54	80	3,724
26 03680	Ash township	Monroe	34.6	7,610	7,388	24	24	17	1	25	131	133	5,516
26 03700	Ashland township	Newaygo	34.9	2,570	2,403	14	13	6	-	92	42	242	1,703
26 03900	Athens township	Calhoun	36.1	2,571	2,492	5	31	2	3	8	30	40	1,869
26 04000	Atlas township	Genesee	35.4	7,257	7,080	24	23	37	9	18	66	78	5,103
26 04040	Attica township	Lapeer	35.8	4,678	4,531	6	27	20	1	55	38	124	3,317
26 04180	Augusta township	Washtenaw	36.7	4,813	4,458	254	16	10	3	8	64	33	3,614
26 04240	Aurelius township	Ingham	36.5	3,318	3,202	21	13	9	-	27	46	120	2,355
26 04780	Bagley township	Otsego	28.6	5,838	5,691	13	32	20	1	7	74	45	4,156
26 04840	Bainbridge township	Berrien	35.2	3,132	2,990	18	21	3	3	60	37	404	2,368
26 05120	Bangor township	Bay	13.9	15,547	14,999	96	69	89	3	106	185	414	11,870
26 05340	Baraga township	Baraga	185.6	3,542	2,393	429	496	14	-	17	193	42	2,705
26 05520	Baroda township	Berrien	17.8	2,880	2,777	7	7	10	2	58	19	74	2,116

[Includes functioning minor civil divisions (MCDs) of 2,500 or more population as of April 1, 2000 in the following 12 states: CT, ME, MA, MI, MN, NH, NJ, NY, PA, RI, VT, and WI. Codes shown are two-digit Federal Information Processing Standards (FIPS) state codes and five-digit FIPS place codes. Place names and codes are those in effect as of January 1, 2000. County refers to the county in which the MCD is located]

State and place code	MCD	County	Land area, 2000 (sq. mi.)	Population, 2000 (April 1) Total	By race— One race White	Black or African American	American Indian and Alaska Native	Asian	Native Hawaiian and Other Pacific Islander	Some other race	Two or more races	Hispanic or Latino (of any race)	18 years and over
26 00000	MICHIGAN—Con.												
26 05560	Barry township	Barry	34.8	3,489	3,404	13	22	15	-	4	31	39	2,563
26 05900	Bath township	Clinton	36.1	7,541	7,179	62	43	68	2	58	129	208	5,414
26 06380	Bear Creek township	Emmet	39.6	5,269	5,075	5	91	31	1	12	54	54	3,819
26 06540	Beaver township	Bay	35.4	2,806	2,773	-	4	5	-	12	12	41	2,092
26 06720	Bedford township	Calhoun	29.4	9,517	7,999	1,151	32	41	6	81	207	142	7,223
26 06740	Bedford township	Monroe	39.1	28,606	27,907	114	56	147	2	118	262	552	20,578
26 07080	Bellevue township	Eaton	36.4	3,144	3,041	15	8	10	5	18	47	74	2,302
26 07280	Bennington township	Shiawassee	36.5	3,017	2,944	5	9	14	-	16	29	52	2,229
26 07400	Benton charter township	Berrien	32.6	16,404	7,235	8,507	61	59	2	242	298	515	11,475
26 07420	Benton township	Cheboygan	58.7	3,080	2,899	1	111	7	2	2	58	18	2,353
26 07440	Benton township	Eaton	33.7	2,712	2,627	12	7	-	-	30	36	97	2,042
26 07600	Benzonia township	Benzie	28.3	2,839	2,732	4	62	7	1	15	18	47	2,269
26 07700	Berlin township	Ionia	41.6	2,787	2,274	385	39	11	-	22	56	62	2,317
26 07720	Berlin charter township	Monroe	32.1	6,924	6,724	34	23	5	1	40	97	99	5,080
26 07760	Berlin township	St. Clair	37.1	3,162	3,073	28	6	7	1	18	29	89	2,250
26 07820	Berrien township	Berrien	35.3	5,075	4,466	276	34	87	3	99	110	339	3,709
26 08020	Bethany township	Gratiot	35.2	3,492	2,257	1,029	46	19	2	51	88	135	3,110
26 08220	Big Creek township	Oscoda	141.5	3,380	3,295	2	17	4	1	5	56	36	2,574
26 08320	Big Rapids township	Mecosta	30.7	3,249	3,056	67	13	62	1	12	38	33	2,503
26 08360	Billings township	Gladwin	21.7	2,715	2,634	3	20	2	-	14	42	40	2,142
26 08400	Bingham township	Clinton	32.3	2,776	2,708	-	9	10	-	30	19	71	2,029
26 08560	Birch Run township	Saginaw	35.6	6,191	6,003	30	24	12	-	37	85	135	4,511
26 08760	Blackman township	Jackson	31.8	22,800	18,116	3,931	86	131	5	251	280	563	18,989
26 08880	Blair township	Grand Traverse	35.6	6,448	6,106	16	106	27	1	98	94	160	4,510
26 08940	Blendon township	Ottawa	36.5	5,721	5,596	10	5	24	-	25	61	111	3,829
26 09020	Blissfield township	Lenawee	21.1	3,915	3,784	2	1	3	-	98	27	234	2,875
26 09040	Bloomer township	Montcalm	35.2	3,039	2,006	862	36	10	-	23	102	125	2,571
26 09110	Bloomfield township	Oakland	24.9	43,023	37,732	1,849	35	2,783	23	125	476	595	32,781
26 09240	Bloomingdale township	Van Buren	34.1	3,364	3,145	59	30	7	-	68	55	172	2,402
26 09680	Boston township	Ionia	35.0	4,961	4,848	12	14	10	3	26	48	96	3,592
26 09780	Bowne township	Kent	35.9	2,743	2,677	5	14	9	2	14	22	51	1,855
26 09920	Brady township	Kalamazoo	34.9	4,263	4,153	7	11	14	-	28	50	43	3,086
26 10040	Brandon township	Oakland	35.1	14,765	14,408	59	35	53	2	58	150	235	10,243
26 10220	Breitung township	Dickinson	65.1	5,930	5,832	2	26	28	-	7	35	26	4,459
26 10460	Bridgeport charter township	Saginaw	34.6	11,709	8,498	2,418	72	38	1	382	300	1,060	8,746
26 10640	Brighton township	Livingston	33.1	17,673	17,194	76	52	146	7	55	143	215	12,366
26 11060	Brooks township	Newaygo	31.8	3,671	3,532	7	17	10	1	63	41	132	2,677
26 11220	Brownstown township	Wayne	22.4	22,989	20,464	878	121	880	-	197	449	824	16,395
26 11300	Bruce township	Macomb	36.4	8,158	7,822	146	30	33	5	35	87	143	5,787
26 11420	Buchanan township	Berrien	32.3	3,510	3,376	42	17	9	-	15	51	44	2,614
26 11560	Buena Vista charter township	Saginaw	36.0	10,318	3,818	5,734	47	13	1	444	261	940	7,194
26 11880	Burns township	Shiawassee	35.5	3,500	3,427	1	15	6	-	2	49	53	2,478
26 11940	Burr Oak township	St. Joseph	35.6	2,739	2,672	11	11	8	-	15	22	44	1,962
26 12020	Burtchville township	St. Clair	15.6	3,956	3,853	12	16	12	1	7	55	71	2,989
26 12240	Byron township	Kent	36.6	17,553	16,638	213	57	186	3	206	250	487	12,459
26 12500	Caledonia township	Kent	35.1	8,964	8,744	22	28	68	3	42	57	111	6,161
26 12520	Caledonia township	Shiawassee	31.7	4,427	4,305	6	14	27	1	30	44	73	3,354
26 12600	Calumet township	Houghton	33.3	6,997	6,883	8	33	9	1	13	50	62	5,190
26 12700	Cambria township	Hillsdale	34.9	2,546	2,471	11	10	15	-	11	28	16	1,864
26 12720	Cambridge township	Lenawee	32.0	5,299	5,156	8	19	14	-	35	67	107	3,934
26 13080	Cannon township	Kent	35.9	12,075	11,794	57	15	41	10	48	110	122	7,949
26 13120	Canton township	Wayne	36.0	76,366	64,045	3,466	224	6,664	17	489	1,461	1,788	54,196
26 13380	Carmel township	Eaton	34.1	2,626	2,566	2	7	4	-	16	31	62	1,902
26 13540	Carrollton township	Saginaw	3.2	6,602	5,452	605	33	45	1	323	143	711	4,771
26 13660	Cascade township	Kent	33.9	15,107	14,284	151	42	462	-	39	129	131	10,673
26 13700	Casco township	Allegan	38.9	3,019	2,661	103	21	12	-	165	57	344	2,239
26 13720	Casco township	St. Clair	37.1	4,747	4,584	24	12	8	4	8	107	44	3,401
26 13780	Caseville township	Huron	13.9	2,723	2,671	9	6	7	2	5	23	29	2,267
26 13840	Casnovia township	Muskegon	35.7	2,652	2,502	-	10	3	-	90	47	148	1,835
26 13960	Castleton township	Barry	35.1	3,475	3,380	3	20	10	-	6	56	31	2,510
26 14000	Cato township	Montcalm	35.3	2,920	2,824	5	12	8	2	19	50	79	2,079
26 14100	Cedar Creek township	Muskegon	35.2	3,109	2,963	38	29	5	-	23	51	64	2,249
26 15160	Chesaning township	Saginaw	34.7	4,861	4,731	12	12	4	1	64	37	206	3,668
26 15340	Chesterfield township	Macomb	27.9	37,405	34,948	1,110	149	284	6	324	584	941	26,255
26 15480	Chikaming township	Berrien	22.1	3,678	3,520	83	14	11	1	13	36	35	2,950
26 15540	China township	St. Clair	34.4	3,340	3,280	11	11	8	1	4	25	36	2,358
26 15580	Chippewa township	Isabella	36.2	4,617	3,716	28	684	12	5	24	148	146	3,238
26 15660	Chocolay township	Marquette	59.7	7,148	6,193	619	144	41	5	21	125	57	5,578
26 16180	Clay township	St. Clair	35.5	9,822	9,618	20	67	11	-	21	85	83	7,601
26 16260	Clayton township	Genesee	34.3	7,546	7,198	85	38	58	-	43	124	153	5,533
26 16500	Clinton township	Lenawee	18.1	3,624	3,555	7	11	4	-	12	35	58	2,638
26 16520	Clinton township	Macomb	28.2	95,648	87,151	4,461	276	1,605	14	391	1,750	1,664	74,266
26 16760	Clyde township	St. Clair	35.9	5,523	5,398	16	19	21	2	19	48	70	4,057
26 16880	Coe township	Isabella	36.2	2,993	2,900	9	20	9	2	21	32	50	2,191
26 16920	Cohoctah township	Livingston	38.1	3,394	3,323	2	16	9	3	13	28	32	2,409
26 17040	Coldwater township	Branch	27.4	3,678	3,571	19	10	22	-	23	33	40	2,804
26 17340	Coloma charter township	Berrien	18.2	5,217	5,036	36	23	31	2	27	62	135	3,954

Table D-2. MCDs — **Area and Population**—Con.

[Includes functioning minor civil divisions [MCDs] of 2,500 or more population as of April 1, 2000 in the following 12 states: CT, ME, MA, MI, MN, NH, NJ, NY, PA, RI, VT, and WI. Codes shown are two-digit Federal Information Processing Standards (FIPS) state codes and five-digit FIPS place codes. Place names and codes are those in effect as of January 1, 2000. County refers to the county in which the MCD is located]

State and place code	MCD	County	Land area, 2000 (sq. mi.)	Population, 2000 (April 1)									
					By race—								
					One race								
				Total	White	Black or African American	American Indian and Alaska Native	Asian	Native Hawaiian and Other Pacific Islander	Some other race	Two or more races	Hispanic or Latino (of any race)	18 years and over
26 00000	MICHIGAN—Con.												
26 17370	Colon township	St. Joseph	34.6	3,405	3,327	17	8	8	-	4	41	23	2,498
26 17400	Columbia township	Jackson	36.6	7,234	7,076	5	22	26	-	28	77	99	5,557
26 17440	Columbia township	Van Buren	34.1	2,714	2,413	83	28	4	-	126	60	205	1,958
26 17520	Columbus township	St. Clair	37.1	4,615	4,477	4	26	17	1	32	58	106	3,198
26 17640	Commerce township	Oakland	27.6	34,764	33,626	175	66	454	4	110	329	404	24,521
26 17680	Comstock township	Kalamazoo	33.0	13,851	12,740	556	60	160	1	97	237	232	10,144
26 17760	Concord township	Jackson	35.9	2,692	2,641	4	9	9	2	13	14	22	1,917
26 17860	Constantine township	St. Joseph	34.6	4,181	4,020	22	9	28	-	19	83	47	2,984
26 17920	Conway township	Livingston	37.8	2,732	2,622	7	39	4	-	15	45	36	1,877
26 17980	Cooper township	Kalamazoo	36.3	8,754	8,418	119	26	39	1	34	117	105	6,410
26 18400	Cottrellville township	St. Clair	21.2	3,814	3,764	3	4	6	3	-	34	29	2,765
26 18500	Courtland township	Kent	35.5	5,817	5,705	11	20	15	-	19	47	75	4,043
26 18560	Covert township	Van Buren	35.0	3,141	1,605	1,107	32	4	-	251	142	478	2,143
26 18800	Crockery township	Ottawa	32.7	3,782	3,653	24	21	4	1	28	51	65	2,737
26 18980	Croton township	Newaygo	34.0	3,042	2,946	12	24	4	-	26	30	50	2,276
26 19080	Crystal township	Montcalm	34.1	2,824	2,754	4	11	6	-	11	38	28	2,094
26 19660	Dalton township	Muskegon	35.7	8,047	7,511	186	105	16	-	75	154	231	5,713
26 19720	Danby township	Ionia	35.3	2,696	2,639	6	10	9	-	5	27	22	1,903
26 19880	Davison city	Genesee	1.8	5,536	5,340	28	32	20	1	24	91	132	4,186
26 19900	Davison township	Genesee	33.5	17,722	16,712	364	65	155	1	90	335	370	13,401
26 21060	Decatur township	Van Buren	35.2	3,916	3,497	181	46	10	4	104	74	195	2,811
26 21140	Deerfield township	Isabella	35.8	3,081	2,998	5	35	12	1	5	25	28	2,204
26 21160	Deerfield township	Lapeer	35.9	5,736	5,567	8	14	12	1	46	88	126	3,947
26 21220	Deerfield township	Livingston	36.4	4,087	4,017	-	21	5	-	4	40	51	2,867
26 21420	Delhi charter township	Ingham	28.8	22,569	20,978	532	110	260	10	213	466	804	16,055
26 21520	Delta charter township	Eaton	34.5	29,682	25,405	2,375	118	765	12	384	623	1,105	22,890
26 21600	Denmark township	Tuscola	35.3	3,249	3,152	1	6	40	-	18	32	79	2,412
26 21640	Denton township	Roscommon	26.4	5,817	5,713	6	57	3	3	3	32	46	4,686
20 22140	De Witt township	Clinton	31.7	12,143	11,434	163	98	105	3	148	192	488	9,106
26 22180	Dexter township	Washtenaw	30.8	5,248	5,118	20	15	32	3	4	56	54	3,753
26 22680	Dorr township	Allegan	36.2	6,579	6,377	34	30	17	-	59	62	137	4,362
26 23160	Dryden township	Lapeer	35.9	4,624	4,524	5	18	10	-	22	45	49	3,316
26 23400	Dundee township	Monroe	48.4	6,341	6,173	31	14	22	-	27	74	79	4,555
26 23800	East Bay township	Grand Traverse	39.9	9,919	9,652	22	86	60	1	29	69	124	7,104
26 23820	East China township	St. Clair	6.7	3,630	3,578	8	10	7	1	2	24	19	2,885
26 24220	Easton township	Ionia	28.4	2,835	2,752	7	6	9	-	31	30	73	2,116
26 24520	Eaton township	Eaton	32.6	4,278	4,120	10	16	38	3	44	47	110	3,115
26 24560	Eaton Rapids township	Eaton	34.1	3,821	3,682	23	22	6	-	31	57	94	2,752
26 24830	Edenville township	Midland	34.8	2,528	2,476	1	13	7	-	6	25	14	1,921
26 25080	Egelston township	Muskegon	35.0	9,537	8,969	100	100	29	-	141	198	380	6,748
26 25160	Elba township	Lapeer	32.8	5,462	5,312	20	36	8	-	28	58	98	4,036
20 25300	Elkland township	Tuscola	35.6	3,659	3,579	9	31	16	-	6	18	40	2,759
26 25340	Elk Rapids township	Antrim	7.1	2,741	2,677	6	22	7	4	11	14	52	2,135
26 25700	Elmwood charter township	Leelanau	20.1	4,264	4,147	12	38	9	-	22	36	102	3,247
26 25935	Emmett township	Calhoun	32.3	11,979	11,201	253	81	154	3	98	189	277	9,041
26 25960	Emmett township	St. Clair	35.3	2,506	2,462	6	3	7	2	16	10	36	1,739
26 26320	Erie township	Monroe	24.1	4,850	4,623	49	29	10	-	69	70	208	3,538
26 26380	Escanaba township	Delta	59.6	3,587	3,475	-	52	15	-	6	39	7	2,611
26 26520	Eureka township	Montcalm	29.6	3,271	3,152	5	18	14	-	44	38	103	2,357
26 26720	Evergreen township	Montcalm	34.7	2,922	2,840	12	24	15	2	9	20	50	2,114
26 26880	Exeter township	Monroe	36.6	3,727	3,422	229	11	14	1	15	35	35	2,694
26 26920	Fabius township	St. Joseph	32.3	3,285	3,178	31	13	18	-	10	35	34	2,540
26 27580	Fayette township	Hillsdale	23.1	3,350	3,230	46	9	6	-	13	46	71	2,433
26 27780	Fenton township	Genesee	23.9	12,968	12,582	36	53	100	4	44	149	153	9,704
26 28120	Fillmore township	Allegan	28.6	2,756	2,621	17	6	34	-	49	29	125	1,904
26 29020	Flint township	Genesee	23.6	33,691	26,200	5,430	205	740	6	252	858	784	25,461
26 29220	Flushing township	Genesee	30.9	10,230	9,813	112	47	59	10	60	129	201	7,490
26 29420	Forest township	Genesee	35.8	4,738	4,609	17	16	10	1	26	59	56	3,535
26 29720	Forsyth township	Marquette	175.2	4,824	4,591	27	73	29	-	20	84	40	3,733
26 29760	Fort Gratiot township	St. Clair	16.1	10,691	10,202	156	28	143	1	56	105	187	8,046
26 30180	Frankenlust township	Bay	22.8	2,530	2,421	16	4	51	-	4	34	38	1,984
26 30320	Franklin township	Lenawee	38.5	2,939	2,881	2	3	9	-	14	30	32	2,140
26 30400	Fraser township	Bay	32.3	3,375	3,300	10	19	12	-	4	30	47	2,569
26 30760	Fremont township	Tuscola	35.9	3,559	3,470	6	18	4	-	2	59	51	2,562
26 30820	Frenchtown township	Monroe	42.1	20,777	19,845	331	85	110	3	94	309	510	15,063
26 30980	Fruitland township	Muskegon	36.5	5,235	5,076	33	34	13	-	13	66	54	3,717
26 31020	Fruitport charter township	Muskegon	30.0	12,533	12,145	82	88	54	-	56	108	211	9,064
26 31220	Gaines township	Genesee	35.2	6,491	6,291	22	26	23	1	31	97	83	4,774
26 31240	Gaines township	Kent	35.9	20,112	17,960	1,058	101	418	5	204	366	567	14,310
26 31360	Ganges township	Allegan	32.5	2,524	2,357	12	19	5	-	104	27	301	1,896
26 31580	Garfield township	Grand Traverse	26.7	13,840	13,334	46	140	99	4	56	161	207	10,789
26 31800	Genesee township	Genesee	29.4	24,125	21,206	1,973	161	72	3	198	512	651	17,428
26 31840	Geneva township	Van Buren	35.3	3,975	3,281	365	55	7	-	172	95	315	2,798
26 31860	Genoa township	Livingston	34.3	15,901	15,472	30	67	113	2	35	182	159	11,578
26 31880	Georgetown township	Ottawa	33.5	41,658	40,403	240	73	378	7	227	330	694	29,421
26 31960	Gerrish township	Roscommon	27.6	3,072	3,018	10	9	5	3	5	22	19	2,458
26 33300	Grand Blanc township	Genesee	32.6	29,827	26,285	1,998	115	749	7	182	491	622	22,216

Table D-2. MCDs — **Area and Population**—Con.

[Includes functioning minor civil divisions [MCDs] of 2,500 or more population as of April 1, 2000 in the following 12 states: CT, ME, MA, MI, MN, NH, NJ, NY, PA, RI, VT, and WI. Codes shown are two-digit Federal Information Processing Standards (FIPS) state codes and five-digit FIPS place codes. Place names and codes are those in effect as of January 1, 2000. County refers to the county in which the MCD is located]

State and place code	MCD	County	Land area, 2000 (sq. mi.)	Population, 2000 (April 1)									
					By race—								
					One race							Hispanic or Latino (of any race)	18 years and over
				Total	White	Black or African American	American Indian and Alaska Native	Asian	Native Hawaiian and Other Pacific Islander	Some other race	Two or more races		
26 00000	MICHIGAN—Con.												
26 33360	Grand Haven township	Ottawa	28.6	13,278	12,900	16	47	74	1	89	151	252	9,236
26 34020	Grand Rapids charter township	Kent	15.4	14,056	13,466	139	25	203	1	75	147	183	9,981
26 34220	Grant township	Clare	33.2	3,034	2,953	4	18	11	-	12	36	16	2,254
26 34380	Grant township	Newaygo	35.9	3,130	2,888	11	13	4	-	160	54	363	2,110
26 34400	Grant township	Oceana	35.4	2,932	2,669	11	51	22	-	147	32	305	2,042
26 34500	Grass Lake charter township	Jackson	47.2	4,586	4,499	23	14	4	2	8	36	49	3,384
26 34560	Grattan township	Kent	35.0	3,551	3,441	25	8	8	-	18	51	91	2,561
26 34660	Grayling township	Crawford	171.1	6,516	6,179	198	31	17	-	5	86	52	4,855
26 34760	Green charter township	Mecosta	36.9	3,209	3,119	28	15	1	-	7	39	33	2,351
26 34960	Green Lake township	Grand Traverse	29.4	5,009	4,856	1	61	21	3	14	53	43	3,687
26 35060	Green Oak township	Livingston	34.7	15,618	14,981	247	73	77	2	32	206	200	11,054
26 35420	Grosse Ile township	Wayne	9.6	10,894	10,374	39	37	299	4	32	109	175	8,183
26 35500	Grosse Pointe township	Wayne	1.0	2,743	2,577	16	5	109	-	12	24	49	2,107
26 35640	Groveland township	Oakland	35.5	6,150	5,947	52	19	33	-	28	71	103	4,451
26 35720	Gunplain township	Allegan	34.1	5,637	5,482	20	19	20	3	22	71	61	4,057
26 35840	Hadley township	Lapeer	35.3	4,655	4,570	2	13	16	-	11	43	53	3,353
26 35860	Hagar township	Berrien	18.6	3,964	3,789	69	28	12	-	33	33	85	3,021
26 36100	Hamburg township	Livingston	32.4	20,627	20,054	211	57	90	6	40	169	236	14,520
26 36200	Hamlin township	Eaton	34.3	2,953	2,859	8	7	8	1	26	44	56	2,078
26 36220	Hamlin township	Mason	27.5	3,192	3,110	2	18	7	-	19	36	57	2,498
26 36260	Hampton township	Bay	27.1	9,902	9,412	132	48	68	-	74	168	255	7,660
26 36340	Handy township	Livingston	34.5	7,004	6,797	13	68	24	1	18	83	75	4,837
26 36400	Hanover township	Jackson	35.0	3,792	3,718	11	8	8	-	5	42	34	2,756
26 36600	Haring township	Wexford	32.5	2,962	2,905	11	17	10	-	4	15	16	2,189
26 36820	Harrison township	Macomb	14.3	24,461	23,123	604	94	141	10	109	380	362	19,109
26 36980	Hartford township	Van Buren	33.7	3,159	2,750	15	38	7	-	281	68	490	2,245
26 37040	Hartland township	Livingston	36.3	10,996	10,769	30	33	41	-	28	95	122	7,656
26 37140	Hastings charter township	Barry	30.2	2,930	2,877	3	5	3	-	23	19	37	2,204
26 37340	Hayes township	Clare	31.5	4,916	4,786	6	39	9	1	26	49	69	3,662
26 37460	Heath township	Allegan	35.5	3,100	2,991	10	5	14	1	35	44	80	2,084
26 37700	Henrietta township	Jackson	36.2	4,483	4,371	19	22	4	3	34	30	83	3,257
26 38080	Highland township	Oakland	33.6	19,169	18,675	58	89	71	3	48	225	244	13,607
26 38660	Holland township	Ottawa	27.2	28,911	22,902	642	118	2,287	8	2,188	766	4,574	19,866
26 38720	Holly township	Oakland	34.8	10,037	9,486	221	46	42	4	83	155	289	7,365
26 38820	Holton township	Muskegon	35.2	2,532	2,431	11	31	6	-	4	49	45	1,776
26 38840	Home township	Montcalm	36.0	2,708	2,611	7	14	2	-	23	51	85	1,936
26 38940	Homer township	Calhoun	35.7	3,010	2,943	6	3	2	-	3	53	51	2,105
26 38980	Homer township	Midland	21.4	3,924	3,858	11	19	4	1	4	27	40	2,864
26 39120	Hope township	Barry	32.6	3,283	3,198	8	25	5	-	9	38	38	2,428
26 39200	Hopkins township	Allegan	35.8	2,671	2,484	11	37	14	-	98	27	141	1,825
26 39480	Howard township	Cass	34.8	6,309	5,922	234	26	11	2	37	77	61	4,860
26 39560	Howell township	Livingston	31.7	5,679	5,551	10	17	14	1	17	69	61	4,091
26 40040	Huron charter township	Wayne	35.6	13,737	13,182	148	88	49	1	72	197	344	9,832
26 40260	Ida township	Monroe	36.7	4,949	4,874	7	8	10	-	25	25	62	3,491
26 40300	Imlay township	Lapeer	33.6	2,713	2,604	5	6	13	-	67	18	242	1,947
26 40400	Independence township	Oakland	35.2	32,581	31,226	274	79	396	3	198	405	818	23,564
26 40440	Indianfields township	Tuscola	34.7	6,392	5,930	181	59	35	2	107	78	258	4,954
26 40620	Ingersoll township	Midland	36.4	3,018	2,948	10	4	8	-	18	30	54	2,230
26 40880	Ionia township	Ionia	33.7	3,669	3,518	5	8	11	-	74	53	143	2,613
26 40900	Iosco township	Livingston	35.5	3,039	2,882	2	15	18	-	88	34	113	2,049
26 40920	Ira township	St. Clair	17.0	6,966	6,748	57	44	18	3	22	74	88	5,028
26 41120	Irving township	Barry	35.9	2,682	2,605	17	11	6	-	11	32	18	1,841
26 41240	Ishpeming township	Marquette	86.5	3,522	3,469	6	15	7	2	5	18	15	2,715
26 41520	Jamestown charter township	Ottawa	35.6	5,062	4,959	23	7	27	-	17	29	57	3,295
26 41620	Jefferson township	Hillsdale	35.6	3,141	3,074	8	14	5	-	13	27	26	2,335
26 41760	Jerome township	Midland	34.0	4,888	4,788	6	24	10	-	15	45	46	3,693
26 41860	Johnstown township	Barry	35.2	3,067	3,008	5	13	1	-	10	30	23	2,345
26 42180	Kalamazoo township	Kalamazoo	11.7	21,675	17,874	2,668	65	254	5	348	461	666	16,822
26 42280	Kalkaska township	Kalkaska	70.4	4,830	4,680	22	50	22	-	3	53	39	3,529
26 42360	Kawkawlin township	Bay	32.7	5,104	4,924	24	29	13	-	31	83	117	3,866
26 42500	Keeler township	Van Buren	34.0	2,601	2,311	35	30	4	-	146	75	587	1,845
26 43160	Kimball township	St. Clair	37.3	8,628	8,352	77	34	13	2	38	112	136	6,339
26 43480	Kinross charter township	Chippewa	120.1	5,922	3,825	1,021	669	36	-	49	322	159	4,701
26 43800	Kochville township	Saginaw	18.8	3,241	2,866	207	7	67	1	44	49	111	2,725
26 44140	La Grange township	Cass	33.5	3,340	2,428	631	14	74	-	36	157	62	2,459
26 44260	Lake charter township	Berrien	18.7	3,148	3,077	21	9	8	1	6	26	29	2,367
26 45160	Laketon township	Muskegon	17.3	7,363	7,052	57	42	48	-	41	123	151	5,336
26 45180	Laketown township	Allegan	21.6	5,561	5,341	28	4	49	6	84	49	206	4,056
26 45560	L'Anse township	Baraga	248.7	3,926	3,253	7	537	7	1	3	118	30	2,984
26 46020	Lansing charter township	Ingham	4.9	8,458	7,014	713	41	175	3	268	244	620	6,691
26 46060	Lapeer township	Lapeer	32.0	5,078	4,933	15	11	32	1	26	60	98	3,701
26 46160	Larkin charter township	Midland	32.8	4,514	4,377	33	8	38	-	9	49	50	3,086
26 46260	La Salle township	Monroe	26.6	5,001	4,899	18	20	13	-	14	37	116	3,729
26 46460	Lawrence township	Van Buren	35.0	3,341	2,822	98	36	12	-	237	136	448	2,371
26 46600	Lawrence township	Allegan	35.3	4,114	3,066	318	39	12	-	529	150	868	2,686
26 46640	Lee township	Midland	36.0	4,411	4,278	8	38	7	-	10	70	45	3,026
26 46760	Leighton township	Allegan	34.9	3,652	3,570	4	34	3	1	16	24	38	2,524

[Includes functioning minor civil divisions (MCDs) of 2,500 or more population as of April 1, 2000 in the following 12 states: CT, ME, MA, MI, MN, NH, NJ, NY, PA, RI, VT, and WI. Codes shown are two-digit Federal Information Processing Standards (FIPS) state codes and five-digit FIPS place codes. Place names and codes are those in effect as of January 1, 2000. County refers to the county in which the MCD is located]

State and place code	MCD	County	Land area, 2000 (sq. mi.)	Population, 2000 (April 1)									
					By race—								
					One race							Hispanic or Latino (of any race)	18 years and over
				Total	White	Black or African American	American Indian and Alaska Native	Asian	Native Hawaiian and Other Pacific Islander	Some other race	Two or more races		
26 00000	MICHIGAN—Con.												
26 46900	Lenox township	Macomb	38.8	8,433	6,662	1,395	62	22	1	57	234	239	6,342
26 46980	Leoni township	Jackson	49.1	13,459	13,060	110	42	44	3	42	158	218	9,969
26 47060	Leroy township	Calhoun	35.9	3,240	3,133	22	14	5	-	21	45	54	2,400
26 47080	Leroy township	Ingham	34.2	3,653	3,545	18	15	9	2	16	48	39	2,606
26 47300	Lexington township	Sanilac	36.2	3,688	3,623	2	11	9	-	25	18	77	2,829
26 47360	Liberty township	Jackson	34.8	2,903	2,844	4	8	11	-	12	24	32	2,158
26 47460	Lima township	Washtenaw	36.2	3,224	3,145	12	7	19	-	7	34	29	2,360
26 47600	Lincoln charter township	Berrien	17.9	13,952	13,341	148	44	194	3	83	139	182	10,316
26 48020	Littlefield township	Emmet	21.7	2,783	2,560	12	129	9	-	7	66	21	2,065
26 49060	Lockport township	St. Joseph	29.6	3,814	3,277	396	16	22	-	34	69	85	2,720
26 49120	Lodi township	Washtenaw	33.7	5,710	5,381	130	18	80	3	15	83	70	4,033
26 49180	London township	Monroe	35.7	3,024	2,569	391	13	1	-	6	44	43	2,129
26 49240	Long Lake township	Grand Traverse	30.1	7,648	7,433	20	55	34	-	20	86	71	5,394
26 49560	Lowell township	Kent	32.6	5,219	5,045	43	21	26	-	28	56	90	3,643
26 49780	Lyndon township	Washtenaw	32.1	2,728	2,451	167	32	9	-	35	34	68	2,085
26 49820	Lyon township	Oakland	31.3	11,041	10,721	39	45	67	4	50	115	162	7,859
26 49920	Lyons township	Ionia	36.2	3,446	3,346	3	21	1	-	17	58	58	2,415
26 50480	Macomb township	Macomb	36.3	50,478	48,518	426	95	713	4	157	565	735	35,222
26 50540	Madison charter township	Lenawee	30.7	8,200	6,694	1,070	22	29	-	273	112	603	6,538
26 50640	Mancelona township	Antrim	71.4	4,100	3,955	9	53	1	2	11	69	61	2,892
26 50680	Manchester township	Washtenaw	38.0	4,102	4,026	15	19	7	-	11	24	47	3,024
26 50740	Manistee township	Manistee	44.5	3,764	3,185	344	80	18	1	42	94	103	3,117
26 50840	Manlius township	Allegan	35.4	2,634	2,476	15	14	15	6	79	29	243	1,813
26 51060	Maple Grove township	Saginaw	35.6	2,640	2,575	23	6	2	-	18	16	39	1,988
26 51420	Marathon township	Lapeer	33.4	4,701	4,545	31	37	12	-	35	41	90	3,381
26 51480	Marcellus township	Cass	33.3	2,712	2,619	22	14	4	-	5	48	31	1,962
26 51640	Marion township	Livingston	35.6	6,757	6,607	2	28	18	1	8	93	70	4,779
26 51920	Marquette township	Marquette	54.7	3,286	3,134	3	58	30	1	6	54	24	2,531
26 51960	Marshall township	Calhoun	31.2	2,922	2,838	8	8	19	3	8	38	49	2,183
26 52000	Martin township	Allegan	35.6	2,514	2,433	4	8	16	-	28	25	53	1,785
26 52140	Mason township	Cass	20.3	2,514	2,437	6	13	18	-	8	32	42	1,877
26 52500	Mayfield township	Lapeer	34.8	7,659	7,462	19	23	30	2	29	94	132	5,562
26 53000	Mendon township	St. Joseph	35.0	2,775	2,678	28	15	3	5	13	33	47	2,018
26 53040	Menominee township	Menominee	72.7	3,939	3,895	1	16	4	-	3	20	18	3,039
26 53140	Meridian charter township	Ingham	31.0	39,116	33,781	1,584	127	2,546	21	271	786	990	29,863
26 53360	Metamora township	Lapeer	34.8	4,184	4,070	7	14	18	-	13	62	50	3,101
26 53980	Milford township	Oakland	33.3	15,271	14,884	65	42	70	-	44	166	182	10,915
26 54240	Millington township	Tuscola	35.8	4,459	4,366	11	17	5	-	11	49	50	3,283
26 54340	Mills township	Ogemaw	34.4	4,005	3,850	11	61	-	-	2	81	50	3,151
26 54460	Milton township	Cass	21.3	2,646	2,517	58	5	10	-	12	44	43	1,955
26 54980	Monitor township	Bay	37.0	10,037	9,819	22	21	37	-	50	88	169	7,895
26 55040	Monroe charter township	Monroe	17.4	13,491	12,807	252	25	111	1	107	188	266	9,954
26 55140	Montcalm township	Montcalm	35.7	3,178	3,122	4	19	3	1	9	20	40	2,288
26 55300	Montrose township	Genesee	34.4	6,336	6,066	112	50	3	-	36	69	107	4,492
26 55600	Morton township	Mecosta	33.1	3,597	3,409	58	11	9	-	12	98	40	2,994
26 55980	Mount Morris township	Genesee	31.4	23,725	12,940	9,526	148	61	9	298	743	722	16,585
26 56160	Mundy township	Genesee	36.0	12,191	11,708	172	27	100	1	54	129	225	9,422
26 56220	Munising township	Alger	202.6	3,125	2,282	593	134	10	1	27	78	48	2,498
26 56340	Muskegon township	Muskegon	23.8	17,737	16,223	822	168	50	1	141	332	569	12,567
26 56380	Mussey township	St. Clair	36.0	3,740	3,511	7	27	10	-	137	48	367	2,562
26 56640	Napoleon township	Jackson	29.4	6,962	6,726	60	22	25	-	48	81	108	5,075
26 56880	Negaunee township	Marquette	42.1	2,707	2,641	2	25	5	1	5	28	13	2,036
26 56920	Nelson township	Kent	36.0	4,192	4,089	15	13	11	-	25	39	70	2,858
26 57780	Niles township	Berrien	37.7	13,325	12,432	404	75	67	2	111	234	256	10,018
26 58090	North Branch township	Lapeer	36.1	3,595	3,492	4	12	5	-	34	48	111	2,451
26 58280	Northfield township	Washtenaw	36.3	8,252	7,933	88	38	47	10	19	117	89	6,142
26 59000	Northville township	Wayne	16.5	21,036	18,787	923	58	905	7	92	264	372	16,537
26 59180	Norvell township	Jackson	30.0	2,922	2,842	18	15	3	-	4	40	20	2,224
26 59400	Nottawa township	St. Joseph	35.8	3,999	3,870	46	10	21	-	10	42	43	2,853
26 59580	Oakfield township	Kent	34.6	5,058	4,955	7	13	17	-	13	53	41	3,629
26 59820	Oakland charter township	Oakland	36.4	13,071	12,305	262	12	342	-	25	125	155	9,079
26 60120	Oceola township	Livingston	36.3	8,362	8,121	10	39	53	2	19	118	96	5,681
26 60200	Odessa township	Ionia	35.8	4,036	3,850	6	20	20	-	88	52	185	2,818
26 60460	Olive township	Ottawa	36.2	4,691	4,191	106	29	52	1	254	58	634	3,133
26 60700	Oneida charter township	Eaton	32.5	3,703	3,585	19	17	11	1	26	44	89	2,720
26 60800	Onondaga township	Ingham	36.5	2,958	2,823	9	8	1	3	57	57	87	2,054
26 60880	Ontonagon township	Ontonagon	192.8	2,954	2,883	-	25	4	-	5	37	17	2,324
26 60900	Ontwa township	Cass	19.5	5,865	5,676	18	49	16	2	15	89	50	4,406
26 60980	Orangeville township	Barry	33.6	3,321	3,205	11	21	3	-	41	40	95	2,470
26 61060	Oregon township	Lapeer	33.2	6,166	6,028	4	26	20	-	34	54	124	4,400
26 61100	Orion township	Oakland	33.4	33,463	31,931	423	89	396	8	203	413	858	23,932
26 61160	Orleans township	Ionia	35.5	2,736	2,690	2	10	4	1	12	17	43	1,950
26 61180	Oronoko charter township	Berrien	32.5	9,843	6,550	1,721	39	692	27	431	383	840	7,681
26 61340	Oscoda township	Iosco	121.8	7,248	6,906	58	74	51	10	30	119	94	5,557
26 61400	Oshtemo township	Kalamazoo	36.0	17,003	14,447	1,597	51	385	4	184	335	397	13,461
26 61640	Otsego township	Allegan	33.3	4,854	4,718	17	15	26	2	14	62	72	3,513
26 61680	Otsego Lake township	Otsego	32.7	2,532	2,489	3	9	-	-	1	30	8	1,967

[Includes functioning minor civil divisions (MCDs) of 2,500 or more population as of April 1, 2000 in the following 12 states: CT, ME, MA, MI, MN, NH, NJ, NY, PA, RI, VT, and WI. Codes shown are two-digit Federal Information Processing Standards (FIPS) state codes and five-digit FIPS place codes. Place names and codes are those in effect as of January 1, 2000. County refers to the county in which the MCD is located]

State and place code	MCD	County	Land area, 2000 (sq. mi.)	Population, 2000 (April 1)									
					By race—								
					One race							Hispanic or Latino (of any race)	18 years and over
				Total	White	Black or African American	American Indian and Alaska Native	Asian	Native Hawaiian and Other Pacific Islander	Some other race	Two or more races		
26 00000	MICHIGAN—Con.												
26 61820	Overisel township	Allegan	35.8	2,594	2,514	1	1	13	-	57	8	88	1,793
26 61880	Ovid township	Clinton	35.8	3,490	3,387	6	15	-	9	29	44	110	2,486
26 61960	Owosso township	Shiawassee	32.4	4,670	4,564	7	13	30	1	16	39	63	3,511
26 62040	Oxford charter township	Oakland	33.9	16,025	15,517	72	42	81	3	100	210	351	11,340
26 62320	Paradise township	Grand Traverse	52.9	4,191	4,068	9	36	8	1	19	50	62	2,808
26 62460	Park township	Ottawa	19.3	17,579	16,446	79	32	376	3	383	260	959	12,140
26 62480	Park township	St. Joseph	35.1	2,699	2,537	64	13	14	-	18	53	59	2,039
26 62760	Parma township	Jackson	36.3	2,696	2,523	98	23	4	2	20	26	52	1,952
26 62960	Pavilion township	Kalamazoo	34.9	5,829	5,573	66	26	17	2	38	107	121	4,168
26 63000	Paw Paw township	Van Buren	35.2	7,091	6,637	172	62	19	2	67	132	246	5,255
26 63340	Peninsula township	Grand Traverse	27.9	5,265	5,122	3	19	31	-	51	39	106	4,050
26 63440	Pennfield charter township	Calhoun	34.8	8,913	8,271	388	42	49	3	43	117	147	6,670
26 63720	Perry township	Shiawassee	31.8	4,438	4,318	13	19	10	3	10	65	57	3,097
26 64040	Pierson township	Montcalm	34.7	2,866	2,759	2	25	8	3	17	52	39	1,996
26 64180	Pinconning township	Bay	36.6	2,608	2,512	-	23	7	-	27	39	49	1,964
26 64280	Pine Grove township	Van Buren	34.4	2,773	2,668	28	13	9	-	17	38	42	2,039
26 64560	Pittsfield charter township	Washtenaw	27.5	30,167	21,229	4,311	132	3,005	14	507	969	1,199	22,939
26 64640	Plainfield township	Iosco	103.8	4,292	4,189	4	25	5	-	4	65	30	3,392
26 64660	Plainfield township	Kent	35.1	30,195	28,892	369	98	282	13	183	358	529	21,139
26 65080	Plymouth township	Wayne	15.9	27,798	25,680	822	76	759	4	110	347	455	21,503
26 65540	Portage township	Houghton	112.6	3,156	3,029	7	13	68	-	8	31	23	2,408
26 65720	Porter township	Cass	51.7	3,794	3,694	24	20	3	-	8	45	51	2,910
26 65840	Port Huron township	St. Clair	12.9	8,615	8,066	298	53	30	2	53	113	212	6,391
26 65940	Port Sheldon township	Ottawa	22.4	4,503	4,209	23	13	50	1	130	77	277	3,176
26 65980	Portsmouth township	Bay	20.0	3,619	3,507	27	15	5	-	33	32	125	2,778
26 66260	Prairieville township	Barry	33.3	3,175	3,087	7	12	11	-	18	40	44	2,391
26 66540	Putnam township	Livingston	34.4	7,500	7,336	13	25	18	4	15	89	68	5,419
26 66660	Quincy township	Branch	35.3	4,411	4,328	8	11	10	3	20	31	50	3,115
26 66840	Raisin township	Lenawee	36.3	6,507	6,247	35	28	32	-	100	65	313	4,638
26 66900	Raisinville township	Monroe	48.2	4,896	4,795	24	8	12	-	15	42	59	3,595
26 67300	Ravenna township	Muskegon	36.3	2,856	2,769	9	9	3	-	43	23	87	1,992
26 67420	Ray township	Macomb	36.8	3,740	3,657	6	11	14	-	17	35	44	2,777
26 67625	Redford township	Wayne	11.2	51,622	45,418	4,410	222	392	10	295	875	1,044	38,544
26 68120	Reynolds township	Montcalm	36.0	4,279	4,118	20	24	6	1	19	91	71	2,951
26 68180	Richfield township	Genesee	35.3	8,170	7,723	201	39	17	-	35	155	128	6,006
26 68200	Richfield township	Roscommon	68.9	4,139	4,056	3	37	8	2	5	28	34	3,340
26 68260	Richland township	Kalamazoo	34.7	6,491	6,064	217	24	61	4	29	92	100	4,606
26 68300	Richland township	Montcalm	35.9	2,868	2,815	7	12	7	-	4	23	52	2,035
26 68340	Richland township	Saginaw	37.1	4,281	4,205	3	10	9	-	34	20	84	3,091
26 68400	Richmond township	Macomb	37.3	3,416	3,311	33	13	6	-	6	47	37	2,458
26 68620	Riley township	St. Clair	38.3	3,046	2,970	15	3	5	-	12	41	48	2,157
26 68920	Rives township	Jackson	35.9	4,725	4,590	9	29	5	3	24	65	83	3,374
26 69000	Robinson township	Ottawa	38.6	5,588	5,232	17	26	41	4	185	83	343	3,853
26 69340	Rollin township	Lenawee	33.9	3,176	3,127	4	4	12	-	4	25	41	2,381
26 69560	Roscommon township	Roscommon	103.9	4,249	4,147	34	26	10	1	2	29	37	3,202
26 69580	Rose township	Oakland	35.0	6,210	6,032	55	14	16	-	30	63	134	4,563
26 69820	Ross township	Kalamazoo	33.3	5,047	4,914	16	28	19	-	15	55	64	3,805
26 70060	Royal Oak charter township	Oakland	0.7	5,446	1,238	3,894	12	79	2	39	182	63	4,084
26 70100	Royalton township	Berrien	18.1	3,888	3,627	79	6	95	-	52	29	133	2,781
26 70420	Rutland charter township	Barry	35.2	3,646	3,558	8	16	13	-	16	35	58	2,659
26 70500	Sage township	Gladwin	34.5	2,617	2,539	1	20	10	-	7	40	10	1,971
26 70540	Saginaw charter township	Saginaw	24.6	39,657	35,205	2,095	108	1,062	2	581	604	1,652	31,288
26 70660	St. Charles township	Saginaw	37.0	3,393	3,282	16	19	9	-	27	40	110	2,473
26 70700	St. Clair township	St. Clair	39.0	6,423	6,306	17	15	19	-	17	49	67	4,641
26 70980	St. Joseph charter township	Berrien	6.7	10,042	8,557	1,152	32	173	3	44	81	105	7,639
26 71100	Salem township	Allegan	35.8	3,486	3,381	5	36	11	-	20	33	64	2,377
26 71130	Salem township	Washtenaw	34.3	5,562	5,338	74	10	38	-	20	82	63	4,059
26 71500	Sandstone township	Jackson	36.3	3,801	3,702	19	15	17	-	11	37	37	2,699
26 71580	Sanilac township	Sanilac	40.9	2,609	2,540	1	18	9	-	9	32	28	2,030
26 71720	Saugatuck township	Allegan	25.3	3,590	3,462	15	11	8	1	45	48	148	2,844
26 71880	Schoolcraft township	Kalamazoo	34.4	7,260	7,039	37	22	48	-	17	97	84	5,270
26 71940	Scio township	Washtenaw	34.0	15,759	14,109	651	43	583	5	63	305	241	11,480
26 72200	Sebewaing township	Huron	32.6	2,944	2,903	2	7	4	-	14	14	93	2,252
26 72820	Shelby charter township	Macomb	34.7	65,159	61,870	553	158	1,374	12	291	901	1,112	48,940
26 72860	Shelby township	Oceana	36.0	3,951	3,431	4	44	3	4	381	84	724	2,745
26 73200	Sherman township	Isabella	34.8	2,616	2,513	11	27	5	-	13	47	42	1,957
26 73300	Sherman township	St. Joseph	33.1	3,248	3,155	21	6	22	1	16	27	47	2,442
26 73520	Shiawassee township	Shiawassee	36.7	2,907	2,827	-	19	3	-	11	47	30	2,099
26 73840	Sidney township	Montcalm	34.1	2,563	2,499	11	19	4	-	11	19	23	1,887
26 73940	Silver Creek township	Cass	32.2	3,491	3,160	29	41	5	-	198	58	352	2,606
26 74460	Solon township	Kent	35.8	4,662	4,490	12	54	13	-	28	65	81	3,319
26 74560	Somerset township	Hillsdale	33.4	4,277	4,187	16	9	7	2	19	37	59	3,293
26 74620	Soo township	Chippewa	50.2	2,652	2,216	3	297	10	-	-	126	10	2,042
26 74920	Southfield township	Oakland	8.0	14,430	13,332	523	19	313	2	42	199	177	10,866
26 75000	South Haven charter township	Van Buren	17.5	4,046	3,322	510	29	17	-	78	90	216	2,945
26 75440	Sparta township	Kent	36.5	8,938	8,592	42	23	27	1	138	115	320	6,305
26 75560	Spencer township	Kent	35.1	3,681	3,564	28	13	15	-	6	55	47	2,677

Table D-2. MCDs — **Area and Population**—Con.

[Includes functioning minor civil divisions (MCDs) of 2,500 or more population as of April 1, 2000 in the following 12 states: CT, ME, MA, MI, MN, NH, NJ, NY, PA, RI, VT, and WI. Codes shown are two-digit Federal Information Processing Standards (FIPS) state codes and five-digit FIPS place codes. Place names and codes are those in effect as of January 1, 2000. County refers to the county in which the MCD is located]

State and place code	MCD	County	Land area, 2000 (sq. mi.)	Population, 2000 (April 1) By race— One race Total	White	Black or African American	American Indian and Alaska Native	Asian	Native Hawaiian and Other Pacific Islander	Some other race	Two or more races	Hispanic or Latino (of any race)	18 years and over
26 00000	MICHIGAN—Con.												
26 75640	Spring Arbor township	Jackson	35.4	7,577	7,353	61	30	38	10	27	58	130	5,659
26 75760	Springfield township	Oakland	35.6	13,338	12,897	146	62	73	1	35	124	264	9,492
26 75840	Spring Lake township	Ottawa	16.5	13,140	12,792	43	55	68	-	57	125	206	9,812
26 76580	Stockbridge township	Ingham	35.6	3,435	3,346	11	17	5	-	15	41	54	2,488
26 77140	Summerfield township	Monroe	42.2	3,233	3,171	8	3	2	-	42	7	90	2,355
26 77200	Summit township	Jackson	29.3	21,534	19,752	906	57	315	17	137	350	398	16,140
26 77360	Sumpter township	Wayne	37.6	11,856	10,040	1,462	62	21	-	59	212	211	8,328
26 77560	Superior township	Washtenaw	35.4	10,740	6,767	3,309	51	247	3	76	287	197	7,634
26 77580	Surrey township	Clare	35.3	3,555	3,474	10	35	10	-	4	22	39	2,755
26 77620	Suttons Bay township	Leelanau	24.6	2,982	2,252	6	567	3	-	103	51	194	2,121
26 77660	Swan Creek township	Saginaw	23.2	2,536	2,478	4	12	1	-	11	30	59	1,919
26 77800	Sylvan township	Washtenaw	35.2	6,425	6,243	43	20	33	3	17	66	82	4,841
26 77980	Tallmadge township	Ottawa	32.4	6,881	6,732	21	22	21	-	30	55	63	4,845
26 79100	Taymouth township	Saginaw	35.6	4,624	4,421	30	31	9	6	38	89	159	3,322
26 79300	Texas township	Kalamazoo	34.5	10,919	10,297	165	19	266	3	46	123	170	7,715
26 79460	Thetford township	Genesee	34.7	8,277	7,815	241	57	20	-	42	102	155	6,054
26 79520	Thomas township	Saginaw	31.5	11,877	11,533	74	26	81	-	73	90	314	8,995
26 79620	Thornapple township	Barry	35.5	6,685	6,477	10	28	31	4	42	93	94	4,565
26 79740	Three Oaks township	Berrien	23.4	2,949	2,855	26	14	3	-	12	39	48	2,195
26 79840	Tittabawassee township	Saginaw	35.2	7,706	6,729	685	41	37	3	60	151	232	5,864
26 79860	Tobacco township	Gladwin	34.0	2,552	2,526	-	3	6	1	1	15	37	1,964
26 79980	Tompkins township	Jackson	36.1	2,758	2,668	14	5	4	-	22	45	37	1,960
26 80620	Trowbridge township	Allegan	34.7	2,519	2,436	27	5	10	-	21	20	51	1,874
26 80880	Tuscarora township	Cheboygan	29.4	3,091	2,990	1	39	2	-	5	54	31	2,422
26 81140	Tyrone township	Kent	36.4	4,304	4,174	5	12	9	-	66	38	212	2,939
26 81160	Tyrone township	Livingston	35.6	8,459	8,274	5	34	52	-	21	73	81	6,027
26 81240	Unadilla township	Livingston	34.0	3,190	3,105	12	14	12	-	2	45	40	2,362
26 81280	Union township	Branch	35.7	3,121	3,012	12	16	10	-	12	59	28	2,239
26 81340	Union charter township	Isabella	28.5	7,615	6,900	138	291	80	*	51	155	180	5,963
26 81660	Van Buren township	Wayne	33.9	23,559	19,468	2,835	128	440	10	121	557	529	17,926
26 81860	Vassar township	Tuscola	35.2	4,356	4,215	20	22	19	-	19	61	97	3,075
26 81880	Venice township	Shiawassee	37.5	2,588	2,528	2	6	2	-	18	32	51	1,928
26 81920	Vergennes township	Kent	34.7	3,611	3,520	23	7	28	-	17	16	78	2,401
26 82040	Vernon township	Shiawassee	33.9	4,980	4,853	6	25	9	-	26	61	89	3,680
26 82220	Vevay township	Ingham	32.2	3,614	3,488	28	11	12	-	37	38	73	2,626
26 82320	Victor township	Clinton	34.6	3,275	3,198	14	6	2	-	22	33	57	2,323
26 82380	Vienna township	Genesee	35.0	13,108	12,583	147	67	45	1	102	163	258	9,856
26 82900	Wales township	St. Clair	37.4	2,986	2,859	97	10	2	-	4	14	32	2,145
26 84120	Washington township	Macomb	35.9	19,080	18,552	94	50	118	4	111	151	458	14,000
26 84240	Waterford township	Oakland	31.3	73,150	67,777	2,114	259	926	9	829	1,236	2,863	56,193
26 84300	Waterloo township	Jackson	47.9	3,069	2,931	88	13	4	-	11	22	22	2,270
26 84400	Watertown township	Clinton	35.7	4,162	4,000	29	8	32	5	48	40	100	3,018
26 84520	Watervliet township	Berrien	13.6	3,392	3,177	58	30	11	-	77	39	143	2,523
26 84900	Wayland township	Allegan	32.7	3,013	2,906	12	44	9	-	24	18	66	2,116
26 84920	Wayne township	Cass	34.3	2,861	2,644	60	39	6	-	60	52	104	2,075
26 85100	Webster township	Washtenaw	35.3	5,198	5,052	32	16	45	-	13	40	60	3,612
26 85240	Wells township	Delta	39.5	5,044	4,866	3	78	17	4	4	72	22	3,687
26 85480	West Bloomfield township	Oakland	27.3	64,860	54,644	3,360	78	5,063	11	246	1,458	905	47,767
26 85600	West Branch township	Ogemaw	34.2	2,628	2,588	4	6	4	-	2	24	21	1,939
26 86620	Wheeler township	Gratiot	35.8	2,785	2,676	1	2	3	1	70	32	153	2,022
26 86740	Whiteford township	Monroe	39.8	4,420	4,217	87	3	9	-	66	38	110	3,261
26 86860	White Lake township	Oakland	33.7	28,219	27,247	219	137	167	6	83	360	510	20,412
26 86940	White Pigeon township	St. Joseph	25.5	3,847	3,711	7	23	26	3	39	38	63	2,869
26 87380	Williams township	Bay	33.5	4,492	4,383	10	15	8	1	25	50	86	3,259
26 87440	Williamstown township	Ingham	29.4	4,834	4,716	30	9	27	-	6	46	50	3,435
26 87840	Windsor charter township	Eaton	34.9	7,340	6,829	222	37	30	5	93	124	251	5,567
26 88400	Woodhull township	Shiawassee	27.1	3,850	3,746	10	25	10	-	15	44	43	2,816
26 88640	Woodstock township	Lenawee	33.9	3,468	3,394	6	8	6	-	14	40	44	2,599
26 88760	Worth township	Sanilac	38.7	4,021	3,923	6	16	3	3	28	42	83	3,041
26 88820	Wright township	Ottawa	36.2	3,286	3,139	9	20	5	-	85	28	141	2,324
26 89020	Yankee Springs township	Barry	31.5	4,219	4,107	11	15	8	1	19	58	66	3,117
26 89100	York charter township	Washtenaw	35.2	7,392	6,191	940	19	77	1	62	102	300	5,726
26 89160	Ypsilanti township	Washtenaw	30.1	49,182	33,202	12,525	239	988	16	590	1,622	1,379	36,249
26 89280	Zeeland charter township	Ottawa	34.4	7,613	6,994	47	29	138	-	289	116	481	5,013
27 00000	MINNESOTA		79,610.1	4,919,479	4,400,282	171,731	54,967	141,968	1,979	65,810	82,742	143,382	3,632,585
27 00946	Alexandria township	Douglas	24.6	4,760	4,682	8	13	17	1	10	29	26	3,491
27 03286	Baldwin township	Sherburne	33.6	4,672	4,596	6	12	11	-	8	39	31	3,162
27 04636	Becker township	Sherburne	55.5	3,605	3,542	4	7	10	-	10	32	23	2,315
27 05086	Bemidji township	Beltrami	21.1	2,934	2,622	6	200	12	-	16	78	25	2,090
27 05770	Big Lake township	Sherburne	42.3	6,785	6,670	12	16	25	8	24	30	61	4,510
27 07246	Bradford township	Isanti	34.5	3,472	3,398	10	18	14	3	4	25	25	2,407
27 07840	Brockway township	Stearns	47.9	2,551	2,532	-	1	8	-	4	6	4	1,750
27 08740	Burns township	Anoka	33.8	3,557	3,505	7	10	6	-	5	24	21	2,393
27 10180	Cascade township	Olmsted	17.4	3,183	2,914	10	-	207	-	23	29	37	2,106
27 11368	Chisago Lake township	Chisago	46.2	3,276	3,249	11	4	2	-	1	9	27	2,282
27 12592	Collegeville township	Stearns	31.6	3,516	3,413	22	2	55	1	12	11	30	2,929

[Includes functioning minor civil divisions [MCDs] of 2,500 or more population as of April 1, 2000 in the following 12 states: CT, ME, MA, MI, MN, NH, NJ, NY, PA, RI, VT, and WI. Codes shown are two-digit Federal Information Processing Standards (FIPS) state codes and five-digit FIPS place codes. Place names and codes are those in effect as of January 1, 2000. County refers to the county in which the MCD is located]

State and place code	MCD	County	Land area, 2000 (sq. mi.)	Population, 2000 (April 1)									
					By race—							Hispanic or Latino (of any race)	18 years and over
					One race						Two or more races		
				Total	White	Black or African American	American Indian and Alaska Native	Asian	Native Hawaiian and Other Pacific Islander	Some other race			
27 00000	MINNESOTA—Con.												
27 12718	Columbus township	Anoka	44.9	3,957	3,862	7	22	22	-	3	41	23	2,856
27 13726	Credit River township	Scott	23.4	3,895	3,824	11	11	29	-	4	16	22	2,665
27 21788	Forest Lake township	Washington	26.9	7,642	7,463	15	19	46	3	24	72	71	5,494
27 22400	Franklin township	Wright	42.8	2,774	2,736	3	9	16	1	4	5	23	2,014
27 24956	Grand Lake township	St. Louis	65.9	2,621	2,506	16	53	5	1	11	29	22	2,006
27 25136	Grand Rapids township	Itasca	33.7	11,747	11,300	27	195	63	2	34	126	86	8,951
27 27296	Harris township	Itasca	31.9	3,328	3,257	7	23	10	-	2	29	7	2,512
27 33992	La Grand township	Douglas	26.4	4,056	4,024	3	3	16	-	1	9	8	3,038
27 37376	Linwood township	Anoka	33.4	4,668	4,549	14	18	14	5	6	62	56	3,269
27 37754	Livonia township	Sherburne	31.8	3,917	3,850	6	12	19	-	10	20	23	2,575
27 40616	Marion township	Olmsted	33.6	6,159	5,879	86	7	56	4	46	81	105	4,419
27 41120	May township	Washington	35.3	2,928	2,862	3	9	22	-	14	18	37	2,078
27 43792	Monticello township	Wright	40.1	4,139	4,030	10	24	22	1	21	31	62	2,836
27 45700	New London township	Kandiyohi	24.8	3,057	3,015	3	5	8	1	14	11	24	2,235
27 45754	New Market township	Scott	33.8	3,057	3,003	6	7	7	1	15	18	33	2,041
27 45952	New Scandia township	Washington	36.0	3,692	3,613	9	7	21	2	10	30	28	2,735
27 46906	Northern township	Beltrami	27.5	4,021	3,695	9	216	29	1	9	62	32	2,809
27 48670	Orrock township	Sherburne	34.9	2,764	2,701	3	14	12	-	14	20	29	1,855
27 51784	Pokegama township	Pine	51.6	2,570	2,526	5	18	-	-	4	17	14	1,948
27 54070	Rice Lake township	St. Louis	32.4	4,139	4,049	12	24	10	4	4	36	17	3,000
27 54898	Rochester township	Olmsted	22.3	2,916	2,794	33	7	49	-	4	29	35	2,077
27 55024	Rockford township	Wright	34.7	3,444	3,345	14	10	17	-	22	36	55	2,462
27 56752	St. Augusta township	Stearns	37.6	3,065	3,028	2	1	16	-	1	17	12	2,096
27 61978	Spring Lake township	Scott	30.3	3,681	3,616	11	12	13	5	2	22	22	2,548
27 62842	Stillwater township	Washington	16.5	2,553	2,509	3	6	26	1	1	7	14	1,773
27 64768	Thomson township	Carlton	39.7	4,361	4,269	9	27	26	-	1	29	18	3,085
27 67630	Wakefield township	Stearns	30.9	3,103	3,009	15	3	2	1	38	35	106	2,108
27 68476	Watab township	Benton	20.3	2,920	2,882	4	4	10	-	5	15	21	2,055
27 69520	West Lakeland township	Washington	12.4	3,547	3,441	12	7	43	-	14	30	53	2,333
27 69898	White township	St. Louis	109.2	3,477	3,412	1	15	11	-	1	37	15	2,738
27 69916	White Bear township	Ramsey	7.5	11,293	10,970	46	25	136	2	37	77	134	8,023
27 72040	Wyoming township	Chisago	29.7	4,379	4,267	9	13	24	-	14	52	46	2,961
33 00000	NEW HAMPSHIRE		8,968.1	1,235,786	1,186,851	9,035	2,964	15,931	371	7,420	13,214	20,489	926,224
33 00660	Allenstown town	Merrimack	20.5	4,843	4,738	24	11	18	-	13	39	57	3,521
33 01060	Alton town	Belknap	63.1	4,502	4,446	3	15	13	2	3	20	24	3,430
33 01300	Amherst town	Hillsborough	34.3	10,769	10,446	46	14	144	2	23	94	109	7,359
33 02340	Atkinson town	Rockingham	11.1	6,178	6,031	16	4	73	-	13	41	43	4,665
33 02820	Auburn town	Rockingham	25.2	4,682	4,602	10	11	19	-	11	29	44	3,327
33 03220	Barnstead town	Belknap	41.9	3,886	3,798	24	12	23	-	2	27	23	2,860
33 03460	Barrington town	Strafford	46.6	7,475	7,334	19	10	31	4	17	60	69	5,418
33 03700	Bartlett town	Carroll	75.3	2,705	2,655	4	8	11	-	17	10	11	2,113
33 04500	Bedford town	Hillsborough	32.8	18,274	17,801	59	11	234	4	23	142	165	13,053
33 04740	Belmont town	Belknap	30.6	6,716	6,550	10	22	35	-	11	88	64	5,038
33 06260	Boscawen town	Merrimack	24.7	3,672	3,589	21	11	17	-	6	28	30	2,832
33 06500	Bow town	Merrimack	28.1	7,138	6,980	9	7	74	-	21	47	35	4,811
33 07220	Brentwood town	Rockingham	16.8	3,197	3,084	27	8	28	2	23	25	47	2,406
33 07700	Bristol town	Grafton	17.3	3,033	2,914	8	12	42	1	15	41	29	2,296
33 08100	Brookline town	Hillsborough	19.8	4,181	4,092	6	8	26	2	9	38	38	2,775
33 08660	Campton town	Grafton	51.9	2,719	2,665	1	1	19	4	-	29	11	2,073
33 08980	Canaan town	Grafton	53.2	3,319	3,257	4	4	12	-	7	35	17	2,422
33 09300	Candia town	Rockingham	30.3	3,911	3,837	17	18	23	1	4	11	34	2,869
33 11380	Charlestown town	Sullivan	35.8	4,749	4,679	15	12	7	-	3	33	28	3,576
33 12100	Chester town	Rockingham	25.9	3,792	3,715	10	16	12	-	6	33	31	2,618
33 12260	Chesterfield town	Cheshire	45.6	3,542	3,464	8	20	6	-	3	41	20	2,623
33 14660	Conway town	Carroll	69.7	8,604	8,383	21	27	67	-	21	85	36	6,672
33 17140	Danville town	Rockingham	11.7	4,023	3,926	23	11	14	1	12	36	34	2,847
33 17460	Deerfield town	Rockingham	50.9	3,678	3,624	6	5	5	-	8	30	11	2,576
33 17940	Derry town	Rockingham	35.8	34,021	32,676	305	71	362	16	205	386	643	23,767
33 19700	Durham town	Strafford	22.4	12,664	11,974	98	27	392	16	34	123	157	11,144
33 24340	Enfield town	Grafton	40.3	4,618	4,523	7	5	34	-	8	41	34	3,609
33 24660	Epping town	Rockingham	26.0	5,476	5,316	15	13	24	-	8	100	42	3,993
33 24900	Epsom town	Merrimack	34.2	4,021	3,966	4	4	13	-	4	30	18	3,037
33 25380	Exeter town	Rockingham	19.6	14,058	13,662	59	24	132	-	41	140	122	10,649
33 26020	Farmington town	Strafford	37.1	5,774	5,670	2	25	7	-	12	58	58	4,151
33 27940	Fremont town	Rockingham	17.2	3,510	3,445	2	2	12	-	18	31	27	2,490
33 28740	Gilford town	Belknap	39.0	6,803	6,689	13	10	35	-	5	51	39	5,190
33 28980	Gilmanton town	Belknap	57.1	3,060	3,017	3	6	4	-	-	30	9	2,319
33 29860	Goffstown town	Hillsborough	36.9	16,929	16,625	43	40	53	2	55	111	141	13,092
33 30260	Gorham town	Coos	31.9	2,895	2,818	2	6	35	1	4	29	9	2,256
33 31700	Greenland town	Rockingham	10.5	3,208	3,137	9	1	39	1	4	17	23	2,357
33 32900	Hampstead town	Rockingham	13.3	8,297	8,170	19	7	45	4	13	39	65	5,901
33 33060	Hampton town	Rockingham	13.0	14,937	14,574	59	26	129	10	37	102	135	11,746
33 33860	Hanover town	Grafton	49.1	10,850	9,546	189	51	734	7	96	227	276	9,211
33 34820	Haverhill town	Grafton	51.1	4,416	4,338	20	11	16	1	9	21	27	3,373
33 35540	Henniker town	Merrimack	44.1	4,433	4,284	20	8	44	1	17	59	37	3,328

Table D-2. MCDs — **Area and Population**—Con.

[Includes functioning minor civil divisions [MCDs] of 2,500 or more population as of April 1, 2000 in the following 12 states: CT, ME, MA, MI, MN, NH, NJ, NY, PA, RI, VT, and WI. Codes shown are two-digit Federal Information Processing Standards (FIPS) state codes and five-digit FIPS place codes. Place names and codes are those in effect as of January 1, 2000. County refers to the county in which the MCD is located]

State and place code	MCD	County	Land area, 2000 (sq. mi.)	Population, 2000 (April 1) Total	By race—One race White	Black or African American	American Indian and Alaska Native	Asian	Native Hawaiian and Other Pacific Islander	Some other race	Two or more races	Hispanic or Latino (of any race)	18 years and over
33 00000	NEW HAMPSHIRE—Con.												
33 36180	Hillsborough town	Hillsborough	43.6	4,928	4,803	9	22	46	-	6	42	26	3,623
33 36660	Hinsdale town	Cheshire	20.7	4,082	3,980	17	8	13	12	9	43	19	3,020
33 37140	Hollis town	Hillsborough	31.7	7,015	6,776	31	8	116	1	12	71	65	4,937
33 37300	Hooksett town	Merrimack	36.2	11,721	11,305	80	28	195	3	23	87	170	8,872
33 37540	Hopkinton town	Merrimack	43.3	5,399	5,316	7	14	14	4	2	42	27	3,967
33 37940	Hudson town	Hillsborough	28.3	22,928	22,091	193	34	255	13	125	217	356	16,460
33 38600	Jaffrey town	Cheshire	38.3	5,476	5,329	23	19	38	-	2	65	31	4,052
33 40100	Kingston town	Rockingham	19.6	5,862	5,743	13	7	24	3	26	46	48	4,357
33 40420	Lancaster town	Coos	50.1	3,280	3,217	2	9	7	-	8	37	21	2,452
33 41460	Lee town	Strafford	19.9	4,145	3,980	23	9	65	8	16	44	49	2,866
33 42260	Litchfield town	Hillsborough	15.1	7,360	7,192	39	21	42	-	11	55	61	4,904
33 42580	Littleton town	Grafton	50.2	5,845	5,643	22	33	49	3	35	60	85	4,405
33 43220	Londonderry town	Rockingham	41.8	23,236	22,521	129	40	269	6	75	196	356	15,593
33 43380	Loudon town	Merrimack	46.8	4,481	4,402	11	9	20	-	5	34	27	3,231
33 47140	Meredith town	Belknap	40.2	5,943	5,819	10	10	34	4	13	53	30	4,607
33 47540	Merrimack town	Hillsborough	32.6	25,119	24,260	184	48	378	10	54	185	272	17,826
33 48020	Milford town	Hillsborough	25.2	13,535	13,096	122	19	125	1	28	144	158	9,780
33 48660	Milton town	Strafford	33.1	3,910	3,826	8	12	10	-	3	51	16	2,853
33 49380	Moultonborough town	Carroll	59.8	4,484	4,416	6	10	25	-	1	26	28	3,537
33 50740	New Boston town	Hillsborough	42.8	4,138	4,056	15	4	15	-	13	35	26	2,880
33 51940	New Ipswich town	Hillsborough	32.7	4,289	4,227	8	5	16	-	6	27	34	2,809
33 52100	New London town	Merrimack	22.5	4,116	4,048	9	2	30	1	8	18	26	3,529
33 52340	Newmarket town	Rockingham	12.6	8,027	7,558	51	16	241	-	34	127	139	6,250
33 52580	Newport town	Sullivan	43.6	6,269	6,144	9	13	22	-	7	74	35	4,610
33 52900	Newton town	Rockingham	9.9	4,289	4,199	29	7	3	1	17	33	56	3,055
33 54260	Northfield town	Merrimack	28.8	4,548	4,465	6	8	19	-	7	43	42	3,281
33 54580	North Hampton town	Rockingham	13.9	4,259	4,191	13	2	27	-	9	17	33	3,265
33 56820	Northwood town	Rockingham	28.0	3,640	3,550	11	11	24	5	7	32	20	2,655
33 57460	Nottingham town	Rockingham	46.5	3,701	3,641	7	7	21	1	10	14	26	2,673
33 58710	Ossipee town	Carroll	71.1	4,211	4,125	6	16	9	-	3	52	14	3,205
33 59940	Pelham town	Hillsborough	26.4	10,914	10,624	48	24	114	-	27	77	105	7,765
33 60020	Pembroke town	Merrimack	22.8	6,897	6,748	26	18	26	-	2	77	30	5,039
33 60580	Peterborough town	Hillsborough	37.7	5,883	5,705	37	9	76	2	16	38	49	4,405
33 61940	Pittsfield town	Merrimack	23.6	3,931	3,828	15	5	4	-	10	69	45	2,821
33 62500	Plaistow town	Rockingham	10.6	7,747	7,618	16	8	39	-	23	43	102	5,746
33 62660	Plymouth town	Grafton	28.4	5,892	5,688	25	8	49	-	30	92	86	4,937
33 64020	Raymond town	Rockingham	28.8	9,674	9,460	54	23	18	5	25	89	76	6,854
33 64580	Rindge town	Cheshire	37.2	5,451	5,299	63	8	18	1	22	40	48	4,137
33 65540	Rollinsford town	Strafford	7.3	2,648	2,589	18	2	14	-	2	23	16	1,982
33 66180	Rye town	Rockingham	12.6	5,182	5,115	7	4	24	-	5	27	32	4,031
33 66660	Salem town	Rockingham	24.7	28,112	26,708	156	59	639	18	232	300	552	21,001
33 67300	Sanbornton town	Belknap	47.5	2,581	2,533	4	4	13	-	3	24	11	1,928
33 67620	Sandown town	Rockingham	13.9	5,143	5,062	11	6	8	1	19	36	29	3,527
33 68260	Seabrook town	Rockingham	8.9	7,934	7,737	27	19	43	-	30	78	68	6,310
33 73860	Strafford town	Strafford	49.2	3,626	3,571	5	5	9	-	2	34	23	2,538
33 74340	Stratham town	Rockingham	15.1	6,355	6,226	10	3	53	-	9	54	41	4,507
33 75060	Sunapee town	Sullivan	21.1	3,055	2,993	6	6	11	1	10	28	14	2,359
33 75700	Swanzey town	Cheshire	45.0	6,800	6,686	12	16	36	1	9	40	38	5,096
33 76100	Tamworth town	Carroll	59.9	2,510	2,461	4	6	5	-	9	25	16	1,916
33 77060	Tilton town	Belknap	11.4	3,477	3,361	2	22	21	3	6	62	34	2,677
33 78180	Wakefield town	Carroll	39.3	4,252	4,176	4	19	8	-	8	37	24	3,160
33 78420	Walpole town	Cheshire	35.6	3,594	3,533	5	9	6	-	3	38	17	2,693
33 78580	Warner town	Merrimack	55.7	2,760	2,714	1	7	6	-	3	29	20	2,085
33 79780	Weare town	Hillsborough	58.8	7,776	7,640	13	17	33	-	17	56	54	5,284
33 85220	Wilton town	Hillsborough	25.8	3,743	3,652	13	5	19	-	17	37	29	2,735
33 85540	Winchester town	Cheshire	54.9	4,144	4,035	13	23	13	-	9	51	34	3,087
33 85780	Windham town	Rockingham	26.8	10,709	10,376	34	7	167	13	37	75	106	7,580
33 86420	Wolfeboro town	Carroll	48.3	6,083	6,030	10	4	22	-	3	14	37	4,741
34 00000	NEW JERSEY		7,417.3	8,414,350	6,104,705	1,141,821	19,492	480,276	3,329	450,972	213,755	1,117,191	6,326,792
34 00000	Aberdeen township	Monmouth	5.5	17,454	13,758	2,098	24	962	1	306	305	1,225	13,185
34 00550	Alexandria township	Hunterdon	27.5	4,698	4,558	37	5	34	2	21	41	81	3,378
34 00670	Allamuchy township	Warren	20.5	3,877	3,702	36	2	72	-	27	38	104	3,142
34 00880	Alloway township	Salem	32.8	2,774	2,516	191	15	12	-	11	29	66	1,995
34 01360	Andover township	Sussex	20.2	6,033	5,698	112	5	139	2	36	41	136	4,522
34 03050	Barnegat township	Ocean	34.7	15,270	14,468	338	14	152	-	107	191	590	11,137
34 04450	Bedminster township	Somerset	26.5	8,302	7,476	145	9	532	2	69	69	319	6,822
34 04695	Belleville township	Essex	3.3	35,928	24,950	1,926	60	4,062	26	3,532	1,372	8,507	28,082
34 05305	Berkeley township	Ocean	42.9	39,991	38,833	519	16	181	4	173	265	932	35,433
34 05320	Berkeley Heights township	Union	6.3	13,407	12,019	149	11	1,055	-	82	91	494	9,812
34 05470	Berlin township	Camden	3.2	5,290	4,362	628	9	143	4	64	80	254	3,926
34 05560	Bernards township	Somerset	24.0	24,575	21,921	354	13	1,928	3	98	258	646	17,770
34 05650	Bethlehem township	Hunterdon	20.8	3,820	3,725	33	4	39	2	1	16	62	2,693
34 06160	Blairstown township	Warren	31.0	5,747	5,642	15	8	32	1	16	33	114	4,278
34 06260	Bloomfield township	Essex	5.3	47,683	33,421	5,573	91	3,998	31	3,061	1,508	6,901	37,644
34 06640	Boonton township	Morris	8.4	4,287	3,987	51	2	175	-	27	45	92	3,221
34 06700	Bordentown township	Burlington	8.5	8,380	7,486	421	17	278	-	57	121	254	6,394
34 07180	Branchburg township	Somerset	20.3	14,566	13,174	284	15	898	4	57	134	392	10,583

Table D-2. MCDs — **Area and Population**—Con.

[Includes functioning minor civil divisions [MCDs] of 2,500 or more population as of April 1, 2000 in the following 12 states: CT, ME, MA, MI, MN, NH, NJ, NY, PA, RI, VT, and WI. Codes shown are two-digit Federal Information Processing Standards (FIPS) state codes and five-digit FIPS place codes. Place names and codes are those in effect as of January 1, 2000. County refers to the county in which the MCD is located]

State and place code	MCD	County	Land area, 2000 (sq. mi.)	Population, 2000 (April 1)									
					By race—							Hispanic or Latino (of any race)	18 years and over
					One race						Two or more races		
				Total	White	Black or African American	American Indian and Alaska Native	Asian	Native Hawaiian and Other Pacific Islander	Some other race			

State and place code	MCD	County	Land area, 2000 (sq. mi.)	Total	White	Black or African American	American Indian and Alaska Native	Asian	Native Hawaiian and Other Pacific Islander	Some other race	Two or more races	Hispanic or Latino (of any race)	18 years and over
34 00000	NEW JERSEY—Con.												
34 07420	Brick township	Ocean	26.2	76,119	72,932	751	76	904	12	650	794	2,930	57,965
34 07720	Bridgewater township	Somerset	32.4	42,940	36,527	931	33	4,525	5	381	538	2,056	31,922
34 08710	Buena Vista township	Atlantic	41.4	7,436	5,751	1,167	16	17	1	303	181	689	5,598
34 08950	Burlington township	Burlington	13.5	20,294	13,742	4,971	33	757	6	296	489	814	14,775
34 09160	Byram township	Sussex	21.1	8,254	7,905	80	5	116	5	53	90	243	5,874
34 10610	Carneys Point township	Salem	17.5	7,684	6,034	1,250	21	70	3	161	145	306	5,927
34 11200	Cedar Grove township	Essex	4.2	12,300	11,076	368	6	667	3	57	123	393	9,934
34 12130	Chatham township	Morris	9.3	10,086	9,452	45	6	485	1	15	82	197	7,392
34 12280	Cherry Hill township	Camden	24.3	69,965	59,240	3,121	71	6,205	24	491	813	1,778	53,495
34 12610	Chester township	Morris	29.3	7,282	6,927	84	1	174	4	19	73	188	5,064
34 12670	Chesterfield township	Burlington	21.4	5,955	2,960	2,225	40	38	5	503	184	735	5,250
34 12940	Cinnaminson township	Burlington	7.6	14,595	13,334	742	24	274	1	72	148	224	11,012
34 13045	City of Orange township	Essex	2.2	32,868	4,337	24,685	113	415	33	1,712	1,573	4,097	23,760
34 13150	Clark township	Union	4.3	14,597	13,956	44	2	402	-	92	101	535	11,562
34 13750	Clinton township	Hunterdon	30.0	12,957	11,365	902	26	304	9	206	145	507	9,559
34 14560	Colts Neck township	Monmouth	31.4	12,331	10,544	973	28	447	1	179	159	520	8,731
34 14710	Commercial township	Cumberland	32.5	5,259	4,364	706	22	12	1	53	101	203	3,773
34 15550	Cranbury township	Middlesex	13.4	3,227	2,865	73	-	239	-	7	43	55	2,245
34 15640	Cranford township	Union	4.8	22,578	21,156	583	9	485	5	151	189	879	17,316
34 16900	Deerfield township	Cumberland	16.8	2,927	2,289	382	45	30	-	89	92	174	2,154
34 17080	Delanco township	Burlington	2.5	3,237	3,104	62	8	13	-	13	37	63	2,430
34 17170	Delaware township	Hunterdon	36.7	4,478	4,375	18	2	46	1	11	25	51	3,429
34 17440	Delran township	Burlington	6.6	15,536	12,875	1,464	27	435	25	253	457	505	11,722
34 17560	Dennis township	Cape May	61.4	6,492	6,325	62	6	28	1	40	30	98	4,656
34 17650	Denville township	Morris	12.1	15,824	14,659	181	12	734	5	70	163	418	12,047
34 17710	Deptford township	Gloucester	17.5	26,763	22,330	3,314	56	410	9	266	378	766	20,383
34 18130	Dover township	Ocean	41.0	89,706	83,939	1,568	117	2,207	21	850	1,004	4,070	68,815
34 18790	Eastampton township	Burlington	5.8	6,202	4,853	730	14	336	-	89	180	293	4,371
34 18820	East Amwell township	Hunterdon	28.7	4,455	4,320	32	6	41	1	21	34	68	3,328
34 19000	East Brunswick township	Middlesex	22.0	46,756	36,265	1,321	42	7,607	5	526	990	1,957	34,588
34 19180	East Greenwich township	Gloucester	14.7	5,430	5,141	177	7	35	-	13	57	76	4,070
34 19210	East Hanover township	Morris	8.2	11,393	9,921	66	3	1,269	-	27	107	312	8,828
34 19780	East Windsor township	Mercer	15.6	24,919	18,545	2,217	49	2,380	31	1,148	549	3,559	18,935
34 20050	Edgewater Park township	Burlington	2.9	7,864	5,353	1,683	13	256	1	252	306	519	6,053
34 20230	Edison township	Middlesex	30.1	97,687	58,116	6,728	132	28,597	37	1,973	2,104	6,226	75,365
34 20290	Egg Harbor township	Atlantic	67.3	30,726	24,404	3,185	66	1,552	15	868	636	2,076	22,142
34 21060	Elk township	Gloucester	19.6	3,514	2,884	501	20	15	-	48	46	103	2,558
34 22110	Evesham township	Burlington	29.5	42,275	38,579	1,313	31	1,721	8	203	420	829	30,790
34 22185	Ewing township	Mercer	15.3	35,707	24,645	8,863	55	811	22	653	658	1,586	29,263
34 22350	Fairfield township	Cumberland	42.3	6,283	2,602	2,980	319	35	2	150	195	557	5,037
34 22385	Fairfield township	Essex	10.5	7,063	6,754	37	7	199	-	28	38	244	5,506
34 23850	Florence township	Burlington	9.7	10,746	9,190	1,047	19	253	1	70	166	253	8,039
34 24810	Frankford township	Sussex	34.1	5,420	5,320	21	3	21	-	27	28	96	4,067
34 24840	Franklin township	Gloucester	56.0	15,466	13,954	1,030	48	63	2	193	176	543	11,185
34 24870	Franklin township	Hunterdon	22.9	2,990	2,916	12	7	23	-	10	22	67	2,244
34 24900	Franklin township	Somerset	46.8	50,903	28,052	13,223	93	6,486	21	1,811	1,217	4,127	39,361
34 24960	Franklin township	Warren	24.0	2,768	2,686	23	2	24	-	3	30	55	1,970
34 25140	Fredon township	Sussex	17.8	2,860	2,779	15	7	24	-	16	19	62	2,099
34 25230	Freehold township	Monmouth	38.5	31,537	27,466	1,616	44	1,623	5	374	409	1,637	23,564
34 25560	Galloway township	Atlantic	90.5	31,209	24,081	3,058	75	2,498	15	807	675	1,924	23,147
34 26760	Gloucester township	Camden	23.2	64,350	53,484	7,432	100	1,688	16	715	915	1,962	47,057
34 27420	Green township	Sussex	16.2	3,220	3,107	30	1	31	-	9	42	103	2,227
34 27510	Green Brook township	Somerset	4.6	5,654	5,000	95	4	452	2	40	61	231	4,278
34 28185	Greenwich township	Gloucester	9.3	4,879	4,613	162	5	33	1	13	52	75	3,767
34 28260	Greenwich township	Warren	10.6	4,365	4,071	108	12	97	3	25	49	166	2,897
34 28740	Haddon township	Camden	2.7	14,651	13,980	173	8	294	6	82	108	226	11,340
34 29010	Hainesport township	Burlington	6.5	4,126	3,882	110	4	70	-	21	39	88	3,042
34 29280	Hamilton township	Atlantic	111.3	20,499	14,646	3,949	60	675	10	682	477	1,621	14,946
34 29310	Hamilton township	Mercer	39.5	87,109	74,173	7,112	121	2,234	31	1,908	1,530	4,471	66,909
34 29490	Hampton township	Sussex	24.6	4,943	4,809	48	1	33	1	15	36	94	3,632
34 29550	Hanover township	Morris	10.7	12,898	11,452	140	7	1,123	1	76	99	452	9,956
34 29700	Harding township	Morris	20.4	3,180	3,091	13	-	34	1	7	34	57	2,379
34 29850	Hardyston township	Sussex	32.1	6,171	5,897	52	10	97	-	30	85	199	4,588
34 30090	Harmony township	Warren	23.8	2,729	2,672	19	2	11	-	5	20	35	2,071
34 30180	Harrison township	Gloucester	19.1	8,788	8,363	260	11	64	-	36	54	156	5,866
34 30690	Hazlet township	Monmouth	5.6	21,378	19,918	235	12	725	1	242	245	1,254	15,932
34 31890	Hillsborough township	Somerset	54.7	36,634	31,491	1,379	32	2,679	23	468	562	1,740	25,963
34 31980	Hillside township	Union	2.8	21,747	8,705	10,122	50	751	17	1,144	958	3,153	16,185
34 32460	Holland township	Hunterdon	23.7	5,124	5,026	22	2	22	-	20	32	87	3,856
34 32640	Holmdel township	Monmouth	18.0	15,781	12,657	102	4	2,753	1	82	182	387	11,279
34 33120	Hopewell township	Cumberland	29.9	4,434	3,862	306	103	25	1	64	73	159	3,430
34 33180	Hopewell township	Mercer	58.1	16,105	14,220	939	20	639	4	107	176	395	11,833
34 33300	Howell township	Monmouth	60.9	48,903	44,008	1,739	58	1,749	5	633	711	2,610	33,815
34 33930	Independence township	Warren	19.8	5,603	5,322	65	3	97	-	44	72	211	4,104
34 34450	Irvington township	Essex	3.0	60,695	5,446	49,566	146	669	59	2,234	2,575	5,086	43,691
34 34680	Jackson township	Ocean	100.1	42,816	39,073	1,670	57	882	3	414	717	2,474	30,114
34 34980	Jefferson township	Morris	40.6	19,717	18,955	163	32	211	10	122	224	672	14,407
34 37065	Kingwood township	Hunterdon	35.2	3,782	3,692	23	3	29	-	7	28	70	2,750

Table D-2. MCDs — **Area and Population**—Con.

[Includes functioning minor civil divisions [MCDs] of 2,500 or more population as of April 1, 2000 in the following 12 states: CT, ME, MA, MI, MN, NH, NJ, NY, PA, RI, VT, and WI. Codes shown are two-digit Federal Information Processing Standards (FIPS) state codes and five-digit FIPS place codes. Place names and codes are those in effect as of January 1, 2000. County refers to the county in which the MCD is located]

State and place code	MCD	County	Land area, 2000 (sq. mi.)	Population, 2000 (April 1)									
					By race—								
					One race							Hispanic or Latino (of any race)	18 years and over
				Total	White	Black or African American	American Indian and Alaska Native	Asian	Native Hawaiian and Other Pacific Islander	Some other race	Two or more races		
34 00000	NEW JERSEY—Con.												
34 37320	Knowlton township	Warren	24.8	2,977	2,901	12	2	19	-	14	29	55	2,154
34 37380	Lacey township	Ocean	84.0	25,346	24,800	91	38	139	2	103	173	545	18,863
34 38550	Lakewood township	Ocean	24.8	60,352	47,542	7,270	105	836	19	2,783	1,797	8,935	41,166
34 39450	Lawrence township	Cumberland	37.5	2,721	2,228	283	29	7	5	93	76	191	1,946
34 39510	Lawrence township	Mercer	22.1	29,159	23,101	2,707	23	2,306	31	523	468	1,344	22,836
34 39660	Lebanon township	Hunterdon	31.7	5,816	5,640	47	6	54	1	22	46	100	4,332
34 40110	Liberty township	Warren	11.8	2,765	2,693	10	3	16	-	15	28	74	1,981
34 40560	Little Egg Harbor township	Ocean	49.1	15,945	15,342	126	41	96	1	156	183	520	12,091
34 40620	Little Falls township	Passaic	2.8	10,855	10,001	71	7	456	2	144	174	579	8,888
34 40890	Livingston township	Essex	13.9	27,391	22,637	328	14	3,982	3	190	237	695	20,107
34 41160	Logan township	Gloucester	22.6	6,032	4,946	815	8	107	1	73	82	165	4,095
34 41250	Long Beach township	Ocean	5.3	3,329	3,280	8	1	12	-	11	17	70	2,940
34 41362	Long Hill township	Morris	12.1	8,777	8,141	34	15	420	3	49	115	303	6,470
34 41490	Lopatcong township	Warren	7.1	5,765	5,550	65	4	94	-	28	24	115	4,351
34 41610	Lower township	Cape May	28.2	22,945	22,088	319	52	121	5	150	210	432	17,504
34 42060	Lumberton township	Burlington	12.9	10,461	8,192	1,438	24	354	2	199	252	539	7,524
34 42090	Lyndhurst township	Bergen	4.6	19,383	17,433	119	9	1,046	1	397	378	1,744	15,690
34 42750	Mahwah township	Bergen	25.9	24,062	21,157	519	169	1,518	7	361	331	1,028	18,717
34 42990	Manalapan township	Monmouth	30.8	33,423	30,687	664	9	1,514	5	177	367	1,183	23,283
34 43140	Manchester township	Ocean	82.6	38,928	36,724	1,190	45	338	10	267	354	1,024	34,744
34 43290	Mansfield township	Burlington	21.7	5,090	4,857	97	9	76	2	11	38	93	4,140
34 43320	Mansfield township	Warren	29.9	6,653	6,048	300	16	81	-	106	102	291	4,857
34 43440	Mantua township	Gloucester	15.9	14,217	13,622	294	28	122	-	40	111	179	10,423
34 43740	Maple Shade township	Burlington	3.8	19,079	15,868	1,376	30	1,164	8	323	310	850	15,382
34 43800	Maplewood township	Essex	3.8	23,868	14,030	7,788	31	682	7	373	957	1,248	17,175
34 44070	Marlboro township	Monmouth	30.6	36,398	30,487	752	17	4,612	5	171	354	1,051	25,409
34 44580	Maurice River township	Cumberland	93.4	6,928	4,062	2,285	54	19	1	307	200	634	6,036
34 45120	Medford township	Burlington	39.3	22,253	21,527	170	26	327	9	63	131	252	16,279
34 45360	Mendham township	Morris	17.9	5,400	5,179	50	5	109	-	19	38	82	3,674
34 45810	Middle township	Cape May	71.3	16,405	13,979	1,781	37	236	4	108	260	347	12,360
34 45990	Middletown township	Monmouth	41.1	66,327	62,819	803	46	1,717	17	353	572	2,265	48,886
34 46380	Millburn township	Essex	9.4	19,765	17,573	217	10	1,660	6	85	214	404	13,789
34 46560	Millstone township	Monmouth	36.8	8,970	8,237	274	9	308	3	55	84	315	6,028
34 46860	Mine Hill township	Morris	3.0	3,679	3,326	126	4	92	3	66	62	319	2,778
34 47250	Monroe township	Gloucester	46.6	28,967	24,573	3,231	72	356	9	286	440	785	21,540
34 47280	Monroe township	Middlesex	41.9	27,999	26,127	820	16	655	24	189	168	666	23,521
34 47430	Montague township	Sussex	44.0	3,412	3,250	61	6	23	-	37	35	112	2,485
34 47500	Montclair township	Essex	6.3	38,977	23,297	12,497	73	1,228	14	688	1,180	1,995	29,013
34 47580	Montgomery township	Somerset	32.6	17,481	14,781	361	15	2,011	2	80	231	387	11,722
34 47670	Montville township	Morris	18.9	20,839	17,703	193	9	2,619	4	74	237	531	15,597
34 47880	Moorestown township	Burlington	14.8	19,017	16,962	1,082	30	621	1	81	240	332	13,797
34 48090	Morris township	Morris	15.8	21,796	19,317	1,189	33	849	3	199	206	830	16,846
34 48900	Mount Holly township	Burlington	2.9	10,728	7,368	2,314	45	147	7	512	335	942	7,905
34 49020	Mount Laurel township	Burlington	21.8	40,221	35,034	2,785	38	1,529	12	256	567	901	30,916
34 49080	Mount Olive township	Morris	30.4	24,193	20,974	918	40	1,452	2	369	438	1,445	17,525
34 49410	Mullica township	Atlantic	56.6	5,912	4,764	371	16	49	7	509	196	975	4,318
34 49890	Neptune township	Monmouth	8.2	27,690	15,485	10,567	46	325	12	547	708	1,537	21,292
34 51510	New Hanover township	Burlington	22.3	9,744	6,249	2,816	41	143	8	259	228	1,890	8,331
34 52470	North Bergen township	Hudson	5.2	58,092	39,131	1,581	235	3,756	28	9,023	4,338	33,260	44,887
34 52560	North Brunswick township	Middlesex	12.0	36,287	22,763	5,542	63	5,152	10	1,707	1,050	3,775	27,934
34 53070	North Hanover township	Burlington	17.3	7,347	5,924	805	35	156	4	160	263	423	4,879
34 53680	Nutley township	Essex	3.4	27,362	24,064	511	15	1,943	10	480	339	1,830	21,396
34 54270	Ocean township	Monmouth	11.0	26,959	22,738	1,529	40	1,689	20	425	518	1,215	20,088
34 54300	Ocean township	Ocean	20.8	6,450	6,278	48	10	27	2	23	62	200	4,807
34 54705	Old Bridge township	Middlesex	38.1	60,456	48,049	3,207	94	6,544	27	1,133	1,402	4,578	44,822
34 56460	Parsippany-Troy Hills township	Morris	23.9	50,649	37,620	1,574	61	9,145	28	963	1,258	3,535	40,034
34 57510	Pemberton township	Burlington	61.7	28,691	18,946	6,632	132	913	23	828	1,217	2,477	20,770
34 57660	Pennsauken township	Camden	10.5	35,737	21,479	8,641	124	1,636	7	2,954	896	5,126	25,925
34 57870	Pennsville township	Salem	23.1	13,194	12,756	127	21	127	2	51	110	211	10,134
34 58110	Pequannock township	Morris	7.1	13,888	13,416	41	17	265	-	69	80	408	10,293
34 58530	Pilesgrove township	Salem	34.9	3,923	3,320	478	11	36	2	42	34	117	2,989
34 59010	Piscataway township	Middlesex	18.8	50,482	24,642	10,254	104	12,519	13	1,553	1,397	4,002	39,430
34 59130	Pittsgrove township	Salem	45.2	8,893	7,838	715	34	52	4	115	135	303	6,523
34 59280	Plainsboro township	Middlesex	11.8	20,215	11,765	1,533	20	6,168	2	275	452	937	15,239
34 59790	Plumsted township	Ocean	40.0	7,275	6,831	167	10	53	1	99	114	280	5,204
34 59820	Pohatcong township	Warren	13.3	3,416	3,348	15	1	10	-	22	20	69	2,621
34 60915	Princeton township	Mercer	16.4	16,027	12,807	852	20	1,599	8	338	403	847	12,121
34 61470	Quinton township	Salem	24.2	2,786	2,286	403	30	9	-	20	38	42	2,128
34 61890	Randolph township	Morris	21.0	24,847	21,293	572	15	2,272	5	326	364	1,208	17,469
34 61920	Raritan township	Hunterdon	37.8	19,809	18,466	244	17	693	2	135	252	552	14,010
34 62250	Readington township	Hunterdon	47.7	15,803	15,035	120	10	405	-	84	149	324	11,618
34 63510	Riverside township	Burlington	1.5	7,911	7,137	351	11	33	1	180	198	325	5,931
34 63690	River Vale township	Bergen	4.1	9,449	8,724	55	-	557	2	41	70	304	6,876
34 63990	Rochelle Park township	Bergen	1.0	5,528	4,980	25	2	333	-	112	76	474	4,497
34 64080	Rockaway township	Morris	42.8	22,930	20,375	565	23	1,295	4	367	301	1,440	16,715
34 64980	Roxbury township	Morris	21.4	23,883	22,110	456	35	855	17	162	248	1,154	17,438
34 65340	Saddle Brook township	Bergen	2.7	13,155	11,936	183	5	623	-	223	185	825	10,499

[Includes functioning minor civil divisions (MCDs) of 2,500 or more population as of April 1, 2000 in the following 12 states: CT, ME, MA, MI, MN, NH, NJ, NY, PA, RI, VT, and WI. Codes shown are two-digit Federal Information Processing Standards (FIPS) state codes and five-digit FIPS place codes. Place names and codes are those in effect as of January 1, 2000. County refers to the county in which the MCD is located]

State and place code	MCD	County	Land area, 2000 (sq. mi.)	Population, 2000 (April 1)									
					By race—								
					One race						Two or more races	Hispanic or Latino (of any race)	18 years and over
				Total	White	Black or African American	American Indian and Alaska Native	Asian	Native Hawaiian and Other Pacific Islander	Some other race			
34 00000	NEW JERSEY—Con.												
34 66060	Scotch Plains township	Union	9.1	22,732	17,931	2,568	21	1,648	3	216	345	895	16,967
34 66810	Shamong township	Burlington	44.8	6,462	6,284	53	7	43	-	20	55	68	4,564
34 68610	Southampton township	Burlington	44.0	10,388	10,086	125	29	65	-	31	52	134	8,534
34 68790	South Brunswick township	Middlesex	40.9	37,734	26,600	2,975	48	6,808	14	518	771	1,918	27,005
34 69274	South Orange Village township	Essex	2.9	16,964	10,248	5,309	16	660	5	266	460	837	13,187
34 69690	Sparta township	Sussex	37.4	18,080	17,481	52	12	252	5	81	197	459	12,544
34 69990	Springfield township	Burlington	30.0	3,227	2,967	104	10	85	-	7	54	57	2,394
34 70020	Springfield township	Union	5.1	14,429	12,946	537	3	676	-	139	128	597	11,463
34 70320	Stafford township	Ocean	46.5	22,532	21,808	166	21	217	7	114	199	542	17,180
34 70890	Stillwater township	Sussex	27.1	4,267	4,180	7	9	20	-	10	41	89	3,072
34 72060	Tabernacle township	Burlington	49.5	7,170	6,904	150	7	52	-	22	35	106	5,166
34 72360	Teaneck township	Bergen	6.1	39,260	22,082	11,298	59	2,798	11	1,633	1,379	4,103	29,139
34 72510	Tewksbury township	Hunterdon	31.6	5,541	5,365	29	-	104	-	15	28	85	4,091
34 74420	Union township	Hunterdon	19.0	6,160	5,041	823	11	98	1	98	88	316	4,980
34 74480	Union township	Union	9.1	54,405	36,809	10,752	80	4,201	13	1,329	1,221	4,861	42,286
34 74810	Upper township	Cape May	63.2	12,115	11,823	83	15	74	7	23	90	155	8,648
34 74870	Upper Deerfield township	Cumberland	31.1	7,556	5,725	1,240	61	231	1	138	160	343	5,455
34 74900	Upper Freehold township	Monmouth	46.9	4,282	4,055	45	6	60	-	36	80	151	3,091
34 75110	Upper Pittsgrove township	Salem	40.4	3,468	3,289	75	18	11	-	45	30	109	2,591
34 75740	Vernon township	Sussex	68.4	24,686	23,837	188	22	173	7	195	264	889	17,126
34 75815	Verona township	Essex	2.8	13,533	12,585	207	3	462	8	96	172	467	10,490
34 76220	Voorhees township	Camden	11.6	28,126	22,011	2,249	38	3,217	8	156	447	694	20,699
34 76460	Wall township	Monmouth	30.6	25,261	24,526	155	26	319	9	80	146	391	18,887
34 76790	Wantage township	Sussex	67.1	10,387	10,086	67	6	70	1	43	114	300	7,337
34 76940	Warren township	Somerset	19.7	14,259	12,303	180	5	1,521	8	59	183	455	10,027
34 77135	Washington township	Bergen	2.9	8,938	8,229	88	4	498	-	39	80	299	6,905
34 77180	Washington township	Gloucester	21.4	47,114	42,497	2,286	39	1,558	6	252	476	955	33,571
34 77210	Washington township	Mercer	20.5	10,275	9,350	297	14	443	-	57	114	279	7,590
34 77240	Washington township	Morris	44.9	17,592	16,917	146	15	329	9	62	114	389	12,281
34 77300	Washington township	Warren	17.6	6,248	5,997	107	4	59	-	31	50	135	4,373
34 77630	Waterford township	Camden	36.2	10,494	9,733	439	22	94	1	70	135	217	7,793
34 77840	Wayne township	Passaic	23.8	54,069	48,687	895	54	3,066	11	631	725	2,754	41,543
34 77930	Weehawken township	Hudson	0.8	13,501	9,862	483	27	630	14	1,882	603	5,487	11,265
34 78200	Westampton township	Burlington	11.0	7,217	5,110	1,535	20	219	3	132	198	448	5,104
34 78510	West Caldwell township	Essex	5.0	11,233	10,541	100	4	432	4	68	84	314	8,463
34 78800	West Deptford township	Gloucester	15.9	19,368	17,875	984	45	219	4	82	159	341	14,807
34 79460	West Milford township	Passaic	75.4	26,410	25,110	326	159	269	4	160	382	893	19,222
34 79800	West Orange township	Essex	12.1	44,943	30,359	7,848	63	3,635	17	1,584	1,437	4,514	34,477
34 80240	West Windsor township	Mercer	26.0	21,907	15,670	605	17	4,986	2	236	391	892	14,939
34 80570	White township	Warren	27.4	4,245	4,090	51	8	26	2	14	54	90	3,299
34 81440	Willingboro township	Burlington	7.7	33,008	8,144	22,021	99	562	12	866	1,304	1,998	23,939
34 81740	Winslow township	Camden	57.7	34,611	22,670	10,154	104	449	10	547	677	1,492	24,646
34 82000	Woodbridge township	Middlesex	23.0	97,203	68,848	8,507	167	14,054	24	3,212	2,391	8,956	75,460
34 82840	Woolwich township	Gloucester	20.9	3,032	2,763	138	-	34	-	59	38	118	2,081
34 83050	Wyckoff township	Bergen	6.5	16,508	15,607	77	25	611	2	74	112	376	11,837
36 00000	NEW YORK		47,213.8	18,976,457	12,893,689	3,014,385	82,461	1,044,976	8,818	1,341,946	590,182	2,867,583	14,286,350
36 00210	Adams town	Jefferson	42.4	4,782	4,685	14	13	17	1	10	42	31	3,465
36 00287	Addison town	Steuben	25.6	2,640	2,599	8	9	1	-	2	21	16	1,924
36 00353	Afton town	Chenango	45.9	2,977	2,937	8	16	2	-	2	12	22	2,209
36 01044	Albion town	Orleans	25.2	8,042	6,181	1,289	59	43	6	345	119	653	6,143
36 01099	Alden town	Erie	34.5	10,470	9,523	709	30	24	6	150	28	285	8,291
36 01176	Alexandria town	Jefferson	73.0	4,097	4,037	12	9	1	2	7	29	26	3,089
36 01209	Alfred town	Allegany	31.5	5,140	4,718	178	13	127	1	49	54	116	4,712
36 01297	Allegany town	Cattaraugus	71.2	8,230	7,934	65	27	109	2	21	72	77	6,616
36 01528	Altamont town	Franklin	117.6	6,137	5,987	78	18	5	-	5	44	35	4,626
36 01583	Altona town	Clinton	101.1	3,160	2,607	378	11	4	-	150	10	256	2,469
36 01693	Amenia town	Dutchess	43.3	4,048	3,781	119	24	19	-	31	74	136	3,090
36 02000	Amherst town	Erie	53.2	116,510	104,018	4,544	146	6,079	29	427	1,267	1,579	90,672
36 02077	Amsterdam town	Montgomery	29.7	5,820	5,690	40	6	14	-	21	49	135	4,645
36 02253	Annsville town	Oneida	60.2	2,956	2,860	69	7	2	-	3	15	26	2,076
36 02418	Arcade town	Wyoming	47.1	4,184	4,122	9	9	16	1	7	20	36	3,047
36 02440	Arcadia town	Wayne	52.0	14,889	13,614	572	45	66	5	314	273	823	10,999
36 02561	Argyle town	Washington	56.7	3,688	3,649	8	1	1	-	10	19	38	2,712
36 02913	Athens town	Greene	26.2	3,991	3,826	39	11	34	2	26	53	68	3,062
36 03012	Attica town	Wyoming	35.7	6,028	4,388	1,270	20	20	-	312	18	552	5,014
36 03166	Aurelius town	Cayuga	30.3	2,936	2,895	10	4	1	-	2	24	35	2,184
36 03199	Aurora town	Erie	36.4	13,996	13,832	19	25	50	2	16	66	82	10,443
36 03221	Au Sable town	Clinton	39.1	3,015	2,948	24	7	9	-	8	19	40	2,231
36 03364	Avon town	Livingston	41.2	6,443	6,177	99	22	46	1	15	83	89	4,756
36 04000	Babylon town	Suffolk	52.3	211,792	161,675	33,137	566	4,007	63	7,123	5,221	21,275	156,653
36 04044	Bainbridge town	Chenango	34.3	3,401	3,345	11	-	8	2	10	25	40	2,513
36 04220	Ballston town	Saratoga	29.6	8,729	8,510	45	20	43	1	44	66	116	6,461
36 04429	Barker town	Broome	41.4	2,738	2,677	21	3	9	-	4	24	16	1,958
36 04671	Barton town	Tioga	59.4	9,066	8,894	35	23	36	-	14	64	93	6,710

Table D-2. MCDs — **Area and Population**—Con.

[Includes functioning minor civil divisions (MCDs) of 2,500 or more population as of April 1, 2000 in the following 12 states: CT, ME, MA, MI, MN, NH, NJ, NY, PA, RI, VT, and WI. Codes shown are two-digit Federal Information Processing Standards (FIPS) state codes and five-digit FIPS place codes. Place names and codes are those in effect as of January 1, 2000. County refers to the county in which the MCD is located]

State and place code	MCD	County	Land area, 2000 (sq. mi.)	Population, 2000 (April 1) Total	White	Black or African American	American Indian and Alaska Native	Asian	Native Hawaiian and Other Pacific Islander	Some other race	Two or more races	Hispanic or Latino (of any race)	18 years and over
36 00000	NEW YORK—Con.												
36 04726	Batavia town	Genesee	48.4	5,915	5,726	50	23	50	2	20	44	39	4,473
36 04770	Bath town	Steuben	96.0	12,097	11,618	217	36	86	4	12	124	85	9,272
36 05320	Bedford town	Westchester	37.2	18,133	15,867	1,291	16	359	14	340	246	1,372	13,340
36 05452	Beekman town	Dutchess	30.0	11,452	10,678	277	21	198	3	108	167	616	7,912
36 05485	Beekmantown town	Clinton	60.5	5,326	5,200	38	9	15	1	13	50	54	3,927
36 05936	Bennington town	Wyoming	55.0	3,349	3,318	2	4	4	-	1	20	9	2,514
36 00002	Benton town	Yates	41.5	2,640	2,610	11	-	4	-	2	13	11	1,891
36 06057	Bergen town	Genesee	27.6	3,182	3,095	10	8	16	-	25	28	32	2,337
36 06211	Berne town	Albany	64.1	2,846	2,786	11	-	11	2	7	29	22	2,123
36 06310	Bethel town	Sullivan	85.4	4,362	3,941	201	8	22	7	122	61	492	3,410
36 06354	Bethlehem town	Albany	48.8	31,304	29,656	706	47	521	13	97	264	544	22,695
36 06475	Big Flats town	Chemung	44.5	7,224	6,960	85	1	110	1	11	56	48	5,348
36 06618	Binghamton town	Broome	25.4	4,969	4,777	62	4	48	2	19	57	55	3,598
36 07003	Blooming Grove town	Orange	34.8	17,351	15,658	659	85	245	3	418	283	1,556	12,124
36 07366	Boonville town	Oneida	71.9	4,572	4,536	3	7	6	1	-	19	8	3,453
36 07454	Boston town	Erie	35.8	7,897	7,811	11	11	16	1	8	39	57	5,910
36 08246	Brighton town	Monroe	15.5	35,588	30,639	1,315	35	2,892	10	223	474	831	28,470
36 08433	Broadalbin town	Fulton	31.7	5,066	4,982	28	12	5	1	11	27	56	3,693
36 10000	Brookhaven town	Suffolk	259.3	448,248	396,381	19,411	1,036	13,019	113	9,902	8,386	36,041	328,627
36 10242	Brownville town	Jefferson	59.3	5,843	5,717	16	32	16	1	16	45	34	4,249
36 10275	Brunswick town	Rensselaer	44.5	11,664	11,242	105	7	187	2	36	85	93	8,918
36 10297	Brutus town	Cayuga	22.1	4,777	4,669	17	16	21	1	3	50	38	3,437
36 11451	Busti town	Chautauqua	47.8	7,760	7,602	40	6	34	-	34	44	55	5,891
36 11649	Cairo town	Greene	60.0	6,355	6,156	35	21	14	-	38	91	233	4,756
36 11715	Caledonia town	Livingston	44.1	4,567	4,298	160	17	24	3	8	57	38	3,285
36 11759	Callicoon town	Sullivan	48.7	3,052	2,924	23	6	21	-	35	43	139	2,346
36 11803	Cambria town	Niagara	39.9	5,393	5,301	14	27	22	1	3	25	28	4,021
36 11858	Camden town	Oneida	54.0	5,028	4,933	19	9	22	-	10	35	40	3,658
36 11913	Camillus town	Onondaga	34.5	23,152	22,331	219	86	255	4	63	194	213	17,556
36 11940	Campbell town	Steuben	40.7	3,691	3,637	16	3	10	1	6	18	13	2,730
36 12122	Canajoharie town	Montgomery	42.9	3,797	3,684	24	15	19	-	12	43	43	2,800
36 12155	Canandaigua town	Ontario	56.9	7,649	7,428	56	18	59	-	21	67	82	5,708
36 12221	Candor town	Tioga	94.5	5,317	5,171	45	14	10	-	4	73	52	3,821
36 12243	Caneadea town	Allegany	35.5	2,694	2,595	27	4	26	-	15	27	61	2,199
36 12265	Canisteo town	Steuben	54.4	3,583	3,520	7	6	19	-	9	22	30	2,643
36 12342	Canton town	St. Lawrence	104.8	10,334	9,776	275	41	70	-	65	107	144	8,383
36 12364	Cape Vincent town	Jefferson	56.5	3,345	2,363	732	13	12	-	210	15	444	2,902
36 12496	Carlton town	Orleans	43.7	2,960	2,792	96	16	3	1	27	25	33	2,163
36 12529	Carmel town	Putnam	36.1	33,006	31,223	362	42	391	3	482	503	1,955	24,009
36 12606	Caroline town	Tompkins	55.0	2,910	2,702	90	17	25	3	11	62	69	2,122
36 12639	Carroll town	Chautauqua	33.4	3,635	3,600	5	8	5	-	6	11	17	2,694
36 12782	Castile town	Wyoming	37.0	2,873	2,828	13	6	9	-	3	14	15	2,168
36 12947	Catlin town	Chemung	38.0	2,649	2,603	12	4	6	-	6	18	9	1,938
36 12969	Cato town	Cayuga	33.6	2,744	2,682	10	11	8	1	2	30	10	1,948
36 13013	Catskill town	Greene	60.5	11,849	10,645	715	38	72	2	102	275	477	9,066
36 13156	Cazenovia town	Madison	49.9	6,481	6,303	71	17	34	1	10	45	96	4,926
36 13717	Champion town	Jefferson	44.3	4,361	4,049	120	27	46	6	39	74	126	3,150
36 13750	Champlain town	Clinton	51.2	5,791	5,660	30	17	21	1	15	47	58	4,346
36 13926	Charlton town	Saratoga	32.8	3,954	3,893	11	6	15	-	2	27	38	2,956
36 14014	Chatham town	Columbia	53.3	4,249	4,079	74	9	30	7	7	43	32	3,252
36 14069	Chautauqua town	Chautauqua	67.2	4,666	4,491	74	11	18	4	9	59	49	3,621
36 14113	Chazy town	Clinton	54.2	4,181	4,095	13	17	21	-	4	31	29	3,063
36 15011	Cheektowaga town	Erie	29.5	94,019	89,266	2,754	154	883	7	252	703	908	74,640
36 15077	Chemung town	Chemung	49.5	2,665	2,602	14	7	5	-	12	25	22	1,919
36 15110	Chenango town	Broome	33.9	11,454	11,161	67	12	61	2	43	108	107	8,566
36 15308	Chester town	Orange	25.2	12,140	10,584	804	41	323	6	234	148	1,231	8,819
36 15319	Chester town	Warren	84.5	3,614	3,532	7	5	23	-	13	34	38	2,896
36 15462	Chili town	Monroe	39.7	27,638	25,188	1,579	67	310	6	143	345	456	20,558
36 15704	Cicero town	Onondaga	48.5	27,982	26,950	333	107	200	5	61	326	245	20,114
36 15825	Clarence town	Erie	53.4	26,123	25,343	169	43	361	11	50	146	208	18,808
36 15880	Clarendon town	Orleans	35.2	3,392	3,272	32	14	17	-	21	36	55	2,426
36 15957	Clarkson town	Monroe	33.2	6,072	5,703	123	15	39	3	85	104	165	4,287
36 15968	Clarkstown town	Rockland	38.5	82,082	65,643	6,459	110	6,486	81	1,635	1,668	5,683	61,768
36 16045	Claverack town	Columbia	47.7	6,401	6,014	212	13	23	4	50	85	158	4,836
36 16067	Clay town	Onondaga	48.0	58,805	54,177	2,060	279	1,182	14	224	869	816	42,488
36 16100	Clayton town	Jefferson	82.6	4,817	4,684	45	17	11	5	23	32	76	3,532
36 16353	Clifton Park town	Saratoga	48.6	32,995	31,309	403	45	820	3	118	297	473	24,274
36 16408	Clinton town	Dutchess	38.5	4,010	3,851	64	14	41	-	9	31	70	3,018
36 16639	Cobleskill town	Schoharie	30.6	6,407	6,071	142	16	65	4	34	75	150	5,227
36 16694	Coeymans town	Albany	50.2	8,151	7,712	174	18	34	2	64	147	264	5,906
36 16738	Cohocton town	Steuben	56.1	2,626	2,560	12	16	7	-	5	26	7	1,870
36 16870	Colden town	Erie	35.6	3,323	3,284	1	7	6	-	3	22	14	2,494
36 17046	Colesville town	Broome	78.5	5,441	5,324	16	17	19	3	1	61	40	3,841
36 17200	Collins town	Erie	48.1	8,307	5,553	1,879	288	16	-	512	57	992	7,203
36 17343	Colonie town	Albany	56.1	79,258	71,771	3,137	119	2,843	13	481	894	1,476	61,956
36 17585	Concord town	Erie	70.1	8,526	8,390	43	14	21	3	16	39	106	6,345
36 17772	Conklin town	Broome	24.5	5,940	5,804	50	8	13	-	17	48	51	4,329

[Includes functioning minor civil divisions (MCDs) of 2,500 or more population as of April 1, 2000 in the following 12 states: CT, ME, MA, MI, MN, NH, NJ, NY, PA, RI, VT, and WI. Codes shown are two-digit Federal Information Processing Standards (FIPS) state codes and five-digit FIPS place codes. Place names and codes are those in effect as of January 1, 2000. County refers to the county in which the MCD is located]

State and place code	MCD	County	Land area, 2000 (sq. mi.)	Population, 2000 (April 1)									
					By race—								
					One race								
				Total	White	Black or African American	American Indian and Alaska Native	Asian	Native Hawaiian and Other Pacific Islander	Some other race	Two or more races	Hispanic or Latino (of any race)	18 years and over
36 00000	NEW YORK—Con.												
36 17904	Constantia town	Oswego	56.9	5,141	5,053	11	34	4	1	4	34	17	3,682
36 18102	Copake town	Columbia	41.0	3,278	3,165	23	15	4	-	19	52	75	2,577
36 18223	Corinth town	Saratoga	56.8	5,985	5,882	12	9	12	6	18	46	47	4,428
36 18267	Corning town	Steuben	36.9	6,426	6,121	158	13	87	-	7	40	43	4,796
36 18300	Cornwall town	Orange	26.8	12,307	11,652	162	20	158	6	144	165	629	8,871
36 18410	Cortlandt town	Westchester	39.7	38,467	34,082	1,765	79	987	5	903	646	2,766	28,264
36 18421	Cortlandville town	Cortland	49.8	7,919	7,676	32	25	56	-	17	113	84	6,082
36 18729	Coxsackie town	Greene	36.9	8,884	6,418	1,806	27	54	2	520	57	991	7,223
36 18916	Crawford town	Orange	40.1	7,875	7,528	94	6	60	1	91	95	404	5,488
36 19081	Croghan town	Lewis	179.4	3,161	3,137	4	2	2	-	7	9	15	2,254
36 19367	Cuba town	Allegany	35.1	3,392	3,321	9	8	13	-	9	32	37	2,521
36 19620	Danby town	Tompkins	53.6	3,007	2,816	81	5	32	-	13	60	51	2,271
36 19653	Dannemora town	Clinton	59.2	5,149	2,899	1,665	28	44	2	461	50	817	4,619
36 19719	Darien town	Genesee	47.5	3,061	3,034	3	9	1	-	-	14	7	2,174
36 19763	Davenport town	Delaware	52.4	2,774	2,718	15	9	7	-	6	19	28	2,083
36 19928	Deerfield town	Oneida	32.9	3,906	3,857	23	2	11	-	1	12	28	2,910
36 19961	Deerpark town	Orange	66.4	7,858	7,506	121	21	45	-	58	107	300	5,699
36 20104	Delaware town	Sullivan	34.7	2,719	2,374	264	6	22	1	27	25	172	1,990
36 20137	Delhi town	Delaware	64.6	4,629	4,254	196	12	58	1	42	66	124	3,888
36 20214	Denmark town	Lewis	50.6	2,747	2,658	14	7	5	1	23	39	50	1,959
36 20478	De Witt town	Onondaga	33.9	24,071	21,592	1,177	135	718	6	63	380	324	18,264
36 20588	Dickinson town	Broome	4.8	5,335	4,976	224	5	33	-	44	53	95	4,321
36 20676	Dix town	Schuyler	36.1	4,197	4,084	22	23	24	1	12	31	46	3,143
36 20819	Dover town	Dutchess	55.7	8,565	7,684	471	28	85	5	130	162	484	6,067
36 20962	Dryden town	Tompkins	93.9	13,532	12,816	201	45	200	4	79	187	223	10,083
36 21006	Duanesburg town	Schenectady	71.2	5,808	5,672	26	17	16	2	16	59	47	4,243
36 21204	Durham town	Greene	49.2	2,592	2,550	2	8	11	-	2	19	35	1,996
36 21699	East Bloomfield town	Ontario	33.2	3,361	3,309	13	6	7	1	6	19	35	2,461
36 21820	Eastchester town	Westchester	4.9	31,318	27,355	878	21	2,144	9	439	472	1,402	23,850
36 21996	East Fishkill town	Dutchess	56.9	25,589	23,679	585	39	716	6	220	344	1,035	17,977
36 22117	East Greenbush town	Rensselaer	24.1	15,560	14,628	443	21	302	3	45	118	207	11,813
36 22194	East Hampton town	Suffolk	74.3	19,719	17,322	706	38	236	5	957	455	2,914	15,531
36 22870	East Rochester town	Monroe	1.4	6,650	6,379	92	17	49	1	24	88	158	5,046
36 23305	Eaton town	Madison	44.7	4,826	4,363	316	22	51	-	22	52	96	3,863
36 23415	Eden town	Erie	39.8	8,076	7,941	33	20	16	1	25	40	83	5,906
36 23800	Elbridge town	Onondaga	37.6	6,091	5,951	23	25	28	-	16	48	67	4,430
36 23976	Ellery town	Chautauqua	47.6	4,576	4,503	9	10	8	-	26	20	39	3,488
36 23998	Ellicott town	Chautauqua	30.5	9,280	9,066	49	24	53	-	24	64	97	7,125
36 24086	Ellisburg town	Jefferson	85.3	3,541	3,465	14	17	13	1	13	18	37	2,498
36 24130	Elma town	Erie	34.5	11,304	11,201	6	6	30	1	8	52	68	8,533
36 24240	Elmira town	Chemung	22.3	7,199	6,933	107	8	88	-	11	52	31	5,514
36 24548	Enfield town	Tompkins	36.9	3,369	3,194	63	12	15	-	17	68	57	2,442
36 24647	Erwin town	Steuben	38.7	7,227	6,658	162	13	332	-	9	53	94	5,430
36 24691	Esopus town	Ulster	37.2	9,331	8,824	203	22	88	-	46	148	178	6,965
36 24801	Evans town	Erie	41.8	17,594	17,209	66	109	35	3	34	138	212	12,959
36 25241	Fallsburg town	Sullivan	77.6	12,234	9,199	1,904	52	143	4	616	316	1,777	9,387
36 25406	Farmington town	Ontario	39.4	10,585	10,218	108	28	100	1	27	103	128	7,543
36 25505	Fayette town	Seneca	55.2	3,643	3,573	19	10	21	-	2	18	33	2,706
36 25604	Fenton town	Broome	32.9	6,909	6,738	60	21	17	-	13	60	55	5,177
36 25978	Fishkill town	Dutchess	27.4	20,258	15,638	2,863	38	605	5	909	200	2,121	16,554
36 26231	Fleming town	Cayuga	21.8	2,647	2,612	4	3	15	-	4	9	21	2,036
36 26308	Florida town	Montgomery	50.4	2,731	2,683	6	4	4	-	5	29	64	2,065
36 26385	Floyd town	Oneida	34.6	3,869	3,772	14	7	16	3	7	50	40	2,784
36 26715	Fort Ann town	Washington	109.5	6,417	4,377	1,545	22	17	2	408	46	801	5,437
36 26781	Fort Edward town	Washington	26.8	5,892	5,809	20	14	13	-	6	30	31	4,456
36 27199	Frankfort town	Herkimer	37.2	7,478	7,323	37	10	10	-	12	86	76	5,705
36 27232	Franklin town	Delaware	81.4	2,621	2,582	18	1	4	-	8	8	19	1,968
36 27342	Franklinville town	Cattaraugus	51.8	3,128	3,079	3	16	7	-	1	22	15	2,236
36 27958	Gaines town	Orleans	34.4	3,740	3,427	165	12	5	-	82	49	155	2,754
36 28013	Galen town	Wayne	59.4	4,439	4,182	149	10	8	-	31	59	60	3,189
36 28112	Galway town	Saratoga	44.0	3,589	3,528	3	-	11	2	19	26	38	2,695
36 28255	Gardiner town	Ulster	44.4	5,238	4,942	92	7	39	2	58	98	240	3,876
36 28442	Gates town	Monroe	15.2	29,275	25,943	1,868	49	691	12	318	394	855	22,652
36 28519	Geddes town	Onondaga	9.2	17,740	17,218	86	102	98	6	31	199	268	13,615
36 28629	Geneseo town	Livingston	44.0	9,654	9,066	143	11	252	4	67	111	211	8,510
36 28651	Geneva town	Ontario	19.1	3,289	3,080	80	2	57	1	17	52	56	2,561
36 28750	German Flatts town	Herkimer	33.7	13,629	13,339	80	15	24	2	27	142	196	10,194
36 28871	Ghent town	Columbia	45.2	5,276	5,114	58	12	10	-	15	67	71	3,998
36 29366	Glenville town	Schenectady	49.9	28,183	27,437	204	35	252	6	39	210	337	21,504
36 29531	Gorham town	Ontario	48.9	3,776	3,714	14	2	5	1	8	32	18	2,782
36 29553	Goshen town	Orange	43.8	12,913	11,452	868	21	221	5	235	111	950	9,756
36 29608	Gouverneur town	St. Lawrence	71.5	7,418	6,337	702	30	29	10	219	91	435	5,603
36 29729	Granby town	Oswego	44.9	7,009	6,839	38	32	16	-	24	60	96	5,024
36 29828	Grand Island town	Erie	28.5	18,621	17,838	308	46	218	2	46	163	203	13,651
36 30037	Granville town	Washington	56.1	6,456	6,332	24	14	18	1	13	54	40	4,750
36 30290	Greece town	Monroe	47.4	94,141	87,903	2,712	227	1,403	24	818	1,054	2,404	70,600
36 30367	Greenburgh town	Westchester	30.5	86,764	62,825	11,344	148	7,608	41	2,547	2,251	7,825	66,204

Table D-2. MCDs — **Area and Population**—Con.

[Includes functioning minor civil divisions (MCDs) of 2,500 or more population as of April 1, 2000 in the following 12 states: CT, ME, MA, MI, MN, NH, NJ, NY, PA, RI, VT, and WI. Codes shown are two-digit Federal Information Processing Standards (FIPS) state codes and five-digit FIPS place codes. Place names and codes are those in effect as of January 1, 2000. County refers to the county in which the MCD is located]

State and place code	MCD	County	Land area, 2000 (sq. mi.)	Population, 2000 (April 1)									
					By race—							Hispanic or Latino (of any race)	18 years and over
					One race						Two or more races		
				Total	White	Black or African American	American Indian and Alaska Native	Asian	Native Hawaiian and Other Pacific Islander	Some other race			
36 00000	NEW YORK—Con.												
36 30422	Greene town	Chenango	75.1	5,729	5,645	14	16	15	1	4	34	33	4,211
36 30444	Greenfield town	Saratoga	67.4	7,362	7,174	48	10	25	-	16	89	83	5,356
36 30565	Greenport town	Columbia	18.8	4,180	3,808	213	10	37	-	35	77	146	3,300
36 30620	Greenville town	Greene	38.9	3,316	3,215	16	5	38	-	9	33	54	2,485
36 30631	Greenville town	Orange	30.3	3,800	3,615	48	11	40	1	43	42	170	2,647
36 30686	Greenwich town	Washington	44.0	4,896	4,789	15	3	40	2	9	38	32	3,629
36 30972	Groton town	Tompkins	49.5	5,794	5,642	37	5	14	-	15	81	46	4,165
36 31016	Groveland town	Livingston	39.2	3,853	2,314	1,250	10	7	-	249	23	587	3,471
36 31104	Guilderland town	Albany	57.9	32,688	30,097	820	47	1,248	4	138	334	585	24,826
36 31148	Guilford town	Chenango	61.7	3,046	2,974	20	5	7	-	7	33	27	2,255
36 31489	Halfmoon town	Saratoga	32.6	18,474	17,539	234	31	350	3	76	241	304	14,104
36 31654	Hamburg town	Erie	41.3	56,259	55,096	277	115	217	5	214	335	876	42,324
36 31720	Hamilton town	Madison	41.4	5,733	5,369	114	4	141	2	26	77	105	4,835
36 31797	Hamlin town	Monroe	43.4	9,355	9,054	102	33	30	1	64	71	150	6,470
36 31907	Hamptonburgh town	Orange	26.8	4,686	4,387	92	9	69	-	51	78	207	3,326
36 31951	Hancock town	Delaware	159.3	3,449	3,335	24	18	21	-	11	40	82	2,618
36 32028	Hannibal town	Oswego	44.8	4,957	4,858	11	22	6	-	23	37	44	3,443
36 32050	Hanover town	Chautauqua	49.3	7,638	7,395	37	69	9	4	58	66	130	5,696
36 32314	Harrietstown town	Franklin	196.8	5,575	5,420	29	19	36	-	12	59	59	4,303
36 32413	Harrison town	Westchester	16.8	24,154	21,686	345	21	1,314	2	383	403	1,618	18,238
36 32490	Hartland town	Niagara	52.4	4,165	4,073	22	13	6	2	9	40	30	3,056
36 32688	Hastings town	Oswego	45.8	8,803	8,605	28	43	26	4	10	87	59	6,406
36 32765	Haverstraw town	Rockland	22.4	33,811	22,398	3,471	138	1,085	33	5,292	1,394	10,729	24,919
36 33073	Hector town	Schuyler	102.5	4,854	4,748	27	19	11	-	7	42	42	3,540
36 34000	Hempstead town	Nassau	120.0	755,924	564,260	111,723	1,453	26,678	240	33,992	17,578	86,657	563,573
36 34099	Henrietta town	Monroe	35.4	39,028	32,890	2,708	105	2,143	11	379	792	1,181	31,084
36 34132	Herkimer town	Herkimer	31.6	9,962	9,646	97	18	103	1	41	56	117	7,947
36 34550	Highlands town	Orange	30.9	12,484	10,259	1,143	61	334	20	283	384	962	9,635
36 35122	Holland town	Erie	35.8	3,603	3,537	18	11	14	-	5	18	13	2,605
36 35287	Homer town	Cortland	50.4	6,363	6,243	26	14	17	1	19	43	54	4,672
36 35463	Hoosick town	Rensselaer	63.0	6,759	6,621	33	20	26	2	23	34	57	5,011
36 35551	Hopewell town	Ontario	35.6	3,346	3,278	26	10	4	1	8	19	61	2,533
36 35683	Hornellsville town	Steuben	43.5	4,042	3,958	21	2	33	-	10	18	31	3,143
36 35705	Horseheads town	Chemung	35.9	19,561	18,757	253	23	300	2	39	187	145	14,974
36 35782	Hounsfield town	Jefferson	49.3	3,323	3,241	19	13	10	-	6	34	38	2,536
36 36178	Hunter town	Greene	90.5	2,721	2,638	16	3	4	1	9	50	57	2,008
36 37000	Huntington town	Suffolk	94.0	195,289	172,459	8,241	263	6,840	37	4,425	3,024	12,844	145,570
36 37143	Hurley town	Ulster	29.9	6,564	6,278	92	8	80	7	20	79	125	5,101
36 37209	Hyde Park town	Dutchess	37.0	20,851	18,978	887	42	290	17	249	388	674	15,697
36 37726	Irondequoit town	Monroe	15.2	52,354	48,707	1,857	79	514	10	533	654	1,602	40,873
36 38000	Islip town	Suffolk	105.3	322,612	249,210	29,110	839	7,005	161	26,841	9,446	65,031	234,307
36 38088	Ithaca town	Tompkins	29.1	18,198	15,312	533	24	1,671	8	251	399	611	15,444
36 38583	Jerusalem town	Yates	58.9	4,525	4,452	25	5	13	1	13	16	30	3,626
36 38792	Johnstown town	Fulton	70.2	7,166	6,624	332	3	51	-	112	44	235	5,663
36 39188	Kendall town	Orleans	32.9	2,838	2,754	18	16	5	-	16	29	34	2,031
36 39331	Kent town	Putnam	40.6	14,009	13,142	198	19	174	2	254	220	808	10,328
36 39573	Kinderhook town	Columbia	31.8	8,296	8,073	56	19	71	3	27	47	117	6,265
36 39650	Kingsbury town	Washington	39.9	11,171	10,967	41	30	23	1	15	94	67	8,378
36 39804	Kirkland town	Oneida	33.8	10,138	9,765	122	7	123	3	27	91	134	8,113
36 39837	Kirkwood town	Broome	31.0	5,651	5,524	34	10	22	1	9	51	36	4,296
36 40002	Knox town	Albany	41.8	2,647	2,579	20	5	13	2	2	26	8	1,910
36 40266	LaFayette town	Onondaga	39.2	4,833	4,605	18	112	28	5	6	59	21	3,533
36 40299	La Grange town	Dutchess	39.7	14,928	13,731	360	18	439	-	170	210	636	10,670
36 40519	Lake George town	Warren	30.2	3,578	3,497	19	9	21	1	6	25	33	2,801
36 40662	Lake Luzerne town	Warren	52.6	3,219	3,148	8	11	9	-	7	36	33	2,418
36 41146	Lancaster town	Erie	37.8	39,019	38,239	315	71	151	2	47	194	262	29,224
36 41234	Lansing town	Tompkins	60.7	10,521	8,847	430	20	932	4	77	211	247	7,779
36 41762	Lee town	Oneida	45.2	6,875	6,697	59	13	32	1	15	58	55	5,041
36 41905	Lenox town	Madison	36.4	8,665	8,462	57	40	21	1	21	63	75	6,436
36 42015	Le Ray town	Jefferson	73.7	19,836	13,980	3,245	156	409	97	1,209	740	2,170	14,314
36 42037	Le Roy town	Genesee	42.2	7,790	7,479	146	21	34	1	16	93	61	5,829
36 42136	Lewisboro town	Westchester	27.9	12,324	11,730	147	7	258	-	60	122	306	8,427
36 42158	Lewiston town	Niagara	37.3	16,257	15,766	149	109	95	2	56	80	148	12,913
36 42235	Liberty town	Sullivan	79.6	9,632	8,062	885	36	138	1	362	148	1,050	7,252
36 42334	Lima town	Livingston	31.9	4,541	4,399	47	13	20	3	15	44	57	3,462
36 42631	Lisbon town	St. Lawrence	108.2	4,047	3,977	5	23	7	-	3	32	21	2,919
36 42653	Lisle town	Broome	46.9	2,707	2,663	12	8	1	-	5	18	9	1,906
36 42917	Livingston town	Columbia	38.2	3,424	3,326	50	4	14	1	11	18	58	2,687
36 42961	Livonia town	Livingston	38.3	7,286	7,122	37	23	25	1	7	71	59	5,145
36 42994	Lloyd town	Ulster	31.7	9,941	8,976	519	16	121	1	129	179	504	7,387
36 43093	Lockport town	Niagara	44.6	19,653	18,250	802	93	202	2	70	234	235	14,690
36 43588	Louisville town	St. Lawrence	48.2	3,195	3,094	8	31	40	-	6	16	49	2,399
36 43731	Lowville town	Lewis	37.8	4,548	4,422	27	15	31	-	26	27	46	3,366
36 43973	Lyons town	Wayne	37.5	5,831	5,134	503	14	24	3	62	91	153	4,410
36 44039	Lysander town	Onondaga	61.9	19,285	18,686	141	56	193	3	47	159	150	13,728
36 44160	Macedon town	Wayne	38.7	8,688	8,432	64	20	62	-	26	84	125	6,195
36 44435	Madison town	Madison	40.9	2,801	2,740	9	3	17	4	6	22	21	2,107

[Includes functioning minor civil divisions [MCDs] of 2,500 or more population as of April 1, 2000 in the following 12 states: CT, ME, MA, MI, MN, NH, NJ, NY, PA, RI, VT, and WI. Codes shown are two-digit Federal Information Processing Standards (FIPS) state codes and five-digit FIPS place codes. Place names and codes are those in effect as of January 1, 2000. County refers to the county in which the MCD is located]

State and place code	MCD	County	Land area, 2000 (sq. mi.)	Population, 2000 (April 1) Total	By race— One race White	Black or African American	American Indian and Alaska Native	Asian	Native Hawaiian and Other Pacific Islander	Some other race	Two or more races	Hispanic or Latino (of any race)	18 years and over
36 00000	NEW YORK—Con.												
36 44611	Maine town	Broome	45.7	5,459	5,344	24	3	29	1	4	54	30	4,024
36 44721	Malone town	Franklin	101.9	14,981	11,028	2,781	74	94	-	937	67	1,677	12,541
36 44743	Malta town	Saratoga	28.0	13,005	12,516	141	36	137	2	67	106	188	9,678
36 44809	Mamakating town	Sullivan	95.9	11,002	10,337	235	36	113	-	98	183	525	8,042
36 44842	Mamaroneck town	Westchester	6.6	28,967	25,759	812	35	905	14	844	598	3,164	21,414
36 44864	Manchester town	Ontario	37.8	9,258	9,044	49	34	19	-	13	99	106	6,960
36 44974	Manheim town	Herkimer	29.0	3,171	3,103	11	15	12	1	2	27	22	2,388
36 45029	Manlius town	Onondaga	49.6	31,872	30,182	277	75	937	4	55	342	310	23,473
36 45458	Marbletown town	Ulster	54.6	5,854	5,588	81	13	41	-	31	100	121	4,497
36 45491	Marcellus town	Onondaga	32.6	6,319	6,212	26	19	14	1	4	43	53	4,535
36 45535	Marcy town	Oneida	33.0	9,469	6,479	2,102	26	57	4	620	181	1,328	8,217
36 45601	Marilla town	Erie	27.6	5,709	5,657	7	4	9	1	8	23	26	4,158
36 45645	Marion town	Wayne	29.2	4,974	4,879	34	8	10	1	13	29	66	3,491
36 45722	Marlborough town	Ulster	24.8	8,263	7,807	233	16	27	1	69	110	329	6,070
36 46030	Massena town	St. Lawrence	44.7	13,121	12,439	40	426	54	4	24	134	141	10,014
36 46217	Mayfield town	Fulton	58.4	6,432	6,303	25	14	27	-	30	33	56	4,808
36 46558	Mendon town	Monroe	39.8	8,370	8,158	60	6	90	-	11	45	80	5,961
36 46822	Mexico town	Oswego	46.3	5,181	5,085	9	23	11	1	10	42	35	3,658
36 46855	Middleburgh town	Schoharie	49.2	3,515	3,436	13	14	5	-	22	25	66	2,594
36 47031	Middletown town	Delaware	96.4	4,051	3,853	26	13	29	-	86	44	260	3,200
36 47207	Milan town	Dutchess	36.1	4,559	2,764	1,241	30	34	2	450	38	715	3,913
36 47240	Milford town	Otsego	46.1	2,938	2,865	21	9	17	-	3	23	56	2,258
36 47504	Milo town	Yates	38.4	7,026	6,841	44	17	20	3	24	77	61	5,180
36 47537	Milton town	Saratoga	35.6	17,103	16,493	175	42	81	3	72	237	299	12,372
36 47614	Minden town	Montgomery	51.0	4,202	4,142	4	8	18	-	12	18	56	3,138
36 47713	Minisink town	Orange	23.1	3,585	3,440	51	1	21	2	37	33	165	2,516
36 47834	Mohawk town	Montgomery	34.7	3,902	3,801	16	12	27	1	9	36	59	2,887
36 47933	Moira town	Franklin	45.2	2,857	2,802	14	16	7	-	4	14	20	2,115
36 47999	Monroe town	Orange	20.1	31,407	29,809	382	80	428	1	362	345	1,543	18,363
36 48153	Montgomery town	Orange	50.4	20,891	19,069	771	53	142	3	491	362	1,620	14,762
36 48252	Mooers town	Clinton	87.7	3,404	3,339	7	19	8	-	8	23	27	2,491
36 48307	Moravia town	Cayuga	29.0	4,040	2,921	864	11	11	-	216	17	403	3,360
36 48318	Moreau town	Saratoga	42.2	13,826	13,006	495	28	52	3	142	100	289	10,528
36 48428	Moriah town	Essex	64.7	4,879	4,621	136	10	23	3	59	27	161	3,780
36 48857	Mount Hope town	Orange	25.2	6,639	5,220	1,096	18	98	2	122	83	970	5,272
36 48895	Mount Kisco town	Westchester	3.1	9,983	7,766	598	28	423	-	901	267	2,450	7,773
36 48956	Mount Morris town	Livingston	50.7	4,567	4,341	42	15	28	-	88	53	205	3,443
36 49011	Mount Pleasant town	Westchester	27.7	43,221	36,415	2,191	104	1,411	18	2,168	914	6,057	32,002
36 49286	Murray town	Orleans	31.0	6,259	5,235	916	18	8	-	41	41	394	4,856
36 49517	Nassau town	Rensselaer	44.5	4,818	4,657	52	12	26	-	5	66	47	3,565
36 49847	Neversink town	Sullivan	82.9	3,553	3,444	20	8	8	-	23	50	78	2,554
36 49913	Newark Valley town	Tioga	50.3	4,097	4,023	15	8	13	1	10	28	27	2,925
36 49935	New Baltimore town	Greene	41.6	3,417	3,328	24	4	13	1	15	32	55	2,591
36 49957	New Berlin town	Chenango	46.4	2,803	2,751	10	4	4	1	7	26	34	2,086
36 50001	New Bremen town	Lewis	55.5	2,722	2,670	21	8	5	2	4	12	9	1,898
36 50045	Newburgh town	Orange	43.7	27,568	23,455	2,083	41	569	7	846	567	2,644	20,354
36 50078	New Castle town	Westchester	23.2	17,491	16,004	240	8	971	3	90	175	487	11,917
36 50232	Newfane town	Niagara	51.8	9,657	9,382	73	52	19	-	49	82	95	7,144
36 50254	Newfield town	Tompkins	58.9	5,108	4,907	55	28	19	-	25	74	53	3,721
36 50309	New Hartford town	Oneida	25.4	21,172	20,332	169	21	496	3	44	107	154	16,581
36 50342	New Haven town	Oswego	31.2	2,930	2,883	5	14	12	-	4	12	26	2,068
36 50562	New Paltz town	Ulster	33.9	12,830	10,541	768	26	521	6	632	336	1,054	10,666
36 50672	New Scotland town	Albany	58.1	8,626	8,468	24	17	43	-	17	57	75	6,482
36 50716	Newstead town	Erie	51.0	8,404	8,253	34	65	10	-	8	34	44	6,386
36 50848	New Windsor town	Orange	34.8	22,866	19,372	1,545	62	396	12	953	526	2,538	16,802
36 51033	Niagara town	Niagara	9.4	8,978	8,349	271	132	50	2	20	154	105	6,877
36 51121	Nichols town	Tioga	33.7	2,584	2,559	10	-	5	1	-	9	21	1,863
36 51264	Niskayuna town	Schenectady	14.1	20,295	18,417	318	19	1,215	5	91	230	333	14,994
36 51330	Norfolk town	St. Lawrence	56.9	4,565	4,431	19	49	22	4	5	35	25	3,414
36 51407	Northampton town	Fulton	21.0	2,760	2,712	9	2	8	-	7	22	30	2,159
36 51693	North Castle town	Westchester	24.1	10,849	10,022	191	3	430	5	68	130	449	7,625
36 51803	North Collins town	Erie	42.9	3,376	3,216	15	51	24	-	15	55	80	2,493
36 51869	North Dansville town	Livingston	9.8	5,738	5,517	61	15	33	-	63	49	102	4,256
36 51891	North East town	Dutchess	43.4	3,002	2,870	63	3	17	1	21	27	98	2,310
36 51935	North Elba town	Essex	151.9	8,661	7,423	875	35	75	17	158	78	564	7,138
36 52100	North Greenbush town	Rensselaer	18.7	10,805	10,460	109	10	82	1	26	117	92	8,364
36 52155	North Harmony town	Chautauqua	42.2	2,521	2,492	3	4	1	-	2	19	20	1,832
36 53000	North Hempstead town	Nassau	53.6	222,611	175,809	14,238	306	20,281	65	6,453	5,459	21,872	170,186
36 53517	North Salem town	Westchester	21.4	5,173	4,937	39	4	50	-	58	85	189	3,820
36 53737	Northumberland town	Saratoga	32.3	4,603	4,515	25	15	13	-	8	27	43	3,220
36 53990	Norwich town	Chenango	42.0	3,836	3,737	19	17	19	-	14	30	54	2,859
36 54089	Nunda town	Livingston	37.1	3,017	2,953	16	7	5	1	10	25	27	2,176
36 54166	Oakfield town	Genesee	23.5	3,203	3,115	33	6	6	-	19	24	33	2,289
36 54474	Ogden town	Monroe	36.5	18,492	17,850	250	39	136	5	53	159	253	13,357
36 54749	Olive town	Ulster	58.7	4,579	4,427	28	8	42	8	22	44	115	3,471
36 54892	Oneonta town	Otsego	33.5	4,994	4,528	307	17	40	2	46	54	169	3,803
36 54958	Onondaga town	Onondaga	57.7	21,063	19,861	413	225	244	8	34	278	221	15,485

[Includes functioning minor civil divisions (MCDs) of 2,500 or more population as of April 1, 2000 in the following 12 states: CT, ME, MA, MI, MN, NH, NJ, NY, PA, RI, VT, and WI. Codes shown are two-digit Federal Information Processing Standards (FIPS) state codes and five-digit FIPS place codes. Place names and codes are those in effect as of January 1, 2000. County refers to the county in which the MCD is located]

State and place code	MCD	County	Land area, 2000 (sq. mi.)	Population, 2000 (April 1) Total	White	Black or African American	American Indian and Alaska Native	Asian	Native Hawaiian and Other Pacific Islander	Some other race	Two or more races	Hispanic or Latino (of any race)	18 years and over
36 00000	NEW YORK—Con.												
36 55013	Ontario town	Wayne	32.2	9,778	9,433	122	19	55	-	33	116	119	6,999
36 55211	Orangetown town	Rockland	24.2	47,711	40,064	2,806	53	3,064	11	792	921	2,873	36,957
36 55277	Orchard Park town	Erie	38.5	27,637	26,965	133	41	292	6	46	154	265	20,667
36 55541	Ossining town	Westchester	11.7	36,534	25,667	5,217	127	1,660	7	2,683	1,173	7,282	28,582
36 55563	Oswegatchie town	St. Lawrence	65.8	4,370	4,304	13	15	14	1	1	22	13	3,231
36 55585	Oswego town	Oswego	27.4	7,287	6,850	179	10	91	2	84	71	146	6,001
36 55629	Otego town	Otsego	44.9	3,183	3,105	32	7	14	-	5	20	38	2,323
36 55651	Otisco town	Onondaga	29.6	2,561	2,491	6	8	16	-	4	36	12	1,762
36 55695	Otsego town	Otsego	54.2	3,904	3,816	25	3	27	-	10	23	60	3,046
36 55827	Ovid town	Seneca	31.0	2,757	2,355	262	13	3	2	82	40	160	2,108
36 55871	Owasco town	Cayuga	20.9	3,755	3,714	4	1	20	-	3	13	12	2,791
36 55893	Owego town	Tioga	104.2	20,365	19,709	143	45	205	4	52	207	226	14,959
36 55959	Oxford town	Chenango	60.1	3,992	3,901	34	13	9	4	3	28	43	3,033
36 56000	Oyster Bay town	Nassau	104.4	293,925	266,983	4,819	201	14,265	52	3,987	3,618	14,877	221,842
36 56099	Palatine town	Montgomery	41.2	3,070	3,003	19	8	16	-	2	22	15	2,261
36 56154	Palermo town	Oswego	40.6	3,686	3,607	14	20	7	-	2	36	18	2,606
36 56198	Palmyra town	Wayne	33.5	7,672	7,477	29	28	38	-	17	83	53	5,679
36 56209	Pamelia town	Jefferson	34.0	2,897	2,729	44	19	35	1	17	52	50	2,057
36 56330	Paris town	Oneida	31.4	4,609	4,531	16	3	10	1	9	39	25	3,349
36 56352	Parish town	Oswego	41.8	2,694	2,657	10	10	2	-	1	14	14	1,890
36 56561	Parma town	Monroe	42.0	14,822	14,389	191	26	77	4	36	99	166	10,625
36 56748	Patterson town	Putnam	32.3	11,306	10,320	402	18	144	3	220	199	792	8,286
36 56825	Pawling town	Dutchess	44.2	7,521	7,102	110	13	96	3	98	99	365	5,617
36 57012	Pelham town	Westchester	2.1	11,866	10,363	542	10	470	-	216	265	714	8,471
36 57078	Pembroke town	Genesee	41.7	4,530	4,445	17	16	7	-	6	39	31	3,264
36 57111	Pendleton town	Niagara	27.2	6,050	5,961	25	10	16	1	2	35	36	4,383
36 57144	Penfield town	Monroe	37.5	34,645	32,386	732	40	1,057	7	104	319	495	25,696
36 57221	Perinton town	Monroe	34.1	46,090	43,278	795	50	1,309	3	209	446	660	33,797
36 57254	Perry town	Wyoming	36.4	6,654	5,272	1,048	19	28	1	220	66	664	5,061
36 57331	Persia town	Cattaraugus	20.9	2,512	2,405	7	63	9	-	1	27	22	1,888
36 57353	Perth town	Fulton	26.1	3,638	3,329	233	8	13	-	21	34	128	2,511
36 57375	Peru town	Clinton	79.4	6,370	6,193	58	5	39	-	10	65	54	4,566
36 57529	Phelps town	Ontario	65.0	7,017	6,883	18	10	19	-	32	55	86	5,118
36 57584	Philipstown town	Putnam	48.8	9,422	9,005	106	14	107	-	87	103	357	7,164
36 57771	Pierrepont town	St. Lawrence	60.4	2,674	2,641	5	4	14	-	-	10	8	1,981
36 58156	Pine Plains town	Dutchess	30.9	2,569	2,473	23	17	17	-	12	27	35	1,904
36 58365	Pittsford town	Monroe	23.2	27,219	25,208	436	23	1,245	5	92	210	353	20,318
36 58398	Pittstown town	Rensselaer	61.7	5,644	5,522	27	25	17	-	9	44	37	4,017
36 58552	Plattekill town	Ulster	35.6	9,892	8,597	457	31	62	3	501	241	1,583	7,166
36 58585	Plattsburgh town	Clinton	45.7	11,190	10,818	120	43	61	1	49	98	116	8,327
36 58695	Pleasant Valley town	Dutchess	32.9	9,066	8,654	175	11	58	2	75	91	240	6,700
36 58805	Poestenkill town	Rensselaer	32.5	4,054	3,987	7	12	14	-	11	23	27	2,903
36 58981	Pomfret town	Chautauqua	43.9	14,703	14,009	305	48	127	3	94	117	342	12,026
36 59036	Pompey town	Onondaga	66.4	6,159	6,009	23	13	59	-	17	38	43	4,337
36 59267	Porter town	Niagara	33.2	6,920	6,758	33	53	32	-	8	36	46	5,221
36 59421	Portland town	Chautauqua	34.3	5,502	4,563	663	27	1	1	193	54	474	4,337
36 59509	Portville town	Cattaraugus	35.6	3,952	3,870	30	6	9	1	8	28	27	2,914
36 59575	Potsdam town	St. Lawrence	101.5	15,957	15,033	254	67	403	2	57	141	200	13,209
36 59652	Poughkeepsie town	Dutchess	28.8	42,777	35,511	3,453	59	2,194	10	695	855	2,254	33,119
36 59685	Pound Ridge town	Westchester	22.8	4,726	4,515	57	3	78	1	15	57	116	3,491
36 60147	Putnam Valley town	Putnam	41.4	10,686	10,103	171	20	91	-	137	164	671	7,834
36 60356	Queensbury town	Warren	63.0	25,441	24,816	141	50	181	4	55	194	285	18,997
36 60510	Ramapo town	Rockland	61.2	108,905	78,996	18,555	348	5,007	77	2,883	3,039	8,923	72,297
36 60587	Randolph town	Cattaraugus	36.2	2,681	2,607	24	13	7	1	4	25	16	1,922
36 60905	Red Hook town	Dutchess	36.7	10,408	9,804	150	8	216	11	68	151	276	7,818
36 61357	Rhinebeck town	Dutchess	36.3	7,762	7,180	280	7	106	-	91	98	306	6,189
36 61533	Richland town	Oswego	57.2	5,824	5,716	11	19	23	-	7	48	38	4,208
36 61544	Richmond town	Ontario	42.4	3,452	3,404	2	3	12	-	-	31	23	2,585
36 61742	Ridgeway town	Orleans	50.0	6,886	6,330	303	31	33	1	66	122	162	4,960
36 61808	Riga town	Monroe	35.2	5,437	5,288	39	8	40	2	5	55	50	3,900
36 61885	Ripley town	Chautauqua	48.9	2,636	2,590	5	3	2	1	9	26	38	1,937
36 61984	Riverhead town	Suffolk	67.4	27,680	23,593	2,913	74	249	24	396	431	1,678	21,308
36 63011	Rochester town	Ulster	88.4	7,018	6,556	176	38	36	3	58	151	339	5,163
36 63176	Rockland town	Sullivan	94.3	3,913	3,573	125	2	35	-	106	72	278	2,918
36 63737	Rosendale town	Ulster	19.9	6,352	6,080	114	18	28	-	27	85	167	4,789
36 63935	Rotterdam town	Schenectady	36.0	28,316	27,541	269	44	162	4	60	236	276	21,774
36 64001	Roxbury town	Delaware	87.2	2,509	2,442	11	13	12	2	7	22	34	1,969
36 64034	Royalton town	Niagara	69.8	7,710	7,492	49	29	41	3	14	82	71	5,669
36 64144	Rush town	Monroe	30.5	3,603	3,337	178	13	30	-	16	29	71	2,546
36 64265	Rutland town	Jefferson	45.2	2,959	2,821	44	12	20	1	25	36	54	2,154
36 64320	Rye town	Westchester	7.0	43,880	31,287	2,256	152	1,262	18	6,762	2,143	14,264	33,571
36 64650	St. Johnsville town	Montgomery	16.8	2,565	2,531	2	10	4	1	3	14	35	1,964
36 64782	Salem town	Washington	52.5	2,702	2,651	25	2	5	1	1	17	15	2,040
36 64815	Salina town	Onondaga	13.8	33,290	31,250	718	173	534	12	136	467	466	26,054
36 65013	Sand Lake town	Rensselaer	35.2	7,987	7,853	17	23	37	-	6	51	66	5,864
36 65079	Sandy Creek town	Oswego	42.3	3,863	3,796	4	14	4	-	7	38	18	2,858
36 65134	Sangerfield town	Oneida	30.8	2,610	2,566	10	8	10	1	1	14	14	1,875

Table D-2. MCDs — **Area and Population**—Con.

[Includes functioning minor civil divisions (MCDs) of 2,500 or more population as of April 1, 2000 in the following 12 states: CT, ME, MA, MI, MN, NH, NJ, NY, PA, RI, VT, and WI. Codes shown are two-digit Federal Information Processing Standards (FIPS) state codes and five-digit FIPS place codes. Place names and codes are those in effect as of January 1, 2000. County refers to the county in which the MCD is located]

State and place code	MCD	County	Land area, 2000 (sq. mi.)	Total	White	Black or African American	American Indian and Alaska Native	Asian	Native Hawaiian and Other Pacific Islander	Some other race	Two or more races	Hispanic or Latino (of any race)	18 years and over
36 00000	NEW YORK—Con.												
36 65211	Saranac town	Clinton	115.7	4,165	4,108	6	14	8	2	10	17	43	2,974
36 65244	Saratoga town	Saratoga	40.7	5,141	5,028	50	3	8	3	12	37	60	3,876
36 65277	Sardinia town	Erie	50.2	2,692	2,627	9	7	9	-	4	36	16	1,943
36 65299	Saugerties town	Ulster	64.5	19,868	18,277	806	47	152	4	328	254	916	15,160
36 65442	Scarsdale town	Westchester	6.6	17,823	14,989	271	3	2,242	3	71	244	467	11,985
36 65486	Schaghticoke town	Rensselaer	49.9	7,456	7,275	94	13	27	-	10	37	49	5,497
36 65541	Schodack town	Rensselaer	62.2	12,536	12,228	85	28	62	-	48	85	187	9,278
36 65596	Schoharie town	Schoharie	29.8	3,299	3,243	12	16	4	-	6	18	32	2,476
36 65618	Schroeppel town	Oswego	42.3	8,566	8,377	33	58	26	-	8	64	72	6,158
36 65695	Schuyler town	Herkimer	39.8	3,385	3,316	17	1	15	2	5	29	21	2,579
36 65717	Schuyler Falls town	Clinton	36.5	5,128	4,982	56	16	19	-	12	43	43	3,681
36 65992	Scriba town	Oswego	40.6	7,331	7,125	28	28	41	2	47	60	134	5,248
36 66289	Seneca town	Ontario	50.4	2,731	2,672	13	4	7	-	13	22	41	1,985
36 66333	Seneca Falls town	Seneca	24.2	9,347	8,960	81	21	142	-	28	115	124	7,143
36 66443	Sennett town	Cayuga	28.8	3,244	3,115	77	6	28	2	1	15	21	2,364
36 66597	Shandaken town	Ulster	119.8	3,235	3,062	39	13	38	4	18	61	99	2,580
36 66674	Shawangunk town	Ulster	56.2	12,022	10,398	978	31	111	1	344	159	837	9,324
36 66751	Shelby town	Orleans	46.3	5,420	4,862	380	24	19	2	63	70	178	3,986
36 66773	Sheldon town	Wyoming	47.3	2,561	2,551	1	-	1	1	4	3	6	1,870
36 66894	Sherburne town	Chenango	43.6	3,979	3,929	9	1	5	2	10	23	31	2,923
36 66916	Sheridan town	Chautauqua	37.3	2,838	2,734	18	12	6	2	29	37	69	2,205
36 67345	Sidney town	Delaware	50.3	6,109	5,886	52	20	47	2	24	78	88	4,556
36 67521	Skaneateles town	Onondaga	42.7	7,323	7,249	7	7	26	-	3	31	31	5,386
36 68000	Smithtown town	Suffolk	53.6	115,715	110,546	748	78	2,763	22	660	898	3,855	85,624
36 68220	Sodus town	Wayne	67.4	8,949	7,856	750	21	45	-	77	200	228	6,603
36 68308	Somers town	Westchester	30.0	18,346	17,400	313	9	341	1	109	173	543	13,823
36 68330	Somerset town	Niagara	37.2	2,865	2,781	21	19	15	-	13	16	37	2,021
36 68473	Southampton town	Suffolk	138.9	54,712	48,133	3,624	224	488	45	1,249	949	4,700	43,147
36 68924	Southeast town	Putnam	32.1	17,316	16,083	323	24	283	16	416	171	1,393	12,750
36 69463	Southold town	Suffolk	53.7	20,599	19,266	600	14	92	14	311	302	982	16,178
36 69617	Southport town	Chemung	46.5	11,185	10,128	758	21	26	4	164	84	326	8,809
36 70178	Spencer town	Tioga	49.5	2,979	2,898	20	6	11	-	14	30	38	2,123
36 70662	Stanford town	Dutchess	50.0	3,544	3,365	54	7	39	1	29	49	94	2,716
36 70816	Starkey town	Yates	32.8	3,465	3,362	40	3	16	-	14	30	47	2,419
36 71102	Stephentown town	Rensselaer	58.0	2,873	2,819	9	6	4	2	11	22	32	2,136
36 71146	Sterling town	Cayuga	45.6	3,432	3,379	3	15	2	-	8	25	17	2,524
36 71333	Stillwater town	Saratoga	41.4	7,522	7,387	31	8	35	1	8	52	47	5,488
36 71410	Stockholm town	St. Lawrence	93.9	3,592	3,517	12	15	7	-	5	36	18	2,602
36 71443	Stockport town	Columbia	11.6	2,933	2,830	47	5	3	-	13	35	53	2,165
36 71674	Stony Point town	Rockland	27.8	14,244	13,437	181	27	184	3	236	176	974	10,526
36 71993	Sullivan town	Madison	73.4	14,991	14,728	49	54	34	-	20	106	81	10,935
36 72455	Sweden town	Monroe	33.5	13,716	12,699	510	28	142	8	146	183	395	10,983
36 73627	Thompson town	Sullivan	84.1	14,189	10,457	2,403	25	262	4	659	379	2,066	10,493
36 73891	Ticonderoga town	Essex	81.8	5,167	5,068	24	16	14	1	-	44	21	3,788
36 73968	Tioga town	Tioga	58.7	4,840	4,741	7	9	15	1	14	53	38	3,510
36 75000	Tonawanda town	Erie	18.8	78,155	75,008	1,103	210	897	15	281	641	1,015	61,056
36 75280	Trenton town	Oneida	43.3	4,670	4,580	18	3	25	-	8	36	16	3,407
36 75319	Triangle town	Broome	38.1	3,032	2,964	6	8	10	3	8	33	26	2,137
36 75638	Tully town	Onondaga	25.9	2,709	2,634	12	6	16	-	6	35	30	1,941
36 75781	Tuxedo town	Orange	47.4	3,334	3,090	41	11	107	-	28	57	142	2,612
36 75935	Ulster town	Ulster	26.8	12,544	11,721	362	21	196	8	45	191	307	9,592
36 75990	Ulysses town	Tompkins	33.0	4,775	4,608	53	5	37	1	18	53	56	3,596
36 76012	Unadilla town	Otsego	46.4	4,548	4,418	39	11	9	1	26	44	55	3,346
36 76056	Union town	Broome	35.2	56,298	52,198	1,377	96	1,509	19	324	775	863	43,963
36 76166	Union Vale town	Dutchess	37.7	4,546	4,284	107	5	54	2	47	47	156	3,233
36 76496	Urbana town	Steuben	41.1	2,546	2,483	19	4	14	-	4	22	9	1,990
36 76760	Van Buren town	Onondaga	35.6	12,667	12,293	101	64	52	2	21	134	95	9,679
36 77123	Vernon town	Oneida	38.1	5,335	5,225	23	22	21	-	4	40	37	3,944
36 77178	Verona town	Oneida	69.3	6,425	6,278	24	41	24	1	3	54	30	4,718
36 77255	Vestal town	Broome	52.2	26,535	23,120	580	41	2,211	1	264	318	637	21,527
36 77310	Veteran town	Chemung	38.4	3,271	3,205	14	5	8	-	8	31	28	2,453
36 77387	Victor town	Ontario	35.9	9,977	9,612	89	18	117	-	48	93	162	7,211
36 77486	Vienna town	Oneida	61.5	5,819	5,672	29	32	31	-	12	43	45	4,237
36 77662	Volney town	Oswego	48.3	6,094	5,977	16	18	17	3	13	50	42	4,367
36 77871	Wales town	Erie	35.6	2,960	2,918	3	11	11	-	6	11	22	2,224
36 77992	Wallkill town	Orange	62.2	24,659	19,899	2,304	75	590	12	1,063	716	3,304	18,192
36 78047	Walton town	Delaware	97.2	5,607	5,484	19	14	28	-	11	51	58	4,291
36 78102	Walworth town	Wayne	33.8	8,402	8,126	76	9	79	4	40	68	127	5,743
36 78157	Wappinger town	Dutchess	27.3	26,274	22,643	1,302	62	1,127	5	642	493	2,068	19,606
36 78300	Warrensburg town	Warren	63.7	4,255	4,176	7	11	21	-	3	37	20	3,197
36 78344	Warsaw town	Wyoming	35.4	5,423	5,276	21	17	51	-	5	53	37	4,127
36 78366	Warwick town	Orange	101.7	30,764	28,015	1,387	96	263	14	493	496	1,991	22,399
36 78388	Washington town	Dutchess	59.1	4,742	4,490	134	3	31	1	37	46	170	3,586
36 78531	Waterford town	Saratoga	6.6	8,515	8,248	63	17	93	-	8	86	80	6,509
36 78564	Waterloo town	Seneca	21.7	7,866	7,622	78	17	29	-	42	78	141	5,936
36 78619	Watertown town	Jefferson	36.0	4,482	3,762	504	15	27	1	152	21	307	3,527
36 78828	Wawarsing town	Ulster	130.7	12,889	9,670	1,605	67	151	1	1,000	395	2,326	9,902

Table D-2. MCDs — **Area and Population**—Con.

[Includes functioning minor civil divisions (MCDs) of 2,500 or more population as of April 1, 2000 in the following 12 states: CT, ME, MA, MI, MN, NH, NJ, NY, PA, RI, VT, and WI. Codes shown are two-digit Federal Information Processing Standards (FIPS) state codes and five-digit FIPS place codes. Place names and codes are those in effect as of January 1, 2000. County refers to the county in which the MCD is located]

State and place code	MCD	County	Land area, 2000 (sq. mi.)	Population, 2000 (April 1)									
					By race—							Hispanic or Latino (of any race)	18 years and over
					One race						Two or more races		
				Total	White	Black or African American	American Indian and Alaska Native	Asian	Native Hawaiian and Other Pacific Islander	Some other race			
36 00000	NEW YORK—Con.												
36 78839	Wawayanda town	Orange	35.0	6,273	5,825	110	23	101	1	119	94	369	4,421
36 78861	Wayland town	Steuben	39.0	4,314	4,205	37	19	18	-	5	30	37	3,110
36 78971	Webster town	Monroe	34.0	37,926	36,013	607	37	740	1	172	356	596	28,039
36 79103	Wellsville town	Allegany	36.7	7,678	7,421	41	20	95	-	16	85	55	5,923
36 79356	West Bloomfield town	Ontario	25.5	2,549	2,505	11	8	3	-	8	14	20	1,931
36 79851	Westerlo town	Albany	57.9	3,466	3,406	19	4	7	-	5	25	32	2,547
00 79950	Westfield town	Chautauqua	47.2	5,232	5,074	14	13	28	-	68	35	138	3,904
36 80500	West Monroe town	Oswego	33.7	4,428	4,312	6	30	15	1	8	56	16	3,135
36 80533	Westmoreland town	Oneida	43.1	6,207	6,092	43	15	18	-	13	26	59	4,492
36 80918	West Seneca town	Erie	21.4	45,920	45,051	213	80	229	4	86	257	405	35,686
36 81380	Wheatfield town	Niagara	27.9	14,086	13,725	139	60	69	5	11	77	82	10,770
36 81402	Wheatland town	Monroe	30.6	5,149	4,788	207	20	42	3	42	47	112	3,787
36 81578	White Creek town	Washington	47.9	3,411	3,326	28	5	17	-	1	34	38	2,545
36 81633	Whitehall town	Washington	57.6	4,035	3,954	8	10	11	-	22	30	49	2,998
36 81754	Whitestown town	Oneida	27.2	18,635	18,126	220	17	90	1	52	129	246	14,379
36 82040	Williamson town	Wayne	34.6	6,777	6,339	252	25	30	-	50	81	117	4,911
36 82348	Wilna town	Jefferson	78.9	6,235	5,788	182	45	57	2	53	108	131	4,482
36 82370	Wilson town	Niagara	49.5	5,840	5,698	22	31	15	2	21	51	49	4,341
36 82403	Wilton town	Saratoga	35.9	12,511	12,142	120	17	66	7	32	127	143	8,895
36 82535	Windsor town	Broome	91.5	6,421	6,288	38	18	14	3	11	49	50	4,527
36 82689	Wolcott town	Wayne	39.3	4,692	4,350	197	29	9	-	59	48	183	3,429
36 82755	Woodbury town	Orange	36.2	9,460	8,531	287	27	246	2	209	158	751	6,541
36 83052	Woodstock town	Ulster	67.5	6,241	5,882	81	13	98	1	49	117	160	5,118
36 83448	Yates town	Orleans	37.5	2,510	2,438	20	7	7	-	7	31	26	1,781
36 84022	York town	Livingston	49.1	3,219	3,136	34	3	18	-	-	28	27	2,359
36 84055	Yorkshire town	Cattaraugus	37.0	4,210	4,160	4	14	12	-	6	14	25	3,065
36 84077	Yorktown town	Westchester	36.7	36,318	32,919	1,103	51	1,251	3	472	519	2,112	26,311
42 00000	PENNSYLVANIA		44,816.6	12,281,054	10,484,203	1,224,612	18,348	219,813	3,417	188,437	142,224	394,088	9,358,833
42 00156	Abington township	Montgomery	15.5	56,103	47,194	6,072	51	1,832	28	288	638	883	42,876
42 00300	Adams township	Butler	22.6	6,774	6,613	54	2	58	1	15	31	53	4,748
42 00308	Adams township	Cambria	46.5	6,495	6,423	3	12	8	5	10	34	49	5,012
42 00852	Allegheny township	Blair	29.4	6,965	6,866	45	-	25	3	1	25	12	5,526
42 00892	Allegheny township	Westmoreland	30.8	8,002	7,871	52	13	9	-	11	46	14	6,087
42 00948	Allen township	Northampton	11.1	2,630	2,595	5	2	2	1	11	14	29	2,060
42 02120	Alsace township	Berks	12.2	3,689	3,631	16	5	19	3	10	5	36	2,886
42 02328	Amity township	Berks	18.3	8,867	8,484	181	17	59	1	34	91	89	6,415
42 02384	Amwell township	Washington	44.8	3,960	3,903	24	5	3	-	-	25	7	3,012
42 02600	Annville township	Lebanon	1.6	4,518	4,310	49	1	56	5	44	53	81	3,781
42 02680	Antis township	Blair	60.8	6,328	6,265	6	11	11	1	5	29	18	4,917
42 02696	Antrim township	Franklin	70.1	12,504	12,243	97	31	36	-	30	67	98	9,055
42 03040	Armagh township	Mifflin	92.8	3,988	3,940	3	-	17	-	8	20	28	2,962
42 03064	Armstrong township	Indiana	37.7	3,090	3,045	11	1	9	-	9	15	21	2,298
42 03336	Aston township	Delaware	5.7	16,203	15,662	239	5	127	3	45	122	163	12,516
42 03400	Athens township	Bradford	43.8	5,058	4,901	20	8	80	-	16	33	34	3,713
42 04320	Barrett township	Monroe	52.6	3,880	3,709	78	4	25	-	26	38	61	2,952
42 04376	Bart township	Lancaster	16.2	3,003	2,961	24	8	-	-	5	5	4	1,880
42 04592	Bear Creek township	Luzerne	66.2	2,580	2,551	8	1	8	-	2	10	20	2,019
42 04952	Bedford township	Bedford	68.6	5,417	5,262	72	3	26	-	13	41	32	4,264
42 04976	Bedminster township	Bucks	30.2	4,804	4,714	28	1	20	1	9	31	44	3,626
42 05608	Benner township	Centre	28.5	5,217	3,970	1,035	12	24	3	149	24	183	4,512
42 05616	Bensalem township	Bucks	20.0	58,434	48,443	4,047	126	3,860	30	961	967	2,505	44,924
42 05816	Bern township	Berks	19.2	6,758	6,255	315	6	97	-	23	62	557	5,637
42 06008	Bethel township	Berks	42.2	4,166	4,056	23	4	27	-	32	24	65	3,033
42 06024	Bethel township	Delaware	5.7	6,421	6,064	140	2	155	1	21	38	124	4,396
42 06040	Bethel township	Lebanon	34.7	4,526	4,442	12	5	11	-	35	21	70	3,265
42 06096	Bethlehem township	Northampton	14.6	21,171	19,747	516	14	465	2	242	185	840	15,849
42 06544	Birmingham township	Chester	6.4	4,221	3,984	24	2	172	2	13	24	50	2,950
42 06872	Blair township	Blair	13.6	4,587	4,536	10	2	20	-	4	15	20	3,534
42 07088	Blooming Grove township	Pike	75.3	3,621	3,345	122	7	26	1	84	36	151	2,889
42 07424	Boggs township	Centre	55.2	2,834	2,796	5	13	1	-	3	16	14	2,154
42 08032	Bradford township	Clearfield	38.3	3,314	3,278	7	13	3	-	1	12	6	2,458
42 08048	Bradford township	McKean	55.6	4,816	4,721	28	25	19	-	8	15	30	3,847
42 08344	Brecknock township	Berks	17.8	4,459	4,363	27	6	10	-	11	42	41	3,239
42 08352	Brecknock township	Lancaster	24.9	6,699	6,545	22	10	50	2	20	50	64	4,487
42 08480	Briar Creek township	Columbia	21.1	3,061	3,036	6	1	3	-	7	8	12	2,375
42 08648	Bridgewater township	Susquehanna	40.5	2,668	2,610	18	5	5	-	9	21	15	2,044
42 08680	Brighton township	Beaver	19.0	8,024	7,860	86	4	35	1	5	33	49	6,171
42 08768	Bristol township	Bucks	16.1	55,521	47,818	4,690	115	1,188	21	863	826	2,139	41,174
42 09256	Brothersvalley township	Somerset	62.7	4,184	2,908	1,033	6	14	-	158	65	235	3,581
42 09288	Brown township	Mifflin	33.2	3,852	3,804	14	5	16	-	1	12	8	2,813
42 09816	Buckingham township	Bucks	33.1	16,442	15,907	171	19	195	2	43	105	220	11,794
42 10000	Buffalo township	Butler	24.2	6,827	6,763	16	8	20	-	1	19	15	5,127
42 10016	Buffalo township	Union	30.6	3,207	3,138	18	3	8	1	12	27	31	2,269
42 10152	Bullskin township	Fayette	43.4	7,782	7,732	4	7	13	3	8	15	13	6,009
42 10352	Burrell township	Indiana	23.7	3,746	3,665	59	3	1	-	4	14	17	2,940
42 10400	Bushkill township	Northampton	25.3	6,982	6,861	13	17	27	-	24	40	70	5,017
42 10456	Butler township	Adams	24.0	2,678	2,560	16	10	3	-	71	18	136	2,014

[Includes functioning minor civil divisions (MCDs) of 2,500 or more population as of April 1, 2000 in the following 12 states: CT, ME, MA, MI, MN, NH, NJ, NY, PA, RI, VT, and WI. Codes shown are two-digit Federal Information Processing Standards (FIPS) state codes and five-digit FIPS place codes. Place names and codes are those in effect as of January 1, 2000. County refers to the county in which the MCD is located]

State and place code	MCD	County	Land area, 2000 (sq. mi.)	Population, 2000 (April 1)									
					By race—								
					One race							Hispanic or Latino (of any race)	18 years and over
				Total	White	Black or African American	American Indian and Alaska Native	Asian	Native Hawaiian and Other Pacific Islander	Some other race	Two or more races		
42 00000	PENNSYLVANIA—Con.												
42 10472	Butler township	Butler	21.5	17,185	16,904	92	9	78	9	12	81	67	13,630
42 10480	Butler township	Luzerne	33.3	7,166	6,642	406	11	36	1	28	42	128	5,479
42 10488	Butler township	Schuylkill	26.1	3,588	3,549	21	1	8	-	4	5	4	2,916
42 10704	Caernarvon township	Lancaster	23.0	4,278	4,231	21	4	11	-	2	9	28	2,915
42 10824	Caln township	Chester	8.8	11,916	9,387	1,878	23	291	6	142	189	386	8,878
42 10880	Cambria township	Cambria	49.3	6,323	6,069	189	7	23	4	5	26	35	5,044
42 11176	Canton township	Washington	14.9	8,826	8,431	266	6	17	-	14	92	41	6,833
42 11416	Carroll township	Perry	34.4	5,095	5,041	13	6	3	1	11	20	31	3,736
42 11424	Carroll township	Washington	13.5	5,677	5,578	62	3	6	3	12	13	42	4,566
42 11432	Carroll township	York	15.0	4,715	4,606	19	3	39	2	8	38	37	3,472
42 11800	Cecil township	Washington	26.3	9,756	9,504	154	8	24	4	13	49	52	7,485
42 12016	Center township	Beaver	15.4	11,492	11,017	341	10	46	-	14	64	80	8,885
42 12024	Center township	Butler	24.4	8,182	8,040	36	3	47	1	20	35	28	6,380
42 12040	Center township	Indiana	40.4	4,876	4,825	25	5	6	-	4	11	22	3,869
42 12344	Centre township	Berks	21.4	3,631	3,557	22	1	15	-	16	20	51	2,735
42 12442	Chadds Ford township	Delaware	8.7	3,170	3,020	34	2	88	-	15	11	45	2,479
42 12584	Chanceford township	York	48.5	5,973	5,850	39	17	22	-	8	37	40	4,373
42 12728	Charleston township	Tioga	52.6	3,233	3,166	6	5	21	2	3	30	35	2,442
42 12744	Charlestown township	Chester	12.5	4,051	3,863	63	7	69	1	10	38	56	3,006
42 12848	Chartiers township	Washington	24.5	7,154	6,825	263	2	9	4	9	42	26	5,688
42 12968	Cheltenham township	Montgomery	9.0	36,875	24,503	9,074	46	2,376	23	290	563	732	28,472
42 13072	Cherryhill township	Indiana	48.8	2,842	2,811	14	2	4	-	-	11	3	2,155
42 13212	Chester township	Delaware	1.4	4,604	1,046	3,376	12	27	1	44	98	95	3,051
42 13328	Chestnuthill township	Monroe	37.5	14,418	13,313	586	19	144	3	149	204	703	10,121
42 13488	Chippewa township	Beaver	15.9	7,021	6,853	65	1	43	2	9	48	19	5,426
42 13808	Clarion township	Clarion	31.5	3,273	3,176	54	2	7	-	4	30	13	2,576
42 13936	Clay township	Butler	25.2	2,628	2,604	6	-	3	-	4	11	21	1,933
42 13960	Clay township	Lancaster	22.2	5,173	5,064	9	2	41	2	10	45	29	3,618
42 14048	Clearfield township	Butler	23.4	2,705	2,673	6	5	2	-	5	14	14	2,022
42 14320	Clinton township	Butler	23.8	2,779	2,739	4	1	3	-	-	32	11	2,080
42 14336	Clinton township	Lycoming	28.0	3,947	3,092	762	7	15	-	60	11	97	3,442
42 14536	Coal township	Northumberland	26.5	10,628	9,506	959	7	28	-	65	63	223	8,772
42 14832	Codorus township	York	33.5	3,646	3,584	3	16	9	-	9	25	8	2,785
42 14984	Colebrookdale township	Berks	8.4	5,270	5,201	10	4	18	7	4	26	18	3,999
42 15056	Colerain township	Lancaster	28.8	3,261	3,190	22	1	4	-	19	25	30	2,080
42 15136	College township	Centre	18.3	8,489	8,000	139	4	228	-	59	59	100	6,702
42 15216	Collier township	Allegheny	14.2	5,265	5,163	39	-	26	-	11	26	19	4,242
42 15488	Concord township	Delaware	13.7	9,933	9,514	101	9	223	-	16	70	65	7,156
42 15568	Conemaugh township	Somerset	41.3	7,452	7,417	3	5	9	1	4	13	31	5,830
42 15592	Conestoga township	Lancaster	14.6	3,749	3,686	12	5	6	8	5	27	37	2,741
42 15632	Conewago township	Adams	10.5	5,709	5,590	30	2	9	-	44	34	90	4,240
42 15640	Conewago township	Dauphin	16.7	2,847	2,779	23	-	11	4	10	20	27	2,093
42 15656	Conewago township	York	24.4	5,278	5,131	71	9	14	-	8	45	35	3,951
42 15672	Conewango township	Warren	30.0	3,915	3,826	24	10	16	2	15	22	23	3,076
42 15736	Conneaut township	Erie	43.3	3,908	2,868	988	18	14	-	2	18	202	3,361
42 15816	Connoquenessing township	Butler	22.5	3,653	3,620	4	5	9	1	5	9	17	2,700
42 15824	Conoy township	Lancaster	14.8	3,067	3,035	1	4	5	1	9	12	26	2,199
42 15960	Coolbaugh township	Monroe	85.7	15,205	10,883	2,384	43	154	11	1,116	614	2,327	10,395
42 16040	Cooper township	Clearfield	40.6	2,731	2,723	-	1	3	-	-	4	7	2,042
42 16232	Cornplanter township	Venango	37.3	2,687	2,655	11	2	1	-	1	17	9	2,040
42 16728	Cowanshannock township	Armstrong	45.6	3,006	2,992	3	2	4	-	5	10	10	2,190
42 16920	Cranberry township	Butler	22.8	23,625	22,869	208	15	320	5	46	162	166	16,376
42 16944	Cranberry township	Venango	70.4	7,014	6,921	22	17	14	-	17	23	46	5,324
42 17144	Cresson township	Cambria	11.8	4,055	3,342	555	8	10	-	120	20	141	3,408
42 17640	Cumberland township	Adams	33.4	5,718	5,366	145	17	83	1	60	46	123	4,539
42 17648	Cumberland township	Greene	38.2	6,564	6,471	18	15	1	-	1	58	33	4,985
42 17720	Cumru township	Berks	20.7	13,816	12,965	265	8	260	6	175	137	389	11,194
42 18056	Dallas township	Luzerne	18.7	8,179	8,052	17	5	59	1	11	34	46	6,455
42 18104	Damascus township	Wayne	79.1	3,662	3,603	22	12	12	-	3	10	37	2,728
42 18160	Darby township	Delaware	1.4	9,622	5,994	3,498	11	23	3	28	65	86	7,108
42 18264	Daugherty township	Beaver	10.0	3,441	3,341	63	6	5	2	-	24	8	2,613
42 18456	Decatur township	Clearfield	38.1	2,974	2,938	4	3	5	-	8	16	19	2,332
42 18464	Decatur township	Mifflin	45.2	3,021	2,985	18	2	5	-	2	9	12	2,256
42 18696	Delaware township	Northumberland	30.4	4,341	4,289	12	8	10	1	6	15	23	3,277
42 18704	Delaware township	Pike	44.0	6,319	6,016	136	9	28	-	54	76	302	4,345
42 18760	Delmar township	Tioga	80.4	2,893	2,858	10	8	3	-	3	11	8	2,139
42 18936	Derry township	Dauphin	27.1	21,273	19,710	355	15	843	5	92	253	297	16,410
42 18944	Derry township	Mifflin	31.1	7,256	7,136	22	1	46	-	18	33	43	5,673
42 18968	Derry township	Westmoreland	95.8	14,726	14,463	174	5	21	1	7	55	69	11,450
42 19144	Dickinson township	Cumberland	45.6	4,702	4,622	23	5	18	1	9	24	22	3,499
42 19272	Dingman township	Pike	58.2	8,788	8,273	200	41	45	-	92	137	450	6,058
42 19664	Douglass township	Berks	12.7	3,327	2,967	310	2	14	1	7	26	20	2,452
42 19672	Douglass township	Montgomery	15.3	9,104	8,901	70	7	65	2	13	46	43	6,441
42 19704	Dover township	York	42.0	18,074	17,577	166	34	78	1	93	125	187	13,702
42 19792	Doylestown township	Bucks	15.5	17,619	16,777	457	11	221	4	36	113	247	13,448
42 20136	DuBois city	Clearfield	3.3	8,123	7,975	24	8	43	4	7	62	34	6,248
42 20224	Dunbar township	Fayette	59.1	7,562	7,378	115	9	16	-	3	41	24	5,821

Table D-2. MCDs — **Area and Population**—Con.

[Includes functioning minor civil divisions [MCDs] of 2,500 or more population as of April 1, 2000 in the following 12 states: CT, ME, MA, MI, MN, NH, NJ, NY, PA, RI, VT, and WI. Codes shown are two-digit Federal Information Processing Standards (FIPS) state codes and five-digit FIPS place codes. Place names and codes are those in effect as of January 1, 2000. County refers to the county in which the MCD is located]

State and place code	MCD	County	Land area, 2000 (sq. mi.)	Population, 2000 (April 1)									
					By race—								
					One race							Hispanic or Latino (of any race)	18 years and over
				Total	White	Black or African American	American Indian and Alaska Native	Asian	Native Hawaiian and Other Pacific Islander	Some other race	Two or more races		
42 00000	PENNSYLVANIA—Con.												
42 20680	Earl township	Berks	13.8	3,050	2,993	22	3	7	1	13	11	22	2,353
42 20688	Earl township	Lancaster	22.0	6,183	6,014	37	-	71	-	12	49	66	4,231
42 20736	East Allen township	Northampton	14.4	4,903	4,788	24	4	27	5	25	30	84	3,808
42 20808	East Bethlehem township	Washington	5.1	2,524	2,426	60	10	1	-	3	24	12	1,973
42 20824	East Bradford township	Chester	15.0	9,405	8,789	328	16	176	5	38	53	132	6,824
42 20864	East Brandywine township	Chester	11.4	5,822	5,625	73	6	67	1	4	46	30	4,140
42 20888	East Buffalo township	Union	15.6	5,730	5,499	69	2	102	4	20	34	107	4,541
42 20920	East Caln township	Chester	3.6	2,857	2,507	176	10	115	1	5	43	54	2,179
42 20984	East Cocalico township	Lancaster	20.6	9,954	9,532	47	11	221	3	53	87	137	7,137
42 21008	East Coventry township	Chester	10.8	4,566	4,492	39	5	10	-	8	12	32	3,496
42 21032	East Donegal township	Lancaster	21.8	5,405	5,253	41	3	31	2	35	40	96	3,897
42 21040	East Drumore township	Lancaster	23.2	3,535	3,477	16	1	5	2	22	12	29	2,554
42 21072	East Earl township	Lancaster	24.6	5,723	5,618	33	3	21	2	7	39	38	3,812
42 21104	East Fallowfield township	Chester	15.7	5,157	4,558	471	7	22	6	24	69	87	3,731
42 21160	East Franklin township	Armstrong	30.9	3,900	3,856	4	8	14	1	1	16	17	3,045
42 21192	East Goshen township	Chester	10.1	16,824	15,880	452	9	331	6	46	100	197	13,083
42 21208	East Hanover township	Dauphin	39.9	5,322	5,160	38	7	22	-	37	58	101	3,872
42 21224	East Hanover township	Lebanon	32.6	2,858	2,767	18	7	15	1	24	26	64	2,223
42 21232	East Hempfield township	Lancaster	21.2	21,399	19,997	324	23	548	1	323	183	595	16,293
42 21304	East Huntingdon township	Westmoreland	32.8	7,781	7,678	37	7	17	2	10	30	23	6,030
42 21344	East Lampeter township	Lancaster	20.0	13,556	12,489	286	9	369	4	251	148	524	10,094
42 21464	East Manchester township	York	16.6	5,078	4,946	53	10	34	-	13	22	47	3,831
42 21480	East Marlborough township	Chester	15.6	6,317	5,963	76	6	147	4	50	71	250	4,366
42 21600	East Norriton township	Montgomery	6.1	13,211	11,730	800	17	507	-	51	106	154	10,728
42 21624	East Nottingham township	Chester	20.0	5,516	5,128	162	14	13	-	128	71	292	3,718
42 21680	East Pennsboro township	Cumberland	10.9	18,254	17,111	268	26	462	5	116	266	281	14,102
42 21696	East Pikeland township	Chester	8.8	6,551	6,306	89	5	113	2	10	26	45	4,858
42 21760	East Rockhill township	Bucks	12.9	5,199	5,053	42	21	20	3	10	50	65	3,703
42 21788	East St. Clair township	Bedford	33.9	3,123	3,074	16	1	21	-	3	8	10	2,010
42 21896	East Taylor township	Cambria	9.0	2,726	2,651	61	1	1	-	3	9	14	2,167
42 21928	Easttown township	Chester	8.2	10,270	9,630	258	11	286	1	21	63	111	7,610
42 22000	East Vincent township	Chester	13.5	5,493	5,086	259	5	51	2	22	68	61	3,913
42 22048	East Wheatfield township	Indiana	26.9	2,607	2,583	1	3	2	1	2	15	9	2,005
42 22056	East Whiteland township	Chester	11.0	9,333	8,360	306	8	465	4	68	122	226	7,089
42 22584	Edgmont township	Delaware	9.8	3,918	3,549	192	5	107	-	15	50	53	2,825
42 22904	Eldred township	Monroe	24.3	2,665	2,604	14	8	5	-	12	22	37	2,005
42 23000	Elizabeth township	Allegheny	22.6	13,839	13,473	234	6	36	2	24	64	51	10,880
42 23008	Elizabeth township	Lancaster	17.6	3,833	3,780	14	1	11	-	14	13	48	2,703
42 23840	Ephrata township	Lancaster	16.2	8,026	7,720	35	6	146	-	61	58	142	5,552
42 24384	Exeter township	Berks	24.4	21,161	20,181	433	22	245	3	116	161	374	15,839
42 24400	Exeter township	Luzerne	12.9	2,557	2,539	2	1	2	4	8	1	9	1,936
42 24592	Fairfield township	Lycoming	11.6	2,659	2,605	16	8	10	-	1	19	14	1,963
42 24608	Fairfield township	Westmoreland	60.5	2,536	2,504	10	7	1	-	2	12	11	1,913
42 24864	Fairview township	Erie	29.2	10,140	9,953	54	8	57	-	14	54	69	7,581
42 24888	Fairview township	Luzerne	9.7	3,995	3,842	33	2	84	-	8	26	42	2,844
42 24936	Fairview township	York	35.6	14,321	13,818	125	17	143	12	72	134	186	10,831
42 25104	Fallowfield township	Washington	21.3	4,461	4,365	64	3	7	-	3	19	28	3,639
42 25112	Falls township	Bucks	22.3	34,865	31,454	1,704	55	899	7	269	477	818	25,887
42 25400	Fawn township	Allegheny	12.9	2,504	2,472	5	1	17	1	2	6	6	1,978
42 25408	Fawn township	York	27.1	2,727	2,667	22	7	11	-	13	7	8	1,956
42 25440	Fayette township	Juniata	39.7	3,252	3,212	11	2	4	5	9	9	23	2,363
42 25624	Ferguson township	Centre	48.1	14,063	12,359	338	15	1,046	4	82	219	256	10,916
42 25648	Fermanagh township	Juniata	32.1	2,544	2,515	8	-	16	-	-	5	14	1,987
42 25904	Findlay township	Allegheny	32.6	5,145	4,948	84	7	57	-	4	45	29	3,825
42 26728	Forks township	Northampton	12.1	8,419	7,991	189	4	117	1	52	65	173	6,098
42 26896	Forward township	Allegheny	18.9	3,771	3,681	41	5	12	1	3	28	12	2,927
42 26904	Forward township	Butler	23.3	2,687	2,654	5	6	15	-	3	4	9	1,946
42 26928	Foster township	Luzerne	44.8	3,323	3,261	37	1	8	-	7	9	26	2,675
42 26936	Foster township	McKean	46.4	4,566	4,498	9	15	22	-	6	16	14	3,438
42 27088	Fox township	Elk	67.3	3,734	3,717	2	3	3	-	2	7	4	2,750
42 27280	Franconia township	Montgomery	13.8	11,523	11,128	99	9	197	1	35	54	103	8,617
42 27320	Franklin township	Adams	68.4	4,590	4,298	80	16	4	-	148	44	264	3,434
42 27336	Franklin township	Beaver	17.6	4,307	4,277	5	5	6	-	3	11	24	3,218
42 27368	Franklin township	Carbon	14.6	4,243	4,195	3	6	15	-	4	20	19	3,336
42 27376	Franklin township	Chester	13.2	3,850	3,724	43	7	29	-	19	28	49	2,529
42 27400	Franklin township	Fayette	29.6	2,628	2,582	23	4	1	-	7	11	3	2,039
42 27408	Franklin township	Greene	40.9	7,694	6,237	1,374	3	40	1	10	29	206	6,386
42 27480	Franklin township	York	19.1	4,515	4,446	8	4	16	3	6	32	26	3,260
42 27600	Frankstown township	Blair	48.7	7,694	7,467	32	3	141	-	6	45	43	5,847
42 27720	Freedom township	Blair	17.4	3,261	3,227	7	7	4	-	-	16	3	2,455
42 28168	Fulton township	Lancaster	25.9	2,826	2,754	36	1	6	-	9	20	34	1,877
42 28792	Georges township	Fayette	47.9	6,752	6,613	68	10	3	-	2	56	19	5,197
42 28856	German township	Fayette	33.3	5,595	5,139	403	11	4	-	5	33	25	4,207
42 29184	Gilpin township	Armstrong	16.5	2,587	2,535	26	1	5	3	1	16	5	2,060
42 29240	Girard township	Erie	31.8	5,133	5,078	10	8	10	2	3	22	14	3,744
42 30480	Granville township	Mifflin	40.2	4,895	4,835	17	9	12	-	5	17	22	3,797
42 30816	Green township	Indiana	52.8	3,995	3,949	7	-	-	-	4	35	21	2,993

Table D-2. MCDs — **Area and Population**—Con.

[Includes functioning minor civil divisions (MCDs) of 2,500 or more population as of April 1, 2000 in the following 12 states: CT, ME, MA, MI, MN, NH, NJ, NY, PA, RI, VT, and WI. Codes shown are two-digit Federal Information Processing Standards (FIPS) state codes and five-digit FIPS place codes. Place names and codes are those in effect as of January 1, 2000. County refers to the county in which the MCD is located]

State and place code	MCD	County	Land area, 2000 (sq. mi.)	Population, 2000 (April 1) Total	White	Black or African American	American Indian and Alaska Native	Asian	Native Hawaiian and Other Pacific Islander	Some other race	Two or more races	Hispanic or Latino (of any race)	18 years and over
42 00000	PENNSYLVANIA—Con.												
42 30920	Greene township	Beaver	24.9	2,705	2,652	7	7	2	1	3	33	21	1,910
42 30936	Greene township	Erie	37.5	4,768	4,729	4	9	3	-	8	15	12	3,559
42 30944	Greene township	Franklin	56.8	12,284	11,841	189	10	87	12	56	89	161	9,476
42 30976	Greene township	Pike	60.2	3,149	3,063	11	6	10	1	20	38	83	2,445
42 31000	Greenfield township	Blair	35.9	3,904	3,863	6	3	1	-	7	24	14	2,943
42 31352	Greenwich township	Berks	31.3	3,386	3,335	12	8	5	-	2	24	23	2,503
42 31480	Gregg township	Union	15.1	4,687	2,586	1,716	14	91	2	16	262	964	4,457
42 31720	Guilford township	Franklin	52.6	13,100	12,565	232	27	75	1	45	155	164	10,171
42 32040	Halifax township	Dauphin	27.9	3,329	3,274	11	-	18	-	9	17	17	2,461
42 32152	Hamilton township	Franklin	35.7	8,949	8,499	230	10	66	7	45	92	127	6,681
42 32176	Hamilton township	Monroe	38.3	8,235	7,817	200	8	82	4	55	69	229	6,273
42 32296	Hampden township	Cumberland	17.8	24,135	22,680	208	33	904	10	89	211	289	18,224
42 32328	Hampton township	Allegheny	16.0	17,526	17,116	118	8	215	1	21	47	93	12,605
42 32392	Hanover township	Beaver	44.9	3,529	3,469	21	7	5	-	7	20	35	2,625
42 32416	Hanover township	Luzerne	18.8	11,488	11,268	110	2	20	-	14	74	69	8,965
42 32432	Hanover township	Northampton	6.7	9,563	8,940	90	10	328	-	81	114	237	7,227
42 32440	Hanover township	Washington	47.6	2,795	2,754	17	4	6	1	6	7	11	2,191
42 32520	Harborcreek township	Erie	34.2	15,178	14,802	183	12	78	2	26	75	86	11,597
42 32624	Harmar township	Allegheny	6.0	3,242	3,169	22	3	32	-	2	14	18	2,689
42 32680	Harmony township	Beaver	2.9	3,373	3,288	49	-	4	4	7	21	19	2,728
42 32792	Harris township	Centre	31.9	4,657	4,437	61	3	76	3	12	65	54	3,334
42 32832	Harrison township	Allegheny	7.3	10,934	10,367	404	6	45	-	12	100	60	8,642
42 33120	Hatfield township	Montgomery	10.0	16,712	13,859	610	24	1,735	6	165	313	400	12,513
42 33144	Haverford township	Delaware	10.0	48,498	45,585	1,028	49	1,338	6	98	394	431	36,401
42 33256	Hayfield township	Crawford	38.9	3,092	3,063	2	6	7	-	2	12	11	2,269
42 33376	Hazle township	Luzerne	44.9	9,000	8,880	15	5	28	-	38	34	92	7,257
42 33584	Hegins township	Schuylkill	32.0	3,519	3,484	3	-	8	2	12	10	20	2,769
42 33608	Heidelberg township	Lebanon	24.2	3,832	3,805	8	-	7	-	5	7	14	2,779
42 33616	Heidelberg township	Lehigh	24.7	3,279	3,236	9	2	10	-	7	15	29	2,411
42 33624	Heidelberg township	York	14.5	2,970	2,908	14	9	4	2	8	25	19	2,204
42 33728	Hellam township	York	27.7	5,930	5,800	44	2	20	2	11	51	55	4,570
42 33784	Hempfield township	Mercer	14.1	4,004	3,952	11	3	20	-	1	17	15	3,144
42 33792	Hempfield township	Westmoreland	76.6	40,721	39,670	451	33	341	18	46	162	154	32,404
42 33944	Hepburn township	Lycoming	16.6	2,836	2,801	10	2	12	-	-	11	6	2,112
42 34016	Hereford township	Berks	15.4	3,174	3,116	6	3	12	-	15	22	41	2,402
42 34952	Hilltown township	Bucks	26.9	12,102	11,611	186	11	131	3	40	120	177	8,812
42 35536	Honey Brook township	Chester	25.1	6,278	6,115	68	15	12	2	18	48	62	4,458
42 35640	Hopewell township	Beaver	16.9	13,254	12,902	240	1	42	2	7	60	65	10,448
42 35704	Hopewell township	York	26.9	5,062	4,959	36	6	17	1	16	27	50	3,585
42 35808	Horsham township	Montgomery	17.3	24,232	21,764	904	42	1,164	3	134	221	387	17,691
42 36296	Hunlock township	Luzerne	21.3	2,568	2,538	3	1	11	-	-	15	1	1,957
42 36776	Independence township	Beaver	22.9	2,802	2,741	5	3	-	-	5	48	17	2,028
42 36808	Indiana township	Allegheny	17.7	6,809	6,514	88	4	147	2	21	33	37	4,960
42 37344	Jackson township	Butler	21.2	3,645	3,573	33	3	10	-	6	20	11	2,824
42 37352	Jackson township	Cambria	48.3	4,925	4,891	2	1	4	-	2	25	5	3,863
42 37392	Jackson township	Lebanon	23.8	6,338	6,249	18	6	23	1	19	22	48	4,822
42 37400	Jackson township	Luzerne	13.3	4,453	3,251	1,098	5	40	1	26	32	185	3,820
42 37424	Jackson township	Monroe	29.4	5,979	5,485	201	18	72	7	115	81	276	4,330
42 37488	Jackson township	York	22.4	6,095	5,991	20	6	23	-	20	35	64	4,580
42 37848	Jefferson township	Butler	23.4	5,690	5,659	9	-	3	-	6	13	15	4,363
42 37888	Jefferson township	Greene	21.6	2,528	2,433	70	8	7	-	-	10	14	2,016
42 37896	Jefferson township	Lackawanna	33.5	3,592	3,545	12	2	9	-	4	20	14	2,714
42 37984	Jenkins township	Luzerne	13.6	4,584	4,537	12	3	7	1	3	21	23	3,667
42 38032	Jenner township	Somerset	64.6	4,054	4,027	-	2	4	-	5	16	10	3,158
42 38912	Keating township	McKean	98.1	3,087	3,043	4	4	7	-	1	28	17	2,346
42 39136	Kelly township	Union	17.1	4,502	3,566	852	11	39	-	8	26	279	3,859
42 39312	Kennedy township	Allegheny	5.4	7,504	7,402	38	1	36	2	3	22	22	5,969
42 39344	Kennett township	Chester	15.5	6,451	5,982	133	2	91	2	178	63	593	4,867
42 39792	Kingston township	Luzerne	13.6	7,145	7,070	17	4	20	-	6	28	27	5,365
42 39968	Kiskiminetas township	Armstrong	40.7	4,950	4,865	24	6	11	-	14	30	25	3,813
42 40760	Lackawannock township	Mercer	20.8	2,561	2,503	22	8	5	1	13	9	20	1,816
42 40776	Lackawaxen township	Pike	78.6	4,154	3,941	107	8	18	-	20	60	113	3,162
42 40936	Lake township	Wayne	28.1	4,361	4,236	70	5	8	-	16	26	69	3,344
42 41208	Lancaster township	Butler	23.4	2,511	2,486	6	-	6	1	2	10	11	1,860
42 41224	Lancaster township	Lancaster	6.0	13,944	11,724	900	13	292	1	731	283	1,346	11,055
42 41672	Latimore township	Adams	21.2	2,528	2,472	3	1	9	1	21	21	47	1,869
42 41952	Lawrence township	Clearfield	83.1	7,712	7,607	31	13	23	-	4	34	35	6,039
42 41984	Lawrence Park township	Erie	1.9	4,048	3,994	21	1	9	-	7	16	33	3,027
42 42080	Leacock township	Lancaster	20.7	4,878	4,786	20	6	35	1	7	23	29	3,118
42 42424	Lehigh township	Northampton	29.7	9,728	9,599	35	19	17	-	16	42	72	7,540
42 42504	Lehman township	Luzerne	21.7	3,206	3,153	15	9	17	-	-	12	5	2,473
42 42512	Lehman township	Pike	48.9	7,515	6,087	856	16	78	1	270	207	881	5,268
42 43240	Ligonier township	Westmoreland	91.8	6,973	6,918	9	3	9	-	5	29	19	5,556
42 43312	Limerick township	Montgomery	22.6	13,534	12,871	285	26	175	-	60	117	179	9,908
42 43832	Little Britain township	Lancaster	27.4	3,514	3,448	23	1	8	-	4	30	42	2,330
42 44328	Logan township	Blair	46.6	11,925	11,736	70	8	50	1	7	53	48	9,483
42 44440	London Britain township	Chester	9.9	2,797	2,700	25	1	26	1	11	33	47	1,989

[Includes functioning minor civil divisions [MCDs] of 2,500 or more population as of April 1, 2000 in the following 12 states: CT, ME, MA, MI, MN, NH, NJ, NY, PA, RI, VT, and WI. Codes shown are two-digit Federal Information Processing Standards (FIPS) state codes and five-digit FIPS place codes. Place names and codes are those in effect as of January 1, 2000. County refers to the county in which the MCD is located]

State and place code	MCD	County	Land area, 2000 (sq. mi.)	Population, 2000 (April 1)									
					By race—								
					One race							Hispanic or Latino (of any race)	18 years and over
				Total	White	Black or African American	American Indian and Alaska Native	Asian	Native Hawaiian and Other Pacific Islander	Some other race	Two or more races		
42 00000	PENNSYLVANIA—Con.												
42 44464	Londonderry township	Dauphin	22.8	5,224	5,106	40	5	13	-	6	54	35	3,914
42 44480	London Grove township	Chester	17.2	5,265	4,812	127	12	23	-	194	97	695	3,665
42 44584	Longswamp township	Berks	22.8	5,608	5,549	18	5	14	-	7	15	47	4,300
42 44832	Lower Allen township	Cumberland	10.3	17,437	14,946	1,889	22	330	10	105	135	641	14,750
42 44840	Lower Alsace township	Berks	4.7	4,478	4,324	31	-	40	-	50	33	127	3,506
42 44872	Lower Chanceford township	York	41.6	2,899	2,839	12	10	16	2	9	11	12	2,544
42 44888	Lower Chichester township	Delaware	1.1	3,591	3,460	73	5	14	-	6	33	49	2,544
42 44912	Lower Frederick township	Montgomery	8.0	4,795	4,580	89	11	39	-	23	53	71	3,383
42 44920	Lower Gwynedd township	Montgomery	9.3	10,422	9,046	811	8	427	1	27	102	109	8,016
42 44928	Lower Heidelberg township	Berks	14.9	4,150	4,038	36	1	49	-	11	15	43	3,045
42 44952	Lower Macungie township	Lehigh	22.6	19,220	18,023	112	22	828	-	93	142	292	14,375
42 44968	Lower Makefield township	Bucks	17.9	32,681	30,498	592	24	1,217	1	95	254	463	23,664
42 44976	Lower Merion township	Montgomery	23.7	59,850	54,047	2,694	45	2,048	41	302	673	956	46,850
42 44992	Lower Milford township	Lehigh	19.7	3,617	3,548	6	9	20	-	4	30	25	2,710
42 45008	Lower Moreland township	Montgomery	7.3	11,281	10,757	60	6	380	-	22	56	103	8,760
42 45016	Lower Mount Bethel township	Northampton	24.2	3,228	3,173	22	2	8	1	8	14	32	2,444
42 45024	Lower Nazareth township	Northampton	13.4	5,259	5,100	47	9	63	-	7	33	73	3,806
42 45040	Lower Oxford township	Chester	18.2	4,319	2,648	1,490	2	11	-	126	42	282	3,356
42 45056	Lower Paxton township	Dauphin	28.1	44,424	38,431	3,680	46	1,194	10	464	599	1,053	34,428
42 45072	Lower Pottsgrove township	Montgomery	7.9	11,213	10,004	921	12	101	4	29	142	137	7,973
42 45080	Lower Providence township	Montgomery	15.3	22,390	19,314	1,624	24	1,045	15	232	136	470	16,573
42 45096	Lower Salford township	Montgomery	14.4	12,893	12,044	379	7	302	6	40	115	183	8,892
42 45104	Lower Saucon township	Northampton	24.1	9,884	9,561	55	16	119	6	68	59	253	7,528
42 45112	Lower Southampton township	Bucks	6.7	19,276	18,571	207	12	264	2	80	140	272	14,870
42 45120	Lower Swatara township	Dauphin	12.1	8,149	7,636	250	4	125	1	47	86	156	6,240
42 45128	Lower Towamensing township	Carbon	21.1	3,173	3,133	-	4	2	-	14	20	33	2,446
42 45152	Lower Windsor township	York	25.1	7,405	7,300	11	8	9	-	29	48	84	5,476
42 45160	Lower Yoder township	Cambria	13.2	3,029	2,980	25	-	10	2	2	10	12	2,580
42 45224	Loyalsock township	Lycoming	21.0	10,876	10,312	287	14	114	1	36	112	93	8,626
42 45560	Luzerne township	Fayette	29.6	4,683	4,442	176	5	5	-	1	54	15	3,697
42 45656	Lynn township	Lehigh	41.4	3,849	3,775	9	4	9	-	16	36	43	2,841
42 45900	McCandless township	Allegheny	16.5	29,022	27,449	375	15	926	2	41	214	202	22,176
42 46224	McKean township	Erie	36.6	4,619	4,536	26	18	5	-	13	21	33	3,326
42 46480	Madison township	Lackawanna	17.0	2,542	2,509	12	3	3	-	3	12	13	1,845
42 46640	Mahoning township	Carbon	23.6	3,978	3,909	9	16	18	-	3	23	16	3,189
42 46648	Mahoning township	Lawrence	24.6	3,447	3,407	10	4	6	-	4	16	12	2,630
42 46656	Mahoning township	Montour	8.2	4,263	4,006	82	1	116	-	26	32	73	3,312
42 46680	Maidencreek township	Berks	13.3	6,553	6,331	58	4	83	-	36	41	150	4,674
42 46872	Manchester township	York	15.9	12,700	11,973	266	15	218	3	110	115	211	9,564
42 46896	Manheim township	Lancaster	24.2	33,697	31,400	491	36	1,056	2	344	368	932	25,894
42 46904	Manheim township	York	21.5	3,119	3,076	-	8	9	-	2	24	8	2,256
42 46976	Manor township	Armstrong	16.6	4,231	4,167	26	5	4	1	4	24	16	3,311
42 46992	Manor township	Lancaster	38.6	16,498	15,779	223	16	208	2	128	142	376	12,532
42 47592	Marlborough township	Montgomery	12.5	3,104	3,028	22	4	5	-	20	25	34	2,370
42 47616	Marple township	Delaware	10.2	23,737	21,980	261	21	1,307	-	28	140	156	18,559
42 47696	Marshall township	Allegheny	15.6	5,996	5,750	65	-	133	1	4	44	41	3,978
42 47824	Martic township	Lancaster	29.0	4,990	4,906	24	12	8	1	10	29	68	3,485
42 48128	Maxatawny township	Berks	26.2	5,982	5,746	119	5	36	8	20	48	87	5,148
42 48608	Menallen township	Adams	42.8	2,974	2,777	27	6	1	1	122	40	273	2,194
42 48616	Menallen township	Fayette	21.2	4,644	4,448	145	6	5	-	-	40	16	3,503
42 49040	Middle Paxton township	Dauphin	54.6	4,823	4,727	13	8	20	1	23	31	34	3,761
42 49056	Middlesex township	Butler	23.0	5,586	5,524	14	8	9	1	11	22	38	4,065
42 49072	Middlesex township	Cumberland	25.9	6,669	6,401	100	7	53	3	29	76	84	5,088
42 49080	Middle Smithfield township	Monroe	53.1	11,495	9,798	881	25	151	1	365	274	990	7,941
42 49120	Middletown township	Bucks	19.1	44,141	41,432	927	65	1,061	2	243	411	757	32,576
42 49136	Middletown township	Delaware	13.5	16,064	15,145	495	5	275	3	25	116	139	12,757
42 49384	Milford township	Bucks	28.1	8,810	8,612	61	8	57	1	28	43	90	6,499
42 49548	Millcreek township	Erie	29.5	52,129	50,332	570	45	698	7	155	322	518	39,581
42 49560	Millcreek township	Lebanon	20.4	2,921	2,857	22	-	5	-	17	20	37	2,075
42 50472	Monroe township	Cumberland	26.1	5,530	5,452	12	2	31	1	1	31	26	4,175
42 50488	Monroe township	Snyder	15.6	4,012	3,920	10	2	43	-	7	30	21	3,105
42 50616	Montgomery township	Franklin	67.1	4,949	4,911	12	6	3	-	8	9	22	3,677
42 50640	Montgomery township	Montgomery	10.7	22,025	18,853	852	16	2,023	3	62	216	279	15,771
42 50784	Moon township	Allegheny	23.7	22,290	20,768	798	14	433	5	56	216	220	17,356
42 50824	Moore township	Northampton	37.5	8,673	8,569	31	4	18	3	19	29	88	6,753
42 50992	Morgan township	Greene	24.5	2,600	2,566	12	6	2	-	1	13	10	2,009
42 51056	Morris township	Clearfield	19.7	3,063	3,046	2	1	5	-	1	8	21	2,316
42 51504	Mount Carmel township	Northumberland	21.8	2,701	2,689	-	-	3	1	1	7	3	2,137
42 51640	Mount Joy township	Adams	25.9	3,232	3,115	47	11	15	-	22	22	64	2,354
42 51664	Mount Joy township	Lancaster	28.0	7,944	7,717	20	11	85	4	57	50	110	5,776
42 51696	Mount Lebanon township	Allegheny	6.1	33,017	31,766	202	23	757	4	61	204	263	24,818
42 51776	Mount Pleasant township	Adams	30.6	4,420	4,351	19	6	17	-	15	12	75	3,234
42 51864	Mount Pleasant township	Washington	35.6	3,422	3,302	102	-	3	-	-	15	3	2,602
42 51888	Mount Pleasant township	Westmoreland	55.8	11,153	11,064	28	1	5	1	11	43	44	8,728
42 52200	Muhlenberg township	Berks	12.0	16,305	15,568	198	6	115	-	271	147	638	12,988
42 52288	Muncy Creek township	Lycoming	20.1	3,487	3,441	6	4	21	-	3	12	8	2,715
42 53064	Neshannock township	Lawrence	17.3	9,216	9,047	31	10	95	1	3	31	39	7,368

[Includes functioning minor civil divisions [MCDs] of 2,500 or more population as of April 1, 2000 in the following 12 states: CT, ME, MA, MI, MN, NH, NJ, NY, PA, RI, VT, and WI. Codes shown are two-digit Federal Information Processing Standards (FIPS) state codes and five-digit FIPS place codes. Place names and codes are those in effect as of January 1, 2000. County refers to the county in which the MCD is located]

State and place code	MCD	County	Land area, 2000 (sq. mi.)	Population, 2000 (April 1)									
					By race—								
					One race							Hispanic or Latino (of any race)	18 years and over
				Total	White	Black or African American	American Indian and Alaska Native	Asian	Native Hawaiian and Other Pacific Islander	Some other race	Two or more races		
42 00000	PENNSYLVANIA—Con.												
42 53104	Nether Providence township	Delaware	4.7	13,456	12,121	824	13	315	5	36	142	152	10,033
42 53304	New Britain township	Bucks	14.7	10,698	10,298	144	13	122	-	46	75	137	7,767
42 53608	New Garden township	Chester	16.1	9,083	7,712	333	37	118	4	733	146	2,065	6,294
42 53664	New Hanover township	Montgomery	21.6	7,369	7,245	23	5	58	1	4	33	56	5,343
42 53816	New London township	Chester	11.9	4,583	4,431	44	4	30	2	41	31	109	2,862
42 53960	Newport township	Luzerne	16.4	5,006	4,514	429	6	15	-	27	15	115	4,199
42 54072	New Sewickley township	Beaver	32.7	7,076	7,004	12	9	11	-	1	39	24	5,458
42 54136	Newton township	Lackawanna	22.4	2,699	2,671	7	3	12	-	5	1	12	2,074
42 54192	Newtown township	Bucks	12.0	18,206	17,052	191	7	734	-	46	176	242	12,946
42 54224	Newtown township	Delaware	10.0	11,700	11,251	77	8	269	-	15	80	81	8,996
42 54576	Nockamixon township	Bucks	22.2	3,517	3,457	18	1	4	4	5	28	21	2,692
42 54688	Northampton township	Bucks	25.8	39,384	38,205	163	14	708	3	64	227	325	28,277
42 54768	North Beaver township	Lawrence	43.1	4,022	3,968	2	1	15	-	5	31	20	3,024
42 54856	North Buffalo township	Armstrong	24.7	2,942	2,926	5	-	6	1	-	4	14	2,259
42 54904	North Codorus township	York	32.3	7,915	7,779	22	8	17	-	34	55	73	5,957
42 54928	North Cornwall township	Lebanon	9.5	6,403	5,897	98	9	146	4	150	99	338	4,845
42 54936	North Coventry township	Chester	13.4	7,381	7,100	132	15	61	-	21	52	67	5,753
42 54960	North East township	Erie	42.4	7,702	7,535	68	2	33	2	19	43	63	5,880
42 55016	North Fayette township	Allegheny	25.1	12,254	11,518	319	15	307	1	20	74	108	9,224
42 55040	North Franklin township	Washington	7.3	4,818	4,642	116	8	19	-	3	30	17	3,834
42 55112	North Hopewell township	York	18.6	2,507	2,465	9	3	6	-	-	24	14	1,891
42 55128	North Huntingdon township	Westmoreland	27.3	29,123	28,780	92	12	113	6	14	106	120	22,780
42 55160	North Lebanon township	Lebanon	16.9	10,629	10,046	118	13	124	-	231	97	570	8,075
42 55176	North Londonderry township	Lebanon	10.8	6,771	6,621	9	-	85	-	14	42	86	5,371
42 55192	North Manheim township	Schuylkill	20.5	3,287	3,229	18	6	18	-	3	13	16	2,561
42 55216	North Middleton township	Cumberland	23.5	10,197	9,488	348	20	158	11	64	108	151	7,825
42 55400	North Sewickley township	Beaver	20.8	6,120	6,010	55	1	12	1	3	38	20	4,637
42 55432	North Strabane township	Washington	27.3	10,057	9,700	209	1	81	2	22	42	61	7,828
42 55464	North Union township	Fayette	38.7	14,140	13,619	368	17	40	2	15	79	60	11,077
42 55488	North Versailles township	Allegheny	8.1	11,125	9,769	1,087	7	85	3	24	150	54	8,910
42 55576	North Whitehall township	Lehigh	28.5	14,731	14,265	123	13	106	2	85	137	244	10,466
42 55712	Nottingham township	Washington	20.3	2,522	2,499	14	-	2	-	-	7	5	1,932
42 55992	Oakland township	Butler	22.9	3,074	3,060	3	5	3	-	-	3	2	2,278
42 56384	O'Hara township	Allegheny	7.0	8,856	8,435	74	4	269	-	23	51	101	6,585
42 56392	Ohio township	Allegheny	6.9	3,086	2,992	26	2	46	2	3	15	14	2,270
42 56608	Old Lycoming township	Lycoming	9.4	5,508	5,364	46	9	43	-	10	36	13	4,301
42 56672	Oley township	Berks	24.2	3,583	3,535	5	1	10	-	7	25	35	2,733
42 57472	Oxford township	Adams	9.7	4,876	4,629	23	6	23	4	151	40	239	3,696
42 57552	Paint township	Somerset	32.0	3,300	3,291	-	-	3	-	3	3	17	2,601
42 57672	Palmer township	Northampton	10.7	16,809	15,854	360	10	308	4	106	167	393	13,182
42 57728	Palmyra township	Pike	34.4	3,145	3,081	17	3	6	-	11	27	50	2,452
42 57848	Paradise township	Lancaster	18.6	4,698	4,621	29	5	5	3	8	27	34	3,277
42 57856	Paradise township	Monroe	21.4	2,671	2,468	96	13	28	1	28	37	85	2,065
42 57872	Paradise township	York	20.2	3,600	3,538	18	3	15	1	12	13	22	2,664
42 58160	Parks township	Armstrong	14.1	2,754	2,622	89	1	-	-	25	17	17	2,138
42 58375	Patterson township	Beaver	1.7	3,197	3,114	47	5	2	-	1	28	21	2,491
42 58440	Patton township	Centre	24.8	11,420	10,191	405	15	512	7	92	198	247	9,236
42 58480	Paupack township	Wayne	28.1	2,959	2,889	25	2	11	1	12	19	74	2,236
42 58560	Peach Bottom township	York	29.2	4,412	4,262	88	16	14	-	4	28	25	3,124
42 58792	Penn township	Butler	24.1	5,210	5,145	13	3	28	2	2	17	22	3,869
42 58808	Penn township	Chester	9.6	2,812	2,622	75	5	9	-	65	36	166	2,121
42 58824	Penn township	Cumberland	29.2	2,807	2,749	7	8	7	1	13	22	20	2,057
42 58840	Penn township	Lancaster	29.6	7,312	7,132	61	11	53	4	17	34	63	5,402
42 58856	Penn township	Perry	21.4	3,013	2,969	9	6	3	1	1	24	10	2,326
42 58864	Penn township	Snyder	17.9	3,781	3,610	98	2	30	-	25	16	82	2,987
42 58880	Penn township	Westmoreland	30.5	19,591	19,310	74	17	88	4	23	75	86	14,251
42 58888	Penn township	York	12.8	14,592	14,221	72	25	119	3	68	84	153	10,811
42 58968	Penn Forest township	Carbon	74.2	5,439	5,030	183	12	29	5	68	112	293	4,025
42 59032	Penn Hills township	Allegheny	19.0	46,809	34,443	11,347	62	255	5	157	540	297	36,669
42 59136	Pennsbury township	Chester	9.9	3,500	3,359	25	4	77	-	7	28	54	2,760
42 59360	Pequea township	Lancaster	13.6	4,358	4,258	21	2	27	2	13	35	45	3,194
42 59392	Perkiomen township	Montgomery	4.8	7,093	6,596	223	8	135	5	44	82	108	4,842
42 59448	Perry township	Berks	18.3	2,517	2,474	9	1	5	-	19	9	30	1,972
42 59464	Perry township	Fayette	19.8	2,786	2,678	84	3	4	-	2	15	6	2,237
42 59600	Peters township	Franklin	55.9	4,251	4,158	38	2	5	-	22	26	56	3,196
42 59608	Peters township	Washington	19.6	17,566	17,181	84	5	191	5	35	65	127	12,407
42 60272	Pine township	Allegheny	16.8	7,683	7,465	61	5	86	2	12	52	57	5,032
42 60336	Pine township	Mercer	25.7	4,493	4,189	243	-	25	4	3	29	47	3,100
42 60360	Pine Creek township	Clinton	14.4	3,184	3,162	8	1	3	2	3	5	2	2,456
42 60464	Pine Grove township	Schuylkill	38.2	3,930	3,899	-	1	10	-	2	18	13	3,020
42 60480	Pine Grove township	Warren	39.7	2,712	2,674	3	5	15	-	2	13	7	2,057
42 61056	Pittston township	Luzerne	14.4	3,450	3,421	10	-	3	-	2	14	12	2,728
42 61088	Plainfield township	Northampton	24.7	5,668	5,603	21	1	16	-	8	19	38	4,408
42 61120	Plains township	Luzerne	13.3	10,906	10,724	52	3	87	-	10	30	56	8,982
42 61208	Pleasant township	Warren	34.3	2,528	2,498	1	4	6	-	1	18	10	2,028
42 61616	Plumstead township	Bucks	27.2	11,409	10,994	81	32	115	1	97	89	226	7,883
42 61664	Plymouth township	Montgomery	8.4	16,045	14,321	669	14	837	2	59	143	201	12,814

Table D-2. MCDs — **Area and Population**—Con.

[Includes functioning minor civil divisions (MCDs) of 2,500 or more population as of April 1, 2000 in the following 12 states: CT, ME, MA, MI, MN, NH, NJ, NY, PA, RI, VT, and WI. Codes shown are two-digit Federal Information Processing Standards (FIPS) state codes and five-digit FIPS place codes. Place names and codes are those in effect as of January 1, 2000. County refers to the county in which the MCD is located]

State and place code	MCD	County	Land area, 2000 (sq. mi.)	Population, 2000 (April 1)									
					By race—							Hispanic or Latino (of any race)	18 years and over
					One race						Two or more races		
				Total	White	Black or African American	American Indian and Alaska Native	Asian	Native Hawaiian and Other Pacific Islander	Some other race			
42 00000	PENNSYLVANIA—Con.												
42 61728	Pocono township	Monroe	34.2	9,607	8,666	394	14	128	7	216	182	548	7,102
42 61800	Pocopson township	Chester	8.3	3,350	2,915	390	1	26	5	-	13	70	2,712
42 61832	Point township	Northumberland	25.2	3,722	3,668	13	8	14	-	4	15	26	2,972
42 61928	Polk township	Monroe	31.0	6,533	6,296	120	13	37	-	21	46	220	4,735
42 62056	Portage township	Cambria	24.3	3,906	3,871	8	1	6	-	4	16	14	3,067
42 62360	Potter township	Centre	58.1	3,339	3,296	13	5	6	1	7	11	15	2,471
42 62632	Price township	Monroe	25.0	2,649	2,413	138	4	31	-	27	36	103	1,885
42 62832	Providence township	Lancaster	20.1	6,651	6,501	41	11	14	1	23	60	61	4,805
42 62904	Pulaski township	Lawrence	30.5	3,658	3,620	10	3	5	-	8	12	11	2,723
42 63008	Pymatuning township	Mercer	16.5	3,782	3,718	24	4	6	-	9	21	25	2,738
42 63200	Quincy township	Franklin	44.6	5,846	5,603	130	7	28	1	40	37	69	4,485
42 63224	Raccoon township	Beaver	18.5	3,397	3,353	13	5	1	-	3	22	24	2,476
42 63264	Radnor township	Delaware	13.8	30,878	27,652	953	24	1,750	5	190	304	628	24,866
42 63328	Ralpho township	Northumberland	18.5	3,764	3,738	3	3	10	-	-	10	16	2,900
42 63440	Rapho township	Lancaster	47.5	8,578	8,382	25	7	69	-	44	51	69	6,251
42 63584	Rayne township	Indiana	47.2	3,292	3,265	8	1	5	-	-	13	8	2,533
42 63616	Reading township	Adams	26.6	5,106	5,017	9	12	9	1	14	44	61	3,592
42 63904	Redstone township	Fayette	22.6	6,397	5,771	515	7	7	3	19	75	19	4,966
42 64240	Reserve township	Allegheny	2.0	3,856	3,775	52	7	11	-	6	5	17	2,998
42 64528	Richland township	Allegheny	14.6	9,231	9,075	43	7	53	-	13	40	60	6,664
42 64536	Richland township	Bucks	20.5	9,920	9,558	92	11	115	-	38	106	131	7,324
42 64544	Richland township	Cambria	20.0	12,598	12,236	98	12	180	-	16	56	65	10,421
42 64592	Richmond township	Berks	23.6	3,500	3,449	5	3	9	2	18	14	34	2,680
42 64792	Ridgway township	Elk	87.3	2,802	2,782	4	1	3	-	3	9	9	2,075
42 64800	Ridley township	Delaware	5.1	30,791	28,626	1,313	21	505	14	66	246	282	23,285
42 65320	Robeson township	Berks	33.9	6,869	6,724	22	14	17	2	45	45	60	5,034
42 65352	Robinson township	Allegheny	14.7	12,289	11,705	234	7	251	3	17	72	90	9,488
42 65400	Rochester township	Beaver	3.8	3,129	2,977	114	3	3	-	-	32	6	2,434
42 65544	Rockland township	Berks	17.1	3,765	3,699	9	2	12	-	13	30	42	2,737
42 66264	Ross township	Allegheny	14.4	32,551	31,225	463	27	586	21	65	164	237	26,246
42 66272	Ross township	Luzerne	43.2	2,742	2,721	1	-	1	-	1	18	13	2,063
42 66280	Ross township	Monroe	22.6	5,435	5,251	59	4	21	-	42	58	119	3,878
42 66376	Rostraver township	Westmoreland	32.2	11,634	11,273	226	14	33	3	19	66	61	8,914
42 66728	Ruscombmanor township	Berks	13.9	3,776	3,730	6	1	9	-	2	28	46	2,847
42 66736	Rush township	Centre	148.7	3,466	3,441	-	6	9	-	-	10	8	2,764
42 66760	Rush township	Schuylkill	22.8	3,957	3,816	93	1	19	1	10	17	44	3,231
42 67080	Sadsbury township	Chester	6.2	2,582	2,419	110	4	16	1	14	18	21	1,889
42 67088	Sadsbury township	Crawford	23.7	2,941	2,922	2	2	2	1	1	11	7	2,326
42 67096	Sadsbury township	Lancaster	19.7	3,025	2,995	8	2	10	-	-	10	12	1,951
42 67400	St. Thomas township	Franklin	51.7	5,775	5,657	38	15	16	-	14	35	43	4,311
42 67456	Salem township	Luzerne	29.0	4,269	4,210	20	1	13	-	11	14	20	3,320
42 67488	Salem township	Wayne	30.8	3,664	3,564	32	6	7	-	10	45	52	2,706
42 67496	Salem township	Westmoreland	47.1	6,939	6,792	84	6	4	1	3	49	11	5,417
42 67568	Salisbury township	Lancaster	41.9	10,012	9,759	76	12	49	4	34	78	108	6,524
42 67576	Salisbury township	Lehigh	11.0	13,498	12,879	204	5	200	5	115	90	289	10,358
42 67640	Saltlick township	Fayette	37.7	3,715	3,690	-	1	3	-	-	21	14	2,761
42 67792	Sandy township	Clearfield	51.8	11,556	11,392	23	7	70	3	8	53	52	8,927
42 68288	Schuylkill township	Chester	8.6	6,960	6,600	116	5	173	2	25	39	88	5,328
42 68388	Scott township	Allegheny	4.0	17,288	15,792	198	14	1,067	2	40	175	117	14,072
42 68392	Scott township	Columbia	7.1	4,768	4,649	14	3	67	3	8	24	30	3,811
42 68400	Scott township	Lackawanna	27.3	4,931	4,850	32	-	18	-	9	22	35	3,774
42 69392	Sewickley township	Westmoreland	26.6	6,230	6,167	10	11	10	1	8	23	36	4,869
42 69448	Shade township	Somerset	67.1	2,886	2,868	2	1	1	-	-	14	15	2,255
42 69584	Shaler township	Allegheny	11.0	29,757	29,139	122	18	268	7	35	168	155	23,206
42 70080	Shenango township	Lawrence	24.4	7,633	7,426	131	3	8	1	31	33	58	5,794
42 70096	Shenango township	Mercer	29.9	4,037	3,933	71	2	4	-	7	20	17	3,106
42 70360	Shippensburg township	Cumberland	2.5	4,504	4,218	168	2	51	2	17	46	51	4,167
42 70400	Shirley township	Huntingdon	58.2	2,526	2,488	16	3	7	-	-	12	18	1,929
42 70576	Shrewsbury township	York	29.2	5,947	5,859	18	2	27	-	12	29	55	4,491
42 70792	Silver Spring township	Cumberland	32.5	10,592	10,184	39	8	244	4	32	81	77	7,885
42 71016	Skippack township	Montgomery	13.8	6,516	6,239	141	18	59	-	26	33	78	4,775
42 71192	Slippery Rock township	Butler	25.9	5,251	5,017	120	3	57	-	7	47	38	4,631
42 71200	Slippery Rock township	Lawrence	30.1	3,179	3,153	2	6	4	-	4	10	12	2,379
42 71288	Smith township	Washington	34.4	4,567	4,449	83	3	5	-	5	22	44	3,480
42 71328	Smithfield township	Huntingdon	5.6	4,466	2,368	1,865	8	10	-	123	92	300	4,173
42 71344	Smithfield township	Monroe	23.2	5,672	4,979	319	25	54	1	170	124	419	4,193
42 71624	Snyder township	Blair	45.2	3,358	3,330	6	1	5	-	-	16	6	2,567
42 71752	Solebury township	Bucks	26.6	7,743	7,520	49	15	66	7	27	59	112	6,037
42 71784	Somerset township	Somerset	63.9	9,319	9,058	138	6	50	-	32	35	46	7,164
42 71792	Somerset township	Washington	32.1	2,701	2,675	5	-	2	-	7	12	11	2,126
42 71872	South Abington township	Lackawanna	9.0	8,638	8,313	63	3	195	1	11	52	94	6,366
42 71904	Southampton township	Cumberland	52.4	4,787	4,693	19	8	15	1	11	40	36	3,376
42 71912	Southampton township	Franklin	38.0	6,138	5,937	90	8	32	2	8	61	39	4,361
42 71928	South Annville township	Lebanon	19.6	2,946	2,884	11	1	22	-	15	13	37	2,254
42 71952	South Beaver township	Beaver	30.0	2,974	2,915	37	3	6	-	3	10	11	2,348
42 72000	South Buffalo township	Armstrong	27.1	2,785	2,763	4	2	1	-	-	17	4	2,149
42 72160	South Fayette township	Allegheny	20.3	12,271	11,526	429	2	195	6	37	76	88	9,557

[Includes functioning minor civil divisions (MCDs) of 2,500 or more population as of April 1, 2000 in the following 12 states: CT, ME, MA, MI, MN, NH, NJ, NY, PA, RI, VT, and WI. Codes shown are two-digit Federal Information Processing Standards (FIPS) state codes and five-digit FIPS place codes. Place names and codes are those in effect as of January 1, 2000. County refers to the county in which the MCD is located]

State and place code	MCD	County	Land area, 2000 (sq. mi.)	Population, 2000 (April 1)									
					By race—								
					One race								
				Total	White	Black or African American	American Indian and Alaska Native	Asian	Native Hawaiian and Other Pacific Islander	Some other race	Two or more races	Hispanic or Latino (of any race)	18 years and over
42 00000	PENNSYLVANIA—Con.												
42 72176	South Franklin township	Washington	20.6	3,796	3,765	7	4	9	-	3	8	19	2,768
42 72200	South Hanover township	Dauphin	11.3	4,793	4,679	16	14	45	-	4	35	38	3,462
42 72208	South Heidelberg township	Berks	13.8	5,491	5,310	80	2	25	-	42	32	86	4,162
42 72256	South Huntingdon township	Westmoreland	45.3	6,175	6,053	56	7	5	1	4	49	23	4,852
42 72288	South Lebanon township	Lebanon	21.8	8,383	8,025	132	8	80	1	83	54	255	6,609
42 72296	South Londonderry township	Lebanon	24.1	5,458	5,341	29	2	39	-	11	36	32	4,078
42 72336	South Middleton township	Cumberland	49.5	12,939	12,571	87	9	122	11	43	96	116	9,859
42 72400	South Park township	Allegheny	9.2	14,340	13,645	460	9	109	6	17	94	79	10,673
42 72440	South Pymatuning township	Mercer	19.3	2,857	2,823	12	-	8	-	3	11	9	2,223
42 72504	South Strabane township	Washington	23.1	7,987	7,775	126	4	39	1	11	31	32	6,334
42 72544	South Union township	Fayette	16.7	11,337	10,758	371	8	95	1	12	92	37	8,779
42 72632	South Whitehall township	Lehigh	17.1	18,028	17,247	184	6	373	-	80	138	272	14,163
42 72824	Spring township	Berks	18.2	21,805	20,399	458	14	470	2	222	240	631	16,706
42 72832	Spring township	Centre	25.8	6,117	6,030	15	4	10	6	9	43	28	4,621
42 72992	Springettsbury township	York	16.7	23,883	21,767	1,022	26	588	8	231	241	661	19,137
42 73016	Springfield township	Bucks	30.8	4,963	4,894	30	5	5	-	9	20	43	3,853
42 73032	Springfield township	Delaware	6.4	23,677	22,868	170	13	466	3	29	128	146	17,997
42 73048	Springfield township	Erie	37.7	3,378	3,306	21	7	9	-	9	26	19	2,476
42 73064	Springfield township	Fayette	59.8	3,111	3,079	-	7	1	-	1	23	20	2,302
42 73088	Springfield township	Montgomery	6.8	19,533	17,294	1,623	25	376	1	66	148	203	15,350
42 73096	Springfield township	York	26.2	3,889	3,842	15	2	14	-	-	16	21	2,929
42 73168	Spring Garden township	York	6.6	11,974	11,514	199	9	101	2	51	98	196	9,685
42 73240	Springhill township	Fayette	33.5	2,974	2,912	28	8	3	2	3	18	16	2,238
42 74432	Stonycreek township	Cambria	3.4	3,204	3,156	21	-	5	-	7	15	26	2,660
42 74648	Stowe township	Allegheny	2.0	6,706	6,065	539	14	11	-	15	62	28	5,374
42 74680	Straban township	Adams	34.4	4,539	4,351	65	8	33	-	41	41	104	3,530
42 74720	Strasburg township	Lancaster	20.0	4,021	3,979	8	1	4	2	3	24	10	2,701
42 74880	Stroud township	Monroe	31.2	13,978	12,067	960	26	232	2	405	286	1,029	10,378
42 75064	Sugarloaf township	Luzerne	21.9	3,652	3,580	10	4	37	-	8	13	26	2,926
42 75144	Summerhill township	Cambria	28.9	2,724	2,712	2	1	-	-	-	9	1	1,991
42 75184	Summit township	Butler	22.3	4,728	4,512	188	1	10	-	1	16	37	3,390
42 75208	Summit township	Erie	23.9	5,529	5,432	31	7	13	-	13	33	19	4,227
42 75528	Susquehanna township	Dauphin	13.4	21,895	16,487	4,241	24	479	4	226	434	492	17,092
42 75672	Swatara township	Dauphin	13.2	22,611	17,680	3,613	28	394	11	392	493	1,071	17,530
42 75680	Swatara township	Lebanon	21.2	3,941	3,835	44	7	23	-	7	25	39	2,929
42 76424	Texas township	Wayne	14.4	2,501	2,441	14	12	15	-	5	14	28	1,901
42 76568	Thornbury township	Chester	3.9	2,678	2,461	69	-	122	1	6	19	21	1,983
42 76576	Thornbury township	Delaware	9.2	7,093	4,588	2,205	8	90	4	149	49	193	5,125
42 76712	Tilden township	Berks	18.9	3,553	3,480	10	4	4	-	37	18	48	2,685
42 76784	Tinicum township	Bucks	30.2	4,206	4,090	32	7	17	2	21	37	57	3,321
42 76792	Tinicum township	Delaware	5.7	4,353	4,226	35	3	19	-	14	56	55	3,339
42 76960	Tobyhanna township	Monroe	50.4	6,152	5,681	245	23	37	1	74	91	312	4,656
42 77152	Towamencin township	Montgomery	9.7	17,597	15,538	611	15	1,097	4	91	241	291	13,156
42 77160	Towamensing township	Carbon	27.0	3,475	3,428	15	3	8	-	6	15	43	2,639
42 77344	Tredyffrin township	Chester	19.8	29,062	26,412	825	33	1,487	4	85	216	350	22,293
42 77752	Tulpehocken township	Berks	23.3	3,290	3,051	125	2	12	-	75	25	131	2,352
42 77776	Tunkhannock township	Monroe	38.6	4,983	4,310	352	12	47	1	119	142	472	3,413
42 77792	Tunkhannock township	Wyoming	31.1	4,298	4,223	19	6	16	1	9	24	33	3,242
42 78264	Union township	Adams	17.5	2,989	2,939	2	7	20	-	4	17	25	2,176
42 78280	Union township	Berks	23.2	3,453	3,385	20	5	4	1	10	28	33	2,707
42 78368	Union township	Lawrence	9.6	5,103	4,844	207	1	8	-	15	28	27	4,140
42 78376	Union township	Lebanon	29.9	2,590	2,542	5	6	8	-	9	20	21	2,023
42 78392	Union township	Mifflin	25.5	3,313	3,289	7	2	3	-	5	7	10	2,392
42 78432	Union township	Washington	15.4	5,599	5,501	38	2	9	-	13	36	30	4,426
42 78656	Unity township	Westmoreland	67.1	21,137	20,740	68	28	181	4	32	84	88	16,594
42 78736	Upper Allen township	Cumberland	13.3	15,338	14,646	197	14	253	5	92	131	219	12,295
42 78744	Upper Augusta township	Northumberland	20.3	2,556	2,509	13	-	2	3	12	17	19	2,045
42 78776	Upper Chichester township	Delaware	6.7	16,842	14,484	1,744	30	340	1	51	192	196	12,870
42 79000	Upper Darby township	Delaware	7.9	81,821	63,222	9,270	102	7,246	21	422	1,538	1,343	61,186
42 79008	Upper Dublin township	Montgomery	13.2	25,878	22,637	1,402	23	1,611	1	49	155	233	18,782
42 79040	Upper Frederick township	Montgomery	10.0	3,141	3,047	45	6	9	-	5	29	16	2,298
42 79056	Upper Gwynedd township	Montgomery	8.1	14,243	12,358	566	11	1,116	-	58	134	207	10,860
42 79064	Upper Hanover township	Montgomery	20.2	4,885	4,790	34	7	15	-	16	23	39	3,672
42 79080	Upper Leacock township	Lancaster	18.0	8,229	7,599	102	12	305	-	106	105	267	5,628
42 79104	Upper Macungie township	Lehigh	26.2	13,895	12,917	164	5	588	-	82	139	235	10,217
42 79128	Upper Makefield township	Bucks	20.9	7,180	6,973	58	5	91	-	17	36	81	5,266
42 79136	Upper Merion township	Montgomery	16.9	26,863	22,767	1,245	34	2,271	14	178	354	481	21,834
42 79160	Upper Milford township	Lehigh	17.9	6,889	6,772	11	6	47	-	14	39	70	5,217
42 79176	Upper Moreland township	Montgomery	8.0	24,993	22,673	1,090	24	793	6	146	261	432	19,473
42 79184	Upper Mount Bethel township	Northampton	43.4	6,063	5,935	42	8	30	-	13	35	84	4,681
42 79192	Upper Nazareth township	Northampton	7.3	4,426	4,337	27	5	18	-	22	17	65	3,459
42 79216	Upper Paxton township	Dauphin	26.0	3,930	3,887	16	5	10	-	4	8	15	3,017
42 79240	Upper Pottsgrove township	Montgomery	5.0	4,102	3,905	103	10	37	-	11	36	42	2,926
42 79248	Upper Providence township	Delaware	5.6	10,509	9,650	410	8	321	-	31	89	112	7,910
42 79256	Upper Providence township	Montgomery	17.8	15,398	14,399	395	15	427	4	41	117	207	11,065
42 79274	Upper St. Clair township	Allegheny	9.8	20,053	18,962	136	5	806	5	15	124	157	14,369
42 79280	Upper Salford township	Montgomery	9.0	3,024	2,935	15	8	26	1	17	22	25	2,214

Table D-2. MCDs — **Area and Population**—Con.

[Includes functioning minor civil divisions (MCDs) of 2,500 or more population as of April 1, 2000 in the following 12 states: CT, ME, MA, MI, MN, NH, NJ, NY, PA, RI, VT, and WI. Codes shown are two-digit Federal Information Processing Standards (FIPS) state codes and five-digit FIPS place codes. Place names and codes are those in effect as of January 1, 2000. County refers to the county in which the MCD is located]

State and place code	MCD	County	Land area, 2000 (sq. mi.)	Population, 2000 (April 1)									
					By race—								
					One race							Hispanic or Latino (of any race)	18 years and over
				Total	White	Black or African American	American Indian and Alaska Native	Asian	Native Hawaiian and Other Pacific Islander	Some other race	Two or more races		
42 00000	PENNSYLVANIA—Con.												
42 79288	Upper Saucon township	Lehigh	24.7	11,939	11,594	83	7	135	1	48	71	128	9,073
42 79296	Upper Southampton township	Bucks	6.6	15,764	15,270	122	10	237	3	30	92	127	12,363
42 79352	Upper Uwchlan township	Chester	10.8	6,850	6,672	48	4	77	-	14	35	66	4,452
42 79360	Upper Yoder township	Cambria	11.9	5,862	5,764	39	9	29	3	4	14	22	4,786
42 79480	Uwchlan township	Chester	10.4	16,576	15,526	306	13	537	1	61	142	206	11,571
42 79544	Valley township	Chester	6.0	5,116	3,663	1,279	6	20	-	61	87	183	3,762
42 80000	Vernon township	Crawford	29.6	5,499	5,359	55	16	25	1	10	33	31	4,356
42 80552	Walker township	Centre	40.5	3,299	3,268	3	2	7	-	4	15	12	2,461
42 80568	Walker township	Juniata	29.0	2,598	2,568	13	1	5	-	6	5	15	1,894
42 80616	Wallace township	Chester	12.0	3,240	3,100	81	1	38	2	11	7	42	2,148
42 80952	Warminster township	Bucks	10.3	31,383	28,558	1,038	35	624	20	695	413	1,454	23,679
42 81048	Warrington township	Bucks	13.8	17,580	16,553	339	12	439	13	93	131	275	12,460
42 81056	Warrington township	York	35.4	4,435	4,367	10	5	19	-	3	31	46	3,381
42 81144	Warwick township	Bucks	11.1	11,977	11,490	124	8	256	6	16	77	123	8,016
42 81160	Warwick township	Chester	19.2	2,556	2,509	6	7	12	-	8	14	17	1,957
42 81168	Warwick township	Lancaster	19.8	15,475	15,049	75	14	132	7	66	132	241	11,139
42 81184	Washington township	Berks	14.0	3,354	3,283	25	3	11	-	8	24	22	2,489
42 81224	Washington township	Erie	45.2	4,526	4,445	14	6	9	-	7	45	34	3,246
42 81232	Washington township	Fayette	9.6	4,461	4,370	59	10	8	-	4	10	9	3,649
42 81240	Washington township	Franklin	38.9	11,559	11,221	117	17	104	4	39	57	93	8,875
42 81280	Washington township	Lehigh	23.7	6,588	6,503	14	5	27	-	16	23	64	5,092
42 81296	Washington township	Northampton	18.1	4,152	4,117	2	3	4	-	13	13	28	3,224
42 81312	Washington township	Schuylkill	31.0	2,750	2,725	5	-	8	1	2	9	5	2,032
42 81336	Washington township	Westmoreland	31.7	7,384	7,310	44	2	7	-	7	14	18	5,740
42 81472	Waterford township	Erie	50.0	3,878	3,823	6	2	3	-	2	42	20	2,733
42 81792	Wayne township	Schuylkill	35.0	4,721	4,661	11	2	23	-	11	13	19	3,599
42 82064	Weisenberg township	Lehigh	26.8	4,144	4,064	22	1	18	-	12	27	52	3,069
42 82544	West Bradford township	Chester	18.6	10,775	9,957	532	34	67	1	56	128	190	7,240
42 82576	West Brandywine township	Chester	13.4	7,153	6,823	234	10	28	-	19	39	50	5,218
42 82632	West Brunswick township	Schuylkill	30.3	3,428	3,313	8	2	76	-	4	25	9	2,665
42 82640	West Buffalo township	Union	38.0	2,795	2,742	12	7	9	-	7	18	27	1,939
42 82664	West Caln township	Chester	21.7	7,054	6,740	185	12	25	3	32	57	69	5,038
42 82712	West Chillisquaque township	Northumberland	12.9	2,846	2,797	16	4	4	2	10	13	12	2,232
42 82728	West Cocalico township	Lancaster	27.6	6,967	6,849	22	6	27	-	29	34	75	4,786
42 82800	West Deer township	Allegheny	29.0	11,563	11,440	34	13	25	-	11	40	49	8,671
42 82816	West Donegal township	Lancaster	15.6	6,539	6,424	18	6	30	3	17	41	46	4,876
42 82824	West Earl township	Lancaster	17.6	6,766	6,538	24	4	144	-	32	24	102	4,821
42 83080	West Goshen township	Chester	11.9	20,495	18,549	871	9	775	2	134	155	410	15,108
42 83128	West Hanover township	Dauphin	23.4	6,505	6,332	75	2	65	2	7	22	35	5,043
42 83152	West Hempfield township	Lancaster	18.9	15,128	14,105	283	14	233	1	316	176	690	10,820
42 83256	West Lampeter township	Lancaster	16.4	13,145	12,797	104	6	79	1	92	66	226	10,185
42 83408	West Mahanoy township	Schuylkill	10.4	6,166	4,284	1,665	5	25	-	176	11	317	5,563
42 83432	West Manchester township	York	20.1	17,035	16,271	286	13	210	3	80	172	206	13,613
42 83440	West Manheim township	York	19.5	4,865	4,771	40	3	19	1	5	26	31	3,611
42 83480	West Mead township	Crawford	18.2	5,227	5,045	108	12	29	-	4	29	26	3,940
42 83696	West Norriton township	Montgomery	5.9	14,901	13,335	909	11	407	8	72	159	236	12,071
42 83712	West Nottingham township	Chester	13.9	2,634	2,494	51	10	7	-	44	28	110	1,897
42 83792	West Penn township	Schuylkill	58.0	3,852	3,805	8	3	9	-	13	14	28	3,005
42 83800	West Pennsboro township	Cumberland	30.5	5,263	5,195	16	8	16	1	4	23	18	3,988
42 83832	West Pikeland township	Chester	10.0	3,551	3,413	44	1	67	-	13	13	36	2,460
42 83912	West Pottsgrove township	Montgomery	2.4	3,815	3,406	275	7	32	1	31	63	83	2,877
42 83920	West Providence township	Bedford	38.5	3,323	3,290	10	1	3	2	3	14	13	2,618
42 83960	West Rockhill township	Bucks	16.3	4,233	4,158	23	6	20	-	6	20	25	3,348
42 83976	West Salem township	Mercer	37.0	3,565	3,525	10	4	3	-	1	22	13	2,806
42 84104	Westtown township	Chester	8.7	10,352	9,728	268	7	251	1	38	59	117	7,563
42 84160	West Vincent township	Chester	17.7	3,170	3,100	19	4	21	1	2	23	18	2,280
42 84192	West Whiteland township	Chester	13.0	16,499	14,742	887	26	598	10	80	156	330	12,367
42 84344	Wharton township	Fayette	91.9	4,145	4,109	4	1	5	1	8	17	17	3,035
42 84368	Wheatfield township	Perry	20.9	3,329	3,301	4	1	7	-	2	14	24	2,415
42 84472	White township	Indiana	42.6	14,034	13,216	348	16	301	-	35	118	97	11,225
42 84496	White Deer township	Union	46.5	4,273	4,194	26	-	9	-	11	33	30	3,246
42 84528	Whitehall township	Lehigh	12.6	24,896	22,545	682	32	902	16	426	293	1,089	19,609
42 84624	Whitemarsh township	Montgomery	14.6	16,702	15,582	369	4	618	-	23	106	165	12,641
42 84888	Whitpain township	Montgomery	12.9	18,562	16,021	870	12	1,452	-	42	165	247	13,916
42 85160	Wilkes-Barre township	Luzerne	3.0	3,235	3,006	76	7	117	-	3	26	25	2,657
42 85184	Wilkins township	Allegheny	2.6	6,917	6,418	303	6	105	4	13	68	31	5,747
42 85256	Williams township	Northampton	18.4	4,470	4,347	36	2	42	1	6	36	47	3,389
42 85352	Willistown township	Chester	18.2	10,011	9,596	214	5	127	10	30	29	81	7,668
42 85504	Wilmington township	Lawrence	20.0	2,760	2,738	8	1	1	-	2	10	15	1,917
42 85736	Windsor township	York	27.2	12,807	12,556	51	12	79	5	29	75	118	9,628
42 85784	Winfield township	Butler	24.4	3,585	3,552	6	6	3	1	6	11	10	2,685
42 85840	Winslow township	Jefferson	45.5	2,591	2,577	2	4	5	-	1	2	15	1,978
42 85984	Wolf township	Lycoming	19.6	2,707	2,685	6	2	4	-	-	10	4	2,023
42 86168	Woodcock township	Crawford	32.5	2,976	2,918	30	7	2	-	3	16	6	2,213
42 86440	Woodward township	Clearfield	22.2	3,550	2,412	955	4	12	-	164	3	169	3,117
42 86496	Worcester township	Montgomery	16.2	7,789	7,177	181	2	345	-	19	65	68	5,662
42 86584	Wright township	Luzerne	13.1	5,593	5,402	31	2	111	-	15	32	66	4,220
42 86624	Wrightstown township	Bucks	9.9	2,839	2,752	24	1	43	-	2	17	17	2,046
42 87056	York township	York	25.5	23,637	22,680	359	33	293	6	86	180	337	18,527

Table D-2. MCDs — **Area and Population**—Con.

[Includes functioning minor civil divisions (MCDs) of 2,500 or more population as of April 1, 2000 in the following 12 states: CT, ME, MA, MI, MN, NH, NJ, NY, PA, RI, VT, and WI. Codes shown are two-digit Federal Information Processing Standards (FIPS) state codes and five-digit FIPS place codes. Place names and codes are those in effect as of January 1, 2000. County refers to the county in which the MCD is located]

State and place code	MCD	County	Land area, 2000 (sq. mi.)	Population, 2000 (April 1) Total	By race— One race White	Black or African American	American Indian and Alaska Native	Asian	Native Hawaiian and Other Pacific Islander	Some other race	Two or more races	Hispanic or Latino (of any race)	18 years and over
44 00000	RHODE ISLAND		1,044.9	1,048,319	891,191	46,908	5,121	23,665	567	52,616	28,251	90,820	800,497
44 05140	Barrington town	Bristol	8.4	16,819	16,209	115	19	297	-	43	136	177	12,074
44 09280	Bristol town	Bristol	10.1	22,469	21,826	140	37	151	10	74	231	289	18,070
44 11800	Burrillville town	Providence	55.6	15,796	15,569	34	31	34	4	40	84	132	11,753
44 14500	Charlestown town	Washington	36.8	7,859	7,565	30	99	48	2	42	73	87	6,147
44 18640	Coventry town	Kent	59.5	33,668	32,859	131	50	187	9	106	326	385	25,279
44 20080	Cumberland town	Providence	26.8	31,840	30,803	180	25	264	8	267	293	667	24,150
44 22240	East Greenwich town	Kent	16.6	12,948	12,383	89	8	324	1	37	106	117	9,384
44 25300	Exeter town	Washington	57.7	6,045	5,825	40	36	45	1	20	78	77	4,456
44 27460	Foster town	Providence	51.1	4,274	4,157	9	10	25	4	11	58	34	3,169
44 30340	Glocester town	Providence	54.8	9,948	9,797	34	15	24	-	10	68	65	7,284
44 35380	Hopkinton town	Washington	43.0	7,836	7,587	48	70	34	-	21	76	83	5,825
44 36820	Jamestown town	Newport	9.7	5,622	5,484	44	12	22	-	13	47	50	4,384
44 37720	Johnston town	Providence	23.7	28,195	27,254	184	37	304	14	155	247	533	22,289
44 41500	Lincoln town	Providence	18.2	20,898	19,967	176	16	366	2	134	237	343	15,741
44 42400	Little Compton town	Newport	20.9	3,593	3,548	2	7	8	3	2	23	31	2,813
44 45460	Middletown town	Newport	13.0	17,334	15,448	819	62	378	19	186	422	508	13,006
44 48340	Narragansett town	Washington	14.1	16,361	15,680	122	148	124	3	55	229	204	13,528
44 51580	North Kingstown town	Washington	43.6	26,326	25,196	256	145	251	9	139	330	465	19,478
44 51760	North Providence town	Providence	5.7	32,411	29,812	859	55	598	7	511	569	1,247	26,475
44 52480	North Smithfield town	Providence	24.0	10,618	10,440	45	22	55	-	8	48	50	8,239
44 57880	Portsmouth town	Newport	23.2	17,149	16,432	201	33	234	6	63	180	249	12,820
44 61160	Richmond town	Washington	40.6	7,222	7,003	29	66	32	-	14	78	89	5,208
44 64220	Scituate town	Providence	48.7	10,324	10,131	30	7	60	3	33	60	77	7,689
44 66200	Smithfield town	Providence	26.6	20,613	20,066	165	25	183	3	26	145	191	16,594
44 67460	South Kingstown town	Washington	57.1	27,921	25,440	437	449	859	15	203	518	493	21,637
44 70880	Tiverton town	Newport	29.4	15,260	14,952	65	26	59	5	33	120	104	11,893
44 73760	Warren town	Bristol	6.2	11,360	10,999	94	26	57	4	33	147	106	8,906
44 77000	Westerly town	Washington	30.1	22,966	21,857	164	130	457	-	77	281	270	17,560
44 77720	West Greenwich town	Kent	50.6	5,085	4,968	14	12	29	-	12	50	35	3,641
44 78440	West Warwick town	Kent	7.9	29,581	27,740	328	105	420	7	425	556	918	22,949
50 00000	VERMONT		9,249.6	608,827	589,208	3,063	2,420	5,217	141	1,443	7,335	5,504	461,304
50 03250	Barre town	Washington	30.6	7,602	7,486	14	7	22	-	14	59	115	5,655
50 03550	Barton town	Orleans	43.7	2,780	2,707	9	11	5	-	2	46	8	2,091
50 04825	Bennington town	Bennington	42.4	15,737	15,258	99	40	150	3	35	152	156	12,039
50 05650	Berlin town	Washington	36.5	2,864	2,773	5	7	15	-	1	63	19	2,191
50 07375	Bradford town	Orange	29.8	2,619	2,559	12	12	6	4	-	26	16	1,934
50 07750	Brandon town	Rutland	40.1	3,917	3,872	4	7	6	-	-	28	8	2,949
50 07900	Brattleboro town	Windham	32.0	12,005	11,292	136	31	201	5	66	274	201	9,330
50 09025	Bristol town	Addison	41.8	3,788	3,728	9	5	15	-	4	27	19	2,738
50 11500	Cambridge town	Lamoille	63.7	3,186	3,075	8	18	4	-	2	79	24	2,409
50 11950	Castleton town	Rutland	39.0	4,367	4,279	4	14	25	1	21	23	47	3,499
50 13300	Charlotte town	Chittenden	41.5	3,569	3,495	7	2	21	-	16	28	25	2,510
50 13675	Chester town	Windsor	55.9	3,044	3,006	10	3	7	-	1	17	21	2,313
50 14500	Clarendon town	Rutland	31.6	2,811	2,757	8	9	16	-	6	15	14	2,162
50 14875	Colchester town	Chittenden	36.9	16,986	16,397	107	29	268	6	43	136	189	13,153
50 17350	Derby town	Orleans	49.6	4,604	4,492	13	22	13	1	5	58	31	3,352
50 21925	East Montpelier town	Washington	32.0	2,578	2,485	20	18	10	1	1	43	29	1,951
50 23875	Enosburg town	Franklin	48.6	2,788	2,671	4	49	8	-	6	50	20	2,006
50 24175	Essex town	Chittenden	39.0	18,626	17,763	164	36	419	4	40	200	158	13,429
50 24925	Fairfax town	Franklin	40.2	3,765	3,680	20	12	11	-	4	38	25	2,674
50 25375	Fair Haven town	Rutland	17.6	2,928	2,867	10	6	9	-	13	23	24	2,150
50 26275	Ferrisburg town	Addison	47.8	2,657	2,595	5	11	13	-	1	32	15	1,995
50 27700	Georgia town	Franklin	39.5	4,375	4,301	11	7	11	1	10	34	25	3,010
50 31825	Hardwick town	Caledonia	38.5	3,174	3,107	2	26	3	-	6	30	13	2,239
50 32275	Hartford town	Windsor	45.2	10,367	10,058	57	32	91	3	17	109	88	7,939
50 32425	Hartland town	Windsor	45.0	3,223	3,177	4	5	14	2	2	19	20	2,383
50 33025	Highgate town	Franklin	51.1	3,397	3,157	1	143	5	1	7	83	5	2,399
50 33475	Hinesburg town	Chittenden	39.8	4,340	4,249	6	9	22	1	7	46	34	3,086
50 35050	Hyde Park town	Lamoille	37.9	2,847	2,783	15	15	11	-	-	23	22	2,143
50 36700	Jericho town	Chittenden	35.4	5,015	4,887	34	7	28	4	15	40	56	3,467
50 37075	Johnson town	Lamoille	45.1	3,274	3,162	20	14	22	-	10	46	24	2,568
50 41725	Lyndon town	Caledonia	39.8	5,448	5,326	14	27	34	1	9	37	24	4,192
50 42850	Manchester town	Bennington	42.2	4,180	4,091	16	7	13	-	18	35	73	3,213
50 44350	Middlebury town	Addison	39.0	8,183	7,714	89	23	153	2	54	148	174	6,752
50 45250	Milton town	Chittenden	51.5	9,479	9,299	20	38	32	2	16	72	59	6,758
50 46675	Morristown town	Lamoille	51.4	5,139	5,011	18	18	24	-	6	62	40	3,897
50 50275	Northfield town	Washington	43.7	5,791	5,525	59	21	77	-	25	84	128	4,665
50 52900	Norwich town	Windsor	44.7	3,544	3,401	17	7	57	1	22	39	28	2,507
50 55600	Pittsford town	Rutland	43.5	3,140	3,111	7	2	6	-	-	14	13	2,412
50 56875	Poultney town	Rutland	43.9	3,633	3,530	25	17	32	-	9	20	21	2,866
50 57025	Pownal town	Bennington	46.7	3,560	3,483	10	15	20	-	7	25	15	2,656
50 57700	Putney town	Windham	26.8	2,634	2,519	27	13	20	1	8	46	41	2,040
50 58075	Randolph town	Orange	47.9	4,853	4,745	10	7	29	4	1	57	26	3,723
50 59275	Richmond town	Chittenden	31.8	4,090	4,023	2	5	21	1	3	35	34	2,893
50 60250	Rockingham town	Windham	41.9	5,309	5,170	18	5	29	3	14	70	61	3,975
50 60850	Royalton town	Windsor	40.4	2,603	2,530	20	11	20	-	-	22	23	2,023

Table D-2. MCDs — Area and Population—Con.

[Includes functioning minor civil divisions (MCDs) of 2,500 or more population as of April 1, 2000 in the following 12 states: CT, ME, MA, MI, MN, NH, NJ, NY, PA, RI, VT, and WI. Codes shown are two-digit Federal Information Processing Standards (FIPS) state codes and five-digit FIPS place codes. Place names and codes are those in effect as of January 1, 2000. County refers to the county in which the MCD is located]

State and place code	MCD	County	Land area, 2000 (sq. mi.)	Population, 2000 (April 1) Total	By race— One race White	Black or African American	American Indian and Alaska Native	Asian	Native Hawaiian and Other Pacific Islander	Some other race	Two or more races	Hispanic or Latino (of any race)	18 years and over
50 00000	VERMONT—Con.												
50 61300	Rutland town	Rutland	19.3	4,038	3,984	15	2	13	-	5	19	30	3,146
50 61750	St. Albans town	Franklin	37.6	5,086	4,931	20	38	17	-	8	72	34	3,714
50 62200	St. Johnsbury town	Caledonia	36.7	7,571	7,303	39	50	47	2	17	113	89	5,842
50 63550	Shaftsbury town	Bennington	43.1	3,767	3,719	8	2	11	-	6	21	34	2,796
50 64300	Shelburne town	Chittenden	24.3	6,944	6,777	16	7	70	-	22	52	60	5,024
50 69550	Springfield town	Windsor	49.3	9,078	8,860	22	13	70	5	16	92	65	6,962
50 70525	Stowe town	Lamoille	72.7	4,339	4,231	12	16	19	-	10	51	46	3,425
50 71725	Swanton town	Franklin	48.4	6,203	5,775	26	211	28	1	11	151	27	4,487
50 72400	Thetford town	Orange	43.6	2,617	2,550	12	6	15	-	5	29	12	1,913
50 73975	Underhill town	Chittenden	51.4	2,980	2,935	8	4	6	-	9	18	21	2,116
50 76975	Waterbury town	Washington	48.2	4,915	4,807	13	6	32	-	13	44	33	3,682
50 77500	Weathersfield town	Windsor	43.8	2,788	2,748	2	8	7	-	-	23	20	2,215
50 81400	Westminster town	Windham	46.1	3,210	3,137	13	9	7	-	11	33	22	2,333
50 82300	West Rutland town	Rutland	18.0	2,535	2,483	11	2	19	1	1	18	11	1,932
50 84175	Williamstown town	Orange	40.2	3,225	3,171	2	9	4	-	8	31	25	2,381
50 84475	Williston town	Chittenden	30.3	7,650	7,455	38	11	92	1	8	45	73	5,544
50 84925	Windsor town	Windsor	19.5	3,756	3,671	9	15	10	-	9	42	40	2,923
50 85975	Woodstock town	Windsor	44.5	3,232	3,170	13	7	20	-	8	14	26	2,564
55 00000	WISCONSIN		54,310.1	5,363,675	4,769,857	304,460	47,228	88,763	1,630	84,842	66,895	192,921	3,994,919
55 00425	Addison town	Washington	36.2	3,341	3,317	5	7	1	1	1	9	32	2,377
55 00950	Alden town	Polk	56.1	2,615	2,580	2	8	4	-	9	12	17	1,910
55 01025	Algoma town	Winnebago	10.0	5,702	5,583	11	8	57	-	8	35	40	3,941
55 02450	Arbor Vitae town	Vilas	62.6	3,153	3,066	1	45	7	1	2	31	27	2,496
55 05050	Barton town	Washington	19.2	2,546	2,505	4	1	10	1	2	23	15	1,891
55 05925	Beaver Dam town	Dodge	34.3	3,440	3,320	2	14	13	-	67	24	134	2,508
55 06350	Bellevue town	Brown	14.3	11,828	11,284	60	99	160	2	130	93	310	8,644
55 06525	Beloit town	Rock	20.0	7,038	6,334	470	20	39	-	68	107	182	5,397
55 08275	Bloomfield town	Walworth	32.6	5,537	5,256	108	6	19	2	65	81	220	3,954
55 09225	Bradley town	Lincoln	55.7	2,573	2,550	2	2	3	1	5	10	8	2,036
55 09775	Bristol town	Dane	34.4	2,698	2,637	14	2	25	-	7	13	20	1,908
55 09825	Bristol town	Kenosha	34.7	4,538	4,422	13	5	41	4	30	23	108	3,364
55 09900	Brockway town	Jackson	47.7	2,580	1,699	370	456	3	2	17	33	74	2,097
55 10050	Brookfield town	Waukesha	5.5	6,390	6,047	53	2	204	1	27	56	80	4,985
55 10750	Buchanan town	Outagamie	16.6	5,827	5,728	9	11	46	-	4	29	40	3,799
55 11150	Burke town	Dane	19.5	2,990	2,875	27	8	31	-	13	36	47	2,273
55 11225	Burlington town	Racine	34.5	6,384	6,234	5	3	27	-	62	53	131	4,739
55 11950	Caledonia town	Racine	45.5	23,614	22,240	470	98	301	11	216	278	736	17,482
55 12300	Campbell town	La Crosse	3.8	4,410	4,255	23	23	48	1	12	48	30	3,362
55 13400	Cedarburg town	Ozaukee	25.6	5,744	5,678	9	10	21	-	6	20	38	4,130
55 13600	Contor town	Outagamie	35.7	3,163	3,128	3	17	3	-	1	11	21	2,307
55 15150	Clayton town	Winnebago	36.5	2,974	2,912	5	9	21	-	10	17	20	2,168
55 17200	Cottage Grove town	Dane	33.4	3,839	3,758	15	4	30	-	6	26	40	2,732
55 19025	Dayton town	Waupaca	35.2	2,734	2,678	3	17	6	-	16	14	36	2,017
55 19425	Delafield town	Waukesha	18.6	7,820	7,346	271	19	60	-	39	85	139	5,285
55 19475	Delavan town	Walworth	25.3	4,559	4,272	32	15	34	1	160	45	345	3,426
55 20625	Dover town	Racine	35.4	3,908	3,571	184	42	20	1	56	34	154	2,893
55 21125	Dunn town	Dane	28.6	5,270	5,154	11	13	26	-	35	31	92	4,046
55 21450	Eagle town	Waukesha	34.6	3,117	3,050	16	5	12	-	12	22	18	2,213
55 21600	Eagle Point town	Chippewa	61.4	3,049	3,019	1	6	12	-	-	11	5	2,315
55 22125	East Troy town	Walworth	30.3	3,830	3,767	9	4	9	-	14	27	44	2,902
55 23425	Ellington town	Outagamie	34.9	2,535	2,496	2	3	17	-	5	12	14	1,743
55 24050	Empire town	Fond du Lac	29.0	2,620	2,571	7	9	17	-	3	13	26	1,869
55 24225	Erin town	Washington	35.9	3,664	3,609	6	10	16	-	6	17	17	2,681
55 25375	Farmington town	Washington	36.4	3,239	3,212	3	7	3	1	-	13	29	2,351
55 25400	Farmington town	Waupaca	34.5	4,148	4,088	2	7	6	1	17	27	33	3,291
55 27575	Fredonia town	Ozaukee	34.7	2,903	2,820	31	8	13	-	18	13	30	2,362
55 27650	Freedom town	Outagamie	35.8	5,241	5,172	-	37	4	3	10	15	42	3,669
55 28075	Fulton town	Rock	31.9	3,158	3,120	5	9	6	-	6	12	21	2,408
55 28487	Genesee town	Waukesha	31.9	7,284	7,161	14	20	21	3	31	34	130	5,132
55 28550	Geneva town	Walworth	29.3	4,099	3,913	25	4	22	-	102	33	191	3,159
55 30025	Grafton town	Ozaukee	19.8	4,132	4,050	14	9	20	4	14	21	46	3,113
55 30075	Grand Chute town	Outagamie	24.9	18,392	17,340	142	74	279	15	344	198	649	14,088
55 30125	Grand Rapids town	Wood	20.8	7,801	7,630	19	40	60	3	11	38	63	5,572
55 31100	Greenbush town	Sheboygan	47.2	2,773	2,060	642	48	5	1	8	9	110	2,326
55 31550	Greenville town	Outagamie	35.8	6,844	6,724	15	20	14	5	27	39	109	4,621
55 32125	Hallie town	Chippewa	21.4	4,703	4,569	8	9	68	-	19	30	42	3,378
55 32800	Harrison town	Calumet	33.5	5,756	5,661	23	7	40	-	9	16	34	3,972
55 33025	Hartford town	Washington	30.2	4,031	3,986	8	4	15	-	6	12	22	2,903
55 33475	Hayward town	Sawyer	57.4	3,279	2,444	3	772	13	2	6	39	21	2,344
55 35150	Hobart town	Brown	33.2	5,090	4,101	5	848	35	4	20	77	44	3,572
55 35350	Holland town	La Crosse	42.5	3,042	2,942	2	6	62	1	3	26	12	2,093
55 36275	Hudson town	St. Croix	25.9	6,213	6,070	21	13	59	1	19	30	61	4,152
55 36350	Hull town	Portage	28.3	5,493	5,371	15	17	32	-	8	50	50	3,968
55 37600	Ixonia town	Jefferson	35.9	2,902	2,860	2	6	9	1	8	16	26	2,164
55 37700	Jackson town	Washington	34.2	3,516	3,479	1	2	12	-	-	22	12	2,527

Table D-2. MCDs — **Area and Population**—Con.

[Includes functioning minor civil divisions [MCDs] of 2,500 or more population as of April 1, 2000 in the following 12 states: CT, ME, MA, MI, MN, NH, NJ, NY, PA, RI, VT, and WI. Codes shown are two-digit Federal Information Processing Standards (FIPS) state codes and five-digit FIPS place codes. Place names and codes are those in effect as of January 1, 2000. County refers to the county in which the MCD is located]

State and place code	MCD	County	Land area, 2000 (sq. mi.)	Population, 2000 (April 1)									
					By race—							Hispanic or Latino (of any race)	18 years and over
					One race						Two or more races		
				Total	White	Black or African American	American Indian and Alaska Native	Asian	Native Hawaiian and Other Pacific Islander	Some other race			
55 00000	WISCONSIN—Con.												
55 37850	Janesville town	Rock	28.1	3,750	3,495	175	10	18	2	25	25	55	2,918
55 40375	Koshkonong town	Jefferson	42.1	3,395	3,324	1	10	6	-	18	36	60	2,535
55 40550	Kronenwetter town	Marathon	51.9	5,369	5,275	11	10	49	4	6	14	28	3,842
55 40687	Lac du Flambeau town	Vilas	100.3	3,004	1,188	6	1,784	-	-	9	17	48	2,108
55 40900	Lafayette town	Chippewa	34.5	5,199	5,124	9	22	14	-	7	23	21	3,819
55 43090	Ledgeview town	Brown	17.6	3,363	3,319	7	6	13	-	7	11	25	2,356
55 44150	Lima town	Sheboygan	36.6	2,948	2,909	4	3	12	-	8	12	27	2,188
55 44525	Lincoln town	Vilas	32.6	2,579	2,537	3	10	5	-	5	19	17	2,055
55 44850	Lisbon town	Waukesha	29.5	9,359	9,230	20	26	35	-	4	44	68	6,764
55 45275	Little Suamico town	Oconto	37.3	3,877	3,794	23	21	10	1	10	18	31	2,715
55 45375	Lodi town	Columbia	27.1	2,791	2,755	4	14	4	1	-	13	13	2,104
55 46725	Lyons town	Walworth	34.5	3,440	3,358	11	8	12	1	15	35	74	2,533
55 48025	Madison town	Dane	3.1	7,005	4,344	1,088	61	328	4	834	346	1,455	5,697
55 48575	Manitowoc Rapids town	Manitowoc	27.4	2,520	2,494	4	4	3	-	12	3	24	1,954
55 50850	Menasha town	Winnebago	12.4	15,858	15,135	62	71	264	6	189	131	493	12,023
55 50975	Menominee town	Menominee	358.0	4,562	528	3	3,981	-	1	15	34	122	2,786
55 51050	Menomonie town	Dunn	41.8	3,174	2,928	3	4	216	-	6	17	17	2,206
55 51275	Merrill town	Lincoln	52.1	2,979	2,940	3	5	8	-	4	19	10	2,205
55 51400	Merton town	Waukesha	25.7	7,988	7,880	12	10	40	4	16	26	81	5,544
55 51600	Middleton town	Dane	17.7	4,594	4,492	17	8	36	-	8	33	32	3,220
55 52225	Milton town	Rock	31.3	2,844	2,789	5	5	9	-	12	24	33	2,096
55 53225	Minocqua town	Oneida	150.8	4,859	4,745	2	50	12	1	11	38	46	3,905
55 54875	Mount Pleasant town	Racine	34.9	23,142	20,635	1,479	60	281	7	423	257	1,149	17,980
55 55025	Mukwa town	Waupaca	31.4	2,773	2,740	4	9	7	-	2	11	16	1,993
55 55075	Mukwonago town	Waukesha	30.9	6,868	6,724	7	11	22	-	12	92	103	4,713
55 55775	Neenah town	Winnebago	9.0	2,657	2,609	1	8	26	-	6	7	20	1,954
55 56425	Newbold town	Oneida	79.1	2,710	2,669	2	13	2	-	15	9	26	2,094
55 58600	Norway town	Racine	33.7	7,600	7,460	20	29	17	3	32	39	145	5,366
55 59125	Oakland town	Jefferson	34.9	3,135	3,084	1	7	5	1	11	26	41	2,340
55 59275	Oconomowoc town	Waukesha	29.3	7,451	7,357	10	10	15	1	14	44	39	5,559
55 59950	Onalaska town	La Crosse	37.0	5,210	5,055	12	32	67	-	6	38	31	3,649
55 60000	Oneida town	Outagamie	60.8	4,001	2,303	10	1,542	6	-	10	130	126	2,671
55 60225	Oregon town	Dane	32.1	3,148	3,094	5	8	13	-	-	28	16	2,165
55 60525	Oshkosh town	Winnebago	10.4	3,234	3,057	61	16	54	-	19	27	30	2,579
55 60700	Ottawa town	Waukesha	34.3	3,758	3,685	10	15	9	-	14	25	27	2,765
55 60925	Pacific town	Columbia	20.3	2,518	2,482	2	2	6	-	3	23	35	1,958
55 60962	Packwaukee town	Marquette	38.1	2,574	1,874	501	115	7	1	2	74	220	2,323
55 61625	Pelican town	Oneida	51.5	2,902	2,846	-	8	15	1	1	31	9	2,170
55 62200	Peshtigo town	Marinette	59.3	3,819	3,778	-	5	14	-	4	18	10	2,924
55 62925	Pine Lake town	Oneida	40.6	2,720	2,651	26	20	9	-	3	11	16	2,104
55 63375	Pleasant Springs town	Dane	33.4	3,053	2,990	18	-	20	-	4	21	18	2,260
55 63400	Pleasant Valley town	Eau Claire	54.2	2,681	2,623	-	8	29	-	16	5	34	1,879
55 63725	Plymouth town	Sheboygan	31.5	3,115	3,055	13	6	8	1	6	26	27	2,328
55 63875	Polk town	Washington	31.9	3,938	3,887	8	6	6	5	13	13	36	2,880
55 66125	Randall town	Kenosha	15.9	2,929	2,867	9	2	8	-	7	36	67	2,109
55 66375	Raymond town	Racine	35.6	3,516	3,444	16	10	18	-	3	25	41	2,580
55 67325	Rib Mountain town	Marathon	24.6	7,556	7,291	9	16	189	-	15	36	36	5,458
55 67375	Rice Lake town	Barron	26.4	3,026	2,973	5	7	8	1	12	20	29	2,208
55 67475	Richfield town	Washington	35.9	10,373	10,195	24	4	69	7	11	63	73	7,614
55 68600	Rock town	Rock	29.5	3,338	3,187	40	10	13	9	36	43	70	2,524
55 69275	Rome town	Adams	54.3	2,656	2,614	-	7	12	-	1	22	7	2,198
55 70825	St. Joseph town	St. Croix	32.1	3,436	3,365	9	9	21	5	8	19	26	2,431
55 71125	Salem town	Kenosha	29.7	9,871	9,607	52	32	30	2	79	69	248	6,947
55 71600	Saratoga town	Wood	49.4	5,383	5,244	9	38	31	-	17	44	29	3,966
55 72200	Scott town	Brown	19.7	3,712	3,568	60	13	24	-	21	26	55	2,858
55 72600	Sevastopol town	Door	51.9	2,667	2,616	1	8	5	-	20	17	36	2,059
55 72675	Seymour town	Eau Claire	31.2	2,978	2,914	3	16	25	1	3	16	25	2,201
55 73000	Sheboygan town	Sheboygan	11.0	5,874	5,646	7	9	145	-	32	35	68	4,242
55 73125	Shelby town	La Crosse	25.6	4,687	4,541	15	13	79	1	5	33	34	3,433
55 74650	Somers town	Kenosha	30.5	9,059	8,295	293	25	112	4	174	156	371	7,105
55 74700	Somerset town	St. Croix	47.9	2,644	2,583	1	8	24	1	3	24	10	1,876
55 75350	Sparta town	Monroe	49.3	2,750	2,717	1	5	12	1	2	12	9	2,030
55 75875	Springfield town	Dane	36.2	2,762	2,698	15	2	15	-	10	22	20	1,932
55 76850	Star Prairie town	St. Croix	31.4	2,944	2,847	45	13	17	1	4	17	24	2,078
55 77000	Stephenson town	Marinette	169.6	3,065	3,011	4	21	3	2	7	17	25	2,495
55 77537	Stockton town	Portage	57.7	2,896	2,834	6	8	15	-	8	25	35	2,054
55 77975	Suamico town	Brown	36.2	8,686	8,510	19	50	33	8	12	54	54	6,118
55 78100	Sugar Creek town	Walworth	33.0	3,331	3,241	4	5	14	-	32	35	89	2,384
55 78375	Summit town	Waukesha	25.8	4,999	4,862	40	7	43	-	17	30	70	3,615
55 79125	Taycheedah town	Fond du Lac	30.0	3,666	3,636	1	4	6	-	2	17	26	2,692
55 80575	Trenton town	Washington	33.4	4,440	4,384	8	9	6	-	17	16	49	3,257
55 80800	Troy town	St. Croix	37.7	3,661	3,597	4	12	14	-	10	24	43	2,559
55 82575	Vernon town	Waukesha	32.2	7,227	7,111	33	15	18	4	6	40	74	5,198
55 83612	Washington town	Eau Claire	56.1	6,995	6,735	24	37	102	-	30	67	74	5,070
55 83850	Waterford town	Racine	31.5	5,938	5,849	24	7	13	1	10	34	85	4,245
55 84275	Waukesha town	Waukesha	22.9	8,596	8,353	24	10	96	5	60	48	172	6,052
55 85275	Wescott town	Shawano	22.7	3,653	3,432	4	158	6	3	7	43	32	2,903

Table D-2. MCDs — **Area and Population**—Con.

[Includes functioning minor civil divisions (MCDs) of 2,500 or more population as of April 1, 2000 in the following 12 states: CT, ME, MA, MI, MN, NH, NJ, NY, PA, RI, VT, and WI. Codes shown are two-digit Federal Information Processing Standards (FIPS) state codes and five-digit FIPS place codes. Place names and codes are those in effect as of January 1, 2000. County refers to the county in which the MCD is located]

State and place code	MCD	County	Land area, 2000 (sq. mi.)	Population, 2000 (April 1)									
					By race—								
					One race							Hispanic or Latino (of any race)	18 years and over
				Total	White	Black or African American	American Indian and Alaska Native	Asian	Native Hawaiian and Other Pacific Islander	Some other race	Two or more races		
55 00000	WISCONSIN—Con.												
55 85375	West Bend town	Washington	16.1	4,834	4,784	1	9	13	3	2	22	27	3,673
55 86125	Westport town	Dane	22.2	3,586	3,503	22	6	31	3	9	12	28	2,841
55 86500	Wheatland town	Kenosha	23.6	3,292	3,230	16	7	8	-	9	22	32	2,407
55 87500	Wilson town	Sheboygan	22.9	3,227	3,124	7	5	44	-	27	20	75	2,438
55 87750	Windsor town	Dane	30.7	5,286	5,112	24	17	49	2	23	59	61	3,773
55 89575	Yorkville town	Racine	34.3	3,291	3,229	8	5	11	-	8	30	47	2,489

Source: U.S. Census Bureau, 2000 Census of Population and Housing, *Race and Hispanic or Latino Summary File on CD-ROM*, PL/00-3, issued April 2001 (related Internet site <http://www.census.gov/clo/www/redistricting.html>).

Source Notes and Explanations

Appendix A

You may visit us on the Web at
http://www.census.gov/statab/www/ccdb.html

Appendix A

Appendix A.
Source Notes and Explanations

This appendix presents general notes on population and economic censuses followed by source notes and explanation of the data items presented in table sets A/B, C, and D of this publication. Tables A/B, state/county contain identical data items, but Table C and D vary in both geographic and data coverage.

GENERAL NOTES

Population

Decennial censuses. The population statistics for 2000 and earlier are based on results from the censuses of population and housing, conducted by the U.S. Census Bureau as of April 1 in each of those years. As provided by Article 1, Section 2, of the U.S. Constitution, adopted in 1787, a census has been taken every 10 years commencing with 1790. The original purposes of the census were to apportion the seats in the U.S. House of Representatives based on the population of each state and to derive an equitable tax on each state for the payment of the Revolutionary War debt. Through the years, the nation's needs and interests have become more complex, and the content of the decennial census has changed accordingly. Presently, census data not only are used to apportion seats in the House and to aid legislators in the realignment of legislative district boundaries but are also used in the distribution of billions of federal dollars each year and are vital to state and local governments and to private firms for such functions as market analysis, site selection, and environmental impact studies.

The decennial census uses both short- and long-form questionnaires to gather information. The short form asks a limited number of basic questions. These questions are asked of all people and housing units and are often referred to as 100-percent questions because they are asked of the entire population. The population items include sex, age, race, Hispanic or Latino, household relationship, and group quarters. Housing items include occupancy status, vacancy status, and tenure (owner occupied or renter occupied). The long form asks more detailed information on a sample basis and includes the 100-percent questions as well as questions on education, employment, income, ancestry, homeowner costs, units in a structure, number of rooms, plumbing facilities, etc. This book only includes data from the short-form questionnaire. For a more detailed discussion of the information available from the 2000 census, see *Introduction to Census 2000 Data Products* available at <http://www.census.gov/mso/www/prodprof/census2000.pdf>.

Persons enumerated in the census were counted as inhabitants of their usual place of residence, which generally means the place where a person lives and sleeps most of the time. This place is not necessarily the same as the legal residence, voting residence, or domicile. In the vast majority of cases, however, the use of these different bases of classification would produce substantially the same statistics, although appreciable differences may exist for a few areas.

The implementation of this usual-residence practice has resulted in the establishment of residence rules for certain categories of persons whose usual place of residence is not immediately apparent (e.g., college students were counted at their college residence). As in the above example, persons were not always counted as residents of the place where they happened to be staying on census day. However, persons without a usual place of residence were counted where they were enumerated.

For information on procedures and concepts used for the 2000 Census of Population and Housing, as well as a facsimile of the questionnaires and descriptions of the data products resulting from the census, see U.S. Census Bureau, *2000 Census of Population and Housing: Summary File 1, Technical Documentation,* Series SF1/01(RV) released June 2001 and available on the Census Bureau Web site at <http://www.census.gov/prod/cen2000/doc/sf1.pdf> and *2000 Census of Population and Housing, Demographic Profiles of General Demographic Characteristics, Technical Documentation,* released May 2001 and available at <http://www.census.gov/prod/cen2000/doc/ProfilesTD.pdf>.

Population estimates. The Census Bureau develops county level population estimates with a demographic procedure called a "component change" method. A major assumption underlying this approach is that the components that constitute population change can be represented by administrative data in a statistical model. In order to build the model, Census Bureau demographers estimated each component of population change separately. For the population residing in households, the components of change are births, deaths, and net migration, including net immigration from abroad. For the nonhousehold population, change is represented by net change in the population in group quarters. For a detailed description of this methodology, see "Methodology for Estimates of State and County Total Population," which was used for the intercensal estimates for 1990 to 1999, found on the Census Web site at <http://www.census.gov/population/methods/stco99.txt>.

The Census Bureau calculates subcounty (cities and places) estimates using a "housing unit" method in which the change in the number of housing units at the subcounty level is used to distribute the county population to subcounty areas. In order to develop these estimates, data on building permits for new residential construction in permit issuing areas, new mobile home placements, and estimated housing loss are developed, utilized, and/or imputed. Varied other assumptions that cover non-permitted areas, occupancy, and group quarters also are intricately involved. For a description of the methodology, see "Subcounty Population Estimates Methodology" found at <http://www.census.gov/population/methods/e98scdoc.txt> on the Census Web site.

Many of the tables in this publication present data expressed as "rates" or on a "per capita" basis. Census population estimates are extensively utilized in these calculations. Population estimates used for 1991 to 1999 do not reflect the results of the 2000 census of population.

Economic Censuses

The economic census is the major source of facts about the structure and functioning of the nation's economy. It provides essential information for government, business, industry, and the general public. It furnishes an important part of the framework for such composite measures as the gross domestic product estimates, input/output measures, production and price indexes, and other statistical series that measure short-term changes in economic conditions. Title 13 of the United States Code (Sections 131, 191, and 224) directs the Census Bureau to take the economic censuses every 5 years, covering years ending in "2" and "7." The economic censuses form an integrated program at 5-year intervals since 1967 and before that for 1963, 1958, and 1954. Prior to that time, the individual censuses were taken separately at varying intervals. Prior to 1997, the census of agriculture was taken by the Census Bureau, but for 1997 was done under the direction of the U.S. Department of Agriculture.

The 1997 Economic Census data found in this publication is the first census to present data based of the new North American Industry Classification System (NAICS). Previous census data were presented based on the Standard Industrial Classification (SIC) system developed some 60 years ago. Due to this change, comparability between census years and data found in previous books will be limited. This new system of industrial classification was developed by experts on classification in government and private industry under the guidance of the Office of Information and Regulatory Affairs, Office of Management and Budget.

There are 20 NAICS sectors, which are subdivided into 96 subsectors (three-digit codes), 313 industry groups (four-digit codes), and, as implemented in the United States, 1,170 industries (five- and six-digit codes). While many of the individual NAICS industries correspond directly to industries as defined under the SIC system, most of the higher level groupings do not.

The economic censuses are collected on an establishment basis. A company operating at more than one location is required to file a separate report for each store, factory, shop, or other location. Each establishment is assigned a separate industry classification based on its primary activity and not that of its parent company. Establishments responding to the establishment survey are classified into industries on the basis of their principal product or activity (determined by annual sales volume) in accordance with the *North American Industry Classification System—United States, 1997* manual available from the National Technical Information Service and the Superintendent of Documents, U.S. Government Printing Office.

More detailed information about the scope, coverage, classification system, data items, and publications for each of the economic censuses and related surveys is published in the *Guide to the Economic Censuses and Related Statistics*. More information on the methodology, procedures, and history of the censuses is available in the *History of the 1997 Economic Census* found on the Census Web site at <http://www.census.gov/prod/ec97/pol00-hec.pdf>.

Data from the 1997 Economic Census were released through the Census Bureau's American FactFinder service, on CD-ROM, and in Adobe Acrobat PDF reports available on the Census Bureau Web site. For more information on these various media of release, see the following page on the Census Web site <http://www.census.gov/epcd/www/econ97.html>.

TABLE A/B—STATES/COUNTIES

Table A presents 13 tables with 191 items of data for each state, the United States as a whole, and the District of Columbia. On the first page of the table, the stub presents Federal Information Processing Standard (FIPS) state codes for the 50 states and the District of Columbia. For a discussion of the codes, see Appendix B, Geographic Information

Table B presents the same 13 tables with the same items of data as in Table A for each state and for each of the 3,142 counties and county equivalents (boroughs, independent cities, parishes, etc.).

Counties and county equivalents are presented in alphabetical order within states, which are also presented in alphabetical order. Independent cities, which are found in Maryland, Missouri, Nevada, and Virginia, are placed at the end of the county listing for those states.

FIPS codes for states and counties, with applicable metropolitan area codes, are shown in tables A-1 and B-1, respectively. These codes are given to facilitate cross-reference with other publications and to provide information for access to data available in electronic format. For more information regarding these code numbers, see Appendix B, Geographic Information.

Table A/B-1. Area and Population

Land area, 2000—Population, 2000: number, rank, per square mile; 1990: number and rank; 1980: number; net change: 1990-2000, 1980-1990; percent change: 1990-2000, 1980-1990; Hispanic or Latino origin, 2000: number and percent.

Source: **Land Area**—U.S. Census Bureau, unpublished data file from Geography Division based on TIGER database.

The Census Bureau provides land area for the decennial censuses. Area was calculated from the specific set of boundaries recorded for the entity (in this case, states and counties) in the Census Bureau's geographic database.

Land area measurements may disagree with the information displayed on census maps and in the TIGER file because, for area measurement purposes, features identified as "intermittent water" and "glacier" are reported as land area. TIGER is an acronym for the new digital (computer-readable) geographic database that automates the mapping and related geographic activities required to support the Census Bureau's census and survey programs; TIGER stands for Topologically Integrated Geographic Encoding and Referencing system.

The accuracy of any area measurement figure is limited by the inaccuracy inherent in (1) the location and shape of the various boundary features in the database, and (2) rounding affecting the last digit in all operations that compute and/or sum the area measurement. Identification of land and inland, coastal, and territorial is for statistical purposes and does not necessarily reflect legal definitions thereof.

Source: **2000 Population**—U.S. Census Bureau, *Census of Population and Housing, Census 2000 Redistricting Data (Public Law 94-171) Summary Files* (related Internet site <http://www.census.gov/dmd/www/2kresult.html >).

These decennial population counts are from the short-form questionnaires that were asked of all people and housing units and are often referred to as 100-percent questions because they are asked of the entire population. For more information on the decennial census, see General Notes.

Persons enumerated in the census were counted as inhabitants of their usual place of residence, which generally means the place where a person lives and sleeps most of the time. This place is not necessarily the same as the legal residence, voting residence, or domicile. In the vast majority of cases, however, the use of these different bases of classification would produce substantially the same statistics, although appreciable differences may exist for a few areas.

The implementation of this usual-residence practice has resulted in the establishment of residence rules for certain categories of persons whose usual place of residence is not immediately apparent (e.g., college students were counted at their college residence). As in the above example, persons were not always counted as residents of the place where they happened to be staying on census day. However, persons without a usual place of residence were counted where they were enumerated.

Rank numbers are assigned on the basis of population size, with each county area placed in descending order, largest to smallest. Where ties occur—two or more areas with identical populations—the same rank is assigned to each of the tied county areas. In such cases, the following rank number(s) is omitted so that the lowest rank is usually equal to the number of county areas ranked.

Persons per square mile, also known as population density, is the average number of inhabitants per square mile of land area. These figures are derived by dividing the total number of residents by the number of square miles of land area in the specified geographic area. To determine population per square kilometer, multiply the population per square mile by .3861.

Percent change represents the increase or decrease between the two years shown as a percentage of the beginning population. Net change represents the increase or decrease between the two years shown.

Hispanic or Latino, 2000. Census 2000 adheres to the federal standards for collecting and presenting data on race and Hispanic origin as established by the Office of Management and Budget (OMB) in October 1997. The OMB defines Hispanic or Latino as a person who classifies themselves in one of the specific Hispanic or Latino categories listed on the questionnaire—"Mexican," "Puerto Rican," or "Cuban"—as well as those who indicate that they are "other Spanish, Hispanic, or Latino." People who identify their origin as Spanish, Hispanic, or Latino may be of any race.

The federal government considers race and Hispanic origin to be two separate and distinct concepts. For Census 2000, the questions on race and Hispanic origin were asked of every individual living in the United States. The question on Hispanic origin asked respondents if they were Spanish, Hispanic, or Latino. The question on race asked respondents to report the race or races they considered themselves to be. Both questions are based on self-identification. The question on Hispanic origin for Census 2000 was similar to the 1990 census question, except for its placement on the questionnaire. For Census 2000, the question on Hispanic origin was asked directly before the question on race.

Source: **1990 Population**—U.S. Census Bureau, "CO-99-8 County Population Estimates and Demographic Components of Population Change: Annual Time Series, July 1, 1990, to July 1, 1999 (includes revised April 1, 1990, Population Estimates Base)"; release date: 9 March 2000; <http://www.census.gov/population/estimates/county/co-99-8/99C8_00.txt>. These data include count resolution corrections through 1997 and adjustments based on

Census 2000 dress rehearsal results. For information on methodology, see "Population estimates" under the General Note.

Source: **1980 Population**—U.S. Census Bureau, "1980-1990 Intercensal Population Estimates by County" on diskette (related Internet site <http://www.census.gov/population/www/estimates/countypop.html>).

Table A/B-2. Population by Age, Sex, and Race

Age, 2000: percent by selected age groups and median age—Males per 100 females, 2000—Race, 2000: White, Black or African American, American Indian and Alaska Native, Asian, Native Hawaiian and Other Pacific Islander, Some other race, Two or more races.

Source: **Population Characteristics, 2000**—U.S. Census Bureau, *2000 Census of Population and Housing,* "Census 2000 Profiles of General Demographic Characteristics" data files, published May 2001 (related Internet site at <http://www.census.gov/mp/www/pub/2000cen/mscen01.html>).

These decennial population counts are from the short-form questionnaires that were asked of all people and housing units and are often referred to as 100-percent questions because they are asked of the entire population. For more information on the decennial census, see General Notes.

Age. The age classification is based on the age of the person in complete years as of April 1, 2000. The age of the person usually was derived from their date of birth information. **Median age** represents the age that divides the age distribution into two equal parts, one-half of the cases falling below the median age and one-half above the median. This measure is rounded to the nearest tenth.

Race. The racial classifications used by the Census Bureau adhere to the October 30, 1997, *Federal Register Notice* entitled, "Revisions to the Standards for the Classification of Federal Data on Race and Ethnicity" issued by the OMB. These standards govern the categories used to collect and present federal data on race and ethnicity. The OMB requires federal agencies to use a minimum of five race categories: White, Black or African American, American Indian and Alaska Native, Asian, and Native Hawaiian and Other Pacific Islander. For respondents unable to identify with any of these five race categories, the OMB approved including a sixth category "Some other race" on the Census 2000 questionnaire.

The question on race for Census 2000 was different from the one for the 1990 census in several ways. Most significantly, respondents were given the option of selecting one or more race categories to indicate their racial identities. Because of these changes, the Census 2000 data on race are not directly comparable with data from the 1990 census or earlier censuses. Caution must be used when interpreting changes in the racial composition of the U.S. population over time.

White refers to people having origins in any of the original peoples of Europe, the Middle East, or North Africa. It includes people who indicated their race or races as White or wrote in entries such as Irish, German, Italian, Lebanese, Near Easterner, Arab, or Polish.

Black or African American refers to people having origins in any of the Black racial groups of Africa. It includes people who indicated their race or races as Black, African American, or Negro or wrote in entries such as African American, Afro American, Nigerian, or Haitian.

American Indian and Alaska Native refers to people having origins in any of the original peoples of North and South America (including Central America) and who maintain tribal affiliation or community attachment. It includes people who indicated their race or races by marking this category or writing in their principal or enrolled tribe, such as Rosebud Sioux, Chippewa, or Navajo.

Asian refers to people having origins in any of the original peoples of the Far East, Southeast Asia, or the Indian subcontinent. It includes people who indicated their race or races as Asian Indian, Chinese, Filipino, Korean, Japanese, Vietnamese, or Other Asian or wrote in entries such as Burmese, Hmong, Pakistani, or Thai.

Native Hawaiian and Other Pacific Islander refers to people having origins in any of the original peoples of Hawaii, Guam, Samoa, or other Pacific Islands. It includes people who indicated their race or races as Native Hawaiian, Guamanian or Chamorro, Samoan, or Other Pacific Islander or wrote in entries such as Tahitian, Mariana Islander, or Chuukese.

Some other race includes all other responses not included in the "White," "Black or African American," "American Indian and Alaska Native," "Asian," and "Native Hawaiian and Other Pacific Islander" race categories described above. Respondents providing write-in entries such as multiracial, mixed, interracial, or a Hispanic/Latino group (for example, Mexican, Puerto Rican, or Cuban) in the "Some other race" write-in space are included in this category.

Two or more races. People may have chosen to provide two or more races either by checking two or more race response check boxes, by providing multiple write-in responses, or by some combination of check boxes and write-in responses. The race response categories shown on the questionnaire were collapsed into the five minimum race groups identified by the OMB, and the Census Bureau "Some other race" category.

Table A/B-3. Group Quarters Population and Households

Group quarters population, 2000: total and institutionalized—Households, 2000: total, percent change 1990-2000, persons per household; percent one-person; family households, total and by type and presence of children; nonfamily households.

These decennial group quarters and household numbers are from the short-form questionnaires that were asked of all people and housing units and are often referred to as 100-percent questions because they are asked of the entire population. For more information on the decennial census, see General Notes.

Source: **Group quarters population, 2000**—U.S. Census Bureau, *2000 Census of Population and Housing,* "Census 2000 Profiles of General Demographic Characteristics" data files, published May 2001 (related Internet site at <http://www.census.gov/mp/www/pub/2000cen/mscen01.html>).

The **group quarters population** includes all people not living in households. Two general categories of people in group quarters are recognized (1) the institutionalized population which includes people under formally authorized, supervised care, or custody in institutions at the time of enumeration (such as correctional institutions, nursing homes, and juvenile institutions) and (2) the noninstitutionalized population which includes all people who live in group quarters other than institutions (such as college dormitories, military quarters, and group homes). The **institutionalized population** includes people under formally authorized, supervised care, or custody in institutions at the time of enumeration.

Source: **Households, 2000**—U.S. Census Bureau, *2000 Census of Population and Housing,* "Census 2000 Profiles of General Demographic Characteristics" data files, published May 2001 (related Internet site at <http://www.census.gov/mp/www/pub/2000cen/mscen01.html>); **Households, 1990**—U.S. Census Bureau, *1990 Census of Population and Housing, Summary Tape File (STF) 1C* on CD-ROM (related Internet site at <http://homer.ssd.census.gov/cdrom/lookup>).

Household. A household includes all of the people who occupy a housing unit. People not living in households are classified as living in group quarters. Persons per household (or average household size) is a measure obtained by dividing the number of people in households by the total number of households (or householders).

Family household (family). A family includes a householder and one or more people living in the same household who are related to the householder by birth, marriage, or adoption. All people in a household who are related to the householder are regarded as members of his or her family. A family household may contain people not related to the householder, but those people are not included as part of the householder's family in census tabulations. Thus, the number of family households is equal to the number of families, but family households may include more members than do families. A household can contain only one family for purposes of census tabulations. Not all households contain families since a household may comprise a group of unrelated people or one person living alone. **Married-couple family** is a family in which the householder and his or her spouse are enumerated as members of the same household. **Female householder, no husband present** is a category where a female maintains a household with no husband of the householder present. **Nonfamily household** is a household in which the householder lives alone or with nonrelatives only.

Own child category is a child under 18 years old who is a son or daughter by birth, marriage (a stepchild), or adoption. For 100-percent tabulations, own children consist of all sons/daughters of householders who are under 18 years of age. For sample data, own children consist of sons/daughters of householders who are under 18 years of age and who have never been married, therefore, numbers of own children of householders may be different in these two tabulations.

Table A/B-4. Vital Statistics and Health

Births, 1997: number and rate—Deaths, 1997: number and rate; infant deaths, number and rate—Physicians, 1999: number and rate—Community hospitals, 1998: number; beds, number and rate—Nursing and personal care facilities, 1997: establishments and employees—Medicare program enrollment, 1999: total and aged.

Source: **Births, 1997,** U.S. National Center for Health Statistics (NCHS), *Vital Statistics of the United States,* Vol. I, "Natality," annual, and unpublished data. **Deaths, 1997,** U.S. National Center for Health Statistics, *Vital Statistics of the United States,* Vol. II, "Mortality," annual, and unpublished data.

Through the National Vital Statistics System, the NCHS collects and publishes data on births and deaths in the United States. The Division of Vital Statistics obtains information on births and deaths from the registration offices of all states, New York City, and the District of Columbia. In most areas, practically all births and deaths are registered. The most recent test of the completeness of birth registration, conducted on a sample of births from 1964 to 1968, showed that 99.3 percent of all births in the United States during that period were registered. No comparable information is available for deaths, but it is generally believed that death registration in the United States is at least as complete as birth registration.

Birth and **death** statistics are limited to events occurring during the year. The data are by place of residence and exclude events occurring to nonresidents of the United States. Births or deaths that occur outside the United States are excluded. **Birth** and **death rates** represent the number of births and deaths per 1,000 resident population estimated as of July 1 for 1997. **Infant death rates** represent the number of deaths of infants under 1 year of age per 1,000 live births. They exclude fetal deaths.

Source: **Physicians, 1999,** American Medical Association, Chicago, IL, *Physician Characteristics and Distribution in the U.S.,* annual (copyright).

The number of physicians covers active, nonfederal physicians, as of December 31 of the year shown. The figures are based on information contained in the AMA Physician Masterfile. The file has been maintained by the AMA since 1906 and includes information on every physician in the country and on those graduates of American medical schools who are temporarily practicing overseas. The file also includes members and nonmembers of the AMA and graduates of foreign medical schools who are in the United States and meet U.S. education standards for primary recognition as physicians. Thus, all physicians comprising the total manpower pool are included on the file. However, this publication excludes data for all federal physicians and nonfederal physicians who are temporarily in foreign locations.

Masterfile data are obtained from both AMA surveys and inputs from physicians, other organizations, and institutions. Primary sources are as follows: medical schools, hospitals, medical societies, national boards, state licensing agencies, Educational Commission for Foreign Medical Graduates, Surgeon General of the U.S. Government, American Board of Medical Specialties, and physicians.

Physician rate is per 100,000 resident population estimated as of July 1, 1999.

Source: **Community hospitals, 1998,** Health Forum, LLC, an American Hospital Association (AHA) Company, Chicago, IL, *Hospital Statistics 2000* edition and unpublished data (copyright).

Community hospitals statistics were compiled by the AHA from surveys of all hospitals in the United States and its outlying areas. AHA surveys include unregistered hospitals, as well as those registered by the AHA. Hospitals were asked to report data for a full year ending September 30.

Community hospitals are defined as nonfederal, short-term (average length of stay less than 30 days), general, or other special hospitals whose facilities and services are available to the public; psychiatric and tuberculosis hospitals and hospital units of institutions are excluded. Data for beds are based on the average number of beds in the facilities over the reporting period. Rate is per 100,000 resident population estimated as of July 1, 1998.

Source: **Nursing and personal care facilities, 1997,** U.S. Census Bureau, *County Business Patterns: 1997* on CD-ROM (related Internet site <http://www.census.gov/epcd/cbp/view/cbpview.html>).

These County Business Patterns (CBP) data are based on the Standard Industrial Classification (SIC) system for SIC's 8051, 8052, and 8059. The **nursing and personal care facilities** presented cover establishments engaged in providing skilled nursing care such as in convalescent homes,

extended care facilities, nursing homes (skilled), and mental retardation hospitals; intermediate care facilities that provide inpatient nursing and rehabilitative services, but not on a continuous basis; and facilities that provide some nursing and/or health-related care to patients who do not require the degree of care and treatment that a skilled or intermediate care facility is designed to provide.

For information on CBP program and definitions of establishments and employees, see Table A/B-7 on Private Business Establishments and Employment.

Source: **Medicare, 1999,** U.S. Health Care Financing Administration, *Medicare County Enrollment as of July 1, 1999 - Aged and Disabled,* March 2000 update, <http://www.hcfa.gov/stats/enroll/default.htm>.

When first implemented in 1966, medicare covered only most persons age 65 and over. By the end of 1966, 3.7 million persons had received at least some health care services covered by medicare. In 1973, other groups became eligible for medicare benefits: persons who are entitled to social security or Railroad Retirement disability benefits for at least 24 months; persons with endstage renal disease (ESRD) requiring continuing dialysis or kidney transplant; and certain otherwise noncovered aged persons who elect to buy into medicare.

Medicare consists of two primary parts: Hospital Insurance (HI), also known as Part A, and Supplementary Medical Insurance (SMI), also known as Part B. Health care services covered under Medicare's Hospital Insurance include, inpatient hospital care, skilled nursing facility care, home health agency care, and Hospice care. SMI coverage is optional and requires payment of a monthly premium.

Table A/B-5. Education, Income, and Poverty

Public school enrollment, 1998-1999, 1994-1995, and 1990—Educational attainment, 1990: high school graduate or higher, bachelor's degree or higher—Median household income, 1997 and 1989: amount and percent change—Persons below poverty level, 1997: all persons, number and percent; persons under 18, number and percent.

Source: **Public school enrollment, 1998-1999 and 1994-1995,** U.S. National Center for Education Statistics, <http://nces.ed.gov/ccd/pubagency.html> (accessed: 16 March 2001); **Public school enrollment, 1990,** U.S. Census Bureau. *1990 Census of Population and Housing, Summary Tape File (STF) 3C.*

Public school enrollment data represent enrollment at all levels taught in a public school system, from prekindergarten through grade 12. Grades 13 and 14 do appear in a few school systems containing vocational education courses, and many operating school systems offer postgraduate courses. In addition, school system enrollment figures are tabulated on the basis of the county in which the superintendent's office is located, although the system many cover some parts of other counties.

Data for public school enrollment are for all public elementary and secondary schools in operation during the year shown. These data are from the Common Core of Data (CCD) which is the National Center for Education Statistics (NCES) primary database on elementary and secondary public education in the United States. The CCD, collected annually, is a comprehensive, national statistical database of all public elementary and secondary schools and school districts that contains data that are comparable across all states.

The CCD is based on a set of surveys sent to state education departments. Most of the data are obtained from administrative records maintained by the State Education Agencies (SEAs). Statistical information is also collected annually from public elementary and secondary schools (approximately 87,000), public school districts (approximately 16,000), and the 50 states, the District of Columbia, and outlying areas. The SEAs compile CCD requested data into prescribed format and transmit the information to NCES. The data presented here were compiled from the school district files. Data were placed in counties based on the location of the superintendent of school districts.

The 1990 data on school enrollment were obtained from a sample of the population as part of the decennial censuses. Persons were classified as enrolled in school if they attended a "regular" public or private school or college at any time since February 1 of the year shown. Enrollment in a trade or business school, company training, or tutoring were not included unless the course would be accepted for credit at a regular elementary school, high school, or college. As with other census data, persons are counted in their current locations. For a discussion of usual place of residence, see text for Table A/B 1.

Source: **Educational attainment, 1990**—U.S. Census Bureau, *1990 Census of Population and Housing, Summary Tape File (STF) 3C* on CD-ROM (related Internet site <http://homer.ssd.census.gov/cdrom/lookup>).

Data on educational attainment in 1990 were derived from answers to the questionnaire, which was asked of a sample of persons. Data are tabulated as attainment for persons 25 years old and over. Persons are classified according to the highest level of school completed or the highest degree received. Respondents were asked to report the level of the previous grade attended or the highest degree received for persons currently enrolled in school. The question included response categories which allowed persons to report completing the 12th grade without receiving a high school diploma and which instructed respondents to report as "high school graduate(s)"— persons who received either a high school diploma or the equivalent, for example, passed the Test of General Educational Development (G.E.D.) and did not attend college. The category "High school graduate or higher" covers persons whose highest degree was a high school diploma or

its equivalent, persons who attended college or professional school, and persons who received a college, university, or professional degree. Persons who reported completing the 12th grade but not receiving a diploma are not included.

Source: **Household income and poverty, 1997**—U.S. Census Bureau, "State and County Income and Poverty Estimates - 1997," published: 22 November 2000, <http://www.census.gov/housing/saipe/estmod97/est97ALL.dat> (related Internet site <http://www.census.gov/hhes/www/saipe/estimatetoc.html>).

Data for 1997 household income and persons below poverty level are based on the Small Area Income and Poverty Estimates (SAIPE) program. This program was started by the Census Bureau with support from other federal agencies in order to provide more current estimates of selected income and poverty statistics than the most recent decennial census. Estimates are created for states, counties, and school districts (not shown in this publication). These updated estimates of income and poverty statistics are used for the administration of federal programs and the allocation of federal funds to local jurisdictions.

The estimates are not direct counts from enumerations or administrative records, nor direct estimates from sample surveys. Data from these sources are not adequate to provide intercensal estimates for all counties. Instead, a model is employed that utilizes the relation between income or poverty and tax and program data for the states and a subset of counties using estimates of income or poverty from the Current Population Survey. The models involve use selected variables based on survey and administrative sources including income and poverty estimates derived from the March Current Population Survey; direct estimates of income and poverty from the 1990 decennial census data; data summarized from federal individual income tax returns; number of food stamp recipients; information from the Bureau of Economic Analysis (BEA), in the form of personal income estimates; Supplemental Security Income recipients; and demographic intercensal estimates of the population of states and counties, by age and group quarters status. For a more detailed discussion of this methodology, see "State and County Estimates" and "Frequently Asked Questions" at <http://www.census.gov/hhes/www/saipe.html>.

Household income is total money income received in a calendar year by all household members 15 years old and over. Total money income is the sum of amounts reported separately for income from wages or salaries; nonfarm self-employment; farm self-employment; social security; public assistance; and all other regularly received income such as veterans' payments, pensions, unemployment compensation, and alimony. Receipts not counted as income include various "lump sum" payments such as capital gains or inheritances. The total represents the amount of income received before deductions for personal income taxes, social security, bond purchases, union dues, medicare deductions, etc. Household income differs from family income by including income received by all household members, not just those related to the householder, and by persons living alone or in other nonfamily households. Income is derived on a sample basis.

Median income figures are based on all families/households and represent the dollar amount that divides the distribution of families/households into two equal parts—one half of the families/households falling below this value and the other half exceeding it.

Poverty is defined in relation to family income. Families and unrelated individuals are classified as above or below the poverty level by comparing their total income to an income cutoff or "poverty threshold." The income cutoffs vary by family size, number of children, and age of the family householder or unrelated individual. Poverty status is determined for all families (and, by implication, all family members). Poverty status is also determined for persons not in families, except for inmates of institutions, members of the Armed Forces living in barracks, college students living in dormitories, and unrelated individuals under 15 years old. Poverty status is derived on a sample basis.

The estimates of poverty for "persons under 18 years" are for related children in families meaning children related to the householder by birth, marriage (stepchildren), or adoption. Foster children and other children not related to the householder by birth, marriage, or adoption are excluded. The estimate of related children covers ages 5 through 17 and excludes people within this age range who maintain households, families, or subfamilies as a householder or spouse. In practice, the difference between the numbers of related children in families and all children is very small.

Source: **Household income and persons below poverty level, 1989,** U.S. Census Bureau, *1990 Census of Population and Housing, Summary Tape File (STF) 3C* on CD-ROM (related Internet site <http://homer.ssd.census.gov/cdrom/lookup>).

Table A/B-6. Crime, Housing, and Building Permits

Serious crimes known to police, 1999: number (total, violent, and property) and rate; 1990: number and rate—Housing, 2000: total units, number and percent change 1990-2000; occupied units, total and owner-occupied—New private housing units authorized by building permits, 2000: number (total and by units in structure) and valuation.

Source: **Crime**—U.S. Federal Bureau of Investigation (FBI), *Crime in the United States,* annual (related Internet site <http://www.fbi.gov/ucr/ucr.htm>).

Data presented on crime are through the voluntary contribution of crime statistics by law enforcement agencies across the United States. The Uniform Crime Reporting (UCR) program provides periodic assessments of crime in the nation as measured by offenses coming to the attention of the law enforcement community. The Committee of Uniform Crime Records of the International Association of Chiefs of Police initiated this voluntary national data-collection effort in 1930. UCR program contributors compile and submit their crime data in one of two means: either directly to the FBI or through the state UCR programs.

Users of these data are cautioned about comparing data between areas based on these respective Crime Index figures. Assessing criminality and law enforcement's responses from area to area should encompass many elements (i.e., population density and urbanization, population composition, stability of population, modes of transportation, commuting patterns and highway systems, economic conditions, cultural conditions, family conditions, climate, effective strength and emphasis of law enforcement agencies, attitudes of citizenry toward crime, and crime reporting practices). These elements may have a significant impact on crime reporting. Also, not all law enforcement agencies provide data for all 12 months of the year and some agencies fail to report at all. Data are as reported to the FBI.

Seven offenses, because of their seriousness, frequency of occurrence, and likelihood of being reported to police, were initially selected to serve as an index for evaluating fluctuations in the volume of crime. These crimes, known as the Crime Index offenses, were murder and nonnegligent manslaughter, forcible rape, robbery, aggravated assault, burglary, larceny-theft, and motor vehicle theft. By congressional mandate, arson was added as the eighth Index offense in 1979. Only the Modified Index (not shown in this publication) includes arson.

Violent crimes include four crime categories: (1) Murder and nonnegligent manslaughter, as defined in the UCR program, is the willful (nonnegligent) killing of one human being by another. This offense excludes deaths caused by negligence, suicide, or accident; justifiable homicides; and attempts to murder or assaults to murder. (2) Forcible rape is the carnal knowledge of a female forcibly and against her will. Assaults or attempts to commit rape by force or threat of force are also included; however, statutory rape (without force) and other sex offenses are excluded. (3) Robbery is the taking or attempting to take anything of value from the care, custody, or control of a person or persons by force or threat of force or violence and/or by putting the victim in fear. (4) Aggravated assault is an unlawful attack by one person upon another for the purpose of inflicting severe or aggravated bodily injury. This type of assault is usually accompanied by the use of a weapon or by means likely to produce death or great bodily harm. Attempts are included since an injury does not necessarily have to result when a gun, knife, or other weapon is used, which could and probably would result in a serious personal injury if the crime were successfully completed.

In general, **property crimes** include four crime categories: (1) Burglary is the unlawful entry of a structure to commit a felony or theft. (2) Larceny-theft is the unlawful taking, carrying, leading, or riding away of property from the possession or constructive possession of another. It includes crimes such as shoplifting, pocket picking, purse snatching, thefts from motor vehicles, thefts of motor vehicle parts and accessories, bicycle thefts, etc., in which no use of force, violence, or fraud occurs. This crime category does not include embezzlement, "con" games, forgery, worthless checks, and motor vehicle theft. (3) Motor vehicle theft is the theft or attempted theft of a motor vehicle. This definition excludes the taking of a motor vehicle for temporary use by those persons having lawful access. (4) Arson is any willful or malicious burning or attempt to burn, with or without intent to defraud, a dwelling house, public building, motor vehicle or aircraft, personal property of another, etc. Only fires determined through investigation to have been willfully or maliciously set are classified as arson. Fires of suspicious or unknown origins are excluded. In this publication, arson is not included in property crime figures or total crimes.

Rates are based on resident population enumerated as of April 1 for decennial census years and estimated as of July 1 for other years. Population figures used for these rates are from the FBI.

Source: **Housing, 2000**—U.S. Census Bureau, *2000 Census of Population and Housing,* "Census 2000 Profiles of General Demographic Characteristics" data files, published May 2001 (related Internet site <http://www. census.gov/mp/www/pub/2000cen/mscen01.html>); **Housing, 1990**—U.S. Census Bureau, *1990 Census of Population and Housing, Summary Tape File (STF) 1C* on CD-ROM (related Internet site <http://homer.ssd.census. gov/cdrom/lookup>).

These decennial housing counts were tabulated from the short-form questionnaires that were asked of all people and housing units and are often referred to as 100-percent questions because they are asked of the entire population. For more information on the decennial census, see General Notes.

A **housing unit** is a house, apartment, mobile home or trailer, group of rooms, or single room occupied or, if vacant, intended for occupancy as separate living quarters. Separate living quarters are those in which the occupants do not live and eat with any other persons in the structure and which have direct access from the outside of the building through a common hall. A housing unit is classified as **occupied** if it is the usual place of residence of the person or group of people living in it at the time of census enumeration or if the occupants are only temporarily absent; that is, away on vacation or business. All occupied housing units are classified as either owner occupied or renter occupied. A housing unit is owner occupied if the owner or co-owner lives in the unit even if it is mortgaged or not fully paid for. All occupied housing

units which are not owner occupied, whether they are rented for cash rent or occupied without payment of cash rent, are classified as renter occupied. The 1990 and 2000 data presented are from the decennial censuses and are based on tabulations of 100-percent or complete counts (i.e. information obtained for all persons and housing units).

Source: **Building permits**—U.S. Census Bureau, "New Residential Construction-Building Permits," e-mail from Manufacturing and Construction Division/Residential Construction Branch, subject: building permits by place 2000, 22 May 2001 (related Internet site <http://www.census. gov/const/www/permitsindex.html>).

Building permits data are based on reports submitted by local building permit officials in response to a Census Bureau mail survey. They are obtained using Form C-404, "Report of New Privately Owned Residential Building or Zoning Permits Issued." Data are collected from individual permit offices, most of which are municipalities; the remainder are counties, townships, or New England and Middle Atlantic-type towns. Currently, there are 19,000 permit-issuing places. When a report is not received, missing data are either (1) obtained from the Survey of Use of Permits, which is used to collect information on housing starts, or (2) imputed. For more information on the methodology, see <http://www.census.gov/const/www/ newresconstdoc.html>.

The data relate to new private housing units intended for occupancy on a housekeeping basis. They exclude mobile homes (trailers), hotels, motels, and group residential structures, such as nursing homes and college dormitories. They also exclude conversions of and alterations to existing buildings. A **housing unit** consists of a room or group of rooms intended for occupancy as separate living quarters by a family, by a group of unrelated persons living together, or by a person living alone. **Valuation** represents the cost of construction as recorded on the building permit. This figure usually excludes the cost of on-site and off-site development and improvements and the cost of heating, plumbing, electrical, and elevator installations.

Table A/B-7. Labor Force and Private Business Establishments and Employment

Civilian labor force, 2000: total and percent change, 1999-2000; unemployment, total and rate— Private nonfarm businesses: establishments and employment, 1998, 1995, and 1990; annual payroll per employee, 1998.

Source: **Civilian labor force**—U.S. Bureau of Labor Statistics (BLS), Local Area Unemployment Statistics, 2000 data published: 2 May 2001; 1999 data published: 30 May 2001; <ftp://ftp.bls.gov/pub/time.series/la/> (related Internet site <http://www.bls.gov/lauhome.htm>).

Civilian labor force data are the product of a federal-state cooperative program in which state employment security agencies prepare labor force and unemployment estimates under concepts, definitions, and technical procedures established by the BLS. These data for substate areas are produced by the BLS primarily for use in allocating funds under various federal legislative programs. Users of these data are cautioned that, because of the small size of many of the areas, as well as limitations of the data inputs, the estimates are subject to considerable, but nonquantifiable, error. An explanation of the technical procedures used to develop monthly and annual local area labor force estimates appears monthly in the Explanatory Note for state and area unemployment data in the BLS periodical, *Employment and Earnings. Information may also be found in the Handbook of Labor Statistics,* which may be found at the BLS Web site at <http://stats.bls. gov/opub/hom/homhome.htm>.

The **civilian labor force** comprises all civilians 16 year old and over classified as employed or unemployed. Employed persons are all civilians who, during the survey week, did any work at all as paid employees, in their own business, profession, or on their own farm or who worked 15 hours or more as unpaid workers in an enterprise operated by a member of the family. It also includes all those who were not working but who had jobs or businesses from which they were temporarily absent because of illness, bad weather, vacation, labor-management disputes, job training, or personal reasons, whether they were paid for the time off or were seeking other jobs. Each employed person is counted only once. Those who held more than one job are counted in the job at which they worked the greatest number of hours during the survey week, the calendar week including the 12th of the month.

Unemployed persons are all civilians 16 years old and over who had no employment during the survey week were available for work, except for temporary illness, and had made specific efforts to find employment some time during the prior 4 weeks. Persons who were laid off or were waiting to report to a new job within 30 days did not need to be looking for work to be classified as unemployed. The unemployment rate for all civilian workers represents the number of unemployed as a percent of the civilian labor force.

Source: **Private business establishments and employment**—U.S. Census Bureau; *County Business Patterns* on CD-ROM; annual (related Internet site <http://www.census.gov/epcd/cbp/view/cbpview.html>).

County Business Patterns (CBP) is an annual series that provides subnational economic data by industry. The series is useful for studying the economic activity of small areas; analyzing economic changes over time; and as a benchmark for statistical series, surveys, and databases between economic censuses. CBP covers most of the country's economic activity. The series excludes data on self-employed individuals, employees of private households, railroad employees, agricultural production employees, and most government employees.

CBP data are extracted from the Business Register, the Census Bureau's file of all known single and multiestablishment companies. The Annual Company Organization Survey and quinquennial economic censuses provide individual establishment data for multilocation firms. Data for single-location firms are obtained from various programs conducted by the Census Bureau, such as the economic censuses, the Annual Survey of Manufactures, and Current Business Surveys, as well as from administrative records of the Internal Revenue Service (IRS), the Social Security Administration (SSA), and the Bureau of Labor Statistics (BLS).

An **establishment** is a single physical location at which business is conducted or services or industrial operations are performed. It is not necessarily identical with a company or enterprise, which may consist of one or more establishments. When two or more activities are carried on at a single location under a single ownership, all activities generally are grouped together as a single establishment. The entire establishment is classified on the basis of its major activity and all data are included in that classification. Establishment counts represent the number of locations with paid employees any time during the year. This series excludes governmental establishments except for wholesale liquor establishments, retail liquor stores, federally-chartered savings institutions, federally-chartered credit unions, and hospitals. Establishments without a fixed location or having an unknown county location within a state are included under a "statewide" geography classification.

Total **payroll** includes all forms of compensation, such as salaries, wages, reported tips, commissions, bonuses, vacation allowances, sick-leave pay, employee contributions to qualified pension plans, and the value of taxable fringe benefits. For corporations, it includes amounts paid to officers and executives; for unincorporated businesses, it does not include profit or other compensation of proprietors or partners. Payroll is reported before deductions for social security, income tax, insurance, union dues, etc. First-quarter payroll consists of payroll during the January-to-March quarter.

Paid employment consists of full- and part-time employees, including salaried officers and executives of corporations, who are on the payroll in the pay period including March 12. Included are employees on paid sick leave, holidays, and vacations; not included are proprietors and partners of unincorporated businesses.

Table A/B-8. Personal Income and Earnings

Personal income, 1998: total, percent change 1990-1998, per capita, transfer payments; earnings, total and percent by selected industry—Manufacturing earnings: 1998, 1997, and 1996.

Source: **Personal income and earnings**—U.S. Bureau of Economic Analysis, *Regional Economic Information System (REIS) 1969-1998* on CD-ROM (related Internet site <http://www.bea.doc.gov/bea/regional/data.htm>).

The **personal income** of an area is defined as the income received by, or on behalf of, all the residents of that area. It consists of the income received by persons from all sources, that is, from participation in production, from both government and business transfer payments, and from government interest. Personal income is the sum of wage and salary disbursements, other labor income, proprietors' income, rental income of persons, personal dividend income, personal interest income, and transfer payments, less personal contributions for social insurance.

Personal income differs by definition from money income, which is prepared by the Census Bureau (see Table A/B-5. Education, Income, and Poverty), in that money income is measured before deduction of personal contributions for social insurance and does not include imputed income, lump sum payments, and income received by quasi-individuals. Money income does include income from private pensions and annuities and from interpersonal transfer, such as child support; therefore, it is not comparable to personal income. Total personal income is adjusted to place of residence.

About 90 percent of the state and county estimates of personal income are based on census data and on administrative-records data that are collected by other federal agencies. The data from censuses are mainly collected from the recipient of the income. The most important sources of census data for the state and county estimates are the census of agriculture and the census of population and housing that are conducted by the Census Bureau. The data from administrative records may originate either from the recipients of the income or from the source of the income. These data are a byproduct of the administration of various federal and state government programs. The most important sources of these data are as follows: The state unemployment insurance programs of the Employment and Training Administration, Department of Labor; the social insurance programs of the Social Security Administration and the Health Care Financing Administration, Department of Health and Human Services; the federal income tax program of the Internal Revenue Service, Department of the Treasury; the veterans benefit programs of the Department of Veterans Affairs; and the military payroll systems of the Department of Defense. The remaining 10 percent of the estimates are based on data from other sources. For example, the estimates of the components of farm proprietors' income, a component of personal income, are partly based on the state estimates of farm income and the county estimates of cash receipts, crop production, and livestock inventory that are prepared by the Department of Agriculture, which uses sample surveys, along with census data and administrative-records data, to derive its estimates. For more information on the methodology, see the following document at the BEA Web site <http://www.bea.doc.gov/bea/articles/regional/persinc/Meth/lapi6992.pdf>.

Per capita personal income is calculated as the total personal income of the residents of an area divided by the population of the area. Per capita personal income is often used as an indicator of the quality of consumer markets and of the economic well-being of the residents of an area.

Transfer payments are income payments persons for which no current services are performed. They are payments by government and business to individuals and nonprofit In this discussion, transfer payments consists of three major components government payments to individuals, government and business payments to nonprofit institutions, and business payments to individuals.

Total **earnings** cover wage and salary disbursements, other labor income, and proprietors' income. Wage and salary disbursements are defined as monetary remuneration of employees, including corporate officers; commissions, tips, and bonuses; and pay-in-kind that represents income to the recipient. They are measured before such deductions as social security contributions and union dues. All disbursements in the current period are covered. Pay-in-kind represents allowances for food, clothing, and lodging paid in kind to employees, which represent income to them, valued at the cost to the employer. Other labor income consists of employer contributions to privately administered pension and welfare funds and a few small items such as directors' fees, compensation of prison inmates, and miscellaneous judicial fees. Proprietors' income is the monetary income and income in-kind of proprietorships and partnerships, including the independent professions, and of tax-exempt cooperatives.

Manufacturing earnings cover earnings by employees in the manufacturing industry, which covers establishments primarily engaged in the mechanical or chemical transformation of substances or materials into new products. The assembly of component parts of products also is considered to be manufacturing if the resulting product is neither a structure nor other fixed improvement. These activities are usually carried on in plants, factories, or mills that characteristically use power-driven machines and materials-handling equipment.

Table A/B-9. Manufacturing and Water Use

Manufacturing, 1997: establishments, all employees, production workers, value added by manufacture, value of shipments—Water use per day, 1995: total, percent ground water, percent by selected major use, consumptive use.

Source: **Manufacturing, 1997**—U.S. Census Bureau, 1997 Economic Census - Manufacturing, generated by Statistical Compendia Branch, using American Factfinder at <http://www.census.gov/> (7 June 2000) (related Internet site <http://www.census.gov/epcd/www/97EC31.HTM>).

Manufacturing data presented are based on the North American Industry Classification System (NAICS) for 1997 and are not entirely comparable with previous data for 1992 and earlier economic censuses (see General Note for the economic censuses). The manufacturing sector (NAICS code 31-33) comprises establishments engaged in the mechanical, physical, or chemical transformation of materials, substances, or components into new products. The assembling of component parts of manufactured products is considered manufacturing, except in cases where the activity is appropriately classified in the construction sector. Establishments in the manufacturing sector are often described as plants, factories, or mills and characteristically use power-driven machines and materials-handling equipment. However, establishments that transform materials or substances into new products by hand or in the worker's home and those engaged in selling to the general public products made on the same premises from which they are sold, such as bakeries, candy stores, and custom tailors, may also be included in this sector. Manufacturing establishments may process materials or may contract with other establishments to process their materials for them. Both types of establishments are included in manufacturing.

An **establishment** is a single physical location at which business is conducted or where services or industrial operations are performed. It is not necessarily identical with the company or enterprise, which may consist of one or more establishments. The count of establishments represents the number in business at any time during the year.

The **all employees** number is the average number of production workers plus the number of other employees in mid-March. Included are all persons on paid sick leave, paid holidays, and paid vacations during the pay period. Officers of corporations are included as employees; proprietors and partners of unincorporated firms are excluded.

Payroll includes all forms of compensation such as salaries, wages, commissions, bonuses, vacation allowances, sick-leave pay, and the value of payments in kind (e.g., free meals and lodgings) paid during the year to all employees. Tips and gratuities received by employees from patrons and reported to employers are included. For corporations, it includes amounts paid to officers and executives; for unincorporated businesses, it does not include profit or other compensation of proprietors or partners. Payroll is reported before deductions for social security, income tax, insurance, union dues, etc. This definition of payroll is the same as that used by the IRS on form 941.

The number of production workers is the average for the payroll periods including the 12th of March, May, August, and November. **Production workers** include workers (up through the line-supervisor level) engaged in fabricating, processing, assembling, inspecting, receiving, storing, handling, packing, warehousing, shipping (but not delivering), maintenance, repair, janitorial and guard services, product development, auxiliary production for plant's own use (e.g., power plant), recordkeeping, and other services closely associated with these production operations. Not included in this classification are all other employees, defined as nonproduction employees, including those engaged in factory supervision above the line-supervisor level.

Value added by manufacture is a measure of manufacturing activity derived by subtracting the cost of materials, supplies, containers, fuel, purchased electricity, and contract work from the value of shipments (products manufactured plus receipts for services rendered). The result of this calculation is adjusted by the addition of value added by merchandising operations (i.e., the difference between the sales value and cost of merchandise sold without further manufacture, processing, or assembly) plus the net change in finished goods and work-in-process between the beginning- and end-of-year inventories. Value added avoids the duplication in the figure for value of shipments that results from the use of products of some establishments as materials by others. Value added is considered to be the best value measure available for comparing the relative economic importance of manufacturing among industries and geographic areas.

Value of shipments covers the received or receivable net selling values, free on board plant (exclusive of freight charges and taxes), of all products shipped, both primary and secondary, as well as all miscellaneous receipts, such as receipts for contract work performed for others, installation and repair, sales of scrap, and sales of products bought and resold without further processing. Included are all items made by or for the establishment from materials owned by it, whether sold, transferred to other plants of the same company, or shipped on consignment. The net selling value of products made in one plant on a contract basis from materials owned by another was reported by the plant providing the materials. In the case of multiunit companies, the manufacturer was requested to report the value of products transferred to other establishments of the same company at full economic or commercial value, including not only the direct costs of production but also a reasonable proportion of "all other costs" (including company overhead) and profit.

Source: **Water use per day, 1995,** U.S. Geological Survey (USGS), *Water Use in the United States,* individual state/county and U.S. by state files from <http://water.usgs.gov/watuse/spread95.html> (accessed: 9 September 1999).

The U.S. Geological Survey's National Water-Use Information Program is responsible for compiling and disseminating the nation's water-use data. The USGS works in cooperation with local, state, and federal environmental agencies to collect water-use information at a site-specific level, such as the amount of water used to produce power at a fossil-fuel power-generation plant in Georgia. USGS also compiles the data from hundreds of thousands of these sites to produce water-use information aggregated up to the county, state, and national levels. Every 5 years, data at the state and hydrologic region level are compiled into a national water-use data system. The data were most recently published in USGS Circular 1200, "Estimated Use of Water in the United States in 1995." For more information on methodology and procedures, see the *National Handbook of Recommended Methods for Water Data Acquisition* found on the USGS Web site at <http://water.usgs.gov/pubs/chapter11/>.

Water use, in the broadest sense, pertains to the interaction of human activity with and their influence on the hydrologic cycle and includes elements such as self-supplied withdrawal, public supply delivery, consumptive use, wastewater release, reclaimed wastewater, return flow, and instream use. In a restrictive sense, water use refers to water that is actually used for a specific purpose, such as for domestic use, irrigation, or industrial processing. The quantity of water use for a specific category is determined by combining self-supplied withdrawals and public water-supply deliveries. **Withdrawals** include water removed from the ground or diverted from a surface-water source for use. **Ground water withdrawals** cover generally all subsurface water as distinct from surface water; specifically, that part of the subsurface water in the saturated zone (a zone in which all voids are filled with water) where the water is under pressure greater than atmospheric.

Data are presented for irrigation, public supply, and industrial water withdrawals. Other water-use categories available from USGS include domestic, commercial, livestock, mining, thermoelectric power, hydroelectric power, and wastewater treatment. **Irrigation water use** covers the artificial application of water on lands to assist in the growing of crops and pastures or to maintain vegetative growth in recreational lands such as parks and golf courses. **Public supply use** covers water withdrawn by public and private water suppliers and delivered to users. Public suppliers provide water for a variety of uses, such as domestic, commercial, thermoelectric power, industrial, and public water use. **Industrial water use** covers water used for industrial purposes such as fabrication, processing, washing, and cooling and includes such industries as steel, chemical and allied products, paper and allied products, mining, and petroleum refining. The water may be obtained from a public supply or may be self supplied. **Consumptive use** represents that part of water withdrawn that is evaporated, transpired, incorporated into products or crops, consumed by humans or livestock, or otherwise removed from the immediate water environment. Also referred to as water consumed.

Table A/B-10. Farm Population, Farm Earnings and Agriculture

Farm population, 1990—Farm earnings, 1998 and 1997—Agriculture, 1997: farms, number and percent by selected acreage; land in farms, total and cropland; value of farm products sold, total and percent from selected product.

Source: **Farm population**—U.S. Census Bureau, *1990 Census of Population and Housing, Summary Tape File (STF) 3C* on CD-ROM (related Internet site <http://homer.ssd.census.gov/cdrom/lookup>).

The data on rural farm population were obtained from a sample of the population as part of the census of population and housing, conducted by the Census Bureau. For more information on the census, see General Notes. **Farm population** covers all persons in households living in farm residence as of April 1. An occupied one-family house or mobile home is classified as a farm residence if: (1) the housing unit is located on a property of 1 acre or more, and (2) at least $1,000 worth of agricultural products were sold from the property (or yard in the case of a tenants household) in 1989. Group quarters and housing units that are in multiunit buildings or vacant are not included as farm residences.

Source: **Farm earnings**—U.S. Bureau of Economic Analysis, *Regional Economic Information System (REIS) 1969-1998* on CD-ROM (related Internet site <http://www.bea.doc.gov/bea/regional/data.htm>).

Farm earnings include the income of farm workers (wages and salaries and other labor income) and farm proprietors. The estimation of farm proprietors' income starts with the computation of the realized net income of all farms, which is derived as farm gross receipts less production expenses. This measure is then modified to reflect current production through a change-in-inventory adjustment and to exclude the income of corporate farms and salaries paid to corporate officers. Farm proprietors' income includes only the income of sole proprietorships and partnerships. Therefore, an adjustment is made to exclude the net farm income of corporate farms, including the salaries of officers of corporate farms. For more information on earnings and personal income, see descriptive text for Table A/B-8. Personal Income and Earnings.

Source: **Agriculture, 1997**—U.S. Department of Agriculture, National Agricultural Statistics Service (NASS), *1997 Census of Agriculture,* Volume 1, Geographic Area Series, 1A, 1B, and 1C CD-ROM set (related Internet site <http://www.nass.usda.gov/census/>).

The census of agriculture was taken every 10 years from 1840 to 1920 and every 5 years from 1925 to 1974. The law was changed to adjust the data reference years to those ending in "2" and "7," beginning with the 1982 Census of Agriculture. The 1997 census is the nation's 25th census of agriculture and the first one conducted by NASS (previous censuses were conducted by the U.S. Census Bureau).

The current definition of a **farm,** in use since 1974, covers any place from which $1,000 or more of agricultural products were produced and sold, or normally would have been sold, during the census year. Farms were classified into selected size groups according to the total land area in the farm. The land area of a farm is an operating unit concept and includes land owned and operated as well as land rented from others. Land rented to or assigned to a tenant was considered the tenant's farm and not the owners.

The acreage designated as **land in farms** consists primarily of agricultural land used for crops, pasture, or grazing. It also includes woodland and wasteland not actually under cultivation or used for pasture or grazing, provided it was part of the farm operator's total operation. Land in farms is an operating-unit concept and includes land owned and operated, as well as land rented from others. Land used rent free was to be reported as land rented from others. Land rented or assigned to a tenant was considered the tenant's farm and not the owner's. All land in Indian reservations used for growing crops or grazing livestock was to be included as land in farms. With few exceptions, the land in each farm was tabulated as being in the operator's principal county. The principal county was defined as the one where the largest value of agricultural products were raised or produced. It was usually the county containing all or the largest proportion of the land in the farm. For a limited number of midwest and western states, this procedure resulted in the allocation of more land in farms to a county than the total land area of the county.

Cropland consists of land from which crops were harvested or hay was cut; land in orchards, citrus groves, vineyards, nurseries, and greenhouses; cropland used only for pasture or grazing; land in cover crops, legumes, and soil-improvement grasses; land on which all crops failed; land in cultivated summer fallow; and idle cropland.

Value of farm products sold represents the gross market value before taxes and production expenses of all agricultural products sold or removed from the place in 1997 regardless of who received the payment. It includes sales by the operator as well as the value of any shares received by partners, landlords, contractors, or others associated with the operation. In addition, it includes receipts from placing commodities in the Commodity Credit Corporation (CCC) loan program. It does not include payments received for participation in federal farm programs, nor does it include income from farm-related sources such as custom work and other agricultural services, or income from nonfarm sources. Data may include sales from crops produced in earlier years and exclude some crops produced in a given year, but held in storage. The value of agricultural products sold was requested of all operators. If the operator failed to report this information, estimates were made based on the amount of crops harvested, livestock or poultry inventory, or number sold. Extensive estimation was required for operators growing crops or livestock under contract.

Table A/B-11. Wholesale Trade and Retail Trade

Wholesale trade, 1997: establishments, sales, paid employees, annual payroll, and operating expenses—Retail trade, 1997: establishments, sales, paid employees, and annual payroll.

Source: **Wholesale trade, 1997**—U.S. Census Bureau, *1997 Economic Census,* ECON 97 Report Series CD-ROM, CD-EC97-1, Disc 1E, issued February 2001 (related Internet site <http://www.census.gov/epcd/www/97EC42. HTM>).

Wholesale trade data presented are based on the North American Industry Classification System (NAICS) for 1997 and are not entirely comparable with previous data for 1992 and earlier economic censuses (see General Note for the Economic Censuses). The data cover only establishments with payroll. The wholesale trade sector (NAICS code 42) comprises establishments engaged in wholesaling merchandise, generally without transformation, and rendering services incidental to the sale of merchandise. The wholesaling process is an intermediate step in the distribution of merchandise. Wholesalers are organized to sell or arrange the purchase or sale of (a) goods for resale (i.e., goods sold to other wholesalers or retailers), (b) capital or durable nonconsumer goods, and (c) raw and intermediate materials and supplies used in production. Wholesalers sell merchandise to other businesses and normally operate from a warehouse or office. These warehouses and offices are characterized by having little or no display of merchandise. In addition, neither the design nor the location of the premises is intended to solicit walk-in traffic. Wholesalers do not normally use advertising directed to the general public.

Merchant wholesalers represent establishments primarily engaged in buying and selling merchandise on their own account. Included are such types of establishments as wholesale merchants or jobbers, industrial distributors, voluntary group wholesalers, importers, exporters, cash-and-carry wholesalers, retailer cooperative warehouses, terminal and country grain elevators, farm products assemblers, wholesale cooperative associations, and petroleum bulk plants and terminals operated by nonrefining companies.

For definitions of establishments, paid employees, and annual payroll, see descriptive text for Table A/B-9. Manufacturing and Water Use.

Wholesale trade sales figures represent sales of all establishments in business at any time during the year. Sales include merchandise sold for cash or credit at wholesale and retail by establishments primarily engaged in wholesale trade; receipts from rental or leasing of vehicles, equipment, instruments, tools, etc.; receipts for delivery, installation, maintenance, repair, alteration, storage, and other services; and gasoline, liquor, tobacco, and other excise taxes that are paid by the manufacturer and passed on to the wholesaler. Sales figures do not include wholesale sales made by manufacturers, retailers, service establishments, or other businesses whose primary activity is other than wholesale trade. They do include receipts other than from the sale of merchandise at wholesale (e.g., service receipts, retail sales, etc.) by establishments primarily engaged in wholesale trade. Further, sales are net after deductions for refunds and allowances for merchandise returned by customers. Trade-in allowances are not deducted from total sales. Total sales do not include carrying or other credit charges; sales (or other) taxes collected from customers and forwarded to taxing authorities; and nonoperating income from such sources as investments, rental or sale of real estate, etc.

Operating expenses include payroll, employee benefits, interest and rent expenses, payroll taxes, cost of supplies used for operation, depreciation expenses, fund raising expenses, contracted or purchased services, and other expenses charged to operations during 1997. Expenses exclude cost of goods sold, income taxes, and interest for wholesale establishments; outlays for the purchase of real estate; construction and all other capital improvements; funds invested; assessments or dues paid to the parent or other chapters of the same organization; and, for fund raising organizations, funds transferred to charities and other organizations.

Source: **Retail trade, 1997**—U.S. Census Bureau, *1997 Economic Census*, ECON 97 Report Series CD-ROM, CD-EC97-1, Disc 1E, issued February 2001 (related Internet site <http://www.census.gov/epcd/www/97EC44.HTM>).

Retail trade data presented are based on the North American Industry Classification System (NAICS) for 1997 and are not entirely comparable with previous data for 1992 and earlier economic censuses (see General Note for the Economic Censuses). The data cover only establishments with payroll. The retail sector (NAICS codes 44-45) comprises establishments engaged in retailing merchandise, generally without transformation, and rendering services incidental to the sale of merchandise. The retailing process is the final step in the distribution of merchandise; retailers are, therefore, organized to sell merchandise in small quantities to the general public. This sector comprises two main types of retailers: store (operate fixed point-of-sale locations, located and designed to attract a high volume of walk-in customers) and nonstore retailers (establishments of this subsector reach customers and market merchandise with methods, such as the broadcasting of "infomercials," the broadcasting and publishing of direct-response advertising, the publishing of paper and electronic catalogs, door-to-door solicitation, in-home demonstration, selling from portable stalls (street vendors, except food), and distribution through vending machines).

For definitions of establishments, paid employees, and annual payroll, see Table A/B-9. Manufacturing and Water Use.

Retail trade sales include merchandise sold for cash or credit at retail and wholesale by establishments primarily engaged in retail trade; amounts received from customers for layaway purchases; receipts from rental or leasing of vehicles, equipment, instruments, tools, etc.; receipts for delivery, installation, maintenance, repair,

alteration, storage, and other services; the total value of service contracts: and gasoline, liquor, tobacco, and other excise taxes which are paid by the manufacturer or wholesaler and passed on to the retailer. Sales are net after deductions for refunds and allowances for merchandise returned by customers. Trade-in allowances are not deducted from total sales. Total sales do not include carrying or other credit charges; sales (or other) taxes collected from customers and forwarded to taxing authorities; commissions from vending machine operators; and nonoperating income from such sources as investments, rental or sale of real estate, etc. Sales figures represent the sales of all establishments in business at any time during the year.

Table A/B-12. Accommodation and Foodservices, Banking, and Federal Funds

Accomodation and foodservices, 1997: establishments, sales, paid employees, and annual payroll—Banking, 1999: offices and deposits—Federal funds and grants, 1999: total, percent change 1990-1999, and per capita, total and by selected type.

Sources: **Accommodation and foodservices, 1997**—U.S. Census Bureau, *1997 Economic Census*, ECON 97 Report Series CD-ROM, CD-EC97-1, Disc 1E, issued February 2001 (related Internet site <http://www.census.gov/epcd/www/97EC72.HTM>).

Accomodation and foodservices data presented are based on the North American Industry Classification System (NAICS) for 1997. The data cover only establishments with payroll. The accomodation and foodservice sector (NAICS code 72) comprises establishments providing customers with lodging and/or prepared meals, snacks, and beverages for immediate consumption. This sector is comprised of hotels and other lodging places that were formerly classified in the Standard Industrial Classification (SIC) system in Division I, Services, and eating and drinking places and mobile foodservices that were classified in SIC Division G, Retail Trade. This new sector includes both accommodation and food services establishments because the two activities are often combined at the same establishment. Excluded from this sector are civic and social organizations, amusement and recreation parks, theaters, and other recreation or entertainment facilities providing food and beverage services.

For definitions of establishments, paid employees, and annual payroll, see Table A/B-9. Manufacturing and Water Use and for sales, see Table A/B-11. Wholesale and Retail Trade. **Sales** in the foodservices sector cover the industries in the Food Services and Drinking Places subsector that prepare meals, snacks, and beverages to customer order for immediate on-premises and off-premises consumption. There is a wide range of establishments in these industries. Some provide food and drink only; while others provide various combinations of seating space, waiter/waitress services, and incidental amenities, such as limited entertainment. The industries in the subsector are grouped based on the type and level of services provided. The industry groups are full-service restaurants; limited-service eating places; special food services, such as food service contractors, caterers, and mobile food services, and drinking places.

Sources: **Banking, 1999**—U.S. Federal Deposit Insurance Corporation (FDIC) and Office of Thrift Supervision (OTS), *1999 Bank and Thrift Branch Office Data Book: Summary of Deposits,* national and six regional data books (related Internet site <http://www2.fdic.gov/sod/>).

The FDIC and OTS collect deposit data on each office of every FDIC-insured bank and saving association as of June 30 of each year in the Summary of Deposits (SOD) survey. The FDIC surveys all FDIC-insured commercial banks, savings banks, and U.S. branches of foreign banks, and the OTS surveys all savings associations. Data presented here exclude U.S. branch offices of foreign banks. For all counties, individual banking offices — not the combined totals of the bank— are the source of the data.

Insured commercial banks include commercial banks insured by the FDIC through either the BIF or SAIF. These institutions are regulated by one of the three federal commercial bank regulators (FDIC, Federal Reserve Board of Office of the Comptroller of the Currency). They submit financial reports to the Federal Reserve (state member banks) or the FDIC (state nonmember banks and national banks). Insured savings institutions include savings institutions insured by either BIF or SAIF that operate under state or federal banking codes applicable to thrift institutions. These institutions are regulated by and submit financial reports to one of two federal regulators (FDIC or Office of Thrift Supervision).

The number of banking offices in any given area includes every location at which deposit business is transacted. Banking **office** is defined to include all offices and facilities that actually hold deposits, but to exclude loan production offices, computer centers, and other nondeposit installations, such as automated teller machines (ATMs). The term "offices" includes both main offices and branches. An institution with four branches operates a total of five offices.

Sources: **Federal funds and grants, 1999**—U.S. Census Bureau, County Aggregate files for each state, <http://www.census.gov/govs/www/cffr99.html> (accessed: August 2000).

Data on federal expenditures and obligations were obtained from a report prepared in accordance with the Consolidated Federal Funds Report (CFFR) Act of 1982 (P.L. 97-326) (1983-1985), amended Act of 1986 (P.L. 99-547) (1986-1994) which specified that the following reporting systems and agencies be used as data sources: Federal Assistance Award Data System (FAADS),

Federal Procurement Data Center (FPDC), Office of Personnel Management (OPM), Department of Defense (DOD), U.S. Postal Service (USPS), Internal Revenue Service (IRS), U.S. Coast Guard (USCG), Public Health Service (PHS), National Oceanic and Atmospheric Administration (NOAA), and Federal Bureau of Investigation (FBI). In addition, several other agencies were requested to provide data, usually for selected programs. For more information on the methodology and sources of data utilized, see the Introduction and Appendix D of the *Consolidated Federal Funds Report for Fiscal Year 1999* found on the Census Bureau Web site at <http://www.census.gov/prod/2000pubs/cffr-99.pdf>.

The CFFR covers federal government expenditures or obligation for direct payments for individuals, procurement, grants, salaries and wages, direct loans, and guaranteed loans and Insurance. The dollar amounts reported under these categories can represent actual expenditures or obligations. The grants and procurement data represent obligated funds, while salaries, wages, and direct payments represent actual expenditures. Data on loan and insurance programs generally represent the contingent liability of the federal government.

Most data covering **direct payments for individuals** were taken from information reported to the Federal Assistance Awards Data System. The two object areas of direct payments for individuals are (1) direct payments for retirement and disability benefits and (2) all other direct payments for individuals.

Data covering **procurement** were provided by the United States Postal Service (USPS) for Postal Service procurement and the Federal Procurement Data Center (FPDC) for procurement actions for all other federal agencies, including the defense department. Amounts provided by the USPS represent actual outlays for contractual commitments while amounts provided by the FPDC represent the value of obligations for contract actions and do not reflect actual federal government expenditures. In general, only current-year contract actions are reported for data provided by the FPDC; however, multiple-year obligations may be reported for contract actions of less than 3 years' duration.

Expenditures reported for **salaries and wages** were obtained from five sources: the Office of Personal Management, Department of Defense, the Postal Service, the Federal Bureau of Investigation, and Department of Transportation. DOD provided information on military payrolls, with separate amounts for active military and inactive military (reserve and National Guard); this excludes amounts for military personnel stationed overseas. Data covering civilian employees of DOD were obtained from OPM. Amounts reported by DOD represent estimates of fiscal year outlays by state and county. Data for uniformed employees of the Coast Guard were obtained from the Department of Transportation. Data for Postal Service employees were provided by the USPS and were based upon place of employment (postal facility). Amounts represent actual outlays during the fiscal year with the national total distributed among the states and counties on an estimated basis. Data on salaries and wages for most other federal government employees were obtained from OPM. National totals represent actual expenditures during the fiscal year; the geographic distribution of these amounts by state and county was estimated based upon place of employment. Salaries and wages for employees of the FBI were obtained separately from that agency. No data are provided for employees of the Central Intelligence, Defense Intelligence, and National Security Agencies.

The principal source of **grants** data was the information submitted to the FAADS. The Census Bureau is the Executive Agent for the OMB and is responsible for the operation of the FAADS reporting system. The FAADS data represent the federal obligation incurred at the time the grant is awarded. The amounts reported do not represent actual expenditures since obligations in one time period may not result in outlays during the same time period. Moreover, initial amounts obligated may be adjusted at a later date, either through enhancements or deobligations. The data were derived by summing the quarterly reports that covered financial assistance awarded between October 1, and September 30. All grant awards were reported by state, county, and city of the initial recipient. For many grants, this recipient is the state government even though the grant monies are subsequently distributed to county, municipal, or township governments. These "pass-through" grants generally appear in the CFFR at the state capital city (and in the associated county). No attempt is made in the CFFR to assign the dollar amounts for these pass-through programs to locations other than the state capital.

Table A/B-13. Government Programs, Employment, and Finances

Social Security Program beneficiaries, 1999: total (number, percent change 1990-1999, rate) and retired workers—Supplemental Security Income Program recipients, 1999—Government employment, 1998: Federal (civilian and military) and state and local—Local government employment, 1997—Local government finances, 1996-1997: general revenue, taxes (total, per capita, percent property), direct general expenditure.

Sources: **Social Security Program, 1999**—U.S. Social Security Administration, *OASDI Beneficiaries by State and County - December 1999*, <http://www.ssa.gov/statistics/oasdi_sc/1999/oasdi_sc99.pdf> (accessed: 7 March 2001) for 1999; for 1990, annual publication of same title.

The Old-age, Survivors, and Disability Insurance Program (OASDI) provides monthly benefits for retired and disabled insured workers and their dependents and to survivors of insured workers. To be eligible for benefits, a worker must have had a specified period of employment in which OASDI taxes were paid. A worker becomes eligible for full retirement benefits at age 65, although reduced benefits may be obtained up to 3 years earlier; the worker's spouse is under the same limitations. Survivor benefits are payable to dependents of deceased insured workers. Disability benefits are payable to an insured worker under age 65 with a prolonged disability and to that person's dependents on the same basis as dependents of a retired worker. Also, disability benefits are payable at age 50 to the disabled widow or widower of a deceased worker who was fully insured at the time of death. A lump-sum benefit is generally payable on the death of an insured worker to a spouse or minor children.

The data were derived from the Master Beneficiary Record (MBR), the principal administrative file of social security beneficiaries. Data for total recipients and retired workers include persons with special age-72 benefits. Special age-72 benefit represents the monthly benefit payable to men who attained age 72 before 1972 and for women who attained age 72 before 1970 and who do not have sufficient quarters to qualify for a retired-worker benefit under either the fully or the transitionally insured status provision.

Sources: **Supplemental Security Income Program, 1999**—U.S. Social Security Administration, *SSI Recipients by State and County - December 1999*, <http://www.ssa.gov/statistics/ssistcty/1999/ssistcty.pdf> (accessed: November 2000). December 2000 data now available at <http://www.ssa.gov/statistics/ssi_st_cty/2000/index.html>.

The Supplemental Security Income (SSI) program provides cash payments in accordance with nationwide eligibility requirements to persons with limited income and resources who are aged, blind, or disabled. Under the SSI program, each person living in his or her own household is provided a cash payment from the federal government that is sufficient, when added to the person's countable income (the total gross money income of an individual less certain exclusions), to bring the total monthly income up to a specified level (the federal benefit rate). If the individual or couple is living in another household, the guaranteed level is reduced by one-third.

An aged person is defined as an individual who is 65 years old or over. A blind person is anyone with vision of 20/200 or less with the use of correcting lens in the better eye or with tunnel vision of 20 degrees or less. The disabled classification refers to any person unable to engage in any substantial gainful activity by reason of any medically determinable physical or mental impairment expected to result in death or that has lasted or can be expected to last for a continuous period of at least 12 months. For a child under 18 years, eligibility is based on disability or severity comparable with that of an adult, since the criterion of "substantial gainful activity" is inapplicable for children.

Sources: **Government employment, 1998**—U.S. Bureau of Economic Analysis (BEA), "Regional Economic Information System (REIS) 1969-1998" on CD-ROM (related Internet site <http://www.bea.doc.gov/bea/regional/data.htm>).

Government employment estimates are a companion series to the personal income estimates (see text, Table A/B88. Personal Income and Earnings) from BEA. The estimates are constructed primarily from the Bureau of Labor Statistics ES-202 program and the Unemployment Compensation for federal employees program. The employment estimates are the average of 12 monthly observations of a number of full-time and part-time employees. BEA adjusts data from these programs based on information from other sources, such as the Department of Defense, Department of Education, and Census Bureau. Government includes the executive, legislative, judicial, administrative, and regulatory activities of federal, state, and local governments.

Sources: **Local government employment, 1997**—U.S. Census Bureau, *1997 Census of Governments, Compendium of Public Employment,* <http://www.census.gov/govs/apes/97coar2.dat> (accessed: 14 January 2000). For more information, see related Internet site <http://www.census. gov/govs/www/apes/oc.html>.

A census of governments is taken at 5-year intervals as required by law under Title 13, United States Code, Section 161. This 1997 census, similar to those taken since 1957, covers three major subject fields—government organization, public employment, and government finances.

The concept of local governments as defined by the Census Bureau covers three general-purpose governments (county, municipal, and township) and two limited-purpose governments (school district and special district). For information on the history, methodology, and concepts for the census of governments, see the *Governments Finance and Employment Classification Manual* found at <http://www.census.gov/govs/www/ class.html>.

The term "full-time equivalent employment" refers to a computed statistic representing the number of full-time employees that could have been employed if the reported number of hours worked by part-time employees had been worked by full-time employees. This statistic is calculated separately for each function of a government by dividing the "part-time hours paid" by the standard number of hours for full-time employees in the particular government and then adding the resulting quotient to the number of full-time employees.

Source: **Local government finances, 1997**—U.S. Census Bureau, *1997 Census of Governments, Compendium of Government Finances,* <http://www.census.gov/prod/gc97/gc974-5.pdf> (accessed: 16 February 2001).

For a brief discussion of the census of governments, see descriptive text under Local government employment.

General revenue covers all government revenue except liquor stores revenue, insurance trust revenue, and utility revenue. **Taxes** are compulsory contributions exacted by a government for public purposes except employee and employer assessments for retirement and social insurance purposes, which are classified as insurance trust revenue. All tax revenue is classified as general revenue and comprises amounts received (including interest and penalties but excluding protested amounts and refunds) from all taxes imposed by a government. Local government tax revenue excludes any amounts from shares of state imposed and collected taxes, which are classified as intergovernmental revenue. Property taxes are taxes conditioned on ownership of property and measured by its value. This category includes general property taxes related to property as a whole, real and personal, tangible or intangible, whether taxed at a single rate or at classified rates, and taxes on selected types of property, such as motor vehicles or on certain or all intangibles. **Direct expenditure** include payments to employees, suppliers, contractors, beneficiaries, and other final recipients of government payment i.e., all expenditure other than intergovernmental expenditure while **general expenditure** cover all government expenditure other than the specifically enumerated kinds of expenditure classified as utility expenditure, liquor stores expenditure, and employee-retirement or other insurance trust expenditure.

TABLE C—CITIES

Table C comprises seven individual tables with 103 items of data. These tables present data for 1,070 cities with populations of 25,000 or more as of April 1, 1990. The stub for Table C-1 presents a "state and place code" comprised of the Federal Information Processing Standard (FIPS) two-digit state codes and five-digit place code. For a discussion of the codes, see Appendix B, Geographic Information.

Table C-1. Area and Population

Land area, 2000—Population, 2000: number, rank, per square mile; 1990: number and rank; 1980: number; net change: 1990-2000, 1980-1990; percent change: 1990-2000, 1980-1990; Hispanic or Latino origin, 2000: number and percent.

Source: **Land area**—U.S. Census Bureau, unpublished data file from Geography Division based on TIGER database.

Source: **2000 Population**—U.S. Census Bureau, *Census of Population and Housing, Census 2000 Redistricting Data (Public Law 94-171) Summary Files* (related Internet site <http://www.census.gov/dmd/www/2kresult.html >).

These decennial numbers are from the short-form questionnaires that were asked of all people and housing units and are often referred to as 100-percent questions because they are asked of the entire population. For more information on the decennial census, see General Notes. For information regarding these concepts, see Table A/B-1.

Rank numbers are assigned on the basis of population size, with each city area placed in descending order, largest to smallest. Where ties occur—two or more areas with identical populations—the same rank is assigned to each of the tied county areas. In such cases, the following rank number(s) is omitted so that the lowest rank is usually equal to the number of city areas ranked.

Source: **1990 Population**—U.S. Census Bureau, "SU-99-7 Population Estimates for Places (Sorted Alphabetically Within State): Annual Time Series, July 1, 1999 (includes April 1, 1990, Population Estimates Base)," release date: 20 October 2000 <http://www.census. gov/population/estimates/metro-city/placebyst/ SC99T7_US.txt>.

Source: **1980 Population**—U.S. Census Bureau, *1990 Census of Population and Housing, Population and Housing Unit Counts*, Series CPH-2-1 through CPH-2-52.

Table C-2. Population by Age, Sex, and Race

Age, 2000: percent by selected age groups and median age—Males per 100 females, 2000—Race, 2000: White, Black or African American, American Indian and Alaska Native, Asian, Native Hawaiian and Other Pacific Islander, Some other race, Two or more races.

Source: **Population Characteristics, 2000**—U.S. Census Bureau, *2000 Census of Population and Housing,* "Census 2000 Profiles of General Demographic Characteristics" data files, published May 2001, (related Internet site at <http://www.census.gov/mp/www/pub/2000cen/ mscen01.html>).

These decennial age, sex, and race numbers are from the short-form questionnaires that were asked of all people and housing units and are often referred to as 100-percent questions because they are asked of the entire population. For more information on the decennial census, see General Notes. For information regarding these concepts, see Table A/B-2.

Table C-3. Group Quarters Population and Households

Group quarters population, 2000: total and institutionalized—Households, 2000: total, percent change 1990-2000, persons per household; percent one-person; family households, total and by type and presence of children; nonfamily households.

Source: **Group quarters population, 2000**—U.S. Census Bureau, *2000 Census of Population and Housing,* "Census 2000 Profiles of General Demographic Characteristics" data files, published May 2001 (related Internet site at <http://www.census.gov/mp/www/pub/2000cen/ mscen01.html>).

Source: **Households, 2000**—U.S. Census Bureau, *2000 Census of Population and Housing,* "Census 2000 Profiles of General Demographic Characteristics" data files, published May 2001 (related Internet site at <http://www. census.gov/mp/www/pub/2000cen/mscen01.html>); **Households, 1990**—U.S. Census Bureau, *1990 Census of Population and Housing, Summary Tape File (STF) 1C* on CD-ROM (related Internet site at <http://homer.ssd. census.gov/cdrom/lookup>).

These decennial group quarters and household numbers are from the short-form questionnaires that were asked of all people and housing units and are often referred to as 100-percent questions because they are asked of the entire population. For more information on the decennial census, see General Notes. For information regarding group quarters and households, see Table A/B-3.

Table C-4. Housing, Crime, and Labor Force

Housing, 2000: total units, percent change 1990-2000, occupied units, percent owner-occupied— Serious crimes known to police, 1999: number (total, violent, property) and rate; 1998: number and rate—Civilian labor force, 2000: total (number and percent change 1999-2000); unemployment (number and rate).

Source: **Housing, 2000**—U.S. Census Bureau, *2000 Census of Population and Housing,* "Census 2000 Profiles of General Demographic Characteristics" data files, published May 2001 (related Internet site <http://www. census.gov/mp/www/pub/2000cen/mscen01.html>).

These decennial housing numbers are from the short-form questionnaires that were asked of all people and housing units and are often referred to as 100-percent questions because they are asked of the entire population. For more information on the decennial census, see General Notes. For information regarding housing, see Table A/B-6.

Source: **Serious crimes known to the police**—U.S. Federal Bureau of Investigation, *Crime in the United States,* annual. See also <http://www.fbi.gov/ucr/ Cius_99/99crime/99c2_01.pdf> (accessed: 20 October 2000) and <http://www.fbi.gov/ucr/Cius_98/98crime/ 98cius05.pdf> (accessed: 9 December 1999).

For information regarding housing and crime, see Table A/B-6.

Source: **Civilian labor force**—U.S. Bureau of Labor Statistics (BLS), Local Area Unemployment Statistics, 2000 data published: 2 May 2001; 1999 data published: 30 May 2001; <ftp://ftp.bls.gov/pub/time.series/la/> (related Internet site: <http://www.bls.gov/lauhome. htm>).

For information regarding civilian labor force, see Table A/B-7.

Table C-5. Manufacturing and Wholesale Trade

Manufacturing, 1997: establishments, all employees, production workers, value added by manufacture, and value of shipments—Wholesale trade,

1997: establishments, sales, paid employees, annual payroll, and operating expenses.

Source: **Manufacturing, 1997**—U.S. Census Bureau, *1997 Economic Census - Manufacturing,* generated by Statistical Compendia Branch, using American Factfinder at <http://www.census.gov/> (07 June 2000) (related Internet site <http://www.census.gov/epcd/www/ 97EC31.HTM>).

For information on the economic censuses, see General Notes. For information regarding manufacturing, see Table A/B-9.

Source: **Wholesale trade, 1997**—U.S. Census Bureau, *1997 Economic Census,* ECON 97 Report Series CD-ROM, CD-EC97-1, Disc 1E, issued February 2001 (related Internet site <http://www.census.gov/epcd/www97EC42. HTM>).

For information on the economic censuses, see General Notes. For information regarding wholesale trade, see Table A/B-11.

Table C-6. Retail Trade and Accommodation and Foodservices

Retail trade, 1997: establishments, sales, paid employees, and annual payroll—Accomodation and foodservices, 1997: establishments, sales, paid employees and annual payroll.

Source: **Retail trade, 1997**—U.S. Census Bureau, *1997 Economic Census,* ECON 97 Report Series CD-ROM, CD-EC97-1, Disc 1E, issued February 2001 (related Internet site <http://www.census.gov/epcd/www/ 97EC44.HTM>).

For information on the economic censuses, see General Notes. For information regarding retail trade, see Table A/B-11.

Sources: **Accommodation and foodservices, 1997**—U.S. Census Bureau, *1997 Economic Census,* ECON 97 Report Series CD-ROM, CD-EC97-1, Disc 1E, issued February 2001 (related Internet site <http://www.census. gov/epcd/www/97EC72.HTM>).

For information on the economic censuses, see General Notes. For information regarding accommodation and foodservices, see Table A/B-12.

Table C-7. City Government Finances and Climate

City government finances, 1996-1997: general revenue (total, per capita and taxes), general expenditure (total and per capita)—Climate, 1961-1990: average daily temperature (January and July), annual precipitation, heating and cooling degree days.

Source: **City government finances, 1997**—U.S. Census Bureau, *1997 Census of Governments, Finances of Municipal and Township Governments,* Volume 4, <http://www.census.gov/prod/gc97/gc974-5.pdf> (accessed: 16 February 2001).

For a brief discussion of the census of governments, see descriptive text for Table A/B-13.

Police protection expenditures are for preservation of law and order and traffic safety and includes police patrols and communications, crime prevention activities, detention and custody of persons awaiting trail, traffic, safety, and vehicular inspection. **Sewerage and solid waste management** expenditures are for provision of sanitary and storm sewers and sewage disposal facilities and services, and payment to other governments for such purposes and for street cleaning, solid wate collection and disposal, and provision of sanitary landfills. **Highway** expenditures are for construction, maintenance, and operation of highways, streets, and related structures, including toll highways, bridges, tunnels, ferries, street lighting, and snow and ice removal.

Source: **Climate,** National Oceanic and Atmospheric Administration, National Climatic Data Center (NCDC), *Climatography of the United States,* Number 81 (January 1992).

All climate data presented are average values for the 30-year period, 1961-1990. The average value of a meteorological element over 30 years is defined as a climatological normal. The normal climate helps in describing the climate and is used as a base to which current conditions can be compared. Every 10 years, NCDC computes new 30-year climate normals for selected temperature and precipitation elements for a large number of U.S. climate and weather stations. Climate normals are a useful way to describe the average weather of a location. Several statistical measures are computed as part of the normals, including measures of central tendency (such as the mean or median), of dispersion or how spread out the values are (such as the standard deviation or inter-quartile range), and of frequency or probability of occurrence. Over the decades the term "normal," to the lay person, has come to be most closely associated with the mean or average. In this context, a "climatic normal" is simply the arithmetic average of the values over a 30-year period (generally, three consecutive decades). A person unfamiliar with climate and climate normals may perceive the normal to be the climate that one should expect to happen. It's important to note that the normal may, or may not, be what one would "expect" to happen. This is especially true with precipitation in dry climates, such as the desert southwestern region of the United States, and with temperature at continental locations which frequently experience large swings from cold air masses to warm air masses.

Mean temperatures for January and July were determined by adding the average daily maximum temperatures and average daily minimum temperatures and dividing by 2. Temperature limits represent average daily minimum for January and average daily maximum for July.

Annual precipitation values are the average annual water equivalent of all precipitation for the 30-year period. The total include accumulated rain, drizzle, and the water equivalent of all forms of freezing and frozen precipitation such as hail, snow, sleet, and freezing rain.

Heating and cooling days are used as relative measures of the energy required for heating and cooling buildings. One **heating-degree day** is accumulated for each whole degree that the mean daily temperature is below 65 F (i.e., a mean daily temperature of 62 F will produce three heating-degree days). **Cooling-degree days** are accumulated in similar fashion for deviations of the mean daily temperature above 65 F.

Please note that the climate normals for the 30-year period, 1971-2000, were released by NCDC in late August 2001, too late to be processed and included in this publication. For more information, see NCDC Internet site <http://wf.ncdc.noaa.gov/oa/climate/normals/usnormals.html>.

TABLE D—PLACES/MCDs

These two tables present the same 11 data items for all places (incorporated places and census designated places) and MCDs (minor civil divisions) of 2,500 persons or more as of April 1, 2000. There are 8,888 places and 2,759 MCDs covered in the two tables. The stub for both tables includes a column with the "state and place codes." The

code is a seven-digit code comprised of a Federal Information Processing Standard (FIPS) two-digit state code and five-digit place code. For a discussion of the codes, see Appendix B, Geographic Information.

Table D-1. Places and D-2. MCDs—Area and Population

Land area, 2000—Population, 2000: total, by race (White, Black or African American, American Indian and Alaska Native, Asian, Native Hawaiian and Other Pacific Islander, Some other race, Two or more races); Hispanic or Latino (of any race); 18 years and over.

Source: **2000 Population**—U.S. Census Bureau, *2000 Census of Population and Housing, Race and Hispanic or Latino Summary File* on CD-ROM, PL00-3, issued April 2001 (related Internet site <http://www.census.gov/clo/www/redistricting.html>).

These decennial numbers are from the short-form questionnaires that were asked of all people and housing units and are often referred to as 100-percent questions because they are asked of the entire population. For more information on the decennial census, see General Notes. For information regarding these concepts, see Table A/B-1 and Table A/B-2.

Geographic Information

Appendix B

You may visit us on the Web at
http://www.census.gov/statab/www/ccdb.html

Appendix B

Appendix B.
Geographic Information

Table A—States

States are the primary governmental divisions of the United States. The District of Columbia is treated as a statistical equivalent of a state for census purposes.

A map showing the United States with census regions and divisions and their constituent states appears on the inside front cover.

Each state and the District of Columbia is assigned a two-digit Federal Information Processing Standards (FIPS) code. The FIPS state code is a sequential numbering, with some gaps, of the alphabetic arrangement of the states and the District of Columbia: Alabama (01) to Wyoming (56). These codes are presented in the first column of table A-1.

FIPS codes are issued by the National Institute of Standards and Technology for a variety of geographical entities, including states, counties, metropolitan areas, and places. The objective of the FIPS codes is to improve the transferability of the data resources within the federal government and to avoid unnecessary duplication and incompatibilities in the collection, processing, and dissemination of data. FIPS code documentation is available from the National Technical Information Service, Springfield, VA, 22161 (703-487-4650). State FIPS codes can be viewed at Internet site <http://www.itl.nist.gov/fipspubs/fip5-2.htm>.

Table B—Counties

The primary legal divisions of most states are termed "counties." In Louisiana, these divisions are known as parishes. In Alaska, which has no counties, the statistically equivalent entities are the "organized boroughs" and "census areas". Census areas are delineated cooperatively for statistical purposes by the state of Alaska and the U.S. Census Bureau.

In four states (Maryland, Missouri, Nevada, and Virginia) there are one or more incorporated places that are independent of any county organization and thus constitute primary divisions of their states; these incorporated places are known as "independent cities" and are treated as equivalent to counties for statistical purposes. Similarly, the portion of Yellowstone National Park in Montana is treated as a county equivalent. The District of Columbia has no primary divisions; the entire area is considered equivalent to a county for statistical purposes.

The 136 areas classified as county equivalents as of January 1, 1992, include 15 organized boroughs and 11 census areas in Alaska; the District of Columbia; the

64 parishes in Louisiana; Baltimore city, Maryland; St Louis city, Missouri; the part of Yellowstone National Park in Montana; Carson City, Nevada; and 41 independent cities in Virginia. Maps for each state showing counties and equivalent areas can be found in Appendix C.

Each county and statistically equivalent entity is assigned a three-digit FIPS code that is unique within state. These codes are assigned in alphabetical order of county or county except for the independent cities, which are assigned codes higher than and following the listing of counties. The combination of a FIPS two-digit state code followed by a FIPS three-digit county code provides a unique geographic identifier for each county and equivalent area. These codes are presented in the second column of table B-1. County codes can be viewed at Internet site <http://www.itl.nist.gov/fipspubs/fip6-4.htm>.

Metropolitan areas. The first column of table B-1 presents the four-digit FIPS code for the metropolitan area (MA) In which the county is located. The codes represent metropolitan areas defined by the Office of Management and Budget as of June 30, 1999. Because New England MSA and CMSA are defined in terms of cities and towns, not counties, the New England county metropolitan area (NECMA) code is shown for counties in these states. For most states, the metropolitan statistical area (MSA) or consolidated metropolitan statistical area (CMSA) code is shown if the county is in a MA. If a county is not in a MA, three dots are shown.

A complete listing of these MAs with their component counties and 2000 population can be found at the end of this appendix in table B-3. For a discussion of metropolitan area concepts, see Internet site <http://www.census.gov/population/www/estimates/ metroarea.html>. Other data for these areas are not presented in this volume but are published in another *Statistical Abstract* supplement, *State and Metropolitan Area Data Book.* For a complete description, see the inside back cover.

County changes. Counties and equivalent areas shown in tables B-1 through B-13 of this publication are the 3,142 counties defined as of January 1, 1992. Between then and Census 2000, one state has had a county name change and four states have had changes in their county boundaries. These changes are summarized below.

In Alaska: effective September 22, 1992, the Yakutat Borough was established; this new borough was created from part of the Skagway-Yakutat-Angoon Census Area

(CA) with the remaining area being renamed the Skagway-Hoonah-Angoon CA. Effective January 1, 1994, Juneau Borough gained territory from Skagway-Hoonah-Angoon Census Area.

In Florida: effective November 13, 1997, Dade County changed its name from Dade to Miami-Dade County; the FIPS code changed from 025 to 086.

In Maryland: effective July 1, 1997, Montgomery County expanded to include all of the former Prince George's County part of Takoma Park city and Prince George's County decreased as a result of the county boundary shift excluding Takoma Park city.

In Montana: effective November 7, 1997, Gallatin County was expanded by addition of territory from the former county equivalent of Yellowsone National Park. Park County was also expanded by addition of territory from the former county equivalent of Yellowsone National Park. This change eliminates Yellowstone National Park as a county equivalent.

In Virginia: effective July 1, 1993, the independent city of Bedford gained area annexed from Bedford County; the independent city of Galax gained area annexed from Carroll County, and the independent city of Fairfax gained area annexed from Fairfax County. Effective June 30, 1995, the independent city of South Boston no longer exists; it became a dependent town within Halifax County. Effective December 31, 1995, the independent city of Franklin gained area annexed from Southampton County.

Table C—Cities

As used in this volume, the term "city" refers to incorporated places with a 1990 population of 25,000 or more. Incorporated places presented in this table are those reported to the U.S. Census Bureau as legally in existence on January 1, 1990, under the laws of their respective states as cities, boroughs, towns, and villages, with the following exceptions: the boroughs in Alaska and New York and the towns in the New England states, New York, and Wisconsin. The boroughs in Alaska are county equivalents and are shown in table B. The five boroughs in New York are presented in table C following New York city. The towns in the states noted above are treated as minor civil divisions for census purposes; data for these areas are presented in table D-2.

The areas for which data are included in table C are the 1,070 incorporated places with a 1990 population of 25,000 or more and the 8 census designated places (CDPs) in Hawaii with a 1990 population of 25,000 or more, as well as the 50 states, the District of Columbia, and the 5 New York city boroughs. CDPs are used for Hawaii as it is the only state with no incorporated places recognized by the U.S. Census Bureau. With the exception of Hilo which is in Hawaii County, the eight CDPs shown for Hawaii are all located in Honolulu County. For a discussion of CDPs, see the section on table D-1.

In table C, the two-digit FIPS state code and five-digit FIPS place codes is presented in the first column of table C-1. Each place is assigned a five-digit FIPS place code that is unique within the state based on alphabetical order within the state. Together with the two-digit FIPS state code, this code provides a unique identifier for each place in the country. To view place codes see Internet site <http:www.itl.nist.gov/fipspubs/55new/nav-top-fr.htm>.

Consolidated cities. For the 1990 census, the Census Bureau recognized six entities that had consolidated their city governmental function with a county or minor civil division (MCD) but continue to contain governmentally active incorporated places within and as part of those consolidated cities. These areas with their components and 1990 population are listed below in table B-1. The data for cities shown in tables C-1 through C-7 of this publication cover only the portion of the consolidated city not in any other place, e.g., "Indianapolis city (remainder)."

Table B-1. Consolidated Cities and Components: 1990

Area name	1990 population
Milford, CT	49,938
(coextensive with Milford town)	
Woodmont borough	1,770
Milford city (remainder)	48,168
Jacksonville, FL	672,971
(coextensive with Duval County)	
Atlantic Beach city	11,636
Baldwin town	1,450
Jacksonville Beach city	17,839
Neptune Beach city	6,816
Jacksonville city (remainder)	635,230
Columbus, GA	179,278
(coextensive with Muscogee County)	
Bibb City town	597
Columbus city (remainder)	178,681
Indianapolis, IN	741,952
(not coextensive with Marion County due to exclusion of following four places:	
Beech Grove city 13,383	
Lawrence city 26,763	
Southport city 1,969	
Speedway town 13,092)	
Castleton town	37
Clermont town	1,678
Crows Nest town	114
Cumberland town (part)	2,933
Homecroft town	758
Meridian Hills town	1,728
North Crows Nest town	57
Rocky Ripple town	751
Spring Hill town	112
Warren Park town	1,763
Williams Creek town	425
Wynnedale town	269
Indianapolis city (remainder)	731,327
Butte-Silver Bow, MT	33,941
(coextensive with Silver Bow County)	
Walkerville city	605
Butte-Silver Bow (remainder)	33,336
Nashville-Davidson, TN	510,784
(coextensive with Davidson County)	
Belle Meade city	2,839
Berry Hill city	802
Forest Hills city	4,231
Goodlettsville city (part)	8,177
Lakewood city	2,009
Oak Hill city	4,301
Ridgetop town (part)	51
Nashville-Davidson (remainder)	488,374

Note: For Census 2000, Jacksonville is no longer a consolidated city. The local governments brought to the Census Bureau's attention that legislation in 1978 and 1992 changed the relationship of Jacksonville city to the other incorporated places in Duval County. It should also be noted that the land area/population of Jacksonville city (remainder) in the 1990 census was 758.7 square miles/635,230 persons and that the land area of Jacksonville city for Census 2000 is 757.7 square miles/735,617 persons. Data published in tables C-1 through C-7 of this publication from Census 2000 are for Jacksonville city, not Jacksonville city (remainder) as designated in the table stub.

Table D-1. Places

Places, for the reporting of decennial census data, include census designated places, consolidated cities, and incorporated places. Places may extend across county boundaries but never across state boundaries. For this publication, places include incorporated places (discussed under table C—Cities) and census designated places (discussed below).

Census designated places (CDPs) are delineated for the decennial census as the statistical counterparts of incorporated places. CDPs are delineated to provide census data for settled concentrations of population that are identifiable by name, but are not legally incorporated under the laws of the state in which they are located. These boundaries are defined in cooperation with local or tribal officials. These boundaries, which usually coincide with visible features or the boundary of an adjacent incorporated place or other legal entity boundary, have no legal status, nor do these places have officials elected to serve traditional municipal functions. CDP boundaries may change with changes in the settlement pattern; a CDP with the same name as in an earlier census does not necessarily have the same boundaries.

Data for table D-1 are presented for the 8,888 incorporated places and CDPs with a April 1, 2000 population of 2,500 or more persons that were reported to the U.S. Census Bureau as legally in existence on January 1, 2000.

Each place is assigned a five-digit FIPS code, based on the alphabetical order of the place name within each state. If place names are duplicated within a state and they represent distinctly different areas, a separate code is assigned to each place name alphabetically by primary county in which each place is located, or if both places are in the same county, alphabetically by their legal description (for example, "city" before "village"). The two-digit FIPS state code and five-digit FIPS place code is presented in the first column of the table.

Also found in table D-1 is the name of the county or counties in which the place is located. This information is shown in the column following the area name. If a place crosses county boundaries, all counties in which the place is located are listed alphabetically.

Consolidated cities. For the 2000 census, the Census Bureau recognized seven entities that have consolidated their city governmental function with a county or minor civil division (MCD) but continue to contain governmentally active incorporated places within and as part of those consolidated cities. These areas with their components and 2000 population are listed below in table B-2. The data for places shown in table D-1 of this publication cover only the portion of the consolidated city not in any other place, e.g., "Nashville-Davidson (balance)."

Table B-2. Consolidated Cities and Components: 2000

Area name	2000 population
Milford, CT	52,305
(coextensive with Milford town)	
Milford city (balance)	50,594
Woodmont borough	1,711
Athens-Clarke County, GA	101,489
(coextensive with Clarke County)	
Athens-Clarke County (balance)	100,266
Bogart town (part)	118
Winterville city	1,068
Augusta-Richmond County, GA	199,775
(coextensive with Richmond County)	
Augusta-Richmond County (balance)	195,182
Blythe city (part)	713
Hephzibah city	3,880
Columbus city, GA	186,291
(coextensive with Muscogee County)	
Bibb city town	510
Columbus city (balance)	185,781
Indianapolis city, IN	791,926
(not coextensive with Marion County due to exclusion of following four places:	
Beech Grove city 14,880	
Lawrence city 38,915	
Southport city 1,852	
Speedway town 12,881)	
Clermont town	1,477
Crows Nest town	96
Cumberland town (part)	2,824
Homecroft town	751
Indianapolis city (balance)	781,870
Meridian Hills town	1,713
North Crows Nest town	42
Rocky Ripple town	712
Spring Hill town	97
Warren Park town	1,656
Williams Creek town	413
Wynnedale town	275
Butte-Silver Bow, MT	34,606
(coextensive with Silver Bow County)	
Butte-Silver Bow (balance)	33,892
Walkerville city	714
Nashville-Davidson, TN	569,891
(coextensive with Davidson County)	
Belle Meade city	2,943
Berry Hill city	674
Forest Hills city	4,710
Goodlettsville city (part)	9,155
Lakewood city	2,341
Nashville-Davidson (balance)	545,524
Oak Hill city	4,493
Ridgetop city (part)	41

Table D-2. MCDs

Table D-2 presents data for the 2,759 functioning minor civil divisions (MCDs) with a April 1, 2000 population of 2,500 or more in the following 12 states: Connecticut, Maine, Massachusetts, Michigan, Minnesota, New Hampshire, New Jersey, New York, Pennsylvania, Rhode Island, Vermont, and Wisconsin. MCDs in these states serve as general-purpose local governments that generally can perform the same governmental functions as incorporated places. The U.S. Census Bureau presents data for these MCDs in all data products in which it provides data for places. They are variously designated as towns, townships, and boroughs.

In table D-2, the two-digit FIPS state code and five-digit FIPS place code is presented in the first column of the table. Each MCD is assigned a five-digit FIPS code that is unique within state based on the alphabetical order of these areas within the state. MCD codes can be viewed at Internet site <http://www.census.gov/population/www/estimates/mcdchg.html>.

Also found in table D-2 is the name of the county in which the MCD is located. The county name is shown in the column following the area name. MCDs do not cross county boundaries.

[Metropolitan areas (MAs) defined as of June 30, 1999. MSA = metropolitan statistical area; CMSA = consolidated MSA; PMSA = primary MSA; NECMA = New England county MA. Geographic codes shown are Federal Information Processing Standards (FIPS) codes]

Geographic codes			Metropolitan area title and geographic component(s)	2000 population	Geographic codes			Metropolitan area title and geographic component(s)	2000 population
MSA/ CMSA/ NECMA	PMSA	State and county			MSA/ CMSA/ NECMA	PMSA	State and county		
0040			Abilene, TX MSA.........................	126,555	0580			Auburn-Opelika, AL MSA..................	115,092
		48441	Taylor County, TX......................	126,555			01081	Lee County, AL........................	115,092
	0080		Akron, OH PMSA......................	694,960	0600			Augusta-Aiken, GA-SC MSA.............	477,441
			(See Cleveland-Akron, OH CMSA)				13073	Columbia County, GA..................	89,288
0120			Albany, GA MSA......................	120,822			13189	McDuffie County, GA..................	21,231
		13095	Dougherty County, GA.................	96,065			13245	Richmond County, GA.................	199,775
		13177	Lee County, GA......................	24,757			45003	Aiken County, SC....................	142,552
							45037	Edgefield County, SC.................	24,595
0160			Albany-Schenectady-Troy, NY MSA.......	875,583	0640			Austin-San Marcos, TX MSA.............	1,249,763
		36001	Albany County, NY....................	294,565			48021	Bastrop County, TX..................	57,733
		36057	Montgomery County, NY................	49,708			48055	Caldwell County, TX.................	32,194
		36083	Rensselaer County, NY................	152,538			48209	Hays County, TX....................	97,589
		36091	Saratoga County, NY.................	200,635			48453	Travis County, TX..................	812,280
		36093	Schenectady County, NY...............	146,555			48491	Williamson County, TX...............	249,967
		36095	Schoharie County, NY.................	31,582	0680			Bakersfield, CA MSA..................	661,645
0200			Albuquerque, NM MSA.................	712,738			06029	Kern County, CA....................	661,645
		35001	Bernalillo County, NM................	556,678		0720		Baltimore, MD PMSA.................	2,552,994
		35043	Sandoval County, NM.................	89,908				(See Washington-Baltimore, DC-MD-VA-WV CMSA)	
		35061	Valencia County, NM.................	66,152	0730			Bangor, ME MSA....................	90,864
0220			Alexandria, LA MSA..................	126,337			23019	Penobscot County (pt.)...............	87,262
		22079	Rapides Parish, LA..................	126,337			23027	Waldo County (pt.)..................	3,602
0240			Allentown-Bethlehem-Easton, PA MSA....	637,958	0733			Bangor, ME NECMA..................	144,919
		42025	Carbon County, PA..................	58,802			23019	Penobscot County, ME...............	144,919
		42077	Lehigh County, PA..................	312,090	0740			Barnstable-Yarmouth, MA MSA..........	162,582
		42095	Northampton County, PA..............	267,066			25001	Barnstable County (pt.)..............	162,582
0280			Altoona, PA MSA....................	129,144	0743			Barnstable-Yarmouth, MA NECMA........	222,230
		42013	Blair County, PA...................	129,144			25001	Barnstable County, MA...............	222,230
0320			Amarillo, TX MSA...................	217,858	0760			Baton Rouge, LA MSA................	602,894
		48375	Potter County, TX..................	113,546			22005	Ascension Parish, LA...............	76,627
		48381	Randall County, TX..................	104,312			22033	East Baton Rouge Parish, LA..........	412,852
0380			Anchorage, AK MSA.................	260,283			22063	Livingston Parish, LA...............	91,814
		02020	Anchorage Borough, AK..............	260,283			22121	West Baton Rouge Parish, LA..........	21,601
	0440		Ann Arbor, MI PMSA.................	578,736	0840			Beaumont-Port Arthur, TX MSA..........	385,090
			(See Detroit-Ann Arbor-Flint, MI CMSA)				48199	Hardin County, TX..................	48,073
0450			Anniston, AL MSA...................	112,249			48245	Jefferson County, TX................	252,051
		01015	Calhoun County, AL.................	112,249			48361	Orange County, TX.................	84,966
0460			Appleton-Oshkosh-Neenah, WI MSA......	358,365	0860			Bellingham, WA MSA................	166,814
		55015	Calumet County, WI.................	40,631			53073	Whatcom County, WA................	166,814
		55087	Outagamie County, WI...............	160,971	0870			Benton Harbor, MI MSA..............	162,453
		55139	Winnebago County, WI...............	156,763			26021	Berrien County, MI.................	162,453
0480			Asheville, NC MSA..................	225,965		0875		Bergen-Passaic, NJ PMSA.............	1,373,167
		37021	Buncombe County, NC...............	206,330				(See New York-Northern New Jersey-Long Island, NY-NJ-CT-PA CMSA)	
		37115	Madison County, NC................	19,635	0880			Billings, MT MSA...................	129,352
0500			Athens, GA MSA....................	153,444			30111	Yellowstone County, MT..............	129,352
		13059	Clarke County, GA..................	101,489	0920			Biloxi-Gulfport-Pascagoula, MS MSA......	363,988
		13195	Madison County, GA.................	25,730			28045	Hancock County, MS................	42,967
		13219	Oconee County, GA.................	26,225			28047	Harrison County, MS................	189,601
0520			Atlanta, GA MSA...................	4,112,198			28059	Jackson County, MS................	131,420
		13013	Barrow County, GA.................	46,144	0960			Binghamton, NY MSA................	252,320
		13015	Bartow County, GA.................	76,019			36007	Broome County, NY.................	200,536
		13045	Carroll County, GA.................	87,268			36107	Tioga County, NY..................	51,784
		13057	Cherokee County, GA...............	141,903	1000			Birmingham, AL MSA................	921,106
		13063	Clayton County, GA.................	236,517			01009	Blount County, AL.................	51,024
		13067	Cobb County, GA..................	607,751			01073	Jefferson County, AL...............	662,047
		13077	Coweta County, GA.................	89,215			01115	St. Clair County, AL...............	64,742
		13089	DeKalb County, GA.................	665,865			01117	Shelby County, AL.................	143,293
		13097	Douglas County, GA................	92,174	1010			Bismarck, ND MSA..................	94,719
		13113	Fayette County, GA.................	91,263			38015	Burleigh County, ND................	69,416
		13117	Forsyth County, GA.................	98,407			38059	Morton County, ND.................	25,303
		13121	Fulton County, GA.................	816,006	1020			Bloomington, IN MSA................	120,563
		13135	Gwinnett County, GA................	588,448			18105	Monroe County, IN.................	120,563
		13151	Henry County, GA..................	119,341	1040			Bloomington-Normal, IL MSA...........	150,433
		13217	Newton County, GA.................	62,001			17113	McLean County, IL..................	150,433
		13223	Paulding County, GA................	81,678	1080			Boise City, ID MSA.................	432,345
		13227	Pickens County, GA................	22,983			16001	Ada County, ID...................	300,904
		13247	Rockdale County, GA...............	70,111			16027	Canyon County, ID.................	131,441
		13255	Spalding County, GA................	58,417					
		13297	Walton County, GA.................	60,687					
	0560		Atlantic-Cape May, NJ PMSA...........	354,878					
			(See Philadelphia-Wilmington-Atlantic City, PA-NJ-DE-MD CMSA)						

[Metropolitan areas (MAs) defined as of June 30, 1999. MSA = metropolitan statistical area; CMSA = consolidated MSA; PMSA = primary MSA; NECMA = New England county MA. Geographic codes shown are Federal Information Processing Standards (FIPS) codes]

Geographic codes			Metropolitan area title and geographic component(s)	2000 population	Geographic codes			Metropolitan area title and geographic component(s)	2000 population
MSA/ CMSA/ NECMA	PMSA	State and county			MSA/ CMSA/ NECMA	PMSA	State and county		
	1120		**Boston, MA-NH PMSA**	**3,406,829**	1305			**Burlington, VT MSA**	**169,391**
			(See Boston-Worcester-Lawrence, MA-NH-ME-CT CMSA)				50007	Chittenden County (pt.)	138,661
1122	1120		**Boston-Worcester-Lawrence, MA-NH-ME-CT CMSA** .	**5,819,100**			50011	Franklin County (pt.)	27,079
			Boston, MA-NH PMSA	**3,406,829**			50013	Grand Isle County (pt.)	3,651
		25005	Bristol County, MA (pt.)	108,350					
		25009	Essex County, MA (pt.)	458,546	1320			**Canton-Massillon, OH MSA**	**406,934**
		25017	Middlesex County, MA (pt.)	1,171,779			39019	Carroll County, OH	28,836
		25021	Norfolk County, MA (pt.)	645,865			39151	Stark County, OH	378,098
		25023	Plymouth County, MA (pt.)	239,872					
		25025	Suffolk County, MA (pt.)	689,807	1350			**Casper, WY MSA**	**66,533**
		25027	Worcester County, MA (pt.)	83,832			56025	Natrona County, WY	66,533
		33015	Rockingham County, NH (pt.)	8,778					
	1200		**Brockton, MA PMSA**	**255,459**	1360			**Cedar Rapids, IA MSA**	**191,701**
		25005	Bristol County (pt.)	34,038			19113	Linn County, IA	191,701
		25021	Norfolk County (pt.)	4,443					
		25023	Plymouth County (pt.)	216,978	1400			**Champaign-Urbana, IL MSA**	**179,669**
	2600		**Fitchburg-Leominster, MA PMSA**	**142,284**			17019	Champaign County, IL	179,669
		25017	Middlesex County (pt.)	2,845					
		25027	Worcester County (pt.)	139,439	1440			**Charleston-North Charleston, SC MSA** . . .	**549,033**
	4160		**Lawrence, MA-NH PMSA**	**396,230**			45015	Berkeley County, SC	142,651
		25009	Essex County, MA (pt.)	264,873			45019	Charleston County, SC	309,969
		33015	Rockingham County, NH (pt.)	131,357			45035	Dorchester County, SC	96,413
	4560		**Lowell, MA-NH PMSA**	**301,686**					
		25017	Middlesex County, MA (pt.)	290,772	1480			**Charleston, WV MSA**	**251,662**
		33011	Hillsborough County, NH (pt.)	10,914			54039	Kanawha County, WV	200,073
	4760		**Manchester, NH PMSA**	**198,378**			54079	Putnam County, WV	51,589
		33011	Hillsborough County (pt.)	149,985					
		33013	Merrimack County (pt.)	16,564	1520			**Charlotte-Gastonia-Rock Hill, NC-SC MSA** . . .	**1,499,293**
		33015	Rockingham County (pt.)	31,829			37025	Cabarrus County, NC	131,063
	5350		**Nashua, NH PMSA**	**190,949**			37071	Gaston County, NC	190,365
		33011	Hillsborough County (pt.)	190,949			37109	Lincoln County, NC	63,780
	5400		**New Bedford, MA PMSA**	**175,198**			37119	Mecklenburg County, NC	695,454
		25005	Bristol County (pt.)	159,226			37159	Rowan County, NC	130,340
		25023	Plymouth County (pt.)	15,972			37179	Union County, NC	123,677
	6450		**Portsmouth-Rochester, NH-ME PMSA**	**240,698**			45091	York County, SC	164,614
		23031	York County, ME (pt.)	41,375					
		33015	Rockingham County, NH (pt.)	94,376	1540			**Charlottesville, VA MSA**	**159,576**
		33017	Strafford County, NH (pt.)	104,947			51003	Albemarle County, VA	79,236
	9240		**Worcester, MA-CT PMSA**	**511,389**			51065	Fluvanna County, VA	20,047
		09015	Windham County, CT (pt.)	8,878			51079	Greene County, VA	15,244
		25013	Hampden County, MA (pt.)	2,407			51540	Charlottesville city, VA	45,049
		25027	Worcester County, MA (pt.)	500,104					
					1560			**Chattanooga, TN-GA MSA**	**465,161**
1123			**Boston-Worcester-Lawrence-Lowell-Brockton, MA-NH NECMA**	**6,057,826**			13047	Catoosa County, GA	53,282
		25005	Bristol County, MA.	534,678			13083	Dade County, GA	15,154
		25009	Essex County, MA.	723,419			13295	Walker County, GA	61,053
		25017	Middlesex County, MA.	1,465,396			47065	Hamilton County, TN	307,896
		25021	Norfolk County, MA.	650,308			47115	Marion County, TN.	27,776
		25023	Plymouth County, MA.	472,822					
		25025	Suffolk County, MA.	689,807	1580			**Cheyenne, WY MSA**	**81,607**
		25027	Worcester County, MA.	750,963			56021	Laramie County, WY	81,607
		33011	Hillsborough County, NH.	380,841					
		33015	Rockingham County, NH.	277,359		1600		**Chicago, IL PMSA**	**8,272,768**
		33017	Strafford County, NH	112,233				(See Chicago-Cary-Kenosha, IL-IN-WI CMSA)	
	1125		**Boulder-Longmont, CO PMSA**	**291,288**	1602			**Chicago-Gary-Kenosha, IL-IN-WI CMSA**	**9,157,540**
			(See Denver-Boulder-Greeley, CO CMSA)			1600		**Chicago, IL PMSA**	**8,272,768**
							17031	Cook County, IL	5,376,741
	1145		**Brazoria, TX PMSA**	**241,767**			17037	DeKalb County, IL	88,969
			(See Houston-Galveston-Brazoria, TX CMSA)				17043	DuPage County, IL	904,161
							17063	Grundy County, IL	37,535
	1150		**Bremerton, WA PMSA**	**231,969**			17089	Kane County, IL.	404,119
			(See Seattle-Tacoma-Bremerton, WA CMSA)				17093	Kendall County, IL	54,544
							17097	Lake County, IL	644,356
	1160		**Bridgeport, CT PMSA**	**459,479**			17111	McHenry County, IL	260,077
			(See New York-Northern New Jersey-Long Island, NY-NJ-CT-PA CMSA)				17197	Will County, IL.	502,266
						2960		**Gary, IN PMSA**	**631,362**
	1200		**Brockton, MA PMSA**	**255,459**			18089	Lake County, IN.	484,564
			(See Boston-Worcester-Lawrence, MA-NH-ME-CT CMSA)				18127	Porter County, IN	146,798
						3740		**Kankakee, IL PMSA**	**103,833**
1240			**Brownsville-Harlingen-San Benito, TX MSA**	**335,227**			17091	Kankakee County, IL.	103,833
		48061	Cameron County, TX	335,227		3800		**Kenosha, WI PMSA**	**149,577**
							55059	Kenosha County, WI.	149,577
1260			**Bryan-College Station, TX MSA**	**152,415**					
		48041	Brazos County, TX.	152,415	1620			**Chico-Paradise, CA MSA**	**203,171**
							06007	Butte County, CA.	203,171
1280			**Buffalo-Niagara Falls, NY MSA**	**1,170,111**					
		36029	Erie County, NY	950,265	1640			**Cincinnati, OH-KY-IN PMSA**	**1,646,395**
		36063	Niagara County, NY.	219,846				(See Cincinnati-Hamilton, OH-KY-IN CMSA)	
1303			**Burlington, VT NECMA**	**198,889**	1642			**Cincinnati-Hamilton, OH-KY-IN CMSA**	**1,979,202**
		50007	Chittenden County, VT	146,571		1640		**Cincinnati, OH-KY-IN PMSA**	**1,646,395**
		50011	Franklin County, VT	45,417			18029	Dearborn County, IN	46,109
		50013	Grand Isle County, VT	6,901			18115	Ohio County, IN	5,623
							21015	Boone County, KY	85,991
							21037	Campbell County, KY	88,616
							21077	Gallatin County, KY	7,870
							21081	Grant County, KY.	22,384
							21117	Kenton County, KY.	151,464

[Metropolitan areas (MAs) defined as of June 30, 1999. MSA = metropolitan statistical area; CMSA = consolidated MSA; PMSA = primary MSA; NECMA = New England county MA. Geographic codes shown are Federal Information Processing Standards (FIPS) codes]

MSA/ CMSA/ NECMA	PMSA	State and county	Metropolitan area title and geographic component(s)	2000 population	MSA/ CMSA/ NECMA	PMSA	State and county	Metropolitan area title and geographic component(s)	2000 population
1642			Cincinnati-Hamilton, OH-KY-IN CMSA—Con.		1960			Davenport-Moline-Rock Island, IA-IL MSA	359,062
	1640		Cincinnati, OH-KY-IN PMSA—Con.				17073	Henry County, IL	51,020
		21191	Pendleton County, KY	14,390			17161	Rock Island County, IL	149,374
		39015	Brown County, OH	42,285			19163	Scott County, IA	158,668
		39025	Clermont County, OH	177,977	2000			Dayton-Springfield, OH MSA	950,558
		39061	Hamilton County, OH	845,303			39023	Clark County, OH	144,742
		39165	Warren County, OH	158,383			39057	Greene County, OH	147,886
	3200		Hamilton-Middletown, OH PMSA	332,807			39109	Miami County, OH	98,868
		39017	Butler County, OH	332,807			39113	Montgomery County, OH.	559,062
1660			Clarksville-Hopkinsville, TN-KY MSA.	207,033	2020			Daytona Beach, FL MSA	493,175
		21047	Christian County, KY	72,265			12035	Flagler County, FL	49,832
		47125	Montgomery County, TN	134,768			12127	Volusia County, FL.	443,343
	1680		Cleveland-Lorain-Elyria, OH PMSA	2,250,871	2030			Decatur, AL MSA.	145,867
			(See Cleveland-Akron, OH CMSA)				01079	Lawrence County, AL	34,803
1692			Cleveland-Akron, OH CMSA.	2,945,831			01103	Morgan County, AL	111,064
	0080		Akron, OH PMSA	694,960	2040			Decatur, IL MSA	114,706
		39133	Portage County, OH	152,061			17115	Macon County, IL	114,706
		39153	Summit County, OH	542,899		2080		Denver, CO PMSA	2,109,282
	1680		Cleveland-Lorain-Elyria, OH PMSA	2,250,871				(See Denver-Boulder-Greeley, CO CMSA)	
		39007	Ashtabula County, OH.	102,728	2082			Denver-Boulder-Greeley, CO CMSA.	2,581,506
		39035	Cuyahoga County, OH	1,393,978		1125		Boulder-Longmont, CO PMSA.	291,288
		39055	Geauga County, OH	90,895			08013	Boulder County, CO	291,288
		39085	Lake County, OH	227,511		2080		Denver, CO PMSA	2,109,282
		39093	Lorain County, OH	284,664			08001	Adams County, CO.	363,857
		39103	Medina County, OH	151,095			08005	Arapahoe County, CO	487,967
1720			Colorado Springs, CO MSA	516,929			08031	Denver County, CO	544,636
		08041	El Paso County, CO.	516,929			08035	Douglas County, CO	175,766
1740			Columbia, MO MSA.	135,454			08059	Jefferson County, CO	527,056
		29019	Boone County, MO	135,454		3060		Greeley, CO PMSA.	180,936
1760			Columbia, SC MSA	536,691			08123	Weld County, CO	180,936
		45063	Lexington County, SC.	216,014	2120			Des Moines, IA MSA	456,022
		45079	Richland County, SC	320,677			19049	Dallas County, IA.	40,750
1800			Columbus, GA-AL MSA	274,624			19153	Polk County, IA	374,601
		01113	Russell County, AL	49,756			19181	Warren County, IA	40,671
		13053	Chattahoochee County, GA	14,882	2160			Detroit, MI PMSA	4,441,551
		13145	Harris County, GA	23,695				(See Detroit-Ann Arbor-Flint, MI CMSA)	
		13215	Muscogee County, GA	186,291	2162			Detroit-Ann Arbor-Flint, MI CMSA	5,456,428
1840			Columbus, OH MSA.	1,540,157		0440		Ann Arbor, MI PMSA	578,736
		39041	Delaware County, OH.	109,989			26091	Lenawee County, MI	98,890
		39045	Fairfield County, OH	122,759			26093	Livingston County, MI	156,951
		39049	Franklin County, OH	1,068,978			26161	Washtenaw County, MI	322,895
		39089	Licking County, OH	145,491		2160		Detroit, MI PMSA	4,441,551
		39097	Madison County, OH	40,213			26087	Lapeer County, MI	87,904
		39129	Pickaway County, OH.	52,727			26099	Macomb County, MI	788,149
1880			Corpus Christi, TX MSA.	380,783			26115	Monroe County, MI	145,945
		48355	Nueces County, TX	313,645			26125	Oakland County, MI	1,194,156
		48409	San Patricio County, TX	67,138			26147	St. Clair County, MI	164,235
1890			Corvallis, OR MSA.	78,153			26163	Wayne County, MI	2,061,162
		41003	Benton County, OR	78,153		2640		Flint, MI PMSA.	436,141
1900			Cumberland, MD-WV MSA	102,008			26049	Genesee County, MI.	436,141
		24001	Allegany County, MD	74,930	2180			Dothan, AL MSA	137,916
		54057	Mineral County, WV	27,078			01045	Dale County, AL	49,129
	1920		Dallas, TX PMSA	3,519,176			01069	Houston County, AL	88,787
			(See Dallas-Fort Worth, TX CMSA)		2190			Dover, DE MSA.	126,697
1922			Dallas-Fort Worth, TX CMSA	5,221,801			10001	Kent County, DE	126,697
	1920		Dallas, TX PMSA	3,519,176	2200			Dubuque, IA MSA	89,143
		48085	Collin County, TX	491,675			19061	Dubuque County, IA.	89,143
		48113	Dallas County, TX	2,218,899	2240			Duluth-Superior, MN-WI MSA	243,815
		48121	Denton County, TX.	432,976			27137	St. Louis County, MN	200,528
		48139	Ellis County, TX.	111,360			55031	Douglas County, WI	43,287
		48213	Henderson County, TX	73,277		2281		Dutchess County, NY PMSA	280,150
		48231	Hunt County, TX	76,596				(See New York-Northern New Jersey-Long Island, NY-NJ-CT-PA CMSA)	
		48257	Kaufman County, TX	71,313	2290			Eau Claire, WI MSA.	148,337
		48397	Rockwall County, TX.	43,080			55017	Chippewa County, WI.	55,195
	2800		Fort Worth-Arlington, TX PMSA.	1,702,625			55035	Eau Claire County, WI	93,142
		48221	Hood County, TX	41,100	2320			El Paso, TX MSA.	679,622
		48251	Johnson County, TX	126,811			48141	El Paso County, TX	679,622
		48367	Parker County, TX	88,495	2330			Elkhart-Goshen, IN MSA	182,791
		48439	Tarrant County, TX	1,446,219			18039	Elkhart County, IN	182,791
	1930		Danbury, CT PMSA	217,980	2335			Elmira, NY MSA	91,070
			(See New York-Northern New Jersey-Long Island, NY-NJ-CT-PA CMSA)				36015	Chemung County, NY.	91,070
1950			Danville, VA MSA	110,156					
		51143	Pittsylvania County, VA.	61,745					
		51590	Danville city, VA	48,411					

[Metropolitan areas (MAs) defined as of June 30, 1999. MSA = metropolitan statistical area; CMSA = consolidated MSA; PMSA = primary MSA; NECMA = New England county MA. Geographic codes shown are Federal Information Processing Standards (FIPS) codes]

MSA/CMSA/NECMA	PMSA	State and county	Metropolitan area title and geographic component(s)	2000 population	MSA/CMSA/NECMA	PMSA	State and county	Metropolitan area title and geographic component(s)	2000 population
2340			Enid, OK MSA..........	57,813	2975			Glens Falls, NY MSA........	124,345
		40047	Garfield County, OK.........	57,813			36113	Warren County, NY........	63,303
2360			Erie, PA MSA...........	280,843			36115	Washington County, NY........	61,042
		42049	Erie County, PA........	280,843	2980			Goldsboro, NC MSA........	113,329
2400			Eugene-Springfield, OR MSA.......	322,959			37191	Wayne County, NC........	113,329
		41039	Lane County, OR........	322,959	2985			Grand Forks, ND-MN MSA........	97,478
2440			Evansville-Henderson, IN-KY MSA.......	296,195			27119	Polk County, MN........	31,369
		18129	Posey County, IN........	27,061			38035	Grand Forks County, ND........	66,109
		18163	Vanderburgh County, IN.......	171,922	2995			Grand Junction, CO MSA........	116,255
		18173	Warrick County, IN........	52,383			08077	Mesa County, CO........	116,255
		21101	Henderson County, KY........	44,829	3000			Grand Rapids-Muskegon-Holland, MI MSA........	1,088,514
2520			Fargo-Moorhead, ND-MN MSA.......	174,367			26005	Allegan County, MI........	105,665
		27027	Clay County, MN........	51,229			26081	Kent County, MI........	574,335
		38017	Cass County, ND........	123,138			26121	Muskegon County, MI........	170,200
2560			Fayetteville, NC MSA........	302,963			26139	Ottawa County, MI........	238,314
		37051	Cumberland County, NC........	302,963	3040			Great Falls, MT MSA........	80,357
2580			Fayetteville-Springdale-Rogers, AR MSA........	311,121			30013	Cascade County, MT........	80,357
		05007	Benton County, AR........	153,406	3060			Greeley, CO PMSA........	180,936
		05143	Washington County, AR........	157,715				(See Denver-Boulder-Greeley, CO CMSA)	
	2600		Fitchburg-Leominster, MA PMSA........	142,284	3080			Green Bay, WI MSA........	226,778
			(See Boston-Worcester-Lawrence, MA-NH-ME-CT CMSA)				55009	Brown County, WI........	226,778
2620			Flagstaff, AZ-UT MSA........	122,366	3120			Greensboro—Winston-Salem—High Point, NC MSA.	1,251,509
		04005	Coconino County, AZ........	116,320			37001	Alamance County, NC........	130,800
		49025	Kane County, UT........	6,046			37057	Davidson County, NC........	147,246
	2640		Flint, MI PMSA........	436,141			37059	Davie County, NC........	34,835
			(See Detroit-Ann Arbor-Flint, MI CMSA)				37067	Forsyth County, NC........	306,067
2650			Florence, AL MSA........	142,950			37081	Guilford County, NC........	421,048
		01033	Colbert County, AL........	54,984			37151	Randolph County, NC........	130,454
		01077	Lauderdale County, AL........	87,966			37169	Stokes County, NC........	44,711
2655			Florence, SC MSA........	125,761			37197	Yadkin County, NC........	36,348
		45041	Florence County, SC........	125,761	3150			Greenville, NC MSA........	133,798
2670			Fort Collins-Loveland, CO MSA........	251,494			37147	Pitt County, NC........	133,798
		08069	Larimer County, CO........	251,494	3160			Greenville-Spartanburg-Anderson, SC MSA........	962,441
	2680		Fort Lauderdale, FL PMSA........	1,623,018			45007	Anderson County, SC........	165,740
			(See Miami-Fort Lauderdale, FL CMSA)				45021	Cherokee County, SC........	52,537
2700			Fort Myers-Cape Coral, FL MSA........	440,888			45045	Greenville County, SC........	379,616
		12071	Lee County, FL........	440,888			45077	Pickens County, SC........	110,757
2710			Fort Pierce-Port St. Lucie, FL MSA........	319,426			45083	Spartanburg County, SC........	253,791
		12085	Martin County, FL........	126,731	3180			Hagerstown, MD PMSA........	131,923
		12111	St. Lucie County, FL........	192,695				(See Washington-Baltimore, DC-MD-VA-WV CMSA)	
2720			Fort Smith, AR-OK MSA........	207,290	3200			Hamilton-Middletown, OH PMSA........	332,807
		05033	Crawford County, AR........	53,247				(See Cincinnati-Hamilton, OH-KY-IN CMSA)	
		05131	Sebastian County, AR........	115,071	3240			Harrisburg-Lebanon-Carlisle, PA MSA........	629,401
		40135	Sequoyah County, OK........	38,972			42041	Cumberland County, PA........	213,674
2750			Fort Walton Beach, FL MSA........	170,498			42043	Dauphin County, PA........	251,798
		12091	Okaloosa County, FL........	170,498			42075	Lebanon County, PA........	120,327
2760			Fort Wayne, IN MSA........	502,141			42099	Perry County, PA........	43,602
		18001	Adams County, IN........	33,625	3280			Hartford, CT MSA........	1,183,110
		18003	Allen County, IN........	331,849			09003	Hartford County (pt.)........	855,171
		18033	DeKalb County, IN........	40,285			09005	Litchfield County (pt.)........	37,163
		18069	Huntington County, IN........	38,075			09007	Middlesex County (pt.)........	104,442
		18179	Wells County, IN........	27,600			09011	New London County (pt.)........	21,458
		18183	Whitley County, IN........	30,707			09013	Tolland County (pt.)........	135,671
	2800		Fort Worth-Arlington, TX PMSA........	1,702,625			09015	Windham County (pt.)........	29,205
			(See Dallas-Fort Worth, TX CMSA)		3283			Hartford, CT NECMA........	1,148,618
2840			Fresno, CA MSA........	922,516			09003	Hartford County, CT........	857,183
		06019	Fresno County, CA........	799,407			09007	Middlesex County, CT........	155,071
		06039	Madera County, CA........	123,109			09013	Tolland County, CT........	136,364
2880			Gadsden, AL MSA........	103,459	3285			Hattiesburg, MS MSA........	111,674
		01055	Etowah County, AL........	103,459			28035	Forrest County, MS........	72,604
2900			Gainesville, FL MSA........	217,955			28073	Lamar County, MS........	39,070
		12001	Alachua County, FL........	217,955	3290			Hickory-Morganton-Lenoir, NC MSA........	341,851
	2920		Galveston-Texas City, TX PMSA........	250,158			37003	Alexander County, NC........	33,603
			(See Houston-Galveston-Brazoria, TX CMSA)				37023	Burke County, NC........	89,148
	2960		Gary, IN PMSA........	631,362			37027	Caldwell County, NC........	77,415
			(See Chicago-Gary-Kenosha, IL-IN-WI CMSA)				37035	Catawba County, NC........	141,685
					3320			Honolulu, HI MSA........	876,156
							15003	Honolulu County, HI........	876,156
					3350			Houma, LA MSA........	194,477
							22057	Lafourche Parish, LA........	89,974
							22109	Terrebonne Parish, LA........	104,503

[Metropolitan areas (MAs) defined as of June 30, 1999. MSA = metropolitan statistical area; CMSA = consolidated MSA; PMSA = primary MSA; NECMA = New England county MA. Geographic codes shown are Federal Information Processing Standards (FIPS) codes]

Geographic codes			Metropolitan area title and geographic component(s)	2000 population	Geographic codes			Metropolitan area title and geographic component(s)	2000 population
MSA/ CMSA/ NECMA	PMSA	State and county			MSA/ CMSA/ NECMA	PMSA	State and county		
	3360		Houston, TX PMSA	4,177,646	3710			Joplin, MO MSA	157,322
			(See Houston-Galveston-Brazoria, TX CMSA)				29097	Jasper County, MO	104,686
3362			Houston-Galveston-Brazoria, TX CMSA	4,669,571			29145	Newton County, MO	52,636
	1145		Brazoria, TX PMSA.	241,767	3720			Kalamazoo-Battle Creek, MI MSA	452,851
		48039	Brazoria County, TX.	241,767			26025	Calhoun County, MI.	137,985
	2920		Galveston-Texas City, TX PMSA	250,158			26077	Kalamazoo County, MI	238,603
		48167	Galveston County, TX.	250,158			26159	Van Buren County, MI	76,263
	3360		Houston, TX PMSA	4,177,646	3740			Kankakee, IL PMSA	103,833
		48071	Chambers County, TX.	26,031				(See Chicago-Gary-Kenosha, IL-IN-WI CMSA)	
		48157	Fort Bend County, TX.	354,452	3760			Kansas City, MO-KS MSA.	1,776,062
		48201	Harris County, TX.	3,400,578			20091	Johnson County, KS	451,086
		48291	Liberty County, TX.	70,154			20103	Leavenworth County, KS.	68,691
		48339	Montgomery County, TX.	293,768			20121	Miami County, KS	28,351
		48473	Waller County, TX.	32,663			20209	Wyandotte County, KS.	157,882
3400			Huntington-Ashland, WV-KY-OH MSA	315,538			29037	Cass County, MO	82,092
		21019	Boyd County, KY.	49,752			29047	Clay County, MO.	184,006
		21043	Carter County, KY	26,889			29049	Clinton County, MO	18,979
		21089	Greenup County, KY	36,891			29095	Jackson County, MO.	654,880
		39087	Lawrence County, OH	62,319			29107	Lafayette County, MO.	32,960
		54011	Cabell County, WV	96,784			29165	Platte County, MO.	73,781
		54099	Wayne County, WV	42,903			29177	Ray County, MO	23,354
3440			Huntsville, AL MSA	342,376	3800			Kenosha, WI MSA	149,577
		01083	Limestone County, AL	65,676				(See Chicago-Gary-Kenosha, IL-IN-WI CMSA)	
		01089	Madison County, AL.	276,700	3810			Killeen-Temple, TX MSA.	312,952
3480			Indianapolis, IN MSA	1,607,486			48027	Bell County, TX.	237,974
		18011	Boone County, IN	46,107			48099	Coryell County, TX.	74,978
		18057	Hamilton County, IN.	182,740	3840			Knoxville, TN MSA	687,249
		18059	Hancock County, IN	55,391			47001	Anderson County, TN.	71,330
		18063	Hendricks County, IN.	104,093			47009	Blount County, TN	105,823
		18081	Johnson County, IN.	115,209			47093	Knox County, TN.	382,032
		18095	Madison County, IN.	133,358			47105	Loudon County, TN.	39,086
		18097	Marion County, IN.	860,454			47155	Sevier County, TN	71,170
		18109	Morgan County, IN.	66,689			47173	Union County, TN	17,808
		18145	Shelby County, IN.	43,445	3850			Kokomo, IN MSA.	101,541
3500			Iowa City, IA MSA	111,006			18067	Howard County, IN	84,964
		19103	Johnson County, IA.	111,006			18159	Tipton County, IN	16,577
3520			Jackson, MI MSA	158,422	3870			La Crosse, WI-MN MSA	126,838
		26075	Jackson County, MI.	158,422			27055	Houston County, MN	19,718
3560			Jackson, MS MSA	440,801			55063	La Crosse County, WI	107,120
		28049	Hinds County, MS	250,800	3880			Lafayette, LA MSA.	385,647
		28089	Madison County, MS	74,674			22001	Acadia Parish, LA	58,861
		28121	Rankin County, MS	115,327			22055	Lafayette Parish, LA.	190,503
3580			Jackson, TN MSA	107,377			22097	St. Landry Parish, LA.	87,700
		47023	Chester County, TN	15,540			22099	St. Martin Parish, LA.	48,583
		47113	Madison County, TN	91,837	3920			Lafayette, IN MSA	182,821
3600			Jacksonville, FL MSA	1,100,491			18023	Clinton County, IN	33,866
		12019	Clay County, FL	140,814			18157	Tippecanoe County, IN	148,955
		12031	Duval County, FL.	778,879	3960			Lake Charles, LA MSA.	183,577
		12089	Nassau County, FL	57,663			22019	Calcasieu Parish, LA.	183,577
		12109	St. Johns County, FL.	123,135	3980			Lakeland-Winter Haven, FL MSA.	483,924
3605			Jacksonville, NC MSA	150,355			12105	Polk County, FL	483,924
		37133	Onslow County, NC	150,355	4000			Lancaster, PA MSA	470,658
3610			Jamestown, NY MSA.	139,750			42071	Lancaster County, PA.	470,658
		36013	Chautauqua County, NY	139,750	4040			Lansing-East Lansing, MI MSA.	447,728
3620			Janesville-Beloit, WI MSA	152,307			26037	Clinton County, MI.	64,753
		55105	Rock County, WI	152,307			26045	Eaton County, MI.	103,655
	3640		Jersey City, NJ PMSA	608,975			26065	Ingham County, MI	279,320
			(See New York-Northern New Jersey-Long Island, NY-NJ-CT-PA CMSA)		4080			Laredo, TX MSA	193,117
3660			Johnson City-Kingsport-Bristol, TN-VA MSA	480,091			48479	Webb County, TX.	193,117
		47019	Carter County, TN	56,742	4100			Las Cruces, NM MSA.	174,682
		47073	Hawkins County, TN	53,563			35013	Dona Ana County, NM	174,682
		47163	Sullivan County, TN	153,048	4120			Las Vegas, NV-AZ MSA	1,563,282
		47171	Unicoi County, TN	17,667			04015	Mohave County, AZ	155,032
		47179	Washington County, TN	107,198			32003	Clark County, NV.	1,375,765
		51169	Scott County, VA	23,403			32023	Nye County, NV.	32,485
		51191	Washington County, VA	51,103	4150			Lawrence, KS MSA	99,962
		51520	Bristol city, VA.	17,367			20045	Douglas County, KS.	99,962
3680			Johnstown, PA MSA	232,621	4160			Lawrence, MA-NH PMSA	396,230
		42021	Cambria County, PA.	152,598				(See Boston-Worcester-Lawrence, MA-NH-ME-CT CMSA)	
		42111	Somerset County, PA.	80,023	4200			Lawton, OK MSA.	114,996
3700			Jonesboro, AR MSA	82,148			40031	Comanche County, OK.	114,996
		05031	Craighead County, AR	82,148					

[Metropolitan areas (MAs) defined as of June 30, 1999. MSA = metropolitan statistical area; CMSA = consolidated MSA; PMSA = primary MSA; NECMA = New England county MA. Geographic codes shown are Federal Information Processing Standards (FIPS) codes]

MSA/ CMSA/ NECMA	PMSA	State and county	Metropolitan area title and geographic component(s)	2000 population
4240			Lewiston-Auburn, ME MSA.	90,830
		23001	Androscoggin County (pt.).	90,830
4243			Lewiston-Auburn, ME NECMA	103,793
		23001	Androscoggin County, ME.	103,793
4280			Lexington, KY MSA.	479,198
		21017	Bourbon County, KY	19,360
		21049	Clark County, KY.	33,144
		21067	Fayette County, KY.	260,512
		21113	Jessamine County, KY	39,041
		21151	Madison County, KY	70,872
		21209	Scott County, KY	33,061
		21239	Woodford County, KY.	23,208
4320			Lima, OH MSA	155,084
		39003	Allen County, OH.	108,473
		39011	Auglaize County, OH	46,611
4360			Lincoln, NE MSA.	250,291
		31109	Lancaster County, NE	250,291
4400			Little Rock-North Little Rock, AR MSA . . .	583,845
		05045	Faulkner County, AR	86,014
		05085	Lonoke County, AR	52,828
		05119	Pulaski County, AR	361,474
		05125	Saline County, AR	83,529
4420			Longview-Marshall, TX MSA.	208,780
		48183	Gregg County, TX	111,379
		48203	Harrison County, TX.	62,110
		48459	Upshur County, TX	35,291
4472			Los Angeles-Riverside-Orange County, CA CMSA . .	16,373,645
	4480		Los Angeles-Long Beach, CA PMSA	9,519,338
		06037	Los Angeles County, CA	9,519,338
	5945		Orange County, CA PMSA.	2,846,289
		06059	Orange County, CA	2,846,289
	6780		Riverside-San Bernardino, CA PMSA	3,254,821
		06065	Riverside County, CA	1,545,387
		06071	San Bernardino County, CA	1,709,434
	8735		Ventura, CA PMSA	753,197
		06111	Ventura County, CA	753,197
	4480		Los Angeles-Long Beach, CA PMSA	9,519,338
			(See Los Angeles-Riverside-Orange County, CA CMSA)	
4520			Louisville, KY-IN MSA	1,025,598
		18019	Clark County, IN	96,472
		18043	Floyd County, IN	70,823
		18061	Harrison County, IN	34,325
		18143	Scott County, IN	22,960
		21029	Bullitt County, KY	61,236
		21111	Jefferson County, KY	693,604
		21185	Oldham County, KY	46,178
	4560		Lowell, MA-NH PMSA	301,686
			(See Boston-Worcester-Lawrence, MA-NH-ME-CT CMSA)	
4600			Lubbock, TX MSA	242,628
		48303	Lubbock County, TX.	242,628
4640			Lynchburg, VA MSA	214,911
		51009	Amherst County, VA	31,894
		51019	Bedford County, VA	60,371
		51031	Campbell County, VA	51,078
		51515	Bedford city, VA	6,299
		51680	Lynchburg city, VA	65,269
4680			Macon, GA MSA	322,549
		13021	Bibb County, GA	153,887
		13153	Houston County, GA	110,765
		13169	Jones County, GA	23,639
		13225	Peach County, GA	23,668
		13289	Twiggs County, GA	10,590
4720			Madison, WI MSA	426,526
		55025	Dane County, WI	426,526
	4760		Manchester, NH PMSA	198,378
			(See Boston-Worcester-Lawrence, MA-NH-ME-CT CMSA)	
4800			Mansfield, OH MSA	175,818
		39033	Crawford County, OH	46,966
		39139	Richland County, OH	128,852
4880			McAllen-Edinburg-Mission, TX MSA	569,463
		48215	Hidalgo County, TX	569,463

MSA/ CMSA/ NECMA	PMSA	State and county	Metropolitan area title and geographic component(s)	2000 population
4890			Medford-Ashland, OR MSA	181,269
		41029	Jackson County, OR	181,269
4900			Melbourne-Titusville-Palm Bay, FL MSA	476,230
		12009	Brevard County, FL.	476,230
4920			Memphis, TN-AR-MS MSA	1,135,614
		05035	Crittenden County, AR	50,866
		28033	DeSoto County, MS	107,199
		47047	Fayette County, TN	28,806
		47157	Shelby County, TN.	897,472
		47167	Tipton County, TN	51,271
4940			Merced, CA MSA.	210,554
		06047	Merced County, CA	210,554
4992			Miami-Fort Lauderdale, FL CMSA	3,876,380
	2680		Fort Lauderdale, FL PMSA	1,623,018
		12011	Broward County, FL	1,623,018
	5000		Miami, FL PMSA	2,253,362
		12086	Miami-Dade County, FL.	2,253,362
5000			Miami, FL PMSA	2,253,362
			(See Miami-Fort Lauderdale, FL CMSA)	
5015			Middlesex-Somerset-Hunterdon, NJ PMSA	1,169,641
			(See New York-Northern New Jersey-Long Island, NY-NJ-CT-PA CMSA)	
5080			Milwaukee-Waukesha, WI PMSA	1,500,741
			(See Milwaukee-Racine, WI CMSA)	
5082			Milwaukee-Racine, WI CMSA	1,689,572
	5080		Milwaukee-Waukesha, WI PMSA	1,500,741
		55079	Milwaukee County, WI.	940,164
		55089	Ozaukee County, WI	82,317
		55131	Washington County, WI	117,493
		55133	Waukesha County, WI.	360,767
	6600		Racine, WI PMSA	188,831
		55101	Racine County, WI	188,831
5120			Minneapolis-St. Paul, MN-WI MSA	2,968,806
		27003	Anoka County, MN	298,084
		27019	Carver County, MN	70,205
		27025	Chisago County, MN	41,101
		27037	Dakota County, MN	355,904
		27053	Hennepin County, MN	1,116,200
		27059	Isanti County, MN	31,287
		27123	Ramsey County, MN	511,035
		27139	Scott County, MN	89,498
		27141	Sherburne County, MN	64,417
		27163	Washington County, MN	201,130
		27171	Wright County, MN	89,986
		55093	Pierce County, WI	36,804
		55109	St. Croix County, WI	63,155
5140			Missoula, MT MSA.	95,802
		30063	Missoula County, MT	95,802
5160			Mobile, AL MSA	540,258
		01003	Baldwin County, AL	140,415
		01097	Mobile County, AL	399,843
5170			Modesto, CA MSA	446,997
		06099	Stanislaus County, CA	446,997
5190			Monmouth-Ocean, NJ PMSA	1,126,217
			(See New York-Northern New Jersey-Long Island, NY-NJ-CT-PA CMSA)	
5200			Monroe, LA MSA.	147,250
		22073	Ouachita Parish, LA.	147,250
5240			Montgomery, AL MSA	333,055
		01001	Autauga County, AL	43,671
		01051	Elmore County, AL	65,874
		01101	Montgomery County, AL	223,510
5280			Muncie, IN MSA	118,769
		18035	Delaware County, IN	118,769
5330			Myrtle Beach, SC MSA.	196,629
		45051	Horry County, SC	196,629
5345			Naples, FL MSA	251,377
		12021	Collier County, FL.	251,377
5350			Nashua, NH PMSA	190,949
			(See Boston-Worcester-Lawrence, MA-NH-ME-CT CMSA)	

[Metropolitan areas (MAs) defined as of June 30, 1999. MSA = metropolitan statistical area; CMSA = consolidated MSA; PMSA = primary MSA; NECMA = New England county MA. Geographic codes shown are Federal Information Processing Standards (FIPS) codes]

MSA/ CMSA/ NECMA	PMSA	State and county	Metropolitan area title and geographic component(s)	2000 population	MSA/ CMSA/ NECMA	PMSA	State and county	Metropolitan area title and geographic component(s)	2000 population
5360			**Nashville, TN MSA.**	**1,231,311**				**Newark, NJ PMSA**	**2,032,989**
		47021	Cheatham County, TN	35,912			34013	Essex County, NJ.	793,633
		47037	Davidson County, TN	569,891			34027	Morris County, NJ.	470,212
		47043	Dickson County, TN	43,156			34037	Sussex County, NJ.	144,166
		47147	Robertson County, TN	54,433			34039	Union County, NJ.	522,541
		47149	Rutherford County, TN	182,023			34041	Warren County, NJ.	102,437
		47165	Sumner County, TN	130,449		5660		**Newburgh, NY-PA PMSA**	**387,669**
		47187	Williamson County, TN	126,638			36071	Orange County, NY	341,367
		47189	Wilson County, TN.	88,809			42103	Pike County, PA.	46,302
	5380		**Nassau-Suffolk, NY PMSA**	**2,753,913**	8040			**Stamford-Norwalk, CT PMSA.**	**353,556**
			(See New York-Northern New Jersey-Long Island, NY-NJ- CT PA CMSA)			09001		Fairfield County (pt.)	353,556
					8480			**Trenton, NJ PMSA**	**350,761**
	5400		**New Bedford, MA PMSA**	**175,198**			34021	Mercer County, NJ.	350,761
			(See Boston-Worcester-Lawrence, MA-NH-ME-CT CMSA)		8880			**Waterbury, CT PMSA**	**228,984**
						09005		Litchfield County (pt.)	41,784
	5480		**New Haven-Meriden, CT PMSA**	**542,149**		09009		New Haven County (pt.)	187,200
			(See New York-Northern New Jersey-Long Island, NY-NJ- CT-PA CMSA)		5640			**Newark, NJ PMSA**	**2,032,989**
5483			**New Haven-Bridgeport-Stamford-Waterbury-Danbury, CT NECMA**	**1,706,575**				(See New York-Northern New Jersey-Long Island, NY-NJ- CT-PA CMSA)	
		09001	Fairfield County, CT.	882,567	5660			**Newburgh, NY-PA PMSA**	**387,669**
		09009	New Haven County, CT	824,008				(See New York-Northern New Jersey-Long Island, NY-NJ- CT-PA CMSA)	
5520			**New London-Norwich, CT-RI MSA.**	**293,566**	5720			**Norfolk-Virginia Beach-Newport News, VA-NC MSA .**	**1,569,541**
		09007	Middlesex County, CT (pt.)	10,367			37053	Currituck County, NC	18,190
		09011	New London County, CT (pt.)	233,086			51073	Gloucester County, VA.	34,780
		09015	Windham County, CT (pt.)	19,311			51093	Isle of Wight County, VA.	29,728
		44009	Washington County, RI (pt.).	30,802			51095	James City County, VA.	48,102
5523			**New London-Norwich, CT NECMA**	**259,088**			51115	Mathews County, VA.	9,207
		09011	New London County, CT	259,088			51199	York County, VA.	56,297
5560			**New Orleans, LA MSA.**	**1,337,726**			51550	Chesapeake city, VA.	199,184
		22051	Jefferson Parish, LA.	455,466			51650	Hampton city, VA.	146,437
		22071	Orleans Parish, LA.	484,674			51700	Newport News city, VA.	180,150
		22075	Plaquemines Parish, LA.	26,757			51710	Norfolk city, VA.	234,403
		22087	St. Bernard Parish, LA.	67,229			51735	Poquoson city, VA.	11,566
		22089	St. Charles Parish, LA.	48,072			51740	Portsmouth city, VA.	100,565
		22093	St. James Parish, LA.	21,216			51800	Suffolk city, VA.	63,677
		22095	St. John the Baptist Parish, LA.	43,044			51810	Virginia Beach city, VA.	425,257
		22103	St. Tammany Parish, LA.	191,268			51830	Williamsburg city, VA.	11,998
	5600		**New York, NY PMSA**	**9,314,235**	5775			**Oakland, CA PMSA**	**2,392,557**
			(See New York-Northern New Jersey-Long Island, NY-NJ- CT-PA CMSA)					(See San Francisco-Oakland-San Jose, CA CMSA)	
					5790			**Ocala, FL MSA.**	**258,916**
5602			**New York-Northern New Jersey-Long Island, NY-NJ- CT-PA CMSA**	**21,199,865**			12083	Marion County, FL.	258,916
	0875		**Bergen-Passaic, NJ PMSA**	**1,373,167**	5800			**Odessa-Midland, TX MSA.**	**237,132**
		34003	Bergen County, NJ.	884,118			48135	Ector County, TX.	121,123
		34031	Passaic County, NJ	489,049			48329	Midland County, TX.	116,009
	1160		**Bridgeport, CT PMSA.**	**459,479**	5880			**Oklahoma City, OK MSA.**	**1,083,346**
		09001	Fairfield County (pt.)	345,708			40017	Canadian County, OK.	87,697
		09009	New Haven County (pt.)	113,771			40027	Cleveland County, OK.	208,016
	1930		**Danbury, CT PMSA.**	**217,980**			40083	Logan County, OK.	33,924
		09001	Fairfield County (pt.)	183,303			40087	McClain County, OK.	27,740
		09005	Litchfield County (pt.)	34,677			40109	Oklahoma County, OK.	660,448
	2281		**Dutchess County, NY PMSA**	**280,150**			40125	Pottawatomie County, OK.	65,521
		36027	Dutchess County, NY	280,150	5910			**Olympia, WA PMSA**	**207,355**
	3640		**Jersey City, NJ PMSA.**	**608,975**				(See Seattle-Tacoma-Bremerton, WA CMSA)	
		34017	Hudson County, NJ.	608,975	5920			**Omaha, NE-IA MSA.**	**716,998**
	5015		**Middlesex-Somerset-Hunterdon, NJ PMSA**	**1,169,641**			19155	Pottawattamie County, IA.	87,704
		34019	Hunterdon County, NJ.	121,989			31025	Cass County, NE.	24,334
		34023	Middlesex County, NJ.	750,162			31055	Douglas County, NE.	463,585
		34035	Somerset County, NJ.	297,490			31153	Sarpy County, NE.	122,595
	5190		**Monmouth-Ocean, NJ PMSA.**	**1,126,217**			31177	Washington County, NE.	18,780
		34025	Monmouth County, NJ.	615,301	5945			**Orange County, CA PMSA**	**2,846,289**
		34029	Ocean County, NJ.	510,916				(See Los Angeles-Riverside-Orange County, CA CMSA)	
	5380		**Nassau-Suffolk, NY PMSA**	**2,753,913**	5960			**Orlando, FL MSA.**	**1,644,561**
		36059	Nassau County, NY.	1,334,544			12069	Lake County, FL.	210,528
		36103	Suffolk County, NY.	1,419,369			12095	Orange County, FL.	896,344
	5480		**New Haven-Meriden, CT PMSA**	**542,149**			12097	Osceola County, FL.	172,493
		09007	Middlesex County (pt.)	19,112			12117	Seminole County, FL.	365,196
		09009	New Haven County (pt.)	523,037	5990			**Owensboro, KY MSA.**	**91,545**
	5600		**New York, NY PMSA.**	**9,314,235**			21059	Daviess County, KY.	91,545
		36005	Bronx County, NY.	1,332,650	6015			**Panama City, FL MSA.**	**148,217**
		36047	Kings County, NY.	2,465,326			12005	Bay County, FL.	148,217
		36061	New York County, NY.	1,537,195	6020			**Parkersburg-Marietta, WV-OH MSA.**	**151,237**
		36079	Putnam County, NY.	95,745			39167	Washington County, OH.	63,251
		36081	Queens County, NY.	2,229,379			54107	Wood County, WV.	87,986
		36085	Richmond County, NY.	443,728					
		36087	Rockland County, NY.	286,753					
		36119	Westchester County, NY.	923,459					

[Metropolitan areas (MAs) defined as of June 30, 1999. MSA = metropolitan statistical area; CMSA = consolidated MSA; PMSA = primary MSA; NECMA = New England county MA. Geographic codes shown are Federal Information Processing Standards (FIPS) codes]

MSA/CMSA/NECMA	PMSA	State and county	Metropolitan area title and geographic component(s)	2000 population
6080			**Pensacola, FL MSA**	**412,153**
		12033	Escambia County, FL	294,410
		12113	Santa Rosa County, FL	117,743
6120			**Peoria-Pekin, IL MSA**	**347,387**
		17143	Peoria County, IL	183,433
		17179	Tazewell County, IL	128,485
		17203	Woodford County, IL	35,469
	6160		**Philadelphia, PA-NJ PMSA**	**5,100,931**
			(See Philadelphia-Wilmington-Atlantic City, PA-NJ-DE-MD CMSA)	
			Philadelphia-Wilmington-Atlantic City, PA-NJ-DE-MD CMSA	**6,188,463**
6162	0560		**Atlantic-Cape May, NJ PMSA**	**354,878**
		34001	Atlantic County	252,552
		34009	Cape May County	102,326
	6160		**Philadelphia, PA-NJ PMSA**	**5,100,931**
		34005	Burlington County, NJ	423,394
		34007	Camden County, NJ	508,932
		34015	Gloucester County, NJ	254,673
		34033	Salem County, NJ	64,285
		42017	Bucks County, PA	597,635
		42029	Chester County, PA	433,501
		42045	Delaware County, PA	550,864
		42091	Montgomery County, PA	750,097
		42101	Philadelphia County, PA	1,517,550
	8760		**Vineland-Millville-Bridgeton, NJ PMSA**	**146,438**
		34011	Cumberland County	146,438
	9160		**Wilmington-Newark, DE-MD PMSA**	**586,216**
		10003	New Castle County, DE	500,265
		24015	Cecil County, MD	85,951
6200			**Phoenix-Mesa, AZ MSA**	**3,251,876**
		04013	Maricopa County, AZ	3,072,149
		04021	Pinal County, AZ	179,727
6240			**Pine Bluff, AR MSA**	**84,278**
		05069	Jefferson County, AR	84,278
6280			**Pittsburgh, PA MSA**	**2,358,695**
		42003	Allegheny County, PA	1,281,666
		42007	Beaver County, PA	181,412
		42019	Butler County, PA	174,083
		42051	Fayette County, PA	148,644
		42125	Washington County, PA	202,897
		42129	Westmoreland County, PA	369,993
6320			**Pittsfield, MA MSA**	**84,699**
		25003	Berkshire County (pt.)	84,699
6323			**Pittsfield, MA NECMA**	**134,953**
		25003	Berkshire County, MA	134,953
6340			**Pocatello, ID MSA**	**75,565**
		16005	Bannock County, ID	75,565
6400			**Portland, ME MSA**	**243,537**
		23005	Cumberland County (pt.)	219,712
		23031	York County (pt.)	23,825
6403			**Portland, ME NECMA**	**265,612**
		23005	Cumberland County, ME	265,612
	6440		**Portland-Vancouver, OR-WA PMSA**	**1,918,009**
			(See Portland-Salem, OR-WA CMSA)	
6442			**Portland-Salem, OR-WA CMSA**	**2,265,223**
	6440		**Portland-Vancouver, OR-WA PMSA**	**1,918,009**
		41005	Clackamas County, OR	338,391
		41009	Columbia County, OR	43,560
		41051	Multnomah County, OR	660,486
		41067	Washington County, OR	445,342
		41071	Yamhill County, OR	84,992
		53011	Clark County, WA	345,238
	7080		**Salem, OR PMSA**	**347,214**
		41047	Marion County	284,834
		41053	Polk County	62,380
	6450		**Portsmouth-Rochester, NH-ME PMSA**	**240,698**
			(See (See Boston-Worcester-Lawrence, MA-NH-ME-CT CMSA)	
6480			**Providence-Fall River-Warwick, RI-MA MSA**	**1,188,613**
		25005	Bristol County, MA (pt.)	233,064
		44001	Bristol County, RI	50,648
		44003	Kent County, RI	167,090
		44005	Newport County, RI (pt.)	24,475
		44007	Providence County, RI	621,602
		44009	Washington County, RI (pt.)	91,734
6483			**Providence-Warwick-Pawtucket, RI NECMA**	**962,886**
		44001	Bristol County, RI	50,648
		44003	Kent County, RI	167,090
		44007	Providence County, RI	621,602
		44009	Washington County, RI	123,546
6520			**Provo-Orem, UT MSA**	**368,536**
		49049	Utah County, UT	368,536
6560			**Pueblo, CO MSA**	**141,472**
		08101	Pueblo County, CO	141,472
6580			**Punta Gorda, FL MSA**	**141,627**
		12015	Charlotte County, FL	141,627
6600			**Racine, WI PMSA**	**188,831**
			(See Milwaukee-Racine, WI CMSA)	
6640			**Raleigh-Durham-Chapel Hill, NC MSA**	**1,187,941**
		37037	Chatham County, NC	49,329
		37063	Durham County, NC	223,314
		37069	Franklin County, NC	47,260
		37101	Johnston County, NC	121,965
		37135	Orange County, NC	118,227
		37183	Wake County, NC	627,846
6660			**Rapid City, SD MSA**	**88,565**
		46103	Pennington County, SD	88,565
6680			**Reading, PA MSA**	**373,638**
		42011	Berks County, PA	373,638
6690			**Redding, CA MSA**	**163,256**
		06089	Shasta County, CA	163,256
6720			**Reno, NV MSA**	**339,486**
		32031	Washoe County, NV	339,486
6740			**Richland-Kennewick-Pasco, WA MSA**	**191,822**
		53005	Benton County, WA	142,475
		53021	Franklin County, WA	49,347
6760			**Richmond-Petersburg, VA MSA**	**996,512**
		51036	Charles City County, VA	6,926
		51041	Chesterfield County, VA	259,903
		51053	Dinwiddie County, VA	24,533
		51075	Goochland County, VA	16,863
		51085	Hanover County, VA	86,320
		51087	Henrico County, VA	262,300
		51127	New Kent County, VA	13,462
		51145	Powhatan County, VA	22,377
		51149	Prince George County, VA	33,047
		51570	Colonial Heights city, VA	16,897
		51670	Hopewell city, VA	22,354
		51730	Petersburg city, VA	33,740
		51760	Richmond city, VA	197,790
6780			**Riverside-San Bernardino, CA PMSA**	**3,254,821**
			(See Los Angeles-Riverside-Orange County, CA CMSA)	
6800			**Roanoke, VA MSA**	**235,932**
		51023	Botetourt County, VA	30,496
		51161	Roanoke County, VA	85,778
		51770	Roanoke city, VA	94,911
		51775	Salem city, VA	24,747
6820			**Rochester, MN MSA**	**124,277**
		27109	Olmsted County, MN	124,277
6840			**Rochester, NY MSA**	**1,098,201**
		36037	Genesee County, NY	60,370
		36051	Livingston County, NY	64,328
		36055	Monroe County, NY	735,343
		36069	Ontario County, NY	100,224
		36073	Orleans County, NY	44,171
		36117	Wayne County, NY	93,765
6880			**Rockford, IL MSA**	**371,236**
		17007	Boone County, IL	41,786
		17141	Ogle County, IL	51,032
		17201	Winnebago County, IL	278,418
6895			**Rocky Mount, NC MSA**	**143,026**
		37065	Edgecombe County, NC	55,606
		37127	Nash County, NC	87,420

Table B-3. **Metropolitan Areas and Component Counties** —Con.

[Metropolitan areas (MAs) defined as of June 30, 1999. MSA = metropolitan statistical area; CMSA = consolidated MSA; PMSA = primary MSA; NECMA = New England county MA. Geographic codes shown are Federal Information Processing Standards (FIPS) codes]

MSA/ CMSA/ NECMA	PMSA	State and county	Metropolitan area title and geographic component(s)	2000 population	MSA/ CMSA/ NECMA	PMSA	State and county	Metropolitan area title and geographic component(s)	2000 population
	6920		Sacramento, CA PMSA	1,628,197	7480			Santa Barbara-Santa Maria-Lompoc, CA MSA	399,347
			(See Sacramento-Yolo, CA CMSA)				06083	Santa Barbara County, CA	399,347
6922			Sacramento-Yolo, CA CMSA.	1,796,857	7485			Santa Cruz-Watsonville, CA PMSA	255,602
	6920		Sacramento, CA PMSA.	1,628,197				(See San Francisco-Oakland-San Jose, CA	
		06017	El Dorado County, CA.	156,299				CMSA)	
		06061	Placer County, CA.	248,399	7490			Santa Fe, NM MSA	147,635
		06067	Sacramento County, CA.	1,223,499			35028	Los Alamos County, NM	18,343
	9270		Yolo, CA PMSA	168,660			35049	Santa Fe County, NM.	129,292
		06113	Yolo County, CA	168,660	7500			Santa Rosa, CA PMSA	458,614
6960			Saginaw-Bay City-Midland, MI MSA.	403,070				(See San Francisco-Oakland-San Jose, CA CMSA)	
		26017	Bay County, MI.	110,157	7510			Sarasota-Bradenton, FL MSA	589,959
		26111	Midland County, MI	82,874			12081	Manatee County, FL.	264,002
		26145	Saginaw County, MI.	210,039			12115	Sarasota County, FL	325,957
6980			St. Cloud, MN MSA	167,392	7520			Savannah, GA MSA.	293,000
		27009	Benton County, MN	34,226			13029	Bryan County, GA.	23,417
		27145	Stearns County, MN.	133,166			13051	Chatham County, GA.	232,048
7000			St. Joseph, MO MSA	102,490			13103	Effingham County, GA.	37,535
		29003	Andrew County, MO.	16,492	7560			Scranton–Wilkes-Barre–Hazleton, PA MSA.	624,776
		29021	Buchanan County, MO	85,998			42037	Columbia County, PA	64,151
7040			St. Louis, MO-IL MSA	2,603,607			42069	Lackawanna County, PA.	213,295
		17027	Clinton County, IL	35,535			42079	Luzerne County, PA.	319,250
		17083	Jersey County, IL	21,668			42131	Wyoming County, PA.	28,080
		17119	Madison County, IL	258,941	7600			Seattle-Bellevue-Everett, WA PMSA	2,414,616
		17133	Monroe County, IL.	27,619				(See Seattle-Tacoma-Bremerton, WA CMSA)	
		17163	St. Clair County, IL	256,082	7602			Seattle-Tacoma-Bremerton, WA CMSA.	3,554,760
		29071	Franklin County, MO	93,807		1150		Bremerton, WA PMSA	231,969
		29099	Jefferson County, MO.	198,099			53035	Kitsap County, WA.	231,969
		29113	Lincoln County, MO	38,944		5910		Olympia, WA PMSA	207,355
		29183	St. Charles County, MO.	283,883			53067	Thurston County, WA	207,355
		29189	St. Louis County, MO.	1,016,315		7600		Seattle-Bellevue-Everett, WA PMSA	2,414,616
		29219	Warren County, MO	24,525			53029	Island County, WA	71,558
		29510	St. Louis city, MO	348,189			53033	King County, WA	1,737,034
	7080		Salem, OR PMSA	347,214			53061	Snohomish County, WA.	606,024
			(See Portland-Salem, OR-WA CMSA)			8200		Tacoma, WA PMSA.	700,820
7120			Salinas, CA MSA.	401,762			53053	Pierce County, WA.	700,820
		06053	Monterey County, CA.	401,762	7610			Sharon, PA MSA	120,293
7160			Salt Lake City-Ogden, UT MSA.	1,333,914			42085	Mercer County, PA.	120,293
		49011	Davis County, UT.	238,994	7620			Sheboygan, WI MSA	112,646
		49035	Salt Lake County, UT.	898,387			55117	Sheboygan County, WI.	112,646
		49057	Weber County, UT.	196,533	7640			Sherman-Denison, TX MSA	110,595
7200			San Angelo, TX MSA.	104,010			48181	Grayson County, TX.	110,595
		48451	Tom Green County, TX.	104,010	7680			Shreveport-Bossier City, LA MSA	392,302
7240			San Antonio, TX MSA	1,592,383			22015	Bossier Parish, LA	98,310
		48029	Bexar County, TX	1,392,931			22017	Caddo Parish, LA	252,161
		48091	Comal County, TX	78,021			22119	Webster Parish, LA	41,831
		48187	Guadalupe County, TX.	89,023	7720			Sioux City, IA-NE MSA.	124,130
		48493	Wilson County, TX.	32,408			19193	Woodbury County, IA.	103,877
7320			San Diego, CA MSA.	2,813,833			31043	Dakota County, NE	20,253
		06073	San Diego County, CA	2,813,833	7760			Sioux Falls, SD MSA	172,412
	7360		San Francisco, CA PMSA	1,731,183			46083	Lincoln County, SD	24,131
			(See San Francisco-Oakland-San Jose, CA CMSA)				46099	Minnehaha County, SD.	148,281
7362			San Francisco-Oakland-San Jose, CA CMSA	7,039,362	7800			South Bend, IN MSA	265,559
	5775		Oakland, CA PMSA	2,392,557			18141	St. Joseph County, IN	265,559
		06001	Alameda County, CA	1,443,741	7840			Spokane, WA MSA	417,939
		06013	Contra Costa County, CA	948,816			53063	Spokane County, WA.	417,939
	7360		San Francisco, CA PMSA	1,731,183	7880			Springfield, IL MSA	201,437
		06041	Marin County, CA.	247,289			17129	Menard County, IL	12,486
		06075	San Francisco County, CA.	776,733			17167	Sangamon County, IL.	188,951
		06081	San Mateo County, CA	707,161	7920			Springfield, MO MSA.	325,721
	7400		San Jose, CA PMSA	1,682,585			29043	Christian County, MO.	54,285
		06085	Santa Clara County, CA	1,682,585			29077	Greene County, MO	240,391
	7485		Santa Cruz-Watsonville, CA PMSA.	255,602			29225	Webster County, MO	31,045
		06087	Santa Cruz County, CA.	255,602	8000			Springfield, MA MSA	591,932
	7500		Santa Rosa, CA PMSA	458,614			25011	Franklin County (pt.)	3,777
		06097	Sonoma County, CA.	458,614			25013	Hampden County (pt.)	444,276
	8720		Vallejo-Fairfield-Napa, CA PMSA	518,821			25015	Hampshire County (pt.).	143,879
		06055	Napa County, CA	124,279	8003			Springfield, MA NECMA	608,479
		06095	Solano County, CA.	394,542			25013	Hampden County, MA	456,228
	7400		San Jose, CA PMSA	1,682,585			25015	Hampshire County, MA	152,251
			(See San Francisco-Oakland-San Jose, CA CMSA)						
			San Luis Obispo-Atascadero-Paso Robles, CA						
7460			MSA.	246,681					
		06079	San Luis Obispo County, CA	246,681					

[Metropolitan areas (MAs) defined as of June 30, 1999. MSA = metropolitan statistical area; CMSA = consolidated MSA; PMSA = primary MSA; NECMA = New England county MA. Geographic codes shown are Federal Information Processing Standards (FIPS) codes]

MSA/ CMSA/ NECMA	PMSA	State and county	Metropolitan area title and geographic component(s)	2000 population
	8040		**Stamford-Norwalk, CT PMSA**	**353,556**
			(See New York-Northern New Jersey-Long Island, NY-NJ-CT-PA CMSA)	
8050			**State College, PA MSA**	**135,758**
		42027	Centre County, PA.	135,758
8080			**Steubenville-Weirton, OH-WV MSA**	**132,008**
		39081	Jefferson County, OH.	73,894
		54009	Brooke County, WV	25,447
		54029	Hancock County, WV.	32,667
8120			**Stockton-Lodi, CA MSA**	**563,598**
		06077	San Joaquin County, CA.	563,598
8140			**Sumter, SC MSA**	**104,646**
		45085	Sumter County, SC	104,646
8160			**Syracuse, NY MSA**	**732,117**
		36011	Cayuga County, NY	81,963
		36053	Madison County, NY	69,441
		36067	Onondaga County, NY	458,336
		36075	Oswego County, NY	122,377
	8200		**Tacoma, WA PMSA**	**700,820**
			(See Seattle-Tacoma-Bremerton, WA CMSA)	
8240			**Tallahassee, FL MSA**	**284,539**
		12039	Gadsden County, FL	45,087
		12073	Leon County, FL	239,452
8280			**Tampa-St. Petersburg-Clearwater, FL MSA**	**2,395,997**
		12053	Hernando County, FL.	130,802
		12057	Hillsborough County, FL.	998,948
		12101	Pasco County, FL	344,765
		12103	Pinellas County, FL.	921,482
8320			**Terre Haute, IN MSA**	**149,192**
		18021	Clay County, IN.	26,556
		18165	Vermillion County, IN	16,788
		18167	Vigo County, IN.	105,848
8360			**Texarkana, TX-Texarkana, AR MSA**	**129,749**
		05091	Miller County, AR.	40,443
		48037	Bowie County, TX	89,306
8400			**Toledo, OH MSA**	**618,203**
		39051	Fulton County, OH	42,084
		39095	Lucas County, OH.	455,054
		39173	Wood County, OH	121,065
8440			**Topeka, KS MSA**	**169,871**
		20177	Shawnee County, KS	169,871
	8480		**Trenton, NJ PMSA**	**350,761**
			(See New York-Northern New Jersey-Long Island, NY-NJ-CT-PA CMSA)	
8520			**Tucson, AZ MSA**	**843,746**
		04019	Pima County, AZ	843,746
8560			**Tulsa, OK MSA**	**803,235**
		40037	Creek County, OK	67,367
		40113	Osage County, OK.	44,437
		40131	Rogers County, OK	70,641
		40143	Tulsa County, OK	563,299
		40145	Wagoner County, OK	57,491
8600			**Tuscaloosa, AL MSA**	**164,875**
		01125	Tuscaloosa County, AL.	164,875
8640			**Tyler, TX MSA**	**174,706**
		48423	Smith County, TX	174,706
8680			**Utica-Rome, NY MSA**	**299,896**
		36043	Herkimer County, NY	64,427
		36065	Oneida County, NY	235,469
	8720		**Vallejo-Fairfield-Napa, CA PMSA**	**518,821**
			(See San Francisco-Oakland-San Jose, CA CMSA)	
	8735		**Ventura, CA PMSA**	**753,197**
			(See Los Angeles-Riverside-Orange County, CA CMSA)	
8750			**Victoria, TX MSA**	**84,088**
		48469	Victoria County, TX	84,088
	8760		**Vineland-Millville-Bridgeton, NJ PMSA**	**146,438**
			(See Philadelphia-Wilmington-Atlantic City, PA-NJ-DE-MD CMSA)	

MSA/ CMSA/ NECMA	PMSA	State and county	Metropolitan area title and geographic component(s)	2000 population
8780			**Visalia-Tulare-Porterville, CA MSA**	**368,021**
		06107	Tulare County, CA.	368,021
8800			**Waco, TX MSA**	**213,517**
		48309	McLennan County, TX	213,517
	8840		**Washington, DC-MD-VA-WV PMSA**	**4,923,153**
			(See Washington-Baltimore, DC-MD-VA-WV CMSA)	
8872			**Washington-Baltimore, DC-MD-VA-WV CMSA**	**7,608,070**
	0720		**Baltimore, MD PMSA**	**2,552,994**
		24003	Anne Arundel County, MD	489,656
		24005	Baltimore County, MD	754,292
		24013	Carroll County, MD.	150,897
		24025	Harford County, MD	218,590
		24027	Howard County, MD	247,842
		24035	Queen Anne's County, MD.	40,563
		24510	Baltimore city, MD	651,154
	3180		**Hagerstown, MD PMSA.**	**131,923**
		24043	Washington County, MD	131,923
	8840		**Washington, DC-MD-VA-WV PMSA.**	**4,923,153**
		11001	District of Columbia	572,059
		24009	Calvert County, MD	74,563
		24017	Charles County, MD	120,546
		24021	Frederick County, MD	195,277
		24031	Montgomery County, MD.	873,341
		24033	Prince George's County, MD	801,515
		51013	Arlington County, VA.	189,453
		51043	Clarke County, VA.	12,652
		51047	Culpeper County, VA.	34,262
		51059	Fairfax County, VA	969,749
		51061	Fauquier County, VA	55,139
		51099	King George County, VA.	16,803
		51107	Loudoun County, VA.	169,599
		51153	Prince William County, VA.	280,813
		51177	Spotsylvania County, VA.	90,395
		51179	Stafford County, VA.	92,446
		51187	Warren County, VA.	31,584
		51510	Alexandria city, VA	128,283
		51600	Fairfax city, VA	21,498
		51610	Falls Church city, VA.	10,377
		51630	Fredericksburg city, VA	19,279
		51683	Manassas city, VA	35,135
		51685	Manassas Park city, VA.	10,290
		54003	Berkeley County, WV	75,905
		54037	Jefferson County, WV	42,190
8880			**Waterbury, CT PMSA**	**228,984**
			(See New York-Northern New Jersey-Long Island, NY-NJ-CT-PA CMSA)	
8920			**Waterloo-Cedar Falls, IA MSA.**	**128,012**
		19013	Black Hawk County, IA.	128,012
8940			**Wausau, WI MSA.**	**125,834**
		55073	Marathon County, WI.	125,834
8960			**West Palm Beach-Boca Raton, FL MSA.**	**1,131,184**
		12099	Palm Beach County, FL.	1,131,184
9000			**Wheeling, WV-OH MSA**	**153,172**
		39013	Belmont County, OH.	70,226
		54051	Marshall County, WV	35,519
		54069	Ohio County, WV.	47,427
9040			**Wichita, KS MSA.**	**545,220**
		20015	Butler County, KS	59,482
		20079	Harvey County, KS	32,869
		20173	Sedgwick County, KS	452,869
9080			**Wichita Falls, TX MSA**	**140,518**
		48009	Archer County, TX	8,854
		48485	Wichita County, TX	131,664
9140			**Williamsport, PA MSA**	**120,044**
		42081	Lycoming County, PA	120,044
	9160		**Wilmington-Newark, DE-MD PMSA**	**586,216**
			(See Philadelphia-Wilmington-Atlantic City, PA-NJ-DE-MD CMSA)	
9200			**Wilmington, NC MSA.**	**233,450**
		37019	Brunswick County, NC	73,143
		37129	New Hanover County, NC	160,307

[Metropolitan areas (MAs) defined as of June 30, 1999. MSA = metropolitan statistical area; CMSA = consolidated MSA; PMSA = primary MSA; NECMA = New England county MA. Geographic codes shown are Federal Information Processing Standards (FIPS) codes]

Geographic codes			Metropolitan area title and geographic component(s)	2000 population	Geographic codes			Metropolitan area title and geographic component(s)	2000 population
MSA/ CMSA/ NECMA	PMSA	State and county			MSA/ CMSA/ NECMA	PMSA	State and county		
	9240		Worcester, MA-CT PMSA	511,389	9320			Youngstown-Warren, OH MSA	594,746
			(See Boston-Worcester-Lawrence, MA-NH-ME-CT CMSA)				39029	Columbiana County, OH	112,075
							39099	Mahoning County, OH	257,555
9260			Yakima, WA MSA.	222,581			39155	Trumbull County, OH	225,116
		53077	Yakima County, WA	222,581	9340			Yuba City, CA MSA	139,149
	9270		Yolo, CA PMSA	168,660			06101	Sutter County, CA	78,930
			(See Sacramento-Yolo, CA CMSA)				06115	Yuba County, CA.	60,219
					9360			Yuma, AZ MSA	160,026
9280			York, PA MSA.	381,751			04027	Yuma County, AZ	160,026
		42133	York County, PA	381,751					

County Maps by State

Appendix C

Page

You may visit us on the Web at

http://www.census.gov/statab/www/ccdb.html

County Maps
by State

C

Appendix C

ALABAMA - Metropolitan Areas, Counties, and Selected Places

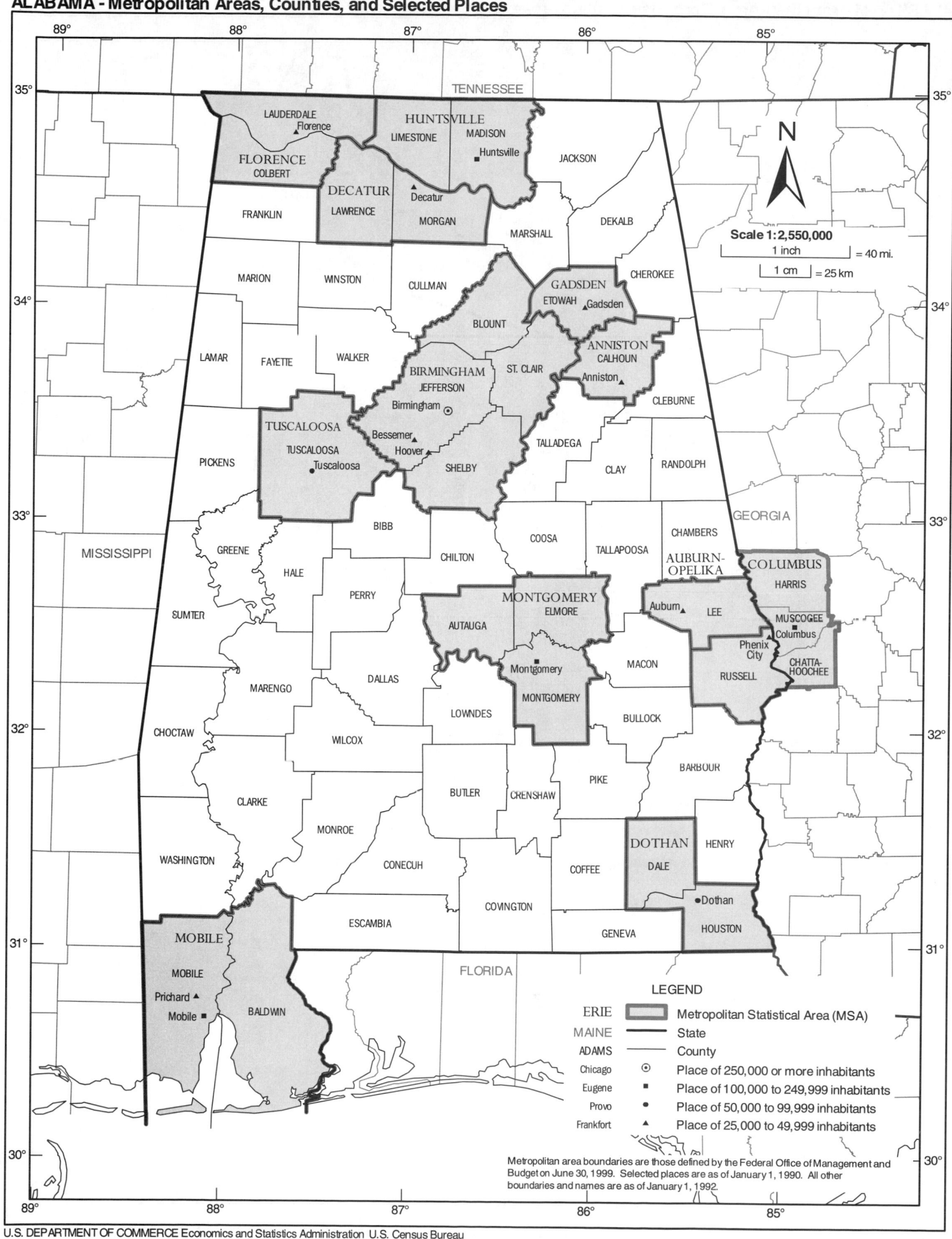

LEGEND

ERIE	Metropolitan Statistical Area (MSA)
MAINE	State
ADAMS	County
Chicago ⊙	Place of 250,000 or more inhabitants
Eugene ■	Place of 100,000 to 249,999 inhabitants
Provo ●	Place of 50,000 to 99,999 inhabitants
Frankfort ▲	Place of 25,000 to 49,999 inhabitants

Metropolitan area boundaries are those defined by the Federal Office of Management and Budget on June 30, 1999. Selected places are as of January 1, 1990. All other boundaries and names are as of January 1, 1992.

Scale 1:2,550,000
1 inch = 40 mi.
1 cm = 25 km

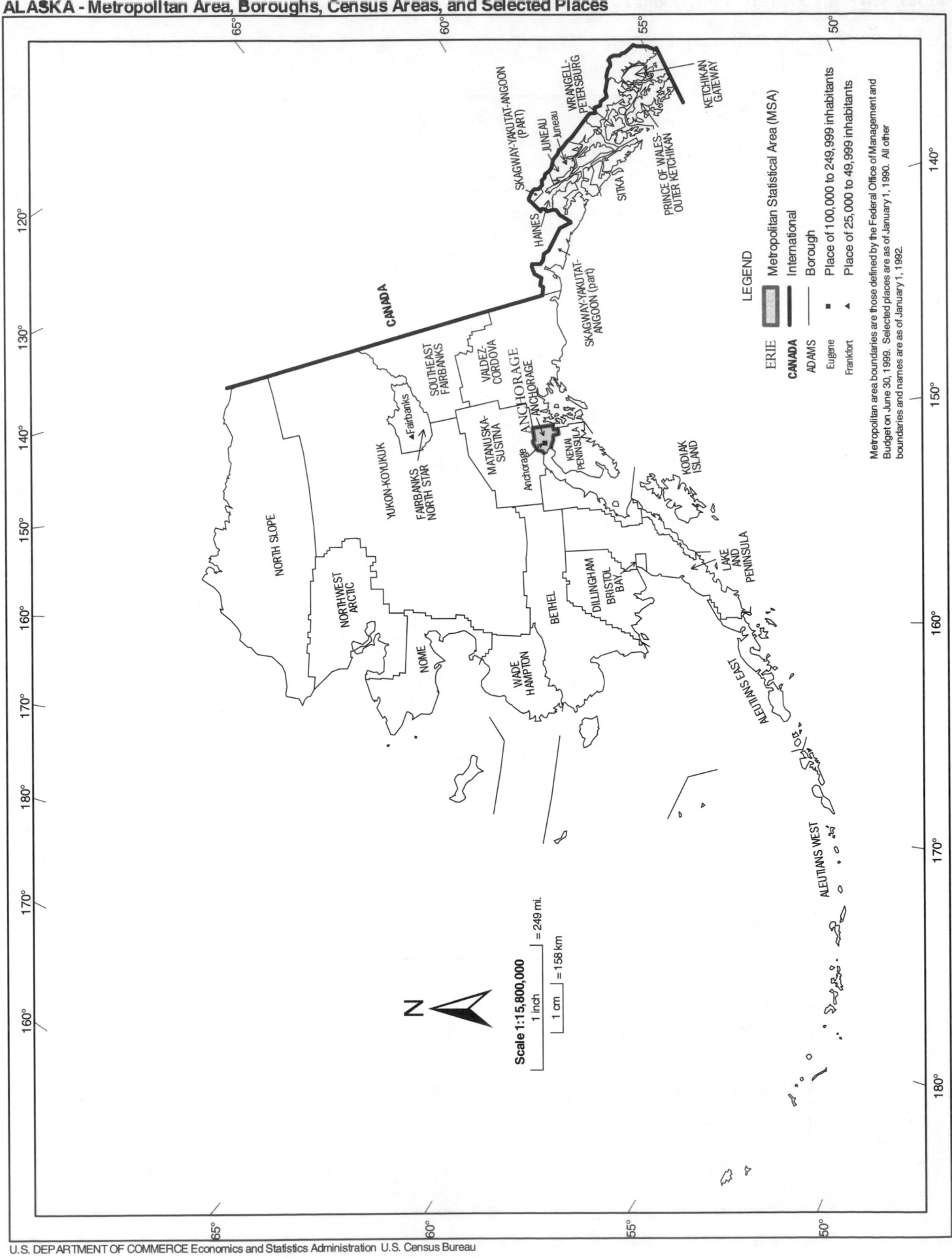

LEGEND

ERIE   Metropolitan Statistical Area (MSA)

CANADA   International

ADAMS   Borough

Eugene   ■ Place of 100,000 to 249,999 inhabitants

Frankfort   ▲ Place of 25,000 to 49,999 inhabitants

Metropolitan area boundaries are those defined by the Federal Office of Management and Budget on June 30, 1999. Selected places are as of January 1, 1990. All other boundaries and names are as of January 1, 1992.

Scale 1:15,800,000

1 inch = 249 mi.

1 cm = 158 km

N

ARIZONA - Metropolitan Areas, Counties, and Selected Places

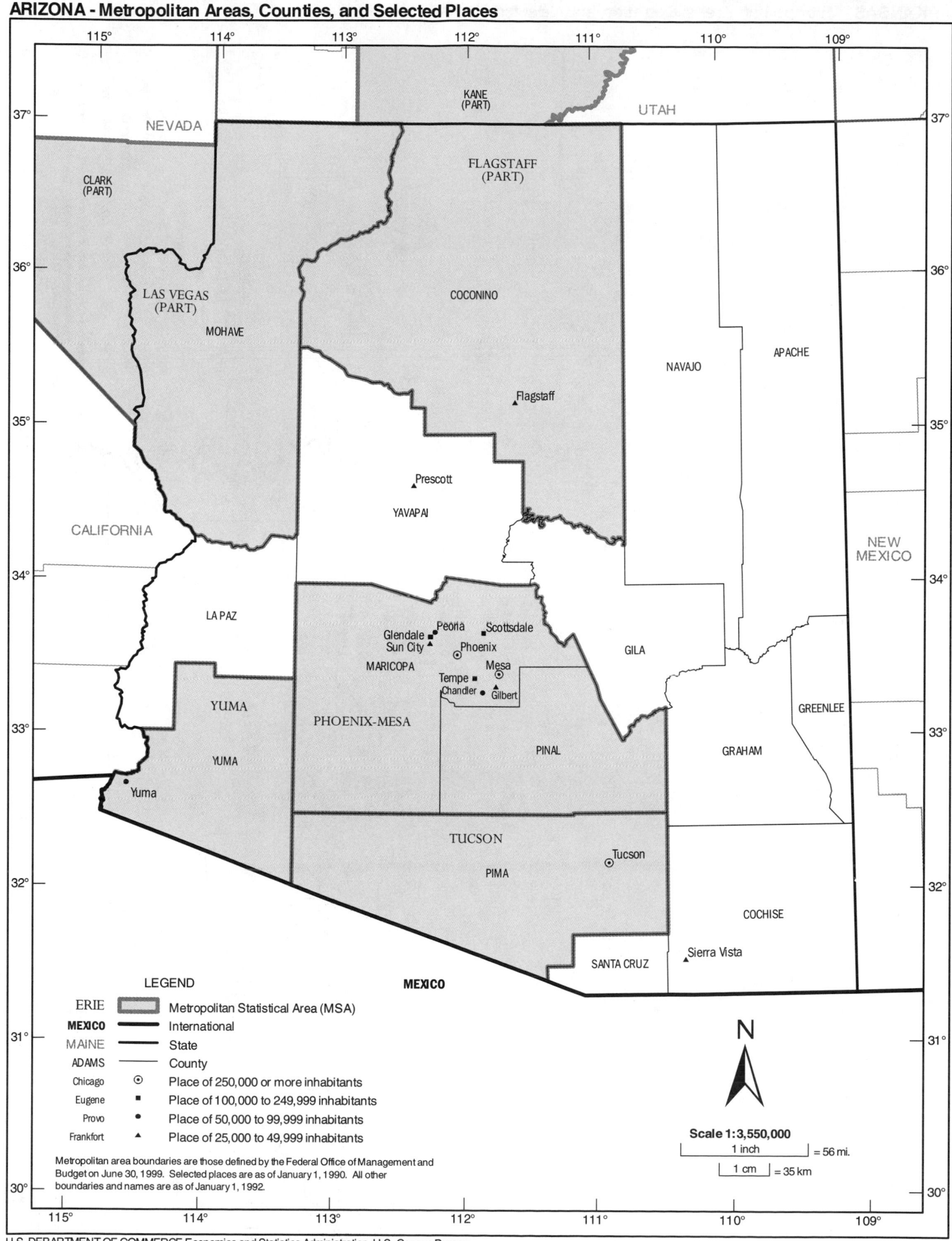

LEGEND

ERIE	Metropolitan Statistical Area (MSA)
MEXICO	International
MAINE	State
ADAMS	County
Chicago ⊙	Place of 250,000 or more inhabitants
Eugene ■	Place of 100,000 to 249,999 inhabitants
Provo ●	Place of 50,000 to 99,999 inhabitants
Frankfort ▲	Place of 25,000 to 49,999 inhabitants

Metropolitan area boundaries are those defined by the Federal Office of Management and Budget on June 30, 1999. Selected places are as of January 1, 1990. All other boundaries and names are as of January 1, 1992.

Scale 1:3,550,000

1 inch = 56 mi.

1 cm = 35 km

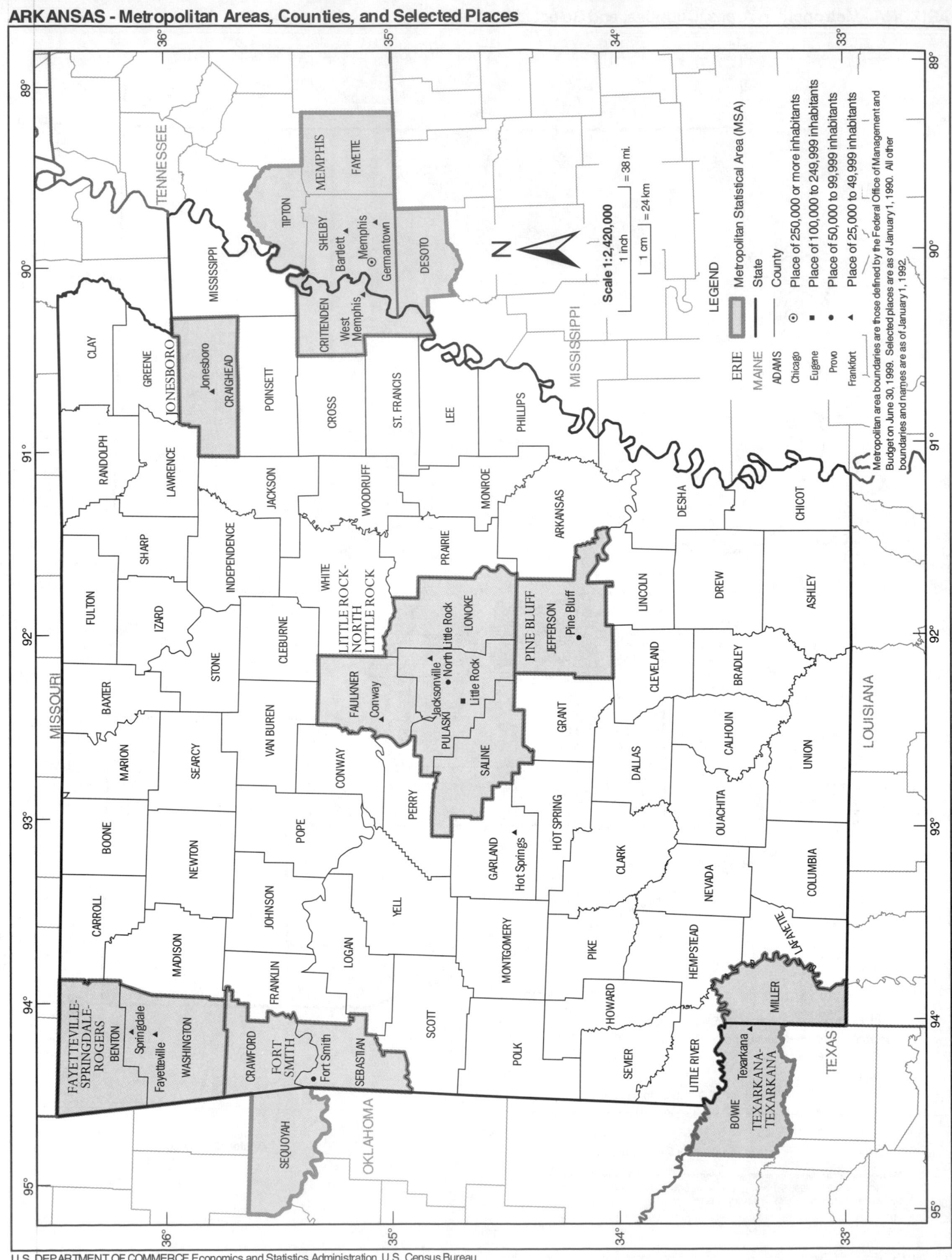

LEGEND

Metropolitan Statistical Area (MSA)
State
County

Place of 250,000 or more inhabitants
Place of 100,000 to 249,999 inhabitants
Place of 50,000 to 99,999 inhabitants
Place of 25,000 to 49,999 inhabitants

ERIE
MAINE
ADAMS
Chicago
Eugene
Provo
Frankfort

Metropolitan area boundaries are those defined by the Federal Office of Management and Budget on June 30, 1999. Selected places are as of January 1, 1990. All other boundaries and names are as of January 1, 1992.

Scale 1:2,420,000
1 inch = 38 mi.
1 cm = 24 km

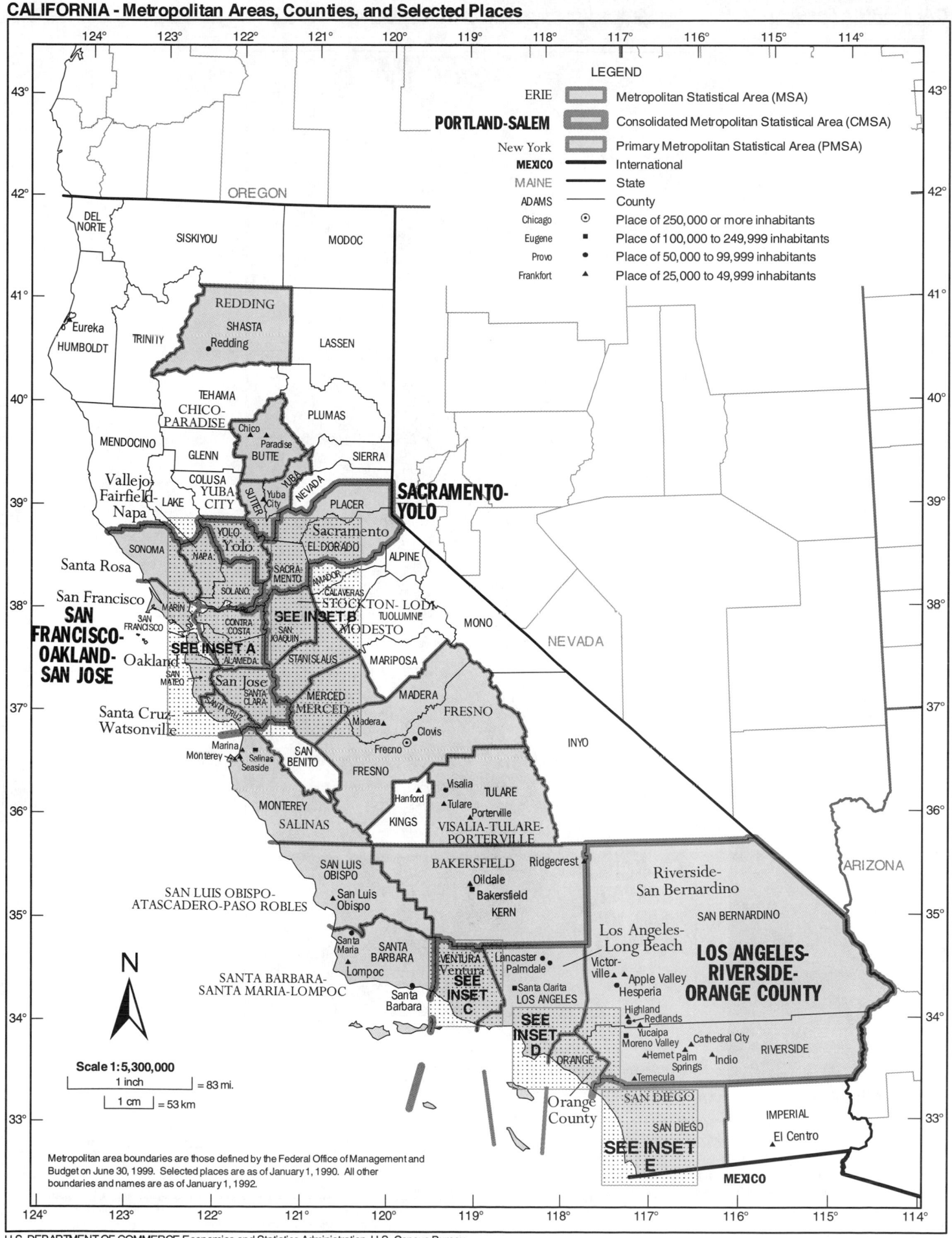

LEGEND

ERIE — Metropolitan Statistical Area (MSA)
PORTLAND-SALEM — Consolidated Metropolitan Statistical Area (CMSA)
New York — Primary Metropolitan Statistical Area (PMSA)
MEXICO — International
MAINE — State
ADAMS — County
Chicago ⊙ Place of 250,000 or more inhabitants
Eugene ■ Place of 100,000 to 249,999 inhabitants
Provo • Place of 50,000 to 99,999 inhabitants
Frankfort ▲ Place of 25,000 to 49,999 inhabitants

Scale 1:5,300,000
1 inch = 83 mi.
1 cm = 53 km

Metropolitan area boundaries are those defined by the Federal Office of Management and Budget on June 30, 1999. Selected places are as of January 1, 1990. All other boundaries and names are as of January 1, 1992.

U.S. DEPARTMENT OF COMMERCE Economics and Statistics Administration U.S. Census Bureau

SACRAMENTO-
YOLO
(PART)

LAKE
(PART)

SUTTER
(PART)

YOLO

Yolo
(Part)

Woodland ▲

Sacramento
(Part)

Davis ▲

West
Sacramento ▲

Vallejo-
Fairfield-
Napa

SONOMA
(PART)

38°30′

■ Santa Rosa

NAPA

Vacaville •

38°30′

▲ Rohnert Park

Santa Rosa
(Part)

Napa •

Fairfield •

Sacramento
(Part)

▲ Petaluma

SOLANO

SACRAMENTO
(PART)

Novato ▲

• Vallejo

San
Francisco
(Part)

38°00′

San
Rafael •

Martinez ▲

Pittsburg ▲

Antioch •

38°00′

MARIN
(PART)

▲ San Pablo

Richmond ■

■ Concord
Pleasant Hill •

Oakland

Berkeley •

• Walnut Creek

SAN FRANCISCO
(PART)

San Francisco
(Part)

CONTRA COSTA

Danville ▲

⊙ Oakland

Alameda •

• San Ramon

Daly City •

South
San
Francisco

San
Leandro •

Castro Valley ▲

Livermore •

SAN JOAQUIN (PART)

San Bruno ▲

▲ Pacifica

Foster
City

• Hayward

Pleasanton •

Burlingame ▲

San Mateo ▲

Union City •

ALAMEDA

Newark •

Fremont ▲

STOCKTON-
LODI (PART)

Redwood City •
San Carlos ▲

37°30′

Menlo Park ▲

37°30′

Palo
Alto •

Mountain
View

Milpitas •

SAN
FRANCISCO-
OAKLAND-
SAN JOSE
(PART)

SAN MATEO

Los Altos ▲

Sunnyvale ■

• Santa Clara

Cupertino •

⊙ San Jose

Saratoga ▲

• Campbell

San Jose
(Part)

• Los Gatos

SANTA CRUZ

SANTA CLARA
(PART)

37°00′

Santa Cruz-
Watsonville

Gilroy ▲

37°00′

▲ Santa Cruz

Watsonville •

SALINAS
(PART)

MONTEREY
(PART)

SAN BENITO
(PART)

122°30′

122°00′

121°30′

N

LEGEND

ERIE — Metropolitan Statistical Area (MSA)

PORTLAND-SALEM — Consolidated Metropolitan Statistical Area (CMSA)

New York — Primary Metropolitan Statistical Area (PMSA)

ADAMS —— County

Chicago ⊙ Place of 250,000 or more inhabitants

Eugene ■ Place of 100,000 to 249,999 inhabitants

Provo • Place of 50,000 to 99,999 inhabitants

Frankfort ▲ Place of 25,000 to 49,999 inhabitants

Scale 1:1,200,000
1 inch = 18 mi.
1 cm = 12 km

Metropolitan area boundaries are those defined by the Federal Office of Management and
Budget on June 30, 1999. Selected places are as of January 1, 1990. All other
boundaries and names are as of January 1, 1992.

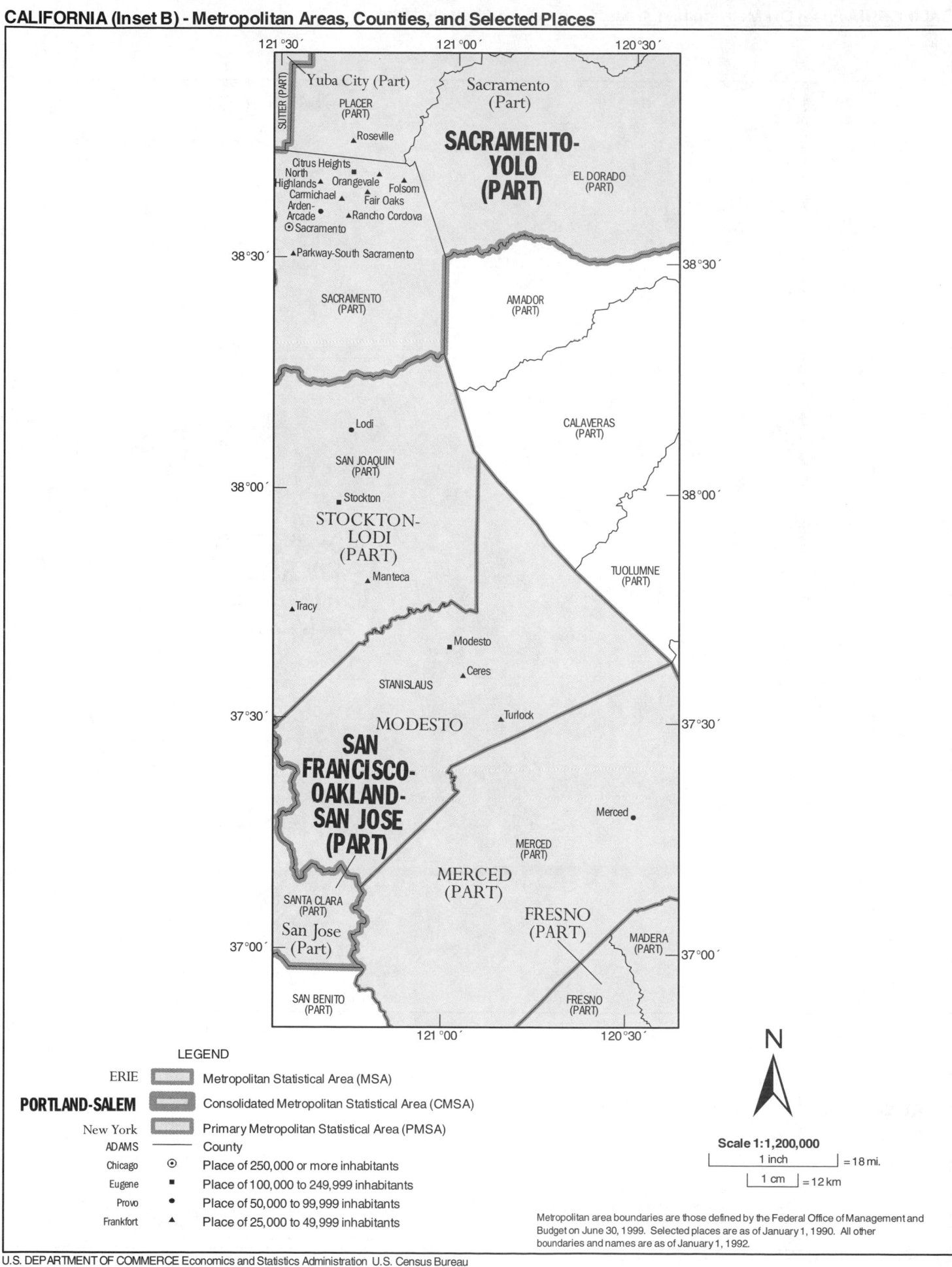

CALIFORNIA (Inset B) - Metropolitan Areas, Counties, and Selected Places

Yuba City (Part)
SUTTER (PART)
Sacramento (Part)
PLACER (PART)
Roseville
SACRAMENTO-YOLO (PART)
EL DORADO (PART)
Citrus Heights
North Highlands
Orangevale
Folsom
Carmichael
Fair Oaks
Arden-Arcade
Rancho Cordova
Sacramento
Parkway-South Sacramento
SACRAMENTO (PART)
AMADOR (PART)
Lodi
CALAVERAS (PART)
SAN JOAQUIN (PART)
Stockton
STOCKTON-LODI (PART)
TUOLUMNE (PART)
Manteca
Tracy
Modesto
Ceres
STANISLAUS
MODESTO
Turlock
SAN FRANCISCO-OAKLAND-SAN JOSE (PART)
Merced
MERCED (PART)
SANTA CLARA (PART)
MERCED (PART)
FRESNO (PART)
San Jose (Part)
MADERA (PART)
SAN BENITO (PART)
FRESNO (PART)

N

LEGEND

ERIE — Metropolitan Statistical Area (MSA)

PORTLAND-SALEM — Consolidated Metropolitan Statistical Area (CMSA)

New York — Primary Metropolitan Statistical Area (PMSA)

ADAMS — County

Chicago ⊙ Place of 250,000 or more inhabitants

Eugene ■ Place of 100,000 to 249,999 inhabitants

Provo • Place of 50,000 to 99,999 inhabitants

Frankfort ▲ Place of 25,000 to 49,999 inhabitants

Scale 1:1,200,000

1 inch = 18 mi.

1 cm = 12 km

Metropolitan area boundaries are those defined by the Federal Office of Management and Budget on June 30, 1999. Selected places are as of January 1, 1990. All other boundaries and names are as of January 1, 1992.

U.S. DEPARTMENT OF COMMERCE Economics and Statistics Administration U.S. Census Bureau

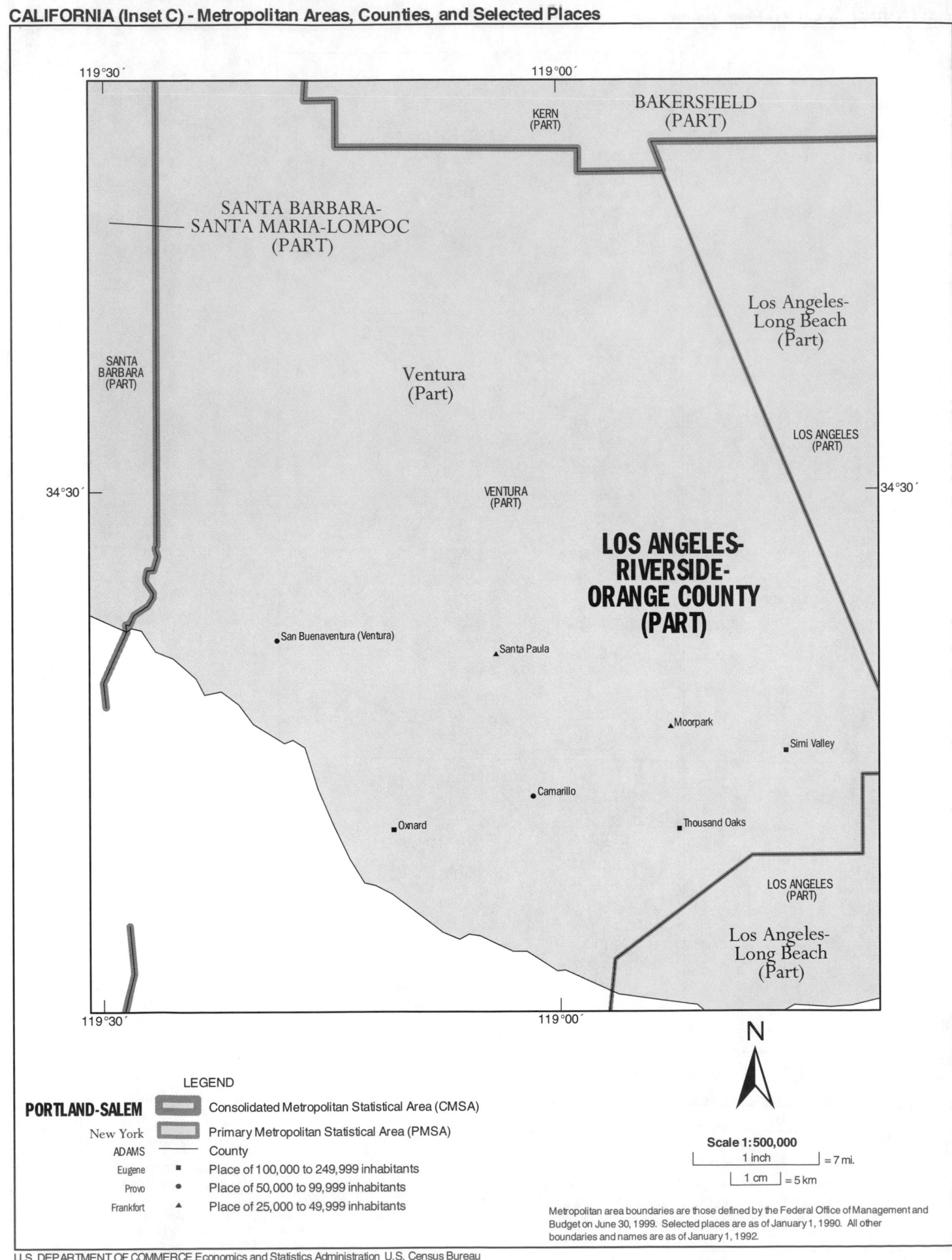

119°30′   119°00′

BAKERSFIELD
(PART)

KERN
(PART)

SANTA BARBARA-
SANTA MARIA-LOMPOC
(PART)

Los Angeles-
Long Beach
(Part)

SANTA
BARBARA
(PART)

Ventura
(Part)

LOS ANGELES
(PART)

34°30′   34°30′

VENTURA
(PART)

**LOS ANGELES-
RIVERSIDE-
ORANGE COUNTY
(PART)**

● San Buenaventura (Ventura)

▲ Santa Paula

▲ Moorpark

■ Simi Valley

● Camarillo

■ Oxnard   ■ Thousand Oaks

LOS ANGELES
(PART)

Los Angeles-
Long Beach
(Part)

119°30′   119°00′

N

LEGEND

PORTLAND-SALEM ▭ Consolidated Metropolitan Statistical Area (CMSA)

New York ▭ Primary Metropolitan Statistical Area (PMSA)

ADAMS ── County

Eugene ■ Place of 100,000 to 249,999 inhabitants

Provo ● Place of 50,000 to 99,999 inhabitants

Frankfort ▲ Place of 25,000 to 49,999 inhabitants

Scale 1:500,000

|⊢ 1 inch ⊣| = 7 mi.

|⊢ 1 cm ⊣| = 5 km

Metropolitan area boundaries are those defined by the Federal Office of Management and
Budget on June 30, 1999. Selected places are as of January 1, 1990. All other
boundaries and names are as of January 1, 1992.

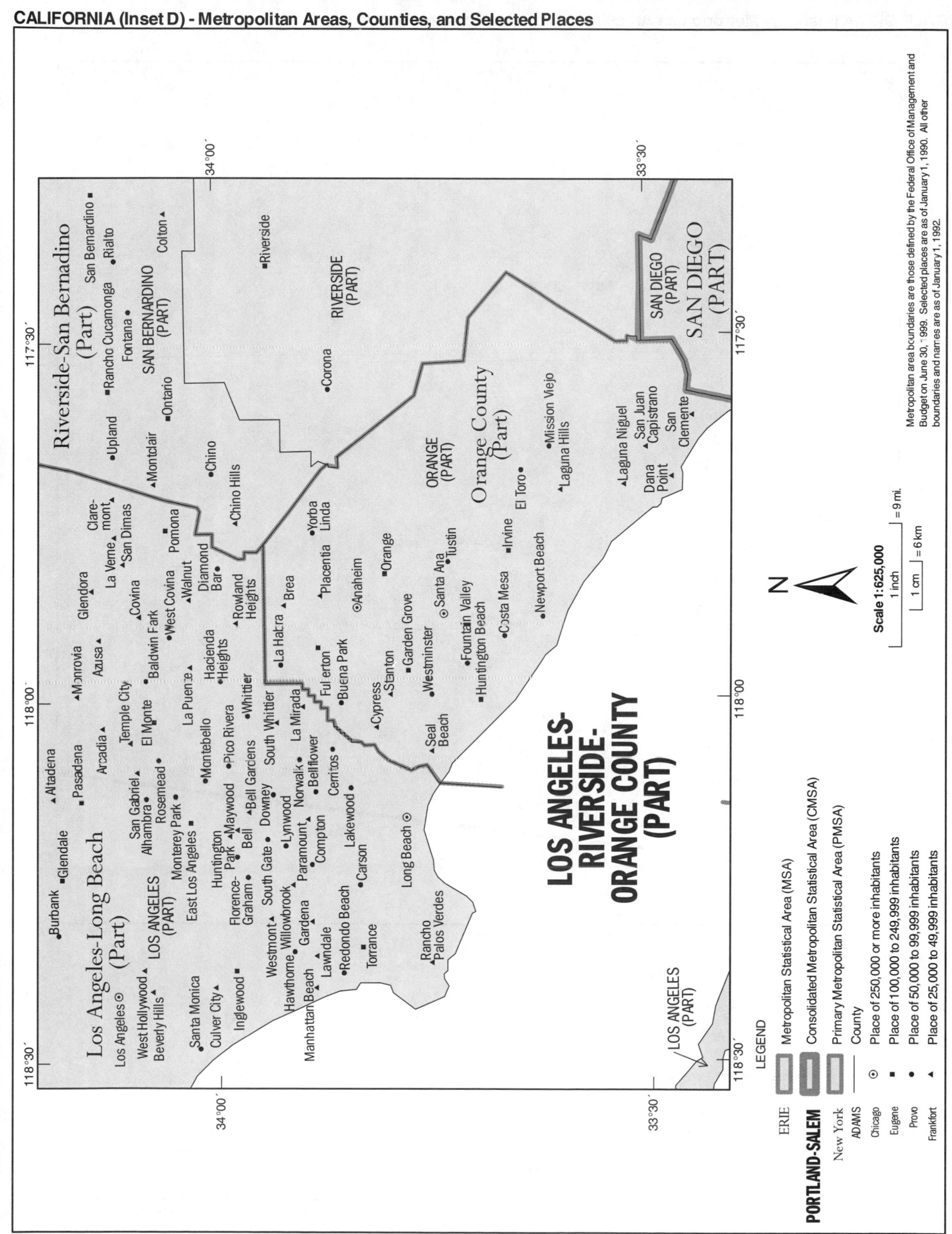

Metropolitan area boundaries are those defined by the Federal Office of Management and Budget on June 30, 1999. Selected places are as of January 1, 1990. All other boundaries and names are as of January 1, 1992.

Scale 1:625,000

1 inch = 9 mi.

1 cm = 6 km

N

LOS ANGELES-RIVERSIDE-ORANGE COUNTY (PART)

LEGEND

ERIE — Metropolitan Statistical Area (MSA)

PORTLAND-SALEM — Consolidated Metropolitan Statistical Area (CMSA)

New York — Primary Metropolitan Statistical Area (PMSA)

ADAMS — County

⊙ Chicago — Place of 250,000 or more inhabitants

■ Eugene — Place of 100,000 to 249,999 inhabitants

● Provo — Place of 50,000 to 99,999 inhabitants

▲ Frankfort — Place of 25,000 to 49,999 inhabitants

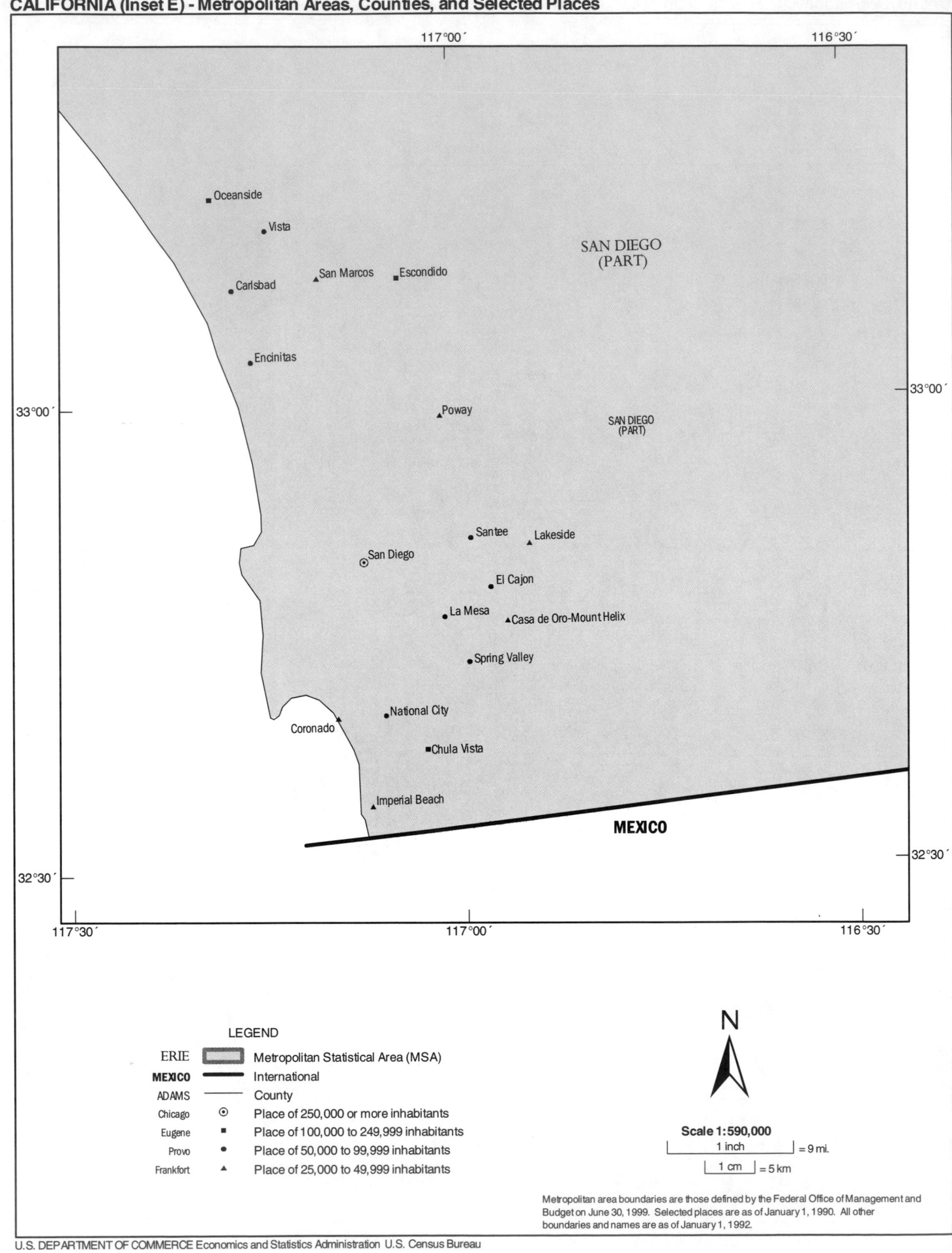

117°00′   116°30′

33°00′

Oceanside

Vista

SAN DIEGO
(PART)

San Marcos   Escondido

Carlsbad

Encinitas

Poway

SAN DIEGO
(PART)

33°00′

Santee   Lakeside

San Diego

El Cajon

La Mesa   Casa de Oro-Mount Helix

Spring Valley

National City

Coronado

Chula Vista

Imperial Beach

MEXICO

32°30′

32°30′

117°30′   117°00′   116°30′

LEGEND

ERIE ☐ Metropolitan Statistical Area (MSA)

MEXICO ▬ International

ADAMS ─── County

Chicago ⊙ Place of 250,000 or more inhabitants

Eugene ■ Place of 100,000 to 249,999 inhabitants

Provo ● Place of 50,000 to 99,999 inhabitants

Frankfort ▲ Place of 25,000 to 49,999 inhabitants

N

Scale 1:590,000
1 inch = 9 mi.
1 cm = 5 km

Metropolitan area boundaries are those defined by the Federal Office of Management and
Budget on June 30, 1999. Selected places are as of January 1, 1990. All other
boundaries and names are as of January 1, 1992.

U.S. DEPARTMENT OF COMMERCE Economics and Statistics Administration U.S. Census Bureau

COLORADO - Metropolitan Areas, Counties, and Selected Places

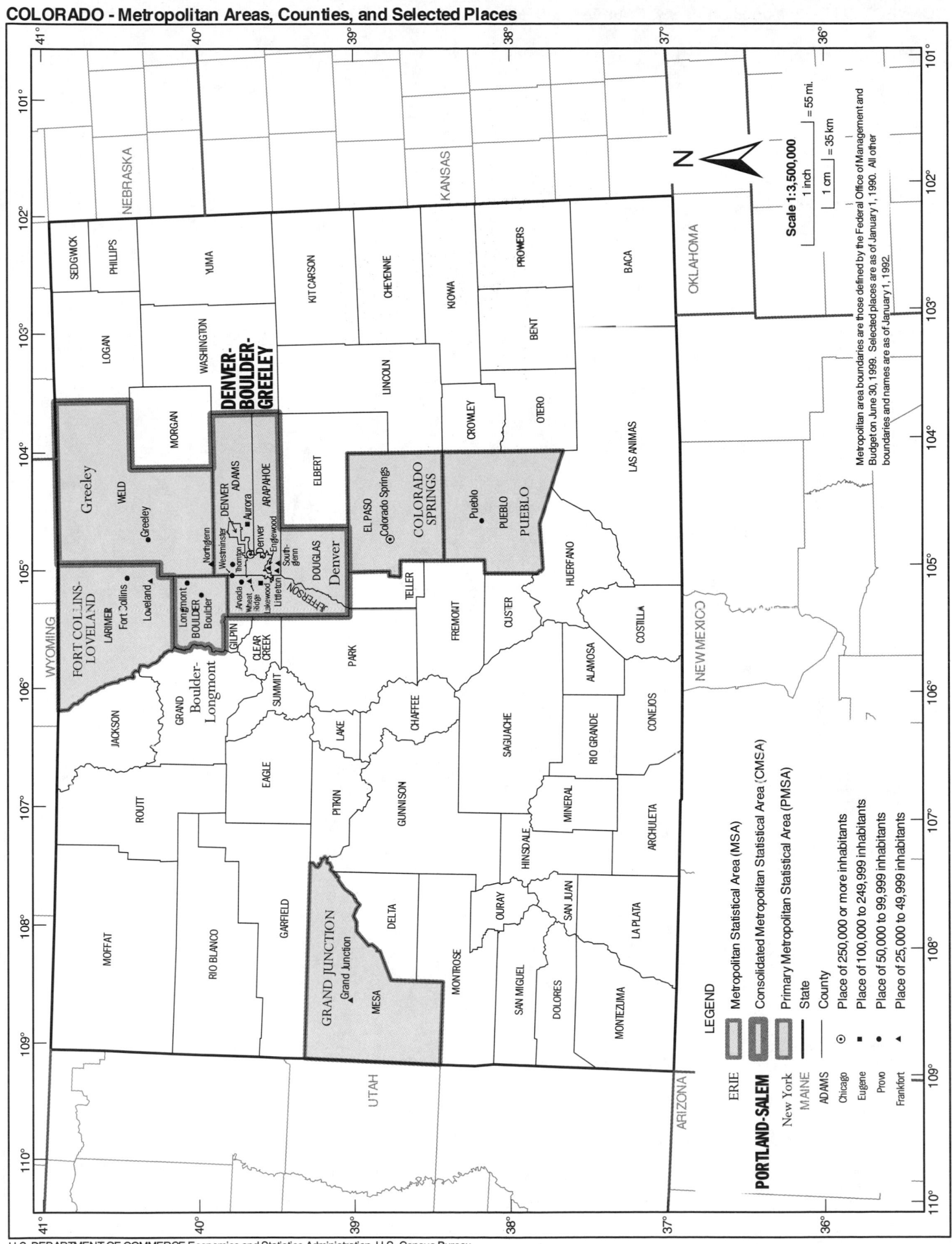

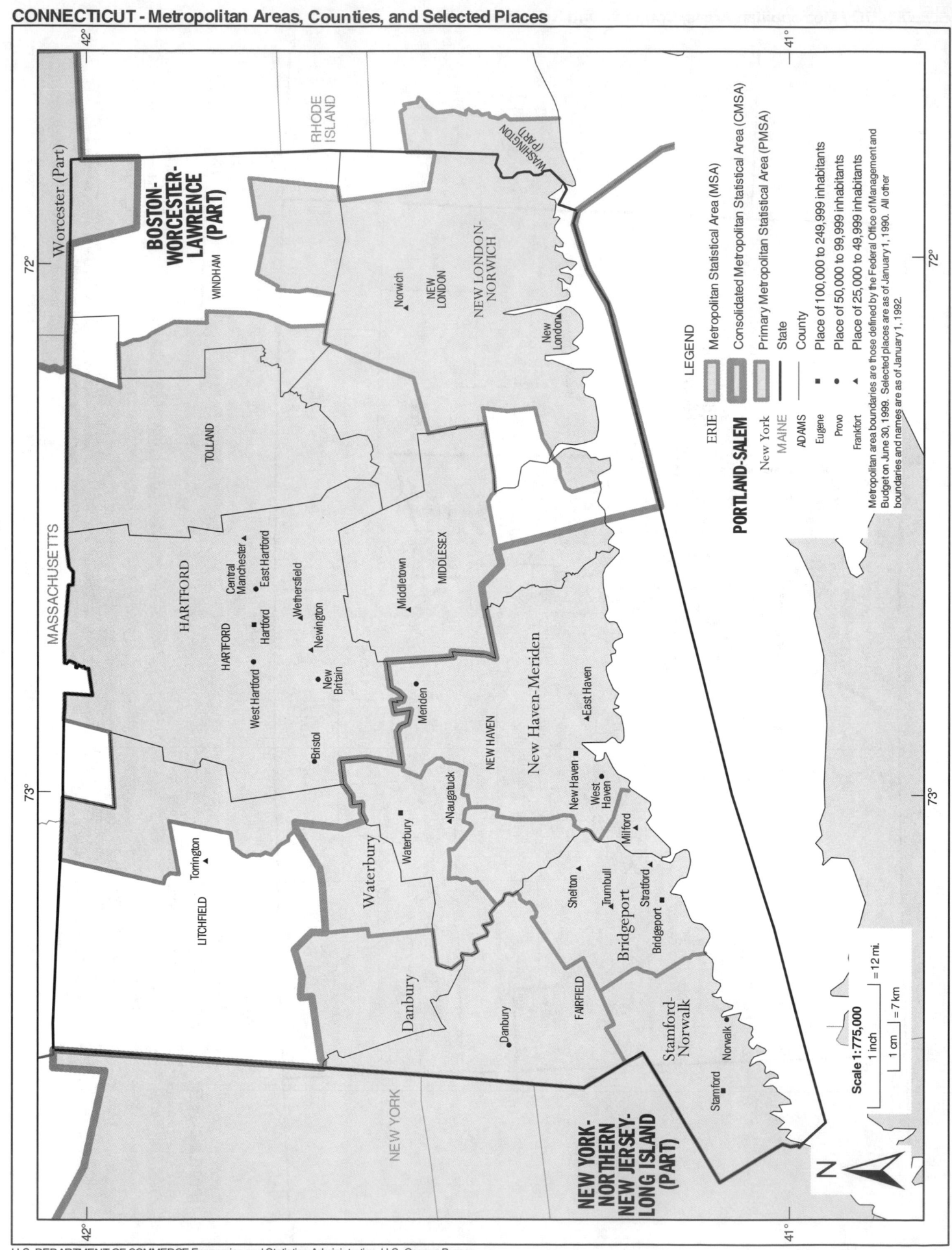

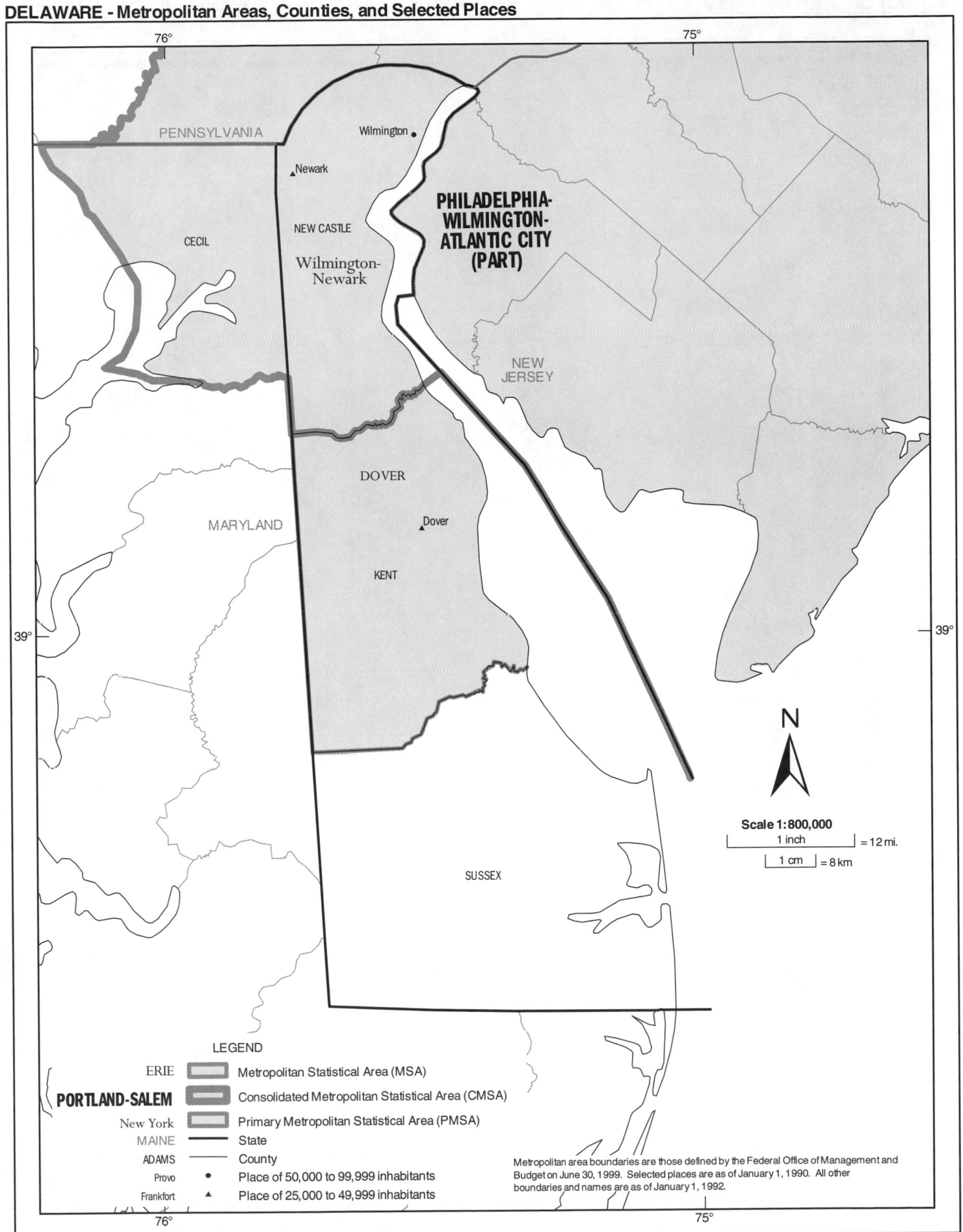

Scale 1:800,000

1 inch = 12 mi.

1 cm = 8 km

LEGEND

ERIE		Metropolitan Statistical Area (MSA)
PORTLAND-SALEM		Consolidated Metropolitan Statistical Area (CMSA)
New York		Primary Metropolitan Statistical Area (PMSA)
MAINE	——	State
ADAMS	——	County
Provo	●	Place of 50,000 to 99,999 inhabitants
Frankfort	▲	Place of 25,000 to 49,999 inhabitants

Metropolitan area boundaries are those defined by the Federal Office of Management and Budget on June 30, 1999. Selected places are as of January 1, 1990. All other boundaries and names are as of January 1, 1992.

DISTRICT OF COLUMBIA - Metropolitan Area, District of Columbia, Counties, Independent Cities, and Selected Places

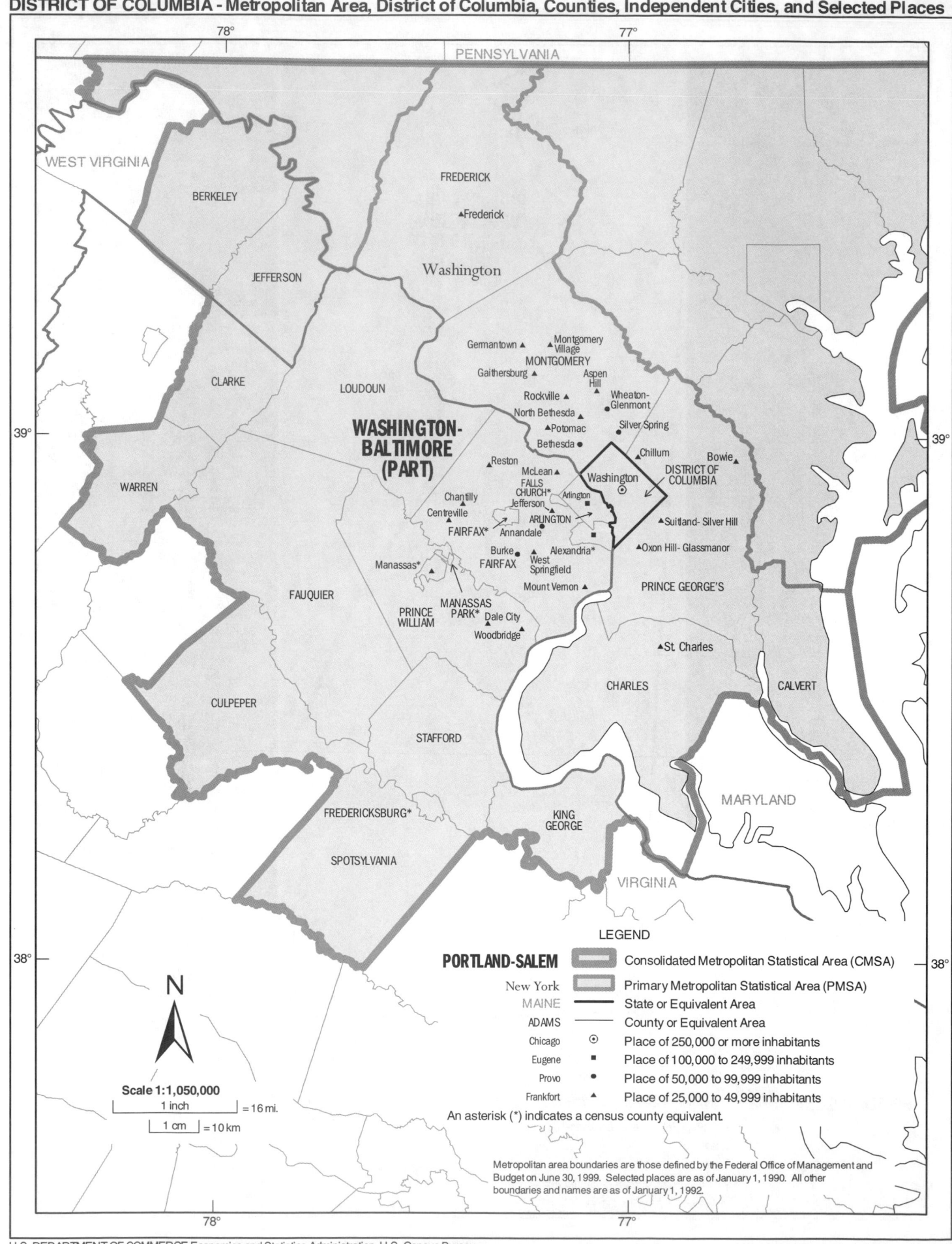

PENNSYLVANIA

WEST VIRGINIA

BERKELEY

JEFFERSON

FREDERICK

▲Frederick

Washington

Germantown ▲   ▲Montgomery Village

MONTGOMERY

Gaithersburg ▲   ▲Aspen Hill

Rockville ▲

North Bethesda ▲   Wheaton-Glenmont ●

▲Potomac   Silver Spring ●

Bethesda ●

CLARKE

LOUDOUN

WASHINGTON-BALTIMORE (PART)

Reston ▲

McLean ▲

FALLS CHURCH*

Jefferson ▲

Chantilly ▲

Centreville ▲

FAIRFAX*

Annandale ▲

Arlington ■

ARLINGTON

Chillum ●

DISTRICT OF COLUMBIA

Washington ⊙

Bowie ▲

▲Suitland- Silver Hill

WARREN

Burke ●

West Springfield ▲

Alexandria* ▲

▲Oxon Hill- Glassmanor

FAIRFAX

Manassas* ▲

Mount Vernon ▲

PRINCE GEORGE'S

FAUQUIER

MANASSAS PARK* ▲   Dale City ▲

PRINCE WILLIAM

Woodbridge ▲

▲St. Charles

CULPEPER

STAFFORD

CHARLES

CALVERT

FREDERICKSBURG*

KING GEORGE

MARYLAND

SPOTSYLVANIA

VIRGINIA

N

Scale 1:1,050,000

1 inch = 16 mi.

1 cm = 10 km

LEGEND

PORTLAND-SALEM   Consolidated Metropolitan Statistical Area (CMSA)

New York   Primary Metropolitan Statistical Area (PMSA)

MAINE   State or Equivalent Area

ADAMS   County or Equivalent Area

Chicago   ⊙   Place of 250,000 or more inhabitants

Eugene   ■   Place of 100,000 to 249,999 inhabitants

Provo   ●   Place of 50,000 to 99,999 inhabitants

Frankfort   ▲   Place of 25,000 to 49,999 inhabitants

An asterisk (*) indicates a census county equivalent.

Metropolitan area boundaries are those defined by the Federal Office of Management and Budget on June 30, 1999. Selected places are as of January 1, 1990. All other boundaries and names are as of January 1, 1992.

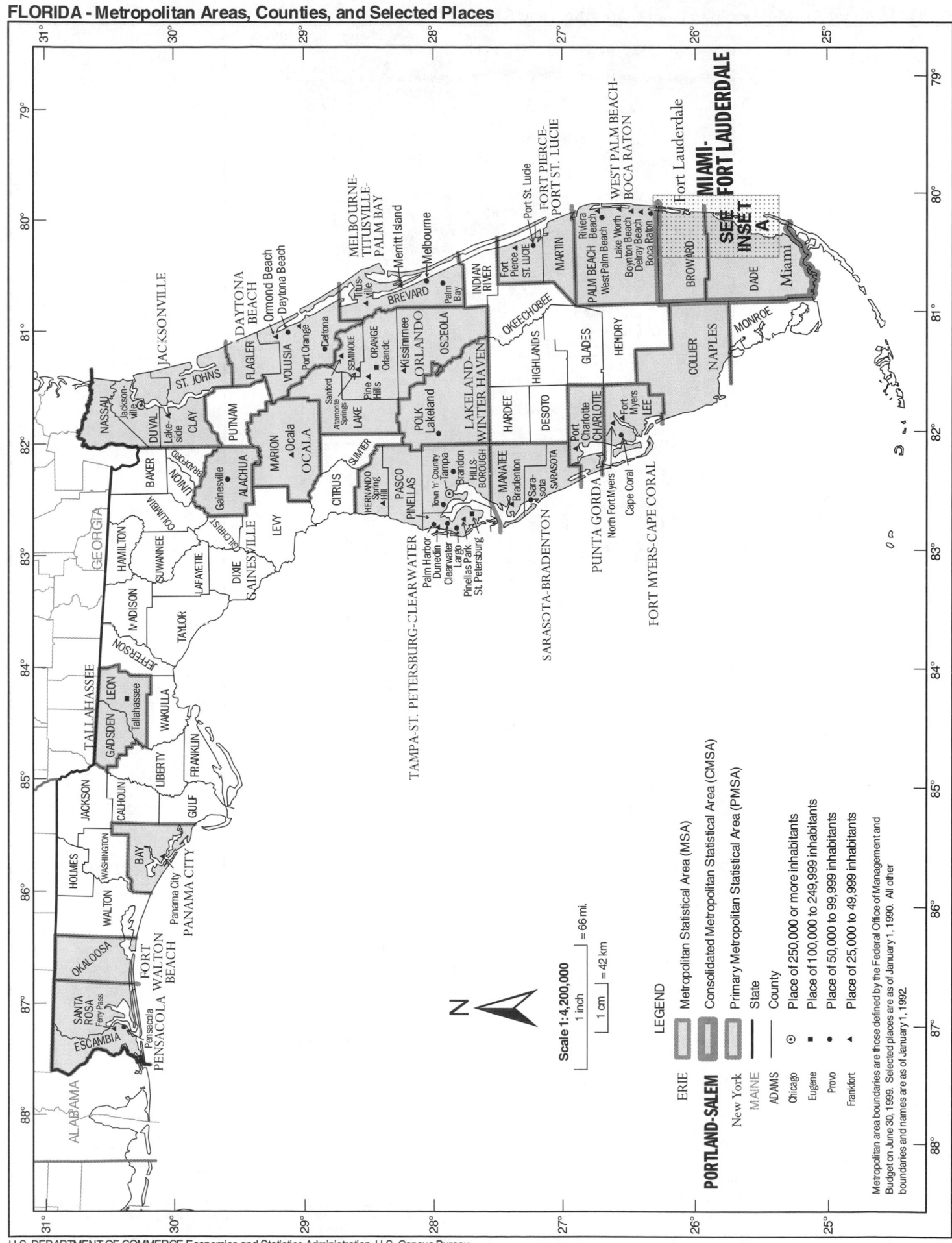

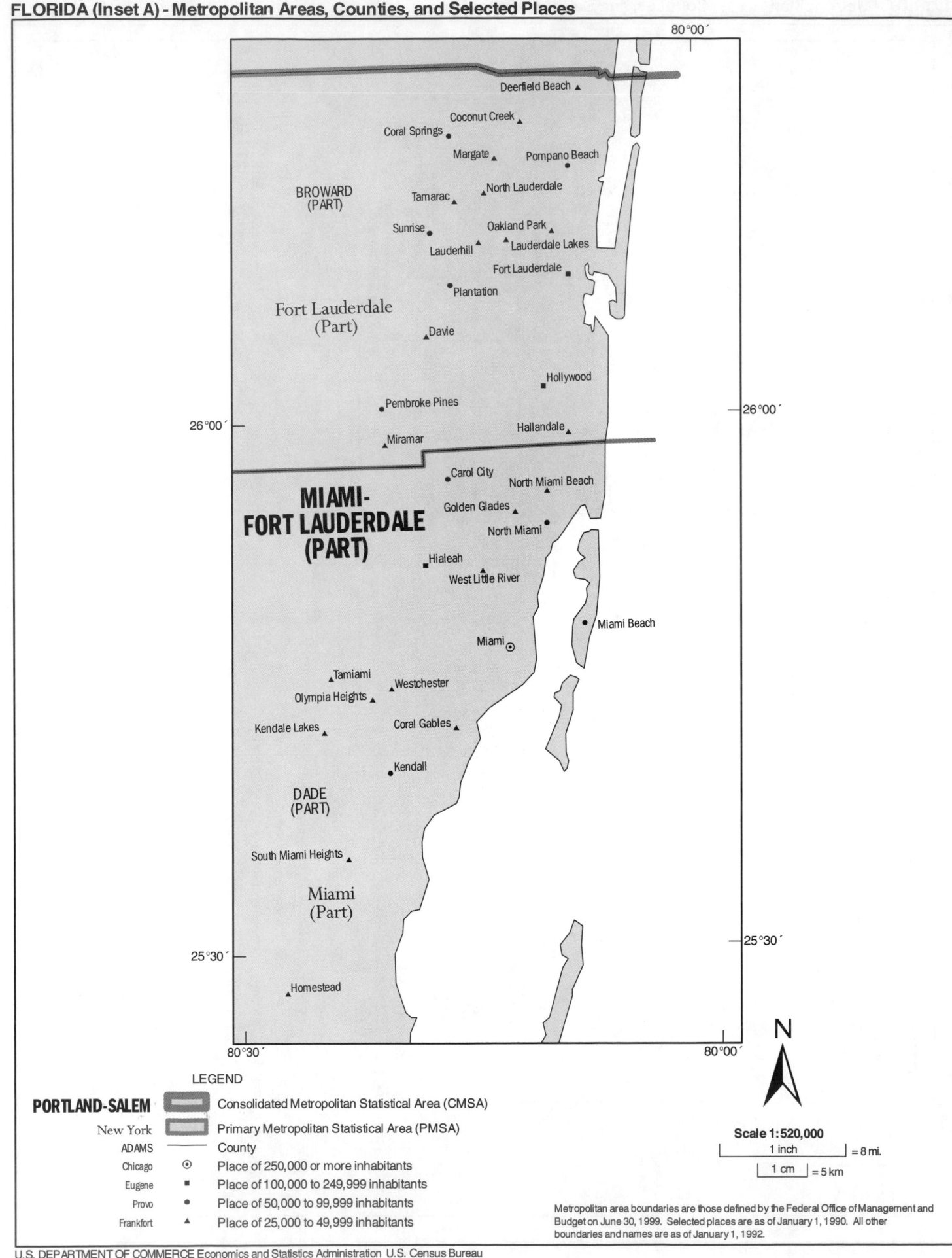

U.S. DEPARTMENT OF COMMERCE Economics and Statistics Administration U.S. Census Bureau

U.S. Census Bureau, County and City Data Book: 2000

GEORGIA - Metropolitan Areas, Counties, and Selected Places

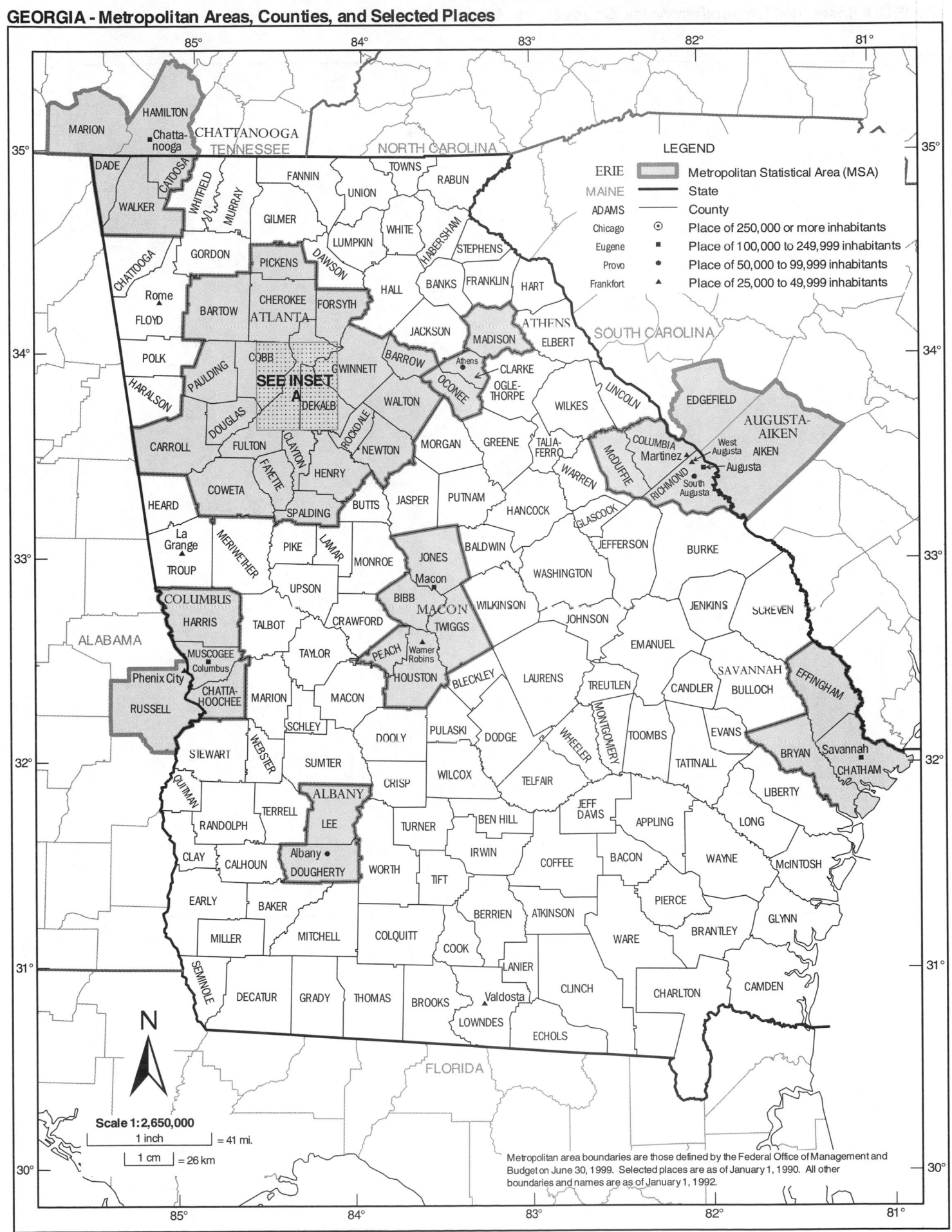

LEGEND

ERIE	Metropolitan Statistical Area (MSA)
MAINE	State
ADAMS	County
Chicago ⊙	Place of 250,000 or more inhabitants
Eugene ■	Place of 100,000 to 249,999 inhabitants
Provo ●	Place of 50,000 to 99,999 inhabitants
Frankfort ▲	Place of 25,000 to 49,999 inhabitants

Scale 1:2,650,000

1 inch = 41 mi.

1 cm = 26 km

Metropolitan area boundaries are those defined by the Federal Office of Management and Budget on June 30, 1999. Selected places are as of January 1, 1990. All other boundaries and names are as of January 1, 1992.

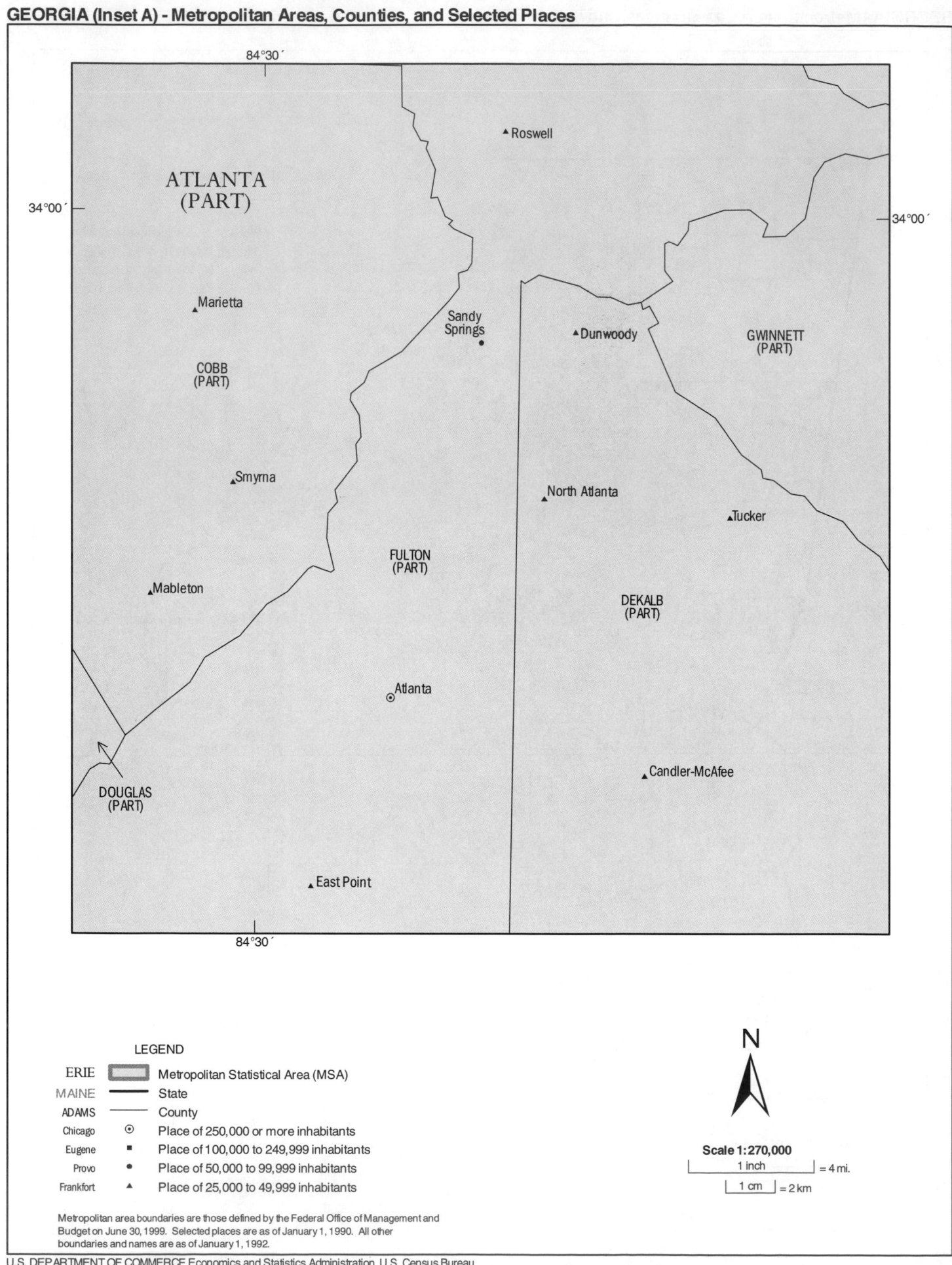

LEGEND

ERIE	▭	Metropolitan Statistical Area (MSA)
MAINE	▬	State
ADAMS	─	County
Chicago	⊙	Place of 250,000 or more inhabitants
Eugene	■	Place of 100,000 to 249,999 inhabitants
Provo	●	Place of 50,000 to 99,999 inhabitants
Frankfort	▲	Place of 25,000 to 49,999 inhabitants

Scale 1:270,000

1 inch = 4 mi.

1 cm = 2 km

Metropolitan area boundaries are those defined by the Federal Office of Management and
Budget on June 30, 1999. Selected places are as of January 1, 1990. All other
boundaries and names are as of January 1, 1992.

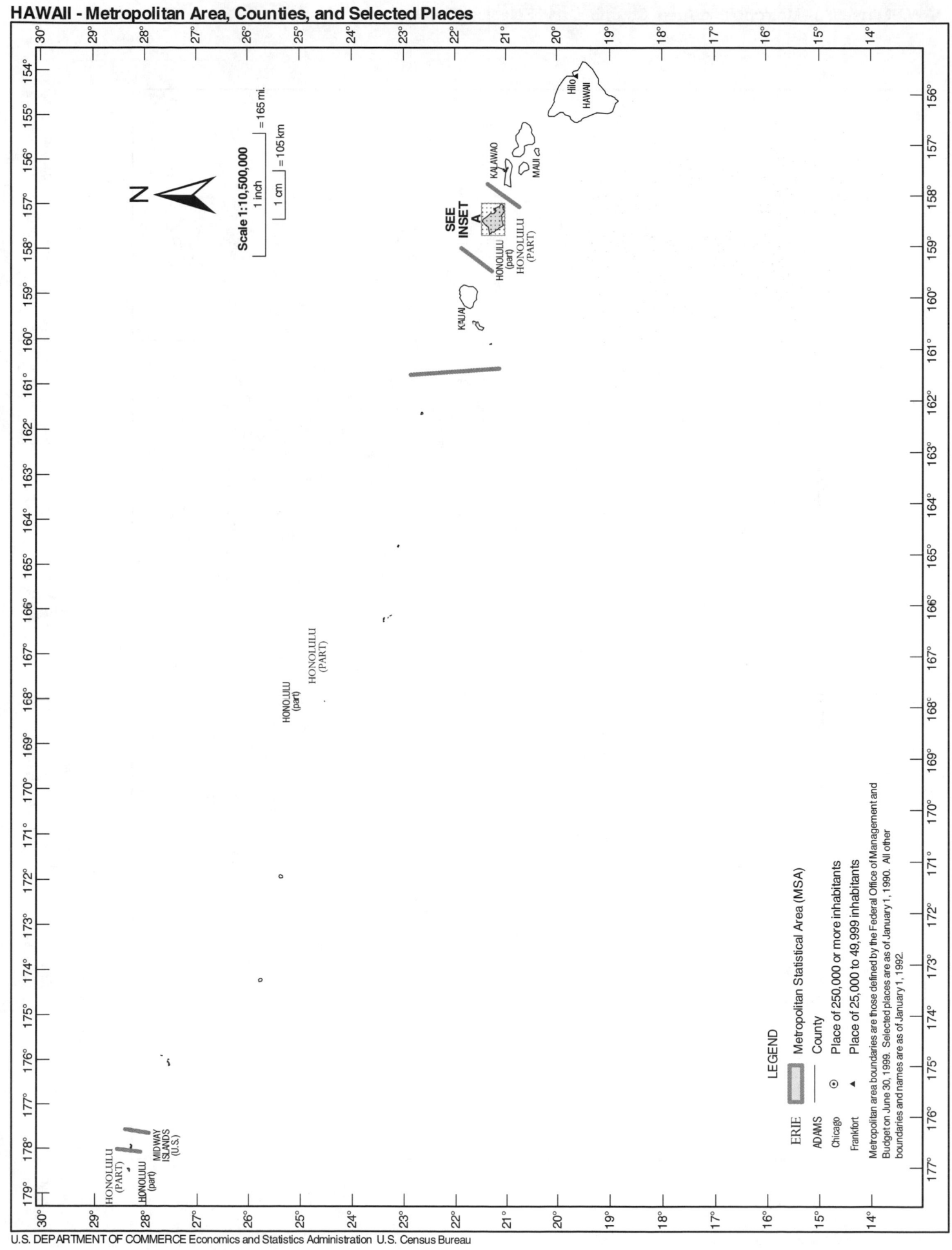

Scale 1:10,500,000

1 inch = 165 mi.

1 cm = 105 km

N

HILO
HAWAII

KALAWAO

MAUI

SEE
INSET
A

HONOLULU
(part)

HONOLULU
(PART)

KAUAI

HONOLULU
(part)

HONOLULU
(PART)

HONOLULU
(PART)

HONOLULU
(part)

MIDWAY
ISLANDS
(U.S.)

LEGEND

ERIE	Metropolitan Statistical Area (MSA)
ADAMS	County
Chicago ⊙	Place of 250,000 or more inhabitants
Frankfort ▲	Place of 25,000 to 49,999 inhabitants

Metropolitan area boundaries are those defined by the Federal Office of Management and Budget on June 30, 1999. Selected places are as of January 1, 1990. All other boundaries and names are as of January 1, 1992.

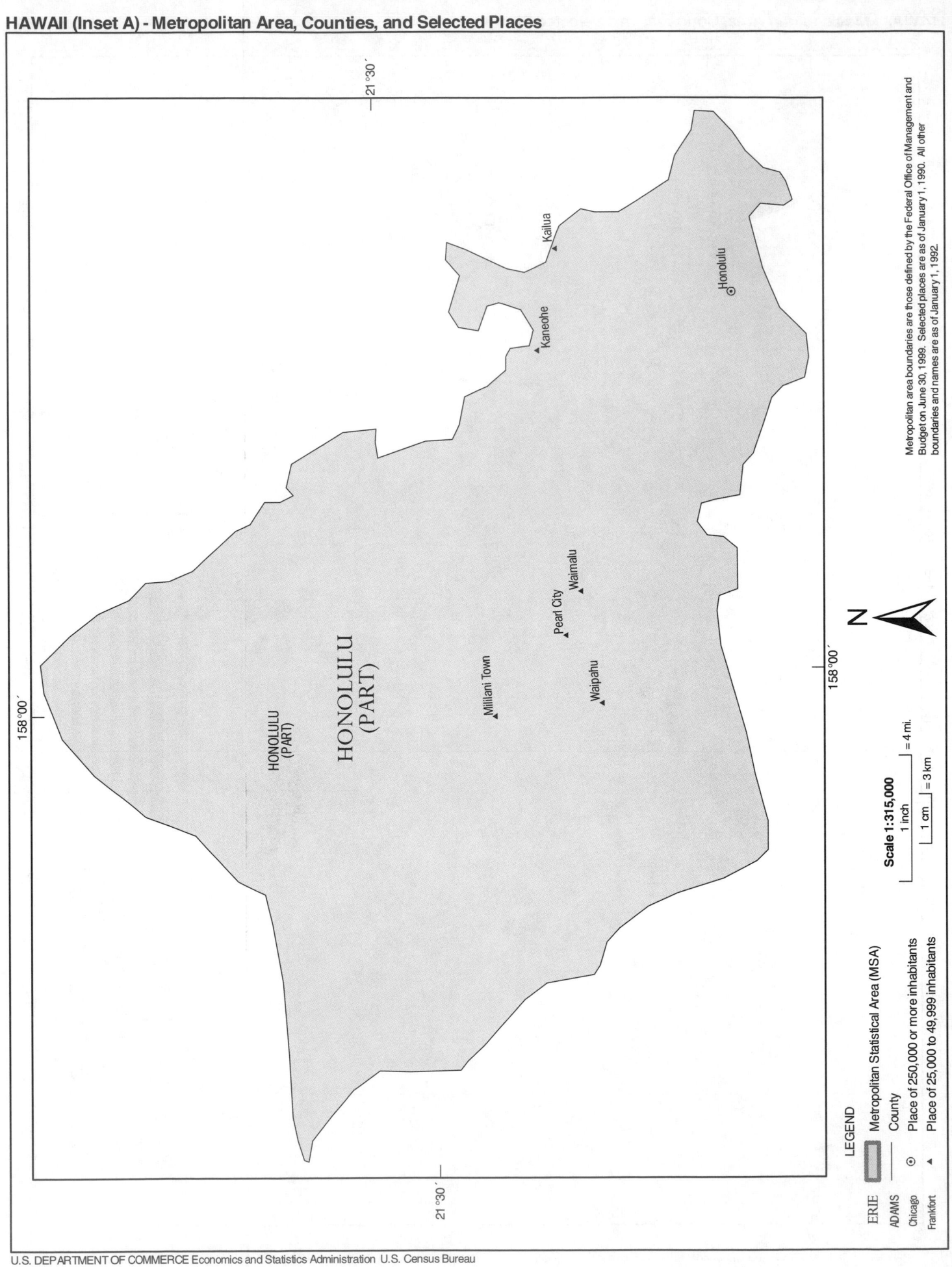

Kailua

Honolulu

Kaneohe

Waimalu

Pearl City

Mililani Town

Waipahu

HONOLULU
(PART)

HONOLULU
(PART)

21°30´

158°00´

158°00´

21°30´

N

Scale 1:315,000

1 inch ⌐ = 4 mi.

1 cm ⌐ = 3 km

Metropolitan area boundaries are those defined by the Federal Office of Management and Budget on June 30, 1999. Selected places are as of January 1, 1990. All other boundaries and names are as of January 1, 1992.

LEGEND

▭ Metropolitan Statistical Area (MSA)

— County

⊙ Place of 250,000 or more inhabitants

▲ Place of 25,000 to 49,999 inhabitants

ERIE

ADAMS

Chicago

Frankfort

IDAHO - Metropolitan Areas, Counties, and Selected Places

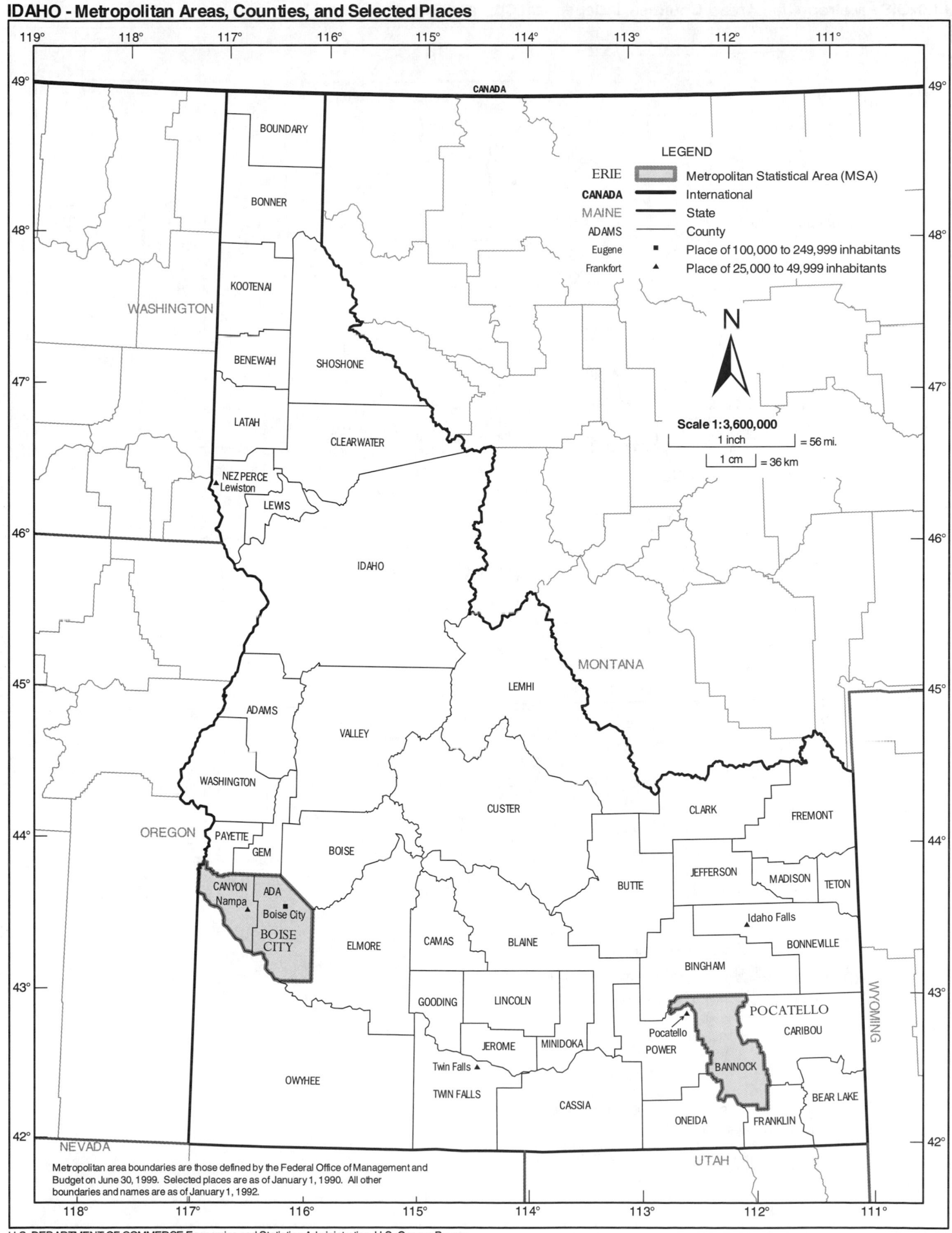

LEGEND

ERIE	Metropolitan Statistical Area (MSA)
CANADA	International
MAINE	State
ADAMS	County
Eugene ■	Place of 100,000 to 249,999 inhabitants
Frankfort ▲	Place of 25,000 to 49,999 inhabitants

Scale 1:3,600,000

1 inch = 56 mi.

1 cm = 36 km

Metropolitan area boundaries are those defined by the Federal Office of Management and Budget on June 30, 1999. Selected places are as of January 1, 1990. All other boundaries and names are as of January 1, 1992.

U.S. DEPARTMENT OF COMMERCE Economics and Statistics Administration U.S. Census Bureau

ILLINOIS - Metropolitan Areas, Counties, Independent City, and Selected Places

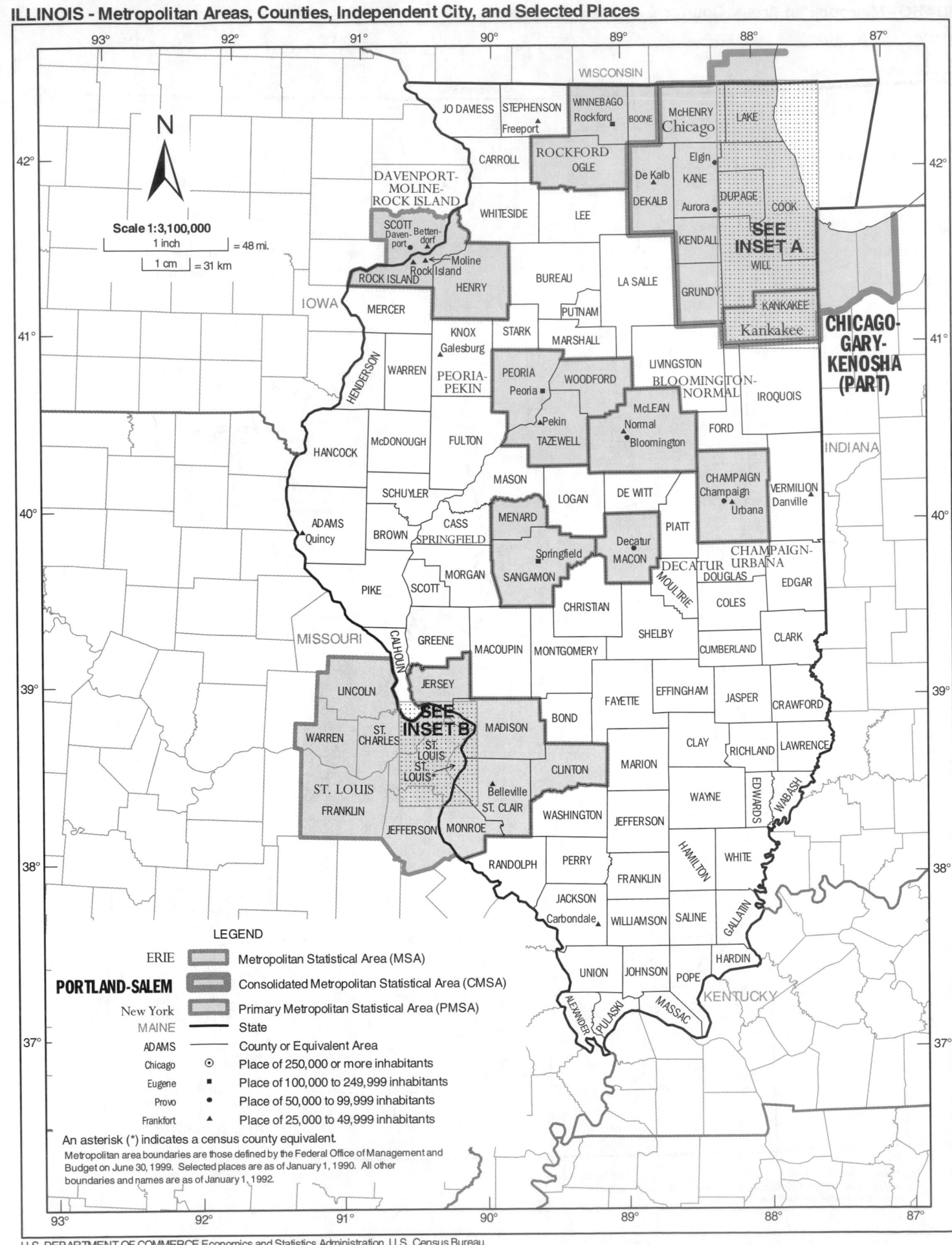

LEGEND

ERIE	Metropolitan Statistical Area (MSA)
PORTLAND-SALEM	Consolidated Metropolitan Statistical Area (CMSA)
New York	Primary Metropolitan Statistical Area (PMSA)
MAINE	State
ADAMS	County or Equivalent Area
Chicago ⊙	Place of 250,000 or more inhabitants
Eugene ▪	Place of 100,000 to 249,999 inhabitants
Provo ●	Place of 50,000 to 99,999 inhabitants
Frankfort ▲	Place of 25,000 to 49,999 inhabitants

An asterisk (*) indicates a census county equivalent.

Metropolitan area boundaries are those defined by the Federal Office of Management and Budget on June 30, 1999. Selected places are as of January 1, 1990. All other boundaries and names are as of January 1, 1992.

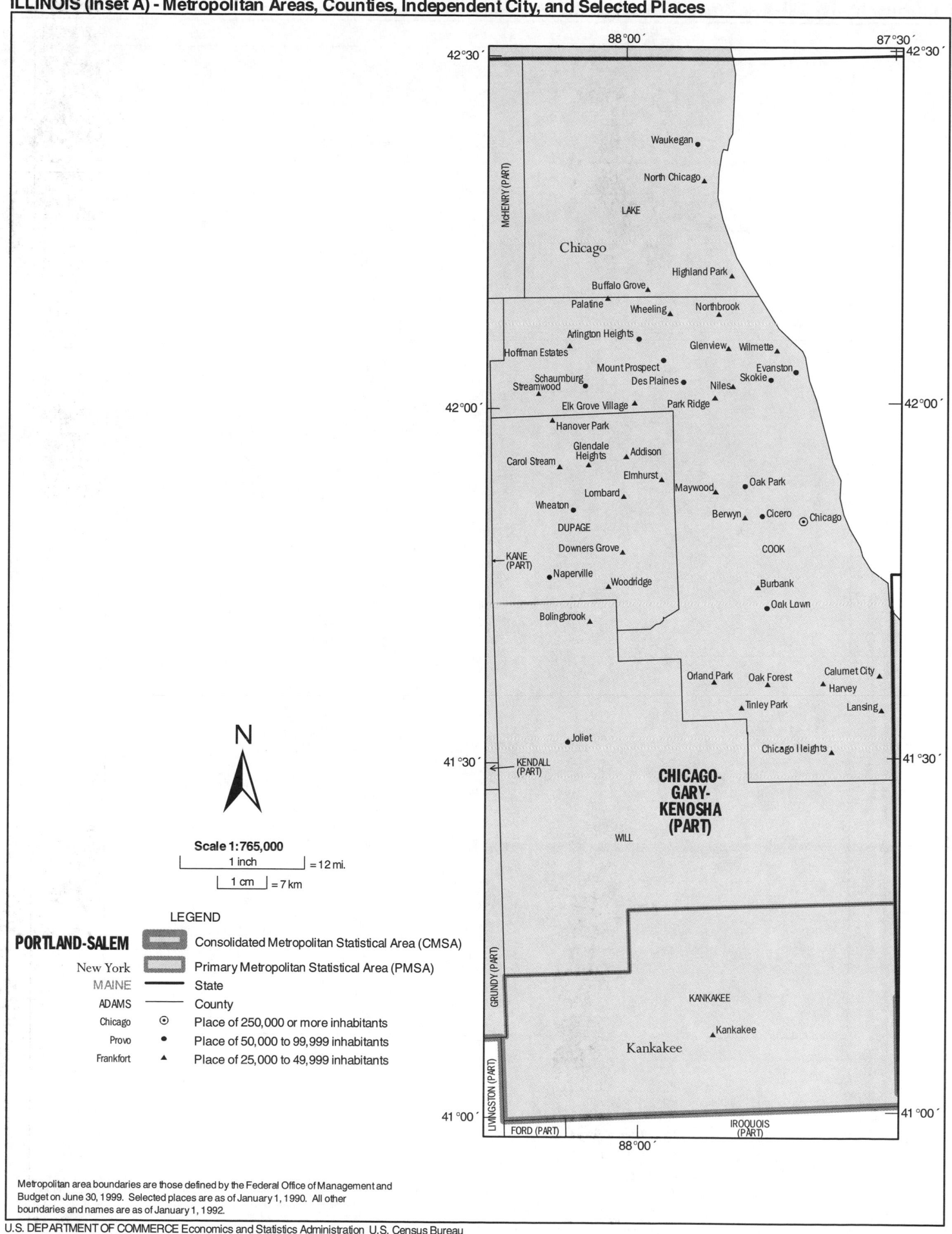

N

Scale 1:765,000

| 1 inch | = 12 mi. |

| 1 cm | = 7 km |

LEGEND

PORTLAND-SALEM ▭ Consolidated Metropolitan Statistical Area (CMSA)

New York ▭ Primary Metropolitan Statistical Area (PMSA)

MAINE ▬ State

ADAMS ▬ County

Chicago ⊙ Place of 250,000 or more inhabitants

Provo ● Place of 50,000 to 99,999 inhabitants

Frankfort ▲ Place of 25,000 to 49,999 inhabitants

Metropolitan area boundaries are those defined by the Federal Office of Management and
Budget on June 30, 1999. Selected places are as of January 1, 1990. All other
boundaries and names are as of January 1, 1992.

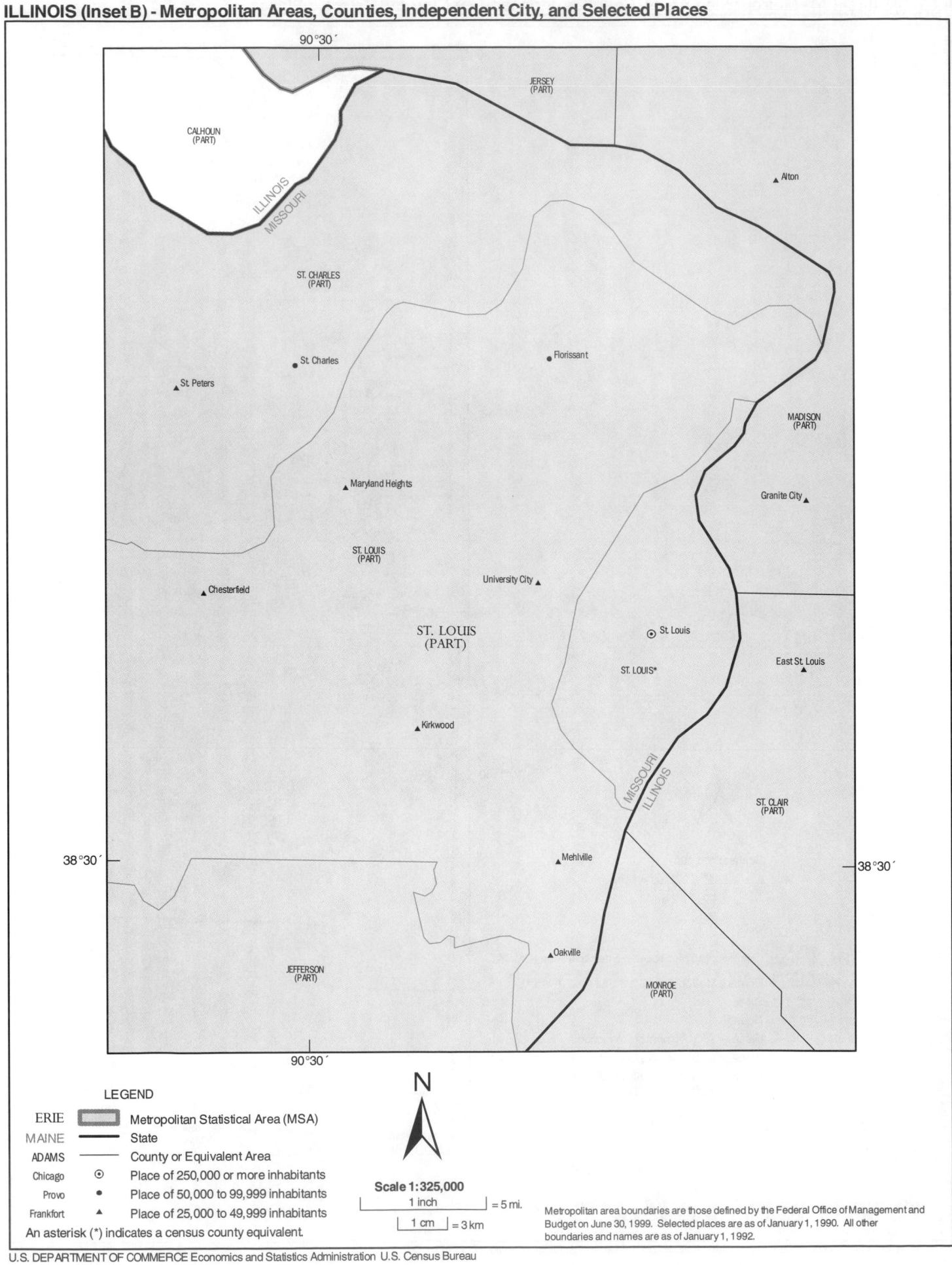

LEGEND

ERIE		Metropolitan Statistical Area (MSA)
MAINE		State
ADAMS		County or Equivalent Area
Chicago	⊙	Place of 250,000 or more inhabitants
Provo	●	Place of 50,000 to 99,999 inhabitants
Frankfort	▲	Place of 25,000 to 49,999 inhabitants

An asterisk (*) indicates a census county equivalent.

N

Scale 1:325,000

1 inch ⊢——⊣ = 5 mi.

1 cm ⊢——⊣ = 3 km

Metropolitan area boundaries are those defined by the Federal Office of Management and Budget on June 30, 1999. Selected places are as of January 1, 1990. All other boundaries and names are as of January 1, 1992.

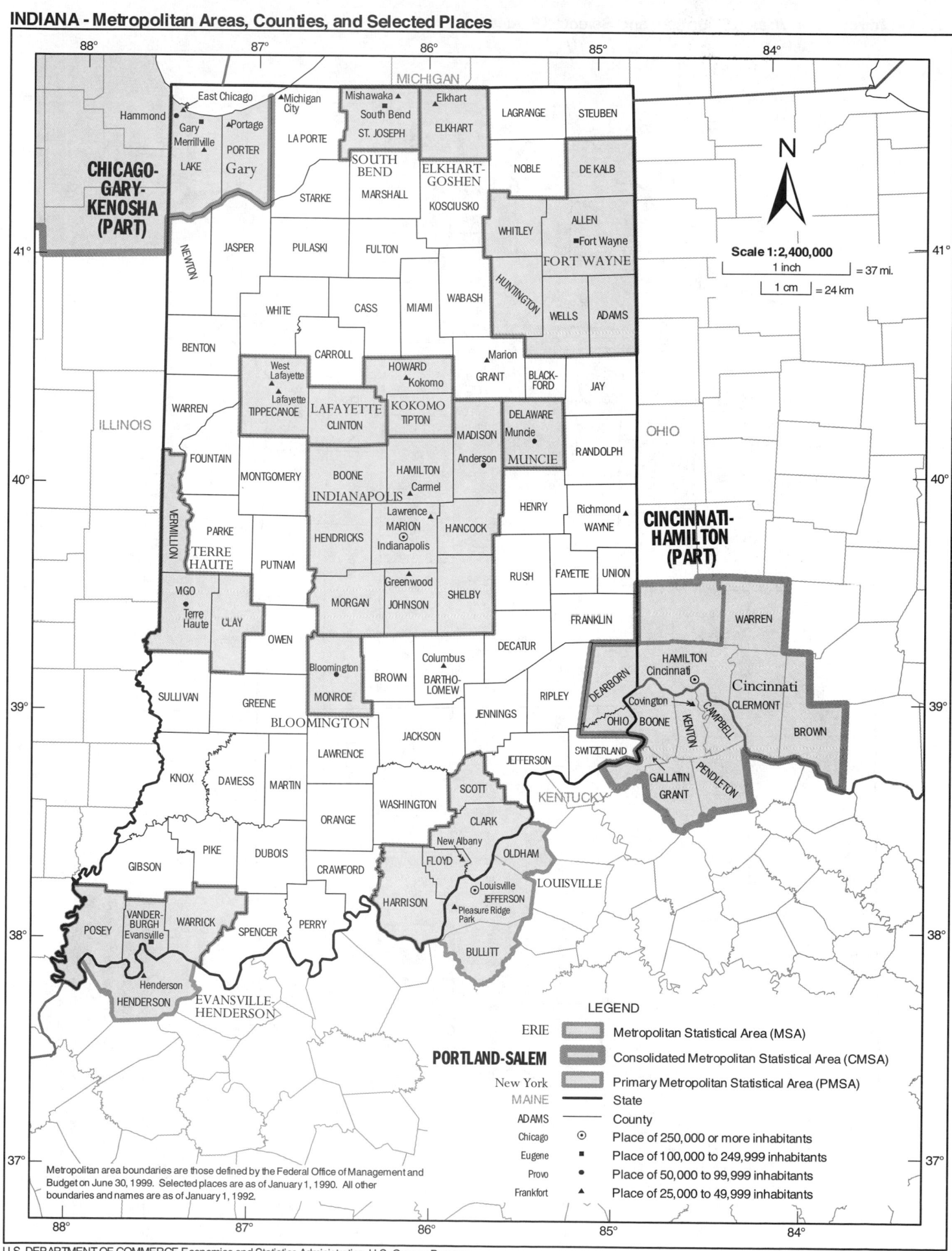

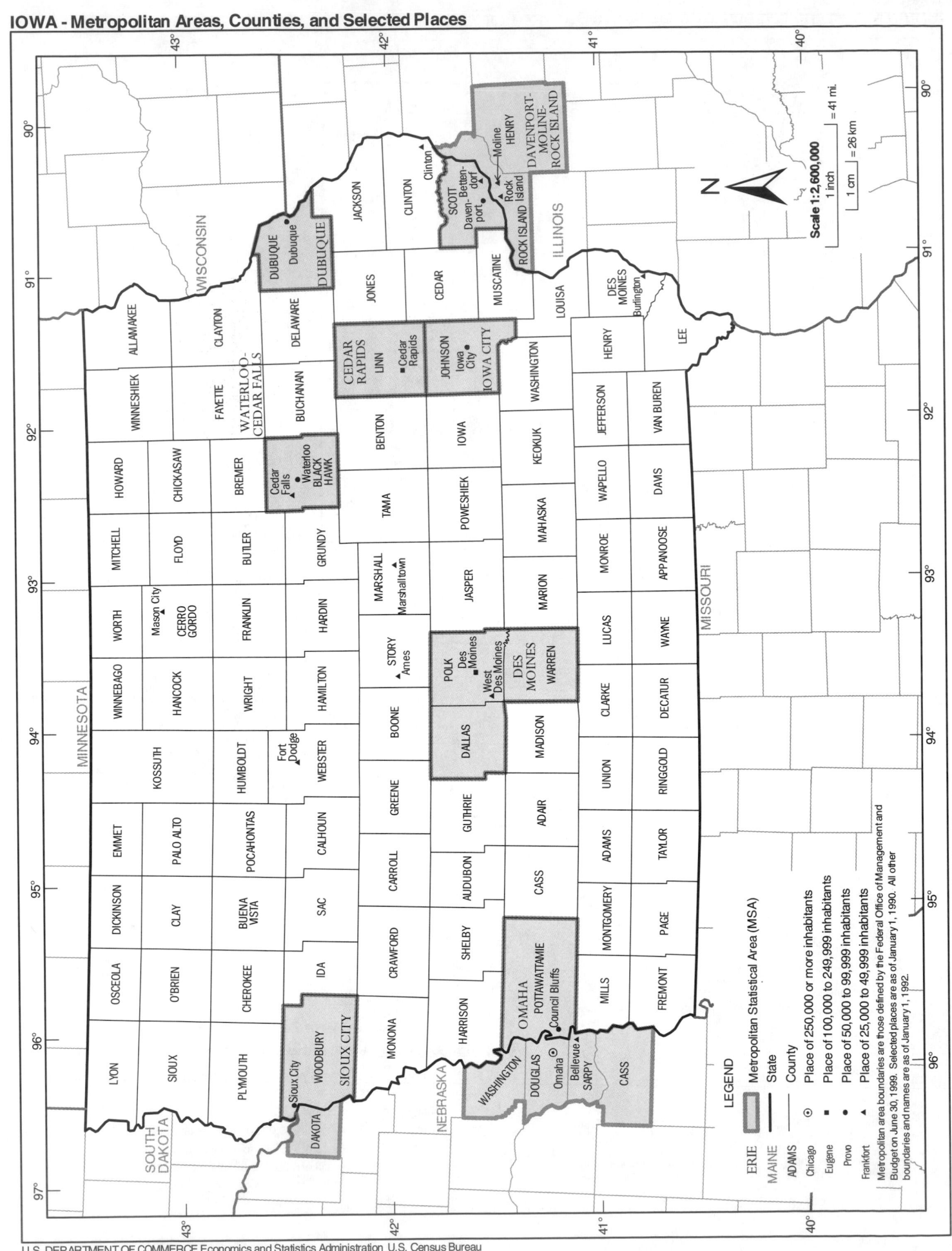

KANSAS - Metropolitan Areas, Counties, and Selected Places

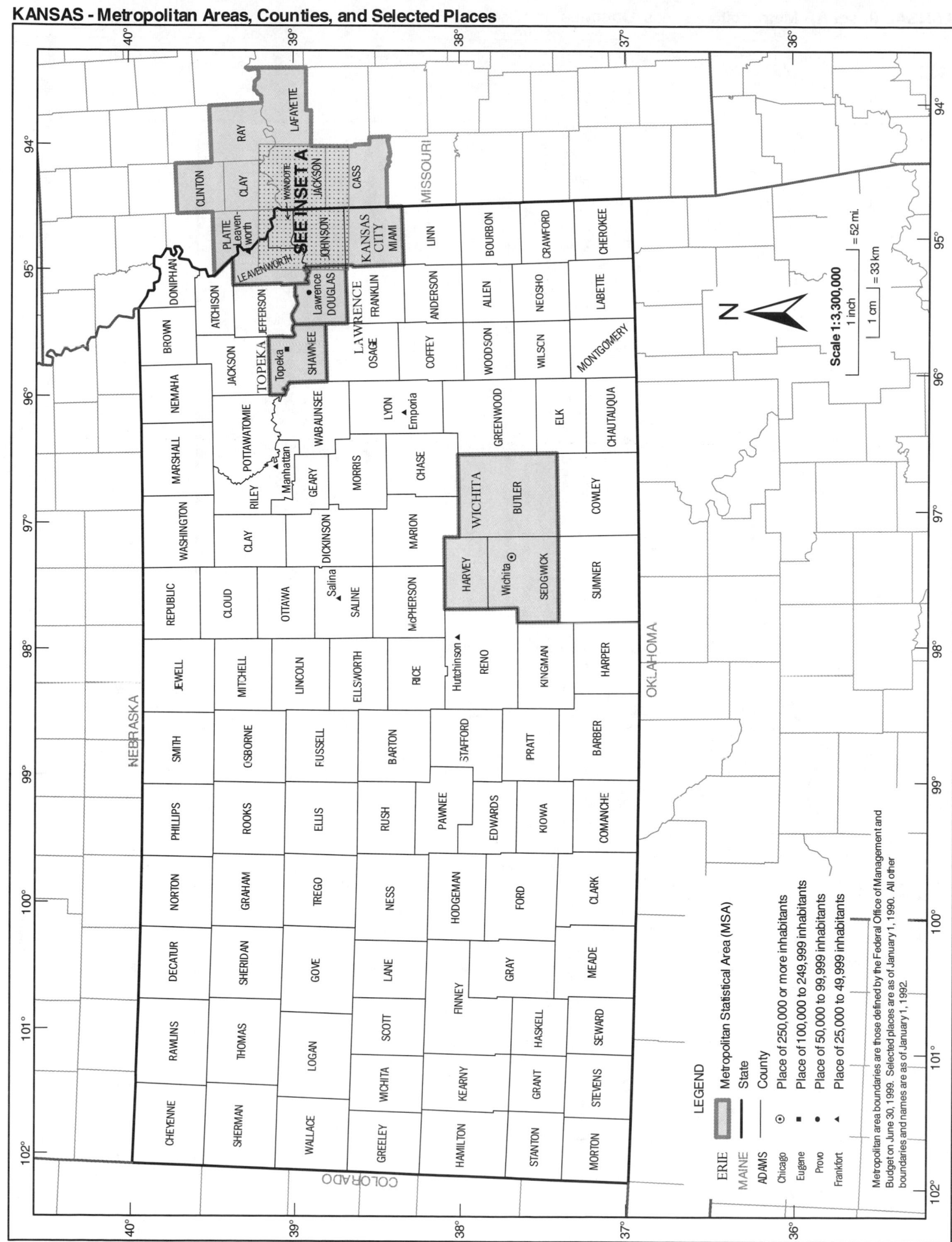

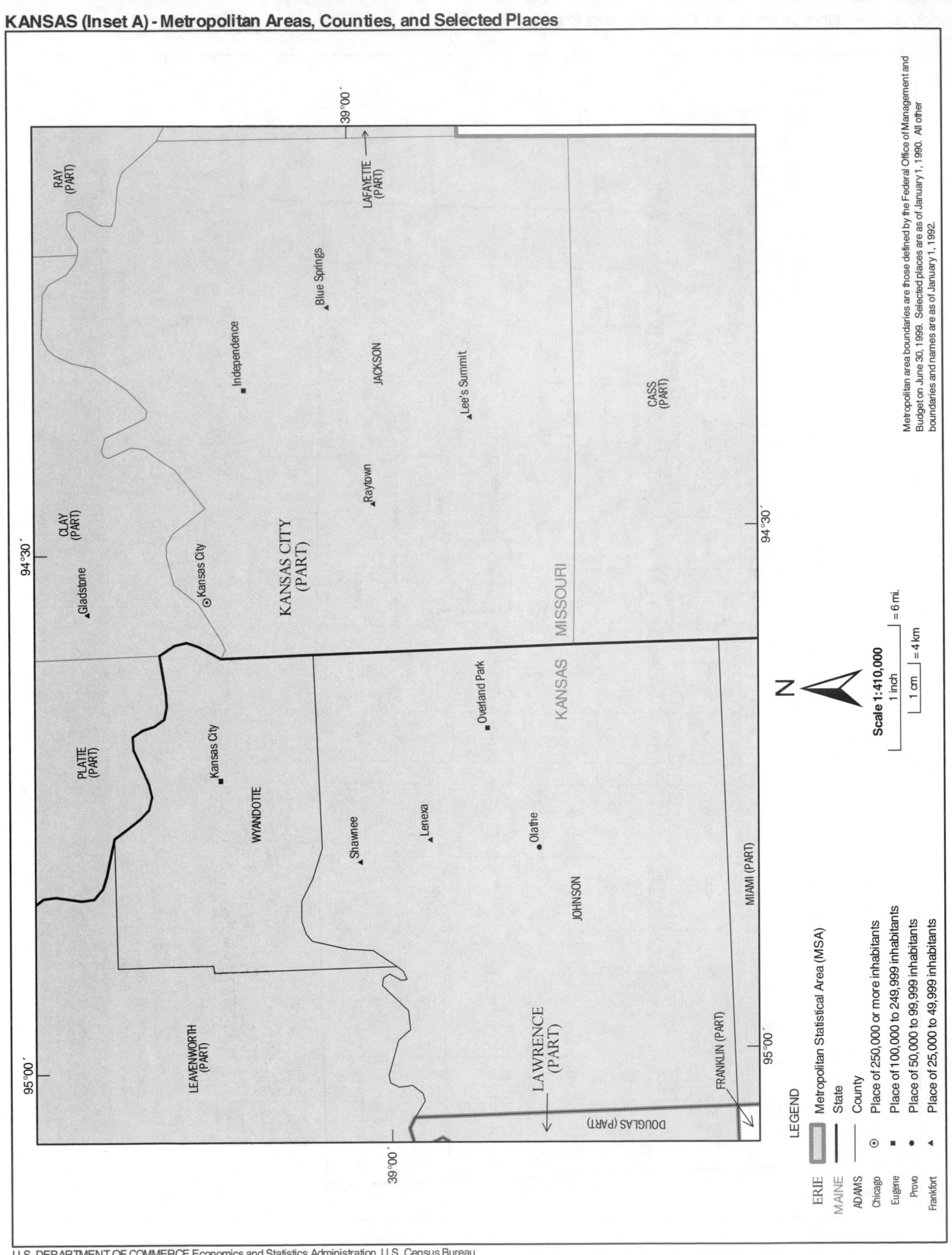

Scale 1:410,000

LEGEND

Metropolitan Statistical Area (MSA)
State
County
⊙ Place of 250,000 or more inhabitants
■ Place of 100,000 to 249,999 inhabitants
● Place of 50,000 to 99,999 inhabitants
▲ Place of 25,000 to 49,999 inhabitants

ERIE
MAINE
ADAMS
Chicago
Eugene
Provo
Frankfort

Metropolitan area boundaries are those defined by the Federal Office of Management and Budget on June 30, 1999. Selected places are as of January 1, 1990. All other boundaries and names are as of January 1, 1992.

KENTUCKY - Metropolitan Areas, Counties, and Selected Places

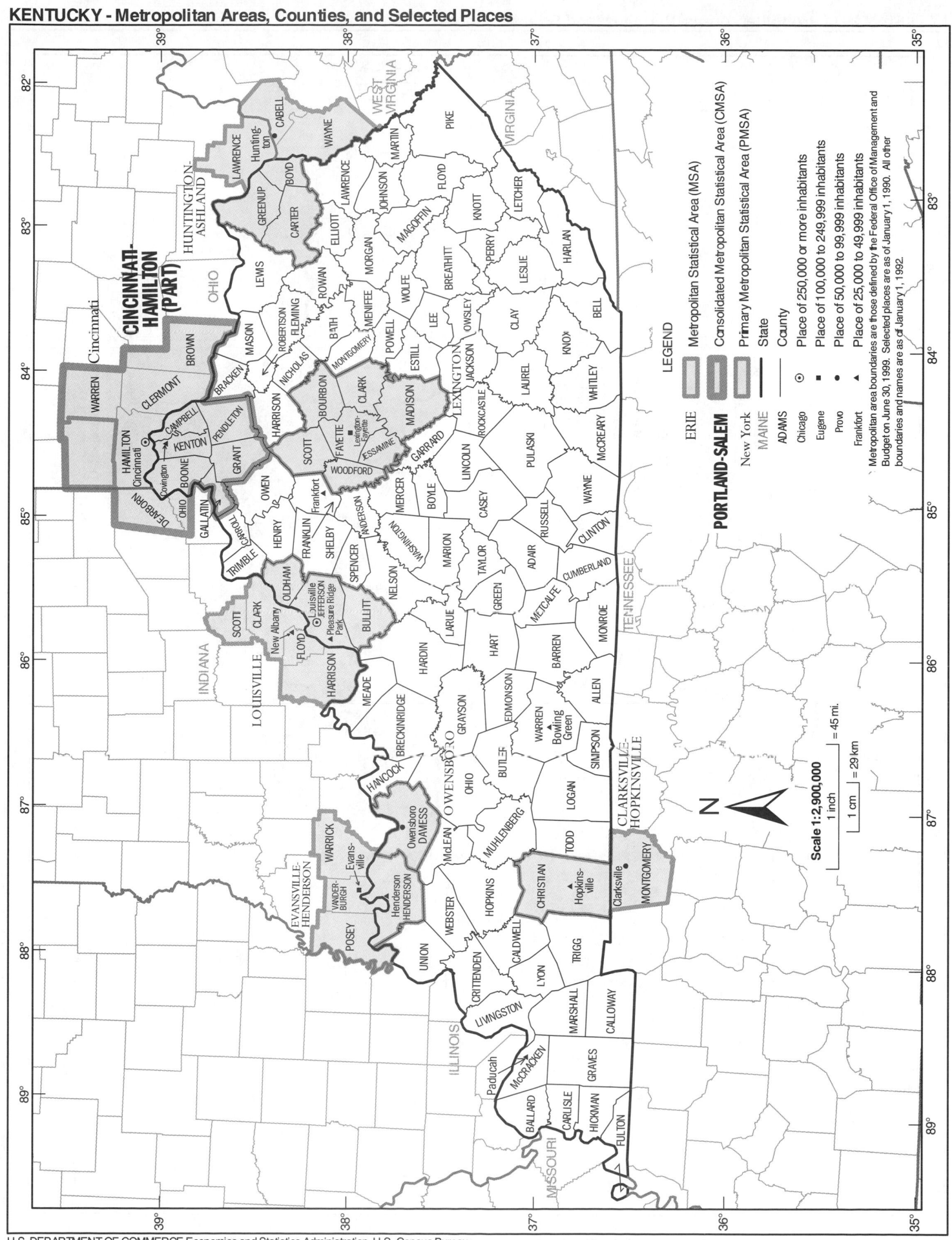

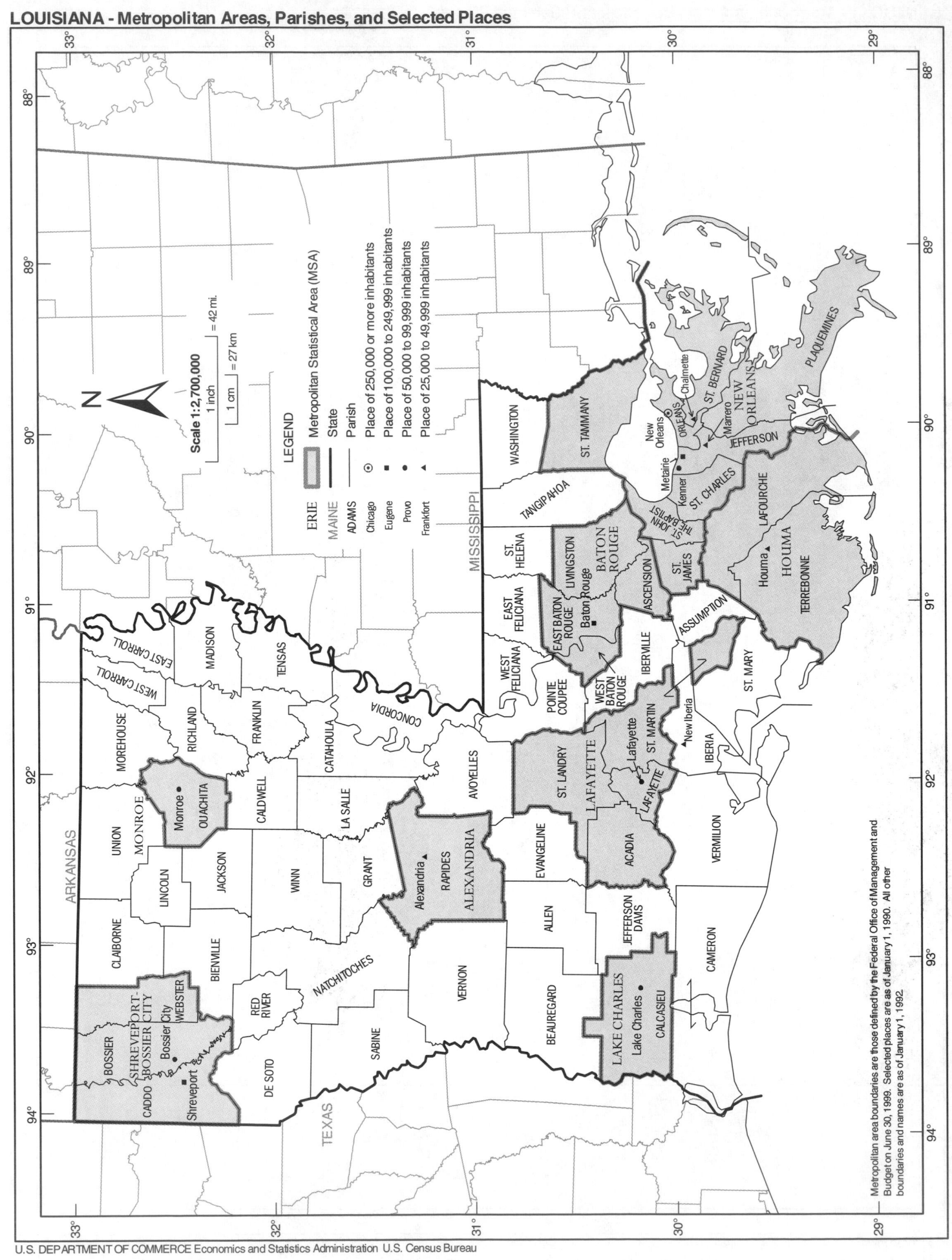

LEGEND

Metropolitan Statistical Area (MSA)
State
Parish

Place of 250,000 or more inhabitants
Place of 100,000 to 249,999 inhabitants
Place of 50,000 to 99,999 inhabitants
Place of 25,000 to 49,999 inhabitants

ERIE
MAINE
ADAMS
Chicago
Eugene
Provo
Frankfort

Scale 1:2,700,000
1 inch = 42 mi.
1 cm = 27 km

Metropolitan area boundaries are those defined by the Federal Office of Management and Budget on June 30, 1999. Selected places are as of January 1, 1990. All other boundaries and names are as of January 1, 1992.

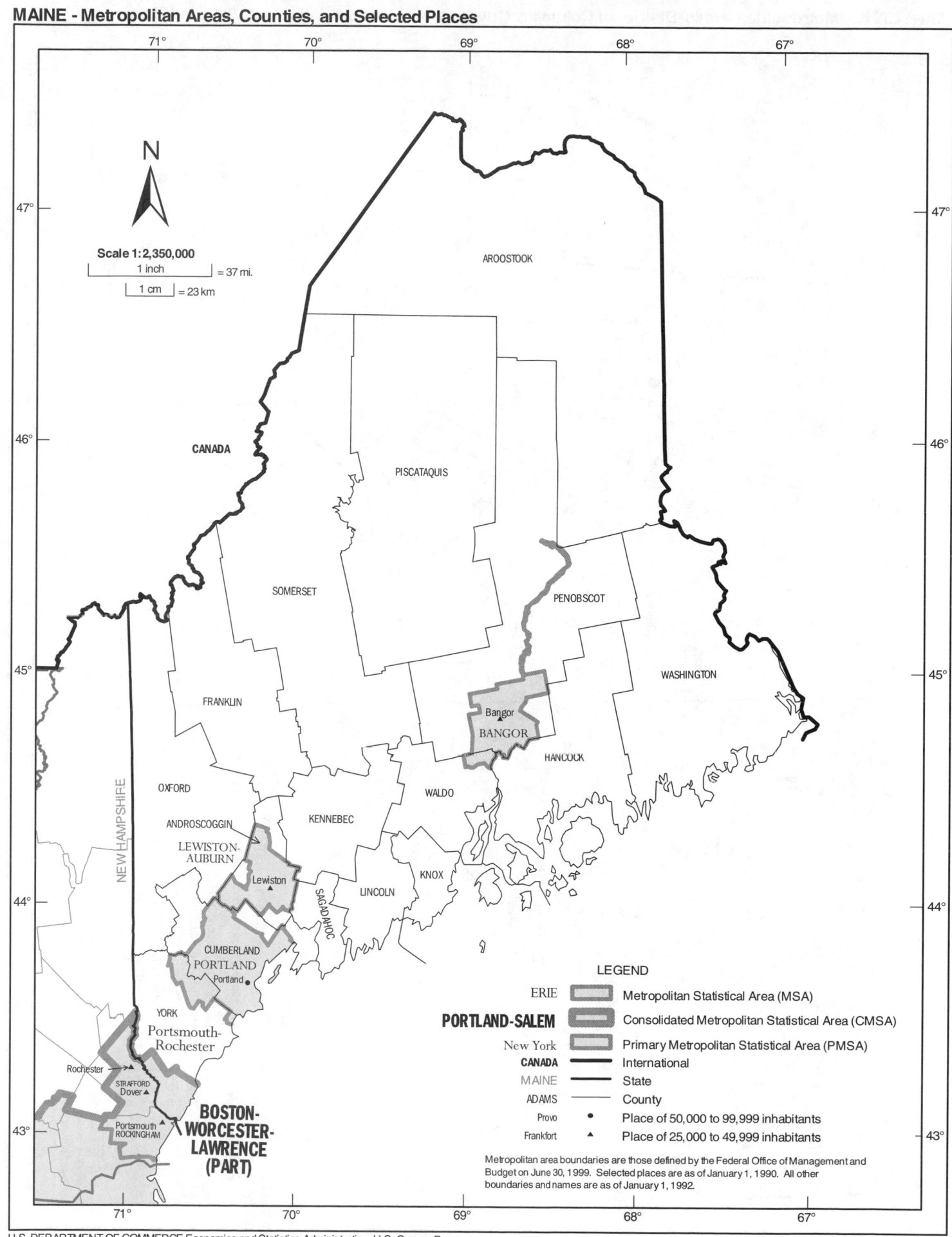

Scale 1:2,350,000

1 inch = 37 mi.

1 cm = 23 km

LEGEND

ERIE	Metropolitan Statistical Area (MSA)
PORTLAND-SALEM	Consolidated Metropolitan Statistical Area (CMSA)
New York	Primary Metropolitan Statistical Area (PMSA)
CANADA	International
MAINE	State
ADAMS	County
Provo ●	Place of 50,000 to 99,999 inhabitants
Frankfort ▲	Place of 25,000 to 49,999 inhabitants

Metropolitan area boundaries are those defined by the Federal Office of Management and Budget on June 30, 1999. Selected places are as of January 1, 1990. All other boundaries and names are as of January 1, 1992.

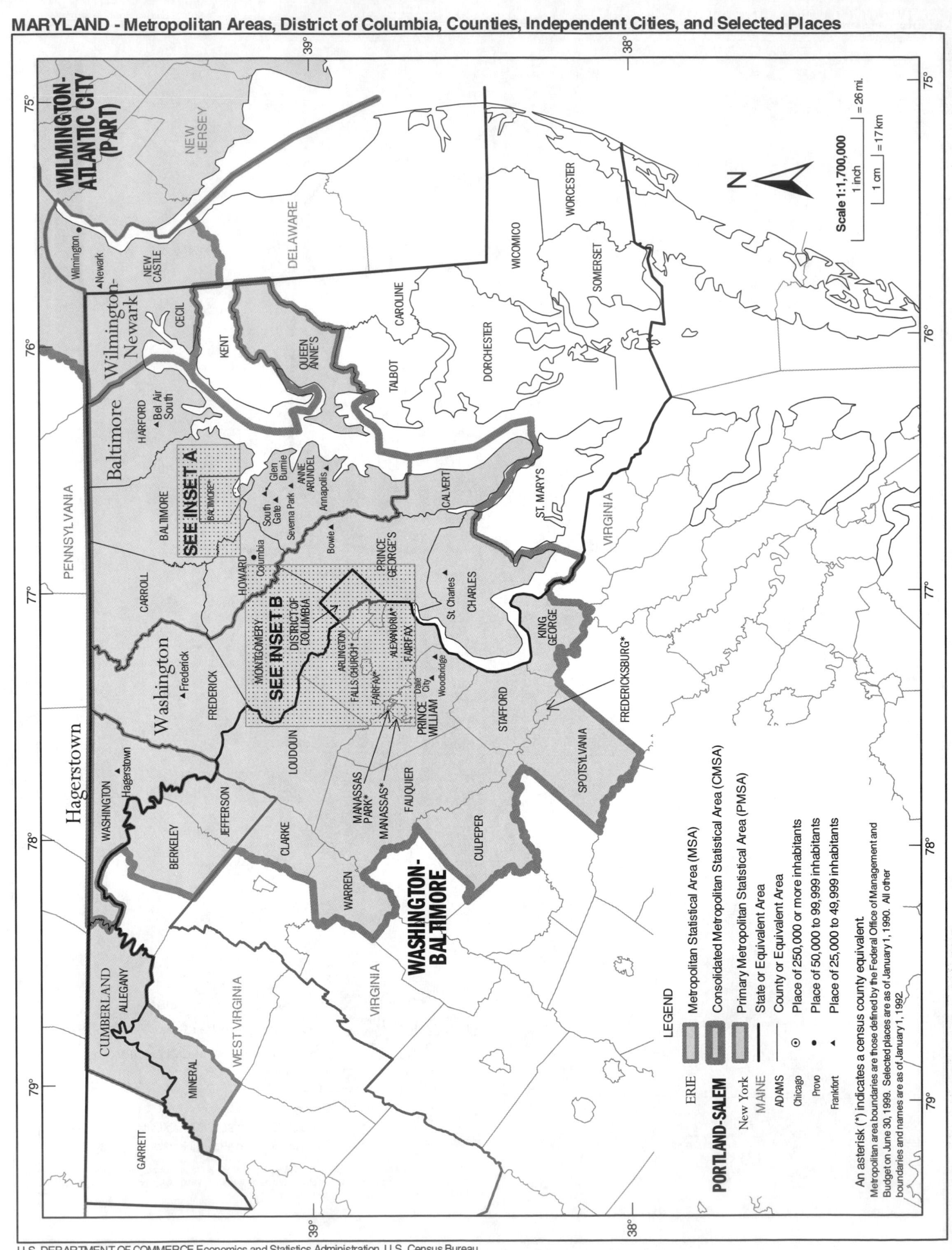

WILMINGTON-ATLANTIC CITY (PART)

WASHINGTON-BALTIMORE

Scale 1:1,700,000

1 inch = 26 mi.

1 cm = 17 km

LEGEND

ERIE	Metropolitan Statistical Area (MSA)
	Consolidated Metropolitan Statistical Area (CMSA)
PORTLAND-SALEM	Primary Metropolitan Statistical Area (PMSA)
New York	State or Equivalent Area
MAINE	County or Equivalent Area
ADAMS	
Chicago ⊙	Place of 250,000 or more inhabitants
Provo ●	Place of 50,000 to 99,999 inhabitants
Frankfort ▲	Place of 25,000 to 49,999 inhabitants

An asterisk (*) indicates a census county equivalent.
Metropolitan area boundaries are those defined by the Federal Office of Management and Budget on June 30, 1999. Selected places are as of January 1, 1990. All other boundaries and names are as of January 1, 1992.

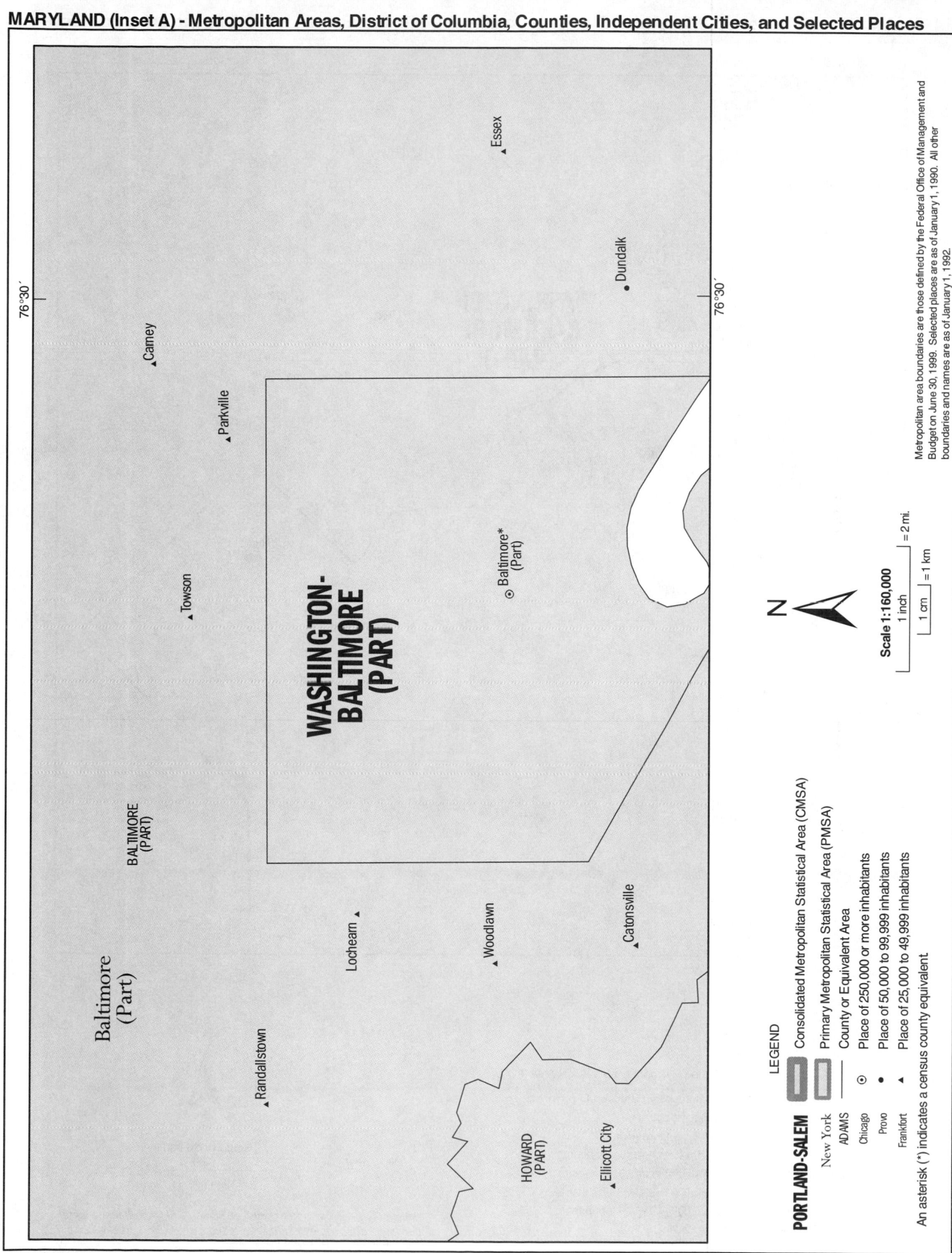

76°30′

76°30′

Essex

Dundalk

Carney

Parkville

Towson

WASHINGTON-BALTIMORE (PART)

BALTIMORE (PART)

Baltimore* (Part)

Baltimore (Part)

Randallstown

Locheam

Woodlawn

Catonsville

HOWARD (PART)

Ellicott City

Scale 1:160,000

1 inch = 2 mi.

1 cm = 1 km

N

Metropolitan area boundaries are those defined by the Federal Office of Management and Budget on June 30, 1999. Selected places are as of January 1, 1990. All other boundaries and names are as of January 1, 1992.

LEGEND

PORTLAND-SALEM   Consolidated Metropolitan Statistical Area (CMSA)

New York   Primary Metropolitan Statistical Area (PMSA)

ADAMS   County or Equivalent Area

Chicago ⊙   Place of 250,000 or more inhabitants

Provo ●   Place of 50,000 to 99,999 inhabitants

Frankfort ▲   Place of 25,000 to 49,999 inhabitants

An asterisk (*) indicates a census county equivalent

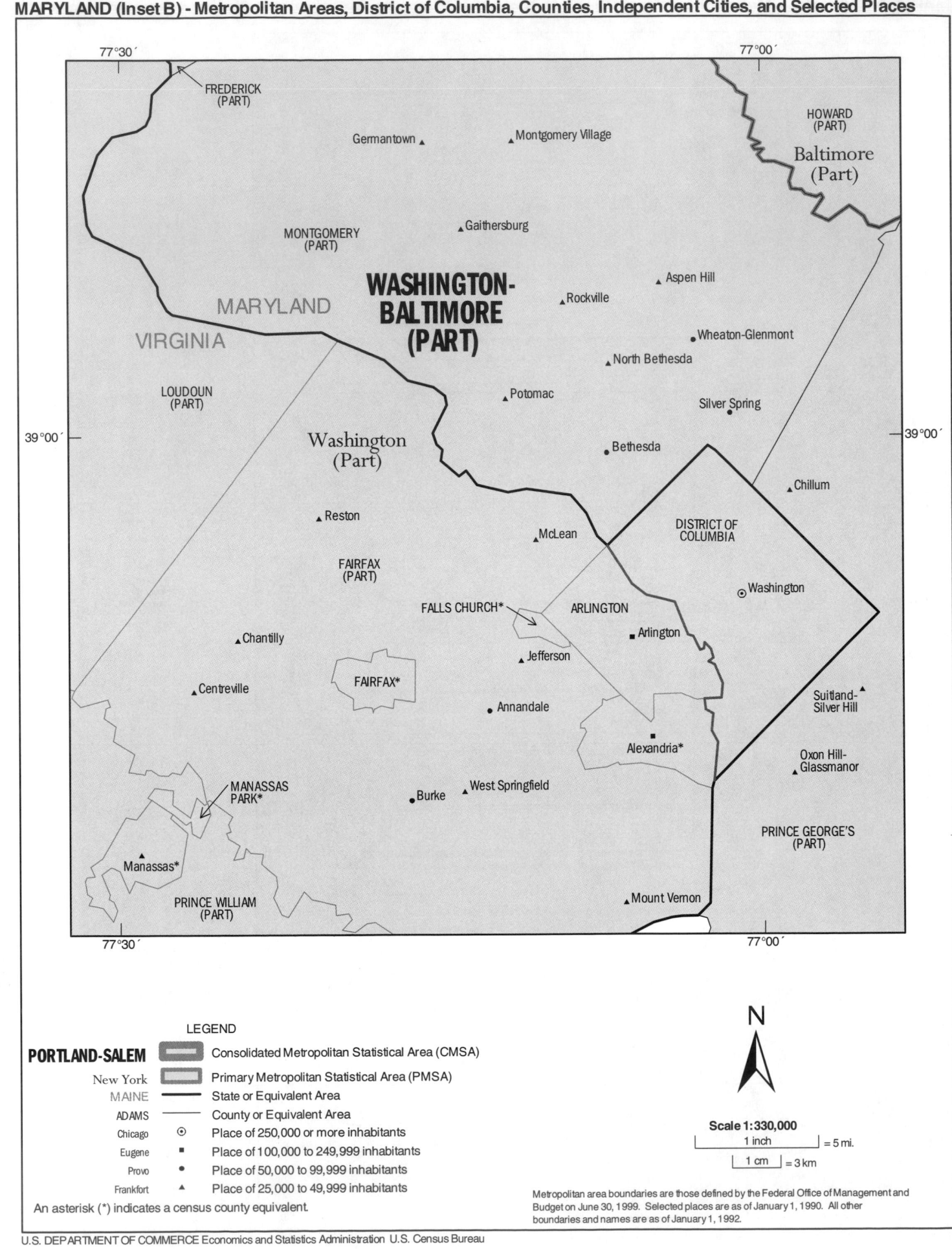

77°30´

FREDERICK (PART)

77°00´

Germantown ▲

Montgomery Village ▲

HOWARD (PART)

Baltimore (Part)

MONTGOMERY (PART)

Gaithersburg ▲

MARYLAND

VIRGINIA

WASHINGTON-BALTIMORE (PART)

Aspen Hill ▲

Rockville ▲

Wheaton-Glenmont ●

LOUDOUN (PART)

North Bethesda ▲

Potomac ▲

Silver Spring ●

39°00´

Washington (Part)

Bethesda ●

Chillum ▲

39°00´

Reston ▲

McLean ▲

DISTRICT OF COLUMBIA

FAIRFAX (PART)

FALLS CHURCH*

ARLINGTON

⊙ Washington

Chantilly ▲

Jefferson ▲

Arlington ■

Suitland-Silver Hill ▲

Centreville ▲

FAIRFAX*

Annandale ●

Centreville ▲

Alexandria* ■

Oxon Hill-Glassmanor ▲

MANASSAS PARK*

Burke ●

West Springfield ▲

PRINCE GEORGE'S (PART)

Manassas* ▲

PRINCE WILLIAM (PART)

Mount Vernon ▲

77°30´

77°00´

N

Scale 1:330,000

1 inch ⊢———⊣ = 5 mi.

1 cm ⊢—⊣ = 3 km

Metropolitan area boundaries are those defined by the Federal Office of Management and Budget on June 30, 1999. Selected places are as of January 1, 1990. All other boundaries and names are as of January 1, 1992.

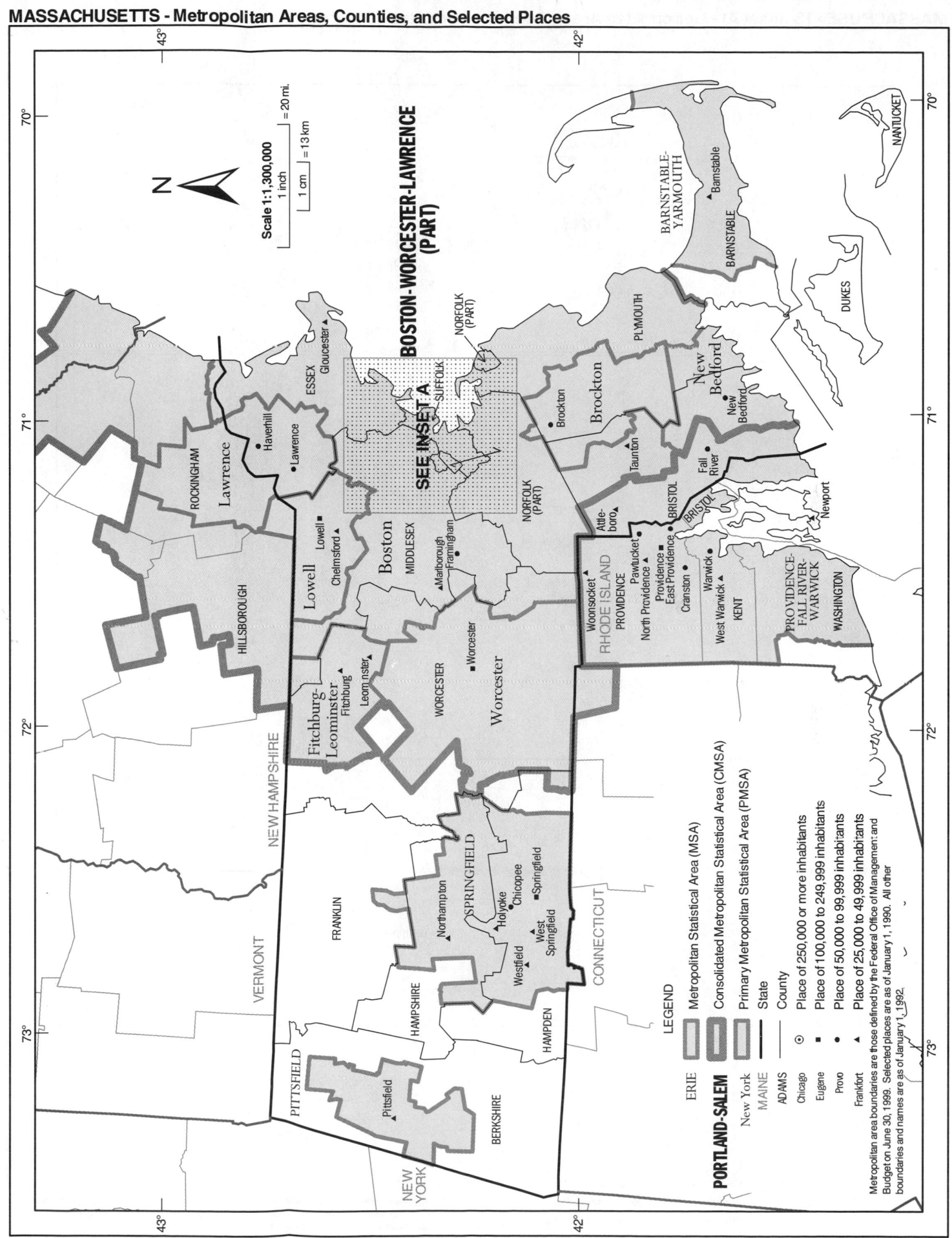

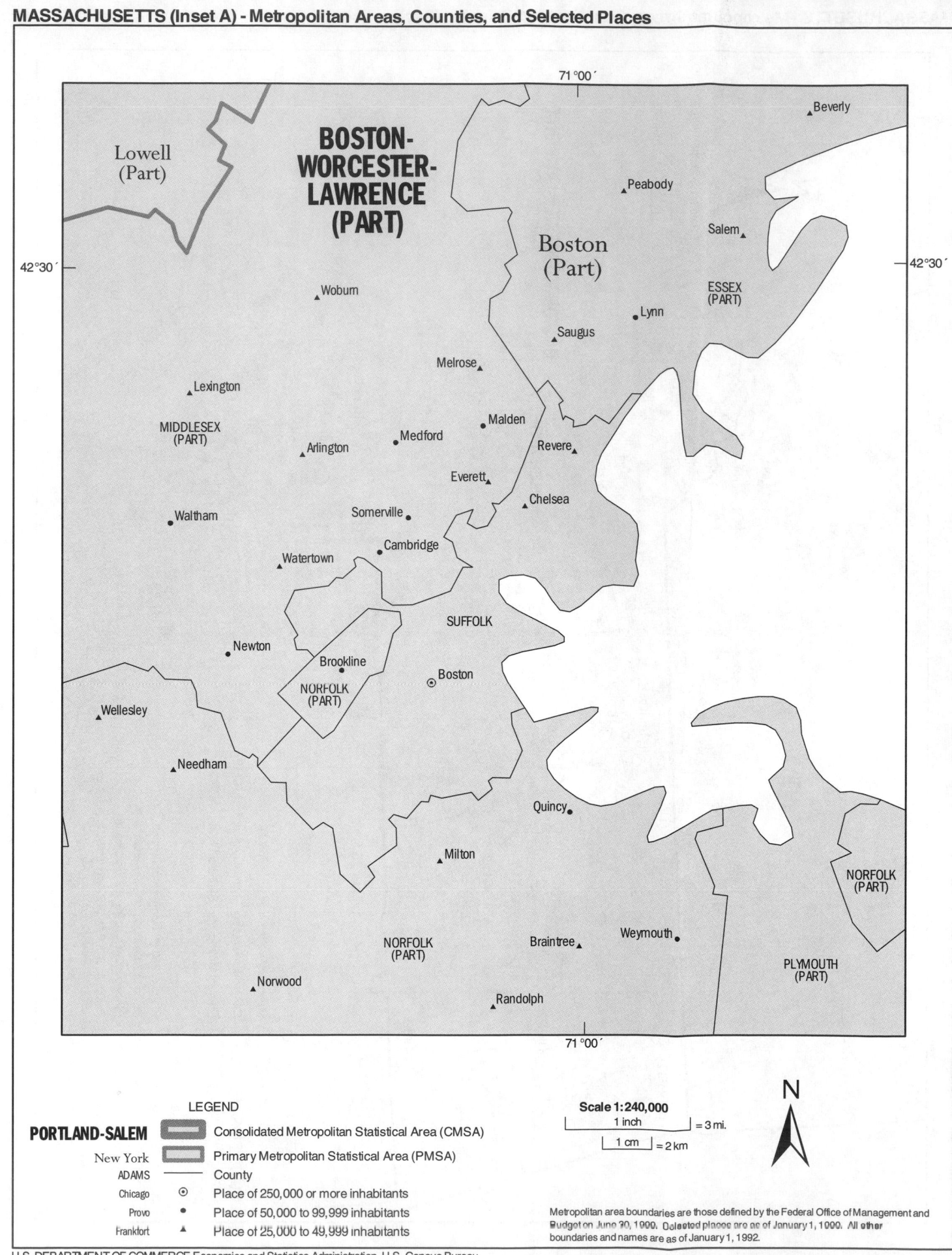

BOSTON-WORCESTER-LAWRENCE (PART)

Boston (Part)

Lowell (Part)

Beverly

Peabody

Salem

ESSEX (PART)

Woburn

Lynn

Saugus

Melrose

Lexington

MIDDLESEX (PART)

Malden

Arlington Medford

Revere

Everett

Waltham

Somerville Chelsea

Watertown Cambridge

SUFFOLK

Newton

Brookline

NORFOLK (PART)

Boston

Wellesley

Needham

Quincy

Milton

NORFOLK (PART)

Braintree Weymouth

NORFOLK (PART)

PLYMOUTH (PART)

Norwood

Randolph

71°00′

42°30′   42°30′

71°00′

LEGEND

PORTLAND-SALEM ▭ Consolidated Metropolitan Statistical Area (CMSA)

New York ▭ Primary Metropolitan Statistical Area (PMSA)

ADAMS — County

Chicago ⊙ Place of 250,000 or more inhabitants

Provo • Place of 50,000 to 99,999 inhabitants

Frankfort ▲ Place of 25,000 to 49,999 inhabitants

Scale 1:240,000

1 inch ⊢———⊣ = 3 mi.

1 cm ⊢—⊣ = 2 km

N

Metropolitan area boundaries are those defined by the Federal Office of Management and Budget on June 30, 1999. Selected places are as of January 1, 1990. All other boundaries and names are as of January 1, 1992.

U.S. DEPARTMENT OF COMMERCE Economics and Statistics Administration U.S. Census Bureau

MICHIGAN - Metropolitan Areas, Counties, and Selected Places

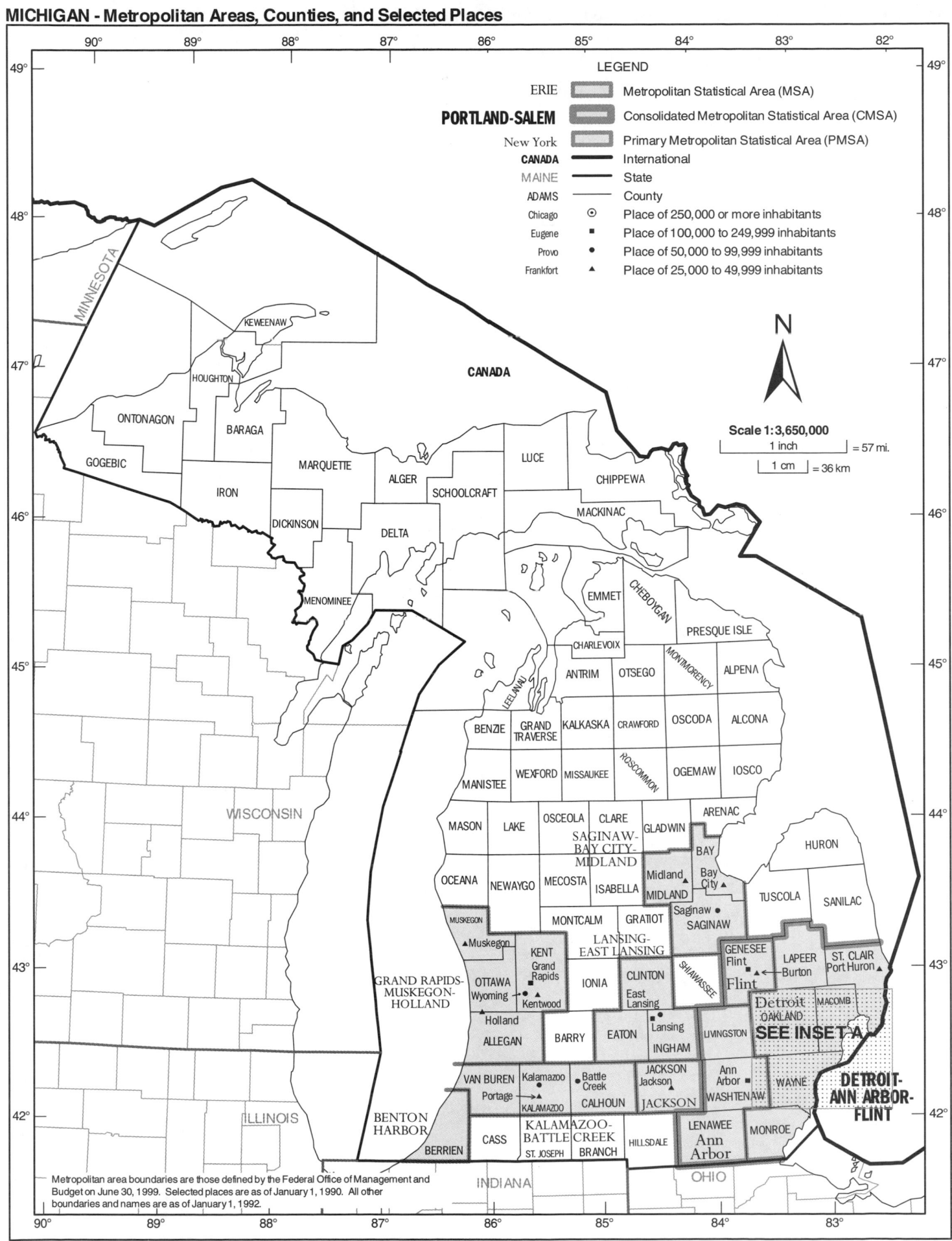

LEGEND

ERIE		Metropolitan Statistical Area (MSA)
PORTLAND-SALEM		Consolidated Metropolitan Statistical Area (CMSA)
New York		Primary Metropolitan Statistical Area (PMSA)
CANADA		International
MAINE		State
ADAMS		County
Chicago	⊙	Place of 250,000 or more inhabitants
Eugene	■	Place of 100,000 to 249,999 inhabitants
Provo	●	Place of 50,000 to 99,999 inhabitants
Frankfort	▲	Place of 25,000 to 49,999 inhabitants

Scale 1:3,650,000

1 inch = 57 mi.

1 cm = 36 km

Metropolitan area boundaries are those defined by the Federal Office of Management and Budget on June 30, 1999. Selected places are as of January 1, 1990. All other boundaries and names are as of January 1, 1992.

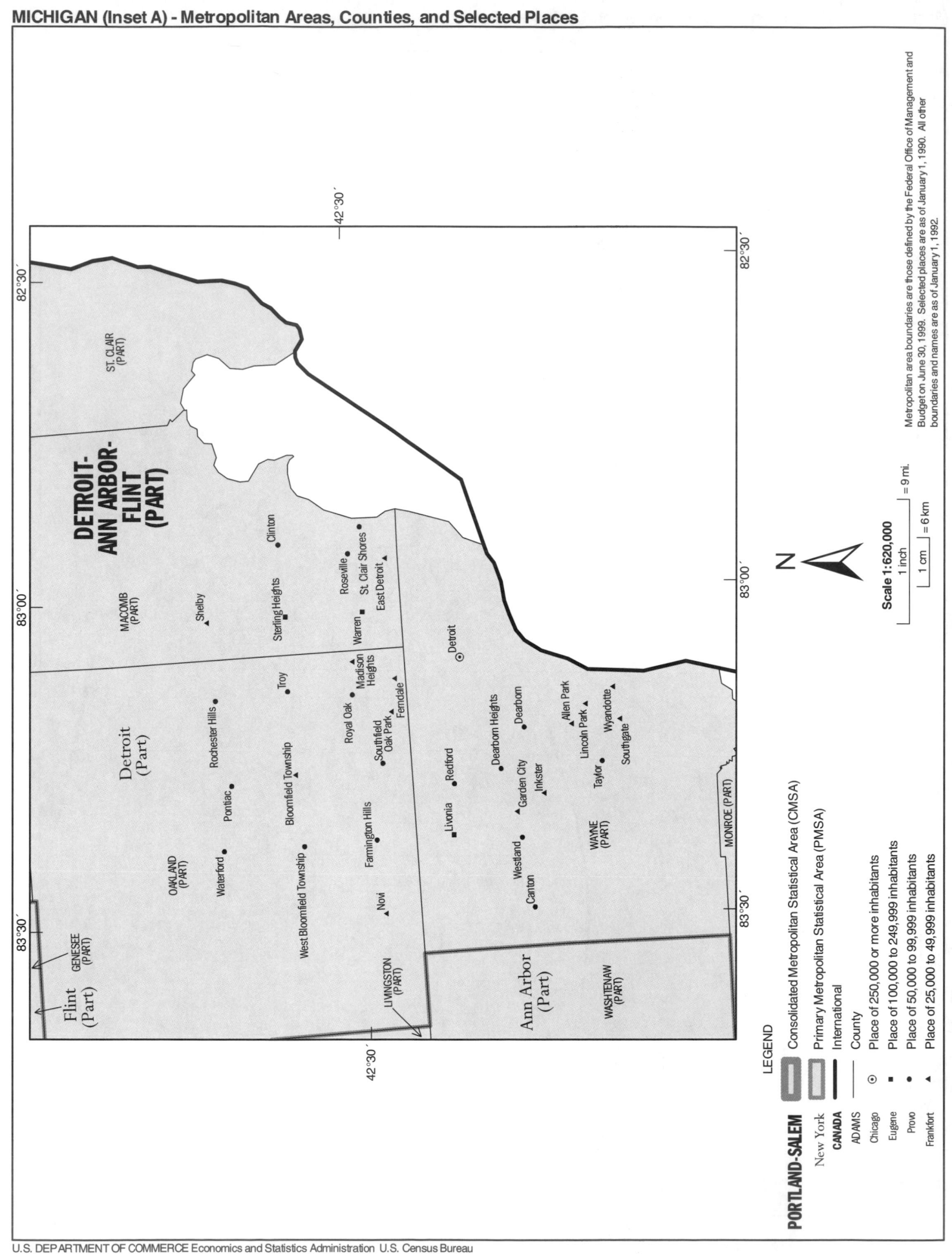

U.S. DEPARTMENT OF COMMERCE Economics and Statistics Administration U.S. Census Bureau

MINNESOTA - Metropolitan Areas, Counties, and Selected Places

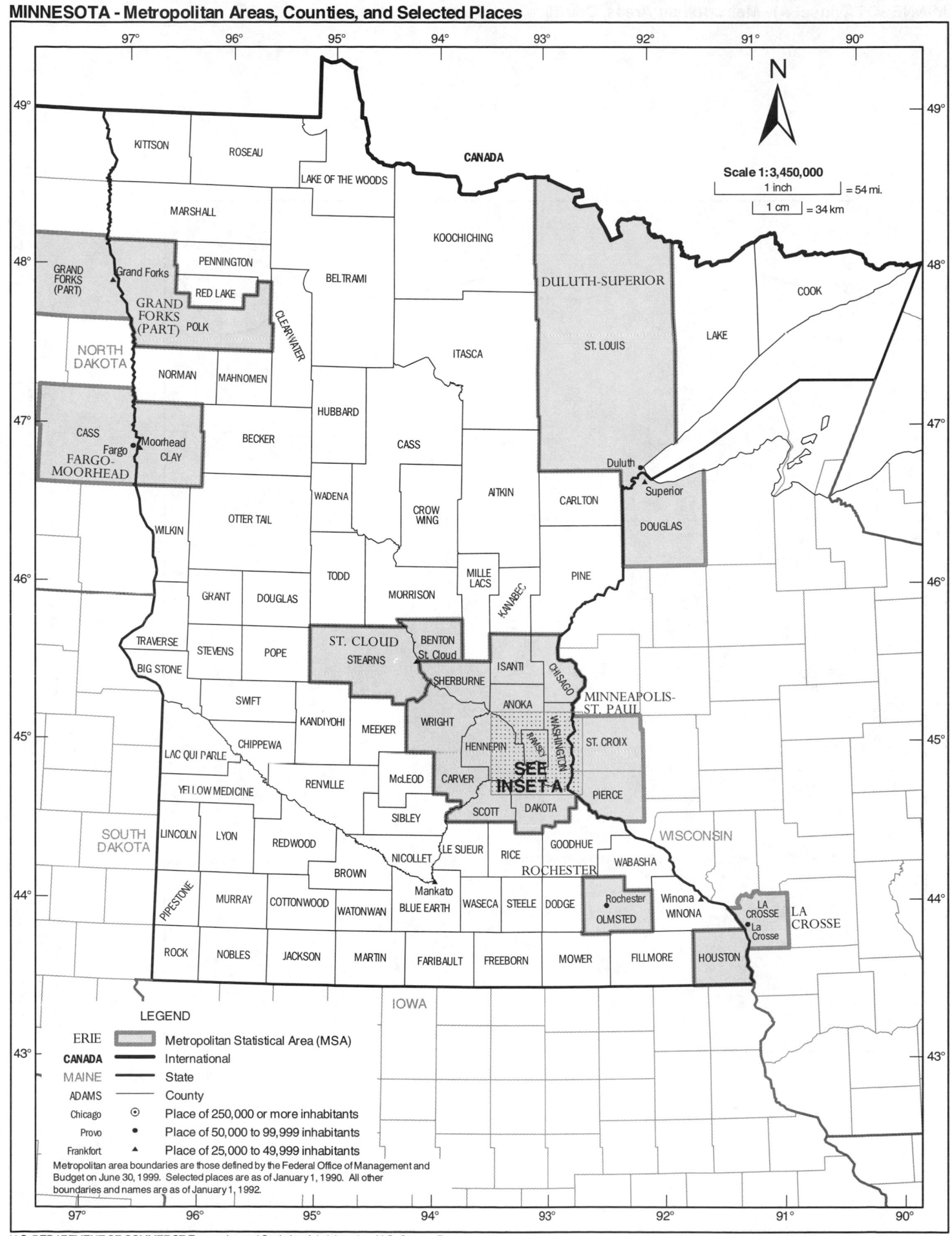

Scale 1:3,450,000

1 inch = 54 mi.

1 cm = 34 km

LEGEND

ERIE	▨	Metropolitan Statistical Area (MSA)
CANADA	▬	International
MAINE	▬	State
ADAMS	—	County
Chicago	⊙	Place of 250,000 or more inhabitants
Provo	•	Place of 50,000 to 99,999 inhabitants
Frankfort	▲	Place of 25,000 to 49,999 inhabitants

Metropolitan area boundaries are those defined by the Federal Office of Management and Budget on June 30, 1999. Selected places are as of January 1, 1990. All other boundaries and names are as of January 1, 1992.

Metropolitan area boundaries are those defined by the Federal Office of Management and Budget on June 30, 1999. Selected places are as of January 1, 1990. All other boundaries and names are as of January 1, 1992.

45°00´

WISCONSIN

ST. CROIX
(PART)

PIERCE
(PART)

WASHINGTON
(PART)

93°00´

93°00´

MINNEAPOLIS-
ST. PAUL
(PART)

Maplewood

DAKOTA
(PART)

RAMSEY

St. Paul

Roseville

ANOKA
(PART)

Eagan

Blaine

Apple Valley

Coon Rapids

Fridley

Minneapolis

Richfield

Bloomington

Burnsville

Brooklyn
Park

Brooklyn Center

HENNEPIN
(PART)

St Louis Park

Edina

Maple Grove

Plymouth

Minnetonka

Eden Prairie

SCOTT
(PART)

45°00´

N

Scale 1:375,000

1 inch | = 5 mi.

1 cm | = 3 km

LEGEND

ERIE | Metropolitan Statistical Area (MSA)

MAINE | State

ADAMS | County

Chicago | ⊙ | Place of 250,000 or more inhabitants

Provo | • | Place of 50,000 to 99,999 inhabitants

Frankfort | ▲ | Place of 25,000 to 49,999 inhabitants

MISSISSIPPI - Metropolitan Areas, Counties, and Selected Places

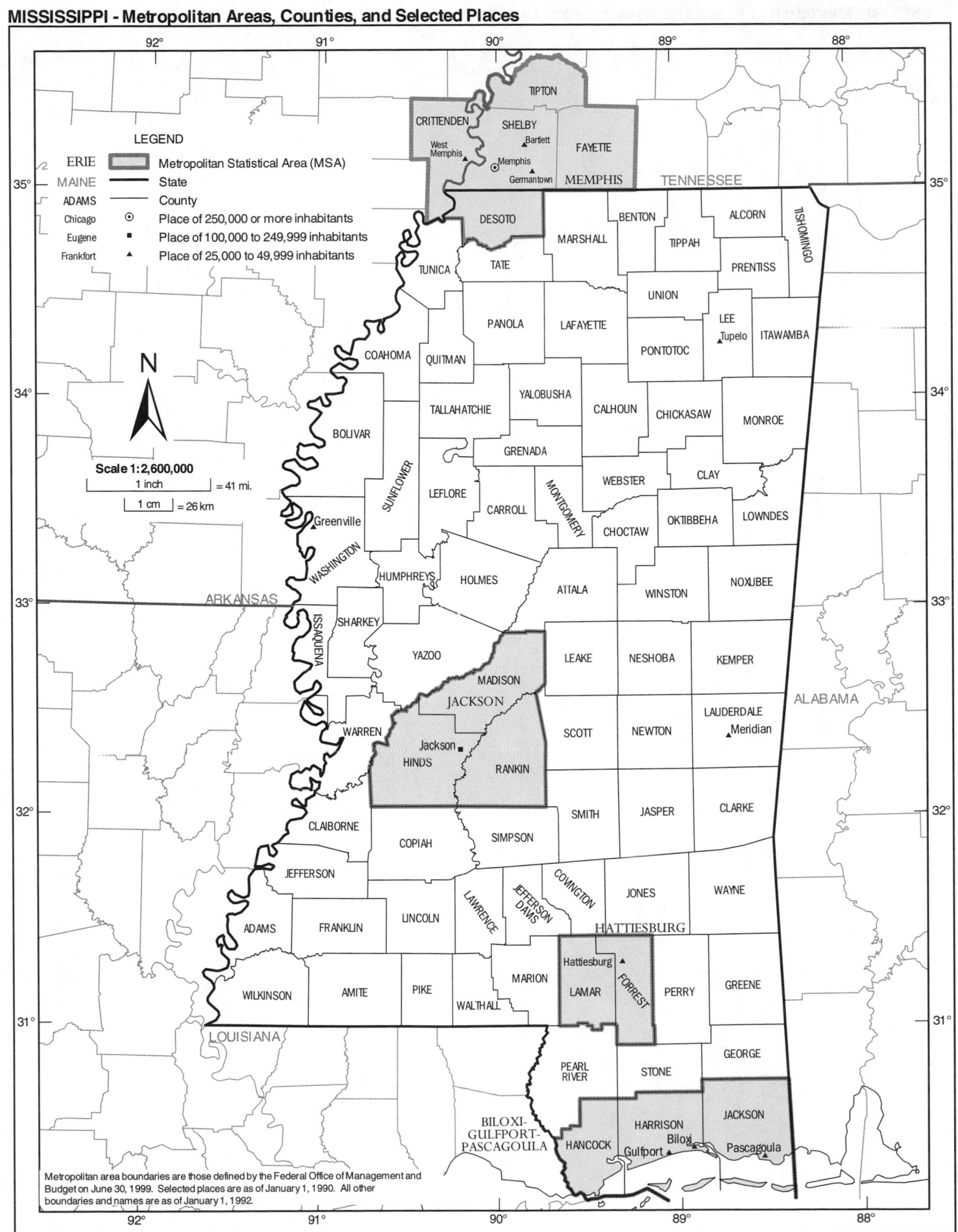

LEGEND

ERIE — Metropolitan Statistical Area (MSA)
MAINE — State
ADAMS — County
Chicago ⊙ Place of 250,000 or more inhabitants
Eugene ■ Place of 100,000 to 249,999 inhabitants
Frankfort ▲ Place of 25,000 to 49,999 inhabitants

Scale 1:2,600,000
1 inch = 41 mi.
1 cm = 26 km

Metropolitan area boundaries are those defined by the Federal Office of Management and Budget on June 30, 1999. Selected places are as of January 1, 1990. All other boundaries and names are as of January 1, 1992.

MISSOURI - Metropolitan Areas, Counties, Independent City, and Selected Places

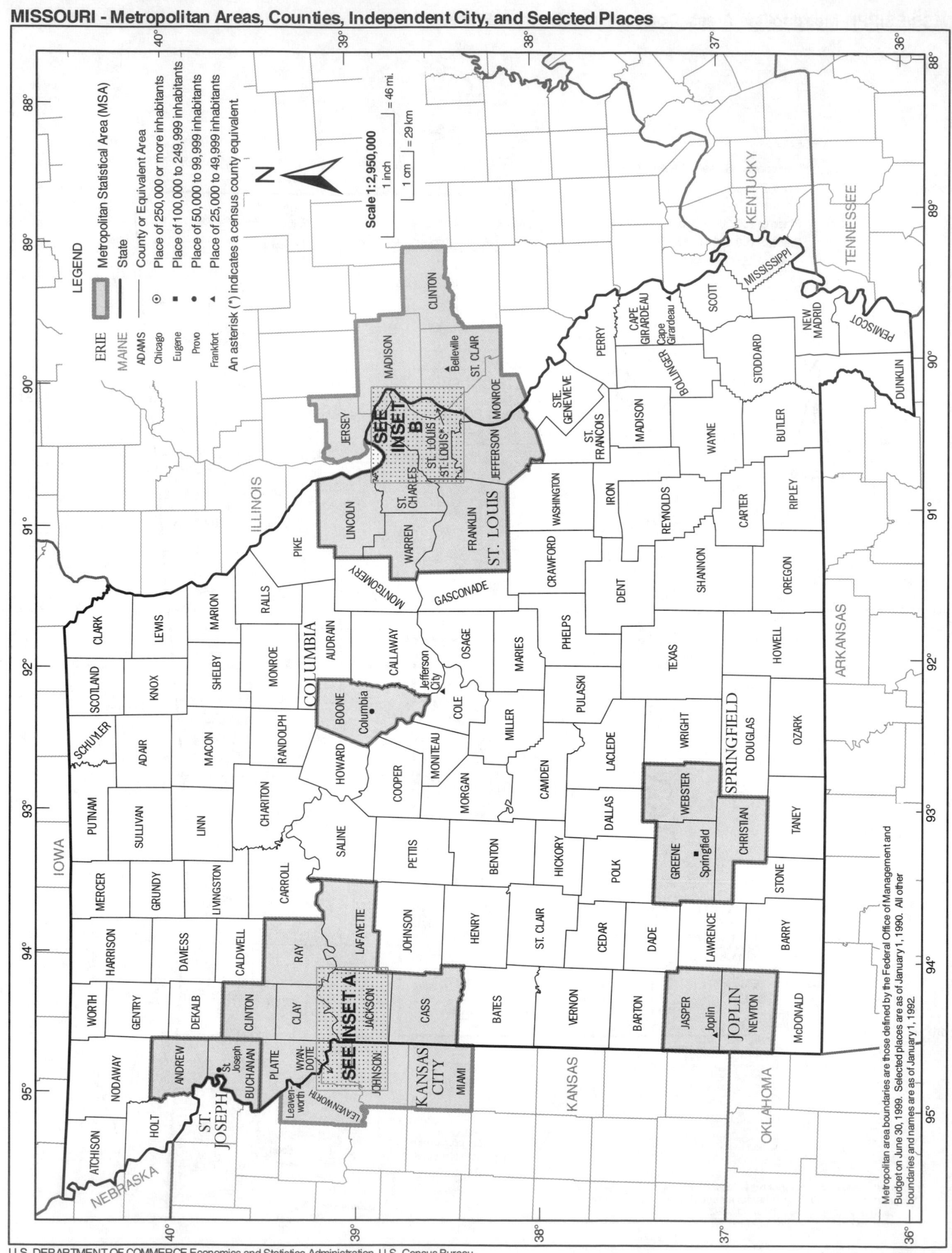

U.S. DEPARTMENT OF COMMERCE Economics and Statistics Administration U.S. Census Bureau

U.S. Census Bureau, County and City Data Book: 2000

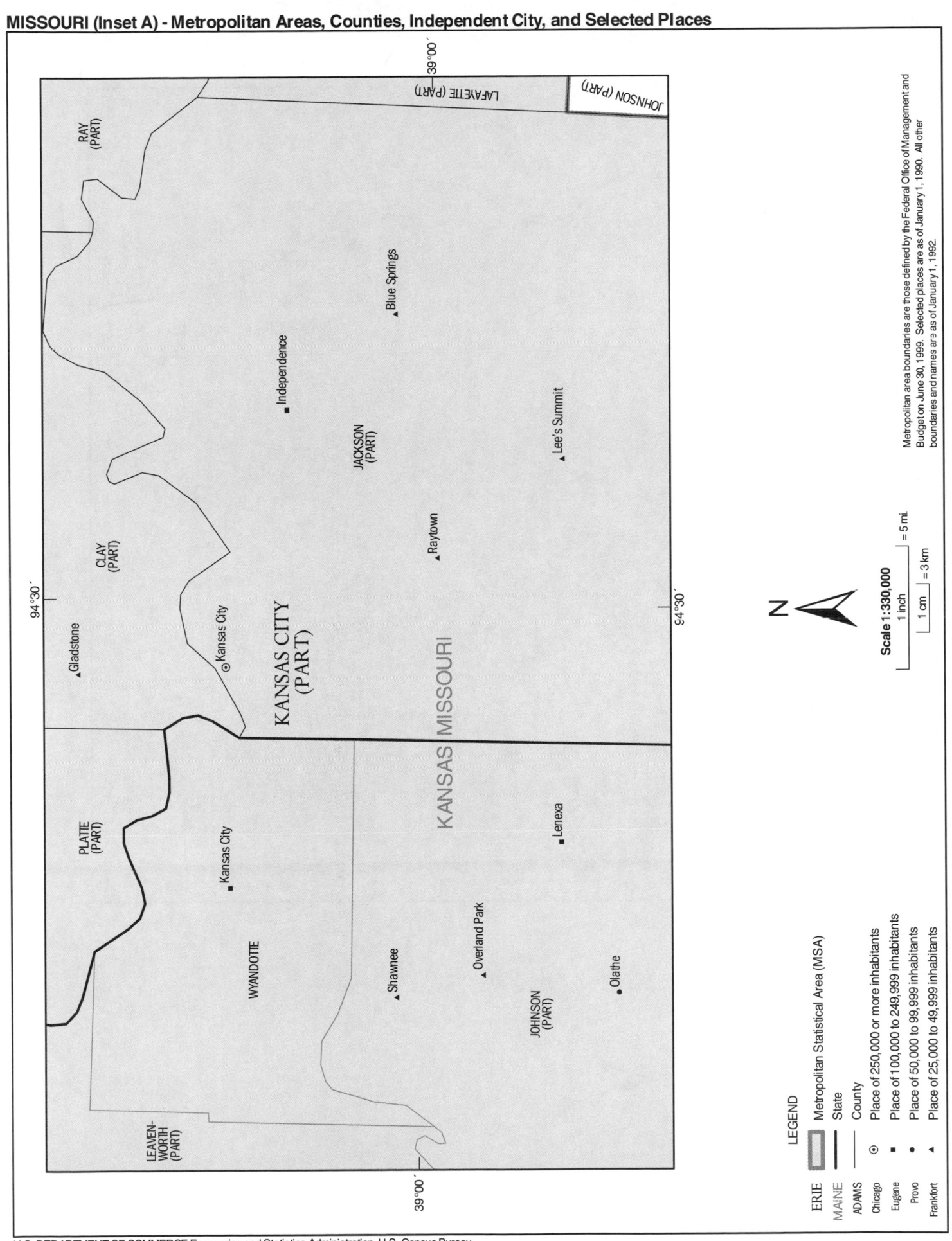

Metropolitan area boundaries are those defined by the Federal Office of Management and Budget on June 30, 1999. Selected places are as of January 1, 1990. All other boundaries and names are as of January 1, 1992.

Scale 1:330,000

1 inch = 5 mi.

1 cm = 3 km

N

LEGEND

ERIE	Metropolitan Statistical Area (MSA)
MAINE	State
ADAMS	County
⊙ Chicago	Place of 250,000 or more inhabitants
■ Eugene	Place of 100,000 to 249,999 inhabitants
● Provo	Place of 50,000 to 99,999 inhabitants
▲ Frankfort	Place of 25,000 to 49,999 inhabitants

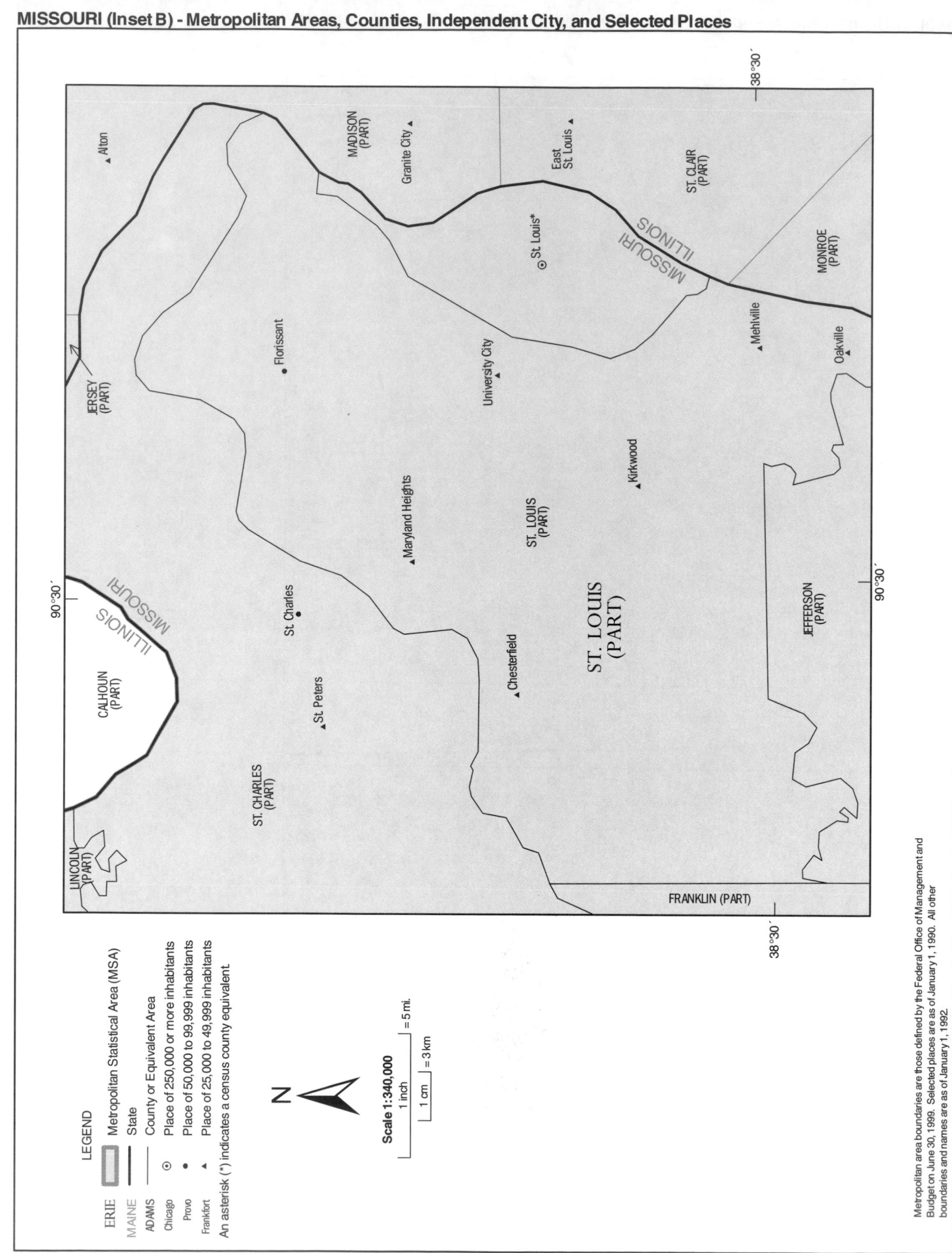

Scale 1:340,000

1 inch = 5 mi.

1 cm = 3 km

N

LEGEND

ERIE — Metropolitan Statistical Area (MSA)

MAINE — State

ADAMS — County or Equivalent Area

⊙ Chicago — Place of 250,000 or more inhabitants

• Provo — Place of 50,000 to 99,999 inhabitants

▲ Frankfort — Place of 25,000 to 49,999 inhabitants

An asterisk (*) indicates a census county equivalent.

Places on map: Alton, MADISON (PART), Granite City, East St. Louis, ST. CLAIR (PART), MONROE (PART), JERSEY (PART), St Louis*, University City, Mehlville, Oakville, Florissant, Kirkwood, ST. LOUIS (PART), Maryland Heights, St Charles, Chesterfield, JEFFERSON (PART), St Peters, ST. CHARLES (PART), CALHOUN (PART), LINCOLN (PART), FRANKLIN (PART)

MISSOURI / ILLINOIS

90°30´   38°30´   38°30´   90°30´

Metropolitan area boundaries are those defined by the Federal Office of Management and Budget on June 30, 1999. Selected places are as of January 1, 1990. All other boundaries and names are as of January 1, 1992.

MONTANA - Metropolitan Areas, Counties, and Selected Places

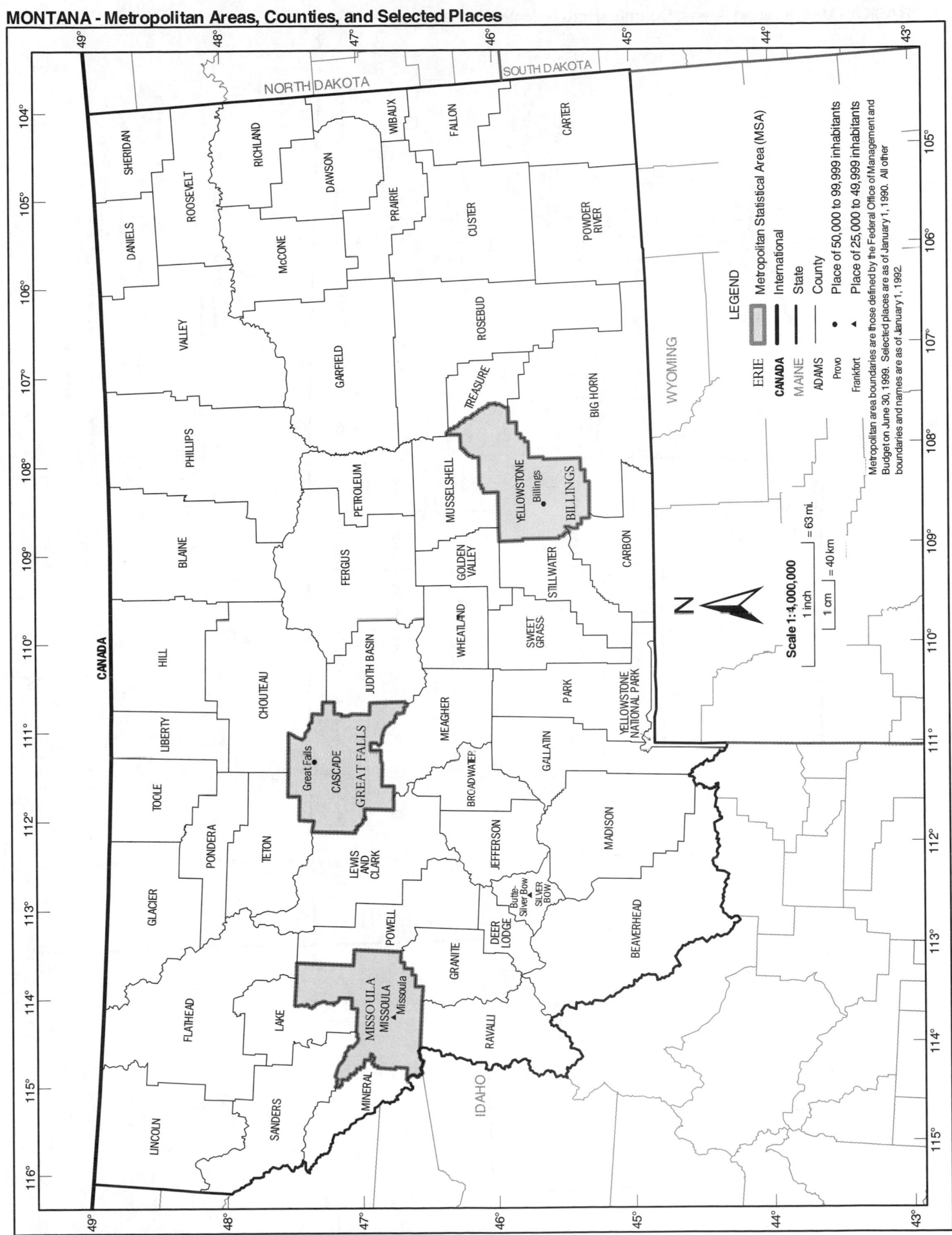

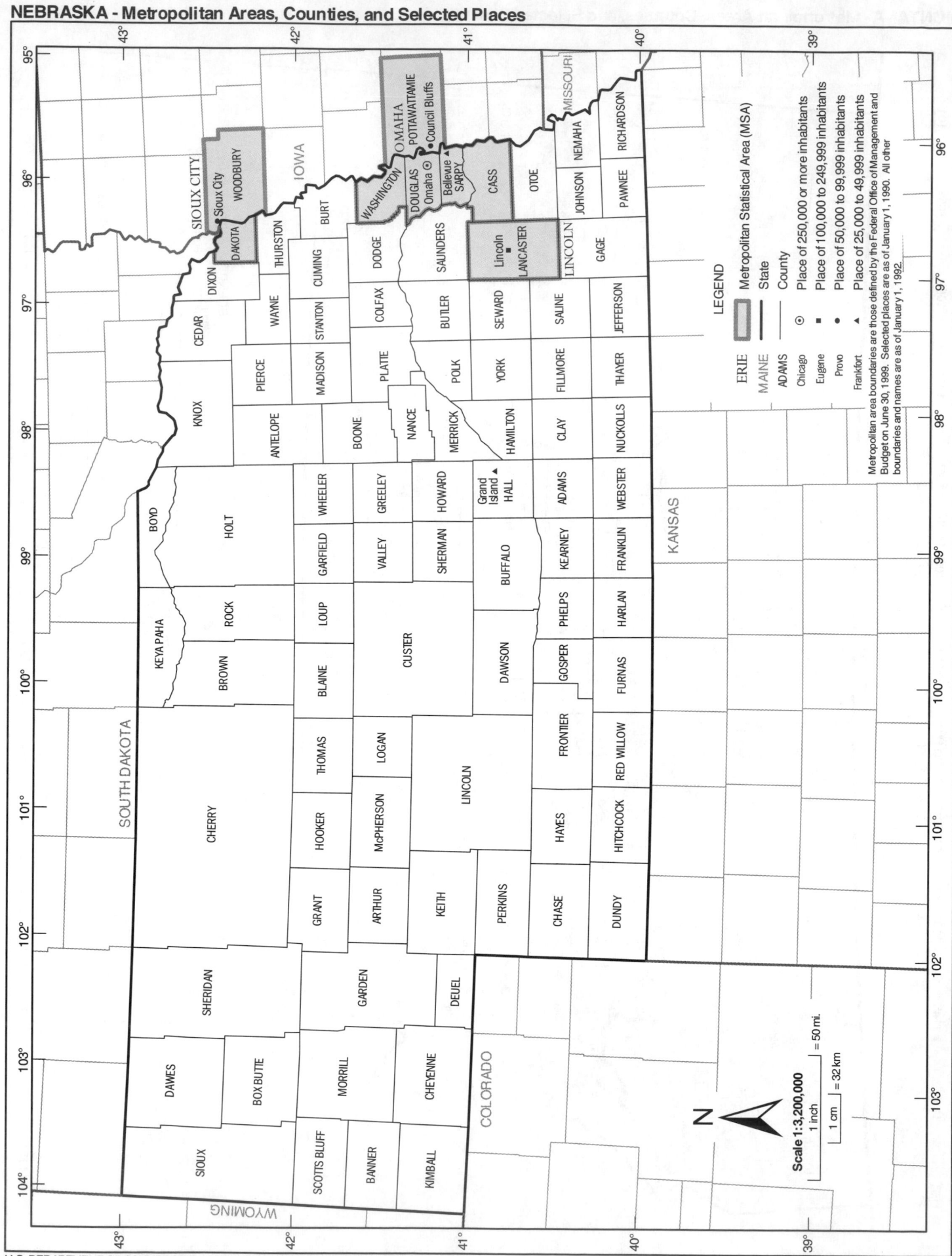

NEVADA - Metropolitan Areas, Counties, Independent City, and Selected Places

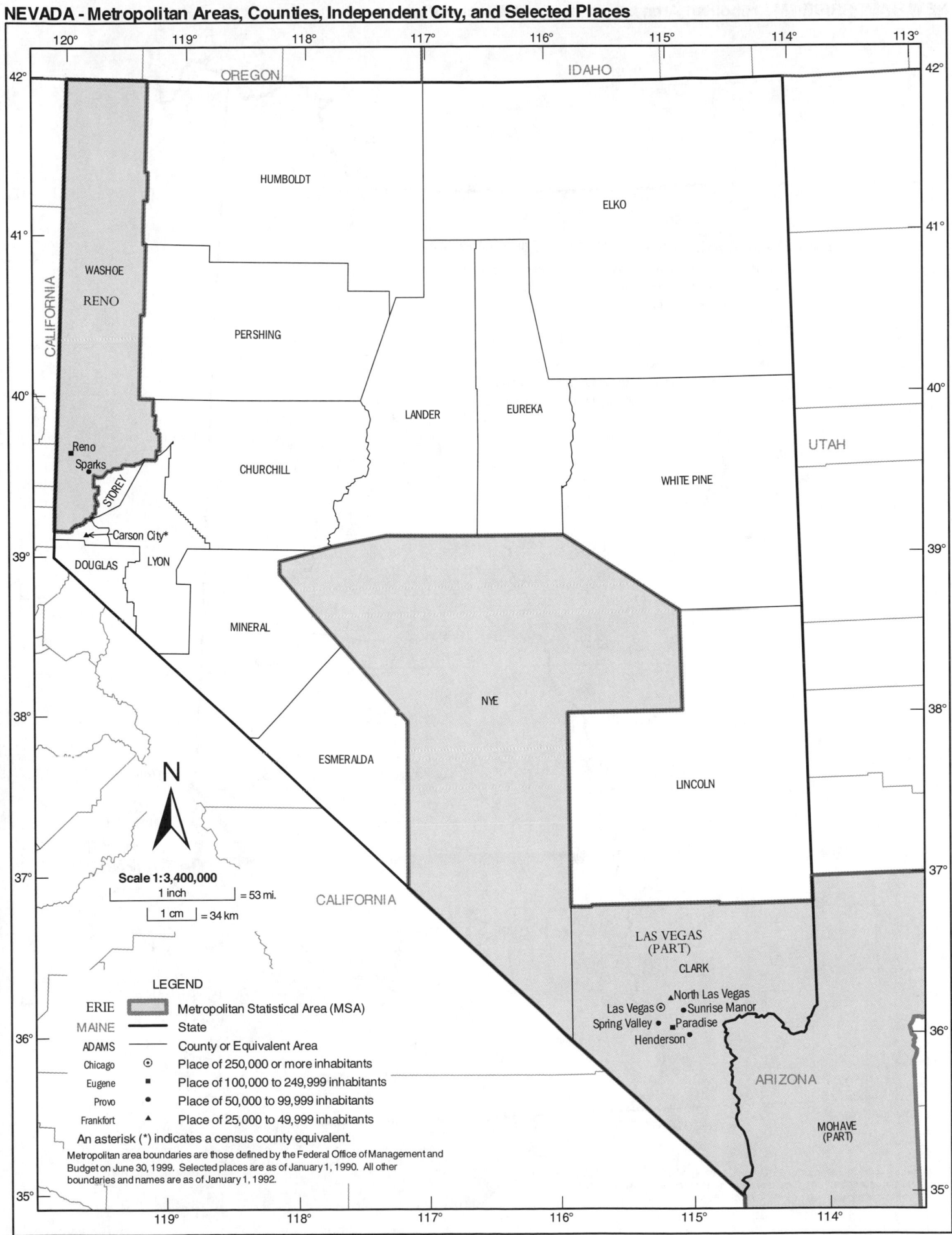

LEGEND

ERIE	▭	Metropolitan Statistical Area (MSA)
MAINE	—	State
ADAMS	—	County or Equivalent Area
Chicago	⊙	Place of 250,000 or more inhabitants
Eugene	■	Place of 100,000 to 249,999 inhabitants
Provo	●	Place of 50,000 to 99,999 inhabitants
Frankfort	▲	Place of 25,000 to 49,999 inhabitants

An asterisk (*) indicates a census county equivalent.

Metropolitan area boundaries are those defined by the Federal Office of Management and Budget on June 30, 1999. Selected places are as of January 1, 1990. All other boundaries and names are as of January 1, 1992.

Scale 1:3,400,000
1 inch = 53 mi.
1 cm = 34 km

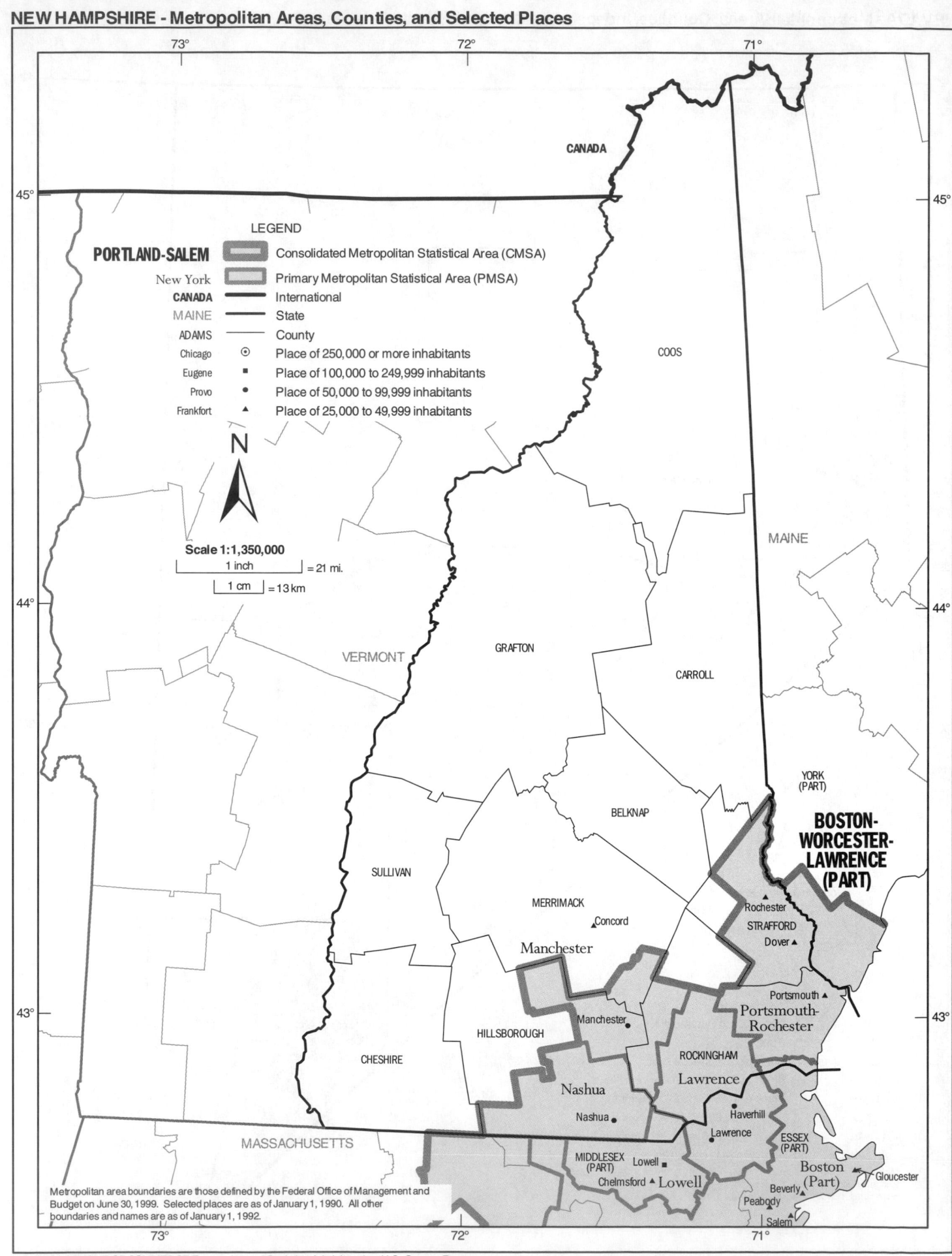

U.S. DEPARTMENT OF COMMERCE Economics and Statistics Administration U.S. Census Bureau

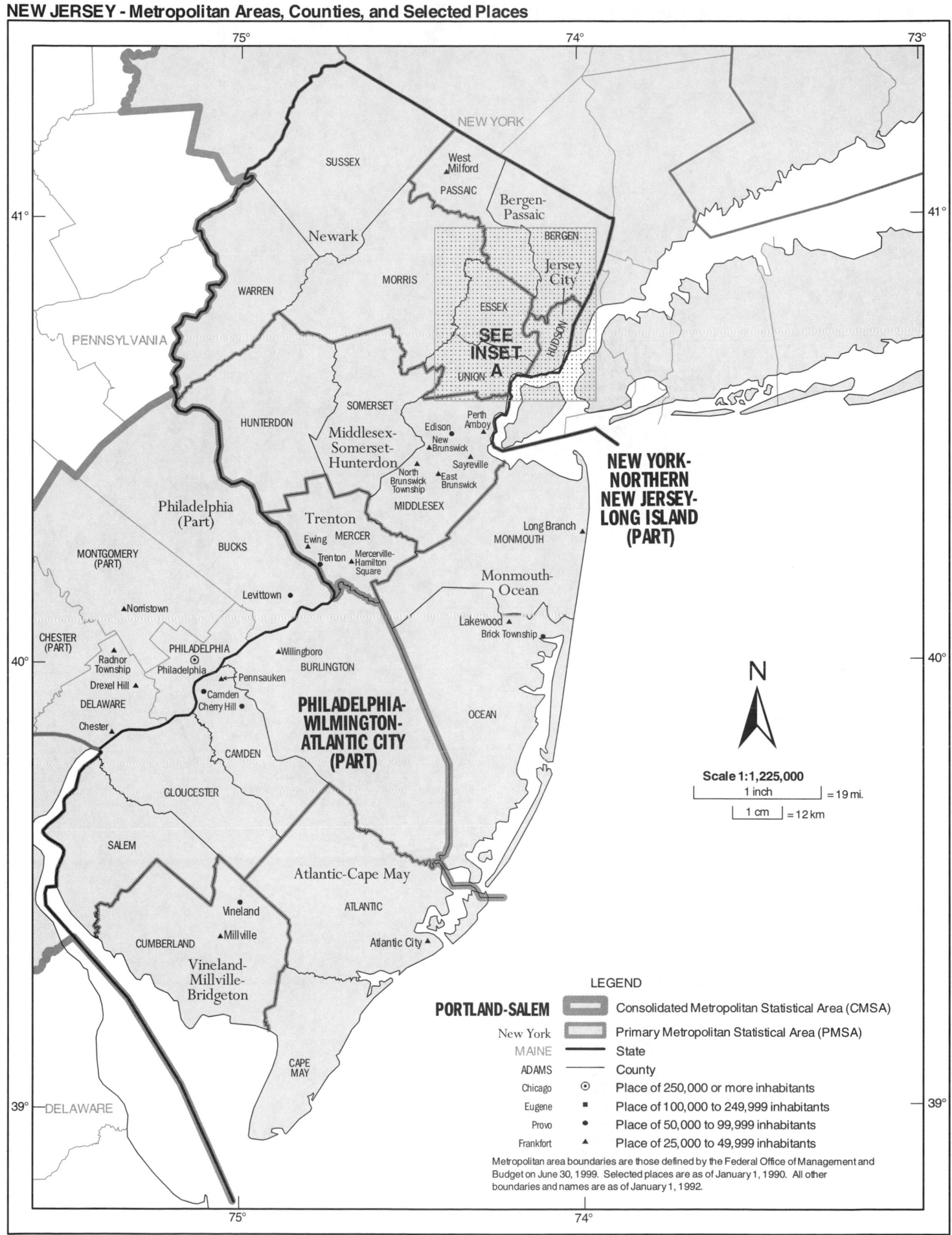

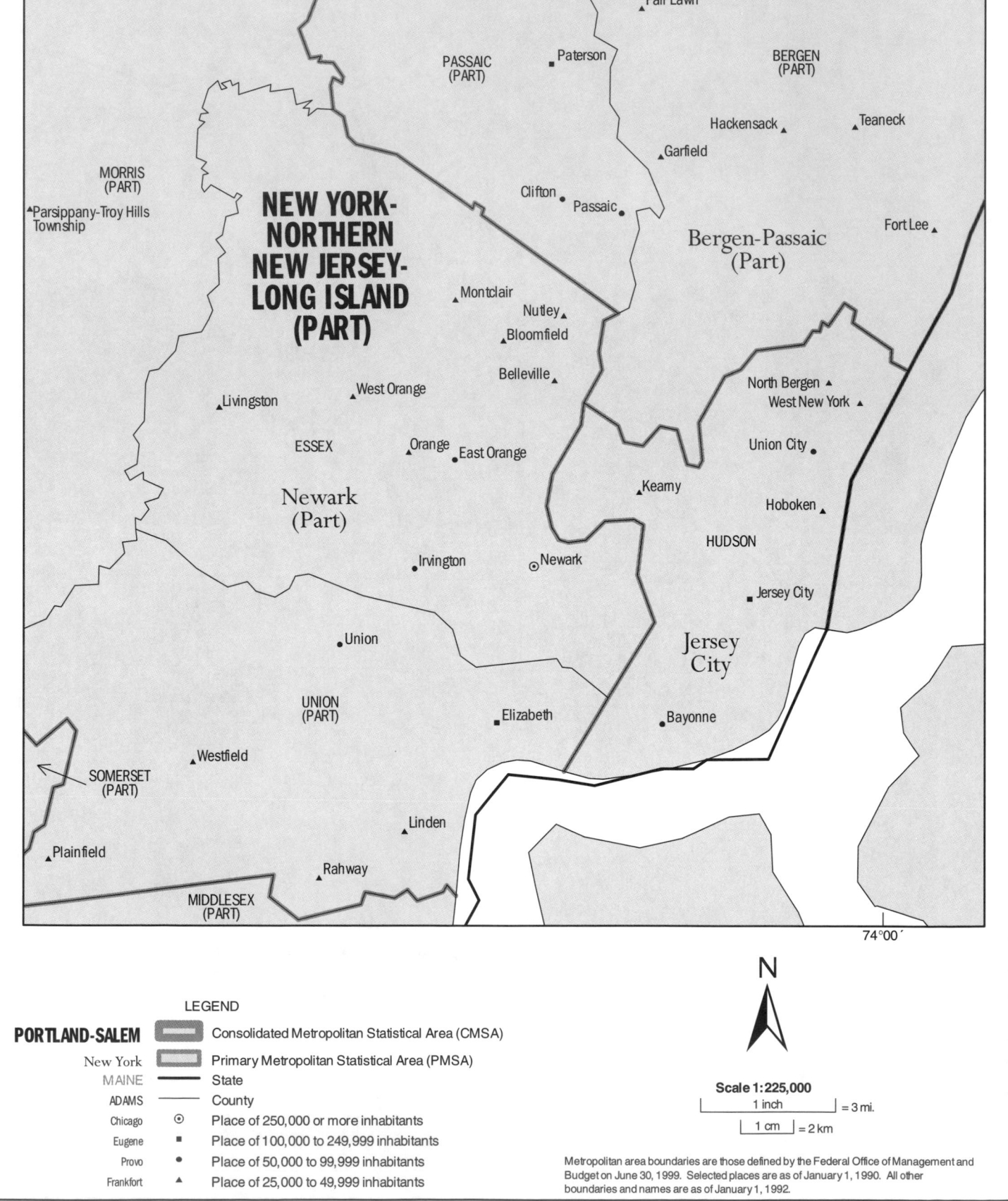

74°00´

MORRIS
(PART)

▲Parsippany-Troy Hills
Township

PASSAIC
(PART)

▲Wayne

▲Fair Lawn

▲Paramus

■Paterson

BERGEN
(PART)

Hackensack▲

▲Teaneck

■Garfield

Clifton●
●Passaic

NEW YORK-
NORTHERN
NEW JERSEY-
LONG ISLAND
(PART)

Bergen-Passaic
(Part)

Fort Lee▲

▲Montclair

Nutley▲

▲Bloomfield

Belleville▲

North Bergen ▲

West New York ▲

●West Orange

▲Livingston

ESSEX

▲Orange
●East Orange

Union City ●

Newark
(Part)

●Kearny

Hoboken ●

HUDSON

●Irvington

⊙Newark

■Jersey City

Jersey
City

●Union

UNION
(PART)

■Elizabeth

●Bayonne

▲Westfield

SOMERSET
(PART)

▲Plainfield

●Linden

●Rahway

MIDDLESEX
(PART)

74°00´

N

Scale 1:225,000

1 inch = 3 mi.

1 cm = 2 km

Metropolitan area boundaries are those defined by the Federal Office of Management and
Budget on June 30, 1999. Selected places are as of January 1, 1990. All other
boundaries and names are as of January 1, 1992.

NEW MEXICO - Metropolitan Areas, Counties, and Selected Places

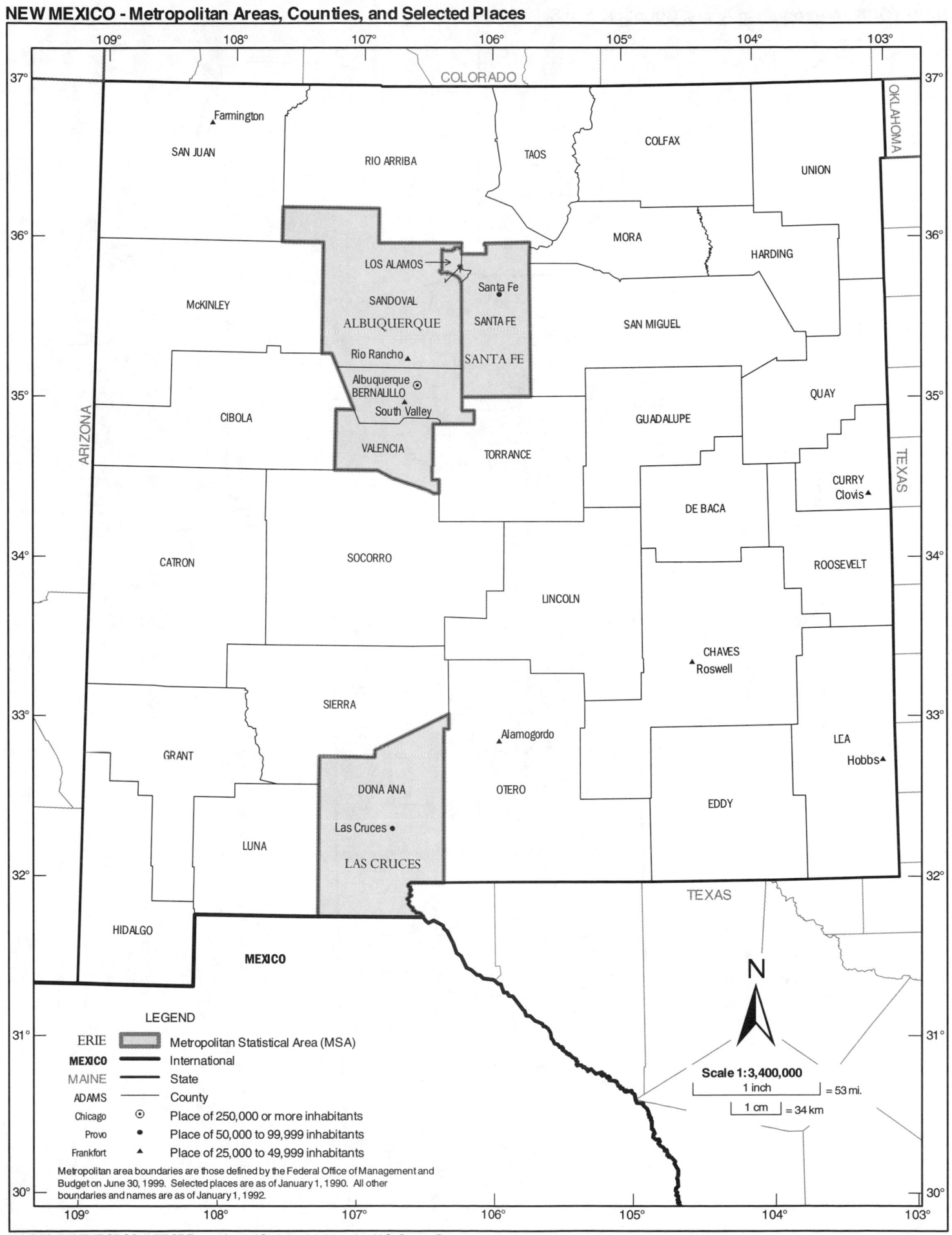

LEGEND

ERIE		Metropolitan Statistical Area (MSA)
MEXICO		International
MAINE		State
ADAMS		County
Chicago	⊙	Place of 250,000 or more inhabitants
Provo	●	Place of 50,000 to 99,999 inhabitants
Frankfort	▲	Place of 25,000 to 49,999 inhabitants

Metropolitan area boundaries are those defined by the Federal Office of Management and Budget on June 30, 1999. Selected places are as of January 1, 1990. All other boundaries and names are as of January 1, 1992.

Scale 1:3,400,000

1 inch = 53 mi.

1 cm = 34 km

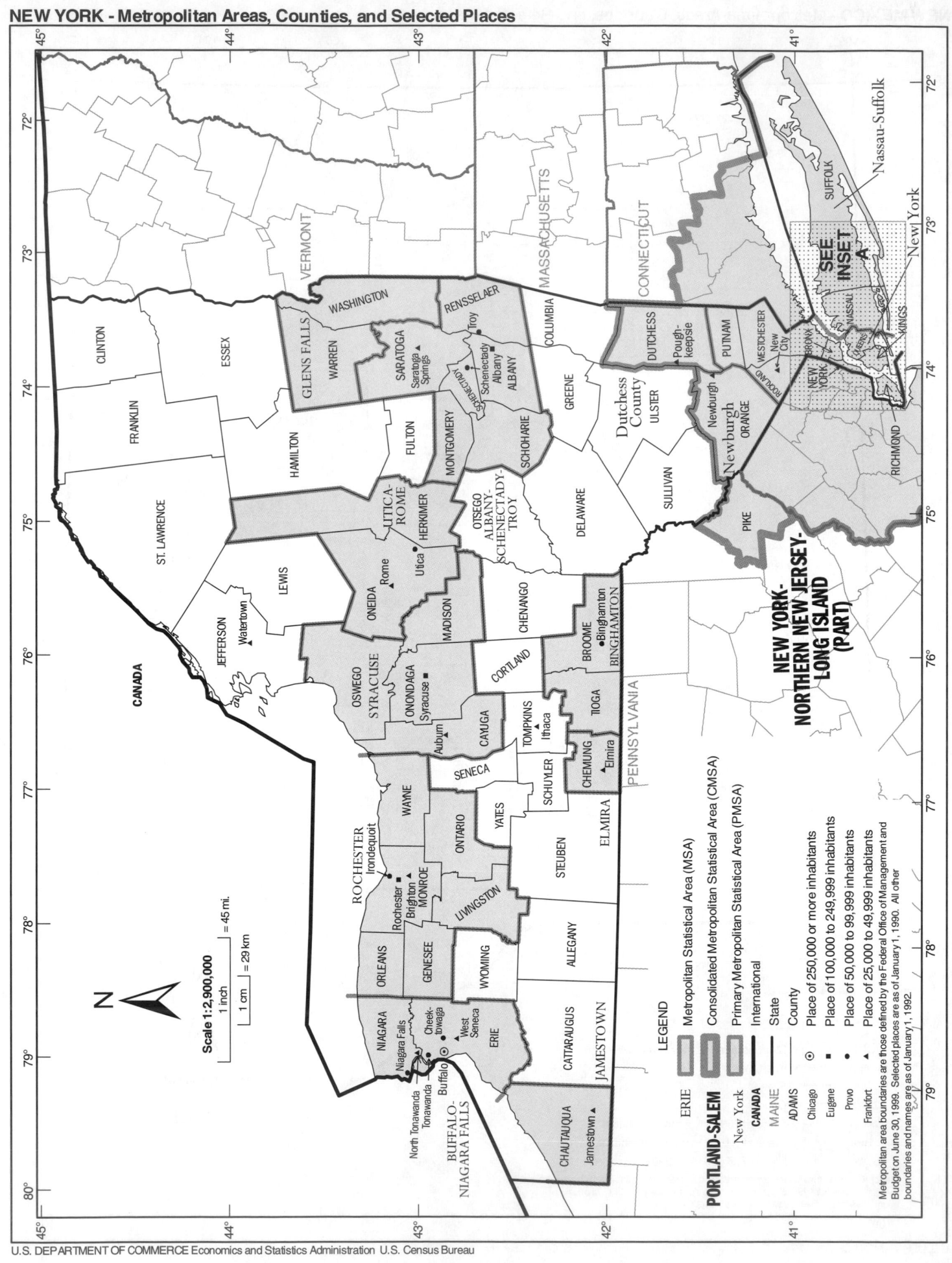

LEGEND

	Metropolitan Statistical Area (MSA)
	Consolidated Metropolitan Statistical Area (CMSA)
	Primary Metropolitan Statistical Area (PMSA)
	International
	State
	County

ERIE New York
PORTLAND-SALEM CANADA
ADAMS MAINE

⊙ Chicago — Place of 250,000 or more inhabitants
■ Eugene — Place of 100,000 to 249,999 inhabitants
● Provo — Place of 50,000 to 99,999 inhabitants
▲ Frankfort — Place of 25,000 to 49,999 inhabitants

Metropolitan area boundaries are those defined by the Federal Office of Management and Budget on June 30, 1999. Selected places are as of January 1, 1990. All other boundaries and names are as of January 1, 1992.

Scale 1:2,900,000
1 inch = 45 mi.
1 cm = 29 km

N

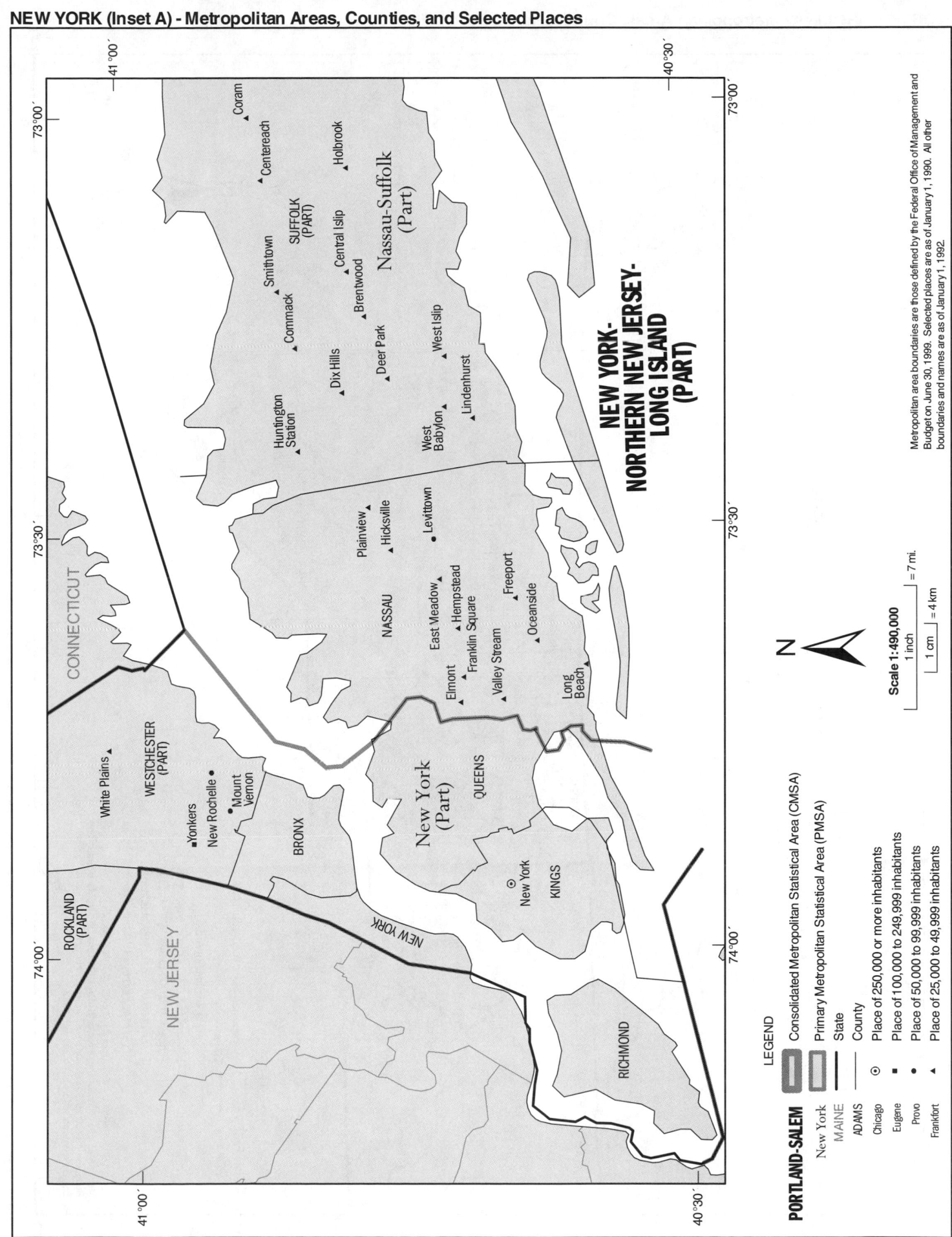

Metropolitan area boundaries are those defined by the Federal Office of Management and Budget on June 30, 1999. Selected places are as of January 1, 1990. All other boundaries and names are as of January 1, 1992.

NEW YORK-NORTHERN NEW JERSEY-LONG ISLAND (PART)

Scale 1:490,000

1 inch = 7 mi.

1 cm = 4 km

N

LEGEND

PORTLAND-SALEM Consolidated Metropolitan Statistical Area (CMSA)

New York Primary Metropolitan Statistical Area (PMSA)

MAINE State

ADAMS County

Chicago ⊙ Place of 250,000 or more inhabitants

Eugene ■ Place of 100,000 to 249,999 inhabitants

Provo ● Place of 50,000 to 99,999 inhabitants

Frankfort ▲ Place of 25,000 to 49,999 inhabitants

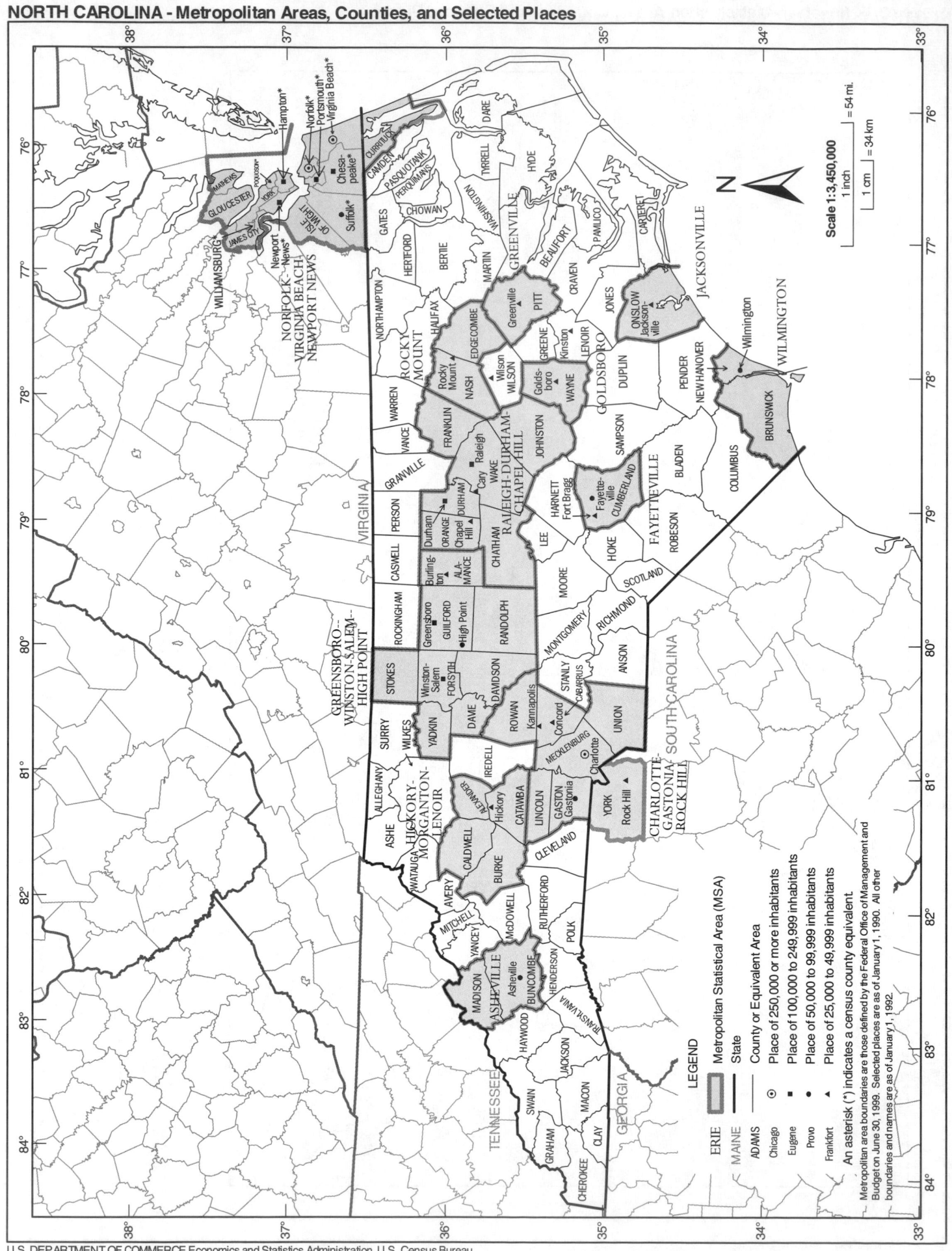

NORTH DAKOTA - Metropolitan Areas, Counties, and Selected Places

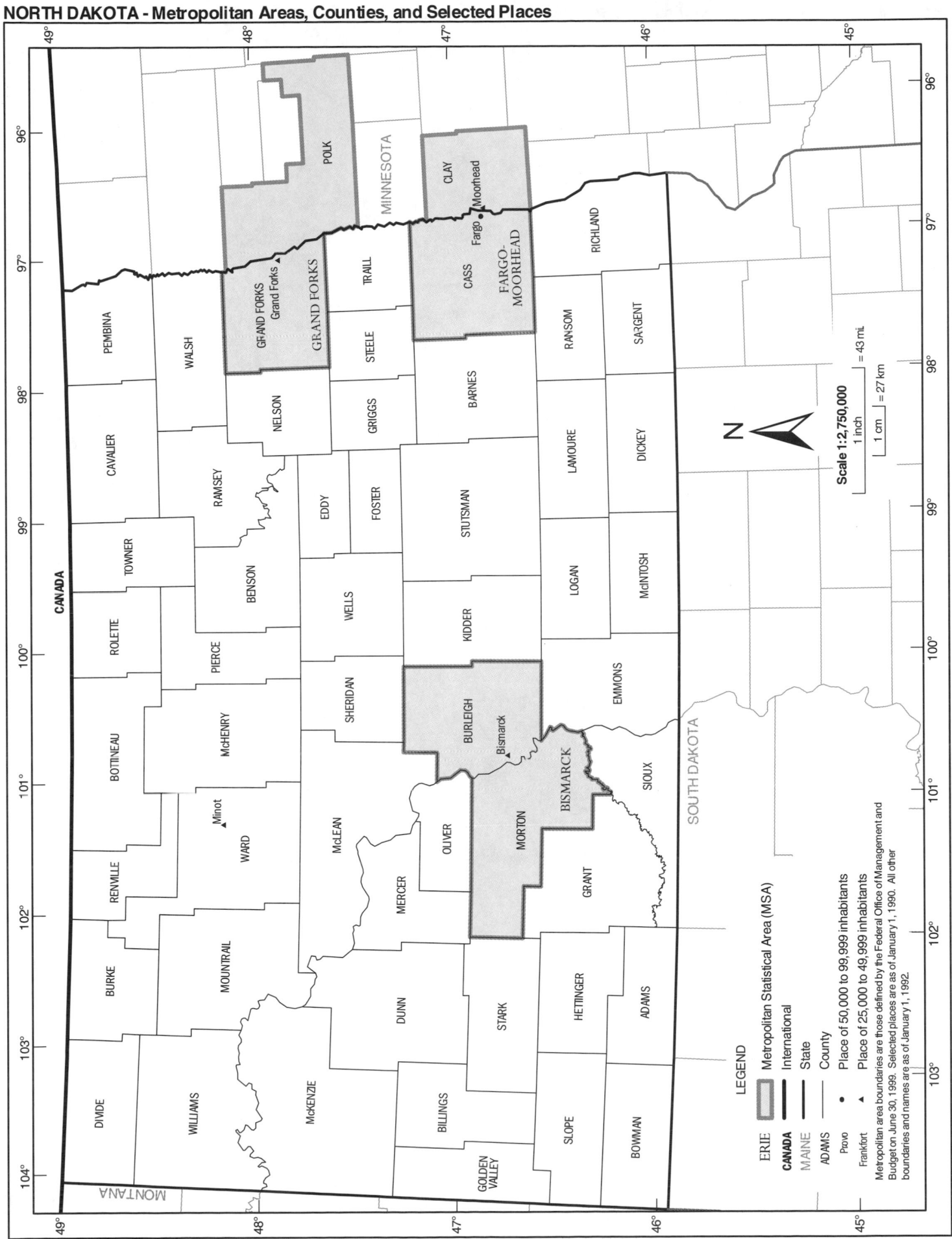

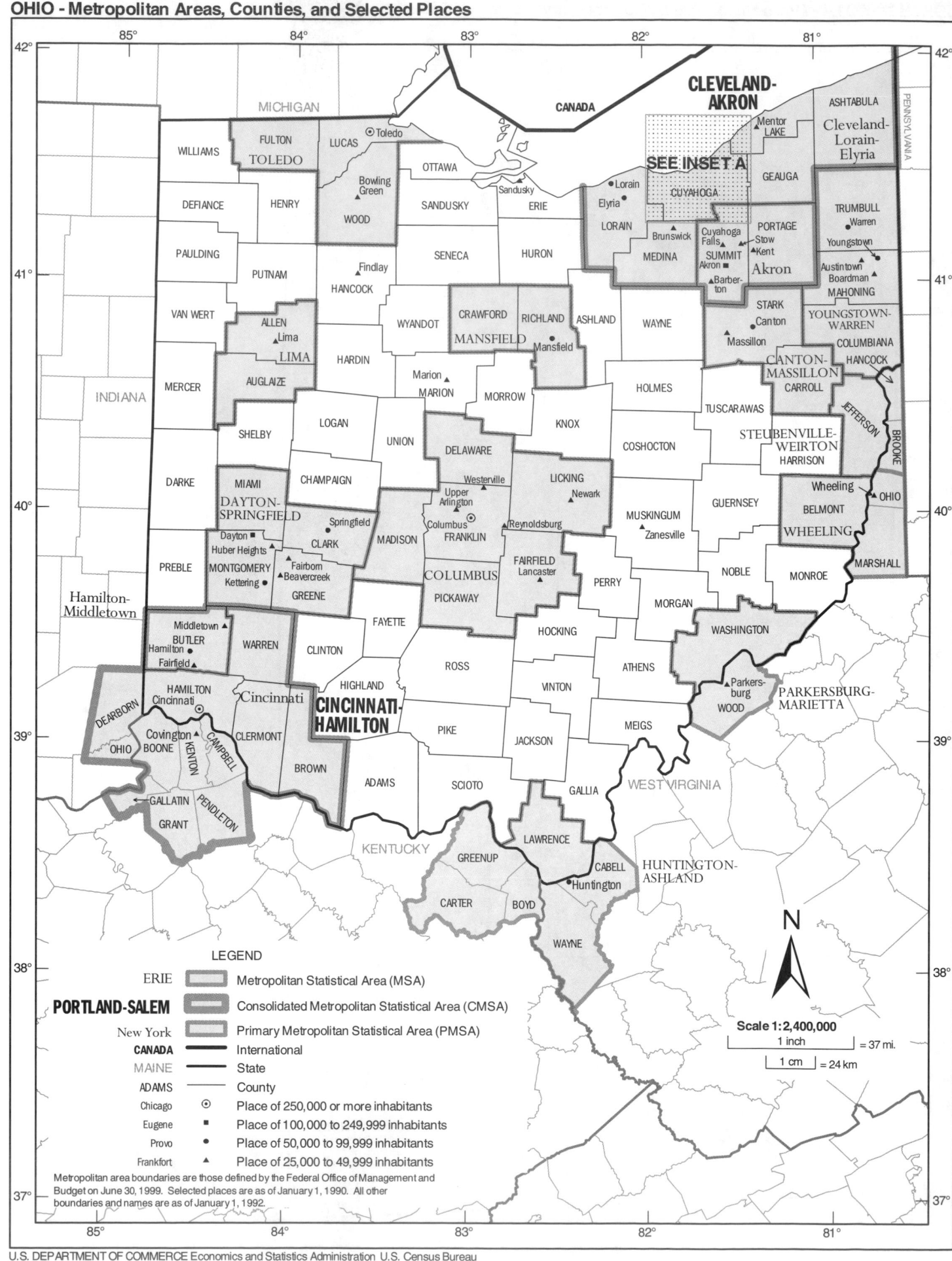

LEGEND

ERIE	Metropolitan Statistical Area (MSA)
PORTLAND-SALEM	Consolidated Metropolitan Statistical Area (CMSA)
New York	Primary Metropolitan Statistical Area (PMSA)
CANADA	International
MAINE	State
ADAMS	County
Chicago ⊙	Place of 250,000 or more inhabitants
Eugene ■	Place of 100,000 to 249,999 inhabitants
Provo ●	Place of 50,000 to 99,999 inhabitants
Frankfort ▲	Place of 25,000 to 49,999 inhabitants

Metropolitan area boundaries are those defined by the Federal Office of Management and Budget on June 30, 1999. Selected places are as of January 1, 1990. All other boundaries and names are as of January 1, 1992.

Scale 1:2,400,000

1 inch = 37 mi.

1 cm = 24 km

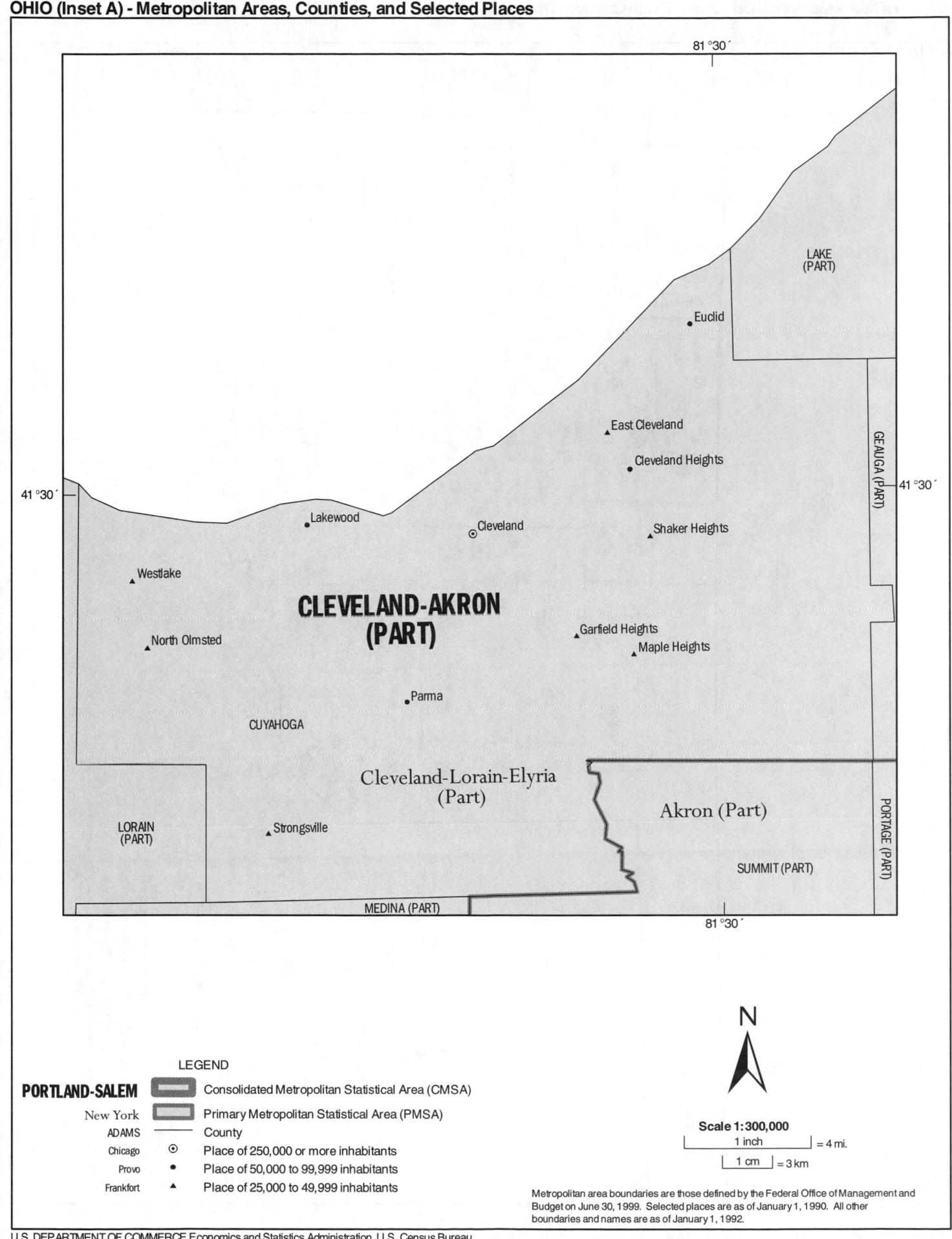

81°30′

LAKE
(PART)

• Euclid

GEAUGA (PART)

41°30′   41°30′

▲ East Cleveland

■ Cleveland Heights

Lakewood

⊙ Cleveland

■ Shaker Heights

▲ Westlake

**CLEVELAND-AKRON
(PART)**

▲ North Olmsted

■ Garfield Heights
▲ Maple Heights

• Parma

CUYAHOGA

Cleveland-Lorain-Elyria
(Part)

Akron (Part)

PORTAGE (PART)

LORAIN
(PART)

▲ Strongsville

SUMMIT (PART)

MEDINA (PART)

81°30′

N

LEGEND

PORTLAND-SALEM   ▭ Consolidated Metropolitan Statistical Area (CMSA)

New York   ▭ Primary Metropolitan Statistical Area (PMSA)

ADAMS   —— County

Chicago   ⊙ Place of 250,000 or more inhabitants

Provo   • Place of 50,000 to 99,999 inhabitants

Frankfort   ▲ Place of 25,000 to 49,999 inhabitants

Scale 1:300,000
| 1 inch | = 4 mi.
| 1 cm | = 3 km

Metropolitan area boundaries are those defined by the Federal Office of Management and
Budget on June 30, 1999. Selected places are as of January 1, 1990. All other
boundaries and names are as of January 1, 1992.

U.S. DEPARTMENT OF COMMERCE Economics and Statistics Administration U.S. Census Bureau

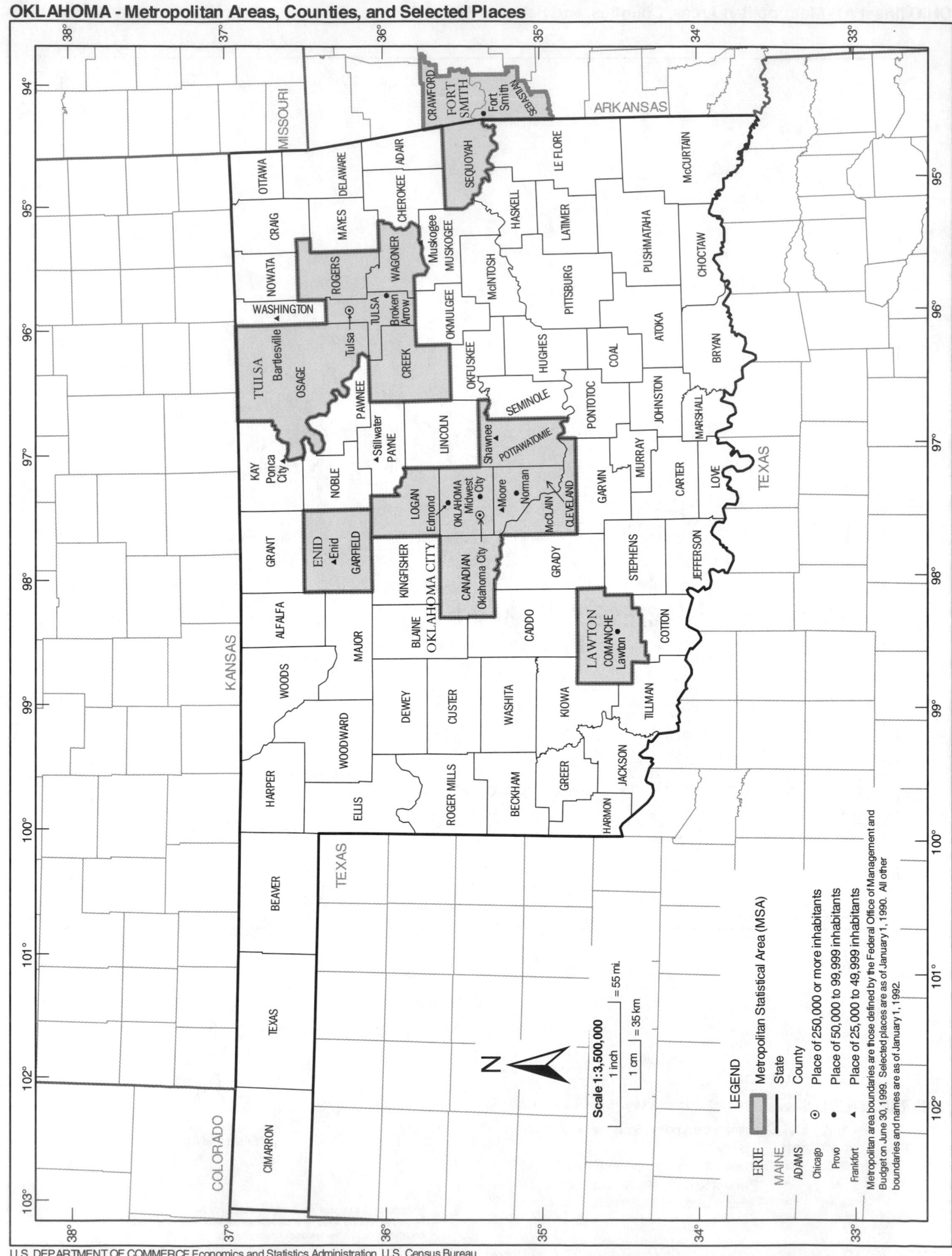

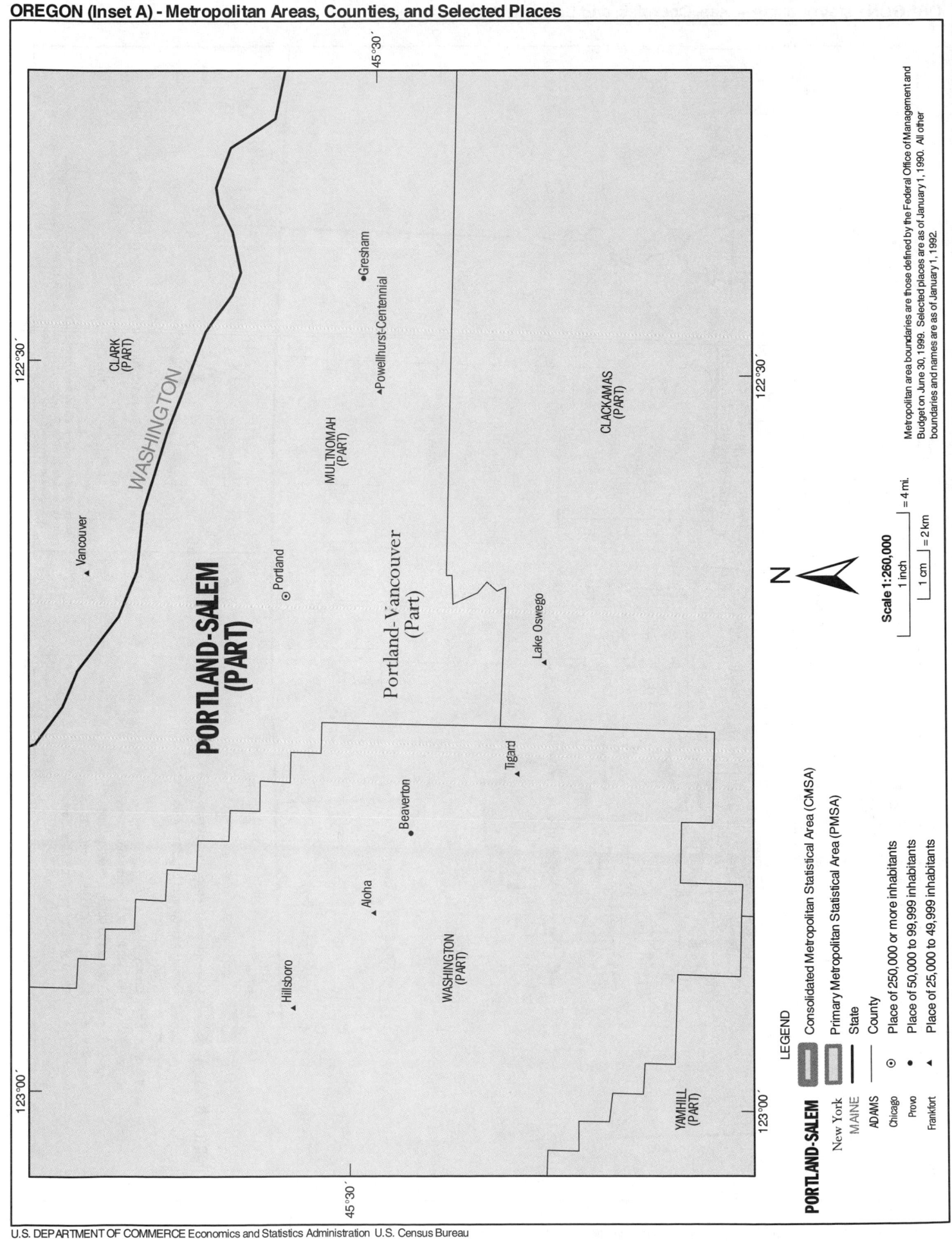

Scale 1:260,000

1 inch [____] = 4 mi.

1 cm [____] = 2 km

Metropolitan area boundaries are those defined by the Federal Office of Management and Budget on June 30, 1999. Selected places are as of January 1, 1990. All other boundaries and names are as of January 1, 1992.

LEGEND

PORTLAND-SALEM ▢ Consolidated Metropolitan Statistical Area (CMSA)

New York ▢ Primary Metropolitan Statistical Area (PMSA)

MAINE —— State

ADAMS —— County

Chicago ⊙ Place of 250,000 or more inhabitants

Provo ● Place of 50,000 to 99,999 inhabitants

Frankfort ▲ Place of 25,000 to 49,999 inhabitants

OREGON - Metropolitan Areas, Counties, and Selected Places

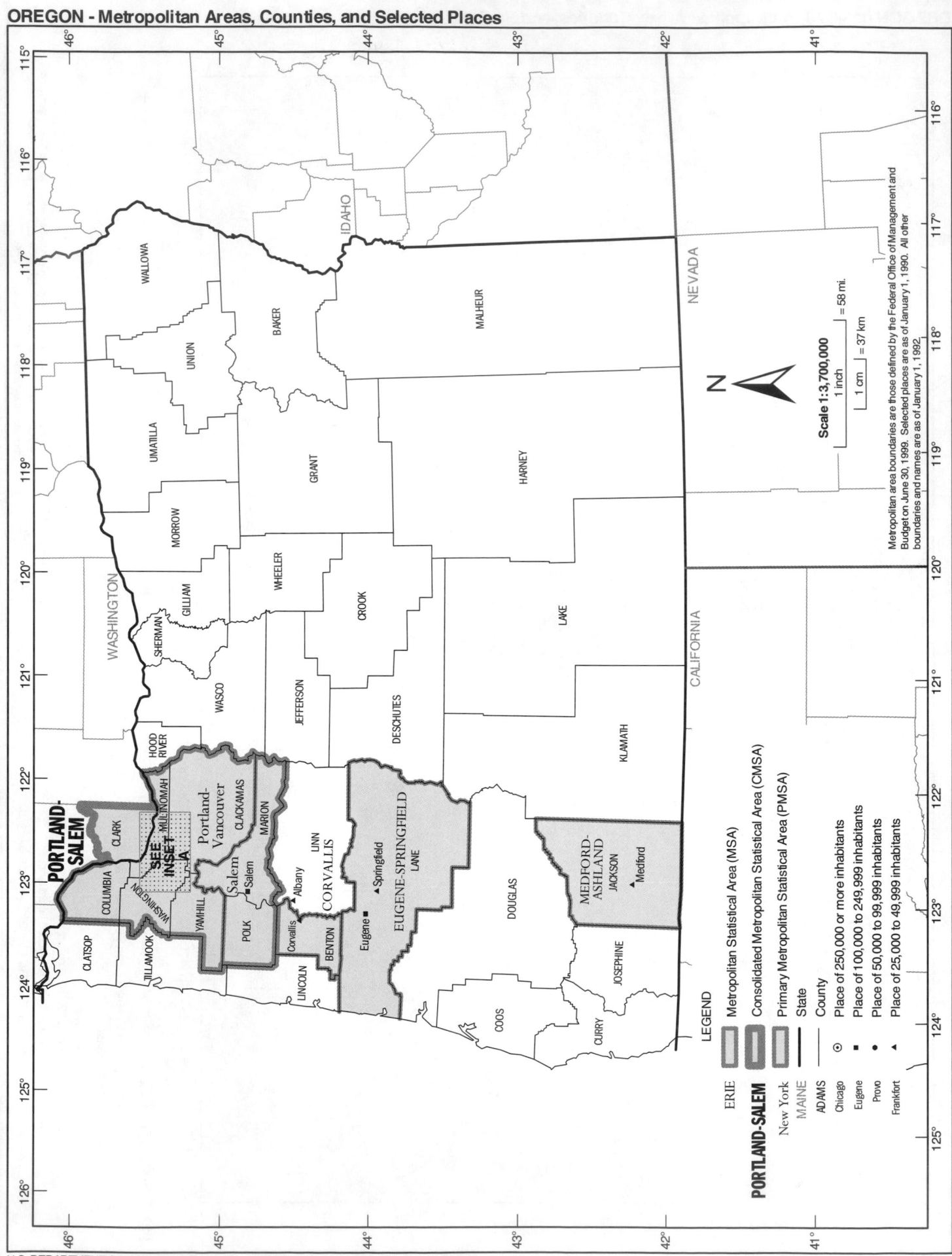

PENNSYLVANIA - Metropolitan Areas, Counties, and Selected Places

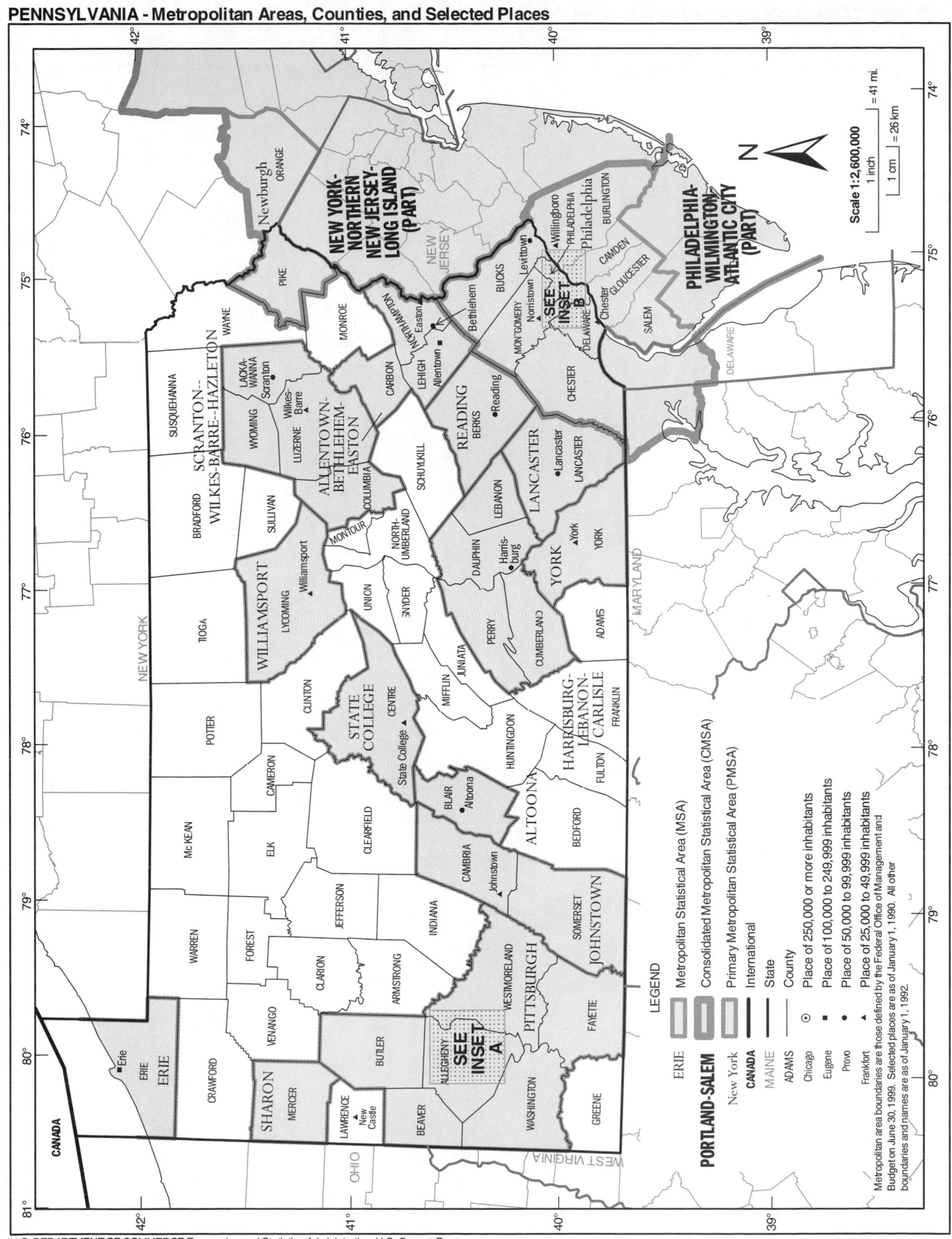

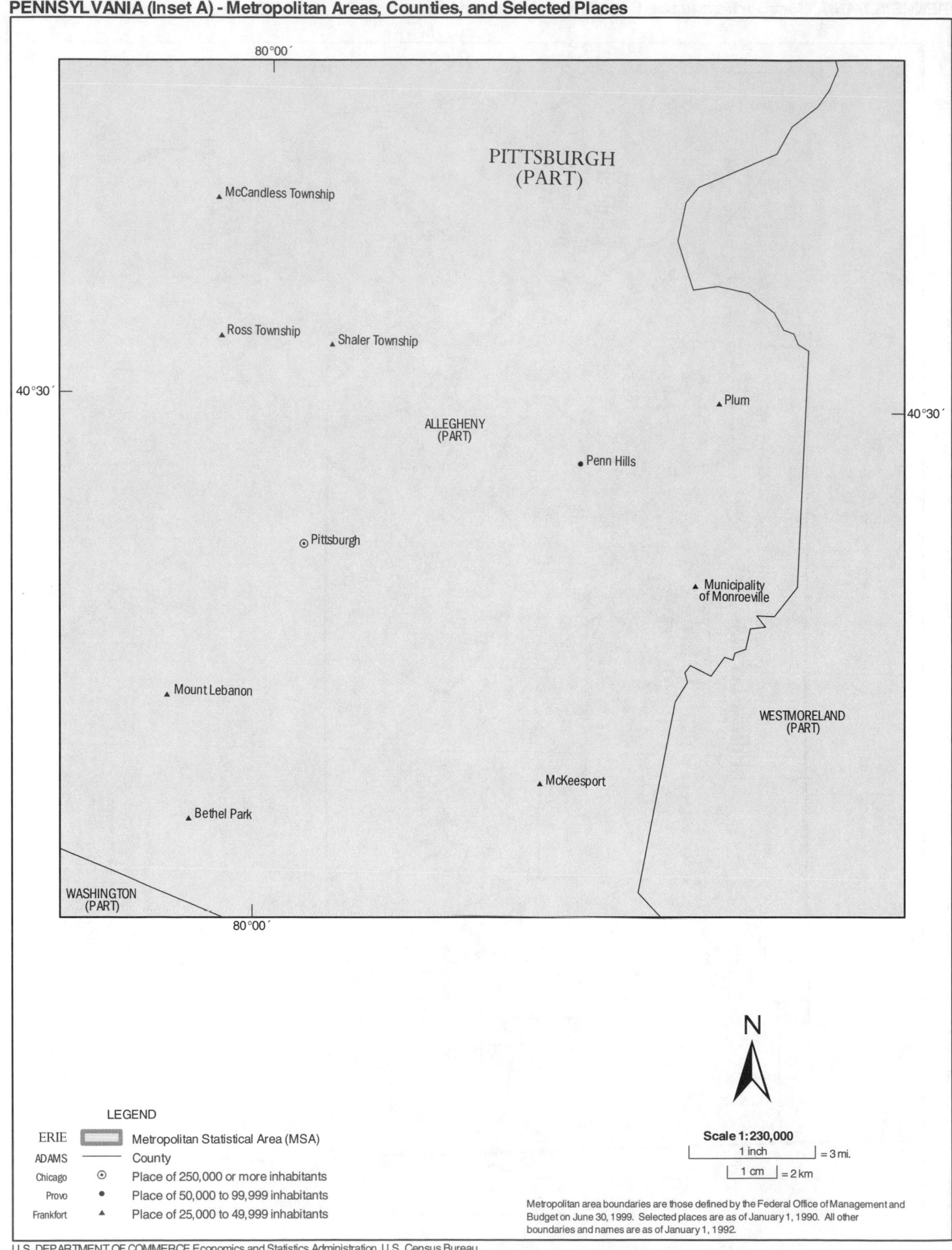

80°00´

PITTSBURGH
(PART)

▲ McCandless Township

40°30´

▲ Ross Township

▲ Shaler Township

40°30´

▲ Plum

ALLEGHENY
(PART)

● Penn Hills

⊙ Pittsburgh

▲ Municipality
of Monroeville

WESTMORELAND
(PART)

▲ Mount Lebanon

▲ McKeesport

▲ Bethel Park

WASHINGTON
(PART)

80°00´

N

LEGEND

ERIE	▭	Metropolitan Statistical Area (MSA)
ADAMS	—	County
Chicago	⊙	Place of 250,000 or more inhabitants
Provo	●	Place of 50,000 to 99,999 inhabitants
Frankfort	▲	Place of 25,000 to 49,999 inhabitants

Scale 1:230,000

| 1 inch | = 3 mi. |
| 1 cm | = 2 km |

Metropolitan area boundaries are those defined by the Federal Office of Management and
Budget on June 30, 1999. Selected places are as of January 1, 1990. All other
boundaries and names are as of January 1, 1992.

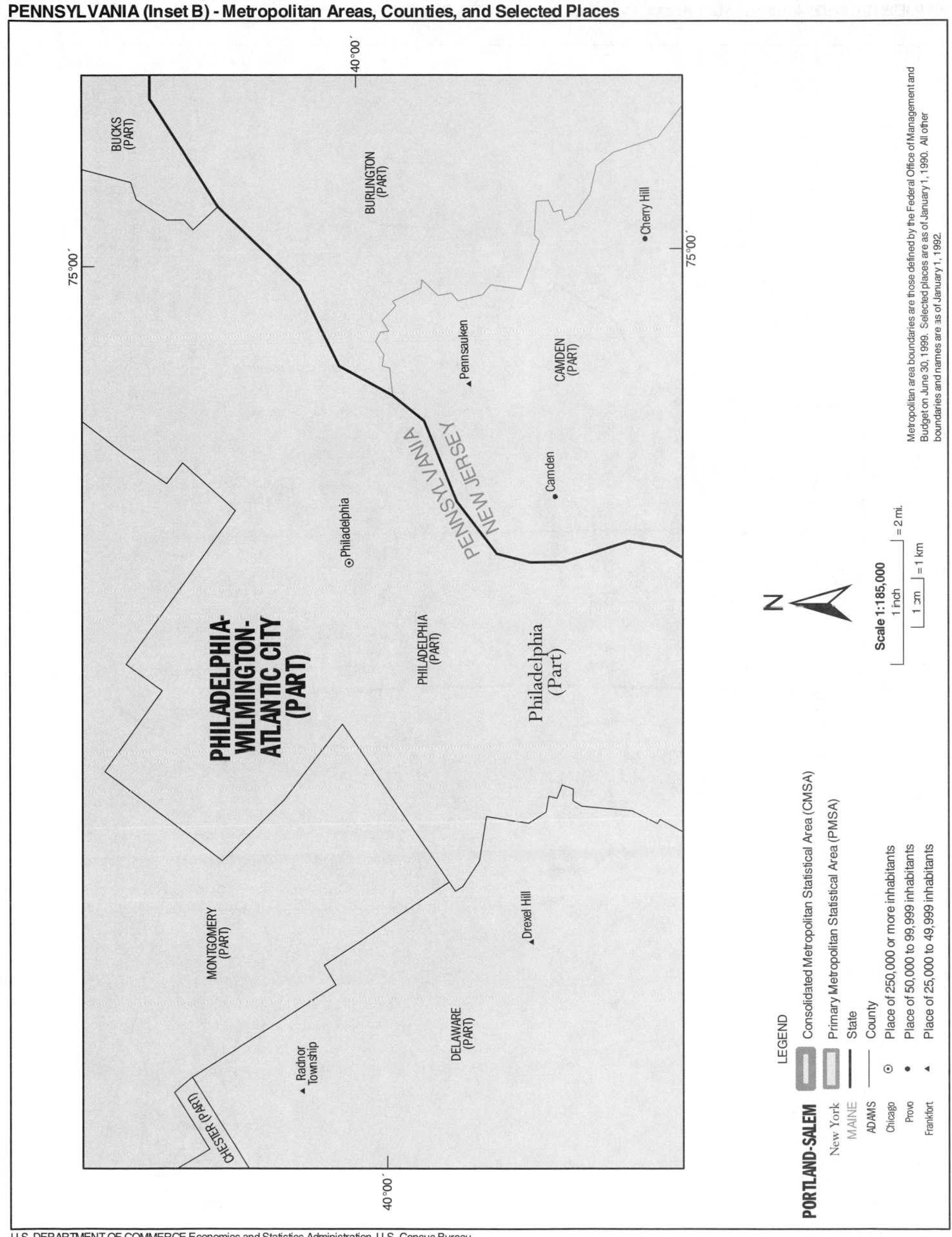

BUCKS
(PART)

BURLINGTON
(PART)

75°00´

75°00´

40°00´

• Cherry Hill

▲ Pennsauken

CAMDEN
(PART)

PENNSYLVANIA

NEW JERSEY

⊙ Philadelphia

• Camden

PHILADELPHIA-
WILMINGTON-
ATLANTIC CITY
(PART)

PHILADELPHIA
(PART)

Philadelphia
(Part)

MONTGOMERY
(PART)

▲ Drexel Hill

DELAWARE
(PART)

▲ Radnor
Township

CHESTER (PART)

40°00´

Scale 1:185,000
1 inch ___ = 2 mi.

1 cm ___ = 1 km

N

Metropolitan area boundaries are those defined by the Federal Office of Management and Budget on June 30, 1999. Selected places are as of January 1, 1990. All other boundaries and names are as of January 1, 1992.

LEGEND

▭▭	Consolidated Metropolitan Statistical Area (CMSA)
▭▭	Primary Metropolitan Statistical Area (PMSA)
—	State
—	County
⊙	Place of 250,000 or more inhabitants
•	Place of 50,000 to 99,999 inhabitants
▲	Place of 25,000 to 49,999 inhabitants

PORTLAND-SALEM

New York

MAINE

ADAMS

Chicago

Provo

Frankfort

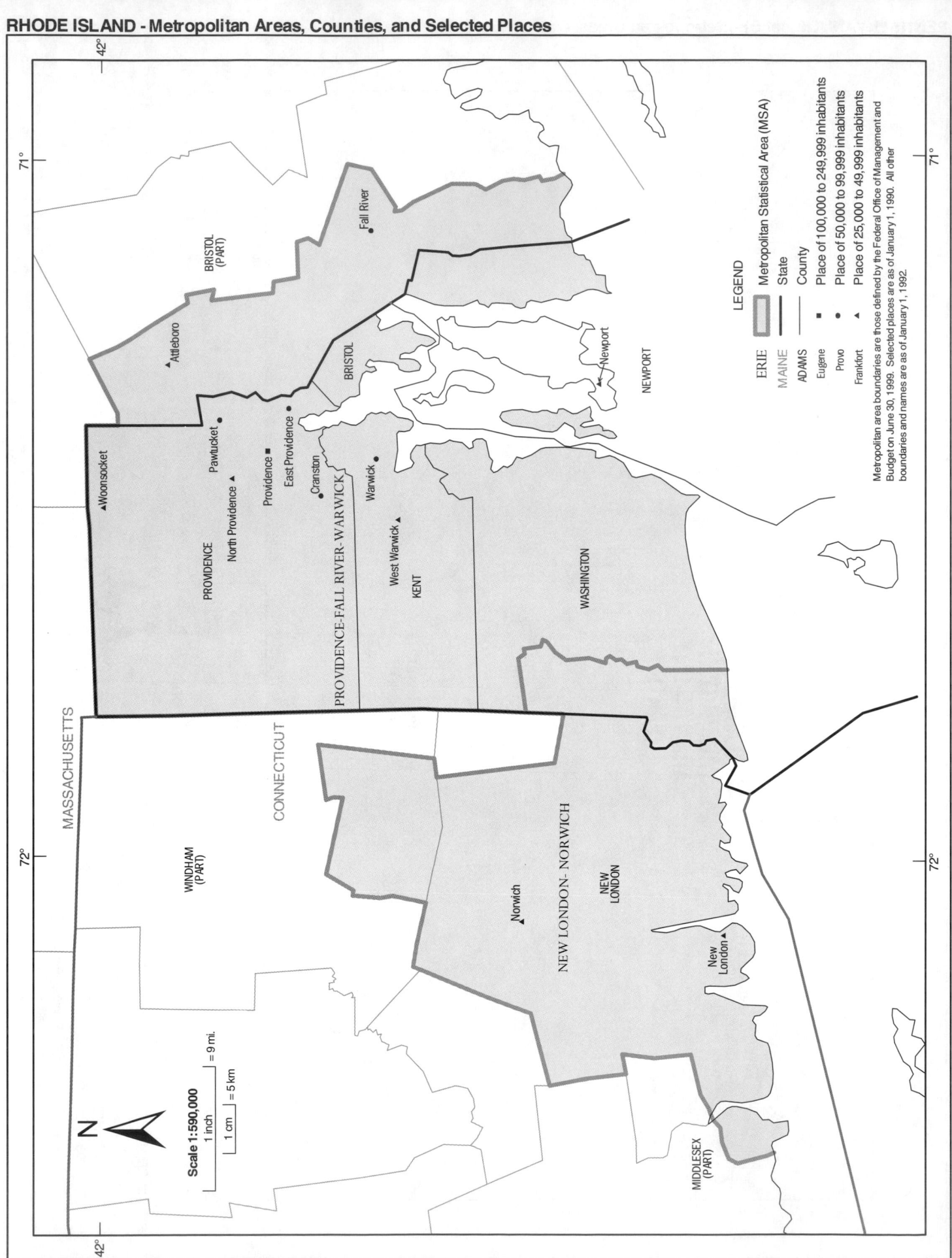

SOUTH CAROLINA - Metropolitan Areas, Counties, and Selected Places

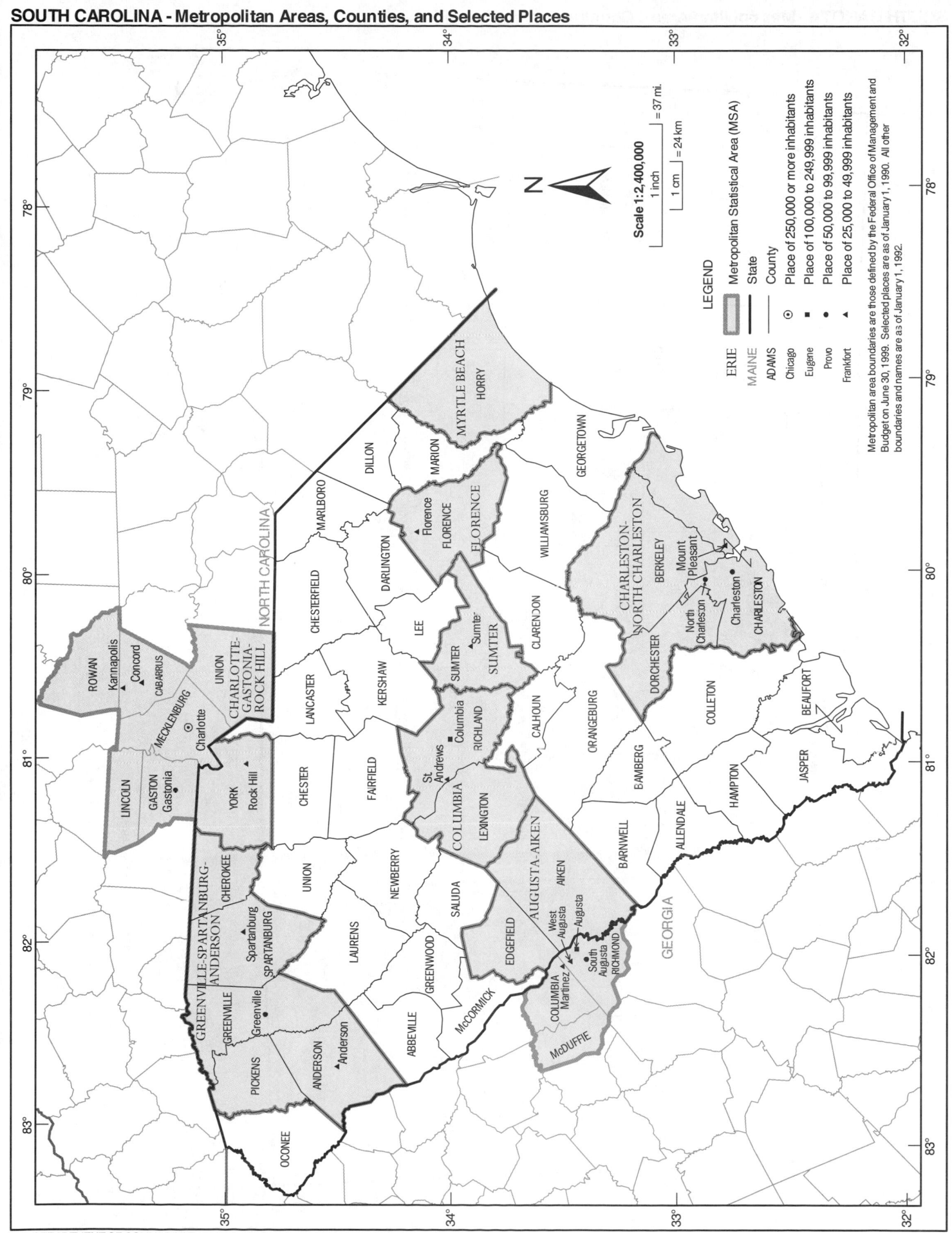

Scale 1:2,400,000

1 inch = 37 mi.

1 cm = 24 km

LEGEND

	Metropolitan Statistical Area (MSA)
ERIE	
MAINE	State
ADAMS	County
Chicago ⊙	Place of 250,000 or more inhabitants
Eugene ■	Place of 100,000 to 249,999 inhabitants
Provo ●	Place of 50,000 to 99,999 inhabitants
Frankfort ▲	Place of 25,000 to 49,999 inhabitants

Metropolitan area boundaries are those defined by the Federal Office of Management and Budget on June 30, 1999. Selected places are as of January 1, 1990. All other boundaries and names are as of January 1, 1992.

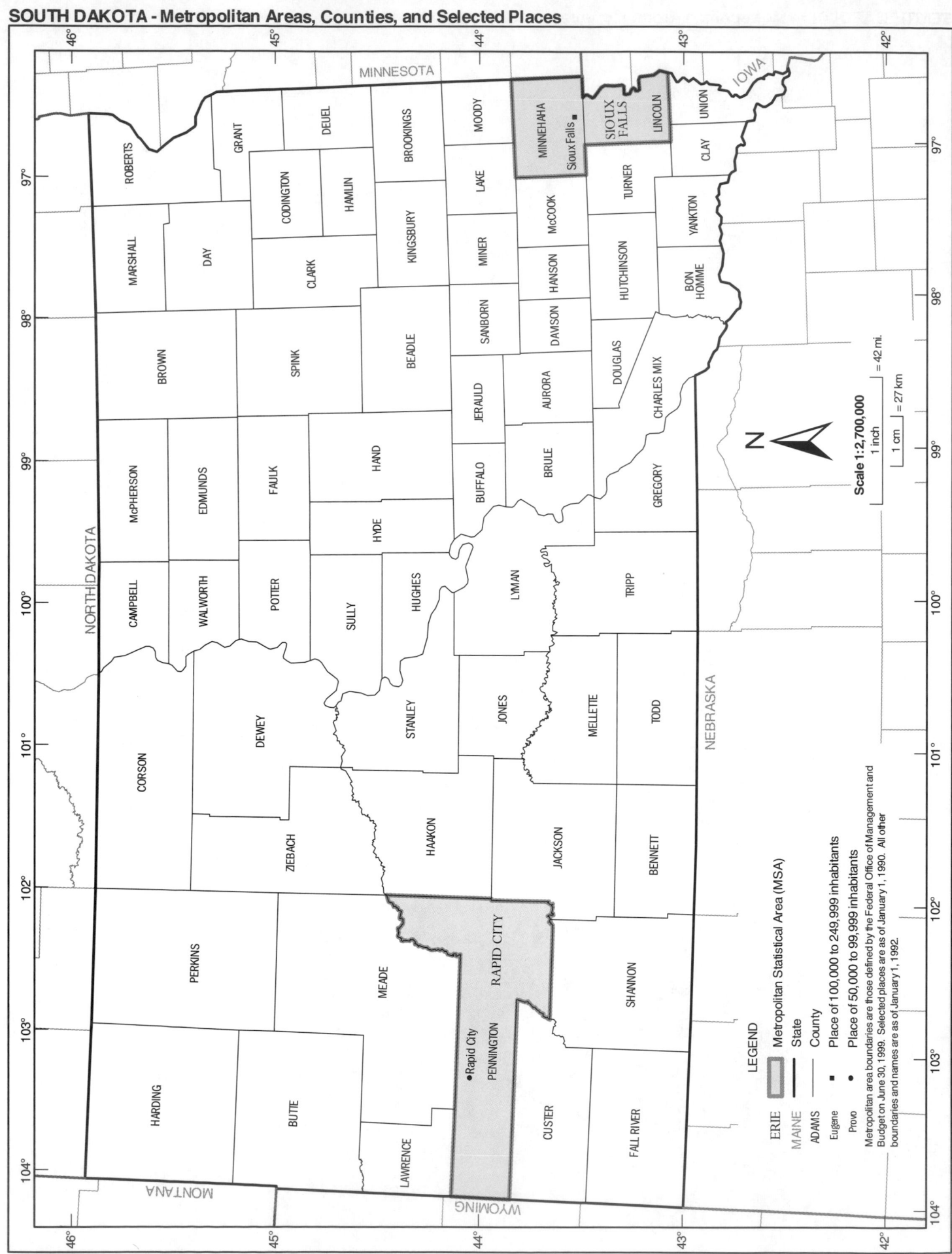

LEGEND

	Metropolitan Statistical Area (MSA)
ERIE	
MAINE	State
ADAMS	County
Eugene	Place of 100,000 to 249,999 inhabitants
Provo	Place of 50,000 to 99,999 inhabitants

Metropolitan area boundaries are those defined by the Federal Office of Management and Budget on June 30, 1999. Selected places are as of January 1, 1990. All other boundaries and names are as of January 1, 1992.

Scale 1:2,700,000
1 inch = 42 mi.
1 cm = 27 km

TENNESSEE - Metropolitan Areas, Counties, Independent City, and Selected Places

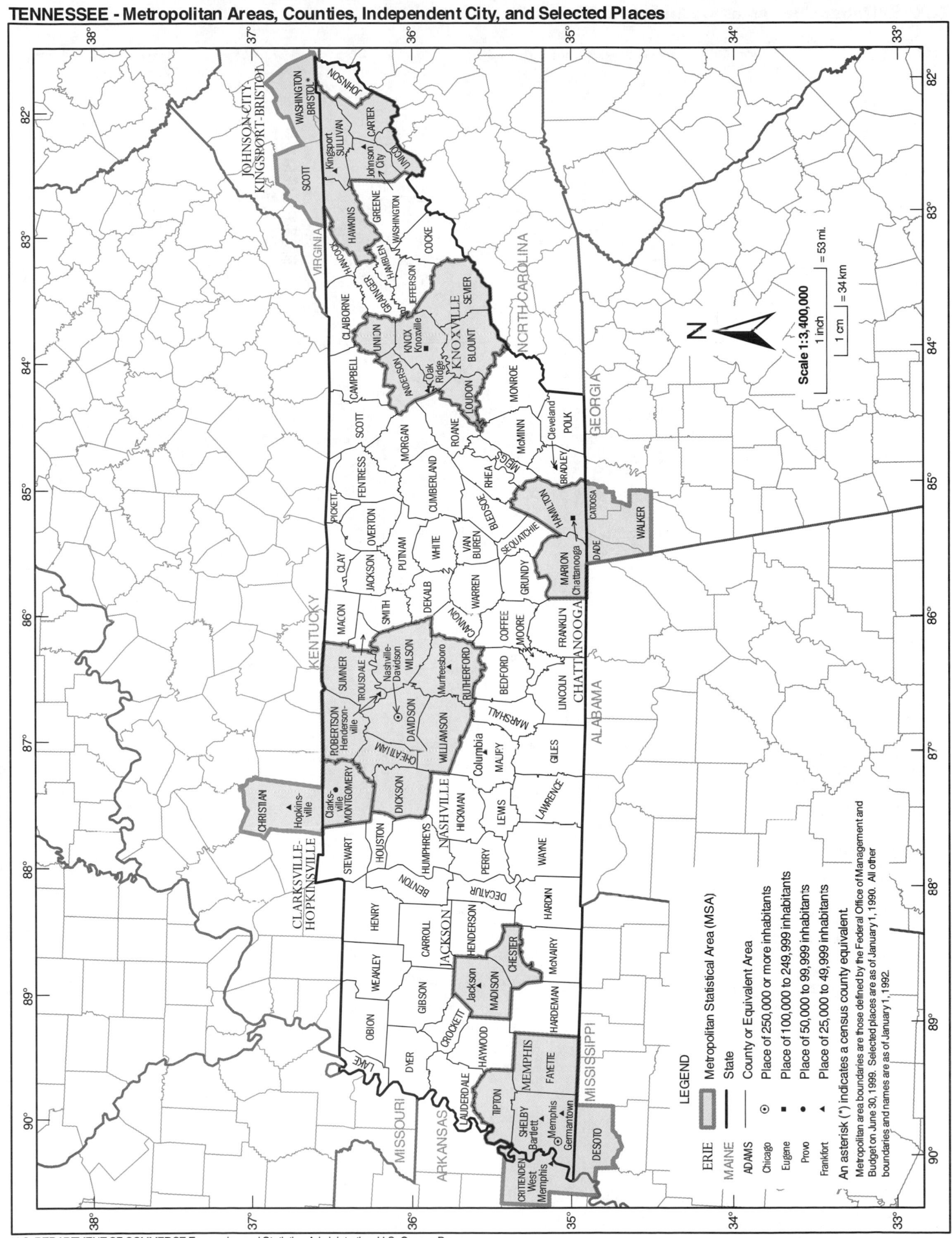

LEGEND

⬚ Metropolitan Statistical Area (MSA)
— State
— County or Equivalent Area

⊙ Place of 250,000 or more inhabitants
■ Place of 100,000 to 249,999 inhabitants
● Place of 50,000 to 99,999 inhabitants
▲ Place of 25,000 to 49,999 inhabitants

ERIE
MAINE
ADAMS
Chicago
Eugene
Provo
Frankfort

An asterisk (*) indicates a census county equivalent.

Metropolitan area boundaries are those defined by the Federal Office of Management and Budget on June 30, 1999. Selected places are as of January 1, 1990. All other boundaries and names are as of January 1, 1992.

Scale 1:3,400,000
1 inch = 53 mi.
1 cm = 34 km

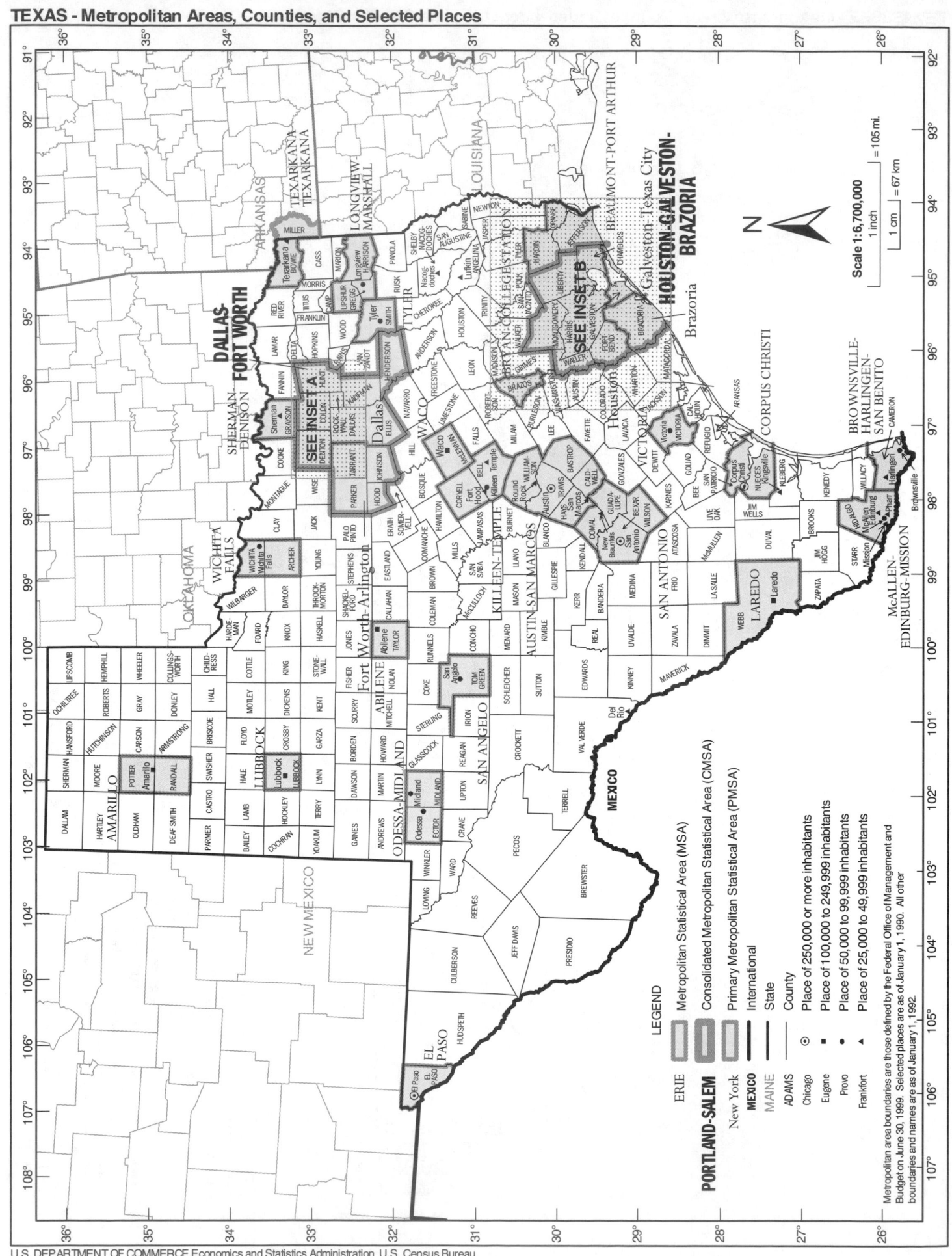

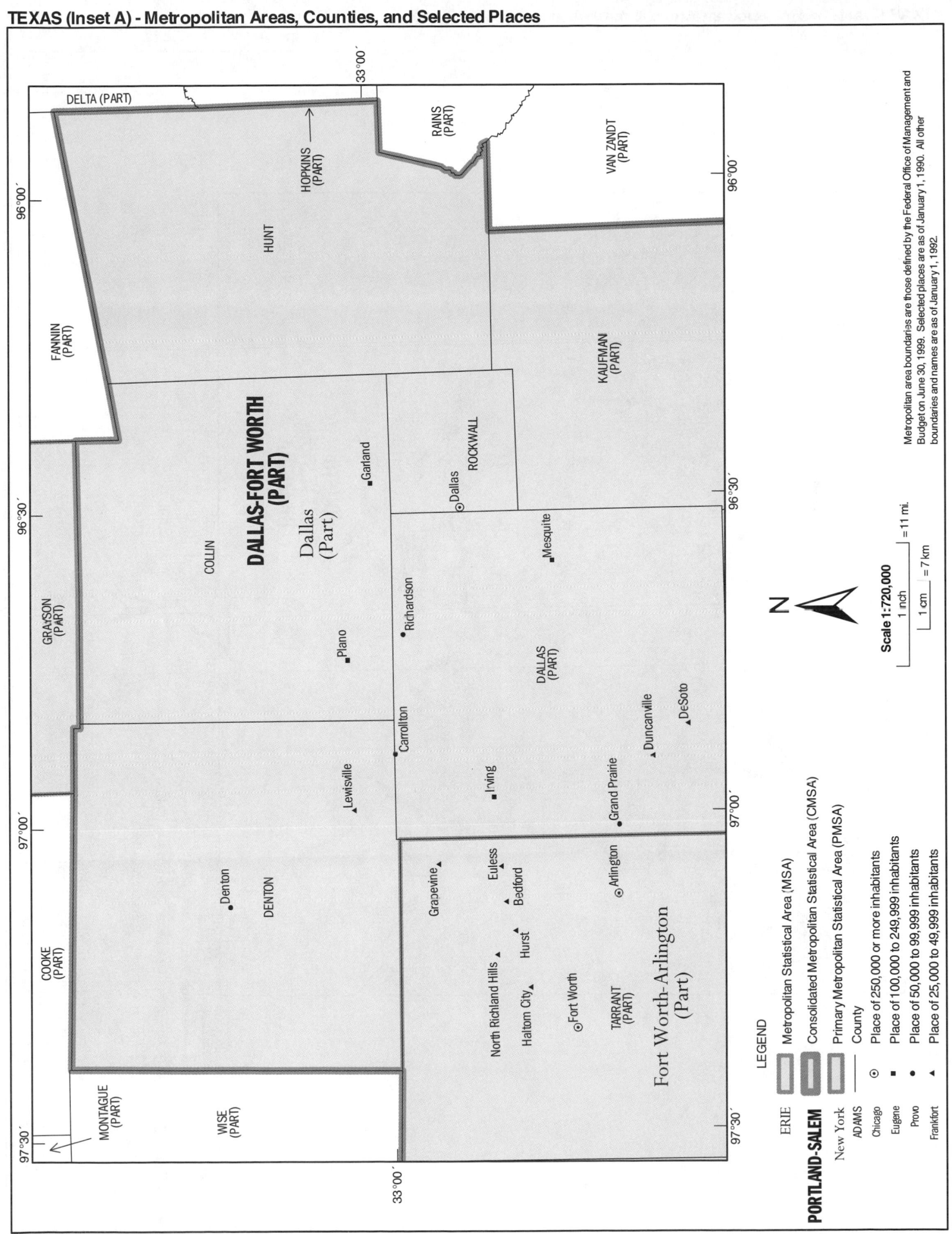

LEGEND

⬚ ERIE	Metropolitan Statistical Area (MSA)
▦ **PORTLAND-SALEM**	Consolidated Metropolitan Statistical Area (CMSA)
⬚ New York	Primary Metropolitan Statistical Area (PMSA)
— ADAMS	County
⊙ Chicago	Place of 250,000 or more inhabitants
▪ Eugene	Place of 100,000 to 249,999 inhabitants
• Provo	Place of 50,000 to 99,999 inhabitants
▲ Frankfort	Place of 25,000 to 49,999 inhabitants

Scale 1:720,000
1 inch = 11 mi.
1 cm = 7 km

Metropolitan area boundaries are those defined by the Federal Office of Management and Budget on June 30, 1999. Selected places are as of January 1, 1990. All other boundaries and names are as of January 1, 1992.

Metropolitan area boundaries are those defined by the Federal Office of Management and Budget on June 30, 1999. Selected places are as of January 1, 1990. All other boundaries and names are as of January 1, 1992.

NEWTON (PART)

JASPER (PART)

ORANGE

LOUISIANA

TEXAS

JEFFERSON

Port Arthur

TYLER (PART)

HARDIN

BEAUMONT-PORT ARTHUR

Beaumont

Galveston-Texas City

POLK (PART)

LIBERTY

CHAMBERS

LIBERTY

TRINITY (PART)

SAN JACINTO

Kingwood

Baytown

Channelview

La Porte

League City

Texas City

GALVESTON

HOUSTON (PART)

Huntsville

WALKER (PART)

Conroe

The Woodlands

Spring

MONTGOMERY

Houston

HARRIS

Pasadena

Deer Park

Galveston

Galveston

HOUSTON-GALVESTON-BRAZORIA

MADISON (PART)

GRIMES

Missouri City

FORT BEND

Brazoria

BRAZORIA

LEON (PART)

BRYAN-COLLEGE STATION

BRAZOS

College Station

Bryan

WALLER

ROBERTSON (PART)

BURLESON (PART)

WASHINGTON (PART)

FAYETTE (PART)

AUSTIN

WHARTON

MATAGORDA (PART)

COLORADO (PART)

LAVACA (PART)

JACKSON (PART)

Scale 1:1,750,000

1 inch = 27 mi.

1 cm = 17 km

N

LEGEND

	Metropolitan Statistical Area (MSA)
	Consolidated Metropolitan Statistical Area (CMSA)
	Primary Metropolitan Statistical Area (PMSA)
	State
	County
⊙	Place of 250,000 or more inhabitants
■	Place of 100,000 to 249,999 inhabitants
●	Place of 50,000 to 99,999 inhabitants
▲	Place of 25,000 to 49,999 inhabitants

ERIE

PORTLAND-SALEM

New York

MAINE

ADAMS

Chicago

Eugene

Provo

Frankfort

UTAH - Metropolitan Areas, Counties, and Selected Places

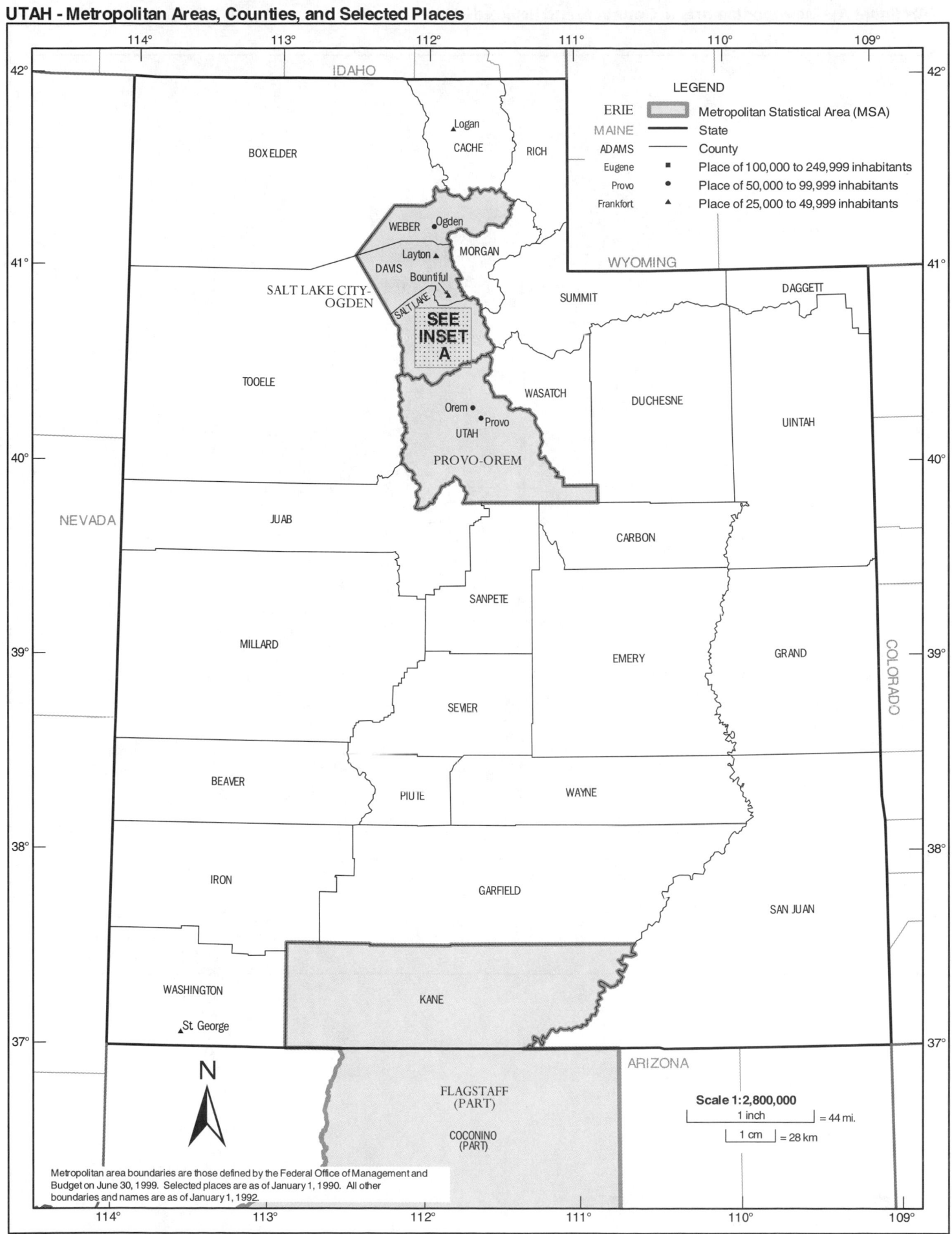

LEGEND

ERIE (shaded box)	Metropolitan Statistical Area (MSA)
MAINE	State
ADAMS	County
Eugene ■	Place of 100,000 to 249,999 inhabitants
Provo ●	Place of 50,000 to 99,999 inhabitants
Frankfort ▲	Place of 25,000 to 49,999 inhabitants

Scale 1:2,800,000

1 inch = 44 mi.

1 cm = 28 km

Metropolitan area boundaries are those defined by the Federal Office of Management and Budget on June 30, 1999. Selected places are as of January 1, 1990. All other boundaries and names are as of January 1, 1992.

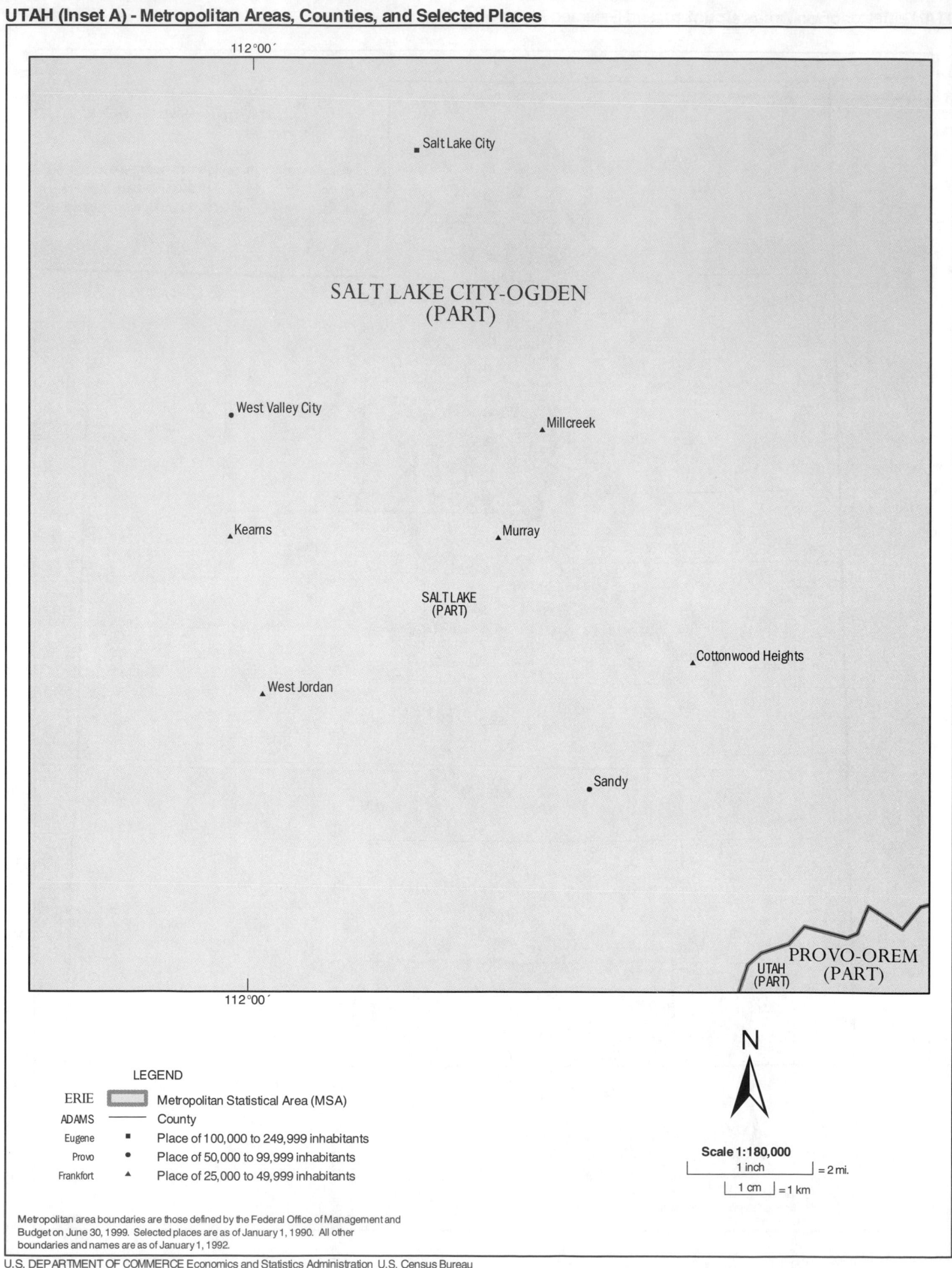

112°00´

SALT LAKE CITY-OGDEN
(PART)

■ Salt Lake City

• West Valley City

▲ Millcreek

▲ Kearns

▲ Murray

SALT LAKE
(PART)

▲ Cottonwood Heights

▲ West Jordan

• Sandy

PROVO-OREM
(PART)

UTAH
(PART)

112°00´

LEGEND

ERIE		Metropolitan Statistical Area (MSA)
ADAMS	——	County
Eugene	■	Place of 100,000 to 249,999 inhabitants
Provo	•	Place of 50,000 to 99,999 inhabitants
Frankfort	▲	Place of 25,000 to 49,999 inhabitants

N

Scale 1:180,000

| 1 inch | = 2 mi. |
| 1 cm | = 1 km |

Metropolitan area boundaries are those defined by the Federal Office of Management and
Budget on June 30, 1999. Selected places are as of January 1, 1990. All other
boundaries and names are as of January 1, 1992.

U.S. DEPARTMENT OF COMMERCE Economics and Statistics Administration U.S. Census Bureau

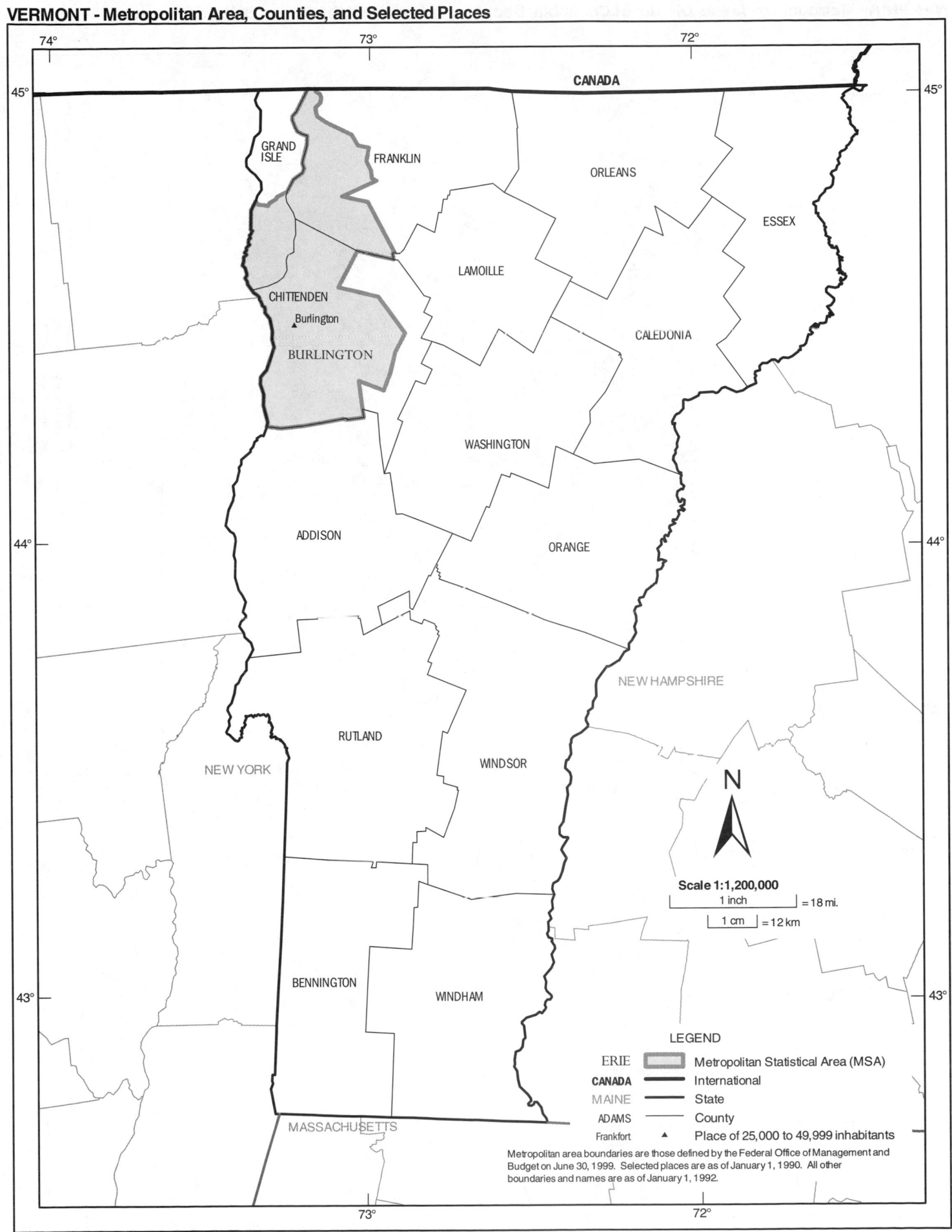

CANADA

74°   73°   72°

45°   45°

GRAND ISLE

FRANKLIN

ORLEANS

ESSEX

LAMOILLE

CHITTENDEN

▲ Burlington

CALEDONIA

BURLINGTON

WASHINGTON

ADDISON

ORANGE

44°   44°

NEW HAMPSHIRE

RUTLAND

NEW YORK

WINDSOR

N

Scale 1:1,200,000

| 1 inch | = 18 mi. |

| 1 cm | = 12 km |

BENNINGTON

WINDHAM

43°   43°

LEGEND

ERIE		Metropolitan Statistical Area (MSA)
CANADA		International
MAINE		State
ADAMS		County
Frankfort	▲	Place of 25,000 to 49,999 inhabitants

MASSACHUSETTS

Metropolitan area boundaries are those defined by the Federal Office of Management and Budget on June 30, 1999. Selected places are as of January 1, 1990. All other boundaries and names are as of January 1, 1992.

73°   72°

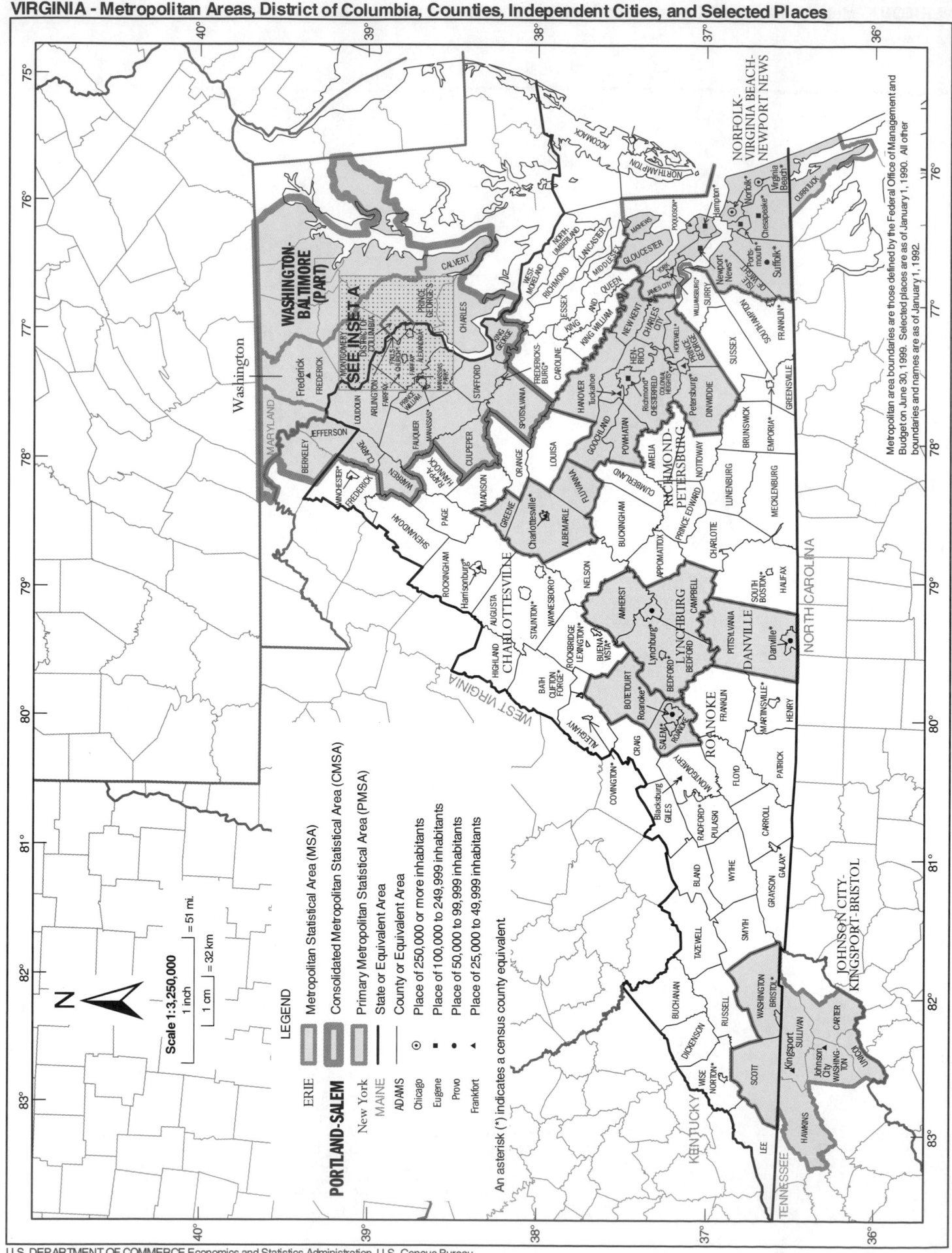

LEGEND

Metropolitan Statistical Area (MSA)

Consolidated Metropolitan Statistical Area (CMSA)

Primary Metropolitan Statistical Area (PMSA)

State or Equivalent Area

County or Equivalent Area

⊙ Place of 250,000 or more inhabitants

■ Place of 100,000 to 249,999 inhabitants

● Place of 50,000 to 99,999 inhabitants

▲ Place of 25,000 to 49,999 inhabitants

An asterisk (*) indicates a census county equivalent

ERIE
New York
MAINE
ADAMS
Chicago
Eugene
Provo
Frankfort

WASHINGTON-BALTIMORE (PART)

PORTLAND-SALEM

Scale 1:3,250,000
1 inch = 51 mi.
1 cm = 32 km

Metropolitan area boundaries are those defined by the Federal Office of Management and Budget on June 30, 1999. Selected places are as of January 1, 1990. All other boundaries and names are as of January 1, 1992.

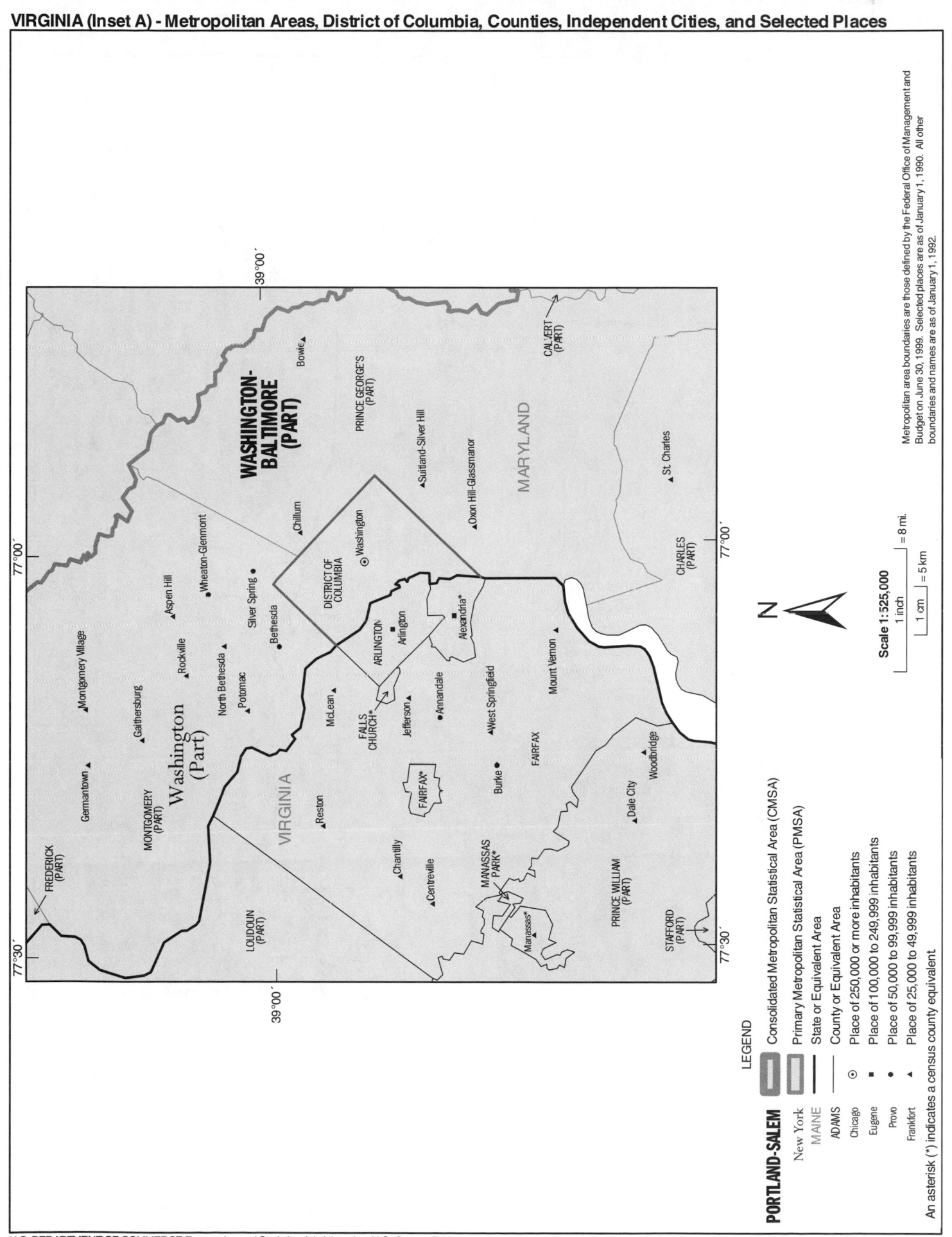

LEGEND

PORTLAND-SALEM ▮▮ Consolidated Metropolitan Statistical Area (CMSA)

New York ▮▮ Primary Metropolitan Statistical Area (PMSA)

MAINE —— State or Equivalent Area

ADAMS —— County or Equivalent Area

Chicago ⊙ Place of 250,000 or more inhabitants

Eugene ■ Place of 100,000 to 249,999 inhabitants

Provo ● Place of 50,000 to 99,999 inhabitants

Frankfort ▲ Place of 25,000 to 49,999 inhabitants

An asterisk (*) indicates a census county equivalent

Scale 1:525,000

1 inch = 8 mi.

1 cm = 5 km

N

Metropolitan area boundaries are those defined by the Federal Office of Management and Budget on June 30, 1999. Selected places are as of January 1, 1990. All other boundaries and names are as of January 1, 1992.

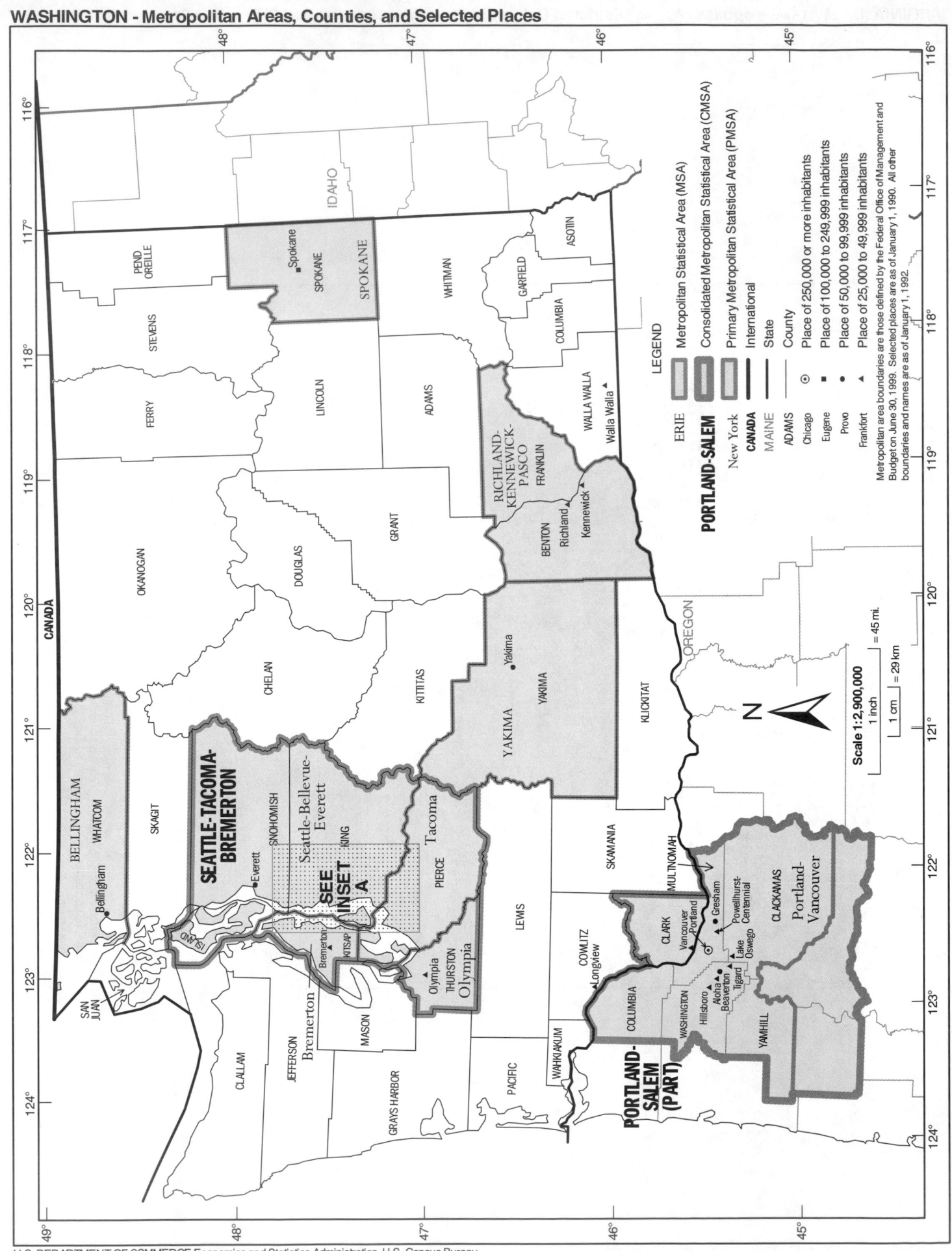

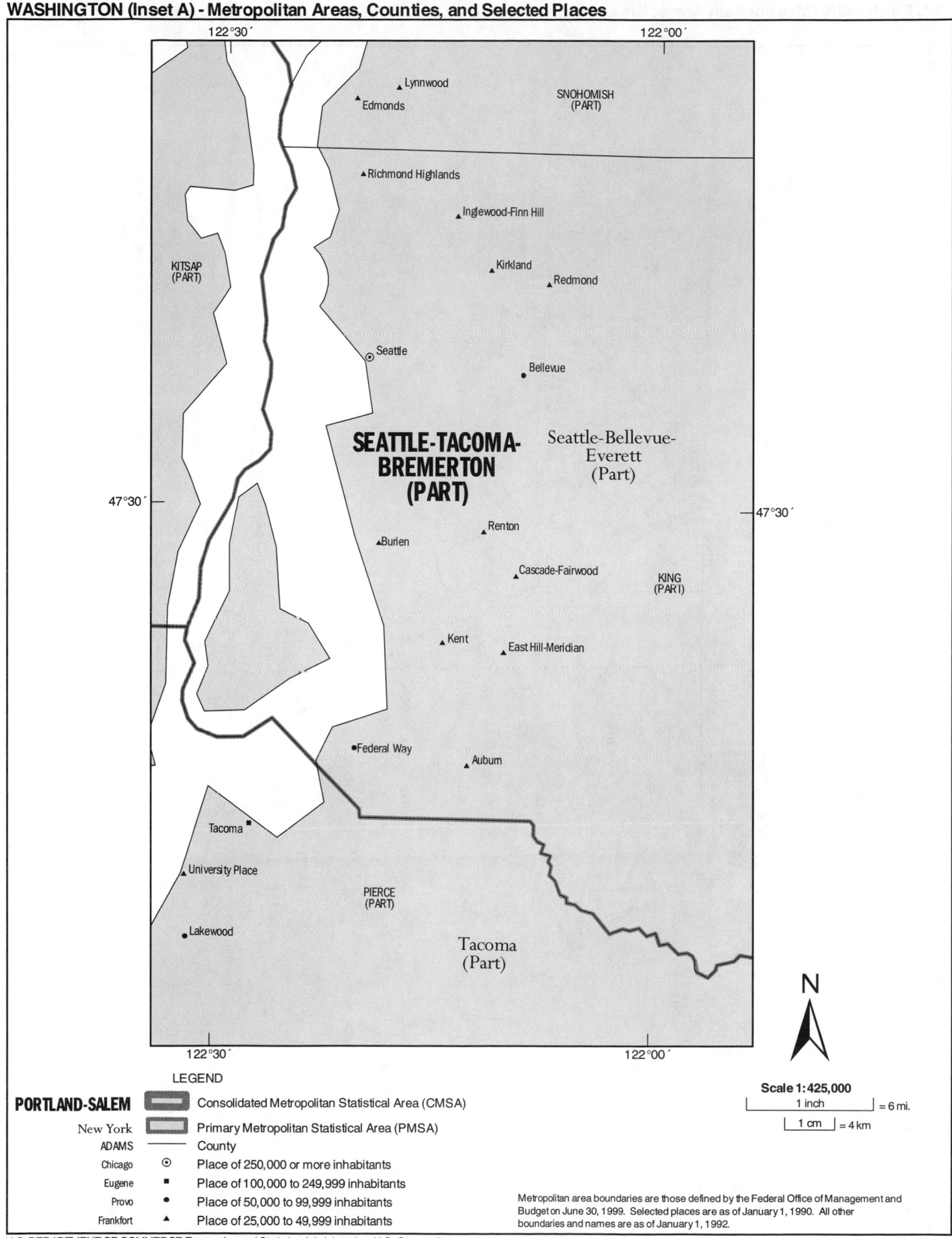

122°30′   122°00′

SNOHOMISH
(PART)

Lynnwood

Edmonds

Richmond Highlands

Inglewood-Finn Hill

KITSAP
(PART)

Kirkland

Redmond

Seattle

Bellevue

**SEATTLE-TACOMA-
BREMERTON
(PART)**

Seattle-Bellevue-
Everett
(Part)

47°30′   47°30′

Renton

Burien

Cascade-Fairwood

KING
(PART)

Kent

East Hill-Meridian

Federal Way

Auburn

Tacoma

University Place

PIERCE
(PART)

Lakewood

Tacoma
(Part)

N

122°30′   122°00′

LEGEND

Scale 1:425,000

| 1 inch | = 6 mi. |

| 1 cm | = 4 km |

PORTLAND-SALEM	Consolidated Metropolitan Statistical Area (CMSA)
New York	Primary Metropolitan Statistical Area (PMSA)
ADAMS	County
Chicago ⊙	Place of 250,000 or more inhabitants
Eugene ■	Place of 100,000 to 249,999 inhabitants
Provo ●	Place of 50,000 to 99,999 inhabitants
Frankfort ▲	Place of 25,000 to 49,999 inhabitants

Metropolitan area boundaries are those defined by the Federal Office of Management and
Budget on June 30, 1999. Selected places are as of January 1, 1990. All other
boundaries and names are as of January 1, 1992.

U.S. DEPARTMENT OF COMMERCE Economics and Statistics Administration U.S. Census Bureau

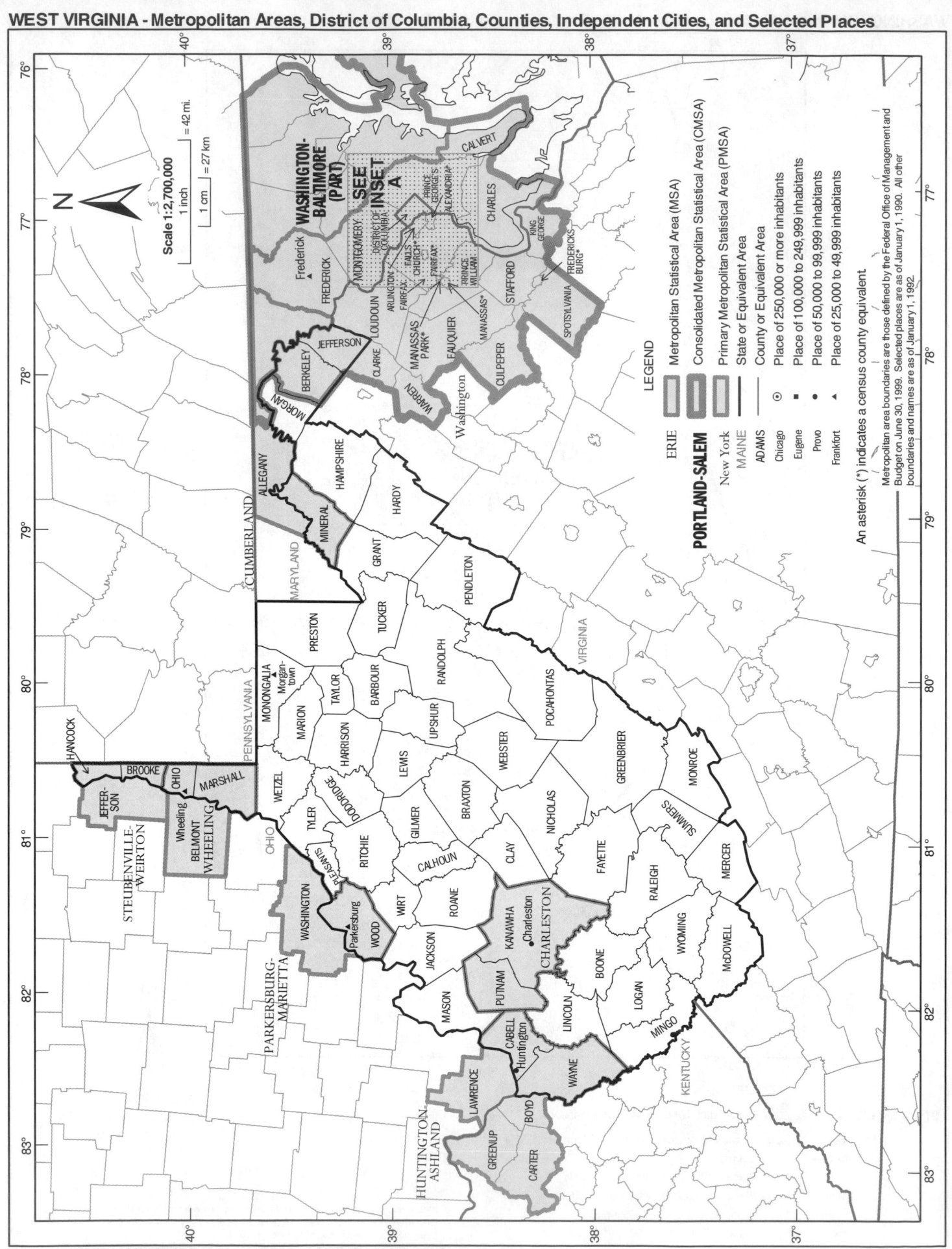

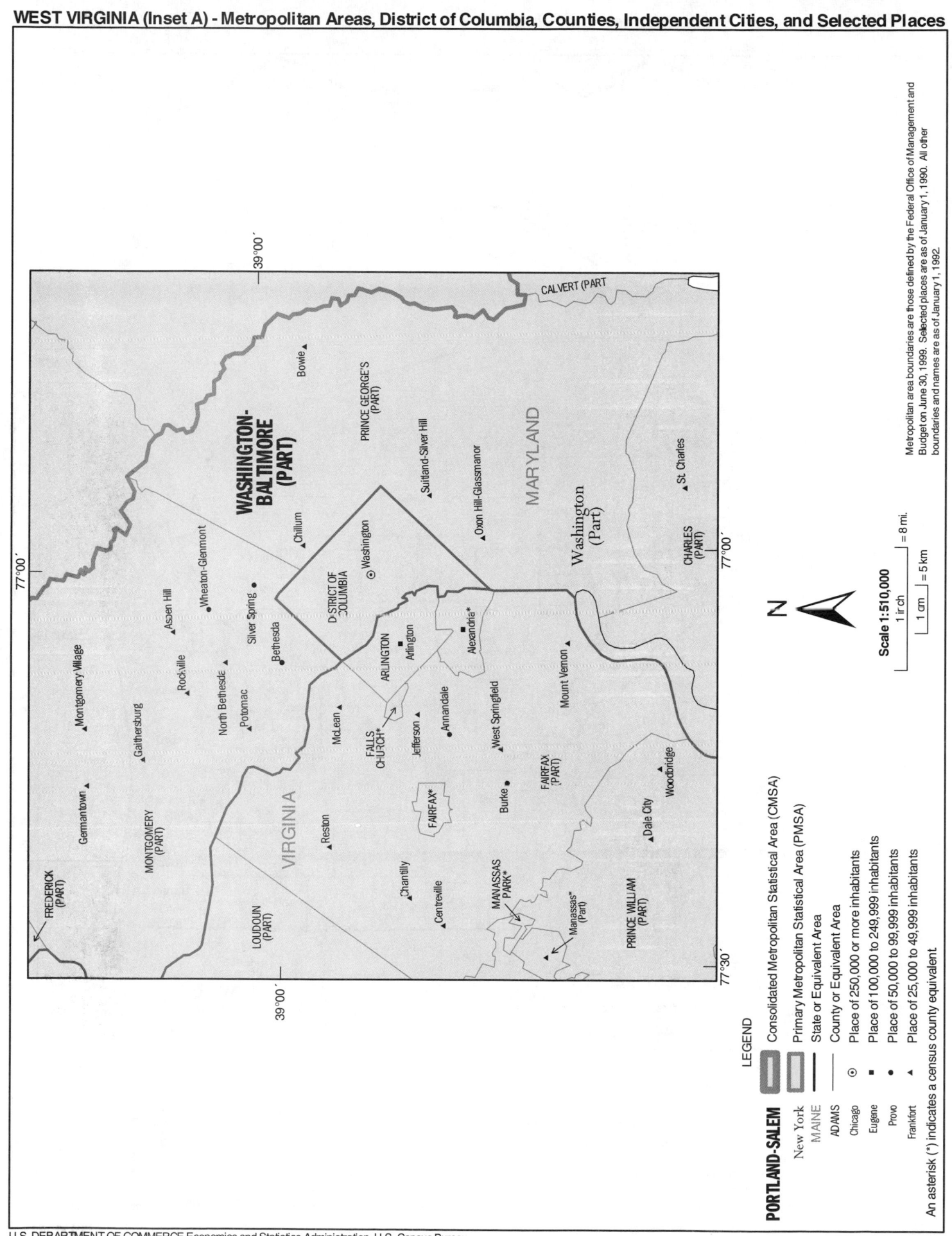

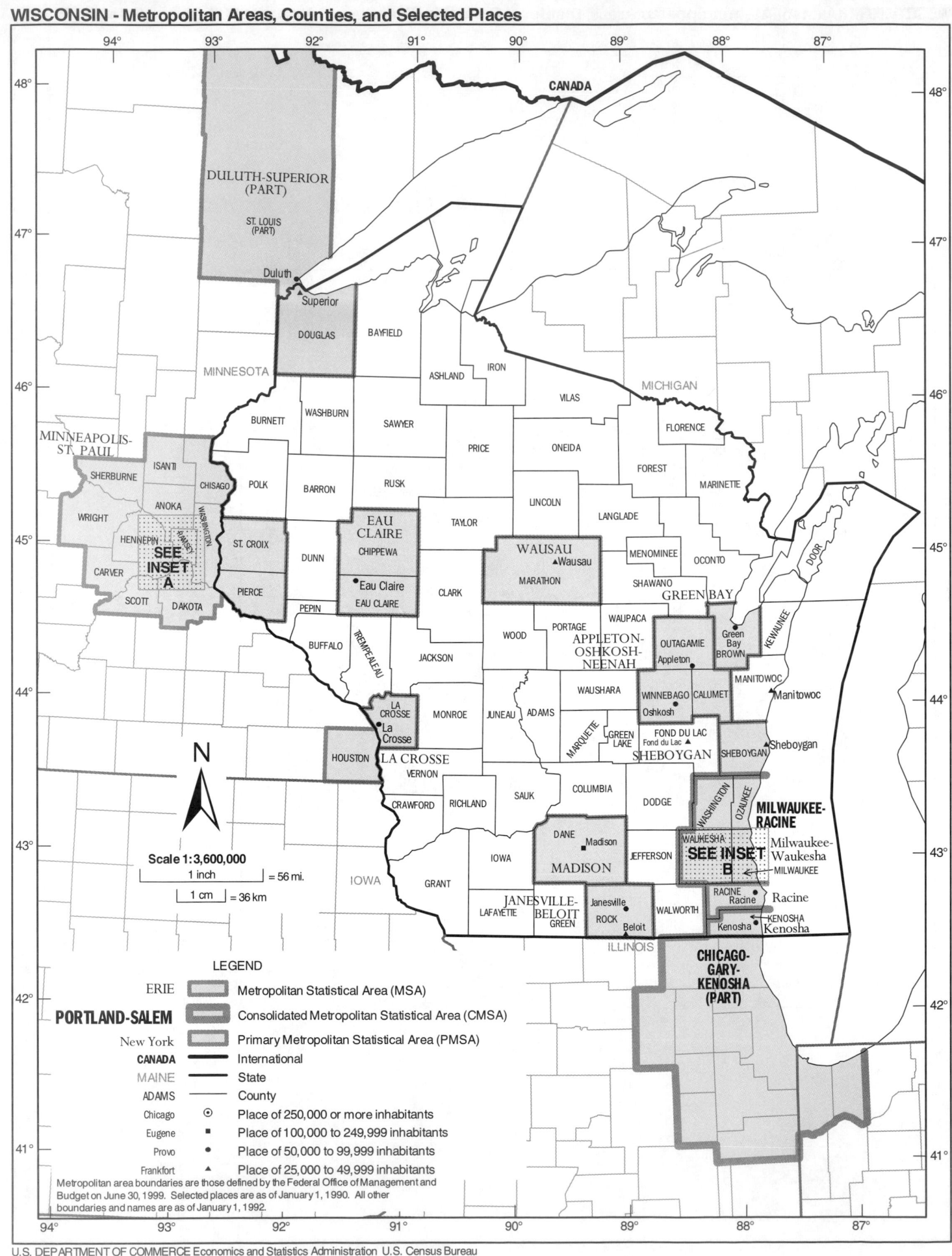

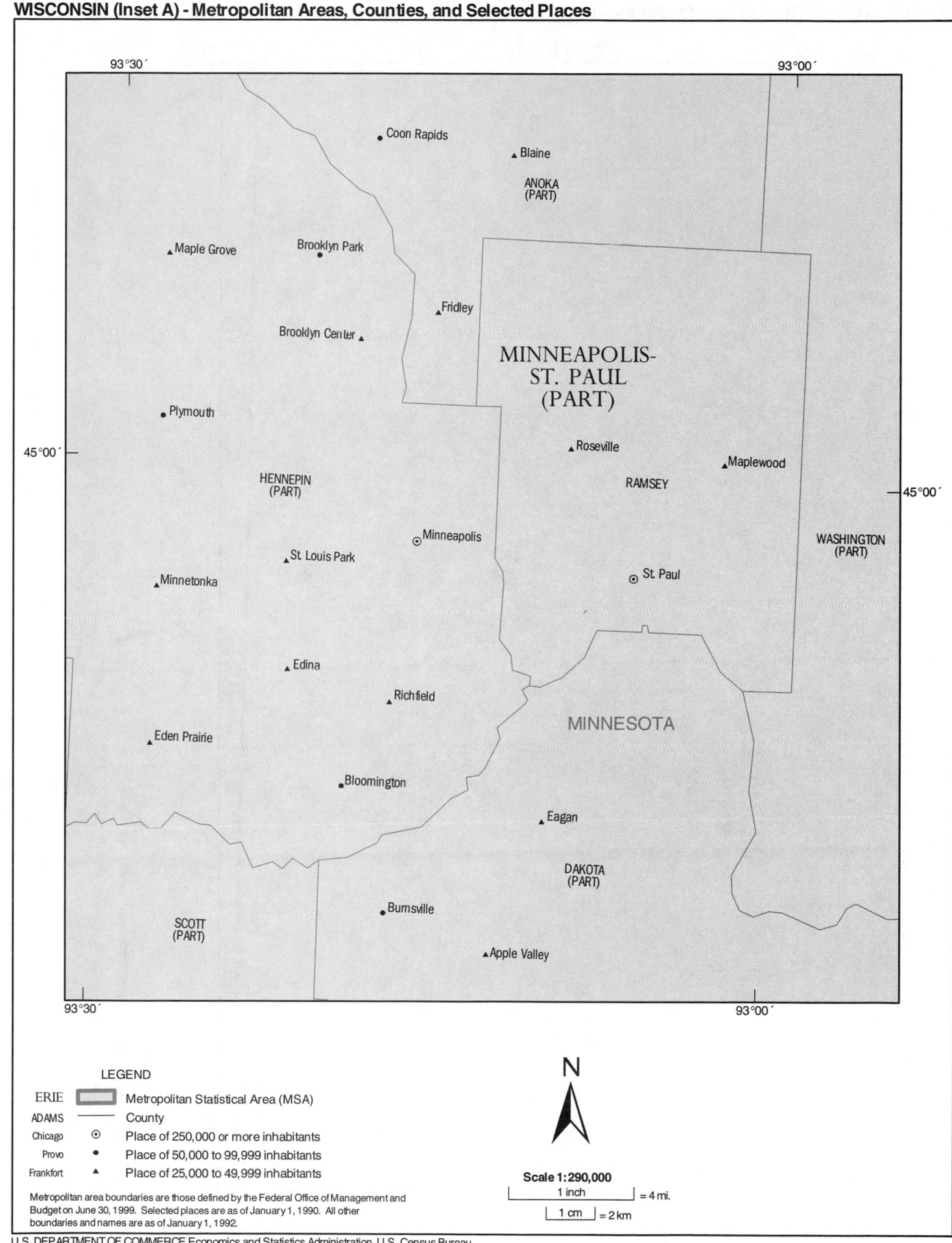

93°30′   93°00′

Coon Rapids
▲ Blaine

ANOKA
(PART)

▲ Maple Grove   Brooklyn Park

▲ Fridley

Brooklyn Center ▲

MINNEAPOLIS-
ST. PAUL
(PART)

• Plymouth

45°00′

▲ Roseville
▲ Maplewood

HENNEPIN
(PART)   RAMSEY   45°00′

⊙ Minneapolis   WASHINGTON
                                                         (PART)
▲ St. Louis Park

▲ Minnetonka   ⊙ St. Paul

▲ Edina

▲ Richfield

MINNESOTA
▲ Eden Prairie

• Bloomington

▲ Eagan

DAKOTA
(PART)

SCOTT   • Burnsville
(PART)

▲ Apple Valley

93°30′   93°00′

N

Metropolitan area boundaries are those defined by the Federal Office of Management and
Budget on June 30, 1999. Selected places are as of January 1, 1990. All other
boundaries and names are as of January 1, 1992.

Scale 1:290,000
1 inch ⊢──────⊣ = 4 mi.
1 cm ⊢──────⊣ = 2 km

U.S. DEPARTMENT OF COMMERCE Economics and Statistics Administration U.S. Census Bureau

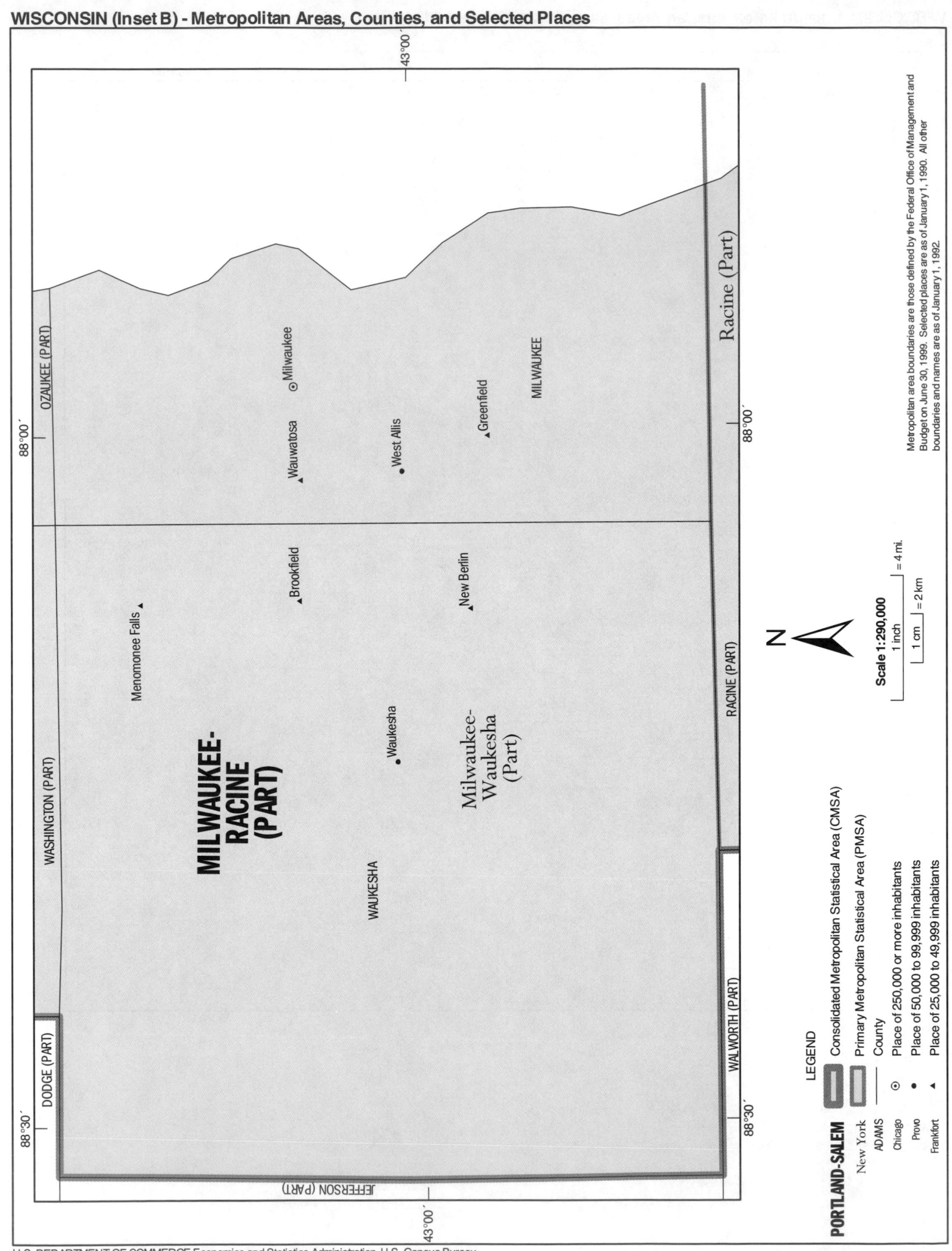

Scale 1:290,000

1 inch = 4 mi.

1 cm = 2 km

Metropolitan area boundaries are those defined by the Federal Office of Management and Budget on June 30, 1999. Selected places are as of January 1, 1990. All other boundaries and names are as of January 1, 1992.

LEGEND

PORTLAND-SALEM Consolidated Metropolitan Statistical Area (CMSA)

New York Primary Metropolitan Statistical Area (PMSA)

ADAMS County

⊙ Chicago Place of 250,000 or more inhabitants

● Provo Place of 50,000 to 99,999 inhabitants

▲ Frankfort Place of 25,000 to 49,999 inhabitants

WYOMING - Metropolitan Areas, Counties, and Selected Places

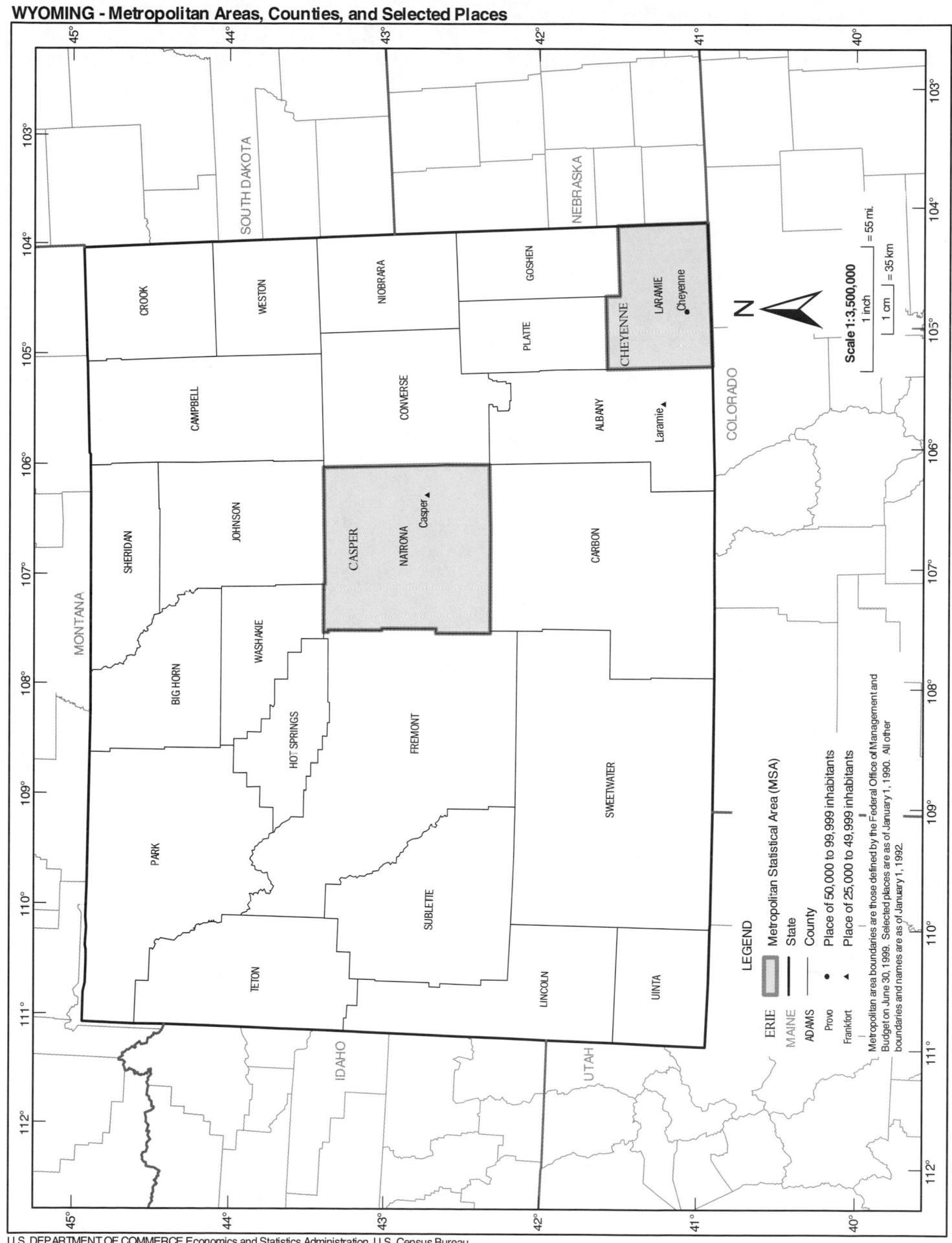

LEGEND

Metropolitan Statistical Area (MSA)

State

County

• Place of 50,000 to 99,999 inhabitants

▲ Place of 25,000 to 49,999 inhabitants

Metropolitan area boundaries are those defined by the Federal Office of Management and Budget on June 30, 1999. Selected places are as of January 1, 1990. All other boundaries and names are as of January 1, 1992.

ERIE

MAINE

ADAMS   Provo

Frankfort

Scale 1:3,500,000

1 inch = 55 mi.

1 cm = 35 km

N

Subject Guide

Appendix D

Subjects covered in this publication are shown down the left side of this guide in alphabetic order. Types of geographic areas are shown across the top. Page and table references are given where applicable. For information on subjects, see Appendix A. For definitions of geographic areas, see Appendix B.

Appendix D

Appendix D. Subject Guide

Item	Table A. States		Table B. Counties		Table C. Cities		Table D-1. Places		Table D-2. MCDs	
	Page	Table	Page	Table	Page	Table	Page	Table	Page	Table
A										
Accommodation and foodservices (NAICS 72):										
Annual payroll	14	A-12	546-593	B-12	734-751	C-6				
Employees, paid	14	A-12	546-593	B-12	734-751	C-6				
Establishments	14	A-12	546-593	B-12	734-751	C-6				
Sales, total	14	A-12	546-593	B-12	734-751	C-6				
Foodservices	14	A-12	546-593	B-12	734-751	C-6				
Acreage, farm	12	A-10	450-497	B-10						
Age groups	4	A-2	66-113	B-2	662-679	C-2	773-893	D-1	895-931	D-2
Agriculture:										
Acreage	12	A-10	450-497	B-10						
Earnings	12	A-10	450-497	B-10						
Farms	12	A-10	450-497	B-10						
Land in farms	12	A-10	450-497	B-10						
Value of farm products sold	12	A-10	450-497	B-10						
American Indian and Alaska Native population	4	A-2	66-113	B-2	662-679	C-2	773-893	D-1	895-931	D-2
Annual payroll:										
Accommodation and foodservices (NAICS 72)	14	A-12	546-593	B-12	734-751	C-6				
Manufacturing (NAICS 31-33)	11	A-9	402-449	B-9	716-733	C-5				
Private nonfarm businesses	9	A-7	306-353	B-7						
Retail sales (NAICS 44-45)	13	A-11	498-545	B-11	734-751	C-6				
Wholesale (NAICS 42)	13	A-11	498-545	B-11	716-733	C-5				
Area, land	3	A-1	18-65	B-1	644-661	C-1	773-893	D-1	895-931	D-2
Asian population	4	A-2	66-113	B-2	662-679	C-2	773-893	D-1	895-931	D-2
B										
Banking:										
Deposits	14	A-12	546-593	B-12	734-751	C-6				
Offices	14	A-12	546-593	B-12	734-751	C-6				
Births and birth rates	6	A-4	162-209	B-4						
Black or African American population	4	A-2	66-113	B-2	662-679	C-2	773-893	D-1	895-931	D-2
Building permits	8	A-6	258-305	B-6						
C										
City government finances:										
General revenue total					752-769	C-7				
Taxes					752-769	C-7				
General expenditure					752-769	C-7				
Civilian labor force	9	A-7	306-353	B-7	698-715	C-4				
Climate:										
Annual precipitation					752-769	C-7				
Average daily temperature (Fahrenheit)					752-769	C-7				
Cooling degree days					752-769	C-7				
Heating degree days					752-769	C-7				
Community hospitals	6	A-4	162-209	B-4						
Crime and crime rates:										
Property crime	8	A-6	258-305	B-6	698-715	C-4				
Violent crime	8	A-6	258-305	B-6	698-715	C-4				
D										
Deaths:										
Infant	6	A-4	162-209	B-4						
Rates	6	A-4	162-209	B-4						
E										
Earnings:										
Farm	12	A-10	450-497	B-10						
Manufacturing	10	A-8	354-401	B-8						
Personal Income	10	A-8	354-401	B-8						
Education:										
Attainment	7	A-5	210-257	B-5						
Enrollment	7	A-5	210-257	B-5						
Elderly:										
Medicare	6	A-4	162-209	B-4						
Population	4	A-2	66-113	B-2	662-679	C-2				
Social Security	15	A-13	594-641	B-13						

Item	Table A. States		Table B. Counties		Table C. Cities		Table D-1. Places		Table D-2. MCDs	
	Page	Table	Page	Table	Page	Table	Page	Table	Page	Table
Establishments:										
Accommodation and foodservices (NAICS 72)...	14	A-12	546-593	B-12						
Manufacturing (NAICS 31-33)	11	A-9	402-449	B-9						
Nursing and personal care facilities	6	A-4	162-209	B-4						
Private nonfarm businesses	9	A-7	306-353	B-7						
Retail (NAICS 44-45).	13	A-11	498-545	B-11						
Wholesale (NAICS 42).	13	A-11	498-545	B-11						
F										
Family households.	5	A-3	114-161	B-3	680-697	C-3				
Married-couple.	5	A-3	114-161	B-3	680-697	C-3				
Female householder	5	A-3	114-161	B-3	680-697	C-3				
Farms and characteristics:										
Acreage	12	A-10	450-497	B-10						
Crops	12	A-10	450-497	B-10						
Farms.	12	A-10	450-497	B-10						
Farm population	12	A-10	450-497	B-10						
Size	12	A-10	450-497	B-10						
Value of farm products sold	12	A-10	450-497	B-10						
Federal Government:										
Civilian employment	15	A-13	594-641	B-13						
Military employment	15	A-13	594-641	B-13						
Federal funds and grants:										
Expenditure, total.	14	A-12	546-593	B-12						
Per capita	14	A-12	546-593	B-12						
Direct payments for individuals.	14	A-12	546-593	B-12						
Grant awards	14	A-12	546-593	B-12						
Procurement contract awards.	14	A-12	546-593	B-12						
Salaries and wages	14	A-12	546-593	B-12						
Females:										
Female householder	5	A-3	114-161	B-3	680-697	C-3				
Males per 100 females	4	A-2	66-113	B-2	662-679	C-2				
Finance, insurance, and real estate:										
Earnings	10	A-8	354-401	B-8						
G										
Goods-related earnings.	10	A-8	354-401	B-8						
Government:										
Earnings.	10	A-8	354-401	B-8						
Employment:										
Federal	15	A-13	594-641	B-13						
Local.	15	A-13	594-641	B-13						
State and local	15	A-13	594-641	B-13						
Finances:										
City.					752-767	C-7				
Local.	15	A-13	594-641	B-13						
H										
Hispanic or Latino population	3	A-1	18-65	B-1	644-661	C-1	773-893	D-1	895-931	D-2
Households:										
Family	5	A-3	114-161	B-3	680-697	C-3				
Median income.	7	A-5	210-257	B-5						
Non-family.	5	A-3	114-161	B-3	680-697	C-3				
Housing:										
New units authorized.	8	A-6	258-305	B-6						
Occupied units	8	A-6	258-305	B-6	698-715	C-4				
Owner-occupied, percent	8	A-6	258-305	B-6	698-715	C-4				
I										
Income:										
Median household	7	A-5	210-257	B-5						
Poverty status	7	A-5	210-257	B-5						
Infant deaths and death rates	6	A-4	162-209	B-4						
Institutionalized population in group quarters.	5	A-3	114-161	B-3	680-697	C-3				
L										
Labor force, civilian	9	A-7	306-353	B-7	698-715	C-4				
Land area:										
Farmland	12	A-10	450-497	B-10						
Total land area.	3	A-1	18-65	B-1	644-661	C-1	773-893	D-1	895-931	D-2
Latino population.	3	A-1	18-65	B-1	644-661	C-1	773-893	D-1	895-931	D-2
Local government employment.	15	A-13	594-641	B-13						
Local government finances:										
Direct general expenditure	15	A-13	594-641	B-13						
General revenue.	15	A-13	594-641	B-13						
Taxes	15	A-13	594-641	B-13						

Item	Table A. States		Table B. Counties		Table C. Cities		Table D-1. Places		Table D-2. MCDs	
	Page	Table	Page	Table	Page	Table	Page	Table	Page	Table
M										
Males per 100 females	4	A-2	66-113	B-2	662-679	C-2				
Manufacturing (NAICS 31-33):										
Annual payroll	11	A-9	402-449	B-9	716-733	C-5				
Earnings	10	A-8	354-401	B-8						
Establishments	11	A-9	402-449	B-9	716-733	C-5				
Private nonfarm business	9	A-7	306-353	B-7						
Production workers	11	A-9	402-449	B-9	716-733	C-5				
Value added	11	A-9	402-449	B-9	716-733	C-5				
Value of shipments	11	A-9	402-449	B-9	716-733	C-5				
Wages	11	A-9	402-449	B-9	716-733	C-5				
Married-couple households	5	A-3	114-161	B-3	680-697	C-3				
N										
Native Hawaiian and Other Pacific Islander population.	4	A-2	66-113	B-2	662-679	C-2	773-893	D-1	895-931	D-2
New private housing units	8	A-6	258-305	B-6						
Valuation.	8	A-6	258-305	B-6						
Nonfamily-households.	5	A-3	114-161	B-3	680-697	C-3				
Nursing and personal care facilities	6	A-4	162-209	B-4						
P										
Payroll:										
Accommodation and foodservices (NAICS 72) . . .	14	A-12	546-593	B-12	734-751	C-6				
Manufacturing (NAICS 31-33)	11	A-9	402-449	B-9	716-733	C-5				
Private nonfarm businesses	9	A-7	306-353	B-7						
Retail trade (NAICS 44-45)	13	A-11	498-545	B-11	734-751	C-6				
Wholesale trade (NAICS 42)	13	A-11	498-545	B-11	716-733	C-5				
Personal income:										
Earnings.	10	A-8	354-401	B-8						
Fire, insurance, and real estate (FIRE)	10	A-8	354-401	B-8						
Government	10	A-8	354-401	B-8						
Manufacturing	10	A-8	354-401	B-8						
Retail trade	10	A-8	354-401	B-8						
Services.	10	A-8	354-401	B-8						
Per capita	10	A-8	354-401	B-8						
Physicians	6	A-4	162-209	B-4						
Population:										
Age groups	4	A-2	66-113	B-2	662-679	C-2				
Density	3	A-1	18-65	B-1	644-661	C-1				
Farm population	12	A-10	450-497	B-10						
Group quarters.	5	A-3	114-161	B-3	680-697	C-3				
Hispanic or Latino population	3	A-1	18-65	B-1	644-661	C-1	773 893	D-1	895-931	D-2
Households	5	A-3	114-161	B-3	680-697	C-3				
Institutionalized population	5	A-3	114-161	B-3	680-697	C-3				
Males per 100 females	4	A-2	66-113	B-2	662-679	C-2				
Median age	4	A-2	66-113	B-2	662-679	C-2				
Race	4	A-2	66-113	B-2	662-679	C-2	773-893	D-1	895-931	D-2
Rank	3	A-1	18-65	B-1	644-661	C-1				
Total population	3	A-1	18-65	B-1	644-661	C-1	773-893	D-1	895-931	D-2
Two or more races	4	A-2	66-113	B-2	680-697	C-2	773-893	D-1	895-931	D-2
Poverty	7	A-5	210-257	B-5						
Private nonfarm business:										
Establishments	9	A-7	306-353	B-7						
Employment.	9	A-7	306-353	B-7						
Annual payroll per employee.	9	A-7	306-353	B-7						
Production workers:										
Manufacturing	11	A-9	402-449	B-9	716-733	C-5				
Wages	11	A-9	402-449	B-9	716-733	C-5				
Property crime.	8	A-6	258-305	B-6	698-715	C-4				
R										
Race.	4	A-2	66-113	B-2	662-679	C-2	773-893	D-1	895-931	D-2
Retail trade (NAICS 44-45):										
Annual payroll	13	A-11	498-545	B-11	734-751	C-6				
Earnings	10	A-8	354-401	B-8						
Employees, paid.	13	A-11	498-545	B-11	734-751	C-6				
Establishments.	13	A-11	498-545	B-11	734-751	C-6				
Sales, total	13	A-11	498-545	B-11	734-751	C-6				
General merchandise	13	A-11	498-545	B-11	734-751	C-6				
S										
Sales:										
Accommodation and foodservices (NAICS 72) . . .	14	A-12	546-593	B-12	734-751	C-6				
Retail trade (NAICS 44-45).	13	A-11	498-545	B-11	734-751	C-6				
Wholesale (NAICS 31-33)	13	A-11	498-545	B-11	716-733	C-5				

Item	Table A. States		Table B. Counties		Table C. Cities		Table D-1. Places		Table D-2. MCDs	
	Page	Table	Page	Table	Page	Table	Page	Table	Page	Table
Service-related earnings	10	A-8	354-401	B-8						
Shipments, value of	11	A-9	402-449	B-9	716-733	C-5				
Social Security beneficiaries	15	A-13	594-641	B-13						
Supplemental Security Income recipients	15	A-13	594-641	B-13						
U										
Unemployment	9	A-7	306-353	B-7	698-715	C-4				
V										
Value added by manufacture	11	A-9	402-449	B-9	716-733	C-5				
Value of shipments.	11	A-9	402-449	B-9	716-733	C-5				
Value of farm products sold	12	A-10	450-497	B-10						
Violent crime.	8	A-6	258-305	B-6						
W										
Water use:										
Consumption	11	A-9	402-449	B-9						
Industrial	11	A-9	402-449	B-9						
Irrigation	11	A-9	402-449	B-9						
Public supply	11	A-9	402-449	B-9						
Withdrawls	11	A-9	402-449	B-9	662-679	C-2				
White population	4	A-2	66-113	B-2	662-679	C-2	773-893	D-1	895-931	D-2
Wholesale trade (NAICS 42):										
Annual payroll	13	A-11	498-545	B-11	716-733	C-5				
Employees, paid.	13	A-11	498-545	B-11	716-733	C-5				
Establishments.	13	A-11	498-545	B-11	716-733	C-5				
Operating expenses	13	A-11	498-545	B-11	716-733	C-5				
Sales, total	13	A-11	498-545	B-11	716-733	C-5				
Merchant wholesalers.	13	A-11	498-545	B-11	716-733	C-5				

U.S. Census Bureau, *County and City Data Book: 2000*